Small Business Sourcebook

ISSN 0883-3397

Small Business Sourcebook

The Entrepreneur's Resource

THIRTY-SECOND EDITION

Volume 4

General Small Business Topics

(Entries 32654-46743)

Virgil L. Burton III
Project Editor

GALE
CENGAGE Learning

Farmington Hills, Mich • San Francisco • New York • Waterville, Maine
Meriden, Conn • Mason, Ohio • Chicago

GALE
CENGAGE Learning®

Small Business Sourcebook, 32nd edition

Project Editor: Virgil L. Burton III

Editorial Support Services: Charles Beaumont

Composition and Electronic Prepress: Gary Leach

Manufacturing: Rita Wimberley

For product information and technology assistance, contact us at
Gale Customer Support, 1-800-877-4253.
For permission to use material from this text or product,
submit all requests online at **www.cengage.com/permissions.**
Further permissions questions can be emailed to
permissionrequest@cengage.com

Gale
27500 Drake Rd.
Farmington Hills, MI, 48331-3535

ISBN-13: 978-1-57302-581-2 (set)
ISBN-13: 978-1-57302-582-9 (vol. 1)
ISBN-13: 978-1-57302-583-6 (vol. 2)
ISBN-13: 978-1-57302-584-3 (vol. 3)
ISBN-13: 978-1-57302-585-0 (vol. 4)
ISBN-13: 978-1-57302-586-7 (vol. 5)
ISBN-13: 978-1-57302-587-4 (vol. 6)

ISSN 0883-3397

Printed in the United States of America
1 2 3 4 5   19 18 17 16 15

Contents

The appeal of small business ownership remains perpetually entrenched in American culture as one of the most viable avenues for achieving the American Dream. To many entrepreneurs going into business for themselves represents financial independence, an increased sense of identity and self-worth, and the fulfillment of personal goals. Small business owners strive to make their mark in today's competitive marketplace by establishing healthy businesses that can, over time, become legacies handed down from one generation to the next. Entrepreneurs from each generation tackle the obstacles and adversities of the current business and economic climate to test their business savvy and generate opportunities. Today's entrepreneurs face many of the problems of their predecessors, as well as some distinctly new challenges.

With the rightsizing, downsizing, and reorganization of corporate America, many individuals have decided to confront the risks of developing and operating their own businesses. Small business ownership is rapidly becoming a viable alternative to what is perceived as an equally unstable corporate environment. These entrepreneurs, many of whom have firsthand experience with the problems and inefficiencies inherent in today's large corporations, seek to improve upon an archaic business model and to capitalize on their own ingenuity and strengths. Led by their zeal, many would-be entrepreneurs let their desire, drive, and determination overshadow the need for business knowledge and skill. Ironically, aids in obtaining these components of entrepreneurial success are widely available, easily accessible, and often free of charge.

Small Business Sourcebook (*SBS*) is a six-volume annotated guide to more than 24,764 listings of live and print sources of information designed to facilitate the start-up, development, and growth of specific small businesses, as well as over 31,877 similar listings on general small business topics. An additional 11,278 state-specific listings and over 1,380 U.S. federal government agencies and offices specializing in small business issues, programs, and assistance are also included. *SBS* covers 340 specific small business profiles and 99 general small business topics.

Features of This Edition

This edition of *Small Business Sourcebook* has been revised and updated, incorporating thousand of changes to names, addresses, contacts, and descriptions of listings from the previous edition.

Contents and Arrangement

The geographical scope of *SBS* encompasses the United States and Canada, with expanded coverage for resources pertaining to international trade and for resources that have a U.S. or Canadian distributor or contact. Internet sites that are maintained outside of the U.S. and Canada are also included if they contain relevant information for North American small businesses. Resources that do not relate specifically to small businesses are generally not included.

The information presented in *SBS* is grouped within four sections: Specific Small Business Profiles, General Small Business Topics, State Listings, and Federal Government Assistance. Detailed outlines of these sections may be found in the Users' Guide following this Introduction. Also included is a Master Index to Volumes 1 through 6.

Specific Small Business Profiles This section includes the following types of resources: start-up information, associations and other organizations, educational programs, directories of educational programs, reference works, sources of supply, statistical sources, trade periodicals, videocassettes/audiocassettes, trade shows and conventions, consultants, franchises and business opportunities, computerized databases, computer systems/software, Internet databases, libraries, and research centers-all arranged by business type. Entries range from Accounting Service to Word Processing Service, and include such businesses as Airbag Replacement Service Centers, Computer Consulting, Damage Restoration Service, and Web Site Design.

General Small Business Topics This section offers such resources as associations, books, periodicals, articles, pamphlets, educational programs, directories of educational programs,videocassettes/audiocassettes, trade shows and conventions, consultants, computerized databases, Internet databases, software, libraries, and research centers, arranged alphabetically by business topic.

State Listings Entries include government, academic, and commercial agencies and organizations, as well as select coverage of relevant state-specific publications; listings are arranged alphabetically by state, territory, and Canadian province. Some examples include small business development consultants, educational programs, financing and loan programs, better business bureaus, and chambers of commerce.

Federal Government Assistance Listings specializing in small business issues, programs, assistance, and policyare arranged alphabetically by U.S. government agency or office; regional or branch offices are listed alphabetically by state.

Master Index All entries in Volumes 1 through 6 are arranged in one alphabetic index for convenience.

Entries in *SBS* include (as appropriate andavailable):

- Organization, institution, or product name

- Contact information, including contact name, address and phone, toll-free, and fax numbers

- Author/editor, date(s), and frequency

- Availability, including price

- Brief description of purpose, services, or content

- Company and/or personal E-mail addresses

- Web site addresses

SBS also features the following:

Guide to Publishers—An alphabetic listing of 2,092 companies, associations, institutions, and individuals that publish the periodicals, directories, guidebooks, and other publications noted in the Small Business Profiles and General Topics sections. Users are provided with full contact information, including address, phone, fax,and e-mail and URL when available. The Guide to Publishers facilitates contact with publishers and provides a one- stop resource for valuable information.

Method of Compilation

SBS was compiled by consulting small business experts and entrepreneurs, as well as a variety of resources, including direct contact with the associations, organizations, and agencies through telephone surveys, Internet research, or through materials provided by those listees; government resources; and data obtained from other relevant Gale directories. *SBS* was reviewed by a team of small business advisors, all of whom have numerous years of expertise in small business counseling and identification of small business information resources. The last and perhaps most important resource we utilize is direct contact with our readers, who provide valuable comments and suggestions to improve our publication. *SBS* relies on these comprehensive market contacts to provide today's entrepreneurs with relevant, current, and accurate informationon all aspects of small business.

Available in Electronic Formats

Licensing. *Small Business Sourcebook* is available for licensing. The complete database is provided in a fielded format and is deliverable on such media as disk or CD-ROM. For more information, contact Gale's Business Development Group at1-800-877-GALE, or visit our website at www.gale.com/bizdev.

Comments and Suggestions Welcome

Associations, agencies, business firms, publishers, and other organizations that provide assistance and information to the small business community are encouraged to submit material about their programs, activities, services, or products. Comments and suggestions from users of this directory are also welcomed and appreciated. Please contact:

Project Editor
Small Business Sourcebook
Gale, Cengage Learning
27500 Drake Rd.
Farmington Hills, MI 48331-3535
Phone: (248) 699-4253
Fax: (248) 699-8070
URL: www.gale.com

Small Business Sourcebook (*SBS*) provides information in a variety of forms and presentations for comprehensive coverage and ease of use. The directory contains four parts within two volumes:

- Specific Small Business Profiles
- General Small Business Topics
- State Listings
- Federal Government Assistance

Information on specific businesses is arranged by type of business; the many general topics that are of interest to the owners, operators, or managers of all small businesses are grouped in a separate section for added convenience. Users should consult the various sections to benefit fully from the information *SBS* offers. For example, an entrepreneur with a talent or interest in the culinary arts could peruse a number of specific small business profiles, such as Restaurant, Catering, Cooking School, Specialty Food/Wine Shop, Bakery/Doughnut Shop, Healthy Restaurant, or Candy/Chocolate Store. Secondly, the General Small Business Topics section could be consulted for any applicable subjects, such as Service Industry, Retailing, Franchising, and other relevant topics. Then, the appropriate state within the State Listings section would offer area programs and offices providing information and support to small businesses, including venture capital firms and small business development consultants. Finally, the Federal Government Assistance section could supply relevant government offices, such as procurement contacts.

Features Included in Volumes 1 through 3

List of Small Business Profiles. This list provides an alphabetic outline of the small businesses profiled, with cross-references for related profiles and for alternate names by which businesses may be identified. The page number for each profile is indicated.

Standard Industrial Classification (SIC) Codes for Profiled Small Businesses. This section lists four-digit SIC codes and corresponding classification descriptions for the small businesses profiled in this edition. The SIC system, which organizes businesses by type, is a product of the Statistical Policy Division of the U.S. Office of Management and Budget. Statistical data produced by government, public, and private organizations is usually categorized according to SIC codes, thereby facilitating the collection, comparison, and analysis of data as well as providing a uniform method for presenting statistical information. Hence, knowing the SIC code for a particular small business increases access and the use of a variety of statistical data from many sources.

Guide to Publishers. This resource lists alphabetically the companies, associations, institutions, and individuals that publish the periodicals, directories, guidebooks, and other publications noted in the "Small Business Profiles" and "General Topics" sections. Users are provided with full contact information, including address, phone, fax, and e-mail and URL when available. The "Guide" facilitates contact with publishers and provides a one-stop resource for valuable information.

Glossary of Small Business Terms. This glossary defines nearly 400 small business terms, including financial, governmental, insurance, procurement, technical, and general business definitions. Cross-references and acronyms are also provided.

Small Business Profiles A-Z. A total of 340 small businesses is represented in volumes 1 through 3. Profiles are listed alphabetically by business name. Entries within each profile are arranged alphabetically by resource type, within up to 17 subheadings. These subheadings are detailed below:

- *Start-up Information*—Includes periodical articles, books, manuals, book excerpts, kits, and other sources of information. Entries offer title; publisher; address; phone, fax, toll-free numbers; company e-mail and URL addresses; and a description. Bibliographic data is provided for cited periodical articles whenever possible.

- *Associations and Other Organizations*—Includes trade and professional associations whose members gather and disseminate information of interest to small business owners. Entries offer the association's name; address; phone, toll-free and fax numbers; company e-mail address; contact name; purpose and objective; a description of membership; telecommunication services; and a listing of its publications, including publishing frequency.

- **Educational Programs**—Includes university and college programs, schools, training opportunities, association seminars, correspondence courses, and other educational programs.Entries offer name of program or institution, sponsor name, address, phone, toll-free and fax numbers, e-mail and URL addresses; and description of program.

- **Directories of Educational Programs**—Includes directories and other publications that list educational programs. Entries offer name of publication; publisher name, address, and phone, toll-free and fax numbers; editor; frequency or date of publication; price; and description of contents, including directory arrangement and indexes.

- **Reference Works**—Includes handbooks, manuals, textbooks, guides, directories, dictionaries, encyclopedias, and other published reference materials. Entries offer name of publication; publisher name, address, and phone, toll-free and fax numbers; e-mail and URL addresses; and, when available, name of author or editor, publication year or frequency, and price. A brief description is often featured.

- **Sources of Supply**—Includes buyer's guides,directories, special issues of periodicals, and other publications that list sources of equipment, supplies, and services related to the operation of the profiled small business. Entries offer publication name; publisher name, address, and phone, toll-free and fax numbers; e-mail and URL addresses; and, when available, editor's name, frequency or publication year, and price. A brief description of the publication, including directory arrangement and indexes, is often provided.

- **Statistical Sources**—Includes books, reports, pamphlets, and other sources of statistical data of interest to an owner, operator or manager of the profiled small business, such as wage, salary, and compensation data; financial and operating ratios; prices and costs; demographics; and other statistical information. Entries offer publication/data source name; publisher (if applicable); address; phone, toll-free and fax numbers of data source; publication date or frequency; and price. A brief description of the publication/data source is often provided.

- **Trade Periodicals**—Includes trade journals, newsletters, magazines, and other serials that offer information about the management and operation of the profiled small business. Such periodicals often contain industry news; trends and developments; reviews; articles about new equipment and supplies;

and other information related to business operations. Entries offer publication name; publisher name, address, phone, toll-free and fax numbers, and e-mail and URL addresses; editor name; publication frequency; andprice. A brief description of the publication's content is also included, when known.

- **Videocassettes/Audiocassettes**—Includes videocassettes, audiocassettes, and other audiovisual media offering information on the profiled small business. Entries offer program title; distributor name, address, phone, toll-free and fax numbers, and e-mail and URL addresses; description of program; release date; price; and format(s).

- **Trade Shows and Conventions**—Includes tradeshows, exhibitions, expositions, conventions, and other industry meetings that provide prospective and existing business owners with the opportunity to meet and exchange information with their peers, review commercial exhibits, establish business or sales contacts, and attend educational programs. Entries offer event name; sponsor or management company name, address, phone, toll-free and fax numbers, and e-mail and URL addresses; a description of the event, including audience, frequency, principal exhibits, and dates and locations of event for as many years ahead as provided by the event's sponsor.

- **Consultants**—Includes consultants and consulting organizations that provide services specifically related to the profiled small business. Entries offer individual consultant or consulting organization name, address, and phone, toll-free and fax numbers; company and individual e-mail addresses; and a brief description of consulting services. (For e-mail and URL addresses, see the Small Business Development Consultants subheadings in the State Listings section in Volume 2.)

- **Franchises and Business Opportunities**—Includes companies granting franchise licenses for enterprises falling within the scope of the profiled small business, as well as other non-franchised business opportunities that operate within a given network or system. Entries offer franchise name, address, phone, toll-free and fax numbers, and e-mail and URL addresses, as well as a description of the franchise or business opportunity, which has been expanded whenever possible to include the number of existing franchises, the founding date of the franchise, franchise fees, equity capital requirements, royalty fees, any managerial assistance offered, and available training.

- **Computerized Databases**—Includes diskettes, magnetic tapes, CD-ROMs, online systems, and other computer-readable databases. Entries offer database name; producer name, address, phone, toll-free and fax numbers, e-mail and URL addresses; description; and available format(s), including vendor name.

(Many university and public libraries offer online information retrieval services that provide searches of databases, including those listed in this category.)

- **Computer Systems/Software**—Includes softwareand computerized business systems designed to assist in the operation of the profiled small business. Entries offer name of the software or system; publisher name, address, phone, toll-free and faxnumbers; price; and description.

- **Libraries**—Includes libraries and special collections that contain material especially applicable to the profiled small business. Entries offer library or collection name; parent organization (where applicable); address; phone, toll-free and fax numbers; e-mail and URL addresses; contact name and title; scope of collection; and description of holdings, subscriptions, and services.

- **Research Centers**—Includes university-related and independently operated research institutes and information centers that generate, through their research programs, data related to the operation of the profiled small business. Also listed are associations and other business-related organizations that conduct research programs. Entries offer name of organization; address; phone, toll-free and fax numbers; company web site address; contact name and personale-mail; a description of principal fields of research or services; publications, including title and frequency; and related conferences.

Features Included in Volumes 2 through 6

General Small Business Topics. This section offers chapters on different topics in the operation of any small business, for example, venture capital and other funding, or compensation. Chapters are listed alphabetically by small business topic; entries within each chapter are arranged alphabetically, within up to 14 subheadings, by resource type:

- **Associations and Other Organizations**—Includes trade and professional associations that gather and disseminate information of interest to small business owners. Entries offer the association's name; address; phone, toll-free and fax numbers; organization e-mail and URL addresses; contact name;purpose and objectives; a description of membership; telecommunication services; and a listing of its publications, including publishing frequency.

- **Educational Programs**—Includes university and college programs, schools, training opportunities, association seminars, correspondence courses, and other educational programs. Entries offer name of program or institution, sponsor name, address, phone, toll-free and fax numbers, e-mail and URL addresses, and description of program.

- **Directories of Educational Programs**—Includes directories and other publications that list educational programs. Entries offer name of publication; publisher name, address, phone, toll-free and fax numbers, and e-mail and URL addresses; editor; frequency or date of publication; price; and description of contents, including arrangement and indexes.

- **Reference Works**—Includes articles, handbooks, manuals, textbooks, guides, directories, dictionaries, encyclopedias, and other published reference materials. Entries offertitle of article, including bibliographic information; name of publication; publisher name, address, phone, toll-free and fax numbers, and e-mail and URL addresses; and, when available, name of author oreditor, publication year or frequency, and price. A brief descriptionis often featured.

- **Sources of Supply**—Includes buyer's guides,directories, special issues of periodicals, and other publications that list sources of equipment, supplies, and services. Entries offer publication name; publisher name, address, phone, toll-free and fax numbers, and e-mail and URL addresses; editor's name, frequency or publication year, price, and a brief description of the publication, when available.

- **Statistical Sources**—Includes books, reports, pamphlets, and other sources of statistical data of interest to an owner, operator, or manager of a small business, such as wage, salary, and compensation data; financial and operating ratios; prices and costs; demographics; and other statistical information. Entries offer publication/data source name; publisher (if applicable); address; phone, toll-free and fax numbers of data source; publication date or frequency; and price. A brief description is often provided.

- **Trade Periodicals**—Includes journals, newsletters, magazines, and other serials. Entries offer name of publication; publisher name, address, phone, toll-free and fax numbers, and e-mail and URL addresses; and name of editor, frequency, and price.A brief description of the periodical's content is included when known.

- **Videocassettes/Audiocassettes**—Includes videocassettes, audiocassettes, and other audiovisual media. Entries offer program title; distributor name, address, phone, toll-free and fax numbers, and e-mail and URL addresses; price; description of program; release date; and format(s).

- **Trade Shows and Conventions**—Includes tradeshows, exhibitions, expositions, seminars, and conventions. Entries offer event name; sponsor or management company name, address, phone, toll-free and fax numbers, and e-mail and URL addresses; frequency of event; and dates and locations of the event for as many years ahead as known.

- **Consultants**—Includes consultants and consulting organizations. Entries offer individual consultant or-consulting organization name, address, and phone, toll-free and fax numbers; company and individual e-mail addresses; and a brief description of consulting services. (See also Consultants in the State Listings section.)

- **Computerized Databases**—Includes diskettes, CD-ROMs, magnetic tape, online systems and other computer-readable databases. Entries offer database name; producer, address, phone, toll-free and fax numbers, and e-mail and URL addresses; description; and available format(s), including vendor name. (Many university and public libraries offer online information retrieval services that provide searches of databases, including those listed in this category.)

- **Computer Systems/Software**—Includes software and computerized business systems. Entries offer name of the software or system; publisher name, address, phone, toll-free and fax numbers, and e-mail and URL addresses; price; and description.

- **Libraries**—Includes libraries and special collections that contain material applicable to the small business topic. Entries offer library or collection name, parent organization (where applicable), address, phone and fax numbers, e-mail and URL addresses, scope of collection, and description of holdings and services.

- **Research Centers**— Includes university-related and independently operated research institutes and information centers that generate, through their research programs, data related to specific small business topics. Entries offer name of organization, address, phone, toll-free and fax numbers, e-mail and URL addresses, a description of principal fields of research or services, and related conferences.

State Listings. This section lists various sources of information and assistance available within given states, territories, and Canadian provinces; entries include governmental, academic, and commercial agencies, and are arranged alphabetically within up to 15 subheadings by resource type:

- **Small Business Development Center Lead Office**— Includes the lead small business development center (SBDC) for each state.

- **Small Business Development Centers**—Includes any additional small business development centers (SBDC) in the state, territory, or province. SBDCs provide support services to small businesses, including individual counseling, seminars, conferences, and learning center activities.

- **Small Business Assistance Programs**—Includes state small business development offices and other programs offering assistance to small businesses.

- **SCORE Offices**—Includes SCORE office(s) for each state. The Service Corps of Retired Executives Association (SCORE), a volunteer program sponsored by the Small Business Administration, offers counseling, workshops, and seminars across the U.S. for small business entrepreneurs.

- **Better Business Bureaus**—Includes various better business bureaus within each state. By becoming a member of the local Better Business Bureau, a small business owner can increase the prestige and credibility of his or her business within the community, as well as make valuable business contacts.

- **Chambers of Commerce**—Includes various chambers of commerce within each state. Chambers of Commerce are valuable sources of small business advice and information; often, local chambers sponsor SCORE counseling several times per month for a small fee, seminars, conferences, and other workshops to its members. Also, by becoming a member of the local Chamber of Commerce, a small business owner can increase the prestige and credibility of his or herbusiness within the community, as well as make valuable business contacts.

- **Minority Business Assistance Programs**—Includes minority business development centers and other sources of assistance for minority-owned business.

- **Financing and Loan Programs**—Includes venture capital firms, small business investment companies (SBIC), minority enterprise small business investment companies (MESBIC), and other programs that provide funding to qualified small businesses.

- **Procurement Assistance Programs**—Includes state services such as counseling, set-asides, and sheltered-market bidding, which are designed to aid small businesses in bidding on government contracts.

- **Incubators/Research and Technology Parks**— Includes small business incubators, which provide newly established small business owners with work sites, business services, training, and consultation; also includes research and technology parks, which sponsor research and facilitate commercialization of new technologies.

- **Educational Programs**—Includes university and college programs, as well as those sponsored by other organizations that offer degree, nondegree, certificate, and correspondence programs in entrepreneurship and in small business development.

- **Legislative Assistance**—Includes committees, subcommittees, and joint committees of each state's senate and house of representatives that are concerned with small business issues and regulations.

- *Consultants*—Includes consultants and consulting firms offering expertise in small business development.

- *Publications*—Includes publications related to small business operations within the profiled state.

- *Publishers*—Includes publishers operating in or for the small business arena within the profiled state.

Federal Government Assistance. This section lists federal government agencies and offices, many with additional listings for specific offices, as well as regional or district branches. Main agencies or offices are listed alphabetically; regional, branch, ordistrict offices are listed after each main office or agency.

Master Index. This index provides an alphabetic listing of all entries contained in Volumes 1 throgh 6. Citations are referenced by their entry numbers. Publication titles are rendered in italics.

The editors would like to extend sincere thanks to the following members of the Small Business Sourcebook advisory board for their expert guidance, recommendations, and suggestions for the ongoing development of this title:

Susan C. Awe
Assistant Director,
William J. Parish Memorial Business Library

Jill Clever
Business Technology Specialist,
Toledo-Lucas County Public Library

Jules Matsoff
District Manager,
Service Corps of Retired Executives (SCORE) Milwaukee Chapter

Ken MacKenzie
President,
Southeast Business Appraisal

The editors would also like to thank the individuals from associations and other organizations who provided information for the compilation of this directory.

List of General Small Business Topics

This section covers sources of assistance applicable to a variety of small businesses. Resources are arranged by topic and include associations, educational programs, directories of educational programs, reference works, sources of supply, statistical sources, periodicals, videocassettes/audiocassettes, trade shows and conventions, consultants, computerized databases, computer systems/software, Internet databases, libraries, and research centers.

START-UP INFORMATION

32654 ■ *"218 More Programs"* in *Entrepreneur (Vol. 35, November 2007, No. 11, pp. 96)*
Description: List of 218 colleges and universities in the U.S. offering entrepreneurship programs is presented.

32655 ■ *"Austin's Connection To Aggies, Angels and Investors"* in *Austin Business Journal (Vol. 32, April 6, 2012, No. 5, pp. A1)*
Pub: American City Business Journals, Inc.
Contact: Whitney Shaw, President
Ed: Christopher Calnan. **Released:** April 6, 2012. **Description:** Texas A and M University System director for new ventures, Jamie Rhodes, has been using his experience as an entrepreneur and angel investor to work with the university's professors, researchers, and new entrepreneurs on commercialization opportunities. Rhodes has a goal to create startups based on research produced at Texas A and M.

32656 ■ *"Campus CEOs: Young and the Restless"* in *Business Journal Portland (Vol. 30, February 21, 2014, No. 50, pp. 4)*
Pub: American City Business Journals
Released: February 14, 2014. **Description:** A number of startups in Portland, Oregon were created by young entrepreneurs while still attending college. The University of Oregon and Portland State University are developing courses designed to launch the entrepreneurial ambitions of their students.

32657 ■ *"Can You Say $1 Million? A Language-Learning Start-Up Is Hoping That Investors Can"* in *Inc. (Vol. 33, November 2011, No. 9, pp. 116)*
Pub: Inc. Magazine
Ed: April Joyner. **Description:** Startup, Verbling is a video platform that links language learners and native speakers around the world. The firm is working to raise money to hire engineers in order to build the product and redesign their Website.

32658 ■ *Entrepreneurship with Online Learning Center Access Card*
Ed: Robert D. Hirich; Michael P. Peters; Dean A. Shepherd. **Released:** October 2006. **Price:** $103.25. **Description:** Book instructs students on entrepreneurial processes that include starting a new business.

32659 ■ *"Franchises with an Eye on Chicago"* in *Crain's Chicago Business (Vol. 34, March 14, 2011, No. 11, pp. 20)*
Pub: Crain Communications Inc.
Contact: Todd Johnson, Publisher
Description: Profiles of franchise companies seeking franchisees for the Chicago area include: Extreme Pita, a sandwich shop; Hand and Stone, offering massage, facial and waxing services; Molly Maid, homecleaning service; Primrose Schools, private accredited schools for children 6 months to 6 hears and after-school programs; Protect Painters, residential

and light-commercial painting contractor; and Wingstop, a restaurant offering chicken wings in nine flavors, fries and side dishes.

32660 ■ *"Fun And Easy Gold Mines"* in *Small Business Opportunities (Fall 2008)*
Description: Twenty-five businesses that cater to the booming children's market are profiled; day care services, party planning, special events videomaking, tutoring, personalized children's toys and products and other services geared toward the kids market are included.

32661 ■ *"John Brownlee, Vidscrip.com"* in *Business Journal (Vol. 32, June 27, 2014, No. 5, pp. 6)*
Pub: American City Business Journals
Released: June 27, 2014. **Description:** John Brownlee, CEO of vidscrip.com, discusses the Minneapolis, Minnesota startup's deal with Partners HealthCare and what it means for the business. Partners HealthCare is using the vidscrip technology to create educational videos for patients.

32662 ■ *"Make Money Selling Products on YouTube"*
Pub: Amazon Digital Services
Released: October 2, 2014. **Price:** $2.99 Kindle. **Description:** Advice is rendered to help individuals sell products such as eBooks, online courses, audio programs, video programs; marketing products such as those found on ClickBank; as well as physical products such as clothing, household accessories and goods, cars, and more on YouTube. Aspects of electronic commerce are covered.

32663 ■ *"May I Help You?"* in *Entrepreneur (September 2014)*
Pub: Entrepreneur Media Inc.
Released: September 2014. **Description:** Entrepreneur magazine lists 114 of the top personal-service franchises in the U.S. These personal-service businesses are among the fastest growing categories in the franchise sector. Included in the list are child care services, children's enrichment programs, fitness businesses, hair care businesses, spa services, senior care, travel agencies, and tutoring services. Data also includes rankings in the 2014 Franchise 500, startup costs and the number of total franchises or co-owned businesses.

32664 ■ *"Online Fortunes"* in *Small Business Opportunities (Fall 2008)*
Description: Fifty hot, e-commerce enterprises for the aspiring entrepreneur to consider are featured; virtual assistants, marketing services, party planning, travel services, researching, web design and development, importing as well as creating an online store are among the businesses featured.

32665 ■ *"Open English Touted as Startup Worth Emulating"* in *South Florida Business Journal (Vol. 34, January 24, 2014, No. 27, pp. 30)*
Pub: American City Business Journals
Released: January 24, 2014. **Description:** Open English, a language education company, received more than $150 million in investments from venture

capitalists. The firm's cloud-based platform is still in its infancy, but the startup's success has shown that entrepreneurs can generate money and grow their businesses in Florida. Open English is the only online English school that offers live classes with native English-speaking teachers.

32666 ■ *"Rehab Will Turn Hospital Into Incubator"* in *The Business Journal-Serving Metropolitan Kansas City (Vol. 26, September 12, 2008)*
Ed: Rob Roberts. **Description:** Independence Regional Health Center will be purchased by CEAH Realtors and be converted into the Independence Regional Entrepreneurial Center, a business incubator that will house startups and other tenants. Other details about the planned entrepreneurial center are provided.

32667 ■ *"SBA Streamlines Loans and Ramps Up Web Presence"* in *Hispanic Business (January-February 2008, pp. 64)*
Description: Federal government's Small Business Administration offers informational resources and tools to individuals wishing to start a new company as well as those managing existing firms. The site consists of over 20,000 pages with information, advice and tips on starting, financing and managing any small business. Free online courses are also provided.

32668 ■ *Start Your Own Tutoring and Test Prep Business: Your Step-by-Step Guide to Success*
Pub: Entrepreneur Press
Contact: Perlman Neil, President
Ed: Rich Mintzer. **Released:** October 01, 2009. **Price:** $17.95, paperback. **Description:** Are you an advocate of higher learning? Do you enjoy teaching others? Are you interested in starting a business that makes money and a positive impact? Keys for starting a successful tutoring and test preparation small business are presented. **Availability:** Print.

32669 ■ *"The Startup of Something Big"* in *Philadelphia Business Journal (Vol. 33, July 11, 2014, No. 22, pp. 4)*
Pub: American City Business Journals
Released: July 11, 2014. **Description:** Philadelphia is slowly emerging as America's leading innovation district. The South Bank Campus is the city's game changer as University of Pennsylvania and Drexel University, along with others are seeking to harness the merging of innovation and academic pursuits that ultimately translate into new business development.

32670 ■ *"Texas State Building a Home for Startups"* in *Austin Business Journal (Vol. 32, April 20, 2012, No. 7, pp. 1)*
Pub: American City Business Journals, Inc.
Contact: Whitney Shaw, President
Ed: Sandra Zaragoza. **Released:** April 20, 2012. **Description:** Texas State University is set to open a new business incubator for technology startups. The incubator will have secure wet labs, clean rooms and office space.

32671 ■ "Top 25 Graduate Programs" in Entrepreneur (Vol. 35, November 2007, No. 11, pp. 92)
Description: List of the top twenty-five graduate entrepreneurship programs of different colleges and universities in the U.S. for 2007, as ranked by Entrepreneur Magazine and the Princeton Review, is presented.

32672 ■ "Top 25 Undergrad Programs" in Entrepreneur (Vol. 35, November 2007, No. 11, pp. 88)
Description: List of the top twenty-five undergraduate entrepreneurship programs of different colleges and universities in the U.S. for 2007, as ranked by Entrepreneur Magazine and the Princeton Review, is highlighted.

32673 ■ "Top of the Class" in Entrepreneur (Vol. 35, November 2007, No. 11, pp. 82)
Pub: Entrepreneur Press
Contact: Perlman Neil, President

Ed: Nichole L. Torres. **Description:** Education in entrepreneurship is being pursued by many students and it is important to understand what entrepreneurship program fits you. Aspiring entrepreneurs should also ask about the program's focus. Considerations searched for by students regarding the particular school they chose to study entrepreneurship are discussed.

32674 ■ "UM-Dearborn to Launch Program for Entrepreneurs" in Crain's Detroit Business (Vol. 24, April 14, 2008, No. 15, pp. 7)
Pub: Crain Communications Inc.
Contact: Rance E. Crain, President

Ed: Chad Halcom. **Description:** Starting this fall the University of Michigan-Dearborn will begin its Product Realization and Technology Commercialization Program for entrepreneurs and innovators with lab-tested, high-technology products. Ultimately, 20 businesses will each work with the university in creating a customer base, commercializing a new high-tech product or process and connecting with venture capitalists who may invest in the new companies.

32675 ■ "Where the Next Big Thing Lives In Our Nation's Research Labs. Hard Part: Turning Scientists Into Entrepreneurs" in Inc. (Vol. 34, September 2012, No. 7, pp. 43)
Pub: Mansueto Ventures L.L.C.
Contact: John Koten, Chief Executive Officer

Ed: Steve Blank. **Released:** September 2012. **Description:** Steve Blank, former entrepreneur, was invited to speak to the National Science Foundation's new rogram called Innovation Corps. The program is designed to help identify and commercialize research projects and involves mentoring from entrepreneurs, venture capitalists and technology developers.

ASSOCIATIONS AND OTHER ORGANIZATIONS

32676 ■ Association to Advance Collegiate Schools of Business (AACSB International)
77 S Harbour Island Blvd., Ste. 750
Tampa, FL 33602
Ph: (813)769-6500
Fax: (813)769-6559
Co. E-mail: events@aacsb.edu
URL: http://www.aacsb.edu
Contact: John J. Fernandes, President
Description: Represents educational institutions, businesses, and other entities devoted to the advancement of management education. Works to advance quality management education worldwide through accreditation. **Founded:** 1916. **Publications:** Global Salary Survey Report (Annual); AACSB Newsline; BizEd: The Leading Voice of Business Education (Bimonthly); AACSB Newsline; International Business Education in the 1990s: A Global Perspective (Irregular); Achieving Quality and Continuous Improvement Through Self-Evaluation and Peer Review (Annual); eNewsline (Monthly); Salary Survey (Annual); AACSB--The International Associa-

tion for Management Education--Membership Directory (Annual). **Educational Activities:** AACSB International Conference (Annual).

32677 ■ ASTD - Information Center [American Society for Training and Development]
1640 King St.
Alexandria, VA 22314-2746
Ph: (703)683-8100
Free: 800-628-2783
Fax: (703)683-1523
Co. E-mail: customercare@astd.org
URL: http://www.astd.org
Contact: Tony Bingham, President
E-mail: tbingham@astd.org
Description: Represents workplace learning and performance professionals. **Scope:** training and development, workplace performance. **Services:** Library open to national members of the Society. **Founded:** 1943. **Holdings:** 3000 bound volumes. **Publications:** ASTD Buyer's Guide (Annual); ASTD Buyer's Guide (Annual); Member Information Exchange (MIX); TRAINET; ATD Buyer's Guide (Annual); Buyer's Guide & Consultant Directory; American Society for Training and Development--Training Video Directory; ASTD Buyer's Guide and Consultants Directory; Who's Who in Training and Development (Annual); ASTD Buyer's Guide and Consultants Directory; American Society Training and Development Buyer's Guide and Consultant Directory (Annual); Technical Training: Learning Technology for Performance Improvement; ASTD Buyer's Guide & Consultant Directory (Annual); TD at Work (Monthly); Learning Circuits (Monthly); T and D Magazine; TD Magazine (Monthly). **Educational Activities:** International Exposition (Annual); American Society for Training and Development Conference (Annual); TechKnowledge Conference and Exposition (Annual). **Awards:** ASTD BEST Award; Excellence in Practice; Awards in the Advancing Workplace Learning and Performance; Gordon M. Bliss Memorial Award; Dissertation Award; Distinguished Contribution Award; Torch Award.

32678 ■ Canadian Accredited Independent Schools (CAIS)
2 Ridley Rd.
Saint Catharines, ON, Canada L2R 7C3
Ph: (905)684-5658
Fax: (905)684-5057
Co. E-mail: execdir@cesi.edu
URL: http://www.cais.ca
Contact: Ms. Anne-Marie Kee, Executive Director
Description: Private schools. Promotes excellence in independent education. Represents members' interests. **Founded:** 1979. **Publications:** Canadian Accredited Independent School--School Directory (Biennial).

32679 ■ Canadian Federation of University Women (CFUW) [Federation Canadienne des Femmes Diplomees des Universites]
331 Cooper St., Ste. 502
Ottawa, ON, Canada K2P 0G5
Ph: (613)234-8252
Fax: (613)234-8221
URL: http://www.cfuw.org
Contact: Robin Jackson, Executive Director
E-mail: cfuwed@rogers.com
Description: Women graduates from accredited universities from around the world. Promotes continuing education for women. Fosters communication and fellowship among members. Advocates for status of women and human rights and equality rights. **Founded:** 1919. **Publications:** The Communicator (Periodic). **Educational Activities:** Tides of Change. **Awards:** Canadian Home Economics Association Fellowships; Elizabeth Massey Awards; Dr. Alice E. Wilson Awards (Annual); Beverley Jackson Fellowship (Annual); Bourse Georgette LeMoyne (Annual); Memorial Fellowship (Annual); Dr. Marion Elder Grant Award (Annual); Margaret Dale Philip Award (Annual); Dr. Margaret McWilliams Pre-Doctoral Fellowship (Annual); Ecole Polytechnique Commemorative Awards (Annual); CFUW Memorial Fellowship Award (Annual).

32680 ■ Canadian Journal of Learning and Technology
260 Dalhousie St., Ste. 204
Ottawa, ON, Canada K1N 7E4
Ph: (613)241-0018
Fax: (613)241-0019
Co. E-mail: cnie-rcie@cnie-rcie.ca
URL: http://www.cnie-rcie.ca
Contact: Marc Imbeault, President
URL(s): www.cjlt.ca/index.php/cjltwww.cnie-rcie.ca/?q=node/119. **Released:** Semiannual **Price:** $40.

32681 ■ Canadian Network for Innovation in Education (CNIE) [Reseau canadien pour l'innovation en education]
260 Dalhousie St., Ste. 204
Ottawa, ON, Canada K1N 7E4
Ph: (613)241-0018
Fax: (613)241-0019
Co. E-mail: cnie-rcie@cnie-rcie.ca
URL: http://www.cnie-rcie.ca
Contact: Marc Imbeault, President
Description: Educators, students, and other individuals with an interest in distance education. Promotes advancement in the field of distance education. Encourages use of new technologies in distance education. **Founded:** 1983. **Publications:** Journal of Distance Education (JDE) (Semiannual); Online Learning; Canadian Journal of Learning and Technology (Semiannual). **Awards:** Awards of Excellence (Biennial); Graduate Student Stipend Award (Annual); Leadership Award (Annual).

32682 ■ A Commitment to Training and Employment for Women (ACTEW)
215 Spadina Ave., Ste. 350
Toronto, ON, Canada M5T 2C7
Ph: (416)599-3590
Fax: (416)599-2043
Co. E-mail: info@actew.org
URL: http://www.ohrc.on.ca/zh-hant/node/8932
Contact: Ursule Critoph, Co-Chairperson
Description: Serves as umbrella organization of agencies, networks, and groups working on the local level to support existing education and training opportunities for women (particularly lower income, refugee, and older women). Encourages the creation of new programs. Conducts research, lobbying, and advocacy. **Founded:** 1987.

32683 ■ The Communicator
331 Cooper St., Ste. 502
Ottawa, ON, Canada K2P 0G5
Ph: (613)234-8252
Fax: (613)234-8221
URL: http://www.cfuw.org
Contact: Robin Jackson, Executive Director
E-mail: cfuwed@rogers.com
Released: Periodic; 7/year. **Price:** C$10, /year.

32684 ■ Community College Business Officers (CCBO)
3 Boar's Head Ln., Ste. B
Charlottesville, VA 22903-4604
Ph: (434)293-2825
Fax: (434)245-8453
Co. E-mail: info@ccbo.org
URL: http://www.ccbo.org
Contact: Jami Van Ess, President
Description: Represents business officers. Works to support business officers. **Awards:** Exemplary Practices Award (Annual); Outstanding Business Officer and Outstanding Chief Business Officer Awards (Annual).

32685 ■ National Black MBA Association (NBMBAA)
1 E Wacker Ste. 3500
Chicago, IL 60601
Ph: (312)236-2622
Fax: (312)236-0390
Co. E-mail: info@nbmbaa.org
URL: http://www.nbmbaa.org
Contact: Jesse J. Tyson, President
Description: Creates educational opportunities to form professional and economic growth of African-Americans. Develops partnerships to its members and provides educational programs to increase the

awareness on business field. **Founded:** 1970. **Publications:** *Black MBA* (Semiannual); *National Black MBA Association--Newsletter* (Monthly). **Educational Activities:** National Black Masters of Business Administration Annual Conference and Exposition (Annual). **Awards:** NBMBAA Graduate Scholarships Program.

32686 ■ National Business Education Association (NBEA)
1914 Association Dr.
Reston, VA 20191-1596
Ph: (703)860-8300
Fax: (703)620-4483
Co. E-mail: nbea@nbea.org
URL: http://www.nbea.org
Contact: Maurice S. Henderson, President
E-mail: maurice.henderson@emich.edu
Description: Teachers of business subjects in secondary and postsecondary schools and colleges; administrators and research workers in business education; businesspersons interested in business education; teachers in educational institutions training business teachers; high school and college students preparing for careers in business. **Founded:** 1892. **Publications:** *Business Education Forum-- Professional Leadership Roster Issue* (Quarterly); *Business Education Forum: Official Journal of the National Business Education Association*; *National Business Education Yearbook* (Annual); *Business Education Forum*; *Keying In* (Quarterly); *NBEA Yearbook* (Annual). **Educational Activities:** National Business Education Association Convention (Annual). **Awards:** Collegiate or University Teacher of the Year (Annual); Distinguished Service Award for an Administrator or Supervisor (Annual); Distinguished Service Award (Annual); Postsecondary Teacher of the Year (Annual); Secondary Teacher of the Year (Annual); Award of Merit (Annual); Distinguished Service Awards (Annual).

32687 ■ Online Learning
260 Dalhousie St., Ste. 204
Ottawa, ON, Canada K1N 7E4
Ph: (613)241-0018
Fax: (613)241-0019
Co. E-mail: cnie-rcie@cnie-rcie.ca
URL: http://www.cnie-rcie.ca
Contact: Marc Imbeault, President
URL(s): onlinelearningconsortium.org/publications/olj_main www.cnie-rcie.ca/?q=node/70. **Released:** 4/year. **Price:** $185, Individuals for print; $49.95, Individuals single issue (print).

EDUCATIONAL PROGRAMS

32688 ■ ACCS - Advanced Cisco Campus Switching (Onsite)
Seminar Information Service Inc.
20 Executive Park, Ste. 120
Irvine, CA 92614
Ph: (949)261-9104
Free: 877-SEM-INFO
Fax: (949)261-1963
Co. E-mail: info@seminarinformation.com
URL: http://www.seminarinformation.com
Price: $199. **Description:** Covers Catalyst 6000 Series Architecture; Catalyst 2948G-L3 Configuration; Layer 2 and Layer3 Forwarding; Switching Quality of Service Fundamentals and Configuration; Dynamic and Private VLANs; VLAN Access Control Lists; MLS and CEF Operation; High Availability Options for the 6000 Series; FlexWAN Configuration and Operation; and Catalyst 6000 Hybrid to Native IOS Conversion. **Audience:** Industry professionals.

32689 ■ Adobe Acrobat I (Onsite)
EEI Communications
8945 Guilford Rd., Ste. 145
Columbia, MD 21046
Ph: (410)309-8200
Free: 888-253-2762
Fax: (410)630-3980
Co. E-mail: train@eeicom.com
URL: http://www.eeicom.com/eei-training-services
URL(s): www.cvent.com. **Description:** Covers creating PDF documents, including using hyperlinks, bookmarks, sound clips, and security. **Audience:**

General public. **Telecommunication Services:** train@eeicom.com.

32690 ■ Adobe After Effects I (Onsite)
EEI Communications
8945 Guilford Rd., Ste. 145
Columbia, MD 21046
Ph: (410)309-8200
Free: 888-253-2762
Fax: (410)630-3980
Co. E-mail: train@eeicom.com
URL: http://www.eeicom.com/eei-training-services
URL(s): www.eeicom.com. **Description:** Covers using After Effects to create digital composites, smooth 2-D animations, and elaborate special effects. **Audience:** General public. **Telecommunication Services:** train@eeicom.com.

32691 ■ Adobe Director I
EEI Communications
8945 Guilford Rd., Ste. 145
Columbia, MD 21046
Ph: (410)309-8200
Free: 888-253-2762
Fax: (410)630-3980
Co. E-mail: train@eeicom.com
URL: http://www.eeicom.com/eei-training-services
URL(s): www.eeicom.com. **Price:** $745.00. **Description:** Covers how to create interactive training applications, electronic marketing pieces, and presentations utilizing Macromedia Director. **Dates and Locations:** Silver Spring, MD; Alexandria, VA; Hunt Valley, MD; and Columbia, MD. **Telecommunication Services:** train@eeicom.com.

32692 ■ Adobe Director II
EEI Communications
8945 Guilford Rd., Ste. 145
Columbia, MD 21046
Ph: (410)309-8200
Free: 888-253-2762
Fax: (410)630-3980
Co. E-mail: train@eeicom.com
URL: http://www.eeicom.com/eei-training-services
URL(s): www.eeicom.com. **Price:** $1,065.00. **Description:** Seminar introduces Lingo, Director's programming language. **Dates and Locations:** Silver Spring, MD; Alexandria, VA; Hunt Valley, MD; and Columbia, MD. **Telecommunication Services:** train@eeicom.com.

32693 ■ Adobe Flash I (Onsite)
EEI Communications
8945 Guilford Rd., Ste. 145
Columbia, MD 21046
Ph: (410)309-8200
Free: 888-253-2762
Fax: (410)630-3980
Co. E-mail: train@eeicom.com
URL: http://www.eeicom.com/eei-training-services
URL(s): www.eeicom.com/eei-training-services/classes/adobe-flash-cs5/. **Price:** $797.00. **Description:** Covers the basics of Flash including creating animation on the Web that downloads fast and takes up less file space. **Audience:** adobe flash users. **Dates and Locations:** Silver Spring, MD; Columbia, MD; and Alexandria, VA. **Telecommunication Services:** train@eeicom.com.

32694 ■ Adobe Flash II (Onsite)
EEI Communications
8945 Guilford Rd., Ste. 145
Columbia, MD 21046
Ph: (410)309-8200
Free: 888-253-2762
Fax: (410)630-3980
Co. E-mail: train@eeicom.com
URL: http://www.eeicom.com/eei-training-services
URL(s): www.eeicom.com/eei-training-services/classes/adobe-flash-cs5/. **Price:** $797.00 2 days; $1,097.00 3 days. **Description:** Covers advanced techniques including planning, organizing, and creating a Flash project. **Audience:** adobe flash users. **Dates and Locations:** Silver Spring, MD; Columbia, MD; and Alexandria, VA. **Telecommunication Services:** train@eeicom.com.

32695 ■ Adobe FrameMaker I (Onsite)
EEI Communications
8945 Guilford Rd., Ste. 145
Columbia, MD 21046
Ph: (410)309-8200
Free: 888-253-2762
Fax: (410)630-3980
Co. E-mail: train@eeicom.com
URL: http://www.eeicom.com/eei-training-services
URL(s): www.eeicom.com. **Description:** Covers paragraph designs, color use, graphics, headers and footers, tables, and advanced editing techniques. **Audience:** General public. **Telecommunication Services:** train@eeicom.com.

32696 ■ Adobe FrameMaker II (Onsite)
EEI Communications
8945 Guilford Rd., Ste. 145
Columbia, MD 21046
Ph: (410)309-8200
Free: 888-253-2762
Fax: (410)630-3980
Co. E-mail: train@eeicom.com
URL: http://www.eeicom.com/eei-training-services
URL(s): www.eeicom.com. **Description:** Covers cross-references, footnotes, creating a book file, hyperlinks, and exporting to HTML and PDF. **Audience:** General public. **Telecommunication Services:** train@eeicom.com.

32697 ■ Adobe Illustrator I (Onsite)
EEI Communications
8945 Guilford Rd., Ste. 145
Columbia, MD 21046
Ph: (410)309-8200
Free: 888-253-2762
Fax: (410)630-3980
Co. E-mail: train@eeicom.com
URL: http://www.eeicom.com/eei-training-services
URL(s): www.cvent.com. **Description:** Covers basic graphic design features, including creating geometric shapes and free forms, using type, creating graphs, and using the manipulation tools. **Audience:** General public. **Telecommunication Services:** train@eeicom.com.

32698 ■ Adobe Illustrator II (Onsite)
EEI Communications
500 Montgomery St., Ste. 400
Alexandria, VA 22314-5507
Ph: (410)309-8200
Free: 888-253-2762
Fax: (703)683-7310
Co. E-mail: info@eeicom.com
URL: http://www.eeicom.com
Contact: James T. DeGraffenreid, President
URL(s): www.cvent.com. **Description:** Covers some advanced features of Illustrator, including custom brush patterns, blending modes, effects and styles, and image maps. **Audience:** General public. **Telecommunication Services:** info@eeicom.com.

32699 ■ Adobe Illustrator III (Onsite)
EEI Communications
8945 Guilford Rd., Ste. 145
Columbia, MD 21046
Ph: (410)309-8200
Free: 888-253-2762
Fax: (410)630-3980
Co. E-mail: train@eeicom.com
URL: http://www.eeicom.com/eei-training-services
URL(s): www.eeicom.com/. **Description:** Covers one- and two-point perspective, shadows, geometric depth, and masking and pathfinders. **Audience:** General public. **Telecommunication Services:** train@eeicom.com.

32700 ■ Adobe InDesign CS4 Master Class for Designers Training (Onsite)
EEI Communications
8945 Guilford Rd., Ste. 145
Columbia, MD 21046
Ph: (410)309-8200
Free: 888-253-2762

Fax: (410)630-3980
Co. E-mail: train@eeicom.com
URL: http://www.eeicom.com/eei-training-services
Description: Master Adobe InDesign CS4's styles, text processing capabilities, table-creation tools, automation features, and in-document creativity enhancements to free up countless hours from smaller tasks and concentrate on designing. **Audience:** Industry professionals.

32701 ■ Adobe InDesign I (Onsite)
EEI Communications
8945 Guilford Rd., Ste. 145
Columbia, MD 21046
Ph: (410)309-8200
Free: 888-253-2762
Fax: (410)630-3980
Co. E-mail: train@eeicom.com
URL: http://www.eeicom.com/eei-training-services
URL(s): www.eeicom.com/eei-training-services/classes/adobe-indesign-cs5/. **Price:** $797.00. **Description:** Covers basic techniques for creating graphic-intensive documents including editing master pages, placeholder frames, applying color, and flowing and threading text. **Audience:** adobe indesign users. **Dates and Locations:** Silver Spring, MD; and Alexandria, VA. **Telecommunication Services:** train@eeicom.com.

32702 ■ Adobe InDesign II (Onsite)
EEI Communications
500 Montgomery St., Ste. 400
Alexandria, VA 22314-5507
Ph: (410)309-8200
Free: 888-253-2762
Fax: (703)683-7310
Co. E-mail: info@eeicom.com
URL: http://www.eeicom.com
Contact: James T. DeGraffenreid, President
URL(s): www.eeicom.com/eei-training-services/classes/adobe-indesign-cs5/. **Price:** $745.00. **Description:** Covers techniques for creating graphic-intensive documents including typography, decorative and special font features, exporting documents, importing and linking graphics, drawing straight and curved segments, and advanced frame techniques. **Audience:** adobe indesign users. **Dates and Locations:** Silver Spring, MD; Alexandria, VA; and Hunt Valley, MD. **Telecommunication Services:** info@eeicom.com.

32703 ■ Adobe InDesign with InCopy for Workgroups Training (Onsite)
EEI Communications
8945 Guilford Rd., Ste. 145
Columbia, MD 21046
Ph: (410)309-8200
Free: 888-253-2762
Fax: (410)630-3980
Co. E-mail: train@eeicom.com
URL: http://www.eeicom.com/eei-training-services
Description: Learn a professional writing and editing program that tightly integrates with Adobe InDesign for a complete solution, including assigning editors to work on parts of pages, spreads, or entire documents in parallel with designers, significantly decreasing the production time for projects. **Audience:** Industry professionals.

32704 ■ Adobe Photoshop I (Onsite)
EEI Communications
8945 Guilford Rd., Ste. 145
Columbia, MD 21046
Ph: (410)309-8200
Free: 888-253-2762
Fax: (410)630-3980
Co. E-mail: train@eeicom.com
URL: http://www.eeicom.com/eei-training-services
URL(s): www.eeicom.com/eei-training-services/classes/adobe-photoshop-cs5/. **Price:** $797.00. **Description:** Covers the basic photo manipulation features of Photoshop. **Audience:** adobe photoshop users. **Dates and Locations:** Silver Spring, MD; Alexandria, VA; and Columbia, MD. **Telecommunication Services:** train@eeicom.com.

32705 ■ Adobe Photoshop II (Onsite)
EEI Communications
8945 Guilford Rd., Ste. 145
Columbia, MD 21046
Ph: (410)309-8200
Free: 888-253-2762
Fax: (410)630-3980
Co. E-mail: train@eeicom.com
URL: http://www.eeicom.com/eei-training-services
URL(s): www.eeicom.com/eei-training-services/classes/adobe-photoshop-cs5/. **Price:** $1,097.00. **Description:** Covers intermediate techniques including channel and masking, paths, layering, spot techniques, proper file formatting, and gamuts and color transition issues. **Audience:** adobe photoshop users. **Dates and Locations:** Silver Spring, MD; and Alexandria, VA. **Telecommunication Services:** train@eeicom.com.

32706 ■ Adobe Photoshop III: Tips and Tricks (Onsite)
EEI Communications
8945 Guilford Rd., Ste. 145
Columbia, MD 21046
Ph: (410)309-8200
Free: 888-253-2762
Fax: (410)630-3980
Co. E-mail: train@eeicom.com
URL: http://www.eeicom.com/eei-training-services
URL(s): www.eeicom.com/eei-training-services/classes/adobe-photoshop-cs5/. **Price:** $497.00. **Description:** Covers advanced Photoshop techniques and effects. **Audience:** adobe photoshop users. **Dates and Locations:** Silver Spring, MD; and Alexandria, VA. **Telecommunication Services:** train@eeicom.com.

32707 ■ Adobe Premiere I (Onsite)
EEI Communications
8945 Guilford Rd., Ste. 145
Columbia, MD 21046
Ph: (410)309-8200
Free: 888-253-2762
Fax: (410)630-3980
Co. E-mail: train@eeicom.com
URL: http://www.eeicom.com/eei-training-services
URL(s): www.eeicom.com/eei-training-services. **Price:** $797.00. **Description:** Covers an introduction to video capture and video editing utilizing Premiere. **Dates and Locations:** Silver Spring, MD. **Telecommunication Services:** train@eeicom.com.

32708 ■ Advanced Grammar Roundtable (Onsite)
EEI Communications
8945 Guilford Rd., Ste. 145
Columbia, MD 21046
Ph: (410)309-8200
Free: 888-253-2762
Fax: (410)630-3980
Co. E-mail: train@eeicom.com
URL: http://www.eeicom.com/eei-training-services
Price: $797.00. **Description:** Discuss various philosophies about grammar, the origins of grammar rules and the case against "rule-based" grammar, diagram sentences, review grammar concepts as needed, examine particles, determiners and interrupters, examine the difference between an absolute phrase and a descriptive one. **Dates and Locations:** Silver Spring, MD; and Alexandria, VA.

32709 ■ Advanced PC Configuration, Troubleshooting and Data Recovery: Hands-On (Onsite)
Seminar Information Service Inc.
20 Executive Park, Ste. 120
Irvine, CA 92614
Ph: (949)261-9104
Free: 877-SEM-INFO
Fax: (949)261-1963
Co. E-mail: info@seminarinformation.com
URL: http://www.seminarinformation.com
URL(s): www.seminarinformation.com. **Description:** Learn how to: Recover lost files and directories; Revive non-bootable floppies and hard disks; Create emergency rescue disks to recover crashed Windows systems; Detect, isolate and contain damage from virus programs; Create full disk images for complete backups; Remove unwanted start-up programs from the Registry; Examine system status with Windows XP Computer Management tools; Install and configure a simple TCP/IP network. **Audience:** Industry professionals. **Telecommunication Services:** info@seminarinformation.com.

32710 ■ Advertising Research (Onsite)
Seminar Information Service Inc.
20 Executive Park, Ste. 120
Irvine, CA 92614
Ph: (949)261-9104
Free: 877-SEM-INFO
Fax: (949)261-1963
Co. E-mail: info@seminarinformation.com
URL: http://www.seminarinformation.com
Price: $1,895.00. **Description:** Provides a practical and a comprehensive framework for classifying various advertising research methods based on what they measure, how they measure it and how good they are at it. Participants will be able to evaluate and select among the numerous procedures used in practice to facilitate key advertising decisions.

32711 ■ Air Conditioning & Refrigeration (Onsite)
American Trainco, Inc.
9785 S Maroon Cir., Ste. 300
Englewood, CO 80112
Ph: (303)531-4560
Free: 877-978-7246
Fax: (303)531-4565
Co. E-mail: Sales@AmericanTrainco.com
URL: http://wwww.americantrainco.com
URL(s): www.americantrainco.com/courses/air%20conditioning/dtlac.aspx. **Price:** $990. **Description:** Course designed for anyone who needs to understand basic operation, maintenance, and troubleshooting of air conditioning and refrigeration systems in order to improve efficiencies and uptime at their industrial plants and large building facilities. **Audience:** Industry professionals.

32712 ■ AMA's PMP Exam Prep Express (Onsite)
American Management Association (AMA)
1601 Broadway
New York, NY 10019-7420
Ph: (212)586-8100
Free: 877-566-9441
Fax: (212)903-8168
Co. E-mail: customerservice@amanet.org
URL: http://www.amanet.org
Contact: Edward T. Reilly, President
URL(s): www.amanet.org/training/seminars/PMP-Exam-Prep-Express.aspx#who_should_attend. **Price:** $2,195, Non-members; $1,995, Members AMA; $1,708, Members GSA. **Description:** Three-day seminar to increase the probability of obtaining your PMP. **Audience:** Project managers, program managers, and project team leaders.

32713 ■ Arc Flash Protection & Electrical Safety 70E
American Trainco, Inc.
9785 S Maroon Cir., Ste. 300
Englewood, CO 80112
Ph: (303)531-4560
Free: 877-978-7246
Fax: (303)531-4565
Co. E-mail: Sales@AmericanTrainco.com
URL: http://www.americantrainco.com
URL(s): www.americantrainco.com/courses/arc%20flash%20training/dtles.aspx. **Price:** $990. **Description:** Training course designed to save lives, prevent disabling injuries, and prevent damage to plants, buildings and equipment. Participants learn about personal safety for working on or around electrical systems and equipment, how to use proper materials and procedures for doing electrical work, and the potential consequences for themselves and others if they don't. **Audience:** Electricians, maintenance supervisors and machine operators.

32714 ■ Assertiveness Training (Onsite)
American Management Association (AMA)
1601 Broadway
New York, NY 10019-7420
Ph: (212)586-8100

Free: 877-566-9441
Fax: (212)903-8168
Co. E-mail: customerservice@amanet.org
URL: http://www.amanet.org
Contact: Edward T. Reilly, President
URL(s): www.amanet.org/training/seminars/onsite/
Assertiveness-Training.aspx. **Description:** Three-day
seminar to enhance your assertiveness skills at all
levels in the organization. **Audience:** Associates,
business professionals, team leaders and individual
contributors.

**32715 ■ Basic Electricity for the Non
Electrician (Onsite)**
American Trainco, Inc.
9785 S Maroon Cir., Ste. 300
Englewood, CO 80112
Ph: (303)531-4560
Free: 877-978-7246
Fax: (303)531-4565
Co. E-mail: Sales@AmericanTrainco.com
URL: http://www.americantrainco.com
URL(s): www.americantrainco.com/courses/
basic%20electricity/dtlbe.aspx. **Price:** $990. **Descrip-
tion:** Understanding and working with industrial
electricity. **Audience:** Mechanics, HVAC technicians,
and machine operators .

**32716 ■ Basic Problem Solving Techniques
(Onsite)**
Seminar Information Service Inc.
20 Executive Park, Ste. 120
Irvine, CA 92614
Ph: (949)261-9104
Free: 877-SEM-INFO
Fax: (949)261-1963
Co. E-mail: info@seminarinformation.com
URL: http://www.seminarinformation.com
Price: Contact for fee. **Description:** With the help of
several qualitative, quantitative, and creative problem
solving methods participants develop their ability to
recognize and solve problems through their own ef-
forts. **Dates and Locations:** Waukesha, WI.

**32717 ■ Basics of Commercial Contracting
(Onsite)**
Seminar Information Service Inc.
20 Executive Park, Ste. 120
Irvine, CA 92614
Ph: (949)261-9104
Free: 877-SEM-INFO
Fax: (949)261-1963
Co. E-mail: info@seminarinformation.com
URL: http://www.seminarinformation.com
Price: $1,095. **Description:** Learn the key practical
and legal principles applicable to business dealings,
as well as a thorough understanding of the Uniform
Commercial Code (UCC). **Audience:** People know
the Uniform Commercial Code. **Dates and Loca-
tions:** Arlington, VA.

**32718 ■ Best Practices in Java
Programming: Hands-On (Onsite)**
Seminar Information Service Inc.
20 Executive Park, Ste. 120
Irvine, CA 92614
Ph: (949)261-9104
Free: 877-SEM-INFO
Fax: (949)261-1963
Co. E-mail: info@seminarinformation.com
URL: http://www.seminarinformation.com
URL(s): www.seminarinformation.com/qqbtlg/best-
practices-in-java-programming-hands-on. **Price:**
$2,990, Onsite. **Description:** Learn how to: Apply
Java best practices to increase productivity and build
fast, secure and reliable applications; Optimize the
compilation, deployment and testing of software applications; Solve architectural problems with proven
design patterns and advanced language features;
Code securely in Java and authenticate with industry-
standard security frameworks; Maximize software
performance; Improve the reliability of threaded applications; Extend application functionality non-
intrusively. **Audience:** Developers, architects and
java programmers. **Dates and Locations:** 2015 Feb
10-13; venue not reported. **Telecommunication Services:** info@seminarinformation.com.

**32719 ■ Boiler Operation, Maintenance &
Safety (Onsite)**
American Trainco, Inc.
9785 S Maroon Cir., Ste. 300
Englewood, CO 80112
Ph: (303)531-4560
Free: 877-978-7246
Fax: (303)531-4565
Co. E-mail: Sales@AmericanTrainco.com
URL: http://www.americantrainco.com
URL(s): www.americantrainco.com/courses/
boiler%20operation/dtlbo.aspx. **Price:** $990. **Descrip-
tion:** Seminar designed to teach building and facility
maintenance personnel how to service their own
boiler safely reducing the need for outside service
contractors, while at the same time increases your
confidence and comfort level in operating and
maintaining your own broilers. **Audience:** Building
maintenance personnel, technicians and engineers .

**32720 ■ Building Applications with Microsoft
Access 2007: Hands-On (Onsite)**
Seminar Information Service Inc.
20 Executive Park, Ste. 120
Irvine, CA 92614
Ph: (949)261-9104
Free: 877-SEM-INFO
Fax: (949)261-1963
Co. E-mail: info@seminarinformation.com
URL: http://www.seminarinformation.com
Description: Learn how to: Develop distributable
applications with Microsoft Access 2007; Incorporate
user specifications to enhance application functionality; Customize applications by dynamically setting
properties and executing methods; Assemble expressions into VBA statements using variables and
intrinsic functions; Control program flow with loops
and decision-making logic; Apply Data Access
Objects (DAO) to incorporate business rules; Central-
ize the error handling process. **Audience:** Industry
professionals.

**32721 ■ Business Process Reengineering for
Competitive Advantage (Onsite)**
Seminar Information Service Inc.
20 Executive Park, Ste. 120
Irvine, CA 92614
Ph: (949)261-9104
Free: 877-SEM-INFO
Fax: (949)261-1963
Co. E-mail: info@seminarinformation.com
URL: http://www.seminarinformation.com
URL(s): www.seminarinformation.com. **Description:**
Learn how to: Select, organize and implement a busi-
ness reengineering project using CLAMBRE/UML;
Achieve competitive advantage by capitalizing on
technology opportunities and the application of UML
tools; Maximize customer satisfaction by matching
process design to customer needs; Identify typical
symptoms of business process dysfunction; Redesign
workflow and structure successfully within the business; Ensure best practice through the application of
business patterns. **Audience:** Industry professionals.
Telecommunication Services: info@seminarinfor-
mation.com.

**32722 ■ C++ Programming for Non-C
Programmers (Onsite)**
Seminar Information Service Inc.
20 Executive Park, Ste. 120
Irvine, CA 92614
Ph: (949)261-9104
Free: 877-SEM-INFO
Fax: (949)261-1963
Co. E-mail: info@seminarinformation.com
URL: http://www.seminarinformation.com
Price: $2,595. **Description:** Provides an accelerated
introduction to the most essential components of the
C language on the first day, followed by four days
focus on object-oriented programming with C. **Audi-
ence:** Programmers. **Dates and Locations:** Cities
throughout the United States.

32723 ■ Certified Ethical Hacker (Onsite)
Seminar Information Service Inc.
20 Executive Park, Ste. 120
Irvine, CA 92614
Ph: (949)261-9104

Free: 877-SEM-INFO
Fax: (949)261-1963
Co. E-mail: info@seminarinformation.com
URL: http://www.seminarinformation.com
Price: $3,395.00. **Description:** Learn to footprint
organizations, perform port scanning, and exploit a
variety of systems and architectures, including
hands-on labs. You'll also receive the CEH study
guide, Certified Ethical Hacker Exam Prep, CDs
packed with security tools, templates, and white
papers, practice exam questions, and an exam
voucher.

32724 ■ Chilled Water Systems (Onsite)
American Trainco, Inc.
9785 S Maroon Cir., Ste. 300
Englewood, CO 80112
Ph: (303)531-4560
Free: 877-978-7246
Fax: (303)531-4565
Co. E-mail: Sales@AmericanTrainco.com
URL: http://www.americantrainco.com
URL(s): www.americantrainco.com/courses/in-house/
dtlih70.aspx. **Description:** Learn to control your
systems and properly maintain them, getting the most
out of them. **Audience:** Technicians, engineers and
managers .

**32725 ■ Creative Problem Solving and
Strategic Thinking (Onsite)**
Fred Pryor Seminars & CareerTrack
5700 Broadmoor St., Ste. 300
Mission, KS 66202
Ph: (800)780-8476
Free: 800-780-8476
Fax: (913)967-8849
Co. E-mail: customerservice@pryor.com
URL: http://www.pryor.com
Contact: Phil Love, Chief Executive Officer
URL(s): www.pryor.com/mkt_info/seminars/desc/PU.
asp. **Price:** $149. **Description:** Learn an innovative
approach to problem solving. **Audience:** Profession-
als.

**32726 ■ Critical Thinking Skills-Strategic
Planning in Action (Onsite)**
Seminar Information Service Inc.
20 Executive Park, Ste. 120
Irvine, CA 92614
Ph: (949)261-9104
Free: 877-SEM-INFO
Fax: (949)261-1963
Co. E-mail: info@seminarinformation.com
URL: http://www.seminarinformation.com
Price: $355, Members; $460, Non-members. **De-
scription:** Seminar provides participants with tools,
techniques and the critical thinking skills to identify
their critical measures of success, the requirements
of internal and external customers, including the
strengths and weaknesses of their staff. **Audience:**
Experienced managers and supervisors . **Dates and
Locations:** Waukesha, WI; and Palatine, IL.

32727 ■ Dealing with Competing Demands
Canadian Management Centre (CMC)
150 York St., 5th Fl.
Toronto, ON, Canada M5H 3S5
Free: 877-262-2519
Fax: (416)214-6047
Co. E-mail: cmcinfo@cmcoutperform.com
URL: http://cmcoutperform.com
Contact: John Wright, President
URL(s): www.cmctraining.org. **Description:** Covers
the skills necessary to manage your objectives with
success, including prioritizing, realistic objectives,
effective use of communication to meet your goals,
and utilize control stress. **Audience:** General public
and industry professionals. **Telecommunication Ser-
vices:** cmcinfo@cmctraining.org.

**32728 ■ Defending Windows Networks
(Onsite)**
Seminar Information Service Inc.
20 Executive Park, Ste. 120
Irvine, CA 92614
Ph: (949)261-9104
Free: 877-SEM-INFO

Fax: (949)261-1963
Co. E-mail: info@seminarinformation.com
URL: http://www.seminarinformation.com
Price: $2,995.00. **Description:** Lab-intensive to illustrate defense techniques against real-world threats, instead of simply addressing software security features, including how attacks are performed, how they can compromise a Windows Server Network Infrastructure, and how you can lock down the network.

32729 ■ Deploying Intrusion Detection Systems: Hands-On (Onsite)
Seminar Information Service Inc.
20 Executive Park, Ste. 120
Irvine, CA 92614
Ph: (949)261-9104
Free: 877-SEM-INFO
Fax: (949)261-1963
Co. E-mail: info@seminarinformation.com
URL: http://www.seminarinformation.com
URL(s): www.seminarinformation.com. **Description:** Learn how to: Detect and respond to network- and host-based intruder attacks; Integrate intrusion detection systems (IDS) into your current network topology; Analyze IDS alerts using the latest tools and techniques; Identify methods hackers use to attack systems; Recognize detection avoidance schemes; Stop attackers with Intrusion Prevention Systems (IPSs). **Audience:** Industry professionals. **Telecommunication Services:** info@seminarinformation.com.

32730 ■ Deploying Virtual Server and Workstation Technology: Hands-On (Onsite)
Seminar Information Service Inc.
20 Executive Park, Ste. 120
Irvine, CA 92614
Ph: (949)261-9104
Free: 877-SEM-INFO
Fax: (949)261-1963
Co. E-mail: info@seminarinformation.com
URL: http://www.seminarinformation.com
URL(s): www.seminarinformation.com. **Description:** Learn how to: Implement VMware and Microsoft virtual machine (VM) technologies; Combine Windows and Linux workstations and servers on a single platform; Leverage VMs to build testing, support and training environments; Partition physical servers to decrease operating costs; Migrate from physical to virtual machines; Manage VMs throughout the enterprise. **Audience:** Industry professionals. **Telecommunication Services:** info@seminarinformation.com.

32731 ■ Designing and Building Great Web Pages: Hands-On (Onsite)
Seminar Information Service Inc.
20 Executive Park, Ste. 120
Irvine, CA 92614
Ph: (949)261-9104
Free: 877-SEM-INFO
Fax: (949)261-1963
Co. E-mail: info@seminarinformation.com
URL: http://www.seminarinformation.com
Price: $2,890.00. **Description:** Learn to build powerful Web content that effectively conveys your message; Create graphical content using Photoshop CS2, Fireworks 8 and Flash 8; Develop Web page content with FrontPage and Dreamweaver 8; Generate complex Web pages using Cascading Style Sheets, tables and layers; and Enhance Web pages with special effects and DHTML.

32732 ■ Developing Effective Software Estimation Techniques (Onsite)
Seminar Information Service Inc.
20 Executive Park, Ste. 120
Irvine, CA 92614
Ph: (949)261-9104
Free: 877-SEM-INFO
Fax: (949)261-1963
Co. E-mail: info@seminarinformation.com
URL: http://www.seminarinformation.com
Description: Learn how to prepare a software project estimate through an iterative process; Develop an initial estimate using the expert judgment method; Apply historical data for greater precision in an estimate; Refine the size or scope estimate using a component-based method; Perform Function Point calculations to determine the magnitude of a project; Translate a size or scope estimate into a time, schedule and cost estimate. **Audience:** Industry professionals.

32733 ■ Developing Effective Training
Seminar Information Service Inc.
20 Executive Park, Ste. 120
Irvine, CA 92614
Ph: (949)261-9104
Free: 877-SEM-INFO
Fax: (949)261-1963
Co. E-mail: info@seminarinformation.com
URL: http://www.seminarinformation.com
Price: $1,495.00. **Description:** Provides less experienced trainers with an overview of the training process and shows them how to make each element yield effective learning results. **Dates and Locations:** New York, NY.

32734 ■ Developing SQL Queries for SQL Server: Hands-On (Onsite)
Seminar Information Service Inc.
20 Executive Park, Ste. 120
Irvine, CA 92614
Ph: (949)261-9104
Free: 877-SEM-INFO
Fax: (949)261-1963
Co. E-mail: info@seminarinformation.com
URL: http://www.seminarinformation.com
Price: $2,990, Onsite. **Description:** Learn how to develop complex and robust SQL queries for SQL Server 2005 and SQL Server 2000; Query multiple tables with inner joins, outer joins and self joins; Transform data with built-in functions; Summarize data using aggregation and grouping; Execute analytic functions to calculate ranks; Build simple and correlated sub-queries. **Audience:** Those who are developing systems using SQL Server databases, or who are using SQL to extract and analyze data from SQL Server databases. **Dates and Locations:** 2015 Feb 03-06; venue not reported.

32735 ■ Digital Photography Techniques (Onsite)
EEI Communications
500 Montgomery St., Ste. 400
Alexandria, VA 22314-5507
Ph: (410)309-8200
Free: 888-253-2762
Fax: (703)683-7310
Co. E-mail: info@eeicom.com
URL: http://www.eeicom.com
Contact: James T. DeGraffenreid, President
URL(s): www.eeicom.com. **Description:** Covers using a digital camera, and manipulating digital pictures with Photoshop. **Audience:** General public. **Telecommunication Services:** info@eeicom.com.

32736 ■ Effective Training Techniques for Group Leaders (Onsite)
Seminar Information Service Inc.
20 Executive Park, Ste. 120
Irvine, CA 92614
Ph: (949)261-9104
Free: 877-SEM-INFO
Fax: (949)261-1963
Co. E-mail: info@seminarinformation.com
URL: http://www.seminarinformation.com
URL(s): www.seminarinformation.com/qqadnm/effective-training-techniques-for-group-leaders. **Description:** Provides group leaders precise and practical methods to train their employees. Leaders also learn to spot worker training needs and provide effective on-the-job training. **Audience:** Team leaders. **Telecommunication Services:** info@seminarinformation.com.

32737 ■ Electrical Ladder Drawings, Schematics & Design (Onsite)
American Trainco, Inc.
9785 S Maroon Cir., Ste. 300
Englewood, CO 80112
Ph: (303)531-4560
Free: 877-978-7246

Fax: (303)531-4565
Co. E-mail: Sales@AmericanTrainco.com
URL: http://www.americantrainco.com
URL(s): www.americantrainco.com/courses/electrical%20ladder%20drawings/dtlscm.aspx. **Price:** $990. **Description:** Training will include exercises where participants create schematic diagrams based on circuit descriptions, as well as interpreting schematic drawings so that they can provide verbal or written circuit descriptions and an understanding of several types of drawings and diagrams including Block, Pictorial, One-line, Wiring, Terminal, and Schematic. **Audience:** Engineers, electricians, plant & facility managers and mechanics.

32738 ■ Electrical Troubleshooting & Preventive Maintenance (Onsite)
American Trainco, Inc.
9785 S Maroon Cir., Ste. 300
Englewood, CO 80112
Ph: (303)531-4560
Free: 877-978-7246
Fax: (303)531-4565
Co. E-mail: Sales@AmericanTrainco.com
URL: http://www.americantrainco.com
Price: $000. **Description:** Two-day seminar designed for anyone who needs to sharpen their electrical troubleshooting skills in order to increase efficiencies and uptime at their industrial plant or building facility. **Audience:** Electricians, Mechanic, HVAC Technicians and students . **Dates and Locations:** 2015 May 28-29; venue not reported.

32739 ■ Electronic Editing (Onsite)
EEI Communications
8945 Guilford Rd., Ste. 145
Columbia, MD 21046
Ph: (410)309-8200
Free: 888-253-2762
Fax: (410)630-3980
Co. E-mail: train@eeicom.com
URL: http://www.eeicom.com/eei-training-services
URL(s): www.eeicom.com. **Description:** Seminar that covers marking copy using style sheets, tracking changes and comparing documents, using the "search and replace" function, analyzing global changes, writing macros to make repetitive tasks simpler, checking references against citations, and develop a systematic approach to electronic manuscripts. **Audience:** Editors and writers. **Telecommunication Services:** train@eeicom.com.

32740 ■ Forensic Photoshop (Onsite)
EEI Communications
8945 Guilford Rd., Ste. 145
Columbia, MD 21046
Ph: (410)309-8200
Free: 888-253-2762
Fax: (410)630-3980
Co. E-mail: train@eeicom.com
URL: http://www.eeicom.com/eei-training-services
Description: Designed for law enforcement and Homeland Security personnel that outlines the processes for using Photoshop in a forensic environment.

32741 ■ Functional Gage Design (Onsite)
Seminar Information Service Inc.
20 Executive Park, Ste. 120
Irvine, CA 92614
Ph: (949)261-9104
Free: 877-SEM-INFO
Fax: (949)261-1963
Co. E-mail: info@seminarinformation.com
URL: http://www.seminarinformation.com
Description: Learn about Gage design principles/tolerances; Ways to avoid commonly used but improper gaging and inspection techniques; Inspection machines; Substitute systems; Surface plate inspection and more.

32742 ■ Generators & Emergency Power (Onsite)
American Trainco, Inc.
9785 S Maroon Cir., Ste. 300
Englewood, CO 80112
Ph: (303)531-4560
Free: 877-978-7246

Fax: (303)531-4565
Co. E-mail: Sales@AmericanTrainco.com
URL: http://wwww.americantrainco.com
URL(s): www.americantrainco.com/courses/generators/dtlgn.aspx. **Price:** $990. **Description:** Learn what you can do, and should do with generators, to make sure your facility will keep running even when the electricity to your facility doesn't. **Audience:** Facility managers, building owners, maintenance managers, building engineers and maintenance technicians.

32743 ■ Hands-On UNIX and Linux Tools and Utilities (Onsite)
Seminar Information Service Inc.
20 Executive Park, Ste. 120
Irvine, CA 92614
Ph: (949)261-9104
Free: 877-SEM-INFO
Fax: (949)261-1963
Co. E-mail: info@seminarinformation.com
URL: http://www.seminarinformation.com
Description: Become an expert builder and user of UNIX/Linux tools and utilities, including how to employ standard, programmable text filters to manipulate text and data, build shell scripts to automate routine tasks, and achieve significant productivity gains by matching the mix of tools to the task at hand. **Audience:** Systems and database administrators, software engineers and programmers.

32744 ■ How to Conduct Your Own Energy Audit (Onsite)
American Trainco, Inc.
9785 S Maroon Cir., Ste. 300
Englewood, CO 80112
Ph: (303)531-4560
Free: 877-978-7246
Fax: (303)531-4565
Co. E-mail: Sales@AmericanTrainco.com
URL: http://www.americantrainco.com
URL(s): www.americantrainco.com/courses/energy%20audit/dtleg.aspx. **Description:** Two-day hands-on seminar shows you how to find quick and inexpensive ways to immediately cut energy costs at your plant or facility. **Audience:** Industry professionals.

32745 ■ HVAC Controls & Air Distribution (Onsite)
American Trainco, Inc.
9785 S Maroon Cir., Ste. 300
Englewood, CO 80112
Ph: (303)531-4560
Free: 877-978-7246
Fax: (303)531-4565
Co. E-mail: Sales@AmericanTrainco.com
URL: http://www.americantrainco.com
URL(s): www.americantrainco.com/courses/hvac%20controls/dtlhve.aspx. **Price:** $990. **Description:** Learn how to "control" their controls, and how to use fundamental air distribution principles for achieving consistent HVAC comfort and efficiency in buildings, plants and facilities. **Audience:** Supervisors, building owners, managers, building maintenance technicians and engineers.

32746 ■ Improving Editing Skills (Onsite)
EEI Communications
8945 Guilford Rd., Ste. 145
Columbia, MD 21046
Ph: (410)309-8200
Free: 888-253-2762
Fax: (410)630-3980
Co. E-mail: train@eeicom.com
URL: http://www.eeicom.com/eei-training-services
URL(s): www.eeicom.com. **Description:** Covers the editorial issues such as active and passive voice, lists, redundancy, and sentence construction. **Audience:** Editors and writers. **Telecommunication Services:** train@eeicom.com.

32747 ■ Installing, Configuring, and Troubleshooting Microsoft SQL Server
Seminar Information Service Inc.
20 Executive Park, Ste. 120
Irvine, CA 92614
Ph: (949)261-9104
Free: 877-SEM-INFO

Fax: (949)261-1963
Co. E-mail: info@seminarinformation.com
URL: http://www.seminarinformation.com
Price: $899.00. **Description:** Learn to manage your database projects efficiently, knowledgeable and effectively. **Dates and Locations:** Cities throughout the United States.

32748 ■ Instrumentation, Process Measurement & Control (Onsite)
American Trainco, Inc.
9785 S Maroon Cir., Ste. 300
Englewood, CO 80112
Ph: (303)531-4560
Free: 877-978-7246
Fax: (303)531-4565
Co. E-mail: Sales@AmericanTrainco.com
URL: http://www.americantrainco.com
URL(s): www.americantrainco.com/courses/instrumentation%20process%20management/dtlia.aspx. **Price:** $990. **Description:** Learn why it is necessary to measure what is going on with your systems and equipment, how to measure it, and what those measurements may mean in terms of action that should be taken to eliminate future downtime and unnecessary expense. **Audience:** Electricians, mechanics, and engineers.

32749 ■ Integrating Forms and Databases on the Web (Onsite)
EEI Communications
500 Montgomery St., Ste. 400
Alexandria, VA 22314-5507
Ph: (410)309-8200
Free: 888-253-2762
Fax: (703)683-7310
Co. E-mail: info@eeicom.com
URL: http://www.eeicom.com
Contact: James T. DeGraffenreid, President
URL(s): www.eeicom.com. **Description:** Covers the basics of integrating a database with the world wide web using a Microsoft Access database, active server pages, or Microsoft's Internet Information Server. **Audience:** General public. **Telecommunication Services:** info@eeicom.com.

32750 ■ Introduction to OS X
URL(s): www.eeicom.com/eei-training-services. **Description:** Seminar designed for beginning MAC users, which serves as the foundation for all MAC courses. **Telecommunication Services:** train@eeicom.com.

32751 ■ Introduction to System and Network Security (Onsite)
Seminar Information Service Inc.
20 Executive Park, Ste. 120
Irvine, CA 92614
Ph: (949)261-9104
Free: 877-SEM-INFO
Fax: (949)261-1963
Co. E-mail: info@seminarinformation.com
URL: http://www.seminarinformation.com
Price: $2,990, Onsite. **Description:** Learn to analyze your exposure to information assurance threats and protect your organization's systems and data; Reduce your susceptibility to an attack by deploying firewalls, data encryption and other countermeasures; Manage risks emanating from inside the organization and from the Internet; Protect network users from hostile applications and viruses; Identify the security risks that need to be addressed within your organization. **Audience:** Industry professionals. **Dates and Locations:** 2015 Feb 03-06; venue not reported.

32752 ■ Introduction to Windows
EEI Communications
8945 Guilford Rd., Ste. 145
Columbia, MD 21046
Ph: (410)309-8200
Free: 888-253-2762
Fax: (410)630-3980
Co. E-mail: train@eeicom.com
URL: http://www.eeicom.com/eei-training-services
URL(s): www.eeicom.com/eei-training-services. **Price:** $425.00. **Description:** Covers introduction to the PC and the basics of Windows. **Dates and Loca-**

tions: Silver Spring, MD; Alexandria, VA; Hunt Valley, MD; and Columbia, MD. **Telecommunication Services:** train@eeicom.com.

32753 ■ Inventory Control for Maintenance (Onsite)
American Trainco, Inc.
9785 S Maroon Cir., Ste. 300
Englewood, CO 80112
Ph: (303)531-4560
Free: 877-978-7246
Fax: (303)531-4565
Co. E-mail: Sales@AmericanTrainco.com
URL: http://www.americantrainco.com
URL(s): www.americantrainco.com/courses/inventory%20control%20for%20maintenance/dtlim.aspx. **Price:** $990. **Description:** Focus on building an inventory management system that will lead to better control through optimization of inventory quantities, organization of inventory and access to inventory. **Audience:** Maintenance, operations & purchasing managers and personnel.

32754 ■ Java for Non-Programmers (Onsite)
EEI Communications
500 Montgomery St., Ste. 400
Alexandria, VA 22314-5507
Ph: (410)309-8200
Free: 888-253-2762
Fax: (703)683-7310
Co. E-mail: info@eeicom.com
URL: http://www.eeicom.com
Contact: James T. DeGraffenreid, President
URL(s): www.eeicom.com. **Description:** Covers the basics of Java and how to use it for developing websites. **Audience:** General public. **Telecommunication Services:** info@eeicom.com.

32755 ■ Macromedia Authorware I
EEI Communications
8945 Guilford Rd., Ste. 145
Columbia, MD 21046
Ph: (410)309-8200
Free: 888-253-2762
Fax: (410)630-3980
Co. E-mail: train@eeicom.com
URL: http://www.eeicom.com/eei-training-services
URL(s): www.eeicom.com/eei-training-services. **Price:** $1,695.00. **Description:** Covers how to utilize Authorware to develop presentations, quizzes, interactive hypertext, Help systems, and glossaries. **Dates and Locations:** Silver Spring, MD; Alexandria, VA; Hunt Valley, MD; and Columbia, MD. **Telecommunication Services:** train@eeicom.com.

32756 ■ Maintenance Welding (Onsite)
American Trainco, Inc.
9785 S Maroon Cir., Ste. 300
Englewood, CO 80112
Ph: (303)531-4560
Free: 877-978-7246
Fax: (303)531-4565
Co. E-mail: Sales@AmericanTrainco.com
URL: http://www.americantrainco.com
URL(s): www.americantrainco.com/courses/maintenance%20welding/dtlwl.aspx. **Price:** $990. **Description:** Learn welding techniques, welding processes, metal and filler selection, cutting processes, new fabrications, troubleshooting defects, welding repair, personal safety, managing costs, record keeping and more. **Audience:** Welders, maintenance and repair personnel, multi-craft technicians, fabricators, maintenance supervisors and managers, and inspectors.

32757 ■ Managing Stress Productively (Onsite)
Seminar Information Service Inc.
20 Executive Park, Ste. 120
Irvine, CA 92614
Ph: (949)261-9104
Free: 877-SEM-INFO
Fax: (949)261-1963
Co. E-mail: info@seminarinformation.com
URL: http://www.seminarinformation.com
URL(s): www.seminarinformation.com/details.cfm?qc=qqabrx. **Price:** $190, Members; $250, Non-members. **Description:** Learn to deal with the pres-

sures of work and to meet the challenges of stress-related problems. **Audience:** Individuals who are experiencing work-related stress.

32758 ■ Mastering Microsoft Project (Onsite)

Seminar Information Service Inc.
20 Executive Park, Ste. 120
Irvine, CA 92614
Ph: (949)261-9104
Free: 877-SEM-INFO
Fax: (949)261-1963
Co. E-mail: info@seminarinformation.com
URL: http://www.seminarinformation.com
Price: $399. **Description:** Learn how to import tasks into your project from any source; how to pull resources from Microsoft Outlook Active Directory and other sources; merge multiple projects into a single master project; and take advantage of templates and Wizards that can reduce your project planning time. **Audience:** Industry professionals. **Dates and Locations:** Cities throughout the United States.

32759 ■ Mastering QuickBooks Seminars and QuickBooks Classes (Onsite)

Seminar Information Service Inc.
20 Executive Park, Ste. 120
Irvine, CA 92614
Ph: (949)261-9104
Free: 877-SEM-INFO
Fax: (949)261-1963
Co. E-mail: info@seminarinformation.com
URL: http://www.seminarinformation.com
URL(s): www.seminarinformation.com/details.cfm?qc=qqbvef. **Price:** $479.95. **Description:** Discover how QuickBooks can make you and your business more successful. **Audience:** Professionals.

32760 ■ Microsoft Access 2003: A Comprehensive Hands-On Introduction - Building a Foundation for Client/Server Database Applications (Onsite)

Seminar Information Service Inc.
20 Executive Park, Ste. 120
Irvine, CA 92614
Ph: (949)261-9104
Free: 877-SEM-INFO
Fax: (949)261-1963
Co. E-mail: info@seminarinformation.com
URL: http://www.seminarinformation.com
Description: Learn how to: Design robust relational database applications using Microsoft Access 2003; Develop client/server database front-ends; Build database applications quickly using Form, Table, Report and Query wizards; Link to ODBC and OLE-DB data sources to leverage enterprise security; Create and integrate macros into your applications; Implement advanced Access reporting features. **Audience:** Professionals.

32761 ■ Microsoft Access 2007: A Comprehensive Hands-On Introduction (Onsite)

Seminar Information Service Inc.
20 Executive Park, Ste. 120
Irvine, CA 92614
Ph: (949)261-9104
Free: 877-SEM-INFO
Fax: (949)261-1963
Co. E-mail: info@seminarinformation.com
URL: http://www.seminarinformation.com
Price: $2,990. **Description:** Learn how to: Utilize Microsoft Access 2007 to design robust database applications; Apply Form, Table, Report and Query wizards to quickly build database applications; Create and integrate macros into your applications; Quickly modify forms and reports with selective filtering, sorting and grouping; Implement advanced Access reporting features; Link to SharePoint and SQL Server data systems. **Audience:** Industry professionals. **Dates and Locations:** 2015 Feb 10-13; venue not reported.

32762 ■ Microsoft Access 2007 - I (Onsite)

EEI Communications
8945 Guilford Rd., Ste. 145
Columbia, MD 21046
Ph: (410)309-8200
Free: 888-253-2762

Fax: (410)630-3980
Co. E-mail: train@eeicom.com
URL: http://www.eeicom.com/eei-training-services
URL(s): www.eeicom.com/eei-training-services/classes/microsoft-office-2007-training/. **Price:** $797.00. **Description:** Covers basic database concepts using Access. **Audience:** microsoft access users. **Dates and Locations:** Columbia, MD; and Silver Spring, MD. **Telecommunication Services:** train@eeicom.com.

32763 ■ Microsoft Access 2007 - II (Onsite)

EEI Communications
8945 Guilford Rd., Ste. 145
Columbia, MD 21046
Ph: (410)309-8200
Free: 888-253-2762
Fax: (410)630-3980
Co. E-mail: train@eeicom.com
URL: http://www.eeicom.com/eei-training-services
URL(s): www.eeicom.com/eei-training-services/classes/microsoft-office-2007-training/. **Price:** $797.00. **Description:** Covers database concepts including table design and relationships, advanced query, functions, and form and report techniques. **Audience:** microsoft access users. **Dates and Locations:** Silver Spring, MD. **Telecommunication Services:** train@eeicom.com.

32764 ■ Microsoft Excel 2007 - I (Onsite)

EEI Communications
8945 Guilford Rd., Ste. 145
Columbia, MD 21046
Ph: (410)309-8200
Free: 888-253-2762
Fax: (410)630-3980
Co. E-mail: train@eeicom.com
URL: http://www.eeicom.com/eei-training-services
URL(s): www.eeicom.com. **Description:** Covers the basics of creating simple spreadsheets, including absolute and relative formulas, formatting cells and cell ranges, control pages, working with multiple sheets, and using templates. **Audience:** General public. **Telecommunication Services:** train@eeicom.com.

32765 ■ Microsoft FrontPage (Onsite)

EEI Communications
8945 Guilford Rd., Ste. 145
Columbia, MD 21046
Ph: (410)309-8200
Free: 888-253-2762
Fax: (410)630-3980
Co. E-mail: train@eeicom.com
URL: http://www.eeicom.com/eei-training-services
URL(s): www.eeicom.com. **Description:** Covers using FrontPage to develop websites. **Audience:** General public. **Telecommunication Services:** train@eeicom.com.

32766 ■ Microsoft Office

Fred Pryor Seminars & CareerTrack
5700 Broadmoor St., Ste. 300
Mission, KS 66202
Ph: (800)780-8476
Free: 800-780-8476
Fax: (913)967-8849
Co. E-mail: customerservice@pryor.com
URL: http://www.pryor.com
Contact: Phil Love, Chief Executive Officer
URL(s): www.pryor.com/mkt_info/seminars/desc/m7.asp. **Description:** Covers using Microsoft Office. **Audience:** General public. **Telecommunication Services:** customerservice@pryor.com.

32767 ■ Microsoft PowerPoint 2007 - I (Onsite)

EEI Communications
8945 Guilford Rd., Ste. 145
Columbia, MD 21046
Ph: (410)309-8200
Free: 888-253-2762
Fax: (410)630-3980
Co. E-mail: train@eeicom.com
URL: http://www.eeicom.com/eei-training-services
URL(s): www.eeicom.com/eei-training-services/classes/microsoft-office-2007-training/. **Price:** $797.00. **Description:** Covers creating slides and electronic presentations utilizing PowerPoint. **Audience:**

microsoft application users. **Dates and Locations:** Silver Spring, MD; and Columbia, MD. **Telecommunication Services:** train@eeicom.com.

32768 ■ Microsoft Project 2007 - I (Onsite)

EEI Communications
8945 Guilford Rd., Ste. 145
Columbia, MD 21046
Ph: (410)309-8200
Free: 888-253-2762
Fax: (410)630-3980
Co. E-mail: train@eeicom.com
URL: http://www.eeicom.com/eei-training-services
URL(s): www.eeicom.com. **Description:** Covers using Project to successfully manage projects, including using Gantt charts, resource leveling, and establishing task dependencies. **Audience:** General public. **Telecommunication Services:** train@eeicom.com.

32769 ■ Microsoft Project: Managing Multiple and Complex Projects (Onsite)

Seminar Information Service Inc.
20 Executive Park, Ste. 120
Irvine, CA 92614
Ph: (949)261-9104
Free: 877-SEM-INFO
Fax: (949)261-1963
Co. E-mail: info@seminarinformation.com
URL: http://www.seminarinformation.com
Description: Learn how to: Leverage Microsoft Project Professional tools and techniques in a multi-project environment; Reorganize large or complex projects into master and subprojects; Optimize resource assignments across projects and resolve over allocations; Track schedule, completeness and budget on complex projects and for distributed teams; Connect project managers, teams and data across the organization; Integrate third-party applications to facilitate data sharing and accessibility. **Audience:** Professionals.

32770 ■ Microsoft Word 2007 - I (Onsite)

EEI Communications
8945 Guilford Rd., Ste. 145
Columbia, MD 21046
Ph: (410)309-8200
Free: 888-253-2762
Fax: (410)630-3980
Co. E-mail: train@eeicom.com
URL: http://www.eeicom.com/eei-training-services
URL(s): www.eeicom.com/eei-training-services/classes/microsoft-office-2007-training/. **Price:** $497.00. **Description:** Covers how to create basic documents using Word. **Audience:** microsoft word users. **Dates and Locations:** Silver Spring, MD. **Telecommunication Services:** train@eeicom.com.

32771 ■ Microsoft Word 2007 - II (Onsite)

EEI Communications
8945 Guilford Rd., Ste. 145
Columbia, MD 21046
Ph: (410)309-8200
Free: 888-253-2762
Fax: (410)630-3980
Co. E-mail: train@eeicom.com
URL: http://www.eeicom.com/eei-training-services
URL(s): www.eeicom.com/eei-training-services/classes/microsoft-office-2007-training/. **Price:** $497.00. **Description:** Covers techniques including creating styles and sections, newspaper-style layouts, creating charts, and adding clip art. **Audience:** microsoft word users. **Dates and Locations:** Silver Spring, MD. **Telecommunication Services:** train@eeicom.com.

32772 ■ Microsoft Word 2007 - III (Onsite)

EEI Communications
8945 Guilford Rd., Ste. 145
Columbia, MD 21046
Ph: (410)309-8200
Free: 888-253-2762
Fax: (410)630-3980
Co. E-mail: train@eeicom.com
URL: http://www.eeicom.com/eei-training-services
URL(s): www.eeicom.com/eei-training-services/classes/microsoft-office-2007-training/. **Price:** $497.00. **Description:** Covers advanced Word skills including running, recording, and running macros,

creating custom toolbars, creating online forms, working with master documents, and creating table of contents and indexes. **Audience:** microsoft word users. **Dates and Locations:** Silver Spring, MD. **Telecommunication Services:** train@eeicom.com.

32773 ■ Motor Selection, Maintenance, Testing & Replacement

American Trainco, Inc.
9785 S Maroon Cir., Ste. 300
Englewood, CO 80112
Ph: (303)531-4560
Free: 877-978-7246
Fax: (303)531-4565
Co. E-mail: Sales@AmericanTrainco.com
URL: http://www.americantrainco.com
URL(s): www.americantrainco.com/courses/one-day/dtlomt.aspx. **Description:** Seminar designed for anyone whose work is affected by motors at their facility, whether they are mechanics doing the work, a supervisor in charge of fixing problems, or purchasing agents responsible for saving money. **Audience:** Mechanics, foremen, supervisors, purchasing agents, and HVAC technicians .

32774 ■ Moving Ahead: Breaking Behavior Patterns That Hold You Back (Onsite)

American Management Association (AMA)
1601 Broadway
New York, NY 10019-7420
Ph: (212)586-8100
Free: 877-566-9441
Fax: (212)903-8168
Co. E-mail: customerservice@amanet.org
URL: http://www.amanet.org
Contact: Edward T. Reilly, President
URL(s): www.amaseminars.org. **Description:** Covers resolution techniques for bad workplace behaviors. **Audience:** General managers, supervisors, team leaders and anyone who has a negative behavior pattern that has created a bad professional image and impeded his or her career success. **Telecommunication Services:** customerservice@amanet.org.

32775 ■ Online Marketing and Search Engine Optimization

EEI Communications
8945 Guilford Rd., Ste. 145
Columbia, MD 21046
Ph: (410)309-8200
Free: 888-253-2762
Fax: (410)630-3980
Co. E-mail: train@eeicom.com
URL: http://www.eeicom.com/eei-training-services
URL(s): www.eeicom.com. **Description:** Covers how to increase traffic to your online site to market your products and services using the Web, including creating and implementation of your plan, setting a budget, redesigning Web site for search engine optimization, tips and tricks, promotion hints, tips, and advice, and how to measure your Internet marketing results. **Audience:** Marketing professionals. **Telecommunication Services:** train@eeicom.

32776 ■ Personal Success Strategies (Onsite)

Seminar Information Service Inc.
20 Executive Park, Ste. 120
Irvine, CA 92614
Ph: (949)261-9104
Free: 877-SEM-INFO
Fax: (949)261-1963
Co. E-mail: info@seminarinformation.com
URL: http://www.seminarinformation.com
URL(s): www.seminarinformation.com/details.cfm?qc=qqbrrs. **Price:** $390. **Description:** Develop a plan to eliminate weaknesses that inhibit success and replace them with positive actions. **Audience:** Individuals who wish to modify behaviors.

32777 ■ PLC Programming & Applications (Onsite)

American Trainco, Inc.
9785 S Maroon Cir., Ste. 300
Englewood, CO 80112
Ph: (303)531-4560
Free: 877-978-7246

Fax: (303)531-4565
Co. E-mail: Sales@AmericanTrainco.com
URL: http://www.americantrainco.com
URL(s): www.americantrainco.com/courses/plc%20programming/dtlpcp.aspx. **Price:** $990. **Description:** Provides skills needed to organize, plan, write, enter, test, and document SLC500 programs using the basic programming instructions and RSLogix software. **Audience:** Apprentice and experienced electricians, instrumentation technicians, and building maintenance personnel .

32778 ■ PLCs for Non-Programmers (Onsite)

American Trainco, Inc.
9785 S Maroon Cir., Ste. 300
Englewood, CO 80112
Ph: (303)531-4560
Free: 877-978-7246
Fax: (303)531-4565
Co. E-mail: Sales@AmericanTrainco.com
URL: http://www.americantrainco.com
URL(s): www.americantrainco.com/courses/plc%20non-programmer/dtlpc.aspx. **Price:** $990. **Description:** Seminar designed for maintenance technicians, electricians, or other non-programmers who need a general understanding of automation and Programmable Logic Controllers. **Audience:** Apprentice and experienced electricians, instrumentation technicians, and all building maintenance Personnel .

32779 ■ Plumbing & Pipefitting for Plants & Buildings (Onsite)

American Trainco, Inc.
9785 S Maroon Cir., Ste. 300
Englewood, CO 80112
Ph: (303)531-4560
Free: 877-978-7246
Fax: (303)531-4565
Co. E-mail: Sales@AmericanTrainco.com
URL: http://www.americantrainco.com
URL(s): www.americantrainco.com/courses/plumbing%20and%20pipefitting/dtlpb.aspx. **Price:** $990. **Description:** Covers the necessary requirements to follow code and safety regulations while providing the student with a practical foundation to quickly identify problems and solve them on their own, whether it's a low-pressure water supply line problem, drippy valve or a clogged drain trap. **Audience:** Plumbing and pipefitting professionals.

32780 ■ Power Excel: Making Better Decisions (Onsite)

Seminar Information Service Inc.
20 Executive Park, Ste. 120
Irvine, CA 92614
Ph: (949)261-9104
Free: 877-SEM-INFO
Fax: (949)261-1963
Co. E-mail: info@seminarinformation.com
URL: http://www.seminarinformation.com
Description: Learn how to: Leverage advanced features of Microsoft Excel to facilitate business decisions; Perform 'what-if' analysis for developing budget and project plans; Predict potential business developments using trend analysis; Consolidate and process multidimensional worksheets; Summarize and analyze large amounts of data using PivotTables and Excel features; Automate Excel processes and enhance worksheet models; Generate interactive Web-based worksheet models. **Audience:** Industry professionals.

32781 ■ Predictive Maintenance and Condition Monitoring (Onsite)

American Trainco, Inc.
9785 S Maroon Cir., Ste. 300
Englewood, CO 80112
Ph: (303)531-4560
Free: 877-978-7246
Fax: (303)531-4565
Co. E-mail: Sales@AmericanTrainco.com
URL: http://www.americantrainco.com
URL(s): www.americantrainco.com/courses/predictive%20maintenance/dtlpdm.aspx. **Price:** $990. **Description:** Provides the fundamentals of PdM and

condition monitoring applicable to plants, facilities, and manufacturing lines. **Audience:** Maintenance, operations, purchasing managers and personnel.

32782 ■ Preparing for the Project Management Professional PMP Exam (Onsite)

Seminar Information Service Inc.
20 Executive Park, Ste. 120
Irvine, CA 92614
Ph: (949)261-9104
Free: 877-SEM-INFO
Fax: (949)261-1963
Co. E-mail: info@seminarinformation.com
URL: http://www.seminarinformation.com
Price: $2,950. **Description:** Learn how to: Prepare to pass the PMP(r) exam; Navigate the process groups and knowledge areas of the PMBOK(r) Guide 3rd Edition; Identify and map the inputs and outputs of the PMBOK(r) Guide processes; Align your project management knowledge with PMBOK(r) Guide terminology and definitions; Analyze PMBOK(r) Guide tools and techniques essential for PMP(r) exam success; Improve your exam-taking techniques through PMP(r)-style practice questions; Create a personalized plan for self-study to focus your efforts after the course. **Audience:** experienced project managers . **Dates and Locations:** Cities throughout the United States and Toronto and Ottawa, CN.

32783 ■ Programming Boot Camp (Onsite)

EEI Communications
500 Montgomery St., Ste. 400
Alexandria, VA 22314-5507
Ph: (410)309-8200
Free: 888-253-2762
Fax: (703)683-7310
Co. E-mail: info@eeicom.com
URL: http://www.eeicom.com
Contact: James T. DeGraffenreid, President
URL(s): www.eeicom.com. **Description:** Covers basic concepts of scripting languages and tools, including JavaScript and Visual Basic. **Audience:** Programmer and general public. **Telecommunication Services:** info@eeicom.com.

32784 ■ C Programming: Hands-On (Onsite)

Seminar Information Service Inc.
20 Executive Park, Ste. 120
Irvine, CA 92614
Ph: (949)261-9104
Free: 877-SEM-INFO
Fax: (949)261-1963
Co. E-mail: info@seminarinformation.com
URL: http://www.seminarinformation.com
URL(s): www.seminarinformation.com/qqbtkn/c-programming-hands-on. **Price:** $2,990, Onsite. **Description:** Learn how to: Create, compile and run C programs using Visual Studio 2005; Write and understand C language constructs, syntax and classes; Leverage the architecture and namespaces of the .NET Framework library; Manage the Common Language Infrastructure (CLI) to integrate C with Visual Basic 2005 and C; Develop .NET components in C for desktop and distributed multi-tier applications. **Audience:** C programmers, developers and engineers. **Dates and Locations:** 2015 Feb 10-13; venue not reported. **Telecommunication Services:** info@seminarinformation.com.

32785 ■ Programming Microsoft Access 2003: Hands-On - Building Database Applications with Access and VBA (Onsite)

Seminar Information Service Inc.
20 Executive Park, Ste. 120
Irvine, CA 92614
Ph: (949)261-9104
Free: 877-SEM-INFO
Fax: (949)261-1963
Co. E-mail: info@seminarinformation.com
URL: http://www.seminarinformation.com
Description: Learn how to: Develop applications with Microsoft Access 2003 using Visual Basic for Applications (VBA); Identify and populate event properties to satisfy design specifications; Modify object properties and invoke object methods to customize applications; Create VBA statements using variables and built-in functions; Build loops and decision logic; Apply Data

Access Objects (DAO) to incorporate business rules; Integrate Access with external applications through automation. **Audience:** Professionals.

32786 ■ The Project Planning Workshop
Canadian Management Centre (CMC)
150 York St., 5th Fl.
Toronto, ON, Canada M5H 3S5
Free: 877-262-2519
Fax: (416)214-6047
Co. E-mail: cmcinfo@cmcoutperform.com
URL: http://cmcoutperform.com
Contact: John Wright, President
Price: $1,995.00 Canadian for non-members; $1,845.00 Canadian for CMC members. **Description:** Two-day seminar covers the applicable tools, templates and proven practices to plan real life work projects.

32787 ■ Pump Repair & Maintenance (Onsite)
American Trainco, Inc.
9785 S Maroon Cir., Ste. 300
Englewood, CO 80112
Ph: (303)531-4560
Free: 877-978-7246
Fax: (303)531-4565
Co. E-mail: Sales@AmericanTrainco.com
URL: http://www.americantrainco.com
URL(s): www.americantrainco.com/courses/in-house/dtlih25.aspx. **Description:** Learn common sense pump maintenance and repair techniques to keep facilities and equipment up and running. **Audience:** Multi-craft technicians, maintenance technicians, plumbers & pipefitters and pump system engineers.

32788 ■ Pumps & Pump Systems: Specification, Installation & Operation (Onsite)
American Trainco, Inc.
9785 S Maroon Cir., Ste. 300
Englewood, CO 80112
Ph: (303)531-4560
Free: 877-978-7246
Fax: (303)531-4565
Co. E-mail: Sales@AmericanTrainco.com
URL: http://www.americantrainco.com
URL(s): www.americantrainco.com/courses/pumps/dtlcp.aspx. **Price:** $990. **Description:** From the pump and pump system, to the people who operate, maintain and design the pump system, this seminar will teach students how to identify the real problems causing pump failure, and how to avoid repeating those problems in the future. **Audience:** Students, maintenance supervisors and engineers.

32789 ■ QuarkXPress I
EEI Communications
8945 Guilford Rd., Ste. 145
Columbia, MD 21046
Ph: (410)309-8200
Free: 888-253-2762
Fax: (410)630-3980
Co. E-mail: train@eeicom.com
URL: http://www.eeicom.com/eei-training-services
URL(s): www.eeicom.com. **Price:** $745.00. **Description:** Covers basic desktop publishing skills including creating and saving documents, formatting text and paragraphs, and manipulating graphics. **Dates and Locations:** Alexandria, VA. **Telecommunication Services:** train@eeicom.com.

32790 ■ QuarkXPress II
EEI Communications
8945 Guilford Rd., Ste. 145
Columbia, MD 21046
Ph: (410)309-8200
Free: 888-253-2762
Fax: (410)630-3980
Co. E-mail: train@eeicom.com
URL: http://www.eeicom.com/eei-training-services
URL(s): www.eeicom.com. **Price:** $745.00. **Description:** Covers desktop publishing skills including paragraph and character style sheets, libraries, master pages, tracking and kerning, and processing colors. **Dates and Locations:** Silver Spring, MD; Alexandria, VA; Hunt Valley, MD; and Columbia, MD. **Telecommunication Services:** train@eeicom.com.

32791 ■ QuarkXPress III
EEI Communications
8945 Guilford Rd., Ste. 145
Columbia, MD 21046
Ph: (410)309-8200
Free: 888-253-2762
Fax: (410)630-3980
Co. E-mail: train@eeicom.com
URL: http://www.eeicom.com/eei-training-services
URL(s): www.eeicom.com. **Price:** $425.00. **Description:** Covers advanced desktop publishing skills including building table of contents and indexes, creating PostScript files, working with books, and synchronizing documents. **Dates and Locations:** Alexandria, VA. **Telecommunication Services:** info@eeicom.com.

32792 ■ Resume Writing (Onsite)
EEI Communications
8945 Guilford Rd., Ste. 145
Columbia, MD 21046
Ph: (410)309-8200
Free: 888-253-2762
Fax: (410)630-3980
Co. E-mail: train@eeicom.com
URL: http://www.eeicom.com/eei-training-services
Description: Learn to create an exceptional resume that helps you compete successfully for the job you want, as well as how to customize your resume and cover letter for each targeted employer in just a few strokes. **Audience:** General public.

32793 ■ Search Engine Optimization Training
EEI Communications
8945 Guilford Rd., Ste. 145
Columbia, MD 21046
Ph: (410)309-8200
Free: 888-253-2762
Fax: (410)630-3980
Co. E-mail: train@eeicom.com
URL: http://www.eeicom.com/eei-training-services
Price: $745.00. **Description:** Learn how to increase traffic to your Web site and get your products and services visible on the Web. **Dates and Locations:** Alexandria, VA.

32794 ■ Speed Reading with Evelyn Wood Reading Dynamics (Onsite)
Fred Pryor Seminars & CareerTrack
5700 Broadmoor St., Ste. 300
Mission, KS 66202
Ph: (800)780-8476
Free: 800-780-8476
Fax: (913)967-8849
Co. E-mail: customerservice@pryor.com
URL: http://www.pryor.com
Contact: Phil Love, Chief Executive Officer
Description: Learn Evelyn Wood's basic concepts, how to increase your reading rate, note-taking, studying and listening skills and develop better memory, recall and comprehension. **Audience:** Industry professionals.

32795 ■ Steam Systems Maintenance, Safety & Optimization (Onsite)
American Trainco, Inc.
9785 S Maroon Cir., Ste. 300
Englewood, CO 80112
Ph: (303)531-4560
Free: 877-978-7246
Fax: (303)531-4565
Co. E-mail: Sales@AmericanTrainco.com
URL: http://www.americantrainco.com
URL(s): www.americantrainco.com/courses/steam%20systems/dtlste.aspx. **Price:** $990. **Description:** This course will teach you how to keep your steam system working efficiently and how to fix common problems and work safely reducing energy loss. **Audience:** Boiler operators, technicians and mechanics, plant engineers, steam drive equipment operators and energy management personnel.

32796 ■ Style Summit (Onsite)
EEI Communications
8945 Guilford Rd., Ste. 145
Columbia, MD 21046
Ph: (410)309-8200
Free: 888-253-2762

Fax: (410)630-3980
Co. E-mail: train@eeicom.com
URL: http://www.eeicom.com/eei-training-services
URL(s): www.eeicom.com. **Description:** Covers simplifying the editorial process, including issues such as nouns used as verbs (E-mail me), e-jargon and acronyms, and informal usages that seem to break the rules (like vs. such as; more vs. over). **Audience:** Industry professionals. **Telecommunication Services:** train@eeicom.com.

32797 ■ Technical Writing: A Comprehensive Hands-On Introduction (Onsite)
Seminar Information Service Inc.
20 Executive Park, Ste. 120
Irvine, CA 92614
Ph: (949)261-9104
Free: 877-SEM-INFO
Fax: (949)261-1963
Co. E-mail: info@seminarinformation.com
URL: http://www.seminarinformation.com
URL(s): www.seminarinformation.com/qqbtkf/technical-writing-a-comprehensive-hands-on-introduction. **Price:** $2,990, Onsite. **Description:** Learn how to: Write clear, effective technical = documents, including user manuals and technical reports; Assess your target audience and develop documents to meet their needs; Choose the appropriate writing style to communicate to specialized audiences; Build effective sentences, paragraphs and sections that explain information clearly; Employ diagrams, tables, charts and other graphical tools effectively; Create informative and interesting content that your readers will comprehend and utilize. **Audience:** Technical writers. **Dates and Locations:** 2015 Feb 24-27; venue not reported. **Telecommunication Services:** info@seminarinformation.com.

32798 ■ Troubleshooting Mechanical Drive Systems & Rotating Equipment (Onsite)
American Trainco, Inc.
9785 S Maroon Cir., Ste. 300
Englewood, CO 80112
Ph: (303)531-4560
Free: 877-978-7246
Fax: (303)531-4565
Co. E-mail: Sales@AmericanTrainco.com
URL: http://www.americantrainco.com
URL(s): www.americantrainco.com/courses/mechanical%20drives/dtlbts.aspx. **Price:** $990. **Description:** Provide a new perspective on troubleshooting mechanical and rotating equipment and learn about basic mechanical applications, failures, life expectancy and maintenance shafts, bearings, couplings, chains, sprockets, bushings, gears, belts, sheaves and other mechanical components. You'll learn what data to measure, track and trend so that when equipment fails you can get quick answers to what is wrong, as well as fix the real problems with your equipment and not just the symptoms. **Audience:** Maintenance technicians, mechanics, HVAC technicians, electricians and machine operators .

32799 ■ Understanding & Troubleshooting Hydraulics (Onsite)
American Trainco, Inc.
9785 S Maroon Cir., Ste. 300
Englewood, CO 80112
Ph: (303)531-4560
Free: 877-978-7246
Fax: (303)531-4565
Co. E-mail: Sales@AmericanTrainco.com
URL: http://www.americantrainco.com
URL(s): www.americantrainco.com/courses/troubleshooting%20hydraulics/dtlhy.aspx. **Price:** $990. **Description:** Provides the basic building blocks and information you need to become proficient in working with industrial hydraulics and fluid power, whether a small mobile unit or large industrial installation. **Audience:** Mechanics, fluid power technicians, machine operators, plant and facility managers and building engineers.

32800 ■ Uninterruptable Power Supply (UPS) Maintenance and Readiness (Onsite)
American Trainco, Inc.
9785 S Maroon Cir., Ste. 300
Englewood, CO 80112
Ph: (303)531-4560

Free: 877-978-7246
Fax: (303)531-4565
Co. E-mail: Sales@AmericanTrainco.com
URL: http://wwww.americantrainco.com

URL(s): www.americantrainco.com/courses/one-day/dtloup.aspx. **Price:** $495. **Description:** Seminar designed for personnel responsible for the UPS systems in industrial plants, public facilities, and commercial buildings. **Audience:** Electricians, maintenance technicians, maintenance managers, supervisors, plant and building engineers.

32801 ■ Variable Frequency Drives (Onsite)
American Trainco, Inc.
9785 S Maroon Cir., Ste. 300
Englewood, CO 80112
Ph: (303)531-4560
Free: 877-978-7246
Fax: (303)531-4565
Co. E-mail: Sales@AmericanTrainco.com
URL: http://wwww.americantrainco.com

URL(s): www.americantrainco.com/courses/variable%20frequency%20drives/dtlvf.aspx. **Price:** $990. **Description:** Learn how to troubleshoot common VFD problems, take care of your own equipment, and avoid costly repairs or service repairs, including how to identify hazards associated with working on VFDs, an understanding of the importance of safe work practices, recognition of the main components of a VFD system, and the different methods of controlling a VFD. **Audience:** Industry professionals.

32802 ■ Visual Design I (Onsite)
EEI Communications
8945 Guilford Rd., Ste. 145
Columbia, MD 21046
Ph: (410)309-8200
Free: 888-253-2762
Fax: (410)630-3980
Co. E-mail: train@eeicom.com
URL: http://www.eeicom.com/eei-training-services

Description: Covers the history of type, typography's role in visual communication, structural line, space and kinetic lines, the elements of line, shape and space, and typography and type anatomy. **Audience:** Professional digital artist.

32803 ■ Visual Design II (Onsite)
EEI Communications
8945 Guilford Rd., Ste. 145
Columbia, MD 21046
Ph: (410)309-8200
Free: 888-253-2762
Fax: (410)630-3980
Co. E-mail: train@eeicom.com
URL: http://www.eeicom.com/eei-training-services

Description: Covers the principles of texture and the diverse approaches to the element of value. Explore monochromatic, analogous and complementary combinations from Itten's color wheel. **Audience:** Digital professional and students.

32804 ■ Visual Design III (Onsite)
EEI Communications
8945 Guilford Rd., Ste. 145
Columbia, MD 21046
Ph: (410)309-8200
Free: 888-253-2762
Fax: (410)630-3980
Co. E-mail: train@eeicom.com
URL: http://www.eeicom.com/eei-training-services

Description: Covers the compositional elements of line, plane, and form combined with neutral tones, and the Bauhaus and Constructivist theory as it relates to compositional tension and movement created by design. **Audience:** Digital professional and Students.

32805 ■ Visual Design IV (Onsite)
EEI Communications
8945 Guilford Rd., Ste. 145
Columbia, MD 21046
Ph: (410)309-8200
Free: 888-253-2762

Fax: (410)630-3980
Co. E-mail: train@eeicom.com
URL: http://www.eeicom.com/eei-training-services
Description: With focus on the works of Malevich and Escher as a foundation, learn the attributes of shape in positive and negative space, organic and geometric differences, metamorphosis, and symbolism. **Audience:** Digital professional and Students.

32806 ■ Water Treatment for Boilers, Chillers & Cooling Towers (Onsite)
American Trainco, Inc.
9785 S Maroon Cir., Ste. 300
Englewood, CO 80112
Ph: (303)531-4560
Free: 877-978-7246
Fax: (303)531-4565
Co. E-mail: Sales@AmericanTrainco.com
URL: http://www.americantrainco.com

URL(s): www.americantrainco.com/courses/in-house/dtlih68.aspx. **Description:** One-day seminar to take the mystery out of creating, and stabilizing high water quality for your HVAC systems. **Audience:** Building maintenance personnel, engineers and plant maintenance technicians .

32807 ■ Windows Vista: A Hands-On Introduction (Onsite)
URL(s): www.seminarinformation.com. **Description:** Learn how to: Install and maintain Windows Vista in a professional environment; Navigate and configure Windows Vista; Create and manage users and groups; Protect resources with rights, access control and encryption; Implement and troubleshoot network and Internet connectivity; Improve application compatibility to maximize user productivity. **Telecommunication Services:** info@seminarinformation.com.

32808 ■ The Women's Conference (Onsite)
Fred Pryor Seminars & CareerTrack
5700 Broadmoor St., Ste. 300
Mission, KS 66202
Ph: (800)780-8476
Free: 800-780-8476
Fax: (913)967-8849
Co. E-mail: customerservice@pryor.com
URL: http://www.pryor.com
Contact: Phil Love, Chief Executive Officer

URL(s): www.pryor.com/mkt_info/seminars/desc/zw.asp. **Description:** Covers the following topics: enhancing your career and professional development; expert communication skills just for women; and the women's professional toolbox. **Audience:** Professional women. **Telecommunication Services:** customerservice@pryor.com.

32809 ■ Writing the Perfect Business E-Mail (Onsite)
EEI Communications
500 Montgomery St., Ste. 400
Alexandria, VA 22314-5507
Ph: (410)309-8200
Free: 888-253-2762
Fax: (703)683-7310
Co. E-mail: info@eeicom.com
URL: http://www.eeicom.com
Contact: James T. DeGraffenreid, President
URL(s): www.eeicom.com/eei-training-services/classes/writing/. **Price:** $425.00. **Frequency:** Periodic. **Description:** Seminar that covers e-mails that get read and are understood, including keeping it short and simple, make it useful, spelling, grammar, and other problems, controlling emotion, writing attachments that get read, progress reports, instructions, and evaluations and recommendations. **Audience:** writers. **Dates and Locations:** Silver Spring, MD; Alexandria, VA; Hunt Valley, MD; and Columbia, MD. **Telecommunication Services:** info@eeicom.com.

REFERENCE WORKS

32810 ■ *"$56M Coming to Cincinnati Children's Hospital, University of Cincinnati, from Stimulus Bill' in Business Courier (Vol.*

26, October 9, 2009, No. 24, pp. 1)
Pub: American City Business Journals, Inc.
Contact: Whitney Shaw, President
Ed: Dan Monk, James Ritchie. **Description:** Cincinnati's Children's Hospital Medical Center and the University of Cincinnati researchers are set to receive at least $56 million from the stimulus bill. The cash infusion has reenergized research scientists and enhances Cincinnati's national clout as a major research center.

32811 ■ *"The 2007 Black Book' in Hawaii Business (Vol. 53, December 2007, No. 6, pp. 43)*
Description: Brief biographies of 364 top executives in Hawaii are presented. Information on their educational achievement, membership in associations, hobbies, family, present position and the company they work for are supplied.

32812 ■ *"2010 Book of Lists" in Austin Business JournalInc. (Vol. 29, December 25, 2009, No. 42, pp. 1)*
Description: Rankings of companies and organizations within the business services, finance, healthcare, hospitality and travel, insurance, marketing and media, professional services, real estate, education and technology industries in Austin, Texas are presented. Rankings are based on sales, business size, and other statistics.

32813 ■ *"2010 Book of Lists" in Business Courier (Vol. 26, December 26, 2009, No. 36, pp. 1)*
Description: Rankings of companies and organizations within the business services, education, finance, health care, hospitality and tourism, real estate, and technology industries in the Cincinnati, Ohio-Northern Kentucky area are presented. Rankings are based on sales, business size, or other statistics.

32814 ■ *"2010 Book of Lists" in Tampa Bay Business Journal (Vol. 30, December 22, 2009, No. 53, pp. 1)*
Description: Rankings of companies and organizations within the human resources, banking and finance, business services, healthcare, real estate, technology, hospitality and travel, and education industries in the Greater Tampa Bay area are presented. Rankings are based on sales, business size, and more.

32815 ■ *"ACC Game Development Program Opens" in Austin Business JournalInc. (Vol. 28, October 31, 2008, No. 33, pp. 1)*
Pub: American City Business Journals
Ed: Sandra Zaragoza. **Description:** Austin, Texas-based Austin Community College has launched its Game Development Institute. The institute was created to meet the gaming industry's demand for skilled workers. One hundred students have enrolled with the institute.

32816 ■ *"Active Duty' in Crain's Cleveland Business (Vol. 28, November 26, 2007, No. 47, pp. 3)*
Pub: Crain Communications Inc.
Ed: David Bennett. **Description:** Discusses the Veteran Workforce Training Program, sponsored by the Volunteers of America - Greater Ohio; the program is meant to provide employment training for military veterans and to assist them in transitioning back into the work force.

32817 ■ *"Advantage Tutoring Center Helps Students of All Levels" in Bellingham Business Journal (Vol. February 2010, pp. 16)*
Pub: Sound Publishing Inc.
Contact: Gloria G. Fletcher, President
Ed: Ashley Mitchell. **Description:** Profile of the newly opened Advantage Tutoring, owned by Mary and Peter Morrison. The center offers programs ranging from basic homework help to subject-specific enrichment.

32818 ■ *Ahead of the Curve: Two Years at Harvard Business School*
Pub: Dutton Children's Books
Contact: Lauri Hornik, President
Ed: Philip Delves Broughton. **Released:** June 30, 2009. **Price:** $16, paperback. **Description:** A behind-the-scenes glimpse at Harvard Business School is

given. The author believes Harvard succeeds in transforming students into business leaders but feels they are failing them in every other way. **Availability:** Print.

32819 ■ "All Fired Up!" in Small Business Opportunities (November 2008)
Ed: Stan Roberts. **Description:** Profile of Brixx Wood Fired Pizza, which has launched a franchising program due to the amount of interest the company's founders received over the years; franchisees do not need experience in the food industry or pizza restaurant service business in order to open a franchise of their own because all franchisees receive comprehensive training in which they are educated on all of the necessary tools to effectively run the business.

32820 ■ """All We've Done is Hire People That Believe In the Direction We're Going"" in Business Journal (Vol. 31, January 31, 2014, No. 36, pp. 9)
Pub: American City Business Journals
Released: January 31, 2014. **Description:** Fastenal founder, Bob Kierline, keeps hiring standards high in order to promote his firm's growth. He also said Fastenal's School of Business employs 40 licensed teachers. Their CEO, Will Oberton, said the company has done a better job in customer relations than its competitors.

32821 ■ "Alpharetta Seeding Startups To Encourage Job Growth" in Atlanta Business Chronicle(June 20, 2014, pp. 3A)
Pub: American City Business Journals, Inc.
Contact: Whitney Shaw, President
Released: June 20, 2014. **Description:** The City of Alpharetta is witnessing several incubators and accelerators that will create the physical and educational infrastructure to convert ideas into sustainable businesses. This will help startups develop a go-to-market strategy, prepare for FDA certification and insurance reimbursement as well as see that the company reaches a point where it can attract private equity or venture capital.

32822 ■ "American Indian College Fund to Support Environmental Science and Sustainability Programs, Fellowships, and Internships" in Ecology, Environment & Conservation Business (April 12, 2014, pp. 21)
Pub: NewsRX
Contact: Susan E. Hasty, Publisher
Released: April 12, 2014. **Description:** Tribal colleges serve communities facing environmental issues, such as water quality, energy development, depletion of natural resources, and agricultural management. The American Indian College Fund has created a new Environmental Science and Sustainability Project of $1.35 million grant money to support tribal colleges and universities in select states that underwrite environmental science and sustainability programs of studies. Details of the project are included.

32823 ■ "The Americans Are Coming" in The Economist (Vol. 390, January 3, 2009, No. 8612, pp. 44)
Description: Student recruitment consultancies, which help place international students at universities in other countries and offer services such as interpreting or translating guidelines, are discussed; American universities who have shunned these agencies in the past; the result has been that America underperforms in relation to its size with a mere 3.5 percent of students on its campuses that are from abroad.

32824 ■ "Angels for the Jobless: Church Volunteer Groups Give Career Guidance" in Crain's Detroit Business (Vol. 24, April 3, 2008, No. 13)
Pub: Crain Communications Inc.
Contact: Rance E. Crain, President
Ed: Sherri Begin. **Description:** St. Andrew Catholic Church, located in Rochester, offers the St. Andrew Career Mentoring Ministry, a program that brings in professionals who volunteer to aid those seeking jobs or, in numerous cases, new careers.

32825 ■ "Applications for Law School Drop" in Philadelphia Business Journal (Vol. 28, June 8, 2012, No. 17, pp. 1)
Pub: American City Business Journal
Description: Law School Admissions Council data for the past two years show the number of applicants have dropped by 25 percent ant the number of people who took the Law School Admissions Test fell by 26 percent. The numbers reflect the national trend that shows the struggling job market has affected decisions to go to law school.

32826 ■ "Applying to Colleges? Consultants Can Demystify the Process" in Palm Beach Post (September 3, 2011)
Pub: Palm Beach Post
Ed: Susan Salisbury. **Description:** More parents are turning to college consultants to help guide them through the process of applying to and choosing the right college or university. These specialized consultants assist with every detail for several years and students can reach them 24/7; costs can vary from several hundred dollars to $10,000 depending on services.

32827 ■ "Apprenticeship: Earn While You Learn" in Occupational Outlook Quarterly (Vol. 54, Fall 2010, No. 3, pp. 24)
Pub: U.S. Department of Labor Bureau of Labor Statistics
Contact: Philip L. Rones, Manager
E-mail: rones.philip@bls.gov
Description: Paid training, or apprenticeships, are examined. Registered apprenticeship programs conform to certain guidelines and industry-established training standards and may be run by businesses, trade or professional associations, or partnerships with business and unions.

32828 ■ "Aquatic Medications Engender Good Health" in Pet Product News (Vol. 64, November 2010, No. 11, pp. 47)
Pub: Bowtie Inc.
Ed: Madelaine Heleine. **Description:** Pet supply manufacturers and retailers have been exerting consumer education and preparedness efforts to help aquarium hobbyists in tackling ornamental fish disease problems. Aquarium hobbyists have been also assisted in choosing products that facilitate aquarium maintenance before disease attacks their pet fish.

32829 ■ "Are There Material Benefits To Social Diversity?" in Hispanic Business (Vol. 30, September 2008, No. 9, pp. 10)
Ed: Brigida Benitez. **Description:** Diversity in American colleges and universities, where students view and appreciate their peers as individuals and do not judge them on the basis of race, gender, or ethnicity is discussed. The benefits of diversity in higher education are also acknowledged by the U.S. Supreme Court and by leading American corporations.

32830 ■ "Artexpo Celebrates 30th Anniversary" in Art Business News (Vol. 34, November 2007, No. 11, pp. 18)
Description: In honor of its 30th anniversary Artexpo New York 2008 will be an unforgettable show offering a collection of fine-art education courses for both trade and consumer attendees and featuring a variety of artists working in all mediums.

32831 ■ "Asterand Eyes Jump to Ann Arbor" in Crain's Detroit Business (Vol. 25, June 22, 2009)
Pub: Crain Communications Inc. - Detroit
Contact: Keith Crain, Chairman
Ed: Tom Henderson. **Description:** Asterand PLC is considering a move to Ann Arbor from its current location as anchor tenant at TechTown, an incubator and technology park associated with Wayne State University. The university believes the Ann Arbor location's rent is too expensive for the tissue bank company.

32832 ■ "ASU Explores Russian Partnership" in The Business Journal - Serving Phoenix

and the Valley of the Sun (Vol. 28, September 5, 2008)
Pub: American City Business Journals, Inc.
Contact: Whitney Shaw, President
Ed: Mike Sunnucks. **Description:** Arizona State University is planning to partner with Russia-based St. Petersburg State University (SPSU) regarding research, faculty and student exchange, and other joint efforts. SPSU is one of Russia's leading scientific and research institutions. Arizona State's partnerships with other foreign colleges are also mentioned.

32833 ■ "At This Bakery, Interns' Hope Rises Along With the Bread" in Chicago Tribune (October 31, 2008)
Pub: McClatchy-Tribune Information Services
Ed: Mary Schmich. **Description:** Profile of Sweet Miss Givings Bakery and its diverse founder, interns and employees; the bakery was founded by Stan Sloan, an Episcopal priest who started the business to help fund his ministry; Sloan saw a need for jobs for those living with HIV and other disabilities and through the bakery the interns learn the skills needed to eventually find work elsewhere.

32834 ■ ATD Buyer's Guide (Internet only)
Pub: ASTD
Contact: Tony Bingham, President
E-mail: tbingham@astd.org
URL(s): webcasts.astd.org/sites. **Released:** Annual; December. **Entries include:** Company name, contact information and name, profile, list of products and services. **Database covers:** Businesses and individual consultants offering products, services, and equipment for sale to persons in corporate training and human resource development. **Arrangement:** Alphabetical. **Indexes:** Subject, geographical, industry focus.

32835 ■ "ATI Now Ready to Pounce on Biotech" in Austin Business JournalInc. (Vol. 28, August 21, 2008, No. 23, pp. 1)
Pub: American City Business Journals
Ed: Laura Hipp. **Description:** Austin Technology Incubator has entered the biotechnology sector through a program of the University of Texas incubator. The company's bioscience program was set off by a grant from the City of Austin worth $125,000. The growth of Austin's biotechnology sector is examined.

32836 ■ "The Balancing Act: How Busy Executives Make Their Lives Work" in Black Enterprise (Vol. 37, February 2007, No. 7, pp. 118)
Pub: Earl G. Graves Publishing Co. Inc.
Contact: Earl G. Graves, Jr., President
Ed: Marcia A. Reed-Woodard. **Description:** More than 70 percent of women with children work outside the home, according to a 2005 survey conducted by the U.S. Department of Labor Bureau. One of the biggest struggles these women face is balancing family with career aspirations and climbing the corporate ranks.

32837 ■ "Banks Deposit Reassurance, Calm Customers" in The Business Journal-Serving Greater Tampa Bay (Vol. 28, August 22, 2008)
Pub: American City Business Journals, Inc.
Contact: Whitney Shaw, President
Description: Community banks in the Tampa Bay Area are training tellers and other customer care workers to help reassure customers that their deposits are safe. Other measures to reassure depositors include joining a network that allows banks to share deposits. Additional information on moves community banks are making to reassure consumers is presented.

32838 ■ "Barshop Leading 'Paradigm Shift' In Aging Research" in San Antonio Business Journal (Vol. 28, September 12, 2014, No. 31, pp. 4)
Pub: American City Business Journals
Released: September 12, 2014. **Description:** The National Institute of Health has given a $7.5 million five-year grant to University of Texas Health Science at San Antonio's Barshop Insitute for Longevity and

Aging Studies. The funding was awarded to help researchers accelerate the discoveries of commercial drugs that slow the aging process.

32839 ■ *"BC Forest Safety Council Unveils Supervisor Course to Respond to Industry Demands" in Marketwired (May 14, 2007)*
Pub: Comtex News Network Inc.
Description: BC Forest Safety Council launched the sector's first supervisor training program that will lead to certification of forest supervisors in response to an industry-wide demand for standardized safety training for supervisors.

32840 ■ *"Bearish Ken Rosen Growls About Tech" in San Francisco Business Times (Vol. 28, May 2, 2014, No. 41, pp. 3)*
Pub: American City Business Journals
Released: May 2, 2014. **Description:** Ken Rose, chairman of the University of California Berkeley's Fisher Center, believes that 50 percent of technology companies will fail. He thinks that these firms will not be able to use all the office space they are taking. However, real estate developers are optimistic about office demand in the technology sector.

32841 ■ *"The Bell Tolls for Thee" in Canadian Business (Vol. 81, March 3, 2008, No. 3, pp. 36)*
Ed: Andrew Wahl. **Description:** Bell Canada has formed the Canadian Coalition for Tomorrow's IT Skills to solve the shortage of technology talent in the country. Canada's total workforce has only around 4%, or 600,000 people employed in information technology-related fields. The aims of the Bell-led coalition, which is supported by different industry associations and 30 corporations, are investigated.

32842 ■ *"Best Foot Forward" in Canadian Business (Vol. 80, October 22, 2007, No. 21, pp. 115)*
Ed: Jeremy Shinewald. **Description:** Jeremy Shinewald's mbaMission admissions consulting business helps prospective MBA students with essay writing, mock interview preparation and school selection. The consulting fee for application to one school is $2,250. Details of the business schools' MBA programs and tuition fees are explored.

32843 ■ *"Better Card Collecting" in Canadian Business (Vol. 80, January 15, 2007, No. 2, pp. 66)*
Ed: Sarah B. Hood. **Description:** Tips on how to collect business cards and use them for enhancing one's business performance are presented. Targeting specific people, taking notes and giving follow ups are some suggestions.

32844 ■ *"The Big Idea: No, Management Is Not a Profession" in Harvard Business Review (Vol. 88, July-August 2010, No. 7-8, pp. 52)*
Pub: Harvard Business School Publishing
Ed: Richard Barker. **Description:** An argument is presented that management is not a profession, as it is less focused on mastering a given body of knowledge than it is on obtaining integration and collaboration skills. Implications for teaching this new approach are also examined.

32845 ■ *"The BIG Picture" in Crain's Cleveland Business (Vol. 30, June 22, 2009, No. 24, pp. 12)*
Pub: Crain Communications Inc.
Ed: Arielle Kass. **Description:** Entrepreneurs are quick to praise their colleges and universities and attribute both personal and business success to them.

32846 ■ *"Biggest UM Landlords" in Crain's Detroit Business (Vol. 25, June 15, 2009, No. 24, pp. 1)*
Pub: Crain Communications Inc. - Detroit
Contact: Keith Crain, Chairman
Description: University of Michigan will purchase the two million-square-foot Pfizer campus in June 2009. The university is the largest occupier of commercial real estate university off campus in and around Ann Arbor, Michigan.

32847 ■ *"BioPark Eyes New Anchor" in Baltimore Business Journal (Vol. 30, June 22, 2012, No. 7, pp. 1)*
Pub: American City Business Journals, Inc.
Contact: Whitney Shaw, President
Ed: Sarah Gantz. **Released:** June 22, 2012. **Description:** University of Maryland BioPark leaders are wooing a biotechnology firm in Boston to become the anchor tenant of the park's third office building. Getting an anchor tenant would start construction of the BioPark's new 200,000 square-foot building. The 12-acre park's recovery from the struggling economy is described.

32848 ■ *"Birmingham: Losing the Mid Game" in Birmingham Business Journal (Vol. 31, February 28, 2014, No. 9, pp. 4)*
Pub: American City Business Journals, Inc.
Contact: Whitney Shaw, President
Released: February 28, 2014. **Description:** Birmingham, Alabama's short supply of college graduates has resulted in economic loss for the city. The city has ranked 77th in a study conducted by American City Business Journals. Economic effects include lost potential income.

32849 ■ *"Biz U: Cool for School" in Entrepreneur (Vol. 35, October 2007, No. 10, pp. 144)*
Pub: Entrepreneur Press
Contact: Perlman Neil, President
Ed: Nichole L. Torres. **Description:** Forming a high technology business while still in college has its advantages such as having information resources nearby and having students from various fields to ask for help and advice. School business competitions are also helpful in building networks with investors. Ways that the college environment can be useful to aspiring entrepreneurs, particularly to those who are into high technology business, are discussed.

32850 ■ *"Blues, BBQ, But Mostly You!" in Women in Business (Vol. 64, Fall 2012, No. 3, pp. 6)*
Released: Fall 2012. **Description:** The National Women's Leadership Conference will be held in Memphis,. Tennessee from October 11-13, 2012. The American Business Women's Association-University of Kansas MBA Essentials courses will be offered at the conference in addition to the Woman as 21st Century Leaders sessions.

32851 ■ *"Bold Goals Will Require Time" in Contractor (Vol. 56, October 2009, No. 10, pp. S2)*
Ed: Ted Lower. **Description:** Offering a broad range of courses is the Radiant Panel Association (RPA), an organization that holds education as its top priority. The RPA must lead the industry by raising the educational bar for future installers.

32852 ■ *"Bond Hill Cinema Site To See New Life" in Business Courier (Vol. 27, October 29, 2010, No. 26, pp. 1)*
Pub: Business Courier
Ed: Dan Monk. **Description:** Avondale, Ohio's Corinthian Baptist Church will redevelop the 30-acre former Showcase Cinema property to a mixed-use site that could feature a college, senior home, and retail. Corinthian Baptist, which is one of the largest African-American churches in the region, is also planning to relocate the church.

32853 ■ *"Book Smart" in Hawaii Business (Vol. 53, December 2007, No. 6, pp. 39)*
Ed: David K. Choo. **Description:** Different parts of a biography entry in the Black Book are examined in relation to their usage in starting a conversation with an executive. The second part, which is the educational background, is considered the most significant of all, due to the amount of information given. The importance of making connections in Hawaii is discussed.

32854 ■ *Boosting Corporate Entrepreneurship Through HRM Practices: Evidence from German SMEs" in Human Resource Management (Vol. 49, July-August 2010, No. 4)*
Pub: John Wiley
Ed: Ralf Schmelter, Rene Mauer, Christiane Borsch, Malte Brettel. **Description:** A study was conducted to determine which human resource management (HRM) practices promote corporate entrepreneurship (CE) in small and medium-sized enterprises (SMEs). Findings indicate that staff selection, staff development, training, and staff rewards on CE have a strong impact on SMEs.

32855 ■ *"Breaking From Tradition Techstyle" in Providence Business News (Vol. 28, March 17, 2014, No. 50, pp. 1)*
Pub: American City Business Journals
Released: March 17, 2014. **Description:** Providence, Rhode Island's Techstyle Haus is being constructed by a group of students from Brown University. The textile house features a flexible exterior that uses high-performance materials and solar cells. Techstyle Haus is one of two entries from the U.S. competing in the Solar Decathlon Europe 2014.

32856 ■ *"Bridging the Academic-Practitioner Divide in Marketing Decision Models" in Journal of Marketing (Vol. 75, July 2011, No. 4, pp. 196)*
Pub: American Marketing Association
Contact: Lucille Pointer, President
Ed: Gary L. Lilien. **Description:** A study to determine the reason for the relatively low level of practical use of the many marketing models is presented. Changing the incentive and reward systems for marketing academics, practitioners, and intermediaries can bring about adoption and implementation improvements. Those changes could be beneficial by bridging the academic-practitioner divide.

32857 ■ *"Bridging the Talent Gap Through Partnership and Innovation" in Canadian Business (Vol. 81, October 27, 2008, No. 18, pp. 88)*
Description: Research revealed that North America is short by more than 60,000 qualified networking professionals. Businesses, educators and communities are collaborating in order to address the shortfall.

32858 ■ *"BRIEF: District Using Bilingual Kiosks to Promote Health Literacy Among Hispanic Families" in Palm Beach Post (August 24, 2012)*
Pub: McClatchy Tribune Information Services
Released: August 24, 2012. **Description:** A partnership between the Palm Beach County School District and United Healthcare provides access to health information, in both English and Spanish in order to promote health literacy.

32859 ■ *"Brown Lab Image of R.I. Innovation" in Providence Business News (Vol. 28, February 24, 2014, No. 47, pp. 1)*
Pub: American City Business Journals
Released: February 24, 2014. **Description:** The Advanced Baby Imaging Lab at Brown University in Rhode Island is studying infant brain development using magnetic resonance imaging (MRI). The lab is attracting attention from researchers from Europe and California who see potential in Sean C. Deoni's technique to take an MRI of an infant without using sedation.

32860 ■ *"Bryan's House Retools for New Funds: Dallas Nonprofit Expands Mission as Money Related to HIV/AIDS Plummets" in Dallas Business Journal (Vol. 35, April 20, 2012, No. 32, pp. 1)*
Description: Nonprofit organization Bryan's House in Dallas, Texas is expanding its HIV/AIDS services to include early childhood education services and other child care programs. New funding includes $315,000 for the early childhood program, $450,000 for an Early Head Start Program for special-needs children and $125,000 for the "Wisdom's Hope Project for homeless special-needs children.

32861 ■ *"Budget Woes Endanger E-Prep Progress" in Crain's Cleveland Business (Vol.*

30, June 22, 2009, No. 24, pp. 6)
Pub: Crain Communications Inc.
Ed: Brian Tucker. **Description:** The future of the Entrepreneurship Preparatory School located in Cleveland is being threatened by State budget concerns. The charter school requires all students to wear uniforms, respect discipline, and attend for longer hours and more weeks.

32862 ■ *Business Black Belt: Develop the Strength, Flexibility and Agility to Run Your Company*
Ed: Burke Franklin. **Released:** November 1, 2010. **Price:** $15.99. **Description:** Manual offering insights that will enable anyone to become successful in small business. Seventy short chapters included topics such as attitude, management, marketing, selling, employees, money, MBAs, lawyers, consultants, and investors.

32863 ■ *"Business Plan Refines Focus" in Business Journal Portland (Vol. 27, December 10, 2010, No. 41, pp. 1)*
Pub: Portland Business Journal
Ed: Wendy Culverwell. **Description:** Organizers of the Oregon Business Plan's Leadership Summit 2010 seek the opinions of nearly 1,000 business, education, political, and civic leaders in an effort to address how to rehabilitate Oregon's economy. The opinion-seeking actions recognize the organizers' belief that the economic fate of the state depends on rural Oregon.

32864 ■ *"CADD Microsystems Launches the CADD Community, Partners with Global eTraining to Provide Online, On-Demand Training for Autodesk Software" in Computer Business Week (August 28, 2014, pp. 24)*
Pub: NewsRX
Contact: Susan E. Hasty, Publisher
Released: August 28, 2014. **Description:** A new on-line customer-only portal the integrates on-demand training, applications and extension, videos and additional value-added content for customers only was developed by CADD Microsystems. The Autodesk Platinum Partner calls this training program, CADD Community.

32865 ■ *The Campus CEO: The Student Entrepreneur's Guide to Launching a Multi-Million Dollar Business*
Ed: Randal Pinkett. **Released:** February 2007. **Price:** , $21.00 (CND). **Description:** Tips for generating income, while attending college is presented to students.

32866 ■ *"Canada Tomorrow" in Canadian Business (Vol. 80, October 8, 2007, No. 20, pp. 14)*
Ed: Donald J. Johnston. **Description:** An assessment of Canada's future in terms of its educational, social, and economic environment is presented. Concerns regarding the country's educational system such as the declining interest in science and technology and the possible lack of teachers in the future are discussed. In terms of its social and economic aspects, the need to support entrepreneurs and other qualified people is explained.

32867 ■ *"Canadian Research Generates Innovation and Prosperity" in Canadian Business (Vol. 81, October 27, 2008, No. 18, pp. 87)*
Description: Universities play a key role in helping Canadians achieve prosperity, competitiveness, and quality of life by conducting more than a third of Canada's research. Research in universities help train graduates to apply sophisticated knowledge to real problems.

32868 ■ *"Cancer-Fighting Entrepreneurs" in Austin Business Journal (Vol. 31, August 5, 2011, No. 22, pp. 1)*
Pub: American City Business Journals
Ed: Sandra Zaragoza. **Description:** Cancer Prevention and Research Institute of Texas has invested $10 million in recruiting known faculty to the University of Texas. The move is seen to bolster Austin's posi-

tion as a major cancer research market. The institute has awarded grants to researchers Jonghwan Kim, Guangbin Dong and Kyle Miller.

32869 ■ *"Capital Campaign Will Boost Local Research" in San Antonio Business Journal (Vol. 28, March 14, 2014, No. 5, pp. 8)*
Pub: American City Business Journals
Released: March 14, 2014. **Description:** The University of Texas Health Science Center at San Antonio's Campaign for the Future of fundraising project has been completed. The Health Science Center is expected to use the money to support research at the South Texas Medical Center. The capital campaign will allow the Health Science Center to become one of the most prominent universities in the U.S.

32870 ■ *"Capital One and Count Me In for Women's Economic Independence to Launch Program to Support Women Veteran-Owned Small Businesses Across the U.S." in Investment Weekly News (June 23, 2012, pp. 210)*
Released: June 23, 2012. **Description:** Capital One Financial Corporation partnered with Count Me In for Women's Economic Independence to help create a new small business training program for women veteran business owners. The not-for-profit providers of business education and resources for women is commited to helping women veterans to succeed.

32871 ■ *"Capitalizing On Our Intellectual Capital" in Harvard Business Review (Vol. 90, May 2012, No. 5, pp. 42)*
Pub: Harvard Business Review Press
Contact: Peter E. Walsh, Director
Ed: Iqbal Quadir. **Released:** May 2012. **Description:** By managing education as an export, the US can benefit not only from revenue received from tuition, but also from the relationships forged with foreign students. The students will import the networks and technologies they used while in the US and their education levels will help create global growth.

32872 ■ *"Captain Planet" in (Vol. 90, June 2012, No. 6, pp. 112)*
Pub: Harvard Business Review Press
Contact: Peter E. Walsh, Director
Ed: Adi Ignatius. **Released:** June 2012. **Description:** Paul Polman, chief executive officer of Unilever N.V., discusses his company's sustainable living plan, which integrates social responsibility with corporate objectives. Topics include sustainable sourcing, abolishing quarterly reporting in favor of long-term perspectives, the impact of the 2008 global economic crisis, and turning a company into a learning organization.

32873 ■ *"Casinos See College as Job Jackpot" in The Business Journal-Serving Metropolitan Kansas City (Vol. 26, August 1, 2008, No. 47)*
Ed: Suzanna Stagemeyer. **Description:** Wyandotte County casino managers revealed plans to develop partnerships with Kansas City Kansas Community College. The planned partnership is expected to include curriculum development and degree programs that would help train employees for the planned casinos. Other views and information on the project are presented.

32874 ■ *"CBC and Chrysler Strike Deal" in Black Enterprise (Vol. 37, December 2006, No. 5, pp. 36)*
Pub: Earl G. Graves Publishing Co. Inc.
Contact: Earl G. Graves, Jr., President
Ed: Kiara Ashanti. **Description:** Congressional Black Foundation and Chrysler Financial have partnered to provide financial education to students at historically black colleges and universities. The prime objective of the program is to reduce the number of college students that graduate with poor credit scores and high debt.

32875 ■ *"Cengage Learning Makes Boston Its Headquarters" in Boston Business Journal (Vol. 34, April 25, 2014, No. 12, pp. 6)*
Pub: American City Business Journals, Inc.
Contact: Whitney Shaw, President
Released: April 25, 2014. **Description:** Cengage Learning's office in Boston, Massachusetts will become the company's new corporate headquarters.

The educational publishing firm, which has more than 400 employees in Boston, is also expected to develop new digital products for higher education.

32876 ■ *"The CEO of Anglo American On Getting Serious About Safety" in (Vol. 90, June 2012, No. 6, pp. 43)*
Pub: Harvard Business Review Press
Contact: Peter E. Walsh, Director
Ed: Cynthia Carroll. **Released:** June 2012. **Description:** The author discusses her decision to shut down Anglo American PLC's platinum mine, the world's largest, for a complete overhaul of the firm's safety procedures. This involved a thorough retraining of the mine's workforce, replacing nearly all of the managers, and promoting the changes throughout the rest of the industry.

32877 ■ *"The China Connection" in Crain's Chicago Business (Vol. 31, March 24, 2008, No. 12, pp. 26)*
Pub: Crain Communications Inc.
Contact: Todd Johnson, Publisher
Ed: Samantha Stainburn. **Description:** Interview with Ben Munoz who studied abroad in Beijing, China for three months to study international economics, e-commerce and global leadership.

32878 ■ *"Cincinnati Business Committee's Tom Williams: Future is Now" in Business Courier (Vol. 27, August 13, 2010, No. 15, pp. 1)*
Pub: Business Courier
Ed: Lucy May. **Description:** Tom Williams, chairman of the Cincinnati Business Committee (CBC), maintains that politicians and business leaders must cooperate to ensure the competitiveness of the city for the 21st Century. Under Williams' leadership, the CBC has put emphasis on initiatives related to government efficiency, economic development, and public education. Williams' views on a proposed inland port are given.

32879 ■ *"A Class Act" in Hawaii Business (Vol. 53, March 2008, No. 9, pp. 25)*
Pub: PacificBasin Communications
Ed: Cathy S. Cruz-George. **Description:** UBoost is a startup company that offers online content for the educational magazine 'Weekly Reader'. The website features quizzes and allows users to accumulate points and redeem rewards afterward. Other details about the company are discussed.

32880 ■ *"Class Management" in Canadian Business (Vol. 80, April 23, 2007, No. 9, pp. 64)*
Ed: Erin Pooley. **Description:** The role of executive MBA programs in improving performance of employees is presented.

32881 ■ *"The Colt Effect" in Hawaii Business (Vol. 53, January 2008, No. 7, pp. 30)*
Pub: PacificBasin Communications
Ed: David K. Choo. **Description:** Participation at the Bowl Championship Games can help the University of Hawaii financially. Playing at a prominent sports event could provoke donations from alumni and increase enrollment at the university. Examples of universities that earned generous income by becoming a part of prestigious sporting events are presented.

32882 ■ *"Companies Urged to Take Steps to Replenish Work Force" in Crain's Cleveland Business (Vol. 28, October 29, 2007, No. 43, pp. 9)*
Pub: Crain Communications Inc.
Ed: Mike Verespej. **Description:** If America wants to stay competitive in the global marketplace, experts say that the education system will need serious improvements. According to Thomas J. Donahue, president and CEO of the U.S. Chamber of Commerce, one-third of the K-through-12 students in the United States don't graduate from high school.

32883 ■ *"The Competitive Imperative Of Learning" in Harvard Business Review (Vol.*

86, July-August 2008, No. 8, pp. 60)
Pub: Harvard Business Review Press
Contact: Peter E. Walsh, Director
Description: Experimentation and reflection are important components for maintaining success in the business world and are the kind of character traits that can help one keep his or her competitive edge.

32884 ■ *"Contractors Debate Maximizing Green Opportunities, Education" in Contractor (Vol. 56, November 2009, No. 11, pp. 3)*
Pub: Penton Media, Inc.
Ed: Robert P. Mader. **Description:** Attendees at the Mechanical Service Contractors Association convention were urged to get involved with their local U.S. Green Building Council chapter by one presenter. Another presenter says that one green opportunity for contractors is the commissioning of new buildings.

32885 ■ *"Conversation: Historian Geoffrey Jones On Why Knowledge Stays Put" in Harvard Business Review (Vol. 86, July-August 2008, No. 8)*
Pub: Harvard Business Review Press
Contact: Peter E. Walsh, Director
Ed: Gardiner Morse. **Description:** Geoffrey Jones, Harvard Business School's professor of business history, discusses factors that cause knowledge to concentrate in particular regions, rather than disperse, such as the location of wealth.

32886 ■ *"Could UNCC Be Home to Future Med School Here?" in Charlotte Business Journal (Vol. 25, July 23, 2010, No. 18, pp. 1)*
Pub: Charlotte Business Journal
Ed: Jennifer Thomas. **Description:** University of North Carolina, Charlotte chancellor Phil Dubois is proposing that a medical school be established at the campus. The idea began in 2007 and Dubois' plan is for students to spend all four years in Charlotte and train at the Carolinas Medical Center.

32887 ■ *"Craning for Workers" in Puget Sound Business Journal (Vol. 35, August 15, 2014, No. 17, pp. 4)*
Pub: American City Business Journals
Released: August 15, 2014. **Description:** The U.S. Department of Labor statistics show that Washington State has 15, 510 laborers in 2013. However, construction companies are having difficulty hiring skilled workers, particularly as apprentices. The Associated General Contractors of Washington's expansion of training slots for crane and other heave equipment operators is discussed.

32888 ■ *"A Crash Course in Global Relations" in Canadian Business (Vol. 87, July 2014, No. 7, pp. 77)*
Pub: George Media Inc.
Released: July 2014. **Description:** Teach Away Inc. is a global education firm based in Toronto, Ontario that recruits English-speaking teachers to work abroad. The firm's revenues have grown by 1,621 percent from 2008 to 2013, placing it in the 37th spot on the 2014 Profit ranking of fastest growing companies in Canada.

32889 ■ *"Crew Training Changes Tactics" in Memphis Business Journal (Vol. 33, March 16, 2012, No. 49, pp. 1)*
Pub: American City Business Journal
Ed: Cole Epley. **Description:** Teamwork and communication training services firm Crew Training International Inc. has revamped its strategy and executive board as it moved from small to mid-tier status. The recalibration of strategy comes along with a renovation at the headquarters in southeast Memphis, Tennessee.

32890 ■ *"Culinary School Puts a Food Truck on the Road" in St. Louis Post-Dispatch (March 21, 2012)*
Pub: McClatchy-Tribune Regional News
Ed: Joe Bonwich. **Released:** March 21, 2012. **Description:** Le Food Truck is a teach tool to help students learn about the fast-growing food truck market. Tony Hedger, instructor at L'Ecole Culinaire,

a career college located in Laude, Missouri, coordinated the new program. The school also operates the Presentation Room, a restaurant used as part of the classroom.

32891 ■ *"David Saunders Q&A" in Canadian Business (Vol. 80, October 22, 2007, No. 21, pp. 11)*
Ed: Erin Pooley. **Description:** David Saunders, chairman of the Federation of Business School Deans, talks about the changes in business education in Canada. He stresses that a master's degree in business administration is vital and a good investment that would reap rewards in a business career.

32892 ■ *"Day Care for Affluent Drawing a Crowd" in Business First Columbus (Vol. 24, August 15, 2008, No. 52, pp. 1)*
Pub: American City Business Journals
Ed: Carrie Ghose. **Description:** Day care centers for affluent families have grown in popularity in Columbus, Ohio. Primrose Schools Franchising Company has opened three such schools in the area. Statistical data included.

32893 ■ *"Day-Care Center Owner to Argue Against Liquor Store Opening Nearby" in Chicago Tribune (March 13, 2008)*
Pub: McClatchy-Tribune Information Services
Ed: Matthew Walberg. **Description:** NDLC's owner feels that Greenwood Liquors should not be granted its liquor license due to the claim that the NDLC is not only a day-care center but also a school that employs state-certified teachers.

32894 ■ *"Deal Made for Pontiac Home of Film Studio" in Crain's Detroit Business (Vol. 25, June 1, 2009, No. 22, pp. 3)*
Pub: Crain Communications Inc. - Detroit
Contact: Keith Crain, Chairman
Ed: Daniel Duggan. **Description:** Details of the $75 million movie production and training facility in Pontiac, Michigan are revealed.

32895 ■ *"Debt Grows At State's Largest Universities as Enrollment Booms" in Birmingham Business Journal (Vol. 29, July 13, 2012, No. 29, pp. 1)*
Pub: American City Business Journals, Inc.
Contact: Whitney Shaw, President
Ed: Nick Bowman. **Released:** July 13, 2012. **Description:** Alabama's largest public universities have reported growing long-term debt as record enrollment drives them to incur more debt to accommodate the high number of students. University of Alabama's debt increase 48 percent to $682 million in 2011, while Auburn University saw its debt jump 25.5 percent to $773 million.

32896 ■ *"Deep Thoughts: Getting Employees to Think Better Requires a Bit of Creative Thinking Itself" in Canadian Business (March 17, 2008)*
Ed: Lauren McKeon. **Description:** Discusses the reason a company needs to make their employees understand that ideas are the stuff of life. For employees to be more creative, they need to cultivate spark moments, play with possibilities, and venture into the unknown.

32897 ■ *"Defensive Training" in Crain's Detroit Business (Vol. 24, September 22, 2008, No. 38, pp. 11)*
Pub: Crain Communications Inc.
Contact: Rance E. Crain, President
Ed: Robert Ankeny. **Description:** Rising retaliation claims in regards to discrimination complaints are creating an atmosphere in which managers must learn how to avoid or deal with these lawsuits as well as the retaliation that often follows. Examples of cases are given as well as advice for dealing with such problems that may arise in the workplace.

32898 ■ *"DePaul To Train Hotel Leaders" in Chicago Tribune (September 22, 2008)*
Pub: McClatchy-Tribune Information Services
Ed: Kathy Bergen. **Description:** With help from a $7.5 million grant from the Conrad N. Hilton Foundation, DePaul University will dramatically expand its role as a training ground for the tourism-industry with the opening of a School of Hospitality.

32899 ■ *"Design program in Athletic Footwear" in Occupational Outlook Quarterly (Vol. 55, Fall 2011, No. 3, pp. 21)*
Pub: U.S. Department of Labor Bureau of Labor Statistics
Contact: Philip L. Rones, Manager
E-mail: rones.philip@bls.gov
Description: The Fashion Institute of Technology offers the only certificate program in performance athletic footwear design in the U.S. The program focuses on conceptualizing and sketching shoe designs and covers ergonomic, anatomical, and material considerations for athletic footwear design.

32900 ■ *"Developers Vie for UWM Dorm" in The Business Journal-Milwaukee (Vol. 25, July 11, 2008, No. 42, pp. A1)*
Pub: American City Business Journals, Inc.
Contact: Whitney Shaw, President
Ed: Rich Kirchen. **Description:** Eight developers are competing to build a 500- to 700-student residence hall for the University of Wisconsin-Milwaukee. The residence hall will probably be developed within two miles of the main campus. It was revealed that the university's real estate foundation will select the successful bidder on July 25, 2008, and construction will begin by January 2009.

32901 ■ *"Dick Haskayne" in Canadian Business (Vol. 81, March 31, 2008, No. 5, pp. 72)*
Pub: Rogers Media Inc.
Contact: Tony Viner, President
Ed: Andy Holloway. **Description:** Dick Haskayne says that he learned a lot about business from his dad who ran a butcher shop where they had to make a decision on buying cattle and getting credit. Haskayne says that family, friends, finances, career, health, and infrastructure are benchmarks that have to be balanced.

32902 ■ *"Digital-Physical Mashups: To Consumers, the Real and Virtual Worlds Are One. The Same Should Go For Your Company" in Harvard Business Review (Vol. 92, September 2014, No. 9, pp. 84)*
Pub: Harvard Business Publishing
Released: September 2014. **Description:** By merging their physical and virtual operations, companies can provide a seamless experience for customers, boosting competitive advantage. These include strengthening customer/engagement links, approaching innovation through complementary expertise, and ensure that chief executive officers possess adequate technological knowledge.

32903 ■ *"Dispelling Rocky Mountain Myths Key to Wellness" in Employee Benefit News (Vol. 25, November 1, 2011, No. 14, pp. 12)*
Pub: SourceMedia Inc.
Contact: James M. Malkin, Chief Executive Officer
Ed: Andrea Davis. **Description:** Andrew Sykes, chairman of Health at Work Wellness Actuaries, states that it is a myth that Colorado is ranked as the healthiest state in America. Sykes helped implement a wellness programs at Brighton School District in the Denver area.

32904 ■ *"Dr. Mark Holder" in Crain's Cleveland Business (Vol. 30, June 29, 2009, No. 25, pp. 14)*
Pub: Crain Communications Inc.
Ed: Kathy Ames Carr. **Description:** Dr. Mark Holder is the director of the financial engineering program at Kent State University. Dr. Holder discusses his role to help teach his students how to market themselves for finance jobs in a down economy.

32905 ■ *"Don't Shoot the Messenger: A Wake-Up Call For Academics" in Academy of Management Journal (Vol. 50, No. 5, October 1, 2007, pp. 1020)*
Pub: Academy of Management
Contact: Ming-Jer Chen, President
Ed: David E. Guest. **Description:** Author evaluates two well-known publications: HR Magazine and People Management, to emphasize the role of U.S. academics in communicating management practice.

32906 ■ *"Downtowns Must Court Young, CEOs for Cities President Says"* in *Crain's Detroit Business (Vol. 24, October 6, 2008, No. 40, pp. 18)*

Ed: Amy Lane. **Description:** It is important to produce more college graduates, and keep them in Michigan, according to CEOs for Cities President Carol Coletta when she spoke to a session at the West Michigan Regional Policy Conference which was held in September in Grand Rapids. Ways in which city leaders can connect students to communities, resulting in employees who have vested interest in the region, are also discussed.

32907 ■ *"Dozens 'Come Alive' in Downtown Chicago"* in *Green Industry Pro (July 2011)*

Pub: Cygnus Business Media

Contact: Paul Mackler, Chief Executive Officer

Ed: Gregg Wartgow. **Description:** Highlights from the Come Alive Outside training event held in Chicago, Illinois July 14-15, 2011 are shared. Nearly 80 people representing 38 landscape companies attended the event that helps contractors review their services and find ways to sell them in new and various ways.

32908 ■ *"The Early Bird Gets the Worm"* in *Black Enterprise (Vol. 37, January 2007, No. 6, pp. 111)*

Ed: Tykisha N. Lundy. **Description:** General Motors hosts the Black Enterprise Conference And Expo: Where Deals Are Made at Walt Disney World's Swan and Dolphin Resort, May 9-12. The conference will offer great information to entrepreneurs.

32909 ■ *"East Coast Solar"* in *Contractor (Vol. 57, February 2010, No. 2, pp. 17)*

Pub: Penton Media, Inc.

Ed: Dave Yates. **Description:** U.S. Department of Energy's Solar Decathlon lets 20 college student-led teams from around the world compete to design and build a solar-powered home. A mechanical contractor discusses his work as an advisor during the competition.

32910 ■ *"The Economics of Well-Being: Have We Found a Better Gauge of Success Than GDP?"* in *Harvard Business Review (Vol. 90, January-February 2012, No.1-2, pp. 78)*

Pub: Harvard Business Review Press

Contact: Peter E. Walsh, Director

Ed: Justin Fox. **Released:** January-February 2012. **Description:** Gross domestic product is no longer a valid means of determining national success. GDP does not take into account factors such as unpaid houswork and sustainability. Other metrics may be more accurate and encompassing, including life expectancy, individual freedom, and educational achievement.

32911 ■ *"An Educated Play on China"* in *Barron's (Vol. 88, June 30, 2008, No. 26, pp. M6)*

Pub: Dow Jones & Co., Inc.

Contact: Clare Hart, President

Ed: Mohammed Hadi. **Description:** New Oriental Education & Technology Group sells English-language courses to an increasingly competitive Chinese workforce that values education. The shares in this company have been weighed down by worries on the impact of the Beijing Olympics on enrollment and the Sichuan earthquake. These shares could be a great way to get exposure to the long-term growth in China.

32912 ■ *"Education Path to Economic Growth in R.I."* in *Providence Business News (Vol. 29, June 23, 2014, No. 12, pp. 1)*

Pub: American City Business Journals

Released: June 23, 2014. **Description:** A gubernatorial candidate in Rhode Island is offering an education-related initiative that involves the creation of a statewide internship program, managed by each local school district and offering high school students the chance to participate in an internship at a local company. The state would provide $2.5 million to set up the "Hope Internships" with the help of nonprofits

and to provide tax incentives for participating firms. Human resource department interest of local firms is also discussed.

32913 ■ *"Embry-Riddle Aeronautical University Opening Alliance Campus"* in *Dallas Business Journal (Vol. 35, May 25, 2012, No. 37, pp. 1)*

Pub: American City Business Journal

Ed: Matt Joyce. **Description:** Embry-Riddle Aeronautical University is set to open a campus at Fort Worth Alliance Airport. The plan is part of the university's efforts to supply the workforce demands of the aviation and aerospace sectors. Comments from university officials are also included.

32914 ■ *"EMU, Spark Plan Business Incubator for Ypsilanti"* in *Crain's Detroit Business (Vol. 23, October 15, 2007, No. 42, pp. 3)*

Pub: Crain Communications Inc. - Detroit

Contact: Keith Crain, Chairman

Ed: Chad Halcom. **Description:** Eastern Michigan University is seeking federal grants and other funding for a new business incubator program that would be in cooperation with Ann Arbor Spark. The site would become a part of a network of three Spark incubator programs with a focus on innovation in biotechnology and pharmaceuticals.

32915 ■ *"Encouraging Study in Critical Languages"* in *Occupational Outlook Quarterly (Vol. 55, Summer 2011, No. 2, pp. 23)*

Pub: U.S. Department of Labor Bureau of Labor Statistics

Contact: Philip L. Rones, Manager

E-mail: rones.philip@bls.gov

Description: Proficiency in particular foreign languages is vital to the defense, diplomacy, and security of the United States. Several federal programs provide scholarships and other funding to encourage high school and college students to learn languages of the Middle East, China, and Russia.

32916 ■ *"The End of RIM"* in *Canadian Business (Vol. 85, August 13, 2012, No. 13, pp. 22)*

Pub: George Media Inc.

Ed: Joe Castaldo. **Released:** August 13, 2012. **Description:** The potential implications of the collapse of Research in Motion (RIM) on the Canadian technology sector are examined. The country is expected to lose its biggest training ground for technology talent without RIM, but the company's decline will not stop Canadians from trying to build and sustain multinational technolgy companies.

32917 ■ *"Endowments for Colleges Hit Hard in '09"* in *Milwaukee Business Journal (Vol. 27, February 12, 2010, No. 20, pp. A1)*

Pub: American City Business Journals

Ed: Corrinne Hess. **Description:** Southeast Wisconsin college endowments declined by as much as 35 percent in 2009 due to the economic downturn. A list of 2009 endowments to colleges in southeast Wisconsin and their percent change from 2008 is presented.

32918 ■ *"Energy Alliance Formed"* in *Austin Business Journal (Vol. 32, Jun 29, 2012, No. 17, pp. 1)*

Pub: American City Business Journals, Inc.

Contact: Whitney Shaw, President

Ed: Christopher Calnan. **Released:** June 29, 2012. **Description:** Texas Battery and Energy Storage Consortium has held an organizational meeting at the Austin Chamber of Commerce in a bid to compete for a $120 million U.S. Department of Energy Hub grant. The grant would team university and industry leaders with the Oak Ridge National Research Laboratory to develop battery and energy storage technology. Insights on the hub are also given.

32919 ■ *"Energy Exec Bankrolls Big-Budget UT Film"* in *Austin Business Journal (Vol. 34, June 6, 2014, No. 16, pp. A8)*

Pub: American City Business Journals, Inc.

Contact: Whitney Shaw, President

Released: June 6, 2014. **Description:** Bud Brigham, CEO of the energy firm Brigham Resources is bankrolling the film, "My All American" that focuses on

University of Texas football coach Darrell K. Royal. The film is about his bond with star player Freddie Steinmark during the 1969 national championship season. Through this film, Brigham hopes to establish himself in Hollywood and dreams of being as big as Disney.

32920 ■ *"Enlightened Leadership: Best Practice Guidelines and Time Tools for Easily Implementing Learning Organizations*

Pub: Learning House Publishing, Inc.

Ed: Ralph LoVuolo; Alan G. Thomas. **Released:** May 2006. **Price:** $79.99. **Description:** Innovation and creativity are essential for any successful small business. The book provides owners, managers, and team leaders with the tools necessary to produce 'disciplined innovation'.

32921 ■ *"Enlightened Leadership: Best Practice Guidelines and Timesaving Tools for Easily Implementing Learning Organizations*

Pub: Learning House Publishing, Inc.

Ed: Alan G. Thomas; Ralph L. LoVuolo; Jeanne C. Hillson. **Released:** September 2006, printable 3 times/year. **Price:** $21.00. **Description:** Book provides the tools required to create a learning organization management model along with a step-by-step guide for team planning and learning. The strategy works as a manager's self-help guide as well as offering continuous learning and improvement for company-wide success.

32922 ■ *"Enphase Energy To Present At Solar Power International 2012"* in *Entertainment Close-Up (September 11, 2012)*

Description: Solar Power International 2012 conference will feature Enphase Energy at the Orange County Convention Center in Orlando, Florida. Visitors can test new installer tools that sync with Enphase Microinverter System and receive live training and more.

32923 ■ *"Enriching the Ecosystem: A Four-Point Plan for Linking Innovation, Enterprises, and Jobs"* in *Harvard Business Review (Vol. 90, March 2012, No. 3, pp. 140)*

Pub: Harvard Business Review Press

Contact: Peter E. Walsh, Director

Ed: Rosabeth Moss Kanter. **Released:** March 2012. **Description:** The four goals for enriching the ecosystem include: linking venture creation and knowledge creation to speed up the idea-to-enterprise transition; revitalizing small-, medium-, and large-sized firms via partnerships; improving matches between education and employment opportunities; and bringing together leaders across different sectors to create regional strategies.

32924 ■ *"Essentially Organic Vending Takes Healthy Snacks to Ohio High School"* in *Entertainment Close-Up (September 13, 2011)*

Pub: Close-Up Media

Description: Essentially Organic Vending is offering students a healthy alternative for their snacking. The vending machines will be stocked with nutritious energy options.

32925 ■ *"Etextbook Space Heats Up"* in *Information Today (Vol. 28, November 2011, No. 10, pp. 10)*

Pub: Information Today, Inc.

Contact: Thomas H. Hogan, President

E-mail: ctuthill@infotoday.com

Ed: Paula J. Hane. **Description:** The use of etextbooks is expected to grow with the use of mobile devices and tablets. A new group of activists is asking students, faculty members and others to sign a petition urging higher education leaders to prioritize affordable textbooks or free ebooks over the traditional, expensive new books required for classes.

32926 ■ *"Etextbooks: Coming of Age"* in *Information Today (Vol. 28, September 2011, No. 8, pp. 1)*

Pub: Information Today, Inc.

Contact: Thomas H. Hogan, President

E-mail: ctuthill@infotoday.com

Ed: Amanda Mulvihill. **Description:** National average for textbooks costs was estimated at $1,137 annually at a 4-year public college for the 2010-2011 school year. Amazon reported selling 105 etextbooks for every 100 print books, while Barnes and Noble announced that their etextbooks were outselling print 3 to 1.

32927 ■ *"EVMS Gets Grant to Train Providers for Elder Care"* in *Virginian-Pilot (October 29, 2010)*
Pub: Virginian-Pilot
Ed: Elizabeth Simpson. **Description:** Eastern Virginia Medical School received a federal grant to train health providers in elder care. Details of the program are provided.

32928 ■ *"Executive Training"* in *Black Enterprise (Vol. 37, December 2006, No. 5, pp. 70)*
Ed: Marcia A. Reed-Woodard. **Description:** Roy N. Gundy Jr. was preparing to introduce a new strategic plan within his division and understood that his plan may fail if not executed properly. He discusses his experience in the Wharton School's executive education workshop Implementing Strategy, at the University of Pennsylvania and gives tips on putting strategy into action.

32929 ■ *"Expanding the Entrepreneurship Class"* in *(Vol. 90, July-August 2012, No. 7-8, pp. 40)*
Pub: Harvard Business Review Press
Contact: Peter E. Walsh, Director
Ed: Carl Schramm. **Released:** July-August 2012. **Description:** Two programs for encouraging entrepreneurship are highlighted. One offers trained facilitators who help participants move through iterations to produce viable business models. Another provides college juniors and seniors with instruction and advice from successful businesspeople.

32930 ■ *"Experts Strive to Educate on Proper Pet Diets"* in *Pet Product News (Vol. 64, November 2010, No. 11, pp. 40)*
Pub: Bowtie Inc.
Ed: John Hustace Walker. **Description:** Pet supply manufacturers have been bundling small mammal food and treats with educational sources to help retailers avoid customer misinformation. This action has been motivated by the customer's quest to seek proper nutritional advice for their small mammal pets.

32931 ■ *"Exploring Supportive and Developmental Career Management Through Business Strategies and Coaching"* in *Human Resource Management (Vol. 51, January-February 2012, No. 1, pp. 99-120)*
Pub: John Wiley & Sons Inc.
Contact: Stephen M. Smith, President
Ed: Jesse Segers, Ilke Inceoglu. **Description:** Coaching and other career practices that are part of supportive and developmental career management are examined. Such practices are found to be most present in organizations with a prospector strategy.

32932 ■ *"Export Initiative Launched"* in *Philadelphia Business Journal (Vol. 28, December 11, 2009, No. 43, pp. 1)*
Pub: American City Business Journals Inc.
Ed: Athena D. Merritt. **Description:** The first initiative that came out of the partnership between the Export-Import Bank of the US, the city of Philadelphia, and the World Trade Center of Greater Philadelphia is presented. A series of export finance workshops have featured Ex-Im Bank resources that can provide Philadelphia businesses with working capital, insurance protection and buyer financing.

32933 ■ *"Facilitating and Rewarding Creativity During New Product Development"* in *Journal of Marketing (Vol. 75, July 2011, No. 4, pp. 53)*
Pub: American Marketing Association
Contact: Lucille Pointer, President
Ed: James E. Burroughs, Darren W. Dahl, C. Page Moreau, Amitava Chattopadhay, Gerald J. Gorn. **Description:** A study to determine the effects of rewards to creativity in the process of new product development is presented. The findings show that the effect of rewards can be made positive if combined with appropriate creativity training.

32934 ■ *"Falcons' Blank Kicking Off 'Westside Works' Job Training Program"* in *Atlanta Business Chronicle (May 30, 2014, pp. 6A)*
Pub: American City Business Journals, Inc.
Contact: Whitney Shaw, President
Released: May 30, 2014. **Description:** Arthur Blank, owner of the Atlanta Falcons, is kicking off 'Westside Works', an initiative to build a world-class football/soccer stadium in Atlanta and transform the adjacent communities. Westside Works, a partnership between The Arthur M. Blank Family Foundation, the Construction Education Foundation of Georgia, and Integrity CDC will provide construction jobs for at least 100 men and women from the Westside neighborhoods in the next 12 months. The program will also provide job training, skills assessment, adult education programs, interview preparedness, and job placement.

32935 ■ *"Feds to Pay University Hospital $20M"* in *Business Courier (Vol. 27, July 23, 2010, No. 12, pp. 3)*
Pub: Business Courier
Ed: James Ritchie. **Description:** The U.S. government is set to pay University Hospital and medical residents who trained there $20 million as part of a tax dispute settlement. Around 1,000 former residents are to receive tax refunds. But the hospital must provide the U.S. Internal Revenue Service with extensive documentation.

32936 ■ *"Fighting the Good Fight"* in *Inc. (Vol. 33, October 2011, No. 8, pp. 8)*
Pub: Inc. Magazine
Ed: Eric Markowitz. **Description:** Rob Roy, former Navy SEAL, runs SOT-G a firm that offers an 80-hour leadership training course inspired by military combat preparations. Details of the program are outlined.

32937 ■ *"Finding Life Behind the Numbers"* in *Crain's Chicago Business (Vol. 31, March 24, 2008, No. 12, pp. 25)*
Pub: Crain Communications Inc.
Contact: Todd Johnson, Publisher
Ed: Samantha Stainburn. **Description:** Interview with Phillip Capodice who is a graduate student at DePaul University's Kellstadt Graduate School of Business and studied abroad in Lima, Peru where he visited a number of companies including some who are trade partners with the United States.

32938 ■ *"Finishing High School Leads to Better Employment Prospects"* in *Occupational Outlook Quarterly (Vol. 55, Summer 2011, No. 2, pp. 36)*
Pub: U.S. Department of Labor Bureau of Labor Statistics
Contact: Philip L. Rones, Manager
E-mail: rones.philip@bls.gov
Description: Students who drop out of high school are more likely to face unemployment than those who finish. Statistical data included.

32939 ■ *"The Firm: The Story of McKinsey and Its Secret Influence on American Business"*
Pub: Simon & Schuster Adult Publishing Group
Contact: Carolyn Reidy, President
E-mail: carolyn.reidy@simonandschuster.com
Released: September 30, 2014. **Price:** $17.00 paperback. **Description:** Profile of McKinsey & Company, the most influential and controversial business consulting firm in the United States. McKinsey consultants have ushered in waves of structural, financial, and technological change to America's best organizations; they've reorganized the power structure within the White House; and they have revolutionized business schools.

32940 ■ *"Five New Scientists Bring Danforth Center $16 Million"* in *Saint Louis Business Journal (Vol. 32, October 7, 2011, No. 6, pp. 1)*
Pub: Saint Louis Business Journal
Ed: E.B. Solomont. **Description:** Donald Danforth Plant Science Center's appointment of five new lead scientists has increased its federal funding by $16 million. Cornell University scientist Tom Brutnell is one of the five new appointees.

32941 ■ *"5 Steps for Handling Independent Contractors"* in *Hawaii Business (Vol. 53, January 2008, No. 7, pp. 49)*
Pub: PacificBasin Communications
Ed: Jason Ubay. **Description:** Small companies should be cautious in dealing with independent contractors. They must understand that they cannot dictate specific operational procedures, job duties, standards of conduct and performance standards to the contractors, and they cannot interfere with the evaluation and training of the contractors' employees. Tips on negotiating with independent contractors are given.

32942 ■ *"Florida Hospital, UCF Affiliation in Danger?"* in *Orlando Business Journal (Vol. 29, September 21, 2012, No. 29, pp. 1)*
Pub: American City Business Journal
Description: Florida Hospital is said to be considering the possibility of terminating its affiliation agreement with the University of Central Florida's (UCF) College of Medicine that ends June 30, 2018. Two of the reasons for the move include UCF's plans for a teaching hospital and a new graduate medical education program that could place Florida Hospital into competition with UCF.

32943 ■ *"Follow the ABCs of Buying a Business"* in *Women Entrepreneur (September 10, 2008)*
Ed: Nina Kaufman. **Description:** Buying a business will likely result in the largest single asset one will ever own. A list of steps one can take in order to educate and protect themselves is provided.

32944 ■ *"For-Profit Medical School Ramping Up for Business"* in *Sacramento Business Journal (Vol. 30, February 21, 2014, No. 52, pp. 6)*
Pub: American City Business Journals
Released: February 21, 2014. **Description:** California Northstate University got full accreditation for the College of Pharmacy at Elk Grove in summer 2013 and hopes to start classes in August or September 2014. The university is in talks to acquire a second building in the area worth $15 million.

32945 ■ *"Fortis College Opens on St. Luke's Medical Center Site"* in *The Business Journal - Serving Phoenix and the Valley of the Sun (Vol. 28, September 7, 2008)*
Pub: American City Business Journals, Inc.
Contact: Whitney Shaw, President
Ed: Angela Gonzales. **Description:** Fortis College is planning to offer classes in Phoenix, Arizona. It has made its home at the St. Luke's Medical Center. Courses to be offered by the college are also provided.

32946 ■ *"Forward Motion"* in *Green Industry Pro (July 2011)*
Pub: Cygnus Business Media
Contact: Paul Mackler, Chief Executive Officer
Ed: Gregg Wartgow. **Description:** Several landscape contractors have joined this publication's Working Smarter Training Challenge over the last year. This process is helping them develop ways to improve work processes, boost morale, drive out waste, reduce costs, improve customer service, and be more competitive.

32947 ■ *"Funbrain Launches Preschool Content"* in *Marketing to Women (Vol. 21, March 2008, No. 3, pp. 3)*
Description: Funbrain.com launches The Moms and Kids Playground, a section of the website devoted to activities and games for moms and kids aged 2 to 6; content aims at building early computer skills and to teach basic concepts such as counting and colors.

32948 ■ *"Future Autoworkers will Need Broader Skills"* in *Crain's Detroit Business (Vol. 25, June 8, 2009, No. 23, pp. 13)*
Pub: Crain Communications Inc. - Detroit
Contact: Keith Crain, Chairman
Ed: Ryan Beene. **Description:** Auto industry observers report that new workers in the industry will need advanced skills and educational backgrounds in

engineering and technical fields because jobs in the factories will become more technology-based and multidisciplinary.

32949 ■ *"The Future Is Another Country; Higher Education"* in The Economist (Vol. 390, January 3, 2009, No. 8612, pp. 43)
Description: Due to the growth of the global corporation, more ambitious students are studying at universities abroad; the impact of this trend is discussed.

32950 ■ *"Ga. PMA Launches Online Education Program"* in Contractor (Vol. 56, October 2009, No. 10, pp. 8)
Pub: Penton Media, Inc.
Description: Plumbing & Mechanical Association of Georgia launched an online program that covers technical and business management that will help contractors run their businesses. Future courses will include math for plumbers, graywater systems, and recession-proofing your business.

32951 ■ *"The Gender Wage Gap: What Local Firms Plan To Do About It"* in Orlando Business Journal (Vol. 30, May 2, 2014, No. 45, pp. 4)
Pub: American City Business Journals
Released: May 2, 2014. **Description:** Reports show that women in Orlando, Florida earn 20 percent less than men. The gender wage gap trend in the city can be attributed to bias and women working in lower-wage positions. Graphs that present information on income gap by education and income gap by industry are also given.

32952 ■ *"Get With the Program"* in Entrepreneur (Vol. 36, April 2008, No. 4, pp. 130)
Ed: Nichole L. Torres. **Description:** Entrepreneurship initiatives help college students get connected with other students, teach them about how to start their own business while still in school, and help with funding. Some of these programs are the Harold Grinspoon Charitable Foundation's Entrepreneurship Initiative and the Syracuse Campus-Community Entrepreneurship Initiative.

32953 ■ *"Give 'Em a Break"* in Entrepreneur (Vol. 35, November 2007, No. 11, pp. 32)
Pub: Entrepreneur Press
Contact: Perlman Neil, President
Ed: J.J. Ramberg. **Description:** Andy Walter and Peer Pedersen founded Blue Orchid Capital, a fund of hedge funds, and Steamboat Foundation a foundation that helps college students find high-profile summer internships. Details on the fund and the foundation are presented.

32954 ■ *"Giving Biotech Startups a Hand"* in Philadelphia Business Journal (Vol. 28, January 8, 2010, No. 47, pp. 1)
Pub: American City Business Journals Inc.
Ed: John George. **Description:** Elkins Park, Pennsylvania-based BioStrategy Partners is a virtual life sciences incubator that is seeking to improve the dull ranking of Philadelphia in the small business vitality index of life sciences. BioStrategy provides technology and business development services to startup life sciences companies and university-based research projects.

32955 ■ *"Glendale Pumping $29 Million Into Redevelopment"* in The Business Journal - Serving Phoenix and the Valley of the Sun (Vol. 28, August 1, 2008, No. 48, pp. 1)
Pub: American City Business Journals, Inc.
Contact: Whitney Shaw, President
Ed: Mike Sunnucks. **Description:** Glendale City is planning to invest $29 million to improve city infrastructure like roadways and water and sewer lines over the next five years. Glendale's city council is also planning to hold a workshop on the redevelopment projects in September 2008. Other views and information on the redevelopment project, are presented.

32956 ■ *"Global Business Speaks English: Why You Need a Language Strategy Now"* in Harvard Business Review (Vol. 90, May 2012,

No. 5, pp. 116)
Pub: Harvard Business Review Press
Contact: Peter E. Walsh, Director
Ed: Tsedal Neeley. **Released:** May 2012. **Description:** English is rapidly becoming the language of businesses regardless of where they are located. To improve efficiency, the author advocates implementing an English-only policy. However, this must be conducted with sufficient training and support, and appropriate cultural sensitivity.

32957 ■ *"Going for the APEX"* in Women In Business (Vol. 62, September 2010, No. 3, pp. 28)
Pub: American Business Women's Association
Contact: Lorie Burch, President
Description: Information about the American Business Women's Association (ABWA) professional development tools, which keep members focused on personal excellence, is presented. The organization recently launched the APEX (Achieving Personal Excellence) Award to honor women who are making a commitment to themselves.

32958 ■ *"Goodbye, Locker Room: Hello, Boardroom"* in Inc. (Vol. 33, October 2011, No. 8, pp. 30)
Pub: Inc. Magazine
Ed: Issie Lapowsky, Kasey Wehrum. **Description:** In 2005, the National Football League started the NFL Business Management and Entrepreneurial Program. Since the onset of the program, 700 players have participated in the program which takes place at the business schools of Harvard, the University of Pennsylvania, Northwestern and Stanford.

32959 ■ *"Gordon College Chief Explores the Secrets of Corporate Leadership"* in Boston Business Journal (Vol. 34, May 23, 2014, No. 16, pp. 4)
Pub: American City Business Journals, Inc.
Contact: Whitney Shaw, President
Released: May 23, 2014. **Description:** Gordon College president, Michael Lindsay, shares his findings on the secrets of corporate leadership in the book, 'View from the Top: An Inside Look at How People in Power See and Shape the World'. Lindsay describes the characteristics of the leaders he interviewed for the book.

32960 ■ *"Grant Could Help Schools Harness Wind"* in Dallas Business Journal (Vol. 37, April 11, 2014, No. 31, pp. 8)
Pub: American City Business Journals
Released: April 11, 2014. **Description:** Five universities led by Texas A&M have received a $2.2 million grant from the Texas Emerging Technologies Fund for use in wind technology research. The research will focus on turbines that feature bigger blades to capture more wind. Technology developed by the universities will eventually be handed to the state.

32961 ■ *"Grant Program Boosting Biomedical Research"* in Providence Business News (Vol. 28, February 24, 2014, No. 47, pp. 3)
Pub: American City Business Journals
Released: February 24, 2014. **Description:** The role played by the Institutional Development Award Network of Biomedical Research Excellence (INBRE) is boosting biomedical research in Rhode Island. According to researcher, Niall G. Howlett, procuring startup funding through INBRE led to receiving other grants and working with graduate students who have the potential to become part of the biomedical workforce.

32962 ■ *"Groomers Eye Profit Growth Through Services"* in Pet Product News (Vol. 64, December 2010, No. 12, pp. 26)
Pub: Bowtie Inc.
Ed: Kathleen M. Mangan. **Description:** Pet groomers can successfully offer add-on services by taking into account insider customer knowledge, store image, and financial analysis in the decision-making process. Many pet groomers have decided to add services such as spa treatments and training due to a slump in the bathing and grooming business. How some pet groomers gained profitability through add-on services is explored.

32963 ■ *"Ground Forces: Insurance Companies Should Help Agents to Build the Skills and Relationships that Translate Into More Business"* in Best's Review (Vol. 113, September 2012, No. 5, pp. 25)
Description: The economic challenges of the past few years required insurance agents and financial professionals to better trained. Insurance companies should help their agents build skills and relationships in order to grow.

32964 ■ *"Group Learning"* in Academy of Management Review (October 2007, pp. 1041)
Pub: ScholarOne Inc.
Contact: William T. Carden, Jr., President
Ed: Jeanne M. Wilson, Paul S. Goodman, Matthew A. Cronin. **Description:** The processes that constitute group learning in order to undertake necessary modifications are covered.

32965 ■ *"Group Thinking"* in Business Strategy Review (Vol. 23, Spring 2012, No. 1, pp. 48)
Released: Spring 2012. **Description:** Conflicts and decision making in groups has long been a subject of fascination for Randall Peterson, Professor of Organizational Behavior at London Business School. He talks to Business Strategy Review about what ignited his interest and his latest research and thinking.

32966 ■ *"Growing Your Business Through BPI Certification"* in Indoor Comfort Marketing (Vol. 70, May 2011, No. 5, pp. 12)
Pub: Industry Publications Inc.
Contact: Shirleen Dorman, Editor
Ed: Scott Vadino. **Description:** Profile of the Building Performance Institute and the ways BPI certification will help grow a heating, ventilation, cooling firm.

32967 ■ *"GSK Creating Pathways From Academia to Industry"* in Philadelphia Business Journal (Vol. 33, March 7, 2014, No. 4, pp. 8)
Pub: American City Business Journals
Released: March 7, 2014. **Description:** The Discovery Fast Track Challenge program of GlaxoSmithKline will expand in 2014 to include scientists in North America and Europe. Scientists will be asked to submit information about their innovative drug research proposals and the winner could be offered a deal with the Discovery Partnerships with Academia team.

32968 ■ *"Guest Speaker: The Real World: Forget the Elaborate Business Plans, Kids With Passion Are Our Next Great Entrepreneurs"* in Inc. (October 2007, pp. 87-88)
Pub: Mansueto Ventures L.L.C.
Contact: John Koten, Chief Executive Officer
Ed: George Gendron. **Description:** George Gendron, founder and executive director of the Innovation and Entrepreneurship Program at Clark University, stresses the importance of encouraging business students in his entrepreneurial program to follow their passion. The program is dedicated to real-world entrepreneurship by creating businesses rather than business plans.

32969 ■ *"Guts Not Included"* in Canadian Business (Vol. 81, March 31, 2008, No. 5, pp. 46)
Pub: Rogers Media Inc.
Contact: Tony Viner, President
Ed: Andrew Wahl. **Description:** Executives need the vision to create a strategy that prepares for an uncertain future in light of growing global competition. Canadian business leaders have the right skills and education but do not have enough tolerance for risk.

32970 ■ *"Head of the Class"* in Hispanic Business (September 2007, pp. 34, 36, 38)
Pub: Hispanic Business Inc.
Contact: Jesus Chavarria, President
Ed: Hildy Medina. **Description:** Stanford's business school recruits Hispanic students through the Charles P. Bonini Partnership for Diversity Fellowship program. A listing of the top schools for business, engineering, law, and medicine for Hispanics are included.

32971 ■ *"Head of the Class" in Entrepreneur (Vol. 37, October 2009, No. 10, pp. 59)*
Pub: Entrepreneur Press
Contact: Perlman Neil, President
Description: Top 25 graduate and undergraduate entrepreneurship programs in the US for 2009 as ranked by The Princeton Review are listed. Babson College in Wellesley, Massachusetts topped both categories.

32972 ■ *"Healthy Start for Medical Kiosks; Lions Kick in $20K" in Crain's Detroit Business" (Vol. 28, June 11, 2012, No. 24, pp. 18)*
Pub: Crain Communications Inc.
Contact: Rance E. Crain, President
Released: June 11, 2012. **Description:** Detroit Lions Charities has given Henry Ford Health System's school-based and community health program money to purchase nine interactive health kiosks. These kiosks will be provided by Medical Imagineering LLC, a spinoff of Henry Ford's Innovation Institute and installed in elementary and middle schools in Detroit.

32973 ■ *"Henry Mintzberg: Still the Zealous Skeptic and Scold" in Strategy and Leadership (Vol. 39, March-April 2011, No. 2, pp. 4)*
Pub: Emerald Group Publishing Inc.
Ed: Robert J. Allio. **Description:** Henry Mintzberg, professor at the McGill University in Montreal, Canada, shares his thoughts on issues such as inappropriate methods in management education and on trends in leadership and management. Mintzberg believes that US businesses are facing serious management and leadership challenges.

32974 ■ *"Higher-Ed Finally in Session" in Business Journal Portland (Vol. 30, February 7, 2014, No. 49, pp. 4)*
Pub: American City Business Journals
Released: February 7, 2014. **Description:** Oregon lawmakers and voters are set to consider several proposals on how higher education is funded, including free community college and free college for a percentage of future earnings. State Treasurer, Ted Wheeler, is proposing a large endowment that would pay for scholarships and vocational training.

32975 ■ *"Higher Education" in Canadian Business (Vol. 79, October 23, 2006, No. 21, pp. 129)*
Ed: Erin Pooley; Laura Bogomolny; Joe Castaldo; Michelle Magnan. **Description:** Details of some Canadian business schools, where students can simultaneously pursue a master of business administration degree and also be employed on a part time basis, are presented.

32976 ■ *"Hire Education" in Canadian Business (Vol. 79, September 11, 2006, No. 18, pp. 114)*
Pub: Rogers Media Inc.
Contact: Tony Viner, President
Ed: Erin Pooley. **Description:** Study results showing the perceptions of students while considering full-time employment and the attributes they look for in their future employers are presented.

32977 ■ *"Hiring Unpaid Interns: Failing To Comply With Labor Laws Can Lead to Legal Trouble" in Black Enterprise (Vol. 44, June 2014, No. 10, pp. 22)*
Pub: Earl G. Graves Publishing Co. Inc.
Contact: Earl G. Graves, Jr., President
Released: June 2014. **Description:** Before hiring an intern for a small business it is critical to study the Department of Labor's legal criteria, determine whether the internship should be paid or unpaid, weigh the pros and cons, focus on the training aspect, and work with local colleges.

32978 ■ *"His Brother's Keeper: A Mentor Learns the True Meaning of Leadership" in Black Enterprise (Vol. 37, December 2006, No. 5, pp. 69)*
Pub: Earl G. Graves Publishing Co. Inc.
Contact: Earl G. Graves, Jr., President
Ed: Laura Egodigwe. **Description:** Interview with Keith R. Wyche of Pitney Bowes Management Services, which discusses the relationship between a mentor and mentee as well as sponsorship.

32979 ■ *"Hit the Books" in Entrepreneur (Vol. 36, April 2008, No. 4, pp. 74)*
Pub: Entrepreneur Press
Contact: Perlman Neil, President
Ed: Nichole L. Torres. **Description:** Lists of the top business schools in different U.S. universities are presented. These lists are categorized according to best professors, best classroom experience, most competitive students, greatest opportunity for women, and greatest opportunity for minority students. The lists, compiled by the Princeton Review, are based on student opinion.

32980 ■ *"Hitting the E-Books" in Inc. (Vol. 33, September 2011, No. 7, pp. 36)*
Pub: Inc. Magazine
Ed: Shivani Vora. **Description:** Textbooks may be getting cheaper for college students now that they can use electronic textbooks that can be read on a laptop or tablet. The market is growing about 50 percent annually. Statistical data included.

32981 ■ *"Holy Wasabi! Sushi Not Just For Parents Anymore" in Chicago Tribune (March 13, 2008)*
Pub: McClatchy-Tribune Information Services
Ed: Christopher Borrelli. **Description:** Wicker Park cooking school, The Kid's Table, specializes in cooking classes for pre-teens; Elena Marre who owns the school was surprised when she was asked to plan a children's party in which she would teach a course in sushi making. More and more adolescents and small children are eating sushi.

32982 ■ *"Home Grown" in Hawaii Business (Vol. 53, November 2007, No. 5, pp. 51)*
Pub: PacificBasin Communications
Ed: Jolyn Okimoto Rosa. **Description:** Discusses a program that focuses on Native Hawaiian entrepreneurs and offers business training at the Kapiolani Community College; upon completion of the program, participants may apply for a loan provided by the Office of Hawaiian Affairs (OHA) to help them start their business. OHA plans to present the restructured loan program in November 2007, with aims of shortening the loan process.

32983 ■ *"Home Instead Senior Care of Seacoast and Southern New Hampshire" in New Hampshire Business Review (Vol. 34, April 6, 2012, No. 7, pp. 45)*
Pub: Business Publications Corp.
Contact: Connie Wimer, President
Released: April 6, 2012. **Description:** Portsmouth, New Hampshire-based Home Instead Senior Care of Seacoast and Southern New Hampshire launched a specialized training program for professional and family caregivers designed to help them improve the quality of life for those living with dementia and the families who support them.

32984 ■ *"Hopkins' Security, Reputation Face Challenges in Wake of Slaying" in Baltimore Business Journal (Vol. 28, August 6, 2010, No. 13)*
Pub: Baltimore Business Journal
Ed: Gary Haber. **Description:** The slaying of Johns Hopkins University researcher Stephen Pitcairn has not tarnished the reputation of the elite school in Baltimore, Maryland among students. Maintaining Hopkins' reputation is important since it is Baltimore's largest employer with nearly 32,000 workers. Insights on the impact of the slaying among the Hopkins' community are also given.

32985 ■ *How to Hire, Train and Keep the Best Employees for Your Small Business*
Pub: Atlantic Publishing Co.
Contact: Amanda Miller, Manager
E-mail: amiller@atlantic-pub.com

Ed: Dianna Podmoroff. **Released:** June 2004. **Price:** $29.95, with companion CD-ROM. **Description:** Costs of hiring, training, and lost productivity costs related to losing employees. **Availability:** Print.

32986 ■ *"How I Became a Serial Entrepreneur" in Baltimore Business Journal (Vol. 31, April 18, 2014, No. 51, pp. 26)*
Pub: American City Business Journals, Inc.
Contact: Whitney Shaw, President
Released: April 18, 2014. **Description:** Dr. Lisa Beth Ferstenberg, a physician by training, teaches a course at the Maryland Center for Entrepreneurship in Columbia to help CEOs attract prospective investors. Dr. Ferstenberg is also the chief medical officer at Sequella Inc. She reflects on the kind of personality required to become a successful entrepreneur and the mistakes entrepreneurs make in raising capital funding.

32987 ■ *"How to Survive This Mess" in Crain's Chicago Business (Vol. 31, April 14, 2008, No. 15, pp. 18)*
Pub: Crain Communications Inc.
Contact: Todd Johnson, Publisher
Ed: Christina Le Beau. **Description:** Small business owners can make it through a possible recession with preparations such as reviewing their balance sheet and cash flow every week and spotting trends then reacting quickly to them.

32988 ■ *"How To Fill Birmingham's Tech Talent Pool" in Birmingham Business Journal (Vol. 31, March 7, 2014, No. 10, pp. 4)*
Pub: American City Business Journals, Inc.
Contact: Whitney Shaw, President
Released: March 7, 2014. **Description:** Discussion on ways the City of Birmingham, Alabama could increase the number of technology workers in the area is presented. The sector should allow more work off-site to attract technology workers. Meanwhile, local schools have been expanding their offerings to cater to the technology sector needs.

32989 ■ *"How To Make Training a Catalyst for Real Change; Too Often, Training Programs Fail To Deliver. Here Are Some Guidelines for Programs That Will Create Meaningful Change In Your Company" in Gallup Business Journal (March 11, 2014)*
Pub: Gallup Press
Released: March 11, 2014. **Description:** Training alone is not enough to transform habits or culture. Training programs often fail to deliver the change a company is seeking. Guidelines for creating meaningful change through comprehensive training programs are provided.

32990 ■ *"How To Prevent Cyber Crime At Your Biz" in Birmingham Business Journal (Vol. 31, March 14, 2014, No. 11, pp. 10)*
Pub: American City Business Journals, Inc.
Contact: Whitney Shaw, President
Released: March 14, 2014. **Description:** Ways businesses can prevent cyber attacks are prevented. Employees should be educated to be aware of cyber crimes. Policies on confidentiality and privacy should also be established in business organizations.

32991 ■ *"How Will You Ever Replace Yourself?" in Canadian Business (Vol. 83, August 17, 2010, No. 13-14, pp. 77)*
Ed: Jacqueline Nelson. **Description:** SoftBank founder and CEO masayoshi Son created his very own school called SoftBank Academia in order to pick a successor that will follow his footprint. Son's strategy is extreme but other corporate leaders should pay attention to succession planning.

32992 ■ *"Human Resource Management: Challenges for Graduate Education" in Business Horizons (Vol. 51, March-April 2008, No. 2, pp. 151)*
Pub: Elsevier Advanced Technology Publications
Ed: James C. Wimbush. **Description:** Human resource management education at the master's and doctoral degree levels is discussed. There is an ever-increasing need to produce human resource managers who understand the value of human resource management as a strategic business contributor. uman.

32993 ■ *"IMPACT Fitness Boot Camp Training Now Approved for NESTA Credits for Personal Trainer Certification" in Marketing Weekly News (January 28, 2012)*

Description: Intense Mixed Performance Accelerated Cross Training (IMPACT) helps personal trainers impact their clients' lives as well as their own income. However, the IMPACT fitness certification program now qualifies trainers for continuing education credits through the National Exercise & Sports Trainers Association's (NESTA) Personal Fitness Trainer program. The online IMPACT fitness training and business systems helps personal trainers create a successful fitness business in any 30x30 foot space.

32994 ■ *"Innovation Station" in Canadian Business (Vol. 80, October 8, 2007, No. 20, pp. 42)*

Ed: Andrew Wahl. **Description:** Study and teaching of entrepreneurship at the University of Waterloo is discussed. Research projects in the university are expected to be influential in Canada's economic development. In spite of the success of these studies, financing is still a problem for the university, especially in technological innovations.

32995 ■ *"The Innovator: Rob McEwen's Unique Vision of Philanthropy and Business" in Canadian Business (Vol. 81, November 10, 2008, No. 19)*

Pub: Rogers Media Inc.

Contact: Tony Viner, President

Ed: Alex Mlynek. **Description:** Rob McEwen says that his donation to the Schulich School of Business is his first large donation. He went to the University Health Network and was told about their pan for regenerative medicine, helping him make the decision. McEwan wants to be involved in philanthropy in the areas of leadership and education.

32996 ■ *"Innovators Critical in Technical Economy" in Crain's Cleveland Business (Vol. 28, November 5, 2007, No. 44, pp. 10)*

Pub: Crain Communications Inc.

Ed: Peter Rea. **Description:** Discusses the importance to attract, develop and retain talented innovators on Ohio's economy. Also breaks down the four fronts on which the international battle for talent is being waged.

32997 ■ *"Integrating Business Core Knowledge through Upper Division Report Composition" in Business Communication Quarterly (December 2007)*

Pub: Pine Forge Press

Contact: Blaise R. Simqu, President

Ed: Joy Roach, Daniel Tracy, Kay Durden. **Description:** An assignment that integrates subjects and encourages the use of business communication report-writing skills is presented. This assignment is designed to complement business school curricula and help develop critical thinking and organizational skills.

32998 ■ *International Entrepreneurship Education: Issues and Newness*

Pub: Edward Elgar Publishing Inc.

Contact: Richard Henning, Vice President

E-mail: kwight@e-elgar.com

Ed: Alain Fayolle, Heinz Klandt. **Released:** 2006. **Price:** £76.50. **Description:** Entrepreneurial education, focusing on economic, political and social needs of a changing world; ideas for reassessing, redeveloping, and renewing curricula and methods for teaching entrepreneurship are offered. **Availability:** Print.

32999 ■ *"International Growth" in Black Enterprise (Vol. 38, July 2008, No. 12, pp. 64)*

Pub: Earl G. Graves Publishing Co. Inc.

Contact: Earl G. Graves, Jr., President

Ed: Marcia A. Reed-Woodard. **Description:** Becoming an increasingly smaller portion of the global business environment is the U.S. economy. Christopher Catlin, an associate with Booz Allen Hamilton, a technology management and strategy-consulting firm, shares what he has learned about the global market.

33000 ■ *"Interning Your Way to the Right Career" in Business Review Albany (Vol. 41, June 20, 2014, No. 12, pp. 9)*

Pub: American City Business Journals, Inc.

Contact: Whitney Shaw, President

Released: June 20, 2014. **Description:** The degree boom has made it increasingly important for students to participate in internship programs in order to stand out. Internship programs also provide companies with several benefits.

33001 ■ *Introduction to Business*

Pub: The McGraw-Hill Companies

Ed: Laura Portolese Dias, Amit J. Shah. **Released:** January 1, 2009. **Price:** $70.94. **Description:** Introduction to business course discusses the changing educational environment for teaching business courses in colleges and universities.

33002 ■ *"Invest in Energy-Efficient Equipment for Your Pet Store" in Pet Product News (Vol. 66, September 2012, No. 9, pp. 72)*

Pub: Bowtie Inc.

Ed: Leila Meyer. **Description:** Aquatic retailers can achieve business growth by offering lighting products, pumps, heaters, filters, and other aquarium supplies that would help customers realize energy efficiency. Aside from offering an education in energy efficiency as a customer service opportunity, retailers are encouraged to determine what supplies are crucial in helping customers achieve energy usage goals.

33003 ■ *"Is Business Ethics Getting Better? A Historical Perspective" in Business Ethics Quarterly (Vol. 21, April 2011, No. 2, pp. 335)*

Pub: Society for Business Ethics

Contact: Dawn Elm, Executive Director

Ed: Joanne B. Ciulla. **Description:** The question 'Is Business Ethics Getting Better?' as a heuristic for discussing the importance of history in understanding business and ethics is answered. The article uses a number of examples to illustrate how the same ethical problems in business have been around for a long time. It describes early attempts at the Harvard School of Business to use business history as a means of teaching students about moral and social values. In the end, the author suggests that history may be another way to teach ethics, enrich business ethics courses, and develop the perspective and vision in future business leaders.

33004 ■ *"Is Formal Ethics Training Merely Cosmetic? A Study of Ethics Training and Ethical Organizational Culture" in Business Ethics Quarterly (Vol. 24, January 2014, No. 1, pp. 85)*

Pub: Business Ethics Quarterly

Released: January 2014. **Description:** U.S. Organizational Sentencing Guidelines provide firms with incentives to develop formal ethics programs that promote ethical organizational cultures and thereby decrease corporate offenses. An examination of the effects of training on ethical organizational culture is discussed.

33005 ■ *"Is It Ever OK to Break a Promise? A Student Must Decide Whether to Leave the Company that Sponsored His MBA for a Dream Job" in Harvard Business Review (Vol. 92, September 2014, No. 9, pp. 119)*

Pub: Harvard Business Publishing

Released: September 2014. **Description:** A fictitious decision making scenario is presented, with contributors providing advice. One notes that change, requiring people to adapt and, in some cases, alter contracts. Another states that the original contract should be honored and that other opportunities are likely to present themselves to the student considering leaving the firm that sponsored his MBA.

33006 ■ *"It's Not Rocket Science" in Hispanic Business (September 2007, pp. 30, 32)*

Pub: Hispanic Business Inc.

Contact: Jesus Chavarria, President

Ed: Hildy Medina. **Description:** Profile of France Cordova, president of Purdue University. Cordova has established many diversity programs at the school.

33007 ■ *"A Jobs Compact for America's Future: Badly Needed Investments In Human Capital Are Not Being Made. What We Can Do - Together - To Jump-Start the Process?" in Harvard Business Review (Vol. 90, March 2012, No. 3, pp. 64)*

Pub: Harvard Business Review Press

Contact: Peter E. Walsh, Director

Ed: Thomas A. Kochan. **Released:** March 2012. **Description:** Obstacles to strengthening US human capital are a lack of focus on obtaining both high wages and high productivity, and a lack of value placed on human capital as a competitive advantage. Business schools are well positioned to address these obstacles via curricula, programs, and partnerships.

33008 ■ *"Jobs: On the Clock" in Canadian Business (Vol. 82, April 27, 2009, No. 7, pp. 28)*

Pub: Rogers Media Inc.

Contact: Tony Viner, President

Ed: Sarka Halas. **Description:** Survey of 100 Canadian executives found that senior managers can be out of a job for about nine months before their careers are adversely affected. The nine month mark can be avoided if job seekers build networks even before they lose their jobs. Job seekers should also take volunteer work and training opportunities to increase their changes of landing a job.

33009 ■ *"John Spencer Ellis Offers Free Video Training On Creating Your Own Personal Trainer, Fitness and Coaching Information Products" in Marketing Weekly News (January 14, 2012, pp. 40)*

Description: John Spencer Ellis helps personal fitness trainers create fitness coaching products such as training videos, audio programs, smartphone apps, membership sites, training courses, ebooks, downloads and more.

33010 ■ *"Kids, Computers and the Social Networking Evolution" in Canadian Business (Vol. 81, October 27, 2008, No. 18, pp. 93)*

Ed: Penny Milton. **Description:** Social networking was found to help educate students in countries like the U.S., Canada and Mexico. Schools that embrace social networking teach students how to use computers safely and responsibly in order to counter threats to children on the Internet.

33011 ■ *"Knocking On the World's Door" in Business Journal Portland (Vol. 31, March 28, 2014, No. 4, pp. 4)*

Pub: American City Business Journals

Released: March 28, 2014. **Description:** A list of things that the City of Portland, Oregon should do to achieve world-class status is provided. Portland must welcome companies as a site selection, build infrastructure, consider the economic and recreational potential of the Willamette River, allocate more education budget and provide greater access to capital.

33012 ■ *"Knowing Is Growing: Five Strategies To Develop You and Your Business" in Black Enterprise (Vol. 38, November 2007, No. 4, pp. 106)*

Pub: Earl G. Graves Publishing Co. Inc.

Contact: Earl G. Graves, Jr., President

Ed: Erinn R. Johnson. **Description:** Five strategies for growing a small business are listed by Andrew Morrison, founder of the Small Business Camp. The camp provides training, coaching, and marketing services to entrepreneurs.

33013 ■ *"Knox County Schools Debate Outsourcing Janitorial Services" in (March 29, 2011)*

Pub: Knoxville News Sentinel Co.

Ed: Lola Alapo. **Description:** Custodial services of Knox County Schools in Tennessee may be outsourced in move to save money for the school district. Details of the proposed program are included.

33014 ■ *"The Labor Crunch is Coming"* in *Canadian Business (Vol. 80, December 25, 2006, No. 1, pp. 74)*
Description: The need for skilled and educated workforce to meet labor shortage in future in Canada is discussed.

33015 ■ *"Law School Not Such a Great Idea?"* in *Philadelphia Business Journal (Vol. 33, February 28, 2014, No. 3, pp. 8)*
Pub: American City Business Journals
Released: February 28, 2014. **Description:** Several law schools in Philadelphia, Pennsylvania saw a 31.5 percent decline in combined first-year enrollment from 2000-2014. The University of Pennsylvania gained less than one percent during the period, while Widener University's Hidener Campus had the biggest drop from 181 first-year students in 2009-2010 to just 74 in 2013-2014.

33016 ■ *The Leadership Challenge: How to Make Extraordinary Things Happen in Organizations*
Pub: Jossey-Bass Publishers
Contact: Matthew Hoover, Manager
E-mail: fwelsch@jbp.com
Ed: James M. Kouzes, Barry Z. Posner. **Released:** Fifth Edition. **Price:** $29.95, hardcover; $16.99. **Description:** According to research by the authors, people can make extraordinary things happen by liberating the leader within everyone around them. This handbook gives practical tips to aspire leaders in retail, manufacturing, government, community, church and school settings. **Availability:** PrintE-book.

33017 ■ *"Leadership Development In the Age of the Algorithm"* in *(Vol. 90, June 2012, No. 6, pp. 86)*
Pub: Harvard Business Review Press
Contact: Peter E. Walsh, Director
Ed: Marcus Buckingham. **Released:** June 2012. **Description:** Guidelines to tailor leadership training to specific individuals include assessing the leadership type for each person, identifying the top leaders for each type, creating practices that are effective for each type, delivering those practices to others, and integrate user feedback to fine-tune the process.

33018 ■ *"Leadership Training"* in *Black Enterprise (Vol. 37, January 2007, No. 6, pp. 56)*
Pub: Earl G. Graves Publishing Co. Inc.
Contact: Earl G. Graves, Jr., President
Ed: Marcia A. Reed-Woodard. **Description:** Profile of Theopolis Holman, Group Vice-President of Duke Energy, who discusses how he prepared for the merger between Duke Energy and Cinergy. Holman oversees a division of 9,000 service contractors and employees.

33019 ■ *"Leaks in the Pipeline"* in *Hispanic Business (September 2007, pp. 18, 20, 22, 24)*
Pub: Hispanic Business Inc.
Contact: Jesus Chavarria, President
Ed: Holly Ocasio Rizzo. **Description:** Graduate schools need to focus on domestic diversity in order to attract Hispanic students in a growing global economy.

33020 ■ *"Learning Before Earning"* in *Pittsburgh Business Times (Vol. 34, August 15, 2014, No. 4, pp. 12)*
Pub: American City Business Journals
Released: August 15, 2014. **Description:** The importance of the Master in Business Administration (MBA) degree in the contemporary U.S. job market, specifically whether the cost of an MBA education is justified in the current economy is discussed. Experts assert that an MBA does not guarantee a job and recommend that undergraduate students join the workforce for a few years before entering and MBA program.

33021 ■ *"Learning by Doing: Engaging Students through Learner-Centered Activities"* in *Business Communication Quarterly (December 2007, pp. 451)*
Pub: Pine Forge Press
Contact: Blaise R. Simqu, President
Ed: Karl L. Smart, Nancy Csapo. **Description:** Active learning techniques, such as the Puzzle Brain Spark activity, allow students to engage in learning activities that allow deeper thinking, critical thinking, and problem solving ability that develop business management skills.

33022 ■ *"Lessons Learned from Instructional Design Theory: An Application in Management Education"* in *Business Communication Quarterly (December 2007, pp. 414)*
Pub: Pine Forge Press
Contact: Blaise R. Simqu, President
Ed: Lisa A. Burke. **Description:** Instructors should present course information to business students in a way that enhances understanding and should use presentation techniques that students may eventually use; course materials should be kept relevant and simple.

33023 ■ *"Liberty Tax Service is Registering Students for Fall Tax Preparation Courses"* in *Economics Week (August 3, 2012)*
Pub: NewsRX
Contact: Susan E. Hasty, Publisher
Released: August 3, 2012. **Description:** Liberty Tax Service is enrolling for fall income tax preparation classes across the nation. The ten-week school teaches students strategies and advantages for personal tax savings. Liberty Tax Service offers a three-tier skill certification examination for its preparers.

33024 ■ *"The Life Changers"* in *Canadian Business (Vol. 81, October 27, 2008, No. 18, pp. 86)*
Description: The first season of 'The Life Changers' was produced in September 2007 to feature stories about research and development (R&D) efforts by universities in Atlantic Canada. The program addresses the need to inform the public about university R&D and its outcomes.

33025 ■ *"Lobster Mania Hits China: They Just Had To Get Used To the Claws"* in *Canadian Business (Vol. 85, July 16, 2012, No. 11-12, pp. 10)*
Pub: George Media Inc.
Ed: Joe Castaldo. **Released:** July 16, 2012. **Description:** Canadian lobster exports to China have tripled to almost $30 million annually since 2010 as a result of marketing efforts by Maritimes governments including pitching lobster to cooking shows and organizing training sessions for Chinese chefs. Canadian exporters must decide whether their lobster is a premium product or a commodity product to solidify its image in China.

33026 ■ *"The Long View: Roberta Bondar's Unique Vision of Science, The Need for Education, and More"* in *Canadian Business (Vol. 81, October 27, 2008, No. 18)*
Pub: Rogers Media Inc.
Contact: Tony Viner, President
Ed: Alex Mlynek. **Description:** Roberta Bondar believes that energy and renewable energy is a critical environmental issue faced by Canada today. Bondar is the first Canadian woman and neurologist in space.

33027 ■ *"Loss of Rutgers Name Causing a Stir for Law School"* in *Philadelphia Business Journal (Vol. 28, April 20, 2012, No. 10, pp. 1)*
Pub: American City Business Journal
Description: The plan to merge Rutgers University-Camden with Rowan University is being opposed by those from Rutgers who feel they will have problems recruiting students if they lose the Rutgers brand. Rowan on the other hand, is more known in the South Jersey area only.

33028 ■ *"Lower Unemployment Hasn't Offset Total Losses"* in *Sacramento Business Journal (Vol. 31, May 23, 2014, No. 13, pp. 6)*
Pub: American City Business Journals
Released: May 23, 2014. **Description:** The decline in Sacramento, California's unemployment rate has not reduced the city's economic losses. Unemployment in the area has decreased by 7.5 percent in April 2014. Meanwhile, educational and health services are expected to be the job growth sectors in the next 12 months.

33029 ■ *"lynda.com Receives Green Business Certification"* in *Benzinga.com (July 11, 2012)*
Pub: Benzinga.com
Contact: Kyle Bazzy, President
Ed: Aaron Wise. **Description:** Online learning firm, lynda.com, earned the Green Business certification from the Green Business Program (GBP) of Santa Barbara, California. The company has reduced energy and water usage, reduced solid waste such as composting food scraps and donating electronics, and created an employee commuter program saving 600 gallons of gas in its first two months.

33030 ■ *"Macomb County, OU Eye Business Incubator"* in *Crain's Detroit Business (Vol. 24, February 11, 2008, No. 6, pp. 1)*
Pub: Crain Communications Inc. - Detroit
Contact: Keith Crain, Chairman
Ed: Chad Halcom. **Description:** Officials in Macomb County, Michigan are discussing plans to create a defense-themed business incubator in the county. Macomb County was awarded $282,000 in federal budget appropriation for the project.

33031 ■ *"Madison Schools To Use $12M Windfall for Tax Relief, Technology Upgrades, Achievement Gap"* in *WI State Journal (September 22, 2012)*
Description: Madison, Wisconsin School District recommends that its School Board use a $12 million state aid payment from a mix of property tax relief on technology upgrades and other new spending initiatives aimed at closing student achievement gaps.

33032 ■ *"Making the Most of Milk to Revive a Falling Market"* in *Farmer's Weekly (March 28, 2008, No. 320)*
Description: DairyCo, eight of whom are working dairy farmers, aim to promote a feeding campaign for better herd health, provide research into efficient labor use, and sponsor discussion groups to enhance business skills.

33033 ■ *"Making Waves"* in *Business Journal Portland (Vol. 27, November 26, 2010, No. 39, pp. 1)*
Pub: Portland Business Journal
Ed: Erik Siemers. **Description:** Corvallis, Oregon-based Columbia Power Technologies LLC is about to close a $2 million Series A round of investment initiated by $750,000 from Oregon Angel Fund. The wave energy startup company was formed to commercialize the wave buoy technology developed by Oregon State University researchers.

33034 ■ *"Managing the Facebookers; Business"* in *The Economist (Vol. 390, January 3, 2009, No. 8612, pp. 10)*
Pub: Economist Newspaper Ltd.
Description: According to a report from PricewaterhouseCoopers, a business consultancy, workers from Generation Y, also known as the Net Generation, are more difficult to recruit and integrate into companies that practice traditional business acumen. 61 percent of chief executive managers say that they have trouble with younger employees who tend to be more narcissistic and more interested in personal fulfillment with a need for frequent feedback and an over-precise set of objectives on the path to promotion which can be hard for managers who are used to a different relationship with their subordinates. Older bosses should prepare to make some concessions to their younger talent since some of the issues that make them happy include cheaper online ways to communicate and additional coaching, both of which are good for business.

33035 ■ *Managing for Success: The Latest in Management Thought and Practice from Canada's Premier Business School*
Ed: Monica Fleck. **Released:** December 2000. **Description:** Canadian business school offers insight into the latest management skills of the nation's business leaders.

33036 ■ *"Mandel Site Favored For UWM Hall" in The Business Journal-Milwaukee (Vol. 25, September 19, 2008, No. 52, pp. A1)*
Pub: American City Business Journals, Inc.
Contact: Whitney Shaw, President
Ed: Pete Millard. **Description:** University of Wisconsin-Milwaukee student residence hall's leading location is a site pushed by Mandel Group Inc. Real estate sources say that the developer's proposal offers the best opportunity for business development and the least conflict with nearby neighborhoods. Plans for the Mandel site are presented.

33037 ■ *"Manufacturers Urged to Adapt to Defense" in Crain's Cleveland Business (Vol. 30, June 22, 2009, No. 24, pp. 3)*
Pub: Crain Communications Inc.
Ed: Dan Shingler. **Description:** Manufacturers in Northeast Ohio are making products for the military from steel, polymers or composite materials. The U.S. Department of Defense is teaching companies to work with titanium and other advanced metals in order to further manufacture for the military.

33038 ■ *"Market Forces" in Canadian Business (Vol. 79, October 23, 2006, No. 21, pp. 93)*
Ed: Erin Pooley. **Description:** The tremendous rise in the number of business schools offering Master of business administration degree in Canada and the depletion in the quality of education provided in these business schools is discussed.

33039 ■ *"Marketing Scholarship 2.0" in Journal of Marketing (Vol. 75, July 2011, No. 4, pp. 225)*
Pub: American Marketing Association
Contact: Lucille Pointer, President
Ed: Richard J. Lutz. **Description:** A study of the implications of changing environment and newer collaborative models for marketing knowledge production and dissemination is presented. Crowdsourcing has become a frequently employed strategy in industry. Academic researchers should collaborate more as well as the academe and industry, to make sure that important problems are being investigated.

33040 ■ *"Mass. STEM Approach and R.I. Model?" in Providence Business News (Vol. 28, March 10, 2014, No. 49, pp. 1)*
Pub: American City Business Journals
Released: March 10, 2014. **Description:** Rhode Island is in the process of developing an educational system that prepares students to excel in science, technology, engineering and math (STEM). Educational services in the state are examining the Massachusetts educational program in order to generate ideas.

33041 ■ *"A Master Chef's Recipe for Business Success" in Business Strategy Review (Vol. 23, Spring 2012, No. 1, pp. 65)*
Released: Spring 2012. **Description:** Often called the world's greatest chef, Ferran Adria, longtime owner of El Built, Spain's three-star Michelin rated revolutionary restaurant, is now embarking on a new venture: the El Built Foundation, a place where chefs can create, interact, and discuss their ideas with researchers from other disciplines. He recently spoke at London Business School as part of his tour of a number of select universities to invite students to enter a competition to design an innovative business model for the new Foundation.

33042 ■ *"MBA Essentials: Real-Life Instruction" in Women In Business (Vol. 61, October-November 2009, No. 5, pp. 28)*
Pub: American Business Women's Association
Contact: Lorie Burch, President
Ed: Leigh Elmore. **Description:** University of Kansas School of Business allied itself with the American Business Women's Association (ABWA) which led to

the formation of the ABWA-KU MBA essentials program. With this program, ABWA members are exposed to graduate-level coursework that delves on business topics, such as strategy and operations.

33043 ■ *"MBA Guide 2008" in Canadian Business (Vol. 81, November 10, 2008, No. 19, pp. 92)*
Ed: Sharda Prashad. **Description:** Escalating tuition costs for an MBA degree means that the return on investment could take longer. One study found that MBA degree holders who graduated during recessionary times earned less than those who graduated during good economic times.

33044 ■ *MBA In A Day: What You Would Learn At Top-Tier Business Schools (If You Only Had The Time!)*
Pub: John Wiley & Sons Inc.
Contact: Stephen M. Smith, President
Ed: Steven Stralser. **Released:** September 2004. **Price:** $34.95, hardcover; $22.99. **Description:** Management professor presents important concepts, business topics and strategies that can be used by anyone to manage a small business or professional practice. Topics covered include: human resources and personal interaction, ethics and leadership skills, fair negotiation tactics, basic business accounting practices, project management, and the fundamentals of economics and marketing. **Availability:** PrintEbook.

33045 ■ *"MBAs by the Hour" in Entrepreneur (August 2014)*
Pub: Entrepreneur Media Inc.
Released: August 2014. **Description:** HourlyNerd started from a classroom project by Pat Petitti and Rob Biederman at Harvard Business School in Boston, Massachusetts in 2003. the temporary-staffing firm recruits business students to act as consultants to small businesses that hire them. Consultants must come from one of the top 40 Master of Business Administration Programs in the U.S. in order to bid on a project. The firm receives 15 percent of the project fee from the hiring company while the business consultants pay 5 percent to the company.

33046 ■ *"MBAs Plus Designers Equals New Life for Business" in Globe & Mail (April 24, 2007, pp. B1)*
Ed: Gordon Pitts. **Description:** The need for Canadian companies to combine the skills of management graduates and designers to achieve corporate growth is discussed.

33047 ■ *"Md. Is a Victim of Its Own STEM Success" in Baltimore Business Journal (Vol. 30, August 10, 2012, No. 14, pp. 1)*
Pub: American City Business Journals, Inc.
Contact: Whitney Shaw, President
Ed: Sarah Gantz. **Released:** August 10, 2012. **Description:** Colleges and universities in Maryland are over filling their capacity to provide science, technology, engineering, and mathematics education. Maryland's success in STEM education has led to its losing students to colleges in other states that offer smaller classes or better facilities. Factors that influence the rising demand for STEM degrees and its impact on state and private universities are discussed.

33048 ■ *"Meet the Next Big Name in Residential Construction" in Houston Business Journal (Vol. 44, February 21, 2014, No. 42, pp. 8)*
Pub: American City Business Journals
Released: February 21, 2014. **Description:** Hillwood Communities of Dallas, Texas will break ground on the Pomona master-planned community in Manvel, 20 miles south of downtown Houston. The development will include 2,100 single-family homes ranging from $250,000 to $400,000, a new elementary school and a new junior high school.

33049 ■ *"Meet UT's New Business Mind" in Austin Business Journal (Vol. 31, May 13, 2011, No. 10, pp. A1)*
Pub: American City Business Journals
Ed: Sandra Zaragoza. **Description:** University of Texas (UT) chief commercialization officer, Dr. Richard Miller, has opened a satellite office in Silicon

Valley, California in the hopes of luring Californian investors to the science and technology at UT. The satellite office is just one of Miller's efforts to reshape and widen the commercialization of UT-Austin. Insights into Miller's long-term view approach to commercialization are also covered.

33050 ■ *"Mentoring Support" in Black Enterprise (Vol. 38, July 2008, No. 12, pp. 64)*
Pub: Earl G. Graves Publishing Co. Inc.
Contact: Earl G. Graves, Jr., President
Description: With his relocation from his multicultural team in New York to the less diverse Scripps Networks' headquarters in Knoxville, Earl Cokley has made it a top priority to push for more diversity and mentoring opportunities within the management of the media and marketing company.

33051 ■ *"Mercyhurst Rolls Out Culinary Cab Food Truck" in Erie Times-News (June 19, 2012)*
Pub: McClatchy-Tribune Information Services
Ed: Erica Erwin. **Released:** June 19, 2012. **Description:** Mercyhurst University's food service company launched a Culinary Cab, or food truck, offering a variety of food choices to the campus community. Details of Parkhurst Dining Services plan for the mobile restaurant are outlined.

33052 ■ *"Mettle Detector" in Canadian Business (Vol. 79, July 17, 2006, No. 14-15, pp. 63)*
Pub: Rogers Media Inc.
Contact: Tony Viner, President
Ed: Calvin Leung. **Description:** The difficulties faced in completing the Certified Financial Analyst course, and the rewards one can expect after its completion, are discussed.

33053 ■ *"MicroPort Wasting No Time To Raise Manufacturing Capacity" in Memphis Business Journal (Vol. 35, January 24, 2014, No. 42, pp. 7)*
Pub: American City Business Journals
Released: January 24, 2014. **Description:** MicroPort Orthopedics has occupied the 250,000-square-foot manufacturing, distribution and office space in Arlington, Tennessee since its acquisition from Wright Medical Group Inc. MicroPort CEO, Ted Davis, plans to add a surgical training facility and increase manufacturing capacity.

33054 ■ *Microtrends: The Small Forces Behind Tomorrow's Big Changes*
Ed: Mark J. Penn. **Released:** 2007. **Price:** $25.99. **Description:** Political pollster and lead presidential campaign strategist for Hillary Clinton, identifies seventy-five microtrends he believes are changing the social and cultural landscape in the U.S. and globally. The book covers the areas of health and wellness, technology, education and more.

33055 ■ *"MindLeaders' Online Training Courses Come to ePath Learning" in Information Today (Vol. 26, February 2009, No. 2, pp. 4)*
Description: MindLeaders has partnered with ePath Learning to provide clients with over 2,200 new online courses. ePath's integrated Learning Management Service (iLMS) allows organizations to create online training programs for employees.

33056 ■ *"Moooove Over, Sodas: Okaloosa to Get Dairy Vending Machines for Two Schools" in Northwest Florida Daily News (September 27, 2001)*
Pub: Freedom Communications
Ed: Katie Tammen. **Description:** Two Okaloosa County high schools will be offering more lunch options by installing refrigerated vending machines featuring dairy-related food.

33057 ■ *"More Cuts On the Way At OSU Ag School" in Business First-Columbus (December 14, 2007, pp. A1)*
Pub: American City Business Journals, Inc.
Ed: Carrie Ghose. **Description:** Program cuts at Ohio State University's Agriculture School are discussed. A voluntary retirement incentive to reduce

staff was approved by the University's trustees. Since 2000, the College of Food, Agricultural and Environmental Sciences' staff have decreased by 21 percent, while the faculty experienced a 25 percent reduction. According to Bobby Moser, the college's dean, the institution is looking for other ways to generate income.

33058 ■ *"More Sales Leads, Please: Or, What Happened When Frontline Selling Started Practicing What It Preaches" in Inc. (November 2007)*
Pub: Mansueto Ventures L.L.C.
Contact: John Koten, Chief Executive Officer
Ed: Beth Kwon. **Description:** Frontline Selling, located in Oakland, New Jersey, helps train sales teams to generate and convert sales leads. The consulting firm doubled their marketing budget to increase their own sales.

33059 ■ *"NASA and Partners Complete Unmanned Aircraft Testing" in Travel & Leisure Close-Up (October 8, 2012)*
Description: A partnership between the government, a not-for-profit research and development organization, and academia tested an unmanned aircraft for 'sense and avoid' technology in order to better integrate unmanned aircraft into the national air technology system.

33060 ■ *"Natalie Peterson; Corporate Counsel, Steris Corp." in Crain's Cleveland Business (Vol. 28, November 19, 2007, No. 46, pp. F-14)*
Pub: Crain Communications Inc.
Ed: Chuck Soder. **Description:** Profile of Natalie Peterson, corporate counsel for Steris Corp., a manufacturer of sterilization products; Peterson's blue-collar background did not detour her from her collegiate goals although she hardly knew how to fill out a college application. After graduating from Stanford Law School in 1997, she opted to return to Cleveland in lieu of more lucrative job offers in San Francisco. She has joined the school board and has participated in the 3Rs program, in which lawyers visit public schools in Cleveland to get students thinking about career choices and talk about constitutional law.

33061 ■ *"National Instruments Connects with Lego" in Austin Business JournalInc. (Vol. 28, August 25, 2008, No. 23, pp. 1)*
Pub: American City Business Journals
Ed: Laura Hipp. **Description:** Austin-based National Instruments Corporation has teamed with Lego Group from Denmark to create a robot that can be built by children and can be used to perform tasks. Lego WeDo, their latest product, uses computer connection to power its movements. The educational benefits of the new product are discussed.

33062 ■ *"Native Wisdom" in Canadian Business (Vol. 80, October 8, 2007, No. 20, pp. 121)*
Ed: Bernd Christmas. **Description:** Roles of Canadian indigenous peoples in the country's economic development are discussed. It is believed that empowering Canadian natives to contribute to the country's economy will positively affect the country's future. The need for education in preparing natives for the global economy is also tackled.

33063 ■ *"Negotiating Tips" in Black Enterprise (Vol. 37, December 2006, No. 5, pp. 70)*
Pub: Earl G. Graves Publishing Co. Inc.
Contact: Earl G. Graves, Jr., President
Ed: Marcia A. Reed-Woodard. **Description:** Sekou Kaalund, head of strategy, mergers & acquisitions at Citigroup Securities & Fund Services, states that 'Negotiation skills are paramount to success in a business environment because of client, employee, and shareholder relationships'. He discusses how the book by George Kohlrieser, Hostage at the Table: How Leaders Can Overcome Conflict, Influence Others, and Raise Performance, has helped him negotiate more powerfully and enhance his skills at conflict-resolution.

33064 ■ *"'Netting Degrees: More Professionals Continuing Their Education Online" in Hispanic Business (September 2007, pp. 62, 64)*
Ed: Hildy Medina. **Description:** Traditional universities and private institutions offer online courses to professionals wishing to further their education.

33065 ■ *"New A.D.'s Task: Grow the Gopher Budget" in Business Journal (Vol. 30, June 29, 2012, No. 5, pp. 1)*
Pub: American City Business Journals, Inc.
Contact: Whitney Shaw, President
Ed: John Vomhof Jr. **Released:** June 29, 2012. **Description:** Norwood Teague, the new athletic director of the University of Minnesota, believes that the school needs to improve its fundraising efforts in order to competitively fund its 25 sports. The university's athletic department ranked eighth out of 21 teams in the Big Ten Conference in terms of revenue.

33066 ■ *"New Approach Could Boost Ivory Tower Innovation" in Business Journal-Portland (Vol. 24, November 16, 2007, No. 37, pp. 1)*
Pub: American City Business Journals, Inc.
Ed: Aliza Earnshaw. **Description:** New approach which aims to help universities move to a corporate structure, secure funds, and find professional managers is being explored. Accelerator Corporation was able to help six companies through its funding. Joe Tanous who is behind Oregon's State University's enhanced commercialization, would like to apply the same approach Accelerator used to help Oregon State University, the University of Oregon, Portland State University and Oregon Health and Science University.

33067 ■ *"New Biz Mixes Paint, Wine; Will It Yield Green?" in Crain's Detroit Business (Vol. 30, September 8, 2014, No. 36, pp. 6)*
Pub: Crain Communications Inc. - Detroit
Contact: Keith Crain, Chairman
Released: September 8, 2014. **Description:** Profile of Leanna Haun, owner of Picasso's Grapevine in downtown Clarkston, Michigan. Haun describes her business as one part wine, one part paint, and one part entertainment. Sessions include as many as ten people who are given instruction to paint a picture while enjoying wine and conversation with others.

33068 ■ *"New Career Center Opens at Right Time: Laid-Off Freightliner Workers Will Need Help" in Charlotte Observer (February 1, 2007)*
Ed: Gail Smith-Arrants. **Description:** Rowan-Cabarrus Community College announced the opening of its new career development center that will help area workers train for new careers.

33069 ■ *"New Generation Deans Lead Atlanta Area Business Schools Into the Future" in Atlanta Business Chronicle (July 25, 2014, pp. 3A)*
Pub: American City Business Journals, Inc.
Contact: Whitney Shaw, President
Released: July 25, 2014. **Description:** An interview with five business school deans from Georgia share their views on the future of business education, changing business education needs, and other issues affecting the Atlanta area business schools. The growing demands for greater global competences, good communication skills across various cultures, and other challenges faced by the students and employers are discussed. Other topics include the role of women in the corporate world.

33070 ■ *"The New Schools" in Black Enterprise (February 2008)*
Pub: Earl G. Graves Publishing Co. Inc.
Contact: Earl G. Graves, Jr., President
Ed: Kingsley Kanu, Jr. **Description:** Ten educational programs to help top executives keep pace with the ever-changing market trends while gaining perspective on innovation and new ideas are examined.

33071 ■ *"New Venture Putting City on Pharma Map" in San Antonio Business Journal (Vol. 26, September 14, 2012, No. 33, pp. 1)*
Released: September 14, 2012. **Description:** The Center for Innovation in Drug Discovery is a joint project of the University of Texas at San Antonio and University of Texas Health Science Center that aims to expand drug development and create new bioscience companies in the city. The institutions have received nearly $4 million in public and private funding and plan to raise additional capital.

33072 ■ *"Next Generation Security Awareness" in Security Management (Vol. 56, September 2012, No. 9, pp. 32)*
Pub: ASIS International
Contact: Joseph R. Granger, President
Released: September 2012. **Description:** Carnegie Mellon University (CMU) has purchased Wombat Security Technologies' PhishGuru to reduce the phishing attacks. CMU also purchased Wombat's two educational games, Anti-Phishing and Anti-Phishing Phyllis, partly due to the PhishGuru's success. Insights on the software-as-a-service solution are also given.

33073 ■ *"Nike, AdPro Investments Up Value of UB Apparel Contract" in Business First of Buffalo (Vol. 30, February 14, 2014, No. 22, pp. 3)*
Pub: American City Business Journals, Inc.
Contact: Whitney Shaw, President
Released: February 14, 2014. **Description:** Amherst, New York-based AdPro Sports has signed an amendment to its contract with University of Buffalo that increased the investments to $161,650. The new agreement includes new commitments from Nike and AdPro, while the marketing for men and women's basketball was increased. Details of the 2012-13 and 2013-14 contracts are examined.

33074 ■ *"No Fast Cash Class" in Black Enterprise (Vol. 37, December 2006, No. 5, pp. 72)*
Pub: Earl G. Graves Publishing Co. Inc.
Contact: Earl G. Graves, Jr., President
Ed: Sonia Alleyne. **Description:** There are no shortcuts to a obtaining a career as a financial planner. The Certified Financial Planner Board of Standards has specific requirements for certification which include having a bachelor's degree from an accredited U.S. school before candidates are even eligible for taking the certification exam. Other criteria and requirements are discussed.

33075 ■ *"No More Ivory Towers: Local Colleges and Universities are Here to Help Your Business" in Orlando Business Journal (Vol. 30, February 28, 2014, No. 36, pp. 4)*
Pub: American City Business Journals
Released: February 28, 2014. **Description:** A number of school leaders in Central Florida share their views on partnering with the business community, boosting science and technology graduates, benefits of a private college, economic development efforts and fixing the higher education construction gridlock. Local universities and colleges have a combined economic impact of $15 billion each year.

33076 ■ *"Nonprofit Ready to Get More Girls into 'STEM' Jobs" in Austin Business JournalInc. (Vol. 29, December 25, 2009, No. 42, pp. 1)*
Pub: American City Business Journals
Ed: Sandra Zaragoza. **Description:** Girlstart has completed its $1.5 million capital campaign to buy the building it will care the Girlstart Tech Center. Girlstart is a nonprofit organization that prepares girls for science, technology, engineering and mathematics or STEM careers. Details of the program are highlighted.

33077 ■ *"Not-So-Rare Workplace Violence" in Baltimore Business Journal (Vol. 31, January 31, 2014, No. 40, pp. 2)*
Pub: American City Business Journals, Inc.
Contact: Whitney Shaw, President
Released: January 31, 2014. **Description:** Advice is given for people to understand about workplace violence. A list of eight important things everyone

needs to know is given. The US Bureau of Labor Statistics reports data showing 551 people per year have died in work-related homicides since 2010. The Columbia mall shooting provided a typical setting for assailant suicides in the sense that the victims were retail employees.

33078 ■ "NSU Seeks Private Partners For New $80M Research Building" in South Florida Business Journal (Vol. 34, February 21, 2014, No. 31, pp. 4)
Pub: American City Business Journals
Released: February 21, 2014. **Description:** The $80 million Center for Collaborative Research at Nova Southeastern University hopes to become the largest incubator and wet laboratory space in Broward County, Florida. The center had its groundbreaking on February 13, 2014, and will be open for lease to private companies when it is ready in 22 months.

33079 ■ "NU Again Offering Free Tax Preparation" in Buffalo News (January 22, 2012)
Pub: The McClatchy Co.
Contact: Peter Tira, Director
Ed: Helen Jones. **Released:** January 22, 2012. **Description:** Niagara University partnered with the Internal Revenue Service 31 years ago to provide the Volunteer Income Tax Assistance program. University students from the College of Business Administration prepare and file electronically federal and state tax returns for the elderly and low-income individuals and families.

33080 ■ Nurses Come To Fore as Care Landscape Shifts
Pub: American City Business Journals, Inc.
Contact: Whitney Shaw, President
Ed: Sarah Gantz. **Released:** July 20, 2012. **Description:** Maryland's healthcare industry is looking to increase the supply of nursesto meet an anticipated growth in demand for primary care services. The industry is working with nursing schools and colleges to increase enrollment and improve the education of existing nurses.

33081 ■ "Nurturing Talent for Tomorrow" in Restaurants and Institutions (Vol. 118, September 15, 2008, No. 14, pp. 90)
Description: Hormel Foods Corporation and The Culinary Institute of America (CIA) have teamed to develop The Culinary Enrichment and Innovation Program that supports future culinary leaders by providing creative and competitive staff development. Sixteen students attend four three-day sessions at the CIA's campus in Hyde Park, New York; sessions include classroom teaching, one-on-one interaction with leading culinarians, and hands-on kitchen time.

33082 ■ "Oakland County to Survey Employers on Needed Skills" in Crain's Detroit Business (Vol. 24, April 14, 2008, No. 15, pp. 30)
Pub: Crain Communications Inc.
Contact: Rance E. Crain, President
Ed: Chad Halcom. **Description:** In an attempt to aid educators and attract talent, Oakland County plans to collect data from 1,000 local employers on workforce skills they need now or will need soon.

33083 ■ The Official Guide for GMAT Verbal Review, 2nd Edition
Ed: Graduate Management Admissions Council. **Released:** August 17, 2009. **Price:** $17.95. **Description:** The only official verbal review for the GMAT from the creators of the test. The guide provides questions, answers, and explanations and targets study and helps improve verbal skills by focusing on the ability to read and comprehend written material, to reason and evaluate arguments, and to correct written material to conform to Standard English.

33084 ■ "Old Freescale Campus in East Austin Will Soon Have a New Life" in Austin Business Journal (Vol. 32, August 17, 2012, No. 24, pp. A1)
Pub: American City Business Journals, Inc.
Contact: Whitney Shaw, President
Ed: Jan Buchholz. **Released:** August 17, 2012. **Description:** Freescale Semiconductor Inc.'s industrial campus in East Austin, Texas has been sold to a

consortium of investors led by JLM Financial Investments LLC. The investors plan to recruit companies to lease space in the nine-building corporate campus. Insight on JLM's involvement in the deal are also given.

33085 ■ "On Beyond Powerpoint: Presentations Get a Wake-Up Call" in Inc. (November 2007, pp. 58-59)
Pub: Mansueto Ventures L.L.C.
Contact: John Koten, Chief Executive Officer
Ed: Michael Fitzgerald. **Description:** New software that allows business presentations to be shared online are profiled, including ProfCast, audio podcasts for sales, marketing, and training; SmartDraw2008, software that creates professional graphics; Dimdim, an open-Web conferencing tool; Empressr, a hosted Web service for creating, managing, and sharing multimedia presentations; Zentation, a free tool that allows users to watch slides and a videos of presenter; Spresent, a Web-based presentation tool for remote offices or conference calls.

33086 ■ "On Their Own: Bronx High School Students Open a Bank Branch" in Black Enterprise (Vol. 38, February 2008, No. 7, pp. 42)
Pub: Earl G. Graves Publishing Co. Inc.
Contact: Earl G. Graves, Jr., President
Ed: Jessica Jones. **Description:** Students at Fordham Leadership Academy for Business and Technology in New York City opened a student-run bank branch at their high school. The business paid high school seniors $11 per hour to work as tellers. Students were also taught interviewing basics.

33087 ■ "One Hundred Years of Excellence in Business Education: What Have We Learned?" in Business Horizons (January-February 2008)
Pub: Elsevier Advanced Technology Publications
Ed: Frank Acito, Patricia M. McDougall, Daniel C. Smith. **Description:** Business schools have to be more innovative, efficient and nimble, so that the quality of the next generation of business leaders is improved. The Kelley School of Business, Indiana University ahs long been a leader in business education. The trends that influence the future of business education and useful success principles are discussed.

33088 ■ "One Laptop Per Child Weighs Going For-Profit" in Boston Business Journal (Vol. 31, May 20, 2011, No. 17, pp. 1)
Pub: Boston Business Journal
Ed: Mary Moore. **Description:** Nonprofit organization One Laptop Per Child is thinking of shifting into a for-profit structure in order to raise as much as $10 million in capital to achieve its goal of distributing more XO laptops to poor children worldwide. The organization has distributed 2 million computers since 2008 with Uruguay, Peru and Rwanda as its biggest markets.

33089 ■ "Online Training Requires Tools, Accessories" in Contractor (Vol. 56, September 2009, No. 9, pp. 67)
Pub: Penton Media, Inc.
Ed: Larry Drake. **Description:** Importance of the right equipment and tools to members of the United States plumbing industry undergoing online training is discussed. Portable devices such as Blackberrys and I-phones could be used for online training. The use of headphones makes listening easier for the trainee.

33090 ■ "Organic Food Industry Goes to College" in USA Today (April 9, 2012)
Pub: Gannett Company Inc.
Contact: Craig A. Dubow, President
Ed: Chuck Raasch. **Description:** With the organic food industry growing the US Department of Agriculture is has pumped $117 million into organic research in the last three years. According to a recent report by the Organic Farming Research Foundation (OFRF), the number of states committing land for organic research has nearly doubled from 2003 to 2011. Universities offering academic programs in organic farming rose from none to nine. The OFRF supports organic farmers and producers.

33091 ■ "The Outcome of an Organization Overhaul" in Black Enterprise (Vol. 41, December 2010, No. 5)
Pub: Earl G. Graves Publishing Co. Inc.
Contact: Earl G. Graves, Jr., President
Ed: Tamara E. Holmes. **Description:** Savvy business owners understand the need for change in order to stay competitive and be successful. This article examines how to manage change as well as what strategies can help employees to get with the program faster.

33092 ■ "Overqualified. Underemployed" in Philadelphia Business Journal (Vol. 33, August 1, 2104, No. 25, pp. 14)
Pub: American City Business Journals
Released: August 1, 2014. **Description:** Overqualified workers often find themselves in employment situations where their education, experience and skills are beyond the requirements of the job. The implications of underemployment for the worker, the organization and the overall U.S. economy are discussed.

33093 ■ "Owner of Skin Care Business Offers Westfield State Scholarships If Ex-President Droops Lawsuit" in Boston Business Journal (Vol. 34, April 25, 2014, No. 12, pp. 5)
Pub: American City Business Journals, Inc.
Contact: Whitney Shaw, President
Released: April 25, 2014. **Description:** John Walsh, CEO of Elizabeth Grady Company, has offered $100,000 in scholarships if Westfield State University President, Evan Dobelle, drops his lawsuits against the university. Dobelle decided to sue the school after he was placed on paid leave by three trustees.

33094 ■ "Palace Adds Marketing Arm: College Sponsorships First Step In New Effort" in Crain's Detroit Business (October 1, 2007)
Pub: Crain Communications Inc. - Detroit
Contact: Keith Crain, Chairman
Ed: Bill Shea. **Description:** Palace Sports and Entertainment is restructuring itself from operating the Detroit Piston's basketball team and concert venues into a marketing company that also runs sports teams and venues. The firm signed a deal to handle sponsorship sales for colleges and universities.

33095 ■ "Past Promises Haunt Project" in The Business Journal-Portland (Vol. 25, August 1, 2008, No. 21, pp. 1)
Pub: American City Business Journals, Inc.
Contact: Whitney Shaw, President
Ed: Aliza Earnshaw. **Description:** Oregon University System and Oregon Health and Science University will face the state Legislature to defend their request for a $250 million in state bonds to fund a life-sciences collaborative research building. The project is meant to help grow the Oregon bioscience industry. Comments from industry observers and legislators are also presented.

33096 ■ "The People Puzzle; Re-Training America's Workers" in The Economist (Vol. 390, January 3, 2009, No. 8612, pp. 32)
Description: With thousands of workers losing their jobs, America is now facing the task of getting them back to work. With an overall unemployment rate of 6.7 percent, the federal government has three main ways for leading workers back to employment: training them for new jobs, providing unemployment insurance in order to replace lost wages during the period of job-hunting; and matching employers who desire a skill with workers who have that skill. Specialized staffing agencies provide employers and potential employees with the help necessary to find a job in some of the more niche markets.

33097 ■ "Perfecting Customer Services" in Pet Product News (Vol. 64, November 2010, No. 11, pp. 18)
Pub: Bowtie Inc.
Description: Pet supply retailers are encouraged to emphasize customer experience and sales representatives' knowledge of the store's product offerings to foster repeat business. Employee protocols could be

implemented to improve customer interaction. Other guidelines on developing a pet supply retail environment that advances repeat business are presented.

33098 ■ *"Personal Trainer Fitness Certification Offers Secrets to Personal Training Business and Career Success"* in *Marketing Weekly News (January 14, 2012, pp. 56)*

Description: The National Exercise and Sports Trainers Association (NESTA) is offering an online NCCA accredited four-year training certification with cost savings over most other certification programs. The program is 100 percent online and self-paced.

33099 ■ *"Pet Store Fish Provide Clue to How Alzheimer's Disease May Start"* in *Internet Wire (July 9, 2012)*

Released: July 9, 2012. **Description:** Western University of Health Sciences in Pomona, California researchers report that studies with zebrafish provided an important clue to understanding how Alzheimer's disease starts. Details of the study are included.

33100 ■ *"Pet Store Pro Adds New Curriculum"* in *Pet Product News (Vol. 66, February 2012, No. 2, pp. 2012)*

Description: Pet Store Pro, the Pet Industry Distributors Association's free online training program, is going to launch chapters of a curriculum intended to assist pet store managers learn effective approaches to motivate employees and boost profitability. Other management-level chapters to be added by Pet Store Pro throughout 2012 are listed.

33101 ■ *"Physics for Females"* in *Occupational Outlook Quarterly (Vol. 55, Summer 2011, No. 2, pp. 22)*

Pub: U.S. Department of Labor Bureau of Labor Statistics

Contact: Philip L. Rones, Manager

E-mail: rones.philip@bls.gov

Description: Free resources to help females investigate careers in medical physics and health physics are available from the American Physical Society. The booklet is designed for girls in middle and high school and describes the work of 15 women who use physics to solve medical mysteries, discover planets, research new materials, and more.

33102 ■ *"A Plea for the Two-Year Degree"* in *Canadian Business (Vol. 85, June 11, 2012, No. 10, pp. 19)*

Pub: George Media Inc.

Ed: Richard Branson. **Released:** June 11, 2012. **Description:** The vision to shorten the duration of undergraduate degrees by a year or more is proposed to allow skilled people to move into the workforce more quickly and with reduced student debt. Universities in North America can maximize the use of facilities by reducing schooling from 100 weeks to 8 weeks over two to three years to accommodate other students during summer breaks.

33103 ■ *"Plenty of Jobs, Will Workers Follow?"* in *Providence Business News (Vol. 28, January 27, 2014, No. 43, pp. 1)*

Pub: American City Business Journals

Released: January 27, 2014. **Description:** Electric Boat announced a plan to hire 650 employees in 2014 for its facility at Quonset Business Park in North Kingstown, Rhode Island. However, meeting the hiring goals will be a challenge because of smaller educational pipeline for welders, electricians, shipfitters, and pipefitters. Rhode Island's internship programs to fill the skills gap are also discussed.

33104 ■ *"Polanco Fellows: A Capital Program that Changes Lives"* in *Hispanic Business (Vol. 30, September 2008, No. 9, pp. 82)*

Pub: Hispanic Business Inc.

Contact: Jesus Chavarria, President

Ed: John Schumacher. **Description:** Launched in 2003, the Polanco fellows program is named after former state Senator Richard Polanco, a founder and chairman of the California Latino Caucus Institute. The program offers young Hispanics a chance to

experience public policy and the functioning of the California Capitol through a 12-month, on-the-job Capitol training.

33105 ■ *The Portable MBA in Entrepreneurship*

Pub: John Wiley & Sons Inc.

Contact: Stephen M. Smith, President

Ed: William D. Bygrave, Andrew Zacharakis. **Released:** 4th Edition. **Price:** $34.95, hardcover. **Description:** An updated and revised new edition of the comprehensive guide to modern entrepreneurship that tracks the core curriculum of leading business schools.

33106 ■ *"Post-Prison Center Idea Rankles Cincinnati's Over-the-Rhine"* in *Business Courier (Vol. 26, November 27, 2009, No. 31, pp. 1)*

Pub: American City Business Journals, Inc.

Contact: Whitney Shaw, President

Ed: Lucy May. **Description:** Cincinnati officials and community leaders oppose Firetree Ltd.'s plan to launch a residential program for federal offenders near the School for the Creative and Performing Arts in Over-the-Rhine. Firetree, a Pennsylvania-based reentry center services firm, proposed a five-year contract with the Federal Bureau of Prisons based on a letter to Cincinnati Police Chief Thomas Streicher.

33107 ■ *"The Power of ABWA"* in *Women In Business (Vol. 62, September 2010, No. 3, pp. 36)*

Pub: American Business Women's Association

Contact: Lorie Burch, President

Ed: Leigh Elmore. **Description:** Information about the internship received by Erica Rockley at American Business Women's Association (ABWA) headquarters is presented. Rockley received heartfelt professional advice the days she spent at the office. She also learned the importance of networking.

33108 ■ *"Pre-K Pressure"* in *Hawaii Business (Vol. 53, October 2007, No. 4, pp. 32)*

Pub: PacificBasin Communications

Ed: David K. Choo. **Description:** Kindergarten admission in Hawaii is becoming more competitive. Parents, for example, prepare their children for the kindergarten admissions process by bringing them to the schools before the interview or by paying for tutorial services. The impacts of increased competition in school admissions on the life of Hawaiian children are discussed.

33109 ■ *"The Preparation Gap"* in *Hawaii Business (Vol. 53, February 2008, No. 8, pp. 37)*

Pub: PacificBasin Communications

Ed: Ashley Hamershock. **Description:** Discussion of the educational gap in Hawaii's workforce is being addressed by educational workshops that aim to improve students' knowledge in science, technology, math, and engineering, and prepare them for their entry into the workforce. Education beyond high school is required for jobs to be filled in the coming years.

33110 ■ *"Prison Farms are Closing, but the Manure Remains"* in *Canadian Business (Vol. 83, August 17, 2010, No. 13-14, pp. 9)*

Pub: Rogers Media Inc.

Contact: Tony Viner, President

Ed: Steve Maich. **Description:** The explanation given by Canada's government ministers on planned closure of the prison farms and scrapping of the long form census are designed by mixing of spin, argument and transparent justification. The defense should have been plausible but the ministers could not handle the simple questions about statistics and prison job training with pretense.

33111 ■ *"Program To Steer Mexican Business Here"* in *Austin Business Journal (Vol. 32, June 8, 2012, No. 14, pp. 1)*

Pub: American City Business Journals, Inc.

Contact: Whitney Shaw, President

Ed: Vicky Garza. **Released:** June 8, 2012. **Description:** The Greater Austin Hispanic Chamber of Commerce has co-launched the Instituto de Empresarios

de Austin (IDEA) to attract Mexican entrepreneurs to Austin. IDEA is a monthlong program that aims to provide Mexican entrepreneurs with necessary information and make it easy for them to invest in the city. The program was formed through a partnership with the University of Texas IC(super 2) Institute.

33112 ■ *"Programs Provide Education and Training"* in *Contractor (Vol. 56, September 2009, No. 9, pp. 56)*

Pub: Penton Media, Inc.

Ed: William Feldman, Patti Feldman. **Description:** Opportunity Interactive's Showroom v2 software provides uses computer graphics to provide education and training on HVAC equipment and systems. It can draw heat pump balance points for a specific home. Meanwhile, Simutech's HVAC Training Simulators provide trainees with 'hands-on' HVACR training.

33113 ■ *"Promoting Academic Programs Using Online Videos"* in *Business Communication Quarterly (December 2007, pp. 478)*

Pub: Pine Forge Press

Contact: Blaise R. Simqu, President

Ed: Thomas Clark, Julie Stewart. **Description:** Xavier Entrepreneurial Center successfully used online videos to promote the effectiveness of its academic programs. Online videos are a cost-effective way of publicizing academic programs.

33114 ■ *"PSU Launches $90 Million Project"* in *The Business Journal-Portland (Vol. 25, July 18, 2008, No. 19, pp. 1)*

Pub: American City Business Journals, Inc.

Contact: Whitney Shaw, President

Ed: Aliza Earnshaw. **Description:** Portland State University (PSU) has launched a $90-million project for a new business school building, which is to be located at Southwest Market and Southwest Park. The business school is expected to move in to its new 130,000-suqare-foot building by 2013. PSU business school needs to raise $30 million for the project.

33115 ■ *"Q&A: Saskatchewan Premier Brad Wall"* in *Canadian Business (Vol. 82, April 27, 2009, No. 7, pp. 9)*

Pub: Rogers Media Inc.

Contact: Tony Viner, President

Ed: Joe Castaldo. **Description:** Saskatchewan Premier Brad Wall believes that the mood in the province is positive, as its economy is one of the few that is expected to post growth in 2009. Wall actively promotes the province in job fairs, offering $20,000 in tuition for recent college and university graduates that relocate in the province for seven years. Wall's views on the province's economy and challenges are presented.

33116 ■ *"Queens' Neighbors Fighting Growth"* in *Charlotte Business Journal (Vol. 27, July 20, 2012, No. 18, pp. 1)*

Pub: American City Business Journals, Inc.

Contact: Whitney Shaw, President

Ed: Susan Stabley. **Released:** July 20, 2012. **Description:** Queens University of Charlotte has been experiencing a rapid growth and has several construction project under way. However, Myers Park Homeowners Association has filed a legal action against the school and the City of Charlotte, North Carolina for changes to the zoning code that allowed the Queens' current expansion.

33117 ■ *"A Quick Guide to NATE"* in *Indoor Comfort Marketing (Vol. 70, February 2011, No. 2, pp. 12)*

Pub: Industry Publications Inc.

Contact: Shirleen Dorman, Editor

Description: Guide for training and certification in the North American Technician Excellence award.

33118 ■ *"Reaching Your Potential"* in *Harvard Business Review (Vol. 86, July-August 2008, No. 8, pp. 45)*

Pub: Harvard Business Review Press

Contact: Peter E. Walsh, Director

Ed: Robert S. Kaplan. **Description:** Being proactive in developing one's career is an important part of entrepreneurship. Keys to successful development include knowing oneself and one's goals, and taking calculated risks.

33119 ■ "Real Estate Ambitions" in Black Enterprise (Vol. 37, January 2007, No. 6, pp. 101)
Pub: Earl G. Graves Publishing Co. Inc.
Contact: Earl G. Graves, Jr., President
Ed: Tanisha A. Sykes. Description: National Real Estate Investors Association is a nonprofit trade association for both advanced as well as novice real estate investors that offers information on builders to contractors to banks. When looking to become a real estate investor utilize this organization, talk to various investors like the president of your local chapter, let people know your aspirations, and see if you can find a partner who has experience in the field. Resources included.

33120 ■ "Real-Life Coursework for Real-Life Business People" in Women In Business (Vol. 63, Summer 2011, No. 2, pp. 22)
Pub: American Business Women's Association
Contact: Lorie Burch, President
Ed: Leigh Elmore. Description: American Business Women's Association National Women's Leadership Conference provides members with academic business training courses. Members can take a variety of MBA-level courses that are taught by University of Kansas School of Business professors. Courses include marketing, management, leadership and communication and decision making.

33121 ■ "Real-Time Computer-Mediated Communication: Email and Instant Messaging Simulation" in Business Communication Quarterly (December 2007, pp. 466)
Pub: Pine Forge Press
Contact: Blaise R. Simqu, President
Ed: Amy Newman. Description: Technology-based simulation for business students to respond to emails and instant messages is presented. The simulation allows students to handle volume business correspondence at work with organizational context and under real-word business situations.

33122 ■ "Rebels' Cause: Adult Stem Cell" in Austin Business Journal (Vol. 31, June 3, 2011, No. 13, pp. 1)
Pub: American City Business Journals
Ed: Sandra Zaragoza. Description: MedRebels Foundation was launched in February 2011 with the goal of providing millions of dollars for research funding, education and advocacy for adult stem cell-focused medicine. The foundation, whose major contributor is SpineSmith LP, is a collaboration of other adult stem cell-related companies and nonprofit partners. It hopes to raise $200,000 by the end of 2011.

33123 ■ "Recovery on Tap for 2010?" in Orlando Business Journal (Vol. 26, January 1, 2010, No. 31, pp. 1)
Pub: American City Business Journals
Ed: Melanie Stawicki Azam, Richard Bilbao, Christopher Boyd, Anjali Fluker. Description: Economic forecasts for Central Florida's leading business sectors in 2010 are presented. These sectors include housing, film and TV, sports business, law, restaurants, aviation, tourism and hospitality, banking and finance, commercial real estate, retail, health care, insurance, higher education, and manufacturing. According to some local executives, Central Florida's economy will slowly recover in 2010.

33124 ■ "Red One and The Rain Chronicles" in Michigan Vue (Vol. 13, July-August 2008, No. 4, pp. 30)
Ed: Evan Cornish. Description: Troy-based film school the Motion Picture Institute (MPI) implemented the latest technology by shooting the second of their trilogy, 'The Rain Chronicles', on the Red One camera. This is the first feature film in Michigan to utilize this exciting new camera, which includes proprietary software for rendering and color correction. Brian K. Johnson heads up the visual effects team as visual effects supervisor and lead CG artist. His company, Dream Conduit Studios, had to tackle the task of employing the new work flow through a post-production pipeline that would allow him to attack complex visual effects shots, many of which

were shot with a moving camera, a technique rarely seen in films at this budgetary level where the camera is traditionally locked off.

33125 ■ "Region to Be Named Innovation Hub" in Business Courier (Vol. 27, July 2, 2010, No. 9, pp. 1)
Pub: Business Courier
Ed: Dan Monk. Description: The selection of Cincinnati's consumer-marketing cluster as a 'Hub of Innovation' by the Ohio Department of Development could boost Cincinnati's chances of receiving $100 million in grants from Ohio's Third Frontier program and other funding sources. Implications of the University of Cincinnati's designation as a Center of Excellence in Advanced Transportation and Aerospace are also discussed.

33126 ■ "Region Ready to Dig Deeper into Tech Fund" in Business Courier (Vol. 26, October 30, 2009, No. 27, pp. 1)
Pub: American City Business Journals, Inc.
Contact: Whitney Shaw, President
Ed: James Ritchie. Description: Southwest Ohio region aims for a bigger share in the planned renewal of Ohio's Third Frontier technology funding program. Meanwhile, University of Cincinnati vice president Sarah Degen will be appointed to the program's advisory board if the renewal proceeds.

33127 ■ "Regional Talent Network Unveils Employment Web Site" in Crain's Cleveland Business (Vol. 30, June 1, 2009, No. 21, pp. 11)
Pub: Crain Communications Inc.
Ed: Chuck Soder. Description: Regional Talent Network launched WhereToFindHelp.org, a Website designed to act as a directory of all Northeast Ohio resources that can help employers recruit and job seekers look for positions. The site also lists organizations offering employment and training services.

33128 ■ "Research, Treatment to Expand" in Philadelphia Business Journal (Vol. 28, June 22, 2012, No. 19, pp. 1)
Pub: American City Business Journal
Description: Fox Chase Cancer Center and Temple University Health System have been planning several projects once their merger is completed. Their plans include the construction of a unit for cancer patients on the third floor of the Founder's Building at Jeanes Hospital and a granting mechanism to fund research collaborations.

33129 ■ "Rethinking School: For the U.S. To Remain Competitive, Its Students Need To Learn Vastly More, Much More Quickly" in Harvard Business Review (Vol. 90, March 2012, No. 3, pp. 76)
Pub: Harvard Business Review Press
Contact: Peter E. Walsh, Director
Ed: Stacey Childress. Released: March 2012. Description: Improving primary education is a key component to future US economic growth. The article emphasizes the importance of personalized learning and educational technology to enhance academic achievement.

33130 ■ "Revisiting Rep Coping Strategies" in Agency Sales Magazine (Vol. 39, December 2009, No. 11, pp. 32)
Ed: Jack Foster. Description: Independent manufacturers representatives should become a well-rounded and complete businessman with continued education. The new type of representative is a problem solver and the resource for answering questions. Employing the concept of synergistic selling is also important to salespeople.

33131 ■ "RhodeMap for State Won't Focus on Finding a 'Big Fix'" in Providence Business News (Vol. 29, June 23, 2014, No. 12, pp. 4)
Pub: American City Business Journals
Released: June 23, 2014. Description: Rhode Island Department of Administration Associate Director, Kevin Flynn, asserts that the new comprehensive plan for land use and economic development, RhodeMap RI, is not focused on one single big fix to solve

the state's economic problems. Flynn notes that RhodeMap RI will address various social disparities, including education and income.

33132 ■ "The Right Stuff" in Canadian Business (Vol. 79, October 23, 2006, No. 21, pp. 151)
Ed: Laura Bogomolny. Description: The profile of Linda Duxbury, the winner of the Sprott MBA Students Society 2003-04 Best teacher award as well as Carleton University Students' Association 2002-03 award, is presented.

33133 ■ "The Right Time for REITs" in Barron's (Vol. 88, July 14, 2008, No. 28, pp. 32)
Pub: Dow Jones & Co., Inc.
Contact: Clare Hart, President
Ed: Mike Hogan. Description: Discusses the downturn in U.S. real estate investment trusts so these are worth considering for investment. Several Websites that are useful for learning about real estate investment trusts for investment purposes are presented.

33134 ■ "Ripple Effect From Solar Frontier May Be Big" in Business First of Buffalo (Vol. 30, April 25, 2014, No. 32, pp. 4)
Pub: American City Business Journals, Inc.
Contact: Whitney Shaw, President
Released: April 25, 2014. Description: A memorandum of understanding was signed by Japanese solar technology manufacturer Solar Frontier K.K. with the State University of New York, College of Nanoscale Science and Engineering in Albany. The agreement is expected to create about 1,000 new jobs in the U.S. and at least $700 million in investments.

33135 ■ "The Role for Canada's Research Universities" in Canadian Business (Vol. 81, October 27, 2008, No. 18, pp. 84)
Description: Great students tend to be the foundation of a great research-intensive university, enabling it to attract great teachers and researchers. Success is likely to attract the brightest graduate students to do research, leading to further success.

33136 ■ "Rosewood Site Faces Big Cleanup Before Stevenson Can Expand" in Baltimore Business Journal (Vol. 27, February 6, 2010, No. 40, pp. 1)
Pub: American City Business Journals
Ed: Daniel J. Sernovitz. Description: Environmental assessment report states that Maryland's Rosewood Center for the Developmentally Disabled has significant amounts of toxic chemicals, which could impact Stevenson University's decision to purchase the property. Senator Robert A. Zirkin believes that the state should pay for the cleanup, which is expected to cost millions.

33137 ■ "SAGE Publications Announced a Partnership with Which Medical Device" in Information Today (Vol. 28, November 2011, No. 10, pp. 15)
Pub: Information Today, Inc.
Contact: Thomas H. Hogan, President
E-mail: ctuthill@infotoday.com
Description: SAGE Publications has partnered with Which Medical Device to offer insights, tutorials, and reviews of medical devices.

33138 ■ "St. Rose Professor Builds Contractors and Micro-Doctors" in Business Review, Albany New York (Vol. 34, December 31, 2007, No. 39)
Pub: American City Business Journals, Inc.
Ed: Robin K. Cooper. Description: Mike Mathews is an associate professor at the College of Saint Rose School of Business and one of the founders of the Center for Micro Enterprises Development, which provides training programs on business planning and management. Details of the business school's curricula and foundations are presented.

33139 ■ "Sales Reps: How Manufacturers and Reps Can Better Work with Each Other for Mutual Gain"
Pub: R & R Publishing
Released: November 19, 2012. Price: $4.99 Kindle.
Description: Advice is given to help manufacturers and sales representatives can create a positive

partnership that will increase revenue, while extending their working relationship. Topics include: reasons to work with a representative, who becomes a rep, reps domain, finding and selecting a rep's services, commission, manufacturer complaints about reps, sales representative training, advice for both parties, and the future of these relationships.

33140 ■ *"San Antonio Researchers Develop New Laser-Based Imaging System" in San Antonio Business Journal (Vol. 26, August 24, 2012, No. 30, pp. 1)*
Pub: American City Business Journal
Description: Researchers at the University of Texas Health Science Center at San Antonio in Texas have developed an optical sensor-dependent medical imaging system, which is ready for commercialization. The laser-based imaging system is expected to improve non-invasive imaging for medical diagnostics.

33141 ■ *"Scholarships for Minority Students" in Occupational Outlook Quarterly (Vol. 54, Fall 2010, No. 3, pp. 25)*
Pub: U.S. Department of Labor Bureau of Labor Statistics
Contact: Philip L. Rones, Manager
E-mail: rones.philip@bls.gov
Description: Gates Millennium Scholars scholarship is awarded to minority students with leadership skills, a good GPA, and college aspirations.

33142 ■ *"School for Tech Skills" in San Antonio Business Journal (Vol. 28, September 5, 2014, No. 30, pp. 4)*
Pub: American City Business Journals
Released: September 5, 2014. **Description:** The Alamo Academies program is a nonprofit partnership between Alamo Colleges, local high schools, local industry groups and the City of San Antonio, Texas aimed at creating skilled workers. The program has been recognized by the Texas Higher Education Coordinating Board for meeting the state's goal of reducing the skills gap in the workforce.

33143 ■ *"SCO Expanding to Meet Optometry Growth" in Memphis Business Journal (Vol. 33, March 2, 2012, No. 47, pp. 1)*
Pub: American City Business Journal
Ed: Christopher Sheffield. **Description:** Southern College of Optometry (SCO) has begun construction of a $9.4 million expansion that will provide new classrooms, a flexible state-of-the-art lecture hall, and a glass atrium and grand hall. The project was designed to secure SCO's position among the top US optometry school as demand for its graduates grow.

33144 ■ *"Selling With Strengths; Talent Trumps Training" in Gallup Management Journal (March 24, 2011)*
Pub: Gallup Inc.
Contact: Jim Clifton, Chief Executive Officer
Description: What are the strengths of salespeople, and how can organizations develop them? What do great sales managers do differently? The authors of, 'Strengths Based Selling' answer these questions and others, including: why money is overrated as a motivator.

33145 ■ *"Senate OKs Funds for Promoting Tourism" in Crain's Detroit Business (Vol. 24, March 31, 2008, No. 13, pp. 6)*
Pub: Crain Communications Inc.
Contact: Rance E. Crain, President
Ed: Amy Lane. **Description:** Discusses the Senate proposal which allocates funds for Michigan tourism and business promotion as well as Michigan's No Worker Left Behind initiative, a program that provides free tuition at community colleges and other venues to train displaced workers for high-demand occupations.

33146 ■ *"Senators Predict Online School Changes" in Puget Sound Business Journal (Vol. 29, September 19, 2008, No. 22, pp. 1)*
Pub: American City Business Journals
Ed: Clay Holtzman. **Description:** State senators promise to create new legislation that would tighten the monitoring and oversight of online public schools.

The officials are concerned about the lack of oversight of the programs as well as lack of knowledge about content of the lessons.

33147 ■ *"The Service Imperative" in Business Horizons (Vol. 51, January-February 2008, No. 1, pp. 39)*
Pub: Elsevier Advanced Technology Publications
Ed: Mary Jo Bitner, Stephen W. Brown. **Description:** The importance of services is growing in developing countries like India and China, but little attention is given to service research, education and innovation. The 'service imperative' seeks to promote the advancement of services. The scope, objectives and philosophy of the service imperative platform are outlined.

33148 ■ *"Sewing Is a Life Skill; Teaching To Sew Is An Art" in Virginia-Pilot (August 31, 2010)*
Pub: Virginian-Pilot
Ed: Jamesetta M. Walker. **Description:** In conjunction with National Sewing Month, the American Sewing Guild is sponsoring a two-day workshop featuring Stephanie Kimura.

33149 ■ *"Sharing's Not Just for Start-ups: What Marriott, GE, and Other Traditiional Companies are Learning About the Collaborative Economy" in Harvard Business Review (Vol. 92, September 2014, No. 9, pp. 23)*
Pub: Harvard Business Publishing
Ed: Rachel Botsman. **Released:** September 2014. **Description:** The collaborative economy answers five basic problems companies face: redundancy, broken trust, limited access, waste, and complexity. Online matches eliminate redundancy; peer-to-peer networks boost trust; online training answers access issues; online services can market what other entities are not utilizing (i.e., excess space); and other services can streamline or provide alternative solutions for complex processes.

33150 ■ *"Skill Seekers" in South Florida Business Journal (Vol. 34, February 7, 2014, No. 29, pp. 15)*
Pub: American City Business Journals
Released: February 7, 2014. **Description:** Executives talk about the need for schools to help businesses find talent to hire. Robin Sandler of Charter School USA reveals that the organization's 'Leading Edge' program allows teachers to participate in leadership opportunities, while Mason Jackson of WorkForce One Employment Solutions believes that schools need to customize the curriculum in order to support internships.

33151 ■ *"Small-Business Agenda: Increase Capital, Education, Tax Breaks" in Crain's Detroit Business (Vol. 24, March 30, 2008)*
Pub: Crain Communications Inc.
Contact: Rance E. Crain, President
Ed: Nancy Kaffer. **Description:** Discusses the policy suggestions detailed in the Small Business Association of Michigan's entrepreneurial agenda which include five main categories of focus: making entrepreneurial education a higher state priority; increasing capital available to entrepreneurs; using the state's tax structure as an incentive for entrepreneurial growth; getting university research from the lab to the market; and limiting government regulation that's burdensome to small businesses and getting legislative support of entrepreneurial assistance efforts.

33152 ■ *"Solar Power Paying Off for PUSD" in Porterville Recorder (September 29, 2012)*
Description: Porterville Unified School District has received $700,000 in rebates after operating its new solar-powered projects at three of five sites over the last six months.

33153 ■ *"Some Good Earners: Preparing Prison Inmates to Start Businesses Upon Their Release" in Inc. (Vol. 31, January-February 2009, No. 1)*
Pub: Mansueto Ventures L.L.C.
Contact: John Koten, Chief Executive Officer
Ed: Mike Hofman. **Description:** Prison Entrepreneurship Program (PEP) is a nonprofit organization that works with the Texas Department of Criminal Justice

to teach entrepreneurship to prison inmates. Profiled is Hans Becker, owner of Armadillo Tree and Shrub in Dallas; Becker studied the PEP program while serving five years in prison and started his successful company when released.

33154 ■ *"Spinout Success: New Leadership Steps In At UW's C4C" in Puget Sound Business Journal (Vol. 35, June 27, 2014, No. 10, pp. 11)*
Pub: American City Business Journals
Released: June 27, 2014. **Description:** University of Washington's Center for Commercialization vice provost, Vikram Jandhyala, talks about his new position with the school. Jandhyala says he plans to build more synergy between the medical school and engineering and between social sciences and computer science. He also says the medical and software industry need to grow to accommodate the volume of data crossing and stored within the Internet.

33155 ■ *"Spotlight; 'Classroom Focus' at Encyclopaedia Britannica" in Crain's Chicago Business (Vol. 34, October 24, 2011, No. 42, pp. 6)*
Pub: Crain Communications Inc.
Contact: Todd Johnson, Publisher
Ed: Paul Merrion. **Description:** Profile of Gregory Healy, product officer for Encyclopaedia Britannica is presented. Healy took the position in May 2010 and is focused on online offerings of their publication and to make them more useful to teachers.

33156 ■ *"Staples Advantage Receives NJPA National Contract for Janitorial Supplies" in Professional Services Close-Up (April 22, 2011)*
Pub: Close-Up Media
Description: Staples Advantage, the business-to-business division of Staples Inc. was awarded a contract for janitorial supplies to members of the National Joint Powers Alliance (NJPA). NJPA is a member-owned buying cooperative serving public and private schools, state and local governments, and nonprofit organizations.

33157 ■ *StartingUp Now Facilitator Guide*
Ed: L. Jenkins. **Released:** September 11, 2011. **Price:** $29.95. **Description:** Guide for those teaching entrepreneurship using StartingUp Now; the guide provides 24 lesson plans for each of the 24 steps/chapters in the book.

33158 ■ *"State Moves to Improve Child Care" in Providence Business News (Vol. 29, April 7, 2014, No. 1, pp. 1)*
Pub: American City Business Journals
Released: April 7, 2014. **Description:** Rhode Island Department of Human Services has been helping to administer BrightStars contracts to child care centers, home-based providers and educational programs to help ensure the availability of high quality child care to the workforce. Part of the BrightStars funding came from the $50 million Race to the Top grant. Insights on BrightStars rating systems are also given.

33159 ■ *"Stay in School: Economy Got You Down?" in Canadian Business (Vol. 81, November 10, 2008, No. 19, pp. 98)*
Ed: Graham F. Scott, Jane Bao. **Description:** A guide to Canadian MBA programs is presented. The tuition and length of each program is provided along with each school. Details on whether the universities offer part-time options, diversity, and co-op/internships are also given.

33160 ■ *"Steel Yard Eyes Funding Balance" in Providence Business News (Vol. 29, May 26, 2014, No. 8, pp. 1)*
Pub: American City Business Journals
Released: May 26, 2014. **Description:** Steel Yard is looking for new revenue to sustain its expansion as a nonprofit, metalwork training organization based in Providence, Rhode Island. The organization is applying for money from a proposed state funding pool of $590,000 for the first time to be used in 2014-2015 fiscal year.

33161 ■ "Stop the Madness" in Hawaii Business (Vol. 53, October 2007, No. 4, pp. 10)
Pub: PacificBasin Communications
Description: Discusses the number of parents paying for kindergarten admissions tutorials for their kids which has increased, as parents want to improve their children's chances of being admitted at a prestigious school. Some schools in Hawaii are not in favor of this trend, and they actually rate an applicant negatively if his or her answers seem to be too rehearsed. Some of the lessons in the admissions tutorials are discussed.

33162 ■ "Storytelling Star of Show for Cincinnati's E.W. Scripps" in Business Courier (Vol. 26, November 13, 2009, No. 29, pp. 1)
Pub: American City Business Journals, Inc.
Contact: Whitney Shaw, President
Ed: Dan Monk. **Description:** Rich Boehne, CEO Of the EW Scripps Company in Cincinnati has authorized a new training program in storytelling for employees at Scripps' 10 television stations. He believes that the training will improve the quality of broadcasting content. His plans to improve quality of newspaper content are also discussed.

33163 ■ "Study Puts Hub On Top of the Tech Heap" in Boston Business Journal (Vol. 30, November 26, 2010, No. 44, pp. 1)
Pub: Boston Business Journal
Ed: Galen Moore. **Description:** The Ewing Marion Kauffman Foundation ranked Massachusetts at the top in its evaluations of states' innovative industries, government leadership, and education. Meanwhile, research blog formDs.com also ranked Massachusetts number one in terms of venture-capital financings per capita.

33164 ■ "Suddenly, Sewing Is Hip Again for Kids, Moms and Crafters" in Atlanta Journal-Constitution (August 29, 2010)
Ed: Rosalind Bentley. **Description:** Across Atlanta, Georgia, along with the entire nation, sewing classes are increasing in popularity.

33165 ■ "Survey: Don't Expect Big Results From Stimulus" in Crain's Detroit Business (Vol. 25, June 1, 2009, No. 22)
Pub: Crain Communications Inc. - Detroit
Contact: Keith Crain, Chairman
Ed: Nancy Kaffer, Chad Halcom. **Description:** In a recent survey, Michigan business owners, operators or managers showed that 48 percent of respondents oppose the President's stimulus package and believe it will have little or no effect on the economy.

33166 ■ "The Sustainability Agenda: Ioannia Ioannou" in Business Strategy Review (Vol. 25, Summer 2014, No. 2, pp. 16)
Pub: Blackwell Publishing Professional
Contact: Stephen M. Smith, President
Released: Summer 2014. **Description:** How should academics keep up to date with issues such as corporate responsibility? Ioannis Ioannou of the London School of Business advocates a more interventionist approach to this issue.

33167 ■ "Tackling Tuition Increases Head On" in Pittsburgh Business Times (Vol. 34, July 25, 2014, No. 1, pp. 6)
Pub: American City Business Journals
Released: July 25, 2014. **Description:** The University of Pittsburgh has tried to contain tuition increases after the state cut funding by about $70 million in the 2012 budget year. The measures include a one-time-only early retirement program offered in 2012, greater focus on sustainability and cutting energy costs, and streamlining operations and sharing services.

33168 ■ "Taking on 911 - and Making a New Tech Biz In the Process" in Orlando Business Journal (Vol. 30, January 24, 2014, No. 31, pp. 3)
Pub: American City Business Journals
Released: January 24, 2014. **Description:** Central Florida-based TapShield LLC is on the path to growth. The firm has developed a mobile application that enables University of Florida students to coordinate with police. Meanwhile, TapShield is in negotiations with large companies for similar deals.

33169 ■ "Talk Story: Mitch D'Olier, President, CEO Kaneohe Ranch" in Hawaii Business (Vol. 53, November 2007, No. 5, pp. 27)
Pub: PacificBasin Communications
Ed: Cathy S. Cruz-George. **Description:** Mitch D'Olier chief executive officer of Kaneohe Ranch/ Harold K.L. Castle Foundation thinks that achievement gaps are a nationwide problem and that the Knowledge is Power Program is one of the programs that focuses on achievement gaps in some communities across the US. He also provides his insights on education in Hawaii and the current shortage of teachers.

33170 ■ "Teachable Moments: Worth Every Penny" in Pet Product News (Vol. 64, December 2010, No. 12, pp. 34)
Pub: Bowtie Inc.
Ed: Cheryl Reeves. **Description:** Pet bird retailers can attain both outreach to customers and enhanced profitability by staging educational events such as the annual Parrot Palooza event of Burlington, New Jersey-based Bird Paradise. Aside from attracting a global audience, Parrot Palooza features seminars, workshops, classes, and bird-related contests.

33171 ■ "Teaching Sales: Great Sales Professionals are Scarce and Getting Scarcer. Why Aren't Universities Working Harder to Create More?" in (Vol. 90, July-August 2012, No. 7-8, pp. 94)
Pub: Harvard Business Review Press
Contact: Peter E. Walsh, Director
Ed: Suzanne Fogel, David Hoffmeister, Richard Rocco, Daniel P. Strunk. **Released:** July-August 2012. **Description:** Partnerships between industry and business schools can improve the quality of new sales education programs, increasing access to funding and talent. Industry input to school curricula and scholarly research informing business decisions will produce mutual benefits.

33172 ■ "Ted Stahl: Executive Chairman" in Inside Business (Vol. 13, September-October 2011, No. 5, pp. NC6)
Pub: Great Lakes Publishing Co.
Ed: Miranda S. Miller. **Description:** Profile of Ted Stahl, who started working in his family's business when he was ten years old is presented. The firm makes dies for numbers and letters used on team uniforms. Another of the family firms manufactures stock and custom heat-printing products, equipment and supplies. It also educates customers on ways to decorate garments with heat printing products and offers graphics and software for customers to create their own artwork.

33173 ■ "Texas State University Poised for Boom" in Austin Business JournalInc. (Vol. 29, January 29, 2010, No. 47, pp. 1)
Pub: American City Business Journals
Ed: Sandra Zaragoza. **Description:** Texas State University, San Marcos has seen its student population grow to 30,800 and the university is set for $633 million in construction projects to address demand for student housing and building expansions and renovations. Details on the buildings and student housing plans for the projects are provided.

33174 ■ "The Thinker" in Canadian Business (Vol. 81, March 31, 2008, No. 5, pp. 52)
Pub: Rogers Media Inc.
Contact: Tony Viner, President
Ed: Andrew Wahl. **Description:** Mihnea Moldoveanu provides much of the academic rigor that underpins Roger Martin's theories on how to improve the way business leaders think. Moldoveanu is also a classically trained pianist and founder of Redline Communications and has a mechanical engineering degree from MIT on top of his astounding knowledge on many academic fields.

33175 ■ "Thinking Aloud: Julian Franks" in Business Strategy Review (Vol. 21, Autumn 2010, No. 3, pp. 35)
Pub: Blackwell Publishers Ltd.
Ed: Stuart Crainer. **Description:** Julian Franks is Academic Director of the Centre for Corporate Governance at London Business School and lead investigator for a 1.4 million (sterling pounds) grand for research into corporate governance.

33176 ■ "Thinking Aloud: Julian Franks" in Business Strategy Review (Vol. 21, Autumn 2010, No. 3, pp. 35)
Pub: John Wiley & Sons Inc. Scientific, Technical, Medical, and Scholarly Div. (Wiley-Blackwell)
Contact: William J. Pesce, Manager
E-mail: wpesce@wiley.com
Ed: Stuart Crainer. **Description:** Julian Franks is academic director of the Centre for Corporate Governance at London Business School and lead investigator for a (pounds sterling) 1.4 million grant for research into corporate governance.

33177 ■ "Those Letters After Your Name Say More Than You Think" in Special Events Magazine (Vol. 31, March 1, 2012, No. 2)
Ed: Sara Hunt. **Released:** March 1, 2012. **Description:** Professional event planners recognize the importance of the letters CSEP after their name. The CSEP exam accreditation signifies the planner's ability in all aspects of event planning, including catering, insurance, AV, risk assessment, marketing, etc. The benefits of earning the CSEP for event planners is discussed.

33178 ■ "Tooling Firm Thinks Being In U.P. Gives It Upper Hand" in Crain's Detroit Business (Vol. 30, October 13, 2014, No. 41, pp. 21)
Pub: Crain Communications Inc. - Detroit
Contact: Keith Crain, Chairman
Released: October 13, 2014. **Description:** Extreme Tool & Engineering is located in a remote region of Michigan's Upper Peninsula. The firm's employees average age is 28 and owner, Mike Zacharias, believes that combination contributes to the mold maker's success. He believes in the power of youth and reinvesting in training. Despite the economic challenges of the area, he employs nearly 80 workers.

33179 ■ "Top Marks" in Canadian Business (Vol. 79, October 23, 2006, No. 21, pp. 143)
Ed: Erin Pooley; Laura Bogomolny. **Description:** Profiles of some top grade master of business administration students like Hogan Mullally and Will mercer, belonging to reputed business schools, are presented.

33180 ■ "Trade Craft: Take Pride in Your Trade, Demand Excellence" in Contractor (Vol. 56, October 2009, No. 10, pp. 24)
Pub: Penton Media, Inc.
Ed: Al Schwartz. **Description:** There is a need for teaching, developing, and encouraging trade craft. An apprentice plumber is not only versed in the mechanical aspects of the trade but he also has a working knowledge of algebra, trigonometry, chemistry, and thermal dynamics. Contractors should be demanding on their personnel regarding their trade craft and should only keep and train the very best people they can hire.

33181 ■ "Train Now to Get the Competitive Edge" in Contractor (Vol. 56, October 2009, No. 10, pp. 58)
Pub: Penton Media, Inc.
Ed: Merry Beth Hall. **Description:** Due to the harsh economic climate, mechanical contractors would be well-served to train their employees while they have time to take them out of the field. This will help ensure that they are not behind when the economic recovery happens. Suggestions on how to choose the best type of training are presented.

33182 ■ "Training Center Wants to be College" in Austin Business JournalInc. (Vol. 29, November 13, 2009, No. 36, pp. A1)
Pub: American City Business Journals
Ed: Sandra Zaragoza. **Description:** Texas-based CyberTex Institute, a job training center, has established technical careers in an effort to obtain federal ac-

creditation as a college. A college status would allow CyperTex to extend financial assistance to students. Aside from potentially having an enlarged student body and expanded campus, CyberTex would be allowed to engage in various training programs.

33183 ■ *"Training Essential For Growth; It Doesn't Have To Cost Much" in Crain's Detroit Business (Vol. 24, January 21, 2008, No. 3, pp. 14)*

Pub: Crain Communications Inc. - Detroit

Contact: Keith Crain, Chairman

Ed: Sheena Harrison. **Description:** Employee training is essential for small companies to achieve growth.

33184 ■ *"Training the Troops: Battlefield Simulations Bring Growth to UNITECH" in Black Enterprise (Vol. 38, February 2008, No. 7, pp. 30)*

Pub: Earl G. Graves Publishing Co. Inc.

Contact: Earl G. Graves, Jr., President

Ed: Cliff Hocker. **Description:** Universal Systems and Technology (UNITECH) received a total of over $45 million U.S. Department of Defense orders during September and October 2007. UNITECH designs and manufactures battlefield simulation devices used to train troops in the Army and Marine Corps.

33185 ■ *"Trend: Tutors to Help You Pump Up the Staff" in Business Week (September 22, 2008, No. 4100, pp. 45)*

Ed: Reena Janaj. **Description:** High-level managers are turning to innovation coaches in an attempt to obtain advice on how to better sell new concepts within their companies. Individuals as well as consulting firms are now offering this service.

33186 ■ *Trump University Entrepreneurship 101*

Pub: John Wiley & Sons Inc.

Contact: Stephen M. Smith, President

Ed: Mike Gordon. **Released:** December 2006. **Price:** $21.95, hardcover. **Description:** Entrepreneurs, past, present or future, will find this book helpful. The book covers three objectives: to energize readers to be courageous when taking steps toward an entrepreneurial goal, works to demystify the entrepreneurial process, and to help individuals improve success. **Availability:** Print.

33187 ■ *"TWU Offers Course in Project Management" in Bellingham Business Journal (Vol. February 2010, pp. 4)*

Pub: Sound Publishing Inc.

Contact: Gloria G. Fletcher, President

Ed: Lance Henderson. **Description:** Trinity Western University in Bellinham, Washington is offering a new certification program in project management. Students who take and pass the certification examination of the International Project Management Institutes will lead to positions in many industries. Details of the program are provided.

33188 ■ *"U Overhauling Its Janitorial Program, but Custodians Taking Exception" in Saint Paul Pioneer Press (August 20, 2011)*

Pub: McClatchy-Tribune Regional News

Ed: Mila Koumpilova. **Description:** University of Minnesota developed a new team cleaning approach for its campus. The new custodian program will save $3.1 million annually while providing a cleaner campus. The union representing the custodians questions both claims.

33189 ■ *"UA, BP Test Unmanned Aircraft" in Alaska Business Monthly (Vol. 27, October 2011, No. 10, pp. 8)*

Pub: Alaska Business Publishing Company Inc.

Contact: Jim Martin, President

Ed: Nancy Pounds. **Description:** University of Alaska Fairbanks Geophysical Institute and BP Exploration Alaska tested the oil-spill capabilities of an unmanned aircraft. The aircraft will be used to gather 3-D ariel data to aid in oil-spill cleanup.

33190 ■ *"UA Pacts With School Teams: By the Numbers" in Baltimore Business Journal (Vol. 31, January 10, 2014, No. 37, pp. 6)*

Pub: American City Business Journals, Inc.

Contact: Whitney Shaw, President

Released: January 10, 2014. **Description:** Under Armour Inc. (UA) has sponsored schools with cash and bonuses for winning national football championships, as well as providing equipment and apparel allowances. Auburn University, University of South Carolina, Texas Tech University, University of Maryland, University of Utah and University of Hawaii share details of their contracts with UA.

33191 ■ *"UA Turns Ann Arbor Green" in Contractor (Vol. 56, September 2009, No. 9, pp. 5)*

Pub: Penton Media, Inc.

Ed: Robert P. Mader. **Description:** Instructors at the United Association of Plumbers and Steamfitters have studied the latest in green and sustainable construction and service at the Washtenaw Community College in Michigan. Classes included building information modeling, hydronic heating and cooling and advanced HVACR troubleshooting. The UA is currently focusing on green training.

33192 ■ *"UAlbany on the Hunt for New Brand" in Business Review, Albany New York (Vol. 34, October 5, 2007, No. 27, pp. 1)*

Pub: American City Business Journals, Inc.

Ed: Richard A. D'Errico. **Description:** State University of New York at Albany is working on a new marketing and branding initiative to help communicate its message better. The initiative is for the school to better understand its target audiences and their perception of the university.

33193 ■ *"UB Program Offers Free Tax Preparation" in Buffalo News (January 29, 2012)*

Pub: McClatchy-Tribune Information Services

Ed: Jonathan D. Epstein. **Released:** January 29, 2012. **Description:** University of Buffalo's Schhol of Management in New York is offering free tax preparation for low-income individuals and families. The program is available on North and South campuses and is designed to help these people save money and collect all refunds in which they are eligible.

33194 ■ *"UC May Expand into Old Ford Plant" in Business Courier (Vol. 26, December 25, 2009, No. 35, pp. 1)*

Pub: American City Business Journals, Inc.

Contact: Whitney Shaw, President

Ed: Dan Monk. **Description:** Developer Stuart Lichter is planning to acquire University of Cincinnati (UC) as a tenant at a two-story office building on a 132-acre site where a vacant Ford transmission plant is located. Details of the transaction are outlined.

33195 ■ *"UMKC, Hospital Drill Down on Deal" in The Business Journal-Serving Metropolitan Kansas City (Vol. 26, July 18, 2008, No. 45, pp. 1)*

Ed: Rob Roberts. **Description:** University of Missouri Kansas City and Children's Mercy Hospital are negotiating the hospital's potential acquisition of the university's School of Dentistry building. The deal would transfer the 240,000-square foot dental school building to Children's Mercy. Plans for a new dental school building for the UMKC are also presented.

33196 ■ *"University Book Store Inc.: an Act of Independence" in Retail Merchandiser (Vol. 51, September-October 2011, No. 5, pp. 68)*

Pub: Phoenix Media Corporation

Ed: Lori Sichtermann. **Description:** University Book Store Inc. is a campus bookstore located at the University of Washington, in Seattle. The book store provides more than $1 million in UW customer rebates and discounts annually and donated more than $800,000 in UW student scholarships.

33197 ■ *"Up Against the Ropes: A Professional Coach May Help" in Black*

Enterprise (Vol. 37, December 2006, No. 5, pp. 72)

Pub: Earl G. Graves Publishing Co. Inc.

Contact: Earl G. Graves, Jr., President

Ed: Karen Chambers. **Description:** Executive coaching is now a $1 billion industry. The coaching process itself and traits to look for in a coach are discussed.

33198 ■ *"An Updated Ranking of Academic Journals in Economics" in Canadian Journal of Economics (Vol. 44, November 2011, No. 4, pp. 1525)*

Pub: Wiley-Blackwell

Contact: Gordon Tibbitts, President

Ed: Pantelis Kalaitzidakis, Theofanis P. Mamuneas, Thanasis Stengos. **Description:** An updated list showing the ranking of economic journals (2003) is presented; however this present study differs methodologically from an earlier study by using a rolling window of years between 2003 and 2008, for each year counting the number of citations of articles published in the previous ten years.

33199 ■ *"Urban League Training Program Finds Jobs for Cincinnati's 'Hard to Serve" in Business Courier (Vol. 27, July 2, 2010, No. 9, pp. 1)*

Pub: Business Courier

Ed: Lucy May. **Description:** Stephen Tucker, director of workforce development for the Urban League of Greater Cincinnati, is an example of how ex-offenders can be given chances for employment after service jail sentences. How the Urban Leagues' Solid Opportunities for Advancement job training program helped Tucker and other ex-offenders is discussed.

33200 ■ *"URI Centre Seen as Bridge From Campus to Employment" in Providence Business News (Vol. 29, June 30, 2014, No. 13, pp. 4)*

Pub: American City Business Journals

Released: June 30, 2014. **Description:** Kimberly S. Washor is the first director of University of Rhode Island's (URIs) new Centre for Career and Experiential Education that combines the missions of Experiential Learning and Community Engagement along with Career Services and Employer Relations. By joining the two offices, URI is implementing a new database that will meet the needs of both career and internship advising, where adviser will be able to track industry human resource partners.

33201 ■ *"Using Teaching Teams to Encourage Active Learning" in Business Communication Quarterly (December 2007, pp. 457)*

Pub: Pine Forge Press

Contact: Blaise R. Simqu, President

Ed: Lisa E. Gueldenzoph. **Description:** The practice of dividing classes into teaching teams to encourage active learning is studied. Students in business management courses become more involved in the learning process with this technique and collaborate to enhance better understanding of course content.

33202 ■ *"USM Focuses on Turning Science Into New Companies, Cash" in Boston Business Journal (Vol. 29, July 1, 2011, No. 8, pp. 1)*

Pub: American City Business Journals, Inc.

Ed: Alexander Jackson. **Description:** University System of Maryland gears up to push for its plan for commercializing its scientific discoveries which by 2020 could create 325 companies and double the $1.4 billion the system's eleven schools garner in yearly research grants. It is talking with University of Utah and University Maryland, Baltimore to explore ways to make this plan a reality.

33203 ■ *"UT Deans Serious about Biz" in Austin Business Journal (Vol. 31, May 20, 2011, No. 11, pp. 1)*

Pub: American City Business Journals

Ed: Sandra Zaragoza. **Description:** Dean Thomas Gilligan of the University of Texas, McCombs School of Business and engineering school Dean Gregory Fenves have partnered to develop a joint engineering and business degree. Their partnership has resulted in an undergraduate course on initiating startups.

33204 ■ *"UTSA Entrepreneur Program Receives Federal Designation"* in San Antonio Business Journal (Vol. 28, June 6, 2014, No. 17, pp. 7)
Pub: American City Business Journals
Released: June 6, 2014. **Description:** The National Science Foundation has designated the University of Texas at San Antonio (UTSA) as an Innovation Corps Site because of its strong entrepreneurial system through the Center for Innovation and Technology Entrepreneurship. The UTSA expects to see an increase in entrepreneurial activity and successful technology commercialization with such designation.

33205 ■ *"UW Wary of WSU's Wish for Spokane Medical School"* in Puget Sound Business Journal (Vol. 35, May 9, 2014, No. 3, pp. 9)
Pub: American City Business Journals
Released: May 9, 2014. **Description:** University of Washington leaders believe that opening a medical school in Washington State University's (WSU) Spokane Campus will create more competition for state funding. However, WSU officials claim that the demand for new doctors demonstrates the need for a second school.

33206 ■ *"The Valuation of Players"* in Canadian Business (Vol. 80, October 22, 2007, No. 21, pp. 39)
Ed: Jeff Sanford. **Description:** Business professionals are supplementing their Masters in Business Administration degrees with CBV or chartered business valuator. CBVs are trained, not only in business tangibles, but also in business intangibles such as market position, reputation, intellectual property, and patent. Details of employment opportunities for chartered business valuators are discussed.

33207 ■ *"Verdict: Few Legal Jobs"* in Boston Business Journal (Vol. 31, June 17, 2011, No. 21, pp. 1)
Pub: Boston Business Journal
Ed: Lisa van der Pool. **Description:** Law school graduates in Massachusetts are finding it harder to find work as the legal job market remains weak. The national employment rate for the 2010 law school class fell to 87.6 percent, while only 68.4 percent held jobs that require passing the bar examination.

33208 ■ *"Veterans Train to Use Military Skills In Civilian Workforce"* in South Florida Business Journal (Vol. 34, April 18, 2014, No. 39, pp. 10)
Pub: American City Business Journals
Released: April 18, 2014. **Description:** United Way of Broward County has launched the Mission United program that offers a one-stop shop of information and resources to meet the needs of military veterans. Mission United aims to reduce the jobless rate among veterans by creating two programs to help veterans and connect them with potential employers who are hiring. Details of the job training program is explored.

33209 ■ *"The View from the Field: Six Leaders Offer Their Perspectives On Sales Success"* in (Vol. 90, July-August 2012, No. 7-8, pp. 101)
Pub: Harvard Business Review Press
Contact: Peter E. Walsh, Director
Ed: Jim Koch, James Farley, Susan Silbermann, Duncan MacNaughton, Phil Guido, Suresh Goklaney. **Released:** July-August 2012. **Description:** Six business leaders provide their perspectives on successful selling. Common themes include engaging customers and seeking their input, personalizing their services, ensuring accountability, implementing community outreach, being mindful of cultural and regulatory issues, providing unique offerings, incorporating experiential learning, and properly identifying a customer's needs.

33210 ■ *"Vision for Camden in Better Focus"* in Philadelphia Business Journal (Vol. 30, September 30, 2011, No. 33, pp. 1)
Pub: American City Business Journals Inc.
Ed: Natalie Kostelni. **Description:** More than $500 million worth of projects aimed at redeveloping the downtown and waterfront areas of Camden, New

Jersey are being planned. These include the construction of residential, commercial, and education buildings.

33211 ■ *"The Way I Work: Kim Kleeman of ShakespeareSquared"* in Inc. (October 2007, pp. 110-112, 114)
Pub: Mansueto Ventures L.L.C.
Contact: John Koten, Chief Executive Officer
Ed: Leigh Buchanan. **Description:** Profile of Kim Kleeman, founder and president of ShakespeareSquared, a firm that develops educational materials, including lesson plans, teacher guides, activity workbooks, and discussion guides for large publishers. Kleeman talks about the challenges she faces running her nearly all-women company while maintaining a balance with her family.

33212 ■ *"A Well-Crafted Employee Handbook Can Make Work Run More Smoothly"* in Idaho Business Review (September 17, 2014)
Pub: Dolan Co.
Contact: James P. Dolan, President
Released: September 17, 2014. **Description:** An employee handbook will provide a complaint process, provide company management flexibility and clarity and keep a company out of legal problems. Training, compensation, benefits, security, health, performance appraisals, and safety issues must be covered. Human resource managers and other mangers should cover basics to help communicate with workers.

33213 ■ *"What Business Schools Can Learn From the Medical Profession"* in Harvard Business Review (Vol. 90, January-February 2012, No.1-2, pp. 38)
Pub: Harvard Business Review Press
Contact: Peter E. Walsh, Director
Ed: Nitin Nohria. **Released:** January-February 2012. **Description:** The author recommends closing the knowing-doing gap by applying health care feedback methods to business school instruction. Hospital residents receive feedback after making their rounds; so too should business school students and faculty assemble on a regular basis so that they can discuss what they are learning.

33214 ■ *"What Businesses Can Do: Growing the Supply of Highly Skilled Graduates"* in Canadian Business (Vol. 81, October 27, 2008, No. 18)
Description: Employers in Canada have expressed concerns over the findings of various studies that revealed current and projected labor shortages in the country. A low birthrate and an aging population is contributing to the problem. Ways businesses can increase the supply of highly skilled workers in Canada is presented.

33215 ■ *"What School Did You Attend?"* in Hawaii Business (Vol. 53, December 2007, No. 6, pp. 14)
Pub: PacificBasin Communications
Ed: Kelli Abe Trifonovitch. **Description:** Discusses the question 'what school did you attend?' which is observed to be the most important inquiry in Hawaiian business discourse. The principle behind the question is based on establishing connections. The relation between the aforementioned inquiry and Hawaiian culture is explained.

33216 ■ *"What's Working Now: In Providing Jobs for North Carolinians"* in Business North Carolina (Vol. 28, February 2008, No. 2, pp. 16)
Pub: Business North Carolina
Ed: Edward Martin, Frank Maley. **Description:** Individuals previously employed in the furniture, tobacco, or textile manufacturing sectors have gone back to school to be trained in new sectors in the area such as life sciences, finances and other emerging sectors.

33217 ■ *"Wheatfield First Choice for Canadian Manufacturer"* in Business First Buffalo (November 26, 2007, pp. 1)
Pub: American City Business Journals, Inc.
Ed: James Fink. **Description:** Niagara County Industrial Development Agency is preparing an enticement program that would lure automotive parts

manufacturer Pop & Lock Corporation to shift manufacturing operations to Wheatfield, Niagara County, New York. The package includes job-training grants and assistance for acquiring new machinery. Details of the plan are included.

33218 ■ *"Where to Buy the Right MBA"* in Canadian Business (Vol. 79, October 23, 2006, No. 21, pp. 99)
Ed: Erin Pooley; Laura Bogomolny; Joe Castaldo; Michelle Magnan; Claire Gagne. **Description:** Details of Canadian graduate business schools offering Master of business administration degree are presented.

33219 ■ *"Where New Economy Initiative Grants Have Gone"* in Crain's Detroit Business (Vol. 25, June 1, 2009, No. 22, pp. M014)
Pub: Crain Communications Inc. - Detroit
Contact: Keith Crain, Chairman
Ed: Sherri Begin Welch. **Description:** Listing of grants totaling $20.5 million focusing on talent development, attraction and retention; innovation and entrepreneurship; and shifting to a culture that values learning, work and innovation, is presented.

33220 ■ *"Why Did Cincinnati Chef Jean-Robert de Cavel Stay in Town?"* in Business Courier (Vol. 27, August 6, 2010, No. 14, pp. 1)
Pub: Business Courier
Ed: Dan Monk. **Description:** Jean-Robert de Cavel will open his new restaurant in Cincinnati, Ohio. The culinary arts program at Cincinnati State Technical and Community College offered him $100,000 to be its 'chef in residence'. He was able to energize students, boost enrollment, and increase the stature of the culinary program.

33221 ■ *"Why Does Firm Reputation In Human Resource Policies Influence College Students? The Mechanisms Underlying Job Pursuit Intentions"* in Human Resource Management (Vol. 51, January-February 2012, No. 1, pp. 121-142)
Pub: John Wiley & Sons Inc.
Contact: Stephen M. Smith, President
Ed: Julie Holliday Wayne, Wendy J. Casper. **Description:** The effects of reputational information about human resource practices of companies on college students seeking employment are examined. The reputation of firms in compensation, work-family, and diversity efforts are found to increase intentions to pursue employment in these firms.

33222 ■ *"Why I Stopped Firing Everyone and Started Being a Better Boss"* in Inc. (Vol. 34, September 2012, No. 7, pp. 86)
Pub: Mansueto Ventures L.L.C.
Contact: John Koten, Chief Executive Officer
Ed: April Joyner. **Released:** September 2012. **Description:** Indigo Johnson, former Marine, discusses her management style when starting her business. She fired employees regularly. Johnson enrolled in a PhD program in leadership and established a better hiring program and learned to utilize her workers' strengths.

33223 ■ *"Why Top Young Managers Are In a Nonstop Job Hunt"* in (Vol. 90, July-August 2012, No. 7-8, pp. 28)
Pub: Harvard Business Review Press
Contact: Peter E. Walsh, Director
Ed: Monika Hamori, Jie Cao, Burak Koyuncu. **Released:** July-August 2012. **Description:** Managers are moving from firm to firm in part because companies are not addressing formal training, coaching, and mentoring needs. While these are costly, companies might benefit from the investment, as managers may tend to stay longer in firms where they are provided.

33224 ■ *"The WIN Library"* in Women In Business (Vol. 61, August-September 2009, No. 4, pp. 36)
Pub: American Business Women's Association
Contact: Lorie Burch, President
Ed: Leigh Elmore. **Description:** Women's Instructional Network (WIN) offers members of the American Business Women's Association with information

about the organization and 15 Team Tools learning modules to help further the learning of business women. Other training programs and services offered by WIN are presented.

33225 ▪ *"A Woman's Advantage"* in *Black Enterprise (Vol. 38, December 2007, No. 5, pp. 86)*

Pub: Earl G. Graves Publishing Co. Inc.

Contact: Earl G. Graves, Jr., President

Ed: Marcia A. Reed-Woodard. **Description:** Leadership development is essential for any small business. Simmons College's Strategic Leadership for Women educational course offers a five-day program for professional women teaching powerful strategies to perform, compete, and win in the workplace.

33226 ▪ *"Women as 21st Century Leaders"* in *Women In Business (Vol. 63, Summer 2011, No. 2, pp. 26)*

Pub: American Business Women's Association

Contact: Lorie Burch, President

Ed: Leigh Elmore. **Description:** American Business Women's Association and Park University have partnered to provide a leadership training program to attendees of the 2011 National Women's Leadership Conference. The courses will incorporate introduction to concepts, development of critical thinking skills and direct application through exercises. Comments from executives are also included.

33227 ▪ *"Women and Higher Education"* in *Montly Labor Review (Vol. 133, September 2010, No. 9, pp. 70)*

Pub: U.S. Department of Labor Bureau of Labor Statistics

Contact: Philip L. Rones, Manager

E-mail: rones.philip@bls.gov

Description: The increase in people going to college has been mostly among women. Statistical data included.

33228 ▪ *"Work Force: In the Mix"* in *Entrepreneur (Vol. 35, October 2007, No. 10, pp. 109)*

Pub: Entrepreneur Press

Contact: Perlman Neil, President

Ed: Mark Henricks. **Description:** A study of 708 companies' diversity programs shows that diversity training alone is not the most effective way of increasing diversity in management. It was found that one effective way of putting minorities and women in management teams is to give a team or a person the task of improving diversity in the company. The reason why accountability succeeds in diversifying the workforce is discussed.

33229 ▪ *"Work Less, Earn More"* in *Canadian Business (Vol. 80, March 12, 2007, No. 6, pp. 30)*

Ed: Erin Pooley. **Description:** Expert advice on ways to work efficiently to complete the job instead of extending work hours is presented.

33230 ▪ *Working Papers, Chapters 1-14 for Needles/Powers/Crosson's Financial and Managerial Accounting*

Pub: Cengage South-Western

Ed: Belverd E. Needles, Marian Powers, Susan V. Crosson. **Released:** May 10, 2010. **Price:** $62.95. **Description:** Appropriate accounting forms for completing all exercises, problems and cases in the text are provided for financial management of a small company.

33231 ▪ *"The World Is Your Oyster"* in *Canadian Business (Vol. 80, October 22, 2007, No. 21, pp. 140)*

Ed: Regan Ray. **Description:** Business graduates are not that keen on working abroad. Fortune 500 companies are requiring executives to have a multi-country focus. The skill required for jobs abroad, as well as employment opportunities are discussed.

33232 ▪ *"The World is Their Classroom"* in *Crain's Chicago Business (Vol. 31, March 24,*

2008, No. 12, pp. 24)

Pub: Crain Communications Inc.

Contact: Todd Johnson, Publisher

Ed: Samantha Stainburn. **Description:** Due to globalization more business students are studying abroad; 89 percent of eligible students in its executive MBA program went overseas in 2007 compared to 15 percent ten years ago.

33233 ▪ *"Wyse Transforms Digital Signage, In-Store Advertising and Retail Kiosks With Cloud Client Computing"* in *Internet Wire (February 1, 2012)*

Released: February 1, 2012. **Description:** Wyse Technology is providing cloud computing services instead of PCs to power their customers' digital signage, in-store advertising and retail kiosks. Wyse is a world leader in cloud client computing is applauded for the security, reliability, affordability, sustainability and ease of use from their customers that include banks, retailers, airports and universities and more.

33234 ▪ *"Young Entrepreneur Gets Some Recognition and Some Help for College"* in *Philadelphia Inquirer (August 30, 2010)*

Pub: Philadelphia Inquirer

Ed: Susan Snyder. **Description:** Profile of Zachary Gosling, age 18, who launched an online auction Website from his bedroom, using advertising and sponsorship funds rather than charging fees to users.

33235 ▪ *"Young Money"*

Pub: Grand Central Publishing

Released: February 18, 2014. **Price:** $27.00. **Description:** How the financial crisis of 2008 changed a generation and remade Wall Street is discussed. The author spent three years following eight entry-level workers at Goldman Sachs, Bank of America Merrill Lynch and other leading investment firms. These young bankers are exposed to the exhausting workloads, huge bonuses, and recreational drugs that have always characterized Wall Street life, but as they get their education and training, they face questions about ethics, prestige and the value of their work.

33236 ▪ *"Zions Offers Step-by-Step Small Business Guidance"* in *Idaho Business Review (September 1, 2014)*

Pub: Dolan Co.

Contact: James P. Dolan, President

Released: September 15, 2014. **Description:** Zions bank provides small business guidance to clients through its Zions Bank Idaho Business Resource Center. The program helps entrepreneurs learn the basic rules of running a small business. Free courses teach the essentials of finance, marketing and selling, .

TRADE PERIODICALS

33237 ▪ *AACE Distinguished Member Series*

Pub: American Association for Career Education

Ed: Pat Nellor Wickwire, Editor. **Released:** Periodic. **Price:** Included in membership. **Description:** Publication of the American Association for Career Education. Provides information on careers, education, and employment.

33238 ▪ *AACSB Newsline*

Pub: Association to Advance Collegiate Schools of Business

Contact: John J. Fernandes, President

URL(s): www.aacsb.edu/. **Ed:** Becky Johnson, Editor. **Released:** 4/yr. **Price:** $25 /year; $35 elsewhere. **Description:** Covers issues and events affecting management education, and Association projects and activities. Recurring features include notices of publications available and news of educational opportunities.

33239 ▪ *The Chemical Educator*

Pub: The Chemical Educator

URL(s): chemeducator.org. **Ed:** Hugh Cartwright. **Released:** Annual. **Price:** $29.95, Individuals; $149.95, Institutions print archive edition available separately; $10, Single issue + shipping.

33240 ▪ *Multimedia Internet@Schools: A Practical Journal of Multimedia, CD-ROM, Online, & Internet in K-12*

Pub: Information Today, Inc.

Contact: Thomas H. Hogan, President

E-mail: ctuthill@infotoday.com

URL(s): www.mmischools.com. **Ed:** David Hoffman. **Released:** Bimonthly **Price:** $45.95, U.S.; $64, Canada and Mexico; $94, Two years; $144, Individuals 3 years; $73, outside north america.

33241 ▪ *School Scene*

Pub: Technology Student Association

Contact: Steven Stokes, President

URL(s): www.tsaweb.org/School-Scene-Newsletters. **Ed:** Jane Wright, Editor. **Released:** 3/year; Spring, Winter and Fall. **Price:** Included in membership. **Description:** Functions as a member newsletter for the Technology Student Association. Dedicated to preparing membership for the challenges of a dynamic world by promoting personal growth and opportunities. Also provides competitive event news and tips, along with conference news. Recurring features include interviews, a calendar of events, reports of meetings, news of educational opportunities, and notices of publications available.

33242 ▪ *Teach Magazine: Education for Today and Tomorrow*

Pub: TEACH Magazine

URL(s): teachmag.com/. **Ed:** Wili Liberman. **Released:** 5/yr. **Price:** $18.95, Individuals.

VIDEOCASSETTES/ AUDIOCASSETTES

33243 ▪ *Adult Learning Video? You've Got to Be Kidding!*

ASTD

1640 King St.

Alexandria, VA 22314-2746

Ph: (703)683-8100

Free: 800-628-2783

Fax: (703)683-1523

Co. E-mail: customercare@astd.org

URL: http://www.astd.org

Contact: Tony Bingham, President

E-mail: tbingham@astd.org

Released: 1989. **Description:** A look at the seven steps to becoming an all-star trainer in business and industry. Describes how to use the principles of learning theory to improve training sessions. Focuses on the issues of the adult learner, including fear of failure, new technology vs. past experience, and bureaucractic systems. **Availability:** VHS; 3/4 U.

33244 ▪ *Basic Techniques in Practical Chemistry*

TMW Media Group

2321 Abbot Kinney Blvd., Ste. 101

Venice, CA 90291-4726

Ph: (310)577-8581

Free: 800-262-8862

Fax: (310)574-0886

Co. E-mail: sale@firslightvideo.com

URL: http://www.tmwmedia.com

Contact: Michael Bennett, President

Released: 1997. **Price:** $395. **Description:** Ten-volume series provide hands on presentations and precise, analytical content that make difficult chemistry understandable for all levels. **Availability:** VHS.

33245 ▪ *Charley Chapters: Contraction Action*

Media, Inc.

PO Box 496

Media, PA 19063

Ph: (610)565-2844

Free: 800-523-0118

Fax: (610)565-3614

URL: http://www.mediaincorporated.com

Released: 1996. **Price:** $225. **Description:** Explains the rules for changing two words into one. **Availability:** VHS.

33246 ■ Charley Chapters: Root Words, Prefixes, and Suffixes
Media, Inc.
PO Box 496
Media, PA 19063
Ph: (610)565-2844
Free: 800-523-0118
Fax: (610)565-3614
URL: http://www.mediaincorporated.com
Released: 1996. **Price:** $225. **Description:** Provides lessons for making spelling easier. **Availability:** VHS.

33247 ■ Charley Chapters: Suffixes and Their Rule Changes
Media, Inc.
PO Box 496
Media, PA 19063
Ph: (610)565-2844
Free: 800-523-0118
Fax: (610)565-3614
URL: http://www.mediaincorporated.com
Released: 1996. **Price:** $225. **Description:** Explains the rules for the ways words change when suffixes are added. **Availability:** VHS.

33248 ■ Charley Chapters: Writing with Synonyms, Antonyms, and the Thesaurus
Media, Inc.
PO Box 496
Media, PA 19063
Ph: (610)565-2844
Free: 800-523-0118
Fax: (610)565-3614
URL: http://www.mediaincorporated.com
Released: 1995. **Price:** $225. **Description:** Explains how to expand vocabulary and writing skills. **Availability:** VHS.

33249 ■ Common Miracles: The New American Revolution in Learning
MPI Media Group
16101 S 108th Ave.
Orland Park, IL 60467
Ph: (708)460-0555
Free: 800-323-0442
Fax: (708)873-3177
Co. E-mail: info@mpimedia.com
URL: http://www.mpimedia.com
Contact: Malik Ali, President
Released: 1997. **Price:** $19.98. **Description:** Peter Jennings examines the future of education. **Availability:** VHS.

33250 ■ Disney Presents Bill Nye the Science Guy Sampler III
Buena Vista Home Entertainment
500 S Buena Vista St.
Burbank, CA 91521-1120
Ph: (818)295-5200
Fax: (818)845-8728
URL: http://www.bvhe.com
Contact: Bob Chapek, President
Released: 19??. **Price:** $199. **Description:** Collection of 10 full-length shows featuring lessons in archeology, volcanoes, inventions, animal locomotion, and more. **Availability:** VHS.

33251 ■ The Eisenhower Era, 1940-1960
Buena Vista Home Entertainment
500 S Buena Vista St.
Burbank, CA 91521-1120
Ph: (818)295-5200
Fax: (818)845-8728
URL: http://www.bvhe.com
Contact: Bob Chapek, President
Released: 19??. **Price:** $699. **Description:** Twenty-volume series covers four thematic units: World War II, The Cold War, The Eisenhower Presidency (Domestic Policy), and The Eisenhower Presidency (Foreign Policy). Includes teacher's guide, companion software, and activities. **Availability:** VHS.

33252 ■ Got a Problem? Solve It!
Sunburst Digital Inc.
1550 Executive Dr.
Elgin, IL 60123-9311
Free: 800-321-7511
Co. E-mail: service@sunburst.com
URL: http://www.sunburst.com
Contact: Dan Figurski, President
Released: 1997. **Price:** $59.95. **Description:** Four vignettes present positive strategies for logical thinking and problem solving. On-screen questions promote classroom discussions. **Availability:** VHS.

33253 ■ Helping Your Child Succeed in School
Tapeworm Video Distributors Inc.
25876 The Old Rd., Ste. 141
Stevenson Ranch, CA 91381
Ph: (661)257-4904
Fax: (661)257-4820
Contact: Connie Figgins, President
E-mail: conrief@tapeworm.com
Released: 19??. **Price:** $18.95. **Description:** Six part video series discussing aspects of all stages of learning and development. **Availability:** VHS.

33254 ■ Hola Amigos Boxed Set
Monterey Home Video
566 St. Charles Dr.
Thousand Oaks, CA 91360-3953
Ph: (805)494-7199
Free: 800-424-2593
Fax: (805)496-6061
Co. E-mail: customerservice@montereymedia.com
URL: http://www.montereymedia.com
Contact: Scott Mansfield, President
Released: 1997. **Price:** $54.95. **Description:** Three-volume set uses songs and games to provide a gentle introduction to the Spanish language. **Availability:** VHS.

33255 ■ Johnny Tremain
Buena Vista Home Entertainment
500 S Buena Vista St.
Burbank, CA 91521-1120
Ph: (818)295-5200
Fax: (818)845-8728
URL: http://www.bvhe.com
Contact: Bob Chapek, President
Released: 1997. **Price:** $99. **Description:** Presents reenactments of historical figures and events such as the Boston Tea Party, Paul Revere, and Samuel Adams. **Availability:** VHS.

33256 ■ Science in Action
TMW Media Group
2321 Abbot Kinney Blvd., Ste. 101
Venice, CA 90291-4726
Ph: (310)577-8581
Free: 800-262-8862
Fax: (310)574-0886
Co. E-mail: sale@firslightvideo.com
URL: http://www.tmwmedia.com
Contact: Michael Bennett, President
Released: 1997. **Price:** $119. **Description:** Six-volume series explains basic scientific concepts and principles in an easy-to-understand manner. **Availability:** VHS.

33257 ■ Something Special
Educational Activities Inc. (EDACT)
1941 Grand Ave.
Baldwin, NY 11510
Ph: (516)223-4666
Free: 800-797-3223
Fax: (516)623-9282
Co. E-mail: learn@edact.com
URL: http://www.edact.com
Contact: Alfred S. Harris, President
Released: 1997. **Price:** $19.95. **Description:** Teaches movement vocabulary skills and promotes self-esteem. **Availability:** VHS.

33258 ■ Table Time for Tots
Tapeworm Video Distributors Inc.
25876 The Old Rd., Ste. 141
Stevenson Ranch, CA 91381
Ph: (661)257-4904
Fax: (661)257-4820
Contact: Connie Figgins, President
E-mail: conrief@tapeworm.com
Released: 1997. **Price:** $14.95. **Description:** Introduces children to the basic food groups using poem and song. **Availability:** VHS.

33259 ■ Training 101: Principles, Processes and People Every Trainer Should Know
ASTD
1640 King St.
Alexandria, VA 22314-2746
Ph: (703)683-8100
Free: 800-628-2783
Fax: (703)683-1523
Co. E-mail: customercare@astd.org
URL: http://www.astd.org
Contact: Tony Bingham, President
E-mail: tbingham@astd.org
Released: 1989. **Description:** A video overview of training, designed to give trainers more competence and confidence. Basic processes and concepts are explained and human resource development experts present descriptions of their work. **Availability:** VHS; 3/4 U.

33260 ■ Transformations: Science, Technology, and Society
Karol Media
Hanover Industrial Estates
375 Stewart Rd.
Wilkes Barre, PA 18773-7600
Ph: (570)822-8899
Free: 800-526-4773
Co. E-mail: sales@karolmedia.com
URL: http://www.karolmedia.com
Contact: Jay Roehrig, Customer Service
Released: 1997. **Price:** $125. **Description:** Eight-volume series designed to motivate learning and enhance science instruction. **Availability:** VHS.

33261 ■ Volcanoes: Cauldrons of Fury
MPI Media Group
16101 S 108th Ave.
Orland Park, IL 60467
Ph: (708)460-0555
Free: 800-323-0442
Fax: (708)873-3177
Co. E-mail: info@mpimedia.com
URL: http://www.mpimedia.com
Contact: Malik Ali, President
Released: 19??. **Price:** $19.98. **Description:** Examines the causes, history and future of volcanoes. **Availability:** VHS.

TRADE SHOWS AND CONVENTIONS

33262 ■ Michigan Association for Computer Users in Learning Conference
Michigan Association for Computer Users in Learning (MACUL)
520 S Creyts Rd.
Lansing, MI 48917
Ph: (517)882-1403
Fax: (517)882-2362
Co. E-mail: macul@macul.org
URL: http://www.macul.org
Contact: Pamela Shoemaker, President
URL(s): www.macul.org. **Frequency:** Annual. **Audience:** Educational technology professionals. **Principal Exhibits:** Computer and educational equipment, supplies, and services. **Dates and Locations:** 2015 Mar 18-20, Cobo Center, Detroit, MI.

CONSULTANTS

33263 ■ American English Academy (AEA) [American English College]
111 N Atlantic Blvd., Ste. 112
Monterey Park, CA 91754
Ph: (626)457-2800

Fax: (626)457-2808
Co. E-mail: info@aec.edu
URL: http://www.aea-usa.com
Contact: Charles Policky, President
Scope: Specializes in providing on-site English language and communication development for corporations and individuals. Also develops and delivers training in speaking, writing, pronunciation, grammar, and idioms with an emphasis on business communication. Offers individual, small group, intensive, and long-distance learning. Programs tailor-made for each client. **Founded:** 1983.

33264 ■ Beeline Learning Solutions (BLS)
14911 Quorum Dr., Ste. 120
Dallas, TX 75254
Free: 866-479-1442
Co. E-mail: info@consultingpartners.com
URL: http://www.beeline.com
Contact: Doug Leeby, President
Scope: Consulting firm offering technology, content and services addressing recruitment and sourcing, talent management and learning and performance optimization. Solutions offered include contingent workforce solutions, vendor management software, talent management solutions, recruitment process outsourcing, performance management, applicant tracking, learning management and eLearning. **Founded:** 1990. **Special Services:** Beeline®.

33265 ■ Blackmon Roberts Group Inc.
902 S S Florida Ave., Ste. 205
Lakeland, FL 33803-1116
Ph: (863)802-1280
Free: 877-450-3237
Fax: (863)802-1290
Co. E-mail: dbeinformation@blackmonroberts.com
URL: http://www.blackmonroberts.com
Contact: Sylvia Blackmon Roberts, President
E-mail: sylvia@blackmonroberts.com
Scope: Technical support consultant in technical writing, planning, research, needs analysis, marketing and training, offers training programs from cultural sensitivity issues to effective listening skills. **Founded:** 1992.

33266 ■ Daniel Bloom and Associates Inc. (DBAI)
11517 128th Ave. N
Largo, FL 33778
Ph: (727)581-6216
Fax: (727)216-8532
Co. E-mail: dan@dbaiconsulting.com
URL: http://www.dbaiconsulting.com
Contact: Sharon Megiel, Consultant
Scope: Human resources management consultant with a specialization in corporate relocation. Offers clients a turn key service aimed at meeting the unique relocation needs of their employees. Develops and implements training programs within the relocation industry. **Founded:** 1980. **Publications:** "Where Have All the Elders Gone," Aug, 2002; "Recoup Your Hiring Investment," Brainbuzz.com, Aug, 2000; "Managing Your Lump Sum Program," Brainbuzz. com, Jun, 2000; "Buyer Value Options," Brainbuzz. com, Apr, 2000; "Just Get Me There". **Seminars:** Chaos in the Workplace: Multiple Generational Interactions; Training Effectiveness: Is the Cost Justified?; Human Capital Resource Management: A Six-Sigma Based Approach to Paving Your Way to the Table; Welcome to My World.

33267 ■ Business Education Associates (BEA) [Ashford Group Inc.]
4 Long Hill Rd.
Bethel, CT 06801
Ph: (203)798-6035
Contact: Robert J. Popp, President
E-mail: bob@ashfordgrp.com
Scope: Offers tailored management education programs. Has been designed to meet the business education needs of companies implementing new systems and companies to re-educate users of existing systems. **Founded:** 1984. **Publications:** "The Ashford Group and TQuist Partner to Provide High Impact Manufacturing Solutions"; "The Future of ERP"; "Winning the Implementation Game". **Special Services:** Building Manufacturing Excellence.

33268 ■ Business Improvement Architects (BIA)
33 Riderwood Dr.
Toronto, ON, Canada M2L 2X4
Ph: (416)444-8225
Free: 866-346-3242
Fax: (416)444-6743
Co. E-mail: info@bia.ca
URL: http://www.bia.ca
Contact: Michael Stanleigh, Chief Executive Officer
E-mail: mstanleigh@bia.ca
Scope: Provider of the following services: strategic planning, leadership development, innovation and project and quality management. Specialize in strategic planning, change management, leadership assessment and development of skills. **Founded:** 1989. **Publications:** "Avoiding Pit falls to Innovation"; "Create a New Dimension of Performance with Innovation"; "The Power of Appreciation in Leadership"; "Why It Makes Sense To Have a Strategic Enterprise Office"; "Burning Rubber at the Start of Your Project"; "Accounting for Quality"; "How Pareto Charts Can Help You Improve the Quality of Business Processes"; "Managing Resistance to Change". **Seminars:** The Innovation Process From Vision to Reality, San Diego, Oct, 2007; Critical Thinking, Kuala Lump or, Sep, 2007; Critical Thinking, Brunei, Sep, 2007; Delivering Project Assurance, Auckland, Jun, 2007; From Crisis to Control: A New Era in Strategic Project Management, Prague, May, 2007; What Project Leaders Need to Know to Help Them Sleep Better At Night, London, May, 2007; Innovation Process. . .From Vision To Reality, Orlando, Apr, 2007. **Special Services:** Project Planning Tool™.

33269 ■ Center for Personal Empowerment
102 N Main St., Ste. 1
Columbia, IL 62236-1702
Ph: (618)281-3565
Contact: Cherri Hendrix, Owner
Scope: Private consultations and trainings to educate on how to determine which emotions, events, beliefs from the past prevent you from achieving success. Methods used include time line therapy, news linguistic programming and hypnosis. Behavior modification through NLP trainings. **Founded:** 1996. **Seminars:** NLP Practitioner Training; Hypnosis Certification Training; Lifemap Seminars.

33270 ■ Competitive Edge Inc.
241 E Crestwood Rd.
Peachtree City, GA 30269
Ph: (770)487-6460
Fax: (770)487-2919
Co. E-mail: judy@competitiveedgeinc.com
URL: http://www.competitiveedgeinc.com
Contact: Judy I. Suiter, President
E-mail: judy@competitiveedgeinc.com
Scope: A human resources consulting firm providing customized training and software solutions to assist clients in optimizing their human intellectual capital through effective selection, coaching, and training. Works with a network of consultants that are located throughout the United States, Canada, and Europe. **Founded:** 1981. **Publications:** "Beteenden och drivkrafter"; "Energizing People: Unleashing The Power of DISC"; "The Ripple Effect: How the Global Model of Endorsement Opens Doors to Success"; "The Journey - Quotes to keep your boat afloat"; "The Universal Language DISC Reference Manual"; "Exploring Values: Releasing the Power of Attitudes"; "Competitive Products Review Book"; "The Mother Of All Minds"; "The Sea of Change: Solutions for Navigating the Disconnects in the Workplace". **Seminars:** How to Recruit and Retain High Performing Employees; The Importance of Values Matching For Sales Selection; How to Build a High Performance Team; Dynamic Communication Skills; Creating Nurturing Customer Relationships; Your Attitude Is Showing; Sales Strategy Index; Validity Study.

33271 ■ Donna Cornell Enterprises Inc. [Cornell Career Center]
68 N Plank Rd., Ste. 204
Newburgh, NY 12550-2122
Ph: (845)565-0088

Fax: (845)565-0084
Scope: Offers services in career consultant, professional search, job placement and national professional search. **Founded:** 1996. **Publications:** "The Power of the Woman Within"; "Juggling it All!"; "Journey: A Woman's Guide to Success"; "Shatter the Traditions".

33272 ■ donphin.com Inc.
1001 B Ave., Ste. 200
Coronado, CA 92118
Ph: (619)550-3533
Free: 800-234-3304
Fax: (619)600-0096
Co. E-mail: don@donphin.com
URL: http://www.donphin.com
Scope: Offers a comprehensive approach to understanding and applying a broad range of business principles: legal compliance issues, management concerns, health and safety, customer service, marketing, information management. Industries served: All developing small businesses. **Founded:** 1983. **Publications:** "Doing Business Right!"; "HR That Works!"; "Lawsuit Free! How to Prevent Employee Lawsuits"; "Building Powerful Employment Relationships!"; "Victims, Villains and Heroes: Managing Emotions in The Workplace". **Seminars:** Doing Business Right!; HR That Works!; Building Powerful Employment Relationships; Lawsuit Free!.

33273 ■ Dorn & Associates Inc.
8506 Bass Lake Rd.
Minneapolis, MN 55428-5304
Ph: (763)533-7689
Contact: John L. Dorn, President
Scope: Services include accounting, marketing, employment partnership, new doctor agreements, personnel issues and human resources assessment, practice management, practice merger acquisition sale and liquidation, practice surveys and valuation, staff development and training.

33274 ■ Full Voice
3217 Broadway Ave., Ste. 300
Kansas City, MO 64111
Ph: (816)941-0011
Free: 800-684-8764
Fax: (816)931-8887
URL: http://www.fullvoice.us
Contact: Garrett Haskell Gardner, Owner
E-mail: garrett@infullvoice.com
Scope: Vocal performance training firm offering consulting services and personal training sessions in the implementation of effective vocal communication techniques for the development of business relationships and career enhancement. Formalizes a program of proven techniques into a practical method of helping individuals improve their ability to better present themselves when speaking in a professional situation. Industries served: All. **Founded:** 1992. **Publications:** "You Can Sound Like You Know What You're Saying". **Seminars:** You Can Sound Like You Know What You're Saying; The Psychology of Vocal Performance; Security. . .the Ability to Accept Change; Knowing. . .the Key to Relaxed Public Communication; The Effective Voice for Customer Service Enhancement; You Can Speak With Conviction; How To Make Yours a Championship Team; Functional English For Foreign Trade. **Special Services:** FULL VOICE™.

33275 ■ Harding & Co.
511 Harvard Ave.
Swarthmore, PA 19081
Ph: (610)544-9005
Co. E-mail: fharding@hardingco.com
URL: http://www.hardingco.com
Contact: Mimi Spangler, President
E-mail: mspangler@hardingco.com
Scope: Specializes in sales management, client development and employee training. **Founded:** 1993. **Publications:** "Cross-Selling Success: A Rainmakers Guide to Professional Account Development," Aug, 2002; "Rain Making: The Professional's Guide to Attracting New Clients"; "Creating Rainmakers: The Managers Guide to Training Professionals to Attract New Clients".

33276 ■ Hills Consulting Group Inc.
6 Partridge Ct.
Novato, CA 94945-1315
Ph: (415)898-3944
Contact: Michael R. Hills, President
Scope: Specializes in strategic planning; marketing surveys; market research; customer service audits; new product development; competitive analysis; and sales forecasting. **Founded:** 1985.

33277 ■ Interpersonal Coaching & Consulting (ICC)
1516 W Lake St., Ste. 2000S
Minneapolis, MN 55408
Ph: (612)381-2494
Co. E-mail: mail@interpersonal-coaching.com
URL: http://www.interpersonal-coaching.com
Contact: Richard J. Studer, Partner
E-mail: mail@interpersonal-coaching.com
Scope: Provider of coaching and consulting to businesses and organizations. Assesses the interpersonal workplace through interviews, assessment instruments and individual group settings. Experienced as a therapist for over a decade. **Publications:** "Sexual Harassment In The Workplace For Newspapers". **Seminars:** More On Relationships; Sexual harassment and discrimination issues.

33278 ■ Mandalay Associates L.L.C.
190 El Cerrito Plz., Ste. 226
El Cerrito, CA 94530-4002
Ph: (510)526-4651
Fax: (510)526-5774
Contact: Kristina Combs, Member
Scope: Business management firm specializes in conflict resolution, employee relations, employment and placement, organizational analysis and development, human resources program development, program and project management and staff development and training.

33279 ■ Milestone Inc. [Blue SuitMilestone Consulting;]
PO Box 630
Dedham, MA 02027
Co. E-mail: bob@milestoneideas.com
URL: http://www.milestoneideas.com
Contact: Robert J. Taraschi, President
E-mail: bob@milestoneideas.com
Scope: Facilitates 100 business creativity and innovation growth sessions per year. Assists to: Discover new growth strategies and planning options; create new ideas, new promises, value propositions, products and programs; identify and integrate customer passions in new and surprising ways; realize higher returns on involvement, interest and investment; refine processes, accelerate innovative growth and build better teams. **Founded:** 1980. **Publications:** "Can your brand tell a bigger story". **Seminars:** Ideas in Action; Double-Gesturing; Growth in a period of no growth; Strike while the iron is cold; Natural Creative Strategies; The Enduring Power of Open Ended Creativity; Ideation Techniques to Drive Brand Value. **Special Services:** Milestone®; IMMERgENT®; SmartAlec.

33280 ■ Art Munin Consulting
c/o Assistant Dean of Students Office
Depaul University, Student Ctr.
Chicago, IL 60614-3673
Ph: (773)316-2276
Co. E-mail: art@artmunin.com
URL: http://www.artmunin.com
Contact: Art Munin, Principal
Scope: Consulting firm committed to advancing multicultural education and imparting advocacy. Expands the opportunities to engage people in conversations about diversity and social justice. Other areas of interest include counseling skills, crisis response, improving the campus climate for bi/multiracial students, sexual assault, GLBT advocacy, team building, and other diversity-related training topics. **Publications:** "Would they still have written if they knew I had to go home and tell my wife?," 2009; "The leadership bookshelf," 2009; "Improving the campus environment for bi/multiracial students," Peter Lang Publishing, 2009; "Empathy: Love the sinner, hate the sin. About Campus," 2007; "Factors influencing the ally development of college students". **Seminars:** White Privilege 101; Locating Justice; Targeting the Majority in Diversity Education; Art of War - Targeting the Majority in Multicultural Education; Higher Education: The Gate-Keeper to the Middle Class; Who Are Our Transgendered Students?; The Basics of Diversity Training; Retreats; Ethics and Leadership: Making Choices for Social Justice; Color by Number.

33281 ■ National Pediculosis Association (NPA)
1005 Boylston St., Ste. 343
Newton, MA 02461
Ph: (617)905-0176
Fax: (800)235-1305
Co. E-mail: npa@headlice.org
URL: http://www.headlice.org
Contact: Deborah Z. Altschuler, President
E-mail: dza@headlice.org
Description: Parents, physicians, school nurses, and individuals representing hospitals and county health departments. Works to eliminate the incidence, particularly among children, of pediculosis (head lice). Conducts public education campaign to make pediculosis control a public health priority; acts as consumer advocate to ensure the quality and safety of products for treating pediculosis and scabies; encourages scientific research to discover methods of treatment that minimize the use of pesticides, which may harm pregnant and nursing women as well as infants and children. Disseminates information on identifying, treating, and preventing pediculosis, with emphasis on finding and removing nits (louse eggs) in the hair. Provides consultations to schools, camps, and other organizations. **Scope:** Consultants in head lice and scabies management, treatment, prevention, and education. Specializes in monitoring health policy administration in schools and trends in the treatment of head lice. Emphasis is on educational activities. Industries served: schools, health professionals, medical professionals, child care centers, health departments, hospitals, HMO's, clinics, libraries, parents, PTA's, camps, military bases, and churches. **Founded:** 1983. **Publications:** "All out Comb out".

33282 ■ ProActive English
4355 SE 29th Ave.
Portland, OR 97202
Ph: (503)231-2906
Co. E-mail: infopae@proactive-english.com
URL: http://www.proactive-english.com
Contact: Margaret Lyman, Manager
E-mail: mlyman@proactive-english.com
Scope: Offers on-site individual and small group language and communication training. Sets up learning plans tailored to the needs and schedules of managers and executives who are non-native English speakers. Serves all industries. **Founded:** 1997. **Seminars:** Communicating in Business Situations; Presentations and Pronunciation; Tailored Curriculum; One-on-One Programs.

33283 ■ Professional Psychological Services (PPS)
4130 Linden Ave., Ste. 309
Dayton, OH 45432-3034
Ph: (937)254-7301
Fax: (937)254-2117
Co. E-mail: ppsdocs@aol.com
Contact: Mary Ann Jones, Partner
Scope: Offers clinical services, human relations training, multicultural and pluralistic training and staff development and training. **Founded:** 1994.

33284 ■ Sandy Corp. [Sandy]
300 E Big Beaver Rd., Ste. 500
Troy, MI 48084-3526
Ph: (248)729-4628
Fax: (248)729-4701
Co. E-mail: info@gpsandy.com
URL: http://www.sandycorp.com
Contact: Raymond A. Ketchledge, President
Scope: It provides the design, development and production of specific consulting, training, communicating and evaluating programs to help clients improve the capabilities of their people to such a level that consistent performance on the job becomes a visible, valued competitive strength. **Founded:** 1911. **Seminars:** Emerging Issues seminars, May, 2012.

33285 ■ Tamayo Consulting Inc.
169 Saxony Rd., Ste. 112
Encinitas, CA 92024-6779
Ph: (760)479-1352
Fax: (760)479-1465
Co. E-mail: info@tamayoconsulting.com
URL: http://www.tamayoconsulting.com
Contact: Jennifer Dreyer, President
E-mail: jdreyer@earthlink.net
Scope: It Provides training and consulting services. And also it specializes in leadership and team development. Industries served: private, non-profit, government, educational. **Founded:** 1986. **Seminars:** Presentation AdvantEdge Program; Lead point Development Program; Supervisor Development Programs.Identify Presentation Objectives; Implement 360-degree presentation assessment; conduct baseline-coaching session; Develop coaching plan; Staying connected.

33286 ■ Training Systems Plus
742 Brent Dr.
Mulvane, KS 67110-1245
Ph: (316)777-1337
Contact: Charles M. Cadwell, Owner
E-mail: chastrain@cox.net
Scope: Provider of management and training systems to businesses to improve operational profitability as well as individual management and employee performance. Activities include consultation, job descriptions, evaluation forms, training seminars, training materials, operations manuals and employee handbooks. **Founded:** 1986. **Seminars:** Effective Classroom Instruction; Training System Design; Interviewing and Selecting; Performance Management, Leadership Skills.

FRANCHISES AND BUSINESS OPPORTUNITIES

33287 ■ Canadian School of Natural Nutrition
11685 Yonge St.
Unit B108
Richmond Hill, ON, Canada L4E 0K7
Ph: (905)737-0284
Fax: (905)737-1994
URL: http://www.csnn.ca
Description: private vocational school offering adult education leading to professional designations: RHN-Reg. Holistic Nutritionist, and RECP-Reg, ElderCare Practitioner. Franchisees are licensed to distribute CSNN curriculum material to students through classroom education. CSNN offers two programs: Natural Nutrition and Elder Care. CSNN is privately owned, incorporated as 3393291 Canada Inc. **No. of Franchise Units:** 4. **No. of Company-Owned Units:** 10. **Founded:** 1994. **Franchised:** 1996. **Equity Capital Needed:** $70,000 Canadian Capital. **Franchise Fee:** $12,000. **Training:** Ongoing.

33288 ■ Club Scientific
106 Hartwood Dr.
Woodstock, GA 30189
Free: 800-399-8309
URL: http://www.clubscientific.com
Description: Science enrichment program. **No. of Franchise Units:** 5. **No. of Company-Owned Units:** 8. **Founded:** 1997. **Franchised:** 2007. **Equity Capital Needed:** $56,825-$84,720. **Franchise Fee:** $20,000-$24,500. **Royalty Fee:** 6%. **Financial Assistance:** Third party financing available. **Training:** Provides 4 days training at headquarters, 4 days at franchisee's location and ongoing support.

33289 ■ Cybertary
1217 Pleasant Grove Blvd., Ste. 100
Roseville, CA 95678
Ph: (916)781-7799
Free: 888-292-8279
Fax: (877)292-8279
URL: http://www.CybertaryFranchise.com
Description: Virtual assistant (VA) industry providing on-demand administrative support to businesses, entrepreneurs, and busy people through a nationwide team network to meet the needs of any business. This home-based B2B service offers low overhead and a flexible schedule. **No. of Franchise Units:** 23. **Founded:** 2005. **Franchised:** 2006. **Equity Capital**

Needed: $39,500-$78,500. **Franchise Fee:** $37,500-$56,250. **Royalty Fee:** 5%. **Training:** Receive 4 days of intensive training.

33290 ■ Drama Kids International, Inc.
525-K E Market St., Ste. 250
Leesburg, VA 20176
Free: 866-809-1055
Co. E-mail: dramakids@starpower.net
URL: http://www.dramakids.com
Description: After-school developmental drama program. Curriculum uses fun and creative drama activities so kids ages 5-17 act confidently and speak clearly. **No. of Franchise Units:** 56. **Founded:** 1979. **Franchised:** 1989. **Equity Capital Needed:** $33,550-38,950. **Franchise Fee:** $29,000. **Royalty Fee:** 8-9%. **Financial Assistance:** Third party financing available. **Training:** Available 5 days at headquarters, 5 days at franchisee's location, 1 day of regional training plus annual conference and ongoing support.

33291 ■ E.nopi
50 Passaic St.
Hackensack, NJ 07601
Ph: (201)498-1212
Free: 888-835-1212
Fax: (201)498-1218
Description: Supplemental education. **No. of Franchise Units:** 125. **No. of Company-Owned Units:** 513. **Founded:** 1976. **Franchised:** 1976. **Equity Capital Needed:** $52,000-$91,000. **Franchise Fee:** $12,000. **Royalty Fee:** $15/student. **Training:** Offers 16 hours training at headquarters, at franchisee's location and ongoing.

33292 ■ Estrada Strategies Franchise Inc.
3400 Inland Empire Blvd., Ste. 101
Ontario, CA 91764
Ph: (909)476-3510
Co. E-mail: info@estradastrategies.com
URL: http://estradastrategies.com
Description: Executive coaching programs. **No. of Franchise Units:** 2. **No. of Company-Owned Units:** 1. **Founded:** 2000. **Franchised:** 2006. **Equity Capital Needed:** $43,300-$77,200. **Franchise Fee:** $25,000. **Royalty Fee:** Varies. **Training:** Training at corporate headquarters, onsite and ongoing support provided.

33293 ■ Fastrackids International, Ltd.
6900 E Belleview Ave., Ste. 320
Greenwood Village, CO 80111
Ph: (303)224-0200
Free: 888-576-6888
Fax: (303)224-0222
Co. E-mail: info@fastrackids.com
URL: http://www.fastrackids.com
Description: An accelerated learning system for children. **No. of Franchise Units:** 150. **Founded:** 1998. **Franchised:** 1998. **Equity Capital Needed:** $33,800-$183,500. **Franchise Fee:** $22,000. **Financial Assistance:** 30-V, FRA handbook. **Training:** Provides initial training, periodic regional seminars, an annual international conference, sales/telemarketing assistance, and classroom facilitation tips.

33294 ■ Frozen Ropes Training Centers
24 Old Black Meadow Rd.
Chester, NY 10918
Ph: (845)469-7331
Fax: (845)469-6742
Co. E-mail: info@frozenropes.com
URL: http://www.frozenropes.com
Description: Baseball & softball instruction. **No. of Franchise Units:** 8. **No. of Company-Owned Units:** 1. **Founded:** 1994. **Franchised:** 2003. **Equity Capital Needed:** $219,800-$276,200. **Franchise Fee:** $45,000. **Royalty Fee:** 3-6%.

33295 ■ Ho Math & Chess Learning Centre
5707 Balsam St.
Vancouver, BC, Canada V6M 2A3
Ph: (604)263-4321
Co. E-mail: mathandchess@telus.net
URL: http://www.mathandchess.com
Contact: Frank Ho, President
Description: Math & chess learning program. **No. of Franchise Units:** 4. **No. of Company-Owned Units:** 1. **No. of Operating Units:** 8. **Founded:** 1995. Fran-

chised: 2004. **Equity Capital Needed:** $25,150. **Franchise Fee:** $2,100. **Royalty Fee:** None. **Training:** 1 week training provided at headquarters.

33296 ■ KidzArt
KidzArt Texas LLC
1001 Laurence Ave., Ste. E
Jackson, MI 49202
Ph: (514)509-1315
Free: 800-379-8302
Co. E-mail: info@kidzart.com
URL: http://www.kidzart.com
Contact: Chris Cruikshank, President
Description: Offers children's products and education services. **No. of Franchise Units:** 65. **Founded:** 1997. **Franchised:** 2002. **Equity Capital Needed:** $15,045-$38,150, includes working capital and franchise fee. **Franchise Fee:** $9,900-$19,900. **Financial Assistance:** Yes. **Training:** Offers 1 week business/operations training and cutting edge franchisee support; conferences, monthly training calls, one on one quick start coaching and ongoing support.

33297 ■ KnowledgePoints Inc.
5 Centerpoint Dr., Ste. 250
Lake Oswego, OR 97035
Ph: (503)270-5100
Fax: (503)270-5117
Description: Tutoring programs. **No. of Franchise Units:** 46. **No. of Company-Owned Units:** 1. **Founded:** 1999. **Franchised:** 2003. **Equity Capital Needed:** $89,350-$150,250. **Franchise Fee:** $22,500. **Royalty Fee:** 8%. **Training:** Provides 6 days training at headquarters, 3 weeks at franchisee's location, and ongoing support for franchisee & managers.

33298 ■ Kumon North America, Inc.
300 Frank W. Burr Blvd., Ste. 6
Teaneck, NJ 07666
Ph: (201)928-0444
Fax: (201)928-0444
URL: http://www.kumonfranchise.com
Description: North America provider of supplemental math and learning material. The learning center caters to all ages and abilities from pre-school through high school. **No. of Franchise Units:** 2,000. **No. of Company-Owned Units:** 24. **Founded:** 1958. **Franchised:** 1980. **Equity Capital Needed:** $70,000 cash, $150,000 net worth; $69,943-$144,050 initial investment. **Franchise Fee:** $1,000. **Training:** Kumon has offices worldwide to provide training, support and onsite consultation to franchisee's.

33299 ■ Language Leaders Franchising LLC
Foreign Language Network, L.L.C.
401 W State St.
Geneva, IL 60134
Ph: (630)232-2001
Description: Foreign language education and interpreting. **No. of Company-Owned Units:** 1. **Founded:** 1998. **Franchised:** 2004. **Equity Capital Needed:** $18,700-$107,000. **Franchise Fee:** $10,000-$90,000. **Royalty Fee:** 15%. **Training:** 2 days training at headquarters.

33300 ■ LearningRX Franchise Corp.
LearningRx, Inc.
5085 List Dr., Ste. 200
Colorado Springs, CO 80919
Ph: (719)264-8808
URL: http://www2.learningrx.com
Description: One on one brain skills and reading training. **No. of Franchise Units:** 80. **No. of Company-Owned Units:** 2. **Founded:** 1987. **Franchised:** 2003. **Equity Capital Needed:** $200,000. **Franchise Fee:** $25,000-$35,000. **Training:** Yes.

33301 ■ The LiceSquad Inc.
Lice Squad Canada Inc.
3A King St.
Cookstown, ON, Canada L0L 1L0
Free: 888-542-3778
Fax: (705)458-8887
URL: http://www.licesquad.com
Description: Join Canada's leading head lice removal and Education Company. Low start up costs and proven potential. Perfect for those in the nursing, hairdressing and child care fields. Our clients include

schools, families, camps and other child care organizations. Our home-based business model allows flexibility. Enjoy both family and career. 15 successful LiceSquad franchises operating in Ontario with master franchises available. **No. of Franchise Units:** 9. **No. of Company-Owned Units:** 20. **Founded:** 2001. **Franchised:** 2002. **Equity Capital Needed:** $42,000-$85,000 investment required; start-up capital required $25,000-$35,000. **Franchise Fee:** $20,000. **Training:** Provides training (excluding travel/hotel costs).

33302 ■ Little City Kids
10127 Northwestern Ave.
Franksville, WI 53126
Ph: (262)884-4226
Co. E-mail: little.city.kids.FS@gmail.com
URL: http://www.littlecitykids.com
Description: Educational playcare for your child. The environment is set into action in an interactive world filled with imagination stations, innovative online curriculum and team teaching methods. We offer two models, the Little City Kids model is for children ages 2-13 years and the Itty Bitty Kids model adds infant and toddler care. **No. of Company-Owned Units:** 1. **Founded:** 1998. **Franchised:** 2004. **Equity Capital Needed:** $118,000-$189,000. **Franchise Fee:** $35,000. **Royalty Fee:** 7%. **Training:** Available at headquarters 30-60 days, 10 days at franchisee's location and ongoing support.

33303 ■ The Mad Science Group
8360 Bougainville St., Ste. 201
Montreal, QC, Canada H4P 2G1
Ph: (514)344-4181
Free: 800-586-5231
Fax: (514)344-6695
Co. E-mail: info@madscience.org
URL: http://www.madscience.org
Description: Mad Science is a service company specializing in fun hands on educational science for children. We send trained instructors with all required materials and supplies to conduct onsite activities to schools and other organizations dealing with kids. Our franchisees are sales marketing oriented individuals who enjoy a hands-on owner operated business that enriches children and contributes to the community. **No. of Franchise Units:** 200. **Founded:** 1985. **Franchised:** 1995. **Equity Capital Needed:** $10,000-$23,500 franchise fee, $25,000 equipment package; $20,000-$30,000 working capital. **Franchise Fee:** $10,000-$23,500. **Financial Assistance:** Yes. **Training:** 6 day training at corporate headquarters followed by 5 day training onsite.

33304 ■ Math Monkey Knowledge Centers
56 Winchester Rd.
Newton, MA 02458
Ph: (954)384-1050
Free: 877-468-6284
Description: After school enrichment program. **No. of Franchise Units:** 14. **No. of Company-Owned Units:** 1. **Founded:** 2006. **Franchised:** 2006. **Equity Capital Needed:** $99,000-$164,000. **Franchise Fee:** $31,500. **Royalty Fee:** 6%. **Training:** 2 weeks training at headquarters included, 2 weeks at franchisee's location, 1 week at existing franchise location, online seminars and ongoing support.

33305 ■ Mathnasium Learning Centers
5120 W Goldleaf Cir., Ste. 300
Los Angeles, CA 90056
Ph: (323)421-8000
Free: 877-531-6284
Fax: (310)943-2111
Co. E-mail: info@mathnasium.com
URL: http://www.mathnasium.com
Description: Mathnasium provides the most effective mathematics in education available to grade school children after school, in an attractive neighborhood learning center environment. The Mathnasium Method, developed over 30 years of hands-on experience, is engaging for students and builds confidence as it builds real understanding. Created to address a real need in the market by a team with unparalleled success in the industry, the business model is strong and the opportunity is now. **No. of Franchise Units:** 389. **No. of Company-Owned Units:** 2. **Founded:** 2002. **Franchised:** 2003. **Equity Capital Needed:**

$82,250-$136,000 initial investment range. **Franchise Fee:** $37,000. **Training:** Initial training 1 week online followed by 1 week in person at corporate headquarters. Support continues with ongoing training, in-the-field regional managers and monthly conference calls.

33306 ■ Motion Golf LLC
55 Lane Rd.
Fairfield, NJ 07004
Free: 866-585-6033
Description: Golf swing analysis, instruction, and club fitting. **No. of Company-Owned Units:** 3. **Founded:** 2006. **Franchised:** 2007. **Equity Capital Needed:** $250,000 (Express/kiosk option available). **Franchise Fee:** $79,500. **Royalty Fee:** 6%. **Training:** 1 week at franchisee's location.

33307 ■ Online Trading Academy
17780 Fitch, Ste. 200
Irvine, CA 92614
Ph: (949)475-5652
Free: 888-841-8418
URL: http://www.tradingacademy.com/irvine
Description: Stock-trading instruction. **No. of Franchise Units:** 16. **Founded:** 1998. **Franchised:** 2004. **Equity Capital Needed:** $209,800-$388,000. **Franchise Fee:** $80,000-$200,000. **Royalty Fee:** 10%. **Training:** Offers 2 weeks training at headquarters, 1 week at franchisees location and ongoing support.

33308 ■ Oxford Learning Centers Inc.
747 Hyde Park Rd., Ste. 230
London, ON, Canada N6H 3S3
Ph: (519)473-1460
Fax: (519)473-6086
URL: http://www.oxfordlearning.com
Description: Oxford is an educational franchise in Canada, which provides extensive training in all fields. **No. of Franchise Units:** 108. **No. of Company-Owned Units:** 5. **Founded:** 1984. **Franchised:** 1991. **Equity Capital Needed:** $140,000-$210,000 plus applicable taxes. **Franchise Fee:** $40,000 plus applicable taxes. **Training:** Provides 2 weeks training and ongoing support.

33309 ■ Parisi Speed School
291 Franklin Ave.
Wyckoff, NJ 07481
Ph: (201)485-8584
URL: http://www.parisischool.com/wyckoff
Description: Youth performance training. **No. of Franchise Units:** 44. **No. of Company-Owned Units:** 5. **Founded:** 1992. **Franchised:** 2005. **Equity Capital Needed:** $132,500-$300,100. **Franchise Fee:** $29,900. **Royalty Fee:** $1,000/month.

33310 ■ Parmasters Golf Training Centers
1500 W Georgia St., 14th Fl.
Vancouver, BC, Canada V6G 2Z6
URL: http://www.franchising.com/parmasters
URL(s): www.parmastersgolf.com. **Description:** Year-round indoor golf training center. **No. of Franchise Units:** 27. **No. of Company-Owned Units:** 7. **Founded:** 2000. **Franchised:** 2001. **Equity Capital Needed:** $300,000-$2,500,000. **Franchise Fee:** $50,000.

33311 ■ Pathways Education and Training Centers, Inc.
333 S Parkside Cir.
Saint George, UT 84770
Ph: (435)674-1331
Fax: (435)674-1831
Description: Brain integration program. **No. of Franchise Units:** 6. **No. of Company-Owned Units:** 1. **Founded:** 2000. **Franchised:** 2005. **Equity Capital Needed:** $20,000. **Training:** Yes.

33312 ■ Spirit of Math Schools
178 Willowdale Ave.
Toronto, ON, Canada M2N 4Y8
Ph: (416)223-1985
Fax: (416)946-1902
Co. E-mail: info@spiritofmath.com
URL: http://www.spiritofmath.com
Contact: Kim Langen, Chief Executive Officer
Description: Offers an after-school classroom program for high performing students. It develops as skill-based understanding of math focusing on

problem solving, co-operation and numeric skills and produces some of the top math students in the nation. **No. of Franchise Units:** 13. **No. of Company-Owned Units:** 13. **Founded:** 1992. **Franchised:** 2006. **Equity Capital Needed:** $32,000-$70,000. **Franchise Fee:** $39,000. **Training:** A comprehensive training and support program is provided.

33313 ■ Thinkertots
Thinkertots Franchise Inc.
22214 Union Tpke.
Bayside, NY 11364
Ph: (718)740-1616
Description: Educational parent/child classes. **No. of Franchise Units:** 4. **No. of Company-Owned Units:** 1. **Founded:** 1998. **Franchised:** 2005. **Equity Capital Needed:** $42,000-$160,000. **Franchise Fee:** $15,000-$25,000. **Training:** Yes.

33314 ■ The Whole Child Learning Co.
2200 Kraft Dr., Ste. 1350
Blacksburg, VA 24060
Ph: (540)443-9252
Fax: (540)242-3214
URL: http://www.wholechild.com
Description: Educational services for children. **No. of Franchise Units:** 6. **No. of Company-Owned Units:** 4. **Founded:** 1996. **Franchised:** 1999. **Equity Capital Needed:** $7,500. **Franchise Fee:** $15,000. **Financial Assistance:** Yes. **Training:** Yes.

33315 ■ Young Rembrandts - The Power Of Drawing
Young Rembrandts
23 N Union St.
Elgin, IL 60123
Ph: (847)742-6966
Co. E-mail: info@youngrembrandts.com
URL: http://www.youngrembrandts.com
Description: Developed a proven method that ensures artistic and academic success for every child. Our unique method and original curriculum teaches drawing, the fundamental skill of visual arts to children ages 3 1/2 to 12. **No. of Franchise Units:** 80. **Founded:** 1988. **Franchised:** 2001. **Equity Capital Needed:** Liquid $50,000; $100,000 net. **Franchise Fee:** $31,500. **Training:** Provides 1 week initial training program for up to 2 people at corporate office. This covers sales, marketing, the Young & Rembrandts method, classroom training and more. We provide complete operation and training manuals, and continual training and coaching calls and an Annual Conference.

LIBRARIES

33316 ■ ASTD - Information Center [American Society for Training and Development]
1640 King St.
Alexandria, VA 22314-2746
Ph: (703)683-8100
Free: 800-628-2783
Fax: (703)683-1523
Co. E-mail: customercare@astd.org
URL: http://www.astd.org
Contact: Tony Bingham, President
E-mail: tbingham@astd.org
Description: Represents workplace learning and performance professionals. **Scope:** training and development, workplace performance. **Services:** Library open to national members of the Society. **Founded:** 1943. **Holdings:** 3000 bound volumes. **Publications:** *ASTD Buyer's Guide* (Annual); *ASTD Buyer's Guide* (Annual); *Member Information Exchange (MIX)*; *TRAINET*; *ATD Buyer's Guide* (Annual); *Buyer's Guide & Consultant Directory; American Society for Training and Development--Training Video Directory; ASTD Buyer's Guide and Consultants Directory; Who's Who in Training and Development* (Annual); *ASTD Buyer's Guide and Consultants Directory; American Society Training and Development Buyer's Guide and Consultant Directory* (Annual); *Technical Training: Learning Technology for Performance Improvement; ASTD Buyer's Guide & Consultant Directory* (Annual); *TD at Work* (Monthly); *Learning Circuits* (Monthly); *T and D Magazine; TD Magazine* (Monthly). **Educational Activities:** Interna-

tional Exposition (Annual); American Society for Training and Development Conference (Annual); TechKnowledge Conference and Exposition (Annual). **Awards:** ASTD BEST Award; Excellence in Practice; Awards in the Advancing Workplace Learning and Performance; Gordon M. Bliss Memorial Award; Dissertation Award; Distinguished Contribution Award; Torch Award.

RESEARCH CENTERS

33317 ■ Center for Entrepreneurial Studies & Development Inc. (CESD)
1062 Maple Dr., Ste. 2
Morgantown, WV 26505
Ph: (304)293-5551
Fax: (304)293-6707
Co. E-mail: info@cesd.wvu.edu
URL: http://www.cesd.wvu.edu
Contact: Jack Byrd, Executive Director
Scope: Business operations improvement, employee training, management, and systems development. Operations improvement studies focus on quality control, materials handling systems, cost reduction, work standards development, facilities utilization and planning, work methods, inventory control systems, and computer applications. Employee training focuses on supervisory development, quality training, and problem solving. Management studies focus on management development programs, organization development, steering committee development, facilitation, incentives, and small business organizations. Systems studies focus on business plan development. **Services:** Competitive and economic development strategies; Market assessment and development; Operational improvements; Performance management; Provides assistance in new product or service development. **Founded:** 1981.

33318 ■ Center for Occupational Research and Development (CORD)
PO Box 21689
Waco, TX 76702-1689
Ph: (254)772-8756
Free: 800-972-2766
Fax: (254)772-8972
Co. E-mail: hinckley@cord.org
URL: http://www.cord.org
Contact: Dr. Richard Hinckley, President
Description: Provides innovative changes in education to prepare students for better chances in career and higher education. Assists educators in secondary schools and colleges through new curricula, teaching strategies, professional development and partnerships with community leaders. Initiates developments in curriculum design, learning tools and creating applications in educational technology and conducting educational research and evaluation. **Scope:** Educational research and evaluation; designs and develops instructional materials and curricula for grades 7-14; creates innovative applications of educational technology. **Services:** Consulting and coordination services; Forms networks and partnerships. **Founded:** 1979. **Publications:** *CORD Newsletter* (Monthly); *White papers; Rigor and Relevance: A New Vision for Career and Technical Education; Teacher Professional Development: It's Not an Event, It's a Process; Teaching Mathematics Contextually; Technology to Improve Texas Education; Tech Prep: The Next Generation.*

33319 ■ Illinois State Board of Education - Data Analysis and Accountability Division
100 N 1st St.
Springfield, IL 62777
Ph: (217)782-3950
Fax: (217)524-7784
Co. E-mail: dsmalley@isbe.net
URL: http://www.isbe.net/research/Default.htm
Contact: David Smalley, Administrator
Scope: Education policy.

33320 ■ Indiana University Bloomington - Center for Evaluation and Education Policy (CEEP)
1900 E 10th St.
Bloomington, IN 47406-7512
Ph: (812)855-4438

Free: 800-511-6575
Fax: (812)856-5890
Co. E-mail: pmuller@indiana.edu
URL: http://ceep.indiana.edu
Contact: Dr. John Hitchcock, Director
Scope: Program evaluation and policy research, primarily on education issues but also in healthcare. **Founded:** 1990. **Publications:** *Policy Bulletins* (Monthly); *Education Policy Briefs* (Occasionally); *Special Reports and Technical Studies.*

33321 ■ Indiana University Bloomington - Center for Postsecondary Research (CPR)
Eigenmann Hall, Ste. 419
1900 E 10th St.
Bloomington, IN 47406-7512
Ph: (812)856-5824
Free: 866-435-6773
Fax: (812)856-5150
Co. E-mail: vatorres@indiana.edu
URL: http://cpr.iub.edu/index.cfm
Contact: Vasti Torres, Director
Scope: Policy issues and issues related to student learning and personal development, including student engagement, student persistence and attrition, institutional advancement, enrollment management and marketing, program evaluation, institutional culture, student learning and personal development, and equity and access in higher education. **Founded:** 1986. **Publications:** *National Survey of Student Engagement* (Annual).

33322 ■ Indiana University Bloomington - Center for the Study of Institutions, Population, and Environmental Change (CIPEC)
408 N Indiana Ave.
Bloomington, IN 47408-3799
Ph: (812)855-2230
Fax: (812)855-2634
Co. E-mail: cipec@indiana.edu
URL: http://www.indiana.edu/~cipec
Contact: Prof. Tom Evans, Director
Scope: Processes of change in forest environments as mediated by institutional arrangements, demographic factors, and other major human driving forces. **Founded:** 1996.

33323 ■ Indiana University-Purdue University at Indianapolis - Center for the Study of Religion and American Culture
425 University Blvd., Rm. 417
Indianapolis, IN 46202-5140
Ph: (317)274-8409
Fax: (317)278-3354
Co. E-mail: raac@iupui.edu
URL: http://raac.iupui.edu
Contact: Dr. Philip K. Goff, Executive Director
Scope: Relationship between religion and aspects of American culture, and how religion has shaped American politics, justice, and society. **Founded:** 1989. **Publications:** *News from the Center for the Study of Religion and American Culture* (Semiannual); *Religion and American Culture: A Journal of Interpretation* (Semiannual). **Educational Activities:** Public lectures, conferences, and symposia; Young Scholars in American Religion Program.

33324 ■ Indiana University-Purdue University at Indianapolis - CyberLab
School of Engineering and Technology, Rm. 245
799 W Michigan St.
Indianapolis, IN 46202
Ph: (317)274-3463
Fax: (317)278-9171
Co. E-mail: cyberlab@iupui.edu
URL: http://cyberlab.iupui.edu/home.php
Contact: Ali Jafari, Director
Scope: Worldwide web applications in teaching and learning, especially course management portals, campus portals, agent-based learning environment, and intelligent user interfaces. **Founded:** 1989.

33325 ■ Indiana University-Purdue University at Indianapolis - Nuclear Magnetic Resonance Laboratory
402 N Blackford St., Rm. 154
Indianapolis, IN 46202

Ph: (317)274-6900
Fax: (317)274-2393
Co. E-mail: bray@iupui.edu
URL: http://webphysics.iupui.edu/nmr/NMR_Center_web/index.html
URL(s): physics.iupui.edu/research/center/nuclear-magnetic-resonance-center. **Scope:** Structure-function relationships of biological macromolecules, using the techniques of nuclear magnetic resonance (NMR). The research is interdisciplinary, bringing together researchers from the School of Science and the School of Medicine. **Founded:** 1992. **Educational Activities:** Nuclear Magnetic Resonance Laboratory Training, for scientists interested in learning or using NMR techniques.

33326 ■ Indiana University-Purdue University at Indianapolis - Peirce Edition Project
0010 Education/Social Work
Indianapolis, IN 46202-5157
Ph: (317)274-3374
Fax: (317)274-2170
Co. E-mail: adetienn@iupui.edu
URL: http://www.iupui.edu/~peirce
Contact: Prof. André De Tienne, Director
Scope: American philosophy and culture, focusing on the writings of scientist and philosopher Charles S. Peirce. **Founded:** 1976. **Publications:** *Peirce Project News* (Periodic); *Writings of Charles S. Peirce: A Chronological Edition* (Occasionally). **Educational Activities:** Indianapolis Peirce Seminar (Periodic), lecture series where the speakers are scholars or researchers that are Peirce Project visitors willing to share the latest stage of their research with the Project's specialists and philosophy students.

33327 ■ Institute for Forensic Imaging (IFI)
9855 Crosspoint Blvd., Ste. 126
Indianapolis, IN 46256-3336
Ph: (317)356-0245
Fax: (317)842-6974
Co. E-mail: jward@ifi-indy.org
URL: http://ifi-indy.org
Contact: Joe Ward, Executive Director
Scope: Forensic imaging in the investigation of crimes and legal questions. **Services:** Consulting; Research. **Founded:** 1995.

33328 ■ Massachusetts Institute of Technology - Center for Technology, Policy and Industrial Development - International Motor Vehicle Program (IMVP)
Bldg. E40-207
1 Amherst St.
Cambridge, MA 02139-4307
Ph: (617)253-8973
Fax: (617)253-7140
Co. E-mail: imvpmail@mit.edu
URL: http://imvp.mit.edu
Contact: John Moavenzadeh, Executive Director
E-mail: moavenza@wharton.upenn.edu
Scope: Product development, supply chain management, manufacturing, organization and human resources, distribution and marketing, environmental issues, and mobility in the motor vehicle industry. **Founded:** 1979. **Publications:** *IMVP Working papers.*

33329 ■ Massachusetts Institute of Technology - Japan Program
MIT Bldg., Rm. E40-455
77 Massachusetts Ave.
Cambridge, MA 02139-4307
Ph: (617)258-2449
Fax: (617)258-7432
Co. E-mail: samuels@mit.edu
URL: http://web.mit.edu/misti/mit-japan
Contact: Dr. Richard J. Samuels, Director
Scope: Japan and Asia, in particular Japanese foreign policy with regard to China, Asian energy and security, the changing role of Japan's technology at home and abroad. **Founded:** 1983. **Publications:** *MIT Japan Science, Technology & Management Report*; *Japan Program Newsletter* (Monthly); *Sponsor Update* (Quarterly); *Working Papers Series.*

33330 ■ Massachusetts Institute of Technology - Program on the Pharmaceutical Industry (POPI)
MIT Center for Biomedical Innovation
77 Massachusetts Ave., E19-604
Cambridge, MA 02139-4307
Ph: (617)324-9640
Fax: (617)253-0687
Co. E-mail: ghirsch@mit.edu
URL: http://cbi.mit.edu/resources/working-papers/popi-working-papers
Contact: Gigi Hirsch, Executive Director
Scope: Competitiveness, performance, and productivity in the pharmaceutical field. **Founded:** 1991.

33331 ■ Rice University - Center for Education
IBC Bldg., Ste. 320
5615 Kirby Dr.
Houston, TX 77005
Ph: (713)348-5145
Fax: (713)348-3715
Co. E-mail: lmcneil@rice.edu
URL: http://centerforeducation.rice.edu
Contact: Prof. Linda McSpadden McNeil, Director
Scope: Teacher development, reorganization of schools, student evaluation methods, and educational policy and urban schools. **Founded:** 1988. **Publications:** *CenterPiece.*

33332 ■ Rice University - Center for Languages and Intercultural Communication
6100 Main St., MS 36
Houston, TX 77005
Ph: (713)348-3156
Fax: (713)348-5846
Co. E-mail: salaberry@rice.edu
URL: http://langcenter.rice.edu
Contact: M. Rafael Salaberry, Director
Scope: Language teaching and learning. **Founded:** 1997.

33333 ■ University of Connecticut - Institute for Teaching and Learning (ITL)
Center for Undergraduate Education
368 Fairfield Rd., Unit 2001
Storrs, CT 06269-2001
Ph: (860)486-2686
Fax: (860)486-1766
Co. E-mail: dan.mercier@uconn.edu
URL: http://www.itl.uconn.edu/itl_web
Contact: Daniel Mercier, Director
Scope: Teaching and learning methods, pedagogy, media use and distance learning, and technology use in the classroom and online. **Services:** Consulting; Instructional design. **Founded:** 1996. **Publications:** *The Journal of Graduate Teaching Assistant Development*; *TA Handbook*. **Educational Activities:** ITL Workshops, conferences.

33334 ■ University of Delaware - Delaware Education Research and Development Center (DERDC)
Pearson Hall
College of Education & Human Development
Newark, DE 19716
Ph: (302)831-4433
Fax: (302)831-4438
Co. E-mail: jbuttram@udel.edu
URL: http://www.rdc.udel.edu
Contact: Joan Buttram, Director
Scope: Educational practice, policy reform, program evaluation. **Founded:** 1992.

33335 ■ University of Toronto - Ontario Institute for Studies in Education - International Centre for Educational Change (ICEC)
252 Bloor St. W
Toronto, ON, Canada M5S 1V6
Fax: (416)978-1156
Co. E-mail: sanderson@oise.utoronto.ca
URL: http://www.oise.utoronto.ca/lhae/Research/Research_Centres/International_Centre_For_Educational_Change.html
Contact: Stephen Anderson, Director (Acting)
Scope: Processes of educational change, including scheduling, teaching, curriculum, caring, assessment

and decision-making; large-scale reform efforts, large-scale assessment, evaluation of programs and

policies. **Services:** Practical field development, professional development activities, and consulting.

Founded: 1997. **Educational Activities:** ICEC Study groups, presentations, discussions, and debates.

START-UP INFORMATION

33336 ■ *101 Internet Businesses You Can Start from Home: How to Choose and Build Your Own Successful E-Business*
Pub: Maximum Press
Contact: James W. Hoskins, President

Ed: Susan Sweeney. **Released:** August 31, 2010. **Price:** $23.31, paperback. **Description:** Guide for starting and growing an Internet business; information for developing a business plan, risk levels, and promotional techniques are included. **Availability:** Print.

33337 ■ *202 Things You Can Buy and Sell for Big Profits*
Pub: Entrepreneur Press
Contact: Perlman Neil, President

Ed: James Stephenson. **Description:** Become an entrepreneur at selling new and used products. This handbook will help individuals cash in on the boom in reselling new and used products online. A new section defines ways to set realistic goals while distinguishing between 'get-rich schemes' and long term, viable businesses. A discussion about targeting and reaching the right customer base is included, along with finding and obtaining the service support needed for starting a new business.

33338 ■ *"Affiliate Marketing: How To Make Your First Sale in 7 Days"*
Pub: Amazon Digital Services

Released: September 29, 2014. **Price:** $3.99 Kindle. **Description:** Book 2 in the Digital Marketing Academy series, explains an easy and cost effective method for entering the world of Internet Marketing. List building to incorporate the art of Affiliate Marketing while building relationships with prospects is covered along with ways to attract customers through effective marketing. A seven day video training series is included to show how to start an online business.

33339 ■ *"Amazon Selling Secrets: How to Make an Extra $1K - $10K a Month Selling Your Own Products on Amazon"*
Pub: Amazon Digital Services

Released: July 19, 2014. **Price:** $7.99 paperback. **Description:** Secrets for finding and selling popular items on Amazon.com are shared. The tools, resources and system for earning extra money each month selling on Amazon are presented.

33340 ■ *"Are We There Yet?" in Entrepreneur (September 2014)*
Pub: Entrepreneur Media Inc.

Released: September 2014. **Description:** Entrepreneurs and small business advocates discuss the progress of Jumpstart Our Business Startups (JOBS) Act two years after it was signed into law in the U.S. in April 2012. The implementation of Title II in September 2013 allowed private companies to publicly advertise their fundraising efforts. Rewards-based crowdfunding also benefited from the publicity

surrounding the JOBS Act. Crowdfunding advocates are looking forward to the finalization of Title III to address their concerns about red tape and compliance costs.

33341 ■ *"The Best Book on How to Sell Anything Online: A Step by Step Guide"*
Pub: ARI Publishing

Released: October 21, 2014. **Price:** $9.95 paperback. **Description:** A guide to help entrepreneurs launch an online service selling anything without startup or overhead costs. Profits for selling software can be as high as 50-75 percent. Tips for Web design is also included.

33342 ■ *The Complete Idiot's Guide to Starting an eBay® Business*
Pub: Penguin Books USA Inc.

Released: February 2008. **Price:** $19.95. **Description:** Guide for starting an eBay business includes information on products to sell, how to price merchandise, and details for working with services like PayPal, and how to organize fulfillment services.

33343 ■ *"Consumer Startup Hub Set for Downtown" in Atlanta Business Chronicle (June 13, 2014, pp. 3A)*
Pub: American City Business Journals, Inc.
Contact: Whitney Shaw, President

Released: June 13, 2014. **Description:** Michael Tavani, co-founder of Scoutmob, believes that Atlanta is fast becoming the hub for consumer- and design-focused startups. He is planning to locate his consumer-focused startup, Switchyards, in a 1920s building downtown, which will become a hive for mobile app, media, and ecommerce startups.

33344 ■ *Design and Launch an E-Commerce Business in a Week*
Pub: Entrepreneur Press
Contact: Perlman Neil, President

Ed: Jason R. Rich. **Released:** June 01, 2008. **Price:** $11.19. **Description:** Guide to help anyone start an online business in one week; included tips for Website design. **Availability:** E-book.

33345 ■ *Design and Launch an Online Boutique in a Week*
Pub: Entrepreneur Press

Ed: Melissa Campanelli. **Released:** July 01, 2008. **Price:** $14.90. **Description:** Tips for starting an online boutique in a short amount of time are given. The books shows how to build the online boutique with designer goods or your own product, ways to create eye-catching content, online tools to handle payments and accept orders, marketing and advertising techniques, and customer service. **Availability:** Print; E-book.

33346 ■ *E-Preneur*
Pub: Career Press Inc.
Contact: Ron Fry, President

Ed: Richard J. Goossen. **Released:** April 2008. **Price:** $15.99, paperback. **Description:** Entrepreneurs in the new virtual marketplace are examined.

The book surveys and explains the field of Web 2.0 and entrepreneurs successfully using the virtual marketplace. **Availability:** Print.

33347 ■ *eBay Business the Smart Way*
Ed: Joseph T. Sinclair. **Released:** June 6, 2007. **Price:** $17.95. **Description:** eBay commands ninety percent of all online auction business. Computer and software expert and online entrepreneur shares information to help online sellers get started and move merchandise on eBay. Tips include the best ways to build credibility, find products to sell, manage inventory, create a storefront Website, and more.

33348 ■ *The eBay Business Start-Up Kit: With 100s of Live Links to All the Information & Tools You Need*
Pub: Nolo
Contact: Ralph Warner, Chief Executive Officer

Ed: Richard Stim. **Released:** July 2008. **Description:** Interactive kit that provides in-depth information and practical advice in launching an eBay business.

33349 ■ *"eBay Selling: 102 Killer Profitable Items To Sell On eBay From Thrift Stores, Flea Markets, Garage Sales and More..."*
Pub: Amazon Digital Services

Released: October 2, 2014. **Price:** $0.99 Kindle. **Description:** eBay is a source of income for entrepreneurs wishing to start an online business. The guide will provide access to 102 research items that will help start a profitable online business on eBay, the auction online store.

33350 ■ *Entrepreneurship with Online Learning Center Access Card*
Ed: Robert D. Hirich; Michael P. Peters; Dean A. Shepherd. **Released:** October 2006. **Price:** $103. 25. **Description:** Book instructs students on entrepreneurial processes that include starting a new business.

33351 ■ *"How to Open and Operate a Financially Successful Florist and Floral Business Online and Off"*
Pub: Atlantic Publishing Group, Inc.

Released: October 22, 2012. **Price:** $24.95 paperback. **Description:** A concise and easy to follow guide for opening a retail florist or floral business online or a traditional brick and mortar store. Knowledge shared includes: cost control systems, retail math and competitive pricing, legal concerns, tax reporting requirements and reporting, profit and loss statements, management skills, sales advertising, and marketing techniques, customer service, direct sales, internal marketing ideas, and more.

33352 ■ *How to Start a Home-Based Mail Order Business*
Pub: Globe Pequot Press Inc.
Contact: Robert Irwin, Manager
E-mail: robert.irwin@globepequot.com

Ed: Georganne Fiumara. **Released:** June 01, 2011. **Price:** $18.95, paperback. **Description:** Step-by-step guide for starting and growing a home-based mail order business. Information about equipment, pricing, online marketing, are included along with worksheets and checklists for planning. **Availability:** Print.

33353 ■ *How to Start a Home-Based Online Retail Business*
Pub: Globe Pequot Press Inc.
Contact: Robert Irwin, Manager
E-mail: robert.irwin@globepequot.com
Ed: Jeremy Shepherd. **Released:** Second Edition. **Price:** $19.95, Paperback. **Description:** Information for starting an online retail, home-based business is shared. **Availability:** Print.

33354 ■ *How to Start an Internet Sales Business Without Making the Government Mad*
Pub: Lulu.com
Ed: Dan Davis. **Released:** September 30, 2011. **Price:** $14.38. **Description:** Small business guide for launching an Internet sales company. Topics include business structure, licenses, and taxes. **Availability:** PDF.

33355 ■ *"Hunger Relief" in Entrepreneur (August 2014)*
Pub: Entrepreneur Media Inc.
Released: August 2014. **Description:** Mobile application NoWait provides assistance to restaurants so they can efficiently manage the lines of customers waiting to be seated. Former employee-benefits director, Robb Meyer, partnered with marketer, Luke Panza, and developers James Belt and Richard Colvin to launch their NoWait host app for the iPad in 2010. Meyer and his team also launched a free consumer version for iOs and Android in February 2014. Restaurants that seat up to 200 parties per month can use NoWait for free.

33356 ■ *"Interest Soaring In 44North Business Competition" in Business First of Buffalo (Vol. 30, February 21, 2014, No. 23, pp. 3)*
Pub: American City Business Journals, Inc.
Contact: Whitney Shaw, President
Released: February 21, 2014. **Description:** The 43North business plan competition has attracted over 200 applications from entrepreneurs coming from various sectors like e-commerce, clean technology, and advanced manufacturing. The winners of the competition will qualify for the Start-Up New York program which eliminates the tax burden for qualified firms.

33357 ■ *"Leading Digital: Turning Technology into Business Transformation"*
Pub: Harvard Business Review Press
Contact: Peter E. Walsh, Director
Released: October 14, 2014. **Price:** $30.00. **Description:** Mobile technology, analytics, social media, sensors, and cloud computing have changed the entire business environment in every industry. A guide to help any small startup business in any industry gain strategic advantage using digital, including where to invest in digital technologies and how to lead the transformation. The guide teaches how to engage better with customers, digitally enhance operations, create a digital vision, and govern digital activities.

33358 ■ *"Make Money Selling Products on YouTube"*
Pub: Amazon Digital Services
Released: October 2, 2014. **Price:** $2.99 Kindle. **Description:** Advice is rendered to help individuals sell products such as eBooks, online courses, audio programs, video programs; marketing products such as those found on ClickBank; as well as physical products such as clothing, household accessories and goods, cars, and more on YouTube. Aspects of electronic commerce are covered.

33359 ■ *"Modern Meal Offers Recipe Inspiration, Curation and Home Delivery" in Orlando Business Journal (Vol. 30, April 4, 2014, No. 41, pp. 3)*
Pub: American City Business Journals
Released: April 4, 2014. **Description:** Modern Meal LLC's CEO, Mark Hudgins, works to get people to the dinner table for a good meal. The social network

with a Pinterest look is in early-beta-launch and users are trying out the features by curating recipes from popular cooking Websites and looking at recipes of other users. Modern' Meal's plan to tap into the e-grocery market is also discussed.

33360 ■ *"No. 105: What I Learned from Steve Jobs" in Inc. (Vol. 36, September 2014, No. 7, pp. 129)*
Pub: Mansueto Ventures L.L.C.
Contact: John Koten, Chief Executive Officer
Released: September 2014. **Description:** Entrepreneur, Matt MacInnis, started his firm that publishes interactive textbooks and manuals. MacInnis got his start working in marketing at Apple before launching the San Francisco-based Inkling. Over five years, he has received almost $50 million in venture capital.

33361 ■ *"No. 369: How I Turned Big Data Into Viral Marketing" in Inc. (Vol. 36, September 2014, No. 7, pp. 134)*
Pub: Mansueto Ventures L.L.C.
Contact: John Koten, Chief Executive Officer
Released: September 2014. **Description:** Six Spoke Media was founded in 2009 by Edward Kim of San Francisco, California. Kim cashed out his 401(K) to fund his startup that makes a marketing campaign go viral on social media to help businesses grow.

33362 ■ *"Online Fortunes" in Small Business Opportunities (Fall 2008)*
Description: Fifty hot, e-commerce enterprises for the aspiring entrepreneur to consider are featured; virtual assistants, marketing services, party planning, travel services, researching, web design and development, importing as well as creating an online store are among the businesses featured.

33363 ■ *"Open English Touted as Startup Worth Emulating" in South Florida Business Journal (Vol. 34, January 24, 2014, No. 27, pp. 30)*
Pub: American City Business Journals
Released: January 24, 2014. **Description:** Open English, a language education company, received more than $150 million in investments from venture capitalists. The firm's cloud-based platform is still in its infancy, but the startup's success has shown that entrepreneurs can generate money and grow their businesses in Florida. Open English is the only online English school that offers live classes with native English-speaking teachers.

33364 ■ *"Other Message Firms Get Lift From WhatsApp" in San Francisco Business Times (Vol. 28, February 28, 2014, No. 32, pp. 6)*
Pub: American City Business Journals
Released: February 28, 2014. **Description:** The $19 billion acquisition of mobile messaging service WhatsApp by Facebook, signaled the growth of mobile computing in the global market. Other startups in San Francisco, California that provide similar creative text, photo and video messaging over the Internet are Tango, Littleinc Labs, and PageBites.

33365 ■ *"Power Up" in Entrepreneur (Vol. 35, November 2007, No. 11, pp. 140)*
Pub: Entrepreneur Press
Contact: Perlman Neil, President
Ed: Amanda C. Kooser. **Description:** PowerSeller is a status in the Internet company eBay, wherein sellers average at least $1,000 in sales per month for three consecutive months. There are five tiers in the PowerSeller status, which ranges from Bronze to Titanium. Launching startups at eBay can help entrepreneurs pick up a wide customer base, but getting and maintaining PowerSeller status is a challenge.

33366 ■ *Scrapbooking for Profit: Cashing in on Retail, Home-Based and Internet Opportunities*
Pub: Allworth Press
Contact: Tad Crawford, Author
Ed: Rebecca Pittman. **Released:** January 02, 2014. **Price:** $16.95, paperback. **Description:** Eleven strategies for starting a scrapbooking business, including brick-and-mortar stores, home-based businesses, and online retail and wholesale outlets. **Availability:** Print.

33367 ■ *"Selling Groceries & More on Amazon: The Ultimate Home Based Business for Families"*
Pub: Amazon Digital Services
Released: October 16, 2014. **Price:** $7.99 Kindle. **Description:** Tips for starting an online grocery store from your home are shared. Grocery inventory, coupons and store promotions, setting up a seller account, application and approval for the grocery category, shipping information, sales techniques and private labeling are all addressed for this family owned type of business.

33368 ■ *"Social Media Bootcamp: How Not To Suck At Social Media"*
Pub: Amazon Digital Services
Released: September 29, 2014. **Price:** $0.99 Kindle. **Description:** Seven steps to build a social media presence are presented in boot camp style. Whether direct sales, multi-level marketing, online store, or another type of online, home-based startup business, this book give tips for would-be entrepreneurs.

33369 ■ *Start Your Own Blogging Business, Second Edition*
Pub: Entrepreneur Press
Contact: Perlman Neil, President
Ed: Jason R. Rich. **Released:** Third Edition. **Price:** $19.95, Paperback. **Description:** Interviews with professional bloggers from some of the most popular blogs on the Internet will help anyone interested in starting their own blogging business.

33370 ■ *Start Your Own Business on eBay*
Pub: Entrepreneur Press
Contact: Perlman Neil, President
Ed: Jacquelyn Lynn. **Released:** Second Edition. **Price:** $17.95, Paperback. **Description:** Tips for starring a new online business on eBay are shared. **Availability:** Print.

33371 ■ *Start Your Own Net Service Business*
Pub: Entrepreneur Press
Contact: Perlman Neil, President
Ed: Liane Cassavoy. **Released:** March 01, 2009. **Price:** $17.95, paperback. **Description:** Web design, search engine marketing, new-media online, and blogging, are currently the four most popular web services available. This book provides information to start a net service business. **Availability:** Print.

33372 ■ *Starting an Ebay Business for Canadians for Dummies*
Pub: John Wiley & Sons Inc.
Contact: Stephen M. Smith, President
Ed: Marsha Collier, Bill Summers. **Released:** January 2007. **Price:** $35.99; $23.99. **Description:** Tips for turning a hobby into a successful online eBay company. **Availability:** PrintE-book.

33373 ■ *Starting an iPhone Application Business for Dummies*
Pub: Wiley Publishing Inc.
Contact: William J. Pesce, President
Ed: Aaron Nicholson, Joel Elad, Damien Stolarz. **Released:** October 2009. **Price:** $24.95, paperback; $16.99. **Description:** Ways to create a profitable, sustainable business developing and marketing iPhone applications are profiled. **Availability:** PrintE-book.

33374 ■ *Starting a Yahoo! Business for Dummies*
Pub: John Wiley & Sons Inc.
Contact: Stephen M. Smith, President
Ed: Rob Snell. **Released:** March 2006. **Price:** $24.95, paperback; 16.99. **Description:** Rob Snell offers advice for turning online browsers into buyers, increase online traffic, and build an online store from scratch. **Availability:** PrintE-book.

33375 ■ *Starting a Yahoo! Business For Dummies*
Pub: John Wiley & Sons Inc.
Contact: Stephen M. Smith, President
Ed: Rob Snell. **Released:** March 2006. **Price:** $24.95, paperback; $16.99. **Description:** Advice helps turn Web browsers into buyers, boost online traffic, and information to launch a profitable online business. **Availability:** PrintE-book.

33376 ■ *"TDP Inc. Aims to Cut Out Coupon Clipping"* in *The Business Journal-Serving Metropolitan Kansas City (Vol. 26, August 15, 2008, No. 49)*
Pub: American City Business Journals, Inc.
Contact: Whitney Shaw, President
Ed: Suzanna Stagemeyer. **Description:** TDP Inc., who started operations 18 months ago, aims to transform stale coupon promotions using technology by digitizing the entire coupon process. The process is expected to enable consumers to hunt coupons online where they will be automatically linked to loyalty cards. Other views and information on TDP and its services are presented.

33377 ■ *"Truthfully Speaking"* in *Entrepreneur (Vol. 35, November 2007, No. 11, pp. 118)*
Pub: Entrepreneur Press
Contact: Perlman Nell, President
Ed: Amanda C. Kooser. **Description:** Internet startup guru Guy Kawasaki talks about his new Web venture Truemors and shares tips on creating a successful Web-based company.

33378 ■ *"Virtual Playground"* in *Entrepreneur (Vol. 36, March 2008, No. 3, pp. 112)*
Pub: Entrepreneur Press
Contact: Perlman Neil, President
Ed: Amanda C. Kooser. **Description:** The growing number of children visiting virtual worlds provides opportunity for entrepreneurs to start online businesses catering to this market. Entrepreneurs need to be aware of the Children's Online Privacy Protection Act with regard to collecting children's information. Details of other things to know about with reference to these businesses are examined.

ASSOCIATIONS AND OTHER ORGANIZATIONS

33379 ■ **Internet Alliance (IA)**
1615 L St. NW, Ste. 1100
Washington, DC 20036-5624
Ph: (202)861-2407
Co. E-mail: tammy@internetalliance.org
URL: http://www.internetalliance.org
Contact: Tammy Cota, Executive Director
Description: Companies offering Internet services. Seeks to "build the confidence and trust necessary for the Internet to become the global mass market medium of the 21st century". Represents members' commercial and regulatory interests; conducts promotional activities; facilitates communication and cooperation among members. **Founded:** 1981. **Holdings:** The Alliance maintains a reference library in its field of interest.

EDUCATIONAL PROGRAMS

33380 ■ **Developing Web E-Commerce Applications**
EEI Communications
8945 Guilford Rd., Ste. 145
Columbia, MD 21046
Ph: (410)309-8200
Free: 888-253-2762
Fax: (410)630-3980
Co. E-mail: train@eeicom.com
URL: http://www.eeicom.com/eei-training-services
Description: Experienced Web producers will learn how to build a shopping cart/order management system for secure transaction processing using the scripting languages ColdFusion and PHP. **Audience:** Industry professionals.

REFERENCE WORKS

33381 ■ *"3Par: Storing Up Value"* in *Barron's (Vol. 90, August 30, 2010, No. 35, pp. 30)*
Pub: Barron's Editorial & Corporate Headquarters
Ed: Mark Veverka. **Description:** Dell and Hewlett Packard are both bidding for data storage company 3Par. The acquisition would help Dell and Hewlett Packard provide customers with a one-stop shop as customers move to a private cloud in the Internet.

33382 ■ *"10 Steps to Successful Social Networking for Business"*
Pub: ASTD
Contact: Tony Bingham, President
E-mail: tbingham@astd.org
Ed: Darin Hartley. **Released:** July 01, 2010. **Price:** $19.95; $17.95, Members. **Description:** Designed for today's fast-paced, need-it-yesterday business environment and for the thousands of workers who find themselves faced with new assignments, responsibilities, and requirements and too little time to learn what they must know.

33383 ■ *"11 Minutes That Rocked the Sneaker World"* in *Business Journal Portland (Vol. 30, February 14, 2014, No. 50, pp. 8)*
Pub: American City Business Journals
Released: February 14, 2014. **Description:** The sale of the Nike Air Yeezy 2, the latest shoes from a partnership with artist Kanye West, sparked a social media debate on the importance of limited edition shoes for the Nike brand. The shoes sold out in 11 minutes and made their way to eBay for as much as $10,000.

33384 ■ *"3.4 Million Votes Cast in 2011 eBay Motors People's Pick Poll ? Winners Announced at SEMA Show"* in *Benzinga.com (, 2011)*
Pub: Benzinga.com
Contact: Kyle Bazzy, President
Ed: Benzinga Staff. **Description:** eBay Motors sponsored the 2011 People's Picks survey, an annual poll inviting car enthusiasts to vote on their favorite auto thing, ranging from the best camshaft, favorite ignition, to favorite muscle car. More than 3.4 million votes were counted this year. A complete profile of eBay Motors is also provided.

33385 ■ *"55-Alive! Wants To Be MySpace for the Baby Boomer Set. Can It Raise $250,000?"* in *Inc. (October 2007, pp. 50)*
Pub: Mansueto Ventures L.L.C.
Contact: John Koten, Chief Executive Officer
Ed: Dalia Fahmy. **Description:** Profile of 55-Alive! The online community created especially for individuals over the age of 50. The Website offers blogs, a dating section, listings for recreational vehicles for sale, movie reviews, advertising and articles of interest to users.

33386 ■ *"2015 Marketing Calendar for Real Estate Pros: Own It"*
Pub: CreateSpace
Contact: Daren Giles, President
Released: October 14, 2014. **Price:** $24.95 paperback. **Description:** Real estate agents, mortgage loan agents, and new home builders and site and listing agents are shown how to use low-cost, high yield, proven marketing techniques to create digital real estate listings, find more customers, and sell more homes. Advice for building a brand and public relations; attracting renters and buyers; developing a good Website; and a digital marketing plan are explained.

33387 ■ *"Advanced Internet Bookselling Techniques"*
Pub: Small Business Press Inc.
Released: October 18, 2014. **Price:** $29.95 paperback. **Description:** Tips for growing a home-based part-time bookselling business into a full-time commercial operation is presented.

33388 ■ *"Advanced Selling for Dummies"*
Ed: Ralph R. Roberts; Joe Kraynak (As told to). **Released:** September 2007. **Price:** $21.99. **Description:** This book explores topics such as: visualizing success (includes exercises), investing and reinvesting in your own success, harnessing media and multi-media outlets, calculating risks that stretch your limits, creating lasting relationships, finding balance to avoid burnout and more. This guide is for salespeople who have already read 'Selling for Dummies' and now want forward-thinking, advanced strategies for recharging and reenergizing their careers and their lives. Blogging, Internet leads and virtual assistants are also discussed.

33389 ■ *"AdWords Direct Response 1"*
Pub: Amazon Digital Services
Released: October 19, 2014. **Price:** $7.77 Kindle. **Description:** Instruction for starting and running Adwords campaigns are provided to help any small business market and advertise their firm.

33390 ■ *"All About Pay Per Click: Learn The Most Effective Way Of Using PPC Advertising"*
Pub: CreateSpace
Contact: Daren Giles, President
Released: October 10, 2014. **Price:** $5.75 paperback. **Description:** Pay Per Click advertising is explained to help businesses develop a marketing campaign and use successful pay per click advertising to increase sales, customers and revenue.

33391 ■ *"AllHipHop.com's Founders Thought a Weeklong Event Would Raise the Company"* in *Inc. (February 2008, pp. 48-51)*
Ed: Kermit Pattison. **Description:** Co-founders Greg Watkins and Chuck Creekmur, planned a weeklong festival to promote their company, AllHipHop.com; the event nearly ruined the firm. The online firm provides news about hip hop artists and the industry and is updated daily.

33392 ■ *"American Chemistry Council Launches Flagship Blog"* in *Ecology,Environment & Conservation Business (October 29, 2011, pp. 5)*
Pub: Highbeam Research
Contact: Patrick Spain, Chief Executive Officer
Description: American Chemistry Council (ACC) launched its blog, American Chemistry Matters, where interactive space allows bloggers to respond to news coverage and to discuss policy issues and their impact on innovation, competitiveness, job creation and safety.

33393 ■ *"Analyzing the Analytics"* in *Entrepreneur (Vol. 37, October 2009, No. 10, pp. 42)*
Pub: Entrepreneur Press
Contact: Perlman Neil, President
Ed: Mikal E. Belicove. **Description:** Startups can maximize Web analytics by using them to monitor traffic sources and identify obstacles to converting them into targeted behaviors. Startups should set trackable Web site goals and continuously track traffic and conversion rates.

33394 ■ *"Ann Arbor Google's Growth Dips"* in *Crain's Detroit Business (Vol. 25, June 8, 2009, No. 23, pp. 3)*
Pub: Crain Communications Inc. - Detroit
Contact: Keith Crain, Chairman
Ed: Bill Shea. **Description:** Global recession has slowed the growth of Google Inc. Three years ago, when Google moved to Ann Arbor, Michigan it estimated it would provide 1,000 new jobs within five years, so far the firm employs 250.

33395 ■ *"Another California Firm On Way"* in *Austin Business Journal (Vol. 31, May 6, 2011, No. 9, pp. 1)*
Pub: American City Business Journals
Ed: Christopher Calnan. **Description:** Main Street Hub Inc. is planning to build a facility in Austin, Texas. The company helps businesses manage their online reputations. Main Street has selected Aquila Commercial LLC as its real estate broker.

33396 ■ *"Anthem Leading the Way in Social Tech Revolution"* in *Inside Business (Vol. 13, September-October 2011, No. 5, pp. 1B3)*
Pub: Great Lakes Publishing Co.
Ed: Ryan Clark. **Description:** Anthem Blue Cross and Blue Shield is leading the way in social technology. The firm's social media initiatives to promote itself are outlined.

33397 ■ *"Anything Could Happen"* in *Inc. (March 2008, pp. 116-123)*
Pub: Mansueto Ventures L.L.C.
Contact: John Koten, Chief Executive Officer
Ed: Max Chafkin. **Description:** Profile of Evan Williams, founder of Blogger and Twitter, a new type of technology idea; Williams answers ten questions and share insight on growing both of his companies.

33398 ■ *"App Helps Consumers Spot Suspicious Charges"* in Black Enterprise (Vol. 44, June 2014, No. 10, pp. 34)
Pub: Earl G. Graves Publishing Co. Inc.
Contact: Earl G. Graves, Jr., President
Released: June 2014. **Description:** BiliGuard is a mobile app used to track activity on credit and debit card accounts. The app allows users to notify a merchant as soon as they see an unfamiliar charge. BiliGuard can also alert users to fees.

33399 ■ *"Aptitudes for Apps"* in Boston Business Journal (Vol. 31, July 1, 2011, No. 23, pp. 3)
Pub: Boston Business Journal
Ed: Kyle Alspach. **Description:** Startups Apperian Inc. and Kinvey Inc. are aiming to accelerate the development and deployment of mobile applications and have received fund pledges from Boston-area venture capital firms.

33400 ■ *"Are Offline Pushes Important to E-Commerce?"* in DM News (Vol. 31, September 14, 2009, No. 23, pp. 10)
Pub: Haymarket Media, Inc.
Description: With the importance of Internet marketing and the popularity of ecommerce increasing experts debate the relevance of more traditional channels of advertising.

33401 ■ *"Are You Ready To Do It Yourself? Discipline and Self-Study Can Help You Profit From Online Trading"* in Black Enterprise (February 1, 2008)
Pub: Earl G. Graves Publishing Co. Inc.
Contact: Earl G. Graves, Jr., President
Ed: Steve Garmhausen. **Description:** Steps to help individuals invest in stocks online is given by an expert broker. Discount brokerage houses can save money for online investors.

33402 ■ *"Area VCs Take Praise, Lumps, on Web site"* in Boston Business Journal (Vol. 27, October 26, 2007, No. 39, pp. 1)
Ed: Jesse Noyes. **Description:** TheFunded.com is a social networking site that allows entrepreneurs to rate venture capitalists and post their comments. Information about venture capitalist firms such as size and the partners behind it are also provided.

33403 ■ *"Art of the Online Deal"* in Farm Industry News (March 25, 2011)
Pub: Penton Business Media Inc.
Contact: David Kieselstein, Chief Executive Officer
Description: Farmers share advice for shopping online for machinery; photos, clean equipment, the price, equipment details, and online sources topped their list.

33404 ■ *"As Technology Changes, So Must African American Business"* in Black Enterprise (Vol. 41, August 2010, No. 1, pp. 61)
Pub: Earl G. Graves Publishing Co. Inc.
Contact: Earl G. Graves, Jr., President
Ed: Sonya A. Donaldson. **Description:** Social media is essential to compete in today's business environment, especially for African American firms.

33405 ■ *"Ask Inc."* in Inc. (October 2007, pp. 73-74)
Description: An online marketing research firm investigates the use of online communities such as MySpace and Second life in order to recruit individuals to answer surveys.

33406 ■ *"Ask Inc.: E-mail and Marketing: Tackling that Overflowing Inbox; Marketing on the Cheap"* in Inc. (January 2008, pp. 60)
Pub: Gruner and Jahr USA Publishing Co.
Contact: J. Russell Denson, President
Description: Ways to manage high volumes of email are examined.

33407 ■ *"Atlific Adds Management of 4 Hotels to Its Portfolio in Fort McMurray"* in Canadian Corporate News (May 16, 2007)
Description: Atlific Hotels & Resorts took over management for Merit Inn & Suites, The Merit Hotel, The Nomad Hotel and The Nomad Suites in Fort Mc-

Murray. The company feels that they will be able to increase the hotels' abilities to promote their services through their vast network of sales personnel and marketing and e-commerce team.

33408 ■ *"Attention, Please"* in Entrepreneur (Vol. 36, April 2008, No. 4, pp. 52)
Pub: Entrepreneur Press
Contact: Perlman Neil, President
Ed: Andrea Cooper. **Description:** Gurbaksh Chahal created his own company ClickAgents at the age of 16, and sold it two years later for $40 million to Value-Click. He then founded BlueLithium, an online advertising network on behavioral targeting, which Yahoo! Inc. bought in 2007 for $300 million. Chahal, now 25, talks about his next plans and describes how BlueLithium caught Yahoo's attention.

33409 ■ *"Attract More Online Customers: Make Your Website Work Harder for You"* in Black Enterprise (Vol. 37, November 2006, No. 4, pp. 66)
Pub: Earl G. Graves Publishing Co. Inc.
Contact: Earl G. Graves, Jr., President
Ed: Sharon Fling. **Description:** Having an impressive presence on the Internet has become crucial. Detailed advice on making your website serve your business in the best way possible is included.

33410 ■ *"Auctions and Bidding: A Guide for Computer Scientists"* in ACM Computing Surveys (Vol. 43, Summer 2011, No. 2, pp. 10)
Pub: Association for Computing Machinery
Contact: Vinton G. Cerf, President
Ed: Simon Parsons, Juan A. Rodriguez-Aguilar, Mark Klein. **Description:** There are various actions: single dimensional, multi-dimensional, single-sided, double-sided, first-price, second-price, English, Dutch, Japanese, sealed-bid, and these have been extensively discussed and analyzed in economics literature. This literature is surveyed from a computer science perspective, primarily from the viewpoint of computer scientists who are interested in learning about auction theory, and to provide pointers into the economics literature for those who want a deeper technical understanding. In addition, since auctions are an increasingly important topic in computer science, the article also looks at work on auctions from the computer science literature. The aim is to identify what both bodies of work tell us about creating electronic auctions.

33411 ■ *"Austin Startup on Cusp of Trend"* in Austin Business JournalInc. (Vol. 29, January 8, 2010, No. 44, pp. 1)
Pub: American City Business Journals
Ed: Christopher Calnan. **Description:** Austin-based Socialware Inc. introduced a new business called social middleware, which is a software that is layered between the company network and social networking Website used by workers. The software was designed to give employers a measure of control over content while allowing workers to continue using online social networks.

33412 ■ *"AVG Introduces Security Software Suite for SMBs 551179"* in eWeek (October 12, 2010)
Pub: Ziff Davis Enterprise
Description: AVG Technologies is offering its AVG Internet Security 2011 Business Edition and AVG Anti-Virus Business Edition designed to give Internet-active SMB owners protection. The system protects online transactions and email communications as well as sensitive customer data and AVG Anti-Virus 2011 Business edition offers real-time protection against the latest online threats.

33413 ■ *"Banking on Twitter"* in Baltimore Business Journal (Vol. 27, February 6, 2010, No. 40, pp. 1)
Pub: American City Business Journals
Ed: Gary Haber. **Description:** Ways that banks are using Twitter, Facebook and other social networking sites to provide customer services is discussed. First Mariner Bank is one of those banks that are finding the social media platform as a great way to reach customers. Privacy issues regarding this marketing trend are examined.

33414 ■ *"The Bankrate Double Play, Bankrate Is Having Its Best Quarter Yet"* in Barron's (Vol. 88, March 24, 2008, No. 12, pp. 27)
Pub: Dow Jones & Co., Inc.
Contact: Clare Hart, President
Ed: Neil A. Martin. **Description:** Shares of Bankrate may rise as much as 25 percent from their level of $45.08 a share due to a strong cash flow and balance sheet. The company's Internet business remains strong despite weakness in the online advertising industry and is a potential takeover target.

33415 ■ *"Banks Fall Short in Online Services for Savvy Traders"* in Barron's (Vol. 88, March 17, 2008, No. 11, pp. 35)
Pub: Dow Jones & Co., Inc.
Contact: Clare Hart, President
Ed: Theresa W. Carey. **Description:** Banc of America Investment Services, WellsTrade, and ShareBuilder are at the bottom of the list of online brokerages because they offer less trading technologies and product range. Financial shoppers miss out on a lot of customized tools and analytics when using these services.

33416 ■ *"Baseline Metrics CEOs Need for Online Brand Oversight"* in South Florida Business Journal (Vol. 34, May 23, 2014, No. 44, pp. 16)
Pub: American City Business Journals
Released: May 23, 2014. **Description:** Chief executive officers have the option to use metrics that will allow them to monitor their online brands. Social media engagement is an effective customer service metric because it presents a clear assessment of a business social media prowess. Reputation management software, on the other hand, ranks a firm's weekly, hourly, and daily sentiments online.

33417 ■ *"BayTSP, NTT Data Corp. Enter Into Reseller Pact to Market Online IP Monitoring"* in Professional Services Close-Up (Sept. 11, 2009)
Description: Due to incredible interest from distributors and content owners across Asia, NTT Data Corp. will resell BayTSP's online intellectual property monitoring, enforcement, business intelligence and monetization services in Japan.

33418 ■ *"BBB Hires Marketing Firm to Attract More Businesses"* in Baltimore Business Journal (Vol. 27, January 1, 2010, No. 35, pp. 1)
Pub: American City Business Journals
Ed: Julekha Dash. **Description:** Better Business Bureau (BBB) of Greater Maryland hired Bystry Carson & Associates Ltd. to assist in its rebranding efforts in order to entice more businesses. Bystry Carson will promote BBB's new mission at lectures, seminars, and networking events, as well as educate businesses about the agency through blogs and Twitter. BBB's services are also outlined.

33419 ■ *"BBVA Offers Medical Practices help that Floats on a Cloud"* in Dallas Business Journal (Vol. 37, May 30, 2014, No. 38, pp. 6)
Pub: American City Business Journals
Released: May 30, 2014. **Description:** BBVA Compass is offering a package of bank services and health care technology for medical practices in Dallas-Fort Worth, Texas in partnership with technology platform provider CareCloud. The innovative cloud-based technology platform will allow the Birmingham, Alabama-based bank to help medical practices affected by the demands of technology and government regulations.

33420 ■ *"BDC Launches New Online Business Advice Centre"* in Marketwired (July 13, 2010)
Pub: COMTEX
Contact: Chip Brian, President
Description: The Business Development Bank of Canada (BDC) offers entrepreneurs the chance to use their new online BDC Advice Centre in order to seek advice regarding the challenges of entrepreneurship. Free online business tools and information to help both startups and established firms are also provided.

33421 ■ *"Before You Hit Send: Crafting Workplace E-Mails to Avoid Mishaps"* in *Black Enterprise (Vol. 38, January 2008, No. 6, pp. 85)*
Pub: Earl G. Graves Publishing Co. Inc.
Contact: Earl G. Graves, Jr., President
Ed: Tennille M. Robinson. **Description:** Tips to use before sending an office email our presented. It is important to keep emails looking professional.

33422 ■ *Behind the Cloud*
Pub: Jossey-Bass
Contact: William J. Pesce, President
Ed: Marc R. Benioff, Carlye Adler. **Released:** 2010. **Price:** $27.95, Hardcover. **Description:** Salesforce.com is the world's most successful business-to-business cloud-computing company that sells an on-line service that helps businesses manage sales, customer service, and marketing functions.

33423 ■ *"Being all a-Twitter"* in *Canadian Business (Vol. 81, December 8, 2008, No. 21, pp. 22)*
Ed: Andrew Wahl. **Description:** Marketing experts suggest that advertising strategies have to change along with new online social media. Companies are advised to find ways to incorporate social software because workers and customers are expected to continue its use.

33424 ■ *"Bellingham-Based Baby Web Site to Shut Down"* in *Bellingham Business Journal (Vol. February 2010, pp. 3)*
Pub: Sound Publishing Inc.
Contact: Gloria G. Fletcher, President
Ed: Lance Henderson. **Description:** Saralee Sky and Jerry Kilgore, owners of Babynut.com will close their online store. The site offered a free online and email newsletter to help mothers through pregnancy and the first three years of their child's life. Products being sold at clearance prices include organic and natural maternity and nursing clothing, baby and toddler clothes, books on pregnancy, and more.

33425 ■ *"Beyond YouTube: New Uses for Video, Online and Off"* in *Inc. (October 2007, pp. 53-54)*
Pub: Mansueto Ventures L.L.C.
Contact: John Koten, Chief Executive Officer
Ed: Leah Hoffmann. **Description:** Small companies are using video technology for embedding messages into email, broadcasting live interactive sales and training seminars, as well as marketing campaigns. Experts offer insight into producing and broadcasting business videos.

33426 ■ *The Big Switch*
Ed: Nicholas Carr. **Released:** January 19, 2009. **Price:** $16.95, paperback. **Description:** Today companies are dismantling private computer systems and tapping into services provided via the Internet. This shift is remaking the computer industry, bringing competitors such as Google to the forefront ant threatening traditional companies like Microsoft and Dell. The book weaves together history, economics, and technology to explain why computing is changing and what it means for the future.

33427 ■ *The Big Switch: Rewiring the World, From Edison to Google*
Pub: W.W. Norton and Company Inc.
Contact: A Malmud, President
Ed: Nicholas Carr. **Released:** June 2013. **Price:** $16.95, paperback. **Description:** Companies such as Google, Microsoft, and Amazon.com are building huge centers in order to create massive data centers. Together these centers form a giant computing grid that will deliver the digital universe to scientific labs, companies and homes in the future. This trend could bring about a new, darker phase for the Internet, one where these networks could operate as a fearsome entity that will dominate the lives of individuals worldwide. **Availability:** Print.

33428 ■ *"Bitcoin 'Killer App' Or the Currency of the Future?"* in *Providence Business News (Vol. 28, January 6, 2014, No. 40, pp. 1)*
Pub: American City Business Journals
Released: January 6, 2014. **Description:** The Providence Bitcoin Meetup has gathered several technology experts to discuss Bitcoin, the popular

digital currency. However, software developers, engineers and entrepreneurs see Bitcoin as the next killer app for the Internet and is changing how information and data is stored, shared and verified. The Bitcoin's impact in Rhode Island is examined.

33429 ■ *"Blacks Go Broadband: High-Speed Internet Adoption Grows Among African Americans"* in *Black Enterprise (Vol. 38, February 2008)*
Pub: Earl G. Graves Publishing Co. Inc.
Contact: Earl G. Graves, Jr., President
Ed: Cliff Hocker. **Description:** Number of black households using broadband Internet services tripled since 2005 according to a survey conducted by Pew Internet and American Life Project.

33430 ■ *"Bloomberg Law Upgraded Its Online Legal Research Platform"* in *Information Today (Vol. 28, September 2011, No. 8, pp. 28)*
Pub: Information Today, Inc.
Contact: Thomas H. Hogan, President
E-mail: ctuthill@infotoday.com
Description: Bloomberg Law upgraded its online legal research platform for law practices. The new services includes a redesigned interface, improved search capabilities, and expanded collaboration and workflow features, while maintaining it comprehensive law resources such as mergers and acquisitions, antitrust, and securities.

33431 ■ *"Book Yourself Solid: The Fastest, Easiest, and Most Reliable System for Getting More Clients Than You Can Handle"*
Pub: John Wiley & Sons Inc.
Contact: Stephen M. Smith, President
Released: November 23, 2010. **Price:** $18.95 paperback. **Description:** Self-promotion is essential for successful selling. Strategies, techniques, and skills necessary for success are presented, covering social media marketing strategies for service professionals; pricing models and sales strategies to simplify selling; new networking and outreach plans that take only minutes a day; and new product launches ideas and tactics.

33432 ■ *"Boom and Bust in the Book Biz"* in *Canadian Business (Vol. 83, August 17, 2010, No. 13-14, pp. 16)*
Pub: Rogers Media Inc.
Contact: Tony Viner, President
Ed: Jordan Timm. **Description:** Electronic book marketplace is booming with Amazon.com's e-book sales for the Kindle e-reader exceeding the hardcover sales. Kobo Inc. has registered early success with its Kobo e-reader and has partnered with Hong Kong telecom giant on an e-book store.

33433 ■ *"Boosting Strategy With An Online Community"* in *Business Strategy Review (Vol. 21, Spring 2010, No. 1, pp. 40)*
Pub: John Wiley & Sons Inc. Scientific, Technical, Medical, and Scholarly Div. (Wiley-Blackwell)
Contact: William J. Pesce, Manager
E-mail: wpesce@wiley.com
Ed: Lynda Gratton, Joel Casse. **Description:** A program that merged online communities with strategic development and implementation at Nokia has provided valuable lessons about new ways employees are able to engage and interact.

33434 ■ *"Boosting Your Merchant Management Services With Wireless Technology"* in *Franchising World (Vol. 42, August 2010, No. 8, pp. 27)*
Pub: International Franchise Association
Contact: Stephen J. Caldeira, President
E-mail: scaldeira@franchise.org
Ed: Michael S. Slominski. **Description:** Franchises should have the capability to accept credit cards away from their businesses. This technology will increase sales.

33435 ■ *"Borders Previews New Web Site"* in *Crain's Detroit Business (Vol. 23, October 8,*

2007, No. 41, pp. 4)
Pub: Crain Communications Inc. - Detroit
Contact: Keith Crain, Chairman
Ed: Sheena Harrison. **Description:** Borders Group Inc. previewed its new Website that allows customers to buy items that include the Magic Shelf, a virtual bookcase that displays available recommended books, movies and music.

33436 ■ *"Bottoms Up!"* in *Entrepreneur (Vol. 36, April 2008, No. 4, pp. 128)*
Pub: Entrepreneur Press
Contact: Perlman Neil, President
Ed: Amanda C. Kooser. **Description:** Jill Bernheimer launched her online alcohol business Domaine547 in 2007, and encountered challenges as legal issues over the licensing and launching of the business took about seven months to finish. Domain547 features blog and forum areas. Marketing strategy that connects to the social community is one of the ways to reach out to customers.

33437 ■ *"Brands' Mass Appeal"* in *ADWEEK (Vol. 51, June 14, 2010, No. 24)*
Pub: Nielsen Business Media Inc.
Contact: Howard Appelbaum, President
Ed: Brian Morrissey. **Description:** Engineering/science crowdsourced projects tend to result from posting and/or publishing interim results as well as from other talents building upon those results to produce even better results. However, the author does not see the same results in the creative world.

33438 ■ *"Breakaway Crowdfunding Launches"* in *San Francisco Business Times (Vol. 28, January 10, 2014, No. 25, pp. 10)*
Pub: American City Business Journals
Released: January 10, 2014. **Description:** Kim Kaselionis, founder of an online crowdfunding platform called Breakaway Funding, reveals that the service will take advantage of companies' relationships with credit unions and community banks. Breakaway wants to focus on firms that report annual revenue of $1 million to $20 million.

33439 ■ *"Bricks vs. Clicks: the Growth of Online Sales Is Changing the Way Many Companies Do Business, But Brick-and-Mortar Retailers are Adapting and Finding Ways to Keep Their Stores Relevant With Customers"* in *Retail Merchandising (Vol. 54, March-April 2014, No. 2, pp. 6)*
Pub: S & R Media Corporation
Released: March-April 2014. **Description:** The increased use in smartphones and tables has boosted the amount of time consumers spend making online purchases. Consumers us their cellular smartphones to research purchases, locate stores and compare price. Electronic commerce continues to grow and consumers are growing more comfortable making larger purchases through online stores. Statistical data included.

33440 ■ *"Brief: US-Business/eBay Earnings Rise 31 Per Cent"* in *Denver Post (July 21, 2011)*
Pub: The Denver Post
Ed: Andy Goldberg. **Description:** eBay's strong performance in second quarter 2011 is being attributed to Paypal online payments division. eBay's online auction sites reported gross merchandise volume up 34 percent. Statistical data included.

33441 ■ *"Brite-Strike Tactical Launches New Internet Marketing Initiatives"* in *Marketwired (September 15, 2009)*
Pub: COMTEX News Network Inc.
Contact: Chip Brian, President
Description: Brite-Strike Tactical Illumination Products, Inc. has enlisted the expertise of Internet marketing guru Thomas J. McCarthy to help revamp the company's Internet campaign. An outline of the Internet marketing strategy is provided.

33442 ■ *"Broadband Reaches Access Limits in Europe"* in *Information Today (Vol. 26,*

February 2009, No. 2, pp. 22)
Pub: Information Today, Inc.
Contact: Thomas H. Hogan, President
E-mail: ctuthill@infotoday.com

Ed: Jim Ashling. **Description:** Eurostat (the Statistical Office of the European communities) reports results from is survey regarding Internet use by businesses throughout its 27-member states. Iceland, Finland and the Netherlands provide the most access at broadband speeds, followed by Belgium, Spain and France.

33443 ■ *"Building a Better Twitter Brand: My Foray Into Social Analytics"* in Inc. (Vol. , pp.)
Pub: Inc. Magazine

Ed: John Brandon. **Description:** A small business using Twitter to research and promote the firm decided to test some Web-based dashboards that allow you to manage and analyze accounts on multiple social media networks including Facebook, Twitter, and LinkedIn.

33444 ■ *"Building Your Business: A Strong Web Presence Is a Must"* in Black Enterprise (Vol. 38, December 2007, No. 5, pp. 74)
Pub: Earl G. Graves Publishing Co. Inc.
Contact: Earl G. Graves, Jr., President

Ed: Tennille M. Robinson. **Description:** Building a strong presence on the Internet is crucial to any growing business. Websites can provide information or sell merchandise, but the site must also make sure the customer knows how to use and navigate around within the site. Common mistakes to avoid when designing a small business Website are outlined.

33445 ■ *"The Business Case for Mobile Content Acceleration"* in Streaming Media (November 2011, pp. 78)
Pub: Information Today, Inc.
Contact: Thomas H. Hogan, President
E-mail: ctuthill@infotoday.com

Ed: Dan Rayburn. **Description:** Last holiday season, eBay became a mobile commerce (m-commerce) giant when sales rose by 134 percent, as most online retailers offered customers the ability to purchase items using their mobile devices.

33446 ■ *"Business Forecast: Stormy and Successful"* in Women In Business (Vol. 62, June 2010, No. 2, pp. 12)
Pub: American Business Women's Association
Contact: Lorie Burch, President

Ed: Kathleen Leighton. **Description:** Stormy Simon, vice president of customer service at Overstock.com is a self-made career woman who started out as a temporary employee in the company in 2001. She was not able to attend college because she had two sons to care for after her divorce. Simon got involved in advertising and media buying and shares her love for business.

33447 ■ *"But We'll Miss the Wrestling Matches Over Dinner Bills"* in Washington Business Journal (Vol. 33, June 6, 2014, No. 7, pp. 6)
Pub: American City Business Journals

Released: June 6, 2014. **Description:** Online reservation service OpenTable launched its mobile payment platform in five local restaurants in Washington DC. The OpenTable reservation system charges about 75 cents per transaction for added convenience to the customer.

33448 ■ *"Buy Local to Land Great Deals"* in Inside Business (Vol. 13, September-October 2011, No. 5, pp. SS8)
Pub: Great Lakes Publishing Co.

Description: Buy Lakewood! Loyalty Program offers residents great bargains for shopping at local retailers. Residents sign up online and the city mails them a letter of appreciations along with a key card. Showing the key card at any participating businesses listed on the Website will provide discounts.

33449 ■ *"Buyout Rumors Have Rackspace Back in the News"* in San Antonio Business

Journal (Vol. 28, September 12, 2014, No. 31, pp. 6)
Pub: American City Business Journals

Released: September 12, 2014. **Description:** Louisiana-based CenturyLink Inc. has offered to buy-out San Antonio, Texas-based Rackspace Hosting in order to boost its Internet and cloud services. The latest stock market valuation of Rackspace was at $5.33 billion. The potential impact of the CenturyLink and Rackspace merger deal on the managed hosting services market is also analyzed.

33450 ■ *"CADD Microsystems Launches the CADD Community, Partners with Global eTraining to Provide Online, On-Demand Training for Autodesk Software"* in Computer Business Week (August 28, 2014, pp. 24)
Pub: NewsRX
Contact: Susan E. Hasty, Publisher

Released: August 28, 2014. **Description:** A new online customer-only portal the integrates on-demand training, applications and extension, videos and additional value-added content for customers only was developed by CADD Microsystems. The Autodesk Platinum Partner calls this training program, CADD Community.

33451 ■ *"Campaigner Survey: 46 Percent of Small Businesses Use Email Marketing"* in Wireless News (November 21, 2009)

Description: Almost half (46 percent) of small businesses surveyed by Campaigner's 2009 State of Small Business Online Marketing, say that they rely on email marketing to help them find new customers, keep existing ones and grow their businesses. The survey also found that 36 percent of small businesses plan to begin using email marketing over the next year. The trend to utilize Internet marketing tools is allowing small businesses to grow faster and generate higher revenues than those that are not using these mediums.

33452 ■ *"Capturing Generation Y: Ready, Set, Transform"* in Credit Union Times (Vol. 21, July 14, 2010, No. 27, pp. 20)
Pub: Summit Professional Networks
Contact: Steve Weitzner, President

Ed: Senthil Kumar. **Description:** The financial services sector recognizes that Generation Y will have a definite impact on the way business is conducted in the future. The mindset of Generation Y is social and companies need to use networking tools such as Facebook in order to reach this demographic.

33453 ■ *"Chafee Eyes Tax On Travel Sites"* in Providence Business News (Vol. 28, March 24, 2014, No. 51, pp. 1)
Pub: American City Business Journals

Released: March 24, 2014. **Description:** Rhode Island Governor, Lincoln D. Chafee's 2015 budget will include new tax rules for travel Websites. State officials claim the new regulations will deal with a loophole that has allowed travel Websites to pay less in taxes. Many hotels enter into partnerships with travel Websites in order to sell rooms in bulk.

33454 ■ *"The China Connection"* in Crain's Chicago Business (Vol. 31, March 24, 2008, No. 12, pp. 26)
Pub: Crain Communications Inc.
Contact: Todd Johnson, Publisher

Ed: Samantha Stainburn. **Description:** Interview with Ben Munoz who studied abroad in Beijing, China for three months to study international economics, e-commerce and global leadership.

33455 ■ *"Choice, TripAdvisor Team Up on Bookings"* in Washington Business Journal (Vol. 33, May 16, 2014, No. 4, pp. 8)
Pub: American City Business Journals

Released: May 16, 2014. **Description:** Choice Hotels International Inc. has formed a partnership with TripAdvisor LLC that will allow potential Choice customers to book rooms through the travel review site's Web pages, featuring the Choice-branded hotels. Robert Dowell of Choice Hotels says the business strategy will enhance the customer experience and increase booking sales to their properties.

33456 ■ *"Chris Curtis Preaches: The Gospel of Internet Success"* in Black Enterprise (Vol. 38, March 1, 2008, No. 8, pp. 56)
Pub: Earl G. Graves Publishing Co. Inc.
Contact: Earl G. Graves, Jr., President

Ed: Anthony Calypso. **Description:** Profile of the Web Business Ownership Series, a collection of 20 free seminars that help small businesses learn about the Web development process.

33457 ■ *"Click Here to Book"* in Caterer & Hotelkeeper (October 28, 2011, No. 288)
Pub: Reed Reference Publishing
Contact: Erik Engstrom, Chief Executive Officer

Ed: Ross Bentley. **Description:** Customers expectations are determined by the quality of a Website when booking hotel rooms.

33458 ■ *"A Click In the Right Direction: Website Teaches Youth Financial Literacy"* in Black Enterprise (Vol. 38, December 2007, No. 5)
Pub: Earl G. Graves Publishing Co. Inc.
Contact: Earl G. Graves, Jr., President

Ed: Nicole Norfleet. **Description:** Profile of Donald Lee Robinson who launched SkillsThatClick, a Website that teaches young individuals ages 12 to 15 about money management. Robinson shares how he used his Navy career as a model for designing the site.

33459 ■ *"Click Your Chicken"* in Canadian Business (Vol. 87, October 2014, No. 10, pp. 11)
Pub: George Media Inc.

Released: October 2014. **Description:** A number of business ideas, products and strategies are ranked from the ingenious to the extremely bizarre. A mobile Web startup called FarmLogs helps farmers track everything from soil conditions to weather to profit forecasts. Kentucky Fried Chicken restaurants awards top Twitter fans in Japan with USB drive, a mouse and a keyboard designed with chicken parts.

33460 ■ *"ClickFuel Unveils Internet Marketing Tools for Small Businesses"* in Marketwired (October 19, 2009)
Pub: COMTEX News Network Inc.
Contact: Chip Brian, President

Description: ClickFuel, a firm that manages, designs and tracks marketing campaigns has unveiled a full software suite of affordable services and technology solutions designed to empower small business owners and help them promote and grow their businesses through targeted Internet marketing campaigns.

33461 ■ *Clicking Through: A Survival Guide for Bringing Your Company Online*
Ed: Jonathan I. Ezor. **Released:** October 1999. **Description:** Summary of legal compliance issues faced by small companies doing business on the Internet, including copyright and patent laws.

33462 ■ *"Clicks For Cash: Earning More From Your Website"* in Inc. (December 2007, pp. 64-65)
Pub: Gruner and Jahr USA Publishing Co.
Contact: J. Russell Denson, President

Ed: Michael Fitzgerald. **Description:** Ways to use a company's Website to generate revenue are discussed. Free services for placing ads include Google AdSense, AdBrite, AuctionAds, Chitika eMiniMalls, Vizu Answers, and Value Click; profiles of each service are presented.

33463 ■ *"Clicks From Round the World: Simplifying International E-Commerce"* in Inc. (Volume 32, December 2010, No. 10, pp. 146)
Pub: Inc. Magazine

Ed: Ryan Underwood. **Description:** By 2014, global e-commerce spending is expected to increase more than 90 percent, with much of that growth coming from Latin America.

33464 ■ *"Cloud City"* in Puget Sound Business Journal (Vol. 34, February 28, 2014, No. 46, pp. 4)
Pub: American City Business Journals

Released: February 28, 2014. **Description:** Seattle, Washington is experiencing an influx of the world's most innovative cloud companies. Businesses are shifting their applications from in-house servers or private data center into public cloud infrastructure, which is less expensive than buying the servers and managing the data systems. Seattle software companies are taking advantage of this trend and developing products.

33465 ■ *"Cloudera Mines Big Data Lode, Raises $900 Million" in San Francisco Business Times (Vol. 28, April 4, 2014, No. 37, pp. 6)*
Pub: American City Business Journals
Released: April 4, 2014. Description: Palo Alto, California-based Cloudera sold an 18 percent stake to Intel in order to raise the latest funding round to $900 million. Cloudera sells Apache Hadoop analytic data management software in the massive big data market that could potentially hit $50-plus billion a year. The application of Cloudera's platform in genomic research is also presented.

33466 ■ *"Cloudy Future for VMware?" in Barron's (Vol. 90, September 13, 2010, No. 37, pp. 21)*
Pub: Barron's Editorial & Corporate Headquarters
Ed: Jonathan R. Laing. Description: VMWare dominated the virtualization market for years, but it may be ending as it faces more competition from rivals that offer cloud computing services. The company's stocks are also expensive and are vulnerable to the smallest mishap.

33467 ■ *"Complete Discovery Source, Inc. (CDS) Receives Minority Owned Business Certification" in Marketwired (December 14, 2010)*
Pub: COMTEX
Contact: Chip Brian, President
Description: Complete Discovery Source Inc. (CDS) was granted Minority-Owned Business Enterprise status by the New York State Department of Economic Development. The certification provides CDS, an end-to-end eDiscovery services provider, with access to contracting opportunities with 130 government agencies throughout New York state.

33468 ■ *The Complete Guide to Google Adwords: Secrets, Techniques, and Strategies You Can Learn to Make Millions*
Pub: Atlantic Publishing Co.
Contact: Amanda Miller, Manager
E-mail: amiller@atlantic-pub.com
Released: December 01, 2010. Price: $24.95. Description: Google AdWords, when it launched in 2002 signaled a fundamental shift in what the Internet was for so many individuals and companies. Learning and understanding how Google AdWords operates and how it can be optimized for maximum exposure, boosting click through rates, conversions, placement, and selection of the right keywords, can be the key to a successful online business.

33469 ■ *"Computer Repair Reno Co., PC Service Center Chooses GLSM LLC as Primary SEO Provider" in Marketing Weekly News (July 21, 2012)*
Released: July 21, 2012. Description: PC Service Center, located in theReno-Sparks area, has partnered with Get Local Search Marketing LLC giving GLSM exclusive online marketing rights which will increase PC Service Center ranking within all search engines, including Google, Yahoo and Bing. PC Service Center offers computer repair, laptop repair, and new and used computer services in the Northern Nevada area.

33470 ■ *"Connections: United We Gab" in Entrepreneur (Vol. 35, October 2007, No. 10, pp. 60)*
Pub: Entrepreneur Press
Contact: Perlman Neil, President
Ed: Mike Hogan. Description: T-Mobile and AT&T introduced dual-mode service to consumers, helping them to switch between cellular and Wi-Fi networks easily. These services, such as Hotspot@Home, reduces the cost of long distance calls by routing them over the Internet with the use of WiFi. Benefits of dual mode service, such as lower hardware price and better call coverage are given.

33471 ■ *"Consumer Electronics: Brick and Mortar Vs. Online" in Retail Merchandiser (Vol. 51, September-October 2011, No. 5, pp. 15)*
Pub: Phoenix Media Corporation
Description: Brick and mortar retailers with Websites are discovering that the Internet is used more for research than purchasing when it comes to electronics products. According to a recent study conducted by The NPD Group shows that 56 percent of consumers research televisions online before purchasing, but only 19 percent actually buy them online.

33472 ■ *"Consumer Trust in E-Commerce Web Sites: a Meta-Study" in ACM Computing Surveys (Vol. 43, Fall 2011, No. 3, pp. 14)*
Pub: Association for Computing Machinery
Contact: Vinton G. Cerf, President
Ed: Patricia Beatty, Ian Reay, Scott Dick, James Miller. Description: Trust is at once an elusive, imprecise concept, and a critical attribute that must be engineered into e-commerce systems. Engineering trust is examined.

33473 ■ *"Contagious: Why Things Catch On"*
Pub: Simon and Schuster Inc.
Contact: Carolyn Reidy, President
E-mail: carolyn.reidy@simonandschuster.com
Released: March 5, 2013. Price: $26.00. Description: Wharton marketing professor, Jonah Berger, reveals the science of successful word-of-mouth and social media marketing that provides greater results than traditional advertising.

33474 ■ *Content Rich: Writing Your Way to Wealth on the Web*
Ed: Jon Wuebben. Released: April 2008. Price: $19.95. Description: A definitive search engine optimization (SEO) copywriting guide for search engine rankings and sales conversion. It includes topics not covered in other books on the subject and targets the small to medium sized business looking for ways to maximize online marketing activities as well as designers and Web developers seeking to incorporate more SEO techniques into design and content.

33475 ■ *"Contests Produce Ad Designs on a Dime" in San Diego Business Journal (Vol. 31, August 23, 2010, No. 31, pp. 1)*
Pub: San Diego Business Journal
Ed: Mike Allen. Description: San Diego-based Prova.fm runs design contests for clients such as the U.S. Postal Service. The client then chooses the best entry from the contest. Prova.fm relies on the Internet to deliver a range of possible graphic solutions and allowing the customer to make the right selection for its business through a process called crowdsourcing.

33476 ■ *"Conversations with Customers" in Business Journal Serving Greater Tampa Bay (Vol. 31, December 31, 2010, No. 1, pp. 1)*
Pub: Tampa Bay Business Journal
Description: Tampa Bay, Florida-based businesses have been using social media to interact with customers. Forty percent of businesses have been found to have at least one social media platform to reach customers and prospects.

33477 ■ *"Coping with the Web" in Agency Sales Magazine (Vol. 39, December 2009, No. 11, pp. 52)*
Ed: Karen Saunders. Description: When branding your company on the Internet, strategy should first be discussed with the website designer and the target and niche audience should also be defined. Describing 'what' and 'how' the product or service is offering is also important. In addition, perception, the logo, and the tag line are some elements that are needed to create a brand.

33478 ■ *"Copyright Clearance Center (CCC) Partnered with cSubs" in Information Today (Vol. 28, November 2011, No. 10, pp. 14)*
Pub: Information Today, Inc.
Contact: Thomas H. Hogan, President
E-mail: ctuthill@infotoday.com
Description: Copyright Clearance Center (CCC) partnered with cSubs to integrate CCC's point-of-content licensing solution RightsLink Basic directly into cSubs workflow. The partnership will allow cSubs' customers a user-friendly process for obtaining permissions. Csubs is a corporate subscription management service for books, newspapers, and econtent.

33479 ■ *"The Copyright Evolution" in Information Today (Vol. 28, November 2011, No. 10, pp. 1)*
Pub: Information Today, Inc.
Contact: Thomas H. Hogan, President
E-mail: ctuthill@infotoday.com
Ed: Nancy Davis Kho. Description: For information professionals, issues surrounding copyright compliance have traditionally been on the consumption side. However, today, content consumption is only half the program because blogging, tweeting, and commenting is a vital part of more standard duties for workers as corporations aim to create authentic communications with customers.

33480 ■ *"CradlePoint Is Adding Workers, Seeking More Space" in Idaho Business Review (September 3, 2014)*
Pub: Dolan Co.
Contact: James P. Dolan, President
Released: September 3, 2014. Description: CradlePoint makes networking routers and software, focusing on security for businesses. The firm is hiring new workers at a rate higher than predicted and is seeking new office space in downtown Boise, Idaho. CradlePoint is a major player in the growing wireless service and cloud platform market and is growing faster than its competitors.

33481 ■ *Crossing the Chasm: Marketing and Selling Disruptive Products to Mainstream Customers*
Pub: HarperCollins Publishers Inc.
Contact: Jane Friedman, President
E-mail: jfriedman@harpercollins.com
Ed: Geoffrey A. Moore. Price: $17.99, paperback; 12.99; C$11.99. Description: A guide for marketing in high-technology industries, focusing on the Internet. Availability: PrintE-book.

33482 ■ *"Crowd Control" in Washington Business Journal (Vol. 33, August 15, 2014, No. 17, pp. 8)*
Pub: American City Business Journals
Released: August 15, 2014. Description: Washington DC's Department of Insurance, Securities and Banking issued a proposal that would create the legal framework by which companies can raise cash through crowdfunding. The DC proposal would allow District-based businesses to crowdfund from District-based backers. The advantages and drawbacks to the plan are examined.

33483 ■ *"Crowdfund Your Way to Millions: LeVar Burton's Kickstarter Campaign Raises $1 Million In Less Than 12 Hours" in Black Enterprise (Vol. 45, July-August 2014, No. 1, pp. 61)*
Pub: Earl G. Graves Publishing Co. Inc.
Contact: Earl G. Graves, Jr., President
Released: July-August 2014. Description: Kickstarted is a viable option for funding a small business. Actor, LeVar Burton launched a Kickstarter campaign to help revive the learning show Reading Rainbow and raised $1 million in less than 12 hours. Information about six crowdfunding sites are listed, including: Kickstarter, Angellist, Rockethub, Crowdtilt, Indiegogo, and Rallyme.

33484 ■ *"Crowdfunding Success for Julep" in Puget Sound Business Journal (Vol. 34, March 21, 2014, No. 49, pp. 3)*
Pub: American City Business Journals
Released: March 21, 2014. Description: Beauty product and cosmetics company, Julep, raised over $140,000 from 6,200 individuals through a crowdfunding campaign. The money will be sued to develop a new nail polish tool called Plie Wand. The firm was able to surpass its funding goal of $75,000 within the first 24 hours of the campaign.

33485 ■ *"Crowdsourcing their Way into One Big Mess"* in Brandweek *(Vol. 51, October 25, 2010, No. 38, pp. 26)*
Ed: Gregg S. Lipman. **Description:** The Gap, was counting on crowdsourcing to provide feedback for its new logo, but it did not prove positive for the retailer. However, a massive outcry of negative opinion, via crowdsourcing, may not always equal valid, constructive criticism.

33486 ■ *Crowdsourcing: Why the Power of the Crowd is Driving the Future of Business*
Pub: Crown Business
Ed: Jeff Howe. **Released:** September 15, 2009. **Price:** $15, paperback. **Description:** Small businesses are shown how to use social networks online to promote goods and services. **Availability:** Print.

33487 ■ *Crush It!: Why NOW Is the Time to Cash In on Your Passion*
Pub: HarperStudio/HarperCollins
Ed: Gary Vaynerchuk. **Released:** October 13, 2009. **Price:** $21.99, hardcover; $14.99; C$13.99. **Description:** Ways the Internet can help entrepreneurs turn their passions into successful companies. **Availability:** PrintE-book.

33488 ■ *"Cyber Thanksgiving Online Shopping a Growing Tradition"* in Marketing Weekly News *(December 12, 2009, pp. 137)*
Pub: Investment Weekly News
Description: According to e-commerce analysts, Thanksgiving day is becoming increasingly important to retailers in terms of online sales. Internet marketers are realizing that consumers are already searching for Black Friday sales and if they find deals on the products they are looking for, they are highly likely to make their purchase on Thanksgiving day instead of waiting.

33489 ■ *"Cyberwise"* in Black Enterprise *(Vol. 41, December 2010, No. 5, pp. 50)*
Ed: Marica Wade Talbert. **Description:** Information is given regarding single platforms that can be used to develop applications for iPhone, Android, Blackberry, and Nokia.

33490 ■ *"Cyberwise"* in Black Enterprise *(Vol. 41, September 2010, No. 2, pp. 49)*
Pub: Earl G. Graves Publishing Co. Inc.
Contact: Earl G. Graves, Jr., President
Ed: Marcia Wade Talbert. **Description:** Advice is given to assist in selling an online store called theupscalegaragesale.com. A listing of business brokers specializing in the sale of Internet businesses is included.

33491 ■ *"Datran Media Executives to Lead Industry Debates Across Q1 Conferences"* in Marketwired *(January 22, 2010)*
Pub: COMTEX News Network Inc.
Contact: Chip Brian, President
Description: Datran Media, an industry-leading digital marketing technology company, will be sending members of its management team to several conferences in the early part of the first quarter of 2010; discussions will include Internet marketing innovations, e-commerce and media distribution.

33492 ■ *"Dealing With Cyber Insecurity"* in Philadelphia Business Journal *(Vol. 33, June 13, 2014, No. 18, pp. 4)*
Pub: American City Business Journals
Released: June 13, 2014. **Description:** The threat of cyber theft or data breach is increasing globally as technology becomes advanced and more companies start storing their important data electronically. Therefore, the importance of cyber security has increased. Although big businesses suffer more from data breaches, small companies can also take a beating if data breach happens. A survey found that small businesses were wary of spending money on security issues; good investment in IT and creating a privacy policy will help companies fight cyber threats.

33493 ■ *"Dear Customer: Managing E-Mail Campaigns"* in Inc. *(March 2008, pp. 58-59)*
Pub: Mansueto Ventures L.L.C.
Contact: John Koten, Chief Executive Officer
Ed: Ryan Underwood. **Description:** Internet services that help firms manage their online business including email marketing, to manage subscriber lists,

comply with spam regulations, monitor bouncebacks, and track potential customers are profiled. Constant Contact, MobileStorm Stun, Campaign Monitor, Pop Commerce, Emma, and StrongMail E-mail Server are among software and services highlighted.

33494 ■ *Designing Websites for Every Audience*
Ed: Ilise Benun. **Released:** January 2003. **Description:** Twenty-five case studies targeting six difference audiences are used to help a business design, or make over, a Website.

33495 ■ *Digital Divide: Civic Engagement, Information Poverty, and the Internet Worldwide*
Pub: Cambridge University Press
Contact: Richard Ziemacki, President
E-mail: rziemacki@cambridge.org
Ed: Pippa Norris. **Released:** September 2001. **Price:** $32.99, paperback; $82, hardback. **Description:** The expansive growth of the Internet is intensifying existing inequalities between the information rich and poor. The book examines the evidence for access and use of the Internet in 179 countries and discusses the global divide that is evident between industrialized and developing societies. **Availability:** Print.

33496 ■ *"Digital Marketing: Integrating Strategy and Tactics with Values, A Guidebook for Executives, Managers, and Students"*
Pub: Routledge
Contact: Kevin Bradley, President
E-mail: kbradley@taylorandfrancis.com
Released: October 22, 2014. **Price:** $38.95 paperback. **Description:** Guidebook filled with information on the latest digital marketing tactics and strategic insights to help small businesses generate sustainable growth and achieve competitive advantage through digital integration. A five-step program: mindset, model, strategy, implementation, and sustainability is explained.

33497 ■ *"The Digital Revolution is Over. Long Live the Digital Revolution!"* in Business Strategy Review *(Vol. 21, Spring 2010, No. 1, pp. 74)*
Pub: John Wiley & Sons Inc. Scientific, Technical, Medical, and Scholarly Div. (Wiley-Blackwell)
Contact: William J. Pesce, Manager
E-mail: wpesce@wiley.com
Ed: Gianvito Lanzolla, Jamie Anderson. **Description:** Many businesses are now involved in the digital marketplace. The authors argue that the new reality of numerous companies offering overlapping products means that it is critical for managers to understand digital convergence and to observe the imperatives for remaining competitive.

33498 ■ *"Do-It-Yourself Portfolio Management"* in Barron's *(Vol. 89, July 13, 2009, No. 28, pp. 25)*
Pub: Dow Jones & Co., Inc.
Contact: Clare Hart, President
Ed: Mike Hogan. **Description:** Services of several portfolio management web sites are presented. These web sites include MarketRiders E.Adviser, TD Ameritrade and E.

33499 ■ *"DocuSign Raises $85 Million for Electronic Signatures"* in San Francisco Business Times *(Vol. 28, March 7, 2014, No. 33, pp. 6)*
Pub: American City Business Journals
Released: March 7, 2014. **Description:** DocuSign, the market leader in electronic signatures, reported that it was able to raise another $85 million in capital. The company is expected to file an initial public offering in 2014 or 2015. CFO, Mike Dinsdale, shares that the firm also wants to expand internationally.

33500 ■ *"Dollar General Selects GSI Commerce to Launch Its eCommerce Business"* in Benzinga.com *(October 29, 2011)*
Pub: Benzinga.com
Contact: Kyle Bazzy, President
Ed: Benzinga Staff. **Description:** Dollar General Corporation chose GSI Commerce, a leading provider

of ecommerce and interactive marketing solutions, to launch its online initiative. GSI Commerce is an eBay Inc. company.

33501 ■ *"Door Knocking 3.0: Two Ways to Find New Customers"* in Inc. *(Vol. 31, January-February 2009, No. 1, pp. 41)*
Pub: Mansueto Ventures L.L.C.
Contact: John Koten, Chief Executive Officer
Description: Latest software programs that help sales staff connect to new leads are profiled. Salesconx provides online leads while Demandbase reports users on a particular Website.

33502 ■ *"Dots Sings To New Tune With Its Radio Station"* in Crain's Cleveland Business *(Vol. 30, June 15, 2009, No. 23, pp. 7)*
Description: Dots LLC, a women's clothing retailer, has launched an online radio station on its Website. The station plays the in-store music to customers while they are shopping online.

33503 ■ *Double or Nothing: How Two Friends Risked It All to Buy One of Las Vegas' Legendary Casinos*
Pub: HarperBusiness
Ed: Tom Breitling, Cal Fussman. **Released:** March 18, 2008. **Price:** $24.95, hardcover; $3.99; C$16.99. **Description:** Founders of a successful Internet travel agency share their experience from startup to selling the company. **Availability:** PrintE-book.

33504 ■ *"Dramatic Results: Making Opera (Yes, Opera) Seem Young and Hip"* in Inc. *(October 2007, pp. 61-62)*
Pub: Mansueto Ventures L.L.C.
Contact: John Koten, Chief Executive Officer
Ed: Stephanie Clifford. **Description:** Profile of Peter Gelb, who turned New York's Metropolitan Opera into one of the most media-savvy organizations in the country, using a multifaceted marketing strategy through the media. Gelb used streaming audio and simulcasts on satellite radio and movie theaters to promote a message that opera is hip.

33505 ■ *"Drive Traffic To Your Blog"* in Women Entrepreneur *(January 13, 2009)*
Ed: Lesley Spencer Pyle. **Description:** Internet social networking has become a vital component to marketing one's business. Tips are provided on how to establish a blog that will attract attention to one's business and keep one's customers coming back for more.

33506 ■ *e-Business, e-Government and Small and Medium-Size Enterprises: Opportunities and Challenges*
Pub: IGI Global
Contact: Dr. Mehdi Khosrow-Pour, President
Released: July 2003. **Price:** $79.95. **Description:** Electronic commerce and information technology research in small and medium-sized enterprises (SMEs). Policymakers, legislators, researchers and professionals address significant issues of importance to the small business sector. **Availability:** Print.

33507 ■ *"E-Commerce: As Seen on TV"* in Canadian Business *(Vol. 80, November 5, 2007, No. 22, pp. 93)*
Pub: Rogers Media Inc.
Contact: Tony Viner, President
Ed: Zena Olijnyk. **Description:** StarBrand Media Inc. is one of the companies providing fans with information on how and where to purchase the items that television characters are using. StarBrand created the style section found on different television shows' Websites, such as that of the Gossip Girl and Smallville. The benefits of using sites like StarBrand are evaluated.

33508 ■ *E-Commerce in Regional Small to Medium Enterprises*
Pub: IGI Global
Contact: Dr. Mehdi Khosrow-Pour, President
Ed: Robert MacGregor, Lejla Vrazalic. **Released:** June 2007. **Price:** $99.95. **Description:** Strategies small to medium enterprises (SMEs) need to implement in order to compete with larger, global businesses and the role electronic commerce plays in this process are outlined. Studies of e-commerce in

multiple regional areas, focusing on the role of business size, business sector, market focus, gender of CEO, and education level of the CEO are discussed. **Availability:** Print; E-book.

33509 ■ *e-Riches 2.0: Next-Generation Marketing Strategies for Making Millions Online*
Pub: AMACOM
Contact: Edward T. Reilly, Manager
Ed: Scott Fox. **Released:** May 2009. **Price:** $25, hardback. **Description:** Beginner's guide to using the Internet to help grow business, including the best ways to use email lists and newsletters, RSS feeds, online viral marketing, social networking, microblogging, online video and radio/podcasts, tele-seminars and webinars, search engine keyword advertising and affiliate program advertising. **Availability:** Print.

33510 ■ *"eBay Business Looking Up" in Zacks (July 26, 2011)*
Pub: COMTEX News Network Inc.
Contact: Chip Brian, President
Ed: Sejuti Banerjea. **Description:** eBay reported solid revenue growth for 2011 second quarter, keeping in line with the Zacks Consensus Estimate, and third quarter earnings are expected to be higher. eBay's new strategy is to direct traffic to bigger sellers with improved customer service, making this good for eBay businesses.

33511 ■ *"EBay Finally Gaining Traction in China" in San Jose Mercury News (October 26, 2011)*
Pub: San Jose Mercury News Inc.
Contact: Barbara Vroman, Manager
E-mail: bvroman@sjmercury.com
Ed: John Boudreau. **Description:** eBay has developed a new strategy in China that allows exporters of every type of merchandise to sell directly to eBays 97 million overseas users.

33512 ■ *EBay Income: How ANYONE of Any Age, Location, and/or Background Can Build a Highly Profitable Online Business with eBay*
Pub: Atlantic Publishing Co.
Contact: Amanda Miller, Manager
E-mail: amiller@atlantic-pub.com
Released: Revised Second Edition. **Price:** $24.95. **Description:** A complete overview of eBay is given and guides any small company through the entire process of creating the auction and auction strategies, photography, writing copy, text and formatting, multiple sales, programming tricks, PayPal, accounting, creating marketing, merchandising, managing email lists, advertising plans, taxes and sales tax, best time to list items and for how long, sniping programs, international customers, opening a storefront, electronic commerce, buy-it now pricing, keywords, Google marketing and eBay secrets.

33513 ■ *"eBay Inc. Completes Acquisition of Zong" in Benzinga.com (October 29, 2011)*
Pub: Benzinga.com
Contact: Kyle Bazzy, President
Ed: Benzinga Staff. **Description:** eBay Inc. acquired Zong, a provider of payments through mobile carrier billing. Terms of the agreement are outlined.

33514 ■ *"eBay Introduces Open Commerce Ecosystem" in Entertainment Close-Up (October 24, 2011)*
Pub: Close-Up Media
Description: eBay's new X.commerce is an open commerce ecosystem that will arm developers and merchants with the technology tools required to keep pace with the ever-changing industry. X.commerce brings together the technology assets and developer communities of eBay, PayPal, Magento and partners to expand on eBays vision for enabling commerce.

33515 ■ *"eBay and Jonathan Adler Team to Launch 'The eBay Inspiration Shop" in Entertainment Close-Up (October 25, 2011)*
Pub: Close-Up Media
Description: Designer Jonathan Adler partnered with eBay to create a collection of new must-have merchandise for the fall season. Top trendsetters, includ-

ing actors, designers, bloggers, stylists, editors, photographers, models and musicians helped curate the items being featured in the windows by sharing their shopping wish lists with users.

33516 ■ *The Ebay Seller's Tax and Legal Answer Book*
Pub: AMACOM
Contact: Edward T. Reilly, Manager
Ed: Cliff Ennico. **Released:** May 2007. **Price:** $19.95, Paper or Softback. **Description:** Helps sellers using Ebay to file taxes properly, while saving money. **Availability:** Print.

33517 ■ *eBay the Smart Way: Selling, Buying, and Profiting on the Web's #1 Auction Site*
Pub: AMACOM
Contact: Edward T. Reilly, Manager
Ed: Joseph T. Sinclair. **Released:** Fifth Edition. **Price:** $17.95, paperback. **Description:** Resource to help individuals sell, buy and profit using the Internet auction site Ebay.

33518 ■ *Effective Web Presence Solutions for Small Businesses: Strategies for Successful Implementation*
Pub: IGI Global
Contact: Dr. Mehdi Khosrow-Pour, President
Ed: Stephen Burgess, Carmine Sellitto, Stan Karanasios. **Released:** February 2009. **Price:** $165. **Description:** Examines business strategies to implement a Web presence for any small business, focusing on website development. **Availability:** Print; E-book.

33519 ■ *"Elanco Challenges Bayer's Advantage, K9 Advantix Ad Claims" in Pet Product News (Vol. 64, November 2010, No. 11, pp. 11)*
Pub: Bowtie Inc.
Description: Elanco Animal Health has disputed Bayer Animal Health's print and Web advertising claims involving its flea, tick, and mosquito control products Advantage and K9 Advantix. The National Advertising Division of the Council of Better Business Bureaus recommended the discontinuation of ads, while Bayer Animal Health reiterated its commitment to self-regulation.

33520 ■ *Electronic Commerce*
Pub: Course Technology
Contact: Manuel Guzman, President (Acting)
Ed: Gary P. Schneider, Bryant Chrzan, Charles McCormick. **Released:** May 01, 2010. **Price:** $149.99. **Description:** E-commerce can open the door to more opportunities than ever before for small business. Packed with real-world examples and cases, the book delivers comprehensive coverage of emerging online technologies and trends and their influence on the electronic marketplace. It details how the landscape of online commerce is evolving, reflecting changes in the economy and how business and society are responding to those changes. Balancing technological issues with the strategic business aspects of successful e-commerce, the new edition includes expanded coverage of international issues, social networking, mobile commerce, Web 2.0 technologies, and updates on spam, phishing, and identity theft. **Availability:** Print.

33521 ■ *Electronic Commerce: Technical, Business, and Legal Issues*
Ed: Oktay Dogramaci; Aryya Gangopadhyay; Yelena Yesha; Nabil R. Adam. **Released:** August 1998. **Description:** Provides insight into the goals of using the Internet to grow a business in the areas of networking and telecommunication, security, and storage and retrieval; business areas such as marketing, procurement and purchasing, billing and payment, and supply chain management; and legal aspects such as privacy, intellectual property, taxation, contractual and legal settlements.

33522 ■ *Email Marketing by the Numbers: How to Use the World's Greatest Marketing*

Tool to Take Any Organization to the Next Level
Pub: John Wiley & Sons Inc.
Contact: Stephen M. Smith, President
Ed: Chris Baggott, Ali Sales. **Released:** April 2007. **Price:** $24.95, hardcover; $16.99. **Description:** Tips for using email to market small business products and services are provided. **Availability:** PrintE-book.

33523 ■ *Emerging Business Online: Global Markets and the Power of B2B Internet Marketing*
Pub: FT Press
Contact: Timothy C. Moore, Vice President
Ed: Lara Fawzy, Lucas Dworski. **Released:** October 04, 2010. **Price:** $49.99. **Description:** An introduction into ebocube (emerging business online), a comprehensive proven business model for Internet B2B marketing in emerging markets.

33524 ■ *"Empowered" in Harvard Business Review (Vol. 88, July-August 2010, No. 7-8, pp. 94)*
Pub: Harvard Business School Publishing
Ed: Josh Bernoff, Ted Schadler. **Description:** HERO concept (highly empowered and resourceful operative) which builds a connection between employees, managers, and IT is outlined. The resultant additional experience and knowledge gained by employees improves customer relationship management.

33525 ■ *"Endeca Gears Up for Likely IPO Bid" in Boston Business Journal (Vol. 31, July 1, 2011, No. 23, pp. 1)*
Pub: Boston Business Journal
Ed: Kyle Alspach. **Description:** Endeca Inc. is readying itself for its plans to register as a public company. The search engine technology leader is enjoying continued growth with revenue up by 30 percent in 2010 while its expansion trend makes it an unlikely candidate for an acquisition.

33526 ■ *The Essential Online Solution: The 5-Step Formula for Small Business Success*
Pub: John Wiley & Sons Inc.
Contact: Stephen M. Smith, President
Ed: Rick Segel, Barbara Callan-Bogia. **Released:** September 2006. **Price:** $22.95; $14.99. **Description:** Strategies to help any small business increase its online presence and compete with big retail chains. Tips for success Web design are included. **Availability:** PrintE-book.

33527 ■ *Essentials of Entrepreneurship and Small Business Management*
Pub: Prentice Hall PTR
Ed: Norman M. Scarborough, Thomas W. Zimmerer, Doug Wilson. **Released:** 7th Edition. **Price:** $199.80. **Description:** New venture creation and the knowledge required to start a new business are shared. The challenges of entrepreneurship, business plans, marketing, e-commerce, and financial considerations are explored.

33528 ■ *"Etextbook Space Heats Up" in Information Today (Vol. 28, November 2011, No. 10, pp. 10)*
Pub: Information Today, Inc.
Contact: Thomas H. Hogan, President
E-mail: ctuthill@infotoday.com
Ed: Paula J. Hane. **Description:** The use of etextbooks is expected to grow with the use of mobile devices and tablets. A new group of activists is asking students, faculty members and others to sign a petition urging higher education leaders to prioritize affordable textbooks or free ebooks over the traditional, expensive new books required for classes.

33529 ■ *"Etextbooks: Coming of Age" in Information Today (Vol. 28, September 2011, No. 8, pp. 1)*
Pub: Information Today, Inc.
Contact: Thomas H. Hogan, President
E-mail: ctuthill@infotoday.com
Ed: Amanda Mulvihill. **Description:** National average for textbooks costs was estimated at $1,137 annually at a 4-year public college for the 2010-2011 school

year. Amazon reported selling 105 etextbooks for every 100 print books, while Barnes and Noble announced that their etextbooks were outselling print 3 to 1.

33530 ■ *"Etiquette, Common Sense Often Lag Behind Smarter Devices" in Crain's Cleveland Business (Vol. 28, October 22, 2007, No. 42, pp. 21)*

Pub: Crain Communications Inc.

Ed: Chrissy Kadleck. **Description:** Discusses the importance of good etiquette in regards to electronic communication both within as well as outside the business world.

33531 ■ *"The Everything Store: Jeff Bezos and the Age of Amazon"*

Pub: Little, Brown and Company

Released: October 17, 2013. **Price:** $28.00. **Description:** Amazon.com started as a bookseller, a company delivering books through the mail. Today, the online store, offers a limitless selection of goods at competitively low prices. Profile of entrepreneur Jeff Bezos that outlines his endless pursuit of new markets and risky new ventures to transform retail.

33532 ■ *"Evolutionary Psychology in the Business Sciences"*

Pub: Springer Publishing Co.

Contact: Ursula Springer, President

Released: September 28, 2014. **Price:** $150.93. **Description:** All individuals operating in the business sphere share a common biological heritage, including consumers, employers, employees, entrepreneurs, or financial traders, to name a few. The evolutionary behavioral sciences and specific business contexts including marketing, consumer behavior, advertising, innovation and creativity and invention, intertemporal choice, negotiations, competition and cooperation in organizational settings, sex differences in workplace patterns, executive leadership, business ethics, store and office design, behavioral decision making, and electronic communications and commerce are all addressed.

33533 ■ *"F1 Makes Room(s) for Aspiring Entrepreneur" in Austin Business Journal (Vol. 31, July 1, 2011, No. 17, pp. 1)*

Pub: American City Business Journals

Ed: Vicky Garza. **Description:** Formula One fan and graphic designer Danielle Crespo cashes in on the June 17, 2012 racing event in Austin, Texas via hosting a Website that allows users to book hotel rooms. She invested less than $100 and long hours on this enterprise which now has 74,000-plus visitors.

33534 ■ *The Facebook Effect: The Inside Story of the Company That Is Connecting the World*

Pub: Simon & Shuster

Ed: David Kirkpatrick. **Released:** February 2011. **Price:** $17, paperback. **Description:** There's never been a Website like Facebook: more than 350 million people have accounts, and if the growth rate continues, by 2013 every Internet user worldwide will have his or her own page. No one's had more access to the inner workings of the phenomenon than Kirkpatrick, a senior tech writer at Fortune magazine. Written with the full cooperation of founder Mark Zuckerberg, the book follows the company from its genesis in a Harvard dorm room through its successes over Friendster and MySpace, the expansion of the user base, and Zuckerberg's refusal to sell. **Availability:** Print.

33535 ■ *The Facebook Era: Tapping Online Social Networks to Build Better Products, Reach New Audiences, and Sell More Stuff*

Ed: Clara Shih. **Price:** $24.99. **Description:** The '90s were about the World Wide Web of information and the power of linking Web pages. Today it's about the World Wide Web of people and the power of the social graph. Online social networks are fundamentally changing the way we live, work, and interact. They offer businesses immense opportunities to transform customer relationships for profit: opportuni-

ties that touch virtually every business function, from sales and marketing to recruiting, collaboration to executive decision-making, product development to innovation.

33536 ■ *"Facebook, Google, LinkedIn Line Up In Patent Case Before Supreme Court" in San Francisco Business Times (Vol. 28, March 28, 2014, No. 36)*

Pub: American City Business Journals

Released: March 28, 2014. **Description:** The U.S. Supreme Court is set to hear a case involving Alice Corporation Pty. Ltd. and CLS Bank International in a dispute over a patented computer-implemented escrow service. The case has larger implications to tech companies concerning whether a business method can be patented if it is made electronic.

33537 ■ *Facebook Marketing: Designing Your Next Marketing Campaign*

Pub: Pearson Education Que Publishing

Ed: Justin R. Levy. **Released:** Second Edition. **Price:** $19.99. **Description:** Detailed steps are given in order to develop, use, and create awareness for any business. The book provides detailed instructions, along with case studies from known brands, for launching marketing campaigns on Facebook. **Availability:** E-book.

33538 ■ *"Facebook Purchased Push Pop Press" in Information Today (Vol. 28, October 2011, No. 9, pp. 12)*

Pub: Information Today, Inc.

Contact: Thomas H. Hogan, President

E-mail: ctuthill@infotoday.com

Description: Facebook purchased Push Pop Press, a digital publishing company that developed a multi-touch interface for ebook publishing on the iPad.

33539 ■ *"Feds Finalize I-9 Form Rules Allowing Electronic Storage" in HR Specialist (Vol. 8, September 2010, No. 9, pp. 5)*

Pub: Capitol Information Group Inc.

Description: U.S. Department of Homeland Security issued regulations that give employers more flexibility to electronically sing and store I-9 employee verification forms.

33540 ■ *"Fifty Percent of Global Online Retail Visits Were to Amazon, eBay and Alibaba in June 2011" in Benzinga.com (October 29, 2011)*

Pub: Benzinga.com

Contact: Kyle Bazzy, President

Ed: Benzinga Staff. **Description:** Current statistics and future forecasts through the year 2015 for Amazon, eBay and Alibaba are explored.

33541 ■ *"Financo Panel Lauds Product, Online Marketing" in Home Textiles Today (Vol. 31, January 25, 2010, No. 3, pp. 1)*

Pub: Reed Elsevier Group plc Reed Business Information

Contact: Mark Kelsey, Chief Executive Officer

Ed: James Mammarella. **Description:** Overview of the Financo Annual Merchandising Industry Chief Executives Event during which there was much discussion on the merits of e-commerce, online marketing as well as the traditional methods of brand recognition and retailing.

33542 ■ *"Five Great Business Tools" in Black Enterprise (Vol. 44, June 2014, No. 10, pp. 24)*

Pub: Earl G. Graves Publishing Co. Inc.

Contact: Earl G. Graves, Jr., President

Released: June 2014. **Description:** Five products to help run a small business are listed: Legal Zoom Business Plan Attorney, provides attorney reviews of contracts and other legal documents; Shopify.com, is a fully hosted and customizable online shopping cart; SurveyMonkey.com, builds free surveys to conduct market research; Expensify.com handles credit card transactions, receipts, and invoices; and Intelius.com which allows companies to browse criminal records and other information for hiring purposes.

33543 ■ *"Five Low-Cost Home Based Startups" in Women Entrepreneur (December 16, 2008)*

Ed: Lesley Spencer Pyle. **Description:** During tough economic times, small businesses have an advantage over large companies because they can adjust to economic conditions more easily and without having to go through corporate red tape that can slow the implementation process. A budding entrepreneur may find success by taking inventory of his or her skills, experience, expertise and passions and utilizing those qualities to start a business. Five low-cost home-based startups are profiled. These include starting an online store, a virtual assistant service, web designer, sales representative and a home staging counselor.

33544 ■ *"Fly Phishing" in Canadian Business (Vol. 80, October 22, 2007, No. 21, pp. 42)*

Pub: Rogers Media Inc.

Contact: Tony Viner, President

Ed: Andy Holloway. **Description:** Symantec Corporation's report shows consumers and companies have effectively installed network defenses that prevent unwanted access. Phishing packages are readily available and are widely used. Other details of the Internet Security Threat Report are presented.

33545 ■ *"For Apple, It's Showtime Again" in Barron's (Vol. 90, August 30, 2010, No. 35, pp. 29)*

Pub: Barron's Editorial & Corporate Headquarters

Ed: Eric J. Savitz. **Description:** Speculations on what Apple Inc. will unveil at its product launch event are presented. These products include a possible new iPhone Nano, a new update to its Apple TV, and possibly a deal with the Beatles to distribute their songs over iTunes.

33546 ■ *"For MySpace, A Redesign to Entice Generation Y" in The New York Times (October 27, 2010, pp. B3)*

Pub: The New York Times Co.

Contact: Darline Jean, President

Ed: Miguel Helft. **Description:** MySpace is redesigning its Website in order to attract individuals within the Generation Y group.

33547 ■ *"ForeSee Finds Satisfaction On Web Sites, Bottom Line" in Crain's Detroit Business (Vol. 24, February 25, 2008, No. 8, pp. 3)*

Pub: Crain Communications Inc. - Detroit

Contact: Keith Crain, Chairman

Ed: Tom Henderson. **Description:** Ann Arbor-based ForeSee Results Inc. evaluates user satisfaction on Web sites. The company expects to see an increase of 40 percent in revenue for 2008 with plans to expand to London, Germany, Italy and France by the end of 2009.

33548 ■ *"Free Speech Vs. Privacy in Data Mining" in Information Today (Vol. 28, September 2011, No. 8, pp. 22)*

Pub: Information Today, Inc.

Contact: Thomas H. Hogan, President

E-mail: ctuthill@infotoday.com

Ed: George H. Pike. **Description:** The U.S. Constitution does not explicitly guarantee the right of privacy. Organizations and businesses that require obtaining and disseminating information can be caught in the middle of privacy rights. The long-term impact on data mining, Internet marketing, and Internet privacy issues are examined.

33549 ■ *Freelancing for Journalists*

Ed: Diana Harris. **Released:** January 1, 2010. **Price:** , $110.00. **Description:** Comprehensive guide showing the specific skills required for those wishing to freelance in newspapers, magazines, radio, television, and as online journalists.

33550 ■ *"Fresh Direct's Crisis" in Crain's New York Business (Vol. 24, January 14, 2008, No. 2, pp. 3)*

Ed: Lisa Fickenscher. **Description:** Freshdirect, an Internet grocery delivery service, finds itself under siege from federal immigration authorities, customers and labor organizations due to its employment practice of hiring illegals. At stake is the grocer's reputation as well as its ambitious growth plans, including an initial public offering of its stock.

33551 ■ *"Fresh Spots" in Entrepreneur (June 2014)*
Pub: Entrepreneur Media Inc.
Released: June 2014. **Description:** Zooppa is an advertising and digital marketing platform that takes advantage of crowdsourcing by setting up competitions for finding new talent. The platform allows its clients to save money that would otherwise be used in advertising campaigns. The Seattle-based company charges a flat fee of at least $50,000 for setting up and managing a contest. Clients retain the rights to all submissions, allowing them to gain access to videos and graphics that could be used for various presentations. Zooppa has expanded its workforce to 20 employees since its launch in 2008.

33552 ■ *"Friendly Ice Cream Corporation" in Ice Cream Reporter (Vol. 23, August 20, 2010, No. 9, pp. 8)*
Description: Friendly Ice Cream Corporation appointed Andrea M. McKenna as vice president of marketing and chief marketing officer.

33553 ■ *From Entrepreneur to Infopreneur: Make Money with Books, eBooks, and Information Products*
Pub: John Wiley & Sons Inc.
Contact: Stephen M. Smith, President
Ed: Stephanie Chandler. **Released:** November 2006. **Price:** $27.95, paperback; $18.99. **Description:** Infopreneurs sell information online in the forms of books, e-books, special reports, audio and video products, seminars, and more. **Availability:** PrintE-book.

33554 ■ *"The Future of Work" in Black Enterprise (Vol. 41, August 2010, No. 1, pp. 65)*
Pub: Earl G. Graves Publishing Co. Inc.
Contact: Earl G. Graves, Jr., President
Ed: Annya M. Lott. **Description:** Technology, globalization, and outsourcing will continue to shape the future of work. Social media is a means for small companies to market goods and services.

33555 ■ *"gdgt: The New Online Home for Gadget Fans" in Hispanic Business (July-August 2009, pp. 15)*
Pub: Hispanic Business Inc.
Contact: Jesus Chavarria, President
Ed: Jeremy Nisen. **Description:** Profile of the new online Website for gadget lovers. The site combines a leek interface, gadget database, and social networking-type features which highlights devices for the consumer.

33556 ■ *"Generation Y Chooses the Mobile Web" in PR Newswire (November 24, 2010)*
Pub: PR Newswire Association L.L.C.
Contact: David B. Armon, President
Description: Generation Y individuals between the ages of 18 - 27 use their mobile phones to browse the Internet more often than a desktop or laptop computer, according to a survey conducted by Opera, a Web browser company.

33557 ■ *"Geo-Location Technology Linking Stores, Shoppers" in Providence Business News (Vol. 29, May 5, 2014, No. 5, pp. 1)*
Pub: American City Business Journals
Released: May 5, 2014. **Description:** Jewelry maker, Alex and Ani LLC of Cranston, Rhode Island, outfitted their 40 retail stores in the U.S. with Bluetooth Low Energy systems called iBeacons to communicate directly with customers' mobile phones when they are in or near the store. The company claims that its stores have not received any negative feedback on hyperlocal messaging since the program started in summer 2013.

33558 ■ *"Get Paid and Get Moving" in Entrepreneur (Vol. 37, October 2009, No. 10, pp. 38)*
Description: GoPayments application from Intuit allows mobile telephones to process payments like credit card terminals. The application costs $19.95 a month and can be used on the Internet browsers of mobile telephones.

33559 ■ *"Get Sold On eBay" in Entrepreneur (Vol. 36, March 2008, No. 3, pp. 94)*
Pub: Entrepreneur Press
Contact: Perlman Neil, President
Ed: Marcia Layton Turner. **Description:** Entrepreneurs are increasingly using eBay to sell products. Some tips to start selling products through eBay include: starting with used items, developing a niche to sell specific products, and researching product pricing. Other tips with regard to starting an eBay business are covered.

33560 ■ *"Get Them Talking" in Entrepreneur (Vol. 36, February 2008, No. 2, pp. 50)*
Pub: Entrepreneur Press
Contact: Perlman Neil, President
Ed: Heather Clancy. **Description:** Yelp.com is an Internet search site that presents businesses across the U.S., sorted according to the number of customer reviews they have received. One to five stars are used by the reviewers, or yelpers, to rate businesses. Details on how the International Orange day spa benefited from Yelp are discussed.

33561 ■ *Getting Clients and Keeping Clients for Your Service Business: A 30-Day Step-By-Step Plan for Building Your Business*
Pub: Atlantic Publishing Co.
Contact: Amanda Miller, Manager
E-mail: amiller@atlantic-pub.com
Ed: M. D. Weems. **Price:** $24.95. **Description:** Tips are offered to help any small service business identify customers, brand and grow the business, as well as development of logos, brochures and Websites.

33562 ■ *"Ghouls, Goblins, and Harry Potter: Cashing In On Halloween" in Inc. (Vol. 33, October 2011, No. 8, pp. 24)*
Pub: Inc. Magazine
Ed: Darren Dahl. **Description:** Costume Craze, an online costume retailer reports $13.2 million in sales last year. Originally the family business started out as a software company called StaticAdvantage, but switched gears.

33563 ■ *Global E-Commerce: Impacts of National Environment and Policy*
Pub: Cambridge University Press
Contact: Richard Ziemacki, President
E-mail: rziemacki@cambridge.org
Released: September 2011. **Price:** $59, paperback; $111, hardback; $47. **Description:** Global assessment of the impact of e-business on companies as well as countries. **Availability:** PrintE-book; PDF.

33564 ■ *Global Electronic Business Research: Opportunities and Directions*
Pub: IGI Global
Contact: Dr. Mehdi Khosrow-Pour, President
Ed: Nabeel A.Y. Al-Qirim. **Released:** December 2005. **Price:** $89.95. **Description:** Importance electronic commerce research plays in small to medium-sized enterprises in various countries. **Availability:** Print.

33565 ■ *"Global Imagery in Online Advertisements" in Business Communication Quarterly (December 2007, pp. 487)*
Pub: Pine Forge Press
Contact: Blaise R. Simqu, President
Ed: Geraldine E. Hynes, Marius Janson. **Description:** Respondents from six countries were interviewed about their reactions to two online ads to determine cultural differences in understanding advertising elements. Universal appeals and cultural values determine the effectiveness of symbols in online advertising.

33566 ■ *"Google Places a Call to Bargain Hunters" in Advertising Age (Vol. 79, September 29, 2008, No. 36, pp. 13)*
Pub: Crain Communications Inc.
Contact: Rance Crain, President
Ed: Abbey Klaassen. **Description:** Google highlighted application developers who have created tools for its Android mobile phone in the device's unveiling; applications such as ShopSavvy and CompareEverywhere help shoppers to find bargains by allowing them to compare prices in their local areas and across the web.

33567 ■ *The Google Story: Inside the Hottest Business, Media, and Technology Success of Our Time*
Pub: Random Housing Publishing Group
Ed: David A. Vise, Mark Malseed. **Released:** September 23, 2008. **Price:** $16. **Availability:** Print.

33568 ■ *"Google's Next Stop: Below 350?" in Barron's (Vol. 88, March 10, 2008, No. 10, pp. 17)*
Pub: Dow Jones & Co., Inc.
Contact: Clare Hart, President
Ed: Jacqueline Doherty. **Description:** Share prices of Google Inc. are expected to drop from their level of $433 each to below $350 per share. The company is expected to miss its earnings forecast for the first quarter of 2008, and its continued aggressive spending on non-core areas will eventually bring down earnings.

33569 ■ *"Googly Eyed" in Entrepreneur (Vol. 36, February 2008, No. 2, pp. 48)*
Pub: Entrepreneur Press
Contact: Perlman Neil, President
Ed: Mike Hogan. **Description:** Linux has developed desktops that boot into the Google toolbar and applications. These desktops include: Zonbu, Everex gPCTC2502, and Asus Eee PC 4G mini laptop. Details on the applications of these desktops are discussed.

33570 ■ *"Government Says Self-Regulation of Online Privacy is Coming Up Short" in Advertising Age (Vol. 81, December 6, 2010, No. 43, pp. 1)*
Pub: Crain Communications Inc.
Contact: Rance Crain, President
Ed: Edmund Lee. **Description:** U.S. Federal Trade Commission and the Department of Commerce are concerned about the current state of digital privacy and stated that self-regulation has not been sufficient to date.

33571 ■ *"The Granary Gains Kudos" in San Antonio Business Journal (Vol. 28, July 18, 2014, No. 23, pp. 3)*
Pub: American City Business Journals
Released: July 18, 2014. **Description:** The Granary 'Cue & Brew in San Antonio, Texas was chosen as one of the top 30 barbeque restaurants in the U.S. by global online restaurant reservation company OpenTable. The list is part of the 2014 Diners' Choice Award program based on the opinions of verified OpenTable diners.

33572 ■ *"Grand Bohemian Hotel in Orlando, Fla. Takes Lead in Wedding Planning" in Benzinga.com (August 4, 2011)*
Pub: Benzinga.com
Contact: Kyle Bazzy, President
Ed: Benzinga Staff. **Description:** MAD-Marketing launched a newly-designed Website for the Grand Bohemian Hotel in Orlando, Florida. The site features the hotel's wedding vanity site to help target prospective couples planning their weddings.

33573 ■ *"Grooming Your Online Persona" in Women In Business (Vol. 62, June 2010, No. 2, pp. 36)*
Pub: American Business Women's Association
Contact: Lorie Burch, President
Ed: Diane Stafford. **Description:** Employees' use of online social networks could become a basis on how their employers, clients, or business partners would judge them. Personal details, pictures and other online data should be filtered to avoid inappropriate or uncomfortable situations and distinguish personal from professional or work life.

33574 ■ *Groundswell: Winning in a World Transformed by Social Technologies*
Pub: Harvard Business Review Press
Contact: Peter E. Walsh, Director
Ed: Charlene Li, Josh Bernoff. **Released:** June 09, 2011. **Price:** $14.95. **Description:** Individuals are using online social technologies such as blogs, social networking sites, YouTube, and podcasts to discuss products and companies, write their own news, and find their own deals. When consumers you've never

met are rating your company's products in public forums with which you have no experience or influence, your company is vulnerable. This book teaches the tools and data necessary to turn this treat into an opportunity. **Availability:** Print; E-book.

33575 ■ *Groundswell: Winning in a World Transformed by Social Technologies*
Pub: Harvard Business Review Press
Contact: Peter E. Walsh, Director
Ed: Charlene Li, Josh Bernoff. **Released:** 2008. **Price:** $29.95. **Description:** Corporate executives are struggling with a new trend: people using online social technologies (blogs, social networking sites, YouTube, podcasts) to discuss products and companies, write their own news, and find their own deals.

33576 ■ *"Group-Buying Site Hones In on Hispanics" in Austin Business Journal (Vol. 31, July 1, 2011, No. 17, pp. 1)*
Pub: American City Business Journals
Ed: Vicky Garza. **Description:** Descuentl Libre is a new group-buying site from Austin, Texas that targets the Hispanic market, offering discounts of practical items and family-friendly activities. The Hispanic market constitutes 17 percent of the U.S. population and spends $23 billion yearly online.

33577 ■ *Grown Up Digital: How the Net Generation Is Changing Your World*
Pub: The McGraw-Hill Companies
Ed: Don Tapscott. **Released:** October 24, 2008. **Price:** $27.95. **Description:** As baby boomers retire, business needs to understand what makes the Internet work for business.

33578 ■ *Guerrilla Marketing for the New Millennium*
Pub: Morgan James Publishing L.L.C.
Contact: Neil Gudovitz, Director
Ed: Jay Conrad Levinson. **Released:** September 01, 2005. **Description:** Steps to successfully market a small business on the Internet.

33579 ■ *Guerrilla Marketing: Put Your Advertising on Steroids*
Pub: Morgan James Publishing L.L.C.
Contact: Neil Gudovitz, Director
Ed: Jay Conrad Levinson. **Released:** September 2005. **Description:** Marketing concepts to successfully advertise any Internet business, featuring the ten most successful advertising campaigns of the 20th Century.

33580 ■ *"Haagen-Dazs Recruits Shop Owners through Facebook" in Ice Cream Reporter (Vol. 23, November 20, 2010, No. 12, pp. 1)*
Description: Haagen-Dazs Shoppe Company is using Facebook, the leading social media, to recruit new franchises.

33581 ■ *"Happy Blogging" in Black Enterprise (Vol. 38, January 2008, No. 6, pp. 47)*
Pub: Earl G. Graves Publishing Co. Inc.
Contact: Earl G. Graves, Jr., President
Ed: Dale Coachman. **Description:** Individual seeks advice for setting up a Website and starting a blog; Squarespace and Weebly both offer Web design.

33582 ■ *"Harlequin Leads the Way" in Marketing to Women (Vol. 22, July 2009, No. 7, pp. 1)*
Pub: EPM Communications Inc.
Contact: Ira Mayer, President
E-mail: imayer@epmcom.com
Description: Although the publishing industry has been slow to embrace new media options, the Internet is now a primary source for reaching women readers. Harlequin has been eager to court their female consumers over the Internet and often uses women bloggers in their campaigns strategies.

33583 ■ *"Harley-Davidson Moves to Unconventional Marketing Plan" in Business Journal-Milwaukee (Vol. 28, November 26,*
2010, No. 8, pp. A1)
Pub: Milwaukee Business Journal
Ed: Rich Rovito. **Description:** Harley Davidson Inc. hired Boulder, Colorado-based Victors & Spoils, an agency that specializes in crowdsourcing, to implement a new creative marketing model. Under the plan, Harley Davidson will draw on the ideas of its brand enthusiasts to help guide the brand's marketing direction.

33584 ■ *"Harness the Internet to Boost Equipment Sales" in Indoor Comfort Marketing (Vol. 70, July 2011, No. 7, pp. 24)*
Pub: Industry Publications Inc.
Contact: Shirleen Dorman, Editor
Ed: Richard Rutigliano. **Description:** Advice is given to increase HVAC/R equipment sales using the Internet.

33585 ■ *"Hatching Twitter: A True Story of Money, Power, Friendship, and Betrayal"*
Pub: Portfolio Hardcover
Released: November 5, 2013. **Price:** $17.00 paperback. **Description:** The first full coverage story covering the four founders of Twitter: Evan Williams, Biz Stone, Jack Dorsey, and Noah Glass, who went from ordinary engineers to wealthy celebrities and entrepreneurs. The story explores their pursuits for money, influence, publicity, and control as Twitter grew larger and more powerful.

33586 ■ *"Health-Care Highway" in Saint Louis Business Journal (Vol. 32, October 14, 2011, No. 7, pp. 1)*
Pub: Saint Louis Business Journal
Ed: Angela Mueller. **Description:** Around $2.6 billion will be invested in health care facilities along the Highway 64/40 corridor in St. Louis, Missouri. Mercy Hospital is planning to invest $19 million in a virtual care center. St. Elizabeth's Hospital on the other hand, will purchase 105 acres in the corridor.

33587 ■ *"Helping Customers Fight Pet Waste" in Pet Product News (Vol. 64, November 2010, No. 11, pp. 52)*
Pub: Bowtie Inc.
Ed: Sandy Robins. **Description:** Pet cleaning products manufacturers have been enjoying high sales figures by paying attention to changing pet ownership trends and environmental awareness. Meanwhile, the inclusion of user-friendly features in these products has also been boosted by the social role of pets and the media attention to pet waste. How manufacturers have been responding to this demand is explored.

33588 ■ *Here Come the Regulars: How to Run a Record Label on a Shoestring Budget*
Pub: Faber & Faber Inc.
Contact: Linda Rosenberg, Director
E-mail: linda.rosenberg@fsgbooks.com
Ed: Ian Anderson. **Released:** October 2009. **Price:** $15, paperback; $7.99. **Description:** Author, Ian Anderson launched his own successful record label, Afternoon Records when he was 18 years old. Anderson shares insight into starting a record label, focusing on label image, budget, blogging, potential artists, as well as legal aspects. **Availability:** PrintE-book.

33589 ■ *"Here's How You Boycott Amazon" in Puget Sound Business Journal (Vol. 35, June 13, 2014, No. 8, pp. 12)*
Pub: American City Business Journals
Released: June 13, 2014. **Description:** Critic, Kimberly Mills, says she boycotted Amazon.com because of its lack of corporate philanthropy and poor working conditions. She also boycotted the firm by purchasing directly from the listed company Websites when purchasing retail products, instead of buying directly from Amazon's site. Other online retailers are increasing customer services corporate social responsibility.

33590 ■ *"HER's: the Future is Free" in Benzinga.com (October 29, 2011)*
Pub: Benzinga.com
Contact: Kyle Bazzy, President
Ed: Benzinga Staff. **Description:** In order to create and maintain electronic health records that connects every physician and hospital it is essential to create a
reliable, easy-to-use, certified Web-based ambulatory ERH using an ad-supported model. eBay seems to be the company showing the most potential for improving services to physicians and consumers, but requires sellers to pay fees based upon sales price.

33591 ■ *"Highway 12 Invests in Crowdsourcing Platform" in Idaho Business Review (September 24, 2010)*
Pub: Dolan Media Newswires
Ed: Simon Shifrin. **Description:** The only venture capital fund in Idaho, Highway 12 Ventures, is funding Kapost a new company that helps news Websites, blogs and other online venues to pull content from a larger network of writers.

33592 ■ *"Hitting the E-Books" in Inc. (Vol. 33, September 2011, No. 7, pp. 36)*
Pub: Inc. Magazine
Ed: Shivani Vora. **Description:** Textbooks may be getting cheaper for college students now that they can use electronic textbooks that can be read on a laptop or tablet. The market is growing about 50 percent annually. Statistical data included.

33593 ■ *"Home Security In a Smartphone" in Denver Business Journal (Vol. 65, March 21, 2014, No. 55, pp. A12)*
Pub: American City Business Journals
Released: March 21, 2014. **Description:** Denver, Colorado-based startup Rentbits developed a home automation application (app) called Remotely that allows people to lock doors, switch the lights on and off, adjust thermostat and monitor home security through a smartphone. The app was built for the security of a 40-million household rental market and for vacation rentals in the U.S.

33594 ■ *"Hoover's Mobile, MobileSP Now Available" in Information Today (Vol. 26, February 2009, No. 2, pp. 29)*
Pub: Information Today, Inc.
Contact: Thomas H. Hogan, President
E-mail: ctuthill@infotoday.com
Description: Hoover's Inc. introduced its Hoover's Mobile for iPhone, BlackBerry and Windows Mobile smartphones along with Hoover's MobileSP for BlackBerry and Windows Mobile. Both products allow users to access customer, prospect, and partner information; analyze competitors; prepare for meetings; and find new opportunities. In addition, MobileSP adds one-click calling to executives, GPS-enabled location searches, advanced search and list building, and a custom call queue and a 'save to contacts' capabilities.

33595 ■ *"Horse Race: Putting the App in Apple" in Inc. (Vol. 30, November 2008, No. 11, pp.)*
Pub: Mansueto Ventures L.L.C.
Contact: John Koten, Chief Executive Officer
Ed: Nitasha Tiku. **Description:** Aftermarket companies are scrambling to develop games and widgets for Apple's iPhone. Apple launched a kit for developers interested in creating iPhone-specific software along with the App Store, and an iTunes spinoff. Profiles of various software programs that may be used on the iPhone are given.

33596 ■ *"Hospital Communication Goes Mobile" in Providence Business News (Vol. 29, July 7, 2014, No. 14, pp. 12)*
Pub: American City Business Journals
Released: July 7, 2014. **Description:** Software company, Care Thread, has designed a mobile health records application that allows providers to share patient e-medical records over a secure network. Care Thread signed a contract for the system with Eastern Connecticut Health Network and Boston's Brigham and Women's Hospital as well as a deal with health care management firm Beacon Partners Inc. to sell and implement the app across the U.S.

33597 ■ *Housecleaning Business: Organize Your Business - Get Clients and Referrals - Set Rates and Services*
Pub: Globe Pequot Press Inc.
Contact: Robert Irwin, Manager
E-mail: robert.irwin@globepequot.com
Ed: Laura Jorstad, Melinda Morse. **Released:** June 24, 2009. **Price:** $18.95, paperback. **Description:** This book shares insight into starting a houseclean-

ing business. It shows how to develop a service manual, screen clients, serve customers, select cleaning products, competition, how to up a home office, using the Internet to grow the business and offering green cleaning options to clients. **Availability:** Print.

33598 ■ *"How to Boost Your Super Bowl ROI" in Advertising Age (Vol. 80, December 7, 2009, No. 41, pp. 3)*
Pub: Crain's Communications
Contact: Keith Crain, Chairman
Ed: Abbey Klaassen. **Description:** Internet marketing is essential, even for the corporations that can afford to spend $3 million on a 30-second Super Bowl spot; last year, Super Bowl advertising reached an online viewership of 99.5 million while 98.7 million people watched the game on television validating the idea that public relations must go farther than a mere television ad campaign. Social media provides businesses with a longer shelf life for their ad campaigns. Advice is also given regarding ways in which to strategize a smart and well-thought plan for utilizing the online marketing options currently available.

33599 ■ *How to Get Rich on the Internet*
Pub: Morgan James Publishing L.L.C.
Contact: Neil Gudovitz, Director
Ed: Ted Ciuba. **Released:** October 01, 2003. **Description:** Interviews with successful Internet entrepreneurs provide insight into marketing products and services online using minimal investment. The importance of a sound marketing ad campaign using the Internet is discussed; maintaining a database and Website will automatically carry out business transactions daily. Suggestions for various types of businesses to run online are given.

33600 ■ *"How Good Advice 'Online' Can Attract Customers" in Indoor Comfort Marketing (Vol. 70, August 2011, No. 8, pp. 20)*
Pub: Industry Publications Inc.
Contact: Shirleen Dorman, Editor
Ed: Richard Rutigilano. **Description:** Online marketing tips for heating and cooling small businesses are explained.

33601 ■ *"How Google Did It: The Secrets of Google's Massive Success"*
Pub: CreateSpace
Contact: Daren Giles, President
Released: October 20, 2014. **Price:** $7.99 paperback. **Description:** Book 24 in the Best Business Books series, Google is profiled. The Internet Search Engine company provides Internet-related services and products such as online advertising, search, cloud computing, and software. The company's impact and growth is examined.

33602 ■ *"How I Did It: Best Buy's CEO On Learning to Love Social Media" in Harvard Business Review (Vol. 88, December 2010, No. 12, pp. 43)*
Pub: Harvard Business School Publishing
Ed: Brian J. Dunn. **Description:** Effective utilization of online social networks to enhance brand identity, connect with consumers, and address bad publicity scenarios is examined.

33603 ■ *"How I Did It: Jack Ma" in Inc. (January 2008, pp. 94-102)*
Pub: Gruner and Jahr USA Publishing Co.
Contact: J. Russell Denson, President
Ed: Rebecca Fannin. **Description:** Profile of Jack Ma, who started as a guide and interpreter for Western tourists in Hangzhou. Ma used the Internet to build Alibaba.com, China's largest business-to-business site and one of the hottest IPOs in years.

33604 ■ *How to Make Money with Social Media: An Insider's Guide to Using New and Emerging Media to Grow Your Business*
Pub: FT Press
Contact: Timothy C. Moore, Vice President
Ed: Jamie Turner, Reshma Shah. **Released:** Second Edition. **Price:** $34.99. **Description:** Marketers, executives, entrepreneurs are shown more effective ways to utilize Internet social media to make money.

This guide brings together both practical strategies and proven execution techniques for driving maximum value from social media marketing. **Availability:** E-book.

33605 ■ *"How to Make Your Website Really Sell" in Entrepreneur (Vol. 37, September 2009, No. 9, pp. 79)*
Pub: Entrepreneur Press
Contact: Perlman Neil, President
Ed: David Port. **Description:** Advice on how to succeed in Internet marketing is presented. Offering visitors purchase incentives on the home page is encouraged. Delivery of customized landing pages and content is also recommended.

33606 ■ *"How to Manage Successful Crowdsourcing Projects" in eWeek (September 29, 2010)*
Pub: Ziff Davis Enterprise
Ed: Lukas Biewald. **Description:** The advantages, challenges and pitfalls faced when using crowdsourcing to improve a business are outlined. Crowdsourcing helps to eliminate the need to rely on an internal workforce and the need to forecast task volume.

33607 ■ *"How to Market and Sell Your Art, Music, Photographs, and Handmade Crafts Online: Turn Your Hobby into a Cash Machine*
Pub: Atlantic Publishing Group, Inc.
Ed: Lee Rowley. **Price:** $24.95. **Description:** The book provides all the basics for starting and running an online store selling arts, crafts, photography or music. There are more than 300 Websites listed to help anyone market and promote their arts and/or crafts online.

33608 ■ *How to Open and Operate a Financially Successful Bookstore on Amazon and Other Web Sites: With Companion CD-ROM*
Pub: Atlantic Publishing Co.
Contact: Amanda Miller, Manager
E-mail: amiller@atlantic-pub.com
Released: December 01, 2010. **Price:** $39.95. **Description:** This book was written for every used book aficionado and bookstore owner who currently wants to take advantage of the massive collection of online resources available to start and run your own online bookstore business.

33609 ■ *How to Start a Home-Based Landscaping Business*
Pub: Globe Pequot Press Inc.
Contact: Robert Irwin, Manager
E-mail: robert.irwin@globepequot.com
Ed: Owen E. Dell. **Released:** January 06, 2010. **Price:** $18.95. **Description:** Guide to starting and running a successful home-based landscaping business, including tips for marketing on the Internet. **Availability:** Print.

33610 ■ *"How To Be a Twitter Ninja" in Canadian Business (Vol. 87, October 2014, No. 10, pp. 51)*
Pub: George Media Inc.
Released: October 2014. **Description:** Robert Palmer, public relations manager at WestJet, shares some rules when it comes to customer engagement on Twitter. He emphasizes the importance of communication when dealing with customer complaints as quickly as possible.

33611 ■ *"How To Get a Loan the Web 2.0 Way" in Black Enterprise (Vol. 41, December 2010, No. 5, pp. 23)*
Pub: Earl G. Graves Publishing Co. Inc.
Contact: Earl G. Graves, Jr., President
Ed: John Simons. **Description:** People are turning to online peer-to-peer network for personal loans as banks are lending less money.

33612 ■ *"How-To Workshops in St. Charles Teach Sewing, Styles" in St. Louis*

Post-Dispatch (September 14, 2010)
Pub: St. Louis Post-Dispatch L.L.C.
Contact: Kevin Mowbray, Publisher
Ed: Kalen Ponche. **Description:** Profile of DIY Style Workshop in St. Charles, Missouri, where sewing, designing and teaching is offered. The shop is home base for DIY Style, a Website created by mother and daughter to teach younger people how to sew.

33613 ■ *How to Use the Internet to Advertise, Promote, and Market Your Business or Web Site: With Little or No Money*
Pub: Atlantic Publishing Co.
Contact: Amanda Miller, Manager
E-mail: amiller@atlantic-pub.com
Ed: Bruce C. Brown. **Released:** Second Edition. **Price:** $24.95. **Description:** Information is given to help build, promote, and make money from your Website or brick and mortar store using the Internet, with minimal costs.

33614 ■ *"Hunhu Healthcare Gets Some Mayo Help" in Business Journal (Vol. 32, August 29, 2014, No. 14, pp. 4)*
Pub: American City Business Journals
Released: August 29, 2014. **Description:** Hunhu Healthcare Inc. has signed a licensing agreement with Mayo Clinic to develop mobile and Web applications that will enable patients to communicate with the company's network using social networking tools. The firm is expected to charge a monthly fee for the service.

33615 ■ *"I Hear You're Interested In a.." in Inc. (January 2008, pp. 40-43)*
Pub: Gruner and Jahr USA Publishing Co.
Contact: J. Russell Denson, President
Ed: Leah Hoffmann. **Description:** Four tips to help any small business generate sales leads online are examined.

33616 ■ *I'm on LinkedIn - Now What?*
Pub: Happy About
Contact: Mitchell Levy, Chief Executive Officer
Ed: Jason Alba. **Released:** Fourth Edition. **Price:** 19.95, paperback; $14.95. **Description:** Designed to help get the most out of LinkedIn, the popular business networking site and follows the first edition and includes the latest and great approaches using LinkedIn. With over 32 million members there is a lot of potential to find and develop relationships to help in your business and personal life, but many professionals find themselves wondering what to do once they sign up. This book explains the different benefits of the system and recommends best practices (including LinkedIn Groups) so that you get the most out of LinkedIn. **Availability:** PrintE-book; PDF.

33617 ■ *"Infectious Behavior" in Entrepreneur (May 2014)*
Pub: Entrepreneur Media Inc.
Released: May 2014. **Description:** Companies use different viral marketing strategies to create campaigns that compel consumers to share content in their social media platforms. Fast-food chain Chipolte Mexican Grill teamed up with Moonbot Studios for an animated short film to raise awareness of its long-running 'Food With Integrity' sustainable farming campaign. The 'Real Beauty Sketches' promotional video of Dove aims to emphasize the difference between how women view themselves and what others see. Evian used the concept of animated babies performing outlandish stunts in its advertisements.

33618 ■ *"Information Technology Changes Roles, Highlights Hiring Needs" in South Florida Business Journal (Vol. 34, February 14, 2014, No. 30, pp. 3)*
Pub: American City Business Journals
Released: February 14, 2014. **Description:** Results of the Steven Douglas Associates survey of 218 senior and mid-level information technology executives in South Florida are presented. About 75 percent of the respondents cited cloud services, mobile technologies, big data and enterprise reporting and planning as having the most profound impact on their roles. The challenges they face with the expected hiring growth are also examined.

33619 ■ *Information Technology for the Small Business: How to Make IT Work For Your Company*
Ed: T.J. Benoit. **Released:** June 2006. **Price:** $17.95. **Description:** Basics of information technology to help small companies maximize benefits are covered. Topics include pitfalls to avoid, email and Internet use, data backup, recovery and overall IT organization.

33620 ■ *"InnoCentive Announces Next Generation Crowdsourcing Platform"* in *Marketwired (June 15, 2010)*
Pub: COMTEX
Contact: Chip Brian, President
Description: InnoCentive, Inc., a world leader in open innovation, is launching InnoCentive@Work3, a third generation of its @Work enterprise platform for collaborative-driven innovation for companies. The product will help clients solve critical business and technical issues by tapping information both inside and outside of a company.

33621 ■ *"Innovation Central: Tech, Tweets, and Trolls"* in *Inc. (Vol. 36, September 2014, No. 7, pp. 102)*
Pub: Mansueto Ventures L.L.C.
Contact: John Koten, Chief Executive Officer
Released: September 2014. **Description:** Results of a survey regarding the ways small business is using technology to grow their businesses is presented. Information covers social media applications, government software patents, trends impacting small business, and the most innovative technology companies.

33622 ■ *Integration Marketing: How Small Businesses Become Big Businesses and Big Businesses Become Empires*
Pub: John Wiley & Sons Inc.
Contact: Stephen M. Smith, President
Ed: Mark Joyner. **Released:** May 2009. **Price:** $22.95, hardcover; $14.99. **Description:** Leading Internet marketing expert offers a marketing methodology to grow any business. **Availability:** PrintE-book.

33623 ■ *"Intentional Networking: Your Guide to Word of Mouth Marketing Greatness"*
Pub: CreateSpace
Contact: Daren Giles, President
Released: October 12, 2014. **Price:** $14.99 paperback. **Description:** Business owners and salespeople know the power of word of mouth marketing to increase sales. Networking, email communications, social media and referrals are techniques to help build revenue.

33624 ■ *"Internet Marketing and Social Media Knowledge Vital for SMBs"* in *Marketwired (November 24, 2009)*
Pub: COMTEX News Network Inc.
Contact: Chip Brian, President
Description: Small and medium-size businesses must learn to market themselves over the Internet in order to succeed and grow in today's marketplace. Web Marketing Today offers the largest source of the most important information concerning doing business on the Internet including e-commerce, email marketing and social networking opportunities.

33625 ■ *"Internet and Mobile Media"* in *MarketingMagazine (Vol. 115, September 27, 2010, No. 13, pp. 60)*
Pub: Rogers Publishing Ltd.
Contact: Edward S. Rogers, President
Description: Market data covering the Internet and mobile media in Canada is given.

33626 ■ *"Internet Translation Service Helps Burmese"* in *News-Sentinel (May 10, 2011)*
Pub: New-Sentinel
Ed: Ellie Bogue. **Description:** Catherine Kasper Place, Parkview Health Community Outreach, Allen County-Fort Wayne Department of Health and Advantage Health have partnered to help the Burmese Community in the area by providing an online service that links doctors' offices with translators in order to provide better healthcare.

33627 ■ *"Israeli Spam Law May Have Global Impact"* in *Information Today (Vol. 26, February 2009, No. 2, pp. 28)*
Pub: Information Today, Inc.
Contact: Thomas H. Hogan, President
E-mail: ctuthill@infotoday.com
Ed: David Mirchin. **Description:** Israels new law, called Amendment 40 of the Communications Law, will regulate commercial solicitations including those sent without permission via email, fax, automatic phone dialing systems, or short messaging technologies.

33628 ■ *"iSymmetry's Technological Makeover: Or, How a Tech Company Finally Grew Up and Discovered the World Wide Web"* in *Inc. (October 2007)*
Pub: Mansueto Ventures L.L.C.
Contact: John Koten, Chief Executive Officer
Ed: Elizabeth S. Bennett. **Description:** Profile of iSymmetry, an Atlanta, Georgia-based IT recruiting firm, covering the issues the company faces keeping its technology equipment up-to-date. The firm has devised a program that will replace its old server-based software systems with on-demand software delivered via the Internet, known as software-as-a-service. Statistical information included.

33629 ■ *"It's Back to Business for the Ravens"* in *Boston Business Journal (Vol. 29, July 29, 2011, No. 12, pp. 1)*
Pub: American City Business Journals, Inc.
Ed: Scott Dance. **Description:** The Baltimore Ravens football team has been marketing open sponsorship packages following the end of the National Football League lockout. Team officials are working to get corporate logos and slogans on radio and television commercials and online advertisements.

33630 ■ *"It's a Hit"* in *Entrepreneur (Vol. 36, March 2008, No. 3, pp. 110)*
Pub: Entrepreneur Press
Contact: Perlman Neil, President
Ed: John Jantsch. **Description:** Entrepreneurs use the Web to market business and keeping relevant content in the Website is important to address questions from customers. Other considerations in marketing businesses online include: interacting with site visitors, using Web applications for project collaboration and file storage, and encouraging customers to post reviews.

33631 ■ *"It's a New Game: Killerspin Pushes Table Tennis to Extreme Heights"* in *Black Enterprise (Vol. 37, October 2006, No. 3, pp. 73)*
Pub: Earl G. Graves Publishing Co. Inc.
Contact: Earl G. Graves, Jr., President
Ed: Bridget McCrea. **Description:** Profile of Robert Blackwell and his company Killerspin L.L.C., which is popularizing the sport of table tennis. Killerspin has hit $1 million in revenues due to product sales primarily generated through the company's website, magazines, DVDs, and event ticket sales.

33632 ■ *"Jab, Jab, Jab, Right Hook: How to Tell Your Story in a Noisy Social World"*
Pub: HarperBusiness
Released: November 26, 2014. **Price:** $29.99. **Description:** Author and social media expert shares advice on ways to connect with customers and beat the competition. Social media strategies for marketers and managers need to convert Internet traffic to sales. Communication is the key to online sales that are adapted to high quality social media platforms and mobile devices.

33633 ■ *"Jo-Ann Fabric and Craft Stores Joins ArtFire.com to Offer Free Online Craft Marketplace"* in *Marketwired (January 26, 2010)*
Pub: COMTEX News Network Inc.
Contact: Chip Brian, President
Description: Jo-Ann Fabric and Craft Stores has entered into a partnership with ArtFire.com which will provide sewers and crafters all the tools they need in order to make and sell their products from an online venue.

33634 ■ *"Joe Wikert, General Manager, O'Reilly Technology Exchange"* in *Information Today (Vol. 26, February 2009, No. 2, pp. 21)*
Ed: Jamie Babbitt. **Description:** Joe Wikert, general manager of O'Reilly Technology Exchange discusses his plans to develop a free content model that will evolve with future needs. O'Reilly's major competitor is Google. Wikert plans to expand the firm's publishing program to include print, online, and in-person products and services.

33635 ■ *"Johnson Publishing Expands: Moving Into Television and Internet To Extend Brand"* in *Black Enterprise (October 1, 2007)*
Pub: Earl G. Graves Publishing Co. Inc.
Contact: Earl G. Graves, Jr., President
Ed: Tamara E. Holmes. **Description:** Johnson Publishing Company has followed the lives of black families in both Ebony and Jet magazines. The media firm has expanded its coverage by developing entertainment content for television, the Internet and other digital arenas.

33636 ■ *"Keep Them Posted"* in *Entrepreneur (Vol. 35, October 2007, No. 10, pp. 39)*
Pub: Entrepreneur Press
Contact: Perlman Neil, President
Ed: Gwen Moran. **Description:** Survey by the Pew Internet and American Life Project found that 12 million American adults maintain blogs, which are created for personal and business reasons. Blogs are effective in giving a business a personal touch while informing the public about its operations and products. Tips on how to create an effective business blog are presented.

33637 ■ *"Kids, Computers and the Social Networking Evolution"* in *Canadian Business (Vol. 81, October 27, 2008, No. 18, pp. 93)*
Ed: Penny Milton. **Description:** Social networking was found to help educate students in countries like the U.S., Canada and Mexico. Schools that embrace social networking teach students how to use computers safely and responsibility in order to counter threats to children on the Internet.

33638 ■ *"Know the Facts About Natural Gas!"* in *Indoor Comfort Marketing (Vol. 70, August 2011, No. 8, pp. 26)*
Pub: Industry Publications Inc.
Contact: Shirleen Dorman, Editor
Description: AEC Activity Update is presented on the American Energy Coalition's Website.

33639 ■ *"Kodak Offers Cloud-Based Operating Option"* in *American Printer (Vol. 128, June 1, 2011, No. 6)*
Pub: Penton Media Inc.
Description: Kodak partnered with VMware to offer its first Virtual Operating Environment option for Kodak Unified Workflow Solutions. The new feature enables cost savings, increased efficiency and failover protection.

33640 ■ *"Kuno Creative to Present B2B Social Media Campaign Webinar"* in *Entertainment Close-Up (August 25, 2011)*
Pub: Close-Up Media
Description: Kuno Creative, an inbound marketing agency, will host Three Steps of a Successful B2B Social Media Campaign. The firm is a provider of Website development, branding, marketing strategy, public relations, Internet marketing, and inbound marketing.

33641 ■ *"Last Founder Standing"* in *Conde Nast Portfolio (Vol. 2, June 2008, No. 6, pp. 124)*
Ed: Kevin Maney. **Description:** Interview with Amazon CEO Jeff Bezos in which he discusses the economy, the company's new distribution center and the hiring of employees for it, e-books, and the overall vision for the future of the firm.

33642 ■ *"Lavante, Inc. Joins Intersynthesis, Holistic Internet Marketing Company"* in

Marketwired (November 5, 2009)
Pub: COMTEX News Network Inc.
Contact: Chip Brian, President
Description: Lavante, Inc., the leading provider of on-demand vendor information and profit recovery audit solutions for Fortune 1000 companies has chosen Intersynthesis, a new holistic Internet marketing firm, as a provider of pay for performance services. Lavante believes that Intersynthesis' expertise and knowledge combined with their ability to develop integrated strategies, will help them fuel more growth.

33643 ■ *"Lawyers Object to New Online Court Fees" in Sacramento Business Journal (Vol. 31, August 8, 2014, No. 24, pp. 3)*
Pub: American City Business Journals
Released: August 8, 2014. **Description:** Lawyers and consumer advocates have complained that the Sacramento County Superior Court's new fee system for online access to online court records hinders access to justice. However, court administrators argue that the charging of fees will only help offset the online record system's maintenance costs.

33644 ■ *"Legislating the Cloud" in Information Today (Vol. 28, October 2011, No. 9, pp. 1)*
Pub: Information Today, Inc.
Contact: Thomas H. Hogan, President
E-mail: ctuthill@infotoday.com
Description: Internet and telecommunications industry leaders are asking for legislation to address the emerging market in cloud computing. Existing communications laws do not adequately govern the modern Internet.

33645 ■ *"Lights, Camera, Action: Tools for Creating Video Blogs" in Inc. (Volume 32, December 2010, No. 10, pp. 57)*
Pub: Inc. Magazine
Ed: John Brandon. **Description:** A video blog is a good way to spread company news, talk about products, and stand out among traditional company blogs. New editing software can create two- to four-minute blogs using a webcam and either Windows Live Essentials, Apple iLife 2011, Powerdirector 9 Ultra, or Adobe Visual Communicator 3.

33646 ■ *"LivingSocial's New 'Glue" in Washington Business Journal (Vol. 33, May 2, 2014, No. 2, pp. 10)*
Pub: American City Business Journals
Released: May 2, 2014. **Description:** LivingSocial Inc. CFO, John Bax, shares his views on the confluence of forces that shaped the company's first quarter results. Bax reports the company is pouring resources into the creation of a new retail merchant solution platform to help market products and services. Bax named the project Glue because it is geared to encouraging customer loyalty to merchants along with repeat business.

33647 ■ *"Looking Out for the Little Guys" in Black Enterprise (Vol. 38, October 1, 2007, No. 3, pp. 58)*
Pub: Earl G. Graves Publishing Co. Inc.
Contact: Earl G. Graves, Jr., President
Description: Biz Tech-Connect is a Web portal that offers free online and social networking, along with four modules that help small businesses with marketing and advertising, communications and mobility, financial management, and customer relationship management.

33648 ■ *"Looking To Leap?" in Black Enterprise (Vol. 38, January 2008, No. 6, pp. 64)*
Pub: Earl G. Graves Publishing Co. Inc.
Contact: Earl G. Graves, Jr., President
Ed: Tennille M. Robinson. **Description:** Websites and organizations providing resources for any young entrepreneur wishing to start a new business are outlined.

33649 ■ *"A Love of Likes" in Boston Business Journal (Vol. 31, July 8, 2011, No. 24, pp. 1)*
Pub: Boston Business Journal
Ed: Lisa van der Pool. **Description:** An increasing number of companies in Boston, Massachusetts have been keen on getting Facebook 'likes' from people.

Business owners realize that Facebook 'likes' could generate sales and based on some studies, equate to specific dollar values.

33650 ■ *Low-Budget Online Marketing for Small Business*
Pub: International Self-Counsel Press, Limited
Ed: Holly Berkley. **Released:** October 15, 2010. **Price:** $20.95. **Description:** Low-cost, effective online marketing tips for small companies selling products or services over the Internet. **Availability:** Print.

33651 ■ *Low-Budget Online Marketing for Small Business*
Pub: Self-Counsel Press Inc.
Ed: Holly Berkley. **Released:** October 15, 2010. **Price:** C$21.95; 12.99. **Description:** Low-budget advertising campaigns are presented to help market any small business. **Availability:** PDFElectronic publishing.

33652 ■ *"Luxe Hotels on a Budget" in Inc. (Volume 32, December 2010, No. 10, pp. 60)*
Pub: Inc. Magazine
Ed: Adam Baer. **Description:** Off & Away Website allows users to vie for discounted hotel rooms at more than 100 luxury properties. To compete, uses buy $1 bids and each time an individual bids the price of the room goes up by 10 cents.

33653 ■ *"MaggieMoo's Ice Cream and Treatery" in Ice Cream Reporter (Vol. 23, September 20, 2010, No. 10, pp. 7)*
Description: MaggieMoo's Ice Cream and Treatery has launched a new Website where visitors can learn about the brands newest ice cream innovations.

33654 ■ *Mail Order in the Internet Age*
Pub: Morgan James Publishing L.L.C.
Contact: Neil Gudovitz, Director
Ed: Ted Ciuba. **Price:** $19.95. **Description:** Direct response market, or mail order, for marketing and selling a product or service is discussed, with emphasis on how direct marketing compares favorably to other methods in terms of speed, ease, profitability, and affordability. Advice is given for writing ads; seminars to attend; and newsletters, mailing lists and magazines in which to subscribe. **Availability:** E-book.

33655 ■ *"Making It Click: Annual Ranking Of the Best Online Brokers" in Barron's (Vol. 88, March 17, 2008, No. 11, pp. 31)*
Pub: Dow Jones & Co., Inc.
Contact: Clare Hart, President
Ed: Theresa W. Carey. **Description:** Listing of 23 online brokers that are evaluated based on their trade experience, usability, range of offerings, research amenities, customer service and access, and costs. TradeStation Securities takes the top spot followed by thinkorswim by just a fraction.

33656 ■ *"Managing Yourself: What's Your Personal Social Media Strategy?" in Harvard Business Review (Vol. 88, November 2010, No. 11, pp. 127)*
Pub: Harvard Business School Publishing
Ed: Soumitra Dutta. **Description:** Identification of four distinct sectors and how they interrelate to social media is given. The sectors are personal and private; professional and private; personal and public; and professional and public. Appropriate topics and types of social media are discussed for each.

33657 ■ *Marketing 2.0: Bridging the Gap between Seller and Buyer through Social Media Marketing*
Pub: Wheatmark Inc.
Ed: Bernie Borges. **Released:** August 15, 2009. **Price:** $22.95, paperback. **Description:** Winning strategies to attract people to your company and your employees using social media site on the Internet are outlined. **Availability:** Print.

33658 ■ *"Marketing in the Digital World: Here's How to Craft a Smart Online Strategy"*

in Black Enterprise (Vol. 40, July 2010, No. 12, pp. 47)
Pub: Earl G. Graves Publishing Co. Inc.
Contact: Earl G. Graves, Jr., President
Ed: Sonya A. Donaldson. **Description:** Social media is an integral part of any small business plan in addressing marketing, sales, and branding strategies.

33659 ■ *"Marketing On Location" in Denver Business Journal (Vol. 65, April 4, 2014, No. 47, pp. A4)*
Pub: American City Business Journals
Released: April 4, 2014. **Description:** A growing number of local software companies in Denver, Colorado are working to make location-based technology useful for consumers, brands and retailers. Roximity is expanding its location-based app initially installed in Ford, Honda, and Subaru cars into mobile phones. PlaceWise Media combines in-store and online marketing for clients like malls and grocery stores.

33660 ■ *"Marketing Scholarship 2.0" in Journal of Marketing (Vol. 75, July 2011, No. 4, pp. 225)*
Pub: American Marketing Association
Contact: Lucille Pointer, President
Ed: Richard J. Lutz. **Description:** A study of the implications of changing environment and newer collaborative models for marketing knowledge production and dissemination is presented. Crowdsourcing has become a frequently employed strategy in industry. Academic researchers should collaborate more as well as the academe and industry, to make sure that important problems are being investigated.

33661 ■ *"Marketing To Go" in Entrepreneur (June 2014)*
Pub: Entrepreneur Media Inc.
Released: June 2014. **Description:** Mobile applications can help entrepreneurs improve their marketing strategies and business productivity. The 30/30 application helps users increase productivity by helping them organize and manage their tasks. The Cal application represents an upgrade to a smartphone's built-in calendar, particularly with its integration with contacts and social media accounts. The Pocket applications allows users to save interesting articles, videos and other online content for later reading or viewing. The Buffer application enables users to manage their social media accounts from a single interface.

33662 ■ *Marketing in a Web 2.0 World - Using Social Media, Webinars, Blogs, and More to Boost Your Small Business on a Budget*
Pub: Atlantic Publishing Co.
Contact: Amanda Miller, Manager
E-mail: amiller@atlantic-pub.com
Ed: Peter VanRysdam. **Released:** June 01, 2010. **Price:** $24.95. **Description:** Web 2.0 technologies have leveled the playing field for small companies trying to boost their presence by giving them an equal voice against larger competitors. Advice is given to help target your audience using social networking hubs.

33663 ■ *Marketing Without Money for Small and Midsize Businesses: 300 FREE and Cheap Ways to Increase Your Sales*
Pub: Halle House Publishing
Contact: Nicholas E. Bade, Publisher
Ed: Nicholas E. Bade. **Released:** July 2005. **Price:** $16.95. **Description:** Three hundred practical low-cost or no-cost strategies to increase sales, focusing on free advertising, free marketing assistance, and free referrals to the Internet.

33664 ■ *Marketing Your Product*
Pub: Self-Counsel Press Inc.
Released: September 15, 2009. **Price:** $21.95. **Description:** Tips for marketing any product in today's competitive consumer environment. One chapter focuses on using the Internet as a marketing tool.

33665 ■ *"Mattel's Got a Monster Holiday Hit, But Will Franchise Have Staying Power?" in Advertising Age (Vol. 81, December 6, 2010, No. 43)*

Pub: Crain Communications Inc.

Contact: Rance Crain, President

Ed: Beth Snyder Bulik. **Description:** Monster High transmedia play expands beyond dolls to merchandise, apparel and entertainment.

33666 ■ *Maximum Marketing, Minimum Dollars: The Top 50 Ways to Grow Your Small Business*

Pub: Kaplan Books

Ed: Kim T. Gordon. **Released:** 2006. **Price:** $18.95; C$24. **Description:** Marketing tips to increase sales are presented. Small business owners will learn to maximize marketing with 50 innovative and affordable methods, including online marketing.

33667 ■ *"Media Giant Remakes Itself: Job Cuts Signal Journal Sentinel's Focus on New Products" in Business Journal-Milwaukee (Oct. 12, 2007)*

Pub: American City Business Journals

Ed: Rich Kirchen. **Description:** Milwaukee Journal Sentinel is reducing its workforce by offering separation pay, and is willing to consider layoffs if the separation program fails. The downsizing is a result of lowered revenue, which was caused by the decline in printed news demand and increase in online competition. Strategies that the Journal Sentinel are employing, such as developing new products, to increase revenue are presented.

33668 ■ *"Media Terminology" in MarketingMagazine (Vol. 115, September 27, 2010, No. 13, pp. 80)*

Pub: Rogers Publishing Ltd.

Contact: Edward S. Rogers, President

Description: Media terminology is provided.

33669 ■ *"Media Wars" in Canadian Business (Vol. 83, August 17, 2010, No. 13-14, pp. 32)*

Ed: Thomas Watson. **Description:** Canada's newspaper industry has changed considerably with The Glove, under Philip Crawley, positioned as corporate Canada's newspaper of record. However, the National Post under Paul Godfrey is making a comeback by re-launching it as the flagship of a national chain of so-called digital first news organizations.

33670 ■ *"Message to the Masses"*

Pub: BK Royston Publishing

Released: October 10, 2014. **Price:** $15.00 paperback. **Description:** Information is offered to help explore ways to get your message to your audience so they not only hear your words, they understand their meaning. Marketing tips for using social media, blogs, the elevator pitch and more are featured.

33671 ■ *"Microsoft Is Cleaning Up the Cloud" in Puget Sound Business Journal (Vol. 35, August 29, 2014, No. 19, pp. 7)*

Pub: American City Business Journals

Released: August 29, 2014. **Description:** Microsoft is forming a partnership with research organizations to conduct pilot projects on new forms of energy for its expanding cloud data centers. One project involves placing fuel cells directly into server racks that is said to be 40 percent more energy efficient than using power off the grid.

33672 ■ *"Microsoft Releases Office Security Updates" in Mac World (Vol. 27, November 2010, No. 11, pp. 66)*

Pub: IDG Consumer & SMB

Ed: David Dahlquist. **Description:** Office for Mac and Mac Business Unit are Microsoft's pair of security- and stability-enhancing updates for Office 2008 and Office 2004. The software will improve the stability and compatibility and fixes vulnerabilities that would allow attackers to overwrite Mac's memory with malicious code.

33673 ■ *Million Dollar Website: Simple Steps to Help You Compete with the Big Boys-Even*

on a Small Business Budget

Pub: Prentice Hall Press

Contact: Susan Petersen Kennedy, President

Ed: Lori Culwell. **Released:** May 09, 2010. **Price:** $19.95, Paperback. **Description:** Resource for any small business owner wishing to build a successful Website in order to compete with big box stores.

33674 ■ *"MindLeaders' Online Training Courses Come to ePath Learning" in Information Today (Vol. 26, February 2009, No. 2, pp. 4)*

Description: MindLeaders has partnered with ePath Learning to provide clients with over 2,200 new online courses. ePath's integrated Learning Management Service (iLMS) allows organizations to create online training programs for employees.

33675 ■ *"Mobility: So Happy Together" in Entrepreneur (Vol. 35, October 2007, No. 10, pp. 64)*

Pub: Entrepreneur Press

Contact: Perlman Neil, President

Ed: Heather Clancy. **Description:** Joshua Burnett, CEO and founder of 9ci, uses index cards to keep track of what he needs to do despite the fact that he has a notebook computer, cell phone and PDA. Kim Hahn, a media entrepreneur, prefers jotting her ideas down in a spiral notebook, has a team that would organize her records for her, and a personal assistant that would keep track of changes to her schedule. Reasons why these entrepreneurs use old-fashioned methods along with new technology are given.

33676 ■ *"The Moment as Currency" in Entrepreneur (September 2014)*

Pub: Entrepreneurial Press

Released: September 2014. **Description:** Young entrepreneur, Brian Wong, recalls how he came up with the idea of launching the mobile rewards network Kiip in 2010. The 23-year-old believed brands could take advantage of the achievements reached by mobile application users by offering rewards through his mobile rewards network. the company's network of 1,000 brands pay on a cost-per-engagement (CPE) basis and earns from 30 cents to $3 per CEP. Wong insists that his technology is not limited to just the smartphone or the application.

33677 ■ *"MoneyGram Hopes Digital Push Will Click With Customers" in Dallas Business Journal (Vol. 37, July 4, 2014, No. 43, pp. 17)*

Pub: American City Business Journals

Released: July 4, 2014. **Description:** Reports on MoneyGram's recent release of a digital monitoring system, which will allow it to work more closely with customers, is profiled. This digital monitoring system will aggregate data from social media platforms and enable the company to identify customer needs and trends across the money transfer industry. It will help MoneyGram outshine its rivals in the money transfer business.

33678 ■ *"More Leading Retailers Using Omniture Conversion Solutions to Boost Sales and Ecommerce Performance" in Marketwired (September 22, 2009)*

Pub: COMTEX News Network Inc.

Contact: Chip Brian, President

Description: Many retailers are utilizing Omniture conversion solutions to improve the performance of their ecommerce businesses; recent enhancements to Omniture Merchandising and Omniture Recommendations help clients drive increased conversion to their Internet ventures.

33679 ■ *"More Leading Retailers Using Omniture Conversion Solutions to Boost Sales and Ecommerce Performance" in Marketwired (September 22, 2009)*

Pub: COMTEX News Network Inc.

Contact: Chip Brian, President

Description: Many retailers are utilizing Omniture conversion solutions to improve the performance of their ecommerce businesses; recent enhancements to Omniture Merchandising and Omniture Recommendations help clients drive increased conversion to their Internet ventures.

33680 ■ *"Moving Into the Digital Space: How New Media Create Opportunities for Minorities" in Black Enterprise (February 2008)*

Pub: Earl G. Graves Publishing Co. Inc.

Contact: Earl G. Graves, Jr., President

Ed: Aisha Sylvester. **Description:** The Internet is becoming an alternative to traditional sources of entertainment; nearly 16 percent of American households who use the Internet watch television online. One such Internet show features a variety of African American lifestyles.

33681 ■ *"My Favorite Tool for Managing Expenses" in Inc. (Volume 32, December 2010, No. 10, pp. 60)*

Pub: Inc. Magazine

Ed: J.J. McCorvey. **Description:** Web-based service called Expensify is outlined. The service allows companies to log expenses while away from the office using the service's iPhone application.

33682 ■ *"Nationwide Bank Ready for December Conversion" in Business First-Columbus (October 15, 2007, pp. A1)*

Pub: American City Business Journals, Inc.

Ed: Adrian Burns. **Description:** Nationwide Bank will increase marketing to its customers, including the 45,000 that came from the acquisition of Nationwide Federal Credit Union in December 2006. Upgrading its online banking system and Website will bring the company and its services closer to clients. The influence of the insurance industry on the bank's marketing strategy is also examined.

33683 ■ *"Navigate to Better Direct Response Messaging Through Search Marketing" in DM News (Vol. 32, January 18, 2010, No. 2, pp. 26)*

Ed: Mark Simon. **Description:** Important lessons to apply when utilizing Internet marketing schemes include telling your customers you have what they want to buy, provide them with discounts or ways to save additional money and drive them to a customized destination like an Online store.

33684 ■ *Nerds on Wall Street: Math, Machines and Wired Markets*

Pub: John Wiley & Sons Inc.

Contact: Stephen M. Smith, President

Ed: David J. Leinweber. **Released:** May 2009. **Price:** $39.95, hardcover; $25.99. **Description:** The history of technology and how it will transform investing and trading on Wall Street is outlined. **Availability:** PrintE-book.

33685 ■ *"Net Profits: Get a Social Life" in Entrepreneur (Vol. 35, October 2007, No. 10, pp. 140)*

Pub: Entrepreneur Press

Contact: Perlman Neil, President

Ed: Amanda C. Kooser. **Description:** Social networking sites such as Facebook and MySpace have millions of users, a sign that social networking is a growing industry. One way to enter this industry is target marketing, like Med3Q, a site for health-conscious individuals had done. How Med3q is earning through online advertising and sponsors is explained.

33686 ■ *"Netflix Gets No Respect" in Barron's (Vol. 89, July 27, 2009, No. 30, pp. 26)*

Pub: Dow Jones & Co., Inc.

Contact: Clare Hart, President

Ed: Tiernan Ray. **Description:** Netflix met expectations when they announced their second quarter sales but their shares still fell by almost 10 percent. Analysts say their entry into the 'streaming video' business is a mixed bag since customers are increasingly buying the cheaper monthly plan and this is dragging the economics of the business.

33687 ■ *"Netting Degrees: More Professionals Continuing Their Education Online" in Hispanic Business (September 2007, pp. 62, 64)*

Ed: Hildy Medina. **Description:** Traditional universities and private institutions offer online courses to professionals wishing to further their education.

33688 ■ *"The New Basics of Marketing"* in *Inc.* (February 2008, pp. 75-81)
Ed: Leigh Buchanan. **Description:** New tools for marketing a business or service include updating or upgrading a Website, using email or texting, or advertising on a social Internet network.

33689 ■ *"The New Face of Social Media"* in *New Generation Latino Consortium* (December 2010)
Pub: Hispanic Business Inc.
Contact: Jesus Chavarria, President
Ed: Gary Fackler. **Description:** Latina bloggers carve out a new niche in social media that helps preserve their unique cultural identities.

33690 ■ *"The New Guard"* in *Entrepreneur* (Vol. 36, February 2008, No. 2, pp. 46)
Pub: Entrepreneur Press
Contact: Perlman Neil, President
Ed: Amanda C. Kooser. **Description:** A natural language search engine is being developed by Powerset for better online searching. Zannel Inc. offers Instant Media Messaging platform, which allows for social networking using phones. Ning is an online platform that allows users to customize and control their social networks.

33691 ■ *"New Sales. Simplified: The Essential Handbook for Prospecting and New Business Development"*
Pub: AMACOM Publishing
Released: September 4, 2012. **Price:** $17.95 paperback. **Description:** The constant flow of new accounts is essential for any small business to grow and thrive. A proven formula for prospecting; customer-focused selling; proactive telephone calling that leads to face-to-face meetings; the use of email, voicemail, and social media; prevent the buyer's anti-salesperson response; build a rapport; winning sales; communicating with clients; plan time for business development activities; and more.

33692 ■ *"New Wave of Business Security Products Ushers in the Kaspersky Anti-Malware Protection System"* in *Internet Wire* (October 26, 2010)
Pub: COMTEX
Contact: Chip Brian, President
Description: Kaspersky Anti-Malware System provides anti-malware protection that requires minimal in-house resources for small businesses. The system offers a full range of tightly integrated end-to-end protection solutions, ensuring unified protection across an entire network, from endpoint and mobile device protection to file server, mail server, network storage and gateway protection. It provides flexible centralized management, immediate threat visibility and a level of responsiveness not seen in other anti-malware approaches.

33693 ■ *"A New Way to Tell When to Fold 'Em"* in *Barron's* (Vol. 88, July 7, 2008, No. 27, pp. 27)
Pub: Dow Jones & Co., Inc.
Contact: Clare Hart, President
Ed: Theresa W. Carey. **Description:** Overview of the Online trading company SmartStops, a firm that aims to tell investors when to sell the shares of a particular company. The company's Web site categorizes stocks as moving up, down, or sideways, and calculates exit points for individual stocks based on an overall market trend.

33694 ■ *"The Next Dimension"* in *Entrepreneur* (Vol. 35, November 2007, No. 11, pp. 62)
Pub: Entrepreneur Press
Contact: Perlman Neil, President
Ed: Heather Clancy. **Description:** Entrepreneurs can make use of virtual worlds like Second Life to promote their products or services. Details and cautions on the use of virtual worlds are discussed.

33695 ■ *"The Next Frontier"* in *San Francisco Business Times* (Vol. 28, February 28, 2014, No. 32, pp. 4)
Pub: American City Business Journals
Released: February 28, 2014. **Description:** The growth of the electronic payments business in San Francisco, California has captured the interest of venture capitalists, entrepreneurs, and other investors. Social media companies like Facebook and Google are expected to expand into electronic payments. Telecommunication companies are also investing in promising startups and joint ventures.

33696 ■ *"Next-Level E-Commerce"* in *Entrepreneur* (June 2014)
Pub: Entrepreneur Media Inc.
Released: June 2014. **Description:** BloomReach's SNAP software enables consumers to see the products they want upon arriving at an e-commerce Website. The software does this by evaluating the users' intent and preferences based on previous site usage. The enterprise-level software, which costs retailers at least $7,500/month, aims to use big data to help consumers choose products based on their intent. The cloud-based service indexes every page on a client's site and automatically generates appropriate content for visitors. The use of machine learning reduces lag time between application and positive results.

33697 ■ *"NMG To Merge Store, Online Leadership Team"* in *Dallas Business Journal* (Vol. 37, April 11, 2014, No. 31, pp. 6)
Pub: American City Business Journals
Released: April 11, 2014. **Description:** Neiman Marcus Group is planning to merge its retail stores and online management teams as part of a restructuring effort. The marketing plan is expected to boost the company's physical and online presence. The company will also open a flagship store in New York City.

33698 ■ *"'Nobody Knows What To Do' To Make Money on the Web"* in *Barron's* (Vol. 88, March 17, 2008, No. 11, pp. 40)
Pub: Dow Jones & Co., Inc.
Contact: Clare Hart, President
Ed: Mark Veverka. **Description:** Attendees of the South by Southwest Interactive conference failed to get an insight on how to make money on the Web from former Walt Disney CEO Michael Eisner when Eisner said there's no proven business model for financing projects. Eisner said he finances his projects with the help of his connections to get product-placement deals.

33699 ■ *"Nowspeed and OneSource to Conduct Webinar: How to Develop Social Media Content That Gets Results"* in *Marketwired* (December 14, 2009)
Pub: COMTEX News Network Inc.
Contact: Chip Brian, President
Description: OneSource, a leading provider of global business information, and Nowspeed, an Internet marketing agency, will conduct a webinar titled 'How to Develop Social Media Content That Gets Results' in order to provide marketers insight into how to develop and optimize effective social media content to get consumer results that translate into purchases and lead generation.

33700 ■ *"No. 83: Tech Service of iCracked"* in *Inc.* (Vol. 36, September 2014, No. 7, pp. 108)
Pub: Mansueto Ventures L.L.C.
Contact: John Koten, Chief Executive Officer
Released: September 2014. **Description:** California-based iCracked employs 600 technicians who repair mobile devices on demand. The company also sells replacement parts and do-it-yourself repair kits online, ranging in price from $9 to $120, as well as instructional videos.

33701 ■ *"Obama Plan May Boost Maryland Cyber Security"* in *Boston Business Journal* (Vol. 29, May 20, 2011, No. 2, pp. 1)
Pub: American City Business Journals, Inc.
Ed: Scott Dance. **Description:** May 12, 2011 outline of the cyber security policies of President Obama may improve the cyber security industry in Maryland as the state is home to large defense and intelligence activities. Details of the proposed policies are discusses as well as their advantages to companies that deal in developing cyber security plans for other companies.

33702 ■ *"Old Spice Guy (Feb.-July 2010)"* in *Canadian Business* (Vol. 83, August 17, 2010, No. 13-14, pp. 23)
Pub: Rogers Media Inc.
Contact: Tony Viner, President
Ed: Andrew Potter. **Description:** Old Spice Guy was played by ex-football player and actor Isaiah Mustafa who made the debut in the ad for Old Spice Red Zone body wash that was broadcast during Super Bowl XLIV in February 2010. Old Spice Guy has become one of social marketing success but was cancelled in July when online viewership started to wane.

33703 ■ *"Oliver Russell Acquiring Social Good Network"* in *Idaho Business Review* (August 29, 2014)
Pub: Dolan Co.
Contact: James P. Dolan, President
Released: August 29, 2014. **Description:** Oliver Russell, owner of a Boise advertising firm, is acquiring the assets of startup Social Good Network, an online fundraising firm that was turned down for additional funding beyond its seed funding. Details of the deal and future plans are discussed.

33704 ■ *"On Beyond Powerpoint: Presentations Get a Wake-Up Call"* in *Inc.* (November 2007, pp. 58-59)
Pub: Mansueto Ventures L.L.C.
Contact: John Koten, Chief Executive Officer
Ed: Michael Fitzgerald. **Description:** New software that allows business presentations to be shared online are profiled, including ProfCast, audio podcasts for sales, marketing, and training; SmartDraw2008, software that creates professional graphics; Dimdim, an open-Web conferencing tool; Empressr, a hosted Web service for creating, managing, and sharing multimedia presentations; Zentation, a free tool that allows users to watch slides and a videos of presenter; Spresent, a Web-based presentation tool for remote offices or conference calls.

33705 ■ *"The One Thing You Must Get Right When Building a Brand"* in *Harvard Business Review* (Vol. 88, December 2010, No. 12, pp. 80)
Pub: Harvard Business School Publishing
Ed: Patrick Barwise, Sean Meehan. **Description:** Four uses for new media include: communicating a clearly defined customer promise, creating trust via delivering on the promise, regularly improving on the promise, and innovating past what is familiar.

33706 ■ *"Online All the Time"* in *Retail Merchandiser* (Vol. 51, July-August 2011, No. 4, pp. 18)
Pub: Phoenix Media Corporation
Description: Ecommerce sales are rising at a steady pace and for cross-channel retailers it is boosting sales in the weak economy. Online sales are expected to reach $188 billion in 2011, boasting a 13.7 rate of growth.

33707 ■ *"Online Book Sales Surpass Bookstores"* in *Information Today* (Vol. 28, September 2011, No. 8, pp. 11)
Pub: Information Today, Inc.
Contact: Thomas H. Hogan, President
E-mail: ctuthill@infotoday.com
Ed: Cindy Martine. **Description:** Online book sales outpaced bookstore purchases in the United States, signaling a shift in the US book industry. Statistical data included.

33708 ■ *"Online Directories: Your Silent Sales Staff"* in *South Florida Business Journal* (Vol. 34, June 20, 2014, No. 48, pp. 14)
Pub: American City Business Journals
Released: June 20, 2014. **Description:** The benefits of using online business directories as an extension of the physical sales personnel are explained. Business owners who plan to use online directories to their advantage need to check their listings and links at least once a year and whenever there is a change to the business.

33709 ■ *"Online Forex Broker Tadawul FX Intros Arabic Website" in Entertainment Close-Up (June 23, 2011)*
Pub: Close-Up Media
Description: Online forex broker, Tadawul FX, launched its Arabic language Website, noting that the Middle East is a key market for the investment firm.

33710 ■ *"Online Pet Medication Store Supports Free Vaccinations for Cats" in Marketwired (August 31, 2010)*
Pub: COMTEX
Contact: Chip Brian, President
Description: Pethealth Inc., The Petango Store will help to support The Humane Society of Tampa Bay's efforts by offering free feline vaccinations for the cat's entire lifetime that is adopted between September 1, 2010 and February 28, 2010. The cat must be one year or older at time of adoption.

33711 ■ *"Online Postings Really Influence Older Women" in Marketing to Women (Vol. 22, July 2009, No. 7, pp. 8)*
Pub: EPM Communications Inc.
Contact: Ira Mayer, President
E-mail: imayer@epmcom.com
Description: Women over the age of 55 are more likely to be swayed to purchase a product by referrals from others, including Online postings by strangers. Another key influence is associated with the brand's ability to address their lifestyle needs.

33712 ■ *"Online Reverse Auctions: Common Myths Versus Evolving Reality" in Business Horizons (September-October 2007, pp. 373)*
Pub: Elsevier Technology Publications
Ed: Tobias Schoenherr, Vincent A. Mabert. **Price:** $35.95. **Description:** Common misconceptions about online reverse auctions are examined based on the data obtained from 30 case study companies. Strategies for maintaining a good buyer-supplier relationship and implications for firms and supply managers are presented.

33713 ■ *"Online Security Crackdown" in Chain Store Age (Vol. 84, July 2008, No. 7, pp. 46)*
Pub: Lebhar-Friedman Inc.
Contact: Roger Friedman, President
Ed: Samantha Murphy. **Description:** Online retailers are beefing up security on their Websites. Cyber thieves use retail systems in order to gain entry to consumer data. David's Bridal operates over 275 bridal showrooms in the U.S. and has a one-stop wedding resource for new brides planning weddings.

33714 ■ *"Online Translation Service Aids Battlefield Troops" in Product News Network (August 30, 2011)*
Pub: Thomas Publishing Company L.L.C.
Contact: C. T. Holst-Knudsen, President
E-mail: hholstknudsen@thomaspublishing.com
Description: Linquist online service, LinGo Link provides real-time interpreter support to military troops overseas. Interpreters skilled in multiple languages and dialects are used in various areas and in multiple instances without requiring physical presence. The service is available through commercial cellular or WiFi services or tactical communications network. The system accommodates exchange of audio, video, photos, and text during conversations via smartphones and mobile peripheral devices.

33715 ■ *"The Open Mobile Summit Opens in San Francisco Today: John Donahoe CEO eBay to Keynote" in Benzinga.com (November 2, 2011)*
Pub: Benzinga.com
Contact: Kyle Bazzy, President
Ed: Benzinga Staff. **Description:** eBay's CEO, John Donahoe was keynote speaker at the 4th Annual Open Mobile Summit held in San Francisco, California. eBay is one of the 130 companies participating as speakers at the event.

33716 ■ *"Open Source Solutions for Small Business Problems*
Pub: Charles River Media Inc.
Contact: Azad Ajamian, President
Ed: John Locke. **Released:** May 15, 2004. **Price:** $39.95. **Description:** Open source software provides solutions to many small business problems such as tracking electronic documents, scheduling, accounting functions, managing contact lists, and reducing spam. **Availability:** Print.

33717 ■ *"Optimize.ca Supplies Free Online Financial Advice" in Entertainment Close-Up (October 9, 2010)*
Description: Optimize.ca provides free online financial advice, focusing on instant savings for their mutual funds and other banking products while improving rates of return and overall financial health.

33718 ■ *"Outsourcing: Information Technology, Original Equipment Manufacturer, Leo, Oursourcing, Offshoring Research Network, Crowdsourcing*
Released: May 01, 2010. **Price:** $14.14. **Description:** Chapters include information for outsourcing firms and how to maintain an outsourcing business.

33719 ■ *"Over and Out" in Entrepreneur (Vol. 36, February 2008, No. 2, pp. 25)*
Pub: Entrepreneur Press
Contact: Perlman Neil, President
Ed: Chris Penttila. **Description:** Ben Wolin, owner of Waterfront Media that operates wellness and health Websites, had employed the services of human resource consulting firm to advise him in regard to overtime pay. Guidelines on how to avoid overtime pay violations are presented.

33720 ■ *"Pagetender LLC Releases Website Design Package for HubSpot Users" in Marketwired (September 30, 2009)*
Pub: COMTEX News Network Inc.
Contact: Chip Brian, President
Description: Profile of Pagetender LLC, a Certified HubSpot partner, who announced a Website Design Package marketed specifically for HubSpot Owner and Marketer users. This packaged was developed for small to medium sized businesses that want a website designed or their current site redesigned on HubSpot's Content Management System. Companies that would like a more robust site have the option of adding Flash development, ecommerce and photo galleries.

33721 ■ *"P&G to Mine E-Commerce Potential" in Business Courier (Vol. 26, September 18, 2009, No. 21, pp. 1)*
Pub: American City Business Journals, Inc.
Contact: Whitney Shaw, President
Ed: Lisa Biank Fasig. **Description:** Procter & Gamble (P&G) is looking to turn the hits to the company's Websites into increased sales. The program will include a shop now option to track all emerging sales.

33722 ■ *"Pandora's Long Strange Trip: Online Radio That's Cool, Addictive, Free, and--Just Maybe--A Lasting Business" In Inc. (October 2007, pp. 100-106, 108)*
Pub: Mansueto Ventures L.L.C.
Contact: John Koten, Chief Executive Officer
Ed: Stephanie Clifford. **Description:** Profile of the Internet radio company, Pandora, whose founder, Tim Westergren discusses his business plans to fruition. The station has over eight million loyal listeners, advertisers and a database of 500,000 songs.

33723 ■ *"Paper a la Carte" in American Printer (Vol. 128, June 1, 2011, No. 6)*
Pub: Penton Media Inc.
Description: Blurb, the online publishing platform, launched ProLine which features Mohawk Superfine and Mohawk proPhoto papers. ProLine papers offer two finishes: Pearl Photo and Uncoated.

33724 ■ *"PC Connection Acquires Cloud Software Provider" in New Hampshire Business Review (Vol. 33, March 25, 2011,*

No. 6, pp. 8)
Pub: Business Publications Inc.
Description: Merrimack-based PC Connection Inc. acquired ValCom Technology, a provider of cloud-based IT service management software. Details of the deal are included.

33725 ■ *"PD Targeting Audience Growth with Web Initiatives" in Crain's Cleveland Business (Vol. 30, June 29, 2009, No. 25, pp. 1)*
Pub: Crain Communications Inc.
Ed: Kathy Ames Carr. **Description:** Plain Dealer's publisher C.Z. Egger has his news organization focusing on online offerings in order to build circulation of its newspaper. The 167-year-old paper boasts 1,305,203 readers in print and online weekly.

33726 ■ *"People; E-Commerce, Online Games, Mobile Apps" in Advertising Age (Vol. 80, October 19, 2009, No. 35, pp. 14)*
Pub: Crain's Communications
Contact: Keith Crain, Chairman
Ed: Nat Ives. **Description:** Profile of People Magazine and the ways in which the publisher is moving its magazine forward by exploring new concepts in a time of declining newsstand sales and advertising pages; among the strategies are e-commerce such as the brand People Style Watch in which consumers are able highlight clothing and jewelry and then connect to retailers' sites and a channel on Taxi TV, the network of video-touch screens in New Your City taxis.

33727 ■ *"People; E-Commerce, Online Games, Mobile Apps: This Isn't Your Mom's People" in Advertising Age (Vol. 80, October 19, 2009, No. 35)*
Pub: Crain's Communications
Contact: Keith Crain, Chairman
Ed: Nat Ives. **Description:** Profile of People Magazine and the ways in which the publisher is moving its magazine forward by exploring new concepts in a time of declining newsstand sales and advertising pages; among the strategies are e-commerce such as the brand People Style Watch in which consumers are able highlight clothing and jewelry and then connect to retailers' sites and a channel on Taxi TV, the network of video-touch screens in New Your City taxis.

33728 ■ *"The Perfect Fit" in Small Business Opportunities (October 2007)*
Pub: Harris Publications Inc.
Description: Launched in 2004, Jigsaw provides an online database of more than 5.5 million business contacts and company information for entrepreneurs.

33729 ■ *"Plan Your Future with My Next Move" in Occupational Outlook Quarterly (Vol. 55, Summer 2011, No. 2, pp. 22)*
Pub: U.S. Department of Labor Bureau of Labor Statistics
Contact: Philip L. Rones, Manager
E-mail: rones.philip@bls.gov
Description: My Next Move, an online tool offering a variety of user-friendly ways to browse more than 900 occupations was created by the National Center for O NET Development for the US Department of Labor's Employment and Training Administration. Clicking on an occupation presents a one-page profile summarizing key information for specific careers.

33730 ■ *Planet Google: One Company's Audacious Plan to Organize Everything We Know*
Pub: Simon and Schuster Inc.
Contact: Carolyn Reidy, President
E-mail: carolyn.reidy@simonandschuster.com
Ed: Randall Stross. **Released:** September 2008. **Price:** $10.93. **Description:** The book examines Google, the leader in Internet search engines. **Availability:** E-book.

33731 ■ *"Play By Play: These Video Products Can Add New Life to a Stagnant Website" in*

Black Enterprise (Vol. 41, December 2010, No. 5)
Pub: Earl G. Graves Publishing Co. Inc.
Contact: Earl G. Graves, Jr., President
Ed: Marcia Wade Talbert. **Description:** Web Visible, provider of online marketing products and services, cites video capability as the fastest-growing Website feature for small business advertisers. Profiles of various devices for adding video to a Website are included.

33732 ■ "Points of Light Sells MissionFish to eBay" in Non-Profit Times (Vol. 25, May 15, 2011, No. 7, pp. May 15, 2011)
Pub: NPT Publishing Group Inc.
Contact: John D. McIlquham, President
E-mail: johnmci2@earthlink.net
Description: eBay purchased MissionFish, a subsidiary of Points of Light Institute for $4.5 million. MissionFish allows eBay sellers to give proceeds from sales to their favorite nonprofit organization and helps nonprofits raise funds by selling on eBay.

33733 ■ "The Power of Negative Thinking" in Inc. (Volume 32, December 2010, No. 10, pp. 43)
Pub: Inc. Magazine
Ed: Jason Fried. **Description:** A Website is software and most businesses have and need a good Website to generate business. Understanding for building a powerful Website is presented.

33734 ■ "The Power of Online" in Advertising Age (Vol. 85, October 13, 2014, No. 21, pp. 4)
Pub: Crain Communications Inc. - Detroit
Contact: Keith Crain, Chairman
Released: October 13, 2014. **Description:** According to Shop.org, online sales could increase by as much as 11 percent this holiday season. Retailers are not only focusing on when customers will start holiday shopping, but whether they will use online stores or shop at brick-and-mortar stores. Many retailers are expanding their online services using digital showrooms on their Websites.

33735 ■ The Power of Social Networking: Using the Whuffie Factor to Build Your Business
Ed: Tara Hunt. **Released:** May 04, 2010. **Price:** $15. **Description:** This book shows how any small business can harness its power by increasing whuffie, the store of social capital that is the currency of the digital world. Blogs and social networks such as Facebook and Twitter are used to help grow any small firm.

33736 ■ "Powering Intelligent Commerce" in Computer Business Week (August 28, 2014, pp. 20)
Pub: NewsRX
Contact: Susan E. Hasty, Publisher
Released: August 28, 2014. **Description:** OrderDynamics, a new global brand created by eCommera, is profiled. The firm will continue to provide an integrated suite of software-as-a-service (SaaS) big data products and service that power intelligent commerce for retailers and brands around the world. Details of the integration of the new brand are included.

33737 ■ "The Pre-Tail Revolution" in Canadian Business (Vol. 87, October 2014, No. 10, pp. 10)
Pub: George Media Inc.
Released: October 2014. **Description:** A number of products that succeeded in security support from crowdfunding platforms, Kickstarter and Indiegogo, and those that failed are presented. Included are the do-it-yourself computer kit Kano, Bluetooth speakers Edge.sound, three-dimensional printer The Micro, Coolest Cooler the insect control device BugASalt, hexacopter Hexo+, and the Ubuntu Edge.

33738 ■ "Pro Livestock Launches Most Comprehensive Virtual Sales Barn for Livestock and Breed Stock" in Benzinga.com

(October 29, 2011)
Pub: Benzinga.com
Contact: Kyle Bazzy, President
Ed: Benzinga Staff. **Description:** Pro Livestock Marketing launched the first online sales portal for livestock and breed stock. The firm has designed a virtual sales barn allowing individuals to purchase and sell cattle, swine, sheep, goats, horses, rodeo stock, show animals, specialty animals, semen and embryos globally. It is like an eBay for livestock and will help ranchers and farmers grow.

33739 ■ "Promote Your Business Through New Media" in Business Week (November 5, 2009)
Pub: The McGraw-Hill Companies Inc.
Contact: Henry Hirschberg, President
Ed: Karen E. Klein. **Description:** Traditional public relations strategies are becoming more and more outdated due to the rapid shift in Internet marketing opportunities. Ideas for marketing your company online are presented.

33740 ■ "Promoting Academic Programs Using Online Videos" in Business Communication Quarterly (December 2007, pp. 478)
Pub: Pine Forge Press
Contact: Blaise R. Simqu, President
Ed: Thomas Clark, Julie Stewart. **Description:** Xavier Entrepreneurial Center successfully used online videos to promote the effectiveness of its academic programs. Online videos are a cost-effective way of publicizing academic programs.

33741 ■ "Promotional Marketing: How to Create, Implement & Integrate Campaigns That Really Work"
Pub: Kogan Page US
Contact: Spencer Smith, Director
Released: September 28, 2014. **Price:** $34.95 paperback. **Description:** Promotional marketing helps companies stay ahead of competition to gain new customers and keep existing ones. The guide includes new developments in the field of marketing, examining the use of digital media such as mobile devices and phones, interactive television, and Web-based advertising, as well as ways to research and evaluate promotional marketing campaigns.

33742 ■ "Promotions Create a Path to Better Profit" in Pet Product News (Vol. 64, December 2010, No. 12, pp. 1)
Pub: Bowtie Inc.
Ed: Joan Hustace Walker. **Description:** Pet store retailers can boost small mammal sales by launching creative marketing and promotions such as social networking and adoption days.

33743 ■ "Protect Your Domain Name From Cybersquatters" in Idaho Business Review (September 1, 2014)
Pub: Dolan Co.
Contact: James P. Dolan, President
Released: September 1, 2014. **Description:** Cybersquatting is the practice of registering, trafficking in or using domain names with the intent to profit from the goodwill of recognizable trade names or trademarks of other companies. Companies can protect their Website domain by following these steps: register domain names, promptly renew registrations, maintain proper records, obtain additional top-level domains, and monitor your site for cybersquatters.

33744 ■ "Providers Ride First Wave of eHealth Dollars" in Boston Business Journal (Vol. 31, June 10, 2011, No. 20, pp. 1)
Pub: Boston Business Journal
Ed: Julie M. Donnelly. **Description:** Health care providers in Massachusetts implementing electronic medical records technology started receiving federal stimulus funds. Beth Israel Deaconess Medical Center was the first hospital to qualify for the funds.

33745 ■ "Punta Gorda Interested in Wi-Fi Internet" in Charlotte Observer (February 1, 2007)
Ed: Steve Reilly. **Description:** Punta Gorda officials are developing plans to provide free wireless Internet services to businesses and residents.

33746 ■ "Puppy Power: Using a New Tool Called a Widget To Boost Your Brand" in Inc. (November 2007, pp. 55-56)
Pub: Mansueto Ventures L.L.C.
Contact: John Koten, Chief Executive Officer
Ed: Dan Brody. **Description:** Widgets look like small television screens posted on Websites, blogs or desktops with a company's brand or logo. It can display any type of information or image, including sports scores, news headlines, weather reports, animated graphics, or a slide show. Profiles of CarDomain Network, Babystrology, DailyPuppy.com, AnchorBank and more are included.

33747 ■ "Putting SogoTrade Through Its Paces" in Barron's (Vol. 89, July 27, 2009, No. 30, pp. 27)
Pub: Dow Jones & Co., Inc.
Contact: Clare Hart, President
Ed: Theresa W. Carey. **Description:** SogoTrade options platform streams options quotes in real time and lets users place a trade in several ways. The site also features notable security tactics and is a reasonable choice for bargain-seekers. OptionsXpress' Xtend platform lets users place trades and get real time quotes.

33748 ■ "Q&A Patrick Pichette" in Canadian Business (Vol. 81, October 13, 2008, No. 17, pp. 6)
Ed: Andrew Wahl. **Description:** Patrick Pichette finds challenge in taking over the finances of an Internet company that has a market cap of about $140 billion. He feels, however, that serving as Google's chief financial officer is nothing compared to running Bell Canada Enterprises (BCE). Pichette's other views on Google and BCE are presented.

33749 ■ "Quickoffice's MobileFiles Pro App Enables Excel Editing On-the-Go" in Information Today (Vol. 26, February 2009, No. 2, pp. 31)
Description: Quickoffice Inc. introduced MobileFiles Pro, which features editable Microsoft Office functionality for the iPone and iPod touch. The application allows users to edit and save Microsoft Excel files in .xls format, transfer files to and from PC and Mac desktops via Wi-Fi, and access and synchronize with Apple MobileMe accounts.

33750 ■ "Real-Time Computer-Mediated Communication: Email and Instant Messaging Simulation" in Business Communication Quarterly (December 2007, pp. 466)
Pub: Pine Forge Press
Contact: Blaise R. Simqu, President
Ed: Amy Newman. **Description:** Technology-based simulation for business students to respond to emails and instant messages is presented. The simulation allows students to handle volume business correspondence at work with organizational context and under real-word business situations.

33751 ■ "Reaping Social-Media Rewards" in Canadian Business (Vol. 83, July 20, 2010, No. 11-12, pp. 19)
Pub: Rogers Media Inc.
Contact: Tony Viner, President
Ed: Lyndsie Bourgon. **Description:** Foursquare is a social network which provides benefits such as discounts to users who show loyalty to a business or a brand. One marketing executive believes Foursquare is a good platform for loyalty programs and is an inexpensive alternative to Aeroplan.

33752 ■ "Recovery 2.0: 'A Work in Progress'" in Tampa Bay Business Journal (Vol. 30, December 18, 2009, No. 52, pp. 3)
Pub: American City Business Journals
Ed: Margaret Cashill. **Description:** The debut of the Recovery.gov 2.0 version has raised questions regarding the Website's price tag, which will cost nearly $18 million. Tampa, Florida-based GSL Solutions Inc. president Michael Gaines believes the Websites created with existing technologies tend to cost less than custom development. The difference between Recovery.org and Recovery.gov are explained.

33753 ■ "Recruiting 2.0" in Entrepreneur (Vol. 35, November 2007, No. 11, pp. 100)
Pub: Entrepreneur Press
Contact: Perlman Neil, President
Ed: Andrea Cooper. **Description:** Technology is becoming a tool to help small companies find the best employees. Firms can look into social networking sites to see recommendations from the applicants' colleagues. Tips on how to select the employees online are listed.

33754 ■ "Regional Talent Network Unveils Employment Web Site" in Crain's Cleveland Business (Vol. 30, June 1, 2009, No. 21, pp. 11)
Pub: Crain Communications Inc.
Ed: Chuck Soder. **Description:** Regional Talent Network launched WhereToFindHelp.org, a Website designed to act as a directory of all Northeast Ohio resources that can help employers recruit and job seekers look for positions. The site also lists organizations offering employment and training services.

33755 ■ "Reinventing Marketing to Manage the Environmental Imperative" in Journal of Marketing (Vol. 75, July 2011, No. 4, pp. 132)
Pub: American Marketing Association
Contact: Lucille Pointer, President
Ed: Philip Kotler. **Description:** Marketers must now examine their theory and practices due to the growing recognition of finite resources and high environmental costs. Companies also need to balance more carefully their growth goals with the need to purse sustainability. Insights on the rise of demarketing and social marketing are also given.

33756 ■ "Remodeled Stores Help Fabric Retailer Stitch Up Profit Growth" in Investor's Business Daily (January 7, 2010, pp. A06)
Pub: Investor's Business Daily, Inc.
Ed: Marilyn Much. **Description:** Overview of the successful plan implemented by Darrell Webb for Jo-Ann Fabric and Craft stores to stimulate growth and generate revenue; changes include better inventory controls and remodeling; statistical data included.

33757 ■ "Remote Control: Working From Wherever" in Inc. (February 2008, pp. 46-47)
Ed: Ryan Underwood. **Description:** New technology allows workers to perform tasks from anywhere via the Internet. Profiles of products to help connect to your office from afar include, LogMein Pro, a Web-based service that allowsaccess to a computer from anywhere; Xdrive, an online service that allows users to store and swap files; Basecamp, a Web-based tools that works like a secure version of MySpace; MojoPac Freedom, is software that allows users to copy their computer's desktop to a removable hard drive and plug into any PC; WatchGuard Firebox X Core e-Series UTM Bundle, hardware that blocks hackers and viruses while allowing employees to work remotely; TightVNC, a free open-source software that lets you control another computer via the Internet.

33758 ■ "Renren Partners With Recruit to Launch Social Wedding Services" in Benzinga.com (June 7, 2011)
Pub: Benzinga.com
Contact: Kyle Bazzy, President
Ed: Benzinga Staff. **Description:** Renren Inc. and Recruit Company Ltd. partnered to build a wedding social media catering to engaged couples and newlyweds in China. The platform will integrate online wedding related social content and offline media such as magazine and wedding exhibitions.

33759 ■ "Renren Partnership With Recruit to Launch Social Wedding Services" in Benzinga.com (June 7, 2011)
Pub: Benzinga.com
Contact: Kyle Bazzy, President
Ed: Benzinga Staff. **Description:** Renren Inc., the leading real name social networking Internet platform in China has partnered with Recruit Company Limited, Japan's largest human resource and classified media group to form a joint venture to build a wedding social media catering to the needs of engaged couples and newlyweds in China.

33760 ■ "Rep. Loretta Sanchez Holds a Hearing on Small Business Cyber Security" in Political/Congressional Transcript Wire (July 29, 2010)
Pub: CQ Roll Call
Description: U.S. House Committee on Armed Services, Subcommittee on Terrorism, Unconventional Threats and Capabilities held a hearing on small business cyber security innovation.

33761 ■ "Research and Markets Adds Report: Asian - Internet Market" in Health and Beauty Close-Up (January 19, 2010)
Description: Overview of Research and Markets new report regarding Internet marketing and e-commerce in the Asian region; statistical data included.

33762 ■ "Research and Markets Adds Report: USA - Internet Market - Analysis, Statistics and Forecasts" in Wireless News (January 15, 2010)
Description: According to Research and Markets new report concerning the United State's Internet market, e-commerce and Online advertising are expected to recover strongly in 2010.

33763 ■ "Retail Product Management: Buying and Merchandising"
Pub: Routledge
Contact: Kevin Bradley, President
E-mail: kbradley@taylorandfrancis.com
Released: October 24, 2014. **Price:** $130.00. **Description:** Due to the rise in Internet use, retailers are facing challenges associated with more informed buyers, technological advances, and the competitive environment. Retail ethics are also examined.

33764 ■ "The Return of the Infomercial" in Canadian Business (Vol. 83, September 14, 2010, No. 15, pp. 19)
Pub: Rogers Media Inc.
Contact: Tony Viner, President
Ed: James Cowan. **Description:** Infomercials or direct response ads have helped some products succeed in the marketplace. The success of infomercials is due to the cheap advertising rates, expansion into retail stores and the products' oddball appeal. Insights into the popularity of infomercial products on the Internet and on television are given.

33765 ■ "Ric Elis/Dan Feldstein" in Charlotte Business Journal (Vol. 25, December 31, 2010, No. 41, pp. 6)
Ed: Ken Elkins. **Description:** Charlotte, North Carolina-based Internet marketing firm Red Ventures has grown significantly. General Atlantic has purchased stakes in Red Ventures.

33766 ■ "Ride-Share Field Has New Player" in Providence Business News (Vol. 29, April 21, 2014, No. 3, pp. 1)
Pub: American City Business Journals
Released: April 21, 2014. **Description:** Lyft is Providence, Rhode Island's newest ride-sharing service. State officials continue to look for ways to regulate Internet vehicle services, taxis and limousines. Nearly all of Lyft's drivers are part-time employees using their own personal vehicles.

33767 ■ "Rise Interactive, Internet Marketing Agency, Now Offers Social Media Services" in Marketwired (November 4, 2009)
Pub: COMTEX News Network Inc.
Contact: Chip Brian, President
Description: Profile of Rise Interactive, a full-service Internet marketing agency which has recently added social media to its list of offerings; the agency touts that its newest service gives their clients the power to have ongoing communication with current and potential customers on the sites they are most actively visiting.

33768 ■ "Ritchie Bros. Breaks Record for Internet Sales at Forth Worth Site During Multi-Million Dollar Unreserved Auction" in Marketwired
Pub: Comtex News Network Inc.
Description: Ritchie Bros. Auctioneers, the world's largest auctioneer of trucks and industrial equipment, conducted a large unreserved auction at its permanent auction facility in Fort Worth, Texas, in which the company broke the record for Internet sales with bidders using the company's online bidding service, rbauctionBid-Live. Internet bidders purchased more than 440 lots in the auction.

33769 ■ "ROIonline Announces Streaming Video Products" in Marketing Weekly News (December 5, 2009, pp. 155)
Pub: Investment Weekly News
Description: ROIonline LLC, an Internet marketing firm serving business-to-business and the industrial marketplace, has added streaming video options to the Internet solutions it offers its clients; due to the huge increase of broadband connections, videos are now commonplace on the Internet and can often convey a company's message in a must more efficient, concise and effective way that will engage a website's visitor thus delivering a high return on a company's investment.

33770 ■ "Rumor Has It" in Entrepreneur (Vol. 35, October 2007, No. 10, pp. 30)
Pub: Entrepreneur Press
Contact: Perlman Neil, President
Ed: Chris Penttila. **Description:** Some entrepreneurs like Ren Moulton and Dan Scudder regard rumor sites and product blogs as great sources of market research. However, there are legal issues that must be studied before using these Internet sites in marketing and product development. The use and limitations of rumor sites and product blogs are provided.

33771 ■ "Ryan Gilbert Wants SBA To Mean Speedy Business Administration" in Philadelphia Business Journal (Vol. 33, May 9, 2014, No. 13, pp. 8)
Pub: American City Business Journals
Released: May 9, 2014. **Description:** Ryan Gilbert, CEO of San Francisco, California-based Better Finance explains that his company uses its financial technology, SmartBiz, to help banks expedite Small Business Administration (SBA) loans. Better Finance, formerly known as BillFloat, helps small business owners receive SBA 7(a) loans between $5,000 and $150,000 within five business days instead of several week, offering easy online access to SBA loans at low interest rates.

33772 ■ "Sales & Use Tax Introduction for USA Internet Retailers"
Pub: Amazon Digital Services
Released: December 23, 2013. **Price:** $9.99 Kindle. **Description:** The guide provides condensed information for online sellers of merchandise and covers various multi-state sales and use taxation topics along with high level awareness of sales and use tax (SUT) compliance for online retailer selling in the United States.

33773 ■ Salesforce.com Secrets of Success: Best Practices for Growth and Profitability
Pub: Prentice Hall Business Publishing
Contact: Jerome Grant, President
Ed: David Taber. **Released:** May 05, 2009. **Price:** $49.99. **Description:** Guide for using Salesforce. com; it provides insight into navigating through user groups, management, sales, marketing and IT departments in order to achieve the best results.

33774 ■ "Same-Day Delivery's Second Act" in Inc. (Vol. 36, March 2014, No. 2, pp. 87)
Pub: Mansueto Ventures L.L.C.
Contact: John Koten, Chief Executive Officer
Released: March 2014. **Description:** New technology is helping electronic commerce to be reliable and profitable while offering same day delivery. Profiles of delivery services competing for retail contracts include Instacart, Zookal, Postmates, to name a few. Statistical data included.

33775 ■ *The Savvy Gal's Guide to Online Networking (Or What Would Jane Austen Do?)*
Pub: Booklocker.com Inc.
Contact: Angela Adair-Hoy, Publisher
Ed: Diane K. Danielson, Lindsey Pollak. **Released:** August 10, 2007. **Description:** The book offers tips, tactics and etiquette for businesswomen wishing to build professional relationships via email, online networks, blogs, and message boards.

33776 ■ *The Savvy Gal's Guide to Online Networking*
Pub: Booklocker.com Inc.
Contact: Angela Adair-Hoy, Publisher
Ed: Diane K. Danielson, Lindsey Pollak. **Description:** It is a truth universally acknowledged that a woman in search of a fabulous career must be in want of networking opportunities. Or so Jane Austen would say if she were writing, or more likely, blogging today. So begins the must-read guide to networking in the 21st Century. Authors and networking experts share the nuts, bolts and savvy secrets that businesswomen need in order to use technology to build professional relationships.

33777 ■ *Say Everything: How Blogging Began, What It's Becoming, and Why It Matters*
Pub: Crown Business
Ed: Scott Rosenberg. **Released:** 2009. **Price:** $15, Paperback. **Description:** A history of Internet blogs that explains how they started and why they matter to any small business. **Availability:** Print.

33778 ■ *"Scientific American Builds Novel Blog Network" in Information Today (Vol. 28, September 2011, No. 8, pp. 12)*
Pub: Information Today, Inc.
Contact: Thomas H. Hogan, President
E-mail: ctuthill@infotoday.com
Ed: Kurt Schiller. **Description:** Scientific American launched a new blog network that joins a diverse lineup of bloggers cover various scientific topics under one banner. The blog network includes 60 bloggers providing insights into the ever-changing world of science and technology.

33779 ■ *"Scitable Puts Nature Education on the Map" in Information Today (Vol. 26, February 2009, No. 2, pp. 29)*
Description: Nature Education, a division of the Nature Publishing Group, released its first product, Scitable, a free online resource for undergraduate biology students and educators. The service includes over 180 overviews of key genetics concepts as well as social networking features, including groups and functionality, that lets students work with classmates and others. Teachers can use the service to set up public or private groups for students.

33780 ■ *"Search and Discover New Opportunities" in DM News (Vol. 31, December 14, 2009, No. 29, pp. 13)*
Pub: Haymarket Media, Inc.
Ed: Chantal Tode. **Description:** Although other digital strategies are gaining traction in Internet marketing, search marketing continues to dominate this advertising forum. Companies like American Greetings, which markets e-card brands online, are utilizing social networking sites and affiliates to generate a higher demand for their products.

33781 ■ *The Search: How Google and Its Rivals Rewrote the Rules of Business and Transformed Our Culture*
Pub: Penguin Group USA
Contact: Phyllis Grann, President
Ed: John Battelle. **Released:** October 03, 2006. **Price:** $17; $13.99. **Description:** Provides a history of Internet search technology. **Availability:** PrintElectronic publishing.

33782 ■ *"Securing our Cyber Status" in San Antonio Business Journal (Vol. 28, May 16, 2014, No. 14, pp. 4)*
Pub: American City Business Journals
Released: May 16, 2014. **Description:** The San Antonio Chamber of Commerce commissioned Deloitte to conduct a study on the local cyber security sector of San Antonio, Texas. Industry insiders are looking forward to securing the status of San Antonio as a top tier cyber city with the results of the study research.

33783 ■ *"The Seller Ledger: An Auction Organizer for Selling on eBay"*
Pub: PerfectBound
Contact: Michael Morrison, President
E-mail: michael.morrison@harpercollins.com
Released: December 1, 2006. **Price:** $6.99 paperback, $44.95 spiral bound. **Description:** The book allows people selling items on the auction site, eBay, to keep track of fees, profits, feedback, addresses, tracking information, shipping and handling costs, and more. This recordkeeping process is essential to run an efficient business using Electronic Commerce.

33784 ■ *Selling Online: Canada's Bestselling Guide to Becoming a Successful E-Commerce Merchant*
Ed: Jim Carroll; Rick Broadhead. **Released:** September 6, 2002. **Description:** Helps individuals build online retail enterprises; this updated version includes current tools, information and success strategies, how to launch an online storefront, security, marketing strategies, and mistakes to avoid.

33785 ■ *"Senators Predict Online School Changes" in Puget Sound Business Journal (Vol. 29, September 19, 2008, No. 22, pp. 1)*
Pub: American City Business Journals
Ed: Clay Holtzman. **Description:** State senators promise to create new legislation that would tighten the monitoring and oversight of online public schools. The officials are concerned about the lack of oversight of the programs as well as lack of knowledge about content of the lessons.

33786 ■ *The SEO Manifesto: A Practical and Ethical Guide to Internet Marketing and Search Engine Optimization*
Ed: Dan Tousignant, Pamela Gobiel. **Released:** December 05, 2011. **Price:** $14.99. **Description:** Comprehensive guide for each phase of launching an online business; chapters include checklists, process descriptions, and examples.

33787 ■ *"Serials Solutions Launches 360 Resource Manager Consortium Edition" in Information Today (Vol. 26, February 2009, No. 2, pp. 32)*
Description: Serials Solutions new Serials Solutions 360 Resource Manager Consortium Edition helps consortia, groups and member libraries with their e-resource management services. The products allows users to consolidate e-resource metadata and acquisition information into one place, which enables groups to manage holdings, subscriptions, licensing, contacts, and cost information and to streamline delivery of information to members.

33788 ■ *"Sharing the Micro Wealth" in Entrepreneur (Vol. 37, July 2009, No. 7, pp. 46)*
Pub: Entrepreneur Press
Contact: Perlman Neil, President
Ed: Jennie Dorris. **Description:** Step-by-step guide is presented on how Kiva.org, a website which allows people to make microloans to entrepreneurs across the world, works. The website, founded by Matt Flannery, raises $1 million weekly and it will add U.S. entrepreneurs to its list of loan recipients in June 2010. Other features of Kiva.org are discussed.

33789 ■ *"Shoestring-Budget Marketing" in Women Entrepreneur (January 5, 2009)*
Ed: Maria Falconer. **Description:** Pay-per-click search engine advertising is the traditional type of e-marketing that may not only be too expensive for certain kinds of businesses but also may not attract the quality customer base a business looking to grow needs to find. Social networking websites have become a mandatory marketing tool for business owners who want to see growth in their sales; tips are provided for utilizing these networking websites in order to gain more visibility on the Internet which can, in turn, lead to the more sales.

33790 ■ *"Silverpop Recognised for Email Marketing Innovations by Econsultancy" in Marketing Weekly News (January 23, 2010, pp. 124)*
Pub: Investment Weekly News
Description: Econsultancy, a respected source of insight and advice on digital marketing and e-commerce, recognized Silverpop, the world's only provider of both marketing automation solutions and email marketing specifically tailored to the unique needs of B2C and B2B marketers at Econsultancy's 2009 Innovation Awards.

33791 ■ *"Simplifying Social Media for Optimum Results" in Franchising World (Vol. 42, August 2010, No. 8, pp. 12)*
Pub: International Franchise Association
Contact: Stephen J. Caldeira, President
E-mail: scaldeira@franchise.org
Ed: Paul Segreto. **Description:** Keys to effective technology usage requires the development of an integrated plan, choosing the most complementary tools and implementing well-planned strategies.

33792 ■ *"Sites Set" in Entrepreneur (Vol. 35, November 2007, No. 11, pp. 112)*
Pub: Entrepreneur Press
Contact: Perlman Neil, President
Ed: Nichole L. Torres. **Description:** Marketing information online can be a good bui9sness if you know who to target. Partnering with other online companies to provide information services that cater to specific groups of people is also helpful.

33793 ■ *"Siteworx Earns 4 Interactive Media Awards in Q1 of 2011" in Entertainment Close-Up (, 2011)*
Pub: Close-Up Media
Description: Details of the four awards Siteworx earned for its achievements in Web development and design are outlined.

33794 ■ *6 Steps to Free Publicity*
Pub: ReadHowYouWant.com, Ltd.
Ed: Marcia Yudkin. **Released:** Third Edition. **Price:** $15.99, paperback. **Description:** Six steps to help promote a small business are given. The history of the Internet and its use to help provide free publicity to small firms is outlined. **Availability:** Print.

33795 ■ *"Skype Ltd. Acquired GroupMe" in Information Today (Vol. 28, October 2011, No. 9, pp. 12)*
Pub: Information Today, Inc.
Contact: Thomas H. Hogan, President
E-mail: ctuthill@infotoday.com
Description: Skype Ltd. acquired GroupMe, a group messaging company that allows users to form impromptu groups where they can text message, share data, and make conference calls for free and is supported on Android, iPhone, BlackBerry, and Windows phones.

33796 ■ *"Small Budget, Big Impact" in Small Business Opportunities (Summer 2010)*
Pub: Harris Publications Inc.
Ed: Hilary J.M. Topper. **Description:** Ways to use social media to get in from of a target audience for small businesses are examined.

33797 ■ *Small Business Clustering Technologies: Applications in Marketing, Management, IT and Economics*
Pub: IGI Global
Contact: Dr. Mehdi Khosrow-Pour, President
Ed: Robert C. MacGregor, Ann T. Hodgkinson. **Released:** September 2006. **Price:** 94.95, hardcover; $145, Institutions. **Description:** An overview of the development and role of small business clusters in disciplines that include economics, marketing, management and information systems. **Availability:** PrintE-book.

33798 ■ *Small Business for Dummies*
Pub: John Wiley & Sons Inc.
Contact: Stephen M. Smith, President
Released: December 2011. **Price:** $22.95. **Description:** Advice for launching and growing a small business; insights into using the Internet as business tool are included. **Availability:** Print.

33799 ■ Small Business Management
Pub: John Wiley & Sons Inc.
Contact: Stephen M. Smith, President
Ed: Margaret Burlingame. Released: March 2007.
Price: $44.95. Description: Advice for starting and running a small business as well as information on the value and appeal of small businesses, is given. Topics include budgets, taxes, inventory, ethics, e-commerce, and current laws.

33800 ■ Small Business Taxes Made Easy: How to Increase Your Deductions, Reduce What You Owe, and Boost Your Profits
Ed: Eva Rosenberg. Released: December 2004.
Price: $16.95. Description: Tax expert gives advice to small business owners regarding tax issues. Tax-Mamma.com, run by Eva Rosenberg, is one of the top seven tax advice Websites on the Internet.

33801 ■ "'Smart' Google Contacts on the Way" in Dallas Business Journal (Vol. 37, July 18, 2014, No. 45, pp. 11)
Pub: American City Business Journals
Released: July 18, 2014. Description: Efforts are being undertaken by Alcon Labs, the Fort Worth-based company along with Google Inc. to develop smart contact lenses with embedded electronics to monitor health and improve vision. Some of the applications of the lenses include monitoring the wearer's blood sugar, correct vision, as well as other ocular capabilities.

33802 ■ SMEs and New Technologies: Learning E-Business and Development
Pub: Palgrave Macmillan
Contact: Lisa Dunn, Manager
E-mail: l.dunn@palgrave.com
Ed: Banji Oyelaran-Oyeyinka, Kaushalesh Lal. Released: July 2006. Price: £84, hardcover; $125. Description: Adoption and learning of new information technologies in developing nations is covered. New technologies are opening opportunities for small companies in these countries. Availability: Print; E-book.

33803 ■ The Social Media Bible: Tactics, Tools, and Strategies for Business Success
Pub: John Wiley & Sons Inc.
Contact: Stephen M. Smith, President
Ed: Lon Safko. Released: Third Edition. Price: $29.95, paperback; $19.99. Description: Information is given to build or transform a business into social media, where customers, employees, and prospects connect, collaborate, and champion products and services in order to increase sales and to beat the competition. Availability: PrintE-book.

33804 ■ "Social Media By the Numbers: Social-Media Marketing Is All the Rage" in Inc. (Vol. 33, November 2011, No. 9, pp. 70)
Pub: Inc. Magazine
Ed: J.J. McCorvey, Issie Lapowsky. Description: Six strategies to help small businesses use social media sites such as Facebook and Twitter to promote their companies are presented.

33805 ■ "Social Media Conference NW 2010" in Bellingham Business Journal (Vol. February 2010, pp. 3)
Pub: Sound Publishing Inc.
Contact: Gloria G. Fletcher, President
Ed: Lance Henderson. Description: Center for Economic Vitality (CEV) and the Technology Alliance Group (TAG) will host the 2010 Social Media Conference at the McIntyre Hall Performing Arts & Conference Center in Mt. Vernon, Washington. The event will provide networking opportunities for attendees.

33806 ■ "Social Networkers for Hire" in Black Enterprise (Vol. 40, December 2009, No. 5, pp. 56)
Pub: Earl G. Graves Publishing Co., Inc.
Ed: Brittany Hutson. Description: Companies are utilizing social networking sites in order to market their brand and personally connect with consumers and are increasingly looking to social media specialists to help with this task. Aliya S. King is one such

web strategist, working for ICED Media by managing their Twitter, Facebook, YouTube and Flickr accounts for one of their publicly traded restaurant clients.

33807 ■ "Social Networks in the Workplace" in Strategy & Leadership (Vol. 38, July-August 2010, No. 4, pp. 50-53)
Pub: Emerald Inc.
Ed: Daniel Burrus. Description: The opinions of futurist Daniel Burrus on a novel trend called 'Business 2.0', which involves the use of social networking applications as business tools, are presented. His suggestion that personal social networking technology can be used by businesses to improve collaboration, problem solving, and leadership communications to achieve continuous value innovation is discussed.

33808 ■ "Social Safety, Thanks to New App" in Providence Business News (Vol. 29, July 21, 2014, No. 16, pp. 10)
Pub: American City Business Journals
Released: July 21, 2014. Description: Middletown-based Vizsafe Inc. has developed the Vizsafe application (app) for public safety and community engagement and is offering it to police departments and to citizens at no cost. Vizsafe president and CEO, Peter Mottur, asserts that the 24/7 crowdsourcing platform is available to smartphone users and can be used as an additional safety resource by individuals and emergency responders.

33809 ■ "Sometimes, Second Impressions Count Most" in Canadian Business (Vol. 83, October 12, 2010, No. 17, pp. 11)
Ed: Richard Branson. Description: Developing a favorable impression at the first point of contact is imperative for businesses. Managers who want their organizations to make positive first and second impressions need to learn to balance the Web's labor-saving efficiencies with human assistants. The importance of considering the customer relations value in company Websites is also explained.

33810 ■ "Sounders Kicking Ball to Fans" in Puget Sound Business Journal (Vol. 29, November 28, 2008, No. 32, pp. 1)
Ed: Greg Lamm. Description: Major League Soccer expansion team, Seattle Sounders FC, hopes to build fan support leading to its inaugural season 2009-2010 by tapping online social networks. The club launched fan clubs with actual powers over its decision making and Websites similar to Facebook.

33811 ■ "Spanish Company to Offer Free Wi-Fi In Miami-Dade County" in South Florida Business Journal (Vol. 34, April 25, 2014, No. 40)
Pub: American City Business Journals
Released: April 25, 2014. Description: GOWEX a Madrid-based company, is offering free Wi-Fi access at 400 public spots in Miami, Florida. The firm will sell advertising over the Wi-Fi network. It has offered similar free access to users in New York, NY and in San Francisco, CA.

33812 ■ "Spinout Success: New Leadership Steps In At UW's C4C" in Puget Sound Business Journal (Vol. 35, June 27, 2014, No. 10, pp. 11)
Pub: American City Business Journals
Released: June 27, 2014. Description: University of Washington's Center for Commercialization vice provost, Vikram Jandhyala, talks about his new position with the school. Jandhyala says he plans to build more synergy between the medical school and engineering and between social sciences and computer science. He also says the medical and software industry need to grow to accommodate the volume of data crossing and stored within the Internet.

33813 ■ "Start: Punch Fear in the Face, Escape Average and Do Work that Matters"
Pub: Ramsey Press
Released: April 23, 2013. Price: $22.99. Description: Three things have occurred that have changed the predictable stages of success. Boomers have started second and third careers. Technology has given access to unprecedented number of people

who are building online empires, thus changing their lives. The days of success first, significance later have ended. All stages must be experienced but there are only two paths in life: average and awesome. Tips for building an awesome life or business are included.

33814 ■ "Startup to Serve Bar Scene" in Austin Business JournalInc. (Vol. 29, December 18, 2009, No. 41, pp. 1)
Ed: Christopher Calnan. Description: Startup ATX Innovation Inc. of Austin, Texas has developed a test version of TabbedOut, a Web-based tool that would facilitate mobile phone-based restaurant and bar bill payment. TabbedOut has been tested by six businesses in Austin and will be available to restaurant and bar owners for free. Income would be generated by ATX through a 99-cent convenience charge per transaction.

33815 ■ Stealing MySpace: The Battle to Control the Most Popular Website in America
Pub: Random House Inc.
Contact: Richard Sarnoff, President
Ed: Julia Angwin. Released: 2009. Price: $13.99. Description: Information regarding Rupert Murdoch's outwitting Viacom's Tom Freston and details of the deal are presented. Availability: E-book.

33816 ■ Success Secrets of Social Media Marketing Superstars
Pub: Entrepreneur Press
Contact: Perlman Neil, President
Ed: Mitch Meyerson. Released: June 01, 2010. Price: $21.95, Paperback. Description: Provides access to the playbooks of social media marketers who reveal their most valuable strategies and tactics for standing out in the new online media environment.

33817 ■ "Sunbrella Engages Consumers Via Social Media" in Home Textiles Today (Vol. 31, May 24, 2011, No. 13, pp. 4)
Pub: Reed Elsevier Group plc Reed Business Information
Contact: Mark Kelsey, Chief Executive Officer
Description: Performance fabric brand Sunbrella is marketing to social media, such as Facebook and Twitter, in order to boost consumer interest and retailer support.

33818 ■ "Sylvie Collection Offers a Feminine Perspective and Voice in Male Dominated Bridal Industry" in Benzinga.com (October 29, 2011)
Pub: Benzinga.com
Contact: Kyle Bazzy, President
Ed: Benzinga Staff. Description: Bridal jewelry designer Sylvie Levine has created over 1,000 customizable styles of engagement rings and wedding bands and is reaching out to prospective new brides through a new Website, interactive social media campaign and monthly trunk show appearances.

33819 ■ "Taking the Steps Into the Clouds" in New Hampshire Business Review (Vol. 33, March 25, 2011, No. 6, pp. 19)
Pub: Business Publications Inc.
Ed: Tim Wessels. Description: Cloud services include Internet and Web security, spam filtering, message archiving, work group collaboration, IT asset management, help desk and disaster recovery backup.

33820 ■ "Tap the iPad and Mobile Internet Device Market" in Franchising World (Vol. 42, September 2010, No. 9, pp. 43)
Pub: International Franchise Association
Contact: Stephen J. Caldeira, President
E-mail: scaldeira@franchise.org
Ed: John Thomson. Description: The iPad and other mobile Internet devices will help franchise owners interact with customers. It will be a good marketing tool for these businesses.

33821 ■ "Targeting Back Pain, With a Big Backer" in Business Journal (Vol. 31, May 2, 2014, No. 49, pp. 6)
Pub: American City Business Journals
Released: May 2, 2014. Description: Orthology, a startup chain of orthopedic-pain clinics, plans to open new facilities. The company's clinics allow patients to

schedule appointments online. Pat Tarnowski, Orthology's director of operations, believes that the company's focus on patient experience will allow the business to differentiate itself from competition.

33822 ■ *"Teacher's Pet" in Entrepreneur (September 2014)*
Pub: Entrepreneur Media Inc.
Released: September 2014. **Description:** Entrepreneur, Andrew Geant, partnered with software developer, Michael Weishuhn, to launch WyzAnt, an online tutoring service based in Chicago, Illinois. Tutors can boost their ranking on the platform by earning positive reviews, their ability to accept electronic payments or use the service's cloud-based schedule system. A tutor's hourly fee ranges from $30 to $60. Geant and Weishuhn are planning for an international expansion of WyzAnt and support development of a series of mobile applications for tutors, students, and parents.

33823 ■ *"Technology Drivers to Boost Your Bottom Line" in Franchising World (Vol. 42, August 2010, No. 8, pp. 15)*
Pub: International Franchise Association
Contact: Stephen J. Caldeira, President
E-mail: scaldeira@franchise.org
Ed: Dan Dugal. **Description:** Technological capabilities are expanding quickly and smart franchises should stay updated on all the new developments, including smart phones, global positioning systems, and social media networks.

33824 ■ *"Technology: What Seems To Be the Problem? Self Service Gets a Tune-Up" in Inc. (February 2008, pp. 43-44)*
Ed: Darren Dahl. **Description:** Self-service software can save companies money when responding to customer service phone calls, text or email messages. More companies are relying on alternatives such as automated Web-based self-service systems.

33825 ■ *"Tee Off Online" in Black Enterprise (Vol. 37, January 2007, No. 6, pp. 52)*
Pub: Earl G. Graves Publishing Co. Inc.
Contact: Earl G. Graves, Jr., President
Ed: James C. Johnson. **Description:** The E-Com Resource Center is one of many resources that are available for those interested in starting an e-commerce business. One of the first steps is to create a business plan, of which there are free samples available at BPlans.com.

33826 ■ *"Tell Us What You Really Think Collecting Customer Feedback" in Inc. (Vol. 30, December 2008, No. 12, pp. 52)*
Pub: Mansueto Ventures L.L.C.
Contact: John Koten, Chief Executive Officer
Ed: Ryan Underwood. **Description:** According to a recent survey, nearly 77 percent of online shoppers review consumer-generated reviews of products before making a purchase.

33827 ■ *"Things Really Clicking for Macy's Online" in Business Courier (Vol. 24, November 29, 2007, No. 33, pp. 1)*
Pub: American City Business Journals, Inc.
Contact: Whitney Shaw, President
Ed: Lisa Biank Fasig. **Description:** Retailer Macy's online division Macys.com are projecting sales at $1billion in 2007, compared to $620 million in 2006. Macy's new online features and products and the growth of online retail sector are also discussed.

33828 ■ *"Thomas Industrial Network Unveils Custom SPEC" in Entertainment Close-Up (March 3, 2011)*
Pub: Close-Up Media
Description: Thomas Industrial Network assists custom manufacturers and industrial service providers a complete online program called Custom SPEC which includes Website development and Internet exposure.

33829 ■ *"Three Ways to Power Up Mobile Marketing" in South Florida Business Journal (Vol. 34, July 18, 2014, No. 52, pp. 12)*
Pub: American City Business Journals
Released: July 18, 2014. **Description:** A number of strategies that companies can apply to prepare for the future reality of mobile marketing are provided.

Companies are encouraged to start the change to accommodate the new mobile world as mobile traffic data is projected to increase in record numbers and mobile connected devices will reach over 10 billion by 2007.

33830 ■ *"Tim Tebow Foundation to Hold Pink 'Cleats for a Cure' Auction" in Travel & Leisure Close-Up (October 20, 2011)*
Pub: Close-Up Media
Description: Tim Tebow Foundation partnered with XV Enterprises to hold the 'Cleats for a Cure' auction on eBay. Tebow is auctioning off a pair of pink cleans he wore during the Denver Broncos vs. Tennessee Titans game October 3, 2010. All funds will go toward finding a cure for breast cancer.

33831 ■ *Titanium eBay: A Tactical Guide to Becoming a Millionaire PowerSeller*
Pub: Penguin Group USA
Contact: Phyllis Grann, President
Ed: Skip McGrath. **Released:** August 2006. **Price:** R 255, paperback. **Description:** Advice is given to help anyone selling items on eBay to become a Power Seller, an award presented based on monthly gross merchandise sales. **Availability:** Print.

33832 ■ *"Tool-o-Rama" in Barron's (Vol. 90, September 6, 2010, No. 36)*
Pub: Barron's Editorial & Corporate Headquarters
Ed: Theresa W. Carey. **Description:** New trading tool features from several online brokers are discussed. The new features from Fidelity, ChoiceTrade, JunoTrade and TradeKing are examined. Investors can now screen exchanged traded funds in the same way as stocks with Fidelity, while ChoiceTrade can run in any browser without the need to install additional plug-ins.

33833 ■ *"Tool Time" in Entrepreneur (Vol. 36, March 2008, No. 3, pp. 90)*
Pub: Entrepreneur Press
Contact: Perlman Neil, President
Ed: Nichole L. Torres. **Description:** DaVinci Institute holds an annual event in Colorado to display new products and inventions. Innovative Design Engineering Animation is a consulting company that helps inventors develop product through various stages. NineSigma Inc. has an online marketplace where inventors can post ideas for clients needing new products.

33834 ■ *"Top 10 Most Viewed Stories, Videos in 2010" in Farm Industry News (January 4, 2011)*
Pub: Penton Business Media Inc.
Contact: David Kieselstein, Chief Executive Officer
Description: The top ten most popularly viewed stories and videos presented on farmindustrynews. com Website are listed.

33835 ■ *"Traffic's Up; Website's Down: Preventing Costly Crashes" in Inc. (March 2008, pp. 55-56)*
Pub: Mansueto Ventures L.L.C.
Contact: John Koten, Chief Executive Officer
Ed: Darren Dahl. **Description:** Grid Web hosting protects a small company's Website when a sudden burst of Internet traffic hits enabling it to continue rather than be crippled. Options can vary in cost from $4 to $1,000 monthly and include using a shared server, grid server, virtual private server, or a dedicated server. The article explains each option.

33836 ■ *"Travel Tech" in Entrepreneur (May 2014)*
Pub: Entrepreneur Media Inc.
Released: May 2014. **Description:** The Goal Zero Sherpa 100 Power Pack includes two USB ports, a 12-volt plug and a proprietary laptop port that can fill a MacBook Air's battery faster on a single charge. The Nomad ChargeKey is lightweight, flexible and allows users to connect their spent smartphones to any full-size USB outlet. The Jawbone Era Bluetooth headset features a sleek carrying case that also functions as a battery-powered charger. The Belkin WeMo Insight Switch is a mobile wall plug that connects to a Wi-Fi and links to smartphones through an application.

33837 ■ *"Try a Little Social Media" in American Printer (Vol. 128, June 1, 2011, No. 6)*
Pub: Penton Media Inc.
Description: Social media helps keep Ussery Printing on customers radar. Jim David, VP of marketing for the firm, states that 350 people following them on Facebook are from the local area.

33838 ■ *"Turnaround Down the Shore" in Philadelphia Business Journal (Vol. 33, May 16, 2014, No. 14, pp. 4)*
Pub: American City Business Journals
Released: May 16, 2014. **Description:** Business owners along the Jersey Shore are looking forward to a strong summer season in 2014, after suffering the devastating effects of Hurricane Sandy in 2012 and bad summer weather in 2013. Shore towns are putting their marketing efforts into full swing, placing emphasis on the use of social media.

33839 ■ *"TW Trade Shows to Offer Seminars On Niche Selling, Social Media" in Travel Weekly (Vol. 69, October 4, 2010, No. 40, pp. 9)*
Pub: NorthStar Travel Media LLC
Contact: Tom Kemp, Chief Executive Officer
Description: Travel Weekly's Leisure World 2010 and Fall Home Based Travel Agent Show focused on niche selling, with emphasis on all-inclusives, young consumers, groups, incentives, culinary vacations, and honeymoon or romance travel.

33840 ■ *"Twitter Hack: Made in Japan? User Says Attack Showed Security Flaw" in Houston Chronicle (September 24, 2010, pp. 3)*
Pub: Houston Chronicle
Contact: Sherry Adams, Director, Library Services
Ed: Tomoko A. Hosaka. **Description:** Details of the attack on Twitter caused by a Japanese computer hacker are revealed.

33841 ■ *Twitterville: How Businesses Can Thrive in the New Global Neighborhoods*
Pub: Portfolio Hardcover
Ed: Shel Israel. **Released:** September 03, 2009. **Price:** $18.99. **Description:** Twitter is the most rapidly adopted communication tool in history, going from zero to ten million users in just over two years. On Twitter, word can spread faster than wildfire. Companies no longer have the option of ignoring the conversation. Unlike other hot social media spaces, Twitterville is dominated by professionals, not students. And despite its size, it still feels like a small town. Twitter allows people to interact much the way they do face-to-face, honestly and authentically. **Availability:** Electronic publishing.

33842 ■ *202 Things You Can Make and Sell for Big Profits*
Pub: Entrepreneur Press
Ed: James Stephenson. **Released:** September 2005. **Description:** Instructions for 202 products that can be made and sold over the Internet.

33843 ■ *The Ultimate Guide to Electronic Marketing for Small Business: Low-Cost/High Return Tools and Techniques That Really Work*
Pub: John Wiley & Sons Inc.
Contact: Stephen M. Smith, President
Ed: Tom Antion. **Released:** May 2005. **Price:** $19.95, paperback. **Description:** Online marketing techniques for small business to grow and increase sales. **Availability:** Print.

33844 ■ *"Ultimate Guide to Google AdWords: How to Access 100 Million People in 10 Minutes"*
Pub: Entrepreneur Press
Released: October 1, 2014. **Price:** $24.95 paperback. **Description:** Google AdWords experts and analytics specialist present the techniques, tools, and tricks for using Google AdWords. The experts help small businesses to write advertising and Website copy design, work into difficult markets, advertise, increase search engine presence, bid strategies for online auctions, financial budgeting and more.

33845 ■ *"Understanding Persuasive Online Sales Messages from eBay Auctions"* in *Business Communication Quarterly (December 2007, pp. 482)*
Pub: Pine Forge Press
Contact: Blaise R. Simqu, President
Ed: Barbara Jo White, Daniel Clapper, Rita Noel, Jenny Fortier, Pierre Grabolosa. **Description:** eBay product listings were studied to determine the requirements of persuasive sales writing. Potential sellers should use the proper keywords and make an authentic description with authentic photographs of the item being auctioned.

33846 ■ *"U.S. Enters BlackBerry Dispute Compromise Sought Over Security Issues"* in *Houston Chronicle (August 6, 2010)*
Pub: Houston Chronicle
Contact: Sherry Adams, Director, Library Services
Ed: Matthew Lee. **Description:** U.S. State Department is working for a compromise with Research in Motion, manufacturer of the BlackBerry, over security issues. The Canadian company makes the smartphones and foreign governments believe they pose a security risk.

33847 ■ *"Universal Music Sues Grooveshark's Parent"* in *Wall Street Journal Eastern Edition (November 22 , 2011, pp. B5)*
Pub: Dow Jones & Co., Inc.
Contact: Clare Hart, President
Ed: Ethan Smith. **Description:** Escape Media Group Inc., the parent company of online-music service Grooveshark, and seven of its executives have been sued by Universal Music Group, which alleges patent infringement involving its sound recordings. The executives are alleged to have uploaded thousands of songs onto Grooveshark.

33848 ■ *"Unlimited Priorities Strengthens Executive Team"* in *Entertainment Close-Up (November 1, 2011)*
Pub: Close-Up Media
Description: Founder and president of Unlimited Priorities Corporation, Iris L. Hanney, added two executive level professionals to her team. The new employees will help increase the firm's capabilities in social media and information technology.

33849 ■ *"Up To Code? Website Eases Compliance Burden for Entrepreneurs"* in *Black Enterprise (Vol. 38, March 1, 2008, No. 8, pp. 48)*
Pub: Earl G. Graves Publishing Co. Inc.
Contact: Earl G. Graves, Jr., President
Ed: Robin White-Goode. **Description:** Business.gov is a presidential E-government project created to help small businesses easily find, understand, and comply with laws and regulations pertaining to a particular industry.

33850 ■ *"UPMC Develops Own Billing Solutions"* in *Pittsburgh Business Times (Vol. 33, January 17, 2014, No. 27, pp. 6)*
Pub: American City Business Journals
Released: January 17, 2014. **Description:** How University of Pittsburgh Medical Center (UPMC) Health System transformed its accounts payable department by passing its process to a subsidiary, Prodigo Solutions, is discussed. UPMC moved suppliers and purchasers to a shared electronic platform and created a digital marketplace. The system's no purchase order, no pay policy has reduced the number of rogue purchases.

33851 ■ *"Uptick in Clicks: Nordstrom's Online Sales Surging"* in *Puget Sound Business Journal (Vol. 29, August 22, 2008, No. 18, pp. 1)*
Ed: Gregg Lamm. **Description:** Nordstrom Inc.'s online division grew its sales by 15 percent in the second quarter of 2008, compared to 2007's 4.3 percent in overall decline. The company expects their online net sales to reach $700 million in 2008 capturing eight percent of overall sales.

33852 ■ *"Utah Technology Council: Social Media Is Here to Stay; Embrace It"* in *Wireless News (December 14, 2009)*
Description: Social media outlets such as Facebook and Twitter are blurring the lines between advertising, public relations, branding and marketing; businesses must stop thinking in terms of traditional marketing versus Internet marketing if they want to succeed in today's marketing climate.

33853 ■ *"A View to a Killer Business Model"* in *Black Enterprise (Vol. 40, December 2009, No. 5, pp. 50)*
Pub: Earl G. Graves Publishing Co., Inc.
Ed: Dale Coachman. **Description:** Profile of Gen2Media Corp., a production, technology and Internet marketing firm based in Florida with offices in New York; Gen2Media is utilizing the advances in technology to now include video in its online marketing offerings.

33854 ■ *"Virgin America Flies with V&S on Web"* in *ADWEEK (Vol. 51, July 12 2010, No. 27, pp. 31)*
Pub: Nielsen Business Media Inc.
Contact: Howard Appelbaum, President
Ed: Brian Morrissey. **Description:** Victors & Spoils, a crowdsourcing agency is examined.

33855 ■ *"Vision Statement: Mapping the Social Internet"* in *Harvard Business Review (Vol. 88, July-August 2010, No. 7-8, pp. 32)*
Pub: Harvard Business School Publishing
Ed: Mikolaj Jan Piskorski, Tommy McCall. **Description:** Chart compares and contrasts online social networks in selected countries.

33856 ■ *"Vistaprint Survey Indicates that Online Marketing Taking Hold Among Small Businesses"* in *Marketwired (December 10, 2009)*
Pub: COMTEX News Network Inc.
Contact: Chip Brian, President
Description: According to a comprehensive survey from Vistaprint N.V., small businesses are very likely to increase their use of Internet marketing strategies such as paid and organic search, email marketing, social media networking and custom websites over the next year. Trends continue to show that more small businesses are indeed adapting to the changing marketplace and are more willing to diversify their marketing strategies than ever before.

33857 ■ *"Wake-Up Call for Taxis"* in *Pittsburgh Business Times (Vol. 33, June 27, 2014, No. 50, pp. 4)*
Pub: American City Business Journals
Released: June 27, 2014. **Description:** Application (app)-based ride shares services Lyft Inc. and Uber Technologies Inc. have entered the Pittsburgh market, giving residents new transportation options that are more reliable than the large taxi services. The competition has forced existing taxi companies to review their service models, with Pittsburgh Transportation Group's Yellow Cab Company launching its own app-based ride sharing service, Yellow X.

33858 ■ *"The Way I Work: Howard Lefkowitz"* in *Inc. (March 2008, pp. 102-104, 106)*
Pub: Mansueto Ventures L.L.C.
Contact: John Koten, Chief Executive Officer
Ed: Hannah Clark Steiman. **Description:** Profile of Howard Lefkowitz, CEO of Vegas.com, a Website that allows visitors to book flights, reserve hotel rooms, buy show tickets, make spa appointments, and coordinate any and all aspects of a trip to Las Vegas. The firm also runs brick-and-mortar box offices and concierge desks at various cities.

33859 ■ *"Web-Based Marketing Excites, Challenges Small Business Use"* in *Colorado Springs Business Journal (January 20, 2010)*
Pub: Dolan Co.
Contact: James P. Dolan, President
Ed: Becky Hurley. **Description:** Business-to-business and consumer-direct firms alike are using the fast-changing Web technologies to increase sales, leads and track consumer behavior but once a company

commits to an Online marketing plan, experts believe, they must be prepared to consistently tweak and overhaul content and distribution vehicles in order to keep up.

33860 ■ *"Web-Preneuring"* in *Small Business Opportunities (July 1, 2007)*
Pub: Harris Publications Inc.
Description: 1&1 Internet provides known servers with more than 6.84 million customers through contracts with both consumer and business users. It operates five secure data centers housing 40,000 servers that process more than 5 billion monthly emails.

33861 ■ *"Web to Print"* in *American Printer (Vol. 128, August 1, 2011, No. 8)*
Pub: Penton Media Inc.
Description: Jerry Kennelly, CEO and founder of Tweak.com believes that Web-to-Design is middleware with no content. His firm offers an easy to use interface that flows right into the printer's workflow with no additional costs.

33862 ■ *"Web Sight: Do You See What I See?"* in *Entrepreneur (Vol. 35, October 2007, No. 10, pp. 58)*
Pub: Entrepreneur Press
Contact: Perlman Neil, President
Ed: Heather Clancy. **Description:** Owners of Trunkt, a boutique in New York that showcases independent designs, have created a new style of Website called Trunkt.org. The Website allows buyers to select the products they want to see and designers can choose anytime which of their items will be displayed on the site. An explanation of the strategy that helped bring Trunkt closer to its clients is presented.

33863 ■ *"Web Traffic Numbers Facing Scrutiny"* in *Boston Business Journal (Vol. 27, November 2, 2007, No. 40, pp. 1)*
Ed: Jesse Noyes. **Description:** Interactive Advertising Bureau (IAB) held a summit meeting with major industry players in an effort to create more transparent standards for measuring Internet traffic. The terms at issue were registered users, unique visitors, time spent and retention.

33864 ■ *"Web Translation Made Simple"* in *Inc. (Vol. 33, October 2011, No. 8, pp. 44)*
Pub: Inc. Magazine
Ed: Adam Baer. **Description:** Smartling is a Web-based service that translates sites into more than 50 foreign languages. The software will begin translation right after setting up the account.

33865 ■ *"Webadvertising"* in *MarketingMagazine (Vol. 115, September 27, 2010, No. 13, pp. 70)*
Pub: Rogers Publishing Ltd.
Contact: Edward S. Rogers, President
Description: Website advertising in Canada is examined.

33866 ■ *"Web.Preneuring: How Local TV Ads and Online Marketing Can Help You Win Big"* in *Small Business Opportunities (January 2008)*
Ed: David Waxman. **Description:** Spot Runner, an Internet-based advertising agency offers low-cost local business television ads. The company secures the ad buy, places and tracks the ads, and analyzes viewership and demographics for clients.

33867 ■ *"What the Future Holds for Consumers"* in *Black Enterprise (Vol. 41, August 2010, No. 1, pp. 47)*
Pub: Earl G. Graves Publishing Co. Inc.
Contact: Earl G. Graves, Jr., President
Ed: Sheiresa Ngo. **Description:** The way people purchase goods and service has changed with technology. With an increased focus on security (as well as privacy and fairness) the U.S. Congress began regulating the credit card industry with the Fair Credit Reporting Act of 1970 and the Credit Card Accountability, Responsibility, and Disclosure (CARD) Act of 2009.

33868 ■ *"What Marketers Misunderstand About Online Reviews: Managers Must Analyze What's Really Driving Buying Decisions - and Adjust Their Strategies Accordingly"* in Harvard Business Review (Vol. 92, January-February 2014, No. 1-2, pp. 23)

Pub: Harvard Business Press

Released: January-February 2014. **Description:** Companies may overestimate the influence of online reviews, as consumers do not turn to reviews for certain products and services (for example, habitual low-involvement purchases such as groceries). Others' opinions matter more for purchases such as independent restaurants and electronics.

33869 ■ *"What Online Brokers Are Doing To Keep Their Customers' Accounts Safe"* in Barron's (Vol. 88, March 10, 2008, No. 10, pp. 37)

Pub: Dow Jones & Co., Inc.

Contact: Clare Hart, President

Ed: Theresa W. Carey. **Description:** Online brokerage firms employ different methods to protect the accounts of their customers from theft. These methods include secure Internet connections, momentary passwords, and proprietary algorithms.

33870 ■ *"What's Your Social Media Strategy?"* in Black Enterprise (Vol. 41, November 2010, No. 4, pp. 75)

Pub: Earl G. Graves Publishing Co. Inc.

Contact: Earl G. Graves, Jr., President

Ed: Denise A. Campbell. **Description:** Advice for using social media sites such as Twitter, Facebook and LinkedIn as a professional networking tool is given.

33871 ■ *"White Cat Media Tells You Where to Get a Bargain: Now It's Shopping for $1.5 Million"* in Inc. (March 2008, pp. 48)

Pub: Mansueto Ventures L.L.C.

Contact: John Koten, Chief Executive Officer

Ed: Athena Schindelheim. **Description:** Profile of White Cat Media which runs two shopping Websites: SheFinds.com for fashion and beauty items, and MomFinds.com for mothers. The New York City firm reported revenues for 2007 at $400,000 and is looking for funding capital in the amount of $1.7 million.

33872 ■ *"Why LinkedIn is the Social Network that Will Never Die"* in Advertising Age (Vol. 81, December 6, 2010, No. 43, pp. 2)

Pub: Crain Communications Inc.

Contact: Rance Crain, President

Ed: Irina Slutsky. **Description:** Despite the popularity of Facebook, LinkIn in will always be a source for professionals who wish to network.

33873 ■ *"Why Some Get Shafted By Google Pricing"* in Advertising Age (Vol. 79, July 14, 2008, No. 7, pp. 3)

Pub: Crain Communications Inc.

Contact: Rance Crain, President

Ed: Abbey Klaassen. **Description:** Google's search advertising is discussed as well as the company's pricing structure for these ads.

33874 ■ *"Why We'll Never Escape Facebook"* in Canadian Business (Vol. 83, June 15, 2010, No. 10, pp. 28)

Pub: Rogers Media Inc.

Contact: Tony Viner, President

Ed: James Cowan, Tamara Shopsin, Jason Fulford. **Description:** Facebook users are growing in numbers despite criticism of the site's privacy policies that have put the onus of keeping anonymous to the user. Facebook's business model and its growing influence on the Internet are discussed.

33875 ■ *"Why You Need a New-Media 'Ringmaster"* in Harvard Business Review (Vol. 88, December 2010, No. 12, pp. 78)

Pub: Harvard Business School Publishing

Ed: Patrick Spenner. **Description:** The concept of ringmaster is applied to brand marketing. This concept includes integrative thinking, lean collaboration skills, and high-speed decision cycles.

33876 ■ *"Wi-Fi On Steroids: Will WiMAX Provide the Juice For Souped-Up Connections?"* in Black Enterprise (November 2007)

Pub: Earl G. Graves Publishing Co. Inc.

Contact: Earl G. Graves, Jr., President

Ed: Fiona Haley. **Description:** WiMAX, Worldwide Interoperability for Microwave Access in the U.S. WiMax is technology that moves data and connects faster and at greater distances than before.

33877 ■ *Wikinomics: How Mass Collaboration Changes Everything*

Pub: Penguin Group USA

Contact: Phyllis Grann, President

Ed: Don Tapscott, Anthony D. Williams. **Released:** September 28, 2010. **Price:** $17, paperback; $13.99. **Description:** Research and information about the every changing world of the Internet is provided to help small businesses. **Availability:** PrintElectronic publishing.

33878 ■ *"Wikinomics: The Sequel"* in Business Strategy Review (Vol. 21, Summer 2010, No. 2, pp. 64)

Pub: Blackwell Publishers Ltd.

Ed: Georgina Peters. **Description:** Ever optimistic Don Tapscott and Anthony Willis, co-authors of Wikinomics (Atlantic Books 2008) as well as various other books that study the Internet and its relationship to society are now working on a new book, one for which they are using the Internet to determine its title.

33879 ■ *"Wikinomics: The Sequel"* in Business Strategy Review (Vol. 21, Summer 2010, No. 2, pp. 64)

Pub: John Wiley & Sons Inc. Scientific, Technical, Medical, and Scholarly Div. (Wiley-Blackwell)

Contact: William J. Pesce, Manager

E-mail: wpesce@wiley.com

Description: Ever-optimistic Don Tapscott and Anthony Williams, coauthors of Wikinomics and individually, of a number of other books that study the Internet and its relation to society, are now working on a new book, one for which they're using the Internet to determine its title.

33880 ■ *"Will mCommerce Make Black Friday Green?"* in Retail Merchandiser (Vol. 51, September-October 2011, No. 5, pp. 8)

Pub: Phoenix Media Corporation

Ed: Scott Miller. **Description:** Retailers speculate the possibilities of mobile commerce and are implementing strategies at their stores. Consumers using mobile devices accounted for only 0.1 percent of visits to retail Websites on Black Friday 2009 and rose to 5.6 percent in 2010; numbers are expected to rise for 2011.

33881 ■ *"Winner: Private Company, Less Than $100M"* in Crain's Detroit Business (Vol. 25, June 22, 2009, No. 25)

Pub: Crain Communications Inc. - Detroit

Contact: Keith Crain, Chairman

Ed: Tom Henderson. **Description:** Profile of ForeSee Results, an Ann Arbor, Michigan-based firm that uses the University of Michigan American Consumer Satisfaction Index to help businesses measure satisfaction with their Websites.

33882 ■ *Winner Take All: How Competitiveness Shapes the Fate of Nations*

Pub: Basic Books

Contact: Elizabeth Maguire, Publisher

Ed: Richard J. Elkus, Jr. **Released:** June 16, 2009. **Price:** $27; C$34; £17.99. **Description:** American government and misguided business practices have allowed the U.S. to fall behind other countries in various market sectors such as cameras and televisions, as well as information technologies. It will take a national strategy for America to regain its lead in crucial industries. **Availability:** E-book.

33883 ■ *"Wireless: Full Service"* in Entrepreneur (Vol. 35, October 2007, No. 10, pp. 60)

Ed: Amanda C. Kooser. **Description:** Palm Foleo, the $599 smart phone enables users to access and compose email, browse the Internet, view documents

and play Powerpoint files. It weighs 2.5 pounds and has a 10-inch screen. Other features, such as built-in WiFi are described.

33884 ■ *"Women Clicking to Earn Virtual Dollars"* in Sales and Marketing Management (November 11, 2009)

Pub: Nielsen Business Media Inc.

Contact: Howard Appelbaum, President

Ed: Stacy Straczynski. **Description:** According to a new report from Internet marketing firm Q Interactive, women are increasingly playing social media games where they are able to click on an ad or sign up for a promotion to earn virtual currency. Research is showing that this kind of marketing may be a potent tool, especially for e-commerce and online stores.

33885 ■ *"Women Workers Spend Lunchtime on Fridays Shopping Online"* in Marketing to Women (Vol. 23, November 2010, No. 11, pp. 8)

Pub: EPM Communications Inc.

Contact: Ira Mayer, President

E-mail: imayer@epmcom.com

Description: Forty percent of women shop online during work hours, particularly on Fridays. The largest number of women make these purchases during their lunch break. Demographics are included.

33886 ■ *"WordStream Announces a Pair of Firsts for SEO & PPC Keyword Research Tools"* in Marketwired (November 10, 2009)

Pub: COMTEX News Network Inc.

Contact: Chip Brian, President

Description: WordSteam, Inc., a provider of pay-per-click (PPC) and search engine optimization (SEO) solutions for continuously expanding and optimizing search marketing efforts has released two new features in their flagship Keyword Management solution; these tools will allow marketers to analyze data from paid search, organic search and estimated totals from keyword suggestion tools side-by-side.

33887 ■ *Work at Home Now: The No-Nonsense Guide to Finding Your Perfect Home-Based Job, Avoiding Scams, and Making a Great Living*

Pub: Career Press Inc.

Contact: Ron Fry, President

Ed: Christine Durst, Michael Haaren. **Released:** November 20, 2009. **Price:** $14.99. **Description:** There are legitimate home-based jobs and projects that can be found on the Internet, but trustworthy guidance is scarce. There is a 58 to 1 scam ratio in work at-home advertising filled with fraud.

33888 ■ *"Xtium Has Its Head in the Clouds"* in Philadelphia Business Journal (Vol. 30, September 23, 2011, No. 32, pp. 1)

Pub: American City Business Journals Inc.

Ed: Peter Key. **Description:** Philadelphia-based cloud computing firm Xtium LLC received an $11.5 million first-round investment from Boston-Massachusetts-based OpenView Venture Partners. Catering to midsize businesses and unit of bigger firms, Xtium offers disaster-recovery, hosting, and managed-information-technology-infrastructure services.

33889 ■ *"The Yahoo Family Tree"* in Conde Nast Portfolio (Vol. 2, June 2008, No. 6, pp. 34)

Pub: Conde Nast Publications

Contact: Charles T. Townsend, President

Ed: Blaise Zerega. **Description:** Yahoo, founded in 1994 by Stanford students Jerry Yang and David Filo, is still an Internet powerhouse. The company's history is also outlined as well as the reasons in which Microsoft desperately wants to acquire the firm.

33890 ■ *"Yahoo! - Microsoft Pact: Alive Again?"* in Barron's (Vol. 89, July 27, 2009, No. 30, pp. 8)

Pub: Dow Jones & Co., Inc.

Contact: Clare Hart, President

Ed: Mark Veverka. **Description:** Yahoo! reported higher than expected earnings in the second quarter of 2009 under CEO Carol Bartz who has yet to articulate her long-term vision and strategy for turning around the company. The media reported that Yahoo! and Microsoft are discussing an advertising-search partnership which should benefit both companies.

33891 ■ *"Yammer Gets Serious"* in *Inc.*
(Volume 32, December 2010, No. 10, pp. 58)
Pub: Inc. Magazine
Ed: Eric Markowitz. **Description:** Yammer, an internal social network for companies, allows coworkers to share ideas and documents in real-time. Details of this service are included.

33892 ■ *"You Are What They Click"* in *Entrepreneur (Vol. 37, July 2009, No. 7, pp. 43)*
Pub: Entrepreneur Press
Contact: Perlman Neil, President
Ed: Mikal E. Belicove. **Description:** Hiring the right website design firm is the first stage in building an online business, and this involves various factors such as price, technical expertise, and talent. Writing a request for proposal (RFP) detailing the website's details, which include purpose, budget and audience, is the first step the process. Other tips in finding the right web designer are given.

33893 ■ *Your First Year in Real Estate: Making the Transition from Total Novice to Successful Professional*
Ed: Dirk Zeller. **Released:** August 03, 2010. **Price:** $20. **Description:** Zeller helps new realtors to select the right company, develop mentor and client relationships, using the Internet and social networking to stay ahead of competition, to set and reach career goals, to stay current in the market, and more.

33894 ■ *"Your Turn in the Spotlight"* in *Inc.*
(Volume 32, December 2010, No. 10, pp. 57)
Pub: Inc. Magazine
Ed: John Brandon. **Description:** Examples of three video blogs created by entrepreneurs to promote their businesses and products are used to show successful strategies. Wine Library TV promotes a family's wine business; SHAMA.TV offers marketing tips and company news; and Will It Blend? promotes sales of a household blender.

33895 ■ *"YourEncore's Corps of Scientists, Engineers Helps Cincinnati's P&G, Others Fight Fires"* in *Business Courier (Vol. 26, November 13, 2009, No. 29, pp. 1)*
Pub: American City Business Journals, Inc.
Contact: Whitney Shaw, President
Ed: Lisa Biank Fasig. **Description:** YourForce has nearly 6,000 retired scientists and researchers who work together in helping Procter & Gamble (P&G) and other companies in addressing various project needs. Operating as an online innovation community, YourEncore is a result of P&G's Connect Develop program.

33896 ■ *YouTube and Video Marketing: An Hour a Day*
Pub: Sybex Inc.
Contact: Scott Kelby, President
Ed: Greg Jarboe. **Released:** Second Edition. **Price:** $29.95, paperback; $19.99. **Description:** The importance of online video marketing for businesses is stressed. Tips for developing and implementing video marketing are outlined. **Availability:** PrintE-book.

33897 ■ *"Zeon Solutions Teams with Endeca for SaaS Version of Endeca InFront"* in *Entertainment Close-Up (October 25, 2011)*
Pub: Close-Up Media
Description: Zeon Solutions, an enterprise e-commerce and Website development firm announced a special licensing partnership with Endeca Technologies. Endeca is an information management software company that provides small and mid-size retailers with high-performance Customer Experience Management technology.

33898 ■ *"The Zero Marginal Cost Society: The Internet of Things, the Collaborative Commons, and the Eclipse of Capitalism"*
Pub: Palgrave Macmillan
Contact: Lisa Dunn, Manager
E-mail: l.dunn@palgrave.com
Released: April 1, 2014. **Price:** $28.00. **Description:** The emerging Internet of things is speeding society to an ear of nearly free goods and services, causing the rise of a global Collaborative Commons and the eclipse of capitalism. Entrepreneurial dynamism of competitive markets that drives productivity up and marginal costs down, enabling businesses to reduce the price of their goods and services to win consumers and market share is slowly dying.

CONSULTANTS

33899 ■ BIA/Kelsey
15120 Enterprise Ct.
Chantilly, VA 20151
Ph: (703)818-2425
Free: 800-331-5086
Co. E-mail: info@bia.com
URL: http://www.biakelsey.com
Contact: Neal Polachek, President
E-mail: npolachek@kelseygroup.com
Description: Description: Publishes market and industry reports for the communications industry. Does not accept unsolicited manuscripts. Reaches market through commission representatives, direct mail, reviews and listings and distributors. **Scope:** A provider of research and fact-based analysis focusing on local advertising and electronic commerce. **Founded:** 1983. **Publications:** "Penetration of Online Media Surpasses Traditional Media for First Time Among Small-Business Advertisers," Aug, 2009; "Rapid Adoption of Advanced Mobile Devices Driving Increased Mobile Local Search Activity, According to The Kelsey Group," Nov, 2008; "Online Consumer Generated Reviews Have Significant Impact on Offline Purchase Behavior," Nov, 2007. **Seminars:** Drilling Down on Local: Marketplaces, The Westin Seattle, Seattle, Washington, Apr, 2008; The Future of Local Search in Europe, Jun, 2007; DDC2006?Directory Driven Commerce Conference, Hyatt Century Plaza, LA, Sep, 2006; Drilling Down on Local: Targeting the On-Demand Marketplace, 2005.

33900 ■ Digital Deli Inc.
3145 Geary Blvd., Ste. 532
San Francisco, CA 94118-3316
Ph: (415)387-7653
Contact: Brian Thomas, Vice President
E-mail: blt@thedeli.com
Scope: Specializes in interactive marketing development. Provides strategic and tactical planning for interactive media. Specializes in marketing communications. **Founded:** 1995.

33901 ■ Digitas
33 Arch St.
Boston, MA 02110
Ph: (617)867-1000
Fax: (617)867-1111
Co. E-mail: info@digitas.com
URL: http://www.digitas.com
Contact: Colin Kinsella, President
Scope: Helps clients determine how to use the Internet and emerging technologies to create new business models and enterprise-wide customer value propositions to gain competitive advantages, improved market share and enhanced profitability. Technology, architecture and infrastructure service marketing and creative services were focused on enabling brands to connect with the right customer at the right time through the right channels in the most effective way possible. Performance measurement provides the ultimate yardstick and continuous feedback mechanisms. **Founded:** 1980.

33902 ■ Organic Inc.
555 Market St., 4th Fl.
San Francisco, CA 94105-2873
Ph: (415)581-5300
Fax: (415)581-5400
Co. E-mail: newbiz-sf@organic.com
URL: http://www.organic.com
Contact: Mark Kingdon, Chief Executive Officer
Scope: Strategic consulting, e-business, marketing solutions, e-commerce website creation, customer service and fulfillment. **Founded:** 1993.

33903 ■ Sapient Corp.
131 Dartmouth St., 3rd Fl.
Boston, MA 02116-5297
Ph: (617)621-0200
Fax: (617)621-1300
Co. E-mail: info@sapient.com
URL: http://www.sapient.com
Contact: Alan J. Herrick, President
Scope: The company offers its services in the areas of business and information technology (IT) strategy, business applications, business intelligence, marketing, and outsourcing. Its business and IT strategy services include business-process consulting, business applications and enterprise architecture planning, e-business and Web strategy, IT governance and advisory services, and program management office. **Founded:** 1990. **Publications:** "Here Today, Gone Tomorrow: How to Get the Most Out of Your Ads," Mar, 2009; "New Media Age," Dec, 2005.

33904 ■ Spherix Inc.
6430 Rockledge Dr., Ste. 503
Bethesda, MD 20817-1886
Ph: (703)992-9325
Co. E-mail: info@spherix.com
URL: http://www.spherix.com
Contact: Anthony Hayes, President
Scope: Provides health sciences consulting services that give scientific and strategic support for suppliers, manufacturers, distributors and retailers of: Conventional foods, biotechnology-derived foods, medical foods, infant formulas, food ingredients, dietary supplements, food contact substances, pharmaceuticals, medical devices, consumer products and industrial chemicals and pesticides. Provides teleservices, ebusinesses, and IT solutions for the health and information industries. **Founded:** 1967. **Publications:** "Viking found no life on Mars, and, just as important, it found why there can be no life". **Special Services:** Naturlose®.

33905 ■ Stratamar Inc.
5661 Seapine Rd.
Hilliard, OH 43026
Ph: (614)946-4614
Fax: (614)529-2945
Co. E-mail: info@stratamar.com
URL: http://www.stratamar.com
Contact: Neil Brown, Principal
E-mail: neilbrown@stratamar.com
Scope: A full-spectrum strategic marketing consulting company. Areas of concentration include product development, product management, strategic planning, development and implementation of tactical marketing plans, and Internet marketing. The primary focus is upon maximizing the benefit, cost ratio of promotions through the use of direct marketing, low cost media, and the like. **Founded:** 1998. **Publications:** "Business Plans," Feb, 2006.

COMPUTERIZED DATABASES

33906 ■ *BtoB*
Crain Communications Inc.
1155 Gratiot Ave.
Detroit, MI 48207-2732
Ph: (313)446-6000
Co. E-mail: info@crain.com
URL: http://www.crain.com
Contact: Rance E. Crain, President
Availability: Online: Crain Communications Inc.
Type: Full-text.

EDUCATIONAL PROGRAMS

33907 ■ Administrative Professionals Retreat
Padgett-Thompson Seminars
Rockhurst University CEC
14502 W 105th St.
Lenexa, KS 66215
Free: 800-349-1935
URL: http://www.findaseminar.com/tpd/Padgett-Thompson-Seminars.asp
URL(s): www.findaseminar.com/event1.asp?eventID=8754. **Price:** $199. **Description:** A two-day seminar for administrative professionals. **Audience:** Administrative professionals and assistants.

33908 ■ Advanced Issues in Employee Relations
Seminar Information Service Inc.
20 Executive Park, Ste. 120
Irvine, CA 92614
Ph: (949)261-9104
Free: 877-SEM-INFO
Fax: (949)261-1963
Co. E-mail: info@seminarinformation.com
URL: http://www.seminarinformation.com
Description: Key topics include coaching managers to more effectively manage high performing employees who consistently demonstrate one serious performance failing, collaborating with managers to assist them in focusing on performance issues without being influenced by employees' personal circumstances, working with managers on dealing more effectively with strong negative employee reactions to direction or feedback, and addressing managers' behavior that is inappropriate and potentially high risk. **Audience:** Professionals.

33909 ■ AMA's Myers-Briggs Type Indicator (MBTI) Certification Program
American Management Association (AMA)
1601 Broadway
New York, NY 10019-7420
Ph: (212)586-8100
Free: 877-566-9441
Fax: (212)903-8168
Co. E-mail: customerservice@amanet.org
URL: http://www.amanet.org
Contact: Edward T. Reilly, President
URL(s): www.amanet.org/Human-Resources.aspx.
Description: Updated MBTI program that focuses on team building, leadership, and individual development. **Audience:** HR professionals, training and OD specialists, career counselors, and line managers .

33910 ■ The Art of Coaching: Enabling Employees to Achieve Their Potential (Onsite)
URL(s): www.seminarinformation.com. **Description:** Learn how to: Apply coaching techniques to unlock employee potential and maximize performance; Harness the art of coaching to forge collaborative relationships; Structure a framework for mutually effective learning and development; Develop the coaching skills, attitudes and behaviors to foster success at all levels; Recognize and adapt to individual and situ-ational differences; Create a positive, supportive environment that generates commitment and enthusiasm. **Telecommunication Services:** info@seminarinformation.com.

33911 ■ Assertive Management (Onsite)
Seminar Information Service Inc.
20 Executive Park, Ste. 120
Irvine, CA 92614
Ph: (949)261-9104
Free: 877-SEM-INFO
Fax: (949)261-1963
Co. E-mail: info@seminarinformation.com
URL: http://www.seminarinformation.com
URL(s): www.seminarinformation.com/qqbeah/positive-assertive. **Description:** Develop the qualities necessary for successful, assertive management. Participants gain confidence and skill in being 'proactive' in communicating with others, including how to use positive, win-win approaches and to defuse emotionally charged situations in order to work more effectively with their fellow workers, supervisors and subordinates. **Audience:** Supervisors and managers. **Telecommunication Services:** info@seminarinformation.com.

33912 ■ Basic Problem Solving Techniques (Onsite)
Seminar Information Service Inc.
20 Executive Park, Ste. 120
Irvine, CA 92614
Ph: (949)261-9104
Free: 877-SEM-INFO
Fax: (949)261-1963
Co. E-mail: info@seminarinformation.com
URL: http://www.seminarinformation.com
Price: Contact for fee. **Description:** With the help of several qualitative, quantitative, and creative problem solving methods participants develop their ability to recognize and solve problems through their own efforts. **Dates and Locations:** Waukesha, WI.

33913 ■ Building Better Work Relationships: New Techniques for Results-oriented Communication
American Management Association (AMA)
1601 Broadway
New York, NY 10019-7420
Ph: (212)586-8100
Free: 877-566-9441
Fax: (212)903-8168
Co. E-mail: customerservice@amanet.org
URL: http://www.amanet.org
Contact: Edward T. Reilly, President
URL(s): www.amanet.org/training/seminars/Building-Better-Work-Relationships-New-Techniques-for-Results-oriented-Communication.aspx. **Price:** $2,345, Non-members; $2,095, Members AMA; $1,794, Members GSA. **Description:** Covers effective work relationships, communication and perceptions, investigating emotions and emotional intelligence, relationship building, relational communication and listening and more. **Audience:** Communication and relationship management professionals.

33914 ■ Business Conversation for Sales and Service (Onsite)
Seminar Information Service Inc.
20 Executive Park, Ste. 120
Irvine, CA 92614
Ph: (949)261-9104
Free: 877-SEM-INFO
Fax: (949)261-1963
Co. E-mail: info@seminarinformation.com
URL: http://www.seminarinformation.com
URL(s): www.seminarinformation.com/qqbmve/business-conversation-for-sales-and-service. **Description:** Participants will learn practical tips and practice conversation. Build common ground with colleagues, customers, and senior managers, including methods to develop a repertoire of topics, make skillful transitions, develop confidence and draw people to you. **Audience:** Business professionals. **Telecommunication Services:** info@seminarinformation.com.

33915 ■ Coaching and Teambuilding Skills for Managers and Supervisors (Onsite)
Seminar Information Service Inc.
20 Executive Park, Ste. 120
Irvine, CA 92614
Ph: (949)261-9104
Free: 877-SEM-INFO
Fax: (949)261-1963
Co. E-mail: info@seminarinformation.com
URL: http://www.seminarinformation.com
URL(s): www.seminarinformation.com/details.cfm?qc=qqbpbe. **Price:** $299. **Description:** Gain team building expertise guaranteed to make your team more cohesive, motivated, and productive. **Audience:** Managers and supervisors.

33916 ■ Creativity and Innovation (Onsite)
Seminar Information Service Inc.
20 Executive Park, Ste. 120
Irvine, CA 92614
Ph: (949)261-9104
Free: 877-SEM-INFO
Fax: (949)261-1963
Co. E-mail: info@seminarinformation.com
URL: http://www.seminarinformation.com
Price: $2,095, Non-members; $1,895, Members AMA. **Description:** Develop creative thinking methods to generate ideas and solutions and learn how to align your ideas with corporate needs to add value and increase recognition. **Audience:** Managers, team leaders, directors, project managers, and supervisors . **Dates and Locations:** New York, NY; and Arlington, VA.

33917 ■ Criticism & Discipline Skills for Managers and Supervisors (Onsite)
Fred Pryor Seminars & CareerTrack
5700 Broadmoor St., Ste. 300
Mission, KS 66202
Ph: (800)780-8476
Free: 800-780-8476

Fax: (913)967-8849
Co. E-mail: customerservice@pryor.com
URL: http://www.pryor.com
Contact: Phil Love, Chief Executive Officer
Description: Learn proven techniques for managing difficult employees without incurring resentment, making enemies, or destroying relationships, including how to discipline employees who have a bad attitude, are chronically tardy, miss work often, refuse to take responsibility and challenge your authority. **Audience:** Industry professionals.

33918 ■ Effective Communication and Motivation (Onsite)
Seminar Information Service Inc.
20 Executive Park, Ste. 120
Irvine, CA 92614
Ph: (949)261-9104
Free: 877-SEM-INFO
Fax: (949)261-1963
Co. E-mail: info@seminarinformation.com
URL: http://www.seminarinformation.com
Description: Gives managerial personnel a sound understanding of the principles of effective communication and the skill to recognize and to resolve communication breakdowns in the workplace. Participants learn to apply communication skills to problem solving, employee relations and performance appraisal. **Audience:** General public.

33919 ■ The Effective Facilitator
Canadian Management Centre (CMC)
150 York St., 5th Fl.
Toronto, ON, Canada M5H 3S5
Free: 877-262-2519
Fax: (416)214-6047
Co. E-mail: cmcinfo@cmcoutperform.com
URL: http://cmcoutperform.com
Contact: John Wright, President
URL(s): www.cmctraining.org. **Description:** Covers achieving positive results in group settings such as meetings, project teams, and group work projects. **Audience:** Industry professionals. **Telecommunication Services:** cmcinfo@cmctraining.org.

33920 ■ The Effective Facilitator: Maximizing Involvement and Results
American Management Association (AMA)
1601 Broadway
New York, NY 10019-7420
Ph: (212)586-8100
Free: 877-566-9441
Fax: (212)903-8168
Co. E-mail: customerservice@amanet.org
URL: http://www.amanet.org
Contact: Edward T. Reilly, President
URL(s): www.amaseminars.org. **Price:** $2,345, Non-members; $2,095, Members; $1,794, Members General Services Administration (GSA). **Description:** Covers achieving positive results in group settings such as meetings, project teams, and group work projects. Held in Chicago, IL; Atlanta, GA; Arlington, VA; and Washington, DC. Also available live online. **Audience:** Managers who must facilitate results in meetings, group work or project teams, managers who have groups under their direction, as well as managers who work as internal consultants. **Dates and Locations:** 2015 Feb 02-04; venue not reported. **Telecommunication Services:** customerservice@amanet.org.

33921 ■ Effective Project Communications, Negotiations and Conflict (Onsite)
EEI Communications
8945 Guilford Rd., Ste. 145
Columbia, MD 21046
Ph: (410)309-8200
Free: 888-253-2762
Fax: (410)630-3980
Co. E-mail: train@eeicom.com
URL: http://www.eeicom.com/eei-training-services
Description: Learn what you need to know to lead projects through their initiation, planning, execution, and control phases, including the skills needed to find common ground, overcome resistance, resolve disputes, and gain commitment to project management efforts. **Audience:** Industry professionals.

33922 ■ Enhancing Your Management Skills (Onsite)
Seminar Information Service Inc.
20 Executive Park, Ste. 120
Irvine, CA 92614
Ph: (949)261-9104
Free: 877-SEM-INFO
Fax: (949)261-1963
Co. E-mail: info@seminarinformation.com
URL: http://www.seminarinformation.com
Description: Learn the critical success factors for driving results through goal alignment, coaching for performance, building trust, and driving committed action through stronger leadership. Receive practical, state-of-the-art tools and techniques for holding conversations that set clear expectations, provide focused feedback, create a motivational environment, and build commitment for needed change. **Audience:** Industry professionals.

33923 ■ Enhancing Your People Skills
Seminar Information Service Inc.
20 Executive Park, Ste. 120
Irvine, CA 92614
Ph: (949)261-9104
Free: 877-SEM-INFO
Fax: (949)261-1963
Co. E-mail: info@seminarinformation.com
URL: http://www.seminarinformation.com
URL(s): www.seminarinformation.com. **Description:** Build awareness and skill in the areas of team dynamics, group problem solving, and group decision making. The critical structural and behavioral dimensions of building and leading an effective work team or task force are fully explored. You will develop leadership skills applicable to many areas, but especially suited to self-directed work teams, employee participation teams, interdepartmental task groups, and other group situations where combined efforts are needed to reach optimal performance levels. **Audience:** General public. **Telecommunication Services:** info@seminarinformation.com.

33924 ■ Essential Skills for the First-Time Manager or Supervisor (Onsite)
Fred Pryor Seminars & CareerTrack
5700 Broadmoor St., Ste. 300
Mission, KS 66202
Ph: (800)780-8476
Free: 800-780-8476
Fax: (913)967-8849
Co. E-mail: customerservice@pryor.com
URL: http://www.pryor.com
Contact: Phil Love, Chief Executive Officer
Description: Gain all the skills and insights you need to lead with confidence and conviction, including how to start producing results right away, what it takes to get productivity from people who aren't used to you being the boss. **Audience:** Industry professionals.

33925 ■ The Exceptional Assistant (Onsite)
Fred Pryor Seminars & CareerTrack
5700 Broadmoor St., Ste. 300
Mission, KS 66202
Ph: (800)780-8476
Free: 800-780-8476
Fax: (913)967-8849
Co. E-mail: customerservice@pryor.com
URL: http://www.pryor.com
Contact: Phil Love, Chief Executive Officer
Price: $99, for groups of 5 or more. **Description:** Covers the necessary skills for success, including prioritizing, problem solving, political and people skills, managing time and resources, crises and decision making. **Audience:** Industry professionals. **Dates and Locations:** Cities throughout the United States.

33926 ■ Greater Productivity Through Improved Work Processes: A Guide for Administrative Professionals (Onsite)
American Management Association (AMA)
1601 Broadway
New York, NY 10019-7420
Ph: (212)586-8100
Free: 877-566-9441

Fax: (212)903-8168
Co. E-mail: customerservice@amanet.org
URL: http://www.amanet.org
Contact: Edward T. Reilly, President
URL(s): www.amaseminars.org. **Description:** Two-day seminar for administrative professionals with three or more years of experience; covers increasing productivity and efficiency, dealing with change, improving your work, and assisting in improving various aspects of the organization. **Telecommunication Services:** customerservice@amanet.org.

33927 ■ How to Be a Dynamic Trainer (Onsite)
Seminar Information Service Inc.
20 Executive Park, Ste. 120
Irvine, CA 92614
Ph: (949)261-9104
Free: 877-SEM-INFO
Fax: (949)261-1963
Co. E-mail: info@seminarinformation.com
URL: http://www.seminarinformation.com
URL(s): www.seminarinformation.com/details. cfm?qc=qqbpgk. **Price:** $249. **Description:** Learn how to motivate reluctant learners and how to engage learners to get them to participate. **Audience:** Trainers, training managers, HR professionals, team leaders, supervisors, managers and educators.

33928 ■ How to Be a Highly Successful Team Leader (Onsite)
Seminar Information Service Inc.
20 Executive Park, Ste. 120
Irvine, CA 92614
Ph: (949)261-9104
Free: 877-SEM-INFO
Fax: (949)261-1963
Co. E-mail: info@seminarinformation.com
URL: http://www.seminarinformation.com
Price: $299. **Description:** Intensive two-day workshop that teaches the many dimensions of effective leadership and develop the skills needed to lead your team to maximum performance. **Audience:** New team leader.

33929 ■ Leadership Skills: Building Success Through Teamwork (Onsite)
Seminar Information Service Inc.
20 Executive Park, Ste. 120
Irvine, CA 92614
Ph: (949)261-9104
Free: 877-SEM-INFO
Fax: (949)261-1963
Co. E-mail: info@seminarinformation.com
URL: http://www.seminarinformation.com
Description: Learn how to: Develop your teams to maximize their strengths and enhance productivity; Optimize organization and work design for success in service delivery teams; Motivate your team with effective performance measurement; Integrate your role as a leader into your management style; Leverage the complementary skills and styles of your team; Eliminate barriers and chokepoints that block teamwork; Apply a diverse and multilevel approach to minimize communication breakdowns. **Audience:** Industry professionals.

33930 ■ Leadership and Team Development for Managerial Success
Canadian Management Centre (CMC)
150 York St., 5th Fl.
Toronto, ON, Canada M5H 3S5
Free: 877-262-2519
Fax: (416)214-6047
Co. E-mail: cmcinfo@cmcoutperform.com
URL: http://cmcoutperform.com
Contact: John Wright, President
URL(s): www.cmctraining.org/leadership-team-development-managerial-success. **Price:** $1,845.00 Canadian for non-members; $1,995.00 Canadian for CMC members. **Frequency:** Bimonthly. **Description:** Covers how to work in a horizontal mode of operation, including when to manage and when to lead your team, distinguishing the three team types, principles that make teams work, differentiating team content and process, and diagnosing work teams.

Audience: executives, managers, team leaders and other business professionals. **Telecommunication Services:** cmcinfo@cmctraining.org.

33931 ■ Leading Effective Teams II - Communicating with Your Teammates (Onsite)
Seminar Information Service Inc.
20 Executive Park, Ste. 120
Irvine, CA 92614
Ph: (949)261-9104
Free: 877-SEM-INFO
Fax: (949)261-1963
Co. E-mail: info@seminarinformation.com
URL: http://www.seminarinformation.com
Price: $350.00 for non-members; $275.00 for MRA members. **Description:** Leaders learn their communication style and how it relates to their team members, as well as how to motivate through communication. **Dates and Locations:** Waukesha, WI.

33932 ■ Leading High Performance Teams
Seminar Information Service Inc.
20 Executive Park, Ste. 120
Irvine, CA 92614
Ph: (949)261-9104
Free: 877-SEM-INFO
Fax: (949)261-1963
Co. E-mail: info@seminarinformation.com
URL: http://www.seminarinformation.com
URL(s): www.seminarinformation.com/qqbtkk/project-leadership-building-high-performance-teams. **Price:** $2,990. **Description:** Builds awareness and skill in the areas of team dynamics, group problem solving, and group decision making. You will develop leadership skills applicable to many areas, but especially suited to self-directed work teams, employee participation teams, interdepartmental task groups, and other group situations where combined efforts are needed to reach optimal performance levels. **Audience:** Team leaders and project managers. **Dates and Locations:** 2015 Mar 17-20; venue not reported. **Telecommunication Services:** info@seminarinformation.com.

33933 ■ Making Successful Business Decisions: Getting it Right the First Time (Onsite)
Seminar Information Service Inc.
20 Executive Park, Ste. 120
Irvine, CA 92614
Ph: (949)261-9104
Free: 877-SEM-INFO
Fax: (949)261-1963
Co. E-mail: info@seminarinformation.com
URL: http://www.seminarinformation.com
Price: $2,490.00. **Description:** Learn how to make intelligent decisions with limited time and information, how to convert conflicting opinions into useful insights, foster efficient and effective group decision making, and ensure decisions are implemented by the organization.

33934 ■ Management Skills for an IT Environment (Onsite)
Seminar Information Service Inc.
20 Executive Park, Ste. 120
Irvine, CA 92614
Ph: (949)261-9104
Free: 877-SEM-INFO
Fax: (949)261-1963
Co. E-mail: info@seminarinformation.com
URL: http://www.seminarinformation.com
Price: $2,810. **Description:** Learn how to apply a proven management model for leading technical staff to excellence; identify key success criteria for leadership in an IT environment; leverage emotion to optimize communication and performance; motivate and empower technical professionals to achieve results; delegate proactively to focus on strengths of IT teams and build accountability. **Audience:** IT managers. **Dates and Locations:** Reston, VA; Ottawa, CN; Schaumburg, IL; Los Angeles, CA; Philadelphia, PA; Toronto, CN; New York, NY; Alexandria, VA; and Rockville, MD.

33935 ■ Managing Today's IT and Technical Professionals (Onsite)
Seminar Information Service Inc.
20 Executive Park, Ste. 120
Irvine, CA 92614
Ph: (949)261-9104
Free: 877-SEM-INFO
Fax: (949)261-1963
Co. E-mail: info@seminarinformation.com
URL: http://www.seminarinformation.com
URL(s): www.seminarinformation.com/details.cfm?qc=qqakqt. **Price:** $2,345. **Description:** Learn how to strengthen, motivate and inspire any group or team. **Audience:** Technical professionals.

33936 ■ Managing in Tough Times (Onsite)
Seminar Information Service Inc.
20 Executive Park, Ste. 120
Irvine, CA 92614
Ph: (949)261-9104
Free: 877-SEM-INFO
Fax: (949)261-1963
Co. E-mail: info@seminarinformation.com
URL: http://www.seminarinformation.com
Price: $2,490.00. **Description:** Learn how to demonstrate authentic and strong leadership to create an atmosphere of confidence and trust in tough times, share your vision and display confidence that the problems your team currently faces will be solved, and minimize stress and maximize productivity and performance during difficult times.

33937 ■ Partnering with Your Boss: Strategic Skills for Administrative Professionals
American Management Association (AMA)
1601 Broadway
New York, NY 10019-7420
Ph: (212)586-8100
Free: 877-566-9441
Fax: (212)903-8168
Co. E-mail: customerservice@amanet.org
URL: http://www.amanet.org
Contact: Edward T. Reilly, President
URL(s): www.amaseminars.org/training/seminars/Partnering-with-Your-Boss-Strategic-Skills-for-Administrative-Professionals.aspx. **Price:** $1,645.00 for non-members; $1,495.00 for AMA members; and $1,280.00 for General Services Administration (GSA) members,. **Description:** Covers skills for setting goals, prioritizing, making decisions, building relationships, and communicating in such a way as to represent your boss authoritatively and gain respect in the workplace. Held in Washington, DC; New York, NY; Arlington, VA; Chicago, IL; San Francisco, CA; and Dallas, TX. Also available live online. **Audience:** senior administrative support staffs, executive secretaries, administrative assistants, staff assistants and executive assistants. **Telecommunication Services:** customerservice@amanet.org.

33938 ■ Project Leadership: Building High-Performance Teams (Onsite)
Seminar Information Service Inc.
20 Executive Park, Ste. 120
Irvine, CA 92614
Ph: (949)261-9104
Free: 877-SEM-INFO
Fax: (949)261-1963
Co. E-mail: info@seminarinformation.com
URL: http://www.seminarinformation.com
Price: $2,990. **Description:** Learn how to: Develop the leadership skills to build and sustain high-performing project teams; Develop effective team performance through the Leadership Services Model; Build a strong team identity through vision, purpose and commitment; Foster positive and productive team communication and define ground rules; Protect the team and convert conflicts into advantages that promote high performance; Maximize your leadership abilities when you return to your organization. **Audience:** Team leaders and project managers. **Dates and Locations:** 2015 Mar 17-20; venue not reported.

33939 ■ Projecting a Positive Professional Image
American Management Association (AMA)
1601 Broadway
New York, NY 10019-7420

Ph: (212)586-8100
Free: 877-566-9441
Fax: (212)903-8168
Co. E-mail: customerservice@amanet.org
URL: http://www.amanet.org
Contact: Edward T. Reilly, President
URL(s): www.amaseminars.org/training/articles/Projecting-a-Positive-Professional-Image.aspx. **Price:** $1,895.00 for non-members; $1,795.00 for AMA members; and $1,537.00 for. **Description:** Covers creating a self-image, including look, dress, and behavior, to project a positive image in your current position and to advance to new positions. **Audience:** Mobile executives, professionals and salespeople. **Dates and Locations:** Washington, DC; San Francisco, CA; Atlanta, GA; Chicago, IL; and New York, NY. **Telecommunication Services:** customerservice@amanet.org.

33940 ■ Responding to Conflict: Creating Resolution and Cooperation (Onsite)
Seminar Information Service Inc.
20 Executive Park, Ste. 120
Irvine, CA 92614
Ph: (949)261-9104
Free: 877-SEM-INFO
Fax: (949)261-1963
Co. E-mail: info@seminarinformation.com
URL: http://www.seminarinformation.com
URL(s): www.seminarinformation.com/qqaaug/responding-to-conflict-strategies-for-improved. **Price:** $2,345, Onsite; $2,095, Members AMA. **Frequency:** Monthly. **Description:** Learn how to: Effectively handle conflict using a powerful conflict resolution method; Anticipate the causes of conflict and respond proactively; Manage strong emotions in a conflict situation; Remove barriers to cooperation; Create productive outcomes and reach a final agreement; Embrace conflict as an opportunity for team and organizational growth. **Audience:** Business professionals. **Dates and Locations:** 2015 Feb 02-03, AMA New York Center, New York, NY. **Telecommunication Services:** info@seminarinformation.com.

33941 ■ Sparking Innovation and Creativity (Onsite)
Seminar Information Service Inc.
20 Executive Park, Ste. 120
Irvine, CA 92614
Ph: (949)261-9104
Free: 877-SEM-INFO
Fax: (949)261-1963
Co. E-mail: info@seminarinformation.com
URL: http://www.seminarinformation.com
URL(s): www.seminarinformation.com/qqbupu/sparking-innovation-and-creativity. **Price:** $199. **Description:** Innovative problem-solving skills to overcome negative thinking habits within the organization to reach the company's goals and objectives. **Audience:** All employees.

33942 ■ Strategic Planning
Canadian Management Centre (CMC)
150 York St., 5th Fl.
Toronto, ON, Canada M5H 3S5
Free: 877-262-2519
Fax: (416)214-6047
Co. E-mail: cmcinfo@cmcoutperform.com
URL: http://cmcoutperform.com
Contact: John Wright, President
URL(s): www.cmctraining.org/strategic-planning. **Description:** Covers the strategic planning process, identifying threats and opportunities for your company, and developing strategies and action plans. **Audience:** Business leaders, executives and other senior managers involved in the formation and implementation of strategy. Line managers in finance, marketing, R&D and manufacturing who are responsible for strategy development and implementation will also benefit from this course. **Telecommunication Services:** cmcinfo@cmctraining.org.

33943 ■ Total Productive Maintenance (TPM) & 5S (Onsite)
American Trainco, Inc.
9785 S Maroon Cir., Ste. 300
Englewood, CO 80112
Ph: (303)531-4560

Free: 877-978-7246
Fax: (303)531-4565
Co. E-mail: Sales@AmericanTrainco.com
URL: http://wwww.americantrainco.com
Price: $990.00. **Description:** Two-day seminar that focuses on getting managers, maintenance personnel and equipment users all working together to prevent equipment problems and reduce expenditures. **Audience:** managers, maintenance personnel and equipment users . **Dates and Locations:** Cities throughout the United States.

REFERENCE WORKS

33944 ■ *"5 Conversations: How to Transform Trust, Engagement and Performance at Work"*
Pub: Panoma Press
Released: October 14, 2014. **Price:** $24.95 paperback. **Description:** Engaged employees help to create successful businesses. The importance of authentic, two-way, human conversations to build relationships, trust, and engagement is stressed to develop a motivated workforce.

33945 ■ *30 Reasons Employees Hate their Managers*
Pub: AMACOM
Contact: Edward T. Reilly, Manager
Ed: Bruce L. Katcher, Adam Snyder. **Released:** March 2007. **Price:** $18.95, Paper or Softback. **Description:** Issues involved in employee negative feelings towards managers are discussed; a survey of more than 50,000 employees in 65 organizations of all types and sizes cited 30 main causes for ill will. **Availability:** Print; E-book.

33946 ■ *"ABCP: Hunter and the Hunted" in Canadian Business (Vol. 81, May 22, 2008, No. 9, pp. 12)*
Pub: Rogers Media Inc.
Contact: Tony Viner, President
Ed: Thomas Watson. **Description:** Brian Hunter, a partner in oil and gas engineering firm Montane Resources, invested his life savings in Vancouver-based Canacord Capital Corp. Details of the asset-backed commercial paper fiasco and Hunter's use of Facebook to encourage other investors to participate in his claim against the mortgage company are presented.

33947 ■ *"The Advantage: Why Organizational Health Trumps Everything Else in Business (J-B Lencioni Series)"*
Pub: Jossey-Bass
Contact: William J. Pesce, President
Released: March 14, 2012. **Price:** $27.95. **Description:** A comprehensive examination of the unique advantage organizational health provides any small business and sets them apart from their competition. A healthy organization is whole, consistent and complete, is free of politics and confusion, and provides an environment where star performers want to stay.

33948 ■ *"All In Good Fun" in Entrepreneur (Vol. 36, May 2008, No. 5, pp. 22)*
Pub: Entrepreneur Press
Contact: Perlman Neil, President
Ed: Christopher Percy Collier. **Description:** According to a study conducted in 2007, humor in the workplace helps people communicate effectively and improves camaraderie. Company leaders and entrepreneurs can also tell humorous stories about themselves, but must also set lines that should not be crossed. The humorous atmosphere in the company YouSendIt is presented.

33949 ■ *"The Alliance: Managing Talent in the Networked Age"*
Pub: Harvard Business Review Press
Contact: Peter E. Walsh, Director
Released: July 8, 2014. **Price:** $25.00. **Description:** It is suggested that management see their workers as allies instead of family or free agents in order to create a realistic loyalty pact between employer and employee. Both sides need to trust each other for the company to succeed and the employee to further their career with the firm.

33950 ■ *Alpha Dogs: How Your Small Business Can Become a Leader of the Pack*
Pub: Harper Business
Ed: Donna Fenn. **Released:** May 08, 2007. **Price:** $14.95, paperback. **Description:** Ways for an entrepreneur to outsmart competitors in the marketplace, to generate higher sales, and earn lasting customer and employee loyalty. **Availability:** Print.

33951 ■ *"Altus Jobs Founders' Unique Operating System Generates Success" in Orlando Business Journal (Vol. 30, April 11, 2014, No. 42, pp. 3)*
Pub: American City Business Journals
Released: April 11, 2014. **Description:** Maitland, Florida-based Altus Jobs founders, Saum Sharifi and Augusto Guevara, have credited their unique operating sytem with their quick success in recruiting talent, specializing in high level engineering positions. The system allows employees to work from 9:30 a.m. to 3:30 p.m. in their casual office and motivates them to show entrepreneurship by offering commission on top of base salary.

33952 ■ *"The Anatomy of a High Potential" in Business Strategy Review (Vol. 21, Autumn 2010, No. 3, pp. 52)*
Pub: Blackwell Publishers Ltd.
Ed: Doug Ready, Jay Conger, Linda Hill, Emily Stecker. **Description:** Companies have long been interested in identifying high potential employees, but few firms know how to convert top talent into game changers, or people who can shape the future of the business. The authors have found the 'x factors' that can make a high-potential list into a strong competitive advantage.

33953 ■ *"The Anatomy of a High Potential" in Business Strategy Review (Vol. 21, Autumn 2010, No. 3, pp. 52)*
Pub: John Wiley & Sons Inc. Scientific, Technical, Medical, and Scholarly Div. (Wiley-Blackwell)
Contact: William J. Pesce, Manager
E-mail: wpesce@wiley.com
Ed: Doug Ready, Jay Conger, Linda Hill, Emily Stecker. **Description:** Companies have long been interested in identifying high-potential employees, but few firms know how to convert top talent into game changers - people who can shape the future of the business. The authors have found the x-factors that can make the high-potential list into a strong competitive advantage.

33954 ■ *"Anatomy of a Rumor" in Entrepreneur (Vol. 37, September 2009, No. 9, pp. 18)*
Pub: Entrepreneur Press
Contact: Perlman Neil, President
Ed: Jason Daley. **Description:** Progression and adverse effect of office rumors on businesses are discussed. The quality of someone's work, tenure and personnel changes are the most prevalent categories of rumors. Workers can lose trust in management and one another as a result of rumors.

33955 ■ *"The Art of Appreciation" in Business Horizons (November-December 2007, pp. 441)*
Pub: Elsevier Technology Publications
Ed: Catherine M. Dalton. **Price:** $35.95. **Description:** The art of appreciation is an art less and less practices by employees. Employers should lead by example and practice this art to inspire employees to do the same. **Availability:** PDF.

33956 ■ *"The Art of the Huddle: How To Run a Prompt, Productive, and Painless Morning Meeting" in Inc. (November 2007, pp. 40, 42-43)*
Pub: Mansueto Ventures L.L.C.
Contact: John Koten, Chief Executive Officer
Ed: Leigh Buchanan. **Description:** Five CEOs describe the ways they use meetings to improve their companies: team building, coordinating, efficiency, motivation, and strategic planning.

33957 ■ *"At Your Career Crossroads" in Women In Business (Vol. 61, December 2009, No. 6, pp. 26)*
Pub: American Business Women's Association
Contact: Lorie Burch, President
Ed: Diane Stafford. **Description:** Guidelines for employees who are considering a job or career change are presented. Among the reasons for lead employees to make these changes are downsizing, job loss, environments that are not conducive to work or unfavorable work relationships with bosses.

33958 ■ *"Baltimore GM Plant Moves Forward" in Baltimore Business Journal (Vol. 32, July 4, 2014, No. 9, pp. 18)*
Pub: American City Business Journals, Inc.
Contact: Whitney Shaw, President
Released: July 4, 2014. **Description:** General Motors (GM) plant at White Marsh represents traditional and modern manufacturing, attracting young employees with the use of advanced technology, but still retaining its loyal, veteran workforce. Most workers at the plant's Allison Transmission facility have been with GM for 25 years or more, while the adjacent facility making electric motors for the Chevy Spark EV is primarily made up of workers in their late 20s.

33959 ■ *"Bank on It: Scouting and Keeping Good Talent in the Workplace" in Hawaii Business (Vol. 53, January 2008, No. 7, pp. 50)*
Pub: PacificBasin Communications
Ed: Christine Dermengian. **Description:** Tips on improving employee selection and retention are presented. The strategies in choosing and keeping the right employees include identifying which type of people the company needs and improving the workplace environment.

33960 ■ *Battling Big Box: How Nimble Niche Companies Can Outmaneuver Giant Competitors*
Pub: Career Press Inc.
Contact: Ron Fry, President
Ed: Henry Dubroff, Susan J. Marks. **Released:** January 2009. **Price:** $15.99. **Description:** Small companies can compete with larger firms through agility, adaptability, customer service, and credibility. Topics include information to help empower employees, build a powerful brand, manage cash flow, and maintaining a business vision. **Availability:** Print.

33961 ■ *"Be a Brilliant Business Writer: Write Well, Write Fast, and Whip the Competition"*
Ed: Jane Curry, Diana Young. **Released:** October 05, 2010. **Price:** $13.99. **Description:** Tools for mastering the art of persuasive writing in every document created, from email and client letters to reports and presentations, this book will help any writer convey their message with clarity and power, increase productivity by reducing rewrites, and provide the correct tone for navigating office politics.

33962 ■ *"Be Nice at Work - Everybody's Watching" in Puget Sound Business Journal (Vol. 34, April 4, 2014, No. 51, pp. 10)*
Pub: American City Business Journals
Released: April 4, 2014. **Description:** Employees can become great co-workers by acknowledging their colleagues, respecting others, avoiding gossip, expressing gratitude and being helpful. Staying positive will also allow staff to deal with demanding bosses and challenging co-workers.

33963 ■ *"Before Happiness: The 5 Hidden Keys to Achieving Success, Spreading Happiness, and Sustaining Positive Change"*
Pub: Crown Business Books
Released: September 10, 2013. **Price:** $26.00. **Description:** Harvard trained researcher explains proven strategies for changing attitudes to positive include, the most valuable reality to see a broader range of ideas and solutions; success mapping, setting goals around things that matter to you most; the x-spot, using success accelerants to propel you more quickly towards goals; noise-canceling, boost the

signal pointing to opportunities and possibilities others miss; and positive inception, transferring your skills to your team, employees and everyone around you.

33964 ■ *"Biblical Secrets to Business Success"*
Pub: CreateSpace
Contact: Daren Giles, President
Released: October 2, 2014. **Price:** $14.99 paperback. **Description:** Bob Diener share insight into his journey as an entrepreneur. He focuses on tough issues like: how to treat employees, how to please customers, whether or not to cut corners, whether to follow temptation of an unethical deal, and provides solutions to these dilemmas. He recommends abiding by the Bible's rules of business in order to prosper long term.

33965 ■ *Big Vision, Small Business: 4 Keys to Success without Growing Big*
Pub: Ivy Sea Inc.
Ed: Jamie S. Walters. **Released:** October 10, 2002. **Price:** $17.95, paperback. **Description:** The power of the small enterprise is examined. The author shares her expertise as an entrepreneur and founder of a business consulting firm to help small business owners successfully run their companies. Interviews with more than seventy small business owners provide insight into visioning, planning, and establishing a small company, as well as strategies for good employee and customer relationships. **Availability:** Print; PDF.

33966 ■ *"Blach Builds on Teamwork"* in *Silicon Valley/San Jose Business Journal (Vol. 30, August 24, 2012, No. 22, pp. 1)*
Pub: American City Business Journal
Description: Blach Construction chief executive, Mike Blach, has grown the firm into a top contractor in San Jose, California. The construction company's earnings have increased to $98 million in 2011.

33967 ■ *"Blast from the Past"* in *Entrepreneur (Vol. 35, November 2007, No. 11, pp. 48)*
Pub: Entrepreneur Press
Contact: Perlman Neil, President
Ed: Robert Kiyosaki. **Description:** Entrepreneurs of today face the challenge of creating new ideas. Collaborating with younger employees provides new perspective, but it also has to be a partnership with old ideas and sharing experiences between the older and the younger to forecast the future.

33968 ■ *Boosting Corporate Entrepreneurship Through HRM Practices: Evidence from German SMEs"* in *Human Resource Management (Vol. 49, July-August 2010, No. 4)*
Pub: John Wiley
Ed: Ralf Schmelter, Rene Mauer, Christiane Borsch, Malte Brettel. **Description:** A study was conducted to determine which human resource management (HRM) practices promote corporate entrepreneurship (CE) in small and medium-sized enterprises (SMEs). Findings indicate that staff selection, staff development, training, and staff rewards on CE have a strong impact on SMEs.

33969 ■ *"Boosting Strategy With An Online Community"* in *Business Strategy Review (Vol. 21, Spring 2010, No. 1, pp. 40)*
Pub: John Wiley & Sons Inc. Scientific, Technical, Medical, and Scholarly Div. (Wiley-Blackwell)
Contact: William J. Pesce, Manager
E-mail: wpesce@wiley.com
Ed: Lynda Gratton, Joel Casse. **Description:** A program that merged online communities with strategic development and implementation at Nokia has provided valuable lessons about new ways employees are able to engage and interact.

33970 ■ *Bottom-Line Training: Performance-Based Results*
Pub: Training Education Management
Contact: Donald J. Ford, President
Ed: Donald J. Ford. **Released:** Second Edition. **Price:** $29. **Description:** Training is critical to any successful enterprise. The key to any successful

training program involves defining and constantly focusing on the desired results of the program. The author provides a training model based on five phases, known as ADDIE: analysis, design, development, implementation and evaluation.

33971 ■ *"Boundaries for Leaders (Enhanced Edition): Results, Relationships, and Being Ridiculously In Charge"*
Pub: Harper Business
Released: April 16, 2013. **Price:** $28.99. **Description:** Clinical psychologist and author explains how the best business leaders set boundaries within their organizations, with their teams and themselves, to improve performance and increase customer and employee satisfaction. Practical advice is given to manage teams, coach direct reports, and create an organization with strong ethics and culture.

33972 ■ *"Breaking Bad: Rid Yourself of Negative Habits"* in *Black Enterprise (Vol. 40, July 2010, No. 12, pp. 104)*
Pub: Earl G. Graves Publishing Co. Inc.
Contact: Earl G. Graves, Jr., President
Ed: Renita Burns. **Description:** Tardiness, procrastination, chronic complaining are among the bad habits that can make people bad employees; tips for breaking these habits are outlined.

33973 ■ *"Brief: Janitorial Company Must Pay Back Wages"* in *Buffalo News (September 24, 2011)*
Pub: The Buffalo News
Contact: Warren T. Colville, President
Ed: Jonathan D. Epstein. **Description:** Knights Facilities Management, located in Michigan, provides grounds maintenance and janitorial services at the Ralph Wilson Stadium in Buffalo, New York. The US Department of Labor ordered the firm to pay $22,000 in back wages and damages to 26 employees for overtime and minimum wage compensation. Details of the company's violation of the Fair Labor Standards Act are included.

33974 ■ *"Bring Out the Best in Your Team"* in *Harvard Business Review Vol. 92, September 2014, No. 9, pp. 26)*
Pub: Harvard Business Publishing
Released: September 2014. **Description:** Social influence often impacts team decision making, as more outgoing members tend to dominate discussion. To replace social influence with informational influence, have team members state at the beginning what knowledge they have regarding the task at hand.

33975 ■ *"Bringing Out the Best in Employees"* in *Business Strategy Review (Vol. 23, Spring 2012, No. 1, pp. 39)*
Released: Spring 2012. **Description:** Employees who find their work frustrating, boring and worthless have found their hero in Scott Adams' Dilbert, the nine-to-five man who lets us know just how bad managers can be at their jobs. Julian Birkinshaw, Vyla Rollins and Stefano Turconi believe that bad bosses can change to become true leaders.

33976 ■ *"Build a Better Bonus"* in *Canadian Business (Vol. 80, January 15, 2007, No. 2, pp. 65)*
Pub: Rogers Media Inc.
Contact: Tony Viner, President
Ed: John Gray. **Description:** The use of employee performance incentives to enhance employee productivity is discussed. Tips for employers, on how to create an effective bonus plan, are presented.

33977 ■ *"Building the Right Culture Can Add Huge Value"* in *South Florida Business Journal (Vol. 34, May 9, 2014, No. 42, pp. 20)*
Pub: American City Business Journals
Released: May 9, 2014. **Description:** Corporate culture has become an afterthought in many companies and this might be the result of viewing operating results purely from a financial perspective. However, it is the people who work for the companies that create value and they would become more effective by defining the culture. The benefits of creating a positive culture are also discussed.

33978 ■ *Business Upgrade: 21 Days to Reignite the Entrepreneurial Spirit in You and Your Team*
Pub: John Wiley & Sons Inc.
Contact: Stephen M. Smith, President
Ed: Richard Parkes Cordock. **Released:** November 2006. **Price:** $18.95, paperback. **Description:** Business consultant works to inspire and guide entrepreneurs to spark growth in their companies while motivating workers. **Availability:** Print.

33979 ■ *"Can People Collaborate Effectively While Working Remotely? Vint Cerf, Co-Creator of the Internet, On How Employees Can Work Together More Productively In An Age When Many Can Work Almost Anywhere"* in *Gallup Business Journal (March 13, 2014)*
Pub: Gallup Press
Released: March 13, 2014. **Description:** Vint Cerf, co-creator of the Internet, discusses ways that employees can work more productively when technology allows them to work from almost anywhere.

33980 ■ *"Can You Hear Me Now?"* in *Harvard Business Review (Vol. 86, July-August 2008, No. 8, pp. 23)*
Pub: Harvard Business Review Press
Contact: Peter E. Walsh, Director
Ed: Katharina Pick. **Description:** Tips for improving communication among boardroom members are presented. These include encouraging frankness via in-meeting leaders, and the ability of directors to meet without managers.

33981 ■ *"Candor, Criticism, Teamwork"* in *Harvard Business Review (Vol. 90, January-February 2012, No.1-2, pp. 40)*
Pub: Harvard Business Review Press
Contact: Peter E. Walsh, Director
Ed: Keith Ferrazzi. **Released:** January-February 2012. **Description:** To ensure honest and effective feedback, meetings should be broken up into smaller groups. Individuals should be selected to be advocates of candor, and techniques for caring criticism should be taught, such as identifying a problem but then suggesting ways to correct it.

33982 ■ *The Carrot Principle: How the Best Managers Use Recognition to Engage Their People, Retain Talent, and Accelerate Performance*
Pub: Simon and Schuster Inc.
Contact: Carolyn Reidy, President
E-mail: carolyn.reidy@simonandschuster.com
Released: April 2009. **Price:** $23.99. **Description:** Book show ways that managers can fail to acknowledge special achievements of employees thereby risking alienating the best workers or losing them to competing firms. **Availability:** Print.

33983 ■ *"Celebrate Success. Embrace Innovation"* in *Black Enterprise (Vol. 37, February 2007, No. 7, pp. 145)*
Description: 2007 Women of Power Summit provides networking opportunities, empowerment sessions, and nightly entertainment. More than 500 executive women of color are expected to attend this inspiring summit in Phoenix, February 7-10.

33984 ■ *"Chameleonic or Consistent? A Multilevel Investigation of Emotional Labor Variability and Self-Monitoring"* in *Academy of Management Journal (Vol. 55, August 1, 2012, No. 4, pp. 905)*
Pub: Academy of Management
Contact: Ming-Jer Chen, President
Ed: Brent A. Scott, Christopher M. Barnes, David T. Wagner. **Description:** The importance of emotional labor variability in association with job satisfaction and work withdrawal is examined. Results indicate that surface acting variability is linked to lower levels of job satisfaction and higher levels of work withdrawal and that self-monitoring influences the impact of surface acting variability on job satisfaction and work withdrawal.

33985 ■ *"Chameloeonic or Consistent? A Multilevel Investigation of Emotional Labor Variability and Self-Monitoring"* in *Academy of Management Journal (Vol. 55, August 2012, No. 4, pp. 905)*
Released: August 2012. **Description:** The importance of emotional labor variability in association with job satisfaction and work withdrawal is examined. Results indicate that surface acting variability is linked to lowe levels of job satisfaction and higher levels of work withdrawal and that self-monitoring influences the impact of surface acting variability on job satisfactionand work withdrawal.

33986 ■ *"Class Management"* in *Canadian Business (Vol. 80, April 23, 2007, No. 9, pp. 64)*
Ed: Erin Pooley. **Description:** The role of executive MBA programs in improving performance of employees is presented.

33987 ■ *"Cloud Computing for a Crowd"* in *CIO (Vol. 24, October 2, 2010, No. 1, pp. 16)*
Pub: CIO
Ed: Stephanie Overby. **Description:** Information about a project which aimed to implement a cloud-based crowdsourcing platform and innovation-management process is provided. Chubb Group of Insurance Companies wanted to mine revenue-generating ideas from its 10,400 employees and hundreds of thousands of external agents. The company hosted its first innovation event using its new system in October 2008.

33988 ■ *"Coffee Breaks Don't Boost Productivity After All"* in *Harvard Business Review (Vol. 90, May 2012, No. 5, pp. 34)*
Pub: Harvard Business Review Press
Contact: Peter E. Walsh, Director
Ed: Charlotte Fritz. **Released:** May 2012. **Description:** Research shows no statistical correlation between taking a short break at work and one's fatigue and vitality levels. However, a link was found between personal productivity and assisting a co-worker. Employees detach from work more successfully during long breaks rather than short ones.

33989 ■ *"Column: Good Decisions. Bad Outcomes"* in *Harvard Business Review (Vol. 88, December 2010, No. 12, pp. 40)*
Pub: Harvard Business School Publishing
Ed: Dan Ariely. **Description:** Suggestions are provided for developing and implementing improved reward systems that in turn produce better decision-making processes. These include documenting critical assumptions and changing mind sets.

33990 ■ *"Column: Work Pray Love"* in *Harvard Business Review (Vol. 88, December 2010, No. 12, pp. 38)*
Pub: Harvard Business School Publishing
Ed: Rosabeth Moss Kanter. **Description:** It is recommended to reinvest in values in order to promote better employee-company engagement and performance.

33991 ■ *"Coming Through When It Matters Most: How Great Teams Do Their Best Work Under Pressure"* in *Harvard Business Review (Vol. 90, April 2012, No. 4, pp. 82)*
Pub: Harvard Business Review Press
Contact: Peter E. Walsh, Director
Ed: Heidi K. Gardner. **Released:** April 2012. **Description:** Teamwork can be enhanced by measuring each member's contribution more deliberately, and by examining every new item of information. This way, teams avoid performance pressure that constricts creativity and innovation.

33992 ■ *"Commitment Issues: Restoring Employee Engagement"* in *Workforce Management (Vol. 88, November 16, 2009, No. 12, pp. 20)*
Pub: Crain Communications Inc.
Contact: Rance E. Crain, President
Ed: Ed Frauenheim. **Description:** Employee engagement refers to how committed workers are to their company and how much extra effort they are willing

to put in on the job; firms could find that they are having a more difficult time coming out of the recession if they lack this important feature in workplace relations.

33993 ■ *"Complaints, Workforce Composition, Productivity, Organizational Values"* in *HRMagazine (Vol. 54, January 2009, No. 1, pp. 29)*
Pub: Society for Human Resource Management
Contact: Henry G. Jackson, President
E-mail: hjackson@shrm.org
Ed: Amy Maingault, Regan Halvorsen, Rue Dooley, Liz Petersen. **Description:** Workforce composition trends that management should monitor are outlined. A goal-development process is discussed.

33994 ■ *"Conquering the Seven Summits of Sales: From Everest to Every Business, Achieving Peak Performance"*
Pub: Harper Business
Released: October 7, 2014. **Price:** $17.95 Audio, $14.44 Kindle. **Description:** Sales professionals are taught to overcome their perceived limitations and strive for success. The guide shows how to define goals, build the right team, commit to a vision, time management, and tracking of progress.

33995 ■ *"Conscious Capitalism: Liberating the Heroic Spirit of Business"*
Released: December 25, 2012. **Price:** $27.00. **Description:** Conscious Capitalism companies include Whole Foods Market, Southwest Airlines, Costco, Google, Patagonia, The Container Store, UPS and others. These firms under the four specific tenants to success: higher purpose, stakeholder integration, conscious leadership, and conscious culture and management. These companies are able to create value for all stakeholders, including customers, employees, suppliers, investors, society, and the environment.

33996 ■ *"The Consequences of Tardiness"* in *Modern Machine Shop (Vol. 84, August 2011, No. 3, pp. 34)*
Pub: Gardner Business Media, Inc.
Contact: Richard G. Kline, President
E-mail: rkline@gardnerweb.com
Ed: Wayne S. Chaneski. **Description:** Five point addressing motivating factors behind employees who are tardy and those who choose to be on time in the workplace are shared.

33997 ■ *"Coolhunting: Chasing Down the Next Big Thing"*
Pub: AMACOM
Contact: Edward T. Reilly, Manager
Ed: Peter A. Gloor, Scott W. Cooper. **Released:** April 2007. **Price:** $24.95, hardback. **Description:** Lessons for unlocking and applying swarm creativity in organizations to increase creativity, productivity, and efficiency. **Availability:** Print; E-book.

33998 ■ *"Corporate Etiquette: The Art of Apology"* in *Canadian Business (Vol. 80, January 29, 2007, No. 3, pp. 62)*
Ed: John Gray. **Description:** The methods of nurturing professional relationships, by apologizing for the mistakes committed by individuals and institutions, are described.

33999 ■ *"Corporate Responsibility"* in *Professional Services Close-Up (July 2, 2010)*
Description: List of firms awarded the inaugural Best Corporate Citizens in Government Contracting by the Corporate Responsibility Magazine is presented. The list is based on the methodology of the Magazine's Best Corporate Citizen's List, with 324 data points of publicly-available information in seven categories which include: environment, climate change, human rights, philanthropy, employee relations, financial performance, and governance.

34000 ■ *"Counting on Engagement at Ernst & Young"* in *Workforce Management (Vol. 88, November 16, 2009, No. 12, pp. 25)*
Pub: Crain Communications Inc.
Contact: Rance E. Crain, President
Ed: Ed Frauenheim. **Description:** Employee engagement has been difficult to maintain through the recession but firms such as Ernst & Young have found that the effort to keep their employees loyal has paid off.

34001 ■ *"Crafting Kinship at Home and Work: Women Miners in Wyoming"* in *WorkingUSA (Vol. 11, December 2008, No. 4, pp. 439)*
Ed: Jessica M. Smith. **Description:** Institutional policies and social dynamics shaping women working in the northeastern Wyoming mining industry are examined. Ethnographic research suggests that the women's successful integration into this nontraditional workplace is predicated on their ability to craft and maintain kin-like social relationships in two spheres. First, women miners have addressed the challenges of managing their home and work responsibilities by cultivating networks of friends and family to care for their children while they are at work. Second, women miners craft close relationships with coworkers in what are called 'crew families'. These relationships make their work more enjoyable and the ways in which they create camaraderie prompt a reconsideration of conventional accounts of sexual harassment in the mining industry.

34002 ■ *"Creating Sustainable Performance: If You Give Your Employees the Chance To Learn and Grow, They'll Thrive - And So Will Your Organization"* in *Harvard Business Review (Vol. 90, January-February 2012, No.1-2, pp. 92)*
Pub: Harvard Business Review Press
Contact: Peter E. Walsh, Director
Ed: Gretchen Spreitzer,Christine Porath. **Released:** January-February 2012. **Description:** Identification of four key factors that increase employee morale and productivity are outlined. These are: providing decision-making capability, sharing information, reducing incivility, and offering performance feedback. All four factors are needed to produce improvements.

34003 ■ *"Creativity, Inc.: Overcoming the Unseen Forces That Stand in the Way of True Inspiration"*
Pub: Random House L.L.C.
Contact: Markus Dohle, Chief Executive Officer
Released: April 8, 2014. **Price:** $28.00. **Description:** Ed Catmull, co-founder of Pixar Animation Studios, reaches out to managers who want to lead their employees to greater heights. Pixar has dominated the world of animated films for twenty years. Catmull addresses philosophies that protect the creative process and defy convention to inspire employees and create a successful small business.

34004 ■ *"Crew Training Changes Tactics"* in *Memphis Business Journal (Vol. 33, March 16, 2012, No. 49, pp. 1)*
Pub: American City Business Journal
Ed: Cole Epley. **Description:** Teamwork and communication training services firm Crew Training International Inc. has revamped its strategy and executive board as it moved from small to mid-tier status. The recalibration of strategy comes along with a renovation at the headquarters in southeast Memphis, Tennessee.

34005 ■ *"Cultural Due Diligence"* in *Canadian Business (Vol. 80, April 23, 2007, No. 9, pp. 60)*
Ed: Graham Lowe. **Description:** The factors to be considered by job seekers during judging good workplace with relation to corporate culture are presented.

34006 ■ *"Culture Club: Effective Corporate Cultures"* in *Canadian Business (Vol. 79, October 9, 2006, No. 20, pp. 115)*
Pub: Rogers Media Inc.
Contact: Tony Viner, President
Ed: Calvin Leung. **Description:** Positive impacts of an effective corporate culture on the employees' productivity and the performance of the business are discussed.

34007 ■ *"Customer Retention is Proportionate to Employee Retention"* in *Green Industry Pro (Vol. 23, September 2011)*
Pub: Cygnus Business Media
Contact: Paul Mackler, Chief Executive Officer
Description: Presented in a question-answer format, information is provided to help retain customers as well as keeping workers happy.

34008 ■ *Cute Little Store: Between the Entrepreneurial Dream and Business Reality*
Pub: Outskirts Press Inc.
Contact: Brent Sampson, President
Ed: Adeena Mignogna. **Released:** July 03, 2006. **Price:** $11.95, paperback; $9.99. **Description:** Challenges of starting and growing a retail business are profiled. **Availability:** PrintE-book.

34009 ■ *"The Darwinian Workplace: New Technology Is Helping Employers Systematically Shift More Work To Their Best Employees" in Harvard Business Review (Vol. 90, May 2012, No. 5, pp. 25)*
Pub: Harvard Business Review Press
Contact: Peter E. Walsh, Director
Ed: Serguei Netessine, Valery Yakubovich. **Released:** May 2012. **Description:** The winners-take-all model is a productivity-based system that shifts work and incentives to a firm's most productive employees. Challenges such as unpredictable pay swings, excessive competition, and unfair comparisons are addressed.

34010 ■ *"Deep Thoughts: Getting Employees to Think Better Requires a Bit of Creative Thinking Itself" in Canadian Business (March 17, 2008)*
Ed: Lauren McKeon. **Description:** Discusses the reason a company needs to make their employees understand that ideas are the stuff of life. For employees to be more creative, they need to cultivate spark moments, play with possibilities, and venture into the unknown.

34011 ■ *"Defend Your Research: It's Not "Unprofessional" to Gossip at Work" in Harvard Business Review (Vol. 88, September 2010, No. 9, pp. 28)*
Pub: Harvard Business School Publishing
Ed: Giuseppe Labianca. **Description:** Gossip can be of value to a company as an exchange of information and its use as a diagnostic tool can enable managers to address problems promptly and even head them off.

34012 ■ *"Demystifying Demotion: A Look at the Psychological and Economic Consequences on the Demotee" in Business Horizons (November-December 2007, pp. 455)*
Pub: Elsevier Technology Publications
Ed: Paula Phillips Carson, Kerry David Carson. **Price:** $35.95. **Description:** A model of employee demotion is developed after conducting personal interviews with more than 20 demotees. The effects of demotion, such as economic harm, lower well-being, underemployment, and grief reactions and identity crises are studied. **Availability:** PDF.

34013 ■ *Design Your Own Effective Employee Handbook: How to Make the Most of Your Staff with Companion CD-ROM*
Pub: Atlantic Publishing Co.
Contact: Amanda Miller, Manager
E-mail: amiller@atlantic-pub.com
Ed: Michelle Devon. **Released:** 2007. **Price:** $39.95. **Description:** An employee handbook should include clearly written policies covering the rights and responsibilities of workers. **Availability:** CD-ROM.

34014 ■ *"Desk-Bound No More" in Charlotte Business Journal (Vol. 25, August 13, 2010, No. 21, pp. 1)*
Pub: Charlotte Business Journal
Ed: Adam O' Daniel. **Description:** Bank of America has launched a program that encourages employees to work on their own schedules. The program encourages productivity and health work-life balance. A survey has also revealed that employees feel more productive under the program.

34015 ■ *"Discipline In Your Business" in South Florida Business Journal (Vol. 34, June 6, 2014, No. 46, pp. 10)*
Pub: American City Business Journals
Released: June 6, 2014. **Description:** Ways a business can maintain a disciplined response to market conditions and achieve success are discussed. Organizations are advised to set clear goals, com-

municate these goals, and establish clear lines of accountability. The importance of compensation to motivate staff is also explained.

34016 ■ *"The Discomfort Zone: How Leaders Turn Difficult Conversations Into Breakthroughs"*
Pub: Berrett-Koehler Communications Inc.
Contact: Steve Piersanti, President
E-mail: spiersanti@bkpub.com
Released: October 13, 2014. **Price:** $18.95 paperback. **Description:** Top leadership coach provides a model for using the Discomfort Zone, which leads people to think through problems, see situations more strategically, and transcend their limitations. The author draws on recent findings in the neuroscience of learning and provides exercises and case studies to use discomfort in business conversations and communication to create lasing changes and a more motivated workforce.

34017 ■ *"Do Something!" in Entrepreneur (Vol. 36, March 2008, No. 3, pp. 79)*
Pub: Entrepreneur Press
Contact: Perlman Neil, President
Ed: Chris Penttila. **Description:** Employers are addressing the cause of employee stress by adjusting work structure. Some of the actions taken to tackle the concern include examples such as the eCast executive having quick one-on-one talks with employees and GlaxoSmithKlline employees taking online stress assessment. Other details on reducing job/ employee stress are discussed.

34018 ■ *"Does Rudeness Really Matter? The Effects of Rudeness on Task Performance and Helpfulness" in Academy of Management Journal (Vol. 50, No. 5, October 1, 2007, pp. 1181)*
Pub: Academy of Management
Contact: Ming-Jer Chen, President
Ed: Christine L. Porath, Amir Erez. **Description:** Study assessing the effect of impoliteness on performance and helpfulness showed rude behavior lowered performance levels and also decreased attitude of helpfulness.

34019 ■ *"The Don't Do Lists" in Inc. (Vol. 33, October 2011, No. 8, pp. 65)*
Pub: Inc. Magazine
Ed: Jennifer Alsever, Adam Bluestein. **Description:** Ten business leaders and experts share their don't do lists, the things that should be avoided when going on sales calls, planning business lunches, motivating employees and more are presented.

34020 ■ *"Don't Leave Employees on the Outside Looking In" in Canadian Business (Vol. 83, July 20, 2010, No. 11-12, pp. 13)*
Ed: Richard Branson. **Description:** Managers should be careful with employee's tendencies to use the word 'they' when problems occur since this shows that employees are not associating themselves with their company. Employees should be involved in the development of the company and improving the flow of information is important in overcoming this communication challenge.

34021 ■ *"Don't Lose That Personal Touch" in Canadian Business (Vol. 85, July 16, 2012, No. 11-12, pp. 18)*
Pub: George Media Inc.
Ed: Richard Branson. **Released:** July 16, 2012. **Description:** There are advantages to running a big company as if it were a small business which can easily adapt to changing circumstances, develop a personal level of customer service and foster a sense of community and committment among employees. These can be achieved through building up team spirit, focusing on customers and delegating tasks.

34022 ■ *"Downturn Tests HCL's Pledge to Employees" in Workforce Management (Vol. 88, November 16, 2009, No. 12, pp. 23)*
Pub: Crain Communications Inc.
Contact: Rance E. Crain, President
Ed: Ed Frauenheim. **Description:** HCL Technologies has kept its promise to keep from laying any employees off during the recession which served as a test

for the tech firm's Employee First program, which seeks to give workers greater income security as well as a stronger voice in the firm.

34023 ■ *The Dream Manager*
Pub: Hyperion
Ed: Matthew Kelly. **Released:** August 09, 2007. **Price:** $19.95; C$24.95. **Description:** A business fable about the virtues of helping those working for and with you to achieve their dreams. Managers can boost morale and control turnover by adopting this policy.

34024 ■ *"Dream Town Launches Organic Food Delivery for Its Employees" in Internet Wire (June 28, 2012)*
Pub: COMTEX
Contact: Chip Brian, President
Description: Local organics were spotlighted by Chicago real estate online firm, Dream Team, who held a special event for its employees and special guests at the Landmark Century Cinema. Robert Kenner's Food Inc. presented Irv and Shelly's Fresh Picks. Dream Team is committed to helping first time home buyers.

34025 ■ *"The Dynamic DUO" in Canadian Electronics (Vol. 23, February 2008, No. 1, pp. 24)*
Description: Citronics Corporation not only aims to proved a good working environment for its employees, it also values the opinions of its personnel. Citronics had its employees test different workbenches before finally purchasing thirty-five of Lista's Align adjustable height workstation, which combines flexibility with aesthetics. The design of the Alin workbench is described.

34026 ■ *"Dynamically Integrating Knowledge in Teams: Transforming Resources Into Performance" in Academy of Management Journal (Vol. 55, August 1, 2012, No. 4, pp. 998)*
Pub: Academy of Management
Contact: Ming-Jer Chen, President
Ed: Heidi K. Gardner, Francesca Gino, Bradley R. Staats. **Description:** A method for developing a knowledge-integration capability to dynamically integrate the resources of team members into higher performance is proposed. Results suggest that the development of this capability is aided by the use of relational, structural, and experiential resources while uncertainty plays a moderating role in these relationships.

34027 ■ *"Easing the Global (and Costly) Problem of Workplace Stress; Stress Is Reportedly the Leading Cause of Long-Term Sickness for Workers Around the World. But Relief Is In Sight" in Gallup Business Journal (March 27, 2014)*
Pub: Gallup Press
Released: March 27, 2014. **Description:** Stress is considered the leading cause of long-term illness for workers globally. According to an employee engagement survey, workplace stress can be reduced through engagement.

34028 ■ *"The Effects of Perceived Corporate Social Responsibility on Employee Attitudes" in Business Ethics Quarterly (Vol. 24, April 2014, No. 2, pp. 165)*
Pub: Business Ethics Quarterly
Released: April 2014. **Description:** The impact on employee attitudes and their perceptions of how others outside the organization are treated (i.e., corporate social responsibility) above and beyond the impact of how employees are directly treated by organizations is addressed. Results of a study of 827 employees in 18 organizations show that employee perceptions of corporation social responsibility (CSR) are positively related to organizational commitment with the relationship being partially mediated by work meaningfulness and perceived organizational support (POS) and job satisfaction with work meaningfulness partially mediating the relationship but not POS.

34029 ■ *"Eight Tips For Leaders On Protecting the Team"* in Puget Sound Business Journal (Vol. 35, August 22, 2014, No. 18, pp. 13)

Pub: American City Business Journals

Released: August 22, 2014. **Description:** Advice on ways to protect corporate teams is given. Unnecessary information and processes should be filtered to avoid distraction of the team. Team action plans must be prioritized.

34030 ■ *"The Employee Brand: Is Yours an All-Star?"* in Business Horizons (September-October 2007, pp. 423)

Pub: Elsevier Technology Publications

Ed: W. Glynn Mangold, Sandra Jeanquart Miles. **Price:** $35.95. **Description:** Employees can influence the brand image either positively or negatively. The typology presented provides guidelines on how employees can reflect a company's brand image. Classifications of organizations into all-star rookies, injured reserves, or strike-out kings are also discussed. **Availability:** PDF.

34031 ■ *"Employee Motivation: A Powerful New Model"* in Harvard Business Review (Vol. 86, July-August 2008, No. 8, pp. 78)

Pub: Harvard Business Review Press

Contact: Peter E. Walsh, Director

Ed: Nitin Nohira, Boris Groysberg, Linda-Eling Lee. **Description:** Four drives underlying employee motivation are discussed as well as processes for leveraging these drives through corporate culture, job design, reward systems, and resource-allocation priorities.

34032 ■ *"Empowered"* in Harvard Business Review (Vol. 88, July-August 2010, No. 7-8, pp. 94)

Pub: Harvard Business School Publishing

Ed: Josh Bernoff, Ted Schadler. **Description:** HERO concept (highly empowered and resourceful operative) which builds a connection between employees, managers, and IT is outlined. The resultant additional experience and knowledge gained by employees improves customer relationship management.

34033 ■ *"The End of Clock-Punching"* in Canadian Business (Vol. 83, September 14, 2010, No. 15, pp. 96)

Pub: Rogers Media Inc.

Contact: Tony Viner, President

Ed: Lyndsie Bourgon. **Description:** Workplace consultant Peter Hadwen is pushing for the transformation of Canada's government departments into results-only work environments (ROWE). ROWE does not require employees to show up to work at a certain time as long as they are meeting goals and achieving results in their jobs. Details of studies regarding ROWE in US companies are examined.

34034 ■ *Enlightened Leadership: Best Practice Guidelines and Timesaving Tools for Easily Implementing Learning Organizations*

Pub: Learning House Publishing, Inc.

Ed: Alan G. Thomas; Ralph L. LoVuolo; Jeanne C. Hillson. **Released:** September 2006, printable 3 times/year. **Price:** $21.00. **Description:** Book provides the tools required to create a learning organization management model along with a step-by-step guide for team planning and learning. The strategy works as a manager's self-help guide as well as offering continuous learning and improvement for company-wide success.

34035 ■ *"Entrepreneurial Human Resource Leadership: A Conversation with Dwight Carlson"* in Human Resource Management (Vol. 49, July-August 2010, No. 4, pp. 793-804)

Pub: John Wiley

Ed: David C. Strubler, Benjamin W. Redekop. **Description:** Dwight Carlson, a visionary entrepreneur, talks about his main role as a leader. He believes that experience can help in making choices between difficult alternatives. He also thinks that leaders do not really motivate people, they actually create an environment where they motivate themselves.

34036 ■ *"Executive Summary: Codeines and Coding"* in Business Strategy Review (Vol. 23, Spring 2012, No. 1, pp. 82)

Released: Spring 2012. **Description:** Adam Powell, Sergei Savin, and Nicos Savva, 'Physician Workload and Hospital Reimbursement: Overworked Servers Generate Lower Income', working paper, August 2011 is examined.

34037 ■ *"Explaining Organizational Responsiveness to Work-Life Balance Issues: the Role of Business Strategy and High-Performance Work Systems"* in Human Resource Management (Vol. 51,May- June 2012, No. 3, pp. 407-432)

Pub: John Wiley & Sons Inc.

Contact: Stephen M. Smith, President

Ed: Jing Wang, Anil Verma. **Description:** The effects of business strategies and high-performance work systems on the adoption of work-life balance programs are examined. Results indicate a mediating role of high-performance work systems in the relationship between business strategies and the adoption of work-life balance programs.

34038 ■ *"Facilitating and Rewarding Creativity During New Product Development"* in Journal of Marketing (Vol. 75, July 2011, No. 4, pp. 53)

Pub: American Marketing Association

Contact: Lucille Pointer, President

Ed: James E. Burroughs, Darren W. Dahl, C. Page Moreau, Amitava Chattopadhay, Gerald J. Gorn. **Description:** A study to determine the effects of rewards to creativity in the process of new product development is presented. The findings show that the effect of rewards can be made positive if combined with appropriate creativity training.

34039 ■ *"Family Dollar Reaches Preliminary Class Action Settlement"* in Benzinga.com (September 12, 2012)

Pub: Benzinga.com

Contact: Kyle Bazzy, President

Description: Family Dollar Stores Inc. has reached a preliminary settlement with New York store managers. The settlement provides 1,700 managers a maximum payment of $14 million. A profile of the Family Dollar Stores company is also included.

34040 ■ *"Feeling the Heat: Effects of Stress, Commitment, and Job Experience On Job Performance"* in Academy of Management Journal (Vol. 50, No. 4, August 1, 2007, pp. 953)

Pub: Academy of Management

Contact: Ming-Jer Chen, President

Ed: Larry W. Hunter, Sherry M.B. Thatcher. **Description:** Links between bank branch employees' felt job stress, organizational commitment, job experience, and performance is analyzed. Results found are uniform with the attention view of stress.

34041 ■ *"Fifth Third Bank's Journey: One of Inclusion and Engagement; The Bank's Investment in Development, Engagement, and Inclusion Has Proven To Be Good for Employees, Customers, and the Bottom Line"* in Gallup Business Journal (July 8, 2014)

Pub: Gallup Press

Released: July 8, 2014. **Description:** Fifth Third Bank is committed to investing in development, engagement, and inclusion in order to benefit employees, customers, and the bottom line. A company is more likely to be engaging if it is inclusive and the same is if it is inclusive it will be engaging.

34042 ■ *"First Class All the Way"* in Entrepreneur (July 2014)

Pub: Entrepreneur Media Inc.

Released: July 2014. **Description:** Entrepreneurs are offered tips on dealing with problem employees and fostering diversity in business. Leaders must be vigilant and proactive when handling an employee who has a sense of entitlement. The culture and values of the company and the reason why his me-first-and-only approach will not work must be explained to him. A healthy business environment in the

21st Century must be open to diversifying its people and ideas. Hiring women employees will help successful businesses grow.

34043 ■ *The Five Dysfunctions of a Team: A Leadership Fable*

Pub: John Wiley & Sons Inc.

Contact: Stephen M. Smith, President

Ed: Patrick M. Lencioni. **Released:** May 2002. **Price:** $24.95, hardcover; $16.99. **Description:** Analysis of a hypothetical tale of the CEO of a struggling, high-profile firm with a dysfunctional executive team. **Availability:** PrintE-book.

34044 ■ *"5 Steps to an Effective Meeting"* in Hawaii Business (Vol. 53, March 2008, No. 9, pp. 55)

Pub: PacificBasin Communications

Ed: Jason Ubay. **Description:** Identifying goals and writing them down can help in knowing what needs get done. Engaging everyone is a way to get cooperation in reaching the goals set. Other tips on how to have an effective meeting are discussed.

34045 ■ *"Forging Her Own Career and Identity"* in Women in Business (Vol. 66, Summer 2014, No. 1, pp. 10)

Pub: Women In Business

Ed: Leigh Elmore. **Released:** Summer 2014. **Description:** Jenna Bush Hager, daughter of former United States President George W. Bush, believes that women who are entering the workforce need to look for mentors who can help them grow. Hager, who works as a correspondent for the "Today" show, also thinks that women employees should become part of a team.

34046 ■ *"Forward Motion"* in Green Industry Pro (July 2011)

Pub: Cygnus Business Media

Contact: Paul Mackler, Chief Executive Officer

Ed: Gregg Wartgow. **Description:** Several landscape contractors have joined this publication's Working Smarter Training Challenge over the last year. This process is helping them develop ways to improve work processes, boost morale, drive out waste, reduce costs, improve customer service, and be more competitive.

34047 ■ *"Friends With (Health) Benefits"* in Canadian Business (Vol. 87, July 2014, No. 7, pp. 32)

Pub: George Media Inc.

Released: July 2014. **Description:** The benefits of turning professional working relationships into real friendships and strong personal bonds are explained. The decision to create warm and respectful culture in the company will pay a lot of dividends in long-term employee motivation and team work.

34048 ■ *"Gain the 'Come Alive Outside' Selling Edge"* in Green Industry Pro (July 2011)

Pub: Cygnus Business Media

Contact: Paul Mackler, Chief Executive Officer

Ed: Jim Paluch. **Description:** Marketing the 'Come Alive Outside' slogan can help landscapers to increase their market share by identifying and applying these elements to each customer as well as their workers.

34049 ■ *The Game-Changer: How You Can Drive Revenue and Profit Growth with Innovation*

Pub: Crown Business

Ed: A.G Lafley, Ram Charan. **Price:** $27.50, Hardcover. **Description:** Management guru Charan and Proctor & Gamble CEO Lafley provide lessons to encourage innovation at all levels, including how to hire for and encourage an environment of communication and tangible work processes.

34050 ■ *"Generalizing Newcomers' Relational and Organizational Identifications: Processes and Prototypicality"* in Academy of Management Journal (Vol. 55, August 1, 2012,

No. 4, pp. 949)
Pub: Academy of Management
Contact: Ming-Jer Chen, President
Ed: David M. Sluss, Robert E. Ployhart, M. Glenn Cobb, Blake E. Ashforth. **Description:** The process in which newcomers identify themselves with a supervisor and with the employing organization is examined. Results suggest that relational identification with a supervisor converges with organizational identification through effective, cognitive and behavioral mechanisms yet only when the relational other is perceived to be prototypical.

34051 ■ *"Get Your Mojo Working" in Small Business Opportunities (March 2011)*
Pub: Harris Publications Inc.
Ed: Holly G. Green. **Description:** Ways to keep employees engaged and productive are discussed.

34052 ■ *"Getting Drowned Out by the Brainstorm" in Canadian Business (Vol. 83, June 15, 2010, No. 10, pp. 91)*
Pub: Rogers Media Inc.
Contact: Tony Viner, President
Ed: Joe Castaldo. **Description:** A study reveals that people generate more ideas when they do it alone rather than as part of a brainstorming group. The limited range of ideas is due to the fixation of group members on the first idea that gets offered.

34053 ■ *"Getting to 'Us'" in Harvard Business Review (Vol. 92, September 2014, No. 9, pp. 38)*
Pub: Harvard Business Publishing
Released: September 2014. **Description:** Employee motivation and satisfaction can be enhanced through leadership that presents a shared goal that emphasizes kinship and relationship to others, rather than citing a common enemy.

34054 ■ *"The Gifts of Summer: Antsy Workers and Wasted Fridays" in Canadian Business (Vol. 85, June 11, 2012, No. 10, pp. 69)*
Pub: George Media Inc.
Ed: Jasmine Budak. **Released:** June 11, 2012. **Description:** Ways to deal with distracted staff and accommodate vacation requests while maintaining productivity during the summer months are suggested. A compressed or flexible work week policy during summer months can help employers deal with anxious employees while workforce management experts say preparation is important when scheduling staff holidays.

34055 ■ *"Gilt Groupe's CEO On Building a Team of A Players" in Harvard Business Review (Vol. 90, January-February 2012, No.1-2, pp. 43)*
Pub: Harvard Business Review Press
Contact: Peter E. Walsh, Director
Ed: Kevin Ryan. **Released:** January-February 2012. **Description:** The author stresses the role of human capital in a firm's success, and the importance of employment references in determining a candidate's talents. Key questions include whether the reference would hire the person, whether people enjoy working with him or her, and what areas could use improvements.

34056 ■ *The Girls' Guide to Building a Million-Dollar Business*
Pub: AMACOM
Contact: Edward T. Reilly, Manager
Ed: Susan Wilson Solovic. **Released:** November 2007. **Price:** $18.95, Paper or Softback. **Description:** Success plan for women business owners; the book includes tips for determination, managing changing relationships, keeping employees and customers happy, getting and maintaining credit, overcoming gender bias, and creating a good business plan and solid brand. **Availability:** Print.

34057 ■ *"Glenmede at Liberty To Show Off Space" in Philadelphia Business Journal (Vol. 32, January 24, 2014, No. 50, pp. 8)*
Pub: American City Business Journals
Released: January 24, 2014. **Description:** Glenmede Trust Company decided to undertake a full office renovation after renewing its lease at One Liberty Place. The investment company decided to replace drywall with glass and more informal meeting places were constructed. The firm, which focuses on employee engagement, aims to improve the work environment.

34058 ■ *Go Put Your Strengths to Work*
Pub: Free Press/Simon & Schuster Inc.
Ed: Marcus Buckingham. **Released:** December 2010. **Price:** $16. **Description:** A guide to being more productive, focused and creative at work.

34059 ■ *"Go Team! Why Building a Cohesive Organization Is a Necessary Exercise" in Black Enterprise (Vol. 38, February 2008, No. 7, pp. 66)*
Pub: Earl G. Graves Publishing Co. Inc.
Contact: Earl G. Graves, Jr., President
Ed: Angeli R. Rasbury. **Description:** Tips to help manage successful as well as productive teams are outlined for small business managers.

34060 ■ *Group Genius: The Creative Power of Collaboration*
Pub: Basic Books/Perseus Books Group
Ed: Keith Sawyer. **Released:** March 04, 2008. **Price:** $16.95, U.S.; C$18.50, Canada; C$32.50, Canada; £11.99, UK. **Description:** Organizations can foster creativity and innovation through discussion, argumentation and group activities. **Availability:** PrintE-book.

34061 ■ *"Group Learning" in Academy of Management Review (October 2007, pp. 1041)*
Pub: ScholarOne Inc.
Contact: William T. Carden, Jr., President
Ed: Jeanne M. Wilson, Paul S. Goodman, Matthew A. Cronin. **Description:** The processes that constitute group learning in order to undertake necessary modifications are covered.

34062 ■ *"HBR Case Study: When the Longtime Star Fades" in Harvard Business Review (Vol. 88, September 2010, No. 9, pp. 117)*
Pub: Harvard Business School Publishing
Ed: Jimmy Guterman. **Description:** A fictitious aging employee scenario is presented, with contributors offering advice. The scenarios focuses on an older employee's match with a rapidly changing industry; suggestions include consolidating a niche business around the employee, and also engaging the older employee in solving the productivity issue.

34063 ■ *"He Said, She Said: Stay Clear of Gossip In the Workplace With a Mature Attitude" in Black Enterprise (February 2008)*
Pub: Earl G. Graves Publishing Co. Inc.
Contact: Earl G. Graves, Jr., President
Ed: Akoto Ofori-Atta. **Description:** It is important for employees to avoid gossip in the workplace because of the negative impact; it is recommended focusing on conversations that will help an individual's professional goals.

34064 ■ *"Health Nuts and Bolts" in Entrepreneur (Vol. 36, April 2008, No. 4, pp. 24)*
Pub: Entrepreneur Press
Contact: Perlman Neil, President
Ed: Jacquelyn Lynn. **Description:** Encouraging employees to develop good eating habits can promote productivity at work. Ways on how to improve employee eating habits include employers setting a good example themselves and offering employees healthy options. Other details about the topic are discussed.

34065 ■ *"A Heart for Software; Led by Its Upbeat CEO, Menlo Spreads Joy of Technology" in Crain's Detroit Business (Vol. 30, October 13, 2014, No. 41, pp. 1)*
Pub: Crain Communications Inc. - Detroit
Contact: Keith Crain, Chairman
Released: October 13, 2014. **Description:** Profile of Rich Sheridan, one of the most prominent names in IT in Ann Arbor, Michigan. Sheridan believes in common-sense solutions and manages his workers to be empowered employees to come up with their own solutions to software coding issues, and he is a consummate salesman and marketer. He runs his company so it goes beyond understanding what the user needs, and managing a great team, to being the front man selling his goods and services.

34066 ■ *"Help Employees Give Away Some Of That Bonus" in Harvard Business Review (Vol. 86, July-August 2008, No. 8, pp. 1)*
Pub: Harvard Business Review Press
Contact: Peter E. Walsh, Director
Ed: Michael I. Norton, Elizabeth W. Dunn. **Description:** Research indicates that how employees spend their bonuses is key to their resultant happiness, rather than simply receiving the bonus itself. Firms that offer donation options can thereby increase employee satisfaction.

34067 ■ *"Help Yourself" in Entrepreneur (September 2014)*
Pub: Entrepreneurial Press
Released: September 2014. **Description:** Employers can create a workplace where mutual trust is possible by expressing clearly what they expect from their employees, giving feedback that reinforces positive behavior and mentoring them to improve customer service. A leader needs to talk to a pregnant worker about her job priorities, deadlines and communicate ways to help her meet expectations. The best way to approach a company for unsolicited ideas is to find out the contact person who would be responsible for inventors or potential collaborators.

34068 ■ *"The Hidden Advantages of Quiet Bosses" in Harvard Business Review (Vol. 88, December 2010, No. 12, pp. 28)*
Pub: Harvard Business School Publishing
Ed: Adam M. Grant, Francesca Gino, David A. Hofmann. **Description:** Research on organizations behavior indicates that, while extroverts most often become managers, introvert managers paired with proactive employees make a highly efficient and effective combination.

34069 ■ *"High Octane Team Building: Adventure Spas for Office Retreats" in Inc. (Vol. 33, September 2011, No. 7, pp. 54)*
Pub: Inc. Magazine
Ed: Adam Baer. **Description:** Adventure spas offer plush accommodations for hosting team-building activities. The Resort at PAWS UP, Topnotch Resort and Spa, Dunton Hot Springs and Miraval Resort and Spa are among the retreats revealed.

34070 ■ *"HireDiversity: Some Companies Developing Affinity for Employee Groups" in Hispanic Business (October 2007, pp. 86-87)*
Ed: Hildy Medina. **Description:** Affinity groups, also known as employee resource networks, help companies identify and recruit candidates.

34071 ■ *"Holiday Shopping Meets Social Media" in Employee Benefit News (Vol. 25, December 1, 2011, No. 15)*
Pub: SourceMedia Inc.
Contact: James M. Malkin, Chief Executive Officer
Ed: Rob J. Thurston. **Description:** Offering employees access to discount shopping using social media sites for Christmas bonuses, could be the gift that keeps on giving.

34072 ■ *"Holidays Should Foster Mutual Respect" in Women In Business (Vol. 61, October-November 2009, No. 5, pp. 33)*
Pub: American Business Women's Association
Contact: Lorie Burch, President
Ed: Diane Stafford. **Description:** Workplaces have modified the way year-end holiday celebrations are held in an effort to promote mutual respect. The workers' varying religious beliefs, political affiliations, and other differences have brought about the modifications. The importance of developing mutual understanding is emphasized as a mechanism to stimulate successful business ties.

34073 ■ *How to Become a Great Boss: The Rules for Getting and Keeping the Best Employees*
Pub: Hyperion
Ed: Jeffrey J. Fox. **Released:** May 15, 2002. **Price:** $17, hardcover; C$19, hardcover. **Description:** The book offers valuable advice to any manager or

entrepreneur to improve leadership and management skills. Topics covered include: hiring, managing, firing, partnership and competition, self and organization, employee performance, attitude, and priorities. **Availability:** Print.

34074 ■ *"How to Divorce Your Office Spouse"* **in Canadian Business (Vol. 83, June 15, 2010, No. 10, pp. 74)**
Pub: Rogers Media Inc.
Contact: Tony Viner, President
Ed: Jacqueline Nelson. **Description:** A work spouse or the platonic relationship between male and female coworkers can increase productivity in some cases, but these friendships can become complicated due to power struggles and sexual tension. When this type of relationship goes sour, it is advised to tell the spouse honestly how you feel.

34075 ■ *"How Employees' Strengths Make Your Company Stronger; Employees Who Use Their Strengths Are More Engaged, Perform Better, Are Less Likely To Leave -- and Boost Your Bottom Line"* **in Gallup Business Journal (February 20, 2014)**
Pub: Gallup Press
Released: February 20, 2014. **Description:** The best way for organizations to maximize their workers' strengths is through their managers. When staff members know and use their strongest skills, they are more engaged and will perform better, have a higher sense of well being, are less likely to seek employment elsewhere, while increasing the firm's bottom line.

34076 ■ *"How the Generation Gap Can Hurt Your Business"* **in Agency Sales Magazine (Vol. 39, November 2009, No. 10, pp. 16)**
Ed: Jack Foster. **Description:** Now that there are four generations of people in the workplace, there is a need to add flexibility to communications for independent manufacturers representatives. Managers can encourage the younger generations to do the research and the boomers to process information and let each side report to the other.

34077 ■ *"How Great Leaders Think: The Art of Reframing"*
Pub: Jossey-Bass
Contact: William J. Pesce, President
Released: July 8, 2014. **Price:** $30.00. **Description:** More complex thinking is the key to better leadership. A guide to help leaders understand four major aspects of organizational life: structure, people, politics, and culture is given. The book's lessons include: how to use structural tools to organize teams and organizations for better results, how to build motivation and morale by aligning organizations and people, how to map the terrain and build a power base to navigate the political dynamics of organizations, and how to develop a leadership story that shapes culture, provides direction, and inspires commitment to excellence.

34078 ■ *"How Pixar Fosters Collective Creativity"* **in Harvard Business Review (Vol. 86, September 2008, No. 9, pp. 64)**
Pub: Harvard Business Review Press
Contact: Peter E. Walsh, Director
Ed: Ed Catmull. **Description:** Pixar Animation Studios illustrates peer-culture methods for fostering product development. These include allowing any employee to communicate with any other employee, providing a safe environment for new ideas, and watching the academic community closely for innovations.

34079 ■ *"How to Protect Your Job in a Recession"* **in Harvard Business Review (Vol. 86, September 2008, No. 9, pp. 113)**
Pub: Harvard Business Review Press
Contact: Peter E. Walsh, Director
Ed: Janet Banks, Diane Coutu. **Description:** Strategies are presented for enhancing one's job security. These include being a team player, empathizing with management, preserving optimism, and concentrating on the customer.

34080 ■ *"How to Recognize and Reward Employees: 150 Ways to Inspire Peak Performance"*
Pub: American Management Association
Contact: Edward T. Reilly, President
Ed: Donna Deeprose. **Released:** 2nd Edition. **Price:** $13.95, paperback. **Availability:** PDF.

34081 ■ *"How To Build a Cool Office (That Makes People Work Harder)"* **in Canadian Business (Vol. 87, October 2014, No. 10, pp. 48)**
Pub: American City Business Journals
Released: October 2014. **Description:** Hootsuite operations manager and vice president of talent, Sepi Bordian and Ambrosia Humphrey respectively, discuss how to design an office space that motivates its employees to work harder. They suggest workstations around multi-purpose spaces that allow the staff to do anything want with the space. This new trend is office design is explored.

34082 ■ *"How To Earn Loyalty From Millenials"* **in Birmingham Business Journal (Vol. 31, February 28, 2014, No. 9, pp. 16)**
Pub: American City Business Journals, Inc.
Contact: Whitney Shaw, President
Released: February 28, 2014. **Description:** Advice for earning loyalty from millennial employees is offered. Management need to create an environment where mistakes are openly admitted and employees should be encouraged to give back to causes that matter most to them.

34083 ■ *"How To Help Your Organization SOAR"* **in Birmingham Business Journal (Vol. 31, February 21, 2014, No. 8, pp. 8)**
Pub: American City Business Journals, Inc.
Contact: Whitney Shaw, President
Released: February 21, 2014. **Description:** Ways to change disruptive behavior of an employee is examined. The SOAR Formula for feedback can help provide the necessary results to address challenging or difficult behavior before an employee can adversely affect productivity and morale in the office.

34084 ■ *"How To Turn Your Efforts Into Results"* **in Green Industry Pro (Vol. 23, September 2011)**
Pub: Cygnus Business Media
Contact: Paul Mackler, Chief Executive Officer
Ed: Bob Coulter. **Description:** Working Smarter Training Challenge teaches that leaders are able to carry out solutions directly into their organization, develop skills and drive business results in key areas by creating a culture of energized workers who are able to take ownership of their performance as well as the performance of the company as a whole.

34085 ■ *"How to Turn Employee Conflict Into a Positive, Productive Force"* **in HR Specialist (Vol. 8, September 2010, No. 9, pp. 6)**
Pub: Capitol Information Group Inc.
Description: Ways to help manage a team of workers are presented, focusing on ways to avoid conflict within the group are discussed.

34086 ■ *"I Quit...Six Months From Now"* **in Canadian Business (Vol. 85, July 16, 2012, No. 11-12, pp. 71)**
Pub: George Media Inc.
Ed: Matthew McClearn. **Released:** July 16, 2012. **Description:** Employees who are planning to resign should consider the notice period, the time it will take for employers to find a replacement and the reason for leaving. Departing employees can use their knowledge and skills to compete directly with their former employer, but they should be wary of unfair competition.

34087 ■ *"Increasing HR's Strategic Participation: the Effect of HR Service Quality and Contribution Expectations"* **in Human Resource Management (Vol. 51, January-February 2012, No. 1, pp. 3-23)**
Pub: John Wiley & Sons Inc.
Contact: Stephen M. Smith, President
Ed: Jin Feng Uen, David Ahlstrom, Shu-Yuan Chen, Pai-Wei Tseng. **Description:** The impact of human resources service quality and human resources

contribution expectations on the strategic participation of human resources in organizations is examined. Human resource professionals are found to increase the organizational value of human resources through improving quality and addressing the needs of potential internal customers.

34088 ■ *"Innovation Despite Reorganization"* **in Journal of Business Strategy (Vol. 35, May-June 2014, No. 3, pp. 18-25)**
Pub: Emerald Group Publishing Inc.
Released: May-June 2014. **Description:** Innovation can be sustained through a downsizing event. The articles shows how prevailing formal and informal networks can be used for reestablishing connections between employees after a company is downsized.

34089 ■ *"Inside the Googleplex"* **in Canadian Business (Vol. 79, November 6, 2006, No. 22, pp. 59)**
Pub: Rogers Media Inc.
Contact: Tony Viner, President
Ed: Christina Campbell. **Description:** The views of Clive Wilkinson, a designer, on the relationship between interior design and employees' productivity are presented.

34090 ■ *"Into the Wild"* **in Inc. (October 2007, pp. 116-120, 122, 124, 126)**
Pub: Mansueto Ventures L.L.C.
Contact: John Koten, Chief Executive Officer
Ed: Alison Stein Wellner. **Description:** Perry Klebahn, CEO of Timbuk2, manufacturer of messenger bags, tells how he took his top executives into the deep Wyoming wilderness in order to build employee team work skills. Other options for this type of team-building include cooking courses, changing a tire together, solving a kidnapping, or discussing ways to survive a nuclear winter.

34091 ■ *"Is the Generation Gap Gone?"* **in Agency Sales Magazine (Vol. 39, November 2009, No. 10, pp. 3)**
Ed: Bryan C. Shirley. **Description:** Four generations are working side-by-side in the workplace for the first time in history and this is a big opportunity to get different perspectives and views on life. In the sales representatives business, there is a need to better understand the upcoming generations and understand their specific abilities to their risk/reward business.

34092 ■ *"It's Not the How or the What but the Who: Succeed by Surrounding Yourself with the Best"*
Pub: Harvard Business Review Press
Contact: Peter E. Walsh, Director
Released: May 13 ,2014. **Price:** $28.00. **Description:** Surrounding yourself with the best matters in every aspect of life and can mean the difference between success and failure. The author draws upon years of experience in global executive search and talent development, as well as the latest management and psychology research, to help improve the choices management makes about employees and mentors, business partners and friends, top corporate leaders and elected officials.

34093 ■ *"It's the People Who Bring the Energy"* **in Boston Business Journal (Vol. 34, June 13, 2014, No. 19, pp. 6)**
Pub: American City Business Journals, Inc.
Contact: Whitney Shaw, President
Released: June 13, 2014. **Description:** Florence Electric, founded in 2004, won the best mid-size company award category in The Boston Business Journal Competition of Best Places to Work. The owner of the company, Eli Florence, attributed this success to the relationships the company built with its customers over the years and the talent and hard work of his employees.

34094 ■ *It's Your Ship*
Ed: Michael Abrashoff. **Released:** May 01, 2002. **Price:** $24.95. **Description:** Naval Captain D. Michael Abrashoff shares management principles he used to shape his ship, the U.S.S. Benfold, into a

model of progressive leadership. Abrashoff revolutionized ways to face the challenges of excessive costs, low morale, sexual harassment, and constant turnover.

34095 ■ *"The Job Survival Equation" in Women in Business (Vol. 65, Winter 2013, No. 3, pp. 36)*
Pub: Women In Business
Released: Winter 2013. **Description:** How combining skills and a positive attitude can improve job survivability after a layoff is discussed. The attitude side of survivability is said to be more difficult than improving one's set of skills, because people do not always see themselves as others see them.

34096 ■ *"Junior Executives Need Hugs Too" in Canadian Business (Vol. 83, October 12, 2010, No. 17, pp. 87)*
Pub: Rogers Media Inc.
Contact: Tony Viner, President
Ed: James Cowan. **Description:** Psychology professor Mark Frame believes that sensitive men fail to meet perceptions of how a chief executive officer (CEO) should act. The results of a study show that communal qualities are highly valued in first-line and middle managers, but these qualities become less important when employees move closer to senior executive roles.

34097 ■ *"Justice In Self-Managing Teams: the Role of Social Networks In the Emergence of Procedural Justice Climates" in Academy of Management Journal (Vol. 55, June 1, 2012, No. 3, pp. 685)*
Pub: Academy of Management
Contact: Ming-Jer Chen, President
Ed: Quinetta M. Roberson, Ian O. Williamson. **Description:** The effect of social network content and structure on organizational justice in self-managing teams is studied using data from 79 project teams. Findings show that team instrumental network density has positive impact on procedural Justice climate strength. Low team functional background diversity was also found to strengthen this relationship.

34098 ■ *"Labor and Management: Working Together for a Stable Future" in Alaska Business Monthly (Vol. 27, October 2011, No. 10, pp. 130)*
Pub: Alaska Business Publishing Company Inc.
Contact: Jim Martin, President
Ed: Nicole A. Bonham Colby. **Description:** Alaska unions and employers are working to ensure a consistent flow of skilled Alaska workers as current the current workforce reaches retirement age.

34099 ■ *"The Last Word Dirty Work Required" in Workforce Management (Vol. 88, November 16, 2009, No. 12, pp. 34)*
Pub: Crain Communications Inc.
Contact: Rance E. Crain, President
Ed: John Hollon. **Description:** Due to salary freezes, pay cuts, layoffs, buyouts and a number of other stress factors brought about by the recession, employee engagement has been difficult to maintain by managers.

34100 ■ *"Lead Like It Matters...Because It Does: Practical Leadership Tools to Inspire and Engage Your People and Create Great Results"*
Pub: McGraw-Hill
Released: September 19, 2014. **Price:** $25.00. **Description:** The Ripple Effect method for increasing employee engagement, reducing turnover, and driving overall business success will help any manager or entrepreneur to lead his company. Important practices like eliminating wasted meetings, addressing conflict, and aligning decisions with business needs are addressed.

34101 ■ *"Leaders Eat Last Deluxe: Why Some Teams Pull Together and Others Don't"*
Pub: Penguin Group USA
Released: January 7, 2014. **Price:** $27.95. **Description:** Author of "Start with Why" returns to help create happier and healthier organizations. Sinek helps us to understand the biology of trust and cooperation

and why they are critical to success and fulfillment. He believes that organizations that develop environments filled with trust and cooperation thrive and outperform competition because employees love working there.

34102 ■ *"The Leadership Equation: 10 Practices That Build Trust, Spark Innovation, and Create High-Performing Organizations"*
Pub: Greenleaf Book Group Press
Released: September 30, 2014. **Price:** $18.95 paperback. **Description:** Entrepreneur and business consultant draws upon his work with corporations, government agencies, and nonprofit organizations and their human resource departments to explain the workings of high-performing organizations with his equation: Trust + Spark = Leadership Culture. He describes the ten more important practices for building trust and spark that improves team performance, the business unit, and the entire organization.

34103 ■ *"Leadership in Flight" in Women In Business (Vol. 63, Fall 2011, No. 3, pp. 24)*
Pub: American Business Women's Association
Contact: Lorie Burch, President
Ed: Leigh Elmore. **Description:** Flight attendants in major airlines are trained to keep passengers comfortable and to calmly deal with emergencies. They also have a significant role in brand image and customer loyalty as they interact with the customers directly. Examples of teamwork leadership for flight attendants are given.

34104 ■ *"Leadership: Growing Pains" in Canadian Business (Vol. 80, November 19, 2007, No. 23, pp. 41)*
Pub: Rogers Media Inc.
Contact: Tony Viner, President
Ed: Lauren McKeon. **Description:** Employee promotions must be done with consideration to the effects of ill-prepared leadership, which include high worker turnover, low morale, and ineffective management. Organizations must handle the transition period involved in promotion by setting clear expectations, providing guidelines on approaching different situations, and by welcoming the promoted employees; impacts are further analyzed.

34105 ■ *"Leadership Is a Conversation: How To Improve Employee Engagement and Alignment In Today's Flatter, More Networked Organizations" in (Vol. 90, June 2012, No. 6, pp. 76)*
Pub: Harvard Business Review Press
Contact: Peter E. Walsh, Director
Ed: Boris Groysberg, Michael Slind. **Released:** June 2012. **Description:** A two-way flow of communication is essential in promoting and maintaining employee motivation. Key points are establishing intimacy through gaining trust, interactivity via dialogue, inclusion by expanding employee roles, and intentionality through establishing an agenda.

34106 ■ *"Leadership: Just Shut The Hell Up" in Canadian Business (Vol. 81, July 22, 2008, No. 12-13, pp. 33)*
Pub: Rogers Media Inc.
Contact: Tony Viner, President
Ed: Jane Bao. **Description:** Employees desire better communication as opposed to more communication from their managers. Advice regarding managing communication in the workplace is given including ways in which speakers can say more with fewer words.

34107 ■ *"Leadership Training" in Black Enterprise (Vol. 37, January 2007, No. 6, pp. 56)*
Pub: Earl G. Graves Publishing Co. Inc.
Contact: Earl G. Graves, Jr., President
Ed: Marcia A. Reed-Woodard. **Description:** Profile of Theopolis Holman, Group Vice-President of Duke Energy, who discusses how he prepared for the merger between Duke Energy and Cinergy. Holman oversees a division of 9,000 service contractors and employees.

34108 ■ *Leading at a Higher Level*
Pub: FT Press
Contact: Timothy C. Moore, Vice President
Ed: Ken Blanchard. **Released:** September 08, 2009. **Price:** $22.39, Members; $27.99, Nonmembers. **Description:** Tips, advice and techniques from a management consultant to help entrepreneurs create a vision for their company; includes information on manager-employee relationships. **Availability:** Print.

34109 ■ *"'Leave Your Ego at the Door" in South Florida Business Journal (Vol. 34, June 20, 2014, No. 43, pp. 13)*
Pub: American City Business Journals
Released: June 20, 2014. **Description:** Doria Camaraza, senior vice president and general manager of American Express Service Centers in Fort Lauderdale, Mexico and Argentina, share advice for successfully running service centers for the credit card company. She describes ways in which she inspires creativity and drive, while promoting employee team building with her workers.

34110 ■ *"Lessons from Turnaround Leaders" in Strategy and Leadership (Vol. 39, May-June 2011, No. 3, pp. 36-43)*
Pub: Emerald Group Publishing Inc.
Ed: David P. Boyd. **Description:** A study analyzes the cases of some successful turnaround leaders to present a strategic model to help firms tackle challenges such as employee inertia, competition and slow organizational renewal. It describes a change model consisting of five major steps to be followed by firms with environmental uncertainty for the purpose.

34111 ■ *"Let the Insults Fly: Want to Learn What Your Employees Really Think?' in Inc. (Vol. 33, October 2011, No. 8, pp. 36)*
Pub: Inc. Magazine
Ed: Jason Fried. **Description:** A company that hosts a Comedy Central-style celebrity roast of its top-selling product was able to improve their business.

34112 ■ *"Let's Go Team: When a Retail Professional Leads by Example, Everyone Benefits" in Black Enterprise (Vol. 41, November 2010, No. 4)*
Pub: Earl G. Graves Publishing Co. Inc.
Contact: Earl G. Graves, Jr., President
Ed: Aisha I. Jefferson. **Description:** Profile of Derek Jenkins, senior vice president of Target Stores Northeast Region is presented. Jenkins oversees the management of 450 retail stores with nearly 75,000 workers. He shares insight into managing by making sure every interaction with his team counts.

34113 ■ *"Life's Work: Ben Bradlee" in Harvard Business Review (Vol. 88, September 2010, No. 9, pp. 128)*
Pub: Harvard Business School Publishing
Ed: Alison Beard. **Price:** $8.95. **Description:** Newspaper publisher Ben Bradlee discusses factors that lead to success, including visible supervisors, enthusiasm, appropriate expansion, and the importance in truth in reporting. **Availability:** PDF.

34114 ■ *"Life's Work: Interview with Alain Ducasse" in Harvard Business Review (Vol. 92, May 2014, No. 5, pp. 136)*
Pub: Harvard Business Press
Released: May 2014. **Description:** Alain Ducasse believes supervision is secondary to shared experience, and emphasizes the importance of communicating with employees to engage them and enable them to perform well. Job satisfaction is dependent on individual growth, appropriate compensation, and harmony.

34115 ■ *"Linking HRM and Knowledge Transfer Via Individual-Level Mechanisms" in Human Resource Management (Vol. 51,May-June 2012, No. 3, pp. 387-405)*
Pub: John Wiley & Sons Inc.
Contact: Stephen M. Smith, President
Ed: Dana B. Minbaeva, Kristina Makela, Larissa Rabbiosi. **Description:** The relationship between human resource management and knowledge transfer and the role of individual-level mechanisms in this

relationship are examined. Results indicate that individual-level perceptions of organizational commitment to knowledge sharing and extrinsic motivation affect internal knowledge exchange among employees.

34116 ■ "Making Diverse Teams Click" in Harvard Business Review (Vol. 86, July-August 2008, No. 8, pp. 20)
Pub: Harvard Business Review Press
Contact: Peter E. Walsh, Director
Ed: Jeffrey T. Polzer. **Description:** 360-degree feedback to increase the efficacy of diverse-member workplace teams, which involves each member providing feedback to the others on the team is discussed.

34117 ■ Management Rewired: Why Feedback Doesn't Work and Other Surprising Lessons from the Latest Brain Science
Pub: Portfolio
Ed: Charles S. Jacobs. **Released:** 2009. **Price:** $12.99; $16, Paperback. **Description:** According to the author, human psychology works better than feedback, praise or criticism when managing employees.
Availability: Electronic publishing.

34118 ■ "Managerial Rudeness: Bad Attitudes Can Demoralize Your Staff" in Black Enterprise (Vol. 37, January 2007, No. 6, pp. 58)
Pub: Earl G. Graves Publishing Co. Inc.
Contact: Earl G. Graves, Jr., President
Ed: Chauntelle Folds. **Description:** Positive leadership in the managerial realm leads to a more productive workplace. Managers who are negative, hostile, arrogant, rude or fail to accept any responsibility for their own mistakes find that employees will not give their all on the job.

34119 ■ The Manager's Guide to Rewards: What You Need to Know to Get the Best of-and-from-Your Employees
Ed: Doug Jensen; Tom McMullen; Mel Stark. **Released:** 2006. **Price:** $24.95.

34120 ■ "Managing Corporate Social Networks" in Harvard Business Review (Vol. 86, July-August 2008, No. 8, pp. 26)
Pub: Harvard Business Review Press
Contact: Peter E. Walsh, Director
Ed: Adam M. Kleinbaum, Michael L. Tushman. **Description:** Tips on how to promote business creativity and foster knowledge building through business social networks are given.

34121 ■ Managing the Older Worker: How to Prepare for the New Organizational Order
Pub: Harvard Business Press
Ed: Peter Cappelli, Bill Novelli. **Released:** August 17, 2010. **Price:** $29.95, hardcover. **Description:** Your organization needs older workers more than ever: They transfer knowledge between generations, transmit your company's values to new hires, make excellent mentors for younger employees, and provide a 'just in time' workforce for special projects.
Availability: Print.

34122 ■ "Meet the 'Googlebusters'" in Austin Business Journal (Vol. 34, February 28, 2014, No. 2, pp. 4)
Pub: American City Business Journals, Inc.
Contact: Whitney Shaw, President
Released: February 28, 2014. **Description:** Executives' views on how companies should retain employees are presented. Sailpoint Technologies CEO, Mark McClain, says companies should give employees the tools and resources they need to be successful. John Cyrier, president of Sabre Commercial Inc., says constant communication with employees is critical.

34123 ■ "The Mobile Workforce Revolution" in Canadian Business (Vol. 81, March 31, 2008, No. 5, pp. 28)
Pub: Rogers Media Inc.
Contact: Tony Viner, President
Ed: Diane Horton. **Description:** Diane Horton explains how a mobile workforce helps companies cut costs, increase productivity, and boost employee

motivation. Horton says that employees believe they usually become more productive by 15 to 30 percent after their companies go mobile.

34124 ■ "The Moderating Effects of Organizational Context On the Relationship Between Voluntary Turnover and Organizational Performance: Evidence from Korea" in Human Resource Management (Vol. 51, January-February 2012, No. 1, pp. 47-70)
Pub: John Wiley & Sons Inc.
Contact: Stephen M. Smith, President
Ed: Kiwook Kwon, Kweontaek Chung, Hyuntak Roh, Clint Chadwick, John J. Lawler. **Description:** The ability of organizational context to moderate the relationship between voluntary employee turnover and organizational performance is examined using data from South Korean firms. The effects of employee involvement practices, investment in employee training and development, and the availability of potential workers on this relationship are studied.

34125 ■ "Monitor Work Productivity" in Business Owner (Vol. 35, July-August 2011, No. 4, pp. 4)
Pub: DL Perkins Company
Description: Tips for tracking employee productivity are explained.

34126 ■ "The Moody Blues" in Entrepreneur (Vol. 36, April 2008, No. 4, pp. 87)
Pub: Entrepreneur Press
Contact: Perlman Neil, President
Ed: Mark Henricks. **Description:** Depression among employees can affect their productivity and cost the company. Businesses with a workforce that is likely to have depression should inform their employees about the health benefits covered by insurance. Other details on how to address depression concerns among employees are discussed.

34127 ■ "More Important than Results" in Business Strategy Review (Vol. 21, Summer 2010, No. 2, pp. 81)
Pub: John Wiley & Sons Inc. Scientific, Technical, Medical, and Scholarly Div. (Wiley-Blackwell)
Contact: William J. Pesce, Manager
E-mail: wpesce@wiley.com
Ed: Bert De Reyck, Zeger Degraeve. **Description:** Managing only for results leads to crises. Reward people for decisions they make, not just for the results they create.

34128 ■ More Than a Pink Cadillac
Pub: McGraw-Hill
Ed: Jim Underwood. **Released:** January 08, 2003. **Price:** Rs 1,389.43, softcover. **Description:** Profile of Mary Kay Ash who turned her $5,000 investment into a billion-dollar corporation. Ash's nine principles that form the foundation of her company's global success are outlined. Stories from her sales force leaders share ideas for motivating employees, impressing customers and building a successful company. The book emphasizes the leadership skills required to drive performance in any successful enterprise. **Availability:** Print.

34129 ■ "Negotiating Tips" in Black Enterprise (Vol. 37, December 2006, No. 5, pp. 70)
Pub: Earl G. Graves Publishing Co. Inc.
Contact: Earl G. Graves, Jr., President
Ed: Marcia A. Reed-Woodard. **Description:** Sekou Kaalund, head of strategy, mergers & acquisitions at Citigroup Securities & Fund Services, states that 'Negotiation skills are paramount to success in a business environment because of client, employee, and shareholder relationships'. He discusses how the book by George Kohlrieser, Hostage at the Table: How Leaders Can Overcome Conflict, Influence Others, and Raise Performance, has helped him negotiate more powerfully and enhance his skills at conflict-resolution.

34130 ■ "A New Challenge Facing Reps: The Generation Gap!" in Agency Sales Magazine (Vol. 39, November 2009, No. 10, pp. 9)
Ed: Roger Ralston. **Description:** Different generations in the workplace is one of the many drivers of change that reps are facing today. Pre-boomers and

boomers historically put work first while Gen-Xers and Millennials think lifestyle before work. A sales rep should listen and learn, while providing a strong sense of flexibility in this environment.

34131 ■ "The New Science of Building Great Teams: The Chemistry of High-Performing Groups Is No Longer a Mystery" in Harvard Business Review (Vol. 90, April 2012, No. 4, pp. 60)
Pub: Harvard Business Review Press
Contact: Peter E. Walsh, Director
Ed: Alex Pentland. **Released:** April 2012. **Description:** Body language and tone of voice are key to the dynamics of a team that works well together. Face-to-face communication is the most valuable. Energy, engagement, and exploration delineate how team members contribute, communicate with other team members, and communicate with other teams respectively.

34132 ■ "The Next 20 Years: How Customer and Workforce Attitudes Will Evolve" in Harvard Business Review (Vol. 85, July-August 2007, No. 7-8)
Pub: Harvard Business School Publishing
Ed: Neil Howe, William Strauss. **Price:** $8.95. **Description:** Identification of social categories inhabited by age groups is used to calculate how consumer and employee opinions and behavior will change, and how this will impact economic development and corporate growth. **Availability:** PDF.

34133 ■ "Nine Paradoxes of Problem Solving" in Strategy and Leadership (Vol. 39, May-June 2011, No. 3, pp. 25-31)
Pub: Emerald Group Publishing Inc.
Ed: Alex Lowy. **Description:** Nine frequently-occurring inherent paradoxes in corporate decision making for solving complex problems are identified. The methods with which these paradoxes and their influence can be recognized and dealt with for firm leaders and management team members to better understand and solve the problems are discussed.

34134 ■ The No Asshole Rule
Ed: Robert I. Sutton PhD. **Released:** February 22, 2007. **Price:** $22.99. **Description:** Problem employees are more than just a nuisance they are a serious and costly threat to corporate success and employee health.

34135 ■ "No Place Like Home? An Identity Strain Perspective On Repatriate Turnover" in Academy of Management Journal (Vol. 55, April 1, 2012, No. 2, pp. 399)
Pub: Academy of Management
Contact: Ming-Jer Chen, President
Ed: Maria L. Kraimer, Margaret A. Shaffer, David A. Harrison, Hong Ren. **Description:** Identity theory is invoked to investigate why employees returning from an international assignment may leave their organizations. Identity strain is attributed to the relation between prior job embeddedness during expatriation and strength of one's identity as an international employee of repatriation. Implications on international role transitions and turnover mechanisms are discussed.

34136 ■ "No Secrets; Businesses Find It Pays to Open Books to Employees" in Crain's Detroit Business (Vol. 26, January 18, 2010, No. 3)
Pub: Crain Communications Inc.
Contact: Rance E. Crain, President
Ed: Dustin Walsh. **Description:** Many businesses are finding that practicing an open-book management wherein employees share financial and decision-making duties that are usually left up to executives of firms creates a transparency within a company that eliminates the us versus them mentality between management and employees. Another benefit to this business model is that employees get to really participate in the business, learning to manage money and run a business entity.

34137 ■ "Not Just for Kids: ADHD can be Debilitating for an Employee, and Frustrating

for Bosses" in Canadian Business (April 14, 2008)
Pub: Rogers Media Inc.
Contact: Tony Viner, President
Ed: Andy Holloway. **Description:** Up to four percent of North American adults continue to feel the effects of Attention Deficit Hyperactivity Disorder or Attention Deficit Disorder. Explaining the value of the task at hand to people who are afflicted with these conditions is one way to keep them engaged in the workplace. Giving them opportunities to create their own working structure is another strategy to manage these people.

34138 ■ Now, Discover Your Strengths
Pub: Free Press/Simon & Schuster Inc.
Ed: Marcus Buckingham, Donald O. Clifton. **Price:** $32. **Description:** How to identify and develop your talents and those of your employees.

34139 ■ "The Office: Good to Great" in Inc. (October 2007, pp. 140)
Pub: Mansueto Ventures L.L.C.
Contact: John Koten, Chief Executive Officer
Ed: Leigh Buchanan. **Description:** Qualities that make a good manager great are explored. Great bosses make their employees feel smart, they know who performs what job, know when to step back, and remember things about each employee such as their families' names.

34140 ■ "On the Edge: The Art of High-Impact Leadership"
Pub: Business Plus/Warner Business Books
Released: January 7, 2014. **Price:** $27.00. **Description:** Alison Levine provides insights into leadership garnered from her various expeditions from Mount Everest to the South Pole. Levine believes that leadership principles that apply in extreme adventure sport also apply in today's extreme business environment. She discusses your survival as well as the survival of the team.

34141 ■ One Foot Out the Door: How to Combat the Psychological Recession That's Alienating Employees and Hurting American Business
Pub: AMACOM
Contact: Edward T. Reilly, Manager
Ed: Judith M. Bardwick. **Released:** October 31, 2007. **Price:** $24.95; C$32.95. **Description:** Drawing on research that indicates Generation X and younger baby boomers feel disconnected from their jobs, the author explores the causes (bad management) of that disengagement. Her pragmatic suggestions about how companies can prove their commitment to employees is beneficial.

34142 ■ The One Minute Entrepreneur: The Secret to Creating and Sustaining a Successful Business
Pub: Doubleday
Contact: Jack Hoeft, President
Ed: Ken Blanchard, Don Hutson, Ethan Willis. **Released:** April 29, 2008. **Price:** $19.95, hardcover; $11.99. **Description:** Four traditional business ideas are covered including: revenue needs to exceed expenses, bill collection, customer service, and employee motivation in order to be successful. **Availability:** PrintE-book.

34143 ■ "Open For Business" in Baltimore Business Journal (Vol. 30, June 22, 2012, No. 7, pp. 1)
Pub: American City Business Journals, Inc.
Contact: Whitney Shaw, President
Ed: James Briggs. **Released:** June 22, 2012. **Description:** The demand for offices with open floor plans has risen as companies look to improve collaboration while cutting costs. Incorporating glass walls and low desks to open office design allow the flow of natural light, which in turn, reduces energy bills. How companies are addressing the challenge of maintaining privacy in an open office design are also discussed.

34144 ■ The Orange Revolution: How One Great Team Can Transform an Entire Organization
Pub: Simon and Schuster Inc.
Contact: Carolyn Reidy, President
E-mail: carolyn.reidy@simonandschuster.com
Ed: Adrian Gostick, Chester Elton. **Released:** September 2010. **Price:** $25, hardcover; $16.99. **Description:** Based on a 350,000-person study by the Best Companies Group, as well as research into exceptional teams at leading companies, including Zappos.com, Pepsi Beverages Company, and Madison Square Garden, the authors have determined a key set of characteristics displayed by members of breakthrough teams, and have identified a set of rules great teams live by, which generate a culture of positive teamwork and led to extraordinary results. Using specific stories from the teams they studied, they reveal in detail how these teams operate and how managers can transform their own teams into such high performers by fostering: stronger clarity of goals, greater trust among team members, more open and honest dialogue, stronger accountability for all team members, and purpose-based recognition of team member contributions. **Availability:** PrintE-book.

34145 ■ Our Iceberg is Melting
Pub: St. Martin's Press
Contact: Sally Richardson, President
E-mail: sally.richardson@stmartins.com
Ed: John P. Kotter, Holger Rathgeber. **Released:** September 2006. **Price:** $19.99, Hardcover. **Description:** A fable about how to bring about change in a group.

34146 ■ "The Outcome of an Organization Overhaul" in Black Enterprise (Vol. 41, December 2010, No. 5)
Pub: Earl G. Graves Publishing Co. Inc.
Contact: Earl G. Graves, Jr., President
Ed: Tamara E. Holmes. **Description:** Savvy business owners understand the need for change in order to stay competitive and be successful. This article examines how to manage change as well as what strategies can help employees to get with the program faster.

34147 ■ Overcoming the Five Dysfunctions of a Team: A Field Guide for Leaders, Managers, and Facilitators
Pub: John Wiley & Sons Inc.
Contact: Stephen M. Smith, President
Ed: Patrick M. Lencioni. **Released:** February 2005. **Price:** $27.95. **Description:** Tools, exercises, assessment, and real-world examples for overcoming the five dysfunctions of a team. **Availability:** Print.

34148 ■ "Pay or Play: Do Nice (Sales) Guys Finish Last?" in Agency Sales Magazine (Vol. 39, August 2009, No. 8, pp. 8)
Ed: Julia M. Rahn. **Description:** How positive interpersonal relationships among salespersons, program coordinators, and other business-related professions will pay in terms of business success is presented. Business people should know the ideal customers, promise only what they can do, refer out when needed, and follow through with any stated promise. Further insight into these ideas is presented.

34149 ■ "Peer Power" in Business Strategy Review (Vol. 23, Spring 2012, No. 1, pp. 60)
Released: Spring 2012. **Description:** In troubled economic times, how do managers keep people engaged and motivated? Christoffer Ilehus suggests the world of sports offers valuable inspiration.

34150 ■ "Pep Talk" in Black Enterprise (Vol. 40, July 2010, No. 12, pp. 104)
Pub: Earl G. Graves Publishing Co. Inc.
Contact: Earl G. Graves, Jr., President
Ed: Tennille M. Robinson. **Description:** Advice for maintaining motivation in any small business is given.

34151 ■ "The Performer: Soulpepper Theatre Company's Albert Shultz" in Canadian Business (Vol. 83, August 17, 2010, No. 13-14, pp. 71)
Pub: Rogers Media Inc.
Contact: Tony Viner, President
Ed: Steve Maich. **Description:** Soulpepper Theater Company founder and actor/director Albert Schultz shares the key ingredient to his success both artisti-

cally and commercially. Schultz believes his success was a combination of passion and persistence, as well as team building. He believes his entrepreneurial impulse came when he began thinking of making opportunities instead of taking them.

34152 ■ "Pet Store Pro Adds New Curriculum" in Pet Product News (Vol. 66, February 2012, No. 2, pp. 2012)
Description: Pet Store Pro, the Pet Industry Distributors Association's free online training program, is going to launch chapters of a curriculum intended to assist pet store managers learn effective approaches to motivate employees and boost profitability. Other management-level chapters to be added by Pet Store Pro throughout 2012 are listed.

34153 ■ "Pete Carroll's Winning Rule: Protect Your Team" in Puget Sound Business Journal (Vol. 35, July 25, 2014, No. 14, pp. 12)
Pub: American City Business Journals
Released: July 25, 2014. **Description:** Seattle Seahawks coach, Pete Carroll, has three simple rules for team success and the first rule is to always protect the team. The rule is also important in every workplace because it will help align the workers attention to their behavior. Seven ways to protect the team are outlined.

34154 ■ "Plays Well With Others: How To Work With People You Can't Stand"
Pub: CreateSpace
Contact: Daren Giles, President
Released: October 19, 2014. **Price:** $6.97 paperback. **Description:** Human resource managers, as well as coworkers, will benefit from this book that helps employees deal with difficult people at work.

34155 ■ "Positive Social Interactions and the Human Body at Work: Linking Organizations and Physiology" in Academy of Management Review (January 2008, pp. 137)
Pub: ScholarOne Inc.
Contact: William T. Carden, Jr., President
Ed: Emily D. Heaphy, Jane E. Dutton. **Description:** Research is recommended for the manner in which positive social interactions in organizational contexts can influence employees' health and physiological resourcefulness.

34156 ■ "Power Play" in Harvard Business Review (Vol. 88, July-August 2010, No. 7-8, pp. 84)
Pub: Harvard Business School Publishing
Ed: Jeffrey Pfeffer. **Description:** Guidelines include in-depth understanding of resources at one's disposal, relentlessness that still provides opponents with opportunities to save face, and a determination not to be put off by the processes of politics.

34157 ■ "Powerlessness Corrupts" in Harvard Business Review (Vol. 88, July-August 2010, No. 7-8, pp. 36)
Pub: Harvard Business School Publishing
Ed: Rosabeth Moss Kanter. **Description:** Studies show that individuals who perceive that they are being treated poorly and denied sufficient freedom for a certain level of autonomy are more likely to act negatively.

34158 ■ "Principles for Creating Growth in Challenging Times" in Agency Sales Magazine (Vol. 39, September-October 2009, No. 9, pp. 35)
Ed: Robert Goshen. **Description:** Creating a productive environment is one vital key for businesses to utilize during the challenging times that arise due to a weak economy; other important factors include maintaining a good relationship with the staff, responding appropriately to challenges and keeping a sense of humor.

34159 ■ "The Profits of Good Works" in Barron's (Vol. 92, September 17, 2012, No. 38, pp. 14)
Description: The nonprofit organization B Lab is responsible for certifying companies as socially conscious and environmentally friendly. B Lab examines the impact of companies on workers, communities, and the environment as well as their internal governance.

34160 ■ *"A Proper Welcome" in Canadian Business (Vol. 79, July 17, 2006, No. 14-15, pp. 67)*
Pub: Rogers Media Inc.
Contact: Tony Viner, President
Ed: Graham Lowe. **Description:** New-employee orientation programs of various companies are highlighted. Useful practices to create a comfortable ambiance for new recruits are elucidated as well.

34161 ■ *"Proud Out Loud" in Canadian Business (Vol. 80, April 23, 2007, No. 9, pp. 52)*
Description: The role of accomplishments of employees in improving workplace conditions is presented.

34162 ■ *"Putting the Service-Profit Chain to Work" in Harvard Business Review (Vol. 86, July-August 2008, No. 8, pp. 118)*
Pub: Harvard Business Review Press
Contact: Peter E. Walsh, Director
Ed: James L. Heskett, Thomas O. Jones, Gary W. Loveman, W. Earl Sasser, Jr., Leonard A. Schlesinger. **Description:** Advice is given on how to foster profitability in service businesses. Topics include the link between employee satisfaction and customer satisfaction, internal service quality, external service value, and revenue growth.

34163 ■ *"QuikTrip Makes Fortune 'Best' List" in Tulsa World (January 22, 2010)*
Pub: Tulsa World
Contact: Debbie Jackson, Director, Library Services
Ed: Kyle Arnold. **Description:** According to a list released by Fortune Magazine, QuikTrip Corp. is once again ranked among the best companies in the country to work for due to the core values and culture held by the company's management.

34164 ■ *Reality-Based Leadership: Ditch the Drama, Restore Sanity to the Workplace, & Turn Excuses into Results*
Pub: Jossey-Bass
Ed: Cy Wakeman. **Released:** August 2010. **Price:** $27.95, hardcover; $18.99. **Description:** Recent polls show that 71 percent of workers think about quitting their jobs every day. That number would be shocking if people actually were quitting. Worse, they go to work, punching time clocks and collecting pay checks, while checked out emotionally. Cy Wakeman reveals how to be the kind of leader who changes the way people think about and perceive their circumstances, one who deals with the facts, clarifies roles, gives clean and direct feedback, and insists that everyone do the same without drama or defensiveness. **Availability:** PrintE-book.

34165 ■ *"Reconsidering Pay Dispersion's Effect On the Performance of Interdependent Work: Reconciling Sorting and Pay Inequality" in Academy of Management Journal (Vol. 55, June 1, 2012, No. 3, pp. 585)*
Pub: Academy of Management
Contact: Ming-Jer Chen, President
Ed: Charlie O. Trevor, Greg Reilly, Barry Gerhart. **Description:** The use of pay dispersion in interdependent work settings to secure valued employee inputs is investigated. Results show that the strategy positively affects interdependent team performance. Potential constraints on the sorting perspective on pay dispersion are also studied.

34166 ■ *"Reinventing Your Rep Training Program" in Agency Sales Magazine (Vol. 39, August 2009, No. 8, pp. 40)*
Description: Tips on how to encourage manufacturer's representatives to attend scheduled training sessions are given. Manufacturers should learn the value of keeping the training program up-to-date and communicate with the sales team to know what needs to be revamped. Problems faced by representatives with inside sales staff should also be addressed by the manufacturer.

34167 ■ *"Research Highlights Disengaged Workforce" in Workforce Management (Vol.*

88, November 16, 2009, No. 12, pp. 22)
Pub: Crain Communications Inc.
Contact: Rance E. Crain, President
Ed: Ed Frauenheim. **Description:** Most researchers have documented a drop in employee engagement during the recession due to such factors as layoffs, restructuring and less job security.

34168 ■ *"Retiring Baby Boomers and Dissatisfied Gen-Xers Cause..Brain Drain" in Agency Sales Magazine (Vol. 39, November 2009, No. 10)*
Ed: Denise Kelly. **Description:** Due to the impending retirement of the baby boomers a critical loss of knowledge and experience in businesses will result. Creating a plan to address this loss of talent centered on the development of the younger generation is discussed.

34169 ■ *"A Reverse-Innovation Playbook: Insights From a Company That Developed Products For Emerging Markets and Then Brought Them Back Home" in Harvard Business Review (Vol. 90, April 2012, No. 4, pp. 120)*
Pub: Harvard Business Review Press
Contact: Peter E. Walsh, Director
Ed: Vijay Govindarajan. **Released:** April 2012. **Description:** An overview is presented on the organizational change implemented by Harman International Industries Inc. to create products for emerging markets and ensure that they would be accepted in already established middle markets. Components include setting radical goals, selecting team leaders with no competing interests, and leveraging global resources.

34170 ■ *"RIM Rocks Out: Billionaire Bosses Sponsor a Free Concert for Deserving Staff" in Canadian Business (Vol. 80, Winter 2007, No. 24)*
Ed: Joe Castaldo. **Description:** Jim Balsillie and Mike Lazaridis of Research in Motion Ltd. (RIM) rented out the Air Canada Centre in Toronto to give their employees a free concert that features performances by the Tragically Hip and Van Halen on November 15, 2007. RIM has sponsored concerts by Aerosmith, Tom Cochrane, and the Barenaked Ladies in past parties that only shows how far the company goes in terms of employee appreciation.

34171 ■ *"The Risks and Rewards of Speaking Up: Managerial Responses to Employee Voice" in Academy of Management Journal (Vol. 55, August 1, 2012, No. 4, pp. 851)*
Pub: Academy of Management
Contact: Ming-Jer Chen, President
Ed: Ethan R. Burris. **Description:** The ways in which managers respond to suggestions made by employees is examined. Positive and negative managerial reactions to employees speaking up depend on whether the type of voice exhibited is challenging or supportive as well as on the psychological mechanisms of loyalty and threat.

34172 ■ *"Say No to Slackers" in Canadian Business (Vol. 79, November 6, 2006, No. 22, pp. 105)*
Pub: Rogers Media Inc.
Contact: Tony Viner, President
Ed: Erin Pooley. **Description:** The effects of underperformers on performance of other colleagues with relation to company productivity are analyzed.

34173 ■ *"Scaling Up Excellence: Getting to More Without Settling for Less"*
Pub: Crown Business Books
Released: February 4, 2014. **Price:** $26.00. **Description:** Authors have dedicated ten years to finding out what it takes to build and discover exemplary performance in businesses to help recharge organizations and help them to grow. They reveal how the best leaders and teams develop, grow, and instill the right mindsets in workers.

34174 ■ *"The Secret Strategy for Meaningful Sales Meetings" in Agency Sales Magazine (Vol. 39, December 2009, No. 11, pp. 40)*
Ed: Dave Kahle. **Description:** Sales meetings can be made more meaningful by focusing on the end results that the meeting seeks to achieve. Describing

the changed behavior that is sought from the sales force and working backwards from there also help make a sales meeting more meaningful.

34175 ■ *"Seven Things Great Employers Do (That Others Don't); Unusual, Innovative, and Proven Tactics To Create Productive and Profitable Working Environments" in Gallup Business Journal (April 15, 2014)*
Pub: Gallup Press
Released: April 15, 2014. **Description:** Seven unusual, innovative, and proven tactics that create productive and profitable working environments are examined through researching 32 companies. These firms represented many industries, including healthcare, financial services, hospitality, manufacturing, and retail throughout the world.

34176 ■ *"Shared Leadership In Teams: An Investigation of Antecedent Conditions and Performance" in Academy of Management Journal (Vol. 50, No. 5, October 1, 2007, pp. 1217)*
Pub: Academy of Management
Contact: Ming-Jer Chen, President
Ed: Jay B. Carson, Paul E. Tesluk, Jennifer A. Marrone. **Description:** Study assessed the advantages of distribution of leadership among team members rather than on a single person revealed advantages that ranged from support and shared functions along with higher ratings from clients on their performance.

34177 ■ *Shop Class as Soulcraft*
Pub: Dutton Children's Books
Contact: Lauri Hornik, President
Ed: Matthew B. Crawford. **Released:** May 28, 2009. **Price:** $25.95, Hardcover; $16, Paperback. **Description:** A philosopher and mechanic argues for the satisfaction and challenges of manual work.

34178 ■ *"Should Managers Focus on Performance or Engagement? Gallup Examined this Question and Found That the Answer Isn't as 'Either/Or' as Many Companies Might Think" in Gallup Business Journal (August 5, 2014)*
Pub: Gallup Press
Released: August 5, 2014. **Description:** A Gallup survey of over 8,000 employees were asked whether managers should focus on performance or engagement. High performance managers create an engaging work environment promoting peak performance in three ways.

34179 ■ *Silos, Politics and Turf Wars: A Leadership Fable about Destroying the Barriers That Turn Colleagues Into Competitors*
Pub: Jossey-Bass
Ed: Patrick M. Lencioni. **Released:** January 2006. **Price:** $24.95, hardcover; $16.99. **Description:** The author addresses management problems through a fable that revolves around a self-employed consultant who has to dismantle silos at an upscale hotel, a technology company and a hospital. The story explains how organizations can use a collective operational vision in order to overcome pride, greed, and tribalism and work as a team with the same goal in mind. **Availability:** PrintE-book.

34180 ■ *"16 Creative and Cheap Ways to Say 'Thank You" in HR Specialist (Vol. 8, September 2010, No. 9, pp. 8)*
Pub: Capitol Information Group Inc.
Description: Tips for starting an employee appreciation program for a small company are presented.

34181 ■ *"Size Does Matter" in International Journal of Globalisation and Small Business (Vol. 4, September 21, 2010, No. 1, pp. 61)*
Pub: Publishers Communication Group
Contact: Doug Wright, Director
Ed: Julia Cornnell, Ranjit Voola. **Description:** Examination of how members of an Australian-based manufacturing and engineering cluster share knowledge through networking as a means to improve competitive advantage.

34182 ■ *"Sleeping with Your Smartphone: How to Break the 24/7 Habit and Change the Way You Work"*
Pub: Harvard Business Review Press
Contact: Peter E. Walsh, Director
Released: May 1, 2012. **Price:** $27.00. **Description:** Harvard Business School professor, Leslie Perlow, reveals ways to become more productive after disconnecting from your smartphone. A six-person team was used in an experiment at The Boston Consulting Group, an elite management consulting firm, where teams changed the way they worked and became more efficient and effective by disconnecting. The team was better able to perform and recruit new talent. A step-by-step guide is offered to change your team.

34183 ■ *Small Business, Big Life: Five Steps to Creating a Great Life with Your Own Small Business*
Pub: Thomas Nelson Inc.
Contact: Michael S. Hyatt, President
Ed: Louis Barajas. **Released:** May 01, 2007. **Price:** $22.99, hardcover. **Description:** Barajas describes his and his father's independent entrepreneurial paths and suggests an inspirational approach to business that relies on four personal greatness cornerstones: truth, responsibility, awareness, and courage, and on keeping in mind your vision and your team's needs. The book provides a new look at achieving a work/life balance. **Availability:** Print.

34184 ■ *"Small Businesses Get Creative to Retain Workers"* in Crain's Detroit Business *(Vol. 24, March 17, 2008, No. 11, pp. 21)*
Ed: Nancy Kaffer. **Description:** Small businesses are often unable to compete with larger firms when it comes to offering employees fringe benefits and such perks as a company gym or an in-house chef; however, many smaller companies have found that the key to gaining employee loyalty lies in creating an atmosphere in which employees feel job satisfaction. Also provides tips on how to keep employees.

34185 ■ *"A Social Context Model of Envy and Social Undermining"* in Academy of Management Journal *(Vol. 55, June 1, 2012, No. 3, pp. 643)*
Pub: Academy of Management
Contact: Ming-Jer Chen, President
Ed: Michelle K. Duffy, Kristin L. Scott, Jason D. Shaw, Bennett J. Tepper, Karl Aquino. **Description:** The relationship between envy and social undermining is investigated using the case of hospital employees. Results show that the impact of envy on social undermining through moral disengagement is higher when social identification ith coworkers is low. The indirect effect of envy is also greater in teams with high team undermining norms and low team identification.

34186 ■ *"Social Intelligence and the Biology of Leadership"* in Harvard Business Review *(Vol. 86, September 2008, No. 9, pp. 74)*
Pub: Harvard Business Review Press
Contact: Peter E. Walsh, Director
Ed: Daniel Goleman, Richard Boyatzis. **Description:** Social intelligence within the framework of corporate leadership is defined and described. Guidelines for assessing one's own capabilities as a socially intelligent leader include empathy, teamwork, inspiration, and influence.

34187 ■ *The Social Media Bible: Tactics, Tools, and Strategies for Business Success*
Pub: John Wiley & Sons Inc.
Contact: Stephen M. Smith, President
Ed: Lon Safko. **Released:** Third Edition. **Price:** $29.95, paperback; $19.99. **Description:** Information is given to build or transform a business into social media, where customers, employees, and prospects connect, collaborate, and champion products and services in order to increase sales and to beat the competition. **Availability:** PrintE-book.

34188 ■ *"Spring Cleaning"* in Entrepreneur *(May 2014)*
Pub: Entrepreneur Media Inc.
Released: May 2014. **Description:** Office designers provide tips for organizing the shared office space model. Jessica Mowery of MOW Design Studio

emphasizes the importance of employee productivity while making changes that result in more efficient and motivated people. Sonya Dufner of Gensler says they design with flexibility while making sure that the office space will work for clients in the long term. Some suggested solutions for decluttering the office are the HP Officejet Pro 8600 e-All-In-One Printer, David Hsu's Desk 117 and Herman Miller's SAYL Work Chair with Suspension Back.

34189 ■ *"A Stalled Culture Change?"* in Workforce Management *(Vol. 88, December 14, 2009, No. 13, pp. 1)*
Pub: Crain Communications Inc.
Contact: Rance E. Crain, President
Ed: Jeremy Smerd. **Description:** General Motors CEO Fritz Henderson's abrupt resignation shocked employees and signaled that Henderson had not done enough to change the company's culture, especially in dealing with its top management.

34190 ■ *The Starbucks Experience*
Ed: Joseph A. Michelli. **Released:** September 14, 2006. **Price:** $24.95. **Description:** Boardroom strategies, employee motivation tips, community involvement, and customer satisfaction are issues addressed, using Starbucks as a model.

34191 ■ *"Start Filling Your Talent Gap - Now"* in Business Strategy Review *(Vol. 21, Spring 2010, No. 1, pp. 56)*
Pub: John Wiley & Sons Inc. Scientific, Technical, Medical, and Scholarly Div. (Wiley-Blackwell)
Contact: William J. Pesce, Manager
E-mail: wpesce@wiley.com
Ed: Alan Bird, Lori Flees, Paul Di Paola. **Description:** As businesses steer their way out of turbulence, they have a unique opportunity to identify their leadership supply and demand and then to close the talent gap in their organization. Authors explain how to take immediate steps to build the right team now and lay the groundwork for a long-term approach for nurturing talent within the organization.

34192 ■ *"Storytelling Star of Show for Cincinnati's E.W. Scripps"* in Business Courier *(Vol. 26, November 13, 2009, No. 29, pp. 1)*
Pub: American City Business Journals, Inc.
Contact: Whitney Shaw, President
Ed: Dan Monk. **Description:** Rich Boehne, CEO Of the EW Scripps Company in Cincinnati has authorized a new training program in storytelling for employees at Scripps' 10 television stations. He believes that the training will improve the quality of broadcasting content. His plans to improve quality of newspaper content are also discussed.

34193 ■ *Streetwise Motivating and Rewarding Employees: New and Better Ways to Inspire Your People*
Ed: Alexander Hiam. **Released:** March 1999. **Description:** Ways for employers and business managers to motivate difficult employees.

34194 ■ *"Stress-Test Your Strategy: the 7 Questions to Ask"* in Harvard Business Review *(Vol. 88, November 2010, No. 11, pp. 92)*
Pub: Harvard Business School Publishing
Ed: Robert Simons. **Description:** Seven questions organizations should use to assess crisis management capabilities are: who is the primary customer, how do core values prioritize all parties, what performance variables are being tracked, what strategic boundaries have been set, how is creative tension being produced, how committed are workers to assisting each other, and what uncertainties are causing worry?.

34195 ■ *"Striving for Self-Verification During Organizational Entry"* in Academy of Management Journal *(Vol. 55, June 2012, No. 2, pp. 360)*
Pub: Academy of Management
Contact: Ming-Jer Chen, President
Ed: Daniel M. Cable, Virginia S. Kay. **Description:** How striving for self-verification relates with self-disclosure, self-monitoring, and core self-evaluations

is explored. Striving refers to bringing others to know who a person is during the organizational entry process. Relations to the validity of interviewers' evaluations, job seekers' ability to find satisfying work, and supervisors' evaluations of newcomers' performance are given.

34196 ■ *"Stylish Successes"* in Women In Business *(Vol. 61, October-November 2009, No. 5, pp. 12)*
Pub: American Business Women's Association
Contact: Lorie Burch, President
Ed: Leigh Elmore; Megan L. Reese. **Description:** Amanda Horan Kennedy, Angela Samuels, Barbara Nast Saletan, and Patty Nast Canton are career women who ventured into entrepreneurship. They are deemed to possess networking and teamwork skills that ensured their success in the garment industry.

34197 ■ *"The Superfluous Position"* in Entrepreneur *(Vol. 37, July 2009, No. 7, pp. 62)*
Pub: Entrepreneur Press
Contact: Perlman Neil, President
Description: Profile of an anonymous editor at a multimedia company that publishes tourism guides who shares his experiences in dealing with an officemate who was promoted as creative manager of content. Everyone was irritated by this person, who would constantly do something to justify his new title. The biggest problem was the fact that this person didn't have a clear job description.

34198 ■ *"The Sustainable Supply Chain"* in Harvard Business Review *(Vol. 88, October 2010, No. 10, pp. 70)*
Pub: Harvard Business School Publishing
Ed: Steven Prokesch. **Description:** Peter Senge, founder of the Society for Organizational Learning, emphasizes the importance of assessing the system as a whole under which one is operating, and learning how to work with individuals with which one has not worked previously. He also points to nongovernmental organizations to provide assistance and legitimacy.

34199 ■ *Switch: How to Change Things When Change Is Hard*
Pub: Broadway Business
Contact: David Drake, Manager
E-mail: ddrake@randomhouse.com
Ed: Chip Heath, Dan Heath. **Released:** February 16, 2010. **Price:** $26, hardcover; $14.99. **Description:** Change is difficult for everyone. This book helps business leaders to motivate employees as well as to help everybody motive themselves and others. **Availability:** PrintE-book.

34200 ■ *"Take Command: Lessons in Leadership: How to Be a First Responder in Business"*
Pub: Crown Business
Released: October 14, 2014. **Price:** $25.00. **Description:** What do elite members of the military, first responders in a disaster zone, and successful business leaders have in common? Clarity of mind and purpose in the midst of chaos. Cofounder and CEO of Team Rubicon and former Marine Sniper Jake Wood, teaches the lessons in leadership and teamwork to help managers and entrepreneurs succeed in this hyper-competitive business environment today.

34201 ■ *"Team Bonding for Fun and Profit"* in Women Entrepreneur *(December 3, 2008)*
Ed: Eve Gumpel. **Description:** Discusses the benefits that competitions such as the 2008 BG U.S. Challenge in Lake Placid, New York, can offer in terms of team building and employee motivation as well as networking and the development of a positive working relationship with partners and competitors alike.

34202 ■ *"Team Implicit Coordination Processes: A Team Knowledge-based Approach"* in Academy of Management

Review (January 2008, pp. 163)
Pub: ScholarOne Inc.
Contact: William T. Carden, Jr., President
Ed: Ramon Rico, Miriam Sanchez-Manzanares, Francisco Gil, Cristina Gibson. **Description:** An integrated theoretical framework is developed to enhance understanding of the functioning of work teams and implicit coordination behaviors; the implications for team coordination theory and effective management of work teams is discussed.

34203 ■ *"Teamwork On the Fly: How To Master the New Art of Teaming" in Harvard Business Review (Vol. 90, April 2012, No. 4, pp. 72)*
Pub: Harvard Business Review Press
Contact: Peter E. Walsh, Director
Ed: Amy C. Edmondson. **Released:** April 2012. **Description:** Description of the concept of 'teaming' or flexible teamwork is given. Teaming brings together expertise from disparate fields and forms temporary groups to identify innovations and address unanticipate problems. Project management and team leadership are important components of success.

34204 ■ *Thank God It's Monday! How to Create a Workplace You and Your Customers Love*
Pub: FT Press
Contact: Timothy C. Moore, Vice President
Ed: Roxanne Emmerich. **Released:** April 22, 2009. **Price:** $19.99, Hardcover. **Description:** Tips on creating a positive environment for both employees and customers.

34205 ■ *"There's Always Something Unexpected" in South Florida Business Journal (Vol. 34, June 6, 2014, No. 46, pp. 13)*
Pub: American City Business Journals
Released: June 6, 2014. **Description:** Hannah Granade, CEO of Advantix Systems, likes how her job allows her to build the business and bring people together. The company, that provides cooling and dehumidification systems for industrial and commercial applications, encourages creative thinking by building an open culture.

34206 ■ *The Thin Book of Naming Elephants: How to Surface Undiscussables for Greater Organizational Success*
Pub: Thin Book Publishing Co.
Contact: Sue Annis Hammond, Owner
E-mail: sue@thinbook.com
Ed: Sue Annis Hammond, Andrea B. Mayfield. **Price:** $10.95. **Description:** Organizational success is of upmost importance to today's entrepreneurs and organizations. The hierarchal system in which people are afraid to speak up in organizations is discussed. The points of view and inability to see things from an overall perspective can cause insecurity among employees. The three elephants present in every organization include: arrogance, hubris, and screamers and the damage caused by these elephants in any organization is examined.

34207 ■ *30 Reasons Employees Hate Their Managers: What Your People May Be Thinking and What You Can Do About It*
Pub: AMACOM
Contact: Edward T. Reilly, Manager
Ed: Bruce L. Katcher, Adam Snyder. **Released:** March 07, 2007. **Price:** $18.95, Paper or Softback. **Description:** Thirty reasons why American employees are unhappy in their jobs are outlined. Each chapter is opened with a reason, an examination of how it creates work difficulties, and makes suggestions to managers on how to best address each issue. **Availability:** Print.

34208 ■ *"Transportation Insight Places in Top 25 North Carolina's 100 Private Companies" in Travel & Leisure Close-Up (October 8, 2012)*
Description: Transportation Insight was ranked 23rd on Business North Carolina Magazine's list of the Top 100 Private Companies in the state. Transportation Insight is a third-party logistics provider and accredits it business model and workers for its success.

34209 ■ *"Truffles & Trifles' Marci Arthur Plans YouTube Channel, Cookbook" in Orlando Business Journal (Vol. 30, May 2, 2014, No. 45, pp. 3)*
Pub: American City Business Journals
Released: May 2, 2014. **Description:** Marci Arthur, founder of Truffles & Trifles Cooking School, plans to create a YouTube channel and publish a cookbook. Arthur believes that the survival of her business can be attributed to the devotion and integrity of her employees. Reports show that the school has been receiving donations from sponsors such as Wolf Appliances and Sub-Zero.

34210 ■ *"Tsingtao's Chairman On Jump-Starting a Sluggish Company" in Harvard Business Review (Vol. 90, April 2012, No. 4, pp. 41)*
Pub: Harvard Business Review Press
Contact: Peter E. Walsh, Director
Ed: Jin Zhiguo. **Released:** April 2012. **Description:** The key challenge Tsingtao Brewery Company Ltd. faced was the focus on pleasing corporate superiors, rather than the firm's customers. By inventing a new model, the brewery was able to boost both employee productivity and product quality. First half profits and revenue for 2011 grew more than 20 percent over the previous year.

34211 ■ *Ubuntu!: An Aspiring Story About an African Tradition of Teamwork and Collaboration*
Pub: Broadway Business
Contact: David Drake, Manager
E-mail: ddrake@randomhouse.com
Ed: Bob Nelson, Stephen Lundin. **Released:** March 30, 2010. **Price:** $19.99, hardcover; $11.99. **Description:** The African tradition of teamwork and collaboration is used to demonstrate these skills to small business leaders. **Availability:** PrintE-book.

34212 ■ *"The Uncompromising Leader" in Harvard Business Review (Vol. 86, July-August 2008, No. 8, pp. 50)*
Pub: Harvard Business Review Press
Contact: Peter E. Walsh, Director
Ed: Russel A. Eisenstat, Michael Beer, Nathaniel Foote, Flemming Norrgren. **Description:** Advice regarding how to drive performance without sacrificing commitment to people is given. Topics include development of shared purpose, organizational engagement, the fostering of collective leadership capability, and maintaining perspective.

34213 ■ *"Vacation, All I Ever Wanted" in Entrepreneur (August 2014)*
Pub: Entrepreneur Media Inc.
Released: August 2014. **Description:** Small business owners can maximize the value of spending time away from work. Paid vacations boost employee productivity and the same effect can also be experienced by owners. Vacation expenses can be managed with creativity and careful planning according to Matt Kepnes, author of 'How to Travel the World on $50 a Day: Travel Cheaper, Longer, Smarter'. The three main vacation expenses that business owners should carefully plan include lodging, transportation, and food and entertainment.

34214 ■ *"The Value of Conversations With Employees; Talk Isn't Cheap" in Gallup Management Journal (June 30, 2011)*
Pub: Gallup Inc.
Contact: Jim Clifton, Chief Executive Officer
Ed: Jessica Tyler. **Description:** When managers have meaningful exchanges with their employees, they don't only show they care, they also add value to their organization's bottom line.

34215 ■ *"The Virgin Way"*
Released: September 9, 2014. **Price:** $29.95. **Description:** Sir Richard Branson, founder of Virgin Group, shares his own style of leadership. He teaches how fun, family, passion, and the dying art of listening are key ingredients to what his employees describe as the "Virgin Way". The entrepreneur reveals insights into his forty years of starting and building his airline company.

34216 ■ *"Virtue and Vice" in Entrepreneur (September 2014)*
Pub: Entrepreneur Media Inc.
Released: September 2014. **Description:** Socially responsible investments (SRI) are rising in the U.S., but many claim that vice funds offer better returns. Vice fund proponents argue that any profitable company deserves a place in a good investment portfolio. SRI proponents emphasize investments that benefit the society. Analysts note that investors who restrict their investment landscape by selecting only vice funds or only SRI funds may lead to lower returns. Other specialized funds attract activist investors supporting advocacies like gender equality or a positive work environment.

34217 ■ *"Voices: More Important than Results" in Business Strategy Review (Vol. 21, Summer 2010, No. 2, pp. 81)*
Pub: Blackwell Publishers Ltd.
Ed: Bert De Reyck, Zeger Degraeve. **Description:** Managing only for results leads to crises. It is important to reward people for the decisions they make, not just for the results they create.

34218 ■ *"Want To Increase Hospital Revenues? Engage Your Physicians. When Doctors Are Frustrated, Patient Care and Hospital Revenues Suffer. Here's How to Boost Physicians' Engagement -- and the Bottom Line" in Gallup Business Journal (June 5, 2014)*
Pub: Gallup Press
Released: June 5, 2014. **Description:** Hospitals need to engage their doctors in order to be successful for both patient care and the bottom line. Four key practices to drive physician engagement are outlined.

34219 ■ *"We Move Forward as a Team" in Women In Business (Vol. 61, December 2009, No. 6, pp. 6)*
Pub: American Business Women's Association
Contact: Lorie Burch, President
Ed: Rene Street. **Description:** Based on her experiences in ABWA's National Board of Directors retreat, an executive director of the American Business Women's Association, shares her belief that interaction is necessary for a successful business enterprise. She believes that the problems presented in the retreat's team-building exercises are similar to challenges which are faced in ABWA, in the workplace, and in the marketplace.

34220 ■ *"We Were Strutting Our Stuff" in Women In Business (Vol. 63, Summer 2011, No. 2, pp. 10)*
Pub: American Business Women's Association
Contact: Lorie Burch, President
Ed: Rene Street, Leigh Elmore. **Description:** American Business Women's Association's STRUT relay race event helped raise awareness of the group in the United States. The event also provided excellent team-building exercises for ABWA chapters. It also helped participants boost their leadership and business skills.

34221 ■ *"A Weak Link Can Break the Chain of Good Service" in Canadian Business (Vol. 83, August 17, 2010, No. 13-14, pp. 11)*
Pub: Rogers Media Inc.
Contact: Tony Viner, President
Ed: Richard Branson. **Description:** Good customer service is a practice that requires the efforts of the entire chain of coworkers that work as a team from beginning to end. The chain of assistance is only as strong as the weakest link when it comes to helping a customer.

34222 ■ *"A Well-Crafted Employee Handbook Can Make Work Run More Smoothly" in Idaho Business Review (September 17, 2014)*
Pub: Dolan Co.
Contact: James P. Dolan, President
Released: September 17, 2014. **Description:** An employee handbook will provide a complaint process, provide company management flexibility and clarity and keep a company out of legal problems. Training, compensation, benefits, security, health, performance

appraisals, and safety issues must be covered. Human resource managers and other mangers should cover basics to help communicate with workers.

34223 ■ *"What Employees Worldwide Have in Common" in Gallup Management Journal (September 22, 2011)*
Pub: Gallup Inc.
Contact: Jim Clifton, Chief Executive Officer
Ed: Steve Crabtree. **Description:** According to a Gallup study, workplace conditions are strongly tied to personal wellbeing, regardless of geographic region. The employee study covered 116 countries.

34224 ■ *"What Your Employees Need to Know; They Probably Don't Know How They're Performing" in Gallup Management Journal (April 13, 2011)*
Pub: Gallup Inc.
Contact: Jim Clifton, Chief Executive Officer
Ed: Steve Crabtree. **Description:** Personalized feedback and recognition aren't just extras that make workers feel good about themselves they are critical predictors of positive performance.

34225 ■ *"What Your Workplace Wellness Programs are Missing; Companies Can Benefit From Taking a Holistic Approach To Their Employees. Here's How" in Gallup Business Journal (July 7, 2014)*
Pub: Gallup Press
Released: July 7, 2014. **Description:** Companies should take a holistic approach to their employees' well being when addressing physical wellness in their workforce. Although employers are working to improve the physical wellness of workers, including weight loss, smoking cessation, and stress management, five essential elements: purpose, social, financial, community and physical issues would round out a good program.

34226 ■ *"What's More Important: Talent or Engagement? A Study With Retailer ANN INC. Seeks To Find the Essential Ingredients To High-Performing Managers and Employees" in Gallup Business Journal (April 22, 2014)*
Pub: Gallup Press
Released: April 22, 2014. **Description:** ANN INC. is a leading women's clothing retailer that is exploring the necessary steps to achieving both high-performing managers and employees. The firm found that hiring people with the right talent and engaging them will maximize performance.

34227 ■ *"When Emotional Reasoning Trumps IQ" in Harvard Business Review (Vol. 88, September 2010, No. 9, pp. 27)*
Pub: Harvard Business School Publishing
Ed: Roderick Gilkey, Ricardo Caceda, Clinton Kilts. **Description:** Strategic reasoning was found to be linked more closely to areas of the brain associated with intuition and emotion, rather than the prefrontal cortex, which is typically thought to be the center of such activity. Implications for management skills are discussed.

34228 ■ *"When Key Employees Clash: How Should a Business Owner Handle a Conflict Between Two Senior Managers?" in Harvard Business Review (Vol. 90, June 2012, No. 6, pp. 135)*
Pub: Harvard Business Review Press
Contact: Peter E. Walsh, Director
Ed: H. Irving Grousbeck. **Released:** June 2012. **Description:** A fictitious employee conflict scenario is presented, with contributors providing suggestions for an effective management plan. The key component is ensuring that both employees receive the coaching and support necessary to enable them to perceive their roles more clearly and to build trust.

34229 ■ *"When R&D Spending Is Not Enough: The Critical Role of Culture When You Really Want to Innovate" in Human Resource Management (Vol. 49, July-August*

2010, No. 4, pp. 767-792)*
Pub: John Wiley
Ed: Sheng Wang, Rebecca M. Guidice, Judith W. Tansky, Zhong-Ming Wang. **Description:** A study was conducted to examine the effect of contextual contingencies on innovation. Findings indicate that Chinese manufacturers with cultures emphasizing innovation and teamwork more effectively utilize financial resources in the innovation process. Results also show that a culture emphasizing outcomes and stability leads to lower levels innovation irrespective of investments.

34230 ■ *"Whole Foods: The King of Pinterest?" in Austin Business Journal (Vol. 32, July 13, 2012, No. 19, pp. A1)*
Pub: American City Business Journals, Inc.
Contact: Whitney Shaw, President
Ed: Vicky Garza. **Released:** July 13, 2012. **Description:** Whole Foods Market Inc. has gained almost 50,000 followers on the Pinterest social network and has been cited for its best practices on the new social media platform. The company's Pinterest account is managed on a national level and allows employees to contribute to the page.

34231 ■ *"Why Creating Organizational Change Is So Hard; Resistance To Change Is Entrenched In Most Companies. Here's How To Overcome Obstacles and Create Change That Lasts" in Gallup Business Journal (May 22, 2014)*
Pub: Gallup Press
Released: May 22, 2014. **Description:** Poorly defined objectives, politics, and unclear metrics are come of the obstacles to implementing meaningful change in any organization. Employees are motivated to change if leaders provide hope and inspiration. Ways that companies can overcome barriers to change are examined.

34232 ■ *"Why Did We Ever Go Into HR?" in Harvard Business Review (Vol. 86, July-August 2008, No. 8, pp. 39)*
Pub: Harvard Business Review Press
Contact: Peter E. Walsh, Director
Ed: Matthew D. Breitfelder, Daisy Wademan Dowling. **Description:** Examines the role of human resource directors and how their jobs foster new ideas and generate optimism.

34233 ■ *"Why Does Firm Reputation In Human Resource Policies Influence College Students? The Mechanisms Underlying Job Pursuit Intentions" in Human Resource Management (Vol. 51, January-February 2012, No. 1, pp. 121-142)*
Pub: John Wiley & Sons Inc.
Contact: Stephen M. Smith, President
Ed: Julie Holliday Wayne, Wendy J. Casper. **Description:** The effects of reputational information about human resource practices of companies on college students seeking employment are examined. The reputation of firms in compensation, work-family, and diversity efforts are found to increase intentions to pursue employment in these firms.

34234 ■ *"Why Good Jobs Are Good for Retailers: Some Companies Are Investing In Their Workers and Reaping Healthy Profits" in Harvard Business Review (Vol. 90, January-February 2012, No.1-2, pp. 124)*
Pub: Harvard Business Review Press
Contact: Peter E. Walsh, Director
Ed: Zeynep Ton. **Released:** January-February 2012. **Description:** Four key operational practices can help retailers sever the trade-off between investing in employees and maintaining low prices. These are: offering fewer promotions and SKUs, cross-training workers rather than varifying their number to match customer traffic, eliminating waste while preserving staff, and empowering workers to make prompt decisions.

34235 ■ *"Why I Stopped Firing Everyone and Started Being a Better Boss" in Inc. (Vol. 34,*

September 2012, No. 7, pp. 86)*
Pub: Mansueto Ventures L.L.C.
Contact: John Koten, Chief Executive Officer
Ed: April Joyner. **Released:** September 2012. **Description:** Indigo Johnson, former Marine, discusses her management style when starting her business. She fired employees regularly. Johnson enrolled in a PhD program in leadership and established a better hiring program and learned to utilize her workers' strengths.

34236 ■ *"Why Motivating People Doesn't Work...and What Does: The New Science of Leading, Energizing, and Engaging"*
Pub: Berrett-Koehler Communications Inc.
Contact: Steve Piersanti, President
E-mail: spiersanti@bkpub.com
Released: September 30, 2014. **Price:** $24.95. **Description:** Leaderehip reccarcher, consultant, and business coach, Susan Fowler, shares the latest research on the nature of human motivation to present a tested model and course of action to help Human Resource leaders and managers guide workers towards motivation that will not only increase productivity and engagement but will provide employees with a sense of purpose and fulfillment.

34237 ■ *"Why To Embrace Positive Leadership" in Birmingham Business Journal (Vol. 31, February 7, 2014, No. 6, pp. 14)*
Pub: American City Business Journals, Inc.
Contact: Whitney Shaw, President
Released: February 7, 2014. **Description:** The benefits achieved from managers' adoption of positive leadership are discussed. Positive leadership motivates employees to achieve higher performance levels. Tips to achieve positive leadership are listed.

34238 ■ *Why Work Sucks and How To Fix It*
Pub: Portfolio Publishing
Contact: Adrian Zackheim, President
Ed: Cali Ressler, Jody Thompson. **Released:** May 01, 2008. **Price:** $12.99; $15, Paperback. **Description:** Results-Only Work Environments (ROWE) not only make employees happier, it also delivers better results. ROWE allows employees to do whatever they want, whenever they want as long as business objectives are met. No more pointless meetings, fighting traffic to be to work on time, or asking for permission for time off. **Availability:** Electronic publishing.

34239 ■ *"Why Your Company Must Be Mission-Driven; A Clear Mission Inspires Employee Engagement, Fosters Customer Engagement, and Helps Boost Company Performance -- Among Other Benefits" in Gallup Business Journal (March 6, 2014)*
Pub: Gallup Press
Released: March 6, 2014. **Description:** It is stressed that executives need a clear mission in order to engage their workers, foster customer engagement, and to help boost their firm's performance.

34240 ■ *"Winners Dream: A Journey from Corner Store to Corner Office"*
Pub: Simon & Schuster Adult Publishing Group
Contact: Carolyn Reidy, President
E-mail: carolyn.reidy@simonandschuster.com
Released: October 14, 2014. **Price:** $28.00. **Description:** Bill McDermott, CEO of the world's largest business software company, SAP, profiles his career. He discusses his career moves, sales strategies, employee incentives to create high performance teams, and the competitive advantages of optimism and hard work. The entrepreneur offers a blueprint for success and the knowledge that the real dream is the journey, not the preconceived destination.

34241 ■ *"Winners & Losers" in Canadian Business (Vol. 85, July 16, 2012, No. 11-12, pp. 22)*
Pub: George Media Inc.
Released: July 16, 2012. **Description:** Canadian Pacific Railway's 4,800 locomotive engineers and conductors walked out in protest of the proposed work rules and pension cuts. Shareholders rejected a $25-million bonus and retention payout to Astral Media chief executive officer Ian Greenburg. The

Dragon spacecraft of Space Exploration Technologies delivered supplies and experiments to the International Space Station.

34242 ■ "Work Buds" in Canadian Business (Vol. 80, April 23, 2007, No. 9, pp. 56)
Ed: Andrew Wahl. **Description:** The role of team work and cooperation in improving workplace environment is presented.

34243 ■ "Work/Life Balance" in Dallas Business Journal (Vol. 37, June 20, 2014, No. 41, pp. 4)
Pub: American City Business Journals
Released: June 20, 2014. **Description:** Younger generations of corporate employees are increasingly looking for a more engaged workplace community. Research firm, Quantum Workplace, identifies several trends that help to attract and retain employees, including jobs that align with the workers' own values, growth opportunities within the firm, social interactions with co-workers, and employee health benefits.

34244 ■ "Working It Out! How a Young Executive Overcomes Obstacles on the Job" in Black Enterprise (Vol. 37, January 2007, No. 6, pp. 55)
Pub: Earl G. Graves Publishing Co. Inc.
Contact: Earl G. Graves, Jr., President
Ed: Laura Egodigwe. **Description:** Interview with Susan Chapman, Global Head of Operations for Citigroup Realty Services, in which she discusses issues such as the important skills necessary for overcoming obstacles in the workplace.

34245 ■ "Workplace Wellness" in Entrepreneurs (June 2014)
Pub: Entrepreneur Media Inc.
Released: June 2014. **Description:** Workplace wellness programs can be started by checking with insurers who may provide program and activity suggestions promotional materials or other resources. Teaming up with others is encouraged. For instance, employees from various departments or nearby companies can get flu shots or blood pressure screening. Management should also get involved in these programs, because it will then be known among employees that wellness is taken seriously. It is also important that workplace wellness programs are kept safe and legally sound.

34246 ■ Ya Gotta Wanna
Pub: Creative Book Publishers
Ed: Malcolm Paice. **Released:** July 2005. **Price:** $12.95. **Description:** Three phases of teamwork are outlined: identifying the people and creating the team, analyzing the components of the team, and implementing the project. The author compares a soccer team to a management team and that a successful soccer team has three main area attributes: a solid defense, a creative midfield, and a potent strike force.

34247 ■ "Your First 100 Days on Your New Job" in Women In Business (Vol. 63, Spring 2011, No. 1, pp. 28)
Pub: American Business Women's Association
Contact: Lorie Burch, President
Ed: Diane Stafford. **Description:** The first 100 days on the job are crucial if the person's permanent hiring is conditional on surviving a probationary period. The new hire must do more than just master the job's technical details to maximize the chance of success. Details of some basic tips to fit into the corporate culture and get along with coworkers are also discussed.

TRADE PERIODICALS

34248 ■ The Journal for Quality and Participation
Pub: American Society for Quality
Contact: Paul E. Borawski, Chief Executive Officer
URL(s): www.asq.org/pub/jqp/. **Released:** Quarterly **Price:** $58, Members domestic, individuals; $90, Members international, individuals; $83, Members includes GST individual, Canada; $99, Nonmembers domestic, individuals; $111, Nonmembers international, individuals; $111, Nonmembers Canadian, includes GST individual.

34249 ■ Teamwork
Pub: Dartnell Publications
URL(s): www.dartnellcorp.com/newsletters/teamwork.php. **Released:** Monthly. **Price:** $179, online only.; $249, print and online. **Description:** Focuses on successful teamwork in manufacturing and corporate businesses. Recurring features include columns titled What Would You Do?, Test Yourself and See, and Teamwork in Action.

VIDEOCASSETTES/AUDIOCASSETTES

34250 ■ Better Productivity Is Not By Chance—Dr. Robert Lorher
Instructional Video
2219 C St.
Lincoln, NE 68502-1745
Ph: (402)475-6570
Free: 800-228-0164
Fax: (402)475-6500
Co. E-mail: orders@insvideo.com
URL: http://www.insvideo.com
Contact: Kathy Damkroger, President
Released: 19??. **Price:** $169. **Description:** Dr. Robert Lorher offers five factors that will improve motivational skills and productivity, and support the importance of setting reachable goals. **Availability:** VHS.

34251 ■ Building Blocks for Team Performance
Instructional Video
2219 C St.
Lincoln, NE 68502-1745
Ph: (402)475-6570
Free: 800-228-0164
Fax: (402)475-6500
Co. E-mail: orders@insvideo.com
URL: http://www.insvideo.com
Contact: Kathy Damkroger, President
Released: 19??. **Price:** $295. **Description:** Teaches the importance of teamwork and offers concepts to be used to build successful teams within your organization, including effective listening, developing top performers, and time management. Includes workbook. **Availability:** VHS.

34252 ■ Building High Performing Teams
Excellence in Training Corp.
c/o ICON Training
804 Roosevelt St.
Polk City, IA 50226
Free: 800-609-0479
Co. E-mail: info@icontraining.com
URL: http://www.icontraining.com
Contact: Linda Russell, Vice President
Released: 1991. **Price:** $995. **Description:** A presentation on the four steps of building an effective management team. **Availability:** VHS; 3/4 U; Special order formats.

34253 ■ Coaching Skills: Developing a Better Employee
Provant Media
4621 121st St.
Urbandale, IA 50323-2311
Ph: (888)776-8268
Free: 888-776-8268
Fax: (515)327-2555
Co. E-mail: custsvc@ammedia.com
URL: http://www.provantmedia.com
Contact: Tiffan Yamen, Manager, Marketing
Released: 19??. **Price:** $495. **Description:** Focuses on ways to coach employees with training, motivation, and delegation to help employees grow in their positions. Two videos discuss coaching methods and show examples of good and bad coaching. A trainer's guide is included. **Availability:** VHS; 3/4 U; 8 mm.

34254 ■ Coaching for Top Performance
Films Media Group of Cos.
132 W 31st St., 17th Fl.
New York, NY 10001-3406
Ph: (609)671-1000
Free: 800-257-5126
Fax: (609)671-0266
Co. E-mail: custserv@films.com
URL: http://www.cambridgeeducational.com
Contact: David Waldherr, President
Released: 1992. **Description:** Get the best work possible out of your team by using these coaching strategies. **Availability:** VHS.

34255 ■ Dealing with Difficult People Volume Two
RMI Media
1365 N. Winchester St.
Olathe, KS 66061-5880
Ph: (913)768-1696
Free: 800-745-5480
Fax: (800)755-6910
Co. E-mail: actmedia@act.org
URL: http://www.actmedia.com
Released: 1993. **Price:** $99. **Description:** Ed Greif explains how to handle very difficult problems with people. **Availability:** VHS.

34256 ■ Developing Strategies for Teamwork
Aspen Publishers, Inc.
7201 McKinney Cir.
Frederick, MD 21704
Ph: (301)698-7100
Free: 800-234-1660
Fax: (800)901-9075
Co. E-mail: customerservice@aspenpublisher.com
URL: http://www.aspenpublishers.com
Contact: Robert Becker, President
Released: 1986. **Price:** $495. **Description:** Strategy tips to teach your supervisors how to get their employees working together and working harder are shown. **Availability:** VHS; 3/4 U; Special order formats.

34257 ■ Discipline: A Matter of Judgment
Encyclopedia Britannica
331 N La Salle St.
Chicago, IL 60654
Ph: (312)347-7000
Free: 800-323-1229
Fax: (312)294-2104
URL: http://www.corporate.britannica.com
Contact: Jacob E. Safra
Released: 1989. **Description:** This video teaches that discipline must educate, not humiliate, and urges fair, prompt, and consistent disciplinary action. **Availability:** VHS; 3/4 U.

34258 ■ Empowering Employees to Claim Their Autonomy
ASTD
1640 King St.
Alexandria, VA 22314-2746
Ph: (703)683-8100
Free: 800-628-2783
Fax: (703)683-1523
Co. E-mail: customercare@astd.org
URL: http://www.astd.org
Contact: Tony Bingham, President
E-mail: tbingham@astd.org
Released: 1989. **Description:** Peter Block shows how to get past the passivity inherent in large organizations and help employees take charge of their individual needs, creating more creativity and energy in the workplace. **Availability:** VHS; 3/4 U.

34259 ■ Empowerment: Communicating with Others
International Training Consultants, Inc.
1838 Park Oaks
Kemah, TX 77565
Free: 800-998-8764
Co. E-mail: itc@trainingitc.com
URL: http://www.trainingitc.com
Contact: Dick Leatherman, Chief Executive Officer
Released: 19??. **Price:** $495. **Description:** Part of the "Empowerment: The Employee Development Series." Provides instructional material for employees which helps them becoming better communicators. Covers both speaking and listening techniques. **Availability:** VHS.

34260 ■ Empowerment: Meeting Change Creatively
International Training Consultants, Inc.
1838 Park Oaks
Kemah, TX 77565
Free: 800-998-8764
Co. E-mail: itc@trainingitc.com
URL: http://www.trainingitc.com
Contact: Dick Leatherman, Chief Executive Officer
Released: 19??. **Price:** $495. **Description:** Part of the "Empowerment: The Employee Development Series." Helps employees learn to cope with change by showing them how to increase their tolerance to change and benefit from it. **Availability:** VHS.

34261 ■ Empowerment: Solving Problems Together
International Training Consultants, Inc.
1838 Park Oaks
Kemah, TX 77565
Free: 800-998-8764
Co. E-mail: itc@trainingitc.com
URL: http://www.trainingitc.com
Contact: Dick Leatherman, Chief Executive Officer
Released: 19??. **Price:** $495. **Description:** Part of the "Empowerment: The Employee Development Series." Illustrates skills which will help employees become better problem solvers. **Availability:** VHS.

34262 ■ Empowerment: Team Skills for Meeting Together
International Training Consultants, Inc.
1838 Park Oaks
Kemah, TX 77565
Free: 800-998-8764
Co. E-mail: itc@trainingitc.com
URL: http://www.trainingitc.com
Contact: Dick Leatherman, Chief Executive Officer
Released: 19??. **Price:** $495. **Description:** Part of the "Empowerment: The Employee Development Series." Teaches employees skills which help them become better meeting and team participants, including those of the group leader, recorder, facilitator, observer, and group member. **Availability:** VHS.

34263 ■ Empowerment: Working Effectively with Others
International Training Consultants, Inc.
1838 Park Oaks
Kemah, TX 77565
Free: 800-998-8764
Co. E-mail: itc@trainingitc.com
URL: http://www.trainingitc.com
Contact: Dick Leatherman, Chief Executive Officer
Released: 19??. **Price:** $495. **Description:** Part of the "Empowerment: The Employee Development Series." Examines methods which help employees work together more effectively. Covers two important areas which affect teamwork: individual behaviors and interaction. **Availability:** VHS.

34264 ■ Everything You Always Wanted to Know about Management
Provant Media
4621 121st St.
Urbandale, IA 50323-2311
Ph: (888)776-8268
Free: 888-776-8268
Fax: (515)327-2555
Co. E-mail: custsvc@ammedia.com
URL: http://www.provantmedia.com
Contact: Tiffan Yamen, Manager, Marketing
Released: 1995. **Price:** $595. **Description:** Outlines the essentials of good management, including the six steps of delegation, employee empowerment, communication, feedback, and goal achievement. Includes course guide with participant exercises and case studies. **Availability:** VHS; CC.

34265 ■ How to Motivate Your People
1st Financial Training Services
1515 E. Woodfield Rd., Ste. 345
Schaumburg, IL 60173
Ph: (847)969-0900
Free: 800-442-8662
Fax: (847)969-0521
URL: http://www.1stfinancialtraining.com
Contact: Lee Marsh, Director, Operations
Released: 1987. **Price:** $250. **Description:** The program answers questions about how to motivate people and why some people are harder to motivate than others. **Availability:** VHS; 3/4 U.

34266 ■ How to Supervise People
Nightingale-Conant Corp.
1400 South Wolf Rd., Bldg. 300, Ste. 103
Wheeling, IL 60090
Ph: (847)647-0300
Free: 800-557-1660
Fax: (847)647-7145
Co. E-mail: sales@nightingale.com
URL: http://www.nightingale.com
Contact: L. Victor Conant, President
Released: 19??. **Price:** $95. **Description:** Eileen Parkinson presents techniques for building a winning team by leading people, as opposed to managing them. Includes an audio cassette and book. **Availability:** VHS.

34267 ■ Motivating/Directing/Leading—The Basics of Winning with People
RMI Media
1365 N. Winchester St.
Olathe, KS 66061-5880
Ph: (913)768-1696
Free: 800-745-5480
Fax: (800)755-6910
Co. E-mail: actmedia@act.org
URL: http://www.actmedia.com
Released: 1989. **Price:** $129. **Description:** Find out how to get other people to do what you want them to do. **Availability:** VHS; 3/4 U.

34268 ■ Motivating Others
American Management Association (AMA)
1601 Broadway
New York, NY 10019-7420
Ph: (212)586-8100
Free: 877-566-9441
Fax: (212)903-8168
Co. E-mail: customerservice@amanet.org
URL: http://www.amanet.org
Contact: Edward T. Reilly, President
Released: 1993. **Price:** $215. **Description:** Provides tips on how to motivate employees to perform better. Contains information on proven, top-rated employee motivators and how to use them. **Availability:** VHS.

34269 ■ Motivating People Toward Peak Performance
Nightingale-Conant Corp.
1400 South Wolf Rd., Bldg. 300, Ste. 103
Wheeling, IL 60090
Ph: (847)647-0300
Free: 800-557-1660
Fax: (847)647-7145
Co. E-mail: sales@nightingale.com
URL: http://www.nightingale.com
Contact: L. Victor Conant, President
Released: 19??. **Price:** $95. **Description:** A look at motivational strategies for encouraging top-notch performance from ordinary people. Includes two audio cassettes and two workbooks. **Availability:** VHS.

34270 ■ Motivation & a Positive Attitude
University of Wisconsin-Madison Center on Education & Work
1025 W. Johnson St., Rm. 964
Madison, WI 53706-1796
Ph: (608)265-6700
Free: 800-862-1071
Co. E-mail: cewmail@education.wisc.edu
URL: http://www.cew.wisc.edu
Released: 1997. **Price:** $79. **Description:** Looks at how to develop motivational behavior and a positive attitude. **Availability:** VHS.

34271 ■ Muppet Sales: Make-a-Buck
Video Arts, Inc.
c/o Aim Learning Group
8238-40 Lehigh
Morton Grove, IL 60053-2615
Free: 877-444-2230
Fax: (416)252-2155
Co. E-mail: service@aimlearninggroup.com
URL: http://www.aimlearninggroup.com
Released: 19??. **Price:** $795. **Description:** Topic-specific selections from "The Muppets Show" provide motivation and humor to meetings and work related obligations. **Availability:** VHS.

34272 ■ Planning a Project and Building Your Project Team
ISA -The International Society of Automation (ISA)
67 Alexander Dr.
Research Triangle Park, NC 27709
Ph: (919)549-8411
Fax: (919)549-8288
Co. E-mail: info@isa.org
URL: http://www.isa.org
Contact: Patrick Gouhin, Chief Executive Officer
Released: 199?. **Price:** $95. **Description:** An instrument technology training program on planning a project and building your project team. Includes a manual. **Availability:** VHS.

34273 ■ Team Building
Excellence in Training Corp.
c/o ICON Training
804 Roosevelt St.
Polk City, IA 50226
Free: 800-609-0479
Co. E-mail: info@icontraining.com
URL: http://www.icontraining.com
Contact: Linda Russell, Vice President
Released: 1991. **Price:** $495. **Description:** A detailed discussion of the ingredients of building an effective work team. A detailed leader's guide is included. **Availability:** VHS; 3/4 U; Special order formats.

34274 ■ Team of Champions
Excellence in Training Corp.
c/o ICON Training
804 Roosevelt St.
Polk City, IA 50226
Free: 800-609-0479
Co. E-mail: info@icontraining.com
URL: http://www.icontraining.com
Contact: Linda Russell, Vice President
Released: 1991. **Price:** $595. **Description:** John Parker Stewart discusses how to combine empowerment, teamwork, and quality improvement to build a more effective working environment. A leader's guide is included. **Availability:** VHS; 3/4 U; Special order formats.

34275 ■ Team Excellence
Home Vision Cinema
c/o Image Entertainment
20525 Nordhoff St., Ste. 200
Chatsworth, CA 91311
URL: http://www.image-entertainment.com
Contact: Gretchen Hagle, Manager, Marketing
Released: 1987. **Price:** $995. **Description:** Walter Cronkite emphasizes the importance of teamwork in the workplace. **Availability:** VHS; 3/4 U.

34276 ■ Team Player
Provant Media
4621 121st St.
Urbandale, IA 50323-2311
Ph: (888)776-8268
Free: 888-776-8268
Fax: (515)327-2555
Co. E-mail: custsvc@ammedia.com
URL: http://www.provantmedia.com
Contact: Tiffan Yamen, Manager, Marketing
Released: 1993. **Price:** $650. **Description:** Features a scene in which the main character develops a team approach to problem-solving in a very realistic way. **Availability:** VHS.

34277 ■ Together!
Provant Media
4621 121st St.
Urbandale, IA 50323-2311
Ph: (888)776-8268
Free: 888-776-8268

Fax: (515)327-2555
Co. E-mail: custsvc@ammedia.com
URL: http://www.provantmedia.com
Contact: Tiffan Yamen, Manager, Marketing
Released: 1990. **Price:** $325. **Description:** Focuses on the importance of teamwork in business using a story about a group of boys and girls working together to perform a complicated task. **Availability:** VHS; 3/4 U; 8 mm.

34278 ■ *Together We Can!*
Provant Media
4621 121st St.
Urbandale, IA 50323-2311
Ph: (888)776-8268
Free: 888-776-8268
Fax: (515)327-2555
Co. E-mail: custsvc@ammedia.com
URL: http://www.provantmedia.com
Contact: Tiffan Yamen, Manager, Marketing
Released: 1991. **Price:** $545. **Description:** Discusses actions individuals can take to ensure good teamwork. Includes a discussion guide. **Availability:** VHS; 3/4 U; 8 mm; CC.

34279 ■ *Trust Your Team*
Excellence in Training Corp.
c/o ICON Training
804 Roosevelt St.
Polk City, IA 50226
Free: 800-609-0479
Co. E-mail: info@icontraining.com
URL: http://www.icontraining.com
Contact: Linda Russell, Vice President
Released: 1987. **Price:** $595. **Description:** This video is designed to help managers open up their management styles, to allow all employees to function better, and take on more responsibility. **Availability:** VHS; 3/4 U.

34280 ■ *Where There's a Will. . .: Leadership and Motivation*
Video Arts, Inc.
c/o Aim Learning Group
8238-40 Lehigh
Morton Grove, IL 60053-2615
Free: 877-444-2230
Fax: (416)252-2155
Co. E-mail: service@aimlearninggroup.com
URL: http://www.aimlearninggroup.com
Released: 1988. **Price:** $790. **Description:** Find out how you can motivate your workers to a higher productivity level. **Availability:** VHS; 8 mm; 3/4 U; Special order formats.

34281 ■ *Working Teams: Helping Your Team Succeed*
American Management Association (AMA)
1601 Broadway
New York, NY 10019-7420
Ph: (212)586-8100
Free: 877-566-9441
Fax: (212)903-8168
Co. E-mail: customerservice@amanet.org
URL: http://www.amanet.org
Contact: Edward T. Reilly, President
Released: 19??. **Price:** $645. **Description:** Outlines the principles of being a contributing team member and not just a team player. **Availability:** VHS; CC.

34282 ■ *Workplace Readiness: Teamwork*
Agency for Instructional Technology (AIT)
8111 Lee Paul Rd.
Bloomington, IN 47404-7916
Ph: (812)339-2203
Free: 800-457-4509
Fax: (812)333-4218
URL: http://www.ait.net
Contact: Sandra L. McBrayer, Chief Executive Officer
Released: 1992. **Price:** $395. **Description:** Series of seven programs introducing students to the idea of teamwork in culturally diverse work forces. Programs deal with specific examples. Comes with guide. **Availability:** VHS; CC.

34283 ■ *Workplace Teams*
American Management Association (AMA)
1601 Broadway
New York, NY 10019-7420
Ph: (212)586-8100
Free: 877-566-9441
Fax: (212)903-8168
Co. E-mail: customerservice@amanet.org
URL: http://www.amanet.org
Contact: Edward T. Reilly, President
Released: 19??. **Price:** $975. **Description:** Contains information on the concept of building productive teams and the use of teamwork. **Availability:** VHS; CC.

CONSULTANTS

34284 ■ Adventure Learning Associates Inc.
567 Hale Rd.
Brattleboro, VT 05302
Ph: (802)254-6160
Free: 800-551-3210
Fax: (802)254-3852
Co. E-mail: info@alrna.com
URL: http://www.alrna.com
Contact: Paul A. Kidder, Owner Founder
E-mail: paul@alrna.com
Scope: Provider of consulting services and training in experiential training and development. Specifically provides team building, communications skills and empowerment skill sessions. Also focuses on needs analysis, strategic planning and visioning for newly developing groups. Firm specializes in training trainers in experiential outdoor programming. Industries served: all including government and can work with intact groups at all levels from line staff to boards and executive committees. **Founded:** 1990. **Seminars:** Train the Adventure Trainer.

34285 ■ Advisory Management Services Inc.
9600 E 129th St., Ste. B
Kansas City, MO 64149-1025
Ph: (816)765-9611
Contact: Hal Wood, Agent
Scope: A management consulting and training firm specializing in employee relations, management and staff training, organizational development, strategic planning and continuous quality improvement. **Founded:** 1979.

34286 ■ Arete Ventures Administration L.L.C.
3 Bethesda Metro Ctr., Ste. 770
Bethesda, MD 20814-5330
Ph: (301)657-6268
Fax: (301)770-2877
Contact: Robert W. Shaw, Jr., President
Scope: Provider of team based management consulting services to organizations of all types. Provides management consulting services by bridging traditional strategic consulting that focuses on the numbers and largely ignores the human side of organizations and typical organization consulting that stresses team development but avoids the pragmatic realities of running an organization. Focuses on strategic planning, organization design and effectiveness, managing human resources and teambuilding or group dynamics. **Founded:** 1983.

34287 ■ The Axelrod Group Inc.
723 Laurel Ave.
Wilmette, IL 60091
Ph: (847)251-7361
Fax: (847)251-7370
Co. E-mail: info@axelrodgroup.com
URL: http://www.axelrodgroup.com
Contact: Thava Govender, Manager
Scope: Provider of organizational development consulting services in the following areas: conference Model approach to redesign, strategic planning, organization assessment, self directed work teams, cultural change and team development, and management. Clients include major corporations and nonprofit organizations. **Founded:** 1981. **Publications:** "Large Group Interventions"; "Future Search"; "Real Time Strategic Change"; "The Path of Least Resistance for Managers"; "Open Space Technology"; "Flawless Consulting"; "Leadership and the New Science"; "The Birth of the Chaordic Age"; "Beyond the Wall of

Resistance"; "Beat the Odds and Succeed in Organizational Change," Consulting to Management Magazine, Jun, 2006; "You Don't Have to Do it Alone," Oct, 2004; "Terms of Engagement," Barrett-Koehler Publishers; "The Conference Model"; "Harnessing Complexity"; "The Philosophy Behind Our Systems"; "Considerations Before You Build a Collaborative Process"; "Making Teams Work"; "Purpose is the Cornerstone"; "How to Build Relationships"; "How to Maximize Information Sharing"; "How to Promote Equity and Fairness"; "How to Create Freedom and Autonomy"; "The Handbook of Large Group Methods"; "The Change Handbook"; "The Intelligence Advantage: Organizing for Complexity"; "Investors Business Daily Leaders and Success: Top 10 Secrets to Success"; "Terms of Engagement: An Interview with Dick Axelrod," Per dido Magazine; "The Beauty of the Beast". **Seminars:** Conference Model Professional Skills; Team Development; Creating Team Based Organizations; Conflict Management for Managers; Working Together; Communications Skills for Improving Productivity and Relationships; Designing for Engagement; Terms of Engagement.

34288 ■ Bloch Consulting Group
2033 Wild Cherry Ln.
Kalamazoo, MI 49009-9168
Ph: (616)375-6849
Fax: (616)375-6849
Contact: Raleigh Bloch, President
E-mail: rbloch@compuserve.com
Scope: Managing creative processes to develop new ideas and products. Firm offers expertise in high performance work systems, teamwork, self-regulated teams, total quality management, employee involvement and creativity session facilitation. **Founded:** 1993.

34289 ■ Business Development Group Inc. (BDG)
29255 Laurel Woods Dr., Ste. 202
Southfield, MI 48034
Ph: (248)358-0121
Fax: (248)350-3025
Co. E-mail: info@busdevgroup.com
URL: http://www.busdevgroup.com
Contact: Guy D. Kolb, Partner
Scope: Consulting firm expertise in leadership development; strategic thinking; organizational transformation; team-based work systems; organizational learning; rapid change; knowledge management; competitive intelligence; crisis management; merger and acquisition integration; product integration and new product development. **Publications:** "Navigating in the Sea of Change," Competitive Intelligence Review Journal; "The Influence of Cultural Aspects of Strategic Information, Analysis and Delivery"; "What Leadership Needs From Competitive Intelligence Professionals," Journal of Association for Global and Strategic Information. **Seminars:** Process of Self-Design for the Evolving Organization; Large System Change Intervention; Self Assessment and the Transformational Process; The Knowledge Exchange - Shared Practices Workshop.

34290 ■ CFI Group USA L.L.C. [Claes Fornell International]
625 Avis Dr.
Ann Arbor, MI 48108
Ph: (734)930-9090
Free: 800-930-0933
Fax: (734)930-0911
Co. E-mail: askcfi@cfigroup.com
URL: http://www.cfigroup.com
Contact: Sheri Petras, Chief Executive Officer
E-mail: steodoru@mail.cfigroup.com
Scope: Management consulting firm that helps its clients worldwide to maximize shareholder value by optimizing customer and employee satisfaction. Clients span a variety of industries, including manufacturing, telecommunications, retail and government. **Founded:** 1988. **Publications:** "Customer Satisfaction and Stock Prices: High Returns, Low Risk," American Marketing Association, Jan, 2006; "Customer Satisfaction Index Climbs," The Wall Street Journal, Feb, 2004; "What's Next? Customer Service is Key to Post-Boom Success," The Bottom Line, Mar, 2003; "Boost Stock Performance, Nation's Economy," Quality Progress, Feb, 2003.

34291 ■ Charismedia
610 W End Ave., Ste. B1
New York, NY 10001
Ph: (212)362-6808
Co. E-mail: charismedia@earthlink.net
URL: http://www.charismedia.net
Contact: Dr. Doe Lang, President
E-mail: charismedia@earthlink.net
Scope: Offers speech and image training as well as speech writing services for effective presentation skills. Conducts workshops like anti-stage fright breathing, psychophysical exercises, transformational success imagery, face reading and body language, EMDR (Eye Movement Desensitization Re-Processing) for Permanent Trauma and Fear Removal, Bach Flower remedies, thought field therapy, cross-cultural communication, speech, voice and diction; regional and foreign accent elimination and acquisition, Positive Perception Management (P.P.M.), Ad-libbing, humor and spontaneity training, fast creative speech preparation, Neuro-Linguistic Programming and Hypnosis. **Founded:** 1974. **Publications:** "Flaunt It"; "Improve Your Sex Life"; "Phone Power"; "Train Your Voice"; "Turning Tinny, Tiny Tones To Gold"; "The New Secrets of Charisma: How to Discover and Unleash your Hidden Powers," McGraw-Hill, Jul, 1999. **Seminars:** Services for Comfortable Effective Speaking.

34292 ■ Cole Financial Service Inc.
3170 E, Lafayette Blvd.
Detroit, MI 48207-4378
Ph: (313)962-7055
Free: 877-972-7055
Fax: (313)962-7815
Co. E-mail: jason.a.cole@colefinancial1.net
URL: http://www.colefinancial1.net
Contact: Patricia Allen Cole, President
E-mail: patricia.a.cole@colefinancial1.net
Scope: A full service human capital development firm providing services in recruiting, coaching, retaining, developing and retiring. Works with front line staff, managers and executive level decision makers that set strategy. Industries served: Engineering, construction, government and other business entities. **Founded:** 1983. **Seminars:** How to Run Your Own Business; 25Ways to stay in Business 25Years; How to Tap Your Potential and Discover Your GENIUS; The Job Ladder Steps to SUCCESS; Making and Keeping a Budget; Records Retention and Disposal; Take Control of Your Life; Time and Priority Management; TQM - Total Quality Management; Leadership 101; Leadership 201; Diversity Agent or Opponent A Personal Development Workshop; Coaching in a Diverse Workplace.

34293 ■ Competitive Edge Inc.
241 E Crestwood Rd.
Peachtree City, GA 30269
Ph: (770)487-6460
Fax: (770)487-2919
Co. E-mail: judy@competitiveedgeinc.com
URL: http://www.competitiveedgeinc.com
Contact: Judy I. Suiter, President
E-mail: judy@competitiveedgeinc.com
Scope: A human resources consulting firm providing customized training and software solutions to assist clients in optimizing their human intellectual capital through effective selection, coaching, and training. Works with a network of consultants that are located throughout the United States, Canada, and Europe. **Founded:** 1981. **Publications:** "Beteenden och drivkrafter"; "Energizing People: Unleashing The Power of DISC"; "The Ripple Effect: How the Global Model of Endorsement Opens Doors to Success"; "The Journey - Quotes to keep your boat afloat"; "The Universal Language DISC Reference Manual"; "Exploring Values: Releasing the Power of Attitudes"; "Competitive Products Review Book"; "The Mother Of All Minds"; "The Sea of Change: Solutions for Navigating the Disconnects in the Workplace". **Seminars:** How to Recruit and Retain High Performing Employees; The Importance of Values Matching For Sales Selection; How to Build a High Performance Team; Dynamic Communication Skills; Creating Nurturing Customer Relationships; Your Attitude Is Showing; Sales Strategy Index; Validity Study.

34294 ■ The Corlund Group L.L.C. (CG)
101 Federal St., Ste. 310
Boston, MA 02110
Ph: (617)423-9364
Fax: (617)423-9371
Co. E-mail: corlund@corlundgroup.com
URL: http://www.corlundgroup.com
Contact: Wilmot J. Gravenslund, Director
E-mail: wgravenslund@corlundgroup.com
Scope: Boutique firm offering services in the areas of leadership, governance, and change with a particular focus on CEO and senior executive succession planning, including assessment, development, and orchestrating succession processes with management and Boards of Directors. Also Board governance effectiveness. **Founded:** 1996. **Publications:** "Are You Rolling the Dice on CEO Succession?" Center for Healthcare Governance, 2006; "Leadership Due Diligence: The Neglected Governance Frontier," Directorship, Sep, 2001; "Leadership Due Diligence: Managing the Risks," The Corporate Board, Aug, 2001; "Succession: The need for detailed insight," Directors and Boards, 2001; "CEO Succession: Who's Doing Due Diligence?," 2001.

34295 ■ The Cradlerock Group
65 High Ridge Rd., Ste. 229
Stamford, CT 06905
Ph: (203)324-0088
Fax: (203)547-7778
Co. E-mail: info@cradlerock.com
URL: http://www.cradlerock.com
Contact: Scott Conley, President
Scope: Provider of teambuilding and personal challenge programs for both corporate and nonprofit groups. Utilizing both team-challenge and personal initiative courses, along with a variety of other outdoor-based adventure activities, participants being encouraged to explore group dynamics and personal abilities. Cradle rock facilitators then help the participants tolerate the outdoor experience to the business, education and social worlds. Industries served: large corporations, school districts, nonprofit organizations and government agencies. **Founded:** 1984. **Seminars:** Team Start; Who Are We?; Who's On First?; Getting Past Stuck; Team Skills; Group Skills; Effective Team Leadership; Leading Global Teams; 360Coaching; The Other Diversity; Harnessing Change; The Art of Sale.

34296 ■ Delta Systems
5621 Somerset Dr.
Brooklyn, MI 49230
Ph: (517)592-5463
Fax: (517)592-5463
Co. E-mail: renee@4deltasystems.com
URL: http://www.4deltasystems.com
Contact: Renee R. Merchant, Owner Founder
E-mail: renee@4deltasystems.com
Scope: Organizational development consultant specializing in team-building training and keynote speeches. Industries served: manufacturing, automotive suppliers, and nuclear power plants. **Publications:** "Teamwork Case"; "Changes, Choices, and Commitment"; "Make Teamwork a Way of Life"; "Checkered Flag Teams: Driving Your Workplace Into the Winners Circle"; "Success is a Team Effort"; "CARStyles™ - A Communication Style Model"; "Face Posters"; "CAR Styles Communication Model and Assessment". **Seminars:** Team Leader Training; Fast Cycle Time and Process Improvement; Change Leadership; Revitalizing Mature Teams; Fast Problem Solving; Pit Crew Challenge; Leadership Skills for Non-Supervisory People; Fast Start Teamwork; The Pit Crew Challenge.

34297 ■ Dimond Hospitality Consulting Group Inc.
5710 Stoneway Trl.
Nashville, TN 37209
Ph: (615)353-0033
Fax: (615)352-5290
Co. E-mail: drew@dimondhotelconsulting.com
URL: http://www.dimondhotelconsulting.com
Contact: Drew W. Dimond, President
E-mail: drew@dimondhotelconsulting.com
Scope: Specializes in strategic planning; start-up businesses; business process re-engineering; team building; competitive analysis; venture capital; competitive intelligence; and due diligence. Offers litigation support. Comprehensive hospitality consulting firm that serves as an adviser to leading hotel companies, independent hotels, lending institutions, trustees, law firms, investment companies and municipalities in the areas of: Asset management, Acquisition due diligence, Arbitration, Disposition advisory services, Exit strategies, Financial review and analysis, Impact studies, Mediation. **Founded:** 1985. **Publications:** "The distressed debt conundrum," Jul, 2009; "How to buy distressed assets," Apr, 2009; "Cmbs Loans: A History and the Future," Apr, 2009; "Opportunity Knocks," Apr, 2009; "Another Reality Check," Mar, 2009; "An Inkling of Hope," Mar, 2009; "Strong World Tourism Growth in 2007," 2007; "Les U.S. Construction Pipeline Sets Another Record at 5011 Hotels with 654503 Rooms"; "Hotel Capitalization Rates Hold for Now"; "Winning Cornell Hotel and Restaurant Administration Quarterly Article Provides Hotel Brand Analysis"; "Breaking News for Lifestyle Hotels. Ian Schrager and Bill Marriott Announce Their Marriage Will the Schrager-Marriott Marriage Lead to Eternal Bliss Or End in Divorce What Will the M Hotels Children Be Named"; "Brands Vs Independents"; "Nyu Conf Takes Industry Temp"; "Economy Hotel Performance Indication of Travel Trends"; "Hotel Sales Continue at Brisk Pace"; "Fundamentals Strong, Weakening Undercurrent"; "Hotel Investments: Where Do We Go From Here"; "On the Road: Aahoa Panel Commits to Change"; "Cuba Not Ready, But Expecting U.S. Tourists".

34298 ■ The DuMond Group
5282 Princeton Ave.
Westminster, CA 92683-2753
Ph: (714)373-0610
Contact: Adrianne H. Geiger-Dumond, Owner
Scope: Human resources and executive search consulting firm that specializes in organizational development; small business management; employee surveys and communication; performance appraisals; and team building. **Founded:** 1992.

34299 ■ Dynamic Firm Management Inc.
4570 Campus Dr., Ste. 60
Newport Beach, CA 92660
Ph: (949)640-2220
Co. E-mail: info@dynamicfirm.com
URL: http://www.dynamicfirm.com
Contact: Dennis McCue, Principal
E-mail: mccue@dynamicfirm.com
Scope: Services: Law, accounting and other consulting. **Founded:** 1987. **Publications:** "Workflow Management," C2M: Consulting to Management - The Journal of Management Consulting, Jun, 2006; "Why Good Partnerships Go Bad," The Journal of Law Office Economics and Management, Feb, 2006; "The Wisdom of Ambulance Chasers," LACBA Update, Feb, 2005; "7 Components to Building A Successful Firm," LACBA Update, Nov, 2004; "Maximize the Productivity of Your Support Team," LACBA Update, Mar, 2004; "Perfect Union," Daily Journal, Mar, 2004; "Future Perfect," Daily Journal, Dec, 2003.

34300 ■ Eastern Point Consulting Group Inc.
36 Glen Ave.
Newton, MA 02464
Ph: (617)965-4141
Fax: (617)965-4172
Co. E-mail: info@eastpt.com
URL: http://www.eastpt.com
Contact: Katherine A. Herzog, President
E-mail: kherzog@eastpt.com
Scope: Specializes in bringing practical solutions to complex challenges. Provides consulting and training in managing diversity; comprehensive sexual-harassment policies and programs; organizational development; benchmarks 360 skills assessment; executive coaching; strategic human resource planning; team building; leadership development for women; mentoring programs; and gender issues in the workplace. **Founded:** 1995. **Seminars:** Leadership Development for Women.

34301 ■ Effective Resources Inc. (ERI)
118 N Peters Rd., Ste. 171
Knoxville, TN 37923
Free: 800-288-6044

Fax: (800)409-2812
Co. E-mail: customerservice@effectiveresources.com
URL: http://www.effectiveresources.com
Contact: Barry L. Brown, President
E-mail: barry@effectiveresources.com
Scope: Human resource consulting firm helping clients in all aspects of planning and implementation, to assure the program meets their objectives and budget considerations. Can work with clients on an interim basis or as consultants on short term assignment. Products and services include salary and benefits surveys, employee satisfaction surveys, performance management, compensation administration, compliance assistance and personality profile testing. Specializes in compensation and incentive plans, performance appraisals, team building and personnel policies and procedures, affirmative action plan preparation. **Founded:** 1988. **Special Services:** DiSC® Personality Profile.

34302 ■ Employee Development Systems Inc. (EDSI)
7308 S Alton Way, Ste. 2J
Centennial, CO 80112
Ph: (303)221-0710
Free: 800-282-3374
Fax: (303)221-0704
Co. E-mail: info@edsiusa.com
URL: http://www.employeedevelopmentsystems.com
Contact: Suzanne Updegraff, President
Scope: Produces training systems that increase employee productivity by motivating employees to take responsibility for their own performance and by showing employees and managers how to improve communications and create productive team relationships. **Founded:** 1979. **Publications:** "Company Connection Life Changing Lessons"; "Why People Skills are Still Being Taught at Work"; "Leading With Credibility Manage Up"; "Words of Peter Drucker"; "Coaching for Results". **Seminars:** Increasing Personal Effectiveness; Communicating to Manage Performance; ProAction: Responding to Change; Just-in-Time Training: Working Successfully in a Changing Environment, Challenging the Status Quo for Continuous Improvement, Assertive Communication and Reaching Agreement; Learning in the 21st Century, Apr, 2007.

34303 ■ Goldore Consulting Inc.
120-5 St. NW, Ste. 1
Linden, AB, Canada T0M 1J0
Ph: (403)546-4208
Fax: (403)546-4208
Contact: Robert A. Orr, President
E-mail: orr@leadershipessentials.com
Description: Description: Publishes materials on leadership and management skills for churches and charitable organizations that provide services to developing countries. Also publishes in Spanish and Portuguese. Does not accept unsolicited manuscripts. Reaches market through direct mail and wholesalers and distributors, including Leadership Training Ministry Foundation, Inc. **Scope:** Provides consulting service in leadership and management skills. Industries served: primarily charities, non-profits; some businesses. **Founded:** 1990. **Seminars:** The Challenge Of Leadership.

34304 ■ Grimmick Consulting Services (GCS)
455 Donner Way
San Ramon, CA 94582
Ph: (925)735-1036
Fax: (925)735-1100
Co. E-mail: hank@grimmickconsulting.com
URL: http://www.grimmickconsulting.com
Contact: Henry Grimmick, President
E-mail: hank@grimmickconsulting.com
Scope: Provider of consulting services in the areas of strategic planning; organizational assessment; organizational development; leadership and management development Baldridge criteria, process improvement and balanced scorecards and team dynamics. **Founded:** 1993.

34305 ■ Interminds & Federer Resources Inc.
106 E 6th St., Ste. 310
Austin, TX 78701-3659

Ph: (512)476-8800
Co. E-mail: yesyoucan@interminds.com
URL: http://www.interminds.com
Contact: Frank Federer, President
E-mail: ffederer@integra100.com
Scope: Specializes in feasibility studies; startup businesses; small business management; mergers and acquisitions; joint ventures; divestitures; interim management; crisis management; turnarounds; production planning; team building; appraisals and valuations. **Founded:** 1985. **Publications:** "Yes You Can: How To Be A Success No Matter Who You Are Or Where You're From".

34306 ■ Interpersonal Communication Programs Inc. (ICP) [Couple Communication]
30772 Southview Dr., Ste. 200
Evergreen, CO 80439
Ph: (303)674-2051
Free: 800-328-5099
Fax: (303)674-4283
Co. E-mail: icp@comskills.com
URL: http://www.couplecommunication.com
Contact: Sheila Boone, Director
E-mail: sheila@comskills.com
Description: Description: Publishes works dealing with communications. Offers instructor and participant materials plus training. Reaches market through direct mail and trade sales. Does not accept unsolicited manuscripts. **Scope:** Provider of team building and interpersonal communication training in small and large corporations. Serves private industries as well as government agencies. **Founded:** 1972. **Publications:** "CC I & II texts"; "Collaborative Marriage Skills and Thriving Together in the Skills Zone"; "Core communication"; "Alive and Aware"; "Straight Talk," Connecting With Self and Others. **Seminars:** Collaborative Team Skills for Intact Work Groups; Core Communication: Skills and Processes for Managers, Supervisors and Employees; Couple communication I and II. **Special Services:** Awareness Wheel®; Styles of Communication® ; Listening Cycle®; Styles of Communication®.

34307 ■ K & T Training [K & T Consulting]
103 Greenville St.
Newnan, GA 30263
Ph: (770)253-5870
Contact: J. R. Tumperi, President
Scope: Specializes in strategic planning; profit enhancement; organizational development; start-up businesses; interim management; crisis management; turnarounds; business process re-engineering; team building; cost controls. **Founded:** 1983.

34308 ■ Ken Blanchard Co.
125 State Pl.
Escondido, CA 92029-1323
Fax: (760)489-8407
URL: http://www.kenblanchard.com
Contact: Howard Farfel, President
Scope: Full service management development-training company known for development of the one minute manager concept. Develops and sells quality products and services that enhance management and leadership skills. Offers seminars, workshops, in house consulting, videos, audio tapes, slides, books, instruments and games. Areas of expertise include management training, team building, attitude and needs assessment, productivity improvement, motivation, and corporate development. Industries served: health, hospitality, financial, food service, telecommunications, retail, utilities, associations, aerospace, automotive, military, education, manufacturing, and government agencies. **Founded:** 1979. **Publications:** "Who Killed Change? Solving the Mystery of Leading People Through Change," 2009; "Helping People Win at Work: A Business Philosophy Called Don't Mark My Paper, Help Me Get An A," 2009; "Leading at a Higher Level," 2009; "The One Minute Entrepreneur," 2008; "Coaching in Organizations," 2008; "Know Can Do! Put Your Know-How Into Action," Oct, 2007; "Hamster Revolution, The: Stop Info Glut-Reclaim Your Life!"; "Leading at a Higher Level: Blanchard on Leadership and Creating High Performing Organizations"; "The Simple Truths of Service"; "Building High Performing Teams"; "Leadership Training for Supervisors"; "Legendary Service"; "The One Minute Manager"; "Whale Done!"; "The Power of Ethi-

cal Management"; "Managing By Values"; "The Leader Within"; "Leverage Your Best, Ditch the Rest"; "High Five". **Seminars:** Situational Leadership II; Situational Team Leadership; The One Minute Manager; Leadership and The One Minute Manager; Putting The One Minute Manager to Work; Ethical Management; Situational Frontline Leadership; The Magic of Situational Self Leadership; DISCovering Self and Others; Coaching Essentials for Leaders; Legendary Service; Whale Done!; GungHo!.

34309 ■ William E. Kuhn & Associates
234 Cook St.
Denver, CO 80206-5305
Ph: (303)322-8233
Fax: (303)331-9032
Scope: Firm specializes in strategic planning; profit enhancement; small business management; mergers and acquisitions; joint ventures; divestitures; human resources management; performance appraisals; team building; sales management; appraisals and valuations. **Founded:** 1980. **Publications:** "Creating a High-Performance Dealership," Office SOLUTIONS and Office DEALER, Jul-Aug, 2006.

34310 ■ LDG Associates
8094 Mission Vista Dr.
San Diego, CA 92120-1537
Ph: (619)583-0261
Fax: (619)583-4608
Co. E-mail: doug144@carolina.rr.com
Contact: Larry D. Gable, Manager
Scope: Consultants in leadership training and development, coaching, 360 degree feedback and team building. Specialize in helping leaders build effective teams. Leaders learn specific skills to help them achieve individual and organizational objectives. Industries served medical manufacturing, aerospace, electrical manufacturing, manufacturing, petroleum and government agencies. **Founded:** 1988. **Seminars:** Leadership Styles and Strategies; Influencing Styles and Strategies; Organizing Yourself and Others; Team Building; 360 Degree Feed back; Executive Coaching; Stress Management; Leadership 2000; Team Building 2000.

34311 ■ May Toy Lukens
3226 NE 26th Ct.
Renton, WA 98056
Scope: Provides training to teach people to think of ways to improve their operations continuously by changing the way they think. Industries served: All, particularly financial. Operational analysis and training. **Founded:** 1996. **Seminars:** Seminars and workshops in maximizing resource utilization and staff potential.

34312 ■ Lupfer & Associates (L&A)
92 Glen St.
Natick, MA 01760-5646
Ph: (508)655-3950
Fax: (508)655-7826
Co. E-mail: donlupfer@aol.com
Contact: Donald Lupfer, Owner
E-mail: donlupfer@europartners.eu.com
Scope: Assists off shore hi-tech companies in entering United States markets and specializes in channel development for all sorts of products. Perform MARCOM support for hi-tech United States clients. **Founded:** 1988. **Publications:** "What's Next For Distribution-Feast or Famine"; "The Changing Global Marketplace"; "Making Global Distribution Work". **Seminars:** How to do Business in the United States.

34313 ■ MAA Consulting Inc.
546 Hillcrest Dr.
Bowling Green, OH 43402
Ph: (419)352-7782
Fax: (419)354-8781
Co. E-mail: maa@wcnet.org
URL: http://www.wcnet.org
Contact: Ruth P. Varney, President
Scope: Offers counsel in organizational diagnosis, development and change, as well as management development, manpower planning and forecasting, performance appraisal, management by objectives, team building, related industrial and human relations areas, and a strong emphasis on self directed work teams. Industries served: energy, health care, auto

parts manufacturers, chemical, financial, petroleum, and government agencies. **Founded:** 1967. **Publications:** "Caribbean Island Survival II"; Alaskan Adventure"; Task Force"; "Group Process Questionnaire"; "Acceleration"; "Contracting for Change"; "The Discipline of Change Management," 2005; "An Operational Definition of Odc," 2004; "Cases in Organization Development," 1999; "Measuring and Improving Teamwork," 1998; "Name Recognition of Master Level Graduate Programs in Organization Development and Change," 1998; "A Critical Examination of a Failed Attempt to Implement Self-Directed Work Teams," 1996; "Organization Development," 1996; "Rethinking the Knowledge Worker: Where Have All the Workers Gone," 1995; "The Primary Determinant of Successful Application of Self-Directed Work Teams," 1994; "Helping a Team Find All the Answers," 1991; "The Caster Case," 1990; "Teamwork Survey and Planning Guide," 1990. **Seminars:** Implementing Self-Directed Work Teams; SDWT Simulation; Managing Team Productivity; Navigating the Mine Fields of Change.

34314 ■ Mandalay Associates L.L.C.
190 El Cerrito Plz., Ste. 226
El Cerrito, CA 94530-4002
Ph: (510)526-4651
Fax: (510)526-5774
Contact: Kristina Combs, Member
Scope: Business management firm specializes in conflict resolution, employee relations, employment and placement, organizational analysis and development, human resources program development, program and project management and staff development and training.

34315 ■ Miller, Hellwig Associates
150 W End Ave.
New York, NY 10023-5713
Contact: Ernest C. Miller, President
Scope: Consulting services in the areas of start-up businesses; small business management; employee surveys and communication; performance appraisals; executive searches; team building; personnel policies and procedures; market research. Also involved in improving cross-cultural and multi-cultural relationships, particularly with Japanese clients. **Founded:** 1984. **Seminars:** Objectives and standards/recruiting for boards of directors.

34316 ■ Jane Moosbruker, Organization Development Consultant
72 Coventry Wood Rd.
Bolton, MA 01740-1123
Ph: (978)779-5423
Fax: (978)779-6036
Co. E-mail: jamoos@ziplink.net
Contact: Jane Moosbruker, Owner
Scope: Offers process-oriented consultation to organizations, in the areas of organizational change, team building, management development and conflict utilization. Industries served include biotechnology, information services, computer technology, aerospace, education, healthcare and environmental. **Founded:** 1970. **Publications:** "Transitioning Work Groups Into High Performing Teams," 1993; "Group Dynamics- History and Future," Vienna: Wuv-Verlag, 1993; "Business Process Redesign and Organization Development-Applied Behavioral Science," 1998; "Forgotten Elements: Including Structure and Process in Recovery Efforts". **Seminars:** Managing Organizational Change; Facilitating and Managing Complex Systems Change; Team Leadership for Developing a High Productivity Team; Building a Team-based Organization; Conflict Utilization; Team Skills.

34317 ■ Murray Dropkin & Associates [Dropkin Consulting]
390 George St.
New Brunswick, NJ 08901
Co. E-mail: murray@dropkin.com
URL: http://www.dropkin.com
Contact: Murray Dropkin, President
E-mail: murray@dropkin.com
Scope: Specializes in feasibility studies; business management; business process re-engineering; and team building, health care and housing. **Founded:** 1969. **Publications:** "Bookkeeping for Nonprofits," Jossey Bass, 2005; "Guide to Audits of Nonprofit

Organizations," PPC; "The Nonprofit Report," Warren, Gorham & Lamont; "The Budget Building Book for Nonprofits," Jossey-Bass; "The Cash Flow Management Book for Nonprofits," Jossey-Bass.

34318 ■ MW Corp.
2538 Crompond Rd.
Yorktown Heights, NY 10598
Ph: (914)528-0888
Contact: Ann Harper, Owner
Scope: Training firm provides training materials books and videos and conducts public workshops and custom-designed on-site training and development in the areas of management development, supervisor technical leader training and development, team development, facilitator training, self-directed work teams, quality customer service workshops and employee involvement programs. Serves all types of organizations. **Founded:** 1983. **Publications:** "Leading a Service Team"; "A Team Leader's Day"; "The Changing Workplace"; "Self-Directed Work Teams"; "Supervisor in Transition". **Seminars:** Self-Directed Work Teams; The Management Workshop; First-line Supervisor/Technical Leader Workshop.

34319 ■ New Commons
545 Pawtucket Ave., Studio 106A
Pawtucket, RI 02860
Ph: (401)351-7110
Fax: (401)351-7158
Co. E-mail: info@newcommons.com
URL: http://www.newcommons.com
Contact: Robert Leaver, Chief Executive Officer
E-mail: rleaver@newcommons.com
Scope: Builder of agile human networks to champion innovation and mobilize change; to pursue business opportunities; to custom design agile organizations and communities, to foster civic engagement. Clients include organizations on-profits, corporations, government agencies, educational institutions; networks- Trade/professional groups, IT services collaborations, service-sharing collectives; and communities- municipalities, states and statewide agencies, regional collaborations. **Founded:** 1982. **Publications:** "Plexus Imperative," Sep, 2005; "Creating 21st Century Capable Innovation Systems," Aug, 2004; "Call to Action: Building Providences Creative and Innovative Economy"; "Getting Results from Meetings"; "The Entrepreneur as Artist," Commonwealth Publications; "Leader and Agent of Change," Commonwealth Publications; "Achieving our Providence: Lessons of City-Building," Commonwealth Publications. **Seminars:** Introduction to Social Computing (Web 2.0), Jan, 2009; Every Company Counts, Jun, 2009; Facilitating for Results; Story-Making and Story-Telling.

34320 ■ Organizational Transformations
PO Box 2553
Aptos, CA 95001-2553
Ph: (831)688-1344
Fax: (831)688-8091
URL: http://www.orgtrans.com
Contact: Rochelle Sjolseth, Director
E-mail: rochelle@orgtrans.com
Scope: A management and organizational consulting firm that provides customized strategies to help companies increase productivity and profit. Specializes in organizational development, executive coaching, team building, conflict resolution and work comp reduction.

34321 ■ P2C2 Group Inc.
4101 Denfeld Ave.
Kensington, MD 20895-1514
Ph: (301)942-7985
Fax: (301)942-7986
Co. E-mail: info@p2c2group.com
URL: http://www.p2c2group.com
Scope: Works with clients on the business side of federal program and project management. Services include program/project planning and optimization; acquisition strategy and work statements; IT Capital Planning and Investment Control (CPIC); business cases - new, revisions, critiques; budget analysis - cost benefits- alternatives; CPIC, SELC, and security documentation; research, metrics, analysis, and case studies. Consulting support helping to: Define or redefine programs; strengthen portfolio management;

identify alternatives for lean budgets; improve capital planning and investment; develop better plans and documentation, and evaluate performance of existing program investments. **Founded:** 1994. **Publications:** "OMB 300s Go Online," Federal Sector Report, Mar, 2007; "Using Risk-Adjusted Costs for Projects," Federal Sector Report, Feb, 2007; "Make Better Decisions Using Case Studies," Federal Sector Report, Jan, 2007; "PMO Performance Measurement & Metrics"; "Executive Sponsors for Projects"; "ABCs of the Presidential Transition"; "Financial Systems and Enterprise Portfolio Management"; "The Future of CPIC"; "Critical Factors for Program and Project Success"; "Using Risk-Adjusted Costs for Projects"; "Tactics for a Successful Year of CPIC"; "Operational Analysis Reviews"; "Successful IT Strategic Planning"; "Information Technology Investment Management". **Seminars:** Requests For Information; Pre Solicitation Marketing; Qualifications Statement Support For The Capital Planning And Investment Control (cpic) Process; How To Hire A Management Consultant And Get The Results You Expect.

34322 ■ Glenn M. Parker Associates Inc. [Glenn Parker Team Building Consultant]
36 Otter Creek Rd.
Skillman, NJ 08558
Ph: (609)333-0203
Fax: (609)333-0204
Co. E-mail: glenn@glennparker.com
URL: http://www.glennparker.com
Contact: Glenn M. Parker, President
E-mail: gparker@glennparker.com
Scope: Provider of the following services: teambuilding without business teams, training workshops in team effectiveness, facilitation skills and meeting management, consulting to help organizations transition to a team-based operation, speaking at professional conferences and corporate meeting and diagnostic services to assess the effectiveness of teams and organizations. **Founded:** 1971. **Publications:** "Women Love Team Players"; "Meeting Excellence: 33 Tools to Lead Meetings That Get Results," Jossey Bass/Wiley, 2006; "Cross Functional Teams: Working with Allies, Enemies and Other Strangers, Completely Revised and Updates," 2003; "Team Depot: A Warehouse of 585 Tools to Reassess, Rehabilitate and Rejuvenate Your Team," Jossey-Bass/Pfeiffer/Wiley, 2002; "Team Workout: A Trainer's Source book of 50 Team Building Games and Activities," Hrd Press, 2001; "Rewarding Teams: Lessons From the Trenches," Jossey-Bass/Wiley, 2000; "Teamwork and Team play: Games and Activities for Building and Training Teams," Jossey-Bass/Pfeiffer, 1999; "25 Instruments for Team Building," Hrd Press, 1998; "Video: Team Building: What Makes a Good Team Player," Crm Learning, 1996; "Cross-Functional Teams Tool Kit," Pfeiffer/Jossey Bass, 1997; "Best Practices for Teams," Hrd Press, 1996; "50 Activities for Self-Directed Teams," Hrd Press, 1994; "50 Activities for Team Building," Hrd Press, 1992; "Instruments: Parker Team Player Survey," Consulting Psychologists Press, 1992; "Team Development Survey," Consulting Psychologists Press, 1992; "Team Players and Teamwork," Jossey-Bass, 1990. **Seminars:** Effective Conflict Resolution; How to Build Strong Teams and Develop Team Players; Effective Meetings; Skills and Techniques for Successful Cross-Functional Teamwork; Boundary Management; How to Plan and Conduct a Successful Team Meeting; Building A Facilitator's Tool Kit.

34323 ■ Parker Consultants Inc.
230 Mason St.
Greenwich, CT 06830-6633
Ph: (203)869-9400
Contact: William P. Hartl, Chief Executive Officer
Scope: Firm specializes in strategic planning; organizational development; small business management; performance appraisals; executive searches; team building; and customer service audits. **Founded:** 1988.

34324 ■ Partnerwerks Inc.
PO Box 1046
Comfort, TX 78013
Ph: (830)995-4853

Fax: (830)995-4854
URL: http://www.christopheravery.com
Scope: Services: Leadership training and executive monitoring. **Founded:** 1991. **Publications:** "Teamwork Is An Individual Skill: Getting Your Work Done When Sharing Responsibility," Berrett-Kohler, 2001; "The Leaders Guide". **Seminars:** Leadership: Simply Solve the Real Problem, Jun, 2010; Project Team Leadership; Managing Teams; Team Planning.

34325 ■ Performance Consulting Associates Inc. (PCA)
3700 Crestwood Pky., Ste. 100
Duluth, GA 30096
Ph: (770)717-2737
Fax: (770)717-7014
Co. E-mail: info@pcaconsulting.com
URL: http://www.pcaconsulting.com
Contact: Richard A. Defazio, President
E-mail: defazio@pcaconsulting.com
Scope: Maintenance consulting and engineering firm specializing in production planning, project management, team building, and re-engineering maintenance. **Founded:** 1976. **Publications:** "Does Planning Pay," Plant Services, Nov, 2000; "Asset Reliability Coordinator," Maintenance Technology, Oct, 2000; "Know What it is You Have to Maintain," Maintenance Technology, May, 2000; "Does Maintenance Planning Pay," Maintenance Technology, Nov, 2000.; "What is Asset Management?"; "Implementing Best Business Practices".

34326 ■ Performance Technologies Inc.
137 N main St., Ste. 1016
Dayton, OH 45402
Ph: (937)296-5060
Fax: (937)890-7853
Contact: Norm Evans, Sr., Principal
Scope: A consulting/training firm that designs and instills sales, leadership and management skills, processes and tools that strengthens overall organizational effectiveness. Services include: organizational transformation, creation of vision, values and operating philosophy, business analysis, impact analysis, innovation technology, succession planning and process mapping. Training services include: Advanced sales strategies, sales coaching and management, training processes, management effectiveness, leadership development, performance management, measurement and assessment. **Founded:** 1982. **Publications:** "Get- Real Selling".

34327 ■ Pilot Consulting Corp.
29 Wildhorse Trl.
Crested Butte, CO 81224-1249
Ph: (970)349-1250
Fax: (970)349-1251
URL: http://www.pilotconsulting.com
Contact: Christopher A. Cappy, President
E-mail: ccappy@pilotconsulting.com
Scope: Specializes in the implementation of strategy, management of transition and development of leadership in companies. **Founded:** 1995. **Publications:** "Leading Beyond the Walls". **Seminars:** Facilitative Leadership Training.

34328 ■ Pioneering Management Possibilities (PMP) [Personal Mastery Programs]
31000 Telegraph Rd., Ste. 260
Bingham Farms, MI 48025
Ph: (248)647-9290
Fax: (248)647-1537
Co. E-mail: bzimmerman@pmpcoach.com
URL: http://www.pioneeringmanagement.com
Contact: Mark B. Stein, President
E-mail: mstein@pmpcoach.com
Scope: A team of management consultants and business coaches specializing in the application of management principles. Areas include team building, strategic planning, personal development, leadership development and management training. **Founded:** 1987. **Publications:** "Accountability - Compliance or Commitment"; "Leadership - The Missing Link"; "Succession Planning: An Imperative for Personal Growth"; "The Soft Stuff Yields Hard Results". **Seminars:** Fomenting Innovation; The Practice of Leader-

ship; Leadership, Culture and Corporate Performance; Transforming Behavioral Health care Through Innovation and Collaboration; Leadership Succession.

34329 ■ Positive Impact Consulting
9845 Horn Rd., Ste. 120
Sacramento, CA 95827
Ph: (916)366-3000
Free: 800-376-7484
Fax: (916)364-9860
Co. E-mail: info@positiveimpact.com
URL: http://www.positiveimpact.com
Contact: Jeff Douglas, Owner
Scope: Management services in executive development, strategic planning, team building, organization-wide surveys, customer surveys, systems and process redesigns, skills assessments, TQM overview training, TQM tools training, positive impact facilitator training, the coaching experience (TQM leadership training), customized course designing. **Founded:** 1985. **Seminars:** The Coaching Experience, Jul, 2007; Facilitator Boot Camp, May, 2007; On-The-Spot Communicating, May, 2007; Cafe de la Facilitation, Apr, 2007; Becoming a Great Recorder, Mar, 2007.

34330 ■ Profit Associates Inc.
26 Hunters Forest Dr.
Charleston, SC 29414
Ph: (843)763-5718
Free: 800-688-6304
Fax: (843)763-5719
Co. E-mail: bobrog@profit-associates.com
URL: http://www.profit-associates.com
Contact: Bob Rogers, Managing Director
E-mail: bobrog@awod.com
Scope: A team of management and turnaround specialists providing consulting services. Focuses on the problems of small to medium-sized businesses in the manufacturing, distribution, construction, software. Specializes in employee productivity and incentives, management reengineering, profit and expense controls, production planning, strategic business planning, marketing and public relations, or ISO 9000 support. **Founded:** 1993. **Seminars:** Essential Elements of a Good Incentive Program; Why Look at Management Re-engineering; The Profit & Expense Control Process; The Executive Coaching Alternative.

34331 ■ Renaissance Leadership
2500 Olde King Cir.
Midlothian, VA 23113-9685
Ph: (804)423-4266
Fax: (804)423-4267
URL: http://www.renlead.com
Contact: Thomas W. Newton, President
E-mail: tomnewton@renlead.com
Scope: Specializes in the strategic building of high performance organizations and culture. Offer strategic consulting, executive coaching, team development and cultural transformation seminars which combine contemporary learning theory, leadership practice and work-related outdoor adventures. Serves all industries in the United States, Europe, Central America and Asia. **Founded:** 1978. **Seminars:** Culture Change Leadership; Creating High Performance Learning Organizations; Life Planning; Thriving on Change; Team Building and Alignment; Creativity, Risk Taking, and Innovation; Creating a High Performance Culture; Servant Leadership; Capitalizing on Diversity; Coaching for Optimal Performance.

34332 ■ Soul Works
3809 County Road E
Swanton, OH 43558-9276
Ph: (419)825-2444
Contact: Robert Anderson, Owner
Scope: Organizational development consulting and training firm that specializes in leadership development and creating high performance work systems. Focuses on organizational system change and work redesign efforts. Also supports system change with an integrated curriculum of leadership development workshops. Provides workshops and consulting services including empowered entrepreneurial leadership, personal and organizational vision, teamwork

and involvement and a whole systems perspective when implementing change. Industries served: private industries including healthcare organizations, manufacturing, service and nonprofit. **Founded:** 1986. **Seminars:** Organizational Control and Dependency; Mastering Leadership; Aligned Teams.

34333 ■ Stier Associates
4 Dunellen
Cromwell, CT 06416-2702
Ph: (860)635-1590
Contact: Dr. Suzanne Stier, President
Scope: Offers personal development consulting. Services include: succession planning, executive coaching, strategic management, team building and board development. Consulting services for public companies include: process consulting, team building, executive coaching, diversity management, strategic management and religious institutions. **Founded:** 1981.

34334 ■ Tamayo Consulting Inc.
169 Saxony Rd., Ste. 112
Encinitas, CA 92024-6779
Ph: (760)479-1352
Fax: (760)479-1465
Co. E-mail: info@tamayoconsulting.com
URL: http://www.tamayoconsulting.com
Contact: Jennifer Dreyer, President
E-mail: jdreyer@earthlink.net
Scope: It Provides training and consulting services. And also it specializes in leadership and team development. Industries served: private, non-profit, government, educational. **Founded:** 1986. **Seminars:** Presentation AdvantEdge Program; Lead point Development Program; Supervisor Development Programs.Identify Presentation Objectives; Implement 360-degree presentation assessment; conduct baseline-coaching session; Develop coaching plan; Staying connected.

34335 ■ Vision Management
149 Meadows Rd.
Lafayette, NJ 07848-3120
Ph: (973)702-1116
Fax: (973)702-8311
Contact: Norman L. Naidish, President
Scope: Firm specializes in profit enhancement; strategic planning; business process reengineering; industrial engineering; facilities planning; team building; inventory management; and total quality management (TQM). **Founded:** 1984. **Publications:** "To increase profits, improve quality," Manufacturing Engineering, May, 2000.

34336 ■ Steve Wilson and Co.
1159 S Creekway Ct.
Columbus, OH 43230
Free: 800-669-5233
Fax: (614)855-4889
Co. E-mail: steve@stevewilson.com
URL: http://www.stevewilson.com
Contact: Steve Wilson, President
E-mail: steve@stevewilson.com
Scope: Specializing in team building, staff development and personal growth, consultant presents the way humor works and awakens new ways of relating to ourselves and others. Consultant carries designation of Certified Speaking Professional (CSP) and is one of seven persons worldwide certified in I Power program instruction. The topics that consultant specializes in are: health and humor, funny business, motivation and productivity, human relations, stress management, team building, communication, and creativity. Industries served: Education, medical, telecommunications, service, allied medical, sales, training, real estate, associations, universities and colleges, temporary services, state and federal government, churches, and manufacturing worldwide. **Founded:** 1985. **Publications:** "Good Hearted Living"; "Birthrights: Your Essence, Purpose & Self-Esteem"; "Toilet Paper, Toothpaste, and Tuna Noodle Casserole"; "The Steve Wilson Report"; "The Art of Mixing Work and Play," Sep, 1992; "Super Humor Power," Oct, 1992; "Remarried with Children," May, 1992; "Eat Dessert First," May, 1990; "CHILL!". **Seminars:** Creating Positive Working Environments™; Putting Humor to Work at Work; Pulling Together Instead of Falling Apart; Winning over Customers

from Hell; The Play shop Lab™; Humor For the Health of It; I-Power; Don't Postpone Joy™; Laughing Matters in the Classroom; The Art of Mixing Work and Play™; and Managing Stress Through Humor.

FRANCHISES AND BUSINESS OPPORTUNITIES

34337 ■ Turbo Leadership Systems (TLS)
36280 NE Willsonville Rd.
Newberg, OR 97132
Ph: (503)625-1867
Free: 800-574-4373
Fax: (503)625-2699
Co. E-mail: turbo@turbols.com
URL: http://www.turboleadershipsystems.com
Contact: Larry W. Dennis, Sr., President
E-mail: larry@turbols.com
Description: Management training and team building training. **Scope:** Leadership, development and training programs, helping clients assess their current culture by using a copyrighted employee opinion survey. Coaches top management team to arrive at greater level of support around a vision and develops breakthrough action plans. Helps structure work timber groups into customer responsive performance teams. Industries served: retail, distribution, paper, manufacturing and construction primarily in the Northwest, also in the Midwest and on the Southwest Coast. **No. of Company-Owned Units:** 1. **Founded:** 1985. **Franchised:** 1995. **Equity Capital Needed:** $49,000. **Franchise Fee:** $39,000. **Publications:** "Empowering Leadership"; "How to Turbo Charge You"; "Repeat Business"; "Making Moments Matter, Information"; "The Turbo Charger"; "15 Leadership Principles and Ronald Reagan"; "Motorcycle Meditations"; "Repeat Business"; "Empowering Leadership"; "Communication For Results"; "The Great Baseball Cap". **Training:** Yes. **Seminars:** Creating Synergistic Teamwork; How To Make Change Work For You; Making Moments Matter; Leadership Insights; Surpassing Past Performance; Communicating for Results.

COMPUTER SYSTEMS/ SOFTWARE

34338 ■ *Facilitation Skills for Team Leaders*
Chris Learning Center, Inc.
3204 Accolade Dr.
Clinton, MD 20735
Ph: (888)534-5556
Free: 800-442-7477
Fax: (888)715-0220
Co. E-mail: courseiltcrisp@thomaslearning.com
URL: http://www.chrislearningcenter.com
Contact: John Winder, President
Price: $13.95. **Description:** Bring out the collaborative voices of your team members. Get started with this simple six-step plan. Increase participation and

team efficiency. Develop feedback and clarification skills. Shortcut the path to team consensus.

34339 ■ *Team Problem Solving*
Chris Learning Center, Inc.
3204 Accolade Dr.
Clinton, MD 20735
Ph: (888)534-5556
Free: 800-442-7477
Fax: (888)715-0220
Co. E-mail: courseiltcrisp@thomaslearning.com
URL: http://www.chrislearningcenter.com
Contact: John Winder, President
Price: $13.95 (VCI CD-ROM). **Description:** Based on the Team Problem-Solving and Decision-Making video and book. Includes book and user's guide.

RESEARCH CENTERS

34340 ■ Riegel and Emory Human Resource Research Center
Darla-Moore School of Business
University of S Carolina at Columbia
1705 College St.
Columbia, SC 29208
Ph: (803)777-3176
URL: http://mooreschool.sc.edu/facultyresearch/re-
    searchcenters/riegelemoryhrcenter.aspx
Contact: Prof. Brian S. Klaas, Director
Scope: Improvement of understanding of how human resource practices can contribute to improved organizational performance, particularly employee values in the workplace, motivation and satisfaction of workers, and management skills. Aims to increase cooperation in the workplace and to preserve the values of the free market system. **Founded:** 1982. **Publications:** *Values Research Project Reprint Series.*

34341 ■ University of North Carolina at Chapel Hill - Frank Hawkins Kenan Institute of Private Enterprise
Campus Box 3440, Kenan Ctr.
Chapel Hill, NC 27599
Ph: (919)962-8201
Fax: (919)962-8202
Co. E-mail: kenan_institute@unc.edu
URL: http://www.kenan-flagler.unc.edu/kenan-
    institute
Contact: John D. Kasarda, Director
Description: National center for private enterprise research focusing on entrepreneurial development, new venture management, and coursework development. **Scope:** Free enterprise, including job creation, changing labor-force skill needs, factors affecting business competitiveness and employment growth, international trade and privatization, management in the financial services industry, policy issues relating to financial services, financial services markets, offshore sourcing in manufacturing, manufacturing quality, manufacturing forecasting, human resources

supervision, team building, compensation, management development, and multidisciplinary research on global economic change and international marketing. **Founded:** 1985. **Educational Activities:** Carolina Challenge Star Program; Carolina Entrepreneurial Initiative; International Executive Series and MBA Enterprise Corps. **Awards:** Citibank International Fellows Program.

34342 ■ University of Southern California - Marshall School of Business - Center for Effective Organizations
Davidson Conference Ctr., Ste. 200
3415 S Figueroa St.
Los Angeles, CA 90089-0871
Ph: (213)740-9814
Fax: (213)740-4354
Co. E-mail: elawler@marshall.usc.edu
URL: http://ceo.usc.edu
Contact: Edward E. Lawler, III, Director
E-mail: elawler@marshall.usc.edu
Scope: Center offers expertise of faculty on critical organizational issues that involve the design and management of complex organizations. Issues include: performance appraisal, careers, organizational learning, job design, knowledge work teams, team performance management and organizational change. Primarily serves human resources executives. **Founded:** 1979. **Publications:** "Beyond HR: The New Science of Human Capital," Harvard Business School Press, 2007; "Achieving Strategic Excellence: An Assessment of Human Resource Organizations," Stanford University Press, 2006; "America at Work: Choices and Challenges," Palgrave-Macmillan, 2006; "Built to Change: How to Achieve Sustained Organizational Effectiveness," Jossey-Bass, 2006. **Educational Activities:** HCEO Certificate Program; Organization Design Workshop and Organization Design Certificate. **Seminars:** Becoming an Organizational Playmaker: Influence Skills for HR Leaders, Mar, 2013; Advanced Topics in Organization Design Workshop, Jun, 2013; Employee Resource Group Leadership Summit, Jun, 2013; Data Coaching Workshop, Jun, 2013; THREE - The HR Emerging Executive, Sep, 2013; Beyond Change Management: Accelerating Transformations and Building Agile Organizations, Oct, 2013; Strategic Partnership with Impact, Oct, 2013; Strategic Organization Design Workshop, Nov, 2013; Talent Management; Leadership Development; Strategic Partnership with Impact, Jun, 2010; Data Coaching Workshop: Optimal Data Strategies to Drive Results, Mar, 2010; The Necessary Art of Constructive Persuasion: How HR Can Be Heard, Mar, 2010; Strategic Organization Design Workshop, Los Angeles, Feb, 2010; Strategy Analysis, New York, Oct, 2008; Strategic Organization Design Workshop, Sep, 2008; Leveraging Leadership, Sep, 2008; Advanced Topics in Organization Design, Jun, 2008; Beyond Change Management: Building and Leading the Continuously Transforming Organization, Apr, 2008; Strategic Partnership with Impact: Strategy Analysis for Organization and Human Resources, Mar, 2008; HR Metrics and Analytics, Feb, 2008.

ASSOCIATIONS AND OTHER ORGANIZATIONS

34343 ■ **International Association of Professional Security Consultants (IAPSC)**
575 Market St., Ste. 2125
San Francisco, CA 94105
Ph: (415)536-0288
Fax: (415)764-4915
Co. E-mail: iapsc@iapsc.org
URL: http://www.iapsc.org
Contact: Frank Pisciotta, President
Description: Security management, technical, training and forensic consultants. Promotes understanding and cooperation among members and industries or individuals requiring such services. Seeks to enhance members' knowledge through seminars, training programs and educational materials. Works to foster public awareness of the security consulting industry; serves as a clearinghouse for consultants' requirements. Maintains code of conduct, ethics and professional standards. Offers consultant referral service; operates speakers' bureau. **Founded:** 1984. **Publications:** *IAPSC Consultants Directory* (Annual); *IAPSC News* (Quarterly). **Educational Activities:** International Association of Professional Security Consultants Convention (Annual); How to Succeed as a Professional Security Consultant. **Awards:** Charles A. Sennewald Distinguished Service Accolade (Annual).

REFERENCE WORKS

34344 ■ *"The Danger from Within: The Biggest Threat to Your Cybersecurity May Be an Employee or a Vendor" in Harvard Business Review (Vol. 92, September 2014, No. 9, pp. 94)*
Pub: Harvard Business Publishing
Released: September 2014. **Description:** Corporate computer crimes involving insiders are on the rise. To reduce vulnerability, firms should incorporate employees into the watchdog process, perform regular audits of distributors and suppliers, and implement security procedures involving both management and information technology personnel.

34345 ■ *"How to Detect and Prevent Employee Fraud" in Contractor (Vol. 56, October 2009, No. 10, pp. 57)*
Pub: Penton Media, Inc.
Ed: James R. Leichter. **Description:** Mechanical contractors can prevent employee fraud by handing out a detailed employment policy manual to their employees and making sure that their invoices are numbered. It is also highly advised to have bank statements reconciled by a third party.

34346 ■ *"Retailers Report 'Shrinkage' - Disappearance of Inventory - on the Rise" in Arkansas Business (Vol. 26, September 28, 2009, No. 39, pp. 17)*
Pub: Arkansas Business Publishing Group
Ed: Mark Friedman. **Description:** According to a National Retail Security Survey report released last June, retailers across the country have lost about $36.5 billion in shrinkage, most of it at the hands of employees and shoplifters alike. Statistical data included.

34347 ■ *"What Has Sergey Wrought?" in Barron's (Vol. 89, July 13, 2009, No. 28, pp. 8)*
Pub: Dow Jones & Co., Inc.
Contact: Clare Hart, President
Ed: Alan Abelson. **Description:** Sergey Aleynikov is a computer expert that once worked for Goldman Sachs but he was arrested after he left the company and charged with theft for bringing with him the code for the company's proprietary software for high-frequency trading. The stock market has been down for four straight weeks as of July 13, 2009 which reflects the reality of how the economy is still struggling.

VIDEOCASSETTES/ AUDIOCASSETTES

34348 ■ *Choices: How to Control Internal Shrink*
Excellence in Training Corp.
c/o ICON Training
804 Roosevelt St.
Polk City, IA 50226
Free: 800-609-0479
Co. E-mail: info@icontraining.com
URL: http://www.icontraining.com
Contact: Linda Russell, Vice President
Released: 1987. **Price:** $550. **Description:** Offers tips for retail stores to cut down employee theft through a look at two new employees: one conscientious, one not. **Availability:** VHS; 3/4 U.

34349 ■ *Stop Business Crime: Shoplifting & Employee Theft*
Instructional Video
2219 C St.
Lincoln, NE 68502-1745
Ph: (402)475-6570
Free: 800-228-0164
Fax: (402)475-6500
Co. E-mail: orders@insvideo.com
URL: http://www.insvideo.com
Contact: Kathy Damkroger, President
Released: 19??. **Price:** $79.95. **Description:** Offers solutions the problems of shoplifting and employee theft. Includes examples of how each is done followed by several alternatives that could be used to prevent them. **Availability:** VHS.

CONSULTANTS

34350 ■ **AlixPartners**
2000 Town Ctr., Ste. 2400
Southfield, MI 48075-1250
Ph: (248)358-4420
Fax: (248)358-1969
Co. E-mail: info@alixpartners.com
URL: http://www.alixpartners.com
Contact: Frederick A. Crawford, Chief Executive Officer
E-mail: fcrawford@alixpartners.com
Scope: Corporate turnaround and crisis management consultants specialize in debt restructuring, chapter 11 reorganizations, workout negotiations, refinancing, litigation support, forensic accounting, fraud investigations, valuation and expert testimony and information technology outsourcing management and realignment. **Founded:** 1981. **Publications:** "Managing Along the Cutting Edge," Newsweek, Feb, 2009; "Mitigating Fcpa Risks When Doing Business in China," Bloomberg Corporate Law Journal, Feb, 2009; "Crisis Management Alix partners," Consulting Magazine, 2008; "Getting The Most Out Of IT C Suite Survey"; "Vestar Minority Deal Turns Into Turnaround"; "The Impact of US Style Regulation in Europe"; "The Corporate Superheroes Who Support Strapped Businesses in Their Hour of Need," the Daily Telegraph, Dec, 2008; "Changes to Claim Objection Rules Go Effective," Dec, 2007; "Squeeze Makes Life Harder," Financial Times, Oct, 2007; "Dialing for Dollars and Other Tactics for Finding Cash for the Estate," Abi Journal, Oct, 2007; "Don't Blame the Tool," Sep, 2007; "Claims Chats Guide to Claims Settlement Letters," Abi Journal, Aug, 2007; "Managing it Through Tough Times," Architecture and Governance, Jul, 2007; "Marketers Must Learn New Brand Imperatives," Cpg Matters, Jun, 2007. **Seminars:** A Business Perspective on Bankruptcy and Insolvency; How to Avoid Corporate Bankruptcy; The Accountant's Role in Bankruptcy and Insolvency.

34351 ■ **Assets Protection Inc. (API)**
421 Eastern Blvd.
Essex, MD 21221-6715
Ph: (410)780-0010
Fax: (410)327-3025
URL: http://www.sasi1968.com/api
Contact: Roger B. Copinger, Jr., President
Scope: Security consultants providing professional loss prevention assistance, development and maintenance of security programs for both small and large businesses in retail and manufacturing. Loss prevention security surveys conducted and cost effective strategies designed to reduce and eliminate security hazards, risks and exposures. **Founded:** 1968.

34352 ■ **Frederick A. Bornhofen & Associates [Bornhofen & Associates]**
220 Isabella Rd.
Elverson, PA 19520-9141
Ph: (610)942-9140
Fax: (610)942-9576
Contact: Frederick A. Bornhofen, President
E-mail: fborn@comcast.net
Scope: Offers commercial and industrial security services, specializes in areas of robbery and violence prevention, business ethics, cargo security, commercial loss prevention techniques and security management. Industries served: retail, convenience store, transportation, manufacturing and energy.

Founded: 1989. **Publications:** "Everything Changes Sometime". **Seminars:** Business Ethics; Fraud in the Business World.

34353 ■ Dale System Inc.
1101 Stewart Ave., Ste. 300
Garden City, NY 11530-4826
Ph: (516)794-2800
Contact: Harvey M. Yaffe, President
Scope: Provider of advice, guidance and services covering internal security to industrial firms, retail stores and theater owners. Loss prevention services include undercover operations, shopping services, polygraph, and recreation or entertainment checking. Also surveys retail operations for price maintenance and product presentation. Additionally provides background investigations for business purposes. Serves private industries as well as government agencies. **Founded:** 1933.

34354 ■ Executive Management Services Inc.
307 4th Ave.
Pittsburgh, PA 15222
Ph: (412)471-8858
Contact: Jodi L. Stofko, Vice President
Scope: Security management loss prevention consulting and service company providing planning services and security awareness programs to its clients. Expertise focuses on providing solutions to internal theft issues and loss prevention contingency planning. **Founded:** 1987.

34355 ■ Fidelity Polygraph & Investigation Consultants Inc.
2163 Pelham Pky., Ste. 218
Pelham, AL 35124
Ph: (205)988-8644
Fax: (205)663-1489
Contact: Albert J. Silvani, President
Scope: Offers pre-employment screening as well as polygraph examinations and specific issue polygraph examinations; in-depth interviewing; loss prevention consulting; lectures on loss prevention; and shopping services interrogation, interviewing and investigations. Serves retail businesses including clothing, hardware, auto, materials and attorneys. **Founded:** 1985.

34356 ■ Greene Group
500 Market St.
Portsmouth, NH 03801
Ph: (603)433-8883
Fax: (973)522-0303
Contact: Ben W. Greene, Jr., President
Scope: Firm specializes in business research and risk assessment: handles discreet, time-sensitive assignments, including site security systems and controls for clients in the United States, Latin America and Southeast Asia. **Founded:** 1977.

34357 ■ Richard Haynes & Associates L.L.C.
1021 Temple St.
Charleston, WV 25312-2153
Ph: (304)346-6228
Fax: (304)346-9135
Contact: Capt. Richard A. Haynes, President
E-mail: captrah@citynet.net
Scope: Security management consultant. Offers the following services: security surveys and audits; security readiness for labor disputes; investigations; security training and awareness programs; special projects. Industries served: mining, petroleum, law

enforcement, private security companies and government agencies. **Founded:** 1980. **Publications:** "Let's Talk Security," Kanawha Valley Business Monthly; "The SWAT Cyclopedia" Aug, 1999. **Seminars:** Personal Protection Workshop: Workplace Violence.

34358 ■ Hub Kelsh Inc.
5312 Claridge Sq.
Atlanta, GA 30338
Ph: (770)730-8575
Fax: (770)730-8575
Contact: Hubert G. Kelsh, President
E-mail: hubkelsh@dscga.com
Scope: Investigations and loss prevention consulting for business (theft, harassment, drug activity, fraud, sabotage, hostile work environment and other inappropriate workplace conduct). Employee involvement programs for loss prevention and a drug-free workplace. Conducts physical security surveys. Inventory shrinkage a specialty. **Founded:** 1985. **Seminars:** Theft By Employees and Outsiders; Substance Abuse in the Workplace; Sexual Harassment; Workplace Violence; Dealing with Diversity Issues. Seminars, keynote speaker on integrity, workplace substance abuse, and employee misconduct.

34359 ■ Kies Intelligence Agency (KIA)
13630 Eldridge Ave.
Sylmar, CA 91342
Ph: (818)367-8416
Fax: (818)367-4983
Co. E-mail: kies@intelligence.org
URL: http://www.intelligence.org
Contact: Rudolf Kies, President
E-mail: kies@intelligence.org
Scope: Offers expertise in civil and criminal investigations, fingerprint analysis, missing persons and embezzlement investigations, employee background investigations and asset searches. Also specializes in messenger services, all kinds of investigative work and undercover assignments. Industries served: insurance companies, corporations and attorneys in United States branch office in Europe. **Founded:** 1976.

34360 ■ Security & Loss Prevention Associates Inc.
4718 Sylvia Ln.
Manvel, TX 77578
Fax: (281)489-8636
Contact: Jack R. Barbour, Director
Scope: Security and loss control consultants in physical security, operating systems and procedures and personnel practices, investigations of internal and external fraud and offers expert witness testimony in negligence litigation. Serve the convenience store industry, chain restaurants and health food industry. **Founded:** 1979.

RESEARCH CENTERS

34361 ■ International Centre for Comparative Criminology (ICCC) [Centre International de Criminologie Comparee]
University of Montreal
Pavillon Lionel-Groulx
3150, rue Jean-Brillant
Suite C-4086
Montreal, QC, Canada H3T 1N8
Ph: (514)343-7065

Fax: (514)343-2269
Co. E-mail: cicc@umontreal.ca
URL: http://www.cicc.umontreal.ca/en
Contact: Prof. Benoît Dupont, Director
Description: Initiates comparative studies and the training of professional personnel and research workers in the field of criminal justice. Disseminates cross-cultural experience and resources; encourages the exchange of information on research and penal reform. Conducts studies on topics such as the adaptation of traditional systems of criminal justice to the demands of modern industrial societies. Organizes refresher courses for practitioners; participants evaluate the criminal justice system of many countries with a view toward initiating reforms in their own system. Conducts seminars on subjects such as crime, and deviance, adolescent delinquency, domestic violence, development of delinquent behavior, enforcement of penal norms, social image of crime, and victimology. **Scope:** Criminal phenomenon as it exists in Quebec and Canada, including prevention of delinquency and protection of youth; delinquency that persists from adolescence to adulthood; female delinquency; victimology, white collar criminality (fraud, forgery, and counterfeiting and business crimes); crimes of violence (terrorism, group violence, and armed robbery); public reaction to various forms of deviance and criminality; functioning of the justice system, including functioning of the juvenile and adult courts; services for the execution of punishment (probation and pre-sentence reports); community participation in measures regarding criminals and delinquents; and clinical criminology and forensic psychiatry. **Founded:** 1969. **Publications:** *ICCC Annual report* (Annual); *CICC-Hebdo* (Weekly); *CICC-Info* (Semiannual); *Proceedings Collaborates in the publication of four specialized reviews: Criminologie* (Semiannual); *ICCC Research Reports*; *Annual reports* (Annual); *Criminologie* (Semiannual). **Educational Activities:** ICCC Conferences (Weekly); ICCC International congresses; ICCC Research seminars (Occasionally). **Awards:** Post-Doctoral Award (Annual); ICCC Grants (Periodic); Postdoctoral Fellowship (Annual).

34362 ■ Vera Institute of Justice - Louis Schweitzer Library
233 Broadway, 12th Fl.
New York, NY 10279-1299
Ph: (212)334-1300
Fax: (212)941-9407
URL: http://www.vera.org
Contact: John F. Savarese, Chairman
Description: Seeks to make government policies and practices more fair and humane. Encourages just practices in public services and aims to improve the quality of urban life. **Scope:** Effects of community policing, alternatives to incarceration programs in New York City courts, the introduction of European dayfines into U.S. criminal courts, speed of felony case processing in New York City, alcohol and drug treatment strategies for parolees in New York City, mental health care in the justice system, policing, relationships between employment and crime, juveniles and the court system, immigration, violence against women, and indigent defense. **Services:** Interlibrary loan; library open to the public by appointment. **Founded:** 1961. **Holdings:** The Institute's library contains an extensive archive of Vera's works.; 2000 articles, books, and periodicals. **Subscriptions:** ; 40 journals and other serials. **Publications:** *Research Department Monographs*; *Research Department Reports*; *Federal Sentencing Reporter* (Bimonthly).

START-UP INFORMATION

34363 ■ *"$44M Father/Son Biz Involved in Major Orlando Projects"* in *Orlando Business Journal (Vol. 31, July 18, 2014, No. 3, pp. 3)*
Pub: American City Business Journals
Released: July 18, 2014. **Description:** Sy and mark Israel, father-son duo of Universal Engineering Sciences, speak about the projects that have been their largest challenges. They also highlight the advice they would give to a family business or a new business startup.

34364 ■ *The 100 Best Businesses to Start When You Don't Want to Work Hard Anymore*
Pub: Career Press Inc.
Contact: Ron Fry, President
Ed: Lisa Rogak. **Price:** $14.99. **Availability:** Print.

34365 ■ *"The $100 Startup: Reinvent the Way You Make a Living, Do What You Love, and Create a New Future"*
Pub: Crown Business
Released: May 8, 2012. **Price:** $23.00. **Description:** Chris Guillebeau shows how to turn good ideas into income in order to pursue a life of adventure and the ability to give back to society. He believes entrepreneurship is about finding the intersection between our expertise and what people will buy.

34366 ■ *101 Businesses You Can Start at With Less Than One Thousand Dollars: For Retirees*
Pub: Atlantic Publishing Co.
Contact: Amanda Miller, Manager
E-mail: amiller@atlantic-pub.com
Ed: Christina Bultinck. **Price:** $21.95. **Description:** Business ideas to help retirees start a home-based business on a low budget.

34367 ■ *101 Businesses You Can Start at With Less Than One Thousand Dollars: For Stay-at-Home Moms & Dads*
Pub: Atlantic Publishing Co.
Contact: Amanda Miller, Manager
E-mail: amiller@atlantic-pub.com
Ed: Christina Bultinck. **Price:** $21.95. **Description:** Business ideas to help stay-at-home moms and dads start a home-based business on a low budget.

34368 ■ *202 Things You Can Buy and Sell for Big Profits*
Pub: Entrepreneur Press
Contact: Perlman Neil, President
Ed: James Stephenson. **Description:** Become an entrepreneur at selling new and used products. This handbook will help individuals cash in on the boom in reselling new and used products online. A new section defines ways to set realistic goals while distinguishing between 'get-rich schemes' and long term, viable businesses. A discussion about targeting and reaching the right customer base is included, along with finding and obtaining the service support needed for starting a new business.

34369 ■ *"218 More Programs"* in *Entrepreneur (Vol. 35, November 2007, No. 11, pp. 96)*
Description: List of 218 colleges and universities in the U.S. offering entrepreneurship programs is presented.

34370 ■ *The 250 Questions Every Self-Employed Person Should Ask*
Pub: Adams Media Corp.
Contact: Scott Watrous, President
E-mail: bobadams@adamsmedia.com
Ed: Mary Mihaly. **Released:** January 01, 2010. **Price:** $5.48. **Description:** Comprehensive information is given for anyone wishing to start their own business. **Availability:** Print.

34371 ■ *The Accidental Entrepreneur: Practical Wisdom for People Who Never Expected to Work for Themselves*
Pub: Career Steps
Ed: Susan Urquhart-Brown. **Released:** October 20, 2005. **Description:** Steps for launching, growing and running a successful small company.

34372 ■ *The Accidental Entrepreneur: The 50 Things I Wish Someone Had Told Me About Starting a Business*
Pub: AMACOM
Contact: Edward T. Reilly, Manager
Ed: Susan Urquhart-Brown. **Released:** May 2008. **Price:** $17.95, Paper or Softback. **Description:** Advice is offered to any would-be entrepreneur, including eight questions to ask before launching a new business, ten traits of a successful entrepreneur, how to obtain licenses and selling permits, best way to create a business plan, ten ways to get referrals, six secrets of marketing, investment and financial information, ways to avoid burnout, and the seven biggest pitfalls to avoid. **Availability:** Print.

34373 ■ *The Accidental Startup: How to Realize Your True Potential by Becoming Your Own Boss*
Pub: Dutton Children's Books
Contact: Lauri Hornik, President
Ed: Danielle Babb. **Released:** May 05, 2009. **Price:** $11.99. **Description:** Advice is given to help would-be entrepreneurs realize their goals for starting and running a successful small business. **Availability:** E-book.

34374 ■ *Advancing Research on Minority Entrepreneurship*
Pub: Pine Forge Press
Contact: Blaise R. Simqu, President
Ed: Timothy Bates, William E. Jackson, James H. Johnson, Jr. **Released:** September 13, 2007. **Price:** $40, paperback; $47, hardcover. **Description:** Although minorities are more likely to engage in start-up businesses than others, minority entrepreneurs are less likely to get their enterprises off the ground or succeed in growing their businesses. The higher failure rates, lower sales and profits and less employment are among topics discussed. **Availability:** Print.

34375 ■ *"Allied Brokers of Texas Looking to Fill Private Lending Gap"* in *San Antonio Business Journal (Vol. 26, March 23, 2012, No. 8, pp. 1)*
Pub: American City Business Journal
Description: San Antonio, Texas-based Allied Brokers of Texas has announced the expansion of its services to offer private lending. The move would provide direct private financing of $250,000 to $5 million to entrepreneurs looking to buy or sell a small business. Insights into the firm's new subsidiary, Allied Lending Services, are also offered.

34376 ■ *Angel Financing: How to Find and Invest in Private Equity*
Pub: John Wiley & Sons Inc.
Contact: Stephen M. Smith, President
Ed: Gerald A. Benjamin, Joel B. Margulis. **Released:** October 1999. **Price:** $73.95, hardcover. **Description:** The book provides a proven strategy to help entrepreneurs find angel investors. Interviews with angel investors as well as information about investors' hedging strategies, risk assessments, syndication orientation, financial return expectations, deal structuring preferences, monitoring investments, harvesting returns, and realist exit strategies are covered. **Availability:** Print.

34377 ■ *"Angel Investing Network Launches"* in *Washington Business Journal (Vol. 31, August 31, 2012, No. 19, pp. 1)*
Pub: American City Business Journal
Description: Dan Mindus, investment director for Virginia's CIT GAP Funds, is launching a network of angel investors, venture capitalists and entrepreneurs. The network, which is expected to have 45 to 50 investors, is in the final stages of formation and could be a source of funds for startups in Washington, DC.

34378 ■ *"Are We There Yet?"* in *Entrepreneur (September 2014)*
Pub: Entrepreneur Media Inc.
Released: September 2014. **Description:** Entrepreneurs and small business advocates discuss the progress of Jumpstart Our Business Startups (JOBS) Act two years after it was signed into law in the U.S. in April 2012. The implementation of Title II in September 2013 allowed private companies to publicly advertise their fundraising efforts. Rewards-based crowdfunding also benefited from the publicity surrounding the JOBS Act. Crowdfunding advocates are looking forward to the finalization of Title III to address their concerns about red tape and compliance costs.

34379 ■ *The Art of the Start: The Time-Tested, Battle-Hardened Guide for Anyone Starting Anything*
Pub: Penguin Books USA Inc.
Ed: Guy Kawasaki. **Released:** September 09, 2004. **Price:** $27.95, hardcover. **Description:** Advice for someone starting a new business covering topics such as hiring employees, building a brand, business competition, and management.

34380 ■ The Art of the Start: The Time-Tested, Battle-Hardened Guide for Anyone Starting Anything
Pub: Portfolio Publishing
Contact: Adrian Zackheim, President
Ed: Guy Kawasaki. **Released:** September 09, 2004. **Price:** $27.95, hardcover; $19.99. **Description:** Apple's Guy Kawasaki offers information to help would-be entrepreneurs create new enterprises. As founder and CEO of Garage Technology Ventures, he has field-tested his ideas with newly hatched companies and he takes readers through every phase of creating a business, from the very basics of raising money and designing a business model through the many stages that eventually lead to success and thus giving back to society. **Availability:** PrintElectronic publishing.

34381 ■ "Austin Welcomes New Program for Entrepreneurs" in Austin Business JournalInc. (Vol. 29, February 12, 2010, No. 29, pp. 1)
Pub: American City Business Journals
Ed: Christopher Calnan. **Description:** Nonprofit group Economic Development Catalyst Organization (ECDO) is formalizing its BizLaunch mentoring program, which was stated in 2009. The program aims to offer support networks to entrepreneurs and assistance regarding early-stage venture capital.

34382 ■ "Austin's Connection To Aggies, Angels and Investors" in Austin Business Journal (Vol. 32, April 6, 2012, No. 5, pp. A1)
Pub: American City Business Journals, Inc.
Contact: Whitney Shaw, President
Ed: Christopher Calnan. **Released:** April 6, 2012. **Description:** Texas A and M University System director for new ventures, Jamie Rhodes, has been using his experience as an entrepreneur and angel investor to work with the university's professors, researchers, and new entrepreneurs on commercialization opportunities. Rhodes has a goal to create startups based on research produced at Texas A and M.

34383 ■ Awakening the Entrepreneur Within: How Ordinary People Can Create Extraordinary Companies
Pub: HarperCollins Publishers Inc.
Contact: Jane Friedman, President
E-mail: jfriedman@harpercollins.com
Ed: Michael E. Gerber. **Released:** December 08, 2009. **Price:** $15.99, paperback. **Description:** Four dimensions of the entrepreneurial personality are explored: dreamer, thinker, performer and leader. **Availability:** Print.

34384 ■ Be Your Own Boss
Pub: Wet Feet, Incorporated
Ed: Marcia Passos Duffy. **Released:** November 2006. **Price:** $14.95. **Description:** Tips for starting a freelance business in any career or industry are covered. **Availability:** PDF.

34385 ■ The Beermat Entrepreneur: Turn Your Good Idea Into a Great Business
Pub: Pearson Education Ltd.
Contact: Rod Bristow, President
Ed: Mike Southon, Chris West. **Released:** 2nd Edition. **Price:** £14.99, paperback; £9.99. **Description:** Information to help start, maintain and grow a small business is given, along with suggestions for working with a bank. **Availability:** PrintElectronic publishing.

34386 ■ "Beyond Bootstrapping" in Inc. (Vol. 36, September 2014, No. 7, pp. 64)
Pub: Mansueto Ventures L.L.C.
Contact: John Koten, Chief Executive Officer
Released: September 2014. **Description:** Dave Lerner, serial entrepreneur, angel investor, B-school professor, and author, explains the challenges entrepreneurs face when self-funding their startup business.

34387 ■ Birthing the Elephant: The Woman's Go-for-It! Guide to Overcoming the Big Challenges of Launching a Business
Pub: Celestial Arts Publishing Co.
Contact: Kristin Casemore, Manager
E-mail: kristin.casemore@tenspeed.com
Ed: Karin Abarbanel, Bruce Freeman. **Released:** March 2008. **Price:** $15.99; $11.99. **Description:** Advice for women entrepreneurs is given. The book

explores the emotional challenges faced by women starting businesses, along with advice for reshaping image. This handbook helps women survive and succeed in business. **Availability:** PrintE-book.

34388 ■ "Breaking Barriers" in Baltimore Business Journal (Vol. 30, June 29, 2012, No. 8, pp. 1)
Pub: American City Business Journals, Inc.
Contact: Whitney Shaw, President
Ed: Jack Lambert. **Released:** June 29, 2012. **Description:** Many Hispanic entrepreneurs have been struggling to start businesses in Baltimore, Maryland. Many necessary documents are available only in English. Hispanic businesses are seen to spark future economic growth in Baltimore.

34389 ■ Breaking Free: How to Quit Your Job and Start Your Own Business
Pub: Greenwood Publishing Group, Inc.
Ed: Chris Lauer. **Released:** March 01, 2009. **Price:** $34.95, hardcover. **Description:** This book helps individuals transition from working for others to starting their own business. **Availability:** Print.

34390 ■ "Breakthrough: How to Build a Million Dollar Business by Helping Others Succeed"
Pub: CreateSpace
Contact: Daren Giles, President
Released: October 23, 2014. **Price:** $14.95 paperback. **Description:** Instruction for starting and growing a thriving business from home is provided. The book teaches how to listing to the small voice within, follow your instincts, deliver effective presentations, attract customers who require your products or services, host home meetings, develop leadership skills, discover purpose, and clarify your entrepreneurial visions and goals.

34391 ■ Brewing Up a Business: Adventures in Beer from the Founder of Dogfish Head Craft Brewery
Pub: John Wiley & Sons Inc.
Contact: Stephen M. Smith, President
Ed: Sam Calagione. **Released:** 2nd Edition. **Price:** $18.95, paperback; $12.99. **Description:** Author shares nontraditional success secrets. Calgione began his business with a home brewing kit and grew it into Dogfish Head Craft Beer, the leading craft brewery in the U.S. **Availability:** PrintE-book.

34392 ■ "Business With Brains" in Canadian Business (Vol. 85, September 17, 2012, No. 14, pp. 41)
Pub: George Media Inc.
Ed: Richard Warnica. **Released:** September 17, 2012. **Description:** The Ontario Brain Institute launched the Entrepreneurs Program to provide funding, business training, and connections to Canadian medical researchers who believe they have great ideas for business. The program aims to close the gap between neuroscience publications and viable projects.

34393 ■ The Campus CEO: The Student Entrepreneur's Guide to Launching a Multi-Million Dollar Business
Ed: Randal Pinkett. **Released:** February 2007. **Price:** , $21.00 (CND). **Description:** Tips for generating income, while attending college is presented to students.

34394 ■ "Campus CEOs: Young and the Restless" in Business Journal Portland (Vol. 30, February 21, 2014, No. 50, pp. 4)
Pub: American City Business Journals
Released: February 14, 2014. **Description:** A number of startups in Portland, Oregon were created by young entrepreneurs while still attending college. The University of Oregon and Portland State University are developing courses designed to launch the entrepreneurial ambitions of their students.

34395 ■ Canadian Small Business Kit for Dummies
Pub: CDG Books Canada Inc.
Contact: Tom Best, President
E-mail: tbest@cdgbooks.com
Ed: Margaret Kerr, JoAnn Kurtz. **Released:** March 2007. **Price:** $37.99 (Canadian). **Description:**

Entrepreneurial guide to starting and running a small business in Canada.

34396 ■ Careers for Self-Starters and Other Entrepreneurial Types
Ed: Blythe Camenson. **Released:** September 2004. **Price:** $9.95 (US).; $13.95 (US). **Description:** Advice to entrepreneurs wishing to start their own small company. Tips for turning hobbies into job skills are included.

34397 ■ Cash In On Cash Flow
Pub: Simon and Schuster Inc.
Contact: Carolyn Reidy, President
E-mail: carolyn.reidy@simonandschuster.com
Ed: Lawrence J. Pino. **Released:** July 2005. **Price:** $19.95. **Description:** Guide to assist entrepreneurs with starting a new business as a cash flow specialist. **Availability:** Print.

34398 ■ "Close-Up: LeVar Burton: They Cancelled His Show; He Started a Business" in Inc. (Vol. 34, September 2012, No. 7, pp. 22)
Pub: Mansueto Ventures L.L.C.
Contact: John Koten, Chief Executive Officer
Ed: Issie Lapowsky. **Released:** September 2012. **Description:** Profile of LeVar Burton, who hosted the PBS children's show, 'Reading Rainbow' has relaunched the program under his new firm, RRKidz. Burton partnered with Mark Wolfe to start a for-profit technology committed to developing educational tools for children.

34399 ■ The Complete Startup Guide for the Black Entrepreneur
Pub: Career Press Inc.
Contact: Ron Fry, President
Ed: Bill Bourdreaux. **Price:** $15.99. **Availability:** Print.

34400 ■ "Confessions Of Serial Entrepreneurs" in Entrepreneur (January 8, 2009)
Pub: Entrepreneur Press
Contact: Perlman Neil, President
Ed: Jennifer Wang. **Description:** Serial entrepreneurs are those individuals that are able to start business after business. These individuals enjoy the process of starting a company then handing off the finished product and starting over with a new endeavor. Several serial entrepreneurs are profiled.

34401 ■ "CrowdFunding Made Simple Conference at University of Utah Ignites Ecosystem of Entrepreneurs and Investors" in Economics Week (June 29, 2012)
Pub: NewsRX
Contact: Susan E. Hasty, Publisher
Released: June 29, 2012. **Description:** The first national conference on crowdfunding was held at the University of Utah Guest House and Conference Center May 31 through June 1, 2012. The event, CrowdFunding Made Simple, gathered entrepreneurs, business owners, professional service providers, investors, government officials and students to provide understanding and potential of crowdfunding, including information on the Jumpstart Our Business Startups (JOBS) Act.

34402 ■ Crush It!: Why NOW Is the Time to Cash In on Your Passion
Pub: HarperStudio/HarperCollins
Ed: Gary Vaynerchuk. **Released:** October 13, 2009. **Price:** $21.99, hardcover; $14.99; C$13.99. **Description:** Ways the Internet can help entrepreneurs turn their passions into successful companies. **Availability:** PrintE-book.

34403 ■ Cute Little Store: Between the Entrepreneurial Dream and Business Reality
Pub: Outskirts Press Inc.
Contact: Brent Sampson, President
Ed: Adeena Mignogna. **Released:** July 03, 2006. **Price:** $11.95, paperback; $9.99. **Description:** Challenges of starting and growing a retail business are profiled. **Availability:** PrintE-book.

34404 ■ *"De la Garza Discusses the Launch of Her New Media Venture" in Boston Business Journal (Vol. 34, June 6, 2014, No. 18, pp. 4)*
Pub: American City Business Journals, Inc.
Contact: Whitney Shaw, President
Released: June 6, 2014. **Description:** News anchor, Bianca de la Garza says career advancement prompted her to form Lucky Gal Productions LLC. She said her entrepreneurial pursuit will develop a television show focusing on lifestyle and entertainment. De la Garza admits she will miss her co-anchor job at WCVB-TV's morning show, 'EyeOpener'.

34405 ■ *"Do Cool Sh*t: Quit Your Day Job, Start Your Own Business, and Live Happily Ever After"*
Pub: Harper Business
Released: August 6, 2013. **Price:** $24.99. **Description:** Serial social entrepreneur, angel investor, and woman business leader, Miki Agrawal, teaches how to start and run a successful new business. She covers all issues from brainstorming, to raising money to getting press without any connections, and still have time to enjoy life. She created WILD, a farm-to-table pizzeria in New York City and Las Vegas; partnered in a children's multimedia company called Super Sprowtz,, a story-driven nutrition program for children; and launched a patented high-tech underware business called THINX. Agrawal also discusses the growth in her businesses.

34406 ■ *The E-Myth Enterprise: How to Turn a Great Idea into a Thriving Business*
Pub: HarperCollins Publishers Inc.
Contact: Jane Friedman, President
E-mail: jfriedman@harpercollins.com
Ed: Michael E. Gerber. **Released:** August 03, 2010. **Price:** $14.99, paperback. **Description:** This book explores the requirement needed to start and run a successful small business. **Availability:** Print.

34407 ■ *E-Preneur*
Pub: Career Press Inc.
Contact: Ron Fry, President
Ed: Richard J. Goossen. **Released:** April 2008. **Price:** $15.99, paperback. **Description:** Entrepreneurs in the new virtual marketplace are examined. The book surveys and explains the field of Web 2.0 and entrepreneurs successfully using the virtual marketplace. **Availability:** Print.

34408 ■ *Enterprise Planning and Development: Small Business and Enterprise Start-Up Survival and Growth*
Pub: Elsevier Science and Technology Books
Ed: David Butler. **Released:** June 2006. **Description:** Innovation, intellectual property, and exit strategies are among the issues discussed in this book involving current entrepreneurship.

34409 ■ *The Entrepreneurial Itch: Don't Scratch Until You Read This Book!*
Pub: Self-Counsel Press Inc.
Ed: David Trahair. **Released:** October 15, 2006. **Price:** $13.95. **Description:** Small business accountant shares a plan for starting a business. **Availability:** Print.

34410 ■ *Entrepreneurial Management*
Pub: McGraw-Hill
Ed: Robert J. Calvin. **Released:** February 28, 2002. **Price:** A$69.95, Hardcover; NZ$82, Hardcover. **Description:** Starting a new business takes careful consideration, determined preparation and a well-developed plan president of an international company that helps startups offers strategies, tools, techniques, models and methodologies for starting a new business. This guidebook covers all aspects of launching a new company as well as hands-on business skills and the motivation to keep new business owners moving towards success while conquering the entrepreneurial challenges along with way. **Availability:** Print.

34411 ■ *"Entrepreneurial StrengthsFinder"*
Pub: Gallup Press
Released: September 30, 2014. **Price:** $29.95. **Description:** The psychology of the entrepreneur is investigated. Research performed by Gallup shows

that decisions and actions, influenced by the personality of the entrepreneur, affect the survival and growth of any small business. The book answers essential questions for anyone thinking about starting a new business or for those already managing a startup. Advice is offered to help grow a new venture.

34412 ■ *"Entrepreneurs: Search Party" in Business Strategy Review (Vol. 21, Autumn 2010, No. 3, pp. 30)*
Pub: John Wiley & Sons Inc. Scientific, Technical, Medical, and Scholarly Div. (Wiley-Blackwell)
Contact: William J. Pesce, Manager
E-mail: wpesce@wiley.com
Ed: Georgina Peters. **Description:** Entrepreneurs tend to be fixated on coming up with a foolproof idea for a new business and then raising money to start it. Raising startup funds is difficult, but it doesn't have to be that way. Search funds offers an innovative alternative, and the results are often impressive.

34413 ■ *"Entrepreneurs Take Different Paths, but Arrive at Same Place" in Business Journal Portland (Vol. 30, February 14, 2014, No. 50, pp. 6)*
Pub: American City Business Journals
Released: February 14, 2014. **Description:** Several young entrepreneurs in Portland, Oregon describe how they started their own businesses while attending college. They discuss the challenges of balancing their studies and their companies.

34414 ■ *Entrepreneurship*
Pub: John Wiley & Sons Inc.
Contact: Stephen M. Smith, President
Ed: William D. Bygrave, Andrew Zacharakis. **Released:** Third Edition. **Price:** $218.95, paperback; $52. **Description:** Information for starting a new business is shared, focusing on marketing and financing a product or service. **Availability:** PrintE-book.

34415 ■ *Entrepreneurship and the Creation of Small Firms: Empirical Studies of New Ventures*
Pub: Edward Elgar Publishing Inc.
Contact: Richard Henning, Vice President
E-mail: kwight@e-elgar.com
Ed: Carin Holmquist, Johan Wiklund. **Released:** 2010. **Price:** £63, hardback. **Description:** Study focuses on the important issue of new venture creation. Using a variety of data sources, methods and theories, the authors demonstrate the factors that aid or hinder new venture creation in a number of settings.

34416 ■ *Entrepreneurship and Effective Small Business Management*
Pub: Prentice Hall Higher Education
Ed: Norman M. Scarborough, Jeffrey R. Cornwall. **Released:** Eleventh Edition. **Price:** $217.40. **Description:** Provides undergraduate and graduate entrepreneurship and/or small business management courses with information to successfully launch a new company. The books offers entrepreneurs the tools required to develop staying power to succeed and grow their new business. **Availability:** Print.

34417 ■ *Entrepreneurship and the Financial Community: Starting Up and Growing New Businesses*
Pub: Edward Elgar Publishing Inc.
Contact: Richard Henning, Vice President
E-mail: kwight@e-elgar.com
Price: $114.30, hardback; $41.60, paperback. **Description:** Understanding the role of private equity providers in the development and growth processes of small business. **Availability:** Print.

34418 ■ *Entrepreneurship with Online Learning Center Access Card*
Ed: Robert D. Hirich; Michael P. Peters; Dean A. Shepherd. **Released:** October 2006. **Price:** $103. 25. **Description:** Book instructs students on entrepreneurial processes that include starting a new business.

34419 ■ *Entrepreneurship Strategy: Changing Patterns in New Venture Creation, Growth, and Reinvention*
Pub: Pine Forge Press
Contact: Blaise R. Simqu, President
Ed: Lisa K. Gundry, Jill R. Kickul. **Released:** 2007. **Price:** $122. **Description:** Entrepreneurial strategies that incorporate new venture emergence, early growth, and reinvention and innovation are examined. **Availability:** Print.

34420 ■ *Entrepreneurship: Successfully Launching New Ventures*
Ed: Bruce Barringer, Duane Ireland. **Released:** October 17, 2011. **Price:** C$198. **Description:** Guide to help any entrepreneur successfully launch a new venture. **Availability:** Print.

34421 ■ *Escape from Corporate America: A Practical Guide to Creating the Career of Your Dreams*
Pub: Ballantine/Random House
Ed: Pamela Skillings. **Released:** May 13, 2008. **Price:** $15; $13.99. **Description:** How to quit your job and start your own business. **Availability:** PrintE-book.

34422 ■ *Escape from Cubicle Nation: From Corporate Prisoner to Thriving Entrepreneur*
Pub: Berkley Publishing Group
Contact: Susan Petersen Kennedy, President
Ed: Pamela Slim. **Released:** April 06, 2010. **Price:** $15, paperback. **Description:** Insight is offered to help anyone wishing to leave their corporate position and start their own small business. **Availability:** Print.

34423 ■ *Essentials of Entrepreneurship and Small Business Management*
Pub: Prentice Hall PTR
Ed: Norman M. Scarborough, Thomas W. Zimmerer, Doug Wilson. **Released:** 7th Edition. **Price:** $199.80. **Description:** New venture creation and the knowledge required to start a new business are shared. The challenges of entrepreneurship, business plans, marketing, e-commerce, and financial considerations are explored.

34424 ■ *Extraordinary Entrepreneurship: The Professional's Guide to Starting an Exceptional Enterprise*
Pub: John Wiley & Sons Inc.
Contact: Stephen M. Smith, President
Ed: Stephen C. Harper. **Released:** October 2006. **Price:** $66.95; $53.99. **Description:** New rules to assist entrepreneurs in the 21st Century. The book focuses on thinking outside the box. **Availability:** PrintE-book.

34425 ■ *"Faces: Q&A with Kevin Huyck, Chef/Owner of R.A. MacSammy's Food Truck Specializing in Mac and Cheese" in Saint Paul Pioneer Press (March 28, 2012)*
Pub: McClatchy-Tribune Regional News
Ed: Kathie Jenkins. **Released:** March 28, 2012. **Description:** Profile of 48 year old Kevin Huyck, chef and owner of his R.A. MacSammy food truck. Huyck specializes in serving a variety of macaroni and cheese dishes. He wanted to own his own restaurant but did not have the capital for such an investment at the time and hopes to expand with either another food truck or possibly a restaurant that features mac and cheese dishes.

34426 ■ *Fast-Track Business Start-Up Kit: California*
Pub: Kaplan Books
Ed: Carolyn Usinger. **Released:** 2006. **Price:** $22.95; C$29. **Description:** Step-by-step guide for starting and running a business in California, including information on sole proprietors, partnerships, limited liability companies, S and C corporations, as well as details concerning business entities, sales taxes, environmental issues, human resources, and more.

34427 ■ *Financial Times Guide to Business Start Up 2007*
Ed: Sara Williams; Jonquil Lowe. **Released:** November 2006. **Price:** $52.50. **Description:** Guide for starting and running a new business is presented. Sections include ways to get started, direct marketing, customer relations, management and accounting.

34428 ■ *"'Find a Customer To Validate Your Idea" in South Florida Business Journal (Vol. 34, May 2, 2014, No. 41, pp. 15)*
Pub: American City Business Journals
Released: May 2, 2014. **Description:** Venture Hive founder, Susan Amat, share her views on her mission to nurture the entrepreneurial ecosystem from South Florida to the Americas. Amat says Venture Hive is a safe space where world-class technologists can learn to scale their businesses. Amat is a 40 Under 40 honoree, a White House Champion of Change, chair of Startup Florida, an Emerging Leader and a Woman to Watch.

34429 ■ *"Find the Upside to a Down Economy" in Women Entrepreneur (September 30, 2008)*
Ed: Tamara Monosoff. **Description:** Starting a new business in this economic crisis may not be as daunting of a pursuit as one might think. Aspiring entrepreneurs may find success by looking for opportunities in unusual places and relying on what they do best.

34430 ■ *"Finding Startups a Place To Take Root" in Business Journal (Vol. 32, August 29, 2014, No. 14, pp. 6)*
Pub: American City Business Journals
Released: August 29, 2014. **Description:** Entrepreneurs David Berglund and Justin Ley have unveiled a new crowdfunding Website called Hoodstarter. The Website gathers business ideas from residents and help entrepreneurs make a pitch. Startups can seek further financing if they can show ample consumer demand.

34431 ■ *"The Food Truck Handbook: Start, Grow, and Succeed in the Mobile Food Business"*
Pub: John Wiley & Sons Inc.
Contact: Stephen M. Smith, President
Released: March 13, 2012. **Price:** $19.95 paperback. **Description:** Food truck businesses have grown so much in popularity, there are actually food truck competitions and was once a television show featuring them. A practical, step-by-step handbook is offered to help an entrepreneur start a mobile food delivery service. Information includes tips on choosing vending locations, opening and closing checklists; creation of a business plan with budget and finding vendor services, daily operation issues; common operating mistakes; and insight into delivery high quality food.

34432 ■ *"Former Boxer Lou Savarese Fits Into New Business Role" in Houston Business Journal (Vol. 40, January 8, 2010, No. 35, pp. 1)*
Pub: American City Business Journals
Ed: Greg Barr. **Description:** Lou Savarese explains how the lessons he learned as a professional boxer help him to manage his new business venture, a gym called Savarese Fight Gym. Customers who desire to learn boxing and to stay fit like a boxer comprise the fitness center's target market.

34433 ■ *Franchising for Dummies*
Pub: John Wiley & Sons Inc.
Contact: Stephen M. Smith, President
Ed: Dave Thomas, Michael Seid. **Released:** 2nd Edition. **Price:** $24.95, paperback; $16.99. **Description:** Advice to help entrepreneurs choose the right franchise, as well as financing, managing and expanding the business. **Availability:** PrintE-book.

34434 ■ *"From the Boardroom to the Drawing Board" in Dallas Business Journal (Vol. 37, July 18, 2014, No. 45, pp. 4)*
Pub: American City Business Journals
Released: July 18, 2014. **Description:** Several former North Texas Executive Directors resigned from their positions at top of the corporate ladder to start their own entrepreneurial ventures. Some of the challenges faced and how they overcame them to succeed are highlighted.

34435 ■ *Getting Rich In Your Underwear: How To Start and Run a Profitable Home-Based Business*
Pub: HCM Publishing
Price: $17.95. **Description:** Book offers insight into starting a home-based business. Entrepreneurs will learn about business models and the home business;

distribution and fulfillment of product or service; marketing and sales; how to overcome the fear of starting a business; personal success characteristics; naming a business; zoning and insurance; intellectual capital; copyrights, trademarks, and patents; limited liability companies and S-corporations; business expenses and accounting; taxes; fifteen basic steps for starting a home-based business, state resources for starting a home company; and seven home-based business ideas.

34436 ■ *The Girl's Guide to Starting Your Own Business: Candid Advice, Frank Talk, and True Stories for the Successful Entrepreneur*
Pub: William Morrow
Ed: Caitlin Friedman, Kimberly Yorio. **Released:** December 07, 2010. **Price:** $15.99, paperback; $11.49; C$11.99. **Description:** Advice is given to help any woman start her own company. Every chapter includes interviews, charts, quizzes and witty directives about self-employment. Topics include, choosing a name and logo, business law, communication and information about business associations. **Availability:** PrintE-book.

34437 ■ *"Gotta Go!" in Entrepreneur (September 2014)*
Pub: Entrepreneur Media Inc.
Released: September 2014. **Description:** Tooshlights is an LED lighting system for public bathrooms developed by entrepreneurs, Allen Klevens and Todd Bermann. The Los Angeles, California-based firm uses a wireless, infrared-based color scheme that allows bathroom users to determine which stalls are unoccupied. The partners funded the company with their own money and are looking for potential investors. The firm is also working on a new product application that will allow spectators to see how many stalls are available at any given time during a concert of sports event.

34438 ■ *Harmonic Wealth: The Secret of Attracting the Life You Want*
Pub: Hyperion Books
Contact: Ellen Archer, President
Ed: James Arthur Ray, Linda Sivertsen. **Released:** 2008. **Price:** $24.95; C$31.50. **Description:** Secrets for attracting the life you want through entrepreneurship; tips for timing a startup are included.

34439 ■ *"Home Is Where Your Startup Is" in Dallas Business Journal (Vol. 37, January 31, 2014, No. 21, pp. 6)*
Pub: American City Business Journals
Released: January 31, 2014. **Description:** Business accelerator Tech Wildcatters is planning to open a startup house in Dallas, Texas. The facility will bring together entrepreneurs, artists, and other creative individuals. A brief description of the facility is also included.

34440 ■ *How I Made It: 40 Successful Entrepreneurs Reveal How They Made Millions*
Pub: Kogan Page, Limited
Contact: Philip Kogan, Chairman of the Board
Ed: Rachel Bridge. **Released:** May 10, 2010. **Price:** £14.99, Paperback. **Description:** Inspiration is given to anyone wishing to become a successful entrepreneur.

34441 ■ *How to Make Big Money in Your Own Small Business: Unexpected Rules Every Small Business Owner Needs to Know*
Pub: Hyperion Books
Contact: Ellen Archer, President
Ed: Jeffrey J. Fox. **Released:** May 12, 2004. **Price:** $16.95; C$24.95. **Description:** Entrepreneur and consultant offer advice to help others create successful startups and prosper. Fox directs new business owners with a counterintuitive style and describes essential methods that beat the competition. Tips include: setting priorities, getting a personal driver, creating a contingency plan for employees, pricing to value, saving money, and getting an office outside of the home.

34442 ■ *How to Start and Run a Small Book Publishing Company: A Small Business Guide to Self-Publishing and Independent Publishing*
Pub: HCM Publishing
Ed: Peter I. Hupalo. **Released:** August 30, 2002. **Price:** $18.95. **Description:** The book teaches all aspects of starting and running a small book publishing company. Topics covered include: inventory accounting in the book trade, just-in-time inventory management, turnkey fulfillment solutions, tax deductible costs, basics of sales and use tax, book pricing, standards in terms of the book industry, working with distributors and wholesalers, cover design and book layout, book promotion and marketing, how to select profitable authors to publish, printing process, printing on demand, the power of a strong backlist, and how to value copyright.

34443 ■ *How to Start Your Own Business for Entrepreneurs*
Pub: FT Press
Contact: Timothy C. Moore, Vice President
Ed: Robert Ashton. **Released:** Second Edition. **Price:** $24.99. **Description:** More than 300,000 individuals start a business every year. That number will rise over the next year or two if the current economic downturn leads to widespread job losses.

34444 ■ *"I Have A Business Idea. What Now?" in Women Entrepreneur (October 15, 2008)*
Ed: Cheryl Isaac. **Description:** Four pre-planning steps to take before launching a new business are discussed in detail.

34445 ■ *"'I'm Going to Prove Everyone Wrong" in South Florida Business Journal (Vol. 34, May 9, 2014, No. 42, pp. 19)*
Pub: American City Business Journals
Released: May 9, 2014. **Description:** New Wave Health Care Ventures managing partners, Alex Gomez, shares his views about leaving medical school to launch his startup. Gomez says he always had the spirit of an entrepreneur and business excites him. He knows what he is looking for in investing at startup companies because of his experience with New Wave Surgical Corporation.

34446 ■ *"Inc. 500" in Inc. (Vol.. 36, September 2014, No. 7, pp. 25)*
Pub: Mansueto Ventures L.L.C.
Contact: John Koten, Chief Executive Officer
Released: September 2014. **Description:** Discussion involving the 500 entrepreneurs selected by this journal who, over the past three years, built fast-growing companies.

34447 ■ *"Innovative Ability and Entrepreneurial Activity: Two Factors to Enhance 'Quality of Life" in Journal of Business & Industrial Marketing (Vol. 29, July 2014, No. 6)*
Pub: Emerald Group Publishing Inc.
Released: July 2014. **Description:** Examination of how aspects of knowledge economy covered by the KEI (Knowledge Economy Index) and those of entrepreneurial activity covered by the GEI (Global Entrepreneurship Index) affect QOL (quality of Life) in a country. KEI, GEI, and QOL data gathered from different countries was analyzed using correlation and regression analyses. It was observed that KEI and GEI feature a momentous effect on QOL, while innovation index and total early stage entrepreneurship improve it.

34448 ■ *"Interest Soaring In 44North Business Competition" in Business First of Buffalo (Vol. 30, February 21, 2014, No. 23, pp. 3)*
Pub: American City Business Journals, Inc.
Contact: Whitney Shaw, President
Released: February 21, 2014. **Description:** The 43North business plan competition has attracted over 200 applications from entrepreneurs coming from various sectors like e-commerce, clean technology,

and advanced manufacturing. The winners of the competition will qualify for the Start-Up New York program which eliminates the tax burden for qualified firms.

34449 ■ International Entrepreneurship: Starting, Developing, and Managing a Global Venture
Pub: Pine Forge Press
Contact: Blaise R. Simqu, President
Ed: Robert D. Hisrich. Released: Second Edition. Price: $79, paperback. Description: International entrepreneurship combines the aspects of domestic entrepreneurship along with other disciplines, including anthropology, economics, geography, history, jurisprudence, and language. Availability: Print.

34450 ■ "The Introvert's Guide to Entrepreneurship: How to Become a Successful Entrepreneur as an Introvert"
Pub: CreateSpace
Contact: Daren Giles, President
Released: October 15, 2014. Price: $9.99 paperback. Description: The five main strengths and the five harmful weaknesses for an introvert wishing to become an entrepreneur are listed. Three key strategies to help an introvert run his new company are examined. Five key attributes of a good business partner are considered. Management tips are also shared for introverted leaders.

34451 ■ "Inverse Economics" in Entrepreneur (May 2014)
Pub: Entrepreneur Media Inc.
Released: May 2014. Description: The bullish economy provides an opportunity for U.S. entrepreneurs to launch their startups because that is the time when venture capitalists start to take notice. A depressed economic downturn increases the number of breakthrough startups to invest in. Venture capitalists and angel investors become more open to backing a startup when the economy declines. Entrepreneurs should consider launching their business when their finances are stable and they feel safe because there will be fewer competitors fighting for investors.

34452 ■ "Lean Branding"
Pub: O'Reilly and Associates Inc.
Contact: Tim O'Reilly, President
E-mail: tim@oreilly.com
Released: September 17, 2014. Price: $29.99. Description: Branding your startup is essential to any small business success. A toolkit is provided to help build dynamic brands that generate conversion. Over 100 do-it-yourself branding tactics and case studies as well as step-by-step instructions for building and measuring 25 essential brand strategy ingredients, from logo design to demonstration day pitches.

34453 ■ Lean In
Pub: Knopf Publishing/Random House
Ed: Sheryl Sandberg. Released: March 11, 2013. Price: $24.95, U.S.; $12.99. Description: The chief operating officer at Facebook examines women's progress in achieving leadership roles and provides solutions to help women fully achieve their goals. Availability: PrintE-book.

34454 ■ Legal Guide for Starting & Running a Small Business
Pub: Nolo
Contact: Ralph Warner, Chief Executive Officer
Ed: Fred S. Steingold. Released: April 2013. Price: $31.99; $27.99. Description: Legal issues any small business owner needs to know for starting and running a successful business are outlined. Availability: PrintE-book; PDF.

34455 ■ Life Entrepreneurs: Ordinary People Creating Extraordinary Lives
Pub: Jossey-Bass
Ed: Christopher Gergen, Gregg Vanourek. Released: February 2008. Price: $24.95, hardcover; $16.99. Description: Consultants Christopher Gergen and Gregg Vanourek present the basic principles for becoming a successful entrepreneur: recognizing opportunity, taking risks, and innovation. Availability: PrintE-book.

34456 ■ "The Little Black Book of Fitness Business Success"
Pub: Fitness Consulting Group
Released: February 1, 2012. Price: $19.95 paperback. Description: Tools and strategies into the essential areas for entrepreneurial fitness professionals, focusing on starting and improving a fitness business.

34457 ■ "Live & Learn: Gordon Stollery" in Canadian Business (Vol. 81, December 19, 2007, No. 1, pp. 76)
Pub: Rogers Media Inc.
Contact: Tony Viner, President
Ed: Michelle Magnan. Description: Gordon Stollery of Highpine Oil and Gas Ltd. talks about being a hard-rock geologist and his move to start his oil and gas business. Other aspects of his business career are discussed.

34458 ■ "Looking To Leap?" in Black Enterprise (Vol. 38, January 2008, No. 6, pp. 64)
Pub: Earl G. Graves Publishing Co. Inc.
Contact: Earl G. Graves, Jr., President
Ed: Tennille M. Robinson. Description: Websites and organizations providing resources for any young entrepreneur wishing to start a new business are outlined.

34459 ■ Low Risk, High Reward: Practical Prescriptions for Starting and Growing Your Business
Pub: R & R Publishing
Ed: Bob Reiss, Jeffrey L. Cruikshank. Released: December 01, 2000. Price: $19.95, paperback. Description: Successful entrepreneur teaches others about creating, growing and maintaining a successful business venture. The book offers a step-by-step approach to helping entrepreneurs minimize the risk involved in a new business while examining the skills and resources needed to succeed. Availability: Print.

34460 ■ Making a Living Without a Job: Winning Ways for Creating Work That You Love
Pub: Random House Publishing Group
Contact: John Irwing, Editor
Ed: Barbara J. Winter. Released: August 09, 2010. Price: $16, Paperback. Description: For all Americans who are out of work, soon to be out of work, or wishing to be freed from unrewarding work: here is the must-have book that shows how to make a living by working when, where, and how you want to work.

34461 ■ Mommy Millionaire: How I Turned My Kitchen Table Idea Into a Million Dollars and How You Can, Too!
Pub: Palgrave Macmillan
Contact: Lisa Dunn, Manager
E-mail: l.dunn@palgrave.com
Ed: Kim Lavine. Released: February 2008. Price: $17.99, paperback; $7.99. Description: Advice, secrets and lessons for making a million dollars from a mom who turned her kitchen into a successful business; tools cover developing and patenting an idea, cold calling, trade shows, QVC, big retailers, manufacturing, and raising venture capital. Availability: PrintE-book.

34462 ■ "Moms Mean Business: A Guide to Creating a Successful Company and Happy Life as a Mom Entrepreneur"
Pub: Career Press Inc.
Contact: Ron Fry, President
Released: October 20, 2014. Price: $15.99. Description: Currently, more women are starting new businesses than men and there are 9 million women-owned businesses in the United States; most of these women are also moms. A guide to help women start and run a successful home-based business is presented.

34463 ■ "Mount Laurel Woman Launches Venture Into Children's Used Clothing" in Philadelphia Inquirer (September 17, 2010)
Pub: Philadelphia Media Network
Contact: Robert J. Hall, Chief Executive Officer
Ed: Maria Panaritis. Description: Profile of Jennifer Frisch, stay-at-home mom turned entrepreneur. Frisch started a used-clothing store Once Upon a Child after opening her franchised Plato's Closet, selling unwanted and used baby clothing and accessories at her new shop, while offering used merchandise to teens at Plato's Closet.

34464 ■ The Mousedriver Chronicles: The True-Life Adventures Of Two First-time Entrepreneurs
Pub: The Perseus Books Group
Contact: David Steinberger, President
E-mail: david.steinberger@perseusbooks.com
Ed: John Lusk, Kyle Harrison. Released: April 29, 2009. Price: $16.95; C$21.50. Description: Entrepreneurial voyage through the startup business of two ivy-league business school graduates and the lessons they learned while developing their idea of a computer mouse that looks like a golf driver into the marketplace. The book is an inspiration for those looking to turn an idea into a company. Availability: E-book.

34465 ■ "The New CEO: 185 Easy-To-Set-Up Businesses for Youth and Adult Entrepreneurs"
Pub: CreateSpace
Contact: Daren Giles, President
Released: October 21, 2014. Price: $12.99 paperback. Description: Regardless of age, this book will help anyone wishing to launch and run a small business.

34466 ■ New Venture Creation: Entrepreneurship for the 21st Century with Online Learning Center Access Card
Pub: McGraw-Hill
Ed: Jeffrey A. Timmons; Stephen Spinelli. Released: November 1, 2008. Price: $71.97. Description: A handbook for students that explores all the concepts necessary for successfully launching a new enterprise.

34467 ■ "The Next Generation: African Americans Are Successfully Launching Businesses Earlier In Life" in Black Enterprise (January 2008)
Pub: Earl G. Graves Publishing Co. Inc.
Contact: Earl G. Graves, Jr., President
Ed: Tennille M. Robinson. Description: According to a survey conducted by OPEN, a team dedicated small business at American Express, Generation Y individuals are three times more likely to start their own company. Three African American individuals who did just that are profiled.

34468 ■ Niche and Grow Rich
Ed: Jennifer Basye Sander; Peter Sander. Released: 2003. Description: Consultants share insight to entrepreneurs wishing to find a profitable niche market. Authors write that good niche businesses are easy to start and easy to defend from competitors. They also report that finding a successful niche can attract and maintain good customers who are willing to pay more for unique goods and services.

34469 ■ "No. 64: Scaling the Business Meant Rebuilding a Bridge" in Inc. (Vol. 36, September 2014, No. 7, pp. 48)
Pub: Mansueto Ventures L.L.C.
Contact: John Koten, Chief Executive Officer
Released: September 2014. Description: Profile of Susan Meitner, mortgage industry veteran who founded Centennial Lending Group, a mortgage lending institution. Meitner and her family helped raise the needed $2.5 million to launch the firm in order to provide loans to new customers.

34470 ■ "No. 407: What I Learned in the Military, and What I Had to Unlearn" in Inc. (Vol. 36, September 2014, No. 7, pp. 80)
Pub: Mansueto Ventures L.L.C.
Contact: John Koten, Chief Executive Officer
Released: September 2014. Description: Profile of William Bailey, who served in the U.S. Army as information manager at the U.S. Military Academy at West Point. Bailey discusses his startup firm, Rapier Solutions, a government contractor providing IT, logistics, and social-work expertise. The firm has developed a new survivor outreach system for the U.S. Army.

34471 ■ *"No. 479: SeaSnax Seaweed Snacks"* *in Inc. (Vol. 36, September 2014, No. 7, pp. 44)*
Pub: Mansueto Ventures L.L.C.
Contact: John Koten, Chief Executive Officer
Released: September 2014. **Description:** SeaSnax make a perfect snack for children's lunchboxes. These crispy sheets of seaweed made the 500 Inc. list of outstanding entrepreneurial startups and are now sold in Whole Foods Stores.

34472 ■ *"Office For One: The Sole Proprietor's Survival Guide"*
Pub: CreateSpace
Contact: Daren Giles, President
Released: October 7, 2014. **Price:** $12.95 paperback. **Description:** Over thirty experts offer advice to any entrepreneur wishing to start a business by themselves. Tips and advice on tuning out negativity, maintaining balance and boundaries, handling legal issues and financial challenges, finding and keeping customers, marketing on a small budge, networking, cracking the media code, growing a sustainable vision, and addressing burnouts.

34473 ■ *"Oh, Grow Up" in Entrepreneur (Vol. 35, October 2007, No. 10, pp. 120)*
Pub: Entrepreneur Press
Contact: Perlman Neil, President
Ed: Mark Henricks. **Description:** Most entrepreneurs are overwhelmed with the idea of expanding their business, forgetting to strategically plan the process of business growth. However, there are certain steps entrepreneurs must take in turning a startup business into a bigger venture. Eight steps to growing a business, such as asking for advice and deciding on a focus are presented.

34474 ■ *"One of the Best Ways to Build Wealth...Is to Take Equity In a Company" in Business Journal (Vol. 31, May 2, 2014, No. 49, pp. 9)*
Pub: American City Business Journals
Released: May 2, 2014. **Description:** Entrepreneur Abir Sen reveals that he was not planning to start a business after selling Bloom Health, but he soon discovered that he wanted to do something productive. He believes that the traditional model of employer-paid health care insurance is dying. His opinion on health care entrepreneurial activity in Minnesota is also examined.

34475 ■ *101 Small Business Ideas for Under $5000*
Pub: John Wiley & Sons Inc.
Contact: Stephen M. Smith, President
Released: April 2005. **Price:** $29; $18.99. **Description:** Entrepreneurial ideas for starting companies that can be run part-time or full-time, and some as an absentee owner. **Availability:** PrintE-book.

34476 ■ *Overcoming Barriers to Entrepreneurship in the United States*
Pub: Lexington Books
Contact: Serena Leigh Kromback, Director
Ed: Diana Furchtgott-Roth. **Released:** March 28, 2008. **Price:** $32.99, Paperback; £19.95, Paperback. **Description:** Real and perceived barriers to the founding and running of small businesses in America are discussed. Each chapter outlines how policy and economic environments can hinder business owners and offers tips to overcome these obstacles. Starting with venture capital access in Silicon Valley during the Internet bubble, the book goes on to question the link between personal wealth and entrepreneurship, examines how federal tax rates affect small business creation and destruction, explains the low rate of self-employment among Mexican immigrants, and suggests ways pension coverage can be increased in small businesses.

34477 ■ *"Passion Is the Key to Accomplishment" in South Florida Business Journal (Vol. 35, August 15, 2014, No. 3, pp. 11)*
Pub: American City Business Journals
Released: August 15, 2014. **Description:** Metro 1 president and CEO, Tony Cho, made his name by shaping neighborho9ods and large-scale urban projects in Miami, Florida. Cho says he got his first job when he was 11 years old working with a maintenance crew. Cho started his real estate firm during the economic downturn and believes surviving during the recession is his greatest entrepreneurial accomplishment to date.

34478 ■ *"Paul Hawken and Other Top Lumnaries to Participate in Green Business BASE CAMP in Los Angeles" in Benzinga.com (April 19, 2012)*
Pub: Benzinga.com
Contact: Kyle Bazzy, President
Ed: Aaron Wise. **Description:** Paul Hawken, environmentalist, entrepreneur and author, is one of many people participating in the Green Business BASE CAMP, a four-day workshop for green business and cleantech entrepreneurs. The event will be held in Los Angeles, California from May 31 through June 3, 2012. Insider guidance will be offered to early-stage entrepreneurs seeking to compete within this sector.

34479 ■ *"Places for People Who Want to Make Things" in Philadelphia Business Journal (Vol. 28, May 4, 2012, No. 23, pp. 1)*
Pub: American City Business Journal
Description: Entrepreneurs in Philadelphia, Pennsylvania have been opening businesses and nonprofits for people who have the urge to work in wood, sculpt or even make robots. Their sudden proliferation has provided people who like making things with their hands but can't afford the tools or don't have the space in which to do it where they live.

34480 ■ *Prepare to Be a Teen Millionaire*
Pub: Health Communications, Inc.
Contact: Peter Vegso, President
Ed: Kimberly Spinks-Burleson, Robyn Collins. **Released:** March 03, 2008. **Price:** $13.56, Members, paperback; $16.95, Nonmembers, paperback. **Description:** Business reference for any teenager wishing to become a successful entrepreneur; advice is given from successful teenage millionaires. Topics covered include: choosing a business name, type, and location; use of the Internet; legal issues; branding, sales, and marketing; funding and financial management; return on investment; retirement; development of a sound business plan; and certification for minority or women-owned companies. **Availability:** Print.

34481 ■ *The Professional Personal Chef: The Business of Doing Business as a Personal Chef*
Pub: John Wiley & Sons Inc.
Contact: Stephen M. Smith, President
Ed: Candy Wallace, Greg Forte. **Released:** February 2007. **Price:** $78.95, hardcover. **Description:** Resources for starting a personal chef business are covered. **Availability:** Print.

34482 ■ *"The Responsible Entrepreneur: Four Game-Changing Archetypes for Founders, Leaders, and Impact Investors"*
Pub: Jossey-Bass
Contact: William J. Pesce, President
Released: July 14, 2014. **Price:** $28.00. **Description:** Responsible entrepreneurs are special people who are able to transform industries as well as society. They challenge and refine cultural assumptions, laws, regulations, along with the processes of governance. They think beyond the status quo of entrepreneurship. Sanford provides the makings for this new type of business leadership, describing the ways in which any entrepreneur can achieve a higher level of work. Four archetypes are cover to help managers and entrepreneurs start and scale any business venture.

34483 ■ *"SABER Research Institute's Steve Nivin" in San Antonio Business Journal (Vol. 28, April 4, 2014, No. 8, pp. 6)*
Pub: American City Business Journals
Released: April 4, 2014. **Description:** SABER Research Institute director and chief economist, Steve Nivin, shares his views on the potential expansion of Google Fiber's broadband Internet network to San Antonio, Texas. Nivin says Google Fiber should encourage entrepreneurs to start businesses in San Antonio. He also says the chances of fast growth companies being created in the city is enhanced with Google Fiber.

34484 ■ *Seed-Stage Venture Investing: An Insider's Guide to Start-Ups for Scientists, Engineers, and Investors*
Ed: William L. Robbins, Jonathan Lasch. **Released:** November 01, 2011. **Price:** $39.96. **Description:** Ideas for starting, funding, and managing technology-based firms, also known as, venture capitalists, are featured. **Availability:** Print.

34485 ■ *"Self-Employment: What To Know To Be Your Own Boss" in Occupational Outlook Quarterly (Vol. 58, Summer 2014, No. 2, pp. 2)*
Pub: Government Printing Office
Released: Summer 2014. **Description:** Information is presented to help would-be entrepreneurs decide if self-employment is for them. The challenges, rewards, and fastest growth sectors are discussed. Whether to incorporate or not is examined, as well as the skills and knowledge to become a successful small business owner is explored.

34486 ■ *"The Self Starting Entrepreneurs Handbook"*
Pub: CreateSpace
Contact: Daren Giles, President
Released: September 24, 2014. **Price:** $17.95 paperback. **Description:** Information for starting a business is provided. Advice is given for writing a business plan, naming your new business, obtaining a business license if required, and building a marketing strategy for entrepreneurs.

34487 ■ *"Should You Choose a Lump-Sum Pension Payout? Here's How Entrepreneur Ramona Harper Decided" in Black Enterprise (Vol. 44, June 2014, No. 10, pp. 27)*
Pub: Earl G. Graves Publishing Co. Inc.
Contact: Earl G. Graves, Jr., President
Released: June 2014. **Description:** Entrepreneur, Ramona Harper, chose a lump sum payout of her pension in order to start a new business. She used $110,000 to start her accessories boutique and put the remaining money into a small business 401(k), which helped her avoid a large tax. Tips to help individuals decide the best way to collect their pension are provided.

34488 ■ *"Slow-Down Startups Hot" in Austin Business JournalInc. (Vol. 28, September 12, 2008, No. 26, pp. 1)*
Pub: American City Business Journals
Ed: Sandra Zaragoza. **Description:** A number of entrepreneurs from Austin, Texas are starting their own small business despite the economic slowdown. The Small Business Development Program in Austin has seen a 50 percent increase in the demand for its services in 2008 as compared to demand in 2007. Other details about the entrepreneurship trend are discussed.

34489 ■ *Small Business, Big Life: Five Steps to Creating a Great Life with Your Own Small Business*
Pub: Thomas Nelson Inc.
Contact: Michael S. Hyatt, President
Ed: Louis Barajas. **Released:** May 01, 2007. **Price:** $22.99, hardcover. **Description:** Barajas describes his and his father's independent entrepreneurial paths and suggests an inspirational approach to business that relies on four personal greatness cornerstones: truth, responsibility, awareness, and courage, and on keeping in mind your vision and your team's needs. The book provides a new look at achieving a work/life balance. **Availability:** Print.

34490 ■ *Small Business for Dummies*
Pub: John Wiley & Sons Inc.
Contact: Stephen M. Smith, President
Ed: Eric Tyson, Jim Schell. **Released:** 4th Edition. **Price:** $22.95; $14.99. **Description:** Guidebook for anyone wanting to start or grow a small business; topics include information financing, budgeting, marketing, management and more. **Availability:** PrintE-book.

34491 ■ *Small Business Entrepreneur: Launching a New Venture and Managing a Business on a Day-to-Day Basis*
Ed: Rory Burke. **Released:** February 2006. **Price:** $19.95. **Description:** Comprehensive guide examining the management skills required to launch and run a small business.

34492 ■ *Small Business Management*
Pub: John Wiley & Sons Inc.
Contact: Stephen M. Smith, President
Ed: Margaret Burlingame. **Released:** March 2007. **Price:** $44.95. **Description:** Advice for starting and running a small business as well as information on the value and appeal of small businesses, is given. Topics include budgets, taxes, inventory, ethics, e-commerce, and current laws.

34493 ■ *Small Business Savvy*
Ed: Norma J. Rist; Katina Z. Jones. **Released:** 2002. **Description:** Advice is given to women wishing to start their own companies using guidance and real-world examples to help position themselves for future growth. Tips to survive through a bad economic environment, breaking into a market, working with less money, accepting change, and ways to balance success with personal life are explored.

34494 ■ *The Small Business Start-Up Kit*
Pub: Nolo
Contact: Ralph Warner, Chief Executive Officer
Ed: Peri Pakroo. **Released:** February 2014. **Price:** $23.99; $20.99. **Description:** Entrepreneurial advice for launching a new business. Topics include compliance with state regulations, sole proprietorships, partnerships, corporations, limited liability companies, as well as accounting and tax information. **Availability:** PrintE-book.

34495 ■ *The Small Business Start-Up Workbook: A Step-by-Step Guide to Starting the Business You've Dreamed Of*
Pub: How To Books
Contact: Giles Lewis, Publisher
Ed: Cheryl D. Rickman. **Released:** May 01, 2005. **Price:** £11.04; £12.99, Nonmembers. **Description:** Book provides practical exercises for starting a small business, including marketing and management strategies. **Availability:** Online.

34496 ■ *Small Business Survival Guide*
Ed: Cliff Ennico. **Price:** $12.95. **Description:** Small business expert provides strategies to start a company and survive in the 21st Century. He shows small business owners how to succeed despite challenges that can defeat any firm. His advice covers suppliers; customers and contractors; competitors and creditors; spouses, family and friends; as well as the ways lawyers, accountants and other can steal an entrepreneur's success. Ennico also describes how startups can comply with local regulations.

34497 ■ *Small Business Tool Kit*
Ed: Linda M. Magoon. **Released:** April 10, 2010. **Price:** $40. **Description:** When starting a business, new managers and entrepreneurs require many resources to get the company up and running successfully. This book covers a wide range of topics that are critical for any new business owner.

34498 ■ *So You Want to Start a Business?*
Ed: Edward D. Hess; Charles Goetz. **Released:** August 30, 2008. **Price:** $18.99. **Description:** Over sixty percent of Americans say they would like to own their own business and more than five million business startups are launched annually. However, fifty to seventy percent of new businesses fail. This book identifies the eight mistakes that cause these business failures and offers entrepreneurs the knowledge, tools, templates, strategies, and hands-on how-to advice needed to avoid these errors and succeed.

34499 ■ *"Some Good Earners: Preparing Prison Inmates to Start Businesses Upon Their Release" in Inc. (Vol. 31, January-February 2009, No. 1)*
Pub: Mansueto Ventures L.L.C.
Contact: John Koten, Chief Executive Officer
Ed: Mike Hofman. **Description:** Prison Entrepreneurship Program (PEP) is a nonprofit organization that works with the Texas Department of Criminal Justice to teach entrepreneurship to prison inmates. Profiled is Hans Becker, owner of Armadillo Tree and Shrub in Dallas; Becker studied the PEP program while serving five years in prison and started his successful company when released.

34500 ■ *Soul Proprietor: 101 Lessons from a Lifestyle Entrepreneur*
Ed: Jane Pollak. **Released:** September 2004. **Description:** More than 100 tips and stores to inspire and guide any would-be entrepreneur to earn a living from a favorite hobby or passion.

34501 ■ *The Spiritual Entrepreneur*
Pub: New Paradigm Media
Ed: Robert Morgen. **Released:** January 1, 2010. **Price:** $16.95. **Description:** Step-by-step guide to start a small business and then use that business to create various streams of passive income to support yourself and charities is presented.

34502 ■ *"Spring Round a Dud for StartUp Kitchen" in Washington Business Journal (Vol. 32, March 21, 2014, No. 49, pp. 8)*
Pub: American City Business Journals
Released: March 21, 2014. **Description:** The latest round of the StartUp Kitchen culinary business incubation program has been canceled due to a lack of eligible candidates. The program, a partnership between Think Local First DC and the nonprofit organization Nurish, received only seven applications compared to the usual 15-25 would-be entrepreneurs applying.

34503 ■ *"Staking Claim as Hub for Design" in Providence Business News (Vol. 28, March 17, 2014, No. 50, pp. 1)*
Pub: American City Business Journals
Released: March 17, 2014. **Description:** Providence, Rhode Island is expected to have two startup accelerators in 2014, even though the city lacks a large technology and venture capital presence. The Providence Design Forward accelerator is a partnership with Rhode Island School of Design and will focus on architecture and interior design entrepreneurship. It is modeled after Boston's MassChallenge.

34504 ■ *Start Business in California, 3E*
Ed: John J. Talamo. **Released:** July 2006. **Price:** $24.95. **Description:** Information required for starting any business in California.

34505 ■ *"Start-Up Pointers" in Inside Business (Vol. 13, September-October 2011, No. 5, pp. Y3)*
Pub: Great Lakes Publishing Co.
Description: Four tips to help entrepreneurs with startup firms are provided by Youngstown Business Incubator.

34506 ■ *"Start-Up! So You Want to Be an Entrepreneur. So You Want to Be Rich"*
Pub: Amazon Digital Services
Released: October 10, 2014. **Price:** $14.99 Kindle. **Description:** Entrepreneur offers a guide for startups. Jim Lewis shares the innovative thinking that helped him launch, grow and sell two successful high-tech companies.

34507 ■ *Start Your Own Business, Fifth Edition*
Pub: Entrepreneur Press
Contact: Perlman Neil, President
Ed: Rieva Lesonsky. **Released:** October 01, 2010. **Price:** $24.95, Paperback. **Description:** Author and the staff of Entrepreneur Magazine provide business resources and information for starting a successful business. The book guides you through the first three years of ownership and provides work sheets and checklists.

34508 ■ *Starting Green: An Ecopreneur's Toolkit for Starting a Green Business From Business Plans to Profits*
Pub: Entrepreneur Press
Contact: Perlman Neil, President
Ed: Glenn E. Croston. **Released:** 2009. **Description:** Entrepreneur and scientist outline green business essentials and helps uncover eco-friendly business opportunities, build a sustainable business plan, and gain the competitive advantage.

34509 ■ *Starting an iPhone Application Business for Dummies*
Pub: Wiley Publishing Inc.
Contact: William J. Pesce, President
Ed: Aaron Nicholson, Joel Elad, Damien Stolarz. **Released:** October 2009. **Price:** $24.95, paperback; $16.99. **Description:** Ways to create a profitable, sustainable business developing and marketing iPhone applications are profiled. **Availability:** PrintE-book.

34510 ■ *Starting a Successful Business in Canada*
Pub: Self-Counsel Press Inc.
Ed: Jack D. James. **Price:** $12.99. **Description:** Provides a framework for entrepreneurs launching a new business in Canada. **Availability:** Electronic publishing.

34511 ■ *"Starting Up All Over Again: Alex Bogusky Backs Bootcamp for Advertising Startup" in Denver Business Journal (Vol. 65, February 7, 2014, No. 39, pp. 8)*
Pub: American City Business Journals
Released: February 7, 2014. **Description:** Once called the Elvis of advertising, Alex Bogusky is now launching a new startup named 'Boomtown' with an aim to cultivate a new generation of advertising, marketing, design, and media related tech companies. The end goal of boomtown will be to figure out the trend in which media as well as the relationship between brands and people is going.

34512 ■ *StartingUp Now Facilitator Guide*
Ed: L. Jenkins. **Released:** September 11, 2011. **Price:** $29.95. **Description:** Guide for those teaching entrepreneurship using StartingUp Now; the guide provides 24 lesson plans for each of the 24 steps/chapters in the book.

34513 ■ *"The Startup Blueprint: The Young Entrepreneur's Step-by-Step Guide To Starting Your Own Business"*
Pub: CreateSpace
Contact: Daren Giles, President
Released: October 21, 2014. **Price:** $8.99 paperback. **Description:** Careful planning and smart execution is required to start a new business. More than 90 percent of new business fail with the first three years. Practical tips and advice are offered to help young entrepreneurs successfully start a new business.

34514 ■ *"Startup Communities: Building an Entrepreneurial Ecosystem in Your City"*
Pub: John Wiley & Sons Inc.
Contact: Stephen M. Smith, President
Released: September 6, 2012. **Price:** $26.95. **Description:** A guide for building supportive entrepreneurial communities that drive innovation and small business energy. Brad Feld, entrepreneur turned-venture capitalist describes what it takes to create an entrepreneurial community in any city, at any time. He details the four critical principles required to form a sustainable startup community.

34515 ■ *Startups That Work: Surprising Research on What Makes or Breaks a New Company*
Pub: Penguin Group USA
Contact: Phyllis Grann, President
Ed: Joel Kurtzman, Glenn Rifkin. **Released:** October 2005. **Price:** $25.95. **Availability:** Print.

34516 ■ *"StartX Med Prescribed for Innovation" in Silicon Valley/San Jose Business Journal (Vol. 30, June 8, 2012, No. 11, pp. 1)*
Pub: American City Business Journal
Description: StartX Med is a program started by entrepreneur Divya Nag along with Stanford student-led nonprofit StartX to help medical startups. Under the program, entrepreneurs will have access to wet and dry laboratory space, animal testing and information related to US Food and Drug Adminstration regulations.

34517 ■ *"Steal Your Success" in Canadian Business (Vol. 87, July 2014, No. 7, pp. 64)*
Pub: George Media Inc.
Released: July 2014. **Description:** The act of borrowing an idea to start a business can be critical to success when its done effectively. Imitation is as important as innovation and entrepreneurs need to realize that great ideas are often borrowed.

34518 ■ *Steps to Small Business Start-Up: Everything You Need to Know to Turn Your Idea into a Successful Business*
Pub: Kaplan Books
Ed: Linda Pinson, Jerry Jinnett. **Released:** 2006. **Price:** $22.95; C$29. **Description:** Tips for starting and running a new company are presented.

34519 ■ *Structuring Your Business*
Pub: Adams Media Corp.
Contact: Scott Watrous, President
E-mail: bobadams@adamsmedia.com
Ed: Michele Cagan. **Released:** 2004. **Price:** $19.95. **Description:** Accountant and author shares insight into starting a new company. The guide assists entrepreneurs through the process, whether it is a corporation, an LLC, a sole proprietorship, or a partnership. Tax codes, accounting practices and legislation affecting every business as well as tips on managing finances are among the topics covered.

34520 ■ *"Survival of the Fittest" in Black Enterprise (November 1, 2007)*
Pub: Earl G. Graves Publishing Co. Inc.
Contact: Earl G. Graves, Jr., President
Ed: Tennille M. Robinson. **Description:** Black Enterprise has developed the Small Business Success Guide for prospective and current entrepreneurs.

34521 ■ *Swimming Against the Stream: Launching Your Business and Making Your Life*
Ed: Tim Waterstone. **Released:** March 2007. **Price:** $17.99. **Description:** Ten rules for launching a new business are outlined using real-life experiences.

34522 ■ *"T-Shirt Business: How To Work From Home Starting your Own Online Business In A Popular Teespring Niche!"*
Pub: Amazon Digital Services
Released: September 12, 2014. **Price:** $5.99. **Description:** Advice is given to launch a T-shirt business without investing a lot of money. Profile of Teespring T-shirts, a company that helps entrepreneurs start a home-based online store, is provided. It teaches how to sell, entice a niche, copyright infringement information, competition, social media marketing and advertising, and more.

34523 ■ *"Take the Money and Run" in Entrepreneur (September 2014)*
Pub: Entrepreneur Media Inc.
Released: September 2014. **Description:** Startup founders are encouraged to ask for more than they think they will need when raising capital. The tendency to think small when it comes to capital or staging rounds to preserve ownership is a mistake for founders. Securing a large amount of capital in the first round could help save the time and costs associated with raising the next round of funds. Venture capitalists welcome founders who ask for more money because they prefer to go bigger on a single bet and their focus is always on valuation.

34524 ■ *Technology Ventures: From Idea to Enterprise*
Pub: McGraw-Hill Higher Education
Contact: Edward Stanford, President
E-mail: ed_stanford@mcgraw-hill.com
Ed: Richard C. Dorf, Thomas H. Byers. **Price:** $181.67, retail; $136.25, wholesale. **Description:** Textbook examining technology entrepreneurship on a global basis; technology management theories are explored. **Availability:** Print.

34525 ■ *Technology Ventures: From Idea to Enterprise*
Pub: McGraw-Hill Higher Education
Contact: Edward Stanford, President
E-mail: ed_stanford@mcgraw-hill.com
Ed: Richard C. Dorf, Thomas H. Byers, Andrew Nelson. **Released:** 2nd Edition. **Description:** An action-approached through the use of examples, exercises,

cases, sample business plans, and recommended sources helps entrepreneurs start and run a technology-base small business.

34526 ■ *"TEDx Talk Puts the Pieces Together" in Philadelphia Business Journal (Vol. 33, April 4, 2014, No. 8, pp. 6)*
Pub: American City Business Journals
Released: April 4, 2014. **Description:** Gabriel Investments managing partner, Richard Vague, shares his views about entrepreneurs wanting to start a company. Vague says they should be relentless because it takes a long time to start and run a business and it is a challenge to recruit customers and grow rapidly. He also states his experience as an entrepreneur enables him to give advice and put things into perspective for the people he mentors.

34527 ■ *There's a Business In Every Woman: A 7-Step Guide to Discovering, Starting, and Building the Business of Your Dreams*
Pub: Ballantine/Random House
Ed: Ann M. Holmes. **Released:** March 25, 2008. **Price:** $16, paperback. **Description:** Economist and workplace expert provides a no-nonsense guide detailing seven steps to creating a successful business, based on her own experiences and on those of her employees. She highlights the importance of understanding and using your core competencies, building an organized infrastructure from the start, and planning for and managing your growth. **Availability:** Print.

34528 ■ *"Think of Start-Ups as Shots On Goal" in (Vol. 90, June 2012, No. 6, pp. 38)*
Pub: Harvard Business Review Press
Contact: Peter E. Walsh, Director
Ed: Robert E. Litan. **Released:** June 2012. **Description:** The importance of start-up businesses to the nation's economic recovery is emphasized. Comprehensive legislation is necessary to improve start-up access to opportunity and talent.

34529 ■ *"Time for a Leap Of Faith?" in Women Entrepreneur (November 18, 2008)*
Ed: Cynthia McKay. **Description:** Starting a new business, despite the downturn in the economy, can prove to be a successful endeavor if one has the time, energy and most importantly a good idea.

34530 ■ *The Toilet Paper Entrepreneur: The Tell-It-Like-It-Is Guide to Cleaning Up In Business, Even If You Are At the End of Your Roll*
Pub: Obsidian Launch LLC
Ed: Mike Michalowicz. **Price:** $24.95. **Description:** The founder of three multimillion-dollar companies, including Obsidian Launch, a company that partners with first-time entrepreneurs to grow their concepts into industry leaders.

34531 ■ *"Top 25 Graduate Programs" in Entrepreneur (Vol. 35, November 2007, No. 11, pp. 92)*
Description: List of the top twenty-five graduate entrepreneurship programs of different colleges and universities in the U.S. for 2007, as ranked by Entrepreneur Magazine and the Princeton Review, is presented.

34532 ■ *"Top 25 Undergrad Programs" in Entrepreneur (Vol. 35, November 2007, No. 11, pp. 88)*
Description: List of the top twenty-five undergraduate entrepreneurship programs of different colleges and universities in the U.S. for 2007, as ranked by Entrepreneur Magazine and the Princeton Review, is highlighted.

34533 ■ *"Top of the Class" in Entrepreneur (Vol. 35, November 2007, No. 11, pp. 82)*
Pub: Entrepreneur Press
Contact: Perlman Neil, President
Ed: Nichole L. Torres. **Description:** Education in entrepreneurship is being pursued by many students and it is important to understand what entrepreneurship program fits you. Aspiring entrepreneurs should

also ask about the program's focus. Considerations searched for by students regarding the particular school they chose to study entrepreneurship are discussed.

34534 ■ *"The Toughest Sell" in Inc. (Vol. 36, September 2014, No. 7, pp. 69)*
Pub: Mansueto Ventures L.L.C.
Contact: John Koten, Chief Executive Officer
Released: September 2014. **Description:** Finding top talent for a new startup company is challenging. It is suggested that entrepreneurs should sell the challenges faced by the new firm when hiring new workers. Startup recruiting is examined.

34535 ■ *"Travel In Style" in Washington Business Journal (Vol. 32, March 28, 2014, No. 50, pp. 5)*
Pub: American City Business Journals
Released: March 28, 2014. **Description:** Entrepreneur, Any Seligman, launched the Royal Sprinter Bus Service, which will operate twice daily between Washington DC and midtown Manhattan. The bus service will commence on April 11, 2014 and will cost $90 each way.

34536 ■ *"Troy Patent Law Firm Launches Rent-Free Tech Incubator" in Crain's Detroit Business (Vol. 25, June 8, 2009, No. 23, pp. 4)*
Pub: Crain Communications Inc. - Detroit
Contact: Keith Crain, Chairman
Ed: Tom Henderson. **Description:** Young Basile Hanlon MacFarlane & Helmholdt PC, a patent law firm located in Troy, Michigan has created a small, rent-free technology incubator on site. The incubator will be called North Woodward Tech Incubator and has room for four or five startups. The incubator is for the earliest or pre-seed stage for entrepreneurs who have not yet gotten significant investment capital.

34537 ■ *Trump University Entrepreneurship 101: How to Turn Your Idea Into a Money Machine*
Pub: John Wiley & Sons Inc.
Contact: Stephen M. Smith, President
Ed: Michael E. Gordon. **Released:** Second Edition. **Price:** $24.95, hardcover; $16.99. **Description:** Current and expanded edition of the Trump guide to starting a business where Trump teams up with Professor Michael Gordon to show how to take a dream and turn it into a successful enterprise. **Availability:** PrintE-book.

34538 ■ *Ultimate Startup Directory: Expert Advice and 1,500 Great Startup Ideas*
Pub: Entrepreneur Press
Contact: Perlman Neil, President
Ed: James Stephenson. **Description:** Startup opportunities in over 30 industries are given, along with information on investment, earning potential, skills, legal requirements and more.

34539 ■ *"UM-Dearborn to Launch Program for Entrepreneurs" in Crain's Detroit Business (Vol. 24, April 14, 2008, No. 15, pp. 7)*
Pub: Crain Communications Inc.
Contact: Rance E. Crain, President
Ed: Chad Halcom. **Description:** Starting this fall the University of Michigan-Dearborn will begin its Product Realization and Technology Commercialization Program for entrepreneurs and innovators with lab-tested, high-technology products. Ultimately, 20 businesses will each work with the university in creating a customer base, commercializing a new high-tech product or process and connecting with venture capitalists who may invest in the new companies.

34540 ■ *Upstarts! How GenY Entrepreneurs Are Rocking the World of Business and 8 Ways You Can Profit from Their Success*
Pub: The McGraw-Hill Companies
Ed: Donna Fenn. **Released:** September 08, 2009. **Price:** $25.95, hardback. **Description:** An inside glance at the GenY startup companies that are changing the way the world conducts business. **Availability:** Print.

34541 ■ "Want Capital? Avoid These 7 Mistakes" in Birmingham Business Journal (Vol. 31, March 7, 2014, No. 10, pp. 10)

Pub: American City Business Journals, Inc.

Contact: Whitney Shaw, President

Released: March 7, 2014. Description: Advice to entrepreneurs to help secure capital for their small business is given. Entrepreneurs should not approach investors prior to having a strong management team or great business potential. It is important to comply with all federal rules and regulations.

34542 ■ Weekend Small Business Start

Ed: Mark Warda. Released: June 2007. Price: $19.95. Description: Information for starting a new business is presented.

34543 ■ What No One Ever Tells You About Starting Your Own Business: Real-Life Start-Up Advice from 101 Successful Entrepreneurs

Pub: Kaplan Publishing

Contact: Julie Marshall, Director

E-mail: julie.marshall@kaplan.com

Ed: Jan Norman. Released: July 2004. Price: $18.95. Description: From planning to marketing, advice is given to entrepreneurs starting new companies. s. Availability: Print.

34544 ■ "Where the Next Big Thing Lives In Our Nation's Research Labs. Hard Part: Turning Scientists Into Entrepreneurs" in Inc. (Vol. 34, September 2012, No. 7, pp. 43)

Pub: Mansueto Ventures L.L.C.

Contact: John Koten, Chief Executive Officer

Ed: Steve Blank. Released: September 2012. Description: Steve Blank, former entrepreneur, was invited to speak to the National Science Foundation's new rogram called Innovation Corps. The program is designed to help identify and commercialize research projects and involves mentoring from entrepreneurs, venture capitalists and technology developers.

34545 ■ "Why High Confidence Is Crucial for Entrepreneurs; It Helps Them Start Businesses, Persist In the Face of Ambiguity and Failure, and Remain Poised In Meeting Challenges" in Gallup Business Journal (July 17, 2014)

Pub: Gallup Press

Released: July 17, 2014. Description: Confidence is the key for entrepreneurs when starting new businesses, it helps them persist in the face of ambiguity and failure and to remain ready to meet any challenges.

34546 ■ Working for Yourself: An Entrepreneur's Guide to the Basics

Pub: Kogan Page, Limited

Contact: Philip Kogan, Chairman of the Board

Ed: Jonathan Reuvid. Released: June 03, 2009. Price: £12.99. Description: Guide for starting a new business venture, focusing on raising financing, legal and tax issues, marketing, information technology, and site location. Availability: Print.

34547 ■ You Can Do It Too: The 20 Essential Things Every Budding Entrepreneur Should Know

Pub: Kogan Page, Limited

Contact: Philip Kogan, Chairman of the Board

Ed: Rachel Bridge. Released: May 10, 2010. Price: £9.99, Paperback. Description: Collective wisdom of successful entrepreneurs in the form of twenty essential elements to focus on when starting a new company is illustrated by real-life entrepreneurial stories.

34548 ■ You Need to be a Little Bit Crazy: The Truth about Starting and Growing Your Business

Ed: Barry J. Moltz. Description: Offers entrepreneurs and small business owners insight into the ups and downs of running a business.

34549 ■ You Need To Be a Little Crazy

Ed: Barry J. Moltz. Released: December 2008. Price: $14.95. Description: Entrepreneur and investor who has founded several successful startups provides a guide using personal experience to help anyone start a new business.

34550 ■ Your Million-Dollar Idea: From Concept to Marketplace

Ed: Sandy Abrams. Released: March 01, 2010. Price: $14.95. Description: Self-taught entrepreneur provides a 12-step plan to make a new product or service a profitable reality.

34551 ■ "Zero to One: Notes on Startups , or How to Build the Future"

Pub: Random House Publishing Group

Contact: John Irwing, Editor

Released: September 16, 2014. Price: $27.00. Description: Entrepreneur and investor, Peter Thiel, covers new frontiers and new inventions yet to be discovered. Progress can be achieved in more industries than information technology, but thinking for one's self is critical to any entrepreneur in order to start and build a new venture. Tomorrow's leaders will avoid competition and create a unique business that will stand on its own.

ASSOCIATIONS AND OTHER ORGANIZATIONS

34552 ■ Canadian Association of Family Enterprise (CAFE) [Association Canadienne des Entreprises Familiales]

465 Morden Rd., Ste. 112

Oakville, ON, Canada L6K 3W6

Ph: (905)337-8375

Free: 866-849-0099

Fax: (905)337-0572

URL: http://www.cafecanada.ca

Contact: Paul MacDonald, Executive Director

E-mail: paul@cafecanada.ca

Description: Family-owned businesses. Seeks to "encourage, educate, and inform members in disciplines unique to the family business." Fosters increased understanding of the importance of family-owned enterprises in the national economy among government agencies and the public. Gathers and disseminates information of interest to members. Conducts educational and lobbying activities. Provides technical support and advisory services to small businesses in areas including succession planning, taxation, family law, and arbitration and mediation. Maintains network of Family Councils, which serve as a forum for discussion of family and business matters. Scope: business, personal wellness, family business. Founded: 1983. Subscriptions: books. Publications: Family Business Magazine (Quarterly); Family Enterpriser (Quarterly); International Magazine for Family Businesses (Bimonthly); Canadian Association of Family Enterprise--Annual Membership Directory. Educational Activities: Family Business Symposium (Biennial). Awards: Family Enterprise of the Year Award (Annual).

34553 ■ Canadian Innovation Centre (CIC)

Waterloo Research and Technology Park

Accelerator Ctre.

295 Hagey Blvd., Ste. 15

Waterloo, ON, Canada N2L 6R5

Ph: (519)885-5870

Fax: (519)513-2421

Co. E-mail: info@innovationcentre.ca

URL: http://innovationcentre.ca

Contact: Josie Graham, Chief Executive Officer

E-mail: jgraham@innovationcentre.ca

Description: Investors, entrepreneurs, and innovative companies. Promotes innovation in economic activity; seeks to ensure that developers of inventions or innovations receive full credit for their discoveries. Provides support and assistance to members. Conducts research and educational programs. Scope: Offers assistance to individuals and companies for the commercial realization of technological innovation by assessing technical strength, conducting market research, evaluating commercial potential, managing development and testing, assisting in venture planning, providing training and transfer

of technology. Services: Invention Assistance Program: which assesses all aspects of an invention and aids in its development; Marketing Services: which provides market research assistance to small, medium, and large companies. Founded: 1981. Subscriptions: books business records clippings periodicals. Publications: "Getting Going on Innovation part 3 in a series of 4: How a Gating System Can Boost Your Innovation Success," 2008; "Aligning the stages of the commercialization process"; "Overestimating the importance of licensing in fostering the Entrepreneurial University"; "Creating a New Model for Technology Commercialization in the Canadian Context"; "The role of Incubators and Contract research Organizations in growing new biotechnology companies"; "The role of Incubators within a University Environment"; "How the Inno-Gate System Can Boost Your Rates of Innovation Success"; "How entrepreneurs-in-residence increase seed investment rates"; "Technology incubators: Facilitating technology transfer or creating regional wealth"; "Pitchers Bible," Oct, 2007; "Making the Pitch - A Guide," Oct, 2006; "What should I include in my pitch? - A Guide," Oct, 2006. Seminars: Big Companies Can't Innovate; Innovation Awareness Seminar, Mar, 2008; First Steps Seminar, Jun, 2006; Government Assistance: Financing and Risk Solutions in Trying Times; First Steps for Innovators, 2006; Services for Innovation Partners; Innovation Workshop, Jun, 2006; Increasing the Rate of Commercialization of technological innovation: the catalytic role of the commerce agent, Jul, 2006; CFA Workshop; The Role of Universities and Colleges in Creating Canada's Wealth, Feb, 2005; Increasing the commercialization yield of Canada's innovation Efforts by Establishing Customer Pull, Jan, 2005; BCIP Presentation, Nov, 2004.

34554 ■ Enactus Canada

920 Yonge St., Ste. 800

Toronto, ON, Canada M4W 3C7

Ph: (416)304-1566

Free: 800-766-8169

Fax: (416)864-0514

URL: http://www.enactus.ca

Contact: Ian Aitken, Chairman

Description: Young people, business owners, or engaged in entrepreneurial activities. Promotes growth and development of members' business interests. Provides support and services to businesses owned by young people; encourages communication and mutual support among collegiate entrepreneurs. Awards: Alumnus or Alumna of the Year (Annual); Most Improved Award (Annual); Most Supportive Business Advisory Board Member of the Year (Annual); Most Supportive Dean or Department Chair of the Year (Annual); Alumnus/Alumna of the Year Award (Annual); Most Improved Award; Most Supportive Business Advisory Board Member of the Year Award; Most Supportive Dean or Department Chair of the Year Award; Student Leader of the Year Award; Student Leader of the Year (Annual).

34555 ■ Family Business Magazine

465 Morden Rd., Ste. 112

Oakville, ON, Canada L6K 3W6

Ph: (905)337-8375

Free: 866-849-0099

Fax: (905)337-0572

URL: http://www.cafecanada.ca

Contact: Paul MacDonald, Executive Director

E-mail: paul@cafecanada.ca

Released: Quarterly

34556 ■ Family Enterpriser

465 Morden Rd., Ste. 112

Oakville, ON, Canada L6K 3W6

Ph: (905)337-8375

Free: 866-849-0099

Fax: (905)337-0572

URL: http://www.cafecanada.ca

Contact: Paul MacDonald, Executive Director

E-mail: paul@cafecanada.ca

Released: Quarterly

34557 ■ National Federation of Filipino American Associations (NaFFAA)

1322 18th St. NW

Washington, DC 20036-1803

Ph: (202)361-0296
Co. E-mail: inquiries@naffaa-national.org
URL: http://naffaa-national.org
Contact: Eduardo Navarra, Chairperson
Description: Filipino American individuals and organizations. Seeks to promote the interests and well-being of the 3 million Filipinos and Filipino Americans residing in the United States by getting them involved as leaders and participants in United States society. Major programs include citizenship and leadership development, voter education, entrepreneurial training, and community development. **Founded:** 1997.

34558 ■ Network for Teaching Entrepreneurship (NFTE)
120 Wall St., 18th Fl.
New York, NY 10005
URL: http://www.nfte.com
Contact: Steve Mariotti, Founder
Description: Devoted to teaching entrepreneurship education to low-income young people, ages 11 through 18. **Founded:** 1987. **Publications:** *NFTE News* (Quarterly).

REFERENCE WORKS

34559 ■ *The 4 Routes to Entrepreneurial Success*
Pub: Berrett-Koehler Communications Inc.
Contact: Steve Piersanti, President
E-mail: spiersanti@bkpub.com
Ed: John B. Miner. **Price:** $18.95, paperback. **Description:** After researching one hundred successful entrepreneurs, the author discovered there are basically four personality types of entrepreneurs: the personal achiever, the super salesperson, the real manager, and the expert idea generator. **Availability:** Print.

34560 ■ *"10 Talents That Drive Entrepreneurial Success; Gallup Has Identified the Behaviors We Have Consistently Observed In Highly Successful Entrepreneurs"* in Gallup Business Journal (May 6, 2014)
Pub: Gallup Press
Released: May 6, 2014. **Description:** Behaviors observed in highly successful entrepreneurs are defined. The ten talents of successful entrepreneurs are listed.

34561 ■ *The 30-Second Commute*
Pub: McGraw-Hill
Ed: Beverley Williams, Donald Cooper. **Released:** June 22, 2004. **Price:** Rs 1,072.93, Softcover. **Description:** Home-based business owners explain how entrepreneurs can avoid long commutes and high costs of working outside the home by starting a home-based company. Essential steps for launching a successful home-based business are covered, including type of business, legal issues, and writing a business plan. **Availability:** Print.

34562 ■ *32 Ways to Be a Champion in Business*
Pub: Three Rivers Press
Contact: Caroline Sincerbeaux, Editor
E-mail: csincerbeaux@randomhouse.com
Ed: Earvin Magic Johnson. **Released:** December 29, 2009. **Price:** $18.94. **Description:** Earvin Johnson discusses his transition from athlete to entrepreneur and discusses the importance of hard work in order to pursue your dreams of starting and running a successful business.

34563 ■ *"100 Brilliant Companies"* in Entrepreneur (May 2014)
Pub: Entrepreneur Media Inc.
Released: May 2014. **Description:** Entrepreneur magazine annually selects 100 companies, ideas, innovations and applications which the editors feel offer unique, simple and high-tech solutions to various everyday problems. These may include design developments, innovations in wearable gadgets, travel applications and other new ideas which represent 21st Century breakthroughs and thinking

outside the box. The list is divided into ten categories, including Fashion, The Human Factor, and Travel and Transportation.

34564 ■ *"The 2007 Black Book"* in Hawaii Business (Vol. 53, December 2007, No. 6, pp. 43)
Description: Brief biographies of 364 top executives in Hawaii are presented. Information on their educational achievement, membership in associations, hobbies, family, present position and the company they work for are supplied.

34565 ■ *"2008 Woman of the Year Event Filled with Hope and Inspiration"* in Hispanic Business (Vol. 30, July-August 2008, No. 7-8, pp. 58)
Pub: Hispanic Business Inc.
Contact: Jesus Chavarria, President
Ed: Brynne Chappell. **Description:** Brief report on the sixth annual Women of the Year Awards gala which was held at JW Marriott Desert Ridge Resort and Spa is given; 20 women were honored with these awards for their professional contribution, commitment to the advancement of the Hispanic community and involvement with charitable organizations.

34566 ■ *"2009: A Call For Vision"* in Women Entrepreneur (January 28, 2009)
Ed: Elinor Robin. **Description:** Providing exemplary customer service, reducing expenses and creating an out-of-the-box niche are three key factors that will help business survive during this economic crisis. Business owners must see potential where others see failure in order to create new opportunities that may not only allow their business to survive during these times but may actually cause some businesses to thrive despite this economic downturn.

34567 ■ *"2009 Corporate Elite - The Complete List"* in Hispanic Business (January-February 2009, pp. 16, 18, 20, 22)
Pub: Hispanic Business Inc.
Contact: Jesus Chavarria, President
Description: Profiles of Hispanic Business Media's 2009 Corporate Elite are presented.

34568 ■ *"2010 American Business Woman of ABWA"* in Women In Business (Vol. 61, October-November 2009, No. 5, pp. 22)
Pub: American Business Women's Association
Contact: Lorie Burch, President
Ed: Doris Brown. **Description:** Achievements of Doris Brown are presented in light of her being named as the 2010 American Business Woman of American Business Women's Association (ABWA). She specializes in the field of client and customer satisfaction for Avue Technologies. Brown believes that her involvement in the ABWA has helped her to see the importance of being a resource for other people.

34569 ■ *The Accidental Millionaire: How to Succeed in Life Without Really Trying*
Pub: BenBella Books
Contact: Aida Herrera, Director
E-mail: aida@benbellabooks.com
Ed: Gary Fong. **Released:** October 2009. **Price:** $8.75. **Description:** Gary Fong shares his memoirs about growing up in poverty in Los Angeles. Fong discusses how he revolutionized wedding photography and invented photography aids. **Availability:** Print.

34570 ■ *"Adapt or Die"* in Black Enterprise (Vol. 38, July 2008, No. 12, pp. 27)
Pub: Earl G. Graves Publishing Co. Inc.
Contact: Earl G. Graves, Jr., President
Ed: Rebecca Frances Rohan. **Description:** Turbulence in the domestic auto industry is hitting auto suppliers hard and black suppliers, the majority of whom contract with the Big Three, are just beginning to establish relationships with import car manufacturers. The more savvy CEOs are adopting new technologies in order to weather the downturn in the economy and in the industry as a whole.

34571 ■ *"Advice at Entrepreneurs Event: Make Fast Decisions, See Trends"* in Crain's Detroit Business (Vol. 30, July 28, 2014, No. 30, pp. 4)
Pub: Crain Communications Inc. - Detroit
Contact: Keith Crain, Chairman
Released: July 28, 2014. **Description:** Crain's entrepreneurial event was held a The Henry Ford in Dearborn, Michigan. Panelists at the event advised entrepreneurs to make fast decisions and to be aware of small business trends in order to be successful. George Matick Chevrolet was honored. Details of the event are covered.

34572 ■ *"Albuquerque Entrepreneurs Selected As Top Participants in USHCC Foundation Green Builds Business Program"* in Marketing Weekly News (April 21, 2012)
Description: Five winners of the 2012 Green Builds Business program was announced by the United States Hispanic Chamber of Commerce Foundation (USHCCF). These winners will receive a combined 24 hours of one-on-one green coaching with Bill Roth, the Green Business Coach for Entrepreneur.com and Founder of Earth 2017. Details are included.

34573 ■ *"All In Good Fun"* in Entrepreneur (Vol. 36, May 2008, No. 5, pp. 22)
Pub: Entrepreneur Press
Contact: Perlman Neil, President
Ed: Christopher Percy Collier. **Description:** According to a study conducted in 2007, humor in the workplace helps people communicate effectively and improves camaraderie. Company leaders and entrepreneurs can also tell humorous stories about themselves, but must also set lines that should not be crossed. The humorous atmosphere in the company YouSendIt is presented.

34574 ■ *Alpha Dogs: How Your Small Business Can Become a Leader of the Pack*
Pub: Harper Business
Ed: Donna Fenn. **Released:** May 08, 2007. **Price:** $14.95, paperback. **Description:** Ways for an entrepreneur to outsmart competitors in the marketplace, to generate higher sales, and earn lasting customer and employee loyalty. **Availability:** Print.

34575 ■ *Alpha Dogs: How Your Small Business Can Become a Leader of the Pack*
Pub: HarperCollins Publishers Inc.
Contact: Jane Friedman, President
E-mail: jfriedman@harpercollins.com
Ed: Donna Fenn. **Released:** May 08, 2007. **Price:** $14.95, paperback; $9.99; C$11.99. **Description:** Profiles of eight successful entrepreneurs along with information for developing customer service, technology and competition. **Availability:** PrintE-book.

34576 ■ *"Altus Jobs Founders' Unique Operating System Generates Success"* in Orlando Business Journal (Vol. 30, April 11, 2014, No. 42, pp. 3)
Pub: American City Business Journals
Released: April 11, 2014. **Description:** Maitland, Florida-based Altus Jobs founders, Saum Sharifi and Augusto Guevara, have credited their unique operating sytem with their quick success in recruiting talent, specializing in high level engineering positions. The system allows employees to work from 9:30 a.m. to 3:30 p.m. in their casual office and motivates them to show entrepreneurship by offering commission on top of base salary.

34577 ■ *"Always Striving"* in Women In Business (Vol. 61, December 2009, No. 6, pp. 28)
Pub: American Business Women's Association
Contact: Lorie Burch, President
Ed: Kathleen Leighton. **Description:** Jennifer Mull discusses her responsibilities and how she attained success as CEO of Backwoods, a gear and clothing store founded by her father in 1973. She places importance on being true to one's words and beliefs, while emphasizing the capacity to tolerate risks in business. Mull defines success as an evolving concept and believes there must always be something to strive for.

34578 ■ The AMA Handbook of Project Management
Pub: AMACOM
Contact: Edward T. Reilly, Manager
Ed: Paul C. Dinsmore, Jeannette Cabanis-Brewin. Released: Third Edition. Price: $79.95, Hardback. Description: A comprehensive reference presenting the critical concepts and theories all project managers must master using essays and advice from the field's top professionals. Availability: Print.

34579 ■ "Amit Wadhwaney" in Canadian Business (Vol. 80, March 12, 2007, No. 6, pp. 22)
Ed: Rachel Pulfer. Description: Manager of Third Avenue International Value Fund, Amit Wadhwaney, shares his views on buying Canadian agricultural and forestry stocks.

34580 ■ "ANATURALCONCEPT" in Crain's Cleveland Business (Vol. 30, June 22, 2009, No. 24, pp. 1)
Pub: Crain Communications Inc.
Ed: Dan Shingler. Description: Cleveland-based Biomimicry Institute, led by Cleveland's Entrepreneurs for Sustainability and the Cuyahoga County Planning Commission, are using biomimicry to incorporate eco-friendliness with industry. Biomimicry studies nature's best ideas then imitates these designs and processes to solve human problems.

34581 ■ "And the Money Comes Rolling In" in Inc. (Vol. 31, January-February 2009, No. 1, pp. 62)
Pub: Mansueto Ventures L.L.C.
Contact: John Koten, Chief Executive Officer
Ed: Max Chafkin. Description: Profile of Markus Frind, founder of the online dating service in British Columbia called Plenty of Fish. Frind works one hour a day and earns $10 million a year by keeping things simple.

34582 ■ "Angels In the Firm" in Entrepreneur (July 2014)
Pub: Entrepreneur Media Inc.
Released: July 2014. Description: Entrepreneurs must remember that a personal investment from an angel investor does not necessarily mean an investment from the venture capital firm owned by the investor. An angel investment could actually mean that the startup does not fit the goals of the venture capital firm. Angel investors face a potential conflict if they lead their venture capital companies into investing in these startups. Angel investors used to be organized groups specific to a region or cause, but later became wealthy individuals who are active in building and funding startups.

34583 ■ "Anja Carroll; Media Director-McDonald's USA" in Advertising Age (Vol. 79, November 17, 2008, No. 34, pp. 6)
Pub: Crain Communications Inc.
Contact: Rance Crain, President
Ed: Emily Bryson York. Description: Profile of Anja Carroll who is the media director for McDonald's USA and has the challenge of choosing the right mix of media for the corporation.

34584 ■ "Another Determinant of Entrepreneurship" in International Journal of Entrepreneurship and Small Business (Vol. 10, July 6, 2010)
Pub: Publishers Communication Group
Contact: Doug Wright, Director
Ed: Felix Pauligard Ntep, Wilton Wilton. Description: Interviews were carried out with entrepreneurs of Douala, Cameroon. These entrepreneurs believe that witchcraft existed and could bring harm to them or their enterprises.

34585 ■ "Anything Could Happen" in Inc. (March 2008, pp. 116-123)
Pub: Mansueto Ventures L.L.C.
Contact: John Koten, Chief Executive Officer
Ed: Max Chafkin. Description: Profile of Evan Williams, founder of Blogger and Twitter, a new type of technology idea; Williams answers ten questions and share insight into growing both of his companies.

34586 ■ "The Apprentice Entrepreneur"
Pub: CreateSpace
Contact: Daren Giles, President
Released: October 9, 2014. Price: $5.38 paperback. Description: An autobiography of an amateur entrepreneur and his journey to succeed in the business world is presented.

34587 ■ "Are You Ernest? How One Man Sincerely Grew His Business"
Pub: Amazon Digital Services
Released: October 2, 2014. Price: $0.99 Kindle. Description: Dr. Ernest Lee profiles his career in healthcare and shares his desire to make his life count. He discusses seven effective tools for growing a business, despite opposition, which are universal to business, charity, or relationship; a must read for anyone involved in public relations or sales.

34588 ■ "The Art of Persuasion: How You Can Get the Edge You Need To Reach Every Goal" in Small Business Opportunities (November 2007)
Ed: Paul Endress. Description: Expert in the field of psychology to business in the areas of communication, hiring and retention discusses a unique approach to solving business problems.

34589 ■ "The Art of War for Women" in Hawaii Business (Vol. 54, July 2008, No. 1, pp. 23)
Pub: PacificBasin Communications
Ed: Chin-Ning Chu. Description: Business consultant Chi-Ning Chu talks about her new book 'The Art of War for Women: Sun Tzu's Ancient Strategies and Wisdom for Winning at Work', which discusses how women can more effectively win in business. She also shares her thoughts about the advantages that women have, which they can use in businesses decisions.

34590 ■ "Attending to the Needs of the Too-Busy" in New York Times (Vol. 158, October 1, 2008, No. 54450, pp. 7)
Pub: New York Times Co./Globe Newspaper Co.
Ed: Ken Belson. Description: Profiles of individuals working as concierges to meet the needs of their clients are presented.

34591 ■ "Attention, Please" in Entrepreneur (Vol. 36, April 2008, No. 4, pp. 52)
Pub: Entrepreneur Press
Contact: Perlman Neil, President
Ed: Andrea Cooper. Description: Gurbaksh Chahal created his own company ClickAgents at the age of 16, and sold it two years later for $40 million to Value-Click. He then founded BlueLithium, an online advertising network on behavioral targeting, which Yahoo! Inc. bought in 2007 for $300 million. Chahal, now 25, talks about his next plans and describes how BlueLithium caught Yahoo's attention.

34592 ■ Attracting Investors: A Marketing Approach to Finding Funds for Your Business
Pub: John Wiley & Sons Inc.
Contact: Stephen M. Smith, President
Released: September 2004. Price: $34.95, hardcover. Description: Marketing experts advise entrepreneurs in ways to find investors in order to raise capital for their companies. Availability: Print.

34593 ■ Awesomely Simple: Essential Business Strategies for Turning Ideas Into Action
Pub: Jossey-Bass
Contact: William J. Pesce, President
Ed: John Spence. Released: September 08, 2009. Price: $24.95, Hardcover. Description: Six key strategies that create a foundation for achieving business excellence include: vivid vision, best people, a performance-oriented culture, robust communication, a sense of urgency, and extreme customer focus.

34594 ■ "Back Talk with Chris Gardner" in Black Enterprise (Vol. 37, January 2007, No. 6, pp. 112)
Ed: Kenneth Meeks. Description: Profile of with Chris Gardner and his Chicago company, Gardner Rich L.L.C., a multimillion-dollar investment firm. Dur-

ing an interview, Gardner discusses his rise from homelessness. His story became a book, The Pursuit of Happyness and was recently released as a film starring Will Smith.

34595 ■ "Backtalk with Terrie M. Williams" in Black Enterprise (Vol. 38, December 2007, No. 5, pp. 204)
Pub: Earl G. Graves Publishing Co. Inc.
Contact: Earl G. Graves, Jr., President
Ed: Tennille M. Robinson. Description: Profile of Terrie M. Williams, president of a public relations agency as well as founder of a youth empowerment organization called Stay Strong Foundation. Williams reflects on her bouts with depression and how the disease impacts sufferers and talks about her book that will inspire others dealing with depression.

34596 ■ Balls!: 6 Rules for Winning Today's Business Game
Pub: John Wiley & Sons Inc.
Contact: Stephen M. Smith, President
Ed: Alexi Venneri. Released: January 2005. Price: $29.95. Description: In order to be successful business leaders must be brave, authentic, loud, lovable, and spunky and they need to lead their competition. Availability: Print.

34597 ■ "Baltimore Entrepreneur Develops an Event-Themed Wish List App" in Baltimore Business Journal (Vol. 32, July 25, 2014, No. 12, pp. 7)
Pub: American City Business Journals, Inc.
Contact: Whitney Shaw, President
Released: July 25, 2014. Description: Baltimore-based entrepreneur Patrick Nagle has developed an online event-themed gift registry named Glist, a mobile application (app) and Website that assists in gift buying. Glist allows users to photograph items they want, put them on the online birthday wish list, or 'glist', and share the registries via social media.

34598 ■ "Barriers to Small Business Creations in Canada" in International Journal of Entrepreneurship and Small Business (Vol. , pp.)
Pub: Publishers Communication Group
Contact: Doug Wright, Director
Ed: Amarjit Gill, Nahum Biger, Vivek Nagpal. Description: Studies of Hatala (2005) and Choo and Wong (2006) related to the barriers to new venture creations in Canada are examined.

34599 ■ Battling Big Box: How Nimble Niche Companies Can Outmaneuver Giant Competitors
Pub: Career Press Inc.
Contact: Ron Fry, President
Ed: Henry Dubroff, Susan J. Marks. Released: January 2009. Price: $15.99. Description: Small companies can compete with larger firms through agility, adaptability, customer service, and credibility. Topics include information to help empower employees, build a powerful brand, manage cash flow, and maintaining a business vision. Availability: Print.

34600 ■ "BDC Launches New Online Business Advice Centre" in Marketwired (July 13, 2010)
Pub: COMTEX
Contact: Chip Brian, President
Description: The Business Development Bank of Canada (BDC) offers entrepreneurs the chance to use their new online BDC Advice Centre in order to seek advice regarding the challenges of entrepreneurship. Free online business tools and information to help both startups and established firms are also provided.

34601 ■ "Be a Better Manager: Live Abroad" in Harvard Business Review (Vol. 88, September 2010, No. 9, pp. 24)
Pub: Harvard Business School Publishing
Ed: William W. Maddux, Adam D. Galinsky, Carmit T. Tadmor. Description: Interrelationship between international experience and entrepreneurship is discussed. Individuals with international experience are likelier to be promoted and to develop new products and businesses.

34602 ■ Be the Elephant: Build a Bigger, Better Business
Pub: Workman Publishing Co.
Contact: Kristina Peterson, Director
E-mail: kristina@workman.com
Ed: Steve Kaplan. **Price:** $19.95. **Description:** Entrepreneur and author sets out an accessible, no-frills plan for business owners, managers, and other industrialists to grow their businesses into elephants: big and strong but also smart. Advice is given on fostering a growth mind-set, assessing risk, and creating unique selling propositions. **Availability:** E-book.

34603 ■ Be the Hero: Three Powerful Ways to Overcome Challenges in Work and In Life
Pub: Berrett-Koehler Communications Inc.
Contact: Steve Piersanti, President
E-mail: spiersanti@bkpub.com
Ed: Noah Blumenthal. **Released:** January 09, 2012. **Price:** $15.95, paperback; $19.95, hardcover. **Description:** Details are given to help individuals perform at their best when challenges are the greatest. It shows how to turn self-defeating thoughts and behavior into heroic actions. **Availability:** Print; PDF.

34604 ■ "Because 10 Million Zumba Lovers Can't Be Wrong" in Inc. (Volume 32, December 2010, No. 10, pp. 106)
Pub: Inc. Magazine
Ed: Christine Lagorio. **Description:** Profile of partners, Alberto Perez, Alberto Perlman, and Alberto Aghion, founders of Zumba, a form of dance used for fitness.

34605 ■ "Because He Is Still Growing: Horst Rechelbacher: Intelligent Nutrients Minneapolis" in Inc. (Volume 32, December 2010, No. 10)
Pub: Inc. Magazine
Ed: Mike Hoffman. **Description:** Horst Hechelbacher, founder of hair care company Aveda, and after selling Aveda to Estee Lauder, he is expanding into a nutraceuticals company offering hair care products that are organically grown.

34606 ■ "Become A Brand" in Women Entrepreneur (September 14, 2008)
Ed: Suzy Girard-Ruttenberg. **Description:** Powerful brands are effective, innovative, exclusive or even socially conscious; it is important for small businesses to understand the power of becoming a brand since it is one of the best ways in which to position one's company and drive its growth.

34607 ■ "Beer Drinkers Wanted More. The Brewer Had No Room to Expand: How Could It Keep the Taps Flowing?" in Inc. (October 2007, pp. 65-66)
Pub: Mansueto Ventures L.L.C.
Contact: John Koten, Chief Executive Officer
Ed: Alex Salkever. **Description:** Profile of John Mc-Donald, founder of Boulevard, the second-largest beer company located in Kansas City, Missouri. McDonald tells how he was able to expand his turn-of-the-century brick building he had imported from Bavaria by developing a 70,000-square-foot building on four acres adjacent to his existing location rather move to a suburb.

34608 ■ "Behind Frenemy Lines" in Entrepreneur (May 2014)
Pub: Entrepreneur Media Inc.
Released: May 2014. **Description:** Entrepreneurs have three options when it comes to socializing with competitors. One is to avoid them socially, another is to socialize with them as if they are not competitors, or they can take the occasionally awkward dance of the two competitors. The dance involves giving up some personal and business information, while protecting proprietary information at the same time. Entrepreneurs should view the competitor as a threat who should not be treated like a threat. They can turn a potentially awkward situation into a social and professional advantage by seeing threat as an opportunity.

34609 ■ "Being Emotional During Decision Making-Good or Bad? An Empirical Investigation" in Academy of Management Journal (Vol. 50, No. 4, August 1, 2007, pp. 923)
Pub: Academy of Management
Contact: Ming-Jer Chen, President
Ed: Myeong-Gu Seo, Lisa Feldman Barrett. **Description:** Relationship between affective experience and decision-making performance is studied.

34610 ■ Ben Franklin: America's Original Entrepreneur, Franklin's Autobiography Adapted for Modern Times
Pub: Entrepreneur Press
Contact: Perlman Neil, President
Ed: Blaine McCormick. **Released:** September 2005. **Price:** $19.95. **Availability:** Print.

34611 ■ "The Best Advice I Ever Got" in Harvard Business Review (Vol. 86, September 2008, No. 9, pp. 29)
Pub: Harvard Business Review Press
Contact: Peter E. Walsh, Director
Ed: Daisy Wademan. **Description:** Bright Horizons Family Solutions founder and chair Linda Mason illustrates how letting one's life passion direct entrepreneurship and business success. She describes how her humanitarian interests and efforts gave her the drive to launch a childcare service.

34612 ■ "The Best Execs in Canada" in Canadian Business (Vol. 79, October 9, 2006, No. 20, pp. 68)
Description: The annual list of the most outstanding and innovative business executives of Canada is presented.

34613 ■ "Best Places to Work; No. 2 Tasty Catering Inc." in Crain's Chicago Business (Vole 35, April 2, 2012, No. 14, pp. 18)
Pub: Crain Communications Inc.
Contact: Todd Johnson, Publisher
Ed: Sachiko Yoshitsugu. **Description:** Tasty Catering Inc., located in Elk Grove Village, Illinois was rated Number 2 in Crain's Best Places to Work category. The event planning and catering firm offers a family style lunch to employees weekly. CEO Tom Walters enjoys this meal with his workers. The company offers an educational program called Tasty Catering University that provides up to 30 hours of paid class time in courses ranging from English to business.

34614 ■ "Better Business By Design" in Entrepreneur (August 2014)
Pub: Entrepreneur Media Inc.
Released: August 2014. **Description:** Designer Yves Behar was born in Switzerland in 1967 and has always been a risk taker since a young age. He earned his bachelor's degree in industrial design at the Art Center College of Design in Los Angeles, California. He is redefining the model of the design business through his agency Fuseproject. His strategy involves establishing integrated and long-term relationships with clients in exchange for an equity stake. Behar believes in the importance of working with entrepreneurs on long-term design projects.

34615 ■ "Better Card Collecting" in Canadian Business (Vol. 80, January 15, 2007, No. 2, pp. 66)
Ed: Sarah B. Hood. **Description:** Tips on how to collect business cards and use them for enhancing one's business performance are presented. Targeting specific people, taking notes and giving follow ups are some suggestions.

34616 ■ "Beverage Brand Vies To Be the Latest Purple Prince" in Brandweek (Vol. 49, April 21, 2008, No. 16, pp. 20)
Pub: Nielsen Business Media Inc.
Contact: Howard Appelbaum, President
Ed: Becky Ebenkamp. **Description:** Profile on the new beverage product Purple and its founder, Ted Farnsworth; Purple is a drink that blends seven antioxidant-rich juices to create what Mr. Farnsworth calls a 'Cascade Effect' that boosts antioxidants' ef-

fectiveness. Mr. Farnsworth is marketing the brand's Oxygen Radical Absorbance Capability (ORAC) which is a value of 7,600 compared with orange juice's 1,200.

34617 ■ "Biblical Secrets to Business Success"
Pub: CreateSpace
Contact: Daren Giles, President
Released: October 2, 2014. **Price:** $14.99 paperback. **Description:** Bob Diener share insight into his journey as an entrepreneur. He focuses on tough issues like: how to treat employees, how to please customers, whether or not to cut corners, whether to follow temptation of an unethical deal, and provides solutions to these dilemmas. He recommends abiding by the Bible's rules of business in order to prosper long term.

34618 ■ The Big Book of Small Business: You Don't Have to Run Your Business by the Seat of Your Pants
Pub: HarperCollins Publishers Inc.
Contact: Jane Friedman, President
E-mail: jfriedman@harpercollins.com
Ed: Tom Gegax, Phil Bolsta. **Released:** February 06, 2007. **Price:** $29.99, hardcover; $16.99; C$19.99. **Description:** Entrepreneur shares his experiences starting and running his small business. **Availability:** PrintE-book.

34619 ■ The Big Payback: The History of the Business of Hip-Hop
Pub: New American Library/Penguin Group
Ed: Dan Charnas. **Released:** November 01, 2011. **Price:** $17, paperback; $13.99. **Description:** The complete history of hip-hop music is presented, by following the money and the relationship between artist and merchant. In its promise of economic security and creative control for black artist-entrepreneurs, it is the culmination of dreams of black nationalists and civil rights leaders. **Availability:** PrintElectronic publishing.

34620 ■ "The BIG Picture" in Crain's Cleveland Business (Vol. 30, June 22, 2009, No. 24, pp. 12)
Pub: Crain Communications Inc.
Ed: Arielle Kass. **Description:** Entrepreneurs are quick to praise their colleges and universities and attribute both personal and business success to them.

34621 ■ The Big Rich: The Rise and Fall of the Greatest Texas Oil Fortunes
Pub: Dutton Children's Books
Contact: Lauri Hornik, President
Ed: Bryan Burrough. **Released:** 2009. **Price:** $14.99; $18, Paperback. **Description:** The story of the great 20th Century oilmen offers lessons on the value of confidence, grit and guile. **Availability:** Electronic publishing.

34622 ■ Big Vision, Small Business: 4 Keys to Success without Growing Big
Pub: Ivy Sea Inc.
Ed: Jamie S. Walters. **Released:** October 10, 2002. **Price:** $17.95, paperback. **Description:** The power of the small enterprise is examined. The author shares her expertise as an entrepreneur and founder of a business consulting firm to help small business owners successfully run their companies. Interviews with more than seventy small business owners provide insight into visioning, planning, and establishing a small company, as well as strategies for good employee and customer relationships. **Availability:** Print; PDF.

34623 ■ "Bill Lee's Auto Repair Business Chugs Along Despite Life's Obstacles" in Bradenton Herald (August 22, 2010)
Pub: Bradenton Herald
Ed: Grace Gagliano. **Description:** Profile of Bill Lee's Professional Automotive Services located in Bradenton, Florida. The auto repair business was opened 26 years ago and provides repair for an assortment of fleet vehicles, including truck repair.

34624 ■ Billions of Entrepreneurs: How China and India Are Reshaping Their Futures and Yours
Pub: Harvard Business Review Press
Contact: Peter E. Walsh, Director
Ed: Tarun Khanna. Released: March 17, 2011. Price: $16.95, paperback. Description: Various success strategies for success in both China and India are examined. Implications of the concurrent economic booms in both countries are cited. Availability: Print.

34625 ■ "Bitcoin 'Killer App' Or the Currency of the Future?" in Providence Business News (Vol. 28, January 6, 2014, No. 40, pp. 1)
Pub: American City Business Journals
Released: January 6, 2014. Description: The Providence Bitcoin Meetup has gathered several technology experts to discuss Bitcoin, the popular digital currency. However, software developers, engineers and entrepreneurs see Bitcoin as the next killer app for the Internet and is changing how information and data is stored, shared and verified. The Bitcoin's impact in Rhode Island is examined.

34626 ■ The Black Swan
Pub: Ballantine/ Del Rey/Fawcett/Ivy Books
Contact: Gilbert Perlman, President
Ed: Nassim Nicholas Taleb. Price: $17, Paperback; $30, Hardcover. Description: A black swan is a highly improbably event with three principle characteristics: it is unpredictable, it carries a massive impact, and after the fact, we concoct an explanation that makes it appear less random and more predictable than it really was. The success of Google was a black swan; so was 9/11. According to the author, black swans underlie almost everything about the world, from the rise of religions to events in personal lives.

34627 ■ The Blackwell Encyclopedia of Management: Entrepreneurship
Pub: Blackwell Publishing Inc.
Contact: Gordon Tibbitts, III, President
Released: Volume 3, 2nd Edition. Price: $165, hardcover. Description: Overview of entrepreneurship through the use of dictionary definitions as well as entries of 2,500 words explaining advanced issues and debates. Availability: Print.

34628 ■ "Blast from the Past" in Entrepreneur (Vol. 35, November 2007, No. 11, pp. 48)
Pub: Entrepreneur Press
Contact: Perlman Neil, President
Ed: Robert Kiyosaki. Description: Entrepreneurs of today face the challenge of creating new ideas. Collaborating with younger employees provides new perspective, but it also has to be a partnership with old ideas and sharing experiences between the older and the younger to forecast the future.

34629 ■ "Blindspot: Hidden Biases of Good People"
Pub: Ballantine/ Del Rey/Fawcett/Ivy Books
Contact: Gilbert Perlman, President
Released: February 12, 2013. Price: $27.00. Description: Perceptions of social groups that shape our likes and dislikes and our judgments about people's character, abilities and potential include exposure to and attitudes about age, gender, race, ethnicity, religion, social class, sexuality, disability status, and nationality are examined. Hidden biases impact everyone, including business leaders, entrepreneurs and managers in decision making.

34630 ■ "Boar Market: Penny-Wise Consumers Favoring Pork" in Crain's Chicago Business (Vol. 31, April 14, 2008, No. 15, pp. 4)
Pub: Crain Communications Inc.
Contact: Todd Johnson, Publisher
Ed: Bruce Blythe. Description: Interview with Alan Cole who is the president of Cedar Hill Associates Inc. and who discusses ways in which his company is taking advantage of the record highs of oil and natural gas as well as his overall outlook on the market.

34631 ■ The Book of Entrepreneurs' Wisdom: Classic Writings by Legendary Entrepreneurs
Pub: John Wiley & Sons Inc.
Contact: Stephen M. Smith, President
Released: September 1999. Price: $44.95, hardcover. Availability: Print.

34632 ■ The Book of Hard Choices: How to Make the Right Decisions at Work and Keep Your Self-Respect
Pub: Broadway Business
Contact: David Drake, Manager
E-mail: ddrake@randomhouse.com
Ed: Peter Roy, James A. Autry. Released: December 2006. Price: $13.99. Availability: E-book.

34633 ■ Boosting Corporate Entrepreneurship Through HRM Practices: Evidence from German SMEs" in Human Resource Management (Vol. 49, July-August 2010, No. 4)
Pub: John Wiley
Ed: Ralf Schmelter, Rene Mauer, Christiane Borsch, Malte Brettel. Description: A study was conducted to determine which human resource management (HRM) practices promote corporate entrepreneurship (CE) in small and medium-sized enterprises (SMEs). Findings indicate that staff selection, staff development, training, and staff rewards on CE have a strong impact on SMEs.

34634 ■ Bo's Lasting Lessons
Ed: Bo Schembechler; John U. Bacon. Price: $13.99. Description: Leadership skills are taught.

34635 ■ Bottom-Line Training: Performance-Based Results
Pub: Training Education Management
Contact: Donald J. Ford, President
Ed: Donald J. Ford. Released: Second Edition. Price: $29. Description: Training is critical to any successful enterprise. The key to any successful training program involves defining and constantly focusing on the desired results of the program. The author provides a training model based on five phases, known as ADDIE: analysis, design, development, implementation and evaluation.

34636 ■ "Bottoms Up!" in Entrepreneur (Vol. 36, April 2008, No. 4, pp. 128)
Pub: Entrepreneur Press
Contact: Perlman Neil, President
Ed: Amanda C. Kooser. Description: Jill Bernheimer launched her online alcohol business Domaine547 in 2007, and encountered challenges as legal issues over the licensing and launching of the business took about seven months to finish. Domain547 features blog and forum areas. Marketing strategy that connects to the social community is one of the ways to reach out to customers.

34637 ■ Brag!: The Art of Tooting Your Own Horn Without Blowing It
Pub: Grand Central Publishing
Contact: Maureen Mahon Egen, President
Ed: Peggy Klaus. Price: $14; C$16; $9.99. Description: A plan to promote a small business by effectively selling one's self. Availability: PrintE-book.

34638 ■ "Branding Specialist" in Black Enterprise (Vol. 38, July 2008, No. 12, pp. 1)
Pub: Earl G. Graves Publishing Co. Inc.
Contact: Earl G. Graves, Jr., President
Ed: Faith Chukwudi. Description: Interview with Wonya Lucas who is the chief marketing officer for Discovery Communications and is known for building strong brands by understanding her audience and generating buy-in throughout the organization; Lucas discusses her role in the corporation, guerilla marketing techniques, and what companies tend to overlook in marketing their products or services.

34639 ■ "Breaking Through" in Inc. (January 2008, pp. 90-93)
Pub: Gruner and Jahr USA Publishing Co.
Contact: J. Russell Denson, President
Ed: Mike Hofman. Description: Entrepreneur Keith R. McFarland, shares insight into why most successful companies eventually plateau, while others keep on growing.

34640 ■ The Breakthrough Company
Pub: Crown Publishing/Random House
Ed: Keith R. McFarland. Released: September 01, 2009. Price: $16, Paperback. Description: Traits of high-growth players that actually make it in business.

34641 ■ The Breakthrough Company: How Everyday Companies Become Extraordinary Performers
Pub: Crown Publishing Group
Ed: Keith R. McFarland. Released: September 01, 2009. Price: $16; $11.99. Description: Author shares five years of building and analyzing the world's largest growth companies performance database and interviews with over 1,500 growth-company executives to help identify the secrets of breakthrough. This book will help any small business learn ways to avoid potential hazards along with way. Availability: PrintE-book.

34642 ■ "Brief: Make a Bigger Impact by Saying Less"
Pub: John Wiley & Sons Inc.
Contact: Stephen M. Smith, President
Released: February 10, 2014. Price: $15.93. Description: Communication is key to any business success. Today, busy executives demand respect and manage their time more efficiently than ever. The author addresses the challenges of inattention, interruptions, and impatience faced by professionals and to help leaders gain the strength required to eliminate wasteful words and stand out from others when communicating.

34643 ■ "Bring It On" in Entrepreneur (Vol. 35, November 2007, No. 11, pp. 52)
Pub: Entrepreneur Press
Contact: Perlman Neil, President
Ed: Guy Kawasaki. Description: Tips on managing corporate competition in order to drive a company to success are presented.

34644 ■ "Bringing Manufacturing Concerns to Springfield" in Crain's Chicago Business (Vol. 31, March 31, 2008, No. 13, pp. 6)
Pub: Crain Communications Inc.
Contact: Todd Johnson, Publisher
Ed: Paul Merrion. Description: Profile of the new executive vice-president of Tooling & Manufacturing Assn., Paul Merrion, a man who plans to grow TMA's membership with an aggressive legislative agenda in Springfield.

34645 ■ "Brock's Lessons for Modern CEOs" in Canadian Business (Vol. 85, June 11, 2012, No. 10, pp. 17)
Pub: George Media Inc.
Ed: Peter Shawn Taylor. Released: June 11, 2012. Description: Modern day executives can learn the characteristics of a great leader from Sir Isaac Brock, who helped win the War of 1812 for Canada. Brock refused to accept defeat, took steps to deal with his weaknesses and was always at the front when decisive action was necessary.

34646 ■ "The Buck Stops Here" in Canadian Business (Vol. 81, November 10, 2008, No. 19, pp. 25)
Pub: Rogers Media Inc.
Contact: Tony Viner, President
Ed: Sarka Halas. Description: Reputation strategist Leslie Gaines-Ross says that minimizing the damage followed by the identification of what went wrong are the first steps that companies need to take when trying to salvage their reputation. Gaines-Ross states that it is up to the CEO to ensure the company's speedy recovery and they need to be at the forefront of the process.

34647 ■ "Budget Woes Endanger E-Prep Progress" in Crain's Cleveland Business (Vol. 30, June 22, 2009, No. 24, pp. 6)
Pub: Crain Communications Inc.
Ed: Brian Tucker. Description: The future of the Entrepreneurship Preparatory School located in Cleveland is being threatened by State budget concerns. The charter school requires all students to wear uniforms, respect discipline, and attend for longer hours and more weeks.

34648 ■ *"Building Alexian Brothers' Clinical Reputation"* in *Crain's Chicago Business (Vol. 31, May 5, 2008, No. 18, pp. 6)*
Pub: Crain Communications Inc.
Contact: Todd Johnson, Publisher
Ed: Mike Colias. Description: Profile of the CEO of Alexian Brothers Medical Center in Elk Grove Village who plans to stabilize Alexian Brothers' financial performance in part by eliminating $20 million in annual costs.

34649 ■ *Building a Business the Buddhist Way*
Ed: Geri Larkin. Released: September 2004. Price: $11.67 (Canadian). Description: Principles of entrepreneurship for starting and growing a business while maintaining a balance between business goals and spiritual goals.

34650 ■ *"Building His Dream"* in *Business Courier (Vol. 24, January 24, 2008, No. 42, pp. 1)*
Pub: American City Business Journals, Inc.
Contact: Whitney Shaw, President
Ed: Laura Baverman. Description: Technology entrepreneur Mahendra Vora plans to build a more than $100 million local IT headquarters for VTech Holdings Ltd by 2010. Acquisition of four $5 million companies within 2008 are part of the owner's plan to expand the office equipment company. Other plans for the IT company are discussed.

34651 ■ *Building Wealth in China: 36 True Stories of Chinese Millionaires and How They Made Their Fortunes*
Ed: Ling, Zhu. Released: April 27, 2010. Price: $15. Description: Thirty-six of China's most successful and innovative entrepreneurs discuss valuable lessons for growing a business in China.

34652 ■ *Built to Last: Successful Habits of Visionary Companies*
Pub: HarperCollins Publishers Inc.
Contact: Jane Friedman, President
E-mail: jfriedman@harpercollins.com
Ed: James C. Collins, Jerry I. Porras. Price: $29.99, hardcover; $17.99, paperback; $12.99; C$11.99. Availability: PrintE-book.

34653 ■ *Business for Beginners*
Pub: Sourcebooks Mediafusion
Ed: Frances McGuckin. Released: March 01, 2005. Price: C$22.99; C$17.99. Description: Small business advice is shared by seven successful entrepreneurs. Availability: PrintE-book.

34654 ■ *Business Black Belt: Develop the Strength, Flexibility and Agility to Run Your Company*
Ed: Burke Franklin. Released: November 1, 2010. Price: $15.99. Description: Manual offering insights that will enable anyone to become successful in small business. Seventy short chapters included topics such as attitude, management, marketing, selling, employees, money, MBAs, lawyers, consultants, and investors.

34655 ■ *Business Fairy Tales*
Pub: South-Western
Contact: Susan Badger, President
Ed: Cecil W. Jackson. Price: £35.99, hardback. Description: The seven most-common business schemes are uncovered.

34656 ■ *Business Management for Entrepreneurs*
Pub: Double Storey Books
Ed: Cecile Nieuwenhuizen. Released: March 1, 2009. Price: $35.95. Description: Lack of good management skills are usually the reason for any small company to fail. This book introduces entrepreneurs and managers of small to medium-sized firms to all functions required to manage successfully.

34657 ■ *Business Plans to Game Plans: A Practical System for Turning Strategies into Action*
Pub: John Wiley & Sons Inc.
Contact: Stephen M. King, President
Ed: Jan B. King. Released: December 2003. Price: $29.95, paperback; $19.99. Description: Information for running a small business are examined, focusing

on action plans and ways to avoid the pitfalls of strategic planning. The book describes how entrepreneurs should set standards, lead by example, look to the future, focus on important details, face reality, grow profitability, and take action. Availability: PrintE-book.

34658 ■ *The Business of Small Business: Succeeding and Prospering in Business for Reasonably Intelligent Entrepreneurs*
Released: August 2006. Price: $27.95. Description: Tips for running a successful company are presented to entrepreneurs.

34659 ■ *Business Stripped Bare: Adventures of a Global Entrepreneur*
Pub: Virgin Books/Random House
Ed: Richard Branson. Released: January 22, 2010. Price: £20, Hardback; £9.99, Paperback. Description: Successful entrepreneur, Sir Richard Branson, shares the inside track on some of his greatest achievements in business and the lessons learned from setbacks.

34660 ■ *Business Unusual*
Ed: Anita Roddick. Price: $24.95.

34661 ■ *Business Upgrade: 21 Days to Reignite the Entrepreneurial Spirit in You and Your Team*
Pub: John Wiley & Sons Inc.
Contact: Stephen M. Smith, President
Ed: Richard Parkes Cordock. Released: November 2006. Price: $18.95, paperback. Description: Business consultant works to inspire and guide entrepreneurs to spark growth in their companies while motivating workers. Availability: Print.

34662 ■ *Business as Usual*
Pub: HarperBusiness
Ed: Anita Roddick. Released: 2005. Price: $12.95. Description: Founder of The Body Shop shares her story and gives her opinion on everything from cynical cosmetic companies to destructive consultants.

34663 ■ *Business Vision: Beyond the Horizon, 2nd Ed.*
Ed: Dennis Wengert. Released: January 2009. Description: Challenges small business owners face when running their companies are addressed in order to position themselves for the future. The book teaches how to envision future direction and measure personal and business activities that provide an indication of personal progress in achieving visionary business leadership.

34664 ■ *Business Warrior: Strategy for Entrepreneurs*
Ed: Sun Tzu. Released: September 2006. Price: $19.95. Description: Advice to help entrepreneurs understand competitive strategies in order to succeed, focusing on sales, marketing, and personnel management.

34665 ■ *"Businessman Legend Passes: Charles H. James II Credited With Transforming Family Business"* in *Black Enterprise (December 2007)*
Ed: Tara C. Walker. Description: Profile of Charles H. James II, president and chairman of The James Corporation, a family-owned multigenerational food distribution company that started as a produce firm.

34666 ■ *Busting the Myth of the Heroic CEO*
Ed: Michel Villette, Catherine Vuillermot. Released: 2010. Price: $24.95. Description: According to the authors, corporate leaders do not get ahead through productive risk-taking and innovation, but through ruthless exploitation of market imperfections and rivals.

34667 ■ *BUZZ: How to Create It and Win With It*
Pub: AMACOM
Contact: Edward T. Reilly, Manager
Ed: Edward I. Koch, Christy Heady. Released: June 2007. Price: $21.95; C$26.95. Description: Former New York City Mayor, Edward Koch demonstrates buss to define a small business image, how to create

buzz with honesty, engage the media, withstand public scrutiny, turn mistakes into opportunities, and create loyal followers.

34668 ■ *"Bye-Bye, Ol' Boys"* in *Canadian Business (Vol. 80, January 15, 2007, No. 2, pp. 16)*
Ed: Michelle Magnan. Description: A profile of Kathy Sendall, senior vice-president of Petro-Canada of the North American division and chairperson of the Canadian Association of Petroleum Producers, is presented.

34669 ■ *"C. Andrew McCartney; President, Owner, Bowden Manufacturing Corp., 37"* in *Crain's Cleveland Business (November 19, 2007)*
Pub: Crain Communications Inc.
Ed: David Bennett. Description: Profile of C. Andrew McCartney who was named president of Bowden Manufacturing Corp., a company that machines and fabricates metal and plastic parts for products ranging from airplanes to medical equipment; Mr. McCartney has since purchased the company, which posted $8 million in sales last year. He feels that part of his success is due to adherence to such policies such as gaining the employees trust and to avoid making promises to customers that Bowden cannot keep.

34670 ■ *"Calendar"* in *Crain's Detroit Business (Vol. 24, March 10, 2008, No. 10, pp. 21)*
Description: Listing of events in the Detroit area include conferences addressing entrepreneurialism, economic development, and women business ownership.

34671 ■ *"Calendar"* in *Crain's Detroit Business (Vol. 24, March 17, 2008, No. 11, pp. 20)*
Description: Listing of events in the Detroit area include conferences addressing entrepreneurialism, economic development, and women business ownership.

34672 ■ *"Calendar"* in *Crain's Detroit Business (Vol. 24, March 24, 2008, No. 12, pp. 25)*
Pub: Crain Communications Inc.
Contact: Rance E. Crain, President
Description: Listing of events in the Detroit area include conferences addressing entrepreneurialism, economic development, and women business ownership.

34673 ■ *"Calendar"* in *Crain's Detroit Business (Vol. 24, March 31, 2008, No. 13, pp. 1)*
Pub: Crain Communications Inc.
Contact: Rance E. Crain, President
Description: Listing of events in the Detroit area include conferences addressing entrepreneurialism, economic development, and minority business ownership.

34674 ■ *"Calendar"* in *Crain's Detroit Business (Vol. 24, April 7, 2008, No. 14, pp. 27)*
Pub: Crain Communications Inc.
Contact: Rance E. Crain, President
Description: Listing of events in the Detroit area include conferences addressing entrepreneurialism, economic development, and minority business ownership.

34675 ■ *"Calendar"* in *Crain's Detroit Business (Vol. 24, April 14, 2008, No. 15, pp. 25)*
Pub: Crain Communications Inc.
Contact: Rance E. Crain, President
Description: Listing of events in the Detroit area include conferences addressing entrepreneurialism, economic development, and ways in which to develop environmentally friendly buildings.

34676 ■ *"Calendar"* in *Crain's Detroit Business (Vol. 24, September 29, 2008, No. 39, pp. 41)*
Pub: Crain Communications Inc.
Contact: Rance E. Crain, President
Description: Listing of events in the Detroit area include conferences addressing entrepreneurialism, economic development, and women business ownership.

34677 ■ *"Calendar" in Crain's Detroit Business (Vol. 24, October 6, 2008, No. 40, pp. 22)*
Pub: Crain Communications Inc.
Contact: Rance E. Crain, President
Description: Listing of events in the Detroit area include conferences addressing entrepreneurialism, economic development, manufacturing, marketing, the housing crisis and women business ownership.

34678 ■ *Call Me Ted*
Pub: Grand Central Publishing
Contact: Maureen Mahon Egen, President
Ed: Ted Turner, Bill Burke. **Released:** 2009. **Price:** $16.99; C$19.99. **Description:** Media mogul, Ted Turner's biography is full of personal and business details from his careers in advertising and broadcasting.

34679 ■ *"Can He Win the Patent Game?" in Globe & Mail (February 20, 2006, pp. B1)*
Ed: Simon Avery, Paul Waldie. **Description:** A profile on managerial abilities of chief executive officer Jim Balsillie of Research In Motion Ltd., who will face the patent case with NTP Inc., is presented.

34680 ■ *"Canada Tomorrow" in Canadian Business (Vol. 80, October 8, 2007, No. 20, pp. 14)*
Ed: Donald J. Johnston. **Description:** An assessment of Canada's future in terms of its educational, social, and economic environment is presented. Concerns regarding the country's educational system such as the declining interest in science and technology and the possible lack of teachers in the future are discussed. In terms of its social and economic aspects, the need to support entrepreneurs and other qualified people is explained.

34681 ■ *"Canada's Uber-Wealthy" in Canadian Business (Vol. 80, Winter 2007, No. 24, pp. 16)*
Description: Statistics of the concentration of millionaire households around the world and the wealth of major cities in Canada are presented. The data reveals that Montreal has the highest concentration of billionaires and that the U.S. has the highest concentration of millionaire households.

34682 ■ *Canadian Entrepreneurship and Small Business Management*
Pub: McGraw-Hill Ryerson Ltd.
Contact: Robert J. Bahash, President
Ed: D. Wesley Balderson. **Price:** C$104.36, Members; C$115.95, Nonmembers. **Description:** Successful entrepreneurship and small business management is shown through the use of individual Canadian small business experiences. **Availability:** Print.

34683 ■ *Canadian Small Business Kit for Dummies*
Pub: John Wiley & Sons Inc.
Contact: Stephen M. Smith, President
Ed: Margaret Kerr, JoAnn Kurtz. **Released:** 3rd Edition. **Description:** Resources include information on changes to laws and taxes for small businesses in Canada.

34684 ■ *"Career Transition" in Crain's Detroit Business (Vol. 26, January 4, 2010, No. 1, pp. 14)*
Pub: Crain Communications Inc.
Contact: Rance E. Crain, President
Description: Profile of Nicole Longhini-McElroy who has opted to radically change her career path from working in the manufacturing sector to becoming a self-published author of 'Charmed Adventures', a book series created to engage children in creative thought.

34685 ■ *Careers for Homebodies & Other Independent Souls*
Pub: McGraw-Hill
Ed: Jan Goldberg. **Released:** August 23, 2010. **Price:** Rs 883.03. **Description:** The books offers insight into choosing the right career for individuals. Jobs range from office to outdoors, job markets, and levels of education requirements. **Availability:** Print.

34686 ■ *"Carving a Niche" in Hawaii Business (Vol. 53, November 2007, No. 5, pp. 58)*
Pub: PacificBasin Communications
Ed: Kyle Galdeira. **Description:** Stephanie Lay created Extreme Surf Fitness which is a program that promotes natural performance enhancement and rehabilitation of surfers using core and balance exercises. Lay's goal is to become a full time coach for a big surf brand and tour the world with the team.

34687 ■ *"Carving Passion, Talent Help Couple Craft Business on Wood-Rich Land" in Crain's Cleveland Business (October 8, 2007)*
Pub: Crain Communications Inc.
Ed: Sharon Schnall. **Description:** Profile of Wood-carved Art Gallery & Studio, a family-owned business which includes several ventures of the husband-and-wife team, Jim Stadtlander and Diane Harto.

34688 ■ *Cash In a Flash*
Ed: Robert G. Allen, Mark Victor Hansen. **Released:** December 28, 2010. **Price:** $15. **Description:** Proven, practical advice and techniques are given to help entrepreneurs make money quickly using skills and resources known to generate permanent and recurring income.

34689 ■ *"The Caterer and Hotelkeeper Interview Patrick Harbour and Nathan Jones" in Caterer & Hotelkeeper (October 28, 2011, No. 288)*
Pub: Reed Reference Publishing
Contact: Erik Engstrom, Chief Executive Officer
Description: Profiles of Patrick Harbour and Nathan Jones who quit their jobs to start their own catering business. The partners discuss their business strategy when launching their boutique catering firm and ways they are adapting to the slow economy in order to remain successful.

34690 ■ *"Celebrate Success. Embrace Innovation" in Black Enterprise (Vol. 37, February 2007, No. 7, pp. 145)*
Description: 2007 Women of Power Summit provides networking opportunities, empowerment sessions, and nightly entertainment. More than 500 executive women of color are expected to attend this inspiring summit in Phoenix, February 7-10.

34691 ■ *"The Center of Success: Author Explores How Confidence Can Take You Further" in Black Enterprise (Vol. 38, March 1, 2008, No. 8)*
Pub: Earl G. Graves Publishing Co. Inc.
Contact: Earl G. Graves, Jr., President
Ed: Ayana Dixon. **Description:** Motivational speaker and author, Valorie Burton, provides a 50-question confidence quotient assessment to help business owners and managers develop confidence in order to obtain goals.

34692 ■ *"CEO Forecast: With Cloudy Economy, Executives Turn to Government Contracting" in Hispanic Business (January-February 2009, pp. 34, 36)*
Pub: Hispanic Business Inc.
Contact: Jesus Chavarria, President
Ed: Jessica Haro, Richard Kaplan. **Description:** As economic uncertainty fogs the future, executives turn to government contracts in order to boost business. Revenue sources, health care challenges, environmental consulting and remediation services, as well as technological strides are discussed.

34693 ■ *"Challenges, Responses and Available Resources" in Journal of Small Business and Entrepreneurship (Vol. 23, Winter 2010, No. 1)*
Pub: Canadian Council for Small Business and Entrepreneurship
Contact: Sandra Altner, President
Ed: Lynne Siemens. **Description:** Rural communities and their residents are exploring the potential of small business and entrepreneurship to address the economic changes they are facing. While these rural areas present many opportunities, business people in these areas face challenges which they must navigate to operate successfully.

34694 ■ *"Changing Society One Organization at a Time" in Hispanic Business (January-February 2008, pp. 55-56)*
Pub: Hispanic Business Inc.
Contact: Jesus Chavarria, President
Ed: Hildy Medina. **Description:** Profile of Jerry Porras, Stanford professor, whose mission is to create a healthier society. Porras discusses what makes any business successful.

34695 ■ *The Checklist Manifesto: How to Get Things Right*
Pub: Metropolitan Books
Contact: Sara Bershtel, Manager
Ed: Atul Gawande. **Released:** December 2009. **Price:** $27, hardcover; $9.99. **Description:** How tragic errors can be sharply reduced with a piece of paper, hand-drawn boxes, and a pencil. **Availability:** PrintE-book.

34696 ■ *China's Rational Entrepreneurs: The Development of the New Private Business Sector*
Pub: Routledge
Contact: Kevin Bradley, President
E-mail: kbradley@taylorandfrancis.com
Ed: Barbara Krug. **Released:** November 2012. **Price:** $54.95, paperback. **Description:** Difficulties faced by entrepreneurs in China are discussed, including analysis for understanding their behavior and relations with local governments in order to secure long-term business success. **Availability:** Print.

34697 ■ *"Choice Bits" in Crain's Cleveland Business (Vol. 30, June 29, 2009, No. 25, pp. 19)*
Pub: Crain Communications Inc.
Description: Ross Farro, Cleveland area restaurateur who was featured in the New York Times story about casual dining chains competing over lunch traffic through pricing.

34698 ■ *"Chuck Hughes" in Canadian Business (Vol. 85, July 16, 2012, No. 11-12, pp. 65)*
Pub: George Media Inc.
Ed: Nancy Won. **Released:** July 16, 2012. **Description:** Celebrity chef Chuck Hughes feels blessed for the opportunity to work on a new cookbook based on the 'Chuck's Day Off' series and to start filming for a new U.S. show called 'Chuck Eats the Street'. For Hughes, cooking at the restaurant is the most rewarding and fulfilling job of all the things he does.

34699 ■ *"Cincinnati Entrepreneur's DotLoop Software Being Tested by Realtors" in Business Courier (Vol. 26, September 11, 2009, No. 20, pp. 1)*
Pub: American City Business Journals, Inc.
Contact: Whitney Shaw, President
Ed: Dan Monk. **Description:** DotLoop Company, owned by entrepreneur Austin Allison, is developing the DotLoop software, which eliminates paperwork in the processing of real estate contracts. The software allows realtors to take control of the negotiation process and is adaptable to the rules of different US states.

34700 ■ *"City Slickers" in Canadian Business (Vol. 81, March 31, 2008, No. 5, pp. 36)*
Pub: Rogers Media Inc.
Contact: Tony Viner, President
Ed: Joe Castaldo. **Description:** Richard Florida believes that the creative class drives the economy and the prosperity of countries depends on attracting and retaining these people. Florida has brought attention to developing livable and economically vibrant cities thanks in part to his promotional skills. However, he has also drawn critics who see his data on his theories as flimsy and inadequate.

34701 ■ *"The Classless Workplace: The Digerati and the New Spirit of Technocapitalism" in WorkingUSA (Vol. 11,*

June 2008, No. 2, pp. 181)
Ed: Eran Fisher. **Description:** Article argues the formation of a new type of economic actor at the intersection of a new capitalism and a new technology: The Dierati. The discourse in based on the analysis of the popular magazine Wired, which registers the culture of contemporary technocapitalism. The suggestion that the new persona of the digerati is constructed as a rejection of the ethics, which dominated the Fordist workplace and Fordist society: Hierarchy and differentiation between workers, on the one hand and capitalists and managers, on the other hand. The transformation of these two categories, workers and capitalists into the digerati worker and the digerati entrepreneur, is described. Set within the context of the structural transformations of capitalism from Fordism to post-Fordism, the article shows the ideological fit of the new ethics of the digerati to the new working arrangements of post-Fordist capitalism, characterized by more privatizes, flexible, and precarious working arrangements.

34702 ■ *"Code Name: Inventors: Go From Golden Idea to Agent of Invention" in Black Enterprise (Vol. 41, November 2010, No. 4, pp. 78)*
Pub: Earl G. Graves Publishing Co. Inc.
Contact: Earl G. Graves, Jr., President
Ed: Renita Burns. **Description:** Profile of Andre Woolery, inventor of a magnetic wristband that holds small nails, screws, drill bits, and small tools, allowing handymen to keep essential tools at hand while working.

34703 ■ *"Collective Wisdom" in Entrepreneur (July 2014)*
Pub: Entrepreneur Media Inc.
Released: July 2014. **Description:** Several entrepreneurs share advice they have received to succeed in business. Foursquare CEO, Dennis Crowley, adheres to his mother's advice to follow his heart in very decision he makes. Skullcandy founder, Rick Alden, says he learned everything he needs to know about startups from the book, "The Art of the Start", by Guy Kawasaki. Peter Relan, founder of technology incubator, 9+, explains how a great entrepreneur can take a bad idea and turn it into something good.

34704 ■ *"Column: Wealth and Jobs: the Broken Link" in Harvard Business Review (Vol. 88, November 2010, No. 11, pp. 44)*
Pub: Harvard Business School Publishing
Ed: Nitin Nohria. **Description:** Rebuilding the link between business and job creation to shore up the middle class is advocated. A blend of government policies and business strategies that foster entrepreneurship and innovation are essential.

34705 ■ *Common Problems; Common Sense Solutions: Practical Advice for Small Business Owners*
Pub: iUniverse Inc.
Contact: Kevin Weiss, President
Ed: Greg Hadley. **Released:** September 14, 2004. **Price:** $14.95, softcover; $6. **Description:** Common sense advice for entrepreneurs running a small business. **Availability:** PrintE-book.

34706 ■ *Common Sense Business: Starting, Operating, and Growing Your Small Business-In Any Economy!*
Pub: Harper Business
Ed: Steve Gottry. **Released:** July 26, 2005. **Price:** $19.95. **Description:** Strategies for starting, operating and growing a small business in any economy. **Availability:** Print.

34707 ■ *The Commonsense Way to Build Wealth: One Entrepreneur Shares His Secrets*
Ed: Jack Chou. **Released:** September 2004. **Price:** $19.95. **Description:** Entrepreneurial tips to accumulate wealth, select the proper business or franchise, choose and manage rental property, and how to negotiate a good lease.

34708 ■ *The Company We Keep: Reinventing Small Business for People, Community, and Place*
Pub: Chelsea Green Publishing Co.
Contact: Margo Baldwin, President
E-mail: mbaldwin@chelseagreen.com
Ed: John Abrams, William Grieder. **Released:** May 15, 2006. **Price:** $18. **Description:** The new business trend in social entrepreneurship as a business plan enables small business owners to meet the triple bottom line of profits for people (employees and owners), community, and the environment. **Availability:** Print.

34709 ■ *"The Competitive Imperative Of Learning" in Harvard Business Review (Vol. 86, July-August 2008, No. 8, pp. 60)*
Pub: Harvard Business Review Press
Contact: Peter E. Walsh, Director
Description: Experimentation and reflection are important components for maintaining success in the business world and are the kind of character traits that can help one keep his or her competitive edge.

34710 ■ *The Complete Idiot's Guide to Finance for Small Business*
Ed: Kenneth E. Little. **Released:** April 2006. **Price:** $19.95. **Description:** Financial experts helps small business owners through strategies for long-term financial success.

34711 ■ *The Complete Small Business Guide: A Sourcebook for New and Small Businesses*
Pub: John Wiley & Sons Inc.
Contact: Stephen M. Smith, President
Ed: Colin Barrow. **Released:** 8th Edition. **Price:** $32. **Description:** Sourcebook for creating new small companies and running established small businesses.

34712 ■ *"Conference Calendar" in Marketing to Women (Vol. 21, March 2008, No. 3, pp. 7)*
Description: Listing of current conferences and events aimed at women entrepreneurs and leaders.

34713 ■ *"Conference Calendar" in Marketing to Women (Vol. 22, July 2009, No. 7, pp. 7)*
Pub: EPM Communications Inc.
Contact: Ira Mayer, President
E-mail: imayer@epmcom.com
Description: Listing of conferences and seminars targeting female entrepreneurs.

34714 ■ *"Conference Calendar" in Marketing to Women (Vol. 22, August 2009, No. 8, pp. 7)*
Pub: EPM Communications Inc.
Contact: Ira Mayer, President
E-mail: imayer@epmcom.com
Description: Listing of conferences and seminars targeting female entrepreneurs.

34715 ■ *Confessions of a Serial Entrepreneur: Why I Can't Stop Starting Over*
Pub: John Wiley & Sons Inc.
Contact: Stephen M. Smith, President
Ed: Stuart Skorman, Catherine Guthrie. **Released:** January 2007. **Price:** $22.95, hardcover; $14.99. **Description:** Profile of Stuart Skorman who was raised in a retail family; Skorman shares his business success. **Availability:** PrintE-book.

34716 ■ *"Congratulations to the 2010 Top Ten Business Women of ABWA" in Women In Business (Vol. 61, August-September 2009, No. 4, pp. 12)*
Pub: American Business Women's Association
Contact: Lorie Burch, President
Description: Listing of the top 10 members of the American Business Women's Association (ABWA) for 2010 is presented. The lists of the top ten 2010 members selected by each of the six ABWA chapters are also provided.

34717 ■ *The Connection Key: Seven Ways the World's Most Successful Entrepreneurs Trounce the Competition and How You Can, Too*
Ed: Maribeth Kuzmeski. **Released:** September 22, 2009. **Price:** $22.95. **Description:** The book is written under the premise that getting ahead in business does not come down to smarts, guts, rare talent, or plain old luck. While those things are helpful, the real missing ingredient is the ability to meaningfully connect with others.

34718 ■ *"Connie Ozan; Founder, Design Director, Twist Creative, 37" in Crain's Cleveland Business (Vol. 28, November 19, 2007, No. 46)*
Pub: Crain Communications Inc.
Ed: John Booth. **Description:** Profile of Connie Ozan, design director and founder of Twist Creative, an advertising agency that she runs with her husband, Michael; Ms. Ozan credits her husband's business sense in bringing a more strategic side to the company in which to complement her art direction.

34719 ■ *"Conversation: Historian Geoffrey Jones On Why Knowledge Stays Put" in Harvard Business Review (Vol. 86, July-August 2008, No. 8)*
Pub: Harvard Business Review Press
Contact: Peter E. Walsh, Director
Ed: Gardiner Morse. **Description:** Geoffrey Jones, Harvard Business School's professor of business history, discusses factors that cause knowledge to concentrate in particular regions, rather than disperse, such as the location of wealth.

34720 ■ *"A Conversation With: Steven Hilfinger, Foley & Lardner L.L.P." in Crain's Detroit Business (Vol. 24, March 24, 2008, No. 12, pp. 1)*
Pub: Crain Communications Inc.
Contact: Rance E. Crain, President
Ed: Tom Henderson. **Description:** Interview with Steven Hilfinger who is a member of Foley & Lardner L.L.P.'s mergers and acquisitions practice and is co-chair of its automotive industry team. Hilfinger discusses such issues as the role a board of directors can play in the M&A process and the future of the auto market.

34721 ■ *Coolhunting: Chasing Down the Next Big Thing*
Pub: AMACOM
Contact: Edward T. Reilly, Manager
Ed: Peter A. Gloor, Scott W. Cooper. **Released:** April 2007. **Price:** $24.95, hardback. **Description:** Lessons for unlocking and applying swarm creativity in organizations to increase creativity, productivity, and efficiency. **Availability:** Print; E-book.

34722 ■ *Corporate Crisis and Risk Management: Modeling, Strategies and SME Application*
Ed: M. Aba-Bulgu; S.M.N. Islam. **Released:** December 2006. **Price:** $115.00. **Description:** Methods and tools for handling corporate risk and crisis management are profiled for small to medium-sized businesses.

34723 ■ *Corporate Entrepreneurship & Innovation*
Pub: South-Western
Contact: Susan Badger, President
Ed: Michael H. Morris, Donald F. Kuratko, Jeffrey G. Covin. **Released:** 3rd Edition. **Price:** A$127.95; NZ$137.95; A$64.95; NZ$69.95. **Description:** Innovation is the key to running a successful small business. The book helps entrepreneurs to develop the skills and business savvy to sustain a competitive edge. **Availability:** PrintE-book.

34724 ■ *Corporate Entrepreneurship: Top Managers and New Business Creation*
Pub: Cambridge University Press
Contact: Richard Ziemacki, President
E-mail: rziemacki@cambridge.org
Ed: Vijay Sathe. **Released:** February 2007. **Price:** $54, Paperback; $45, hardback; $43. **Description:** Studies covering entrepreneurship and business growth are examined. **Availability:** PrintE-book; PDF.

34725 ■ *"Corporate Etiquette: The Art of Apology" in Canadian Business (Vol. 80, January 29, 2007, No. 3, pp. 62)*
Ed: John Gray. **Description:** The methods of nurturing professional relationships, by apologizing for the mistakes committed by individuals and institutions, are described.

34726 ■ "Corporate Responsibility" in Professional Services Close-Up (July 2, 2010)
Description: List of firms awarded the inaugural Best Corporate Citizens in Government Contracting by the Corporate Responsibility Magazine is presented. The list is based on the methodology of the Magazine's Best Corporate Citizen's List, with 324 data points of publicly-available information in seven categories which include: environment, climate change, human rights, philanthropy, employee relations, financial performance, and governance.

34727 ■ Country Studies in Entrepreneurship: A Historical Perspective
Pub: Palgrave Macmillan
Contact: Lisa Dunn, Manager
E-mail: l.dunn@palgrave.com
Released: May 2006. **Price:** £90. **Description:** Comparison of eight national entrepreneurial ventures, covering three continents, is discussed. **Availability:** Print.

34728 ■ Creating Success from the Inside Out: Develop the Focus and Strategy to Uncover the Life You Want
Pub: John Wiley & Sons Inc.
Contact: Stephen M. Smith, President
Ed: Ephren W. Taylor, Emerson Brantley. **Released:** November 2007. **Price:** $24.95, hardcover; $16.99. **Description:** Ephren Taylor founded his first business at age 12 and was a multimillionaire CEO ten years later. Taylor explains how he and other successful young entrepreneurs think about success and achievement. **Availability:** PrintE-book.

34729 ■ Creativity and Innovation: Breaking New Ground..Without Breaking the Bank
Ed: Janice Armstrong. **Released:** March 1, 2009. **Price:** $12.95. **Description:** Advice is given to help small business owners be creative in order to compete in their sector.

34730 ■ "Crimes of Passion" in Entrepreneur (July 2014)
Pub: Entrepreneur Media Inc.
Released: July 2014. **Description:** Entrepreneurs can be passionate about a business, a new product or an idea without clouding the message and overshadowing the mission. When talking passionately about a product, an idea or a business, entrepreneurs need to tone down their enthusiasm to make their proposition more appealing to the audience. Passion must be inclusive, allowing the audience to understand why the proposition is good for them. Passion has to be tempered in a way that it still seems connected to reality and to the mission.

34731 ■ "Crisis Management" in Black Enterprise (Vol. 38, October 1, 2007, No. 3, pp. 69)
Pub: Earl G. Graves Publishing Co. Inc.
Contact: Earl G. Graves, Jr., President
Ed: Faith Chukwudi. **Description:** Shirley W. Bridges, chief information officer for Delta Air Lines, discusses leadership skills that establish trust within an organization.

34732 ■ "Crucible: Losing the Top Job - And Winning It Back" in Harvard Business Review (Vol. 88, October 2010, No. 10, pp. 136)
Pub: Harvard Business School Publishing
Ed: Alison Beard. **Description:** Michael Mack chronicles the changes in perspectives that occurred when he was fired from Garden Fresh, a restaurant firm he co-owned. Once again at the company helm, he is now more receptive to outside input and acknowledges the importance of work-life balance.

34733 ■ Crunch Point: The 21 Secrets to Succeeding When it Matters Most
Pub: American Management Association
Contact: Edward T. Reilly, President
Ed: Brian Tracy. **Price:** $17.95, Hardback. **Availability:** Print.

34734 ■ "Customized Before Custom Was Cool" in Green Industry Pro (July 2011)
Pub: Cygnus Business Media
Contact: Paul Mackler, Chief Executive Officer
Ed: Gregg Wartgow. **Description:** Profile of Turf Care Enterprises and owner Kevin Vogeler, who discusses his desire to use more natural programs using little or

no chemicals in 1986. At that time, that sector represented 20 percent of his business, today it shares 80 percent.

34735 ■ Dare to Prepare - How to Win Before You Begin
Pub: Crown Publishing/Random House
Ed: Ronald M. Shapiro, Gregory Jordan. **Released:** February 24, 2009. **Price:** $15.99, Paperback. **Description:** Shapiro uses his experience as one of America's top negotiators and lawyers to show how meticulous planning can raise the odds of success in business as well as in life.

34736 ■ "Datebook" in Crain's Chicago Business (Vol. 31, March 24, 2008, No. 12, pp. 18)
Pub: Crain Communications Inc.
Contact: Todd Johnson, Publisher
Description: Listing of events in the Chicago area, including conferences addressing entrepreneurialism, economic development, secrets of getting hired, and women business ownership.

34737 ■ "Datebook" in Crain's Chicago Business (Vol. 31, March 31, 2008, No. 13, pp. 1)
Pub: Crain Communications Inc.
Contact: Todd Johnson, Publisher
Description: Listing of events in the Detroit area include conferences addressing entrepreneurialism, economic development, secrets of getting hired, and women business ownership.

34738 ■ "Datebook" in Crain's Chicago Business (Vol. 31, April 28, 2008, No. 17, pp. 18)
Pub: Crain Communications Inc.
Contact: Todd Johnson, Publisher
Description: Listing of events in the Detroit area include conferences addressing entrepreneurialism, economic development, and women business ownership.

34739 ■ "David Low" in Hawaii Business (Vol. 53, October 2007, No. 4, pp. 38)
Pub: PacificBasin Communications
Ed: Cathy S. Cruz-George. **Description:** Hawaii Capital Management managing director David Low ranked first in the 2007 competition for fittest male executives in Hawaii. This 5-foot-9 executive, who weighed 225 lbs. in 2003, weighs 150 lbs. in 2007. The activities that improved Low's fitness, such as weight training, swimming, biking, and running, are discussed.

34740 ■ Dead on Arrival: How the Anti-Business Backlash is Destroying Entrepreneurship in America and What We Can Still Do About It!
Ed: Bernie Marcus; Steve Gottry. **Released:** November 2006. **Price:** $23.95. **Description:** Bernie Marcus, Home Depot leader, addresses regulations hurting small businesses in America.

34741 ■ Dealing with the Tough Stuff: Practical Wisdom for Running a Values-Driven Business
Pub: Berrett-Koehler Communications Inc.
Contact: Steve Piersanti, President
E-mail: spiersanti@bkpub.com
Ed: Margot Fraser, Lisa Lorimer. **Released:** November 01, 2009. **Price:** $16.95. **Description:** Advice is given to help small firms run a value-driven business. **Availability:** Print; PDF.

34742 ■ "Defend Your Research: The Early Bird Really Does Get the Worm" in Harvard Business Review (Vol. 88, July-August 2010, No. 7-8, pp. 30)
Pub: Harvard Business School Publishing
Ed: Christoph Randler. **Price:** $6. **Description:** Research indicates that those who identify themselves as 'morning people' tend to be more proactive, and thus have a career-development advantage over those who identify themselves as 'night people'. Implications of the research are also discussed. **Availability:** PDF.

34743 ■ The Definitive Drucker: Challenges for Tomorrow's Executives -- Final Advice from the Father of Modern Management
Pub: McGraw-Hill
Ed: Elizabeth Haas Edersheim. **Released:** January 2007. **Price:** £17.99, paperback. **Availability:** Print.

34744 ■ "Describing the Entrepreneurial Profile" in International Journal of Entrepreneurship and Small Business (Vol. 11, November 1, 2010)
Pub: Publishers Communication Group
Contact: Doug Wright, Director
Ed: Serena Cubico, Elisa Bortolani, Giuseppe Favretto, Riccardo Sartori. **Description:** An illustration of metric characteristics and selected research applications of an instrument that can be used to define aptitude for an entrepreneurial profile (created in the 1990s) is examined. The entrepreneurial aptitude test (TAI) describes entrepreneurial potential with regard to eight factors.

34745 ■ "The Design of Things to Come" in Business Horizons (Vol. 51, January-February 2008, No. 1, pp. 74)
Ed: Mimi Dollinger. **Description:** Review of the book that helps entrepreneurs develop and market new products, 'The Design of Things to Come: How Ordinary People Create Extraordinary Products'.

34746 ■ Developmental Entrepreneurship: Adversity, Risk, and Isolation
Pub: Emerald Group Publishing Ltd.
Contact: Peter Shelley, Director
Released: July 05, 2006. **Price:** £67.95. **Description:** Volume five of the series, this book focuses on the fields of entrepreneurship, sociology, and economics. Fifteen articles related to entrepreneurship and small business development within a global environment are included. **Availability:** Print.

34747 ■ "Diana Sands: Vice-President of Investor Relations, Boeing Co." in Crain's Chicago Business (Vol. 31, May 5, 2008, No. 18, pp. 32)
Pub: Crain Communications Inc.
Contact: Todd Johnson, Publisher
Ed: John Rosenthal. **Description:** Profile of Diana Sands who is the vice-president of investor relations at Boeing Co. which entails explaining the company's performance to securities analysts and institutional investors.

34748 ■ "Diary of a Short-Seller" in Conde Nast Portfolio (Vol. 2, June 2008, No. 6, pp. 44)
Ed: Jesse Eisinger. **Description:** Profile of David Einhorn who is a fund manager that spoke out against finance company Allied Capital whose stock fell nearly 20 percent the day after Einhorn's critique; Einhorn subsequently had to contend with attacks against his credibility as well as investigations by the S.E.C.; Einhorn's experience illuminates our current economic crisis.

34749 ■ "Dick Haskayne" in Canadian Business (Vol. 81, March 31, 2008, No. 5, pp. 72)
Pub: Rogers Media Inc.
Contact: Tony Viner, President
Ed: Andy Holloway. **Description:** Dick Haskayne says that he learned a lot about business from his dad who ran a butcher shop where they had to make a decision on buying cattle and getting credit. Haskayne says that family, friends, finances, career, health, and infrastructure are benchmarks that have to be balanced.

34750 ■ "Did I Do That?" in Entrepreneur (Vol. 35, November 2007, No. 11, pp. 144)
Pub: Entrepreneur Press
Contact: Perlman Neil, President
Ed: Romanus Wolter. **Description:** Entrepreneurs need to watch habits as some bad habits can affect business operations. Tips on ways to identify bad habits and how to address them are presented.

34751 ■ *"A Different Breed of Deal Maker is Emerging"* in *Globe & Mail (January 14, 2006, pp. B2)*
Pub: CTVglobemedia Publishing Inc.
Ed: Eric Reguly. **Description:** The managerial strategies of chief executive officers in business acquisitions of companies, such as Dofasco Inc., are presented.

34752 ■ *"Digging Deep for Gold"* in *Barron's (Vol. 88, March 24, 2008, No. 12, pp. 49)*
Pub: Dow Jones & Co., Inc.
Contact: Clare Hart, President
Ed: Suzanne McGee. **Description:** David Iben, manager of the Nuveen Tradewinds Value Opportunities Fund, looks for value in companies and industries where the consensus of analysts is negative. He started investing in gold stocks well before gold prices started to rise.

34753 ■ *"Disrupt Yourself: Four Principles for Finding the Career Path You Really Want"* in *(Vol. 90, July-August 2012, No. 7-8, pp. 147)*
Pub: Harvard Business Review Press
Contact: Peter E. Walsh, Director
Ed: Whitney Johnson. **Released:** July-August 2012. **Description:** The four principles are: target needs that need to be met more effectively; identify one's own disruptive strengths; step down or step aside to aside to achieve growth; and allow one's strategy to emerge.

34754 ■ *Divas Doing Business: What the Guidebooks Don't Tell You About Being A Woman Entrepreneur*
Pub: Nouveau Connoisseurs Corporation
Ed: Monique Hayward. **Released:** February 14, 2009. **Price:** $17.96, Paperback; $19.96, Kindle. **Description:** A must-read for any woman who's currently running a business or is thinking of starting one.

34755 ■ *Divine Wisdom at Work: 10 Universal Principles for Enlightened Entrepreneurs*
Pub: Aha! House
Ed: Tricia Molloy. **Released:** July 2006. **Price:** $20.00. **Description:** Entrepreneurial advice for managing a small enterprise is given using inspiration, anecdotes and exercises.

34756 ■ *Do You! 12 Laws to Access the Power in You to Achieve Happiness and Success*
Pub: Gotham/Penguin Group Incorporated
Ed: Russell Simmons, Chris Morrow. **Released:** April 10, 2008. **Price:** $15, paperback; 12.99. **Description:** Hip-Hop mogul describes his successful visions and ventures. **Availability:** PrintElectronic publishing.

34757 ■ *"Do You Really Know Your Problems: Entrepreneurs Have a Tendency To See What They Want To See"* in *Inc. (December 2007, pp. 95-96)*
Pub: Gruner and Jahr USA Publishing Co.
Contact: J. Russell Denson, President
Ed: Norm Brodsky. **Description:** Information is offered to help entrepreneurs diagnose and resolve company issues.

34758 ■ *Doing Business with Beauty: Black Women, Hair Salons, and the Racial Enclave Economy*
Pub: Rowman and Littlefield Publishers Inc.
Contact: Jason Aronson, President
Ed: Adia Harvey Wingfield. **Released:** July 2009. **Price:** $19.95, paperback; £11.95, paperback. **Description:** Factors that draw black women into the hair industry are examined. Interviews with hair salon owners explore aspects of owning a salon, owner-employee relationships, and the black female owner's struggle for autonomy and success in entrepreneurship.

34759 ■ *"Doing It Right"* in *Black Enterprise (Vol. 38, October 1, 2007, No. 3, pp. 53)*
Pub: Earl G. Graves Publishing Co. Inc.
Contact: Earl G. Graves, Jr., President
Ed: Sheiresa Ngo. **Description:** One of the hardest things for every entrepreneur to do is delegate responsibility to employees; Anthony Samuels offers tips on the art of delegating.

34760 ■ *"Don's Pomeroy House a Strongsville Staple"* in *Crain's Cleveland Business (Vol. 30, June 1, 2009, No. 21, pp. 12)*
Pub: Crain Communications Inc.
Ed: Kathy Ames Carr. **Description:** Profile of Don's Pomeroy House, an upscale restaurant inside a 162-year-old brick mansion. The building is listed on the National Register of Historic Places and features a main restaurant, pub and outdoor patio.

34761 ■ *Don't Bitch, Just Get Rich*
Ed: Toney Fitzgerald. **Released:** June 2006. **Price:** $16.00. **Description:** Advice is given to business leaders to help them shift from the position whereby money has power over you to taking responsibility for life choices in order to meet new challenges.

34762 ■ *"The Don't Do Lists"* in *Inc. (Vol. 33, October 2011, No. 8, pp. 65)*
Pub: Inc. Magazine
Ed: Jennifer Alsever, Adam Bluestein. **Description:** Ten business leaders and experts share their don't do lists, the things that should be avoided when going on sales calls, planning business lunches, motivating employees and more are presented.

34763 ■ *"Don't Quit When The Road Gets Bumpy"* in *Women Entrepreneur (November 25, 2008)*
Ed: Bonnie Price. **Description:** Discusses techniques four women entrepreneurs are utilizing to keep their businesses successful despite the credit crunch and the economic downturn.

34764 ■ *"The Doodle Revolution: Unlock the Power to Think Differently"*
Pub: Portfolio Hardcover
Released: January 9, 2014. **Price:** $28.95. **Description:** Powerhouse minds like Albert Einstein, John F. Kennedy, Marie Curie, Thomas Edison, and Henry Ford were all doodlers. Doodling has led to countless discoveries in science, technology, medicine, architecture, literature, and art. Brown guides us through basic doodling to the infodoodle, in other words, a higher level of thinking and empowerment for anyone, especially entrepreneurs and managers.

34765 ■ *Double or Nothing: How Two Friends Risked It All to Buy One of Las Vegas' Legendary Casinos*
Pub: HarperBusiness
Ed: Tom Breitling, Cal Fussman. **Released:** March 18, 2008. **Price:** $24.95, hardcover; $3.99; C$16.99. **Description:** Founders of a successful Internet travel agency share their experience from startup to selling the company. **Availability:** PrintE-book.

34766 ■ *The Dream Manager*
Pub: Hyperion
Ed: Matthew Kelly. **Released:** August 09, 2007. **Price:** $19.95; C$24.95. **Description:** A business fable about the virtues of helping those working for and with you to achieve their dreams. Managers can boost morale and control turnover by adopting this policy.

34767 ■ *Dreams with a Deadline: How to Turn a Strategy for Tomorrow Into a Plan for Today*
Ed: Jacques Horovitz; Anne-Valerie Ohlsson-Corboz. **Released:** November 2006. **Price:** $54.00. **Description:** Tips for successful entrepreneurship are covered.

34768 ■ *"Driving Passion"* in *Small Business Opportunities (April 2008)*
Pub: Harris Publications Inc.
Ed: Chuck Green. **Description:** Profile of Joe Assell, founder of Golftec, a company offering golf instruction that uses the latest technology with professional teachers.

34769 ■ *Driving With No Brakes: How a Bunch of Hooligans Built the Best Travel Company in the World*
Pub: Grand Circle Corporation
Ed: Alan Lewis, Harriet Lewis. **Released:** August 20, 2010. **Price:** $6.94. **Description:** Inspirational book about how two courageous leaders built a remark-

able company that can thrive in change and succeed in an unpredictable world. Important lessons for any business leader trying to create value in the 21st Century are included.

34770 ■ *"The Duty of Wealth: Canadian Business Leaders on Nepotism and Philanthropy"* in *Canadian Business (Vol. 80, Winter 2007, No. 24)*
Ed: Joe Castaldo. **Description:** Fifty-one percent of the respondents in a survey of business leaders say that the decision to allow adult children to join a family firm should be based on the circumstances at the time. He CEOs that were surveyed also believed that billionaires should donate an average of forty percent of their estates and keep the rest for their family.

34771 ■ *E-Myth Mastery: The Seven Essential Disciplines for Building a World Class Company*
Pub: HarperCollins Publishers Inc.
Contact: Jane Friedman, President
E-mail: jfriedman@harpercollins.com
Ed: Michael E. Gerber. **Released:** February 20, 2007. **Price:** $18.99, paperback; $11.99. **Description:** Leadership, marketing, money, management, lead conversion, lead generation, client fulfillment are the seven keys to successful entrepreneurship. **Availability:** PrintE-book.

34772 ■ *The E Myth Revisited: Why Most Small Businesses Don't Work and What to Do About It*
Pub: HarperCollins Publishers Inc.
Contact: Jane Friedman, President
E-mail: jfriedman@harpercollins.com
Ed: Michael E. Gerber. **Released:** January 18, 2010. **Price:** $20.99, Paperback; $14.99. **Description:** The book dispels the myths surrounding starting a business and shows how traditional assumptions can get in the way of running a small company. Topics cover entrepreneurship from infancy to growth and covers franchising. **Availability:** E-book.

34773 ■ *"The Early Bird Gets the Worm"* in *Black Enterprise (Vol. 37, January 2007, No. 6, pp. 111)*
Ed: Tykisha N. Lundy. **Description:** General Motors hosts the Black Enterprise Conference And Expo: Where Deals Are Made at Walt Disney World's Swan and Dolphin Resort, May 9-12. The conference will offer great information to entrepreneurs.

34774 ■ *"Eat, Drink and Be a Success"* in *Entrepreneur (Vol. 37, August 2009, No. 8, pp. 70)*
Pub: Entrepreneur Press
Contact: Perlman Neil, President
Ed: Joel Holland. **Description:** Profile of Fritz Brogan, who is a full time student but also runs a successful bar and restaurant named Gin & Tonic and Kitchen. The bar was built with their target audience in mind which happens to be Brogan's college friends.

34775 ■ *Eco Barons: The New Heroes of Environmental Activism*
Pub: Ecco/HarperCollins
Ed: Edward Humes. **Released:** January 19, 2010. **Price:** $14.99, paperback. **Description:** Profiles of business leaders who have dedicated their lives to saving the planet from ecological devastation. **Availability:** Print.

34776 ■ *Economic Freedom and the American Dream*
Pub: Palgrave Macmillan
Contact: Lisa Dunn, Manager
E-mail: l.dunn@palgrave.com
Ed: Joseph Shaanan. **Released:** February 2010. **Price:** £46, hardcover; $70. **Description:** An exploration into the effects of economic freedom on American in several areas such as markets, politics, and opportunities for would-be entrepreneurs. **Availability:** PrintE-book.

34777 ■ *The Economics of Entrepreneurship*
Pub: Edward Elgar Publishing Inc.
Contact: Richard Henning, Vice President
E-mail: kwight@e-elgar.com
Ed: Simon C. Parker. **Released:** 2006. **Price:** £136,
Hardback. **Description:** Previously published articles
influencing research into the economic structure of
entrepreneurship are examined. **Availability:** Print.

**34778 ■ *The Economics of Self-Employment
and Entrepreneurship***
Pub: Cambridge University Press
Contact: Richard Ziemacki, President
E-mail: rziemacki@cambridge.org
Ed: Simon C. Parker. **Released:** November 2006.
Price: $78, paperback; $146, hardback; $62. **De-
scription:** The importance of self-employment and
entrepreneurship in a modern economy is explored.
Availability: PrintE-book.

**34779 ■ *Ecopreneuring: Putting Purpose and
the Planet Before Profits***
Pub: New Society Publishers
Contact: Sue Custance, Director
Ed: John Ivanko, Lisa Kivirist. **Released:** July 01,
2008. **Price:** $17.95, paperback; $11.65. **Description:** Ecopreneurs in America are shifting profits and
market share towards green living. The book provides
a guideline for ecopreneurs in the areas of eco-
business basics, purposeful management, marketing
in the green economy, and running a lifestyle business. **Availability:** PrintE-book.

**34780 ■ *"Ed Otto, Director of Biotechnology
at RCCC" in Charlotte Observer (February 8,
2007)***
Ed: Gail Smith-Arrants. **Description:** Profile of Ed
Otto, director of biotechnology at Rowan-Cabarrus
Community College. Before taking the position at
RCCC, Otto directed the Food and Drug Administration office responsible for regulating cellular, tissue
and gene therapies products.

**34781 ■ *Edgewalkers: People and
Organizations That Take Risks, Build
Bridges, and Break New Ground***
Pub: Greenwood Publishing Group Inc.
Contact: Janann Sherman, Manager
Ed: Judi Neal. **Released:** October 2006. **Price:** $39.
95. **Description:** Profiles of entrepreneurs who thrive
on change and challenge in order to create success-
ful companies in today's complex business climate.
Availability: Print.

**34782 ■ *"EF, Community Foundation Join
Forces For Good" in Silicon Valley/San Jose
Business Journal (Vol. 30, June 15, 2012, No.
12, pp. 1)***
Pub: American City Business Journal
Description: Nonprofits Entrepreneurs Foundation
and Community Foundation are set to merge. The
plan is in line with the nonprofits' push to better serve
the philanthropic needs of the Bay Area.

**34783 ■ *Effective Operations and Controls
for the Small Privately Held Business***
Pub: John Wiley & Sons Inc.
Contact: Stephen M. Smith, President
Ed: Rob Reider. **Released:** December 2007. **Price:**
$74.95, hardcover; $48.99. **Description:** Guide for
implementing effective operations and controls for
non-regulated small businesses with the least cost
possible is presented. **Availability:** PrintE-book.

34784 ■ *Effectuation*
Pub: Edward Elgar Publishing Inc.
Contact: Richard Henning, Vice President
E-mail: kwight@e-elgar.com
Ed: Saras D. Sarasvathy. **Price:** $37.60, paperback;
$150.30, hardback. **Description:** Effectuation is the
idea that the future is unpredictable while being
controllable. A study of 27 entrepreneurs shows effec-
tive effectuators. **Availability:** Print.

**34785 ■ *"Eight Bucks an Hour" in South
Florida Business Journal (Vol. 34, July 11,
2014, No. 51, pp. 13)***
Pub: American City Business Journals
Released: July 11, 2014. **Description:** Tips on ways
to improve entrepreneurial selling behavior are listed.
A number of potential activities that entrepreneurs

can and should be doing to build business include
cold calling, attending networking events, and creating business alliances.

**34786 ■ *Embedded Entrepreneurship: The
Institutional Dynamics of Innovation***
Pub: Routledge
Contact: Kevin Bradley, President
E-mail: kbradley@taylorandfrancis.com
Ed: Alexander Ebner. **Released:** April 10, 2010.
Price: $160, Hardback. **Description:** In this book,
Alexander Ebner reconstructs the theory of entrepre-
neurship from an institutional perspective.

**34787 ■ *The Emerging Digital Economy:
Entrepreneurship, Clusters, and Policy***
Pub: Springer
Contact: Derk Haank, Chief Executive Officer
E-mail: derk.haank@springer.com
Released: 2006. **Price:** €149.99, hardcover or soft-
cover; €124.94. **Description:** The new economy, or
digital economy, and its impact on the way industries
and firms choose to locate and cluster geographi-
cally. **Availability:** PrintE-book.

**34788 ■ *"Empathy: An Entrepreneur's Killer
App" in Women Entrepreneur (February 3,
2009)***
Ed: Kristi Hedges. **Description:** It is just as important
to treat employees with courtesy and respect during
bad economic times as it is in a good economy.
Employers sometimes take advantage of such bad
economic times since they realize that employees
are grateful to have a job and cannot just quit and
easily find work elsewhere. The importance of
empathy in a company's leadership personnel is
discussed.

**34789 ■ *"Empire of Pixels" in Entrepreneur
(Vol. 37, September 2009, No. 9, pp. 50)***
Pub: Entrepreneur Press
Contact: Perlman Neil, President
Ed: Jason Daley. **Description:** Entrepreneur Jack
Levin has successfully grown Imageshack, an image-
hosting Web service. The Website currently gets 50
million unique visitors a month. Levin has launched
Y-Frog, an application that uses Imageshack to allow
Twitter users to add images to their posts.

**34790 ■ *Employee Management for Small
Business***
Pub: Self-Counsel Press Inc.
Ed: Lin Grensing-Pophal. **Released:** October 15,
2009. **Price:** $20.95. **Description:** Management tools
to help entrepreneurs maintain an effective human
resources plan for a small company. **Availability:**
Print.

**34791 ■ *"Employee Motivation: A Powerful
New Model" in Harvard Business Review (Vol.
86, July-August 2008, No. 8, pp. 78)***
Pub: Harvard Business Review Press
Contact: Peter E. Walsh, Director
Ed: Nitin Nohira, Boris Groysberg, Linda-Eling Lee.
Description: Four drives underlying employee
motivation are discussed as well as processes for
leveraging these drives through corporate culture, job
design, reward systems, and resource-allocation
priorities.

34792 ■ *Encyclopedia of Small Business*
Pub: Cengage Learning
Ed: Arsen Darnay, Monique D. Magee, Kevin Hillstrom. **Released:** 4th Edition. **Price:** $763. **Descrip-
tion:** Concise encyclopedia of small business information. **Availability:** Print.

**34793 ■ *"The Endless Flow of Russell
Simmons" in Entrepreneur (Vol. 37,
September 2009, No. 9, pp. 24)***
Pub: Entrepreneur Press
Contact: Perlman Neil, President
Ed: Josh Dean. **Description:** Entrepreneur Russell
Simmons has successfully grown his businesses by
focusing on underserved markets. Simons has never
given up on any business strategy. He has also
entered the music, clothing and television industries.

**34794 ■ *The Engine of America: The Secrets
to Small Business Success from
Entrepreneurs Who Have Made It!***
Pub: John Wiley & Sons Inc.
Contact: Stephen M. Smith, President
Ed: Hector Barreto. **Released:** September 2007.
Price: $24.95, hardcover; $16.99. **Description:** Successful business strategies from CEOs of fifty small
businesses (some of which are now large corporations) are shared to help entrepreneurs start or grow
an existing company. **Availability:** PrintE-book.

**34795 ■ *"Engineering Business Success:
Essential Lessons In Building A Thriving
Company"***
Pub: Advantage Media
Contact: Daniel Amos, Chief Executive Officer
Released: October 6, 2014. **Price:** $14.99 paper-
back. **Description:** The structure of success is
examined offering detail about business systems. As
an engineer and businessperson, the author, discusses business opportunities and how so many
businesses fail. He believes seizing the responsibility
to serve your industry, your clients, and our stakeholders is key to any successful business venture.
Entrepreneurial enthusiasm is also explored.

**34796 ■ *Enlightened Leadership: Best
Practice Guidelines and Time Tools for Easily
Implementing Learning Organizations***
Pub: Learning House Publishing, Inc.
Ed: Ralph LoVuolo; Alan G. Thomas. **Released:** May
2006. **Price:** $79.99. **Description:** Innovation and
creativity are essential for any successful small business. The book provides owners, managers, and
team leaders with the tools necessary to produce
'disciplined innovation'.

**34797 ■ *Enlightened Leadership: Best
Practice Guidelines and Timesaving Tools for
Easily Implementing Learning Organizations***
Pub: Learning House Publishing, Inc.
Ed: Alan G. Thomas; Ralph L. LoVuolo; Jeanne C.
Hillson. **Released:** September 2006, printable 3
times/year. **Price:** $21.00. **Description:** Book pro-
vides the tools required to create a learning organization management model along with a step-by-step
guide for team planning and learning. The strategy
works as a manager's self-help guide as well as offering continuous learning and improvement for
company-wide success.

**34798 ■ *"Enterpreneur Thorkil Sonne on
What You Can Learn from Employees with
Autism" in Harvard Business Review (Vol. 86,
September 2008, No. 9, pp. 32)***
Pub: Harvard Business Review Press
Contact: Peter E. Walsh, Director
Ed: Susan Donovan. **Description:** Danish software
entrepreneur Thorkil Sonne has helped improve
employment for individuals with autism after discover-
ing the perception of detail and remarkable memory
skills in his own son, who has autism. His company,
Specialisterne, was built via focusing on these
strengths.

**34799 ■ *Enterprise, Entrepreneurship and
Innovation: Concepts, Context and
Commercialization***
Pub: Elsevier Science and Technology Books
Ed: Robin Lowe, Sue Marriott. **Released:** May 2006.
Description: Application of enterprise, innovation
and entrepreneurship are discussed to help compa-
nies grow.

**34800 ■ *Enterprise and Small Business:
Principles, Practice and Policy***
Pub: Pearson Education Inc.
Contact: Steven A. Dowling, President
Ed: Sara Carter, Dylan Jones-Evans. **Released:** 3rd
Edition. **Price:** £49.99. **Description:** Introduction to
small business, challenges of a changing environ-
ment, and the nature of entrepreneurship are among
the issues covered. **Availability:** Print.

**34801 ■ *Enterprising Women in Urban
Zimbabwe: Gender, Microbusiness, and***

Globalization
Pub: Indiana University Press
Contact: Robert Sloan, Director
E-mail: rjsloan@indiana.edu
Ed: Mary Johnson Osirim. **Released:** May 01, 2009.
Price: $23.97, cloth. **Description:** An investigation into the business and personal experiences of women entrepreneurs in the microenterprise sector in Zimbabwe. Many of these women work as market traders, crocheters, seamstresses, and hairdressers. **Availability:** Print.

34802 ■ *The Entrepreneur Next Door: Discover the Secrets to Financial Independence*
Ed: William F. Wagner. **Released:** May 2006. **Price:** , $19.95. **Description:** Traits required to become a successful entrepreneur are highlighted.

34803 ■ *"Entrepreneur Says Spirituality Has Been a Key to Her Success" in Business First Columbus (Vol. 25, October 17, 2008, No. 8, pp. 1)*
Ed: Scott Rawdon. **Description:** Profile of Carolyn Williams Francis, CEO of Williams Interior Designs Inc. She outlines her mantra for success in her furniture design business, but emphasizes that faith has taken her business to greater heights.

34804 ■ *The Entrepreneur and Small Business Problem Solver*
Pub: John Wiley & Sons Inc.
Contact: Stephen M. Smith, President
Ed: William A. Cohen. **Released:** November 2005. **Price:** $31.95; C$26.99. **Description:** Revised edition of the resource for entrepreneurs and small business owners that covers everything from start-up financing and loans to new product promotion and more. **Availability:** Print.

34805 ■ *"Entrepreneur: Suite Expansion For Niche Business" in Boston Business Journal (Vol. 34, April 18, 2014, No. 11)*
Pub: American City Business Journals, Inc.
Contact: Whitney Shaw, President
Released: April 18, 2014. **Description:** Report on a Boston-based short-term corporate housing company, Northeast Suites and investigate its business model. Founded by Patrick Flynn, the company leases available apartment units from property management companies, fully furnishes them, and again rents them to business travelers and relocated employees for a shorter period. The rent may vary depending upon the age of the building, its location, and the amenities provided.

34806 ■ *The Entrepreneurial Author*
Ed: David L. Hancock. **Released:** October 2009. **Price:** $17.95. **Description:** Handbook to help entrepreneurs author and publish a book based on their expertise in their chosen field.

34807 ■ *The Entrepreneurial Culture: Network Advantage Within Chinese and Irish Software Firms*
Pub: Edward Elgar Publishing Inc.
Contact: Richard Henning, Vice President
E-mail: kwight@e-elgar.com
Ed: Denise Tsang. **Released:** 2006. **Price:** £66.60. **Description:** Ways national cultural heritage influences entrepreneurial ventures are discussed. **Availability:** Print.

34808 ■ *Entrepreneurial Decision-Making: Individuals, Tasks and Cognitions*
Pub: Edward Elgar Publishing Inc.
Contact: Richard Henning, Vice President
E-mail: kwight@e-elgar.com
Ed: Veronica Gustafsson. **Released:** December 2006. **Price:** $107.10, hardback. **Description:** Entrepreneurial decision-making is examined by comparing various individuals with differing levels of expertise and potential. **Availability:** Print.

34809 ■ *Entrepreneurial Finance*
Pub: Pearson Education Inc.
Contact: Steven A. Dowling, President
Ed: Philip J. Adelman, Alan M. Marks. **Released:** Sixth Edition. **Price:** $129.60. **Description:** Financial aspects of running a small business are covered; topics include sole proprietorships, partnerships, limited liability companies, and private corporations.

34810 ■ *Entrepreneurial Finance: A Casebook*
Pub: John Wiley & Sons Inc.
Contact: Stephen M. Smith, President
Ed: Paul A. Gompers, William Sahlman. **Released:** December 2001. **Price:** $142.95, paperback. **Description:** Investment analysis, entrepreneurial financing, harvesting, and renewal in the entrepreneurial firm are among the topics discussed. **Availability:** Print.

34811 ■ *"Entrepreneurial Human Resource Leadership: A Conversation with Dwight Carlson" in Human Resource Management (Vol. 49, July-August 2010, No. 4, pp. 793-804)*
Pub: John Wiley
Ed: David C. Strubler, Benjamin W. Redekop. **Description:** Dwight Carlson, a visionary entrepreneur, talks about his main role as a leader. He believes that experience can help in making choices between difficult alternatives. He also thinks that leaders do not really motivate people, they actually create an environment where they motivate themselves.

34812 ■ *The Entrepreneurial Imperative: How America's Economic Miracle Will Reshape the World*
Pub: HarperCollins Publishers Inc.
Contact: Jane Friedman, President
E-mail: jfriedman@harpercollins.com
Ed: Carl J. Schramm. **Released:** October 10, 2006. **Price:** $24.95. **Description:** Carl Schramm, president of Kauffman Foundation discusses the secret to America's economy. **Availability:** Print.

34813 ■ *"Entrepreneurial Orientation and Firm Performance" in Journal of Small Business and Entrepreneurship (Vol. 23, Winter 2010, No. 1)*
Pub: Canadian Council for Small Business and Entrepreneurship
Contact: Sandra Altner, President
Description: The article develops a theoretical model of the relationship between firm-level entrepreneurship and firm performance. This model is intended to further clarify the consequences of an 'entrepreneurial orientation', paying particular attention to the differential relationship that exists between the three sub-dimensions of entrepreneurial orientation and firm performance. Included in the theoretical model are other important variables (such as organizational structure and environmental characteristics) that may impact the EO-performance relationship. Propositions are developed regarding the various configurations of the sub-dimensions of EO and organizational structure that would be most appropriate in a given environmental context. Future research may also benefit from considering the important role that organizational strategy and life cycle stage play in this model. The implications of this model for both researchers and managers are discussed.

34814 ■ *Entrepreneurial Skills: 2nd Edition*
Pub: Double Storey Books
Ed: Cecile Nieuwenhuizen. **Released:** March 1, 2009. **Price:** $32.00. **Description:** Entrepreneurial skills are examined, showing how entrepreneurship differs from management mostly in attitude and approach.

34815 ■ *Entrepreneurial Small Business*
Pub: McGraw-Hill Higher Education
Contact: Edward Stanford, President
E-mail: ed_stanford@mcgraw-hill.com
Ed: Jerome A. Katz, Richard P. Green. **Released:** Fourth Edition. **Price:** $259. **Description:** Students are able to get a clear vision of small enterprise in today's business climate. The textbook helps focus on the goal of having personal independence with financial security as an entrepreneur.

34816 ■ *Entrepreneurial Strategies: New Technologies and Emerging Markets*
Pub: Blackwell Publishing Inc.
Contact: Gordon Tibbitts, III, President
Released: August 2006. **Price:** $100; $80.99. **Description:** Ideas to help a small business expand into emerging market economies (EMEs) are discussed. Despite the high failure rate, this book helps a small firm develop a successful plan. **Availability:** PrintE-book.

34817 ■ *Entrepreneurial Strategy: Emerging Businesses in Declining Industries*
Pub: Edward Elgar Publishing Inc.
Contact: Richard Henning, Vice President
E-mail: kwight@e-elgar.com
Ed: Lucio Cassia, Michael Fattore, Stefano Paleari. **Released:** 2006. **Price:** £76.50. **Description:** Role of entrepreneurship in context of older and declining industries is explored. The book offers insight into entrepreneurial dynamics behind emerging businesses in declining industries, especially the roles of resources processes and people. **Availability:** Print.

34818 ■ *The Entrepreneur's Almanac: Fascinating Figures, Fundamentals and Facts You Need to Run and Grow Your Business*
Ed: Jacquelyn Lynn. **Released:** October 2007. **Price:** , $24.95. **Description:** Reference containing a collection of tips, ideas and wisdom required to run and grow a successful business. Short articles, anecdotes, powerful lists and checklists, charts, and profiles of successful entrepreneurs are included.

34819 ■ *"Entrepreneurs Conference" in Black Enterprise (Vol. 38, February 2008, No. 7, pp. 163)*
Description: Black Enterprise Entrepreneurs Conference and Expo will be held May 14-17, 2008 at the Charlotte Westin Hotel and Charlotte Convention Center in North Carolina. Entrepreneurs are given the opportunity to present their business ideas in the Bevator Pitch Competition for a chance to win products and services.

34820 ■ *The Entrepreneur's Edge: Finding Money, Making Money, Keeping Money*
Ed: Daniel Hogan. **Released:** October 2006. **Price:** $24.95. **Description:** Advice for starting, running and growing a new business is given.

34821 ■ *The Entrepreneur's Guide to Managing Growth and Handling Crises*
Pub: Greenwood Publishing Group Inc.
Contact: Janann Sherman, Manager
Ed: Theo J. Van Dijk. **Released:** December 2007. **Price:** $39.95, hardcover. **Description:** The author explains how entrepreneurs can overcome crisis by changing the way they handle customers, by putting new processes and procedures in place, and managing employees in a professional manner. The book includes appendices with tips for hiring consultants, creating job descriptions, and setting up systems to chart cash flow as well as worksheets, tables and figures and a listing of resources. **Availability:** Print.

34822 ■ *Entrepreneurs in the Southern Upcountry: Commercial Culture in Spartanburg, South Carolina, 1845-1880*
Pub: University of Georgia Press
Contact: Nicole Mitchell, Director
Ed: Bruce W. Eelman. **Released:** February 15, 2008. **Price:** $46.95; $44.95. **Description:** Historical account of the entrepreneurial culture in a nineteenth-century southern community outside the plantation belt is given. **Availability:** PrintE-book.

34823 ■ *The Entrepreneur's Strategy Guide: Ten Keys for Achieving Marketplace Leadership and Operational Excellence*
Pub: Greenwood Publishing Group Inc.
Contact: Janann Sherman, Manager
Ed: Tom Cannon. **Released:** September 2006. **Price:** $44.95. **Description:** Ten principles of marketplace leadership are explored. The book provides a plan for small businesses, including diagnostics, checklists, and other interactive exercises to study both external and internal principles. **Availability:** Print.

34824 ■ *Entrepreneurship*
Pub: McGraw-Hill Higher Education
Contact: Edward Stanford, President
E-mail: ed_stanford@mcgraw-hill.com
Ed: Robert D. Hisrich, Michael P. Peters, Dean A. Shepherd. **Released:** 9th Edition. **Price:** $254.67, retail; $191, wholesale. **Description:** Advice is offered to entrepreneurs in formulating, planning, and implementing a business plan. **Availability:** Print.

34825 ■ *Entrepreneurship*
Pub: Greenwood Publishing Group Inc.
Contact: Janann Sherman, Manager
Ed: Alan L. Carsrud, Malin E. Brannback. **Released:** March 30, 2007. **Price:** $55, Hardcover. **Description:** Entrepreneurial process is profiles, examining how these individuals identify opportunity and ways they address the personal, social, and financial risks involved in starting a new business venture. **Availability:** Print; E-book.

34826 ■ *Entrepreneurship: A Process Perspective*
Pub: South-Western
Contact: Susan Badger, President
Ed: Robert A. Baron, Scott A. Shane. **Released:** 2nd Edition. **Price:** $259.95, Hardcover. **Description:** Entrepreneurial process covering team building, finances, business plan, legal issues, marketing, growth and exit strategies. **Availability:** Print.

34827 ■ *Entrepreneurship: A Small Business Approach*
Pub: McGraw-Hill Higher Education
Contact: Edward Stanford, President
E-mail: ed_stanford@mcgraw-hill.com
Ed: Charles E. Bamford, Garry D. Bruton. **Released:** January 10, 2010. **Description:** This text takes a hands-on, problem-based learning approach that works through real problems faced by entrepreneurs and small business owners.

34828 ■ *"Entrepreneurship: As Cool As It Gets" in Canadian Business (Vol. 80, January 29, 2007, No. 3, pp. 10)*
Ed: Norman de Bono. **Description:** The proposed construction of a restaurant with ice in Dubai by the Canadian firm Iceculture Inc. for the Sharaf Group is discussed. The growth of the clientele of Iceculture Inc. is described.

34829 ■ *Entrepreneurship As Social Change: A Third Movements in Entrepreneurship Book*
Pub: Edward Elgar Publishing Inc.
Contact: Richard Henning, Vice President
E-mail: kwight@e-elgar.com
Ed: Chris Steyaert, Daniel Hjorth. **Released:** 2007. **Price:** £28.80, paperback. **Description:** Third book in a series, the edition examines entrepreneurship as a societal phenomenon. **Availability:** Print; E-book.

34830 ■ *Entrepreneurship and Economic Growth*
Pub: Edward Elgar Publishing Inc.
Contact: Richard Henning, Vice President
E-mail: kwight@e-elgar.com
Ed: Martin Carree, A.R. Thurik. **Released:** 2006. **Price:** £117. **Description:** Historic and country-specific studies and articles regarding entrepreneurship and innovation, growth models, competition and productivity, and empirical evidence. **Availability:** Print.

34831 ■ *Entrepreneurship and Economic Progress*
Pub: Routledge
Contact: Kevin Bradley, President
E-mail: kbradley@taylorandfrancis.com
Ed: Randall Holcombe. **Price:** $54.95, paperback; $170, hardback. **Description:** Economic models of economic growth and the ways entrepreneurial progress are highlighted. **Availability:** Print.

34832 ■ *Entrepreneurship: Frameworks and Empirical Investigations from Forthcoming Leaders of European Research*
Pub: Emerald Group Publishing Ltd.
Contact: Peter Shelley, Director
Released: May 25, 2006. **Price:** £67.95. **Description:** Entrepreneurial research and theory cover the early growth of research-based startups and the role of learning in international entrepreneurship, focusing on Europe. **Availability:** Print.

34833 ■ *Entrepreneurship: From Opportunity to Action*
Pub: Palgrave Macmillan
Contact: Lisa Dunn, Manager
E-mail: l.dunn@palgrave.com
Ed: David Rae. **Released:** January 2007. **Price:** £39. 99, paperback. **Description:** Learning enterprise

theory is discussed, focusing on the individual as an entrepreneur and ways to create and take advantage of opportunities. **Availability:** Print; E-book.

34834 ■ *Entrepreneurship, Geography, and American Economic Growth*
Pub: Cambridge University Press
Contact: Richard Ziemacki, President
E-mail: rziemacki@cambridge.org
Ed: Zoltan Acs, Catherine Armington. **Released:** July 2011. **Price:** $54, paperback; $43. **Description:** Knowledge among college-educated workers was among the key reasons for economic growth throughout the U.S. in the 1990s. **Availability:** PrintE-book.

34835 ■ *Entrepreneurship and the Growth of Firms*
Pub: Edward Elgar Publishing Inc.
Contact: Richard Henning, Vice President
E-mail: kwight@e-elgar.com
Released: December 2006. **Price:** $107.10, hardback; $41.60, paperback. **Description:** Relationships between entrepreneurial skills and business growth are explored. **Availability:** Print.

34836 ■ *Entrepreneurship and How to Establish Your Own Business*
Pub: Double Storey Books
Ed: Johan Strydon. **Released:** March 1, 2009. **Price:** , $37.95. **Description:** Guidelines are given to help develop a small business idea and to establish a successful enterprise. .

34837 ■ *Entrepreneurship, Innovation and Economic Growth*
Pub: Edward Elgar Publishing Inc.
Contact: Richard Henning, Vice President
E-mail: kwight@e-elgar.com
Ed: David B. Audretsch. **Released:** 2006. **Price:** £117. **Description:** Links between entrepreneurship, innovation and economic growth are examined. **Availability:** Print.

34838 ■ *Entrepreneurship, Innovation and the Growth Mechanism of the Free-Enterprise Economies*
Pub: Princeton University Press
Contact: Shirley M. Tilghman, President
Released: January 2007. **Price:** $97.50, hardcover; £68, hardcover. **Description:** Scholars address the free-enterprise Western economies. **Availability:** Print.

34839 ■ *Entrepreneurship, Investment and Spatial Dynamics: Lessons and Implications for an Enlarged EU*
Pub: Edward Elgar Publishing Inc.
Contact: Richard Henning, Vice President
E-mail: kwight@e-elgar.com
Ed: Peter Nijkamp, Ronald L. Moomaw, Iulia Traistaru-Siedschlag. **Released:** 2006. **Price:** £67. 50. **Description:** Understanding the impact and interaction between investment, knowledge and entrepreneurship with an expanding European Union. **Availability:** Print.

34840 ■ *"Entrepreneurship and Service Innovation" in Journal of Business & Industrial Marketing (Vol. 29, July 2014, No. 6)*
Pub: Emerald Group Publishing Inc.
Released: July 2014. **Description:** An overview of entrepreneurship and service innovation and the association between entrepreneurial orientation, innovation, and entrepreneurship or new entry. Analysis of secondary data was performed and observed that EO (entrepreneurial orientation), innovation, and entrepreneurship feature a triadic connect. EO supports innovation, innovation endorses new venture creation, and it in turn commercializes innovations.

34841 ■ *Entrepreneurship and Small Business*
Pub: Palgrave Macmillan
Contact: Lisa Dunn, Manager
E-mail: l.dunn@palgrave.com
Ed: Paul Burns. **Released:** 3rd Edition . **Price:** $78, paperback; £44.99, paperback. **Description:** Entrepreneurial skills, focusing on good management practices are discussed. Topics include family businesses, corporate, international and social entrepreneurship.

34842 ■ *Entrepreneurship and Small Business Development in the Former Soviet Bloc*
Ed: David Smallbone, Friederike Welter. **Released:** January 10, 2010. **Price:** $140. **Description:** Examination of entrepreneurship and small business in Russia and other key countries of Eastern Europe, showing how far small businesses have developed in the region.

34843 ■ *Entrepreneurship and SMEs in the Euro-Zone*
Pub: Imperial College Press
Ed: Leo-Paul Dana. **Description:** Information regarding entrepreneurship and SMEs in Europe is presented.

34844 ■ *Entrepreneurship and Technology Policy*
Pub: Edward Elgar Publishing Inc.
Contact: Richard Henning, Vice President
E-mail: kwight@e-elgar.com
Released: 2006. **Price:** £108. **Description:** Journal articles focusing how and the ways small businesses' technical contributions are affecting business. The book is divided into four parts: Government's Direct Support of R&D, Government's Leveraging of R&D, Government's Infrastructure Policies; and Knowledge Flows from Universities and Laboratories. **Availability:** Print.

34845 ■ *Entrepreneurship: The Engine of Growth*
Pub: Greenwood Publishing Group Inc.
Contact: Janann Sherman, Manager
Released: November 2006. **Price:** $300, hardcover. **Description:** Dynamics of entrepreneurship are examined. **Availability:** Print.

34846 ■ *Entrepreneurship: Theory, Process, and Practice*
Pub: South-Western
Contact: Susan Badger, President
Ed: Donald F. Kuratko. **Released:** 9th Edition. **Price:** $249.99; $49.99, rental; $232, wholesale; $93.49. **Description:** Understanding the process of entrepreneurship. **Availability:** PrintE-book.

34847 ■ *Entrepreneurship in the U.S.: The 2005 Assessment*
Ed: Paul Reynolds. **Released:** March 2007. **Price:** $79.95. **Description:** Entrepreneurship and its role in the U.S. economy is discussed, examining new business creation and its impact on job growth, productivity enhancements, innovation, and social mobility.

34848 ■ *"Entreprenewers" in Birmingham Business Journal (Vol. 31, April 18, 2014, No. 16, pp. 4)*
Pub: American City Business Journals, Inc.
Contact: Whitney Shaw, President
Released: April 18, 2014. **Description:** Innovations from winners of Birmingham, Alabama's 2014 Entrepreneur Spotlight are discussed. Ice Coffee owners John Wright and Jeff Hooker said their product gradually garnered local support until Barber Companies agreed to distribute it. Securing funding continues to be the greatest challenge for entrepreneurs.

34849 ■ *"EPG Security Group" in Business Journal (Vol. 31, May 16, 2014, No. 51, pp. 10)*
Pub: American City Business Journals
Released: May 16, 2014. **Description:** Profile of Erik Bergling, a former Marine, and owner of EPG Security Group. The firm provides security guards for special events, music venues, and executive protection. Bergling was forced to retire early from the Marines due to a hip injury.

34850 ■ *Ethnic Solidarity for Economic Survival: Korean Greengrocers in New York City*
Pub: Russell Sage Foundation Publications
Contact: David Haproff, Director, Communications
E-mail: david@rsage.org
Ed: Pyong Gap Min. **Released:** February 2011. **Price:** $24.95, paperback. **Description:** Investigations into the entrepreneurial traditions of Korean immigrant families in New York City running ethnic

businesses, particularly small grocery stores and produce markets. Social, cultural and economic issues facing these retailers are discussed. **Availability:** Print.

34851 ■ *"Everett Dowling" in Hawaii Business (Vol. 54, August 2008, No. 2, pp. 32)*
Pub: PacificBasin Communications

Ed: Jason Ubay. **Description:** Real estate developer Everett Dowling, president of Dowling Company Inc., talks about the company's sustainable management and services. The company's office has been retrofitted to earn a Leadership in Energy and Environmental Design (LEED) certification. Dowling believes that real estate development can be part of the sustainable solution.

34852 ■ *Everything I Know About Business I Learned from My Mama: A Down-Home Approach to Business and Personal Success*
Pub: John Wiley & Sons Inc.

Contact: Stephen M. Smith, President

Ed: Tim Knox. **Released:** May 2007. **Price:** $22.95; $14.99. **Description:** Part memoir, part self-help, and part business how-to manual designed to help any small business owner/entrepreneur. **Availability:** Print E-book.

34853 ■ *Everything is Possible: Life and Business Lessons from a Self-Made Billionaire and the Founder of Slim-Fast*
Ed: S. Daniel Abraham. **Released:** February 10, 2010. **Price:** $24.95. **Description:** A profile of the founder of Slim-Fast nutritional diet drink used to help people lose weight.

34854 ■ *"The Evolution of Corporate Social Responsibility" in Business Horizons (November-December 2007, pp. 449)*
Pub: Elsevier Technology Publications

Ed: Philip L. Cochran. **Price:** $35.95. **Description:** Corporate social responsibility is now perceived as vital in enhancing the profitability of businesses while improving their reputation. It has changed business practices such as philanthropy, investment, and entrepreneurship. **Availability:** PDF.

34855 ■ *"Evolutionary Psychology in the Business Sciences"*
Pub: Springer Publishing Co.

Contact: Ursula Springer, President

Released: September 28, 2014. **Price:** $150.93. **Description:** All individuals operating in the business sphere share a common biological heritage, including consumers, employers, employees, entrepreneurs, or financial traders, to name a few. The evolutionary behavioral sciences and specific business contexts including marketing, consumer behavior, advertising, innovation and creativity and invention, intertemporal choice, negotiations, competition and cooperation in organizational settings, sex differences in workplace patterns, executive leadership, business ethics, store and office design, behavioral decision making, and electronic communications and commerce are all addressed.

34856 ■ *"Ex-Medical Student Stages Career In Event Planning: Barcelona Owner Makes Inroads With Luxury Car Dealerships" in Los Angeles Business Journal (Vol. 34, June 18, 2012, No. 25, pp. 10)*
Pub: CBJ, L.P.

Description: Barcelona Enterprises started as a company designing menus for restaurants, organizing food shows, to planning receptions for luxury car dealers. The fim will be launching the first Las Vegas Chocolate Festival & Pastry Show in July 2012. Presently, the company runs 24 wine and food festivals, organizes events for an upscale dog shampoo maker, and sports car dealerships.

34857 ■ *Execution: The Discipline of Getting Things Done*
Ed: Larry Bossidy, Ram Charan, Charles Burck. **Released:** June 15, 2002. **Price:** $27.50. **Description:** The book shows how to get things done and deliver results whether you are running an entire company or in your first management position.

34858 ■ *"The Executive Brain" in Canadian Business (Vol. 80, October 22, 2007, No. 21, pp. 41)*
Ed: Rachel Pulfer. **Description:** Studies by Jordan Petersen, Frank Schmidt, and John Hunter show that leaders have highly evolved capacities to think using the prefrontal cortex of the brain. Inspirational leadership ability is located in the parietal lobe. Other details of the research are discussed.

34859 ■ *"Executive Summary: How Smart Firms Create Productive Ties" in Business Strategy Review (Vol. 23, Spring 2012, No. 1, pp. 83)*
Released: Spring 2012. **Description:** Benjamin L. Hallen and Kathleen M. Eisenhardt wrote, 'Catalyzing Strategies and Efficient Tie Formation: How Entrepreneurial Firms Obtain Investment Ties', May 3, 2011. The report is examined.

34860 ■ *"Executive of the Year: Sullivan Led Bucyrus through Unforgettable Year" in Business Journal-Milwaukee (Vol. 28, December 17, 2010, No. 11, pp. A1)*
Pub: Milwaukee Business Journal

Ed: Rich Rovito. **Description:** Bucyrus International's president and CEO, Tim Sullivan, was chosen as Milwaukee's Executive of the Year for 2010. Sullivan led Bucyrus through a year of dramatic change which started with the acquisition of the mining business of Terex Corporation and culminating with a deal to sell Caterpillar Inc.

34861 ■ *"Expanding the Entrepreneurship Class" in (Vol. 90, July-August 2012, No. 7-8, pp. 40)*
Pub: Harvard Business Review Press

Contact: Peter E. Walsh, Director

Ed: Carl Schramm. **Released:** July-August 2012. **Description:** Two programs for encouraging entrepreneurship are highlighted. One offers trained facilitators who help participants move through iterations to produce viable business models. Another provides college juniors and seniors with instruction and advice from successful businesspeople.

34862 ■ *"Expanding Middleby's Food Processing Biz" in Crain's Chicago Business (Vol. 31, April 21, 2008, No. 16, pp. 6)*
Pub: Crain Communications Inc.

Contact: Todd Johnson, Publisher

Ed: David Sterrett. **Description:** Profile of the executive vice-president of the food processing company, Middleby Corp, whose business plan is to develop new products, begin looking for acquisitions and simplify operations in order to expand the firm.

34863 ■ *The Facebook Effect: The Inside Story of the Company That Is Connecting the World*
Pub: Simon & Shuster

Ed: David Kirkpatrick. **Released:** February 2011. **Price:** $17, paperback. **Description:** There's never been a Website like Facebook: more than 350 million people have accounts, and if the growth rate continues, by 2013 every Internet user worldwide will have his or her own page. No one's had more access to the inner workings of the phenomenon than Kirkpatrick, a senior tech writer at Fortune magazine. Written with the full cooperation of founder Mark Zuckerberg, the book follows the company from its genesis in a Harvard dorm room through its successes over Friendster and MySpace, the expansion of the user base, and Zuckerberg's refusal to sell. **Availability:** Print.

34864 ■ *"Facing the Future" in Canadian Business (Vol. 81, March 31, 2008, No. 5, pp. 69)*
Pub: Rogers Media Inc.

Contact: Tony Viner, President

Ed: John Gray. **Description:** Discusses a web poll of 122 Canadian CEOs which shows that these leaders are convinced that the U.S. economy is slowing but are split on the impact that this will have on the Canadian economy. The aging and retiring workforce and the strong Canadian dollar are other concerns by these leaders.

34865 ■ *"A Failed Promise: A Dream Job Gone..or Just Delayed?" in Restaurant Business (Vol. 107, September 2008, No. 9, pp. 34)*
Pub: Ideal Media

Description: Profile of Jeremy Lycan, executive chef who taught at the California Culinary Academy. Lycan tells of accepting a position as executive chef from his mentor, and later started his own restaurant.

34866 ■ *"The Family Tools" in Canadian Business (Vol. 80, March 26, 2007, No. 7, pp. 14)*
Description: A few strategies for running family businesses successfully are presented.

34867 ■ *"Fashion Forward - Frugally" in Entrepreneur (Vol. 37, July 2009, No. 7, pp. 18)*
Pub: Entrepreneur Press

Contact: Perlman Neil, President

Ed: Jason Daley. **Description:** Staci Deal, a Fayetteville-based franchisee of fashion brand Plato's Closet, shares her experiences on the company's growth. Deal believes that the economy, and the fact that Fayetteville is a college town, played a vital role in boosting the used clothing store's popularity. Her thoughts on being a young business owner, and the advantages of running a franchise are also given.

34868 ■ *Fast Company's Greatest Hits: 10 Years of the Most Innovative Ideas in Business*
Pub: Penguin Group USA

Contact: Phyllis Grann, President

Ed: Mark N. Vamosand, David Lidsky, Jim Collins. **Released:** July 2006. **Price:** $24.95. **Description:** Offering of Fast Company's best articles covering business ideas and profiles of successful firms and their leaders. **Availability:** Print.

34869 ■ *Fast-Track Employer's Kit: California*
Pub: Kaplan Books

Ed: Carolyn Usinger. **Released:** 2006. **Price:** $29.95; C$37. **Description:** Requirements for running a small business in California re outlined.

34870 ■ *"Fearless Leaders: Sharpen Your Focus: How the New Science of Mindfulness Can Help You Reclaim Your Confidence"*
Pub: Waterfront Digital Press

Released: August 21, 2014. **Price:** $14.95 paperback. **Description:** Executive coaches explain the principles that make managers and entrepreneurs and business leaders fearless.

34871 ■ *Female Entrepreneurship in East and South-East Asia: Opportunities and Challenges*
Pub: Woodhead Publishing Ltd.

Ed: Philippe Debroux. **Released:** February 10, 2010. **Price:** $145. **Description:** A detailed study of female entrepreneurship in Asia, where public authorities are slowly realizing the importance of women as workers and entrepreneurs. **Availability:** Print; E-book.

34872 ■ *Fierce Conversations*
Pub: Berkley Trade

Ed: Susan Scott. **Released:** January 06, 2004. **Price:** $16, Paperback. **Description:** Seven Principles of Fierce Conversations are addressed to help readers become effective conversationalists in both business and social settings.

34873 ■ *Fierce Leadership*
Ed: Susan Scott. **Released:** January 11, 2011. **Price:** $15. **Description:** A bold alternative to the worst 'best' practices of business in the 21st Century.

34874 ■ *"The File On..Skoda Minotti" in Crain's Cleveland Business (Vol. 28, October 8, 2007, No. 40, pp. 26)*
Pub: Crain Communications Inc.

Ed: Kimberly Bonvissuto. **Description:** Overview of Skoda Minotti, the accounting and financial services firm located in Mayfield Village; the company has 140 employees and an expanded slate of services.

34875 ■ *"Filling the Gap" in Canadian Business (Vol. 80, March 12, 2007, No. 6, pp. 62)*
Pub: Rogers Media Inc.
Contact: Tony Viner, President
Ed: Andrew Wahl. Description: The chief executive officer of GAP, Bruce Poon Tip, shares his experience and efforts in the growth of the company to a leading position in Canada.

34876 ■ *"Finding A Higher Gear" in Harvard Business Review (Vol. 86, July-August 2008, No. 8, pp. 68)*
Pub: Harvard Business Review Press
Contact: Peter E. Walsh, Director
Ed: Thomas A. Stewart, Anand P. Raman. Description: Anand G. Mahindra, the chief executive officer of Mahindra and Mahindra Ltd., discusses how his company fosters innovation, drawn from customer centricity, and how this will grow the company beyond India's domestic market.

34877 ■ *"Finding Good Bets Down on the Farm" in Crain's Chicago Business (Vol. 31, March 24, 2008, No. 12, pp. 4)*
Pub: Crain Communications Inc.
Contact: Todd Johnson, Publisher
Ed: Daniel Rome Levine. Description: Interview with money manager Jeff James, the portfolio manager for Driehaus Capital Management LLC, who discusses the Federal Reserve and recommends several companies in which to make investments.

34878 ■ *"Finding Success in Small Businesses" in Women in Business (Vol. 66, Summer 2014, No. 1, pp. 16)*
Pub: Women In Business
Released: Summer 2014. Description: Television host J.J. Ramberg reveals that she is inspired by everyday people who succeed in business. She mentions that good entrepreneurs tend to focus on the things that matter. Her views about her personal and professional responsibilities are also discussed.

34879 ■ *"Finishing Touches: the Fashion Statement is in the Detail" in Black Enterprise (Vol. 37, January 2007, No. 6, pp. 106)*
Pub: Earl G. Graves Publishing Co. Inc.
Contact: Earl G. Graves, Jr., President
Ed: Sonia Alleyne. Description: Men are discovering the importance of dressing for success. Paying attention to the details such as shoes, socks, cuffs, and collars are just as important as finding the right suit.

34880 ■ *"First Class All the Way" in Entrepreneur (July 2014)*
Pub: Entrepreneur Media Inc.
Released: July 2014. Description: Entrepreneurs are offered tips on dealing with problem employees and fostering diversity in business. Leaders must be vigilant and proactive when handling an employee who has a sense of entitlement. The culture and values of the company and the reason why his me-first-and-only approach will not work must be explained to him. A healthy business environment in the 21st Century must be open to diversifying its people and ideas. Hiring women employees will help successful businesses grow.

34881 ■ *"Fiscally Fit" in Entrepreneur (Vol. 37, October 2009, No. 10, pp. 130)*
Pub: Entrepreneur Press
Contact: Perlman Neil, President
Ed: Jason Daley. Description: Landrie Peterman, owner of an Anytime Fitness franchise in Oregon, describes how she turned her business around. The franchise, located in an industrial park, saw growth after six months with the help of corporate clients.

34882 ■ *"Five Low-Cost Home Based Startups" in Women Entrepreneur (December 16, 2008)*
Ed: Lesley Spencer Pyle. Description: During tough economic times, small businesses have an advantage over large companies because they can adjust to economic conditions more easily and without having to go through corporate red tape that can slow the implementation process. A budding entrepreneur may find success by taking inventory of his or her skills,

experience, expertise and passions and utilizing those qualities to start a business. Five low-cost home-based startups are profiled. These include starting an online store, a virtual assistant service, web designer, sales representative and a home staging counselor.

34883 ■ *"Five More Great Books on Entrepreneurship" in Entrepreneur (Vol. 37, July 2009, No. 7, pp. 19)*
Pub: Entrepreneur Press
Contact: Perlman Neil, President
Ed: Jennifer Wang. Description: 800-CEO-Read founder, Jack Covert, and president, Todd Stattersten, share five books that would have been included in the book, 'The 100 Business Books of All Time' if space was not an issue. 'You Need to Be a Little Crazy,' 'Oh, the Places You'll Go!,' 'Founders at Work,' 'The Innovator's Dilemma,' and 'Purple Cow' are highly recommended for entrepreneurs.

34884 ■ *"Five Reasons Why Florida Is a Great Place for Business" in Orlando Business Journal (Vol. 30, June 27, 2014, No. 53, pp. 5)*
Pub: American City Business Journals
Released: June 27, 2014. Description: The article discusses five reasons why Florida is a great place to do business. Florida has No. 1 tax climate in the Southeast, it ranks among the nation's top ten in entrepreneurial success, is home to 19 commercial airports, 15 deepwater seaports and three spaceports, is home to two major bioresearch centers, and exports about $65 billion in goods annually.

34885 ■ *"Five Steps to the Corner Office" in Canadian Business (Vol. 80, March 12, 2007, No. 6, pp. 36)*
Ed: Marlene Rego. Description: Chief executive of Rona Retail Canada Inc., Robert Dutton, and chief executive of Sysco Food Services Winnipeg, Kim Doherty explain the way they reached the top of their careers.

34886 ■ *"Floral-Design Kiosk Business in Colorado Springs Blossoming" in Colorado Springs Business Journal (September 24, 2010)*
Pub: Dolan Media Newswires
Ed: Monica Mendoza. Description: Profile of Shellie Greto and her mother Jackie Martin who started a wholesale flower business in their garage. The do-it-yourself floral arrangement firm started a kiosk business in supermarkets called Complete Design.

34887 ■ *"For Developer, a Boulevard of Golden Dreams" in Globe & Mail (February 10, 2007, pp. B3)*
Ed: Elizabeth Church. Description: A profile of Ian Gillespie, president of Westbank Projects Corp., including his achievements in the real estate industry are presented.

34888 ■ *"For Giving Us a Way To Say Yes To Solar: Lynn Jurich and Edward Fenster" in Inc. (Volume 32, December 2010, No. 10, pp. 110)*
Pub: Inc. Magazine
Description: Profile of entrepreneurs Lynn Jurich and Edward Fenster, cofounders of SunRun. The firm installs solar panels at little or no cost and homeowners sign 20-year contracts to buy power at a fixed price.

34889 ■ *"For His Bigness of Heart: Larry O'Toole: Gentle Giant Moving, Somerville, Massachusetts" in Inc. (Volume 32, December 2010)*
Pub: Inc. Magazine
Description: Profile of Larry O'Toole, owners of Gentle Giant Moving Company, where his company charges more, but in return consumers receive a higher quality service.

34890 ■ *"For Staying True: Bobby Flam: Jumbo's Restaurant, Miami" in Inc. (Volume 32, December 2010, No. 10, pp. 102)*
Pub: Inc. Magazine
Ed: Leigh Buchanan. Description: Profile of Bobby Flam, owner of Jumbo's Restaurant in Miami, Florida.

34891 ■ *"Forces of Fortune: The Rise of the New Muslim Middle Class and What It Will Mean for Our World*
Ed: Vali Nasr. Released: September 10, 2009. Price: $26. Description: The author argues that entrepreneurial, religiously conservative contingents in such countries as Turkey, Pakistan, and Iran can propel the Middle East into democratic and prosperous times.

34892 ■ *"Former Apprentice Candidate Launches Jewelry Line" in Black Enterprise (Vol. 37, October 2006, No. 3, pp. 36)*
Pub: Earl G. Graves Publishing Co. Inc.
Contact: Earl G. Graves, Jr., President
Ed: Philana Patterson. Description: Star of the second season of NBC's The Apprentice, Stacie J, has launched a line of jewelry and accessories which will be sold at Claire's stores nationwide.

34893 ■ *"Former Chrysler Dealers Build New Business Model" in Crain's Detroit Business (Vol. 25, June 22, 2009, No. 25, pp. 3)*
Pub: Crain Communications Inc. - Detroit
Contact: Keith Crain, Chairman
Ed: Daniel Fuggan. Description: Joe Ricci is one of 14 Detroit area dealerships whose franchises have been terminated. Ricci and other Chrysler dealers in the area are starting new businesses or switching to new franchises. Ricci's All American Buyer's Service will be located in Dearborn and will sell only used cars.

34894 ■ *"Former Dell Exec Turns Entrepreneur, Buys Travel Agency" in Austin Business Journal (Vol. 34, May 9, 2014, No. 12, pp. 9)*
Pub: American City Business Journals, Inc.
Contact: Whitney Shaw, President
Released: May 9, 2014. Description: Robin Goad, former sales executive for Dell Inc., is buying Tramex Travel of Austin, Texas. She hopes to reinvent the travel agency into a corporate powerhouse it once was when she worked there in the 1990s before working for Dell.

34895 ■ *"The Formula for Growth: Through a Mixture of Vision and Partnerships, Leon Richardson has ChemicoMays in Expansion Mode" in Black Enterprise (Vol. 44, June 2014, No. 10, pp. 66)*
Pub: Earl G. Graves Publishing Co. Inc.
Contact: Earl G. Graves, Jr., President
Released: June 2014. Description: Profile of Leon Richardson, who has his family-owned business poised for growth. At the age of 13, Leon helped his family in their convenience store located in West Haven, Connecticut. He has gone from managing storefronts to overseeing a chemical management business during his entrepreneurial career.

34896 ■ *"Formula for Success: Dispelling the Age-Old Myths" in Agency Sales Magazine (Vol. 39, July 2009, No. 7, pp. 26)*
Ed: Douglas Smith. Description: Common misperceptions about selling and salespeople include the idea that anyone can be successful in selling if they work hard enough and that successful salespeople are born that way. In fact, top performers take risks and they invest in themselves.

34897 ■ *The Foundations of Female Entrepreneurship: Enterprise, Home and Household in London, c. 1800-1870*
Pub: Routledge
Contact: Kevin Bradley, President
E-mail: kbradley@taylorandfrancis.com
Ed: Alison Kay. Released: March 16, 2012. Price: $54.95, paperback. Description: This book argues that active business did not exclude women from 1747 to 1880, although careful representation was necessary and this has obscured the similarities of women's businesses to those of many male business owners. Availability: Print.

34898 ■ *Foundations of Small Business Enterprise*
Pub: Routledge
Contact: Kevin Bradley, President
E-mail: kbradley@taylorandfrancis.com
Ed: Gavin Reid. Released: December 2006. Price: $210, hardback. Description: Insight is given into

the life cycle of entrepreneurial ventures; 150 new firms are tracked through early years. **Availability:** Print.

34899 ■ Founders at Work: Stories of Startups' Early Days
Pub: Apress L.P.
Contact: Dominic Shakeshaft, Director
E-mail: dominic.shakeshaft@apress.com
Ed: Jessica Livingston. **Released:** September 18, 2008. **Price:** $17.99; $12.99. **Description:** Through interviews with founders of companies such as Apple, Flickr and PayPal, the book shows the qualities required to be a successful entrepreneur. **Availability:** PrintE-book.

34900 ■ 401 Questions Every Entrepreneur Should Ask
Pub: Career Press Inc.
Contact: Ron Fry, President
Ed: James L. Silvester. **Price:** $17.99. **Description:** Review of 25 functional areas of running a small business are covered along with questions entrepreneurs should ask in order to correct and avoid unwanted issues. **Availability:** Print.

34901 ■ "Four Lessons in Adaptive Leadership" in Harvard Business Review (Vol. 88, November 2010, No. 11, pp. 86)
Pub: Harvard Business School Publishing
Ed: Michael Useem. **Description:** Four key factors to effective leadership are presented. These are establishing a personal link, making sound and timely decisions, developing a common purpose while avoiding personal gain, and ensuring that objectives are clear without micromanaging those implementing them.

34902 ■ The Four Routes to Entrepreneurial Success
Pub: Berrett-Koehler Communications Inc.
Contact: Steve Piersanti, President
E-mail: spiersanti@bkpub.com
Ed: John B. Miner. **Released:** January 01, 1996. **Price:** $18.95, paperback. **Description:** Insight is provided to help entrepreneurs run their business successfully. **Availability:** Print; E-book.

34903 ■ "Francois Coutu" in Canadian Business (Vol. 80, March 12, 2007, No. 6, pp. 66)
Ed: Erin Pooley. **Description:** Pharmacist Francois Coutu shares his passion for the work of a pharmacist and sports.

34904 ■ "Francois Joly" in Canadian Business (Vol. 79, September 11, 2006, No. 18, pp. 146)
Pub: Rogers Media Inc.
Contact: Tony Viner, President
Ed: Andy Holloway. **Description:** President and chief operating officer of Desjardins Financial Security, Francois Joly speaks about his interests and emphasizes the need to be passionate about work.

34905 ■ "From the Battlefield to the Boardroom" in Business Horizons (Vol. 51, March-April 2008, No. 2, pp. 79)
Pub: Elsevier Advanced Technology Publications
Ed: Catherine M. Dalton. **Description:** Effective intelligence gathering, a thorough understanding of the mission, efficient use of resources, and strategic leadership are vital to achieving success in business as well as in the battlefield. Examples of effective leadership in the battle of Gettysburg are cited.

34906 ■ From Entrepreneur to Infopreneur: Make Money with Books, eBooks, and Information Products
Pub: John Wiley & Sons Inc.
Contact: Stephen M. Smith, President
Ed: Stephanie Chandler. **Released:** November 2006. **Price:** $27.95, paperback; $18.99. **Description:** Infopreneurs sell information online in the forms of books, e-books, special reports, audio and video products, seminars, and more. **Availability:** PrintE-book.

34907 ■ "Fueling Change" in Entrepreneur (Vol. 35, November 2007, No. 11, pp. 46)
Pub: Entrepreneur Press
Contact: Perlman Neil, President
Ed: Carol Tice. **Description:** Creativity guru John Kao says the United States is complacent when it comes to business. He talks about how entrepreneurs should think innovatively in terms of big changes.

34908 ■ The Future Arrived Yesterday: The Rise of the Protean Corporation and What It Means for You
Pub: Crown Business
Ed: Michael S. Malone. **Released:** 2009. **Price:** $15.99. **Description:** Reasons why dominant companies of the next decade will behave like perpetual entrepreneurial startups are investigated. **Availability:** E-book.

34909 ■ "Gail Lissner: Vice-President, Appraisal Research Counselors" in Crain's Chicago Business (Vol. 31, May 5, 2008, No. 18, pp. 28)
Pub: Crain Communications Inc.
Contact: Todd Johnson, Publisher
Ed: Phuong Ly. **Description:** Profile of Gail Lissner who is the vice-president of the Appraisal Research Counselors, a company that puts out the quarterly 'Residential Benchmark Report,' in which Ms. Lissner co-authors and is considered a must-read in the industry. Ms. Lissner has risen to become one of the most sought-after experts on the Chicago market considering real estate.

34910 ■ "Galvanizing the Scientific Community" in Information Today (Vol. 26, February 2009, No. 2, pp. 20)
Pub: Information Today, Inc.
Contact: Thomas H. Hogan, President
E-mail: ctuthill@infotoday.com
Ed: Barbara Brynko. **Description:** Profile of John Haynes, newly appointed vice president of publishing for the American Institute of Physics; the Institute consists of ten organizations specializing in STM publishing as well as providing publishing services for over 170 science and engineering journals.

34911 ■ "A Gambling Man: Career Transitions that Put a Vegas Hotshot on Top" in Black Enterprise (Vol. 37, October 2006, No. 3, pp. 89)
Pub: Earl G. Graves Publishing Co. Inc.
Contact: Earl G. Graves, Jr., President
Ed: Laura Egodigwe. **Description:** Interview with Lorenzo Creighton, president and chief operating officer of MGM Mirage's New York-New York Hotel and Casino. Creighton talks about his history and the challenges he faced since he didn't come from the casino industry.

34912 ■ "Game On at Jordan's New Spot" in Crain's Chicago Business (Vol. 34, October 24, 2011, No. 42, pp. 34)
Pub: Crain Communications Inc.
Contact: Todd Johnson, Publisher
Ed: Laura Bianchi. **Description:** Michael Jordan partnered with Cornerstone Restaurant Group to launch Michael Jordan's Steakhouse in Chicago. Details are included.

34913 ■ "Gary Honcoop Honored as BIAWC's Builder of the Year" in Bellingham Business Journal (Vol. February 2010, pp. 17)
Pub: Sound Publishing Inc.
Contact: Gloria G. Fletcher, President
Description: Gary Honcoop, co-owner and president of Roosendaal-Honcoop Construction Inc. was honored by the Building Industry Association of Whatcom County as Builder of the Year. The construction company was founded in 1979.

34914 ■ "Generation Entrepreneur" in Business Strategy Review (Vol. 25, Summer 2014, No. 2, pp. 41)
Pub: Blackwell Publishing Professional
Contact: Stephen M. Smith, President
Released: Summer 2014. **Description:** The early days of entrepreneurial ventures are often recorded in rose-tinted retrospect. In this special section, ideas, hopes, dreams and fears of entrepreneurs in the early stages of their journeys are featured.

34915 ■ Get in the Game: 8 Elements of Perseverance that Make the Difference
Pub: Gotham/Penguin Group Incorporated
Ed: Cal Ripken, Donald T. Phillips. **Released:** April 10, 2008. **Price:** $15, paperback; $12.99. **Description:** Guidebook written by superstar athlete Cal Ripken to help managers and entrepreneurs achieve success. **Availability:** PrintElectronic publishing.

34916 ■ "Get With the Program" in Entrepreneur (Vol. 36, April 2008, No. 4, pp. 130)
Ed: Nichole L. Torres. **Description:** Entrepreneurship initiatives help college students get connected with other students, teach them about how to start their own business while still in school, and help with funding. Some of these programs are the Harold Grinspoon Charitable Foundation's Entrepreneurship Initiative and the Syracuse Campus-Community Entrepreneurship Initiative.

34917 ■ Get Your Business to Work!: 7 Steps to Earning More, Working Less and Living the Life You Want
Pub: BenBella Books
Contact: Aida Herrera, Director
E-mail: aida@benbellabooks.com
Ed: George Hedley. **Released:** May 2014. **Price:** $12.56, paperback. **Description:** Complete step-by-step guide for the small business owner to realize profits, wealth and freedom. **Availability:** Print.

34918 ■ Getting to Innovation: How Asking the Right Questions Generates the Great Ideas Your Company Needs
Pub: AMACOM
Contact: Edward T. Reilly, Manager
Ed: Arthur B. VanGundy. **Released:** July 2007. **Price:** $29.95, hardback. **Description:** Guide to achieving the critical first step in formulating creative and useful ideas that lead to results for any small company. **Availability:** Print; E-book.

34919 ■ "Getting Inventive With..Ed Spellman" in Crain's Cleveland Business (Vol. 28, October 22, 2007, No. 42, pp. 18)
Pub: Crain Communications Inc.
Ed: Kimberly Bonvissuto. **Description:** Profile featuring Ed Spellman, a mechanical engineer who decided to quit his job at Invacare Corp., a medical equipment manufacturer and distributor, in order to devote his full attention to promoting his numerous inventions, including the DV-Grip, a vehicle mount for portable DVD players.

34920 ■ "Getting Inventive With..John Nottingham and John Spirk" in Crain's Cleveland Business (Vol. 28, October 22, 2007, No. 42, pp. 19)
Pub: Crain Communications Inc.
Ed: Kimberly Bonvissuto. **Description:** Profile featuring John Spirk and John Nottingham of the Cleveland-based firm, Nottingham-Spirk Design Associates; the company holds 486 issued and commercialized patents and has reported over $30 billion in new product sales.

34921 ■ "Getting Inventive With..Richard Brindisi and Gregory Vittardi" in Crain's Cleveland Business (Vol. 28, October 22, 2007, No. 42)
Pub: Crain Communications Inc.
Ed: Kimberly Bonvissuto. **Description:** Profile of the SmartShopper, a handheld, voice-recognition device for dictating shopping and errand lists, and its creators, Richard G. Brindisi and Gregory Vittardi.

34922 ■ "Getting It Sold" in Black Enterprise (Vol. 38, November 2007, No. 4, pp. 54)
Pub: Earl G. Graves Publishing Co. Inc.
Contact: Earl G. Graves, Jr., President
Ed: Tennille M. Robinson. **Description:** Artist is given advice for marketing and selling paintings, as well as getting artwork published.

34923 ■ "Getting Others To Take Your Startup Seriously" in Women Entrepreneur (August 1, 2008)
Ed: Tamara Monosoff. **Description:** Writing a serious business plan is essential if you want others to take your startup endeavor seriously. As friends, fam-

ily and acquaintances see you taking positive steps toward your goal they will begin to lend their support and may even help get the business off the ground.

34924 ■ *Getting to Scale: Growing Your Business Without Selling Out*
Pub: Berrett-Koehler Communications Inc.
Contact: Steve Piersanti, President
E-mail: spiersanti@bkpub.com
Ed: Jill Bamburg. **Released:** July 2006. **Price:** $14.95. **Description:** Ways for entrepreneurs to preserve the value of their company while maintaining growth and competitiveness. **Availability:** Print; PDF.

34925 ■ *Getting Things Done*
Ed: David Allen. **Released:** December 2002. **Price:** $16. **Description:** Methods for reducing stress and increasing performance are described.

34926 ■ *"Gillette Creamery" in Ice Cream Reporter (Vol. 23, September 20, 2010, No. 10, pp. 8)*
Description: Gillette family of Gillette Creamery in Ellenville have been Entrepreneurs of the Year in Ulster County, New York. Gillette is the largest supplier of ice cream products in Eastern New York.

34927 ■ *The Girl's Guide to Being a Boss (Without Being a Bitch): Valuable Lessons, Smart Suggestions, and True Stories for Succeeding as the Chick-in-Charge*
Pub: Random Housing Publishing Group
Ed: Caitlin Friedman, Kimberly Yorio. **Released:** May 01, 2007. **Price:** $13.99. **Availability:** Print.

34928 ■ *"Give 'Em a Boost" in Entrepreneur (Vol. 36, April 2008, No. 4, pp. 120)*
Pub: Entrepreneur Press
Contact: Perlman Neil, President
Ed: Kristen Henning. **Description:** Amir Levin of Kaboost Corp. markets a plastic booster system that attaches to the bottom of a regular chair and raises it. He thought of the idea of creating the product after seeing his young cousins refusing to sit in their booster seats. Levin started his company in 2006.

34929 ■ *"The Globe: A Cautionary Tale for Emerging Market Giants" in Harvard Business Review (Vol. 88, September 2010, No. 9, pp. 99)*
Pub: Harvard Business School Publishing
Ed: J. Stewart Black, Allen J. Morrison. **Description:** Key factors that negatively affected Japan corporate growth and organizational effectiveness include: devotion to established path, isolated domestic markets, homogenous executive teams, and a non-contentious labor force. Solutions include leadership development programs, multicultural input, and cross-cultural training.

34930 ■ *"Gloria Christiansen: Tennessee's Unselfish Citizen" in Women In Business (Vol. 61, December 2009, No. 6, pp. 10)*
Pub: American Business Women's Association
Contact: Lorie Burch, President
Description: Gloria Christiansen, a Colombian-born secretary of the Knoxville Area American Business Women's Association (ABWA) Council, shares her experiences as an immigrant in Tennessee who has been provided with the opportunity to grow professionally through ABWA. Aside from participating in community development projects, she deems her American citizenship as an inspiring and honorable experience.

34931 ■ *"Go Beyond Visionary. Be a Leader: Having a Grand Vision Isn't Enough to Build Your Business. You Have to Take the Reins and Actually Run Your Startup" in Inc. (Vol. 36, February 2014, No. 1, pp. 43)*
Pub: Mansueto Ventures L.L.C.
Contact: John Koten, Chief Executive Officer
Released: February 2014. **Description:** Entrepreneurs must be visionaries, leaders and focus on running and growing their small business. Tips for going from visionary to leader include building trust with

talented people, determining what's important, and being transparent. Vision is the reason you started your firm, leadership will be the reason for its success.

34932 ■ *"Go East" in Canadian Business (Vol. 80, February 26, 2007, No. 5, pp. 21)*
Pub: Rogers Media Inc.
Contact: Tony Viner, President
Ed: Claire Gagne. **Description:** The managerial strategies followed by Doug Doust, who left Wal-Mart to take over the position of senior vice-president of supply chain at the struggling Seiyu of Japan are presented.

34933 ■ *The Go-Giver: A Little Story About a Powerful Business Idea*
Pub: Penguin Group USA
Contact: Phyllis Grann, President
Ed: Bob Burg, John David Mann. **Released:** December 27, 2007. **Price:** $21.95, hardcover; $17.99. **Description:** Story of an ambitious young man named Joe who years for success. The book is a heartwarming tale that brings new relevance to the old proverb, 'Give and you shall receive'. **Availability:** PrintElectronic publishing.

34934 ■ *"Go Green Or Go Home" in Black Enterprise (Vol. 41, August 2010, No. 1, pp. 53)*
Pub: Earl G. Graves Publishing Co. Inc.
Contact: Earl G. Graves, Jr., President
Ed: Tennille M. Robinson. **Description:** The green economy has become an essential part of every business, however, small business owners need to learn how to participate, including minority owned entrepreneurs.

34935 ■ *Going to Extremes: How Like Minds Unite and Divide*
Pub: Oxford University Press
Contact: Niko Pfund, President
Ed: Cass R. Sustein. **Released:** 2009. **Price:** £14.99. **Description:** Solutions to marketplace problems are examined.

34936 ■ *"Gold Medal" in Canadian Business (Vol. 79, October 9, 2006, No. 20, pp. 57)*
Ed: Andrew Wahl. **Description:** Creativity skills and management strategies of Rob McEwen, founder and chief executive officer of Goldcorp Inc., are presented.

34937 ■ *"A Good Book Is Worth a Thousand Blogs" in Barron's (Vol. 88, July 14, 2008, No. 28, pp. 42)*
Pub: Dow Jones & Co., Inc.
Contact: Clare Hart, President
Ed: Gene Epstein. **Description:** Nine summer book suggestions on economics are presented. The list includes 'The Revolution' by Ron Paul, 'The Forgotten Man' by Amity Shales, 'The Commitments of Traders Bible' by Stephen Briese, and 'Economic Facts and Fallacies' by Thomas Sowell.

34938 ■ *Good to Great*
Pub: Harper Business
Ed: Jim Collins. **Released:** 2001. **Price:** $29.99, hardcover; $19.99; C$18.99. **Availability:** PrintE-book.

34939 ■ *"Good to Grow" in Entrepreneur (May 2014)*
Pub: Entrepreneur Media Inc.
Released: May 2014. **Description:** Entrepreneurs should look for indications that their startup is ready to expand before undertaking an expansion. They must ensure that their startups have the right people in place, from the management to the employees. Their business should be reaching a level of awareness that is suitable for growth. They should also ensure there is enough cash flow to sustain growth and they can meet business goals.

34940 ■ *"Goodbye, Locker Room: Hello, Boardroom" in Inc. (Vol. 33, October 2011, No. 8, pp. 30)*
Pub: Inc. Magazine
Ed: Issie Lapowsky, Kasey Wehrum. **Description:** In 2005, the National Football League started the NFL Business Management and Entrepreneurial Program.

Since the onset of the program, 700 players have participated in the program which takes place at the business schools of Harvard, the University of Pennsylvania, Northwestern and Stanford.

34941 ■ *"Got Skills?" in Entrepreneur (Vol. 35, October 2007, No. 10, pp. 31)*
Pub: Entrepreneur Press
Contact: Perlman Neil, President
Ed: Laura Tiffany. **Description:** Entrepreneurs such as Jim Mousner, Hugh Briathwaite, and Joi Ito, has been known to apply their skills and interests in other fields on their business operations. Knowing something outside the realm of their industry helps entrepreneurs think of fresh ideas that are beneficial not only to them but also to their clients. Details of how having a different kind of interest helped Mousner, Braithwaite and Ito are presented.

34942 ■ *Goventure: Live the Life of an Entrepreneur*
Pub: Houghton Mifflin College Div.
Contact: June Smith, President
Description: Challenges of operating a small business are presented with more than 6,000 graphics, audio, and interactive video. **Availability:** CD-ROM.

34943 ■ *"A Graceful (and Lucrative) Exit" in Black Enterprise (Vol. 38, November 2007, No. 4, pp. 108)*
Pub: Earl G. Graves Publishing Co. Inc.
Contact: Earl G. Graves, Jr., President
Ed: Tamara E. Holmes. **Description:** BlueKey Business Brokerage M&A helps clients buy, grow or sell a business. Four key points are examined in order to successfully exit a business.

34944 ■ *Great Big Book of Business Lists*
Pub: Entrepreneur Press
Contact: Perlman Neil, President
Ed: Courtney Thurman, Ashlee Gardner. **Released:** April 25, 2006. **Description:** Reference guide for small business that includes information for starting and running a small business; lists are organized for easy access and cover every aspect of small business.

34945 ■ *Great Tips for Your Small Business: Increase Your Profit and Joy in Your Work*
Pub: Dundurn Press Ltd.
Contact: Kirk Howard, President
Ed: Julie V. Watson. **Released:** September 2006. **Price:** $24.99, paperback; $11.99. **Description:** Tips and hints for home-based, micro, and small businesses are presented. **Availability:** PrintE-book.

34946 ■ *Green to Gold: How Smart Companies Use Environmental Strategy to Innovate, Create Value, and Build Competitive Advantage*
Pub: Yale University Press
Contact: John D. Rollins, Chief Financial Officer
E-mail: john.rollins@yale.edu
Ed: Daniel C. Esty, Andrew S. Winston. **Released:** October 09, 2006. **Price:** $27.50. **Description:** Examples are given for small businesses to beat competition while tackling sustainability, engage stakeholders, develop NGO partnerships, and work environmental stewardship into corporate culture.

34947 ■ *"Ground Floor Opportunity" in Small Business Opportunities (July 2008)*
Pub: Entrepreneur Press
Contact: Perlman Neil, President
Description: Profile of Doug Disney, the founder of the booming franchise Tile Outlet Always in Stock, which sells ceramic and porcelain tile and stone products at wholesale prices; Disney found inspiration in a book he read in two days and that motivated him to expand his venture into a huge franchise opportunity.

34948 ■ *Groups in Context: Leadership and Participation in Small Groups*
Pub: McGraw Hill Financial Inc.
Contact: Douglas L. Peterson, President
Ed: Gerald L. Wilson. **Released:** June 2004. **Description:** Small group communication skills for the workplace, in churches, social groups, or civic organizations.

34949 ■ The Growing Business Handbook: Inspiration and Advice from Successful Entrepreneurs and Fast Growing UK Companies
Pub: Kogan Page, Limited
Contact: Philip Kogan, Chairman of the Board
Ed: Adam Jolly. Released: April 03, 2014. Price: £29.99, hardback. Description: Tips for growing and running a successful business are covered, focusing on senior managers in middle market and SME companies. Availability: Print.

34950 ■ Growing Local Value: How to Build Business Partnerships That Strengthen Your Community
Pub: Berrett-Koehler Communications Inc.
Contact: Steve Piersanti, President
E-mail: spiersanti@bkpub.com
Ed: Laury Hammel, Gun Denhart. Price: $16.95. Description: Advice and examples are provided for building socially responsible entrepreneurship. Availability: Print; PDF.

34951 ■ Growing and Managing a Small Business: An Entrepreneurial Perspective
Pub: Houghton Mifflin College Div.
Contact: June Smith, President
Ed: Kathleen R. Allen. Released: 2007. Price: A$159.95; NZ$167.95. Description: Introduction to business ownership and management from startup through growth. Availability: Print.

34952 ■ Growing Your Business
Pub: Routledge
Contact: Kevin Bradley, President
E-mail: kbradley@taylorandfrancis.com
Released: January 2008. Price: $93.95, paperback; $205, hardback. Description: Growth strategies for small businesses are presented. Availability: Print.

34953 ■ Growth-Oriented Women Entrepreneurs and Their Businesses: A Global Research Perspective
Pub: Edward Elgar Publishing Inc.
Contact: Richard Henning, Vice President
E-mail: kwight@e-elgar.com
Ed: Candida G. Brush, Nancy M. Carter, Elizabeth J. Gatewood, Patricia G. Greene, Myra M. Hart. Released: 2006. Price: £89.10. Description: Roles women play in entrepreneurship globally and their economic impact are examined. Availability: Print.

34954 ■ "Guest Speaker: The Real World: Forget the Elaborate Business Plans, Kids With Passion Are Our Next Great Entrepreneurs" in Inc. (October 2007, pp. 87-88)
Pub: Mansueto Ventures L.L.C.
Contact: John Koten, Chief Executive Officer
Ed: George Gendron. Description: George Gendron, founder and executive director of the Innovation and Entrepreneurship Program at Clark University, stresses the importance of encouraging business students in his entrepreneurial program to follow their passion. The program is dedicated to real-world entrepreneurship by creating businesses rather than business plans.

34955 ■ Habitual Entrepreneurs
Pub: Edward Elgar Publishing Inc.
Contact: Richard Henning, Vice President
E-mail: kwight@e-elgar.com
Released: December 2006. Price: $107.10, hardback. Description: Habitual entrepreneurship is explored. Tools for developing a plan for successful leadership are offered. Availability: Print.

34956 ■ "Halls Give Hospital Drive $11 Million Infusion" in The Business Journal-Serving Metropolitan Kansas City (Vol. 26, July 18, 2008)
Ed: Rob Roberts. Description: Don Hall, chairman of Hallmark Cards Inc., and eight family members have announced that they will give $11 million to Children's Mercy Hospitals and Clinics for its $800 million expansion plan. Hall Family Foundation president Bill Hall that contributions such as that for

Children's Mercy reflect the charitable interests of the foundation's board and founders. The possible impacts of the Hall's donation are analyzed.

34957 ■ The Halo Effect: And the Eight Other Business Delusions That Deceive Managers
Pub: Free Press/Simon & Schuster Inc.
Ed: Phil Rosenzweig. Released: June 2014. Price: $17, paperback; $12.38. Description: Nine common business delusions, including the halo effect (which the author describes as the need to attribute positive qualities to successful individuals and companies), are illustrated using case studies of Lego, Cisco, and Nokia to show how adhering to myths can be bad for any business. Availability: PrintE-book.

34958 ■ Handbook of Qualitative Research Methods In Entrepreneurship
Pub: Edward Elgar Publishing Inc.
Contact: Richard Honning, Vice President
E-mail: kwight@e-elgar.com
Ed: Helle Neergaard, John Parm Ulhoi. Price: £139.50, hardback; £41.60, paperback. Description: Advice for researchers to make informed choices and to design more stringent and sophisticated studies in the field of entrepreneurship. Availability: Print.

34959 ■ Happy About Joint-Venturing: The 8 Key Critical Factors of Success
Pub: Happy About
Contact: Mitchell Levy, Chief Executive Officer
Ed: Valerie Orsoni-Vauthey. Price: $19.95, paperback; $14.95. Description: An overview of joint venturing is presented. Availability: PrintE-book; PDF.

34960 ■ "Hatching Twitter: A True Story of Money, Power, Friendship, and Betrayal"
Pub: Portfolio Hardcover
Released: November 5, 2013. Price: $17.00 paperback. Description: The first full coverage story covering the four founders of Twitter: Evan Williams, Biz Stone, Jack Dorsey, and Noah Glass, who went from ordinary engineers to wealthy celebrities and entrepreneurs. The story explores their pursuits for money, influence, publicity, and control as Twitter grew larger and more powerful.

34961 ■ "Having Words with Matt Maroni: Chef-Owner, Gaztro-Wagon, Chicago" in Nation's Restaurant News (Vol. 45, April 4, 2011, No. 7, pp. 62)
Pub: Penton Media, Inc.
Ed: Mike Dempsey. Description: Profile of Matt Maroni, chef and owner of Gaztro-Wagon in Chicago, Illinois is presented. Maroni tells how he found his niche in the food truck industry.

34962 ■ "He Has a Sky-High Outlook on His Business" in Charlotte Observer (February 4, 2007)
Ed: Stella M. Hopkins. Description: Profile of Chuck Boyle, former Army pilot; Boyle patrols over construction sites in the Charlotte, North Carolina area. The firm's team of engineers and geologists specialize in services such as: rock blasting, roads, testing concrete and other construction materials, and more.

34963 ■ "Head of the Class" in Entrepreneur (Vol. 37, October 2009, No. 10, pp. 59)
Pub: Entrepreneur Press
Contact: Perlman Neil, President
Description: Top 25 graduate and undergraduate entrepreneurship programs in the US for 2009 as ranked by The Princeton Review are listed. Babson College in Wellesley, Massachusetts topped both categories.

34964 ■ Heart: Building a Great Brand in the Digital Age
Pub: CreateSpace
Contact: Daren Giles, President
Released: September 29, 2014. Price: $7.95 paperback. Description: Business leader and consultant who works with designers, contractors and service providers in the green industry helps business owners develop and implement company systems and increase revenue. His is a third-generation horticulturist and small business owner and share the challenges of being an entrepreneur.

34965 ■ "A Heavy Burden" in Crain's Cleveland Business (Vol. 30, June 8, 2009, No. 22, pp. 13)
Pub: Crain Communications Inc.
Ed: Cuck Soder. Description: Small business owners are making sacrifices in the tight economy. In a recent survey conducted by American Express, 30 percent of the 727 small business owners questioned said they no longer take salaries from their firms.

34966 ■ "Help Yourself" in Entrepreneur (September 2014)
Pub: Entrepreneurial Press
Released: September 2014. Description: Employers can create a workplace where mutual trust is possible by expressing clearly what they expect from their employees, giving feedback that reinforces positive behavior and mentoring them to improve customer service. A leader needs to talk to a pregnant worker about her job priorities, deadlines and communicate ways to help her meet expectations. The best way to approach a company for unsolicited ideas is to find out the contact person who would be responsible for inventors or potential collaborators.

34967 ■ Here Come the Regulars: How to Run a Record Label on a Shoestring Budget
Pub: Faber & Faber Inc.
Contact: Linda Rosenberg, Director
E-mail: linda.rosenberg@fsgbooks.com
Ed: Ian Anderson. Released: October 2009. Price: $15, paperback; $7.99. Description: Author, Ian Anderson launched his own successful record label, Afternoon Records when he was 18 years old. Anderson shares insight into starting a record label, focusing on label image, budget, blogging, potential artists, as well as legal aspects. Availability: PrintE-book.

34968 ■ "Here's How Buffett Spent 2007" in Barron's (Vol. 88, March 10, 2008, No. 10, pp. 48)
Ed: Andrew Bary. Description: Earnings of Berkshire Hathaway may decline in 2008 due to a tighter insurance market, but its portfolio is expected to continue growing. Warren Buffett purchased $19.1 billion worth of stocks in 2007.

34969 ■ "The High-Intensity Entrepreneur" in Harvard Business Review (Vol. 88, September 2010, No. 9, pp. 74)
Pub: Harvard Business School Publishing
Ed: Anne S. Habiby, Deirdre M. Coyle, Jr. Description: Examination of the role of small companies in promoting global economic growth is presented. Discussion includes identifying entrepreneurial capability.

34970 ■ High Performance with High Integrity
Pub: Harvard Business Review Press
Contact: Peter E. Walsh, Director
Ed: Ben W. Heineman, Jr. Released: June 03, 2008. Price: $22, hardcover. Description: The dark side of today's free-market capitalist system is examined. Under intense pressure to make the numbers, executives and employees are tempted to cut corners, falsify accounts, or worse. In today's unforgiving environment that can lead to catastrophe for a small company.

34971 ■ High-Tech Entrepreneurship: Managing Innovation, Variety and Uncertainty
Pub: Routledge
Contact: Kevin Bradley, President
E-mail: kbradley@taylorandfrancis.com
Ed: Michel Bernasconi, Simon Harris, Mette Moensted. Released: August 02, 2006. Price: $57.95, paperback; $190, hardback. Description: Profiles of successful high tech companies is included; high tech companies are driving innovation globally. Availability: Print.

34972 ■ "His Banking Industry Software Never Caught On, so Bill Randle is Now Targeting the Health Care Market" in Inc.

(March 2008)
Pub: Mansueto Ventures L.L.C.
Contact: John Koten, Chief Executive Officer
Ed: Alex Salkever. **Description:** Profile of Bill Randle, bank executive turned entrepreneur; Randle tells how he changed his focus for his company from banking software to healthcare software. The firm employs ten people who secure online billing and recordkeeping systems for hospitals and insurers. Randle discusses critical decisions that will impact his firm in the coming year. Three experts offer advice.

34973 ■ *"His Brother's Keeper: A Mentor Learns the True Meaning of Leadership"* in Black Enterprise (Vol. 37, December 2006, No. 5, pp. 69)
Pub: Earl G. Graves Publishing Co. Inc.
Contact: Earl G. Graves, Jr., President
Ed: Laura Egodigwe. **Description:** Interview with Keith R. Wyche of Pitney Bowes Management Services, which discusses the relationship between a mentor and mentee as well as sponsorship.

34974 ■ *"His Way"* in Inc. (February 2008, pp. 90-97)
Ed: Stephanie Clifford. **Description:** Profile of Chris Reed, founder of a natural soda company, who undertook an initial public offering (IPO). Reed discusses the challenges he faced mediating with the Securities Exchange Commission regarding his firm's IPO.

34975 ■ *"The Hispanic Business 100 Most Influential Hispanics"* in Hispanic Business (October 2007, pp. 30)
Pub: Hispanic Business Inc.
Contact: Jesus Chavarria, President
Description: Profiles of the one hundred Hispanic business leaders are presented.

34976 ■ *"Hispanic Executives Continue Their Rise to Power Amid a Shaky Economy"* in Hispanic Business (January-February 2009, pp. 12-14)
Pub: Hispanic Business Inc.
Contact: Jesus Chavarria, President
Ed: Michael Bowker. **Description:** Hispanic Business Media's 2009 Corporate Elite winners defied expectations and a tough economy and rose to the top of their industries; innovation being cited as key to growth of Hispanic-owned companies.

34977 ■ *"Home Depot Co-Founder Ken Langone Talks About Business"* in Atlanta Business Chronicle (April 11, 2014)
Pub: American City Business Journals, Inc.
Contact: Whitney Shaw, President
Released: April 11, 2014. **Description:** Ken Langone spoke on April 7, 2014 at Fairfield University in Connecticut. He is one of the co-founders of Home Depot home improvement chain. He provided the funds to start the chain in 1978 after Arthur Blank and Bernie Marcus were let go from their jobs at Handy Dan.

34978 ■ *"Home Grown"* in Hawaii Business (Vol. 53, November 2007, No. 5, pp. 51)
Pub: PacificBasin Communications
Ed: Jolyn Okimoto Rosa. **Description:** Discusses a program that focuses on Native Hawaiian entrepreneurs and offers business training at the Kapiolani Community College; upon completion of the program, participants may apply for a loan provided by the Office of Hawaiian Affairs (OHA) to help them start their business. OHA plans to present the restructured loan program in November 2007, with aims of shortening the loan process.

34979 ■ *"Homelessness, Hair Care and 12,000 Bottles of Tequila"* in Entrepreneur (Vol. 37, July 2009, No. 7, pp. 5)
Pub: Entrepreneur Press
Contact: Perlman Neil, President
Ed: Dennis Romero. **Description:** John Paul DeJoria believes that the biggest hurdle he has faced in business is rejection, and that the successful people will do whatever is required in order to succeed. DeJoria is the man behind Paul Mitchell Systems and Patron Tequila. He was recently included in Forbes magazine's list of global billionaires.

34980 ■ *"Honoring Creativity"* in Playthings (Vol. 107, January 1, 2009, No. 1, pp. 28)
Pub: Reed Elsevier Group plc Reed Business Information
Contact: Mark Kelsey, Chief Executive Officer
Ed: Cliff Annicelli. **Description:** Toy & Game Inventors Expo is held annually in conjunction with the Chicago Toy & Game Fair. The event honors toy inventors in the categories of Game Design, Toy Design and Rising Stars, plus a lifetime achievement award. Profile of the company, Toying With Games, founded by Joyce Johnson and Colleen McCarthy-Evans are included in the article.

34981 ■ *Hoover's Vision*
Ed: Gary Hoover. **Description:** Founder of Bookstop Inc. and Hoover's Inc. provides a plan to turn an enterprise into a success by showing entrepreneurs how to address inputs with an open mind in order to see more than what other's envision. Hoover pushes business owners to create and feed a clear and consistent vision by recognizing the importance of history and trends, then helps them find the essential qualities of entrepreneurial leadership.

34982 ■ *Hoover's Vision: Original Thinking for Business Success*
Pub: Thomson South-Western/Texere
Ed: Gary Hoover. **Price:** $26.95. **Description:** Three keys to business success are to observe and understand other people, serve others while making their lives better, and develop a business style that expresses your5 own passions while serving others.

34983 ■ *How to Be an Entrepreneur and Keep Your Sanity: The African-American Guide to Owning, Building and Maintaining Successfully Your Own Small Business*
Pub: Amber Books
Contact: Tony Rose, Publisher
E-mail: amberbk@aol.com
Ed: Paula McCoy Pinderhughes. **Released:** June 2003. **Price:** $7.95. **Description:** Ten easy steps to becoming a successful African-American entrepreneur.

34984 ■ *How to Be an Entrepreneur: The Six Secrets of Self-Made Success*
Pub: Pearson Education Inc.
Contact: Steven A. Dowling, President
Ed: Steve Parks. **Released:** August 2006. **Price:** £14.99, paperback; £9.99. **Description:** Entrepreneurial creativity is examined. Statistical data covering failure rates of small businesses is included. **Availability:** PrintE-book; Electronic publishing.

34985 ■ *How to Become a Great Boss: The Rules for Getting and Keeping the Best Employees*
Pub: Hyperion
Ed: Jeffrey J. Fox. **Released:** May 15, 2002. **Price:** $17, hardcover; C$19, hardcover. **Description:** The book offers valuable advice to any manager or entrepreneur to improve leadership and management skills. Topics covered include: hiring, managing, firing, partnership and competition, self and organization, employee performance, attitude, and priorities. **Availability:** Print.

34986 ■ *"How Fast Can This Thing Go, Anyway?"* in Inc. (March 2008, pp. 94-101)
Pub: Mansueto Ventures L.L.C.
Contact: John Koten, Chief Executive Officer
Ed: Stephanie Clifford. **Description:** Founder of Zipcar, an auto rental company, tell how he brought a new CEO into the company to boost revenue. The new CEO instituted a seven-step strategy to increase business.

34987 ■ *How to Get Rich*
Pub: Ebury Press
Ed: Felix Dennis. **Released:** August 02, 2009. **Price:** £8.99, paperback. **Description:** The author, publisher of Maxim, The Week, and Stuff magazines, discusses the mistakes he made running his companies. He didn't understand that people who buy computer gaming magazines wanted a free game with each

copy, as one of his rivals was offering. And he laments not diversifying into television and exploiting the Internet. **Availability:** Print; E-book; Electronic publishing.

34988 ■ *How to Get Rich on the Internet*
Pub: Morgan James Publishing L.L.C.
Contact: Neil Gudovitz, Director
Ed: Ted Ciuba. **Released:** October 01, 2003. **Description:** Interviews with successful Internet entrepreneurs provide insight into marketing products and services online using minimal investment. The importance of a sound marketing ad campaign using the Internet is discussed; maintaining a database and Website will automatically carry out business transactions daily. Suggestions for various types of businesses to run online are given.

34989 ■ *"How Great Leaders Think: The Art of Reframing"*
Pub: Jossey-Bass
Contact: William J. Pesce, President
Released: July 8, 2014. **Price:** $30.00. **Description:** More complex thinking is the key to better leadership. A guide to help leaders understand four major aspects of organizational life: structure, people, politics, and culture is given. The book's lessons include: how to use structural tools to organize teams and organizations for better results, how to build motivation and morale by aligning organizations and people, how to map the terrain and build a power base to navigate the political dynamics of organizations, and how to develop a leadership story that shapes culture, provides direction, and inspires commitment to excellence.

34990 ■ *"How Hard Could It Be? Why the Most Important Innovations Are Often Those That Appear To Be Fatally Flawed"* in Inc. (February 2008)
Ed: Joel Spolsky. **Description:** Many times, things that seemed silly or impossible have become great innovations.

34991 ■ *"How I Became a Serial Entrepreneur"* in Baltimore Business Journal (Vol. 31, April 18, 2014, No. 51, pp. 26)
Pub: American City Business Journals, Inc.
Contact: Whitney Shaw, President
Released: April 18, 2014. **Description:** Dr. Lisa Beth Ferstenberg, a physician by training, teaches a course at the Maryland Center for Entrepreneurship in Columbia to help CEOs attract prospective investors. Dr. Ferstenberg is also the chief medical officer at Sequella Inc. She reflects on the kind of personality required to become a successful entrepreneur and the mistakes entrepreneurs make in raising capital funding.

34992 ■ *"How I Did It: George Naddaff: From Spit 'n' Shine Boy To Boston Chicken and Beyond"* in Inc. (February 2008, pp. 98-101)
Ed: Leigh Buchanan. **Description:** Profile of George Naddaff, founder of Boston Chicken as well as numerous other business ventures.

34993 ■ *"How I Did It: Jack Ma"* in Inc. (January 2008, pp. 94-102)
Pub: Gruner and Jahr USA Publishing Co.
Contact: J. Russell Denson, President
Ed: Rebecca Fannin. **Description:** Profile of Jack Ma, who started as a guide and interpreter for Western tourists in Hangzhou. Ma used the Internet to build Alibaba.com, China's largest business-to-business site and one of the hottest IPOs in years.

34994 ■ *"How I Did It: Mel Zuckerman"* in Inc. (December 2007, pp. 140-142)
Pub: Gruner and Jahr USA Publishing Co.
Contact: J. Russell Denson, President
Ed: Daniel McGinn. **Description:** Profile of Mel Zuckerman, who tells how transformed his life as a middle-aged, overweight homebuilder to a healthy addition to the fitness and spa industry with his posh Canyon Ranch retreats.

34995 ■ *"How I Did It: Richard Schaps, CEO, Van Wagner Communications"* in Inc. (October 2007, pp. 128)
Pub: Mansueto Ventures L.L.C.
Contact: John Koten, Chief Executive Officer
Ed: Stephanie Clifford. Description: Richard Schaps shares the story of selling his outdoor-advertising firm, Van Wagner for $170 million and sharing the wealth with his employees. Schaps then started another outdoor-sign company.

34996 ■ *"How I...Smash Chick Peas Into a Business"* in Baltimore Business Journal (Vol. 32, May 30, 2014, No. 4, pp. 23)
Pub: American City Business Journals, Inc.
Contact: Whitney Shaw, President
Released: May 30, 2014. Description: Blake Wollman, owner and executive chef of Wild Pea Hummous, explains that he started making hummous in his Desert Café in Mount Washington until it evolved into a popular product in 300 flavors. Wollman notes that distribution of the product is a big challenge.

34997 ■ *"How Ivanah Thomas Founded a $5 Million Business - While Working Nights"* in Orlando Business Journal (Vol. 30, April 18, 2014, No. 43, pp. 3)
Pub: American City Business Journals
Released: April 18, 2014. Description: Caring First Inc. founder, Ivanah Thomas, says her drive to serve people in their home rather than them being institutionalized lead to the establishment of her firm. She added that she ran the home care business by herself during its early years. Thomas also stated her social status posed challenges for the company.

34998 ■ *How to Make Money with Social Media: An Insider's Guide to Using New and Emerging Media to Grow Your Business*
Pub: FT Press
Contact: Timothy C. Moore, Vice President
Ed: Jamie Turner, Reshma Shah. Released: Second Edition. Price: $34.99. Description: Marketers, executives, entrepreneurs are shown more effective ways to utilize Internet social media to make money. This guide brings together both practical strategies and proven execution techniques for driving maximum value from social media marketing. Availability: E-book.

34999 ■ *How the Mighty Fall: And Why Some Companies Never Give In*
Pub: HarperCollins Publishers Inc.
Contact: Jane Friedman, President
E-mail: jfriedman@harpercollins.com
Ed: Jim Collins. Released: May 19, 2009. Price: $23.99, hardcover; $12.99; C$16.99. Description: Companies fail in stages and their decline can be detected and reversed. Availability: PrintE-book.

35000 ■ *How to Persuade and Influence People: Powerful Techniques to Get your Own Way More Often*
Pub: John Wiley & Sons Inc.
Contact: Stephen M. Smith, President
Ed: Philip Hesketh. Released: August 2010. Price: $24, paperback. Description: Seven psychological reasons behind why and how people are persuaded and how to use these reasons to your advantage in both your personal and business life. Availability: Print.

35001 ■ *How Remarkable Women Lead: A Breakthrough Model for Work and Life*
Pub: Crown Business
Ed: Joanna Barsh, Susie Cranston. Released: September 24, 2009. Price: $27.50, Hardcover. Description: An introduction to remarkable women, from Time Inc.'s Ann Moore to Xerox's Anne Mulcahy, who recount their inspiring struggles.

35002 ■ *How to Run Your Business Like a Girl: Successful Strategies from Entrepreneurial Women Who Made It Happen*
Ed: Elizabeth Cogswell Baskin. Released: September 2005. Description: Tour of three women entrepreneurs and their successful companies.

35003 ■ *How to Salvage More Millions from Your Small Business*
Pub: Mike French and Company Inc.
Contact: Ron Sturgeon, Editor
Ed: Ron Sturgeon. Price: $19.95. Description: Entrepreneurs in any industry will learn how strong work ethics and sound business principles will make any small business successful.

35004 ■ *How to Start and Run Your Own Corporation: S-Corporations For Small Business Owners*
Pub: HCM Publishing
Ed: Peter I. Hupalo. Released: Second Edition. Price: $22.46, paperback. Description: Basics of corporate business structure are explained. Topics include discovering the best business structure for your company; how to decided between an S-Corporation and LLC; choosing the state in which to incorporate, how to form a corporation, angel investing, special issues for one-person corporations, the role of bylaws and corporate minutes, board of directors, taxes, workers' compensation issues, retirement plans, and more. Availability: Print.

35005 ■ *How to Succeed As a Lifestyle Entrepreneur*
Ed: Gary Schine. Price: $18.95.

35006 ■ *"How to Survive This Mess"* in Crain's Chicago Business (Vol. 31, April 14, 2008, No. 15, pp. 18)
Pub: Crain Communications Inc.
Contact: Todd Johnson, Publisher
Ed: Christina Le Beau. Description: Small business owners can make it through a possible recession with preparations such as reviewing their balance sheet and cash flow every week and spotting trends then reacting quickly to them.

35007 ■ *"How Tender Green Turns Top Chefs Into Fast-Food Cooks: a Quick-Serve Chain Lures Kitchen Starts by Treating Them Like Entrepreneurs"* in Inc. (Vol. 36, March 2014, No. 2, pp. 28)
Pub: Mansueto Ventures L.L.C.
Contact: John Koten, Chief Executive Officer
Released: March 2014. Description: Chefs Erik Oberholtzer, David Dressier and Matt Lyman launched Tender Greens, a series of quick-service restaurants serving fresh organic dishes made from local produce, cheeses and meats. The three partners set out to hire fine-dining chefs to run each location. The used their entrepreneurial skills to inspire great chefs into entrepreneur type control by allowing them to run their restaurant individually, including operations, culture and menu items. Tender Greens has grown to 12 locations with an estimated $40 million annual revenue. Their business vision and strategy is examined.

35008 ■ *How To Change the World*
Pub: Oxford University Press
Contact: Niko Pfund, President
Ed: David Bornstein. Released: September 2007. Price: $15.95, paperback. Description: Social entrepreneurs are individuals with powerful ideas that improve other people's lives and have implemented these ideas across cities, countries and in some cases, around the world. These are doctors, lawyers, engineers, teachers, journalists and parents who solve social problems on a large scale and have a profound effect on society. Availability: Print.

35009 ■ *"How To Overcome the Jitters and Not Choke"* in South Florida Business Journal (Vol. 34, July 25, 2014, No. 53, pp. 10)
Pub: American City Business Journals
Released: July 25, 2014. Description: Recommended tips for controlling performance anxiety are presented. The fear of failure for entrepreneurs is paralyzing and prevents owners from taking necessary risks to succeed.

35010 ■ *How We Decide*
Ed: Jonah Lehrer. Released: February 2009. Price: $25. Description: Insights for entrepreneurs to help with decision making; the book describes potential traps such as negative information and how it carries more weight than positive information.

35011 ■ *How: Why How We Do Anything Means Everything*
Pub: John Wiley & Sons Inc.
Contact: Stephen M. Smith, President
Ed: Dov L. Seidman. Released: September 2011. Price: $27.95, hardcover; $18.99. Description: Author shares his unique approach to building successful companies using case studies, anecdotes, research, and interviews to help entrepreneurs succeed in the 21st Century. Availability: PrintE-book.

35012 ■ *"How Will You Ever Replace Yourself?"* in Canadian Business (Vol. 83, August 17, 2010, No. 13-14, pp. 77)
Ed: Jacqueline Nelson. Description: SoftBank founder and CEO masayoshi Son created his very own school called SoftBank Academia in order to pick a successor that will follow his footprint. Son's strategy is extreme but other corporate leaders should pay attention to succession planning.

35013 ■ *How to Win Friends and Influence People*
Pub: Simon and Schuster Inc.
Contact: Carolyn Reidy, President
E-mail: carolyn.reidy@simonandschuster.com
Ed: Dale Carnegie. Released: February 15, 1990. Price: $7.99, Paperback. Description: First published in 1937, this book helps people to understand human nature. The book teaches skills through underlying principles of dealing with people so that they feel important and appreciated.

35014 ■ *How Women Make Money: Inspirational Stories and Practical Advice from Canadian Women*
Pub: Dundurn Press Ltd.
Contact: Kirk Howard, President
Ed: Julie V. Watson. Released: April 2004. Price: C$22.99, paperback; C$4.99. Description: Collection of profiles, anecdotes, and practical advice and guides to help women take control of their lives, start a new business, and reach financial goals. Availability: PrintE-book; Electronic publishing.

35015 ■ *I Can't Believe I Get Paid to Do This*
Pub: Gold Leaf Publishing
Ed: Stacey Mayo. Price: $16.95, plus shipping and handling. Description: This book is targeted to anyone unhappy in their current position. It is designed to help everyone feel good about their job. Availability: Print; E-book.

35016 ■ *"I Fought the Law: a Brewery Comes Out on Top"* in Inc. (Vol. 33, November 2011, No. 9, pp. 28)
Pub: Inc. Magazine
Ed: Darren Dahl. Description: Profile of Omar Ansari, founder of Surly Brewing is presented. Ansari credits fans on Facebook and Twitter for contacting legislators with phone calls and emails to allow him to sell his beer to customers on site.

35017 ■ *If Harry Potter Ran General Electric*
Pub: Doubleday Publishing Group
Contact: Stephen Rubin, President
E-mail: mpalgon@randomhouse.com
Ed: Tom Morris. Released: May 16, 2006. Price: $14.99; C$15.99. Description: The values and timeless truths that underlie J.K. Rowling's popular Harry Potter books are discussed showing the lessons they offer to all individuals in their careers and daily lives. Availability: E-book.

35018 ■ *"I'll Be Back: For Entrepreneurs, Retirement Doesn't Mean Forever"* in Inc. (February 2008, pp. 35-36)
Ed: Leigh Buchanan. Description: Many entrepreneurs return to business after selling their companies and retiring. Advice is given to company owners for retirement planning.

35019 ■ *"I'm Going To Need a Bit More Time"* in Entrepreneur (September 2014)
Pub: Entrepreneur Media Inc.
Released: September 2014. Description: Entrepreneurs have a number of rules to follow when it comes to missing a deadline. The first thing for them to do is to acknowledge that they are missing the deadline and to avoid explaining reasons for not delivering on time.

35020 ■ *Immigrant, Inc.: Why Immigrant Entrepreneurs Are Driving the New Economy*
Pub: John Wiley & Sons Inc.
Contact: Stephen M. Smith, President
Ed: Richard T. Herman, Robert L. Smith. **Released:** 2009. **Price:** $19.99; $29.95, Hardcover. **Description:** Immigrant entrepreneurs are driving the new economy and will play a role in saving American jobs. **Availability:** E-book.

35021 ■ *"The Impact of Immigrant Entrepreneurs" in Business Week (February 7, 2007)*
Ed: Kerry Miller. **Description:** Overview of immigrant entrepreneur's impact on economic development and their status as a driving force for the U.S. economy.

35022 ■ *In the Company of Women: Canadian Women Talk About What It Takes to Start and Manage a Successful Business*
Ed: Katherine Gay. **Released:** 1998. **Description:** Information to help women start and run a small business in Canada.

35023 ■ *"In the Know?" in Entrepreneur (Vol. 37, July 2009, No. 7, pp. 30)*
Pub: Entrepreneur Press
Contact: Perlman Neil, President
Ed: Brad Feld. **Description:** Tips on what entrepreneurs should and should not share with their venture capitalists (VCs) are given. Entrepreneurs must be transparent with their VCs, but they should not bombard VCs with too many details. The aspect of a business that a VC is concerned with varies from one VC to another, and it is important that entrepreneurs understand the best way to communicate with their VC.

35024 ■ *"In My Shoes: A Memoir"*
Pub: Portfolio Hardcover
Released: September 30, 2014. **Price:** $18.00 paperback. **Description:** Profile of Tamara Mellon, woman entrepreneur who built Jimmy Choo into a premier name in the global fashion industry. She addresses her family life, her battles with anxiety and depression, as well as time spend in rehabilitation. She shares her entire life story from her work as a young editor at Vogue to her partnership with shoemaker, Jimmy Choo to her public relationships. She confides what it was like working with an obstinate business partner but also her ability to understand what customers want.

35025 ■ *Influence without Authority*
Pub: John Wiley & Sons Inc.
Contact: Stephen M. Smith, President
Ed: Allan R. Cohen, David L. Bradford. **Released:** 2nd Edition. **Price:** $34.95, hardcover; $22.99. **Availability:** PrintE-book.

35026 ■ *"Info Junkie" in Crain's Chicago Business (Vol. 34, October 24, 2011, No. 42, pp. 35)*
Pub: Crain Communications Inc.
Contact: Todd Johnson, Publisher
Ed: Christina Le Beau. **Description:** Greg Colando, president of Flor Inc., an eco-friendly carpet company located I Chicago discusses his marketing program to increase sales.

35027 ■ *"Infomercial King on TeleBrands, Going Broke, Making Millions" in Philadelphia Business Journal (Vol. 33, July 11, 2014, No. 22, pp. 3)*
Pub: American City Business Journals
Released: July 11, 2014. **Description:** Ajit "A.J." Khubani is CEO of TeleBrands, the Fairfield, New Jersey company that brings to the American mainstream market novelty products by using infomercials, including AmberVision sunglasses and PedEgg. Though the marketing/advertising firm is worth $1 billion, Khubani's entrepreneurship career has gone through ups and downs and he has been close to bankruptcy three times.

35028 ■ *Innovation And Entrepreneurship In Biotechnology: An International Perspective*
Pub: Edward Elgar Publishing Inc.
Contact: Richard Henning, Vice President
E-mail: kwight@e-elgar.com
Ed: Damian Hine, John Kapeleris. **Price:** £72, hardback; £33.60, paperback. **Description:** Innova-

tion processes underlying successful entrepreneurship in the biotechnology sector are explored. **Availability:** Print.

35029 ■ *Innovation and Entrepreneurship*
Ed: Peter F. Drucker. **Released:** May 2007. **Price:** $27.95. **Description:** Profile of entrepreneurial innovation.

35030 ■ *Innovation and Entrepreneurship*
Pub: Harper Business
Ed: Peter F. Drucker. **Released:** May 09, 2006. **Price:** $16.99. **Description:** Innovation and entrepreneurship in America's new economy. **Availability:** Print.

35031 ■ *Innovation and Entrepreneurship*
Pub: HarperCollins Publishers Inc.
Contact: Jane Friedman, President
E-mail: jfriedman@harpercollins.com
Ed: Peter F. Drucker. **Released:** May 09, 2006. **Price:** $16.99; $12.49; C$11.99. **Description:** Presentation of entrepreneurship and innovation and a purposeful and systematic discipline and the challenges and opportunities of the American entrepreneurial economy. **Availability:** PrintE-book.

35032 ■ *Innovation Nation: Canadian Leadership from Java to Jurassic Park*
Pub: John Wiley & Sons Inc.
Contact: Stephen M. Smith, President
Ed: Leonard Brody, Wendy Cukier, Ken Grant, Matt Holland, Catherine Middleton, Denise Shortt. **Released:** October 2002. **Price:** $38, paperback; $24.99. **Description:** Canadian's have risen to the top of the largest technology firms, from development of the Java and the Blackberry to defining specifications for XML. **Availability:** PrintE-book.

35033 ■ *"Innovation Station" in Canadian Business (Vol. 80, October 8, 2007, No. 20, pp. 42)*
Ed: Andrew Wahl. **Description:** Study and teaching of entrepreneurship at the University of Waterloo is discussed. Research projects in the university are expected to be influential in Canada's economic development. In spite of the success of these studies, financing is still a problem for the university, especially in technological innovations.

35034 ■ *"The Innovator: Rob McEwen's Unique Vision of Philanthropy and Business" in Canadian Business (Vol. 81, November 10, 2008, No. 19)*
Pub: Rogers Media Inc.
Contact: Tony Viner, President
Ed: Alex Mlynek. **Description:** Rob McEwen says that his donation to the Schulich School of Business is his first large donation. He went to the University Health Network and was told about their pan for regenerative medicine, helping him make the decision. McEwan wants to be involved in philanthropy in the areas of leadership and education.

35035 ■ *The Innovators: How a Group of Hackers, Geniuses, and Geeks Created the Digital Revolution*
Pub: Simon and Schuster Inc.
Contact: Carolyn Reidy, President
E-mail: carolyn.reidy@simonandschuster.com
Released: October 7, 2014. **Price:** $35.00. **Description:** Profiles of the individuals who created the computer and the Internet are provided describing the talents of certain inventors and entrepreneurs who are able to turn their business visions and goals into realities, while others have failed. The author begins with Ada Lovelace, Lord Byron's daughter, who pioneered computer programming back in the 1840s and continues by exploring the minds of Vannevar Bush, Alan Turing, John von Neumann, J.C.R. Licklider, Doug Englebart, Robert Noyce, Bill Gates, Steve Wozniak, Steve Jobs, Tim Berners-Lee and Larry Page.

35036 ■ *"The Innovator's Solution: Creating and Sustaining Successful Growth"*
Pub: Harvard Business Review Press
Contact: Peter E. Walsh, Director
Released: October 22, 2013. **Price:** $30.00. **Description:** Even in today's hyper-accelerated business environment any small company can transform

their business. Advice on business decisions crucial to achieving truly disruptive growth and purpose guidelines for developing their own disruptive growth engine is given. The forces that cause managers to make bad decisions as they plan new ideas for their company are identified and new frameworks to help develop the right conditions, at the right time, for a disruption to succeed. Managers and business leaders responsible for innovation and growth will benefit their business and their teams with this information.

35037 ■ *"The Inside and Outside Scoop on CEO Succession" in Globe & Mail (January 2, 2006, pp. B8)*
Pub: CTVglobemedia Publishing Inc.
Ed: Shirley Won. **Description:** The career profile of Randy Eresman as the chief executive officer of Encana Corp. is presented.

35038 ■ *Instant Income: Strategies That Bring in the Cash*
Pub: McGraw Hill Financial Inc.
Contact: Douglas L. Peterson, President
Ed: Janet Switzer. **Released:** November 28, 2013. **Price:** A$28.95, Softcover; NZ$33, Softcover. **Description:** Book covers small business advertising techniques, marketing, joint ventures, and sales. **Availability:** Print.

35039 ■ *Instinct: Tapping Your Entrepreneurial DNA to Achieve Your Business Goals*
Ed: Mary H. Frakes; Thomas L. Harrison. **Released:** September 2006. **Price:** $15.99. **Description:** Research shows that entrepreneurs may attribute their success to genetics.

35040 ■ *"The Intel Trinity: How Robert Noyce, Gordon Moore, and Andy Grove Built the World's Most Important Company"*
Pub: Harper Business
Released: July 15, 2014. **Price:** , $34.99. **Description:** A complete history of Intel Corporation, the essential company of the digital age, is presented. After over four decades Intel remains the most important company in the world, a defining company of the global digital economy. The inventors of the microprocessor that powers nearly every intelligent electronic device worldwide are profiled. These entrepreneurs made the personal computer, Internet, telecommunications, and personal electronics all possible. The challenges and successes of the company and its ability to maintain its dominance, its culture and its legacy are examined.

35041 ■ *International Entrepreneurship*
Pub: Edward Elgar Publishing Inc.
Contact: Richard Henning, Vice President
E-mail: kwight@e-elgar.com
Ed: Benjamin M. Oviatt, Patricia Phillips McDougall. **Released:** 2007. **Price:** £175.50, hardback. **Description:** Universities are focusing research efforts on international entrepreneurship. The book features critical articles on the topic. **Availability:** Print.

35042 ■ *International Entrepreneurship Education: Issues and Newness*
Pub: Edward Elgar Publishing Inc.
Contact: Richard Henning, Vice President
E-mail: kwight@e-elgar.com
Ed: Alain Fayolle, Heinz Klandt. **Released:** 2006. **Price:** £76.50. **Description:** Entrepreneurial education, focusing on economic, political and social needs of a changing world; ideas for reassessing, redeveloping, and renewing curricula and methods for teaching entrepreneurship are offered. **Availability:** Print.

35043 ■ *International Entrepreneurship in Small and Medium Size Enterprises: Orientation, Environment and Strategy*
Pub: Edward Elgar Publishing Inc.
Contact: Richard Henning, Vice President
E-mail: kwight@e-elgar.com
Ed: Hamid Etemad. **Released:** October 2004. **Price:** $123.30, hardback. **Description:** Issues involved in internationalizing small and medium sized (SME) businesses. Topics include an investigation into the emerging patterns of SME growth and international expansion in response to the changing competitive

environment, dynamics of competitive behavior, entrepreneurial processes and a formulation of strategy. **Availability:** Print.

35044 ■ *"International Growth" in Black Enterprise (Vol. 38, July 2008, No. 12, pp. 64)*
Pub: Earl G. Graves Publishing Co. Inc.
Contact: Earl G. Graves, Jr., President
Ed: Marcia A. Reed-Woodard. **Description:** Becoming an increasingly smaller portion of the global business environment is the U.S. economy. Christopher Catlin, an associate with Booz Allen Hamilton, a technology management and strategy-consulting firm, shares what he has learned about the global market.

35045 ■ *International Handbook of Entrepreneurship and HRM*
Pub: Edward Elgar Publishing Inc.
Contact: Richard Henning, Vice President
E-mail: kwight@e-elgar.com
Ed: Rowena Barrett, Susan Mayson. **Released:** 2010. **Price:** £31.20, paperback. **Description:** Conceived on the basis that there is a growing recognition of the interplay between human resource management and entrepreneurship, this volume offers insights into the role of HRM and entrepreneurial firms. **Availability:** Print.

35046 ■ *International Handbook of Women and Small Business Entrepreneurship*
Pub: Edward Elgar Publishing Inc.
Contact: Richard Henning, Vice President
E-mail: kwight@e-elgar.com
Ed: Sandra L. Fielden, Marilyn J. Davidson. **Price:** £107.10, hardback; £28.80, paperback. **Description:** Practical initiatives and strategies for women entering small business entrepreneurial ventures are examined. **Availability:** Print.

35047 ■ *"Internationalization of Australian Family Businesses: A Managerial Capabilities Perspective" in Family Business Review (Vol. 19, No.3, September 2006, pp. 207)*
Pub: Family Firm Institute
Contact: Judy L. Green, President
Ed: Chris Graves, Jill Thomas. **Description:** Concept that managerial capabilities of family firms lag behind those of non-family counterparts as they expand is discussed.

35048 ■ *"Into the Groove: Fine-Tune Your Biz By Getting Into the Good Habit Groove" in Small Business Opportunities (Spring 2008)*
Description: Profile of Ty Freyvogel and his consulting firm Freyvogel Communications. Freyvogel serves the telecommunications need of Fortune 500 and mid-sized businesses.

35049 ■ *"Into the Wild" in Inc. (October 2007, pp. 116-120, 122, 124, 126)*
Pub: Mansueto Ventures L.L.C.
Contact: John Koten, Chief Executive Officer
Ed: Alison Stein Wellner. **Description:** Perry Klebahn, CEO of Timbuk2, manufacturer of messenger bags, tells how he took his top executives into the deep Wyoming wilderness in order to build employee team work skills. Other options for this type of team-building include cooking courses, changing a tire together, solving a kidnapping, or discussing ways to survive a nuclear winter.

35050 ■ *"Intrepid Souls: Meet a Few Who've Made the Big Leap" in Crain's Chicago Business (Vol. 31, November 10, 2008, No. 45, pp. 26)*
Ed: Meredith Landry. **Description:** Advice is given from entrepreneurs who have launched businesses in the last year despite the economic crisis. Among the types of businesses featured are a cooking school, a child day-care center, a children's clothing store and an Internet-based company.

35051 ■ *"Irene Rosenfeld: Chairman and CEO, Kraft Foods Inc." in Crain's Chicago Business (Vol. 31, May 5, 2008, No. 18, pp. 31)*
Pub: Crain Communications Inc.
Contact: Todd Johnson, Publisher
Ed: David Sterrett. **Description:** Profile of Irene Rosenfeld who is the chairman and CEO of Kraft Foods Inc. and is entering the second year of a three-

year plan to boost sales of well-known brands such as Oreo, Velveeta and Oscar Mayer while facing soaring commodity costs and a declining market-share. Ms. Rosenfeld's turnaround strategy also entails spending more on advertising and giving managers more control over their budgets and product development.

35052 ■ *"Is Entrepreneurship Right For You?" in Women Entrepreneur (July 25, 2008)*
Ed: Bonnie Price. **Description:** Assessing the marketplace, evaluating your skills and sizing up your passions are three necessary elements to examine before starting a business.

35053 ■ *"It Takes More Than One" in Black Enterprise (Vol. 38, July 2008, No. 12, pp. 38)*
Pub: Earl G. Graves Publishing Co. Inc.
Contact: Earl G. Graves, Jr., President
Ed: James A. Anderson. **Description:** Interview with Eric Small, the CEO of SBK-Brooks Investment Corp., whom discusses the importance of versatility when trying to find the best investment choices; the primary factors investors should be mindful of; his current stock picks; and recommendations for investing in an uncertain and volatile market.

35054 ■ *"It Was a Very Good Year..To Be Ted Rogers" in Canadian Business (Vol. 80, Winter 2007, No. 24, pp. 121)*
Ed: Andrew Wahl. **Description:** Ted Rogers had a banner year in 2007 as Rogers Communications Inc. (RCI) took in huge profits from its phone and wireless business and his personal wealth grew sixty-seven percent to $7.6 billion. Rogers has record of betting on technologies that get the best returns relative to the investment in the marketplace such as its use of the GSM network and its cable hybrid fiber coaxial network.

35055 ■ *"It's In the Bag" in Entrepreneur (Vol. 36, April 2008, No. 4, pp. 122)*
Pub: Entrepreneur Press
Contact: Perlman Neil, President
Ed: Celeste Hoang. **Description:** Sandy Stein launched Alexx Inc in 2004, which markets keychains, called Finders Key Purse, with unique designs to help find keys easier inside the purse. Some of the key ring designs are hearts, sandals, and crowns. The company has approximately $6 million worth of sales in 2007.

35056 ■ *"It's a New Game: Killerspin Pushes Table Tennis to Extreme Heights" in Black Enterprise (Vol. 37, October 2006, No. 3, pp. 73)*
Pub: Earl G. Graves Publishing Co. Inc.
Contact: Earl G. Graves, Jr., President
Ed: Bridget McCrea. **Description:** Profile of Robert Blackwell and his company Killerspin L.L.C., which is popularizing the sport of table tennis. Killerspin has hit $1 million in revenues due to product sales primarily generated through the company's website, magazines, DVDs, and event ticket sales.

35057 ■ *It's Not Who You Know - It's Who Knows You!: The Small Business Guide to Raising Your Profits by Raising Your Profile*
Pub: John Wiley & Sons Inc.
Contact: Stephen M. Smith, President
Ed: David Arvin. **Released:** November 09, 2010. **Description:** When it comes to promoting a small business or a brand, it is essential to know how valuable high-profile attention can be. But for most small companies, the cost of hiring an outside firm to increase attention can be too expensive. **Availability:** E-book.

35058 ■ *It's Your Ship*
Ed: Michael Abrashoff. **Released:** May 01, 2002. **Price:** $24.95. **Description:** Naval Captain D. Michael Abrashoff shares management principles he used to shape his ship, the U.S.S. Benfold, into a model of progressive leadership. Abrashoff revolutionized ways to face the challenges of excessive costs, low morale, sexual harassment, and constant turnover.

35059 ■ *"I've Always Been an Entrepreneur" in South Florida Business Journal (Vol. 34, June 13, 2014, No. 47, pp. 11)*
Pub: American City Business Journals
Released: June 13, 2014. **Description:** Modernizing Medicine CEO, Daniel Cane, says he started doing business at age six when he opened a lemonade stand. His firm helps physicians increase efficiencies in their practices while improving both business and treatment outcomes. He surrounds himself with talented people, which is what he likes most about his job. Cane added that dividing time between work and family is difficult for entrepreneurs.

35060 ■ *"Janet Froetscher: CEO, United Way of Metropolitan Chicago" in Crain's Chicago Business (Vol. 31, May 5, 2008, No. 18, pp. 26)*
Pub: Crain Communications Inc.
Contact: Todd Johnson, Publisher
Ed: Emily Stone. **Description:** Profile of Janet Froetscher who is the CEO of United Way of Metropolitan Chicago who organized the country's largest-ever merger of non-profits with 53 smaller suburban chapters consolidating with the Chicago one. The consolidation saves $4 million a year with departments such as finance, information technology and communications which allows that money be spent funding job training, after-school programs and aid for 7,000 Hurricane Katrina evacuees living in the Chicago area.

35061 ■ *"Java Computing: Second Cup?" in Canadian Business (Vol. 81, June 11, 2008, No. 11, pp. 50)*
Pub: Rogers Media Inc.
Contact: Tony Viner, President
Ed: Calvin Leung. **Description:** Profile of James Gosling who is credited as the inventor of the Java programming language; however, the 53-year-old software developer feels ambivalent for being credited as inventor since many people contributed to the language. Netscape and Sun Microsystems incorporation of the programming language into Java is presented.

35062 ■ *"J.C. Penney Head Shops for Shares" in Barron's (Vol. 88, July 7, 2008, No. 27, pp. 29)*
Pub: Dow Jones & Co., Inc.
Contact: Clare Hart, President
Ed: Teresa Rivas. **Description:** Myron Ullman III, chairman and chief executive officer of J.C. Penney, purchased $1 million worth of shares of the company. He now owns 393,140 shares of the company and an additional 1,282 on his 401(k) plan.

35063 ■ *"J.C. Watts First Black John Deere Dealer" in Black Enterprise (Vol. 37, November 2006, No. 4, pp. 36)*
Pub: Earl G. Graves Publishing Co. Inc.
Contact: Earl G. Graves, Jr., President
Ed: Kiara Ashanti. **Description:** Profile of former Congressman J.C. Watts Jr., a man who grew up in rural America and is the first African American to own a John Deere dealership.

35064 ■ *"Jennifer Hernandez Helps Developers Transform Contaminated Properties" in Hispanic Business (Vol. 30, April 2008, No. 4, pp. 32)*
Pub: Hispanic Business Inc.
Contact: Jesus Chavarria, President
Ed: Hildy Medina. **Description:** Jennifer Hernandez is a partner and head of the law firm of Holland & Knight's environmental practice which specializes in the restoration of polluted land where former industrial and commercial buildings once stood, known as brownfields. Brownfield redevelopment can be lucrative but costly due to the cleaning up of contaminated land and challenging because of federal and state environmental laws.

35065 ■ *The Jewish Century*
Pub: Princeton University Press
Contact: Shirley M. Tilghman, President
Ed: Yuri Slezkine. **Released:** 2006. **Price:** $31.95; £21.95. **Description:** Success and vulnerability of individuals of Jewish descent is discussed, uncovering the 'Jewish Revolution' within the Russian Revolution. **Availability:** Print.

35066 ■ *"The Jobs Man: Working with Cincinnati's Unemployed" in Business Courier (Vol. 26, December 25, 2009, No. 35, pp. 1)*
Pub: American City Business Journals, Inc.
Contact: Whitney Shaw, President
Ed: Lucy May. **Description:** Entrepreneur Bob Messer, a volunteer for Jobs Plus Employment Network in Cincinnati's Over-the-Rhine neighborhood, regularly conducts a seminar that aims to help attendees prepare for employment. Jobs Plus founder Burr Robinson asked Messer to create the seminar in order to help unemployed jobseekers. So far, the program has helped 144 individuals with full time jobs in 2009.

35067 ■ *John F. Kennedy on Leadership: The Lessons and Legacy of a President*
Pub: AMACOM
Contact: Edward T. Reilly, Manager
Ed: John A. Barnes. **Released:** May 2007. **Price:** $16, paperback/softback. **Description:** The author provides concept-based chapters on the life and presidency of John F. Kennedy and his visions. Using his inaugural address, Barnes reflects on JFKs vision and his relationship with his staff. **Availability:** Print.

35068 ■ *"John H. Sykes Shifts from GunnAllen to New Venture" in Tampa Bay Business Journal (Vol. 30, December 18, 2009, No. 52, pp. 1)*
Pub: American City Business Journals
Ed: Margie Manning. **Description:** Tampa, Florida's entrepreneur John H. Sykes acquired Pointe Capital Inc., a GunnAllen Holdings Inc. subsidiary, through his JHS Capital Holdings Inc. and changed the name to JHS Capital Advisors Inc. Sykes will become president and CEO of JHS Capital Advisors and will relocate its corporate headquarters to Tampa, Florida.

35069 ■ *"John Risley" in Canadian Business (Vol. 80, February 26, 2007, No. 5, pp. 70)*
Pub: Rogers Media Inc.
Contact: Tony Viner, President
Ed: Calvin Leung. **Description:** John Risley, co-founder of Clearwater Fine Foods, shares few managerial strategies that helped him to achieve success in various businesses.

35070 ■ *"Julie Holzrichter: Managing Director of Operations, CME Group Inc." in Crain's Chicago Business (Vol. 31, May 5, 2008, No. 18)*
Pub: Crain Communications Inc.
Contact: Todd Johnson, Publisher
Ed: Ann Saphir. **Description:** Profile of Julie Holzrichter who works as the managing director of operations for CME Group Inc. and is known as a decisive leader able to intercept and solve problems.

35071 ■ *"Karen Case: President of Commercial Real Estate Lending, Privatebancorp Inc." in Crain's Chicago Business (May 5, 2008)*
Pub: Crain Communications Inc.
Contact: Todd Johnson, Publisher
Ed: Dee Gill. **Description:** Profile of Karen Case who was hired by PrivateBancorp Inc. to turn its minor share of the city's commercial real estate lending market into a major one.

35072 ■ *"Kid-Friendly Business Sources" in Black Enterprise (Vol. 37, January 2007, No. 6, pp. 40)*
Pub: Earl G. Graves Publishing Co. Inc.
Contact: Earl G. Graves, Jr., President
Ed: Carolyn M. Brown. **Description:** Financial or business camps are a great way to encourage a child who interested in starting his or her own business. A number of these camps are available each year including Kidpreneurs Conference and Bull and Bear Investment Camp. Other resources are available online. Resources included.

35073 ■ *"Kid Rock" in Canadian Business (Vol. 81, Summer 2008, No. 9, pp. 54)*
Ed: John Gray. **Description:** Damien Reynolds is the founder, chairman and chief executive officer of Vancouver-based Longview Capital Partners. The

investment bank, founded in 2005, is one of the fastest-growing companies in British Columbia. The recent economic downturn has battered the stocks of the company and its portfolio of junior miners.

35074 ■ *King of Capital: Sandy Weill and the Making of Citigroup*
Pub: John Wiley & Sons Inc.
Contact: Stephen M. Smith, President
Ed: Amey Stone, Mike Brewster. **Released:** March 2004. **Price:** $16.95, paperback. **Description:** Biography of Sandy Weill describes how he became a billionaire business giant by creating successful companies from smaller, sometimes failing firms; creating successful new products where none previously existed; and making deals no one thought possible. He is also responsible for changing the landscape of the banking industry and insurance business when he created Citigroup in 1998, the world's largest financial services firm. **Availability:** Print.

35075 ■ *The King of Vodka: The Story of Pyotr Smirnov and the Upheaval of an Empire*
Pub: HarperCollins Publishers Inc.
Contact: Jane Friedman, President
E-mail: jfriedman@harpercollins.com
Ed: Linda Himelstein. **Released:** 2009. **Price:** $15.99, Paperback. **Description:** Biography of Pyotr Smirnov and how his determination took him from serf to the head of Smirnov Vodka. Smirnov's marketing techniques are defined and show how he expanded the drink worldwide.

35076 ■ *Kitchen Table Entrepreneurs: How Eleven Women Escaped Poverty and Became Their Own Bosses*
Pub: Westview Press
Contact: David Steinberger, President
E-mail: david.steinberger@perseusbooks.com
Released: March 12, 2004. **Price:** $16.95; C$20.50; £11.99. **Description:** Profile of eleven successful women entrepreneurs. **Availability:** Print.

35077 ■ *"A Knack for Entrepreneurship" in Hispanic Business (January-February 2008, pp. 42, 44-45)*
Pub: Hispanic Business Inc.
Contact: Jesus Chavarria, President
Ed: Hildy Medina. **Description:** Profile of Carlos Antonio Garcia, CEO of Kira, is investing in young companies.

35078 ■ *Knockout Entrepreneur*
Pub: Thomas Nelson Inc.
Contact: Michael S. Hyatt, President
Ed: George Foreman. **Released:** December 14, 2010. **Price:** $22.99, hardcover; $14.99, paperback. **Description:** George Foreman offers ten key strategies for running a successful small business.

35079 ■ *Know-How: The 8 Skills That Separate People Who Perform from Those Who Don't*
Pub: Clarkson N. Potter Publishers
Contact: Jenny Frost, President
Ed: Ram Charan. **Released:** January 02, 2007. **Price:** $13.99. **Description:** Know-how is what separates leaders who perform and deliver good results from those who don't.

35080 ■ *Know-Who Based Entrepreneurship: From Knowledge Creation to Business Implementation*
Pub: Edward Elgar Publishing Inc.
Contact: Richard Henning, Vice President
E-mail: kwight@e-elgar.com
Ed: Sigvald J. Harryson. **Price:** £90.90, hardback; £33.60, paperback. **Description:** Analysis of the knowledge and interconnected areas of entrepreneurship and networking across various levels is presented. Best practice companies are profiled. **Availability:** Print.

35081 ■ *"Knowing Is Growing: Five Strategies To Develop You and Your Business" in Black Enterprise (Vol. 38,*

November 2007, No. 4, pp. 106)
Pub: Earl G. Graves Publishing Co. Inc.
Contact: Earl G. Graves, Jr., President
Ed: Erinn R. Johnson. **Description:** Five strategies for growing a small business are listed by Andrew Morrison, founder of the Small Business Camp. The camp provides training, coaching, and marketing services to entrepreneurs.

35082 ■ *"Koneco Building Services Inc. to Add Theme Park Division" in Orlando Business Journal (Vol. 30, April 25, 2014, No. 44, pp. 3)*
Pub: American City Business Journals
Released: April 25, 2014. **Description:** Koneco Building Services Inc. operations director, Ernie Falco and sales director Wolf Adler, discuss plans to add a theme park division to the Florida-based facility maintenance firm. They offer advice to other entrepreneurs and share the sacrifices they made as their business was growing.

35083 ■ *"Labor of Love" in Green Industry Pro (Vol. 23, March 2011, No. 3, pp. 14)*
Pub: Cygnus Business Media
Contact: Paul Mackler, Chief Executive Officer
Ed: Gregg Wartgow. **Description:** Profile of CLS Landscape Management in Chino, California and its owner who started the company when he was 21 years old. Kevin Davis built his landscape firm into a $20 million a year business without using any dedicated salesperson.

35084 ■ *"Lafley Gives Look At His Game Plan" in Business Courier (Vol. 24, March 21, 2008, No. 50, pp. 1)*
Pub: American City Business Journals, Inc.
Contact: Whitney Shaw, President
Ed: Lisa Biank Fasig. **Description:** Overview of A.G. Lafley's book entitled 'The Game-Changer', is presented. Lafley, Procter & Gamble Co.'s chief executive officer, documented his philosophy and strategy in his book. His work also includes Procter & Gamble's hands-on initiatives such as mock-up grocery stores and personal interviews with homeowners.

35085 ■ *"Last Founder Standing" in Conde Nast Portfolio (Vol. 2, June 2008, No. 6, pp. 124)*
Ed: Kevin Maney. **Description:** Interview with Amazon CEO Jeff Bezos in which he discusses the economy, the company's new distribution center and the hiring of employees for it, e-books, and the overall vision for the future of the firm.

35086 ■ *"Laurent Beaudoin Interview: Deja Vu" in Canadian Business (Vol. 81, July 22, 2008, No. 12-13, pp. 38)*
Pub: Rogers Media Inc.
Contact: Tony Viner, President
Ed: Joe Castaldo. **Description:** Laurent Beaudoin has retired as chief executive officer for Bombardier Inc.'s, a manufacturer of regional and business aircraft, but kept a role in the firm as a non-executive chairman. Beaudoin first resigned from the company in 1999, but had to return in 2004 to address challenging situations faced by the company. Beaudoin's views on management and the company are presented.

35087 ■ *"Lead Like It Matters...Because It Does: Practical Leadership Tools to Inspire and Engage Your People and Create Great Results"*
Pub: McGraw-Hill
Released: September 19, 2014. **Price:** $25.00. **Description:** The Ripple Effect method for increasing employee engagement, reducing turnover, and driving overall business success will help any manager or entrepreneur to lead his company. Important practices like eliminating wasted meetings, addressing conflict, and aligning decisions with business needs are addressed.

35088 ■ *The Leader of the Future 2: Visions, Strategies, and Practices for the New Era*
Pub: Jossey-Bass
Released: August 2006. **Price:** $27.95, hardcover; $18.99. **Description:** Wisdom is lent to any small business owner or leader of a nonprofit organization. **Availability:** PrintE-book.

35089 ■ *"Leaders in Denial" in Harvard Business Review (Vol. 86, July-August 2008, No. 8, pp. 18)*
Pub: Harvard Business Review Press
Contact: Peter E. Walsh, Director
Ed: Richard S. Tedlow. **Description:** Identifying denial in the corporate arena is discussed, along with its impact on business and how to prevent it from occurring.

35090 ■ *Leadership 101: What Every Leader Needs to Know*
Pub: Nelson Business
Ed: John C. Maxwell. **Released:** September 10, 2002. **Price:** $9.99, hardcover. **Description:** Ways to enhance leadership skills focusing on following a vision and bringing others along. **Availability:** Print.

35091 ■ *The Leadership Challenge: How to Make Extraordinary Things Happen in Organizations*
Pub: Jossey-Bass Publishers
Contact: Matthew Hoover, Manager
E-mail: fwelsch@jbp.com
Ed: James M. Kouzes, Barry Z. Posner. **Released:** Fifth Edition. **Price:** $29.95, hardcover; $16.99. **Description:** According to research by the authors, people can make extraordinary things happen by liberating the leader within everyone around them. This handbook gives practical tips to aspire leaders in retail, manufacturing, government, community, church and school settings. **Availability:** PrintE-book.

35092 ■ *"Leadership Development In the Age of the Algorithm" in (Vol. 90, June 2012, No. 6, pp. 86)*
Pub: Harvard Business Review Press
Contact: Peter E. Walsh, Director
Ed: Marcus Buckingham. **Released:** June 2012. **Description:** Guidelines to tailor leadership training to specific individuals include assessing the leadership type for each person, identifying the top leaders for each type, creating practices that are effective for each type, delivering those practices to others, and integrate user feedback to fine-tune the process.

35093 ■ *Leadership in the Era of Economic Uncertainty: Managing in a Downturn*
Ed: Ram Charan. **Released:** December 2008. **Price:** $22.95. **Description:** Management consultant gives advice on how to weather the economic storm, focusing on cash flow and foregoing expansion.

35094 ■ *"Leadership Is...: (Dot, Dot, Dot)"*
Pub: CreateSpace
Contact: Daren Giles, President
Released: October 9, 2014. **Price:** $19.95 paperback. **Description:** A leader makes others aware of the possibilities that exist and inspiring them to achieve them. The book shows through stories and personal experiences the true traits of a good leader. Managers and entrepreneurs, alike, will benefit from the information offered.

35095 ■ *The Leadership Secrets of Colin Powell*
Pub: McGraw Hill Financial Inc.
Contact: Douglas L. Peterson, President
Ed: Oren Harari. **Released:** August 2003. **Price:** £11.99, paperback. **Description:** Profile of Colin Powell, stressing his abilities as a world leader. **Availability:** Print.

35096 ■ *"Leadership Training" in Black Enterprise (Vol. 37, January 2007, No. 6, pp. 56)*
Pub: Earl G. Graves Publishing Co. Inc.
Contact: Earl G. Graves, Jr., President
Ed: Marcia A. Reed-Woodard. **Description:** Profile of Theopolis Holman, Group Vice-President of Duke Energy, who discusses how he prepared for the merger between Duke Energy and Cinergy. Holman oversees a division of 9,000 service contractors and employees.

35097 ■ *Leading with Character: Stories of Valor and Virtue and the Principles They Teach*
Pub: Information Age Publishing Inc.
Contact: Justin Loeber, Director
E-mail: justin@carvertech.ne
Ed: John J. Sosik. **Released:** 2006. **Price:** $39.99, paperback; $73.99, hardcover. **Description:** Examination of the kind of character that leaders develop in themselves and others in order to create and sustain extraordinary organizational growth and performance.

35098 ■ *Leading the Charge: Leadership Lessons from the Battlefield to the Boardroom*
Pub: Palgrave Macmillan
Contact: Lisa Dunn, Manager
E-mail: l.dunn@palgrave.com
Ed: Tony Zinni, Tony Koltz. **Released:** October 2010. **Price:** £13.99, paperback. **Description:** General Anthony Zinni recalls a lifetime of competition on the battlefield and in corporate boardrooms and is leading the call to action to restore American leadership and greatness. **Availability:** Print.

35099 ■ *Leading at a Higher Level*
Pub: FT Press
Contact: Timothy C. Moore, Vice President
Ed: Ken Blanchard. **Released:** September 08, 2009. **Price:** $22.39, Members; $27.99, Nonmembers. **Description:** Tips, advice and techniques from a management consultant to help entrepreneurs create a vision for their company; includes information on manager-employee relationships. **Availability:** Print.

35100 ■ *"Learning Charisma: Transform Yourself Into the Person Others Want to Follow" in Harvard Business Review (Vol. 90, June 2012, No. 6, pp. 127)*
Pub: Harvard Business Review Press
Contact: Peter E. Walsh, Director
Ed: John Antonakis, Marika Fenley, Sue Liechti. **Released:** June 2012. **Description:** Chrismatic leadership tactics include gestures, facial expressions, and an animated voice, all of which can enhance the receptiveness of a given message. Tips include engaging listeners and distilling points, and demonstrating passion, authority, and integrity.

35101 ■ *"Leaving a Legacy: Patricia Latimore and Bourdi Apreala Build a Comprehensive Estate Plan" in Black Enterprise (January 2008)*
Pub: Earl G. Graves Publishing Co. Inc.
Contact: Earl G. Graves, Jr., President
Ed: Cliff Hocker. **Description:** Estate planning is critical for anyone, especially small business owners.

35102 ■ *"Lessons I Learned in the Army: A General's Pep Talk Taught Me That a Leader Can't Lose Sight of What It Means To Be a Grunt" in Inc. (March 2008, pp. 85-86)*
Pub: Mansueto Ventures L.L.C.
Contact: John Koten, Chief Executive Officer
Ed: Joel Spolsky. **Description:** An Israeli general offers leadership advice to entrepreneurs.

35103 ■ *"Lessons Learned From Animals, Part II" in South Florida Business Journal (Vol. 35, September 19, 2014, No. 8, pp. 11)*
Pub: American City Business Journals
Released: September 19, 2014. **Description:** Advice on how to achieve business growth is given. Striving to be in environments that offer mental, spiritual and physical growth to entrepreneurs is encouraged. Businesses should be consistent in practices that promote business growth.

35104 ■ *Lessons of a Lipstick Queen: Finding and Developing the Great Idea That Can Change Your Life*
Pub: Simon and Schuster Inc.
Contact: Carolyn Reidy, President
E-mail: carolyn.reidy@simonandschuster.com
Ed: Poppy King. **Released:** May 2009. **Price:** $22.99, paperback. **Description:** Poppy King tells how she started her lipstick brand at age eighteen. She reveals how she managed to launch her business using a good idea and finding financing, marketing the product and how she became successful. **Availability:** Print.

35105 ■ *"Lessons from Turnaround Leaders" in Strategy and Leadership (Vol. 39, May-June 2011, No. 3, pp. 36-43)*
Pub: Emerald Group Publishing Inc.
Ed: David P. Boyd. **Description:** A study analyzes the cases of some successful turnaround leaders to present a strategic model to help firms tackle challenges such as employee inertia, competition and slow organizational renewal. It describes a change model consisting of five major steps to be followed by firms with environmental uncertainty for the purpose.

35106 ■ *"Let It Shine: Organization Helps Disadvantaged Girls See Their Worth" in Black Enterprise (Vol. 38, February 2008, No. 7, pp. 142)*
Pub: Earl G. Graves Publishing Co. Inc.
Contact: Earl G. Graves, Jr., President
Ed: George Alexander. **Description:** Wilson Mourning, founder of the clothing label Honey Child, attributes her success to her mother and other positive women who helped her through her adolescence. Mourning created a mentoring organization that helps young girls in the Miami, Florida, area to develop life skills.

35107 ■ *Liespotting: Proven Techniques to Detect Deception*
Pub: St. Martins Press/Macmillan
Ed: Pamela Meyer. **Released:** September 2011. **Price:** $14.99, paperback. **Description:** Liespotting links three disciplines: facial recognition training, interrogation training, and a comprehensive survey of research in the field - into a specialized body of information developed specifically to help business leaders detect deception and get the information they need to successfully conduct their most important interactions and transactions. **Availability:** Print.

35108 ■ *"The Life of a Builder" in Birmingham Business Journal (Vol. 31, July 4, 2014, No. 27, pp. 14)*
Pub: American City Business Journals, Inc.
Contact: Whitney Shaw, President
Released: July 4, 2014. **Description:** Rob Burton, CEO of Hoar Construction, one of Birmingham's largest contractors talks about his company and his management style. According to Burton, keeping a long-term perspective helps him make better decisions and has helped him in his job. He mentions that his management style is collaborative, and his belief in his faith is the one thing that helped him overcome a serious illness and mad him realize how much he loves his job.

35109 ■ *The Life Cycle of Entrepreneurial Ventures*
Pub: Springer
Contact: Derk Haank, Chief Executive Officer
E-mail: derk.haank@springer.com
Released: 2007. **Price:** €309, hardcover, softcover; €260.61. **Description:** Issues involved in creating a new business are explored, including venture creation, development and performance. **Availability:** PrintE-book.

35110 ■ *"Life's Work: Ben Bradlee" in Harvard Business Review (Vol. 88, September 2010, No. 9, pp. 128)*
Pub: Harvard Business School Publishing
Ed: Alison Beard. **Price:** $8.95. **Description:** Newspaper publisher Ben Bradlee discusses factors that lead to success, including visible supervisors, enthusiasm, appropriate expansion, and the importance in truth in reporting. **Availability:** PDF.

35111 ■ *"Life's Work: James Dyson" in Harvard Business Review (Vol. 88, July-August 2010, No. 7-8, pp. 172)*
Pub: Harvard Business School Publishing
Ed: Alison Beard. **Description:** The founder of appliance company Dyson Ltd. discusses the role of making mistakes in learning and innovation, and emphasizes the importance of hands-on involvement to make a company successful.

35112 ■ *"Life's Work: Manolo Blahnik"* in *Harvard Business Review (Vol. 88, December 2010, No. 12, pp. 144)*
Pub: Harvard Business School Publishing
Ed: Alison Beard. **Description:** Shoe designer Manolo Blahnik recounts his beginnings in the shoe industry and the influence art has had on his work, as well as balancing art and commerce. He also discusses the importance of quality materials and craftsmanship and the benefits of managing an independent, family-owned business.

35113 ■ *"Life's Work: Oliver Sacks"* in *Harvard Business Review (Vol. 88, November 2010, No. 11, pp. 152)*
Pub: Harvard Business School Publishing
Ed: Lisa Burrell. **Description:** Neurologist and author Oliver Sacks discusses whether different types of minds tend toward certain skills, physician-patient communication, and his own perspectives from being a patient himself.

35114 ■ *"A Lifetime of Giving: Food Bank CEO Fights Hunger One Mouth At a Time"* in *Black Enterprise (Vol. 41, November 2010, No. 4, pp. 86)*
Pub: Earl G. Graves Publishing Co. Inc.
Contact: Earl G. Graves, Jr., President
Ed: Tamara E. Holmes. **Description:** Profile of Valerie Traore, CEO of Food Bank of South Jersey. Traore stresses the importance of volunteerism that she learned from her grandparents. Hunger relief became her passion when she served as a temp office worker for the Maryland Food Bank in Baltimore. She earned her Bachelor's of Science in management and has dedicated herself to a career in nonprofit service.

35115 ■ *"A Lifetime of Making Deals"* in *Crain's Detroit Business (Vol. 24, March 24, 2008, No. 12, pp. 11)*
Pub: Crain Communications Inc.
Contact: Rance E. Crain, President
Ed: Tom Henderson. **Description:** Profile of Walter 'Bud' Aspatore who received Crain's Lifetime Achievement Award for mergers and acquisitions; Aspatore is chairman and co-founder of Amherst Partners L.L.C., an investment banking firm that does evaluations and financings, specializes in turnarounds and advises private and public companies on mergers and acquisitions.

35116 ■ *"A Light Bulb Came On, and It Was Energy Efficient"* in *Globe & Mail (January 27, 2007, pp. B3)*
Ed: Shawn McCarthy. **Description:** A brief profile of Edward Weinstein, chief executive officer of the Montreal-based family-run lighting firm Globe Electric Co., is presented The firm's management strategies are described.

35117 ■ *"Like All Great Visionaries, Steve Jobs has a Dark Side"* in *Canadian Business (Vol. 83, July 20, 2010, No. 11-12, pp. 11)*
Ed: Steve Maich. **Description:** All the adoration piled onto Apple can go to a man's head, especially its CEO Steve Jobs. Jobs is a true visionary but his leadership comes with an autocratic side that is worth watching out for; this is shown by his condescending response to the reported reception problems of the iPhone 4.

35118 ■ *Linchpin: Are you Indispensable?*
Pub: Portfolio
Ed: Seth Godin. **Released:** April 26, 2011. **Price:** $18.50, paperback; $32.50, hardcover. **Description:** The best way to get what you're worth, according to the author, is to exert emotional labor, to be seen as indispensable, and to produce interactions that organizations and people care about. **Availability:** Print.

35119 ■ *Lincoln on Leadership: Executive Strategies for Tough Times*
Pub: Grand Central Publishing
Contact: Maureen Mahon Egen, President
Ed: Donald T. Phillips. **Released:** 1993. **Price:** $16, paperback; C$18, paperback. **Description:** Using President Abraham Lincoln's example of leadership, the author sets out to help business leaders adopt winning strategies.

35120 ■ *"Lines of Communication"* in *Entrepreneur (Vol. 37, October 2009, No. 10, pp. 80)*
Pub: Entrepreneur Press
Contact: Perlman Neil, President
Ed: Brad Feld. **Description:** Entrepreneurial companies should establish a clear and open communication culture between their management teams and their venture capital backers. Chief executive officers should trust their leadership teams when it comes to communicating with venture capitalists.

35121 ■ *"Live and Learn"* in *Canadian Business (Vol. 80, April 23, 2007, No. 9, pp. 76)*
Ed: Chris Buck. **Description:** Paul Anka, a musician, feels that ground work is essential before establishing a company.

35122 ■ *"Live & Learn: Brett Wilson"* in *Canadian Business (Vol. 81, July 22, 2008, No. 12-13, pp. 80)*
Pub: Rogers Media Inc.
Contact: Tony Viner, President
Ed: Michelle Magnan. **Description:** Interview with Brett Wilson who believes he became a 'capitalist with a heart' because he had a father who sold cars and a mother who was a social worker. He feels that being accelerated a grade was one of the biggest opportunities and challenges in his life. Brett Wilson's other views on business and on his family are presented.

35123 ■ *"Clay Riddell"* in *Canadian Business (Vol. 80, February 12, 2007, No. 4, pp. 86)*
Pub: Rogers Media Inc.
Contact: Tony Viner, President
Ed: Michelle Magnan. **Description:** Chief executive officer of Paramount Resources Clay Riddell shares his passion for oil and gas business.

35124 ■ *"Donald Tarlton"* in *Canadian Business (Vol. 80, March 26, 2007, No. 7, pp. 70)*
Pub: Rogers Media Inc.
Contact: Tony Viner, President
Ed: Andy Holloway. **Description:** Donald Tarlton, owner of Donald K Donald Entertainment Group, shares few things about his childhood and career.

35125 ■ *"Live and Learn: George Cohon"* in *Canadian Business (Vol. 79, November 20, 2006, No. 23, pp. 70)*
Pub: Rogers Media Inc.
Contact: Tony Viner, President
Ed: Zena Olijnyk. **Description:** George Cohon, the founder of McDonald's in Canada and Russia, speaks about the Canadian market and the experience of starting McDonald's in Canada.

35126 ■ *"Live & Learn: Ian Delaney"* in *Canadian Business (Vol. 81, Summer 2008, No. 9, pp. 168)*
Pub: Rogers Media Inc.
Contact: Tony Viner, President
Ed: Joe Castaldo. **Description:** Interview with Ian Delaney who is the executive chairman of chemical company Sherritt International Corp.; Delaney previously worked as chief executive for a holding company owned by Peter Munk. Details of his beliefs, profession and family life are discussed.

35127 ■ *"Laurent Beaudoin"* in *Canadian Business (Vol. 80, April 9, 2007, No. 8, pp. 68)*
Pub: Rogers Media Inc.
Contact: Tony Viner, President
Ed: Thomas Watson. **Description:** Chief executive officer of Bombardier Inc., Laurent Beaudoin, talks about his personal life and career.

35128 ■ *"Live and Learn: Lionel Hurtubise"* in *Canadian Business (Vol. 80, January 29, 2007, No. 3, pp. 64)*
Ed: Andy Holloway. **Description:** The views of Lionel Hurtubise, the chairman of SR Telecom, PolarSat, and STP, on his life and the growth of the Canadian telecommunications industry are presented.

35129 ■ *"Live & Learn: Madeleine Paquin"* in *Canadian Business (Vol. 81, February 12, 2008, No. 3, pp. 92)*
Pub: Rogers Media Inc.
Contact: Tony Viner, President
Ed: Regan Ray. **Description:** Madeleine Paquin, chief executive officer and president of Logistec Corp., talks about how she balanced her career and her life as a mother to two girls. Paquin thinks that working mothers need to focus on some things instead of trying to do everything. Her career in the marine cargo handling industry is also discussed.

35130 ■ *"Live and Learn: Penny Chapman"* in *Canadian Business (Vol. 79, July 17, 2006, No. 14-15, pp. 75)*
Pub: Rogers Media Inc.
Contact: Tony Viner, President
Ed: Erin Pooley. **Description:** Interview with Penny Chapman, president of Chapman's Ice Cream, who speaks about her journey from rags to riches.

35131 ■ *"Live & Learn: Philip Kives"* in *Canadian Business (Vol. 79, October 23, 2006, No. 21, pp. 160)*
Pub: Rogers Media Inc.
Contact: Tony Viner, President
Ed: Joe Castaldo. **Description:** Philip Kives, founder and chief executive officer of K-Tel International Inc. discusses his professional achievements.

35132 ■ *"Live & Learn: Savvas Chamberlain"* in *Canadian Business (Vol. 81, February 26, 2008, No. 4, pp. 92)*
Pub: Rogers Media Inc.
Contact: Tony Viner, President
Ed: Andrew Wahl. **Description:** Savvas Chamberlain says he feels cheated during his teenage years because life was not normal for him growing up in Cyprus with all the uprisings against Britain. Chamberlain says he runs Dalsa like he plays chess because all his positions are shown all the time but he keeps his strategy to himself.

35133 ■ *"Live & Learn: Seymour Schulich"* in *Canadian Business (Vol. 79, December 4, 2006, No. 24, pp. 144)*
Pub: Rogers Media Inc.
Contact: Tony Viner, President
Ed: John Gray. **Description:** The views of the Canadian billionaire Seymour Schulich, on the evaluation of donations and gifts, are presented.

35134 ■ *"Live & Learn: Thomas D'Aquino"* in *Canadian Business (Vol. 80, November 19, 2007, No. 23, pp. 92)*
Pub: Rogers Media Inc.
Contact: Tony Viner, President
Ed: Calvin Leung. **Description:** Thomas D'Aquino is the CEO and president of the Canadian Council of Chief Executives since 1981. D'Aquino thinks he has the best job in Canada because he can change the way policies are made and the way people think. Details of his career as a lawyer and CEO and his views on Canada's economy are provided.

35135 ■ *"Live & Learn: WestJet Co-Founder Don Bell"* in *Canadian Business (Vol. 80, November 5, 2007, No. 22, pp. 164)*
Pub: Rogers Media Inc.
Contact: Tony Viner, President
Ed: Michelle Magnan. **Description:** Don Bell was not able to finish his degree at University of Calgary, however, he managed to build companies such as WestJet. Bell hates bureaucracy and believes in the importance of a good corporate culture. Details on his life as a father and a pilot along with his advice for entrepreneurs are given.

35136 ■ *Living Above the Store: Building a Business That Creates Value, Inspires Change, and Restores Land and Community*
Pub: Chelsea Green Publishing Co.
Contact: Margo Baldwin, President
E-mail: mbaldwin@chelseagreen.com
Ed: Martin Melaver. **Released:** May 07, 2009. **Description:** Martin Melaver shares insight into building a business plan that utilizes diversity, shared values, common purpose and land-community ethics that are restorative for humankind and nature.

35137 ■ *"The Long Game" in Business Strategy Review (Vol. 21, Summer 2010, No. 2, pp. 36)*
Pub: John Wiley & Sons Inc. Scientific, Technical, Medical, and Scholarly Div. (Wiley-Blackwell)
Contact: William J. Pesce, Manager
E-mail: wpesce@wiley.com

Ed: Stuart Crainer. **Description:** Profile of Alibaba.com and its CEO David Wei.

35138 ■ *Longaberger: An American Success Story*
Pub: HarperBusiness

Ed: David H. Longaberger, Robert L. Shook. **Released:** August 14, 2003. **Price:** $15.99, paperback. **Description:** J.W. Longaberger, founder of the J.W. Longaberger Handwoven Basket Company offers his personal story of business challenges, mistakes and successes, dreams and accomplishments.

35139 ■ *"Looking Back" in Entrepreneur (Vol. 36, March 2008, No. 3, pp. 118)*
Pub: Entrepreneur Press
Contact: Perlman Neil, President

Ed: Romanus Wolter. **Description:** Entrepreneurs can learn from their mistakes and improve current operations by documenting new strategies and ideas from them, evaluating information and its possible effects, and integrating what has been learned with future plans.

35140 ■ *"Looking Like a Million Bucks" in Entrepreneur (Vol. 37, August 2009, No. 8, pp. 102)*
Pub: Entrepreneur Press
Contact: Perlman Neil, President

Ed: Jason Daley. **Description:** Sunset Tan's Jeff Bozz says he and Devin Haman are executive producers of the show and that they want to stretch the truth a bit and make fun of it. Haman says the business is all about VIP service for everyone and that they want all their clients to feel like celebrities.

35141 ■ *"The Lords of Ideas" in Business Strategy Review (Vol. 21, Autumn 2010, No. 3, pp. 57)*
Pub: John Wiley & Sons Inc. Scientific, Technical, Medical, and Scholarly Div. (Wiley-Blackwell)
Contact: William J. Pesce, Manager
E-mail: wpesce@wiley.com

Ed: Stuart Crainer. **Description:** True originators of modern business strategy are interviewed.

35142 ■ *"Lots More Mr. Nice Guy" in Canadian Business (Vol. 80, October 22, 2007, No. 21, pp. 58)*
Ed: Zena Olijnyk. **Description:** Galen Weston Jr., executive chairman of Loblaw and heir to the Weston family business, has his hands full running the company. Details of his turnaround strategies and ambitious plans to increase profitability of the business are discussed.

35143 ■ *"Lynn Johnson, President: Dowland-Bach" in Alaska Business Monthly (Vol. 27, October 2011, No. 10, pp. 11)*
Pub: Alaska Business Publishing Company Inc.
Contact: Jim Martin, President

Ed: Peg Stomierowski. **Description:** Profile of Lynn C. Johnson cofounder of Dowland-Bach Corporation, a manufacturing and distribution company is presented. The firms primary products are wellhead control and chemical injection systems for corrosion control, UL industrial control panels, and specialty stainless steel sheet metal fabrication.

35144 ■ *Made in China: Secrets of China's Dynamic Entrepreneurs*
Pub: John Wiley & Sons Inc.
Contact: Stephen M. Smith, President

Ed: Winter Nie, Katherine Xin, Lily Zhang. **Released:** December 2008. **Price:** $24.95, paperback. **Description:** Insight and analysis of the strategies leading to China's rapidly growing economy are profiled. **Availability:** Print.

35145 ■ *Made to Stick: Why Some Ideas Survive and Others Die*
Pub: Doubleday Publishing Group
Contact: Stephen Rubin, President
E-mail: mpalgon@randomhouse.com

Ed: Chip Heath, Dan Heath. **Released:** January 02, 2007. **Price:** $26, hardcover; $13.99. **Description:** Entertaining, practical guide to effective business communication; information is derived form psychosocial studies on memory, emotion and motivation. **Availability:** PrintE-book.

35146 ■ *"The Mailman" in Canadian Business (Vol. 80, April 9, 2007, No. 8, pp. 14)*
Pub: Rogers Media Inc.
Contact: Tony Viner, President

Ed: Zena Olijnyk. **Description:** Chief executive officer of Pitney Bowes Inc. Murray Martin's entrepreneurial skills in managing the company and his personal career are discussed.

35147 ■ *Make It Big With Yuvi: How to Achieve Poolside Living by Growing Your Small Business*
Pub: AuthorHouse
Contact: Bryan Smith, President

Ed: Ron Peltier. **Released:** March 23, 2006. **Price:** $16, softcover. **Description:** Successful entrepreneurship is profiled.

35148 ■ *Make Your Business Survive and Thrive!: 100+ Proven Marketing Methods to Help You Beat the Odds and Build a Successful Small or Home-Based Enterprise*
Pub: John Wiley & Sons Inc.
Contact: Stephen M. Smith, President

Ed: Priscilla Y. Huff. **Released:** November 2006. **Price:** $19.95, paperback; $12.99. **Description:** Small business and entrepreneurial expert gives information to help small and home-based businesses grow. **Availability:** PrintE-book.

35149 ■ *"Making the Cut: Osprey Takes Undervalued Courses to the Leader Board" in Crain's Detroit Business (Vol. 24, April 7, 2008, No. 14)*
Pub: Crain Communications Inc.
Contact: Rance E. Crain, President

Ed: Jason Deegan. **Description:** Profile of Osprey Management Co., a diverse real estate company that continues to expand its golf portfolio through the company's recreation division; although many developers are getting out of the field due to Michigan's sluggish golf industry, Osprey has found success by purchasing properties in turmoil for more affordable prices.

35150 ■ *Making Difficult Decisions: How to Be Decisive and Get the Business Done*
Pub: John Wiley & Sons Inc.
Contact: Stephen M. Smith, President

Ed: Peter Shaw. **Released:** June 2008. **Price:** $29.95, paperback. **Description:** Experience of others can help entrepreneurs and managers make difficult business decisions. The strategies set forth in this book have been used successfully in public, private and voluntary sectors. **Availability:** Print.

35151 ■ *Making a Living Without a Job: Winning Ways For Creating Work That You Love*
Pub: Bantam Books

Ed: Barbara Winter. **Released:** July 22, 2009. **Price:** $11.99. **Description:** Winter gives advice to help anyone turn an interest or hobby into a lucrative business. **Availability:** E-book.

35152 ■ *"Making Sure the Doctor Is Always In" in Austin Business Journal (Vol. 34, June 6, 2014, No. 16, pp. B12)*
Pub: American City Business Journals, Inc.
Contact: Whitney Shaw, President

Released: June 6, 2014. **Description:** John Erwin, CEO of Carenet feels that the investment his company has made in finding the best talent in high-performing professionals who share a passion for and dedication to positively impacting the country's health care system is the reason behind the compa-

ny's success. He believes that failure is a big part of success and that one learns from the mistakes more than one learns from doing things right.

35153 ■ *Management Rewired: Why Feedback Doesn't Work and Other Surprising Lessons from the Latest Brain Science*
Pub: Portfolio

Ed: Charles S. Jacobs. **Released:** 2009. **Price:** $12.99; $16, Paperback. **Description:** According to the author, human psychology works better than feedback, praise or criticism when managing employees. **Availability:** Electronic publishing.

35154 ■ *The Management of Small and Medium Enterprises*
Pub: Routledge
Contact: Kevin Bradley, President
E-mail: kbradley@taylorandfrancis.com

Released: March 16, 2011. **Price:** $54.95, paperback. **Description:** Investigation into the underlying mechanisms and practices of management within small and medium enterprises is provided. **Availability:** Print.

35155 ■ *Managing for Results*
Pub: HarperCollins Publishers Inc.
Contact: Jane Friedman, President
E-mail: jfriedman@harpercollins.com

Ed: Peter F. Drucker. **Released:** October 03, 2006. **Price:** $16.99, paperback. **Description:** Entrepreneurs running successful small companies focus on opportunity rather than problems. **Availability:** Print.

35156 ■ *Managing a Small Business Made Easy*
Pub: Entrepreneur Press
Contact: Perlman Neil, President

Ed: Martin E. Davis. **Released:** September 2005. **Description:** Examination of the essential elements for an entrepreneur running a business, including advice on leadership, customer service, financials, and more.

35157 ■ *Managing for Success: The Latest in Management Thought and Practice from Canada's Premier Business School*
Ed: Monica Fleck. **Released:** December 2000. **Description:** Canadian business school offers insight into the latest management skills of the nation's business leaders.

35158 ■ *"The Marathon Club: Building a Bridge to Wealth" in Hispanic Business (March 2008, pp. 24)*
Pub: Hispanic Business Inc.
Contact: Jesus Chavarria, President

Ed: Hildy Medina. **Description:** Minority businesses find it more difficult to secure venture capital for entrepreneurial pursuits. Joe Watson, CEO of Without Excuses and Strategic Hire, suggests Hispanics and African Americans collaborate on issues of importance to minority entrepreneurs.

35159 ■ *"Market Forces" in Canadian Business (Vol. 79, October 23, 2006, No. 21, pp. 93)*
Ed: Erin Pooley. **Description:** The tremendous rise in the number of business schools offering Master of business administration degree in Canada and the depletion in the quality of education provided in these business schools is discussed.

35160 ■ *Marketing for Entrepreneurs*
Pub: FT Press
Contact: Timothy C. Moore, Vice President

Ed: Jurgen Wolff. **Released:** December 07, 2009. **Price:** $22.39, Members; $27.99, Nonmembers; $23.99, Members; $29.99, Nonmembers. **Description:** This text identifies marketing as the entire process of researching, creating, distributing and selling a product or service. It isn't about theory and metrics, rather it is a practical guide that starts with the basics of all marketing aspects. **Availability:** PrintE-book.

35161 ■ *"Marketing: 'Twill be the Season" in Entrepreneur (Vol. 35, October 2007, No. 10, pp. 108)*
Pub: Entrepreneur Press
Contact: Perlman Neil, President

Ed: Kim T. Gordon. **Description:** Entrepreneurs should plan ahead in order to promote products for the holiday season, since it is peak sales time. They can unify their business theme, use customer incentives, advertise early using TV or radio, and reorganize the company Website. Other ways to market for the holiday season are provided.

35162 ■ *Marketing that Works: How Entrepreneurial Marketing Can Add Sustainable Value to Any Sized Company*
Pub: Wharton School Publishing
Ed: Leonard M. Lodish, Howard Morgan, Shellye Archambeau. **Released:** March 2009. **Price:** £22.99, paperback. **Description:** Entrepreneurial marketing techniques are shared in order to help a new company position and target products and services. **Availability:** Print.

35163 ■ *"Marketing: You Are On the Air: Radio and TV Producers Are Looking For Shows Starring Smart CEOs" in Inc. (December 2007, pp. 67-69)*
Pub: Gruner and Jahr USA Publishing Co.
Contact: J. Russell Denson, President
Ed: Sarah Goldstein. **Description:** Many successful entrepreneurs are being hired to host television and radio shows in order to share business expertise.

35164 ■ *Martha, Inc.*
Ed: Christopher Byron. **Released:** 2002. **Price:** $28. **Description:** Profile of Martha Stewart's rise from working class to a billionaire businesswoman is presented. The book covers Stewart's power struggles and personal conflicts as well as her triumphs.

35165 ■ *The Martha Rules: 10 Essentials for Achieving Success as You Start, Build, or Manage a Business*
Ed: Martha Stewart. **Released:** October 2006. **Price:** , $15.95. **Description:** Martha Stewart offers insight into starting, building and managing a successful business.

35166 ■ *The Martha Rules: 10 Essentials for Achieving Success as You Start, Grow, or Manage a Business*
Ed: Martha Stewart. **Released:** October 2005.

35167 ■ *"Massage the Message" in Canadian Business (Vol. 79, December 4, 2006, No. 24, pp. 137)*
Pub: Rogers Media Inc.
Contact: Tony Viner, President
Ed: Erin Pooley. **Description:** The methods adopted by Canadian billionaires to manage their public images are described.

35168 ■ *"Master of His Domain" in Canadian Business (Vol. 81, December 8, 2008, No. 21, pp. S17)*
Ed: Andy Holloway. **Description:** L'Oreal Canada chief executive Javier San Juan believes in being close to consumers and travels to one of his company's fifteen locations in Canada about once a month. San Juan's job is to build the L'Oreal brand in Canada.

35169 ■ *Mastering Business Negotiation: A Working Guide to Making Deals and Resolving Conflict*
Pub: Jossey-Bass Publishers
Contact: Matthew Hoover, Manager
E-mail: fwelsch@jbp.com
Ed: Roy J. Lewicki, Alexander Hiam. **Released:** April 2010. **Price:** $31.95, paperback; $20.99. **Description:** Provides extensive insight into practical strategies and ideas for conducting business negotiations. **Availability:** PrintE-book.

35170 ■ *Mastering Business Negotiation: A Working Guide to Making Deals and Resolving Conflict*
Pub: Jossey-Bass
Ed: Roy J. Lewicki, Alexander Hiam. **Released:** April 2010. **Price:** $31.95, paperback; $20.99. **Description:** Resource guide for any manager requiring practical strategies and ideas for negotiating in business; the book shows how to understand the game to better control the situation, predict the sequence of negotiations, identify tactics of others, and to apply the rules of the game. **Availability:** PrintE-book.

35171 ■ *"MBA Essentials: Real-Life Instruction" in Women In Business (Vol. 61, October-November 2009, No. 5, pp. 28)*
Pub: American Business Women's Association
Contact: Lorie Burch, President
Ed: Leigh Elmore. **Description:** University of Kansas School of Business allied itself with the American Business Women's Association (ABWA) which led to the formation of the ABWA-KU MBA essentials program. With this program, ABWA members are exposed to graduate-level coursework that delves on business topics, such as strategy and operations.

35172 ■ *MBA In A Day: What You Would Learn At Top-Tier Business Schools (If You Only Had The Time!)*
Pub: John Wiley & Sons Inc.
Contact: Stephen M. Smith, President
Ed: Steven Stralser. **Released:** September 2004. **Price:** $34.95, hardcover; $22.99. **Description:** Management professor presents important concepts, business topics and strategies that can be used by anyone to manage a small business or professional practice. Topics covered include: human resources and personal interaction, ethics and leadership skills, fair negotiation tactics, basic business accounting practices, project management, and the fundamentals of economics and marketing. **Availability:** PrintE-book.

35173 ■ *"Me First! Putting Others' Needs Before Your Own Can Be Hazardous to Your Career and Your Health" in Black Enterprise (Vol. 38, December 2007, No. 5, pp. 107)*
Pub: Earl G. Graves Publishing Co. Inc.
Contact: Earl G. Graves, Jr., President
Ed: Tamara E. Holmes. **Description:** Profile of Andrew J. Milisits Jr., entrepreneur and operating manager of an information technology firm; Milisits shares his experiences when taking on increasing responsibilities and his inability to balance the conflicting demands of career and family.

35174 ■ *Medici Effect*
Ed: Frans Johansson. **Released:** October 30, 2006. **Price:** $16. **Description:** Examples of how ideas can be turned into path-breaking innovations.

35175 ■ *Medium-Sized Firms and Economic Growth*
Pub: Nova Science Publishers Inc.
Contact: Frank Columbus, President
Ed: Janez Prasniker. **Released:** April 2005. **Price:** $117, hardcover. **Description:** Medium sized companies should have a more definitive presence in modern microeconomic theory, the theory of entrepreneurship, and the theory of financial markets. **Availability:** Print.

35176 ■ *"Meet the Class of 2014, In their Own Words" in South Florida Business Journal (Vol. 34, June 27, 2014, No. 49, pp. 18)*
Pub: American City Business Journals
Released: June 27, 2014. **Description:** Several business leaders and entrepreneurs under the age of 40 who have achieved success and contributed to their community are presented. The honorees of the 40 Under 40 Class of 2014 share their views about personal and professional lives and social responsibilities to their communities.

35177 ■ *"Megachurch Movie Mogul" in Dallas Business Journal (Vol. 37, June 6, 2014, No. 39, pp. 4)*
Pub: American City Business Journals
Released: June 6, 2014. **Description:** Ordained minister and entrepreneur T.D. Jakes hopes to use the faith-based filmmaking business in Dallas-Fort Worth, Texas as a ministry tool while making huge profits. Jakes says Christian filmmaking represents about 60 percent of his revenue at TDJ Enterprises.

35178 ■ *"Michael Doesn't Live Here Anymore" in Canadian Business (Vol. 80, October 8, 2007, No. 20, pp. 52)*
Ed: Andrew Wahl. **Description:** Michael Treacy's career in the U.S. is discussed. Treacy, a Canadian entrepreneur, believes that Canada has few comparative advantages aside from its natural resources.

Because of this, he also believes that it would not be feasible to do business in the country. Economic factors influenced him to do business in the U.S. instead.

35179 ■ *"Michigan Means Growth: Sustaining Growth Through Thick and Thin: Michigan Companies Sustain Growth with Well-Timed Access to Capital" in Inc. (Vol. 36, September 2014, No. 7, pp. 164)*
Pub: Mansueto Ventures L.L.C.
Contact: John Koten, Chief Executive Officer
Released: September 2014. **Description:** Successful companies possess flexibility, foresight and resources to turn adversity into opportunity. The small businesses in Michigan who have sustained experienced sales growth despite the recession of 2007. The Michigan Economic Development Corporation has introduced three initiatives to help Michigan businesses grow, including venture capital, collateral support and loan participation through the State Small Business Credit Initiative, and cash incentives for businesses looking to invest in urban communities or grow jobs.

35180 ■ *Microfranchising: Creating Wealth at the Bottom of the Pyramid*
Pub: Edward Elgar Publishing Inc.
Contact: Richard Henning, Vice President
E-mail: kwight@e-elgar.com
Price: £20.80, paperback; £72, hardback. **Description:** Ideas from researchers and social entrepreneurs discusses the movement that moves microfranchising into a mechanism for sustainable poverty reduction on a scale to match microfinance. **Availability:** Print.

35181 ■ *"Midas Touch" in Entrepreneur (Vol. 36, April 2008, No. 4, pp. 160)*
Pub: Entrepreneur Press
Contact: Perlman Neil, President
Ed: Sara Wilson. **Description:** Lana Fertelmeister is a model-turned-jewelry designer. Her company, Lana Jewelry, designs fine jewelry for women. Her jewelry line is available in more than 100 stores worldwide and has been worn by celebrities like Cameron Diaz and Sandra Bullock.

35182 ■ *The Middle Class Millionaire: The Rise of the New Rich and How They Are Changing America*
Ed: Russ Alan Prince; Lewis Schiff. **Released:** February 26, 2008. **Price:** $23.95. **Description:** Examination of the far-reaching impact of the middle class millionaires with net worth ranging from one million to ten million dollars and have earned rather than inherited their wealth.

35183 ■ *Millionaire Upgrade: Lessons in Success from Those Who Travel at the Sharp End of the Plane*
Pub: John Wiley & Sons Inc.
Contact: Stephen M. Smith, President
Ed: Richard Parkes Cordock. **Released:** January 2006. **Price:** $19.95; $12.99. **Description:** Interviews with fifty successful millionaire entrepreneurs are used to help a frustrated employee understand the science and secrets behind their successful business ventures. **Availability:** PrintE-book.

35184 ■ *"Minority Entrepreneurs, Business Advocate of the Year Named" in Daily News (November 1, 2010)*
Ed: Aniesa Holmes. **Description:** Jacksonville-Onslow Chamber of Commerce Minority Enterprise Development Day honored outstanding entrepreneurs from the region. Candidates were chosen based on criteria such as business accomplishments, chamber involvement and dedication as well as their commitment to serving people in the community.

35185 ■ *"Mobility: So Happy Together" in Entrepreneur (Vol. 35, October 2007, No. 10, pp. 64)*
Pub: Entrepreneur Press
Contact: Perlman Neil, President
Ed: Heather Clancy. **Description:** Joshua Burnett, CEO and founder of 9ci, uses index cards to keep track of what he needs to do despite the fact that he has a notebook computer, cell phone and PDA. Kim

Hahn, a media entrepreneur, prefers jotting her ideas down in a spiral notebook, has a team that would organize her records for her, and a personal assistant that would keep track of changes to her schedule. Reasons why these entrepreneurs use old-fashioned methods along with new technology are given.

35186 ■ *"Model Citizen" in Entrepreneur (Vol. 36, February 2008, No. 2, pp. 42)*
Pub: Entrepreneur Press
Contact: Perlman Neil, President
Ed: Guy Kawasaki. **Description:** A mensch is a person of noble character, as defined by Leo Rosten. Tips on how to be a mensch and a better person, in relation to being an entrepreneur, are given. These include: helping others without expecting something in return, giving back to society, and knowing the line between right and wrong.

35187 ■ *The Mommy Manifesto: How to Use Our Power to Think Big, Break Limitations and Achieve Success*
Pub: John Wiley & Sons Inc.
Contact: Stephen M. Smith, President
Ed: Kim Lavine. **Released:** August 2009. **Price:** $24.95, hardcover; $16.99. **Description:** A new women's revolution will help women take control of their careers, their lives, and their economic future. The book shows how mom's control the economy and have the power to become successful entrepreneurs. **Availability:** PrintE-book.

35188 ■ *"Money Man" in Canadian Business (Vol. 80, January 15, 2007, No. 2, pp. 67)*
Pub: Rogers Media Inc.
Contact: Tony Viner, President
Ed: Jeff Sanford. **Description:** A profile of Donald A. Guloien, chief investment officer of Manulife Financial and chief executive officer of Global Investment Management, is presented.

35189 ■ *"More Power to Your Presentation" In Business Strategy Review (Vol. 21, Spring 2010, No. 1, pp. 50)*
Pub: John Wiley & Sons Inc. Scientific, Technical, Medical, and Scholarly Div. (Wiley-Blackwell)
Contact: William J. Pesce, Manager
E-mail: wpesce@wiley.com
Ed: Roly Grimshaw. **Description:** You might wonder what similarities there can be between a Russian oligarch and an entrepreneur. When it comes to persuading people to invest, there are plenty.

35190 ■ *"More Than a Feeling" in Entrepreneur (Vol. 36, April 2008, No. 4, pp. 10)*
Ed: Rieva Lesonsky. **Description:** It is said that emotion has no place when it comes to business matters, but it may not be the case as entrepreneurs and other people in business feel passionate about what they do. Emotions can help bring out a positive outlook in them. Other details on the topic are discussed.

35191 ■ *More Than a Pink Cadillac*
Pub: McGraw-Hill
Ed: Jim Underwood. **Released:** January 08, 2003. **Price:** Rs 1,389.43, softcover. **Description:** Profile of Mary Kay Ash who turned her $5,000 investment into a billion-dollar corporation. Ash's nine principles that form the foundation of her company's global success are outlined. Stories from her sales force leaders share ideas for motivating employees, impressing customers and building a successful company. The book emphasizes the leadership skills required to drive performance in any successful enterprise. **Availability:** Print.

35192 ■ *"Morgan Spurlock" in Canadian Business (Vol. 85, June 11, 2012, No. 10, pp. 63)*
Pub: George Media Inc.
Description: Documentary filmmaker Morgan Spurlock believes that filmmakers should have some level of personal integrity in everything theydo and explains that he directs commercials for money and experience that he gains from it. He recalls the biggest risk he had taken in his career beore making the McDonald's documentary 'Super Size Me'.

35193 ■ *"Mover and Sheika" in Conde Nast Portfolio (Vol. 2, June 2008, No. 6, pp. 104)*
Ed: John Arlidge. **Description:** Profile of Princess Sheika Lubna who is the first female foreign trade minister in the Middle East, the United Arab Emirates biggest business envoy, paving the way for billions in new investment, and also a manufacturer of her own perfume line.

35194 ■ *"Murdoch Lifer Mans Main Street Journal" in Advertising Age (Vol. 79, July 7, 2008, No. 26, pp. 1)*
Pub: Crain Communications Inc.
Contact: Rance Crain, President
Ed: Nat Ives. **Description:** Profile of Les Hinton, the U.K. executive who was chosen by Rupert Murdoch to run Dow Jones and The Wall Street Journal; Hinton discusses The Wall Street Journal's unique spot in American business which has helped it survive a dwindling newspaper industry.

35195 ■ *"My Bad: Sometimes, Even CEOs Have to Say They're Sorry" in Inc. (October 2007, pp. 37-38)*
Pub: Mansueto Ventures L.L.C.
Contact: John Koten, Chief Executive Officer
Ed: Donna Fenn. **Description:** A leader's stature with his employees can be elevated if he can admit a mistake simply with sincerity. Unfortunately for large companies, these blunders sometimes make the news.

35196 ■ *My Big Idea: 30 Successful Entrepreneurs Reveal How They Found Inspiration*
Pub: Kogan Page, Limited
Contact: Philip Kogan, Chairman of the Board
Ed: Rachel Bridge. **Released:** April 03, 2010. **Price:** £9.99. **Description:** Thirty successful entrepreneurs share insight into starting and running a small business. **Availability:** Print.

35197 ■ *"My Day" in Business Strategy Review (Vol. 21, Autumn 2010, No. 3, pp. 77)*
Pub: Blackwell Publishers Ltd.
Ed: Julie Meyer. **Description:** Profile of Julie Meyer, who rose to prominence as cofounder of the entrepreneurial network, First Tuesday; Meyer sold the firm for $50 million in 2000.

35198 ■ *"My Day" in Business Strategy Review (Vol. 21, Autumn 2010, No. 3, pp. 77)*
Pub: John Wiley & Sons Inc. Scientific, Technical, Medical, and Scholarly Div. (Wiley-Blackwell)
Contact: William J. Pesce, Manager
E-mail: wpesce@wiley.com
Ed: Julie Meyer. **Description:** Julie Meyer shot to prominence as cofounder of the entrepreneurial network, First Tuesday. The firm was sold for $50 million in 2000.

35199 ■ *"My Inglorious Road to Success" in Harvard Business Review (Vol. 88, July-August 2010, No. 7-8, pp. 38)*
Pub: Harvard Business School Publishing
Ed: Warren Bennis. **Description:** The author discusses the intersection of fortune and opportunity in his career success, and emphasizes the important role of awareness when taking advantage of both.

35200 ■ *My So-Called Freelance Life: How to Survive and Thrive as a Creative Professional for Hire*
Pub: Seal Press
Contact: Christina Henry de Tessan, Editor
E-mail: christina@avalonpub.com
Ed: Michelle Goodman. **Released:** October 2008. **Price:** $15.95. **Description:** Guidebook for women wishing to start a freelancing business; tips, advice, how-to's and all the information needed to survive working from home are included.

35201 ■ *My Start-Up Life: What a (Very) Young CEO Learned on His Journey Through*

Silicon Valley
Pub: Jossey-Bass Publishers
Contact: Matthew Hoover, Manager
E-mail: fwelsch@jbp.com
Ed: Ben Casnocha. **Released:** May 2007. **Price:** $24.95, hardcover; $16.99. **Description:** Profile of Ben Casnocha, a young entrepreneur who shares insight into starting a running a new business. **Availability:** PrintE-book.

35202 ■ *"Natalie Peterson; Corporate Counsel, Steris Corp." in Crain's Cleveland Business (Vol. 28, November 19, 2007, No. 46, pp. F-14)*
Pub: Crain Communications Inc.
Ed: Chuck Soder. **Description:** Profile of Natalie Peterson, corporate counsel for Steris Corp., a manufacturer of sterilization products; Peterson's blue-collar background did not detour her from her collegiate goals although she hardly knew how to fill out a college application. After graduating from Stanford Law School in 1997, she opted to return to Cleveland in lieu of more lucrative job offers in San Francisco. She has joined the school board and has participated in the 3Rs program, in which lawyers visit public schools in Cleveland to get students thinking about career choices and talk about constitutional law.

35203 ■ *"Nation of Islam Businessman Who Became Manager for Muhammad Ali Dies" in Chicago Tribune (August 28, 2008)*
Pub: McClatchy-Tribune Information Services
Ed: Trevor Jensen. **Description:** Profile of Jabir Herbert Muhammad who died on August 25, after heart surgery; Muhammad lived nearly all his life on Chicago's South Side and ran a number of small businesses including a bakery and a dry cleaners before becoming the manager to famed boxer Mohammad Ali.

35204 ■ *Navigating Your Way to Business Success: An Entrepreneur's Journey*
Pub: FreeBridge Publishing, Inc.
Ed: Kathryn B. Freeland. **Price:** $24.95. **Description:** Learn first-hand from a successful entrepreneur about assessing skills and talent, envisioning your company, planning a path to success, and then tapping into available government agencies to make your business become a reality.

35205 ■ *"A Network of One: Local Writer Adds Web Interviews to Creative Output" in La Crosse Tribune (September 14, 2009)*
Pub: La Crosse Tribune
Ed: Geri Parlin. **Description:** Profile of Andrew Revels, a freelance and aspiring writer, who has created a website in order to help gain attention for his own writing as well as for other local artists, musicians and comedians. His latest endeavor includes interviewing local talent and broadcasting the interviews on his site each week.

35206 ■ *Never Bet the Farm: How Entrepreneurs Take Risks, Make Decisions and How You Can, Too*
Pub: Jossey-Bass
Ed: Anthony Iaquinto, Stephen Spinelli, Jr. **Released:** March 2006. **Price:** $24.95, paperback; $16.99. **Description:** Two successful entrepreneurs offer advice for others launching new businesses. The authors show that preparing for setbacks and using a framework to reduce risks and simplify decision making can increase chances for success. **Availability:** PrintE-book.

35207 ■ *Never Eat Alone: And Other Secrets to Success, One Relationship at a Time*
Ed: Keith Ferrazzi, Tahl Raz. **Released:** February 2005. **Description:** Business networking strategies are offered.

35208 ■ *"New Beginnings for VIBE" in Black Enterprise (Vol. 37, November 2006, No. 4, pp. 34)*
Pub: Earl G. Graves Publishing Co. Inc.
Contact: Earl G. Graves, Jr., President
Ed: Mashaun D. Simon. **Description:** Danyel Smith replaced Mimi Valdes as editor-in-chief of VIBE magazine after the Wicks Group, private equity firm

focused on selected segments of the media, communications, and information industries, purchased the magazine.

35210 ■ "A New Breed of Entrepreneurs" in Black Enterprise (Vol. 37, November 2006, No. 4, pp. 16)
Description: Black entrepreneurs are an important part of the chain for providing economic opportunities within the community. Many black business owners are more likely to hire black employees and apply innovative strategies in building their businesses rather than taking the traditional route.

35210 ■ "The New Orleans Saints" in Entrepreneur (Vol. 37, August 2009, No. 8, pp. 40)
Pub: Entrepreneur Press
Contact: Perlman Neil, President
Ed: Jason Meyers. **Description:** Idea Village is a nonprofit group that fosters entrepreneurship in New Orleans, Louisiana. Entrepreneurship is indeed growing in the city during a time when the city is still recovering from the damage of hurricane Katrina.

35211 ■ "The New Orleans Saints" in Entrepreneur (Vol. 37, August 2009, No. 8, pp. 40)
Pub: Entrepreneur Press
Contact: Perlman Neil, President
Ed: Jason Meyers. **Description:** Idea Village is a nonprofit group that fosters entrepreneurship in New Orleans, Louisiana. Entrepreneurship is indeed growing in the city during a time when the city is still recovering from the damage of hurricane Katrina.

35212 ■ "New Project? Don't Analyze - Act: Entrepreneurs Take Small, Quick Steps To Get Initiatives Off the Ground. You Can Do the Same In Your Organization" in Harvard Business Review (Vol. 90, March 2012, No. 3, pp. 154)
Pub: Harvard Business Review Press
Contact: Peter E. Walsh, Director
Ed: Leonard A. Schlesinger, Charles F. Kiefer, Paul B. Brown. **Released:** March 2012. **Description:** Guidelines for acting on a new project include using the means at hand, securing only the commitments needed for the next step, staying within an acceptable loss range, focusing on producing early results, and managing expectations.

35213 ■ The New Social Entrepreneurship: What Awaits Social Entrepreneurial Ventures?
Pub: Edward Elgar Publishing Inc.
Contact: Richard Henning, Vice President
E-mail: kwight@e-elgar.com
Ed: Francesco Perrini. **Released:** 2006. **Price:** £88. 20. **Description:** Social entrepreneurship seeks to improve societal well-being within entrepreneurial organizations. **Availability:** Print.

35214 ■ "New Work Order" in Black Enterprise (Vol. 38, March 1, 2008, No. 8, pp. 60)
Pub: Earl G. Graves Publishing Co. Inc.
Contact: Earl G. Graves, Jr., President
Ed: Marcia A. Reed-Woodward. **Description:** Today's management challenges includes issues of more competition, globalization, outsourcing and technological advances. Suggestions to help create progressive leadership in small business that sustains a competitive edge are listed.

35215 ■ "The Next Frontier" in San Francisco Business Times (Vol. 28, February 28, 2014, No. 32, pp. 4)
Pub: American City Business Journals
Released: February 28, 2014. **Description:** The growth of the electronic payments business in San Francisco, California has captured the interest of venture capitalists, entrepreneurs, and other investors. Social media companies like Facebook and Google are expected to expand into electronic payments. Telecommunication companies are also investing in promising startups and joint ventures.

35216 ■ Nirvana in a Cup: The Founding of Oregon Chai
Pub: Moby Press
Ed: Tedde McMillen; Heather Hale. **Released:** July 2006. **Price:** $12.99. **Description:** Profile of a mother-daughter team who founded Oregon Chai, a tea company.

35217 ■ Non-Standard Employment under Globalization: Flexible Work and Social Security in the Newly Industrializing Countries
Pub: Palgrave Macmillan
Contact: Lisa Dunn, Manager
E-mail: l.dunn@palgrave.com
Ed: Koichi Usami. **Released:** December 2009. **Price:** £84, hardcover; $115. **Description:** Expansion of non-standard employment under globalization is being recognized in all of the newly industrialized countries. The book examines deregulation of labor markets, social protection for nonstandard workers, and social security reforms in accordance with the transformation of employment. **Availability:** PrintE-book.

35218 ■ "Noodles Founder Becomes Colorado's Chief Marketing Officer" in Denver Business Journal (Vol. 64, August 24, 2012, No. 14, pp. 1)
Pub: American City Business Journal
Description: Governor John Hickenlooper has hired Aaron Kennedy to become the first chief marketing officer of the state of Colorado. The founder of restaurant, Noodles & Company will begin his job on August 6, 2012 of creating a state brand to attract more entrepreneurs and businesses entreprises to invest in Colorado.

35219 ■ "Nothing But Net: Fran Harris Offers Advice On Winning the Game of Business" in Black Enterprise (Vol. 38, March 1, 2008, No. 8, pp. 50)
Pub: Earl G. Graves Publishing Co. Inc.
Contact: Earl G. Graves, Jr., President
Ed: Chana Garcia. **Description:** Fran Harris, certified life coach, business consultant, and CEO of her business, a multimedia development company, reveals five tips to ensure entrepreneurial success.

35220 ■ "Now Entering A Secure Area" in Women Entrepreneur (January 14, 2009)
Ed: Aliza Sherman. **Description:** Despite the fact that the field of government intelligence and security is dominated by males, many women entrepreneurs are finding opportunities for their products and services in homeland security. Profiles of several women who have found such opportunities are included.

35221 ■ Nudge: Improving Decisions About Health, Wealth, and Happiness
Pub: Dutton Children's Books
Contact: Lauri Hornik, President
Ed: Richard H. Thaler, Cass R. Sunstein. **Released:** February 24, 2009. **Price:** $17, paperback; $13.99. **Description:** Advice is given to help improve the decision-making process in order to become a successful entrepreneur. **Availability:** PrintElectronic publishing.

35222 ■ "No. 123: Protecting People, From the Bronx to the Beltway" in Inc. (Vol. 36, September 2014, No. 7, pp. 106)
Pub: Mansueto Ventures L.L.C.
Contact: John Koten, Chief Executive Officer
Released: September 2014. **Description:** Profile of Michael S. Rogers, founder of Securityhunter, located in Baltimore, Maryland. The firm installs security systems for military bases and government agencies. The company developed a security system that was used to protect Colin Powell while traveling.

35223 ■ "No. 423: How a Date Led To al Bowling Juggernaut" in Inc. (Vol. 36, September 2014, No. 7, pp. 42)
Pub: Mansueto Ventures L.L.C.
Contact: John Koten, Chief Executive Officer
Released: September 2014. **Description:** Profile of Tom Shannon, entrepreneur who got the idea to buy a bowling alley following a date with a girl. The New

York City-based Bowlmor is a 262-location bowling and entertainment venue that recently became an AMF bowling company.

35224 ■ "The Obstacle Is the Way: The Timeless Art of Turning Trials into Triumph"
Pub: Portfolio Hardcover
Released: May 1, 2014. **Price:** $24.95. **Description:** The formula for success is taking any obstacle and turning it into a business opportunity. Successful leaders throughout history are profiled to show how any entrepreneur can succeed.

35225 ■ "Off the Wall: Keith Collins' Larger-Than-Life Designs" in Black Enterprise (Vol. 37, February 2007, No. 7, pp. 138)
Pub: Earl G. Graves Publishing Co. Inc.
Contact: Earl G. Graves, Jr., President
Ed: Sonia Alleyne. **Description:** Profile of Keith Collins, an entrepreneur who makes carpets for the likes of Jay Leno, Nicolas Cage, Arnold Schwarzenegger, Janet Jackson, and Will Smith. Collins is passionate about this ancient art form and saw a future in it despite the negative feedback from those around him.

35226 ■ "The Office: Do Not Disturb" in Inc. (November 2007, pp. 144)
Pub: Gruner and Jahr USA Publishing Co.
Contact: J. Russell Denson, President
Ed: Leigh Buchanan. **Description:** The importance for any CEO to be accessible to his employees is stressed.

35227 ■ "The Office: Good to Great" in Inc. (October 2007, pp. 140)
Pub: Mansueto Ventures L.L.C.
Contact: John Koten, Chief Executive Officer
Ed: Leigh Buchanan. **Description:** Qualities that make a good manager great are explored. Great bosses make their employees feel smart, they know who performs what job, know when to step back, and remember things about each employee such as their families' names.

35228 ■ "Oil Markets: A Nasty Russian Tale" in Canadian Business (Vol. 81, March 3, 2008, No. 3, pp. 85)
Pub: Rogers Media Inc.
Contact: Tony Viner, President
Ed: Andrew Nikiforuk. **Description:** Billionaires Alex Shnaider and Michael Shtaif entered a partnership for an oil venture which ended in a slew of litigations. Cases of breach of contract, injurious falsehood and other related lawsuits were filed against Shnaider. Details of the lawsuits and the other parties involved in the disputes are presented.

35229 ■ "On Their Own" in Crain's Cleveland Business (Vol. 28, November 12, 2007, No. 45, pp. 19)
Pub: Crain Communications Inc.
Ed: Eileen Beal. **Description:** Discusses the reasons more physicians with entrepreneurial spirit are opening their own practices as well the added challenges and responsibilities that comes with owning one's own practice.

35230 ■ The One Minute Entrepreneur: The Secret to Creating and Sustaining a Successful Business
Pub: Doubleday
Contact: Jack Hoeft, President
Ed: Ken Blanchard, Don Hutson, Ethan Willis. **Released:** April 29, 2008. **Price:** $19.95, hardcover; $11.99. **Description:** Four traditional business ideas are covered including: revenue needs to exceed expenses, bill collection, customer service, and employee motivation in order to be successful. **Availability:** PrintE-book.

35231 ■ The One Minute Manager
Pub: William Morrow
Ed: Kenneth H. Blanchard, Spencer Johnson. **Released:** October 07, 2003. **Price:** $22.99, hardcover. **Description:** Managers of small businesses as well as Fortune 500 companies have been following the management techniques described in this book. Results have shown increased productivity, job satisfaction, and personal prosperity. **Availability:** Print.

35232 ■ *"Online Self-Publishing Services" in Black Enterprise (Vol. 37, November 2006, No. 4, pp. 90)*
Description: Profiles of five online self-publishing services.

35233 ■ *"Operation Fusion" in Black Enterprise (Vol. 38, November 2007, No. 4, pp. 30)*
Pub: Earl G. Graves Publishing Co. Inc.
Contact: Earl G. Graves, Jr., President
Ed: Tara Walker. **Description:** Entrepreneur Albert H. Frazier tells how he combined three separate acquisitions in order to create Goods Movement Inc.:- W&H Systems Inc., a systems integrator and material handler supplier and North American Conveyor Inc. which fabricates and installs conveyor and sort equipment systems for the U.S. Postal Service and Total Transportation Services, a third-party logistics provider.

35234 ■ *The Opposable Mind: How Successful Leaders Win Through Integrative Thinking*
Pub: Harvard Business Review Press
Contact: Peter E. Walsh, Director
Ed: Roger L. Martin. **Released:** December 04, 2007. **Price:** $32, hardcover; $22, paperback; $22. **Description:** The importance of integrative thinking for successful management is discussed. **Availability:** PrintE-book.

35235 ■ *Other Essentials of Business Ownership and Management Development*
Pub: PublishAmerica, Incorporated
Contact: Willem Meiners, Chief Executive Officer
Ed: Charles E. Shaw. **Price:** $24.95, Softcover. **Description:** Things a business owner, entrepreneur, or manager must be aware of in order to successfully manage a small business. **Availability:** Print.

35236 ■ *Out of the Comfort Zone: Learning to Expect the Unexpected*
Ed: Lisbeth Borbye. **Released:** May 10, 2010. **Price:** $35. **Description:** A collection of lectures covering technology, management and entrepreneurship.

35237 ■ *"Out of This World" in Black Enterprise (November 2007)*
Pub: Earl G. Graves Publishing Co. Inc.
Contact: Earl G. Graves, Jr., President
Ed: Anthony Calypso. **Description:** Profile of Noah Samara, CEO of WorldSpace Inc. who raised $1 billion to help create the technological architecture for satellite radio.

35238 ■ *Outliers: The Story of Success*
Pub: Little, Brown and Company
Ed: Malcolm Gladwell. **Released:** November 18, 2008. **Price:** $30, hardcover; C$33, hardcover; $9.99. **Description:** The book explores reasons for individual success. **Availability:** PrintE-book.

35239 ■ *Own Your Own Corporation: Why the Rich Own Their Own Companies and Everyone Else Works for Them*
Pub: Business Plus
Ed: Garrett Sutton; Robert T. Kiyosaki; Ann Blackman. **Released:** June 2008. **Price:** $17.99 paperback. **Description:** Part of the Rich Dad Advisor's Series, this edition shows how individuals can incorporate themselves and their businesses to save thousands of dollars in taxes and protect against financial disaster.

35240 ■ *"Ownership Form, Managerial Incentives, and the Intensity of Rivalry" in Academy of Management Journal (Vol. 50, No. 4, August 1, 2007, pp. 901)*
Pub: Academy of Management
Contact: Ming-Jer Chen, President
Ed: Govert Vroom, Javier Gimeo. **Description:** Ways in which differences in ownership form between franchised and company-owned units alter managerial incentives and competitive pricing in different oligopolistic contexts, or following competitors into foreign markets, is presented.

35241 ■ *The Oxford Handbook of Entrepreneurship*
Pub: Oxford University Press
Contact: Niko Pfund, President
Released: August 15, 2008. **Price:** $62, paperback. **Description:** Research covering entrepreneurship is presented by an international team of leading scholars. **Availability:** Print.

35242 ■ *The Oz Principle*
Ed: Roger Connors. **Released:** 1994. **Price:** $24.95. **Description:** The role of personal and organizational accountability in getting business results is profiled.

35243 ■ *The Pampered Chef: The Story of One of America's Most Beloved Companies*
Pub: Doubleday Publishing Group
Contact: Stephen Rubin, President
E-mail: mpalgon@randomhouse.com
Ed: Doris Christopher. **Released:** July 05, 2005. **Price:** $14.99. **Description:** The Pampered Chef has been selling high quality kitchen tools through in-home cooking demonstration for twenty-five years. CEO and founder explains how she turned her one woman company into a business with sales approaching $1 billion. Christopher shares her story by providing the foundation, strategies for entrepreneurs, setting priorities, knowing when to expand and when to slow growth, and dealing with adversity. **Availability:** E-book.

35244 ■ *"A Panel Study of Copreneurs In Business: Who Enters, Continues, and Exits?" in Family Business Review (Vol. 19, September 2006, No. 3, pp. 193)*
Pub: Family Firm Institute
Contact: Judy L. Green, President
Ed: Glenn Muske, Margaret A. Fitzgerald. **Description:** Analysis of three groups of copreneurs of family businesses, and their entrepreneurial impact on business success is presented.

35245 ■ *"Panera Breadwinner Tries on Tattu Designer Jeans" in Houston Business Journal (Vol. 40, December 18, 2009, No. 32, pp. 1)*
Pub: American City Business Journals
Ed: Allison Wollam. **Description:** Chuck Cain, the franchisee who introduced Panera Bread to Houston, Texas has partnered with tax accountant Jim Jacobsen to introduce custom-make Tattu Jeans. As more Tattu Jeans outlets are being planned, Cain is using entrepreneurial lessons learned from Panera Bread in the new venture. Both Panera Bread and Tattu Jeans were opened by Cain during economic downturns.

35246 ■ *"Paradise Lost" in Inc. (February 2008, pp. 102-109)*
Ed: Bo Burlingham. **Description:** Profile of Bo Burlingham, founder of Precision Manufacturing, a firm cited in books, magazines and newspaper articles for its people-centered culture and success.

35247 ■ *"Patricia Hemingway Hall: President, Chief Operating Officer, Health Care Service Corp." in Crain's Chicago Business (May 5, 2008)*
Pub: Crain Communications Inc.
Contact: Todd Johnson, Publisher
Ed: Mike Colias. **Description:** Profile of Patricia Hemingway Hall who is the president and chief operating officer of Health Care Service Corp., a new strategy launched by Blue Cross & Blue Shield of Illinois; the new endeavor will emphasize wellness rather than just treatment across its four health plans.

35248 ■ *Payback: Reaping the Rewards of Innovation*
Pub: Harvard Business School Publishing
Ed: James P. Andrew, Harold L. Sirkin, John Butman. **Released:** January 09, 2007. **Price:** $29.95, hardcover. **Description:** Three different business innovation models are presented: integration, orchestration, and serving as licensor.

35249 ■ *The Peebles Principles: Tales and Tactics from an Entrepreneur's Life of Winning Deals, Succeeding in Business, and*

Creating a Fortune from Scratch
Pub: John Wiley & Sons Inc.
Contact: Stephen M. Smith, President
Ed: R. Donahue Peebles, J. P. Faber. **Released:** March 2007. **Price:** $24.95, hardcover; $16.99. **Description:** Successful entrepreneur shares his business experience. Peebles went from CEO of the nation's largest Black-owned real estate development firm to founding his own firm. **Availability:** PrintE-book.

35250 ■ *"The Perfect Fit" in Small Business Opportunities (October 2007)*
Pub: Harris Publications Inc.
Description: Launched in 2004, Jigsaw provides an online database of more than 5.5 million business contacts and company information for entrepreneurs.

35251 ■ *"Perfecting the Process: Creating a More Efficient Organization On Your Terms" in Black Enterprise (Vol. 41, October 2010, No. 3)*
Pub: Earl G. Graves Publishing Co. Inc.
Contact: Earl G. Graves, Jr., President
Ed: Tamara E. Holmes. **Description:** More than ever, entrepreneurs need to identify new ways of doing business in a cost-effective manner in order to expand their companies, while remaining true to their customer demands.

35252 ■ *"The Performer: Chess Prodigy Magnus Carlsen" in Canadian Business (Vol. 83, October 12, 2010, No. 17, pp. 79)*
Pub: Rogers Media Inc.
Contact: Tony Viner, President
Description: Magnus Carlsen, chess prodigy, talks about the importance of having a good feel for the game. He thinks that there are some similarities between chess and business, as both are about making good decisions in a limited amount of time. His views about motivation are also discussed.

35253 ■ *"The Performer: Soulpepper Theatre Company's Albert Shultz" in Canadian Business (Vol. 83, August 17, 2010, No. 13-14, pp. 71)*
Pub: Rogers Media Inc.
Contact: Tony Viner, President
Ed: Steve Maich. **Description:** Soulpepper Theater Company founder and actor/director Albert Schultz shares the key ingredient to his success both artistically and commercially. Schultz believes his success was a combination of passion and persistence, as well as team building. He believes his entrepreneurial impulse came when he began thinking of making opportunities instead of taking them.

35254 ■ *"Personal File: Dean Williams" in Canadian Business (Vol. 80, April 23, 2007, No. 9, pp. 55)*
Description: A brief profile of Dean Williams, architect at Softchoice Corp., including his services to the company, is presented.

35255 ■ *"Personal File: Esther Colwill" in Canadian Business (Vol. 80, April 23, 2007, No. 9, pp. 48)*
Description: A brief profile of Esther Colwill, senior manager at Deloitte & Touche LLP, including her achievements which are also presented.

35256 ■ *"Personal File: Laura Laing" in Canadian Business (Vol. 80, April 23, 2007, No. 9, pp. 58)*
Description: A brief profile of Laura Laing, director of public relations at AdFarm, including her services, is presented.

35257 ■ *"Personal File: Malcolm Smillie" in Canadian Business (Vol. 80, April 23, 2007, No. 9, pp. 44)*
Description: A brief profile of Malcolm Smillie, marketing manager of 1-800-Got-Junk?, including his achievements which are also presented.

35258 ■ *Personal Success and the Bottom Line*
Pub: Successful Publishing
Ed: Mark C. Middleton. **Released:** March 2006. **Price:** $24.95. **Description:** Retired certified public accountant provides a primer for those wishing to achieve a balance between career and their personal life.

35259 ■ "Peter Bynoe Trades Up" in Black Enterprise (Vol. 38, July 2008, No. 12, pp. 30)
Pub: Earl G. Graves Publishing Co. Inc.
Contact: Earl G. Graves, Jr., President
Description: Chicago-based Loop Capital Markets L.L.C. has named Peter Bynoe managing director of corporate finance. Bynoe was previously a senior partner at the law firm DLA Piper U.S. L.L.P., where he worked on stadium deals.

35260 ■ "Peter French Tapped to Lead Cafe Commerce" in San Antonio Business Journal (Vol. 28, May 30, 2014, No. 16, pp. 6)
Pub: American City Business Journals
Released: May 30, 2014. **Description:** Entrepreneur Peter French was appointed as the first president of Café Commerce, the new one-stop small business development center in San Antonio, Texas. French is bringing his diverse business experience and entrepreneurial mindset to the business center.

35261 ■ "Peter Gilgan" in Canadian Business (Vol. 82, April 27, 2009, No. 7, pp. 58)
Pub: Rogers Media Inc.
Contact: Tony Viner, President
Ed: Calvin Leung. **Description:** Mattamy Homes Ltd. president and chief executive officer Peter Gilgan believes that their business model of building communities in an organized way brings advantages to the firm and for their customers. He also believes in adopting their product prices to new market realities. Gilgan considers the approvals regime in Ontario his biggest challenge in the last 20 years.

35262 ■ Petty Capitalists and Globalization: Flexibility, Entrepreneurship, and Economic Development
Pub: State University of New York Press
Contact: James Peltz, Director
E-mail: james.peltz@sunypress.edu
Price: $29.95, paperback; $70, hardcover. **Description:** Investigation into ways small businesses in Europe, Asia, and Latin America are required to operate and compete in the fast-growing transnational economy. **Availability:** Print.

35263 ■ "Philanthropy Good For Business" in Crain's Detroit Business (Vol. 24, February 18, 2008, No. 7, pp. 14)
Pub: Crain Communications Inc. - Detroit
Contact: Keith Crain, Chairman
Ed: Sheena Harrison. **Description:** Profile of Burce McCully, founder of Dynamic Edge Inc., and his views on philanthropy as a key to any small company's success. The Ann Arbor, Michigan information technology firm has volunteered and raised funds for many causes since 1999 when the company was founded.

35264 ■ "Phillip Frost: 'Technology Is the Future'" in South Florida Business Journal (Vol. 34, June 20, 2014, No. 48, pp. 16)
Pub: American City Business Journals
Released: June 20, 2014. **Description:** Entrepreneur, Phillip Frost, shares his strategies and perspectives on the business climate of Miami, Florida. He describes investment strategy for the diverse holdings of Opko Health and his criteria for buying companies and licensing technologies.

35265 ■ "Picture of Success" in Black Enterprise (Vol. 38, December 2007, No. 5, pp. 71)
Pub: Earl G. Graves Publishing Co. Inc.
Contact: Earl G. Graves, Jr., President
Ed: Sheiresa Ngo. **Description:** Profile of Kenya Cagle, president and CEO of Caglevision Inc., an independent motion picture production company. Cagle, former off-Broadway child actor, kept his company afloat with financial backing and support from friends, employees, and business colleagues.

35266 ■ "A Piece of the Action: To Attract Top Chefs to His Sushi Restaurant, This Entrepreneur Used Equity as an Incentive" in Black Enterprise (Vol. 38, January 2008, No. 6, pp. 42)
Pub: Earl G. Graves Publishing Co. Inc.
Contact: Earl G. Graves, Jr., President
Ed: Alan Hughes. **Description:** Andre Williams, owner of Kaze Sushi restaurant, offered generous incentive plan-equity in the business in order to acquire Chef Kaze Chan and Chef Hari Chan. Williams' entrepreneurial pursuits are discussed.

35267 ■ "Pioneering Strategies for Entrepreneurial Success" in Business Horizons (Vol. 51, January-February 2008, No. 1, pp. 21)
Pub: Elsevier Advanced Technology Publications
Ed: Candida G. Brush. **Description:** Entrepreneurs are known for new products, services, processes, markets and industries. In order to achieve success, they have to develop a clear vision, creatively manage finances, and use social skills to persuade others to commit to the venture. Pioneering strategies and their implementation are examined.

35268 ■ The Pixar Touch: The Making of a Company
Pub: Pantheon Books Inc.
Contact: Dan Frank, Director
Ed: David A. Price. **Released:** May 05, 2009. **Price:** $16.95, paperback. **Description:** Profile of how Pixar's founders turned their computer-animated films into a successful movie studio. **Availability:** Print.

35269 ■ The Platinum Rule for Small Business Success
Ed: Scott Zimmerman; Tony Allesandra; Ron Finklestein. **Released:** August 2006. **Description:** Rules for running a successful and profitable small business are shared.

35270 ■ "Playing to Win" in Entrepreneur (Vol. 36, May 2008, No. 5, pp. 40)
Pub: Entrepreneur Press
Contact: Perlman Neil, President
Ed: Robert Kiyosaki. **Description:** Four personality types needed by entrepreneurs to drive their leadership in business are given. 'I must be liked' are social directors and go-betweens; 'I must be comfortable' are those who seek job security and are not at ease with deadlines; I must be right are those strong in opinion; and 'I must win' are people in charge.

35271 ■ Poker Winners are Different
Pub: Kensington Publishing Corp.
Contact: Steven Zacharius, President
E-mail: szacharius@atskensingtonbooks.com
Ed: Alan N. Schoonmaker. **Released:** 2009. **Price:** $11.17, Paperback. **Description:** Poker success requires reading the context and reading people, two skills every entrepreneur needs to possess.

35272 ■ "Politicians Who Really Get Business: Meet Four of the Entrepreneurs Running for Congress" in Inc. (Vol. 34, September 2012, No. 7, pp. 21)
Pub: Mansueto Ventures L.L.C.
Contact: John Koten, Chief Executive Officer
Ed: Ryan Underwood. **Released:** September 2012. **Description:** Businessman Mitt Romney is running for President of the United States. Profiles of three entrepreneurs running for Congress and one for the Senate in the 2012 elections include: John Dennis (Rep.), 12th District, California; Jim Graves (Dem.), 6th District, Minnesota; Thomas Massie (Rep.), 4th District, Kentucky; and Linda McMahon (Rep.), US Senate, Connecticut.

35273 ■ The Portable MBA in Entrepreneurship
Pub: John Wiley & Sons Inc.
Contact: Stephen M. Smith, President
Ed: William D. Bygrave, Andrew Zacharakis. **Released:** 4th Edition. **Price:** $34.95, hardcover. **Description:** An updated and revised new edition of the comprehensive guide to modern entrepreneurship that tracks the core curriculum of leading business schools.

35274 ■ Power Ambition Glory: The Stunning Parallels between Great Leaders of the Ancient World and Today... and the Lessons You Can Learn
Pub: Crown Business
Ed: Steve Forbes, John Prevas. **Released:** June 01, 2010. **Price:** $16, paperback; $13.99. **Description:** An examination into the lives of the ancient world's greatest leaders and the lessons they have for today's business leaders. **Availability:** PrintE-book.

35275 ■ The Power of Body Language
Pub: Simon and Schuster Inc.
Contact: Carolyn Reidy, President
E-mail: carolyn.reidy@simonandschuster.com
Ed: Tonya Reiman. **Released:** December 2008. **Price:** $16.99, paperback; $12.38. **Description:** Body language expert describes the hidden meaning behind specific gestures, facial cues, stances, and body movements to help anyone communicate in business. **Availability:** PrintE-book.

35276 ■ "The Power of Commitment: Mere Motivation Is Often Not Enough To Achieve Your Goals" in Black Enterprise (November 1, 2007)
Pub: Earl G. Graves Publishing Co. Inc.
Contact: Earl G. Graves, Jr., President
Ed: Tamara E. Holmes. **Description:** Profile of Michelle Tucker Kirk who opened her bridal shop in 2006. Kirk explains how her commitment and determination were keys to the company's success. Five signs to help any would-be entrepreneur discover if they are truly committed to a business idea are listed.

35277 ■ "Power Cues: The Subtle Science of Leading Groups, Persuading Others, and Maximizing Your Personal Impact"
Pub: Harvard Business Review Press
Contact: Peter E. Walsh, Director
Released: April 22, 2014. **Price:** $25.00. **Description:** Renowned speaking coach and communication expert, Nick Morgan, shows how humans are programmed to respond to the nonverbal cues of others. He teaches business leaders and entrepreneurs how to take control of their communications in order to communicate more effectively while commanding influence.

35278 ■ The Power of Full Engagement: Managing Energy, Not Time, is the Key to High Performance and Personal Renewal
Pub: Free Press/Simon & Schuster Inc.
Ed: Jim Loehr, Tony Schwartz. **Released:** January 2005. **Price:** $15.99, paperback. **Description:** The book presents a program to help stressed individuals find more purpose in their work and ways to better handle overburdened relationships. **Availability:** Print.

35279 ■ "The Power of Fun" in Canadian Business (Vol. 79, November 6, 2006, No. 22, pp. 58)
Pub: Rogers Media Inc.
Contact: Tony Viner, President
Ed: Zena Olijnyk. **Description:** The creative efforts of Philippe Starck in designing condos are analyzed.

35280 ■ The Power of Many: Values for Success in Business and in Life
Pub: Crown Business
Ed: Meg Whitman, Joan O'C Hamilton. **Released:** January 26, 2010. **Price:** $11.99. **Description:** Meg Whitman discusses the important values for success in business and in life: integrity, accountability, authenticity and courage. **Availability:** E-book.

35281 ■ The Power of Nice: How to Conquer the Business World with Kindness
Pub: Doubleday
Contact: Jack Hoeft, President
Ed: Linda Kaplan Thaler, Robin Koval. **Released:** September 19, 2006. **Price:** $17.95, hardcover; $11.99. **Description:** The key principles to running a business through thoughtfulness and kindness are exhibited with the use of success stories. **Availability:** PrintE-book.

35282 ■ "The Power of Noticing: What the Best Leaders See"
Pub: Simon & Schuster Adult Publishing Group
Contact: Carolyn Reidy, President
E-mail: carolyn.reidy@simonandschuster.com
Released: August 5, 2014. **Price:** $28.00. **Description:** A guide to help entrepreneurs and managers gain the advantage in negotiations, decision making, and leadership skills. Instruction is given to see and evaluate information that others overlook.

35283 ■ *The Power of a Positive No: How to Say No and Still Get to Yes*
Pub: Random Housing Publishing Group
Ed: William Ury. **Released:** December 26, 2007. **Price:** $16; C$19.95. **Description:** According to the author, a positive no begins with yes and ends with yes. **Availability:** Print; E-book.

35284 ■ *The Power of Pull: How Small Moves, Smartly Made, Can Set Big Things in Motion*
Pub: Basic Books
Contact: Elizabeth Maguire, Publisher
Ed: John Hagel, III, John Seely Brown, Lang Davison. **Price:** $27.50, hardcover; C$33, hardcover. **Description:** Examination of how we can effectively address the most pressing challenges in a rapidly changing and increasingly interdependent world is addressed. New ways in which passionate thinking, creative solutions, and committed action can and will make it possible for small businesses owners to seize opportunities and remain in step with change. **Availability:** Print.

35285 ■ *The Power of Social Innovation: How Civic Entrepreneurs Ignite Community Networks for Good*
Pub: John Wiley & Sons Inc.
Contact: Stephen M. Smith, President
Ed: Stephen Goldsmith, Tim Burke, Gigi Georges. **Released:** 2010. **Price:** $36.95, Hardcover; $29.99. **Description:** This seminal book provides tools for civic entrepreneurs to create healthier communities and promote innovative solutions to public and social problems. It shows how to effectively tackle the intractable issues facing the country. **Availability:** E-book.

35286 ■ *Predictable Results in Unpredictable Times*
Pub: RosettaBooks LLC
Contact: Marshall Sonenshine, Director
Ed: Stephen R. Covey, Bob Whitman, Breck England. **Released:** August 07, 2009. **Price:** $12.41, hardcover. **Description:** Four essentials for getting great performance in good times and bad are outlined for any small business. **Availability:** Print.

35287 ■ *"Preparing for Weed Control" in Farmer's Weekly (March 28, 2008, No. 320)*
Description: Profile of Richard Beachell who farms in a joint venture with his neighbor. Beachell discusses nitrogen applications, fungicides and the reduction of pesticides.

35288 ■ *Prescriptive Entrepreneurship*
Pub: Edward Elgar Publishing Inc.
Contact: Richard Henning, Vice President
E-mail: kwight@e-elgar.com
Ed: James O. Fiet. **Released:** 2010. **Price:** £22.40, paperback. **Description:** In the only known program of prescriptive entrepreneurship, the author provides a marked contrast to the standard descriptive focus of entrepreneurship studies. **Availability:** Print.

35289 ■ *"Priority: In Memoriam" in Inc. (December 2007, pp. 25-26, 28, 30)*
Pub: Gruner and Jahr USA Publishing Co
Contact: J. Russell Denson, President
Ed: Ryan McCarthy. **Description:** Profiles of entrepreneurs who died in 2007; these individuals helped to create some major business trends in the last fifty years, from the advent of socially responsible business to development of quality manufacturing.

35290 ■ *"Priority: Recessionade" in Inc. (February 2008, pp. 19-20)*
Ed: Amy Feldman. **Description:** Despite signs of inflation, entrepreneurs see these tough economic times as an opportunity to start or grow their businesses. Five entrepreneurs share insight into ways this economic downturn can work to grow their businesses.

35291 ■ *"Profile: Charles Handy" in Business Strategy Review (Vol. 21, Summer 2010, No. 2, pp. 86)*
Pub: Blackwell Publishers Ltd.
Ed: Stuart Crainer. **Description:** In a new series, profiles of a major thinker who has made a significant difference in how organizations are managed and how business careers are shaped are presented.

35292 ■ *"The Profit Recipe: Top Restaurant Trends and How to Use Them to Boost Your Profits"*
Pub: CreateSpace
Contact: Daren Giles, President
Released: September 22, 2014. **Price:** $17.50 paperback. **Description:** Restaurant entrepreneur shares information about food industry trends that will help make a food business more profitable.

35293 ■ *"Program for Women Entrepreneurs: Tips for Surviving this Economy" in Crain's Detroit Business (Vol. 25, June 22, 2009, No. 25)*
Pub: Crain Communications Inc. - Detroit
Contact: Keith Crain, Chairman
Description: Michigan Leadership Institute for Women Entrepreneurs will hold its third and final program, 'Tough Times are Temporary, but Tough People are Permanent' at the Davenport University in Livonia, Michigan.

35294 ■ *Progress-Driven Entrepreneurs, Private Equity Finance and Regulatory Issues*
Pub: Palgrave Macmillan
Contact: Lisa Dunn, Manager
E-mail: l.dunn@palgrave.com
Ed: Zuhayr Mikdashi. **Released:** December 2009. **Price:** £79, hardcover. **Description:** Durable business performance is critically dependent on a stakeholder's strategy along with accessible entrepreneurial financing availability within macro-economic and economic regulatory environments. **Availability:** Print; Electronic publishing.

35295 ■ *"Proof That Good Entrepreneurs Can Make Bad Investors" in Inc. (October 2007, pp. 77-78)*
Pub: Mansueto Ventures L.L.C.
Contact: John Koten, Chief Executive Officer
Ed: Norm Brodsky. **Description:** Information for small business owners is offered to help decide which investments are right for them.

35296 ■ *"Protect Your Trade Secrets" in Business Owner (Vol. 35, July-August 2011, No. 4, pp. 11)*
Pub: DL Perkins Company
Description: Every business has secret information which can include customer lists and contracts or secret formulas and methods used in production of goods vital to the operation. A list of things every small business owner should do to protect these secrets is outlined.

35297 ■ *The Psychology of Entrepreneurship*
Pub: Taylor & Francis Ltd.
Contact: Peter Rigby, Chief Executive Officer
Price: $49.95, paperback; $100, hardback. **Description:** Psychology as the basis for understanding successful entrepreneurship is used to discuss how these small firms impact international social and economic well-being and how they are the main source of job creation, market innovation, and economic growth in most societies. **Availability:** Print.

35298 ■ *"The Pumpkin Plan: A Simple Strategy to Grow a Remarkable Business in Any Field"*
Pub: Portfolio Hardcover
Released: July 5, 2012. **Price:** $26.95. **Description:** One million new businesses are started every year in America and nearly 80 percent of them fail within the first five years. Entrepreneur, Mike Michalowicz discovered the inspiration he needed to successfully grow his business when reading an article about a pumpkin farmer who was committed to growing giant pumpkins. Michalowicz applied the same process to his small business and transformed his company into a multimillion dollar success. The pumpkin plan includes: planting the right seeds, weeding out the losers, and nurturing the winners.

35299 ■ *Purple Cow: Transform Your Business by Being Remarkable*
Pub: Dutton Children's Books
Contact: Lauri Hornik, President
Ed: Seth Godin. **Released:** November 12, 2009. **Price:** $22.95, hardcover; $17.99. **Description:** Being a purple cow means you are exciting, phenomenal and unforgettable, the traits required to be a successful entrepreneur. **Availability:** PrintElectronic publishing.

35300 ■ *The Pursuit of Happyness*
Pub: HarperCollins Publishers Inc.
Contact: Jane Friedman, President
E-mail: jfriedman@harpercollins.com
Ed: Chris Gardner. **Price:** $25.99, hardcover; $14.99, paperback; $10.99; C$11.99. **Description:** Rags-to-riches saga of a homeless father who raised and cared for his son on the streets of San Francisco and worked to become a powerful leader on Wall Street. **Availability:** PrintE-book.

35301 ■ *"Put Down the Phone!" in Entrepreneur (August 2014)*
Pub: Entrepreneur Media Inc.
Released: August 2014. **Description:** Entrepreneurs are advised to not use their mobile phones during business meetings because it would appear they are disengaged and it is insulting to other people in the room. Cognitive psychologist, Ira Hyman, explains that people who are trying to track a social interaction they are in engaged in while tracking their mobile phones will do both things poorly.

35302 ■ *Put Your Business on Autopilot: The 7-Step System to Create a Business That Works So Well That You Don't Have To*
Pub: Morgan James Publishing L.L.C.
Contact: Neil Gudovitz, Director
Ed: Greg Roworth. **Released:** April 01, 2009. **Description:** Failure rates still remain as high as 80 percent within five years of starting a small business despite the hard work by their owners. The author suggests that working harder doesn't necessarily equate to a successful enterprise.

35303 ■ *"Q&A: Crescent Points Scott Saxberg" in Canadian Business (Vol. 81, August 18, 2008, No. 12-13, pp. 8)*
Pub: Rogers Media Inc.
Contact: Tony Viner, President
Ed: Michelle Magnan. **Description:** Interview with Scott Saxberg who discusses Crescent Point Energy Trust's discovery of resources in Saskatchewan and believes that this is a once-in-a-lifetime type of event. Crescent Point holds 75 percent of its resources in Saskatchewan; this new finding being considered the second-largest pool discovered since the 1950s. Saxberg's other views as well as information on Crescent Point's services are presented.

35304 ■ *"Q&A: David Labistour" in Canadian Business (Vol. 81, March 17, 2008, No. 4, pp. 10)*
Pub: Rogers Media Inc.
Contact: Tony Viner, President
Ed: Lauren McKeon. **Description:** David Labistour says that the difference between being a co-op retailer and a corporate-owned retailer in the case of Mountain Equipment Co-op (MEC) is that the company is owned by their customers and not by shareholders. Labistour also says that MEC works with their factories to ensure that these maintain ethical standards in the manufacturing process.

35305 ■ *"Q&A: Joseph Ribkoff" in Canadian Business (Vol. 81, March 31, 2008, No. 5, pp. 4)*
Pub: Rogers Media Inc.
Contact: Tony Viner, President
Ed: Zena Olijnyk. **Description:** Joseph Ribkoff started his career in the garment trade by sweeping floors and running deliveries for a dress manufacturer called Town & Country and earned $16 a week. Ribkoff says that the key to controlling costs in Canada is to invest in the latest equipment and technology to stay competitive.

35306 ■ *"Quality Performance of SMEs in a Developing Economy: Direct and Indirect Effects of Service Innovation and Entrepreneurial Orientation" in Journal of Business & Industrial Marketing (Vol. 29, July*

2014, No. 6)
Pub: Emerald Group Publishing Inc.
Released: July 2014. **Description:** A study was conducted to investigate the effects of innovation and EO (entrepreneurial orientation) on organizational performance in Asian small enterprise context. Strategic management literature and the relationship between EO, innovation, and quality performance was tested. The results indicated that a noteworthy direct and indirect positive relationship exists between EO dimensions, innovation, and quality performance.

35307 ■ Race and Entrepreneurial Success: Black-, Asian-, and White-Owned Businesses in the United States
Pub: The MIT Press
Contact: Ellen W. Faran, Director
E-mail: ewfaran@mit.edu
Ed: Robert W. Fairlie, Alicia M. Robb. **Released:** August 2010. **Price:** $19, paperback; £13.95. **Description:** Trends in minority small business ownership are explored, focusing on the importance of human capital, financial capital, and family business background in successful business ownership.

35308 ■ "Radio Roots Run Deep: Palec Mixes Music with Real Estate" in The Business Journal-Milwaukee (Vol. 25, July 4, 2008, No. 41, pp. A1)
Pub: American City Business Journals, Inc.
Contact: Whitney Shaw, President
Ed: Rich Kirchen. **Description:** Profile of Steve Palec, a real estate broker at CB Richard Ellis, also works as a radio host for shows 'Rock & Roll Roots' and 'Legends of Rock'. Palec shares that real estate is still his top priority, even with his radio gig. Palec's career as a broker and as a radio host is discussed.

35309 ■ "Reaching Your Potential" in Harvard Business Review (Vol. 86, July-August 2008, No. 8, pp. 45)
Pub: Harvard Business Review Press
Contact: Peter E. Walsh, Director
Ed: Robert S. Kaplan. **Description:** Being proactive in developing one's career is an important part of entrepreneurship. Keys to successful development include knowing oneself and one's goals, and taking calculated risks.

35310 ■ "Ready To Take Your Business Global?" in Black Enterprise (Vol. 41, August 2010, No. 1, pp. 89)
Pub: Earl G. Graves Publishing Co. Inc.
Contact: Earl G. Graves, Jr., President
Ed: Alan Hughes. **Description:** The 2010 Black Enterprise Entrepreneurs Conference held in May stressed the need for all small firms to promote a global agenda in order to stay competitive.

35311 ■ "Real Estate Ambitions" in Black Enterprise (Vol. 37, January 2007, No. 6, pp. 101)
Pub: Earl G. Graves Publishing Co. Inc.
Contact: Earl G. Graves, Jr., President
Ed: Tanisha A. Sykes. **Description:** National Real Estate Investors Association is a nonprofit trade association for both advanced as well as novice real estate investors that offers information on builders to contractors to banks. When looking to become a real estate investor utilize this organization, talk to various investors like the president of your local chapter, let people know your aspirations, and see if you can find a partner who has experience in the field. Resources included.

35312 ■ "Real Estate Reinventions: Black Lotus Brewing Co." in Crain's Detroit Business (Vol. 23, October 1, 2007, No. 40, pp. 13)
Pub: Crain Communications Inc. - Detroit
Contact: Keith Crain, Chairman
Ed: Leah Boyd. **Description:** Profile of Black Lotus Brewing Company and owner, Mike Allan who converted a drug store location into a brewery while restoring the building's original architecture.

35313 ■ The Real Leadership Lessons of Steve Jobs: Six Months After Jobs' Death, the Author Of His Best-Selling Biography

Identifies the Practices That Every CEO Can Try to Emulate
Pub: Harvard Business Review Press
Contact: Peter E. Walsh, Director
Ed: Walter Isaacson. **Description:** Fourteen separate leadership practices of Steve Jobs are listed. These include focus, simplify, assume end-to-end responsibility, leapfrog when behind, place products ahead of profits, engage in face-to-face, understood both the details and the big picture, blend the sciences with the humanities, push for perfection, and stay hungry.

35314 ■ Reality-Based Leadership: Ditch the Drama, Restore Sanity to the Workplace, & Turn Excuses into Results
Pub: Jossey-Bass
Ed: Cy Wakeman. **Released:** August 2010. **Price:** $27.95, hardcover; $18.99. **Description:** Recent polls show that 71 percent of workers think about quitting their jobs every day. That number would be shocking if people actually were quitting. Worse, they go to work, punching time clocks and collecting pay checks, while checked out emotionally. Cy Wakeman reveals how to be the kind of leader who changes the way people think about and perceive their circumstances, one who deals with the facts, clarifies roles, gives clean and direct feedback, and insists that everyone do the same without drama or defensiveness. **Availability:** PrintE-book.

35315 ■ "Recent Austin Deals Signal an M&A Resurgence" in Austin Business JournalInc. (Vol. 29, January 22, 2010, No. 46, pp. 1)
Pub: American City Business Journals
Ed: Jacob Dirr. **Description:** The acquisition of at least six Austin, Texas technology companies reflects the growing acquisition activity in the US. Corporations have bought 86 companies and spent $7.3 billion during the fourth quarter of 2009. Insights into the impact of the acquisition activity to Austin's entrepreneurial energy are also given.

35316 ■ "Recession-Proof Your Startup" in Crain's Chicago Business (Vol. 31, November 10, 2008, No. 45, pp. 24)
Description: Detailed information concerning ways in which to start a business during an economic crisis is provided. Ways in which to find financing, the importance of a solid business plan, customer service, problem-solving and finding the right niche for the region are also discussed.

35317 ■ "Red McCombs, Partner Rolling Out New Venture Capital Fund" in San Antonio Business Journal (Vol. 26, April 20, 2012, No. 12, pp. 1)
Pub: American City Business Journal
Description: Entrepreneur Red McCombs has partnered with businessman Chase Fraser to create a new venture capital fund. This new fund will focus on technology startups in the automotive sector.

35318 ■ "Reinventing the Cheeseburger" in Inc. (November 2007, pp. 124-125)
Pub: Gruner and Jahr USA Publishing Co.
Contact: J. Russell Denson, President
Ed: Chris Lydgate. **Description:** Profile of Burgerville's Tom Mears, who turned his drive-through burger restaurant green.

35319 ■ "Reinventing Management" in Harvard Business Review (Vol. 88, July-August 2010, No. 7-8, pp. 167)
Ed: Roberta Fusaro. **Description:** Review of the book, 'Reinventing Management' is presented.

35320 ■ "The Reinvention of Management" in Strategy and Leadership (Vol. 39, March-April 2011, No. 2, pp. 9)
Pub: Emerald Group Publishing Inc.
Ed: Stephen Denning. **Description:** An examination found that critical changes in management practice involves five shifts. These shifts involve the firm's goals, model of coordination, the role of managers and values practiced. Other findings of the study are discussed.

35321 ■ Remarkable Leadership
Ed: Kevin Eikenberry. **Released:** August 30, 2007. **Price:** $27.95. **Description:** Handbook for anyone wishing to be an outstanding business leader; the framework and a mechanism for learning new things and applying current knowledge in a practical to any business situation is outlined.

35322 ■ "A Renewed Sisterhood" in Women in Business (Vol. 64, Summer 2012, No. 2, pp. 6)
Pub: American Business Women's Association
Contact: Lorie Burch, President
Ed: Rene Street. **Released:** Summer 2012. **Description:** The American Business Women's Association (ABWA) regional conference highlighted a new sense of enthusiasm and sisterhood as well as effective visioning exercise and breakout sessions. The ABWA National Women's Leadership Conference in October 2012 will feature the graduates of the Kansas University MBA Essentials Program and keynote speakers Bob Eubanks and Francine Ward.

35323 ■ Renovate Before You Innovate: Why Doing the New Thing Might Not Be the Right Thing
Pub: Portfolio Publishing
Contact: Adrian Zackheim, President
Ed: Sergio Zyman, with Armin A Brott. **Released:** Octobr 4, 2004. **Description:** The author uses his experience as the manager behind the introduction to the New Coke as an example of a lazy business growth strategy. He offers insight into successful growth strategies for any small business owner.

35324 ■ "Resource Line" in Black Enterprise (Vol. 37, January 2007, No. 6, pp. 6)
Description: Interactive Media Editor, Philana Patterson, writes a column for blackenterprise.com that offers advice and provides resources for entrepreneurs, corporate executives, business owners, and budding investors.

35325 ■ "Reviving Entrepreneurship: Policy Decisions in 12 Areas Could Nurture - Or Cripple - America's Greatest Asset" in Harvard Business Review (Vol. 90, March 2012, No. 3, pp. 116)
Pub: Harvard Business Review Press
Contact: Peter E. Walsh, Director
Ed: Josh Lerner, William Sahlman. **Released:** March 2012. **Description:** Government policies should address entrepreneurship as a process, rather than an act. Several key areas for policymaking include basic and translational science, supply and quality of human capital, information availability, tax treatment of rewards and risks, intellectual property rights, workforce healthcare, and mobility of financial and human capital.

35326 ■ Rework
Pub: Crown Business
Ed: Jason Fried, David Heinemeier Hansson. **Released:** March 09, 2010. **Price:** $23, hardcover; $11.99. **Description:** Works to help entrepreneurs and business owners to rethink strategy, customers, and getting things accomplished. **Availability:** PrintE-book.

35327 ■ The Rhythm of Success: How an Immigrant Produced His Own American Dream
Pub: Dutton Children's Books
Contact: Lauri Hornik, President
Ed: Emilio Estefan. **Released:** January 10, 2010. **Price:** $15, Paperback. **Description:** Emilio Estefan, husband to singer Gloria Estefan and founder of the Latin pop legend Miami Sound Machine, is the classic example of the American dream. He shares his guiding principles that entrepreneurs need to start and grow a business.

35328 ■ "The Rich 100" in Canadian Business (Vol. 79, Winter 2006, No. 24, pp. 78)
Pub: Rogers Media Inc.
Contact: Tony Viner, President
Description: The rankings of the 100 richest billionaires in Canada are presented, along with the description of their achievements and their net worth.

35329 ■ *"The Rich 100: Like Father?"* in *Canadian Business (Vol. 79, December 4, 2006, No. 24, pp. 38)*
Pub: Rogers Media Inc.
Contact: Tony Viner, President
Ed: Zena Olijnyk. **Description:** The achievements of the chairman of Thomson Corp., David Thomson, are discussed. The plans of David Thomson to diversify into different areas of business are discussed.

35330 ■ *"The Rich 100: The Frugal Billionaire"* in *Canadian Business (Vol. 79, December 4, 2006, No. 24, pp. 63)*
Pub: Rogers Media Inc.
Contact: Tony Viner, President
Ed: Joe Castaldo. **Description:** The achievements of David Cheriton are described, along with his investments in various firms, including Google Inc.

35331 ■ *"The Rich 100: The Man Behind Brascan"* in *Canadian Business (Vol. 79, December 4, 2006, No. 24, pp. 64)*
Pub: Rogers Media Inc.
Contact: Tony Viner, President
Ed: Andy Holloway. **Description:** The role of Jack Cockwell in the growth of Brookfield Asset Management Inc. is described.

35332 ■ *"The Rich 100: The Oilman"* in *Canadian Business (Vol. 79, December 4, 2006, No. 24, pp. 64)*
Pub: Rogers Media Inc.
Contact: Tony Viner, President
Ed: Michelle Magnan. **Description:** The achievements of David Werklund, the chairman of the CCS Income Trust, are described.

35333 ■ *"Riding High"* in *Small Business Opportunities (November 2008)*
Ed: Stan Roberts. **Description:** Profile of David Sanborn who found a way to turn his passion for biking into a moneymaking opportunity by opening his own bicycle shops; Sanborn's goal is to become the largest independent bike retailer in the United States.

35334 ■ *"The Right Remedy: Entrepreneur's Success Is a Matter of Life and Death"* in *Black Enterprise (Vol. 38, February 2008, No. 7, pp. 46)*
Pub: Earl G. Graves Publishing Co. Inc.
Contact: Earl G. Graves, Jr., President
Ed: Tamara E. Holmes. **Description:** Profile of Leah Brown, whose company conducts clinical trials to determine if specific drugs will relieve particular symptoms. Her company will also visit physician's offices to make certain doctors are following proper protocol for a clinical trial or will collect data from patients.

35335 ■ *"The Right Stuff"* in *Canadian Business (Vol. 79, October 23, 2006, No. 21, pp. 151)*
Ed: Laura Bogomolny. **Description:** The profile of Linda Duxbury, the winner of the Sprott MBA Students Society 2003-04 Best teacher award as well as Carleton University Students' Association 2002-03 award, is presented.

35336 ■ *Risk-Free Entrepreneur*
Ed: Don Debelak. **Released:** June 2006. **Price:** $14.95. **Description:** Information is offered to help entrepreneurs to develop an idea for a product or service and have other companies provide the marketing, manufacturing and staff.

35337 ■ *Risk Takers and Innovators, Great Canadian Business Ventures Since 1950*
Pub: Altitude Publishing
Ed: Sandra Phinney. **Released:** June 15, 2004. **Price:** $7.95. **Description:** Successful business leaders share their creativity, technology skills, and entrepreneurship.

35338 ■ *"Road Warriors: How To Survive Business Travel"* in *Crain's Detroit Business (Vol. 24, February 4, 2008, No. 5, pp. 11)*
Pub: Crain Communications Inc. - Detroit
Contact: Keith Crain, Chairman
Ed: Maureen McDonald. **Description:** Entrepreneurs share tips that help save time and energy at airports when traveling for business.

35339 ■ *"Rob McEwen"* in *Canadian Business (Vol. 80, Winter 2007, No. 24, pp. 138)*
Pub: Rogers Media Inc.
Contact: Tony Viner, President
Ed: John Gray. **Description:** Rob McEwen's interest in gold started with his father who was in the investment industry and was always talking about the value of gold. McEwen believes that there is a lot of room to innovate in mining and that Canada should be a leader in this field.

35340 ■ *"Rob Ritchie"* in *Canadian Business (Vol. 80, January 15, 2007, No. 2, pp. 70)*
Ed: Michelle Magnan. **Description:** The former president of the Canadian Pacific Railway, Rob Ritchie, reveals facts about his personal and professional life.

35341 ■ *"Robert S. McNamara and the Evolution of Modern Management"* in *Harvard Business Review (Vol. 88, December 2010, No. 12, pp. 86)*
Pub: Harvard Business School Publishing
Ed: Phil Rosenzweig. **Description:** A chronicle of the emergence and development of Robert S. McNamara's management skills and perspectives, focusing on the role of his idealism. Lessons learned during the course of the Vietnam Ware are also delineated.

35342 ■ *"Roger Hickel Contracting: Smoothing the Road for Owners"* in *Alaska Business Monthly (Vol. 27, October 2011, No. 10, pp. 114)*
Pub: Alaska Business Publishing Company Inc.
Contact: Jim Martin, President
Ed: Gail West. **Description:** Profile of Roger Hickel and his contracting company that reports nearly $60 million annually in gross revenue. The firm focuses on customer service.

35343 ■ *"Roger Rechler Played Major Role in Long Island's Evolution"* in *Commercial Property News (March 17, 2008)*
Description: Profile of Roger Rechler, real estate developer on Long Island, New York, is presented. Rechler, who died in March 2008, was instrumental in the development, ownership and operations of the largest commercial real estate portfolio on Long Island.

35344 ■ *The Role of the Non-Executive Director in the Small to Medium-Sized Business*
Pub: Palgrave Macmillan
Contact: Lisa Dunn, Manager
E-mail: l.dunn@palgrave.com
Ed: John Smithson. **Released:** November 2003. **Price:** $145, hardcover. **Description:** The role of the non-executive director in a small to medium-sized business is examined. **Availability:** Print.

35345 ■ *"The Romance of Good Deeds: a Business With a Cause Can Do Good in the World"* in *Inc. (Volume 32, December 2010, No. 10, pp. 47)*
Pub: Inc. Magazine
Ed: Meg Cadoux Hirshberg. **Description:** Entrepreneurship and family relationships are discussed. When a small business has a passion for philanthropy it can help any marriage by creating even greater passion for each other.

35346 ■ *"Running the Franchise Numbers"* in *Entrepreneur (Vol. 37, July 2009, No. 7, pp. 87)*
Pub: Entrepreneur Press
Contact: Perlman Neil, President
Ed: Carol Tice. **Description:** Ways in which entrepreneurs can assess if they are ready to be a multi-unit franchisee are presented. Choosing the right locations, knowing how much assistance they can get from the franchisor, and financing are the key considerations when planning additional franchise units. Examples of success in multi-unit operations and multi-unit terms are also presented.

35347 ■ *"Sage Advice"* in *Canadian Business (Vol. 80, October 22, 2007, No. 21, pp. 70)*
Ed: John Gray. **Description:** Seymour Schulich, one of Canada's richest men and generous philanthropist, wrote the book, 'Get Smarter: Life and Business Lessons'. The business book sold more than 50,000 copies and now sits on Canada's bestseller's list. Its popularity is attributed to the marketing efforts of the entrepreneur and author.

35348 ■ *Science Lessons: What the Business of Biotech Taught Me About Management*
Pub: Harvard Business Review Press
Contact: Peter E. Walsh, Director
Ed: Gordon Binder, Philip Bashe. **Released:** April 15, 2008. **Price:** $35, hardcover. **Description:** Former CFO of biotechnology startup Amgen and veteran of Ford Motor Company provides a universal guide to management based on some of the same scientific principles used to create new drugs. **Availability:** Print.

35349 ■ *"Scoring Music"* in *Canadian Business (Vol. 81, December 8, 2008, No. 21, pp. S3)*
Ed: Jay Somerset. **Description:** Boyd Devereaux, who plays with the Toronto Maple Leafs, collaborates with musicians through his record label Elevation Records. Devereaux won a Stanley Cup with the Detroit Red Wings in 2002 and has released five limited edition discs through Elevation records.

35350 ■ *"Screen Time"* in *Canadian Business (Vol. 81, October 13, 2008, No. 17, pp. 93)*
Ed: Calvin Leung. **Description:** Young Canadian entertainment business up-and-comers like Ari Lantos and Brian Mossof plan to produce movies that cold earn and entertain audiences rather than focusing on winning awards. English movies continue to struggle in Canada, while French-language films continue to thrive. Details on Canada's movie industry are furnished.

35351 ■ *The Secret Language of Competitive Intelligence: How to See Through and Stay Ahead of Business Disruptions, Distortions, Rumors, and Smoke*
Ed: Leonard M. Fuld. **Released:** May 2006. **Price:** $24.95.

35352 ■ *"The Secret Life of a Serial CEO"* in *Inc. (January 2008, pp. 80-88)*
Pub: Gruner and Jahr USA Publishing Co.
Contact: J. Russell Denson, President
Ed: David H. Freedman. **Description:** Profile of Bob Cramer, who has lead six successful companies and is now searching for a new business venture and thinks he's found it. Cramer shares his journey from wooing venture capital, handling founders and his hunt for his newest venture.

35353 ■ *Secrets of Millionaire Moms*
Pub: McGraw-Hill
Ed: Tamara Monosoff. **Released:** April 2007. **Price:** £11.99. **Description:** Profiles of successful women/mother entrepreneurs are presented, including Julie Clark, Lane Nemeth, Lillian Vernon, Victoria Knight, Rachel Ashwell and other powerful businesswomen. **Availability:** Print.

35354 ■ *"SEEing an Opportunity: Golden's Eyewear Chain Has a National Vision"* in *Crain's Detroit Business (Vol. 24, January 7, 2008, No. 1)*
Pub: Crain Communications Inc. - Detroit
Contact: Keith Crain, Chairman
Ed: Sheena Harrison. **Description:** Richard Golden, who recently sold D.O.C. Optics Corporation is planning to build a new national eyewear chain called SEE Inc., which stands for Selective Eyewear Elements. SEE will sell expensive-looking glasses at lower prices than designer styles.

35355 ■ *"The Self-Destructive Habits of Good Companies"* in *Harvard Business Review (Vol. 85, July-August 2007, No. 7-8)*
Pub: Harvard Business School Publishing
Ed: John T. Landry. **Description:** Review of the book that helps companies break bad habits and develop new ones for growth and success.

35356 ■ "Sell Out" in Entrepreneur (May 2014)
Pub: Entrepreneur Media Inc.
Released: May 2014. Description: Startup owners should consider a number of less quantifiable, yet equally important reasons to sell their business. The dysfunctional relationship with shareholders or investors is one valid reason to leave the business. David Bloom of Ordr.in says another reason is when the founders have run out of ideas for their current business. Entrepreneur-turned-investor, Sarah Kunst, advises entrepreneurs to examine market interest, the amount of money potential acquirers have, and assess the mergers and acquisitions market as a whole to determine when to sell.

35357 ■ Sell Your Business Your Way: Getting Out, Getting Rich, and Getting on with Your Life
Pub: American Management Association
Contact: Edward T. Reilly, President
Ed: Rick Rickertsen. Released: November 26, 2007.

35358 ■ "Sellers Shift Gears" in Crain's Detroit Business (Vol. 25, June 22, 2009, No. 25, pp. 3)
Pub: Crain Communications Inc. - Detroit
Contact: Keith Crain, Chairman
Description: Of the 14 new car Chrysler dealerships in the Detroit area who had franchises terminated, Joe Ricci of Dearborn will sell used cars at his new business called All American Buyer's Service; Lochmoor Automotive Group in Detroit will focus on Mahindra & Mahindra trucks; Mt. Clemens Dodge, Clinton Township is also selling Mahindra & Mahindra trucks; and Monicatti Chrysler Jeep, Sterling Heights, will offer service along with selling used cars.

35359 ■ "Serial Starter" in Entrepreneur (Vol. 36, April 2008, No. 4, pp. 17)
Pub: Entrepreneur Press
Contact: Perlman Neil, President
Ed: Andrea Cooper. Description: Some entrepreneurs are engaged in serial entrepreneurship as they feel that they are no longer satisfied with their business and they decide to sell it. Others start out new businesses because they believe they can try out and be successful in different kinds of businesses. Details on how to identify and handle new entrepreneurial opportunities are discussed.

35360 ■ Setting the Table
Pub: HarperCollins Publishers Inc.
Contact: Jane Friedman, President
E-mail: jfriedman@harpercollins.com
Ed: Danny Meyer. Released: 2006. Price: $27.99, hardcover. Description: Renowned restauranteur profiles his success in the hospitality business. Availability: Print.

35361 ■ Setting the Table: The Transforming Power of Hospitality in Business
Pub: HarperCollins Publishers Inc.
Contact: Jane Friedman, President
E-mail: jfriedman@harpercollins.com
Ed: Danny Meyer. Released: October 03, 2006. Price: $27.99, hardcover; $11.49; C$11.99. Availability: PrintE-book.

35362 ■ "75 Most Powerful Blacks on Wall Street" in Black Enterprise (Vol. 37, November 7, 2011, No. 3, pp. 136)
Pub: Earl G. Graves Publishing Co. Inc.
Contact: Earl G. Graves, Jr., President
Ed: Alan Hughes. Description: Profiles of seventy-five African American top executives. The listing is a compilation of the brightest and best venture capitalists, asset managers, CEOs, traders, and investment bankers.

35363 ■ "Shape Up! Jamal Williams Develops KIDFIT App to Combat Childhood Obesity" in Black Enterprise (Vol. 41, August 2010, No. 1, pp. 62)
Pub: Earl G. Graves Publishing Co. Inc.
Contact: Earl G. Graves, Jr., President
Ed: Sonya A. Donaldson. Description: Profile of Jamal Williams who developed KIDFIT, an app that helps to combat childhood obesity by offering 150 various exercises for children, with an emphasis on training, conditioning, coordination, and flexibility.

35364 ■ "Shared Leadership In Teams: An Investigation of Antecedent Conditions and Performance" in Academy of Management Journal (Vol. 50, No. 5, October 1, 2007, pp. 1217)
Pub: Academy of Management
Contact: Ming-Jer Chen, President
Ed: Jay B. Carson, Paul E. Tesluk, Jennifer A. Marrone. Description: Study assessed the advantages of distribution of leadership among team members rather than on a single person revealed advantages that ranged from support and shared functions along with higher ratings from clients on their performance.

35365 ■ "Shining a Light on Entrepreneurial Opportunities" in San Antonio Business Journal (Vol. 28, July 11, 2014, No. 22, pp. 4)
Pub: American City Business Journals
Released: July 11, 2014. Description: Café Commerce is a small business and entrepreneurship development program launched by the City of San Antonio in partnership with microlender Accion Texas. The goal of the new resource center is to make entrepreneurship easier by complementing existing programs and serving as a platform to introduce new ones to the business community.

35366 ■ "Shoe's On Other Foot" in Business Courier (Vol. 24, November 29, 2007, No. 33, pp. 1)
Pub: American City Business Journals, Inc.
Contact: Whitney Shaw, President
Ed: Lucy May. Description: Ronald Hummons was fresh out of prison for felony in 2000, and through the help of spiritual non-profit group the Lord's Gym he was able to turn his life around and start his own company Grapevine Ltd. LLC, which makes C-town athletic shoes.

35367 ■ "Should I Stay or Should I Go?" in Entrepreneur (August 2014)
Pub: Entrepreneur Media Inc.
Released: August 2014. Description: The timing of meeting clients in person is critical to the success of a business venture. Entrepreneurs can save time and money if they know when it is worth seeing the client in person. For Jackie Kimzey of the Institute for Innovation and Entrepreneurship, the best time for a face-to-face meeting with clients is when a business relationship is starting to flourish. Kimzey advises entrepreneurs to consider their budget, the amount of time they have been working together, and the importance of the client to the business.

35368 ■ "Siemens Boss on Big Scandals, Bullet-Proof Limos" in Globe & Mail (March 5, 2007, pp. B11)
Description: Interview with Klaus Kleinfeld, the chief executive officer of Siemens AG, in which he shares his views on the job challenges faced by him.

35369 ■ "Sign Up To Grow Your Business, Generate Jobs" in Women Entrepreneur (November 25, 2008)
Ed: Eve Gumpel. Description: Nell Merlino has announced the new Make Mine A Million-Dollar Race, which aims to encourage hundreds of thousands of women entrepreneurs to grow their business to revenue goals of $250,00, $500,000 or $1 million and more as well as create 800,000 new jobs in an attempt to stimulate the nation's economy.

35370 ■ Silos, Politics and Turf Wars: A Leadership Fable about Destroying the Barriers That Turn Colleagues Into Competitors
Pub: Jossey-Bass
Ed: Patrick M. Lencioni. Released: January 2006. Price: $24.95, hardcover; $16.99. Description: The author addresses management problems through a fable that revolves around a self-employed consultant who has to dismantle silos at an upscale hotel, a technology company and a hospital. The story explains how organizations can use a collective operational vision in order to overcome pride, greed, and tribalism and work as a team with the same goal in mind. Availability: PrintE-book.

35371 ■ The Six Sigma Manual for Small and Medium Businesses: What You Need to Know Explained Simply
Pub: Atlantic Publishing Co.
Contact: Amanda Miller, Manager
E-mail: amiller@atlantic-pub.com
Ed: Marsha R. Ford. Price: $24.95. Description: The Six Sigma set of practices used to systematically improve business practices by eliminating defects. To be Six Sigma compliant, a company must produce no more than 3.4 defects per one million products, and if achieved will save the firm millions of dollars. The two main methodologies of Six Sigma are outlined.

35372 ■ "Size Matters" in Entrepreneur (Vol. 36, April 2008, No. 4, pp. 44)
Pub: Entrepreneur Press
Contact: Perlman Neil, President
Ed: Robert Kiyosaki. Description: Entrepreneurs planning to expand their business face challenges when it comes to employing more people and addressing internal relationships, communications and procedures. People skills, organizational skills and leadership skills are some of the things to consider before adding employees.

35373 ■ "Skinner's No Drive-Thru CEO" in Crain's Chicago Business (Vol. 31, April 28, 2008, No. 17, pp. 1)
Pub: Crain Communications Inc.
Contact: Todd Johnson, Publisher
Ed: David Sterrett. Description: Profile of James Skinner who was named CEO for McDonald's Corp. in November 2004 and has proved to be a successful leader despite the number of investors who doubted him when he came to the position. Mr. Skinner has overseen three years of unprecedented sales growth and launched the biggest menu expansion in 30 years.

35374 ■ Small Business: An Entrepreneur's Business Plan
Pub: South-Western
Contact: Susan Badger, President
Ed: Gail P. Hiduke, J. D. Ryan. Released: 2009. Price: $160.25, paperback. Description: Assistance in preparing a business plan that identifies opportunities and ways to target a customer market.

35375 ■ Small Business: An Entrepreneur's Plan
Pub: Nelson Education Ltd.
Contact: Greg Nordal, President
Ed: Ronald A. Knowles. Released: 7th Canadian Edition. Price: C$107.95, paperback; C$62.95. Description: Entrepreneur's guide to planning a small business. Availability: PrintE-book.

35376 ■ Small Business, Big Life: Five Steps to Creating a Great Life with Your Own Small Business
Ed: Louis Barajas. Released: May 2007. Price: $22.99. Description: Five steps for planning, starting and running a small business, while maintaining a good life, are presented.

35377 ■ Small Business and Entrepreneurship
Pub: Pine Forge Press
Contact: Blaise R. Simqu, President
Ed: Robert Blackburn. Released: 2008. Price: $1,200, hardcover, Five-Volume Set. Description: Research covering small business and entrepreneurship.

35378 ■ Small Business Management in Canada
Ed: Robert M. Knight. Released: June 1981. Description: Small business management in Canada.

35379 ■ Small-Business Management Guide: Advice from the Brass-Tacks Entrepreneur
Ed: Jim Schell. Released: October 1995. Description: Entrepreneurs offer advice for managing a small business.

35380 ■ *Small-Business Management Guide: Advice from the Brass-Tacks Entrepreneur*
Ed: Jim Schell. **Released:** 1995. **Description:** Collection of stories, tales and snippets from the perspective of a small business owner.

35381 ■ *Small Business Survival Guide: Starting, Protecting, and Securing Your Business for Long-Term Success*
Pub: Adams Media Corp.
Contact: Scott Watrous, President
E-mail: bobadams@adamsmedia.com
Ed: Cliff Ennico. **Released:** October 2005. **Price:** $12.95. **Description:** Entrepreneurship in the new millennium. Topics include creditors, taxes, competition, business law, and accounting.

35382 ■ *"Smart Investor's Shopping List: Coke, Walgreen, Drill Bits" in Crain's Chicago Business*
Pub: Crain Communications Inc.
Contact: Todd Johnson, Publisher
Ed: Bruce Blythe. **Description:** Interview with Paula Dorion-Gray, president of Dorion-Gray Retirement Planning Inc., discusses the state of the investing environment, favored industries, industries to avoid, and her approach towards investing.

35383 ■ *"Smartcuts: How Hackers, Innovators, and Icons Accelerate Success"*
Pub: HarperBusiness
Released: September 9, 2014. **Price:** $26.99. **Description:** Entrepreneur and journalist describes how some startups go from zero to billions in months by analyzing the lives of the entrepreneurs and their successful companies. He reveals that they do it like computer hackers, they use lateral thinking to rethink convention and break rules that aren't really rules.

35384 ■ *"Smoke Signals: Johnny Drake On What To Expect In a Fine Cigar" in Black Enterprise (Vol. 38, December 2007, No. 5, pp. 195)*
Pub: Earl G. Graves Publishing Co. Inc.
Contact: Earl G. Graves, Jr., President
Ed: Alan Hughes. **Description:** Profile of Johnny Drake, co-owner of the retail tobacco company Renaissance Cigar Emporium. According to the Retail Tobacco Dealers of America, 320 million handmade cigars are sold in the U.S. annually.

35385 ■ *The Snowball: Warren Buffett and the Business of Life*
Pub: Bantam Books
Ed: Alice Schroeder. **Released:** October 27, 2009. **Price:** $20, paperback; $37, hardcover. **Description:** The first authorized biography of Warren Buffett provides deep and timely insight into the psyche of the billionaire investor. **Availability:** Print.

35386 ■ *"So You Want to Start a Brewery? The Lagunitas Story"*
Pub: Chicago Review Press Inc.
Contact: Caroline Robbins, President
Released: October 1, 2014. **Price:** $17.95 paperback. **Description:** Profile of Tony Magee, who founded a brewery in 1993, based in Petaluma, California. The entrepreneur describes the business story of his firm, Lagunitas Brewing Company that makes craft bee that he says defies categorization.

35387 ■ *Social Enterprise in Europe*
Ed: Marthe Nyssens. **Released:** August 2006. **Price:** , $145.00 hardcopy; $46.95 paperback. **Description:** Social enterprises in Europe are examined through three ideas: that they have a complex mixture of goals, that they mobilize various kinds of markets and non-market resources, and that they are embedded in the political context.

35388 ■ *Social Entrepreneurship*
Pub: Palgrave Macmillan
Contact: Lisa Dunn, Manager
E-mail: l.dunn@palgrave.com
Ed: Johanna Mair, Jeffrey Robinson, Kai Hockerts. **Released:** April 2006. **Price:** £88, hardcover. **Description:** Social entrepreneurship is the process involving innovative approaches to solving social problems while creating economic value. **Availability:** Print; E-book.

35389 ■ *Social Entrepreneurship For Dummies*
Pub: John Wiley & Sons Inc.
Contact: Stephen M. Smith, President
Ed: Mark Durieux, Robert Stebbins. **Released:** March 2010. **Price:** $24.95, Paperback; $16.99. **Description:** Discover ways to bring social entrepreneurship to a small company in today's business environment. Today, a company is not measured by financial performance alone, but also on social entrepreneurship. **Availability:** E-book.

35390 ■ *Social Entrepreneurship: What Everyone Needs to Know*
Pub: Oxford University Press
Contact: Niko Pfund, President
Ed: David Bornstein, Susan Davis. **Released:** April 10, 2010. **Price:** $16.95, Paperback. **Description:** In development circles, there is now a widespread consensus that social entrepreneurs represent a far better mechanism to respond to needs than we have ever had before, a decentralized and emergent force that remains the best hope for solutions.

35391 ■ *"Social Intelligence and the Biology of Leadership" in Harvard Business Review (Vol. 86, September 2008, No. 9, pp. 74)*
Pub: Harvard Business Review Press
Contact: Peter E. Walsh, Director
Ed: Daniel Goleman, Richard Boyatzis. **Description:** Social intelligence within the framework of corporate leadership is defined and described. Guidelines for assessing one's own capabilities as a socially intelligent leader include empathy, teamwork, inspiration, and influence.

35392 ■ *"Social (Networking) Butterfly" in Entrepreneur (Vol. 37, September 2009, No. 9, pp. 48)*
Pub: Entrepreneur Press
Contact: Perlman Neil, President
Ed: Jason Daley. **Description:** Entrepreneur Ashley Qualls has successfully grown Whateverlife.com. The site was originally created to share Qualls' custom MySpace.com templates with friends and family. Qualls is planning to redesign the site as a social network focused on Web design.

35393 ■ *"Souled Out" in Canadian Business (Vol. 81, March 3, 2008, No. 3, pp. 35)*
Ed: Calvin Leung. **Description:** According to a survey of over 100 entrepreneurs, 78 percent responded that selling their business was emotionally draining for them. Greig Clark, for example, says that one of the toughest times of his life was selling College Pro Painters, after putting 18 years into that business. The economic impacts of selling out are also examined.

35394 ■ *"A Sound Setup" in Black Enterprise (Vol. 38, November 2007, No. 4, pp. 100)*
Ed: Anthony Calypso. **Description:** Choosing the right corporate identity can ensure that a business has the right foundation on which to build and grow.

35395 ■ *"Speak Better: Five Tips for Polished Presentations" in Women Entrepreneur (September 19, 2008)*
Ed: Suzannah Baum. **Description:** Successful entrepreneurs agree that exemplary public speaking skills are among the core techniques needed to propel their business forward. A well-delivered presentation can result in securing a new distribution channel, gaining new customers, locking into a new referral stream or receiving extra funding.

35396 ■ *"Speed Reader" in Crain's Chicago Business (Vol. 30, February 2007, No. 6, pp. 58)*
Ed: Laura Bianchi. **Description:** Interview with Paul Tamraz, president and CEO of Motor Werkes, which carries luxury vehicle lines like BMW, Porsche, and Mercedes-Benz. Tamraz discusses the importance of keeping up to speed with not only U.S. business but what is happening around the world.

35397 ■ *"Speed Traps: Every Fast-Growth Company Eventually Runs Into At Least One of These All-Too-Common Obstacles. How You Handle Them Can Make the Difference*

Between Success and a High-Speed Smashup" in Inc. (Vol. 34, September 2012, No. 7, pp. 53)
Pub: Mansueto Ventures L.L.C.
Contact: John Koten, Chief Executive Officer
Ed: Kimberly Weisul. **Released:** September 2012. **Description:** Obstacles encountered by fast growing companies and suggestions to avoid falling into these traps are covered. According to a recent study conducted by Gary Kunkle, an economist and research fellowwith Edward Lowe Foundation's Institute for Exceptional Growth Companies, shows that fast growing companies share the same issues, which are different from those of industry peers or businesses of the same size.

35398 ■ *The Speed of Trust: The One Thing that Changes Everything*
Pub: Simon and Schuster Inc.
Contact: Carolyn Reidy, President
E-mail: carolyn.reidy@simonandschuster.com
Ed: Stephen R. Covey, Rebecca R. Merrill. **Released:** February 2008. **Price:** $16.99, paperback. **Description:** Advice is given to help cultivate trust in business, politics and personal relationships. **Availability:** Print.

35399 ■ *The SPEED of Trust: The One Thing That Changes Everything*
Pub: Free Press/Simon & Schuster Inc.
Ed: Stephen M.R. Covey, Rebecca R. Merrill. **Released:** February 05, 2008. **Price:** $16.99. **Description:** Because of recent business scandals, trust and a desire for accountability is addressed by the author. **Availability:** Print.

35400 ■ *The Spirit of Entrepreneurship: Exploring the Essence of Entrepreneurship Through Personal Stories*
Pub: Springer
Contact: Derk Haank, Chief Executive Officer
E-mail: derk.haank@springer.com
Ed: Sharda S. Nandram, Karel J. Samson. **Released:** 2006. **Price:** €89.99, hardcover; €74.96. **Description:** Case studies involving 60 entrepreneurs and executives explores the fundamentals in starting a new business, techniques and mindsets. **Availability:** PrintE-book.

35401 ■ *"The Spirit of a Man: Kedar Massenburg's Intoxicating Style of Conducting Business" in Black Enterprise (Vol. 38, March 1, 2008)*
Pub: Earl G. Graves Publishing Co. Inc.
Contact: Earl G. Graves, Jr., President
Ed: Sonia Alleyne. **Description:** Profile of Kedar Massenburg, personal trainer at The Gym in Montvale, New Jersey. Massenburg also operates an independent record label and management company as well as Kedar Beverages LLC founded in 2005. His latest venture is winemaking.

35402 ■ *"Spread Your Wings" in Canadian Business (Vol. 81, March 17, 2008, No. 4, pp. 31)*
Ed: Megan Harman. **Description:** Financing from angel investors is one avenue that should be explored by startups. Angel investors are typically affluent individuals who invest their own money. Angel investors usually want at least 10 times their initial investment within eight years but they benefit the businesses through their help in decision-making and the industry expertise they provide.

35403 ■ *The Starfish and the Spider*
Pub: Portfolio
Ed: Ori Brafman, Rod A. Beckstrom. **Released:** July 29, 2008. **Price:** $16, paperback; $12.99. **Availability:** PrintElectronic publishing.

35404 ■ *The Starfish and the Spider: The Unstoppable Power of Leaderless Organizations*
Pub: Portfolio Publishing
Contact: Adrian Zackheim, President
Ed: Ori Brafman, Rod A. Beckstrom. **Released:** July 29, 2008. **Price:** $16, Paperback; $12.99. **Description:** Through their experiences promoting peace and economic development through decentralizing net-

working, the authors offer insight into ways that decentralizing can change organizations. Three techniques for combating a decentralized competitor are examined. **Availability:** PrintElectronic publishing.

35405 ■ *"The Stars Align: Trail Blazers, Headline Makers on 2007 List Set Example for Others" in Hispanic Business (October 2007, pp. 22)*
Pub: Hispanic Business Inc.
Contact: Jesus Chavarria, President
Description: Top one hundred most influential Hispanic business leaders comprise of 66 percent men and 34 percent women, distributed by 27 percent in government, 42 percent corporate, 11 percent education, five percent art and entertainment, and 15 percent in other sectors. Statistical data included.

35406 ■ *"Start or Buy? It's a Tough Question for Eager Entrepreneurs" in Crain's Cleveland Business (Vol. 28, October 8, 2007, No. 40, pp. 24)*
Pub: Crain Communications Inc.
Ed: David Prizinsky. **Description:** Discusses different approaches to becoming a small business owner.

35407 ■ *Start, Run, & Grow a Successful Small Business*
Pub: Toolkit Media Group
Ed: John L. Duoba, Joel Handelsman, Alice H. Magos, Catherine Gordon. **Released:** Sixth Edition. **Price:** $18.70. **Availability:** Print.

35408 ■ *Start Small, Finish Big*
Ed: Fred DeLuca with John P. Hayes. **Released:** April 2009. **Price:** $16.95. **Description:** Fred DeLuca is profiled; after founding the multi-billion dollar chain of Subway sandwich restaurants, DeLuca is committed to helping microentrepreneurs, people who start successful small businesses with less than $1,000.

35409 ■ *"Staying Engaged: Location, Location" in Black Enterprise (Vol. 38, February 2008, No. 7, pp. 64)*
Pub: Earl G. Graves Publishing Co. Inc.
Contact: Earl G. Graves, Jr., President
Ed: Marcia A. Reed-Woodard. **Description:** Rules to help business leaders construct networking contacts in order to maximize professional success are outlined.

35410 ■ *"Steve Meginniss Helped Reinvent the Toothbrush. Can He Do the Same Thing for Wheels?" in Inc. (February 2008, pp. 32)*
Ed: Dalia Fahmy. **Description:** Profile of Steve Meginniss, co-inventor of Sonicare Toothbrush and inventor of a two-gear wheel for wheelchairs. Mgeinniss discusses his need to raid $1 million to promote and cut manufacturing costs for this new product that helps reduce pain for users.

35411 ■ *"Still on the Block" in Entrepreneur (Vol. 35, November 2007, No. 11, pp. 22)*
Pub: Entrepreneur Press
Contact: Perlman Neil, President
Ed: Laura Tiffany. **Description:** Neighborhoods where business enterprises are located sometimes go into decline, particularly in low-income communities with high crime rates. Some entrepreneurs share stories about getting involved to help revive the community and keep their businesses thriving.

35412 ■ *"Stitching Cincinnati Together" in Business Courier (Vol. 24, February 7, 2008, No. 44, pp. 1)*
Pub: American City Business Journals, Inc.
Contact: Whitney Shaw, President
Ed: Lucy May. **Description:** Nancy Zimpher, University of Cincinnati president, has been given vital leadership posts in regional development organizations in the area. She sees this as part of her job and of the university's mission of serving the community.

35413 ■ *"Stop the Fear of Success From Holding You Back" in South Florida Business Journal (Vol. 34, May 30, 2014, No. 45, pp. 20)*
Pub: American City Business Journals
Released: May 30, 2014. **Description:** Advice is given to help entrepreneurs overcome the fear of success.

35414 ■ *Stop Working: Start a Business, Globalize It, and Generate Enough Cash Flow to Get Out of the Rat Race*
Pub: Eye Contact Media Inc.
Contact: Rohan Hall, Chief Executive Officer
Ed: Rohan Hall. **Released:** November 2004. **Price:** $15.99. **Description:** Advice is given to small companies to compete in the global marketplace by entrepreneur using the same strategy for his own business.

35415 ■ *Strategic Entrepreneurship*
Ed: Philip A. Wickham. **Released:** September 2006. **Price:** $90.00. **Description:** Conceptual and practical ideas for managing a small business are explored.

35416 ■ *Strategic Partnerships: An Entrepreneur's Guide to Joint Ventures and Alliances*
Pub: Kaplan Publishing
Ed: Robert Wallace. **Released:** September 2004. **Price:** $22. **Description:** Ways to develop and execute joint venture relationships with larger business entities for small company owners.

35417 ■ *"Street Bistro Brings Food Truck Treats to Bangor" in Bangor Daily News (June 26, 2012)*
Pub: McClatchy-Tribune Information Services
Ed: Emily Burnham. **Released:** June 26, 2012. **Description:** Chef Kim Smith launched her food truck, Street Bistro in Bangor, Maine. Smith took a year off after closing her two restaurants called Unbridled Bistro and Bennett's Market. Smith and her husband purchased a Snap-On truck and redesigned it into a kitchen. Menu items range from French to Tex-Mex to Thai to American.

35418 ■ *Strengths Based Leadership*
Pub: Gallup Press
Ed: Tom Rath, Barry Conchie. **Price:** $15.99. **Description:** Three keys to being a more effective leader. **Availability:** Print.

35419 ■ *Strengthsfinder 2.0*
Pub: Gallup Press
Ed: Tom Rath. **Released:** 2007. **Description:** Author helps people uncover their talents in order to achieve their best each day.

35420 ■ *"Stress-Test Your Strategy: the 7 Questions to Ask" in Harvard Business Review (Vol. 88, November 2010, No. 11, pp. 92)*
Pub: Harvard Business School Publishing
Ed: Robert Simons. **Description:** Seven questions organizations should use to assess crisis management capabilities are: who is the primary customer, how do core values prioritize all parties, what performance variables are being tracked, what strategic boundaries have been set, how is creative tension being produced, how committed are workers to assisting each other, and what uncertainties are causing worry?.

35421 ■ *"Strive for 100 Percent Satisfaction" in South Florida Business Journal (Vol. 34, June 27, 2014, No. 49, pp. 13)*
Pub: American City Business Journals
Released: June 27, 2014. **Description:** Allied Kitchen & Bath president and CEO, Bill Feinberg, is profiled. The entrepreneur discusses his advocacy for helping to find a cure for leukemia and lymphoma. He enjoys cooking and traveling with family.

35422 ■ *"Strivers and High Fliers" in Dallas Business Journal (Vol. 37, February 7, 2014, No. 22, pp. 4)*
Pub: American City Business Journals
Released: February 7, 2014. **Description:** The winners of the 2014 Minority Business Leader Award in Dallas, Texas, all share significant entrepreneurial traits like taking the lessons they learned as a child in their careers. Each of the award winners have achieved success using very particular and personal sets of benchmarks.

35423 ■ *Studies in Entrepreneurship, Business and Government in Hong Kong: The Economic Development of a Small Open Economy*
Pub: Edwin Mellen Press
Contact: Kazimierz Braun, Director
Ed: Fu-Lai Tony Yu. **Released:** November 2006. **Price:** $139.95; £94.95. **Description:** Institutional and Austrian theories are used to analyze the transformation taking place in Hong Kong's economy.

35424 ■ *Success Built to Last: Creating a Life That Matters*
Pub: Penguin Group USA
Contact: Phyllis Grann, President
Ed: Jerry Porras, Stewart Emery, Mark Thompson. **Released:** August 28, 2007. **Price:** $17, paperback. **Description:** Interviews with successful individuals are presented to help any entrepreneur or manager. **Availability:** Print.

35425 ■ *"Success Products" in Black Enterprise (Vol. 37, February 2007, No. 7, pp. 135)*
Pub: Earl G. Graves Publishing Co. Inc.
Contact: Earl G. Graves, Jr., President
Ed: Tanisha A. Sykes. **Description:** Offers tips for breaking into the motivational products industry. Suggestions include starting an e-newsletter to let people know about your products, and attending such conferences as the Motivation Show, the world's largest exhibition of motivational products and services related to performance in business.

35426 ■ *The Successful Entrepreneur's Guidebook: Where You Are Now, Where You Want to Be and How to Get There*
Ed: Colin Barrow; Robert Brown. **Released:** January 2007. **Price:** $35.00. **Description:** Characteristics of successful entrepreneurship are examined. The book helps new business owners to develop and grow a business.

35427 ■ *"Survive the Small-to-Big Transition" in Entrepreneur (November 4, 2008)*
Pub: Entrepreneur Press
Contact: Perlman Neil, President
Ed: Elizabeth Wilson. **Description:** Transitioning a small company to a large company can be a challenge, especially during the time when it is too big to be considered small and too small to be considered big. Common pitfalls during this time are discussed as well as techniques business owners should implement when dealing with this transitional period.

35428 ■ *"The Sweet Spot: A Sugar-Coated Pitch Paid Off Big Time" in Black Enterprise (Vol. 37, November 2006, No. 4, pp. 71)*
Pub: Earl G. Graves Publishing Co. Inc.
Contact: Earl G. Graves, Jr., President
Ed: Laura Egodigwe. **Description:** In an interview with Debra Sandler, president of McNeil Nutritionals L.L.C., Sandler talks about the challenges of bringing a new product to the marketplace, how her personal experiences effect her business decisions, and the difficulties of re-entering the workforce.

35429 ■ *Swimming Against the Tide*
Ed: Tim Waterstone. **Released:** October 2006. **Price:** , $29.95. **Description:** Tim Waterstone shares ten rules for creating successful small businesses.

35430 ■ *Switch: How to Change Things When Change Is Hard*
Pub: Broadway Business
Contact: David Drake, Manager
E-mail: ddrake@randomhouse.com
Ed: Chip Heath, Dan Heath. **Released:** February 16, 2010. **Price:** $26, hardcover; $14.99. **Description:** Change is difficult for everyone. This book helps business leaders to motivate employees as well as to help everybody motive themselves and others. **Availability:** PrintE-book.

35431 ■ *"Synthesis: From Lone Hero to a Culture of Leadership" in Harvard Business Review (Vol. 88, November 2010, No. 11, pp. 146)*
Pub: Harvard Business School Publishing
Ed: Charles J. Palus, John B. McGuire. **Description:** Review of the book, 'Working Together: Why Great Partnerships Succeed', is given.

35432 ■ *Tactical Entrepreneur: The Entrepreneur's Game Plan*

Pub: Sortis Publishing

Ed: Brian J. Hazelgren. **Price:** $24.95, plus $3.99 for shipping and handling. **Description:** A smart, realistic business plan is essential for any successful entrepreneur. Besides offering products or services, small business owners must possess skills in accounting, planning, human resources management, marketing, and information technology.

35433 ■ *"Take Command: Lessons in Leadership: How to Be a First Responder in Business"*

Pub: Crown Business

Released: October 14, 2014. **Price:** $25.00. **Description:** What do elite members of the military, first responders in a disaster zone, and successful business leaders have in common? Clarity of mind and purpose in the midst of chaos. Cofounder and CEO of Team Rubicon and former Marine Sniper Jake Wood, teaches the lessons in leadership and teamwork to help managers and entrepreneurs succeed in this hyper-competitive business environment today.

35434 ■ *"Take Down the Swat Team"* in *Entrepreneur (August 2014)*

Pub: Entrepreneur Media Inc.

Released: August 2014. **Description:** Advice is given to entrepreneurs engaged in a business partnership. When a partner is not interested in feedback should be made to understand that his behavior discourages employee vigilance and discussion of ethical issues could damage reputation. Organization leaders should discuss policies on all issues.

35435 ■ *"Take the Plunge"* in *Small Business Opportunities (July 2008)*

Pub: Entrepreneur Press

Contact: Perlman Neil, President

Description: Resources are provided for starting a new business venture for under $500 as well as fifteen different suggestions for different kinds of businesses that can be created with minimal expense.

35436 ■ *"Taking the Right Road"* in *Entrepreneur (Vol. 37, October 2009, No. 10, pp. 104)*

Pub: Entrepreneur Press

Contact: Perlman Neil, President

Ed: Jason Daley. **Description:** Joe Grubb's franchise of BrightStar Healthcare, a home health care provider, in Knoxville, Tennessee has grown into a $1 million business. Grubb, a former sales agent, experienced slow growth for his franchise and had to deal with cash flow issues during its first few months.

35437 ■ *"Taking on the World"* in *Canadian Business (Vol. 79, November 22, 2006, No. 23, pp. 43)*

Pub: Rogers Media Inc.

Contact: Tony Viner, President

Ed: Zena Olijnyk, Claire Gagne. **Description:** The rankings of the top Canadian business executives are presented.

35438 ■ *"A Tale of Two Brothers"* in *Canadian Business (Vol. 80, March 26, 2007, No. 7, pp. 18)*

Description: The successful business strategies followed by Tyler Gompf and Kirby Gompf, owners of Tell Us About Us Inc., are presented.

35439 ■ *The Talent Masters: Why Smart Leaders Put People Before Numbers*

Ed: Bill Conaty, Ram Charan. **Released:** November 09, 2010. **Price:** $27.50. **Description:** This book helps leaders recognize talent in their employees, and to put that talent to work to help achieve business success.

35440 ■ *"Talk, Inc.: How Trusted Leaders Use Conversation to Power Their Organizations"* in *Canadian Business (Vol. 85, August 13, 2012, No. 13, pp. 59)*

Pub: George Media Inc.

Ed: Sarah Barmak. **Released:** August 13, 2012. **Description:** Review of the book entitled, "Talk, Inc.: How Trusted Leaders Use Conversation to Power

Their Organizations". As the title states, this book will help business leaders deliver their messages concisely and effectively.

35441 ■ *"Tao of Downfall"* in *International Journal of Entrepreneurship and Small Business (Vol. 11, August 31, 2010, No. 2, pp. 121)*

Pub: Publishers Communication Group

Contact: Doug Wright, Director

Ed: Wenxian Zhang, Ilan Alon. **Description:** Through historical reviews and case studies, this research seeks to understand why some initially successful entrepreneurs failed in the economic boom of past decades. Among various factors contributing to their downfall are a unique political and business environment, fragile financial systems, traditional cultural influences and personal characteristics.

35442 ■ *"Tap Into Food Truck Trend to Rev Up Sales, Build Buzz"* in *Nation's Restaurant News (Vol. 45, February 7, 2011, No. 3, pp. 18)*

Pub: Penton Media, Inc.

Ed: Brian Sacks. **Description:** Food truck trend is growing, particularly in New York City, Philadelphia, Washington DC, and Los Angeles, California. Man entrepreneurs are using a mobile food component to market their food before opening a restaurant.

35443 ■ *"The Tapestry of Life"* in *Women In Business (Vol. 61, December 2009, No. 6, pp. 8)*

Pub: American Business Women's Association

Contact: Lorie Burch, President

Ed: Kathleen Leighton. **Description:** Suzanne Fanch, co-owner of the Devil's Thumb Ranch, discusses the family and career-related influences that helped her to achieve success as a small business proprietor. She advises that opportunities should be treated as building blocks towards success. Fanch's involvement in advocacies that take care of the welfare of community, children, and environment is also discussed.

35444 ■ *"Tastee-Freez Celebrates 60th Anniversary"* in *Ice Cream Reporter (Vol. 23, July 20, 2010, No. 8, pp. 2)*

Description: Tastee-Freez founders, Leo Moranz (inventor) and Harry Axene, an inventor partnered to market the soft-serve pump and freezer for serving frozen treats back in 1950.

35445 ■ *"The Tea Bag Test"* in *Canadian Business (Vol. 79, October 23, 2006, No. 21, pp. 83)*

Pub: Rogers Media Inc.

Contact: Tony Viner, President

Ed: Clive Mather. **Description:** Tips for business executives, on how to manage leadership skills to attain optimal business growth, are presented.

35446 ■ *"Tech Giving 2.0"* in *Boston Business Journal (Vol. 31, August 5, 2011, No. 28, pp. 1)*

Pub: Boston Business Journal

Ed: Mary Moore. **Description:** Entrepreneurs and venture capitalists in Boston have launched Technology Underwriting Greater Good, the tech industry's answer to the criticism that they are not charitable. The foundation finances nonprofits that aid young people through entrepreneurship, education and life experience. Other tech firms in Boston doing charitable works are discussed.

35447 ■ *"TechLift Strives to Fill in Gaps in Entrepreneurial Support Efforts"* in *Crain's Cleveland Business (November 12, 2007)*

Pub: Crain Communications Inc.

Ed: Marsha Powers. **Description:** Profile of the program, TechLift, a new business model launched by NorTech, that is aiming to provide assistance to technology-based companies that may not be a good fit for other entrepreneurial support venues.

35448 ■ *Technological Entrepreneurship*

Pub: Edward Elgar Publishing Inc.

Contact: Richard Henning, Vice President

E-mail: kwight@e-elgar.com

Released: October 2006. **Price:** $238.50, hardback. **Description:** Technological entrepreneurship at universities is discussed. The book covers four

related topics: university licensing and patenting; science parks and incubators; university-based startups; and the role of academic science in entrepreneurship. **Availability:** Print.

35449 ■ *"Technology-Market Combinations and the Identification of Entrepreneurial Opportunities: an Investigation of the Opportunity-Individual Nexus"* in *Academy of Management Journal (Vol. 55, August 1, 2012, No. 4, pp. 753)*

Pub: Academy of Management

Contact: Ming-Jer Chen, President

Ed: Denis A. Gregoire, Dean A. Shepherd. **Description:** The effects of differences among opportunity ideas on entrepreneurs' opportunity beliefs are investigated. Results indicate that the formation of opportunity beliefs is influenced by the superficial and structural similarities of technology-market combinations and individual differences pay a significant role in moderating these relationships.

35450 ■ *"Ted Stahl: Executive Chairman"* in *Inside Business (Vol. 13, September-October 2011, No. 5, pp. NC6)*

Pub: Great Lakes Publishing Co.

Ed: Miranda S. Miller. **Description:** Profile of Ted Stahl, who started working in his family's business when he was ten years old is presented. The firm makes dies for numbers and letters used on team uniforms. Another of the family firms manufactures stock and custom heat-printing products, equipment and supplies. It also educates customers on ways to decorate garments with heat printing products and offers graphics and software for customers to create their own artwork.

35451 ■ *"Teeling and Gallagher: A Textbook for Success"* in *Agency Sales Magazine (Vol. 39, September-October 2009, No. 9, pp. 20)*

Pub: Manufacturers' Agents National Association

Contact: Charles Cohon, President

Ed: Jack Foster. **Description:** Profile of Teeling & Gallagher, a manufacturing firm that was founded in 1946 as the D.G. Teeling Company and continued as a one-person agency until 1960 when Tom Gallagher joined the company. Tom Gallagher talks about how things have changed and his work with his son Bob in the agency.

35452 ■ *"Tell Me Why"* in *Business Strategy Review (Vol. 25, Summer 2014, No. 2, pp. 50)*

Pub: Blackwell Publishing Professional

Contact: Stephen M. Smith, President

Released: Summer 2014. **Description:** Successful entrepreneurs constantly ask why their ideas will or won't work to help with business visions and goals.

35453 ■ *The Ten Faces of Innovation*

Pub: Doubleday Publishing Group

Contact: Stephen Rubin, President

E-mail: mpalgon@randomhouse.com

Ed: Tom Kelley. **Price:** $29.95, hardcover. **Availability:** Print.

35454 ■ *The Ten Laws of Enduring Success*

Ed: Maria Bartiromo, Catherine Whitney. **Released:** March 01, 2011. **Price:** $15. **Description:** A new meaning for success is described by financial expert, Maria Bartiromo, with advice on how to adapt with the changing times.

35455 ■ *"The Ten Worst Leadership Habits"* in *Canadian Business (Vol. 81, March 31, 2008, No. 5, pp. 63)*

Pub: Rogers Media Inc.

Contact: Tony Viner, President

Ed: Michael Stern. **Description:** Ten leadership behaviors that aspiring leaders need to avoid are presented. These include expecting colleagues and subordinates to be like themselves, attending too many meetings, being miserly when it comes to recognition and praise, and giving an opinion often.

35456 ■ *"Tenacious Trailblazer: Sandra Hernandez, Public Health Pioneer, is Hispanic Business Woman of the Year®"* in *Hispanic*

Business (Vol. 30, April 2008, No. 4, pp. 26)
Pub: Hispanic Business Inc.
Contact: Jesus Chavarria, President
Ed: Melinda Burns. **Description:** Dr. Sandra Hernandez has been named as Hispanic Business Woman of the Year for her pioneering work in health care reform. Dr. Hernandez is the first Hispanic and the first woman to serve as public health director for the city and county of San Francisco.

35457 ■ *"There's Risk, Reward for Business in Baltimore's Edgier Areas: Taking a Chance" in Baltimore Business Journal (Vol. 28, July 16, 2010, No. 10, pp. 1)*
Pub: Baltimore Business Journal
Ed: Scott Dance. **Description:** North Avenue in Baltimore, Maryland is considered a rough neighborhood due to the dangers of prostitution and drug dealing. However, some entrepreneurs have taken the risk of building their businesses on North Avenue as revitalization efforts grow. One of the challenges for businesses in rough neighborhoods is bringing customers to their stores or offices.

35458 ■ *"These Are the Women Who Really Mean Business" in Canadian Business (Vol. 87, October 2014, No. 10, pp. 67)*
Pub: George Media Inc.
Released: October 2014. **Description:** A list of the top 100 women entrepreneurs in Canada are ranked, based on sales, three-year revenue growth rate, and profitability of their businesses is presented. Included in the list are Janet Stimpson of White House Design Company, Inc.; builder, Allison Grafton of Rockwood Custom Homes Inc.; and Janet Jing Di Zhang of Vancouver, BC of New Immigrants Information Services Inc.

35459 ■ *They Made America: From the Steam Engine to the Search Engine: Two Centuries of Innovators*
Pub: Little Brown Company/Time Warner Book Group
Ed: Harold Evans, Gail Buckland, David Lefer. **Released:** March 03, 2009. **Price:** $50, hardcover; $18.95, paperback; $9.99. **Description:** Coffee table book highlighting entrepreneurship; this book is filled with interesting illustrated portraits of entrepreneurs and innovators like Thomas Edison, George Doriot (a venture capital pioneer), and Ida Rosenthal (inventor of the Maidenform bra). **Availability:** PrintE-book.

35460 ■ *The Thin Book of Naming Elephants: How to Surface Undiscussables for Greater Organizational Success*
Pub: Thin Book Publishing Co.
Contact: Sue Annis Hammond, Owner
E-mail: sue@thinbook.com
Ed: Sue Annis Hammond, Andrea B. Mayfield. **Price:** $10.95. **Description:** Organizational success is of upmost importance to today's entrepreneurs and organizations. The hierarchal system in which people are afraid to speak up in organizations is discussed. The points of view and inability to see things from an overall perspective can cause insecurity among employees. The three elephants present in every organization include: arrogance, hubris, and screamers and the damage caused by these elephants in any organization is examined.

35461 ■ *"Think Again: What Makes a Leader?" in Business Strategy Review (Vol. 21, Autumn 2010, No. 3, pp. 64)*
Pub: John Wiley & Sons Inc. Scientific, Technical, Medical, and Scholarly Div. (Wiley-Blackwell)
Contact: William J. Pesce, Manager
E-mail: wpesce@wiley.com
Ed: Rob Goffee, Gareth Jones. **Description:** Leadership cannot be faked and all the self-help books in the world won't make you a leader - but there are four characteristics any leader must possess and they are outlined.

35462 ■ *Think Big and Kick Ass in Business and Life*
Pub: HarperBusiness
Ed: Donald J. Trump, Bill Zanker. **Price:** $29.95; $26.95, Paperback. **Description:** The philosophy of thinking big and acting aggressively on the path to prosperity is examined. **Availability:** CD-I.

35463 ■ *"The Thinker" in Canadian Business (Vol. 81, March 31, 2008, No. 5, pp. 52)*
Pub: Rogers Media Inc.
Contact: Tony Viner, President
Ed: Andrew Wahl. **Description:** Mihnea Moldoveanu provides much of the academic rigor that underpins Roger Martin's theories on how to improve the way business leaders think. Moldoveanu is also a classically trained pianist and founder of Redline Communications and has a mechanical engineering degree from MIT on top of his astounding knowledge on many academic fields.

35464 ■ *"This CEO's Mom Taught Him Everything He Needs to Know" in Globe & Mail (February 19, 2007, pp. B9)*
Ed: Gordon Pitts. **Description:** Interview with Paul House, chairman and chief executive officer of Tim Hortons Inc., who shares a few things about his entrepreneurial life and career.

35465 ■ *"Thomas Morley; President, The Lube Stop Inc., 37" in Crain's Cleveland Business (Vol. 28, November 19, 2007, No. 46, pp. F-12)*
Pub: Crain Communications Inc.
Ed: David Bennett. **Description:** Profile of Thomas Morley, president of The Lube Stop Inc., who is dedicated to promoting the company's strong environmental record as an effective way to differentiate Lube Stop from its competition. Since Mr. Morley came to the company in 2004, Lube Stop has increased sales by 10 percent and has boosted its operating profits by 30 percent.

35466 ■ *Three Moves Ahead: What Chess Can Teach You About Business*
Pub: John Wiley & Sons Inc.
Contact: Stephen M. Smith, President
Ed: Bob Rice. **Released:** March 30, 2008. **Price:** $24.95. **Description:** Things the game of chess can teach about business are explored.

35467 ■ *"Three Weeks To Startup" in Entrepreneur (December 19, 2008)*
Pub: Entrepreneur Press
Contact: Perlman Neil, President
Ed: Tim Berry, Sabrina Parsons. **Description:** Breakdown for realistically starting a business in three weeks is provided in detail.

35468 ■ *"Tim Armstrong" in Canadian Business (Vol. 81, July 21, 2008, No. 11, pp. 10)*
Ed: Calvin Leung. **Description:** Interview with Tim Armstrong who is the president of advertising and commerce department of Google Inc. for North America; the information technology company executive talked about the emerging trends and changes to YouTube made by the company since its acquisition in 2006.

35469 ■ *"Times are Tough, I Figure I'm Tougher" in Inc. (Vol. 33, September 2011, No. 7, pp. 92)*
Pub: Inc. Magazine
Ed: April Joyner. **Description:** Profile of Frank Campanaro and his company, Trillacorpe Construction located in Bingham Farms, Michigan. Campanaro has partnered with other companies that have bonding in reserve and lets them take the lion's share.

35470 ■ *"Tips From a Turnaround Expert" in Business Owner (Vol. 35, July-August 2011, No. 4, pp. 8)*
Pub: DL Perkins Company
Description: The book, 'The Six Month Fix: Adventures in Rescuing Failing Companies' by Gary Sutton is summarized. It provides lessons for finding and building profits in failing firms.

35471 ■ *"To Build for the Future, Reach Beyond the Skies" in Canadian Business (Vol. 83, June 15, 2010, No. 10, pp. 11)*
Pub: Rogers Media Inc.
Contact: Tony Viner, President
Ed: Richard Branson. **Description:** Richard Branson says that tackling an engineering challenge or a scientific venture is a real adventure for an entrepreneur. Branson discusses Virgin's foray into the aviation business and states that at Virgin, they build for the future.

35472 ■ *"To Live and Thrive in L.A." in Canadian Business (Vol. 81, October 13, 2008, No. 17, pp. 78)*
Ed: Rachel Pulfer. **Description:** Toronto entrepreneur Shereen Arazm thrived in Los Angeles, California as the queen of nightlife. Arazm holds or has held ownership stakes in bars, nightspots and restaurants that include the Geisha House, Concorde, Shag, Parc and Central, and Terroni L.A.

35473 ■ *"To Sell Is Human: The Surprising Truth About Moving Others"*
Pub: Riverhead Books
Contact: Sarah McGrath, Vice President
Released: February 7, 2013. **Price:** $26.95. **Description:** The U.S. Bureau of Labor Statistics reports that one in nine Americans form the work sales force. Whether an employee or an entrepreneur, everyone is selling something. The entrepreneur is looking for funders to invest. Pink describes the six successors to the elevator pitch, the three rules for understanding another's perspective, the five frames that can make a message clearer and more persuasive, and more.

35474 ■ *"Tom Gaglardi" in Canadian Business (Vol. 82, April 27, 2009, No. 7, pp. 56)*
Pub: Rogers Media Inc.
Contact: Tony Viner, President
Ed: Calvin Leung. **Description:** Northland Properties Corporation president Tom Gaglardi believes that their business model of keeping much of operations in-house allows the firm to crate assets at a lesser price while commanding higher margins than their competitors. He believes that it is an ideal time to invest in the hospitality industry because of opportunities to purchase properties at low prices.

35475 ■ *"Tony Hawk Carves a New Niche" in Entrepreneur (Vol. 37, October 2009, No. 10, pp. 26)*
Pub: Entrepreneur Press
Contact: Perlman Neil, President
Ed: Gary Cohn. **Description:** Professional skateboarder Tony Hawk discusses the growth of Birdhouse, the skateboard company he founded. He is excited about the release of Tony Hawk Ride, a videogame with a skateboard controller.

35476 ■ *"Too Much Information?" in Black Enterprise (Vol. 37, December 2006, No. 5, pp. 59)*
Pub: Earl G. Graves Publishing Co. Inc.
Contact: Earl G. Graves, Jr., President
Ed: James C. Johnson. **Description:** African American business owners often face the dilemma of whether or not to divulge their minority status when soliciting new customers and financial institutions. The quality of the products or services is always the key factor and race should never define one's business; however, it is appropriate to market oneself as a minority- or women-owned business, especially if the company is in an industry where those clients are offered top-tier contracts.

35477 ■ *"Top Marks" in Canadian Business (Vol. 79, October 23, 2006, No. 21, pp. 143)*
Ed: Erin Pooley; Laura Bogomolny. **Description:** Profiles of some top grade master of business administration students like Hogan Mullally and Will mercer, belonging to reputed business schools, are presented.

35478 ■ *"Top Ten" in Women in Business (Vol. 65, Winter 2013, No. 3, pp. 38)*
Pub: Women In Business
Released: Winter 2013. **Description:** Profiles of the 2013 Top Ten Business Women of American Business Women's Association include Kimberly Andreadis, Eileen Caspers, Melanie Brown, Sue McGee-Chiodini, Diane Stewart, Christine Struwe, Julie Sullivan, Tracy Sweet, Karen Williams, and Jane Winkler.

35479 ■ *Tough Choices: A Memoir*
Pub: Penguin Group USA
Contact: Phyllis Grann, President
Ed: Carly Florina. **Released:** September 25, 2007. **Price:** $15, paperback; $12.99. **Description:** Former woman CEO at Hewlett-Packard is profiled. **Availability:** PrintElectronic publishing.

35480 ■ *"Tough Times for the Irving Clan"* in *Canadian Business (Vol. 83, August 17, 2010, No. 13-14, pp. 14)*
Pub: Rogers Media Inc.
Contact: Tony Viner, President
Ed: Dean Jobb. **Description:** The death of John E. Irving and reported health problems of his nephew Kenneth Irving was a double blow to the billionaire Irving clan. Kenneth suddenly left his job as CEO of Fort Reliance, holding company for Irving Oil and new energy ventures, wherein the explanation was for personal reasons.

35481 ■ *The Towering World of Jimmy Choo: A Story of Power, Profits, and the Pursuit of the Perfect Shoe*
Pub: Bloomsbury USA
Ed: Lauren Goldstein Crowe, Sagra Maceira de Rosen. **Released:** 2009. **Price:** £11.69, Paperback. **Description:** Profile of Jimmy Choo and his pursuit to manufacture the perfect shoe.

35482 ■ *"Transcendent Leadership"* in *Business Horizons (Vol. 51, March-April 2008, No. 2, pp. 131)*
Pub: Elsevier Advanced Technology Publications
Ed: Mary Crossan, Daina Mazutis. **Description:** Transcendent leadership is framework integrating the leadership of self, others, and organizations. Much of the discourse regarding leadership has focused on leadership of others and the organization, while leadership of self is rarely tackled. Successful leaders are able to integrate these three levels of leadership.

35483 ■ *"Transform Your Life"* in *Black Enterprise (Vol. 37, January 2007, No. 6, pp. 14)*
Description: Through the magazine, television and radio programs, events, and the website, the various platforms of Black Enterprise will provide the tools necessary to achieve success in business ventures, career aspirations, and personal goals.

35484 ■ *"Transportation Enterprise"* in *Advertising Age (Vol. 79, June 9, 2008, No. 23, pp. S10)*
Pub: Crain Communications Inc.
Contact: Rance Crain, President
Ed: Jean Halliday. **Description:** Overview of Enterprise rent-a-car's plan to become a more environmentally-friendly company. The family-owned business has spent $1 million a year to plant trees since 2006 and has added more fuel-efficient cars, hybrids and flex-fuel models.

35485 ■ *True to Yourself: Leading a Values-Based Business*
Pub: Berrett-Koehler Communications Inc.
Contact: Steve Piersanti, President
E-mail: spiersanti@bkpub.com
Ed: Mark S. Albion. **Price:** $16.95, paperback, free shipping. **Description:** Pressures faced by entrepreneurs running small companies are discussed. Advice is offered to help grow and maintain a profitable business. **Availability:** Print; PDF.

35486 ■ *The Trump Card: Playing to Win in Work and Life*
Ed: Ivanka Trump. **Released:** October 12, 2009. **Price:** $24.99. **Description:** Profile of Ivanka Trump, the daughter of Donald and Ivana Trump; she shares the life lessons and hard-won insights that have made her successful in the business world.

35487 ■ *Trump University Entrepreneurship 101*
Pub: John Wiley & Sons Inc.
Contact: Stephen M. Smith, President
Ed: Mike Gordon. **Released:** December 2006. **Price:** $21.95, hardcover. **Description:** Entrepreneurs, past, present or future, will find this book helpful. The book covers three objectives: to energize readers to be courageous when taking steps toward an entrepreneurial goal, works to demystify the entrepreneurial process, and to help individuals improve success. **Availability:** Print.

35488 ■ *"The Trust Edge: How Top Leaders Gain Faster Results, Deeper Relationships"*
Pub: Free Press Inc.
Released: October 9, 2012. **Price:** $25.99. **Description:** David Horsager provides the eight Pillars of Trust to business leaders, including managers and entrepreneurs. Those eight trusts are based on research and are practical for today's leaders. They include: clarity, compassion, character, competency, commitment, connection, contribution, and consistency.

35489 ■ *"Truthfully Speaking"* in *Entrepreneur (Vol. 35, November 2007, No. 11, pp. 118)*
Pub: Entrepreneur Press
Contact: Perlman Neil, President
Ed: Amanda C. Kooser. **Description:** Internet startup guru Guy Kawasaki talks about his new Web venture Truemors and shares tips on creating a successful Web-based company.

35490 ■ *"Turning Bright Ideas Into Profitable Businesses"* in *Inside Business (Vol. 13, September-October 2011, No. 5, pp. SS6)*
Pub: Great Lakes Publishing Co.
Ed: Susan Keen Flynn. **Description:** Startup Lakewood was launched by Mickie Rinehart. She provides free resources to entrepreneurs in the city in order to help them turn their small business vision into reality.

35491 ■ *"20 Years of Advocacy and Education"* in *Women Entrepreneur (January 18, 2009)*
Pub: Entrepreneur Press
Contact: Perlman Neil, President
Ed: Eve Gumpel. **Description:** Profile of Sharon Hadary who served as executive director of the Center for Women's Business Research for two decades; Hadary discusses what she has learned about women business owners, their impact on the economy and what successful business owners share in common.

35492 ■ *"Two of a Kind"* in *Entrepreneur (Vol. 35, November 2007, No. 11, pp. 103)*
Pub: Entrepreneur Press
Contact: Perlman Neil, President
Ed: Chris Penttila. **Description:** Entrepreneurs need support and advice once in a while as pressure from work gets to them. It is good to have people from the same industry to give advice on particular topics when needed.

35493 ■ *"2008 SmallBiz Success Awards"* in *Hawaii Business (Vol. 53, February 2008, No. 8, pp. 43)*
Pub: PacificBasin Communications
Ed: Colette P. Fox, Gail Miyasaki, Cathy S. Cruz-George, Lance Tominaga. **Description:** Winners in the Hawaii Business 2008 SB Success Awards are presented; the awards give recognition for Hawaii small businesses with less than 100 employees and are based on four criteria, namely: unique service or product; rapid expansion or sales growth; longevity; and competency in overcoming challenges.

35494 ■ *"2009 Boardroom Elite"* in *Hispanic Business (January-February 2009, pp. 24, 28)*
Pub: Hispanic Business Inc.
Contact: Jesus Chavarria, President
Description: Three percent of those serving as directors of Fortune 500 companies in America are Hispanic. A listing of forty of these directors is included.

35495 ■ *Ubuntu!: An Aspiring Story About an African Tradition of Teamwork and Collaboration*
Pub: Broadway Business
Contact: David Drake, Manager
E-mail: ddrake@randomhouse.com
Ed: Bob Nelson, Stephen Lundin. **Released:** March 30, 2010. **Price:** $19.99, hardcover; $11.99. **Description:** The African tradition of teamwork and collaboration is used to demonstrate these skills to small business leaders. **Availability:** PrintE-book.

35496 ■ *"The Ultimate Business Tune-Up: For Times Like These"* in *Inc. (Vol. 31, January-February 2009, No. 1, pp. 70)*
Pub: Mansueto Ventures L.L.C.
Contact: John Koten, Chief Executive Officer
Ed: Adam Bluestein, Leigh Buchanan, Max Chafkin, Jason Del Rey, April Joyner, Ryan McCarthy. **Description:** Twenty-three things do energize a small business in tough economic times are outlined with insight from successful entrepreneurs.

35497 ■ *The Ultimate Competitive Advantage*
Pub: Berrett-Koehler Communications Inc.
Contact: Steve Piersanti, President
E-mail: spiersanti@bkpub.com
Ed: Donald Mitchell, Carol Coles, B. Thomas Golisano. **Released:** March 12, 2003. **Price:** $36.95, hardcover. **Description:** Results of a ten-year study of companies that experienced fast growth over a three year period shows that while unsuccessful companies apply outdated business models, the successful ones improve their business models every two to four years. **Availability:** Print.

35498 ■ *Ultimate Small Business Advisor*
Ed: Andi Axman. **Released:** May 2007. **Price:** $30.95. **Description:** Tip for starting and running a small business, including new tax rulings and laws affecting small business, are shared.

35499 ■ *Understanding Small Business*
Pub: Tate Publishing and Enterprises, LLC
Contact: Ryan Tate, President
Ed: Edward McMahon. **Price:** $20.95, paperback. **Description:** Three step process to help an entrepreneur build a basic business plan and an effective cash flow statement to minimize risk.

35500 ■ *"U.S. Attorney Post the Latest Twist in A. Brian Albritton's Odyssey"* in *The Business Journal-Serving Greater Tampa Bay (Vol. 28, July 28, 2008, No. 31, pp. 1)*
Pub: American City Business Journals, Inc.
Contact: Whitney Shaw, President
Ed: Jane Meinhardt. **Description:** Tampa, Florida-based lawyer A. Brian Albritton has been nominated to be the U.S. Attorney for the Middle District of Florida. He is an expert in cases involving white-collar crime, secret theft, noncompete agreements, and other agreements.

35501 ■ *"Unretirement: How Baby Boomers are Changing the Way We Think About Work, Community, and the Good Life"*
Pub: Bloomsbury Press
Released: September 2, 2014. **Price:** $26.00. **Description:** Baby boomers are transforming American economics and society in a positive way. Because boomers are living longer in better health and are extending their work lives, may times with new careers, entrepreneurial ventures, and socially responsible volunteering service. This trend will enrich the American workplace, economy, and the society as a whole for future generations.

35502 ■ *"Unveiling the Secrets Behind Hispanic Business' 100 Fastest-Growing Companies"* in *Hispanic Business (Vol. 30, July-August 2008, No. 7-8, pp. 22)*
Pub: Hispanic Business Inc.
Contact: Jesus Chavarria, President
Ed: Michael Bowker. **Description:** CEO's of the five fastest growing Hispanic-owned companies discuss the success of their companies; most of them attribute their success to proper investment and diversification, effective innovations and seeing growth opportunities where others see roadblocks.

35503 ■ *"Up To Code? Website Eases Compliance Burden for Entrepreneurs"* in *Black Enterprise (Vol. 38, March 1, 2008, No. 8, pp. 48)*
Pub: Earl G. Graves Publishing Co. Inc.
Contact: Earl G. Graves, Jr., President
Ed: Robin White-Goode. **Description:** Business.gov is a presidential E-government project created to help small businesses easily find, understand, and comply with laws and regulations pertaining to a particular industry.

35504 ■ *Use What You've Got & Other Business Lessons I Learned from my Mom*
Pub: Portfolio Publishing
Contact: Adrian Zackheim, President
Ed: Barbara Corcoran, Bruce Littlefield. **Released:** February 2003. **Price:** $24.95, hardcover. **Description:** Founder and chairman of New York's premier real estate company, the Corcoran Group, shares her successes in the real estate industry. The book offers tips and pointers to salespeople, entrepreneurs and business people alike. Corcoran explains how she went from waiting tables and borrowed $1,000 from a boyfriend to build her real estate company into the industry's powerhouse. **Availability:** Print.

35505 ■ *"Used to Being Courted" in Business Courier (Vol. 24, March 14, 2008, No. 49, pp. 1)*
Pub: American City Business Journals, Inc.
Contact: Whitney Shaw, President
Ed: Dan Monk. **Description:** College basketball coach Sean Miller is reported to be earning up to $900,000 a year. A look into the contract at regional universities show Thad Matta makes over $2 million in a year and that UK's Billy Gillispie makes over $2.7 million.

35506 ■ *"UTSA Entrepreneur Program Receives Federal Designation" in San Antonio Business Journal (Vol. 28, June 6, 2014, No. 17, pp. 7)*
Pub: American City Business Journals
Released: June 6, 2014. **Description:** The National Science Foundation has designated the University of Texas at San Antonio (UTSA) as an Innovation Corps Site because of its strong entrepreneurial system through the Center for Innovation and Technology Entrepreneurship. The UTSA expects to see an increase in entrepreneurial activity and successful technology commercialization with such designation.

35507 ■ *"Valuation: Confusing and Misunderstood" in Business Owner (Vol. 35, July-August 2011, No. 4, pp. 10)*
Pub: DL Perkins Company
Description: Business valuation is explained to help small business owners realize the value of their company.

35508 ■ *Values-Centered Entrepreneurs and Their Companies*
Pub: Routledge
Contact: Kevin Bradley, President
E-mail: kbradley@taylorandfrancis.com
Ed: David Y. Choi, Edmund Gray. **Released:** August 10, 2010. **Price:** $48.95, Paperback; $165, Hardback. **Description:** A new brand of entrepreneurs has arrived on the business scene, carrying with them a new set of values. They possess a sense of social responsibility, the need to protect the planet, and to do the right thing for all stakeholders.

35509 ■ *Values and Opportunities in Social Entrepreneurship*
Pub: Palgrave Macmillan
Contact: Lisa Dunn, Manager
E-mail: l.dunn@palgrave.com
Released: September 2010. **Price:** £72, hardcover. **Description:** Social entrepreneurship has grown as a research field. This book discusses social entrepreneurship as well as the identification and exploitation of social venturing opportunities. **Availability:** Print; E-book; Electronic publishing; PDF.

35510 ■ *"VC Firm Expands Michigan Reach" in Pittsburgh Business Times (Vol. 33, March 7, 2014, No. 34, pp. 4)*
Pub: American City Business Journals
Released: March 7, 2014. **Description:** Draper Triangle Ventures managing director, Jay Katarincic, says the company opened a facility in Michigan due to its similarities to the markets the company serves. He also said the area's research institutions makes it an ideal place of operation. Katarincic added that the company also considered Michigan's entrepreneurial environment in opening the office.

35511 ■ *The Venture Cafe: Secrets, Strategies, and Stories from America's High-Tech Entrepreneurs*
Pub: Business Plus
Ed: Teresa Esser. **Released:** March 2002. **Price:** $24.95, hardcover. **Description:** Research covering the types of entrepreneurs who build new, high-technology ventures from the ground up. Author interviewed over 150 high-tech professionals in order to gather information to help others start high-tech companies. **Availability:** Print.

35512 ■ *"Victoria Colligan; Co-Founder, Ladies Who Launch Inc., 38' in Crain's Cleveland Business (Vol. 28, November 19, 2007, No. 46)*
Pub: Crain Communications Inc.
Ed: Jay Miller. **Description:** Profile of Victoria Colligan who is the co-founder of Ladies Who Launch Inc., an organization with franchises in nearly 50 cities; the company offers women entrepreneurs workshops and a newsletter to help women balance their businesses with other aspects of their lives. Ms. Colligan found that women were learning about being business owners differently than men and she felt that there was a need to create opportunities for networking for women launching businesses that had more of a lifestyle purpose.

35513 ■ *"The Virgin Way"*
Released: September 9, 2014. **Price:** $29.95. **Description:** Sir Richard Branson, founder of Virgin Group, shares his own style of leadership. He teaches how fun, family, passion, and the dying art of listening are key ingredients to what his employees describe as the "Virgin Way". The entrepreneur reveals insights into his forty years of starting and building his airline company.

35514 ■ *Wake Up and Smell the Zeitgeist*
Ed: Grand McCracken. **Released:** 2010. **Price:** $26.95. **Description:** Insight is given into an element of corporate success that's often overlooked and valuable suggestions are offered for any small business to pursue.

35515 ■ *"Walking Through Failure" in Women in Business (Vol. 64, Summer 2012, No. 2, pp. 10)*
Pub: American Business Women's Association
Contact: Lorie Burch, President
Ed: Leigh Elmore. **Released:** Summer 2012. **Description:** Attorney, author and life-coach Francine Ward will relate her own story of success in her keynote address at the American Business Women's Association National Women's Leadership Conference that will be held in Memphis, Tennessee in October 2012. Ward considers self-esteem as something that must be earned and thinks that having the courage to risk failure is an esteemable act.

35516 ■ *The Wall Street Journal. Complete Small Business Guidebook*
Pub: Three Rivers Press
Contact: Caroline Sincerbeaux, Editor
E-mail: csincerbeaux@randomhouse.com
Ed: Colleen DeBaise. **Released:** December 29, 2009. **Price:** $15. **Description:** The mechanics of building, running and growing a profitable business are outlined, teaching how to write a business plan, ways to finding money during lean years, how to keep stress in check, time management, investment in technology, hiring, marketing, management basics, angel investing and venture capital, as well as an exit strategy.

35517 ■ *"Waste Management Exec First 'Undercover Boss' in Series Kicking Off on Super Bowl Sunday" in Houston Business Journal (Vol. 40, January 22, 2010, No. 37, pp. A1)*
Pub: American City Business Journals
Ed: Christine Hall. **Description:** Houston, Texas-based Waste Management Inc.'s president and chief operation officer, Larry O'Donnell shares some of his experience as CBS Television Network reality show 'Undercover Boss' participant. O'Donnell believes the

show was a great way to show the customers how tough their jobs are and reveals that the most difficult job was being a sorter at the recycling center.

35518 ■ *"Watchful Eye: Entrepreneur Protects Clients and His Bottom Line" in Black Enterprise (Vol. 38, March 1, 2008, No. 8, pp. 46)*
Pub: Earl G. Graves Publishing Co. Inc.
Contact: Earl G. Graves, Jr., President
Ed: Tennille M. Robinson. **Description:** Profile of Elijah Shaw, founder of Icon Services Corporation, a full service security and investigative service; Shaw shares his plans to protect clients while growing his business.

35519 ■ *"Wattles Plugs Back Into State" in Business Journal Portland (Vol. 27, November 19, 2010, No. 38, pp. 1)*
Pub: Portland Business Journal
Ed: Wendy Culverwell. **Description:** Denver, Colorado-based Ultimate Electronics Inc.'s first store in Oregon was opened in Portland and the 46th store in the chain of electronic superstores is expected to employ 70-80 workers. The venture is the latest for Mark Wattles, one of Oregon's most successful entrepreneurs, who acquired Ultimate from bankruptcy.

35520 ■ *"The Way of the Seal: Think Like an Elite Warrior to Lead and Succeed"*
Pub: Reader's Digest
Contact: Mary G. Berner, President
Released: December 26, 2013. **Price:** $21.99. **Description:** Ex-Navy Commander, Mark Divine, teaches how to lead from the front so others will work for you. He reveals exercises, meditations, and focusing techniques train your mind for mental toughness, emotional resilience and uncanny intuition. His experience in America's elite forces provides a guide for business leaders to succeed.

35521 ■ *We Are Smarter Than Me: How to Unleash the Power of Crowds in Your Business*
Pub: Wharton School Publishing
Ed: Barry Libert, Jon Spector, Don Tapscott. **Released:** September 25, 2007. **Price:** $24.99, Non-members; $19.99, Members; $17.59, Members; $21.99, Nonmembers. **Description:** Ways to use social networking and community in order to make decisions and plan your business, with a focus on product development, manufacturing, marketing, customer service, finance, management, and more. **Availability:** PrintE-book.

35522 ■ *Wealth Without a Job: The Entrepreneur's Guide to Freedom and Security Beyond the 9 to 5 Lifestyle*
Pub: John Wiley & Sons Inc.
Contact: Stephen M. Smith, President
Ed: Phil Laut, Andy Fuehl. **Released:** August 2004. **Price:** $31.95, hardcover; $20.99. **Description:** Strategies for successful business ownership and job security are explored. **Availability:** PrintE-book.

35523 ■ *"Wear More Hats" in Canadian Business (Vol. 80, March 12, 2007, No. 6, pp. 39)*
Ed: Michael Stern. **Description:** The need on the part of managers to volunteer to accept more responsibilities for their growth as well as that of company's is discussed.

35524 ■ *The Weather Channel: The Improbable Rise of a Media Phenomenon*
Pub: Harvard Business Review Press
Contact: Peter E. Walsh, Director
Ed: Frank Batten, Jeffrey L. Cruikshank. **Released:** May 02, 2002. **Price:** $29.95, hardcover. **Description:** Frank Batten illustrates the power of a resourceful growth strategy along with details the journey he successfully took his small, private newspaper into the cable industry. **Availability:** Print.

35525 ■ *A Weekend with Warren Buffett: And Other Shareholder Meeting Adventures*
Pub: Basic Books/Perseus Books Group
Ed: Randy Cepuch. **Released:** April 13, 2009. **Price:** $23.95; C$30.50. **Description:** Financial writer and personal investor relates his experiences attending

various shareholder meetings, reviewing each meeting and grading its educational value. The book is essential for those hoping to learn more about the way companies invest and do business. **Availability:** E-book.

35526 ■ *"The Weeks Ahead" in Crain's New York Business (Vol. 24, January 7, 2008, No. 1, pp. 26)*
Description: Listing of events in the Detroit area include conferences addressing entrepreneurialism, economic development, and women business ownership.

35527 ■ *"The Weeks Ahead" in Crain's New York Business (Vol. 24, January 14, 2008, No. 2, pp. 20)*
Description: Listing of events in the Detroit area include conferences addressing entrepreneurialism, economic development, and women business ownership.

35528 ■ *"The Welcome Mat" in Entrepreneur (July 2014)*
Pub: Entrepreneur Media Inc.
Released: July 2014. **Description:** Entrepreneurs should follow certain guidelines when writing the content for their company homepages. The content should be written and designed with customers in mid to impart to them a sense of why they belong there. The main headline should communicate how the business can help its customers while keeping the layout simple and less overwhelming to the audience. The words used in the page, the layout and its usability and the free offerings are some of the primary considerations when designing the calls to action.

35529 ■ *"Welcome to a New Kind of Cubicle Culture" in Boston Business Journal (Vol. 29, August 19, 2011, No. 15, pp. 1)*
Pub: American City Business Journals, Inc.
Ed: Alexander Jackson. **Description:** Beehive Baltimore offers a co-working space where independent freelancers and entrepreneurs can work. There are two other companies that provide the same service and the value of these services to these professional is that it provides them with an office that is both convenient and affordable aside from letting them network with peers.

35530 ■ *The Well-Timed Strategy: Managing Business Cycle for Competitive Advantage*
Pub: Wharton School Publishing
Ed: Peter Navarro. **Released:** January 13, 2006. **Price:** $39.99, Nonmembers; $31.99, Members. **Description:** An overview of business cycles and risks is presented. Recession is a good time to find key personnel for a small business. Other issues addressed include investment, production, and marketing in order to maintain a competitive edge. **Availability:** Print; E-book.

35531 ■ *"Wendy Turner; Vice-President and General Manager, Vocalo.org" in Crain's Chicago Business (Vol. 31, May 5, 2008, No. 18, pp. 22)*
Pub: Crain Communications Inc.
Contact: Todd Johnson, Publisher
Ed: Kevin Mckeough. **Description:** Profile of Wendy Turner who is a leader at Vocalo, a combination of talk radio and Web site, where listeners can set up profile pages similar to those on Facebook.

35532 ■ *"We're Falling Behind the Rest of the Country" in Canadian Business (Vol. 85, August 13, 2012, No. 13, pp. 46)*
Pub: George Media Inc.
Ed: Joe Castaldo. **Released:** August 13, 2012. **Description:** Clearwater Seafoods cofounder John Risley is concerned about the future of the Canadian economy, particularly the Atlantic Provinces, with high unemployment rates and demographic shift. He believes that Atlantic Canadians are great entrepreneurs and workers.

35533 ■ *A Whack on the Side of the Head: How You Can Be More Creative*
Pub: Business Plus
Ed: Roger von Oech. **Released:** May 05, 2008. **Price:** $17, paperback; C$19, paperback. **Descrip-**

tion: The author, a consultant, shares insight into increasing entrepreneurial creativity. **Availability:** Print.

35534 ■ *"Wham-O's Wisdom" in Playthings (Vol. 107, January 1, 2009, No. 1, pp. 13)*
Pub: Reed Elsevier Group plc Reed Business Information
Contact: Mark Kelsey, Chief Executive Officer
Ed: Tim Walsh. **Description:** Toy historian Tim Walsh discusses the history of the toy industry and shares secrets to his success. Walsh is the creator of toys and board games.

35535 ■ *"What Are You Afraid Of?" in Entrepreneur (Vol. 37, July 2009, No. 7, pp. 79)*
Pub: Entrepreneur Press
Contact: Perlman Neil, President
Ed: Lindsay Holloway. **Description:** According to a survey of entrepreneurs in the US, failure, economic uncertainty, not having enough personal time, being their own boss, and staying afloat are the biggest fears when starting a business. Advice on how to deal with these fears is also given.

35536 ■ *"What CEOs Will Admit Out of the Office" in Inc. (November 2007, pp. 30)*
Pub: Mansueto Ventures L.L.C.
Contact: John Koten, Chief Executive Officer
Ed: Sarah Goldstein. **Description:** Thirty CEOs from the fastest growing companies in the U.S. answer questions about their firms.

35537 ■ *"What Dead Zone?" in Entrepreneur (Vol. 37, October 2009, No. 10, pp. 128)*
Pub: Entrepreneur Press
Contact: Perlman Neil, President
Ed: Jason Daley. **Description:** Joe Purifico, Halloween Adventure franchises co-owner and chief executive officer, discusses the Halloween superstore phenomenon. Malls allow seasonal leasing for Halloween stores due to the high number of customers these stores attract.

35538 ■ *What Got You Here Won't Get You There*
Pub: Hyperion Books
Contact: Ellen Archer, President
Ed: Marshall Goldsmith, Mark Reiter. **Released:** January 09, 2007. **Price:** $23.95; C$32.95. **Description:** Executive coach teaches how to climb the ladder to upper levels of management.

35539 ■ *"What Kind of Golfer Are You?" in Baltimore Business Journal (Vol. 29, May 4, 2012, No. 53, pp. 1)*
Pub: American City Business Journals, Inc.
Contact: Whitney Shaw, President
Ed: Gary Haber. **Released:** May 4, 2012. **Description:** Businesspeople playing golf are classified into different profiles according to style. These profiles also describe the behavior of businessmen during and after playing golf.

35540 ■ *"What Kind of Leader Are You?" in Inc. (Vol. 36, September 2014, No. 7, pp. 76)*
Pub: Mansueto Ventures L.L.C.
Contact: John Koten, Chief Executive Officer
Released: September 2014. **Description:** Ranking of leadership skills for entrepreneurs and managers is presented, with being a visionary leading each category.

35541 ■ *What Losing Taught Me about Winning: The Ultimate Guide for Success in Small and Home-Based Business*
Pub: Simon & Schuster Adult Publishing Group
Contact: Carolyn Reidy, President
E-mail: carolyn.reidy@simonandschuster.com
Ed: Fran Tarkenton, Wes Smith. **Released:** April 1999. **Price:** $17.95, paperback. **Description:** Provides insight into running a successful small business.

35542 ■ *What Men Don't Tell Women about Business: Opening Up the Heavily Guarded Alpha Male Playbook*
Pub: John Wiley & Sons Inc.
Contact: Stephen M. Smith, President
Ed: Christopher V. Flett. **Released:** October 2007. **Price:** $29.95, hardcover; $19.99. **Description:** Valuable guide for any woman in business, this book helps reveal everything a woman needs to know in order to understand, communicate, and compete with men in business. **Availability:** PrintE-book.

35543 ■ *What Self-Made Millionaires Really Think, Know and Do: A Straight-Talking Guide to Business Success and Personal Riches*
Pub: John Wiley & Sons Inc.
Contact: Stephen M. Smith, President
Ed: Richard Dobbins, Barrie Pettman. **Released:** January 2006. **Price:** $24.95; $16.99. **Description:** Guide for understanding the concepts of entrepreneurial success; the book offers insight into bringing an idea into reality, marketing, time management, leadership skills, and setting clear goals. **Availability:** PrintE-book.

35544 ■ *What Works: Success in Stressful Times*
Pub: Harper Press
Ed: Hamish McRae. **Released:** November 30, 2001. **Price:** $14.95, paperback. **Description:** Exploration of success stories from across the glove, and what Michelle Obama referred to as 'the flimsy difference between success and failure.' Why do some initiatives take off while others flounder? How have communities managed to achieve so much while others struggle? What distinguishes the good companies from the bad? What lessons can be learned from the well-ordered Mumbai community made famous by 'Slumdog Millionaire'? Why have Canadian manners helped Whistler become the most popular ski resort in North America?. **Availability:** Print.

35545 ■ *"What's Your Business Really Worth?" in Black Enterprise (Vol. 44, June 2014, No. 10, pp. 24)*
Pub: Earl G. Graves Publishing Co. Inc.
Contact: Earl G. Graves, Jr., President
Released: June 2014. **Description:** Experts provide information to help small businesses determine their valuation. Many times entrepreneurs value their company at a higher rate than actual value. Earnings before interest, taxes, depreciation, and amortization (EBITDA) is used as a profitability gauge; a multiplier of the EBITDA is used as a barometer; and qualitative vs. quantitative factors are to be considered.

35546 ■ *When Growth Stalls: How It Happens, Why You're Stuck, and what To Do About It*
Pub: John Wiley & Sons Inc.
Contact: Stephen M. Smith, President
Ed: Steve McKee. **Released:** February 2009. **Price:** $27.95, hardcover; $18.99. **Description:** Marketing expert presents evidence that demonstrates that slow growth experienced by a firm is usually not the cause of mismanagement or blundering, but by natural market forces and destructive internal dynamics that are often unrecognized. **Availability:** PrintE-book.

35547 ■ *"Where Are They Now?" in Canadian Business (Vol. 79, October 9, 2006, No. 20, pp. 71)*
Pub: Rogers Media Inc.
Contact: Tony Viner, President
Ed: Jeff Sanford, Zena Olijnyk, Andrew Wahl, Andy Holloway, John Gray. **Description:** The profile of the top chief executive officers of Canada for the year 2005 is discussed.

35548 ■ *"Where to be an Entrepreneur: Ten Startup-Friendly Cities" in Entrepreneur (Vol. 37, August 2009, No. 8, pp. 49)*
Pub: Entrepreneur Press
Contact: Perlman Neil, President
Ed: Jason Daley. **Description:** Ten U.S. cities that embody the entrepreneurial spirit are presented. These cities are ideal for startup companies and profiles of businesses that are making it in these cities are discussed.

35549 ■ Where Have All the Leaders Gone?
Pub: Simon and Schuster Inc.
Contact: Carolyn Reidy, President
E-mail: carolyn.reidy@simonandschuster.com
Ed: Lee Iacocca. Released: April 2008. Price: $15.
Description: Lee Iacocca discusses the principles of great leadership. Availability: Print.

35550 ■ Who's Got Your Back
Pub: Broadway Books, a Division of Random House
Ed: Keith Ferrazzi. Price: $25, Hardcover. Description: Achieving goals by building close relationships with a small circle of trusted individuals.

35551 ■ "Who's Who In Marketing?" in Entrepreneur (September 2014)
Pub: Entrepreneur Media Inc.
Released: September 2014. Description: Marketers can recruit influencers to help with their marketing efforts in various ways. The key is to cultivate relationships with influencers who have the trust and respect of their audiences. Potential influencers can be found through business networks, social media and industry events. Amanda Maksymiw, content marketing manager at Lattice Engines, suggests engaging and targeting different types of influencers depending on the goal. Lee Odden of TopRank Online Marketing advises helping upcoming talent to become influential.

35552 ■ "Why Business Focus Is a Crucial Entrepreneurial Talent; Successful Entrepreneurs are Profit-Oriented and Judge the Value of Decisions and Relationships By Their Effect On Business" in Gallup Business Journal (June 10, 2014)
Pub: Gallup Press
Released: June 10, 2014. Description: Entrepreneurial traits and skills are highlighted. Successful business owners focus on profit and understand the value of an opportunity, relationship, or a decision can impact their business. It is critical, while focusing on profit, to never underestimate the value of a customer.

35553 ■ "Why Entrepreneurs Matter More Than Innovators" in Gallup Management Journal (November 22, 2011)
Pub: Gallup Inc.
Contact: Jim Clifton, Chief Executive Officer
Ed: Jim Clifton. Description: In the race to create good jobs, leaders are not paying enough attention to cultivating talented entrepreneurs, rather they invest too much attention on innovation.

35554 ■ "Why Is It So Hard To Find Good People? The Problem Might Be You" in Inc. (Vol. 33, November 2011, No. 9, pp. 100)
Pub: Inc. Magazine
Ed: April Joyner. Description: Entrepreneurs sometimes struggle to find good workers. A recent survey shows hiring as their top concern. Four common mistakes that can occur during the hiring process our outlined.

35555 ■ "Why Successful Entrepreneurs Are Effective Delegators; Shifting from a Do-It-Yourself Executive Style to a More Hands-Off Approach is Essential When They're Growing a Business" in Gallup Business Journal (August 26, 2014)
Pub: Gallup Press
Released: August 26, 2014. Description: It is critical for entrepreneurs to step away from a do-it-yourself executive style to a more hands-off approach when a company begins to grow.

35556 ■ Why We Want You to be Rich: Two Men - One Message
Pub: Rich Publishing LLC
Released: 2006. Description: Authors explain why some people get rich while others don't.

35557 ■ "Wilderness Leadership - On the Job: Five Principles From Outdoor Exploration That Will Make You a Better Manager" in Harvard Business Review (Vol.
90, April 2012, No. 4, pp. 127)
Pub: Harvard Business Review Press
Contact: Peter E. Walsh, Director
Ed: John Kanengieter, Aparna Rajagopal-Durbin. Released: April 2012. Description: Five principles of wilderness leadership are: practicing leadership, leading from everywhere, behaving well, remaining calm, and disconnecting to connect. Key points include knowing when to offer leadership to another member, and taking a break from technological devices that can distract from critical thinking.

35558 ■ Wiley Pathways Small Business Management
Pub: John Wiley & Sons Inc.
Contact: Stephen M. Smith, President
Ed: Richard M. Hodgetts, Donald F. Kuratko, Margaret Burlingame, Don Gulbrandsen. Released: March 2007. Price: $76.95, paperback; $42.50. Description: Tips for starting and running a successful small business are given, including advice on writing a business plan, financing, and the law. Availability: PrintE-book.

35559 ■ "William Barr III; President, Co-Founder, Universal Windows Direct, 33" in Crain's Cleveland Business (November 19, 2007)
Pub: Crain Communications Inc.
Ed: David Bennett. Description: Profile of William Barr III, the president and co-founder of Universal Windows Direct, a manufacturer of vinyl windows and siding, whose successful salesmanship and leadership has propelled his company forward.

35560 ■ Winner Takes All: Steve Wynn, Kirk Kerkorian, Gary Loveman, and the Race to Own Las Vegas
Pub: Hyperion
Ed: Christina Binkley. Released: March 10, 2009. Price: $25.95, hardcover; $15.95; C$17.25. Description: The story of three men, Steve Wynn, Kirk Kerkorian, and Gary Loveman, each with different backgrounds are reinventing Las Vegas. Availability: Print.

35561 ■ "Winners Dream: A Journey from Corner Store to Corner Office"
Pub: Simon & Schuster Adult Publishing Group
Contact: Carolyn Reidy, President
E-mail: carolyn.reidy@simonandschuster.com
Released: October 14, 2014. Price: $28.00. Description: Bill McDermott, CEO of the world's largest business software company, SAP, profiles his career. He discusses his career moves, sales strategies, employee incentives to create high performance teams, and the competitive advantages of optimism and hard work. The entrepreneur offers a blueprint for success and the knowledge that the real dream is the journey, not the preconceived destination.

35562 ■ Winning: The Answers
Pub: HarperCollins Publishers Inc.
Contact: Jane Friedman, President
E-mail: jfriedman@harpercollins.com
Ed: Jack Welch, Suzy Welch. Price: $12.95, paperback; $8.99; C$11.99. Availability: PrintE-book.

35563 ■ "Wise Guy: Get In Good" in Entrepreneur (Vol. 35, October 2007, No. 10, pp. 46)
Pub: Entrepreneur Press
Contact: Perlman Neil, President
Ed: Guy Kawasaki. Description: Good public relations are a requirement for business entrepreneurs, and it can be achieved through proper communication. Giving of and asking for favors are some of the ways to build relationships in the business world. Other tips on how to build good business relationships are provided.

35564 ■ "Women as 21st Century Leaders" in Women In Business (Vol. 63, Summer 2011, No. 2, pp. 26)
Pub: American Business Women's Association
Contact: Lorie Burch, President
Ed: Leigh Elmore. Description: American Business Women's Association and Park University have partnered to provide a leadership training program to
attendees of the 2011 National Women's Leadership Conference. The courses will incorporate introduction to concepts, development of critical thinking skills and direct application through exercises. Comments from executives are also included.

35565 ■ "Women: the Alpha Advantage" in Entrepreneur (Vol. 36, February 2008, No. 2, pp. 34)
Pub: Entrepreneur Press
Contact: Perlman Neil, President
Ed: Aliza Sherman. Description: Women entrepreneurs are said to be mistaken with the belief that they need to display aggression and compete with other women to gain power. Workshops and books address this issue and discuss how women could be alpha entrepreneurs. Recommendations with regard to the topic are explored.

35566 ■ Women Entrepreneurs in The Global Marketplace
Pub: Edward Elgar Publishing Inc.
Contact: Richard Henning, Vice President
E-mail: kwight@e-elgar.com
Ed: Andrea E. Smith-Hunter. Released: 2013. Price: £85.50, hardback. Description: Focus is on women entrepreneurs; information includes human capital, network structures and financial capital, with comparative analysis across racial lines. Availability: Print.

35567 ■ "Women's Initiative for Self Employment Honors Home Instead Senior Care Owner as 2012 Woman Entrepreneur of the Year" in Marketwired (September 11, 2012)
Pub: COMTEX
Contact: Chip Brian, President
Ed: Michelle Rogers. Description: Women's Initiative for Self Employment has bestowed its 2012 Woman Entrepreneur of the Year award on Michelle Rogers, owner of Home Instead Senior Care. The Women's Initiative is a nonprofit organization celebrating eight female business owners in the Silicon Valley Region annually. Home Instead Senior Care provides in-home care for seniors in the Bay Area of northern California.

35568 ■ "Work Is An Action Word" in Black Enterprise (Vol. 38, December 2007, No. 5, pp. 86)
Pub: Earl G. Graves Publishing Co. Inc.
Contact: Earl G. Graves, Jr., President
Ed: Marcia A. Reed-Woodard. Description: Understanding your company's culture, knowing the importance of networking, and connecting with the right mentors to guide you are the ingredients required for any entrepreneur.

35569 ■ "Work Naked" in Canadian Business (Vol. 80, March 12, 2007, No. 6, pp. 33)
Ed: Andrew Wahl. Description: The disadvantages of teleworking for both employees and the company, in view of lack of an office environment and self-discipline on the part of workers, are discussed.

35570 ■ "Work Together" in Entrepreneur (Vol. 35, November 2007, No. 11, pp. 34)
Pub: Entrepreneur Press
Contact: Perlman Neil, President
Ed: Aliza Sherman. Description: Marsha Firestone founded Women Presidents' Organization, creating small groups of women who head their own businesses. The idea was for each chapter of the organization to have businesswomen share experiences to help others learn from running their own business.

35571 ■ "Working It Out! How a Young Executive Overcomes Obstacles on the Job" in Black Enterprise (Vol. 37, January 2007, No. 6, pp. 55)
Pub: Earl G. Graves Publishing Co. Inc.
Contact: Earl G. Graves, Jr., President
Ed: Laura Egodigwe. Description: Interview with Susan Chapman, Global Head of Operations for Citigroup Realty Services, in which she discusses issues such as the important skills necessary for overcoming obstacles in the workplace.

35572 ■ *Working for Yourself: Law & Taxes for Independent Contractors, Freelancers & Consultants*
Pub: NOLO Publications
Ed: Stephen Fishman. Released: February 2014. Price: $34.99; $27.99. Description: In-depth information is shared for contractors, freelancers and consultants involving business law and small business taxes. Availability: PrintE-book.

35573 ■ *"World's Best CEOs" in Barron's (Vol. 88, March 24, 2008, No. 12, pp. 33)*
Pub: Dow Jones & Co., Inc.
Contact: Clare Hart, President
Ed: Andrew Bary. Description: Listing of the 30 best chief executive officers worldwide which was compiled through interviews with investors and analysts, analysis of financial and stock market performance, and leadership and industry stature.

35574 ■ *"The Worm Lady" in Hawaii Business (Vol. 53, October 2007, No. 4, pp. 57)*
Pub: PacificBasin Communications
Ed: Jolyn Okimoto Rosa. Description: Mindy Jaffe, also known as the worm lady, founded the Waikiki Worm Company in 2004 and sells composting worms. The company, which received much attention from the media, has earned $54,000 in revenue in 2004, and $92,000 and $120,000 in 2005 and 2006, respectively. Jaffe's past ventures and the challenges she is facing with her new company are discussed.

35575 ■ *"Worth His Salt" in Hawaii Business (Vol. 53, January 2008, No. 7, pp. 45)*
Pub: PacificBasin Communications
Ed: Jolyn Okimoto Rosa. Description: Bryan Zada owns three PretzelMaker franchises, whose total loss amounted to $40,000 in 2003. Zada believes that listening to employees was one of the key steps in turning the business around. The efforts made to improve the franchises' products are also given.

35576 ■ *"Wowing Her Customers" in Women In Business (Vol. 61, August-September 2009, No. 4, pp. 34)*
Pub: American Business Women's Association
Contact: Lorie Burch, President
Ed: Kathleen Leighton. Description: Gail Worth, together with her brother, bought her parents' Harley-Davidson motorcycle dealership in Grandview, Missouri. She eventually had the dealership to herself when her brother broke out of the partnership. Gail says she is comfortable in a man's world kind of business and has expanded the business with a 10-acre site.

35577 ■ *"Wrap It Up" in Entrepreneur (Vol. 36, April 2008, No. 4, pp. 84)*
Pub: Entrepreneur Press
Contact: Perlman Neil, President
Ed: Barry Farber. Description: Tips on how to manage and get through the closing of a business sale are presented. Focus on what solutions you can bring and not on emotional attachments that can show your eagerness for the sale. Having a track of positive accomplishments can also help.

35578 ■ *Ya Gotta Wanna*
Pub: Creative Book Publishers
Ed: Malcolm Paice. Released: July 2005. Price: $12.95. Description: Three phases of teamwork are outlined: identifying the people and creating the team, analyzing the components of the team, and implementing the project. The author compares a soccer team to a management team and that a successful soccer team has three main area attributes: a solid defense, a creative midfield, and a potent strike force.

35579 ■ *"Yamana's Golden Boy" in Canadian Business (Vol. 80, November 19, 2007, No. 23, pp. 49)*
Pub: PacificBasin Communications
Ed: John Gray. Description: Profile of Peter Marrone, founder of the gold-producing company Yamana Gold Inc. in 2003. Yamana has grown since its 2003 launch, with $110 million reported earnings for the first three quarters in 2007. Marrone's career and how he built Yamana are discussed.

35580 ■ *"You Can Rebuild It" in Entrepreneur (Vol. 37, July 2009, No. 7, pp. 28)*
Pub: Entrepreneur Press
Contact: Perlman Neil, President
Ed: Robert Kiyosaki. Description: Entrepreneurs, during tough times, should melt down old business strategies and start rebuilding the business. The business and its customers should be redefined in order to maximize marketing efforts and stay afloat when business slows down. Personal experiences in melting down a business and starting over are also given.

35581 ■ *Young Bucks: How to Raise a Future Millionaire*
Pub: Aylesbury Publishing
Ed: Troy Dunn. Released: November 13, 2007. Price: $19.95, Hardcover. Description: Advice is given to parents to teach their children how to save money, invest wisely and even start their own business. Availability: Print.

35582 ■ *"Young Giants" in Canadian Business (Vol. 79, August 14, 2006, No. 16-17, pp. 47)*
Ed: Brad Purdy. Description: New generations of young chiefs of oil and gas companies in Canada, are featured.

35583 ■ *"Young-Kee Kim: Deputy Director, Fermi National Accelerator Laboratory" in Crain's Chicago Business (Vol. 31, May 5, 2008, No. 18)*
Pub: Crain Communications Inc.
Contact: Todd Johnson, Publisher
Ed: Phuong Ly. Description: Profile of Young-Kee Kim who is the deputy director of Fermilab, a physics lab where scientists study the smallest particles in the universe; Ms. Kim was a researcher at Fermilab before becoming deputy director two years ago; Fermilab is currently home to the most powerful particle accelerator in the world and is struggling to compete with other countries despite cuts in federal funding.

35584 ■ *"Young Millionaires" in Entrepreneur (Vol. 35, October 2007, No. 10, pp. 76)*
Pub: Entrepreneur Press
Contact: Perlman Neil, President
Ed: Jessica Chen, Lindsay Holloway, Amanda C. Kooser, Kim Orr, James Park, Nichole L. Torres, Sara Wilson. Description: Young successful entrepreneurs of 2007 were chosen to talk about their success story and their business strategies in the past and those for the future. Among those featured are Kelly Flatley, Brendan Synnott, Herman Flores, Myles Kovacs, Haythem Haddad, Jim Wetzel, Lance Lawson, Jacob DeHart, Jake Nickell, Tim Vanderhook, Chris Vanderhook, Russell Vanderhook, Megan Duckett, Brad Sugars, John Vechey, Brian Fiete, Jason Kapalka, Nathan Jones, Devon Rifkin, Ryan Black, Ed Nichols, Jeremy Black, Amy Smilovic, Bob Shallenberger, and John Cavanagh.

35585 ■ *"Your Annual Business Tune-Up" in Business Week (December 28, 2006)*
Ed: Karen E. Klein. Description: Interview with entrepreneurial expert, Ty Freyvogel, founder of EntrpreneursLab.com. Freyvogel gives tips on how a thorough review of existing systems, vendors, customers, and employees could help keep an entrepreneur's business not only safe but highly successful in the upcoming year.

35586 ■ *Your Business, Your Future: How to Predict and Harness Growth*
Pub: Allen & Unwin Pty., Limited
Ed: Linda Hailey. Released: June 2006. Price: A$29.99. Description: Four distinct phases every small companies faces during growth are profiled. Availability: Print.

35587 ■ *"Your Turn in the Spotlight" in Inc. (Volume 32, December 2010, No. 10, pp. 57)*
Pub: Inc. Magazine
Ed: John Brandon. Description: Examples of three video blogs created by entrepreneurs to promote their businesses and products are used to show successful strategies. Wine Library TV promotes a family's wine business; SHAMA.TV offers marketing tips and company news; and Will It Blend? promotes sales of a household blender.

35588 ■ *"The Zero Marginal Cost Society: The Internet of Things, the Collaborative Commons, and the Eclipse of Capitalism"*
Pub: Palgrave Macmillan
Contact: Lisa Dunn, Manager
E-mail: l.dunn@palgrave.com
Released: April 1, 2014. Price: $28.00. Description: The emerging Internet of things is speeding society to an ear of nearly free goods and services, causing the rise of a global Collaborative Commons and the eclipse of capitalism. Entrepreneurial dynamism of competitive markets that drives productivity up and marginal costs down, enabling businesses to reduce the price of their goods and services to win consumers and market share is slowly dying.

35589 ■ *"Zions Offers Step-by-Step Small Business Guidance" in Idaho Business Review (September 1, 2014)*
Pub: Dolan Co.
Contact: James P. Dolan, President
Released: September 15, 2014. Description: Zions bank provides small business guidance to clients through its Zions Bank Idaho Business Resource Center. The program helps entrepreneurs learn the basic rules of running a small business. Free courses teach the essentials of finance, marketing and selling, .

TRADE PERIODICALS

35590 ■ *The Small Business Advisor*
Pub: Small Business Advisors Inc.
Contact: Arthur VanDam, President
URL(s): smallbusinessadvice.com. Ed: Ann Liss, Editor. Released: Monthly Price: $45, print or soft copy. Description: Seeks to help emerging growth companies increase profits. Considers small business issues, including marketing sales, finance, taxes, organizing, competition, management, and human resources. Recurring features include letters to the editor, interviews, and columns titled Info Bank, In the Mail Box, Taxes, Human Resources, Marketing, Insurance, and Law. Remarks: Publication suspended in 1980; resumed publication Fall 1993.

VIDEOCASSETTES/ AUDIOCASSETTES

35591 ■ *The Achievement Challenge*
4th Generation Systems
113 N Grant St.
Barrington, IL 60010
Ph: (847)381-7797
Free: 800-227-4332
Fax: (847)381-7301
Co. E-mail: cari@dirkbeveridge.com
URL: http://www.4thgenerationsystems.com
Contact: Dirk Beveridge, President
E-mail: dirk@4thgenerationsystems.com
Released: 1988. Price: $995. Description: A series of programs that explain things to be done and attitudes to be taken to do better in business. Availability: VHS.

35592 ■ *The American Entrepreneur Today*
Released: 1991. Price: $785. Description: A 14-part course focuses on the creativity and dedication needed to making a good idea work. Six successful entrepreneurs offer insight into their business success. Course text is "New Venture Creation: Entrepreneurship in the 1990s" by Jeffry A. Timmons. Availability: VHS.

35593 ■ *The Applied Management Series*
SkillSoft
107 Northeastern Blvd.
Nashua, NH 03062
Ph: (603)324-3000
Free: 877-545-5763
Fax: (603)324-3009
Co. E-mail: information@skillsoft.com
URL: http://www.skillsoft.com
Contact: Chuck Moran, President
Released: 1984. Description: This series of four six hour programs will train people in current effective management techniques. Availability: 3/4 U.

35594 ■ Business, Careers, and Lifestyle Series
RMI Media
1365 N. Winchester St.
Olathe, KS 66061-5880
Ph: (913)768-1696
Free: 800-745-5480
Fax: (800)755-6910
Co. E-mail: actmedia@act.org
URL: http://www.actmedia.com
Released: 1984. **Description:** In this series of 56 half-hour programs, host Dick Goldberg interviews top business leaders in various fields to find out what it takes to be successful in business. **Availability:** VHS; 3/4 U.

35595 ■ Creativity in Business
Advantage Media
c/o Kantola Productions
55 Sunnyside Ave.
Mill Valley, CA 94941
Free: 800-280-1180
Co. E-mail: kantola@kantola.com
URL: http://www.kantola.com/d/advantage.htm
Contact: Daniel Amos, Chief Executive Officer
Released: 1998. **Price:** $95. **Description:** Dr. Michael Ray demonstrates how to apply the principles of consciousness expansion, intuition and creativity to business ventures. **Availability:** VHS.

35596 ■ Decision Making: How to Make Better, Faster, Smarter Decisions
Instructional Video
2219 C St.
Lincoln, NE 68502-1745
Ph: (402)475-6570
Free: 800-228-0164
Fax: (402)475-6500
Co. E-mail: orders@insvideo.com
URL: http://www.insvideo.com
Contact: Kathy Damkroger, President
Released: 19??. **Price:** $59.95. **Description:** Profiles effective decision-making techniques. Includes interactive guidebook. **Availability:** VHS.

35597 ■ Empowerment: How to Receive Work Assignments
International Training Consultants, Inc.
1838 Park Oaks
Kemah, TX 77565
Free: 800-998-8764
Co. E-mail: itc@trainingitc.com
URL: http://www.trainingitc.com
Contact: Dick Leatherman, Chief Executive Officer
Released: 19??. **Price:** $495. **Description:** Part of the "Empowerment: The Employee Development Series." Teaches employees proper procedures in receiving work assignments from their superiors. Includes instruction on how to obtain task objectives, ask for needed details, determine resources available, analyze contraints, ask for training, offer suggestions, and establish performance measures. Emphasis is placed on the employee's knowledge that it is their responsibility to finish the assignment correctly and on time. **Availability:** VHS.

35598 ■ Empowerment: Moving from Criticism to Feedback
International Training Consultants, Inc.
1838 Park Oaks
Kemah, TX 77565
Free: 800-998-8764
Co. E-mail: itc@trainingitc.com
URL: http://www.trainingitc.com
Contact: Dick Leatherman, Chief Executive Officer
Released: 19??. **Price:** $495. **Description:** Part of the "Empowerment: The Employee Development Series." Illustrates proper ways of giving and receiving criticism. Teaches a six-step method which helps turn criticism into constructive feedback. Also discusses methods which help an individual receive criticism without becoming defensive. Comes with leader's guide, self-study instructions, and five participant booklets. **Availability:** VHS.

35599 ■ Empowerment: The Employee Development Series
International Training Consultants, Inc.
1838 Park Oaks
Kemah, TX 77565
Free: 800-998-8764
Co. E-mail: itc@trainingitc.com
URL: http://www.trainingitc.com
Contact: Dick Leatherman, Chief Executive Officer
Released: 19??. **Price:** $10,350. **Description:** Employee development series which prepares employees to meet the demands of today's workplace with skill and confidence. Covers such topics as time management, team work, communication, career advancement, working together, and problem solving. Comes with leader's guide, overhead transparencies, five participant booklets, and a complete participant's manual. **Availability:** VHS.

35600 ■ Everything You Always Wanted to Know about Management
Provant Media
4621 121st St.
Urbandale, IA 50323-2311
Ph: (888)776-8268
Free: 888-776-8268
Fax: (515)327-2555
Co. E-mail: custsvc@ammedia.com
URL: http://www.provantmedia.com
Contact: Tiffan Yamen, Manager, Marketing
Released: 1995. **Price:** $595. **Description:** Outlines the essentials of good management, including the six steps of delegation, employee empowerment, communication, feedback, and goal achievement. Includes course guide with participant exercises and case studies. **Availability:** VHS; CC.

35601 ■ The Good Business Basics Series: The Basics of Entrepreneuring
Films Media Group of Cos.
132 W 31st St., 17th Fl.
New York, NY 10001-3406
Ph: (609)671-1000
Free: 800-257-5126
Fax: (609)671-0266
Co. E-mail: custserv@films.com
URL: http://www.cambridgeeducational.com
Contact: David Waldherr, President
Released: 1992. **Price:** $98. **Description:** So you think you have a good idea. How do you get started in business? This program overviews the basics of getting a business off the ground, from finding a niche in the marketplace, building a staff, learning from others' mistakes, and much more. **Availability:** VHS.

35602 ■ How You Can Start, Build, Manage, or Turn Around Any Business
Nightingale-Conant Corp.
1400 South Wolf Rd., Bldg. 300, Ste. 103
Wheeling, IL 60090
Ph: (847)647-0300
Free: 800-557-1660
Fax: (847)647-7145
Co. E-mail: sales@nightingale.com
URL: http://www.nightingale.com
Contact: L. Victor Conant, President
Released: 19??. **Price:** $395. **Description:** Brian Tracy presents a mini-course in business management. **Availability:** VHS.

35603 ■ I Can Do It! Ed Lewis
Direct Cinema Ltd.
PO Box 10003
Santa Monica, CA 90410-1003
Ph: (310)636-8200
Fax: (310)636-8228
URL: http://www.directcinema.com
Contact: Cathie Christie
Released: 1984. **Description:** The creator of GMS explains the art, drive and knowledge necessary for successful entrepreneurism. **Availability:** VHS; 3/4 U; Special order formats.

35604 ■ Leadership: Building Rainbows
Geographical Studies and Research Center (EKU)
Department of Geography and Planning
521 Lancaster Ave., 103 Roark Bldg.
Richmond, KY 40475-3120

Ph: (859)622-1273
URL: http://www.geography.eku.edu
Contact: Alice L. Jones, Director
E-mail: alice.jones@eku.edu
Released: 1984. **Description:** Professionals in leadership positions looking to gain personal and organizational goals are acquainted with effective persuasive communication skills. **Availability:** VHS.

35605 ■ Product Strategy: All the Right Moves
RMI Media
1365 N. Winchester St.
Olathe, KS 66061-5880
Ph: (913)768-1696
Free: 800-745-5480
Fax: (800)755-6910
Co. E-mail: actmedia@act.org
URL: http://www.actmedia.com
Released: 1991. **Price:** $89.95. **Description:** Presents a case study of Carushka, a dance and exercise wear manufacturer, to demonstrate successful methods for increasing product use and customers; finding new uses for existing products; and broadening the product appeal to old and new markets. **Availability:** VHS.

35606 ■ Speaking of Success
RMI Media
1365 N. Winchester St.
Olathe, KS 66061-5880
Ph: (913)768-1696
Free: 800-745-5480
Fax: (800)755-6910
Co. E-mail: actmedia@act.org
URL: http://www.actmedia.com
Released: 1988. **Price:** $69.95. **Description:** A series of business-oriented programs endeavoring to help the viewer improve his or her self, relations with others, and various manipulative techniques useful in business transactions. **Availability:** VHS; 3/4 U.

35607 ■ Why Study Business?: Skills For the 21st Century
Films Media Group of Cos.
132 W 31st St., 17th Fl.
New York, NY 10001-3406
Ph: (609)671-1000
Free: 800-257-5126
Fax: (609)671-0266
Co. E-mail: custserv@films.com
URL: http://www.cambridgeeducational.com
Contact: David Waldherr, President
Released: 1990. **Price:** $98. **Description:** Introduces the various facets of the business world, and profiles careers in business which utilize several different skills. **Availability:** VHS.

CONSULTANTS

35608 ■ Beacon Management - Management Consultants
1000 W McNab Rd.
Pompano Beach, FL 33069
Ph: (954)782-1119
Co. E-mail: md@beaconmgmt.com
URL: http://www.beaconmgmt.com
Contact: Barbara L. Donnelly, Director
E-mail: bdonnelly@browardhealth.org
Scope: Specializes in change management, organized workplaces, multicultural negotiations and dispute resolutions and internet based decision making. **Founded:** 1985. **Publications:** "Sun-Sentinel Article," Oct, 2012.

35609 ■ Donna Cornell Enterprises Inc. [Cornell Career Center]
68 N Plank Rd., Ste. 204
Newburgh, NY 12550-2122
Ph: (845)565-0088
Fax: (845)565-0084
Scope: Offers services in career consultant, professional search, job placement and national professional search. **Founded:** 1996. **Publications:** "The Power of the Woman Within"; "Juggling it All!"; "Journey: A Woman's Guide to Success"; "Shatter the Traditions".

35610 ■ Entrepreneurial Strategies
107 S Yellowstone Ave., Ste. C
Bozeman, MT 59715
Ph: (406)587-5664
Fax: (406)586-0396
Co. E-mail: nfkrueger@rocketmail.com
Contact: Norris F. Krueger, Jr., Principal
E-mail: nfkrueger@hotmail.com
Scope: Academic consultants helping organizations become more entrepreneurial; helping communities become more entrepreneurial; providing market assessments for 'really new' products and technologies; offering strategic planning and marketing planning.

35611 ■ Third Sector New England Inc. (TSNE)
89 South St., Ste. 700
Boston, MA 02111
Ph: (617)523-6565
Fax: (617)523-2070
Co. E-mail: info@tsne.org
URL: http://www.tsne.org
Contact: Jonathan Spack, Executive Director
Scope: A team of faculty, consultants, project managers, researchers and a variety of strategic alliances provide leadership training, consulting, seminars, educational programs, research and conferences. **Founded:** 1959. **Publications:** "Executive Directors Guide"; "Creative Disruption: Sabbaticals for Capacity Building and Leadership Development in the Nonprofit Sector"; "A Step-by-Step Guide to Achieving Diversity in the Workplace"; "Valuing Our Nonprofit Workforce 2010: A Compensation Survey of and for Nonprofits in Massachusetts and Adjoining Communities"; "Shared Services: A Guide to Collaborative Solutions for Nonprofits"; "TSNe-Bulletin". **Seminars:** Supporting Nonprofits and Communities Through the Rough Times.

LIBRARIES

35612 ■ Canadian Federation of Independent Business Research Library
401-4141 Yonge St.
Toronto, ON, Canada M2P 2A6
Ph: (416)222-8022
Free: 888-234-2232
Fax: (416)222-6103
Co. E-mail: cfib@cfib.ca
URL: http://www.cfib-fcei.ca/english/index.html
Scope: Small business, entrepreneurship, economic policy, politics and government. **Services:** Interlibrary loan; copying; Library open to the public by appointment. **Founded:** 1980. **Holdings:** 4000 volumes; 32 VF drawers of subject files; Annual reports. **Subscriptions:** 100 journals and other serials; 4 newspapers.

RESEARCH CENTERS

35613 ■ Baylor University - Center for Private Enterprise
PO Box 98003
Waco, TX 76798

Ph: (254)710-2263
Fax: (254)710-1092
Co. E-mail: kimberly_mencken@baylor.edu
URL: http://www.baylor.edu/business
Contact: Kimberly Mencken, Director

URL(s): www.baylor.edu/business/index.php-p?id=86674. **Scope:** Pedagogical methods for teaching economics in high school and college levels, development of new active learning lessons for kindergarten through college economics. **Founded:** 1978. **Educational Activities:** Economic Forecast Conference; Leaderships programs, for high school seniors; Seminars, in-service workshops, and programs to teach economics, personal finance, and consumer economics, for elementary and secondary teachers.

35614 ■ Boston University - Institute for Technology Entrepreneurship and Commercialization (ITEC)
595 Commonwealth Ave.
Boston, MA 02215
Ph: (617)353-9391
Fax: (617)353-1695
Co. E-mail: pmcmanus@bu.edu
URL: http://www.bu.edu/itec
Contact: Paul McManus, Managing Director
Scope: Entrepreneurship, global entrepreneurship in healthcare, clean energy, and information systems, women entrepreneurs, management policy, and marketing. **Founded:** 2006. **Publications:** *ITEC Newsletter* (Monthly). **Educational Activities:** Annual Business Plan Competition; Business Plan Boot Camp; Entrepreneurial Research Lab.

35615 ■ Lehigh University - Small Business Development Center (SBDC)
125 Goodman Dr.
Bethlehem, PA 18015
Ph: (610)758-3980
Fax: (610)758-5205
Co. E-mail: insbdc@lehigh.edu
URL: http://www.lehigh.edu/~insbdc/index.html
Contact: Sandra F. Holsonback, Executive Director
Scope: Problems faced by small businesses, the impact of the general economy on the formation and operation of small business, and characteristics on entrepreneurs. **Services:** Administers various loan pools for lending to small businesses; Consulting and research in management assistance, international trade, government marketing, and financing assistance; Lehigh University Management Assistance Counseling (LUMAC) Program: a field studies course for senior students. **Founded:** 1978. **Publications:** *Export Planning Guide*; *Financing Guide for Northampton*; *Financing Your Business*; *Lehigh and Berks County*; *Lehigh Valley Business Support Services*; *Market Planning Guide*. **Educational Activities:** SBDC Seminars.

35616 ■ New York University - Berkley Center for Entrepreneurial Studies (BCES)
NYU Stern School of Business, Ste. 7-150, KMC
44 W 4th St.
New York, NY 10012
Ph: (212)998-0070
Fax: (212)995-4211
Co. E-mail: jeffrey.carr@stern.nyu.edu
URL: http://w4.stern.nyu.edu/berkley
Contact: Jeffrey A. Carr, Executive Director
URL(s): www.stern.nyu.edu. **Scope:** Factors that promote entrepreneurship and lead to the creation of new wealth and business revenues; business venturing within established firms. Topics include the major pitfalls and obstacles to start-ups, securing of venture capital, psychology and sociology of entrepreneurship, valuation and management of new ventures, technological innovation and new product development, emerging and creative industries, and cross-cultural environments that stimulate entrepreneurship. **Founded:** 1984. **Publications:** *Case series*; *BCES Working papers*. **Educational Activities:** BCES Business Plan Competition; BCES Conferences; BCES Entrepreneur in Residence Program; BCES Forums and workshops. **Awards:** Harold Price Entrepreneurship Award; Rennert Entrepreneurial Prize; Gloria Appel Fellowship.

35617 ■ Southern Methodist University - Caruth Institute for Entrepreneurship
Fincher Bldg., Rm. 143
Cox School of Business
Dallas, TX 75275-0333
Ph: (214)768-3689
Fax: (214)768-3604
Co. E-mail: jwhite@cox.smu.edu
URL: http://www.cox.smu.edu/web/caruth-institute
Contact: Prof. Jerry F. White, Director
Scope: Entrepreneurs as managers. **Founded:** 1970. **Publications:** *Caruth Institute of Entrepreneurship Newsletter* (Monthly). **Educational Activities:** Southwest Venture Forum; Caruth Institute for Entrepreneurship Bimonthly Breakfast Meeting. **Awards:** Dallas 100 Awards (Annual).

35618 ■ University of British Columbia - Sauder School of Business - W. Maurice Young Centre Entrepreneurship and Venture Capital Research
2053 Main Mall
Vancouver, BC, Canada V6T 1Z2
Ph: (604)822-8476
Fax: (604)822-8477
Co. E-mail: hellmann@sauder.ubc.ca
URL: http://www.sauder.ubc.ca/Faculty/Research_
    Centres/W_Maurice_Young_Centre_for_
    Entrepreneurship_and_Venture_Capital_Research
Contact: Thomas F. Hellman, Director
Scope: Entrepreneurship and venture capital. **Founded:** 1992. **Publications:** *Industry reports*. **Educational Activities:** Entrepreneurship Luncheon (Annual).

START-UP INFORMATION

35619 ■ *"8 Ways to Make Your Crowdfunding Campaign Stand Out" in Entrepreneur (June 2014)*
Pub: Entrepreneur Media Inc.
Released: June 2014. **Description:** Business experts offer some tips to launch a successful crowdfunding campaign for startups. Entrepreneurs should create a solid plan and reach out to prospective backers before launching their campaigns. Richard Swart of the University of California, suggest hosting launch parties, organizing round table discussions, and establishing a presence at community events to garner support. A series of small campaigns builds brand loyalty over time and provides fans with additional opportunities to support the startup at different stages.

35620 ■ *"Advantage: Early Adopters" in Entrepreneur (July 2014)*
Pub: Entrepreneur Media Inc.
Released: July 2014. **Description:** Franchising is one of the business models that stand to benefit from cloud computing and other digital solutions. A number of innovations are already transforming the franchise community and it remains to be seen how franchisees will respond to these changes. Among the innovations available for franchisees are fleet-management applications, improved customer loyalty programs, and digital signboards. The advent of cloud-based point-of-sale systems are also gaining popularity among some small franchisees.

35621 ■ *"Begslist.org Launches Crowdfunding On Its Website" in Computer Business Week (August 2, 2012)*
Pub: NewsRX
Contact: Susan E. Hasty, Publisher
Released: August 2, 2012. **Description:** Donation Website called Begslist has added crowdfunding to its site. Crowdfunding and begging are popular among small startups wishing to procure funding for their new companies.

35622 ■ *"The Best Book on How to Sell Anything Online: A Step by Step Guide"*
Pub: ARI Publishing
Released: October 21, 2014. **Price:** $9.95 paperback. **Description:** A guide to help entrepreneurs launch an online service selling anything without startup or overhead costs. Profits for selling software can be as high as 50-75 percent. Tips for Web design is also included.

35623 ■ *"CrowdFunding Platform, START.ac, Announces It Is Expanding Its International Scope From the US, Canada and the UK to 36 Countries Including Australia, India, Israel, Italy and Africa" in Benzinga.com (July 11, 2012)*
Pub: Benzinga.com
Contact: Kyle Bazzy, President
Released: July 11, 2012. **Description:** START.ac is expanding its CrowdFunding site to include 36 countries and increasing its scope to include busi-

ness startups, teen projects, as well as medical products. START.ac projects are in the fundraising stage at this point, with 23 percent located outside the United States.

35624 ■ *"Crowdfunding Site Targets Jan. Launch" in Crain's Detroit Business (July 9, 2012)*
Pub: Crain Communications Inc.
Contact: Rance E. Crain, President
Ed: Meghana Keshavan. **Released:** July 9, 2012.
Description: Michigan based RelayFund Inc. incorporates social media with fundraising private equity form small businesses. Before the JOBS Act legislation, it was difficult for small firms to raise money. Crowdfunding connects groups of investors with small startup businesses.

35625 ■ *"Don't Tell Me!" in Entrepreneur (June 2014)*
Pub: Entrepreneur Media Inc.
Released: June 2014. **Description:** Spoiler Shield is a mobile application that allows users to block social media messages pertaining to popular television programs and sports teams. Spoiler Shield, developed by Josh Solt and Matthew Loew, uses a proprietary algorithm to block social media messages that could be spoilers. A virtual gold shield covers spoiler social media posts, which users can reveal on a case-to-case basis. The applications has generated buzz within the mass media industry and has been praised as useful for television viewers. Solt and Loew plan to realize revenues from data mining and white labeling.

35626 ■ *"eBay Selling: 102 Killer Profitable Items To Sell On eBay From Thrift Stores, Flea Markets, Garage Sales and More..."*
Pub: Amazon Digital Services
Released: October 2, 2014. **Price:** $0.99 Kindle.
Description: eBay is a source of income for entrepreneurs wishing to start an online business. The guide will provide access to 102 research items that will help start a profitable online business on eBay, the auction online store.

35627 ■ *"Equity 'Crowdfunding' Platform, RelayFund, Launched by Michigan Investor Group" in Economics Week (July 20, 2012)*
Pub: NewsRX
Contact: Susan E. Hasty, Publisher
Released: July 20, 2012. **Description:** RelayFund was launched by a group of Michigan venture capitalists, entrepreneurs, and investment bankers to link small investors with startup firms under the new JOBS (Jumpstart Our Business Startups) Act. Crowdfunding is money raised for charities, projects or pre-selling products or services and allows online micro investments for startup companies.

35628 ■ *"Finding Startups a Place To Take Root" in Business Journal (Vol. 32, August 29, 2014, No. 14, pp. 6)*
Pub: American City Business Journals
Released: August 29, 2014. **Description:** Entrepreneurs David Berglund and Justin Ley have unveiled a new crowdfunding Website called Hoodstarter. The

Website gathers business ideas from residents and help entrepreneurs make a pitch. Startups can seek further financing if they can show ample consumer demand.

35629 ■ *"Full-Speed Ahead" in Entrepreneur (September 2014)*
Pub: Entrepreneurial Press
Released: September 2014. **Description:** Entrepreneurs, Jessica Scorpio and Sam Zaid, launched their San Francisco, California-based startup Getaround in 2011 based on the business model of car-sharing service Zipcar. Scorpio recalls how she came up with the idea of creating a peer-to-peer car sharing marketplace that would connect individual car owners with renters. Statistical data included.

35630 ■ *"Fundable.com, Crowdfunding for Startups, Chooses WePay's Marketplace API to Power Payments" in Internet Wire (June 20, 2012)*
Released: June 20, 2012. **Description:** Fundable.com has partnered with WePay to allow users to start accepting payments from funding sources immediately and does not require users to have a pre-existing merchant account. The Crowdfunding Bill creates a massive change or accessing capital for starting a new business venture.

35631 ■ *"Interest Soaring In 44North Business Competition" in Business First of Buffalo (Vol. 30, February 21, 2014, No. 23, pp. 3)*
Pub: American City Business Journals, Inc.
Contact: Whitney Shaw, President
Released: February 21, 2014. **Description:** The 43North business plan competition has attracted over 200 applications from entrepreneurs coming from various sectors like e-commerce, clean technology, and advanced manufacturing. The winners of the competition will qualify for the Start-Up New York program which eliminates the tax burden for qualified firms.

35632 ■ *"Kickstarter Funds the Future; Crowdfunding Services Such as Kickstarter Have Been Hailed as a New Way To Get Started In Business and Cut Out the Traditional Money Men" in Telegraph Online (June 24, 2012)*
Pub: Telegraph Media Group Ltd.
Contact: Murdoch MacLennan, Chief Executive Officer
Ed: Monty Munford. **Released:** June 24, 2012. **Description:** More than 530 crowdfunding services are expected to his the net by the end of the year. Crowdfunding helps companies raise money from investors for specific projects. A musician was able to raise over $1 million to fund a new record.

35633 ■ *"Leading Digital: Turning Technology into Business Transformation"*
Pub: Harvard Business Review Press
Contact: Peter E. Walsh, Director
Released: October 14, 2014. **Price:** $30.00. **Description:** Mobile technology, analytics, social media, sensors, and cloud computing have changed the

entire business environment in every industry. A guide to help any small startup business in any industry gain strategic advantage using digital, including where to invest in digital technologies and how to lead the transformation. The guide teaches how to engage better with customers, digitally enhance operations, create a digital vision, and govern digital activities.

35634 ■ *"Legal Matters: 'Crowdfunding' a Boon for Entrepreneurs, If They Clear Regulatory Hurdles" in Finance and Commerce (July 17, 2012)*
Pub: Dolan Co.
Contact: James P. Dolan, President
Ed: Dan Heilman. Released: July 17, 2012. Description: Part of the Jumpstart Our Business Startups Act (JOBS) is crowdfunding, which allows the funding of a company by selling small parts of equity to a group of investors. Kickstarter, a Website for raising funds for business entitites, is primarily used for film and book projects. Most businesses cannot adopt Kickstarter's model because of the legality of receiving investor funds without offering security.

35635 ■ *"MicroVentures: New Crowdfunding Game Makes Startups the Stars, Prepares Players for a New Kind of Investing" in Health & Beauty Close-Up (July 31, 2012)*
Pub: Close-Up Media
Released: July 31, 2012. Description: MicroVentures created the MicroVentures Investor Challenge as a game on Facebook. The game features real startups such as AirBnB, Etsy, and Pinterest and players invest in these firms. The game has real startups face off in six weekly rounds and the players act as venture capitalists. One startup and one investor will win the game.

35636 ■ *"Modern Meal Offers Recipe Inspiration, Curation and Home Delivery" in Orlando Business Journal (Vol. 30, April 4, 2014, No. 41, pp. 3)*
Pub: American City Business Journals
Released: April 4, 2014. Description: Modern Meal LLC's CEO, Mark Hudgins, works to get people to the dinner table for a good meal. The social network with a Pinterest look is in early-beta-launch and users are trying out the features by curating recipes from popular cooking Websites and looking at recipes of other users. Modern' Meal's plan to tap into the e-grocery market is also discussed.

35637 ■ *"MovieHatch.com: Crowdfunding Added to Services for Filmmakers" in Wireless News (June 25, 2012)*
Pub: Close-Up Media
Released: June 25, 2012. Description: MovieHatch.com launched a funding platform offing an opportunity for projects to be introduced to over 50 key industry decision-makers. Participants receive funds and projects getting over $10,000 can position themselves for fan voting, with the top three fan favorites each month winning an introduction to judges/partners for collaboration consideration.

35638 ■ *"No. 105: What I Learned from Steve Jobs" in Inc. (Vol. 36, September 2014, No. 7, pp. 129)*
Pub: Mansueto Ventures L.L.C.
Contact: John Koten, Chief Executive Officer
Released: September 2014. Description: Entrepreneur, Matt MacInnis, started his firm that publishes interactive textbooks and manuals. MacInnis got his start working in marketing at Apple before launching the San Francisco-based Inkling. Over five years, he has received almost $50 million in venture capital.

35639 ■ *"No. 369: How I Turned Big Data Into Viral Marketing" in Inc. (Vol. 36, September 2014, No. 7, pp. 134)*
Pub: Mansueto Ventures L.L.C.
Contact: John Koten, Chief Executive Officer
Released: September 2014. Description: Six Spoke Media was founded in 2009 by Edward Kim of San Francisco, California. Kim cashed out his 401(K) to fund his startup that makes a marketing campaign go viral on social media to help businesses grow.

35640 ■ *"No. 381: Metallica and Other Forms of Hardware" in Inc. (Vol. 36, September 2014, No. 7, pp. 107)*
Pub: Mansueto Ventures L.L.C.
Contact: John Koten, Chief Executive Officer
Released: September 2014. Description: Profile of Mikhail Orlov, who stayed in American instead of fighting a war he did not believe in while living in Chechnya, Russia. Orlov discovered his entrepreneurial spirit when he began importing Russian army surplus gear. He operates his startup online store selling guns, ammo, and hunting accessories.

35641 ■ *"Open English Touted as Startup Worth Emulating" in South Florida Business Journal (Vol. 34, January 24, 2014, No. 27, pp. 30)*
Pub: American City Business Journals
Released: January 24, 2014. Description: Open English, a language education company, received more than $150 million in investments from venture capitalists. The firm's cloud-based platform is still in its infancy, but the startup's success has shown that entrepreneurs can generate money and grow their businesses in Florida. Open English is the only online English school that offers live classes with native English-speaking teachers.

35642 ■ *"PeoplesVC Becomes the 1st Stock-Based Crowdfunding Site to Open Its Doors to Investors" in Investment Weekly (June 23, 2012)*
Pub: NewsRX
Contact: Susan E. Hasty, Publisher
Released: June 23, 2012. Description: Peoples VC is the first equity-based crowdfunding site to invite public investors to set up individual crowdfunding investment accounts. Equity-based crowdfunding allows funders to receive stock in return for their investment into companies. In the past, this process was only available to venture capitalists and accredited investors.

35643 ■ *"Perfect Harmony" in Entrepreneur (June 2014)*
Pub: Entrepreneur Media Inc.
Released: June 2014. Description: Bop.fm is a Web-based service that allows users to share music from competing on-demand streaming services. The service, founded by Shehzad Daredia and Stefan Gomez, detects a user's streaming service and streams a desired song from that service or from free streaming platforms. The service enables the sharing of songs through sending of links and allows users to purchase the track. Bop.fm reports more than 35 million song plays and grows by more than 100,000 plays a day. The company's founders are concentrating on getting more people aware of the service before monetizing it.

35644 ■ *"A Picture Is Worth a Thousand Words" in Entrepreneur (July 2014)*
Pub: Entrepreneur Media Inc.
Released: July 2014. Description: Goodhatch of Los Angeles, California, started a desktop application (app) called Skitch for tracking and communicating notes and design changes of new products for retail customers. Skitch allows the design-driven business incubator to make annotations and quick sketches directly on product images for everyone to see and easily understand the proposed changes. The no-cost Skitch mobile app also allows the Goodhatch team to track notes and changes to products on their smartphones in real time.

35645 ■ *"A Piece of the Action" in Entrepreneur (May 2014)*
Pub: Entrepreneur Media Inc.
Released: May 2014. Description: Franchisor, Mandy Calara of Forever Yogurt explains how his online crowdfunding platform called CrowdFranchise can help potential franchisees find investors. He details the successful opening of their first Forever Yogurt store at Wicker Park in Chicago, Illinois through the CrowdFranchise. He explains the incubator program called Velocity and the use of Crowd-Franchise to measure support. He believes that emerging franchisors and startups with fewer than 20 units will be interested in their concept.

35646 ■ *"Rants and Raves" in Entrepreneur (July 2014)*
Pub: Entrepreneur Media Inc.
Released: July 2014. Description: Industry experts offer tips on ways entrepreneurs can maximize the marketing benefits of user-generated review sites. Jennifer Grappone of Gravity Search Marketing, suggests developing a Web presence with as many details as possible. Michael Dash of CarPartKings.com, emphasizes the importance of reading the terms of the contract before signing up for the site's programs. Startups need to solidify their presence on the Web by accumulating as many reviews as possible as this will help them improve their search results.

35647 ■ *"Recipe for Success" in Business Strategy Review (Vol. 25, Summer 2014, No. 2, pp. 54)*
Pub: Blackwell Publishing Professional
Contact: Stephen M. Smith, President
Released: Summer 2014. Description: Corrado Accardi used crowdfunding to back his business plan and raise capital for his quality pizza carryout restaurant.

35648 ■ *"The Right Way to Start an Online Business: The Untold Truths of What it Takes AFTER Your First Sale to Succeed"*
Pub: Amazon Digital Services
Released: October 4, 2014. Price: $9.99 Kindle. Description: Seven of the top methods for starting an online business are listed. Instruction is given to sell products or services for immediate payment to begin entrepreneurship on the Web. Financial investment in the online startup is covered. Web design and optimization of Search Engines, worksheets, sales page outlines, email templates, sales contracts and more are included.

35649 ■ *"SEC, NASAA Tell Small Businesses: Wait To Join the 'Crowd': Crowdfunding Is 'Not Yet Legal Until the Commission Appoints Rules', Says SEC's Kim" in Investment Advisor (Vol. 3, August 2012, No. 8, pp. 13)*
Pub: Summit Professional Networks
Contact: Steve Weitzner, President
Ed: Melanie Waddell. Released: August 2012. Description: Securities and Exchange Commission along with state regulators have advised small businesses and entrepreneurs to wait until the SEC has produced rules governing crowdfunding practices. Until that happens, federal and state securities laws prohibit publicly accessible Internet securities offerings. An overview of crowdfunding and the JOBS Act is included.

35650 ■ *"Social Media Bootcamp: How Not To Suck At Social Media"*
Pub: Amazon Digital Services
Released: September 29, 2014. Price: $0.99 Kindle. Description: Seven steps to build a social media presence are presented in boot camp style. Whether direct sales, multi-level marketing, online store, or another type of online, home-based startup business, this book give tips for would-be entrepreneurs.

ASSOCIATIONS AND OTHER ORGANIZATIONS

35651 ■ **The Entrepreneurship Institute (TEI)**
3700 Corporate Dr., Ste. 145
Columbus, OH 43231
Ph: (614)895-1153
URL: http://www.tei.net
Description: Provides encouragement and assistance to entrepreneurs who operate companies with revenue in excess of $1 million. Unites financial, legal, and community resources to help foster the success of companies. Promotes sharing of information and interaction between members. Operates President's forums and projects which are designed to improve communication between businesses, develop one-to-one business relationships between small and mid-size businesses and local resources, provide networking, and stimulate the growth of existing companies. **Scope:** growth strategies, account-

ing, finance, investments 401K. **Founded:** 1976. **Subscriptions:** audiovisuals books software. **Publications:** *The President's Forum* (Monthly). **Educational Activities:** The Entrepreneurship Institute Meeting (Periodic).

EDUCATIONAL PROGRAMS

35652 ■ Building XML Web Services with Java- Hands-On (Onsite)
Seminar Information Service Inc.
20 Executive Park, Ste. 120
Irvine, CA 92614
Ph: (949)261-9104
Free: 877-SEM-INFO
Fax: (949)261-1963
Co. E-mail: info@seminarinformation.com
URL: http://www.seminarinformation.com
URL(s): www.seminarinformation.com/qqbtmk/building-xml-web-services-with-java-hands-on. **Price:** $2,990, Onsite. **Description:** Learn how to: Develop and deploy Web services with Java and XML; Describe the functionality of Web services using WSDL; Write interoperable SOAP-based services and clients using JAX-RPC; Generate Java source files for services from WSDL and XML schemas; Customize SOAP messages using SAAJ; Implement strategies to secure your Web services; Locate Web services in XML registries using JAXR. **Audience:** Java programmers, professionals and general public. **Dates and Locations:** 2015 Feb 10-13; venue not reported. **Telecommunication Services:** info@seminarinformation.com.

35653 ■ Building XML Web Services with .NET: Hands-On (Onsite)
Seminar Information Service Inc.
20 Executive Park, Ste. 120
Irvine, CA 92614
Ph: (949)261-9104
Free: 877-SEM-INFO
Fax: (949)261-1963
Co. E-mail: info@seminarinformation.com
URL: http://www.seminarinformation.com
URL(s): www.seminarinformation.com. **Description:** Learn how to: Develop highly scalable distributed applications with XML Web services; Process XML documents with System.Xml library classes; Describe and publish Web services using standard protocols (SOAP, WSDL); Leverage ASP.NET for rapid development and monitoring of Web services; Build high-performance multithreaded and Web clients; Secure XML Web services using encryption and authentication. **Audience:** Industry professionals. **Telecommunication Services:** info@seminarinformation.com.

35654 ■ Cascading Style Sheets CSS for Web Page Development (Onsite)
Seminar Information Service Inc.
20 Executive Park, Ste. 120
Irvine, CA 92614
Ph: (949)261-9104
Free: 877-SEM-INFO
Fax: (949)261-1963
Co. E-mail: info@seminarinformation.com
URL: http://www.seminarinformation.com
URL(s): www.seminarinformation.com/qqbtln/cascading-style-sheets-css-for-web-page-development.
Price: $2,650, Onsite. **Description:** Learn how to: Develop fast, efficient, accessible and attractive Web pages using CSS; Generate table page layouts with pure CSS; Structure site layout and content to make your site faster and more maintainable; Apply best practices to develop cross-browser compatible Web pages and avoid pitfalls; Implement menu designs for effective site navigation; Create Web sites that meet Section 508 and W3C accessibility standards. **Audience:** Web establishers, web designers and web developers and general public. **Dates and Locations:** 2015 Feb 24-27; venue not reported. **Telecommunication Services:** info@seminarinformation.com.

35655 ■ Cisco Networking Introduction: Hands-On (Onsite)
Seminar Information Service Inc.
20 Executive Park, Ste. 120
Irvine, CA 92614

Ph: (949)261-9104
Free: 877-SEM-INFO
Fax: (949)261-1963
Co. E-mail: info@seminarinformation.com
URL: http://www.seminarinformation.com
URL(s): www.seminarinformation.com. **Description:** Learn how to: Successfully install and configure Cisco routers and switches to build internetworks; Create Cisco device configurations from scratch; Configure IP routing protocols; Troubleshoot complex IP routing problems; Perform software and hardware upgrades; Effectively manage and maintain Cisco routers with SNMP. **Audience:** Industry professionals. **Telecommunication Services:** info@seminarinformation.com.

35656 ■ Database Design for Web Development
EEI Communications
8945 Guilford Rd., Ste. 145
Columbia, MD 21046
Ph: (410)309-8200
Free: 888-253-2762
Fax: (410)630-3980
Co. E-mail: train@eeicom.com
URL: http://www.eeicom.com/eei-training-services
Description: Web designers learn how to design and structure a database efficiently. **Audience:** Programmer, professionals.

35657 ■ Developing AJAX Web Applications: Hands-On - Enhancing the Web User Experience (Onsite)
Seminar Information Service Inc.
20 Executive Park, Ste. 120
Irvine, CA 92614
Ph: (949)261-9104
Free: 877-SEM-INFO
Fax: (949)261-1963
Co. E-mail: info@seminarinformation.com
URL: http://www.seminarinformation.com
URL(s): www.seminarinformation.com. **Description:** Learn how to: Develop AJAX-powered interactive and dynamic Web sites; Design accessible interfaces for cross-browser compatibility; Integrate frameworks for data exchange on multiple server environments; Leverage toolkits to rapidly create rich user-friendly interfaces; Optimize and strengthen code to build stable applications; Protect vital information from interception. **Audience:** Professionals and general public. **Telecommunication Services:** info@seminarinformation.com.

35658 ■ Developing a Web Site: Hands-On (Onsite)
Seminar Information Service Inc.
20 Executive Park, Ste. 120
Irvine, CA 92614
Ph: (949)261-9104
Free: 877-SEM-INFO
Fax: (949)261-1963
Co. E-mail: info@seminarinformation.com
URL: http://www.seminarinformation.com
URL(s): www.seminarinformation.com/qqayzx/developing-a-web-site-hands-on. **Price:** $2,990, Onsite. **Description:** Learn how to: Establish, configure and maintain an intranet or Internet Web site; Develop and publish Web pages using HyperText Markup Language (HTML); Create image maps to allow easy navigation of your Web site; Configure a Web server; Capture, retrieve and display information via a database; Produce dynamic Web pages using server-side and client-side scripts. **Audience:** Web programmers, developers and designers. **Dates and Locations:** 2015 Mar 03-06; venue not reported. **Telecommunication Services:** info@seminarinformation.com.

35659 ■ Internet Marketing
EEI Communications
8945 Guilford Rd., Ste. 145
Columbia, MD 21046
Ph: (410)309-8200
Free: 888-253-2762

Fax: (410)630-3980
Co. E-mail: train@eeicom.com
URL: http://www.eeicom.com/eei-training-services
URL(s): www.eeicom.com/eei-training-services. **Price:** $745.00. **Description:** Covers how businesses can use the Internet to market products, including increasing traffic to your site, and measuring results. **Dates and Locations:** Alexandria, VA. **Telecommunication Services:** train@eeicom.com.

35660 ■ SharePoint I (Onsite)
EEI Communications
8945 Guilford Rd., Ste. 145
Columbia, MD 21046
Ph: (410)309-8200
Free: 888-253-2762
Fax: (410)630-3980
Co. E-mail: train@eeicom.com
URL: http://www.eeicom.com/eei-training-services
Description: Learn how to simplify team collaboration using Windows SharePoint Services. **Audience:** Industry professionals.

35661 ■ SharePoint II (Onsite)
EEI Communications
8945 Guilford Rd., Ste. 145
Columbia, MD 21046
Ph: (410)309-8200
Free: 888-253-2762
Fax: (410)630-3980
Co. E-mail: train@eeicom.com
URL: http://www.eeicom.com/eei-training-services
Description: Learn skills to design, maintain, and publish a custom SharePoint site. **Audience:** Industry professionals.

35662 ■ SharePoint III (Onsite)
EEI Communications
8945 Guilford Rd., Ste. 145
Columbia, MD 21046
Ph: (410)309-8200
Free: 888-253-2762
Fax: (410)630-3980
Co. E-mail: train@eeicom.com
URL: http://www.eeicom.com/eei-training-services
Price: . **Description:** Learn how to create and make modifications that can be applied to all users on the site or to individual users using Microsoft SharePoint controls, as well as how to apply personalization to Web pages so that when users modify pages and controls, the settings can be saved to retain a user's personal preferences. **Audience:** Industry professionals.

35663 ■ Web Design
EEI Communications
8945 Guilford Rd., Ste. 145
Columbia, MD 21046
Ph: (410)309-8200
Free: 888-253-2762
Fax: (410)630-3980
Co. E-mail: train@eeicom.com
URL: http://www.eeicom.com/eei-training-services
URL(s): www.eeicom.com. **Price:** $745.00. **Description:** Covers various aspects of graphic interface design for World Wide Web sites, including site conception; navigational and schematic design; processes from delivery of content to page layout for HTML; editorial, informational, and navigational graphics; and related topics. **Audience:** web designers and developers. **Dates and Locations:** Silver Spring, MD; Alexandria, VA; Hunt Valley, MD; and Columbia, MD. **Telecommunication Services:** train@eeicom.com.

35664 ■ Webinars with a WOW Factor: Creating Memorable Meeting Across the Globe (Onsite)
Seminar Information Service Inc.
20 Executive Park, Ste. 120
Irvine, CA 92614
Ph: (949)261-9104
Free: 877-SEM-INFO

Fax: (949)261-1963
Co. E-mail: info@seminarinformation.com
URL: http://www.seminarinformation.com
URL(s): www.seminarinformation.com/details. cfm?qc=qqcxmj. **Price:** $1,595. **Description:** Discover techniques that will make your material come to life on the screen and over the phone. **Audience:** Veteran and apprentice trainers.

35665 ■ Writing for the Web I (Onsite)
EEI Communications
8945 Guilford Rd., Ste. 145
Columbia, MD 21046
Ph: (410)309-8200
Free: 888-253-2762
Fax: (410)630-3980
Co. E-mail: train@eeicom.com
URL: http://www.eeicom.com/eei-training-services
URL(s): www.eeicom.com/eei-training-services/ classes/writing/. **Price:** $797.00. **Description:** Covers how to write and edit for sites on the World Wide Web, including understanding the Web's strengths and limitations, providing your audience the information it needs, organizing information with flowcharts and site maps, and using techniques of multimedia writing. **Audience:** writers and editors. **Dates and Locations:** Columbia, MD; and Silver Spring. **Telecommunication Services:** train@eeicom.com.

35666 ■ (X)HTML and CSS I (Onsite)
EEI Communications
8945 Guilford Rd., Ste. 145
Columbia, MD 21046
Ph: (410)309-8200
Free: 888-253-2762
Fax: (410)630-3980
Co. E-mail: train@eeicom.com
URL: http://www.eeicom.com/eei-training-services
URL(s): www.cvent.com/events/web-development-eei-training-classes/agenda-184c1fdbc5694fadb784e04629977899.aspx. **Price:** $497.00. **Description:** Covers the fundamentals of Web page design, including formatting text, using graphics in a Web page, creating links, making simple tables in HTML, and avoiding common page design flaws. **Audience:** web developers and programmers. **Dates and Locations:** Columbia, MD; Silver Spring, MD; and Alexandria, VA. **Telecommunication Services:** train@eeicom.com.

35667 ■ (X)HTML and CSS II (Onsite)
EEI Communications
8945 Guilford Rd., Ste. 145
Columbia, MD 21046
Ph: (410)309-8200
Free: 888-253-2762
Fax: (410)630-3980
Co. E-mail: train@eeicom.com
URL: http://www.eeicom.com/eei-training-services
URL(s): www.cvent.com/events/web-development-eei-training-classes/agenda-184c1fdbc5694fadb784e04629977899.aspx. **Price:** $497.00. **Description:** Covers intermediate Web page design techniques, including creating forms, including radio buttons and check boxes, creating transparent and interlaced GIFs, using tables for page layout, and creating client-side image maps. **Audience:** web developers and programmers. **Dates and Locations:** Columbia, MD; Silver Spring, MD; and Alexandria, VA. **Telecommunication Services:** train@eeicom.com.

35668 ■ (X)HTML and CSS III (Onsite)
EEI Communications
8945 Guilford Rd., Ste. 145
Columbia, MD 21046
Ph: (410)309-8200
Free: 888-253-2762
Fax: (410)630-3980
Co. E-mail: train@eeicom.com
URL: http://www.eeicom.com/eei-training-services
URL(s): www.cvent.com/events/web-development-eei-training-classes/agenda-184c1fdbc5694fadb784e04629977899.aspx. **Price:** $497.00. **Description:** Covers advanced Web page development techniques, including using frames, animated GIFs, cascading style sheets, and Java Script. **Audience:** Web developers and program-

mers. **Dates and Locations:** Columbia, MD; Silver Spring, MD; and Alexandria, VA. **Telecommunication Services:** train@eeicom.com.

REFERENCE WORKS

35669 ■ "2015 Marketing Calendar for Real Estate Pros: Own It"
Pub: CreateSpace
Contact: Daren Giles, President
Released: October 14, 2014. **Price:** $24.95 paperback. **Description:** Real estate agents, mortgage loan agents, and new home builders and site and listing agents are shown how to use low-cost, high yield, proven marketing techniques to create digital real estate listings, find more customers, and sell more homes. Advice for building a brand and public relations; attracting renters and buyers; developing a good Website; and a digital marketing plan are explained.

35670 ■ "All About Pay Per Click: Learn The Most Effective Way Of Using PPC Advertising"
Pub: CreateSpace
Contact: Daren Giles, President
Released: October 10, 2014. **Price:** $5.75 paperback. **Description:** Pay Per Click advertising is explained to help businesses develop a marketing campaign and use successful pay per click advertising to increase sales, customers and revenue.

35671 ■ "BofA Fights To Keep Top Spot in Mobile Banking" in Charlotte Business Journal (Vol. 27, June 15, 2012, No. 13, pp. 1)
Pub: American City Business Journals, Inc.
Contact: Whitney Shaw, President
Ed: Adam O'Daniel. **Released:** June 15, 2012. **Description:** Bank of America has been fighting to maintain its lead in mobile banking services. Financial institutions, payment processors and e-commerce firms have started offering mobile banking services.

35672 ■ "Chic, Cheap -- And Honest" in Entrepreneur (September 2014)
Pub: Entrepreneurial Press
Released: September 2014. **Description:** Michael Preysman, founder and CEO of online apparel company, Everlane, admits to experiencing difficulties when launching the site in 2011. The 29-year-old entrepreneur started Everlane based on the principle that consumer education is the way to build the brand. he explains how they keep prices low and why clothing never goes on sale.

35673 ■ "Connect: 100 Mind-Blowing Strategies to Use Social Media and Drive Business Growth"
Pub: Amazon Digital Services
Released: September 29, 2014. **Price:** $2.99. **Description:** Marketing and sales strategies to help small businesses grow using social media are presented. Interviews with hundreds of entrepreneurs using the Internet to drive sales are included.

35674 ■ "Crowdfunding Author Thinks Google Will Beat Facebook to the Punch on InvestP2P Acquisition" in GlobeNewswire (July 17, 2012)
Released: July 17, 2012. **Description:** Author, Mark Kanter, explores the potentials of crowdfunding Websites, especially InvestP2P (aka: peer to peer lending) in his new book, "Street Smart CEO". Invest P2P has social networking tools built into its system. Kanter predicts Google to acquire InvestP2P.

35675 ■ "CrowdFunding Made Simple Conference at University of Utah Ignites Ecosystem of Entrepreneurs and Investors" in Economics Week (June 29, 2012)
Pub: NewsRX
Contact: Susan E. Hasty, Publisher
Released: June 29, 2012. **Description:** The first national conference on crowdfunding was held at the University of Utah Guest House and Conference Center May 31 through June 1, 2012. The event, CrowdFunding Made Simple, gathered entrepreneurs, business owners, professional service providers, investors, government officials and students to

provide understanding and potential of crowdfunding, including information on the Jumpstart Our Business Startups (JOBS) Act.

35676 ■ "Digital Marketing: Integrating Strategy and Tactics with Values, A Guidebook for Executives, Managers, and Students"
Pub: Routledge
Contact: Kevin Bradley, President
E-mail: kbradley@taylorandfrancis.com
Released: October 22, 2014. **Price:** $38.95 paperback. **Description:** Guidebook filled with information on the latest digital marketing tactics and strategic insights to help small businesses generate sustainable growth and achieve competitive advantage through digital integration. A five-step program: mindset, model, strategy, implementation, and sustainability is explained.

35677 ■ "Edmond Business iCelebrateDiversity.com Tries Crowdfunding" in Journal Record (July 5, 2012)
Pub: Dolan Media
Ed: Brian Brus. **Released:** July 5, 2012. **Description:** iCelebrateDiversity helped a jelly-bean supplier secure $10,000 in donations through an online crowdfunding site called IndieGoGo.com. Entrepreneurial startups, charities, filmmakers, and other artists are receiving funding through the crowdfunding site. Details of recent crowdfunding projects by IndieGoGo.com are explained.

35678 ■ "Equity Crowdfunding Platform Initial Crowd Offering, Inc. Closes Equity Financing with Third-Party Investor" in GlobeNewswire (July 18, 2012)
Pub: COMTEX News Network Inc.
Contact: Chip Brian, President
Released: July 18, 2012. **Description:** Initial Crowd Offering Inc. closed third-party equity financing round hat provided capital to finish development of its equity crowdfunding portal to the Website. A private angel investor provided development costs to promote the firm's marketing program. Discussion on equity crowdfunding is included.

35679 ■ "The Everything Store: Jeff Bezos and the Age of Amazon"
Pub: Little, Brown and Company
Released: October 17, 2013. **Price:** $28.00. **Description:** Amazon.com started as a bookseller, a company delivering books through the mail. Today, the online store, offers a limitless selection of goods at competitively low prices. Profile of entrepreneur Jeff Bezos that outlines his endless pursuit of new markets and risky new ventures to transform retail.

35680 ■ "Fortunetellers" in Entrepreneur (July 2014)
Pub: Entrepreneur Media Inc.
Released: July 2014. **Description:** Mike Leikin, manager of data and cloud operations for iSeatz, explains how to make predictive analytics work for business. Leikin says the goal of predictive analytics is to maximize every sales opportunity by understanding customer needs. Predictive analytics should focus on incremental improvements and business intelligence software should be used. Interested business owners must make sure data is accurate, the analysis is correct and the outcomes actively monitored.

35681 ■ "FutureDash Launches IndieGoGo Crowdfunding Campaign for the EnergyBuddy Home Energy Monitoring System" in Benzinga.com (June 21, 2012)
Pub: Benzinga.com
Contact: Kyle Bazzy, President
Released: June 21, 2012. **Description:** FutureDash launched its campaign on IndieGoGo to promote its home energy monitoring system called EnergyBuddy. The system monitors the amount of electricity being used in the home or building. Information and control is available through an iPhone, iPad, Android smartphone or computer screen or anywhere on a secure Internet connection.

35682 ■ "H&R Block Launches One-of-a-Kind Tax Preparation Solution: Block Live" in Investment Weekly News (February 4, 2012, pp. 384)
Pub: NewsRX
Contact: Susan E. Hasty, Publisher
Released: February 4, 2012. Description: Block Live, H&R Blocks latest offering, allows taxpayers to have their tax return prepared by an H&R Block tax professional in real time usng an online video conferencing or chat venue. H&R Block is offering a $100 discount for those using virtual tax preparation service. Details of the new program are provided.

35683 ■ "Hoop Culture Opens Showroom, Expands Reach Globally" in Orlando Business Journal (Vol. 30, February 28, 2014, No. 36, pp. 3)
Pub: American City Business Journals
Released: February 28, 2014. Description: Hoop Culture Inc. president, Mike Brown, shares how the online basketball apparel retailer/wholesaler online store has expanded globally. He mentions that Orlando, Florida is one of their biggest markets.

35684 ■ "How I Started an Online Furniture Business" in Baltimore Business Journal (Vol. 31, April 25, 2014, No. 52, pp. 26)
Pub: American City Business Journals, Inc.
Contact: Whitney Shaw, President
Released: April 25, 2014. Description: Andrew Lalia, CEO and founder of Kids Furniture Solutions, explains how he has slowly created a successful business selling children's furniture online. Lalia, who is also a school teacher, asserts that managing shipping costs is the biggest challenge facing his Internet retail business.

35685 ■ "Infectious Behavior" in Entrepreneur (May 2014)
Pub: Entrepreneur Media Inc.
Released: May 2014. Description: Companies use different viral marketing strategies to create campaigns that compel consumers to share content in their social media platforms. Fast-food chain Chipolte Mexican Grill teamed up with Moonbot Studios for an animated short film to raise awareness of its long-running 'Food With Integrity' sustainable farming campaign. The 'Real Beauty Sketches' promotional video of Dove aims to emphasize the difference between how women view themselves and what others see. Evian used the concept of animated babies performing outlandish stunts in its advertisements.

35686 ■ "Information Technology Changes Roles, Highlights Hiring Needs" in South Florida Business Journal (Vol. 34, February 14, 2014, No. 30, pp. 3)
Pub: American City Business Journals
Released: February 14, 2014. Description: Results of the Steven Douglas Associates survey of 218 senior and mid-level information technology executives in South Florida are presented. About 75 percent of the respondents cited cloud services, mobile technologies, big data and enterprise reporting planning as having the most profound impact on their roles. The challenges they face with the expected hiring growth are also examined.

35687 ■ "Initial Crowd Offering, Inc. Announces Launch of Equity Crowdfunding Intermediary Site" in GlobeNewswire (June 21, 2012)
Released: June 21, 2012. Description: Initial Crowd Offering is the IPO for small and emerging businesses and is the most current process to invest and raise capital. The site allows direct, real-time investments in exchange for equity ownership.

35688 ■ "Marketing To Go" in Entrepreneur (June 2014)
Pub: Entrepreneur Media Inc.
Released: June 2014. Description: Mobile applications can help entrepreneurs improve their marketing strategies and business productivity. The 30/30 application helps users increase productivity by helping them organize and manage their tasks. The Cal application represents an upgrade to a smartphone's built-in calendar, particularly with its integration with contacts and social media accounts. The Pocket applications allows users to save interesting articles, videos and other online content for later reading or viewing. The Buffer application enables users to manage their social media accounts from a single interface.

35689 ■ "The Mechanics of Sharing" in Entrepreneur (May 2014)
Pub: Entrepreneur Media Inc.
Released: May 2014. Description: Jonah Berger, marketing professor and author of 'Contagious: Why Things Catch On', explains the science behind viral media success. He identifies six key drivers of going viral online which are social currency, triggers, emotion, public, practical value and stories. He notes that many companies and organizations make the mistake of chasing good content without understanding how it will benefit the brand. He advises small business owners to understand why people share regardless of the technology they are using.

35690 ■ "The Moment as Currency" in Entrepreneur (September 2014)
Pub: Entrepreneurial Press
Released: September 2014. Description: Young entrepreneur, Brian Wong, recalls how he came up with the idea of launching the mobile rewards network Kiip in 2010. The 23-year-old believed brands could take advantage of the achievements reached by mobile application users by offering rewards through his mobile rewards network. the company's network of 1,000 brands pay on a cost-per-engagement (CPE) basis and earns from 30 cents to $3 per CEP. Wong insists that his technology is not limited to just the smartphone or the application.

35691 ■ "A Neat Social Trade" in (Vol. 92, July 23, 2012, No. 30, pp. 23)
Pub: Dow Jones & Co., Inc.
Contact: Clare Hart, President
Ed: Theresa W. Carey. Released: July 23, 2012. Description: SocialTrade is a Website that allows users to exchange ideas and data with each other through video. Online broker DittoTrade launched a mobile applications that allows investors to connect to other traders and follow their trades.

35692 ■ "Online Directories: Your Silent Sales Staff" in South Florida Business Journal (Vol. 34, June 20, 2014, No. 48, pp. 14)
Pub: American City Business Journals
Released: June 20, 2014. Description: The benefits of using online business directories as an extension of the physical sales personnel are explained. Business owners who plan to use online directories to their advantage need to check their listings and links at least once a year and whenever there is a change to the business.

35693 ■ "PeoplesVC Links Its Stock Crowdfunding Site with LinkedIn" in Health & Beauty Close-Up (July 5, 2012)
Pub: Close-Up Media
Released: July 5, 2012. Description: PeoplesVC has introduced crowdfunding into its LinkedIn professional networking tool. PeoplesVC developed an online calculator tool that helps investors invest in Crownfunded businesses. The JOBS Act has legalized stock offerings up to $1 million from startups and existing small businesses directly to the public.

35694 ■ "Publicity Turns Colorado Springs-based Toy-Rental Business Marketing Into Child's Play" in Colorado Springs Business Journal (January 20, 2012)
Pub: Dolan Media
Ed: Amy Gillentine. Released: January 20, 2012. Description: Profile of Stephanie Weber and her Internet toy rental business she launched in 2007. The firm operates on the Netflix model, where customers purchase memberships costing approximately $20 per month. Toys are selected, shipped and returned. Weber's husband partnered with her in this business venture.

35695 ■ "Putting Down Roots" in Entrepreneur (August 2014)
Pub: Entrepreneur Media Inc.
Released: August 2014. Description: Entrepreneur Justin Hartfield and partner Doug Francis created Weedmaps.com, an online portal for marijuana dispensaries, after California legalized the sale of medical marijuana. Hartfield is looking forward to a billion-dollar business once the federal prohibition of marijuana is ended. Local dispensaries pay a monthly subscription of $420 to appear on the site while doctors pay $295 to be featured on the site. Harfield is seeking partnerships with lboratories that will provide marijuana testing and other services.

35696 ■ "Spanish Company to Offer Free Wi-Fi In Miami-Dade County" in South Florida Business Journal (Vol. 34, April 25, 2014, No. 40)
Pub: American City Business Journals
Released: April 25, 2014. Description: GOWEX a Madrid-based company, is offering free Wi-Fi access at 400 public spots in Miami, Florida. The firm will sell advertising over the Wi-Fi network. It has offered similar free access to users in New York, NY and in San Francisco, CA.

35697 ■ "Truffles & Trifles' Marci Arthur Plans YouTube Channel, Cookbook" in Orlando Business Journal (Vol. 30, May 2, 2014, No. 45, pp. 3)
Pub: American City Business Journals
Released: May 2, 2014. Description: Marci Arthur, founder of Truffles & Trifles Cooking School, plans to create a YouTube channel and publish a cookbook. Arthur believes that the survival of her business can be attributed to the devotion and integrity of her employees. Reports show that the school has been receiving donations from sponsors such as Wolf Appliances and Sub-Zero.

35698 ■ "Ultimate Guide to Google AdWords: How to Access 100 Million People in 10 Minutes"
Pub: Entrepreneur Press
Released: October 1, 2014. Price: $24.95 paperback. Description: Google AdWords experts and analytics specialist present the techniques, tools, and tricks for using Google AdWords. The experts help small businesses to write advertising and Website copy design, work into difficult markets, advertise, increase search engine presence, bid strategies for online auctions, financial budgeting and more.

35699 ■ "What Makes a Great Tweet" in Harvard Business Review (Vol. 90, May 2012, No. 5, pp. 36)
Pub: Harvard Business Review Press
Contact: Peter E. Walsh, Director
Ed: Paul Andre, Kurt Luther. Released: May 2012. Description: A chart uses readership approval percentages to identify the most effective uses of Twitter. Best tweets include amusing random thoughts and self promotion; worst include complaints and presence maintenance.

35700 ■ "Wooing Money From THE MASSES" in Baltimore Business Journal (Vol. 32, July 4, 2014, No. 9, pp. 12)
Pub: American City Business Journals, Inc.
Contact: Whitney Shaw, President
Released: July 4, 2014. Description: Crowdfunding is a new fundraising trend for entrepreneurs and artists where users post their projects online, allowing any interested party to contribute to a business idea. Crowdfunding investment sites like Crowdfunder and AngelList allow contributors to become investors or shareholders, while Websites like Kickstarter and Indiegogo are donation-based.

35701 ■ "Yodle To Hire Hundreds Here" in Austin Business Journal (Vol. 32, July 20, 2012, No. 20, pp. 1)
Pub: American City Business Journals, Inc.
Contact: Whitney Shaw, President
Ed: Jan Buchholz. Released: July 20, 2012. Description: Internet marketing firm Yodle Inc. plans to employ more than 800 people in the Austin, Texas

area as part of its expansion plan. The company, which already employs nearly 400 people, leased nearly 100,000 square feet at Plaza 35 in North Austin.

35702 ■ *"Your Facebook Posts, Optimized' in Inc. (Vol. 34, September 2012, No. 7, pp. 46)*
Pub: Mansueto Ventures L.L.C.
Contact: John Koten, Chief Executive Officer
Ed: Jillian D'Onfro. **Released:** September 2012. **Description:** PostRocket is a new service that increases awareness on Facebook. The software will analyze which posts get the most Likes, Shares, and Comments and offers suggestions on when and how often posts should be published, subject matter to feature, and whether to include links, videos, and photos.

35703 ■ *"The Zero Marginal Cost Society: The Internet of Things, the Collaborative Commons, and the Eclipse of Capitalism"*
Pub: Palgrave Macmillan
Contact: Lisa Dunn, Manager
E-mail: l.dunn@palgrave.com
Released: April 1, 2014. **Price:** $28.00. **Description:** The emerging Internet of things is speeding society to an ear of nearly free goods and services, causing the rise of a global Collaborative Commons and the eclipse of capitalism. Entrepreneurial dynamism of competitive markets that drives productivity up and marginal costs down, enabling businesses to reduce the price of their goods and services to win consumers and market share is slowly dying.

CONSULTANTS

35704 ■ Creative Computer Resources Inc. (CCR)
5001 Horizons Dr., Ste. 200
Columbus, OH 43220-5291
Ph: (614)384-7557
Free: 866-720-0209
Fax: (614)573-6331
Co. E-mail: team@planet-ccr.com
URL: http://www.planet-ccr.com
Contact: M. Erik Mueller, President
E-mail: merikm@planet-ccr.com
Scope: Offers information systems support, custom software development, website design, development and implementation. Provides information technology support and management services to small and mid-size businesses. **Founded:** 1996.

RESEARCH CENTERS

35705 ■ Corporation for Enterprise Development (CFED)
1200 G St. NW, Ste. 400
Washington, DC 20005
Ph: (202)408-9788
Fax: (202)408-9793
Co. E-mail: info@cfed.org
URL: http://www.cfed.org
Contact: Andrea Levere, President
E-mail: alevere@cfed.org
Description: Provides assistance to public and private organizations concerned with increasing economic opportunity of individuals through the encouragement and support of enterprise development; serves as a forum for the exchange of ideas. Strives to research, develop, and disseminate entrepreneurial policy initiatives at the local, state, and federal levels. Conducts consulting services and compiles statistics. **Scope:** Offers expertise in economic research. Offers services as identify promising ideas, test and refine them in communities to find out what works, craft policies and products to help good ideas reach scale, and foster new markets to achieve greater economic impact. **Founded:** 1979. **Publications:** "Children's Savings Accounts and Financial Aid"; "Linking Youth Savings and Entrepreneurship". **Educational Activities:** CFED Assets Learning Conference (Biennial). **Seminars:** Fighting Poverty: The Role of Asset Building in Public Policy; IDAS and Microenterprise; Self-Sustaining IDA Initiatives; Serving Multi-Cultural Markets; Asset Purchase Effective Practices; Policy Proposals, Opportunities, and Barriers for Youth Savings.

35706 ■ University of California, Los Angeles - Anderson Graduate School of Management - Harold and Pauline Price Center for

Entrepreneurial Studies
110 Westwood Plz., Rm. C305
Los Angeles, CA 90095-1481
Ph: (310)825-2985
Fax: (310)206-9102
Co. E-mail: esctr@anderson.ucla.edu
URL: http://www.anderson.ucla.edu/centers/price
Contact: Elaine K. Hagan, Executive Director
E-mail: elaine.hagan@anderson.ucla.edu
Scope: Entrepreneurship, venture initiation, family business, and interdisciplinary studies of business development, including finance, operations, information systems, organization, behavior, and oral histories of entrepreneurs. Sponsors certificate programs in management development for entrepreneurs in various industries. **Founded:** 1987. **Educational Activities:** Annual entrepreneurship conference for business people and students, in the spring; Research grants for selected faculty members for entrepreneurially related work; Roundtable sessions, entrepreneur-in-residence series, mentor programs, speaker series, venture proposal competitions, and student investment fund; Venture Fellows Program.

35707 ■ University of South Florida - Small Business Development Center (SBDC)
1101 Channelside Dr., Ste. 210
Tampa, FL 33602
Ph: (813)905-5800
Fax: (813)905-5801
URL: http://www.sbdctampabay.com
Contact: Eileen Rodriguez, Director
Scope: Small business operations, entrepreneurship, and success and failure factors for small business development and management, including developing business plans, marketing strategy, and loan packages. **Services:** Counseling. **Founded:** 1980. **Publications:** *Entrepreneurial Training Schedule* (Monthly); *Minding Your Own Business* (3/year). **Educational Activities:** SBDC Entrepreneurship seminars; SBDC Government contracting trade fair; SBDC Seminars on Small Business Management (Monthly); SBDC Small Business Trade Conference; SBDC Training; SBDC Women Executive Forum.

START-UP INFORMATION

35708 ■ *75 Green Businesses You Can Start to Make Money and Make a Difference*
Pub: Entrepreneur Press
Ed: Glenn Croston. **Released:** August 01, 2008.
Price: $19.95, paperback. **Description:** Descriptions of seventy-five environmentally-friendly business start-ups are presented.

35709 ■ *"EDCO Doling Out Capital Along Border" in Austin Business JournalInc. (Vol. 28, August 1, 2008, No. 20, pp. 1)*
Pub: American City Business Journals
Ed: Sandra Zaragoza. **Description:** Non-profit business incubator Economic Development Catalyst Organization Ventures is searching for promising startup companies. The company is targeting startups in green energy, technology and consumer markets. EDCO has partnered with consumer electronics repair company CherryFusion and technology firm MiniDonations.

35710 ■ *"Green Acre$ Tope 10 Green Biz To Start Right Now" in Small Business Opportunities (September 2010)*
Pub: Harris Publications Inc.
Description: A list of the top ten green businesses to start in 2010 is provided.

35711 ■ *"Green Clean Machine" in Small Business Opportunities (Winter 2010)*
Pub: Harris Publications Inc.
Description: Eco-friendly maid franchise plans to grow its $62 million sales base. Profile of Maid Brigade, a green-cleaning franchise is planning to expand across the country.

35712 ■ *Starting Green: An Ecopreneur's Toolkit for Starting a Green Business From Business Plans to Profits*
Pub: Entrepreneur Press
Contact: Perlman Neil, President
Ed: Glenn E. Croston. **Released:** 2009. **Description:** Entrepreneur and scientist outline green business essentials and helps uncover eco-friendly business opportunities, build a sustainable business plan, and gain the competitive advantage.

35713 ■ *"Sustainable Advantage" in Inc. (Vol. 36, September 2014, No. 7, pp. 86)*
Pub: Mansueto Ventures L.L.C.
Contact: John Koten, Chief Executive Officer
Released: September 2014. **Description:** Four startup companies committed to providing sustainable, eco-friendly products and services while protecting the environment and bettering human health are profiled. Holganix(TM) offers organic lawn care products; Motiv Power Systems electrifies large vehicles; Clean Energy Collective Solar Power builds lareg community solar panel arrays; and Protein Bar offers healthy alternatives to fast food in its chain of restaurants. The company also works with nonprofits focused on wellness and education and has created 167 Learning Gardens nationwide.

ASSOCIATIONS AND OTHER ORGANIZATIONS

35714 ■ *Between the Issues*
2705 Fern Ln.
Halifax, NS, Canada B3K 4L3
Ph: (902)429-2202
Fax: (902)405-3716
Co. E-mail: info@ecologyaction.ca
URL: http://www.ecologyaction.ca
Contact: Maggy Burns, Director
URL(s): www.ecologyaction.ca/between-issues. **Released:** Periodic **Price:** included in membership dues.

35715 ■ **Canadian Association on Water Quality (CAWQ) [Association canadienne sur la qualite de l'eau (ACQE)]**
PO Box 5050
Burlington, ON, Canada L7R 4A6
Ph: (289)780-0378
Co. E-mail: members@cawq.ca
URL: http://www.cawq.ca
Contact: Mr. Clayton Tiedemann, President
E-mail: ctiedema@epcor.ca
Description: Corporations, learned societies, universities, organizations, and individuals. Promotes research on water quality and water pollution. Furthers the exchange of information and practical application of such research for public benefit. **Founded:** 1967. **Publications:** *Water Quality Research Journal of Canada* (Quarterly). **Awards:** Philip H. Jones Award (Annual).

35716 ■ **Canadian Environmental Network (CEN) [Reseau canadien de l'environment (RCEN)]**
1 Nicholas St., Ste. 1510
Ottawa, ON, Canada K1N 7B7
Ph: (613)728-9810
Free: 855-200-2463
Co. E-mail: info@rcen.ca
URL: http://www.rcen.ca
Contact: Josh Brandon, Chairman
Description: Environmental organizations. Seeks to advance the projects and activities of members. Promotes ecologically sustainable development. Serves as a clearinghouse on environmental issues; provides support and assistance to members. **Founded:** 1988. **Publications:** *Canadian Environmental Network News* (Periodic). **Awards:** Caucus Achievement Award (Annual).

35717 ■ *Canadian Environmental Network News*
1 Nicholas St., Ste. 1510
Ottawa, ON, Canada K1N 7B7
Ph: (613)728-9810
Free: 855-200-2463
Co. E-mail: info@rcen.ca
URL: http://www.rcen.ca
Contact: Josh Brandon, Chairman
Released: Periodic

35718 ■ **Canadian Water Resources Association (CWRA) [Association Canadienne des Resources Hydriques (ACRH)]**
9 Corvus Ct.
Ottawa, ON, Canada K2E 7Z4
Ph: (613)237-9363
Fax: (613)594-5190
Co. E-mail: services@aic.ca
URL: http://www.cwra.org
Contact: Andre Saint-Hilaire, President
E-mail: andre_st-hilaire@ete.inrs.ca
Description: Corporations, government agencies, public libraries, and individuals with an interest in water resources. Seeks to increase public awareness and understanding of water resources; serves as a forum for the exchange of information relating to their management and use. Encourages governments at all levels to recognize the importance of water as a resource and supports formulation of appropriate water use policies. Conducts educational programs. **Founded:** 1947. **Publications:** *Canadian Water Resources Journal* (Quarterly); *CWRA Water News* (Quarterly). **Educational Activities:** Canadian Water Resources Association Conference (Annual). **Awards:** Hoskin Scientific Award (Annual); Canadian Water Resources Association Scholarships; Ken Thomson Scholarships; CWRA Scholarships in Water Resources (Annual); Ken Thompson Scholarship (Annual).

35719 ■ *Canadian Water Resources Journal*
9 Corvus Ct.
Ottawa, ON, Canada K2E 7Z4
Ph: (613)237-9363
Fax: (613)594-5190
Co. E-mail: services@aic.ca
URL: http://www.cwra.org
Contact: Andre Saint-Hilaire, President
E-mail: andre_st-hilaire@ete.inrs.ca
Released: Quarterly **Price:** C$25, /copy; Free to members; online.

35720 ■ **Compost Council of Canada [Conseil Canadien du Compost]**
16, rue Northumberland St.
Toronto, ON, Canada M6H 1P7
Ph: (416)535-0240
Free: 877-571-4769
Fax: (416)536-9892
Co. E-mail: info@compost.org
URL: http://www.compost.org
Contact: Susan Antler, Executive Director
Description: Serves to advocate and advance composting and compost usage across Canada. Serves as the central resource and network for the composting industry in Canada. Contributes to the environmental sustainability of communities. Sponsors International Composting Awareness Week; "Plant a Row Grow a Row". Conducts seminars and educational programs. Compiles statistics, maintains speakers' bureau. **Founded:** 1991. **Publications:** *Compost Council of Canada Communique.*

35721 ■ _Compost Council of Canada Communique_
16, rue Northumberland St.
Toronto, ON, Canada M6H 1P7
Ph: (416)535-0240
Free: 877-571-4769
Fax: (416)536-9892
Co. E-mail: info@compost.org
URL: http://www.compost.org
Contact: Susan Antler, Executive Director

35722 ■ _CWRA Water News_
9 Corvus Ct.
Ottawa, ON, Canada K2E 7Z4
Ph: (613)237-9363
Fax: (613)594-5190
Co. E-mail: services@aic.ca
URL: http://www.cwra.org
Contact: Andre Saint-Hilaire, President
E-mail: andre_st-hilaire@ete.inrs.ca
Released: Quarterly **Price:** C$5, /copy.

35723 ■ Ecology Action Centre (EAC) [Centre d'Action Écologique]
2705 Fern Ln.
Halifax, NS, Canada B3K 4L3
Ph: (902)429-2202
Fax: (902)405-3716
Co. E-mail: info@ecologyaction.ca
URL: http://www.ecologyaction.ca
Contact: Maggy Burns, Director
Description: Works to develop solutions to ecological problems. Fosters communication between members. **Scope:** Environmental issues, including acid rain, deforestation, hazardous wastes, recycling, nuclear power, ecosystem stability, species extinction, global warming, pesticides, and waste management. **Services:** Briefs preparation and research: on ocean habitat and biodiversity. **Founded:** 1971. **Publications:** _Between the Issues_ (Periodic); _Between the Issues Newsletter_ (Bimonthly). **Educational Activities:** Educational workshops, on environmental and science topics; Diverse volunteer opportunities; Environment and Development Group Meetings.

35724 ■ _Enviro Business Guide_
PO Box 23
Bluffton, AB, Canada T0C 0M0
Ph: (403)843-6563
Fax: (403)843-4156
Co. E-mail: info@recycle.ab.ca
URL: http://www.recycle.ab.ca
Contact: Sharon Howland, President
URL(s): www.recycle.ab.ca/ebguide. **Price:** free for members.

35725 ■ _For R Information_
127 Wyndham St. N, Ste. 100
Guelph, ON, Canada N1H 4E9
Ph: (519)823-1990
Fax: (519)823-0084
Co. E-mail: mwa@municipalwaste.ca
URL: http://www.municipalwaste.ca
Contact: Sue McCrae, Director
Released: Quarterly

35726 ■ Green Hotels Association
1611 Mossy Stone Dr.
Houston, TX 77077-4109
Ph: (713)789-8889
Fax: (713)789-9786
Co. E-mail: green@greenhotels.com
URL: http://greenhotels.com
Contact: Patricia Griffin, President
Description: Hotels, motels, inns, bed and breakfasts, and all other lodging establishments with an interest in protecting the environment. Encourages, promotes and supports ecological consciousness in the hospitality industry. **Founded:** 1993. **Publications:** _Greening Newsletter_ (Bimonthly); _Membership Conservation Guidelines and Ideas_ (Quadrennial).

35727 ■ Municipal Waste Association (MWA)
127 Wyndham St. N, Ste. 100
Guelph, ON, Canada N1H 4E9
Ph: (519)823-1990

Fax: (519)823-0084
Co. E-mail: mwa@municipalwaste.ca
URL: http://www.municipalwaste.ca
Contact: Sue McCrae, Director
Description: Municipal waste management professionals. Promotes more effective and environmentally sustainable removal of solid wastes. Facilitates sharing of municipal waste management, reduction, recycling, and reuse information and facilities. Conducts continuing professional education courses for members; operates job hotline; represents members' interests before government agencies and the public. Sponsors research; compiles statistics. **Founded:** 1987. **Publications:** _For R Information_ (Quarterly). **Awards:** Promotion and Education Awards (Annual).

35728 ■ Pellet Fuels Institute (PFI)
1901 N Moore St., Ste. 600
Arlington, VA 22209-1708
Ph: (703)522-6778
Fax: (703)522-0548
Co. E-mail: pfimail@pelletheat.org
URL: http://www.pelletheat.org
Contact: Scott Jacobs, President
E-mail: sjacobs1@agrirecycle.com
Description: Pellet and briquette manufacturers; processors of wood, and agricultural fuels; pellet burner manufacturers and distributors; combustion and handling equipment manufacturers and distributors; industry suppliers; and companies and organizations that use wood, agricultural residues, and paper as fuel. Promotes the increased use of pellets, briquettes, chips, and other renewable fiber fuels. Supports lobbying efforts promoting fiber fuels. Acts as an information clearinghouse among members. **Founded:** 1982. **Publications:** _PFI Newsletter_ (Quarterly).

35729 ■ Pembina Institute
219-19 St. NW
Calgary, AB, Canada T2N 2H9
Ph: (403)269-3344
Fax: (403)269-3377
Co. E-mail: info@pembina.org
URL: http://www.pembina.org
Contact: Ed Whittingham, Executive Director
Description: Organizations and individuals with an interest in environmental protection and global development. Promotes increased public awareness of environmental and development issues. Conducts environmental research and educational programs; provides corporate environmental strategic management services, sponsors charitable activities. **Scope:** Sustainable energy. **Founded:** 1985. **Publications:** _Electronic newsletter_ (Monthly); _Pembina Institute Annual report_ (Annual).

35730 ■ Planetary Association for Clean Energy (PACE) - Clean Energy Centre [Societe Planetaire pour l'Assainissement de l'Energie]
100 Bronson Ave., Ste. 1001
Ottawa, ON, Canada K1R 6G8
Ph: (613)236-6265
Fax: (613)235-5876
Co. E-mail: paceincnet@gmail.com
URL: http://pacenet.homestead.com
Contact: Andrew Michrowski, President
Description: Researchers, individuals, corporations, and institutions worldwide seeking to facilitate research, development, demonstration, and evaluation of clean energy systems. Defines clean energy systems as those that utilize natural sources, and are inexpensive, non-polluting, and universally applicable. Concerns include the bioeffects of low-level electromagnetics, bioenergetics, new energy technology, decontamination of nuclear and toxic wastes, production of clean water from ambient air, and pesticide and fertilizer-free ultra-productive agricultural practices. Tests and recommends products that facilitate the implementation of clean energy systems. Serves as a consultant to governments and other agencies. Maintains speaker's bureau. **Scope:** New energy technologies; bioeffects of electromagnetic fields. **Services:** Interlibrary loan; copying; center

open to the public. **Founded:** 1975. **Holdings:** 10,000 books; 500 bound periodical volumes; emerging energy science and technology manuscripts.

35731 ■ Pollution Probe Foundation
150 Ferrand Dr., Ste. 208
Toronto, ON, Canada M3C 3E5
Ph: (416)926-1907
Free: 877-926-1907
Fax: (416)926-1601
Co. E-mail: pprobe@pollutionprobe.org
URL: http://www.pollutionprobe.org
Contact: Bob Oliver, Chief Executive Officer
Description: Works to define environmental problems through research; seeks to raise public awareness of environmental issues through education; lobbies for environmental protection and remediation before government agencies and industrial associations. Focuses on smog and climate change, reduction and elimination of mercury in water, child health and the environment, indoor air quality, and water quality. **Scope:** Environmental problems. **Founded:** 1969. **Publications:** _ProbeAbilities_ (Quarterly); _Pollution Probe Reports_; _Probe Post: Canada's Environmental Magazine_ (Quarterly); _P2 - Exclusive Donor Newsletter_ (Quarterly).

35732 ■ _ProbeAbilities_
150 Ferrand Dr., Ste. 208
Toronto, ON, Canada M3C 3E5
Ph: (416)926-1907
Free: 877-926-1907
Fax: (416)926-1601
Co. E-mail: pprobe@pollutionprobe.org
URL: http://www.pollutionprobe.org
Contact: Bob Oliver, Chief Executive Officer
Released: Quarterly **Price:** available to members only.

35733 ■ _RCA Connector_
PO Box 23
Bluffton, AB, Canada T0C 0M0
Ph: (403)843-6563
Fax: (403)843-4156
Co. E-mail: info@recycle.ab.ca
URL: http://www.recycle.ab.ca
Contact: Sharon Howland, President
URL(s): www.recycle.ab.ca/connector. **Released:** Quarterly **Price:** Included in membership.

35734 ■ Recycling Council of Alberta (RCA)
PO Box 23
Bluffton, AB, Canada T0C 0M0
Ph: (403)843-6563
Fax: (403)843-4156
Co. E-mail: info@recycle.ab.ca
URL: http://www.recycle.ab.ca
Contact: Sharon Howland, President
Description: Promotes and facilitates waste reduction, recycling and resource conservation in the province of Alberta. **Founded:** 1987. **Publications:** _RCA Connector_ (Quarterly); _Enviro Business Guide_. **Awards:** R's of Excellence (Annual); Rs of Excellence Awards (Annual).

35735 ■ Resource Efficient Agricultural Production - Canada (REAPC)
21, 111 Lakeshore Rd.
Centennial Ctre. CCB13
Sainte-Anne-de-Bellevue, QC, Canada H9X 3V9
Ph: (514)398-7743
Fax: (514)398-7972
Co. E-mail: info@reap-canada.com
URL: http://www.reap-canada.com
Contact: Roger Samson, Executive Director
Description: Agricultural researchers and educators. Promotes development and implementation of environmentally sustainable and economically viable agricultural techniques in Canada and internationally. Conducts research and disseminates results in areas including ecology, energy, agri-fibre, and food production. Maintains on-farm research programs. **Founded:** 1986. **Educational Activities:** International Agriculture Program.

35736 ■ Saskatchewan Environmental Society (SES)
PO Box 1372
Saskatoon, SK, Canada S7K 3N9

Ph: (306)665-1915
Fax: (306)665-2128
Co. E-mail: info@environmentalsociety.ca
URL: http://www.environmentalsociety.ca
Contact: Allyson Brady, Executive Director
E-mail: allysonb@environmentalsociety.ca
Description: Seeks to support and encourage the creation of a global community in which all needs are met in sustainable ways. **Founded:** 1970. **Publications:** *SES Newsletter* (Bimonthly).

35737 ■ *SES Newsletter*
PO Box 1372
Saskatoon, SK, Canada S7K 3N9
Ph: (306)665-1915
Fax: (306)665-2128
Co. E-mail: info@environmentalsociety.ca
URL: http://www.environmentalsociety.ca
Contact: Allyson Brady, Executive Director
E-mail: allysonb@environmentalsociety.ca
Released: Bimonthly **Price:** C$40, /subscription; free for members.

35738 ■ Society Promoting Environmental Conservation (SPEC) - Library
2060-B Pine St.
Vancouver, BC, Canada V6J 4P8
Ph: (604)736-7732
Fax: (604)736-7115
Co. E-mail: admin@spec.bc.ca
URL: http://www.spec.bc.ca
Contact: Rob Baxter, President
Description: Promotes environmental research, advocacy, and education. **Scope:** Environmental issues. **Services:** Library open to the public. **Founded:** 1969. **Holdings:** 5000 books, reports, and periodicals. **Publications:** *SPECTRUM* (Quarterly).

35739 ■ *SPECTRUM*
Calzada Mexico-Xochimilco 4985, Colonia Arenal Tepepan
14610 Mexico, Mexico
Ph: 52 55 5227 1800
Fax: 52 55 5227 1891
Contact: Johan de Praeter, Director
Released: Quarterly **Price:** free.

35740 ■ *Walk Softly*
302 Hawkins St.
Whitehorse, YT, Canada Y1A 1X6
Ph: (867)668-5678
Fax: (867)668-6637
Co. E-mail: ycs@ycs.yk.ca
URL: http://www.yukonconservation.org
Contact: Mary Whitley, President
URL(s): www.yukonconservation.org/newsletters.htm. **Released:** Quarterly **Price:** Included in membership; $25, Nonmembers.

35741 ■ *Water Quality Research Journal of Canada*
PO Box 5050
Burlington, ON, Canada L7R 4A6
Ph: (289)780-0378
Co. E-mail: members@cawq.ca
URL: http://www.cawq.ca
Contact: Mr. Clayton Tiedemann, President
E-mail: ctiedema@epcor.ca
URL(s): www.iwaponline.com/wqrjc/aims.htm. **Released:** Quarterly

35742 ■ *Women and Environments*
215 Spadina Ave., Ste. 400
Toronto, ON, Canada M5T 2C7
Ph: (416)928-0880
Fax: (416)644-0116
Co. E-mail: office@womenshealthyenvironments.ca
URL: http://www.womenshealthyenvironments.ca
Contact: Enida Kule, Treasurer
Released: Quarterly **Price:** C$8, /issue; C$21.97, /year.

35743 ■ Women's Healthy Environments Network (WHEN)
215 Spadina Ave., Ste. 400
Toronto, ON, Canada M5T 2C7
Ph: (416)928-0880

Fax: (416)644-0116
Co. E-mail: office@womenshealthyenvironments.ca
URL: http://www.womenshealthyenvironments.ca
Contact: Enida Kule, Treasurer
Description: Women experts in environmental studies and issues. Works to implement community development projects to improve the environment. Provides a forum for discussion, information exchange, and the conducting of research related to women in the fields of planning, health, workplace, design, economy, urban and rural sociology, and community development. Initiates and organizes community projects. Advocates environmental protection, anti-discriminatory zoning practices, and the development of affordable housing. **Founded:** 1994. **Publications:** *Women and Environments* (Quarterly).

35744 ■ Yukon Conservation Society (YCS) - Library
302 Hawkins St.
Whitehorse, YT, Canada Y1A 1X6
Ph: (867)668-5678
Fax: (867)668-6637
Co. E-mail: ycs@ycs.yk.ca
URL: http://www.yukonconservation.org
Contact: Mary Whitley, President
Description: Seeks to protect Canada's natural environment; particularly that of the Yukon region. Encourages the conservation of Yukon wilderness, wildlife and natural resources. **Scope:** Yukon conservation, wildlife conservation, the ecosystem, pollution, climate change. **Services:** Library open to the public for reference use only (books can be borrowed by members). **Founded:** 1968. **Holdings:** 350 books; 20 serials; 900 reports; 50 vertical files; 20 audio/visual items. **Subscriptions:** 5 journals and other serials; 5 newspapers. **Publications:** *Walk Softly* (Quarterly). **Awards:** Ted Parnell Scholarship (Annual).

EDUCATIONAL PROGRAMS

35745 ■ ASTM Phase I & Phase II Environmental Site Assessment Processes (Onsite)
Seminar Information Service Inc.
20 Executive Park, Ste. 120
Irvine, CA 92614
Ph: (949)261-9104
Free: 877-SEM-INFO
Fax: (949)261-1963
Co. E-mail: info@seminarinformation.com
URL: http://www.seminarinformation.com
Description: Gain an understanding how to use the standards and how the standards affect the way you do business. The 'Innocent Landowner Defense' under the Comprehensive Environmental Response, Compensation and Liability Act (CERCLA) and why due diligence is necessary will be covered. **Audience:** Industry professionals.

35746 ■ Climatic Test Techniques (Onsite)
Seminar Information Service Inc.
20 Executive Park, Ste. 120
Irvine, CA 92614
Ph: (949)261-9104
Free: 877-SEM-INFO
Fax: (949)261-1963
Co. E-mail: info@seminarinformation.com
URL: http://www.seminarinformation.com
Description: An introduction to climatic testing with an overview of field test measurement and analysis, with primary emphasis on understanding the physics of each environment, and available measurement and control techniques. **Audience:** Environmental engineering specialists .

35747 ■ Comprehensive 5-Day Training Program For Energy Managers (Onsite)
Seminar Information Service Inc.
20 Executive Park, Ste. 120
Irvine, CA 92614
Ph: (949)261-9104
Free: 877-SEM-INFO

Fax: (949)261-1963
Co. E-mail: info@seminarinformation.com
URL: http://www.seminarinformation.com
Description: Provides detailed coverage of all of the six training areas specified for energy managers in the Energy Policy Act, and offers a comprehensive learning and problem-solving forum for those who want a broader understanding of the latest energy cost reduction techniques and strategies. **Audience:** Industry professionals.

35748 ■ Crude Oil: Sampling, Testing, and Evaluation (Onsite)
Seminar Information Service Inc.
20 Executive Park, Ste. 120
Irvine, CA 92614
Ph: (949)261-9104
Free: 877-SEM-INFO
Fax: (949)261-1963
Co. E-mail: info@seminarinformation.com
URL: http://www.seminarinformation.com
URL(s): www.seminarinformation.com/qqbruu/crude-oil-sampling-testing-and-evaluation. **Description:** Learn how to obtain representative samples of crude oil using automatic and manual methods. Learn the test methods available for obtaining the basic data necessary to determine quantity for custody transfer purposes and conformance to expected quality. **Audience:** Laboratory technicians and chemists. **Telecommunication Services:** info@seminarinformation.com.

35749 ■ DOT Hazardous Materials Training (Onsite)
Seminar Information Service Inc.
20 Executive Park, Ste. 120
Irvine, CA 92614
Ph: (949)261-9104
Free: 877-SEM-INFO
Fax: (949)261-1963
Co. E-mail: info@seminarinformation.com
URL: http://www.seminarinformation.com
URL(s): www.seminarinformation.com/qqaubm/dot-hazardous-materials-training. **Price:** $449. **Description:** DOT is changing virtually all of the rules for hazardous materials containers, labeling, shipping papers, placards, and shipping names. Learn how to comply with the regulations. **Audience:** Shipping supervisors, purchasing managers, traffic managers, plant managers, shipping clerks, dispatchers, purchasing agents, drivers, and compliance managers .

35750 ■ Energy Auditing 101: Identifying Cost Saving Opportunities in Plants & Buildings (Onsite)
Seminar Information Service Inc.
20 Executive Park, Ste. 120
Irvine, CA 92614
Ph: (949)261-9104
Free: 877-SEM-INFO
Fax: (949)261-1963
Co. E-mail: info@seminarinformation.com
URL: http://www.seminarinformation.com
Description: Seminar designed to provide you with the knowledge you need to identify where energy consumption can be reduced, and utilize the latest methods and technologies to accomplish real savings, with emphasis on providing useful calculation methods and practical examples. **Audience:** Industry professionals.

35751 ■ Fundamentals of Carbon Reduction (Onsite)
Seminar Information Service Inc.
20 Executive Park, Ste. 120
Irvine, CA 92614
Ph: (949)261-9104
Free: 877-SEM-INFO
Fax: (949)261-1963
Co. E-mail: info@seminarinformation.com
URL: http://www.seminarinformation.com
URL(s): 15109169. **Price:** $1,450.00. **Description:** First step for organizations that want to become more environmentally-friendly, including how to conduct a 'carbon audit' and how to begin a carbon reduction program.

35752 ■ Gasoline: Specifications, Testing, and Technology (Onsite)
Seminar Information Service Inc.
20 Executive Park, Ste. 120
Irvine, CA 92614
Ph: (949)261-9104
Free: 877-SEM-INFO
Fax: (949)261-1963
Co. E-mail: info@seminarinformation.com
URL: http://www.seminarinformation.com
Description: Covers the properties and specifications of gasoline and how they affect its performance in a spark ignition engine, including a tour of a gasoline testing laboratory. **Audience:** Petroleum company employees, regulatory personnel, and fuel marketing personnel.

35753 ■ Hazardous Waste Management: The Complete Course
Seminar Information Service Inc.
20 Executive Park, Ste. 120
Irvine, CA 92614
Ph: (949)261-9104
Free: 877-SEM-INFO
Fax: (949)261-1963
Co. E-mail: info@seminarinformation.com
URL: http://www.seminarinformation.com
Description: Covers how to meet your annual training requirement and learn a systematic approach to understanding and complying with the latest state and federal regulations. **Audience:** Environmental coordinators, hazardous waste managers and plant managers .

35754 ■ Marine Fuels: Specifications, Testing, Purchase & Use
Seminar Information Service Inc.
20 Executive Park, Ste. 120
Irvine, CA 92614
Ph: (949)261-9104
Free: 877-SEM-INFO
Fax: (949)261-1963
Co. E-mail: info@seminarinformation.com
URL: http://www.seminarinformation.com
Description: Learn how the properties of marine fuels affect fuel handling, combustion, and cost, including a detailed understanding of fuel quality requirements, and why they are necessary for good handling and combustion performance. **Audience:** Supervisors and managers in laboratory operations.

35755 ■ Risk-Based Corrective Action RBCA Applied at Petroleum Release Sites (Onsite)
Seminar Information Service Inc.
20 Executive Park, Ste. 120
Irvine, CA 92614
Ph: (949)261-9104
Free: 877-SEM-INFO
Fax: (949)261-1963
Co. E-mail: info@seminarinformation.com
URL: http://www.seminarinformation.com
Description: Receive the same RBCA training your state regulators are receiving from the organization that developed the RBCA standard from RBCA process overview and risk assessment to fate and transport and policy decisions. **Audience:** Environmental engineers, underground storage tank owners, managers, attorneys and insurance underwriters, and petroleum marketers.

DIRECTORIES OF EDUCATIONAL PROGRAMS

35756 ■ Recycling in America: A Reference Handbook
Pub: ABC-Clio Inc.
Contact: Ron Boehm, President
E-mail: rboehm@abc-clio.com
URL(s): www.abc-clio.com. **Released:** Latest edition 2nd, November 1997. **Price:** $45; $29. **Publication includes:** Lists of private, state, and federal agencies and organizations, and online sources. Principal content of publication is a history of recycling; brief biographical section; facts on recycled materials; and laws and regulations.

REFERENCE WORKS

35757 ■ "3M Sues Law Firm For 'Breach of Loyalty" in Business Journal (Vol. 30, August 3, 2012, No. 10, pp. 1)
Pub: American City Business Journals, Inc.
Contact: Whitney Shaw, President
Ed: Jim Hammerand. **Released:** August 3, 2012. **Description:** 3M Company filed a lawsuit against Covington & Burling for breach of loyalty after seeking to disqualify the law firm from representing the state of Minnesota in a case alleging 3M of polluting water across the eastern Twin Cities metro area with fluorochemicals. 3M claims the law firm switched its position from arguing on their behalf to arguing on behalf of the state.

35758 ■ "$40M Fund Created for Big Energy Project' in Austin Business JournalInc. (Vol. 29, November 27, 2009, No. 38, pp. 1)
Pub: American City Business Journals
Ed: Christopher Calnan. **Description:** A group of Texas businessmen, called Republic Power Partners LP, is planning to raise $40 million in order to launch an alternative energy project. The 6,000-megawatt initiative would generate solar, biomass and wind power in West Texas and could cost as much as $10 billion.

35759 ■ "$600 Million, 270-Megawatt South Kent Wind Project Example of Investments Sought by Ontario Clean Technology Alliance at WINDPOWER 2012' in Investment Business Weekly (June 24, 2012, pp. 49)
Description: WINDPOWER 2012 will be held in Atlanta, Georgia. The event will announce news of the completed plans for a $600 million, 270-megawatt South Kent Wind joint venture between Pattern Energy Group LP and Samsung Renewable Energy Inc. A group of 11 regional and municipal partners called Ontario Clean Technology Alliance, partnered with federal and provincial trade and innovation ministries to attract more wind industry companies to the province.

35760 ■ "2008 Woman of the Year Event Filled with Hope and Inspiration' in Hispanic Business (Vol. 30, July-August 2008, No. 7-8, pp. 58)
Pub: Hispanic Business Inc.
Contact: Jesus Chavarria, President
Ed: Brynne Chappell. **Description:** Brief report on the sixth annual Women of the Year Awards gala which was held at JW Marriott Desert Ridge Resort and Spa is given; 20 women were honored with these awards for their professional contribution, commitment to the advancement of the Hispanic community and involvement with charitable organizations.

35761 ■ "2010: Important Year Ahead for Waterfront' in Bellingham Business Journal (Vol. March 2010, pp. 2)
Ed: Isaac Bonnell. **Description:** A tentative timeline has been established for the environmental impact statement (EIS) slated for completion in May 2010. The plan for the Waterfront District includes detailed economic and architectural analysis of the feasibility of reusing remaining structures and retaining some industrial icons.

35762 ■ "2011 FinOvation Awards" in Farm Industry News (January 19, 2011)
Pub: Penton Business Media Inc.
Contact: David Kieselstein, Chief Executive Officer
Ed: Karen McMahon, Jodie Wehrspann. **Description:** The 2011 FinOvation Award winners are announced, covering new products that growers need for corn and soybean crops. Winners range from small turbines and a fuel-efficient pickup to a Class 10 combine and drought-tolerant hybrids.

35763 ■ "2011 a Record Year for New Wind Energy Installations in Canada' in CNW Group (September 26, 2011)
Pub: CNW Group Ltd.
Contact: Carolyn McGill-Davidson, President
Description: Canada reports a record for new wind energy projects in 2011 with about 1,338 MW of newly installed wind energy capacity expected to come on line, compared to 690 MW installed in 2010. Statistical data included.

35764 ■ "2011 U.S. Smart Grid ? Saving Energy/Saving Money" in Ecology,Environment & Conservation Business (October 8, 2011, pp. 3)
Pub: Highbeam Research
Contact: Patrick Spain, Chief Executive Officer
Description: Highlights of the '2011 U.S. Smart Grid—Saving Energy/Saving Money Customers' Prospective Demand-Response assesses residential energy consumers' willingness to decrease their power consumption in order to mitigate power issues. Statistical details included.

35765 ■ "A123-Fisker Deal May Mean 540 Jobs" in Crain's Detroit Business (Vol. 26, January 18, 2010, No. 3, pp. 4)
Pub: Crain Communications Inc.
Contact: Rance E. Crain, President
Ed: Dustin Walsh. **Description:** Manufacturing plants in Livonia and Romulous may be hiring up to 540 skilled workers due to a contract that was won by A123 Systems Inc. that will result in the company supplying lithium-ion batteries to Fisker Automotive Inc. to be used in their Karma plug-in hybrid electric vehicle.

35766 ■ "The ABCs of a Good Show" in Playthings (Vol. 106, October 1, 2008, No. 9, pp. 18)
Pub: Reed Elsevier Group plc Reed Business Information
Contact: Mark Kelsey, Chief Executive Officer
Ed: Karyn Peterson. **Description:** ABC Kids Expo 2008 made a strong showing with products for babies, kids and new/expecting parents. The new Naturally Kids section promoting eco-friendly products was the highlight of the show.

35767 ■ "Abt Electronics and Appliances Announces the Second Annual Earth Day Recycle Drive" in Ecology, Environment & Conservation Business (May 3, 2014, pp. 3)
Pub: NewsRX
Contact: Susan E. Hasty, Publisher
Released: May 3, 2014. **Description:** Abt Electronics and Appliances is the largest independent, single-store appliance and electronics retailer in the U.S. In honor of Earth Day, Abt has partnered with the City of Chicago to help local residents recycle e-waste, such as electronics and appliances, in an environmentally friendly way for the second year in a row.

35768 ■ "Accessorize Small Animal Habitats for Profit' in Pet Product News (Vol. 66, September 2012, No. 9, pp. 87)
Pub: Bowtie Inc.
Description: Pet supplies retailers can offer accessories that help in maintaining the accessibility, freshness, and cleanliness of small mammals' food and water inside habitats. Aside from these features, the accessories should also promote eco-friendliness to ensure sales growth and repeat business. Tips on marketing these accessories are presented.

35769 ■ "Acciona Windpower to Supply 3-Megawatt Turbines to Prince Edward Island Energy" in Professional Close-Up (September 11, 2012)
Description: Acciona Windpower and Prince Edward Island Energy Corporation (PEIEC) have partnered to supply turbines for the Hermanville & Clear Springs Wind Project that will provide 10 Acciona Windpower AW3000/116 wind turbine generators with capacity of 3 megawatts and a rotor diameter of 116 meters. Acciona will operate and maintain the turbines for the first 15 years.

35770 ■ "ACE Commits $300,000 to Support Environmental Conservation Initiatives and Green Business Entrepreneurs" in Insurance Business Weekly (March 2, 2012, pp. 13)
Pub: NewsRX
Contact: Susan E. Hasty, Publisher
Description: ACE Charitable Foundation has committed to a two-year, $300,000 funding of The Conservation Fund for new initiatives that protect key watersheds, expand wildlife migration corridors and investment in local green economies in the United States.

35771 ■ *"Acing the Test" in Contractor (Vol. 57, January 2010, No. 1, pp. 32)*
Pub: Intertec Publishing
Contact: John French, President
Ed: Robert P. Mader. **Description:** A ward winning mechanical system retrofitting of a middle school in Ohio is discussed. The school now operates at 37,800 Btu/sq. ft and reduced a significant amount of pollutants from being emitted into the environment.

35772 ■ *"Actiontec and Verizon Team Up for a Smarter Home" in Ecology,Environment & Conservation Business (November 5, 2011, pp. 3)*
Pub: Highbeam Research
Contact: Patrick Spain, Chief Executive Officer
Description: Verizon is implementing Actiontec Electronics' SG200 Service Gateway as a basic component of its Home Monitoring and Control service. This new smart home service allows customers to remotely check their homes, control locks and appliances, view home-energy use and more using a smartphone, PC, or FiOS TV.

35773 ■ *"Adventures at Hydronicahh" in Contractor (Vol. 56, September 2009, No. 9, pp. 52)*
Pub: Penton Media, Inc.
Ed: Mark Eatherton. **Description:** Installation of the heating system of a lakeview room are described. The room's radiant windows are powered by electricity from a solar PV array and a propane-powered hydrogen fuel cell. The system will be programmed to use the most energy available.

35774 ■ *"Adventures at Hydronicahh" in Contractor (Vol. 56, November 2009, No. 11, pp. 36)*
Pub: Penton Media, Inc.
Ed: Mark Eatherton. **Description:** Part 6 of the installation of a five stage ground-source heat pump for a hydronic heating system is discussed. The heat exchanger will be bidirectional in the plan described.

35775 ■ *"Adventures at Hydronicahh" in Contractor (Vol. 56, October 2009, No. 10, pp. 42)*
Pub: Penton Media, Inc.
Ed: Mark Eatherton. **Description:** Design and installation of a solar thermal system for a hydronic heating project is described. This portion has two 32-square feet of flat plate glazed solar collectors that are tied to a 120-gallon reverse indirect DHW heater.

35776 ■ *"AF Expands in New Green Building in Gothenburg" in Ecology,Environment & Conservation Business (September 24, 2011, pp. 2)*
Pub: Highbeam Research
Contact: Patrick Spain, Chief Executive Officer
Description: AF signed a ten-year tenancy contract with Skanska for the premises of its new green building in Gothenburg, Sweden. AF offers qualified services and solutions for industrial processes, infrastructure projects and the development of products and IT systems.

35777 ■ *"Agana To Bottle Rain for Whole Foods" in Austin Business Journal (Vol. 32, March 30, 2012, No. 4, pp. 1)*
Pub: American City Business Journals, Inc.
Contact: Whitney Shaw, President
Ed: Vicky Garza. **Released:** March 30, 2012. **Description:** Agana Rainwater has signed a deal to bottle rainwater for Whole Foods Market Inc. Rainwater bottling is seen as a conservation tools as it does not deplete the lake or aquifer.

35778 ■ *"AgraQuest Deal Signals Growth for Biopesticide Makers" in Sacramento Business Journal (Vol. 29, July 13, 2012, No. 20, pp. 1)*
Pub: American City Business Journal
Description: Industry observes claim that biotechnology irm Bayer CropScience's upcoming acquisition of AgraQuest Inc. could signal the growth of biopesticide manufacturing chemical methods for agricultural crop protection could then be complemented with environmentally friendly approaches allowed by biopesticides.

35779 ■ *"Agricultural Community Implements Green Technologies, Building Team" in Contractor (Vol. 56, September 2009, No. 9, pp. 5)*
Pub: Penton Media, Inc.
Ed: Candace Roulo. **Description:** John DeWald and Associates has initiated a residential development project which uses green technologies in Illinois. The community features a community center, organic farm and recreational trails. Comments from executives are also provided.

35780 ■ *"Ahead of the Pack" in Small Business Opportunities (Fall 2010)*
Pub: Harris Publications Inc.
Description: Profile of an organic fast-food business that is carving out a niche that is gaining favor. Elevation Burger is a unique concept offering healthier burgers in sustainable buildings.

35781 ■ *"Air Emissions Plunge in Birmingham" in Birmingham Business Journal (Vol. 29, June 15, 2012, No. 25, pp. 1)*
Pub: American City Business Journals, Inc.
Contact: Whitney Shaw, President
Ed: Nick Bowman. **Released:** June 15, 2012. **Description:** Air emissions in Birmingham, Alabama have declined in 2012. Birmingham has been struggling with air pollution owing its topography and steel production. But US Environmental Protection Agency standards have been accused of limiting industrial growth in the area.

35782 ■ *"Albuquerque Entrepreneurs Selected As Top Participants in USHCC Foundation Green Builds Business Program" in Marketing Weekly News (April 21, 2012)*
Description: Five winners of the 2012 Green Builds Business program was announced by the United States Hispanic Chamber of Commerce Foundation (USHCCF). These winners will receive a combined 24 hours of one-on-one green coaching with Bill Roth, the Green Business Coach for Entrepreneur.com and Founder of Earth 2017. Details are included.

35783 ■ *"Alcoa: 'Going Where No Materials Scientist Has Gone Before'" in Pittsburgh Business Times (Vol. 33, July 18, 2014, No. 53, pp. 5)*
Pub: American City Business Journals
Released: July 18, 2014. **Description:** Alcoa Inc. has signed a $1.1 billion supply agreement with Pratt & Whitney to build the forging for aluminum jet-engine fan blades as well as other parts made with aluminum lithium. This partnership brings together Alcoa's proprietary alloys and unique manufacturing processes with Pratt & Whitney's design, thus forging an aluminum fan blade that is lighter and enables better fuel efficiency.

35784 ■ *"Allowing Ethanol Tax Incentive to Expire Would Risk Jobs, RFA's Dinneen Says" in Farm Industry News (November 3, 2010)*
Pub: Penton Business Media Inc.
Contact: David Kieselstein, Chief Executive Officer
Ed: Lynn Grooms. **Description:** Jobs would be at risk if the ethanol tax incentive expires.

35785 ■ *"Alstom Launches te ECO 122 ? 2.7MW Wind Turbine for Low Wind Sites" in CNW Group (September 28, 2011)*
Pub: CNW Group Ltd.
Contact: Carolyn McGill-Davidson, President
Description: Alstom is launching its new ECO 122, a 2.7MW onshore wind turbine that combines high power and high capacity factor (1) to boost energy yield in low wind regions around the world. The ECO 122 will produce about 25 percent increased wind farm yield that current turbines and fewer turbines would be installed in areas.

35786 ■ *"Altera Ranks Among Top 25 Greenest Companies in U.S." in Ecology, Environment & Conservation Business (August 9, 2014, pp. 2)*
Pub: NewsRX
Contact: Susan E. Hasty, Publisher
Released: August 9, 2014. **Description:** Altera Corporation was ranked 24 on the Newsweek Magazine 2014 Green Rankings of over 500 companies in the United States. These rankings are one of the world's most recognized assessments of corporate sustainability and environmental impact. Eight specific indicators were used, including conservation and sustainability efforts in the areas of energy, carbon, water, and waste productivity.

35787 ■ *"Alternative Energy Calls for Alternative Marketing" in Indoor Comfort Marketing (Vol. 70, June 2011, No. 6, pp. 8)*
Pub: Industry Publications Inc.
Contact: Shirleen Dorman, Editor
Ed: Richard Rutigliano. **Description:** Advice for marketing solar energy products and services is given.

35788 ■ *"Alternative Energy is a Major Topic at Agritechnica 2011" in Farm Industry News (November 16, 2011)*
Pub: Penton Business Media Inc.
Contact: David Kieselstein, Chief Executive Officer
Ed: Mark Moore. **Description:** Sustainable agricultural systems were a hot topic at this year's Agritechnia 2011, held in Germany. Germany is a leader in the development of on-farm biogas systems.

35789 ■ *"Alternative Energy: The Lithium Deficit" in Canadian Business (Vol. 82, April 27, 2009, No. 7, pp. 17)*
Pub: Rogers Media Inc.
Contact: Tony Viner, President
Ed: Joe Castaldo. **Description:** Experts are concerned that there may not be enough lithium available to support the expected rise in demand for the natural resource. Lithium is used in lithium ion batteries, the standard power source for electric and hybrid vehicles. Experts believe that the demand for lithium can only be measured once the technology is out in the market.

35790 ■ *"Alternative Fuels Take Center Stage at Houston Auto Show" in Houston Business Journal (Vol. 44, January 31, 2014, No. 39, pp. 8)*
Pub: American City Business Journals
Released: January 31, 2014. **Description:** An energy summit was held at the Houston Auto Show in Texas on January 22, 2014, where energy executives discussed new technology and initiatives. They considered the market for electric and natural gas-fueled vehicles as well as other options including hydrogen, fuel cells, and biofuels.

35791 ■ *"American Chemistry Council Launches Flagship Blog" in Ecology,Environment & Conservation Business (October 29, 2011, pp. 5)*
Pub: Highbeam Research
Contact: Patrick Spain, Chief Executive Officer
Description: American Chemistry Council (ACC) launched its blog, American Chemistry Matters, where interactive space allows bloggers to respond to news coverage and to discuss policy issues and their impact on innovation, competitiveness, job creation and safety.

35792 ■ *"American Farmland Trust Profiles In Stewardship, How California Farmers and Ranchers are Producing a Better Environment" in Ecology, Environment & Conservation Business (January 4, 2014, pp. 2)*
Pub: NewsRX
Contact: Susan E. Hasty, Publisher
Released: January 4, 2014. **Description:** Forty-five Profiles In Stewardship were presented by the American Farmland Trust showing how farmers and ranchers in 25 California counties are improving the environment by adopting conservation practices that serve examples for others to follow in order to promote sound farming practices and improve the environment by protecting land, air and water.

35793 ■ *"ANATURALCONCEPT" in Crain's Cleveland Business (Vol. 30, June 22, 2009, No. 24, pp. 1)*
Pub: Crain Communications Inc.
Ed: Dan Shingler. **Description:** Cleveland-based Biomimicry Institute, led by Cleveland's Entrepreneurs for Sustainability and the Cuyahoga County Planning Commission, are using biomimicry to incorporate eco-friendliness with industry. Biomimicry studies nature's best ideas then imitates these designs and processes to solve human problems.

35794 ■ *"Ann Alexander: Senior Attorney, Natural Resources Defense Council" in Crain's Chicago Business (Vol. 31, May 5, 2008, No. 18)*
Pub: Crain Communications Inc.
Contact: Todd Johnson, Publisher
Ed: Emily Stone. **Description:** Profile of Ann Alexander who is the senior attorney at the Natural Resources Defense Council and is known for her dedication to the environment and a career spent battling oil companies, steelmakers and the government to change federal regulations. One recent project aims to improve the Bush administration's fuel economy standards for SUVs. Past battles include her work to prevent permits from slipping through the cracks such as the proposal by London-based BP PLC to dump 54 percent more ammonia and 35 percent more suspended solids from its Whiting, Indiana refinery into Lake Michigan-the source of drinking water for Chicago and its surrounding communities.

35795 ■ *"Another Blow To Advertisers?" in Austin Business Journal (Vol. 32, April 27, 2012, No. 8, pp. A1)*
Pub: American City Business Journals, Inc.
Contact: Whitney Shaw, President
Ed: Vicky Garza. **Released:** April 27, 2012. **Description:** A partnership between Austin Resource Recovery and Catalog Choice to reduce the amount of waste paper could cut into the business of direct mail providers in Austin, Texas. The partnership allows the city's residents to opt out of mail they no longer wish to receive.

35796 ■ *"Answers About Commercial Wind Farms Could Come from Downstate" in Erie Times-News (September 27, 2011)*
Pub: Erie Times News
Ed: Valerie Myers. **Description:** Texas-based Pioneer Green Energy is measuring wind and leasing land in North East Township, Pennsylvania. The firm plans to build a 7,000-acre wind farm along wine-country ridges. About 70 turbines would harness wind in order to generate electricity that would be sold into the eastern power grid.

35797 ■ *"Aquarium's Solar Demonstration Project Exceeds Expectations" in Contractor (Vol. 57, February 2010, No. 2, pp. 1)*
Pub: Intertec Publishing
Contact: John French, President
Ed: Candace Roulo. **Description:** Seattle Aquarium cafe installed flat-plate solar collectors to preheat water and data has shown that the system has allowed them to off-set almost double their expected consumption of natural gas. It is estimated that rthe solar panels will shrink the aquarium's carbon footprint by 2.5 tons of carbon dioxide each year.

35798 ■ *"Are You Looking for an Environmentally Friendly Dry Cleaner?" in Inc. (Vol. 30, December 2008, No. 12, pp. 34)*
Pub: Mansueto Ventures L.L.C.
Contact: John Koten, Chief Executive Officer
Ed: Shivani Vora. **Description:** Greenopia rates the greenness of 52 various kinds of businesses, including restaurants, nail salons, dry cleaners, and clothing stores. The guidebooks are sold through various retailers including Barnes & Noble and Amazon.com.

35799 ■ *"Areva Diversifies Further Into Wind" in Wall Street Journal Eastern Edition (November 29, 2011, pp. B7)*
Pub: Dow Jones & Co., Inc.
Contact: Clare Hart, President
Ed: Max Colchester, Noemie Bisserbe. **Description:** French engineering company Areva SA is diversifying and moving away from nuclear energy projects. One

sign of that is its recent discussion to construct 120 wind turbines to be located at two German wind farms. Such a deal, if signed, would be worth about US$1.59 billion.

35800 ■ *"Arise Windpower AB Reports Buy Back of Company Shares" in Manufacturing Close-Up (August 9, 2012)*
Description: Arise Windpower AB's Board of Directors are buying back company shares. This move applies until the next Annual General Meeting and are limited to 10 percent of the total number of outstanding shares.

35801 ■ *"Art Institute of Chicago Goes Green" in Contractor (Vol. 56, July 2009, No. 7, pp. 1)*
Pub: Penton Media, Inc.
Ed: Candace Roulo. **Description:** Art Institute of Chicago's Modern Wing museum addition will receive a certification that makes them one of the most environmentally sound museum expansions in the U.S. A modified variable-air-volume system is being used to meet temperature and humidity requirements in the building and it also has a double curtain wall to capture summer heat.

35802 ■ *"Austin to Buy $1.1B of Wind Power from Two" in Austin Business Journal (Vol. 31, August 19, 2011, No. 24, pp. A1)*
Pub: American City Business Journals
Ed: Vicky Garza. **Description:** Austin City Council is set to approve contracts to purchase wind energy from Duke Energy Corporation and MAP Royalty Inc. The city will get 200MW from Duke and 91MW from MAP and the total contract is estimated to be worth $1.1 million.

35803 ■ *"Austin Energy May Build $2.3B Biomass Plant" in Austin Business JournalInc. (Vol. 28, July 25, 2008, No. 19, pp. A1)*
Pub: American City Business Journals
Ed: Kate Harrington. **Description:** An approval from the Austin City Council is being sought by Austin Energy for a 20-year supply contract with Nacogdoches Power LLC to build a $2.3 billion biomass plant in East Texas. The 100-megawatt biomass plant, which is to run on waste wood, will have Austin Energy as its sole buyer.

35804 ■ *"Auto Show Aims to Electrify" in Crain's Detroit Business (Vol. 26, January 11, 2010, No. 2, pp. 1)*
Pub: Crain Communications Inc.
Contact: Rance E. Crain, President
Ed: Ryan Beene. **Description:** Overview of the North American International Auto show include sixteen production and concept vehicles including eight from the Detroit 3. High-tech battery suppliers as well as hybrid and electric vehicles will highlight the show.

35805 ■ *"Automaker Foundations Run Leaner" in Crain's Detroit Business (Vol. 26, January 11, 2010, No. 2, pp. 1)*
Pub: Crain Communications Inc.
Contact: Rance E. Crain, President
Ed: Sherri Welch. **Description:** Overview of the Detroit automobile industry includes restoring profitability, smarter marketing strategies and philanthropy. Each company comprising the Big 3 is examined, as is their vision for the future.

35806 ■ *"AV Concept Expands Into Green Energy Storage" in Wireless News (January 25, 2010)*
Description: Electronics distributor and manufacturer AV Concept Holdings Limited announced a marketing partnership with Boston-Power, a provider of lithium-ion batteries, with a focus in the Chinese and Korean markets.

35807 ■ *"Avoid the Stress of Traffic and Pollution with House Call Doctor Los Angeles" in Ecology, Environment & Conservation Business (May 24, 2014)*
Pub: NewsRX
Contact: Susan E. Hasty, Publisher
Released: May 24, 2014. **Description:** Record levels of air pollution in the Los Angeles, California area pose serious risks to those suffering from illness or

injury. Michael Farzam and his team at House Call Doctor Los Angeles provides telephone medicine for those unable or unwilling to visit a physician in person. The mobile doctor in Los Angeles offers individuals throughout the area with concierge care without leaving home.

35808 ■ *"Avon Ups Green Performance" in Costmetics International (Vol. 36, June 22, 2012, No. 809, pp. 4)*
Pub: Communications International Group
Released: June 22, 2012. **Description:** Avon constructed its corporate headquarters on Third Avenue in New York using the gold level of the LEED (Leadership in Energy and Environmental Design) rating system. The cosmetics firm is committed to 'green' all future buildings along with 'green' cars and using only 'green' cleaning products and has a team to evaluate raw materials.

35809 ■ *"Award Win Highlights Slingsby's Green Credentials" in Ecology,Environment & Conservation Business (August 20, 2011, pp. 3)*
Pub: Highbeam Research
Contact: Patrick Spain, Chief Executive Officer
Description: Slingsby, an industrial and commercial equipment supplier, was joint winner with Hallmark Cards of the Baildon Business in the Community's Yorkshire and Humber Long Term Environmental Improvement Award. The firm cites its commitment to reducing environmental impact.

35810 ■ *"Baby Business Goes Green" in Northwest Florida Daily News (April 21, 2012)*
Description: Cindi Denbow combined her two companies, child birthing center Gentle Birth Options and mom and baby-focused retail store called Growing Green Bums in Niceville, Florida. Denbow is committed to the environment and running a green business.

35811 ■ *"Back to Business for Bishop Museum" in Hawaii Business (Vol. 54, August 2008, No. 2, pp. 53)*
Ed: Shara Enay. **Description:** Bishop Museum, ranked 224 in Hawaii Business' top 250 companies for 2008, had $29.5 million in gross sales for 2007, up 52.8 percent from the $19.3 million gross sales in 2006. The company has cut 24 positions in a restructuring effort for the museum's sustainability. Grants, artifacts and plans for sustainable operations are discussed.

35812 ■ *"Bank On It: The Many Ways of Giving" in Hawaii Business (Vol. 53, November 2007, No. 5, pp. 60)*
Pub: PacificBasin Communications
Ed: Kathleen Bryan. **Description:** Many Baby Boomers that are preparing to retire would like to give back and make a difference. One way is to make gifts of Individual Retirement Assets (IRA). During 2007 people over 70 years can make withdrawals from an IRA and donate it without realizing the income as taxable.

35813 ■ *"BARS+TONE Achieves Green Business Certification by the City and County of San Francisco" in Benzinga.com (April 26, 2012)*
Pub: Benzinga.com
Contact: Kyle Bazzy, President
Ed: Aaron Wise. **Description:** City and County of San Francisco, California presented a Green Business certification to BARS+TONE, a creative video agency. The certification is part of an ongoing effort to reduce environmental impact.

35814 ■ *"Be Wary of Dual-Flush Conversion Kits" in Contractor (Vol. 56, September 2009, No. 9, pp. 66)*
Pub: Penton Media, Inc.
Ed: John Koeller, Bill Gauley. **Description:** Recommendation of untested dual-flush conversion devices for tank-type toilets in the United States have been questioned. The products are being advertised as having the ability to convert single-flush to a dual-flush toilet. No evidence of water conservation from using such devices has been recorded.

35815 ■ *"Bellingham-Based Baby Web Site to Shut Down" in Bellingham Business Journal (Vol. February 2010, pp. 3)*
Pub: Sound Publishing Inc.
Contact: Gloria G. Fletcher, President
Ed: Lance Henderson. **Description:** Saralee Sky and Jerry Kilgore, owners of Babynut.com will close their online store. The site offered a free online and email newsletter to help mothers through pregnancy and the first three years of their child's life. Products being sold at clearance prices include organic and natural maternity and nursing clothing, baby and toddler clothes, books on pregnancy, and more.

35816 ■ *"BETC Backers Plot Future" in Business Journal Portland (Vol. 27, December 10, 2010, No. 41, pp. 1)*
Pub: Portland Business Journal
Ed: Erik Siemers. **Description:** A coalition of clean energy groups and industrial manufacturers have spearheaded a campaign aimed at persuading Oregon legislators that the state's Business Energy Tax Credit (BETC) is vital in job creation. Oregon's BETC grants tax credits for 50 percent of an eligible renewable or clean energy project's cost. However, some legislators propose BETC's abolition.

35817 ■ *"Beware of E15" in Rental Product News (Vol. 33, October 2011)*
Pub: Cygnus Business Media
Contact: Paul Mackler, Chief Executive Officer
Ed: Curt Bennink. **Description:** Environmental Protection Agency (EPA) set a new regulation that grants partial waivers to allow gasoline containing up to 15 percent ethanol (E15) to be introduced into commerce for use in model year 2001 and newer light-duty motor vehicles, subject to certain conditions.

35818 ■ *"Beyond Meat (R) Completes Largest Financing Round to Date" in Ecology, Environment & Conservation Business (August 16, 2014, pp. 4)*
Pub: NewsRX
Contact: Susan E. Hasty, Publisher
Released: August 16, 2014. **Description:** Beyond Meat (R) is the first company to recreate meat from plants and is dedicated to improving human health, positively impacting climate change, conserving natural resources and respecting animal welfare. The firm has completed its Series D financing round, which will also help the company promote consumer awareness and increase capacity at its manufacturing facility to meet demand.

35819 ■ *"Big-Box Swindle: The True Cost of Mega-Retailers and the Fight for America's Independent Businesses*
Pub: Beacon Press
Contact: Richard Landry, Executive Director
Ed: Stacy Mitchell. **Released:** October 01, 2007. **Price:** $20, paperback. **Description:** Examination of the economic, environmental, and social damage done by big-box retailers like Wal-Mart, Costco, and Home Depot. Labor policies of these retailers, particularly those enforced by Wal-Mart, are discussed at length. **Availability:** Print.

35820 ■ *"Big Energy Deals Power OptiSolar's Local Growth" in Sacramento Business Journal (Vol. 25, August 22, 2008, No. 25, pp. 1)*
Pub: American City Business Journals, Inc.
Contact: Whitney Shaw, President
Ed: Celia Lamb. **Description:** Solar energy projects are driving Sacramento, California-based OptiSolar's growth. The company is set to begin construction of its first photovoltaic project in Ontario. It also plans to build the world largest photovoltaic project in San Luis Obispo County.

35821 ■ *"Big Energy Ideas for Our Times" in Canadian Business (Vol. 83, August 17, 2010, No. 13-14, pp. 49)*
Description: Five ideas Canada must consider in the production of energy are explored. These ideas are run-off-river hydroelectric projects, the tapping of

natural gas inside shale formation, the water's role in creating energy, the development of a smart grid, and the reduction of energy consumption.

35822 ■ *"Bigger is Definitely Not Better When It Comes to Cooling" in Indoor Comfort Marketing (Vol. 70, May 2011, No. 5, pp. 49)*
Pub: Industry Publications Inc.
Contact: Shirleen Dorman, Editor
Ed: Eugene Silberstein. **Description:** Efficiency is more important when installing air conditioning equipment over size of the unit. Details are provided.

35823 ■ *"Billboard Co.'s HQ In Limbo" in Austin Business Journal (Vol. 32, April 6, 2012, No. 5, pp. A1)*
Pub: American City Business Journals, Inc.
Contact: Whitney Shaw, President
Ed: Vicky Garza. **Released:** April 6, 2012. **Description:** Reagan National Advertising has been awaiting the Austin City Council decision on whether it would be allowed to build a new headquarters that was on the drawing board for more than five years. However, approval of Reagan's plan would cut down several trees and that would violate the Heritage tree ordinance.

35824 ■ *"Biodiesel Poised to Regain Growth" in Farm Industry News (January 21, 2011)*
Pub: Penton Business Media Inc.
Contact: David Kieselstein, Chief Executive Officer
Ed: Lynn Grooms. **Description:** According to Gary Haer, vice president of sales and marketing for Renewable Energy Group, the biodiesel industry is positioned to regain growth in 2011 with the reinstatement of the biodiesel blendersa tax credt of $1 per gallon.

35825 ■ *"Bioheat ? Alternative for Fueling Equipment" in Indoor Comfort Marketing (Vol. 70, May 2011, No. 5, pp. 14)*
Pub: Industry Publications Inc.
Contact: Shirleen Dorman, Editor
Ed: Gary Hess. **Description:** Profile of Worley and Obetz, supplier of biofuels used as an alternative for fueling industry equipment.

35826 ■ *"Bitumen Oilsands: Slick Science" in Canadian Business (Vol. 81, September 15, 2008, No. 14-15, pp. 55)*
Pub: Rogers Media Inc.
Contact: Tony Viner, President
Ed: Andrew Nikiforuk. **Description:** N-Solv Corp's John Nenniger has discovered a better alternative to steam-assisted gravity drainage methods for extracting bitumen. Nenniger's technique also relies on gravity but replaces steam with propane, which leaves behind impurities like asphaltenes and heavy metals that are too dirty to burn.

35827 ■ *"Blackwater is LEED Golden for Port of Portland Building" in Contractor (Vol. 56, October 2009, No. 10, pp. 3)*
Pub: Penton Media, Inc.
Ed: Robert P. Mader. **Description:** Worrel Water Technologies' Tidal Wetlands Living Machine recycles blackwater from the toilets and sends it right back to flush the toilets. The Technology is being installed in the new headquarters of the Port of Portland which aims to get awarded a gold certificate from the Leadership in Energy and Environmental Design.

35828 ■ *"A Blueprint for Improving the Quality of Home Construction Through Conservation" in Real Estate Review (Vol. 41, Summer 2012, No. 2, pp. 87)*
Released: Summer 2012. **Description:** Book review of the title, 'Retooling the Industry:How It Got Here, Why It's Broken, and Hot to Fix It' is provided.

35829 ■ *"Board This Powertrain" in Barron's (Vol. 89, July 27, 2009, No. 30, pp. 30)*
Ed: Naureen S. Malik. **Description:** Siemens' American Depositary Receipts have risen 60 percent from their March 2009 low and they should continue heading higher. The company has solid earnings and revenue growth since they lead in growing markets such as alternative energy and health-care infrastructure. Their shares also look cheap at 1.9 times book value.

35830 ■ *"Boatyard Expansion 8-Year Odyssey" in Providence Business News (Vol. 28, March 31, 2014, No. 52, p. 1)*
Pub: American City Business Journals
Released: March 31, 2014. **Description:** Bristol Marine owner, Andy Tyska, has found it challenging to operate and improve the boatyard due to lack of available coastal land and restrictive environmental regulations. Tyska made a large investment in plans for expanding the property he purchased in 1998. Tyska discusses the challenges faced while trying to improve his boatyard.

35831 ■ *"Boeing Partnership to Preserve Thousands of Acres of Threatened Wetlands in South Carolina" in Ecology, Environment & Conservation Business (August 2, 2014, pp. 3)*
Pub: NewsRX
Contact: Susan E. Hasty, Publisher
Released: August 2, 2014. **Description:** U.S. Army Corps of Engineers approved Boeing's comprehensive wetlands mitigation plan to preserve about 4,000 acres of land, including more than 2,000 acres of wetlands near the Francis Marion National Forest in South Carolina Lowcountry. Boeing worked in partnership with federal, state and local agencies and conservation organizations to identify the tracts for preservation in order to achieve conservation goals of regional and national significance.

35832 ■ *"Bold Goals Will Require Time" in Contractor (Vol. 56, October 2009, No. 10, pp. S2)*
Ed: Ted Lower. **Description:** Offering a broad range of courses is the Radiant Panel Association (RPA), an organization that holds education as its top priority. The RPA must lead the industry by raising the educational bar for future installers.

35833 ■ *"Bonefish Grill Debuts New Cocktail to Benefit Conservation Foundation" in Ecology, Environment & Conservation Business (May 17, 2014, pp. 5)*
Pub: NewsRX
Contact: Susan E. Hasty, Publisher
Released: May 17, 2014. **Description:** Bonefish Grill has introduced the Ocean Trust Tropic Heat Martini to support the Ocean Trust, an ocean conservation foundation. The new drink contains house-made infused pineapple Absolut vodka, with fresh mango and a thin slice of jalapeno and served at their restaurants nationwide.

35834 ■ *"Boston Cab Association Gets 2012 Green Business Award" in Professional Close-Up (April 28, 2012)*
Description: Boston Cab Association was awarded the 2012 Green Business Award for its conversion to all hybrid vehicles in its fleet. The company was the first to commit to the purchase of hybrids in 2006 as part of the City of Boston's Clean Air Cab program.

35835 ■ *"Boston Mayor Menino Awards Digital Lumens for Green Business" in Entertainment Close-Up (April 28, 2012)*
Description: Mayor Thomas Menino presented the 2012 Green Business award to Digital Lumens in Boston, Massachusetts. Digital Lumens provides intelligent LED lighting systems and supports clean technology.

35836 ■ *"The Brick Companies Converts Entire Maryland Portfolio to 100 Percent WGES CleanSteps WindPower and Reduces Its Carbon Footprint" in Benzinga.com (September 25, 2012)*
Pub: Benzinga.com
Contact: Kyle Bazzy, President
Description: Properties included the The Brick Companies are six commercial buildings, two golf clubs and two marinas. All of these properties are powered by 100 percent CleanSteps(R) WindPower from Washington Gas Energy Services (WGES) and will reduce greenhouse gases equaling the removal of 1,500 cars off the road for one year.

35837 ■ *"Brown At Center of Local CleanTech Lobbying Efforts"* in *Boston Business Journal (Vol. 30, October 15, 2010, No. 36, pp. 1)*
Pub: Boston Business Journal
Ed: Kyle Alspach. **Description:** U.S. Senator Scott Brown has been active in lobbying for energy reform in Massachusetts. Brown has been meeting with business groups seeking the reforms.

35838 ■ *"Burner Handles Everything From #2 to B100"* in *Indoor Comfort Marketing (Vol. 70, May 2011, No. 5, pp. 24)*
Pub: Industry Publications Inc.
Contact: Shirleen Dorman, Editor
Description: A new oil burner being offered by AMERIgreen Energy is profiled.

35839 ■ *"Burning Issues: Four of Today's Hottest Energy Topics"* in *Canadian Business (Vol. 83, August 17, 2010, No. 13-14, pp. 45)*
Description: A look at four issues dominating Canada's energy industry is presented. These issues are lack of transmission capacity and difficulty in transferring power across provincial boundaries, the management of intermittency of renewable generation, techniques that would clean up the Alberta's oil sands, and the impending massive use of electric cars in North America.

35840 ■ *"The Business of Activism"* in *Entrepreneur (Vol. 37, September 2009, No. 9, pp. 43)*
Pub: Entrepreneur Press
Contact: Perlman Neil, President
Ed: Mary Catherine O'Connor. **Description:** San Francisco, California-based business incubator Virgance has been promoting sustainable projects by partnering with businesses. The company has launched campaigns which include organizing homeowners in negotiating with solar installers. The company is also planning to expand its workforce.

35841 ■ *"Buy the Pants, Save the Planet?"* in *Globe & Mail (February 5, 2007, pp. B1)*
Ed: Keith McArthur. **Description:** The marketing campaign of the clothing company Diesel S.p.A. is discussed. The company has based its latest collection of T-shirt designs on the problem of global warming.

35842 ■ *"Buyer Sought for Clipper Windpower"* in *Gazette (March 16, 2012)*
Pub: McClatchy Tribune Information Services
Ed: Dave DeWitte. **Description:** United Technologies is seeking a buy for its Clipper Windpower, the wind turbine manufacturer located in Cedar Rapids, Iowa. Economic slowdown, tighter credit conditions, and uncertainty over renewal of federal wind energy tax credits are all contributors to the move by UT.

35843 ■ *"Caber Engineering Helps to Reduce Canada's Carbon Footprint"* in *Ecology,Environment & Conservation Business (July 16, 2011, pp. 7)*
Pub: Highbeam Research
Contact: Patrick Spain, Chief Executive Officer
Description: Calgary-based Caber Engineering Inc. will assist in the engineering design of the Alberta Carbon Trunk Line (ACTL). The ACTL is Alberta's first sizable commercial carbon capture and storage project focusing on the reduction of environmental impacts while being economically beneficial.

35844 ■ *"Calendar"* in *Crain's Detroit Business (Vol. 24, April 14, 2008, No. 15, pp. 25)*
Pub: Crain Communications Inc.
Contact: Rance E. Crain, President
Description: Listing of events in the Detroit area include conferences addressing entrepreneurialism, economic development, and ways in which to develop environmentally friendly buildings.

35845 ■ *"Campaign Not Stirred by Wind Issue in Roanoke County"* in *Roanoke Times (September 18, 2011)*
Pub: The Roanoke Times
Contact: Debbie Meade, President
Ed: Katelyn Polantz. **Description:** Wind energy has brought citizens of the Roanoke area into activism this year. Comments from citizen on both sides of the issue are provided.

35846 ■ *"Canada in 2020 Energy: Mr. Clean"* in *Canadian Business (Vol. 81, October 27, 2008, No. 18, pp. 74)*
Pub: Rogers Media Inc.
Contact: Tony Viner, President
Ed: Rachel Pulfer. **Description:** Profile of Nicholas Parker, co-founder of Cleantech Group LLC, a pioneer in clean technology investing. Cleantech, now a global industry, accounts for 10 percent of all venture capital investments made by U.S. companies in 2007.

35847 ■ *"Canada in 2020 Environment: Dirty Realities"* in *Canadian Business (Vol. , pp.)*
Pub: Rogers Media Inc.
Contact: Tony Viner, President
Ed: Matthew McClearn. **Description:** Efforts by Canada's industrial polluters to reduce emissions are examined. Syncrude Canada plans to reduce sulphur emissions by 60 percent in 2011, while TransAlta invests in emission reduction programs. Environmental groups, however, claim that companies are not doing enough to protect the environment.

35848 ■ *"Canada's Clean Energy Advantages Offer a Bright Future"* in *Canadian Business (Vol. 83, August 17, 2010, No. 13-14, pp. 38)*
Ed: Don McKinnon. **Description:** Canada has clean energy advantages in the greenhouse gas emission-free CANada Deuterium Uranium reactor technology and carbon neutral biomass fuels that were continuously ignored by policy makers. Both are proven to significantly reduce emissions while providing reliable, affordable and secure electricity.

35849 ■ *"Canada's Largest Bakery Officially Opened Today"* in *Ecology,Environment & Conservation Business (October 15, 2011, pp. 7)*
Pub: Highbeam Research
Contact: Patrick Spain, Chief Executive Officer
Description: Maple Leaf Foods opened Canada's largest commercial bakery in Hamilton, Ontario. The firm's 385,000 square foot Trillium bakery benefits from efficient design flow and best-in-class technologies.

35850 ■ *"Canadian Hydronics Businesses Promote 'Beautiful Heat'"* in *Indoor Comfort Marketing (Vol. 70, September 2011, No. 9, pp. 20)*
Pub: Industry Publications Inc.
Contact: Shirleen Dorman, Editor
Description: Canadian hydronics companies are promoting their systems as beautiful heat. Hydronics is the use of water as the heat-transfer medium in heating and cooling system.

35851 ■ *"Canadian Hydropower Firm Places Its Bets On Massachusetts Market"* in *Boston Business Journal (Vol. 34, May 9, 2014, No. 14, pp. 3)*
Pub: American City Business Journals, Inc.
Contact: Whitney Shaw, President
Released: May 9, 2014. **Description:** Nalcor Energy has started work on its 824-megawatt Muskrat Falls hydroelectric plant that would supply the Provinces of Newfoundland and Labrador with electricity from renewable sources by the end of 2017. Nalcor is interested in getting longer-term contracts in Massachusetts as part of the state's clean energy legislation.

35852 ■ *"Canadian Wind Farm Sued Due to Negative Health Effects"* in *PC Magazine Online (September 22, 2011)*
Pub: PC Magazine
Description: Suncor Energy is being sued by a family in Ontario, Canada. The family claims that Suncor's wind turbines have created health problems for them, ranging from vertigo and sleep disturbance to depression and suicidal thoughts. The family's home is over 1,000 meters from the eight wind turbines, and according to Ontario officials, wind turbines must be a minimum of 550 meters from existing homes.

35853 ■ *"Candidates Differ On State's Green Streak"* in *Business Journal Portland (Vol. 27, October 22, 2010, No. 34, pp. 1)*
Pub: Portland Business Journal
Ed: Andy Giegerich. **Description:** The views of Oregon gubernatorial candidates Chris Dudley and John Kitzhaber on the state's economy and on environmental policies are presented. Both Dudley, who is a Republican, and his Democratic challenger believe that biomass could help drive the state's economy. Both candidates also pledged changes in Oregon's business energy tax credit (BETC) program.

35854 ■ *"CanWEA Unveils WindVision for BC: 5,250 MW of Wind Energy by 2025"* in *CNW Group (October 4, 2011)*
Pub: CNW Group Ltd.
Contact: Carolyn McGill-Davidson, President
Description: Wind industry leaders are asking British Columbia, Canada policy makers to created conditions to further develop and integrate wind energy in accordance with greenhouse gas emission targets and projected economic growth. Statistical data included.

35855 ■ *"Carbon Capture Hits a Wall: Alberta's Favoured Emissions-Control Plan is Falling Apart"* in *Canadian Business (Vol. 85, June 11, 2012, No. 10, pp. 13)*
Pub: George Media Inc.
Ed: Matthew McClearn. **Released:** June 11, 2012. **Description:** The emissions-control plan of Alberta suffered a major setback following cancellations of major carbon capture and storage (CCS) pilot projects. Project Pioneer was cancelled because the saving did not justify the operating costs while discontinuation of Heartland Area Redwater Project was due to the uncertainty surrounding the province's changing CCS rules.

35856 ■ *"Carbon Capture and Storage: Grave Concerns"* in *Canadian Business (Vol. 81, July 21 2008, No. 11, pp. 25)*
Pub: Rogers Media Inc.
Contact: Tony Viner, President
Ed: Andrew Nikiforuk. **Description:** Air pollution control regulations to reduce greenhouse gasses have been implemented by the Canadian government. The federal government is planning to construct a carbon funeral industry that will store the global warming gases, however the expenditure for the project will be shifted to the taxpayers. Details of the Bruce Peachy's initiative on how to reduce GHGs are presented.

35857 ■ *"The Carbon Equation"* in *Canadian Business (Vol. 81, October 27, 2008, No. 18, pp. 109)*
Pub: Rogers Media Inc.
Contact: Tony Viner, President
Ed: Jack Mintz. **Description:** Economic and environmental impacts of the likely rejection of a carbon tax for the cap-and-trade system in Canada are discussed. The Conservative Party is expected tow in the 2008 elections and would likely pursue the cap-and-trade system.

35858 ■ *"Carbon Trading: Current Schemes and Future Developments"* in *Energy Policy (Vol. 39, October 2011, No. 10, pp. 6040-6054)*
Pub: Reed Elsevier Reference Publishing
Ed: Slobodan Perdan, Adisa Azapagic. **Description:** Current and future developments regarding carbon trading is highlighted.

35859 ■ *"Caribou Coffee Kick-Starts Spring Planting with New Grounds for Your Ground Program in Time for Earth Day"* in *Ecology, Environment and Conservation Business (May 3, 2014, pp. 5)*
Pub: NewsRX
Contact: Susan E. Hasty, Publisher
Released: May 3, 2014. **Description:** Caribou Coffee is providing customers and local gardening clubs in Minnesota free used espresso ground for their

gardens. The Grounds for Your Grounds program allows customers to pick up five-pound recycled bags of used grounds from retail locations for use in their home garden or community garden. The firm is committed to supporting local gardens and gardening organizations with existing reusable resource-espresso grounds.

35860 ■ "Carrington Co. LLC Revolutionizes the Hot Tea Market with First-Ever, Organic Tea in Eco-Friendly Packaging" in Ecology, Environment & Conservation Business (May 3, 2014, pp. 6)
Pub: NewsRX
Contact: Susan E. Hasty, Publisher
Released: May 3, 2014. **Description:** Carrington Company makes organic non-genetically modified products including flax seeds, hemp, chia, and organic coconut oil and teas. The firm is launching its Carrington Organics Tea to its lineup of healthy products, packed in a 100 percent eco-friendly packaging that will fully and safely biodegrade when composted. It is the first tea available packaged in fully recyclable packaging.

35861 ■ "Cascades Awarded 'Innovative Product of the Year' and 'Environmental Strategy of the Year' by Pulp & Paper International PPI" in Ecology, Environment & Conservation Business (January 4, 2014, pp. 4)
Pub: NewsRX
Contact: Susan E. Hasty, Publisher
Released: January 4, 2014. **Description:** Cascades Tissue Group was awarded 'Innovative Product of the Year' for its bathroom and facial tissues made from unbleached recycled fiber, the first of its kind in the U.S. Cascades also won the 'Environmental Strategy of the Year' based on its commitment to reducing its ecological impact through continuous improvement of processes, unique recycling infrastructure, and use of recycled fibers in packaging and tissue products. Pulp and Paper recognizes companies for these efforts annually.

35862 ■ "Case IH Announces Strategy to Meet 2014 Clean Air Standards" in Farm Industry News (September 15, 2011)
Pub: Penton Business Media Inc.
Contact: David Kieselstein, Chief Executive Officer
Ed: Jodie Wehrspann. **Description:** Case IH will meet EPA's stringent engine emissions limits imposed in 2014, called Tier 4. The limits call for a 90 percent reduction in particulate matter and nitrogen oxides (NOx) over the Tier 3 requirements from a few years ago.

35863 ■ "Cash for Appliances Targets HVAC Products, Water Heaters" in Contractor (Vol. 56, October 2009, No. 10, pp. 1)
Pub: Penton Media, Inc.
Ed: Candace Roulo. **Description:** States and territories would need to submit a full application that specifies their implementation plans if they are interested in joining the Cash for Appliances program funded by the American Recovery and Reinvestment Act. The Department of Energy urges states to focus on heating and cooling equipment, appliances and water heaters since these offer the greatest energy savings potential.

35864 ■ "Catch the Wind Announces Filing of Injunction Against Air Data Systems LLC and Philip Rogers" in CNW Group (September 30, 2011)
Pub: CNW Group Ltd.
Contact: Carolyn McGill-Davidson, President
Description: Catch the Wind, providers of laser-based wind sensor products and technology, filed an injunction against Optical Air Data Systems (OADS) LLC and its former President and CEO Philip L. Rogers. The complaint seeks to have OADS and Rogers return tangible and intangible property owned by Catch the Wind, which the firm believes to be critical to the operations of their business.

35865 ■ "Catch the Wind to Hold Investor Update Conference Call on October 18, 2011" in CNW Group (October 4, 2011)
Pub: CNW Group Ltd.
Contact: Carolyn McGill-Davidson, President
Description: Catch the Wind Ltd., providers of laser-based wind sensor products and technology, held a conference call for analysts and institutional investors. The high-growth technology firm is headquartered in Manassas, Virginia.

35866 ■ "CE2 Carbon Capital and Dogwood Carbon Solutions Partner with Missouri Landowners to Generate High Quality Carbon Offsets from 300,000 Acres of Forest" in Nanotechnolgy Business Journal (January 25, 2010)
Pub: Investment Weekly News
Description: Dogwood Carbon Solutions, a developer of agriculture and forestry based conservation projects, has partnered with CE2 Carbon Capital, one of the largest investors and owners of U.S. carbon commodities and carbon emissions reduction projects, to develop high-quality carbon offsets from over 30,000 acres of privately-owned non-industrial forest in the Ozark mountain region of Arkansas and Missouri.

35867 ■ "CEO Forecast: With Cloudy Economy, Executives Turn to Government Contracting" in Hispanic Business (January-February 2009, pp. 34, 36)
Pub: Hispanic Business Inc.
Contact: Jesus Chavarria, President
Ed: Jessica Haro, Richard Kaplan. **Description:** As economic uncertainty fogs the future, executives turn to government contracts in order to boost business. Revenue sources, health care challenges, environmental consulting and remediation services, as well as technological strides are discussed.

35868 ■ "The CEO Poll: Fuel for Thought II Canadian Business Leaders on Energy Policy" in Canadian Business (Vol. 81, September 15, 2008, No. 14-15, pp. 12)
Pub: Rogers Media Inc.
Contact: Tony Viner, President
Ed: Joe Castaldo. **Description:** Most Canadian business leaders worry about the unreliability of the oil supply but feel that Canada is in a better position to benefit from the energy supply crisis than other countries. Many respondents also highlighted the need to invest in renewable energy sources.

35869 ■ "The CEO Poll: Hot Air" in Canadian Business (Vol. 81, July 22, 2008, No. 12-13, pp. 16)
Pub: Rogers Media Inc.
Contact: Tony Viner, President
Ed: Joe Castaldo. **Description:** Over half of 101 business leaders who were recently surveyed oppose Liberal leader Stephane Dion's carbon-tax proposal, saying that manufacturers in Canada are likely to suffer from the plan. Additional key results of the survey are presented.

35870 ■ "Certification Experts Germanischer Lloyd Wind Energy Assist NaiKun's Offshore Wind Project" in Marketwired (May 14, 2007)
Pub: Comtex News Network Inc.
Description: Germanischer Lloyd Wind Energy (GL Wind) will examine, inspect, and provide quality management services for the engineering, design, and construction of the offshore wind project planned by NaiKun Wind Development Inc. in northwest British Columbia.

35871 ■ "Changing Fuel Compositions: What It Means To You and Your Business" in Indoor Comfort Marketing (Vol. 70, June 2011, No. 6, pp. 30)
Pub: Industry Publications Inc.
Contact: Shirleen Dorman, Editor
Ed: Paul Nazzaro. **Description:** Biofuels are outlined and the way it is changing the HVAC/R industry are discussed.

35872 ■ "Charged Up for Sales" in Charlotte Business Journal (Vol. 25, October 15, 2010, No. 30, pp. 1)
Pub: Charlotte Business Journal
Ed: Susan Stabley. **Description:** Li-Ion Motors Corporation is set to expand its production lines of electric cars in Sacramento, California. The plan is seen to create up to 600 jobs. The company's total investment is seen to reach $500 million.

35873 ■ "Chicago Botanic Garden Builds Green Research Facility" in Contractor (Vol. 56, December 2009, No. 12, pp. 5)
Pub: Intertec Publishing
Contact: John French, President
Ed: Candace Roulo. **Description:** Chicago Botanic Garden has built a laboratory and research facility in Illinois. The facility is set to receive a United States Green Building Council LEED Gold certification. The building features a solar photovoltaic array, radiant flooring and water-conserving plumbing products.

35874 ■ "Chicago Public Schools District Builds Green" in Contractor (Vol. 56, October 2009, No. 10, pp. 5)
Pub: Penton Media, Inc.
Ed: Candace Roulo. **Description:** Chicago Public Schools district has already built six U.S. Green Building Council LEED certified schools and one addition in five years and will continue to build new green buildings. The district has an Environmental Action Plan that strives to reduce energy usage, improve indoor air quality, and reduce contribution to climate change.

35875 ■ "China Wind Power Generates Stronger First Quarter Results" in Marketwire Canada (September 28, 2011)
Pub: MarketWired Canada
Description: China Wind Power International Corporation, an independent wind power producer in China reported strong growth for the first quarter 2011. Details of the company and its future developments are highlighted.

35876 ■ "China's Transition to Green Energy Systems" in Energy Policy (Vol. 39, October 2011, No. 10, pp. 5909-5919)
Pub: Reed Elsevier Reference Publishing
Ed: Wei Li, Guojun Song, Melanie Beresford, Ben Ma. **Description:** The economics of home solar water heaters and their growing popularity in Dezhous City, China is discussed.

35877 ■ "Chinese Solar Panel Manufacturer Scopes Out Austin" in Austin Business JournalInc. (Vol. 29, October 30, 2009, No. 34, pp. 1)
Pub: American City Business Journals
Ed: Jacob Dirr. **Description:** China's Yingli Green Energy Holding Company Ltd. is looking for a site in order to construct a $20 million photovoltaic panel plant. Both Austin and San Antonio are vying to house the manufacturing hub. The project could create about 300 jobs and give Austin a chance to become a player in the solar energy market. Other solar companies are also considering Central Texas as an option to set up shop.

35878 ■ "Christmas Trees Keep Giving in St. Louis Area" in St. Louis Post-Dispatch (January 11, 2012
Pub: McClatchy-Tribune Information Services
Released: January 11, 2012. **Description:** Missouri state law prohibiting disposing of Christmas trees into area lakes has forced citizens to find new ways to use their old trees. Saint Louis and other municipalities offers ways to recycle Christmas trees while creating a good habitat for fish. Cities have sunk a portion of the trees, then created mulch and is offered free to residents.

35879 ■ "Cincinnati City Council Power Shift Could Benefit Business" in Business Courier (Vol. 26, November 6, 2009, No. 28, pp. 1)
Pub: American City Business Journals, Inc.
Contact: Whitney Shaw, President
Ed: Lucy May, Dan Monk. **Description:** A majority in the Cincinnati City Council, which is comprised of reelected members, might be created by Charlie Winburn's impending return to the council. It would be

empowered to decide on public safety, stock options taxes, and environmental justice. How the presumed majority would affect the city's economic progress is discussed.

35880 ■ *"City's New Energy Audits to Spawn 'Fantastic' Market" in Austin Business JournalInc. (Vol. 28, November 14, 2008, No. 35, pp. 1)*
Pub: American City Business Journals

Ed: Jean Kwon. **Description:** A new law requiring older homes to undergo energy use audits is seen to provide new business for some companies in the Austin, Texas area. The new law is seen to create a new industry of performance testers. Details of the new ordinance are also given.

35881 ■ *"Clean Power Finance Gets Green Business Certification from City and County of San Francisco" in Professional Services Close-Up (August 23, 2012)*
Description: Clean Power Finance was recognized at a San Francisco Green Business from the City and County of San Francisco, Calfornia. Clean Power Finance is an online marketplace for residential solar financing and provider of solar sales software.

35882 ■ *"Clean-Tech Focus Sparks Growth" in Philadelphia Business Journal (Vol. 28, January 15, 2010, No. 48, pp. 1)*
Pub: American City Business Journals Inc.

Ed: Peter Key. **Description:** Keystone Redevelopment Group and economic development organization Ben Franklin Technology Partners of Southeastern Pennsylvania have partnered in supporting the growth of new alternative energy and clean technology companies. Keystone has also been developing the Bridge Business Center.

35883 ■ *"Clean Wind Energy Tower Transitions from R&D Stage Company" in Professional Services Close-Up (September 30, 2011)*
Pub: Close-Up Media

Description: Clean Wind Energy designed and is developing large downdraft towers that use benevolent, non-toxic natural elements to generate electricity and clean water. The firm is closing its internally staffed engineering office in Warrenton, Virginia and transitioning a development team to oversee and coordinate industry consultants and advisors to construct their first dual renewable energy tower.

35884 ■ *"Cleaner and Greener" in Canadian Business (Vol. 80, February 12, 2007, No. 4, pp. 45)*
Pub: Rogers Media Inc.
Contact: Tony Viner, President

Ed: Zena Olijnyk. **Description:** Canadian research and government investments in clean coal technology are discussed.

35885 ■ *"Climate Law Could Dig into our Coal-Dusted Pockets" in Business Courier (Vol. 26, November 20, 2009, No. 30, pp. 1)*
Pub: American City Business Journals, Inc.
Contact: Whitney Shaw, President

Ed: Lucy May. **Description:** Passage of federal climate legislation into law is set to increase household cost for Greater Cincinnati, according to the calculation by the Brookings Institute. The increase for residents of the area will amount to $244 in 2020 and the city was ranked the sixth-highest rate in the nation, behind Indianapolis.

35886 ■ *"Co-Op Launches Revolving Loan Program for Farmers" in Bellingham Business Journal (Vol. February 2010, pp. 3)*
Pub: Sound Publishing Inc.
Contact: Gloria G. Fletcher, President

Ed: Lance Henderson. **Description:** Community Food Co-op's Farm Fund received a $12,000 matching grant from the Sustainable Whatcom Fund of the Whatcom Community Foundation. The Farm Fund will create a new revolving loan program for local farmers committed to using sustainable practices.

35887 ■ *"CO2 Emissions Embodied in China-US Trade" in Energy Policy (Vol. 39, October 2011, No. 10, pp. 5980-5987)*
Pub: Reed Elsevier Reference Publishing

Ed: Huibin Du, Guozhu Mao, Alexander M. Smith, Xuxu Wang, Yuan Wang, Jianghong Guo. **Description:** Input and output analysis based on the energy per dollar ratio for carbon dioxide emissions involved in China-United States trade is outlined.

35888 ■ *"Coal Train Crush Feared" in Puget Sound Business Journal (Vol. 33, July 6, 2012, No. 11, pp. 1)*
Pub: American City Business Journal

Ed: Steve Wilhelm. **Description:** Coal exports are seen to take up more rail capacity in Washington. The issue was raised in connection with the proposed Gateway Pacific Terminal at Cherry Point. The planned terminal has been opposed by environmental groups.

35889 ■ *"Collection Agency to Exhibit at the Northeast's Leading Horticulture and Green Industry Tradeshow" in Internet Wire (January 23, 2012)*
Released: January 23, 2012. **Description:** American Profit Recovery will be exhibiting at New England Grows, held February 1-3, 2012. The tradeshow is one of the biggest horticultural and green industry events in the northeast region. American Profit Recovery, a collection agency based in Michigan and Massachusetts, focuses on collections in the lawn care and landscaping sector.

35890 ■ *"Combo Dorm-Field House Built to Attain LEED Gold" in Contractor (Vol. 56, September 2009, No. 9, pp. 1)*
Pub: Penton Media, Inc.

Ed: Candace Roulo, Robert P. Mader. **Description:** North Central College in Illinois has built a new dormitory that is expected to attain Leadership in Energy and Environmental Design Gold certification from the United States Green Building Council. The structure features a geo-exchange heat pump system and radiant floor heat. A description of the facility is also provided.

35891 ■ *"Coming Soon: Electric Tractors" in Farm Industry News (November 21, 2011)*
Pub: Penton Business Media Inc.
Contact: David Kieselstein, Chief Executive Officer

Ed: Jodie Wehrspann. **Description:** The agricultural industry is taking another look at electric farm vehicles. John Deere Product Engineering Center said that farmers can expect to see more diesel-electric systems in farm tractors, sprayers, and implements.

35892 ■ *"Commercial Water Efficiency Initiatives Announced" in Contractor (Vol. 56, November 2009, No. 11, pp. 5)*
Pub: Penton Media, Inc.

Ed: Robert P. Mader. **Description:** Plumbing engineers John Koeller and Bill Gauley are developing a testing protocol for commercial toilets. The team said commercial toilets should have a higher level of flush performance than residential toilets for certification. The Environmental Protection Agency's WaterSense program wants to expand the program into the commercial/institutional sector.

35893 ■ *"CommScope and Comsearch to Showcase Innovative Wind Power Solutions at WINDPOWER 2012 in Atlanta" in Benzinga.com (May 31, 2012)*
Pub: Benzinga.com
Contact: Kyle Bazzy, President

Ed: Aaron Wise. **Description:** CommScope Inc. and its subsidiary CommScope will highlight their complete wind power solution products during the WINDPOWER 2012 Conference and Exhibition in Atlanta, Georgia this year. CommScope's wind power products include fiber optic cabling solutions, while Comsearch offers wind energy services that address the siting challenges resulting from complex telecommunications issues.

35894 ■ *The Company We Keep: Reinventing Small Business for People, Community, and Place*
Pub: Chelsea Green Publishing Co.
Contact: Margo Baldwin, President
E-mail: mbaldwin@chelseagreen.com

Ed: John Abrams, William Grieder. **Released:** May 15, 2006. **Price:** $18. **Description:** The new business trend in social entrepreneurship as a business plan enables small business owners to meet the triple bottom line of profits for people (employees and owners), community, and the environment. **Availability:** Print.

35895 ■ *"Conscious Capitalism: Liberating the Heroic Spirit of Business"*
Released: December 25, 2012. **Price:** $27.00. **Description:** Conscious Capitalism companies include Whole Foods Market, Southwest Airlines, Costco, Google, Patagonia, The Container Store, UPS and others. These firms under the four specific tenants to success: higher purpose, stakeholder integration, conscious leadership, and conscious culture and management. These companies are able to create value for all stakeholders, including customers, employees, suppliers, investors, society, and the environment.

35896 ■ *"Consignment Sales Planned for Monona" in Wisconsin State Journal (March 9, 2012)*
Pub: Capital Newspapers

Ed: Karen Rivedal. **Released:** March 9, 2012. **Description:** Monona, Wisconsin Community Center will promote recycling by offering donated children's clothing, toys, strollers, baby carriers and other things to help local families by quality items for lower prices.

35897 ■ *"Consumers Like Green, But Not Mandates" in Business Journal-Milwaukee (Vol. 28, December 10, 2010, No. 10, pp. A1)*
Pub: Milwaukee Business Journal

Ed: Sean Ryan. **Description:** Milwaukee, Wisconsin consumers are willing to spend more on green energy, a survey has revealed. Respondents also said they will pay more for efficient cars and appliances. Support for public incentives for homeowners and businesses that reduce energy use has also increased.

35898 ■ *"Consumers Want to Learn More About Green Business Efforts Despite Deep Doubt" in Benzinga.com (May 1, 2012)*
Pub: Benzinga.com
Contact: Kyle Bazzy, President

Ed: Aaron Wise. **Description:** According to the third annual Gibbs & Soell Sense & Sustainability Study, 21 percent of Americans think the majority of businesses are working toward sustainable development, while 71 percent of consumer desire more knowledge about things corporations are doing to become sustainable and green. A majority of respondents believe the media is more likely to report green business when they can report bad news.

35899 ■ *"Contractors Debate Maximizing Green Opportunities, Education" in Contractor (Vol. 56, November 2009, No. 11, pp. 3)*
Pub: Penton Media, Inc.

Ed: Robert P. Mader. **Description:** Attendees at the Mechanical Service Contractors Association convention were urged to get involved with their local U.S. Green Building Council chapter by one presenter. Another presenter says that one green opportunity for contractors is the commissioning of new buildings.

35900 ■ *"Convert New Customers to Long Term Accounts" in Indoor Comfort Marketing (Vol. 70, February 2011, No. 2, pp. 22)*
Pub: Industry Publications Inc.
Contact: Shirleen Dorman, Editor

Description: Marketing to new customers and suggestions for retaining them is covered.

35901 ■ *"Corporate Park Retrofits for Water Savings"* in *Contractor (Vol. 56, October 2009, No. 10, pp. 5)*

Pub: Penton Media, Inc.

Description: Merrit Corporate Park in Norwalk, Connecticut has been interested in improving building efficiency and one of their buildings has been retrofitted with water-efficient plumbing systems which will allow them to save as much as two million gallons of water. ADP Service Corp. helped the park upgrade their plumbing system.

35902 ■ *Corporate Radar: Tracking the Forces That Are Shaping Your Business*

Ed: Karl Albrecht. **Released:** December 2008. **Price:** , $24.95. **Description:** Ways for a business to assess the forces operating in the external environment that can affect the business and solutions to protect from outside threats.

35903 ■ *"Corporate Responsibility"* in *Professional Services Close-Up (July 2, 2010)*

Description: List of firms awarded the inaugural Best Corporate Citizens in Government Contracting by the Corporate Responsibility Magazine is presented. The list is based on the methodology of the Magazine's Best Corporate Citizen's List, with 324 data points of publicly-available information in seven categories which include: environment, climate change, human rights, philanthropy, employee relations, financial performance, and governance.

35904 ■ *"The Cost of Energy"* in *Canadian Business (Vol. 83, August 17, 2010, No. 13-14, pp. 39)*

Description: Canada's cheap energy has bred complacency among Canadian companies and most have not strived to conserve or develop other forms of energy. However, even costs of traditional energy such as oil are set to rise, fueled by recent events in Saudi Arabia and the Gulf of Mexico.

35905 ■ *"Cost Remains Top Factor In Considering Green Technology"* in *Canadian Sailings (June 30, 2008)*

Ed: Julie Gedeon. **Description:** Improving its environmental performance remains a priority in the shipping industry; however, testing new technologies can prove difficult due to the harsh conditions that ships endure as well as installation which usually requires a dry dock.

35906 ■ *"Could This Be Your Next Office Building?"* in *Austin Business Journal (Vol. 31, May 13, 2011, No. 10, pp. A1)*

Pub: American City Business Journals

Ed: Cody Lyon. **Description:** Falcon Containers moved to a 51-acre site in Far East Austin, Texas and started construction of a 2,500-square-foot headquarters made from eight 40-foot shipping containers. Falcon's CEO Stephen Shang plans to use his headquarters building as a showroom to attract upscale, urban hipsters. Insights on the construction's environmental and social impact are shared.

35907 ■ *"Crude Awakening"* in *Canadian Business (Vol. 81, October 27, 2008, No. 18, pp. 14)*

Ed: Jeff Sanford. **Description:** Jim Grays believes that a global liquid fuels crisis is coming and hopes the expected transition from oil dependence will be smooth. Charles Maxwell, on the other hand, predicts that a new world economy will arrive in three waves. Views of both experts are examined.

35908 ■ *"Customized Before Custom Was Cool"* in *Green Industry Pro (July 2011)*

Pub: Cygnus Business Media

Contact: Paul Mackler, Chief Executive Officer

Ed: Gregg Wartgow. **Description:** Profile of Turf Care Enterprises and owner Kevin Vogeler, who discusses his desire to use more natural programs using little or no chemicals in 1986. At that time, that sector represented 20 percent of his business, today it shares 80 percent.

35909 ■ *"Data Center Goes Off-Grid, Is Research Test Bed"* in *Contractor (Vol. 57, February 2010, No. 2, pp. 1)*

Pub: Intertec Publishing

Contact: John French, President

Ed: Candace Roulo. **Description:** Syracuse University's Green Data Center has gone off-grid through the use of natural gas fired turbines. It is expected to use 50 percent less energy than a typical computer center. The center's heating and cooling system setup is also discussed.

35910 ■ *"David Robinson Column"* in *Buffalo News (October 2, 2011)*

Pub: The Buffalo News

Contact: Warren T. Colville, President

Ed: David Robinson. **Description:** New York Power Authority ceased development of an offshore wind farm project. Wind farming in the waters of Lake Erie or Lake Ontario would be too costly. Details of the project are discussed.

35911 ■ *"A Day Late and a Dollar Short"* in *Indoor Comfort Marketing (Vol. 70, March 2011, No. 3, pp. 30)*

Pub: Industry Publications Inc.

Contact: Shirleen Dorman, Editor

Ed: Philip J. Baratz. **Description:** A discussion involving futures options and fuel oil prices is presented.

35912 ■ *"Deal Snapshot: United Technologies Finalizes Clipper Windpower Sale"* in *M & A Navigator (August 30, 2012)*

Description: United TechnologiesCorporation (UTC) sold its subsidiary Clipper Windpower PLC, a wind turbine maker in the United Kingdom, to private equity firm Platinum Equity LLC.

35913 ■ *"DEM Says River Needs Cleanup"* in *Providence Business News (Vol. 28, January 6, 2014, No. 40, pp. 1)*

Pub: American City Business Journals

Released: January 6, 2014. **Description:** Rhode Island's Department of Environmental Management (DEM) called a meeting to gather information for its Ten Mile River water-quality-restoration plan. DEM announced the failure of the Ten Mile River and its impoundments to meet state water quality standards. The government grant received by Attleboro for the cleanup efforts is examined.

35914 ■ *"Denton To Consider Texas' First Ban"* in *Dallas Business Journal (Vol. 37, July 11, 2014, No. 44, pp. 12)*

Pub: American City Business Journals

Released: July 11, 2014. **Description:** The process of hydraulic fracturing or fracking and its disadvantages is discusses, focusing on Denton City Council's plan to declare the first fracking ban in Texas. The ban is expected to make oil and gas companies to file legal challenges. It is reported that Denton residents had to be relocated after oil well were re-drilled and transformed into deeper and horizontal Barnett Shale natural gas wells.

35915 ■ *"Design Programs for HVAC Sizing Solutions"* in *Contractor (Vol. 57, January 2010, No. 1, pp. 44)*

Pub: Intertec Publishing

Contact: John French, President

Ed: William Feldman, Patti Feldman. **Description:** Rhvac 8 is an HVAC design program that lets users calculate peak heating and cooling load requirements for rooms, zones, systems, and entire buildings. The HVAC Pipe Sizer software for the iPhone enables quick sizing of a simple piping system.

35916 ■ *"Despite Economic Upheaval Generation Y is Still Feeling Green: RSA Canada Survey"* in *CNW Group (October 28, 2010)*

Pub: CNW Group Ltd.

Contact: Carolyn McGill-Davidson, President

Description: Canadian Generation Y individuals believe it is important for their company to be environmentally-friendly and one-third of those

surveyed would quit their job if they found their employer was environmentally irresponsible, despite the economy.

35917 ■ *"Detroit Hosts Conferences on Green Building, IT, Finance"* in *Crain's Detroit Business (Vol. 25, June 1, 2009, No. 22, pp. 9)*

Pub: Crain Communications Inc. - Detroit

Contact: Keith Crain, Chairman

Ed: Tom Henderson. **Description:** Detroit will host three conferences in June 2009, one features green technology, one information technology and the third will gather black bankers and financial experts from across the nation.

35918 ■ *"DeWind Delivering Turbines to Texas Wind Farm"* in *Professional Services Close-Up (September 25, 2011)*

Pub: Close-Up Media

Description: DeWind Company has begun shipment of turbines to the 20 MW Frisco Wind Farm located in Hansford County, Texas. DeWind is a subsidiary of Daewoo Shipbuilding and Marine Engineering Company. Details of the project are discussed.

35919 ■ *"DOE Proposes New Water Heater Efficiency Standards"* in *Contractor (Vol. 57, January 2010, No. 1, pp. 3)*

Pub: Intertec Publishing

Contact: John French, President

Ed: Robert P. Mader. **Description:** U.S. Department of Energy is proposing higher efficiency standards for gas and electric water heaters which will not take effect until 2015. The proposal calls for gas-fired storage water heaters less than 60 gallons to have an Energy Factor of 0.675 and those larger than 60 gallons to have an Energy Factor of 0.717.

35920 ■ *"Doing Good: Fair Fashion"* in *Entrepreneur (Vol. 35, October 2007, No. 10, pp. 36)*

Pub: Entrepreneur Press

Contact: Perlman Neil, President

Ed: J.J. Ramberg. **Description:** Indigenous Designs was launched in 1993, when organic clothing was not yet popular. However, the company has become successful in the industry, with $4 million dollars in revenue, owing to the growing environment awareness of consumers. A history of how the company was formed and an overview of their production process are provided.

35921 ■ *"Doing the Right Thing: Enterpreneurs Make Social Responsibility Part of their Business"* in *Black Enterprise (Vol. 38, July 2008, No. 12, pp. 50)*

Pub: Earl G. Graves Publishing Co. Inc.

Contact: Earl G. Graves, Jr., President

Ed: Tamara E. Holmes. **Description:** More business owners are trying to become more environmentally friendly, either due to their belief in social responsibility or for financial incentives or for both reasons. Tips for making one's business more environmentally responsible are included as well as a listing of resources that may be available to help owners in their efforts.

35922 ■ *"Dorset Feed Mill First in the Country To Use 100 Percent Green Energy"* in *Farmers Weekly (August 17, 2012, No. 774)*

Pub: Reed Elsevier Group plc Reed Business Information

Contact: Mark Kelsey, Chief Executive Officer

Released: August 17, 2012. **Description:** Eco Sustainable Solutions owns and operates the Weltec anaerobic digester togeneral 498kWh of power for the Dorchester Feed Mill, which is a farmer coop Mole Valley Farmers. Mole Valley Farmers history shows a strong investment in renewable energy production.

35923 ■ *"Dow Champions Innovative Energy Solutions for Auto Industry at NAIAS"* in *Business of Global Warming (January 25, 2010, pp. 7)*

Description: This year's North American International Auto Show in Detroit will host the 'Electric Avenue' exhibit sponsored by the Dow Chemical Company. The display will showcase the latest in innovative energy solutions from Dow as well as electric vehicles and the technology supporting them. This marks the first time a non-automotive manufacturer is part of the main floor of the show.

35924 ■ "Driving a Green Agenda" in Charlotte Business Journal (Vol. 27, June 1, 2012, No. 11, pp. 1)
Pub: American City Business Journals, Inc.
Contact: Whitney Shaw, President

Ed: Susan Stabley. **Released:** June 1, 2012. **Description:** NASCAR has become a model for corporate sustainability. NASCAR launched its sustainability program in 2008. Meanwhile, Charlotte Motor Speedway has secured a portable processing center to sort recycled materials.

35925 ■ "Drop in the Bucket Makes a lot of Waves" in Globe & Mail (March 22, 2007, pp. B1)
Pub: CTVglobemedia Publishing Inc.

Ed: Greg Keenan. **Description:** The concern of several auto makers in Canada over the impact of providing heavy rebates to customers buying energy-efficient cars is discussed.

35926 ■ "Dry Idea" in Entrepreneur (Vol. 36, April 2008, No. 4, pp. 20)
Pub: Entrepreneur Press
Contact: Perlman Neil, President

Ed: Tiffany Meyers. **Description:** Lucky Earth LLC is an Inglewood, California-based company that markets 'Waterless' Carwash, an organic product that is sprayed on to the car and wiped down without using water. Businesses related to water conservation are being created, as water shortage is anticipated in 36 states in the U.S. by 2013.

35927 ■ "DTE Energy Foundation Expands 'Greening' Programs at Michigan Festivals" in Ecology, Environment & Conservation Business (June 28, 2014, pp. 3)
Pub: NewsRX
Contact: Susan E. Hasty, Publisher

Released: June 28, 2014. **Description:** DTE Energy Foundation is expanding its support for its 'Greening' or recycling programs to the GrandJazz Fest in Grand Rapids and the Lakeshore Art Festival in Michigan. The Foundation already supports recycling programs at the Detroit Jazz Festival and the National Cherry Festival in Traverse City. The foundation is committed to reduce the carbon footprint at these events by recycling plastic, aluminum cans, glass and other materials.

35928 ■ "Earth Angels" in Playthings (Vol. 106, September 1, 2008, No. 8, pp. 10)
Pub: Reed Elsevier Group plc Reed Business Information
Contact: Mark Kelsey, Chief Executive Officer

Ed: Karyn Peterson. **Description:** ImagiPlay toy company has partnered with Whole Foods Market to distribute the company's wooden playthings across the country. The company's Earth-friendly business model is outlined.

35929 ■ Earth: The Sequel: The Race to Reinvent Energy and Stop Global Warming
Pub: W. W. Norton & Company, Inc.
Contact: Rachel Comerford, Manager

Ed: Miriam Horn, Fred Krupp. **Released:** March 2009. **Price:** $15.95, paperback. **Description:** President of the Environmental Defense Fund offers suggestions for small businesses to help solve global warming. Investigation into the new industries, jobs, and opportunities is provided.

35930 ■ "East Coast Solar" in Contractor (Vol. 57, February 2010, No. 2, pp. 17)
Pub: Penton Media, Inc.

Ed: Dave Yates. **Description:** U.S. Department of Energy's Solar Decathlon lets 20 college student-led teams from around the world compete to design and build a solar-powered home. A mechanical contractor discusses his work as an advisor during the competition.

35931 ■ Eco Barons: The New Heroes of Environmental Activism
Pub: Ecco/HarperCollins
Ed: Edward Humes. **Released:** January 19, 2010. **Price:** $14.99, paperback. **Description:** Profiles of business leaders who have dedicated their lives to saving the planet from ecological devastation. **Availability:** Print.

35932 ■ "Eco-Preneuring" in Small Business Opportunities (July 2008)
Ed: Mary C. Pearl. **Description:** Profile of Wildlife Trust, a rapidly growing global organization dedicated to innovative conservation science linking health and ecology. With partners in nearly twenty countries, Wildlife Trust draws on global strengths in order to respond to well-defined local needs. In the Dominican Republic, they are working with the community and local biologists in order to restore fishing and create jobs in the field of ecotourism.

35933 ■ Ecopreneuring: Putting Purpose and the Planet Before Profits
Pub: New Society Publishers
Contact: Sue Custance, Director
Ed: John Ivanko, Lisa Kivirist. **Released:** July 01, 2008. **Price:** $17.95, paperback; $11.65. **Description:** Ecopreneurs in America are shifting profits and market share towards green living. The book provides a guideline for ecopreneurs in the areas of eco-business basics, purposeful management, marketing in the green economy, and running a lifestyle business. **Availability:** PrintE-book.

35934 ■ "Ecovative Moves Beyond Packaging" in Business Review Albany (Vol. 41, August 1, 2014, No. 19, pp. 12)
Pub: The Business Journals
Released: August 1, 2014. **Description:** Ecovative Design of Green Island, NY has started making new packaging materials to add to its biodegradable product line, including the Myco Board, a material similar to particleboard. Clients range from computer manufacturers to furniture retailers.

35935 ■ "Editor's Note" in Canadian Business (Vol. 81, March 17, 2008, No. 4, pp. 7)
Pub: Rogers Media Inc.
Contact: Tony Viner, President
Ed: Joe Chidley. **Description:** Canadian Consolidated government expenditures increased by an average of 4.5 percent annually from 2003 to 2007. Health care, housing, and the environment were some of the areas which experienced higher spending. However, government spending in labor, employment, and immigration dropped 6.6 percent.

35936 ■ "Election Could Undo Renewable Energy Quotas" in The Business Journal - Serving Phoenix and the Valley of the Sun (Vol. 28, July 11, 2008, No. 45, pp. 1)
Pub: American City Business Journals, Inc.
Contact: Whitney Shaw, President
Ed: Patrick O'Grady. **Description:** Competition for the three open seats in the Arizona Corporation Commission is intense, with 12 candidates contesting for the three slots. The commission's mandates for renewable energy and infrastructure investment will also be at stake.

35937 ■ "Electronic Design and a Greener Environment" in Canadian Electronics (Vol. 23, June-July 2008, No. 4, pp. 6)
Pub: Action Communication Inc.
Ed: Nicholas Deeble. **Description:** Companies seeking to minimize their environmental impact are using Design methodologies of Cadence Design Systems Ltd. The company's Low Power Format and Low Power Design Flow help reduce carbon dioxide emissions.

35938 ■ "Eleni Reed: C&W Gets Green Star" in Crain's New York Business (Vol. 24, January 6, 2008, No. 1, pp. 25)
Pub: Crain Communications Inc.
Contact: Rance Crain, President
Ed: Theresa Agovino. **Description:** Cushman & Wakefield Inc. has hired Eleni Reed as director of sustainability strategies; the real estate firm wants to ensure that the 500 million square feet of office space it manages around the globe meets environmental standards.

35939 ■ "Elon Musk's Solar Firm Is Nearly Doubling Its Massachusetts Workforce" in Boston Business Journal (Vol. 34, May 30, 2014, No. 17, pp. 3)
Pub: American City Business Journals, Inc.
Contact: Whitney Shaw, President
Released: May 30, 2014. **Description:** SolarCity is planning to add 100 jobs to its Massachusetts operations. The solar panel firm opened a second operations center in the state. State business incentives have enabled the company to expand presence in the area.

35940 ■ "EMC Greens Its Machines" in Boston Business Journal (Vol. 31, July 15, 2011, No. 25, pp. 3)
Pub: Boston Business Journal
Ed: Kyle Alspach. **Description:** Hopkinton, Massachusetts-based EMC Corporation has been pursuing a sustainability strategy even though it would not directly pay back money to the company or customers who use the products. EMC has been increasingly requiring sustainable practices from its suppliers and evaluating the full lifecycle impacts of its products.

35941 ■ "Emissions: Cloudy Skies" in Canadian Business (Vol. 81, October 27, 2008, No. 18, pp. 101)
Pub: Rogers Media Inc.
Contact: Tony Viner, President
Ed: Andrew Wahl. **Description:** Canada's federal government is expected to implement its regulations on greenhouse-gas emissions by January 1, 2010, but companies are worried because the plan took so long and some details are yet to be revealed. Corporate Canada wants a firm, long-range plan similar to the European Union Emissions Trading Scheme in dealing with greenhouse-gas emissions.

35942 ■ "Encore Container, Manufacturer of Plastic Drums and IBC Totes, Leads the Way in Environmental Sustainability" in Ecology, Environment & Conservation Business (January 25, 2014, pp. 33)
Pub: NewsRX
Contact: Susan E. Hasty, Publisher
Released: January 25, 2014. **Description:** Encore Container, a leading reconditioner of IBC totes and manufacturer and reconditioner of plastic drums describes its efforts to promote environmental sustainability within the company: container reconditioning, plastic and steel recycling, water conservation and waste minimization.

35943 ■ "Energy Consulting Company to Expand" in Austin Business JournalInc. (Vol. 28, November 7, 2008, No. 34, pp. A1)
Pub: American City Business Journals
Ed: Kate Harrington. **Description:** CLEAResult Consulting Inc. is planning to increase its workforce and move its headquarters to a larger office. The company has posted 1,000 percent increase in revenues. The company's adoption of best practices and setting of benchmark goals are seen as the reason for its growth.

35944 ■ "Energy Efficiency Ordinance Softened" in Austin Business JournalInc. (Vol. 28, October 3, 2008, No. 29)
Pub: American City Business Journals
Ed: Jean Kwon. **Description:** City of Austin has eliminated mandatory energy efficiency upgrades to single-family housing as a condition for selling or renting homes or buildings. The new law proposes that an energy performance audit be conducted on single-family homes before being sold and the results of the audit disclosed to perspectives buyers.

35945 ■ "Energy Is Put to Good Use in Antarctica" in Contractor (Vol. 56, July 2009, No. 7, pp. 32)
Pub: Intertec Publishing
Contact: John French, President
Ed: Carol Fey. **Description:** Recapturing waste heat is an important part of the heating system at the McMurdo Station in Antarctica. The radiators of generators are the heat source and this is supplemented by

modular boilers when seasonal demands for heat increase. Waste heat is also used to make 55,000 gallons of fresh water a day.

35946 ■ "Enriching the Ecosystem: A Four-Point Plan for Linking Innovation, Enterprises, and Jobs" in Harvard Business Review (Vol. 90, March 2012, No. 3, pp. 140)
Pub: Harvard Business Review Press
Contact: Peter E. Walsh, Director
Ed: Rosabeth Moss Kanter. **Released:** March 2012. **Description:** The four goals for enriching the ecosystem include: linking venture creation and knowledge creation to speed up the idea-to-enterprise transition; revitalizing small-, medium-, and large-sized firms via partnerships; improving matches between education and employment opportunities; and bringing together leaders across different sectors to create regional strategies.

35947 ■ "Environment: Green Counting" in Canadian Business (Vol. 81, October 13, 2008, No. 17, pp. 27)
Pub: Rogers Media Inc.
Contact: Tony Viner, President
Ed: Joe Castaldo. **Description:** Procter and Gamble research revealed that only 10 percent of North American consumers are willing to accept trade-offs for a greener product. Three out of four North American consumers will not accept a higher price or a decrease in a product's performance for an environmental benefit. Details on green marketing are also discussed.

35948 ■ Environmental Guide to the Internet
Pub: Government Institutes
Contact: Judith Rothman, Director
URL(s): rowman.com/ISBN/9780865876439. **Ed:** Carol Briggs-Erickson, Toni Murphy. **Released:** Latest edition 4th. **Price:** $83, Individuals Paperback; £51.95, Individuals Paperback. **Covers:** 1,200 resources covering the environment on the Internet, including organizations, products, and resources, including discussion groups, electronic journals, newsgroups, and discussion groups. **Entries include:** Name, online address, description, e-mail address. **Arrangement:** Categories.

35949 ■ "Environmental Working Group Names Whole Foods Market (R) Leading National Retailer for 'Green' Sunscreen" in Ecology, Environment & Conservation Business (June 14, 2014, pp. 5)
Pub: NewsRX
Contact: Susan E. Hasty, Publisher
Released: June 14, 2014. **Description:** Whole Foods Market has been named as the leading retailer selling the largest selection of 'green' rated sunscreen to shoppers.

35950 ■ "EPA Finalizes WaterSense for Homes" in Contractor (Vol. 57, January 2010, No. 1, pp. 70)
Pub: Penton Media, Inc.
Ed: Robert P. Mader. **Description:** U.S. Environmental Protection Agency released its 'final' version of the WaterSense for Homes standard. The standard's provisions that affect plumbing contractors includes the specification that everything has to be leak tested and final service pressure cannot exceed 60 psi.

35951 ■ "EPA Grants E15 Waiver for 2001-2006 Vehicles" in Farm Industry News (January 21, 2011)
Pub: Penton Business Media Inc.
Contact: David Kieselstein, Chief Executive Officer
Ed: Lynn Grooms. **Description:** U.S. Environmental Protection Agency waived a limitation on selling gasoline that contains more than 10 percent ethanol for model year 2001-2006 cars and light trucks, allowing fuel to contain up to 15 percent ethanol (E15) for these vehicles.

35952 ■ "EPA to Tighten Energy Star Standards for 2011" in Contractor (Vol. 56, September 2009, No. 9, pp. 6)
Pub: Penton Media, Inc.
Description: United States Environmental Protection Agency will tighten standards for its Energy Star for Homes program in 2011. The green trend in the

construction industry has been cited as reason for the plan. The agency is adding requirements for energy-efficient equipment and building techniques.

35953 ■ "ESolar Partners With Penglai on Landmark Solar Thermal Agreement for China" in Business of Global Warming (January 25, 2010, pp. 8)
Description: Penglai Electric, a privately-owned Chinese electrical power equipment manufacturer, and eSolar, a global provider of cost-effective and reliable solar power plants, announced a master licensing agreement in which eSolar will build at least 2 gigawatts of solar thermal power plants in China over the next 10 years.

35954 ■ "Everett Dowling" in Hawaii Business (Vol. 54, August 2008, No. 2, pp. 32)
Pub: PacificBasin Communications
Ed: Jason Ubay. **Description:** Real estate developer Everett Dowling, president of Dowling Company Inc., talks about the company's sustainable management and services. The company's office has been retrofitted to earn a Leadership in Energy and Environmental Design (LEED) certification. Dowling believes that real estate development can be part of the sustainable solution.

35955 ■ "Executive Session: Mike Bergey, Bergey Windpower" in Journal Record (June 1, 2012)
Pub: Dolan Media Inc.
Ed: Sarah Terry-Cobo. **Description:** Cofounder and president of Bergey Windpower located in Norman, Oklahoma, is working to keep manufacturing going in the US. His firm manufactures small wind turbines for homes and businesses. He addresses aggressive government programs in the European Union that are increasing sales in the United Kingdom and other countries in the region. California, New York, Ohio and Vermont are the strongest markets in the United States.

35956 ■ "Expansions Signal Growing Interest in Waste-to-Energy Plants" in Crain's Cleveland Business (Vol. 28, November 5, 2007, No. 44, pp. 9)
Pub: Crain Communications Inc.
Ed: Bruce Geiselman. **Description:** According to industry insiders, concerns about greenhouse gas emissions as well as escalating energy and waste disposal prices are fueling increased interest in waste-to-energy plants. Many plants are expanding and considering building new trash-burning plants; this marks the first growth in capacity in more than a decade.

35957 ■ "Family Takes Wind Turbine Companies to Court Over Gag Clauses on Health Effects of Turbines" in CNW Group (September 12, 2011)
Pub: CNW Group Ltd.
Contact: Carolyn McGill-Davidson, President
Description: Shawn and Trisha Drennan are concerned about the negative experiences other have had with wind turbines close to their homes, including adverse health effects. The couple's home will be approximately 650 meters from the Kingsbridge II wind farm project in Ontario, Canada.

35958 ■ Fast-Track Business Start-Up Kit: California
Pub: Kaplan Books
Ed: Carolyn Usinger. **Released:** 2006. **Price:** $22.95; C$29. **Description:** Step-by-step guide for starting and running a business in California, including information on sole proprietors, partnerships, limited liability companies, S and C corporations, as well as details concerning business entities, sales taxes, environmental issues, human resources, and more.

35959 ■ "Fed May Ban Amphibian Trade" in Pet Product News (Vol. 64, November 2010, No. 11, pp. 13)
Pub: Bowtie Inc.
Description: U.S. Fish and Wildlife Service is seeking public input on a petition submitted by the conservation activist group Defenders of Wildlife. The petition involves possible classification of chytrid

fungus-infected amphibians and amphibian eggs as 'injurious wildlife' under the Lacey Act. Interstate trading or importation of injurious wildlife into the U.S. is not allowed.

35960 ■ "Federal Buildings to Achieve Zero-Net Energy by 2030" in Contractor (Vol. 56, December 2009, No. 12, pp. 5)
Pub: Penton Media, Inc.
Ed: Candace Roulo. **Description:** United States president Barack Obama has issued sustainable goals for federal buildings. Federal agencies are also required to increase energy efficiency, conserve water and support sustainable communities. Obama has also announced a $3.4 billion investment in a smart energy creed.

35961 ■ "The Final Frontier" in Canadian Business (Vol. 80, October 8, 2007, No. 20, pp. 127)
Ed: Andy Holloway. **Description:** Effects of economic development in Northern Canada's natural environment are discussed. The caribou, which are still a primary source of food and clothing in the region, are dying. It is assumed that mining and petroleum projects are affecting the migration patterns of the animals inhabiting the region. The need to maintain a balance between the needs of resource companies and traditional businesses is also discussed.

35962 ■ "Find Private Money for FutureGen Plant" in Crain's Chicago Business (Vol. 34, September 12, 2011, No. 37, pp. 18)
Pub: Crain Communications Inc.
Contact: Todd Johnson, Publisher
Description: FutureGen is a clean-coal power plant being developed in Southern Illinois. The need for further funding is discussed.

35963 ■ "First Sustainability Standard for Household Portable and Floor Care Appliances Developed to Identify Environmentally Responsible Products" in Ecology, Environment & Conservation Business (September 13, 2014, pp. 39)
Pub: NewsRX
Contact: Susan E. Hasty, Publisher
Released: September 13, 2014. **Description:** the Association of Home Appliance Manufacturers (AHAM), CSA Group, and the UL Environment released the AHAM 7002-2014/CSA SPE-7002-14/UL 7002, Sustainability Standard for Household Portable and Floor Care Appliances. This is the first voluntary sustainability standards for these appliances and is the third in a unit of product sustainability standards under development by the group. These standards are intended for use by manufacturers, governments, retailers, and others to identify products conforming to these standards in six key areas: materials, manufacturing and operations, energy consumption during use, end-of-life, consumables, and innovation.

35964 ■ "First Suzlon S97 Turbines Arrive in North America for Installation" in PR Newswire (September 28, 2011)
Pub: UBM L.L.C.
Contact: Kate Spellman, President
E-mail: kspellman@cmp.com
Description: Suzlon Energy Ltd., the world's fifth largest manufacturer of wind turbines, will install its first S97 turbine at the Amherst Wind Farm Project. These turbines will be installed on 90-meter hub height towers and at full capacity, will generate enough electricity to power over 10,000 Canadian homes.

35965 ■ "First Venture Reports Proprietary Yeasts Further Reduce Ethyl Carbamate in Sake" in Canadian Corporate News (May 16, 2007)
Description: First Ventures Technologies Corp., a biotechnology company that develops and commercializes advanced yeast products, confirmed that two of their proprietary yeasts used in the making of sake have yielded reductions in ethyl carbamate compared to previous sake brewing trials.

35966 ■ *"Five-Ring Circus" in Entrepreneur (Vol. 35, November 2007, No. 11, pp. 76)*
Pub: Entrepreneur Press
Contact: Perlman Neil, President
Ed: Scott Bernard Nelson. **Description:** China's economy is growing and is expected to do well even after the 2008 Olympics, but growth could slow from eleven percent to eight or nine percent. Chinese portfolio concerns with regard to health and environmental records and bureaucratic fraud are discussed.

35967 ■ *The Flaw of Averages: Why We Underestimate Risk in the Face of Uncertainty*
Pub: John Wiley & Sons Inc.
Contact: Stephen M. Smith, President
Ed: Sam L. Savage. **Released:** March 2012. **Price:** $19.95, paperback; $12.99. **Description:** Personal and business plans are based on uncertainties on a daily basis. The common avoidable mistake individuals make in assessing risk in the face of uncertainty is defined. The explains why plans based on average assumptions are wrong, on average, in areas as diverse as finance, healthcare, accounting, the war on terror, and climate change. **Availability:** PrintE-book.

35968 ■ *"Floyd County Considers Wind Farms" in Roanoke Times (September 19, 2011)*
Pub: The Roanoke Times
Contact: Debbie Meade, President
Ed: Jeff Sturgeon. **Description:** German firm, Nordex USA Inc. is proposing a $100 million, 30-50 megawatt wind farm atop Wills Ridge, Virginia within the next four years. This project is one of several large wind project considered in the Roanoke and New River valleys of Virginia.

35969 ■ *"Flue Vaccines are Going Green" in Canadian Business (Vol. 83, September 14, 2010, No. 15, pp. 24)*
Pub: Rogers Media Inc.
Contact: Tony Viner, President
Ed: Angelia Chapman. **Description:** Quebec-based Medicago has found a solution to the bottleneck in the production of influenza vaccines by using plant-based processes instead of egg-based systems. Medicago's US Department of Defense funded research has produced the technology that speeds up the production time for vaccines by almost two-thirds. Insights into Medicago's patented process are also given.

35970 ■ *"For Giving Us a Way To Say Yes To Solar: Lynn Jurich and Edward Fenster" in Inc. (Volume 32, December 2010, No. 10, pp. 110)*
Pub: Inc. Magazine
Description: Profile of entrepreneurs Lynn Jurich and Edward Fenster, cofounders of SunRun. The firm installs solar panels at little or no cost and homeowners sign 20-year contracts to buy power at a fixed price.

35971 ■ *"For One Homebuilder, It's Pretty Easy Being Green, Even in Houston" in Houston Business Journal (Vol. 44, April 11, 2014, No. 49, pp. 7)*
Pub: American City Business Journals
Released: April 11, 2014. **Description:** Frankel Building Group vice president, Scott Frankel, says new housing projects in Houston, Texas have been getting bigger. He also said that industry members are facing the problem of lack of residential lots in the region. Frankel added that the company builds its homes to LEED-certified standards.

35972 ■ *"For Putting Down Roots in Business: Amy Norquist: Greensulate, New York City" in Inc. (Volume 32, December 2010, No. 10, pp. 106)*
Pub: Inc. Magazine
Ed: Christine Lagorio. **Description:** Profile of Amy Norquist who left her position at an environmental nonprofit organization to found Greensulate. Her firm insulates rooftops with lavender, native grasses and succulents called sedum in order to eliminate carbon from the atmosphere.

35973 ■ *"Forum at UNCW to Explore Offshore Wind Farming" in Star-News (October 4, 2011)*
Pub: StarNews Media
Contact: Diane Keenan, Director of Marketing and Sales
Ed: Kate Elizabeth Queram. **Description:** North Carolina is poised to profit from offshore wind farming, according to regional environmental experts. The Sierra Club, in conjunction with the University of North Carolina Wilmington and Oceana are hosting an offshore wind forum featuring five panelists, focusing on potential impacts on birds and sea life, tourism and cost, as well as other pertinent issues.

35974 ■ *"Fossil Fuel, Renewable Fuel Shares Expected to Flip Flop" in Farm Industry News (April 29, 2011)*
Pub: Penton Business Media Inc.
Contact: David Kieselstein, Chief Executive Officer
Ed: Lynn Grooms. **Description:** Total energy use of fossil fuels is predicted to fall 5 percent by the year 2035, with renewable fuel picking it up.

35975 ■ *"Franchising's Green Scene" in Entrepreneur (Vol. 37, August 2009, No. 8, pp. 85)*
Pub: Entrepreneur Press
Contact: Perlman Neil, President
Ed: Gwen Moran. **Description:** Trends in favor of environmentally friendly franchises have been growing for about 25 years but have now become mainstream. The challenges for a prospective green franchisee is that these companies may be tricky to evaluate and they need to ask franchisors a lot of questions to weed out ones that falsely claim to be green.

35976 ■ *"Free 'Green Business' Workshops Set for Boynton Beach and Lake Worth" in Palm Beach Post (April 14, 2012)*
Pub: McClatchy Tribune Information Services
Ed: Eliot Kleinberg. **Description:** Florida Green Energy workshops will be held to assist companies to become certified as a green business and to also receive public money for energy-saving projects. The workshops will be held in Boynton Beach and Lake Worth, Florida.

35977 ■ *"From Scarcity to Plenty" in Inc. (Vol. 36, March 2014, No. 2, pp. 76)*
Pub: Mansueto Ventures L.L.C.
Contact: John Koten, Chief Executive Officer
Released: March 2014. **Description:** Profile of Mom's Organic Market which started in Scott Nash's mom's garage. Nash describes the healthy food choices offered at the store as well as its Environmental Restoration program which addressed issues including carbon offsets, recycling, and composting.

35978 ■ *"FSU's OGZEB Is Test Bed for Sustainable Technology" in Contractor (Vol. 56, October 2009, No. 10, pp. 1)*
Pub: Penton Media, Inc.
Ed: Candace Roulo. **Description:** Florida State University has one of 14 off-grid zero emissions buildings (OGZEB) in the U.S.; it was built to research sustainable and alternative energy systems. The building produces electricity from 30 photovoltaic panels and it also has three AET water heating solar panels on the roof.

35979 ■ *"FTC Issues Final Version of Green Guides: Revision Target Broad Claims, Force More Proof On Smaller Ones" in Advertising Age (Vol. 83, October 1, 2012, No. 36, pp. 5)*
Pub: Crain Communications Inc.
Contact: Rance E. Crain, President
Ed: Jack Neff. **Description:** Federal Trade Commission issued its final version of its Green Guides regulations to eliminate unclear, unsubstantiated or misleading environmental claims. The final Green Guides do not address two common words used in green marketing: sustainable and natural. However, the words green and eco-friendly qualified as specific claims.

35980 ■ *"Fuel King: The Most Fuel-Efficient Tractor of the Decade is the John Deere 8295R" in Farm Industry News (November 10, 2011)*
Pub: Penton Business Media Inc.
Contact: David Kieselstein, Chief Executive Officer
Description: Farm Industry News compiled a list of the most fuel-efficient tractors with help from the Nebraska Tractor Test Lab, with the John Deere 8295R PTO winner of the most fuel-efficient tractor of the decade.

35981 ■ *"Funeral Directors Get Creative As Boomers Near Great Beyond" in Advertising Age (Vol. 79, October 13, 2008, No. 38, pp. 30)*
Pub: Crain Communications Inc.
Contact: Rance Crain, President
Ed: Lenore Skenazy. **Description:** Despite the downturn in the economy, the funeral business is thriving due to the number of baby boomers who realize the importance of making preparations for their death. Marketers are getting creative in their approach and many companies have taken into consideration the need for a more environmental friendly way to dispose of bodies and thus have created innovative businesses that reflect this need.

35982 ■ *"Game On: The Hunt Is On for Nation's Top Keeper" in Farmer's Weekly (March 28, 2008, No. 320)*
Description: Gamekeepers must strike the natural balance that encourages wildlife and protects game. CLA Game Fair and Farmer's Weekly are holding a competition for Gamekeeper of the Year 2008.

35983 ■ *"GE Announces New Projects, Technology Milestone and New Service Program at AWEA Windpower 2012" in News Bites US (June 6, 2012)*
Pub: Financial Times Ltd.
Contact: John Ridding, Chief Executive Officer
Released: June 6, 2012. **Description:** General Electric announced plans at the AWEA Windpower 2012 for its two new wind turbine projects to be located in Michigan and Iowa. Details of these new wind turbine projects are included.

35984 ■ *"GE Milestone: 1,000th Wind Turbine Installed in Canada" in CNW Group (October 4, 2011)*
Pub: CNW Group Ltd.
Contact: Carolyn McGill-Davidson, President
Description: GE installed its 1,000th wind turbine in Canada at Cartier Wind Energy's Gros Morne project in the Gaspesie Region of Quebec, Canada. As Canada continues to expand its use of wind energy, GE plans to have over 1,100 wind turbines installed in the nation by the end of 2011.

35985 ■ *"General Electric Touts Going Green for Business Fleet Services" in America's Intelligence Wire (June 1, 2012)*
Pub: Financial Times Ltd.
Contact: John Ridding, Chief Executive Officer
Released: June 1, 2012. **Description:** General Capital Fleet Services if featuring alternative-fuel vehicles in Eden Prairie for its corporate customers. GE Capital is the world's largest fleet management service and is offering its customers the first of its kind service that allows corporate lease customers to test drive alternative fuel cars from 20 different manufacturers.

35986 ■ *"Germans Win Solar Decathlon Again" in Contractor (Vol. 56, November 2009, No. 11, pp. 1)*
Pub: Penton Media, Inc.
Ed: Robert P. Mader. **Description:** Students from Technische Universtat Darmstadt won the U.S. Department of Energy's Solar Decathlon by designing and building the most attractive and efficient solar-powered home. The winner's design produced a surplus of power even during three days of rain and photovoltaic panels covered nearly every exterior surface.

35987 ■ *"Getting the Bioheat Word Out" in Indoor Comfort Marketing (Vol. 70, September 2011, No. 9, pp. 32)*
Pub: Industry Publications Inc.
Contact: Shirleen Dorman, Editor
Description: Ways to market advanced liquid fuels to the public are outlined.

35988 ■ *"Getting Going on Going Green" in HRMagazine (Vol. 53, August 2008, No. 8, pp. 8)*
Pub: Society for Human Resource Management
Contact: Henry G. Jackson, President
E-mail: hjackson@shrm.org
Ed: Rita Zeidner. **Description:** Being eco-friendly can help recruit and retain workers. Resources to help firms create green initiatives are presented.

35989 ■ *"Getting NORA reauthorized is high priority" in Indoor Comfort Marketing (Vol. 70, February 2011, No. 2, pp. 14)*
Pub: Industry Publications Inc.
Contact: Shirleen Dorman, Editor
Description: The importance of reauthorizing the National Oilheat Research Alliance is stressed.

35990 ■ *"The GHG Quandary: Whose Problem Is It Anyway?" in Canadian Business (Vol. 81, September 15, 2008, No. 14-15, pp. 72)*
Ed: Matthew McClearn. **Description:** Nongovernmental organizations were able to revoke the permit for Imperial Oil Ltd's Kearl oilsands project on the grounds of its expected greenhouse gas emission but the court's ruling was rendered irrelevant by bureaucratic paper-shuffling shortly after. The idea of an environmental impact assessment as a guide to identify the consequences of a project is also discussed.

35991 ■ *"GIV Mobile Announces New Partnership with American Forests, the Oldest National Nonprofit Conservation Organization in the Country" in Ecology, Environment & Conservation Business (January 25, 2014, pp. 34)*
Pub: NewsRX
Contact: Susan E. Hasty, Publisher
Released: January 25, 2014. **Description:** GIV Mobile has partnered with American Forests to restore and protect urban and rural forests in the nation. GIV is the first consumer conscious wireless network and operates on the 4G network of T-Mobile USA cellular service.

35992 ■ *"The Global Environment Movement is Bjorn Again" in Canadian Business (Vol. 83, September 14, 2010, No. 15, pp. 11)*
Pub: Rogers Media Inc.
Contact: Tony Viner, President
Ed: Steve Maich. **Description:** Danish academic Bjorn Lomborg is in favor of decisive action to combat climate change in his new book and was given front page treatment by a London newspaper. Environmentalist groups see this as a victory since Lomborg had not previously considered climate change an immediate issue.

35993 ■ *"GM's Volt Woes Cast Shadow on E-Cars" in Wall Street Journal Eastern Edition (November 28, 2011, pp. B1)*
Pub: Dow Jones & Co., Inc.
Contact: Clare Hart, President
Ed: Sharon Terlep. **Description:** The future of electric cars is darkened with the government investigation by the National Highway Traffic Safety Administration into General Motor Company's Chevy Volt after two instances of the car's battery packs catching fire during crash tests conducted by the Agency.

35994 ■ *"Go Green Or Go Home" in Black Enterprise (Vol. 41, August 2010, No. 1, pp. 53)*
Pub: Earl G. Graves Publishing Co. Inc.
Contact: Earl G. Graves, Jr., President
Ed: Tennille M. Robinson. **Description:** The green economy has become an essential part of every business, however, small business owners need to learn how to participate, including minority owned entrepreneurs.

35995 ■ *"Going Green: Cut Energy Waste" in Inc. (Vol. 31, January-February 2009, No. 1, pp. 42)*
Pub: Mansueto Ventures L.L.C.
Contact: John Koten, Chief Executive Officer
Description: Carbon Control, Edison, and Saver software programs help companies cut carbon emissions by reducing the amount of energy consumed by computers while they are idle.

35996 ■ *"Going Green, Going Slowly" in Playthings (Vol. 106, September 1, 2008, No. 8, pp. 17)*
Pub: Reed Elsevier Group plc Reed Business Information
Contact: Mark Kelsey, Chief Executive Officer
Ed: Nancy Zweirs. **Description:** Sustainability and greener materials for both product and packaging in the toy industry has become important for protecting our environment. However, in a recent survey nearly 60 percent of responders stated environmental issues did not play a part in purchasing a toy or game for their children.

35997 ■ *"Golden Valley, Fling Hills Plan LNG Plant" in Alaska Business Monthly (Vol. 27, October 2011, No. 10, pp. 9)*
Pub: Alaska Business Publishing Company Inc.
Contact: Jim Martin, President
Ed: Nancy Pounds. **Description:** Golden Valley Electric Association and Flint Hills Resources have partnered on a natural gas liquefaction facility on the North Slope. The deal will deliver gas at cost to GVEA and Flint Hills and Flint Hills will become more competitive and efficient by burning LNG instead of refined crude oil at the refinery.

35998 ■ *Good Green Guide for Small Businesses: How to Change the Way Your Business Works for the Better*
Pub: A. & C. Black
Ed: Impetus Consulting Ltd. Staff. **Released:** September 1, 2009. **Price:** $19.95. **Description:** Guide for small businesses to take an environmental audit of their company and shows how to minimize the impact of office essentials such as utilities, insulation, recycling and waste, electrical equipment, water systems, lighting options, food and drink, and office cleaning arrangements and products.

35999 ■ *"Got to be Smarter than the Average Bear" in Contractor (Vol. 56, September 2009, No. 9, pp. 82)*
Pub: Penton Media, Inc.
Ed: Robert P. Mader. **Description:** International Association of Plumbing and Mechanical Officials Green Technical Committee has debated the need for contractors to have certifications in installing green plumbing. Some have argued that qualifications would discourage homeowners from improving their properties. Comments from executives are also included.

36000 ■ *"Gov. Kasich to Put DOD On Short Leash" in Business Courier (Vol. 27, November 26, 2010, No. 30, pp. 1)*
Pub: Business Courier
Ed: Dan Monk. **Description:** Ohio Governor-elect John Kasich proposed the privatization of the Ohio Department of Development in favor of a nonprofit corporation called JobsOhio. Kasich believes that the department has lost its focus by adding to its mission issues such as energy efficiency and tourism.

36001 ■ *"Grainger Show Highlights Building Green, Economic Recovery" in Contractor (Vol. 57, February 2010, No. 2, pp. 3)*
Pub: Penton Media, Inc.
Ed: Candace Roulo. **Description:** chief U.S. economist told attendees of the Grainger's 2010 Total MRO Solutions National Customer Show that the economic recovery would be subdued. Mechanical contractors who attended the event also learned about building sustainable, green products, and technologies, and economic and business challenges.

36002 ■ *"Greater Cincinnati Green Business Council Releases Composting Toolkit" in Health & Beauty Close-Up (April 2, 2012)*
Pub: Close-Up Media
Released: April 2, 2012. **Description:** The Greater Cincinnati Green Business Council worked with a local waste hauler called Rumpke, to provide a Workplace Composting Toolkit to support composting services in the city.

36003 ■ *"Green Acres" in Hawaii Business (Vol. 54, September 2008, No. 3, pp. 48)*
Pub: PacificBasin Communications
Ed: Jan Tenbruggencate. **Description:** Bill Cowern's Hawaiian Mahogany is a forestry business that processes low-value trees to be sold as wood chips, which can be burned to create biodiesel. Cowern is planning to obtain certification to market carbon credits and is also working with Green Energy Hawaii for the permit of a biomass-fueled power plant. Other details about Cowern's business are discussed.

36004 ■ *"Green Assets Powering Boralex Shares" in Globe & Mail (March 30, 2007, pp. B10)*
Pub: CTVglobemedia Publishing Inc.
Ed: Richard Blackwell. **Description:** The impact of econ-friendly power plant portfolio on the stock performance of Kingsey Falls-based Boralex Inc. is analyzed.

36005 ■ *Green Business: A Five-Part Model for Creating an Environmentally Responsible Company*
Pub: Schiffer Publishing Ltd.
Contact: Jeffrey B. Snyder, Manager
E-mail: juffs@schifferbooks.com
Ed: Amy K. Townsend. **Price:** $29.95, hardcover. **Description:** Five-part model for small companies to become a green business; the book discusses the advantages to following the current trend using environmentally-friendly practices. **Availability:** Print.

36006 ■ *"Green Business Owners Share Secrets of Success In This Business Guide" in PRNewsChannel.com (March 1, 2012)*
Released: March 1, 2012. **Description:** Business guide to help companies become sustainable and work to be a green business.

36007 ■ *"Green Business Plan Competition" in Chemical & Engineering News (Vol. 90, July 9, 2012, No. 28, pp. 34)*
Pub: American Chemical Society, Philadelphia Section
Contact: Steven Fleming, Chairman
Ed: Stephen K. Ritter. **Description:** Startup anticorrosion coatings firm AnCatt Inc. won the inaugural chemistry business plan competition at the Green Chemistry & Engineering Conference held in July 2012 in Washington, DC. AnCatt was honored for its conducting-polymer-based anticorrosion paint system aimed at replacing chromate, lead, and cadmium paint pigments.

36008 ■ *Green Business Practices for Dummies*
Ed: Lisa Swallow. **Released:** January 2009. **Price:** $21.99. **Description:** The book provides information for any small business to help reduce environmental impact without reducing their company's bottom line.

36009 ■ *"Green Business Push Blooms" in Charlotte Observer (February 7, 2007)*
Ed: Christopher D. Kirkpatrick. **Description:** Many energy companies are capitalizing on corporate guild about global warming. Companies offering environmental peace of mind are discussed.

36010 ■ *"Green and Clean" in Retail Merchandiser (Vol. 51, July-August 2011, No. 4, pp. 56)*
Pub: Phoenix Media Corporation
Description: Green Valley Grocery partnered with Paragon Solutions consulting firm to make their stores environmentally green.

36011 ■ *"'Green' Cleaners Buys Seattle Firm"* in *Puget Sound Business Journal (Vol. 29, December 19, 2008, No. 35, pp. 3)*
Pub: American City Business Journals
Ed: Greg Lamm. **Description:** Washington-based Blue Sky Cleaners has purchased Four Seasons Cleaners. The green company also purchased Queen Anne store and Four Seasons' routes fro Snohomish County through Seattle.

36012 ■ *The Green Collar Economy: How One Solution Can Fix Our Two Biggest Problems*
Pub: HarperCollins Publishers Inc.
Contact: Jane Friedman, President
E-mail: jfriedman@harpercollins.com
Ed: Van Jones. **Released:** September 29, 2009.
Price: $14.99, paperack; $10.99; C$11.99. **Description:** This book offers insight into rebuilding the nation's infrastructure and creating alternative energy sources that could boost the economy through increased employment and higher wages while decreasing our dependence on fossil fuels. **Availability:** PrintE-book.

36013 ■ *"Green Collar: Green Buildings Support Job Creation, Workforce Transformation and Economic Recovery"* in *Environmental Design and Construction (Vol. 15, July 2012, No. 7, pp. 31)*
Pub: BNP Media
Contact: Tagg Henderson, Chief Executive Officer
Ed: Maggie Comstock. **Description:** Despite construction being at an all-time low, green building construction has maintained its hold on nonresidential buildings. It has even shown growth in some sectors and accounts for over one-third of all nonresidential design and construction jobs and is expected to show further growth through 2014. Statistical details included.

36014 ■ *"The Green Conversation"* in *Harvard Business Review (Vol. 86, September 2008, No. 9, pp. 58)*
Pub: Harvard Business Review Press
Contact: Peter E. Walsh, Director
Ed: Andrew J. Hoffman, John Woody, Judith Samuelson, Steve Bishop, Rakesh Khurana, Nitin Nohria, Sir Stuart Rose, Brian Walker. **Description:** Six guidelines are presented for addressing and benefiting from environmentally conscious corporate decision making and practices. Topics covered include marketing, supply chain, and leadership.

36015 ■ *"Green Energy Exec Hits State Policy"* in *Boston Business Journal (Vol. 30, December 3, 2010, No. 45, pp. 1)*
Pub: Boston Business Journal
Ed: Kyle Alspach. **Description:** American Superconductor Corporation President Dan McGahn believes that the state government of Massachusetts is not proactive enough to develop the state into a manufacturing hub for wind power technology. McGahn believes that while Governor Deval Patrick campaigned for wind turbines in the state, his administration does not have the focus required to build the turbines in the state.

36016 ■ *Green to Gold: How Smart Companies Use Environmental Strategy to Innovate, Create Value, and Build Competitive Advantage*
Pub: Yale University Press
Contact: John D. Rollins, Chief Financial Officer
E-mail: john.rollins@yale.edu
Ed: Daniel C. Esty, Andrew S. Winston. **Released:** October 09, 2006. **Price:** $27.50. **Description:** Examples are given for small businesses to beat competition while tackling sustainability, engage stakeholders, develop NGO partnerships, and work environmental stewardship into corporate culture.

36017 ■ *The Green Guide for Business: The Ultimate Environment for Businesses of All Sizes*
Pub: Profile Books Limited
Ed: Chris Goodball, Roger East, Hannah Bullock. **Released:** May 10, 2010. **Price:** £9.99. **Description:** Everyone wants to go green these days, but for small

businesses that's easier said than done. How do you measure a company's carbon footprint? Are dryers or hand towels more eco-friendly? Recycled paper or FSC-certified? All these questions and more are explored. **Availability:** E-book.

36018 ■ *"Green Housing for the Rest of Us"* in *Inc. (November 2007, pp. 128-129)*
Pub: Gruner and Jahr USA Publishing Co.
Contact: J. Russell Denson, President
Ed: Nitasha Tiku. **Description:** Profile of Full Spectrum NY, real estate developer firm, offering residences at the Kalahari, a green high-rise with state-of-the-art features at a reasonable price.

36019 ■ *"Green It Like You Mean It"* in *Special Events Magazine (Vol. 28, February 1, 2009, No. 2)*
Ed: Christine Landry. **Description:** Eco-friendly party planners offer advice for planning and hosting green parties or events. Tips include information for using recycled paper products, organic food and drinks. The Eco Nouveau Fashion Show held by Serene Star Productions reused old garments to create new fashions as well as art pieces from discarded doors and window frames for the show; eco-friendly treats and gift bags were highlighted at the event.

36020 ■ *"Green Light"* in *The Business Journal-Portland (Vol. 25, July 11, 2008, No. 18, pp. 1)*
Ed: Erik Siemers. **Description:** Ecos Consulting, a sustainability consulting company based in Portland, Oregon, is seeing a boost in revenue as more businesses turn to sustainable practices. The company's revenue rose by 50 percent in 2007 and employees increased from 57 to 150. Other details about Ecos' growth are discussed.

36021 ■ *"Green Manufacturer Scouts Sites in Greater Cincinnati"* in *Business Courier (Vol. 27, July 23, 2010, No. 12, pp. 1)*
Pub: Business Courier
Ed: Dan Monk. **Description:** CresaPartners is searching for a manufacturing facility in Cincinnati, Ohio. The company is set to tour about ten sites in the area.

36022 ■ *"Green Pipe Helps Miners Remove the Black"* in *Contractor (Vol. 57, January 2010, No. 1, pp. 1)*
Pub: Intertec Publishing
Contact: John French, President
Description: Lyons Co. Mechanical Contractors and Engineers installed a piping system for the River View Coal Mine facility's shower rooms. Lyons used Aquatherm's polypropylene piping system which creates seamless connections in the piping.

36023 ■ *"Green Rules To Drive Innovation: Charging for Carbon Can Inspire Conservation, Fuel Competition, and Enhance Competitiveness"* in *Harvard Business Review (Vol. 90, March 2012, No. 3, pp. 120)*
Pub: Harvard Business Review Press
Contact: Peter E. Walsh, Director
Ed: Daniel C. Esty, Steve Charnovitz. **Released:** March 2012. **Description:** Along with carbon emissions charges, other green policy recommendations include expanding domestic renewable power and the use of natural gas, increasing federal funding of clean-energy research, utilizing incentive-based approaches to encourage the adoption of renewable energy, and implementing the World Trade Organization's Doha negotiations on sustainable development.

36024 ■ *"Green Shift Sees Red"* in *Canadian Business (Vol. 81, September 29, 2008, No. 16)*
Ed: Jeff Sanford. **Description:** Green Shift Inc. is suing the Liberal Party of Canada in an $8.5 million lawsuit for using the phrase 'green shift' when they rolled out their carbon tax and climate change policy. The company has come to be recognized as a consultant and provider of green products such as non-toxic, biodegradable cups, plates, and utensils for events.

36025 ■ *"The Green Trap"* in *Canadian Business (Vol. 80, April 9, 2007, No. 8, pp. 19)*
Ed: Al Rosen. **Description:** Expert advice to companies on investing in environmental-friendly measures is presented.

36026 ■ *Green Your Small Business: Profitable Ways to Become an Ecopreneur*
Pub: McGraw-Hill
Ed: Scott Cooney. **Released:** November 2008. **Price:** A$29.95; NZ$35. **Description:** Advice and guidance is given to help any entrepreneur start, build or grow a green business, focusing on green business basics, market research and financing, as well as handling legal and insurance issues.

36027 ■ *"Greenhouse Announces Reverse Merger With Custom Q, Inc."* in *Investment Weekly (January 30, 2010, pp. 338)*
Pub: Investment Weekly News
Description: In accordance with an Agreement and Plan of Share Exchange, GreenHouse Holdings, Inc., an innovative green solutions provider, has gone public via a reverse merger with Custom Q, Inc.

36028 ■ *"Greening the Auto Industry"* in *Business Journal-Serving Phoenix & the Valley of the Sun (Vol. 30, July 23, 2010, No. 46, pp. 1)*
Pub: Phoenix Business Journal
Ed: Patrick O'Grady. **Description:** Thermo Fluids Inc. has been recycling used oil products since 1993 and could become Arizona's first home for oil filter recycling after retrofitting its Phoenix facility to include a compaction machine. The new service could help establish Thermo Fluids as a recycling hub for nearby states.

36029 ■ *"The Greening of Lunch"* in *Entrepreneur (Vol. 37, October 2009, No. 10, pp. 44)*
Pub: Entrepreneur Press
Contact: Perlman Neil, President
Ed: Deborah Song. **Description:** Kids Konserve is a self-funded online business selling reusable and recycled lunch kits for kids. The company also aims to increase awareness about waste reduction.

36030 ■ *"Greening the Manscape"* in *Canadian Business (Vol. 81, October 13, 2008, No. 17, pp. S19)*
Ed: David Lackie. **Description:** Buyer's guide of environmentally friendly grooming products for men is provided. Improved formulations have solved the problems of having synthetic ingredients in grooming products. Details about a face scrub, after shave conditioner, and a nourishing cream made of 91 percent organic ingredients are given, including prices.

36031 ■ *Greening Your Small Business: How to Improve Your Bottom Line, Grow Your Brand, Satisfy Your Customers and Save the Planet*
Ed: Jennifer Kaplan. **Released:** November 03, 2009.
Price: $19.95. **Description:** A definitive resource for anyone who wants their small business to be cutting-edge, competitive, profitable, and eco-conscious. Stories from small business owners address every aspect of going green, from basics such as recycling waste, energy efficiency, and reducing information technology footprint, to more in-depth concerns such as green marketing and communications, green business travel, and green employee benefits.

36032 ■ *"GreenTech Gears Up for Production"* in *Memphis Business Journal (Vol. 33, April 6, 2012, No. 52, pp. 1)*
Pub: American City Business Journals
Description: GreenTech Automotive has broken ground for construction of a new production facility in Tunica, Tennessee. The company will focus its manufacturing operations in the new facility.

36033 ■ *"Groups Seek Donations to Recycle Christmas Trees"* in *The Register-Guard*

(January 7, 2012, pp. B11)
Pub: McClatchy-Tribune Regional News
Released: January 7, 2012. **Description:** Groups wishing to recycle used Christmas trees in the Eugene, Oregon area are listed. Some of the groups offer incentives as well as free pickup. Contact information for each group is provided.

36034 ■ *"A Growing Concern" in Canadian Business (Vol. 79, October 9, 2006, No. 20, pp. 90)*
Ed: Jeff Sanford. **Description:** With rich dividends being harvested by companies producing ethanol, after ethanol became a petrol additive, is discussed.

36035 ■ *Guerrilla Marketing Goes Green: Winning Strategies to Improve Your Profits and Your Planet*
Pub: John Wiley & Sons Inc.
Contact: Stephen M. Smith, President
Ed: Jay Conrad Levinson, Shel Horowitz. **Released:** January 2010. **Price:** $21.95, paperback; $14.99. **Description:** The latest tips on green marketing and sustainable business strategies are shared. **Availability:** PrintE-book.

36036 ■ *"Guide to Carbon Footprinting" in American Printer (Vol. 128, June 1, 2011, No. 6)*
Pub: Penton Media Inc.
Description: PrintCity Alliance published its new report, 'Carbon Footprint & Energy Reduction for Graphic Industry Value Chain.' The report aims to help improve the environmental performance of printers, converters, publishers, brand owners and their suppliers.

36037 ■ *"Habitat, Home Depot Expand Building Program" in Contractor (Vol. 56, September 2009, No. 9, pp. 16)*
Pub: Penton Media, Inc.
Description: Habitat for Humanity International and The Home Depot Foundation are planning to expand their Partners in Sustainable Building program. The program will provide funds to help Habitat affiliates build 5,000 homes. Comments from executives are also included.

36038 ■ *"Handling Recycling with PaintCare" in Business Journal Portland (Vol. 30, February 28, 2014, No. 52, pp. 10)*
Pub: American City Business Journals
Released: February 28, 2014. **Description:** PaintCare Oregon program manager, Roy Weedman, says the program has achieved permanent status. He also said the program will continue collecting used paint from residents and businesses for free. Weedman added that the program has increased the number of its used paint drop off sites.

36039 ■ *"Hard Rock on Pike" in Puget Sound Business Journal (Vol. 29, September 5, 2008, No. 20, pp. 1)*
Ed: Jeanne Lang Jones. **Description:** A branch of the Hard Rock Cafe is opening in 2009 in the Liberty Building on Pike Street in downtown Seattle, Washington. The location is being renovated as a green building; the restaurant and concert venue will seat 300 patrons and has a rooftop deck and memorabilia shop.

36040 ■ *"Harpoon Brewery Wins Boston Green Business Award for Sustainability and EnerNOC Energy Management Programs" in Investment Weekly News (May 12, 2012, No. 543)*
Description: Harpoon Brewery was awarded a 2012 Boston Green Business Award by Mayor Thomas Menino of Boston, Massachusetts. The brewery was cited for having an exceptional sustainability program that includes waste reduction, responsible chemical usage, and operational efficiency measures combined with energy management initiatives with EnerNOC. EnerNOC is a leading provider of energy management applications for commercial, industrial, and institutional energy users, including Harpoon.

36041 ■ *"Helping Customers Fight Pet Waste" in Pet Product News (Vol. 64, November 2010, No. 11, pp. 52)*
Pub: Bowtie Inc.
Ed: Sandy Robins. **Description:** Pet cleaning products manufacturers have been enjoying high sales figures by paying attention to changing pet ownership trends and environmental awareness. Meanwhile, the inclusion of user-friendly features in these products has also been boosted by the social role of pets and the media attention to pet waste. How manufacturers have been responding to this demand is explored.

36042 ■ *"Hey, You Can't Do That" in Green Industry Pro (Vol. 23, September 2011)*
Pub: Cygnus Business Media
Contact: Paul Mackler, Chief Executive Officer
Ed: Rod Dickens. **Description:** Manufacturers of landscape equipment are making better use of energy resources, such as the use of fuel-injection systems instead of carburetors, lightweight materials, better lubricants, advanced battery technology, and innovative engine designs.

36043 ■ *"High Energy: Gaurdie Banister Joins Aera As President and CEO" in Black Enterprise (Vol. 38, July 2008, No. 12, pp. 30)*
Pub: Earl G. Graves Publishing Co. Inc.
Contact: Earl G. Graves, Jr., President
Ed: Brenda Porter. **Description:** Gaurdie Banister Jr. has been appointed president and CEO of Aera Energy L.L.C., becoming one of the first African Americans in the nation to run a major energy corporation. His plans for the firm include utilizing new, sophisticated technologies in order to unlock the 3-1/2 billion barrels of resources the company has on their books in a safe and environmentally friendly way. He also hopes to increase production and maintain cost leadership.

36044 ■ *"Homing In On the Future" in Black Enterprise (Vol. 38, October 1, 2007, No. 3, pp. 61)*
Pub: Earl G. Graves Publishing Co. Inc.
Contact: Earl G. Graves, Jr., President
Ed: Sean Drakes. **Description:** More and more people are wanting new homes wired automated systems that integrate multiple home devices such as computers, audio/visual entertainment, security, communications, utilities, and lighting and environmental controls.

36045 ■ *"Hoping To Make a Big Splash" in Austin Business Journal (Vol. 34, June 20, 2014, No. 18, pp. 14)*
Pub: American City Business Journals, Inc.
Contact: Whitney Shaw, President
Released: June 20, 2014. **Description:** Austin-based Hydro Toys LLC launched ZORBZ in May 2014, a self-sealing balloon made out of Goodyear latex. ZORBZ balloons are manufactured in specially designed molds made from aircraft-quality aluminum, while a proprietary, natural, non-toxic and biodegradable material is used to make the valve system.

36046 ■ *"Hot Air: On Global Warming and Carbon Tax" in Canadian Business (Vol. 81, October 13, 2008, No. 17, pp. 12)*
Ed: Joe Castaldo. **Description:** Survey of Canadian business leaders revealed that the environment is a key issue in Canada's federal elections. Respondents believe that Prime Minister Stephen Harper's views on global warming and climate change are closer to their own views. Other key information on the survey is presented.

36047 ■ *Hot, Flat and Crowded: Why We Need a Green Revolution - and How It Can Renew America*
Pub: Noonday Press Farrar, Straus & Giroux Inc.
Contact: Jonathan Galassi, President
E-mail: Jonathan.galassi@fsgbooks.com
Ed: Thomas L. Friedman. **Released:** September 08, 2008. **Price:** $27.95, Hardcover. **Description:** Author explains how global warming, rapidly growing populations, and the expansion of the world's middle class through globalization have impacted the environment.

36048 ■ *Housecleaning Business: Organize Your Business - Get Clients and Referrals - Set Rates and Services*
Pub: Globe Pequot Press Inc.
Contact: Robert Irwin, Manager
E-mail: robert.irwin@globepequot.com
Ed: Laura Jorstad, Melinda Morse. **Released:** June 24, 2009. **Price:** $18.95, paperback. **Description:** This book shares insight into starting a housecleaning business. It shows how to develop a service manual, screen clients, serve customers, select cleaning products, competition, how to up a home office, using the Internet to grow the business and offering green cleaning options to clients. **Availability:** Print.

36049 ■ *"How Bad Is It?" in Hawaii Business (Vol. 54, July 2008, No. 1, pp. 35)*
Pub: PacificBasin Communications
Ed: Jolyn Okimoto Rosa. **Description:** Donald G. Horner, chief executive officer of First Hawaiian Bank, says that the current Hawaiian economic situation is a cyclical slowdown. Maurice Kaya, an energy consultant, says the slowdown is due to overdependence on imported fuels. Other local leaders, such as Constance H. Lau, also discuss their view on the current economic situation in Hawaii.

36050 ■ *"How Green Is The Valley?" in Barron's (Vol. 88, July 4, 2008, No. 28, pp. 13)*
Description: San Jose, California has made a good start towards becoming a leader in alternative energy technology through the establishment of United Laboratories' own lab in the city. The certification process for photovoltaic cells will be dramatically shortened with this endeavor.

36051 ■ *"How I Did It: Timberland's CEO On Standing Up to 65,000 Angry Activists" in Harvard Business Review (Vol. 88, September 2010, No. 9, pp. 39)*
Pub: Harvard Business School Publishing
Ed: Jeff Swartz. **Description:** Timberland Company avoided a potential boycott by taking a two-way approach. It addressed a supplier issue that posed a threat to the environment, and launched an email campaign to keep Greenpeace activists informed of the development of a new supplier agreement.

36052 ■ *"How to Reuse Or Recycle Your Old Tech: eWaste Is On the Rise But You Can Help Combat It By Using Old PCs and Electronics In Different Ways" in PC Magazine (Vol. 31, February 2012, No. 2, pp. 108)*
Description: US recycling businesses employ 30,000 workers to recycle 3.5 million tons of electronic waste, that does not include the number of devices that go to landfills. Simple and cheap ways to recycle or put old electronics to work are examined.

36053 ■ *"How to... Harness Green Power" in The Caterer (July 20, 2012, No. 325)*
Pub: Reed Business Information Ltd.
Description: Roger and Emma Stevens discuss their success as at winning the Considerate Hoteliers Association's award for Best Green Marketing Initiative. The couple discusses their restaurant and its partnership with tow nearby guesthouses.

36054 ■ *"Hybrid Popularity Pushes Automakers to Add to Offerings" in Crain's Cleveland Business (Vol. 28, November 12, 2007, No. 45, pp. 30)*
Ed: David Sedgwick. **Description:** Due in part to Toyota's innovative marketing, automotive hybrids have caught on with consumers thus forcing other automakers to add hybrids to their product plans.

36055 ■ *"Hydronicahh - Everything in Modulation" in Contractor (Vol. 56, December 2009, No. 12, pp. 24)*
Pub: Intertec Publishing
Contact: John French, President
Ed: Mark Eatherton. **Description:** Management and the environmental impact of a home hydronic system are discussed. Radiant windows have the potential to reduce energy consumption. A variable speed delta T pump is required for the construction of a hydronic wood pit.

36056 ■ *"IAPMO GTC Debates Supplement"* in *Contractor (Vol. 56, September 2009, No. 9, pp. 3)*

Pub: Penton Media, Inc.

Ed: Robert P. Mader. Description: Green Technical Committee of the International Association of Plumbing and Mechanical Officials is developing a Green Plumbing and Mechanical Supplement. The supplement provides for installation of systems by licensed contractors and installers. Comments from officials are also presented.

36057 ■ *"IAPMO GTC Finalizes Green Supplement"* in *Contractor (Vol. 57, January 2010, No. 1, pp. 1)*

Pub: Intertec Publishing

Contact: John French, President

Ed: Candace Roulo. Description: International Association of Plumbing and Mechanical Officials' Green Technical Committee finalized the Green Plumbing & Mechanical Code Supplement. The supplement was created to provide a set of provisions that encourage sustainable practices and work towards the design and construction of plumbing and mechanical systems.

36058 ■ *"IAPMO GTC Votes to Limit Showers to 2.0-GPM"* in *Contractor (Vol. 56, September 2009, No. 9, pp. 1)*

Ed: Robert P. Mader. Description: Green Technical Committee of the International Association of Plumbing and Mechanical Officials has voted to limit showers to 2.0 GPM. It is also developing a Green Plumbing and Mechanical Supplement. Comments from executives are also supplied.

36059 ■ *"ICC Works on Prescriptive Green Construction Code"* in *Contractor (Vol. 56, October 2009, No. 10, pp. 1)*

Pub: Penton Media, Inc.

Ed: Robert P. Mader. Description: International Code Council launched an initiative to create a green construction code that focuses on existing commercial buildings. The initiative's timeline will include public meetings leading up to a final draft that will be available in 2010.

36060 ■ *"Ill. Residential Building Legislation Includes New HVAC Requirements"* in *Contractor (Vol. 56, July 2009, No. 7, pp. 3)*

Pub: Intertec Publishing

Contact: John French, President

Ed: Candace Roulo. Description: Illinois' Energy Efficient Building Act will require all new buildings and houses to conform to the International Energy Conservation Code. The code includes a duct leakage requirement followed by a post-construction test to verify leakage rates and requires programmable thermostats on all houses.

36061 ■ *"Illinois Bets On Recycling Programs"* in *Chicago Tribune (November 29, 2008)*

Pub: McClatchy-Tribune Information Services

Ed: Joel Hood. Description: Traditionally the holiday gift-giving season is one of the most wasteful times of year and the state of Illinois is granting $760,000 to small businesses and cities in an attempt to expand curbside recycling programs and hire additional workers to address electronic waste.

36062 ■ *"Independence Station Utilizes Sustainable Technologies"* in *Contractor (Vol. 56, September 2009, No. 9, pp. 3)*

Pub: Penton Media, Inc.

Ed: Candace Roulo. Description: Independence Station building in Oregon is seen to receive the most LEED points ever awarded by the United States Green Building Council. The building will use an ice-based cooling storage system, biofuel cogeneration system and phovoltaic system. Other building features and dimensions are also supplied.

36063 ■ *"IndieCompanyDk Offers Eco-Friendly Furniture That Stands Out"* in *Ecology, Environment & Conservation*

Business (September 6, 2014, pp. 39)

Pub: NewsRX

Contact: Susan E. Hasty, Publisher

Released: September 6, 2014. Description: A new manufacturer of eco-friendly furniture and interiors, IndieCompanyDk, is offering a new concept in sustainable furniture design, using exclusive and affordable smooth designs, which maintain the natural and raw look of quality reclaimed materials.

36064 ■ *"Indoor Air Quality ? a Tribute to Efficiency"* in *Indoor Comfort Marketing (Vol. 70, August 2011, No. 8, pp. 8)*

Pub: Industry Publications Inc.

Contact: Shirleen Dorman, Editor

Ed: Matthew Maleske. Description: Efficiency of new HVAC/R equipment has helped improve indoor air quality.

36065 ■ *"Industry Escalates Lobbying Efforts For Loan Program"* in *Crain's Detroit Business (Vol. 24, September 22, 2008, No. 38, pp. 22)*

Pub: Crain Communications Inc.

Contact: Rance E. Crain, President

Ed: Jay Greene, Ryan Beene, Harry Stoffer. Description: Auto suppliers such as Lear Corp., which is best known for vehicle seating, also supplies high-voltage wiring for Ford hybrids and is developing other hybrid components. These suppliers are joining automakers in lobbying for the loan program which would promote the accelerated development of fuel-efficient vehicles.

36066 ■ *"Info Junkie"* in *Crain's Chicago Business (Vol. 34, October 24, 2011, No. 42, pp. 35)*

Pub: Crain Communications Inc.

Contact: Todd Johnson, Publisher

Ed: Christina Le Beau. Description: Greg Colando, president of Flor Inc., an eco-friendly carpet company located I Chicago discusses his marketing program to increase sales.

36067 ■ *"Insider: Peak Oil"* in *Canadian Business (Vol. 81, Summer 2008, No. 9, pp. 170)*

Pub: Rogers Media Inc.

Contact: Tony Viner, President

Ed: Jeff Sanford, Thomas Watson. Description: Oil peak theory posits that the world has consumed half of the non-renewable resources is indicated by the surging oil prices. However, critics argued that the high oil prices are effects of market speculation and not the depletion of the supply. Ten reasons on why to buy and not buy peak oil are presented.

36068 ■ *"Integral USA Magazine Sponsors Eco-Fashion in the Park"* in *Entertainment Close-Up (September 2, 2011)*

Pub: Close-Up Media

Description: Integral Magazine sponsored Eco-Fashion in the Park, a fashion show for the fashion conscious. Eleven independent designers will show their eco-friendly fashions at the event.

36069 ■ *"Interested in 12 Billion Dollars?"* in *Indoor Comfort Marketing (Vol. 70, March 2011, No. 3, pp. 18)*

Pub: Industry Publications Inc.

Contact: Shirleen Dorman, Editor

Ed: Matthew Maleske. Description: Trends in the indoor quality industry are cited, with insight into expanding an existing indoor heating and cooling business.

36070 ■ *"Invest in Energy-Efficient Equipment for Your Pet Store"* in *Pet Product News (Vol. 66, September 2012, No. 9, pp. 72)*

Pub: Bowtie Inc.

Ed: Leila Meyer. Description: Aquatic retailers can achieve business growth by offering lighting products, pumps, heaters, filters, and other aquarium supplies that would help customers realize energy efficiency. Aside from offering an education in energy efficiency as a customer service opportunity, retailers are encouraged to determine what supplies are crucial in helping customers achieve energy usage goals.

36071 ■ *"Iogen in Talks to Build Ethanol Plant in Canada"* in *Globe & Mail (March 21, 2007, pp. B7)*

Pub: CTVglobemedia Publishing Inc.

Ed: Shawn McCarthy. Description: Ottawa based Iogen Corp. is planning to construct a cellulosic ethanol plant in Saskatchewan region. The company will be investing an estimated $500 million for this purpose.

36072 ■ *"Iogen, VW Look to Build Ethanol Plant"* in *Globe & Mail (January 9, 2006, pp. B3)*

Pub: CTVglobemedia Publishing Inc.

Ed: Simon Tuck. Description: Iogen Corp. and Volkswagen AG plan cellulose ethanol plant in Germany. The details of the project are presented.

36073 ■ *"Iron Man Forges New Path"* in *Canadian Business (Vol. 80, February 12, 2007, No. 4, pp. 41)*

Ed: Rachel Pulfer. Description: The research of Donald Sadoway of Massachusetts Institute of Technology in making iron in an environmentally friendly method using electrolysis is discussed.

36074 ■ *"Is Mulcair Good for Business?"* in *Canadian Business (Vol. 85, June 11, 2012, No. 10, pp. 20)*

Pub: George Media Inc.

Ed: Sarah Barmak. Released: June 11, 2012. Description: Some of the pronouncements made by New Democratic Party leader Thomas Mulcair suggest that he may be both a friend and an enemy of the Canadian business community. He expressed supportto the energy sector and endorsed lower taxes but also commented on the negative effect of oilsands development.

36075 ■ *"It's Always 55 Degrees F"* in *Contractor (Vol. 56, September 2009, No. 9, pp. 38)*

Pub: Penton Media, Inc.

Ed: Carol Fey. Description: Geothermal-exchange heating and cooling systems can save businesses up to 60 percent on energy costs for heating and cooling. Geothermal systems get heat from the earth during winter. Design, features and installation of geothermal systems are also discussed.

36076 ■ *"It's Not Easy Investing Green"* in *Entrepreneur (Vol. 37, August 2009, No. 8, pp. 64)*

Pub: Entrepreneur Press

Contact: Perlman Neil, President

Ed: Rosalind Resnick. Description: Some venture capitalists remain bullish on green investing despite signs of stagnation. One way for an investor to cash in on green investing is to invest in large public companies that are investing big in green initiatives. Being an angel investor to a local clean-tech company is another avenue.

36077 ■ *"Jennifer Hernandez Helps Developers Transform Contaminated Properties"* in *Hispanic Business (Vol. 30, April 2008, No. 4, pp. 32)*

Pub: Hispanic Business Inc.

Contact: Jesus Chavarria, President

Ed: Hildy Medina. Description: Jennifer Hernandez is a partner and head of the law firm of Holland & Knight's environmental practice which specializes in the restoration of polluted land where former industrial and commercial buildings once stood, known as brownfields. Brownfield redevelopment can be lucrative but costly due to the cleaning up of contaminated land and challenging because of federal and state environmental laws.

36078 ■ *"Johnston Landfill Again Subject of Legal Dispute"* in *Providence Business News (Vol. 28, January 20, 2014, No. 42, pp. 1)*

Pub: American City Business Journals

Released: January 20, 2014. Description: The Conservation Law Foundation filed a lawsuit against the operators and owners of the Central landfill in Johnston, Rhode Island in December 2013 due to alleged violations of the Clean Air Act. Homeowners are also concerned about the possible hazardous impact of the landfill on the value of their property.

36079 ■ "KC Sewer Solutions May Overflow With Green Ideas" in The Business Journal-Serving Metropolitan Kansas City (August 22, 2008)

Pub: American City Business Journals, Inc.

Contact: Whitney Shaw, President

Ed: Suzanna Stagemeyer. **Description:** Adding green solutions such as small, dispersed basins to catch runoffs and the use of deep rooted natural plants to fix the sewer system of Kansas could probably justify the $2.3 billion worth of funds needed for the project. The city has been ordered by the EPA and the Missouri Department of Natural Resources to fix their sewer systems that are overwhelmed by significant rains.

36080 ■ "Keene: Nominations are Being Sought by the Keene Cities for Climate Protection Committee for the Monadnock Green Business of the Year Award" in New Hampshire Business Review (Vol. 34, February 24, 2012, No. 4, pp. 7)

Pub: Business Publications Corp.

Contact: Connie Wimer, President

Released: February 24, 2012. **Description:** Nominations are being sought by the Keene Cities for Climate Protection Committee for the Monadnock Green Business of the Year Award. The award recognizes socially and environmentally responsible companies in the region that have developed innovative practices or programs while contributing to the economic growth of the area.

36081 ■ "Keeping the Faith in Fuel-Tech" in Barron's (Vol. 88, March 24, 2008, No. 12, pp. 20)

Pub: Dow Jones & Co., Inc.

Contact: Clare Hart, President

Ed: Christopher C. Williams. **Description:** Shares of air pollution control company Fuel-Tech remain on track to reach $40 each from their $19 level due to a continued influx of contracts. The stock has suffered from lower-than-expected quarterly earnings and tougher competition but stand to benefit from increased orders.

36082 ■ "Kelvin Taketa, President, CEO Hawaii Community Foundation" in Hawaii Business (Vol. 53, October 2007, No. 4, pp. 30)

Pub: PacificBasin Communications

Ed: Scott Radway. **Description:** Hawaii Community Foundation chief executive officer Kelvin Taketa believes that the leadership shortage for nonprofit sector in Hawaii is a result of leaders retiring or switching to part-time work. Taketa adds that the duties of a nonprofit organization leader are very challenging, with the organizations being usually thinly staffed. His opinion on the prospects of young leadership in Hawaii is also given.

36083 ■ "Know the Facts About Natural Gas!" in Indoor Comfort Marketing (Vol. 70, August 2011, No. 8, pp. 26)

Pub: Industry Publications Inc.

Contact: Shirleen Dorman, Editor

Description: AEC Activity Update is presented on the American Energy Coalition's Website.

36084 ■ "Kohler Building Earns LEED Silver Certification" in Contractor (Vol. 56, September 2009, No. 9, pp. 12)

Pub: Penton Media, Inc.

Description: United States Green Building Council has awarded Kohler Co. with the Silver Leadership in Energy and Environmental Design Status. The award has highlighted the company's work to transform its building into a more environmentally efficient structure. A description of the facility is also provided.

36085 ■ "Kroger Releases Annual Sustainability Report" in Ecology, Environment & Conservation Business (July

26, 2014, pp. 46)

Pub: NewsRX

Contact: Susan E. Hasty, Publisher

Released: July 26, 2014. **Description:** Kroger Company published its eighth annual sustainability report. The company is committed to reducing water consumption in its grocery stores by 5 percent in 2014. The report also provides a progress report on moving retail locations toward 'zero waste' and sourcing 100 percent certified palm oil. Statistical data included.

36086 ■ "The Lap of Eco-Luxury" in Entrepreneur (Vol. 37, August 2009, No. 8, pp. 38)

Pub: Entrepreneur Press

Contact: Perlman Neil, President

Ed: Dina Mishev. **Description:** Founder Rob DesLauriers of the Terra Resort Group says that the natural world has taken very good care of him and that he wants to do his part to take care of it. The mattresses that their hotel uses are made from recycled steel springs and their TVs are Energy Star-approved. Their linens are made from organically grown cottons and their walls use by-products from coal burning.

36087 ■ "Large Homes can be Energy Efficient Too" in Contractor (Vol. 56, October 2009, No. 10, pp. 5)

Pub: Penton Media, Inc.

Ed: Candace Roulo. **Description:** Eco Estate at Briggs Chaney subdivision in Silver Spring, Maryland has model houses that use sustainable technologies and products and the homes that will be built on the subdivision will feature some of the technologies featured on the model home. The energy efficient HVAC system of the model homes are discussed.

36088 ■ "Legislation Introduced" in Indoor Comfort Marketing (Vol. 70, July 2011, No. 7, pp. 6)

Pub: Industry Publications Inc.

Contact: Shirleen Dorman, Editor

Description: New industry legislation is examined by the National Oilheat Research Alliance.

36089 ■ "Lessons Burma Taught Me" in Canadian Business (Vol. 85, July 16, 2012, No. 11-12, pp. 17)

Pub: George Media Inc.

Ed: Michael Lavergne. **Released:** July 16, 2012. **Description:** The decision of the Canadian government to allow trade with Burma presents Canadian firms with the challenge of ensuring that their projects benefit its people and its economy. Companies are advised to follow international monitoring agreements related to labor, ethnic rights, and environmental protection.

36090 ■ "Let's Put On a Show" in Inc. (November 2007, pp. 127)

Pub: Gruner and Jahr USA Publishing Co.

Contact: J. Russell Denson, President

Ed: Elaine Appleton Grant. **Description:** Profile of Jeff Baker, CEO of Image 4, designer of trade show exhibits. Baker shares details of the firm's commitment to being green.

36091 ■ "A Light Bulb Came On, and It Was Energy Efficient" in Globe & Mail (January 27, 2007, pp. B3)

Ed: Shawn McCarthy. **Description:** A brief profile of Edward Weinstein, chief executive officer of the Montreal-based family-run lighting firm Globe Electric Co., is presented The firm's management strategies are described.

36092 ■ "Lincoln Electric Installs Large Wind Tower" in Modern Machine Shop (Vol. 84, October 2011, No. 5, pp. 42)

Pub: Gardner Business Media, Inc.

Contact: Richard G. Kline, President

E-mail: rkline@gardnerweb.com

Description: Lincoln Electric, a welding product manufacturer, constructed a 443-foot-tall wind tower at its plant in Euclid, Ohio. The tower is expected to

generate as much as 10 percent of the facility's energy and save as much as $500,000 annually in energy costs.

36093 ■ "Lining Up at the Ethanol Trough (Ethanol Production in Canada)" in Globe & Mail (January 25, 2007, pp. B2)

Pub: CTVglobemedia Publishing Inc.

Ed: Eric Reguly. **Description:** The future of ethanol production in Canada is discussed; alternate fuel market is expected to reach 35 billion gallons by 2017.

36094 ■ "A Little Less Hot Air" in Canadian Business (Vol. 81, March 17, 2008, No. 4, pp. 9)

Pub: Rogers Media Inc.

Contact: Tony Viner, President

Description: British Columbia will levy an extra tax on all carbon-emitting fuels starting July 1, 2008. The tax will raise $1.8 billion in three years and in effect, the province will reduce general corporate income tax from 12 percent to 11 percent. The tax on small businesses and personal income will also be reduced.

36095 ■ "Local Green Technology on Display" in Crain's Detroit Business (Vol. 26, January 18, 2010, No. 3, pp. 1)

Pub: Crain Communications Inc.

Contact: Rance E. Crain, President

Ed: Ryan Beene. **Description:** Detroit's 2010 North American International Auto Show put the newest, most innovative green technologies on display showing that the Southeast Michigan automobile industry is gaining traction with its burgeoning e-vehicle infrastructure. Think, a Norwegian electric city-car manufacturer is eyeing sites in Southeast Michigan in which to locate its corporate headquarters and technical center for its North American branch.

36096 ■ "Long Live Rock" in Inc. (November 2007, pp. 130)

Pub: Gruner and Jahr USA Publishing Co.

Contact: J. Russell Denson, President

Ed: Nitasha Tiku. **Description:** Profile of a family business using chemistry to recycle concrete products.

36097 ■ "The Long View: Roberta Bondar's Unique Vision of Science, The Need for Education, and More" in Canadian Business (Vol. 81, October 27, 2008, No. 18)

Pub: Rogers Media Inc.

Contact: Tony Viner, President

Ed: Alex Mlynek. **Description:** Roberta Bondar believes that energy and renewable energy is a critical environmental issue faced by Canada today. Bondar is the first Canadian woman and neurologist in space.

36098 ■ "Lunch Box Maker Gives Back" in Marketing to Women (Vol. 23, November 2010, No. 11, pp. 5)

Pub: EPM Communications Inc.

Contact: Ira Mayer, President

E-mail: imayer@epmcom.com

Description: Female entrepreneurs launched a new program called, 'Share Your Lunch Project' that encourages mothers to give back and replace their child's lunchbox with their eco-friendly lunch boxes, which are available at select retailers. All proceeds from the project will benefit the World Food Program USA, which feeds children in developing countries.

36099 ■ "lynda.com Receives Green Business Certification" in Benzinga.com (July 11, 2012)

Pub: Benzinga.com

Contact: Kyle Bazzy, President

Ed: Aaron Wise. **Description:** Online learning firm, lynda.com, earned the Green Business certification from the Green Business Program (GBP) of Santa Barbara, California. The company has reduced energy and water usage, reduced solid waste such as composting food scraps and donating electronics, and created an employee commuter program saving 600 gallons of gas in its first two months.

36100 ■ "Magpower May Build Solar Panels Here" in Austin Business Journal (Vol. 31, May 13, 2011, No. 10, pp. A1)

Pub: American City Business Journals

Ed: Christopher Calnan. Description: RRE Austin Solar LLC CEO Doven Mehta has revealed plans to partner with Portugal-based Magpower SA, only if Austin energy buys electricity from planned solar energy farm in Pflugerville. Austin Energy has received 100 bids from 35 companies to supply 200 megawatts of solar- and wind-generated electricity.

36101 ■ "Major Auto Makers Take Aim at Toyota in Battle for Green Market Shares" in Hispanic Business (Vol. 30, September 2008, No. 9, pp. 90)

Pub: Hispanic Business Inc.

Contact: Jesus Chavarria, President

Ed: Daniel Soussa. Description: Three major car manufacturers, Chevrolet, BMW, and Honda, are giving market leader Toyota competition for the next generation of eco-friendly car. The latest and most advanced of the gasoline-less cars designed by the three firms, namely, the Chevrolet Volt, BMW's Hydrogen 7, and the Honda FCX Clarity, are reviewed.

36102 ■ "Making Waves" in Business Journal Portland (Vol. 27, November 26, 2010, No. 39, pp. 1)

Pub: Portland Business Journal

Ed: Erik Siemers. Description: Corvallis, Oregon-based Columbia Power Technologies LLC is about to close a $2 million Series A round of investment initiated by $750,000 from Oregon Angel Fund. The wave energy startup company was formed to commercialize the wave buoy technology developed by Oregon State University researchers.

36103 ■ "Manufacturers Become Part of Coalition" in Contractor (Vol. 56, July 2009, No. 7, pp. 40)

Pub: Penton Media, Inc.

Description: Bradford White Water Heaters, Rheem Water Heating, Rinnai America Corp., and A.O. Smith Water Heaters have joined the Consortium for Energy Efficiency in the Coalition for Energy Star Water Heaters. The coalition seeks to increase the awareness of Energy Star water heaters.

36104 ■ "Marine Act Amendments Gain Parliamentary Approval" in Canadian Sailings (July 7, 2008)

Ed: Alex Binkley. Description: Changes to the Canada Marine Act provides better borrowing deals as well as an ability to tap into federal infrastructure funding for environmental protection measures, security improvements and other site enhancements.

36105 ■ "Market Takes Shape for Emissions Credits" in Globe & Mail (April 16, 2007, pp. B3)

Ed: Shawn McCarthy. Description: The effort of Canadian companies to prepare for emissions trading after the government imposes climate change regulations is discussed.

36106 ■ "Loan Dollars Sit Idle for Energy Plan" in Baltimore Business Journal (Vol. 28, September 10, 2010, No. 18, pp. 1)

Pub: Baltimore Business Journal

Ed: Scott Dance. Description: The Maryland Energy Administration has millions of dollars in Federal stimulus and state energy efficiency cash sitting idle and might be lost once the window for stimulus spending is gone. However, businesses have no interest in betting on renewable energy because some cannot afford to take out more loans. Other challenges faced by these businesses are presented.

36107 ■ "Meet the Jetsons" in Entrepreneur (Vol. 35, November 2007, No. 11, pp. 21)

Pub: Entrepreneur Press

Contact: Perlman Neil, President

Ed: Amanda C. Kooser. Description: An overview of modern home devices is presented, including an organic light-emitting diode (OLED) wall display with changeable artwork, networked appliances like refrigerators, biometric door locks, and a television that can serve as a computer monitor.

36108 ■ "Mexican Companies to Rent Space in TechTown, Chinese Negotiating" in Crain's Detroit Business (Vol. 24, September 29, 2008, No. 39)

Pub: Crain Communications Inc.

Contact: Rance E. Crain, President

Ed: Tom Henderson. Description: Wayne State University's TechTown, the business incubator and research park, has signed an agreement with the Mexican government that will provide temporary office space to 25 Mexican companies looking to find customers or establish partnerships in Michigan. TechTown's executive director is negotiating with economic development officials from China. To accommodate foreign visitors the incubator is equipping offices with additional equipment and resources.

36109 ■ "MFG Wind Launched at AWEA WindPower 2012 Conference and Exhibition" in Marketing Weekly News (June 23, 2012, pp. 169)

Description: American Wind Energy Association's Conference & Exhibition was held in Atlanta, Georgia. The Molded Fiber Glass Companies (MFG) introduced MFG Wind, a new brand that stands for comprehensive wind-focused set of capabilities that it is bringing to the marketplace.

36110 ■ "Microsoft Is Cleaning Up the Cloud" in Puget Sound Business Journal (Vol. 35, August 29, 2014, No. 19, pp. 7)

Pub: American City Business Journals

Released: August 29, 2014. Description: Microsoft is forming a partnership with research organizations to conduct pilot projects on new forms of energy for its expanding cloud data centers. One project involves placing fuel cells directly into server racks that is said to be 40 percent more energy efficient than using power off the grid.

36111 ■ "Minnesota Firms Plug Into Solar" in Business Journal (Vol. 31, April 25, 2014, No. 48, pp. 10)

Pub: American City Business Journals

Released: April 25, 2014. Description: Minneapolis, Minnesota-based companies have been benefiting from the increase in solar energy projects. Xcel Energy Inc.'s demand for more power is expected to lure national solar companies to the city. Meanwhile, Geronimo Energy is planning a $250 million solar project in the state.

36112 ■ "Minnesota State Park Building Exemplifies Sustainability" in Contractor (Vol. 56, November 2009, No. 11, pp. 5)

Pub: Penton Media, Inc.

Ed: Candace Roulo. Description: Camden State Park's newly remodeled information/office building in Lynd, Minnesota features a 10 kw wind turbine which is capable of offsetting most of the facility's electricity and a geothermal heat pump system. The heat pump is a 4-ton vertical closed-loop ground source heat pump by ClimateMaster.

36113 ■ "Missouri Public Service Commission Chooses APX" in Wireless News (January 22, 2010)

Description: Missouri Public Service Commission, with the help of APX Inc., an infrastructure provider for environmental and energy markets, has selected the North American Registry as the renewable energy certificate management system for Missouri Renewable Energy Standard compliance. APX will continue to support the state's renewable energy programs and manage their environmental assets.

36114 ■ "Mixing Business and Pleasure On the Green" in Black Enterprise (Vol. 41, October 2010, No. 3, pp. 65)

Ed: Annya M. Lott. Description: Glow Golf, sponsored by Glow Sports, will offer instruction to 150 female corporate executives and entrepreneurs to learn the fundamentals of the game of golf.

36115 ■ "Molycorp Funds Wind Energy Technology Company" in Manufacturing Close-Up (September 19, 2011)

Pub: Close-Up Media

Description: Molycorp Inc., producer of rare earth oxides (REO) and a REO producer outside of China, announced it will invest in Boulder Wind Power, which has designed a rare earth magnet powered wind turbine generator. This new generator can produce electricity as low as $0.04 per Kilowatt Hour. Boulder Wind Power's patented wind turbine technology allows for use of rare earth permanent magnets that do not require dysprosium, which is relatively scarce.

36116 ■ "More Aid, Please: Letting the Sunshine In" in Barron's (Vol. 89, July 6, 2009, No. 27, pp. 11)

Pub: Dow Jones & Co., Inc.

Contact: Clare Hart, President

Ed: Katherine Cheng. Description: Solar energy industry leaders believe the industry needs aid from the US government regarding the funding of its research efforts and lowering solar energy costs. The climate change bill passed by the US House of Representatives signifies the US government's desire to significantly reduce carbon dioxide emissions.

36117 ■ "Motorola's New Cell Phone Lineup Includes Green Effort" in Chicago Tribune (January 14, 2009)

Pub: McClatchy-Tribune Information Services

Ed: Eric Benderoff. Description: Motorola Inc. introduced a new line of mobile phones at the Consumer Electronics Show in Las Vegas; the phones are made using recycled water bottles for the plastic housing.

36118 ■ "Natural Oils Key in Woman's Cleaning Service" in Charleston Gazette (January 22, 2012)

Pub: McClatchy Tribune Information Services

Released: January 22, 2012. Description: Profile of Darlene Rose who uses natural oils in her cleaning service called Smelling Like a Rose. She uses a holistic approach and has studied natural products for over 15 years. Aroma therapy enhances the cleaning process by her firm. Details of various oils and their use are covered.

36119 ■ The Necessary Revolution: Working Together to Create a Sustainable World

Pub: Broadway Business

Contact: David Drake, Manager

E-mail: ddrake@randomhouse.com

Ed: Peter M. Senge, Bryan Smith, Nina Kruschwitz, Joe Laur, Sara Schley. Released: April 06, 2010. Price: $18, paperback. Description: The book outlines various examples for companies to implement sustainable change and go green in the process. Availability: Print.

36120 ■ "N.E.'s Largest Solar Site Set for Scituate Landfill" in Boston Business Journal (Vol. 30, December 17, 2010, No. 47, pp. 1)

Pub: Boston Business Journal

Ed: Kyle Alspach. Description: A closed 12-acre landfill in Scituate, Massachusetts is the proposed site for a 2.4-megawatt solar power plant. The town government will buy the power at a discounted rate, saving it $200,000 annually.

36121 ■ "The New Alchemists" in Canadian Business (Vol. 81, October 27, 2008, No. 18, pp. 22)

Ed: Joe Castaldo. Description: Ethanol industry expects second-generation ethanol or cellulosic biofuels to provide ecologically friendly technologies than the ethanol made from food crops. Government and industries are investing on producing cellulosic biofuels.

36122 ■ "A New Alliance For Global Change" in Harvard Business Review (Vol. 88, September 2010, No. 9, pp. 56)

Pub: Harvard Business School Publishing

Ed: Bill Drayton, Valeria Budinich. Description: Collaboration between social organizations and for-profit firms through the development of hybrid value chains to target complex global issues is promoted. While social organizations offer links to communities and consumers, firms provide financing and scale expertise.

36123 ■ "New Book Takes Alternate View on Ontario's Wind Industry" in CNW Group (September 19, 2011)
Pub: CNW Group Ltd.
Contact: Carolyn McGill-Davidson, President

Description: Dirty Business: The Reality Behind Ontario's Rush to Wind Power, was written by editor and health care writer Jane Wilson of Ottawa, Ontario, Canada along with contributing editor Parker Gallant. The book contains articles and papers on the wind business, including information on illnesses caused from the environmental noise.

36124 ■ "A New Day is Dawning" in Indoor Comfort Marketing (Vol. 70, August 2011, No. 8, pp. 18)
Pub: Industry Publications Inc.
Contact: Shirleen Dorman, Editor

Ed: Paul Nazzaro. **Description:** New trends in the HVAC/R industry regarding biofuels and bioheat are explored.

36125 ■ "New Hydronic Heating Technologies Work" in Contractor (Vol. 57, January 2010, No. 1, pp. 58)
Pub: Intertec Publishing
Contact: John French, President

Ed: Carol Fey. **Description:** Technology behind hydronic heating systems is reviewed. These technologies include radiant and geothermal hydronic heating. System requirements for installing these greener forms of heating are discussed.

36126 ■ "New No. 1 at Element 8" in Puget Sound Business Journal (Vol. 35, September 19, 2014, No. 22, pp. 6)
Pub: American City Business Journals

Released: September 19, 2014. **Description:** Element 8 executive director, Kristi Growdon, says the company continues to find investment opportunities in the Pacific Northwest's clean technology sector. She also said the agricultural sector is a potentially lucrative investment destination. Growdon added that the company bases decisions on clean technology.

36127 ■ "A New World" in Canadian Business (Vol. 80, October 8, 2007, No. 20, pp. 136)
Ed: Deborah Harford. **Description:** Effects of climate change in Canada's economy are presented. A report published by Natural Resources Canada's Climate Change Impacts and Adaptation Program shows severe weather events such as droughts and storms will cause severe economic problems. Canada's infrastructure could also be affected by the rise in sea level over the next century.

36128 ■ "The Next Great Canadian Idea: Peripiteia Generator" in Canadian Business (Vol. 81, July 21, 2008, No. 11, pp. 45)
Pub: Rogers Media Inc.
Contact: Tony Viner, President

Ed: Sharda Prashad. **Description:** Thane Heins has invented a generator that produces energy in an isolated system which contradicts the law of conservation of energy. Perepiteia generator is referred to as a 'perpetual motion machine.' Other inventions slated for the Canadian invention competition include Rob Matthies' batteries and Frank Naumann's Smart Trap.

36129 ■ "Next Stage of Green Building will be Water Efficiency" in Contractor (Vol. 56, July 2009, No. 7, pp. 41)
Pub: Penton Media, Inc.

Description: One market report says that water efficiency and conservation will become critical factors in green design, construction, and product selection in the next five years from 2009. The report outlines how critical it will be for the construction industry to address responsible water practices in the future.

36130 ■ "N.H. Near the LEED in Green Space" in New Hampshire Business Review (Vol. 33, March 25, 2011, No. 6, pp. 30)
Pub: Business Publications Inc.

Description: New Hamphire's architects, contractors and suppliers are among the leaders with LEED-certified space per capita.

36131 ■ "Niche Markets, Green Will Be Ok in 2010" in Contractor (Vol. 57, January 2010, No. 1, pp. 1)
Pub: Intertec Publishing
Contact: John French, President

Ed: Robert P. Mader. **Description:** Mechanical contractors will see most of their work stemming from niche markets, such as green work, as well as service work in 2010. It is said that things will turn around for the industry in 2012 and 2013 and one forecast believes that anything outside of the institutional or more public sector work could be down 15 to 30 percent.

36132 ■ "Nothing But Green Skies" in Inc. (November 2007, pp. 115-120)
Pub: Gruner and Jahr USA Publishing Co.
Contact: J. Russell Denson, President

Ed: Alison Stein Wellner. **Description:** Profile of Enterprise Rent-A-Car, one of the largest family-owned businesses in the U.S. Andy Taylor, CEO, discusses the company's talks about the idea of offering carbon off-sets for a few years.

36133 ■ "NStar Feels the Heat" in Cape Cod Times (September 30, 2011)
Pub: Cape Cod Media Group
Ed: Patrick Cassidy. **Description:** Massachusetts energy officials wish to delay a merger between NStar and Northeast Utilities until it is clear how the partnership would meet the state's green energy goals. Governor Deval Patrick supports the proposed Nantucket Sound wind farm.

36134 ■ "Nuclear Renaissance" in Canadian Business (Vol. 83, August 17, 2010, No. 13-14, pp. 46)
Description: Nuclear energy has come back into the public's favor in Canada because it has virtually no emissions and is always available anytime of the day. Canada's nuclear industry has also achieved an incomparable record of safe, economic and reliable power generation in three provinces for 48 years.

36135 ■ "Oilsands: Environmental Disaster?" in Canadian Business (Vol. 83, October 12, 2010, No. 17, pp. 52)
Pub: Rogers Media Inc.
Contact: Tony Viner, President

Ed: Michael McCullough. **Description:** Studies which were commissioned by the Alberta Energy Research Institute in 2008 found that the life-cycle carbon emissions of oil derived from oilsands was 10 percent greater than the average from all sources. Synthetic crude from the oilsands is 38 percent less carbon-intensive than it was 20 years ago due to productivity improvements.

36136 ■ "On Growth Path of Rising Star" in Boston Business Journal (Vol. 31, June 24, 2011, No. 22, pp. 3)
Pub: Boston Business Journal
Ed: Kyle Alspach. **Description:** 1366 Technologies Inc. of Lexington, Massachusetts is considered a rising solar power technology company. The firm secured $150 million loan guarantee from the US Department of Energy that could go to the construction of a 1,000 megawatt solar power plant.

36137 ■ "One on One With SEIA's President, CEO" in Contractor (Vol. 57, January 2010, No. 1, pp. 40)
Pub: Intertec Publishing
Contact: John French, President

Ed: Dave Yates. **Description:** Solar Energy Industries Association President and CEO Rhone Resch says that the deployment of solar systems in the U.S. has exploded since 2005 and that there is a need to make inroads for shaping the U.S. energy policy. Resch says one of the hurdles they face is that there are no universal standards.

36138 ■ "OPEC Exposed" in Hawaii Business (Vol. 54, September 2008, No. 3, pp. 2)
Ed: Serena Lim. **Description:** Organization of the Petroleum Exporting Countries (OPEC) has said that their effort in developing an alternative energy source has driven prices up. The biofuel sector is criticizing the statement, saying that a research study found that biofuels push petroleum prices down by 15 percent. Details on the effect of rising petroleum prices are discussed.

36139 ■ "Open For Business" in Baltimore Business Journal (Vol. 30, June 22, 2012, No. 7, pp. 1)
Pub: American City Business Journals, Inc.
Contact: Whitney Shaw, President

Ed: James Briggs. **Released:** June 22, 2012. **Description:** The demand for offices with open floor plans has risen as companies look to improve collaboration while cutting costs. Incorporating glass walls and low desks to open office design allow the flow of natural light, which in turn, reduces energy bills. How companies are addressing the challenge of maintaining privacy in an open office design are also discussed.

36140 ■ "Organic Food Takes a Hit, But Boosters Say Study Misses Point" in Advertising Age (Vol. 83, September 10, 2012, No. 32, pp. 5)
Pub: Crain Communications Inc.
Contact: Rance E. Crain, President

Description: Proponents of organic food responded to a Standford University study that reports organic food having no more nutrition than conventional food by stating that consumers purchase organic food because it has less pesticides, hormones and other chemicals, not for added nutrition. Growing organic is better for the environment, too.

36141 ■ "Ottawa Advised to Underwrite Carbon Technology" in Globe & Mail (March 10, 2007, pp. B3)
Ed: Shawn McCarthy. **Description:** A federal panel's suggestion that carbon tax in Canada was not adequate to encourage oil companies and utilities to take up costly technologies to reduce carbon emissions is discussed.

36142 ■ "Our Company is Dedicated to the Environment, But We Work With Vendors that Aren't" in Inc. (March 2008, pp. 78)
Pub: Mansueto Ventures L.L.C.
Contact: John Koten, Chief Executive Officer

Ed: Myra Goodman. **Description:** Insight into working with vendors, such as construction and janitorial contractors, to comploy with your company's environmental policies is given.

36143 ■ "Out of Juice?" in Canadian Business (Vol. 81, October 27, 2008, No. 18, pp. 32)
Ed: Joe Castaldo. **Description:** Alternative energy experts suggest Canada should be more aggressive and should make major policy changes on energy alternatives despite an Ernst & Young research that rated the country high on renewable energy.

36144 ■ "Overheating Taking Place? Pay Attention to Details.." in Indoor Comfort Marketing (Vol. 70, March 2011, No. 3, pp.)
Pub: Industry Publications Inc.
Contact: Shirleen Dorman, Editor

Ed: George R. Carey. **Description:** Boiler facts are outlined to help the small HVAC company when servicing customers.

36145 ■ "An Overview of Energy Consumption of the Globalized World Economy" in Energy Policy (Vol. 39, October 2011, No. 10, pp. 5920-2928)
Pub: Reed Elsevier Reference Publishing
Ed: Z.M. Chen, G.Q. Chen. **Description:** Energy consumption and its impact on the global world economy is examined.

36146 ■ "Paul Hawken and Other Top Lumnaries to Participate in Green Business BASE CAMP in Los Angeles" in

Benzinga.com (April 19, 2012)
Pub: Benzinga.com
Contact: Kyle Bazzy, President
Ed: Aaron Wise. Description: Paul Hawken, environmentalist, entrepreneur and author, is one of many people participating in the Green Business BASE CAMP, a four-day workshop for green business and cleantech entrepreneurs. The event will be held in Los Angeles, California from May 31 through June 3, 2012. Insider guidance will be offered to early-stage entrepreneurs seeking to compete within this sector.

36147 ■ *"Pennsylvania DEP To Conduct Natural Gas Vehicle Seminar" in Travel & Leisure Close-Up (October 8, 2012)*
Description: Pennsylvania Department of Environmental Protection is holding a Natural Gas Vehicle seminar at the Bayfront Convention Center in Erie, PA, as well as other locations throughout the state. The seminars will help municipal and commercial fleet owners make better informed decisions when converting fleets from compressed natural gas and liquefied natural gas.

36148 ■ *"Pet Waste Products Pick Up Sales" in Pet Product News (Vol. 66, September 2012, No. 9, pp. 58)*
Pub: Bowtie Inc.
Ed: Sandi Cain. Description: Pet supplies manufacturers are developing dog waste pickup bags and other convenient cleanup tools characterized by environment-friendliness and fashion. The demand for these cleanup tools has been motivated by dog owners' desire to minimize their and their dogs' environmental footprints.

36149 ■ *"Phoenix Conference Reveals Opportunities are Coming" in Indoor Comfort Marketing (Vol. 70, March 2011, No. 3, pp. 24)*
Pub: Industry Publications Inc.
Contact: Shirleen Dorman, Editor
Ed: Paul J. Nazzaro. Description: Advanced liquid fuels were spotlighted at the Phoenix conference revealing the opportunities for using liquid fuels.

36150 ■ *"Planned CO2 Regulations Could Hit Region Hard" in Pittsburgh Business Times (Vol. 33, June 6, 2014, No. 47, pp. 9)*
Pub: American City Business Journals
Released: June 6, 2014. Description: The U.S. Environmental Protection Agency's (EPA's) proposed rules to cut carbon dioxide (CO2) emissions by 30 percent over 16 years could have an adverse impact on southwestern Pennsylvania. The draft regulations, announced June 2, 2014, will affect the Pennsylvania region's power-generation sector as well as its coal industry, thereby impacting the regional economy.

36151 ■ *"Plans for Coal-Fired Electricity Could Go Up in Smoke" in Globe & Mail (March 5, 2007, pp. B7)*
Ed: Steve James. Description: The coal-fired power project initiated by Texas-based utility company TXU Corp. is receiving legal challenges from green groups. The possible disasters caused by the coal-fired plant are presented.

36152 ■ *"Positive Transformational Change" in Indoor Comfort Marketing (Vol. 70, April 2011, No. 4, pp. 30)*
Pub: Industry Publications Inc.
Contact: Shirleen Dorman, Editor
Ed: Blaine Fox. Description: Management changes taking place at Shark Bites HVAC firm are discussed.

36153 ■ *"Power Ranger" in Inc. (November 2007, pp. 131)*
Pub: Gruner and Jahr USA Publishing Co.
Contact: J. Russell Denson, President
Ed: Nitasha Tiku. Description: Surveyor software is designed to power down computers when not in use, in order to save energy.

36154 ■ *"PPC's Major Commitment to Biofuel Infrastructure" in Indoor Comfort Marketing (Vol. 70, April 2011, No. 4, pp. 6)*
Pub: Industry Publications Inc.
Contact: Shirleen Dorman, Editor
Description: Petroleum Products Corporation's commitment to the biofuel infrastructure is outlined.

36155 ■ *"Pre-Certified LEED Hotel Prototype Reduces Energy Use, Conserves Water" in Contractor (Vol. 57, January 2010, No. 1, pp. 3)*
Pub: Intertec Publishing
Contact: John French, President
Ed: Candace Roulo. Description: Marriott International Inc.'s LEED pre-certified prototype hotel will reduce a hotel's energy and water consumption by 25 percent and save owners approximately $100,000. Their Courtyard Settler's Ridge in Pittsburgh will be the first hotel built based on the prototype.

36156 ■ *"Preparing for Weed Control" in Farmer's Weekly (March 28, 2008, No. 320)*
Description: Profile of Richard Beachell who farms in a joint venture with his neighbor. Beachell discusses nitrogen applications, fungicides and the reduction of pesticides.

36157 ■ *"Professional Grooming Marketplace: Cash In On Green Products and Services" in Pet Product News (Vol. 66, September 2012, No. 9, pp. 84)*
Pub: Bowtie Inc.
Ed: Lizett Bond. Description: Pet grooming salons can build customer reputation by providing sustainable and environment-friendly products and services. Energy efficiency and electricity conservation can also be focused upon as pet grooming salons aspire for green marketing goals.

36158 ■ *"The Profits of Good Works" in Barron's (Vol. 92, September 17, 2012, No. 38, pp. 14)*
Description: The nonprofit organization B Lab is responsible for certifying companies as socially conscious and environmentally friendly. B Lab examines the impact of companies on workers, communities, and the environment as well as their internal governance.

36159 ■ *"Provinces Tackle E-Waste Problem" in Canadian Electronics (Vol. 23, June-July 2008, No. 4, pp. 1)*
Pub: Action Communication Inc.
Ed: Ken Manchen. Description: Canadian provinces are implementing measures concerning the safe and environmentally friendly disposal of electronic waste. Alberta, British Columbia, Nova Scotia, and Saskatchewan impose an e-waste recycling fee on electronic equipment purchases.

36160 ■ *"PSC Approves $130M TECO Solar Project" in Tampa Bay Business Journal (Vol. 30, December 18, 2009, No. 52, pp. 1)*
Pub: American City Business Journals
Ed: Michael Hinman. Description: Florida's Public Service Commission has endorsed Tampa Electric Company's plan to add 25 megawatts of solar energy to its portfolio. TECO's plan needed the approval by PSC to defray additional costs for the project through ratepayers.

36161 ■ *"PSC Decision Could Help Bolster a Solar Market Supernova" in Tampa Bay Business Journal (Vol. 29, November 6, 2009, No. 46, pp. 1)*
Pub: American City Business Journals
Ed: Michael Hinman. Description: Florida's Public Service Commission (PSC) decision on a power purchase agreement that could add 25 megawatts of solar energy on Tampa Electric Company's offerings is presented. The decision could support the growing market for suppliers and marketers of renewable energy such as Jabil Circuit Inc., which manufactures photovoltaic modules. Details of the agreement are discussed.

36162 ■ *"PSEG Queen Creek Solar Farm in Arizona Begins Commercial Operation" in Benzinga.com (October 4, 2012)*
Pub: Benzinga.com
Contact: Kyle Bazzy, President
Description: PSEG Solar Source will launch the commercial operation of the 25.2 megawatt DC (19 megawatt AC) Queen Creek Solar Farm in Queen Creek, Arizona. The Salt River Project (SRP) has a 20-year agreement to acquire acquire all of the solar energy generated by the project. More details are included.

36163 ■ *"PSI Repair Services to Showcase at Windpower Conference and Exhibition" in Entertainment Close-Up (May 19, 2012)*
Description: Subsidiary of Phillips Service Industries, PSI Repair Services, will highlight its off-warranty repair support for wind energy operations at the Windpower 2012 Conference and Exhibition.

36164 ■ *"A Quick Guide to NATE" in Indoor Comfort Marketing (Vol. 70, February 2011, No. 2, pp. 12)*
Pub: Industry Publications Inc.
Contact: Shirleen Dorman, Editor
Description: Guide for training and certification in the North American Technician Excellence award.

36165 ■ *"A Race Fueled By Natural Gas: B.C. Fights the Clock (and Australia) To Supply a New Market" in Canadian Business (Vol. 85, July 16, 2012, No. 11-12, pp. 13)*
Pub: George Media Inc.
Ed: Michael McCullough. Released: July 16, 2012. Description: Power consumption and carbon tax issues associated with the new liquefied natural gas (LNG) projects in British Columbia should be addressed as soon as possible to take advantage of the growing LNG market. Royal Dutch Shell is leading the $12 billion LNG Canada terminal project in Kitimat while three other LNG plants are proposed.

36166 ■ *"Radiant ? the Hottest Topic in .. Cooling" in Indoor Comfort Marketing (Vol. 70, February 2011, No. 2, pp. 8)*
Pub: Industry Publications Inc.
Contact: Shirleen Dorman, Editor
Description: Examination of radiant cooling systems, a new trend in cooling homes and buildings.

36167 ■ *"Radiant Commences In-Lab Testing for US Air Mobility Command" in Canadian Corporate News (May 16, 2007)*
Description: The Boeing Company will be conducting in-lab infrared material testing for the Radiant Energy Corporation, developer and marketer of InfraTek, the environmentally friendly, patented infrared pre-flight aircraft deicing system.

36168 ■ *"Recycling 202: How to Take Your Recycling Practices to the Next Level" in Black Enterprise (Vol. 41, September 2010, No. 2, pp. 38)*
Pub: Earl G. Graves Publishing Co. Inc.
Contact: Earl G. Graves, Jr., President
Ed: Tamara E. Holmes. Description: Consumer Electronics Association and other organizations, manufacturers and retailers list ways to recycle all household items.

36169 ■ *"Red Diesel Cost Sparks a Move to Home-Grown Fuel" in Farmer's Weekly (March 28, 2008, No. 320)*
Description: Due to the rising cost of red diesel, the idea of growing one's own tractor fuel has an undeniable attraction for many farmers. A growing pressure is weighing on engine manufacturers to produce designs that can run on both SVO as well as biodiesel.

36170 ■ *"Red, Pink and More: Cause Marketing Surges as a Prime Tactic to Reach Female Customers" in Marketing to Women (April 2008)*
Description: According to the American Marketing Association, forty percent of women say they are more likely to purchase a product or service if they know a certain amount of the price is being donated directly to a cause or campaign that they believe in supporting.

36171 ■ *"Reduce or Repay" in Canadian Business (Vol. 80, November 5, 2007, No. 22, pp. 35)*
Ed: Regan Ray. Description: The new greenhouse gas (GHG) policy of Alberta, Canada requires about 100 industrial facilities that emit over 100,000 tons of

GHG per year to reduce emissions by 12 percent by the end of 2007. Facilities that fail to comply will pay $15 per ton of GHG emission beyond target. The economic impacts of the regulation are evaluated.

36172 ■ "Reducing the Book's Carbon Footpring" in American Printer (Vol. 128, July 1, 2011, No. 7)
Pub: Penton Media Inc.
Description: Green Press Initiative's Book Industry Environmental Council is working to achieve a 20 percent reduction in the book industry's carbon footprint by 2020. The Council is made up of publishers, printers, paper suppliers, and non-governmental organizations.

36173 ■ "Reinventing the Cheeseburger" in Inc. (November 2007, pp. 124-125)
Pub: Gruner and Jahr USA Publishing Co.
Contact: J. Russell Denson, President
Ed: Chris Lydgate. **Description:** Profile of Burgerville's Tom Mears, who turned his drive-through burger restaurant green.

36174 ■ "Reinventing Marketing to Manage the Environmental Imperative" in Journal of Marketing (Vol. 75, July 2011, No. 4, pp. 132)
Pub: American Marketing Association
Contact: Lucille Pointer, President
Ed: Philip Kotler. **Description:** Marketers must now examine their theory and practices due to the growing recognition of finite resources and high environmental costs. Companies also need to balance more carefully their growth goals with the need to purse sustainability. Insights on the rise of demarketing and social marketing are also given.

36175 ■ "Renewable Energy Adoption in an Aging Population" in Energy Policy (Vol. 39, October 2011, No. 10, pp. 6021-6029)
Pub: Reed Elsevier Reference Publishing
Ed: Ken Willis, Riccardo Scarpa, Rose Gilroy, Neveen Hamza. **Description:** Attitudes and impacts of renewable energy adoption on an aging population is examined.

36176 ■ "Renewable Energy Market Opportunities: Wind Testing" in PR Newswire (September 22, 2011)
Pub: UBM L.L.C.
Contact: Kate Spellman, President
E-mail: kspellman@cmp.com
Description: Global wind energy test systems markets are discussed. Research conducted covers both non-destructive test equipment and condition monitoring equipment product segments.

36177 ■ "Research and Markets Offers Report on US Business Traveler's Green, New Technology Views" in Airline Industry Information (July 30, 2012)
Pub: Normans Media Ltd.
Released: July 30, 2012. **Description:** The US Business Traveler Expectations of Green and Technology Initiatives in Hotels in 2012 contains comprehensive analysis on US business travelers views on green and technology initiative and socially responsible measures geared towards the business traveler.

36178 ■ Resource and Environmental Management in Canada
Pub: Oxford University Press
Contact: Niko Pfund, President
Ed: Bruce Mitchell. **Released:** Fourth Edition. **Price:** $49.95, paperback. **Description:** Discusses resource management in Canada, focusing on business and industry, environmental groups, First Nations, the public, local communities with resource-based economies. **Availability:** Print.

36179 ■ "Return to Wild for R.I. Oysters?" in Providence Business News (Vol. 29, August 25, 2014, No. 21, pp. 1)
Pub: American City Business Journals
Released: August 25, 2014. **Description:** The Nature Conservancy is working to return wild oyster populations that have almost disappeared from Rhode Island waters and to restore the region's nearly extinct oyster reefs. The group's Oysters Gone

Wild project collects hundreds of tons of oyster shells from participating Rhode Island restaurants and returns them into protected waters to build new oyster reefs.

36180 ■ "ReVenture Plan Appears Close to Landing Key Legislative Deal" in Charlotte Business Journal (Vol. 25, July 9, 2010, No. 16, pp. 1)
Pub: Charlotte Business Journal
Ed: John Downey. **Description:** North Carolina lawmakers acted on special legislation that would boost development of Forsite Development 667-acre ReVenture Energy Park. The legislation could also improve chances that Duke Energy Carolinas will contract to purchase the power from the planned 50-megawatt biomass power plant located at the park. How utilities would benefit from the legislation is also discussed.

36181 ■ "R.I. Lags in Solar Incentives" in Providence Business News (Vol. 29, May 26, 2014, No. 8, pp. 1)
Pub: American City Business Journals
Released: May 26, 2014. **Description:** The state of Rhode Island has offered less in government renewable energy incentives than its neighboring states and has yet to experience the growth of residential solar energy projects. The Rhode Island Renewable Energy Fund allocated $800,000 to the small scale solar program in 2014.

36182 ■ "Richard Faulk Covers Climate in Copenhagen" in Houston Business Journal (Vol. 40, December 25, 2009, No. 33, pp. 1)
Pub: American City Business Journals
Ed: Ford Gunter. **Description:** Houston environmental attorney Richard Faulk talks to the United Nations Climate Change Conference in Copenhagen, Denmark. Faulk believes the conference failed due to political differences between countries like US and China. Faulk believed the discussion of developed and developing countries on verification and limits on carbon emissions is something good that came from the conference.

36183 ■ "Rivals Blow In" in Crain's Cleveland Business (Vol. 30, June 1, 2009, No. 21, pp. 1)
Pub: Crain Communications Inc.
Ed: Chuck Soder. **Description:** U.S. and Canadian competitors are hoping to start construction of offshore wind farm project proposed by Cuyahoga County's Great Lakes Energy Development Task Force. Details of the project are included.

36184 ■ "Rosewood Site Faces Big Cleanup Before Stevenson Can Expand" in Baltimore Business Journal (Vol. 27, February 6, 2010, No. 40, pp. 1)
Pub: American City Business Journals
Ed: Daniel J. Sernovitz. **Description:** Environmental assessment report states that Maryland's Rosewood Center for the Developmentally Disabled has significant amounts of toxic chemicals, which could impact Stevenson University's decision to purchase the property. Senator Robert A. Zirkin believes that the state should pay for the cleanup, which is expected to cost millions.

36185 ■ "Rough Headwinds" in Boston Business Journal (Vol. 30, November 12, 2010, No. 42, pp. 1)
Pub: Boston Business Journal
Ed: Kyle Alspach. **Description:** Views of residents, as well as key information on First Wind's plan to install wind power turbines in Brimfield, Massachusetts are presented. Residents believe that First Wind's project will devalue properties, compromise quality of life, and ruin the rural quality of Brimfield. First Wind expects to produce 2,000 megawatts of power from wind by 2020.

36186 ■ "Sacramento Businesses Must Cut Water Use 20 Percent" in Sacramento Business Journal (Vol. 30, January 17, 2014, No. 47, pp. 5)
Pub: American City Business Journals
Released: January 17, 2014. **Description:** The Sacramento, California City, California Council's decision to reduce water use by 20 percent could have a

big impact on businesses. Hotels and restaurants are among the biggest commercial users of water, while golf courses generally use well water. The need for businesses to purchase more efficient fixtures is also discussed.

36187 ■ "Sales of What's Under Feet Add Up Fast" in Pet Product News (Vol. 66, September 2012, No. 9, pp. S8)
Description: Pet supplies retailers and manufacturers have been emphasizing the type of substances in creating new approaches to developing environment-friendly natural litters and beddings for small mammals and cats. Some of these approaches are highlighted, along with marketing strategies retailers have implemented.

36188 ■ "San Antonio's Clean-Energy Push May Need More Peddle Power" in San Antonio Business Journal (Vol. 26, February 10, 2012, No. 2, pp. 1)
Pub: American City Business Journal
Ed: Sanford Nowlin, W. Scott Bailey, Tamarind Phinisee. **Description:** CPS Energy said the government of San Antonio, Texas should form a green-energy coalition to ensure the success of its push for the use of renewable energy. Prospective coalition members include utility, research and industry officials.

36189 ■ "San Diego Museum Receives LEED Certification" in Contractor (Vol. 57, January 2010, No. 1, pp. 14)
Pub: Intertec Publishing
Contact: John French, President
Description: San Diego Natural History Museum received an LEED certification for existing buildings. The certification process began when they committed to displaying the Dead Sea Scrolls in 2007 and they had to upgrade their buildings' air quality and to control for air moisture, temperature, and volume. They reduced their energy consumption by upwards of 20 percent.

36190 ■ "Sandvik Expands Energy-Saving Program" in Modern Machine Shop (Vol. 84, September 2011, No. 4, pp. 48)
Pub: Gardner Business Media, Inc.
Contact: Richard G. Kline, President
E-mail: rkline@gardnerweb.com
Description: Sandvik Coromant, based in Fair Lawn, New Jersey, expanded its Sustainable Manufacturing Program that originally was developed to help Japanese-based firms reduce electricity consumption by 15 percent after the recent earthquake that cause loss of electrical power. The program now provides energy reduction through the Sandvick cutting tool technology, application techniques and productivity increases.

36191 ■ "Saudi Overtures" in The Business Journal-Portland (Vol. 25, August 15, 2008, No. 23, pp. 1)
Pub: American City Business Journals, Inc.
Contact: Whitney Shaw, President
Ed: Aliza Earnshaw. **Description:** Saudi Arabia's huge revenue from oil is creating opportunities for Oregon companies as the country develops new cities, industrial zones, and tourism centers. Oregon exported only $46.8 million worth of goods to Saudi Arabia in 2007 but the kingdom is interested in green building materials and methods, renewable energy and water quality control, and nanotechnology all of which Oregon has expertise in.

36192 ■ "Saving the Planet: A Tale of Two Strategies: Thomas Malthus Advised Restraint; Robert Solow Promotes Innovation. Let's Pursue Both To Solve the Environmental Crisis" in Harvard Business Review (Vol. 90, April 2012, No. 4, pp. 48)
Pub: Harvard Business Review Press
Contact: Peter E. Walsh, Director
Ed: Roger Martin, Alison Kemper. **Released:** April 2012. **Description:** Theories of economists Thomas Malthus and Robert Solow are merged to address specific environmental problems. Malthusian restraint includes fuel economy, refillable bottles, and recycling. Solovian innovation includes water supply chlorination, solar cooking, and geothermal energy.

36193 ■ *"Scorched Earth: Will Environmental Risks in China Overwhelm Its Opportunities?"* in *Harvard Business Review (Vol. 85, June 2007, No. 6)*

Pub: Harvard Business School Publishing

Ed: Elizabeth Economy, Kenneth Lieberthal. **Price:** $6.93. **Description:** Environmental risks for business in China include water supply access, energy needs, pollution, and soil erosion. However, the nation's government is investing money to develop green technology and alternative energy sources. **Availability:** PDF.

36194 ■ *"The Second Most Fuel-Efficient Tractor of the Decade: John Deere 8320R"* in *Farm Industry News (November 10, 2011)*

Pub: Penton Business Media Inc.

Contact: David Kieselstein, Chief Executive Officer

Description: John Deere's 8320R Tractor was ranked second in the Farm Industry News listing of the top 40 most fuel-efficient tractors of the decade, following the winner, John Deere's 8295R PTO tractor.

36195 ■ *"Seeing Green in Going Green"* in *The Business Journal-Serving Greater Tampa Bay (Vol. 28, July 7, 2008, No. 28, pp. 1)*

Pub: American City Business Journals, Inc.

Contact: Whitney Shaw, President

Ed: Janet Leiser. **Description:** Atlanta, Georgia-based developer IDI Corp. is pushing for Leadership in Energy and Environmental Design certification for the warehouse that is currently under construction at Madison Business Center along Port Sutton and U.S. 41. The industrial building is the first in Tampa Bay to seek certification for LEED as set by the U.S. Green Building Council.

36196 ■ *"S.F.'s Drop in the Bucket"* in *San Francisco Business Times (Vol. 28, April 11, 2014, No. 38, pp. 4)*

Pub: American City Business Journals

Released: April 11, 2014. **Description:** San Francisco has been planning to build a pair of water recycling plants that could recycle up to 4 million gallons of water daily, even if many Southern California communities produce more. The city does not need to exert more effort into water recycling because it owns the Hetch Hetchy system that assures its water supply. Impacts of the statewide drought are examined.

36197 ■ *"Shaw Joins Green Institute Launch"* in *Home Textiles Today (Vol. 31, May 24, 2011, No. 13, pp. 4)*

Pub: Reed Elsevier Group plc Reed Business Information

Contact: Mark Kelsey, Chief Executive Officer

Description: Shaw Industries Group joined the Green Products Innovation Institute, the first nonprofit institute of its kind in America. The institute promotes the concepts of reverse engineering, elimination of waste, safe chemistries, and closed loop technical nutrients.

36198 ■ *"Shifting Gears"* in *Business Journal-Serving Phoenix & the Valley of the Sun (Vol. 31, November 12, 2010, No. 10, pp. 1)*

Pub: Phoenix Business Journal

Ed: Patrick O'Grady. **Description:** Automotive parts recyclers in Arizona are benefiting from the challenging national economic conditions as well as from the green movement. Recyclers revealed that customers prefer recycled parts more because they are cheaper and are more environmentally friendly. Other information about the automotive parts recycling industry is presented.

36199 ■ *"Shotgun Christy's Frontier Justice"* in *Canadian Business (Vol. 85, September 17, 2012, No. 14, pp. 18)*

Pub: George Media Inc.

Ed: Peter Shawn Taylor. **Released:** September 17, 2012. **Description:** The economic benefit of the prospect of a Northern Gateway pipeline from the oilsands of Alberta to the port of Kirimat, British Columbia is examined. British Columbia Premier Christy Clark's claim that they get little benefit and more risk of an oil spill has created uncertainty for the project.

36200 ■ *"Should I or Shouldn't I?"* in *Indoor Comfort Marketing (Vol. 70, February 2011, No. 2, pp. 30)*

Pub: Industry Publications Inc.

Contact: Shirleen Dorman, Editor

Ed: Philip J. Baratz. **Description:** Investment tips are shared for investing in futures options.

36201 ■ *"Six Arkansas Construction Projects Get LEED Certification"* in *Arkansas Business (Vol. 29, July 23, 2012, No. 30, pp. 19)*

Pub: Arkansas Business Publishing Group

Ed: Lance Turner. **Description:** State of Arkansas has bestowed its Leadership in Energy and Environmental Design certification on 55 projects throughout the state. Six projects are identified and described. A list of all projects is included.

36202 ■ *"Sizing Up Bentley"* in *Barron's (Vol. 92, September 17, 2012, No. 38, pp. 16)*

Description: The energy efficiencies of cars produced by Bentley Motors have shown little improvement over time. The company needs to invest in improving the fuel efficiencies of its vehicles to attract new customers and remain competitive.

36203 ■ *"Sky Harvest Windpower Corp. - Operational Update"* in *Investment Weekly News (March 10, 2012, pp. 744)*

Pub: NewsRX

Contact: Susan E. Hasty, Publisher

Released: March 10, 2012. **Description:** Sky Harvest Windpower Corporation is rebranding its focus on gas and power activities both nationally and internationally. The firm's Canadian projects are outlined as well as its commitment to purse the Green Options Partners Program in 2012.

36204 ■ *"Sky Harvest Windpower Corp. - Operational Update"* in *Benzinga.com (October 5, 2012)*

Pub: Benzinga.com

Contact: Kyle Bazzy, President

Released: October 5, 2012. **Description:** Solar power is the fastest growing technology in the nation's energy industry and US utility-scale solar power market has grown over the last three years due to rising energy prices, volatility of fuel costs, and government incentives for renewable energy.

36205 ■ *"Small Changes Can Mean Big Energy Savings"* in *Crain's Cleveland Business (Vol. 28, November 5, 2007, No. 44, pp. 21)*

Pub: Crain Communications Inc.

Ed: Harriet Tramer. **Description:** Many Northeast Ohio businesses are taking their cues from the residential real estate market to draw and capitalize on interest in energy efficiency and is regularly taken into account by local architects.

36206 ■ *"Small Wind Power Market to Double by 2015 at $634 Million"* in *Western Farm Press (September 30, 2011)*

Pub: Penton Media, Inc.

Description: Small wind power provides cost-effective electricity on a highly localized level, in both remote settings as well as in conjunction with power from the utility grid. Government incentives are spurring new growth in the industry.

36207 ■ *"Smart Car Sales Take Big Hit in Recession"* in *Business Journal-Milwaukee (Vol. 28, December 10, 2010, No. 10, pp. A1)*

Pub: Milwaukee Business Journal

Ed: Stacy Vogel Davis. **Description:** Sales of smart cars in Milwaukee declined in 2010. Smart Center Milwaukee sold only 52 new cars through October 2010. Increased competition is seen as a reason for the decline in sales.

36208 ■ *"Snow Melt Systems Offer Practical Solutions"* in *Contractor (Vol. 56, October 2009, No. 10, pp. S6)*

Ed: Lisa Murton Beets. **Description:** Cases are discussed in which the installation of a snow melt system becomes a necessity. One example describes how limited space means there would be no place to put plowed snow; snow melt systems can also resolve problems that arise due to an excess of melting snow.

36209 ■ *"Software Solutions from Trane and Carrier"* in *Contractor (Vol. 56, July 2009, No. 7, pp. 38)*

Pub: Intertec Publishing

Contact: John French, President

Ed: William Feldman, Patti Feldman. **Description:** Trane Trace 700 software helps HVAC contractors optimize the design of a building's HVAC system and aids in the evaluation of various key energy-saving concepts, including daylighting, high-performance glazing, and other optimization strategies. Carrier's E20-II family of software programs lets contractors increase the accuracy of an HVAC system estimate.

36210 ■ *"Solar Credit Lapse Spur Late Demand"* in *The Business Journal - Serving Phoenix and the Valley of the Sun (Vol. 28, July 18, 2008)*

Pub: American City Business Journals, Inc.

Contact: Whitney Shaw, President

Ed: Patrick O'Grady. **Description:** Businesses looking to engage in the solar energy industry are facing the problems of taxation and limited solar panel supply. Solar panels manufacturers are focusing more on the European market. Political issues surrounding the federal tax credit policy on solar energy users are also discussed.

36211 ■ *"Something Different in the Air? The Collapse of the Schwarzenegger Health Plan in Calfornia"* in *WorkingUSA (June 2008)*

Ed: Daniel J.B. Mitchell. **Description:** In January 2007, California Governor Arnold Schwarzenegger proposed a state universal health care plan modeled after the Massachusetts individual mandate program. A year later, the plan was dead. Although some key interest groups eventually backed the plan, it was overwhelmed by a looming state budget crisis and a lack of gubernatorial focus. Although much acclaimed for his stance on greenhouse gases, stem cells, hydrogen highways, and other Big Ideas, diffused gubernatorial priorities and a failure to resolve California's chronic fiscal difficulties let the clock run out on universal health care.

36212 ■ *"Star Power Versus (Somewhat) Green Power"* in *Globe & Mail (January 18, 2007, pp. B2)*

Pub: CTVglobemedia Publishing Inc.

Ed: Konrad Yakabuski. **Description:** The views of the Canadian actor Roy Dupuis on the trends of energy consumption by Quebeckers are presented, along with statistics of energy consumption in the Quebec region.

36213 ■ *"Start Connecting Today"* in *Indoor Comfort Marketing (Vol. 70, May 2011, No. 5, pp. 34)*

Pub: Industry Publications Inc.

Contact: Shirleen Dorman, Editor

Ed: Paul Nazzaro. **Description:** An in-depth discussion regarding the use of biofuels on bioheat use and dealership.

36214 ■ *"Start Moving Toward Advanced Fuels"* in *Indoor Comfort Marketing (Vol. 70, March 2011, No. 3, pp. 4)*

Pub: Industry Publications Inc.

Contact: Shirleen Dorman, Editor

Ed: Michael L. SanGiovanni. **Description:** Commentary on advanced fuels is presented.

36215 ■ *"Start Thinking About Carbon Assets - Now"* in *Harvard Business Review (Vol. 86,*

September 2008, No. 9, pp. 28)
Pub: Harvard Business Review Press
Contact: Peter E. Walsh, Director

Ed: Alex Rau, Robert Toker. **Description:** Economic and strategic benefits of adopting a corporate carbon assets policy are discussed. Topics include renewable energy and capturing waste energy.

36216 ■ *"State Investment Goes Sour" in Business Journal Portland (Vol. 26, December 4, 2009, No. 39, pp. 1)*
Pub: American City Business Journals, Inc.

Ed: Erik Siemers. **Description:** Oregon might recoup only $500,000 of a $20 million loan to Vancouver-based Cascade Grain Products LLC. Cascade Grain's ethanol plant in Clatskanie, OR will be put into auction under the supervision of a bankruptcy court.

36217 ■ *"Stimulus 'Loser' Won't Build Plant in Mass." in Boston Business Journal (Vol. 30, November 5, 2010, No. 41, pp. 1)*
Pub: Boston Business Journal

Ed: Kyle Alspach. **Description:** Boston-Power Inc. no longer plans to build an electric vehicle battery plant in Massachusetts after it failed to obtain stimulus funds from the federal government. The company is instead looking to build a lithium-ion battery plant in China and possibly Europe.

36218 ■ *"Stock Car Racing" in Canadian Business (Vol. 81, September 15, 2008, No. 14-15, pp. 29)*
Ed: Thomas Watson. **Description:** Some analysts predict a Chapter 11-style tune-up making GM and Ford a speculative turnaround stock. However, the price of oil could make or break the shares of the Big Three U.S. automobile manufacturers and if oil goes up too high then a speculative stock to watch is an electric car company called Zenn Motor Co.

36219 ■ *"Store Front: Invest in Energy-Efficient Equipment for Your Pet Store" in Pet Product News (Vol. 66, September 2012, No. 9, pp. 43)*
Pub: Bowtie Inc.

Ed: Leila Meyer. **Description:** Developments in energy-efficient lighting, heating, and air conditioning have allowed pet supplies stores to conduct upgrades that result in savings. Pet supplies stores have also been impressing customers by obtaining Energy Start or LEED certification.

36220 ■ *"The Superpower Dilemma" in Canadian Business (Vol. 83, August 17, 2010, No. 13-14, pp. 42)*
Description: Canada has been an energy superpower partly because it controls the energy source and the production means, particularly of fossil fuels. However, Canada's status as superpower could diminish if it replaces petroleum exports with renewable technology for using sources of energy available globally.

36221 ■ *"Sustainability Is Top Priority for GreenTown Chicago" in Contractor (Vol. 56, November 2009, No. 11, pp. 1)*
Pub: Penton Media, Inc.

Ed: Candace Roulo. **Description:** GreenTown Chicago 2009 conference tackled energy-efficient practices and technologies, green design and building, and sustainable policies. Water conservation was also a topic at the conference and one mayor who made a presentation said that reducing the water loss in the system is a priority in the city's endeavor.

36222 ■ *"Sustainability On the Subcontinent: Efficiency Lessons from India's Greenest Buildings" in Real Estate Review (Vol. 41, Spring 2012, No. 1, pp. 67)*
Released: Spring 2012. **Description:** India's adoption of green design in building construction is examined. The country's CLL Godrej Green Building Centre was the first building to earn LEED's highest rating outside the United States. Several buildings in the country return more water to the local aquifer than they use.

36223 ■ *"The Sustainable Organization: Blueprint for an Integrated Model" in Journal of Business Strategy (Vol. 35, May-June 2014, No. 3, pp. 26-37)*
Pub: Emerald Group Publishing Inc.

Released: May-June 2014. **Description:** For senior executives to understand the role of sustainability in their organization's future strategy and structure, a new organizational sustainability model that includes the economic dimension is presented. It is developed based on the existing Dunphy, Griffiths, and Benn model which featured only social and environmental dimensions. This integrated and comprehensive sustainability stage model can assist executives in building more sustainable organizations.

36224 ■ *"Sustaining Supply" in Crain's Cleveland Business (Vol. 28, November 19, 2007, No. 46, pp. 3)*
Pub: Crain Communications Inc.

Ed: David Bennett. **Description:** Local firms are playing key roles in preparing Wal-Mart suppliers to develop sustainable, or ecologically conscious, packaging. New products such as the innovative 'eco-bottle' - a collapsed container made of recyclable plastic that will expand to its traditional size and shape once water is added and would transform to such items as window cleaner when the water mixes with the container's dry contents - are being designed by firms such as Nottingham Spirk.

36225 ■ *"Suzlon S88-Powered Wind Farm in Minnesota Secures Long-Term Financing" in PR Newswire (September 21, 2011)*
Pub: UBM L.L.C.
Contact: Kate Spellman, President
E-mail: kspellman@cmp.com

Description: Suzlon Energy Limited is the world's fifth largest manufacturer of wind turbines. Owners of the Grant County Wind Farm in Minnesota have secured a long-term financing deal for the ten Suzlon S88 2.1 MW wind turbines that generate enough electricity to power 7,000 homes.

36226 ■ *"Taiwan Technology Initiatives Foster Growth" in Canadian Electronics (Vol. 23, February 2008, No. 1, pp. 28)*
Description: A study conducted by the Market Intelligence Center shows that currently, Taiwan is the world's larges producer of information technology products such as motherboards, servers, and LCD monitors. In 2006, Taiwan's LED industry reached a production value of NTD 21 billion. This push into the LED sector shows the Ministry of Economic Affairs' plan to target industries that are environmentally friendly.

36227 ■ *"The Tapestry of Life" in Women In Business (Vol. 61, December 2009, No. 6, pp. 8)*
Pub: American Business Women's Association
Contact: Lorie Burch, President

Ed: Kathleen Leighton. **Description:** Suzanne Fanch, co-owner of the Devil's Thumb Ranch, discusses the family and career-related influences that helped her to achieve success as a small business proprietor. She advises that opportunities should be treated as building blocks towards success. Fanch's involvement in advocacies that take care of the welfare of community, children, and environment is also discussed.

36228 ■ *"Taxis Are Set to Go Hybrid" in Philadelphia Business Journal (Vol. 30, September 16, 2011, No. 31, pp. 1)*
Pub: American City Business Journals Inc.

Ed: Natalie Kostelni. **Description:** Taxis are going hybrid in several major states such as New York, California and Maryland where it is mandated, but it is yet to happen in Philadelphia, Pennsylvania with the exception of one taxi company. Freedom Taxi is awaiting Philadelphia Parking Authority's sign off.

36229 ■ *"Taylor Tests Land Grant Program" in Austin Business Journal (Vol. 31, June 3, 2011, No. 13, pp. 1)*
Pub: American City Business Journals

Ed: Vicky Garza. **Description:** Taylor Economic Development Corporation implemented a land grant program called Build On Our Lot to lure businesses

to Taylor City, Austin, Texas. They are targeting small businesses, especially those in the renewable energy, advanced manufacturing, technical services and food products. Program details are included.

36230 ■ *"Telecom Expense Management Firm, vCom Solutions, Certified as a Green Business" in Marketwired (February 27, 2012)*
Pub: COMTEX
Contact: Chip Brian, President

Description: vCom Solutions has been named a Certified Green Business by the Bay Area Green Business Program in San Francisco, California. The certification shows that vCom is in full compliance with local environmental regulatory agencies.

36231 ■ *"Thirsty? Now There's a Water Cooler to Suit Every Taste" in Inc. (Vol. 33, October 2011, No. 8, pp. 43)*
Pub: Inc. Magazine

Ed: John Brandon. **Description:** Brita's Hydration Station is a wall-mounted unit with a touch-free sensor for dispensing water. This water cooler cuts down on landfill waste and offers special features.

36232 ■ *"Thomas Morley; President, The Lube Stop Inc., 37" in Crain's Cleveland Business (Vol. 28, November 19, 2007, No. 46, pp. F-12)*
Pub: Crain Communications Inc.

Ed: David Bennett. **Description:** Profile of Thomas Morley, president of The Lube Stop Inc., who is dedicated to promoting the company's strong environmental record as an effective way to differentiate Lube Stop from its competition. Since Mr. Morley came to the company in 2004, Lube Stop has increased sales by 10 percent and has boosted its operating profits by 30 percent.

36233 ■ *"Three Megatrends to Help Your Business Compete in 2014" in South Florida Business Journal (Vol. 34, January 3, 2014, No. 24, pp. 10)*
Pub: American City Business Journals

Released: January 3, 2014. **Description:** Businesses can improve their competitive edge in 2014 by adapting several mega small business trends in marketing and communications. Brands can use brand bridging to get customers attention, use wearable technology to increase their value, and adapt environmental sustainability and corporate social responsibility to keep their customers.

36234 ■ *The Three Secrets of Green Business: Unlocking Competitive Advantage in a Low Carbon Economy*
Pub: Earthscan

Ed: Gareth Kane. **Released:** December 08, 2009. **Price:** $33.95, paperback; $135, hardback. **Description:** Small business is coming under increasing pressure from government, customers and campaigning groups to improve environmental performance. Soaring utility and compliance costs are critical financial burdens on small companies. **Availability:** Print.

36235 ■ *"Time to Green Your Business" in Gallup Management Journal (April 22, 2011)*
Pub: Gallup Inc.
Contact: Jim Clifton, Chief Executive Officer

Ed: Bryant Ott. **Description:** It's Earth Day, so expect to hear companies touting their commitment to the environment. However, according to Gallup, more companies are finding it more interested to talk about being green than actually taking the steps to become a green business.

36236 ■ *"Timken Features Solutions at AWEA WINDPOWER 2012" in PR Newswire (June 3, 2012)*
Pub: PR Newswire Association L.L.C.
Contact: David B. Armon, President

Description: The Timken Company plans to highlight its products and aftermarket solutions for the wind industry at the AWEA WINDPOWER 2012 Conference and Exhibition. Timken products help to maximize the performance of wind energy equipment.

36237 ■ *"Too Much Precaution About Biotech Corn"* in Barron's *(Vol. 88, March 17, 2008, No. 11, pp. 54)*
Pub: Dow Jones & Co., Inc.
Contact: Clare Hart, President
Ed: Mark I. Schwartz. **Description:** In the U.S., 90 percent of cultivated soybeans are biotech varietals as well as 60 percent of the corn. Farmers have significantly reduced their reliance on pesticides in the growing of biotech corn. Biotech cotton cultivation has brought hundreds of millions of dollars in net financial gains to farmers. The European Union has precluded the cultivation or sale of biotech crops within its border.

36238 ■ *"Toolmakers' New Tack: Firms' Goal -- Advance Wind-Turbine Technology"* in Crain's Detroit Business *(Vol. 25, June 8, 2009,)*
Pub: Crain Communications Inc. - Detroit
Contact: Keith Crain, Chairman
Ed: Ryan Beene, Amy Lane. **Description:** MAG Industrial Automation Systems LLC and Dowding Machining Inc. have partnered to advance wind-turbine technology. The goal is to cut costs of wind energy to the same level as carbon-based fuel.

36239 ■ *"Top 50 Exporters: In Volatile Market, Food and Green Companies Lead the List"* in Hispanic Business *(Vol. 30, July-August 2008, No. 7-8, pp. 42)*
Pub: Hispanic Business Inc.
Contact: Jesus Chavarria, President
Ed: Hildy Medina. **Description:** Increases in exports revenues reported by food exporters and green companies in a time of economic slowdown in the U.S are described. Food exporters have benefited from the growth of high-volume grocery stores in underdeveloped countries and the German governments' promotion of solar energy has benefited the U.S. solar heating equipment and solar panel manufactures.

36240 ■ *"Tory Green?"* in Canadian Business *(Vol. 80, January 15, 2007, No. 2, pp. 72)*
Ed: Joe Chidley. **Description:** The need for the government to participate actively in protecting the environment through proper enforcement of the Tories Clean Air Act, is discussed.

36241 ■ *"Toward a Better Future"* in Canadian Business *(Vol. 83, August 17, 2010, No. 13-14, pp. 51)*
Description: A look at certain realities in order to build a better future for Canada's energy industry is presented. Canada must focus on making the oil cleaner, instead of replacing it with another source since dependency on oil will remain in this lifetime. Canada must also develop solutions toward clean technology power sources.

36242 ■ *"Traer Turning to Wind Power to Meet Long-Term Energy Needs"* in Waterloo Courier *(September 20, 2011)*
Pub: Lee Enterprises Inc.
Contact: Mary E. Junck, President
Ed: Josh Nelson. **Description:** Traer Municipal Utilities is working with Clark Thompson, a Story City wind turbine developer, to erect a wind turbine to supply electrical energy to the city. Details are included.

36243 ■ *"Transportation Enterprise"* in Advertising Age *(Vol. 79, June 9, 2008, No. 23, pp. S10)*
Pub: Crain Communications Inc.
Contact: Rance Crain, President
Ed: Jean Halliday. **Description:** Overview of Enterprise rent-a-car's plan to become a more environmentally-friendly company. The family-owned business has spent $1 million a year to plant trees since 2006 and has added more fuel-efficient cars, hybrids and flex-fuel models.

36244 ■ *"Tritium: A Hot Topic in Canada"* in Canadian Business *(Vol. 80, January 29, 2007, No. 3, pp. 8)*
Ed: Marlene Rego. **Description:** The views of Canadian environmental activists, on the effects of the release of tritium into the Ottwa river, are presented.

36245 ■ *"True Green at Work: 100 Ways You Can Make the Environment Your Business"*
Pub: National Geographic
Contact: John M. Fahey, Jr., Chief Executive Officer
Ed: Kim McKay, Jenny Bonnin, Tim Wallace. **Released:** February 19, 2008. **Price:** $9.95, Softcover. **Description:** Manual to help any small business minimize its carbon footprint by reducing waste. **Availability:** Print.

36246 ■ *"Tucson Tech Column"* in AZ Daily Star *(September 27, 2011)*
Pub: Arizona Daily Star
Contact: John Humenik, President
E-mail: jhumenik@azstarnet.com
Ed: David Wichner. **Description:** Western Wind Energy, based in Vancouver, British Columbia, Canada is able to harness energy from the sun when the wind is not blowing at the Kingman I Project wind farm. Details of this technology are outlined.

36247 ■ *"Turning Green Ink to Black"* in The Business Journal-Serving Metropolitan Kansas City *(Vol. 26, August 8, 2008, No. 48, pp. 1)*
Ed: James Dornbrook. **Description:** InkCycle has introduced grenk, a line of environmentally-friendly printer toner and ink cartridges. The cartridges are collected and recycled after use by the company, which separates them into their metal, cardboard, and plastic components.

36248 ■ *"Tweaking On-Board Activities, Equipment Saves Fuel, Reduces CO2"* in Canadian Sailings *(June 30, 2008)*
Description: Optimizing ship activities and equipment uses less fuel and therefore reduces greenhouse gas emissions. Ways in which companies are implementing research and development techniques in order to monitor ship performance and analyze data in an attempt to become more efficient are examined.

36249 ■ *"21st Century Filling Station"* in Austin Business JournalInc. *(Vol. 29, December 11, 2009, No. 40, pp. 1)*
Pub: American City Business Journals
Ed: Jacob Dirr. **Description:** Clean Energy Fuels Corporation announced plans for the construction of a $1 million, 17,000 square foot compressed natural gas fueling station at or near the Austin-Bergstrom International Airport (ABIA). Clean Energy Fuels hopes to encourage cab and shuttle companies in the ABIA to switch from gasoline to natural gas.

36250 ■ *"UA Turns Ann Arbor Green"* in Contractor *(Vol. 56, September 2009, No. 9, pp. 5)*
Pub: Penton Media, Inc.
Ed: Robert P. Mader. **Description:** Instructors at the United Association of Plumbers and Steamfitters have studied the latest in green and sustainable construction and service at the Washtenaw Community College in Michigan. Classes included building information modeling, hydronic heating and cooling and advanced HVACR troubleshooting. The UA is currently focusing on green training.

36251 ■ *"The Ultimate Comfort System"* in Contractor *(Vol. 56, July 2009, No. 7, pp. 30)*
Pub: Intertec Publishing
Contact: John French, President
Ed: Mark Eatherton. **Description:** Retrofitting of a hydronic heating system to an existing home is presented. The project approaches near net-zero energy production.

36252 ■ *"Ultra Green Energy Services Opens NJ Biodiesel Transload Facility"* in Indoor Comfort Marketing *(Vol. 70, June 2011, No. 6, pp. 35)*
Pub: Industry Publications Inc.
Contact: Shirleen Dorman, Editor
Description: Profile of Ultra Green Energy Services and the opening of their new biodiesel facility in New Jersey is discussed.

36253 ■ *"Ultra Low Sulfur Diesel: The Promise and the Reality"* in Indoor Comfort Marketing *(Vol. 70, July 2011, No. 7, pp. 22)*
Pub: Industry Publications Inc.
Contact: Shirleen Dorman, Editor
Ed: Ed Kitchen. **Description:** Impacts of ultra low sulfur diesel are examined.

36254 ■ *"Unilever to Sustainably Source All Paper and Board Packaging"* in Ice Cream Reporter *(Vol. 23, July 20, 2010, No. 8, pp. 1)*
Description: Unilever, a leader in the frozen dessert market, has developed a new sustainable paper and board packaging sourcing policy that will reduce environmental impact by working with suppliers to source 75 percent of paper and board packaging from sustainably managed forests or from recycled material. Unilever is parent company to Breyers, Haagen-Dazs, Klondike, Popsicle and other ice cream brands.

36255 ■ *"Unstable Atmosphere: Survey Finds State Execs Cool On Climate Change"* in The Business Journal-Milwaukee *(Vol. 25, August 8, 2008, No. 46, pp. A1)*
Pub: American City Business Journals, Inc.
Contact: Whitney Shaw, President
Ed: David Doege. **Description:** According to a survey of business executives in Wisconsin, business leaders do not see climate change as a pressing concern, but businesses are moving toward more energy-efficient operations. The survey also revealed that executives believe that financial incentives can promote energy conservation. Other survey results are provided.

36256 ■ *"Uranium Energy Corp Provides an Update on Its Goliad Operations"* in Canadian Corporate News *(May 16, 2007)*
Description: Complaints against Uranium Energy Corp. and its Goliad Project in South Texas have been dismissed. The Railroad Commission of Texas (RRC), the regulatory authority which oversees mineral exploration in Texas, concluded that Uranium Energy Corp.'s drilling activities on the Goliad Project have not contaminated certain water wells or the related aquifier.

36257 ■ *"USHCC Applauds Bank of America for Investment in Green Business Practices"* in Manufacturing Close-Up *(July 11, 2012)*
Description: Bank America has been recognized by the United States Hispanic Chamber of Commerce (USHCC) for its commitment to green business practices. Bank of America has established a 10-year, $50 billion environmental goal to help businesses address climate change, to reduce demands on natural resources, and to advance lower-carbon economic solutions, while reducing their own environmental impact.

36258 ■ *"Valener Announces that Gaz Metro has Achieved a Key Step in Acquiring CVPS"* in CNW Group *(September 30, 2011)*
Pub: CNW Group Ltd.
Contact: Carolyn McGill-Davidson, President
Description: Valener Inc., which owns about 29 percent of Gaz Metro Ltd. Partnership, announced that Gaz Metro welcomes the sale of Central Vermont Public Service Corporation (CVPS). Valener owns an indirect interest of 24.5 percent in the wind power projects jointly developed by Beaupre Eole General Partnership and Boralex Inc. on private lands in Quebec. Details of the deal are included.

36259 ■ *Values-Centered Entrepreneurs and Their Companies*
Pub: Routledge
Contact: Kevin Bradley, President
E-mail: kbradley@taylorandfrancis.com
Ed: David Y. Choi, Edmund Gray. **Released:** August 10, 2010. **Price:** $48.95, Paperback; $165, Hardback. **Description:** A new brand of entrepreneurs has arrived on the business scene, carrying with them a new set of values. They possess a sense of social responsibility, the need to protect the planet, and to do the right thing for all stakeholders.

36260 ■ *"Vinyl Recycling Scheme Wins Green Business Award" in Contract Flooring Journal (August 2012, pp. 12)*
Released: August 2012. **Description:** RECOFLOOR won the Business Commitment to Environment Award for their innovative and sustainable work practices by collecting and recycling waste vinyl flooring.

36261 ■ *"Volunteers Needed" in Canadian Business (Vol. 81, October 27, 2008, No. 18, pp. 60)*
Ed: Megan Harman. **Description:** Emissions-targeting regulations focus on the biggest polluters, missing out on other companies that leave carbon footprints in things such as shipping and travel. Some companies in Canada have initiated programs to offset their carbon emissions. Critics claim that offsetting does not reduce emissions and the programs merely justify pollution.

36262 ■ *"Volvo: Logistics Agreement to Reduce Environmental Impact" in Ecology, Environment & Conservation Business (July 19, 2014, pp. 28)*
Pub: NewsRX
Contact: Susan E. Hasty, Publisher
Released: July 19, 2014. **Description:** Scandinavian Logistics Partners AB (Scanlog) will sell surplus capacity in rail transport from Belgium to Sweden to the Volvo Group. The partnership benefits both costs and environmental impact. The Volvo group is committed to optimizing transport of their manufactured cars and trucks.

36263 ■ *"Warm Floors Make Warm Homes" in Contractor (Vol. 56, October 2009, No. 10, pp. S18)*
Ed: Lisa Murton Beets. **Description:** Three award winning radiant floor-heating installations are presented. The design and the equipment used for these systems are discussed.

36264 ■ *"Was Mandating Solar Power Water Heaters For New Homes Good Policy?" in Hawaii Business (Vol. 54, August 2008, No. 2, pp. 28)*
Pub: PacificBasin Communications
Description: Senator Gary L. Kooser of District 7 Kauai-Niihau believes that the mandating of energy-efficient water heaters for new single-family homes starting in 2010 will help cut Hawaii's oil consumption. Ron Richmond of the Hawaii Solar Energy Association says that the content of SB 644 has negative consequences as it allows for choice of energy and not just solar, and it also eliminates tax credits for new homebuyers.

36265 ■ *"Washington Business Owners Get National Green Builds Business Program" in Manufacturing Close-Up (January 23, 2012)*
Description: Five business owners from Pasco, Washington were awarded the United States Hispanic Chamber of Commerce Foundation's national Green Builds Business Program. The Green Builds Business is a two-day program that helps business owners incorporate sustainability measures by teaching methods for lowering operating costs, increasing revenues and motivating workers with green initiatives.

36266 ■ *"Waste Management Exec First 'Undercover Boss' in Series Kicking Off on Super Bowl Sunday" in Houston Business Journal (Vol. 40, January 22, 2010, No. 37, pp. A1)*
Pub: American City Business Journals
Ed: Christine Hall. **Description:** Houston, Texas-based Waste Management Inc.'s president and chief operation officer, Larry O'Donnell shares some of his experience as CBS Television Network reality show 'Undercover Boss' participant. O'Donnell believes the show was a great way to show the customers how tough their jobs are and reveals that the most difficult job was being a sorter at the recycling center.

36267 ■ *"Waste Not" in Entrepreneur (Vol. 36, April 2008, No. 4, pp. 21)*
Pub: Entrepreneur Press
Contact: Perlman Neil, President
Ed: JJ Ramberg. **Description:** RecycleBank is a company that provides homes with carts in which

recyclables are thrown. An identification chip measures the amount of recyclables and converts them into points, which can be redeemed in stores, such as Starbucks and Whole Foods. RecycleBank earns revenue from cities that save landfill waste spending with the use of the program.

36268 ■ *"Water Conservation Helps GC's Building Attain LEED Gold Status" in Contractor (Vol. 56, September 2009, No. 9, pp. 5)*
Pub: Penton Media, Inc.
Description: Green contractor Marshall Erdman has built a new office building using green design. The facility is seen to become a prime Leadership in Energy and Environmental Design (LEED) building model. Details of the building's design and features are also provided.

36269 ■ *"Water Distiller" in Canadian Business (Vol. 81, September 29, 2008, No. 16, pp. 52)*
Ed: Matthew McClearn. **Description:** Les Fairn's invention of a water distiller called a Solarsphere was recognized in the Great Canadian Invention Competition. Fairn's invention resembles a buoy that uses the sun's energy to vaporize dirty water then leaves the impurities behind in a sump. The invention has an application for producing potable water in impoverished countries.

36270 ■ *"Water Efficiency Bills Move Through Congress" in Contractor (Vol. 56, July 2009, No. 7, pp. 20)*
Pub: Penton Media, Inc.
Ed: Kevin Schwalb. **Description:** National Association, a plumbing-heating-cooling contractor, was instrumental in drafting the Water Advanced Technologies for Efficient Resource Use Act of 2009 and they are also backing the Water Accountability Tax Efficiency Reinvestment Act. The first bill promotes WaterSense-labeled products while the other promotes water conservation through tax credits.

36271 ■ *"Water Woes Force Big Brewers to Tighten the Tap" in Idaho Business Review (June 11, 2014)*
Pub: Dolan Co.
Contact: James P. Dolan, President
Released: June 11, 2014. **Description:** As drought or wildfires threated watersheds, large brewers across the nation are seeking to reduce their water-to-beer ratio in order to conserve the nation's water supply. Craft beer makers have expanded to its highest level since the 1870s. Statistical data included.

36272 ■ *"Watershed Solution" in Business Courier (Vol. 24, December 13, 2007, No. 35, pp. 1)*
Pub: American City Business Journals, Inc.
Contact: Whitney Shaw, President
Ed: Dan Monk. **Description:** Discusses the Metropolitan Sewer District of Greater Cincinnati which is planning to spend around $128 million for its 20-year green-infrastructure improvement projects. Part of the project involves construction of green roofs, rain gardens and restored wetlands to manage water overflows.

36273 ■ *"Wave of Resale, Consignment Shops Pop Up In Springs" in Gazette (March 19, 2012)*
Ed: Bill Radford. **Released:** March 19, 2012. **Description:** The depressed economy has spurred the growth of consignment shops across the nation. Colorado Springs, Colorado area urges people to shop at these resale locations because they promote green initiatives by recycling goods. WeeCycle, Knit Wits, Once Upon a Child and Re-Generation, Moutain Equipment Recyclers, and Gearonimo, are among the established consignment stores in the area.

36274 ■ *"Western Wind Energy Corporation" in CNW Group (October 4, 2011)*
Pub: CNW Group Ltd.
Contact: Carolyn McGill-Davidson, President
Description: Profile of Western Wind Energy Corporation will complete the installation of 60 wind turbines by the end of 2011. The first 106MW are ready for pre-commissioning with the ability to sell power in November when the site is interconnected.

36275 ■ *"What Is a Geothermal Heat Pump" in Indoor Comfort Marketing (Vol. 70, August 2011, No. 8, pp. 14)*
Pub: Industry Publications Inc.
Contact: Shirleen Dorman, Editor
Ed: George Carey. **Description:** Examination of geothermal heat pumps is provided, citing new trends in the industry.

36276 ■ *"What Keeps Global Leaders Up at Night" in Harvard Business Review (Vol. 90, April 2012, No. 4, pp. 32)*
Pub: Harvard Business Review Press
Contact: Peter E. Walsh, Director
Released: April 2012. **Description:** A chart uses colored squares to portray economic, environmental, geopolitical, societal, and technological concerns of industry leaders, and ranks them according to likelihood and impact.

36277 ■ *"What's In That Diaper?" in Inc. (November 2007, pp. 126)*
Pub: Gruner and Jahr USA Publishing Co.
Contact: J. Russell Denson, President
Ed: Nitasha Tiku. **Description:** Profile of Jason and Kimberly Graham-Nye, inventors of the gDiaper, consisting of a washable cotton elastine outer pant and an insert made of fluffed wood pulp and viscose rayon, both harvested from trees certified by the Sustainable Forestry Initiative.

36278 ■ *"Where the Future is Made" in Indoor Comfort Marketing (Vol. 70, May 2011, No. 5, pp. 48)*
Pub: Industry Publications Inc.
Contact: Shirleen Dorman, Editor
Description: Research being performed at Brookhaven National Laboratory, located in Upton, New York, is discussed, focusing on new energy sources for our nation.

36279 ■ *"Where Rubber Meets Road" in Canadian Business (Vol. 80, March 13, 2007, No. 6, pp. 15)*
Pub: Rogers Media Inc.
Contact: Tony Viner, President
Ed: Michelle Magnan. **Description:** The partnership between Engineered Drilling Solutions Inc. and En-Cana Corp. to build road from rubber wastes and follow environment-friendly methods in work is discussed.

36280 ■ *"The Whole Package" in Entrepreneur (Vol. 36, February 2008, No. 2, pp. 24)*
Pub: Entrepreneur Press
Contact: Perlman Neil, President
Ed: Laura Tiffany. **Description:** Holy Bohn, owner of The Honest Statute, developed an environmentally-friendly packaging for her pet food products. The company hired a packaging consultant and spent $175,000. Big corporations also spend money and plunge into the latest trends in packaging ranging from lighter and flexible to temperature-sensitive labels.

36281 ■ *"Why Don't Businesses Buy Solar Panels? Commercial Installations Down Noticeably" in Austin Business Journal (Vol. 32, May 4, 2012, No. 9, pp. 1)*
Pub: American City Business Journals, Inc.
Contact: Whitney Shaw, President
Ed: Christopher Calnan. **Released:** May 4, 2012. **Description:** Commercial solar panel installations in Austin, Texas declined in 2011, a trend attributed to industry experts to the restructuring of Austin Energy's rebate program but utility officials cited market demand and recession as contributing factors. The solar energy advisory committee of the Austin City Council is developing ways to promote solar energy use in commercial projects.

36282 ■ *"Why the Ethanol King Loves Driving his SUV" in Globe & Mail (January 29, 2007, pp. B17)*
Ed: Gordon Pitts. **Description:** Ken Field, chairman of Canada's leading ethanol manufacturer GreenField Ethanol, talks about the cars he drives, the commercial use of cellulose, ethanol's performance as an alternative to gasoline and about the plans of his firm to go public.

36283 ■ *"Will Home Buyers Pay for Green Features?" in Contractor (Vol. 56, October 2009, No. 10, pp. 70)*
Pub: Penton Media, Inc.
Ed: Robert P. Mader. Description: National Association of Home Builders commissioned a survey which shows that homeowners are interested in green as long as they do no have to pay much for it. The association did not allow a board member to read the survey which raises questions about how the questions were phrased and how the sample was selected.

36284 ■ *"Wind Farm Is Planned for Yolo Farmland" in Sacramento Business Journal (Vol. 29, September 21, 2012, No. 30, pp. 1)*
Pub: American City Business Journal
Ed: Melanie Turner. Description: Austin, Texas-based Pioneer Green Energy LLC has been planning to build as many as 400 wind turbines in Yolo County, California that could potentially generate up to 600 megawatts. The company has already raised $20 and it is expected to formally propose the project in early 2013. The economic impact on the farmers and landowners in the region is explored.

36285 ■ *"Wind Gets Knocked Out of Energy Farm Plan" in Buffalo News (September 28, 2011)*
Pub: The Buffalo News
Contact: Warren T. Colville, President
Ed: David Robinson. Description: New York Power Authority formally killed the proposal for a wind energy farm off the shores of Lake Erie and Lake Ontario. The Authority cited high subsidy costs would be required to make the wind farm economically feasible. Details of the proposal are outlined.

36286 ■ *"WindPower Innovations Releases Statement to Their Stockholders" in Internet Wire (July 2, 2012)*
Released: July 2, 2012. Description: WindPower Innovations Inc. released a letter stating corporate growth and strategy. WindPower, a small wind farm, was granted a special energy credit by the federal government. Statistical data included.

36287 ■ *"WindPower Solutions Announces Its Best In Class 'Next Gen' 85kw Wind Turbine" in Marketwired (June 6, 2012)*
Pub: COMTEX
Contact: Chip Brian, President
Description: WinPower Innovations Inc.'s subsidiary, WindPower Solutions, unveiled its next generation 85kw wind turbines that are available for sale. They are perfect for remote locations where there is a lot of wind and can be used locally or the site owner, if near the power grid, could sell the energy to the market.

36288 ■ *"Winning Gold" in The Business Journal-Milwaukee (Vol. 25, August 8, 2008, No. 46, pp. A1)*
Pub: American City Business Journals, Inc.
Contact: Whitney Shaw, President
Ed: Rich Rovito. Description: Johnson Controls Inc. of Milwaukee, Wisconsin is taking part in the 2008 Beijing Olympics with the installation of its sustainable control equipment and technology that monitor over 58,000 points in 18 Olympic venues. Details of Johnson Controls' green products and sustainable operations in China are discussed.

36289 ■ *"Women Up: Kathleen Ligocki of Harvest Power Inc." in Boston Business Journal (Vol.. 34, April 11, 2014, No. 10)*
Pub: American City Business Journals, Inc.
Contact: Whitney Shaw, President
Released: April 11, 2014. Description: Kathleen Ligocki is the CEO of Harvest Power Inc. of Massachusetts. The company diverts organic waste destined for landfills and produces green energy and soil enrichment products. The company was founded in 2008 and reported sales of over $130 million in 2013.

36290 ■ *"Wood Increasingly Used in School Construction" in Arkansas Business (Vol. 29,*
July 23, 2012, No. 30, pp. 11)
Pub: Arkansas Business Publishing Group
Ed: Jan Cottingham. Description: Arkansas state guidelines have increased the use of wood in school building construction. Wood is believed to provide strength and durability along with cost effectiveness and environmental benefits.

36291 ■ *"WQA's Leadership Conference Tackles Industry Issues" in Contractor (Vol. 56, October 2009, No. 10, pp. 3)*
Pub: Penton Media, Inc.
Ed: Candace Roulo. Description: Water Quality Association's Mid-Year Leadership Conference held in Bloomingdale, Illinois in September 2009 tackled lead regulation, water softeners, and product efficiency. The possibility of a WQA green seal was discussed by the Water Sciences Committee and the Government Relations Committee meeting.

36292 ■ *"Xerox Diverts Waste from Landfills" in Canadian Electronics (Vol. 23, February 2008, No. 1, pp. 1)*
Description: Xerox Corporation revealed that it was able to divert more than two billion pounds of electronic waste from landfills through waste-free initiatives. The company's program, which was launched in 1991, covers waste avoidance in imaging supplies and parts reuse. Environmental priorities are also integrated into manufacturing operations.

36293 ■ *"Yates Helps Turn Log Home Green" in Contractor (Vol. 56, December 2009, No. 12, pp. 40)*
Pub: Penton Media, Inc.
Description: Upgrading and greening of a log home's HVAC system in Pennsylvania is discussed. F. W. Behler Inc. president Dave Yates was chosen to manage the project. A large coil of R-flex was used to connect the buffer tank to the garage's radiant heat system.

36294 ■ *"Yates Helps Turn Log Home Green" in Contractor (Vol. 56, November 2009, No. 11, pp. 1)*
Pub: Penton Media, Inc.
Description: Dave Yates of F.W. Behler Inc. helped homeowners from James Creek, Pennsylvania achieve energy efficiency on the heating system of their log cabin. The mechanical system installed on the cabin had high-temp 'THW' water-to-water geothermal system by ClimateMaster, two twin-coil indirect water heaters, and several pre-assembled, pre-engineered Hydronex panels by Watts Radiant.

36295 ■ *"Yates Turns Log Home Green - Part Three" in Contractor (Vol. 57, January 2010, No. 1, pp. 5)*
Pub: Intertec Publishing
Contact: John French, President
Description: Dave Yates of F.W. Behler Inc. discusses remodeling a log home's HVAC system with geo-to-radiant heat and thermal-solar systems. The solar heater's installation is discussed.

36296 ■ *"You're a What? Wind Turbine Service Technician" in Occupational Outlook Quarterly (Vol. 54, Fall 2010, No. 3, pp. 34)*
Pub: U.S. Department of Labor Bureau of Labor Statistics
Contact: Philip L. Rones, Manager
E-mail: rones.philip@bls.gov
Ed: Drew Liming. Description: Profile of Brandon Johnson, former member of the Air Force, found a career as a wind turbine service technician.

36297 ■ *"Yudelson Challenges San Antonio Groups" in Contractor (Vol. 56, October 2009, No. 10, pp. 6)*
Pub: Penton Media, Inc.
Description: Green building consultant and author Jerry Yudelson made a presentation for the Central Texas Green Building Council and Leadership San Antonio where he discussed the European approach to sustainability and how it can be used for designing green buildings. Yudelson also discussed how to use sustainable practices for planning 25 years into the future.

TRADE PERIODICALS

36298 ■ *Composting News*
Pub: McEntee Media Corp.
URL(s): www.compostingnews.com/. Ed: Ken McEntee, Editor, ken@recycle.cc. Released: Monthly Price: $83, Individuals; $93, Canada and Mexico; $105, Other countries. Description: Covers news and trends in the composting industry. Also reports on compost product prices. Recurring features include letters to the editor, interviews, news of research, a calendar of events, reports of meetings, and notices of publications available.

36299 ■ *Inside Cal/EPA*
Pub: Inside Washington Publishers
Contact: Korila Malecha, Manager
URL(s): iwpnews.com/IWP-General/Inside-Washington-Publishers-General/products/menu-id-812.html. Released: Weekly (Fri.) Price: $685, U.S. and Canada; $735, Elsewhere. Description: Reports on environmental legislation, regulation, and litigation.

36300 ■ *Water Policy Report*
Pub: Inside Washington Publishers
Contact: Korila Malecha, Manager
URL(s): iwpnews.com/IWP-General/Inside-Washington-Publishers-General/products/menu-id-812.html. Released: Biweekly; every other Monday. Price: $700, U.S. and Canada; $750, Elsewhere. Description: Reports on federal water quality programs and policies. Covers topics such as drinking water, toxics, enforcement, monitoring, and state/EPA relations.

36301 ■ *Wind Energy Weekly*
Pub: American Wind Energy Association
Contact: Edward Zaelke, President
URL(s): www.awea.org/wew/. Ed: Thomas O. Gray, Editor, tom_gray@igc.org. Released: Weekly. Price: Included in membership; $595, nonmembers. Description: Provides wind energy trade news, plus covers energy and environmental policy. Recurring features include news of research, reports of meetings, job listings, and notices of publications available. Remarks: Available only via E-mail account.

VIDEOCASSETTES/ AUDIOCASSETTES

36302 ■ *Cleaning Up Toxics*
The Video Project
PO Box 411376
San Francisco, CA 94141-1376
Ph: (415)241-2514
Free: 800-4-PLANET
Fax: (888)562-9012
Co. E-mail: support@videoproject.com
URL: http://www.videoproject.com
Contact: Steve Michelson, President
Released: 1990. Price: $59.95. Description: A series containing practical suggestions on reducing the amount of hazardous substances introduced into the environment from homes and businesses. Availability: VHS; 3/4 U; Special order formats.

36303 ■ *Free Energy: The Race to Zero Point*
Lightworks Audio & Video
PO Box 661593
Los Angeles, CA 90066
Ph: (310)398-4949
Free: 800-795-8273
Fax: (310)397-4401
Co. E-mail: sales1@lightworksav.com
URL: http://www.lightworksav.com
Released: 1998. Price: $29.95. Description: Documentary takes a look at the quest to find safe non-polluting energy sources that are available to everyone. Features segments on Nikola Tesla's method of "broadcasting" free energy, electric cars, zero-point "space" energy and cold fusion. Availability: DVD.

36304 ■ *Greenbucks: The Challenge of Sustainable Development*
The Video Project
PO Box 411376
San Francisco, CA 94141-1376
Ph: (415)241-2514
Free: 800-4-PLANET

Fax: (888)562-9012
Co. E-mail: support@videoproject.com
URL: http://www.videoproject.com
Contact: Steve Michelson, President
Released: 1992. **Price:** $195. **Description:** Major corporations change their attitudes and look for environmental solutions. Designed to inspire other businesses to higher ecological awareness. **Availability:** VHS.

36305 ■ *Grime Goes Green: Your Business & the Environment*
Video Arts, Inc.
c/o Aim Learning Group
8238-40 Lehigh
Morton Grove, IL 60053-2615
Free: 877-444-2230
Fax: (416)252-2155
Co. E-mail: service@aimlearninggroup.com
URL: http://www.aimlearninggroup.com
Released: 1991. **Price:** $435. **Description:** How to implement effective organizational environmental policies. Shows how to avoid waste, use resources more efficiently, and institute re-cycling systems. **Availability:** VHS; 8 mm; 3/4 U; Special order formats.

36306 ■ *The Impact of Environmental Regulations on Business Transactions*
Practising Law Institute (PLI)
1177 Avenue of the Americas
New York, NY 10036
Ph: (212)824-5700
Free: 800-260-4754
Fax: (212)824-5733
Co. E-mail: info@pli.edu
URL: http://www.pli.edu
Contact: Victor J. Rubino, President
Released: 1988. **Price:** $245. **Description:** A look at how environmental standards affect business dealings. **Availability:** VHS.

36307 ■ *Nuclear Power: The Hot Debate*
Released: 19??. **Price:** $395. **Description:** Looks at the pros and cons of nuclear power and at possible energy alternatives. **Availability:** VHS.

CONSULTANTS

36308 ■ GE Energy [Mostardi-Platt Enviornmental]
4200 Wildwood Pkwy.
Atlanta, GA 30309
Ph: (678)844-6000
Co. E-mail: daniel.grabowski@ge.com
URL: http://www.gepower.com
Contact: John Krenicki, Jr., President
Scope: Provides environmental compliance, permitting and site assessment services including compliance management systems, environmental outsourcing, remediation design and management, asbestos project management, wetlands investigations, risk management planning, OSHA Compliance, and indoor air quality. **Founded:** 2008. **Publications:** "Energy consulting".

36309 ■ Occusafe Inc.
608 S Washington St., Ste. 9
Naperville, IL 60540
Ph: (630)851-3255
Free: 800-323-7597
Fax: (630)851-9339
Co. E-mail: info@occusafe-inc.com
Contact: Robert K. McKinley, President
E-mail: rkm@occusafe-inc.com
Scope: Assist clients in resolving employee safety, health or environmental problems or concerns by providing practical and economical solutions. **Founded:** 1972.

36310 ■ Prindle Hinds Environmental Inc.
7208 Jefferson St. NE
Albuquerque, NM 87109
Ph: (505)345-8732
Fax: (505)345-0393
Contact: William V. Hinds, Vice President
Scope: Provides environmental engineering/consulting services needed by clients to prevent/solve regulatory compliance problems and/or reduce their potential liabilities. Services include: geology, hydrology and engineering; hazardous waste management; non-hazardous waste management; permit preparation/delisting; site/risk assessments; and site characterization/remedial action planning and training. Additional specialized expertise includes underground storage tanks, regulatory negotiations and expert witness testimony. **Seminars:** Firm has presented over a hundred specialized seminars/workshops, most pertaining to hazardous waste management.

36311 ■ SENES Consultants Ltd.
121 Granton Dr., Ste. 12
Richmond Hill, ON, Canada L4B 3N4
Ph: (905)764-9380
Fax: (905)764-9386
Co. E-mail: info@senes.ca
URL: http://www.senes.ca
Contact: Donald Gorber, President
Scope: Provider of environmental and solid waste management solutions. It offers site investigations, air quality assessment, preparation of solid waste management master plans and data management services. **Founded:** 1980. **Seminars:** Risk assessments; Environmental audits and other environmental matters.

36312 ■ Smyth Fivenson Co.
8513 Irvington Ave.
Bethesda, MD 20817-3815
Ph: (301)493-6600
URL: http://www.smythfivenson.com
Contact: Frank Sterrett, Jr., Manager
E-mail: fsterrett@smythfivenson.com
Scope: A Human Resources consulting firm providing services to two business areas, both nationally. First, provides temporary human resource professionals to all industries. Second, Smyth Fivenson Co. performs recruiting and placement services for the environmental industry. **Founded:** 1982.

36313 ■ Versar Inc.
6850 Versar Ctr.
Springfield, VA 22151
Ph: (703)750-3000
Free: 800-283-7727
Fax: (703)642-6825
URL: http://www.versar.com
Contact: Jeffrey A. Wagonhurst, President
Scope: Consultants offering environmental services; complete regulatory assistance to industry; applied research services to industry and government, emergency planning services; nuclear power plant emergency plan development; engineering services; atmospheric and meteorological modeling; and recent experience in evaluation of off site consequences of chemical accidents. Versar serves private industries as well as government agencies. **Founded:** 1969.

LIBRARIES

36314 ■ Environmental Bankers Association (EBA) - Library
510 King St., Ste. 410
Alexandria, VA 22314
Ph: (703)549-0977

Fax: (703)548-5945
Co. E-mail: eba@envirobank.org
URL: http://www.envirobank.org
Contact: Rick Ferguson, President
Description: Banks and financial services organizations, law firms, consultants, and insurers interested in environmental risk management and liability issues. Aims to help members preserve net income and assets from environmental liability issues resulting from lending and trust activities. Updates members on environmental risk management programs, auditing procedures, legislation and government regulation, environmental banking case law, and environmental insurance/risk management procedures. **Scope:** environmental lender liability insurance, EPA and FDIC regulations, environment risk management. **Services:** Library not open to the public. **Founded:** 1994. **Holdings:** 50 books, periodicals, and clippings. **Subscriptions:** 50 books clippings periodicals; 125 journals and other serials. **Educational Activities:** Environmental Bankers Association Meeting (Annual).

RESEARCH CENTERS

36315 ■ Colorado State University - Industrial Assessment Center (IAC)
Department of Mechanical Engineering
Fort Collins, CO 80523-1374
Ph: (970)491-8617
Fax: (970)491-3827
Co. E-mail: hittle@engr.colostate.edu
URL: http://www.engr.colostate.edu/IAC/
Contact: Prof. Douglas C. Hittle, Director
Scope: Pollution prevention and energy conservation in manufacturing. **Services:** Pollution prevention, energy conservation & productivity improvement: to industry. **Founded:** 1984.

36316 ■ Tarleton State University - Texas Institute for Applied Environmental Research (TIAER)
Box T-0410
Stephenville, TX 76402
Ph: (254)968-9567
Fax: (254)968-9336
Co. E-mail: dhunter@tiaer.tarleton.edu
URL: http://tiaer.tarleton.edu
Contact: Dan Hunter, Executive Director
Scope: Environmental issues of state and national significance, focusing on the interface between the private sector and government as environmental policy is developed and implemented.

36317 ■ University of California, Davis - Information Center for the Environment (ICE)
1 Shields Ave.
Davis, CA 95616
Ph: (530)752-8027
Fax: (530)752-8027
Co. E-mail: jfquinn@ucdavis.edu
URL: http://ice.ucdavis.edu
Contact: Prof. James F. Quinn, Director
Scope: Environmental protection. **Founded:** 1991.

36318 ■ University of Florida - Powell Center for Construction and Environment
342 Rinker Hall
Gainesville, FL 32611-5703
Ph: (352)273-1172
Co. E-mail: ckibert@ufl.edu
URL: http://www.cce.ufl.edu
Contact: Dr. Charles J. Kibert, Director
Scope: Environmental problems associated with planning and architecture activities, and the determination of the optimum materials and methods for use in minimizing environmental damage. **Services:** Continuing education courses. **Founded:** 1991. **Publications:** *Powell Center for Construction and Environment Conference proceedings*; *Powell Center for Construction and Environment Research reports*. **Educational Activities:** Powell Center for Construction and Environment Conferences; Powell Center for Construction and Environment Workshops.

ASSOCIATIONS AND OTHER ORGANIZATIONS

36319 ■ *Communique*
160 Elgin St., 9th Fl.
Ottawa, ON, Canada K1A 0W9
Ph: (613)954-1800
Co. E-mail: ethics-ethique@cihr-irsc.gc.ca
URL: http://www.ncehr-cnerh.org
Contact: Glenn Griener, President
Released: Annual **Price:** free.

36320 ■ **Council for Ethical Leadership (CEE)**
1 College and Main
Columbus, OH 43209
Ph: (614)236-7222
URL: http://www.businessethics.org
Contact: Barbara Barresi, Director
Description: Leaders in business, education, and the professions. Seeks to "strengthen the ethical fabric of business and economic life". Facilitates the development of international networks of business-people interested in economic ethics; sponsors educational programs and develops and distributes educational materials; advises and supports communities wishing to implement character educational programs; makes available consulting services. **Founded:** 1982. **Publications:** *Ethical Leadership* (3/year).

36321 ■ **National Council on Ethics in Human Research (NCEHR) [Conseil national d'ethique en recherche chez l'humain]**
160 Elgin St., 9th Fl.
Ottawa, ON, Canada K1A 0W9
Ph: (613)954-1800
Co. E-mail: ethics-ethique@cihr-irsc.gc.ca
URL: http://www.ncehr-cnerh.org
Contact: Glenn Griener, President
Description: Encourages high ethical standards research involving human subjects. Consults with universities, government agencies and businesses engaged in human research; recommends standards for research projects using human subjects. Conducts educational programs. **Founded:** 1989. **Subscriptions:** books periodicals. **Publications:** *Communique* (Annual).

36322 ■ **Society for Business Ethics (SBE)**
University of New Brunswick
PO Box 4400
Fredericton, NB, Canada E3B 5A3
URL: http://sbeonline.org
Contact: Dawn Elm, Executive Director
Description: Philosophy and theology professors, business school professors, and business executives. Facilitates information exchange regarding research and activities in business ethics. **Founded:** 1980. **Publications:** *Society For Business Ethics Newsletter* (Quarterly). **Educational Activities:** Society for Business Ethics Annual Meeting (Annual).

REFERENCE WORKS

36323 ■ *"The Accountability Lens: A New Way to View Management Issues"* in *Business Horizons (September-October 2007, pp. 405)*
Pub: Elsevier Technology Publications
Ed: Angela T. Hall, Michael G. Bowen, Gerald R. Ferris, M. Todd Royle, Dale E. Fitzgibbons. **Price:** $35.95. **Description:** Organizations are viewed through an accountability lens in terms of source, focus, salience, and intensity to explain issues on corporate governance and ethics. Accountability environment, the individual's immediate work environment that directly affects the subjective experience of felt accountability, and its four main aspects are discussed. **Availability:** PDF.

36324 ■ *"Accountants Get the Hook"* in *Canadian Business (Vol. 80, October 22, 2007, No. 21, pp. 19)*
Ed: John Gray. **Description:** Chartered Accountants of Ontario handed down the decision on Douglas Barrington, Anthony Power and Claudio Russo's professional misconduct case. The three accountants of Deloitte & Touche LLP must pay C$100,000 in fines and C$417,000 in costs. Details of the disciplinary case are presented.

36325 ■ *"As Fake Reviews Rise, Yelp, Others Crack Down on Fraudsters; Value of This Essential Local-Marketing Tool Can Breed Bad Actors"* in *Advertising Age (Vol. 83, October 1, 2012, No. 35, pp. 11)*
Pub: Crain Communications Inc.
Contact: Rance E. Crain, President
Ed: Michael Learmonth. **Description:** Online reviews can help or hinder any small business. These reviews have created an incentive for unethical people to cheat with paid-for, malicious or fraudulent reviews. TripAdvisor, Google Local, and Yelp are using a mix of algorithms and human moderators to distinguish fraudulent reviews from genuine reviews. Details on this issue are outlined.

36326 ■ *"Biblical Secrets to Business Success"*
Pub: CreateSpace
Contact: Daren Giles, President
Released: October 2, 2014. **Price:** $14.99 paperback. **Description:** Bob Diener share insight into his journey as an entrepreneur. He focuses on tough issues like: how to treat employees, how to please customers, whether or not to cut corners, whether to follow temptation of an unethical deal, and provides solutions to these dilemmas. He recommends abiding by the Bible's rules of business in order to prosper long term.

36327 ■ *"Biovail Hits SAC With $4.6 Billion Suit"* in *Globe & Mail (February 23, 2006, pp. B1)*
Ed: Shawn McCarthy. **Description:** The details of Biovail Corp.'s securities fraud case against SAC Management LLC are presented.

36328 ■ *"Blood Diamonds are Forever"* in *Canadian Business (Vol. 83, August 17, 2010, No. 13-14, pp. 59)*
Ed: Matthew McClearn. **Description:** The failed case against Donald McKay who was found in possession of rough diamonds in a raid by Royal Canadian Mounted Police has raised doubts about Kimberley Process (KP) attempts to stop the illicit global trade in diamonds. KP has managed to reduce total global trade of blood diamonds by 1 percent in mid-2000.

36329 ■ *The Board Book: An Insider's Guide for Directors and Trustees*
Pub: W.W. Norton and Company Inc.
Contact: A Malmud, President
Ed: William G. Bowen. **Released:** April 2012. **Price:** $16.95, paperback. **Description:** A primer for all directors and trustees that provides suggestions for getting back to good-governance basics in business. **Availability:** Print.

36330 ■ *"Boards That Lead: When to Take Charge, When to Partner, and When to Stay Out of the Way"*
Pub: Harvard Business Review Press
Contact: Peter E. Walsh, Director
Released: March 4, 2014. **Price:** $26.00. **Description:** As boards take a more active role in decision making at companies, leadership at the top is being redefined. Boardroom veterans describe the successes and pitfalls of this new leadership style and explain how to define the central idea of the company, ensure that the right CEO is in place and potential successors are identified, recruit directors who add value, root out board dysfunction, select a board leader who bridges the divide between management and the board, and to set a high bar on ethics and risk.

36331 ■ *"Boundaries for Leaders (Enhanced Edition): Results, Relationships, and Being Ridiculously In Charge"*
Pub: Harper Business
Released: April 16, 2013. **Price:** $28.99. **Description:** Clinical psychologist and author explains how the best business leaders set boundaries within their organizations, with their teams and themselves, to improve performance and increase customer and employee satisfaction. Practical advice is given to manage teams, coach direct reports, and create an organization with strong ethics and culture.

36332 ■ *"Bridging Diverging Perspectives and Repairing Damaged Relationships in the Aftermath of Workplace Transgressions"* in *Business Ethics Quarterly (Vol. 24, July 2014, No. 3, pp. 443)*
Pub: Business Ethics Quarterly
Released: July 2014. **Description:** Workplace transgressions elicit a variety of opinions about their meaning and what is required to address them. This diversity in views makes it difficult for managers to identify a mutually satisfactory response and to enable repair of the relationships between the affected

parties. A conceptual model is developed for understanding how to bridge these diverging perspectives and foster relationship repair.

36333 ■ "Bridging the Gap: Contextualizing Professional Ethics in Collaborative Writing Projects" in Business Communication Quarterly (December 2007)
Pub: Pine Forge Press
Contact: Blaise R. Simqu, President
Ed: J. A. Rice. **Description:** A classroom activity for business management students integrates ethical concepts with business writing strategies, while increasing understanding of writing ethics by emphasizing its rhetorical, contingent, and public nature.

36334 ■ "Business Ethics, Strategic Decision Making, and Firm Performance" in Business Horizons (September-October 2007, pp. 353)
Pub: Elsevier Technology Publications
Ed: Michael A. Hitt, Jaime D. Collins. **Price:** $35.95. **Description:** Strategic management and decision-making process are linked to business ethics. The Strengths, Weakness, Opportunities, and Threats (SWOT) analysis model is employed to design an effective strategy for companies. **Availability:** PDF.

36335 ■ Business Fairy Tales
Pub: South-Western
Contact: Susan Badger, President
Ed: Cecil W. Jackson. **Price:** £35.99, hardback. **Description:** The seven most-common business schemes are uncovered.

36336 ■ "The Case for Treating the Sex Trade as an Industry" in Canadian Business (Vol. 83, October 12, 2010, No. 17, pp. 9)
Pub: Rogers Media Inc.
Contact: Tony Viner, President
Ed: Steve Maich. **Description:** It is believed that the worst aspects of prostitution in Canada are exacerbated by the fact that it must take place in secret. The laws that deal with the market for sex have led to an unsafe working environment. Prostitutes believe their industry needs to be sanctioned and regulated rather than ignored and reviled.

36337 ■ "Chino Valley Ranches: a Family of Farmers" in Retail Merchandiser (Vol. 51, September-October 2011, No. 5, pp. 79)
Pub: Phoenix Media Corporation
Ed: Angela Forsyth. **Description:** Charles B. Nichols and his wife Isabella purchased their ranch in Beaumont, California in the early 1950s. The family has been raising their chickens, producing eggs with quality, integrity and honesty the foundation of their business.

36338 ■ "Citi Ruling Could Chill SEC, Street Legal Pacts" in Wall Street Journal Eastern Edition (November 29, 2011, pp. C1)
Pub: Dow Jones & Co., Inc.
Contact: Clare Hart, President
Ed: Jean Eaglesham, Chad Bray. **Description:** A $285 million settlement was reached between the Securities and Exchange Commission and Citigroup Inc. over allegations the bank misled investors over a mortgage-bond deal. Now, Judge Jed S. Rakoff has ruled against the settlement, a decision that will affect the future of such attempts to prosecute Wall Street fraud. Rakoff said that the settlement was 'neither fair, nor reasonable, nor adequate, nor in the public interest.'.

36339 ■ "The Classless Workplace: The Digerati and the New Spirit of Technocapitalism" in WorkingUSA (Vol. 11, June 2008, No. 2, pp. 181)
Ed: Eran Fisher. **Description:** Article argues the formation of a new type of economic actor at the intersection of a new capitalism and a new technology: The Dierati. The discourse in based on the analysis of the popular magazine Wired, which registers the culture of contemporary technocapitalism. The suggestion that the new persona of the digerati is constructed as a rejection of the ethics, which dominated the Fordist workplace and Fordist society: Hierarchy and differentiation between workers, on the one hand and capitalists and managers, on the other

hand. The transformation of these two categories, workers and capitalists into the digerati worker and the digerati entrepreneur, is described. Set within the context of the structural transformations of capitalism from Fordism to post-Fordism, the article shows the ideological fit of the new ethics of the digerati to the new working arrangements of post-Fordist capitalism, characterized by more privatizes, flexible, and precarious working arrangements.

36340 ■ "Column: It's Time to Take Full Responsibility" in Harvard Business Review (Vol. 88, October 2010, No. 10, pp. 42)
Pub: Harvard Business School Publishing
Ed: Rosabeth Moss Kanter. **Description:** A case for corporate responsibility is cited, focusing on long-term impact and the effects of public accountability.

36341 ■ "Corporate Responsibility" in Professional Services Close-Up (July 2, 2010)
Description: List of firms awarded the inaugural Best Corporate Citizens in Government Contracting by the Corporate Responsibility Magazine is presented. The list is based on the methodology of the Magazine's Best Corporate Citizen's List, with 324 data points of publicly-available information in seven categories which include: environment, climate change, human rights, philanthropy, employee relations, financial performance, and governance.

36342 ■ "CR Magazine Taps ITT As a 'Best Corporate Citizen' in Government Contracting" in Profesisonal Services Close-Up (July 30, 2010)
Description: ITT Corporation was named by Corporate Responsibility Magazine as a Best Corporate Citizen in Government Contracting. The list recognizes publicly-traded companies that exemplify transparency and accountability while serving the U.S. government.

36343 ■ "Crime and Punishment" in Canadian Business (Vol. 81, December 24, 2007, No. 1, pp. 21)
Ed: Joe Castaldo. **Description:** Cmpass Inc.'s survey of 137 Canadian chief executive officers showed that they want tougher imposition of sentences on white-collar criminals, as they believe that the weak enforcement of securities laws gives an impression that Canada is a country where it is easy to get away with fraud.

36344 ■ "Critics Target Bribery Law" in Wall Street Journal Eastern Edition (November 28, 2011, pp. B1)
Pub: Dow Jones & Co., Inc.
Contact: Clare Hart, President
Ed: Joe Palazzuolo. **Description:** Concern about how the Foreign Corrupt Practices Act, the United States' anti-bribery law, is enforced has drawn the focus of corporate lobbyists. Corporations have paid some $4 billion in penalties in cases involving the law, which prohibits companies from paying foreign officials bribes. The US Chamber of Commerce believes amending the act should be a priority.

36345 ■ "Crucible: Battling Back from Betrayal" in Harvard Business Review (Vol. 88, December 2010, No. 12, pp. 130)
Pub: Harvard Business School Publishing
Ed: Daniel McGinn. **Description:** Stephen Greer's scrap metal firm, Hartwell Pacific, lost several million dollars due to a lack of efficient and appropriate inventory audits, accounting procedures, and new-hire reference checks for his foreign operations. Greer believes that balancing growth with control is a key component of success.

36346 ■ Data Driven Investing: Professional Edition
Pub: Data Driven Publishing, LLC
Ed: Mitchell R. Hardy, Bill Matson. **Released:** 2004. **Description:** Investment concepts and trading techniques are explored in a simple and practical way. The book covers the unreliability of financial markets due to malpractices, appalling analysis, insider training and more. Information is based on data and common sense and easy to use for beginner as well as professional.

36347 ■ "Dating Games" in Canadian Business (Vol. 79, September 25, 2006, No. 19, pp. 23)
Ed: John Gray. **Description:** Increasing stock option scandals in Canada and American companies is discussed.

36348 ■ "Decent Termination: A Moral Case for Severance Pay" in Business Ethics Quarterly (Vol. 24, April 2014, No. 2, pp. 203)
Pub: Business Ethics Quarterly
Released: April 2014. **Description:** People are often involuntarily laid off from their jobs through no fault of their own. Employees who are dismissed in this manner cannot always legitimately hold employers accountable for these miserable situations because the decision to implement layoffs is often the best possible outcome given the context. Even in circumstances in which layoffs qualify as 'necessary evils', morality demands that employers respect the dignity of those whose employment is involuntarily terminated. This paper argues that to preserve the dignity of the employees involuntarily terminated, in most cases employers have a substantial reason to offer a special unemployment benefit or severance pay.

36349 ■ "Defend Your Research: People Often Trust Eloquence More Than Honesty" in Harvard Business Review (Vol. 88, November 2010, No. 11, pp. 36)
Pub: Harvard Business School Publishing
Ed: Todd Rogers, Michael I. Norton. **Description:** The article shows how deftly side-stepping a ques tion in an eloquent manner generates a more positive response in an audience than does a direct answer that is ineffectively delivered. Implications for both politics and business are discussed.

36350 ■ "Diary of a Short-Seller" in Conde Nast Portfolio (Vol. 2, June 2008, No. 6, pp. 44)
Ed: Jesse Eisinger. **Description:** Profile of David Einhorn who is a fund manager that spoke out against finance company Allied Capital whose stock fell nearly 20 percent the day after Einhorn's critique; Einhorn subsequently had to contend with attacks against his credibility as well as investigations by the S.E.C.; Einhorn's experience illuminates our current economic crisis.

36351 ■ "Do the Math" in Canadian Business (Vol. 79, October 9, 2006, No. 20, pp. 17)
Ed: Al Rosen. **Description:** Faulty practices followed by regulators in Canadian stock market are discussed. The need for authorities to protect investors against these frauds are emphasized.

36352 ■ Doing Business Anywhere: The Essential Guide to Going Global
Pub: John Wiley & Sons Inc.
Contact: Stephen M. Smith, President
Ed: Tom Travis. **Description:** Plans are given for new or existing businesses to organize, plan, operate and execute a business on a global basis. Trade agreements, brand protection and patents, ethics, security as well as cultural issues are among the issues addressed. **Availability:** E-book.

36353 ■ "Don't Let the Door Hit You" in Entrepreneur (May 2014)
Pub: Entrepreneur Media Inc.
Released: May 2014. **Description:** An ethics coach offers advice on the proper way of managing exit strategies. A company policy saying that if sales-people make a sale, but leave the company before the deal closes, will not be paid the commission is unethical and not a good business strategy. An ethical way of getting references for the new business is to line up a few small jobs and even consider the possibility of offering discounts. The main motivation for taking a business partner must be carefully considered so that the partnership will not suffer if things went wrong.

36354 ■ "Don't Lie To Me: Dishonesty Can Ruin Professional and Personal Relationships" in Black Enterprise (Vol. 38,

January 2008)
Pub: Earl G. Graves Publishing Co. Inc.
Contact: Earl G. Graves, Jr., President
Ed: Marcia A. Reed-Woodard. Description: Consequences of lying can be devastating in any business environment. When a person lies he loses integrity, credibility, confidence and self-esteem.

36355 ■ "easyhome Ltd. Discovers Employee Fraud at an Easyfinancial Kiosk Company" in Internet Wire (October 14, 2010)
Pub: COMTEX
Contact: Chip Brian, President
Description: Canada's leading merchandise leasing company and provider of financial services, easyhome Ltd., reported employee fraud totaling $3.4 million that was perpetrated against the firm's easyfinancial services business.

36356 ■ The Economics of Integrity: From Dairy Farmers to Toyota, How Wealth Is Built on Trust and What That Means for Our Future
Pub: HarperStudio/HarperCollins
Ed: Anna Bernasek. Released: February 23, 2010. Price: $13.99. Description: Integrity is built over time and the importance of trust in starting and building business relationships is stressed. Availability: E-book.

36357 ■ "Errors in Tax Preparation by Mo' Money Taxes Cited" in Commerical Appeal (March 30, 2012)
Pub: McClatchy-Tribune Information Services
Ed: Ted Evanoff. Released: March 30, 2012. Description: Mo' Money LLC is facing fraud and excessive fee charges by Attorney Generals in both Illinois and Missouri along with its sister firm MoneyCo USA LLC. Details of complaints filed against the company that is claiming software problems as the culprit.

36358 ■ The Ethical Executive: Becoming Aware of the Root Causes of Unethical Behavior: 45 Psychological Traps that Every One of Us Falls Prey To
Pub: Stanford University Press
Contact: Geoffrey Burn, Director
E-mail: grhburn@stanford.edu
Ed: Robert Hoyk, Paul Hersey. Released: 2008. Price: $18.95, paperback; $24.95, cloth. Description: Forty-five lessons to help avoid becoming a victim to day-to-day ethical traps are outlined using moral lapses at Enron, Tyco International, Adelphia, World Com and other businesses as examples. Availability: Print; E-book.

36359 ■ "Ethics Commission May Hire Collection Agency" in Tulsa World (August 21, 2010)
Pub: World Publishing Co.
Ed: Barbara Hoberock. Description: Oklahoma Ethics Commission is considering a more to hire a collection agency or law firm in order to collect fees from candidates owing money for filing late financial reports.

36360 ■ "Ethics and the End of Life" in Crain's Chicago Business (Vol. 34, October 24, 2011, No. 42, pp. 31)
Pub: Crain Communications Inc.
Contact: Todd Johnson, Publisher
Ed: Lisa Bertagnoli. Description: Technology has enabled doctors to provide more and better methods for helping patients, however end of life issues faced by medical ethicists are discussed.

36361 ■ "The Ethics of Price Discrimination" in Business Ethics Quarterly (Vol. 21, October 2011, No. 4, pp. 633)
Pub: Society for Business Ethics
Contact: Dawn Elm, Executive Director
Ed: Juan M. Elegido. Description: Price discrimination is the practice of charging different customers different prices for the same product. Many people consider price discrimination unfair, but economists argue that in many cases price discrimination is more likely to lead to greater welfare than is the uniform pricing alternative, sometimes even for every party in the transaction.

36362 ■ "The Evolution of Corporate Social Responsibility" in Business Horizons (November-December 2007, pp. 449)
Pub: Elsevier Technology Publications
Ed: Philip L. Cochran. Price: $35.95. Description: Corporate social responsibility is now perceived as vital in enhancing the profitability of businesses while improving their reputation. It has changed business practices such as philanthropy, investment, and entrepreneurship. Availability: PDF.

36363 ■ "Evolutionary Psychology in the Business Sciences"
Pub: Springer Publishing Co.
Contact: Ursula Springer, President
Released: September 28, 2014. Price: $150.93. Description: All individuals operating in the business sphere share a common biological heritage, including consumers, employers, employees, entrepreneurs, or financial traders, to name a few. The evolutionary behavioral sciences and specific business contexts including marketing, consumer behavior, advertising, innovation and creativity and invention, intertemporal choice, negotiations, competition and cooperation in organizational settings, sex differences in workplace patterns, executive leadership, business ethics, store and office design, behavioral decision making, and electronic communications and commerce are all addressed.

36364 ■ "Extortion: How Politicians Extract Your Money, Buy Votes, and Line Their Own Pockets"
Pub: Mariner Books
Contact: Barry O'Callaghan, Chief Executive Officer
Released: October 7, 2014. Price: $14.95 paperback. Description: Politicians and lawmakers have developed a new set of legislative tactics designed to extort wealthy industries and donors into huge contributions. This money is then funneled into the pockets of their friends and family members. Schweizer reveals the secret 'fees' each political party charges politicians for top committee assignments; how fourteen members of Congress received hundreds of thousands of dollars using a self-loan loophole; how PAC money is used to bankroll their lavish lifestyles; and more. The first time these unethical issues have been reported to the public.

36365 ■ Extraordinary Circumstances: The Journey of a Corporate Whistleblower
Pub: John Wiley & Sons Inc.
Contact: Stephen M. Smith, President
Ed: Cynthia Cooper. Released: March 2009. Price: $16.95, paperback; $11.99. Description: Cynthia Cooper offers details of the events that led to the implosion of telecom giant WorldCom. Availability: PrintE-book.

36366 ■ "FBI Initiates Fraud Inquiry Into Mortgage Lenders" in Miami Daily Business Review (March 26, 2008)
Description: FBI has launched investigations into Countrywide Financial, the nation's largest mortgage lender, along with sixteen other firms, tied to the subprime mortgage crisis.

36367 ■ "Final Player In Big Mortgage Fraud Operation Gets Jail Time" in Boston Business Journal (Vol. 31, May 27, 2011, No. 18, pp. 3)
Pub: Boston Business Journal
Ed: Galen Moore. Description: Real estate broker Ralp Appolon has been sentenced to 70 months in prison for wire fraud. Appolon was part of a group that falsified information about property purchase prices. A total of ten mortgage lenders have become victims of the group.

36368 ■ "Finally, Justice" in Canadian Business (Vol. 82, April 27, 2009, No. 7, pp. 12)
Ed: John Gray. Description: Former investment adviser Alex Winch feels that he was vindicated with the Canadian Court's ruling that Livent Inc. founders Garth Drabinsky and Myron Gottlieb were guilty of fraud. Drabinsky filed a libel case on Winch over Winch's letter that complained over Livent's account-

ing procedures. Winch also criticized the inconsistent accounting during Drabinsky's term as chief executive of another firm.

36369 ■ "Five-Ring Circus" in Entrepreneur (Vol. 35, November 2007, No. 11, pp. 76)
Pub: Entrepreneur Press
Contact: Perlman Neil, President
Ed: Scott Bernard Nelson. Description: China's economy is growing and is expected to do well even after the 2008 Olympics, but growth could slow from eleven percent to eight or nine percent. Chinese portfolio concerns with regard to health and environmental records and bureaucratic fraud are discussed.

36370 ■ "From the Editors: Plagiarism Policies and Screening at AMJ" in Academy of Management Journal (Vol. 55, August 2012, No. 4, pp. 749)
Pub: Academy of Management
Contact: Ming-Jer Chen, President
Description: The plagiarism policies and practices of the Academy of Management Journal (AMJ) based on the Committee on Publications Ethics and AOM guidelines are described. The function of the Cross-Check software tool for screening manuscripts for plagiarism is explained.

36371 ■ Guerrilla Marketing Goes Green: Winning Strategies to Improve Your Profits and Your Planet
Pub: Accurate Writing & More
Ed: Jay Conrad Levinson, Shel Horowitz. Price: $21.95. Description: The importance for companies to market ethically and honestly is stressed. Quality marketing will build customer loyalty and that will translate into new customers and repeat business. A customer-retention strategy is outlined along with ideas to increase profits of any small business.

36372 ■ "A Hacker in India Hijacked His Website Design and Was Making Good Money Selling It" in Inc. (December 2007, pp. 77-78, 80)
Ed: Darren Dahl. Description: John Anton, owner of an online custom T-shirt business and how a company in India was selling software Website templates identical to his firm's Website.

36373 ■ "Hello, and Goodbye" in Entrepreneur (June 2014)
Pub: Entrepreneur Media Inc.
Released: June 2014. Description: Companies must implement strategies to ensure the creation of an ethical workplace. They must be able to deal with clients that experience problems and try to bully their counterparts as a result. Executive search firms must be responsible for compensating new executive hires by helping them find new jobs. Businesses must communicate to their employees about their importance as a way of making them feel appreciated and, thus, contribute to ethical behavior.

36374 ■ High Performance with High Integrity
Pub: Harvard Business Review Press
Contact: Peter E. Walsh, Director
Ed: Ben W. Heineman, Jr. Released: June 03, 2008. Price: $22, hardcover. Description: The dark side of today's free-market capitalist system is examined. Under intense pressure to make the numbers, executives and employees are tempted to cut corners, falsify accounts, or worse. In today's unforgiving environment that can lead to catastrophe for a small company.

36375 ■ "Home Builder, Four Others, Face Sentencing" in Business Courier (Vol. 27, November 26, 2010, No. 30, pp. 1)
Pub: Business Courier
Ed: Jon Newberry. Description: Home builder Bernie Kurlemann was convicted on November 10, 2010 on six felony counts and faces up to 65 years in prison due to his part in a 2006 Warren County mortgage fraud scheme. Four other business people have pleaded guilty to related charges, and all are awaiting sentencing in early 2011.

36376 ■ House of Cards: A Tale of Hubris and Wretched Excess on Wall Street
Ed: William D. Cohan. **Released:** February 09, 2010. **Price:** $16.95. **Description:** A historical account of the events leading up to the Bear Stearns implosion.

36377 ■ How to Salvage More Millions from Your Small Business
Pub: Mike French and Company Inc.
Contact: Ron Sturgeon, Editor
Ed: Ron Sturgeon. **Price:** $19.95. **Description:** Entrepreneurs in any industry will learn how strong work ethics and sound business principles will make any small business successful.

36378 ■ How to Start a Home-Based Senior Care Business: Develop a Winning Business Plan
Pub: Globe Pequot Press Inc.
Contact: Robert Irwin, Manager
E-mail: robert.irwin@globepequot.com
Ed: James L. Ferry. **Released:** January 06, 2010. **Price:** $18.95, paperback. **Description:** Everything needed to know in order to start and run a profitable, ethical, and satisfying senior care business from your home. Information covers writing a good business plan, marketing services to families, creating a fee structure, and developing a network of trusted caregivers and service providers. **Availability:** Print.

36379 ■ "How To Detect a Liar (Even One as Big as Bernie Madoff)" in South Florida Business Journal (Vol. 34, May 2, 2014, No. 41, pp. 16)
Pub: American City Business Journals
Released: May 2, 2014. **Description:** Ways to avoid pitfalls of con artists is discussed. To detect a deception and unethical behavior requires paying attention and watch out for signs of lying because awkward speech patterns are a good indicator of deception. Liars are more likely to repeat the questions of their target victim or rephrase it when they answer.

36380 ■ "Identity Thieves Hit a New Low" in Information Today (Vol. 26, February 2009, No. 2, pp. 1)
Pub: Information Today, Inc.
Contact: Thomas H. Hogan, President
E-mail: ctuthill@infotoday.com
Ed: Phillip Britt. **Description:** Identity thieves are opening credit lines after reading obituaries. Actual identity theft cases are examined.

36381 ■ "In the Afternoon, the Moral Slope Gets Slipperier" in Harvard Business Review (Vol. 92, May 2014, No. 5, pp. 34)
Pub: Harvard Business Publishing
Released: May 2014. **Description:** Research indicates that psychological stress accumulated as the day goes on can make individuals cognitively weaker, and therefore more susceptible to engaging in unethical behavior.

36382 ■ "Individual and Organizational Reintegration After Ethical or Legal Transgressions: Challenges and Opportunities" in Business Ethics Quarterly (Vol. 24, July 2014, No. 3, pp. 315)
Pub: Business Ethics Quarterly
Released: July 2014. **Description:** Individual and organizational reintegration in the aftermath of transgressions that violate ethical and legal boundaries are explored.

36383 ■ "Institutional Logics in the Study of Organizations" in Business Ethics Quarterly (Vol. 21, July 2011, No. 3, pp. 409)
Pub: Society for Business Ethics
Contact: Dawn Elm, Executive Director
Ed: Marc Orlitzky. **Description:** Examination into whether the empirical evidence on the relationship between corporate social performance (CSP) and corporate financial performance (CFP) differs depending on the publication outlet in which that evidence appears.

36384 ■ "Internal Auditor Wants Ethics Review of City's Billy Casper Golf Contract" in Business Courier (Vol. 27, September 10, 2010, No. 19, pp. 1)
Pub: Business Courier
Ed: Dan Monk. **Description:** Mark Ashworth, an internal auditor for Cincinnati, Ohio is pushing for an ethics review of management contract for seven city-owned golf courses. Ashworth wants the Ohio Ethics Commission to investigate family ties between a superintendent for the Cincinnati Recreation Commission and Billy Casper Golf.

36385 ■ "Investment Manager Disciplined" in Sacramento Business Journal (Vol. 25, July 9, 2008, No. 18, pp. 1)
Pub: American City Business Journals, Inc.
Contact: Whitney Shaw, President
Ed: Mark Anderson. **Description:** Community Capital Management's David A. Zwick is permanently barred by the Securities and Exchange Commission (SEC) from associating with any broker or dealer, after investigations revealed that he took part in paying kickbacks to a bond trader. Other views and information on Community Capital, and on the SEC investigation on Zwick, are presented.

36386 ■ "Is Business Ethics Getting Better? A Historical Perspective" in Business Ethics Quarterly (Vol. 21, April 2011, No. 2, pp. 335)
Pub: Society for Business Ethics
Contact: Dawn Elm, Executive Director
Ed: Joanne B. Ciulla. **Description:** The question 'Is Business Ethics Getting Better?' as a heuristic for discussing the importance of history in understanding business and ethics is answered. The article uses a number of examples to illustrate how the same ethical problems in business have been around for a long time. It describes early attempts at the Harvard School of Business to use business history as a means of teaching students about moral and social values. In the end, the author suggests that history may be another way to teach ethics, enrich business ethics courses, and develop the perspective and vision in future business leaders.

36387 ■ "Is Formal Ethics Training Merely Cosmetic? A Study of Ethics Training and Ethical Organizational Culture" in Business Ethics Quarterly (Vol. 24, January 2014, No. 1, pp. 85)
Pub: Business Ethics Quarterly
Released: January 2014. **Description:** U.S. Organizational Sentencing Guidelines provide firms with incentives to develop formal ethics programs that promote ethical organizational cultures and thereby decrease corporate offenses. An examination of the effects of training on ethical organizational culture is discussed.

36388 ■ "Is It Ever OK to Break a Promise? A Student Must Decide Whether to Leave the Company that Sponsored His MBA for a Dream Job" in Harvard Business Review (Vol. 92, September 2014, No. 9, pp. 119)
Pub: Harvard Business Publishing
Released: September 2014. **Description:** A fictitious decision making scenario is presented, with contributors providing advice. One notes that change, requiring people to adapt and, in some cases, alter contracts. Another states that the original contract should be honored and that other opportunities are likely to present themselves to the student considering leaving the firm that sponsored his MBA.

36389 ■ "Is the Ponzi Pond Dry?" in Denver Business Journal (Vol. 65, March 28, 2014, No. 46, pp. A5)
Pub: American City Business Journals
Released: March 28, 2014. **Description:** The number of Ponzi schemes in Colorado has decreased in recent years because of efforts to expose scams. However, experts believe that investors need to be wary of deals because a strong economy can mask Ponzi schemes. Figures show that investors lost a total of $159 million in four of the highest profile cases in Colorado.

36390 ■ "It's Time to Wise Up: Income Trusts" in Canadian Business (Vol. 79, November 6, 2006, No. 22, pp. 24)
Ed: Mark Rosen. **Description:** The effects bogus financial reporting of income trusts on investors are analyzed.

36391 ■ "Kraft Not Alone" in Crain's Chicago Business (Vol. 30, February 2007, No. 6, pp. 8)
Description: Consumer watchdog group, The Center for Science in the Public Interest, has been putting pressure on food companies to be more truthful on their product labels. Listing of companies who have had misleading claims on their products is included.

36392 ■ Liespotting: Proven Techniques to Detect Deception
Pub: St. Martins Press/Macmillan
Ed: Pamela Meyer. **Released:** September 2011. **Price:** $14.99, paperback. **Description:** Liespotting links three disciplines: facial recognition training, interrogation training, and a comprehensive survey of research in the field - into a specialized body of information developed specifically to help business leaders detect deception and get the information they need to successfully conduct their most important interactions and transactions. **Availability:** Print.

36393 ■ "Life's Work: Ben Bradlee" in Harvard Business Review (Vol. 88, September 2010, No. 9, pp. 128)
Pub: Harvard Business School Publishing
Ed: Alison Beard. **Price:** $8.95. **Description:** Newspaper publisher Ben Bradlee discusses factors that lead to success, including visible supervisors, enthusiasm, appropriate expansion, and the importance in truth in reporting. **Availability:** PDF.

36394 ■ "Life's Work: Interview With Kareem Abdul-Jabbar" in Harvard Business Review (Vol. 90, January-February 2012, No.1-2, pp. 156)
Pub: Harvard Business Review Press
Contact: Peter E. Walsh, Director
Ed: Alison Beard. **Released:** January-February 2012. **Description:** Former basketball player Kareem Abdul-Jabbar believes that a solid work ethic and practice always wins over lazy, undeveloped talent. Although he was known as a strictly-focused athlete, he now feels he relates to others on a more personal level than before. His interests in history and writing have made him a multidimensional individual.

36395 ■ "Lying"
Pub: Four Elephant Press
Released: October 23, 2013. **Price:** $16.99. **Description:** Author and neuroscientist, Sam Harris, argues that lives can be simplified and society improved just by telling the truth, whether in business or personal lives. The ethics of white lies is examined.

36396 ■ "Making the Tough Call: Great Leaders Recognize When Their Values Are On the Line" in Inc. (November 2007, pp. 36, 38)
Pub: Mansueto Ventures L.L.C.
Contact: John Koten, Chief Executive Officer
Ed: Noel M. Tichy, Warren G. Bennis. **Description:** Good judgment by company leaders is a process involving preparation, making the call, and executing the process. Character provides a moral compass for these decision makers.

36397 ■ MBA In A Day: What You Would Learn At Top-Tier Business Schools (If You Only Had The Time!)
Pub: John Wiley & Sons Inc.
Contact: Stephen M. Smith, President
Ed: Steven Stralser. **Released:** September 2004. **Price:** $34.95, hardcover; $22.99. **Description:** Management professor presents important concepts, business topics and strategies that can be used by anyone to manage a small business or professional practice. Topics covered include: human resources and personal interaction, ethics and leadership skills, fair negotiation tactics, basic business accounting practices, project management, and the fundamentals of economics and marketing. **Availability:** PrintE-book.

36398 ■ "Medicare Fraudsters Turn to Pharmacies" in South Florida Business Journal (Vol. 32, June 15, 2012, No. 47, pp. 1)
Pub: American City Business Journal
Description: U.S. Department of Health and Human Services, Office of Inspector General reports indicate that 2,637 retail pharmacies, or 4.4 percent of all

pharmacies, had dubious Part D practices in 2009. However, the Miami area led the nation with 19.4 percent of its retail pharmacies submitting dubious claims as unethical frauds turn them in.

36399 ■ "Messing with Corporate Heads? Psychological Contracts and Leadership Integrity" in Journal of Business Strategy (Vol. 35, May-June 2014, No. 3, pp. 38-46)
Pub: Emerald Group Publishing Inc.
Released: May-June 2014. **Description:** A model of leadership, i.e. the leadership psychological contract (LPC) and investigation of the contribution of psychological contract (PC) to the leadership domain is investigated. Contemporary literature on leadership and PC is reviewed and it was observed that the LPC is a predictive model consisting of three dependent variables namely trust, fairness, and fulfillment of expectations. The LPC model seeks to augment the value of ethical and effective leadership approaches.

36400 ■ "Millions of Senior Citizens Swindled by Financial Fraud" in Black Enterprise (Vol. 41, September 2010, No. 2, pp. 24)
Pub: Earl G. Graves Publishing Co. Inc.
Contact: Earl G. Graves, Jr., President
Description: One of every five citizens over the age of 65 have been victims of financial fraud. Statistical data included.

36401 ■ "Missing MF Global Funds Could Top $1.2 Billion" in Wall Street Journal Eastern Edition (November 22 , 2011, pp. A1)
Pub: Dow Jones & Co., Inc.
Contact: Clare Hart, President
Ed: Aaron Lucchetti, Dan Strumpf. **Description:** As the investigation into the collapse of securities brokerage MF Global Holdings Ltd. continues, the question of what happened to customers' funds has to be answered. Now, it is believed that the actual amount of missing funds is much more than the $600 million originally thought, and could be well over $1.2 billion.

36402 ■ "Model Citizen" in Entrepreneur (Vol. 36, February 2008, No. 2, pp. 42)
Pub: Entrepreneur Press
Contact: Perlman Neil, President
Ed: Guy Kawasaki. **Description:** A mensch is a person of noble character, as defined by Leo Rosten. Tips on how to be a mensch and a better person, in relation to being an entrepreneur, are given. These include: helping others without expecting something in return, giving back to society, and knowing the line between right and wrong.

36403 ■ "The Moral Legitimacy of NGOs as Partners of Corporations" in Business Ethics Quarterly (Vol. 21, October 2011, No. 4, pp. 579)
Pub: Society for Business Ethics
Contact: Dawn Elm, Executive Director
Ed: Dorothea Baur, Guido Palazzo. **Description:** Partnerships between companies and NGOs have received considerable attention in CSR in the past years. However, the role of NGO legitimacy in such partnerships has thus far been neglected. The article argues that NGOs assume a status as special stakeholders of corporations which act on behalf of the common good. This role requires a particular focus on their moral legitimacy. An introduction to the conceptual framework analyzing the moral legitimacy of NGOs along three dimensions, building on the theory of deliberative democracy.

36404 ■ "The Murky Tale of a Failed Fund" in Globe & Mail (January 3, 2006, pp. B1)
Pub: CTVglobemedia Publishing Inc.
Ed: Bertrand Marotte. **Description:** The opinions of chief executive officer John Xanthoudakis of Norshield Financial Group, on controversy surrounding the company's handling of investors' money, are presented.

36405 ■ "'No Snitch' Culture in American Business" in Business Owner (Vol. 35, September-October 2011, No. 5, pp. 7)
Pub: DL Perkins Company
Description: It is important to make known the fact that a businessman is performing unethical or illegal activities in his firm.

36406 ■ "Now That's Rich" in Canadian Business (Vol. 80, February 12, 2007, No. 4, pp. 92)
Ed: Thomas Watson. **Description:** The effort of chief executive officer of Stelco Inc. Rodney Mott in resolving the issue of financial loss of the company by taking up backdating options for share price is discussed.

36407 ■ "One-Time Area Trust Executive Finds Trouble in N.H." in The Business Journal-Serving Metropolitan Kansas City (September 12, 2008)
Ed: Steve Vockrodt. **Description:** About 200 investors, some from Missouri's Kansas City area, claim that they had conducted business with Noble Trust Co. The trust company was placed under New Hampshire Banking Department's conservatorship after $15 million was discovered to be missing from its account. It is alleged that the money was lost in a Colorado Ponzi scheme.

36408 ■ "Only in Canada, Eh?" in Canadian Business (Vol. 79, November 6, 2006, No. 22, pp. 17)
Ed: Al Rosen. **Description:** The ethics of corporate spying with relation to competitive information leakage are analyzed.

36409 ■ "Organizational Virtue Orientation and Family Firms" in Business Ethics Quarterly (Vol. 21, April 2011, No. 2, pp. 257)
Pub: Society for Business Ethics
Contact: Dawn Elm, Executive Director
Ed: G. Tyge Payne, Keith H. Brigham, J. Christian Broberg, Todd W. Moss, Jeremy C. Short. **Description:** The concept of organizational virtue orientation (OVO) and the differences between family and non-family firms on six organizational virtue dimensions of Integrity, Empathy, Warmth, Courage, Conscientiousness, and Zeal are examined.

36410 ■ "Paging Dr. Phil" in Canadian Business (Vol. 79, September 25, 2006, No. 19, pp. 21)
Ed: John Gray. **Description:** Increasing corporate crimes in software industry is discussed by focusing on recent case of Hewlett and Packard.

36411 ■ "Pet Food Insider Sold Shares Before Recall" in Globe & Mail (April 10, 2007, pp. B1)
Ed: Keith McArthur. **Description:** The issue related the selling of share units by Mark Weins, chief financial officer of pet food firm Menu Foods Income Fund, just before the recall of contaminated pet food is discussed.

36412 ■ The Power of Many: Values for Success in Business and in Life
Pub: Crown Business
Ed: Meg Whitman, Joan O'C Hamilton. **Released:** January 26, 2010. **Price:** $11.99. **Description:** Meg Whitman discusses the important values for success in business and in life: integrity, accountability, authenticity and courage. **Availability:** E-book.

36413 ■ "Practices, Governance, and Politics: Applying MacIntyre's Ethics to Business" in Business Ethics Quarterly (Vol. 24, April 2014, No. 2, pp. 229)
Pub: Business Ethics Quarterly
Released: April 2014. **Description:** An argument to apply MacIntyre's positive moral theory to business ethics is problematic due to the cognitive closure of MacIntyre's concept of practice. The paper begins by outlining the notion of a practice, before turning Moore's attempt to provide a MacIntyrean account of corporate governance. It argues that Moore's attempt is mismatched with MacIntyre's account of moral education. Because the notion of practices resists general application it is argued that a negative application, which focuses on regulation, is more plausible. Large-scale regulation, usually thought anti-ethical to MacIntyre's advocacy of small-scale politics, has the potential to facilitate practice-based work and reveals that MacIntyre's own work can be used against his pessimism about the modern order.

Furthermore, the conception of regulation can show how management is more amenable to ethical understanding than MacIntyre's work is often taken to imply.

36414 ■ "Proactive Elder-Care Workshop Scheduled" in News-Sentinel (February 15, 2012)
Description: Proactive Elder Care has partnered with IPFW to provide an educational workshop open to caregivers, seniors, family members, employed caregivers and employers. Breakout sessions cover when to begin care, finances, law, healthcare, housing, community services, and bioethics.

36415 ■ "A Property Rights Analysis of Newly Private Firms" in Business Ethics Quarterly (Vol. 21, July 2011, No. 3, pp. 445)
Pub: Society for Business Ethics
Contact: Dawn Elm, Executive Director
Ed: Marguerite Schneider, Alix Valenti. **Description:** A key factor in the decision to convert a publicly owned company to private status is the expectation that value will be create, providing the firm with rent. These rents have implications regarding the property rights of the firm's capital-contributing constituencies. The article identifies and analyzes the types of rent associated with the newly private firm. Compared to public firms, going private allows owners the potential to partition part of the residual risk to bond holders and employees, rendering them to be co-residual risk bearers with owners.

36416 ■ "Q&A: David Labistour" in Canadian Business (Vol. 81, March 17, 2008, No. 4, pp. 10)
Pub: Rogers Media Inc.
Contact: Tony Viner, President
Ed: Lauren McKeon. **Description:** David Labistour says that the difference between being a co-op retailer and a corporate-owned retailer in the case of Mountain Equipment Co-op (MEC) is that the company is owned by their customers and not by shareholders. Labistour also says that MEC works with their factories to ensure that these maintain ethical standards in the manufacturing process.

36417 ■ "Regulator Issues Warning On Reverse Mortgage Loans" in Retirement Advisor (Vol. 13, October 2012, No. 10, pp. 28)
Pub: Summit Professional Networks
Contact: Steve Weitzner, President
Description: Reverse mortgages were first introduced in 1961 and are becoming popular now with aging baby boomers. The new Consumer Financial Protection Bureau warns the public to look closing before entering a reverse mortgage contract. The National Ethics Association encourages financial advisors to use the same caution and offers advise for advisors to help educate their clients about reverse mortgages.

36418 ■ "A Research Firm With More Than One Foe" in Globe & Mail (February 24, 2006, pp. B1)
Ed: Shawn McCarthy. **Description:** The details of Biovail Corp.'s securities fraud case against Gradient Analytics Inc. are presented.

36419 ■ "A Responsive Approach to Organizational Misconduct: Rehabilitation, Reintegration, and the Reduction of Reoffense" in Business Ethics Quarterly (Vol. 24, July 2014, No. 3, pp. 343)
Pub: Business Ethics Quarterly
Released: July 2014. **Description:** Examination of ways regulators, prosecutors, and courts might support and encourage the efforts of organizations to not only reintegrate after misconduct, but to also improve their conduct in a way that reduces their likelihood of re-offense (rehabilitation). An experiment in creative sentencing in Alberta, Canada that aimed to try to change the behavior of an industry by publicly airing the root causes of a failure of one of the industry's leaders is examined. A model for a responsive and restorative approach to organizational misconduct

that balances the punitive role of regulators and courts with new roles in supporting and overseeing rehabilitation are observed.

36420 ■ "Retail Product Management: Buying and Merchandising"
Pub: Routledge
Contact: Kevin Bradley, President
E-mail: kbradley@taylorandfrancis.com
Released: October 24, 2014. **Price:** $130.00. **Description:** Due to the rise in Internet use, retailers are facing challenges associated with more informed buyers, technological advances, and the competitive environment. Retail ethics are also examined.

36421 ■ "Ringgold Computer Repair Owner Accused of Swindling Customers" in Chattanooga Times/Free Press (February 15, 2012)
Released: February 15, 2012.

36422 ■ "Risk Management Starts at the Top" in Business Strategy Review (Vol. 21, Spring 2010, No. 1, pp. 18)
Pub: John Wiley & Sons Inc. Scientific, Technical, Medical, and Scholarly Div. (Wiley-Blackwell)
Contact: William J. Pesce, Manager
E-mail: wpesce@wiley.com
Ed: Paul Strebel, Hongze Lu. **Description:** Authors question why, at the end of 2008, Citigroup, Merrill Lynch and UBS had well over $40 billion in sub-prime write-downs and credit losses, while some of their competitors were much less exposed. Their research into the situation revealed correlations of great import to today's firms.

36423 ■ "Rogue's Gallery" in Canadian Business (Vol. 81, November 10, 2008, No. 19, pp. 44)
Pub: Rogers Media Inc.
Contact: Tony Viner, President
Ed: Rachel Pulfer. **Description:** Laissez-faire capitalism or poor oversight of Fannie Mae and Freddie Mac are causes for the financial crisis in the U.S., depending or Democrat or Republican viewpoint. Events leading up to the 2008 financial crisis are covered.

36424 ■ Rogues' Gallery: The Secret Story of the Lust, Lies, Greed, and Betrayals That Made the Metropolitan Museum of Art
Ed: Michael Gross. **Released:** May 11, 2010. **Price:** $16.99. **Description:** Michael Gross, leading chronicler of the American rich, looks at the saga of the nation's largest museum, the Metropolitan Museum of Art.

36425 ■ "Save the Date" in Barron's (Vol. 90, September 13, 2010, No. 37, pp. 35)
Pub: Barron's Editorial & Corporate Headquarters
Ed: Mark Veverka. **Description:** Mark Hurd is the new Co-President of Oracle after being forced out at Hewlett-Packard where he faced a harassment complaint. HP fired Hurd due to expense account malfeasance. Hurd is also set to speak at an Oracle trade show in San Francisco on September 20, 2010.

36426 ■ "Scott Rothstein Ponzi Reveals Ethics Issues in Jewelry Biz" in South Florida Business Journal (Vol. 33, September 14, 2012, No. 7, pp. 1)
Pub: American City Business Journal
Description: JR Dunn Jewelers of Florida is suing New York jewelry company JB International for an 8.91 carat diamond it claims is tainted because it was allegedly sold offby Ponzi schemer Scott Rothstein or his wife Kimberly. Dunn is being sued for $748,000 in the bankruptcy of Rothstein Rosenfelt Adler, Rothstein's former law firm.

36427 ■ "Search Engine Optimization is Becoming a Must for Businesses, But Unethical Companies Can Hurt Worse than Help" in Idaho Business Review (August 3, 2012)
Pub: Dolan Media
Ed: Sean Olson. **Released:** August 3, 2012. **Description:** Search engine optimization increases presence on the Internet for any small business wishing to

market a service or product. It is critical to choose an ethical company that has experience in creating Web sites that will get noticed.

36428 ■ The SEO Manifesto: A Practical and Ethical Guide to Internet Marketing and Search Engine Optimization
Ed: Dan Tousignant, Pamela Gobiel. **Released:** December 05, 2011. **Price:** $14.99. **Description:** Comprehensive guide for each phase of launching an online business; chapters include checklists, process descriptions, and examples.

36429 ■ Small Business Desk Reference
Pub: Penguin Books USA Inc.
Released: December 2004. **Price:** $29.95. **Description:** Comprehensive guide for starting or running a successful small business, focusing on buying a business or franchise, writing a business plan, financial management, accounting, legal issues, human resources management, operations, marketing, sales, customer service, taxes, insurance, and ethics. Information for launching a restaurant, property management firm, retail outlet, consulting firm, and service business is included.

36430 ■ Small Business Management
Pub: John Wiley & Sons Inc.
Contact: Stephen M. Smith, President
Ed: Margaret Burlingame. **Released:** March 2007. **Price:** $44.95. **Description:** Advice for starting and running a small business as well as information on the value and appeal of small businesses, is given. Topics include budgets, taxes, inventory, ethics, e-commerce, and current laws.

36431 ■ "Soldiering On to Remake the SBA" in Inc. (February 2008, pp. 21)
Description: Steven Preston discusses efforts to improve the Small Business Administration's processes to improve services to small businesses. Topics covered include customer service issues, loans, and fraud.

36432 ■ "Soldiers as Consumers: Predatory and Unfair Business Practices Harming the Military Community"
Pub: CreateSpace
Contact: Daren Giles, President
Released: October 5, 2014. **Price:** $15.95 paperback. **Description:** Soldiers, airmen, sailors, and marines are young consumers and are appealing targets for unscrupulous businesses. There are lending organizations that prey upon our military offering products to help them bridge financial problems. Unethical elements of these loans includes higher interest rates and/or high fees or waivers of certain rights in fine print of contracts. A Federal Law called the Military Lending Act is supposed to protect service members from this kind of abuse, but the law only covers loans with terms of six months or less.

36433 ■ The SPEED of Trust: The One Thing That Changes Everything
Pub: Free Press/Simon & Schuster Inc.
Ed: Stephen M.R. Covey, Rebecca R. Merrill. **Released:** February 05, 2008. **Price:** $16.99. **Description:** Because of recent business scandals, trust and a desire for accountability is addressed by the author. **Availability:** Print.

36434 ■ "Stan Chesley Fighting Kentucky Disbarment" in Business Courier (Vol. 27, September 10, 2010, No. 19, pp. 1)
Pub: Business Courier
Ed: Jon Newberry. **Description:** Stan Chesley, a Cincinnati attorney, has been accused of making false statements to the courts and bar officials, self-dealing in violation of the bar's conflict of interest rules, and failing to adequately inform clients. Kentucky Bar Association officials will seek to have Chesley permanently disbarred.

36435 ■ "Stent Cases at Md. Hospitals Falling" in Baltimore Business Journal (Vol. 28, November 12, 2010, No. 27, pp. 1)
Pub: Baltimore Business Journal
Ed: Emily Mullin. **Description:** Cardiologists believe that the recent drop in cardiac stent procedures in Maryland can be associated with the ongoing investi-

gation of Dr. Mark G. Midei and St. Joseph Medical Center. Midei is accused of performing unnecessary stent procedures on patients and was let go from the clinical practice in St. Joseph in 2009.

36436 ■ "Synthesis: Business Through Hollywood's Lens" in Harvard Business Review (Vol. 88, October 2010, No. 10, pp. 146)
Pub: Harvard Business School Publishing
Ed: Batia Wiesenfeld, Gino Cattani. **Description:** The authors contend that businesses are likely to be portrayed as villains in movies because corruption has higher entertainment draw. However, movies also depict popular opinion, which encourages businesses to be accountable and to help build communities.

36437 ■ "Take Down the Swat Team" in Entrepreneur (August 2014)
Pub: Entrepreneur Media Inc.
Released: August 2014. **Description:** Advice is given to entrepreneurs engaged in a business partnership. When a partner is not interested in feedback should be made to understand that his behavior discourages employee vigilance and discussion of ethical issues could damage reputation. Organization leaders should discuss policies on all issues.

36438 ■ "Talent Scout: How This Exec Finds and Develops Leaders Internally" in Black Enterprise (Vol. 38, November 2007, No. 4, pp. 63)
Pub: Earl G. Graves Publishing Co. Inc.
Contact: Earl G. Graves, Jr., President
Ed: Faith Chukwudi. **Description:** Profile of Bernard Bedon, director at Public Group Media. Bedon helps attract, develop, retain, and reward talent in his media group of 10,000 employees worldwide.

36439 ■ "The Ten Commandments of Legal Risk Management" in Business Horizons (Vol. 51, January-February 2008, No. 1, pp. 13)
Pub: Elsevier Advanced Technology Publications
Ed: Michael B. Metzger. **Description:** Effective legal risk management is tightly linked with ethical and good management, and managers' behaviors have to be professional and based on ethically defensible principles of action. Basic human tendencies cannot be used in justifying questionable decisions in court. Guidelines for legal risk management are presented.

36440 ■ "Toward a Theory of Stakeholder Salience in Family Firms" in Business Ethics Quarterly (Vol. 21, April 2011, No. 2, pp. 235)
Pub: Society for Business Ethics
Contact: Dawn Elm, Executive Director
Ed: Ronald K. Mitchell, Bradley R. Agle, James J. Chrisman, Laura J. Spence. **Description:** The notion of stakeholder salience based on attributes (e.g. power, legitimacy, urgency) is applied in the family business setting.

36441 ■ Trade-Off: The Ever-Present Tension Between Quality and Conscience
Ed: Kevin Maney. **Released:** August 17, 2010. **Price:** $15. **Description:** The tension between fidelity (the quality of a consumer's experience) and convenience (the ease of getting and paying for a product) are shown to be the forces that determine the success or failure of new products and services in the marketplace.

36442 ■ "Trial of Enron Ex-Bosses to Begin Today" in Globe & Mail (January 30, 2006, pp. B1)
Ed: Shawn McCarthy. **Description:** The details of the case against former executives Kenneth L. Lay and Jeffrey Skilling of Enron Corp. are presented.

36443 ■ "Twilight of the 'Banksters': the Barclays Scandal Could Finally Spark Serious Banking Reform" in Canadian Business (Vol. 85, August 13, 2012, No. 13, pp. 11)
Pub: George Media Inc.
Ed: Richard Warnica. **Released:** August 13, 2012. **Description:** Potential banking reform is anticipated after British bank Barclays PLC admitted fixing the London Interbank Offered Rate and agreed to pay

$451 million in fines for its wrongdoing. The separation of investment and retail banking was endorsed by conservative 'Financial Times' newspaper.

36444 ■ *"Union Ethics Training: Building the Legitimacy and Effectiveness of Organized Labor" in WorkingUSA (Vol. 11, September 2008, No. 3)*
Ed: Maggie Cohen. **Description:** Arguments are presented for the implementation of serious ethics training at all levels of labor unions and their contribution to union effectiveness by enhancing union legitimacy-understood as an amalgam of legal, pragmatic, and moral legitimacy and by paving the way to stable recognition of the labor movement as an integral part of American society, necessary to economic prosperity and the realization of fundamental American moral and social values.

36445 ■ *Values-Centered Entrepreneurs and Their Companies*
Pub: Routledge
Contact: Kevin Bradley, President
E-mail: kbradley@taylorandfrancis.com
Ed: David Y. Choi, Edmund Gray. **Released:** August 10, 2010. **Price:** $48.95, Paperback; $165, Hardback. **Description:** A new brand of entrepreneurs has arrived on the business scene, carrying with them a new set of values. They possess a sense of social responsibility, the need to protect the planet, and to do the right thing for all stakeholders.

36446 ■ *"Voice: Rebuilding Trust" in Business Strategy Review (Vol. 21, Summer 2010, No. 2, pp. 79)*
Pub: Blackwell Publishers Ltd.
Ed: David De Cremer. **Description:** An examination of the financial sector's attempt to rebuild trust is given. Three steps to jump start the process are explored.

36447 ■ *"Voices: Breaking the Corruption Habit" In Business Strategy Review (Vol. 21, Autumn 2010, No. 3, pp. 67)*
Pub: John Wiley & Sons Inc. Scientific, Technical, Medical, and Scholarly Div. (Wiley-Blackwell)
Contact: William J. Pesce, Manager
E-mail: wpesce@wiley.com
Ed: David De Cremer. **Description:** In times of crisis, it seems natural that people will work together for the common good. David De Cremer cautions that, on the contrary, both economic and social research prove otherwise. He proposes steps for organizations to take to prevent corrupt behaviors.

36448 ■ *"Voices: Climategate Leads Nowhere" in Business Strategy Review (Vol. 21, Summer 2010, No. 2, pp. 76)*
Pub: Blackwell Publishers Ltd.
Ed: Mick Blowfield. **Description:** An examination of the recent Climategate scandal that explores the damage caused by managers who are too easily mystified or misled.

36449 ■ *"Werner's Legacy: 'His Word Meant Something" in Pittsburgh Business Times (Vol. 33, June 6, 2014, No. 47, pp. 3)*
Pub: American City Business Journals
Released: June 6, 2014. **Description:** Public relations expert, Lawrence Werner, was highly respected for his professional skills as well as his honesty and integrity. Werner's former colleague, John Verbanac, asserts 'His word meant something', as several large Pittsburgh companies and nonprofit organizations sought his advice to improve image, particularly on crisis management.

36450 ■ *"When You Need Strong Millennials in Your Workplace" in Agency Sales Magazine (Vol. 39, November 2009, No. 10, pp. 22)*
Ed: Joanne G. Sujansky. **Description:** Millennials are bringing a new set of skills and a different kind of work ethics to the workplace. This generation is used to receiving a great deal of positive feedback and they expect to continue receiving this on the job. Expectations should be made clear to this generation and long-term career plans and goals should also be discussed with them.

36451 ■ *"Why Business Ethics Needs Rhetoric: an Aristotelian Perspective" in Business Ethics Quarterly (Vol. 24, January 2014, No. 1, pp. 119)*
Pub: Business Ethics Quarterly
Released: January 2014. **Description:** If the ultimate purpose of ethical argument is to persuade people to act a certain way, the point of doing business ethics is to persuade others about what constitutes proper ethical behavior.

36452 ■ *Work at Home Now: The No-Nonsense Guide to Finding Your Perfect Home-Based Job, Avoiding Scams, and Making a Great Living*
Pub: Career Press Inc.
Contact: Ron Fry, President
Ed: Christine Durst, Michael Haaren. **Released:** November 20, 2009. **Price:** $14.99. **Description:** There are legitimate home-based jobs and projects that can be found on the Internet, but trustworthy guidance is scarce. There is a 58 to 1 scam ratio in work at-home advertising filled with fraud.

36453 ■ *"Young Money"*
Pub: Grand Central Publishing
Released: February 18, 2014. **Price:** $27.00. **Description:** How the financial crisis of 2008 changed a generation and remade Wall Street is discussed. The author spent three years following eight entry-level workers at Goldman Sachs, Bank of America Merrill Lynch and other leading investment firms. These young bankers are exposed to the exhausting workloads, huge bonuses, and recreational drugs that have always characterized Wall Street life, but as they get their education and training, they face questions about ethics, prestige and the value of their work.

TRADE PERIODICALS

36454 ■ *Business Ethics: The Magazine of Corporate Responsibility*
Pub: Business Ethics
URL(s): business-ethics.com. **Ed:** Michael Connor. **Released:** Quarterly

36455 ■ *Ethics Today*
Pub: Ethics Resource Center
Contact: Patricia Harned, President
URL(s): www.ethics.orgwww.ethics.org/ethics-today. **Ed:** Lauren Larsen, Editor, lauren@ethics.org. **Released:** Monthly **Price:** free. **Description:** .

36456 ■ *Issues in Ethics*
Pub: Santa Clara University Markkula Center for Applied Ethics
Contact: Kirk O. Hanson, Executive Director
URL(s): www.scu.edu/ethics/publications/iie/. **Ed:** Miriam Schulman, Editor. **Released:** Semiannual **Price:** $30, Individuals. **Description:** Covers ethics in fields of education, business, biotech, healthcare, and technology. Recurring features include letters to the editor, interviews, news of research, and book reviews.

36457 ■ *Poynter Center Newsletter*
Pub: Poynter Center for the Study of Ethics and American Institutions
Contact: David Smith, Director
URL(s): www.indiana.edu. **Ed:** Glenda Murray, Editor, glmurray@indiana.edu. **Released:** Semiannual. **Price:** Free. **Description:** Focuses on Center programs in American ethics and institutions, such as political institutions, research ethics and biomedical ethics.

VIDEOCASSETTES/ AUDIOCASSETTES

36458 ■ *Concerns Quarterly with Footage from CBS News: General Business*
Harcourt Brace College Publishers
301 Commerce St., Ste. 3700
Fort Worth, TX 76102
Ph: (817)334-7500
Free: 800-237-2665

Fax: (817)334-0947
Co. E-mail: info@harcourt.com
URL: http://www.hmhco.com
Released: 1995. **Price:** $80. **Description:** Video newsletter containing footage from such CBS programs as CBS Evening News, 48 Hours, Street Stories, and CBS This Morning. Provides information on such topics as ethical responsibilities in business, people in business, competition, manufacturing, and marketing. Comes with instructor's guide. Available at an annual subscription rate of $300.00. **Availability:** VHS.

36459 ■ *Ethics in American Business*
Phoenix Learning Group
2349 Chaffee Dr.
Saint Louis, MO 63146-3306
Ph: (314)569-0211
Free: 800-221-1274
Fax: (314)569-2834
URL: http://www.phoenixlearninggroup.com
Released: 1988. **Price:** $475. **Description:** This video provides suggestions for formulating a legal code of business ethics. **Availability:** VHS; 3/4 U.

CONSULTANTS

36460 ■ Frederick A. Bornhofen & Associates [Bornhofen & Associates]
220 Isabella Rd.
Elverson, PA 19520-9141
Ph: (610)942-9140
Fax: (610)942-9576
Contact: Frederick A. Bornhofen, President
E-mail: fborn@comcast.net
Scope: Offers commercial and industrial security services, specializes in areas of robbery and violence prevention, business ethics, cargo security, commercial loss prevention techniques and security management. Industries served: retail, convenience store, transportation, manufacturing and energy. **Founded:** 1989. **Publications:** "Everything Changes Sometime". **Seminars:** Business Ethics; Fraud in the Business World.

36461 ■ Siebrand-Wilton Associates Inc.
PO Box 369
Marlboro, NJ 07746-0369
Ph: (732)917-0239
Fax: (732)972-0214
Co. E-mail: clientsvcs@s-wa.com
URL: http://www.s-wa.com
Contact: John S. Sturges, President
E-mail: bencomp@s-wa.com
Scope: Assesses, plans and implements human resources aspects of mergers and acquisitions. Offers human resources consulting in compensation and benefit plan design, mergers and acquisitions (HR aspects), business ethics assessment and development, editing, writing and association management services, and contract professionals and interim executives. **Founded:** 1986. **Publications:** "Should Government or Business Try to Save Medicare," HR News; "Executive Temping," HR Horizons; "When is an Employee Truly an Employee," HR Magazine; "Examining Your Insurance Carrier," HR Magazine.

LIBRARIES

36462 ■ Ethics Centre CA Library
1 Yonge St., Ste. 1801
Toronto, ON, Canada M5E 1W7
Ph: (416)368-7525
Fax: (416)369-0515
Co. E-mail: info@ethicscentre.ca
URL: http://www.ethicscentre.ca
Contact: Helene Yaremko-Jarvis, Executive Director
Scope: Ethics, business, corporate policy. **Services:** Library open to the public for reference use only. **Holdings:** Books; periodicals; videocassettes.

36463 ■ University of South Florida, Saint Petersburg - Nelson Poynter Memorial Library and Special Collections
140 7th Ave. S
Saint Petersburg, FL 33701-5016

Ph: (727)873-4405
Fax: (727)873-4196
URL: http://lib.usfsp.edu
Contact: Jim Schnur, Librarian, Special Collections
Scope: Marine science and ichthyology, local and regional history, oral history, journalism and media studies, campus archives, ethics. **Services:** Interlibrary loan; copying; library open to the public by appointment. **Founded:** 1968. **Holdings:** 4,750 books; 200 bound periodical volumes; 100 reports; 500 lin.ft. of archival material; 1,700 audio/visual materials.

RESEARCH CENTERS

36464 ■ Josephson Institute of Ethics
9841 Airport Blvd., No. 300
Los Angeles, CA 90045
Ph: (310)846-4800
Free: 800-711-2670
Fax: (310)846-4858
URL: http://josephsoninstitute.org
Contact: Michael S. Josephson, President
Scope: Ethical decision making and behavior, focusing on improving the ethical quality of personal, corporate, and governmental conduct by stimulating moral aspirations, reinforcing the motivation and abilities necessary to perceive the ethical dimensions of choices, and formulating optimal ethical responses. **Services:** Radio commentaries. **Founded:** 1987.

Publications: *Ethics in Action*; *Good Ideas Books—The Power of Character*. **Educational Activities:** Aspen Summit Conference; Josephson Institute of Ethics Character Counts!, youth education project; Character Development Seminars; Ethics in the Workplace training; Pursuing Victory with Honor, sportsmanship campaign; Character Counts! Coalition Meeting.

36465 ■ Loyola University Chicago - Center for Ethics and Social Justice
6525 N Sheridan Rd.
Chicago, IL 60626
Ph: (773)508-8349
Fax: (773)508-8879
Co. E-mail: ethics@luc.edu
URL: http://www.luc.edu/ethics
Contact: William French, Director
Scope: Ethics, particularly in the fields of business, health care, dental care, organizations, and journalism. **Services:** Consulting. **Founded:** 1991. **Educational Activities:** Ethics Breakfast Series; Integration Courses; Moral Reasoning Workshop; Nursing Ethics Workshops; Center for Ethics and Social Justice Short courses, about health care ethics for ethics committees.

36466 ■ San Jose State University - Institute for Social Responsibility, Ethics, and

Education (ISREE)
1 Washington Sq.
San Jose, CA 95192-0096
Ph: (408)924-5563
Fax: (408)924-4527
Co. E-mail: lawrence.quill@sjsu.edu
URL: http://www.sjsu.edu/isree
Contact: Prof. Lawrence Quill, Director
URL(s): csr-news.net/directory/san-jose-state-institute-for-social-responsibility-ethics-and-education-isree. **Scope:** Social responsibility, including professional and business ethics. **Founded:** 1987. **Educational Activities:** Lecture series, corporate roundtables, seminars, training session, and workshops.

36467 ■ Western Michigan University - Center for the Study of Ethics in Society
3024 Moore Hall
Kalamazoo, MI 49008-5328
Ph: (269)387-4397
Fax: (269)387-4390
Co. E-mail: michael.pritchard@wmich.edu
URL: http://www.wmich.edu/ethics
Contact: Michael S. Pritchard, Director
Scope: Applied and professional ethics in all fields. **Services:** Consulting. **Founded:** 1985. **Publications:** *Occasional papers* (Quarterly). **Educational Activities:** Center for the Study of Ethics in Society Colloquia; Public presentations, 20 per academic year.

START-UP INFORMATION

36468 ■ "Aubry & Kale Walch" in Business Journal (Vol. 32, August 29, 2014, No. 14, pp. 6)

Pub: American City Business Journals

Released: August 29, 2014. **Description:** Kale and Aubry Walch, founders of family-owned The Herbivorous Butcher, reveal that the process of formulating recipes for their shop took years. Aubry said that she and her brother used to make fake meats for themselves. Their plan to open a full-scale vegan butcher shop is also discussed.

36469 ■ "Dining Notes: The Salty Fig is Jacksonville's Newest Food Truck" in Florida Times-Union (July 13, 2012)

Pub: McClatchy-Tribune Information Services

Ed: Gary T. Mills. **Released:** July 13, 2012. **Description:** Jeff and John Stanford has selected locations throughout the city of Jacksonville, Florida to operate the food truck operation called, The Salty Fig. The brothers serve New American Southern style food along with a bar drink menu. The Salty Fig is named after the trees the boys enjoyed at their grandparent's home.

36470 ■ "Family Dynamics and Family Business Financial Performance: Spousal Commitment" in Family Business Review (Vol. 19, No. 1, March 2006, pp. 49)

Pub: Family Firm Institute

Contact: Judy L. Green, President

Ed: Howard Van Auken, James Werbel. **Description:** Study examining the effect of spousal commitment on launch and survival of family-owned businesses is presented.

36471 ■ "Hand-Held Heaven: Smallcakes Cupcakery" in Tulsa World (February 15, 2011)

Pub: The McClatchy Co.

Contact: Peter Tira, Director

Description: Franchisee Carolyn Archer displays her products at Smallcakes Cupcakery, a Jenks shop that's the first to be co-branded with FreshBerry under the Beautiful Brands International banner. The shop's launch is part of a franchise deal between BBI and Jeff and Brandy Martin, co-owners of Smallcakes; twelve concepts have been developed and marketed already by Tulsa-based BBI.

36472 ■ "Military Vet Uses SBA Program to Help Fund His Business" in Philadelphia Business Journal (Vol. 33, May 9, 2014, No. 13, pp. 6)

Pub: American City Business Journals

Released: May 9, 2014. **Description:** Colonel Richard Elam and his wife Kimberly, both with the Florida Army National Guard, secured funding through the Small Business Administration's (SBA's) Veterans Advantage program to launch iPlay, which rents mobile entertainment equipment such as rock walls and laser-tag setups for group events. The

capital access initiative, launched in January 2014, waives the origination fee for SBA Express loans to qualified veteran entrepreneurs.

36473 ■ "No. 359: FlexGround: Recreational Surfaces" in Inc. (Vol. 36, September 2014, No. 7, pp. 130)

Pub: Mansueto Ventures L.L.C.

Contact: John Koten, Chief Executive Officer

Released: September 2014. **Description:** Flex-Ground was co-founded by Bill Stafford and his father, Bill Stafford Sr. The company makes flooring used on playgrounds that provides both grip and safety padding. FlexGround flowing is poured into place like concrete, but feels like a mix of a rubber mat and a trampoline and maintains its thickness no matter how high the traffic.

36474 ■ "Securing a Fortune" in Small Business Opportunities (Fall 2010)

Pub: Harris Publications Inc.

Description: Profile of Whelan Security based in Saint Louis and is a private security company operating in 17 states. The family owned business started as a safety patrol unit.

36475 ■ "Selling Groceries & More on Amazon: The Ultimate Home Based Business for Families"

Pub: Amazon Digital Services

Released: October 16, 2014. **Price:** $7.99 Kindle. **Description:** Tips for starting an online grocery store from your home are shared. Grocery inventory, coupons and store promotions, setting up a seller account, application and approval for the grocery category, shipping information, sales techniques and private labeling are all addressed for this family owned type of business.

36476 ■ "Should You Go Into Business With Your Spouse?" in Women Entrepreneur (September 1, 2008)

Ed: Tamara Monosoff. **Description:** Things to consider before starting a business with one's spouse are discussed. Compatible work ethics, clear expectations of one another, long-term goals for the company and the status of the relationship are among the things to consider before starting a business endeavor with a spouse.

36477 ■ "Street Bistro Brings Food Truck Treats to Bangor" in Bangor Daily News (June 26, 2012)

Pub: McClatchy-Tribune Information Services

Ed: Emily Burnham. **Released:** June 26, 2012. **Description:** Chef Kim Smith launched her food truck, Street Bistro in Bangor, Maine. Smith took a year off after closing her two restaurants called Unbridled Bistro and Bennett's Market. Smith and her husband purchased a Snap-On truck and redesigned it into a kitchen. Menu items range from French to Tex-Mex to Thai to American.

ASSOCIATIONS AND OTHER ORGANIZATIONS

36478 ■ Canadian Association of Family Enterprise (CAFE) [Association Canadienne

des Entreprises Familiales]

465 Morden Rd., Ste. 112
Oakville, ON, Canada L6K 3W6
Ph: (905)337-8375
Free: 866-849-0099
Fax: (905)337-0572
URL: http://www.cafecanada.ca
Contact: Paul MacDonald, Executive Director
E-mail: paul@cafecanada.ca
Description: Family-owned businesses. Seeks to "encourage, educate, and inform members in disciplines unique to the family business." Fosters increased understanding of the importance of family-owned enterprises in the national economy among government agencies and the public. Gathers and disseminates information of interest to members. Conducts educational and lobbying activities. Provides technical support and advisory services to small businesses in areas including succession planning, taxation, family law, and arbitration and mediation. Maintains network of Family Councils, which serve as a forum for discussion of family and business matters. **Scope:** business, personal wellness, family business. **Founded:** 1983. **Subscriptions:** books. **Publications:** Family Business Magazine (Quarterly); Family Enterpriser (Quarterly); International Magazine for Family Businesses (Bimonthly); Canadian Association of Family Enterprise--Annual Membership Directory. **Educational Activities:** Family Business Symposium (Biennial). **Awards:** Family Enterprise of the Year Award (Annual).

36479 ■ Family Business Magazine

465 Morden Rd., Ste. 112
Oakville, ON, Canada L6K 3W6
Ph: (905)337-8375
Free: 866-849-0099
Fax: (905)337-0572
URL: http://www.cafecanada.ca
Contact: Paul MacDonald, Executive Director
E-mail: paul@cafecanada.ca
Released: Quarterly

36480 ■ Family Enterpriser

465 Morden Rd., Ste. 112
Oakville, ON, Canada L6K 3W6
Ph: (905)337-8375
Free: 866-849-0099
Fax: (905)337-0572
URL: http://www.cafecanada.ca
Contact: Paul MacDonald, Executive Director
E-mail: paul@cafecanada.ca
Released: Quarterly

36481 ■ Focus on the Family (FOTF)

8605 Explorer Dr.
Colorado Springs, CO 80920
Free: 800-232-6459
Fax: (719)548-5947
Co. E-mail: pastors@fotf.org
URL: http://www.focusonthefamily.com
Contact: James Daly, President
Description: Promotes traditional Judeo-Christian values and strong family ties. Gathers and disseminates practical resource information on marriage, parenting, and other subjects related to family life.

Produces fourteen different radio programs, aired in 96 countries. Conducts research and educational programs; sponsors charitable activities; makes available children's services; maintains speakers' bureau. Broadcasts and resources are also available in Hebrew, Hungarian, Indonesian, Italian, Japanese, Korean, Lithuanian, Norwegian, Polish, Portuguese, Romanian, Russian, Slovakian, Spanish, Swedish, Thai, Ukrainian and Zulu. **Founded:** 1977. **Publications:** *Citizen* (Weekly (Thurs.)); *Boundless* (Weekly); *Breakaway* (Monthly); *Clubhouse* (Monthly); *Clubhouse, Jr.* (Monthly); *LifeWise* (Bimonthly); *Citizen*; *Clubhouse Jr.* (Monthly); *Brio Magazine* (Monthly); *Breakaway Magazine* (Monthly); *Teachers in Focus Magazine*; *Focus on the Family Magazine* (Monthly); *Brio* (Monthly); *Focus on the Family Citizen* (Monthly); *Physician Magazine: A Publication of Focus on the Family* (Bimonthly); *Plugged In* (Monthly); *Focus on the Family Clubhouse* (Monthly). **Educational Activities:** Pillars (Annual); Counseling Enrichment Program (Periodic); Crisis Pregnancy Center Directors Conference.

EDUCATIONAL PROGRAMS

36482 ■ Kennesaw State University - Cox Family Enterprise Center
1000 Chastain Rd.
Kennesaw, GA 30144
Ph: (770)423-6045
Fax: (770)423-6721
Co. E-mail: cfec@kennesaw.edu
URL: http://coles.kennesaw.edu/centers/cox-family-enterprise
Contact: Gaia Marchisio, Executive Director

Description: Four-day course covering family business. Topics include: strategic and family business planning, leadership and management, conflict resolutions, total quality management (TQM), working with boards and other advisors, family and business values, and succession.

REFERENCE WORKS

36483 ■ *"$44M Father/Son Biz Involved in Major Orlando Projects"* in Orlando Business Journal (Vol. 31, July 18, 2014, No. 3, pp. 3)
Pub: American City Business Journals

Released: July 18, 2014. **Description:** Sy and mark Israel, father-son duo of Universal Engineering Sciences, speak about the projects that have been their largest challenges. They also highlight the advice they would give to a family business or a new business startup.

36484 ■ *"Achieving Sustained Competitive Advantage: A Family Capital Theory"* in Family Business Review (Vol. 19, June 2006, No. 2, pp. 135)
Pub: Family Firm Institute
Contact: Judy L. Green, President

Ed: James Hoffman, Mark Hoelscher, Ritch Sorenson. **Description:** Impact of capital assets on performance of family businesses is discussed.

36485 ■ *"Advantage Tutoring Center Helps Students of All Levels"* in Bellingham Business Journal (Vol. February 2010, pp. 16)
Pub: Sound Publishing Inc.
Contact: Gloria G. Fletcher, President

Ed: Ashley Mitchell. **Description:** Profile of the newly opened Advantage Tutoring, owned by Mary and Peter Morrison. The center offers programs ranging from basic homework help to subject-specific enrichment.

36486 ■ *"After the Storm: Following a Tragic Loss, the Chambers Family Is Starting To See the Light"* in Black Enterprise (November 2007)
Pub: Earl G. Graves Publishing Co. Inc.
Contact: Earl G. Graves, Jr., President

Ed: Sheryl Nance-Nash. **Description:** A family law firm filed bankruptcy after the death of a daughter.

36487 ■ *"All In The Family: Weston Undergoes a Shakeup"* in Canadian Business (Vol. 79, September 22, 2006, No. 19, pp. 75)
Pub: Rogers Media Inc.
Contact: Tony Viner, President

Ed: Zena Olijnyk. **Description:** Continuing ownership of Weston dynasty on Canada's largest chain Loblaw Co. is discussed.

36488 ■ *"Always Striving"* in Women In Business (Vol. 61, December 2009, No. 6, pp. 28)
Pub: American Business Women's Association
Contact: Lorie Burch, President

Ed: Kathleen Leighton. **Description:** Jennifer Mull discusses her responsibilities and how she attained success as CEO of Backwoods, a gear and clothing store founded by her father in 1973. She places importance on being true to one's words and beliefs, while emphasizing the capacity to tolerate risks in business. Mull defines success as an evolving concept and believes there must always be something to strive for.

36489 ■ *"Auction Company Grows with Much Smaller Sites"* in Automotive News (Vol. 86, October 31, 2011, No. 6488, pp. 23)
Pub: Crain Communications Inc.
Contact: Rance E. Crain, President

Ed: Arlena Sawyers. **Description:** Auction Broadcasting Company has launched auction sites and is expanding into new areas. The family-owned business will provide auctions half the size traditionally used. The firm reports that 40 percent of the General Motors factory-owned vehicles sold on consignment were purchased by online buyers, up 30 percent over 2010.

36490 ■ *"Avoid the Traps That Can Destroy Family Businesses: An Emerging Set of Best Practices Can Turn the Age-Old Problem of Generational Succession Into an Opportunity To Thrive"* in Harvard Business Review (Vol. 90, January-February 2012, No.1, pp. 25)
Pub: Harvard Business Review Press
Contact: Peter E. Walsh, Director

Ed: George Stalk, Henry Foley. **Released:** January-February 2012. **Description:** Tips to effective succession planning in family-owned businesses include proper screening and training for family members, managing family-member entry with company growth, and appointing non-family mentors to provide cross training.

36491 ■ *"B. Jannetta"* in Ice Cream Reporter (Vol. 21, August 20, 2008, No. 9, pp. 8)
Description: B. Jannetta ice cream parlor, run by Owen and Nicola Hazel, is celebrating its 100th Anniversary. The ice cream parlor is believed to be the oldest business still operating in its original shop in Saint Andrews. Owen and Nicola are the fourth generation to run the shop since Hazel's grandfather founded the business in 1908.

36492 ■ *"Baxter Baker Wins in Hot Finale of 'Cupcake Wars"* in Fort Mill Times (September 13, 2011)
Pub: McClatchy Company

Ed: Jenny Overmann. **Description:** Heather McDonnell, owner of Cupcrazed Cakery, and her assistant Debbie McDonnell, vied for a chance to win $10,000 on the cable network show called 'Cupcake Wars', and to serve cupcakes at the album release party for country singer Jennette McCurdy. At the end of the show, the sisters-in-law won the top prize.

36493 ■ *"Bellingham Boatbuilder Norstar Yachts Maintains Family Tradition"* in Bellingham Business Journal (Vol. February 2010, pp. 12)

Ed: Isaac Bonnell. **Description:** Profile of Norstar Yachts and brothers Gary and Steve Nordtvedt who started the company in 1994. The company recently moved its operations to a 12,000 square foot space in the Fairhaven Marine Industrial Park.

36494 ■ *"Better Than New Runs on Tried-and-True Model"* in Bellingham Business Journal (Vol. February 2010, pp. 16)
Pub: Sound Publishing Inc.
Contact: Gloria G. Fletcher, President

Ed: Ashley Mitchell. **Description:** Profile of family owned Better Than New clothing store that sells overstock items from department stores and clothing manufacturers. The stores location makes it easy to miss and its only advertising is a large sign posted outside. This is the sixth store owned by the couple, Keijeo and Sirba Halmekanqas.

36495 ■ *"Bienvenido, Mercadito"* in Washington Business Journal (Vol. 33, September 12, 2014, No. 21, pp. 8)
Pub: American City Business Journals

Released: September 12, 2014. **Description:** Restaurateur, Alfredo Sandoval, partnered with brothers Felipe and Patricio to open Mercadito, an upscale casual Mexican restaurant at the Marriott Marquis Hotel in Washington DC. The restaurant is geared to attract customers between 25 and 40 years of age.

36496 ■ *"Boston Printer Celebrates 60th Anniversary"* in American Printer (Vol. 128, August 1, 2011, No. 8)
Pub: Penton Media Inc.

Description: Shawmut printing is celebrating its 60th anniversary. The family business plans to increase efficiency through automation, monitoring job progress online from start to finish.

36497 ■ *"Brewing a Love-Haiti Relationship"* in The Business Journal - Serving Phoenix and the Valley of the Sun (Vol. 28, July 4, 2008, No. 44)

Ed: Yvonne Zusel. **Description:** Jean and Alicia Marseille have ventured into a coffee distribution company called Ka Bel LLC which markets Marabou brand of coffee imported from Haiti. Part of the proceeds of the business is donated to entrepreneurs from Jean's country, Haiti. Details of the Marseille's startup business and personal mission to help are discussed.

36498 ■ *"Bro Deals"* in Entrepreneur (August 2014)
Pub: Entrepreneur Media Inc.

Released: August 2014. **Description:** Brothers Joe and Allen Hertzman, owners of six Long John Silver's, 13 Rally's and 24 Papa John's Pizza units, share the secret behind their success in the restaurant franchising business. Allen offers advice to franchisees and emphasizes the importance of finding good operating partners who can help the business succeed. They describe their management styles and how growing up in the family's franchising business benefitted them.

36499 ■ *"Builders Land Rutenberg Deal"* in Charlotte Observer (February 2, 2007)

Ed: Bob Fliss. **Description:** Jim and Larry Sanders purchased a franchise from builder, Arthur Rutenberg Homes. The brothers will build custom homes in the area.

36500 ■ *"Business for Sale: For the Seasoned Buyer"* in Inc. (Vol. 30, November 2008, No. 11, pp. 32)
Pub: Mansueto Ventures L.L.C.
Contact: John Koten, Chief Executive Officer

Ed: Darren Dahl. **Description:** Dominick Fimiano shares his plans to sell his ten-year-old business that manufactures and sells frozen pizza dough and crusts as well as a variety of topped pizzas. Products are purchased by schools, hospitals, bowling alleys and amusement parks. The business sale includes the buyer's taking on Fimiano's son the firm's most senior employee.

36501 ■ *"Business Succession Planning"* in New Jersey Law Review (December 7, 2007)
Pub: New Jersey Law Journal
Contact: Ronald J. Fleury, Manager

Ed: Robert W. Cockren, Elga A. Goodman. **Description:** Ninety percent of American businesses are family-owned. The importance of estate planning for family-owned or controlled firms is covered.

36502 ■ *"A Business That Cares: Dale and Diana Bevington Purchased Their Home Instead Senior Care Franchise in 2007 and Have Seen It Grow From Strength to Strength"* in *Business Franchise (Vol. 213, May 2012, pp. 98)*
Pub: Circle Publishing
Contact: Robert Perry, President
Description: Dale and Diana Bevington have run their Home Instead Senior Care franchise since 2007. The Bevington's launched their company after watching Dale's father, who lived in Canada, was diagnosed with vascular dementia. They feel their franchise business offers everything they needed while caring for Dale's father.

36503 ■ *"Businessman Legend Passes: Charles H. James II Credited With Transforming Family Business"* in *Black Enterprise (December 2007)*
Ed: Tara C. Walker. **Description:** Profile of Charles H. James II, president and chairman of The James Corporation, a family-owned multigenerational food distribution company that started as a produce firm.

36504 ■ *"Carving Passion, Talent Help Couple Craft Business on Wood-Rich Land"* in *Crain's Cleveland Business (October 8, 2007)*
Pub: Crain Communications Inc.
Ed: Sharon Schnall. **Description:** Profile of Wood-carved Art Gallery & Studio, a family-owned business which includes several ventures of the husband-and-wife team, Jim Stadtlander and Diane Harto.

36505 ■ *"Changing Prescriptions"* in *Business North Carolina (Vol. 28, March 2008, No. 3, pp. 52)*
Description: Profile of Moose Drug Company, founded by Archibald Walter Moose in 1882. Family owners share how they focus on pharmacoeconomics (cost-benefit analyses of drugs or drug therapy) and customer service.

36506 ■ *"Chino Valley Ranches: a Family of Farmers"* in *Retail Merchandiser (Vol. 51, September-October 2011, No. 5, pp. 79)*
Pub: Phoenix Media Corporation
Ed: Angela Forsyth. **Description:** Charles B. Nichols and his wife Isabella purchased their ranch in Beaumont, California in the early 1950s. The family has been raising their chickens, producing eggs with quality, integrity and honesty the foundation of their business.

36507 ■ *"Cleaning Up"* in *Small Business Opportunities (Get Rich At Home 2010)*
Pub: Harris Publications Inc.
Description: Break into the $23 billion pro car wash business with no experience needed. Profile of Team Blue, founded by father and son team, Jeff and Jason Haas along with franchise opportunities is included.

36508 ■ *The Complete Idiot's Guide to a Successful Family Business*
Pub: Dutton Children's Books
Contact: Lauri Hornik, President
Ed: Neil Raphel. **Released:** August 04, 2009. **Price:** $18.95. **Description:** Guide to running a family business includes information for expanding beyond the original family firm and family versus hired management. **Availability:** Print.

36509 ■ *"Concrete Company Makes Lasting Impression in Valley"* in *Silicon Valley/San Jose Business Journal (Vol. 30, August 10, 2012, No. 20, pp. 1)*
Pub: American City Business Journal
Ed: Gloria Wang Shawber. **Description:** Joseph J. Albanese Inc. has made a lasting impression on projects throughout Silicon Valley for nearly 60 years. President and CEO, John Albanese, started his family owned concrete company as concrete contractors and it was often selected as the subcontractor for various general contractors in the valley.

36510 ■ *"Connie Ozan; Founder, Design Director, Twist Creative, 37"* in *Crain's Cleveland Business (Vol. 28, November 19,*

2007, No. 46)
Pub: Crain Communications Inc.

Ed: John Booth. **Description:** Profile of Connie Ozan, design director and founder of Twist Creative, an advertising agency that she runs with her husband, Michael; Ms. Ozan credits her husband's business sense in bringing a more strategic side to the company in which to complement her art direction.

36511 ■ *"Cupcake Craze"* in *Mail Tribune (March 2, 2011)*
Pub: Southern Oregon Media Group
Contact: Dena DeRose, Director, Advertising

Ed: Sarah Lemon. **Description:** Gourmet cupcake shops are sprouting up in large cities in Oregon. The Cupcake Company, a family business, is profiled.

36512 ■ *"Cupcake Maker Grabs Outpost"* in *Crain's New York Business (Vol. 27, August 15, 2011, No. 33, pp. 16)*
Pub: Crain Communications Inc.
Contact: Rance Crain, President

Ed: Jermaine Taylor. **Description:** Family-owned miniature cupcake maker, Baked by Melissa, singed a ten-year lease, expanding their stores to five. The business was started three years ago by advertising executive Melissa Bushell.

36513 ■ *"Dancing With Giants: Acquisition and Survival of the Family Firm"* in *Family Business Review (Vol. 19, December 2006, No. 4, pp. 289)*
Pub: Family Firm Institute
Contact: Judy L. Green, President

Ed: Adam Steen, Lawrence S. Welch. **Description:** Responses of family firms to mergers and acquisitions are analyzed taking the example of the takeover of an Australian wine producer and family firm.

36514 ■ *"Davis Family Expands Cable Empire"* in *St. Louis Business Journal (Vol. 32, June 15, 2012, No. 43, pp. 1)*
Pub: American City Business Journal

Description: Missouri-based Fidelity Communications has become a standout in the $98 billion cable industry through low-profile management of the Davis family, with the help of John Colbert. Fidelity has made five acquisitions since 1992 and has grown its subscriber base to more than 115,000 customers or revenue generating units.

36515 ■ *"Detroit Pawn Shop to be Reality TV Venue"* in *UPI NewsTrack (July 10, 2010)*
Pub: United Press International
Contact: Nicholas Chiaia, President
E-mail: president@upi.com

Description: TruTV will present a new series called 'Hardcore Pawn' to compete with the History Channel's successful show 'Pawn Stars'. The show will feature American Jewelry and Loan in Detroit, Michigan and its owner Les Gold, who runs the store with his wife and children.

36516 ■ *"The Duty of Wealth: Canadian Business Leaders on Nepotism and Philanthropy"* in *Canadian Business (Vol. 80, Winter 2007, No. 24)*
Ed: Joe Castaldo. **Description:** Fifty-one percent of the respondents in a survey of business leaders say that the decision to allow adult children to join a family firm should be based on the circumstances at the time. He CEOs that were surveyed also believed that billionaires should donate an average of forty percent of their estates and keep the rest for their family.

36517 ■ *"The Effect of Cunfucian Values On Succession In Family Business"* in *Family Business Review (Vol. 19, September 2006, No. 3)*
Pub: Family Firm Institute
Contact: Judy L. Green, President

Ed: Jun Yan, Ritch Sorenson. **Description:** Position of family business in a social context using Confucian values is examined.

36518 ■ *Entrepreneurship and Small Business*
Pub: Palgrave Macmillan
Contact: Lisa Dunn, Manager
E-mail: l.dunn@palgrave.com
Ed: Paul Burns. **Released:** 3rd Edition . **Price:** $78, paperback; £44.99, paperback. **Description:** Entrepreneurial skills, focusing on good management practices are discussed. Topics include family businesses, corporate, international and social entrepreneurship.

36519 ■ *Ethnic Solidarity for Economic Survival: Korean Greengrocers in New York City*
Pub: Russell Sage Foundation Publications
Contact: David Haproff, Director, Communications
E-mail: david@rsage.org
Ed: Pyong Gap Min. **Released:** February 2011. **Price:** $24.95, paperback. **Description:** Investigations into the entrepreneurial traditions of Korean immigrant families in New York City running ethnic businesses, particularly small grocery stores and produce markets. Social, cultural and economic issues facing these retailers are discussed. **Availability:** Print.

36520 ■ *"Fairfax Announces Acquisition of William Ashley"* in *Benzinga.com (August 16, 2011)*
Pub: Benzinga.com
Contact: Kyle Bazzy, President
Ed: Benzinga Staff. **Description:** Fairfax Financial Holdings Limited acquired the family-owned William Ashley China company, leader within the dinnerware and wedding registry industries and was the first company in North America to introduce a computerized wedding registry system.

36521 ■ *Family Business*
Pub: Cengage South-Western
Ed: Ernesto J. Poza. **Released:** 4th Edition. **Price:** $119, wholesale; $63.99. **Description:** Family-owned businesses face unique challenges in today's economy. This book provides the next generation of knowledge and skills required for profitable management and leadership in a family enterprise. **Availability:** PrintE-book.

36522 ■ *Family Business Models: Practical Solutions for the Family Business*
Pub: Palgrave Macmillan
Contact: Lisa Dunn, Manager
E-mail: l.dunn@palgrave.com
Ed: Alberto Gimeno, Gemma Baulenas, Joan Coma-Cros. **Released:** June 10, 2010. **Price:** £34. **Description:** A unique new model for understanding family businesses gives readers the potential to build better managed and more stable family firms and to plan for a success future.

36523 ■ *"Family Business Research"* in *International Journal of Entrepreneurship and Small Business (Vol. 12, December 3, 2010, No. 1)*
Pub: Publishers Communication Group
Contact: Doug Wright, Director
Ed: A. Bakr Ibrahim, Jean B. McGuire. **Description:** Assessment of the growing field of family business and suggestions for an integrated framework. The paper addresses a number of key issues facing family business research.

36524 ■ *"Family Feud: Pawn Shop Empire Stalls with Transition to Second Generation"* in *Billings Gazette (December 19, 2010)*
Pub: The Billings Gazette
Ed: Jan Falstad. **Description:** Profile of Ben L. Brown Sr. and his pawn shop located in Billings, Montana is presented. Brown discusses his plan to transition his business to his children.

36525 ■ *"Family Firm Performance: Further Evidence"* in *Family Business Review (Vol. 19, June 2006, No. 2, pp. 103)*
Pub: Family Firm Institute
Contact: Judy L. Green, President
Ed: Jim Lee. **Description:** Empirical results of regression analysis, which is used to examine the competitiveness of family owned businesses and non-family firms are presented.

36526 ■ *"Family Governance and Firm Performance: Agency, Stewardship, and Capabilities" in Family Business Review (Vol. 19, March 2006)*
Pub: Family Firm Institute
Contact: Judy L. Green, President
Ed: Danny Miller, Isabelle Le Breton-Miller. **Description:** Study examining the effect of governance, agency perspective, and stewardship perspective on performances of major publicly-traded family-controlled businesses in the U.S. is presented.

36527 ■ *Family Limited Partnership Deskbook*
Pub: American Bar Association
Contact: Carolyn Lamm, President
Ed: David T. Lewis, Andrea C. Chomakos. **Released:** 2007. **Price:** $169.95, Paperback. **Description:** Forming and funding a family limited partnership or limited liability company is complicated. In-depth analysis of all facets of this business entity are examined using detailed guidance on the basic principles of drafting, forming, funding, and valuing an FLP or LLC and also covers tax concerns. Examples and extensive sample forms are included on a CD-ROM included with the book.

36528 ■ *The Family Limited Partnership Deskbook: Forming and Funding FLPs and Other Closely Held Business Entities*
Pub: American Bar Association
Contact: Carolyn Lamm, President
Ed: Andrea Chomakos, David Tyler Lewis. **Released:** April 2007. **Price:** $169.95, CD-ROM included, paperback. **Description:** Forming and funding a family limited partnership (FLP) or limited liability company (LLC) is common and complicated. This handbook offers in-depth analysis of issues facing these types of businesses. Guidance is given on the principles of drafting, forming, funding, and valuing an FLP or LLC as well as tax matters. Examples and sample forms are included on a CD-ROM. **Availability:** Print.

36529 ■ *"Family Matters: Founding Family Firms and Corporate Political Activity" in Business and Society (December 2007, pp. 395-428)*
Pub: Pine Forge Press
Contact: Blaise R. Simqu, President
Ed: Michael Hadani. **Description:** The impact of publicly traded family founding firms and their inclination for corporate political activity is examined. Publicly traded family founding firms are more predisposed to engage in corporate political activity when the founder is in an executive position. Details of these findings are reported.

36530 ■ *"Family Matters: Founding Family Firms and Corporate Political Activity" in Business and Society (Vol. 46, December 7, 2007, No. 4)*
Pub: Pine Forge Press
Contact: Blaise R. Simqu, President
Ed: Michael Hadani. **Description:** The impact of publicly traded family founding firms and their inclination for corporate political activity is examined. Publicly traded family founding firms are more predisposed to engage in corporate political activity when the founder is in an executive position.

36531 ■ *"Family-Owned Train Service Offers a Ride for Your Raft" in Idaho Business Review (June 11, 2014)*
Pub: Dolan Co.
Contact: James P. Dolan, President
Released: June 11, 2014. **Description:** Payette River Flyer's run between Smith's Ferry and Cascade is part of Thunder Mountain's Line new rail service that allows rafters to leave their vehicles at Smith's Ferry and load whitewater gear onto the train. The train provides a scenic ride along the Payette River. Details of this family-operated tourist train service is profiled.

36532 ■ *"The Family-Run Business" in Small Business Opportunities (Get Rich At Home 2010)*
Pub: Harris Publications Inc.
Ed: Gene Siciliano. **Description:** The good, the bad and the ugly of succession planning for any small business is spotlighted.

36533 ■ *"Family Throne" in Hawaii Business (Vol. 53, March 2008, No. 9, pp. 51)*
Pub: PacificBasin Communications
Ed: Cathy S. Cruz-George. **Description:** Jeanette and George Grace inherited Paradise Lua Inc., a portable toilet company founded by George's father. The toilets are rented by Aloha Stadium during football season and St. Patrick's Day block party among others. The company has 2,500 toilets and 20 pumping trucks and had earnings of $1.3 million in 2007.

36534 ■ *"The Family Tools" in Canadian Business (Vol. 80, March 26, 2007, No. 7, pp. 14)*
Description: A few strategies for running family businesses successfully are presented.

36535 ■ *Family Wars*
Pub: Kogan Page Ltd.
Ed: Nigel Nicholson, Grant E. Gordon. **Released:** April 01, 2010. **Price:** $16.95. **Description:** Family feuding, sibling rivalries, and petty jealousies are among the greatest issues faced by family owned companies. Family Wars explores behind the scenes issues of some of the largest family-run firms in the world, and shows how family in-fighting has threatened their downfall. Ford, Gucci, McCain, Guinness, Fallo, and Restone are among the families discussed. Advice is given to anyone involved in a family business and offers suggestions to avoid problems.

36536 ■ *"A Family's Fortune" in Canadian Business (Vol. 80, Winter 2007, No. 24, pp. 103)*
Ed: Graham F. Scott. **Description:** James Richardson started as a tailor before moving into the grain business because his clients paid him in sacks of wheat and barley. The James Richardson and Sons Ltd. entered the radio business in 1927 but later sold it off in 1951.

36537 ■ *"Finalist: Private Company, Less Than $100M" in Crain's Detroit Business (Vol. 25, June 22, 2009, No. 25)*
Pub: Crain Communications Inc. - Detroit
Contact: Keith Crain, Chairman
Ed: Sherri Begin Welch. **Description:** Profile of family-owned Guardian Alarm Company is presented. The firm has expanded to include medical monitoring and video equipment of doors and windows.

36538 ■ *"Firm Stays In the 'Family'; After Owner's Death, Employees Buy Company" in Crain's Detroit Business (Vol. 24, January 28, 2008)*
Pub: Crain Communications Inc. - Detroit
Contact: Keith Crain, Chairman
Ed: Chad Halcom. **Description:** Sterling Office Systems Inc., distributor of photocopiers and other office machines was purchased from the owner's family after his demise. The new owners would like to hit $1.75 million in sales their first year.

36539 ■ *"Food Biz Grows On Its President" in Denver Business Journal (Vol. 66, June 27, 2014, No. 6, pp. B6)*
Pub: American City Business Journals
Released: June 27, 2014. **Description:** Kristy Taddonio Mullins, president of Mile Hi, a family business and a regional distributor for McDonald's throughout the Midwest, has helped the company expand. When she joined in 2013, she believed that growth was critical to the continued success of the company and started a $22 million LEED Gold Bakery with double the production capacity.

36540 ■ *"Former NFL Player Tackles a New Restaurant Concept" in Inc. (Vol. 33, September 2011, No. 7, pp. 32)*
Pub: Inc. Magazine
Ed: Nadine Heintz. **Description:** Matt Chatham, former NFL player, launched SkyCrepers, a chain of fast-serve crepe shops with his wife Erin. Chatham entered Babson College's MBA program after retiring from football.

36541 ■ *"Freeman Beauty Labs" in Retail Merchandiser (Vol. 51, September-October 2011, No. 5, pp. 74)*
Pub: Phoenix Media Corporation
Description: Profile of Freeman Beauty Labs, the family owned beauty product developer supplying retailers and salons with quality products. The firm promotes its bath, foot care, hair care, and skincare brands as a whole, not as individual products.

36542 ■ *"Fromm Family Foods Converts Old Feed Mill Into Factory for Gourmet Pet Food" in Wisconsin State Journal (August 3, 2011)*
Pub: Capital Newspapers
Ed: Barry Adams. **Description:** Fromm Family Foods, a gourmet cat and dog food company spent $10 million to convert an old feed mill into a pet food manufacturing facility. The owner forecasts doubling or tripling its production of 600 tons of feed per week in about five years.

36543 ■ *"Generational Savvy" in Hawaii Business (Vol. 54, August 2008, No. 2, pp. 135)*
Pub: PacificBasin Communications
Ed: Jolyn Okimoto Rosa. **Description:** Lawrence Takeo Kagawa founded Security Insurance Agency, later renamed Occidental Underwriters of Hawaii Ltd., in 1933 to provide insurance to Asian-Americans in Hawaii at lower premiums. Details on the company's history, growth investment products and Transamerica Life products and 75 years of family-run business are discussed.

36544 ■ *"Get On the Shelf: Selling Your Product In Retail Stores" in Black Enterprise (Vol. 44, February 2014, No. 6, pp. 18)*
Pub: Earl G. Graves Publishing Co. Inc.
Contact: Earl G. Graves, Jr., President
Released: February 2014. **Description:** Profile of Arsha and Charles Jones, Washington DC natives, who are selling their Capital City Mumbo Sauce to local retailers as well as big box retailers. The husband and wife team share tips for getting your product into retail establishments.

36545 ■ *"Gillette Creamery" in Ice Cream Reporter (Vol. 23, September 20, 2010, No. 10, pp. 8)*
Description: Gillette family of Gillette Creamery in Ellenville have been Entrepreneurs of the Year in Ulster County, New York. Gillette is the largest supplier of ice cream products in Eastern New York.

36546 ■ *"Good Price, Best Brands" in Retail Merchandiser (Vol. 51, July-August 2011, No. 4, pp. 58)*
Pub: Phoenix Media Corporation
Description: Flemington Department Store has been a family-owned and operated retailer for over 50 years. Customer service is key to the store's success.

36547 ■ *"Grape Expectations" in Canadian Business (Vol. 80, Winter 2007, No. 24, pp. 57)*
Ed: Joe Castaldo. **Description:** Laura McCain-Jensen bought a 15-acre vineyard in the Niagara wine country after a trip to Ontario for her husband's hair transplant. The vineyard has since been renamed Creekside Estate Winery and now produces two celebrity-branded wines under the name of golfer Mike Weir and hockey player Wayne Gretsky.

36548 ■ *"'Groundhog Day' B&B Likely Will Be Converted Into One In Real Life" in Chicago Tribune (October 21, 2008)*
Pub: McClatchy-Tribune Information Services
Ed: Carolyn Starks. **Description:** Everton Martin and Karla Stewart Martin have purchased the Victorian house that was featured as a bed-and-breakfast in the 1993 hit move 'Groundhog Day'; the couple was initially unaware of the structure's celebrity status when they purchased it with the hope of fulfilling their dream of owning a bed-and-breakfast.

36549 ■ *"Guidelines For Family Business Boards of Directors" in Family Business*

Review (Vol. 19, June 2006, No. 2, pp. 147)
Pub: Family Firm Institute
Contact: Judy L. Green, President
Ed: Suzanne Lane, Joseph Astrachan, Andrew Keyt, Kristi McMillan. **Description:** Effective corporate governance standards for boards of directors of family businesses are examined.

36550 ■ *"Halls Give Hospital Drive $11 Million Infusion" in The Business Journal-Serving Metropolitan Kansas City (Vol. 26, July 18, 2008)*
Ed: Rob Roberts. **Description:** Don Hall, chairman of Hallmark Cards Inc., and eight family members have announced that they will give $11 million to Children's Mercy Hospitals and Clinics for its $800 million expansion plan. Hall Family Foundation president Bill Hall that contributions such as that for Children's Mercy reflect the charitable interests of the foundation's board and founders. The possible impacts of the Hall's donation are analyzed.

36551 ■ *"Healthful, Organic Food is the Name of the Game at Renee's" in AZ Daily Star (May 10, 2012)*
Pub: McClatchy Tribune Information Services
Ed: Kristen Cook. **Description:** Profile of Renee's Organic Oven offer organic and locally grown foods at their restaurant. The eatery is owned by husband and wife team, Steve and Renee Kreager.

36552 ■ *"Hometown Value" in Retail Merchandiser (Vol. 51, July-August 2011, No. 4, pp. 50)*
Pub: Phoenix Media Corporation
Ed: Todd Vowell. **Description:** Profile of family-owned Vowell's Marketplace located in Noxapater, Mississippi. The 10-store chain caters to its Southern roots and is run by the third generation of the Vowell family.

36553 ■ *"How to... Harness Green Power" in The Caterer (July 20, 2012, No. 325)*
Pub: Reed Business Information Ltd.
Description: Roger and Emma Stevens discuss their success as at winning the Considerate Hoteliers Association's award for Best Green Marketing Initiative. The couple discusses their restaurant and its partnership with tow nearby guesthouses.

36554 ■ *"How-To Workshops in St. Charles Teach Sewing, Styles" in St. Louis Post-Dispatch (September 14, 2010)*
Pub: St. Louis Post-Dispatch L.L.C.
Contact: Kevin Mowbray, Publisher
Ed: Kalen Ponche. **Description:** Profile of DIY Style Workshop in St. Charles, Missouri, where sewing, designing and teaching is offered. The shop is home base for DIY Style, a Website created by mother and daughter to teach younger people how to sew.

36555 ■ *"Husband-Wife Team Opens Somali Interpreting Business in Willmar, Minn." in West Central Tribune (May 22, 2012)*
Pub: McClatchy-Tribune Regional News
Ed: Linda Vanderwerf. **Released:** May 22, 2012. **Description:** Profile of husband and wife team who launched an interpreting service in Somali. Details of the business are included.

36556 ■ *"Impact of Family Relationships On Attitudes of the Second Generation In Family Business" in Family Business Review (September 2006)*
Pub: Family Firm Institute
Contact: Judy L. Green, President
Ed: Jean Lee. **Description:** Relationship of family functioning with organizational variables, with particular attention given to family cohesion and family adaptability is examined.

36557 ■ *In-N-Out Burger: A Behind-the-Counter Look at the Fast-Food Chain That Breaks All the Rules*
Pub: HarperCollins Publishers Inc.
Contact: Jane Friedman, President
E-mail: jfriedman@harpercollins.com
Ed: Stacy Perman. **Released:** April 2009. **Price:** $14.99, Paperback. **Description:** Business analysis of the factors that helped In-N-Out Burgers, a family owned burger chain in California, along with a history of its founding family, the Synders.

36558 ■ *"In a Twist, Pretzel Vendors Will Be Selling Pizza: Wetzels to Launch Blaze Fast-Fire'd Concept with Two SoCal Locations" in Los Angeles Business Journal (Vol. 34, June 4, 2012, No. 23, pp. 12)*
Pub: CBJ, L.P.
Ed: Bethany Firnhaber. **Description:** Rick and Elise Wetzel, cofounders of Wetzel's Pretzels is launching its new restaurants featuring fast-casual pizza. The concept is of an assembly line process where customers can make 11-inch personalized pizzas with toppings like artichokes, gorgonzola cheese, roasted red peppers and arugula. The pizzas bake in two minutes.

36559 ■ *"Internationalization of Australian Family Businesses: A Managerial Capabilities Perspective" in Family Business Review (Vol. 19, No.3, September 2006, pp. 207)*
Pub: Family Firm Institute
Contact: Judy L. Green, President
Ed: Chris Graves, Jill Thomas. **Description:** Concept that managerial capabilities of family firms lag behind those of non-family counterparts as they expand is discussed.

36560 ■ *"It All Comes Back to Trust" in Canadian Business (Vol. 80, March 26, 2007, No. 7, pp. S11)*
Description: Eileen Fischer, family business expert at York University, shares her views on the challenges involved in running family businesses.

36561 ■ *"JK Lasser's New Rules for Estate, Retirement, and Tax Planning"*
Pub: John Wiley & Sons Inc.
Contact: Stephen M. Smith, President
Released: October 20, 2014. **Price:** $24.95 paperback. **Description:** The authoritative guide to estate, retirement and tax planning is fully updated and reflects the new changes and legal updates. Estate planning section covers: planning, taxation, investing, wills, executors, trusts, life insurance, retirement planning, Social Security, business planning, succession, asset protection and family limited partnerships.

36562 ■ *"Kennedy Mansion Bed & Breakfast Faces Threat of Closure" in Tulsa World (February 12, 2012)*
Pub: World Publishing Co.
Released: February 12, 2012. **Description:** Darell Christoper and his wife Francoise opened their Kennedy Mansion B&B in Tulsa in 2007. The couple is having difficulty saving their business because their request to the city's Board of Adjustment for special exceptions and variances to the zoning code have not been met. The Christophers would like to host special events on their property.

36563 ■ *"A Life of Spice" in Entrepreneur (Vol. 37, September 2009, No. 9, pp. 46)*
Pub: Entrepreneur Press
Contact: Perlman Neil, President
Ed: Jason Daley. **Description:** Matt and Bryan Walls have successfully grown their Atlanta, Georgia-based Snorg Tees T-shirt company. The company has expanded its product offering and redesigned its Website to be more user-friendly. The company has registered between $5 and 10 million in 2008.

36564 ■ *"Life's Work: Manolo Blahnik" in Harvard Business Review (Vol. 88, December 2010, No. 12, pp. 144)*
Pub: Harvard Business School Publishing
Ed: Alison Beard. **Description:** Shoe designer Manolo Blahnik recounts his beginnings in the shoe industry and the influence art has had on his work, as well as balancing art and commerce. He also discusses the importance of quality materials and craftsmanship and the benefits of managing an independent, family-owned business.

36565 ■ *"Like Mom, Like Son" in Washington Business Journal (Vol. 33, May 9, 2014, No. 3, pp. 6)*
Pub: American City Business Journals
Released: May 9, 2014. **Description:** Chef Victor Albisu convinced his mother, Rosa Susinski, to open the Taco Bamba restaurant in Falls Church, Virginia

even though they are not Mexican. The taqueria is near Plaza Latina, Rose's market, so the mother and son will alternate management of the restaurant. Their goal is to open another location.

36566 ■ *"Long Live Rock" in Inc. (November 2007, pp. 130)*
Pub: Gruner and Jahr USA Publishing Co.
Contact: J. Russell Denson, President
Ed: Nitasha Tiku. **Description:** Profile of a family business using chemistry to recycle concrete products.

36567 ■ *"Lots More Mr. Nice Guy" in Canadian Business (Vol. 80, October 22, 2007, No. 21, pp. 58)*
Ed: Zena Olijnyk. **Description:** Galen Weston Jr., executive chairman of Loblaw and heir to the Weston family business, has his hands full running the company. Details of his turnaround strategies and ambitious plans to increase profitability of the business are discussed.

36568 ■ *"Marketing is Everything, But Timing Helps" in Idaho Business Review (September 9, 2014)*
Pub: Dolan Co.
Contact: James P. Dolan, President
Released: September 9, 2014. **Description:** Profile of Ladd Family Pharmacy, founded by husband and wife Kip and Elaine, who borrowed money from Idaho Banking Company to start their pharmacy. The firm has expanded from three workers in 2008 to 22 to date and reported $6.2 million in revenue for 2013.

36569 ■ *"Mars Advertising's Orbit Grows as Other Ad Segments Fall" in Crain's Detroit Business (Vol. 25, June 1, 2009, No. 22, pp. 10)*
Pub: Crain Communications Inc. - Detroit
Contact: Keith Crain, Chairman
Ed: Bill Shea. **Description:** An electrical fire burned at Mars Advertising's headquarters in Southfield, Michigan. The company talks about its plans for regrouping and rebuilding. The family firm specializes in in-store marketing that targets consumers already in the buying mode.

36570 ■ *"McIntosh Family Sells Car Dealership" in Black Enterprise (Vol. 38, December 1, 2007, No. 5)*
Pub: Earl G. Graves Publishing Co. Inc.
Contact: Earl G. Graves, Jr., President
Ed: Brenda Porter. **Description:** Seattle's McIntosh family sold its Kirkland Chrysler Jeep dealership to private equity firm Cerberus Capital Management. Details of the deal are given.

36571 ■ *"Measuring Success In Family Businesses: The Concept of Configurational Fit" in Family Business Review (Vol. 19, No. 2, June 2006, pp. 115)*
Pub: Family Firm Institute
Contact: Judy L. Green, President
Ed: Christoph Hienerth, Alexander Kessler. **Description:** Strategic benchmarking, which are used to examine business success of family-owned enterprises are investigated.

36572 ■ *"Minnesota State Fair Vendors Accept Big Risks for Big Rewards" in Business Journal (Vol. 32, August 22, 2014, No. 13, pp. 10)*
Pub: American City Business Journals
Released: August 22, 2014. **Description:** Food and beverage concessionaires compete for booths at the Minnesota State Fair and there are many vendors that wait for years to get one, especially a large booth with room for tables and a beer garden. The State Fair has been a good business opportunity and a family bonding experience for most of the vendors.

36573 ■ *"The Molson Way" in Canadian Business (Vol. 80, April 16, 2007, No. 8, pp. 36)*
Pub: Rogers Media Inc.
Contact: Tony Viner, President
Ed: Andy Holloway. **Description:** The success of the seventh generation of Molson family in running the Molson Coors Brewing Co. since it was established 221 years ago by John Molson is discussed.

36574 ■ The Mom & Pop Store: How the Unsung Heroes of the American Economy Are Surviving and Thriving
Pub: Walker Publishing Company Inc.
Contact: Peter Miller, Manager
E-mail: pmiller@walkerbooks.com
Ed: Robert Spector. Released: September 22, 2009. Price: $26, hardback. Description: The history of small independent retail enterprises and how mom and pop stores in the U.S. continue to thrive through customer service and renewed community support for local businesses. Availability: Print.

36575 ■ "MPI Expansion Goes Back to Family Roots" in Crain's Detroit Business (Vol. 25, June 1, 2009, No. 22, pp. M007)
Pub: Crain Communications Inc. - Detroit
Contact: Keith Crain, Chairman
Ed: Sherri Begin Welch. Description: William Parfet, grandson of Upjohn Company founder, is expanding MPI Research's clinical and early clinical research operations into two buildings in Kalamazoo, land which was once part of his grandfather's farm.

36576 ■ "Muirhead Farmhouse B&B Owners Get Hospitality Wright" in Chicago Tribune (July 31, 2008)
Pub: McClatchy-Tribune Information Services
Ed: Glenn Jeffers. Description: Profile of the Muirhead Farmhouse, a bed-and-breakfast owned by Mike Petersdorf and Sarah Muirhead Petersdorf; Frank Lloyd Wright designed the historic farmhouse which blends farm life and history into a unique experience that is enhanced by the couple's hospitality.

36577 ■ "Muzzle & Fitness" in Washington Business Journal (Vol. 33, July 25, 2014, No. 14, pp. 8)
Pub: American City Business Journals
Released: July 25, 2014. Description: Couple, Kevin and Kim Gilliam, founded their family business, Frolick Dogs in Alexandria, Virginia to offer obedience or agility training services to dog owners. A self-serve dog washing station is also available after the dog's workout.

36578 ■ "The Natural Environment, Innovation, and Firm Performance" in Family Business Review (Vol. 19, December 2006, No. 4)
Pub: Family Firm Institute
Contact: Judy L. Green, President
Ed: Justin Craig, Clay Dibrell. Description: Comparative study of the impact of firm-level natural environment-related policies on innovation and performance of family and non-family firms is presented.

36579 ■ "A New Perspective On the Development Model for Family Business" in Family Business Review (Vol. 19, December 2006, No. 4, pp. 317)
Pub: Family Firm Institute
Contact: Judy L. Green, President
Ed: Matthew W. Rutherford, Lori A. Muse, Sharon L. Oswald. Description: Empirical test model of the developmental model for family business is proposed and owner, firm and family characteristics which have an impact on the development model are examined.

36580 ■ Nirvana in a Cup: The Founding of Oregon Chai
Pub: Moby Press
Ed: Tedde McMillen; Heather Hale. Released: July 2006. Price: $12.99. Description: Profile of a mother-daughter team who founded Oregon Chai, a tea company.

36581 ■ "Nothing But Green Skies" in Inc. (November 2007, pp. 115-120)
Pub: Gruner and Jahr USA Publishing Co.
Contact: J. Russell Denson, President
Ed: Alison Stein Wellner. Description: Profile of Enterprise Rent-A-Car, one of the largest family-owned businesses in the U.S. Andy Taylor, CEO, discusses the company's talks about the idea of offering carbon off-sets for a few years.

36582 ■ "No. 156: Divorced, But Still Running the Company Together" in Inc. (Vol. 36, September 2014, No. 7, pp. 78)
Pub: Mansueto Ventures L.L.C.
Contact: John Koten, Chief Executive Officer
Released: September 2014. Description: Co-founders, Lacy Starling and Tony Coutsoftides, of Legion Logistics discuss the challenges of running their family-owned business after their divorce.

36583 ■ "Oberweis Tests Home Ice Cream Delivery" in Ice Cream Reporter (Vol. 21, November 20, 2008, No. 12, pp. 1)
Description: Oberwies Dairy launched its Treat Delivery Program in the Saint Louis area. The program allows customers to order milkshakes, ice cream cones, sundaes and scoops of ice cream and they are delivered to their home or office. Oberweis is a fourth generation family run business.

36584 ■ "Organic Food Business Opening" in Clovis News Journal (August 2, 2012)
Pub: McClatchy Tribune Information Services
Description: Bill and Rhonda Bargman will open their new market that will offer organic and gourmet foods. The Bargmans have more than 34 years of experience in the grocery business. Free range meats, pesticide free produce, bread made with unbleached flour along with a choice of gluten-free products will stock the store shelves.

36585 ■ "Organizational Virtue Orientation and Family Firms" in Business Ethics Quarterly (Vol. 21, April 2011, No. 2, pp. 257)
Pub: Society for Business Ethics
Contact: Dawn Elm, Executive Director
Ed: G. Tyge Payne, Keith H. Brigham, J. Christian Broberg, Todd W. Moss, Jeremy C. Short. Description: The concept of organizational virtue orientation (OVO) and the differences between family and non-family firms on six organizational virtue dimensions of Integrity, Empathy, Warmth, Courage, Conscientiousness, and Zeal are examined.

36586 ■ "Ownership Preferences, Competitive Heterogeneity, and Family-Controlled Businesses" in Family Business Review (June 2006)
Pub: Family Firm Institute
Contact: Judy L. Green, President
Ed: David G. Hoopes, Danny Miller. Description: Impact of ownership structure and corporate governance choices on competition among family-owned businesses is explored.

36587 ■ "A Panel Study of Copreneurs In Business: Who Enters, Continues, and Exits?" in Family Business Review (Vol. 19, September 2006, No. 3, pp. 193)
Pub: Family Firm Institute
Contact: Judy L. Green, President
Ed: Glenn Muske, Margaret A. Fitzgerald. Description: Analysis of three groups of copreneurs of family businesses, and their entrepreneurial impact on business success is presented.

36588 ■ "Perry's Goes Organic" in Ice Cream Reporter (Vol. 22, December 20, 2008, No. 1, pp. 1)
Description: Family-owned Perry's Ice Cream is starting a new line of organic ice cream in both vanilla and chocolate flavors. All Perry's products are made with milk and cream from local dairy farmers.

36589 ■ "A Pioneer of Paying With Plastic" in Crain's Chicago Business (Vol. 31, April 28, 2008, No. 17, pp. 39)
Pub: Crain Communications Inc.
Contact: Todd Johnson, Publisher
Ed: Phuong Ly. Description: Profile of Perfect Plastic Printing Corp., a family-owned company which manufactures credit cards, bank cards and gift cards and whose sales hit $50.1 million last year, a 16 percent jump from 2006.

36590 ■ "Please Pass the Mayo" in Crain's Chicago Business (Vol. 31, April 28, 2008, No. 17, pp. 32)
Pub: Crain Communications Inc.
Contact: Todd Johnson, Publisher
Ed: Samantha Stainburn. Description: Fort Dearborn Co. has come a long way since it started as on

one-press print shop; the family-owned company was struggling to keep up with the technology of making consumer product labels for curvy bottles of products like V8 V-Fusion juice and in 2006 sold off to Genstar Capital LLC which has pushed for acquisitions; last year, Fort Derborn bought its biggest competitor, Renaissance Mark Inc., doubling its size and adding spirit and wine makers to its client roster.

36591 ■ "Printing Company Edwards Brothers Grapples With a Shrinking Market" in Crain's Detroit Business (Vol. 26, Jan. 4, 2010)
Pub: Crain Communications Inc.
Contact: Rance E. Crain, President
Ed: Bill Shea. Description: Overview of the publishing industry, which has seen a huge decline in revenue; Edwards Brothers, Inc., a family printing business that was founded 117 years ago is struggling due to a variety of factors, many of which are explored.

36592 ■ "Publicity Turns Colorado Springs-based Toy-Rental Business Marketing Into Child's Play" in Colorado Springs Business Journal (January 20, 2012)
Pub: Dolan Media
Ed: Amy Gillentine. Released: January 20, 2012. Description: Profile of Stephanie Weber and her Internet toy rental business she launched in 2007. The firm operates on the Netflix model, where customers purchase memberships costing approximately $20 per month. Toys are selected, shipped and returned. Weber's husband partnered with her in this business venture.

36593 ■ Race and Entrepreneurial Success: Black-, Asian-, and White-Owned Businesses in the United States
Pub: The MIT Press
Contact: Ellen W. Faran, Director
E-mail: ewfaran@mit.edu
Ed: Robert W. Fairlie, Alicia M. Robb. Released: August 2010. Price: $19, paperback; £13.95. Description: Trends in minority small business ownership are explored, focusing on the importance of human capital, financial capital, and family business background in successful business ownership.

36594 ■ "Ready To Ride the 'Silver Tsunami'" in Austin Business Journal (Vol. 34, May 30, 2014, No. 15, pp. 8)
Pub: American City Business Journals, Inc.
Contact: Whitney Shaw, President
Released: May 30, 2014. Description: Profiles of Seniors Real Estate Inc. Institute founders Nikki and Bruce Buckelew are presented. Nikki has focused on providing real estate agents with training and Webinars. Their career achievements are also included.

36595 ■ "The Real Estate Success Formula: 19 Proven Strategies to Making Money in Real Estate"
Pub: CreateSpace
Contact: Daren Giles, President
Released: September 28, 2014. Price: $19.99 paperback. Description: Nineteen proven strategies for selling real estate are provided by husband and wife real estate team. The book teaches how to buy, hold and sell houses quickly without using your money or your credit. Tactics for marketing, systematizing and managing your real estate business are outlined.

36596 ■ "The Relationship Between Boards and Planning In Family Businesses" in Family Business Review (Vol. 19, March 2006, No. 1, pp. 65)
Pub: Family Firm Institute
Contact: Judy L. Green, President
Ed: Timothy Blumentritt. Description: Study determining the extent of control exercised by board of directors and advisory boards on business planning within family-owned businesses is covered.

36597 ■ "The Romance of Good Deeds: a Business With a Cause Can Do Good in the World" in Inc. (Volume 32, December 2010,

No. 10, pp. 47)
Pub: Inc. Magazine

Ed: Meg Cadoux Hirshberg. **Description:** Entrepreneurship and family relationships are discussed. When a small business has a passion for philanthropy it can help any marriage by creating even greater passion for each other.

36598 ■ *"Root, Root, Root for the P.A. Hutchison Co." in American Printer (Vol. 128, August 1, 2011, No. 8)*
Pub: Penton Media Inc.

Description: The P.A. Hutchison Company celebrate 100 years in the printing business. President and CEO Chris Hutchison presented awards to employees, however employees also presented awards to Chris and his father as Employer of the Century.

36599 ■ *"Rudy's Tortillas Wraps Up Expansion Plan in Carrollton" in Dallas Business Journal (Vol. 35, August 31, 2012, No. 51, pp. 1)*
Pub: American City Business Journal

Ed: Candace Carlisle. **Description:** Rudy's Tortillas Corporation, a 67-year old family business based in Dallas, Texas, is moving into a new plant on Belt Line Road, Carrollton. The expansion will also involve the hiring of 150 new workers and enable the company to expand its operations. Rudy's will spend $14 million dollars on construction and equipment on the new tortilla plant.

36600 ■ *"Savvy Solutions" in Black Enterprise (Vol. 41, October 2010, No. 3, pp. 52)*
Pub: Earl G. Graves Publishing Co. Inc.
Contact: Earl G. Graves, Jr., President

Ed: Tennille M. Robinson. **Description:** Husband and wife team seek advice for expanding their catering business. They are also seeking funding resources.

36601 ■ *"Sawatdee Rethinks Express Eatery Model" in Business Journal (Vol. 31, January 10, 2014, No. 33, pp. 4)*
Pub: American City Business Journals

Released: January 10, 2014. **Description:** The two Sawatdee Express restaurants owned by Supenn Harrison closed their uptown and downtown locations in Minneapolis, Minnesota in December 2013. Harrison and her family own six other traditional, sit-down models of the Sawatdee restaurants.

36602 ■ *Small Business Survival Guide*
Ed: Cliff Ennico. **Price:** $12.95. **Description:** Small business expert provides strategies to start a company and survive in the 21st Century. He shows small business owners how to succeed despite challenges that can defeat any firm. His advice covers suppliers; customers and contractors; competitors and creditors; spouses, family and friends; as well as the ways lawyers, accountants and other can steal an entrepreneur's success. Ennico also describes how startups can comply with local regulations.

36603 ■ *Sneaker Wars: The Enemy Brothers Who Founded Adidas and Puma and the Family Feud that Forever Changed the Business of Sports*
Pub: HarperCollins Ecco

Ed: Barbara Smit. **Released:** March 17, 2009. **Price:** $15.99, paperback. **Description:** A history of Puma and Adidas shoes and the two German brothers who built the empires. **Availability:** Print.

36604 ■ *"Social Networking: Growing Pains" in Canadian Business (Vol. 81, July 22, 2008, No. 12-13, pp. 35)*
Pub: Rogers Media Inc.
Contact: Tony Viner, President

Ed: Alex Mlynek. **Description:** Laughing Stock Vineyards' Cynthia Enns and David Enns plan to target young buyers by using social media. The Enns however, are concerned that targeting younger buyers may affect Laughing Stock's image as a premium brand. Additional information regarding the company's future plans is presented.

36605 ■ *"Solutions to Family Business Problems" in Contractor (Vol. 56, October 2009, No. 10, pp. 51)*
Pub: Penton Media, Inc.

Ed: Irving L. Blackman. **Description:** Several common business problems that family owned firms face are presented together with their solutions. These problems include giving the children stock bonus options while another discusses the tax burden when a father wants to transfer the business to his son.

36606 ■ *"Son of Sandman: Can Tom Gaglardi Really Outdo His Old Man?" in Canadian Business (Vol. 80, Winter 2007, No. 24, pp. 106)*
Ed: Calvin Leung. **Description:** Bob Gagliardi of Northland Properties started to learn about his family's business by working at a construction site at one of the high-rise buildings in downtown Vancouver. Gagliardi wants to expand their Moxie's restaurant chain and increase the market share of their Sandman hotel by 2018.

36607 ■ *"Soured Relationship Plays Out in Courts" in The Business Journal-Serving Greater Tampa Bay (Vol. 28, September 19, 2008, No. 39)*
Pub: American City Business Journals, Inc.
Contact: Whitney Shaw, President

Ed: Janet Leiser. **Description:** Heirs of developer Julian Hawthorne Lifset won a court battle to end a 50-year lease with Specialty Restaurants Corp. in Rocky Point. The decision opens the Tampa Bay prime waterfront property for new development.

36608 ■ *"Spouses Plan for the Return of the Company Doctor" in Philadelphia Business Journal (Vol. 33, May 2, 2014, No. 12, pp. 4)*
Pub: American City Business Journals

Released: May 2, 2014. **Description:** Nephrologist, Scott Bralow and primary care physician, Vick Bralow, started a company called Affordable Care Options in Philadelphia, Pennsylvania. The couple's company will provide physicians to the workplace to monitor the health of employees for a monthly fee.

36609 ■ *"Stockerts Open Repair Business" in Dickinson Press (July 13, 2010)*
Pub: The Dickinson Press
Contact: Jerry Obrigewitsch, Director
E-mail: jerryo@thedickinsonpress.com

Ed: Ashley Martin. **Description:** Ed Stockert is opening his new appliance repair firm in Dickinson, North Dakota with his wife Anna.

36610 ■ *"Swedes Swoop In To Save Time4 Media" in Advertising Age (Vol. 78, January 29, 2007, No. 5, pp. 4)*
Pub: Crain Communications Inc.
Contact: Rance Crain, President

Ed: Nat Ives. **Description:** Overview of Stockholm's Bonnier Group, a family-owned publisher that is looking to expand its U.S. presence; Bonnier recently acquired a number of Time Inc. magazines.

36611 ■ *"A Tale of Two Brothers" in Canadian Business (Vol. 80, March 26, 2007, No. 7, pp. 18)*
Description: The successful business strategies followed by Tyler Gompf and Kirby Gompf, owners of Tell Us About Us Inc., are presented.

36612 ■ *"Ted Stahl: Executive Chairman" in Inside Business (Vol. 13, September-October 2011, No. 5, pp. NC6)*
Pub: Great Lakes Publishing Co.

Ed: Miranda S. Miller. **Description:** Profile of Ted Stahl, who started working in his family's business when he was ten years old is presented. The firm makes dies for numbers and letters used on team uniforms. Another of the family firms manufactures stock and custom heat-printing products, equipment and supplies. It also educates customers on ways to decorate garments with heat printing products and offers graphics and software for customers to create their own artwork.

36613 ■ *"Teeling and Gallagher: A Textbook for Success" in Agency Sales Magazine (Vol. 39, September-October 2009, No. 9, pp. 20)*
Pub: Manufacturers' Agents National Association
Contact: Charles Cohon, President

Ed: Jack Foster. **Description:** Profile of Teeling & Gallagher, a manufacturing firm that was founded in 1946 as the D.G. Teeling Company and continued as a one-person agency until 1960 when Tom Gallagher joined the company. Tom Gallagher talks about how things have changed and his work with his son Bob in the agency.

36614 ■ *"Termite Trouble" in Arkansas Business (Vol. 28, March 28, 2011, No. 13, pp. 5)*
Pub: Arkansas Business Publishing Group

Description: Thomas Pest Control of Little Rock, Arkansas has had liens placed against it by the Internal Revenue Service. The owner's daughter took over the business after her father passed away and is trying to rectify the situation.

36615 ■ *"To Sell or Not To Sell" in Inc. (December 2007, pp. 80)*
Pub: Gruner and Jahr USA Publishing Co.
Contact: J. Russell Denson, President

Ed: Patrick J. Sauer. **Description:** Owner of a private equity discusses the challenges he faces when deciding to sell his family's business.

36616 ■ *"Toward a Theory of Stakeholder Salience in Family Firms" in Business Ethics Quarterly (Vol. 21, April 2011, No. 2, pp. 235)*
Pub: Society for Business Ethics
Contact: Dawn Elm, Executive Director

Ed: Ronald K. Mitchell, Bradley R. Agle, James J. Chrisman, Laura J. Spence. **Description:** The notion of stakeholder salience based on attributes (e.g. power, legitimacy, urgency) is applied in the family business setting.

36617 ■ *"Transportation Enterprise" in Advertising Age (Vol. 79, June 9, 2008, No. 23, pp. S10)*
Pub: Crain Communications Inc.
Contact: Rance Crain, President

Ed: Jean Halliday. **Description:** Overview of Enterprise rent-a-car's plan to become a more environmentally-friendly company. The family-owned business has spent $1 million a year to plant trees since 2006 and has added more fuel-efficient cars, hybrids and flex-fuel models.

36618 ■ *"Trouble With Transport" in Farmer's Weekly (March 28, 2008, No. 320)*
Description: Profile of Richard Crewe and his wife Jane who farm alongside a main trans-Canadian railway line but keep getting pushed back on their delivery of malt barley.

36619 ■ *"UC's Goering Center to Get New Director" in Business Courier (Vol. 24, February 14, 2008, No. 45, pp. 3)*
Pub: American City Business Journals, Inc.
Contact: Whitney Shaw, President

Ed: Dan Monk. **Description:** Kent Lutz, director of University of Cincinnati Goering (UC) Center for Family & Private Business is to leave the resource center in June 2008 after nine years of service. Changes in the UC-affiliated institute include the expansion of the board from three to seven members and developing new programs related to family businesses.

36620 ■ *"Ultimate Business of the Week: McDougals Sewing Center" in Houston Chronicle (December 2, 2010)*
Description: Profile of family owned, McDouglas Sewing Center located in Houston, Texas. The shop offers computerized sewing machines, supplies, classes and repairs.

36621 ■ *"Up, Up and Away" in Small Business Opportunities (November 2007)*
Ed: Stan Roberts. **Description:** Profile of Miniature Aircraft USA, a mail order business providing kits to build flying machines priced from $500 to $2,500.

36622 ■ *"Variations in R&D Investments of Family and Nonfamily Firms: Behavioral Agency and Myopic Loss Aversion Perspectives"* in *Academy of Management Journal (Vol. 55, August 1, 2012, No. 4, pp. 976)*
Pub: Academy of Management
Contact: Ming-Jer Chen, President
Ed: James J. Chrisman, Pankaj C. Patel. **Description:** The variability in the behavior of family firms is analyzed using the behavioral agency model and the myopic loss aversion framework. Results show that family firms tend to invest less in research and development than nonfamily businesses but the variability of their investments is influenced by family goals and economic goals of the firm.

36623 ■ *"We All Scream for Ice Cream"* in *Crain's Chicago Business (Vol. 31, April 28, 2008, No. 17, pp. 48)*
Pub: Crain Communications Inc.
Contact: Todd Johnson, Publisher
Ed: Phuong Ly. **Description:** Profile of Oberweis' ice cream shops which has expanded its business by delivering dairy products to grocery stores.

36624 ■ *"We Do: Copreneurs Simultaneously Build Happy Marriages and Thriving Enterprises"* in *Black Enterprise (Vol. 38, February 1, 2008)*
Pub: Earl G. Graves Publishing Co. Inc.
Contact: Earl G. Graves, Jr., President
Ed: Krissah Williams. **Description:** Of the 2.7 million businesses in the U.S. that are equally owned by male-female partnerships, about 79,000 are black-owned. One couple shares their experiences of working and growing their business together.

36625 ■ *"Wegmans Adding 1,600-Plus Jobs Here Over the Next Year"* in *Boston Business Journal (Vol. 34, February 14, 2014, No. 2, pp. 3)*
Pub: American City Business Journals, Inc.
Contact: Whitney Shaw, President
Released: February 14, 2014. **Description:** Wegmans, a family-owned grocery chain, is planning to add the most jobs of any firm in Massachusetts in 2014. The company will create more than 1,600 full- and part-time positions by opening three stores. Bill Congdon, Wegmans' New England division manager, reveals that the company is also planning to open a store in the city of Boston.

36626 ■ *"West Palm Beach Bed and Breakfast is a Labor of Love"* in *Palm Beach Post (April 7, 2012)*
Pub: McClatchy-Tribune Information Services
Released: April 7, 2012. **Description:** Profile of Cheryl and Kirk Grantham, husband and wife team who run a bed and breakfast in West Palm Beach, Florida. The couple discusses their move to the community and why they decided to open their inn. Their property offers five bed and breakfast guest suites along with another five suites in an Art Deco building. Cheryl talks about her love for entertaining along with the four diamond rating of their establishment.

36627 ■ *"When Family Businesses are Best: The Parallel Planning Process for Family Harmony and Business Success"*
Pub: Palgrave Macmillan
Contact: Lisa Dunn, Manager
E-mail: l.dunn@palgrave.com
Ed: Randel S. Carlock, John L. Ward. **Released:** October 2010. **Price:** £34, hardcover. **Description:** An exploration into effective planning and communication to help small businesses grow into multigeneration family enterprises. **Availability:** Print; Electronic publishing; E-book; PDF.

36628 ■ *"Wowing Her Customers"* in *Women In Business (Vol. 61, August-September 2009, No. 4, pp. 34)*
Pub: American Business Women's Association
Contact: Lorie Burch, President
Ed: Kathleen Leighton. **Description:** Gail Worth, together with her brother, bought her parents' Harley-Davidson motorcycle dealership in Grandview, Missouri. She eventually had the dealership to herself

when her brother broke out of the partnership. Gail says she is comfortable in a man's world kind of business and has expanded the business with a 10-acre site.

36629 ■ *"Wrigley's Juicy Feud"* in *Crain's Chicago Business (Vol. 31, May 5, 2008, No. 18, pp. 1)*
Pub: Crain Communications Inc.
Contact: Todd Johnson, Publisher
Ed: David Sterrett. **Description:** Discusses the sale of Wm. Wrigley Jr. Co. to Mars Inc. and Warren Buffett for $23 billion as well as the intra-family feuding which has existed for nearly a decade since William Wrigley Jr. took over as CEO of the company following his father's death.

36630 ■ *"Your Lawyer: An Owner's Manual, a Business Owner's Guide to Managing Your Lawyer"* in *Family Business Review (Vol. 19, No. 2, June 2006, pp. 171)*
Pub: Family Firm Institute
Contact: Judy L. Green, President
Ed: Jane Hilburt-Davis. **Description:** Profile of the guide for managing a lawyer for a family-owned small business.

36631 ■ *"Your Turn in the Spotlight"* in *Inc. (Volume 32, December 2010, No. 10, pp. 57)*
Pub: Inc. Magazine
Ed: John Brandon. **Description:** Examples of three video blogs created by entrepreneurs to promote their businesses and products are used to show successful strategies. Wine Library TV promotes a family's wine business; SHAMA.TV offers marketing tips and company news; and Will It Blend? promotes sales of a household blender.

TRADE PERIODICALS

36632 ■ *Estate Planners Alert*
Pub: Thomson RIA
Contact: Mark Schlageter, President
E-mail: mark.schlageter@thomsonreuters.com
URL(s): ria.thomson.com/. **Released:** Monthly. **Price:** $210. **Description:** Spotlights critical developments in estate and financial planning.

36633 ■ *Family Business Advisor*
Pub: Family Enterprise Publishers
URL(s): www.thefbcg.com/publications/newsletter.
Ed: Craig E. Aronoff, Ph.D., Editor. **Released:** Monthly; . **Price:** $195, U.S.; $210, Canada; $225, elsewhere. **Description:** Covers business management, family relations, and asset protection. Addresses succession planning, estate planning, conflict management, compensation, family meetings, strategic planning, and board composition. Recurring features include news of research.

VIDEOCASSETTES/ AUDIOCASSETTES

36634 ■ *The Agony and the Ecstasy—The Special Problems of Running a Closely-Held or Family Business*
RMI Media
1365 N. Winchester St.
Olathe, KS 66061-5880
Ph: (913)768-1696
Free: 800-745-5480
Fax: (800)755-6910
Co. E-mail: actmedia@act.org
URL: http://www.actmedia.com
Released: 1989. **Price:** $149. **Description:** About 90% of American businesses are family-owned. Find out their disadvantages and advantages and what makes them so special. **Availability:** VHS; 3/4 U.

CONSULTANTS

36635 ■ **Calmas Associates**
62 Fairway Rd.
Chestnut Hill, MA 02467
Ph: (617)277-9244

Fax: (617)277-2021
Co. E-mail: wcalmas@calmasassociates.com
URL: http://www.calmasassociates.com
Contact: Paul Mazonson, President
Scope: Offers sales productivity services, specializing in intra-corporate communications, employee relations and motivation. Offers unique coaching program for increasing sales force productivity. Also serves in resolving family conflicts. Industries served: all, but primarily insurance and stock brokerage in New England. Executive coach. **Founded:** 1984. **Publications:** "Overcoming People Problems"; "How to Combat High Sales Force Turnover," Boston Business Journal. **Seminars:** How to Communicate with Difficult People, Jan, 2009; Succession Issues for Family Owned Businesses; Role of Psychoanalysis in the Succession Process; The Sports Approach for Success in Sales.

36636 ■ **Dean Fowler Associates Inc.**
200 S Executive Dr., Ste. 101
Brookfield, WI 53005
Ph: (262)271-5979
Co. E-mail: dean@deanfowler.com
URL: http://www.deanfowler.com
Contact: Henry Landes, President
Scope: Offers management services in family dynamics in family owned businesses. Services include: management development and peer interaction, maintaining family harmony and business success, and resolving personal and interpersonal issues. Industries served: Family businesses, all industries. **Founded:** 1999. **Publications:** "Forums for Family Business," 2006; "The Family Forum," 2005; "The Bermuda Triangle," 2003; "Love, Power and Money: Family Business Between Generations," Glengrove Publishing, May, 2002.

36637 ■ **Family Business Institute Inc.**
904 Steffi Ct.
Lawrenceville, GA 30044-6933
Ph: (770)952-4085
URL: http://www.family-business-experts.com
Contact: Wayne Rivers, President
Scope: Assists families in business to achieve personal, family and organizational goals by meeting challenges that are unique to family-owned businesses. Provides coordinated and integrated assessments and solutions for family issues and needs; for company finance and for human resource and operational requirements. **Founded:** 1985. **Publications:** "Professional Intervention in the Family Owned Business"; "Building Consensus in a Family Business"; "Professionalizing Family Business Management"; "Recognizing generations - know them by their weekends"; "Succession planning tactics"; "Succession Planning Obstacles in Family Business"; "Succession: three ways to ease the transition"; "Pruning the family business tree"; "Responsibility diffusion - the most critical impediment to successfully growing any kind of business"; "Breaking Up is Hard to Do: Divorce in the Family Business".

36638 ■ **Frankel and Topche P.C.**
1700 Galloping Hill Rd.
Kenilworth, NJ 07033
Ph: (908)298-7700
Fax: (908)298-7701
Co. E-mail: info@frankelandtopche.com
URL: http://www.frankelandtopche.com
Contact: Lawrence N. Frankel, Owner
E-mail: lnfcpa@aol.com
Scope: Offers financial consulting for closely held businesses. Assists in mergers and acquisitions, tax planning, strategic business planning, family succession planning, accounting, auditing and obtaining financing. The firm serves small businesses in the service, retail, wholesale and manufacturing industries. Specializes in real estate, lumber and building materials and service businesses. **Founded:** 1990. **Seminars:** Annual Tax Seminar.

36639 ■ **Management Growth Institute (MGI)**
27 Chelmsford Rd.
Rochester, NY 14618
Ph: (585)461-1353

Fax: (585)461-5266
Co. E-mail: kbalbertini@managementgrowth.com
URL: http://www.managementgrowth.com
Contact: Kathleen Barry Albertini, President
E-mail: kbalbertini@managementgrowth.com
Scope: Offers assistance in the specification, design and implementation of management development programs. Clients include individuals, small businesses, national trade associations and government agencies. **Founded:** 1961. **Publications:** "Cost Reduction Is Your Company the Target," InFocus Magazine, Apr, 2010; "Fall-I hired this great person," The Canadian Mover, Dec, 2009; "Profit Strategies," Direction Magazine, Jul, 2009; "Customer Loyalty," InFocus Magazine, Jul, 2009; "Cash Management," The Portal Magazine, Jul, 2009; "What is Customer Loyalty," In FOCUS Magazine, Dec, 2008; "Strategies to Improve Profits," Aug, 2008; "A Question of Management," Moving World. **Seminars:** Profit Enhancement; Family-Owned Businesses; Strategic Planning; Survival and Growth in a Down Economy.

36640 ■ Profit Planning Consultants
617 Fields Dr.
Lafayette Hill, PA 19444-1511
Ph: (610)828-1999
Contact: Martin Feinberg, Owner
Scope: Strengthening the Family Firm; Increasing the value of the business and preserving the heritage; Provides a full range of management services to independently-owned companies; Services cover such areas as operations analysis, planning and budgeting, marketing and sales, organizational development, succession planning, debt and equity financing, employee training and motivation as well as acquisitions, mergers and sales of business. Client's sales range from over $1 million to $50 million; Client base covers a broad range of family-owned businesses in all industries; Teaches the entrepreneur survival and growth techniques that become his own and develop with him/her the company's succession plan. **Founded:** 1982. **Seminars:** How to Enter International Markets; Time Management; Leadership, Professional Selling Skills; Managing a Family Owned Business; Profit Opportunities for Your Business; Family vs. Business; Doubling Your Net Profit; Transferring Management in a Family Owned Business.

36641 ■ ReGENERATION Partners
3811 Turtle Creek Blvd., Ste. 300
Dallas, TX 75219
Ph: (214)559-3999
Fax: (214)559-4299
Co. E-mail: info@regeneration-partners.com
URL: http://www.regeneration-partners.com
Contact: James Olan Hutcheson, President
E-mail: jim@regeneration-partners.com
Scope: Specializes in business expertise growth strategies, competitive planning, crisis intervention, dispute resolution, interim management, bridge management, strategic planning, team selection, transitional management, employee assessment, business planning, management skills training, profit enhancement, family perspective, conflict management, communication barriers, family meetings, wealth preservation, succession planning, management mentoring, family values, family retreats. **Founded:** 1995. **Publications:** "When Siblings Share Leadership," May, 2007; "The End of a 1400-Year-Old Business," Apr, 2007; "Building a Family Business to Last," Mar, 2007; "Dealing with Death in a Family Business," Feb, 2007; "Best Practices for Family Business," Dec, 2006; "Resolving Family Business Conflicts," Nov, 2006; "Coping with Family-Business Ills," Oct, 2006; "Should You Join the Family Business," Sep, 2006; "A Transfer Tsunami for Family Biz," Jun, 2006; "When Kids Play the Guilt Card," Apr, 2006.

36642 ■ Schneider Consulting Group Inc.
2801 E 4th Ave.
Denver, CO 80206
Ph: (303)320-4413
Fax: (303)320-5795
Co. E-mail: info@schneiderconsultinggroup.com
URL: http://www.consultscg.com
Contact: Kim Schneider Malek, Founder
Scope: Assists family-owned and privately-held business transition to the next generation and/or to a more professionally managed company, turn around consulting for small and medium size companies. **Founded:** 1987. **Seminars:** Family Business Council; Impact of the Energy Renaissance.

36643 ■ Stier Associates
4 Dunellen
Cromwell, CT 06416-2702
Ph: (860)635-1590
Contact: Dr. Suzanne Stier, President
Scope: Offers personal development consulting. Services include: succession planning, executive coaching, strategic management, team building and board development. Consulting services for public companies include: process consulting, team building, executive coaching, diversity management, strategic management and religious institutions. **Founded:** 1981.

36644 ■ The Titens Consulting Group
12612 Cedar St.
Leawood, KS 66209-3148
Ph: (913)469-5279
Fax: (913)469-5192
Co. E-mail: sherman@redzeus.com
URL: http://www.redzeus.com
Contact: Sherman Titens, Owner
E-mail: sherman.titens@gmail.com
Scope: Provider of market positioning, strategic planning and continuing education design, standards, certification for trade associations, professional societies and professional service providers and family businesses. Industries served include banking, financial services, automotive, jewellery, health care, law, materials, joining, retail, environmental programs and distribution. **Founded:** 1993. **Publications:** "NFP"; "Applied Research at the Graduate Level," Parkway Press; "123 Secrets for Success in Your Family Business". **Seminars:** Making Family Business Work; Getting Started With Strategic Planning; Using the Internet as an Educational Tool.

36645 ■ Turnaround Inc.
3415 A St. NW
Gig Harbor, WA 98335
Ph: (253)857-6730
Fax: (253)857-6344
Co. E-mail: info@turnround-inc.com
URL: http://www.turnaround-inc.com
Contact: Miles Stover, President
E-mail: mstover@turnaround-inc.com
Scope: Provider of interim executive management assistance and management advisory to small, medium and family-owned businesses that are not meeting their goals. Services include acting as an interim executive or on-site manager. Extensive practices in arena of bankruptcy management. **Founded:** 1997. **Publications:** "How to Identify Problem and Promising Management"; "How to Tell if Your Company is a Bankruptcy Candidate"; "Signs that Your Company is in Trouble"; "The Turnaround Specialist: How to File a Petition Under 11 USC 11". **Seminars:** Competitive Intelligence Gathering.

START-UP INFORMATION

36646 ■ *"Beyond Bootstrapping" in Inc. (Vol. 36, September 2014, No. 7, pp. 64)*
Pub: Mansueto Ventures L.L.C.
Contact: John Koten, Chief Executive Officer
Released: September 2014. **Description:** Dave Lerner, serial entrepreneur, angel investor, B-school professor, and author, explains the challenges entrepreneurs face when self-funding their startup business.

36647 ■ *Entrepreneurship and the Financial Community: Starting Up and Growing New Businesses*
Pub: Edward Elgar Publishing Inc.
Contact: Richard Henning, Vice President
E-mail: kwight@e-elgar.com
Price: $114.30, hardback; $41.60, paperback. **Description:** Understanding the role of private equity providers in the development and growth processes of small business. **Availability:** Print.

36648 ■ *How to Get the Financing for Your New Small Business: Innovative Solutions from the Experts Who Do It Every Day*
Pub: Atlantic Publishing Co.
Contact: Amanda Miller, Manager
E-mail: amiller@atlantic-pub.com
Ed: Sharon L. Fullen. **Released:** May 2006. **Price:** $39.95, Includes companion CD-Rom. **Description:** Ready capital is essential for starting and expanding a small business. Topics include traditional financing methods, financial statements, and a good business plan. **Availability:** Print.

36649 ■ *How to Start a Bankruptcy Forms Processing Service*
Ed: Victoria Ring. **Released:** September 2004. **Price:** , $39.00. **Description:** Due to the increase in bankruptcy filings, attorneys are outsourcing related jobs in order to reduce overhead.

36650 ■ *"Office For One: The Sole Proprietor's Survival Guide"*
Pub: CreateSpace
Contact: Daren Giles, President
Released: October 7, 2014. **Price:** $12.95 paperback. **Description:** Over thirty experts offer advice to any entrepreneur wishing to start a business by themselves. Tips and advice on tuning out negativity, maintaining balance and boundaries, handling legal issues and financial challenges, finding and keeping customers, marketing on a small budge, networking, cracking the media code, growing a sustainable vision, and addressing burnouts.

36651 ■ *"The Right Way to Start an Online Business: The Untold Truths of What it Takes AFTER Your First Sale to Succeed"*
Pub: Amazon Digital Services
Released: October 4, 2014. **Price:** $9.99 Kindle. **Description:** Seven of the top methods for starting an online business are listed. Instruction is given to sell products or services for immediate payment to begin entrepreneurship on the Web. Financial invest-

ment in the online startup is covered. Web design and optimization of Search Engines, worksheets, sales page outlines, email templates, sales contracts and more are included.

36652 ■ *Working for Yourself: An Entrepreneur's Guide to the Basics*
Pub: Kogan Page, Limited
Contact: Philip Kogan, Chairman of the Board
Ed: Jonathan Reuvid. **Released:** June 03, 2009. **Price:** £12.99. **Description:** Guide for starting a new business venture, focusing on raising financing, legal and tax issues, marketing, information technology, and site location. **Availability:** Print.

EDUCATIONAL PROGRAMS

36653 ■ **Advanced Auditing for In-Charge Auditors (Onsite)**
Seminar Information Service Inc.
20 Executive Park, Ste. 120
Irvine, CA 92614
Ph: (949)261-9104
Free: 877-SEM-INFO
Fax: (949)261-1963
Co. E-mail: info@seminarinformation.com
URL: http://www.seminarinformation.com
Price: $2,050. **Description:** Learn all of the elements involved in traditional and operational auditing from the unique perspective of the in-charge position, while reviewing concepts such as audit program flexibility, risk assessment, priority setting during fieldwork, and effective oral and written communications of audit findings. **Audience:** Financial, operational, IT and external auditors . **Dates and Locations:** Chicago, IL; Las Vegas, NV; Atlanta, GA; and New York, NY.

36654 ■ **Advanced Collection Strategies (Onsite)**
Seminar Information Service Inc.
20 Executive Park, Ste. 120
Irvine, CA 92614
Ph: (949)261-9104
Free: 877-SEM-INFO
Fax: (949)261-1963
Co. E-mail: info@seminarinformation.com
URL: http://www.seminarinformation.com
URL(s): www.seminarinformation.com/details. cfm?qc=qqbvad. **Price:** $369. **Description:** Learn the secrets to getting what's owed while complying with strict debtor protection laws, including strategies for defending against collection harassment claims should they arise. **Audience:** Attorneys, in-house counsel, creditors, third-party debt collectors and debt buyers.

36655 ■ **Advanced Cost Accounting (Onsite)**
Description: Learn to incorporate Activity-Based Costing with advanced traditional costing methodologies determining true product cost information.

36656 ■ **AMA's Finance Workshop for Nonfinancial Executives (Onsite)**
American Management Association (AMA)
1601 Broadway
New York, NY 10019-7420

Ph: (212)586-8100
Free: 877-566-9441
Fax: (212)903-8168
Co. E-mail: customerservice@amanet.org
URL: http://www.amanet.org
Contact: Edward T. Reilly, President
URL(s): www.amanet.org/training/seminars/Finance-Workshop-for-Nonfinancial-Executives.aspx. **Price:** $2,645, Non-members; $2,395, Members AMA; $2,051, Members GSA. **Description:** Comprehensive four-day seminar covering all aspects of corporate finance. **Audience:** Experienced managers, general managers, directors, vice presidents and top executives in sales.

36657 ■ **Collections Law (Onsite)**
Fred Pryor Seminars & CareerTrack
5700 Broadmoor St., Ste. 300
Mission, KS 66202
Ph: (800)780-8476
Free: 800-780-8476
Fax: (913)967-8849
Co. E-mail: customerservice@pryor.com
URL: http://www.pryor.com
Contact: Phil Love, Chief Executive Officer
Price: $139, for groups of 5 or more. **Description:** Ensure your organization is legally compliant, including strategies and techniques to gain quicker results in collecting money. **Audience:** Industry professionals. **Dates and Locations:** Cities throughout the United States.

36658 ■ **Corporate Cash Management (onsite)**
Seminar Information Service Inc.
20 Executive Park, Ste. 120
Irvine, CA 92614
Ph: (949)261-9104
Free: 877-SEM-INFO
Fax: (949)261-1963
Co. E-mail: info@seminarinformation.com
URL: http://www.seminarinformation.com
URL(s): www.seminarinformation.com/details. cfm?qc=qqagsa. **Price:** $1,795, Members; $1,995, Non-members. **Description:** Introductory course that covers how money moves, how to accelerate cash receipts, how to select the right cash management bank, and how to make better use of excess funds through short-term investments. **Audience:** Professionals.

36659 ■ **Creative Ways to Cut and Control Costs (Onsite)**
Fred Pryor Seminars & CareerTrack
5700 Broadmoor St., Ste. 300
Mission, KS 66202
Ph: (800)780-8476
Free: 800-780-8476
Fax: (913)967-8849
Co. E-mail: customerservice@pryor.com
URL: http://www.pryor.com
Contact: Phil Love, Chief Executive Officer
URL(s): www.pryor.com/mkt_info/seminars/desc/CZ. asp. **Price:** $149. **Description:** Learn how to control business expenses to create an organization that is

competitive, profitable, and growth focused. **Audience:** Professionals.

36660 ■ The Essentials of Cash Flow Forecasting (Onsite)

Fred Pryor Seminars & CareerTrack
5700 Broadmoor St., Ste. 300
Mission, KS 66202
Ph: (800)780-8476
Free: 800-780-8476
Fax: (913)967-8849
Co. E-mail: customerservice@pryor.com
URL: http://www.pryor.com
Contact: Phil Love, Chief Executive Officer
URL(s): www.pryor.com/mkt_info/seminars/desc/KF.
asp. **Price:** $249. **Description:** Learn to make better budget decisions through proven strategies and techniques. **Audience:** Business professionals.

36661 ■ Export/Import Procedures and Documentation (Onsite)

American Management Association (AMA)
1601 Broadway
New York, NY 10019-7420
Ph: (212)586-8100
Free: 877-566-9441
Fax: (212)903-8168
Co. E-mail: customerservice@amanet.org
URL: http://www.amanet.org
Contact: Edward T. Reilly, President
URL(s): www.amaseminars.org/training/seminars/
Import-Export-Procedures-and-Documentation.aspx.
Price: $2,195.00 for non-members; $1,995.00 for AMA members; and $1,708.00 for General Services Administration (GSA) members. **Description:** Covers export and import guidelines and regulations, business documentation practices, using foreign trade zones, and financial aspects of importing and exporting. **Audience:** Import and export managers, traffic managers, shipping department personnels, international marketing mangers, customer service staffs, credit managers, controllers, purchasing managers and procurement directors. **Dates and Locations:** Chicago, IL; and New York, NY. **Telecommunication Services:** customerservice@amanet.org.

36662 ■ Financial & Accounting Concepts, Statements & Terminology: 2 Day (Onsite)

Seminar Information Service Inc.
20 Executive Park, Ste. 120
Irvine, CA 92614
Ph: (949)261-9104
Free: 877-SEM-INFO
Fax: (949)261-1963
Co. E-mail: info@seminarinformation.com
URL: http://www.seminarinformation.com
URL(s): www.seminarinformation.com/details.
cfm?qc=qqbvtb. **Price:** $399. **Description:** Financial and accounting training in plain English. **Audience:** Nonfinancial managers.

36663 ■ Financial Modeling and Forecasting

Canadian Management Centre (CMC)
150 York St., 5th Fl.
Toronto, ON, Canada M5H 3S5
Free: 877-262-2519
Fax: (416)214-6047
Co. E-mail: cmcinfo@cmcoutperform.com
URL: http://cmcoutperform.com
Contact: John Wright, President
URL(s): cmcoutperform.com/ama-advanced-financial-modeling-forecasting-online. **Price:** $2,295, Members; $2,545, Non-members. **Description:** This highly interactive course helps you build more powerful and accurate forecasting models that fast-track decision making and improve end results. **Audience:** Analysts, executive-level managers and financial professionals.

36664 ■ Financial Statement Analysis (Onsite)

Seminar Information Service Inc.
20 Executive Park, Ste. 120
Irvine, CA 92614
Ph: (949)261-9104
Free: 877-SEM-INFO

Fax: (949)261-1963
Co. E-mail: info@seminarinformation.com
URL: http://www.seminarinformation.com
Price: $199.00. **Description:** Enhance your ability to read, analyze and use financial statements to manage, drive and stay on top of your company's growth, including how to understand the specialized language of finance and quickly scan a financial report and pick out the numbers that matter and detect variance while there's time to take corrective action. **Dates and Locations:** Cities throughout the United States.

36665 ■ How to Implement Effective Internal Controls (Onsite)

Fred Pryor Seminars & CareerTrack
5700 Broadmoor St., Ste. 300
Mission, KS 66202
Ph: (800)780-8476
Free: 800-780-8476
Fax: (913)967-8849
Co. E-mail: customerservice@pryor.com
URL: http://www.pryor.com
Contact: Phil Love, Chief Executive Officer
URL(s): www.pryor.com/mkt_info/seminars/desc/ci.
asp. **Price:** $199. **Description:** Learn to protect, maintain, and control your financial structure while streamlining your business. **Audience:** Financial professionals, business leaders, managers, and supervisors.

36666 ■ How to Manage & Organize Accounts Payable (Onsite)

Fred Pryor Seminars & CareerTrack
5700 Broadmoor St., Ste. 300
Mission, KS 66202
Ph: (800)780-8476
Free: 800-780-8476
Fax: (913)967-8849
Co. E-mail: customerservice@pryor.com
URL: http://www.pryor.com
Contact: Phil Love, Chief Executive Officer
URL(s): www.pryor.com/mkt_info/seminars/desc/ap.
asp. **Price:** $199. **Description:** Learn how to organize your files, records, and workspace for maximum organization and flow. **Audience:** Financial management professionals.

36667 ■ How to Read and Understand Financial Statements (Onsite)

Fred Pryor Seminars & CareerTrack
5700 Broadmoor St., Ste. 300
Mission, KS 66202
Ph: (800)780-8476
Free: 800-780-8476
Fax: (913)967-8849
Co. E-mail: customerservice@pryor.com
URL: http://www.pryor.com
Contact: Phil Love, Chief Executive Officer
URL(s): www.pryor.com/site/webinar-audio/how-to-read-and-understand-financial-statements. **Price:** $199. **Description:** Learn how to read financial statements, interpret their data, and put that information to positive use. **Audience:** Small business owners, mid-to upper-level managers, department heads, and non-financial professionals .

36668 ■ The Nonfinancial Manager's Guide to Understanding Financial Statements (Onsite)

Padgett-Thompson Seminars
Rockhurst University CEC
14502 W 105th St.
Lenexa, KS 66215
Free: 800-349-1935
URL: http://www.findaseminar.com/tpd/Padgett-Thompson-Seminars.asp
URL(s): www.findaseminar.com/event1.asp?eventID=3403. **Description:** Comprehensive, fast-paced, one-day seminars that covers all the essentials of understanding financial statements. **Audience:** Managers and professionals.

36669 ■ Principles of Cost and Finance for Engineers (Onsite)

Description: Learn to make and justify financial decisions using sound economic principles, including how to use current economic strategies to reduce costs and improve productivity, estimate capital and

manufacturing or service costs, identify the relationship between direct and marginal costs in the decision making process, and execute strategies for resource allocation and cost-control measures.

36670 ■ Successful Inventory Management (Onsite)

Fred Pryor Seminars & CareerTrack
5700 Broadmoor St., Ste. 300
Mission, KS 66202
Ph: (800)780-8476
Free: 800-780-8476
Fax: (913)967-8849
Co. E-mail: customerservice@pryor.com
URL: http://www.pryor.com
Contact: Phil Love, Chief Executive Officer
URL(s): www.pryor.com/mkt_info/seminars/desc/iv.
asp. **Price:** $199. **Description:** Learn proven cost saving methods that improve inventory and cycle count accuracy. **Audience:** Professionals.

REFERENCE WORKS

36671 ■ "3 Reasons To Invest In Energy" in Black Enterprise (Vol. 45, July-August 2014, No. 1, pp. 26)

Pub: Earl G. Graves Publishing Co. Inc.
Contact: Earl G. Graves, Jr., President
Released: July-August 2014. **Description:** According to experts, energy is currently the most valuable market segment. The energy sector is valued at $7 trillion worldwide and generates more revenues than any other industry. Projected investment information is provided.

36672 ■ "4 Things You Need To Know About Credit Scores: What Millennials Don't Know Can Hurt Their Finances" in Black Enterprise (Vol. 45, July-August 2014, No. 1, pp. 64)

Pub: Earl G. Graves Publishing Co. Inc.
Contact: Earl G. Graves, Jr., President
Released: July-August 2014. **Description:** The Consumer Federation of America and VantageScore Solutions LLC report their fourth annual survey on consumers' understanding of credit scores. Six types of businesses using credit scores, include electric company, cell phone company, home insurer, landlord, mortgage lender, and credit card issuer. Age, payment history, debt, years of having credit, last credit application date, and type of credit all factor into scores.

36673 ■ "13D Filings" in Barron's (Vol. 88, March 24, 2008, No. 12, pp. M13)

Pub: Dow Jones & Co., Inc.
Contact: Clare Hart, President
Description: HealthCor Management called as problematic the plan of Magellan Health Services to use its high cash balances for acquisitions. Carlson Capital discussed with Energy Partners possible changes in the latter's board. Investor Carl Icahn suggested that Enzon Pharmaceuticals consider selling itself or divest some of its assets.

36674 ■ "13D Filings" in Barron's (Vol. 88, March 17, 2008, No. 11, pp. M11)

Pub: Dow Jones & Co., Inc.
Contact: Clare Hart, President
Description: Nanes Delorme wants Vaalco Energy to keep an investment bank to start an open-bid process to sell the company. West Creek Capital plans to nominate two directors at the 2008 annual meeting of the Capital Senior Living just as ValueVest Management wants to nominate the same number of people at Ampex's annual meeting.

36675 ■ "13D Filings" in Barron's (Vol. 88, March 10, 2008, No. 10, pp. M11)

Pub: Dow Jones & Co., Inc.
Contact: Clare Hart, President
Description: Barington Capital and Clinton Group sent a letter to Dillard's demanding a list of the company's stockholders. Elliott Associates announced that it is prepared to take over Packeteer for $5.50 a share. Strongbow capital suggested a change in leadership in Duckwall-ALCO Stores.

36676 ■ *"13D Filings" in Barron's (Vol. 89, July 13, 2009, No. 28, pp. M9)*
Pub: Dow Jones & Co., Inc.
Contact: Clare Hart, President
Description: Bulldog Investors wants Hicks Acquisition Co. to liquidate and return money to shareholders and they believe that the acquisition of Graham Packaging by Hicks will not be completed in a timely manner. Discovery Group raised their holdings to 5.2 percent of Nobel Learning Communities.

36677 ■ *"13D Filings" in Barron's (Vol. 89, July 27, 2009, No. 30, pp. M14)*
Pub: Dow Jones & Co., Inc.
Contact: Clare Hart, President
Description: Duquesne Capital Management is opposed to Alpha Natural Resources' proposed merger with Foundation Coal Holdings since it is against the long-term interest of shareholders. Lime Rock Partners increased their holdings of Tesco to 5,234,516 shares while Nova A/S increased their holdings of BioMimetic Therapeutics to 3,729,065 shares.

36678 ■ *"13D Filings: Investors Report to the SEC" in Barron's (Vol. 88, March 31, 2008, No. 13, pp. M10)*
Description: Obrem Capital Management wants Micrel to rescind Micrel's shareholder-rights plan and to boost its board to six members from five. Patricia L. Childress plans to nominate herself to the board of Sierra Bancorp, and Luther King Capital Management may consider a competing acquisition proposal for Industrial Distribution Group.

36679 ■ *"A 16-Year Housing Slump? It Could Happen" in Barron's (Vol. 88, March 17, 2008, No. 11, pp. 27)*
Pub: Dow Jones & Co., Inc.
Contact: Clare Hart, President
Ed: Gene Epstein. **Description:** Housing remains a good protection against inflation but over very long periods. Inflation-adjusted stock prices did even better but have greater volatility. Commodities, on the other hand, underperformed both housing and stocks as inflation hedges. House prices tend to rise faster than the consumer price index is because land is inherently limited.

36680 ■ *"18 Percent of Banks Based Here at Risk, Study Says" in Philadelphia Business Journal (Vol. 31, February 17, 2012, No. 1, pp. 1)*
Description: Around 18 percent of Philadelphia-based banks may close or fail in the next two years, the Invictus Consulting Group has reported. Correction action to raise capital funds or mergers are seen to prevent bank closures.

36681 ■ *"The 100 Most Bullish Stocks" in Canadian Business (Vol. 81, Summer 2008, No. 9, pp. 81)*
Ed: Megan Harman; Lauren McKeon. **Description:** 100 of the most bullish stocks are taken from the list of the 500 best-performing stocks. The idea is to narrow the list help investors in their investment decisions since it is difficult to choose from a large list. Analysts rate the companies with 5 being the most bullish and 1 the least. Other details of the roster are presented.

36682 ■ *"401(k) Keys to Stable Value" in Barron's (Vol. 88, March 10, 2008, No. 10, pp. 40)*
Pub: Dow Jones & Co., Inc.
Contact: Clare Hart, President
Ed: Tom Sullivan. **Description:** Stable-value funds offer investors stability in a period of volatility in financial markets, attracting $888 million in funds. The Securities and Exchange Commission approved the launch of actively managed exchange-traded funds.

36683 ■ *"529.com Wins Outstanding Achievement in Web Development" in Investment Weekly (November 14, 2009, pp. 152)*
Pub: Investment Weekly News
Description: Web Marketing Association's 2009 WebAward for Financial Services Standard of Excellence and Investment Standard of Excellence was won by 529.com, the website from Upromise Investments, Inc., the leading administrator of 529 college savings plans.

36684 ■ *"2010 Book of Lists" in Tampa Bay Business Journal (Vol. 30, December 22, 2009, No. 53, pp. 1)*
Description: Rankings of companies and organizations within the human resources, banking and finance, business services, healthcare, real estate, technology, hospitality and travel, and education industries in the Greater Tampa Bay area are presented. Rankings are based on sales, business size, and more.

36685 ■ *Access to Finance*
Ed: Barr. **Released:** December 2006. **Price:** $39.95. **Description:** Challenges to help make financial systems more inclusive to promote successful venture in new markets while utilizing new technologies and government policies to expand financial access to smaller companies.

36686 ■ *The Accidental Entrepreneur: The 50 Things I Wish Someone Had Told Me About Starting a Business*
Pub: AMACOM
Contact: Edward T. Reilly, Manager
Ed: Susan Urquhart-Brown. **Released:** May 2008. **Price:** $17.95, Paper or Softback. **Description:** Advice is offered to any would-be entrepreneur, including eight questions to ask before launching a new business, ten traits of a successful entrepreneur, how to obtain licenses and selling permits, best way to create a business plan, ten ways to get referrals, six secrets of marketing, investment and financial information, ways to avoid burnout, and the seven biggest pitfalls to avoid. **Availability:** Print.

36687 ■ *Accounting and Finance for Your Small Business*
Pub: John Wiley & Sons Inc.
Contact: Stephen M. Smith, President
Ed: Steven M. Bragg, Edwin James Burton. **Released:** 2nd Edition. **Price:** $71.95, hardcover; $57.99. **Description:** Financial procedures and techniques for establishing and maintaining a profitable small company are outlined. **Availability:** PrintEbook.

36688 ■ *"Accrual vs. Cash Accounting, Explained" in Business Owner (Vol. 35, July-August 2011, No. 4, pp. 13)*
Pub: DL Perkins Company
Description: Cash method versus accrual accounting methods are examined, using hypothetical situations.

36689 ■ *"After Price Cuts, Competition GPS Makers Lose Direction" in Brandweek (Vol. 49, April 21, 2008, No. 16, pp. 16)*
Pub: Nielsen Business Media Inc.
Contact: Howard Appelbaum, President
Ed: Steve Miller. **Description:** Garmin and TomTom, two of the leaders in portable navigation devices, have seen lowering revenues due to dramatic price cuts and unexpected competition from the broadening availability of personal navigation on mobile phones. TomTom has trimmed its sales outlook for its first quarter while Garmin's stock dropped 40 percent since February.

36690 ■ *"Ag Firms Harvest Revenue Growth" in The Business Journal-Serving Metropolitan Kansas City (Vol. 26, July 18, 2008, No. 45, pp. 1)*
Ed: Steve Vockrodt. **Description:** Five of the biggest agricultural companies in the Kansas City area, except one, reported multibillion-dollar revenue increases in 2007. The companies, which include Lansing Trade Group, posted a combined $9.5 billion revenue growth. The factors that affected the revenue increase in the area's agricultural companies, such as prices and high demand, are also examined.

36691 ■ *"AIG Fixed; Is Michigan Next?" in Crain's Detroit Business (Vol. 24, September 22, 2008, No. 38, pp. 1)*
Pub: Crain Communications Inc.
Contact: Rance E. Crain, President
Ed: Jay Greene. **Description:** Michigan's economic future is examined as is the mortgage buyout plan and American International Group Inc.'s takeover by the U.S. government.

36692 ■ *"All Eyes On Iris" in Canadian Business (Vol. 81, July 22, 2008, No. 12-13, pp. 20)*
Ed: Jack Mintz. **Description:** Provincial governments in Canada are believed to be awaiting Alberta Finance Minister Iris Evans' financial and investment policies as well as Evans' development of a new saving strategy. Alberta is the only Canadian province that is in position to invest in sovereign wealth funds after it eliminated its debt in 2005.

36693 ■ *All the Money in the World: How the Forbes 400 Make - and Spend - Their Fortunes*
Ed: Peter W. Bernstein; Annalyn Swan. **Released:** September 2007. **Description:** A fascinating and historical breakdown of the 400 richest Americans according to Forbes magazine. The book examines how the list's members actually make and spend their money. Illustrating the text with charts and informational sidebars, readers are given the opportunity to look at both production and consumption and insights in social and historical context.

36694 ■ *American Bar Association Legal Guide for Small Business: Everything You Need to Know About Small Business*
Ed: American Bar Association. **Released:** June 10, 2010. **Description:** The American Bar Association provides insight into financial, health and family issues affecting small business, including start up issues, employment laws, financing a business, and selling a business.

36695 ■ *"American Water's Ed Vallejo Chosen for 2012 Minority Business Leader Awards" in Manufacturing Close-Up (July 30, 2012)*
Description: Ed Vallejo, vice presient of investor relations at American Water, has been awarded the 2012 Minority Business Leader Award from the Philadelphia Business Journal. Vallejo is responsible for developing investor relations strategies for the publicly traded water and wastewater utility firm. He also serves as the company's liaison with financial analyst and investor communities.

36696 ■ *"The Annual Entitlement Lecture Medicare Elephantiasis" in Barron's (March 31, 2008)*
Pub: Dow Jones & Co., Inc.
Contact: Clare Hart, President
Ed: Thomas G. Donlan. **Description:** Expenditures on Medicare hospital insurance and the revenues available to pay for it have led to a gap of capital valued at $38.6 trillion. Slashing the benefits or raising taxes will not solve the gap which exists unless the government saves the money and invests it in private markets.

36697 ■ *"Antwerpen Takes on Chrysler Financial Over Foreclosure Sales" in Baltimore Business Journal (Vol. 28, July 30, 2010, No. 12, pp. 1)*
Pub: Baltimore Business Journal
Ed: Gary Haber. **Description:** Antwerpen Motorcars Ltd. aims to fight the scheduled foreclosure sale of real estate it leases in Baltimore County, including the showroom for its Hyundai dealership on Baltimore National Pike in Catonsville, Maryland. The company is planning to file papers in court to stop the scheduled August 11, 2010 auction sought by Chrysler Financial Services Americas LLC.

36698 ■ *Are the Rich Necessary? Great Economic Arguments and How They Reflect Our Personal Values*
Pub: Axios Press
Contact: Stephanie Bosserman, President
Ed: Hunter Lewis. **Released:** 2007. **Price:** $10.80, paperback. **Description:** Investment advisor argues whether today's economic system promotes greed. Each chapter of the book poses a question and then he answers. **Availability:** Print.

36699 ■ *"Are You Ready for Dow 20,000?"* in *Barron's* (Vol. 88, March 24, 2008, No. 12, pp. 26)
Pub: Dow Jones & Co., Inc.
Contact: Clare Hart, President
Ed: Jonathan R. Laing. **Description:** Stock strategist James Finucane forecasts that the Dow Jones Industrial Average will rise from its 12,361 level to as high as 20,000 from 2008 to 2009. He believes that stock liquidation and a buildup of cash provide the perfect conditions for a huge rally.

36700 ■ *"Are You Ready To Do It Yourself? Discipline and Self-Study Can Help You Profit From Online Trading"* in *Black Enterprise* (February 1, 2008)
Pub: Earl G. Graves Publishing Co. Inc.
Contact: Earl G. Graves, Jr., President
Ed: Steve Garmhausen. **Description:** Steps to help individuals invest in stocks online is given by an expert broker. Discount brokerage houses can save money for online investors.

36701 ■ *"The Art of Disclosure: Function Over Forms?"* in *Barron's* (Vol. 88, June 30, 2008, No. 26, pp. 17)
Pub: Dow Jones & Co., Inc.
Contact: Clare Hart, President
Ed: Eric Savitz. **Description:** Securities and Exchange Commission (SEC) chairman Christopher Cox wants the SEC to consider an overhaul of the forms used to meet the agency's disclosure requirements. Cox also said that the U.S. Generally Accepted Accounting Standards has too many rules with exceptions and alternative interpretations.

36702 ■ *The Ascent of Money: A Financial History of the World*
Pub: Dutton Children's Books
Contact: Lauri Hornik, President
Ed: Niall Ferguson. **Released:** 2009. **Price:** $29.95, Hardcover. **Description:** How financial considerations prompted the Crusades and other surprising explanations of famous events are uncovered.

36703 ■ *"Asia Breathes a Sigh of Relief"* in *Business Week* (September 22, 2008, No. 4100, pp. 32)
Ed: Bruce Einhorn; Theo Francis; Chi-Chu Tschang; Moon Ihlwan; Hiroko Tashiro. **Description:** Foreign bankers, such as those in Asia, that had been investing heavily in the United States began to worry as the housing crisis deepened and the impact on Freddie Mac and Fannie Mae became increasingly clear. Due to the government bailout, however, central banks will most likely continue to buy American debt.

36704 ■ *"ATS Secures Investment From Goldman Sachs"* in *The Business Journal - Serving Phoenix and the Valley of the Sun* (Vol. 29, September 28, 2008, No. 4, pp. 1)
Pub: American City Business Journals, Inc.
Contact: Whitney Shaw, President
Ed: Patrick O'Grady. **Description:** Goldman Sachs made an investment to American Traffic Solutions Inc. (ATS) which will allow it to gain two seats on the board of the red-light and speed cameras maker. The investment will help ATS maintain its rapid growth which is at 83 percent over the past 18 months leading up to September 2008.

36705 ■ *"Attend To Your Corporate Housekeeping"* in *Women Entrepreneur* (December 4, 2008)
Ed: Nina Kaufman. **Description:** Business owners can lose all the benefits and privileges of the corporate form if they do not follow proper corporate formalities such as holding an annual meeting, electing officers and directors and adopting or passing corporate resolutions. Creditors are able to take from one's personal assets if such formalities have not been followed.

36706 ■ *"Au Revoir Or Goodbye?"* in *Barron's* (Vol. 88, July 14, 2008, No. 28, pp. 5)
Pub: Dow Jones & Co., Inc.
Contact: Alan Abelson. **Description:** Former Senator Phil Gramm's opinion that the U.S. is a 'nation of whiners' as they moan about recession is another ex-ample of the disconnection between Washington and Wall Street on one hand and the real world on the other. It would be a catastrophe for most of the world if Fannie Mae and Freddie Mac were to go under and take their trillions of mortgage debt with them.

36707 ■ *"Auction-Rate Cash Frees Up"* in *The Business Journal-Portland* (Vol. 25, August 15, 2008, No. 23, pp. 1)
Pub: American City Business Journals, Inc.
Contact: Whitney Shaw, President
Ed: Aliza Earnshaw. **Description:** FEI Co. and Radi-Sys Corp. have received notices that UBS AG will buy back the auction-rate securities that were sold to them in around two years from 2008. FEI had $110.1 million invested in auction-rate securities while Radi-Sys holds $62.8 million of these securities.

36708 ■ *"Auto Supplier Stock Battered In Wake Of Wall Street Woes"* in *Crain's Detroit Business* (Vol. 24, September 29, 2008, No. 39, pp. 4)
Pub: Crain Communications Inc.
Contact: Rance E. Crain, President
Ed: Ryan Beene. **Description:** Due to the volatility of the stock market and public perception of the $700 billion banking bailout, auto suppliers are now facing a dramatic drop in their shares. Statistical data included.

36709 ■ *"BABs in Bond Land"* in *Barron's* (Vol. 89, July 6, 2009, No. 27, pp. 14)
Pub: Dow Jones & Co., Inc.
Contact: Clare Hart, President
Ed: Jim McTague. **Description:** American Recovery and Reinvestment Act has created taxable Build America Bonds (BAB) to finance new construction projects. The issuance of the two varieties of taxable BABs is expected to benefit the municipal bond market.

36710 ■ *"Baby's Room Franchisee Files Bankruptcy"* in *Crain's Detroit Business* (Vol. 25, June 22, 2009, No. 25, pp. 15)
Pub: Crain Communications Inc. - Detroit
Contact: Keith Crain, Chairman
Ed: Gabe Nelson. **Description:** Emery L, a franchisee of USA Baby Inc. and ran the franchised Baby's Room Nursery Furniture stores in the area has filed for bankruptcy. Details of the bankruptcy are included.

36711 ■ *"Back In the Black, Maryland Zoo Upgrades"* in *Baltimore Business Journal* (Vol. 32, July 25, 2014, No. 12, pp. 4)
Pub: American City Business Journals, Inc.
Contact: Whitney Shaw, President
Released: July 25, 2014. **Description:** Maryland Zoo has stabilized its finances after several years of budgetary problems that nearly caused the zoo to lose its accreditation from the Association of Zoos and Aquariums. President Donald P. Hutchinson reveals the zoo has increased the number of private and corporate donors and is carrying out several upgrades, including new penguin and flamingo exhibits.

36712 ■ *"Back in the Race. New Fund Manager Has Whipped Sentinel International Equity Back into Shape"* in *Barron's* (Vol. 88, March 17, 2008, No. 11, pp. 43)
Pub: Dow Jones & Co., Inc.
Contact: Clare Hart, President
Ed: Leslie P. Norton. **Description:** Katherine Schapiro was able to get Sentinel International Equity's Morningstar classification to blended fund from a value fund rating after joining Sentinel from her former jobs at Strong Overseas Fund. Schapiro aims to benefit from the global rebalancing as the U.S.'s share of the world economy shrinks.

36713 ■ *"Back Talk with Chris Gardner"* in *Black Enterprise* (Vol. 37, January 2007, No. 6, pp. 112)
Ed: Kenneth Meeks. **Description:** Profile of with Chris Gardner and his Chicago company, Gardner Rich L.L.C., a multimillion-dollar investment firm. During an interview, Gardner discusses his rise from homelessness. His story became a book, The Pursuit of Happyness and was recently released as a film starring Will Smith.

36714 ■ *"Back-Tested ETFs Draw Assets, Flub Returns"* in *(Vol. 92, July 23, 2012, No. 30, pp. 26)*
Pub: Dow Jones & Co., Inc.
Contact: Clare Hart, President
Ed: Janet Paskin. **Released:** July 23, 2012. **Description:** New exchange-traded funds are attracting investors by using 'back-tested' data offered by the indexes they track. Investors are substituting real performance for these hypothetical returns, which measure past performance of indexes had they been in existence.

36715 ■ *"Back on Track-Or Off the Rails?"* in *Business Week* (September 22, 2008, No. 4100, pp. 22)
Pub: Bloomberg L.P.
Contact: Matthew Winkler, Manager
Ed: Peter Coy, Tara Kalwarski. **Description:** Discusses the possible scenarios the American economy may undergo due to the takeover of Fannie Mae and Freddie Mac. Statistical data included.

36716 ■ *"Bad-Loan Bug Bites Mid-Tier Banks"* in *Crain's Chicago Business* (May 5, 2008)
Pub: Crain Communications Inc.
Contact: Todd Johnson, Publisher
Ed: Steve Daniels. **Description:** Mid-sized commercial banks form the bedrock of Chicago's financial-services industry and they are now feeling the results of the credit crisis that has engulfed the nation's largest banks and brokerages. Commercial borrowers are seeing tighter terms on loans and higher interest rates while bank investors are unable to forecast lenders' earnings performance from quarter to quarter. Statistical data included.

36717 ■ *"Bad Loans Start Piling Up"* in *Crain's New York Business* (Vol. 24, January 6, 2008, No. 1, pp. 2)
Pub: Crain Communications Inc.
Contact: Rance Crain, President
Ed: Tom Fredrickson. **Description:** Problems in the subprime mortgage industry have extended to other lending activities as evidenced by bank charge-offs on bad commercial and industrial loans which have more than doubled in the third quarter.

36718 ■ *Bad Money*
Ed: Kevin Phillips. **Released:** April 15, 2008. **Description:** How the financial sector has hijacked the American economy, aided by Washington's ruinous faith in the efficiency of markets.

36719 ■ *"The Bad News Bulls"* in *Barron's* (Vol. 92, July 23, 2012, No. 30, pp. 7)
Pub: Dow Jones & Co., Inc.
Contact: Clare Hart, President
Ed: Alan Abelson. **Released:** July 23, 2012. **Description:** Revelations of banking scandals have spurred the so-called 'bad news bulls' into buying US equities. Russell Wasendorf Sr. of Peregrine Financial Group has been charged regarding his involvement in a Ponzi scheme. An estimated $400 billion in corporate pension plans and $4 trillion in government pension plans in the US are underfunded.

36720 ■ *"Bailey Banks & Biddle Loses Street Sparkle"* in *Houston Business Journal* (Vol. 40, November 27, 2009, No. 29, pp. 1)
Pub: American City Business Journals
Ed: Allison Wollam. **Description:** High-end jeweler Bailey Banks & Biddle's 7,000 square foot prototype store in Houston, Texas' CityCentre will be ceasing operations despite its parent company's filing for Chapter 11 protection from creditors. According to the bankruptcy filing, parent company Finlay Enterprises Inc. of New York intends to auction off its business and assets. Finlay has 67 Bailey Banks locations throughout the US.

36721 ■ *"Bailout Forgets the 'Little Guys'"* in *The Business Journal-Milwaukee (Vol. 25, September 26, 2008, No. 53, pp. A1)*
Pub: American City Business Journals, Inc.
Contact: Whitney Shaw, President
Ed: Rich Kirchen. **Description:** Community Bankers of Wisconsin and the Wisconsin Bankers Association are urging members to approach congressional representatives and remind them to include local banks in building the $700 billion bailout plan. WBA president and CEO Kurt Bauer thinks that it is only fair to include smaller institutions in the bailout. The initial bailout plan and its benefit for the smaller banks are examined.

36722 ■ *"Bailout May Force Cutbacks, Job Losses"* in *The Business Journal - Serving Phoenix and the Valley of the Sun (Vol. 29, September 26, 2008, No. 4, pp. 1)*
Ed: Mike Sunnucks. **Description:** Economists say the proposed $700 billion bank bailout could affect Arizona businesses as banks could be forced to reduce the amount and number of loans it has thereby forcing businesses to shrink capital expenditures and then jobs. However, the plan could also stimulate the economy by taking bad loans off banks balance sheets according to another economist.

36723 ■ *"Balancing Risk and Return in a Customer Portfolio"* in *Journal of Marketing (Vol. 75, May 2011, No. 3, pp. 1)*
Pub: American Marketing Association
Contact: Lucille Pointer, President
Ed: Crina O. Tarasi, Ruth N. Bolton, Michael D. Hutt, Beth A. Walker. **Description:** A framework for reducing the vulnerability and volatility of cash flows in customer portfolios is presented. The efficient portfolios of firms are identified and tested against their current portfolios and hypothetical profit maximization portfolios.

36724 ■ *"Baltimore Car Dealers Have One More Shot to Get Their Franchises Back: Fighting Detroit"* in *Baltimore Business Journal (Vol. 27, January 22, 2010, No. 38, pp. 1)*
Pub: American City Business Journals
Ed: Daniel J. Sernovitz. **Description:** Baltimore, Maryland-based car dealers could retrieve their franchises from car manufacturers, Chrysler LLC and General Motors Corporation, through a forced arbitration. A provision in a federal budget mandates the arbitration. The revoking of franchises has been attributed to the car manufacturers' filing of bankruptcy protection.

36725 ■ *"BancVue to Expand"* in *Austin Business JournalInc. (Vol. 29, November 27, 2009, No. 38, pp. 1)*
Pub: American City Business Journals
Ed: Kate Harrington. **Description:** Significant growth of BancVue in the past six years has prompted the company to look for a site that could increase its office space from 25,000 square feet to 65,000 square feet. BancVue offers bank and credit union software solutions and is planning to lease or buy a property in Austin, Texas.

36726 ■ *"Bank Bullish on Austin"* in *Austin Business JournalInc. (Vol. 29, November 13, 2009, No. 36, pp. A1)*
Pub: American City Business Journals
Ed: Kate Harrington. **Description:** American Bank's presence in Austin, Texas has been boosted by new management and a new 20,000 square foot building. This community bank intends to focus on building relationship with commercial banking customers. American Bank also plans to extend investment banking, treasury management, and commercial lending services.

36727 ■ *The Bank Directory*
Pub: Accuity Inc.
Contact: Hugh M. Jones, IV, President
URL(s): store.accuitysolutions.com/order.html. **Released:** Semiannual; June and December. **Price:** $1,670, Individuals. **Covers:** In five volumes, about 11,000 banks and 50,000 branches of United States banks, and 60,000 foreign banks and branches

engaged in foreign banking; Federal Reserve system and other United States government and state government banking agencies; 500 largest North American and International commercial banks; paper and automated clearinghouses. Volumes 1 and 2 contain North American listings; volumes 3 and 4, international listings (also cited as 'Thomson International Bank Directory; volume 5, Worldwide Correspondents Guide containing key correspondent data to facilitate funds transfer. **Entries include:** For domestic banks--Bank name, address, phone, telex, cable, date established, routing number, charter type, bank holding company affiliation, memberships in Federal Reserve System and other banking organizations, principal officers by function performed, principal correspondent banks, and key financial data (deposits, etc.). For international banks--Bank name, address, phone, fax, telex, cable, SWIFT address, transit or sort codes within home country, ownership, financial data, names and titles of key personnel, branch locations. For branches--Bank name, address, phone, charter type, ownership and other details comparable to domestic bank listings. **Database includes:** Bank operations information, asset ranking in state and country, bank routing numbers in numeric sequence, discontinued or changed bank names in geographical sequence. **Arrangement:** Geographical. **Indexes:** Alphabetical, geographical.

36728 ■ *"Bank Expects Profit After Rough Start"* in *Austin Business Journal (Vol. 32, April 20, 2012, No. 7, pp. 1)*
Pub: American City Business Journals, Inc.
Contact: Whitney Shaw, President
Ed: Christopher Calnan. **Released:** April 20, 2012. **Description:** Libertad Bank SSB has projected profitability in 2012 after it was fined by federal regulators for poor financial performance. The bank is being monitored for its compliance management plans.

36729 ■ *"Bank Forces Brooke Founder To Sell His Holdings"* in *The Business Journal-Serving Metropolitan Kansas City (October 10, 2008)*
Pub: American City Business Journals, Inc.
Contact: Whitney Shaw, President
Ed: James Dornbrook. **Description:** Robert Orr who is the founder of Brooke Corp., a franchise of insurance agencies, says that he was forced to sell virtually all of his stocks in the company by creditors. First United Bank held the founder's stock as collateral for two loans worth $5 million and $7.9 million, which were declared in default in September 2008. Details of the selling of the company's stocks are provided.

36730 ■ *"Bank On It: New Year, New Estate Plan"* in *Hawaii Business (Vol. 53, February 2008, No. 8, pp. 54)*
Pub: PacificBasin Communications
Ed: Antony M. Orme. **Description:** Discusses the start of the new year which can be a time to revise wills and estate plans as failure to do so may create problems of unequal inheritance and increase in estate tax exemption, which could disinherit beneficiaries. Other circumstances that can prompt changes in wills and estate plans are presented.

36731 ■ *"Bank On It: The Many Ways of Giving"* in *Hawaii Business (Vol. 53, November 2007, No. 5, pp. 60)*
Pub: PacificBasin Communications
Ed: Kathleen Bryan. **Description:** Many Baby Boomers that are preparing to retire would like to give back and make a difference. One way is to make gifts of Individual Retirement Assets (IRA). During 2007 people over 70 years can make withdrawals from an IRA and donate it without realizing the income as taxable.

36732 ■ *"Bank Takes Charge: Who Gets Last Laugh?"* in *Barron's (Vol. 88, March 31, 2008, No. 13, pp. 17)*
Pub: Dow Jones & Co., Inc.
Contact: Clare Hart, President
Ed: Leslie P. Norton. **Description:** Nord/LB will take a charge of 82.5 million euros to cover potential losses apparently related to Vatas' refusal to take the shares of Remote MDx Inc. after buying the shares. Remote MDx's main product is an ankle bracelet to

monitor criminals; the firm has lost over half of its market cap due to the Nord/LB troubles and questions about its revenues.

36733 ■ *"Banking Bailout: Boost or Bust? Economic Insiders Mixed on Impact to State"* in *Crain's Detroit Business (Vol. 24, September 29, 2008, No. 39, pp. 1)*
Pub: Crain Communications Inc.
Contact: Rance E. Crain, President
Ed: Amy Lane. **Description:** Economic insiders discuss the banking bailout and how it might impact the state of Michigan.

36734 ■ *"A Banking Play Without Banking Plagues"* in *Barron's (Vol. 88, March 31, 2008, No. 13, pp. 26)*
Ed: Jack Willoughby. **Description:** Fiserv's shares have been dragged down by about 20 percent which presents an appealing entry point since the shares could rise by 30 percent or more by 2009. The company enables banks to post and open new checks and keeps track of loans which are not discretionary processes of banks.

36735 ■ *"Banking Sector To See Moderate Growth in 2014"* in *Houston Business Journal (Vol. 44, January 3, 2014, No. 35, pp. 5)*
Pub: American City Business Journals
Released: January 3, 2014. **Description:** The Greater Houston Partnership reported that Houston, Texas' finance industry recovered 50.9 percent of the 5,500 jobs it lost compared to the nation's recovery rate of 34.4 percent. However, Houston's banking sector remains strong and deposits have almost doubled since 2008. The banks that established or expanded operations in Houston are also presented.

36736 ■ *"Banking on Twitter"* in *Baltimore Business Journal (Vol. 27, February 6, 2010, No. 40, pp. 1)*
Pub: American City Business Journals
Ed: Gary Haber. **Description:** Ways that banks are using Twitter, Facebook and other social networking sites to provide customer services is discussed. First Mariner Bank is one of those banks that are finding the social media platform as a great way to reach customers. Privacy issues regarding this marketing trend are examined.

36737 ■ *"The Bankrate Double Play, Bankrate Is Having Its Best Quarter Yet"* in *Barron's (Vol. 88, March 24, 2008, No. 12, pp. 27)*
Pub: Dow Jones & Co., Inc.
Contact: Clare Hart, President
Ed: Nell A. Martin. **Description:** Shares of Bankrate may rise as much as 25 percent from their level of $45.08 a share due to a strong cash flow and balance sheet. The company's Internet business remains strong despite weakness in the online advertising industry and is a potential takeover target.

36738 ■ *"Bankruptcies Shoot Up 68 Percent"* in *Sacramento Business Journal (Vol. 25, July 18, 2008, No. 20, pp. 1)*
Pub: American City Business Journals, Inc.
Contact: Whitney Shaw, President
Ed: Kathy Robertson. **Description:** Personal bankruptcy in the Sacramento area rose by 88 percent for the first half of 2008 while business bankruptcies rose by 50 percent for the same period. The numbers of consumer bankruptcy reflects the effect of high debt, rising mortgage costs, and declining home values on U.S. households.

36739 ■ *"Bankruptcy Blowback"* in *Business Week (September 22, 2008, No. 4100, pp. 36)*
Pub: Bloomberg L.P.
Contact: Matthew Winkler, Manager
Ed: Jessica Silver-Greenberg. **Description:** Changes to bankruptcy laws which were enacted in 2005 after banks and other financial institutions lobbied hard for them are now suffering the consequences of the laws which force more troubled borrowers to let their homes go into foreclosure; lenders suffer financially every time they have to take on a foreclosure and the laws in which they lobbied so hard to see enacted

are now becoming a problem for these lending institutions. Details of the changes in the laws are outlined as are the affects on the consumer, the economy and the lenders.

36740 ■ Bankruptcy for Small Business
Pub: Sphinx Legal Inc.
Contact: Todd Stocke, Director
E-mail: todd.stocke@sourcebooks.com
Ed: Wendell Schollander. **Released:** July 1, 2008. **Price:** $22.95 paperback. **Description:** Bankruptcy laws can be used to save a small business, homes or other property. The book provides general information for small business owners regarding the reasons for money problems, types of bankruptcy available and their alternatives, myths about bankruptcy, and the do's and don'ts for filing for bankruptcy.

36741 ■ Bankruptcy for Small Business, 2E: Know Your Legal Rights and Recover from Mistakes and Start Over Successfully
Ed: Wendell Schollander; Wes Schollander. **Released:** July 2008. **Price:** $22.95. **Description:** Bankruptcy laws can actually help small business owners save their companies, homes and other property. This book offers general information regarding reasons for money problems, types of bankruptcy available to small business owners as well as alternatives to bankruptcy and more.

36742 ■ "Banks" in Black Enterprise (Vol. 44, June 2014, No. 10, pp. 86)
Pub: Earl G. Graves Publishing Co. Inc.
Contact: Earl G. Graves, Jr., President
Released: June 2014. **Description:** A listing o f the top 100 banks in the U.S.

36743 ■ "Banks Continue March Out of Bad-Loan Numbers: Total Loans Up, Non-Performing Loans Decline" in Memphis Business Journal (Vol. 34, August 24, 2012, No. 19, pp. 1)
Pub: American City Business Journal
Description: Banks in Memphis, Tennessee continue to improve their capital status throughout the second quarter of 2012. The twenty-five banks observed showed improvements in total loan volume, as well as in non-performing loans and real estate. Total loans grew $723.26 million, while non-performing loans and real-estate-owned assets fell $322.4 million.

36744 ■ "Banks Deposit Reassurance, Calm Customers" in The Business Journal-Serving Greater Tampa Bay (Vol. 28, August 22, 2008)
Pub: American City Business Journals, Inc.
Contact: Whitney Shaw, President
Description: Community banks in the Tampa Bay Area are training tellers and other customer care workers to help reassure customers that their deposits are safe. Other measures to reassure depositors include joining a network that allows banks to share deposits. Additional information on moves community banks are making to reassure consumers is presented.

36745 ■ "Banks Fall Short in Online Services for Savvy Traders" in Barron's (Vol. 88, March 17, 2008, No. 11, pp. 35)
Pub: Dow Jones & Co., Inc.
Contact: Clare Hart, President
Ed: Theresa W. Carey. **Description:** Banc of America Investment Services, WellsTrade, and ShareBuilder are at the bottom of the list of online brokerages because they offer less trading technologies and product range. Financial shoppers miss out on a lot of customized tools and analytics when using these services.

36746 ■ "Banks Find Borrowers Off the Beaten Path" in Boston Business Journal (Vol. 30, December 3, 2010, No. 45, pp. 1)
Pub: Boston Business Journal
Ed: Tim McLaughlin. **Description:** Banks in Boston have found unlikely applicants for bank loans in organizations such as the Dorchester Collegiate Academy. Dorchester is a charter school in its second year of operation, but qualified for $1.08 million to finance its own building. Other information, as well as views on the unexpected borrowers in Boston, is presented.

36747 ■ "Banks Fret About Gist Of Bailout" in The Business Journal-Serving Metropolitan Kansas City (Vol. 27, September 26, 2008, No. 2)
Pub: American City Business Journals, Inc.
Contact: Whitney Shaw, President
Ed: James Dornbrook. **Description:** Banks from the Kansas City area hope that the proposed $700 billion bailout will not send the wrong message. UMB Financial Corp. chairman says that he hopes that the bailout would benefit companies that were more risk restrained and punish those that took outsized risk. Other bank executives' perceptions on the planned bailout are given.

36748 ■ "Banks Lower Rates on CDs, Deposits" in Baltimore Business Journal (Vol. 27, January 1, 2010, No. 35, pp. 1)
Pub: American City Business Journals
Ed: Gary Haber. **Description:** Greater Baltimore area banks in Maryland have lowered their rates on certificates of deposits (CDs) and money market accounts, which could indicate the incoming trend for the first half of 2010. A banking industry forecast shows that lower Federal Funds rate, low inflation, and a new Federal Deposit Insurance Corporation (FDIC) rule might cause the rates to drop even further. Details on the FDIC rule are given.

36749 ■ "Banks, Retailers Squabble Over Fees" in Baltimore Business Journal (Vol. 28, June 18, 2010, No. 6, pp. 1)
Pub: Baltimore Business Journal
Ed: Gary Haber. **Description:** How an amendment to the financial regulatory reform bill would affect the bankers' and retailers' conflict over interchange fees is discussed. Interchange fees are paid for by retailers every time consumers make purchases through debit cards. Industry estimates indicate that approximately $50 million in such fees are paid by retailers.

36750 ■ "Banks Seeing Demand for Home Equity Loans Slowing" in Crain's Cleveland Business (Vol. 28, December 3, 2007, No. 48, pp. 1)
Pub: Crain Communications Inc.
Ed: Shawn A. Turner. **Description:** Discusses the reasons for the decline in demand for home equity loans and lines of credit. Statistical data included.

36751 ■ "Bargain Hunting In Vietnam" in Barron's (Vol. 88, July 14, 2008, No. 28, pp. M6)
Pub: Dow Jones & Co., Inc.
Contact: Clare Hart, President
Ed: Elliot Wilson. **Description:** Vietnam's economy grew by just 6.5 percent for the first half of 2008 and its balance of payments ballooned to $14.4 billion. The falling stock prices in the country is a boon for bargain hunters and investing in the numerous domestic funds is one way of investing in the country. Some shares that investors are taking an interest in are also discussed.

36752 ■ "Barron's Lipper Fund Listings" in Barron's (Vol. 89, July 13, 2009, No. 28, pp. 19)
Description: Statistical tables are presented which show the assets and return of mutual funds up to a ten year period. The listing covers funds with at least $200 million in assets.

36753 ■ "Basel3 Quick Fix Actually Neither" in Canadian Business (Vol. 83, October 12, 2010, No. 17, pp. 19)
Pub: Rogers Media Inc.
Contact: Tony Viner, President
Ed: Thomas Watson. **Description:** Information about the so-called Basel 3 standards, which will require banks to hold top-quality capital totaling at least 7 percent of their risk-bearing assets is provided. The rules' supporters believe that a good balance has been reached between improving the Basel 2 framework and maintaining enough lending capital to stimulate an economic growth.

36754 ■ "Battle of the Titans" in Canadian Business (Vol. 81, March 17, 2008, No. 4, pp. 15)
Pub: Rogers Media Inc.
Contact: Tony Viner, President
Ed: Rachel Pulfer. **Description:** Regulatory authorities in Canada gave Thomson Corp and Reuters Group PLC the permission to go ahead with their merger. The merged companies could eclipse Bloomberg LP's market share of 33 percent. Authorities also required Thomson and Reuters to sell some of their databases to competitors.

36755 ■ Battling Big Box: How Nimble Niche Companies Can Outmaneuver Giant Competitors
Pub: Career Press Inc.
Contact: Ron Fry, President
Ed: Henry Dubroff, Susan J. Marks. **Released:** January 2009. **Price:** $15.99. **Description:** Small companies can compete with larger firms through agility, adaptability, customer service, and credibility. Topics include information to help empower employees, build a powerful brand, manage cash flow, and maintaining a business vision. **Availability:** Print.

36756 ■ "Baupost Group Pours Money into Charlotte Real Estate Projects" in Charlotte Business Journal (Vol. 25, December 3, 2010, No. 37, pp. 1)
Pub: Charlotte Business Journal
Ed: Will Boye. **Description:** Boston-based hedge fund Baupost Group has been financing real estate project in Charlotte, North Carolina including more than 80 acres just north of uptown. Aside from purchasing the $23.8 million note for the Rosewood Condominiums from Regions Financial Corporation, the Baupost Group is also negotiating with Regions to buy the $93.9 million debt of the EipCentre real estate project.

36757 ■ "BBVA Compass To Open Loan Office In Chicago" in Birmingham Business Journal (Vol. 29, July 20, 2012, No. 30, pp. 1)
Pub: American City Business Journals, Inc.
Contact: Whitney Shaw, President
Ed: Antrenise Cole. **Released:** July 20, 2012. **Description:** Birmingham, Alabama-based BBVA Compass plans to open a commercial loan production office in Chicago, Illinois and has filed an application with the State of Alabama Banking Department. The company intends to serve companies of all sizes but plans to focus on firms with $500 million to $2 billion in revenue.

36758 ■ "BBVA Offers Medical Practices help that Floats on a Cloud" in Dallas Business Journal (Vol. 37, May 30, 2014, No. 38, pp. 6)
Pub: American City Business Journals
Released: May 30, 2014. **Description:** BBVA Compass is offering a package of bank services and health care technology for medical practices in Dallas-Fort Worth, Texas in partnership with technology platform provider CareCloud. The innovative cloud-based technology platform will allow the Birmingham, Alabama-based bank to help medical practices affected by the demands of technology and government regulations.

36759 ■ "BDC Launches New Online Business Advice Centre" in Marketwired (July 13, 2010)
Pub: COMTEX
Contact: Chip Brian, President
Description: The Business Development Bank of Canada (BDC) offers entrepreneurs the chance to use their new online BDC Advice Centre in order to seek advice regarding the challenges of entrepreneurship. Free online business tools and information to help both startups and established firms are also provided.

36760 ■ "The Bear Arrives - With Bargain Hunters" in Barron's (Vol. 88, July 7, 2008,

No. 27, pp. M3)
Pub: Dow Jones & Co., Inc.
Contact: Clare Hart, President
Ed: Kopin Tan. **Description:** US stock markets have dropped 20 percent below their highs, entering the bear market at the end of June 2008. It was also the worst performance of the stock markets during June. Wine maker Constellation Brands, however, reported a 50 percent rise in net income for the first quarter of 2008.

36761 ■ *"Bear Market Tough On Investors"* in *The Business Journal-Milwaukee* (Vol. 25, July 4, 2008, No. 41, pp. A1)
Pub: American City Business Journals, Inc.
Contact: Whitney Shaw, President
Ed: Rich Kirchen. **Description:** Public companies and their investors in the Milwaukee area suffered as the bear market took hold of the Wisconsin stock market. There were 18 stocks out of the 36 publicly traded stocks that have fallen into the bear market, meaning a 20 percent decline from the market peak in the fall of 2007. The impacts of the bear market on investors are evaluated.

36762 ■ *"The Bear Stearns-JPMorgan Deal - Rhymes with Steal - Of A Lifetime"* in *Barron's* (Vol. 88, March 24, 2008, No. 12, pp. 24)
Pub: Dow Jones & Co., Inc.
Contact: Clare Hart, President
Ed: Andrew Bary. **Description:** JPMorgan Chase's impending acquisition of Bear Stearns for $2.50 a share is a huge steal for the former. JPMorgan is set to acquire a company with a potential annual earnings of $1 billion while the Federal Reserve funds Bear's illiquid assets by providing $30 billion in nonrecourse loans.

36763 ■ *"The Bear's Back"* in *Barron's* (Vol. 88, July 7, 2008, No. 27, pp. 17)
Pub: Dow Jones & Co., Inc.
Contact: Clare Hart, President
Ed: Randall W. Forsyth, Vito Racanelli. **Description:** US stock markets have formally entered the bear market after the Dow Jones Industrial Average dropped 20 percent from its high as of June 2008. Investors remain uncertain as to how long the bear market will persist, especially with the US economy on the edge of recession.

36764 ■ *"Beat the Buck: Bartering Tips from In-The-Know Authors"* in (June 23, 2010)
Pub: The Telegraph
Description: The Art of Barter is a new book to help small businesses learn this art form in order to expand customer base and reserve cash flow.

36765 ■ *"Beaumont Outsources Purchasing as Route to Supply Cost Savings"* in *Crain's Detroit Business* (Vol. 25, June 1, 2009, No. 22)
Pub: Crain Communications Inc. - Detroit
Contact: Keith Crain, Chairman
Ed: Jay Greene. **Description:** William Beaumont Hospitals in Royal Oak have begun outsourcing the purchasing of supplies in order to cut costs. So far, Beaumont is the only hospital in southeast Michigan to outsource its purchasing department. Other hospitals employ their own purchasing supply workers.

36766 ■ *"The Beauty of Banking's Big Ugly"* in *Barron's* (Vol. 89, July 27, 2009, No. 30, pp. 31)
Pub: Dow Jones & Co., Inc.
Contact: Clare Hart, President
Ed: Andrew Bary. **Description:** Appeal of the shares of Citigroup comes from its sharp discount to its tangible book value and the company's positive attributes include a strong capital position, high loan-loss reserves, and their appealing global-consumer. The shares have the potential to generate nice profits and decent stock gains as the economy turns.

36767 ■ *"Behind the Numbers: When It Comes to Earnings, Look for Quality, Not Just Quantity"* in *Black Enterprise* (Vol. 38,

July 2008, pp. 35)
Pub: Earl G. Graves Publishing Co. Inc.
Contact: Earl G. Graves, Jr., President
Description: It is important for investors to examine the quality of a company's earnings rather than fixate on the quantity of those earnings. Advice is given regarding issues investors can look at when trying to determine the potential growth of a firm.

36768 ■ *"Bertha's Birth Stirs Juice"* in *Barron's* (Vol. 88, July 14, 2008, No. 28, pp. M11)
Pub: Dow Jones & Co., Inc.
Contact: Clare Hart, President
Ed: Tom Sellen. **Description:** Price of frozen concentrated orange juice, which has risen to four-month highs of $1.3620 in July 2008 is due, in part, to the hurricane season that has come earlier than normal in the far eastern Atlantic thereby possibly harming the 2008-2009 Florida orange crop. Future tropical-storm development will affect the prices of this commodity.

36769 ■ *"Best Cash Flow Generators"* in *Canadian Business* (Vol. 81, Summer 2008, No. 9, pp. 73)
Ed: Calvin Leung. **Description:** Table showing the five-year annualized growth rate and one-year stock performance of companies that have grown their cash flow per share at an annualized rate of 15 percent or more over the past five years. Analysts project that the cash flow trend will continue. Other details of the stock performance index are presented.

36770 ■ *"Best Cash Flow Generators"* in *Canadian Business* (Vol. 82, Summer 2009, No. 8, pp. 40)
Ed: Calvin Leung. **Description:** Agrium Inc. and FirstService Corporation are in the list of firms that are found to have the potential to be the best cash flow generators in Canada. The list also includes WestJet Airlines Ltd., which accounts for 385 flights each day. More than 80 percent of analysts rate the airline stocks a Buy.

36771 ■ *"Best Defensive Stocks"* in *Canadian Business* (Vol. 81, Summer 2008, No. 9, pp. 67)
Ed: Calvin Leung. **Description:** Stocks of the companies presented have market capitalization of greater than $1 billion and dividend gains of at least 2 percent. A table showing the average one-year total return of the stocks is provided.

36772 ■ *"The Best Five-Month Run Since 1938"* in *Barron's* (Vol. 89, August 3, 2009, No. 31, pp. M3)
Pub: Dow Jones & Co., Inc.
Contact: Clare Hart, President
Ed: Kopin Tan, Andrew Bary. **Description:** US stock markets ended July 2009 registering the highest five-month rise since 1938. The shares of Cablevision could rise as the company simplifies its structure and spins off its Madison Square Garden unit. The shares of Potash Corp. could fall as the company faces lower earnings due to falling potash purchases.

36773 ■ *"Best Growth Stocks"* in *Canadian Business* (Vol. 81, Summer 2008, No. 9, pp. 61)
Ed: Calvin Leung. **Description:** Table showing the one-year performance of growth stocks is presented. Edmonton-based Stantec Inc. expects to advance its sales and profits by 15 percent to 20 percent per year through tapping international markets and acquisitions. Analysts forecast a 17.1 percent growth rate annually over the next 3 to 5 years.

36774 ■ *"Best Growth Stocks"* in *Canadian Business* (Vol. 82, Summer 2009, No. 8, pp. 28)
Pub: Rogers Media Inc.
Contact: Tony Viner, President
Ed: Calvin Leung. **Description:** Canadian stocks that are considered as the best growth stocks, and whose price-earnings ratio is less than their earnings growth rate, are suggested. Suggestions include pharmaceu-

tical firm Paladin Labs, which was found to have 13 consecutive years of revenue growth. Paladin Labs acquires or licenses niche drugs and markets them in Canada.

36775 ■ *"Best Income Trust"* in *Canadian Business* (Vol. 81, Summer 2008, No. 9, pp. 69)
Ed: Calvin Leung. **Description:** Table showing five-year annualized growth rate and one-year stock performance of real estate investment trusts firms in Canada is presented. Calgary-based Boardwalk REIT is projected to grow the fastest among North American REITs over the next two years. Other details on the stock performance analysis are presented.

36776 ■ *"Best Managed Companies"* in *Canadian Business* (Vol. 81, Summer 2008, No. 9, pp. 71)
Ed: Calvin Leung. **Description:** Table showing the five-year annualized growth rate and one-year stock performance of companies that have grown their cash flow per share at an annualized rate of 15 percent or more over the past five years. Analysts project that the cash flow trend will continue. Other details of stock performance index are presented.

36777 ■ *"Best Turnaround Stocks"* in *Canadian Business* (Vol. 81, Summer 2008, No. 9, pp. 65)
Ed: Calvin Leung. **Description:** Share prices of Sierra Wireless Inc. and EXFO Electro Optical Engineering Inc. have fallen over the past year but have good chance at a rebound considering that the companies have free cash flow and no long-term debt. One-year stock performance analysis of the two companies is presented.

36778 ■ *"Best Value Stocks"* in *Canadian Business* (Vol. 81, Summer 2008, No. 9, pp. 63)
Ed: Calvin Leung. **Description:** Table showing the one-year performance of bargain or best-value stocks is presented. These stocks are undervalued compared to their North American peers, but it is projected that their five-year average return on equity is greater.

36779 ■ *"Best Value Stocks"* in *Canadian Business* (Vol. 82, Summer 2009, No. 8, pp. 30)
Pub: Rogers Media Inc.
Contact: Tony Viner, President
Ed: Calvin Leung. **Description:** Canadian companies that are believed to have the best value stocks are suggested. Suggestions include publishing firm Glacier Media, which has reported a four-fold growth in sales in the last three years. While publishers like Glacier Media face challenges such as declining circulation, the firm's industry diversification is expected to help it weather the economic downturn.

36780 ■ *"Bet on the Subcontinent"* in *Canadian Business* (Vol. 81, April 14, 2008, No. 6, pp. 27)
Pub: Rogers Media Inc.
Contact: Tony Viner, President
Ed: Calvin Leung. **Description:** Morgan Stanley Capital International India Index is down 28 percent for the first half of 2008 but this index rebounded 6 percent in 2002 then skyrocketed 65 percent in 2003. The economic reforms in the 1990's have created a growing middle class and households that can afford discretionary items will grow from eight million to 94 million by 2025. India's equity market could outperform developed markets if its economy grows at its current rate.

36781 ■ *"Betsey Johnson LLC (1978-2012): Johnson's Iconic Label Refined the CBGB Look for the Masses"* in *Canadian Business* (Vol. 85, June 11, 2012, No. 10, pp. 14)
Pub: George Media Inc.
Ed: Sarah Barmak. **Released:** June 11, 2012. **Description:** Fashion label Betsey Johnson LLC filed for Chapter 11 bankruptcy protection in April 2012 that would result in 350 layoffs and closure of most of its 63 stores. The company cited severe liquidity constraints and $4.1 million in outstanding unsecured obligations to creditors in its filing.

36782 ■ *"A Better Way to Tax U.S. Businesses"* in (Vol. 90, July-August 2012, No. 7-8, pp. 134)
Pub: Harvard Business Review Press
Contact: Peter E. Walsh, Director
Ed: Mihir A. Desai. **Released:** July-August 2012. **Description:** Correcting the US corporate tax code will require ending the disconnect between earnings stated to investors and taxable income, implementing rate reductions, eliminating the taxing of overseas income, and securing an agreement by business leaders to acknowledge taxes as a responsibility.

36783 ■ *"Betting Big, Winning Big: Interview With Bruce Berkowitz, CEO of Fairholme Capital Management"* in Barron's (Vol. 88, March 17, 2008, No. 11, pp. 49)
Pub: Dow Jones & Co., Inc.
Contact: Clare Hart, President
Ed: Lawrence C. Strauss. **Description:** Bruce Berkowitz explains that the reason that his portfolio is concentrated is because getting more positions makes the portfolio more average compared to putting the money into your 10th or 20th-best idea. Berkowitz' picks include Berkshire Hathaway, WellCare Health Plus, Sears Holdings, and Mohawk Industries.

36784 ■ *"Betting on a Happy Ending"* in Barron's (Vol. 88, July 7, 2008, No. 27, pp. 14)
Pub: Dow Jones & Co., Inc.
Contact: Clare Hart, President
Ed: Dimitra DeFotis. **Description:** Shares of Time Warner, priced at $14.69 each, appear under-priced as financial analysts discount the value of the company. The company should be worth more than $20 a share as the company is spinning off Time Warner Cable.

36785 ■ *"Betting On Volatile Materials"* in Barron's (Vol. 88, July 14, 2008, No. 28, pp. M11)
Pub: Dow Jones & Co., Inc.
Contact: Clare Hart, President
Ed: John Marshall. **Description:** Economic slowdowns in the U.S., Europe and China could cause sharp short-term declines in the materials sector. The S&P Materials sector is vulnerable to shifts in the flow of funds. Statistical data included.

36786 ■ *"Beware, Complacent Bankers"* in Canadian Business (Vol. 85, September 17, 2012, No. 14, pp. 9)
Pub: George Media Inc.
Ed: Sarah Barmak. **Released:** September 17, 2012. **Description:** Canadian Finance Minister Jim Flaherty has released draft rules that would allow credit unions to go national and compete with major banks. Approval of the rules would see a fianancial services mix that includes a few credit unions with coast-to-coast ATM networks.

36787 ■ *"Beware the Ides of March"* in Canadian Business (Vol. 81, April 14, 2008, No. 6, pp. 13)
Pub: Rogers Media Inc.
Contact: Tony Viner, President
Ed: Jeff Sanford. **Description:** Financial troubles of Bear Stearns in March, 2008 was part of the credit crunch that started in the summer of 2007 in the U.S. when subprime mortgages that were written for people who could barely afford the payments started defaulting. The bankruptcy protection given to 20 asset backed commercial paper trusts is being fought by the investors in these securities who could stand to lose 40 percent of their money under the agreement.

36788 ■ *"Beware of Rotting Money"* in Barron's (Vol. 89, July 13, 2009, No. 28, pp. 31)
Pub: Dow Jones & Co., Inc.
Contact: Clare Hart, President
Ed: Thomas G. Donlan. **Description:** Inflation can take hold of a country and do it great harm; it is caused by people, most particularly central bankers in charge of the world's reserve currency. Arrogant economists pushed the belief that the government can engineer the economy and it is argued that there is trouble ahead when the government tries to control the economy.

36789 ■ *"Beyond Microsoft and Yahoo!: Some M&A Prospects"* in Barron's (Vol. 88, March 17, 2008, No. 11, pp. 39)
Pub: Dow Jones & Co., Inc.
Contact: Clare Hart, President
Ed: Eric J. Savitz. **Description:** Weak quarterly earnings report for Yahoo! could pressure the company's board to cut a deal with Microsoft. Electronic Arts is expected to win its hostile $26-a-share bid for Take-Two Interactive Software. Potential targets and buyers for mergers and acquisitions are mentioned.

36790 ■ *"The Big 50"* in Canadian Business (Vol. 81, Summer 2008, No. 9, pp. 125)
Description: Large publicly held corporations are ranked based on market capitalization and stock performance. Potash Corp. of Saskatchewan topped the roster with 169.3 percent of return and even surpassing its 2007 result of 107 percent. A table showing the 2008 rankings of the companies is presented.

36791 ■ *"The Big Idea: The Judgment Deficit"* in Harvard Business Review (Vol. 88, September 2010, No. 9, pp. 44)
Pub: Harvard Business School Publishing
Ed: Amar Bhide. **Description:** The importance of individual, decentralized initiative and judgment in the capitalist system is outlined. While financial models have their use, they cannot always account appropriately for the inherent uncertainty in economic decision making.

36792 ■ *"Big Losses Mount for Baltimore's Hospitals"* in Baltimore Business Journal (Vol. 27, October 23, 2009, No. 24, pp. 1)
Pub: American City Business Journals
Ed: Scott Graham. **Description:** Reported losses by nine of the 22 hospitals in the Greater Baltimore area during fiscal 2009 have proven that the health care industry is not immune to the recession. The rising costs of doing business and losses in the stock market have strongly affected the financial status of hospitals.

36793 ■ *The Big Squeeze: Tough Times for the American Worker*
Pub: Pantheon Books Inc.
Contact: Dan Frank, Director
Ed: Steven Greenhouse. **Released:** February 10, 2009. **Price:** $16, paperback. **Description:** Labor correspondent for the New York Times reports on the bleak condition of the current workplace environment, citing violations of child labor laws and forced slave labor conditions in third world countries and robber baron era occurring often here in America that are expanding the number of working poor. **Availability:** Print.

36794 ■ *"Big Trouble at Sony Ericsson"* in Barron's (Vol. 88, March 24, 2008, No. 12, pp. M9)
Pub: Dow Jones & Co., Inc.
Contact: Clare Hart, President
Ed: Angelo Franchini. **Description:** Sony Ericsson is facing trouble as it warned that its sales and net income before taxes will fall by nearly half for the first quarter of 2008. The joint venture of Sony and Ericsson has a global mobile phone market share of nine percent as of 2007, fourth largest in the world.

36795 ■ *"Bill to Roll Back Banking Regulations Faces Tough Odds"* in San Antonio Business Journal (Vol. 28, April 18, 2014, No. 10, pp. 6)
Pub: American City Business Journals
Released: April 18, 2014. **Description:** U.S. Representative Henry Cuellar is co-sponsoring legislation that will ease some of the regulations governing community banks. The Community Lending Enhancement and Regulatory Relief Act has 129 co-sponsors in the House of Representatives.

36796 ■ *"Blackstone's Outlook Still Tough"* in Barron's (Vol. 88, March 17, 2008, No. 11, pp. 19)
Pub: Dow Jones & Co., Inc.
Contact: Clare Hart, President
Ed: Andrew Bary. **Description:** Earnings for the Blackstone Group may not recover soon since the company's specialty in big leveraged buyouts is floundering and may not recover until 2009. The company earns lucrative incentive fees on its funds but those fees went negative in the fourth quarter of 2007 and there could be more fee reversals in the future.

36797 ■ *"Bloody Monday for Bear?"* in Barron's (Vol. 88, March 17, 2008, No. 11, pp. M14)
Pub: Dow Jones & Co., Inc.
Contact: Clare Hart, President
Ed: Steven M. Sears. **Description:** Shares of Bear Stearns could slip further at the start of the trading week unless the company is bought out or bolstered by some other development over the weekend. Prices of the company's shares in the options market suggests about a 30 percent chance that the stock falls below $20 before March expirations expire.

36798 ■ *"BMO Harris Plans Boost In Local Biz Banking Unit"* in Business Journal (Vol. 30, June 29, 2012, No. 5, pp. 1)
Pub: American City Business Journals, Inc.
Contact: Whitney Shaw, President
Ed: Jim Hammerand. **Released:** June 29, 2012. **Description:** BMO Harris Bank plans to bulk up its commercial banking group in Minnesota. The company, which is a subsidiary of Bank of Montreal, is assigning Todd Senger to oversee commercial banking operations and strategy. It is believed that BMO Harris' expansion will drive growth in other business lines.

36799 ■ *"BMW Revs Up for a Rebound"* in Barron's (Vol. 89, July 13, 2009, No. 28, pp. M7)
Pub: Dow Jones & Co., Inc.
Contact: Clare Hart, President
Ed: Jonathan Buck. **Description:** Investors may like BMW's stocks because the company has maintained its balance sheet strength and has an impressive production line of new models that should boost sales in the next few years. The company's sales are also gaining traction, although their vehicle delivery was down 1.7 percent year on year on June 2009, this was still the best monthly sales figure for 2009.

36800 ■ *"Boar Market: Penny-Wise Consumers Favoring Pork"* in Crain's Chicago Business (Vol. 31, April 14, 2008, No. 15, pp. 4)
Pub: Crain Communications Inc.
Contact: Todd Johnson, Publisher
Ed: Bruce Blythe. **Description:** Interview with Alan Cole who is the president of Cedar Hill Associates Inc. and who discusses ways in which his company is taking advantage of the record highs of oil and natural gas as well as his overall outlook on the market.

36801 ■ *"Board This Powertrain"* in Barron's (Vol. 89, July 27, 2009, No. 30, pp. 30)
Ed: Naureen S. Malik. **Description:** Siemens' American Depositary Receipts have risen 60 percent from their March 2009 low and they should continue heading higher. The company has solid earnings and revenue growth since they lead in growing markets such as alternative energy and health-care infrastructure. Their shares also look cheap at 1.9 times book value.

36802 ■ *"Boeing Earns Its Wings With Strong Quarter"* in Crain's Chicago Business (Vol. 31, April 28, 2008, No. 17, pp. 4)
Pub: Crain Communications Inc.
Contact: Todd Johnson, Publisher
Ed: Daniel Rome Levine. **Description:** Interview with Michael A. Crowe, the senior managing director at Mesirow Financial Investment Management, who discusses highlights from the earnings season so far,

his outlook for the economy and the stock market as well as what his company is purchasing. Mr. Crowe also recommends shares of five companies.

36803 ■ *"BofA Fights To Keep Top Spot in Mobile Banking" in Charlotte Business Journal (Vol. 27, June 15, 2012, No. 13, pp. 1)*
Pub: American City Business Journals, Inc.
Contact: Whitney Shaw, President
Ed: Adam O'Daniel. **Released:** June 15, 2012. **Description:** Bank of America has been fighting to maintain its lead in mobile banking services. Financial institutions, payment processors and e-commerce firms have started offering mobile banking services.

36804 ■ *"BofA Goes for Small Business" in Austin Business Journal (Vol. 31, July 22, 2011, No. 20, pp. A1)*
Pub: American City Business Journals
Ed: Christopher Calnan. **Description:** Bank of America is planning to target small businesses as new customers. The bank lost its number one market share in Austin, Texas in 2010.

36805 ■ *"BofA May Part With U.S. Trust" in Boston Business Journal (Vol. 31, May 20, 2011, No. 17, pp. 1)*
Pub: Boston Business Journal
Ed: Tim McLaughlin. **Description:** Bank of America Corporation is willing to sell its U.S. Trust private banking division to improve its capital ratio. The unit remains to be the corporation's core asset and posted $696 million revenue in the first quarter 2010 in contract with Merrill Lynch Global Wealth Management's $3.5 billion. Analysts say that U.S. Trust would fetch more than $3 billion.

36806 ■ *"The Bogleheads' Guide to Investing"*
Pub: John Wiley & Sons Inc.
Contact: Stephen M. Smith, President
Released: August 18, 2014. **Price:** $26.95. **Description:** Advice that provides the first step to successful financial investments includes new information of backdoor Roth IRAs and ETFs as mainstream buy and hold investments, estate taxes and gifting, along with information on the changes in laws regarding Traditional and Roth IRAs and 401k and 403b retirement plans. The author teaches how to craft proven individual investment strategies.

36807 ■ *Bonds: The Other Market*
Pub: AuthorHouse
Contact: Bryan Smith, President
Ed: George L. Fulton. **Released:** March 16, 2005. **Price:** $16.75, softcover; $27.50, hardcover. **Description:** Professional bond broker provides fundamental information to help investors choose the bond market an alternative to the stock market. The book describes the various types of bonds available, including treasury bonds, issued by the U.S. Government; municipal bonds, issued by a municipal authority of a local or state government; and corporate bonds, issued by corporations. Risk vs. reward in bond investing is also covered. **Availability:** Print.

36808 ■ *"Bonds v. Stocks: Who's Right About Recession?" in Barron's (Vol. 90, August 23, 2010, No. 34, pp. M3)*
Pub: Barron's Editorial & Corporate Headquarters
Ed: Kopin Tan. **Description:** The future of treasury securities and stocks should the U.S. enter or avoid a recession are discussed. The back to school business climate and BHP Billiton's bid for Potash Corporation of Saskatchewan are also discussed.

36809 ■ *"Book of Lists 2010" in Philadelphia Business Journal (Vol. 28, December 25, 2009, No. 45, pp. 1)*
Pub: American City Business Journals Inc.
Description: Rankings of companies and organizations within the banking, biotechnology, economic development, healthcare, hospitality, law and accounting, marketing and media, real estate, and technology industries in the Philadelphia, Pennsylvania area are presented. Rankings are based on sales, business size, and more.

36810 ■ *"The Book On Indigo" in Canadian Business (Vol. 81, July 22, 2008, No. 12-13, pp. 29)*
Ed: Thomas Watson. **Description:** Indigo Books & Music Inc. reported record sales of $922 million resulting in a record net profit of $52.8 million for the 2008 fiscal year ended March 29, 2008. Earnings per share were $2.13, greater than Standard & Poor's expected $1.70 per share. Additional information concerning Indigo Books is presented.

36811 ■ *"Bookkeeping For Dummies"*
Pub: For Dummies
Released: May 21, 2007. **Price:** $19.99 paperback. **Description:** Because accurate and concise bookkeeping is critical to any small business, information for managing finances to save money while growing your business is offered. The guide covers the basics of bookkeeping, from recording transactions to producing balance sheets and year-end reports.

36812 ■ *"Boomers' Spending Hurts Retirement" in Employee Benefit News (Vol. 25, November 1, 2011, No. 14, pp. 18)*
Pub: SourceMedia Inc.
Contact: James M. Malkin, Chief Executive Officer
Ed: Ann Marsh. **Description:** Financial planners and employers need to educate clients and employees about retirement planning. Boomers are spending money that should be saved for their retirement.

36813 ■ *"Bottler Will Regain Its Pop" in Barron's (Vol. 88, March 17, 2008, No. 11, pp. 56)*
Ed: Alexander Eule. **Description:** Discusses he 30 percent drop in the share price of PepsiAmericas Inc. from their 2007 high which presents an opportunity to buy into the company's dependable U.S. market and fast growing Eastern European business. The bottler's Eastern European operating profits in 2007 grew to $101 million from $21 million in 2006.

36814 ■ *"Bottom-Fishing and Speed-Dating in India-How Investors Feel About the Indian Market" in Barron's (Vol. 88, March 24, 2008, No. 12, pp. M12)*
Pub: Dow Jones & Co., Inc.
Contact: Clare Hart, President
Ed: Elliot Wilson. **Description:** Indian stocks have fallen hard in 2008, with Mumbai's Sensex 30 down 30 percent from its January 2008 peak of 21,000 to 14,995 in March. The India Private Equity Fair 2008 attracted 140 of the world's largest private equity firms and about 24 of India's fastest-growing corporations. Statistical data included.

36815 ■ *"Bountiful Barrels: Where to Find $140 Trillion" in Barron's (Vol. 88, July 14, 2008, No. 28, pp. 40)*
Pub: Dow Jones & Co., Inc.
Contact: Clare Hart, President
Ed: Andrew Bary. **Description:** Surge in oil prices has caused a large transfer of wealth to oil-producing countries thereby reshaping the global economy. Oil reserves of oil exporting countries are now valued at $140 trillion. Economist Stephen Jen believes that this wealth will be transformed into paper assets as these countries invest in global stocks and bonds.

36816 ■ *"Bracing for a Bear of a Week" in Barron's (Vol. 88, March 17, 2008, No. 11, pp. 24)*
Pub: Dow Jones & Co., Inc.
Contact: Clare Hart, President
Ed: Jacqueline Doherty. **Description:** JPMorgan Chase and the Federal Reserve Bank of New York's opening of a line of credit to Bear Stearns cut the stock price of Bear Stearns by 47 percent to 30 followed by speculation of an imminent sale. JP Morgan may be the only potential buyer for the firm and some investors say Bears could be sold at $20 to $30. Bears prime assets include its enormous asset base worth $395 billion.

36817 ■ *Bridging the Equity Gap for Innovative SMEs*
Pub: Palgrave Macmillan
Contact: Lisa Dunn, Manager
E-mail: l.dunn@palgrave.com
Ed: Elisabetta Gualandri, Valeria Venturelli. **Released:** October 2008. **Price:** £90, hardcover. **Description:** This book addresses the evaluation of financial constraints faced by innovative and startup companies and explores ways for bridging the financing and equity gap faced by small to medium business enterprises. **Availability:** Print; E-book; Electronic publishing.

36818 ■ *"Brooke Agents Claim Mistreatment" in The Business Journal-Serving Metropolitan Kansas City (Vol. 27, October 24, 2008, No. 7, pp. 1)*
Pub: American City Business Journals, Inc.
Contact: Whitney Shaw, President
Ed: James Dornbrook. **Description:** Franchisees of Brooke Corp., an insurance franchise, face uncertainty as their bills remain unpaid and banks threaten to destroy their credit. The company bundled and sold franchisee loans to different banks, but the credit crunch left the company with massive debts and legal disputes.

36819 ■ *"Building Fast-Growing Companies" in South Florida Business Journal (Vol. 35, September 19, 2014, No. 8, pp. 16)*
Pub: American City Business Journals
Released: September 19, 2014. **Description:** Members of Florida's construction industry have registered continuous growth in 2014. Recovery from the economic crisis is driving the construction growth. Economic resilience and proper debt management have also contributed to the sector's growth.

36820 ■ *"Building Portfolios for a World of 2.5 Percent Gains" in Barron's (Vol. 88, July 7, 2008, No. 27, pp. L9)*
Pub: Dow Jones & Co., Inc.
Contact: Clare Hart, President
Ed: Karen Hube. **Description:** Interview with Harold Evenski whom is a financial planner running a fee-only planning practice; he continues to caution investors against pursuing short-term gains and focusing on long-term trends. He advises investors against investing in commodity and real estate stocks and is concerned about the possible effects of high inflation.

36821 ■ *"Building the Right Culture Can Add Huge Value" in South Florida Business Journal (Vol. 34, May 9, 2014, No. 42, pp. 20)*
Pub: American City Business Journals
Released: May 9, 2014. **Description:** Corporate culture has become an afterthought in many companies and this might be the result of viewing operating results purely from a financial perspective. However, it is the people who work for the companies that create value and they would become more effective by defining the culture. The benefits of creating a positive culture are also discussed.

36822 ■ *"A Bull Market in Finger-Pointing" in Barron's (Vol. 88, March 10, 2008, No. 10, pp. 9)*
Pub: Dow Jones & Co., Inc.
Contact: Clare Hart, President
Ed: Michael Santoli. **Description:** Discusses who is to blame for the financial crisis brought about by the credit crunch in the United States; the country's financial markets will eventually digest this crisis but will bottom out first before the situation improves.

36823 ■ *Business Black Belt: Develop the Strength, Flexibility and Agility to Run Your Company*
Ed: Burke Franklin. **Released:** November 1, 2010. **Price:** $15.99. **Description:** Manual offering insights that will enable anyone to become successful in small business. Seventy short chapters included topics such as attitude, management, marketing, selling, employees, money, MBAs, lawyers, consultants, and investors.

36824 ■ *"Business Execs Await Walker's Tax Cut Plan" in Business Journal-Milwaukee (Vol. 28, December 17, 2010, No. 11, pp. A1)*
Pub: Milwaukee Business Journal
Ed: Rich Kirchen. **Description:** Wisconsin governor-elect Scott Walker has to tackle the state's projected $3.3 billion budget deficit, which became the subject of speculation among business groups and state

politic watchers. Walker has pledged to reduce the state taxes without driving costs down to the local government and school district level.

36825 ■ *"Business Guide and Employment Role"*
Pub: AuthorHouse
Contact: Bryan Smith, President
Released: October 10, 2014. **Price:** $15.18 paperback. **Description:** Financial expert discusses the importance of economic and business and their role in employment. The business and finance manager is crucial to any small business. The guide is an essential tool for any entrepreneur, the investor in business enterprise, the individual businessman, the human resources manager, and the business and finance professional to learn the merits to do business and play a role in employment.

36826 ■ *Business Management for Tropical Dairy Farmers*
Pub: CSIRO Publishing
Contact: Megan Clark, Chief Executive Officer
Ed: John Moran. **Released:** 2009. **Price:** A$49.95, paperback. **Description:** Business management skills required for dairy farmers are addressed, focusing on financial management and ways to improve cattle housing and feeding systems. **Availability:** Print.

36827 ■ *"But Who's Counting.."* in Canadian Business (Vol. 79, December 4, 2006, No. 24, pp. 27)
Pub: Rogers Media Inc.
Contact: Tony Viner, President
Ed: David Wolf. **Description:** The analysis of the debt management policies of the Canadian government is presented. The plans of the Canadian government to repay all of its debts by the year 2020 are discussed.

36828 ■ *"Buyers' Market"* in Baltimore Business Journal (Vol. 27, November 20, 2009, No. 28, pp. 1)
Ed: Daniel J. Sernovitz. **Description:** Some business owners in Maryland are removing their leases and purchasing buildings due to the lower costs of real estate. This trend has enabled small business owners to avoid rent hikes, while setting equity into their companies. The pros and cons of owning buildings and how business owners assess their return on investment are examined.

36829 ■ *"C.A. Bancorp Inc. (TSX:BKP) Announces First Quarter 2007 Financial Results"* in Canadian Corporate News (May 16, 2007)
Description: Financial report for the first quarter of 2007 for C.A. Bancorp Inc., a publicly traded Canadian merchant bank and asset manager providing investors access to a range of private equity and alternative asset class investment opportunities. Statistical data and highlights included.

36830 ■ *"Calming Customers"* in The Business Journal-Portland (Vol. 25, August 29, 2008, No. 25, pp. 1)
Pub: American City Business Journals, Inc.
Contact: Whitney Shaw, President
Ed: Kirsten Grind, Rob Smith. **Description:** Credit unions and banks in the Portland area are reaching out to clients in an effort to reassure them on the security of their money and the firms' financial stability. Roy Whitehead of Washington Federal Savings, for instance, wrote 41,000 customers of the bank to reassure them. The strategies of different banks and credit unions to answer their client's worries are discussed.

36831 ■ *"Cambodia Calls"* in Barron's (Vol. 89, July 27, 2009, No. 30, pp. M7)
Pub: Dow Jones & Co., Inc.
Contact: Clare Hart, President
Ed: Leslie P. Norton. **Description:** Interest in frontier markets could jump if enthusiasm about growth in the developed world gathers steam. Cambodia is the latest market to get attention where a handful of

investors are trying to set up funds. One investor believes that Cambodia is back open for business but others are still cautious about investing in the country.

36832 ■ *Canadian Multinationals and International Finance*
Pub: Taylor & Francis Ltd.
Contact: Peter Rigby, Chief Executive Officer
Ed: Gregory P. Marchildon, Duncan McDowall. **Released:** September 30, 1992. **Price:** C$206, hardback. **Description:** Seven stories that explore the role of Canadian multinational enterprise in world finance, trade and direct investment. **Availability:** Print.

36833 ■ *"Candidates Won't Bash Fed; Rate Cuts Bash Savers"* in Barron's (Vol. 88, March 24, 2008, No. 12, pp. 31)
Pub: Dow Jones & Co., Inc.
Contact: Clare Hart, President
Ed: Jim McTague. **Description:** Candidates in the 2008 US presidential election, like the current administration, do not and will not bash the Federal Reserve. The Federal Reserve's aggressive interest rate cuts hurt the incomes of people depending on their savings accounts.

36834 ■ *"Capturing Generation Y: Ready, Set, Transform"* in Credit Union Times (Vol. 21, July 14, 2010, No. 27, pp. 20)
Pub: Summit Professional Networks
Contact: Steve Weitzner, President
Ed: Senthil Kumar. **Description:** The financial services sector recognizes that Generation Y will have a definite impact on the way business is conducted in the future. The mindset of Generation Y is social and companies need to use networking tools such as Facebook in order to reach this demographic.

36835 ■ *"CareFirst To Reward Doctors for Reducing Costs, Improving Care"* in Baltimore Business Journal (Vol. 28, June 4, 2010, No. 4, pp. 1)
Pub: Baltimore Business Journal
Ed: Scott Graham. **Description:** CareFirst Blue Cross Blue Shield plans to introduce a program that dangles big financial rewards to physicians who change the way they deliver primary care by improving the health of their sickest patients while reducing costs. The company will soon begin recruiting primary care physicians in Maryland, Washington DC, and Northern Virginia.

36836 ■ *Cash In a Flash*
Ed: Robert G. Allen, Mark Victor Hansen. **Released:** December 28, 2010. **Price:** $15. **Description:** Proven, practical advice and techniques are given to help entrepreneurs make money quickly using skills and resources known to generate permanent and recurring income.

36837 ■ *"Catch Up To Your Dream Retirement"* in Canadian Business (Vol. 85, July 16, 2012, No. 11-12, pp. 46)
Pub: George Media Inc.
Ed: David Aston. **Released:** July 16, 2012. **Description:** Tips on how to save for retirement during the early saving years, family years, and pre-retirement years are provided. Priority for those in their early saving years is to pay off debts first then consider employer pension plans and registered retirement savings plans. Those in their family years can save bonuses while those in pre-retirement should start by taking stock.

36838 ■ *"Cautions On Loans With Your Business"* in Business Owner (Vol. 35, July-August 2011, No. 4, pp. 5)
Pub: DL Perkins Company
Description: Caution must be used when borrowing from or lending to any small business. Tax guidelines for the borrowing and lending practice are also included.

36839 ■ *"Cemex Paves a Global Road to Solid Growth"* in Barron's (Vol. 88, March 10,

2008, No. 10, pp. 24)
Pub: Dow Jones & Co., Inc.
Contact: Clare Hart, President
Ed: Sandra Ward. **Description:** Shares of Cemex are expected to perform well with the company's expected strong performance despite fears of a US recession. The company has a diverse geographical reach and benefits from a strong worldwide demand for cement.

36840 ■ *"Centrue Sets Down New Roots in St. Louis"* in Crain's Chicago Business (May 5, 2008)
Pub: Crain Communications Inc.
Contact: Todd Johnson, Publisher
Ed: H. Lee Murphy. **Description:** Centrue Financial Corp. has moved its headquarters from Ottawa to suburban St. Louis in search of higher-growth markets. The banks acquisitions and expansion plans are also discussed.

36841 ■ *"The CEO Poll: A Say on Pay"* in Canadian Business (Vol. 82, April 27, 2009, No. 7, pp. 14)
Pub: Rogers Media Inc.
Contact: Tony Viner, President
Ed: Joe Castaldo. **Description:** A COMPAS Inc. survey of 134 Canadian chief executive officers found that 44 percent agree that CEO compensation should be subject to a non-binding vote. The respondents were also divided on whether to allow shareholders to exercise retroactive clawbacks on executive compensation if firm performance turns out to be worse than projected.

36842 ■ *"Change of Plans"* in Entrepreneur (Vol. 35, November 2007, No. 11, pp. 74)
Pub: Entrepreneur Press
Contact: Perlman Neil, President
Ed: C.J. Prince. **Description:** Companies should provide 401K plans that meet employee needs and demographics, with new technology allowing providers to lower their own costs. Details on finding a plans that appeal to employees are examined.

36843 ■ *The Changing Geography of Banking and Finance*
Pub: Springer Publishing Co.
Contact: Ursula Springer, President
Released: 2009. **Price:** €129.99, hardcover, softcover; €107.09. **Description:** The two contrasting trends that have emerged from the integration and consolidation processes of the banking industry in both Europe and the United States in the 1990s is examined. **Availability:** PrintE-book.

36844 ■ *"Chasing Credit"* in Canadian Business (Vol. 81, November 10, 2008, No. 19, pp. 59)
Pub: Rogers Media Inc.
Contact: Tony Viner, President
Ed: Joe Castaldo. **Description:** Small and medium sized companies are dealing with tightening credit because they appear riskier than usual. Some of these businesses are turning to private investors, but this is not easy since many have invested everything in the stock market. The sector is expected to weaken with the broader Canadian market in the next six months from October 2008.

36845 ■ *"Cheap Deposits Fuel Bank Profits"* in Boston Business Journal (Vol. 31, July 29, 2011, No. 27, pp. 1)
Pub: Boston Business Journal
Ed: Tim MacLaughlin. **Description:** Massachusetts-are banks increased profits primarily due to inexpensive deposits. The cheaper deposits have provided profit stability and fuel loan growth in an environment of historically low interest rates and uncertain economic recovery. Details of the banks' move to shed the more expensive certificates of deposit in favor of money market accounts are discussed.

36846 ■ *"Chuck's Big Chance"* in Barron's (Vol. 89, July 13, 2009, No. 28, pp. L3)
Pub: Dow Jones & Co., Inc.
Contact: Clare Hart, President
Ed: Leslie P. Norton. **Description:** Charles Schwab is cutting prices and rolling out new products to lure customers and the company is well positioned to

benefit from Wall Street's misery. Their shares are trading at just 17 times earnings, which should be at least at a multiple of 20.

36847 ■ *"Cincinnati Hospitals Feel Pain from Slow Economy" in Business Courier (Vol. 27, September 3, 2010, No. 18, pp. 1)*
Pub: Business Courier
Ed: James Ritchie. **Description:** Hospitals in Cincinnati, Ohio have suffered from decreased revenues owing to the economic crises. Declining patient volumes and bad debt have also adversely impacted hospitals.

36848 ■ *"Cincinnati's First Financial Bancorp Aiming for Banking Big Leagues" in Business Courier (Vol. 26, December 4, 2009, No. 32, pp. 1)*
Pub: American City Business Journals, Inc.
Contact: Whitney Shaw, President
Ed: Steve Watkins. **Description:** First Financial Bancorp could dominate the community banking market of Greater Cincinnati after buying failed banks with the supervision of the FDIC. Details of the transactions are presented.

36849 ■ *"Citadel Hires Three Lehman Execs" in Chicago Tribune (October 2, 2008)*
Ed: James P. Miller. **Description:** Citadel Investment Group LLC, Chicago hedge-fund operator, has hired three former senior executives of bankrupt investment banker Lehman Brothers Holding Inc. Citadel believes that the company's hiring spree will help them to further expand the firm's capabilities in the global fixed income business.

36850 ■ *"Citi Ruling Could Chill SEC, Street Legal Pacts" in Wall Street Journal Eastern Edition (November 29, 2011, pp. C1)*
Pub: Dow Jones & Co., Inc.
Contact: Clare Hart, President
Ed: Jean Eaglesham, Chad Bray. **Description:** A $285 million settlement was reached between the Securities and Exchange Commission and Citigroup Inc. over allegations the bank misled investors over a mortgage-bond deal. Now, Judge Jed S. Rakoff has ruled against the settlement, a decision that will affect the future of such attempts to prosecute Wall Street fraud. Rakoff said that the settlement was 'neither fair, nor reasonable, nor adequate, nor in the public interest.'.

36851 ■ *"Citizens Unveils Mobile App for Business Customers" in New Hampshire Business Review (Vol. 33, March 25, 2011, No. 6, pp. 27)*
Pub: Business Publications Inc.
Description: Citizens Financial Group offers a new mobile banking application that allows business customers to manage cash and payments from a mobile device.

36852 ■ *"Clearwire Struggling, Banks on Deals with Competitors" in Puget Sound Business Journal (Vol. 33, August 24, 2012, No. 18, pp. 1)*
Pub: American City Business Journal
Ed: Emily Parkhurst, Alyson Raletz. **Description:** Clearwire Corporation's chief executive, Erik Prusch, is planning to lease the wireless spectrum of the company to major mobile providers that run out of their own supply. At issue is whether the Bellevue, Washington-based telecommunication company can manage its $4 billion debt and maximize the value of its technology while managing its partners all at the same time.

36853 ■ *"A Click In the Right Direction: Website Teaches Youth Financial Literacy" in Black Enterprise (Vol. 38, December 2007, No. 5)*
Pub: Earl G. Graves Publishing Co. Inc.
Contact: Earl G. Graves, Jr., President
Ed: Nicole Norfleet. **Description:** Profile of Donald Lee Robinson who launched SkillsThatClick, a Website that teaches young individuals ages 12 to 15 about money management. Robinson shares how he used his Navy career as a model for designing the site.

36854 ■ *"Climbing the Wall of Worry, Two Steps at a Time" in Barron's (Vol. 89, July 13, 2009, No. 28, pp. L16)*
Pub: Dow Jones & Co., Inc.
Contact: Clare Hart, President
Ed: Brian Blackstone. **Description:** Statistical table that shows the performance of different mutual funds for the second quarter of 2009 is presented. The data shows that on average, the 8,272 diversified equity funds gained 17 percent for this quarter.

36855 ■ *"Clock Ticks On Columbia Sussex Debt" in Business Courier (Vol. 27, July 30, 2010, No. 13, pp. 1)*
Pub: Business Courier
Ed: Dan Monk. **Description:** Cincinnati, Ohio-based Columbia Sussex Corporation has made plans to restructure a $1 billion loan bundle that was scheduled to mature in October 2010. The privately held hotel has strived in a weak hotel market to keep pace with its $3 billion debt load.

36856 ■ *"CN 'Extremely Optimistic' After Record Profit" in Globe & Mail (January 24, 2007, pp. B3)*
Pub: CTVglobemedia Publishing Inc.
Ed: Brent Jang. **Description:** The increase in Canadian National Railway Co.'s profits to $2.1 billion despite a harsh winter is discussed.

36857 ■ *"Coca-Cola Looks Ready to Pause" in Barron's (Vol. 88, March 10, 2008, No. 10, pp. 18)*
Pub: Dow Jones & Co., Inc.
Contact: Clare Hart, President
Ed: Michael Santoli. **Description:** Shares of Coca-Cola are expected to turn sideways or experience a slight drop from $59.50 each to the mid-50 level. The company has seen its shares jump 40 percent since 2006, when it was in a series of measures to improve profitability.

36858 ■ *Code of Federal Regulations: Title 13: Business Credit and Assistance*
Pub: U. S. Government Printing Office
Contact: Veronica Meter, Director
E-mail: tpriebe@gpo.gov
Ed: Department of Commerce Staff. **Released:** January 2014. **Price:** $61. **Description:** Title 13 covers regulations governing the activities of the Small Business Administration and the Department of Commerce. Book covers information on business credit, finance, and economic development. **Availability:** Print.

36859 ■ *"Column: Want People to Save? Force Them" in Harvard Business Review (Vol. 88, September 2010, No. 9, pp. 36)*
Pub: Harvard Business School Publishing
Ed: Dan Ariely. **Description:** Contrasts in U.S. attitudes towards savings and government regulation with those of Chile, where all employees are required to save 11 percent of their salary in a retirement account, are highlighted.

36860 ■ *"Coming: Cheaper Oil and a Stronger Buck" in Barron's (Vol. 88, March 24, 2008, No. 12, pp. 53)*
Pub: Dow Jones & Co., Inc.
Contact: Clare Hart, President
Ed: Lawrence C. Strauss. **Description:** Carl C. Weinberg, the chief economist of High Frequency Economics, forecasts that Chinese economic growth will slow down and that oil prices will drop to $80 a barrel in 2008. He also believes that the US dollar will start rising the moment the Federal Reserve stops cutting interest rates.

36861 ■ *"Coming Soon: Bailouts of Fannie and Freddie" in Barron's (Vol. 88, July 14, 2008, No. 28, pp. 14)*
Pub: Dow Jones & Co., Inc.
Contact: Clare Hart, President
Ed: Jonathan R. Laing. **Description:** Assurances from the government that Fannie Mae and Freddie Mac are adequately capitalized and able to carry on their duties as guarantors or owners of over $5 trillion of U.S. home mortgages are designed to keep both entities afloat until they attempt to raise $10 billion in

new equity. The government would assume any losses in a bailout and owners of the banks' papers would profit as yields drop.

36862 ■ *"Coming: The End of Fiat Money" in (Vol. 92, July 23, 2012, No. 30, pp. 32)*
Pub: Dow Jones & Co., Inc.
Contact: Clare Hart, President
Ed: Leslie Norton. **Released:** July 23, 2012. **Description:** Stephanie Pomboy, founder of MicroMavens, discusses her views on the global financial system. She believes that the global fiat currency system may collapse within five years and be replaced by a gold-backed currency system.

36863 ■ *"A Comment on 'Balancing Risk and Return in a Customer Portfolio" in Journal of Marketing (Vol. 75, May 2011, No. 3, pp. 18)*
Pub: American Marketing Association
Contact: Lucille Pointer, President
Ed: Fred Selnes. **Description:** Issues regarding the use of approaches to managing customer portfolios are described. These are related to assumptions in modern financial portfolio theory and return and risk.

36864 ■ *"Commentary. Small Business Economic Trends" in Small Business Economic Trends (March 2008, pp. 3)*
Pub: National Federation of Independent Business
Contact: Caitlin McDevitt, Program Manager
Ed: William C. Dunkelberg, Holly Wade. **Description:** Commentary on the economic trends for small businesses in the U.S. is presented. Analysis of the labor market and low interest rates is given. The effect of the Federal Reserve's policy announcement on small business owner optimism is also discussed.

36865 ■ *"Commentary. Small Business Economic Trends" in Small Business Economic Trends (February 2008, pp. 3)*
Pub: National Federation of Independent Business
Contact: Caitlin McDevitt, Program Manager
Ed: William C. Dunkelberg, Holly Wade. **Description:** Commentary on the economic trends for small businesses in the U.S. is presented. Analysis of the U.S. Federal Reserve Board's efforts to prevent a recession is given. Reduction in business inventories is also discussed.

36866 ■ *"Commentary. Small Business Economic Trends" in Small Business Economic Trends (January 2008, pp. 3)*
Pub: National Federation of Independent Business
Contact: Caitlin McDevitt, Program Manager
Description: Federal Reserve cut interest rates and announced its economic outlook on September 18, 2007 to stimulate spending. The cut in interest rates, however, may not help in supporting consumer spending because savers may lose interest income. The expected economic impact of the interest rate cuts and the U.S. economic outlook are also discussed.

36867 ■ *"Commodities: Who's Behind the Boom?" in Barron's (Vol. 88, March 31, 2008, No. 13, pp. 3)*
Pub: Dow Jones & Co., Inc.
Contact: Clare Hart, President
Ed: Gene Epstein. **Description:** Proliferation of mutual funds and exchange traded funds tied to commodities indexes has helped speculative buying reach unusual levels. Index funds are estimated to account for 40 percent of all bullish bets on commodities. Commodities could drop by 30 percent as speculators retreat. Statistical data included.

36868 ■ *"Commodity Speculation: Over the Top?" in Barron's (Vol. 89, July 13, 2009, No. 28, pp. 22)*
Pub: Dow Jones & Co., Inc.
Contact: Clare Hart, President
Ed: Gene Epstein. **Description:** Commodity Futures Trading Commission is planning to consider position limits on speculators of oil and other commodities as energy costs rebound from their lows. These regulations make much sense and these position limits would greatly diminish the cash commitment of the commodity index traders if these were imposed on speculators and swaps dealers properly.

36869 ■ *"Compelling Opportunities for Investors in Emerging Markets"* in *Barron's (Vol. 88, March 10, 2008, No. 10, pp. 39)*
Pub: Dow Jones & Co., Inc.
Contact: Clare Hart, President

Ed: Neil A. Martin. **Description:** Michael L. Reynal, portfolio manager of Principal International Emerging Markets Fund, is bullish on the growth prospects of stocks in emerging markets. He is investing big on energy, steel, and transportation companies.

36870 ■ *"Competitors Line Up to Save Failing Banks"* in *The Business Journal - Serving Phoenix and the Valley of the Sun (Vol. 28, July 25, 2008, No. 47, pp. 1)*
Pub: American City Business Journals, Inc.
Contact: Whitney Shaw, President

Ed: Chris Casacchia. **Description:** Financial institutions in Arizona are positioning themselves as possible buyers in the event of failure of one of their competitors. These banks have already approached the Federal Deposit Insurance Corp. about their ability to take over their more troubled competitors.

36871 ■ *The Complete Idiot's Guide to Finance for Small Business*
Ed: Kenneth E. Little. **Released:** April 2006. **Price:** $19.95. **Description:** Financial experts helps small business owners through strategies for long-term financial success.

36872 ■ *"Comtech's Winning Streak"* in *Crain's New York Business (Vol. 24, January 6, 2008, No. 1, pp. 3)*
Pub: Crain Communications Inc.
Contact: Rance Crain, President

Description: Comtech Telecommunications Corp., a designer and manufacturer of equipment that helps military track troops and vehicles on the field, has been one of the stock market's biggest winners over the past decade. Statistical data included.

36873 ■ *"Conquering Your Fear of Fees"* in *Entrepreneur (Vol. 37, October 2009, No. 10, pp. 86)*
Pub: Entrepreneur Press
Contact: Perlman Neil, President

Ed: Rosalind Resnick. **Description:** Entrepreneurs should study money management charges carefully before investing. They should understand how different forms of investments work and how much money managers and mutual funds charge for their services.

36874 ■ *"Consumer Contagion? A Bleak Earnings View"* in *Barron's (Vol. 88, March 10, 2008, No. 10, pp. 15)*
Pub: Dow Jones & Co., Inc.
Contact: Clare Hart, President

Ed: Robin Goldwyn Blumenthal. **Description:** Analysts expect consumer discretionary profits in the S&P 500 to drop 8.4 percent in the first quarter of 2008. A less confident consumer is expected to pull profits down, putting forecasts of earnings growth in the S&P 500 at risk. Statistical data included.

36875 ■ *"Consumers Are Still Wary; Here's How To Win Them. The Great Recession Has Left Consumers Worried About Their Financial Future. But the Right Strategies Can Engage Leery Spenders"* in *Gallup Business Journal (June 24, 2014)*
Pub: Gallup Press

Released: June 24, 2014. **Description:** Because consumers are concerned about their financial futures, they are less likely to spend money. Strategies to increase sales while increasing consumer confidence are outlined.

36876 ■ *"Consumers Finding It Harder to Get and Keep Credit"* in *Chicago Tribune (January 10, 2009)*
Pub: McClatchy-Tribune Information Services

Ed: Susan Chandler. **Description:** Five tips to maintain a good credit rating in these economic times are outlined and discussed.

36877 ■ *"Consumers Seek to Redo Rate Structure: Smaller Biz Paid Big Rates"* in *Crain's Detroit Business (Vol. 25, June 22, 2009)*
Pub: Crain Communications Inc. - Detroit
Contact: Keith Crain, Chairman

Ed: Amy Lane. **Description:** Consumers Energy Company charged small business customers disproportionately higher rates on June 2009 electric bills than other consumers.

36878 ■ *"Consumers Turned Off? Not at Best Buy"* in *Barron's (Vol. 88, March 24, 2008, No. 12, pp. 29)*
Pub: Dow Jones & Co., Inc.
Contact: Clare Hart, President

Ed: Sandra Ward. **Description:** Shares of Best Buy, trading at $42.41 each, are expected to rise to an average of $52 a share due to the company's solid fundamentals. The company's shares have fallen 20 percent from their 52-week high and are attractive given the company's bright prospects in the video game sector and high-definition video.

36879 ■ *"Controlling Costs: Update Your Information Technology Program"* in *Franchising World (Vol. 42, August 2010, No. 8, pp. 18)*
Pub: International Franchise Association
Contact: Stephen J. Caldeira, President
E-mail: scaldeira@franchise.org

Ed: Jeff Dumont. **Description:** It is imperative for any franchise to understand its technology needs in order to control costs. Needs analysis; creating a Request for Proposal; and information regarding the choices between renting, buying or building technology are covered. Relationship contingency in franchised organizations is also covered.

36880 ■ *"Conversation Starters for the Holiday"* in *Barron's (Vol. 89, July 6, 2009, No. 27, pp. 7)*
Pub: Dow Jones & Co., Inc.
Contact: Clare Hart, President

Ed: Michael Santoli. **Description:** Investors are concerned that the US will experience high inflation due to low interest rates and improved money supply. US consumer spending has increased to 70 percent of gross domestic product, brought by health-care spending increases, while savings rates have risen to 6.9 percent.

36881 ■ *"A Conversation With Money Manager William Vellon"* in *Crain's Chicago Business (Vol. 31, November 17, 2008, No. 46, pp. 4)*

Ed: Mike Colias. **Description:** Interview with William Vellon, the executive vice-president of Kingsbury Capital Investment Advisors; Vellon discusses ways in which the government can help the financial sector, his client base and bargains that investors should consider.

36882 ■ *"A Conversation With; Ron Gantner, Jones Lang LaSalle"* in *Crain's Detroit Business (Vol. 24, October 6, 2008, No. 40, pp. 9)*
Pub: Crain Communications Inc.
Contact: Rance E. Crain, President

Description: Interview with Ron Gantner who is a corporate real estate adviser with the real estate company Jones Lang LaSalle as well as the company's executive vice president and part of the tenant advisory team; Gantner speaks about the impact that the Wall Street crisis is having on the commercial real estate market in Detroit.

36883 ■ *"Copy Karachi?"* in *Barron's (Vol. 88, June 30, 2008, No. 26, pp. 5)*
Pub: Dow Jones & Co., Inc.
Contact: Clare Hart, President

Ed: Randall W. Forsyth. **Description:** Karachi bourse had a historic 8.6 percent one-day gain because the bourse banned short-selling for a month and announced a 30 billion rupee fund to stabilize the market. The shares of General Motors are trading within the same values that it had in 1974. The reasons for this decline are discussed.

36884 ■ *"Corn May Get Shucked By Soy"* in *Barron's (Vol. 88, March 31, 2008, No. 13, pp. M12)*
Pub: Dow Jones & Co., Inc.
Contact: Clare Hart, President

Ed: Angie Pointer. **Description:** Acreage allotted to soybeans could jump by 12 percent from 2007's 63.6 million as the price for soybeans reaches record highs. Corn acreage could drop by 6.7 percent as other crops expand and higher fertilizer prices shift farmers away from corn.

36885 ■ *"Cornerstone Seeks Investors for Hedge Fund"* in *Baltimore Business Journal (Vol. 32, June 20, 2014, No. 7, pp. 10)*
Pub: American City Business Journals, Inc.
Contact: Whitney Shaw, President

Released: June 20, 2014. **Description:** Cornerstone Advisory LLP is looking for investors to create a hedge fund that ties returns to various indices, real estate or commodity prices. Cornerstone hopes to raise between $30 million to $50 million and are planning a fall launch for the fund. They have hired New York law firm Thompson Hine LLP to draft the subscription agreement and NebraskaEs Gimini Fund Services LLC to run as third party administrator.

36886 ■ *"Corporate Elite Show Resilience"* in *The Business Journal-Serving Greater Tampa Bay (Vol. 28, August 4, 2008, No. 32, pp. 1)*
Pub: American City Business Journals, Inc.
Contact: Whitney Shaw, President

Ed: Margie Manning, Alexis Muellner. **Description:** Stocks of the largest public companies in Tampa Bay, Florida, outperformed the S&P 500 index by 28 percent in the first half of 2008. The escalation is attributed to the growth orientation of the companies in the area and the lack of exposure to the real estate and financial services sectors.

36887 ■ *"Corporate Responsibility"* in *Professional Services Close-Up (July 2, 2010)*
Description: List of firms awarded the inaugural Best Corporate Citizens in Government Contracting by the Corporate Responsibility Magazine is presented. The list is based on the methodology of the Magazine's Best Corporate Citizen's List, with 324 data points of publicly-available information in seven categories which include: environment, climate change, human rights, philanthropy, employee relations, financial performance, and governance.

36888 ■ *"Corus Eases Off Ailing Condo Market"* in *Crain's Chicago Business (April 28, 2008)*
Pub: Crain Communications Inc.
Contact: Todd Johnson, Publisher

Ed: H. Lee Murphy. **Description:** Corus Bankshares Inc., a specialist in lending for the condominium high-rise construction market, is diversifying its portfolio by making loans to office developers and expects to be investing in hotels through the rest of the year. Corus' $7.57 billion loan portfolio is also discussed in detail as well as the company's earnings and share price. Statistical data included.

36889 ■ *"COSE Turns On To Electricity Market"* in *Crain's Cleveland Business (Vol. 30, June 22, 2009, No. 24, pp. 4)*
Pub: Crain Communications Inc.

Ed: Jay Miller. **Description:** Council of Smaller Enterprises is working to offer small businesses and their employees electricity at discount prices set at auction by the Public Utilities Commission of Ohio and even lower prices from the Northern Ohio Public Energy Council. Details of the program are offered.

36890 ■ *"Cost of Creating Health Insurance Exchange in Md. 'Largely Unknown"* in *Baltimore Business Journal (Vol. 28, September 3, 2010, No. 17, pp. 1)*
Pub: Baltimore Business Journal

Ed: Emily Mullin. **Description:** United States health reform is seen to result in increased health insurance prices in Maryland. However, health care reform advocates claim a new marketplace and increased competition will help keep costs down.

36891 ■ *"Cost of Md.'s Business Banking May Soon Go Up"* in Baltimore Business Journal (Vol. 28, October 29, 2010, No. 25, pp. 1)

Pub: Baltimore Business Journal

Ed: Gary Haber. **Description:** Experts in the financial industry expect banks to charge credit card transactions, especially to small business owners and consumers to recover about $11 million in lost revenue annually. Banks are expected to charge old fees and new ones, including $5 to $10 a month for a checking account.

36892 ■ *"Countdown"* in Canadian Business (Vol. 81, March 3, 2008, No. 3, pp. 27)

Ed: Al Rosen. **Description:** According to a recent poll only 42 percent of portfolio managers in Canada are aware that the country is planning to adopt the International Financial Reporting Standards beginning 2011. The shift to the new standards will have significant impacts on investment values and will be the biggest revolution in Canadian financial reporting. The effects of the transition on portfolio managers and investors are analyzed.

36893 ■ *"Crain's Picks Top '08 Stocks"* in Crain's New York Business (Vol. 24, January 6, 2008, No. 1, pp. 3)

Pub: Crain Communications Inc.

Contact: Rance Crain, President

Ed: Aaron Elstein. **Description:** Listing of five stocks that Crain's believes can deliver solid gains for shareholders.

36894 ■ *"Crash Landing? Serious Signal Flashing"* in Barron's (Vol. 88, July 7, 2008, No. 27, pp. 11)

Pub: Dow Jones & Co., Inc.

Contact: Clare Hart, President

Description: Discusses the Hindenburg Omen, named after the airship disaster of May 1937, which is considered a predictor of market crashes and has appeared twice in June 2008. There is a 25 percent probability that the US stock market will suffer a crash in the July-October 2008 period.

36895 ■ *Crash Proof 2.0: How to Profit From the Economic Collapse*

Pub: John Wiley & Sons Inc.

Contact: Stephen M. Smith, President

Ed: Peter D. Schiff, John Downes. **Released:** Second Edition. **Price:** $16.95, paperback; $11.99. **Description:** Factors that will affect financial stability in the coming years are explained. A three step plan to battle the current economic downturn is also included. **Availability:** PrintE-book.

36896 ■ *Creating a World without Poverty: Social Business and the Future of Capitalism*

Pub: Basic Books

Contact: Elizabeth Maguire, Publisher

Ed: Muhammad Yunus. **Released:** April 26, 2009. **Price:** $15.99, Paperback; C$18.50; £9.99. **Description:** Explanation of how microcredit lending practices and more collaborative business strategies can be used to alleviate poverty worldwide.

36897 ■ *"Creative In-Sourcing Boosts Franchisee Performance"* in Franchising World (Vol. 42, September 2010, No. 9, pp. 16)

Pub: International Franchise Association

Contact: Stephen J. Caldeira, President

E-mail: scaldeira@franchise.org

Ed: Daniel M. Murphy. **Description:** Operational training and support is usually provided by franchisors. To be successful in this process it is important to balance the reality of limited financial and human resources.

36898 ■ *"The Credit Crisis Continues"* in Barron's (Vol. 88, March 10, 2008, No. 10, pp. M12)

Pub: Dow Jones & Co., Inc.

Contact: Clare Hart, President

Ed: Randall W. Forsyth. **Description:** Short-term Treasury yields dropped to new cyclical lows in early March 2008, with the yield for the two-year Treasury note falling to 1.532 percent. Spreads of the mortgage-backed securities of Fannie Mae and Freddie Mac rose on suspicion of collapses in financing.

36899 ■ *"Credit Crisis Puts Market in Unprecedented Territory"* in Crain's New York Business (Vol. 24, January 6, 2008, No. 1, pp. 14)

Pub: Crain Communications Inc.

Contact: Rance Crain, President

Ed: Aaron Elstein. **Description:** Banks are being forced to take enormous losses due to investors who are refusing to buy anything linked to subprime mortgages and associated securities.

36900 ■ *"Credit Crunch Takes Bite Out Of McDonald's"* in Advertising Age (Vol. 79, September 29, 2008, No. 36, pp. 1)

Pub: Crain Communications Inc.

Contact: Rance Crain, President

Ed: Emily Bryson York. **Description:** McDonald's will delay its launch of coffee bars inside its restaurants due to the banking crisis which has prompted Bank of America to halt loans to the franchise chains.

36901 ■ *"Credit Reporting Myths and Reality"* in Black Enterprise (Vol. 41, December 2010, No. 5, pp. 34)

Pub: Earl G. Graves Publishing Co. Inc.

Contact: Earl G. Graves, Jr., President

Ed: Denise A. Campbell. **Description:** It is critical to understand all the factors affecting credit scores before making any major purchase.

36902 ■ *"Credit Unions Cast Wary Eye at Paulson Plan, But Not Panicking Yet"* in The Business Review Albany (Vol. 35, April 11, 2008, No. 1)

Pub: The Business Review

Ed: Barbara Pinckney. **Description:** Credit unions are suspicious of US Treasury Secretary Henry Paulson's plan to establish a single federally insured depository institution charter for all institutions covered by federal deposit insurance. The charter would replace national banks, federal savings associations, and federal credit union charters.

36903 ■ *"Cummins Is a Engine of Growth"* in Barron's (Vol. 88, July 14, 2008, No. 28, pp. 43)

Pub: Dow Jones & Co., Inc.

Contact: Clare Hart, President

Ed: Shirley A. Lazo. **Description:** Engine maker Cummins increased its quarterly common dividend by 40 percent to 17.5 cents per share from 12.5 cents. CVS Caremark's dividend saw a hike of 18.4 percent from 9.5 cents to 11.25 cents per share while its competitor Walgreen is continuing its 75th straight year of dividend distribution and its 33rd straight year of dividend hikes.

36904 ■ *"Currency: I'm Outta Here"* in Entrepreneur (Vol. 35, October 2007, No. 10, pp. 72)

Pub: Entrepreneur Press

Contact: Perlman Neil, President

Ed: C.J. Prince. **Description:** Liberum Research revealed that 193 chief financial officers (CFOs) at small companies have either resigned or retired during the first half of 2007. A survey conducted by Tatum found that unreasonable expectations from the management and compliance to regulations are the main reasons why CFOs are leaving small firms. The chief executive officer's role in making CFOs stay is also discussed.

36905 ■ *Currency Internationalization: Global Experiences and Implications for the Renminbi*

Pub: Palgrave Macmillan

Contact: Lisa Dunn, Manager

E-mail: l.dunn@palgrave.com

Released: November 2009. **Price:** £79; $115. **Description:** A collection of academic studies relating to the potential internationalization of China's remninbi. It also discusses the increasing use of China's remninbi currency in international trade and finance. **Availability:** PrintE-book; PDF.

36906 ■ *"Cyclicals, Your Day Is Coming"* in Barron's (Vol. 89, July 27, 2009, No. 30, pp. 24)

Pub: Dow Jones & Co., Inc.

Contact: Clare Hart, President

Ed: Dimitra DeFotis. **Description:** Cyclical stocks are likely to be big winners when the economy improves and 13 stocks that have improving earnings, decent balance sheets, and dividends are presented. These candidates include U.S. Steel, Alcoa, Allegheny Tech, Dow Chemical, and Nucor.

36907 ■ *"Dallas-Foth Worth Banks Debate Need to Grow Branches"* in Dallas Business Journal (Vol. 35, April 13, 2012, No. 31, pp. 1)

Pub: American City Business Journal

Description: Dallas-Fort Worth Metropolitan Area (DFW)-based banks have been debating whether to add more branches as more customers go online to handle their finances. The Federal Deposit Insurance Corporation (FDIC) has reported the number of bank and thrift branches in DFW fell 5 percent to 1.717 in June 2011 from 1,809 in June 2009. Details of the FDIC report are also discussed.

36908 ■ *"Daniel Snook"* in Sacramento Business Journal (Vol. 31, April 11, 2014, No. 7, pp. 6)

Pub: American City Business Journals

Released: April 11, 2014. **Description:** DKS Inc. president and chief financial officer, Daniel Snook, shares his views about his plumbing company. Snook believes it is just a philosophy and attitude they had that enabled the company to grow quickly. He also says cost control is one of the dangers in growing so fast and they are now carefully watching their financial reinvestment.

36909 ■ *"Data Dispel Some Notions About Value of Stock Buybacks"* in Crain's Cleveland Business (Vol. 28, November 19, 2007, No. 46, pp. 9)

Pub: Crain Communications Inc.

Ed: Megan Johnston. **Description:** According to new research on buybacks and their benefits, companies engaged in stock buybacks frequently do not enjoy a nice boost in their share prices despite the conventional wisdom that states that investors like stock buybacks.

36910 ■ *Data Driven Investing: Professional Edition*

Pub: Data Driven Publishing, LLC

Ed: Mitchell R. Hardy, Bill Matson. **Released:** 2004. **Description:** Investment concepts and trading techniques are explored in a simple and practical way. The book covers the unreliability of financial markets due to malpractices, appalling analysis, insider training and more. Information is based on data and common sense and easy to use for beginner as well as professional.

36911 ■ *"Deal Braces Cramer for Growth Run"* in The Business Journal-Serving Metropolitan Kansas City (Vol. 26, July 4, 2008, No. 43, pp. 1)

Ed: James Dornbook. **Description:** Gardner, Kansas-based Cramer Products Inc. bought 100 percent of the stocks of Louisville, Kentucky-based Active Ankle Inc. from 26 private investors increasing its revenue by 20 percent. The latter is the second largest vendor of Cramer. Other details of the merger are presented.

36912 ■ *"Deal Snapshot: Americanwest Bank Closes Acquistion of Security Business Bancorp"* in M & A Navigator (July 9, 2012)

Pub: Normans Media Ltd.

Released: July 19, 2012. **Description:** American-West Bank has purchased Security Business Bancorp (SBBC), the parent company of San Diego-based Security Business Bank. AmericanWest Bank is a subsidiary of American West Bancorporation.

36913 ■ *"Dealers Leasing Changes Name, Hopes to Stoke National Growth"* in Wichita Business Journal (Vol. 27, January 27, 2012,

No. 4, pp. 1)
Pub: American City Business Journal
Description: Wichita, Kansas-based Dealers Financing has changed its name to Lease Finance Partners as part of its plans to expand the market it serves. The name change was designed to better reflect the kind of business the company does, which is financing the leasing of fleet vehicles and heavy equipment.

36914 ■ *"Debt Grows At State's Largest Universities as Enrollment Booms"* in Birmingham Business Journal (Vol. 29, July 13, 2012, No. 29, pp. 1)
Pub: American City Business Journals, Inc.
Contact: Whitney Shaw, President
Ed: Nick Bowman. **Released:** July 13, 2012. **Description:** Alabama's largest public universities have reported growing long-term debt as record enrollment drives them to incur more debt to accommodate the high number of students. University of Alabama's debt increase 48 percent to $682 million in 2011, while Auburn University saw its debt jump 25.5 percent to $773 million.

36915 ■ *"Decline in Assets Is Costly for Advisers"* in The Business Journal-Serving Metropolitan Kansas City (Vol. 27, October 24, 2008)
Ed: James Dornbrook. **Description:** Financial advisers in the Kansas City, Missouri area are forced to cut costs as their assets have decreased sharply due to the huge drop in stock prices. American Century Investments was forced to diversify into foreign assets and cut 90 jobs as its assets dropped to $84 billion. Diversification has softened the impact of the steep decline in stock prices for Waddell & Reed Financial Inc.

36916 ■ *"Deutsche Bank Joins the Club Of Banks With Problems"* in Barron's (Vol. 88, March 31, 2008, No. 13, pp. M6)
Pub: Dow Jones & Co., Inc.
Contact: Clare Hart, President
Ed: Arindam Nag. **Description:** Deutsche Bank's tangible leverage has worsened sharply in the past year from 2.1 percent to 2.3 percent during 2002-2006 to only 1.6 percent. The bank has also been accumulating a lot of illiquid assets and its Level-3 assets are three times its tangible equity.

36917 ■ *"Developers Compete for APG Project"* in Baltimore Business Journal (Vol. 27, October 16, 2009, No. 23, pp. 1)
Ed: Daniel J. Sernovitz. **Description:** Corporate Office Properties Trust has lost the case in Delaware bankruptcy court to prevent rival St. John Properties Inc. from going ahead with its plans to develop the 400 acres at Aberdeen Proving Ground (APG) in Maryland. Both developers have competed for the right to develop the two million square foot business park in APG.

36918 ■ *The Dhandho Investor: The Low-Risk Value Method to High Returns*
Pub: John Wiley & Sons Inc.
Contact: Stephen M. Smith, President
Ed: Mohnish Pabrai. **Released:** March 2007. **Price:** $29.95, hardcover; $19.99. **Description:** Value investing is described using the Dhandho capital allocation framework for successfully investing in the stock market. **Availability:** PrintE-book.

36919 ■ *"Diary of a Short-Seller"* in Conde Nast Portfolio (Vol. 2, June 2008, No. 6, pp. 44)
Ed: Jesse Eisinger. **Description:** Profile of David Einhorn who is a fund manager that spoke out against finance company Allied Capital whose stock fell nearly 20 percent the day after Einhorn's critique; Einhorn subsequently had to contend with attacks against his credibility as well as investigations by the S.E.C.; Einhorn's experience illuminates our current economic crisis.

36920 ■ *"Dick Haskayne"* in Canadian Business (Vol. 81, March 31, 2008, No. 5, pp. 72)
Pub: Rogers Media Inc.
Contact: Tony Viner, President
Ed: Andy Holloway. **Description:** Dick Haskayne says that he learned a lot about business from his

dad who ran a butcher shop where they had to make a decision on buying cattle and getting credit. Haskayne says that family, friends, finances, career, health, and infrastructure are benchmarks that have to be balanced.

36921 ■ *Dictionary of Finance, Investment and Banking*
Pub: Palgrave Macmillan
Contact: Lisa Dunn, Manager
E-mail: l.dunn@palgrave.com
Ed: Erik Banks. **Released:** December 2009. **Price:** £33.99. **Description:** Comprehensive dictionary covering terms used in finance, investment and banking sectors. **Availability:** Print; E-book; Electronic publishing.

36922 ■ *"Different This Time?"* in Canadian Business (Vol. 81, April 14, 2008, No. 6, pp. 38)
Pub: Rogers Media Inc.
Contact: Tony Viner, President
Ed: Matthew McClearn. **Description:** Irving Fisher believed that the low interest rates of the 1920's spurred investors to borrow and use the money to speculate with the proceeds thereby increasing the debt to unmanageable levels prior to the stock market crash in Oct. 29, 1929. The U.S. economic conditions in 1929 and U.S. economic conditions in 2008 are discussed.

36923 ■ *"Digging Deep for Gold"* in Barron's (Vol. 88, March 24, 2008, No. 12, pp. 49)
Pub: Dow Jones & Co., Inc.
Contact: Clare Hart, President
Ed: Suzanne McGee. **Description:** David Iben, manager of the Nuveen Tradewinds Value Opportunities Fund, looks for value in companies and industries where the consensus of analysts is negative. He started investing in gold stocks well before gold prices started to rise.

36924 ■ *"Dividing to Conquer"* in Barron's (Vol. 88, March 31, 2008, No. 13, pp. 22)
Ed: Andrew Bary. **Description:** Altria's spin off of Philip Morris International could unlock substantial value for both domestic and international cigarette concerns. The strong brands and ample payouts from both companies will most likely impress investors.

36925 ■ *"Do-It-Yourself Portfolio Management"* in Barron's (Vol. 89, July 13, 2009, No. 28, pp. 25)
Pub: Dow Jones & Co., Inc.
Contact: Clare Hart, President
Ed: Mike Hogan. **Description:** Services of several portfolio management web sites are presented. These web sites include MarketRiders E.Adviser, TD Ameritrade and E.

36926 ■ *"The Dogs of TSX"* in Canadian Business (Vol. 81, Summer 2008, No. 9, pp. 77)
Ed: Calvin Leung. **Description:** Table showing the one-year stock performance of the ten highest dividend-yielding stocks on the S&P/TSX 60 Composite Index is presented. This technique is similar to the 'Dogs of the Dow' approach. The idea in this investment strategy is to buy equal amounts of stocks from these companies and selling them a year later, and then repeat the process.

36927 ■ *"The Dominance of Doubt"* in Barron's (Vol. 89, July 13, 2009, No. 28, pp. M3)
Pub: Dow Jones & Co., Inc.
Contact: Clare Hart, President
Ed: Jay Palmer. **Description:** Five straight down days leading up to July 10, 2009 in the U.S. stock market reminds one strategist of 1982 when there was a feeling that things could never be the same again. One analyst is bullish on the stocks of Apple Inc. and sees the stocks rising to at least 180 in 12 months. The prospects of the shares of GM and Ford are also discussed.

36928 ■ *"Don't Bet Against The House"* in Barron's (Vol. 88, July 14, 2008, No. 28, pp. 20)
Pub: Dow Jones & Co., Inc.
Contact: Clare Hart, President
Ed: Sandra Ward. **Description:** Shares of Nasdaq OMX have lost more than 50 percent of their value from November 2007 to July 2008 but the value of these shares could climb 50 percent on the strength of world security exchanges. Only 15 percent of the company's revenues come from the U.S. and the shares are trading at 12.5 times the amount expected for 2008.

36929 ■ *"Don't Expect Quick Fix"* in The Business Journal-Serving Metropolitan Kansas City (Vol. 27, October 3, 2008, No. 3, pp. 1)
Pub: American City Business Journals, Inc.
Contact: Whitney Shaw, President
Ed: James Dornbrook. **Description:** United States governmental entities cannot provide a quick fix solution to the current financial crisis. The economy requires a systemic change in the way people think about credit. The financial services industry should also focus on core lending principles.

36930 ■ *"Don't Get Lulled by the Calm"* in Barron's (Vol. 89, July 27, 2009, No. 30, pp. M13)
Pub: Dow Jones & Co., Inc.
Contact: Clare Hart, President
Ed: Steven M. Sears. **Description:** Options traders expect volatility to return in the fall of 2009 and to bring correlation with it. September and October are typically the most volatile months and the trick is to survive earnings season.

36931 ■ *"Don't' Hang Up On FairPoint"* in Barron's (Vol. 88, July 7, 2008, No. 27, pp. M5)
Ed: Fleming Meeks. **Description:** Shares of FairPoint Communications, priced at $6.63 each, are undervalued and should be worth over $12 each. The company increased its size by more than five times by acquiring Verizon's local telephone operations in Vermont, New Hampshire, and Maine, but must switch customers in those areas into their system by the end of September 2007.

36932 ■ *"Downtown Bank Got High Marks for Irwin Purchase, Is Looking For More"* in Business Courier (Vol. 27, September 3, 2010, No. 18, pp. 1)
Pub: Business Courier
Ed: Steve Watkins. **Description:** First Financial Bancorp is looking to acquire more troubled banks following its purchase of Irwin Union Bank. The bank has reported a $383 million bargain purchase gain during the third quarter of 2009.

36933 ■ *"Drilling Deep and Flying High"* in Barron's (Vol. 88, June 30, 2008, No. 26, pp. 34)
Pub: Dow Jones & Co., Inc.
Contact: Clare Hart, President
Ed: Kenneth Rapoza. **Description:** Shares of Petrobras could rise another 25 percent if the three deepwater wells that the company has found proves as lucrative as some expect. Petrobras will become an oil giant if the reserves are proven.

36934 ■ *"Drug-Maker Plans IPO"* in Business Courier (Vol. 24, November 23, 2008, No. 32, pp. 1)
Ed: James Ritchie; Steve Watkins. **Description:** Xanodyne Pharmaceuticals Inc. filed plans with the Securities and Exchange Commission on November 9, 2007 for an initial public offering. The company, with annual sales of $75 million, had lost $222 million since it was founded in 2001.

36935 ■ *"Drug, Seed Firms Offer Antidote For Inflation"* in Crain's Chicago Business (Vol. 31, April 21, 2008, No. 16, pp. 4)
Pub: Crain Communications Inc.
Contact: Todd Johnson, Publisher
Ed: Daniel Rome Levine. **Description:** Interview with Jerrold Senser, the CEO of Institutional Capital LLC in Chicago, in which he discusses the ways that the

company is adjusting to the economic slowdown and rising inflation, his favorite firms for investment and his prediction of an economic turnaround; he also recommends five companies he feels are worth investing in.

36936 ■ *"Ducking the New Health-Care Taxes"* **in Barron's (Vol. 92, September 15, 2012, No. 38, pp. 34)**
Pub: Dow Jones & Co., Inc.
Contact: Clare Hart, President
Ed: Elizabeth Ody. **Description:** Strategies that investors can use to avoid paying higher taxes starting January 2013 are discussed. These include selling assets by December 2012, distributing dividends, purchasing private-placement life insurance and converting individual retirement accounts.

36937 ■ *"Dueling Visions"* **in Barron's (Vol. 89, July 27, 2009, No. 30, pp. 13)**
Pub: Dow Jones & Co., Inc.
Contact: Clare Hart, President
Ed: Michael Santoli. **Description:** Goldman Sachs' market strategists believe the stock market has entered a 'sustained-rally' mode while Morgan Stanley's strategist believes this is a 'rally to sell into'. What is not known in the stock market is how much of a 'V'-shaped recovery in earning the market rebound has already priced in.

36938 ■ *"Dynamic Duo: Payouts Rise at General Dynamics, Steel Dynamics"* **in Barron's (Vol. 88, March 10, 2008, No. 10, pp. 45)**
Pub: Dow Jones & Co., Inc.
Contact: Clare Hart, President
Ed: Shirley A. Lazo. **Description:** General Dynamics, the world's sixth-largest military contractor, raised its dividend payout by 20.7 percent from 29 cents to 35 cents a share. Steel Dynamics, producer of structural steel and steel bar products, declared a 2-for-1 stock split and raised its quarterly dividend by 33 percent to a split-adjusted 10 cents a share.

36939 ■ *"Easier Options Orders"* **in Barron's (Vol. 92, August 25, 2012, No. 35, pp. 28)**
Pub: Dow Jones & Co., Inc.
Contact: Clare Hart, President
Ed: Theresa W. Carey. **Description:** Online brokerage optionsXpress introduced the Walk Limit, a service that allows traders to improve pricing for options and save money. Online brokerage TradeMonster introduced portfolio margining to qualified customers.

36940 ■ *"Eastern Market's New Bite?"* **in Washington Business Journal (Vol. 33, August 8, 2014, No. 16, pp. 6)**
Pub: American City Business Journals
Released: August 8, 2014. **Description:** Eastern Market continues to operate despite allegations of financial mismanagement on the part of Washington DC auditors. Many of the market's vendors have been operating their stands with expired leases for more than five years. However, the Department of General Services has vowed to draw a new standard contract for renting and renegotiate new leases.

36941 ■ *"Economic Recovery Prognosis: Four More Years"* **in Barron's (Vol. 89, July 13, 2009, No. 28, pp. 11)**
Pub: Dow Jones & Co., Inc.
Contact: Clare Hart, President
Ed: Karen Hube. **Description:** Loomis Sayles Bond Fund manager Dan Fuss believes that the economy is bottoming and that recovery will be long and drawn out. Fuss guesses that the next peak in 10-year Treasury yields will be about 6.25% in around 4 and a half or five years ahead of 2009.

36942 ■ *"Economic Woes Portend Consumer Shift"* **in The Business Journal-Serving Metropolitan Kansas City (Vol. 27, September 26, 2008, No. 2, pp. 1)**
Pub: American City Business Journals, Inc.
Contact: Whitney Shaw, President
Ed: Suzanna Stagemeyer. **Description:** Black Bamboo owner Tim Butt believes that prolonged tightening of the credit market will result in consumer

spending becoming more cash-driven that credit card driven. The financial crisis has already constricted spending among consumers. Forecasts for the US economy are provided.

36943 ■ *"Edging Toward Disaster"* **in Canadian Business (Vol. 85, July 16, 2012, No. 12, pp. 9)**
Pub: George Media Inc.
Ed: Graham F. Scott. **Released:** July 16, 2012. **Description:** The possibility that Green may default and exit from the Eurozone could trigger a series of bank runs in Europe and not even the solvenc of the European Central Bank is guaranteed, having already spent over trillion Euro in bailouts. Greek banks have lost 72 billion Euro in deposits since 2010 while clients withdrew 97 billion Euro from Spanish banks in the first quarter 2012.

36944 ■ *"An Educated Play on China"* **in Barron's (Vol. 88, June 30, 2008, No. 26, pp. M6)**
Pub: Dow Jones & Co., Inc.
Contact: Clare Hart, President
Ed: Mohammed Hadi. **Description:** New Oriental Education & Technology Group sells English-language courses to an increasingly competitive Chinese workforce that values education. The shares in this company have been weighed down by worries on the impact of the Beijing Olympics on enrollment and the Sichuan earthquake. These shares could be a great way to get exposure to the long-term growth in China.

36945 ■ *"Effect of Oil Prices on the Economy"* **in Canadian Business (Vol. 81, September 15, 2008, No. 14-15, pp. 5)**
Ed: Joe Chidley. **Description:** Rise of oil prices above $100 in February 2008 and $140 in July signals the birth of a 'new economy' according to commentators; this shift is causing uneasiness from oil industry professionals who are unsure of how this trend could be sustained. Oil dropped below $120 in August, which could slow down global economic growth followed by oil demand, then oil prices.

36946 ■ *"Egg Fight: The Yolk's on the Shorts"* **in Barron's (Vol. 88, July 7, 2008, No. 27, pp. 20)**
Pub: Dow Jones & Co., Inc.
Contact: Clare Hart, President
Ed: Christopher C. Williams. **Description:** Shares of Cal-Maine Foods, the largest egg producer and distributor in the US, are due for a huge rise because of the increase in egg prices. Short sellers, however, continue betting that the stock, priced at $31.84 each, will eventually go down.

36947 ■ *"Elder Care Costs Surge"* **in National Underwriter Life & Health (Vol. 114, November 8, 2020, No. 21, pp. 25)**
Pub: Summit Professional Networks
Contact: Steve Weitzner, President
Ed: Trevor Thomas. **Description:** Nursing home and assisted living rates rose from 2009 to 2010, according to MetLife Mature Market Institute. Statistical data included.

36948 ■ *"End of an Era"* **in Barron's (Vol. 88, July 7, 2008, No. 27, pp. 3)**
Pub: Dow Jones & Co., Inc.
Contact: Clare Hart, President
Ed: Alan Abelson. **Description:** June 2008 was a very bad month for US stocks, with investors losing as much as 41.9 percent in the first half of 2008 signaling an end to the financial environment that prevailed around the world since the 1980's. The US job market lost 62,000 jobs in June 2008.

36949 ■ *"The End of the Line for Line Extensions?"* **in Advertising Age (Vol. 79, July 7, 2008, No. 26, pp. 3)**
Pub: Crain Communications Inc.
Contact: Rance Crain, President
Ed: Jack Neff. **Description:** After years of double-digit growth, some of the most heavily extended personal-care products have slowed substantially or

even declined in the U.S. Unilever's Dove and P&G's Pantene and Olay are two such brands that have been affected. Statistical data included.

36950 ■ *"Energy MPLs: Pipeline to Profits"* **in Barron's (Vol. 89, July 27, 2009, No. 30, pp. 9)**
Pub: Dow Jones & Co., Inc.
Contact: Clare Hart, President
Ed: Dimitra DeFotis. **Description:** Energy master limited partnership stocks are range-bound in the next few months from July 2009 but there are there are some opportunities that remain. These include Energy Transfer Equity, Enterprise GP holdings, NuStar GP Holdings, and Plains All American Pipeline.

36951 ■ *Entrepreneurial Finance*
Pub: Pearson Education Inc.
Contact: Steven A. Dowling, President
Ed: Philip J. Adelman, Alan M. Marks. **Released:** Sixth Edition. **Price:** $129.60. **Description:** Financial aspects of running a small business are covered; topics include sole proprietorships, partnerships, limited liability companies, and private corporations.

36952 ■ *Entrepreneurial Finance: A Casebook*
Pub: John Wiley & Sons Inc.
Contact: Stephen M. Smith, President
Ed: Paul A. Gompers, William Sahlman. **Released:** December 2001. **Price:** $142.95, paperback. **Description:** Investment analysis, entrepreneurial financing, harvesting, and renewal in the entrepreneurial firm are among the topics discussed. **Availability:** Print.

36953 ■ *Entrepreneurial Small Business*
Pub: McGraw-Hill Higher Education
Contact: Edward Stanford, President
E-mail: ed_stanford@mcgraw-hill.com
Ed: Jerome A. Katz, Richard P. Green. **Released:** Fourth Edition. **Price:** $259. **Description:** Students are able to get a clear vision of small enterprise in today's business climate. The textbook helps focus on the goal of having personal independence with financial security as an entrepreneur.

36954 ■ *The Entrepreneur's Edge: Finding Money, Making Money, Keeping Money*
Ed: Daniel Hogan. **Released:** October 2006. **Price:** $24.95. **Description:** Advice for starting, running and growing a new business is given.

36955 ■ *"Equal Weighting's Heavy Allure"* **in (Vol. 92, July 23, 2012, No. 30, pp. 27)**
Pub: Dow Jones & Co., Inc.
Contact: Clare Hart, President
Ed: Brendan Conway. **Released:** July 23, 2012. **Description:** Equal weight index exchange-traded funds are attracting investors due to their strong returns. This strategy gives investors a greater exposure to mid-capitalization companies and could provide strong returns over longer stretches.

36956 ■ *"An Equity Fund of Their Own"* **in Entrepreneur (Vol. 35, October 2007, No. 10, pp. 68)**
Pub: Entrepreneur Press
Contact: Perlman Neil, President
Ed: Lee Gimpel. **Description:** About 100 new private equity funds have formed since 2002, proof that private equity investing is becoming popular among companies. There is also an increase in competition to close deals owing to the large number of investors that companies can choose; advantages of smaller funds over the larger one is explained.

36957 ■ *"Essential Releases Record First Quarter Results"* **in Marketwired (May 14, 2007)**
Pub: Comtex News Network Inc.
Description: The first quarter of 2007 saw record financial performance despite numerous challenges for Essential Energy Services Trust. Statistical data included.

36958 ■ *Essentials of Entrepreneurship and Small Business Management*
Pub: Prentice Hall PTR
Ed: Norman M. Scarborough, Thomas W. Zimmerer, Doug Wilson. **Released:** 7th Edition. **Price:** $199.80.
Description: New venture creation and the knowledge required to start a new business are shared. The challenges of entrepreneurship, business plans, marketing, e-commerce, and financial considerations are explored.

36959 ■ *"ETF Score Card" in Barron's (Vol. 89, July 13, 2009, No. 28, pp. 51)*
Pub: Dow Jones & Co., Inc.
Contact: Clare Hart, President
Description: Statistical table is presented which shows the net assets of various exchange-traded funds is presented. The table also shows the total return of these funds up to a three-year time period.

36960 ■ *"Ethics Commission May Hire Collection Agency" in Tulsa World (August 21, 2010)*
Pub: World Publishing Co.
Ed: Barbara Hoberock. **Description:** Oklahoma Ethics Commission is considering a more to hire a collection agency or law firm in order to collect fees from candidates owing money for filing late financial reports.

36961 ■ *"European Stocks on Deck" in Barron's (Vol. 89, July 27, 2009, No. 30, pp. M7)*
Pub: Dow Jones & Co., Inc.
Contact: Clare Hart, President
Ed: Vito J. Racanelli. **Description:** European stocks are cheap and these trade at a discount to U.S. equities rarely seen in the past 40 years. This represents an opportunity for Americans and trends show that Europe's stocks outperform when there is a discrepancy between the price to earnings ratio in European stocks versus U.S. stocks and when sentiment on European equities are downbeat.

36962 ■ *"Even Gold Gets Tarnished When Everyone Wants Cash" in Globe & Mail (February 28, 2007, pp. B1)*
Ed: John Partridge. **Description:** The impact of fall in Chinese equities on the United States stock market and metal prices, including gold, is discussed.

36963 ■ *"Everyone Out of the Pool" in Barron's (Vol. 89, July 20, 2009, No. 29, pp. 18)*
Pub: Dow Jones & Co., Inc.
Contact: Clare Hart, President
Ed: Sandra Ward. **Description:** Shares of Pool Corp. could drop as continued weakness in the housing market weakens the market for swimming pool equipment. The company's shares are trading at $18.29, about 20 times projected 2009 earnings of $0.91 a share.

36964 ■ *"An Exit Without an Exit" in Washington Business Journal (Vol. 33, June 6, 2014, No. 7, pp. 8)*
Pub: American City Business Journals
Released: June 6, 2014. **Description:** Investment research firm Morningstar Inc. has acquired financial guidance software company HelloWallet in a $52.5 million deal that would make Morningstar the owner of the remaining shares of the company. Morningstar's existing stake in HelloWallet is valued at $13.5 million and is expected to pay $39 million under the deal.

36965 ■ *"Expect a Rally as Waders Dive In" in Barron's (Vol. 89, July 20, 2009, No. 29, pp. 11)*
Pub: Dow Jones & Co., Inc.
Contact: Clare Hart, President
Ed: Vito J. Racanelli. **Description:** US stock markets may experience a rally in the autumn of 2009 as skeptical investors start to return to the market. The Standard & Poor's Index may jump to the 1025-1050 point levels during this rally.

36966 ■ *"Experts: Market Shaky But Resilient" in The Business Journal-Serving Metropolitan Kansas City (Vol. 27, September 19, 2008, No. 1)*
Pub: American City Business Journals, Inc.
Contact: Whitney Shaw, President
Ed: Steve Vockrodt. **Description:** Investment advisers believe that the local investors in Kansas City who have a long-term approach towards their portfolios may come out even or even experience gains despite the Wall Street financial crisis. The impacts of the crisis are expected to take time to reach the area of Kansas City. The potential impacts of the Wall Street meltdown are examined further.

36967 ■ *"Export Initiative Launched" in Philadelphia Business Journal (Vol. 28, December 11, 2009, No. 43, pp. 1)*
Pub: American City Business Journals Inc.
Ed: Athena D. Merritt. **Description:** The first initiative that came out of the partnership between the Export-Import Bank of the US, the city of Philadelphia, and the World Trade Center of Greater Philadelphia is presented. A series of export finance workshops have featured Ex-Im Bank resources that can provide Philadelphia businesses with working capital, insurance protection and buyer financing.

36968 ■ *"Extra Rehab Time Boosts M-B's Off-Lease Profits" in Automotive News (Vol. 86, October 31, 2011, No. 6488, pp. 22)*
Pub: Crain Communications Inc.
Contact: Rance E. Crain, President
Ed: Arlena Sawyers. **Description:** Mercedes-Benz Financial Services USA is holding on to off-lease vehicles in order to recondition them and the move is boosting profits for the company.

36969 ■ *Facing Financial Dysfunction*
Ed: Bert Whitehead. **Released:** April 2004. **Description:** Handbook to help individuals manage their finances, investments, taxes and retirement.

36970 ■ *"Fair Exchange" in Food and Drink (Winter 2010, pp. 84)*
Pub: Schofield Media Group
Ed: Don Mardak. **Description:** Bartering can assist firms in the food and beverage industry to attract new customers, maximize resources, and reduce cash expenses.

36971 ■ *"Falling Local Executive Pay Could Suggest a Trend" in Tampa Bay Business Journal (Vol. 30, January 15, 2010, No. 4, pp. 1)*
Pub: American City Business Journals
Ed: Margie Manning. **Description:** Tampa Bay, Florida-based Raymond James Financial Inc. and MarineMax Inc.'s proxy statements have shown the decreasing compensation of the companies' highest paid executives. The falling trend in executive compensation was a result of intensified shareholder scrutiny and the economy.

36972 ■ *"Falling Markets' Nastiest Habit" in Barron's (Vol. 88, July 7, 2008, No. 27, pp. 7)*
Pub: Dow Jones & Co., Inc.
Contact: Clare Hart, President
Ed: Michael Santoli. **Description:** US market conditions reflect a bear market, with the S&P 500 index falling 20 percent below its recent high as of June 2008. The bear market is expected to persist in the immediate future, although bear market rallies are likely to occur.

36973 ■ *A Family Matter: A Guide To Organizing Your Personal Estate*
Pub: Brown Books Publishing Group
Contact: Mili A. Brown, Chief Executive Officer
Ed: William A. Verkest. **Price:** $20, includes a CD. **Description:** Guidebook to financial management of personal assets is presented. Important documents must be maintained in a safe, secure place for family members or attorneys to access when necessary. The author suggests that a personal diary be kept with important information regarding records of investment accounts and financial summaries for every year in order to calculate taxes and manage financial matters more efficiently.

36974 ■ *"Fannie and Freddie: How They'll Change" in Business Week (September 22, 2008, No. 4100, pp. 30)*
Ed: Jane Sasseen. **Description:** Three possible outcomes of the fate of struggling mortgage giants Freddie Mac and Fannie Mae after the government bailout are outlined.

36975 ■ *"Fast Revival Unlikely For Indian 'Net Stocks" in Barron's (Vol. 88, July 7, 2008, No. 27, pp. 12)*
Pub: Dow Jones & Co., Inc.
Contact: Clare Hart, President
Ed: Leslie P. Norton. **Description:** Shares of Indian Internet companies Rediff.com and Sify are not likely to stage a rebound due to weak financial results. Rediff.com shares have declined 39.2 percent in 2008, while Sify shares are down 35.8 percent.

36976 ■ *"The Fatal Bias" in Business Strategy Review (Vol. 25, Summer 2014, No. 2, pp. 34)*
Pub: Blackwell Publishing Professional
Contact: Stephen M. Smith, President
Released: Summer 2014. **Description:** The prevailing managerial bias towards cost efficiency is harmful to corporate performance. Management's fatal bias is discussed.

36977 ■ *"February Hot for Mutual Fund Sales" in Globe & Mail (March 3, 2006, pp. B10)*
Ed: Keith Damsell. **Description:** The details on Canadian mutual fund sector, which posted $4.7 billion for February 2005, are presented.

36978 ■ *"Fed Tackles Bear of a Crisis" in Barron's (Vol. 88, March 17, 2008, No. 11, pp. M10)*
Pub: Dow Jones & Co., Inc.
Contact: Clare Hart, President
Ed: Randall W. Forsyth. **Description:** Emergency funding package for Bear Stearns from the Federal Reserve Bank of New York through JPMorgan Chase is one of the steps taken by the central bank shore up bank liquidity. Prior to the emergency funding, the central bank announced the Term Securities Lending Facility to allow dealers to borrow easily saleable Treasuries in exchange for less-liquid issues.

36979 ■ *"Fees Come Down; Markets Come Down More" in Barron's (Vol. 89, July 13, 2009, No. 28, pp. L8)*
Pub: Dow Jones & Co., Inc.
Contact: Clare Hart, President
Ed: J.R. Brandstrader. **Description:** Investors spent less on mutual fund fees in 2009 than they did in the last 25 years. These fees include administration, accounting, and legal expense. Despite the popularity of money market funds which has contributed to this decline, the short-term yields of these funds fell in the last year.

36980 ■ *"A Few Points of Contention" in Barron's (Vol. 88, July 14, 2008, No. 28, pp. 3)*
Pub: Dow Jones & Co., Inc.
Contact: Clare Hart, President
Ed: Michael Santoli. **Description:** Headline inflation tends to revert to the lower core inflation, which excludes food and energy in its calculation over long periods. Prominent private equity figures believe that regulators should allow more than the de facto 10 percent to 25 percent limit of commercial banks to hasten the refunding of the financial sector.

36981 ■ *"Fewer Banks Offer Big Gifts to Lure Clients" in Globe & Mail (March 14, 2006, pp. D1)*
Ed: Chris Reidy. **Description:** Fewer banks are offering gifts to lure the customers in this year in the wake of less favorable interest rates in the spring season. The market climate is analyzed.

36982 ■ *"Fifth Third CEO Kabat: A World of Difference" in Business Courier (Vol. 26, January 1, 2010, No. 37, pp. 1)*
Pub: American City Business Journals, Inc.
Contact: Whitney Shaw, President
Ed: Steve Watkins. **Description:** CEO Kevin Kabat of Cincinnati-based Fifth Third Bancorp believes that the bank's assets of $111 billion and stock value of

more than $10 indicate the recovery from the low stock prices posted in February 2009. He attributes the recovery from the federal government's stress test finding in May 2009 that Fifth Third needs to generate $1.1 billion.

36983 ■ *"Fifth Third Grapples With Account Snafu" in Business Courier (Vol. 24, December 6, 2007, No. 34, pp. 1)*
Pub: American City Business Journals, Inc.
Contact: Whitney Shaw, President

Ed: Jon Newberry. **Description:** Fifth Third Bank's vendor committed an error which led to a badly damaged credit score for Brett and Karen Reloka. The couple reported the incident to the bank and are still waiting for action to be taken. A major outourced services vendor caused paid-off mortgages to be reported delinquent.

36984 ■ *"Fifth Third Spinoff Eyes More Space" in Business Courier (Vol. 27, July 16, 2010, No. 11, pp. 1)*
Pub: Business Courier

Ed: Dan Monk, Steve Watkins. **Description:** Electronic-funds transfer company Fifth Third Solutions (FTPS), a spinoff of Fifth Third Bancorp, is seeking as much as 200,000 square feet of new office space in Ohio. The bank's sale of 51 percent ownership stake to Boston-based Advent International Corporation has paved the way for the growth of FTPS. How real estate brokers' plans have responded to FTPS' growth mode is discussed.

36985 ■ *"The File On..Skoda Minotti" in Crain's Cleveland Business (Vol. 28, October 8, 2007, No. 40, pp. 26)*
Pub: Crain Communications Inc.

Ed: Kimberly Bonvissuto. **Description:** Overview of Skoda Minotti, the accounting and financial services firm located in Mayfield Village; the company has 140 employees and an expanded slate of services.

36986 ■ *"Finalist: BlackEagle Partners L.L.C." in Crain's Detroit Business (Vol. 24, March 24, 2008, No. 12, pp. 12)*
Pub: Crain Communications Inc.
Contact: Rance E. Crain, President

Ed: Brent Snavely. **Description:** Overview of private-equity firm, BlackEagle Partners L.L.C., an upstart that acquired Rockford Products Corp. in order to improve the performance of the company who does business with several major tier-one automotive suppliers; Rockford manufactures highly engineered chassis and suspension components for automakers and the automotive aftermarket.

36987 ■ *Finance & Accounting: How to Keep Your Books and Manage Your Finances with an MBA, a CPA, or a Ph.D*
Ed: Suzanne Caplan. **Price:** $19.95.

36988 ■ *"The Finance Function In A Global Corporation" in Harvard Business Review (Vol. 86, July-August 2008, No. 8, pp. 108)*
Pub: Harvard Business Review Press
Contact: Peter E. Walsh, Director

Ed: Mihir A. Desai. **Description:** Designing and implementing a successful finance function in a global setting is discussed. Additional topics include the internal capital market, managing risk and budgeting capital internationally.

36989 ■ *"Finance: Peak Performer" in Canadian Business (Vol. 81, October 13, 2008, No. 17, pp. 30)*
Pub: Rogers Media Inc.
Contact: Tony Viner, President

Ed: Andrea Jezovit. **Description:** Jerry Del Missier's promotion as president of Barclays Capital (BarCap) has made him the likely successor to BarCap chief executive Bob Diamond. Diamond believes the technology Jerry Del Missier built on BarCap is producing record performance for the company. Public opinion on Jerry Del Missier, as well as his views, is discussed.

36990 ■ *Financial Management 101: Get a Grip on Your Business Numbers*
Pub: Self-Counsel Press Inc.
Ed: Angie Mohr. **Released:** September 15, 2007. **Price:** $16.95. **Description:** An overview of business planning, financial statements, budgeting and advertising for small businesses. s.

36991 ■ *Financial Management for the Small Business*
Pub: Kogan Page, Limited
Contact: Philip Kogan, Chairman of the Board
Ed: Colin Barrow. **Description:** Keys to successful financial management are presented to help small business owners to address the principles and problems associated with financial planning.

36992 ■ *"Financial Planning and Advisory Firms" in Business Review Albany (Vol. 41, August 15, 2014, No. 21, pp. 8)*
Pub: The Business Journals
Released: August 15, 2014. **Description:** Rankings of financial planning and advisory firms in the Albany, New York area are presented. Rankings are based on the 2013 year-end assets under management in Capital Region offices.

36993 ■ *"Financial Stability: Fraud, Confidence, and the Wealth of Nations"*
Pub: John Wiley & Sons Inc.
Contact: Stephen M. Smith, President
Released: September 29, 2014. **Price:** $59.84. **Description:** Instruction is provided to help modern investors and finance professionals to learn from past successes and failures and to gauge future market threats. Insight into today's financial markets and the political economy will help craft a strategy that leads to financial stability. Topics covered include: capital; forecasting; political reaction; and past, present, and future applications within all areas of business. A companion Website offers additional data and research, providing a comprehensive resource for those wishing a better understanding of risk factors in investing.

36994 ■ *"Finding Good Bets Down on the Farm" in Crain's Chicago Business (Vol. 31, March 24, 2008, No. 12, pp. 4)*
Pub: Crain Communications Inc.
Contact: Todd Johnson, Publisher
Ed: Daniel Rome Levine. **Description:** Interview with money manager Jeff James, the portfolio manager for Driehaus Capital Management LLC, who discusses the Federal Reserve and recommends several companies in which to make investments.

36995 ■ *"Fine Wine, Poor Returns" in Barron's (Vol. 92, September 17, 2012, No. 38, pp. 11)*
Description: Investing in wines in not considered a good idea due to irrationally high wine prices. Wine collectors buying wines at very high prices are not expected to make money and are charged with a 28 percent 'collectibles' tax.

36996 ■ *"First Mariner's New Ads No Passing Fancy" in Boston Business Journal (Vol. 29, September 16, 2011, No. 19, pp. 1)*
Pub: American City Business Journals, Inc.
Ed: Gary Haber. **Description:** Baltimore, Maryland-based First Mariner Bank replaced Ed Hale, the bank's CEO and founder, as the pitchman for its television ads with Ravens quarterback Joe Flacco. Hales' exit from the advertisements is the result of First Mariner's struggle to raise money for recapitalization.

36997 ■ *"FirstMerit's Top Executive Turns Around Credit Quality" in Crain's Cleveland Business (Vol. 28, October 15, 2007, No. 41, pp. 3)*
Pub: Crain Communications Inc.
Ed: Shawn A. Turner. **Description:** Discusses the ways in which chairman and CEO Paul Greig has been able to improve FirstMerit Corp.'s credit quality and profit margin. Strategies included selling more than $70 million in bad loans, hiring a new chief credit

officer and redirecting its focus on cross-selling its wealth and investment services to its commercial customers. Statistical data included.

36998 ■ *"Fiscal Cliff Notes" in Barron's (Vol. 92, September 15, 2012, No. 38, pp. 27)*
Pub: Dow Jones & Co., Inc.
Contact: Clare Hart, President
Ed: Mike Hogan. **Description:** Websites and blogs dedicated to providing information on the economic effects of the 'fiscal cliff' are described. These sites discuss possible effects on the US economy, budget, and personal finances.

36999 ■ *"5 Things You Should Know If Your Bank Fails" in Black Enterprise (Vol. 41, December 2010, No. 5, pp. 29)*
Pub: Earl G. Graves Publishing Co. Inc.
Contact: Earl G. Graves, Jr., President
Ed: John Simons. **Description:** The Federal Deposit Insurance Corporation announced that the number of banks in trouble has reached the highest level since March 1993. Advice from the FDIC is cited. Statistical data included.

37000 ■ *The Flaw of Averages: Why We Underestimate Risk in the Face of Uncertainty*
Pub: John Wiley & Sons Inc.
Contact: Stephen M. Smith, President
Ed: Sam L. Savage. **Released:** March 2012. **Price:** $19.95, paperback; $12.99. **Description:** Personal and business plans are based on uncertainties on a daily basis. The common avoidable mistake individuals make in assessing risk in the face of uncertainty is defined. The explains why plans based on average assumptions are wrong, on average, in areas as diverse as finance, healthcare, accounting, the war on terror, and climate change. **Availability:** PrintE-book.

37001 ■ *"A Flawed Yardstick for Banks" in Barron's (Vol. 88, July 14, 2008, No. 28, pp. M6)*
Pub: Dow Jones & Co., Inc.
Contact: Clare Hart, President
Ed: Arindam Nag. **Description:** Return on equity is no longer the best measure for investors to judge banks by in a post-subprime-crises world. Investors should consider the proportion of a bank's total assets that are considered risky and look out for any write-downs of goodwill when judging a bank's financial health.

37002 ■ *"Florida's Housing Gloom May Add To Woes of National City" in Crain's Cleveland Business (Vol. 28, October 29, 2007, No. 43, pp. 1)*
Pub: Crain Communications Inc.
Ed: Shawn A. Turner. **Description:** Already suffering by bad loans in the troubled mortgage market, National City Corp. is attempting to diversify its geographic presence beyond the slow-growth industrial Midwest by acquiring two Florida firms. Analysts worry that the acquisitions may end up making National City vulnerable to a takeover if the housing slump continues and credit quality becomes more of an issue for the bank.

37003 ■ *Fooling Some of the People All of the Time*
Pub: John Wiley & Sons Inc.
Contact: Stephen M. Smith, President
Ed: David Einhorn. **Released:** April 2008. **Price:** $29.95, Hardcover; $16.95, Paperback. **Description:** A chronicle of the ongoing saga between author, David Einhorn's hedge fund, Greenlight Capital, and Allied Capital, a leader in the private finance industry.

37004 ■ *"For Baxter, A Lingering PR Problem" in Crain's Chicago Business (April 21, 2008)*
Pub: Crain Communications Inc.
Contact: Todd Johnson, Publisher
Ed: Mike Colias. **Description:** Baxter International Inc.'s recall of the blood-thinning medication heparin has exposed the company to costly litigation and put the perils of overseas drug manufacturing in the spotlight. Wall Street investors predict that an

indefinite halt in production of the drug should not hurt the company's bottom line since heparin represents a tiny sliver of the business. Since Baxter began recalling the drug in January its shares have continued to outpace most other medical stocks.

37005 ■ *"For Buffett Fans, the Price Is Right"* in Barron's (Vol. 89, July 13, 2009, No. 28, pp. 17)
Pub: Dow Jones & Co., Inc.
Contact: Clare Hart, President
Ed: Andrew Bary. **Description:** Shares of Warren Buffett's Berkshire Hathaway have fallen to $85,000 and these are cheap since they are trading at just 1.2 times estimated book value and are well below its peak of $149,000. One fan of the stock expects it to top $110,000 in the next year from June 2009.

37006 ■ *"For Gilead, Growth Beyond AIDS"* in Barron's (Vol. 88, June 30, 2008, No. 26, pp. 18)
Pub: Dow Jones & Co., Inc.
Contact: Clare Hart, President
Ed: Jay Palmer. **Description:** First-quarter 2008 revenue for Gilead Sciences grew by 22 percent and an earnings gain of 19 percent thanks to their HIV-treatment drugs that comprised over two-thirds of the company's sales in 2007. An analyst has a 12-month target from June, 2008 of 65 per share. The factors behind the company's prospects are also discussed.

37007 ■ *"Ford: Down, Not Out, and Still a Buy"* in Barron's (Vol. 92, July 23, 2012, No. 30, pp. 14)
Pub: Dow Jones & Co., Inc.
Contact: Clare Hart, President
Ed: Vito J. Racanelli. **Released:** July 23, 2012. **Description:** Stocks of Ford Motor Company could gain value as the company continues to improve its finances despite fears of slower global economic growth. The company's stock prices could double from $9.35 per share within three years.

37008 ■ *"Foreclosure Crisis Expected to Significantly Drain Wealth"* in Black Enterprise (Vol. 41, September 2010, No. 2, pp. 24)
Pub: Earl G. Graves Publishing Co. Inc.
Contact: Earl G. Graves, Jr., President
Description: African American communities will lose billions in wealth because of the current foreclosure crisis. Statistical data included.

37009 ■ *"Foreign (In)Direct Investment and Corporate Taxation"* in Canadian Journal of Economics (Vol. 44, November 2011, No. 4, pp. 1497)
Pub: Wiley-Blackwell
Contact: Gordon Tibbitts, President
Ed: Georg Wamser. **Description:** Foreign investments of multinational firms are often complex in that they involve conduit entities. In particular, a multinational can pursue either a direct or an indirect investment strategy, where the latter involves an intermediate corporate entity and is associated with enhanced opportunities for international tax planning. As a consequence, in the case of indirect investments, the role of corporate taxation in destination countries may change. An investigation into the effects of corporation taxation on foreign investment decisions of German multinationals, taking explicitly into account that firms choose in a first stage the investment regime, (direct vs. indirect) is provided.

37010 ■ *"Former Mayor, Paul Johnson, Driving $500M Real Estate Equity Fund"* in The Business Journal - Serving Phoenix and the Valley of the Sun (Vol. 28, August 15, 2008, No. 50, pp. 1)
Pub: American City Business Journals, Inc.
Contact: Whitney Shaw, President
Ed: Jan Buchholz. **Description:** Paul John, the former mayor of Phoenix, is establishing a $500 million real estate asset management fund. The fund is dubbed Southwest Next Capital Management and has attracted three local partners, namely Joseph Meyer, Jay Michalowski, and James Mullany, who all have background in finance and construction.

37011 ■ *"Forward Motion"* in Green Industry Pro (July 2011)
Pub: Cygnus Business Media
Contact: Paul Mackler, Chief Executive Officer
Ed: Gregg Wartgow. **Description:** Several landscape contractors have joined this publication's Working Smarter Training Challenge over the last year. This process is helping them develop ways to improve work processes, boost morale, drive out waste, reduce costs, improve customer service, and be more competitive.

37012 ■ *"The Four Cheapest Plays in Emerging Markets"* in Barron's (Vol. 89, July 27, 2009, No. 30, pp. 34)
Pub: Dow Jones & Co., Inc.
Contact: Clare Hart, President
Ed: Lawrence C. Strauss. **Description:** Portfolio manager Arjun Divecha of the GMO Emerging Markets III Fund says that the main thing in investing in emerging markets is getting the country right since getting it wrong makes it harder to add value. Divecha says that the four countries that they are positive on are Turkey, Russia, South Korea, and Thailand.

37013 ■ *"Four Ways to Fix Banks: a Wall Street Veteran Suggests How To Cut Through the Industry's Complexity"* in (Vol. 90, June 2012, No. 6, pp. 106)
Pub: Harvard Business Review Press
Contact: Peter E. Walsh, Director
Ed: Sallie Krawcheck. **Released:** June 2012. **Description:** Despite new regulations in the post-global economic crisis of 2008, banks are sill too complex for effective management of their boards. Recommendations for improving governance include incorporating bank debt in executive compensation to increase their sensitivity to risk, and paying dividends as a percentage of company earnings to maintain capital.

37014 ■ *"Four Ways Hospitals Can Reduce Patient Readmissions; Hospitals Have a Powerful Financial Incentive to Reduce Readmissions. Here Are the Most Effective Strategies"* in Gallup Business Journal (July 2, 2014)
Pub: Gallup Press
Released: July 2, 2014. **Description:** The Centers for Medicare and Medicaid Services (CMS) report readmissions as hospitalizations that occur within 30 days of discharge. Hospitals need to identify and implement the right strategies to reduce readmissions.

37015 ■ *"From Buyout to Busted"* in Business Week (September 22, 2008, No. 4100, pp. 18)
Pub: Bloomberg L.P.
Contact: Matthew Winkler, Manager
Ed: Emily Thornton, Deborah Stead. **Description:** Bankruptcy filings by private equity-backed companies are at a record high with 134 American firms taken private (or invested in) by buyout firms that have filed for protection this year under Chapter 11; this is 91 percent higher than the previous year, which had set a record when 70 of such companies filed for protection under Chapter 11.

37016 ■ *"From Fastenal, a Boost"* in Barron's (Vol. 89, July 20, 2009, No. 29, pp. M13)
Pub: Dow Jones & Co., Inc.
Contact: Clare Hart, President
Ed: Shirley A. Lazo. **Description:** Fastenal increased its semi-annual common payout from $0.35 to $0.37 a share. Core Laboratories declared a special dividend of $0.75 a share along with its quarterly payout of $0.10. Ryder System and Landstar System raised their payouts to $0.23 and $0.045 a share respectively.

37017 ■ *"Fuel Costs Curb Food Truck Trend"* in Tampa Tribune (March 26, 2012)
Pub: Media General Business Communications Inc.
Ed: Jeff Houck. **Released:** March 26, 2012. **Description:** Owner of Maggie on the Move food truck, Margaret Loflin, has had to raise the cost of drinks served in order to cover the increased cost of gasoline to run her business. She also added smaller, less costly items to her menu. Her husband has gone back to a part-time job in he hopes of keeping their food truck running.

37018 ■ *"Full-Court Press for Apple"* in Barron's (Vol. 88, March 24, 2008, No. 12, pp. 47)
Pub: Dow Jones & Co., Inc.
Contact: Clare Hart, President
Ed: Mark Veverka. **Description:** Apple Inc. is facing more intellectual property lawsuits in 2008, with 30 patent lawsuits filed compared to 15 in 2007 and nine in 2006. The lawsuits, which involve products such as the iPod and the iPhone, present some concern for Apple's shareholders.

37019 ■ *"Funds "Friend" Facebook"* in Barron's (Vol. 89, July 27, 2009, No. 30, pp. 30)
Pub: Dow Jones & Co., Inc.
Contact: Clare Hart, President
Ed: Leslie P. Norton. **Description:** Mutual-fund companies are the latest entrants to the 'social media' space and several companies have already set up Facebook and Twitter pages. The use of this technology pose special challenges for compliance and regulators especially since the Financial Industry Regulatory Authority reminds companies that advertising, sales and literature are governed by regulations.

37020 ■ *"Future's Brighter for Financial Stocks"* in Barron's (Vol. 89, July 20, 2009, No. 29, pp. 14)
Pub: Dow Jones & Co., Inc.
Contact: Clare Hart, President
Ed: Jacqueline Doherty. **Description:** Shares of US financial companies are projected to rise as their earnings start to normalize. Earnings of these companies have been hurt by credit losses but have been bolstered by one-time gains.

37021 ■ *"Futures Shock for the CME"* in Crain's Chicago Business (Vol. 31, November 10, 2008, No. 45, pp. 8)
Pub: Crain Communications Inc.
Contact: Todd Johnson, Publisher
Ed: Ann Saphir. **Description:** Chicago-based CME Group Inc., the largest futures exchange operator in the U.S., is facing a potentially radically altered regulatory landscape as Congress weighs sweeping reform of financial oversight. The possible merger of the CFTC and the Securities and Exchange Commission are among CME's concerns. Other details of possible regulatory measures are provided.

37022 ■ *"Futures of the Street"* in Barron's (Vol. 88, June 30, 2008, No. 26, pp. 27)
Pub: Dow Jones & Co., Inc.
Contact: Clare Hart, President
Ed: Michael Santoli. **Description:** Prospects of the securities industry in terms of jobs and profit sources are discussed. Suggestions on what the industry needs with regards to its use of capital are also discussed.

37023 ■ *"Garden Bargains: Restaurant Cut Costs With Homegrown Foods"* in Washington Business Journal (Vol. 33, August 22, 2014, No. 18, pp. 6)
Pub: American City Business Journals
Released: August 22, 2014. **Description:** A number of chefs and restaurants in Washington DC are seeing the benefits of growing their own healthy kitchen gardens. The Urbana restaurant is saving $250 monthly in herbs since it started planting them in 2014 and chef, Ethan McKee expects to increase that savings to $75 monthly in 2015.

37024 ■ *"Gas Glut Pummels Prices"* in Barron's (Vol. 89, July 27, 2009, No. 30, pp. M8)
Pub: Dow Jones & Co., Inc.
Contact: Clare Hart, President
Ed: Christine Buurma. **Description:** Natural gas-futures prices have fallen 73 percent and the glut of output from onshore gas fields and the weak demand

signals that a rebound is not near. An analyst expects U.S. production to show increasingly steep declines but the oversupply situation is not good for prices.

37025 ■ *"Gateway Delays Start" in The Business Journal-Serving Metropolitan Kansas City (Vol. 27, October 31, 2008, No. 8, pp. 1)*

Ed: Rob Roberts. **Description:** Economic problems caused, in part, by the Wall Street crisis has resulted in the setback of a proposed mixed-use redevelopment project, The Gateway. The $307 million project, which includes the Kansas Aquarium, will be delayed due to financing problems. Details of the project are given.

37026 ■ *"GE Looking to Extend Hot Streak" in Business Courier (Vol. 24, January 24, 2008, No. 42, pp. 1)*

Pub: American City Business Journals, Inc.

Contact: Whitney Shaw, President

Ed: Jon Newberry. **Description:** GE Aviation has enjoyed strong revenues and sales due to increase aircraft engine orders. It has an engine backlog order of $19 million as of the end of 2007. Data on the aviation company's revenues, operating profit and total engine orders for the year 2004 to 2007 are presented.

37027 ■ *"General Motors Can't Kick Incentives-But They Work" in Advertising Age (Vol. 79, July 7, 2008, No. 26, pp. 3)*

Pub: Crain Communications Inc.

Contact: Rance Crain, President

Ed: Jean Halliday. **Description:** General Motors Corp. was able to maintain their market share just as Toyota Motor Corp. was beginning to pass the manufacturer; GM lured in customers with a sales incentive that they heavily advertised and subsequently helped build demand; investors, however, were not impressed and GM shares were hammered to their lowest point in 50 years after analysts speculated the company might go bankrupt.

37028 ■ *"Generation Y - An Opportunity for a Fresh Financial Start" in (September 11, 2010, pp. 241)*

Pub: VerticalNews

Description: Eleanor Blayney, the consumer advocate for the Certified Financial Planner Board of Standards, offers a financial strategy for Generation Y individuals starting their financial planning. The first segment of the non-profit's Lifelong Financial Strategies initiative is called 'Starting Out', and focuses on ways Generation Y people can avoid pitfalls of earlier generations by making smart financial decisions.

37029 ■ *"Genzyme: Underrated Oversold" in Barron's (Vol. 88, March 24, 2008, No. 12, pp. 58)*

Ed: Johanna Bennett. **Description:** Shares of biotechnology company Genzyme appear oversold and underrated at their $71.86 level. The company's finances are on a solid foundation, with revenues over $3.8 billion in 2007 and forecasts of $4.5-4.7 billion in revenue for 2008.

37030 ■ *"Get Off The Rollercoaster" in Michigan Vue (Vol. 13, July-August 2008, No. 4, pp. 19)*

Ed: Donald N. Hobley Jr. **Description:** Benefits of creating and implementing a solid financial plan during these rocky economic times are examined. Things to keep in mind before meeting with a financial planner include risk assessment, investment goals, the length of time required to meet those goals and the amount of money one has available to invest.

37031 ■ *"Getting In on the Ground Floor" in Barron's (Vol. 89, July 27, 2009, No. 30, pp. 32)*

Pub: Dow Jones & Co., Inc.

Contact: Clare Hart, President

Ed: Jacqueline Doherty. **Description:** Shares of AvalonBay Communities have fallen 61 percent in the past two and a half years to July 2009 but at $56, the stock is trading near the asset value. The shares

could rise as the economy improves and if the recovery takes longer, investors will be rewarded with a yield of 3.5 percent.

37032 ■ *"Getting More Out of Retirement" in Agency Sales Magazine (Vol. 39, November 2009, No. 10, pp. 48)*

Ed: Joshua D. Mosshart. **Description:** Overview of the Tax Increase Prevention and Reconciliation Act, which lets employees convert to a Roth IRA in 2010. The benefits of conversion depend on age and wealth and it is best to consult a tax advisor to determine the best strategy for retirement planners.

37033 ■ *"Getting Out of an IRS Mess" in Black Enterprise (Vol. 37, December 2006, No. 5, pp. 53)*

Pub: Earl G. Graves Publishing Co. Inc.

Contact: Earl G. Graves, Jr., President

Ed: Carolyn M. Brown. **Description:** Owing back taxes to the IRS can lead to huge penalties and interest. Here are some tips on how to handle paying the IRS what you owe them.

37034 ■ *Getting Rich In Your Underwear: How To Start and Run a Profitable Home-Based Business*

Pub: HCM Publishing

Price: $17.95. **Description:** Book offers insight into starting a home-based business. Entrepreneurs will learn about business models and the home business; distribution and fulfillment of product or service; marketing and sales; how to overcome the fear of starting a business; personal success characteristics; naming a business; zoning and insurance; intellectual capital; copyrights, trademarks, and patents; limited liability companies and S-corporations; business expenses and accounting; taxes; fifteen basic steps for starting a home-based business, state resources for starting a home company; and seven home-based business ideas.

37035 ■ *"Giants Now Admit They Roam Planet Earth; Time To Buy?" in Barron's (Vol. 88, March 31, 2008, No. 13, pp. 39)*

Pub: Dow Jones & Co., Inc.

Contact: Clare Hart, President

Ed: Eric J. Savitz. **Description:** Oracle's third-quarter results showed that top-line growth fell short of expectations but the company is expected to fare better than most applications companies in the downturn. Google had a flat growth in the number of people who click their online ads. The time for investors in the tech sector with a long-term horizon has arrived.

37036 ■ *"A Gift From Interactive Brokers" in Barron's (Vol. 92, July 23, 2012, No. 30, pp. M11)*

Pub: Dow Jones & Co., Inc.

Contact: Clare Hart, President

Ed: Steven M. Sears. **Released:** July 23, 2012. **Description:** Investors are advised to sell put options of Interactive Brokers stock in anticipation of lower share prices. This trade is also a hedge against a possible takeover but allows investors to buy into a company that pays regular dividends and is managed well.

37037 ■ *Girl, Get Your Credit Straight!: A Sister's Guide to Ditching Your Debt, Mending Your Credit, and Building a Strong Financial Future*

Pub: Broadway Business

Contact: David Drake, Manager

E-mail: ddrake@randomhouse.com

Ed: Glinda Bridgforth. **Released:** December 31, 2007. **Price:** $13.99, paperback; $9.99. **Description:** Third book in the series is aimed primarily at African American women and offers helpful and understandable information for a larger audience. The sidebars on how women in particular tend to get into credit trouble and ways they can increase their financial knowledge and reign in their spending habits are especially notable. **Availability:** PrintE-book.

37038 ■ *"Give Me Liberty With DirecTV" in Barron's (Vol. 89, July 13, 2009, No. 28, pp. M5)*

Ed: Fleming Meeks. **Description:** Shares of Liberty Entertainment look cheap at $25.14 and the same goes for DirecTV at $23.19. A merger between the

two companies was announced and the deal will likely close by September 2009. Barclays Capital has a target of $30 for Liberty Media and $32 for DirecTV.

37039 ■ *"The Globe: Singapore Airlines' Balancing Act" in Harvard Business Review (Vol. 88, July-August 2010, No. 7-8, pp. 145)*

Pub: Harvard Business School Publishing

Ed: Loizos Heracleous, Jochen Wirtz. **Description:** Singapore Airlines is used as an illustration of organizational effectiveness. The article includes the firm's 4-3-3 rule of spending, its promotion of centralized as well as decentralized innovation, use of technology, and strategic planning.

37040 ■ *"Go Big or Go Home" in Entrepreneur (July 2014)*

Pub: Entrepreneur Media Inc.

Released: July 2014. **Description:** Business owners can achieve financial success by managing their personal finance the same as running their small business. Many people tend to put more energy into small financial payoffs, but to maximize on financial success, they need to look for opportunities that will pay off in the long term.

37041 ■ *"Gold Still Has That Glitter" in Barron's (Vol. 89, July 20, 2009, No. 29, pp. M8)*

Pub: Dow Jones & Co., Inc.

Contact: Clare Hart, President

Ed: Allen Sykora. **Description:** Gold prices appear to be ready for an increase starting in the fall of 2009 due to an increase in demand. The price of the August 2009 gold contract fell to as low as $904.08 an ounce before recovering to $937.50.

37042 ■ *"A Good Book Is Worth a Thousand Blogs" in Barron's (Vol. 88, July 14, 2008, No. 28, pp. 42)*

Pub: Dow Jones & Co., Inc.

Contact: Clare Hart, President

Ed: Gene Epstein. **Description:** Nine summer book suggestions on economics are presented. The list includes 'The Revolution' by Ron Paul, 'The Forgotten Man' by Amity Shales, 'The Commitments of Traders Bible' by Stephen Briese, and 'Economic Facts and Fallacies' by Thomas Sowell.

37043 ■ *"Good Going, Partners" in Barron's (Vol. 89, July 27, 2009, No. 30, pp. M8)*

Pub: Dow Jones & Co., Inc.

Contact: Clare Hart, President

Ed: Shirley A. Lazo. **Description:** Four master limited partnerships boosted their dividends. Sunoco Logistics raised theirs by 11.2 percent, El Paso Pipeline by 12 percent, Holly Energy upped their dividends by a penny, and Western Gas hiked their dividend to 31 cents per unit.

37044 ■ *"A Good Step, But There's a Long Way to Go" in Business Week (September 22, 2008, No. 4100, pp. 10)*

Ed: James C. Cooper. **Description:** Despite the historic action by the U.S. government to nationalize the mortgage giants Freddie Mac and Fannie Mae, rising unemployment rates may prove to be an even bigger roadblock to bringing back the economy from its downward spiral. The takeover is meant to restore confidence in the credit markets and help with the mortgage crisis but the rising rate in unemployment may make many households unable to take advantage of any benefits which arise from the bailout. Statistical data included.

37045 ■ *"Google's Next Stop: Below 350?" in Barron's (Vol. 88, March 10, 2008, No. 10, pp. 17)*

Pub: Dow Jones & Co., Inc.

Contact: Clare Hart, President

Ed: Jacqueline Doherty. **Description:** Share prices of Google Inc. are expected to drop from their level of $433 each to below $350 per share. The company is expected to miss its earnings forecast for the first quarter of 2008, and its continued aggressive spending on non-core areas will eventually bring down earnings.

37046 ▪ *"Graduates to the TSX in 2008"* in *Canadian Business (Vol. 81, Summer 2008, No. 9, pp. 79)*

Ed: Calvin Leung. **Description:** Table showing the market capitalization and stock performance of the companies that jumped to the TSX Venture Exchange is presented. The 17 companies that made the leap to the list will have an easier time raising capital, although leeway must be made in investing since they are still new businesses.

37047 ▪ *"The Great Fall: Here Comes The Humpty Dumpty Economy"* in *Barron's (Vol. 88, March 10, 2008, No. 10, pp. 5)*

Pub: Dow Jones & Co., Inc.

Contact: Clare Hart, President

Ed: Alan Abelson. **Description:** Discusses the US economy is considered to be in a recession, with the effects of the credit crisis expected to intensify as a result. Inflation is estimated at 4.3 percent in January 2008, while 63,000 jobs were lost in February 2008.

37048 ▪ *The Great Inflation and Its Aftermath: The Past and Future of American Affluence*

Pub: Random House Inc.

Contact: Richard Sarnoff, President

Ed: Robert J. Samuelson. **Released:** January 26, 2010. **Price:** $17, paperback. **Description:** How inflation has shaped the economics in today's United States is examined. **Availability:** Print.

37049 ▪ *"A Greenish Light for Financial-Sector Funds"* in *Barron's (Vol. 88, March 24, 2008, No. 12, pp. 52)*

Pub: Dow Jones & Co., Inc.

Contact: Clare Hart, President

Ed: Tom Sullivan. **Description:** Financial sector funds have lost value in 2008 through 17 March, and investors are advised to reduce investments in the financial sector. Exchange-traded funds present a good way to own financial stocks.

37050 ▪ *"A Gripping Read: Bargains & Noble"* in *Barron's (Vol. 88, March 17, 2008, No. 11, pp. 20)*

Pub: Dow Jones & Co., Inc.

Contact: Clare Hart, President

Ed: Jonathan R. Laing. **Description:** Barnes & Noble's earnings forecast for the fiscal year ending in January, 2008 to be $1.70 to $1.90 per share which is way lower than the $2.12 analyst consensus. The company also said that sales at stores one-year old or older dropped 0.5 percent in the fourth quarter. However, the shares are now cheap at 4.9 times enterprise value with some analysts putting a price target of 41 per share.

37051 ▪ *Grow Your Money: 101 Easy Tips to Plan, Save and Invest*

Pub: HarperBusiness

Ed: Jonathan D. Pond. **Released:** December 04, 2007. **Price:** $26.95, hardcover. **Description:** In what should be required reading for anyone entering the work world, the author offers helpful investment and financial definitions, debt-management strategies, retirement and home ownerships considerations and more. **Availability:** Print.

37052 ▪ *"Growth Back on CIBC's Agenda"* in *Globe & Mail (March 3, 2006, pp. B1)*

Ed: Sinclair Stewart. **Description:** The details on business growth of Canadian Imperial Bank of Commerce, which posted $547 million profit for first quarter 2006, are presented.

37053 ▪ *The Handbook of Financing Growth: Strategies, Capital Structure, and M&A Transactions*

Pub: John Wiley & Sons Inc.

Contact: Stephen M. Smith, President

Released: August 2009. **Price:** $99.95, hardcover. **Description:** Using empirical data and actual case studies, strategies are presented to illustrate capital structures and fund raising techniques for emerging growth and middle-market companies. **Availability:** Print.

37054 ▪ *The Handbook of Financing Growth: Strategies, Capital Structure, and M&A Transactions*

Pub: John Wiley & Sons Inc.

Contact: Stephen M. Smith, President

Ed: Kenneth H. Marks, Larry E. Robbins, Gonzalo Fernandez, John P. Funkhouser, D. L. Williams. **Released:** August 2009. **Price:** $100, hardcover; $65.99. **Description:** Guide for emerging growth and middle market companies includes information to help understand and apply the basics of corporate finance using empirical data and actual company cases to illustrate capital structures and financing approaches. **Availability:** PrintE-book.

37055 ▪ *"Handleman Liquidation Leaves Questions For Shareholders"* in *Crain's Detroit Business (Vol. 24, October 6, 2008, No. 40, pp. 4)*

Pub: Crain Communications Inc.

Contact: Rance E. Crain, President

Ed: Nancy Kaffer. **Description:** Discusses Handleman Co., a Troy-based music distribution company, and their plan of liquidation and dissolution as well as how shareholders will be affected by the company's plan. Handleman filed its plan to liquidate and dissolve assets with the Securities and Exchange Commission in mid-August, following several quarters of dismal earnings.

37056 ▪ *"Hank and Ben: Hedgies' BFFs"* in *Barron's (Vol. 88, March 31, 2008, No. 13, pp. 50)*

Pub: Dow Jones & Co., Inc.

Contact: Clare Hart, President

Ed: Tom Sullivan. **Description:** David Ballin of Alternative Investment Solutions says that everything in the financial markets is tainted and beaten-up which presents an extraordinary opportunity for hedge funds as long as they back up their decisions with sharp and intensive research. He adds that money managers should short suspect stocks and go long on undeservedly battered stocks in the same sector.

37057 ▪ *"Hank Paulson On the Housing Bailout and What's Ahead"* in *Business Week (September 22, 2008, No. 4100, pp. 19)*

Ed: Maria Bartiromo. **Description:** Interview with Treasury Secretary Henry Paulson in which he discusses the bailout of Fannie Mae and Freddie Mac as well as the potential impact on the American economy and foreign interests and investments in the country. Paulson has faith that the government's actions will help to stabilize the housing market.

37058 ▪ *"A Harbinger? Insiders Stocking Up on M&I, MGIC Shares"* in *The Business Journal-Milwaukee (Vol. 25, August 29, 2008, No. 49, pp. A1)*

Pub: American City Business Journals, Inc.

Contact: Whitney Shaw, President

Ed: Rich Kirchen. **Description:** Stock prices of Marshall & Ilsley Corp. (M&I) and MGIC Investment Corp. are expected to rebound after insiders were reported to have bought stocks of the companies. M&I director David Lubar bought $4.3 million, while MGIC CEO and chairman Curt Culver bought 20,000 stocks of MGIC. Other views and information on the insiders' purchase of stocks are presented.

37059 ▪ *"The Hard Thing About Hard Things: Building a Business When There Are No Easy Answers"*

Pub: HarperCollins Publishers

Released: March 4, 2014. **Price:** $29.99. **Description:** Cofounder of Andreessen Horowitz and well-respected Silicon Valley entrepreneur, offers advice for building and running a startup small business. Horowitz analyzes issues confronting startup leaders daily and shares insights he gained from managing, selling, buying investing in, and supervising technology firms.

37060 ▪ *"Hartco Income Fund Announces the Completion of the CompuSmart Strategic Review"* in *Marketwired (May 14, 2007)*

Pub: Comtex News Network Inc.

Description: Hartco Income Fund announced that it has completed the process of exploring strategic options for CompuSmart and found that it should imple-

ment a plan to sell select stores and assets while consolidating remaining CompuSmart locations over the next sixty days.

37061 ▪ *"Has Microsoft Found a Way to Get at Yahoo?"* in *Advertising Age (Vol. 79, July 7, 2008, No. 26, pp. 4)*

Pub: Crain Communications Inc.

Contact: Rance Crain, President

Ed: Abbey Klaassen. **Description:** Microsoft's attempt to acquire Yahoo's search business is discussed as is Yahoo's plans for the future at a time when the company's shares have fallen dangerously low.

37062 ▪ *"Hastily Enacted Regulation Will Not Cure Economic Crisis"* in *Crain's Chicago Business (Vol. 31, May 5, 2008, No. 18, pp. 18)*

Pub: Crain Communications Inc.

Contact: Todd Johnson, Publisher

Ed: Stephen P. D'Arcy. **Description:** Policymakers are looking for ways to respond to what is possibly the greatest financial crisis of a generation due to the collapse of the housing market, the credit crisis and the volatility of Wall Street.

37063 ▪ *"Hawaii's Identity Crisis"* in *Hawaii Business (Vol. 53, November 2007, No. 5, pp. 10)*

Ed: Kelli Abe Trifonovitch. **Description:** Some Hawaiians have shown that the Superferry controversy makes it seem to the rest of the world as if they do not know what they are doing, and intensifies several issues regarding the stability of investing in Hawaii. With or without the Superferry, there is still no evidence that investors are afraid to put their money in Hawaii.

37064 ▪ *"Hawaii's Top Twenty Financial Advisors"* in *Hawaii Business (Vol. 53, February 2008, No. 8, pp. 32)*

Pub: PacificBasin Communications

Description: Listing of Hawaii's top 20 financial advisors is presented. Details on the methodology used to create the rankings are discussed.

37065 ▪ *"HBDiversityStockIndex"* in *Hispanic Business (October 2009, pp. 1)*

Description: Data covering the Hispanic Business Diversity Stock Index is highlighted. The HBDSI was up 0.12 percent through September 3, 2009. Statistical data included.

37066 ▪ *"Headwinds From the New Sod Slow Aer Lingus"* in *Barron's (Vol. 88, March 10, 2008, No. 10, pp. M6)*

Pub: Dow Jones & Co., Inc.

Contact: Clare Hart, President

Ed: Sean Walters, Arindam Nag. **Description:** Aer Lingus faces a drop in its share prices with a falling US market, higher jet fuel prices, and lower long-haul passenger load factors. British media companies Johnston Press and Yell Group are suffering from weaker ad revenue and heavier debt payments due to the credit crunch.

37067 ▪ *"The 'Health' of a Senior's Retirement Plan"* in *Senior Market Advisor (Vol. 13, October 2012, No. 10, pp. 48)*

Description: Seniors are the fastest growing demographic, accounting for 16 percent of the population. Medicare changes taking place with the implementation of Obamacare make it essential for Americans 62 years of age and older to understand how to navigate the system. Medicare recipients will experience a reduction of access to doctors, hospitals, diagnostic facilities and other medical centers.

37068 ▪ *"The Heat Is On"* in *Crain's Chicago Business (Vol. 31, April 28, 2008, No. 17, pp. 4)*

Pub: Crain Communications Inc.

Contact: Todd Johnson, Publisher

Ed: Steve Daniels. **Description:** Discusses Nicor Inc., a natural-gas utility with million customers in Chicago's suburbs, and its potential acquirers; shares of the company have dropped 17 percent this year making Nicor the second-worst among 31 utilities in an index tracked by Standrd & Poor's. Statistical data included.

37069 ■ "A Heavy Burden" in Crain's Cleveland Business (Vol. 30, June 8, 2009, No. 22, pp. 13)
Pub: Crain Communications Inc.
Ed: Cuck Soder. Description: Small business owners are making sacrifices in the tight economy. In a recent survey conducted by American Express, 30 percent of the 727 small business owners questioned said they no longer take salaries from their firms.

37070 ■ "Hedge Funds for the Average Joe" in Canadian Business (Vol. 85, August 13, 2012, No. 13, pp. 51)
Pub: George Media Inc.
Ed: Bryan Borzykowski. Released: August 13, 2012. Description: The benefits of the Horizons Morningstar Hedge Fund Index ETF over traditional hedge funds are examined. Retail investors should avoid buying hedge fund exchange-traded funds (ETFs) because they are not actually buying into a hedge fund, the fund is just trying to emulate strategies that popular hedge funds use with derivatives.

37071 ■ "Hello, 9000! The Dow's Run Is Far From Over" in Barron's (Vol. 89, July 27, 2009, No. 30, pp. 20)
Pub: Dow Jones & Co., Inc.
Contact: Clare Hart, President
Ed: Andrew Bary. Description: Another 10 percent gain is possible for the rest of 2009 as the Dow Jones Industrial Average moved above 9000 level for the week ending July 24, 2009. Blue chip stocks could do well in the next 10 years.

37072 ■ Here Come the Regulars: How to Run a Record Label on a Shoestring Budget
Pub: Faber & Faber Inc.
Contact: Linda Rosenberg, Director
E-mail: linda.rosenberg@fsgbooks.com
Ed: Ian Anderson. Released: October 2009. Price: $15, paperback; $7.99. Description: Author, Ian Anderson launched his own successful record label, Afternoon Records when he was 18 years old. Anderson shares insight into starting a record label, focusing on label image, budget, blogging, potential artists, as well as legal aspects. Availability: PrintE-book.

37073 ■ "Here are the Stocks of the Decade" in Business Courier (Vol. 26, December 18, 2009, No. 34, pp. 1)
Ed: Steve Watkins. Description: Listing of companies with stocks that made big gains since December 1999 to November 30, 2009 is presented.

37074 ■ "Here's How Buffett Spent 2007" in Barron's (Vol. 88, March 10, 2008, No. 10, pp. 48)
Ed: Andrew Bary. Description: Earnings of Berkshire Hathaway may decline in 2008 due to a tighter insurance market, but its portfolio is expected to continue growing. Warren Buffett purchased $19.1 billion worth of stocks in 2007.

37075 ■ "The Hidden Tax" in Canadian Business (Vol. 81, April 14, 2008, No. 6, pp. 28)
Pub: Rogers Media Inc.
Contact: Tony Viner, President
Ed: Al Rosen. Description: Accounting fraud could take out a sizable sum from one's retirement fund when computed over a long period of time. The much bigger tax on savings is the collective impact of the smaller losses that do not attract the attention they deserve. Ensuring that investors are not unnecessarily taxed 2 percent of their total investments every year outweighs the benefit of a 2 percent reduction in personal tax rates.

37076 ■ "High Hopes: Ralph Mitchell's Picks Have Growth Potential" in Black Enterprise (Vol. 37, February 2007, No. 7, pp. 42)
Pub: Earl G. Graves Publishing Co. Inc.
Contact: Earl G. Graves, Jr., President
Ed: Carolyn M. Brown. Description: Ralph Mitchell, president and senior financial advisor of Braintree-Carthage Financial Group, offers three recommendations: Toll Brothers, Home Depot, and Lowe's.

37077 ■ High Wire: The Precarious Financial Lives of American Families
Pub: Basic Books
Contact: Elizabeth Maguire, Publisher
Ed: Peter Gosselin. Released: June 09, 2009. Price: $16.95; C$21.50; £11.99; C$18.50. Description: Despite the general prosperity in America, household finances are growing more precarious making people more anxious about their economic prospects in the future. Availability: PrintE-book.

37078 ■ "High-Yield Turns Into Road Kill" in Barron's (Vol. 88, July 7, 2008, No. 27, pp. M7)
Pub: Dow Jones & Co., Inc.
Contact: Clare Hart, President
Ed: Emily Barrett. Description: High-yield bonds have returned to the brink of collapse after profits have recovered from the shock brought about by the collapse of Bear Stearns. The high-yield bond market could decline again due to weakness in the automotive sector, particularly in Ford and General Motors.

37079 ■ "Higher Payouts Should Be In the Cards" in Barron's (Vol. 92, July 23, 2012, No. 30, pp. 14)
Pub: Dow Jones & Co., Inc.
Contact: Clare Hart, President
Ed: Michael Santoli. Released: July 23, 2012. Description: Credit card companies Visa and Master-Card should be more generous to shareholders and pay higher dividends. Both have low dividend yields, with Visa paying $0.88/share a year and MasterCard paying $1.20/share annually.

37080 ■ "Hispantelligence Report" in Hispanic Business (July-August 2009, pp. 8)
Description: After forty years, Hispanic-owned businesses have grown to more than three million, according to a U.S. Census report. The Hispanic business stock index is also presented. Statistical data included.

37081 ■ "Hit the Books" in Black Enterprise (Vol. 38, July 2008, No. 12, pp. 42)
Pub: Earl G. Graves Publishing Co. Inc.
Contact: Earl G. Graves, Jr., President
Ed: Mellody Hobson. Description: Four books that deal with investing are discussed as is the idea that reading even 15 minutes a day from one of these books will give you tools that far exceed what you can learn from magazines and the business section of your daily newspaper.

37082 ■ "Hitting Bottom? Several Banks and Brokerages Are Ready to Pop Up for Air" in Barron's (Vol. 88, March 24, 2008, No. 12, pp. 21)
Pub: Dow Jones & Co., Inc.
Contact: Clare Hart, President
Ed: Jacqueline Doherty. Description: Brokerage houses and banks may stabilize in 2008 as a result of regulatory responses brought about by the near-collapse of Bear Stearns. Some of their shares may rise by as much as 20 percent from 2008 to 2009.

37083 ■ "Hollinger Shares Plummet on Reports" in Globe & Mail (March 10, 2007, pp. B5)
Ed: Richard Blackwell. Description: The fall in the share prices of Hollinger Inc. to 49 percent soon after the company filed its annual statements is discussed.

37084 ■ Home-Based Business for Dummies
Pub: John Wiley & Sons Inc.
Contact: Stephen M. Smith, President
Ed: Paul Edwards, Sarah Edwards, Peter Economy. Released: 3rd Edition. Price: $19.95, paperback; $12.99. Description: Provides all the information needed to start and run a home-based business. Topics include: selecting the right business; setting up a home office; managing money, credit, and financing; marketing; and ways to avoid distractions while working at home. Availability: PrintE-book.

37085 ■ "A Home of Her Own" in Hawaii Business (Vol. 53, October 2007, No. 4, pp. 51)
Pub: PacificBasin Communications
Ed: Maria Torres-Kitamura. Description: It was observed that the number of single women in Hawaii purchasing their own home has increased, as that in

the whole United States where the percentage has increased from 14 percent in 1995 to 22 percent in 2006. However, First Hawaiian Bank's Wendy Lum thinks that the trend will not continue in Hawaii due to lending restrictions. The factors that women consider in buying a home of their own are presented.

37086 ■ "Homebuilders Continue to be Our Nemesis" in Contractor (Vol. 56, July 2009, No. 7, pp. 50)
Pub: Penton Media, Inc.
Ed: Robert P. Mader. Description: Homebuilders rank high on the greed scale along with Wall Street brokers. There is this one instance when a builder gave copies of another contractor's quotes that have just been blackened out and another instance when one builder let other bidders visit a site while the current mechanical contractor is working.

37087 ■ "Hong Kong's Boom in IPOs" in Barron's (Vol. 89, July 13, 2009, No. 28, pp. M7)
Pub: Dow Jones & Co., Inc.
Contact: Clare Hart, President
Ed: Nick Lord. Description: Hong Kong's IPO (initial public offering) market is booming with 13 Chinese IPOs already on the market for the year as July 2009. One of them is Bawang International which raised $214 million after generating $9 billion in order which makes it 42 times oversubscribed.

37088 ■ "Hospital Revenue Healthier in 2009" in Orlando Business Journal (Vol. 26, February 5, 2010, No. 36, pp. 1)
Pub: American City Business Journals
Ed: Melanie Stawicki Azam. Description: Orlando Health, Health Central and Adventist Health System are Florida-based hospital systems that generated the most profits in 2009. Orlando Health had the highest profit in 2009 at $73.3 million, contrary to about $31 million in losses in 2008. The increased profits are attributed to stock market recovery, cost-cutting initiatives, and rising patient volumes.

37089 ■ "Hospitals Try to Buy Smarter" in Crain's Detroit Business (Vol. 25, June 1, 2009, No. 22, pp. M025)
Pub: Crain Communications Inc. - Detroit
Contact: Keith Crain, Chairman
Ed: Jay Greene. Description: Hospitals in southeast Michigan are using bulk discount purchasing of medical and non-medical supplies through group purchasing organizations in order to cut costs.

37090 ■ House of Cards: A Tale of Hubris and Wretched Excess on Wall Street
Ed: William D. Cohan. Released: February 09, 2010. Price: $16.95. Description: A historical account of the events leading up to the Bear Stearns implosion.

37091 ■ "Housing Hedge" in Canadian Business (Vol. 79, July 17, 2006, No. 14-15, pp. 66)
Pub: Rogers Media Inc.
Contact: Tony Viner, President
Ed: Jeff Sanford. Description: The idea of starting a hedge scheme for housing is presented using the advent of pension schemes as an example to follow.

37092 ■ "How to Avold the Most Common and Costliest Mistakes in Retirement Portfolio Investing" in Barron's (Vol. 88, March 10, 2008, No. 10, pp. 30)
Pub: Dow Jones & Co., Inc.
Contact: Clare Hart, President
Ed: Karen Hube. Description: Investors, particularly those having retirement investments, are advised to diversify their investments, refrain from market timing, and minimize payments to maximize investment gains. An investor committing these mistakes could lose as much as $375,000 dollars over ten years.

37093 ■ "How to Beat the Pros" in Canadian Business (Vol. 81, Summer 2008, No. 9, pp. 59)
Ed: Calvin Leung. Description: Table showing the results of the Investor 500 beat the S&P/TSX composite index is presented. The average total return, best performing stocks and total return of the 2007 stock screen are provided.

37094 ■ *How Come That Idiot's Rich and I'm Not?*

Pub: Crown Publishing/Random House

Ed: Robert Shemin. **Released:** April 2009. **Price:** $14.99. **Description:** The book shows the average person not only how to get rich, but to create, connect and contribute greatly.

37095 ■ *"How High Can Soybeans Fly?" in Barron's (Vol. 88, March 10, 2008, No. 10, pp. M14)*

Pub: Dow Jones & Co., Inc.

Contact: Clare Hart, President

Ed: Kenneth Rapoza. **Description:** Prices of soybeans have risen to $14.0875 a bushel, up 8.3 percent for the week. Increased demand, such as in China and in other developing economies, and the investment-driven commodities boom are boosting prices.

37096 ■ *"How Interest Rate Changes Affect You" in Agency Sales Magazine (Vol. 39, September-October 2009, No. 9, pp. 50)*

Ed: Lee Eisinberg. **Description:** Falling interest rates make the prices of previously issued bonds rise and new issues are offered at lower rates. For stock investors, rising interest rates can have a positive or negative effect. Terminologies related to investing are explained.

37097 ■ *How to Make Big Money in Your Own Small Business: Unexpected Rules Every Small Business Owner Needs to Know*

Pub: Hyperion Books

Contact: Ellen Archer, President

Ed: Jeffrey J. Fox. **Released:** May 12, 2004. **Price:** $16.95; C$24.95. **Description:** Entrepreneur and consultant offer advice to help others create successful startups and prosper. Fox directs new business owners with a counterintuitive style and describes essential methods that beat the competition. Tips include: setting priorities, getting a personal driver, creating a contingency plan for employees, pricing to value, saving money, and getting an office outside of the home.

37098 ■ *How to Make Money in Stocks: A Winning System in Good Times and Bad*

Pub: The McGraw-Hill Companies

Ed: William J. O'Neil. **Released:** Fourth Edition. **Price:** A$32.95; NZ$37; C$20.95. **Description:** The bestselling guide to buying stocks, from the founder of Investor's Business Daily. The technique is based on a study of the greatest stock market winners dating back to 1953 and includes a seven-step process for minimizing risk, maximizing return, and finding stocks that are ready to perform.

37099 ■ *"How Not to Raise Bank Capital" in Barron's (Vol. 88, June 30, 2008, No. 26, pp. M6)*

Pub: Dow Jones & Co., Inc.

Contact: Clare Hart, President

Ed: Sean Walters. **Description:** French bank Natixis wants to raise 1 billion euros from cash provided by their two major owners. Natixis will reimburse Banque Populaire and Caisses d'Epargne with hybrid securities so this move will not benefit Natixis' core Tier 1 ratio. This has also given the impression that the company is afraid of a full rights issue which could shake investors' faith in the bank.

37100 ■ *"How Our Picks Beat The Bear" in Barron's (Vol. 88, July 14, 2008, No. 28, pp. 18)*

Pub: Dow Jones & Co., Inc.

Contact: Clare Hart, President

Ed: Andrew Bary. **Description:** Performance of the stocks that Barron's covered in the first half of 2008 is discussed; some of the worst picks and most rewarding pans have been in the financial sector while the best plays were in the energy, materials, and the transportation sectors.

37101 ■ *How to Protect and Manage Your 401K: Shield, Save, and Grow Your Money, Guard Against Corporate Corruption, Do*

What It Takes Now to Protect Your Future

Pub: Career Press Inc.

Contact: Ron Fry, President

Ed: Elizabeth Opalka. **Released:** April 16, 2003. **Price:** $45.58. **Description:** Ways to protect and manage 401(K) investments.

37102 ■ *"How to Retire: Do's and Don'ts" in Canadian Business (Vol. 79, July 17, 2006, No. 14-15, pp. 29)*

Pub: Rogers Media Inc.

Contact: Tony Viner, President

Ed: Andy Holloway, Erin Pooley, Thomas Watson. **Description:** Strategic tips for planning systematic investments, in order to make life more enjoyable after retirement, are elucidated.

37103 ■ *How to Start a Small Business in Canada: Your Road Map to Financial Freedom*

Pub: Self-Help Publishers

Ed: Tariq Nadeem. **Released:** 2nd Edition. **Price:** C$19.95, paperback; C$34.50, hardcover; C$14.95. **Description:** Provides information for starting and managing a small business in Canada. **Availability:** PrintE-book.

37104 ■ *"How Sweet It Will Be" in Barron's (Vol. 89, July 13, 2009, No. 28, pp. M13)*

Pub: Dow Jones & Co., Inc.

Contact: Clare Hart, President

Ed: Debbie Carlson. **Description:** Raw sugar experienced a rally in the first half of 2009 and the long term outlook for sugar prices is still good. However, there is a likely near-term correction due to the onset of Brazilian harvest that could be 20.7 percent higher for 2009 as compared to the previous year and October contracts could fall to 15.61 cents per pound.

37105 ■ *"How To: Manage Your Cash Better" in Inc. (Volume 32, December 2010, No. 10, pp. 69)*

Pub: Inc. Magazine

Description: A monthly guide to policies, procedures and practices for managing cash for a small business.

37106 ■ *"How To Save More" in Canadian Business (Vol. 85, August 13, 2012, No. 13, pp. 33)*

Pub: George Media Inc.

Released: August 13, 2012. **Description:** The top-down approach and the bottom-up approach are two cash-management strategies that are proven to make a person richer. The top-down approach to saving is best suitable to an analytical, detail-oriented person while the bottom-up approach can be effective to people who are having difficulties in keeping track of their spending.

37107 ■ *How to Use the Internet to Advertise, Promote, and Market Your Business or Web Site: With Little or No Money*

Pub: Atlantic Publishing Co.

Contact: Amanda Miller, Manager

E-mail: amiller@atlantic-pub.com

Ed: Bruce C. Brown. **Released:** Second Edition. **Price:** $24.95. **Description:** Information is given to help build, promote, and make money from your Website or brick and mortar store using the Internet, with minimal costs.

37108 ■ *How to Write a Great Business Plan for Your Small Business in 60 Minutes or Less*

Pub: Atlantic Publishing Co.

Contact: Amanda Miller, Manager

E-mail: amiller@atlantic-pub.com

Ed: Sharon L. Fullen. **Released:** January 2006. **Price:** $39.95, Includes CD-Rom. **Description:** A good business plan outlines goals and works as a company's resume to obtain funding, credit from suppliers, management of the operations and finances, promotion and marketing, and more. **Availability:** Print.

37109 ■ *Hug Your Customers: The Proven Way to Personalize Sales and Achieve Astounding Results*

Pub: Hyperion Books

Contact: Ellen Archer, President

Ed: Jack Mitchell. **Released:** June 09, 2003. **Price:** $19.95; C$29.95. **Description:** The CEO of Mitchells/Roberts, two very successful clothing stores, professes his belief in showering customers with attention. His secrets for long-term business success include advice about attracting a good staff, lowering marketing costs, and maintaining higher gross margins and revenues.

37110 ■ *"Huntington's Future At a Crossroads" in Crain's Cleveland Business (Vol. 30, June 22, 2009, No. 24, pp. 1)*

Pub: Crain Communications Inc.

Ed: Arielle Kass. **Description:** Despite Huntington Bancshares plans to expand in the Cleveland, Ohio area, experts wonder if the bank will be able to take advantage of the area's growth in the long run. Statistical data included.

37111 ■ *"Iconic Boise Skateboard Shop to Close" in Idaho Business Review (August 19, 2014)*

Pub: Dolan Co.

Contact: James P. Dolan, President

Released: August 19, 2014. **Description:** Lori Wright and Lori Ambur have owned Newt & Harold's for over 30 years. The partners are closing the firm that sold skateboards and snowboards. Wright focused on the marketing and inventory aspects of the retail shop, while Ambur ran the organizational and financial end. Wright and Ambur say they are leaving retail because the industry has faced so many changes since they first opened, particularly competing with online stores.

37112 ■ *"Ideas at Work: The Reality of Costs" in Business Strategy Review (Vol. 21, Summer 2010, No. 2, pp. 40)*

Pub: John Wiley & Sons Inc. Scientific, Technical, Medical, and Scholarly Div. (Wiley-Blackwell)

Contact: William J. Pesce, Manager

E-mail: wpesce@wiley.com

Ed: Jules Goddard. **Description:** If you think that cost cutting is the surest way to business success, the author wants to challenge every assumption you hold. Costs are an outcome of sound strategy, never the goal of strategy. He offers a new perspective on what counts when it comes to costs.

37113 ■ *"Identity Crisis: The Battle For Your Data" in Canadian Business (Vol. 81, March 17, 2008, No. 4, pp. 12)*

Pub: Rogers Media Inc.

Contact: Tony Viner, President

Description: Nigel Brown explains that businesses must protect their data through encryption and tightening up access to data. Brown also points out that banks and merchants bear most of the costs for identity fraud and leaves individuals with a lot of pain and heartache in clearing their name.

37114 ■ *"If You Go Into the Market Today.." in Canadian Business (Vol. 82, Summer 2009, No. 8, pp. 18)*

Ed: Jeff Sanford. **Description:** Opinions of experts and personalities who are known to have bear attitudes towards the economy were presented in the event 'A Night with the Bears' in Toronto in April 2009. Known bears that served as resource persons in the event were Nouriel Roubini, Eric Sprott, Ian Gordon, and Meredith Whitney. The bears were observed to have differences regarding consumer debt.

37115 ■ *"I'll Have What She's Having" in Canadian Business (Vol. 85, September 17, 2012, No. 14, pp. 17)*

Pub: George Media Inc.

Ed: Andrew Hallam. **Released:** September 17, 2012. **Description:** Studies show that women have the higher tendency to follow responsible investing rules than men, earning more money in the process. Women were also found to perform better in bull markets as well as in the male-dominated hedge fund sector.

37116 ■ *"Immigration Issues Frustrate Owners From Overseas"* in The Business Journal-Serving Greater Tampa Bay (Vol. 28, August 18, 2008)

Pub: American City Business Journals, Inc.

Contact: Whitney Shaw, President

Ed: Margie Manning. **Description:** Investors who availed the E-2 visa program believe that the tightened restrictions on the visa program has trapped them in the United States. The E-2 investor visa program was designed to attract investors into the U.S., but restrictions were tightened after the September 11, 2001 attacks. Other views and information on E-2 and its impact on investors are presented.

37117 ■ *"In 2011, Wichita-Area Banks Cleaned Up Books, Grew Earnings"* in Wichita Business Journal (Vol. 27, February 17, 2012, No. 7, pp. 1)

Pub: American City Business Journal

Description: Wichita, Kansas-based banks have reported smaller loan portfolios and higher loan-loss allowances at the end of 2011 compared to the previous year. The earnings of the 35 banks in the metro area also grew strongly both for the quarter and for the year, while their assets increased. How the banks managed to generate positive earnings results is also discussed.

37118 ■ *"In the Bag?"* in Canadian Business (Vol. 81, March 3, 2008, No. 3, pp. 57)

Ed: Calvin Leung. **Description:** American stocks are beginning to appear cheap amidst the threat of a worldwide economic slowdown, United States economic crisis and declining stock portfolios. Investors looking for bargain stocks should study the shares of Apple and Oshkosh Corp. Evaluation of other cheap-looking stocks such as the shares of Coach and 3M is also given.

37119 ■ *"In China, Railways to Riches"* in Barron's (Vol. 88, July 7, 2008, No. 27, pp. M9)

Pub: Dow Jones & Co., Inc.

Contact: Clare Hart, President

Ed: Assif Shameen. **Description:** Shares of Chinese railway companies look to benefit from multimillion-dollar investments aimed at upgrading the Chinese railway network. Investment in the sector is expected to reach $210 billion for the 2006-2010 period.

37120 ■ *"In the Hot Finance Jobs, Women Are Still Shut Out"* in (Vol. 90, July-August 2012, No. 7-8, pp. 30)

Pub: Harvard Business Review Press

Contact: Peter E. Walsh, Director

Ed: Nori Gerardo Lietz. **Released:** July-August 2012. **Description:** Although women constitute a significant proportion of business school graduates, the percentage of senior investment professionals who are female remain in a single-digit figure. Active effort will be needed to change corporate culture and industry awareness to raise this figure.

37121 ■ *"In India, A Gold-Price Threat?"* in Barron's (Vol. 88, June 30, 2008, No. 26, pp. M12)

Pub: Dow Jones & Co., Inc.

Contact: Clare Hart, President

Ed: Melanie Burton. **Description:** Gold purchases in India are falling as record prices take its toll on demand. Gold imports to India fell by 52 percent in May 2008 from the previous year and local prices are higher by one-third from the previous year to 12,540 rupees for 10 grams.

37122 ■ *"In the Options Market, Financial-Sector Trading Is Moody and Paranoid"* in Barron's (Vol. 88, March 10, 2008, No. 10, pp. M14)

Pub: Dow Jones & Co., Inc.

Contact: Clare Hart, President

Ed: Steven M. Sears. **Description:** Discusses the options market which remains liquid but is cautious of possible failures, especially for financial companies. Investors are in absolute fear when trading with options involving the financial sector.

37123 ■ *"In Praise of How Not to Invest"* in Barron's (Vol. 89, July 13, 2009, No. 28, pp. 11)

Pub: Dow Jones & Co., Inc.

Contact: Clare Hart, President

Ed: Vito J. Racanelli. **Description:** One research study found that the shares of companies that have growing market shares and expanding asset bases underperform. This is contrary to the widely held premise that stock prices for these companies rise. It is argued that this result is caused by these companies' tendency to sacrifice profitability to grab market share and this is reflected in their stock prices.

37124 ■ *"In the Public Eye"* in Entrepreneur (Vol. 35, November 2007, No. 11, pp. 75)

Pub: Entrepreneur Press

Contact: Perlman Neil, President

Ed: David Worrell. **Description:** The market for initial public offerings (IPOs) was booming in 2007 and strong fundamentals for companies that would like to go public are needed. The basics that companies should review before planning an IPO are outlined.

37125 ■ *"In Sickness and In Wealth Management"* in Hispanic Business (Vol. 30, March 2008, No. 3, pp. 28)

Pub: Hispanic Business Inc.

Contact: Jesus Chavarria, President

Ed: Rick Munarriz. **Description:** Discusses the investment and wealth management firms owned and operated by Hispanics. There are only a handful of these firms owned by Hispanics, as most of them prefer capital preservation by investing in hard assets like cash and real estate than in capital appreciation.

37126 ■ *"In Sickness and in Wealth Management"* in Hispanic Business (March 2008, pp. 28, 30)

Pub: Hispanic Business Inc.

Contact: Jesus Chavarria, President

Ed: Rick Munarriz. **Description:** Financial advice is offered by experts, Myrna Rivera and Samuel Ramirez Jr., with an overview of Hispanic-owned investment firms.

37127 ■ *"In Surging Oil Industry, Good Fortune Comes In Stages"* in Barron's (Vol. 88, July 7, 2008, No. 27, pp. 12)

Pub: Dow Jones & Co., Inc.

Contact: Clare Hart, President

Ed: Sandra Ward. **Description:** Shares of US land oil and gas driller Helmerich and Payne, priced at $69 each, are estimated to be at peak levels. The shares are trading at 17 times 2008 earnings and could be in for some profit taking.

37128 ■ *"Inch by Inch, Employees Lose Ground"* in Business Courier (Vol. 26, November 13, 2009, No. 29, pp. 1)

Pub: American City Business Journals, Inc.

Contact: Whitney Shaw, President

Ed: James Ritchie. **Description:** Employees in Ohio who retained their jobs have suffered losses in salary and other benefits, as companies exert efforts to save money. Thirty-four percent of employees experienced pay cuts. Statistical data included.

37129 ■ *"Inesoft Cash Organizer Desktop: A New Approach to Personal Accounts Bookkeeping"* in America's Intelligence Wire (August 7, 2012)

Pub: Financial Times Ltd.

Contact: John Ridding, Chief Executive Officer

Released: August 7, 2012. **Description:** Inesoft Cash Organizer Desktop application is offering a new product for financial management on a home PC and mobile devices. The program supports the classification of money transactions by category, sub-category, project, sub-project, budget planning, and world currencies (including current exchange rates), credit calculators, special reports, and more. Multiple users in the family can use the application. Details of the program are outlined.

37130 ■ *"Inflation Woes: Secure Your Portfolio Against Rising Prices"* in Black Enterprise (Vol. 37, January 2007, No. 6, pp. 40)

Pub: Earl G. Graves Publishing Co. Inc.

Contact: Earl G. Graves, Jr., President

Ed: Donald Jay Korn. **Description:** Inflation has a huge impact on investing and it is important to take the steady increase on cost into account when looking at your financial goals and investing in your future. Statistical data included.

37131 ■ *"Infomercial King on TeleBrands, Going Broke, Making Millions"* in Philadelphia Business Journal (Vol. 33, July 11, 2014, No. 22, pp. 3)

Pub: American City Business Journals

Released: July 11, 2014. **Description:** Ajit "A.J." Khubani is CEO of TeleBrands, the Fairfield, New Jersey company that brings to the American mainstream market novelty products by using infomercials, including AmberVision sunglasses and PedEgg. Though the marketing/advertising firm is worth $1 billion, Khubani's entrepreneurship career has gone through ups and downs and he has been close to bankruptcy three times.

37132 ■ *"Inland Snaps Up Rival REITs"* in Crain's Chicago Business (Vol. 31, November 17, 2008, No. 46, pp. 3)

Pub: Crain Communications Inc.

Contact: Todd Johnson, Publisher

Ed: Alby Gallun. **Description:** Discusses Inland American Real Estate Trust Inc., a real estate investment trust that is napping up depressed shares of publicly traded competitors, a possible first step toward taking over these companies; however, with hotel and retail properties accounting for approximately 70 percent of its portfolio, the company could soon face its own difficulties.

37133 ■ *"Insider"* in Canadian Business (Vol. 81, March 31, 2008, No. 5, pp. 76)

Pub: Rogers Media Inc.

Contact: Tony Viner, President

Ed: John Gray. **Description:** Discusses a comparison of an average Canadian family's finances in 1990 with the data from 2007. The average family in 2007 has over $80,000 in debt compared to just under $52,000 in 1990. However, Canadians have also been accumulating solid assets such as homes and stocks. This means that Canadian debt load has fallen from 22 percent in 1990 to 20 percent in 2007 when taken as a percentage of total net worth.

37134 ■ *"Insider"* in Canadian Business (Vol. 81, March 3, 2008, No. 3, pp. 96)

Description: History of gold usage and gold trading is presented in a timeline. Gold was a symbol of power and wealth in 2500 B.C., and in 1500 B.C., it became the first currency to be recognized internationally. Other remarkable events in the gold industry and laws that covered gold are discussed.

37135 ■ *Instant Cashflow: Hundreds of Proven Strategies to Win Customers, Boost Margins and Take More Money Home*

Ed: Bradley J. Sugars. **Released:** December 2005. **Price:** $17.95 (US), $22.95 (Canadian). **Description:** Nearly 300 proven marketing and sales strategies are shared by the author, a self-made millionaire. Advice on creating the proper mindset, generating new leads, boosting the conversion rate of leads to sales, maximizing the value of the average sale, and measuring results is included.

37136 ■ *Instant Profit: Successful Strategies to Boost Your Margin and Increase the Profitability of Your Business*

Ed: Bradley J. Sugars. **Released:** December 2005. **Price:** $16.95 (US), $22.95 (Canadian). **Description:** Advice on management, money, marketing, and merchandising a successful small business is offered.

37137 ■ *"An Insurance Roll-Up In Danger of Unraveling"* in Barron's (Vol. 88, March 17, 2008, No. 11, pp. 51)

Pub: Dow Jones & Co., Inc.

Contact: Clare Hart, President

Ed: Bill Alpert. **Description:** Shares of National Financial Partners have fallen below their initial offering price as sputtering sales and management turnover leave many investors wondering. One of the company's star brokers is being sued for their 'life settlement' contracts while another broker is being pursued by the IRS for unpaid taxes.

37138 ■ *"International ETFs: Your Passport to the World"* in Barron's (Vol. 89, July 13, 2009, No. 28, pp. L10)
Pub: Dow Jones & Co., Inc.
Contact: Clare Hart, President
Ed: John Hintze. **Description:** International exchange traded funds give investors more choices in terms of investment plays and there are 174 U.S. ETF listings worth $141 billion as of July 2009. Suggestions on how to invest in these funds based on one's conviction on how the global economy will unfold are presented.

37139 ■ *"Invest Like Harvard"* in Barron's (Vol. 92, September 15, 2012, No. 38, pp. 32)
Pub: Dow Jones & Co., Inc.
Contact: Clare Hart, President
Ed: Andrew Bary. **Description:** Asset management firms are offering endowment-style investment services that allow investors to invest in funds in the same way as foundations and endowments. High-Vista Strategies with $3.6 billion in assets under management, has produced a total return of 43.5 percent after fees from October 2005 to June 2012 using this strategy.

37140 ■ *"Investment Funds: Friends with Money"* in Canadian Business (Vol. 81, May 22, 2008, No. 9, pp. 22)
Pub: Rogers Media Inc.
Contact: Tony Viner, President
Ed: Jeff Stanford. **Description:** Two of the most well connected managers in Canadian capital markets Rob Farquharson and Brian Gibson will launch Panoply Capital Asset Management in June. The investment management company aims to raise a billion dollars from institutions and high-net worth individuals.

37141 ■ *"Investment Manager Disciplined"* in Sacramento Business Journal (Vol. 25, July 9, 2008, No. 18, pp. 1)
Pub: American City Business Journals, Inc.
Contact: Whitney Shaw, President
Ed: Mark Anderson. **Description:** Community Capital Management's David A. Zwick is permanently barred by the Securities and Exchange Commission (SEC) from associating with any broker or dealer, after investigations revealed that he took part in paying kickbacks to a bond trader. Other views and information on Community Capital, and on the SEC investigation on Zwick, are presented.

37142 ■ *"Investors Shrug Off the Turmoil"* in Globe & Mail (March 1, 2007, pp. B1)
Ed: Geoffrey York. **Description:** The decision of Chinese investors to continue to buy stocks despite the decade's biggest market crash is discussed. The rise in the stock price indexes of China is described.

37143 ■ *"Iowa Tax Case Could Cost Nation's Franchises"* in Franchising World (Vol. 42, September 2010, No. 9, pp. 38)
Pub: International Franchise Association
Contact: Stephen J. Caldeira, President
E-mail: scaldeira@franchise.org
Ed: Bruce A. Ackerman, Adam B. Thimmesch. **Description:** Ruling by the Iowa Supreme Court could have a financial impact on franchisors across the U.S. Iowa asserted that Kentucky Fried Chicken is subject to Iowa corporate income tax based solely on the fact that it received royalties from franchises in the state.

37144 ■ *"IRS Rules Could Affect Foreign Bank Deposits"* in Dallas Business Journal (Vol. 35, February 24, 2012, No. 24, pp. 1)
Released: February 24, 2012. **Description:** IRS has proposed a rule that requires US banks to disclose foreign depositors' account information. However, bankers and trade groups believe the regulation could prompt deposit runs at banks across Texas since foreign nationals are afraid that information might be used against them.

37145 ■ *"Is Fannie Mae the Next Government Bailout?"* in Barron's (Vol. 88, March 10, 2008, No. 10, pp. 21)
Pub: Dow Jones & Co., Inc.
Contact: Clare Hart, President
Ed: Jonathan R. Laing. **Description:** Fannie Mae may need a government bailout as it faces huge hits brought about by the effects of the housing crisis. The shares of the government-sponsored enterprise have dropped 65 percent since the housing crisis began.

37146 ■ *"Is Fierce Competition Loosening Standards?"* in Birmingham Business Journal (Vol. 31, February 14, 2014, No. 7, pp. 6)
Pub: American City Business Journals, Inc.
Contact: Whitney Shaw, President
Released: February 14, 2014. **Description:** Bankers have been seeing an intense competition for business loans in the Birmingham, Alabama market because of the limited number of qualified borrowers. However, some bankers expressed concerns that the trend signals a return to pre-recession habits for lenders.

37147 ■ *"Is It OK To Expense a Parking Ticket? Straight Answers To Some Common Expense Report Conundrums"* in Canadian Business (Vol. 85, June 11, 2012, No. 10, pp. 70)
Pub: George Media Inc.
Ed: Sarah Barmak. **Released:** June 11, 2012. **Description:** Human resource experts Andrea Fraser of DAC Group and Fiorella Callocchia of Deloitte offer advice to employees on personal costs and when to charge the company for travel expenses. The experts say expense claims should be reasonable and should depend on the firm's culture.

37148 ■ *"Is Raising CPP Premiums a Good Idea?"* in Canadian Business (Vol. 83, July 20, 2010, No. 11-12, pp. 37)
Description: Big labor is pushing for an increase in Canada Pension Plan premiums but pension consultants believe this system is not broken and that the government needs to focus on addressing the low rate of personal retirement savings. If the premiums go up, even those with high savings will be forced to pay more and it could block other plans that really address the real issue.

37149 ■ *"Is There a Doctor In the House?"* in Black Enterprise (Vol. 41, December 2010, No. 5, pp. 42)
Pub: Earl G. Graves Publishing Co. Inc.
Contact: Earl G. Graves, Jr., President
Ed: Renita Burns. **Description:** Health insurance premiums have increased between 15 percent and 20 percent for small business owners, making it one of the most expensive costs. Ways to evaluate a health plan's costs and effectiveness are examined.

37150 ■ *"Is the VIX in Denial?"* in Barron's (Vol. 88, July 7, 2008, No. 27, pp. M12)
Pub: Dow Jones & Co., Inc.
Contact: Clare Hart, President
Ed: Lawrence McMillan. **Description:** Volatility Index (VIX) of the Chicago Board Options Exchange did not rise significantly despite the drop in the US stock markets, rising to near 25. This market decline, however, will eventually result in investor panic and the rise of the VIX.

37151 ■ *"Islamic Banks Get a 'Libor' of Their Own"* in Wall Street Journal Eastern Edition (November 25 , 2011, pp. C4)
Pub: Dow Jones & Co., Inc.
Contact: Clare Hart, President
Ed: Katy Burne. **Description:** The London interbank offered rate, or Libor, has been used by banks internationally for years. It is the rate at which banks lend money to each other. The rate has not been used by Islamic banks, but now sixteen banks have come up with the Islamic Interbank Benchmark Rate.

37152 ■ *"It Could Be Worse"* in Barron's (Vol. 89, July 27, 2009, No. 30, pp. 5)
Pub: Dow Jones & Co., Inc.
Contact: Clare Hart, President
Ed: Alan Abelson. **Description:** Media sources are being fooled by corporate America who is peddling

an economic recovery rather than reality as shown by the report of a rise in existing home sales which boosted the stock market even if it was a seasonal phenomenon. The phrase 'things could be worse' sums up the reigning investment philosophy in the U.S. and this has been stirring up the market.

37153 ■ *"It May Be Cheaper to Manufacture At Home"* in Harvard Business Review (Vol. 88, October 2010, No. 10, pp. 84)
Pub: Harvard Business School Publishing
Ed: Suzanne de Treville, Lenos Trigeorgis. **Description:** Using a real options framework rather than a discounted cash flow model to assess and value supply chain processes is examined. This enables companies to assess costs for a variety of situations, not just ideal or normal circumstances, which can make the difference between domestic and foreign manufacturing decisions.

37154 ■ *"It Takes More Than One"* in Black Enterprise (Vol. 38, July 2008, No. 12, pp. 38)
Pub: Earl G. Graves Publishing Co. Inc.
Contact: Earl G. Graves, Jr., President
Ed: James A. Anderson. **Description:** Interview with Eric Small, the CEO of SBK-Brooks Investment Corp., whom discusses the importance of versatility when trying to find the best investment choices; the primary factors investors should be mindful of; his current stock picks; and recommendations for investing in an uncertain and volatile market.

37155 ■ *"It's Good to be Goldman"* in Barron's (Vol. 89, July 20, 2009, No. 29, pp. 5)
Pub: Dow Jones & Co., Inc.
Contact: Clare Hart, President
Ed: Randall W. Forsyth. **Description:** Profits of Goldman Sachs rose to $3.44 billion in the second quarter of 2009, aided by federal financial stimulus programs. CIT Group is facing bankruptcy and may need up to $6 billion to survive. The federal economic stimulus programs are benefiting Wall Street more than the US economy itself.

37156 ■ *"It's Good To Be a CEO: Top Execs Pull Millions In Raises for 2013"* in Atlanta Business Chronicle (June 20, 2014, pp. 22A)
Pub: American City Business Journals, Inc.
Contact: Whitney Shaw, President
Released: June 20, 2014. **Description:** Discussion regarding the highest paid CEOs in Georgia in 2013, with an average of 8.8 percent increase from 2012. The largest increase went to Jeffrey C. Sprecher, chairman and CEO of Intercontinental Exchange Inc., followed by John F. Brock, chairman and CEO of Coca-Cola Enterprises Inc.

37157 ■ *It's Your Ship*
Ed: Michael Abrashoff. **Released:** May 01, 2002. **Price:** $24.95. **Description:** Naval Captain D. Michael Abrashoff shares management principles he used to shape his ship, the U.S.S. Benfold, into a model of progressive leadership. Abrashoff revolutionized ways to face the challenges of excessive costs, low morale, sexual harassment, and constant turnover.

37158 ■ *"J.C. Evans Seeks Bankruptcy Protection"* in Austin Business Journal (Vol. 31, August 12, 2011, No. 23, pp. A1)
Pub: American City Business Journals
Ed: Vicky Garza. **Description:** J.C. Evans Construction Holdings Inc., as well as its affiliated companies, has filed for Chapter 11 bankruptcy following its continued financial breakdown which it blames on the tough economy. Details are included.

37159 ■ *"J.C. Penney Head Shops for Shares"* in Barron's (Vol. 88, July 7, 2008, No. 27, pp. 29)
Pub: Dow Jones & Co., Inc.
Contact: Clare Hart, President
Ed: Teresa Rivas. **Description:** Myron Ullman III, chairman and chief executive officer of J.C. Penney, purchased $1 million worth of shares of the company. He now owns 393,140 shares of the company and an additional 1,282 on his 401(k) plan.

37160 ■ "JK Lasser's New Rules for Estate, Retirement, and Tax Planning"
Pub: John Wiley & Sons Inc.
Contact: Stephen M. Smith, President
Released: October 20, 2014. Price: $24.95 paperback. Description: The authoritative guide to estate, retirement and tax planning is fully updated and reflects the new changes and legal updates. Estate planning section covers: planning, taxation, investing, wills, executors, trusts, life insurance, retirement planning, Social Security, business planning, succession, asset protection and family limited partnerships.

37161 ■ "JoS. A. Bank Suits Look Better Than Its Shares" in Barron's (Vol. 88, March 31, 2008, No. 13, pp. 25)
Pub: Dow Jones & Co., Inc.
Contact: Clare Hart, President
Ed: Bill Alpert. Description: Jos. A. Bank's inventory has increased sharply raising questions about the company's growth prospects. The company's shares have already dropped significantly from 46 to 23 and could still continue its slide. The company is also battling a class action suit where plaintiffs allege that the Bank inventories were bloated.

37162 ■ "The Joy of Overseas Calling" in Canadian Business (Vol. 85, August 13, 2012, No. 13, pp. 49)
Pub: George Media Inc.
Ed: Bryan Borzykowski. Released: August 13, 2012. Description: Investors should consider growth prospects, regulation and wireless penetration when investing in foreign telecommunications companies. Investment opportunities are available in Europe, Asia, and Latin America and investors should look into dividends, debt and the mix of product offerings.

37163 ■ "Juiced on Energy" in Barron's (Vol. 88, July 14, 2008, No. 28, pp. 33)
Pub: Dow Jones & Co., Inc.
Contact: Clare Hart, President
Ed: Leslie P. Norton. Description: Brad Evans and his team at Heartland Value Plus were able to outperform their peers by significantly under-committing to financials and overexposing themselves with energy stocks. Brad Evans believes that there is a lot of value left in energy stocks such as natural gas.

37164 ■ "Julie Holzrichter: Managing Director of Operations, CME Group Inc." in Crain's Chicago Business (Vol. 31, May 5, 2008, No. 18)
Pub: Crain Communications Inc.
Contact: Todd Johnson, Publisher
Ed: Ann Saphir. Description: Profile of Julie Holzrichter who works as the managing director of operations for CME Group Inc. and is known as a decisive leader able to intercept and solve problems.

37165 ■ "Just Hang Up" in Barron's (Vol. 88, March 10, 2008, No. 10, pp. 45)
Ed: Tiernan Ray. Description: Sprint's shares are expected to continue falling while the company attempts to attract subscribers by cutting prices, cutting earnings in the process. The company faces tougher competition from better-financed AT&T and Verizon Communications.

37166 ■ "Keeping the Faith in Fuel-Tech" in Barron's (Vol. 88, March 24, 2008, No. 12, pp. 20)
Pub: Dow Jones & Co., Inc.
Contact: Clare Hart, President
Ed: Christopher C. Williams. Description: Shares of air pollution control company Fuel-Tech remain on track to reach $40 each from their $19 level due to a continued influx of contracts. The stock has suffered from lower-than-expected quarterly earnings and tougher competition but stand to benefit from increased orders.

37167 ■ "Kenyans Embrace Moving Money By Text Message" in Chicago Tribune (October 7, 2008)
Pub: McClatchy-Tribune Information Services
Ed: Laurie Goering. Description: Cell phone banking services are becoming more common, especially for foreign residents; customers are able to establish a virtual cell phone bank account through companies such as M-Pesa which allows their customers to pay bills, withdraw cash, pay merchants or text money to relatives.

37168 ■ "Key Challenges Dog International Banking in South Florida" in South Florida Business Journal (Vol. 35, August 1, 2014, No. 1, pp. 4)
Pub: American City Business Journals
Released: August 1, 2014. Description: Florida International Bankers Association president, Roberto R. Munoz, discusses the challenges and opportunities in the South Florida international banking market. He explains the impact on international banks with the loss of the Export-Import Bank of the United States charter and the Base1 III rules and regulations regarding higher capital requirements.

37169 ■ "KeyBank CEO Sees Value In Branches" in Business First of Buffalo (Vol. 30, April 25, 2014, No. 32, pp. 6)
Pub: American City Business Journals, Inc.
Contact: Whitney Shaw, President
Released: April 25, 2014. Description: KeyBank CEO, Beth Mooney, wants to drive more revenues across their existing branches because these are an important part of their value ;proposition. She adds that KeyBank continues to invest in digital and mobile banking in response to the transformation of the banking industry.

37170 ■ "Kid Rock" in Canadian Business (Vol. 81, Summer 2008, No. 9, pp. 54)
Ed: John Gray. Description: Damien Reynolds is the founder, chairman and chief executive officer of Vancouver-based Longview Capital Partners. The investment bank, founded in 2005, is one of the fastest-growing companies in British Columbia. The recent economic downturn has battered the stocks of the company and its portfolio of junior miners.

37171 ■ "Know Your Numbers" in Inc. (Volume 32, December 2010, No. 10, pp. 39)
Pub: Inc. Magazine
Ed: Norm Brodsky. Description: Ways to maximize profit and minimize tax burden are presented.

37172 ■ "The Latin Beat Goes On" in Barron's (Vol. 88, July 7, 2008, No. 27, pp. L5)
Pub: Dow Jones & Co., Inc.
Contact: Clare Hart, President
Ed: Tom Sullivan. Description: Latin American stocks have outperformed other regional markets due to rising commodities prices and favorable economic climate. Countries such as Brazil, Mexico, Chile, and Peru provide investment opportunities, while Argentina and Venezuela are tougher places to invest.

37173 ■ "Laugh or Cry? How to Look at the Current State of the Market" in Barron's (Vol. 88, March 24, 2008, No. 12, pp. 7)
Pub: Dow Jones & Co., Inc.
Contact: Clare Hart, President
Ed: Alan Abelson. Description: Discusses the American economy which is just starting to feel the effect of the credit and housing crises. JPMorgan Chase purchased Bear Stearns for $2 a share, much lower than its share price of $60, while quasi-government entities Fannie Mae and Freddie Mac are starting to run into trouble.

37174 ■ Law for the Small and Growing Business
Ed: P. Bohm. Released: February 2007. Price: $59.98. Description: Legal and regulatory issues facing small businesses, including employment law, health and safety, commercial property, company law and finance are covered.

37175 ■ "Leaders and Lagards" in Barron's (Vol. 89, July 13, 2009, No. 28, pp. 14)
Ed: J.R. Brandstrader. Description: Statistical table that shows the returns of different mutual funds in different categories that include U.S. stock funds, sector funds, world equity funds, and mixed equity funds is presented. The data presented is for the second quarter of 2009.

37176 ■ "Leaders and Lagards" in Barron's (Vol. 89, July 13, 2009, No. 28, pp. 14)
Ed: J.R. Brandstrader. Description: Statistical table that shows the returns of different mutual funds in different categories that include U.S. stock funds, sector funds, world equity funds, and mixed equity funds is presented. The data presented is for the second quarter of 2009.

37177 ■ "Leaders Weigh In On Fannie Mae, Freddie Mac Failure, Fed Bailout" in The Business Journal - Serving Phoenix and the Valley of the Sun (Vol. 28, September 14, 2008, No. 53, pp. 1)
Pub: American City Business Journals, Inc.
Contact: Whitney Shaw, President
Ed: Chris Casacchia, Mike Sunnucks, Jan Buchholz. Description: Fannie Mae and Freddie Mac's federal takeover was a move to help stabilize the financial market and it helped bring down interest rates in the past week. Local executives from Arizona's Phoenix area share their thoughts on the immediate effect of the takeover and its upside and downside.

37178 ■ "Leasing: Welcome Back" in Canadian Business (Vol. 82, April 27, 2009, No. 7, pp. 25)
Pub: Rogers Media Inc.
Contact: Tony Viner, President
Ed: Sarka Halas. Description: Some Canadian companies such as Gennum Corporation have taken advantage of corporate sale-leasebacks to raise money at a time when credit is hard to acquire. Corporate sale-leasebacks allow companies to sell their property assets while remaining as tenants of the building. Sale-leasebacks allow firms to increase capital while avoiding the disruptions that may result with moving.

37179 ■ "Legg's Compensation Committee Chair Defends CEO Fetting's Pay" in Boston Business Journal (Vol. 29, July 22, 2011, No. 11, pp. 1)
Pub: American City Business Journals, Inc.
Ed: Gary Haber. Description: Legg Mason Inc. CEO Mark R. Fetting has been awarded $5.9 million pay package and he expects to receive questions regarding it in the coming shareholders meeting. However, Baltimore, Maryland-based RKTL Associates chairman emeritus Harold R. Adams believes Fetting has done a tremendous job in bringing Legg's through a tough market.

37180 ■ "Lehman's Hail Mary Pass" in Business Week (September 22, 2008, No. 4100, pp. 28)
Ed: Matthew Goldstein; David Henry; Ben Levison. Description: Overview of Lehman Brothers' CEO Richard Fuld's plan to keep the firm afloat and end the stock's plunge downward; Fuld's strategy calls for selling off a piece of the firm's investment management business.

37181 ■ "Lenders Capitalize on a Thinning Bulge Bracket" in Mergers & Acquisitions: The Dealmaker's Journal (March 1, 2008)
Pub: SourceMedia Inc.
Contact: James M. Malkin, Chief Executive Officer
Ed: Carol J. Clouse. Description: Regardless of what the economic markets look like, private equity firms will continue to invest capital and mid-market finance firms are becoming very attractive acquisition opportunities since not as much capital is needed to buy them.

37182 ■ "Lenders: Private Equity Funding Most Commercial Real Estate Deals" in The Business Journal - Serving Phoenix and the Valley of the Sun (Vol. 28, July 25, 2008, No. 47, pp. 1)
Pub: American City Business Journals, Inc.
Contact: Whitney Shaw, President
Ed: Jan Buchholz. Description: Private equity lender Investor Mortgage Holdings Inc. has continued growing despite the crisis surrounding the real estate and financial industries and has accumulated a $700 million loan portfolio. Private lending has become increasingly important in financing real estate deals as commercial credit has dried up.

37183 ■ *"Lending Stays Down at Cincinnati Banks"* in *Business Courier* (Vol. 27, October 1, 2010, No. 22, pp. 1)
Pub: Business Courier

Ed: Steve Watkins. **Description:** Greater Cincinnati's largest banks have experienced decreases in loans in the past year due to weak economy and sagging loan demands. Analysis of mid-year data has shown that loans drop by a total of $3.6 billion or 4 percent at the ten largest banks as of June 30, 2010 compared to same period in 2009.

37184 ■ *"Less Malaise in Malaysia"* in *Barron's* (Vol. 88, March 17, 2008, No. 11, pp. M12)
Pub: Dow Jones & Co., Inc.
Contact: Clare Hart, President

Ed: Assif Shameen. **Description:** Shares of Malaysia's Bursa have been in freefall while the Malaysia government prolongs its pitch to sell a 10 percent stake of the exchange to NYSE Euronext. Asian bourses had produced very good returns for five years and charge some of the highest fees for exchanges. A key growth driver for Asian bourses could be the derivatives markets and exchange-traded funds.

37185 ■ *"Let Us Count the Ways"* in *Barron's* (Vol. 88, July 7, 2008, No. 27, pp. M10)
Pub: Dow Jones & Co., Inc.
Contact: Clare Hart, President

Ed: Bennet Sedacca. **Description:** Investors are advised to remain cautious after the drop in stock prices in June 2008. The stock markets remain in the downtrend after reaching a peak in October 2007 and are on the verge of a collapse.

37186 ■ *"Let's Make a Deal"* in *Pittsburgh Business Times* (Vol. 33, July 18, 2014, No. 53, pp. 10)
Pub: American City Business Journals

Released: July 18, 2014. **Description:** The low interest rate, combined with regulation have reduced fixed income trading for banks, thus reducing their profits and increasing the volatility of quarterly earnings. Banks are being forced to consider new ways to make money as the low rates are a function of a Federally-structured government yield curve, reflecting lower economic growth and inflation expectations.

37187 ■ *"Lifesavers"* in *Black Enterprise* (Vol. 41, December 2010, No. 5, pp. 38)
Pub: Earl G. Graves Publishing Co. Inc.
Contact: Earl G. Graves, Jr., President

Ed: Tamara E. Holmes. **Description:** Profile of Interventional Nephrology Specialists Access Center and founders Dr. Omar Davis and Dr. Natarsha Grant; the center generated $5.5 million in revenue for 2009. Details on how they run their successful center are included.

37188 ■ *"A Lifetime of Making Deals"* in *Crain's Detroit Business* (Vol. 24, March 24, 2008, No. 12, pp. 11)
Pub: Crain Communications Inc.
Contact: Rance E. Crain, President

Ed: Tom Henderson. **Description:** Profile of Walter 'Bud' Aspatore who received Crain's Lifetime Achievement Award for mergers and acquisitions; Aspatore is chairman and co-founder of Amherst Partners L.L.C., an investment banking firm that does evaluations and financings, specializes in turnarounds and advises private and public companies on mergers and acquisitions.

37189 ■ *"Lifetime Planning with a Twist"* in *Contractor* (Vol. 56, July 2009, No. 7, pp. 40)
Pub: Intertec Publishing
Contact: John French, President

Ed: Irving L. Blackman. **Description:** Private Placement Life Insurance lets wealthy investors make their investment gains tax-free and can be set up so investors can make tax-free loans from the policy. This can be used on a younger member of the family as a wealth-building strategy if the investor is uninsurable.

37190 ■ *"Like Mom and Apple Pie"* in *Canadian Business* (Vol. 79, October 9, 2006, No. 20, pp. 19)
Pub: Rogers Media Inc.
Contact: Tony Viner, President

Ed: Peter Shawn Taylor. **Description:** Impact of paying huge tax bills on the social benefits of family income is discussed. Income splitting as an effective way to lower household's overall tax bill is presented.

37191 ■ *"Listen Up: There's a Revolution in the Cubicle"* in *Barron's* (Vol. 89, July 27, 2009, No. 30, pp. 18)
Pub: Dow Jones & Co., Inc.
Contact: Clare Hart, President

Ed: Jay Palmer. **Description:** Plantronics will be among the first beneficiaries when the unified communications revolution arrives in the office. Plantronics' shares could rise to around 30 in 2009 from the 20s as of July 2009. Unified communications could create a huge new multimillion-dollar market for Plantronics.

37192 ■ *"The Little Biotech that Could"* in *Barron's* (Vol. 89, July 27, 2009, No. 30, pp. 19)
Pub: Dow Jones & Co., Inc.
Contact: Clare Hart, President

Ed: Christopher C. Williams. **Description:** OSI Pharmaceuticals' shares is a compelling investment bet among small biotech firms due to its Tarceva anticancer drug which has a 23 percent market share as well as their strong balance sheet. OSI is planning to expand the use of Tarceva which could re-ignite sales and one analyst expects the shares to trade in the 40s one year from July 2009.

37193 ■ *"Littleton Firm Chips In On Security Solution"* in *Denver Business Journal* (Vol. 65, May 9, 2014, No. 52, pp. A6)
Pub: American City Business Journals

Released: May 9, 2014. **Description:** CPI Card Group of Littleton, Colorado has been preparing for the nationwide transition to computer chip cards to secure credit and debit cards in the U.S. Banks and merchants in the country need to make the switch by October 2015 or risk being financially liable for fraud if not using the chipped cards in their retail establishments.

37194 ■ *"LLC vs. S-Corp vs. C-Corp: Explained in 100 Pages or Less"*
Pub: Simple Subjects LLC

Released: August 20, 2014. **Price:** $15.00 paperback. **Description:** Whether to form or business as an LLC, S-Corporation or C-Corporation is examined to help any small business owner save money on taxes, know personal assets are protected from lawsuits against your firm, as well as saving money on accounting and legal fees.

37195 ■ *"A Load of Bull?"* in *Canadian Business* (Vol. 82, Summer 2009, No. 8, pp. 12)

Ed: Joe Castaldo. **Description:** Some experts and analysts believe that the improvement of some economic indicators in Canada suggest an economic recovery. A survey of Russell Investment in March 2009 found that 60 percent of investment managers are bullish on Canadian stocks. Some experts like Mike Zyblock, however, remain cautious on the economy.

37196 ■ *"Local Firms Will Feel Impact Of Wall St. Woes"* in *The Business Journal-Milwaukee* (Vol. 25, September 19, 2008, No. 52, pp. A1)
Pub: American City Business Journals, Inc.
Contact: Whitney Shaw, President

Ed: Rich Kirchen. **Description:** Wall Street's crisis is expected to affect businesses in Wisconsin, in terms of decreased demand for services and products and increased financing costs. Businesses in Milwaukee area may face higher interest rates and tougher loan standards. The potential impacts of the Wall Street crisis on local businesses are examined further.

37197 ■ *"Locally Based Stocks Escape Worst of Market's Turmoil"* in *Crain's Detroit Business* (Vol. 24, September 22, 2008, No. 38, pp. 4)
Pub: Crain Communications Inc.
Contact: Rance E. Crain, President

Ed: Daniel Duggan. **Description:** Locally-based companies did not take as big a hit as might be expected with the shock to the financial markets last week; this is due mainly to the fact that the region does not have heavy exposure to energy or capital markets.

37198 ■ *"Long And Leery"* in *Barron's* (Vol. 88, March 31, 2008, No. 13, pp. 47)
Pub: Dow Jones & Co., Inc.
Contact: Clare Hart, President

Ed: Jack Willoughby. **Description:** Tom Claugus' Bay Resource Partners hedge fund has returned 20 percent annually since it started in 1993. Claugus says that he is as aggressively long as he has ever been despite the dangers of the U.S. market. Claugus' stock picks include Canadian Natural Resources, NII Holdings, and Discover Financial.

37199 ■ *"Loonie Tunes: When Will the Dollar Rise Again?"* in *Canadian Business* (Vol. 81, November 10, 2008, No. 19, pp. 62)
Pub: Rogers Media Inc.
Contact: Tony Viner, President

Ed: Joe Castaldo. **Description:** The Canadian dollar has weakened against the U.S. Dollar as the U.S. financial crisis rocked global markets. A currency strategist says that the strength of the U.S. dollar is not based on people's optimism on the U.S. economy but on a structural demand where U.S. non-financial corporations have been repatriating greenbacks from foreign subsidiaries.

37200 ■ *"A Losing Card"* in *Denver Business Journal* (Vol. 65, May 9, 2014, No. 52, pp. A4)
Pub: American City Business Journals

Released: May 9, 2014. **Description:** Banks and retailers in the U.S. find themselves in an ongoing debate about who should pay for the high costs associated with identity theft involving credit and debit cards. Janet Sanders of Denver, Colorado-based In-Com Direct advises banks, retailers and consumers to be more vigilant and proactive about preventing data breaches and fraud.

37201 ■ *"Lots of Explanations, Not Much Growth"* in *Barron's* (Vol. 92, August 25, 2012, No. 35, pp. 38)
Pub: Dow Jones & Co., Inc.
Contact: Clare Hart, President

Ed: Gene Epstein. **Description:** The slow growth of the US economy culd be due to the insufficiency of US fiscal and monetary policy. It could also be attributed to the effects of the recession in Europe, the banking and financial crises, and to the decline in economic freedom.

37202 ■ *"Lotus Starts Slowly, Dodges Subprime Woes"* in *Crain's Detroit Business* (Vol. 24, April 14, 2008, No. 15, pp. 3)
Pub: Crain Communications Inc.
Contact: Rance E. Crain, President

Ed: Tom Henderson. **Description:** Discusses Lotus Bancorp Inc. and their business plan, which although is not right on target due to the subprime mortgage meltdown, is in a much better position than its competitors due to the quality of their loans.

37203 ■ *"Loyalty Cards Score Points"* in *Crain's Cleveland Business* (Vol. 30, June 8, 2009, No. 22, pp. 1)
Pub: Crain Communications Inc.

Ed: Chuck Soder. **Description:** Northeast Ohio retailers are promoting loyalty and rewards programs in order to attract and maintain loyal customers.

37204 ■ *"Loyalty Pays"* in *Entrepreneur* (Vol. 36, February 2008, No. 2, pp. 63)
Pub: Entrepreneur Press
Contact: Perlman Neil, President

Description: Michael Vadini, chief executive officer of Titan Technology Partners looks after his stockholders and investors by making sure that they are protected from risk. Having been affected by the downturn in the technology industry between 2001 and 2004, Vadini granted his investors a liquidity preference. Details regarding his actions to retain investor loyalty are discussed.

37205 ■ "Make Money in 2011" in Small Business Opportunities (January 2011)
Pub: Harris Publications Inc.
Description: Top twenty ways to pick up extra cash, boost your income and generate new revenue. There has never been a better time to start a small business.

37206 ■ "Making Automated Royalty Payments Work for Your Franchise" in Franchising World (Vol. 42, October 2010, No. 10, pp. 30)
Pub: International Franchise Association
Contact: Stephen J. Caldeira, President
E-mail: scaldeira@franchise.org
Ed: J.P. O'Brien. **Description:** In the past, royalty payments were sent by franchisees through regular postal mail and accompanied by a single slip of paper with handwritten notes indicating the month's revenue numbers and royalty amounts.

37207 ■ "Making It Click: Annual Ranking Of the Best Online Brokers" in Barron's (Vol. 88, March 17, 2008, No. 11, pp. 31)
Pub: Dow Jones & Co., Inc.
Contact: Clare Hart, President
Ed: Theresa W. Carey. **Description:** Listing of 23 online brokers that are evaluated based on their trade experience, usability, range of offerings, research amenities, customer service and access, and costs. TradeStation Securities takes the top spot followed by thinkorswim by just a fraction.

37208 ■ Managing Business Growth: Get a Grip on the Numbers That Count
Pub: Self-Counsel Press Inc.
Ed: Angie Mohr. **Released:** 2003. **Description:** Fourth book in the Numbers 101 for Small Business Series, teaches how small company owners can expand their businesses using sound financial planning.

37209 ■ Managing a Small Business Made Easy
Pub: Entrepreneur Press
Contact: Perlman Neil, President
Ed: Martin E. Davis. **Released:** September 2005. **Description:** Examination of the essential elements for an entrepreneur running a business, including advice on leadership, customer service, financials, and more.

37210 ■ "Managing Your Innovation Portfolio: People Throughout Your Organization Are Energetically Pursuing the New. But Does All That Add Up To a Strategy?' in Harvard Business Review (Vol. 90, May 2012, No. 5, pp. 66)
Pub: Harvard Business Review Press
Contact: Peter F. Walsh, Director
Ed: Bansi Nagji, Geoff Tuff. **Released:** May 2012. **Description:** Returns on innovation are higher with transformational initiatives than with core or adjacent pursuits, but require unique management methods. These include establishing a diverse talent set, separating teams from daily operations, and obtaining funding from outside the regular budget cycle.

37211 ■ "M&T On the March?' in Baltimore Business Journal (Vol. 28, November 12, 2010, No. 27, pp. 1)
Pub: Baltimore Business Journal
Ed: Gary Haber. **Description:** Information on the growth of M&T Bank, as well as its expansion plans are presented. M&T recently acquired Wilmington Trust and took over $500 million in deposits from the failed K Bank. Analysts believe that M&T would continue its expansion through Washington DC and Richmond, Virginia, especially after a bank executive acknowledged that the markets in those areas are attractive.

37212 ■ "Many Boomers Skip IRA Contributions" in Retirement Advisor (Vol. 13, October 2012, No. 10, pp. 30)
Pub: Summit Professional Networks
Contact: Steve Weitzner, President
Ed: Warren S. Hersch. **Description:** Only 46 percent of non-retired baby boomers contribute to Individual Retirement Accounts (IRAs), according to new research. The study also revealed that 35 percent of boomers have no plans to retire.

37213 ■ "Many Roads Lead to Value Says David J. Williams, Manager of Excelsior Value & Restructuring Fund" in Barron's (Vol. 88, March 10, 2008, No. 10, pp. 46)
Pub: Dow Jones & Co., Inc.
Contact: Clare Hart, President
Ed: Lawrence C. Strauss. **Description:** David J. Williams, lead manager of Excelsior Value & Restructuring Fund, invests in struggling companies and those companies whose turnarounds show promise. Morgan Stanley, Lehman Brothers, and Petroleo Brasileiro are some of the companies he holds shares in, while he has unloaded shares of Citigroup, Freddie Mac, and Sallie Mae.

37214 ■ "Mapping the Gender Gap" in Business Journal Portland (Vol. 31, April 25, 2014, No. 8, pp. 4)
Pub: American City Business Journals
Released: April 25, 2014. **Description:** The level of gender equality in the health care, banking, technology and commercial real estate industries of Oregon is examined. Gender bias in the workplace is one significant reason behind the wage gap and the lack of women in leadership positions.

37215 ■ "Market Recoups Its Losses - And Its Optimism" in Barron's (Vol. 89, July 20, 2009, No. 29, pp. M3)
Pub: Dow Jones & Co., Inc.
Contact: Clare Hart, President
Ed: Kopin Tan. **Description:** US stock markets gained heavily in the third week of July 2009, rising by about 7 percent during the week. The shares of human resource management companies could be overpriced as they are trading at very high price-earnings multiples. Baxter International faces a class-action suit due to its alleged conspiracy with CSL to fix blood-plasma product prices.

37216 ■ "Market Swings Intensify Yearning for Bonds" in Globe & Mail (March 9, 2007, pp. B9)
Ed: Keith Damsell. **Description:** The rise in demand for proper fixed-income bonds in Canada as a result of uncertainties in the equity market is discussed. Some big Canadian fixed-income funds are presented.

37217 ■ "Market Volatility and Your Retirement" in Agency Sales Magazine (Vol. 39, August 2009, No. 8, pp. 48)
Ed: Joshua D. Mosshart. **Description:** Strategies for retirees in managing investments amid market volatility are presented. Retirees should keep their withdrawal assumptions conservative, maintain sensible asset allocation, review and rebalance their portfolio and allow a financial professional to guide them. Insights on market volatility are also given.

37218 ■ "Market Watch" in Barron's (Vol. 88, March 24, 2008, No. 12, pp. M18)
Pub: Dow Jones & Co., Inc.
Contact: Clare Hart, President
Ed: Ashraf Laidi, Marc Pado, David Kotok. **Description:** Latest measures implemented by the Federal Reserve to address the credit crisis did not benefit the US dollar, with the Japanese yen and the euro recouping earlier losses against the dollar. Goldman Sachs reported earnings of $3.23 per share, claiming a stronger liquidity position. The US markets bottomed early on 22 January 2007, according to evidence.

37219 ■ "Market Watch" in Barron's (Vol. 89, July 20, 2009, No. 29, pp. M10)
Pub: Dow Jones & Co., Inc.
Contact: Clare Hart, President
Ed: Peter Greene, Michael Darda, Ian Wyatt, Stephanie Pomboy. **Description:** Concerns about a possible increase in US inflation rates are overblown

as the country remains in a deflationary environment. Goldman Sachs's second quarter 2009 earnings have already been priced in as its shares rose. Germany's plans of a possible dollar bond sale are in anticipation of a rise in the euro's value.

37220 ■ "Market Watch: A Sampling of Advisory Opinion" in Barron's (Vol. 88, March 17, 2008, No. 11, pp. M10)
Pub: Dow Jones & Co., Inc.
Contact: Clare Hart, President
Ed: Paul Schatz, William Gibson, Michael Darda. **Description:** S&P 500 bank stocks were down 46 percent from their 2007 peak while the peak to through fall in 1989-1990 was just over 50 percent. This suggests that the bottom on the bank stocks could be near. The Federal Reserve Board announced they will lend up to $200 billion to primary lenders in exchange other securities.

37221 ■ "Market Watch: A Sampling of Advisory Opinion US Stock Price Trends, Economic Effects of Global Trade, Chinese Economic Trends" in Barron's (Vol. 92, July 23, 2012, No. 30, pp. M14)
Pub: Dow Jones & Co., Inc.
Contact: Clare Hart, President
Ed: Richard M. Salsman, Jack Ablin, Francois Sicart. **Released:** July 23, 2012. **Description:** US stocks are considered inexpensive due to their low price-earnings ratios compared to levels before the global financial crisis. The US economy is becoming more dependent on the rest of the worldas a result of global trade. The Chinese economy continues to have strong economic growth despite a slowdown.

37222 ■ Marketing in a Web 2.0 World - Using Social Media, Webinars, Blogs, and More to Boost Your Small Business on a Budget
Pub: Atlantic Publishing Co.
Contact: Amanda Miller, Manager
E-mail: amiller@atlantic-pub.com
Ed: Peter VanRysdam. **Released:** June 01, 2010. **Price:** $24.95. **Description:** Web 2.0 technologies have leveled the playing field for small companies trying to boost their presence by giving them an equal voice against larger competitors. Advice is given to help target your audience using social networking hubs.

37223 ■ "Markets Defy the Doomsayers" in Barron's (Vol. 88, March 24, 2008, No. 12, pp. M5)
Pub: Dow Jones & Co., Inc.
Contact: Clare Hart, President
Ed: Leslie P. Norton. **Description:** US stock markets registered strong gains, with the Dow Jones Industrial Average rising 3.43 percent on the week to close at 12,361.32, in a rally that may be seen as short-covering. Shares of Hansen Natural are poised for further drops with a slowdown in the energy drink market.

37224 ■ "The Markets' Tender Spring Shoots, But a Swift Rebound Is Unlikely" in Barron's (Vol. 88, March 31, 2008, No. 13, pp. M3)
Pub: Dow Jones & Co., Inc.
Contact: Clare Hart, President
Ed: Kopin Tan. **Description:** Expansion in price-earnings multiples and a lower credit-default risk index has encouraged fans of the spring-awakening theory. Shares of industrial truckers have gone up 32 percent in 2008 and some shares are pushing five-year highs brought on by higher efficiency and earnings from more load carried. The prospects of the shares of Foot Locker are also discussed.

37225 ■ "Mary Kramer: Good Things Happen When We Buy Local" in Crain's Detroit Business (Vol. 24, October 6, 2008, No. 40, pp. 7)
Pub: Crain Communications Inc.
Contact: Rance E. Crain, President
Description: Michigan is facing incredibly difficult economic times. One way in which each one of us can help the state and the businesses located here is by purchasing our goods and services from local vendors. The state Agriculture Department projected

that if Michigan households earmarked $10 per week in their grocery purchases to made-in-Michigan products, this would generate $30 million a week in economic impact.

37226 ■ *"A Matter of Interest: Payday Loans"* *in Canadian Business (Vol. 79, July 17, 2006, No. 14-15, pp. 21)*
Pub: Rogers Media Inc.
Contact: Tony Viner, President
Ed: Jeff Sanford. **Description:** With the steady decrease in savings, the need for growth in Canada's payloan industry is discussed. Also emphasized are the challenges faced by payloan operators.

37227 ■ *"McDonald's Loses Its Sizzle"* *in Barron's (Vol. 88, March 17, 2008, No. 11, pp. 47)*
Description: McDonald's has promised to return $15 billion to $17 billion to shareholders in 2007-2009 but headwinds are rising for the company. December, 2007 same-store sales were flat and the company's traffic growth in the U.S. is slowing. Its shares are likely to trade in tandem with the market until recession fears recede.

37228 ■ *"Md. Banks Beef Up Deposits, But Lending Lags"* *in Baltimore Business Journal (Vol. 28, October 29, 2010, No. 25, pp. 1)*
Pub: Baltimore Business Journal
Ed: Gary Haber. **Description:** Bank deposits in the Greater Baltimore area have increased but commercial loans have not. Small business owners complain that banks do not help them expand their businesses, but banks argue that they want to lend but the borrowers have to meet standard qualifications.

37229 ■ *"The Medium 150"* *in Canadian Business (Vol. 81, Summer 2008, No. 9, pp. 129)*
Description: Medium-sized companies are ranked based on market capitalization and stock performance. Timminico Ltd. topped the roster with 1,294.2 percent returns, while Petrominerales Ltd. ranked second with 325.4 percent. A table showing the 2008 rankings of the companies is presented.

37230 ■ *"Merrill Lynch in Talks to Buy BlackRock Stake"* *in Globe & Mail (February 13, 2006, pp. B4)*
Ed: Dennis K. Breman; Randall Smith. **Description:** Financial services firm Merrill Lynch and Co. Inc. is planning to acquire money managing company BlackRock Inc. for 8 million dollars. Sources report that this deal would create 1-trillion dollar huge fund management venture.

37231 ■ *"Mettle Detector"* *in Canadian Business (Vol. 79, July 17, 2006, No. 14-15, pp. 63)*
Pub: Rogers Media Inc.
Contact: Tony Viner, President
Ed: Calvin Leung. **Description:** The difficulties faced in completing the Certified Financial Analyst course, and the rewards one can expect after its completion, are discussed.

37232 ■ *"MF Global Moved Clients' Funds to BNY Mellon"* *in Wall Street Journal Eastern Edition (November 19 , 2011, pp. B2)*
Pub: Dow Jones & Co., Inc.
Contact: Clare Hart, President
Ed: Aaron Lucchetti. **Description:** Since the collapse of securities brokerage MF Global Holdings Ltd., one question has remained: where did the hundreds of millions of dollars in customers' accounts go? It has been revealed that MF Global moved these millions from its own brokerage unit to Bank of New York Mellon Corporation in August of this year, just two months before filing for bankruptcy protection.

37233 ■ *"MFS Survey: Generation X/Y Perplexed and Conservative about Future Investing"* *in Wireless News (November 16, 2010)*
Description: Generation X and Y tend to have a conservative approach to investing according to a survey conducted by MFS Investment Management. Statistical data included.

37234 ■ *"Micro-Cap Companies"* *in Canadian Business (Vol. 81, Summer 2008, No. 9, pp. 157)*
Description: Micro-cap companies have lower than $221 million in terms of market capitalization. Burnaby, British Columbia-based Fancamp Exploration Ltd. topped the roster with 1,116.7 percent in return. A table showing the 2008 rankings of the companies is presented.

37235 ■ *"Micro-Finance Agencies and SMEs"* *in International Journal of Entrepreneurship and Small Business (Vol. 11, August 3, 2010)*
Pub: Publishers Communication Group
Contact: Doug Wright, Director
Ed: Patricia A. Rowe, Michael J. Christie, Frank Hoy. **Description:** Institutional preparedness of economic development agencies for developing small and medium-sized enterprises (SMEs) is discussed. The cases presented illustrate variations in the microfinance lender agency-enterprise development of processes for sharing vision and interdependence.

37236 ■ *Microfinance*
Pub: Palgrave Macmillan
Contact: Lisa Dunn, Manager
E-mail: l.dunn@palgrave.com
Ed: Mario La Torre, Gianfranco A. Vento, Philip Molyneux. **Released:** July 2006. **Price:** £84, hardcover; $120. **Description:** Microfinance involves the analysis of operational, managerial and financial aspects of a small business. **Availability:** Print; E-book.

37237 ■ *"Microsoft's Big Gamble"* *in Canadian Business (Vol. 81, March 3, 2008, No. 3, pp. 13)*
Ed: Andrew Wahl. **Description:** Microsoft Corp. is taking a big risk in buying Yahoo, as it is expected to pay more than $31 a share to finalize the acquisition. The deal would be seven and a half times bigger than any other that Microsoft has entered before, an execution of such deal is also anticipated to become a challenge for Microsoft. Recommendations on how Microsoft should handle the integration of the two businesses are given.

37238 ■ *The Middle Class Millionaire: The Rise of the New Rich and How They Are Changing America*
Ed: Russ Alan Prince; Lewis Schiff. **Released:** February 26, 2008. **Price:** $23.95. **Description:** Examination of the far-reaching impact of the middle class millionaires with net worth ranging from one million to ten million dollars and have earned rather than inherited their wealth.

37239 ■ *"Millennial Money: How Young Investors Can Build a Fortune"*
Pub: Palgrave Macmillan
Contact: Lisa Dunn, Manager
E-mail: l.dunn@palgrave.com
Released: October 14, 2014. **Price:** $25.00. **Description:** Because the millennial generation won't be able to depend on pensions or social security for their retirement security, it is stressed that they save and invest their money wisely. As a generation, though, they are skeptical of advice from their elders, but are committed to passing wealth to future generations. A strategy for wise investments to help overcome shortcomings is included.

37240 ■ *"Millennial Spending Influences County Budget"* *in Puget Sound Business Journal (Vol. 35, September 26, 2014, No. 23, pp. 6)*
Pub: American City Business Journals
Released: September 26, 2014. **Description:** Washington State's tax system has been blamed by King County executive Dow Constantine for its proposed 2015-16 budget that cuts 500 positions. The millennial generation's spending was also partially blamed for the drop in sales tax revenue because they don't buy houses and cars as frequently compared to previous generations. How the millennial generation spends their money is also discussed.

37241 ■ *Millionaire Republican*
Pub: Penguin Group USA
Contact: Phyllis Grann, President
Ed: Wayne Allyn Root. **Released:** September 14, 2006. **Price:** $5.99. **Description:** Eighteen steps to create personal wealth in a Republican-dominated era. **Availability:** Electronic publishing.

37242 ■ *"Millions of Senior Citizens Swindled by Financial Fraud"* *in Black Enterprise (Vol. 41, September 2010, No. 2, pp. 24)*
Pub: Earl G. Graves Publishing Co. Inc.
Contact: Earl G. Graves, Jr., President
Description: One of every five citizens over the age of 65 have been victims of financial fraud. Statistical data included.

37243 ■ *Minding Her Own Business, 4th Ed.*
Pub: Sphinx Legal Inc.
Contact: Todd Stocke, Director
E-mail: todd.stocke@sourcebooks.com
Ed: Jan Zobel. **Released:** January 1, 2005. **Price:** $16.95. **Description:** A guide to taxes and financial records for women entrepreneurs is presented.

37244 ■ *"Mine Woes Could Rouse Zinc"* *in Barron's (Vol. 88, July 7, 2008, No. 27, pp. M12)*
Pub: Dow Jones & Co., Inc.
Contact: Clare Hart, President
Ed: Andrea Hotter. **Description:** Prices of zinc could increase due to supply problems in producing countries such as Australia and China. London Metal Exchange prices for the metal have dropped about 36 percent in 2008.

37245 ■ *"Mining Goldman for Insight"* *in Barron's (Vol. 89, July 20, 2009, No. 29, pp. M8)*
Pub: Dow Jones & Co., Inc.
Contact: Clare Hart, President
Ed: Steven M. Sears. **Description:** Methods of investing in options for companies with earnings estimates from Goldman Sachs are discussed. These methods take advantage of increased volatility generated by earnings revisions.

37246 ■ *"Misguided"* *in Canadian Business (Vol. 81, July 22, 2008, No. 12-13, pp. 30)*
Ed: Al Rosen. **Description:** Canada's securities regulations are discussed; differing views on using principles-based and rules-based securities regulations are also presented.

37247 ■ *"A Mixed-Bag Quarter"* *in Barron's (Vol. 88, July 7, 2008, No. 27, pp. 19)*
Ed: Shirley A. Lazo. **Description:** Seven component companies of the Dow Jones Industrial Average increased their dividend payouts in the second quarter of 2008 despite the weak performance of the index. Five companies in the Dow Jones Transportation index and three in the Dow Jones Utilities also increased their dividends.

37248 ■ *"Mobile Homeowners in the Southwest: Financial Behaviors and Economic Mobility Aspirations During Tough Times"* *in Real Estate Review (Vol. 41, Spring 2012, No. 1, pp. 43)*
Released: Spring 2012. **Description:** The financial behaviors of low-income, mobile homeowners in the southwestern United States are examined. Low-income mobile homeowners in the region have been found to display similar patterns of financial behaviors with non-manufactured home owners. Mobile home owners' allocation of lump sum tax refunds are also discussed.

37249 ■ *The Mommy Manifesto: How to Use Our Power to Think Big, Break Limitations and Achieve Success*
Pub: John Wiley & Sons Inc.
Contact: Stephen M. Smith, President
Ed: Kim Lavine. **Released:** August 2009. **Price:** $24. 95, hardcover; $16.99. **Description:** A new women's revolution will help women take control of their careers, their lives, and their economic future. The

book shows how mom's control the economy and have the power to become successful entrepreneurs. **Availability:** PrintE-book.

37250 ■ "Moms Mull Money" in Marketing to Women (Vol. 21, February 2008, No. 2, pp. 6)
Description: According to a survey by Countrywide Bank, women, especially mothers, are more concerned about their financial fitness than men.

37251 ■ "Money Basics: How to Handle a Bank Error" in Black Enterprise (Vol. 41, December 2010, No. 5)
Pub: Earl G. Graves Publishing Co. Inc.
Contact: Earl G. Graves, Jr., President
Ed: Sheiresa Ngo. **Description:** Contact your bank or financial institution immediately after discovering an error in your account.

37252 ■ "MoneyGram Hopes Digital Push Will Click With Customers" in Dallas Business Journal (Vol. 37, July 4, 2014, No. 43, pp. 17)
Pub: American City Business Journals
Released: July 4, 2014. **Description:** Reports on MoneyGram's recent release of a digital monitoring system, which will allow it to work more closely with customers, is profiled. This digital monitoring system will aggregate data from social media platforms and enable the company to identify customer needs and trends across the money transfer industry. It will help MoneyGram outshine its rivals in the money transfer business.

37253 ■ "Mont MN Banks In Black; A Few Fall Back" in August 17, 2012 (Vol. 30, August 17, 2012, No. 12, pp. 1)
Pub: American City Business Journals, Inc.
Contact: Whitney Shaw, President
Ed: Jim Hammerand, Evelina Smirnitskaya. **Released:** August 17, 2012. **Description:** Federal Deposit Insurance Corporation filings by 105 banks within the Twin Cities Metropolitan Area had shown 79 percenter were profitable at the end of the second quarter. The ratio of profitable banks was a slight increase from the same time in 2011 and the last quarter.

37254 ■ "More Gains in the Pipeline" in Barron's (Vol. 89, August 3, 2009, No. 31, pp. M5)
Ed: Fleming Meeks. **Description:** Shares of El Paso Corp. could recover as the company concludes a deal with a private-equity group to fund pipeline construction. The company's shares are trading at $10.06 and could move up to $12 as bad news has already been priced into the stock.

37255 ■ "More Jobs Moving Out of City" in Business Courier (Vol. 24, March 14, 2008, No. 49, pp. 1)
Pub: American City Business Journals, Inc.
Contact: Whitney Shaw, President
Ed: Steve Watkins; Laura Baverman. **Description:** UBS Financial Services Inc. is moving Gradison to Kenwood Town Place in Sycamore Township a year after UBS acquired Gradison. The township does not have a tax on earnings so the move will save Gradison's employees the 2.1 percent Cincinnati tax.

37256 ■ "More Pain" in Canadian Business (Vol. 81, December 24, 2007, No. 1, pp. 12)
Ed: Lauren McKeon. **Description:** Manufacturing sector in Canada is sinking with a forecast by as much as 23 percent for 2008, which can be offset as manufacturers say they plan to increase productivity by 25 percent. Details on the sector's competitiveness, workforce, importing of machinery from the U.S. and financial needs for research and development are examined.

37257 ■ "Mortgage Securities Drop Hits Home" in The Business Journal-Serving Metropolitan Kansas City (Vol. 27, October 17, 2008, No. 5)
Pub: American City Business Journals, Inc.
Contact: Whitney Shaw, President
Ed: Rob Roberts. **Description:** Sale of commercial mortgage-backed securities (CMBS) in Kansas City, Missouri have declined. The area may avoid layoffs if

the United States government succeeds in stabilizing the economy. Major CMBS players in the area include Midland Loan Services Inc. and KeyBank Real Estate Capital.

37258 ■ "Mortgages Going Under" in Black Enterprise (Vol. 41, December 2010, No. 5, pp. 20)
Description: Nearly one-fifth of the country's homeowners are underwater in their mortgages, which means they owe more on their home than the home's worth. Statistical data included.

37259 ■ "Mover and Sheika" in Conde Nast Portfolio (Vol. 2, June 2008, No. 6, pp. 104)
Ed: John Arlidge. **Description:** Profile of Princess Sheika Lubna who is the first female foreign trade minister in the Middle East, the United Arab Emirates biggest business envoy, paving the way for billions in new investment, and also a manufacturer of her own perfume line.

37260 ■ "Mr. Deeds" in Canadian Business (Vol. 81, March 31, 2008, No. 5, pp. 24)
Pub: Rogers Media Inc.
Contact: Tony Viner, President
Ed: Thomas Watson. **Description:** Ron Sandler has the right experience to save Northern Rock PLC get through its liquidity problems. Sandler is known for saving Lloyd's of London in the mid-90's and he is not afraid to make enemies. Ron Sandler's assignment to help Northern Rock comes at a time when the health of the U.K. housing is not great.

37261 ■ "MTI Faces Touch Choices" in The Business Review Albany (Vol. 35, April 4, 2008, No. 53, pp. 1)
Pub: The Business Review
Ed: Richard A. D'Errico. **Description:** Mechanical Technology Inc.'s auditor, PricewaterhouseCoopers LLP is concerned about the company's limited current cash and its $105 million accumulated deficit. MTI has already sold 1.45 million of its PlugPower Inc. shares, but still considers to sell more of the Plug stock. The problems at MTI and the difficult decisions it has to face to solve them are examined.

37262 ■ "Muddy Portfolio Raises a Question: Just What Is National City Worth?" in Crain's Detroit Business (Vol. 24, April 7, 2008, No. 14)
Pub: Crain Communications Inc.
Contact: Rance E. Crain, President
Ed: Jay Miller. **Description:** National City Bank is looking at strategies to help it deal with its credit and loan problems which are reflected in its falling stock price. One possible solution is a merger with another bank, however most national banks are facing their own home-loan portfolio issues and may be unable to tackle another company's unresolved problems. Statistical data included.

37263 ■ "My Favorite Tool for Managing Expenses" in Inc. (Volume 32, December 2010, No. 10, pp. 60)
Pub: Inc. Magazine
Ed: J.J. McCorvey. **Description:** Web-based service called Expensify is outlined. The service allows companies to log expenses while away from the office using the service's iPhone application.

37264 ■ "Nanoready?" in Entrepreneur (Vol. 36, May 2008, No. 5, pp. 20)
Ed: Andrea Cooper. **Description:** Experts predict that the medicine and energy sectors are among those that will see nanotechnology innovations in the coming years, and that nanotechnology will produce significant commercial value in new products. Some entrepreneurs are investing in nanotech and are partnering with universities. Details on nanotech funding concerns are discussed.

37265 ■ "N.C. Foreclosure Regulation Papered Over" in Charlotte Business Journal (Vol. 25, November 5, 2010, No. 33, pp.)
Pub: Charlotte Business Journal
Ed: Adam O'Daniel. **Description:** County courts in North Carolina are having challenges coping with its oversight and regulation duties as it becomes too

busy with foreclosure cases. Clerks in some county courts have presided over foreclosure hearings because of the flooding of foreclosure cases.

37266 ■ "A Neat Social Trade" in (Vol. 92, July 23, 2012, No. 30, pp. 23)
Pub: Dow Jones & Co., Inc.
Contact: Clare Hart, President
Ed: Theresa W. Carey. **Released:** July 23, 2012. **Description:** SocialTrade is a Website that allows users to exchange ideas and data with each other through video. Online broker DittoTrade launched a mobile applications that allows investors to connect to other traders and follow their trades.

37267 ■ "Need Grub? Start Texting at Kroger" in Business Courier (Vol. 24, December 20, 2007, No. 36, pp. 1)
Pub: American City Business Journals, Inc.
Contact: Whitney Shaw, President
Ed: Laura Baverman. **Description:** Discusses the University of Cincinnati which is teaming up to release a technology platform called Macopay that would link a cell phone to a bank account and allow a person to make payments at participating retailers by sending a text message. Details with regard to the new service and its growth potential are discussed.

37268 ■ "Needed: A Strategy; Banking In China" in The Economist (Vol. 390, January 3, 2009, No. 8612, pp. 54)
Description: International banks are competing for a role in China but are finding obstacles in their paths such as a reduction in the credit their operations may receive from Chinese banks and the role they can play in the public capital markets which remain limited.

37269 ■ "Netflix Gets No Respect" in Barron's (Vol. 89, July 27, 2009, No. 30, pp. 26)
Pub: Dow Jones & Co., Inc.
Contact: Clare Hart, President
Ed: Tiernan Ray. **Description:** Netflix met expectations when they announced their second quarter sales but their shares still fell by almost 10 percent. Analysts say their entry into the 'streaming video' business is a mixed bag since customers are increasingly buying the cheaper monthly plan and this is dragging the economics of the business.

37270 ■ Never Bet the Farm: How Entrepreneurs Take Risks, Make Decisions - and How You Can, Too
Pub: Jossey-Bass Publishers
Contact: Matthew Hoover, Manager
E-mail: fwelsch@jbp.com
Released: March 2006. **Price:** $24.95, paperback; $16.99. **Availability:** PrintE-book.

37271 ■ "A New Approach to Funding Social Enterprises: Unbundling Societal Benefits and Financial Returns Can Dramatically Increase Investment" in Harvard Business Review (Vol. 90, January-February 2012, No.1-2, pp. 118)
Pub: Harvard Business Review Press
Contact: Peter E. Walsh, Director
Ed: Antony Bugg-Levine, Bruce Kogut, Nalin Kulatilaka. **Released:** January-February 2012. **Description:** Identification of a range of financing arrangements that can maximize benefits delivered by social organizations. These include equity, quasi-equity debt, charitable giving, convertible debt, and securitized debt. The claims on assets and types of return for each are defined.

37272 ■ "The New Arsenal of Risk Management" in Harvard Business Review (Vol. 86, September 2008, No. 9, pp. 92)
Pub: Harvard Business Review Press
Contact: Peter E. Walsh, Director
Ed: Kevin Buehler, Andrew Freeman, Ron Hulme. **Description:** Goldman Sachs Group Inc. is used to illustrate methods for successful risk management. The investment bank's business principles, partnerships, and oversight practices are discussed.

37273 ■ "New Century's Fall Has a New Culprit" in Barron's (Vol. 88, March 31, 2008, No. 13, pp. 20)
Pub: Dow Jones & Co., Inc.
Contact: Clare Hart, President
Ed: Jonathan R. Laing. **Description:** Court examiner Michael Missal reports that New Century Financial's auditor contributed to New Century's demise by its negligence in permitting improper and imprudent practices related to New Century's accounting processes. New Century's bankruptcy filing is considered the start of the subprime-mortgage crisis.

37274 ■ "New Drug Could Revitalize Amgen" in Barron's (Vol. 88, July 7, 2008, No. 27, pp. 23)
Ed: Johanna Bennett. **Description:** Shares of the biotechnology company Amgen could receive a boost from the release of the anti-osteoporosis drug denosumab. The shares, priced at $48.84 each, are trading at 11 times expected earnings for 2008 and could also be boosted by cost cutting measures.

37275 ■ "A New Kid on the Block" in Barron's (Vol. 88, March 17, 2008, No. 11, pp. 58)
Pub: Dow Jones & Co., Inc.
Contact: Clare Hart, President
Ed: Thomas G. Donlan. **Description:** Discusses the Federal Reserve which has offered to lend $100 billion in cash to banks and $200 billion in Treasuries to Wall Street investment banks that have problems with liquidity. The reluctance of the banks to lend money to meet a margin call on securities that could still depreciate is the reason why the agency is going into the direct loan business.

37276 ■ "New Money" in Entrepreneur (Vol. 36, February 2008, No. 2, pp. 62)
Pub: Entrepreneur Press
Contact: Perlman Neil, President
Ed: C.J. Prince. **Description:** Tips on how to handle business finance, with regard to the tightened credit standards imposed by leading institutions, are provided. These include: selling receivables, margining blue chips, and selling purchase orders.

37277 ■ "The New Risk Tolerance" in Entrepreneur (Vol. 37, September 2009, No. 9, pp. 66)
Pub: Entrepreneur Press
Contact: Perlman Neil, President
Ed: Rosalind Resnick. **Description:** Offers advice on where to invest personal money in the United States. One could lose money from investing in gold and treasuries. High-quality corporate bonds and Treasury Inflation-Protected Securities are seen as ideal investments.

37278 ■ "New Rule Rankles In Jersey" in Philadelphia Business Journal (Vol. 30, September 16, 2011, No. 31, pp. 1)
Pub: American City Business Journals Inc.
Ed: Jeff Blumenthal. **Description:** A new rule in New Jersey which taxes out-of-state companies that conduct business in the state earned the ire of several banks, mortgage lenders and credit card companies and prompted opponents to threaten to file lawsuits. The new rule is an amendment to New Jersey Division of Taxation's corporate business tax regulation and is retroactive to 2002. Details are given.

37279 ■ "New Thinking for a New Financial Order" in Harvard Business Review (Vol. 86, September 2008, No. 9, pp. 26)
Pub: Harvard Business Review Press
Contact: Peter E. Walsh, Director
Ed: Diana Farrell. **Description:** Factors driving the current global economy are analyzed with a focus on the influence of new public and private sectors and the impact of unregulated markets.

37280 ■ "A New Way to Tell When to Fold 'Em" in Barron's (Vol. 88, July 7, 2008, No. 27, pp. 27)
Pub: Dow Jones & Co., Inc.
Contact: Clare Hart, President
Ed: Theresa W. Carey. **Description:** Overview of the Online trading company SmartStops, a firm that aims to tell investors when to sell the shares of a particular

company. The company's Web site categorizes stocks as moving up, down, or sideways, and calculates exit points for individual stocks based on an overall market trend.

37281 ■ "The Next Economic Disaster: Why It's Coming and How to Avoid It"
Pub: University of Pennsylvania Press
Contact: Katherine McGuire, Director
E-mail: mcgk@upenn.edu
Released: July 9, 2014. **Price:** $15.95. **Description:** Findings from a team of economists show that the financial crisis of 2008 was from the rapid growth of private rather than public debt. Credit expert, Richard Vague, also argues that economic collapse over history and other economic downturns around the world were all preceded by a rise in privately held debt. He predicts China may soon be facing economic disaster. If banks in the U.S. do not embrace a policy of debt restructuring, economic growth will suffer.

37282 ■ "Nightmare on Wall Street" in Canadian Business (Vol. 81, October 13, 2008, No. 17, pp. 9)
Ed: Rachel Pulfer. **Description:** Information on events that happened on Wall Street on the week that started September 15, 2008, as well on its effect on financial markets around the world, are presented. Lehman Brothers filed for bankruptcy on September 15, 2008 after negotiations with Barclays Group and Bank of America failed. Details on AIG and Morgan Stanley are also presented.

37283 ■ "No Fast Cash Class" in Black Enterprise (Vol. 37, December 2006, No. 5, pp. 72)
Pub: Earl G. Graves Publishing Co. Inc.
Contact: Earl G. Graves, Jr., President
Ed: Sonia Alleyne. **Description:** There are no shortcuts to a obtaining a career as a financial planner. The Certified Financial Planner Board of Standards has specific requirements for certification which include having a bachelor's degree from an accredited U.S. school before candidates are even eligible for taking the certification exam. Other criteria and requirements are discussed.

37284 ■ "No More Debt" in Black Enterprise (Vol. 37, November 2006, No. 4, pp. 159)
Pub: Earl G. Graves Publishing Co. Inc.
Contact: Earl G. Graves, Jr., President
Ed: Tanisha A. Sykes. **Description:** Eliminating debt is not necessarily easy and can be overwhelming. Here are some tips for reducing and eventually getting out of debt.

37285 ■ "Nonprofits Pressured to Rein in Fundraising Events" in Crain's Detroit Business (Vol. 25, June 15, 2009, No. 24, pp. 1)
Pub: Crain Communications Inc. - Detroit
Contact: Keith Crain, Chairman
Ed: Sherri Begin Welch. **Description:** Local corporations have asked nonprofits to limit fundraising events in order to cut costs during the recession.

37286 ■ North American Financial Institutions Directory
Pub: Accuity Inc.
Contact: Hugh M. Jones, IV, President
URL(s): www.accuity.com/directories/financial-institution-directories/store.accuitysolutions.com/order.html.
Released: Semiannual; January and July. **Price:** $1,430, Individuals. **Covers:** 15,000 banks and their branches; over 2,000 head offices, and 15,500 branches of savings and loan associations; over 5,500 credit unions with assets over $5 million; Federal Reserve System and other U.S. government and state government banking agencies; bank holding, commercial finance, and leasing companies; coverage includes the United States, Canada, Mexico, and Central America. **Entries include:** Bank name, address, phone, fax, telex, principal officers and directors, date established, financial data, association memberships, attorney or counsel, correspondent banks, out-of-town branch, holding company affiliation, ABA transit number and routing symbol, MICR number with check digit, credit card(s) issued, trust powers, current par value and dividend

of common stock, kind of charter. **Database includes:** Bank routing numbers in numeric sequence; maps; discontinued banks. **Arrangement:** Geographical. **Indexes:** Alphabetical.

37287 ■ "Not In My Backyard" in Entrepreneur (Vol. 36, May 2008, No. 5, pp. 42)
Pub: Entrepreneur Press
Contact: Perlman Neil, President
Ed: Farnoosh Torabi. **Description:** More investors are turning to overseas real estate investments as the U.S. market sees a slowdown. Analysts say that risk-averse investors opt for funds with record of strong returns and U.S. real estate investment trusts that partner with foreign businesses for transparency purposes. Other details about foreign real estate investments are discussed.

37288 ■ "A Novel Fix for the Credit Mess" in Barron's (Vol. 88, March 31, 2008, No. 13, pp. 10)
Pub: Dow Jones & Co., Inc.
Contact: Clare Hart, President
Ed: Michael Santoli. **Description:** Due to the common bank-leverage factor of 10, the $250 billion of lost bank capital would have supported $2.5 trillion in lending capacity. Jeffrey Lewis suggests onerous regulations on bank-holding companies that own 10 to 25 percent, as they are partly to blame. Statistical data included.

37289 ■ "Now You See It.." in Canadian Business (Vol. 81, November 10, 2008, No. 19, pp. 20)
Pub: Rogers Media Inc.
Contact: Tony Viner, President
Ed: Sharda Prashad. **Description:** Total return swaps were offered by Deutsche Bank AG and UBS AG to foreign investors for them to avoid paying taxes on the proceeds of their shares of Fording Canadian Coal Trust when Teck Cominco offered to buy the company. This means that the Canadian government is losing tax revenue from foreigners and it is argued that a simpler tax system would avoid this practice.

37290 ■ "Number of Mechanic's Liens Triple Since 2005" in The Business Journal - Serving Phoenix and the Valley of the Sun (Vol. 28, August 22, 2008, No. 51, pp. 1)
Pub: American City Business Journals, Inc.
Contact: Whitney Shaw, President
Ed: Jan Buchholz. **Description:** Experts are blaming the mortgage and banking industries for the tripling of mechanic's liens that were filed in Arizona from 2005 through August 6, 2008. The rise in mechanic's liens is believed to indicate stress in the real estate community. Other views and information on the rise of mechanic's liens filed in Arizona are presented.

37291 ■ "The Numbers Speak For Themselves" in Barron's (Vol. 88, July 14, 2008, No. 28, pp. 16)
Pub: Dow Jones & Co., Inc.
Contact: Clare Hart, President
Ed: Bill Alpert. **Description:** Discusses quant fund managers versus traditional long-short equity funds after quants outperformed traditional funds in the year 2000. Causes for the underperformance are outlined and statistical data is included.

37292 ■ "Nvidia Shares Clobbered After Gloomy Warning" in Barron's (Vol. 88, July 7, 2008, No. 27, pp. 25)
Pub: Dow Jones & Co., Inc.
Contact: Clare Hart, President
Ed: Eric J. Savitz. **Description:** Shares of graphics chip manufacturer Nvidia suffered a 30 percent drop in its share price after the company warned that revenue and gross margin forecasts for the quarter ending July 27, 2008 will be below expectations. Stan Glasgow, chief operating officer of Sony Electronics, believes the US economic slowdown will not affect demand for the company's products. Statistical data included.

37293 ■ *"Nvidia's Picture Brighter Than Stock Price Indicates"* in Barron's (Vol. 88, March 24, 2008, No. 12, pp. 46)
Pub: Dow Jones & Co., Inc.
Contact: Clare Hart, President
Ed: Eric J. Savitz. **Description:** Shares of graphics chip maker Nvidia, priced at $18.52 each, do not indicate the company's strong position in the graphics chip market. The company's shares have dropped due to fears of slower demand for PCs, but the company is not as exposed to broader economic forces.

37294 ■ *"Nymex Dissidents Rattle Sabers"* in Crain's Chicago Business (Vol. 31, April 21, 2008, No. 16, pp. 2)
Pub: Crain Communications Inc.
Contact: Todd Johnson, Publisher
Ed: Ann Saphir. **Description:** Two groups of New York Mercantile Exchange members say they have more than enough votes to stop CME Group Inc.'s $10 billion deal to acquire the oil and metals exchange and they are threatening a proxy fight if the Chicago exchange doesn't raise its offer.

37295 ■ *"October 2009: Recovery Plods Along"* in Hispanic Business (October 2009, pp. 10-11)
Ed: Dr. Juan Solana. **Description:** Economist reports on a possible economic recovery which will not be allowed to rely on a strong domestic demand in order to sustain it. Consumers, looking to counterbalance years of leverage financing based on unrealistic, ever-increasing home and portfolio valuations, are saving rather than spending money.

37296 ■ *"Office Market May Turn Down"* in Crain's New York Business (Vol. 24, January 13, 2008, No. 2, pp. 26)
Pub: Crain Communications Inc.
Contact: Rance Crain, President
Description: Although still dominated by Wall Street, the downturn in the economy is raising fears that the continuing fallout from the subprime mortgage crisis could result in layoffs that will derail the office market.

37297 ■ *"Ohio Commerce Draws Closer to Profitability"* in Crain's Cleveland Business (Vol. 28, October 29, 2007, No. 43, pp. 14)
Pub: Crain Communications Inc.
Ed: Shawn A. Turner. **Description:** Overview of the business plan of Ohio Commerce Bank, a de novo, or startup bank that is close to turning the corner to profitability. The bank opened in November 2006 and focuses on dealing with small businesses totaling $5 million or less in annual revenues.

37298 ■ *"Ok, So Now What?"* in Canadian Business (Vol. 79, November 6, 2006, No. 22, pp. 113)
Ed: Calvin Leung. **Description:** Details of healthy income-generating corporations, such as Cedar Fair L.P., are presented.

37299 ■ *"Older, But Not Wiser"* in Canadian Business (Vol. 85, July 16, 2012, No. 11-12, pp. 54)
Pub: George Media Inc.
Ed: Matthew McClearn, Michael McCullough. **Released:** July 16, 2012. **Description:** Data from Statistics Canada revealed that two-thirds of workers aged 55 and above have some form of debt from mortgage to credit card balance while its one-third among the retired. Some factors contributing to the trend are the decline in borrowing costs, real estate, and older Canadians' car purchasing behavior.

37300 ■ *"On the Trail of the Bear"* in Canadian Business (Vol. 81, March 17, 2008, No. 4, pp. 28)
Ed: Thomas Watson. **Description:** Discusses the conservative rule of thumb which is to invest in equity markets when a five to ten percent market rally is sustained for more than a few months. Bear markets on the S&P 500 bear markets in the 20th century only lasts over a year based on average. It is also good to remember that bear markets are followed by bulls that exceed the previous market highs.

37301 ■ *"The One Minute Entrepreneur: The Secret to Creating and Sustaining a Successful Business*
Pub: Doubleday
Contact: Jack Hoeft, President
Ed: Ken Blanchard, Don Hutson, Ethan Willis. **Released:** April 29, 2008. **Price:** $19.95, hardcover; $11.99. **Description:** Four traditional business ideas are covered including: revenue needs to exceed expenses, bill collection, customer service, and employee motivation in order to be successful. **Availability:** PrintE-book.

37302 ■ *"One-Time Area Trust Executive Finds Trouble in N.H."* in The Business Journal-Serving Metropolitan Kansas City (September 12, 2008)
Ed: Steve Vockrodt. **Description:** About 200 investors, some from Missouri's Kansas City area, claim that they had conducted business with Noble Trust Co. The trust company was placed under New Hampshire Banking Department's conservatorship after $15 million was discovered to be missing from its account. It is alleged that the money was lost in a Colorado Ponzi scheme.

37303 ■ *"Opportunity Now Lies at Short End of the Market"* in Barron's (Vol. 88, June 30, 2008, No. 26, pp. M9)
Pub: Dow Jones & Co., Inc.
Contact: Clare Hart, President
Ed: Michael S. Derby. **Description:** Renewed credit concerns and the lesser chance of a Federal Reserve interest rate hike boosted the bond market. Some portfolio managers are more bullish on short-dated securities as they expect the market to adjust to a more appropriate outlook.

37304 ■ *"An Opportunity for Patience"* in Barron's (Vol. 88, June 30, 2008, No. 26, pp. M5)
Pub: Dow Jones & Co., Inc.
Contact: Clare Hart, President
Ed: Fleming Meeks. **Description:** Shares of Louisiana-Pacific are near their 52-week low at $8.95 per share making them look like a better buy than they were at $11.51 in May, 2008. The company is a to player in a cyclical business and its balance sheet is sound compared to its peers with net debt at just $84 million or 20 percent of total capital.

37305 ■ *"Optimism Index"* in Black Enterprise (Vol. 41, September 2010, No. 2, pp. 24)
Pub: Earl G. Graves Publishing Co. Inc.
Contact: Earl G. Graves, Jr., President
Description: According to a Pew Research Center report, 81 percent of African Americans expect to improve their finances in 2011. Blacks have carried a disproportionate share of job losses and housing foreclosures in the recession that began in 2007.

37306 ■ *"Optimize.ca Supplies Free Online Financial Advice"* in Entertainment Close-Up (October 9, 2010)
Description: Optimize.ca provides free online financial advice, focusing on instant savings for their mutual funds and other banking products while improving rates of return and overall financial health.

37307 ■ *"Oracle: No Profit of Doom"* in Barron's (Vol. 88, March 31, 2008, No. 13, pp. 40)
Pub: Dow Jones & Co., Inc.
Contact: Clare Hart, President
Ed: Mark Veverka. **Description:** Oracle's revenues grew by 21 percent but fell short of expectation and their profits came in at the low-end of expectations. The company's shares dropped 8 percent but investors are advised to pay more attention to the company's earnings expansion rather than revenue growth in a slow economy. Nokia's Rick Simonson points out that their markets in Asia and particularly India is growing so they are not as affected by the U.S. economic conditions.

37308 ■ *"Our Rich Past: a Guide to Some of Canada's Historic Fortunes"* in Canadian

Business (Vol. 80, Winter 2007, No. 24, pp. 131)
Ed: Graham F. Scott. **Description:** Donald Alexander Smith rose through the ranks at Hudson's Bay Company to become the company's principal shareholder. John Wilson McConnell started his career at the Standard Chemical Company but later shifted to selling stocks and receiving equity stocks in return for his endorsement. Bud McDougald is well known for his deal making skills before he died in 1978.

37309 ■ *"Outlook In Other Industries"* in Crain's Detroit Business (Vol. 30, January 6, 2014, No. 1, pp. 3)
Pub: Crain Communications Inc. - Detroit
Contact: Keith Crain, Chairman
Released: January 6, 2014. **Description:** Outlook for industries in the Detroit area are listed, including small business growth, restaurants, defense contracts, nonprofits, transportation, auto suppliers, healthcare, bankruptcy, and government.

37310 ■ *"Over A Barrel"* in Canadian Business (Vol. 81, July 21, 2008, No. 11, pp. 13)
Ed: Thomas Watson. **Description:** Analysts predict that the skyrocketing price of fuel will cause a crackdown in the market as purported in the peak oil theory. It is forecasted that the price of oil will reach $200 per barrel. Details of the effect of the increasing oil prices on the market are presented.

37311 ■ *Own Your Own Corporation: Why the Rich Own Their Own Companies and Everyone Else Works for Them*
Pub: Business Plus
Ed: Garrett Sutton; Robert T. Kiyosaki; Ann Blackman. **Released:** June 2008. **Price:** $17.99 paperback. **Description:** Part of the Rich Dad Advisor's Series, this edition shows how individuals can incorporate themselves and their businesses to save thousands of dollars in taxes and protect against financial disaster.

37312 ■ *"Owning the Right Risks"* in Harvard Business Review (Vol. 86, September 2008, No. 9, pp. 102)
Pub: Harvard Business Review Press
Contact: Peter E. Walsh, Director
Ed: Kevin Buehler, Andrew Freeman, Ron Hulme. **Description:** TXU Corp. is used to illustrate methods for successful risk management. The electric utility's practices include determining which risks are natural, embedding risk in all processes and decisions, and organizing corporate governance around risk.

37313 ■ *"Packaging Firm Wraps Up Remake: Overseas Plants Help Firm Fatten Margins"* in Crain's New York Business (January 6, 2008)
Pub: Crain Communications Inc.
Contact: Rance Crain, President
Description: Sealed Air Corp., a packaging manufacturer, has seen its share price fall nearly 20 percent over the past two years, making it one of the worst performers in the packaging sector.

37314 ■ *"Pain Ahead as Profit Pressure Increases"* in Crain's Chicago Business (Vol. 31, May 5, 2008, No. 18, pp. 4)
Pub: Crain Communications Inc.
Contact: Todd Johnson, Publisher
Ed: Daniel Rome Levine. **Description:** Interview with David Klaskin, the chairman and chief investment officer at Oak Ridge Investments LLC, who discusses the outlook for the economy and corporate earnings, particularly in the housing and auto industries, the impact of economic stimulus checks, the weakness of the dollar and recommendations of stocks that individual investors may find helpful.

37315 ■ *"The Pain Drain: A Tonic for Irrationality?"* in Barron's (Vol. 89, July 13, 2009, No. 28, pp. 12)
Pub: Dow Jones & Co., Inc.
Contact: Clare Hart, President
Ed: Robin Goldwyn Blumenthal. **Description:** Financial-personality assessment being introduced by Barclays Wealth, measures six personality aspects related to financial behavior through a profile that

measures such traits including risk tolerance, composure and perceived financial expertise. The profile helps the company create a portfolio that are structured to meet their client's personality needs.

37316 ■ *Panic! The Story of Modern Financial Insanity*
Pub: W.W. Norton and Company Inc.
Contact: A Malmud, President
Released: 2009. **Price:** $18.95, Paperback. **Description:** Two decades of stock market crashes are outlined.

37317 ■ *Paper Fortunes: Modern Wall Street: Where It's Been and Where It's Going*
Pub: Palgrave Macmillan
Contact: Lisa Dunn, Manager
E-mail: l.dunn@palgrave.com
Ed: Roy C. Smith. **Released:** 2010. **Price:** $7.99. **Description:** Comprehensive history of Wall Street and lessons learned with insight into ways Wall Street will reinvent itself in this new economy. **Availability:** E-book.

37318 ■ *"Paradise Banquet Hall of Toronto: Breaking Traditions Can Keep a Wedding Budget Intact" in Internet Wire (June 12, 2012)*
Released: June 12, 2012. **Description:** Average wedding costs can reach nearly $27,000 and that amount does not inclue honeymoon, wedding shower, engagement party, or bachelor/bachelorette parties. Paradise Banquet Hall of Toronto uses Donna Freedman's approach to planning a wedding on a budget. Details are included.

37319 ■ *"Passing It On: Using Life Insurance as an Estate Planning Tool" in Inc. (October 2007, pp. 47-49)*
Pub: Mansueto Ventures L.L.C.
Contact: John Koten, Chief Executive Officer
Ed: Elaine Appleton Grant. **Description:** Permanent life insurance policies can be used to cover estate taxes for hcirs inheriting large estates, while allowing them time to sell any small business. Six tips are included to assist in choosing the right policy.

37320 ■ *"Paying for the Recession: Rebalancing Economic Growth" in Montana Business Quarterly (Vol. 49, Spring 2011, No. 1, pp. 2)*
Pub: University of Montana Bureau of Business and Economic Research
Contact: Patrick Barkey, Director
E-mail: patrick.barkey@business.umt.edu
Ed: Patrick M. Barkey. **Description:** Four key issues required to address in order to rebalance economic growth in America are examined. They include: savings rates, global trade imbalances, government budgets and most importantly, housing price correction.

37321 ■ *"Perry Ellis and G-III Apparel -- Out of Fashion, But Still in Style" in Barron's (Vol. 88, March 17, 2008, No. 11, pp. 48)*
Pub: Dow Jones & Co., Inc.
Contact: Clare Hart, President
Ed: Robin Goldwyn Blumenthal. **Description:** Shares of Perry Ellis International and G-III Apparel Group have taken some beating in the market despite good growth earnings prospects. Perry Ellis sees earnings growth of 8 to 11 percent for fiscal 2009, while G-III Apparel expects earnings growth of 25 percent.

37322 ■ *Personal Success and the Bottom Line*
Pub: Successful Publishing
Ed: Mark C. Middleton. **Released:** March 2006. **Price:** $24.95. **Description:** Retired certified public accountant provides a primer for those wishing to achieve a balance between career and their personal life.

37323 ■ *"Peter Bynoe Trades Up" in Black Enterprise (Vol. 38, July 2008, No. 12, pp. 30)*
Pub: Earl G. Graves Publishing Co. Inc.
Contact: Earl G. Graves, Jr., President
Description: Chicago-based Loop Capital Markets L.L.C. has named Peter Bynoe managing director of corporate finance. Bynoe was previously a senior partner at the law firm DLA Piper U.S. L.L.P., where he worked on stadium deals.

37324 ■ *"PhotoMedex Bouncing Back from Brink of Bankruptcy" in Philadelphia Business Journal (Vol. 30, January 6, 2012, No. 47, pp. 1)*
Pub: American City Business Journal
Description: PhotoMedex Inc. has managed to avoid bankruptcy through reorganization. The company appointed Dennis McGrath as president and chief executive. Details of the business reorganization plans are covered.

37325 ■ *"Pioneering Strategies for Entrepreneurial Success" in Business Horizons (Vol. 51, January-February 2008, No. 1, pp. 21)*
Pub: Elsevier Advanced Technology Publications
Ed: Candida G. Brush. **Description:** Entrepreneurs are known for new products, services, processes, markets and industries. In order to achieve success, they have to develop a clear vision, creatively manage finances, and use social skills to persuade others to commit to the venture. Pioneering strategies and their implementation are examined.

37326 ■ *"Place Restrictions on Your Stock Shares" in Business Owner (Vol. 35, July-August 2011, No. 4, pp. 14)*
Pub: DL Perkins Company
Description: It is critical for any small business owner to be certain that the buyer or recipient of any part of the company represents that the stock is being acquired or given for investment purposes only.

37327 ■ *"A Place in the Sun" in Canadian Business (Vol. 81, July 22, 2008, No. 12-13, pp. 56)*
Description: Experts believe that it is the best time for Canadians to own a retirement home in the U.S., where real estate prices are up to 50 percent below their peak. Other views concerning the economic conditions occurring in the United States, as well as on the implications for Canadians planning to invest in the country are presented.

37328 ■ *"Plan Targets Small Banks" in Business Journal Portland (Vol. 26, December 11, 2009, No. 40, pp. 1)*
Pub: American City Business Journals, Inc.
Ed: Courtney Sherwood. **Description:** Senator Jeff Merkley of Oregon has proposed an expansion of the Troubled Assets Relief Program to accommodate banks with capital levels of less than 10 percent. In his proposal, affected banks would be mandated on a stress test to evaluate capital requirements.

37329 ■ *"Planning Ahead: Steven Taylor Mulls a Second Career After Retirement" in Black Enterprise (Vol. 37, November 2006, No. 4, pp. 82)*
Pub: Earl G. Graves Publishing Co. Inc.
Contact: Earl G. Graves, Jr., President
Ed: Sheryl Nance-Nash. **Description:** Many workers are unprepared for retirement. Profile of Steven Taylor, a soon to retire dietary correctional officer who looked to Walt Clark, president of Clark Capital Financial in Maryland, to assess his retirement goals. Detailed advice and statistical data included.

37330 ■ *"Playing Citigroup's Woes" in Barron's (Vol. 88, March 31, 2008, No. 13, pp. M7)*
Pub: Dow Jones & Co., Inc.
Contact: Clare Hart, President
Ed: Steven M. Sears. **Description:** Citigroup's first-quarter earnings estimate was slashed to a $1.15-per-share-loss from 28 cents. A strategist recommends buying the company's shares at Sept. 20, 2008 put and selling a Sept. 17.50 put with a maximum profit of $166 if the shares is at or below $17.50 at expiration.

37331 ■ *"Playing Defense" in Crain's Chicago Business (Vol. 31, November 10, 2008, No. 45, pp. 4)*
Pub: Crain Communications Inc.
Contact: Todd Johnson, Publisher
Ed: Monee Fields-White. **Description:** Chicago's money managers are increasingly investing in local companies such as Caterpillar Inc., a maker of

construction and mining equipment, Kraft Foods Inc. and Baxter International Inc., a manufacturer of medical products, in an attempt to bolster their portfolios. These companies have a history of surviving tough economic times.

37332 ■ *"PNC Begins Search for New Baltimore-Area Headquarters" in Baltimore Business Journal (Vol. 28, June 4, 2010, No. 4, pp. 1)*
Pub: Baltimore Business Journal
Ed: Daniel J. Sernovitz. **Description:** PNC Financial Services Group Inc. is searching for a new headquarters building in Greater Baltimore, Maryland. The company is seeking about 150,000 square feet for its regional operations. However, PNC could also end up moving out of Baltimore for space in the surrounding suburbs.

37333 ■ *"Point, Click, Buy" in Barron's (Vol. 90, September 6, 2010, No. 36, pp. 11)*
Pub: Barron's Editorial & Corporate Headquarters
Ed: Vito J. Racanelli. **Description:** Non-travel online retail sales from January to July 2010 increased nine percent which indicates that online shopping for the coming holidays will be good. Online sales are outpacing traditional shopping, but pricing is still critical.

37334 ■ *"Portfolio: Written in the Polls" in Entrepreneur (Vol. 35, October 2007, No. 10, pp. 74)*
Pub: Entrepreneur Press
Contact: Perlman Neil, President
Ed: Scott Bernard Nelson. **Description:** Ibbotsen Associates looked at trends in the U.S. presidential elections to see if the election has something to do with stock market behavior. It was found that election years beat non-election years in the stock market by nearly three percentage points each year. Details of the presidential elections' impact on the stock market are given.

37335 ■ *"Powder River Reports First Quarter Revenues Over 5 Million" in Canadian Corporate News (May 16, 2007)*
Description: Financial report for Powder River Basin Gas Corp., a revenue generating producer, marketer, and acquirer of crude oil and natural gas properties. Statistical data included.

37336 ■ *Prepare to Be a Teen Millionaire*
Pub: Health Communications, Inc.
Contact: Peter Vegso, President
Ed: Kimberly Spinks-Burleson, Robyn Collins. **Released:** March 03, 2008. **Price:** $13.56, Members, paperback; $16.95, Nonmembers, paperback. **Description:** Business reference for any teenager wishing to become a successful entrepreneur; advice is given from successful teenage millionaires. Topics covered include: choosing a business name, type, and location; use of the Internet; legal issues; branding, sales, and marketing; funding and financial management; return on investment; retirement; development of a sound business plan; and certification for minority or women-owned companies. **Availability:** Print.

37337 ■ *"Private Equity Firms Shopping Valley For Deals" in The Business Journal - Serving Phoenix and the Valley of the Sun (Vol. 29, September 21, 2008, No. 3, pp. 1)*
Pub: American City Business Journals, Inc.
Contact: Whitney Shaw, President
Ed: Mike Sunnucks. **Description:** Private equity firms from California, Boston, New York, and overseas are expected to invest in growth-oriented real estate markets that include Phoenix. Real estate experts revealed that privately held investment and acquisition firms are looking to invest in real estate markets hit by the housing crisis. Views and information on private equity firms' real estate investments are presented.

37338 ■ *"Proactive Elder-Care Workshop Scheduled" in News-Sentinel (February 15, 2012)*
Description: Proactive Elder Care has partnered with IPFW to provide an educational workshop open to caregivers, seniors, family members, employed

caregivers and employers. Breakout sessions cover when to begin care, finances, law, healthcare, housing, community services, and bioethics.

37339 ■ *"Profit Predictions Look Too Plump"* **in Barron's (Vol. 88, March 31, 2008, No. 13, pp. 37)**
Ed: Johanna Bennett. **Description:** Full-year forecast points to a 14 percent gain for 2008 but the second-half profit increases would have to grow at a fast rate and peak at 61 percent in the fourth quarter to achieve this. Trends in the U.S. economic conditions are also discussed.

37340 ■ *Profits Aren't Everything. They're the Only Thing: No-Nonsense Rules from the Ultimate Contrarian and Small Business Guru*
Pub: HarperCollins Publishers Inc.
Contact: Jane Friedman, President
E-mail: jfriedman@harpercollins.com
Ed: George Cloutier. **Released:** September 07, 2010. **Price:** $14.99, paperback. **Description:** In difficult economic times, the only way for small businesses to survive is to maximize profits. Thirteen steps to maximize profits in a slow economy are outlined. **Availability:** Print.

37341 ■ *"Profits Without Prosperity: Stock Buybacks Manipulate the Market and Leave Most Americans Worse Off"* **in Harvard Business Review (Vol. 92, September 2014, No. 9, pp. 46)**
Pub: Harvard Business Publishing
Released: September 2014. **Description:** While stock prices rise due to stock buybacks, the long-term effects of buybacks are job instability, sluggish growth, and income inequality. Firms should not be permitted to repurchase their shares, and restrictions should be placed on stock-based pay. Profits should be invested in innovation.

37342 ■ *Progress-Driven Entrepreneurs, Private Equity Finance and Regulatory Issues*
Pub: Palgrave Macmillan
Contact: Lisa Dunn, Manager
E-mail: l.dunn@palgrave.com
Ed: Zuhayr Mikdashi. **Released:** December 2009. **Price:** $79, hardcover. **Description:** Durable business performance is critically dependent on a stakeholder's strategy along with accessible entrepreneurial financing availability within macro-economic and economic regulatory environments. **Availability:** Print; Electronic publishing.

37343 ■ *"Proof That Good Entrepreneurs Can Make Bad Investors"* **in Inc. (October 2007, pp. 77-78)**
Pub: Mansueto Ventures L.L.C.
Contact: John Koten, Chief Executive Officer
Ed: Norm Brodsky. **Description:** Information for small business owners is offered to help decide which investments are right for them.

37344 ■ *"Public Opinion"* **in Entrepreneur (Vol. 36, April 2008, No. 4, pp. 28)**
Pub: Entrepreneur Press
Contact: Perlman Neil, President
Description: According to a 2007 report from Group and Organization Management, women in top positions can lead publicly traded companies to stock price and earnings growth. Some women business owners say that going public has provided them with the capital to grow. Details on the potential of women-managed publicly traded companies are discussed.

37345 ■ *"Put It on MasterCard"* **in Barron's (Vol. 89, July 27, 2009, No. 30, pp. 16)**
Pub: Dow Jones & Co., Inc.
Contact: Clare Hart, President
Ed: Bill Alpert. **Description:** Shares of MasterCard trade at a discount at just 15 times its anticipated earnings and some believe that these shares may be a better play in an economic recovery. The prospects of these shares are compared with those of Visa.

37346 ■ *"Putting SogoTrade Through Its Paces"* **in Barron's (Vol. 89, July 27, 2009, No. 30, pp. 27)**
Pub: Dow Jones & Co., Inc.
Contact: Clare Hart, President
Ed: Theresa W. Carey. **Description:** SogoTrade options platform streams options quotes in real time

and lets users place a trade in several ways. The site also features notable security tactics and is a reasonable choice for bargain-seekers. OptionsXpress' Xtend platform lets users place trades and get real time quotes.

37347 ■ *"Putting the World at Your Fingertips"* **in Barron's (Vol. 88, July 7, 2008, No. 27, pp. L13)**
Pub: Dow Jones & Co., Inc.
Contact: Clare Hart, President
Ed: Neil A. Martin. **Description:** Currency-traded exchange funds allow investors to diversify their assets and take advantage of investment opportunities such as speculation and hedging. Investors can use these funds to build positions in favor of or against the US dollar.

37348 ■ *"Q&A: Bolder Investment Partners' Ian Gordon"* **in Canadian Business (Vol. 81, May 22, 2008, No. 9, pp. 10)**
Pub: Rogers Media Inc.
Contact: Tony Viner, President
Ed: Matthew McClearn. **Description:** Bolder Investment Partners' Ian Gordon discussed the economic theory promulgated by Russian economist Nikolai Kondratieff. The cycle begins with a rising economy then followed by deflationary depression. Details of his views on the Kondratieff cycle and its application to the current economy are presented.

37349 ■ *"Q&A: David Labistour"* **in Canadian Business (Vol. 81, March 17, 2008, No. 4, pp. 10)**
Pub: Rogers Media Inc.
Contact: Tony Viner, President
Ed: Lauren McKeon. **Description:** David Labistour says that the difference between being a co-op retailer and a corporate-owned retailer in the case of Mountain Equipment Co-op (MEC) is that the company is owned by their customers and not by shareholders. Labistour also says that MEC works with their factories to ensure that these maintain ethical standards in the manufacturing process.

37350 ■ *"Q&A Patrick Pichette"* **in Canadian Business (Vol. 81, October 13, 2008, No. 17, pp. 6)**
Ed: Andrew Wahl. **Description:** Patrick Pichette finds challenge in taking over the finances of an Internet company that has a market cap of about $140 billion. He feels, however, that serving as Google's chief financial officer is nothing compared to running Bell Canada Enterprises (BCE). Pichette's other views on Google and BCE are presented.

37351 ■ *"Q&A: Take a Load Off Your HR"* **in Entrepreneur (May 2014)**
Pub: Entrepreneur Media Inc.
Released: May 2014. **Description:** A Professional Employer Organization (PEO) manages all the human resource (HR) needs of a small business. The PEO can help the business save money by purchasing insurance and benefit plans at significant savings, assist with employment-regulatory compliance and ensure effective management and access to personnel records, among other things. Business owners should consider hiring PEOs who are financially responsible and stable. A business needs a PEO when the accounting department asks for a dedicated HR person to handle all the paperwork.

37352 ■ *"Q&A: The CAPP's Greg Stringham"* **in Canadian Business (Vol. 81, February 12, 2008, No. 3, pp. 8)**
Pub: Rogers Media Inc.
Contact: Tony Viner, President
Ed: Michelle Magnan. **Description:** Canadian Association of Petroleum Producers' Greg Stringham thinks that the new royalty plan will result in companies pulling out their investments for Alberta's conventional oil and gas sector. Stringham adds that Alberta is losing its competitive advantage and companies must study their cost profiles to retrieve that advantage. The effects of the royalty system on Alberta's economy are examined further.

37353 ■ *"Qualcomm Could Win Big as the IPhone 3G Calls"* **in Barron's (Vol. 88, July 4, 2008, No. 28, pp. 30)**
Pub: Dow Jones & Co., Inc.
Contact: Clare Hart, President
Ed: Eric J. Savitz. **Description:** Apple iPhone 3G's introduction could widen the smartphone market thereby benefiting handset chipmaker Qualcomm in the process. Qualcomm Senior V.P., Bill Davidson sees huge potential for his company's future beyond phones with their Snapdragon processor. The prospects of Sun Microsystems' shares are also discussed.

37354 ■ *The Quants*
Ed: Scott Patterson. **Released:** January 25, 2011. **Price:** $16. **Description:** The story of four rich and powerful men, along with Jim Simons, the founder of the most successful hedge fund in history and how they felt and what they thought in the days and weeks during the crash of Wall Street.

37355 ■ *"Quarreling Parties Keep Schenectady Redevelopment Plan In Limbo"* **in The Business Review Albany (Vol. 35, April 4, 2008, No. 53)**
Pub: The Business Review
Ed: Michael DeMasi. **Description:** First National Bank of Scotia chairman Louis H. Buhrmaster opposes the Erie Boulevard design project. as it could negatively affect access to the bank. Buhrmaster, aslo a vice president for Schenectady Industrial Corp, prohibits environmental assessment at the former American Locomotive property. The issues affecting the progress of the planned redevelopment at Schenectady are analyzed.

37356 ■ *"A Questionable Chemical Romance"* **in Barron's (Vol. 88, July 14, 2008, No. 28, pp. 28)**
Pub: Dow Jones & Co., Inc.
Contact: Clare Hart, President
Ed: Andrew Bary. **Description:** Dow Chemical paid $78-a-share for the surprise takeover of Rohm & Haas. The acquisition is reducing Dow Chemical's financial flexibility at a time when chemical companies are being affected by high costs and a weak U.S. economy.

37357 ■ *"Quick Earnings Revival Unlikely"* **in Barron's (Vol. 88, June 30, 2008, No. 26, pp. 31)**
Pub: Dow Jones & Co., Inc.
Contact: Clare Hart, President
Ed: Johanna Bennett. **Description:** Analysts are pushing back their prediction of a U.S. economy turnaround to 2009. A recession in the first half of 2008 may not have happened but unemployment is rising and house prices continue to fall.

37358 ■ *"Quicken Starter Edition 2008"* **in Black Enterprise (Vol. 38, March 1, 2008, No. 8, pp. 54)**
Pub: Earl G. Graves Publishing Co. Inc.
Contact: Earl G. Graves, Jr., President
Ed: Dale Coachman. **Description:** Profile of Quicken Starter Edition 2008 offering programs that track spending; it will also categorize tax deductible expenses.

37359 ■ *"Raytheon Stock Up, Will Pay New Quarterly Dividend"* **in Barron's (Vol. 88, March 31, 2008, No. 13)**
Pub: Dow Jones & Co., Inc.
Contact: Clare Hart, President
Ed: Shirley A. Lazo. **Description:** Raytheon hiked their quarterly dividend to 28 cents per share from 25.5 cents. Aircastle slashed their quarterly common dividend by 64 percent for them to retain additional capital that can be used to increase their liquidity position.

37360 ■ *"The RBC Dynasty Continues"* **in Globe & Mail (January 30, 2006, pp. B1)**
Ed: Gordon Pitts. **Description:** The details on business growth of Royal Bank of Canada, under chief executive officer Gordon Nixon, are presented.

37361 ■ *Reading Financial Reports for Dummies*
Pub: John Wiley & Sons Inc.
Contact: Stephen M. Smith, President
Ed: Lita Epstein. **Released:** 3rd Edition. **Price:** $22.95, paperback; $14.99. **Description:** This second edition contains more new and updated information, including new information on the separate accounting and financial reporting standards for private/small businesses versus public/large businesses; updated information reflecting 2007 laws on international financial reporting standards; new content to match SEC and other governmental regulatory changes over the last three years; new information about how the analyst-corporate connection has changed the playing field; the impact of corporate communications and new technologies; new examples that reflect the current trends; and updated Websites and resources. **Availability:** PrintE-book.

37362 ■ *"Ready for a Rally?" in The Economist (Vol. 390, January 3, 2009, No. 8612, pp. 54)*
Description: Analysts predict that the recession could end by 2010. The current economic crisis is presented in detail.

37363 ■ *"Real Estate Defaults Top $300M" in Business Courier (Vol. 26, January 15, 2010, No. 39, pp. 1)*
Ed: Dan Monk. **Description:** Cincinnati commercial real estate owners defaulting in securitized loans reached $306 million at the end of 2009. The trend has lifted the region's default rate to nearly 9 percent. National average for commercial real estate default is examined.

37364 ■ *"Real Opportunities: Don't Let Mortgage Mayhem Steer You Away From Sound Investments" in Black Enterprise (December 2007)*
Pub: Earl G. Graves Publishing Co. Inc.
Contact: Earl G. Graves, Jr., President
Ed: James A. Anderson. **Description:** Real estate investment trusts (REITs) that operate office buildings, industrial parks, shopping malls, hotels, hospitals, or other commercial properties may be a sound investment, despite the mortgage crisis facing the U.S. financial sector.

37365 ■ *"Recession Fears Power Gold" in Barron's (Vol. 88, March 17, 2008, No. 11, pp. M14)*
Pub: Dow Jones & Co., Inc.
Contact: Clare Hart, President
Ed: Melanie Burton. **Description:** Gold prices have been more attractive as the U.S. dollar weakens and the Dow Jones Industrial Average has slipped almost 10 percent in 2008. The rate cuts from the Federal Reserve Board has also spurred inflation fears adding upward pressure to the price of the metal.

37366 ■ *"Recession Management" in Canadian Business (Vol. 81, March 3, 2008, No. 3, pp. 62)*
Ed: Joe Castaldo. **Description:** Some companies such as Capital One Financial Corp. are managing their finances as if a recession has already taken place to prepare themselves for the looming economic downturn. Intel Corp., meanwhile shows how increasing its investments during a recession could be advantageous. Tips on how companies can survive a recession are provided.

37367 ■ *"Recovery Starts to Set Roots in R.I." in Providence Business News (Vol. 28, January 20, 2014, No. 42, pp. 1)*
Pub: American City Business Journals
Released: January 20, 2014. **Description:** The results of a survey indicate that 84 percent of businesses in Rhode Island are expecting the state's economy to improve in 2014. Businesspeople had doubted the state's ability to recover because of fiscal crises. The impact of local firms' strong financial results on the economic recovery are discussed.

37368 ■ *"Reduce the Risk of Failed Financial Judgments" in Harvard Business Review (Vol.*

86, July-August 2008, No. 8, pp. 24)
Pub: Harvard Business Review Press
Contact: Peter E. Walsh, Director
Ed: Robert G. Eccles, Edward J. Riedl. **Description:** Utilization of business consultants, evaluators, appraisers, and actuaries to decrease financial management risks is discussed.

37369 ■ *"Reflecting State Economy, Banks Less Profitable in 1Q" in Providence Business News (Vol. 29, July 14, 2014, No. 15, pp. 8)*
Pub: American City Business Journals
Released: July 14, 2014. **Description:** Rhode Island banks posted an aggregate return on assets (ROA) of 0.60 percent for the first quarter (1Q) of 2014, slightly lower than the 0.66 percent in the same quarter 2013, reflecting the downturn in the state's economy and its high unemployment rate. However, two Rhode Island banks, Union Federal Savings Bank and The Washington Trust Company, reported higher ROA for 1Q than the national average at 3.98 percent and 1.19 percent respectively.

37370 ■ *"Reform Law Spares Community Banks from FDIC Fee Hike" in Baltimore Business Journal (Vol. 28, July 23, 2010, No. 11, pp. 1)*
Pub: Baltimore Business Journal
Ed: Gary Haber. **Description:** A new financial regulator bill has exempted community banks from increased Federal Insurance Deposit Corporation fees. Large banks with assets of $10 billion and above will be required to pay the higher fee in 2010. Small banks are seen to hold bank fees at bay owing to the exemption.

37371 ■ *"Reforms Equal Smaller 401(k)s" in Employee Benefit News (Vol. 25, December 1, 2011, No. 15, pp. 19)*
Pub: SourceMedia Inc.
Contact: James M. Malkin, Chief Executive Officer
Ed: Lisa V. Gillespie. **Description:** According to a new analysis by the Employee Benefit Research Institute, two recent proposals to change existing tax treatment of 401(k) retirement plans could cost workers because they would lower their account balances towards retirement.

37372 ■ *"Regions Fourth for Branch Closures, Following Trend" in Birmingham Business Journal (Vol. 29, August 3, 2012, No. 32, pp. 1)*
Pub: American City Business Journals, Inc.
Contact: Whitney Shaw, President
Ed: Antrenise Cole. **Released:** August 3, 2012. **Description:** Birmingham-based Regions Financial Corporation ranked as the fourth most active branch closer in the US. The bank closed 48 branches and opened only one branch within the period of July 1, 2011 to June 30, 2012. Banks are shifting marketing focus from transactions to sales to counter the trend of bank closures.

37373 ■ *"Regulator Issues Warning On Reverse Mortgage Loans" in Retirement Advisor (Vol. 13, October 2012, No. 10, pp. 28)*
Pub: Summit Professional Networks
Contact: Steve Weitzner, President
Description: Reverse mortgages were first introduced in 1961 and are becoming popular now with aging baby boomers. The new Consumer Financial Protection Bureau warns the public to look closing before entering a reverse mortgage contract. The National Ethics Association encourages financial advisors to use the same caution and offers advise for advisors to help educate their clients about reverse mortgages.

37374 ■ *"Reports of Banks' Revival were Greatly Exaggerated" in Barron's (Vol. 88, July 7, 2008, No. 27, pp. L14)*
Pub: Dow Jones & Co., Inc.
Contact: Clare Hart, President
Ed: Jack Willoughby. **Description:** Performance of mutual funds improved for the second quarter of 2008 compared to the previous quarter, registering an aver-

age gain of 0.13 percent; funds focusing on natural resources rose the highest, their value rising by an average of 24.50 percent.

37375 ■ *"Research Reports" in Barron's (Vol. 88, March 24, 2008, No. 12, pp. M10)*
Pub: Dow Jones & Co., Inc.
Contact: Clare Hart, President
Ed: Anita Peltonen. **Description:** Investors are recommending purchasing shares of Ampco Pittsburgh due to an expected surge in earnings. Deteriorating credit quality presents problems for the shares of BankAtlantic Bancorp, whose price targets have been lowered from $7 to $5 each. Shares of Helicos Biosciences are expected to move sideways from their $6 level. Statistical data included.

37376 ■ *"Research Reports" in Barron's (Vol. 88, March 10, 2008, No. 10, pp. M13)*
Pub: Dow Jones & Co., Inc.
Contact: Clare Hart, President
Ed: Anita Peltonen. **Description:** Research reports on different company stocks by investment analysts are given. Shares of Cal Dive are rated Outperform by analysts, citing the shares' continued attractiveness and the company's acquisition of Horizon. Analysts recommend buying the shares of California Water Service Group.

37377 ■ *"Research Reports" in Barron's (Vol. 89, July 20, 2009, No. 29, pp. M12)*
Pub: Dow Jones & Co., Inc.
Contact: Clare Hart, President
Ed: Anita Peltonen. **Description:** Shares of Bank of the Ozarks, Broadpoint Gleacher Securities Group, Halozyme Therapeutics, and Take Two Interactive are rated as Buy. The shares of Fluor and PetMed Express are rated as Outperform, while those of Humana and Janus Capital Group are rated as Hold and Underweight respectively.

37378 ■ *"Research Reports: How Analysts Size Up Companies" in Barron's (Vol. 88, March 31, 2008, No. 13, pp. M13)*
Pub: Dow Jones & Co., Inc.
Contact: Clare Hart, President
Ed: Anita Peltonen. **Description:** Sirius Satellite's shares are ranked Outperform as it awaits approval from the Federal Communications Commission in its merger with XM. TiVo's shares are ranked Avoid as the company is in a sector that's being commoditized. Verizon Communications' rising dividend yield earns it a Focus List ranking. The shares of Bear Stearns, Churchill Downs, Corning, and Deerfield Triarc Capital are also reviewed. Statistical data included.

37379 ■ *"Research Reports: How Analysts Size Up Companies" in Barron's (Vol. 88, March 17, 2008, No. 11, pp. M13)*
Pub: Dow Jones & Co., Inc.
Contact: Clare Hart, President
Ed: Anita Peltonen. **Description:** Shares of Applied Industrial Technologies are ranked Market Perform while the shares of Google get a buy rating. Salix Pharmaceuticals gets a Sell/Above-Average risk rating. The shares of Dune Energy, Franklin Resources, Internet Brands, Piper Jaffray, and Texas Instruments are also rated.

37380 ■ *"Research Reports: How Analysts Size Up Companies" in Barron's (Vol. 88, June 30, 2008, No. 26, pp. M11)*
Pub: Dow Jones & Co., Inc.
Contact: Clare Hart, President
Ed: Anita Peltonen. **Description:** Shares of Developers Diversified Realty Corp. get a 'Long-Term Buy' rating while the shares of HealthSouth Corp. and Onyx Pharmaceutical get a rating of 'Underperform' and a 'Buy' rating respectively. The shares of American Capital Agency, American Public Education, Bankrate, and Werner Enterprises are also ranked.

37381 ■ *"Research Reports: How Analysts Size Up Companies" in Barron's (Vol. 88, July 14, 2008, No. 28, pp. M13)*
Pub: Dow Jones & Co., Inc.
Contact: Clare Hart, President
Ed: Anita Peltonen. **Description:** Shares of Bankrate and AutoZone both get a 'Buy' rating from analysts while Zions Bancorporation's shares are downgraded

from 'Outperform' to 'Neutral'. The shares of Jet Blue Airline and Deckers Outdoor, a manufacturer of innovative footwear, are also rated and discussed. Statistical data included.

37382 ■ "Research Reports: How Analysts Size Up Companies" in Barron's (Vol. 89, July 13, 2009, No. 28, pp. M11)
Pub: Dow Jones & Co., Inc.
Contact: Clare Hart, President
Ed: Anita Peltonen. Description: Shares of Alaska Air Group get a 'Hold' rating while the shares of Art Technology Group and Cathay General Bancorp both get a 'Buy' rating. The shares of HCC Insurance Holdings, HMS Holdings, H&R Block, Intel, McDonald's, People's United Financial, Pride International, Sino Forest, and Virgin Media are also given ratings.

37383 ■ "Research Reports: How Analysts Size Up Companies" in Barron's (Vol. 89, July 27, 2009, No. 30, pp. M12)
Pub: Dow Jones & Co., Inc.
Contact: Clare Hart, President
Ed: Anita Peltonen. Description: Shares of Allscripts-Misys gets an 'Outperform' rating while the shares of M&T Bank and Precision Castparts get a 'Sell' and 'Hold' rating respectively. The shares of Supervalu, Syniverse Holdings, Valley National Bancorp, Volterra, and Wesco are also rated.

37384 ■ "Retail Woes: The Shoe Doesn't Fit for Gerald Loftin's Stock Picks" in Black Enterprise (Vol. 38, July 2008, No. 12, pp. 40)
Ed: Steve Garmhausen. Description: Each of the three stocks that Gerald Loftin picked in May 2007 have lost money; DSW, the designer shoe retailer, fell by 63.7 percent; paint and coatings retailer Sherwin-Williams Co. fell by 7.2 percent; and Verizon Communications Inc. fell by 1.4 percent. Statistical data included.

37385 ■ Retire Dollar Smart
Pub: Trafford Publishing
Contact: Steen Marcussen, Manager
Ed: Jim Miller. Released: July 30, 2004. Price: $25.99, softcover. Description: The difference between savings and investments and their importance is examined, along with four rules for converting good investments into even greater ones. Contingency plans for healthcare costs as well as ways to manage taxes on investments are discussed. Five methods to control the costs of investing and saving include the use of smart strategies; getting independent, accurate, complete information; investing passively; asking for a discount; and taking off your blinders. Ten steps for designing a foolproof retirement investment portfolio are also provided. Availability: Print.

37386 ■ "Retirement Plans in a Quandary" in Employee Benefit News (Vol. 25, December 1, 2011, No. 15, pp. 18)
Pub: SourceMedia Inc.
Contact: James M. Malkin, Chief Executive Officer
Ed: Terry Dunne. Description: Complex issues arise when employees don't cash their 401(k) balance checks. The US Department of Labor permits plans to cash out accounts of former employees with less than $1,000 to reduce the cost and time required to manage them.

37387 ■ The Return of Depression Economics and the Crisis of 2008
Pub: W. W. Norton & Company, Inc.
Contact: Rachel Comerford, Manager
Ed: Paul Krugman. Price: $16.95, Paperback. Description: The recipient of the 2008 Nobel Memorial Prize in Economics revises his earlier work from 1999 to reflect the current economic crisis of 2008.

37388 ■ "The Return of the War Dividend" in Canadian Business (Vol. 87, July 2014, No. 7, pp. 25)
Pub: George Media Inc.
Released: July 2014. Description: Investors interested in defense industry stocks are advised to avoid any company with large ties to a single big-ticket project. The stability and good dividends generated by large defense companies are recommended for buy-and-hold investors.

37389 ■ "Return to Wealth; Bank Strategy" in The Economist (Vol. 390, January 3, 2009, No. 8612, pp. 56)
Description: UBS' strategy to survive these trying economic times is presented. Statistical data included. UBS has a stronger balance-sheet than most of its investment-banking peers and has reduced its portfolio.

37390 ■ "Reviving Entrepreneurship: Policy Decisions in 12 Areas Could Nurture - Or Cripple - America's Greatest Asset" in Harvard Business Review (Vol. 90, March 2012, No. 3, pp. 116)
Pub: Harvard Business Review Press
Contact: Peter E. Walsh, Director
Ed: Josh Lerner, William Sahlman. Released: March 2012. Description: Government policies should address entrepreneurship as a process, rather than an act. Several key areas for policymaking include basic and translational science, supply and quality of human capital, information availability, tax treatment of rewards and risks, intellectual property rights, workforce healthcare, and mobility of financial and human capital.

37391 ■ "The Rich 100: The Man Behind Brascan" in Canadian Business (Vol. 79, December 4, 2006, No. 24, pp. 64)
Pub: Rogers Media Inc.
Contact: Tony Viner, President
Ed: Andy Holloway. Description: The role of Jack Cockwell in the growth of Brookfield Asset Management Inc. is described.

37392 ■ Rich Dad, Poor Dad
Ed: Robert Kiyosaki with Sharon Lechter. Price: $16.95. Description: What the wealthy teach their children about money that others do not.

37393 ■ Rich Dad, Poor Dad: What the Rich Teach Their Kids About Money-That the Poor and Middle Class Do Not!
Ed: Robert T. Kiyosaki; Sharon L. Lechter. Released: December 5, 2002. Price: $16.95. Description: Personal finance expert shares his economic perspective through exposure to a pair of disparate influences: his own highly education but fiscally unstable father and the multimillionaire eighth-grade dropout father of his closest friend.

37394 ■ Rich Dad's Increase Your Financial IQ
Pub: Business Plus
Ed: Robert T. Kiyosaki. Price: $16.99, paperback. Description: Author describes his five key principles of financial knowledge to help readers build wealth.

37395 ■ "The Right Time for REITs" in Barron's (Vol. 88, July 14, 2008, No. 28, pp. 32)
Pub: Dow Jones & Co., Inc.
Contact: Clare Hart, President
Ed: Mike Hogan. Description: Discusses the downturn in U.S. real estate investment trusts so these are worth considering for investment. Several Websites that are useful for learning about real estate investment trusts for investment purposes are presented.

37396 ■ "Risk and Reward" in Canadian Business (Vol. 81, October 13, 2008, No. 17, pp. 21)
Ed: Calvin Leung. Description: Macro-economist and currency analyst Mark Venezia believes that stable financial institutions, free-market reforms, and the role of central banks in keeping inflation and exchange rates stable could make emerging-market bonds strong performers for better future returns. Venezia's other views on emerging-market bonds are discussed.

37397 ■ "Risky Business" in Canadian Business (Vol. 79, October 23, 2006, No. 21, pp. 153)
Ed: C.J. Burton. Description: Tips for Canadian managers on how to handle business risks are presented.

37398 ■ "Rock Festival: High Spirited Conventioneers Celebrate Their Good Fortune" in Canadian Business (Vol. 81, March 31, 2008, No. 5)
Pub: Rogers Media Inc.
Contact: Tony Viner, President
Ed: Jeff Sanford. Description: Soaring prices of commodities in the mining industry have been very good for the attendees of the 76th annual conference of the Prospectors & Developers Association of Canada. A speaker at the conference expects commodity prices to come off a bit but not fall dramatically as it did in the 1980's.

37399 ■ "Ryder's Shock Absorbers Are In Place" in Barron's (Vol. 88, March 24, 2008, No. 12, pp. 19)
Pub: Dow Jones & Co., Inc.
Contact: Clare Hart, President
Ed: Christopher C. Williams. Description: Shares of Ryder System Inc. are expected to continue rising on the back of rising earnings, forecast at $5.20 a share for 2009. The shares of the truck freight company hit a 52-week high of $62.27 each and may reach $70 a share.

37400 ■ "Sacred Success: A Course in Financial Miracles"
Pub: BenBella Books
Contact: Aida Herrera, Director
E-mail: aida@benbellabooks.com
Released: October 7, 2014. Price: $24.95. Description: A leading expert on women and money helps women to take control of the finances and lose their fear or ambivalence towards it. It is a tutorial for taking charge of a woman's life along with financial investing success.

37401 ■ Safety Net
Ed: James Glassman. Released: February 22, 2011. Price: $23. Description: Ways to build a financial investment strategy that protects you, while ensuring growth in a strong financial future are presented.

37402 ■ "Sales Gave W&S Record '07" in Business Courier (Vol. 24, March 14, 2008, No. 49, pp. 1)
Pub: American City Business Journals, Inc.
Contact: Whitney Shaw, President
Ed: Jon Newberry. Description: Western & Southern Financial Group was able to achieve a record $365 million in net income thanks in large part to the double-digit increases in profits by its W&S Agency Group field offices and non-insurance businesses. The sale of their Integrated Investment Services Subsidiary and shares in several Marriot hotels also added to the record profit.

37403 ■ Sarbanes-Oxley for Dummies
Pub: John Wiley & Sons Inc.
Contact: Stephen M. Smith, President
Ed: Jill Gilbert Welytok. Released: 2nd Edition. Price: $21.95, paperback; $14.99. Description: Provides the latest Sarbanes-Oxley (SOX) legislation with procedures to safely and effectively reduce compliance costs. Topics include way to: establish SOX standards for IT professionals, minimize compliances costs for every aspect of a business, survive a Section 404 audit, avoid litigation under SOX, anticipate future rules and trends, create a post-SOX paper trail, increase a company's standing and reputation, work with SOX in a small business, meet new SOX standards, build a board that can't be bought, and to comply with all SOX management mandates. Availability: PrintE-book.

37404 ■ Save Your Small Business: 10 Crucial Strategies to Survive Hard Times or Close Down & Move On
Pub: Nolo
Contact: Ralph Warner, Chief Executive Officer
Ed: Ralph Warner, Bethany Laurence. Price: $23.99; $20.99. Description: According to a study among 500 businesses, 44 percent used credit cards in order to meet their firm's needs in the previous six months. Written by a business owner, this book provides twelve strategies to protect personal assets from creditors and survive the current recession. Availability: PrintE-book.

37405 ■ *"SBA Can Improve Your Cash Flow"
in Business Owner (Vol. 35,
September-October 2011, No. 5, pp. 3)*
Pub: DL Perkins Company
Description: Federal assistance available to small
business is examined. The Small Business Administration loan guarantee program is designed to
improve availability and attractiveness of small business loans.

37406 ■ *Schaum's Outline of Financial
Management*
Pub: McGraw-Hill
Ed: Jae K. Shim, Joel G. Siegel. **Released:** Third
Edition. **Price:** $21. **Description:** Rules and regulations governing corporate finance, including the
Sarbanes-Oxley Act are discussed. **Availability:**
Print.

37407 ■ *"Schlotzky's Tries for Twin Cities
Revival" in Business Journal (Vol. 31,
January 17, 2014, No. 34, pp. 4)*
Pub: American City Business Journals
Released: January 17, 2014. **Description:** Austin,
Texas-based Schlotzky's announced plans to open
six Minnesota locations as it tries to regain its national
prominence. The bankruptcy in 2004 and the reduction of its restaurant count had wiped out eight Minnesota restaurants and left only the Edina location.
Schlotzky's six-restaurant deal with the local franchisees is examined.

37408 ■ *"Schwab: Lower Returns Ahead" in
Barron's (Vol. 89, July 13, 2009, No. 28, pp.
L4)*
Pub: Dow Jones & Co., Inc.
Contact: Clare Hart, President
Ed: Leslie P. Norton. **Description:** Charles Schwab
says that 8 percent to 10 percent equity-market
returns are not realistic these days and that 4 percent
to 5 percent are more realistic in the next four to five
years from 2009. Schwab expects inflation to be
close to 10 percent per annum in a couple of years.

37409 ■ *"Score One for Barron's" in Barron's
(Vol. 89, July 13, 2009, No. 28, pp. 14)*
Pub: Dow Jones & Co., Inc.
Contact: Clare Hart, President
Ed: Andrew Bary. **Description:** 57 companies that
were bullishly covered on 'Barron's' for the first half
of 2009 were up an average of 20.4 percent compared to the 10.2 percent gain in the relevant market
indexes. The bearish stock picks by 'Barron's' were
down 3.4 percent compared to a 6.4 percent for the
benchmarks.

37410 ■ *"Scottsdale Business Bank Plans 4Q
Opening" in The Business Journal - Serving
Phoenix and the Valley of the Sun (Vol. 28,
August 15, 2008, No. 50)*
Pub: American City Business Journals, Inc.
Contact: Whitney Shaw, President
Ed: Chris Casacchia. **Description:** Arizona's Department of Financial Institutions has approved Scottsdale Business Bank, a community bank which plans
to open in the fourth quarter of 2008. The bank, which
is to be located near McCormick Ranch in Scottsdale, Arizona, will cater to small business owners in
the professional sector, such as accountants and doctors.

37411 ■ *"Screening for the Best Stock
Screens" in Barron's (Vol. 90, September 13,
2010, No. 37, pp. 36)*
Pub: Barron's Editorial & Corporate Headquarters
Ed: Mike Hogan. **Description:** Pros and cons of the
new and revised stock screening tools from Zack,
Finviz.com, and GuruFocus are discussed. FinVix.
com is more capable for screening through stocks
and the service is free.

37412 ■ *"SEC Doesn't Buy Biovail's Claims"
in Barron's (Vol. 88, March 31, 2008, No. 13,
pp. 20)*
Pub: Dow Jones & Co., Inc.
Contact: Clare Hart, President
Ed: Bill Alpert. **Description:** Overstatement of earnings and chronic fraudulent conduct has led the SEC
to file a stock fraud suit against Biovail, Eugene Mel-

nyk and three others present or former employees of
Biovail. Melnyk had the firm file suit in 2006 that
blames short-sellers and stock researchers for the
company's drop in share price.

37413 ■ *"SEC Report On Rating Agencies
Falls Short" in Barron's (Vol. 88, July 14,
2008, No. 28, pp. 35)*
Pub: Dow Jones & Co., Inc.
Contact: Clare Hart, President
Ed: Jack Willoughby. **Description:** The Securities
and Exchange Commissions report on credit-rating
firms should have drawn attention to the slipshod
practices in the offerings of collateralized debt obligations. The report fell short of prescribing correctives
for the flawed system of these agencies' relationship
with their clients.

37414 ■ *"A Security Risk?" in Canadian
Business (Vol. 80, October 22, 2007, No. 21,
pp. 36)*
Ed: Joe Castaldo. **Description:** Garda World Security
Corporation declared a C$1.5 million loss in the
second quarter of 2007. The company's securities
have been falling since June and hit a 52-week low
of $15.90 in September. Details of the physical and
cash-handling firm's strategy to integrate its acquisitions are discussed.

37415 ■ *"SECU's Tax Preparation Services
Net Members More Than $86 Million in
Refunds" in Economics Week (May 11, 2012)*
Pub: NewsRX
Contact: Susan E. Hasty, Publisher
Released: May 11, 2012. **Description:** State Employees' Credit Union (SECU) helped nearly 65,000 North
Carolina members file their income taxes in 2012.
SECU reports $86 million in refunds and saving
members more than $8 million in preparation fees.
The credit union promotes its tax preparation services
so members can avoid the high fees paid to tax preparers.

37416 ■ *"Selling Pressures Rise in China" in
Barron's (Vol. 88, March 10, 2008, No. 10, pp.
M9)*
Pub: Dow Jones & Co., Inc.
Contact: Clare Hart, President
Ed: Mohammed Hadi. **Description:** There are about
1.6 trillion yuan worth of shares up for sale in Chinese
stock markets in 2008, adding to the selling pressures in these markets. The Chinese government
has imposed restrictions to prevent a rapid rise in
selling stocks.

37417 ■ *"Sense and Consensus" in Canadian
Business (Vol. 81, October 13, 2008, No. 17,
pp. 22)*
Ed: David Wolf. **Description:** Stock analysts' agree
that earning estimates are seen to be optimistic in
relation to their global economic outlook. Analysts are
expected to cut earnings projections by fall because
it may negatively affect the Canadian stock market.
Other view on market analysis are presented.

37418 ■ *"Sentiment Split on Financials: Is the
Worse Over or Still to Come?" in Barron's
(Vol. 88, March 24, 2008, No. 12, pp. M14)*
Pub: Dow Jones & Co., Inc.
Contact: Clare Hart, President
Ed: Steven M. Sears. **Description:** Experts in the
financial sector are split as to whether or not the worst
of the financial crisis brought on by the credit crunch
is over. Some options traders are trading on are
defensive puts, expecting the worst, while investors
buying calls are considered as bullish.

37419 ■ *"ServisFirst Expands Into Tough Fla.
Market" in Birmingham Business Journal
(Vol. 29, May 25, 2012, No. 22, pp. 1)*
Pub: American City Business Journals, Inc.
Contact: Whitney Shaw, President
Ed: Antrenise Cole. **Released:** May 25, 2012. **Description:** ServisFirst Bank is planning to open a
branch in Pensacola, Florida. The company has
reached profitability after only a year in business.

37420 ■ *"A Shallow Pool" in Canadian
Business (Vol. 81, Summer 2008, No. 9, pp.
44)*
Ed: Joe Castaldo. **Description:** Bank of Canada
projected in its 'Monetary Policy Report' a growth
rate of 1.4 percent in 2008 and does not expect the
economy to fully recover until mid-2010. The Canadian stock market has been recovering although
slowly with just a 1.6 percent gain by April 30. Other
details on the Canadian equity market are presented.

37421 ■ *"Shopped Out; Retailing Gloom" in
The Economist (Vol. 390, January 3, 2009, No.
8612, pp. 26)*
Description: Economic volatility in the retail sector is
having an impact on a number of countries around
the globe. Europe is experiencing hard economic
times as well and unless businesses have a strong
business plan banks feel unable to lend the money
necessary to tide the retailers over. The falling pound
has increased the cost of imported goods and small
to midsize retail chains may not be able to weather
such an unforgiving economic climate.

37422 ■ *"Shoppes of Kenwood Files Chap.
11" in Business Courier (Vol. 26, December
18, 2009, No. 34, pp. 1)*
Pub: American City Business Journals, Inc.
Contact: Whitney Shaw, President
Ed: Jon Newberry. **Description:** Shoppes of Kenwood filed for Chapter 11 reorganization in US
Bankruptcy Court just as the property was scheduled
to be offered at a sheriff's auction. Details of the filing
are included.

37423 ■ *"Short Alert: Darkness Falling.." in
Barron's (Vol. 89, July 20, 2009, No. 29, pp.
13)*
Pub: Dow Jones & Co., Inc.
Contact: Clare Hart, President
Ed: Robin Goldwyn Blumenthal. **Description:** Newsletter writer Arch Crawford believes that market
indicators signal a possible downturn in US stock
markets. High risk areas also include China and
Japan.

37424 ■ *"Shorts Story" in Barron's (Vol. 89,
July 6, 2009, No. 27, pp. 16)*
Pub: Dow Jones & Co., Inc.
Contact: Clare Hart, President
Ed: Gene Epstein. **Description:** Shares of Compass
Minerals, J2 Global Communications, K12, Middleby,
and Pactiv should be shorted by investors. These
companies suffer from weaknesses in their business
models, making them vulnerable to a share price
decline.

37425 ■ *"Shorts Story" in Barron's (Vol. 89,
July 6, 2009, No. 27, pp. 16)*
Pub: Dow Jones & Co., Inc.
Contact: Clare Hart, President
Ed: Gene Epstein. **Description:** Shares of Compass
Minerals, J2 Global Communications, K12, Middleby,
and Pactiv should be shorted by investors. These
companies suffer from weaknesses in their business
models, making them vulnerable to a share price
decline.

37426 ■ *"Should the Fed Regulate Wall
Street?" in Barron's (Vol. 88, March 24, 2008,
No. 12, pp. M15)*
Pub: Dow Jones & Co., Inc.
Contact: Clare Hart, President
Ed: Randall W. Forsyth. **Description:** Greater regulation of the financial sector by the Federal Reserve is
essential for it to survive the crisis it is experiencing.
The resulting regulation could be in complete contrast
with the deregulation the sector previously experienced.

37427 ■ *"Should I or Shouldn't I?" in Indoor
Comfort Marketing (Vol. 70, February 2011,
No. 2, pp. 30)*
Pub: Industry Publications Inc.
Contact: Shirleen Dorman, Editor
Ed: Philip J. Baratz. **Description:** Investment tips
are shared for investing in futures options.

37428 ■ "Should You Choose a Lump-Sum Pension Payout? Here's How Entrepreneur Ramona Harper Decided" in Black Enterprise (Vol. 44, June 2014, No. 10, pp. 27)
Pub: Earl G. Graves Publishing Co. Inc.
Contact: Earl G. Graves, Jr., President
Released: June 2014. **Description:** Entrepreneur, Ramona Harper, chose a lump sum payout of her pension in order to start a new business. She used $110,000 to start her accessories boutique and put the remaining money into a small business 401(k), which helped her avoid a large tax. Tips to help individuals decide the best way to collect their pension are provided.

37429 ■ "Silver Standard Reports First Quarter 2007 Results" in Marketwired (May 14, 2007)
Pub: Comtex News Network Inc.
Description: Silver Standard Resources Inc. reports a first quarter loss of $1.6 million compared with the first quarter of 2006 in which the loss was $1.1 million. Statistical data included.

37430 ■ "Siri Creator SRI International Hopes Lola Cashes In, Too" in Silicon Valley/San Jose Business Journal (Vol. 30, July 6, 2012, No. 15, pp. 1)
Pub: American City Business Journal
Description: Software developer and SRI and BBVA have partnered to create virtual personal assistant Lola. The program assists customers with their banking needs. Program features and dimensions are also included.

37431 ■ "Six Great Stock Funds for the Long Haul" in Barron's (Vol. 89, July 13, 2009, No. 28, pp. L5)
Pub: Dow Jones & Co., Inc.
Contact: Clare Hart, President
Ed: Lawrence C. Strauss, Tom Sullivan. **Description:** Six mutual funds that have solid long-term performance, transparency, savvy stock picking, and discipline are presented. The managers of these funds are also evaluated. These funds include the T. Rowe Price Emerging Market Stock Fund, Fairholme, and Dodge & Cox Stock.

37432 ■ Six SIGMA for Small Business
Pub: Entrepreneur Press
Contact: Perlman Neil, President
Ed: Greg Brue. **Description:** Jack Welch's Six SIGMA approach to business covers accounting, finance, sales and marketing, buying a business, human resource development, and new product development.

37433 ■ "Six Things You Can Do To Ride Out A Turbulent Market" in Hispanic Business (Vol. 30, March 2008, No. 3, pp. 20)
Pub: Hispanic Business Inc.
Contact: Jesus Chavarria, President
Ed: Hildy Medina, Michael Bowker. **Description:** Top financial experts' views on managing investment portfolios during turbulent periods in the stock market are reported. Experts prefer investing in health care, short term investments, international bonds and preferred stocks or just maintain cash until such times as the market settles.

37434 ■ "A Slice of Danish; Fixing Finance" in The Economist (Vol. 390, January 3, 2009, No. 8612, pp. 55)
Description: Denmark's mortgage-holders and the county's lending system is presented.

37435 ■ "The Small 300" in Canadian Business (Vol. 81, Summer 2008, No. 9, pp. 137)
Description: Small cap-companies are ranked based on market capitalization and stock performance. Calgary-based Grande Cache Coal Corp. topped the roster with 1,000 percent of return resulting from strong sales. A table showing the 2008 rankings of the companies is presented.

37436 ■ The Small Business Bible: Everything You Need to Know to Succeed in Your Small Business
Pub: John Wiley & Sons Inc.
Contact: Stephen M. Smith, President
Ed: Steven D. Strauss. **Released:** March 2012. **Price:** $22.95. **Description:** Comprehensive guide to starting and running a successful small business. Topics include bookkeeping and financial management, marketing, publicity, and advertising. **Availability:** Print.

37437 ■ "Small Business Capital Outlays" in Small Business Economic Trends (April 2008, pp. 16)
Pub: National Federation of Independent Business
Contact: Caitlin McDevitt, Program Manager
Ed: William C. Dunkelberg, Holly Wade. **Description:** Graphs and tables that present the capital outlays of small businesses in the U.S. are provided. The tables include figures on planned and actual capital expenditures, and type and amount of capital expenditures.

37438 ■ "Small Business Capital Outlays" in Small Business Economic Trends (March 2008, pp. 16)
Pub: National Federation of Independent Business
Contact: Caitlin McDevitt, Program Manager
Ed: William C. Dunkelberg, Holly Wade. **Description:** Graphs and tables that present the capital outlays of small businesses in the U.S. are provided. The tables include figures on planned and actual capital expenditures, and type and amount of capital expenditures.

37439 ■ "Small Business Capital Outlays" in Small Business Economic Trends (February 2008, pp. 16)
Pub: National Federation of Independent Business
Contact: Caitlin McDevitt, Program Manager
Ed: William C. Dunkelberg, Holly Wade. **Description:** Graphs and tables that present the capital outlays of small businesses in the U.S. are provided. The tables include figures on planned and actual capital expenditures, and type and amount of capital expenditures.

37440 ■ "Small Business Capital Outlays" in Small Business Economic Trends (January 2008, pp. 16)
Pub: National Federation of Independent Business
Contact: Caitlin McDevitt, Program Manager
Ed: William C. Dunkelberg, Holly Wade. **Description:** Graph representing actual and planned capital expenditures among small businesses surveyed in the U.S. from January 1986 to December 2007 is given. Tables showing actual capital expenditures, type of capital expenditures made, amount of capital expenditures made, and capital expenditure plans are also presented.

37441 ■ "Small Business Capital Outlays" in Small Business Economic Trends (September 2010, pp. 16)
Pub: National Federation of Independent Business
Contact: Caitlin McDevitt, Program Manager
Ed: William C. Dunkelberg, Holly Wade. **Description:** A graph representing actual and planned expenditures among small businesses surveyed in the U.S. from January 1986 to August 2010 is given. Tables showing actual capital expenditures, type of capital expenditures made, amount of capital expenditures made, and capital expenditure plans are also presented.

37442 ■ "Small Business Capital Outlays" in Small Business Economic Trends (July 2010, pp. 16)
Pub: National Federation of Independent Business
Contact: Caitlin McDevitt, Program Manager
Description: A graph representing actual and planned capital expenditures among small businesses surveyed in the U.S. from January 1986 to June 2010 is given. Tables showing actual capital expenditures, type of capital expenditures made, amount of capital expenditures made, and capital expenditure plans are also presented.

37443 ■ "Small Business Capital Outlays" in Small Business Economic Trends (July 2014, pp. 16)
Pub: National Federation of Independent Business
Contact: Caitlin McDevitt, Program Manager
Released: July 2014. **Description:** A graph representing actual and planned capital expenditures among small businesses surveyed in the U.S. from January 1986 to June 2014 is given. Table showing actual capital expenditures, type of capital expenditures made, amount of capital expenditures made and capital expenditure plans are also presented.

37444 ■ Small Business Cash Flow: Strategies for Making Your Business a Financial Success
Pub: John Wiley & Sons Inc.
Contact: Stephen M. Smith, President
Ed: Denise O'Berry. **Released:** October 2006. **Price:** $31.95, paperback; $20.99. **Description:** Tips to help small businesses manage money are given. **Availability:** PrintE-book.

37445 ■ Small Business Clustering Technologies: Applications in Marketing, Management, IT and Economics
Pub: IGI Global
Contact: Dr. Mehdi Khosrow-Pour, President
Ed: Robert C. MacGregor, Ann T. Hodgkinson. **Released:** September 2006. **Price:** 94.95, hardcover; $145, Institutions. **Description:** An overview of the development and role of small business clusters in disciplines that include economics, marketing, management and information systems. **Availability:** PrintE-book.

37446 ■ "Small Business Credit Conditions" in Small Business Economic Trends (July 2014, pp. 12)
Pub: National Federation of Independent Business
Contact: Caitlin McDevitt, Program Manager
Released: July 2014. **Description:** Graphs representing loan availability and interest rates among U.S. small businesses surveyed from January 1986 to June 2014 are given. Tables showing regular borrowers, availability of loans, satisfied borrowing needs, expected credit conditions, relative interest rate paid by regular borrowers, and actual interest rate paid on short-term loans by borrowers are also presented.

37447 ■ Small Business Desk Reference
Pub: Penguin Books USA Inc.
Released: December 2004. **Price:** $29.95. **Description:** Comprehensive guide for starting or running a successful small business, focusing on buying a business or franchise, writing a business plan, financial management, accounting, legal issues, human resources management, operations, marketing, sales, customer service, taxes, insurance, and ethics. Information for launching a restaurant, property management firm, retail outlet, consulting firm, and service business is included.

37448 ■ Small Business for Dummies
Pub: John Wiley & Sons Inc.
Contact: Stephen M. Smith, President
Ed: Eric Tyson, Jim Schell. **Released:** 4th Edition. **Price:** $22.95; $14.99. **Description:** Guidebook for anyone wanting to start or grow a small business; topics include information financing, budgeting, marketing, management and more. **Availability:** PrintE-book.

37449 ■ "Small Business Earnings" in Small Business Economic Trends (March 2008, pp. 6)
Pub: National Federation of Independent Business
Contact: Caitlin McDevitt, Program Manager
Ed: William C. Dunkelberg, Holly Wade. **Description:** Two tables and a graph representing the earnings of small businesses in the U.S. are presented. Statistics for actual earnings changes are provided. The figures in the graph include data from 1986 to 2008.

37450 ■ "Small Business Earnings" in Small Business Economic Trends (February 2008, pp. 6)

Pub: National Federation of Independent Business

Contact: Caitlin McDevitt, Program Manager

Ed: William C. Dunkelberg, Holly Wade. **Description:** Two tables and a graph representing the earnings of small businesses in the U.S. are presented. Statistics for actual earnings changes are provided. The figures in the graph include data from 1974 to 2008.

37451 ■ "Small Business Earnings" in Small Business Economic Trends (January 2008, pp. 6)

Pub: National Federation of Independent Business

Contact: Caitlin McDevitt, Program Manager

Ed: William C. Dunkelberg, Holly Wade. **Description:** Graph from a survey of small businesses in the U.S. is given, representing actual small business earnings from January 1986 to December 2007. Tables showing actual earnings changes and most important reason for lower earnings are also presented.

37452 ■ "Small Business Earnings" in Small Business Economic Trends (September 2010, pp. 6)

Pub: National Federation of Independent Business

Contact: Caitlin McDevitt, Program Manager

Ed: William C. Dunkelberg, Holly Wade. **Description:** A graph from a survey of small businesses in the U.S. is given, representing actual small business earnings from January 1986 to August 2010. Tables showing actual earnings changes and most important reason for lower earnings are also presented.

37453 ■ The Small Business Savings Plan: 101 Tactics for Controlling Costs and Boosting the Bottom Line

Pub: Kaplan Books

Ed: Timothy R. Gase. **Released:** 2007. **Price:** $21.95; C$27. **Description:** Strategies for small business owners to develop a savings plan and increase profits are outlined.

37454 ■ "Small Fortunes: How are Cincinnati's Small Banks Faring?" in Business Courier (Vol. 27, July 23, 2010, No. 12, pp. 1)

Pub: Business Courier

Ed: Steve Watkins. **Description:** Small banks in Cincinnati, Ohio have been faring well despite the economic crisis, a survey has revealed. Sixty percent of local small banks have capital levels above 15.8 percent median. But regulators are seen to close more banks in 2010 than since the financial crises began.

37455 ■ "Smart Investor's Shopping List: Coke, Walgreen, Drill Bits" in Crain's Chicago Business

Pub: Crain Communications Inc.

Contact: Todd Johnson, Publisher

Ed: Bruce Blythe. **Description:** Interview with Paula Dorion-Gray, president of Dorion-Gray Retirement Planning Inc., discusses the state of the investing environment, favored industries, industries to avoid, and her approach towards investing.

37456 ■ "The Smell of Fear: Is a Bottom Near?" in Barron's (Vol. 88, March 17, 2008, No. 11, pp. M3)

Pub: Dow Jones & Co., Inc.

Contact: Clare Hart, President

Ed: Kopin Tan. **Description:** Liquidity problems at Bear Stearns frightened investors in markets around the world due to the fear of the prospects of a big bank's failure. Shares of health maintenance organizations got battered led by WellPoint, and Humana but longer-term investors who could weather short-term volatility may find value here. The value of J. Crew shares is also discussed.

37457 ■ "SNAP Grant and Rebuilding Together-Houston Provide New Roof for Elderly Homeowner" in Benzinga.com

(September 21, 2012)

Pub: Benzinga.com

Contact: Kyle Bazzy, President

Released: September 21, 2012. **Description:** Green Bank and the Federal Home Loan Bank of Dallas (FHLB Dallas), Rebuilding Together-Houston replaced an elderly woman's roof in order to keep her in her home. She qualified for a grant program that helps low-income seniors make repairs to their homes.

37458 ■ "A Socko Payout Menu: Rural Phone Carrier Plots to Supercharge Its Shares" in Barron's (Vol. 88, June 30, 2008, No. 26, pp. M5)

Ed: Shirley A. Lazo. **Description:** CenturyTel boosted its quarterly common payout to 70 cents from 6.75 cents per share due to its strong cash flows and solid balance sheet. Eastman Kodak's plan for a buyback will be partially funded by its $581 million tax refund. CME Group will buyback stocks through 2009 worth $1.1 billion.

37459 ■ "Solace for the Freshly Flaherty'd" in Canadian Business (Vol. 79, November 6, 2006, No. 22, pp. 114)

Ed: Ian McGugan. **Description:** Tips to manage investments with relation to cash distribution tax on income trusts are presented.

37460 ■ "Solar Power Paying Off for PUSD" in Porterville Recorder (September 29, 2012)

Description: Porterville Unified School District has received $700,000 in rebates after operating its new solar-powered projects at three of five sites over the last six months.

37461 ■ "Some Big Biotechs Buying Own Stock" in Boston Business Journal (Vol. 30, November 5, 2010, No. 41, pp. 1)

Ed: Julie M. Donnelly. **Description:** Biotechnology companies such as Biogen Idec and Genzyme Corporation are conducting stock buybacks as they look to invest their cash holdings. Other analysts see the buybacks as reluctance in committing to longer-term investments.

37462 ■ "Some Relief Possible Following Painful Week" in Barron's (Vol. 88, July 14, 2008, No. 28, pp. M3)

Pub: Dow Jones & Co., Inc.

Contact: Clare Hart, President

Ed: Kopin Tan. **Description:** Dow Chemical is offering a 74 percent premium to acquire Rohm & Haas' coatings and electronics materials operations. Frontline amassed a 5.6 percent stake in rival Overseas Shipholding Group and a merger between the two would create a giant global fleet with pricing power. Highlights of the U.S. stock market during the week that ended in July 11, 2008 are discussed. Statistical data included.

37463 ■ "Something to Like" in Canadian Business (Vol. 81, April 14, 2008, No. 6, pp. 22)

Pub: Rogers Media Inc.

Contact: Tony Viner, President

Ed: Jack Mintz. **Description:** Jim Flaherty's policy on tax-free savings account (TFSA) will allow Canadians to accumulate wealth at a much faster rate and these accounts could be especially good for people who are subject to high effective taxes on savings. Investors should put their money into a Registered Retirement Savings Plan (RRSP) when it comes to risky investments but the TFSA is better than an RRSP if investors expect very high taxes on withdrawals from their RRSP.

37464 ■ "Spotlight on Pensions" in Business Horizons (Vol. 51, March-April 2008, No. 2, pp. 105)

Pub: Elsevier Advanced Technology Publications

Ed: Laureen A. Maines. **Description:** Perceptions of pension burden and risk among financial statement users is likely to increase with changes in pension accounting. These perceptions might affect decisions on pension commitments and investments.

37465 ■ "Spread Your Wings" in Canadian Business (Vol. 81, March 17, 2008, No. 4, pp. 31)

Ed: Megan Harman. **Description:** Financing from angel investors is one avenue that should be explored by startups. Angel investors are typically affluent individuals who invest their own money. Angel investors usually want at least 10 times their initial investment within eight years but they benefit the businesses through their help in decision-making and the industry expertise they provide.

37466 ■ "Sprint Tries to Wring Positives from Quarterly Report" in The Business Journal-Serving Metropolitan Kansas City (Vol. 26, August 8, 2008, No. 48)

Pub: American City Business Journals, Inc.

Contact: Whitney Shaw, President

Ed: Suzanna Stagemeyer. **Description:** Sprint Nextel Corp. reported that 901,000 subscribers left the company in the quarter ending June 30, 2008; fewer than the nearly 1.1 million it lost in the previous quarter. Customer turnover also dropped to just less than 2 percent, compared to 2.45 percent in the first quarter of 2008.

37467 ■ "Staffing Firm Grows by Following Own Advice-Hire a Headhunter" in Crain's Detroit Business (Vol. 24, October 6, 2008, No. 40, pp. 1)

Pub: Crain Communications Inc.

Contact: Rance E. Crain, President

Ed: Sherri Begin. **Description:** Profile of Venator Holdings L.L.C., a staffing firm that provides searches for companies in need of financial-accounting and technical employees; the firm's revenue has increased from $1.1 million in 2003 to a projected $11.5 million this year due to a climate in which more people are exiting the workforce than are coming in with those particular specialized skills and the need for a temporary, flexible workforce for contract placements at companies that do not want to take on the legacy costs associated with permanent employees. The hiring of an external headhunter to find the right out-of-state manager for Venator is also discussed.

37468 ■ "Stand-Up Guy: From Bear Stearns to Bear Market" in Barron's (Vol. 88, July 7, 2008, No. 27, pp. L11)

Pub: Dow Jones & Co., Inc.

Contact: Clare Hart, President

Ed: Suzanne McGee. **Description:** James O'Shaughnessy, a mutual fund manager with O'Shaughnessy Asset Management, is bullish on both financial and energy stocks. He was formerly involved with Bear Stearns until he left the firm in March 2008.

37469 ■ "State Shock Prices Take Large Tumble" in The Business Journal-Milwaukee (Vol. 25, September 12, 2008, No. 51, pp. A1)

Ed: Rich Rovito. **Description:** Weak economic times have caused the stocks of most publicly traded companies in Wisconsin to dip in 2008. Companies that appeared on the worst performing stocks list also experienced drops in share price to as much as 70 percent. Information about the companies that experienced increases in stock prices is also presented. Statistical data included.

37470 ■ "State of the States" in Barron's (Vol. 92, August 27, 2012, No. 38, pp. 23)

Pub: Dow Jones & Co., Inc.

Contact: Clare Hart, President

Ed: Andrew Bary. **Description:** The strength of finances of US states are ranked based on their debt ad unfunded pensions compared with their gross domestic products. South Dakota is considered to have the healthiest finances, while those of Connecticut are the weakest.

37471 ■ "Stay Calm, Bernanke Urges Markets" in Globe & Mail (March 1, 2007, pp. B1)

Ed: Brian McKenna. **Description:** The views of Ben Bernanke, the chief of the United States Federal Reserve Board, on the future trends of the United

States' economy are presented. The effect of the global stock market trends on the American stock markets is discussed.

37472 ■ *"Stock Analysts' Pans" in Canadian Business (Vol. 81, Summer 2008, No. 9, pp. 75)*
Ed: Calvin Leung. **Description:** Table showing the one-year stock performance of companies that are least loved by analysts and are rated either to be a Hold or Sell. These companies should not be included in the investment portfolio, at least in the short term.

37473 ■ *"Stock Car Racing" in Canadian Business (Vol. 81, September 15, 2008, No. 14-15, pp. 29)*
Ed: Thomas Watson. **Description:** Some analysts predict a Chapter 11-style tune-up making GM and Ford a speculative turnaround stock. However, the price of oil could make or break the shares of the Big Three U.S. automobile manufacturers and if oil goes up too high then a speculative stock to watch is an electric car company called Zenn Motor Co.

37474 ■ *"Stock Delisting Could Hamper First Mariner" in Boston Business Journal (Vol. 29, July 29, 2011, No. 12, pp. 1)*
Pub: American City Business Journals, Inc.
Ed: Gary Haber. **Description:** Possible delisting of First Mariner Bancorp from the Nasdaq stock exchange could adversely impact the bank's ability to attract institutional investors. Some institutions limit their investments to companies trading on the Nasdaq.

37475 ■ *"Strategy Migration In a Changing Climate" in Harvard Business Review (Vol. 92, May 2014, No. 5, pp. 42)*
Pub: Harvard Business Publishing
Released: May 2014. **Description:** The CEO of World Wildlife Fund discusses the importance of ensuring reliable source supplies and mitigating reputational and financial risk in promoting corporate sustainability. Forging alliances to achieve goals is also key.

37476 ■ *Streetwise Finance and Accounting for Entrepreneurs: Set Budgets, Manage Costs, Keep Your Business Profitable*
Ed: Suzanne Caplan. **Released:** November 2006.
Price: $25.95. **Description:** Book offers a basic understanding of accounting and finance for small businesses, including financial statements, credits and debits, as well as establishing a budget. Strategies for small companies in financial distress are included.

37477 ■ *"Stressed Out: 7 Banks Rated 'At Riks" in Saint Louis Business Journal (Vol. 32, September 16, 2011, No. 3, pp. 1)*
Pub: Saint Louis Business Journal
Ed: Greg Edwards. **Description:** St. Louis, Missouri has seven banks that are well above the 100 percent level that is considered 'at risk' based on a risk measurement called the Texas ratio. The banks are the Sun Security bank, 1st Advantage Bank, Superior Bank, Truman Bank, Reliance Bank, St. Louis Bank and Meramec Valley Bank.

37478 ■ *"Stretch Your Last Dollar Or Invest It?" in Business Owner (Vol. 35, November-December 2011, No. 6, pp. 4)*
Pub: DL Perkins Company
Description: Should small business owners cut expenses or invest in a downturned economy? Difficult times can be an opportunity to build a business brad.

37479 ■ *Structuring Your Business*
Pub: Adams Media Corp.
Contact: Scott Watrous, President
E-mail: bobadams@adamsmedia.com
Ed: Michele Cagan. **Released:** 2004. **Price:** $19.95.
Description: Accountant and author shares insight into starting a new company. The guide assists entrepreneurs through the process, whether it is a corporation, an LLC, a sole proprietorship, or a partnership. Tax codes, accounting practices and legislation affecting every business as well as tips on managing finances are among the topics covered.

37480 ■ *"Struggling Community Banks Find Little Help In Wall Street Bailout" in Crain's Detroit Business (Vol. 24, September 29, 2008, pp. 48)*
Pub: Crain Communications Inc.
Contact: Rance E. Crain, President
Ed: Tom Henderson. **Description:** Both public and private Michigan bands have been hit hard by poorly performing loan portfolios and although their problems were not caused by high-risk securities but by a longtime statewide recession and a housing slump, these community banks have little hope of seeing any of the bailout money that has been allotted for the larger institutions.

37481 ■ *"A Study in Diversity: What Women Want: There Are Fundamental Differences Between How Men and Women View Retirement Planning" in Senior Market Advisor (Vol. 13, October 2012, No. 10, pp. 36)*
Description: An overview of women's attitudes towards finances and retirement planning is provided. Contrasting views are even held by male and female financial advisors.

37482 ■ *"Sudden Shift Leaves Wells Vendor Scrambling" in Charlotte Business Journal (Vol. 25, July 9, 2010, No. 16, pp. 1)*
Pub: Charlotte Business Journal
Ed: Adam O'Daniel. **Description:** Rubber stamps vendor Carolina Marking Devices is facing a 30 percent drop in business after banking firm Wells Fargo & Company decided to buy its rubber stamps from another vendor. Carolina Marking Devices had provided rubber to First Union Corporation and its successor Wachovia Corporation, which was eventually acquired by Wells Fargo. Other reactions from Carolina Marking Device owners are given.

37483 ■ *"SunTrust Builds a New Team" in Charlotte Business Journal (Vol. 27, July 13, 2012, No. 17, pp. 1)*
Pub: American City Business Journals, Inc.
Contact: Whitney Shaw, President
Ed: Adam O'Daniel. **Released:** July 13, 2012. **Description:** SunTrust Banks Inc. hired new bankers from competing banks as part of its continued effort to grow its market share in Charlotte, North Carolina. Regional president Bill Peele, is focused on serving commercial accounts and he believes professional services have the most promising prospects for growth.

37484 ■ *"Surprise Package" in Business Courier (Vol. 27, June 25, 2010, No. 8, pp. 1)*
Pub: Business Courier
Ed: Dan Monk, Jon Newberry, Steve Watkins. **Description:** More than 60 percent of the chief executive officers (CEOs) in Greater Cincinnati's 35 public companies took a salary cut in 2009, but stock grants resulted in large paper gains for the CEOs. The salary cuts show efforts of boards of directors to observe austerity. Statistics on increased values of stock awards for CEOs, median pay for CEOs, and median shareholder return are also presented.

37485 ■ *"Survey Distorts Cost of Capitals" in Canadian Business (Vol. 83, October 12, 2010, No. 17, pp. 22)*
Pub: Rogers Media Inc.
Contact: Tony Viner, President
Ed: Matthew McClearn. **Description:** Swiss bank UBS publishes a study comparing the costs of goods and services in megalopolises every three years. The study ranked Toronto and Montreal outside the Top 30 in 2009, but the two cities jumped to eighth and ninth in a recent update. This change can be contributed to the conversion of prices into Euros before making comparisons.

37486 ■ *"A Survival Guide for Crazy Times" in Canadian Business (Vol. 81, March 3, 2008, No. 3, pp. 61)*
Ed: David Wolf. **Description:** Investors should ensure that their portfolios are positioned defensively more than the average as the U.S. and Canadian markets face turbulent times. They should not assume that U.S. residential property is a good place to

invest only because prices have dropped and the Canadian dollar is showing strength. Other tips that investors can use during unstable periods are supplied.

37487 ■ *"Surviving the Storm" in Canadian Business (Vol. 81, July 22, 2008, No. 12-13, pp. 50)*
Ed: Jeff Sanford. **Description:** Investment adviser Harry Dent and finance professor Paul Marsh discuss their views and forecasts on the United States' economic condition. Dent believes advisors should concentrate on wealth preservation rather than on returns. Other views regarding U.S. economic conditions are also presented.

37488 ■ *"The Sweet Spot for REITs" in Canadian Business (Vol. 87, July 2014, No. 7, pp. 27)*
Pub: George Media Inc.
Released: July 2014. **Description:** Some tips for investors interested in stocks in the industrial real estate investment trust (REIT) sector are provided. Investors need to decide whether they want to won a pure play industrial operation or a diversified REIT with good exposure to such property type.

37489 ■ *"A Swifter, Better Marketplace" in Barron's (Vol. 89, July 13, 2009, No. 28, pp. M13)*
Pub: Dow Jones & Co., Inc.
Contact: Clare Hart, President
Ed: Eric W. Noll. **Description:** Listed-derivatives market is moving towards greater trading through computerized systems with an emphasis on speed and innovation. The market for listed options is also being changed by new techniques from other markets such as algorithmic trading, dark pools, and new-order priority systems.

37490 ■ *"Sykes Group Targets GunnAllen" in The Business Journal-Serving Greater Tampa Bay (Vol. 28, September 5, 2008, No. 37, pp. 1)*
Pub: American City Business Journals, Inc.
Contact: Whitney Shaw, President
Ed: Margie Manning. **Description:** GAH Holdings LLC. a newly formed investment company by John H. Sykes of Sykes Enterprises Inc., will add capital to Tampa Bay Area investment banking firm GunnAllen Holdings Inc. The capital infusion is to aid GunnAllen Holdings in expanding and diversifying as GAH becomes its largest shareholder.

37491 ■ *"Tackling Tuition Increases Head On" in Pittsburgh Business Times (Vol. 34, July 25, 2014, No. 1, pp. 6)*
Pub: American City Business Journals
Released: July 25, 2014. **Description:** The University of Pittsburgh has tried to contain tuition increases after the state cut funding by about $70 million in the 2012 budget year. The measures include a one-time-only early retirement program offered in 2012, greater focus on sustainability and cutting energy costs, and streamlining operations and sharing services.

37492 ■ *"Take Control of Your Company's Finances" in Green Industry Pro (Vol. 23, March 2011, No. 3, pp. 24)*
Pub: Cygnus Business Media
Contact: Paul Mackler, Chief Executive Officer
Ed: Gregg Wartgow. **Description:** Understanding that when certain leading indicators that affect the outcome of certain lagging indicators are aligned, companies will be able to take control of their firm's finances. Ways to improve the processes that drive financial performance for landscape firms are outlined.

37493 ■ *"Take It to the Bank" in Barron's (Vol. 89, July 13, 2009, No. 28, pp. 20)*
Pub: Dow Jones & Co., Inc.
Contact: Clare Hart, President
Ed: Jim McTague. **Description:** Banks are one of the safest place to put one's principal due to the temporary increase in the Federal Deposit Insurance Corp.'s insurance of bank accounts up to $250,000 and also because of the Cdars (Certificates of

Deposit Registry Service) program which spreads the deposit to several banks thereby making the account covered as if it the money was deposited at multiple banks.

37494 ■ "Take the Wheel: the Pension Protection Act Doesn't Mean You Can Sit Back and Relax" in Black Enterprise (October 1, 2007)
Pub: Earl G. Graves Publishing Co. Inc.
Contact: Earl G. Graves, Jr., President
Ed: Mellody Hobson. Description: Pension Protection Act provides multiple benefits and tax advantages for retirement, however the investment options and contribution rates are very conservative.

37495 ■ "Taking the Over-the-Counter Route to U.S." in Barron's (Vol. 88, July 7, 2008, No. 27, pp. 24)
Pub: Dow Jones & Co., Inc.
Contact: Clare Hart, President
Ed: Eric Uhlfelder. Description: Many multinational companies have left the New York Stock Exchange and allowed their shares to trade over-the-counter. The companies have taken advantage of a 2007 SEC rule allowing publicly listed foreign companies to change trading venues if less than 5 percent of global trading volume in the past 12 months occurred in the US.

37496 ■ "Tanganyika Announces First Quarter 2007 Results" in Marketwired (May 14, 2007)
Pub: Comtex News Network Inc.
Description: Tanganyika Oil Company Ltd. announced the interim operating and financial results for the first quarter ending March 31, 2007. Statistical data included.

37497 ■ "Tao of Downfall" in International Journal of Entrepreneurship and Small Business (Vol. 11, August 31, 2010, No. 2, pp. 121)
Pub: Publishers Communication Group
Contact: Doug Wright, Director
Ed: Wenxian Zhang, Ilan Alon. Description: Through historical reviews and case studies, this research seeks to understand why some initially successful entrepreneurs failed in the economic boom of past decades. Among various factors contributing to their downfall are a unique political and business environment, fragile financial systems, traditional cultural influences and personal characteristics.

37498 ■ "TD Pares in U.S., Still Aims for Growth" in Globe & Mail (March 24, 2007, pp. B6)
Pub: CTVglobemedia Publishing Inc.
Ed: Tara Perkins. Description: The decision of TD Banknorth Inc. to close some of its branches and remove 400 jobs, with a view to cutting down operational expenses, is discussed.

37499 ■ "TerraVest Income Fund Releases 2007 First Quarter Financial Results" in Marketwired (May 14, 2007)
Pub: Comtex News Network Inc.
Description: Overview of TerraVest Income Fund's financial results for the quarter ended March 31, 2007 in which the net earnings increased 36.7 percent to $3.7 million from the 2006 first quarter. Statistical data included.

37500 ■ "That's About It for Quantitative Easing" in Barron's (Vol. 89, July 20, 2009, No. 29, pp. M11)
Pub: Dow Jones & Co., Inc.
Contact: Clare Hart, President
Ed: Brian Blackstone. Description: US Federal Reserve appears to have decided to halt quantitative easing, causing bond prices to drop and yields to rise. The yield for the 1-year Treasury bond rose more than 0.3 percentage point to about 3.65 percent.

37501 ■ "TheStreet.com: Study Abroad" in Entrepreneur (Vol. 35, October 2007, No. 10, pp. 44)
Pub: Entrepreneur Press
Contact: Perlman Neil, President
Ed: Farnoosh Torabi. Description: Businessmen who wish to pursue foreign investments should study the country in which they will operate. Some inves-

tors do their research by completely exposing themselves to their prospective country, while others prefer studying the market home-based. Details of how investors pick their country and the different ways of investing in foreign land are presented.

37502 ■ "They've Fallen, But Can Senior-Housing Stocks Get Up" in Barron's (Vol. 88, March 10, 2008, No. 10, pp. 43)
Pub: Dow Jones & Co., Inc.
Contact: Clare Hart, President
Ed: Kopin Tan. Description: Shares of senior housing companies present buying opportunities to investors because of their low prices. Companies such as Brookdale Senior Living are not as dependent on housing prices but have suffered declines in share prices.

37503 ■ "THL Credit Is Hunting In Middle Market" in Boston Business Journal (Vol. 30, October 22, 2010, No. 39, pp. 1)
Pub: Boston Business Journal
Ed: Tim McLaughlin. Description: THL Credit has been supplying capital to middle market companies in Massachusetts. The company has reported investment income of $2.44 million at the end of June 2010.

37504 ■ The Three Secrets of Green Business: Unlocking Competitive Advantage in a Low Carbon Economy
Pub: Earthscan
Ed: Gareth Kane. Released: December 08, 2009. Price: $33.95, paperback; $135, hardback. Description: Small business is coming under increasing pressure from government, customers and campaigning groups to improve environmental performance. Soaring utility and compliance costs are critical financial burdens on small companies. Availability: Print.

37505 ■ "Time to Leave the Party? Re-Evaluating Commodities" in Barron's (Vol. 88, March 24, 2008, No. 12, pp. M16)
Pub: Dow Jones & Co., Inc.
Contact: Clare Hart, President
Ed: Andrea Hotter. Description: Prices of commodities such as gold, copper, crude oil, sugar, cocoa, and wheat have fallen from their all-time highs set in the middle of March 2008. Analysts, however, caution that this decline in prices may be temporary, and that a banking crisis may trigger new price rises in commodities.

37506 ■ "Time for a Little Pruning?" in Barron's (Vol. 89, July 6, 2009, No. 27, pp. 13)
Pub: Dow Jones & Co., Inc.
Contact: Clare Hart, President
Ed: Dimitra DeFotis. Description: Investors are advised to avoid the shares of Whole Foods, American Tower, T. Rowe Price, Iron Mountain, Intuitive Surgical, Salesforce.com, and Juniper Networks due to their high price to earnings ratios. The shares of Amazon.com, Broadcom, and Expeditors International of Washington remain attractive to investors despite their high price to earnings ratios due to their strong growth.

37507 ■ "Time for the Offense to Take Over" in Barron's (Vol. 92, July 23, 2012, No. 30, pp. 11)
Pub: Dow Jones & Co., Inc.
Contact: Clare Hart, President
Ed: Michael Santoli. Released: July 23, 2012. Description: The rise in the US stock market was led by defensive stocks that typically thrive in bear markets. Large-capitalization stocks in the telecommunications and utilities sectors have also outperformed, while cyclical stocks have lagged behind.

37508 ■ "Time to Tweet: Banks and Fun, Benefits in Social Media" in Philadelphia Business Journal (Vol. 31, February 24, 2012, No. 2, pp. 1)
Pub: American City Business Journal
Description: Pennsylvania-based banks have benefited from the use of social media to market their services. TD Bank used Twitter to respond to customer complaints. Citizens Bank uses Twitter to provide customers with financial tips.

37509 ■ "Time Value of Money Rate of Return" in Business Owner (Vol. 35, September-October 2011, No. 5, pp. 8)
Pub: DL Perkins Company
Description: Estimating value of an income-generating asset or group of assets requires the small business owner to consider concepts such as the time value of money, risk and required rate of return. A brief summary explaining this theory is presented.

37510 ■ "A Timely Boon for Small Investors" in Barron's (Vol. 88, March 24, 2008, No. 12, pp. 48)
Pub: Dow Jones & Co., Inc.
Contact: Clare Hart, President
Ed: Theresa W. Carey. Description: Nasdaq Data Store's new program called Market Replay allows investors to accurately track stock price movements. The replay can be as long as a day of market time and allows investors to determine whether they executed stock trades at the best possible price.

37511 ■ "Tiptoeing Beyond Treasuries" in Barron's (Vol. 88, March 31, 2008, No. 13, pp. M6)
Ed: Michael S. Derby. Description: Risk-free assets like treasuries are still a good place for cash even if market conditions have calmed down and Treasury yields are low. Investors looking for yield and safety might want to consider Treasury inflation-indexed securities that are attractive given new inflation pressures.

37512 ■ "To Give and Receive: How to Pass On 401k Assets and Manage an Inheritance" in Black Enterprise (Vol. 38, October 1, 2007, No. 3)
Pub: Earl G. Graves Publishing Co. Inc.
Contact: Earl G. Graves, Jr., President
Ed: Steve Garmhausen. Description: Without proper planning, heirs could pay large tax bills to the government unless assets are managed properly. A common error is to avoid updating account records to reflect the names of designated beneficiaries.

37513 ■ "To Thine Own Self" in Entrepreneur (Vol. 35, November 2007, No. 11, pp. 50)
Pub: Entrepreneur Press
Contact: Perlman Neil, President
Ed: Farnoosh Torabi. Description: Self-directed individual retirement account (IRA) provides more investment options as payoff from this can be higher than an average mutual fund. Details on how to manage self-directed IRAs are discussed.

37514 ■ "Too Much Information?" in Black Enterprise (Vol. 37, December 2006, No. 5, pp. 59)
Pub: Earl G. Graves Publishing Co. Inc.
Contact: Earl G. Graves, Jr., President
Ed: James C. Johnson. Description: African American business owners often face the dilemma of whether or not to divulge their minority status when soliciting new customers and financial institutions. The quality of the products or services is always the key factor and race should never define one's business; however, it is appropriate to market oneself as a minority- or women-owned business, especially if the company is in an industry where those clients are offered top-tier contracts.

37515 ■ "Too Much Precaution About Biotech Corn" in Barron's (Vol. 88, March 17, 2008, No. 11, pp. 54)
Pub: Dow Jones & Co., Inc.
Contact: Clare Hart, President
Ed: Mark I. Schwartz. Description: In the U.S., 90 percent of cultivated soybeans are biotech varietals as well as 60 percent of the corn. Farmers have significantly reduced their reliance on pesticides in the growing of biotech corn. Biotech cotton cultivation has brought hundreds of millions of dollars in net financial gains to farmers. The European Union has precluded the cultivation or sale of biotech crops within its border.

37516 ■ "Too Much too Soon" in Barron's (Vol. 89, July 27, 2009, No. 30, pp. 33)
Pub: Dow Jones & Co., Inc.
Contact: Clare Hart, President
Ed: Leslie P. Norton. Description: Shares of hhgregg have risen 85 percent in the year leading up to July 2009 and analysts believe the stock could hit 25. However, their 113 outlets are concentrated in states where unemployment is above 10 percent and expanding into areas already overstored. Competition is also rife and credit availability is still tight.

37517 ■ "Top 10 Retirement Mistakes and How to Avoid Them" in Canadian Business (Vol. 83, July 20, 2010, No. 11-12, pp. 39)
Pub: Rogers Media Inc.
Contact: Tony Viner, President
Ed: Jacqueline Nelson, Angelina Chapin. Description: Some of the top retirement mistakes is relying on selling one's house to find a retirement. Other mistakes are paying too much for investments and planning to work in retirement since no one can be sure that they will be healthy enough to accomplish this. Suggestions to avoid these pitfalls are discussed.

37518 ■ "Top 40 Wealth Managers" in Barron's (Vol. 92, September 17, 2012, No. 38, pp. 28)
Pub: Dow Jones & Co., Inc.
Contact: Clare Hart, President
Description: The 40 largest wealth managers in the US are ranked according to client assets held in accounts worth $5 million or more as of June 30, 2012. Bank of America Global Wealth and Investment Management remained the largest, with $792 billion in assets under management.

37519 ■ "Top 50 By 1-Year Return" in Canadian Business (Vol. 81, Summer 2008, No. 9, pp. 121)
Description: Table showing the top 50 Canadian companies ranked in terms of one-year return is presented. Toronto, Canada-based Timminco Ltd. topped the roster with a 1,294.2 percent in one-year return. However, the share prices of the company were affected by the recent controversy in its silicon purification process.

37520 ■ "Top 50 By 5-Year Return" in Canadian Business (Vol. 81, Summer 2008, No. 9, pp. 123)
Description: Table showing the rankings of the top 50 Canadian companies in terms of five-year return is presented. Silver Wheaton Corp. topped the roster with a 178.5 percent in five-year return. The company's share prices have skyrocketed despite increasing silver prices.

37521 ■ "Top 50 in the Capital Market" in Canadian Business (Vol. 81, Summer 2008, No. 9, pp. 117)
Description: Research in Motion Ltd. topped the list of companies in Canada in terms of market capitalization. The company's share prices surge to 119.8 percent in the year ended April 4. A table showing the top 50 Canadian companies in terms of market capitalization is presented.

37522 ■ "Top 50 In Profits" in Canadian Business (Vol. 81, Summer 2008, No. 9, pp. 116)
Description: Royal Bank of Canada topped the Investor 500 by profits list despite the slower economic growth in Canada and the U.S. The bank was in the runner-up position in the 2007. RBC's growth strategy is through hefty acquisitions in the U.S. A table ranking the top 50 companies in Canada in terms of profits is presented.

37523 ■ "Top 50 In Total Revenue" in Canadian Business (Vol. 81, Summer 2008, No. 9, pp. 119)
Description: Table showing the top 50 Canadian companies in terms of total revenue is presented. Manulife Financial Corp. topped the list with revenue of 34.5 billion. The financial services firm is the 6th largest provider of life insurance in the world and the second largest in North America.

37524 ■ "Top 100 Indy Advisors" in Barron's (Vol. 92, August 25, 2012, No. 38, pp. S2)
Pub: Dow Jones & Co., Inc.
Contact: Clare Hart, President
Ed: Suzanne McGee. Description: Profiles of five independent financial advisors included the Barron's Top 100 independent financial advisor rankings for 2012 are included. Their investment strategies are also discussed.

37525 ■ "Top Law Firms Join Forces" in Business Journal Portland (Vol. 27, December 3, 2010, No. 40, pp. 1)
Pub: Portland Business Journal
Ed: Andy Giegerich. Description: Law Firms Powell PC and Roberts Kaplan LLP will forge a collaboration, whereby 17 Roberts Kaplan attorneys will join the Portland, Oregon-based office of Lane Powell. The partnership is expected to strengthen the law firms' grip on Portland's banking clients.

37526 ■ "Top Pension Fund Sends a Warning" in Barron's (Vol. 92, July 23, 2012, No. 30, pp. M9)
Pub: Dow Jones & Co., Inc.
Contact: Clare Hart, President
Ed: Michael Aneiro. Released: July 23, 2012. Description: The California Public Employees' Retirement System reported a 1 percent return on investments for the fiscal year ended June 30, 2012. It lost 7.2 percent on stock investments, 11 percent on forest-land holdings and 2 percent on absolute-return assets, negating a 12.7 percent gain on its fixed-income investments.

37527 ■ The Total Money Makeover: A Proven Plan For Financial Fitness
Pub: Nelson Education Ltd.
Contact: Greg Nordal, President
Ed: Dave Ramsey. Released: September 10, 2013. Price: $24.99, hardcover. Description: How to get rid of debt and build up your rainy-day reserves. Availability: Print.

37528 ■ "Trade Groups Push for Delay In Minimum Wage Hike" in Boston Business Journal (Vol. 34, June 13, 2014, No. 19, pp. 6)
Pub: American City Business Journals, Inc.
Contact: Whitney Shaw, President
Released: June 13, 2014. Description: Trade groups from Massachusetts, the Retailers Association of Massachusetts and Associated Industries of Massachusetts, have requested legislatures to delay the proposed hike to the state minimum wage. They have asked the process be delayed until January 1, 2015. The House Bill that would bring the minimum wage up from $8 an hour to $10.50 an hour over three years, and the Senate Bill, which would bring the floor up to $11 an hour, would take effect with an increase to $9 an hour on July 1, 2014.

37529 ■ "A Trader Gets a Better Deal From the IRS Than an Investor" in Barron's (Vol. 88, March 31, 2008, No. 13, pp. 56)
Pub: Dow Jones & Co., Inc.
Contact: Clare Hart, President
Ed: Dan McGuire. Description: There is a $3,000 a year annual limit to deducting investor's losses and normal investment expenses are purportedly deductible as miscellaneous expenses on Schedule A only to the extent that they exceed two percent of adjusted gross income. Professional gamblers who can use Schedule C are unable deduct a net gaming loss against income from any other sources.

37530 ■ "Traditional vs. Roth IRA" in Black Enterprise (Vol. 37, October 2006, No. 3, pp. 58)
Pub: Earl G. Graves Publishing Co. Inc.
Contact: Earl G. Graves, Jr., President
Ed: K. Parker, Carolyn M. Brown. Description: Government taxes the traditional IRAs different than it taxes Roth IRAs.

37531 ■ "Treasuries Buffeted by Stocks" in Barron's (Vol. 89, July 27, 2009, No. 30, pp. M9)
Ed: Randall W. Forsyth. Description: Warren Buffett favors equities over long-term government bonds or stocks even with the Dow index at an eight-month

high. The 10-year Treasury was up two basis points to 3.67 percent as of July 24, 2009. Corporate bond issuance hit a record $1.79 trillion for the first half of 2009.

37532 ■ "Treasuries Rally Despite Huge Supply" in Barron's (Vol. 89, July 13, 2009, No. 28, pp. M10)
Pub: Dow Jones & Co., Inc.
Contact: Clare Hart, President
Ed: Randall W. Forsyth. Description: Prices of U.S. Treasuries were sent higher and their yields lower despite four auctions of coupon securities because of the strong appetite for government securities around the world. The reopening of the 10-year note in the week ending July 10, 2009 drew the strongest bidding since 1995.

37533 ■ "A Trend Is His Friend" in Barron's (Vol. 89, July 27, 2009, No. 30, pp. 28)
Pub: Dow Jones & Co., Inc.
Contact: Clare Hart, President
Ed: Eric Uhlfelder. Description: Global Diversified Program fund under Quality Capital Management is managed through a trading system called the Advanced Resource Allocator which rebalances short-term tactical moves to gather quick profits. CEO Aref Karim's allocations are based on risk and he says their sentiments toward the market conditions are agnostic.

37534 ■ "The Trials of Brian Hunter" in Canadian Business (Vol. 81, March 3, 2008, No. 3, pp. 64)
Ed: Thomas Watson. Description: Brian Hunter was a considered a brilliant trader in Wall Street before he was blamed for the fall of the Amaranth hedge fund. Some people blame Hunter for placing bets based on unpredictable weather when he was a trader for Amaranth Advisors LLC. The accusation against Hunter that he conspired to manipulate natural gas prices is also discussed.

37535 ■ "Trilogy Metals Inc.: Private Placement" in Canadian Corporate News (May 16, 2007)
Description: Trilogy Metals Inc. announces a private placement of 10,000,000 units at $0.08 per unit in an effort to raise total gross proceeds of $800,000 which will be allocated to working capital, new acquisitions, and to service existing debt.

37536 ■ "Try, Try Again" in Baltimore Business Journal (Vol. 28, August 20, 2010, No. 15, pp. 1)
Ed: Gary Haber. Description: Customers' refinancing of mortgages has boosted Baltimore, Maryland mortgage banking business. The housing decline has resulted in a decrease in the number of people looking for new mortgages.

37537 ■ "Tuesday Morning's Corporate Clearance Rack" in Dallas Business Journal (Vol. 37, February 28, 2014, No. 25, pp. 4)
Pub: American City Business Journals
Released: February 28, 2014. Description: Tuesday Morning CEO, Michael Rouleau, has been working to help the company recover from its financial problems. Rouleau has improved the shopping experience from garage sale to discount showroom. The company has also been hiring different executives in the past few years.

37538 ■ "TUSK Announces 2007 First Quarter Results" in Marketwired (May 14, 2007)
Pub: Comtex News Network Inc.
Description: TUSK Energy Corp. announced its financial and operating results for the first quarter ending March 31, 2007.

37539 ■ "Twilight of the 'Banksters': the Barclays Scandal Could Finally Spark Serious Banking Reform" in Canadian Business (Vol. 85, August 13, 2012, No. 13, pp. 11)
Pub: George Media Inc.
Ed: Richard Warnica. Released: August 13, 2012. Description: Potential banking reform is anticipated after British bank Barclays PLC admitted fixing the London Interbank Offered Rate and agreed to pay

$451 million in fines for its wrongdoing. The separation of investment and retail banking was endorsed by conservative 'Financial Times' newspaper.

37540 ■ "UB Program Offers Free Tax Preparation" in Buffalo News (January 29, 2012)
Pub: McClatchy-Tribune Information Services
Ed: Jonathan D. Epstein. **Released:** January 29, 2012. **Description:** University of Buffalo's Schhol of Management in New York is offering free tax preparation for low-income individuals and families. The program is available on North and South campuses and is designed to help these people save money and collect all refunds in which they are eligible.

37541 ■ "Understanding the Fed: Get a Handle on How Ben Bernanke's Decisions Affect Your Wallet" in Black Enterprise (Vol. 38, December 2007, No. 5, pp. 66)
Pub: Earl G. Graves Publishing Co. Inc.
Contact: Earl G. Graves, Jr., President
Ed: Steve Garmhausen. **Description:** The Federal Reserve System along with twelve regional banks regulates the value of money through the law of supply and demand. The Feds increase or decrease the supply of dollars in circulation which makes them cheap or expensive.

37542 ■ "Unemployment Tax Surge Could Hit Businesses Hard" in Orlando Business Journal (Vol. 26, January 1, 2010, No. 31, pp. 1)
Pub: American City Business Journals
Ed: Christopher Boyd. **Description:** Consequences of the almost 1,100 percent increase in Florida's minimum unemployment compensation insurance tax to businesses in the state are discussed. Employers pay for the said tax, which is used to fund the state's unemployment claims.

37543 ■ "An Unfair Knock on Nokia" in Barron's (Vol. 88, March 10, 2008, No. 10, pp. 36)
Pub: Dow Jones & Co., Inc.
Contact: Clare Hart, President
Ed: Mark Veverka. **Description:** Discusses the decision by the brokerage house Exane to recommend a Sell on Nokia shares, presumably due to higher inventories, which is unfounded. The news that the company's inventories are rising is not an indicator of falling demand for its products. The company is also benefiting from solid management and rising market share.

37544 ■ "Unify Corp. Back in the Black, Poised to Grow" in Sacramento Business Journal (Vol. 25, August 29, 2008, No. 26, pp. 1)
Pub: American City Business Journals, Inc.
Contact: Whitney Shaw, President
Ed: Melanie Turner. **Description:** It was reported that Unify Corp. returned to profitability in the fiscal year ended April 30, 2008 with a net income of $1.6 million, under the guidance of Todd Wille. Wille, who took over as the company's chief executive officer in October 2000, was named as Turnaround CEO of the Year in June 2008 for his efforts.

37545 ■ "Universal Energy Group Releases March 31, 2007 Financial Statements" in Marketwired (May 14, 2007)
Pub: Comtex News Network Inc.
Description: Universal Energy Group Ltd., a company that sells electricity and natural gas to small to mid-size commercial and small industrial customers as well as residential customers, announced the release of its March 31, 2007 financial statements. Management's analysis and discussion of the company's financial condition and results of operations are listed. Statistical data included.

37546 ■ "Univest Charter Switch Signals Banking Trend" in Philadelphia Business Journal (Vol. 30, September 2, 2011, No. 29, pp. 1)
Pub: American City Business Journals Inc.
Ed: Jeff Blumenthal. **Description:** Univest Corporation of Pennsylvania changed from a federal to state charter because of cost savings and state agency

has greater understanding of the intricacies of the local economy. The Pennsylvania Department of Banking has also received inquiries from seven other banks about doing the same this year.

37547 ■ "Unpleasant Surprise - When a Stock Distribution is Taxed as Dividend Income" in Barron's (Vol. 88, March 24, 2008, No. 12, pp. 60)
Pub: Dow Jones & Co., Inc.
Contact: Clare Hart, President
Ed: Shirley A. Lazo. **Description:** Discusses the $175 million that footwear company Genesco received in a settlement with Finish Line and UBS is considered as a stock distribution and is taxable as dividend income. Railroad company CSX raised its quarterly common payout from 15 cents to 18 cents.

37548 ■ "The Upside of Fear and Loathing" in Barron's (Vol. 88, March 24, 2008, No. 12, pp. 11)
Pub: Dow Jones & Co., Inc.
Contact: Clare Hart, President
Ed: Michael Santoli. **Description:** Fear and risk aversion prevalent among investors may actually serve to cushion the decline and spark a rally in US stock prices. Surveys of investors indicate rising levels of anxiety and bearishness, indicating a possible positive turnaround.

37549 ■ "USAmeriBank, Liberty Deal Spells Merger Trend" in The Business Journal-Serving Greater Tampa Bay (Vol. 28, September 26, 2008, No. 40, pp. 1)
Pub: American City Business Journals, Inc.
Contact: Whitney Shaw, President
Ed: Margie Manning. **Description:** It is believed that the pending $14.9 million purchase of Liberty Bank by USAmeriBank could be at the forefront of a trend. Executives of both companies expect the deal to close by the end of 2008. USAmeriBank will have $430 million in assets and five offices in Pinellas, Florida once the deal is completed.

37550 ■ "USHCC Applauds Bank of America for Investment in Green Business Practices" in Manufacturing Close-Up (July 11, 2012)
Description: Bank America has been recognized by the United States Hispanic Chamber of Commerce (USHCC) for its commitment to green business practices. Bank of America has established a 10-year, $50 billion environmental goal to help businesses address climate change, to reduce demands on natural resources, and to advance lower-carbon economic solutions, while reducing their own environmental impact.

37551 ■ Using Other People's Money to Get Rich: Secrets, Techniques, and Strategies Investors Use Every Day Using OPM to Make Millions
Pub: Atlantic Publishing Co.
Contact: Amanda Miller, Manager
E-mail: amiller@atlantic-pub.com
Ed: Eric J. Leech. **Price:** $24.95. **Description:** Discussion showing individuals how to invest using other people's money. **Availability:** Print.

37552 ■ "Using Quantile Regression to Understand Visitor Spending" in Journal of Travel Research (Vol. 51, May 2012, No. 3, pp. 278)
Pub: Pine Forge Press
Contact: Blaise R. Simqu, President
Ed: Alan A. Lew, Pin T. Ng. **Description:** Several analyses are carried out to discuss the benefits extended by the use of quantile regression analysis approach for the indentification of the tourist spending patterns and market segments. The methodology shown is not impacted by the outlier values, thus giving accurate results.

37553 ■ "Valenti: Roots of Financial Crisis Go Back to 1998" in Crain's Detroit Business (Vol. 24, October 6, 2008, No. 40, pp. 25)
Pub: Crain Communications Inc.
Contact: Rance E. Crain, President
Ed: Tom Henderson, Nathan Skid. **Description:** Interview with Sam Valenti III who is the chairman and CEO of Valenti Capital L.L.C., a wealth-

management firm; Valenti discusses in detail the history that led up to the current economic crisis as well as his prediction for the future of the country.

37554 ■ Valuing the Closely Held Firm
Pub: Oxford University Press
Contact: Niko Pfund, President
Ed: Michael S. Long, Thomas A. Bryant. **Released:** November 26, 2007. **Price:** $78, Hardcover. **Description:** The differences between a large and small firm and their ability to generate future cash flow are discussed. **Availability:** Print.

37555 ■ "Virtue and Vice" in Entrepreneur (September 2014)
Pub: Entrepreneur Media Inc.
Released: September 2014. **Description:** Socially responsible investments (SRI) are rising in the U.S., but many claim that vice funds offer better returns. Vice fund proponents argue that any profitable company deserves a place in a good investment portfolio. SRI proponents emphasize investments that benefit the society. Analysts note that investors who restrict their investment landscape by selecting only vice funds or only SRI funds may lead to lower returns. Other specialized funds attract activist investors supporting advocacies like gender equality or a positive work environment.

37556 ■ "Virtus.com Wins 'Best of Industry' WebAward for Excellence in Financial Services" in Investment Weekly News (October 24, 2009)
Pub: Investment Weekly News
Description: Web Marketing Association honored Virtus.com, the Website of Virtus Investment Partners, Inc., for Outstanding Achievement in Web Development and Acsys Interactive was awarded the Financial Services Standard of Excellence Award for developing the site. The site was part of a rebranding effort and is a one-stop portal for both financial advisors and their investors.

37557 ■ "Virtus.com Wins 'Best of Industry' WebAward for Excellence in Financial Services" in Investment Weekly News (October 24, 2009, pp. 227)
Pub: Investment Weekly News
Description: Web Marketing Association honored Virtus.com, the Website of Virtus Investment Partners, Inc., for Outstanding Achievement in Web Development and Acsys Interactive was awarded the Financial Services Standard of Excellence Award for developing the site. The site was part of a rebranding effort and is a one-stop portal for both financial advisors and their investors.

37558 ■ "Vital Signs: The Big Picture" in Canadian Business (Vol. 81, Summer 2008, No. 9, pp. 153)
Description: Results of the Investor 500 showing percentage of companies with positive returns, most actively traded companies over the past six months and market capitalization by industry are presented. Stock performance and revenues of publicly held corporations in Canada are also provided.

37559 ■ "WashTrust Profits Up, as Wealth Assets Pass $5B" in Providence Business News (Vol. 29, July 28, 2014, No. 17, pp. 8)
Pub: American City Business Journals
Released: July 28, 2014. **Description:** The Washington Trust Company posted a 9.1 percent income growth year-on-year in the second quarter of 2014, with total earnings at $9.8 million as compared to the previous year. Washington Trust Chairman and CEO, Joseph J. MacAurele attributed the community bank's success to continued market expansion, corporate business growth, and its wealth management team.

37560 ■ "Watchful Eye: Entrepreneur Protects Clients and His Bottom Line" in Black Enterprise (Vol. 38, March 1, 2008, No. 8, pp. 46)
Pub: Earl G. Graves Publishing Co. Inc.
Contact: Earl G. Graves, Jr., President
Ed: Tennille M. Robinson. **Description:** Profile of Elijah Shaw, founder of Icon Services Corporation, a full service security and investigative service; Shaw shares his plans to protect clients while growing his business.

37561 ■ *The Way We'll Be: The Zogby Report on the Transformation of the American Dream*
Pub: Crown Business
Ed: John Zogby. **Released:** August 12, 2008. **Price:** $13.99. **Description:** According to a recent poll, the next generation of Americans are not as concerned about making money as they are about making a difference in the world. **Availability:** E-book.

37562 ■ *We Are Smarter Than Me: How to Unleash the Power of Crowds in Your Business*
Pub: Wharton School Publishing
Ed: Barry Libert, Jon Spector, Don Tapscott. **Released:** September 25, 2007. **Price:** $24.99, Non-members; $19.99, Members; $17.59, Members; $21.99, Nonmembers. **Description:** Ways to use social networking and community in order to make decisions and plan your business, with a focus on product development, manufacturing, marketing, customer service, finance, management, and more. **Availability:** PrintE-book.

37563 ■ *"Website for Women 50 Launches"* in *Marketing to Women (Vol. 21, April 2008, No. 4, pp. 5)*
Description: Vibrantnation.com is an online community targeting women over age 50; members can share recommendations on a variety of topics such as vacation spots, retailers and financial issues.

37564 ■ *"A Week of the Worst Kind of Selling"* in *Barron's (Vol. 88, June 30, 2008, No. 26, pp. M3)*
Pub: Dow Jones & Co., Inc.
Contact: Clare Hart, President
Ed: Kopin Tan. **Description:** In the week that ended in June 27, 2008 the selloff in the U.S. stock market was brought on by mounting bank losses and the spread of economic slowdown on top of high oil prices. The 31 percent decrease in the share price of Ingersoll-Rand since October 2007 may have factored in most of its risks. The company has completed its acquisition of Trane to morph into a refrigeration-equipment company.

37565 ■ *A Weekend with Warren Buffett: And Other Shareholder Meeting Adventures*
Pub: Basic Books/Perseus Books Group
Ed: Randy Cepuch. **Released:** April 13, 2009. **Price:** $23.95; C$30.50. **Description:** Financial writer and personal investor relates his experiences attending various shareholder meetings, reviewing each meeting and grading its educational value. The book is essential for those hoping to learn more about the way companies invest and do business. **Availability:** E-book.

37566 ■ *"Welcome to the Neighborhood"* in *Hawaii Business (Vol. 53, October 2007, No. 4, pp. 48)*
Pub: PacificBasin Communications
Ed: Jolyn Okimoto Rosa. **Description:** Finance Factors is planning to build branches in Manoa, and Liliha, as part of its strategy to position itself in high-yield areas. The company chose Manoa and Liliha due to thee sites' rich deposits. Its strategy with regards to the branches' location and to the building design is discussed.

37567 ■ *"Well-Timed Entrance"* in *(Vol. 92, July 23, 2012, No. 30, pp. 24)*
Pub: Dow Jones & Co., Inc.
Contact: Clare Hart, President
Ed: Michael Aneiro. **Released:** July 23, 2012. **Description:** Dan Ivascyn, portfolio manager of Pimco Income Fund, discusses the fund's investment bonds. The fund is heavily invested in mortgage-backed securities and is positioned for a low-interest-rate environment well into 2014 or 2015.

37568 ■ *"Wenzel Downhole Tools Ltd. Announces First Quarter Results for 2007"* in *Marketwired (May 14, 2007)*
Pub: Comtex News Network Inc.
Description: Wenzel Downhole Tools Ltd., a manufacturer, renter, and seller of drilling tools used in gas and oil exploration, announced its financial results for the first quarter ended March 31, 2007 which includes achieved revenues of $14.5 million. Statistical data included.

37569 ■ *"Western & Southern to Trim Rich Retirement Plan"* in *Business Courier (Vol. 27, October 15, 2010, No. 24, pp. 1)*
Pub: Business Courier
Ed: Dan Monk. **Description:** Insurance firm Western & Southern Financial Group announced that it will reduce the pension benefits of its 4,000 associates by more than 30 percent starting January 1, 2011. The move is expected to reduce annual retirement payments by several thousand dollars per associate. Western is a Fortune 500 company and has $34 billion in total assets.

37570 ■ *"We've Got Questions, RadioShack"* in *Dallas Business Journal (Vol. 37, May 2, 2014, No. 34, pp. 4)*
Pub: American City Business Journals
Released: May 2, 2014. **Description:** The former executives of RadioShack Corporation during the 1980s share their perspectives on the current financial woes of the company. The Fort Worth, Texas-based retailer is planning to close 1,100 retail stores as it continues to suffer from declining sales.

37571 ■ *"Weyerhaeuser's REIT Decision Shouldn't Scare Investors Away"* in *Barron's (Vol. 88, June 30, 2008, No. 26, pp. 18)*
Pub: Dow Jones & Co., Inc.
Contact: Clare Hart, President
Ed: Christopher Williams. **Description:** Weyerhaeuser Co.'s management said that a conversion to a real estate investment trust was not likely in 2009 since the move is not tax-efficient as of the moment and would overload its non-timber assets with debt. The company's shares have fallen by 19.5 percent. However, the company remains an asset-rich outfit and its activist shareholder is pushing for change.

37572 ■ *"What Has Sergey Wrought?"* in *Barron's (Vol. 89, July 13, 2009, No. 28, pp. 8)*
Pub: Dow Jones & Co., Inc.
Contact: Clare Hart, President
Ed: Alan Abelson. **Description:** Sergey Aleynikov is a computer expert that once worked for Goldman Sachs but he was arrested after he left the company and charged with theft for bringing with him the code for the company's proprietary software for high-frequency trading. The stock market has been down for four straight weeks as of July 13, 2009 which reflects the reality of how the economy is still struggling.

37573 ■ *"What Most Banks Fail to See; New and Complex Financial Regulations Can be Daunting"* in *Gallup Management Journal (March 10, 2011)*
Pub: Gallup Inc.
Contact: Jim Clifton, Chief Executive Officer
Ed: Sean Williams, Daniel Porcelli. **Description:** New financial regulations are complicated and politically charged. But banks that move beyond the fear of those regulations will find a new opportunity to engage customers.

37574 ■ *"What Online Brokers Are Doing To Keep Their Customers' Accounts Safe"* in *Barron's (Vol. 88, March 10, 2008, No. 10, pp. 37)*
Pub: Dow Jones & Co., Inc.
Contact: Clare Hart, President
Ed: Theresa W. Carey. **Description:** Online brokerage firms employ different methods to protect the accounts of their customers from theft. These methods include secure Internet connections, momentary passwords, and proprietary algorithms.

37575 ■ *"Whatever Happened to TGIF? How Much Of the Recession Is Priced into Stocks?"* in *Barron's (Vol. 88, March 10, 2008, No. 10, pp. M3)*
Pub: Dow Jones & Co., Inc.
Contact: Clare Hart, President
Ed: Kopin Tan. **Description:** US stock markets fell in early March 2008 to their lowest level in 18 months, venturing close to entering a bear market phase. The S&P 500 has dropped an average of 0.78 percent on Fridays for 2008.

37576 ■ *"What'll You Have Tonight?"* in *Barron's (Vol. 88, July 4, 2008, No. 28, pp. 22)*
Pub: Dow Jones & Co., Inc.
Contact: Clare Hart, President
Ed: Neil A. Martin. **Description:** Shares of Diageo could rise by 30 percent a year from June 2008 after it slipped due to U.S. sales worries. The company also benefits from the trend toward more premium alcoholic beverage brands worldwide especially in emerging markets.

37577 ■ *"What's At Stake In Ex-Im Fight"* in *Puget Sound Business Journal (Vol. 35, July 4, 2014, No. 11, pp. 8)*
Pub: American City Business Journals
Released: July 4, 2014. **Description:** Boeing claims that it is at risk for being placed at a competitive disadvantage against rival Airbus if Congress declines to reauthorize the Export-Import Bank. The possibility of this scenario has increased since House Majority Leader, Eric Cantor, was replaced by Kevin McCarthy. The issue of the government's regulations is addressed.

37578 ■ *"What's In a Name? Fed's Latest Move Should Be Called 'Bankers and Brokers Relief Program"* in *Barron's (Vol. 88, March 17, 2008, No. 11, pp. 7)*
Pub: Dow Jones & Co., Inc.
Contact: Clare Hart, President
Ed: Alan Abelson. **Description:** Eliot Spitzer's resignation incidentally caused the stock market to go up by 400 points. The Federal Reserve Board's new Term Securities Lending Facility provides liquidity to the big lenders by funneling $200 billion in the form of 28-day loans of Treasuries. The analysis of Paul Brodsky and Lee Quaintance of QB Partners on the demand for commodities is also discussed.

37579 ■ *"What's More Important: Stag or Flation?"* in *Barron's (Vol. 88, July 14, 2008, No. 28, pp. M8)*
Pub: Dow Jones & Co., Inc.
Contact: Clare Hart, President
Ed: Randall W. Forsyth. **Description:** Economists are divided on which part of stagflation, an economic situation in which inflation and economic stagnation occur simultaneously and remain unchecked for a period of time, is more important. Some economists say that the Federal government is focusing on controlling inflation while others see the central bank as extending its liquidity facilities to the financial sector.

37580 ■ *"When Dov Cries"* in *Canadian Business (Vol. 83, June 15, 2010, No. 10, pp. 71)*
Pub: Rogers Media Inc.
Contact: Tony Viner, President
Ed: Joe Castaldo. **Description:** American Apparel disclosed that they will have problems meeting one of its debt covenants which could trigger a chain reaction that could lead to bankruptcy. The prospects look bleak, but eccentric company founder Dov Charney, has always defied expectations.

37581 ■ *"When R&D Spending Is Not Enough: The Critical Role of Culture When You Really Want to Innovate"* in *Human Resource Management (Vol. 49, July-August 2010, No. 4, pp. 767-792)*
Pub: John Wiley
Ed: Sheng Wang, Rebecca M. Guidice, Judith W. Tansky, Zhong-Ming Wang. **Description:** A study was conducted to examine the effect of contextual contingencies on innovation. Findings indicate that Chinese manufacturers with cultures emphasizing innovation and teamwork more effectively utilize financial resources in the innovation process. Results also show that a culture emphasizing outcomes and stability leads to lower levels innovation irrespective of investments.

37582 ■ *"When to Roll Over"* in *Black Enterprise (Vol. 37, November 2006, No. 4, pp. 50)*
Pub: Earl G. Graves Publishing Co. Inc.
Contact: Earl G. Graves, Jr., President
Ed: Carolyn M. Brown. **Description:** Being proactive and rolling over your funds if you own stock of your

former employee will give you more control over your money, especially if the company merges or is sold.

37583 ■ *"Where the Money Is" in Conde Nast Portfolio (Vol. 2, June 2008, No. 6, pp. 113)*
Description: Revenue generated from treatments for common brain disorders that are currently on the market are listed.

37584 ■ *"Where Oil-Rich Nations Are Placing Their Bets" in Harvard Business Review (Vol. 86, September 2008, No. 9, pp. 119)*
Pub: Harvard Business Review Press
Contact: Peter E. Walsh, Director
Ed: Rawi Abdelal, Ayesha Khan, Tarun Khanna. **Description:** Investment strategies of the Gulf Cooperation Council nations are examined in addition to how these have impacted the global economy and capitalism.

37585 ■ *"Where Small Biz Gets a 'Yes' More Often" in Denver Business Journal (Vol. 65, February 28, 2014, No. 42, pp. A10)*
Pub: American City Business Journals
Released: February 28, 2014. **Description:** The Biz2Credit Small Business Lending Index has found that alternative lenders granted 66.9 percent of funding requests in Colorado compared to the 15.1 percent approval of loans requests by big banks. The big banks' low approval rates were attributed to their less aggressive lending efforts and the state's fewer restrictions on alternative lending. Other findings from the study are discussed.

37586 ■ *"Where to Stash Your Cash" in Barron's (Vol. 88, March 17, 2008, No. 11, pp. 41)*
Pub: Dow Jones & Co., Inc.
Contact: Clare Hart, President
Ed: Mike Hogan. **Description:** Investors are putting their money in money-market mutual funds seeking fractionally better yields and a safe haven from the uncertainties that was brought about by subprime lending. These funds, however, are hovering near 3.20 percent which is less than the 4 percent inflation rate.

37587 ■ *"Where To Look for Income" in Women In Business (Vol. 63, Summer 2011, No. 2, pp. 50)*
Pub: American Business Women's Association
Contact: Lorie Burch, President
Ed: William J. Lynott. **Description:** Advice on ways to invest in the US market are presented, with information on Certificates of Deposit and Money Markets included.

37588 ■ *"Whiplashed? That's a Bullish Sign Now Is the Time to Buy, Not Sell" in Barron's (Vol. 88, March 31, 2008, No. 13, pp. 34)*
Pub: Dow Jones & Co., Inc.
Contact: Clare Hart, President
Ed: Richard W. Arms. **Description:** Huge volatility often occurs just ahead of a substantial rally, according to an analysis of the volatility in the Dow Jones Index since 2000. The Average Percentage Change based on a 10-day moving average of volatility is a way to measure the level of fear in the market and reveals when buying or selling have been overdone.

37589 ■ *"Whistling Past the Graveyard? Higher Quality Stocks Beckon to Investors?" in Barron's (Vol. 88, March 17, 2008, No. 11, pp. 15)*
Pub: Dow Jones & Co., Inc.
Contact: Clare Hart, President
Ed: Michael Santoli. **Description:** Discusses the Federal Reserve's move to provide $200 billion to the system which can be seen as an effort to avoid the liquidity problems that Bear Stearns suffered. The Federal Reserve's move seems to frighten investors rather than reassure them.

37590 ■ *"A Whole New Way To Beat the Market" in Canadian Business (Vol. 85, June 11, 2012, No. 10, pp. 57)*
Pub: George Media Inc.
Ed: Andrew Hallam. **Released:** June 11, 2012. **Description:** Michael O'Higgings Absolute Return (MOAR) is a diversified, indexed portfolio recom-mended for investors who want decent returns but lower risk. In 2011, the MOAR strategy gained 8.6 percent while most stock market indexes suffered double-digit losses.

37591 ■ *"Why Asset Allocation Is Important: Don't Only Focus On Your Client's Finances, Start With Their Goals" in Retirement Advisor (Vol. 13, October 2012, No. 10, pp. 20)*
Pub: Summit Professional Networks
Contact: Steve Weitzner, President
Ed: Lloyd Lofton. **Description:** Asset allocation can help investors, particularly seniors, to manage risk when planning investments. Diversity means spreading assets into three major classes of stocks, bonds and fixed products. These investments should be reviewed annually.

37592 ■ *"Why Intel Should Dump Its Flash-Memory Business" in Barron's (Vol. 88, March 10, 2008, No. 10, pp. 35)*
Pub: Dow Jones & Co., Inc.
Contact: Clare Hart, President
Ed: Eric J. Savitz. **Description:** Intel Corp. must sell its NAND flash-memory business as soon as it possibly can to the highest bidder to focus on its PC processor business and take advantage of other business opportunities. Apple should consider a buyback of 10 percent of the company's shares to lift its stock.

37593 ■ *"Why the Rally Should Keep Rolling..for Now" in Barron's (Vol. 89, July 27, 2009, No. 30, pp. M3)*
Pub: Dow Jones & Co., Inc.
Contact: Clare Hart, President
Ed: Kopin Tan. **Description:** Stocks rallied for the second straight week as of July 24, 2009 and more companies reported better than expected earnings but the caveat is that companies are beating estimates chiefly by slashing expenses and firing workers. The regulatory risks faced by CME Group and the IntercontinentalExchange are discussed as well as the shares of KKR Private Equity Investors LP.

37594 ■ *"Why the Rout in Financials Isn't Over" in Barron's (Vol. 88, June 30, 2008, No. 26, pp. 23)*
Pub: Dow Jones & Co., Inc.
Contact: Clare Hart, President
Ed: Robin Goldwyn Blumenthal. **Description:** Top market technician Louise Yamada warns that the retreat in the shares of financial services is not yet over based on her analysis of stock charts. Yamada's analysis of the charts of Citigroup, Fifth Third Bancorp and Merrill Lynch are discussed together with the graphs for these shares. Statistical data included.

37595 ■ *"Why This Investing Expert Is Bullish On the Energy Sector: William Heard Expects the Changing Landscape to Lead to Greater Opportunities" in Black Enterprise (Vol. 45, July-August 2014, No. 1, pp. 25)*
Pub: Earl G. Graves Publishing Co. Inc.
Contact: Earl G. Graves, Jr., President
Released: July-August 2014. **Description:** Profile of William Heard and his firm Heard Capital, LLC, the Chicago-based investment company that invests in telecommunications, media, technology, financials, industrials, and energy. Heard shares his investment philosophy and current investments.

37596 ■ *Why We Want You to be Rich: Two Men - One Message*
Pub: Rich Publishing LLC
Released: 2006. **Description:** Authors explain why some people get rich while others don't.

37597 ■ *"Wielding a Big Ax" in Barron's (Vol. 89, July 13, 2009, No. 28, pp. 26)*
Pub: Dow Jones & Co., Inc.
Contact: Clare Hart, President
Ed: Shirley A. Lazo. **Description:** Weyerhaeuser cut their quarterly common payout by 80 percent from 25 cents to a nickel a share which they say will help them preserve their long-term value and improve their performance. Paccar also cut their quarterly dividend by half to nine cents a share. Walgreen however, boosted their quarterly dividend by 22.2 percent to 13.75 cents a share.

37598 ■ *"Will the Force Be With Salesforce? Unlikely" in Barron's (Vol. 88, March 24, 2008, No. 12, pp. 20)*
Pub: Dow Jones & Co., Inc.
Contact: Clare Hart, President
Ed: Mark Veverka. **Description:** Shares of Sales-force.com are likely to drop from the $44.83-a-share level in the face of a deteriorating economy and financial sector and thus lower demand for business software. The company is unlikely to deliver on its ambitious earnings forecasts for 2008 especially with strengthening competition from Oracle.

37599 ■ *"Wind Point Partners Closes Southfield HQ" in Crain's Detroit Business (Vol. 26, January 18, 2010, No. 3, pp. 18)*
Pub: Crain Communications Inc.
Contact: Rance E. Crain, President
Ed: Tom Henderson. **Description:** Wind Point Partners, a private-equity firm that expanded its headquarters to Southfield in 1997, has closed down its Michigan operations opting to move its headquarters back to Illinois.

37600 ■ *Wine Investment for Portfolio Diversification: How Collecting Fine Wines Can Yield Greater Returns than Stocks and Bonds*
Pub: Wine Appreciation Guild
Contact: Jeff Szczesney, Contact
E-mail: jeff@wineappreciation.com
Ed: Mahesh Kumar. **Price:** $45, hardbound. **Description:** Analysis of the performance of investments in fine wines, particularly Bordeaux, is presented. History verifies that wine has traditionally been a sound investment offering a higher expected return over the market relative to its overall contribution of risk. Wine can be used as an effective means of diversifying one's portfolio.

37601 ■ *"WNY Cashing In On Loonie's Climb" in Business First Buffalo (November 26, 2007, pp. 1)*
Pub: American City Business Journals, Inc.
Ed: G. Scott Thomas. **Description:** Economy of Western New York has rebounded since the 9/11 recession and the rise of the Canadian dollar, which has contributed to the areas economic growth. Canadian shoppers are frequenting markets in the area due to the parity of the U.S. and Canadian dollar. Details of the cross-border shopping and its impact in WNY are discussed.

37602 ■ *"Wobbling Economy has a KC Wary" in The Business Journal-Serving Metropolitan Kansas City (Vol. 27, September 26, 2008, No. 2, pp. 1)*
Pub: American City Business Journals, Inc.
Contact: Whitney Shaw, President
Ed: Rob Roberts. **Description:** Real estate developers in Kansas City Metropolitan Area are worried of the possible impacts of the crisis at Wall Street. They expect tightening of the credit market, which will result in difficulty of financing their projects. The potential effects of the Wall Street crisis are examined further.

37603 ■ *The Working Man and Woman's Guide to Becoming a Millionaire*
Pub: Prentiss Publishing
Ed: Al Herron. **Released:** November 2006. **Description:** President and CEO of a Century 21 office in Dallas, Texas shares insight into financial security and commitment to community.

37604 ■ *Working Papers, Chapters 1-14 for Needles/Powers/Crosson's Financial and Managerial Accounting*
Pub: Cengage South-Western
Ed: Belverd E. Needles, Marian Powers, Susan V. Crosson. **Released:** May 10, 2010. **Price:** $62.95. **Description:** Appropriate accounting forms for completing all exercises, problems and cases in the text are provided for financial management of a small company.

37605 ■ *"A World of Opportunity: Foreign Markets Offer Diversity to Keen Investors"* in *Canadian Business (Vol. 81, Summer 2008, No. 9)*
Ed: Andrew Wahl. **Description:** International Monetary Fund projected in its 'World Economy Outlook' that there is a 25 percent chance that a global recession will occur in 2008 and 2009. Global growth rate is forecasted at 3.7 percent in 2008. Inflation in Asia emerging markets and forecasts on stock price indexes are presented.

37606 ■ *"World's Best CEOs"* in *Barron's (Vol. 88, March 24, 2008, No. 12, pp. 33)*
Pub: Dow Jones & Co., Inc.
Contact: Clare Hart, President
Ed: Andrew Bary. **Description:** Listing of the 30 best chief executive officers worldwide which was compiled through interviews with investors and analysts, analysis of financial and stock market performance, and leadership and industry stature.

37607 ■ *The Worst-Case Scenario Business Survival Guide: How to Survive the Recession, Handle Layoffs, Raise Emergency Cash, Thwart an Employee Coup, and Avoid Other Potential Disasters*
Pub: John Wiley & Sons Inc.
Contact: Stephen M. Smith, President
Ed: David Borgenicht, Mark Joyner. **Released:** September 28, 2009. **Price:** $17.95. **Description:** Since 1999, the Worst-Case Scenario survival handbooks have provided readers with real answers for the most extreme situations. Now, in a time of economic crisis, the series returns with a new, real-world guide to avoiding the worst business cataclysms.

37608 ■ *"The Worst Lies Ahead for Wall Street: More Losses Certain; More Expensive Capital to Be Needed"* in *Crain's New York Business (Vol. 24, January 20, 2008, No. 3, pp. 1)*
Pub: Crain Communications Inc.
Contact: Rance Crain, President
Ed: Aaron Elstein. **Description:** Due to the weakening economy, many financial institutions will face further massive losses forcing them to borrow more at higher interest rates and dragging down their earnings for years to come. The effects on commercial real estate and credit card loans are also discussed as well as the trend to investing in Asia and the Middle East.

37609 ■ *"Wyse Transforms Digital Signage, In-Store Advertising and Retail Kiosks With Cloud Client Computing"* in *Internet Wire (February 1, 2012)*
Released: February 1, 2012. **Description:** Wyse Technology is providing cloud computing services instead of PCs to power their customers' digital signage, in-store advertising and retail kiosks. Wyse is a world leader in cloud client computing is applauded for the security, reliability, affordability, sustainability and ease of use from their customers that include banks, retailers, airports and universities and more.

37610 ■ *"Yahoo! - Microsoft Pact: Alive Again?"* in *Barron's (Vol. 89, July 27, 2009, No. 30, pp. 8)*
Pub: Dow Jones & Co., Inc.
Contact: Clare Hart, President
Ed: Mark Veverka. **Description:** Yahoo! reported higher than expected earnings in the second quarter of 2009 under CEO Carol Bartz who has yet to articulate her long-term vision and strategy for turning around the company. The media reported that Yahoo! and Microsoft are discussing an advertising-search partnership which should benefit both companies.

37611 ■ *"YoCream"* in *Ice Cream Reporter (Vol. 23, September 20, 2010, No. 10, pp. 6)*
Description: YoCream reported a sales increase for third quarter 2010 at 15.6 percent and net income increasing 25 percent to $2,141,000 for that quarter.

37612 ■ *"You Won't Go Broke Filling Up On The Stock"* in *Barron's (Vol. 88, July 14, 2008, No. 28, pp. 38)*
Pub: Dow Jones & Co., Inc.
Contact: Clare Hart, President
Ed: Assif Shameen. **Description:** Due to high economic growth, pro-business policies and a consumption boom, the Middle East is a good place to look for equities. The best ways in which to gain exposure to this market include investing in the real estate industry and telecommunications markets as well as large banks that serve corporations and consumers.

37613 ■ *Young Bucks: How to Raise a Future Millionaire*
Pub: Aylesbury Publishing
Ed: Troy Dunn. **Released:** November 13, 2007. **Price:** $19.95, Hardcover. **Description:** Advice is given to parents to teach their children how to save money, invest wisely and even start their own business. **Availability:** Print.

37614 ■ *"Young People Speak Out On Credit Union Board Involvement"* in *Credit Union Times (Vol. 21, July 14, 2010, No. 27, pp. 20)*
Pub: Summit Professional Networks
Contact: Steve Weitzner, President
Ed: Myriam DiGiovanni. **Description:** Results of a Credit Union Times survey of Generation Y individuals about serving on Credit Union boards across the country are examined.

37615 ■ *"Your 2010 Windfall"* in *Small Business Opportunities (July 2010)*
Pub: Harris Publications Inc.
Description: Make this a year of fiscal health and wealth. A survey says most will strive to save this year.

37616 ■ *"Your Exposure to Bear Stearns"* in *Barron's (Vol. 88, March 17, 2008, No. 11, pp. 45)*
Pub: Dow Jones & Co., Inc.
Contact: Clare Hart, President
Ed: Tom Sullivan, Jack Willoughby. **Description:** Bear Stearns makes up 5.5 percent of Pioneer Independence's portfolio, 1.4 percent of Vanguard Windsor II's portfolio, 1.2 percent of Legg Mason Value Trust, about 1 percent of Van Kampen Equity & Income, and 0.79 percent of Putnam Fund for Growth & Income. Ginnie Mae securities are now trading at 1.78 percentage points over treasuries due to the mortgage crises.

37617 ■ *Your Guide to Arranging Bank & Debt Financing for Your Own Business in Canada*
Pub: Productive Publications
Contact: Iain Williamson, Manager
Ed: Iain Williamson. **Released:** August 2013. **Price:** C$81.95, softcover. **Description:** Bank financing for small businesses in Canada is discussed. **Availability:** Print.

37618 ■ *Your Guide to Canadian Export Financing: Successful Techniques for Financing Your Exports from Canada*
Pub: Productive Publications
Contact: Iain Williamson, Manager
Ed: Iain Williamson. **Released:** August 2013. **Price:** C$59.95, softcover. **Description:** Canadian export financing is covered. **Availability:** Print.

37619 ■ *Your Guide to Preparing a Plan to Raise Money for Your Own Business*
Pub: Productive Publications
Contact: Iain Williamson, Manager
Ed: Iain Williamson. **Released:** August 2013. **Price:** C$46.95, softcover. **Description:** A good business plan is essential for raising money for any small business. **Availability:** Print.

37620 ■ *"Zions Offers Step-by-Step Small Business Guidance"* in *Idaho Business Review (September 1, 2014)*
Pub: Dolan Co.
Contact: James P. Dolan, President
Released: September 15, 2014. **Description:** Zions bank provides small business guidance to clients through its Zions Bank Idaho Business Resource

Center. The program helps entrepreneurs learn the basic rules of running a small business. Free courses teach the essentials of finance, marketing and selling, .

TRADE PERIODICALS

37621 ■ *CFO & Controller Alert*
Pub: American Future Systems Inc.
Contact: Tom Schubert, Manager
E-mail: tschubert@pbp.com
URL(s): www.pbp.com/divisions/publishing/newsletters/financial-management/cfo-controller-alert/. **Ed:** John Hiatt, Editor, hiatt@pbp.com. **Released:** Semi-monthly; 23/yr. **Price:** $299, Individuals. **Description:** Assists busy financial executives to boost cash flow, control expenses, manage resources, and comply with changing regulations. Recurring features include case studies, success stories, financial and tax developments, cost-saving ideas and columns titled Management and Sharpen Your Judgment.

37622 ■ *Financial Services Review: The Journal of Individual Financial Management*
Pub: Cadmus Journal Services
URL(s): academyfinancial.org/financial-services-review/. **Ed:** Stuart Michelson. **Released:** Quarterly **Price:** Included in membership.

37623 ■ *Financial Studies of the Small Business*
Pub: Financial Research Association Inc.
Contact: Karen E. Klein, Manager
URL(s): aern.cba.ua.edu. **Released:** Annual

37624 ■ *Quarterly Journal of Finance and Accounting*
Pub: University of Nebraska
Contact: James B. Milliken, President
URL(s): www.qjbe.unl.edu. **Ed:** Robert R. Johnson. **Released:** Quarterly **Price:** $35, Individuals; $55, Institutions; $47, Other countries; $65, Institutions, other countries.

VIDEOCASSETTES/ AUDIOCASSETTES

37625 ■ *Accounting and Finance for Non-Financial Managers*
SmartPros Ltd.
12 Skyline Dr.
Hawthorne, NY 10532-2133
Ph: (914)345-2620
Co. E-mail: admin@smartpros.com
URL: http://www.smartpros.com
Contact: Jack Fingerhut, President
Released: 1986. **Description:** This tape shows non-financial executives how to handle and process business finances. **Availability:** VHS; 3/4 U.

37626 ■ *American Institute of Small Business: Your Personal Financial Guide to Success, Power & Security*
American Institute of Small Business (AISB)
23075 Hwy. 7, Ste. 200
Shorewood, MN 55331-3168
Ph: (952)545-7001
Free: 800-328-2906
Fax: (952)545-7020
Co. E-mail: info@aisb.biz
URL: http://www.aisb.biz
Contact: Kris Solie-Johnson, President
E-mail: kris@aisb.biz
Released: 199?. **Price:** $69.95. **Description:** Covers money management, financial planning, budgeting, record keeping, and spending and savings plans. **Availability:** VHS.

37627 ■ *Corporate Financial Management: Emerging Trends and Recent Developments*
Bisk Education
9417 Princess Palm Ave.
Tampa, FL 33619

Free: 800-874-7877
URL: http://www.bisk.com
Contact: William D. Feinberg, Contact
Released: 19??. **Price:** $179. **Description:** Discusses financial management techniques and recent developments in corporate finance. Furnishes information on Activity-Based Cost Management (ABC), Total Quality Management (TQM), and Internal Controls and Management Accounting. Includes workbook and quizzer. **Availability:** VHS.

37628 ■ Financial Success Strategies for the 1990s
Films Media Group of Cos.
132 W 31st St., 17th Fl.
New York, NY 10001-3406
Ph: (609)671-1000
Free: 800-257-5126
Fax: (609)671-0266
Co. E-mail: custserv@films.com
URL: http://www.cambridgeeducational.com
Contact: David Waldherr, President
Released: 1992. **Price:** $99. **Description:** Best-selling financial author Charles J. Givens gives advice that could save or earn viewers thousands of dollars. **Availability:** VHS.

37629 ■ Money in America
Ambrose Video Publishing, Inc.
145 W. 45th St., Ste. 1115
New York, NY 10036
Ph: (212)768-7373
Free: 800-526-4663
Fax: (212)768-9282
Co. E-mail: customerservice@ambrosevideo.com
URL: http://www.ambrosevideo.com
Contact: William Ambrose, President
Released: 1989. **Price:** $795. **Description:** A video series which explains everything about banks and banking. **Availability:** VHS.

37630 ■ Reading Financial Reports: The Income Statement
Phoenix Learning Group
2349 Chaffee Dr.
Saint Louis, MO 63146-3306
Ph: (314)569-0211
Free: 800-221-1274
Fax: (314)569-2834
URL: http://www.phoenixlearninggroup.com
Released: 1985. **Description:** An explanation of the income statement-how to read it and use it. **Availability:** VHS; 3/4 U; Special order formats.

37631 ■ Return on Investment
Video Arts, Inc.
c/o Aim Learning Group
8238-40 Lehigh
Morton Grove, IL 60053-2615
Free: 877-444-2230
Fax: (416)252-2155
Co. E-mail: service@aimlearninggroup.com
URL: http://www.aimlearninggroup.com
Released: 1986. **Price:** $790. **Description:** For the business owner, a look at assessing and justifying capital expenditures. **Availability:** VHS; 8 mm; 3/4 U; Special order formats.

TRADE SHOWS AND CONVENTIONS

37632 ■ ABA/BMA National Conference for Community Bankers
American Bankers Association (ABA)
1120 Connecticut Ave. NW
Washington, DC 20036
Ph: (202)663-5268
Free: 800-226-5377
Fax: (202)828-5053
Co. E-mail: custserv@aba.com
URL: http://www.aba.com
Contact: Frank Keating, President
URL(s): www.aba.com/Training/Conferences/Pages/community.aspx. **Frequency:** Annual. **Audience:** Chairmen and presidents, community bank CEOs, bank directors, and other community bank executives. **Principal Exhibits:** Products and services

related to investment management, customer service improvements, advertising, asset/liability management, bank management, electronic data interchange, employee recruitment/training, insurance, strategic planning models, including preparation for the 21st century, new revenue sources, cost control techniques, mainframe computers, market research, MCIF technology, minicomputers in community banking applications, software: platform, optical disk, and loan pricing, sweep accounts, and relationship banking for community bankers.

37633 ■ Financial Managers Society Annual Conference
Financial Managers Society (FMS)
1 N La Salle St., Ste. 3100
Chicago, IL 60602-4003
Ph: (312)578-1300
Free: 800-275-4367
Fax: (312)578-1308
Co. E-mail: info@fmsinc.org
URL: http://www.fmsinc.org
Contact: Dick Yingst, President
E-mail: dyingst@fmsinc.org
URL(s): www.fmsinc.org. **Audience:** Financial managers. **Principal Exhibits:** Companies offering products/services to CEOs, CFOs, treasurers, controllers, investment officers, and internal auditors of banks, thrifts, and credit unions. **Telecommunication Services:** info@fmsinc.org.

37634 ■ Marketing and Retail Conference
American Bankers Association (ABA)
1120 Connecticut Ave. NW
Washington, DC 20036
Ph: (202)663-5268
Free: 800-226-5377
Fax: (202)828-5053
Co. E-mail: custserv@aba.com
URL: http://www.aba.com
Contact: Frank Keating, President
URL(s): www.aba.com/Training/Conferences/Pages/MKTG.aspx. **Frequency:** Annual. **Audience:** Bankers including community bank CEOs, marketing directors, sales managers, advertising directors, and public relations managers. **Principal Exhibits:** Financial services marketing offering banking solutions in advertising services, bank equipment/systems, computer software, database marketing, direct marketing/sales, incentive/premium programs, insurance services, investment services, marketing consulting, merchandising, publishing, research, retail delivery, sales training, service quality, signage, and telemarketing. **Dates and Locations:** 2015 Oct 04-06; venue not reported.

37635 ■ National Agricultural Bankers Conference
American Bankers Association (ABA)
1120 Connecticut Ave. NW
Washington, DC 20036
Ph: (202)663-5268
Free: 800-226-5377
Fax: (202)828-5053
Co. E-mail: custserv@aba.com
URL: http://www.aba.com
Contact: Frank Keating, President
URL(s): www.aba.com. **Frequency:** Annual. **Audience:** Bank CEOs, mainly from community banks in rural areas, executive vice presidents, senior vice presidents, economists, analysts. **Principal Exhibits:** The latest developments in the agricultural lending business, as well as strategies for better market share, profitability and customer service. **Telecommunication Services:** jblanchf@aba.com.

37636 ■ Wealth Management and Trust Conference
American Bankers Association (ABA)
1120 Connecticut Ave. NW
Washington, DC 20036
Ph: (202)663-5268
Free: 800-226-5377

Fax: (202)828-5053
Co. E-mail: custserv@aba.com
URL: http://www.aba.com
Contact: Frank Keating, President
URL(s): www.aba.com/Training/Conferences/Pages/WMT.aspx. **Frequency:** Annual. **Audience:** Trust, private banking and asset management officers, bank brokerage managers, sales managers, business development managers, and regional department managers. **Principal Exhibits:** Events for the wealth management and trust banking community. **Dates and Locations:** 2015 Mar 01-03, Hyatt Regency Grand Cypress, Orlando, FL.

CONSULTANTS

37637 ■ 2010 Fund 5
24351 Spartan St.
Mission Viejo, CA 92691-3920
Ph: (949)583-1992
Fax: (949)583-0474
Contact: Wally Eater, Principal
Scope: Funds in formation that will invest in technologies licensed from 30 universities. **Founded:** 1982.

37638 ■ ADG Group
4261 Northside Dr. NW, Ste. 200
Atlanta, GA 30327-3647
Ph: (404)264-9301
Fax: (404)261-3439
Contact: Cameron Adair, Chairman of the Board
E-mail: camadair@aol.com
Scope: Corporate finance advisory firm specializing in arranging venture capital financing for emerging companies. Assists with mergers, acquisitions and divestitures. Offers balance sheet restructuring services for bankrupt and financially troubled companies. Also offers independent due diligence investigations. **Founded:** 1986.

37639 ■ Aurora Management Partners Inc.
4485 Tench Rd., Ste. 340
Suwanee, GA 30024
Ph: (770)904-5209
Fax: (770)904-5226
Co. E-mail: rturcotte@auroramp.com
URL: http://www.auroramp.com
Contact: Laura C. Kendall, Director
E-mail: lkendall@auroramp.com
Scope: Specializes in turnaround management and reorganization consulting. Firm develop strategic initiatives, organize and analyze solutions, deal with creditor issues, review organizational structure and develop time frames for decision making. Turnaround services offered include Recovery plans and their implementation, Viability analysis, Crisis management, Financial restructuring, Corporate and organizational restructuring, Facilities rationalization, Liquidation management, Loan workout, Litigation support and Expert testimony, Contract renegotiation, Sourcing loan refinancing and Sourcing equity investment. **Founded:** 2005. **Publications:** "TMA Turnaround of the Year Award, Small Company, Honorable Mention," Nov, 2005; "Back From The Brink - Bland Farms," Progressive Farmer, Oct, 2004; "New Breed of Turnaround Managers," Catalyst Magazine, Aug, 2004; "Key Performance Drivers - Bland Farms," The Produce News, Apr, 2004; "Corporate Governance: Averting Crisis's Before They Happen," ABJ journal, Feb, 2004.

37640 ■ Beacon Management - Management Consultants
1000 W McNab Rd.
Pompano Beach, FL 33069
Ph: (954)782-1119
Co. E-mail: md@beaconmgmt.com
URL: http://www.beaconmgmt.com
Contact: Barbara L. Donnelly, Director
E-mail: bdonnelly@browardhealth.org
Scope: Specializes in change management, organized workplaces, multicultural negotiations and dispute resolutions and internet based decision making. **Founded:** 1985. **Publications:** "Sun-Sentinel Article," Oct, 2012.

37641 ■ Benchmark Consulting Group Inc.
[Benchmark Advisors]
283 Franklin St., Ste. 400
Boston, MA 02110-3100
Ph: (617)482-7661
Contact: Walter E. Robb, III, President
E-mail: werobb35@aol.com
Scope: Provides financial and management services to companies. Helps companies grow through debt, equity sourcing and restructuring, business valuation, acquisition and divestiture, computer information systems and improved operation profitability. **Founded:** 1978.

37642 ■ Samuel E. Bodily Associates
172, 100 Darden Blvd.
Charlottesville, VA 22903
Ph: (434)924-4813
Fax: (434)243-7677
Contact: Samuel E. Bodily, Principal
E-mail: bodilys@virginia.edu
Scope: Consultant specializes in financial analysis, capital investment, business/product/market planners, financial risk analysis and decision sciences. **Founded:** 1977. **Publications:** "I Can't Get No Satisfaction: How Bundling and Multi-Part Pricing Can Satisfy Consumers and Suppliers," Feb, 2006; "Organizational Use of Decision Analysis," Oct, 2004; "Real Options," Oct, 2004.

37643 ■ The Business Guide Inc.
Torbay Rd.
Saint John, NL, Canada A1A 5B8
Free: 877-754-8433
Fax: (709)754-8434
Co. E-mail: info@businessguide.net
URL: http://www.businessguide.net
Contact: Sharon Monahan, President
E-mail: sharon@businessguide.net
Scope: Assists private sector firms in acquiring financial assistance to start or expand a business. **Founded:** 1998. **Publications:** "Accessing Government Funding".

37644 ■ CBIZ Inc.
6050 Oak Tree Blvd. S, Ste. 500
Cleveland, OH 44131
Ph: (216)525-1947
Fax: (216)447-9007
URL: http://www.cbizinc.com
Contact: David J. Sibits, President
Scope: A business consulting and tax services firm providing financial, consulting, tax and business services through seven groups: Financial management, tax advisory, construction and real estate, health-care, litigation support, capital resource and CEO outsource. **Founded:** 1996. **Publications:** "FAS 154: Changes in the Way We Report Changes," 2006; "Equity-Based Compensation: How Much Does it Really Cost Your Business," 2006; "Preventing Fraud - Tips for Nonprofit Organizations"; "Today's Workforce and Nonprofit Organizations: Meeting a Critical Need"; "IRS Highlights Top Seven Form 990 Errors". **Seminars:** Health Care - What the Future Holds; Consumer Driven Health Plans; Executive Plans; Health Savings Accounts; Healthy Wealthy and Wise; Legislative Update; Medicare Part D; Retirement Plans.

37645 ■ C.C. Comfort Consulting
3370 N Hayden Rd., Ste. 123-127
Scottsdale, AZ 85251
Ph: (480)483-8364
Contact: Clifton C. Comfort, Jr., Principal
Scope: Evaluates, develops and implements financial, operational and compliance management systems strategies, programs and practices. Has professional recognition as certified public accountant, internal auditor, cost analyst and fraud examiner plus investigatory, law enforcement and court experience ensure confidential handling of sensitive and legal matters. Works with management, audit, legal, security and outside personnel to evaluate and improve compliance, efficiency and effectiveness. **Founded:** 1983.

37646 ■ Chartered Management Co.
10 S Riverside Plz., Ste. 1800
Chicago, IL 60606

Ph: (312)214-2575
Contact: William B. Avellone, President
Scope: Operations improvement consultants. Specializes in strategic planning; feasibility studies; management audits and reports; profit enhancement; start-up businesses; mergers and acquisitions; joint ventures; divestitures; interim management; crisis management; turnarounds; business process re-engineering; venture capital; and due diligence. **Founded:** 1985.

37647 ■ Clayton/Curtis/Cottrell
1722 Madison Ct.
Louisville, CO 80027-1121
Ph: (303)665-2005
Contact: Robert Cottrell, President
Scope: Market research firm specializes in providing consultations for packaged goods, telecommunications, direct marketing and printing and packaging industries. Services include strategic planning; profit enhancement; startup businesses; mergers and acquisitions; joint ventures; divestitures; interim management; crisis management; turnarounds; market size, segmentation and rates of growth; competitor intelligence; image and reputation and competitive analysis. **Founded:** 1981. **Publications:** "Turn an attitude into a purchase," Jul, 1995; "Mixed results for private label; price assaults by the national brands are getting heavy, but there's still a place for private label," Jun, 1995; "In-store promotion goes high-tech: is the conventional coupon destined for obsolescence?," Jun, 1995.

37648 ■ John Alan Cohan
433 N Camden Dr., Ste. 600
Beverly Hills, CA 90210
Ph: (310)278-0203
Free: 888-903-7512
Fax: (310)859-8656
Co. E-mail: johnalancohan@aol.com
URL: http://www.johnalancohan.com
Contact: John Alan Cohan, President
E-mail: johnalancohan@aol.com
Scope: Consultant assists in the development of business plans for startups in the fields of livestock, horses, farming, or aviation. Also provides tax consultations and tax opinion letters to support deductions. **Founded:** 1981.

37649 ■ Colmen Menard Company Inc.
(CMCI)
The Woods, 994 Old Eagle School Rd., Ste. 1000
Wayne, PA 19087
Ph: (484)367-0300
Fax: (484)367-0305
Co. E-mail: cmci@colmenmenard.com
URL: http://www.colmenmenard.com
Contact: David W. Menard, President
E-mail: dmenard@colmenmenard.com
Scope: Merger and acquisition corporate finance and business advisory services for public and private companies located in North America. **Founded:** 1982. **Publications:** "Success in Selling a Troubled Company," Nov, 2002; "Savvy Dealmakers," May, 2001; "Success in Selling a Troubled Company feature article from The Technology Times bimonthly newspaper," Apr, 2002; "Truisms," M&A Today, Nov, 2000.

37650 ■ Community Development Consulting
73 Michelle Ave.
Cotuit, MA 02635-2429
Ph: (508)420-9661
Fax: (508)420-4444
Co. E-mail: bobibanez@comcast.net
Contact: Robert Ibanez, Executive
Scope: A consulting practice offering business planning, financial management, organizational assessments and capital formation to non-profit, community development organizations. **Founded:** 2001.

37651 ■ Comprehensive Business Services
3201 Lucas Cir.
Lafayette, CA 94549
Ph: (925)283-8272

Fax: (925)283-8272
Contact: Walter H. Diebold, President
Scope: Business/financial consultants with related experience in marketing, finance, organization, business planning and profit development. Industries served include construction, manufacturing and wholesale. **Founded:** 1985.

37652 ■ Comprehensive Professional
Management Inc.
222 E Dundee Rd.
Wheeling, IL 60090-3009
Ph: (847)520-1301
Contact: M. Katherine Stumpf, Owner
E-mail: mkstumpf@aol.com
Scope: Services include accounting, financial planning, litigation support, pension profit sharing administration, practice surveys, professional corporation issues, retirement and estate planning and tax advice.

37653 ■ Controlled Resources
1021 E 1st Ave., Apt. 822
Broomfield, CO 80020
Ph: (708)798-2978
Fax: (727)532-3955
Scope: Firm offers business and management consultancy services.

37654 ■ Corporate Consulting Inc.
3333 Belcaro Dr.
Denver, CO 80209-4912
Ph: (303)698-9292
Contact: Gray Josephs, Manager
Scope: Specializes in feasibility studies, organizational development, small business management, mergers and acquisitions, joint ventures, divestitures, interim management, crisis management, turnarounds, financing, appraisals valuations and due diligence studies. **Founded:** 1983.

37655 ■ Crystal Clear Communications Inc.
1633 W Winslow Dr., Ste. 210
Mequon, WI 53092
Ph: (262)240-0072
Fax: (262)240-0073
Co. E-mail: barbwoods@crystalclear1.com
URL: http://www.crystalclear1.com
Contact: Barry J. Moze, Partner
E-mail: barrymoze@crystalclearl.com
Scope: Services: Management consulting and executive coaching. **Founded:** 1986. **Publications:** "Weakest Link"; "Aware Leadership"; "Integrity"; "When Your Plate is Full"; "Problem Solving"; "Strategic Thinking".

37656 ■ Effective Compensation Inc. (ECI)
30792 Southview Dr., Ste. 101
Evergreen, CO 80439
Ph: (303)854-1000
Free: 877-746-4324
Fax: (303)854-1030
Co. E-mail: eci@effectivecompensation.com
URL: http://www.effectivecompensation.com
Contact: Kathleen Piper, Vice President, Technical Services
Scope: Independent compensation consulting firm specializing in working with clients on a collaborative basis to improve their organization's efficiency through competitive, focused total compensation processes. Helps organizations determine how to competitively pay their employees. Provides quality, culture sensitive, compensation consulting assistance to all types of employers. Specializes in surveys like drilling industry compensation surveys, environmental industry compensation surveys, liquid pipeline round table compensation surveys; and oil and gas E and P industry compensation surveys. **Founded:** 1991. **Publications:** "Alternative Job Evaluation Approaches"; "Broad Banding: A Management Overview"; "Job Evaluation: Understanding the Issues"; "Industry Compensation Surveys"; "Skill Based Pay"; "Four Levels of Team Membership"; "Factors in Designing an Incentive Plan"; "Key Stock Allocation Issues"; "Stock Plans Primer". **Seminars:** Alternative Job Evaluation Approaches; Broad Banding: A Management Overview; Skill Based Pay; Job Evalua-

tion: Understanding the Issues; Designing Compensation Programs that Motivate Employees; Master the Compensation Maze; Base Salary Administration Manual.

37657 ■ Everett & Co.
3126 S Franklin St.
Englewood, CO 80113
Ph: (303)761-7999
Contact: Peter C. Everett, Owner
Scope: Provides strategic real estate solutions and project management. **Founded:** 1993.

37658 ■ Steven S. Feinbert
412 Beacon St.
Boston, MA 02115
Ph: (617)247-2881
Fax: (617)247-2881
Scope: Offers small business consulting with emphasis on budgeting and financial management needs of small manufacturing firms. Also offers plant layout and work simplification services. Serves private industries. **Founded:** 1980.

37659 ■ Financial Management Solutions Inc. (FMSI)
1720 Windward Condourse, Ste. 200
Alpharetta, GA 30005-1727
Ph: (770)619-3443
Free: 877-887-3022
Fax: (770)619-3095
Co. E-mail: gordonw@fmsi.com
URL: http://www.fmsi.com
Contact: Walter M. Scott, President
Scope: Provider of staff models, industry comparative and benchmark data, measurement and monitoring systems. Also offers data processing evaluations, process improvements and operational reviews. They have also developed resource management and sales management systems. Industries served: communications, banking, insurance, retail. **Founded:** 1990. **Publications:** "Teller Management System and Empowered Process Improvement". **Seminars:** Staff Productivity: Effective Use of Databases to Improve Performance and Statistical Models - the New Wave of Management; Micro-Analysis process to Profitability in the Financial Services Industry. **Special Services:** The Teller Management System™; The Resource ManagementSystem™; The Sales Management System™.

37660 ■ The Foster Group Inc.
180 N Stetson, Ste. 3470
Chicago, IL 60601
Ph: (312)609-1009
Fax: (312)609-1109
Co. E-mail: info@thefostergroup.com
URL: http://www.thefostergroup.com
Contact: John L. Foster, Jr., Managing Partner
E-mail: rpike@thefostergroup.com
Scope: Offers information systems and data security, financial accounting services, and management consulting. **Founded:** 1986.

37661 ■ Frankel and Topche P.C.
1700 Galloping Hill Rd.
Kenilworth, NJ 07033
Ph: (908)298-7700
Fax: (908)298-7701
Co. E-mail: info@frankelandtopche.com
URL: http://www.frankelandtopche.com
Contact: Lawrence N. Frankel, Owner
E-mail: lnfcpa@aol.com
Scope: Offers financial consulting for closely held businesses. Assists in mergers and acquisitions, tax planning, strategic business planning, family succession planning, accounting, auditing and obtaining financing. The firm serves small businesses in the service, retail, wholesale and manufacturing industries. Specializes in real estate, lumber and building materials and service businesses. **Founded:** 1990. **Seminars:** Annual Tax Seminar.

37662 ■ Global Technology Transfer L.L.C.
1500 Dixie Hwy.
Park Hills, KY 41011-2819

Ph: (859)431-1262
Contact: Anthony Zembrodt, President
Scope: Firm specializes in product development; quality assurance; new product development; and total quality management focusing on household chemical specialties, especially air fresheners. Utilizes latest technology from global resources. Specializes in enhancement products for home and automobile. **Founded:** 1992.

37663 ■ Joseph Goldsten & Associates Inc.
401 Jackson Ave.
Lexington, VA 24450-1905
Ph: (540)463-4593
Contact: Joseph Goldsten, President
Scope: Offers counsel to financial institutions, corporations and individuals on planning, financial management, new ventures, small business development, investment counseling, real estate and banking. Active in mergers, acquisitions and valuations. Primarily clients: Financial institutions and manufacturers. **Founded:** 1996.

37664 ■ Gordian Concepts & Solutions
16 Blueberry Ln.
Lincoln, MA 01773-2210
Ph: (617)259-8341
Contact: Stephen R. Low, President
Scope: Engineering and management consultancy offering general, financial and valuation services, civil and tax litigation support. Assists clients in entering new businesses, planning new products and services and evaluating feasibility. Targets industrial concerns engaged in manufacturing, assembly, warehousing, energy production, process systems and biotechnology, steel, paper and electronics. Serves businesses such as retailing, financial services, health care, satellite broadcasting and cable television, outdoor advertising and professional practices. **Founded:** 1990. **Publications:** "Establishing Rural Cellular Company Values," Cellular Business.

37665 ■ Herpers Gowling L.L.P. [310 DEBT Herpers Chagani Gowling Inc.]
4 Hughson St. S, Ste. 300
Hamilton, ON, Canada L8N 3Z1
Ph: (905)529-3328
Free: 888-735-9909
Fax: (905)529-3980
Contact: David Gowling, President
E-mail: dgowling@herpersgowling.com
Scope: Provides services to small and medium size businesses in the areas of financial management, strategic planning, mergers and acquisitions and re-engineering/restructuring. **Founded:** 1996. **Special Services:** 310 DEBT®.

37666 ■ Hewitt Development Enterprises (HDE)
1717 N Bayshore Dr., Ste. 2154
Miami, FL 33132
Ph: (305)372-0941
Fax: (305)372-0941
Co. E-mail: info@hewittdevelopment.com
URL: http://www.hewittdevelopment.com
Contact: Robert G. Hewitt, Principal
E-mail: bob@hewittdevelopment.com
Scope: Specializes in strategic planning; profit enhancement; start-up businesses; interim management; crisis management; turnarounds; production planning; just-in-time inventory management; and project management. Serves senior management (CEOs, CFOs, division presidents, etc.) and acquirers of distressed businesses. **Founded:** 1985.

37667 ■ Hickey & Hill Inc.
1009 Oak Hill Rd., Ste. 201
Lafayette, CA 94549-3812
Ph: (925)283-7802
Contact: Edwin L. Hill, Chief Executive Officer
Scope: Firm provides management consulting services to companies in financial distress. Expertise area: Corporate restructuring and turnaround. **Founded:** 1984.

37668 ■ C. W. Hines and Associates Inc. [C&W Associates Inc.]
344 Churchill Cir., Sanctuary Bay
White Stone, VA 22578

Ph: (804)435-8844
Fax: (804)435-8855
Co. E-mail: turtlecwh@aol.com
URL: http://www.cwhinesassociates.org
Contact: William A. Hines, Jr., Vice President
Scope: Management consultants with expertise in the following categories: advertising and public relations; health and human resources; management sciences; organizational development; computer sciences; financial management; behavioral sciences; environmental design; technology transfer; project management; facility management; program evaluation; and business therapy. Also included are complementary areas such as sampling procedures; job training; managerial effectiveness; corporate seminars; gender harassment; training for trainers and leadership and management skills development. **Founded:** 1979. **Publications:** "Money Muscle, 120 Exercises To Build Spiritual And Financial Strength," 2004; "Inside Track: Executives Coaching Executives"; "Money Muscle: 122 Exercises to Build Financial Strength"; "Nuts and Bolts of Work Force Diversity"; "Legal Issues, published in the Controllers Business Advisor"; "Identifying Racism: Specific Examples"; "BOSS Spelled Backwards is double SSOB! Or is it?"; "A No-Nonsense Guide to Being Stressed". **Seminars:** Career Development; Coaching and Counseling for Work Success; Communicating More Effectively in a Diverse Work Environment; Communications 600: Advanced Skills for Relationship Building; Customer Service: Building a Caring Culture.

37669 ■ Hollingsworth & Associates
395 Wellington Rd. S, Ste. 101
London, ON, Canada N6C 5Z6
Ph: (519)649-2001
Fax: (519)649-7880
Co. E-mail: jack@hollingsworth.net
URL: http://www.appointmentquest.com/scheduler/ 2140113024
Contact: Jack Hollingsworth, President
E-mail: jack@hollingsworth.net
Scope: Acts as management accountants, tax and management consultants and offsite controllers. Consulting services include software selection and financial information systems. Accounting and tax preparation. **Founded:** 1993.

37670 ■ Holt Capital
1916 Pike Pl., Ste. 12-344
Seattle, WA 98101
Ph: (206)484-0403
Fax: (206)789-8034
Co. E-mail: info@holtcapital.com
URL: http://www.holtcapital.com
Contact: Marilyn J. Holt, Principal
Scope: Registered investment advisory firm. Services include: Debt planning, private equity, mergers, divestitures and acquisitions, transaction support services. Connects companies with capital. **Founded:** 1980. **Publications:** "Early Sales Key to Early-Stage Funding"; "Financial Transactions: Who Should Be At Your Table"; "Get the Deal Done: The Four Keys to Successful Mergers and Acquisitions"; "Is Your First Paragraph a Turn-off"; "Bubble Rubble: Bridging the Price Gap for an Early-Stage Business"; "Are You Ready For The new Economy"; "Could I Get Money or Jail Time With That The Sarbanes-Oxley Act Of 2002 gives early-stage companies More Risks". **Seminars:** Attracting Private Investors; Five Proven Ways to Finance Your Company; How to Get VC Financing; Venture Packaging; How to Finance Company Expansion.

37671 ■ Human Capital Research Corp. (HCRC)
1560 Sherman Ave., Ste. 1010
Evanston, IL 60201
Ph: (847)475-7580
Fax: (847)475-7584
URL: http://www.humancapital.com
Contact: Brian Zucker, President
Scope: provides colleges and universities with a wide range of services, including enrollment management, market development, long-term strategic planning, program evaluation, institutional research and learning outcomes assessment. **Founded:** 1991.

37672 ■ InfoSource Management Services Inc.
PO Box 590
Sicamous, BC, Canada V0E 2V0
Ph: (250)804-6113
Fax: (250)836-3667
Contact: Sherry Leggett, President
Scope: Firm provides customized financial reports that highlight the areas where change will improve the bottom line. Founded: 1995.

37673 ■ Integrated Financial Consultants
3625 Dufferin St., Ste. 340
Toronto, ON, Canada M3K 1Z2
Ph: (416)630-4000
Free: 800-263-4570
Fax: (416)630-4022
Co. E-mail: qfs@qfscanada.com
URL: http://www.qfscanada.com
Contact: Nick Simone, President
Scope: Designs and implements a financial plan for the shareholders partners of small businesses. Services include investment management, tax planning risk management in the form of structuring and funding shareholders agreements estate planning and creditor protection. Founded: 1999.

37674 ■ Interminds & Federer Resources Inc.
106 E 6th St., Ste. 310
Austin, TX 78701-3659
Ph: (512)476-8800
Co. E-mail: yesyoucan@interminds.com
URL: http://www.interminds.com
Contact: Frank Federer, President
E-mail: ffederer@integra100.com
Scope: Specializes in feasibility studies; startup businesses; small business management; mergers and acquisitions; joint ventures; divestitures; interim management; crisis management; turnarounds; production planning; team building; appraisals and valuations. Founded: 1985. Publications: "Yes You Can: How To Be A Success No Matter Who You Are Or Where You're From".

37675 ■ Johnston Co.
78 Bedford St.
Lexington, MA 02420
Ph: (781)862-7595
Fax: (781)862-9066
Co. E-mail: info@johnstoncompany.com
URL: http://www.johnstoncompany.com
Contact: Claire Sehringer, Chief Executive Officer
Scope: Services: Business consulting, financial management, strategic and advisory services. Founded: 1987. Publications: "Why are board meetings such a waste of time," Boston Business Journal, Apr, 2004.

37676 ■ Keiei Senryaku Corp.
19191 S Vermont Ave., Ste. 530
Torrance, CA 90502-1049
Ph: (310)366-3331
Fax: (310)366-3330
Contact: Kurt Miyamoto, President
Scope: Offers consulting services in the areas of strategic planning; feasibility studies; profit enhancement; organizational development; start-up businesses; mergers and acquisitions; joint ventures; divestitures; executive searches; sales management; and competitive analysis. Founded: 1989.

37677 ■ Charles A. Krueger [Scheree L. Krueger]
1908 Innsbrooke Dr.
Sun Prairie, WI 53590
Ph: (608)837-5247
Fax: (608)825-7538
Co. E-mail: ckrueger@bus.wisc.edu
Contact: Charles Krueger, Owner
Scope: Financial management consultant specializing in professional education programs for managers and executives. Programs include: Finance and accounting for nonfinancial executives, financial management for executives and developing and using financial information for decision making. Major industries served include manufacturing, service, healthcare and insurance. Founded: 1982. Publications: "Monitoring Financial Results, chapter in Corporate Controllers Manual," Warren Gorham and

Lamont. Seminars: Finance and Accounting for Non-financial Executives; Financial Management for Health Care Executives; Financial Management for Insurance Executives; Direct Costing; Flexible Budgeting; Contribution Reporting; Building Value and Driving Profits - A Business Simulation.

37678 ■ William E. Kuhn & Associates
234 Cook St.
Denver, CO 80206-5305
Ph: (303)322-8233
Fax: (303)331-9032
Scope: Firm specializes in strategic planning; profit enhancement; small business management; mergers and acquisitions; joint ventures; divestitures; human resources management; performance appraisals; team building; sales management; appraisals and valuations. Founded: 1980. Publications: "Creating a High-Performance Dealership," Office SOLUTIONS and Office DEALER, Jul-Aug, 2006.

37679 ■ LaCloche Manitoulin Business Assistance Corp.
30 Meredith St.
Gore Bay, ON, Canada P0P 1H0
Ph: (705)282-3215
Free: 800-461-5131
Fax: (705)282-2989
URL: http://www.lambac.org
Contact: John Foster, Principal
E-mail: louise@lambac.org
Scope: Encourages a strong, vibrant, sustainable, environmentally-friendly, business community through financial investment and support services. Founded: 1986. Publications: "Packed Panniers on Manitoulin," Sep, 2005; "One Wind Farm Gains License, Another Proposes 60 Windmills," Jul, 2005; "The Great Spirit Circle Trail," Jan, 2005.

37680 ■ Management Resource Partners
181 2nd Ave., Ste. 542
San Mateo, CA 94401
Ph: (650)401-5850
Contact: John C. Roberts, Partner
Scope: Firm specializes in strategic planning; small business management; mergers and acquisitions; joint ventures; divestitures; interim management; crisis management; turn around; venture capital; appraisals and valuations. Founded: 1981.

37681 ■ McShane Group L.L.C.
2345 York Rd., Ste. 102
Timonium, MD 21093
Ph: (410)560-0077
Fax: (410)560-2718
URL: http://www.mcshanegroup.com
Contact: Thomas P. McShane, President
E-mail: tmcshane@mcshanegroup.com
Scope: Turnaround consulting and crisis management firm. Specializes in due diligence services; interim management, strategic business realignments, business sale and asset depositions and debt restructuring. Industries served: technology, financial, retail, distribution, medical, educational, manufacturing, contracting, environmental and health care. Founded: 1987.

37682 ■ Mefford, Knutson & Associates Inc. (MK)
6437 Lyndale Ave. S, Ste. 103
Richfield, MN 55423-1465
Ph: (612)869-8011
Free: 800-831-0228
Fax: (612)869-8004
Co. E-mail: info@mkaonline.net
URL: http://www.mkaonline.net
Contact: Sally Knutson, Director
Scope: A consulting and licensed business brokerage firm specializing in start-up businesses; strategic planning; mergers and acquisitions; joint ventures; divestitures; business process re-engineering; personnel policies and procedures; market research; new product development and cost controls. Founded: 1990.

37683 ■ Merrimac Associates Inc.
190 N Evergreen Ave., Ste. 100
Woodbury, NJ 08096-1862
Ph: (856)428-4350

Free: 888-777-5215
Fax: (856)848-7770
Co. E-mail: mo@merrimac.com
Contact: David B. Shaffer, President
E-mail: dbs@merrimac.com
Scope: Offers financial management consulting to help with financial problems of small or medium sized businesses of any type on a long or short term basis. Assists with a wide variety of management problems. Founded: 1992. Special Services: XtremePM™.

37684 ■ Metro Accounting Services Inc.
167 Oxmoor Blvd.
Homewood, AL 35209
Ph: (205)916-0900
Fax: (205)945-1784
Co. E-mail: info@metroaccountingservice.com
URL: http://www.metroaccountingservice.com
Contact: James Waligora, President
E-mail: jim@metroaccountingservice.com
Scope: Consults on tax planning, retirement planning, investment analysis and personal financial planning on a fee basis for individuals and small businesses and on real estate partnerships. Also specializes in employee benefit analysis, pension investment analysis and investment management for small businesses. Founded: 1982. Seminars: How to Win the Money Game; Using Mutual Funds for Financial Independence; IRA's, Keogh and Other Retirement Plans; How to Quit Paying Income Taxes. Special Services: IRS problem solving, Quick Books® installation and training.

37685 ■ Miller/Cook & Associates Inc.
20 Marco Lake Dr., Ste. 12
Marco Island, FL 34145-3644
Ph: (239)394-5040
Free: 800-591-1141
Fax: (239)394-2652
Co. E-mail: info@millercook.com
URL: http://www.millercook.com
Contact: William B. Miller, President
Scope: Specializes in all areas of enrollment management, admissions and financial aid. Involves in institutional and enrollment analysis, strategic positioning/institutional image, enrollment integration/operation, re-recruitment, financial aid and planning, integrated communications, training and workshops and on-site management. Founded: 1988. Publications: "Capital gains: Surviving in an increasingly for profit world"; "Making steps to a brighter future". Seminars: Admissions: An overview of a changing profession; Admission practices: Managing the admissions office; Admission practices: Internal operations often make the difference; Effective communication and the enrollment process; Telemarketing or Tele counseling: How to use the telephone to effectively enroll and re-enroll students; Graduate and professional program recruitment: An overview Re-Recruitment: What is it? Is it necessary?; The effective use of electronic mediums in the recruitment process; The use of alumni to support and sustain your recruiting efforts.

37686 ■ Mitchell and Titus L.L.P. [Mitchell/Titus]
1 Battery Park Plz., 27th Fl.
New York, NY 10004-1405
Ph: (212)709-4500
Fax: (212)709-4680
URL: http://www.mitchelltitus.com
Contact: Bert N. Mitchell, Chief Executive Officer
Scope: Firm provides assurance, advisory business services, transaction support and tax services. Specializes in auditing and accounting services, tax planning and preparation services management and business advisory services. Founded: 1974. Publications: "ITEM Club Budget preview report," 2010; "Year end personal planning," 2010; "Steering towards the future using the Pre Budget Report to help the UK rebound," 2009; "Be careful what you wish for," 2009; "Year end personal planning," 2009. Seminars: Budget Seminar 2010, Mar, 2010.

37687 ■ Partners for Market Leadership L.L.C.
400 Galleria Pky., Ste. 1500
Atlanta, GA 30339
Ph: (770)850-1409

Free: 800-984-1110
Co. E-mail: dcarpenter@market-leadership.com
URL: http://www.market-leadership.com
Contact: Nancy Surdyka, Manager
E-mail: nsurdyka@market-leadership.com
Scope: Boutique consulting firm focused on assisting clients to develop sustainable market leadership in geographic, practice area and/or industry markets. Provides consulting on market leadership, revenue enhancement, strategic development and change facilitation. Additional services are offered to legal, accounting, valuation and financial firms. **Founded:** 1995.

37688 ■ Penny & Associates Inc.
2748 Bur Oak Ave., Unit 2
Markham, ON, Canada L6B 1K4
Ph: (416)907-7158
Fax: (866)370-0703
Co. E-mail: info@pennyinc.com
URL: http://www.pennyinc.com
Contact: Betty Penny, President
E-mail: betty@pennyinc.com
Scope: Accounting and management firm that offers accounting and business solutions. Assistance in preparation of financial reports, reconciliation of inter company accounts, foreign currency transactions, investment trades and auditor working paper files and assistance in developing accounting policies and procedures. Provides part-time controllers to prepare financial statements, cash flow management, credit negotiations and give financial management advice or oversee accounting staff. **Founded:** 1994. **Seminars:** Quick Books, Aug, 2001; How to Stand Up to People Without Being a Jerk; How to Build Influence and Rapport With Almost Anyone; Dealing With Dissatisfied, Different and Difficult People; Effective Public Speaking; How to Incorporate Yourself; Company Perks: Attracting & Retaining Good People; FIRST AID. **Special Services:** Quickbooks®.

37689 ■ Queens Business Consulting (QBC)
Queens School of Business, Goodes Hall, 143 Union St.
Kingston, ON, Canada K7L 3N6
Ph: (613)533-2309
Fax: (613)533-2370
Co. E-mail: qbc@business.queensu.ca
URL: http://www.qsbc.com
Contact: Jacline Abray-Nyman, Director
E-mail: jabray-nyman@business.queensu.ca
Scope: Provides business plans, feasibility studies, financial planning, competitor analysis, market research, marketing strategies, production planning and systems implementation. **Founded:** 1973. **Publications:** "Information technology, network structure and competitive action. Information Systems Research," 2010; "The role of dominance in the appeal of violent media depictions. Journal of Advertising," 2010; "Great expectations and broken promises: Misleading claims, product failure, expectancy disconfirmation and consumer distrust. Journal of the Academy of Marketing Science," 2010; "Development and psychometric properties of the Transformational Teaching Questionnaire. Journal of Health Psychology," 2010; ". Predicting workplace aggression: myths, realities, and remaining questions," 2009; "The Inconvenient Truth about Improving Vehicle Fuel Efficiency: An MultiAttribute Analysis of the Efficient Frontier of the U.S. Automobile Industry, Transportation Research-Part," 2009; "Fraud in Canadian Nonprofit Organizations as Seen through the Eyes of Canadian Newspapers," 2009; "Disentangling the Indirect Links between SES and Health: The Dynamic Roles of Work Stressors and Personal Contro," 2009; "The strong situation hypothesis. Personality and Social Psychology Review," 2009; " Planning Your Next Crisis Decisively and Effectively. Ivey Business Journal," 2009. **Seminars:** Enabling Innovation Discussion Highlights, 2011; Intellectual Capital, 2010; On the diffusion of knowledge inside the organization, 2010; A model of the tacit knowledge lifecycle for decision-making: From creation to utilization, 2010; Individual, group, and organizational learning; A knowledge management perspective, 2010; Political economies of knowledge, with an example, 2009; The alignment of business and knowledge strategies and structures, 2009; Using IT To Support

the Discovery of Novel Knowledge in Organizations, 2008; Leadership: Knowledge Management by a New Name?, 2007; Every User Tells a Story, 2007.

37690 ■ Rainwater Gish & Associates
317 3rd St., Ste. 3
Eureka, CA 95501
Ph: (707)443-0030
Fax: (707)443-5683
Contact: Joan Rainwater Gish, President
Scope: Offers financial management for small business: includes asset management (controlling cash, inventory, A/R), cash flow control, credit policies and securing/structuring financing for growth. Also offers assistance in business planning, preparing proforma statements and other loan documents to secure financing. Majority of financial loan packages have been SBA loans. Firm provides SBA marketing and portfolio management services to banks. **Founded:** 1986.

37691 ■ Scannell & Kurz Inc.
71-B Munroe Ave.
Pittsford, NY 14534
Ph: (585)381-1120
Fax: (585)381-2383
Co. E-mail: info@scannellkurz.com
URL: http://www.scannellkurz.com
Contact: Tracy Brown, Manager
Scope: Provides pricing and financial aid strategies, admissions market analysis, enrollment management and retention strategies. **Founded:** 1996. **Publications:** "Financial Aid Strategies in Tough Economic Times," Jan, 2010; "Financial Aid Trends in the Current Economy: Lessons for the Future," Dec, 2009; "Data-Driven Retention Strategies," Feb, 2009; "Enrollment Management 101," Mar, 2008; "Don't Get Distracted: Top Audit Issues in Financial Aid," Sep, 2007; "Financial Aid and the Business Office," Jul, 2007; "Understanding the Value of Transfers," May, 2007; "Financial Aid Appeal Pitfalls," Mar, 2007; "Is Affordability Really the Issue," Nov, 2006; "Building a Financial Fundraising Case," Jul, 2006; "Enrollment Management Grows Up," May, 2006; "Just One Stop, But Many Potential Pitfalls," Mar, 2006; "Bond Rating: Beyond the Balance," Jan, 2006; "Strategy and Operations in Financial Aid," Nov, 2005; "The Evolution of a Successful Admissions Director"; "Profile of an Effective Enrollment Manager". **Seminars:** 2009 Enrollment and Financial Aid Results: Lessons for the Future, Presidents Institute, Jan, 2010; The Bottom Line on Student Retention: Data-Driven Approaches that Work, Nov, 2009; Thriving Without Deep Pockets--Achieving Enrollment Success on an Uneven Playing Field, Feb, 2009.

37692 ■ Harvey C. Skoog
7151 E Addis Ave.
Prescott Valley, AZ 86314
Ph: (928)772-1448
Scope: Firm has expertise in taxes, payroll, financial planning, budgeting, buy/sell planning, business start-up, fraud detection, troubled business consulting, acquisition and marketing. Serves the manufacturing, construction and retailing industries in Arizona. **Founded:** 1977.

37693 ■ The Stillwater Group [Stillwater Consulting Group Inc.]
920 E Shore Dr.
Stillwater, NJ 07875
Ph: (973)579-7080
Fax: (973)579-7970
Co. E-mail: education@stillwater.com
URL: http://www.stillwater.com
Contact: David Woodward, Consultant
Scope: Provides strategic planning, budget and financial management, process improvement, organizational design and assessment and college student services operations. **Founded:** 1993. **Publications:** "Integrated Resource Planning (Irp)," Business Officer Magazine, 2005; "The Economic Risk Conundrum," University Business Magazine; "Revenue Analysis and Tuition Strategy"; "Managing Advancement Services: Processes and Paper".

37694 ■ Swigert & Associates Inc.
505 Chicago Ave.
Evanston, IL 60202-2916

Ph: (847)864-4690
Fax: (847)864-0802
Co. E-mail: ryan@swigert.biz
URL: http://www.swigert.biz
Contact: Nancy Swigert, Director
Scope: Offers assistance to businesses and individuals on matters related to finance, investment decisions, taxes and general management concerns. **Founded:** 1970.

37695 ■ Value Creation Group Inc.
7820 Scotia Dr., Ste. 2000
Dallas, TX 75248-3115
Ph: (972)980-7407
Fax: (972)980-4619
Co. E-mail: john.antos@valuecreationgroup.com
URL: http://www.valuecreationgroup.com
Contact: John Antos, Manager
Scope: General business experts offering predictive strategic planning, Activity Based Costing ABC, Activity Based Management ABM, mergers and acquisitions, outsourcing, re engineering, process management, web enabling technology, bench marking, installation of financial systems, executive search, training, teams, activity based budgeting, operational auditing, feature costing. Industries served financial services, food, health care, insurance, manufacturing, electronics, real estate, consumer products, nonprofit, telecommunication, oil, service, data processing, hotel and resort and government agencies. **Founded:** 1984. **Publications:** "Handbook of Process Management Based Predictive Accounting," Alcpa 2002; "Cost Management for Today's Manufacturing Environment and Activity Based Management for Service Environments, Government Entities and Nonprofit Organizations"; "Risks and Opportunities in International Finance and Treasury"; "Driving Value Using Activity Based Budgeting"; "Process Based Accounting Leveraging Processes to Predict Results"; "Handbook of Supply Chain Management"; "Economic Value Management Applications and Techniques"; "The Change Handbook": "Group Methods for Creating the Future"; "Why Value Management and Performance Measurement Through U.S. Binoculars," Journal of Strategic Performance Measurement; "Real Options, Intangibles Measurement and the Benefits of Human Capital Investment to Power the Organization," Journal of Strategic Performance Measurement. **Seminars:** Activity Based Management; Predictive Accounting; Performance measures; ABM for Manufacturing; ABM for Service Organizations; Finance and Accounting for Non-Financial Executives; Return on Investment/Capital Expenditure Evaluation; Planning and Cost Control; The Next Step Intermediate Finance and Accounting for Nonfinancial Managers; Activity-Based Budgeting; Friendly Finance for Fund Raisers; Strategic Outsourcing.

37696 ■ ValueNomics Value Specialists
50 W San Fernando St., Ste. 600
San Jose, CA 95113
Fax: (408)200-6401
Co. E-mail: info@amllp.com
Contact: Gary E. Jones, Chief Executive Officer
Scope: Consulting is offered in the areas of financial management, process re-engineering, growth business services; governance, risk/compliance, SOX readiness and compliance, SAS 70, enterprise risk management, system security, operational and internal audit; business advisory services; valuation services; CORE assessment; contract assurance; transaction advisory services, IT solutions and litigation support services. **Founded:** 1993. **Publications:** "Dueling Appraisers: How Differences in Input and Assumptions May Control the Value," Apr, 2005; "The Business of Business Valuation and the CPA as an expert witness"; "The Business of Business Valuation," McGraw-Hill Professional Publishers Inc.

37697 ■ Mark Vanderstelt
9831 Gulfstream Ct.
Fishers, IN 46037
Ph: (317)576-9328
Fax: (317)576-9328
Contact: Mark Vanderstelt, Owner
Scope: Consulting services include financial planning and analysis, inventory control, cash management, return on investment, budgeting, pricing,

system design and analysis, mergers and acquisitions, feasibility studies, data processing, cost systems and controls and performance measurement. Also performs operational and financial reviews. **Founded:** 1985.

37698 ■ VelociTel Inc.
200 N Glebe Rd., Ste. 1000
Arlington, VA 22203-3728
Ph: (703)558-2200
Fax: (703)276-1169
Contact: Jim Estes, Chief Executive Officer
Scope: Provides expertise in developing wireless networks. Services include: project management; site acquisition; land use planning; architecture and engineering; construction and construction management. **Founded:** 1987. **Special Services:** VelociTel®.

37699 ■ VenturEdge Corp.
4711 Yonge St., Ste. 1105
Toronto, ON, Canada M2N 6K8
Ph: (416)224-2000
Fax: (416)224-2376
Contact: Mark Klingbaum, Manager
E-mail: klingbaum@venturedge.com
Scope: Provides services including strategy formulation; business planning; financial management; business coaching; performance improvement; information management; merger, acquisitions and divestitures; family succession planning; competitive intelligence. **Founded:** 1972. **Publications:** "Reputation," Harvard Business School Press, 1996; "Competing for the Future," Harvard Business School Press, 1994; "The Fifth Discipline," 1990.

37700 ■ Verbit & Co.
19 Bala Ave.
Bala Cynwyd, PA 19004-3202
Ph: (610)668-9840
Co. E-mail: verbitcompany@earthlink.net
Contact: Alan C. Verbit, President
Scope: Management consulting firm to assist executives and managers fulfill their mission and to assure that adequate planning of day-to-day operations occurs; that controls sufficient to safeguard valuable resources; and that results of decisions reviewed in sufficient time to effect continuing action. Financial planning and control-to develop accounting, budgeting, forecasting and other information systems for the management of resources and evaluation of strategies. Services also include: Evaluation of desk-top computer systems for small firms; CAD/CAM implementation plan and orderly introduction of CAD/CAM. Industries served: manufacturing, distribution, metals casting, equipment and components, professional services, health care, retail, nonprofit and government. **Founded:** 1981. **Seminars:** Integrating Manufacturing Management Systems with Business Systems; Negotiating Information Systems Agreements with Suppliers.

37701 ■ Vision Management
149 Meadows Rd.
Lafayette, NJ 07848-3120
Ph: (973)702-1116
Fax: (973)702-8311
Contact: Norman L. Naidish, President
Scope: Firm specializes in profit enhancement; strategic planning; business process reengineering; industrial engineering; facilities planning; team building; inventory management; and total quality management (TQM). **Founded:** 1984. **Publications:** "To increase profits, improve quality," Manufacturing Engineering, May, 2000.

37702 ■ WestCap Partners Inc.
750 Lexington Ave., 24th Fl.
New York, NY 10022
Ph: (212)949-1825
Fax: (212)223-7363
Contact: Charles J. Cernansky, Owner
Scope: Business and financial consultants provide corporate finance (debt, equity, private placements) and advisory services to emerging and medium-sized companies; investment and merchant banking; trade assistance, planning, strategy and financing and financial consulting. Also temporarily assist growing companies in operational roles. Offer troubled

company assistance through work-outs and turnarounds. Industries served: All including environmental, manufacturing, information technology (hardware, software, systems integration and implementation) direct marketing, sales service/wholesaling/distribution, construction materials and services, advertising, financial services and emerging technologies. **Seminars:** Financial Negotiations for Mergers, Acquisitions and Projects.

37703 ■ Western Capital Holdings Inc.
10050 E Applewood Dr.
Parker, CO 80138
Ph: (303)841-1022
Scope: Specialists in all phases of financial and management consulting. Provide strong emphasis in strategic planning and corporate development, financial analysis, acquisitions, investment banking and corporate finance. Projects range in size and duration to fit clients needs. Services can be applied to many diverse financial projects that may include the following: Business plan development, budgeting and forecasting, strategic planning, cash flow analysis, cash flow management, corporate development, banking relations, asset management and financial analysis. Industries served: Food industry, manufacturing, distribution, retailing, computer services, agribusiness, financial services, insurance and government agencies. **Founded:** 1986. **Seminars:** Buy Low, Sell High, Collect Early and Pay Late; Preparing Your Company for Sale; Venture Capital - Finding an Angel.

37704 ■ Westlife Consultants & Counsellors
95 October Ln.
Aurora, ON, Canada L4G 7A1
Ph: (905)867-0686
Fax: (416)799-5242
Co. E-mail: westlifeconsultant@hotmail.com
URL: http://www.westlifeconsultants.com
Contact: Dr. Syed N. Hussain, President
E-mail: westlifeconsultant@hotmail.com
Scope: Provider of entrepreneurs and businesses with a highly commercial and global perspectives on the international business development ideas under consideration. **Founded:** 1990. **Publications:** "Innovative Management"; "Team Building and Leadership"; "Financial Planning"; "Estate Planning"; "Risk Management"; "Export/Import Trade Finance Mechanics"; "Marketing and Sales Management"; "What Your Banker Needs to Know"; "Building A Successful Financial Plan".

37705 ■ Donald C. Wright CPA
3906 Lawndale Ln. N
Plymouth, MN 55446-2940
Ph: (763)478-6999
Co. E-mail: donaldwright@compuserve.com
URL: http://www.donaldwrightcpa.com
Contact: Donald C. Wright, President
E-mail: donaldwright@compuserve.com
Scope: Offers accounting, tax and small business consulting services. Services include cash flow and budgeting analysis; financial forecast and projections; financial statements; reviews and compilations; tax planning, tax preparation; IRS and state/local representation; international taxation; estate, gift and trust tax return preparation; benefit plan services; business succession planning; estate planning; financial planning; management advisory services; pension and profit sharing plans, retirement planning, expert witness services and employee benefits plans. Serves individuals, corporations, partnerships and non-profit organizations. **Founded:** 1968. **Seminars:** Qualified pension plans and employee welfare benefit plans.

COMPUTERIZED DATABASES

37706 ■ e-JEP
American Economic Association
2014 Broadway, Ste. 305
Nashville, TN 37203
Ph: (615)322-2595

Fax: (615)343-7590
Co. E-mail: aeainfo@vanderbilt.edu
URL: http://www.aeaweb.org
Contact: Richard H. Thaler, President
Availability: Online: American Economic Association; Thomson Reuters - Westlaw. CD-ROM: American Economic Association. **Type:** Full-text.

37707 ■ InvestmentNews
Crain Communications Inc.
711 3rd Ave.
New York, NY 10017
Ph: (212)210-0100
Co. E-mail: info@crain.com
URL: http://www.crain.com
Contact: Rance Crain, President
URL(s): www.investmentnews.com/. **Availability:** Online: Crain Communications Inc. **Type:** Full-text; Numeric.

37708 ■ Offshore Money Fund Report™
iMoneyNet Inc.
1 Research Dr., Ste. 400A
Westborough, MA 01581-5193
Ph: (508)616-6600
Fax: (508)616-5511
URL: http://www.imoneynet.com
Contact: Paul DiCenso, Manager
Availability: Online: iMoneyNet Inc. **Type:** Full-text; Numeric.

37709 ■ Vickers Weekly Insider Report
Vickers Stock Research Corp.
61 Broadway St., Ste. 1700
New York, NY 10006
Ph: (516)945-0020
Free: 800-645-5043
Co. E-mail: sales@vickers-stock.com
URL: http://www.vickers-stock.com
Availability: Online: Vickers Stock Research Corp. **Type:** Full-text; Numeric.

LIBRARIES

37710 ■ Business Development Bank of Canada Research & Information Centre
5 Place Ville Marie, Ste. 300
Montreal, QC, Canada H3B 5E7
Free: 877-232-2269
Fax: (877)329-9232
URL: http://www.bdc.ca
Scope: Small business; management; Canadian business and industry; banking and finance; development banking. **Services:** Interlibrary loan; library not open to the public. **Founded:** 1977. **Holdings:** 5000 books. **Subscriptions:** 100 journals and other serials; 7 newspapers.

37711 ■ Carnegie Library of Pittsburgh - Downtown & Business
612 Smithfield St.
Pittsburgh, PA 15222-2506
Ph: (412)281-7141
Fax: (412)471-1724
Co. E-mail: downtown@carnegielibrary.org
URL: http://www.carnegielibrary.org/locations/downtown
Contact: Karen Rossi, Department Head
Scope: Investments, small business, entrepreneurship, management, marketing, insurance, advertising, personal finance, accounting, real estate, job and career, International business. **Services:** Library open to the public. **Founded:** 1924. **Holdings:** 13,000 business volumes; VF materials; microfilm; looseleaf services; AV materials.

37712 ■ Nichols College - Conant Library
124 Center Rd.
Dudley, MA 01571-6310
Ph: (508)213-2333
Free: 800-470-3379
Co. E-mail: jim.douglas@nichols.edu
URL: http://www.nichols.edu/academics/academics/Library
Contact: Jim Douglas, Director, Library Services
Scope: Management, advertising, finance and accounting, small business, marketing, taxation, economics, International trade, humanities. **Services:**

Interlibrary loan; copying; information service to groups; document delivery; library open to Dudley and Webster residents. **Founded:** 1962. **Holdings:** 48,000 volumes; 1677 audio/visual titles; 3804 reels of microfilm. **Subscriptions:** 278 journals and electronic subscriptions.

37713 ■ Strategic Account Management Association (SAMA) - Resource Search Library
10 N Dearborn St.
Chicago, IL 60602
Ph: (312)251-3131
Fax: (312)251-3132
URL: http://www.strategicaccounts.org
Contact: Bernard Quancard, President
Description: Corporation sales executives concerned with strategic account sales. Holds seminars on strategic account management. Serves as an information provider on strategic customer-supplier relationship resources. **Scope:** Account management, cross-functional teams, strategic partnering and alliances, channel conflict, national and global account management programs, supply chain management, value-added selling. **Services:** Library not open to the public (numerous sample documents available to non-members, and most can be purchased). **Founded:** 1964. **Holdings:** 1500 documents, periodicals, audiocassettes, case studies, white papers, research studies, books, reports, archives, PDFs, and presentation materials. **Subscriptions:** 500 archival material audio recordings books clippings monographs periodicals; 1 journal; 3 newsletters. **Publications:** *Velocity* (Quarterly); *Focus: Account Manager* (Semiannual); *Velocity* (Quarterly; Bimonthly); *Velocity* (Quarterly). **Educational Activities:** Strategic Account Management Association Conference (Annual).

37714 ■ University of Kentucky - Business & Economics Information Center
B&E Info. Ctr., Rm. 116
335-BA Gatton College of Business & Economics
Lexington, KY 40506-0034
Ph: (859)257-8936
Fax: (859)257-1333
Co. E-mail: provost@email.uky.edu
URL: http://www.uky.edu//Provost/academicprograms.html
URL(s): gatton.uky.edu/. **Scope:** Business, economics, business management, marketing, finance, accounting. **Services:** Library open to the public for reference use only. **Founded:** 1993.

RESEARCH CENTERS

37715 ■ University of Oklahoma - Center for Financial Studies (CFS)
Price College of Business
307 W Brooks, Ste. 205A
Norman, OK 73019
Ph: (405)325-5591
Fax: (405)325-5491
Co. E-mail: pyadav@ou.edu
URL: http://www.ou.edu/price/finance/cfs.html
Contact: Prof. Pradeep Yadav, Director
Scope: Finance. **Founded:** 1990. **Educational Activities:** CFS Seminar.

Franchising

START-UP INFORMATION

37716 ■ *"Advantage: Early Adopters" in Entrepreneur (July 2014)*
Pub: Entrepreneur Media Inc.
Released: July 2014. **Description:** Franchising is one of the business models that stand to benefit from cloud computing and other digital solutions. A number of innovations are already transforming the franchise community and it remains to be seen how franchisees will respond to these changes. Among the innovations available for franchisees are fleet-management applications, improved customer loyalty programs, and digital signboards. The advent of cloud-based point-of-sale systems are also gaining popularity among some small franchisees.

37717 ■ *"Batteries Plus Bulbs Debuts Multi-Unit Franchise Operator Development" in Wireless News (September 16, 2014)*
Pub: Close-Up Media
Released: September 16, 2014. **Description:** Batteries Plus is launching a new Multi-Unit Franchise Operator Development Initiative, offering Batteries Plus Bulbs. The new program will provide support, including discounted fees, to assist qualified multi-franchisees from other non-competing brands.

37718 ■ *"Biz Pays Tribute: Franchise Helps Owners Grieve and Honor Their Beloved Pets" in Small Business Opportunities (November 2007)*
Description: Paws and Remember is a franchise company that provides pet cremation and memorial products while assisting veterinary clinics and other pet specialists to help clients when they lose a pet.

37719 ■ *"Blaze Pizza Adds Nine Franchise Groups" in FastCasual.com (September 2, 2014)*
Pub: Networld Media Group
Released: September 2, 2014. **Description:** Blaze Fast Fire'd Pizza has signed nine new San Diego area development agreements that will add 67 franchise restaurants to its firm. The company will also open 315 company-owned and franchised pizza restaurants in 33 states by the end of 2015.

37720 ■ *"Building a Business: Directbuild Helps Clients Build Their Own Home" in Small Business Opportunities (Winter 2007)*
Description: Mike New, founder of Directbuild, a franchise company that helps individuals with no construction knowledge build their own home.

37721 ■ *Building a Dream: A Canadian Guide to Starting Your Own Business*
Pub: McGraw-Hill Ryerson Ltd.
Contact: Robert J. Bahash, President
Ed: Walter S. Good. **Released:** 9th Edition. **Price:** C$74. **Description:** Topics covered include evaluating business potential, new business ideas, starting or buying a business, franchise opportunities, business organization, protecting an idea, arranging financing, and developing a business plan. **Availability:** Print.

37722 ■ *The Canadian Small Business Survival Guide: How to Start and Operate Your Own Successful Business*
Pub: Dundurn Group
Contact: Kirk Howard, President
E-mail: khoward@dundurn.com
Ed: Benj Gallander. **Released:** April 2002. **Price:** $26.99, paperback; $12.99. **Description:** Ideas for starting and running a successful small business. Topics include selecting a business, financing, government assistance, locations, franchises, and marketing ideas. **Availability:** PrintE-book.

37723 ■ *"A Cheap Ticket to Startup" in Entrepreneur (Vol. 35, November 2007, No. 11, pp. 126)*
Pub: Entrepreneur Press
Contact: Perlman Neil, President
Description: List of 69 franchises that can be started for less than $25,000 is spotlighted.

37724 ■ *"Chem-Dry Carpet Cleaning Franchise on Pace for 120 New Locations In 2014" in Internet Wire (September 16, 2014)*
Pub: COMTEX News Network Inc.
Contact: Chip Brian, President
Released: September 16, 2014. **Description:** Chem-Dry carpet cleaning franchise is poised to record-setting growth for 2014 with 120 new franchisees. Entrepreneur Magazine named Chem-Dry as the No. 1 carpet cleaning franchise, as well as a top home-based business opportunity with low startup-costs.

37725 ■ *"Cleaning Up" in Small Business Opportunities (Get Rich At Home 2010)*
Pub: Harris Publications Inc.
Description: Break into the $23 billion pro car wash business with no experience needed. Profile of Team Blue, founded by father and son team, Jeff and Jason Haas along with franchise opportunities is included.

37726 ■ *"Courier Service Delivers Big Profits and Top-Notch Customer Service" in Small Business Opportunities (November 2007)*
Description: Profile of Relay Express, a courier franchising business started by three friends in 1986. The company focuses on customer service and calls them every 19 minutes to report on progress of a parcel until it is delivered.

37727 ■ *"Driving Home Success: Stamped Asphalt for Driveways and Paths is Hottest New Trend" in Small Business Opportunities (Winter 2007)*
Description: Profile of technology that turns asphalt into three-dimensional replicas of hand-laid brick, slate, cobblestone and other design effects. Profiles of franchise opportunities in this industry are included.

37728 ■ *"Fast-Growing Office Pride Franchise Targets Louisville For Expansion" in Internet Wire (September 9, 2014)*
Pub: COMTEX News Network Inc.
Contact: Chip Brian, President
Released: September 9, 2014. **Description:** Office Pride is a commercial cleaning service that is built on principles that include: honesty, trustworthy service,

excellence, and treating everyone with dignity and respect. The commercial cleaning franchise is seeking a developer to help expand its business in Louisville, Kentucky.

37729 ■ *Franchise: Freedom or Fantasy: How to Know if a Franchise is Right for You After Your Corporate Career*
Pub: iUniverse Inc.
Contact: Kevin Weiss, President
E-mail: kevin.gray@iuniverse.com
Ed: Mitchell York. **Released:** June 24, 2009. **Price:** $23.95, hardcover; $13.95, softcover; $6. **Description:** Successful franchisee and professional certified coach guides individuals through the many steps involved in deciding whether or not to buy a franchise and how to do it correctly. **Availability:** PrintE-book.

37730 ■ *"Franchisee to Smash Way Into Orlando's Better Burger Race" in Orlando Business Journal (Vol. 30, January 31, 2014, No. 32, pp. 3)*
Pub: American City Business Journals
Released: January 31, 2014. **Description:** Palm Coast, Florida-based Two Spurs LLC, the new franchisee for Smashburger, has announced plans to put its first of 12 restaurants in Orlando in 2014. Two Spurs executives, Wellesley Broomfield and Ray Ruiz, have been touring potential sites in the area. Detailed requirements for owning a Smash Burger franchise are provided.

37731 ■ *Franchising for Dummies*
Pub: John Wiley & Sons Inc.
Contact: Stephen M. Smith, President
Ed: Dave Thomas, Michael Seid. **Released:** 2nd Edition. **Price:** $24.95, paperback; $16.99. **Description:** Advice to help entrepreneurs choose the right franchise, as well as financing, managing and expanding the business. **Availability:** PrintE-book.

37732 ■ *"Geo-Marketing: Site Selection by the Numbers" in Franchising World (Vol. 42, September 2010, No. 9, pp.)*
Pub: International Franchise Association
Contact: Stephen J. Caldeira, President
E-mail: scaldeira@franchise.org
Ed: Kellen Vaughn. **Description:** Site location is critical when starting a new franchise. Information to help franchisees choose the right location is included.

37733 ■ *"Hand-Held Heaven: Smallcakes Cupcakery" in Tulsa World (February 15, 2011)*
Pub: The McClatchy Co.
Contact: Peter Tira, Director
Description: Franchisee Carolyn Archer displays her products at Smallcakes Cupcakery, a Jenks shop that's the first to be co-branded with FreshBerry under the Beautiful Brands International banner. The shop's launch is part of a franchise deal between BBI and Jeff and Brandy Martin, co-owners of Smallcakes; twelve concepts have been developed and marketed already by Tulsa-based BBI.

37734 ■ *"Home: Where the Money Is!" in Small Business Opportunities (May 1, 2008)*
Pub: Harris Publications Inc.
Description: Profile of ComForcare, a franchise company that serves the senior population in America; a franchise can be started with one owner and add and build a team as it grows.

37735 ■ *"Hot Market Opportunity" in Small Business Opportunities (January 2011)*
Pub: Harris Publications Inc.
Description: Mobility products for seniors give this small business a $3 million lift. Profile of 101 Mobility, the nation's first full-service sales, service and installation provider of mobility and accessibility products and equipment including stair lifts, auto lifts, ramps, porch lifts, power wheelchairs and scooters as well as other medical equipment such as walkers, hospital beds and more.

37736 ■ *"It's Tea-Riffic! Natural Bottled Tea Satisfies Void In Beverage Market" in Small Business Opportunities (November 2007)*
Description: Profile of Skae Beverage International LLC, offering franchise opportunities for its New Leaf all-natural tea beverage, available in eight flavors of green, white and blue tea.

37737 ■ *"Making Money? Child's Play!" in Small Business Opportunities (March 1, 2008)*
Pub: Harris Publications Inc.
Description: Proven system helps launch a successful child care business.

37738 ■ *"May I Help You?" in Entrepreneur (September 2014)*
Pub: Entrepreneur Media Inc.
Released: September 2014. **Description:** Entrepreneur magazine lists 114 of the top personal-service franchises in the U.S. These personal-service businesses are among the fastest growing categories in the franchise sector. Included in the list are child care services, children's enrichment programs, fitness businesses, hair care businesses, spa services, senior care, travel agencies, and tutoring services. Data also includes rankings in the 2014 Franchise 500, startup costs and the number of total franchises or co-owned businesses.

37739 ■ *"The Melting Pot Targets Calgary, Canada For Franchise Expansion" in CNW Group (September 9, 2014)*
Pub: COMTEX News Network Inc.
Contact: Chip Brian, President
Released: September 9, 2014. **Description:** The Melting Pot, a premier fondue restaurant, is seeking franchisees in the Calgary, Canada region. The restaurants offer posh, casual interactive dining to their guests. The franchise is also offering franchise opportunities in the Vancouver and Greater Toronto areas. Details covering Melting Pot restaurants are included.

37740 ■ *Microfranchising: Creating Wealth at the Bottom of the Pyramid*
Pub: Edward Elgar Publishing Inc.
Contact: Richard Henning, Vice President
E-mail: kwight@e-elgar.com
Price: £20.80, paperback; £72, hardback. **Description:** Ideas from researchers and social entrepreneurs discusses the movement that moves microfranchising into a mechanism for sustainable poverty reduction on a scale to match microfinance. **Availability:** Print.

37741 ■ *"New Wave" in Entrepreneur (Vol. 36, March 2008, No. 3, pp. 100)*
Pub: Entrepreneur Press
Contact: Perlman Neil, President
Description: List of top new franchise opportunities is presented. The list ranks the franchises according to their order in Entrepreneur Magazine's 2008 Franchise 500 issue.

37742 ■ *"A Piece of the Action" in Entrepreneur (May 2014)*
Pub: Entrepreneur Media Inc.
Released: May 2014. **Description:** Franchisor, Mandy Calara of Forever Yogurt explains how his online crowdfunding platform called CrowdFranchise can help potential franchisees find investors. He details the successful opening of their first Forever Yogurt store at Wicker Park in Chicago, Illinois through the CrowdFranchise. He explains the incubator program called Velocity and the use of Crowd-Franchise to measure support. He believes that emerging franchisors and startups with fewer than 20 units will be interested in their concept.

37743 ■ *"Planet Smoothie Introduces New Franchise Information Website" in Wireless News (September 10, 2014)*
Pub: Close-Up Media
Released: September 10, 2014. **Description:** Planet Smoothie introduced its new Website that provides details about the smoothie industry, particularly the franchise Planet Smoothie business model which offers healthier food choices for people.

37744 ■ *"Proven Success Pays Off" in Small Business Opportunities (January 2011)*
Pub: Harris Publications Inc.
Description: Industry pioneers of the fast-casual restaurant launch new venture with sales of $43 million. Profile of Newk's Express Cafe and its founders is included.

37745 ■ *"Pump Up the Profits" in Small Business Opportunities (Summer 2010)*
Pub: Harris Publications Inc.
Description: New fitness franchise offers customized personal training at bargain rates. Profile of Alan Katz, president of EduFit, a concept that allows small groups of people to workout with customized training is provided.

37746 ■ *"Pump Up the Profits: Teaching Small Biz How to Handle Fuel and Reduce Costs!" in Small Business Opportunities (March 2008)*
Description: Profile of 4Refuel, a company that delivers diesel and biodiesel fuel to customers individual fuelings.

37747 ■ *"Rev Up Your Engine" in Small Business Opportunities (Fall 2010)*
Pub: Harris Publications Inc.
Description: Industry giant Meineke is adding franchisees whose average sales top $500,000 annually. Profile of Meineke is also included.

37748 ■ *"Revel in Riches!" in Small Business Opportunities (May 1, 2008)*
Pub: Harris Publications Inc.
Description: Profile of Proforma, a business-to-business franchise firm providing print and promotional products.

37749 ■ *"Riches In Recreation" in Small Business Opportunities (March 2011)*
Pub: Harris Publications Inc.
Description: Making money is child's play thanks to new gym concept that makes parents and franchisors happy. Profile of Great Play, the franchised children's gym is provided.

37750 ■ *"Savvy Solutions" in Black Enterprise (Vol. 40, July 2010, No. 12, pp. 44)*
Pub: Earl G. Graves Publishing Co. Inc.
Contact: Earl G. Graves, Jr., President
Ed: Tennille M. Robinson. **Description:** Advice is offered to an African American interested in starting a franchise operation.

37751 ■ *"Secure Fortune: New Twist In Security: The Marketplace Is Going Digital" in Small Business Opportunities (November 2007)*
Description: Profile of EYESthere, providing digital video security franchise opportunities.

37752 ■ *"Sloan's Ice Cream Inks First Franchise Deal In San Diego" in FastCasual.com (September 12, 2014)*
Pub: Networld Media Group
Released: September 12, 2014. **Description:** Sloan's Ice Cream announced that is has awarded the first franchise location outside of South Florida to Ali Hajisattari of San Diego, California.

37753 ■ *Start Small, Finish Big*
Ed: Fred DeLuca with John P. Hayes. **Released:** April 2009. **Price:** $16.95. **Description:** Fred DeLuca is profiled; after founding the multi-billion dollar chain of Subway sandwich restaurants, DeLuca is committed to helping microentrepreneurs, people who start successful small businesses with less than $1,000.

37754 ■ *"Stepping Out" in Small Business Opportunities (Get Rich At Home 2010)*
Pub: Harris Publications Inc.
Description: Earn $1 million a year selling flip flops? A Flip Flop Shop franchise will help individuals start their own business.

37755 ■ *"Victoria Colligan; Co-Founder, Ladies Who Launch Inc., 38" in Crain's Cleveland Business (Vol. 28, November 19, 2007, No. 46)*
Pub: Crain Communications Inc.
Ed: Jay Miller. **Description:** Profile of Victoria Colligan who is the co-founder of Ladies Who Launch Inc., an organization with franchises in nearly 50 cities; the company offers women entrepreneurs workshops and a newsletter to help women balance their businesses with other aspects of their lives. Ms. Colligan found that women were learning about being business owners differently than men and she felt that there was a need to create opportunities for networking for women launching businesses that had more of a lifestyle purpose.

37756 ■ *"What's the Latest?" in Entrepreneur (July 2014)*
Pub: Entrepreneur Media Inc.
Released: July 2014. **Description:** Entrepreneur magazine selects the top 15 new and 15 established franchises in the U.S. to show that franchising and innovation can be a successful combination. The selection includes companies with services that have never been franchised before or with surprise twists on old ideas. Established franchisors like Arby's Restaurants Group are taking risks with unusual menu items, new technologies and creative marketing strategies. New franchises on the list include Baby Bodyguards, Bio-One and Chocolate Works.

37757 ■ *"WIN Home Inspection Garners Recognition as 2012 Military Friendly Franchise by G.I. Jobs Magazine" in Entertainment Close-Up (May 21, 2012)*
Pub: Close-Up Media
Released: May 21, 2012. **Description:** G.I. Jobs Magazine ranked WIN Home Inspection in the top ten franchises thoughout the United States on its 2012 Military Friendly Franchises. Veterans represent 1/4 of the firm's franchisee base, offering realistic opportunities for vets to become successful. Details of the training and skills involved and what it takes to be selected to launch a WIN franchise are included.

37758 ■ *"Woman Decides to Try Her Hand at Running Maid Service" in News-Sentinel (May 1, 2012)*
Released: May 1, 2012. **Description:** Profile of Denise Lyons, 38 year old owner of a Molly Maid franchise. Lyons discusses her move into purchasing the franchise last year. After investigating other franchises she felt Molly Maid's focus on customer service was her priorty. She has built her business to about 65 recurring customers and five employees.

ASSOCIATIONS AND OTHER ORGANIZATIONS

37759 ■ **American Association of Franchisees and Dealers (AAFD)**
PO Box 10158
Palm Desert, CA 92255-0158
Ph: (619)209-3775
Free: 800-733-9858
Fax: (866)855-1988
URL: http://www.aafd.org
Contact: Robert L. Purvin, Jr., Chief Executive Officer
Description: Franchisees and business services. **Scope:** A nonprofit organization providing referrals and other member benefits and services for franchi-

sees. **Founded:** 1992. **Publications:** "Nsights the Art of Positive Emotions," Sep-Oct, 2003; "Nsights Understanding Basic Human Behaviors at Work," Aug, 2003; "Nsights Pinkerton," Aug, 2002. **Educational Activities:** Total Quality Franchising (Annual). **Awards:** Fair Franchising Seal (Periodic). **Seminars:** Driving Your Association to the Next Level; Keeping your Association on the Fairway: Re-Model and Re-Imaging in Today's Economy; Avoid being an Association duffer: Recruiting and Retaining Membership Dos and Don'ts!; Clubhouse Chatter: The Most Cost Effective Ways to Communicate.

37760 ■ American Franchisee Association (AFA)

53 W Jackson Blvd., Ste. 1256
Chicago, IL 60604
Ph: (312)431-0545
Fax: (312)431-1469
Co. E-mail: spkezios@franchisee.org
URL: http://www.franchisee.org
Contact: Susan P. Kezios, President
Description: Works to promote and enhance the economic interests of small business franchisees; promote the growth and development of members' enterprises; assist in the formation of independent franchisee associations; offer support, assistance, and legal referral services to members. **Scope:** Offers expertise to potential franchise business opportunity buyers. **Founded:** 1993. **Publications:** E-news (Monthly).

37761 ■ Canadian Franchise Association (CFA) [Association Canadienne de la Franchise]

5399 Eglinton Ave. W, Ste. 116
Toronto, ON, Canada M9C 5K6
Ph: (416)695-2896
Free: 800-665-4232
Fax: (416)695-1950
Co. E-mail: info@cfa.ca
URL: http://www.cfa.ca
Contact: Lorraine Mclachlan, President
Description: Franchise businesses. Represents the shared interests of businesses and professionals active in the Canadian franchise sector. Provides information and guidance to aspiring franchisees. **Scope:** franchising. **Founded:** 1967. **Subscriptions:** 30. **Publications:** FranchiseCanada (Bimonthly); FranchiseCanada (Bimonthly). **Awards:** Award of Excellence (Annual).

37762 ■ FranchiseCanada

5399 Eglinton Ave. W, Ste. 116
Toronto, ON, Canada M9C 5K6
Ph: (416)695-2896
Free: 800-665-4232
Fax: (416)695-1950
Co. E-mail: info@cfa.ca
URL: http://www.cfa.ca
Contact: Lorraine Mclachlan, President
Released: Bimonthly **Price:** C$4.99, /issue; C$17.35, /year.

37763 ■ International Franchise Association (IFA)

1501 K St. NW, Ste. 350
Washington, DC 20005
Ph: (202)628-8000
Free: 800-543-1038
Fax: (202)628-0812
Co. E-mail: ifa@franchise.org
URL: http://www.franchise.org
Contact: Stephen J. Caldeira, President
E-mail: scaldeira@franchise.org
Description: Firms in 100 countries utilizing the franchise method of distribution for goods and services in all industries. **Founded:** 1960. **Publications:** Franchising World (Monthly); International Franchise Association--Franchise Opportunities Guide (Semiannual); Franchise Opportunities Guide (Semiannual). **Educational Activities:** Legal Symposium (Annual); International Franchise Association Convention (Annual). **Awards:** Entrepreneur of the Year (Annual); Bonny LeVine Award (Annual); Hall of Fame Award (Annual); Don Debolt Franchising Scholarship Program; Franchise Law Diversity Scholarship Awards.

37764 ■ Women in Franchising (WIF)

53 W Jackson Blvd., Ste. 1157
Chicago, IL 60604
Ph: (312)431-1467
Fax: (312)431-1469
Co. E-mail: spkezios@womeninfranchising.com
Contact: Susan P. Kezios, President
E-mail: spkezios@womeninfranchising.com
Description: Assists women interested in all aspects of franchise business development including those buying a franchised business and those expanding their businesses via franchising. Provides franchise technical assistance in both of these areas. Surveys the industry on the status of women. **Scope:** The firm offers franchise consulting services for women and minorities interested in becoming franchisees or franchisors. Also Offers a number of consulting services including presenting workshops and seminars that teach prospective franchisees the skills and knowledge needed to evaluate, finance and purchase a franchise, providing one-on-one assistance to persons considering buying a franchise by conducting a UFOC (Uniform Franchise Offering Circular) Review and feasibility studies. Provides a variety of tools and one-on-one assistance to prospective franchisees and franchisors including audio seminars, a detailed Operations Manual and sales guidance and national public relations contracts for recruiting franchisees. **Founded:** 1987. **Seminars:** Buying a Franchise: How To Make The Right Choice; Growing Your Business: The Franchise Option.

DIRECTORIES OF EDUCATIONAL PROGRAMS

37765 ■ Bond's Franchise Guide

Pub: Source Book Publications
Contact: Robert E. Bond, Chief Executive Officer
Ed: Robert E. Bond, Michelle Yang. **Released:** 20th Edition. **Price:** $34.95, paperback. **Description:** Comprehensive directory offering prospective franchise owners a current and detailed profile of 1,000 franchises, as well as supplemental profiles of franchise attorneys and consultants; companies are divided into 45 categories for easy comparison. **Availability:** Print.

37766 ■ Bond's Franchise Guide 2007

Pub: Source Book Publications
Contact: Robert E. Bond, Chief Executive Officer
Ed: Robert E. Bond. **Released:** 18th Edition. **Price:** $34.95, paperback. **Description:** Directory of 1,000 franchise opportunities, includes supplemental profiles on franchise attorneys and consultants. The companies are divided into 45 business categories with comparisons. **Availability:** Print.

REFERENCE WORKS

37767 ■ "Affordable Financing for Acquisitions" in Franchising World (Vol. 42, September 2010, No. 9, pp. 47)

Pub: International Franchise Association
Contact: Stephen J. Caldeira, President
E-mail: scaldeira@franchise.org
Ed: Gene Cerrotti. **Description:** Acquisition pricing is reasonable and interest rates are low and quality franchised resale opportunities are priced 4.5 times EBITDA. Information about Small Business Administration loans is also included.

37768 ■ "All Fired Up!" in Small Business Opportunities (November 2008)

Ed: Stan Roberts. **Description:** Profile of Brixx Wood Fired Pizza, which has launched a franchising program due to the amount of interest the company's founders received over the years; franchisees do not need experience in the food industry or pizza restaurant service business in order to open a franchise of their own because all franchisees receive comprehensive training in which they are educated on all of the necessary tools to effectively run the business.

37769 ■ "All Fired Up" in Entrepreneur (September 2014)

Pub: Entrepreneur Media Inc.
Released: September 2014. **Description:** Entrepreneur, Bryan Weinstein, discusses the barbecue-cleaning franchise he started in Southern California,

called Bar-B-Clean. the franchise owner explains why it is necessary to clean barbecue grills. His franchise business targets homes on the Sunbelt with outdoor kitchens that are used year round. Weinstein also mentions several plans for add-on services such as patio furniture pressure washing and possibly oven cleaning.

37770 ■ "All Those Applications, and Phone Users Just Want to Talk" in Advertising Age (Vol. 79, August 11, 2008, No. 31, pp. 18)

Pub: Crain Communications Inc.
Contact: Rance Crain, President
Ed: Mike Vorhaus. **Description:** Although consumers are slowly coming to text messaging and other data applications, a majority of those Americans surveyed stated that they simply want to use their cell phones to talk and do not care about other activities. Statistical data included.

37771 ■ "Allied Brands Loses Baskin-Robbins Franchise Down Under" in Ice Cream Reporter (Vol. 23, November 20, 2010, No. 12, pp. 2)

Description: Dunkin Brands, worldwide franchisor of Baskin-Robbins, terminated the master franchise agreement for Australia held by the food marketer Allied Brands Services.

37772 ■ "Ampm Focus Has BP Working Overtime" in Crain's Chicago Business (April 28, 2008)

Pub: Crain Communications Inc.
Contact: Todd Johnson, Publisher
Ed: John T. Slania. **Description:** Britian's oil giant BP PLC is opening its ampm convenience stores in the Chicago market and has already begun converting most of its 78 Chicago-area gas stations to ampms. The company has also started to franchise the stores to independent operators. BP is promoting the brand with both traditional and unconventional marketing techniques such s real or simulated 3D snacks embedded in bus shelter ads and an in-store Guitar Hero contest featuring finalists from a recent contest at the House of Blues.

37773 ■ "Apple's iPhone 3G: A Marketing 50 Case Study" in Advertising Age (Vol. 79, November 17, 2008, No. 43, pp. 15)

Pub: Crain Communications Inc.
Contact: Rance Crain, President
Ed: Beth Snyder Bulik. **Description:** Review of Apple's new iPhone 3G which includes the addition of smart-phone applications as well as a price drop; the new functionalities as well as the lower price seems to be paying off for Apple who reported sales of 6.9 million iPhones in its most recent quarter, in which the 3G hit store shelves.

37774 ■ "Area Small Businesses Enjoy Benefits of Bartering Group" in News-Herald (August 22, 2010)

Pub: The News Herald
Ed: Brandon C. Baker. **Description:** ITEX is a publicly traded firm that spurs cashless, business-to-business transactions within its own marketplace. Details of the bartering of goods and services within the company are outlined.

37775 ■ "Attracting Veteran-Franchisees To Your System" in Franchising World (Vol. 42, November 2010, No. 11, pp. 53)

Pub: International Franchise Association
Contact: Stephen J. Caldeira, President
E-mail: scaldeira@franchise.org
Ed: Mary Kennedy Thompson. **Description:** As military servicemen and women return home, the franchising industry expects an increase in veterans as franchise owners. The Veterans Transition Franchise Initiative, also known as VetFran, is described.

37776 ■ "Baby's Room Franchisee Files Bankruptcy" in Crain's Detroit Business (Vol. 25, June 22, 2009, No. 25, pp. 15)

Pub: Crain Communications Inc. - Detroit
Contact: Keith Crain, Chairman
Ed: Gabe Nelson. **Description:** Emery L, a franchisee of USA Baby Inc. and ran the franchised Baby's Room Nursery Furniture stores in the area has filed for bankruptcy. Details of the bankruptcy are included.

37777 ■ *"Baltimore Car Dealers Have One More Shot to Get Their Franchises Back: Fighting Detroit"* in *Baltimore Business Journal (Vol. 27, January 22, 2010, No. 38, pp. 1)*
Pub: American City Business Journals
Ed: Daniel J. Sernovitz. **Description:** Baltimore, Maryland-based car dealers could retrieve their franchises from car manufacturers, Chrysler LLC and General Motors Corporation, through a forced arbitration. A provision in a federal budget mandates the arbitration. The revoking of franchises has been attributed to the car manufacturers' filing of bankruptcy protection.

37778 ■ *"Bank Forces Brooke Founder To Sell His Holdings"* in *The Business Journal-Serving Metropolitan Kansas City (October 10, 2008)*
Pub: American City Business Journals, Inc.
Contact: Whitney Shaw, President
Ed: James Dornbrook. **Description:** Robert Orr who is the founder of Brooke Corp., a franchise of insurance agencies, says that he was forced to sell virtually all of his stocks in the company. First United Bank held the founder's stock as collateral for two loans worth $5 million and $7.9 million, which were declared in default in September 2008. Details of the selling of the company's stocks are provided.

37779 ■ *"Bankruptcy Claims Brooke, Gives Franchisees Hope"* in *The Business Journal-Serving Metropolitan Kansas City (October 31, 2008)*
Pub: American City Business Journals, Inc.
Contact: Whitney Shaw, President
Ed: James Dornbrook, Steve Vockrodt. **Description:** Insurer Brooke Corp. was required to file for Chapter 11 bankruptcy for a deal to sell all of its assets to businessmen Terry Nelson and Lysle Davidson. The new Brooke plans to share contingency fees with franchisees. The impacts of the bankruptcy case on Brooke franchisees are discussed.

37780 ■ *"Bark Up The Right Tree"* in *Small Business Opportunities (Winter 2009)*
Description: Profile of Central Bark, a daycare company catering to pets that offers franchise opportunities and is expanding rapidly despite the economic downturn; the company's growth strategy is also discussed.

37781 ■ *"Baskin-Robbins Expanding to South Texas"* in *Ice Cream Reporter (Vol. 23, July 20, 2010, No. 8, pp. 4)*
Pub: Ice Cream Reporter
Description: Baskin-Robbins will develop six new shops in south Texas after signing agreements with two franchisees.

37782 ■ *"Baskin-Robbins: New in U.S., Old in Japan"* in *Ice Cream Reporter (Vol. 23, August 20, 2010, No. 9, pp. 2)*
Description: Baskin-Robbins is celebrating its first franchise in Japan.

37783 ■ *"Best Practices: Developing a Rewards Program"* in *Franchising World (Vol. 42, September 2010, No. 9, pp. 13)*
Pub: International Franchise Association
Contact: Stephen J. Caldeira, President
E-mail: scaldeira@franchise.org
Ed: Leah Templeton. **Description:** Rewards for a job well done are examined in order to recognize franchisees for outstanding performance. Ways to customize a rewards program are outlined.

37784 ■ *"The Big Leap"* in *Entrepreneur (June 2014)*
Pub: Entrepreneur Media Inc.
Released: June 2014. **Description:** Several franchises used their frontline experience and took advantage of the opportunities they saw to start their own franchises. Cory Wiedel's experience as a GNC nutritional supplement franchisee helped him run Complete Nutrition as a 100 percent franchised system. Michael Debenham of American Title Loans says he gained confidence to start his own franchise business by observing Liberty Tax Service as a

franchisee. Ashley Morris thinks being a franchisee of Capriotti's Sandwich Shop gave him the advantage when he became the franchisor of the restaurant.

37785 ■ *"BK Franchisees Lose Sleep Over Late-Night Rule"* in *Advertising Age (Vol. 79, August 11, 2008, No. 31, pp. 1)*
Pub: Crain Communications Inc.
Contact: Rance Crain, President
Ed: Emily Bryson York. **Description:** Burger King's corporate headquarters mandates that franchisees remain open until at least 2 a.m. Three Miami operators have filed a lawsuit that alleges the extended hours can be dangerous, do not make money and overtax the workforce.

37786 ■ *"BK Menu Gives Casual Dining Reason to Worry"* in *Advertising Age (Vol. 79, November 17, 2008, No. 43, pp. 12)*
Pub: Crain Communications Inc.
Contact: Rance Crain, President
Ed: Emily Bryson York. **Description:** Burger King is beginning to compete with such casual dining restaurants as Applebees and the Cheesecake Factory with new premium menu items, including thicker burgers and ribs; statistical data regarding the casual dining segment which continues to fall and Burger King, whose sales continue to rise is included.

37787 ■ *"Blog Buzz Heralds Arrival of IPhone 2.0"* in *Advertising Age (Vol. 79, June 9, 2008, No. 40, pp. 8)*
Pub: Crain Communications Inc.
Contact: Rance Crain, President
Ed: Abbey Klaassen. **Description:** Predictions concerning the next version of the iPhone include a global-positioning-system technology as well as a configuration to run on a faster, 3G network.

37788 ■ *"Blueprint for Profit: Family-Run Lumberyard Sets Sites On Sales of $100 Million a Year"* in *Small Business Opportunities (Jan. 2008)*
Ed: Stan Roberts. **Description:** Profile of family-run lumberyard whose owner shares insight into the challenges of competing with big box operations like Home Depot and Lowe's.

37789 ■ *Bond's Franchise Guide*
Pub: Source Book Publications
Contact: Robert E. Bond, Chief Executive Officer
Ed: Robert E. Bond. **Released:** 20th Edition. **Price:** $34.95, paperback. **Description:** Comprehensive directory of franchise opportunities, divided into 45 categories. **Availability:** Print.

37790 ■ *"Bookkeeping Service Opens First Sacramento Franchise"* in *Sacramento Bee (April 13, 2011)*
Pub: The Sacramento Bee
Ed: Mark Glover. **Description:** Franchise bookkeeping service called BookKeeping Express opened its new office in Roseville, California; its first shop in the area.

37791 ■ *"Boosting Your Merchant Management Services With Wireless Technology"* in *Franchising World (Vol. 42, August 2010, No. 8, pp. 27)*
Pub: International Franchise Association
Contact: Stephen J. Caldeira, President
E-mail: scaldeira@franchise.org
Ed: Michael S. Slominski. **Description:** Franchises should have the capability to accept credit cards away from their businesses. This technology will increase sales.

37792 ■ *"Breaking the Mold"* in *Entrepreneur (Vol. 37, September 2009, No. 9, pp. 87)*
Pub: Entrepreneur Press
Contact: Perlman Neil, President
Ed: Tracy Stapp Herold. **Description:** Profiles of top franchise businesses in the United States are presented. Hey Buddy! Pet Supply Vending Co. offers pet supply vending machines. Home Health Mates, on the other hand, provides professional medical care at home.

37793 ■ *"Bro Deals"* in *Entrepreneur (August 2014)*
Pub: Entrepreneur Media Inc.
Released: August 2014. **Description:** Brothers Joe and Allen Hertzman, owners of six Long John Silver's, 13 Rally's and 24 Papa John's Pizza units, share the secret behind their success in the restaurant franchising business. Allen offers advice to franchisees and emphasizes the importance of finding good operating partners who can help the business succeed. They describe their management styles and how growing up in the family's franchising business benefitted them.

37794 ■ *"Brooke Agents Claim Mistreatment"* in *The Business Journal-Serving Metropolitan Kansas City (Vol. 27, October 24, 2008, No. 7, pp. 1)*
Pub: American City Business Journals, Inc.
Contact: Whitney Shaw, President
Ed: James Dornbrook. **Description:** Franchisees of Brooke Corp., an insurance franchise, face uncertainty as their bills remain unpaid and banks threaten to destroy their credit. The company bundled and sold franchisee loans to different banks, but the credit crunch left the company with massive debts and legal disputes.

37795 ■ *"Builders Land Rutenberg Deal"* in *Charlotte Observer (February 2, 2007)*
Ed: Bob Fliss. **Description:** Jim and Larry Sanders purchased a franchise from builder, Arthur Rutenberg Homes. The brothers will build custom homes in the area.

37796 ■ *"Burger King's Whopper: A Marketing 50 Case Study"* in *Advertising Age (Vol. 79, November 17, 2008, No. 43, pp. S10)*
Pub: Crain Communications Inc.
Contact: Rance Crain, President
Ed: Emily Bryson York. **Description:** Burger King has seen a double digit increase in the sales of its Whopper hamburger despite the economic recession that has hit many in the restaurant industry particularly hard. For most of the spring, U.S. same-store-sales gains beat McDonald's.

37797 ■ *"Burritos New Bag for Shopping Developer"* in *Houston Business Journal (Vol. 40, December 4, 2009, No. 30, pp. 4A)*
Pub: American City Business Journals
Ed: Allison Wollam. **Description:** Houston, Texas-based Rob Johnson is the newest franchisee for Bull-ritos and plans to open eight area locations to market the quick-casual burrito concept. The former shopping center developer was looking for a new business sector after selling off his shopping center holdings.

37798 ■ *"A Business That Cares: Dale and Diana Bevington Purchased Their Home Instead Senior Care Franchise in 2007 and Have Seen It Grow From Strength to Strength"* in *Business Franchise (Vol. 213, May 2012, pp. 98)*
Pub: Circle Publishing
Contact: Robert Perry, President
Description: Dale and Diana Bevington have run their Home Instead Senior Care franchise since 2007. The Bevington's launched their company after watching Dale's father, who lived in Canada, was diagnosed with vascular dementia. They feel their franchise business offers everything they needed while caring for Dale's father.

37799 ■ *"Business Thriller or Romantic Fantasy?"* in *Canadian Business (Vol. 85, April 16, 2012, No. 6, pp. 14)*
Pub: Rogers Media Inc.
Contact: Tony Viner, President
Released: April 16, 2012. **Description:** Planet DVD president, Jim Gormley, announced his intention to fill Blockbuster's exit in the rental market with new made in Canada vending machines. Gromely will roll-out Canada's first franchised video rental kiosks and Planet DVD. The first kiosk was installed in fron of Mississauga, Ontario-based Sobeys.

37800 ■ *"Carvel Offers Franchisee Discount"*
in Ice Cream Reporter (Vol. 21, August 20,
2008, No. 9, pp. 2)
Description: Carvel Ice Cream is offering new
franchise opportunities in Florida, New Jersey, and
New York. The company will offer incentive for new
franchise owners.

37801 ■ *"Children's Place Retail Stores Put*
Call Ratio Increases 6.0 Percent, Stock Dips
0.2 Percent" in News Bites US (August 20,
2012)
Pub: Financial Times Ltd.
Contact: John Ridding, Chief Executive Officer
Released: August 20, 2012. **Description:** Invest-
ment information regarding Children's Place Retail
Stores Inc., the largest children's specialty apparel
retailer in the United States, is provided. Thefirm has
signed a 10-year franchise agreement with Apparel
Group to open shops in the Arab Gulf States of the
UAE, Kuwait, Qatar, Bahrain and Oman.

37802 ■ *"Cincinnati Hospitals Face Big*
Whammy From State Fees" in Business
Courier (Vol. 26, October 2, 2009, No. 23, pp.
1)
Pub: American City Business Journals, Inc.
Contact: Whitney Shaw, President
Ed: James Ritchie. **Description:** Ohio hospitals are
facing losses of nearly $145 million in franchise fees
which are set to be levied by the state. Ohio hospitals
will be responsible for a total of $718 million franchise
fees as required by 2010-2011 state budget but will
recover only 80 percent of the amount in increased
Medicaid fees. Possible effects of anticipated losses
to Ohio hospitals are examined.

37803 ■ *"Cold Stone Creamery" in Ice Cream*
Reporter (Vol. 22, January 20, 2009, No. 2, pp.
8)
Description: Franchise News reports that Cold Stone
Creamery is looking for master franchisees to support
its expansion into the North German market. The
report notes that following its successful launch in
Denmark, the firm is also preparing for expansion
into France.

37804 ■ *The Commonsense Way to Build*
Wealth: One Entrepreneur Shares His Secrets
Ed: Jack Chou. **Released:** September 2004. **Price:**
$19.95. **Description:** Entrepreneurial tips to ac-
cumulate wealth, select the proper business or
franchise, choose and manage rental property, and
how to negotiate a good lease.

37805 ■ *"Community Commitment*
Safeguards Franchising Industry" in
Franchising World (Vol. 42, November 2010,
No. 11, pp. 38)
Pub: International Franchise Association
Contact: Stephen J. Caldeira, President
E-mail: scaldeira@franchise.org
Description: Individuals who are dedicated to com-
mitting time and resources to bring to the attention of
legislators those laws and proposals affecting fran-
chise small businesses are highlighted in a monthly
format.

37806 ■ *"Controlling Costs: Update Your*
Information Technology Program" in
Franchising World (Vol. 42, August 2010, No.
8, pp. 18)
Pub: International Franchise Association
Contact: Stephen J. Caldeira, President
E-mail: scaldeira@franchise.org
Ed: Jeff Dumont. **Description:** It is imperative for
any franchise to understand its technology needs in
order to control costs. Needs analysis; creating a
Request for Proposal; and information regarding the
choices between renting, buying or building technol-
ogy are covered. Relationship contingency in franchised organizations is also covered.

37807 ■ *"Convention Budgeting Best*
Practices" in Franchising World (Vol. 42,

November 2010, No. 11, pp. 11)
Pub: International Franchise Association
Contact: Stephen J. Caldeira, President
E-mail: scaldeira@franchise.org
Ed: Steve Friedman. **Description:** Franchise conventions can offer benefits to both franchisor and
franchisee in terms of culture-building, professional
education and networking. However, these conventions can be costly. Tips for planning a successful
franchising convention on a budget are outlined.

37808 ■ *"Corner Bakery Readies Its Recipes*
for Growth" in Dallas Business Journal (Vol.
35, February 17, 2012, No. 23, pp. 1)
Pub: American City Business Journal
Description: Corner Bakery Cafe is planning to add
10 corporate locations and 15-20 franchise locations
in 2012. The company was acquired by Roark
Capital.

37809 ■ *"Creative In-Sourcing Boosts*
Franchisee Performance" in Franchising
World (Vol. 42, September 2010, No. 9, pp. 16)
Pub: International Franchise Association
Contact: Stephen J. Caldeira, President
E-mail: scaldeira@franchise.org
Ed: Daniel M. Murphy. **Description:** Operational
training and support is usually provided by fran-
chisors. To be successful in this process it is important
to balance the reality of limited financial and human
resources.

37810 ■ *"Credit Crunch Takes Bite Out Of*
McDonald's" in Advertising Age (Vol. 79,
September 29, 2008, No. 36, pp. 1)
Pub: Crain Communications Inc.
Contact: Rance Crain, President
Ed: Emily Bryson York. **Description:** McDonald's will
delay its launch of coffee bars inside its restaurants
due to the banking crisis which has prompted Bank
of America to halt loans to the franchise chains.

37811 ■ *"Culture, Community and Chicken*
Fingers" in Entrepreneur (Vol. 37, July 2009,
No. 7, pp. 96)
Pub: Entrepreneur Press
Contact: Perlman Neil, President
Ed: Jason Daley. **Description:** Raising Cane's
Chicken Fingers founder Todd Graves shares his
experiences in running the company - from getting
funding to plans for company. Graves believes that
the company wants franchisees to live and breathe
the brand, and that the key to its success is doing
one thing and doing it right. Cane's Pillar Program, a
financial support program for franchisees, is also
discussed.

37812 ■ *"Customer Loyalty: Making Your*
Program Excel" in Franchising World (Vol. 42,
August 2010, No. 8, pp. 47)
Pub: International Franchise Association
Contact: Stephen J. Caldeira, President
E-mail: scaldeira@franchise.org
Ed: Steve Baxter. **Description:** Customer loyalty is
key to any franchise operation's growth. Tips for
identifying preferred customers are outlined.

37813 ■ *"Day Care for Affluent Drawing a*
Crowd" in Business First Columbus (Vol. 24,
August 15, 2008, No. 52, pp. 1)
Pub: American City Business Journals
Ed: Carrie Ghose. **Description:** Day care centers for
affluent families have grown in popularity in Columbus, Ohio. Primrose Schools Franchising Company
has opened three such schools in the area. Statistical data included.

37814 ■ *"Daycare Dollars" in Small Business*
Opportunities (Winter 2009)
Description: Profile of Maui Playcare, a franchise
that provides parents drop-in daycare for their
children without having to purchase a membership,
make reservations or pay costly dues; the company
is expanding beyond its Hawaiian roots onto the
mainland and is expected to have between 40 and
50 locations signed by the end of 2010.

37815 ■ *"Dig In!" in Entrepreneur (June 2014)*
Pub: Entrepreneur Media Inc.
Released: June 2014. **Description:** Entrepreneur
magazine annually selects the top food franchises
that are staying on trend by focusing on the demands
of health-conscious consumers. More than one-
quarter of the companies in the 2014 Franchise 500
are quick-service restaurants, full-service restaurants
and retail food businesses. The companies included
in the list offer information on the type of services
they provide as well as their startup costs. Interested
investors can use the annual listing guide for entering the food business.

37816 ■ *"Dollar Thrifty Adds Franchises" in*
Journal Record (December 7, 2010)
Pub: Dolan Media Newswires
Ed: D. Ray Tuttle. **Description:** Dollar Thrifty Auto-
motive Group Inc. opened 31 franchise locations in
2010 as part of its expansion plan in the U.S.

37817 ■ *"Dunkin' Donuts Franchise Looking*
Possible for 2011" in Messenger-Inquirer
(January 2, 2010)
Ed: Joy Campbell. **Description:** Dunkin' Donuts has
approved expansion of their franchises in the Owens-
boro, Kentucky region.

37818 ■ *The E Myth Revisited: Why Most*
Small Businesses Don't Work and What to
Do About It
Pub: HarperCollins Publishers Inc.
Contact: Jane Friedman, President
E-mail: jfriedman@harpercollins.com
Ed: Michael E. Gerber. **Released:** January 18, 2010.
Price: $20.99, Paperback; $14.99. **Description:** The
book dispels the myths surrounding starting a busi-
ness and shows how traditional assumptions can get
in the way of running a small company. Topics cover
entrepreneurship from infancy to growth and covers
franchising. **Availability:** E-book.

37819 ■ *"Eat Up!" in Entrepreneur (Vol. 36,*
April 2008, No. 4, pp. 104)
Pub: Entrepreneur Press
Contact: Perlman Neil, President
Ed: Tracy Stapp. **Description:** Provides a list of the
top restaurant franchises. The restaurant franchises
presented are picked out from the 2008 Franchise
500 ranking and are listed according to category.

37820 ■ *"Economic Loss Rule and Franchise*
Attorneys" in Franchise Law Journal (Vol. 27,
Winter 2008, No. 3, pp. 192)
Pub: American Bar Association
Contact: Carolyn Lamm, President
Ed: Christian C. Burden, Scott Trende. **Description:**
Economic loss rule prohibits recovery of damages in
tort when the subject injury is unaccompanied by
either property damage or personal injury.

37821 ■ *Entrepreneur Magazine--Franchise*
500 Survey Issue
Pub: Entrepreneur Press
Contact: Perlman Neil, President
URL(s): www.entrepreneur.com. **Ed:** Rieva Lesonsky. **Released:** Annual; Latest edition 2012. **Publication includes:** Listing and ranking of top 500 franchises in the United States and Canada. **Entries
include:** Company name, address, and, in tabular
form, key statistics. **Arrangement:** Classified by
industry and ranking.

37822 ■ *"Espirito Santo Bank Mulls Potential*
Buyers" in South Florida Business Journal
(Vol. 35, August 22, 2014, No. 4, pp. 4)
Pub: American City Business Journals
Released: August 22, 2014. **Description:** G. Freder-
ick Reinhardt is looking for potential buyers of his
$735 million asset Espirito Santo Bank in Miami,
Florida. Reinhardt says the bank would be a good
franchise for buyers interested in international bank-
ing.

37823 ■ *"Explosive Growth: Wings Over To*
Triple In Size By 2010" in Small Business
Opportunities (Fall 2007)
Ed: Michael L. Corne. **Description:** Profile of Wings
Over, a franchised chain of restaurants offering
chicken wings in 22 flavors; all items are cooked to
order.

37824 ■ *"Fashion Forward - Frugally"* in *Entrepreneur (Vol. 37, July 2009, No. 7, pp. 18)*
Pub: Entrepreneur Press
Contact: Perlman Neil, President
Ed: Jason Daley. **Description:** Staci Deal, a Fayetteville-based franchisee of fashion brand Plato's Closet, shares her experiences on the company's growth. Deal believes that the economy, and the fact that Fayetteville is a college town, played a vital role in boosting the used clothing store's popularity. Her thoughts on being a young business owner, and the advantages of running a franchise are also given.

37825 ■ *"First Franchising Census Report Highlights Industry's Economic Role"* in *Franchising World (Vol. 42, November 2010, No. 11, pp. 41)*
Pub: International Franchise Association
Contact: Stephen J. Caldeira, President
E-mail: scaldeira@franchise.org
Ed: John Reynolds. **Description:** Franchise businesses accounted for 10.5 percent of businesses with paid employees in the year 2007.

37826 ■ *"Fiscally Fit"* in *Entrepreneur (Vol. 37, October 2009, No. 10, pp. 130)*
Pub: Entrepreneur Press
Contact: Perlman Neil, President
Ed: Jason Daley. **Description:** Landrie Peterman, owner of an Anytime Fitness franchise in Oregon, describes how she turned her business around. The franchise, located in an industrial park, saw growth after six months with the help of corporate clients.

37827 ■ *"Flexible Fun"* in *Entrepreneur (September 2014)*
Pub: Entrepreneur Media Inc.
Released: September 2014. **Description:** Jessica McClintic, yoga instructor and business director of Imagination Yoga, shares some of the lessons she learned from running a business that teaches yoga to children. McClintic explains that she loves working with children so she still teaches yoga instead of focusing on running the franchise. She hopes that future franchisees will be fully committed to teach yoga classes themselves. She looks for franchisees who love working with children.

37828 ■ *"Flurry of Activity from Restaurant Groups as Industry Strengthens"* in *Wichita Business Journal (Vol. 27, February 17, 2012, No. 7, pp. 1)*
Pub: American City Business Journal
Description: Atlanta, Georgia-based Chick-fil-A chain is set to open two restaurants in Wichita, Kansas and those additions were highly anticipated. However, there were other local management groups and franchisees that are investing on new buildings and refurbishing stores. Insights on the increasing restaurant constructions are also given.

37829 ■ *"Former Chrysler Dealers Build New Business Model"* in *Crain's Detroit Business (Vol. 25, June 22, 2009, No. 25, pp. 3)*
Pub: Crain Communications Inc. - Detroit
Contact: Keith Crain, Chairman
Ed: Daniel Fuggan. **Description:** Joe Ricci is one of 14 Detroit area dealerships whose franchises have been terminated. Ricci and other Chrysler dealers in the area are starting new businesses or switching to new franchises. Ricci's All American Buyer's Service will be located in Dearborn and will sell only used cars.

37830 ■ *Franchise Handbook*
Pub: Enterprise Magazines Inc.
Contact: Rob Masson, Controller
URL(s): www.franchisehandbook.com. **Ed:** Michael J. McDermott. **Released:** Quarterly; Latest edition 2014. **Price:** $6.99, Single issue; $22.95, Individuals 1 year subscription (4 issues); $42.95, Individuals 2 years (4 issues); $60.95, Individuals 3 years (4 issues). **Covers:** Firms offering franchises. **Entries include:** Franchisor name, headquarters address, phone, president or other contact, description of operation, number of franchises, year founded, and equity capital needed, financial assistance available,

training provided, managerial assistance available. **Arrangement:** Classified by line of business, alphabetical. **Indexes:** Franchising company name.

37831 ■ *"Franchise Law in China: Law, Regulations, and Guidelines"* in *Franchise Law Journal (Vol. 27, Summer 2007, No. 1, pp. 57)*
Pub: American Bar Association
Contact: Carolyn Lamm, President
Ed: Paul Jones, Erik B. Wulff. **Description:** Issues faced by foreign franchising are discussed, with a focus on China.

37832 ■ *"Franchisee to Add 10 New Applebee's"* in *Memphis Business Journal (Vol. 34, June 8, 2012, No. 8, pp. 1)*
Pub: American City Business Journal
Ed: Andy Ashby. **Description:** Apple Investor Group LLC seeks to open 10 more Applebee's restaurants in Memphis over the next two years. The franchisee purchased the 70-county market from DineEquity for $23 million in early 2012. The group is upgrading 17 Mid-South Applbee's units.

37833 ■ *"Franchisees Lose Battle Against BK"* in *Advertising Age (Vol. 79, June 2, 2008, No. 22, pp. 46)*
Pub: Crain Communications Inc.
Contact: Rance Crain, President
Ed: Emily Bryson York. **Description:** Burger King has had continuing litigation with former franchisees from New York, Luan and Elizabeth Sadik, who claim that Burger King's double cheeseburger, along with additional problems, created the environment for their eventual insolvency. Burger King has since terminated its test of selling the double cheeseburger for $1, although the company declined to comment on the reason for this decision.

37834 ■ *"Franchises with an Eye on Chicago"* in *Crain's Chicago Business (Vol. 34, March 14, 2011, No. 11, pp. 20)*
Pub: Crain Communications Inc.
Contact: Todd Johnson, Publisher
Description: Profiles of franchise companies seeking franchisees for the Chicago area include: Extreme Pita, a sandwich shop; Hand and Stone, offering massage, facial and waxing services; Molly Maid, home-cleaning service; Primrose Schools, private accredited schools for children 6 months to 6 hours and after-school programs; Protect Painters, residential and light-commercial painting contractor; and Wingstop, a restaurant offering chicken wings in nine flavors, fries and side dishes.

37835 ■ *"Franchising Lures Boomers"* in *Business Journal-Portland (Vol. 24, November 9, 2007, No. 36, pp. 1)*
Pub: American City Business Journals, Inc.
Ed: Wendy Culverwell. **Description:** Popularity of franchising has increased, and investors belonging to the baby boom generation contribute largely to this growth. The number of aging baby boomers is also increasing, particularly in Oregon, which means further growth of franchises can be expected. Reasons why franchising is a good investment for aging baby boomers are given.

37836 ■ *"Franchising's Green Scene"* in *Entrepreneur (Vol. 37, August 2009, No. 8, pp. 85)*
Pub: Entrepreneur Press
Contact: Perlman Neil, President
Ed: Gwen Moran. **Description:** Trends in favor of environmentally friendly franchises have been growing for about 25 years but have now become mainstream. The challenges for a prospective green franchiser is that these companies may be tricky to evaluate and they need to ask franchisors a lot of questions to weed out ones that falsely claim to be green.

37837 ■ *"Fries With That?"* in *Canadian Business (Vol. 81, September 29, 2008, No. 16, pp. 33)*
Ed: Calvin Leung. **Description:** Profile of Toronto-based New York Fries, which has four stores in South Korea, is planning to expand further as well as into

Hong Kong and Macau; the company also has a licensee in the United Arab Emirates whom is also planning to expand.

37838 ■ *"From War Zone to Franchise Zone"* in *Entrepreneur (Vol. 37, August 2009, No. 8, pp. 104)*
Pub: Entrepreneur Press
Contact: Perlman Neil, President
Ed: Jason Daley. **Description:** Ross Paterson says that he realized that the material he used in the Growth Coach franchise could give the people of Afghanistan the systematic model they need. Paterson says that the Afghans are very business-oriented people but that they work in a different system than Americans.

37839 ■ *"Getting In On the Ground Floor"* in *Entrepreneur (Vol. 37, September 2009, No. 9, pp. 90)*
Pub: Entrepreneur Press
Contact: Perlman Neil, President
Description: Franchise businesses in the United States are listed. Franchise services are mentioned. Statistical data and contact information included.

37840 ■ *"The Global Economy, the Labor Force and Franchising's Future"* in *Franchising World (Vol. 42, September 2010, No. 9, pp. 35)*
Pub: International Franchise Association
Contact: Stephen J. Caldeira, President
E-mail: scaldeira@franchise.org
Ed: Jeffrey A. Rosensweig. **Description:** Point forecasting and the methodology called scenario analysis are presented looking at the global economy and future of franchising in the U.S. and abroad.

37841 ■ *"GM's Decision to Boot Dealer Prompts Sale"* in *Baltimore Business Journal (Vol. 27, November 6, 2009, No. 26, pp. 1)*
Pub: American City Business Journals
Ed: Daniel J. Sernovitz. **Description:** General Motors Corporation's (GM) decision to strip Baltimore's Anderson Automotive Group Inc. of its GM franchise has prompted the owner, Bruce Mortimer, to close the automotive dealership and sell the land to a developer. The new project could make way for new homes, a shopping center and supermarket.

37842 ■ *"Golden Spoon Accelerates Expansion Here and Abroad"* in *Ice Cream Reporter (Vol. 22, December 20, 2008, No. 1, pp. 2)*
Description: Golden Spoon frozen yogurt franchise chain is developing 35 more locations in the Phoenix, Arizona area along with plans to open a store in Japan.

37843 ■ *"Ground Floor Opportunity"* in *Small Business Opportunities (July 2008)*
Pub: Entrepreneur Press
Contact: Perlman Neil, President
Description: Profile of Doug Disney, the founder of the booming franchise Tile Outlet Always in Stock, which sells ceramic and porcelain tile and stone products at wholesale prices; Disney found inspiration in a book he read in two days and that motivated him to expand his venture into a huge franchise opportunity.

37844 ■ *"Haagen-Dazs Recruits Shop Owners through Facebook"* in *Ice Cream Reporter (Vol. 23, November 20, 2010, No. 12, pp. 1)*
Description: Haagen-Dazs Shoppe Company is using Facebook, the leading social media, to recruit new franchises.

37845 ■ *"Happy Trails: RV Franchiser Gives Road Traveling Enthusiasts a Lift"* in *Black Enterprise (Vol. 38, July 2008, No. 12, pp. 47)*
Pub: Earl G. Graves Publishing Co. Inc.
Contact: Earl G. Graves, Jr., President
Ed: Tamara E. Holmes. **Description:** Overview of Bates International Motor Home Rental Systems Inc., a growing franchise that gives RV owners the chance to rent out their big-ticket purchases to others when they are not using them; Sandra Williams Bate launched the company as a franchise in July 1997

and now has a fleet of 30 franchises across the country. She expects the company to reach 2.2 million for 2008 due to a marketing initiative that will expand the company's presence.

37846 ■ "Home Improvement Service Chain Had to Fix Its Own House" in Crain's Detroit Business (Vol. 30, October 13, 2014, No. 41, pp. 15)
Pub: Crain Communications Inc. - Detroit
Contact: Keith Crain, Chairman
Released: October 13, 2014. **Description:** Mr. Handyman International LLC is the franchising arm for the Mr. Handyman home improvement service chain. The franchises provide smaller home repair and improvement projects, mostly residential with only 15 percent of the jobs being commercial. Statistical data included.

37847 ■ "How BBQ Can Be Birmingham's Secret Sauce" in Birmingham Business Journal (Vol. 31, May 9, 2014, No. 19, pp. 4)
Pub: American City Business Journals, Inc.
Contact: Whitney Shaw, President
Released: May 9, 2014. **Description:** Local barbecue joints in Birmingham, Alabama are branching out to new markets and extending distinct barbecue brand of the city through franchises and corporate expansions across the U.S. Experts say this trend is contributing to more brand awareness and tourists for Birmingham.

37848 ■ "Hyannis Mercedes Franchise Sold" in Cape Cod Times (December 2, 2010)
Pub: Cape Cod Times
Contact: Peter Meyer, President
Ed: Sarah Shemkus. **Description:** Trans-Atlantic Motors franchise has been sold to Mercedes-Benz of Westwood.

37849 ■ "IFA-AAG Professional Athlete Franchise Summit Scores" in Franchising World (Vol. 42, August 2010, No. 8, pp. 56)
Pub: International Franchise Association
Contact: Stephen J. Caldeira, President
E-mail: scaldeira@franchise.org
Ed: Miriam L. Brewer. **Description:** The first International Franchise Association-Allied Athlete Group Franchise summit spotlighted athletes turned business owners addressing peers on franchising. The summit is expected to become an annual event.

37850 ■ "In Radical Change-Up, P&G Streamlines How it Promotes Brands" in Business Courier (Vol. 26, October 2, 2009, No. 23, pp. 1)
Pub: American City Business Journals, Inc.
Contact: Whitney Shaw, President
Ed: Lisa Biank Fasig. **Description:** Procter & Gamble (P&G) revised the way it works with marketing, design and public relations firms. Creative discussions will be managed by only two representatives, the franchise leader and the brand agency leader in order for P&G to simplify operations as it grows larger and more global.

37851 ■ "Integrating Your Compliance Program" in Franchising World (Vol. 42, November 2010, No. 11, pp. 49)
Pub: International Franchise Association
Contact: Stephen J. Caldeira, President
E-mail: scaldeira@franchise.org
Ed: Melanie Bergeron. **Description:** Compliance is integral to every part of any business operation and it is necessary for a company to make standards and compliance to those standards a priority.

37852 ■ International Franchise Association--Franchise Opportunities Guide
Pub: International Franchise Association
Contact: Stephen J. Caldeira, President
E-mail: scaldeira@franchise.org
URL(s): www.franchise.org/industrysecondary.aspx?id=3466. **Released:** Semiannual; Latest Edition Spring/Summer 2014. **Price:** $20, Nonmembers plus $10.00 shipping; $12, Members plus $10.00 shipping. **Covers:** Over 5,000 companies offering franchises. **Entries include:** Company name, address, phone, type of business, contact, number of fran-

chised and company-owned outlets, years in business, qualifications expected of prospective franchisees, investment required, training & support provided. **Arrangement:** Classified.

37853 ■ "Iowa Tax Case Could Cost Nation's Franchises" in Franchising World (Vol. 42, September 2010, No. 9, pp. 38)
Pub: International Franchise Association
Contact: Stephen J. Caldeira, President
E-mail: scaldeira@franchise.org
Ed: Bruce A. Ackerman, Adam B. Thimmesch. **Description:** Ruling by the Iowa Supreme Court could have a financial impact on franchisors across the U.S. Iowa asserted that Kentucky Fried Chicken is subject to Iowa corporate income tax based solely on the fact that it received royalties from franchises in the state.

37854 ■ "It's Good To Be King" in South Florida Business Journal (Vol. 35, August 29, 2014, No. 5, pp. 12)
Pub: American City Business Journals
Released: August 29, 2014. **Description:** The $11.4 billion deal that will create a new holding company for Burger King Worldwide and Tim Hortons will be based in Oakville, Ontario, Canada and was met with public outrage. Burger King declares that the merger with the Canadian coffee and doughnut franchise chain was about global growth, not a strategy to avoid millions of dollars in corporate income tax payments to the U.S. government.

37855 ■ "Learn New Ideas from Experienced Menu Makers" in Nation's Restaurant News (Vol. 45, June 27, 2011, No. 13, pp. 82)
Pub: Intertec Publishing
Contact: John French, President
Ed: Nancy Kruse. **Description:** National Restaurant Association Restaurant, Hotel-Motel Show featured the Food Truck Spot, a firm committed to all aspects of mobile catering, foodtruck manufacturers, leasers of fully equipped truck and a food-truck franchising group.

37856 ■ "Lifetime Achievement" in Entrepreneur (July 2014)
Pub: Entrepreneur Media Inc.
Released: July 2014. **Description:** Dawn Lafreeda discusses how she came to be the largest single-owner franchisee of 75 Denny's restaurants in the U.S. Lafreeda recalls her decision to purchase a Denny's restaurant in the small mining town of Globe, Arizona when she was 23. The former Denny's waitress describes how she was received as a young, female business owner and shares her love for the restaurant business. She explains why she remained loyal to Denny's for 30 years and her decision not to diversify her multi-unit franchise.

37857 ■ "Live and Learn: George Cohon" in Canadian Business (Vol. 79, November 20, 2006, No. 23, pp. 70)
Pub: Rogers Media Inc.
Contact: Tony Viner, President
Ed: Zena Olijnyk. **Description:** George Cohon, the founder of McDonald's in Canada and Russia, speaks about the Canadian market and the experience of starting McDonald's in Canada.

37858 ■ "Local Firm Snaps up 91 Area Pizza Huts" in Orlando Business Journal (Vol. 26, January 8, 2010, No. 32, pp. 1)
Pub: American City Business Journals
Ed: Alexis Muellner, Anjali Fluker. **Description:** Orlando, Florida-based CFL Pizza LLC bought the 91 Orlando-area Pizza Hut restaurants for $35 million from parent company Yum! Brands Inc. CFL Pizza plans to distribute parts of the business to Central Florida vendors and the first business up for grabs is the advertising budget.

37859 ■ "Magellan Companies Establishes Century 21 Beachhead in Boise" in Idaho Business Review (September 15, 2014)
Pub: Dolan Co.
Contact: James P. Dolan, President
Released: September 15, 2014. **Description:** New Jersey-based Century 21, the largest real estate franchise worldwide, has entered the Idaho market

under the name Century 21 Magellan Realty with five agents. Wesley Flacker, builder, home renovator, broker, and property manager purchased the franchise and expects to have 60 agents by 2015.

37860 ■ "Making Automated Royalty Payments Work for Your Franchise" in Franchising World (Vol. 42, October 2010, No. 10, pp. 30)
Pub: International Franchise Association
Contact: Stephen J. Caldeira, President
E-mail: scaldeira@franchise.org
Ed: J.P. O'Brien. **Description:** In the past, royalty payments were sent by franchisees through regular postal mail and accompanied by a single slip of paper with handwritten notes indicating the month's revenue numbers and royalty amounts.

37861 ■ "Marketers Push for Mobile Tuesday as the New Black Friday" in Advertising Age (Vol. 79, December 1, 2008, No. 44, pp. 21)
Pub: Crain Communications Inc.
Contact: Rance Crain, President
Ed: Natalie Zmuda. **Description:** Marketers are using an innovative approach in an attempt to stimulate business on the Tuesday following Thanksgiving by utilizing consumer's cell phones to alert them of sales or present them with coupons for this typically slow retail business day; with this campaign both advertisers and retailers are hoping to start Mobile Tuesday, another profitable shopping day in line with Black Friday and Cyber Monday.

37862 ■ "Mattel's Got a Monster Holiday Hit, But Will Franchise Have Staying Power?" in Advertising Age (Vol. 81, December 6, 2010, No. 43)
Pub: Crain Communications Inc.
Contact: Rance Crain, President
Ed: Beth Snyder Bulik. **Description:** Monster High transmedia play expands beyond dolls to merchandise, apparel and entertainment.

37863 ■ "Maximize Your Marketing Results In a Down Economy" in Franchising World (Vol. 42, November 2010, No. 11, pp. 45)
Pub: International Franchise Association
Contact: Stephen J. Caldeira, President
E-mail: scaldeira@franchise.org
Ed: Loren Rakich. **Description:** Strategies to help any franchisee to maximize their marketing efforts in a slow economy are outlined.

37864 ■ "MBA Project Turns on Tastebuds" in The Business Journal - Serving Phoenix and the Valley of the Sun (Vol. 28, August 15, 2008, No. 50)
Ed: Angela Gonzales. **Description:** Amol Khade, Venkat Nallapati and Govind Arora, master of businesss administration graduates from Thunderbird School of Global Management, have opened an Indian restaurant, called The Daba, in Tempe, Arizona. The Indian name of the restaurant means 'a place for travelers to stop for rest and food'. Franchise plans for the restaurant are discussed.

37865 ■ "McDonald's Loses Its Sizzle" in Barron's (Vol. 88, March 17, 2008, No. 11, pp. 47)
Description: McDonald's has promised to return $15 billion to $17 billion to shareholders in 2007-2009 but headwinds are rising for the company. December, 2007 same-store sales were flat and the company's traffic growth in the U.S. is slowing. Its shares are likely to trade in tandem with the market until recession fears recede.

37866 ■ "McD's Dollar-Menu Fixation Sparks Revolt" in Advertising Age (Vol. 79, June 2, 2008, No. 22, pp. 1)
Pub: Crain Communications Inc.
Contact: Rance Crain, President
Ed: Emily Bryson York. **Description:** McDonald's franchisees say that low-cost dollar-menu offerings are impacting their bottom line and many have discontinued the dollar-menu altogether due to rising commodity costs, an increase in minimum wage and consumers trading down to the lower-price items.

37867 ■ *"McD's Picks a Soda Fight; Takes on 7-Eleven With $1 Pop as Economy Softens"* in *Crain's Chicago Business (April 14, 2008)*
Ed: David Sterrett. **Description:** McDonald's Corp. is urging franchise owners to slash prices on large soft drinks to one dollar this summer to win customers from convenience store chains like 7-Eleven.

37868 ■ *"McD's Tries to Slake Consumer Thirst for Wider Choice of Drinks"* in *Advertising Age (Vol. 79, June 9, 2008, No. 23, pp. 1)*
Pub: Crain Communications Inc.
Contact: Rance Crain, President
Ed: Natalie Zmuda. **Description:** McDonald's is testing the sale of canned and bottled drinks in about 150 locations in an attempt to offer more options to consumers who are going elsewhere for their beverage choices.

37869 ■ *"McD's Warms Up For Olympics Performance"* in *Advertising Age (Vol. 79, July 7, 2008, No. 26, pp. 8)*
Pub: Crain Communications Inc.
Contact: Rance Crain, President
Ed: Emily Bryson York. **Description:** Overview of McDonald's marketing plans for the company's sponsorship of the Olympics which includes a website, an alternate-reality game, names featured on U.S. athletes and on-the-ground activities.

37870 ■ *"Menchie's Tops Restaurant Business' Future 50 List"* in *Ice Cream Reporter (Vol. 23, August 20, 2010, No. 9, pp. 4)*
Description: Menchie's, frozen yogurt shop, announced it placed first in the Restaurant Business Magazine's Future 50, ranking the franchise the fastest-growing in the food industry.

37871 ■ *"Mistakes Were Made"* in *Entrepreneur (August 2014)*
Pub: Entrepreneur Media Inc.
Released: August 2014. **Description:** Industry experts consider the financial struggles of some big-name franchises in the U.S. and offer advice on what they need to do to stay in business. New York pizzeria, Sbarro, should focus on making its existing units more operationally successful than trying out a new concept like fast-casual dining. Irrelevance is the main issue that Texas electronics store RadioShack should try to address. The supply-chain markup structure and weak marketing contributed to the bankruptcy of Colorado sandwich maker Quiznos.

37872 ■ *"Mount Laurel Woman Launches Venture Into Children's Used Clothing"* in *Philadelphia Inquirer (September 17, 2010)*
Pub: Philadelphia Media Network
Contact: Robert J. Hall, Chief Executive Officer
Ed: Maria Panaritis. **Description:** Profile of Jennifer Frisch, stay-at-home mom turned entrepreneur. Frisch started a used-clothing store Once Upon a Child after opening her franchised Plato's Closet, selling unwanted and used baby clothing and accessories at her new shop, while offering used merchandise to teens at Plato's Closet.

37873 ■ *"A New Way to Arrive in Style"* in *Inc. (Vol. 33, September 2011, No. 7, pp. 54)*
Pub: Inc. Magazine
Ed: Matthew Rist. **Description:** EagleRider is a franchise offering various two-wheeled rentals, including BMWs and Harley-Davidsons at more than 100 locations worldwide.

37874 ■ *"New Ways To Think About Data Loss: Data Loss Is Costly and Painful"* in *Franchising World (Vol. 42, August 2010, No. 8, pp. 21)*
Pub: International Franchise Association
Contact: Stephen J. Caldeira, President
E-mail: scaldeira@franchise.org
Ed: Ken Colburn. **Description:** Information for maintaining data securely for franchised organizations, including smart phones, tablets, copiers, computers and more is given.

37875 ■ *"NexCen Brands Sells Chains and Will Liquidate"* in *Ice Cream Reporter (Vol. 23, August 20, 2010, No. 9, pp. 1)*
Description: NexCen Brands is closing the sale of its franchise businesses, which include the frozen dessert chains MaggieMoo's and Marbel Slab Creamery, to Global Franchise Group.

37876 ■ *"NFL Labor, Legal Issues Hang Over Detroit Lions' Rebuilding Efforts"* in *Crain's Detroit Business (Vol. 26, January 11, 2010, No. 2)*
Pub: Crain Communications Inc.
Contact: Rance E. Crain, President
Ed: Bill Shea. **Description:** Overview of the possible outcomes regarding labor talks with Detroit Lion's players as well as the outcome of a U.S. Supreme Court decision that could boost franchise values but at the expense of fans and corporate sponsors.

37877 ■ *"Nothing But the Best"* in *Entrepreneur (May 2014)*
Pub: Entrepreneur Media Inc.
Released: May 2014. **Description:** A total of 97 franchises have been ranked at the top of their industry categories in Entrepreneur's 2014 Franchise 500. The list includes Maaco Franchising for automotive appearance services category, Jiffy Lube International for oil change services category, RNR Custom Wheels for wheels and tires category, Novus Glass for windshield repair category and Midas International for miscellaneous repair and maintenance services. Also included are Coffee News and Valpak Direct Marketing Systems for advertising categories.

37878 ■ *"Nurse Next Door Home Health Care Franchise Meets Growing Challenges of Senior Care"* in *Benzinga.com (September 11, 2012)*
Pub: Benzinga.com
Contact: Kyle Bazzy, President
Description: The need for home health care services in the United States is revealed through federal data. Responding to the lack of services, Nurse Next Door, a Canadian home health care franchise, has begun a program to aggressively expand services in the US market. Statistical data included.

37879 ■ *"Ohio Franchisee Buys 21 Jacksonville-Area Papa John's"* in *Florida Times-Union (December 20, 2010)*
Pub: Florida Times-Union
Ed: Mark Basch. **Description:** Ohio-based Papa John's pizza franchise acquired 21 of the restaurants in Duval, Clay and St. Johns counties in Jacksonville, Florida.

37880 ■ *"Open Price Agreements: Good Faith Pricing in the Franchise Relationship"* in *Franchise Law Journal (Vol. 27, Summer 2007, No. 1, pp. 45)*
Pub: American Bar Association
Contact: Carolyn Lamm, President
Ed: Douglas C. Berry, David M. Byers, Daniel Oates. **Description:** Open price term contracts are important to franchise businesses. Details of open price contracts are examined.

37881 ■ *"Opportunity Knocks"* in *Small Business Opportunities (September 2008)*
Description: Profile of YourOffice USA, a franchise that provides home-based and small businesses cost-effective and efficient support through 'virtual' offices that are available as much or as little as the client needs it; they also supply necessary tools such as a professional business address, private mailbox service, personalized telephone answering and more that supports clients who want to look, act and operate with an advanced business image.

37882 ■ *"Ordering Pizza Hut From Your Facebook Page? It's on the Way"* in *Advertising Age (Vol. 79, November 10, 2008, No. 42, pp. 50)*
Pub: Crain Communications Inc.
Contact: Rance Crain, President
Ed: Emily Bryson York. **Description:** Fast-food chains are experimenting with delivery/takeout services via social networks such as Facebook and iPhone applications. This also allows the chains to build valuable databases of their customers.

37883 ■ *"Ownership Form, Managerial Incentives, and the Intensity of Rivalry"* in *Academy of Management Journal (Vol. 50, No. 4, August 1, 2007, pp. 901)*
Pub: Academy of Management
Contact: Ming-Jer Chen, President
Ed: Govert Vroom, Javier Gimeo. **Description:** Ways in which differences in ownership form between franchised and company-owned units alter managerial incentives and competitive pricing in different oligopolistic contexts, or following competitors into foreign markets, is presented.

37884 ■ *"Panera Breadwinner Tries on Tattu Designer Jeans"* in *Houston Business Journal (Vol. 40, December 18, 2009, No. 32, pp. 1)*
Pub: American City Business Journals
Ed: Allison Wollam. **Description:** Chuck Cain, the franchisee who introduced Panera Bread to Houston, Texas has partnered with tax accountant Jim Jacobsen to introduce custom-make Tattu Jeans. As more Tattu Jeans outlets are being planned, Cain is using entrepreneurial lessons learned from Panera Bread in the new venture. Both Panera Bread and Tattu Jeans were opened by Cain during economic downturns.

37885 ■ *"Personal Pizza Goes Franchise Route"* in *Atlanta Journal-Constitution (December 22, 2010)*
Ed: Bob Townsend. **Description:** Your Pie, developer of the personal-size pizza franchise concept is profiled.

37886 ■ *"Pizza or Beer? Why Kalil Made Right Call"* in *Business Journal (Vol. 31, January 31, 2014, No. 36, pp. 6)*
Pub: American City Business Journals
Released: January 31, 2014. **Description:** Businessman, Matt Kalil, purchased the Pieology franchise rights for Minnesota. Kalil will open his first locations in Maple Grove and Saint Paul's Highland Park. The restaurant franchise is expected to have six locations by the end of 2014.

37887 ■ *"Pizza Chain Enters Boston"* in *Boston Business Journal> (Vol. 34, April 25, 2014, No. 12, pp. 3)*
Pub: American City Business Journals, Inc.
Contact: Whitney Shaw, President
Released: April 25, 2014. **Description:** Mitch Roberts and David Peterman have decided to sign a franchise agreement with Blaze Pizza. The two restaurateurs will bring the California-based restaurant chain to Boston, Massachusetts.

37888 ■ *"Practical Approach to Addressing Holdover Ex-Franchisee Trademark Issues"* in *Franchise Law Journal (Vol. 27, Summer 2007, No. 1, pp. 30)*
Pub: American Bar Association
Contact: Carolyn Lamm, President
Ed: Christopher P. Bussert, William Bryner. **Description:** Franchisor-franchisee relationships can become legally complicated when they are terminated. Laws governing trademarks and other proprietary materials are examined.

37889 ■ *"Prepaid Cards and State Unclaimed Property Laws"* in *Franchise Law Journal (Vol. 27, Summer 2007, No. 1, pp. 23)*
Pub: American Bar Association
Contact: Carolyn Lamm, President
Ed: Phillip Bohl, Kathryn Bergstrom, Kevin Moran. **Description:** Unredeemed value of electronic prepaid stored-value credit cards for retail purchases is known as breakage. Laws governing unclaimed property as it relates to these gift cards is covered.

37890 ■ *"The Profitability of Mobility"* in *Entrepreneur (Vol. 37, September 2009, No. 9, pp. 98)*
Pub: Entrepreneur Press
Contact: Perlman Neil, President
Ed: John Daley. **Description:** Wireless Zone franchisee Jonah Engler says he manages the business by hiring managers that could do the job. He has given

his employees small equity ownership in the company. He also says great service and referrals have contributed to his business' growth.

37891 ■ "Prominent Hispanic Businessman Signs With Choice Hotels" in Hispanic Business (Vol. 30, March 2008, No. 3, pp. 36)

Ed: Melinda Burns. **Description:** Chairman of the board of Lopez Food Inc., John C. Lopez signs the agreement with Choice Hotels International to build five new Cambria suites in the USA. This is his first hotel venture and also the first Hispanic franchisee to enter into business with Choice Hotels.

37892 ■ "Q&A With Devin Ringling: Franchise's Services Go Beyond Elder Care" in Gazette (October 2, 2010)

Pub: The Gazette

Ed: Bill Radford. **Description:** Profile of franchise, Interim HealthCare, in Colorado Springs, Colorado; the company offers home care services that include wound care and specialized feedings to shopping and light housekeeping. It also runs a medical staffing company that provides nurses, therapists and other health care workers to hospitals, prisons, schools and other facilities.

37893 ■ "Quiznos Franchisees Walloped by Recession" in Advertising Age (Vol. 79, October 20, 2008, No. 39, pp. 3)

Pub: Crain Communications Inc.

Contact: Rance Crain, President

Ed: Emily Bryson York. **Description:** While the recession has taken a toll on the entire restaurant industry, a number of Quiznos franchisees claim to have been disproportionately affected due to lackluster marketing, higher-than-average commodity costs, competition with Subway and a premium-pricing structure that is incompatible with a tight economy.

37894 ■ "Report: McD's Pepsi Score Best With Young Hispanics" in Brandweek (Vol. 49, April 21, 2008, No. 16, pp. 8)

Pub: Nielsen Business Media Inc.

Contact: Howard Appelbaum, President

Ed: Della de Lafuente. **Description:** According to a new report, in order to reach Hispanic Gen Yers, marketing strategists need to understand this demographic's 'bi-dentity,' something which has proved an elusive task to many marketers. Another trend is the emergence of Latinas who have careers, as opposed to just jobs. There is an opportunity to tap this new, young and empowered female market with innovative messaging. Statistical data included.

37895 ■ "Retail Franchises to Start Now" in Entrepreneur (Vol. 37, August 2009, No. 8, pp. 88)

Pub: Entrepreneur Press

Contact: Perlman Neil, President

Ed: Tracy Stapp Herold. **Description:** Listing of retail franchises is presented and is categorized based on their products sold. The total cost of the franchise and the website are also included as well as additional statistical data.

37896 ■ "Right at Home China Celebrates 1 Year Anniversary as U.S. In-Home Senior Care Master Franchise" in Professional Service Close-Up (June 24, 2012)

Description: Franchisor, Right at Home International Inc., provides in-home senior care and assistance and has experienced a one year franchise license agreement in China. Right at Home China predicts growth because China has 200 million adults over 65 years of age.

37897 ■ "Road Map to the New FTC Franchise Rule" in Franchise Law Journal (Vol. 27, Fall 2007, No. 2, pp. 105)

Pub: American Bar Association

Contact: Carolyn Lamm, President

Ed: Gerald C. Wells, Dennis E. Wieczorek. **Description:** Information about the Federal Trade Commission's revised Franchise Rule (16 C.F.R. Part 436 Disclosure Requirements and Prohibitions Concerning Franchising) (the New Rule) which replaces the

original 1978 Franchise Rule (the Old Rule) is given; a comprehensive overview of the New Rule and its implications for the franchise industry is included.

37898 ■ "Rooting for Hispanic Dollars" in Hispanic Business (October 2007, pp. 76, 80)

Pub: Hispanic Business Inc.

Contact: Jesus Chavarria, President

Ed: Mike Traphagen. **Description:** Sports franchises are working to gain and retain the Hispanic market.

37899 ■ "Running the Franchise Numbers" in Entrepreneur (Vol. 37, July 2009, No. 7, pp. 87)

Pub: Entrepreneur Press

Contact: Perlman Neil, President

Ed: Carol Tice. **Description:** Ways in which entrepreneurs can assess if they are ready to be a multi-unit franchisee are presented. Choosing the right locations, knowing how much assistance they can get from the franchisor, and financing are the key considerations when planning additional franchise units. Examples of success in multi-unit operations and multi-unit terms are also presented.

37900 ■ "Salad Creations To Open 2nd Location" in Crain's Detroit Business (Vol. 24, March 3, 2008, No. 9, pp. 26)

Ed: Brent Snavely. **Description:** Salad Creations, a franchise restaurant that allows customers to create their own salads and also offers soups and sandwiches; Salad Creations plans to open a total of five locations by the end of 2008.

37901 ■ "SBA Lauds Anchorage DQ Franchise" in Alaska Business Monthly (Vol. 27, October 2011, No. 10, pp. 9)

Pub: Alaska Business Publishing Company Inc.

Contact: Jim Martin, President

Ed: Nancy Pounds. **Description:** US Small Business Administration (SBA) honored Greg Todd, operator of four DQ Grill and Chill eateries in Anchorage, Alaska. The firm has created 100 jobs since receiving SBA assistance.

37902 ■ "Schlotzky's Tries for Twin Cities Revival" in Business Journal (Vol. 31, January 17, 2014, No. 34, pp. 4)

Pub: American City Business Journals

Released: January 17, 2014. **Description:** Austin, Texas-based Schlotzky's announced plans to open six Minnesota locations as it tries to regain its national prominence. The bankruptcy in 2004 and the reduction of its restaurant count has wiped out eight Minnesota restaurants and left only the Edina location. Schlotzky's six-restaurant deal with the local franchisees is examined.

37903 ■ "Seasonal Franchises: Strategies to Advance" in Franchising World (Vol. 42, August 2010, No. 8, pp. 50)

Pub: International Franchise Association

Contact: Stephen J. Caldeira, President

E-mail: scaldeira@franchise.org

Ed: Jennifery Lemcke. **Description:** Seasonal franchises, such as tax businesses can be slow during the summer months. Restaurants are slow during the months of January and February. The various challenges faced by seasonal franchises are examined.

37904 ■ "Sellers Shift Gears" in Crain's Detroit Business (Vol. 25, June 22, 2009, No. 25, pp. 3)

Pub: Crain Communications Inc. - Detroit

Contact: Keith Crain, Chairman

Description: Of the 14 new car Chrysler dealerships in the Detroit area who had franchises terminated, Joe Ricci of Dearborn will sell used cars at his new business called All American Buyer's Service; Lochmoor Automotive Group in Detroit will focus on Mahindra & Mahindra trucks; Mt. Clemens Dodge, Clinton Township is also selling Mahindra & Mahindra trucks; and Monicatti Chrysler Jeep, Sterling Heights, will offer service along with selling used cars.

37905 ■ "Serious Growth Ahead for Tokyo Joe's" in Denver Business Journal (Vol. 65, April 4, 2014, No. 47, pp. A9)

Pub: American City Business Journals

Released: April 4, 2014. **Description:** Tokyo Joe's founder and chief innovation officer, Larry Leith, shares his perspective on the franchising and expansion of the Colorado-based Asian fast food chain. Leith describes the fast-casual chain market in Denver and considers the possibility of going public in the future.

37906 ■ "Setting Out on Your Own? Think Franchises" in Crain's Cleveland Business (Vol. 28, October 8, 2007, No. 40, pp. 20)

Pub: Crain Communications Inc.

Description: Franchisers are targeting baby boomers due to their willingness to put up some of their own money to open their own business. According to local franchising expert, Joel Libava, entrepreneurs should expect to pay about 15 to 30 percent of the total cost of starting the franchise out of their own pocket.

37907 ■ "Shout and Devour" in Tulsa World (November 7, 2009)

Ed: Kyle Arnold. **Description:** Profile of convenience store Shout and Sack whose owners have distanced themselves from the corporate fray of the chain stores by offering homemade lunches served at a counter; the store recently gained national exposure that highlighted the popularity despite a market share heavily dominated by franchises and chains.

37908 ■ "Silver Dollars" in Small Business Opportunities (September 2008)

Description: Profile of Always Best Care Senior Services, a franchise created by Michael Newman, which offers non-medical In-Home Care, Personal Emergency Response Systems, and Assisted Living Placement Services to seniors; the company offers franchisees the opportunity to fill what is oftentimes a void for the seniors and their families in the community.

37909 ■ "Simplifying Social Media for Optimum Results" in Franchising World (Vol. 42, August 2010, No. 8, pp. 12)

Pub: International Franchise Association

Contact: Stephen J. Caldeira, President

E-mail: scaldeira@franchise.org

Ed: Paul Segreto. **Description:** Keys to effective technology usage requires the development of an integrated plan, choosing the most complementary tools and implementing well-planned strategies.

37910 ■ "Skinner's No Drive-Thru CEO" in Crain's Chicago Business (Vol. 31, April 28, 2008, No. 17, pp. 1)

Pub: Crain Communications Inc.

Contact: Todd Johnson, Publisher

Ed: David Sterrett. **Description:** Profile of James Skinner who was named CEO for McDonald's Corp. in November 2004 and has proved to be a successful leader despite the number of investors who doubted him when he came to the position. Mr. Skinner has overseen three years of unprecedented sales growth and launched the biggest menu expansion in 30 years.

37911 ■ Small Business Desk Reference

Pub: Penguin Books USA Inc.

Released: December 2004. **Price:** $29.95. **Description:** Comprehensive guide for starting or running a successful small business, focusing on buying a business or franchise, writing a business plan, financial management, accounting, legal issues, human resources management, operations, marketing, sales, customer service, taxes, insurance, and ethics. Information for launching a restaurant, property management firm, retail outlet, consulting firm, and service business is included.

37912 ■ "State High Court Gives Franchisors a Win" in Sacramento Business Journal (Vol. 31, September 5, 2014, No. 28, pp. 3)

Pub: American City Business Journals

Released: September 5, 2014. **Description:** The California Supreme Court ruled that Domino's Pizza is not responsible for a sexual harassment charge against the manager of one of its franchisees. The ruling counters the recent decision of the National Labor Relations Board that McDonald's could be considered a joint employer in a franchise case involving reaction to employee protests.

37913 ■ *"Steering Toward Profitability" in Black Enterprise (Vol. 41, December 2010, No. 5, pp. 72)*
Pub: Earl G. Graves Publishing Co. Inc.
Contact: Earl G. Graves, Jr., President
Ed: Alan Hughes. **Description:** Systems Electro Coating LLC had to make quick adjustments when auto manufacturers were in a slump. The minority father-daughter team discuss their strategies during the auto industry collapse.

37914 ■ *"Subway Launches Expanded Cafes, Drive-Thru Window Locations" in South Florida Business Journal (Vol. 33, August 10, 2012, No. 2, pp. 1)*
Pub: American City Business Journal
Description: Subway launched its larger cafe concept at Florida Atlantic University and plans to open more drive-thru restaurants in South Florida. This could change preferred leasing locations to Subway franchisees, which are also moving into nontraditional locations. Site selection issues are covered.

37915 ■ *"Sun Capital Partners Affiliate Acquires Timothy's Coffees" in Miami Daily Business Review (March 26, 2008)*
Description: An affiliate of Sun Capital Partners acquired Timothy's Coffees of the World. Timothy's operates and franchises 166 stores offering coffees, muffins, and Michel's Baguette products.

37916 ■ *"Sweet Tea From McDonald's: A Marketing 50 Case Study" in Advertising Age (Vol. 79, November 17, 2008, No. 43, pp. 4)*
Pub: Crain Communications Inc.
Contact: Rance Crain, President
Ed: Emily Bryson York. **Description:** McDonald's launch of iced coffee and sweat tea, which were promoted via price cuts over the summer, helped to boost sales at the fast-food chain.

37917 ■ *"Taco Bell Late-Night: A Marketing 50 Case Study" in Advertising Age (Vol. 79, November 17, 2008, No. 43, pp. S2)*
Pub: Crain Communications Inc.
Contact: Rance Crain, President
Ed: Emily Bryson York. **Description:** Due to the addition of new products such as a low-calorie, low-fat Fresco menu; a fruity iced beverage; and a value initiative, Taco Bell now accounts for half of Yum Brands' profits. The chain has also benefited from a new chief marketing officer, David Ovens, who oversees ad support.

37918 ■ *"Taking the Right Road" in Entrepreneur (Vol. 37, October 2009, No. 10, pp. 104)*
Pub: Entrepreneur Press
Contact: Perlman Neil, President
Ed: Jason Daley. **Description:** Joe Grubb's franchise of BrightStar Healthcare, a home health care provider, in Knoxville, Tennessee has grown into a $1 million business. Grubb, a former sales agent, experienced slow growth for his franchise and had to deal with cash flow issues during its first few months.

37919 ■ *"Tap the iPad and Mobile Internet Device Market" in Franchising World (Vol. 42, September 2010, No. 9, pp. 43)*
Pub: International Franchise Association
Contact: Stephen J. Caldeira, President
E-mail: scaldeira@franchise.org
Ed: John Thomson. **Description:** The iPad and other mobile Internet devices will help franchise owners interact with customers. It will be a good marketing tool for these businesses.

37920 ■ *"Tasti D-Lite Has Franchise Agreement for Australia" in Ice Cream Reporter (Vol. 23, November 20, 2010, No. 12, pp. 3)*
Description: Tasti D-Lite signed an international master franchise agreement with Friezer Australia Pty. Ltd. and will open 30 units throughout Australia over the next five years.

37921 ■ *"Technology Drivers to Boost Your Bottom Line" in Franchising World (Vol. 42, August 2010, No. 8, pp. 15)*
Pub: International Franchise Association
Contact: Stephen J. Caldeira, President
E-mail: scaldeira@franchise.org
Ed: Dan Dugal. **Description:** Technological capabilities are expanding quickly and smart franchises should stay updated on all the new developments, including smart phones, global positioning systems, and social media networks.

37922 ■ *"Thinking Strategically About Technology" in Franchising World (Vol. 42, August 2010, No. 8, pp. 9)*
Pub: International Franchise Association
Contact: Stephen J. Caldeira, President
E-mail: scaldeira@franchise.org
Ed: Bruce Franson. **Description:** Nearly 25 percent of companies waste money from their technology budget. Most of the budget is spent on non-strategic software. Ways to spend money on technology for any franchise are examined.

37923 ■ *"Thriving DFW Big Target for Franchisors" in Dallas Business Journal (Vol. 35, March 30, 2012, No. 29, pp. 1)*
Description: Dallas-Fort Worth Metropolitan Area has attracted outside franchisors looking to expand as Texas continues to fare better than other states during the recession. The Internation Franchising Association estimates that there will be 21,772 franchise establishments in DFW in 2012.

37924 ■ *"Tims Aims for Breakfast Breakout" in Globe & Mail (February 13, 2006, pp. B3)*
Ed: Andy Hoffman. **Description:** Fast food chain Tim Hortons will be launching its new breakfast menu with more combinations that include bacons, eggs and coffee. Tim Horton is subsidiary of Wendy's International Inc and has 290 outlets in America.

37925 ■ *"Top IPhone Apps" in Advertising Age (Vol. 79, December 15, 2008, No. 46, pp. 17)*
Pub: Crain Communications Inc.
Contact: Rance Crain, President
Ed: Marissa Miley. **Description:** Free and low cost applications for the iPhone are described including Evernote, an application that allows users to outsource their memory to keep track of events, notes, ides and more; Handshake, a way for users to exchange business cards and pictures across Wi-Fi and 3G; CityTransit, an interactive map of the New York subway system that uses GPS technology to find nearby stations and also tells the user if a train is out of commission that day; and Stage Hand which allows users to deliver a presentation, control timing and slide order on the spot.

37926 ■ *"Training: an Investment in Performance Improvement" in Franchising World (Vol. 42, September 2010, No. 9, pp. 22)*
Pub: International Franchise Association
Contact: Stephen J. Caldeira, President
E-mail: scaldeira@franchise.org
Ed: Catherine Monson. **Description:** Advantages of training provided by franchisors that are available to franchisees and their employees is discussed.

37927 ■ *"Turn, Turn, Turn" in Entrepreneur (September 2014)*
Pub: Entrepreneur Media Inc.
Released: September 2014. **Description:** A number of franchises in the U.S. remodeled their brands in anticipation of the changes in the marketplace. Meineke rebranded its stores from Meineke Discount Muffler Shops to Meineke Care Care Centers and started offering other automotive services. Popeye's Chicken and Biscuits changes its name to Popeye's Louisiana Kitchen to showcase its Louisiana heritage. Dairy Queen promoted its hot foods and salads alongside the sweet treats to boost sales. Madeleine Country French Café decided to open the business to franchising.

37928 ■ *"U-Swirl Added to SBA's Franchise Registry" in Ice Cream Reporter (Vol. 23, September 20, 2010, No. 10, pp. 1)*
Description: Healthy Fast Food Inc., parent to the U-SWIRL Frozen Yogurt cafe chain announced that the U.S. Small Business Administration listed U-SWIRL Frozen Yogurt on its official franchise registry. This move will allow U-SWIRL the benefits of a streamlined review process for SBA financing.

37929 ■ *"U-Swirl To Open in Salt Lake City Metro Market" in Ice Cream Reporter (Vol. 23, November 20, 2010, No. 12, pp. 4)*
Description: Healthy Fast Food Inc., parent company to U-SWIRL International Inc., the owner and franchisor of U-SWIRL Frozen Yogurt cafes signed a franchising area development agreement for the Salt Lake City metropolitan area with Regents Management and will open 5 cafes over a five year period.

37930 ■ *Ultimate Guide to Buying or Selling Your Business*
Ed: Ira N. Nottonson. **Released:** September 2004. **Price:** $24.95 (US), $35.95 (Canadian). **Description:** Proven strategies to evaluate, negotiate, and buy or sell a small business. Franchise and family business succession planning is included.

37931 ■ *"Valuation of Intangible Assets in Franchise Companies and Multinational Groups: A Current Issue" in Franchise Law Journal (Vol. 27, No. 3, Winter 2008)*
Pub: American Bar Association
Contact: Carolyn Lamm, President
Ed: Bruce D. Schaeffer, Susan J. Robins. **Description:** Intangible assets, also known as intellectual properties are the most valuable assets for companies today. Legal intellectual property issues faced by franchises firms are discussed.

37932 ■ *"V&J Scores Partnership with Shaq" in Business Journal-Milwaukee (Vol. 25, October 12, 2007, No. 2, pp. A1)*
Pub: American City Business Journals
Ed: Rich Kirchen. **Description:** O'Neal Franchise Group has agreed to a partnership with V&J Foods of Milwaukee to handle Auntie Anne's shops in New York, South Africa, Michigan, and the Caribbean. V&J O'Neal Enterprises will open six Auntie Anne's soft pretzel shops in Detroit towards the end of 2007. Planned international ventures of the partnership are presented.

37933 ■ *"Visionary Riches" in Small Business Opportunities (Winter 2009)*
Description: Profile of Sterling Optical, which was included in a recent listing of 25 franchise high performers in The Wall Street Journal and is poised for mega-growth due to its offerings of professional eye exams, impeccable customer service, convenient locations and a great selection of eyewear.

37934 ■ *"V's Barbershop Opening in Bakerview Square" in Bellingham Business Journal (Vol. March 2010, pp. 2)*
Pub: Sound Publishing Inc.
Contact: Gloria G. Fletcher, President
Description: Upscale barbershop franchise catering to men, V's Barbershop, will open a new location in Bakerview Square (its first in Washington) in 2010. The new location will include six chairs and will appear like an old-time barbershop with a contemporary flavor featuring real barber chairs, flat-screen TVs, and hot lather shaves using a straight-edge razor.

37935 ■ *"Want Leverage? Multi-Unit Franchisees Deliver Substantial Savings" in Franchising World (Vol. 42, October 2010, No. 10, pp. 39)*
Pub: International Franchise Association
Contact: Stephen J. Caldeira, President
E-mail: scaldeira@franchise.org
Ed: Aziz Hashim. **Description:** Many retail franchises selling the same product are able to buy in bulk. Volume-buying can save money for any franchise.

37936 ■ *"Wendy's Mulls Total Hortons Selloff" in Globe & Mail (January 7, 2006, pp. B5)*
Pub: CTVglobemedia Publishing Inc.
Ed: Sinclair Stewart, Omar El Akkad. **Description:** The plans of Wendy's International Inc. to spin off Tim Hortons are presented.

37937 ■ *"Wendy's Speeds Up Tims Spinout" in Globe & Mail (January 11, 2006, pp. B1)*
Pub: CTVglobemedia Publishing Inc.
Ed: Andrew Willis. **Description:** The reasons behind the decision of Wendy's International Inc. to bid Tim Hortons are presented.

37938 ■ *"What Dead Zone?" in Entrepreneur (Vol. 37, October 2009, No. 10, pp. 128)*
Pub: Entrepreneur Press
Contact: Perlman Neil, President
Ed: Jason Daley. **Description:** Joe Purifico, Halloween Adventure franchises co-owner and chief executive officer, discusses the Halloween superstore phenomenon. Malls allow seasonal leasing for Halloween stores due to the high number of customers these stores attract.

37939 ■ *"When Are Sales Representatives Also Franchisees?" in Franchise Law Journal (Vol. 27, Winter 2008, No. 3, pp. 151)*
Pub: American Bar Association
Contact: Carolyn Lamm, President
Ed: John R.F. Baer, David A. Beyer, Scott P. Weber. **Description:** Review of the traditional definitions of sales representatives along with information on how these distribution models could fit into various legal tests for a franchise.

37940 ■ *"When Worlds Collide: The Enforceability of Arbitration Agreements in Bankruptcy" in Franchise Law Journal (Vol. 27, Summer 2007)*
Pub: American Bar Association
Contact: Carolyn Lamm, President
Ed: Mark Salzberg, Gary Zinkgraf. **Description:** Most franchise agreements carry broad arbitration clauses requiring arbitration of nearly all disputes between franchisor and franchisee; how these clauses govern issues of bankruptcy are explored.

37941 ■ *"While Competitors Shut Doors, Subway Is Still Growing" in Advertising Age (Vol. 79, July 21, 2008, No. 28, pp. 4)*
Pub: Crain Communications Inc.
Contact: Rance Crain, President
Ed: Emily Bryson York. **Description:** Subway, the largest fast-food chain, with 22,000 U.S. locations, is adding 800 this year, despite the economic downturn that has caused competitors such as Starbucks to close stores and McDonald's to focus its expansion abroad.

37942 ■ *"Wild-Goose Chaser" in Entrepreneur (Vol. 37, September 2009, No. 9, pp. 96)*
Pub: Entrepreneur Press
Contact: Perlman Neil, President
Ed: Jason Daley. **Description:** Geese Police owner David Marcks says he discovered that trained collies could chase geese off golf courses, which started his business. He gives new franchises two dogs to start their business. The company has fared well even during the economic crisis.

37943 ■ *"Worth His Salt" in Hawaii Business (Vol. 53, January 2008, No. 7, pp. 45)*
Pub: PacificBasin Communications
Ed: Jolyn Okimoto Rosa. **Description:** Bryan Zada owns three PretzelMaker franchises, whose total loss amounted to $40,000 in 2003. Zada believes that listening to employees was one of the key steps in turning the business around. The efforts made to improve the franchises' products are also given.

37944 ■ *"Yogun Fruz Adds First Location in Southern New York State" in Ice Cream Reporter (Vol. 23, September 20, 2010, No. 10, pp. 2)*
Description: Yogen Fruz signed a master franchise agreement to expand into the southern counties of New York State. The firm offers a healthy and beneficial option to fast food and typical dessert choices.

TRADE PERIODICALS

37945 ■ *Business Opportunities Journal*
Pub: Business Service Corp.
URL(s): www.boj.com. **Ed:** Mark Adkins. **Released:** Monthly

37946 ■ *Canadian Pizza Magazine*
Pub: Annex Publishing & Printing Inc.
Contact: Martin McAnulty, Director
URL(s): www.canadianpizzamag.comwww.annex-web.com/. **Ed:** Laura Aiken. **Released:** 8/year **Price:** $19, Canada; $35, U.S.; $45, Other countries.

37947 ■ *Franchise News*
Pub: Franchise News
Ed: C. Richey, Editor. **Released:** Quarterly. **Price:** Included in membership. **Description:** Provides information about franchising. Recurring features include letters to the editor, interviews, news of research, a calendar of events, news of educational opportunities, reports of meetings, notices of publications available, and legal and global franchising news.

37948 ■ *Franchising World*
Pub: International Franchise Association
Contact: Stephen J. Caldeira, President
E-mail: scaldeira@franchise.org
URL(s): franchisingworld.comwww.franchise.org/Franchise-Industry-Fran-World.aspx. **Released:** Monthly **Price:** $50, Individuals.

VIDEOCASSETTES/ AUDIOCASSETTES

37949 ■ *The Franchising Explosion*
Released: 1989. **Price:** $29.95. **Description:** The business phenomenon of franchising is explained by the experts at the University of Nebraska-Lincoln. **Availability:** VHS; 3/4 U.

37950 ■ *How to Buy a Franchise*
Chesney Communications
2302 Martin St., Ste. 125
Irvine, CA 92612
Ph: (949)263-5500
Free: 800-223-8878
Fax: (949)263-5506
Contact: G. Kroll, General Manager
Released: 1987. **Price:** $39.95. **Description:** Find out how to become a francisee. **Availability:** VHS; 3/4 U.

TRADE SHOWS AND CONVENTIONS

37951 ■ Franchising Conference & Expo
E.J. Krause and Associates Inc.
6430 Rockledge Dr., Ste. 200
Bethesda, MD 20817
Ph: (301)493-5500
Fax: (301)493-5705
Co. E-mail: info@ejkrause.com
URL: http://www.ejkrause.com
Contact: Ned Krause, President
URL(s): www.franquiciaweb.com. **Frequency:** Annual. **Audience:** General public and industry professionals. **Principal Exhibits:** Franchise systems and conference about purchasing a franchise. **Telecommunication Services:** centro@franquiciaweb.com.

CONSULTANTS

37952 ■ Damas & Associates
6810 S Cedar St., Ste. 2B
Lansing, MI 48911-6961
Ph: (517)694-0910
Fax: (517)694-1377
Contact: Raymond J. Damas, Owner
Scope: Franchise developers and consultants for franchisers in such areas as structuring the franchise, drafting agreements and disclosures statements, registering the franchise offerings where necessary, advising on matters pertaining to anti-trust trade name and trademark protection and rights and

corporate matters, developing marketing materials and operating manuals and marketing franchises. **Founded:** 1979.

37953 ■ Follow-Up News
185 Pine St., Ste. 818
Manchester, CT 06040-5882
Ph: (860)647-7542
Free: 800-708-0696
Fax: (860)646-6544
Co. E-mail: followupnews@aol.com
Contact: Mark Merrill, Owner
Scope: Offers low cost, low volume, target marketing solutions, to small and medium size businesses that never thought before, they had the time or money to advertise and implement loyalty, referral, frequency, retention, reference, name recognition and new customer prospecting programs. **Special Services:** Database management.

37954 ■ Franchise Architects
250 Parkway Dr., Ste. 150
Lincolnshire, IL 60069
Ph: (847)465-3400
Fax: (847)325-5566
Co. E-mail: info@franchisearchitects.com
URL: http://www.franchisearchitects.com
Contact: Craig S. Slavin, President
E-mail: craig@franchisearchitects.com
URL(s): www.franchisecentralusa.com. **Scope:** Creates and manages indirect channels of distribution, which include franchising, licensing, dealerships and distributorships. Development and consulting services include strategic planning, positioning, naming, creation or refinement of training programs, operational manuals, marketing strategies and collateral brochures; organizational surveys and development; and human resource assessment. Industries served: retail, transportation, food service, technology, service and communications. **Founded:** 1980. **Seminars:** Making the Transition from Entrepreneurial to a Professionally Managed Company; Franchising - Is It for You?; The Franchise Success System.

37955 ■ Franchise Brokers Network
3617 Silverside Rd., Ste. A
Wilmington, DE 19810-5117
Ph: (302)478-0200
Contact: N. Norman Schutzman, President
Scope: Serves companies that interested in expanding their business by way of franchising. Provides all services including feasibility studies, contracts, disclosure statement, brochure, marketing plan, advertising program and a sales organization to bring the franchise to market. Active with manufacturing, sales, service, retail and food and beverage companies. Services individuals who: interested into going into their own business. **Founded:** 1976.

37956 ■ Franchise Developments Inc. (FDI)
5001 Baum Blvd., Ste. 660
Pittsburgh, PA 15213
Ph: (412)687-8484
Fax: (412)687-0541
Co. E-mail: franchise-dev@earthlink.net
URL: http://www.franchise-dev.com
Contact: Kenneth Franklin, President
Description: Develop, implement and launch franchise programs. **Scope:** Offers clients full development services for the purpose of designing and implementing a total franchise program. **Founded:** 1970. **Publications:** "Franchising Your Business," May/Jun, 2003; "Female Entrepreneur," May/Jun, 2003; "Franchising World," May/Jun, 2003; "Canadian Business Franchise," Jul/Aug, 2000. **Seminars:** Has presented franchising seminars under auspices of American Management Association, Management Center Europe and International Franchise Association. Recent programs include Expanding Your Business by Franchising; Writing Effective Franchise Operations Manuals. Also has franchise seminar on Prodigy.

37957 ■ Franchise Masters Inc. (FMI)
8301 Golden Valley Rd.
Golden Valley, MN 55427-4435
Ph: (763)541-1385
Free: 800-328-4158

Fax: (763)542-2246
Co. E-mail: johncampbell@franchisemasters.com
URL: http://www.franchisemasters.com
Contact: David Mitchell, President
Scope: Provider of franchise development and consulting services that include franchise legal services, advertising brochures and media advertising, manual preparation, video presentation, training programs, franchiser franchisee relations, franchise sales and marketing, venture capital funding, business planning and human resource evaluation and planning. **Founded:** 1981. **Seminars:** How to Choose a Business or a Franchise.

37958 ■ Francorp Inc.
20200 Governors Dr.
Olympia Fields, IL 60461
Ph: (708)481-2900
Free: 800-372-6244
Fax: (708)481-5885
Co. E-mail: info@francorp.com
URL: http://www.francorp.com
Contact: Ramon Vinay, President
Description: Offers consultancy on franchising business. Consultants have provided full development programs, including feasibility studies, business plans, legal documents, operations manuals, and marketing materials for clients since 1976. **Scope:** A management consulting firm specializing in franchise development. Provides full development programs, including feasibility studies, business plans, legal documents, operations manuals and marketing materials. Also provides post-development services for established franchisers including lead generation programs, franchise brochures, videotapes, international brokerage, public relations and expert witness services. **Founded:** 1976. **Training:** Provides post-development services for establishing franchisors, including lead generation programs, brochures, videotapes, international brokerage, PR, and expert witness service. **Seminars:** Franchise Your Business, Sep, 2006; A review of both Federal and State laws which govern franchising; An overview of different franchise strategies available for expansion, as well as guidance in choosing the right one for your business; A comparison of the cost of various growth strategies; An overview of revenue streams through franchising; The estimated costs of franchising your business; Calculating returns on franchise development and support costs.

37959 ■ General Business Services Corp.
1020 N University Parks Dr.
Waco, TX 76707
Ph: (817)745-2525
Free: 800-583-6181
Fax: (817)745-2544
Contact: Gary Mattson, Principal
Scope: Provider of financial management, business counseling, and tax-related products and services to business owners and professionals. Additional services include proper record-keeping systems, accurate tax return preparation, computer software services, and financial planning services. Initial and continuous training is available to franchisees in all areas: Business and tax counseling, client acquisition and business operations. **Founded:** 1962. **Publications:** "Tax Tips for the Small Business Owner and Professional," 1993.

37960 ■ ISO Healthcare Consulting [Intelligence Strategy Organization]
650 Madison Ave., 9th Fl.
New York, NY 10022
Ph: (212)940-6000
Fax: (212)940-6100
Co. E-mail: info@isohc.com
Contact: David Amar, President
E-mail: damar@isohc.com
Scope: Provides strategic management consulting services to major pharmaceutical, medical device and biotech companies worldwide. ISO helps its clients create and implement strategies that drive top-line growth, performance and competitiveness. The company provides customized services that enhance commercial and R and D performance and alignment. The firm's areas of focus include corporate, functional and brand strategy; marketing and sales effectiveness; R and D portfolio management;

R and D productivity; life cycle management; franchise planning; and organizational effectiveness design. **Founded:** 1975. **Seminars:** Strategy workshops are customized to specific client needs.

37961 ■ JC Ventures Inc.
4 Arnold St.
Old Greenwich, CT 06870
Ph: (203)698-1990
Free: 800-698-1997
Fax: (203)698-2638
Contact: James O. Campbell, President
Scope: Specialize in business strategy consulting services to the middle market and provide venture management services. Venture management services include development of business plans, franchise advisory services and assistance in attaining financing. Industries served: Financial services and high-technology. **Founded:** 1988. **Publications:** "The Commandants of Franchising". **Seminars:** Provide seminars for individuals looking for franchise opportunities.

37962 ■ Harold L. Kestenbaum P.C. [Harold L. Kestenbaum and Kick Solutions]
1425 Rexcorp Plz., E Twr., 15th Fl.
Uniondale, NY 11556
Ph: (516)745-0099
Fax: (516)745-0293
Co. E-mail: hkestenbaum@farrellfritz.com
URL: http://www.franchiseatty.com
Contact: Harold L. Kestenbaum, Attorney
Scope: Provider of consulting services for startup and existing franchisors. Services include feasibility studies, determination of franchise format, business plan development, capital resources, manual preparation and legal services. Practices franchise law and provides marketing services as well. Serves all industries. **Founded:** 1977. **Publications:** "Four tips to starting a successful franchise".

37963 ■ Koach Enterprises
5529 N 18th St.
Arlington, VA 22205
Ph: (703)241-8361
Fax: (703)241-8623
Co. E-mail: info@koach.com
Contact: Joseph L. Koach, President
Scope: Business consultants specializing in franchise development, distribution and small business start-ups. Services include business development plans, preparation of operations manuals, marketing programs and training programs. Serves private industries as well as government agencies. **Founded:** 1981. **Publications:** "How to Franchise Your Business and How to Buy a Franchise". **Seminars:** Taking the Mystique Out of Franchising; Franchising in the 1990's; Franchising Internationally; How to Avoid Bankruptcy; International Franchising.

37964 ■ Lupfer & Associates (L&A)
92 Glen St.
Natick, MA 01760-5646
Ph: (508)655-3950
Fax: (508)655-7826
Co. E-mail: donlupfer@aol.com
Contact: Donald Lupfer, Owner
E-mail: donlupfer@europartners.eu.com
Scope: Assists off shore hi-tech companies in entering United States markets and specializes in channel development for all sorts of products. Perform MARCOM support for hi-tech United States clients. **Founded:** 1988. **Publications:** "What's Next For Distribution-Feast or Famine"; "The Changing Global Marketplace"; "Making Global Distribution Work". **Seminars:** How to do Business in the United States.

37965 ■ Management Action Programs Inc. (MAP)
14140 Ventura Blvd., Ste. 208
Sherman Oaks, CA 91423
Free: 888-834-3040
Co. E-mail: rkwacker@mapconsulting.com
URL: http://www.mapconsulting.com
Contact: Lee Froschheiser, President
E-mail: lfroschheiser@mapconsulting.com
Scope: Counsels distributors of products and services in improving productivity and profitability through the MAP management system. Also special-

izes in dealer and distributor systems, franchised companies, strategic planning and business planning to use investment capital. **Founded:** 1960. **Publications:** "Vital Factors," Oct, 2006. **Seminars:** How to Finance a Growing Business; Venture Capital for Growing Business; Franchise Relations for the Large Accounting Firm; Should You Franchise Your Business; The Pitfalls of TQM; Productivity in the Manufacturing Sector and Re-engineering to Get Results; Management Development Workshop. **Special Services:** Vital Factor®.

37966 ■ Marketing Resources Group Franchise Consulting
7158 Austin St.
Forest Hills, NY 11375
Ph: (718)261-8882
Contact: Bill Alexander, President
Scope: Provider of franchise sales, development and consulting solutions. It offers sales prospecting, competitive analysis, customer evaluation and strategic planning services.

37967 ■ National Cooperative Bank, Corporate Banking Div. (NCB)
2011 Crystal Dr., Ste. 800
Arlington, VA 22202
Ph: (703)302-8000
Free: 800-955-9622
Fax: (703)647-3460
Co. E-mail: marcom@ncb.coop
URL: http://www.ncb.coop
Contact: Charles E. Snyder, President
Scope: In addition to offering various banking services to franchise cooperatives, this Division consults on the establishment of employee stock ownership plans within the franchising system.

37968 ■ National Franchise Associates Inc.
240 Lake View Ct.
Lavonia, GA 30553
Ph: (770)945-0660
Fax: (770)356-5180
Co. E-mail: nfa@nationalfranchise.com
URL: http://www.nationalfranchise.com
Contact: Stephen S. Raines, President
Description: Full service consulting and developmental firm with expertise in feasibility studies, Franchise agreements and UFOC's, advertising and public relations campaigns, operations and training manuals, franchise sales programs, and ongoing franchise consulting. **Scope:** An international franchise consulting firm providing full-service program to franchise companies. Services include: Feasibility studies, franchise plans, venture capital, franchise agreement, FTC disclosure document, state registration applications, operations manuals, training materials, advertising and public relations, computer software programs and sales and marketing of franchises. **Founded:** 1981. **Publications:** "Keys To Successful Franchising: Franchise Marketing Reflections Of A Franchise Consultant"; "Keys To A Successful Franchise Training"; "Keys To Successful Franchise Development: Will The Franchise Generate Sufficient Money? Reflections Of A Franchise Consultant"; "Focus on Operations Manuals & Marketing"; "Keys To Successful Franchising: Will Your Franchise Program Make Enough Money?"; "Keys To Successful Franchise Planning: Selecting The Right Franchisees"; "DePalma's expanding into Asia"; "Spirit Of Ingenuity"; "Why a Franchise Consultant Can Be Helpful". **Seminars:** Franchise Training Program.

37969 ■ National Franchise Sales (NFS)
1601 Dove St., Ste. 150
Newport Beach, CA 92660
Ph: (949)428-0480
Fax: (949)428-0490
Co. E-mail: pp@nationalfranchisesales.com
URL: http://www.nationalfranchisesales.com
Contact: Mike Deegan, President
E-mail: md@nationalfranchisesales.com
Scope: A business brokerage firm specializing in the resale of franchise businesses and small chains. Assists in the asset recovery of non-performing franchise businesses in bankruptcy, foreclosure, or default, by re-franchising the businesses. **Founded:**

1978. **Publications:** "Franchise National Connection Franchise Sales". **Seminars:** Franchising - How to Start a Franchise; Franchising - How to Market Your Franchise.

37970 ■ Nationwide Franchise Marketing Services
18715 Gibbons Dr.
Dallas, TX 75287-4045
Ph: (972)733-9942
Free: 866-740-5815
Fax: (972)733-9942
Co. E-mail: fmmigdol@tx.rr.com
Contact: Marvin J. Migdol, President
E-mail: marvmigdol@aol.com
Description: Full service franchise development evaluations. **Scope:** Helps franchisors in areas such as food services, automotive products and services, apparel, education, personnel, health and beauty aids, maintenance, entertainment and service businesses. **Founded:** 1971. **Publications:** "Starting a Business"; "Winning in the 90S"; "How to Get Organized in 30Days"; "25 Tips for Producing an Effective Direct Mail Brochure"; "How to Land That Job"; "How to Keep a Job"; "How to Buy the Right Franchise"; "Fund-Raising for Business"; "Fund-Raising for Non-Profit Organizations, Public Relations: A Growing Management Function for Today"; "How to Prevent Legal Problems in Hiring"; "Comics As a Public Relations Tool in Communications and Greater Virility".

37971 ■ Sommers Consultants Inc. [Sommers Financial Group Inc.]
301 N Main St., Ste. 5
New City, NY 10956
Ph: (845)638-4111
Contact: Leslie Sommers, President
Scope: Provider of the full scope of services necessary for planning, designing and implementing franchise programs. Industries presently served include: juvenile furniture, uniforms and maternity, fashion and footwear, instant shoe repair and specialty baking and foods. Other services provided include: Business forms and systems, marketing programs and services, real estate site selection and lease negotiations and small business development. **Founded:** 1982. **Publications:** "Estate Planning"; "Living Trusts"; "Avoiding Probate"; "Charitable Gifts"; "Controlling the Distribution"; "Paying Estate Taxes"; "Benefits of A-B Trusts"; "Gifting Strategies"; "Charitable Lead Trusts"; "Charitable Remainder Trusts"; "Wealth Replacement Trusts"; "Family Limited Partnerships"; "Property Ownership"; "Eliminating the Estate Tax".

37972 ■ Tarbutton Associates Inc.
1072 Laskin Rd.
Virginia Beach, VA 23451-6364
Ph: (757)422-2020
Contact: Kenton L. Tarbutton, President
Scope: A consulting firm specializing in franchise consulting worldwide for expert witness court and legislative testimony as well as the sale or acquisition of franchising parent companies. **Founded:** 1962. **Publications:** "Franchising: The How-To Book," Prentice-Hall Inc. **Seminars:** 21st Century Management Techniques; Developing Your Business for Franchising; Developing People into Producers; The Franchising Possibilities.

37973 ■ Venture Marketing Associates L.L.C.
800 Palisade Ave., Ste. 907
Fort Lee, NJ 07024
Ph: (201)924-7435
Co. E-mail: venturemkt@aol.com
URL: http://www.venturemarketingassociates.com
Description: Business development/franchise consultants. **Scope:** Provider of consulting services in business development and franchising. Provides hands-on assistance in planning and implementing strategic marketing/management plans. Clients include franchisers, small business owners and individuals. Cost-effective fees for those in transition, facing unemployment, researching a franchise or starting a business. Industries served: service, retail and distribution. **Founded:** 1976. **Seminars:** Franchise Your Business; How to Research a Franchise Services.

FRANCHISES AND BUSINESS OPPORTUNITIES

37974 ■ Aloha Hotels and Resorts
PO Box 3347
Princeville, HI 96722
Ph: (808)826-6244
URL: http://www.franchisedirectory.ca
Description: Provides independent Inn, Hotel and Resort owners with the ability to obtain new sources of revenue. Membership in the Aloha Hotels and Resort chain brings a wide variety of benefits to the property owner. Aloha Hotel and Resort president has over 25 years of enhancing financial performance for 3 major hotel and resort chains. **Equity Capital Needed:** $1,000-$200,000 total investment; $1,000-$200,000 required cash liquidity. **Training:** Provides training an support programs. There is one assigned management team member to your property that is available to answer any questions and take you through the steps to become an Aloha Hotel and Resort member. There are many training and support areas that are included in your membership.

37975 ■ Dorsey & Whitney, LLP
701 5th Ave., Ste. 6100
Seattle, WA 98104
Ph: (206)903-8701
Fax: (206)903-8820
Co. E-mail: mceachern.connie@dorsey.com
URL: http://www.dorsey.com
Contact: Kimberley Anderson, Committee Management Officer
Description: Franchise Lawyers.

37976 ■ FD & MG Franchise Company Inc.
949 E Pioneer Rd., Ste. B-2
Draper, UT 84020
Ph: (801)352-1400
Fax: (801)619-4038
Description: Franchise consulting. **No. of Franchise Units:** 2. **No. of Company-Owned Units:** 1. **Founded:** 2003. **Franchised:** 2007. **Equity Capital Needed:** $120,500-$152,100. **Franchise Fee:** $75,000. **Royalty Fee:** 6%. **Financial Assistance:** Third party financing and limited in-house financing available. **Training:** Includes 2 weeks training at headquarters and ongoing support.

37977 ■ Franchise Development International - LLC
370 SE 15 Ave.
Pompano Beach, FL 33060
Ph: (954)942-9424
Fax: (954)783-5177
URL: http://www.busop1.com/catno13.htm
Description: Franchise development and marketing. **Founded:** 1991.

37978 ■ Franchise Development & Marketing Group, Inc.
949 E Pioneer Rd., Ste. 2B
Draper, UT 84020
Ph: (801)352-1400
Fax: (801)619-4038
Description: Assist businesses in all franchise phase. **Founded:** 2003.

37979 ■ Franchise Developments Inc. (FDI)
5001 Baum Blvd., Ste. 660
Pittsburgh, PA 15213
Ph: (412)687-8484
Fax: (412)687-0541
Co. E-mail: franchise-dev@earthlink.net
URL: http://www.franchise-dev.com
Contact: Kenneth Franklin, President
Description: Develop, implement and launch franchise programs. **Scope:** Offers clients full development services for the purpose of designing and implementing a total franchise program. **Founded:** 1970. **Publications:** "Franchising Your Business," May/Jun, 2003; "Female Entrepreneur," May/Jun, 2003; "Franchising World," May/Jun, 2003; "Canadian Business Franchise," Jul/Aug, 2000. **Seminars:** Has presented franchising seminars under auspices of American Management Association, Management Center Europe and International Franchise Associa-

tion. Recent programs include Expanding Your Business by Franchising; Writing Effective Franchise Operations Manuals. Also has franchise seminar on Prodigy.

37980 ■ Franchise Foundations
Franchise Foundations
4157 23rd St.
San Francisco, CA 94114
Free: 877-561-3625
Co. E-mail: info@franchisefoundations.biz
URL: http://www.franchisefoundations.biz
Description: Franchise consulting. **Founded:** 1980.

37981 ■ Franchise Recruiters Ltd.
Saddlebrooke Country Club
63284 E Flower Ridge Dr.
Tucson, AZ 85739
Ph: (520)825-9588
Description: Placement of franchise management professionals. **Founded:** 1977.

37982 ■ Franchise Sales
1315 S Villa Ave.
Villa Park, IL 60181
Ph: (630)819-2418
Description: Self franchisees in business now. **Founded:** 1991.

37983 ■ Franchise Search Inc.
Kushell Associates Inc.
48 Burd St., Ste. 101
Nyack, NY 10960
Ph: (845)727-4103
Contact: Douglas T. Kushell, Founder
Description: International executive search firm for franchisors. **Scope:** An international search firm specializing in executive searching for franchisers. Works exclusively for franchise organizations that need experienced franchise specialists in President, CEO, COO, Sales, Operations, Training, Marketing and Advertising, Legal, Finance, Real Estate and Construction and International Development. **Founded:** 1982.

37984 ■ Franchise Specialists, Inc.
1234 Maple St. Ext.
Moon Township, PA 15108
Ph: (412)262-5055
Co. E-mail: info@franchisespecialistsinc.com
URL: http://www.franchisespecialistsinc.com
Contact: Dr. Bill Repack, Chief Executive Officer
Description: Professional franchise development and sales. **Founded:** 1978.

37985 ■ FranchiseInc!
2148 Pelham Pkwy., Bldg. 300
Pelham, AL 35124
Free: 800-961-0420
Fax: (205)682-2939
Description: Franchise consulting service. **No. of Franchise Units:** 24. **No. of Company-Owned Units:** 1. **Founded:** 1995. **Franchised:** 2006. **Equity Capital Needed:** $36,600-$48,500. **Franchise Fee:** $29,500. **Training:** Includes 5 days training at headquarters, 52 weeks mentoring via teleconference and ongoing support.

37986 ■ FranchiseMart / Biz1Brokers
2121 Vista Pkwy.
West Palm Beach, FL 33411
Free: 888-721-1020
Co. E-mail: jmalmuth@tworld.com
URL: http://www.franchisemart.com
Description: Franchise consulting services. **No. of Franchise Units:** 5. **Founded:** 2006. **Franchised:** 2007. **Equity Capital Needed:** $30,000-$35,000 initial, total investment $110,000-$115,000. **Franchise Fee:** $29,500. **Financial Assistance:** Yes. **Training:** Yes.

37987 ■ Franchises Unlimited Network LLC
PO Box 518
Sterling Heights, MI 48311
Free: 866-583-5311
Fax: (586)264-4910
Co. E-mail: tnoga@franchisefun.com
URL: http://www.franchisefun.com
Description: Franchise consulting service.

37988 ■ FranChoice Inc.
7500 Flying Cloud Dr., Ste. 600
Eden Prairie, MN 55344
Ph: (952)345-8400
Free: 877-396-4238
Co. E-mail: info@franchoice.com
URL: http://www.franchoice.com
Contact: Jeffery C. Elgin, Chief Executive Officer
E-mail: jelgin@franchoice.com
Description: Provides consumers with free guidance and advice to help them select a franchise that matches their individual interests and financial qualifications. **Scope:** Firm provides consumers with free guidance and advice to help them select a franchise opportunity that matches their individual interests and financial qualifications. Matches prospective franchisees with franchisors. Assists franchisors with their nationwide expansion. **Founded:** 1999. **Publications:** "VYPE High School Sports Magazine". **Seminars:** How to Evaluate a Franchise.

37989 ■ Francorp Inc.
20200 Governors Dr.
Olympia Fields, IL 60461
Ph: (708)481-2900
Free: 800-372-6244
Fax: (708)481-5885
Co. E-mail: info@francorp.com
URL: http://www.francorp.com
Contact: Ramon Vinay, President
Description: Offers consultancy on franchising business. Consultants have provided full development programs, including feasibility studies, business plans, legal documents, operations manuals, and marketing materials for clients since 1976. **Scope:** A management consulting firm specializing in franchise development. Provides full development programs, including feasibility studies, business plans, legal documents, operations manuals and marketing materials. Also provides post-development services for established franchisers including lead generation programs, franchise brochures, videotapes, international brokerage, public relations and expert witness services. **Founded:** 1976. **Training:** Provides post-development services for establishing franchisors, including lead generation programs, brochures, videotapes, international brokerage, PR, and expert witness service. **Seminars:** Franchise Your Business, Sep, 2006; A review of both Federal and State laws which govern franchising; An overview of different franchise strategies available for expansion, as well as guidance in choosing the right one for your business; A comparison of the cost of various growth strategies; An overview of revenue streams through franchising; The estimated costs of franchising your business; Calculating returns on franchise development and support costs.

37990 ■ The iFranchise Group Inc.
905 W 175th St., 2nd Fl.
Homewood, IL 60430
Ph: (708)957-2300
Fax: (708)957-2395
Co. E-mail: info@ifranchisegroup.com
URL: http://www.ifranchisegroup.com
Contact: David E. Hood, President
E-mail: dhood@ifranchise.net
URL(s): www.ifranchise.com. **Description:** Offers services on strategic planning, franchise law, operations documentation, marketing and sales, and executive recruiting for franchisors. **Scope:** Franchise consulting for new and established franchisers. Services include franchise feasibility, franchise structure, legal documentation, operations and training materials and assistance with franchise sales and franchise feasibility. Franchise development for start-up franchisors. Franchise marketing and sales. Franchise implementation assistance. **Founded:** 1998. **Publications:** "Is Your Business Franchisable?"; "The Right Marketing Materials". **Seminars:**

Franchise Sales and Marketing Techniques; Minimizing Franchise Litigation; How to Franchise a Business; Developing and Maintaining Good Franchisee Relations.

37991 ■ Jones & Co.
365 Bay St., 2nd Fl.
Toronto, ON, Canada M5H 2V1
Ph: (416)703-5716
Fax: (416)703-6180
URL: http://www.jonesco-law.ca
Contact: Paul Jones, Contact
Description: Law firm experienced in franchising and distribution. **Founded:** 2004.

37992 ■ Kanouse & Walker, P.A.
One Boca Pl.
2255 Glades Rd., Ste. 324
Atrium
Boca Raton, FL 33431
Ph: (561)451-8090
Fax: (561)451-8089
URL: http://www.kanouse.com
Description: Represents franchisees in buying a franchise. **Founded:** 1974.

37993 ■ Kaufman & Canoles, P.C.
PO Box 3037
Norfolk, VA 23514
Ph: (757)624-3000
Fax: (757)624-3169
URL: http://www.kaufmanandcanoles.com
Contact: William R. Van Buren, III, Chairman
Description: Franchise attorneys. **Founded:** 1974.

37994 ■ L. Michael Schwartz, P.A.
10561 Barkley Pl., Ste. 510
Overland Park, KS 66212
Ph: (913)341-1919
Co. E-mail: lmschwartz@lmschwartzlaw.com
URL: http://www.lmschwartzlaw.com
Description: Franchise consulting and full legal services.

37995 ■ Marketing Resources Group
83-26 Lefferts Blvd.
Kew Gardens, NY 11415
Ph: (718)261-8882
Description: Franchise development, marketing, and sales.

37996 ■ National Franchise Associates Inc.
240 Lake View Ct.
Lavonia, GA 30553
Ph: (770)945-0660
Fax: (770)356-5180
Co. E-mail: nfa@nationalfranchise.com
URL: http://www.nationalfranchise.com
Contact: Stephen S. Raines, President
Description: Full service consulting and developmental firm with expertise in feasibility studies, Franchise agreements and UFOC's, advertising and public relations campaigns, operations and training manuals, franchise sales programs, and ongoing franchise consulting. **Scope:** An international franchise consulting firm providing full-service program to franchise companies. Services include: Feasibility studies, franchise plans, venture capital, franchise agreement, FTC disclosure document, state registration applications, operations manuals, training materials, advertising and public relations, computer software programs and sales and marketing of franchises. **Founded:** 1981. **Publications:** "Keys To Successful Franchising: Franchise Marketing Reflections Of A Franchise Consultant"; "Keys To A Successful Franchise Training"; "Keys To Successful Franchise Development: Will The Franchise Generate Sufficient Money? Reflections Of A Franchise Consultant"; "Focus on Operations Manuals & Marketing"; "Keys To Successful Franchising: Will Your Franchise Program Make Enough Money?"; "Keys To

Successful Franchise Planning: Selecting The Right Franchisees"; "DePalma's expanding into Asia"; "Spirit Of Ingenuity"; "Why a Franchise Consultant Can Be Helpful". **Seminars:** Franchise Training Program.

37997 ■ Oxford Business Consulting Group, LLC
19 Beech Pl.
Huntington, NY 11743
Ph: (631)423-8570
Fax: (631)423-8580
Description: Outsourced franchise sales & development. **Founded:** 2000.

37998 ■ Webber Consulting Group, Inc.
3506 SW Sawgrass Pky.
Ankeny, IA 50023
Ph: (515)419-6122
Fax: (253)679-4351
Description: Franchise development and accounting service.

LIBRARIES

37999 ■ Alberta Securities Commission Library
250-5th St. SW, Ste. 600
Calgary, AB, Canada T2P 0R4
Ph: (403)297-6454
Free: 877-355-0585
Fax: (403)297-6156
Co. E-mail: inquiries@asc.ca
URL: http://www.albertasecurities.com
Contact: Yanming Fei, Librarian
Scope: Securities legislation, corporate law. **Services:** Library not open to the public. **Holdings:** Figures not available.

38000 ■ Franchise Consultants International Association Library
5147 S. Angela Rd.
Memphis, TN 38117
Ph: (901)368-3361
Fax: (901)368-1144
Co. E-mail: franmark@msn.com
URL: http://www.FranchiseStores.com
Contact: R. Richey
URL(s): www.FranchiseStores.Net, consultantsamerica.net. **Scope:** Franchise law, demographics, statistics, logistics, suppliers, technology, advertising, management, legal consulting. **Services:** Members only participants for reference use. **Founded:** 1976. **Holdings:** 2800 books, periodicals, clippings, audio/visuals, and audio recordings; reports; manuscripts; archives; patents. **Subscriptions:** 143 magazines.

RESEARCH CENTERS

38001 ■ The Nature Conservancy - New Jersey Chapter Office
200 Pottersville Rd.
Chester, NJ 07930
Ph: (908)879-7262
Fax: (908)879-2172
Co. E-mail: newjersey@tnc.org
URL: http://www.nature.org/ourinitiatives/regions/northamerica/unitedstates/newjersey
Contact: Barbara Brummer, Director
Scope: Identifies rare plants and animals and the lands where they live; protects land through acquisition by gift or purchase and managing it using staff and volunteer land stewards. Also uses innovative strategies involving community and corporate partnerships. **Founded:** 1988. **Publications:** Brochures and fact sheets; Nature Conservancy Magazine; The Oak Leaf. **Educational Activities:** New Jersey Chapter Office Field trips and special events throughout the state; New Jersey Chapter Office Annual Members Meeting, each fall.

START-UP INFORMATION

38002 ■ *75 Green Businesses You Can Start to Make Money and Make a Difference*
Pub: Entrepreneur Press
Ed: Glenn Croston. **Released:** August 01, 2008. **Price:** $19.95, paperback. **Description:** Descriptions of seventy-five environmentally-friendly business startups are presented.

38003 ■ *The 100 Best Businesses to Start When You Don't Want to Work Hard Anymore*
Pub: Career Press Inc.
Contact: Ron Fry, President
Ed: Lisa Rogak. **Price:** $14.99. **Availability:** Print.

38004 ■ *"The $100 Startup: Reinvent the Way You Make a Living, Do What You Love and Create a New Future" in Canadian Business (Vol. 85, July 16, 2012, No. 11-12, pp. 68)*
Pub: George Media Inc.
Ed: James Cowan. **Released:** July 16, 2012. **Description:** Review of the book entitled, 'The $100 Startup: Reinvent the Way You Make a Living, Do What You Love and Create a New Future is presented.

38005 ■ *101 Businesses You Can Start at With Less Than One Thousand Dollars: For Retirees*
Pub: Atlantic Publishing Co.
Contact: Amanda Miller, Manager
E-mail: amiller@atlantic-pub.com
Ed: Christina Bultinck. **Price:** $21.95. **Description:** Business ideas to help retirees start a home-based business on a low budget.

38006 ■ *101 Businesses You Can Start at With Less Than One Thousand Dollars: For Stay-at-Home Moms & Dads*
Pub: Atlantic Publishing Co.
Contact: Amanda Miller, Manager
E-mail: amiller@atlantic-pub.com
Ed: Christina Bultinck. **Price:** $21.95. **Description:** Business ideas to help stay-at-home moms and dads start a home-based business on a low budget.

38007 ■ *202 Things You Can Buy and Sell for Big Profits*
Pub: Entrepreneur Press
Contact: Perlman Neil, President
Ed: James Stephenson. **Description:** Become an entrepreneur at selling new and used products. This handbook will help individuals cash in on the boom in reselling new and used products online. A new section defines ways to set realistic goals while distinguishing between 'get-rich schemes' and long term, viable businesses. A discussion about targeting and reaching the right customer base is included, along with finding and obtaining the service support needed for starting a new business.

38008 ■ *"218 More Programs" in Entrepreneur (Vol. 35, November 2007, No. 11, pp. 96)*
Description: List of 218 colleges and universities in the U.S. offering entrepreneurship programs is presented.

38009 ■ *The 250 Questions Every Self-Employed Person Should Ask*
Pub: Adams Media Corp.
Contact: Scott Watrous, President
E-mail: bobadams@adamsmedia.com
Ed: Mary Mihaly. **Released:** January 01, 2010. **Price:** $5.48. **Description:** Comprehensive information is given for anyone wishing to start their own business. **Availability:** Print.

38010 ■ *The Accidental Entrepreneur: Practical Wisdom for People Who Never Expected to Work for Themselves*
Pub: Career Steps
Ed: Susan Urquhart-Brown. **Released:** October 20, 2005. **Description:** Steps for launching, growing and running a successful small company.

38011 ■ *The Accidental Entrepreneur: The 50 Things I Wish Someone Had Told Me About Starting a Business*
Pub: AMACOM
Contact: Edward T. Reilly, Manager
Ed: Susan Urquhart-Brown. **Released:** May 2008. **Price:** $17.95, Paper or Softback. **Description:** Advice is offered to any would-be entrepreneur, including eight questions to ask before launching a new business, ten traits of a successful entrepreneur, how to obtain licenses and selling permits, best way to create a business plan, ten ways to get referrals, six secrets of marketing, investment and financial information, ways to avoid burnout, and the seven biggest pitfalls to avoid. **Availability:** Print.

38012 ■ *The Accidental Startup: How to Realize Your True Potential by Becoming Your Own Boss*
Pub: Dutton Children's Books
Contact: Lauri Hornik, President
Ed: Danielle Babb. **Released:** May 05, 2009. **Price:** $11.99. **Description:** Advice is given to help would-be entrepreneurs realize their goals for starting and running a successful small business. **Availability:** E-book.

38013 ■ *"Ailing Economy Nibbling at Tech-Sector Jobs" in Puget Sound Business Journal (Vol. 29, November 7, 2008, No. 29, pp. 1)*
Ed: Eric Engleman, John Cook. **Description:** Seattle-area tech start-up companies including Redfin, Zillow, WildTangent, Daptiv, Avelle, and Intrepid Learning Solutions have cut staff as the nation's economy staggers. The layoffs are reminiscent of the tech bubble era, but most startups these days have been more prudent about spending and hiring as compared to that period.

38014 ■ *"Alpharetta Seeding Startups To Encourage Job Growth" in Atlanta Business Chronicle(June 20, 2014, pp. 3A)*
Pub: American City Business Journals, Inc.
Contact: Whitney Shaw, President
Released: June 20, 2014. **Description:** The City of Alpharetta is witnessing several incubators and accelerators that will create the physical and educational

infrastructure to convert ideas into sustainable businesses. This will help startups develop a go-to-market strategy, prepare for FDA certification and insurance reimbursement as well as see that the company reaches a point where it can attract private equity or venture capital.

38015 ■ *American Bar Association Legal Guide for Small Business: Everything You Need to Know About Small Business*
Ed: American Bar Association. **Released:** June 10, 2010. **Description:** The American Bar Association provides insight into financial, health and family issues affecting small business, including start up issues, employment laws, financing a business, and selling a business.

38016 ■ *"Angel Investors Across State Collaborate" in Austin Business Journal (Vol. 31, May 20, 2011, No. 11, pp. 1)*
Pub: American City Business Journals
Ed: Christopher Calnan. **Description:** Texas' twelve angel investing groups are going to launch the umbrella organization Alliance of Texas Angel Networks (ATAN) to support more syndicated deals and boost investments in Texas. In 2010, these investing groups infused more than $24 million to startups in 61 deals.

38017 ■ *The Art of the Start: The Time-Tested, Battle-Hardened Guide for Anyone Starting Anything*
Pub: Penguin Books USA Inc.
Ed: Guy Kawasaki. **Released:** September 09, 2004. **Price:** $27.95, hardcover. **Description:** Advice for someone starting a new business covering topics such as hiring employees, building a brand, business competition, and management.

38018 ■ *The Art of the Start: The Time-Tested, Battle-Hardened Guide for Anyone Starting Anything*
Pub: Portfolio Publishing
Contact: Adrian Zackheim, President
Ed: Guy Kawasaki. **Released:** September 09, 2004. **Price:** $27.95, hardcover; $19.99. **Description:** Apple's Guy Kawasaki offers information to help would-be entrepreneurs create new enterprises. As founder and CEO of Garage Technology Ventures, he has field-tested his ideas with newly hatched companies and he takes readers through every phase of creating a business, from the very basics of raising money and designing a business model through the many stages that eventually lead to success and thus giving back to society. **Availability:** PrintElectronic publishing.

38019 ■ *"Austin Welcomes New Program for Entrepreneurs" in Austin Business JournalInc. (Vol. 29, February 12, 2010, No. 29, pp. 1)*
Pub: American City Business Journals
Ed: Christopher Calnan. **Description:** Nonprofit group Economic Development Catalyst Organization (ECDO) is formalizing its BizLaunch mentoring

program, which was stated in 2009. The program aims to offer support networks to entrepreneurs and assistance regarding early-stage venture capital.

38020 ■ *Awakening the Entrepreneur Within: How Ordinary People Can Create Extraordinary Companies*
Pub: HarperCollins Publishers Inc.
Contact: Jane Friedman, President
E-mail: jfriedman@harpercollins.com

Ed: Michael E. Gerber. **Released:** December 08, 2009. **Price:** $15.99, paperback. **Description:** Four dimensions of the entrepreneurial personality are explored: dreamer, thinker, performer and leader. **Availability:** Print.

38021 ■ *"Barriers to Small Business Creations in Canada" in International Journal of Entrepreneurship and Small Business (Vol. , pp.)*
Pub: Publishers Communication Group
Contact: Doug Wright, Director

Ed: Amarjit Gill, Nahum Biger, Vivek Nagpal. **Description:** Studies of Hatala (2005) and Choo and Wong (2006) related to the barriers to new venture creations in Canada are examined.

38022 ■ *"BDC Launches New Online Business Advice Centre" in Marketwired (July 13, 2010)*
Pub: COMTEX
Contact: Chip Brian, President

Description: The Business Development Bank of Canada (BDC) offers entrepreneurs the chance to use their new online BDC Advice Centre in order to seek advice regarding the challenges of entrepreneurship. Free online business tools and information to help both startups and established firms are also provided.

38023 ■ *Be the Elephant: Build a Bigger, Better Business*
Pub: Workman Publishing Co.
Contact: Kristina Peterson, Director
E-mail: kristina@workman.com

Ed: Steve Kaplan. **Price:** $19.95. **Description:** Entrepreneur and author sets out an accessible, no-frills plan for business owners, managers, and other industrialists to grow their businesses into elephants: big and strong but also smart. Advice is given on fostering a growth mind-set, assessing risk, and creating unique selling propositions. **Availability:** E-book.

38024 ■ *Be Your Own Boss*
Pub: Wet Feet, Incorporated

Ed: Marcia Passos Duffy. **Released:** November 2006. **Price:** $14.95. **Description:** Tips for starting a freelance business in any career or industry are covered. **Availability:** PDF.

38025 ■ *Become Your Own Boss in 12 Months: A Month-by-Month Guide to a Business that Works*
Pub: Adams Media Corp.
Contact: Scott Watrous, President
E-mail: bobadams@adamsmedia.com

Ed: Melinda F. Emerson. **Price:** $11.96, paperback. **Description:** Realistic planning guide to help would-be entrepreneurs transition from working for someone else to working for themselves is given. The key to successfully starting a new company lies in thoughtful preparation at least a year and a half before quitting a job.

38026 ■ *The Beermat Entrepreneur: Turn Your Good Idea Into a Great Business*
Pub: Pearson Education Ltd.
Contact: Rod Bristow, President

Ed: Mike Southon, Chris West. **Released:** 2nd Edition. **Price:** £14.99, paperback; £9.99. **Description:** Information to help start, maintain and grow a small business is given, along with suggestions for working with a bank. **Availability:** PrintElectronic publishing.

38027 ■ *Boss of You: Everything a Woman Needs to Know to Start, Run, and Maintain Her Own Business*
Pub: Seal Press
Contact: Christina Henry de Tessan, Editor
E-mail: christina@avalonpub.com

Ed: Emira Mears, Lauren Bacon. **Released:** May 2008. **Price:** $15.95. **Description:** Women entrepreneurs start businesses at twice the rate of male counterparts. Information is shared to help a woman start, run and maintain a successful company.

38028 ■ *"Brand Storytelling Becomes a Booming Business" in Entrepreneur (April 2012)*
Pub: Entrepreneur Press
Contact: Perlman Neil, President

Released: April 2012. **Description:** San Francisco-based Story House Creative engages in helping small businesses connect with their audience in communicating their brand identity. Web content, bios and tag lines are some of the marketing materials Story House Creative creates for its clients. The company also does search engine optimization, video, design, and copywriting. The Brandery, another brand-building company, helps startups promote their business. Eight to ten Brandery mentors are assigned to assist each startup client. Meanwhile, Brand Journalists is a Tennessee-based company focusing on corporate storytelling. It offers Web and blog content, human stories reporting and ghostwriting services.

38029 ■ *Breaking Free: How to Quit Your Job and Start Your Own Business*
Pub: Greenwood Publishing Group, Inc.

Ed: Chris Lauer. **Released:** March 01, 2009. **Price:** $34.95, hardcover. **Description:** This book helps individuals transition from working for others to starting their own business. **Availability:** Print.

38030 ■ *Brewing Up a Business: Adventures in Beer from the Founder of Dogfish Head Craft Brewery*
Pub: John Wiley & Sons Inc.
Contact: Stephen M. Smith, President

Ed: Sam Calagione. **Released:** 2nd Edition. **Price:** $18.95, paperback; $12.99. **Description:** Author shares nontraditional success secrets. Calgione began his business with a home brewing kit and grew it into Dogfish Head Craft Beer, the leading craft brewery in the U.S. **Availability:** PrintE-book.

38031 ■ *Building a Dream: A Canadian Guide to Starting Your Own Business*
Pub: McGraw-Hill Ryerson Ltd.
Contact: Robert J. Bahash, President

Ed: Walter S. Good. **Released:** 9th Edition. **Price:** C$74. **Description:** Topics covered include evaluating business potential, new business ideas, starting or buying a business, franchise opportunities, business organization, protecting an idea, arranging financing, and developing a business plan. **Availability:** Print.

38032 ■ *Business for Beginners*
Pub: Sourcebooks Mediafusion

Ed: Frances McGuckin. **Released:** March 01, 2005. **Price:** C$22.99; C$17.99. **Description:** Small business advice is shared by seven successful entrepreneurs. **Availability:** PrintE-book.

38033 ■ *A Business of My Own? 21 Steps to Successfully Starting and Running a Small Business*
Pub: Enfield Publishing

Ed: Marjorie Cleveland Fisher. **Released:** January 2005. **Price:** $14.95. **Description:** New ideas to start or grow a small business, including ideas for writing business plans with examples, adopting a business structure, and setting goals and objectives.

38034 ■ *Canadian Small Business Kit for Dummies*
Pub: CDG Books Canada Inc.
Contact: Tom Best, President
E-mail: tbest@cdgbooks.com

Ed: Margaret Kerr, JoAnn Kurtz. **Released:** March 2007. **Price:** $37.99 (Canadian). **Description:** Entrepreneurial guide to starting and running a small business in Canada.

38035 ■ *The Canadian Small Business Survival Guide: How to Start and Operate Your Own Successful Business*
Pub: Dundurn Group
Contact: Kirk Howard, President
E-mail: khoward@dundurn.com

Ed: Benj Gallander. **Released:** April 2002. **Price:** $26.99, paperback; $12.99. **Description:** Ideas for starting and running a successful small business. Topics include selecting a business, financing, government assistance, locations, franchises, and marketing ideas. **Availability:** PrintE-book.

38036 ■ *Careers for Self-Starters and Other Entrepreneurial Types*

Ed: Blythe Camenson. **Released:** September 2004. **Price:** $9.95 (US).; $13.95 (US). **Description:** Advice to entrepreneurs wishing to start their own small company. Tips for turning hobbies into job skills are included.

38037 ■ *Cash In On Cash Flow*
Pub: Simon and Schuster Inc.
Contact: Carolyn Reidy, President
E-mail: carolyn.reidy@simonandschuster.com

Ed: Lawrence J. Pino. **Released:** July 2005. **Price:** $19.95. **Description:** Guide to assist entrepreneurs with starting a new business as a cash flow specialist. **Availability:** Print.

38038 ■ *Coin Laundries - Road to Financial Independence: A Complete Guide to Starting and Operating Profitable Self-Service Laundries*

Ed: Emerson G. Higdon. **Released:** June 2001. **Description:** Guide to starting and operating a self-service laundry.

38039 ■ *Common Sense Business: Starting, Operating, and Growing Your Small Business-In Any Economy!*
Pub: Harper Business

Ed: Steve Gottry. **Released:** July 26, 2005. **Price:** $19.95. **Description:** Strategies for starting, operating and growing a small business in any economy. **Availability:** Print.

38040 ■ *The Complete Idiot's Guide to Starting an eBay® Business*
Pub: Penguin Books USA Inc.

Released: February 2008. **Price:** $19.95. **Description:** Guide for starting an eBay business includes information on products to sell, how to price merchandise, and details for working with services like PayPal, and how to organize fulfillment services.

38041 ■ *The Complete Startup Guide for the Black Entrepreneur*
Pub: Career Press Inc.
Contact: Ron Fry, President

Ed: Bill Bourdreaux. **Price:** $15.99. **Availability:** Print.

38042 ■ *Corporation: Small Business Start-Up Kit*

Ed: Daniel Sitarz. **Released:** February 2005. **Price:** $29.95. **Description:** Guidebook to help entrepreneurs start up and run a small business corporation. Book includes state and federal forms with instructions.

38043 ■ *Crush It!: Why NOW Is the Time to Cash In on Your Passion*
Pub: HarperStudio/HarperCollins

Ed: Gary Vaynerchuk. **Released:** October 13, 2009. **Price:** $21.99, hardcover; $14.99; C$13.99. **Description:** Ways the Internet can help entrepreneurs turn their passions into successful companies. **Availability:** PrintE-book.

38044 ■ *The E-Myth Enterprise: How to Turn a Great Idea into a Thriving Business*
Pub: HarperCollins Publishers Inc.
Contact: Jane Friedman, President
E-mail: jfriedman@harpercollins.com

Ed: Michael E. Gerber. **Released:** August 03, 2010. **Price:** $14.99, paperback. **Description:** This book explores the requirement needed to start and run a successful small business. **Availability:** Print.

38045 ■ *The Elements of Small Business*
Pub: Silver Lake Publishing L.L.C.
Contact: Connie Nitzschner, Manager
Ed: John Thaler. **Released:** October 2004. **Price:** $12.95, paperback. **Description:** Concepts, markets, worksheets, letters, business plans, and sample legal forms for starting and running a small business are included. **Availability:** Print.

38046 ■ *Enterprise Planning and Development: Small Business and Enterprise Start-Up Survival and Growth*
Pub: Elsevier Science and Technology Books
Ed: David Butler. **Released:** June 2006. **Description:** Innovation, intellectual property, and exit strategies are among the issues discussed in this book involving current entrepreneurship.

38047 ■ *The Entrepreneurial Itch: Don't Scratch Until You Read This Book!*
Pub: Self-Counsel Press Inc.
Ed: David Trahair. **Released:** October 15, 2006. **Price:** $13.95. **Description:** Small business accountant shares a plan for starting a business. **Availability:** Print.

38048 ■ *Entrepreneurial Management*
Pub: McGraw-Hill
Ed: Robert J. Calvin. **Released:** February 28, 2002. **Price:** A$69.95, Hardcover; NZ$82, Hardcover. **Description:** Starting a new business takes careful consideration, determined preparation and a well-developed plan president of an international company that helps startups offers strategies, tools, techniques, models and methodologies for starting a new business. This guidebook covers all aspects of launching a new company as well as hands-on business skills and the motivation to keep new business owners moving towards success while conquering the entrepreneurial challenges along with way. **Availability:** Print.

38049 ■ *The Entrepreneur's Edge: Finding Money, Making Money, Keeping Money*
Ed: Daniel Hogan. **Released:** October 2006. **Price:** $24.95. **Description:** Advice for starting, running and growing a new business is given.

38050 ■ *"Entrepreneurs: Search Party" in Business Strategy Review (Vol. 21, Autumn 2010, No. 3, pp. 30)*
Pub: John Wiley & Sons Inc. Scientific, Technical, Medical, and Scholarly Div. (Wiley-Blackwell)
Contact: William J. Pesce, Manager
E-mail: wpesce@wiley.com
Ed: Georgina Peters. **Description:** Entrepreneurs tend to be fixated on coming up with a foolproof idea for a new business and then raising money to start it. Raising startup funds is difficult, but it doesn't have to be that way. Search funds offers an innovative alternative, and the results are often impressive.

38051 ■ *Entrepreneurship: A Small Business Approach*
Pub: McGraw-Hill Higher Education
Contact: Edward Stanford, President
E-mail: ed_stanford@mcgraw-hill.com
Ed: Charles E. Bamford, Garry D. Bruton. **Released:** January 10, 2010. **Description:** This text takes a hands-on, problem-based learning approach that works through real problems faced by entrepreneurs and small business owners.

38052 ■ *Entrepreneurship and the Creation of Small Firms: Empirical Studies of New Ventures*
Pub: Edward Elgar Publishing Inc.
Contact: Richard Henning, Vice President
E-mail: kwight@e-elgar.com
Ed: Carin Holmquist, Johan Wiklund. **Released:** 2010. **Price:** £63, hardback. **Description:** Study focuses on the important issue of new venture creation. Using a variety of data sources, methods and theories, the authors demonstrate the factors that aid or hinder new venture creation in a number of settings.

38053 ■ *Entrepreneurship and Effective Small Business Management*
Pub: Prentice Hall Higher Education
Ed: Norman M. Scarborough, Jeffrey R. Cornwall. **Released:** Eleventh Edition. **Price:** $217.40. **Description:** Provides undergraduate and graduate entrepreneurship and/or small business management courses with information to successfully launch a new company. The books offers entrepreneurs the tools required to develop staying power to succeed and grow their new business. **Availability:** Print.

38054 ■ *Entrepreneurship: Successfully Launching New Ventures*
Ed: Bruce Barringer, Duane Ireland. **Released:** October 17, 2011. **Price:** C$198. **Description:** Guide to help any entrepreneur successfully launch a new venture. **Availability:** Print.

38055 ■ *Escape from Corporate America: A Practical Guide to Creating the Career of Your Dreams*
Pub: Ballantine/Random House
Ed: Pamela Skillings. **Released:** May 13, 2008. **Price:** $15; $13.99. **Description:** How to quit your job and start your own business. **Availability:** PrintE-book.

38056 ■ *Escape from Cubicle Nation: From Corporate Prisoner to Thriving Entrepreneur*
Pub: Berkley Publishing Group
Contact: Susan Petersen Kennedy, President
Ed: Pamela Slim. **Released:** April 06, 2010. **Price:** $15, paperback. **Description:** Insight is offered to help anyone wishing to leave their corporate position and start their own small business. **Availability:** Print.

38057 ■ *Extraordinary Entrepreneurship: The Professional's Guide to Starting an Exceptional Enterprise*
Pub: John Wiley & Sons Inc.
Contact: Stephen M. Smith, President
Ed: Stephen C. Harper. **Released:** October 2006. **Price:** $66.95; $53.99. **Description:** New rules to assist entrepreneurs in the 21st Century. The book focuses on thinking outside the box. **Availability:** PrintE-book.

38058 ■ *Fast-Track Business Start-Up Kit: California*
Pub: Kaplan Books
Ed: Carolyn Usinger. **Released:** 2006. **Price:** $22.95; C$29. **Description:** Step-by-step guide for starting and running a business in California, including information on sole proprietors, partnerships, limited liability companies, S and C corporations, as well as details concerning business entities, sales taxes, environmental issues, human resources, and more.

38059 ■ *Financial Times Guide to Business Start Up 2007*
Ed: Sara Williams; Jonquil Lowe. **Released:** November 2006. **Price:** $52.50. **Description:** Guide for starting and running a new business is presented. Sections include ways to get started, direct marketing, customer relations, management and accounting.

38060 ■ *Foreclosure Cleanout Business: High Profits — Low Start Up Cost*
Ed: James Tolliver. **Released:** October 11, 2011. **Price:** $17.99. **Description:** Foreclosure cleanout business is booming. This manual teaches how to start a foreclosure firm, who to contact, what to charge, services provided and more.

38061 ■ *Franchising for Dummies*
Pub: John Wiley & Sons Inc.
Contact: Stephen M. Smith, President
Ed: Dave Thomas, Michael Seid. **Released:** 2nd Edition. **Price:** $24.95, paperback; $16.99. **Description:** Advice to help entrepreneurs choose the right franchise, as well as financing, managing and expanding the business. **Availability:** PrintE-book.

38062 ■ *The Girl's Guide to Starting Your Own Business: Candid Advice, Frank Talk, and True Stories for the Successful*

Entrepreneur
Pub: William Morrow
Ed: Caitlin Friedman, Kimberly Yorio. **Released:** December 07, 2010. **Price:** $15.99, paperback; $11.49; C$11.99. **Description:** Advice is given to help any woman start her own company. Every chapter includes interviews, charts, quizzes and witty directives about self-employment. Topics include, choosing a name and logo, business law, communication and information about business associations. **Availability:** PrintE-book.

38063 ■ *Harmonic Wealth: The Secret of Attracting the Life You Want*
Pub: Hyperion Books
Contact: Ellen Archer, President
Ed: James Arthur Ray, Linda Sivertsen. **Released:** 2008. **Price:** $24.95; C$31.50. **Description:** Secrets for attracting the life you want through entrepreneurship; tips for timing a startup are included.

38064 ■ *Home-Based Business for Dummies*
Pub: John Wiley & Sons Inc.
Contact: Stephen M. Smith, President
Ed: Paul Edwards, Sarah Edwards, Peter Economy. **Released:** 3rd Edition. **Price:** $19.95, paperback; $12.99. **Description:** Provides all the information needed to start and run a home-based business. Topics include: selecting the right business; setting up a home office; managing money, credit, and financing; marketing; and ways to avoid distractions while working at home. **Availability:** PrintE-book.

38065 ■ *How to Form Your Own California Corporation*
Pub: Nolo
Contact: Ralph Warner, Chief Executive Officer
Ed: Anthony Mancuso. **Released:** February 2013. **Price:** $31.99; $27.99. **Description:** Instructions and forms required to incorporate any business in the State of California. **Availability:** PrintE-book.

38066 ■ *How to Get the Financing for Your New Small Business: Innovative Solutions from the Experts Who Do It Every Day*
Pub: Atlantic Publishing Co.
Contact: Amanda Miller, Manager
E-mail: amiller@atlantic-pub.com
Ed: Sharon L. Fullen. **Released:** May 2006. **Price:** $39.95, Includes companion CD-Rom. **Description:** Ready capital is essential for starting and expanding a small business. Topics include traditional financing methods, financial statements, and a good business plan. **Availability:** Print.

38067 ■ *How I Made It: 40 Successful Entrepreneurs Reveal How They Made Millions*
Pub: Kogan Page, Limited
Contact: Philip Kogan, Chairman of the Board
Ed: Rachel Bridge. **Released:** May 10, 2010. **Price:** £14.99, Paperback. **Description:** Inspiration is given to anyone wishing to become a successful entrepreneur.

38068 ■ *How to Make Big Money in Your Own Small Business: Unexpected Rules Every Small Business Owner Needs to Know*
Pub: Hyperion Books
Contact: Ellen Archer, President
Ed: Jeffrey J. Fox. **Released:** May 12, 2004. **Price:** $16.95; C$24.95. **Description:** Entrepreneur and consultant offer advice to help others create successful startups and prosper. Fox directs new business owners with a counterintuitive style and describes essential methods that beat the competition. Tips include: setting priorities, getting a personal driver, creating a contingency plan for employees, pricing to value, saving money, and getting an office outside of the home.

38069 ■ *How to Start a Home-Based Mail Order Business*
Pub: Globe Pequot Press Inc.
Contact: Robert Irwin, Manager
E-mail: robert.irwin@globepequot.com
Ed: Georganne Fiumara. **Released:** June 01, 2011. **Price:** $18.95, paperback. **Description:** Step-by-step guide for starting and growing a home-based mail

order business. Information about equipment, pricing, online marketing, are included along with worksheets and checklists for planning. **Availability:** Print.

38070 ■ *How to Start an Internet Sales Business Without Making the Government Mad*
Pub: Lulu.com
Ed: Dan Davis. **Released:** September 30, 2011. **Price:** $14.38. **Description:** Small business guide for launching an Internet sales company. Topics include business structure, licenses, and taxes. **Availability:** PDF.

38071 ■ *How to Start, Operate and Market a Freelance Notary Signing Agent Business*
Ed: Victoria Ring. **Released:** September 2004. **Price:** , $8.18. **Description:** Due to the changes in the 2001 Uniform Commercial Code allowing notary public agents to serve as a witness to mortgage loan closings (eliminating the 2-witness requirement under the old code), notaries are working directly for mortgage, title and signing companies as mobile notaries.

38072 ■ *How to Start and Run a Small Book Publishing Company: A Small Business Guide to Self-Publishing and Independent Publishing*
Pub: HCM Publishing
Ed: Peter I. Hupalo. **Released:** August 30, 2002. **Price:** $18.95. **Description:** The book teaches all aspects of starting and running a small book publishing company. Topics covered include: inventory accounting in the book trade, just-in-time inventory management, turnkey fulfillment solutions, tax deductible costs, basics of sales and use tax, book pricing, standards in terms of the book industry, working with distributors and wholesalers, cover design and book layout, book promotion and marketing, how to select profitable authors to publish, printing process, printing on demand, the power of a strong backlist, and how to value copyright.

38073 ■ *How to Start and Run Your Own Corporation: S-Corporations For Small Business Owners*
Pub: HCM Publishing
Ed: Peter I. Hupalo. **Released:** Second Edition. **Price:** $22.46, paperback. **Description:** Basics of corporate business structure are explained. Topics include discovering the best business structure for your company; how to decided between an S-Corporation and LLC; choosing the state in which to incorporate, how to form a corporation, angel investing, special issues for one-person corporations, the role of bylaws and corporate minutes, board of directors, taxes, workers' compensation issues, retirement plans, and more. **Availability:** Print.

38074 ■ *How to Start a Small Business in Canada: Your Road Map to Financial Freedom*
Pub: Self-Help Publishers
Ed: Tariq Nadeem. **Released:** 2nd Edition. **Price:** C$19.95, paperback; C$34.50, hardcover; C$14.95. **Description:** Provides information for starting and managing a small business in Canada. **Availability:** PrintE-book.

38075 ■ *How to Start Your Own Business for Entrepreneurs*
Pub: FT Press
Contact: Timothy C. Moore, Vice President
Ed: Robert Ashton. **Released:** Second Edition. **Price:** $24.99. **Description:** More than 300,000 individuals start a business every year. That number will rise over the next year or two if the current economic downturn leads to widespread job losses.

38076 ■ *"Hype: If You Build It.." in Entrepreneur (Vol. 35, October 2007, No. 10, pp. 138)*
Pub: Entrepreneur Press
Contact: Perlman Neil, President
Ed: John Jantsch. **Description:** Marketing strategy can be achieved by determining what a company's target market is, and how that company is unique in its industry. Narrowing the market will make promoting the company's products or services easier, and

identifying the company's unique qualities will help in sending out a uniform message to the clients. Details of how to develop a marketing strategy are provided.

38077 ■ *"The Innovator's Method: Bringing the Lean Start-up into Your Organization"*
Pub: Harvard Business Review Press
Contact: Peter E. Walsh, Director
Released: August 19, 2014. **Price:** $30.00. **Description:** The innovator's method was developed using research inside corporations and successful startups to create, refine, and bring ideas and inventions to the marketplace. Advice is provided to test, validate and commercialize ideas with the lean, design, and agile techniques used by successful startups.

38078 ■ *"It's Not Perfect; But Illinois a Good Home for Business" in Crain's Chicago Business (Vol. 34, October 24, 2011, No. 42, pp. 18)*
Pub: Crain Communications Inc.
Contact: Todd Johnson, Publisher
Description: Focusing on all factors that encompass Illinois' business environment, findings show that Illinois is a good place to start and grow a business. The study focused on corporate income tax rates and the fact that talent, access to capital and customers along with transportation connections are among the important factors the state has for small businesses.

38079 ■ *Kick Start Your Dream Business: Getting it Started and Keeping You Going*
Ed: Romanus Wolter. **Released:** March 2004. **Description:** Comprehensive guide covering the start-up process for any new company.

38080 ■ *"Lean Branding"*
Pub: O'Reilly and Associates Inc.
Contact: Tim O'Reilly, President
E-mail: tim@oreilly.com
Released: September 17, 2014. **Price:** $29.99. **Description:** Branding your startup is essential to any small business success. A toolkit is provided to help build dynamic brands that generate conversion. Over 100 do-it-yourself branding tactics and case studies as well as step-by-step instructions for building and measuring 25 essential brand strategy ingredients, from logo design to demonstration day pitches.

38081 ■ *Legal Guide for Starting & Running a Small Business*
Pub: Nolo
Contact: Ralph Warner, Chief Executive Officer
Ed: Fred S. Steingold. **Released:** April 2013. **Price:** $31.99; $27.99. **Description:** Legal issues any small business owner needs to know for starting and running a successful business are outlined. **Availability:** PrintE-book; PDF.

38082 ■ *Life Entrepreneurs: Ordinary People Creating Extraordinary Lives*
Pub: Jossey-Bass
Ed: Christopher Gergen, Gregg Vanourek. **Released:** February 2008. **Price:** $24.95, hardcover; $16.99. **Description:** Consultants Christopher Gergen and Gregg Vanourek present the basic principles for becoming a successful entrepreneur: recognizing opportunity, taking risks, and innovation. **Availability:** PrintE-book.

38083 ■ *"Live & Learn: Gordon Stollery" in Canadian Business (Vol. 81, December 19, 2007, No. 1, pp. 76)*
Pub: Rogers Media Inc.
Contact: Tony Viner, President
Ed: Michelle Magnan. **Description:** Gordon Stollery of Highpine Oil and Gas Ltd. talks about being a hardrock geologist and his move to start his oil and gas business. Other aspects of his business career are discussed.

38084 ■ *"Looking To Leap?" in Black Enterprise (Vol. 38, January 2008, No. 6, pp. 64)*
Pub: Earl G. Graves Publishing Co. Inc.
Contact: Earl G. Graves, Jr., President
Ed: Tennille M. Robinson. **Description:** Websites and organizations providing resources for any young entrepreneur wishing to start a new business are outlined.

38085 ■ *Low Risk, High Reward: Practical Prescriptions for Starting and Growing Your Business*
Pub: R & R Publishing
Ed: Bob Reiss, Jeffrey L. Cruikshank. **Released:** December 01, 2000. **Price:** $19.95. **Description:** Successful entrepreneur teaches others about creating, growing and maintaining a successful business venture. The book offers a step-by-step approach to helping entrepreneurs minimize the risk involved in a new business while examining the skills and resources needed to succeed. **Availability:** Print.

38086 ■ *"Make Money in 2011" in Small Business Opportunities (January 2011)*
Pub: Harris Publications Inc.
Description: Top twenty ways to pick up extra cash, boost your income and generate new revenue. There has never been a better time to start a small business.

38087 ■ *Making a Living Without a Job: Winning Ways for Creating Work That You Love*
Pub: Random House Publishing Group
Contact: John Irwing, Editor
Ed: Barbara J. Winter. **Released:** August 09, 2010. **Price:** $16, Paperback. **Description:** For all Americans who are out of work, soon to be out of work, or wishing to be freed from unrewarding work: here is the must-have book that shows how to make a living by working when, where, and how you want to work.

38088 ■ *Making a Living Without a Job: Winning Ways For Creating Work That You Love*
Pub: Bantam Books
Ed: Barbara Winter. **Released:** July 22, 2009. **Price:** $11.99. **Description:** Winter gives advice to help anyone turn an interest or hobby into a lucrative business. **Availability:** E-book.

38089 ■ *"Making Social Ventures Work" in Harvard Business Review (Vol. 88, September 2010, No. 9, pp. 66)*
Pub: Harvard Business School Publishing
Ed: James D. Thompson, Ian C. MacMillan. **Description:** Five steps are to define, examine the political aspects, focus on discovery-driven planning, develop an appropriate exit strategy, and anticipate unexpected consequences when starting a new social venture.

38090 ■ *MBA In A Day: What You Would Learn At Top-Tier Business Schools (If You Only Had The Time!)*
Pub: John Wiley & Sons Inc.
Contact: Stephen M. Smith, President
Ed: Steven Stralser. **Released:** September 2004. **Price:** $34.95, hardcover; $22.99. **Description:** Management professor presents important concepts, business topics and strategies that can be used by anyone to manage a small business or professional practice. Topics covered include: human resources and personal interaction, ethics and leadership skills, fair negotiation tactics, basic business accounting practices, project management, and the fundamentals of economics and marketing. **Availability:** PrintE-book.

38091 ■ *Mobile Office: The Essential Small Business Guide to Office Technology*
Pub: Double Storey Books
Ed: Arthur Goldstruck, Steven Ambrose. **Released:** September 1, 2009. **Price:** $6.95. **Description:** Essential pocket guide for startup businesses and entrepreneurs which provides information to create a mobile office in order to maximize business potential while using current technologies.

38092 ■ *"The New Face of Detroit" in Inc. (Vol. 33, October 2011, No. 8, pp. 6)*
Pub: Inc. Magazine
Ed: Elizabeth Sile. **Description:** Basketball legend Magic Johnson has joined Detroit Venture Partners and Detroit will be one of the firm's three inaugural cities to host fellows from Venture for America, a new organization that places recent college graduates in start-up companies.

38093 ■ New Venture Creation: Entrepreneurship for the 21st Century with Online Learning Center Access Card
Pub: McGraw-Hill

Ed: Jeffrey A. Timmons; Stephen Spinelli. **Released:** November 1, 2008. **Price:** $71.97. **Description:** A handbook for students that explores all the concepts necessary for successfully launching a new enterprise.

38094 ■ Niche and Grow Rich
Ed: Jennifer Basye Sander; Peter Sander. **Released:** 2003. **Description:** Consultants share insight to entrepreneurs wishing to find a profitable niche market. Authors write that good niche businesses are easy to start and easy to defend from competitors. They also report that finding a successful niche can attract and maintain good customers who are willing to pay more for unique goods and services.

38095 ■ "Oh, Grow Up" in Entrepreneur (Vol. 35, October 2007, No. 10, pp. 120)
Pub: Entrepreneur Press
Contact: Perlman Neil, President
Ed: Mark Henricks. **Description:** Most entrepreneurs are overwhelmed with the idea of expanding their business, forgetting to strategically plan the process of business growth. However, there are certain steps entrepreneurs must take in turning a startup business into a bigger venture. Eight steps to growing a business, such as asking for advice and deciding on a focus are presented.

38096 ■ 101 Businesses You Can Start at With Less Than One Thousand Dollars: For Stay-at-Home Moms & Dads
Pub: Atlantic Publishing Co.
Contact: Amanda Miller, Manager
E-mail: amiller@atlantic-pub.com
Ed: Heather Lee Shepherd. **Released:** August 2007. **Price:** $21.95. **Description:** Over 100 business ideas are detailed to help stay-at-home parents earn extra money to add to the family income. These businesses can be started with minimum training and investment and most can be easily operated by one person and eventually be sold for an additional profit; many are started with less than one hundred dollars and can be run from home. **Availability:** Print.

38097 ■ 101 Businesses You Can Start at With Less Than One Thousand Dollars: For Retirees
Pub: Atlantic Publishing Co.
Contact: Amanda Miller, Manager
E-mail: amiller@atlantic-pub.com
Ed: Heather Lee Shepherd. **Released:** September 2007. **Price:** $21.95. **Description:** According to a study by the U.S. Department of Health and Human Resources, people starting their work careers will face the following situation when they retire at the age of 65: they will have annual incomes between $4,000 and $26,000. According to the Social Security Administration, today's retirees can count on corporate pensions and Social Security for 61 percent of their retirement income. The remainder must come from other sources. Therefore, if this holds true for the future, today's workers need to accumulate enough in personal savings to make up the 39 percent shortfall in retirement income. The solution for many will be to start a small part-time business. **Availability:** Print.

38098 ■ 101 Businesses You Can Start at With Less Than One Thousand Dollars: For Students
Pub: Atlantic Publishing Co.
Contact: Amanda Miller, Manager
E-mail: amiller@atlantic-pub.com
Ed: Heather Lee Shepherd. **Released:** September 2007. **Price:** $21.95. **Description:** More than 100 business ideas for busy students; these ideas can be started for very little money yet provide striving students with more money than they would make working a job paying an hourly wage. Web links for additional information are provides along with detailed instruction and examples for starting a successful business. **Availability:** Print.

38099 ■ 101 Small Business Ideas for Under $5000
Pub: John Wiley & Sons Inc.
Contact: Stephen M. Smith, President
Released: April 2005. **Price:** $29; $18.99. **Description:** Entrepreneurial ideas for starting companies that can be run part-time or full-time, and some as an absentee owner. **Availability:** PrintE-book.

38100 ■ The Owners Manual for Small Business
Pub: Planning Shop
Contact: Rhonda Abrams, Chief Executive Officer
Ed: Rhonda Abrams. **Released:** December 2005. **Price:** $19.95. **Description:** Reference book offering tips for starting a small business, low-cost marketing, and communicating effectively.

38101 ■ Partnership: Small Business Start-Up Kit
Ed: Daniel Sitarz. **Released:** November 2005. **Price:** , $29.95. **Description:** Guidebook detailing partnership law by state covering the formation and use of partnerships as a business form. Information on filing requirements, property laws, legal liability, standards, and the new Revised Uniform Partnership Act is covered.

38102 ■ Running Your Small Business on a MAC
Ed: Doug Hanley. **Released:** November 2007. **Price:** , $29.99. **Description:** Information to effectively start and run a small business using a MAC, including setting up a network and accounting.

38103 ■ "Self-Employment: What To Know To Be Your Own Boss" in Occupational Outlook Quarterly (Vol. 58, Summer 2014, No. 2, pp. 2)
Pub: Government Printing Office
Released: Summer 2014. **Description:** Information is presented to help would-be entrepreneurs decide if self-employment is for them. The challenges, rewards, and fastest growth sectors are discussed. Whether to incorporate or not is examined, as well as the skills and knowledge to become a successful small business owner is explored.

38104 ■ "Slow-Down Startups Hot" in Austin Business JournalInc. (Vol. 28, September 12, 2008, No. 26, pp. 1)
Pub: American City Business Journals
Ed: Sandra Zaragoza. **Description:** A number of entrepreneurs from Austin, Texas are starting their own small business despite the economic slowdown. The Small Business Development Program in Austin has seen a 50 percent increase in the demand for its services in 2008 as compared to demand in 2007. Other details about the entrepreneurship trend are discussed.

38105 ■ Small Business, Big Life: Five Steps to Creating a Great Life with Your Own Small Business
Pub: Thomas Nelson Inc.
Contact: Michael S. Hyatt, President
Ed: Louis Barajas. **Released:** May 01, 2007. **Price:** $22.99, hardcover. **Description:** Barajas describes his and his father's independent entrepreneurial paths and suggests an inspirational approach to business that relies on four personal greatness cornerstones: truth, responsibility, awareness, and courage, and on keeping in mind your vision and your team's needs. The book provides a new look at achieving a work/life balance. **Availability:** Print.

38106 ■ Small Business for Dummies
Pub: John Wiley & Sons Inc.
Contact: Stephen M. Smith, President
Released: December 2011. **Price:** $22.95. **Description:** Advice for launching and growing a small business; insights into using the Internet as business tool are included. **Availability:** Print.

38107 ■ Small Business for Dummies
Pub: John Wiley & Sons Inc.
Contact: Stephen M. Smith, President
Ed: Eric Tyson, Jim Schell. **Released:** 4th Edition. **Price:** $22.95; $14.99. **Description:** Guidebook for anyone wanting to start or grow a small business; topics include information financing, budgeting, marketing, management and more. **Availability:** PrintE-book.

38108 ■ Small Business Entrepreneur: Launching a New Venture and Managing a Business on a Day-to-Day Basis
Ed: Rory Burke. **Released:** February 2006. **Price:** $19.95. **Description:** Comprehensive guide examining the management skills required to launch and run a small business.

38109 ■ Small Business Legal Tool Kit
Pub: Entrepreneur Press
Contact: Perlman Neil, President
Ed: Ira Nottonson, Theresa A. Pickner. **Description:** Legal expertise is provided by two leading entrepreneurial attorneys. Issues covered include forming and operating a business: taxes, contracts, leases, bylaws, trademarks, small claims court, etc.

38110 ■ Small Business Management: Launching and Growing New Ventures
Pub: Nelson Education Ltd.
Contact: Greg Nordal, President
Ed: Justin G. Longenecker. **Released:** 5th Edition. **Price:** $136.95, paperback; $79.95. **Description:** Tips for starting and running a successful new company are provided. **Availability:** PrintE-book.

38111 ■ The Small Business Owner's Manual: Everything You Need to Know to Start Up and Run Your Business
Pub: Career Press Inc.
Contact: Ron Fry, President
Ed: Joe Kennedy. **Released:** June 2005. **Price:** $19.99. **Description:** Comprehensive guide for starting a small business, focusing on twelve ways to obtain financing, business plans, selling and advertising products and services, hiring and firing employees, setting up a Web site, business law, accounting issues, insurance, equipment, computers, banks, financing, customer credit and collection, leasing, and more. **Availability:** Print.

38112 ■ The Small Business Start-Up Kit
Pub: Nolo
Contact: Ralph Warner, Chief Executive Officer
Ed: Peri Pakroo. **Released:** February 2014. **Price:** $23.99; $20.99. **Description:** Entrepreneurial advice for launching a new business. Topics include compliance with state regulations, sole proprietorships, partnerships, corporations, limited liability companies, as well as accounting and tax information. **Availability:** PrintE-book.

38113 ■ The Small Business Start-Up Kit for California
Pub: Nolo
Contact: Ralph Warner, Chief Executive Officer
Ed: Peri Pakroo. **Released:** February 2014. **Price:** $23.99; $20.99. **Description:** Handbook covering all aspects of starting a business in California, including information about necessary fees, forms, and taxes. **Availability:** PrintE-book.

38114 ■ The Small Business Start-Up Workbook: A Step-by-Step Guide to Starting the Business You've Dreamed Of
Pub: How To Books
Contact: Giles Lewis, Publisher
Ed: Cheryl D. Rickman. **Released:** May 01, 2005. **Price:** £11.04; £12.99, Nonmembers. **Description:** Book provides practical exercises for starting a small business, including marketing and management strategies. **Availability:** Online.

38115 ■ Small Business Survival Guide
Ed: Cliff Ennico. **Price:** $12.95. **Description:** Small business expert provides strategies to start a company and survive in the 21st Century. He shows small business owners how to succeed despite challenges that can defeat any firm. His advice covers suppliers; customers and contractors; competitors and creditors; spouses, family and friends; as well as the ways lawyers, accountants and other can steal an entrepreneur's success. Ennico also describes how startups can comply with local regulations.

38116 ■ Small Time Operator: How to Start Your Own Business, Keep Your Books, Pay

Your Taxes, and Stay Out of Trouble
Pub: Bell Springs Publishing
Contact: Bernard B. Kamoroff, President
E-mail: kamaroff@bellsprings.com
Ed: Bernard B. Kamoroff. **Released:** 13th Edition.
Price: $17.95, plus $4.00 shipping. **Description:**
Comprehensive guide for starting any kind of business.

38117 ■ *So You Want to Start a Business?*
Ed: Edward D. Hess; Charles Goetz. **Released:**
August 30, 2008. **Price:** $18.99. **Description:** Over
sixty percent of Americans say they would like to own
their own business and more than five million business startups are launched annually. However, fifty to
seventy percent of new businesses fail. This book
identifies the eight mistakes that cause these business failures and offers entrepreneurs the knowledge,
tools, templates, strategies, and hands-on how-to
advice needed to avoid these errors and succeed.

38118 ■ *Soul Proprietor: 101 Lessons from a
Lifestyle Entrepreneur*
Ed: Jane Pollak. **Released:** September 2004. **Description:** More than 100 tips and stores to inspire
and guide any would-be entrepreneur to earn a living
from a favorite hobby or passion.

38119 ■ *The Spirit of Entrepreneurship:
Exploring the Essence of Entrepreneurship
Through Personal Stories*
Pub: Springer
Contact: Derk Haank, Chief Executive Officer
E-mail: derk.haank@springer.com
Ed: Sharda S. Nandram, Karel J. Samson. **Released:**
2006. **Price:** €89.99, hardcover; €74.96. **Description:** Case studies involving 60 entrepreneurs and
executives explores the fundamentals in starting a
new business, techniques and mindsets. **Availability:**
PrintE-book.

38120 ■ *The Spiritual Entrepreneur*
Pub: New Paradigm Media
Ed: Robert Morgen. **Released:** January 1, 2010.
Price: $16.95. **Description:** Step-by-step guide to
start a small business and then use that business to
create various streams of passive income to support
yourself and charities is presented.

38121 ■ *Start Business in California, 3E*
Ed: John J. Talamo. **Released:** July 2006. **Price:**
$24.95. **Description:** Information required for starting
any business in California.

38122 ■ *Start and Run a Bookkeeping
Business*
Pub: Self-Counsel, Incorporated
Ed: Angie Mohr. **Released:** October 2005. **Price:**
C$22.95; $17.95; C$12.99, EPUB. **Description:**
Advice for starting and running a bookkeeping service
business. Includes MS Word and PDF formats for
use in Windows-based PC.

38123 ■ *Start, Run, & Grow a Successful
Small Business*
Pub: Toolkit Media Group
Ed: John L. Duoba, Joel Handelsman, Alice H. Magos, Catherine Gordon. **Released:** Sixth Edition.
Price: $18.70. **Availability:** Print.

38124 ■ *"Start-Up Pointers" in Inside
Business (Vol. 13, September-October 2011,
No. 5, pp. Y3)*
Pub: Great Lakes Publishing Co.
Description: Four tips to help entrepreneurs with
startup firms are provided by Youngstown Business
Incubator.

38125 ■ *Start Your Own Business, Fifth
Edition*
Pub: Entrepreneur Press
Contact: Perlman Neil, President
Ed: Rieva Lesonsky. **Released:** October 01, 2010.
Price: $24.95, Paperback. **Description:** Author and
the staff of Entrepreneur Magazine provide business
resources and information for starting a successful
business. The book guides you through the first three
years of ownership and provides work sheets and
checklists.

38126 ■ *Start Your Own Lawn Care or
Landscaping Business: Your Step-by-Step
Guide to Success*
Pub: Entrepreneur Press
Ed: Ciree Linsenman. **Released:** Third Edition. **Price:**
$19.95, paperback. **Description:** Steps for starting
and running a lawn care service. **Availability:** Print.

38127 ■ *Start Your Own Wedding Consultant
Business*
Pub: Entrepreneur Press
Ed: Eileen Figure Sandlin. **Released:** Third Edition.
Price: $19.95, paperback. **Description:** Advice for
starting and running a wedding consulting business.
Availability: Print.

38128 ■ *Starting Green: An Ecopreneur's
Toolkit for Starting a Green Business From
Business Plans to Profits*
Pub: Entrepreneur Press
Contact: Perlman Neil, President
Ed: Glenn E. Croston. **Released:** 2009. **Description:** Entrepreneur and scientist outline green business essentials and helps uncover eco-friendly business opportunities, build a sustainable business plan,
and gain the competitive advantage.

38129 ■ *Starting and Running a Coaching
Business*
Pub: How To Books
Contact: Giles Lewis, Publisher
Ed: Aryanne Oade. **Released:** August 9, 2010. **Price:**
, $26.00. **Description:** Guide for the comprehensive,
practical and personalized process of starting and
running a coaching business is presented.

38130 ■ *Starting a Successful Business in
Canada*
Pub: Self-Counsel Press Inc.
Ed: Jack D. James. **Price:** $12.99. **Description:**
Provides a framework for entrepreneurs launching a
new business in Canada. **Availability:** Electronic
publishing.

38131 ■ *StartingUp Now Facilitator Guide*
Ed: L. Jenkins. **Released:** September 11, 2011.
Price: $29.95. **Description:** Guide for those teaching entrepreneurship using StartingUp Now; the guide
provides 24 lesson plans for each of the 24 steps/
chapters in the book.

38132 ■ *"Startup Activity Among Jobless
Execs is the Highest Since 2009, Survey
Says" in South Florida Business Journal (Vol.
34, February 21, 2014, No. 31, pp. 3)*
Pub: American City Business Journals
Released: February 21, 2014. **Description:** The
percentage of startup activity among former managers and executives in the U.S. increased 31 percent
in 2013 according to consulting firm Challenger, Gray
& Christmas. According to the survey, 5.5 percent of
job-seeking executive launched their own business
during each quarter in 2013, compared with 4.2
percent in 2012 and 3.2 percent in 2011.

38133 ■ *"Startup Communities: Building an
Entrepreneurial Ecosystem in Your City"*
Pub: John Wiley & Sons Inc.
Contact: Stephen M. Smith, President
Released: September 6, 2012. **Price:** $26.95. **Description:** A guide for building supportive entrepreneurial communities that drive innovation and small
business energy. Brad Feld, entrepreneur turned-
venture capitalist describes what it takes to create an
entrepreneurial community in any city, at any time.
He details the four critical principles required to form
a sustainable startup community.

38134 ■ *Startups That Work: Surprising
Research on What Makes or Breaks a New
Company*
Pub: Penguin Group USA
Contact: Phyllis Grann, President
Ed: Joel Kurtzman, Glenn Rifkin. **Released:** October
2005. **Price:** $25.95. **Availability:** Print.

38135 ■ *Steps to Small Business Start-Up:
Everything You Need to Know to Turn Your
Idea into a Successful Business*
Pub: Kaplan Books
Ed: Linda Pinson, Jerry Jinnett. **Released:** 2006.
Price: $22.95; C$29. **Description:** Tips for starting
and running a new company are presented.

38136 ■ *Stop Working: Start a Business,
Globalize It, and Generate Enough Cash Flow
to Get Out of the Rat Race*
Pub: Eye Contact Media Inc.
Contact: Rohan Hall, Chief Executive Officer
Ed: Rohan Hall. **Released:** November 2004. **Price:**
$15.99. **Description:** Advice is given to small companies to compete in the global marketplace by entrepreneur using the same strategy for his own business.

38137 ■ *Straight Talk About Small Business
Success in New Jersey: How to Maximize the
Growth, Cash Flow and Profitability of Your
Small Business*
Pub: Business Success Systems, Incorporated
Ed: Salim Omar. **Released:** April 2004. **Description:**
Small business information geared to new and existing small businesses in New Jersey.

38138 ■ *"Survival of the Fittest" in Black
Enterprise (November 1, 2007)*
Pub: Earl G. Graves Publishing Co. Inc.
Contact: Earl G. Graves, Jr., President
Ed: Tennille M. Robinson. **Description:** Black
Enterprise has developed the Small Business Success Guide for prospective and current entrepreneurs.

38139 ■ *Swimming Against the Stream:
Launching Your Business and Making Your
Life*
Ed: Tim Waterstone. **Released:** March 2007. **Price:**
$17.99. **Description:** Ten rules for launching a new
business are outlined using real-life experiences.

38140 ■ *"Think of Start-Ups as Shots On
Goal" in (Vol. 90, June 2012, No. 6, pp. 38)*
Pub: Harvard Business Review Press
Contact: Peter E. Walsh, Director
Ed: Robert E. Litan. **Released:** June 2012. **Description:** The importance of start-up businesses to the
nation's economic recovery is emphasized. Comprehensive legislation is necessary to improve start-up
access to opportunity and talent.

38141 ■ *The Toilet Paper Entrepreneur: The
Tell-It-Like-It-Is Guide to Cleaning Up In
Business, Even If You Are At the End of Your
Roll*
Pub: Obsidian Launch LLC
Ed: Mike Michalowicz. **Price:** $24.95. **Description:**
The founder of three multimillion-dollar companies,
including Obsidian Launch, a company that partners
with first-time entrepreneurs to grow their concepts
into industry leaders.

38142 ■ *"Top 25 Graduate Programs" in
Entrepreneur (Vol. 35, November 2007, No.
11, pp. 92)*
Description: List of the top twenty-five graduate
entrepreneurship programs of different colleges and
universities in the U.S. for 2007, as ranked by
Entrepreneur Magazine and the Princeton Review, is
presented.

38143 ■ *"Top 25 Undergrad Programs" in
Entrepreneur (Vol. 35, November 2007, No.
11, pp. 88)*
Description: List of the top twenty-five undergraduate entrepreneurship programs of different colleges
and universities in the U.S. for 2007, as ranked by
Entrepreneur Magazine and the Princeton Review, is
highlighted.

38144 ■ *"Top of the Class" in Entrepreneur
(Vol. 35, November 2007, No. 11, pp. 82)*
Pub: Entrepreneur Press
Contact: Perlman Neil, President
Ed: Nichole L. Torres. **Description:** Education in
entrepreneurship is being pursued by many students
and it is important to understand what entrepreneur-

ship program fits you. Aspiring entrepreneurs should also ask about the program's focus. Considerations searched for by students regarding the particular school they chose to study entrepreneurship are discussed.

38145 ■ *"Troy Patent Law Firm Launches Rent-Free Tech Incubator" in Crain's Detroit Business (Vol. 25, June 8, 2009, No. 23, pp. 4)*
Pub: Crain Communications Inc. - Detroit
Contact: Keith Crain, Chairman
Ed: Tom Henderson. **Description:** Young Basile Hanlon MacFarlane & Helmholdt PC, a patent law firm located in Troy, Michigan has created a small, rent-free technology incubator on site. The incubator will be called North Woodward Tech Incubator and has room for four or five startups. The incubator is for the earliest or pre-seed stage for entrepreneurs who have not yet gotten significant investment capital.

38146 ■ *Trump University Entrepreneurship 101: How to Turn Your Idea Into a Money Machine*
Pub: John Wiley & Sons Inc.
Contact: Stephen M. Smith, President
Ed: Michael E. Gordon. **Released:** Second Edition. **Price:** $24.95, hardcover; $16.99. **Description:** Current and expanded edition of the Trump guide to starting a business where Trump teams up with Professor Michael Gordon to show how to take a dream and turn it into a successful enterprise. **Availability:** PrintE-book.

38147 ■ *"Turning Bright Ideas Into Profitable Businesses" in Inside Business (Vol. 13, September-October 2011, No. 5, pp. SS6)*
Pub: Great Lakes Publishing Co.
Ed: Susan Keen Flynn. **Description:** Startup Lakewood was launched by Mickie Rinehart. She provides free resources to entrepreneurs in the city in order to help them turn their small business vision into reality.

38148 ■ *Ultimate Startup Directory: Expert Advice and 1,500 Great Startup Ideas*
Pub: Entrepreneur Press
Contact: Perlman Neil, President
Ed: James Stephenson. **Description:** Startup opportunities in over 30 industries are given, along with information on investment, earning potential, skills, legal requirements and more.

38149 ■ *The Unofficial Guide to Starting a Small Business*
Pub: John Wiley & Sons Inc.
Contact: Stephen M. Smith, President
Ed: Marcia Layton Turner. **Released:** October 2004. **Description:** Information and tools for starting a small business, covering the start-up process, from market research, to business plans, to marketing programs.

38150 ■ *Up and Running: Opening a Chiropractic Office*
Pub: PageFree Publishing, Incorporated
Ed: John L. Reizer. **Released:** March 2002. **Price:** $30.00. **Description:** Tips for starting a chiropractic business.

38151 ■ *"USM Focuses on Turning Science Into New Companies, Cash" in Boston Business Journal (Vol. 29, July 1, 2011, No. 8, pp. 1)*
Pub: American City Business Journals, Inc.
Ed: Alexander Jackson. **Description:** University System of Maryland gears up to push for its plan for commercializing its scientific discoveries which by 2020 could create 325 companies and double the $1.4 billion the system's eleven schools garner in yearly research grants. It is talking with University of Utah and University Maryland, Baltimore to explore ways to make this plan a reality.

38152 ■ *"UT Deans Serious about Biz" in Austin Business Journal (Vol. 31, May 20, 2011, No. 11, pp. 1)*
Pub: American City Business Journals
Ed: Sandra Zaragoza. **Description:** Dean Thomas Gilligan of the University of Texas, McCombs School of Business and engineering school Dean Gregory

Fenves have partnered to develop a joint engineering and business degree. Their partnership has resulted in an undergraduate course on initiating startups.

38153 ■ *Valuing Early Stage and Venture Backed Companies*
Pub: John Wiley & Sons Inc.
Contact: Stephen M. Smith, President
Ed: Neil J. Beaton. **Released:** March 2010. **Price:** $109.95, hardcover; $71.99. **Description:** Valuation techniques that can be used to value early stage companies with complex capital structures are examined. **Availability:** PrintE-book.

38154 ■ *"Virtual Playground" in Entrepreneur (Vol. 36, March 2008, No. 3, pp. 112)*
Pub: Entrepreneur Press
Contact: Perlman Neil, President
Ed: Amanda C. Kooser. **Description:** The growing number of children visiting virtual worlds provides opportunity for entrepreneurs to start online businesses catering to this market. Entrepreneurs need to be aware of the Children's Online Privacy Protection Act with regard to collecting children's information. Details of other things to know about with reference to these businesses are examined.

38155 ■ *Weekend Small Business Start*
Ed: Mark Warda. **Released:** June 2007. **Price:** $19.95. **Description:** Information for starting a new business is presented.

38156 ■ *What No One Ever Tells You About Starting Your Own Business: Real-Life Start-Up Advice from 101 Successful Entrepreneurs*
Pub: Kaplan Publishing
Contact: Julie Marshall, Director
E-mail: julie.marshall@kaplan.com
Ed: Jan Norman. **Released:** July 2004. **Price:** $18.95. **Description:** From planning to marketing, advice is given to entrepreneurs starting new companies. s. **Availability:** Print.

38157 ■ *Working for Yourself: An Entrepreneur's Guide to the Basics*
Pub: Kogan Page, Limited
Contact: Philip Kogan, Chairman of the Board
Ed: Jonathan Reuvid. **Released:** June 03, 2009. **Price:** £12.99. **Description:** Guide for starting a new business venture, focusing on raising financing, legal and tax issues, marketing, information technology, and site location. **Availability:** Print.

38158 ■ *"The Y Factor" in Entrepreneur (Vol. 35, November 2007, No. 11, pp. 58)*
Pub: Entrepreneur Press
Contact: Perlman Neil, President
Ed: Sara Wilson. **Description:** Venture capital company Y Combinator hosts a three-month program wherein the firm's founders select technology entrepreneurs from across the U.S. to help and to mentor them on starting a business.

38159 ■ *You Can Do It Too: The 20 Essential Things Every Budding Entrepreneur Should Know*
Pub: Kogan Page, Limited
Contact: Philip Kogan, Chairman of the Board
Ed: Rachel Bridge. **Released:** May 10, 2010. **Price:** £9.99, Paperback. **Description:** Collective wisdom of successful entrepreneurs in the form of twenty essential elements to focus on when starting a new company is illustrated by real-life entrepreneurial stories.

38160 ■ *You Need to be a Little Bit Crazy: The Truth about Starting and Growing Your Business*
Ed: Barry J. Moltz. **Description:** Offers entrepreneurs and small business owners insight into the ups and downs of running a business.

38161 ■ *You Need To Be a Little Crazy*
Ed: Barry J. Moltz. **Released:** December 2008. **Price:** $14.95. **Description:** Entrepreneur and investor who has founded several successful startups provides a guide using personal experience to help anyone start a new business.

38162 ■ *Your First Business Plan: A Simple Question-and-Answer Format Designed to Help You Write Your Own Plan*
Pub: Sourcebooks Inc.
Contact: Dominique M. Raccah, President
Ed: Joseph A. Covello. **Released:** May 01, 2005. **Price:** $21.99, paperback; $19.99. **Description:** Writing a good first business plan outlines successful business growth. **Availability:** PrintE-book; PDF.

38163 ■ *Your Million-Dollar Idea: From Concept to Marketplace*
Ed: Sandy Abrams. **Released:** March 01, 2010. **Price:** $14.95. **Description:** Self-taught entrepreneur provides a 12-step plan to make a new product or service a profitable reality.

38164 ■ *"Zero to One: Notes on Startups , or How to Build the Future"*
Pub: Random House Publishing Group
Contact: John Irwing, Editor
Released: September 16, 2014. **Price:** $27.00. **Description:** Entrepreneur and investor, Peter Thiel, covers new frontiers and new inventions yet to be discovered. Progress can be achieved in more industries than information technology, but thinking for one's self is critical to any entrepreneur in order to start and build a new venture. Tomorrow's leaders will avoid competition and create a unique business that will stand on its own.

ASSOCIATIONS AND OTHER ORGANIZATIONS

38165 ■ **Association for Enterprise Information (AFEI)**
2111 Wilson Blvd., Ste. 400
Arlington, VA 22201
Ph: (703)247-9474
Fax: (703)522-3192
Co. E-mail: dchesebrough@afei.org
URL: http://www.afei.org/Pages/default.aspx
Contact: Margaret E. Myers, Board Member
Description: Strives to advance enterprise integration and electronic business practices for industries and governments. **Founded:** 1998.

38166 ■ **BC Innovation Council**
1188 W Georgia St., 9th Fl.
Vancouver, BC, Canada V6E 4A2
Ph: (604)683-2724
Free: 800-665-7222
Fax: (604)683-6567
Co. E-mail: info@bcic.ca
URL: http://www.bcic.ca
Contact: Greg Caws, President
E-mail: gcaws@bcic.ca
Description: Provides support and access to companies and institutions by using research results, development projects and programs to further enhance in creating innovations.

38167 ■ **Canadian Federation of Independent Business (CFIB) [Federation Canadienne de l'Entreprise Independante]**
401-4141 Yonge St.
Toronto, ON, Canada M2P 2A6
Ph: (416)222-8022
Free: 888-234-2232
Fax: (416)222-6103
Co. E-mail: cfib@cfib.ca
URL: http://www.cfib-fcei.ca/english/index.html
Contact: Danny Kelly, President
Description: Independent businesses. Promotes economic well-being of members and seeks to maintain a healthy domestic business climate. Represents members' interests before government agencies, labor and industrial organizations, and the public. **Scope:** entrepreneurship, economic policy, small business, public policy. **Founded:** 1971. **Subscriptions:** 4000 books periodicals reports. **Publications:** *Mandate* (Quarterly); *Quarterly Business Barometer* (3/year).

38168 ■ International Council for Small Business (ICSB)
Funger Hall, Ste. 315
2201 G. St. NW
Washington, DC 20052
Ph: (202)994-0704
Fax: (202)994-4930
Co. E-mail: info@icsb.org
URL: http://www.icsb.org
Contact: Ruben Ascua, President
Description: Management educators, researchers, government officials and professionals in 80 countries. Fosters discussion of topics pertaining to the development and improvement of small business management. **Founded:** 1955. **Publications:** *Journal of Small Business Management* (Quarterly).

38169 ■ Mandate
401-4141 Yonge St.
Toronto, ON, Canada M2P 2A6
Ph: (416)222-8022
Free: 888-234-2232
Fax: (416)222-6103
Co. E-mail: cfib@cfib.ca
URL: http://www.cfib-fcei.ca/english/index.html
Contact: Danny Kelly, President
Released: Quarterly

38170 ■ National Association for Business Organizations (NAFBO)
5432 Price Ave.
Baltimore, MD 21215
Ph: (410)367-5309
Co. E-mail: nahbb@msn.com
URL: http://www.ameribizs.com/global
Contact: Rudolph Lewis, President
Description: Business organizations that develop and support small businesses that have the capability to provide their products or services on a national level. Promotes small business in a free market system; represents the interests of small businesses to government and community organizations on small business affairs; monitors and reviews laws that affect small businesses; promotes a business code of ethics. Supplies members with marketing and management assistance; encourages joint marketing services between members. Operates a Home Based Business Television Network that provides an affordable audio/visual media for small and home based businesses. **Founded:** 1986. **Awards:** Entrepreneur Certificate.

38171 ■ National Small Business Association (NSBA)
1156 15th St. NW, Ste. 1100
Washington, DC 20005
Ph: (202)293-8830
Free: 800-345-6728
Fax: (202)872-8543
Co. E-mail: info@nsba.biz
URL: http://www.nsba.biz
Contact: Todd McCracken, President
Description: Small businesses including manufacturing, wholesale, retail, service, and other firms. Works to advocate at the federal level on behalf of smaller businesses. **Founded:** 1937. **Publications:** *Advocate* (Bimonthly). **Educational Activities:** Small Business Meetup Day. **Awards:** Lewis A. Shattuck Small Business Advocate of the Year Award (Annual).

38172 ■ Quarterly Business Barometer
401-4141 Yonge St.
Toronto, ON, Canada M2P 2A6
Ph: (416)222-8022
Free: 888-234-2232
Fax: (416)222-6103
Co. E-mail: cfib@cfib.ca
URL: http://www.cfib-fcei.ca/english/index.html
Contact: Danny Kelly, President
URL(s): www.cfib-fcei.ca/english/research/canada/34-business-barometer.html. **Released:** 3/year

38173 ■ SCORE
1175 Herndon Pkwy., Ste. 900
Herndon, VA 20170
Free: 800-634-0245
Co. E-mail: help@score.org
URL: http://www.score.org
Contact: Kenneth W. Yancey, Jr., Chief Executive Officer
Description: Serves as volunteer program sponsored by U.S. Small Business Administration in which working and retired business management professionals provide free business counseling to men and women who are considering starting a small business, encountering problems with their business, or expanding their business. Offers free one-on-one counseling, online counseling and low cost workshops on a variety of business topics. **Scope:** business. **Founded:** 1964. **Subscriptions:** books clippings periodicals. **Publications:** *SCORE eNews* (Monthly); *SCORE Today* (Monthly). **Awards:** SCORE Chapter of the Year Award (Annual); Outstanding Woman-owned Small Business Award (Annual).

38174 ■ Small Business Investor Alliance (SBIA)
1100 H St. NW, Ste. 610
Washington, DC 20005
Ph: (202)628-5055
Co. E-mail: membership@sbia.org
URL: http://www.sbia.org
Contact: Brett Palmer, President
E-mail: bpalmer@nasbic.org
Description: Firms licensed as Small Business Investment Companies (SBICs) under the Small Business Investment Act of 1958. **Founded:** 1958. **Publications:** *NASBIC Membership Directory* (Annual); *NASBIC Membership Directory* (Annual); *NASBIC News* (Quarterly); *Today's SBICs: Investing in America's Future*; *Venture Capital: Where to Find It* (Annual). **Educational Activities:** Venture Capital Institute for Entrepreneurs (Annual); Venture Capital Institute for Entrepreneurs (Annual); Small Business Investor Alliance Private Equity Conference. **Awards:** Portfolio Company of the Year Award (Annual).

REFERENCE WORKS

38175 ■ "4 Big Fat Business Plan Lies" in Entrepreneur (December 11, 2008)
Pub: Entrepreneur Press
Contact: Perlman Neil, President
Ed: Tim Berry. **Description:** Business plans are essential for every business and do not necessarily have to be a complex document containing a full list of components. Other misconceptions concerning business plans are also discussed.

38176 ■ The 4-Hour Workweek
Pub: Crown Publishing/Random House
Ed: Timothy Ferriss. **Released:** April 24, 2007. **Price:** $22, Hardcover. **Description:** Examination of ways to cut the hours you work and find more enjoyment in your life.

38177 ■ The 4 Routes to Entrepreneurial Success
Pub: Berrett-Koehler Communications Inc.
Contact: Steve Piersanti, President
E-mail: spiersanti@bkpub.com
Ed: John B. Miner. **Price:** $18.95, paperback. **Description:** After researching one hundred successful entrepreneurs, the author discovered there are basically four personality types of entrepreneurs: the personal achiever, the super salesperson, the real manager, and the expert idea generator. **Availability:** Print.

38178 ■ The 5 Big Lies About American Business: Combating Smears Against the Free-Market Economy
Ed: Michael Medved. **Released:** November 02, 2010. **Price:** $15. **Description:** Michael Medved, talk-radio personality and bestselling author, argues for capitalism. He presents popular myths about the free market system and discusses why each myth is instead good for Americans and our economy.

38179 ■ The 7 Irrefutable Rules of Small Business Growth
Pub: John Wiley & Sons Inc.
Contact: Stephen M. Smith, President
Ed: Steven S. Little. **Released:** February 2005. **Price:** $18.95. **Description:** Proven strategies to maintain small business growth are outlined, covering topics such as technology, business plans, hiring, and more. **Availability:** Print.

38180 ■ The 29% Solution
Pub: Greenleaf Book Group Press
Ed: Ivan R. Misner, Michele R. Donovan. **Released:** September 01, 2008. **Price:** $21.95. **Description:** It is true that some people are better connected than others. That means that connecting is a skill that can be acquired. Networking skills used to increase business connections are highlighted. **Availability:** Print.

38181 ■ 32 Ways to Be a Champion in Business
Pub: Three Rivers Press
Contact: Caroline Sincerbeaux, Editor
E-mail: csincerbeaux@randomhouse.com
Ed: Earvin Magic Johnson. **Released:** December 29, 2009. **Price:** $18.94. **Description:** Earvin Johnson discusses his transition from athlete to entrepreneur and discusses the importance of hard work in order to pursue your dreams of starting and running a successful business.

38182 ■ "The 40-Year-Old Intern" in Entrepreneur (Vol. 37, October 2009, No. 10, pp. 90)
Pub: Entrepreneur Press
Contact: Perlman Neil, President
Ed: Kristin Ladd. **Description:** Brian Kurth's VocationVacation is an internship program aimed at helping people experience their dream job. The website, launched in January 2004, matches people with businesses that allow them to experience their fantasy jobs.

38183 ■ "2009: A Call For Vision" in Women Entrepreneur (January 28, 2009)
Ed: Elinor Robin. **Description:** Providing exemplary customer service, reducing expenses and creating an out-of-the-box niche are three key factors that will help business survive during this economic crisis. Business owners must see potential where others see failure in order to create new opportunities that may not only allow their business to survive during these times but may actually cause some businesses to thrive despite this economic downturn.

38184 ■ "2010 Book of Lists" in Business Courier (Vol. 26, December 26, 2009, No. 36, pp. 1)
Description: Rankings of companies and organizations within the business services, education, finance, health care, hospitality and tourism, real estate, and technology industries in the Cincinnati, Ohio-Northern Kentucky area are presented. Rankings are based on sales, business size, or other statistics.

38185 ■ "Abaddon Acquires Pukaskwa Uranium Properties in NW Ontario" in Canadian Corporate News (May 16, 2007)
Description: Rubicon Minerals Corp. has entered into an Option Agreement with Consolidated Abaddon Resources Inc. for the acquisition of Pukaskwa uranium properties and plans to conduct an extensive exploration program to prove out the resource and geological potential of the area. Statistical data included.

38186 ■ "Ace Every Introduction" in Women Entrepreneur (September 10, 2008)
Ed: Cynthia McKay. **Description:** Making a powerful first impression is one of the most important marketing tools a business owner can possess. Advice about meeting new business contacts is given.

38187 ■ The Age Curve: How to Profit from the Coming Demographic Storm
Pub: AMACOM
Contact: Edward T. Reilly, Manager
Ed: Kenneth W. Gronbach. **Released:** June 2008. **Price:** $19.95, Paper or Softback. **Description:** Reveals how America's largest generations are redefining consumer behavior and how businesses can anticipate their growing needs more effectively. **Availability:** Print.

38188 ■ *"Aging Boomers to Slow Growth, Study Says"* in *Globe & Mail (March 15, 2006, pp. B5)*
Ed: Heather Scoffield. **Description:** Acording to a research study by economic forecasters at Global Insight (Canada) Inc., an issue about Canada controlling its economy, as the country's population is aging, is discussed.

38189 ■ *Ahead of the Curve: Two Years at Harvard Business School*
Pub: Dutton Children's Books
Contact: Lauri Hornik, President
Ed: Philip Delves Broughton. **Released:** June 30, 2009. **Price:** $16, paperback. **Description:** A behind-the-scenes glimpse at Harvard Business School is given. The author believes Harvard succeeds in transforming students into business leaders but feels they are failing them in every other way. **Availability:** Print.

38190 ■ *"Alberta: Help Wanted, Badly"* in *Globe & Mail (March 11, 2006, pp. B5)*
Ed: Patrick Brethour, Dawn Walton. **Description:** The issue of unemployment rate, which fell by 3.1 percent in Alberta, is discussed.

38191 ■ *"Alberta Slashes Tax Rate to Ten Percent"* in *Globe & Mail (March 23, 2006, pp. B1)*
Ed: Patrick Brethour. **Description:** Alberta province has slashed its corporate taxes from 11.5 to 10 percent to draw more business to the state. Details of the tax cut and its impact is analyzed.

38192 ■ *"Alcan Statement on Water Rights Could Encourgage Bid"* in *Globe & Mail (April 25, 2007, pp. B5)*
Ed: Andy Hoffman. **Description:** The possibility for a foreign firm to bid for Alcan Inc. in the light of its agreement with Canadian government over water rights is discussed.

38193 ■ *"All In The Family: Weston Undergoes a Shakeup"* in *Canadian Business (Vol. 79, September 22, 2006, No. 19, pp. 75)*
Pub: Rogers Media Inc.
Contact: Tony Viner, President
Ed: Zena Olijnyk. **Description:** Continuing ownership of Weston dynasty on Canada's largest chain Loblaw Co. is discussed.

38194 ■ *Alpha Dogs: How Your Small Business Can Become a Leader of the Pack*
Pub: Harper Business
Ed: Donna Fenn. **Released:** May 08, 2007. **Price:** $14.95, paperback. **Description:** Ways for an entrepreneur to outsmart competitors in the marketplace, to generate higher sales, and earn lasting customer and employee loyalty. **Availability:** Print.

38195 ■ *Alpha Dogs: How Your Small Business Can Become a Leader of the Pack*
Pub: HarperCollins Publishers Inc.
Contact: Jane Friedman, President
E-mail: jfriedman@harpercollins.com
Ed: Donna Fenn. **Released:** May 08, 2007. **Price:** $14.95, paperback; $9.99; C$11.99. **Description:** Profiles of eight successful entrepreneurs along with information for developing customer service, technology and competition. **Availability:** PrintE-book.

38196 ■ *America's Corporate Families*
Pub: Dun & Bradstreet Inc.
Contact: Bob Carrigan, President
URL(s): www.dnb.com. **Released:** Annual **Covers:** Approximately 12,700 U.S. corporations. Ultimate companies must meet all of the following criteria for inclusion: two or more business locations, 250 or more employees at that location or in excess of $25 million in sales volume or a tangible net worth greater than $500,000, and controlling interest in one or more subsidiary company. **Entries include:** D&B D-U-N-S number, company name, address, phone, state of incorporation, line of business, primary/secondary SIC codes, sales volume, net worth, number of employees, current ownership date, year started, number of sites, key executives' names/titles, directors and officers, primary bank and accounting firm, import/export designation, stock exchange symbol

and indicator for publicly owned companies, parent company and location. **Arrangement:** Alphabetical, geographical, industry classification. **Indexes:** Geographical, SIC code (both with address and SIC code).

38197 ■ *"Angels for the Jobless: Church Volunteer Groups Give Career Guidance"* in *Crain's Detroit Business (Vol. 24, April 3, 2008, No. 13)*
Pub: Crain Communications Inc.
Contact: Rance E. Crain, President
Ed: Sherri Begin. **Description:** St. Andrew Catholic Church, located in Rochester, offers the St. Andrew Career Mentoring Ministry, a program that brings in professionals who volunteer to aid those seeking jobs or, in numerous cases, new careers.

38198 ■ *"Arcelor Bid Wins Dofasco Board's Blessing"* in *Globe & Mail (January 17, 2006, pp. B1)*
Pub: CTVglobemedia Publishing Inc.
Ed: Greg Keenan. **Description:** The details surrounding Arcelor SA's proposed acquisition of Dofasco Inc., for $5.5 billion, are presented.

38199 ■ *Are Government Purchasing Policies Failing Small Business?: Roundtable Before the Committee on Small Business & Entrepreneurship, U.S. Senate*
Pub: DIANE Publishing Co.
Contact: Dorothy J. Perkins, Manager
E-mail: dorothyjperkins@hotmail.com
Released: September 2002. **Price:** $35, Paperback. **Description:** Covers Congressional hearing: Steven App, Treasury Department; Fred Armendariz and Major Clark, Small Business Administration; Susan Allen, Pan Asian American Chamber of Commerce; Stephen Denlinger, Latin American Management Association; Charles Henry, National Veteran's Business Development Corporation; Morris Hudson, MO Procurement Technology Assistance Centers; Bar Kasoff, Women Impact, Public Policy; Pam Mazza, Piliero, Massa and Pargament; Ron Newlan, HubZone Contract National Council; Pat Parker, Native American Management Service; Joann Payne, Women First National Legislative Commission; Mike Robinson, MA Small Business Development Centers; Ramon Rodriguez, Hispanic Chamber of Commerce; Angela Styles, Office of Management and Budget; Ralph Thomas, NASA; John Turner, MN Business Enterprise Legal Defense Fund; James Turpin, American Subcontractor's Association, Inc.; and Henry Wilfong, National Association of Small Disadvantaged Business.

38200 ■ *"Are There Material Benefits To Social Diversity?"* in *Hispanic Business (Vol. 30, September 2008, No. 9, pp. 10)*
Ed: Brigida Benitez. **Description:** Diversity in American colleges and universities, where students view and appreciate their peers as individuals and do not judge them on the basis of race, gender, or ethnicity is discussed. The benefits of diversity in higher education are also acknowledged by the U.S. Supreme Court and by leading American corporations.

38201 ■ *"Are You Rich? How Much of a Nest Egg Do You Need to Join the True Elite"* in *Barron's (Vol. 88, March 10, 2008, No. 10, pp. 27)*
Pub: Dow Jones & Co., Inc.
Contact: Clare Hart, President
Ed: Tom Sullivan. **Description:** Discusses the minimum net worth of people considered as rich in America is now at $25 million. There are about 125,000 households in America that meet this threshold, while 49,000 households have a net worth between $25 million and $ 500 million, and about 1,400 US households have a net worth over $500 million.

38202 ■ *"The Art of War for Women"* in *Hawaii Business (Vol. 54, July 2008, No. 1, pp. 23)*
Pub: PacificBasin Communications
Ed: Chin-Ning Chu. **Description:** Business consultant Chi-Ning Chu talks about her new book 'The Art of War for Women: Sun Tzu's Ancient Strategies and

Wisdom for Winning at Work', which discusses how women can more effectively win in business. She also shares her thoughts about the advantages that women have, which they can use in businesses decisions.

38203 ■ *"At Your Career Crossroads"* in *Women In Business (Vol. 61, December 2009, No. 6, pp. 26)*
Pub: American Business Women's Association
Contact: Lorie Burch, President
Ed: Diane Stafford. **Description:** Guidelines for employees who are considering a job or career change are presented. Among the reasons for lead employees to make these changes are downsizing, job loss, environments that are not conducive to work or unfavorable work relationships with bosses.

38204 ■ *"Attend To Your Corporate Housekeeping"* in *Women Entrepreneur (December 4, 2008)*
Ed: Nina Kaufman. **Description:** Business owners can lose all the benefits and privileges of the corporate form if they do not follow proper corporate formalities such as holding an annual meeting, electing officers and directors and adopting or passing corporate resolutions. Creditors are able to take from one's personal assets if such formalities have not been followed.

38205 ■ *"Austin's GMP Growth Top in Nation"* in *Austin Business JournalInc. (Vol. 29, January 8, 2010, No. 44, pp. 1)*
Pub: American City Business Journals
Ed: Jacob Dirr. **Description:** Austin's gross metropolitan product (GMP) has grown by 2 percent, putting it in the top 5 for GMP growth among the largest 100 American metropolitan areas. Insights into the area's business and technology services are examined.

38206 ■ *"The Bad Dresser"* in *Canadian Business (Vol. 80, April 23, 2007, No. 9, pp. 66)*
Ed: Calvin Leung. **Description:** The need of maintaining formal dressing to fit into corporate culture is emphasized.

38207 ■ *Balls!: 6 Rules for Winning Today's Business Game*
Pub: John Wiley & Sons Inc.
Contact: Stephen M. Smith, President
Ed: Alexi Venneri. **Released:** January 2005. **Price:** $29.95. **Description:** In order to be successful business leaders must be brave, authentic, loud, lovable, and spunky and they need to lead their competition. **Availability:** Print.

38208 ■ *"Bank On It: New Year, New Estate Plan"* in *Hawaii Business (Vol. 53, February 2008, No. 8, pp. 54)*
Pub: PacificBasin Communications
Ed: Antony M. Orme. **Description:** Discusses the start of the new year which can be a time to revise wills and estate plans as failure to do so may create problems of unequal inheritance and increase in estate tax exemption, which could disinherit beneficiaries. Other circumstances that can prompt changes in wills and estate plans are presented.

38209 ■ *"Bank On It: Year-End Tax Tips"* in *Hawaii Business (Vol. 53, December 2007, No. 6, pp. 136)*
Pub: PacificBasin Communications
Ed: Kathleen Bryan. **Description:** Tax planning tips for the end of 2007, in relation to the tax breaks that are scheduled to expire, are presented. Among the tax breaks that will be expiring at the 2007 year-end are sales tax deduction in the state and local level, premiums on mortgage insurance, and deduction on tuition. The impacts of these changes are discussed.

38210 ■ *"Bankruptcies"* in *Crain's Detroit Business (Vol. 24, March 24, 2008, No. 12, pp. 6)*
Pub: Crain Communications Inc.
Contact: Rance E. Crain, President
Description: Current list of business that filed for Chapter 7 or 11 protection in U.S. Bankruptcy Court in Detroit include a construction company, a medical care company, a physical therapy firm and a communications firm.

38211 ■ *Bankruptcy for Small Business*
Pub: Sphinx Legal Inc.
Contact: Todd Stocke, Director
E-mail: todd.stocke@sourcebooks.com
Ed: Wendell Schollander. **Released:** July 1, 2008.
Price: $22.95 paperback. **Description:** Bankruptcy laws can be used to save a small business, homes or other property. The book provides general information for small business owners regarding the reasons for money problems, types of bankruptcy available and their alternatives, myths about bankruptcy, and the do's and don'ts for filing for bankruptcy.

38212 ■ *Beans: Four Principles for Running a Business in Good Times or Bad*
Pub: John Wiley & Sons Inc.
Contact: Stephen M. Smith, President
Ed: Leslie Yerkes, Charles Decker, Bob Nelson. **Released:** June 2003. **Price:** $24.95; $16.99. **Description:** Profile of Monorail Espresso, the popular Seattle coffee company that has become prosperous by intentionally staying small and building a strong customer service program. **Availability:** PrintE-book.

38213 ■ *Being Self-Employed: How to Run a Business Out of Your Home, Claim Travel and Depreciation and Earn a Good Income Well into Your 70s or 80s*
Pub: Allyear Tax Guides
Ed: Holmes F. Crouch, Irma Jean Crouch, Barbara J. MacRae. **Released:** September 2004. **Price:** $24.95 (US), $37.95 (Canadian). **Description:** Guide for small business to keep accurate tax records.

38214 ■ *Ben Franklin: America's Original Entrepreneur, Franklin's Autobiography Adapted for Modern Times*
Pub: Entrepreneur Press
Contact: Perlman Neil, President
Ed: Blaine McCormick. **Released:** September 2005. **Price:** $19.95. **Availability:** Print.

38215 ■ *"Best Companies for Diversity" in Black Enterprise (Vol. 38, July 2008, No. 12, pp. 12)*
Pub: Earl G. Graves Publishing Co. Inc.
Contact: Earl G. Graves, Jr., President
Description: Maintaining excellence in a company's diversity efforts requires critical challenges such as recruiting, retaining and developing talent in the executive pipeline. Top young and diverse emerging executives in corporate America are featured.

38216 ■ *"The Best Execs in Canada" in Canadian Business (Vol. 79, October 9, 2006, No. 20, pp. 68)*
Description: The annual list of the most outstanding and innovative business executives of Canada is presented.

38217 ■ *The Big Book of Small Business: You Don't Have to Run Your Business by the Seat of Your Pants*
Pub: HarperCollins Publishers Inc.
Contact: Jane Friedman, President
E-mail: jfriedman@harpercollins.com
Ed: Tom Gegax, Phil Bolsta. **Released:** February 06, 2007. **Price:** $29.99, hardcover; $16.99; C$19.99. **Description:** Entrepreneur shares his experiences starting and running his small business. **Availability:** PrintE-book.

38218 ■ *"The Big Idea: No, Management Is Not a Profession" in Harvard Business Review (Vol. 88, July-August 2010, No. 7-8, pp. 52)*
Pub: Harvard Business School Publishing
Ed: Richard Barker. **Description:** An argument is presented that management is not a profession, as it is less focused on mastering a given body of knowledge than it is on obtaining integration and collaboration skills. Implications for teaching this new approach are also examined.

38219 ■ *"The Big Idea: The Case for Professional Boards" in Harvard Business Review (Vol. 88, December 2010, No. 12, pp. 50)*
Pub: Harvard Business School Publishing
Ed: Robert C. Pozen. **Description:** A professional directorship model can be applied to corporate governance. Suggestions for this include the reduc-tion of board size to seven members in order to improve the effectiveness of decision making, along with the requirement that directors have industry expertise.

38220 ■ *Big Vision, Small Business: 4 Keys to Success without Growing Big*
Pub: Ivy Sea Inc.
Ed: Jamie S. Walters. **Released:** October 10, 2002. **Price:** $17.95, paperback. **Description:** The power of the small enterprise is examined. The author shares her expertise as an entrepreneur and founder of a business consulting firm to help small business owners successfully run their companies. Interviews with more than seventy small business owners provide insight into visioning, planning, and establishing a small company, as well as strategies for good employee and customer relationships. **Availability:** Print; PDF.

38221 ■ *Bigger Isn't Always Better*
Ed: Robert M. Tomasko. **Price:** $24.95.

38222 ■ *"Billion-Dollar Impact: Nonprofit Sector is Economic Powerhouse" in Business First Buffalo (November 12, 2007, pp. 1)*
Pub: American City Business Journals, Inc.
Ed: Tracey Drury. **Description:** Western New York has thousands of nonprofit organizations, 240 of which have collective revenue of $1.74 billion based on federal tax returns for the 2005 and 2006 fiscal years. The nonprofit sector has a large impact on WNY's economy, but it is not highly recognized. The financial performance of notable nonprofit organizations is given.

38223 ■ *The Black Swan*
Pub: Ballantine/ Del Rey/Fawcett/Ivy Books
Contact: Gilbert Perlman, President
Ed: Nassim Nicholas Taleb. **Price:** $17, Paperback; $30, Hardcover. **Description:** A black swan is a highly improbably event with three principle characteristics: it is unpredictable, it carries a massive impact, and after the fact, we concoct an explanation that makes it appear less random and more predictable than it really was. The success of Google was a black swan; so was 9/11. According to the author, black swans underlie almost everything about the world, from the rise of religions to events in personal lives.

38224 ■ *The Blackwell Encyclopedia of Management: Entrepreneurship*
Pub: Blackwell Publishing Inc.
Contact: Gordon Tibbitts, III, President
Released: Volume 3, 2nd Edition. **Price:** $165, hardcover. **Description:** Overview of entrepreneurship through the use of dictionary definitions as well as entries of 2,500 words explaining advanced issues and debates. **Availability:** Print.

38225 ■ *The Board Book: An Insider's Guide for Directors and Trustees*
Pub: W.W. Norton and Company Inc.
Contact: A Malmud, President
Ed: William G. Bowen. **Released:** April 2012. **Price:** $16.95, paperback. **Description:** A primer for all directors and trustees that provides suggestions for getting back to good-governance basics in business. **Availability:** Print.

38226 ■ *"Bombardier Wins Chinese Rail Deal" in Globe & Mail (March 20, 2006, pp. B1)*
Ed: Geoffrey York. **Description:** Bombardier Inc. has won a $68 million (U.S) contract to provide railway cars for rapid transit-link between Beijing and its international airport for 2008 Olympics in China. Details of the contract are presented.

38227 ■ *The Book of Entrepreneurs' Wisdom: Classic Writings by Legendary Entrepreneurs*
Pub: John Wiley & Sons Inc.
Contact: Stephen M. Smith, President
Released: September 1999. **Price:** $44.95, hard-cover. **Availability:** Print.

38228 ■ *"Book of Lists 2010" in Philadelphia Business Journal (Vol. 28, December 25, 2009, No. 45, pp. 1)*
Pub: American City Business Journals Inc.
Description: Rankings of companies and organizations within the banking, biotechnology, economic development, healthcare, hospitality, law and accounting, marketing and media, real estate, and technology industries in the Philadelphia, Pennsylvania area are presented. Rankings are based on sales, business size, and more.

38229 ■ *"The Bottom Line: Did CN Push Too Hard?" in Globe & Mail (February 23, 2007, pp. B1)*
Ed: Brett Jang. **Description:** The effect of the efficiency drive started by Hunter Harrison at Canadian National Railway Company on the company's labor relations is discussed.

38230 ■ *Brag!: The Art of Tooting Your Own Horn Without Blowing It*
Pub: Grand Central Publishing
Contact: Maureen Mahon Egen, President
Ed: Peggy Klaus. **Price:** $14; C$16; $9.99. **Description:** A plan to promote a small business by effectively selling one's self. **Availability:** PrintE-book.

38231 ■ *The Breakthrough Company*
Pub: Crown Publishing/Random House
Ed: Keith R. McFarland. **Released:** September 01, 2009. **Price:** $16, Paperback. **Description:** Traits of high-growth players that actually make it in business.

38232 ■ *"Bridging the Ingenuity Gap" in Canadian Business (Vol. 79, November 6, 2006, No. 22, pp. 12)*
Pub: Rogers Media Inc.
Contact: Tony Viner, President
Ed: Rachel Pulfer. **Description:** The views of Patrick Whitney, director of Illinois Institute of Technology's Institute of Design, on globalization and business design methods are presented.

38233 ■ *"Bryan Berg, Target Corp., Senior Vice President, Region 1" in Hawaii Business (Vol. 53, March 2008, No. 9, pp. 28)*
Pub: PacificBasin Communications
Ed: David K. Choo. **Description:** Bryan Berg, senior vice president at Target Corp.'s Region 1, shares his thoughts about entering the Hawaiian market and Target representatives bringing malasadas when visiting a business in the state. Berg finds the state's aloha spirit interesting and feels that it is important to be respectful of the Hawaiian culture and traditions in doing their business there.

38234 ■ *Building a Business the Buddhist Way*
Ed: Geri Larkin. **Released:** September 2004. **Price:** $11.67 (Canadian). **Description:** Principles of entrepreneurship for starting and growing a business while maintaining a balance between business goals and spiritual goals.

38235 ■ *Built to Last: Successful Habits of Visionary Companies*
Pub: HarperCollins Publishers Inc.
Contact: Jane Friedman, President
E-mail: jfriedman@harpercollins.com
Ed: James C. Collins, Jerry I. Porras. **Price:** $29.99, hardcover; $17.99, paperback; $12.99; C$11.99. **Availability:** PrintE-book.

38236 ■ *Business Diagnostics*
Pub: Trafford Publishing
Contact: Steen Marcussen, Manager
Ed: Michael Thompson, Richard Mimick. **Released:** April 10, 2002. **Price:** C$70. **Description:** Business management skills are outlined. **Availability:** Print.

38237 ■ *"Business Diary" in Crain's Detroit Business (Vol. 24, October 6, 2008, No. 40, pp. 23)*
Pub: Crain Communications Inc.
Contact: Rance E. Crain, President
Description: Detailed listing of acquisitions, expansions, new products, new services, business contracts and startups from the Detroit area is provided.

38238 ■ *"The Business End of Climate"* in Puget Sound Business Journal (Vol. 35, May 2, 2014, No. 2, pp. 9)
Pub: American City Business Journals
Released: May 2, 2014. **Description:** The business community, government and military leaders in Puget Sound, Washington are taking actions to cope with climate change. Data from the University of Washington Center for Climate Change offers projections on the impact of climate change in Washington over the next four decades.

38239 ■ *Business Fairy Tales*
Pub: South-Western
Contact: Susan Badger, President
Ed: Cecil W. Jackson. **Price:** £35.99, hardback. **Description:** The seven most-common business schemes are uncovered.

38240 ■ *Business Know-How: An Operational Guide for Home-Based and Micro-Sized Businesses with Limited Budgets*
Ed: Janet Attard. **Price:** $17.95.

38241 ■ *"Business Looks for Results in Congress"* in Baltimore Business Journal (Vol. 28, November 5, 2010, No. 26, pp. 1)
Pub: Baltimore Business Journal
Ed: Kent Hoover. **Description:** Republican candidates in the 2010 Congressional elections were overwhelmingly supported by the business community. Republican John Boehner, who will be the next Speaker of the House, says that the party's victory would end economic uncertainty and would assist small businesses to rehire workers.

38242 ■ *Business, Occupations, Professions, & Vocations in the Bible*
Pub: ABC Book Publishing
Ed: Rich Brott. **Released:** July 26, 2007. **Price:** $18.55, paperback; $19.99, softcover. **Description:** The important role small business has played in all societies and cultures throughout history is examined. The ingenuity of individuals and their ability to design, craft, manufacture and harvest has kept countries and kingdoms prosperous. **Availability:** Print.

38243 ■ *"The Business Owner's Flight Plan"* in Entrepreneur (Vol. 37, July 2009, No. 7, pp. 22)
Pub: Entrepreneur Press
Contact: Perlman Neil, President
Ed: Jason Daley. **Description:** Greg Rosner, author of 'The Road Warrior Survival Guide: Practical Tips for the Business Traveler,' shares insights on the stages of a typical business trip. Delegating a trusted colleague who can assume certain tasks that you cannot deal with remotely, expecting that the trip is not a vacation, and taking a Thursday night flight are some of the tips given to business travelers.

38244 ■ *Business Plans Kit for Dummies*
Pub: John Wiley & Sons Inc.
Contact: Stephen M. Smith, President
Ed: Steven D. Peterson, Peter E. Jaret, Barbara Findlay Schenck. **Released:** Fourth Edition. **Price:** $34.95; $22.99. **Availability:** PrintE-book.

38245 ■ *Business Plans That Work: A Guide for Small Business*
Pub: McGraw Hill Financial Inc.
Contact: Douglas L. Peterson, President
Released: April 14, 2011. **Price:** $20. **Description:** Guide for preparing a small business plan along with an analysis of potential business opportunities. **Availability:** Print.

38246 ■ *The Business of Small Business: Succeeding and Prospering in Business for Reasonably Intelligent Entrepreneurs*
Released: August 2006. **Price:** $27.95. **Description:** Tips for running a successful company are presented to entrepreneurs.

38247 ■ *"Business Still Expected to Take Hit in 2008"* in Business Journal-Serving Phoenix and the Valley of the Sun (December 28, 2007)
Ed: Chris Casacchia. **Description:** Community banks in 2008 are still projected to suffer from the repercussions of the subprime mortgage and credit crises.

Meanwhile, the asset devaluation of big banks and global investment companies are higher than that of smaller banks. The third quarter and fourth quarter losses of banks such as Bear Stearns are discussed as well.

38248 ■ *"Business Travel Can be a Trip if Structured Right"* in Globe & Mail (February 3, 2007, pp. B11)
Ed: Roma Luciw. **Description:** The importance of arranging a proper business trip for executives by employers, in order to achieve good benefits for the company, is discussed.

38249 ■ *Business Unusual*
Ed: Anita Roddick. **Price:** $24.95.

38250 ■ *Business Warrior: Strategy for Entrepreneurs*
Ed: Sun Tzu. **Released:** September 2006. **Price:** $19.95. **Description:** Advice to help entrepreneurs understand competitive strategies in order to succeed, focusing on sales, marketing, and personnel management.

38251 ■ *Business Week--Corporate Scoreboard Issue (Internet only)*
Pub: The McGraw-Hill Companies Inc.
Contact: Henry Hirschberg, President
URL(s): search.businessweek.com. **Released:** Quarterly; March, May, August, November. **Publication includes:** List of sales and profits for 900 major U.S. Companies in all business, industrial, and financial categories, with extensive analytical text. **Entries include:** Company name, several types of sales and earnings data. **Arrangement:** Alphabetical within line of business categories.

38252 ■ *BUZZ: How to Create It and Win With It*
Pub: AMACOM
Contact: Edward T. Reilly, Manager
Ed: Edward I. Koch, Christy Heady. **Released:** June 2007. **Price:** $21.95; C$26.95. **Description:** Former New York City Mayor, Edward Koch demonstrates buss to define a small business image, how to create buzz with honesty, engage the media, withstand public scrutiny, turn mistakes into opportunities, and create loyal followers.

38253 ■ *"Calgary East"* in Canadian Business (Vol. 80, January 15, 2007, No. 2, pp. 13)
Ed: Charles Mandel. **Description:** The positive impact on the economy of Saint John city of New Brunswick province of Canada, due to the establishment of oil refineries by Irving Oil Ltd. in the area, is discussed.

38254 ■ *"A Call to Make SOX More Elastic"* in Canadian Business (Vol. 80, February 12, 2007, No. 4, pp. 14)
Ed: Rachel Pulfer. **Description:** The suggestion of New York City Governor Eliot Spitzer to relax the Sarbanes-Oxley Act of 2002 due to its 'excessive' regulation is discussed.

38255 ■ *"Can America Invent Its Way Back?"* in Business Week (September 22, 2008, No. 4100, pp. 52)
Pub: Bloomberg L.P.
Contact: Matthew Winkler, Manager
Ed: Michael Mandel. **Description:** Business leaders as well as economists agree that innovative new products, services and ways of doing business may be the only way in which America can survive the downward spiral of the economy; innovation economics may be the answer and may even provide enough growth to enable Americans to prosper in the years to come.

38256 ■ *"Can the State Afford a Big Time College Football Program?"* in Hawaii Business (Vol. 53, March 2008, No. 9, pp. 26)
Pub: PacificBasin Communications
Description: Jill Nunokawa, civil rights at University of Hawaii, believes that athletics are extra-curricular and that the state needs to focus on priorities. State representative K. Mark Takai says that a football program brings pride and inspiration and can generate revenue and provide economic opportunities.

38257 ■ *"Can We Talk?"* in Canadian Business (Vol. 79, September 11, 2006, No. 18, pp. 131)
Pub: Rogers Media Inc.
Contact: Tony Viner, President
Ed: Sarah B. Hood. **Description:** The importance of informal communications and steps to build strong social networks within the organizations are discussed.

38258 ■ *"Can You Hear Me Now?"* in Harvard Business Review (Vol. 86, July-August 2008, No. 8, pp. 23)
Pub: Harvard Business Review Press
Contact: Peter E. Walsh, Director
Ed: Katharina Pick. **Description:** Tips for improving communication among boardroom members are presented. These include encouraging frankness via in-meeting leaders, and the ability of directors to meet without managers.

38259 ■ *"Canada Tops Again in G7: Study"* in Globe & Mail (March 22, 2006, pp. B8)
Ed: Roma Luciw. **Description:** Canada is still the cheapest place to do business among G7 countries, even though the rising dollar has eroded some of its advantages over the United States. The survey is detailed.

38260 ■ *Canadian Small Business Kit for Dummies*
Pub: John Wiley & Sons Inc.
Contact: Stephen M. Smith, President
Ed: Margaret Kerr, JoAnn Kurtz. **Released:** 3rd Edition. **Description:** Resources include information on changes to laws and taxes for small businesses in Canada.

38261 ■ *"Capitol Ideas: Regions to Lansing: Focus on Taxes, Reform, Keeping Talent"* in Crain's Detroit Business (Vol. 24, October 6, 2008)
Pub: Crain Communications Inc.
Contact: Rance E. Crain, President
Ed: Amy Lane. **Description:** Michigan must make bold and dramatic changes in public policy regarding business legislation. The tax structure, unemployment issues and attracting and retaining talent are among the issues the state must confront, especially in this tough economic climate.

38262 ■ *"Cashing in Before You Join: Negotiating a Signing Bonus"* in Black Enterprise (Vol. 37, October 2006, No. 3, pp. 90)
Pub: Earl G. Graves Publishing Co. Inc.
Contact: Earl G. Graves, Jr., President
Ed: Chauntelle Folds. **Description:** Information on how to research and negotiate a signing deal, including how to avoid a tax hit.

38263 ■ *"Cashing In: Gleaning an Education from Our Economic State"* in Agency Sales Magazine (Vol. 39, August 2009, No. 8, pp. 22)
Ed: John Graham. **Description:** Businesses have learned that cutting price can kill business and being tough is normal. The recession has also taught that getting the right vision and gaining the confidence and trust of consumers are important.

38264 ■ *Catalyst Code: The Strategies Behind the World's Most Dynamic Companies*
Pub: Harvard Business Review Press
Contact: Peter E. Walsh, Director
Ed: David S. Evans, Richard Schmalensee. **Released:** May 09, 2007. **Price:** $29.95, hardcover. **Description:** Economic catalysts businesses can bring consumers and merchants together in order to survive in an economy where markets, consumers and technology are always changing.

38265 ■ *CCH Toolkit Tax Guide 2007*
Ed: Paul Gada. **Released:** January 2007. **Price:** $17.95. **Description:** Guide for filing 2007 tax forms for both personal and small businesses with expert line-by-line explanations.

38266 ■ *"Centerra Caught in Kyrgyzstan Dispute"* in Globe & Mail (April 19, 2007, pp. B5)

Ed: Andy Hoffman. **Description:** The details of the demonstrations carried against government proposal to nationalize Centerra Gold Inc.'s assets are presented.

38267 ■ *"C'est Bon"* in Canadian Business (Vol. 79, September 25, 2006, No. 19, pp. 39)

Ed: Benoit Aubin. **Description:** Economic development of Quebec City are evaluated on the eve of its formation anniversary.

38268 ■ *Change in SMEs: The New European Capitalism*

Pub: Palgrave Macmillan

Contact: Lisa Dunn, Manager

E-mail: l.dunn@palgrave.com

Ed: Katharina Bluhm, Rudi Schmidt. **Released:** September 2008. **Price:** £77, hardcover. **Description:** Effects of global change on corporate governance, management, competitive strategies and labor relations in small-to-medium sized enterprises in various European countries are discussed. **Availability:** Print; E-book; Electronic publishing.

38269 ■ *"The China Syndrome"* in Canadian Business (Vol. 79, July 17, 2006, No. 14-15, pp. 25)

Pub: Rogers Media Inc.

Contact: Tony Viner, President

Ed: Peter Diekmeyer. **Description:** Contrasting pace of growth in China and India are presented. Reasons for the slow pace of growth of Canadian companies like CAE Inc. and Magna in India are also discussed.

38270 ■ *China's Rational Entrepreneurs: The Development of the New Private Business Sector*

Pub: Routledge

Contact: Kevin Bradley, President

E-mail: kbradley@taylorandfrancis.com

Ed: Barbara Krug. **Released:** November 2012. **Price:** $54.95, paperback. **Description:** Difficulties faced by entrepreneurs in China are discussed, including analysis for understanding their behavior and relations with local governments in order to secure long-term business success. **Availability:** Print.

38271 ■ *"Choosing Strategies For Change"* in Harvard Business Review (Vol. 86, July-August 2008, No. 8, pp. 130)

Pub: Harvard Business Review Press

Contact: Peter E. Walsh, Director

Ed: John P. Kotter, Leonard A. Schlesinger. **Description:** Methods for implementing organizational change include identifying potential areas of resistance, providing the necessary skills and information to counteract resistance, and assessing situational factors that may influence results.

38272 ■ *Cities from the Arabian Desert: The Building of Jubail and Yambu in Saudi Arabia*

Pub: Turnaround Associates

Contact: Andrea H. Pampanini, Founder

Ed: Andrea H. Pampanini. **Description:** An overview of Saudi Arabia's government to take control of the nation's natural resources and change the government, educational system, and its culture by evolving into a modern industrial society.

38273 ■ *"City Struggles to Iron Out Tangled Transportation"* in Crain's New York Business (Vol. 24, January 13, 2008, No. 2, pp. 33)

Pub: Crain Communications Inc.

Contact: Rance Crain, President

Ed: Judith Messina. **Description:** Discusses the possible solutions to improve lower Manhattan's transportation infrastructure including the construction of three new transit centers, an expansion in ferry service and the plan to get parked buses off the street.

38274 ■ *"The Classless Workplace: The Digerati and the New Spirit of Technocapitalism"* in WorkingUSA (Vol. 11,

June 2008, No. 2, pp. 181)

Ed: Eran Fisher. **Description:** Article argues the formation of a new type of economic actor at the intersection of a new capitalism and a new technology: The Dierati. The discourse in based on the analysis of the popular magazine Wired, which registers the culture of contemporary technocapitalism. The suggestion that the new persona of the digerati is constructed as a rejection of the ethics, which dominated the Fordist workplace and Fordist society: Hierarchy and differentiation between workers, on the one hand and capitalists and managers, on the other hand. The transformation of these two categories, workers and capitalists into the digerati worker and the digerati entrepreneur, is described. Set within the context of the structural transformations of capitalism from Fordism to post-Fordism, the article shows the ideological fit of the new ethics of the digerati to the new working arrangements of post-Fordist capitalism, characterized by more privatizes, flexible, and precarious working arrangements.

38275 ■ *"CN Rail Strike Ends With Fragile Truce"* in Globe & Mail (February 26, 2007, pp. B1)

Ed: Brent Jang. **Description:** The agreement between Canadian National Railway Co. and the United Transportation Union on wage increase that ended employee strike is discussed.

38276 ■ *Code of Federal Regulations: Title 13: Business Credit and Assistance*

Pub: U. S. Government Printing Office

Contact: Veronica Meter, Director

E-mail: tpriebe@gpo.gov

Ed: Department of Commerce Staff. **Released:** January 2014. **Price:** $61. **Description:** Title 13 covers regulations governing the activities of the Small Business Administration and the Department of Commerce. Book covers information on business credit, finance, and economic development. **Availability:** Print.

38277 ■ *"Column: Redefining Failure"* in Harvard Business Review (Vol. 88, September 2010, No. 9, pp. 34)

Pub: Harvard Business School Publishing

Ed: Seth Godin. **Description:** Specific forms of failure, including design failure, failure of priorities, failure of opportunity, and failure to quit are examined. The negative implications of maintaining the status quo are discussed.

38278 ■ *"Column: To Win, Create What's Scarce"* in Harvard Business Review (Vol. 88, November 2010, No. 11, pp. 46)

Pub: Harvard Business School Publishing

Ed: Seth Godin. **Description:** It is recommended to identify what is scarce yet valuable and applying this principle to business in order to be successful.

38279 ■ *"Commentary. Economic Trends for Small Business"* in Small Business Economic Trends (April 2008, pp. 3)

Ed: William C. Dunkelberg, Holly Wade. **Description:** Commentary on the economic trends for small businesses in the U.S. is presented. Analysis of recession possibilities is given. Reports indicate that the number of business owners citing inflation as their number one problem is at its highest point since 1982.

38280 ■ *Common Problems; Common Sense Solutions: Practical Advice for Small Business Owners*

Pub: iUniverse Inc.

Contact: Kevin Weiss, President

Ed: Greg Hadley. **Released:** September 14, 2004. **Price:** $14.95, softcover; $6. **Description:** Common sense advice for entrepreneurs running a small business. **Availability:** PrintE-book.

38281 ■ *The Commonsense Way to Build Wealth: One Entrepreneur Shares His Secrets*

Ed: Jack Chou. **Released:** September 2004. **Price:** , $19.95. **Description:** Entrepreneurial tips to accumulate wealth, select the proper business or franchise, choose and manage rental property, and how to negotiate a good lease.

38282 ■ *"Companies Must Set Goals for Diversity"* in Crain's Detroit Business (Vol. 24, April 14, 2008, No. 15, pp. 16)

Pub: Crain Communications Inc.

Contact: Rance E. Crain, President

Ed: Laura Weiner. **Description:** Diversity programs should start with a plan that takes into account exactly what the company wants to accomplish; this may include wanting to increase the bottom line with new contracts or wanting a staff that is more innovative in their ideas due to their varied backgrounds.

38283 ■ *"Companies Urged to Take Steps to Replenish Work Force"* in Crain's Cleveland Business (Vol. 28, October 29, 2007, No. 43, pp. 9)

Pub: Crain Communications Inc.

Ed: Mike Verespej. **Description:** If America wants to stay competitive in the global marketplace, experts say that the education system will need serious improvements. According to Thomas J. Donahue, president and CEO of the U.S. Chamber of Commerce, one-third of the K-through-12 students in the United States don't graduate from high school.

38284 ■ *"The Companies We Love"* in Canadian Business (Vol. 85, September 17, 2012, No. 14, pp. 43)

Pub: George Media Inc.

Released: September 17, 2012. **Description:** The 2012 annual survey of the brands Canadians trust and respect the most revealed that only six of the top 60 international brands are based in Canada. Sony was the number one favorite brand of Canadians, while the highest-ranked Canadian Brand, Tim Hortons, is in the number 29 spot.

38285 ■ *The Company We Keep: Reinventing Small Business for People, Community, and Place*

Pub: Chelsea Green Publishing Co.

Contact: Margo Baldwin, President

E-mail: mbaldwin@chelseagreen.com

Ed: John Abrams, William Grieder. **Released:** May 15, 2006. **Price:** $18. **Description:** The new business trend in social entrepreneurship as a business plan enables small business owners to meet the triple bottom line of profits for people (employees and owners), community, and the environment. **Availability:** Print.

38286 ■ *"Competing On Resources"* in Harvard Business Review (Vol. 86, July-August 2008, No. 8, pp. 140)

Pub: Harvard Business Review Press

Contact: Peter E. Walsh, Director

Ed: David J. Collis, Cynthia A. Montgomery. **Description:** Guidelines regarding assessing the value of resources, such as slow depreciation and superiority to competitors' similar resources are discussed.

38287 ■ *"The Competitive Imperative Of Learning"* in Harvard Business Review (Vol. 86, July-August 2008, No. 8, pp. 60)

Pub: Harvard Business Review Press

Contact: Peter E. Walsh, Director

Description: Experimentation and reflection are important components for maintaining success in the business world and are the kind of character traits that can help one keep his or her competitive edge.

38288 ■ *The Complete Idiot's Guide to Finance for Small Business*

Ed: Kenneth E. Little. **Released:** April 2006. **Price:** , $19.95. **Description:** Financial experts helps small business owners through strategies for long-term financial success.

38289 ■ *The Complete Small Business Guide: A Sourcebook for New and Small Businesses*

Pub: John Wiley & Sons Inc.

Contact: Stephen M. Smith, President

Ed: Colin Barrow. **Released:** 8th Edition. **Price:** $32. **Description:** Sourcebook for creating new small companies and running established small businesses.

38290 ■ *"Confessions Of Serial Entrepreneurs"* in Entrepreneur (January 8, 2009)
Pub: Entrepreneur Press
Contact: Perlman Neil, President
Ed: Jennifer Wang. **Description:** Serial entrepreneurs are those individuals that are able to start business after business. These individuals enjoy the process of starting a company then handing off the finished product and starting over with a new endeavor. Several serial entrepreneurs are profiled.

38291 ■ *"Congratulations to the 2010 Top Ten Business Women of ABWA"* in Women In Business (Vol. 61, August-September 2009, No. 4, pp. 12)
Pub: American Business Women's Association
Contact: Lorie Burch, President
Description: Listing of the top 10 members of the American Business Women's Association (ABWA) for 2010 is presented. The lists of the top ten 2010 members selected by each of the six ABWA chapters are also provided.

38292 ■ *"Convention Calendar"* in Black Enterprise (Vol. 37, February 2007, No. 7, pp. 68)
Description: Listing of conventions and trade show of interest to minority and women business leaders.

38293 ■ *Coolhunting: Chasing Down the Next Big Thing*
Pub: AMACOM
Contact: Edward T. Reilly, Manager
Ed: Peter A. Gloor, Scott W. Cooper. **Released:** April 2007. **Price:** $24.95, hardback. **Description:** Lessons for unlocking and applying swarm creativity in organizations to increase creativity, productivity, and efficiency. **Availability:** Print; E-book.

38294 ■ *Corporate Affiliations Library: Who Owns Whom*
Pub: LexisNexis
Contact: Michael Walsh, President
URL(s): www.corporateaffiliations.com. **Released:** Annual; Latest Edition 2013. **Description:** A 8-volume set listing public and private companies worldwide. Comprises the following: Master Index (volumes 1 and 2); U.S. Public Companies (volume 3 and 4), listing 6,200 parent companies and 52,000 subsidiaries, affiliates, and divisions worldwide; U.S. Private Companies (volume 5), listing 15,000 privately held companies and 70,000 U.S. and international subsidiaries; and International Public and Private Companies (volume 7 and 8), listing 4,800 parent companies and 69,000 subsidiaries worldwide. **Entries include:** Parent company name, address, phone, fax, telex, e-mail addresses, names and titles of key personnel, financial data, fiscal period, type and line of business, SIC codes; names and locations of subsidiaries, divisions, and affiliates, outside service firms (accountants, legal counsel, etc.). **Arrangement:** Alphabetical within each volume. **Indexes:** Each volume includes company name index; separate Master Index volumes list all company names in the set in one alphabetic sequence in five indexes including private, public, international, alphabetical, geographical, brand name, SIC, and corporate responsibilities.

38295 ■ *"Corporate Canada Eyes Retiree Health Benefit Cuts"* in Globe & Mail (March 8, 2006, pp. B3)
Ed: Virginia Galt. **Description:** A survey on Canadian companies reveals that due to rising health care costs and increasing number of baby boomer retirements, these companies are to cut down on health benefits they are providing to these retired employees.

38296 ■ *Corporate Crisis and Risk Management: Modeling, Strategies and SME Application*
Ed: M. Aba-Bulgu; S.M.N. Islam. **Released:** December 2006. **Price:** , $115.00. **Description:** Methods and tools for handling corporate risk and crisis management are profiled for small to medium-sized businesses.

38297 ■ *"Corporate Diversity Driving Profits"* in Hispanic Business (Vol. 30, September 2008, No. 9, pp. 12)
Ed: Michael Bowker. **Description:** U.S. businesses are beginning to appreciate the importance of diversity and are developing strategies to introduce a diverse workforce that reflects the cultural composition of their customers. The realization that diversity increases profits and the use of professional networks to recruit and retain skilled minority employees are two other new trends impacting corporate diversity in the U.S.

38298 ■ *Corporate Entrepreneurship & Innovation*
Pub: South-Western
Contact: Susan Badger, President
Ed: Michael H. Morris, Donald F. Kuratko, Jeffrey G. Covin. **Released:** 3rd Edition. **Price:** A$127.95; NZ$137.95; A$64.95; NZ$69.95. **Description:** Innovation is the key to running a successful small business. The book helps entrepreneurs to develop the skills and business savvy to sustain a competitive edge. **Availability:** PrintE-book.

38299 ■ *"Corporate Etiquette: The Art of Apology"* in Canadian Business (Vol. 80, January 29, 2007, No. 3, pp. 62)
Ed: John Gray. **Description:** The methods of nurturing professional relationships, by apologizing for the mistakes committed by individuals and institutions, are described.

38300 ■ *Corporate Radar: Tracking the Forces That Are Shaping Your Business*
Ed: Karl Albrecht. **Released:** December 2008. **Price:** , $24.95. **Description:** Ways for a business to assess the forces operating in the external environment that can affect the business and solutions to protect from outside threats.

38301 ■ *"Crafting Kinship at Home and Work: Women Miners in Wyoming"* in WorkingUSA (Vol. 11, December 2008, No. 4, pp. 439)
Ed: Jessica M. Smith. **Description:** Institutional policies and social dynamics shaping women working in the northeastern Wyoming mining industry are examined. Ethnographic research suggests that the women's successful integration into this nontraditional workplace is predicated on their ability to craft and maintain kin-like social relationships in two spheres. First, women miners have addressed the challenges of managing their home and work responsibilities by cultivating networks of friends and family to care for their children while they are at work. Second, women miners craft close relationships with coworkers in what are called 'crew families'. These relationships make their work more enjoyable and the ways in which they create camaraderie prompt a reconsideration of conventional accounts of sexual harassment in the mining industry.

38302 ■ *"Credit Crunch Gives, Takes Away"* in The Business Journal-Serving Metropolitan Kansas City (Vol. 27, October 17, 2008, No. 5, pp. 1)
Ed: Suzanna Stagemeyer. **Description:** Although many Kansas City business enterprises have been adversely affected by the U.S. credit crunch, others have remained relatively unscathed. Examples of how local businesses are being impacted by the crisis are provided including: American Trailer & Storage Inc., which declared bankruptcy after failing to pay a long-term loan; and NetStandard, a technology firm who, on the other hand, is being pursued by prospective lenders.

38303 ■ *Crunch Point: The 21 Secrets to Succeeding When it Matters Most*
Pub: American Management Association
Contact: Edward T. Reilly, President
Ed: Brian Tracy. **Price:** $17.95, Hardback. **Availability:** Print.

38304 ■ *"Culture Club: Effective Corporate Cultures"* in Canadian Business (Vol. 79,

October 9, 2006, No. 20, pp. 115)
Pub: Rogers Media Inc.
Contact: Tony Viner, President
Ed: Calvin Leung. **Description:** Positive impacts of an effective corporate culture on the employees' productivity and the performance of the business are discussed.

38305 ■ *"Cutting Credit Card Processing Costs"* in Hawaii Business (Vol. 53, March 2008, No. 9, pp. 56)
Ed: Robert K.O. Lum. **Description:** Accepting credit card payments offers businesses with profits from the discount rate. The discount rate includes processing fee, VISA & MasterCard assessment and interchange. Details regarding merchant service cost and discount rate portions are discussed. Statistical data included.

38306 ■ *"Danger, Will Robinson!"* in Business Owner (Vol. 35, July-August 2011, No. 4, pp. 3)
Pub: DL Perkins Company
Description: Critical measures each small business owner must take to ensure the success of their company are outlined.

38307 ■ *Dare to Prepare - How to Win Before You Begin*
Pub: Crown Publishing/Random House
Ed: Ronald M. Shapiro, Gregory Jordan. **Released:** February 24, 2009. **Price:** $15.99, Paperback. **Description:** Shapiro uses his experience as one of America's top negotiators and lawyers to show how meticulous planning can raise the odds of success in business as well as in life.

38308 ■ *"Dark Horse Murphy Means Business In Md. Gubernatorial Race"* in Baltimore Business Journal (Vol. 28, June 25, 2010, No. 7, pp. 1)
Pub: Baltimore Business Journal
Ed: Scott Dance. **Description:** Maryland gubernatorial candidate Brian Murphy has claimed better knowledge in helping small business owners than the other candidates, Governor Martin O'Malley and former Governor Robert Ehrlich. Murphy, who faces off against Ehrlich in the Republican primary, is banking on the benefit of his business background.

38309 ■ *"David Saunders Q&A"* in Canadian Business (Vol. 80, October 22, 2007, No. 21, pp. 11)
Ed: Erin Pooley. **Description:** David Saunders, chairman of the Federation of Business School Deans, talks about the changes in business education in Canada. He stresses that a master's degree in business administration is vital and a good investment that would reap rewards in a business career.

38310 ■ *Dead on Arrival: How the Anti-Business Backlash is Destroying Entrepreneurship in America and What We Can Still Do About It!*
Ed: Bernie Marcus; Steve Gottry. **Released:** November 2006. **Price:** , $23.95. **Description:** Bernie Marcus, Home Depot leader, addresses regulations hurting small businesses in America.

38311 ■ *Dealing with the Tough Stuff: Practical Wisdom for Running a Values-Driven Business*
Pub: Berrett-Koehler Communications Inc.
Contact: Steve Piersanti, President
E-mail: spiersanti@bkpub.com
Ed: Margot Fraser, Lisa Lorimer. **Released:** November 01, 2009. **Price:** $16.95. **Description:** Advice is given to help small firms run a value-driven business. **Availability:** Print; PDF.

38312 ■ *"Deals Still Get Done at Drake's Coq d'Or"* in Crain's Chicago Business (Vol. 31, November 17, 2008, No. 46, pp. 35)
Pub: Crain Communications Inc.
Contact: Todd Johnson, Publisher
Ed: Shia Kapos. **Description:** Chicago's infamous Coq d'Or, a restaurant and lounge located at the Drake Hotel, is still a favorite establishment for noted executives but the eatery is now trying to cater to

younger professionals through marketing and offering new beverages that appeal to that demographic. Many find it the perfect environment in which to close deals, relax or network.

38313 ■ *"The Dean of Design" in Canadian Business (Vol. 79, November 6, 2006, No. 22, pp. 42)*
Pub: Rogers Media Inc.
Contact: Tony Viner, President
Ed: Erin Pooley. **Description:** The need of a good business design to increase the business in saturated markets with relation to customer satisfaction is emphasized.

38314 ■ *"Dedge Rejects Inflation Concerns" in Globe & Mail (January 26, 2007, pp. B3)*
Ed: Heather Scoffield. **Description:** The rejection of concern over inflation by Governor of the Bank of Canada David Dodge and his views on checking inflation in Alberta are discussed.

38315 ■ *Delivering Knock Your Socks Off Service*
Pub: American Management Association
Contact: Edward T. Reilly, President
Released: Fifth Edition. **Price:** $18.95, Paper or Softback. **Availability:** Print.

38316 ■ *"Did I Do That?" in Entrepreneur (Vol. 35, November 2007, No. 11, pp. 144)*
Pub: Entrepreneur Press
Contact: Perlman Neil, President
Ed: Romanus Wolter. **Description:** Entrepreneurs need to watch habits as some bad habits can affect business operations. Tips on ways to identify bad habits and how to address them are presented.

38317 ■ *"Director Elections Campaign Pays Off" in Globe & Mail (March 9, 2006, pp. B1)*
Ed: Janet McFarland. **Description:** The details pertaining to the introduction of new voting standards by electing company directors by 20 major Canadian companies, after the Canadian Coalition for Good Governance campaigned for it, are presented.

38318 ■ *Divine Wisdom at Work: 10 Universal Principles for Enlightened Entrepreneurs*
Pub: Aha! House
Ed: Tricia Molloy. **Released:** July 2006. **Price:** , $20.00. **Description:** Entrepreneurial advice for managing a small enterprise is given using inspiration, anecdotes and exercises.

38319 ■ *Do You! 12 Laws to Access the Power in You to Achieve Happiness and Success*
Pub: Gotham/Penguin Group Incorporated
Ed: Russell Simmons, Chris Morrow. **Released:** April 10, 2008. **Price:** $15, paperback; 12.99. **Description:** Hip-Hop mogul describes his successful visions and ventures. **Availability:** PrintElectronic publishing.

38320 ■ *"Dodge Frets Over Flood of Fast Money" in Globe & Mail (May 2, 2007, pp. B1)*
Ed: Heather Scoffield. **Description:** The concern of governor of Bank of Canada, David Dodge, over the increase in global liquidity due to growth in the business of private equity, is discussed.

38321 ■ *Doing Business Anywhere: The Essential Guide to Going Global*
Pub: John Wiley & Sons Inc.
Contact: Stephen M. Smith, President
Ed: Tom Travis. **Description:** Plans are given for new or existing businesses to organize, plan, operate and execute a business on a global basis. Trade agreements, brand protection and patents, ethics, security as well as cultural issues are among the issues addressed. **Availability:** E-book.

38322 ■ *"Don't Expect Quick Fix" in The Business Journal-Serving Metropolitan Kansas City (Vol. 27, October 3, 2008, No. 3, pp. 1)*
Pub: American City Business Journals, Inc.
Contact: Whitney Shaw, President
Ed: James Dornbrook. **Description:** United States governmental entities cannot provide a quick fix solution to the current financial crisis. The economy

requires a systemic change in the way people think about credit. The financial services industry should also focus on core lending principles.

38323 ■ *"Don't Quit When The Road Gets Bumpy" in Women Entrepreneur (November 25, 2008)*
Ed: Bonnie Price. **Description:** Discusses techniques four women entrepreneurs are utilizing to keep their businesses successful despite the credit crunch and the economic downturn.

38324 ■ *"Don't Touch My Laptop, If You Please Mr. Customs Man" in Canadian Electronics (Vol. 23, June-July 2008, No. 4, pp. 6)*
Ed: Mark Borkowski. **Description:** Canadian businessmen bringing electronic devices to the US can protect the contents of their laptops by hiding their data from US border agents. They can also choose to clean up the contents of their laptop using file erasure programs.

38325 ■ *"Down a 'Peg" in Canadian Business (Vol. 79, September 25, 2006, No. 19, pp. 41)*
Ed: Bryan Borzykowski. **Description:** Economic development in Canada's Winnipeg city is evaluated.

38326 ■ *The Dynamic Small Business Manager*
Pub: Lulu.com
Ed: Frank Vickers. **Released:** October 01, 2011. **Price:** $19.95. **Description:** Practical advice is given to help small business owners successfully manage their company. **Availability:** Download; PDF.

38327 ■ *e-Business, e-Government and Small and Medium-Size Enterprises: Opportunities and Challenges*
Pub: IGI Global
Contact: Dr. Mehdi Khosrow-Pour, President
Released: July 2003. **Price:** $79.95. **Description:** Electronic commerce and information technology research in small and medium-sized enterprises (SMEs). Policymakers, legislators, researchers and professionals address significant issues of importance to the small business sector. **Availability:** Print.

38328 ■ *The E-Myth Revisited: Why Most Small Businesses Don't Work and What to Do About It*
Pub: HarperCollins Publishers Inc.
Contact: Jane Friedman, President
E-mail: jfriedman@harpercollins.com
Ed: Michael E. Gerber. **Price:** $20.99, paperback; $14.99; C$13.99. **Description:** Keys for developing a prosperous small business is presented in an updated version of the author's best-seller published in the nineties. **Availability:** PrintE-book.

38329 ■ *The E Myth Revisited: Why Most Small Businesses Don't Work and What to Do About It*
Pub: HarperCollins Publishers Inc.
Contact: Jane Friedman, President
E-mail: jfriedman@harpercollins.com
Ed: Michael E. Gerber. **Released:** January 18, 2010. **Price:** $20.99, Paperback; $14.99. **Description:** The book dispels the myths surrounding starting a business and shows how traditional assumptions can get in the way of running a small company. Topics cover entrepreneurship from infancy to growth and covers franchising. **Availability:** E-book.

38330 ■ *Earth: The Sequel: The Race to Reinvent Energy and Stop Global Warming*
Pub: W. W. Norton & Company, Inc.
Contact: Rachel Comerford, Manager
Ed: Miriam Horn, Fred Krupp. **Released:** March 2009. **Price:** $15.95, paperback. **Description:** President of the Environmental Defense Fund offers suggestions for small businesses to help solve global warming. Investigation into the new industries, jobs, and opportunities is provided.

38331 ■ *The Economics of Integrity: From Dairy Farmers to Toyota, How Wealth Is Built*

on Trust and What That Means for Our Future
Pub: HarperStudio/HarperCollins
Ed: Anna Bernasek. **Released:** February 23, 2010. **Price:** $13.99. **Description:** Integrity is built over time and the importance of trust in starting and building business relationships is stressed. **Availability:** E-book.

38332 ■ *The Economics of Small Firms: An Introduction*
Pub: Routledge
Contact: Kevin Bradley, President
E-mail: kbradley@taylorandfrancis.com
Ed: Peter Johnson. **Released:** March 2007. **Price:** $58.95, paperback; $180, hardback. **Description:** Introduction to the economics of small business, covering both theoretical and empirical issues. **Availability:** Print.

38333 ■ *Edgewalkers: People and Organizations That Take Risks, Build Bridges, and Break New Ground*
Pub: Greenwood Publishing Group Inc.
Contact: Janann Sherman, Manager
Ed: Judi Neal. **Released:** October 2006. **Price:** $39.95. **Description:** Profiles of entrepreneurs who thrive on change and challenge in order to create successful companies in today's complex business climate. **Availability:** Print.

38334 ■ *"The Effect of Cunfucian Values On Succession In Family Business" in Family Business Review (Vol. 19, September 2006, No. 3)*
Pub: Family Firm Institute
Contact: Judy L. Green, President
Ed: Jun Yan, Ritch Sorenson. **Description:** Position of family business in a social context using Confucian values is examined.

38335 ■ *"Effect of Oil Prices on the Economy" in Canadian Business (Vol. 81, September 15, 2008, No. 14-15, pp. 5)*
Ed: Joe Chidley. **Description:** Rise of oil prices above $100 in February 2008 and $140 in July signals the birth of a 'new economy' according to commentators; this shift is causing uneasiness from oil industry professionals who are unsure of how this trend could be sustained. Oil dropped below $120 in August, which could slow down global economic growth followed by oil demand, then oil prices.

38336 ■ *Effective Operations and Controls for the Small Privately Held Business*
Pub: John Wiley & Sons Inc.
Contact: Stephen M. Smith, President
Ed: Rob Reider. **Released:** December 2007. **Price:** $74.95, hardcover; $48.99. **Description:** Guide for implementing effective operations and controls for non-regulated small businesses with the least cost possible is presented. **Availability:** PrintE-book.

38337 ■ *Effectuation*
Pub: Edward Elgar Publishing Inc.
Contact: Richard Henning, Vice President
E-mail: kwight@e-elgar.com
Ed: Saras D. Sarasvathy. **Price:** $37.60, paperback; $150.30, hardback. **Description:** Effectuation is the idea that the future is unpredictable while being controllable. A study of 27 entrepreneurs shows effective effectuators. **Availability:** Print.

38338 ■ *The Emerging Markets Century: How a New Breed of World-Class Companies is Overtaking the World*
Ed: Antoine van Agtmael. **Released:** 2007. **Price:** , $29.00. **Description:** An exploration of how companies like Lenovo and Haier who are presently in emerging economies are already competing with household name brands like Ford and Sony, thus proving globalization is here to stay.

38339 ■ *"Employee Motivation: A Powerful New Model" in Harvard Business Review (Vol. 86, July-August 2008, No. 8, pp. 78)*
Pub: Harvard Business Review Press
Contact: Peter E. Walsh, Director
Ed: Nitin Nohira, Boris Groysberg, Linda-Eling Lee. **Description:** Four drives underlying employee

motivation are discussed as well as processes for leveraging these drives through corporate culture, job design, reward systems, and resource-allocation priorities.

38340 ■ *Encyclopedia of Small Business*
Pub: Cengage Learning

Ed: Arsen Darnay, Monique D. Magee, Kevin Hillstrom. **Released:** 4th Edition. **Price:** $763. **Description:** Concise encyclopedia of small business information. **Availability:** Print.

38341 ■ *"Energy Slide Slows 4th-Quarter Profits" in Globe & Mail (April 13, 2007, pp. B9)*

Ed: Angela Barnes. **Description:** The decrease in the fourth quarter profits of several companies across various industries in Canada, including mining and manufacturing, due to global decrease in oil prices, is discussed.

38342 ■ *Enterprise, Entrepreneurship and Innovation: Concepts, Context and Commercialization*
Pub: Elsevier Science and Technology Books

Ed: Robin Lowe, Sue Marriott. **Released:** May 2006. **Description:** Application of enterprise, innovation and entrepreneurship are discussed to help companies grow.

38343 ■ *Enterprise and Small Business: Principles, Practice and Policy*
Pub: Pearson Education Inc.
Contact: Steven A. Dowling, President

Ed: Sara Carter, Dylan Jones-Evans. **Released:** 3rd Edition. **Price:** £49.99. **Description:** Introduction to small business, challenges of a changing environment, and the nature of entrepreneurship are among the issues covered. **Availability:** Print.

38344 ■ *The Entrepreneur Next Door: Discover the Secrets to Financial Independence*

Ed: William F. Wagner. **Released:** May 2006. **Price:** , $19.95. **Description:** Traits required to become a successful entrepreneur are highlighted.

38345 ■ *The Entrepreneur and Small Business Problem Solver*
Pub: John Wiley & Sons Inc.
Contact: Stephen M. Smith, President

Ed: William A. Cohen. **Released:** November 2005. **Price:** $31.95; C$26.99. **Description:** Revised edition of the resource for entrepreneurs and small business owners that covers everything from start-up financing and loans to new product promotion and more. **Availability:** Print.

38346 ■ *Entrepreneurial Small Business*
Pub: McGraw-Hill Higher Education
Contact: Edward Stanford, President
E-mail: ed_stanford@mcgraw-hill.com

Ed: Jerome A. Katz, Richard P. Green. **Released:** Fourth Edition. **Price:** $259. **Description:** Students are able to get a clear vision of small enterprise in today's business climate. The textbook helps focus on the goal of having personal independence with financial security as an entrepreneur.

38347 ■ *"Entrepreneurs Save the World" in Women In Business (Vol. 61, December 2009, No. 6, pp. 12)*
Pub: American Business Women's Association
Contact: Lorie Burch, President

Ed: Leigh Elmore. **Description:** American economic growth is attributed to small businesses but more than one-third of these businesses have had to cut jobs in 2009, while only five percent have increased workforces. This trend motivated organizations, such as the Ewing Marion Kauffman Foundation, to bring together entrepreneurs and assist them in having greater participation in public dialogues about America's economy.

38348 ■ *Entrepreneurs in the Southern Upcountry: Commercial Culture in*

Spartanburg, South Carolina, 1845-1880
Pub: University of Georgia Press
Contact: Nicole Mitchell, Director

Ed: Bruce W. Eelman. **Released:** February 15, 2008. **Price:** $46.95; $44.95. **Description:** Historical account of the entrepreneurial culture in a nineteenth-century southern community outside the plantation belt is given. **Availability:** PrintE-book.

38349 ■ *Entrepreneurship*
Pub: Greenwood Publishing Group Inc.
Contact: Janann Sherman, Manager

Ed: Alan L. Carsrud, Malin E. Brannback. **Released:** March 30, 2007. **Price:** $55, Hardcover. **Description:** Entrepreneurial process is profiles, examining how these individuals identify opportunity and ways they address the personal, social, and financial risks involved in starting a new business venture. **Availability:** Print; E-book.

38350 ■ *Entrepreneurship: A Process Perspective*
Pub: South-Western
Contact: Susan Badger, President

Ed: Robert A. Baron, Scott A. Shane. **Released:** 2nd Edition. **Price:** $259.95, Hardcover. **Description:** Entrepreneurial process covering team building, finances, business plan, legal issues, marketing, growth and exit strategies. **Availability:** Print.

38351 ■ *Entrepreneurship: From Opportunity to Action*
Pub: Palgrave Macmillan
Contact: Lisa Dunn, Manager
E-mail: l.dunn@palgrave.com

Ed: David Rae. **Released:** January 2007. **Price:** £39.99, paperback. **Description:** Learning enterprise theory is discussed, focusing on the individual as an entrepreneur and ways to create and take advantage of opportunities. **Availability:** Print; E-book.

38352 ■ *Entrepreneurship and How to Establish Your Own Business*
Pub: Double Storey Books

Ed: Johan Strydon. **Released:** March 1, 2009. **Price:** , $37.95. **Description:** Guidelines are given to help develop a small business idea and to establish a successful enterprise. .

38353 ■ *Entrepreneurship and Small Business*
Pub: Palgrave Macmillan
Contact: Lisa Dunn, Manager
E-mail: l.dunn@palgrave.com

Ed: Paul Burns. **Released:** 3rd Edition . **Price:** $78, paperback; £44.99, paperback. **Description:** Entrepreneurial skills, focusing on good management practices are discussed. Topics include family businesses, corporate, international and social entrepreneurship.

38354 ■ *Entrepreneurship and Small Business Development in the Former Soviet Bloc*

Ed: David Smallbone, Friederike Welter. **Released:** January 10, 2010. **Price:** $140. **Description:** Examination of entrepreneurship and small business in Russia and other key countries of Eastern Europe, showing how far small businesses have developed in the region.

38355 ■ *Entrepreneurship: Theory, Process, and Practice*
Pub: South-Western
Contact: Susan Badger, President

Ed: Donald F. Kuratko. **Released:** 9th Edition. **Price:** $249.99; $49.99, rental; $232, wholesale; $93.49. **Description:** Understanding the process of entrepreneurship. **Availability:** PrintE-book.

38356 ■ *The Ethical Executive: Becoming Aware of the Root Causes of Unethical Behavior: 45 Psychological Traps that Every One of Us Falls Prey To*
Pub: Stanford University Press
Contact: Geoffrey Burn, Director
E-mail: grhburn@stanford.edu

Ed: Robert Hoyk, Paul Hersey. **Released:** 2008. **Price:** $18.95, paperback; $24.95, cloth. **Description:** Forty-five lessons to help avoid becoming a

victim to day-to-day ethical traps are outlined using moral lapses at Enron, Tyco International, Adelphia, World Com and other businesses as examples. **Availability:** Print; E-book.

38357 ■ *"Even Money on Recession" in Barron's (Vol. 88, March 10, 2008, No. 10, pp. M9)*
Pub: Dow Jones & Co., Inc.
Contact: Clare Hart, President

Ed: Gene Epstein. **Description:** Discusses the US unemployment rate which was steady in February 2008 at 4.8 percent, while nonfarm payroll employment decreased by 63,000 in the same month, with the private sector losing 101,000 jobs. The economic indicators showed mixed signals on whether or not the US economy is in a recession.

38358 ■ *Everything I Know About Business I Learned from My Mama: A Down-Home Approach to Business and Personal Success*
Pub: John Wiley & Sons Inc.
Contact: Stephen M. Smith, President

Ed: Tim Knox. **Released:** May 2007. **Price:** $22.95; $14.99. **Description:** Part memoir, part self-help, and part business how-to manual designed to help any small business owner/entrepreneur. **Availability:** PrintE-book.

38359 ■ *"The Evolution of the Mobile Entrepreneur" in Entrepreneur (Vol. 37, August 2009, No. 8, pp. 31)*
Pub: Entrepreneur Press
Contact: Perlman Neil, President

Ed: Dan O'Shea. **Description:** Covers the timeline of important events that led to the mobile businessperson today; includes the first cell phone call made by Martin Cooper in 1973 and the invention of Apple and the Newton in 1989. The first BlackBerry appeared in 1999 and the iPod was launched in 2001.

38360 ■ *Falling Behind: How Rising Inequality Harms the Middle Class*
Pub: University of California Press
Contact: Alison Mudditt, Director

Ed: Robert H. Frank. **Released:** September 2013. **Price:** $24.95, Paperback; £16.95, Paperback. **Description:** Economist argues that though middle-class American families aren't earning much more than they were a few decades ago, they are spending considerably more, a pattern attributed primarily to the context of seeing and emulating the spending habits of the rich. **Availability:** Print.

38361 ■ *"Family Matters: Founding Family Firms and Corporate Political Activity" in Business and Society (Vol. 46, December 7, 2007, No. 4)*
Pub: Pine Forge Press
Contact: Blaise R. Simqu, President

Ed: Michael Hadani. **Description:** The impact of publicly traded family founding firms and their inclination for corporate political activity is examined. Publicly traded family founding firms are more predisposed to engage in corporate political activity when the founder is in an executive position.

38362 ■ *Fast Company's Greatest Hits: 10 Years of the Most Innovative Ideas in Business*
Pub: Penguin Group USA
Contact: Phyllis Grann, President

Ed: Mark N. Vamosand, David Lidsky, Jim Collins. **Released:** July 2006. **Price:** $24.95. **Description:** Offering of Fast Company's best articles covering business ideas and profiles of successful firms and their leaders. **Availability:** Print.

38363 ■ *Fast-Track Employer's Kit: California*
Pub: Kaplan Books

Ed: Carolyn Usinger. **Released:** 2006. **Price:** $29.95; C$37. **Description:** Requirements for running a small business in California re outlined.

38364 ■ *"Festivals Press on Despite Loss of Sponsors" in Crain's Detroit Business (Vol.*

25, June 22, 2009, No. 25, pp. 3)
Pub: Crain Communications Inc. - Detroit
Contact: Keith Crain, Chairman
Ed: Sherri Begin Welch. **Description:** Organizers of local festivals are experiencing a decrease in sponsorship this summer due to the slow economy. These events help keep areas vibrant and stress the importance of community and cultural events.

38365 ■ *Financial Management 101: Get a Grip on Your Business Numbers*
Pub: Self-Counsel Press Inc.
Ed: Angie Mohr. **Released:** September 15, 2007. **Price:** $16.95. **Description:** An overview of business planning, financial statements, budgeting and advertising for small businesses. s.

38366 ■ *Financing Your Business: Get a Grip on Finding the Money*
Pub: Self-Counsel Press Inc.
Ed: Angie Mohr. **Released:** 2005. **Description:** Recommendations to help raise capital for a new or expanding small company.

38367 ■ *"Finishing Touches: the Fashion Statement is in the Detail" in Black Enterprise (Vol. 37, January 2007, No. 6, pp. 106)*
Pub: Earl G. Graves Publishing Co. Inc.
Contact: Earl G. Graves, Jr., President
Ed: Sonia Alleyne. **Description:** Men are discovering the importance of dressing for success. Paying attention to the details such as shoes, socks, cuffs, and collars are just as important as finding the right suit.

38368 ■ *First, Break All the Rules: What the World's Greatest Managers Do Differently*
Pub: Simon and Schuster Inc.
Contact: Carolyn Reidy, President
E-mail: carolyn.reidy@simonandschuster.com
Ed: Marcus Buckingham, Curt Coffman. **Released:** May 1999. **Price:** $32. **Description:** Great managers break virtually every rule revered by conventional wisdom.

38369 ■ *"Five More Great Books on Entrepreneurship" in Entrepreneur (Vol. 37, July 2009, No. 7, pp. 19)*
Pub: Entrepreneur Press
Contact: Perlman Neil, President
Ed: Jennifer Wang. **Description:** 800-CEO-Read founder, Jack Covert, and president, Todd Stattersten, share five books that would have been included in the book, 'The 100 Business Books of All Time' if space was not an issue. 'You Need to Be a Little Crazy,' 'Oh, the Places You'll Go!,' 'Founders at Work,' 'The Innovator's Dilemma,' and 'Purple Cow' are highly recommended for entrepreneurs.

38370 ■ *5 Steps to an Effective Meeting" in Hawaii Business (Vol. 53, March 2008, No. 9, pp. 55)*
Pub: PacificBasin Communications
Ed: Jason Ubay. **Description:** Identifying goals and writing them down can help in knowing what needs get done. Engaging everyone is a way to get cooperation in reaching the goals set. Other tips on how to have an effective meeting are discussed.

38371 ■ *"5 Steps for Handling Independent Contractors" in Hawaii Business (Vol. 53, January 2008, No. 7, pp. 49)*
Pub: PacificBasin Communications
Ed: Jason Ubay. **Description:** Small companies should be cautious in dealing with independent contractors. They must understand that they cannot dictate specific operational procedures, job duties, standards of conduct and performance standards to the contractors, and they cannot interfere with the evaluation and training of the contractors' employees. Tips on negotiating with independent contractors are given.

38372 ■ *"Five Steps to Killer Business Ideas" in Hawaii Business (Vol. 53, December 2007, No. 6, pp. 135)*
Pub: PacificBasin Communications
Ed: Jason Ubay. **Description:** Five ways to formulating good business concepts are presented. The importance of keeping an open mind and analyzing the market is discussed.

38373 ■ *"Five Things" in Hawaii Business (Vol. 53, November 2007, No. 5, pp. 20)*
Ed: Jason Ubay. **Description:** Discusses products that are allowed to be carried on board airplane flights by business travelers.

38374 ■ *"Five Tips for New Managers" in Hawaii Business (Vol. 53, November 2007, No. 5, pp. 59)*
Pub: PacificBasin Communications
Ed: Jason Ubay. **Description:** New managers should remember to know what their roles are, learn from others, build an infrastructure according to the customer's needs, communicate professionally and have consideration.

38375 ■ *"Follow the ABCs of Buying a Business" in Women Entrepreneur (September 10, 2008)*
Ed: Nina Kaufman. **Description:** Buying a business will likely result in the largest single asset one will ever own. A list of steps one can take in order to educate and protect themselves is provided.

38376 ■ *Forbes--Platinum 400-America's Best Big Companies*
Pub: Forbes Inc.
Contact: Malcolm S. Forbes, Jr., President
URL(s): www.forbes.com. **Ed:** William Baldwin. **Released:** Annual; Latest edition 2009. **Publication includes:** List of 400 leading publicly owned corporations. **Entries include:** Company name, sales and net income growth rates, return on capital, debt/capital, net profit margin, and operating margin. **Arrangement:** Classified alphabetically by industry. **Indexes:** Alphabetical.

38377 ■ *Forbes--Up-and-Comers 200: Best Small Companies in America Issue*
Pub: Forbes Inc.
Contact: Malcolm S. Forbes, Jr., President
URL(s): www.forbes.com. **Ed:** Steve Kichen. **Released:** Weekly; Latest edition October, 2007. **Publication includes:** List of 200 small companies judged to be high quality and fast-growing on the basis of 5-year return on equity and other qualitative measurements. Also includes a list of the 100 best small companies outside the U.S. **Note:** Issue does not carry address or CEO information for the foreign companies. **Entries include:** Company name, shareholdings data on chief executive officer; financial data. **Arrangement:** Alphabetical. **Indexes:** Ranking.

38378 ■ *"Fortis College Opens on St. Luke's Medical Center Site" in The Business Journal - Serving Phoenix and the Valley of the Sun (Vol. 28, September 7, 2008)*
Pub: American City Business Journals, Inc.
Contact: Whitney Shaw, President
Ed: Angela Gonzales. **Description:** Fortis College is planning to offer classes in Phoenix, Arizona. It has made its home at the St. Luke's Medical Center. Courses to be offered by the college are also provided.

38379 ■ *Foundations of Small Business Enterprise*
Pub: Routledge
Contact: Kevin Bradley, President
E-mail: kbradley@taylorandfrancis.com
Ed: Gavin Reid. **Released:** December 2006. **Price:** $210, hardback. **Description:** Insight is given into the life cycle of entrepreneurial ventures; 150 new firms are tracked through early years. **Availability:** Print.

38380 ■ *401 Questions Every Entrepreneur Should Ask*
Pub: Career Press Inc.
Contact: Ron Fry, President
Ed: James L. Silvester. **Price:** $17.99. **Description:** Review of 25 functional areas of running a small business are covered along with questions entrepreneurs should ask in order to correct and avoid unwanted issues. **Availability:** Print.

38381 ■ *Free Lunch: How the Wealthiest Americans Enrich Themselves at Government Expense (and Stick You with the Bill)*
Pub: Portfolio
Ed: David Cay Johnston. **Released:** December 30, 2008. **Price:** $16, paperback. **Description:** Johnston uses the case of the Texas Rangers as an example to support his belief that the nation's monied elite bend the rules of capitalism for their own benefit. **Availability:** Print.

38382 ■ *The Future Arrived Yesterday: The Rise of the Protean Corporation and What It Means for You*
Pub: Crown Business
Ed: Michael S. Malone. **Released:** 2009. **Price:** $15.99. **Description:** Reasons why dominant companies of the next decade will behave like perpetual entrepreneurial startups are investigated. **Availability:** E-book.

38383 ■ *"The Future of Work" in Black Enterprise (Vol. 41, August 2010, No. 1, pp. 65)*
Pub: Earl G. Graves Publishing Co. Inc.
Contact: Earl G. Graves, Jr., President
Ed: Annya M. Lott. **Description:** Technology, globalization, and outsourcing will continue to shape the future of work. Social media is a means for small companies to market goods and services.

38384 ■ *"The Future of Work" in Business Strategy Review (Vol. 21, Autumn 2010, No. 3, pp. 16)*
Pub: Blackwell Publishers Ltd.
Ed: Lynda Gratton. **Description:** Work is universal. But how, why, where and when we work has never been so open to individual interpretation. The certainties of the past have been replaced by ambiguity, questions and the steady hum of technology. Now, in a groundbreaking research project covering 21 global companies and more than 200 executives, the author is making sense of the future of work.

38385 ■ *Gen X*
Ed: Brian O'Connell. **Price:** , $17.95.

38386 ■ *Gendered Processes: Korean Immigrant Small Business Ownership*
Pub: LFB Scholarly Publishing LLC
Ed: Eunju Lee. **Released:** November 2005. **Price:** $60, hardcover. **Description:** Examination of the gender processes among Korean immigrants becoming small business owners in the New York City metropolitan area. **Availability:** Print.

38387 ■ *"Generation Y Goes To Work; Management" in The Economist (Vol. 390, January 3, 2009, No. 8612, pp. 48)*
Description: Unemployment rates among people in their 20s has increased significantly and there is a lower turnover in crisis-hit firms, which has made it more difficult to simply find another job if one is unsatisfied with the management style of his or her company. Managers are adopting a more command-and-control approach which is the antithesis of the open, collaborative style that younger employees prefer.

38388 ■ *The Geography of Small Firm Innovation*
Pub: Springer-Verlag New York Inc.
Contact: Ruediger Gebauer, President
Ed: Grant Black. **Released:** January 2005. **Price:** $179; $139. **Description:** Concentration of high-tech innovation across metropolitan areas in the U.S. during the 1990s and the role geography plays in innovation. **Availability:** PrintE-book.

38389 ■ *Get in the Game: 8 Elements of Perseverance that Make the Difference*
Pub: Gotham/Penguin Group Incorporated
Ed: Cal Ripken, Donald T. Phillips. **Released:** April 10, 2008. **Price:** $15, paperback; $12.99. **Description:** Guidebook written by superstar athlete Cal Ripkin to help managers and entrepreneurs achieve success. **Availability:** PrintElectronic publishing.

38390 ■ *"Get in Line" in Canadian Business (Vol. 79, September 25, 2006, No. 19, pp. 43)*
Ed: Andy Holloway. **Description:** The needs of economically developing Canada's urban regions are discussed.

38391 ■ *"Get More Time Off" in Canadian Business (Vol. 80, March 12, 2007, No. 6, pp. 32)*
Ed: June Morrow. **Description:** Expert advice to employees to make use of leaves of absence to improve their career instead of working continuously for a long period is presented.

38392 ■ *Get Your Business to Work!: 7 Steps to Earning More, Working Less and Living the Life You Want*
Pub: BenBella Books
Contact: Aida Herrera, Director
E-mail: aida@benbellabooks.com
Ed: George Hedley. **Released:** May 2014. **Price:** $12.56, paperback. **Description:** Complete step-by-step guide for the small business owner to realize profits, wealth and freedom. **Availability:** Print.

38393 ■ *"Getting in the Swing" in Canadian Business (Vol. 80, February 26, 2007, No. 5, pp. 67)*
Ed: Andrew Wahl. **Description:** The economic issues associated with the acquisition of Adams, Harkness and Hill Inc. by Canaccord Capital are presented. A large number of Canadian companies are entering into the United States.

38394 ■ *Getting Things Done: The Art of Stress-Free Productivity*
Pub: Penguin Books USA Inc.
Ed: David Allen. **Released:** December 31, 2002. **Price:** $24.95, hardcover; $12.99. **Description:** Coach and management consultant recommends methods for stress-free performance under the premise that productivity is directly related to our ability to relax. **Availability:** PrintElectronic publishing.

38395 ■ *"Glamis Reserves Get Boost With Western Silver Deal" in Globe & Mail (February 25, 2006, pp. B3)*
Ed: Wendy Stueck. **Description:** The details on Glamis Gold Ltd.'s proposed acquisition of Western Silver Corp., for $1.2 billion, are presented.

38396 ■ *Global Economic Crisis: Impact on Small Business*
Pub: Cengage South-Western
Released: March 01, 2009. **Description:** A discussion of the historical context of the global economic crisis is presented, along with a discussion on the impact of this crisis on small businesses. It also provides learning goals, questions, key terms, and digital access to the Global Economic Crisis Resource Center.

38397 ■ *The Go-Giver: A Little Story About a Powerful Business Idea*
Pub: Penguin Group USA
Contact: Phyllis Grann, President
Ed: Bob Burg, John David Mann. **Released:** December 27, 2007. **Price:** $21.95, hardcover; $17.99. **Description:** Story of an ambitious young man named Joe who years for success. The book is a heartwarming tale that brings new relevance to the old proverb, 'Give and you shall receive'. **Availability:** PrintElectronic publishing.

38398 ■ *Going to Extremes: How Like Minds Unite and Divide*
Pub: Oxford University Press
Contact: Niko Pfund, President
Ed: Cass R. Sustein. **Released:** 2009. **Price:** £14.99. **Description:** Solutions to marketplace problems are examined.

38399 ■ *Good to Great*
Pub: Harper Business
Ed: Jim Collins. **Released:** 2001. **Price:** $29.99, hardcover; $19.99; C$18.99. **Availability:** PrintE-book.

38400 ■ *Good to Great: Why Some Companies Make the Leap..and Others Don't*
Pub: HarperCollins Publishers Inc.
Contact: Jane Friedman, President
E-mail: jfriedman@harpercollins.com
Ed: Jim Collins. **Price:** $29.99; $19.99; C$18.99. **Description:** Management styles for growing a modern business. **Availability:** PrintE-book.

38401 ■ *"Got Skills?" in Entrepreneur (Vol. 35, October 2007, No. 10, pp. 31)*
Pub: Entrepreneur Press
Contact: Perlman Neil, President
Ed: Laura Tiffany. **Description:** Entrepreneurs such as Jim Mousner, Hugh Briathwaite, and Joi Ito, has been known to apply their skills and interests in other fields on their business operations. Knowing something outside the realm of their industry helps entrepreneurs think of fresh ideas that are beneficial not only to them but also to their clients. Details of how having a different kind of interest helped Mousner, Braithwaite and Ito are presented.

38402 ■ *Goventure: Live the Life of an Entrepreneur*
Pub: Houghton Mifflin College Div.
Contact: June Smith, President
Description: Challenges of operating a small business are presented with more than 6,000 graphics, audio, and interactive video. **Availability:** CD-ROM.

38403 ■ *"Grand Action Makes Grand Changes in Grand Rapids" in Crain's Detroit Business (Vol. 25, June 1, 2009, No. 22, pp. M012)*
Pub: Crain Communications Inc. - Detroit
Contact: Keith Crain, Chairman
Ed: Amy Lane. **Description:** Businessman Dick De-Vos believes that governments are not always the best to lead certain initiatives. That's why, in 1991, he gathered 50 west Michigan community leaders and volunteers to look consider the construction of an arena and expanding or renovating local convention operations. Grand Action has undertaken four major projects in the city.

38404 ■ *"The Grass is Greener" in Canadian Business (Vol. 79, August 14, 2006, No. 16-17, pp. 43)*
Pub: Rogers Media Inc.
Contact: Tony Viner, President
Ed: Thomas Watson. **Description:** Owner of New Image Plans LLC, Joe White, shares his views on the Canadian market for the marijuana drug.

38405 ■ *Great Big Book of Business Lists*
Pub: Entrepreneur Press
Contact: Perlman Neil, President
Ed: Courtney Thurman, Ashlee Gardner. **Released:** April 25, 2006. **Description:** Reference guide for small business that includes information for starting and running a small business; lists are organized for easy access and cover every aspect of small business.

38406 ■ *Great Tips for Your Small Business: Increase Your Profit and Joy in Your Work*
Pub: Dundurn Press Ltd.
Contact: Kirk Howard, President
Ed: Julie V. Watson. **Released:** September 2006. **Price:** $24.99, paperback; $11.99. **Description:** Tips and hints for home-based, micro, and small businesses are presented. **Availability:** PrintE-book.

38407 ■ *Green Business Practices for Dummies*
Ed: Lisa Swallow. **Released:** January 2009. **Price:** , $21.99. **Description:** The book provides information for any small business to help reduce environmental impact without reducing their company's bottom line.

38408 ■ *The Gridlock Economy: How Too Much Ownership Wrecks Markets, Stops Innovation, and Costs Lives*
Pub: Basic Books
Contact: Elizabeth Maguire, Publisher
Ed: Michael Heller. **Released:** February 23, 2010. **Price:** C$21.50, paperback; $16.95; C$27.95; £11.99. **Description:** While private ownership generally cre-ates wealth, the author believes that economic grid-lock results when too many people own pieces of one thing, which results in too many people being able to block each other from creating or using a scarce source. **Availability:** PrintE-book.

38409 ■ *"A Growing Concern" in Canadian Business (Vol. 79, October 9, 2006, No. 20, pp. 90)*
Ed: Jeff Sanford. **Description:** With rich dividends being harvested by companies producing ethanol, after ethanol became a petrol additive, is discussed.

38410 ■ *Growing Local Value: How to Build Business Partnerships That Strengthen Your Community*
Pub: Berrett-Koehler Communications Inc.
Contact: Steve Piersanti, President
E-mail: spiersanti@bkpub.com
Ed: Laury Hammel, Gun Denhart. **Price:** $16.95. **Description:** Advice and examples are provided for building socially responsible entrepreneurship. **Availability:** Print; PDF.

38411 ■ *Growing and Managing a Small Business: An Entrepreneurial Perspective*
Pub: Houghton Mifflin College Div.
Contact: June Smith, President
Ed: Kathleen R. Allen. **Released:** 2007. **Price:** A$159.95; NZ$167.95. **Description:** Introduction to business ownership and management from startup through growth. **Availability:** Print.

38412 ■ *"Growth Seen Climbing Out of a Trough" in Globe & Mail (March 3, 2007, pp. B5)*
Ed: Tavia Grant. **Description:** The economic condition of Canada in the fourth quarter 2006 is analyzed. The gross domestic product rose 1.4 percent in the fourth quarter.

38413 ■ *A Guide to the Project Management Body of Knowledge*
Pub: Project Management Institute
Contact: Peter Monkhouse, Director
Released: Fifth Edition. **Price:** $49.50, Members, student; $65.95, Nonmembers. **Description:** A guide for project management using standard language, with new data flow diagrams; the Identify Stakeholders and Collect Requirements processes defined; and with greater attention placed on how knowledge areas integrate in the context of initiating, planning, executing, monitoring and controlling, and closing process groups. **Availability:** Print.

38414 ■ *Happy About Joint-Venturing: The 8 Key Critical Factors of Success*
Pub: Happy About
Contact: Mitchell Levy, Chief Executive Officer
Ed: Valerie Orsoni-Vauthey. **Price:** $19.95, paperback; $14.95. **Description:** An overview of joint venturing is presented. **Availability:** PrintE-book; PDF.

38415 ■ *"Heavy Duty: The Case Against Packing Lightly" in Crain's Chicago Business (Vol. 31, April 21, 2008, No. 16, pp. 29)*
Pub: Crain Communications Inc.
Contact: Todd Johnson, Publisher
Ed: Sarah A. Klein. **Description:** Penelope Biggs, a Northern Trust executive who manages sales teams in North America, Europe and Asia gives advice on traveling abroad for business including time management skills, handling time-zone hops and avoiding jet-lag.

38416 ■ *"Help for Job Seekers" in Crain's Detroit Business (Vol. 26, January 18, 2010, No. 3, pp. 14)*
Pub: Crain Communications Inc.
Contact: Rance E. Crain, President
Description: CareerWorks is aimed at helping those who are in career transition or are looking for new jobs; this weekly collection of news, advertising and information includes weekly stories, events and the highlighting of a person who has successfully made the transition from one profession to another. On the Website, readers are welcome to post an anonymous resume in order to attract employers.

38417 ■ *"Higher Education" in Canadian Business (Vol. 79, October 23, 2006, No. 21, pp. 129)*
Ed: Erin Pooley; Laura Bogomolny; Joe Castaldo; Michelle Magnan. **Description:** Details of some Canadian business schools, where students can simultaneously pursue a master of business administration degree and also be employed on a part time basis, are presented.

38418 ■ *"Hire Education" in Canadian Business (Vol. 79, September 11, 2006, No. 18, pp. 114)*
Pub: Rogers Media Inc.
Contact: Tony Viner, President
Ed: Erin Pooley. **Description:** Study results showing the perceptions of students while considering full-time employment and the attributes they look for in their future employers are presented.

38419 ■ *"Hispanic Representation in Boardrooms Remains Static" in Hispanic Business (January-February 2008, pp. 36, 38, 40)*
Pub: Hispanic Business Inc.
Contact: Jesus Chavarria, President
Description: Estimated 3 percent of Hispanic representation in corporate boardroom in America has remained the same, despite the growth in the Hispanic population. Statistical data and board member names are included.

38420 ■ *History of Canadian Business 1867-1914*
Pub: University of Toronto Press
Ed: R. T. Naylor. **Released:** 1997. **Price:** C$28.99, paperback; C$57.99, hardcover. **Description:** Covers the growth of business in Canada. **Availability:** Print.

38421 ■ *A History of Small Business in America*
Pub: University of North Carolina Press
Contact: Kate Douglas Torrey, Director
E-mail: kate_torrey@unc.edu
Ed: Mansel G. Blackford. **Released:** Second Edition. **Price:** $32.50. **Description:** History of American small business from the colonial era to present, showing how it has played a role in the nation's economic, political, and cultural development across manufacturing, sales, services and farming. **Availability:** Print.

38422 ■ *"Holidays Should Foster Mutual Respect" in Women In Business (Vol. 61, October-November 2009, No. 5, pp. 33)*
Pub: American Business Women's Association
Contact: Lorie Burch, President
Ed: Diane Stafford. **Description:** Workplaces have modified the way year-end holiday celebrations are held in an effort to promote mutual respect. The workers' varying religious beliefs, political affiliations, and other differences have brought about the modifications. The importance of developing mutual understanding is emphasized as a mechanism to stimulate successful business ties.

38423 ■ *Hoover's Vision*
Ed: Gary Hoover. **Description:** Founder of Bookstop Inc. and Hoover's Inc. provides a plan to turn an enterprise into a success by showing entrepreneurs how to address inputs with an open mind in order to see more than what other's envision. Hoover pushes business owners to create and feed a clear and consistent vision by recognizing the importance of history and trends, then helps them find the essential qualities of entrepreneurial leadership.

38424 ■ *"How Innovative Is Michigan? Index Aims To Keep Track" in Crain's Detroit Business (Vol. 24, February 4, 2008, No. 5, pp. 1)*
Pub: Crain Communications Inc. - Detroit
Contact: Keith Crain, Chairman
Ed: Chad Halcom. **Description:** Profile of the newly created 'Innovation Index', released by the University of Michigan-Dearborn. The report showed a combination of indicators that gauged innovation activity in the state slightly lower for second quarter 2007, but ahead of most levels for most of 2006. Statistical data included.

38425 ■ *How to Make Big Money in Your Own Small Business: Unexpected Rules Every Small Business Owner Needs to Know*
Pub: Hyperion Press
Ed: Jeffrey J. Fox. **Released:** May 12, 2004. **Price:** $16.95; C$24.95. **Description:** Former sales and marketing pro offers advice on growing a small business.

38426 ■ *How the Mighty Fall: And Why Some Companies Never Give In*
Pub: HarperCollins Publishers Inc.
Contact: Jane Friedman, President
E-mail: jfriedman@harpercollins.com
Ed: Jim Collins. **Released:** May 19, 2009. **Price:** $23.99, hardcover; $12.99; C$16.99. **Description:** Companies fail in stages and their decline can be detected and reversed. **Availability:** PrintE-book.

38427 ■ *"How to Pick an All-Star" in Canadian Business (Vol. 79, October 9, 2006, No. 20, pp. 15)*
Ed: Andy Holloway. **Description:** Factors that determine the competency levels o f individuals are discussed. The need for firms to take into consideration the right selection factors while hiring an employee is presented.

38428 ■ *How to Raise Capital: Techniques and Strategies for Financing and Valuing Your Small Business*
Ed: Jeffrey A. Timmons, Stephen Spinelli, Andrew Zacharakis. **Released:** May 2004. **Price:** , $16.95 (US), $24.95 (Canadian). **Description:** Small business financing process is examined. Tips for identifying the financial life cycle of new ventures, developing a framework for financial strategies, and understanding an investor's prospective.

38429 ■ *How to Run Your Business Like a Girl: Successful Strategies from Entrepreneurial Women Who Made It Happen*
Ed: Elizabeth Cogswell Baskin. **Released:** September 2005. **Description:** Tour of three women entrepreneurs and their successful companies.

38430 ■ *How to Succeed As a Lifestyle Entrepreneur*
Ed: Gary Schine. **Price:** , $18.95.

38431 ■ *"How To Live To Be 100: John E. Green Co. Grows Through Diversification" in Crain's Detroit Business (February 18, 2008)*
Pub: Crain Communications Inc. - Detroit
Contact: Keith Crain, Chairman
Ed: Chad Halcom. **Description:** Continuity, name recognition, and inventiveness are keys to continuing growth for Highland Park, Michigan's John E. Green Company, designer of pipe systems and mechanical contractor.

38432 ■ *How Walmart is Destroying America (And the World): And What You Can Do About It*
Pub: Celestial Arts Publishing Co.
Contact: Kristin Casemore, Manager
E-mail: kristin.casemore@tenspeed.com
Ed: Bill Quinn. **Released:** April 2005. **Description:** Wal-Mart employs 1.5 million employees and operates more than 3,500 stores, making it the largest private employer globally. Wal-Mart's impact on mom-and-pop business is discussed.

38433 ■ *How: Why How We Do Anything Means Everything*
Pub: John Wiley & Sons Inc.
Contact: Stephen M. Smith, President
Ed: Dov L. Seidman. **Released:** September 2011. **Price:** $27.95, hardcover; $18.99. **Description:** Author shares his unique approach to building successful companies using case studies, anecdotes, research, and interviews to help entrepreneurs succeed in the 21st Century. **Availability:** PrintE-book.

38434 ■ *How to Write a Business Plan*
Pub: Nolo
Contact: Ralph Warner, Chief Executive Officer
Ed: Mike McKeever. **Released:** 11th Edition. **Price:** $27.99; $24.49. **Description:** Author, teacher and financial manager shows how to write an effective business plan. Examples and worksheets are included. **Availability:** Print; PDFE-book; Download.

38435 ■ *How to Write a Great Business Plan for Your Small Business in 60 Minutes or Less*
Pub: Atlantic Publishing Co.
Contact: Amanda Miller, Manager
E-mail: amiller@atlantic-pub.com
Ed: Sharon L. Fullen. **Released:** January 2006. **Price:** $39.95, Includes CD-Rom. **Description:** A good business plan outlines goals and works as a company's resume to obtain funding, credit from suppliers, management of the operations and finances, promotion and marketing, and more. **Availability:** Print.

38436 ■ *"How to Write a Report" in Canadian Business (Vol. 80, November 5, 2007, No. 22, pp. 41)*
Ed: Gabriel Fuchs. **Description:** Basic rule in writing a report is the so-called USNA, which stands for Use Synonyms, No Acronyms. Synonyms make the report seem more interesting while acronyms increase the chance of being misunderstood. Details of how to write an impressive business report are given.

38437 ■ *HRD in Small Organizations: Research and Practice*
Pub: Routledge
Contact: Kevin Bradley, President
E-mail: kbradley@taylorandfrancis.com
Released: March 26, 2007. **Price:** $54.95, paperback. **Description:** Approaches to human resource development in small organizations are evaluated. **Availability:** Print.

38438 ■ *"The Human Factor" in Canadian Business (Vol. 80, October 8, 2007, No. 20, pp. 22)*
Ed: Alex Mynek. **Description:** David Foot, a demographer and an economics professor at the University of Toronto, talks about Canada's future, including economic and demographic trends. He discusses activities that should be done by businessmen in order to prepare for the future. He also addresses the role of the Canadian government in economic development.

38439 ■ *Human Resources for Small Business Made Easy*
Ed: Ruth Zimmerman. **Released:** November 2006. **Description:** Guide for human resource development for small businesses.

38440 ■ *"The 'In-Crowd' Online: Professionals Take Networking To New Levels" in Black Enterprise (Vol. 38, January 2008, No. 6, pp. 47)*
Pub: Earl G. Graves Publishing Co. Inc.
Contact: Earl G. Graves, Jr., President
Ed: Alwin A.D. Jones. **Description:** The Internet is providing new ways for professionals to network with others. New sites like LinkedIn.com provide entrepreneurs with access to others with a business life similar to theirs.

38441 ■ *"In Everyone's Interests" in Canadian Business (Vol. 80, April 23, 2007, No. 9, pp. 62)*
Ed: Rachel Pulfer. **Description:** The need of strategic negotiations during a labor contract to prevent disputes with employer is emphasized.

38442 ■ *Inc.--The Inc. 500 Issue (Fastest growing +private +companies)*
Pub: Gruner & Jahr USA Publishing
Contact: Donald C. Berg, Executive Vice President
URL(s): www.inc.com/inc5000/2009/index.htmlwww.inc.com. **Released:** Annual; Latest edition 2010. **Publication includes:** List of 500 fastest-growing privately held companies based on percentage increase in sales over the five year period prior to compilation of current year's list. **Entries include:** Company name, headquarters city, description of business, year founded, number of employees, sales five years earlier and currently, profitability range, and growth statistics. **Arrangement:** Ranked by sales growth.

38443 ■ Information Technology And Small Businesses: Antecedents and Consequences of Technology Adoption
Pub: Edward Elgar Publishing Inc.
Contact: Richard Henning, Vice President
E-mail: kwight@e-elgar.com
Ed: Andrea Ordanini. Released: 2006. Price: £66.60, hardback. Description: Issues involving information communication technology adoption among small and medium-sized firms are discussed. Availability: Print.

38444 ■ Innovation Methodologies in Enterprise Research
Pub: Edward Elgar Publishing Inc.
Contact: Richard Henning, Vice President
E-mail: kwight@e-elgar.com
Ed: Damian Hine. Price: £81, hardback; £33.60, paperback. Description: The importance of qualitative, interpretist research in the field of enterprise research is discussed. The book stresses how enterprise research is a new method and permits a wide scope for new and innovative research studies. Availability: Online.

38445 ■ Innovative Approaches to Global Sustainability
Pub: Palgrave Macmillan
Contact: Lisa Dunn, Manager
E-mail: l.dunn@palgrave.com
Released: March 2011. Price: £22.99, paperback. Description: Examples are given to help businesses become sustainable as we move towards a sustainable world. Availability: Print.

38446 ■ "The Inside and Outside Scoop on CEO Succession" in Globe & Mail (January 2, 2006, pp. B8)
Pub: CTVglobemedia Publishing Inc.
Ed: Shirley Won. Description: The career profile of Randy Eresman as the chief executive officer of Encana Corp. is presented.

38447 ■ "Interview Advisory; Warning! Do YOU Have VD?" in Canadian Corporate News (May 18, 2007)
Description: Interview with Beverly Beuermann-King, a stress and wellness specialist, who provides insights on the problems associated with Vacation Deprivation.

38448 ■ Introduction to Business
Pub: The McGraw-Hill Companies
Ed: Laura Portolese Dias, Amit J. Shah. Released: January 1, 2009. Price: , $70.94. Description: Introduction to business course discusses the changing educational environment for teaching business courses in colleges and universities.

38449 ■ "Is Globalization Threatening U.S. Hispanic Progress?" in Hispanic Business (Vol. 30, September 2008, No. 9, pp. 16)
Ed: Jessica Haro. Description: Talented Hispanic employees are making progress within the increasingly diverse American corporate scenario. However, while some experts believe the induction of foreign professionals through globalization will not impact this progress, others feel it could hamper opportunities for American Hispanics.

38450 ■ "Is It Time to Move to a Real Office?" in Women Entrepreneur (December 30, 2008)
Ed: Aliza Sherman. Description: Before moving a company from a home-office to a real office it is important to make sure that the additional overhead that will be incurred by the move is comfortably covered and that the move is being done for the right reasons. Several women entrepreneurs who have moved their businesses from their homes to an actual rental space are profiled.

38451 ■ "Is the Sun Setting on Oil Sector's Heydey?" in Globe & Mail (January 25, 2007, pp. B3)
Ed: Shawn McCarthy. Description: The effects of fuel efficiency management policies of the United States on Canadian petroleum industry are discussed. Canada is the largest exporter of crude oil to America after the Middle East.

38452 ■ "Is That the Best You Can Do?" in Entrepreneur (Vol. 37, October 2009, No. 10, pp. 85)
Pub: Entrepreneur Press
Contact: Perlman Neil, President
Ed: Jennifer Wang. Description: Small business owners can deal with hagglers better by setting parameters in advance. They should convince hagglers by offering the best value and separating this from price.

38453 ■ "Is Your Company Ready to Succeed" in Business Strategy Review (Vol. 21, Spring 2010, No. 1, pp. 68)
Pub: John Wiley & Sons Inc. Scientific, Technical, Medical, and Scholarly Div. (Wiley-Blackwell)
Contact: William J. Pesce, Manager
E-mail: wpesce@wiley.com
Ed: Srikumar Rao. Description: The author asked thousands of students about the ideal company of the future, the kind of place where they would want to spend their lives.

38454 ■ "Is Your Supply Chain Sustainable?" in Harvard Business Review (Vol. 88, October 2010, No. 10, pp. 74)
Pub: Harvard Business School Publishing
Description: Charts and models are presented to help a firm assess its sustainability.

38455 ■ "It All Comes Back to Trust" in Canadian Business (Vol. 80, March 26, 2007, No. 7, pp. S11)
Description: Eileen Fischer, family business expert at York University, shares her views on the challenges involved in running family businesses.

38456 ■ It's Not Just Who You Know: Transform Your Life (and Your Organization) by Turning Colleagues and Contacts into Lasting Relationships
Ed: Tommy Spaulding. Released: August 10, 2010. Price: $23. Description: Tommy Spaulding teaches the reader how to reach out to others in order to create lasting relationships that go beyond superficial contacts.

38457 ■ "Jobless Rate Climbs Unexpectedly in December" in Globe & Mail (January 7, 2006, pp. B5)
Description: The reasons behind increase in unemployment rate by 6.5 percent, in Canada, are presented.

38458 ■ "Jobs Boom Ramps Up in March" in Globe & Mail (April 7, 2007, pp. B1)
Ed: Tara Perkins. Description: The increase in the number of jobs by 54,900 in Canada and 180,000 in the United States In March 2007 is discussed.

38459 ■ "Jobs, Export Surge Confirm Recovery" in Globe & Mail (March 10, 2007, pp. B5)
Ed: Heather Scoffield. Description: The increase in the number of jobs and exports that is forecast to reverse the slowdown in the Canadian economy is discussed.

38460 ■ "Keith Crain: Business Must Stand Up And Be Counted" in Crain's Detroit Business (Vol. 24, October 6, 2008, No. 40, pp. 6)
Pub: Crain Communications Inc.
Contact: Rance E. Crain, President
Description: Discusses the challenges that the new mayor of Detroit faces concerning business, the state of the economy and the exceptionally tight budget the city is running on, which includes a lot of red ink. It is very likely that the city is going to see tax revenues fall substantially in the next few months and business leaders may find it in their favor to lend their support to the new mayor as well as provide him with the executive talent necessary to overcome some of these crucial issues.

38461 ■ "Key Budgeting Tips: For Your Management Team" in Agency Sales Magazine (Vol. 39, December 2009, No. 11, pp. 49)
Ed: Gene Siciliano. Description: Constructing a budget must be the result of coordinated input and effort. Practice is also important in creating a budget

and accurately predicting actual results is not the objective but giving the company a direction for course correction.

38462 ■ "Kinross Holds Firm on Offer for Bema" in Globe & Mail (January 20, 2007, pp. B5)
Pub: CTVglobemedia Publishing Inc.
Ed: Andy Hoffman. Description: The acquisition of Bema Gold Corp. by Kinross Gold Corp. is discussed.

38463 ■ Kiss Theory Good Bye: Five Proven Ways to Get Extraordinary Results in Any Company
Pub: Gold Pen Publishing
Ed: Bob Prosen. Released: August 01, 2006. Price: $15.62, hardcover. Description: Author provides wisdom from his career as a high-level executive at AT&T Global Information Solutions, Sabre, and Hitachi, as well as his consulting firm. The book focuses on business execution rather than processes or theory of business management and provides step-by-step instructions allowing organizations to maximize profitability and results.

38464 ■ Knockout Entrepreneur
Pub: Thomas Nelson Inc.
Contact: Michael S. Hyatt, President
Ed: George Foreman. Released: December 14, 2010. Price: $22.99, hardcover; $14.99, paperback. Description: George Foreman offers ten key strategies for running a successful small business.

38465 ■ "Knowledge Workers" in Canadian Business (Vol. 79, October 9, 2006, No. 20, pp. 59)
Ed: Doug Cooper. Description: Knowledge workers as an integral part of organizations and the need for business leaders to effectively manage and recognize the talent of knowledge workers is discussed.

38466 ■ "The Labor Crunch is Coming" in Canadian Business (Vol. 80, December 25, 2006, No. 1, pp. 74)
Description: The need for skilled and educated workforce to meet labor shortage in future in Canada is discussed.

38467 ■ "The Last Word Dirty Work Required" in Workforce Management (Vol. 88, November 16, 2009, No. 12, pp. 34)
Pub: Crain Communications Inc.
Contact: Rance E. Crain, President
Ed: John Hollon. Description: Due to salary freezes, pay cuts, layoffs, buyouts and a number of other stress factors brought about by the recession, employee engagement has been difficult to maintain by managers.

38468 ■ Law (in Plain English) for Small Business
Pub: Sourcebooks Inc.
Contact: Dominique M. Raccah, President
Ed: Leonard D. DuBoff. Released: March 01, 2007. Price: $22.99. Description: Small business law is described in easy to read format.

38469 ■ "Leaders in Denial" in Harvard Business Review (Vol. 86, July-August 2008, No. 8, pp. 18)
Pub: Harvard Business Review Press
Contact: Peter E. Walsh, Director
Ed: Richard S. Tedlow. Description: Identifying denial in the corporate arena is discussed, along with its impact on business and how to prevent it from occurring.

38470 ■ Lean Six Sigma That Works: A Powerful Action Plan for Dramatically Improving Quality, Increasing Speed, and Reducing Waste
Pub: American Management Association
Contact: Edward T. Reilly, President
Ed: Bill Carreira, Bill Trudell. Price: $21.95, paperback. Availability: Print.

38471 ■ *"Leave It Behind" in Crain's Chicago Business (Vol. 31, April 21, 2008, No. 16, pp. 32)*
Pub: Crain Communications Inc.
Contact: Todd Johnson, Publisher
Ed: Sarah A. Klein. Description: Patrick Brady who investigates possible violations of the Foreign Corrupt Practices Act has a novel approach when traveling to frequent destinations which allows him to travel with only a carry-on piece of luggage: he leaves suits at dry cleaners in the places he visits most often and since he mainly stays at the same hotels, he also leaves sets of workout clothes and running shoes with hotel staff.

38472 ■ *"Legal Aid: Sample Legal Documents can Lower Your Attorney Fees" in Black Enterprise (Vol. 37, October 2006, No. 3, pp. 210)*
Pub: Earl G. Graves Publishing Co. Inc.
Contact: Earl G. Graves, Jr., President
Ed: Tamara E. Holmes. Description: FreeLegal-Forms.net provides thousands of free legal forms. These forms are not a substitute for consultation with an attorney but the sample documents can help save you time and money.

38473 ■ *Lessons in Service From Charlie Trotter*
Pub: Celestial Arts Publishing Co.
Contact: Kristin Casemore, Manager
E-mail: kristin.casemore@tenspeed.com
Ed: Edmund Lawler. Released: November 28, 2001. Price: $24.99, hardcover. Description: Chef Charlie Trotter, owner of a restaurant, shares insight into managing any business successfully. Availability: Print.

38474 ■ *The Life Cycle of Entrepreneurial Ventures*
Pub: Springer
Contact: Derk Haank, Chief Executive Officer
E-mail: derk.haank@springer.com
Released: 2007. Price: €309, hardcover, softcover; €260.61. Description: Issues involved in creating a new business are explored, including venture creation, development and performance. Availability: PrintE-book.

38475 ■ *"Lines of Communication" in Entrepreneur (Vol. 37, October 2009, No. 10, pp. 80)*
Pub: Entrepreneur Press
Contact: Perlman Neil, President
Ed: Brad Feld. Description: Entrepreneurial companies should establish a clear and open communication culture between their management teams and their venture capital backers. Chief executive officers should trust their leadership teams when it comes to communicating with venture capitalists.

38476 ■ *"Live & Learn: Brett Wilson" in Canadian Business (Vol. 81, July 22, 2008, No. 12-13, pp. 80)*
Pub: Rogers Media Inc.
Contact: Tony Viner, President
Ed: Michelle Magnan. Description: Interview with Brett Wilson who believes he became a 'capitalist with a heart' because he had a father who sold cars and a mother who was a social worker. He feels that being accelerated a grade was one of the biggest opportunities and challenges in his life. Brett Wilson's other views on business and on his family are presented.

38477 ■ *"Live & Learn: Dick Evans" in Canadian Business (Vol. 82, April 27, 2009, No. 7, pp. 78)*
Pub: Rogers Media Inc.
Contact: Tony Viner, President
Ed: Sean Silcoff. Description: Former Rio Tinto Alcan chief executive officer Dick Evans believes that the 1982 downturn was worse than the current recession, at least for the mining sector. He also believes that while people are anxious, there is confidence that the economy will recover in two to three years. Key information on Evans, as well as his other views on being a CEO is presented.

38478 ■ *"Donald Tarlton" in Canadian Business (Vol. 80, March 26, 2007, No. 7, pp. 70)*
Pub: Rogers Media Inc.
Contact: Tony Viner, President
Ed: Andy Holloway. Description: Donald Tarlton, owner of Donald K Donald Entertainment Group, shares few things about his childhood and career.

38479 ■ *"Live & Learn: Ian Delaney" in Canadian Business (Vol. 81, Summer 2008, No. 9, pp. 168)*
Pub: Rogers Media Inc.
Contact: Tony Viner, President
Ed: Joe Castaldo. Description: Interview with Ian Delaney who is the executive chairman of chemical company Sherritt International Corp.; Delaney previously worked as chief executive for a holding company owned by Peter Munk. Details of his beliefs, profession and family life are discussed.

38480 ■ *"Laurent Beaudoin" in Canadian Business (Vol. 80, April 9, 2007, No. 8, pp. 68)*
Pub: Rogers Media Inc.
Contact: Tony Viner, President
Ed: Thomas Watson. Description: Chief executive officer of Bombardier Inc., Laurent Beaudoin, talks about his personal life and career.

38481 ■ *"Live & Learn: Maurice Strong" in Canadian Business (Vol. 81, December 8, 2008, No. 21, pp. 70)*
Pub: Rogers Media Inc.
Contact: Tony Viner, President
Ed: Andrew Wahl. Description: Peking University honorary professor Maurice Strong believes that a lot of Westerners, including Canadians, do not take time to understand the business culture in China.

38482 ■ *"Live & Learn: Philip Kives" in Canadian Business (Vol. 79, October 23, 2006, No. 21, pp. 160)*
Pub: Rogers Media Inc.
Contact: Tony Viner, President
Ed: Joe Castaldo. Description: Philip Kives, founder and chief executive officer of K-Tel International Inc. discusses his professional achievements.

38483 ■ *"Local Knowledge" in Hawaii Business (Vol. 53, December 2007, No. 6, pp. 40)*
Ed: David K. Choo. Description: Rules and facts business professionals need to know about the local life in Hawaii are presented. The important components in island life include knowledge Hawaiian high schools' histories and image, the local sports scene, special events, potluck ethics, and locals' favorite destination, which is Las Vegas.

38484 ■ *"Local M&A Activity Sputters in 1Q" in Crain's Chicago Business (Vol. 31, April 21, 2008, No. 16, pp. 20)*
Pub: Crain Communications Inc.
Contact: Todd Johnson, Publisher
Ed: H. Lee Murphy. Description: Local mergers-and-acquisitions activity is down by 34 percent in the first quarter compared to the fourth quarter of last year due to the credit crisis making financing harder to obtain.

38485 ■ *The Logic of Life: The Rational Economics of an Irrational World*
Pub: Ballantine/ Del Rey/Fawcett/Ivy Books
Contact: Gilbert Perlman, President
Ed: Tim Harford. Released: February 10, 2009. Price: $15, paperback; $11.99. Description: Harford excels at making economists' studies palatable for discerning but non-expert readers. The uses hard data to show why promiscuous teens are actually health-conscious, divorce hasn't gotten a fair shake, corporate bosses will always be overpaid and job prospects for minorities continue to be grim. Availability: PrintE-book.

38486 ■ *"Look Before You Lease" in Women Entrepreneur (February 3, 2009)*
Ed: Nina L. Kaufman. Description: Top issues to consider before leasing an office space are discussed including: additional charges that may be expected

on top of the basic rental price; determining both short- and long-term goals; the cost of improvements to the space; the cost of upkeep; and the conditions of the lease.

38487 ■ *"Looking For Financing? The Five Things You Should Know First" in Hispanic Business (Vol. 30, July-August 2008, No. 7-8, pp. 16)*
Pub: Hispanic Business Inc.
Contact: Jesus Chavarria, President
Ed: Frank Nelson. Description: Investment firms want to know about businesses that need funding for either expansion or acquisition; companies fitting this profile are interviewed and their perceptions are discussed. Investment firms need businesses to be realistic in their expectations and business plans which show spending of funds and expected benefits, long term goals, track record and strong management teams.

38488 ■ *"Lost in America? An Economic Slowdown May Be Coming" in Canadian Business (Vol. 79, October 23, 2006, No. 21, pp. 23)*
Pub: Rogers Media Inc.
Contact: Tony Viner, President
Ed: David Wolf. Description: The impact of a decline in the economy of the United States on global economy is analyzed.

38489 ■ *"Lots of Qualified Women, But Few Sit on Boards" in Globe & Mail (March 2, 2006, pp. B1)*
Ed: Virginia Galt. Description: The findings of Catalyst Canada survey on the rise in women executives on boards of directors are presented.

38490 ■ *"Magna Banks on Big Cash Hoard" in Globe & Mail (March 1, 2006, pp. B3)*
Ed: Greg Keenan. Description: The details on Magna International Inc., which posted decline in profits at $639 million for 2005, are presented.

38491 ■ *Make It Big With Yuvi: How to Achieve Poolside Living by Growing Your Small Business*
Pub: AuthorHouse
Contact: Bryan Smith, President
Ed: Ron Peltier. Released: March 23, 2006. Price: $16, softcover. Description: Successful entrepreneurship is profiled.

38492 ■ *Make Your Business Survive and Thrive!: 100+ Proven Marketing Methods to Help You Beat the Odds and Build a Successful Small or Home-Based Enterprise*
Pub: John Wiley & Sons Inc.
Contact: Stephen M. Smith, President
Ed: Priscilla Y. Huff. Released: November 2006. Price: $19.95, paperback; $12.99. Description: Small business and entrepreneurial expert gives information to help small and home-based businesses grow. Availability: PrintE-book.

38493 ■ *"Making Diverse Teams Click" in Harvard Business Review (Vol. 86, July-August 2008, No. 8, pp. 20)*
Pub: Harvard Business Review Press
Contact: Peter E. Walsh, Director
Ed: Jeffrey T. Polzer. Description: 360-degree feedback to increase the efficacy of diverse-member workplace teams, which involves each member providing feedback to the others on the team is discussed.

38494 ■ *"Making Your Mark: Five Steps To Brand Your Success" in Black Enterprise (Vol. 38, November 2007, No. 4, pp. 106)*
Ed: Erinn R. Johnson. Description: Founder of Velvet Suite Marketing Consulting Group, Melissa D. Johnson, assists clients in building brands. Johnson offers tips to develop and build a sold brand in her new book, 'Brand Me! Make Your Mark: Turn Passion Into Profit'.

38495 ■ *"Managing Corporate Social Networks"* in *Harvard Business Review (Vol. 86, July-August 2008, No. 8, pp. 26)*
Pub: Harvard Business Review Press
Contact: Peter E. Walsh, Director
Ed: Adam M. Kleinbaum, Michael L. Tushman. **Description:** Tips on how to promote business creativity and foster knowledge building through business social networks are given.

38496 ■ *Managing Labour in Small Firms*
Pub: Routledge
Contact: Kevin Bradley, President
E-mail: kbradley@taylorandfrancis.com
Released: November 25, 2004. **Price:** $180, hardback. **Description:** Essays addressing conditions of workers in small business. **Availability:** Print.

38497 ■ *Managing a Small Business Made Easy*
Pub: Entrepreneur Press
Contact: Perlman Neil, President
Ed: Martin E. Davis. **Released:** September 2005.
Description: Examination of the essential elements for an entrepreneur running a business, including advice on leadership, customer service, financials, and more.

38498 ■ *"Many Sectors Lost Jobs In Detroit Area, State"* in *Crain's Detroit Business (Vol. 24, February 11, 2008, No. 6, pp. 3)*
Pub: Crain Communications Inc. - Detroit
Contact: Keith Crain, Chairman
Ed: Amy Lane. **Description:** Southeast Michigan reported its highest jobless rate since 1992 in fourth quarter 2007. Statistical data included.

38499 ■ *"Market Forces"* in *Canadian Business (Vol. 79, October 23, 2006, No. 21, pp. 93)*
Ed: Erin Pooley. **Description:** The tremendous rise in the number of business schools offering Master of business administration degree in Canada and the depletion in the quality of education provided in these business schools is discussed.

38500 ■ *The Martha Rules: 10 Essentials for Achieving Success as You Start, Build, or Manage a Business*
Ed: Martha Stewart. **Released:** October 2006. **Price:** , $15.95. **Description:** Martha Stewart offers insight into starting, building and managing a successful business.

38501 ■ *The Martha Rules: 10 Essentials for Achieving Success as You Start, Grow, or Manage a Business*
Ed: Martha Stewart. **Released:** October 2005.

38502 ■ *"Mary Kramer: Good Things Happen When We Buy Local"* in *Crain's Detroit Business (Vol. 24, October 6, 2008, No. 40, pp. 7)*
Pub: Crain Communications Inc.
Contact: Rance E. Crain, President
Description: Michigan is facing incredibly difficult economic times. One way in which each one of us can help the state and the businesses located here is by purchasing our goods and services from local vendors. The state Agriculture Department projected that if Michigan households earmarked $10 per week in their grocery purchases to made-in-Michigan products, this would generate $30 million a week in economic impact.

38503 ■ *Mastering Business Growth and Change Made Easy*
Pub: Entrepreneur Press
Contact: Perlman Neil, President
Ed: Jeffrey A. Hansen. **Released:** October 2005.
Description: Tips for growing a small business, regardless of state or environment.

38504 ■ *"MBA Essentials: Real-Life Instruction"* in *Women In Business (Vol. 61, October-November 2009, No. 5, pp. 28)*
Pub: American Business Women's Association
Contact: Lorie Burch, President
Ed: Leigh Elmore. **Description:** University of Kansas School of Business allied itself with the American Business Women's Association (ABWA) which led to

the formation of the ABWA-KU MBA essentials program. With this program, ABWA members are exposed to graduate-level coursework that delves on business topics, such as strategy and operations.

38505 ■ *"MBT Add-On: Gone by 2012?"* in *Crain's Detroit Business (Vol. 24, October 6, 2008, No. 40, pp. 1)*
Pub: Crain Communications Inc.
Contact: Rance E. Crain, President
Ed: Amy Lane. **Description:** Discusses the Michigan Business Tax (MBT), which has angered many businesses in the state due to the addition of a 21.99 percent surcharge. Although the tax policy will cut taxes on 63 percent of businesses in the state and represent no tax liability change for another nine percent of firms, other businesses will see increases of 100 percent or more. This increase means that many business owners will be forced to relocate or close their establishment and others will have to eliminate jobs. Lawmakers are attempting to find a solution to this problem.

38506 ■ *"MBT 'Sticker Shock' Surprises Business; Reaction? 'You Can't Print It,' Owner Says"* in *Crain's Detroit Business (March 16, 2008)*
Pub: Crain Communications Inc.
Contact: Rance E. Crain, President
Ed: Amy Lane. **Description:** Overview of the new Michigan Business Tax which is raising many middle-sized businesses' taxes by up to 400 percent.

38507 ■ *"McClatchy Believed Front-Runner in Knight Ridder Sale"* in *Globe & Mail (March 13, 2006, pp. B6)*
Ed: Joseph T. Hallinan; Dennis K. Berman. **Description:** The details on proposed acquisition of Knight Ridder Inc. by McClatchy Co. are presented.

38508 ■ *"Measure Your Business Plan Results"* in *Entrepreneur (January 6, 2009)*
Pub: Entrepreneur Press
Contact: Perlman Neil, President
Ed: Tim Berry. **Description:** Although no business plan is ever right on target, it is still essential for every business owner to create one; the way in which to analyze the actual results compared to the plan are discussed.

38509 ■ *"Measuring Success In Family Businesses: The Concept of Configurational Fit"* in *Family Business Review (Vol. 19, No. 2, June 2006, pp. 115)*
Pub: Family Firm Institute
Contact: Judy L. Green, President
Ed: Christoph Hienerth, Alexander Kessler. **Description:** Strategic benchmarking, which are used to examine business success of family-owned enterprises are investigated.

38510 ■ *Medium-Sized Firms and Economic Growth*
Pub: Nova Science Publishers Inc.
Contact: Frank Columbus, President
Ed: Janez Prasniker. **Released:** April 2005. **Price:** $117, hardcover. **Description:** Medium sized companies should have a more definitive presence in modern microeconomic theory, the theory of entrepreneurship, and the theory of financial markets. **Availability:** Print.

38511 ■ *Memos to the Prime Minister: What Canada Could Be in the 21st Century*
Ed: Harvey Schacter. **Released:** April 11, 2003.
Price: , $16.95. **Description:** A look into the business future of Canada. Topics include business, healthcare, think tanks, policy groups, education, the arts, economy, and social issues.

38512 ■ *Microtrends*
Ed: Mark J. Pen with E. Kinney Zalesne. **Released:** September 2007. **Price:** $25.99. **Description:** Detecting small patterns the great impact they can have on business.

38513 ■ *"The Middle Ages"* in *Hawaii Business (Vol. 53, October 2007, No. 4, pp. 42)*
Pub: PacificBasin Communications
Ed: Cathy S. Cruz-George. **Description:** Starcom Builders Inc.'s Theodore 'Ted' Taketa, School Kine Cookies' Steven Gold And Sharon Serene of Sharon Serene Creative are among the participants in Hawaii's Fittest CEO competition for executives over 50 years old. Taketa takes yoga classes, and also goes to the gym while Serne has Mike Hann as her professional trainer. Eating habits of the aforementioned executives are also described.

38514 ■ *"Mind the Gap"* in *Canadian Business (Vol. 80, November 5, 2007, No. 22, pp. 21)*
Ed: Matthew McCleam. **Description:** The average difference in median wages between men and women who have full-time jobs, according to the Organization Co-operation and Development is over 15 percent and that number is above 20 percent in Canada. The difference in earnings has become smaller since the 1960s, as more women have joined the labor market. The reasons for the wage gap are examined.

38515 ■ *"Molson Coors Ends Ill-Fated Foray Into Brazil"* in *Globe & Mail (January 17, 2006, pp. B1)*
Pub: CTVglobemedia Publishing Inc.
Ed: Andy Hoffman. **Description:** The details of loss incurred by Molson Coors Brewing Co., from the sale of Cervejarias Kaiser SA to Fomento Economico Mexicano S.A. de C.V., are presented.

38516 ■ *"More Than a Feeling"* in *Entrepreneur (Vol. 36, April 2008, No. 4, pp. 10)*
Ed: Rieva Lesonsky. **Description:** It is said that emotion has no place when it comes to business matters, but it may not be the case as entrepreneurs and other people in business feel passionate about what they do. Emotions can help bring out a positive outlook in them. Other details on the topic are discussed.

38517 ■ *"Most See Gloomy Year For Michigan Business"* in *Crain's Detroit Business (Vol. 24, October 6, 2008, No. 40, pp. 4)*
Pub: Crain Communications Inc.
Contact: Rance E. Crain, President
Ed: Amy Lane. **Description:** Michigan residents are extremely concerned about the economic climate and business conditions in the state. According to the latest quarterly State of the State Survey, conducted by Michigan State University's Institute for Public Policy and Social Research, 63.9 percent of those surveyed anticipate bad times for Michigan businesses over the next year. Additional findings from the survey are also included.

38518 ■ *Never Bet the Farm: How Entrepreneurs Take Risks, Make Decisions - and How You Can, Too*
Pub: Jossey-Bass Publishers
Contact: Matthew Hoover, Manager
E-mail: fwelsch@jbp.com
Released: March 2006. **Price:** $24.95, paperback; $16.99. **Availability:** PrintE-book.

38519 ■ *"New BMO Boss Set to Cut 1,000 Jobs"* in *Globe & Mail (February 1, 2007, pp. B3)*
Ed: Andrew Willis. **Description:** The decision of the new chief executive officer of the Bank of Montreal, Bill Downe, to cut down 1,000 jobs, to boost the company's performance is discussed.

38520 ■ *"A New Era for Raiders"* in *Harvard Business Review (Vol. 88, November 2010, No. 11, pp. 34)*
Pub: Harvard Business School Publishing
Ed: Guhan Subramanian. **Description:** The article presents evidence that Section 203 is vulnerable, and a new wave of corporate takeovers may develop.

The authors suggest that since no bidders have able to use the 85 percent stipulation over the last 19 years, it does not present a meaningful opportunity for success.

38521 ■ *No Man's Land: A Survival Manual for Growing Midsize Companies*
Pub: Penguin Group USA
Contact: Phyllis Grann, President
Ed: Doug Tatum. **Released:** January 13, 2009. **Price:** $16, paperback. **Description:** Tips for managing a small business.

38522 ■ *No Man's Land: What to Do When Your Company Is Too Big to Be Small but Too Small to Be Big*
Ed: Doug Tatum. **Released:** September 13, 2007. **Price:** $24.95. **Description:** Insight to help fast-growing companies navigate the fatal trap of no-man's land, a perilous zone where they have outgrown the habits and practices that fueled their early growth but have not yet adopted new practices and resources in order to cope with new situations and challenges.

38523 ■ *"Northern Overexposure" in Canadian Business (Vol. 79, August 14, 2006, No. 16-17, pp. 36)*
Pub: Rogers Media Inc.
Contact: Tony Viner, President
Ed: Calvin Leung. **Description:** Fall in revenue from foreign film productions in Canada due to its overexposure, and incentives offered by other nations to foreign film productions, are discussed.

38524 ■ *"Not Your Dad's Business Card" in Small Business Opportunities (July 2008)*
Ed: Rob Schlacter. **Description:** Provides tips on how to effectively design and use business cards.

38525 ■ *"Note to Leonard: Swim Fast" in Canadian Business (Vol. 80, January 15, 2007, No. 2, pp. 29)*
Ed: Zena Olijnyk. **Description:** The decision of CanWest Entertainment Inc and Goldman Sachs Capital Partners to collectively acquire Toronto-based Alliance Atlantis Communications Inc. is discussed.

38526 ■ *"Nothing But Net: Fran Harris Offers Advice On Winning the Game of Business" in Black Enterprise (Vol. 38, March 1, 2008, No. 8, pp. 50)*
Pub: Earl G. Graves Publishing Co. Inc.
Contact: Earl G. Graves, Jr., President
Ed: Chana Garcia. **Description:** Fran Harris, certified life coach, business consultant, and CEO of her business, a multimedia development company, reveals five tips to ensure entrepreneurial success.

38527 ■ *"Ocean Choice in Running to Acquire Assets of FPI" in Globe & Mail (March 15, 2007, pp. B9)*
Pub: CTVglobemedia Publishing Inc.
Contact: Keith McArthur. **Description:** Ocean Choice International is bidding vigorously for acquiring assets St. Johns based of FPI Ltd. Complete details of these bids are discussed.

38528 ■ *Off-Ramps and On-Ramps: Keeping Talented Women on the Road to Success*
Pub: Harvard Business Review Press
Contact: Peter E. Walsh, Director
Ed: Sylvia Ann Hewlett. **Released:** May 15, 2007. **Price:** $29.95, hardcover. **Description:** Hewlett (founding president for the Center for Work-Life Policy) examines why many women exit their careers, taking 'off-ramps' (leaving altogether) or 'scenic routes' (opting to work part-time), often during critical, competitive times. She also provides valuable suggestions for companies hoping to retain talented employees of any gender. **Availability:** Print.

38529 ■ *"Office Party Attire" in Women In Business (Vol. 61, October-November 2009, No. 5, pp. 27)*
Pub: American Business Women's Association
Contact: Lorie Burch, President
Ed: Leigh Elmore. **Description:** Office holiday party attire should conform to factors such as time, location, scheduled events, and other company-furnished

details. Observing this guideline can help in upholding the business nature of the party. Party attendees are also encouraged to network with other attendees, while tips on how to behave during the party are also presented.

38530 ■ *"Office Pests" in Canadian Business (Vol. 79, October 9, 2006, No. 20, pp. 122)*
Ed: Calvin Leung. **Description:** Personality traits of employees and strategies for managers to effectively handle them are discussed.

38531 ■ *"O'Malley, Ehrlich Court Business Vote" in Baltimore Business Journal (Vol. 28, October 1, 2010, No. 21, pp. 1)*
Pub: Baltimore Business Journal
Ed: Scott Dance. **Description:** Maryland Governor Martin O'Malley and former Governor Robert Ehrlich reveal their business plans and platforms as they court business-minded votes in the state. Ehrlich, a Republican and O'Malley, a Democrat have both initiated programs that helped small businesses, but both have also introduced programs that made it more expensive and difficult to do business in the state.

38532 ■ *"Omniplex on the Case" in Black Enterprise (Vol. 37, December 2006, No. 5, pp. 38)*
Pub: Earl G. Graves Publishing Co. Inc.
Contact: Earl G. Graves, Jr., President
Ed: Glenn Townes. **Description:** Office of Personnel Management in Washington D.C. recently awarded a service contract to Omniplex World Services Corp. This Virginia-based company will perform security investigations and background checks on current and prospective federal employees and military personnel and contractors.

38533 ■ *"On Track" in Canadian Business (Vol. 79, July 17, 2006, No. 14-15, pp. 51)*
Pub: Rogers Media Inc.
Contact: Tony Viner, President
Ed: John Gray. **Description:** Results of the annual survey conducted by CanadaEs boards, to measure the levels of corporate governance of firms in Canada, which are presented.

38534 ■ *101 Secrets to Building a Winning Business*
Pub: Allen & Unwin Pty. Ltd.
Contact: Paul Donovan, Managing Director
Ed: Andrew Griffiths. **Released:** July 2008. **Price:** A$24.99, paperback. **Description:** Provides expert information for running and growing a small business. **Availability:** Print.

38535 ■ *"One Hundred Years of Excellence in Business Education: What Have We Learned?" in Business Horizons (January-February 2008)*
Pub: Elsevier Advanced Technology Publications
Ed: Frank Acito, Patricia M. McDougall, Daniel C. Smith. **Description:** Business schools have to be more innovative, efficient and nimble, so that the quality of the next generation of business leaders is improved. The Kelley School of Business, Indiana University ahs long been a leader in business education. The trends that influence the future of business education and useful success principles are discussed.

38536 ■ *Organizations Alive!: Six Things That Challenge - Seven That Bring Success*
Pub: Yuill & Associates
Ed: Jan Yuill. **Price:** C$18.95, paperback. **Description:** New insight into understanding how organizations function as individuals is presented by an international consultant. Customer service, resource management, outsourcing, and management are among the issues covered.

38537 ■ *"Our Gadget of the Week: Business Buddy" in Barron's (Vol. 88, July 7, 2008, No. 27, pp. 26)*
Pub: Dow Jones & Co., Inc.
Contact: Clare Hart, President
Ed: Jay Palmer. **Description:** Review and evaluation of the Lenovo X300 laptop computer which offers executives a variety of features despite its smaller

size and weight. The laptop is about 0.73 inch thick, comes with a 64-gigabyte solid-state drive from Samsung, and weighs less than three pounds.

38538 ■ *Outfoxing the Small Business Owner*
Ed: Gene Marks. **Released:** January 2005. **Description:** Special skill sets are required to sell, service or deal with small business customers.

38539 ■ *Outliers: The Story of Success*
Pub: Little, Brown and Company
Ed: Malcolm Gladwell. **Released:** November 18, 2008. **Price:** $30, hardcover; C$33, hardcover; $9.99. **Description:** The book explores reasons for individual success. **Availability:** PrintE-book.

38540 ■ *"Overview - Small Business Optimism" in Small Business Economic Trends (April 2008, pp. 4)*
Ed: William C. Dunkelberg, Holly Wade. **Description:** Graph and table representing the optimism index for small businesses in the U.S., based on ten survey indicators, are presented. The index values include data from 1986 to 2008.

38541 ■ *"Overview - Small Business Optimism" in Small Business Economic Trends (July 2009, pp. 4)*
Pub: National Federation of Independent Business
Contact: Caitlin McDevitt, Program Manager
Ed: William C. Dunkelberg, Holly Wade. **Description:** Small businesses surveyed in the United States regarding their optimism index from 1986 to 2009 shows a marked difference as is presented in a graph. A small business optimism index from January 2004 to June 2009 is also given in tabular form. The index value was seasonally adjusted at 1986=100.

38542 ■ *Own Your Own Corporation: Why the Rich Own Their Own Companies and Everyone Else Works for Them*
Pub: Business Plus
Ed: Garrett Sutton; Robert T. Kiyosaki; Ann Blackman. **Released:** June 2008. **Price:** , $17.99 paperback. **Description:** Part of the Rich Dad Advisor's Series, this edition shows how individuals can incorporate themselves and their businesses to save thousands of dollars in taxes and protect against financial disaster.

38543 ■ *"Owning the Right Risks" in Harvard Business Review (Vol. 86, September 2008, No. 9, pp. 102)*
Pub: Harvard Business Review Press
Contact: Peter E. Walsh, Director
Ed: Kevin Buehler, Andrew Freeman, Ron Hulme. **Description:** TXU Corp. is used to illustrate methods for successful risk management. The electric utility's practices include determining which risks are natural, embedding risk in all processes and decisions, and organizing corporate governance around risk.

38544 ■ *The Oxford Handbook of Entrepreneurship*
Pub: Oxford University Press
Contact: Niko Pfund, President
Released: August 15, 2008. **Price:** $62, paperback. **Description:** Research covering entrepreneurship is presented by an international team of leading scholars. **Availability:** Print.

38545 ■ *"Pau Hana" in Hawaii Business (Vol. 53, December 2007, No. 6, pp. 118)*
Pub: PacificBasin Communications
Ed: Cathy S. Cruz-George. **Description:** Presented are the hobbies of four Hawaii executives as well as the reason these hobbies are an important part of their lives and add to their ability to manage effectively. Mike Wilkins, for example, is not only Turtle Bay Resort's director of sales and marketing, but is also a glider pilot, while Aubrey Hawk Public Relations president Aubrey Hawk loves baking. The interests of Queen Liliuokalani Trust's Thomas K. Kaulukukui Jr., Reyn Spooner's Tim McCullough, and Heide and Cook Ltd.'s Dexter S. Kekua, are discussed.

38546 ■ "People and Places" in Entrepreneur (Vol. 36, February 2008, No. 2, pp. 12)
Ed: Rieva Lesonsky. Description: Websites of different organizations that can provide entrepreneurs with business help are presented. Business-related events such as the Women in Charge conference and Xerox Smart Business Symposium are mentioned.

38547 ■ "Personal File: Dean Williams" in Canadian Business (Vol. 80, April 23, 2007, No. 9, pp. 55)
Description: A brief profile of Dean Williams, architect at Softchoice Corp., including his services to the company, is presented.

38548 ■ Petty Capitalists and Globalization: Flexibility, Entrepreneurship, and Economic Development
Pub: State University of New York Press
Contact: James Peltz, Director
E-mail: james.peltz@sunypress.edu
Price: $29.95, paperback; $70, hardcover. Description: Investigation into ways small businesses in Europe, Asia, and Latin America are required to operate and compete in the fast-growing transnational economy. Availability: Print.

38549 ■ "Pick A Trademark You Can Protect" in Women Entrepreneur (November 3, 2008)
Ed: Nina L. Kaufman. Description: Provides information regarding trademarks, how to choose a name that will win approval from the U.S. Patent and Trademark Office, and how to choose a trademark that one can protect.

38550 ■ A Piece of the Pie
Pub: Outskirts Press Inc.
Contact: Brent Sampson, President
Released: July 2005. Description: Examination of the U.S. Small Business Administration's program 8(a), designed to help disadvantaged individuals grow their small businesses.

38551 ■ "Pioneers Get All The Perks" in Canadian Business (Vol. 81, March 3, 2008, No. 3, pp. 18)
Description: Suncor Energy Inc. will face royalty payments from 25% to 30% of net profits as it signs a new deal with Alberta. Biovail Corp., meanwhile, is under a U.S. grand jury investigation for supposed improprieties in Cardizem LA heart drug launch. The Conference Board of Canada's proposal to impose taxes on greenhouse gas emissions and other developments in the business community are discussed.

38552 ■ "Plan: Put Health Centers in ERs" in Crain's Detroit Business (Vol. 25, June 22, 2009, No. 25, pp. 1)
Pub: Crain Communications Inc. - Detroit
Contact: Keith Crain, Chairman
Ed: Jay Greene. Description: It has been suggested by top CEOs in the Detroit, Michigan area to put satellites of federally qualified health centers within emergency room departments. The plan would have the health centers pay a monthly fee for each patient treated.

38553 ■ The Platinum Rule for Small Business Success
Ed: Scott Zimmerman; Tony Allesandra; Ron Finklestein. Released: August 2006. Description: Rules for running a successful and profitable small business are shared.

38554 ■ "Playing to Win" in Entrepreneur (Vol. 36, May 2008, No. 5, pp. 40)
Pub: Entrepreneur Press
Contact: Perlman Neil, President
Ed: Robert Kiyosaki. Description: Four personality types needed by entrepreneurs to drive their leadership in business are given. 'I must be liked' are social directors and go-betweens; 'I must be comfortable' are those who seek job security and are not at ease with deadlines; I must be right are those strong in opinion; and 'I must win' are people in charge.

38555 ■ Poker Winners are Different
Pub: Kensington Publishing Corp.
Contact: Steven Zacharius, President
E-mail: szacharius@atskensingtonbooks.com
Ed: Alan N. Schoonmaker. Released: 2009. Price: $11.17, Paperback. Description: Poker success requires reading the context and reading people, two skills every entrepreneur needs to possess.

38556 ■ "Polanco Fellows: A Capital Program that Changes Lives" in Hispanic Business (Vol. 30, September 2008, No. 9, pp. 82)
Pub: Hispanic Business Inc.
Contact: Jesus Chavarria, President
Ed: John Schumacher. Description: Launched in 2003, the Polanco fellows program is named after former state Senator Richard Polanco, a founder and chairman of the California Latino Caucus Institute. The program offers young Hispanics a chance to experience public policy and the functioning of the California Capitol through a 12-month, on-the-job Capitol training.

38557 ■ PPC's Guide to Compensation Planning for Small Business
Pub: Thomson Reuters
Contact: Rich Alsano, President
Released: Annual. Price: $165; $180. Description: Technical guide for developing a compensation system for small business. Forms and letters included. Availability: Print; DVDOnline.

38558 ■ "The Preparation Gap" in Hawaii Business (Vol. 53, February 2008, No. 8, pp. 37)
Pub: PacificBasin Communications
Ed: Ashley Hamershock. Description: Discussion of the educational gap in Hawaii's workforce is being addressed by educational workshops that aim to improve students' knowledge in science, technology, math, and engineering, and prepare them for their entry into the workforce. Education beyond high school is required for jobs to be filled in the coming years.

38559 ■ Prepare for the Worst, Plan for the Best: Disaster Preparedness and Recovery for Small Businesses
Pub: John Wiley & Sons Inc.
Contact: Stephen M. Smith, President
Ed: Donna R. Childs. Released: 2nd Edition. Price: $24.95, paperback; $44.95, hardcover. Description: Guide to help small businesses protect themselves from disasters. New information is presented on Redundant Arrays of Independent Disk (RAID) hardware backups, calling trees and the Internet, power outages and suppliers, as well as wireless networks. Availability: Print.

38560 ■ Prescriptive Entrepreneurship
Pub: Edward Elgar Publishing Inc.
Contact: Richard Henning, Vice President
E-mail: kwight@e-elgar.com
Ed: James O. Fiet. Released: 2010. Price: £22.40, paperback. Description: In the only known program of prescriptive entrepreneurship, the author provides a marked contrast to the standard descriptive focus of entrepreneurship studies. Availability: Print.

38561 ■ Principles of Private Firm Valuation
Pub: John Wiley & Sons Inc.
Contact: Stephen M. Smith, President
Ed: Stanley J. Feldman. Released: March 2005. Price: $84.95, hardcover. Description: Tools and techniques to correctly perform private firm valuation, including value and how to measure it, valuing control, determining the size of the marketability discount, creating transparency and the implications for value, the value of tax pass-through entities versus a C corporation, etc. Availability: Print.

38562 ■ Print Solutions--Buyers' Guide Issue
Pub: Print Services and Distribution Association
Contact: Robert Whitman, President
URL(s): www.psda.org/?page=nmk_annbuygu. Released: Annual; October; Latest edition 2011. Price: $49, Individuals. Publication includes: List of about 600 suppliers of business forms and other business printing, such as ad specialties, bar-coded forms & labels, commercial printing calendars, tags, cards, labels, and printed stationery. Entries include: name, address, phone, fax, capabilities, product/service. Arrangement: Alphabetical. Indexes: Product/service.

38563 ■ "Priority: In Memoriam" in Inc. (December 2007, pp. 25-26, 28, 30)
Pub: Gruner and Jahr USA Publishing Co.
Contact: J. Russell Denson, President
Ed: Ryan McCarthy. Description: Profiles of entrepreneurs who died in 2007; these individuals helped to create some major business trends in the last fifty years, from the advent of socially responsible business to development of quality manufacturing.

38564 ■ "Private Equity Party Fuelled by Cheap Debt" in Globe & Mail (February 27, 2007, pp. B1)
Ed: Sinclair Stewart. Description: The funding of private equity fund Kohlberg Kravis through cheap debt, during the buyout of the TXU Corp. is discussed.

38565 ■ "Profit Predictions Look Too Plump" in Barron's (Vol. 88, March 31, 2008, No. 13, pp. 37)
Ed: Johanna Bennett. Description: Full-year forecast points to a 14 percent gain for 2008 but the second-half profit increases would have to grow at a fast rate and peak at 61 percent in the fourth quarter to achieve this. Trends in the U.S. economic conditions are also discussed.

38566 ■ Project Management for Small Business Made Easy
Pub: Entrepreneur Press
Contact: Perlman Neil, President
Ed: Sid Kemp. Released: 2006. Description: Strategies for implementing project management for small business are offered.

38567 ■ Purple Cow: Transform Your Business by Being Remarkable
Pub: Dutton Children's Books
Contact: Lauri Hornik, President
Ed: Seth Godin. Released: November 12, 2009. Price: $22.95, hardcover; $17.99. Description: Being a purple cow means you are exciting, phenomenal and unforgettable, the traits required to be a successful entrepreneur. Availability: PrintElectronic publishing.

38568 ■ The Pursuit of Happyness
Pub: HarperCollins Publishers Inc.
Contact: Jane Friedman, President
E-mail: jfriedman@harpercollins.com
Ed: Chris Gardner. Price: $25.99, hardcover; $14.99, paperback; $10.99; C$11.99. Description: Rags-to-riches saga of a homeless father who raised and cared for his son on the streets of San Francisco and worked to become a powerful leader on Wall Street. Availability: PrintE-book.

38569 ■ Put Your Business on Autopilot: The 7-Step System to Create a Business That Works So Well That You Don't Have To
Pub: Morgan James Publishing L.L.C.
Contact: Neil Gudovitz, Director
Ed: Greg Roworth. Released: April 01, 2009. Description: Failure rates still remain as high as 80 percent within five years of starting a small business despite the hard work by their owners. The author suggests that working harder doesn't necessarily equate to a successful enterprise.

38570 ■ "Randy Perreira, Hawaii Government Employees Association (HGEA), Executive Director" in Hawaii Business (Vol. 53, February 2008, No. 8, pp. 28)
Pub: PacificBasin Communications
Ed: David K. Choo. Description: Randy Perreira is recently named executive director of Hawaii Government Employees Association. He talks about how he was shaped growing up with a father who was a labor leader and how the challenges in 2008 compare with those in the time of his father. He also shares his thoughts about the importance of employees fighting for their rights.

38571 ■ *Re-Imagine! Business Excellence in a Disruptive Age*

Ed: Tom Peters. **Released:** 2006. **Price:** $20. **Description:** Examination of today's business order. Peters urges business owners to re-imagine business.

38572 ■ *"Reaching Your Potential" in Harvard Business Review (Vol. 86, July-August 2008, No. 8, pp. 45)*

Pub: Harvard Business Review Press

Contact: Peter E. Walsh, Director

Ed: Robert S. Kaplan. **Description:** Being proactive in developing one's career is an important part of entrepreneurship. Keys to successful development include knowing oneself and one's goals, and taking calculated risks.

38573 ■ *"The Real Job of Boards" in Business Strategy Review (Vol. 21, Autumn 2010, No. 3, pp. 36)*

Pub: John Wiley & Sons Inc. Scientific, Technical, Medical, and Scholarly Div. (Wiley-Blackwell)

Contact: William J. Pesce, Manager

E-mail: wpesce@wiley.com

Ed: Harry Korine, Marcus Alexander, Pierre-Yves Gomez. **Description:** Widely seen as the key for ensuring quality in corporate governance, the board of directors has been a particular focal point for reform. The authors believe that more leadership at board level could avert many corporate crises in the future.

38574 ■ *Reality Check: The Irreverent Guide to Outsmarting, Outmanaging, and Outmarketing Your Competition*

Pub: Dutton Children's Books

Contact: Lauri Hornik, President

Ed: Guy Kawasaki. **Price:** $18, Paperback. **Description:** Marketing guru and entrepreneur, Guy Kawasaki, provides a compilation of his blog posts on all aspects of starting and operating a business.

38575 ■ *"Recession Drags Down CEO Pay: Full Impact May Not Have Played Out" in Crain's Detroit Business (Vol. 25, June 22, 2009, No. 25)*

Pub: Crain Communications Inc. - Detroit

Contact: Keith Crain, Chairman

Ed: Ryan Beene. **Description:** Median overall compensation package for Detroit's top-compensated 50 CEOs was down 10.67 percent from $2.3 million in 2007 to $2.06 million in 2008. Statistical data included.

38576 ■ *"The Recession: Problem or Opportunity" in Women In Business (Vol. 61, October-November 2009, No. 5, pp. 34)*

Pub: American Business Women's Association

Contact: Lorie Burch, President

Ed: J. Douglas Bate. **Description:** Business organizations' success during a recession is based on how management views the economic situation. The recession may be deemed as a setback or may be visualized as an opportunity that has to be grabbed for the organization. Suggestions on what management should do in the opportunity-creating or proactive approach are also highlighted.

38577 ■ *"Reduce the Risk of Failed Financial Judgments" in Harvard Business Review (Vol. 86, July-August 2008, No. 8, pp. 24)*

Pub: Harvard Business Review Press

Contact: Peter E. Walsh, Director

Ed: Robert G. Eccles, Edward J. Riedl. **Description:** Utilization of business consultants, evaluators, appraisers, and actuaries to decrease financial management risks is discussed.

38578 ■ *"Region and City Need Influx of Youth" in Crain's Detroit Business (Vol. 24, April 14, 2008, No. 15, pp. 8)*

Pub: Crain Communications Inc.

Contact: Rance E. Crain, President

Description: Discusses an upcoming report from Michigan Future Inc. which finds that young professionals, including those with children, are interested

in living in an active urban environment. It also states that because many of those young professionals are entrepreneurial in nature, oftentimes businesses follow.

38579 ■ *"Relocation, Relocation, Relocation" in Conde Nast Portfolio (Vol. 2, June 2008, No. 6, pp. 36)*

Ed: Michelle Leder. **Description:** Perks regarding executive relocation are discussed.

38580 ■ *"A Research Firm With More Than One Foe" in Globe & Mail (February 24, 2006, pp. B1)*

Ed: Shawn McCarthy. **Description:** The details of Biovail Corp.'s securities fraud case against Gradient Analytics Inc. are presented.

38581 ■ *Resource and Environmental Management in Canada*

Pub: Oxford University Press

Contact: Niko Pfund, President

Ed: Bruce Mitchell. **Released:** Fourth Edition. **Price:** $49.95, paperback. **Description:** Discusses resource management in Canada, focusing on business and industry, environmental groups, First Nations, the public, local communities with resource-based economies. **Availability:** Print.

38582 ■ *The RFA at 25: Needed Improvements for Small Business Regulatory Relief*

Pub: U. S. Government Printing Office

Contact: Veronica Meter, Director

E-mail: tpriebe@gpo.gov

Description: Information regarding the hearing on needed improvements for small business regulatory relief before the Committee on Small Business, House of Representatives, One Hundred Ninth Congress, First Session, Washington, DC, March 16, 2005 is provided.

38583 ■ *"The Rich 100" in Canadian Business (Vol. 79, Winter 2006, No. 24, pp. 78)*

Pub: Rogers Media Inc.

Contact: Tony Viner, President

Description: The rankings of the 100 richest billionaires in Canada are presented, along with the description of their achievements and their net worth.

38584 ■ *"The Right Stuff" in Canadian Business (Vol. 79, October 23, 2006, No. 21, pp. 151)*

Ed: Laura Bogomolny. **Description:** The profile of Linda Duxbury, the winner of the Sprott MBA Students Society 2003-04 Best teacher award as well as Carleton University Students' Association 2002-03 award, is presented.

38585 ■ *Risk Takers and Innovators, Great Canadian Business Ventures Since 1950*

Pub: Altitude Publishing

Ed: Sandra Phinney. **Released:** June 15, 2004. **Price:** , $7.95. **Description:** Successful business leaders share their creativity, technology skills, and entrepreneurship.

38586 ■ *The Road from Ruin: How to Revive Capitalism and Put America Back on Top*

Pub: Crown Business

Ed: Matthew Bishop, Michael Green. **Released:** November 29, 2011. **Price:** $15, paperback. **Description:** Authors show why American companies must respond to the economic crisis with long term vision and a renewed emphasis on values. **Availability:** Print.

38587 ■ *"Rob Ritchie" in Canadian Business (Vol. 80, January 15, 2007, No. 2, pp. 70)*

Ed: Michelle Magnan. **Description:** The former president of the Canadian Pacific Railway, Rob Ritchie, reveals facts about his personal and professional life.

38588 ■ *"Sage Advice" in Canadian Business (Vol. 80, October 22, 2007, No. 21, pp. 70)*

Ed: John Gray. **Description:** Seymour Schulich, one of Canada's richest men and generous philanthropist, wrote the book, 'Get Smarter: Life and Business Lessons'. The business book sold more than 50,000 cop-

ies and now sits on Canada's bestseller's list. Its popularity is attributed to the marketing efforts of the entrepreneur and author.

38589 ■ *Save Your Small Business: 10 Crucial Strategies to Survive Hard Times or Close Down & Move On*

Pub: Nolo

Contact: Ralph Warner, Chief Executive Officer

Ed: Ralph Warner, Bethany Laurence. **Price:** $23.99; $20.99. **Description:** According to a study among 500 businesses, 44 percent used credit cards in order to meet their firm's needs in the previous six months. Written by a business owner, this book provides twelve strategies to protect personal assets from creditors and survive the current recession. **Availability:** PrintE-book.

38590 ■ *"Say Goodbye to Shy" in Canadian Business (Vol. 79, September 11, 2006, No. 18, pp. 125)*

Pub: Rogers Media Inc.

Contact: Tony Viner, President

Ed: Alex Mlynek. **Description:** Tips and practices for effective communications at workplaces are presented.

38591 ■ *"Say No to Slackers" in Canadian Business (Vol. 79, November 6, 2006, No. 22, pp. 105)*

Pub: Rogers Media Inc.

Contact: Tony Viner, President

Ed: Erin Pooley. **Description:** The effects of underperformers on performance of other colleagues with relation to company productivity are analyzed.

38592 ■ *"Scotiabank Tapped as Likely Buyer in Puerto Rico" in Globe & Mail (January 30, 2007, pp. B3)*

Ed: Andrew Willis. **Description:** Speculation over Bank of Nova Scotia's proposed acquisition of First BanCorp is discussed.

38593 ■ *"The Search for Big Oil" in Canadian Business (Vol. 80, April 9, 2007, No. 8, pp. 10)*

Ed: Joe Castaldo. **Description:** The continuing effort of Canmex Minerals Corp. to explore for oil in Somalia despite the failure of several other companies is discussed.

38594 ■ *The Secret of Exiting Your Business Under Your Terms!*

Ed: Gene H. Irwin. **Released:** August 2005. **Price:** , $29.95. **Description:** Topics include how to sell a business for the highest value, tax laws governing the sale of a business, finding the right buyer, mergers and acquisitions, negotiating the sale, and using a limited auction to increase future value of a business.

38595 ■ *"The Secret's Out About Kansas City" in Women In Business (Vol. 61, August-September 2009, No. 4, pp. 26)*

Pub: American Business Women's Association

Contact: Lorie Burch, President

Ed: Leigh Elmore. **Description:** Missouri's Kansas City offers various attractions, such as public fountains, the 18th and Vine Historic Districts for jazz enthusiasts, and the Crossroads Arts District with a variety of art galleries. Details on other cultural attractions and neighborhoods in the city are presented.

38596 ■ *"Secrets To Trade Show Success" in Women Entrepreneur (September 12, 2008)*

Ed: Lesley Spencer Pyle. **Description:** Trade shows require an enormous amount of work, but they are an investment that can pay off handsomely because they allow a business to get their product or service in front of their target market. Advice regarding trade shows is given including selecting the correct venue, researching the affair and following up on leads obtained at the event.

38597 ■ *Serves You Right!*

Pub: Serves You Right!, Incorporated

Ed: Susan Brooks. **Released:** May 2004. **Price:** $14. **Description:** Profile of excellence in customer service.

38598 ■ *Services in Canada*
Pub: Routledge
Contact: Kevin Bradley, President
E-mail: kbradley@taylorandfrancis.com
Ed: W. R. Frisbee, M. S. Sommers. **Released:** March 28, 1990. **Price:** C$230. **Description:** Profiles of the services industry in Canada. **Availability:** Print.

38599 ■ *Setting the Table: The Transforming Power of Hospitality in Business*
Pub: HarperCollins Publishers Inc.
Contact: Jane Friedman, President
E-mail: jfriedman@harpercollins.com
Ed: Danny Meyer. **Released:** October 03, 2006. **Price:** $27.99, hardcover; $11.49; C$11.99. **Availability:** PrintE-book.

38600 ■ *"Seven Ways to Fail Big" in Harvard Business Review (Vol. 86, September 2008, No. 9, pp. 82)*
Pub: Harvard Business Review Press
Contact: Peter E. Walsh, Director
Ed: Paul B. Carroll, Chunka Mui. **Description:** Seven factors involved in business failures are identified, and ways to avoid them are described. These factors include flawed financial engineering, hurrying into consolidation, and investing in technology that is not a good fit.

38601 ■ *Shop Class as Soulcraft*
Pub: Dutton Children's Books
Contact: Lauri Hornik, President
Ed: Matthew B. Crawford. **Released:** May 28, 2009. **Price:** $25.95, Hardcover; $16, Paperback. **Description:** A philosopher and mechanic argues for the satisfaction and challenges of manual work.

38602 ■ *"Shopping Around for New Ideas" in Canadian Business (Vol. 79, July 17, 2006, No. 14-15, pp. 76)*
Description: Pensions should be a win-win situation for both the employer and the employee. The perspective of both parties concerning pension plans is explored as well as the need to amend laws in order to make sure that one class of merchant does not suffer at the cost of another.

38603 ■ *Simplified Incorporation Kit*
Ed: Daniel Sitarz. **Released:** March 2007. **Price:** , $19.95. **Description:** Kit includes all the forms, instructions, and information necessary for incorporating any small business in any state (CD-ROM included).

38604 ■ *"Simply Therapeutic" in Women In Business (Vol. 61, December 2009, No. 6, pp. 34)*
Pub: American Business Women's Association
Contact: Lorie Burch, President
Ed: Maureen Sullivan. **Description:** Steps on minimizing office clutter are presented in an effort to also eliminate clutter from the office worker's mind. Allotting time for clutter reduction, setting realistic goals, file organization, labeling, and sticking to a clutter reduction system are suggested. Clutter reduction is expected to contribute to increased productivity in the workplace.

38605 ■ *"Single Most Important Problem" In Small Business Economic Trends (April 2008, pp. 18)*
Pub: National Federation of Independent Business
Contact: Caitlin McDevitt, Program Manager
Ed: William C. Dunkelberg, Holly Wade. **Description:** Two graphs and a table presenting the economic problems encountered by small businesses in the U.S. are provided. The figures presented in the graphs include data from 1986 to 2008.

38606 ■ *"Single Most Important Problem" in Small Business Economic Trends (March 2008, pp. 18)*
Pub: National Federation of Independent Business
Contact: Caitlin McDevitt, Program Manager
Ed: William C. Dunkelberg, Holly Wade. **Description:** Two graphs and a table representing the economic problems encountered by small businesses in the U.S. are presented. The figures presented in the graphs include data from 1986 to 2008.

38607 ■ *"Single Most Important Problem" in Small Business Economic Trends (February 2008, pp. 18)*
Pub: National Federation of Independent Business
Contact: Caitlin McDevitt, Program Manager
Ed: William C. Dunkelberg, Holly Wade. **Description:** Two graphs and a table representing the economic problems encountered by small businesses in the U.S. are presented. The figures presented in the graphs include data from 1974 to 2008.

38608 ■ *"Single Most Important Problem" in Small Business Economic Trends (January 2008, pp. 18)*
Pub: National Federation of Independent Business
Contact: Caitlin McDevitt, Program Manager
Ed: William C. Dunkelberg, Holly Wade. **Description:** Table of the single most important problem among small businesses surveyed in the U.S. in December 2007 is presented. Taxes were selected by 21 percent of firms as the single most important problem, followed by cost and availability of insurance at 16 percent. Graphs comparing selected single most important problem from January 1986 to December 2007 are also given.

38609 ■ *"Single Most Important Problem" in Small Business Economic Trends (September 2010, pp. 18)*
Pub: National Federation of Independent Business
Contact: Caitlin McDevitt, Program Manager
Ed: William C. Dunkelberg, Holly Wade. **Description:** A table of the single most important problem among small businesses surveyed in the U.S. in August 2010 is presented. 'Poor sales' was selected by 31 percent of firms as the single most important problem, followed by taxes at 21 percent. Graphs comparing selected single most important problem from January 1986 to August 2010 are also provided.

38610 ■ *The Six Sigma Manual for Small and Medium Businesses: What You Need to Know Explained Simply*
Pub: Atlantic Publishing Co.
Contact: Amanda Miller, Manager
E-mail: amiller@atlantic-pub.com
Ed: Marsha R. Ford. **Price:** $24.95. **Description:** The Six Sigma set of practices used to systematically improve business practices by eliminating defects. To be Six Sigma compliant, a company must produce no more than 3.4 defects per one million products, and if achieved will save the firm millions of dollars. The two main methodologies of Six Sigma are outlined.

38611 ■ *Six SIGMA for Small Business*
Pub: Entrepreneur Press
Contact: Perlman Neil, President
Ed: Greg Brue. **Description:** Jack Welch's Six SIGMA approach to business covers accounting, finance, sales and marketing, buying a business, human resource development, and new product development.

38612 ■ *"A Skimmer's Guide to the Latest Business Books" in Inc. (Volume 32, December 2010, No. 10, pp. 34)*
Pub: Inc. Magazine
Ed: Leigh Buchanan. **Description:** A list of new books published covering all aspects of small business is offered.

38613 ■ *Small Business: An Entrepreneur's Business Plan*
Pub: South-Western
Contact: Susan Badger, President
Ed: Gail P. Hiduke, J. D. Ryan. **Released:** 2009. **Price:** $160.25, paperback. **Description:** Assistance in preparing a business plan that identifies opportunities and ways to target a customer market.

38614 ■ *Small Business: An Entrepreneur's Plan*
Pub: Nelson Education Ltd.
Contact: Greg Nordal, President
Ed: Ronald A. Knowles. **Released:** 7th Canadian Edition. **Price:** C$107.95, paperback; C$62.95. **Description:** Entrepreneur's guide to planning a small business. **Availability:** PrintE-book.

38615 ■ *The Small Business Bible: Everything You Need to Know to Succeed in Your Small Business*
Pub: John Wiley & Sons Inc.
Contact: Stephen M. Smith, President
Ed: Steven D. Strauss. **Released:** March 2012. **Price:** $22.95. **Description:** Comprehensive guide to starting and running a successful small business. Topics include bookkeeping and financial management, marketing, publicity, and advertising. **Availability:** Print.

38616 ■ *Small Business, Big Life: Five Steps to Creating a Great Life with Your Own Small Business*
Ed: Louis Barajas. **Released:** May 2007. **Price:** , $22.99. **Description:** Five steps for planning, starting and running a small business, while maintaining a good life, are presented.

38617 ■ *"Small Business Compensation" in Small Business Economic Trends (April 2008, pp. 10)*
Pub: National Federation of Independent Business
Contact: Caitlin McDevitt, Program Manager
Ed: William C. Dunkelberg, Holly Wade. **Description:** Graphs and tables that present compensation plans and compensation changes of small businesses in the U.S. are provided. The figures include data from 1986 to 2008.

38618 ■ *"Small Business Compensation" in Small Business Economic Trends (March 2008, pp. 10)*
Pub: National Federation of Independent Business
Contact: Caitlin McDevitt, Program Manager
Ed: William C. Dunkelberg, Holly Wade. **Description:** Graphs and tables that present compensation plans and compensation changes of small businesses in the U.S. are provided. The figures include data from 1968 to 2008.

38619 ■ *"Small Business Compensation" in Small Business Economic Trends (February 2008, pp. 10)*
Pub: National Federation of Independent Business
Contact: Caitlin McDevitt, Program Manager
Ed: William C. Dunkelberg, Holly Wade. **Description:** Graphs and tables that present compensation plans and compensation changes of small businesses in the U.S. are provided. The figures include data from 1974 to 2008.

38620 ■ *"Small Business Compensation" in Small Business Economic Trends (January 2008, pp. 10)*
Pub: National Federation of Independent Business
Contact: Caitlin McDevitt, Program Manager
Ed: William C. Dunkelberg, Holly Wade. **Description:** Graph from a survey of small businesses in the U.S. is given, representing small business compensation from January 1986 to December 2007. Tables showing actual compensation changes and compensation plans are also presented. A graph comparing small business prices and labor compensation is supplied.

38621 ■ *Small Business Desk Reference*
Pub: Penguin Books USA Inc.
Released: December 2004. **Price:** $29.95. **Description:** Comprehensive guide for starting or running a successful small business, focusing on buying a business or franchise, writing a business plan, financial management, accounting, legal issues, human resources management, operations, marketing, sales, customer service, taxes, insurance, and ethics. Information for launching a restaurant, property management firm, retail outlet, consulting firm, and service business is included.

38622 ■ *Small Business and Entrepreneurship*
Pub: Pine Forge Press
Contact: Blaise R. Simqu, President
Ed: Robert Blackburn. **Released:** 2008. **Price:** $1,200, hardcover, Five-Volume Set. **Description:** Research covering small business and entrepreneurship.

38623 ■ Small Business: Innovation, Problems and Strategy
Pub: Nova Science Publishers Inc.
Contact: Frank Columbus, President
Released: 2009. **Price:** $117, hardcover; $79. **Description:** Innovation is a fundamental determinant of value creation in businesses and can also be a key to successful economic growth. The innovative process and innovative effort of small companies are examined and evaluated, along with alternative strategies. **Availability:** PrintE-book.

38624 ■ Small Business Legal Strategies
Pub: Aspatore Books Inc.
Released: July 2004. **Price:** , $37.95. **Description:** Corporate Chairs and Partners from top firms in the U.S. offering insight into selecting, engaging, employing, and benefiting from external corporate counsel for the small business owner or executive.

38625 ■ "Small Business Outlook" in Small Business Economic Trends (July 2009, pp. 4)
Pub: National Federation of Independent Business
Contact: Caitlin McDevitt, Program Manager
Description: Outlook among small businesses surveyed in the United States from January 1986 to June 2009 is presented. Tables showing small business outlook for expansion and outlook for general business conditions from January 2004 to June 2009 and the most important reasons for expansion outlook are also given.

38626 ■ Small Business Sourcebook
Pub: Cengage Learning
Released: 2014. **Price:** $747, paperback. **Description:** Two-volume guide to more than 27,300 listings of live and print sources for small business startups as well as small business growth and development. Over 30,500 topics are included. **Availability:** Print.

38627 ■ Small Business Survival Guide
Ed: Cliff Ennico. **Price:** , $12.95.

38628 ■ Small Business Survival Guide: Starting, Protecting, and Securing Your Business for Long-Term Success
Pub: Adams Media Corp.
Contact: Scott Watrous, President
E-mail: bobadams@adamsmedia.com
Ed: Cliff Ennico. **Released:** October 2005. **Price:** $12.95. **Description:** Entrepreneurship in the new millennium. Topics include creditors, taxes, competition, business law, and accounting.

38629 ■ Small Business Taxes 2006: Your Complete Guide to a Better Bottom Line
Pub: John Wiley & Sons Inc.
Contact: Stephen M. Smith, President
Ed: Barbara Weltman. **Released:** January 2006. **Price:** $11.99. **Description:** Detailed information on new tax laws and IRS rules for small businesses. **Availability:** E-book.

38630 ■ Small Business Taxes Made Easy: How to Increase Your Deductions, Reduce What You Owe, and Boost Your Profits
Ed: Eva Rosenberg. **Released:** December 2004. **Price:** , $16.95. **Description:** Tax expert gives advice to small business owners regarding tax issues. TaxMamma.com, run by Eva Rosenberg, is one of the top seven tax advice Websites on the Internet.

38631 ■ Small Business Turnaround
Ed: Marc Kramer. **Price:** , $17.95 paperback.

38632 ■ Small Businesses and Workplace Fatality Risk: An Exploratory Analysis
Pub: RAND Corp.
Contact: Michael D. Rich, President
E-mail: michael_rich@rand.org
Ed: John Mendeloff, Christopher Nelson, Kilkon Ko. **Released:** 2006. **Price:** $16, paperback; $20, Nonmembers. **Description:** According to previous research, small business worksites report higher rates of deaths or serious injuries than larger corporations. Statistical data included. **Availability:** Print.

38633 ■ Small Giants: Companies that Choose to Be Great Instead of Big
Pub: Penguin Group USA
Contact: Phyllis Grann, President
Ed: Bo Burllingham. **Released:** March 27, 2007. **Price:** $16, paperback; $12.99. **Availability:** Print-Electronic publishing.

38634 ■ Small Giants: Companies That Choose to Be Great Instead of Big
Pub: Penguin Group USA
Contact: Phyllis Grann, President
Ed: Bo Burlingham. **Released:** March 27, 2007. **Price:** $16, paperback; $12.99. **Description:** Profiles of privately held companies that have become huge in their field without becoming large corporations. **Availability:** PrintElectronic publishing.

38635 ■ Small and Medium-Sized Enterprises in Countries in Transition
Released: January 2005. **Price:** , $18.00. **Description:** Characteristics of small and medium enterprise (SME) sector in transition countries and emerging market economies.

38636 ■ "Smart Businesses See Value, and Profit, in Promoting Women" in Crain's Chicago Business (Vol. 30, February 2007, No. 6, pp. 30)
Ed: Marc J. Lane. **Description:** Despite U.S. corporations making little progress in advancing women to leadership positions over the past ten years, enlightened corporate decision makers understand that gender diversity is good business as the highest percentages of women officers yielded, on average, a 34 percent higher total return to shareholders and a 35.1 percent higher return on equity than those firms with the lowest percentages of women officers, according to a 2004 Catalyst study of Fortune 500 companies.

38637 ■ SME Cluster Development: A Dynamic View on Survival Clusters in Developing Countries
Pub: Palgrave Macmillan
Contact: Lisa Dunn, Manager
E-mail: l.dunn@palgrave.com
Ed: Mario Davide Parrilli. **Released:** February 2007. **Price:** £84, hardcover. **Description:** Survival clustering in developing countries is discussed in order to increase effectiveness of policy-making and development operations in local contexts. **Availability:** Print; E-book; Electronic publishing.

38638 ■ "Social Intelligence and the Biology of Leadership" in Harvard Business Review (Vol. 86, September 2008, No. 9, pp. 74)
Pub: Harvard Business Review Press
Contact: Peter E. Walsh, Director
Ed: Daniel Goleman, Richard Boyatzis. **Description:** Social intelligence within the framework of corporate leadership is defined and described. Guidelines for assessing one's own capabilities as a socially intelligent leader include empathy, teamwork, inspiration, and influence.

38639 ■ "Sound Advice From Dr. Sleep" in Crain's Chicago Business (Vol. 31, April 21, 2008, No. 16, pp. 30)
Pub: Crain Communications Inc.
Contact: Todd Johnson, Publisher
Ed: Sarah A. Klein. **Description:** James K. Wyatt, the director of the Sleep Disorders Centers at Rush University Medical Center in Chicago, gives advice to business executives concerning what to eat, how to nap and which drugs to take or avoid in order to ease the strain of air travel, particularly on overseas flights.

38640 ■ "Speak Better: Five Tips for Polished Presentations" in Women Entrepreneur (September 19, 2008)
Ed: Suzannah Baum. **Description:** Successful entrepreneurs agree that exemplary public speaking skills are among the core techniques needed to propel their business forward. A well-delivered presentation can result in securing a new distribution channel, gaining new customers, locking into a new referral stream or receiving extra funding.

38641 ■ The SPEED of Trust: The One Thing That Changes Everything
Pub: Free Press/Simon & Schuster Inc.
Ed: Stephen M.R. Covey, Rebecca R. Merrill. **Released:** February 05, 2008. **Price:** $16.99. **Description:** Because of recent business scandals, trust and a desire for accountability is addressed by the author. **Availability:** Print.

38642 ■ "Spin Zone: Where Hawaii's Leaders Face Off, What Are Your Party's Legislative Priorities for 2008??" in Hawaii Business (Vol. 53, January 2008, No. 7, pp. 22)
Pub: PacificBasin Communications
Description: Discusses the Democratic Party of Hawaii which will prioritize giving more opportunities to earn a living a wage in 2008, according to the party chairwoman Jeani Withington. The Republican Party chairman Willes K. Lee, meanwhile, states that his party will seek to enhance the local business climate. The political parties' plans for Hawaii for the year 2008 are presented in detail.

38643 ■ "Stains Still Set After SBA Scrub" in Black Enterprise (March 1, 2008)
Pub: Earl G. Graves Publishing Co. Inc.
Contact: Earl G. Graves, Jr., President
Ed: Marcia A. Wade. **Description:** Small Business Administration's attempt to ensure that federal contracts were legitimately rewarded to small businesses, however the report filed showed that $4.6 billion in incorrectly coded contracts were removed from the SBA database. Critics contend the report is filled with inaccuracies. Statistical data included.

38644 ■ "Standard-of-Living Gap With U.S. Closing" in Globe & Mail (March 27, 2007, pp. B3)
Pub: CTVglobemedia Publishing Inc.
Ed: Heather Scoffield. **Description:** According to latest report released by Statistics Canada, standard-of-living in Canada has increased considerably in last decade to match-up with American economy. Complete analysis in this context is presented.

38645 ■ "Star Power" in Small Business Opportunities (September 2008)
Pub: Entrepreneur Press
Contact: Perlman Neil, President
Description: Employee retention is an important factor for corporate executives to consider because the impact of excessive turnovers can be devastating to a company causing poor morale, unemployment claims, hiring costs, lost production and customer loss. Although there is no specific formula for retaining employees, there are several things every organization can do to keep their workers happy and increase the chances that they will stay loyal and keep working for the company for years to come; tips aimed at management regarding good employee relationships are included.

38646 ■ "Star Power Versus (Somewhat) Green Power" in Globe & Mail (January 18, 2007, pp. B2)
Pub: CTVglobemedia Publishing Inc.
Ed: Konrad Yakabuski. **Description:** The views of the Canadian actor Roy Dupuis on the trends of energy consumption by Quebeckers are presented, along with statistics of energy consumption in the Quebec region.

38647 ■ The Starfish and the Spider
Pub: Portfolio
Ed: Ori Brafman, Rod A. Beckstrom. **Released:** July 29, 2008. **Price:** $16, paperback; $12.99. **Availability:** PrintElectronic publishing.

38648 ■ The Starfish and the Spider: The Unstoppable Power of Leaderless Organizations
Pub: Portfolio Publishing
Contact: Adrian Zackheim, President
Ed: Ori Brafman, Rod A. Beckstrom. **Released:** July 29, 2008. **Price:** $16, Paperback; $12.99. **Description:** Through their experiences promoting peace and economic development through decentralizing networking, the authors offer insight into ways that

decentralizing can change organizations. Three techniques for combating a decentralized competitor are examined. **Availability:** PrintElectronic publishing.

38649 ■ "Stay Calm, Bernanke Urges Markets" in Globe & Mail (March 1, 2007, pp. B1)

Ed: Brian McKenna. **Description:** The views of Ben Bernanke, the chief of the United States Federal Reserve Board, on the future trends of the United States' economy are presented. The effect of the global stock market trends on the American stock markets is discussed.

38650 ■ "Step Up to Help Regionalism Step Forward" in Crain's Cleveland Business (Vol. 28, November 12, 2007, No. 45, pp. 10)

Pub: Crain Communications Inc.

Ed: Rob Briggs, William Currin. **Description:** Discusses the importance of regionalism for Northeast Ohio as being a broad, collaborative approach to spur economic development.

38651 ■ Strategic Entrepreneurship

Ed: Philip A. Wickham. **Released:** September 2006. **Price:** , $90.00. **Description:** Conceptual and practical ideas for managing a small business are explored.

38652 ■ Strategizing, Disequilibrium, and Profit

Pub: Stanford University Press

Ed: John A. Mathews. **Released:** 2006. **Price:** $27.95, paper; $70, cloth. **Description:** Author proposes the use of a conceptual framework that is consistent with real economies instead of equilibrium-based foundations when creating a business strategy. **Availability:** Print.

38653 ■ "Streaming Hot Currie" in Canadian Business (Vol. 80, April 23, 2007, No. 9, pp. 10)

Ed: Paul Brent. **Description:** The views of Richard Currie, former president of Loblow Cos. Ltd., on the human resource policy of the company are presented.

38654 ■ Streetwise Small Business Book of Lists: Hundreds of Lists to Help You Reduce Costs, Increase Revenues, and Boost Your Profits!

Ed: Gene Marks. **Released:** September 2006. **Price:** , $25.95. **Description:** Strategies to help small business owners locate services, increase sales, and lower expenses.

38655 ■ Strengthsfinder 2.0

Pub: Gallup Press

Ed: Tom Rath. **Released:** 2007. **Description:** Author helps people uncover their talents in order to achieve their best each day.

38656 ■ "Stronach Confirms Magna Eyeing Chrysler" in Globe & Mail (March 9, 2007, pp. B1)

Ed: Greg Keenan. **Description:** The decision of auto parts manufacturing firm Magna International Inc. to participate in the take-over bid for Chrysler Group, as announced by its founder Frank Stronach, is discussed.

38657 ■ "Succeed at a New Job" in Canadian Business (Vol. 79, November 20, 2006, No. 23, pp. 65)

Pub: Rogers Media Inc.

Contact: Tony Viner, President

Ed: Claire Gagne. **Description:** Collections of questions that job-seekers can ask the interviewer during employment interviews are presented.

38658 ■ "Success Fees" in Canadian Business (Vol. 80, March 12, 2007, No. 6, pp.)

Ed: David Baines. **Description:** Legal issues regarding payment of lawyer fees termed 'fair fee' in Canada are discussed with an instance of Inmet Mining Corp.'s dealing with lawyer Irwin Nathanson.

38659 ■ Success Secrets to Maximize Business in Canada

Pub: Graphic Arts Center Publishing Co.

Contact: Charles M. Hopkins, President

E-mail: mike@gacpc.com

Ed: Ken Coates. **Released:** October 5, 2000. **Description:** Part of the Culture Shock! Series that helps companies maximize business opportunities in Canada.

38660 ■ The Successful Entrepreneur's Guidebook: Where You Are Now, Where You Want to Be and How to Get There

Ed: Colin Barrow; Robert Brown. **Released:** January 2007. **Price:** , $35.00. **Description:** Characteristics of successful entrepreneurship are examined. The book helps new business owners to develop and grow a business.

38661 ■ Successful Proposal Strategies for Small Businesses: Using Knowledge Management to Win Government, Private-Sector, and International Contracts

Pub: Artech House Inc.

Contact: Joan Bazzy Egan, Director

Ed: Robert S. Frey. **Released:** 2012. **Price:** $139, CD-ROM Included. **Description:** Front-end proposal planning and storyboarding, focusing on the customer mission in proposals, along with the development of grant proposals. **Availability:** Print; E-book.

38662 ■ "Surprise Offer for Dofasco Puts Heat on Arcelor" in Globe & Mail (January 16, 2006, pp. B1)

Pub: CTVglobemedia Publishing Inc.

Ed: Greg Keenan. **Description:** The details of competition between ThyssenKrupp AG and Arcelor SA to bid Dofasco Inc. are presented.

38663 ■ "Survey Profile" in Small Business Economic Trends (April 2008, pp. 19)

Pub: National Federation of Independent Business

Contact: Caitlin McDevitt, Program Manager

Ed: William C. Dunkelberg, Holly Wade. **Description:** Two graphs and a table presenting the profile of small businesses that participated in the National Federation of Independent Business (NFIB) survey are provided. The actual number of firms, their industry types, and the number of full and part-time employees are also given.

38664 ■ "Survey Profile" in Small Business Economic Trends (March 2008, pp. 19)

Pub: National Federation of Independent Business

Contact: Caitlin McDevitt, Program Manager

Ed: William C. Dunkelberg, Holly Wade. **Description:** Two graphs and a table that present the profile of small businesses that participated in the National Federation of Independent Business (NFIB) survey are provided. The actual number of firms, their industry types, and the number of full and part-time employees are also given.

38665 ■ "Survey Profile" in Small Business Economic Trends (February 2008, pp. 19)

Pub: National Federation of Independent Business

Contact: Caitlin McDevitt, Program Manager

Ed: William C. Dunkelberg, Holly Wade. **Description:** Two graphs and a table that present the profile of small businesses that participated in the National Federation of Independent Business (NFIB) survey are provided. The actual number of firms, their industry types, and the number of full and part-time employees are also given.

38666 ■ "Survey Profile" in Small Business Economic Trends (September 2010, pp. 19)

Pub: National Federation of Independent Business

Contact: Caitlin McDevitt, Program Manager

Ed: William C. Dunkelberg, Holly Wade. **Description:** Two graphs and a table presenting the profile of small businesses that participated in the National Federation of Independent Business (NFIB) survey are provided. The actual number of firms, their industry types, and the number of full and part-time employees are presented.

38667 ■ "Survive the Small-to-Big Transition" in Entrepreneur (November 4, 2008)

Pub: Entrepreneur Press

Contact: Perlman Neil, President

Ed: Elizabeth Wilson. **Description:** Transitioning a small company to a large company can be a challenge, especially during the time when it is too big to be considered small and too small to be considered big. Common pitfalls during this time are discussed as well as techniques business owners should implement when dealing with this transitional period.

38668 ■ "Surviving the Storm" in Canadian Business (Vol. 81, July 22, 2008, No. 12-13, pp. 50)

Ed: Jeff Sanford. **Description:** Investment adviser Harry Dent and finance professor Paul Marsh discuss their views and forecasts on the United States' economic condition. Dent believes advisors should concentrate on wealth preservation rather than on returns. Other views regarding U.S. economic conditions are also presented.

38669 ■ Swimming Against the Tide

Ed: Tim Waterstone. **Released:** October 2006. **Price:** , $29.95. **Description:** Tim Waterstone shares ten rules for creating successful small businesses.

38670 ■ "Talk Story: Mitch D'Olier, President, CEO Kaneohe Ranch" in Hawaii Business (Vol. 53, November 2007, No. 5, pp. 27)

Pub: PacificBasin Communications

Ed: Cathy S. Cruz-George. **Description:** Mitch D'Olier chief executive officer of Kaneohe Ranch/ Harold K.L. Castle Foundation thinks that achievement gaps are a nationwide problem and that the Knowledge is Power Program is one of the programs that focuses on achievement gaps in some communities across the US. He also provides his insights on education in Hawaii and the current shortage of teachers.

38671 ■ The Ten Faces of Innovation

Pub: Doubleday Publishing Group

Contact: Stephen Rubin, President

E-mail: mpalgon@randomhouse.com

Ed: Tom Kelley. **Price:** $29.95, hardcover. **Availability:** Print.

38672 ■ "Ten Ways to Save on Business Travel" in Women Entrepreneur (November 21, 2008)

Ed: Julie Moline. **Description:** Advice regarding ways in which to save money when traveling for business is given.

38673 ■ "The Ten Worst Leadership Habits" in Canadian Business (Vol. 81, March 31, 2008, No. 5, pp. 63)

Pub: Rogers Media Inc.

Contact: Tony Viner, President

Ed: Michael Stern. **Description:** Ten leadership behaviors that aspiring leaders need to avoid are presented. These include expecting colleagues and subordinates to be like themselves, attending too many meetings, being miserly when it comes to recognition and praise, and giving an opinion often.

38674 ■ They Made America: From the Steam Engine to the Search Engine: Two Centuries of Innovators

Pub: Little Brown Company/Time Warner Book Group

Ed: Harold Evans, Gail Buckland, David Lefer. **Released:** March 03, 2009. **Price:** $50, hardcover; $18.95, paperback; $9.99. **Description:** Coffee table book highlighting entrepreneurship; this book is filled with interesting illustrated portraits of entrepreneurs and innovators like Thomas Edison, George Doriot (a venture capital pioneer), and Ida Rosenthal (inventor of the Maidenform bra). **Availability:** PrintE-book.

38675 ■ Think Big and Kick Ass in Business and Life

Pub: HarperBusiness

Ed: Donald J. Trump, Bill Zanker. **Price:** $29.95; $26.95, Paperback. **Description:** The philosophy of thinking big and acting aggressively on the path to prosperity is examined. **Availability:** CD-I.

38676 ■ *"The Thinker" in Canadian Business (Vol. 81, March 31, 2008, No. 5, pp. 52)*
Pub: Rogers Media Inc.
Contact: Tony Viner, President
Ed: Andrew Wahl. **Description:** Mihnea Moldoveanu provides much of the academic rigor that underpins Roger Martin's theories on how to improve the way business leaders think. Moldoveanu is also a classically trained pianist and founder of Redline Communications and has a mechanical engineering degree from MIT on top of his astounding knowledge on many academic fields.

38677 ■ *This Is Not Your Parents' Retirement: A Revolutionary Guide to Investment for a Revolutionary Generation*
Pub: Entrepreneur Press
Contact: Perlman Neil, President
Ed: Patrick P. Astre. **Released:** 2005. **Price:** $19.95. **Description:** Mutual funds, stocks, bonds, insurance products, and tax strategies for retirement planning.

38678 ■ *"Three Funds Look to Join CPP, Bypassing Teachers in BCE Hunt" in Globe & Mail (April 23, 2007, pp. B1)*
Ed: Sinclair Stewart. **Description:** The plans of the Ontario Municipal Employees Retirement Board, British Columbia Investment Management Corp. and the Alberta Investment Corp. to join the bidding consortium led by Canadian Pension Plan Investment Board, for the buyout of BCE Inc. are discussed. The efforts of the Ontario Teachers Pension Plan Board to form a bidding consortium for the same purpose are discussed.

38679 ■ *Three Moves Ahead: What Chess Can Teach You About Business*
Pub: John Wiley & Sons Inc.
Contact: Stephen M. Smith, President
Ed: Bob Rice. **Released:** March 30, 2008. **Price:** $24.95. **Description:** Things the game of chess can teach about business are explored.

38680 ■ *"Top 49ers Alphabetical Listing with Five Years Rank and Revenue" in Alaska Business Monthly (Vol. 27, October 2011, No. 10, pp. 100)*
Pub: Alaska Business Publishing Company Inc.
Contact: Jim Martin, President
Description: A listing of Alaska's top 49 performing companies ranked by revenue for years 2010 and 2011.

38681 ■ *"Top Male and Female Fittest CEO" in Hawaii Business (Vol. 53, October 2007, No. 4, pp. 40)*
Pub: PacificBasin Communications
Ed: Cathy S. Cruz-George. **Description:** Discusses the outcome of the fittest chief executive officers in Hawaii competition for 2007. Hawaii Capital Management's David Low leads the list while Group Pacific (Hawaii) Inc.'s Chip Doyle and Greater Good Inc.'s Kari Leong placed second and third, respectively. The CEO's routines, eating habits, and inspirations for staying fit are provided.

38682 ■ *"Top Marks" in Canadian Business (Vol. 79, October 23, 2006, No. 21, pp. 143)*
Ed: Erin Pooley; Laura Bogomolny. **Description:** Profiles of some top grade master of business administration students like Hogan Mullally and Will mercer, belonging to reputed business schools, are presented.

38683 ■ *"Tough Sell" in Black Enterprise (Vol. 37, October 2006, No. 3, pp. 92)*
Pub: Earl G. Graves Publishing Co. Inc.
Contact: Earl G. Graves, Jr., President
Ed: Sonia Alleyne. **Description:** Career coaches can evaluate your talents and skills. In an era where more companies are downsizing, a coach can help you decide if you are suited for your industry or should try switching careers.

38684 ■ *"Tough Ticket Call at Fenway: Economics at Play When Allocating Seats to Series" in Boston Business Journal (Vol. 27,*
October 26, 2007, No. 39, pp. 1)
Ed: Jesse Noyes; Naomi R. Kooker. **Description:** Business executives are trying to obtain as many baseball tickets to the World Series as possible. Allocating corporate seats to the Series is about maintaining tight relationships and influence clients. It is a key to business relationships.

38685 ■ *Trading Places - Smes In The Global Economy: A Critical Research Handbook*
Pub: Edward Elgar Publishing Inc.
Contact: Richard Henning, Vice President
E-mail: kwight@e-elgar.com
Ed: Lester Lloyd-Reason, Leigh Sear. **Released:** 2007. **Price:** £88.20, hardback. **Description:** An overview of international research for small and medium-sized companies wishing to expand in the global economy. **Availability:** Print; E-book.

38686 ■ *"TransCanada Builds on Proud Olympic History by Joining Vancouver 2010" in Marketwired (May 14, 2007)*
Pub: Comtex News Network Inc.
Description: TransCanada is the official supplier in the Natural Gas Pipeline Operator category for the Vancouver 2010 Olympic and Paralympic Winter Games.

38687 ■ *"Trimming Costs, But Not Looking It" in Crain's Chicago Business (Vol. 31, November 17, 2008, No. 46, pp. 35)*
Pub: Crain Communications Inc.
Contact: Todd Johnson, Publisher
Ed: Shia Kapos. **Description:** Advice is given concerning ways in which to keep up appearances of success during these troubled financial times.

38688 ■ *"The Trouble With $150,000 Wine" in Barron's (Vol. 88, July 7, 2008, No. 27, pp. 33)*
Pub: Dow Jones & Co., Inc.
Contact: Clare Hart, President
Ed: Jay Palmer. **Description:** Review of the book, 'The Billionaire's Vinegar: The Mystery of the World's Most Expensive Bottle of Wine,' which discusses vintners along with the marketing and distribution of wine as well as the winemaking industry as a whole.

38689 ■ *"The Trusty Sidekick" in Canadian Business (Vol. 81, March 31, 2008, No. 5, pp. 33)*
Pub: Rogers Media Inc.
Contact: Tony Viner, President
Ed: John Gray. **Description:** Being second-in-command is a good opportunity to be mentored by the boss and puts the executive in the position to see the whole organization and have influence to make changes. However, the chief operating officer has the unenviable task of trying to achieve unattainable goals. Executives who want to become the right hand man must go beyond their job description.

38690 ■ *The Truth About Middle Managers: Who They Are, How They Work, Why They Matter*
Pub: Harvard Business School Publishing
Ed: Paul Osterman. **Released:** 2009. **Price:** $35. **Description:** The alienation of middle managers is bad for a company.

38691 ■ *"TSX Linkup Sets Stage for Battle" in Globe & Mail (March 6, 2007, pp. B1)*
Ed: Boyd Erman; Sinclair Stewart. **Description:** The strategic alliance between TSX Group Inc. and International Securities Exchange Holdings Inc. for the establishment of a derivatives exchange in Canada is discussed. The prospects of competition between the new exchange and the Montreal Exchange are discussed.

38692 ■ *"A Turn in the South" in The Economist (Vol. 390, January 3, 2009, No. 8612, pp. 34)*
Description: Overview of Charleston, South Carolina, a region that lost its navy base in 1996, which had provided work for more than 22,000 people; the city developed a plan called Noisette in order to redevelop the area and today the economy is healthier and more diversified than it was a decade ago. Charleston was described as among the best cities for doing business by Inc. Magazine and seems

to be handling the downturn of the economy fairly well. Statistical data regarding growth, business and population is included.

38693 ■ *"20 Years of Advocacy and Education" in Women Entrepreneur (January 18, 2009)*
Pub: Entrepreneur Press
Contact: Perlman Neil, President
Ed: Eve Gumpel. **Description:** Profile of Sharon Hadary who served as executive director of the Center for Women's Business Research for two decades; Hadary discusses what she has learned about women business owners, their impact on the economy and what successful business owners share in common.

38694 ■ *"Two of a Kind" in Entrepreneur (Vol. 35, November 2007, No. 11, pp. 103)*
Pub: Entrepreneur Press
Contact: Perlman Neil, President
Ed: Chris Penttila. **Description:** Entrepreneurs need support and advice once in a while as pressure from work gets to them. It is good to have people from the same industry to give advice on particular topics when needed.

38695 ■ *"2008 SmallBiz Success Awards" in Hawaii Business (Vol. 53, February 2008, No. 8, pp. 43)*
Pub: PacificBasin Communications
Ed: Colette P. Fox, Gail Miyasaki, Cathy S. Cruz-George, Lance Tominaga. **Description:** Winners in the Hawaii Business 2008 SB Success Awards are presented; the awards give recognition for Hawaii small businesses with less than 100 employees and are based on four criteria, namely: unique service or product; rapid expansion or sales growth; longevity; and competency in overcoming challenges.

38696 ■ *Ugly Truth about Small Business*
Pub: Sourcebooks Inc.
Contact: Dominique M. Raccah, President
Ed: Ruth King. **Released:** September 01, 2005. **Price:** $14.95. **Description:** More than 50 percent of small businesses fail within their first year and 95 percent fail within the first five years. **Availability:** E-book; PDF.

38697 ■ *"The Ultimate Business Tune-Up: For Times Like These" in Inc. (Vol. 31, January-February 2009, No. 1, pp. 70)*
Pub: Mansueto Ventures L.L.C.
Contact: John Koten, Chief Executive Officer
Ed: Adam Bluestein, Leigh Buchanan, Max Chafkin, Jason Del Rey, April Joyner, Ryan McCarthy. **Description:** Twenty-three things do energize a small business in tough economic times are outlined with insight from successful entrepreneurs.

38698 ■ *Ultimate Guide to Project Management*
Pub: Entrepreneurial Press
Ed: Sid Kemp. **Price:** $29.95. **Description:** Project management strategies including writing a business plan and developing a good advertising campaign.

38699 ■ *Ultimate Small Business Advisor*
Ed: Andi Axman. **Released:** May 2007. **Price:** , $30. 95. **Description:** Tip for starting and running a small business, including new tax rulings and laws affecting small business, are shared.

38700 ■ *"The Uncompromising Leader" in Harvard Business Review (Vol. 86, July-August 2008, No. 8, pp. 50)*
Pub: Harvard Business Review Press
Contact: Peter E. Walsh, Director
Ed: Russel A. Eisenstat, Michael Beer, Nathaniel Foote, Flemming Norrgren. **Description:** Advice regarding how to drive performance without sacrificing commitment to people is given. Topics include development of shared purpose, organizational engagement, the fostering of collective leadership capability, and maintaining perspective.

38701 ■ *"Under Pressure" in Canadian Business (Vol. 81, July 21, 2008, No. 11, pp. 18)*

Ed: Joe Castaldo. **Description:** According to a survey conducted by COMPASS Inc., meeting revenue targets is the main cause of job stress for chief executive officers. Staffing and keeping expenditures lower also contribute to the workplace stress experienced by business executives. Other results of the survey are presented.

38702 ■ *"Unemployment Rates" in The Economist (Vol. 390, January 3, 2009, No. 8612, pp. 75)*

Description: Countries that are being impacted the worst by rising unemployment rates are those that have also been suffering from the housing market crisis. Spain has been the hardest hit followed by Ireland. America and Britain are also seeing levels of unemployment that indicate too much slack in the economy.

38703 ■ *"Unmasking Manly Men" in Harvard Business Review (Vol. 86, July-August 2008, No. 8, pp. 20)*

Pub: Harvard Business Review Press

Contact: Peter E. Walsh, Director

Ed: Robin J. Ely, Debra Meyerson. **Description:** Oil rig work is used to explore how focusing on job requirements and performance successfully challenged stereotypical views of masculinity and competence.

38704 ■ *"Unstable Atmosphere: Survey Finds State Execs Cool On Climate Change" in The Business Journal-Milwaukee (Vol. 25, August 8, 2008, No. 46, pp. A1)*

Pub: American City Business Journals, Inc.

Contact: Whitney Shaw, President

Ed: David Doege. **Description:** According to a survey of business executives in Wisconsin, business leaders do not see climate change as a pressing concern, but businesses are moving toward more energy-efficient operations. The survey also revealed that executives believe that financial incentives can promote energy conservation. Other survey results are provided.

38705 ■ *"Unveiling the Secrets Behind Hispanic Business' 100 Fastest-Growing Companies" in Hispanic Business (Vol. 30, July-August 2008, No. 7-8, pp. 22)*

Pub: Hispanic Business Inc.

Contact: Jesus Chavarria, President

Ed: Michael Bowker. **Description:** CEO's of the five fastest growing Hispanic-owned companies discuss the success of their companies; most of them attribute their success to proper investment and diversification, effective innovations and seeing growth opportunities where others see roadblocks.

38706 ■ *"The Upside of Fear and Loathing" in Barron's (Vol. 88, March 24, 2008, No. 12, pp. 11)*

Pub: Dow Jones & Co., Inc.

Contact: Clare Hart, President

Ed: Michael Santoli. **Description:** Fear and risk aversion prevalent among investors may actually serve to cushion the decline and spark a rally in US stock prices. Surveys of investors indicate rising levels of anxiety and bearishness, indicating a possible positive turnaround.

38707 ■ *"Use Common Sense in Office Gift-Giving" in Women In Business (Vol. 61, October-November 2009, No. 5, pp. 32)*

Pub: American Business Women's Association

Contact: Lorie Burch, President

Ed: Maureen Sullivan. **Description:** Tips on office gift-giving during the Christmas season are discussed. Aside from ensuring appropriateness of the gift with respect to the recipient, a fixed giving budget must be adhered to. Gifts that can be used by anyone may be selected and those with religious overtones must be avoided.

38708 ■ *"Valenti: Roots of Financial Crisis Go Back to 1998" in Crain's Detroit Business (Vol. 24, October 6, 2008, No. 40, pp. 25)*

Pub: Crain Communications Inc.

Contact: Rance E. Crain, President

Ed: Tom Henderson, Nathan Skid. **Description:** Interview with Sam Valenti III who is the chairman and CEO of Valenti Capital L.L.C., a wealth-management firm; Valenti discusses in detail the history that led up to the current economic crisis as well as his prediction for the future of the country.

38709 ■ *"Valuation: Confusing and Misunderstood" in Business Owner (Vol. 35, July-August 2011, No. 4, pp. 10)*

Pub: DL Perkins Company

Description: Business valuation is explained to help small business owners realize the value of their company.

38710 ■ *"The Valuation of Players" in Canadian Business (Vol. 80, October 22, 2007, No. 21, pp. 39)*

Ed: Jeff Sanford. **Description:** Business professionals are supplementing their Masters in Business Administration degrees with CBV or chartered business valuator. CBVs are trained, not only in business tangibles, but also in business intangibles such as market position, reputation, intellectual property, and patent. Details of employment opportunities for chartered business valuators are discussed.

38711 ■ *Wake Up and Smell the Zeitgeist*

Ed: Grand McCracken. **Released:** 2010. **Price:** $26.95. **Description:** Insight is given into an element of corporate success that's often overlooked and valuable suggestions are offered for any small business to pursue.

38712 ■ *"Walker Seeks More Business Participation" in Business Journal-Milwaukee (Vol. 28, December 10, 2010, No. 10, pp. A1)*

Pub: Milwaukee Business Journal

Ed: Rich Kirchen. **Description:** Wisconsin governor Scott Walker is seeking the aid of Milwaukee business leaders to participate in resolving the challenges posed by the economic crisis. Walker is aiming to create 250,000 jobs. He is also planning to call a special session of the legislature to enact strategies to jumpstart the economy.

38713 ■ *The Wall Street Journal. Complete Small Business Guidebook*

Pub: Three Rivers Press

Contact: Caroline Sincerbeaux, Editor

E-mail: csincerbeaux@randomhouse.com

Ed: Colleen DeBaise. **Released:** December 29, 2009. **Price:** $15. **Description:** The mechanics of building, running and growing a profitable business are outlined, teaching how to write a business plan, ways to finding money during lean years, how to keep stress in check, time management, investment in technology, hiring, marketing, management basics, angel investing and venture capital, as well as an exit strategy.

38714 ■ *Ward's Business Directory of U.S. Private and Public Companies*

Pub: Cengage Learning Inc.

Contact: Michael Hansen, Chief Executive Officer

URL(s): www.cengage.com/search/productOverview. do?Ntt=2677896851550767518288621891942626816&N=197+4294904996&Ntk=P_EPI. **Released:** Annual; 56th edition. **Price:** Edition 56, 8-vol. set, $4,485.00 (includes inter-edition supplement). Some individual volumes also sold separately.; $3,627, Individuals five-volume set; $3,205, Individuals four-volume set; $1,697, Individuals volumes 5, 6, or 7; $1,149, Individuals volume 8. **Covers:** Approximately 112,000 companies, 90% of which are privately owned, representing all industries. **Entries include:** Company name, address, phone, fax, toll-free, e-mail, URL, names and titles of up to five officers, up to four Standard Industrial Classification (SIC) codes, NAICS code, revenue figure, number of employees, year founded, ticker symbol, stock exchange, immediate parent, fiscal year end, import/export, type of company (public, private, subsidiary, etc.). In Vol. 4, lists of top 1,000 privately held companies ranked by sales vol., top 1,000

publicly held companies ranked by sales volume, and top 1,000 employers ranked by number of employees; analyses of public and private companies by state, revenue per employee for top 1,000 companies, public and private companies by SIC code and NAICS code. In volume 5, national Standard Industrial Classification (SIC) code rankings are listed, while volumes 6 and 7 lists Standard Industrial Classification (SIC) code rankings by state. In all volumes, guide to abbreviations, codes, and symbols; explanation of classification system; numerical and alphabetical listings of SIC and NAICS codes. In volume 8, NAICS rankings. In the supplement, 10,000 new listings not contained in the main edition are included. **Arrangement:** Volumes 1, 2, and 3, alphabetical; volume 4 is geographical by state, then ascending zip; volume 5 is classified by 4-digit SIC code, then ranked by sales; volumes 6 and 7 are classified by Standard Industrial Classification (SIC) code within state; volume 8 classified by NAICS, then ranked; supplement arranged alphabetical and Standard Industrial Classification (SIC) code. **Indexes:** Company name index in volumes 5, 7, and 8. **Availability:** Online: Cengage Learning Inc. CD-ROM: Cengage Learning Inc. **Type:** Directory; Numeric.

38715 ■ *"We Move Forward as a Team" in Women In Business (Vol. 61, December 2009, No. 6, pp. 6)*

Pub: American Business Women's Association

Contact: Lorie Burch, President

Ed: Rene Street. **Description:** Based on her experiences in ABWA's National Board of Directors retreat, an executive director of the American Business Women's Association, shares her belief that interaction is necessary for a successful business enterprise. She believes that the problems presented in the retreat's team-building exercises are similar to challenges which are faced in ABWA, in the workplace, and in the marketplace.

38716 ■ *"WestJet Hires a New CFO After Lengthy Search" in Globe & Mail (January 23, 2007, pp. B8)*

Pub: CTVglobemedia Publishing Inc.

Ed: Brent Jang. **Description:** Vito Culmone, formerly vice of Malson Canada, is appointed as chief financial officer.

38717 ■ *What Losing Taught Me about Winning: The Ultimate Guide for Success in Small and Home-Based Business*

Pub: Simon & Schuster Adult Publishing Group

Contact: Carolyn Reidy, President

E-mail: carolyn.reidy@simonandschuster.com

Ed: Fran Tarkenton, Wes Smith. **Released:** April 1999. **Price:** $17.95, paperback. **Description:** Provides insight into running a successful small business.

38718 ■ *What Men Don't Tell Women about Business: Opening Up the Heavily Guarded Alpha Male Playbook*

Pub: John Wiley & Sons Inc.

Contact: Stephen M. Smith, President

Ed: Christopher V. Flett. **Released:** October 2007. **Price:** $29.95, hardcover; $19.99. **Description:** Valuable guide for any woman in business, this book helps reveal everything a woman needs to know in order to understand, communicate, and compete with men in business. **Availability:** PrintE-book.

38719 ■ *"What School Did You Attend?" in Hawaii Business (Vol. 53, December 2007, No. 6, pp. 14)*

Pub: PacificBasin Communications

Ed: Kelli Abe Trifonovitch. **Description:** Discusses the question 'what school did you attend?' which is observed to be the most important inquiry in Hawaiian business discourse. The principle behind the question is based on establishing connections. The relation between the aforementioned inquiry and Hawaiian culture is explained.

38720 ■ *What Works: Success in Stressful Times*

Pub: Harper Press

Ed: Hamish McRae. **Released:** November 30, 2001. **Price:** $14.95, paperback. **Description:** Exploration of success stories from across the glove, and what

Michelle Obama referred to as 'the flimsy difference between success and failure.' Why do some initiatives take off while others flounder? How have communities managed to achieve so much while others struggle? What distinguishes the good companies from the bad? What lessons can be learned from the well-ordered Mumbai community made famous by 'Slumdog Millionaire'? Why have Canadian manners helped Whistler become the most popular ski resort in North America?. **Availability:** Print.

38721 ■ *"When Good Deals Go Bad: How to Renegotiate a Contract" in Inc. (November 2007, pp. 33-34)*
Pub: Mansueto Ventures L.L.C.
Contact: John Koten, Chief Executive Officer
Ed: Dee Gill. **Description:** Ways to renegotiate contracts are discussed. Robb Corwin of Gorilla Fuel discusses how he was able to renegotiate contracts in order to save his business

38722 ■ *"When Profit Is Not the Incentive" in Business North Carolina (Vol. 28, February 2008, No. 2, pp. 42)*
Pub: Business North Carolina
Ed: Amamda Parry. **Description:** Novant Health is North Carolina's fifth-largest private-sector employer and one of the largest nonprofit companies. Nonprofits grew 35 percent in North Carolina from 1995 to 2003.

38723 ■ *"When Virtue Is A Vice" in Harvard Business Review (Vol. 86, July-August 2008, No. 8, pp. 22)*
Pub: Harvard Business Review Press
Contact: Peter E. Walsh, Director
Ed: Anat Keinan, Ran Kivetz. **Description:** Negative consequences of habitually denying self-indulgence, from work and life balance to consumer shopping behaviors are discussed.

38724 ■ *"Where Are They Now?" in Canadian Business (Vol. 79, October 9, 2006, No. 20, pp. 71)*
Pub: Rogers Media Inc.
Contact: Tony Viner, President
Ed: Jeff Sanford, Zena Olijnyk, Andrew Wahl, Andy Holloway, John Gray. **Description:** The profile of the top chief executive officers of Canada for the year 2005 is discussed.

38725 ■ *"Where to Buy the Right MBA" in Canadian Business (Vol. 79, October 23, 2006, No. 21, pp. 99)*
Ed: Erin Pooley; Laura Bogomolny; Joe Castaldo; Michelle Magnan; Claire Gagne. **Description:** Details of Canadian graduate business schools offering Master of business administration degree are presented.

38726 ■ *Who's Got Your Back*
Pub: Broadway Books, a Division of Random House
Ed: Keith Ferrazzi. **Price:** $25, Hardcover. **Description:** Achieving goals by building close relationships with a small circle of trusted individuals.

38727 ■ *"Why Did We Ever Go Into HR?" in Harvard Business Review (Vol. 86, July-August 2008, No. 8, pp. 39)*
Pub: Harvard Business Review Press
Contact: Peter E. Walsh, Director
Ed: Matthew D. Breitfelder, Daisy Wademan Dowling. **Description:** Examines the role of human resource directors and how their jobs foster new ideas and generate optimism.

38728 ■ *"Why LinkedIn is the Social Network that Will Never Die" in Advertising Age (Vol. 81, December 6, 2010, No. 43, pp. 2)*
Pub: Crain Communications Inc.
Contact: Rance Crain, President
Ed: Irina Slutsky. **Description:** Despite the popularity of Facebook, LinkIn in will always be a source for professionals who wish to network.

38729 ■ *"Why Oil Fell, and How It May Rise" in Globe & Mail (January 18, 2007, pp. B2)*
Pub: CTVglobemedia Publishing Inc.
Ed: Eric Reguly. **Description:** The causes of the decline in oil prices in Canada are discussed, along with prospects of an increase in the same.

38730 ■ *"Will Business be Stimulated?" in Entrepreneur (Vol. 37, July 2009, No. 7, pp. 18)*
Pub: Entrepreneur Press
Contact: Perlman Neil, President
Ed: Jennifer Wang. **Description:** Steven Strauss, Alberto G. Alvarado, Jeff Rosenweig, Al Gordon, and Theresa Alfaro Daytner share their views on how the American Recovery and Reinvestment Act of 2009, also known as the economic stimulus, will affect small businesses. Their backgrounds are also provided.

38731 ■ *"Will Focus on Maryland Businesses Continue?" in Baltimore Business Journal (Vol. 28, November 5, 2010, No. 26, pp. 1)*
Pub: Baltimore Business Journal
Ed: Scott Dance. **Description:** The 2010 election may call for new efforts to teach new lawmakers to assure that the viewpoints of businesses are considered and accurately delivered. The Greater Baltimore Committee and similar groups have gathered reports on the competitiveness of Maryland and are planning to use them to make a case of keeping business a top priority.

38732 ■ *Winner Take All: How Competitiveness Shapes the Fate of Nations*
Pub: Basic Books
Contact: Elizabeth Maguire, Publisher
Ed: Richard J. Elkus, Jr. **Released:** June 16, 2009. **Price:** $27; C$34; £17.99. **Description:** American government and misguided business practices have allowed the U.S. to fall behind other countries in various market sectors such as cameras and televisions, as well as information technologies. It will take a national strategy for America to regain its lead in crucial industries. **Availability:** E-book.

38733 ■ *Winning: The Answers*
Pub: HarperCollins Publishers Inc.
Contact: Jane Friedman, President
E-mail: jfriedman@harpercollins.com
Ed: Jack Welch, Suzy Welch. **Price:** $12.95, paperback; $8.99; C$11.99. **Availability:** PrintE-book.

38734 ■ *The Wisdom of Crowds: Why the Many Are Smarter Than the Few and How Collective Wisdom Shapes Business, Economies, Societies and Nations*
Pub: Doubleday Canada, Limited
Ed: James Surrowiecki. **Released:** August 16, 2005. **Price:** C$17.95. **Description:** The premise that the many are smarter than the few and its impact on business, economics, societies and nations is discussed. **Availability:** Print.

38735 ■ *"Women Draw Less Pension Income" in Marketing to Women (Vol. 21, March 2008, No. 3, pp. 6)*
Description: According to a study by the Employee Benefit Research Institute, women over the age of 50 are much less likely to receive annuity and/or pension income. Statistical data included.

38736 ■ *"Work Buds" in Canadian Business (Vol. 80, April 23, 2007, No. 9, pp. 56)*
Ed: Andrew Wahl. **Description:** The role of team work and cooperation in improving workplace environment is presented.

38737 ■ *"Work Is An Action Word" in Black Enterprise (Vol. 38, December 2007, No. 5, pp. 86)*
Pub: Earl G. Graves Publishing Co. Inc.
Contact: Earl G. Graves, Jr., President
Ed: Marcia A. Reed-Woodard. **Description:** Understanding your company's culture, knowing the importance of networking, and connecting with the right mentors to guide you are the ingredients required for any entrepreneur.

38738 ■ *"Work Less, Earn More" in Canadian Business (Vol. 80, March 12, 2007, No. 6, pp. 30)*
Ed: Erin Pooley. **Description:** Expert advice on ways to work efficiently to complete the job instead of extending work hours is presented.

38739 ■ *"Work Naked" in Canadian Business (Vol. 80, March 12, 2007, No. 6, pp. 33)*
Ed: Andrew Wahl. **Description:** The disadvantages of teleworking for both employees and the company, in view of lack of an office environment and self-discipline on the part of workers, are discussed.

38740 ■ *"Working His Magic at Home" in Business Courier (Vol. 24, February 21, 2008, No. 46, pp. 1)*
Pub: American City Business Journals, Inc.
Contact: Whitney Shaw, President
Ed: Lucy May. **Description:** Rob Portman has left his position at the White House as budget director and decided to practice law at Squire, Sanders & Dempsey in Cincinnati. However, analysts believe that Portman's political career is not finished yet, as some expect him to become a gubernatorial or senatorial candidate in 2010. Portman's impacts on Cincinnati's business community are also evaluated.

38741 ■ *"Working It Out! How a Young Executive Overcomes Obstacles on the Job" in Black Enterprise (Vol. 37, January 2007, No. 6, pp. 55)*
Pub: Earl G. Graves Publishing Co. Inc.
Contact: Earl G. Graves, Jr., President
Ed: Laura Egodigwe. **Description:** Interview with Susan Chapman, Global Head of Operations for Citigroup Realty Services, in which she discusses issues such as the important skills necessary for overcoming obstacles in the workplace.

38742 ■ *Working Together: Why Great Partnerships Succeed*
Pub: HarperBusiness
Ed: Michael D. Eisner, Aaron Cohen. **Released:** July 31, 2012. **Price:** $14.99, paperback. **Description:** Michael D. Eisner, former CEO of the Walt Disney Company interviews corporate partners from various industries, including Bill and Melinda Gates and Warren Buffet and Charlie Munger. Why certain business partnerships succeed in the corporate world is discussed. **Availability:** Print.

38743 ■ *The World Is Flat: A Brief History of the Twenty-First Century*
Pub: Picador USA
Contact: Frances Coady, Publisher
Ed: Thomas L. Friedman. **Released:** July 2007. **Price:** $17. **Description:** Globalization's impact on business. **Availability:** Print.

38744 ■ *Ya Gotta Wanna*
Pub: Creative Book Publishers
Ed: Malcolm Paice. **Released:** July 2005. **Price:** , $12.95. **Description:** Three phases of teamwork are outlined: identifying the people and creating the team, analyzing the components of the team, and implementing the project. The author compares a soccer team to a management team and that a successful soccer team has three main area attributes: a solid defense, a creative midfield, and a potent strike force.

38745 ■ *"Your Guide to Local Style Business" in Hawaii Business (Vol. 53, December 2007, No. 6, pp. 36)*
Pub: PacificBasin Communications
Ed: David K. Choo. **Description:** Discusses the importance of studying the Hawaiian culture when doing business locally. It was observed that geographical aspects increase emphasis on culture and lifestyle more than the need to rectify false imaging do. Details of how locals adhere to their culture are supplied.

38746 ■ *Your Lawyer: An Owner's Manual*
Pub: Agate Publishing
Contact: Doug Seibold, President
E-mail: seibold@agatepublishing.com
Ed: Henry C. Krasnow. **Released:** October 01, 2005. **Price:** $14, paperback. **Description:** Small business guide that assists owners and managers to find, work with, and inspire attorneys. Includes an overview of the legal processes involved in running a small company.

TRADE PERIODICALS

38747 ■ *Business Periodicals Index (BPI)*
Pub: H.W. Wilson Co.
Contact: Harold Regan, President
URL(s): www.hwwilson.com/dd/bus_i.htmwww.hwwil-
son.com/business.html. Ed: Hiyol Yang. Released:
Monthly; with annual cumulation. Price: An annual
subscription is $1,495.00. Covers: Index of articles
in business periodicals. Entries include: Publisher
name, address, subscription rate, and frequency.
Principal content of publication is annotated index of
articles from 400 business periodicals, including book
reviews.

38748 ■ *Business Week*
Pub: The McGraw-Hill Companies Inc.
Contact: Henry Hirschberg, President
URL(s): www.businessweek.com. Released: Weekly
Price: $5, Individuals 12 issues; $35, Individuals 50
issues; $9, Individuals print and online; $40, Individu-
als print and online.

38749 ■ *Cincy Business Magazine: The
Magazine for Business Professionals*
Pub: Great Lakes Publishing Co.
URL(s): cincymagazine.com. Released: Bimonthly
Price: Free to qualified professionals.

38750 ■ *Forbes*
Pub: Forbes Inc.
Contact: Malcolm S. Forbes, Jr., President
URL(s): www.forbes.com. Ed: John Chamberlain,
Scott DeCarlo. Released: Biweekly Price: $29.99,
Individuals; $22.25, Canada. Availability: Online:
LexisNexis; Forbes Inc. Type: Full-text.

38751 ■ *Fortune*
Pub: Time Inc.
Contact: Wayne Powers, President
URL(s): money.cnn.com/magazines/fortunewww.
timeinc.com/brands/international.php. Released: 25/
yr. Price: $19.99, Individuals; $39.98, Two years;
$59.97, Individuals 3 years.

38752 ■ *Independent Operations*
Pub: American Financial Services Association
Contact: Chris Stinebert, President
URL(s): www.afsonline.org. Ed: Thomas L. Thomas,
Editor. Released: Quarterly. Price: Included in
membership; $15, nonmembers. Description: Fur-
nishes members with news of the financial services
industry, small business, and other areas of concern
to the members of the Association's Section on
Independent Operations. Provides news of current
legislation, regulations, and individual/company
profiles. Recurring features include letters to the editor, interviews, reports of meetings, news of Association events and conferences, and notices of publications available. Also contains columns titled
Chairman's Report, Profile, Marketplace, Want Ads,
For Your Information, and Question and Answer.

38753 ■ *Print Solutions: Award-Winning
Coverage of the Printing Industry*
Pub: Print Services and Distribution Association
Contact: Robert Whitman, President
URL(s): www.printsolutionsmag.com. Ed: John Dela-
van. Released: 10/year Price: Free to members;
$199, Nonmembers.

38754 ■ *Review of Business Information
Systems*
Pub: The Clute Institute for Academic Research
Contact: Diane Pielat, Director
URL(s): www.cluteinstitute.com/journals/review-of-
business-information-systems-rbis/. Released:
Quarterly Price: $300, Institutions.

VIDEOCASSETTES/ AUDIOCASSETTES

38755 ■ *The Business File*
PBS Home Video
2100 Crystal Dr.
Arlington, VA 22202-3784
URL: http://www.pbs.org
Contact: Pat Mitchell, President
Released: 1985. Price: $130. Description: An
extensive course for college students, introducing
them to the basic concepts of business. Availability:
VHS; 3/4 U.

38756 ■ *Career Insights*
RMI Media
1365 N. Winchester St.
Olathe, KS 66061-5880
Ph: (913)768-1696
Free: 800-745-5480
Fax: (800)755-6910
Co. E-mail: actmedia@act.org
URL: http://www.actmedia.com
Released: 1987. Description: Describes 50 occupa-
tions, including skill requirements and interviews with
people employed in these fields. Availability: VHS;
3/4 U.

38757 ■ *Managing the Emerging Company*
411 Video Information
PO Box 1223
Pebble Beach, CA 93953
Ph: (831)656-0553
Free: 877-292-3010
Fax: (831)656-0555
Co. E-mail: leslie@411videoinfo.com
URL: http://www.411videoinfo.com
Released: 1997. Price: $990. Description: Ten-
volume set deals with the functions of developing
and running a business. Availability: VHS.

38758 ■ *Take It from the Top: The Business
of Business Success*
Video Arts, Inc.
c/o Aim Learning Group
8238-40 Lehigh
Morton Grove, IL 60053-2615
Free: 877-444-2230
Fax: (416)252-2155
Co. E-mail: service@aimlearninggroup.com
URL: http://www.aimlearninggroup.com
Released: 1991. Price: $295. Description: David
Frost interviews three of England's most successful
businessmen, who share their secrets of success. In
the first tape, Lord Hanson talks about organization
and change. In the second, Sir John Harvey-Jones
tells the difference between leadership and management. In the third, Sir James Goldsmith shares his
business philosophy. Availability: VHS; 8 mm; 3/4
U; Special order formats.

TRADE SHOWS AND CONVENTIONS

**38759 ■ Sydney Morning Herald Small
Business Show**
Frequency: Annual. Principal Exhibits: Small Busi-
ness equipment, supplies, and services.

CONSULTANTS

38760 ■ Shriner-Midland Co.
7347 Stuart Cir.
Warrenton, VA 20187
Ph: (540)349-8193
Contact: Robert D. Shriner, Manager
E-mail: rshriner@aol.com
Scope: Business and economic analysis for corporations, investors, associations and law firms. Services
include development of management strategies,
financial management and analysis, financial due
diligence, turnaround and work-out support. Also
provides analysis and expert testimony for legislative,
regulatory and trial proceedings. Specializes in high-
tech, services and nonprofit organizations. Founded:
1976. Publications: "Economic Impact Estimates of
the Clinton Health Plan"; "Modeling Product Liability
Costs in Large Class Action Cases"; "Minimum Wage
Research Review"; "Cost Analysis for Nonprofit
Organizations".

38761 ■ Value Creation Group Inc.
7820 Scotia Dr., Ste. 2000
Dallas, TX 75248-3115
Ph: (972)980-7407

Fax: (972)980-4619
Co. E-mail: john.antos@valuecreationgroup.com
URL: http://www.valuecreationgroup.com
Contact: John Antos, Manager
Scope: General business experts offering predictive
strategic planning, Activity Based Costing ABC, Activity Based Management ABM, mergers and acquisitions, outsourcing, re engineering, process management, web enabling technology, bench marking,
installation of financial systems, executive search,
training, teams, activity based budgeting, operational
auditing, feature costing. Industries served financial
services, food, health care, insurance, manufacturing, electronics, real estate, consumer products,
nonprofit, telecommunication, oil, service, data
processing, hotel and resort and government agencies. Founded: 1984. Publications: "Handbook of
Process Management Based Predictive Accounting,"
Alcpa 2002; "Cost Management for Today's Manufacturing Environment and Activity Based Management
for Service Environments, Government Entities and
Nonprofit Organizations"; "Risks and Opportunities in
International Finance and Treasury"; "Driving Value
Using Activity Based Budgeting"; "Process Based
Accounting Leveraging Processes to Predict Results";
"Handbook of Supply Chain Management"; "Economic Value Management Applications and Techniques"; "The Change Handbook": "Group Methods
for Creating the Future"; "Why Value Management
and Performance Measurement Through U.S. Binoculars," Journal of Strategic Performance Measurement; "Real Options, Intangibles Measurement and
the Benefits of Human Capital Investment to Power
the Organization," Journal of Strategic Performance
Measurement. Seminars: Activity Based Management; Predictive Accounting; Performance measures;
ABM for Manufacturing; ABM for Service Organizations; Finance and Accounting for Non-Financial
Executives; Return on Investment/Capital Expenditure Evaluation; Planning and Cost Control; The Next
Step Intermediate Finance and Accounting for Non-
financial Managers; Activity-Based Budgeting;
Friendly Finance for Fund Raisers; Strategic Outsourcing.

COMPUTERIZED DATABASES

38762 ■ *Academic OneFile*
Cengage Learning Inc.
20 Channel Center St.
Boston, MA 02210
Ph: (617)289-7700
Free: 800-487-8488
Fax: (617)289-7844
Co. E-mail: investors@cengage.com
URL: http://www.cengage.com
Contact: Michael Hansen, Chief Executive Officer
Availability: Online: Cengage Learning Inc. Type:
Full-text.

38763 ■ *Bloomberg BusinessWeek*
McGraw-Hill Education
The Woodlands, Woodlands Dr., Woodmead
Sandton 2191, South Africa
Ph: 27 011 802 3582
Fax: 011 802 3579
URL: http://www.mcgraw-hill.com
Availability: Online: ProQuest LLC; Bloomberg L.P.
Type: Full-text.

38764 ■ *BtoB*
Crain Communications Inc.
1155 Gratiot Ave.
Detroit, MI 48207-2732
Ph: (313)446-6000
Co. E-mail: info@crain.com
URL: http://www.crain.com
Contact: Rance E. Crain, President
Availability: Online: Crain Communications Inc.
Type: Full-text.

38765 ■ *Business Periodicals Index
Retrospective™: 1913-1982*
EBSCO Publishing Inc.
10 Estes St.
Ipswich, MA 01938-2106
Ph: (978)356-6500
Free: 800-653-2726

Fax: (978)356-6565
Co. E-mail: information@ebscohost.com
URL: http://www.ebscohost.com
Contact: Tim Collins, President
E-mail: tcollins@ebscohost.com
Availability: Online: EBSCO Publishing Inc. **Type:** Bibliographic; Full-text.

38766 ■ Business Source® Alumni Edition
EBSCO Publishing Inc.
10 Estes St.
Ipswich, MA 01938-2106
Ph: (978)356-6500
Free: 800-653-2726
Fax: (978)356-6565
Co. E-mail: information@ebscohost.com
URL: http://www.ebscohost.com
Contact: Tim Collins, President
E-mail: tcollins@ebscohost.com
URL(s): www.ebscohost.com/academic/business-source-alumni-edition. **Database covers:** Marketing, Management, Management Information Systems, Production and Operations Management, Accounting, Finance, Econometrics and Economics. **Availability:** Online: EBSCO Publishing Inc. **Type:** Full-text.

38767 ■ The CorpTech Directory of Technology Companies
infoUSA Inc. Corporate Technology Information Services Inc.
1020 E 1st St.
Papillin, NE 68046
Free: 800-835-5856
URL: http://www.corptech.com
Availability: Online: infoUSA Inc. - Corporate Technology Information Services Inc. CD-ROM: infoUSA Inc. - Corporate Technology Information Services Inc. **Type:** Full-text; Directory.

38768 ■ NewsEdge™
Acquire Media Corp.
3 Becker Farm Rd., Ste. 401
Roseland, NJ 07068-1726
Ph: (973)422-0800
Fax: (973)422-0028
Co. E-mail: info@acquiremedia.com
URL: http://www.acquiremedia.com
Contact: Bradley Scher, President
Availability: Online: Acquire Media Corp. **Type:** Full-text; Numeric; Statistical.

38769 ■ Small Business Resource Center
Cengage Learning Inc.
20 Channel Center St.
Boston, MA 02210
Ph: (617)289-7700
Free: 800-487-8488
Fax: (617)289-7844
Co. E-mail: investors@cengage.com
URL: http://www.cengage.com
Contact: Michael Hansen, Chief Executive Officer
Availability: Online: Cengage Learning Inc. **Type:** Full-text.

38770 ■ Vente et Gestion
EBSCO Publishing Inc.
10 Estes St.
Ipswich, MA 01938-2106
Ph: (978)356-6500
Free: 800-653-2726
Fax: (978)356-6565
Co. E-mail: information@ebscohost.com
URL: http://www.ebscohost.com
Contact: Tim Collins, President
E-mail: tcollins@ebscohost.com
Database covers: Accounting and tax, administration, industry and manufacturing, logistics, marketing and technology. **Availability:** Online: EBSCO Publishing Inc. **Type:** Full-text.

LIBRARIES

38771 ■ Broome County Public Library - J. Donald Ahearn Business Resource Center
185 Court St., Rm. 138
Binghamton, NY 13901-3503

Ph: (607)778-6400
Co. E-mail: reference@bclibrary.info
URL: http://www.bclibrary.info/content/ahearn-business-center
Contact: Sherry Kowalski, Director, Information Services
E-mail: skowalski@co.broome.ny.us
Scope: Business. **Services:** Center open to the public. **Holdings:** Audio and video tapes; CD-ROMs.

38772 ■ College of William and Mary - Mason School of Business - McLeod Business Library
Alan B. Miller Hall, 2nd Fl.
101 Ukrop Way
Williamsburg, VA 23187
Ph: (757)221-2916
Co. E-mail: charlotte.brown@mason.wm.edu
URL: http://mason.wm.edu/about/library
Contact: Charlotte Davis Brown, Director
URL(s): mason.wm.edu/about/library/index.php. **Scope:** Business. **Founded:** 1985. **Holdings:** Reference materials; corporation records; videocassettes; periodicals and serials; reserve materials.

38773 ■ Community Futures Development Corporation of Greater Trail - Kootenay Regional Business Library
825 Spokane St.
Trail, BC, Canada V1R 3W4
Ph: (250)364-2595
Fax: (250)364-2728
URL: http://communityfutures.com/cms/resources/business-resources/skbc-business-centre
Scope: Business. **Services:** Library open to the public. **Founded:** 1994. **Holdings:** Books; publications. **Subscriptions:** 4 journals and other serials.

38774 ■ Charles Darwin University - Palmerston Campus Library
University Ave.
Palmerston, NT 0830, Australia
Ph: 61 8 89467870
Co. E-mail: referencedesk@cdu.edu.au
URL: http://www.cdu.edu.au/library/about/campuses.html
Scope: Business; cookery; computing; ESL (English as a Second Language); hospitality; tourism. **Holdings:** Books; park guides; magazines; restaurant menus; travel brochures; videos.

38775 ■ East Baton Rouge Parish Library - Main Library - Special Collections
7711 Goodwood Blvd.
Baton Rouge, LA 70806
Ph: (225)231-3700
Co. E-mail: dfarrar@brgov.com
URL: http://www.ebr.lib.la.us/libcollections.htm
Contact: David Farrar, Director, Library Services
Scope: Louisiana history and genealogy, business, automobile repair. **Services:** Library open to the public. **Holdings:** Books; government publications; microfilm; vertical files.

38776 ■ Florida State University - Panama Branch Library
PO Box 0819-05390
Panama City, Panama
Ph: 507 314 0374
Fax: 507 314 0366
URL: http://www.lib.fsu.edu/panama
Contact: Anthony Blackie, Librarian
E-mail: ablackie@mailer.fsu.edu
Scope: Business; computer science; engineering; environmental studies; information science; international affairs; Latin America and Caribbean studies; mathematics. **Services:** Interlibrary loan; copying. **Holdings:** Figures not available.

38777 ■ The New Library at New Hampshire Technical Institute, Concord
31 College Dr
Concord, NH 03301-7412
Ph: (603)230-4028

Fax: (603)230-9310
Co. E-mail: nhtilibrary@ccsnh.edu
URL: http://www.nhti.edu/student-resources/library
Contact: Stephen Ambra, Director, Library Services
E-mail: sambra@ccsnh.edu
URL(s): www.nhti.edu. **Scope:** Full-range community college Library including: business, computers, education, engineering, health, justice/legal studies, architecture, autism, nursing, dental assisting, anthropology, film studies, gaming, sports management. **Services:** Interlibrary loan; library open to the public with restrictions. **Founded:** 1968. **Holdings:** 62,000 titles, including over 140,000 e-books; 50,000 microfilms, DVDs and videocassettes, recordings, CDs, and other media. **Subscriptions:** 191 journals and other serials.

38778 ■ Oxford Brookes University - Wheatley Library
Wheatley
Oxford OX33 1HX, United Kingdom
Ph: 44 1865 485869
Co. E-mail: cmjeffery@brookes.ac.uk
URL: http://www.brookes.ac.uk/library/wheatle.html
Contact: Claire Jeffery, Director, Education
Scope: Business, computing, engineering, mathematics. **Holdings:** Books; company reports; dissertations and theses; exam papers; journals; statistics.

38779 ■ Southern Methodist University - Cox School of Business - Business Information Center
150 Maguire Bldg.
6214 Bishop Blvd.
Dallas, TX 75275
Ph: (214)768-4496
Co. E-mail: bicstaff@cox.smu.edu
URL: http://www.cox.smu.edu/web/business-information-center
Contact: Sandy Miller, Director
Scope: Business. **Services:** Instructional workshops; classroom instruction; group presentation room; multimedia studio; Investing and Trading Center; copying and printing; center not open to public. **Founded:** 1987. **Holdings:** Reference materials; faculty papers. **Subscriptions:** 36 journals and other serials; 480 e-journals.

38780 ■ Texas Southern University - Robert James Terry Library - Business Library
3100 Cleburne St.
Houston, TX 77004
Ph: (713)313-4379
Co. E-mail: west_lg@tsu.edu
URL: http://www.tsu.edu/academics/Robert_J_Terry_Library
Contact: Louis G. West, Librarian
Scope: Business, economics. **Holdings:** 50,000 bound periodical volumes, periodicals, and microforms, CD-ROM. **Subscriptions:** 500 journals and other serials.

38781 ■ Touro College - Bensonhurst Library
1870 Stillwell Ave., No. 86
Brooklyn, NY 11223
Ph: (718)265-6534
Fax: (718)265-0616
URL: http://www.tourolib.org/about/libraries/bensonhurst
Contact: Miriam Magill, Library Assistant
E-mail: miriam.magill@touro.edu
Scope: Business; computer science; human services; ESL. **Services:** Computer access; library open to college affiliates. **Holdings:** Books; diskettes; audio and video tapes; CD-ROMs; DVDs; microfiche.

38782 ■ Touro College - Boro Park Library
1273 53rd St.
Brooklyn, NY 11219
Ph: (718)871-6187
Fax: (718)686-7071
URL: http://www.tourolib.org/about/libraries/boro-park-53
Contact: Leib Klein, Librarian
E-mail: leibk@touro.edu
Scope: Business, computer science, human services, ESL. **Holdings:** Books; diskettes; audio and video

tapes; CD-ROMs; DVDs; microfiche.; Books; diskettes; audio and video tapes; CD-ROMs; DVDs; microfiche.

38783 ■ Touro College - Brighton Beach Library
532 Neptune Ave.
Brooklyn, NY 11224
Ph: (718)449-6160
Fax: (718)265-6341
URL: http://www.tourolib.org/about/libraries/brighton-beach
Contact: Bella Reytblat, Library Assistant
E-mail: bella.reytblat@touro.edu
Scope: Business, computer science, human services, ESL. **Services:** Research and reference; copying; computer access; library open to college students, staff and affiliates. **Holdings:** Books; diskettes; audio and video tapes; CD-ROMs; DVDs; microfiche.

38784 ■ Touro College - Flushing Library
133-35 Roosevelt Ave.
Flushing, NY 11354
Ph: (718)353-6400, x112
Fax: (718)495-3809
Co. E-mail: xuanwen.huang@touro.edu
URL: http://www.tourolib.org/about/libraries/flushing
Contact: Xuan Wen Huang
Scope: Business, computer science, human services, ESL. **Services:** Interlibrary loan; copying. **Holdings:** Books; diskettes; audio and video tapes; CD-ROMs; DVDs; microfiche.

38785 ■ Touro College - Forest Hills Library
71-02 113th St.
Forest Hills, NY 11375
Ph: (718)520-5107
Fax: (718)793-3610
URL: http://www.tourolib.org/about/libraries/forest-hills
Contact: Dora Isakova, Library Assistant
E-mail: dorai@touro.edu
Scope: Business; computer science; human services; ESL. **Services:** Copying; computer access for research purposes; library open to college student, staff and alumni only. **Holdings:** Books; diskettes; audio and video tapes; CD-ROMs; DVDs; microfiche.

38786 ■ Touro College - Lander College of Liberal Arts & Sciences - Midwood Library
1602 Ave. J
Brooklyn, NY 11230
Ph: (718)252-7800
Fax: (718)338-7732
URL: http://www.tourolib.org/about/libraries/midwood
Contact: Bashe Simon, Director, Library Services
E-mail: bashe.simon@touro.edu
Scope: Business; computer science; education; human services; neuroscience; political science; psychology; speech pathology; Judaica. **Services:** Copying; research services; library open to student and staff only. **Holdings:** Books; CD-ROMs; DVDs; microfiche; audio and video tapes.

38787 ■ Touro College - Lander College for Men Library
75-31 150th St.
Kew Gardens Hills, NY 11367
Ph: (718)820-4894

Fax: (718)495-3824
URL: http://www.tourolib.org/about/libraries/kew-gardens-hills
Contact: Joan Wagner, Librarian
E-mail: joan.wagner2@touro.edu
Scope: Biology; business; computer science; management information science; political science; psychology; social sciences Judaica. **Services:** Interlibrary loan; copying; library open to college staff and students. **Holdings:** Books; diskettes; audio and video tapes; CD-ROMs; DVDs; microfiche.

38788 ■ Touro College - Midtown Library
43 W 23rd St.
New York, NY 10010
Ph: (212)463-0400
Fax: (212)627-3696
URL: http://www.tourolib.org/about/libraries/midtown
Contact: Marina Zilberman, Librarian
E-mail: marina.zilberman@touro.edu
Scope: Business; education; ethnic studies; psychology; pre-clinical and clinical medicine; occupational and physical therapy; physician assistant; Oriental medicine. **Services:** Copying; computer access; research and reference; library open to college staff and students only. **Holdings:** Books; diskettes; audio and video tapes; CD-ROMs; DVDs; microfiche.

38789 ■ Touro College - Starrett City Library
1390 Pennsylvania Ave.
Brooklyn, NY 11239
Ph: (718)642-6562
Fax: (718)642-6807
URL: http://www.tourolib.org/about/libraries/starett-city
Contact: Rita Hilu, Library Assistant
E-mail: rita.hilu@touro.edu
Scope: Business, computer science, human services, ESL. **Services:** Interlibrary loan; computer access for research and reference; library open to college staff and students only. **Holdings:** Books; diskettes; audio and video tapes; CD-ROMs; DVDs; microfiche.

38790 ■ Touro College - Sunset Park Library
475 53rd St.
Brooklyn, NY 11220
Ph: (718)748-2776
Fax: (718)492-9031
URL: http://www.tourolib.org/about/libraries/sunset-park
Contact: Faina G. Katsnelson, Contact
E-mail: faina.katsnelson@touro.edu
Scope: Business; computer science; human services; ESL. **Services:** Interlibrary loan; library open to college students and staff. **Holdings:** Books; diskettes; audio and video tapes; CD-ROMs; DVDs; microfiche.

38791 ■ University of Nevada, Reno - Mathewson-IGT Knowledge Center
1664 N. Virginia St.
Mail Stop 322
Reno, NV 89557-0001
Ph: (775)682-4636
Fax: (775)784-4398
Co. E-mail: ragains@unr.edu
URL: http://knowledgecenter.unr.edu
Contact: Patrick Ragains, Librarian, Business Librarian, Government Documents
Scope: Business, government. **Holdings:** Regional Federal Depository Library Collection; Presidential Papers; Indian Agency Correspondence; Census Materials, Patent & Trademark Depository Library Materials; Nevada State and Local Publications.

38792 ■ University of Northampton - Park Campus Library
Boughton Green Rd.
Northampton NN2 7AL, United Kingdom
Ph: 44 1604 893089
Co. E-mail: libraryhelp@northampton.ac.uk
URL: http://www.northampton.ac.uk/about-us/services-and-facilities/library
Contact: Jenny Townend
E-mail: jenny.townend@northampton.ac.uk
Scope: Business; education; health; humanities; law; local history; natural sciences; waste management. **Services:** Interlibrary loan. **Holdings:** 375,000 books. **Subscriptions:** 15,000 journals and other serials.

38793 ■ University of Nottingham - Business Library
Business School South, Top Fl.
Jubilee Campus
Wollaton Rd.
Nottingham NG8 1BB, United Kingdom
Ph: 44 115 8468069
URL: http://www.nottingham.ac.uk/library/libraries/locations/business/businesslibrary.aspx
Scope: Business. **Services:** Copying; scanning; laptop loan. **Holdings:** Figures not available.

38794 ■ University of Queensland - Graduate Economics and Business Library
Colin Clark Bldg., Level 2
Saint Lucia, QLD 4072, Australia
Ph: 61 7 33463553
URL: http://www.library.uq.edu.au/locations/graduate-economics-and-business-library
Contact: Dale Drysdale, Librarian
Scope: Business; economics. **Founded:** 1996. **Holdings:** 9500 books; 12,000 bound periodical volumes; theses. **Subscriptions:** 80 journals and other serials; 16,000 e-journals.

38795 ■ University of the West of Scotland - Ayr Campus Library
University Ave.
Ayr KA8 0SX, United Kingdom
Ph: 44 1292 886324
Co. E-mail: libraryayr@uws.ac.uk
URL: http://www.uws.ac.uk/library
Contact: Neal Buchanan, Librarian
E-mail: neal.buchanan@uws.ac.uk
Scope: Business; primary and secondary education; media; commercial music; nursing. **Founded:** 1965. **Holdings:** Books; journals; audio/visual item; articles.

38796 ■ Winthrop University - Small Business Development Center Library
118 Thurmond Bldg.
Rock Hill, SC 29733
Ph: (803)323-2283
Fax: (803)323-4281
Co. E-mail: stevensl@winthrop.edu
URL: http://cba.winthrop.edu/sbdc/help2.htm
Contact: Larry Stevens, Director
Scope: Business. **Services:** Performs searches on fee basis. **Holdings:** Books; audio/visual items.

START-UP INFORMATION

38797 ■ *"Austin Welcomes New Program for Entrepreneurs"* in Austin Business JournalInc. (Vol. 29, February 12, 2010, No. 29, pp. 1)
Pub: American City Business Journals
Ed: Christopher Calnan. **Description:** Nonprofit group Economic Development Catalyst Organization (ECDO) is formalizing its BizLaunch mentoring program, which was stated in 2009. The program aims to offer support networks to entrepreneurs and assistance regarding early-stage venture capital.

38798 ■ *The Canadian Small Business Survival Guide: How to Start and Operate Your Own Successful Business*
Pub: Dundurn Group
Contact: Kirk Howard, President
E-mail: khoward@dundurn.com
Ed: Benj Gallander. **Released:** April 2002. **Price:** $26.99, paperback; $12.99. **Description:** Ideas for starting and running a successful small business. Topics include selecting a business, financing, government assistance, locations, franchises, and marketing ideas. **Availability:** PrintE-book.

38799 ■ *"Crowdfunding Roadshow Makes Memphis Stop, Pitching the Possibilities of the New JOBS Act"* in Commercial Appeal (August 7, 2012)
Pub: McClatchy-Tribune Information Services
Ed: James Dowd. **Released:** August 7, 2012. **Description:** EarlyShares founder, Maurice Lopes, is touring 24 cities across the US featuring his crowdfunding roadshow which meets with entrepreneurs and investors. The Jumpstart Our Business Startups (JOBS) Act, a nonpartisan program should help small money investors pool resources in order to fund, or crowdfund, startup small businesses. Details of the roadshow are covered.

38800 ■ *Getting Rich In Your Underwear: How To Start and Run a Profitable Home-Based Business*
Pub: HCM Publishing
Price: $17.95. **Description:** Book offers insight into starting a home-based business. Entrepreneurs will learn about business models and the home business; distribution and fulfillment of product or service; marketing and sales; how to overcome the fear of starting a business; personal success characteristics; naming a business; zoning and insurance; intellectual capital; copyrights, trademarks, and patents; limited liability companies and S-corporations; business expenses and accounting; taxes; fifteen basic steps for starting a home-based business, state resources for starting a home company; and seven home-based business ideas.

38801 ■ *"Interest Soaring In 44North Business Competition"* in Business First of Buffalo (Vol. 30, February 21, 2014, No. 23, pp. 3)
Pub: American City Business Journals, Inc.
Contact: Whitney Shaw, President
Released: February 21, 2014. **Description:** The 43North business plan competition has attracted over 200 applications from entrepreneurs coming from various sectors like e-commerce, clean technology, and advanced manufacturing. The winners of the competition will qualify for the Start-Up New York program which eliminates the tax burden for qualified firms.

38802 ■ *"Military Vet Uses SBA Program to Help Fund His Business"* in Philadelphia Business Journal (Vol. 33, May 9, 2014, No. 13, pp. 6)
Pub: American City Business Journals
Released: May 9, 2014. **Description:** Colonel Richard Elam and his wife Kimberly, both with the Florida Army National Guard, secured funding through the Small Business Administration's (SBA's) Veterans Advantage program to launch iPlay, which rents mobile entertainment equipment such as rock walls and laser-tag setups for group events. The capital access initiative, launched in January 2014, waives the origination fee for SBA Express loans to qualified veteran entrepreneurs.

38803 ■ *"Motus Motorcycles To Take Old Barber Sport in Lakeview"* in Birmingham Business Journal (Vol. 29, July 20, 2012, No. 30, pp. 1)
Pub: American City Business Journals, Inc.
Contact: Whitney Shaw, President
Ed: Ryan Poe. **Released:** July 20, 2012. **Description:** Startup luxury motorcycle maker Motus Motorcycles plans to lease the former Barber Vintage Motorsports Museum in Birmingham, Alabama. The startup is expected to get $75,000 in city tax rebates over four years as it stays in Birmingham and plans to create 15 new jobs.

38804 ■ *"SBA Program Helped New Company Survive As It Built Company Base"* in Philadelphia Business Journal (Vol. 33, May 9, 2014, No. 13, pp. 4)
Pub: American City Business Journals
Released: May 9, 2014. **Description:** The Small Business Administration (SBA) Indiana District Business Office helped Netwise Resources set up its information technology (IT) consulting business with a six-month SBA-backed loan and the 8(a) Business Development Program for small disadvantaged businesses. Owner, Mark Gibson, attributes Netwise Resources' success to its focus on branding, recruiting skilled staff, and establishing relationships with clients within the target market.

38805 ■ *"SBA Streamlines Loans and Ramps Up Web Presence"* in Hispanic Business (January-February 2008, pp. 64)
Description: Federal government's Small Business Administration offers informational resources and tools to individuals wishing to start a new company as well as those managing existing firms. The site consists of over 20,000 pages with information, advice and tips on starting, financing and managing any small business. Free online courses are also provided.

38806 ■ *"Should State Invest in Startups?"* in Providence Business News (Vol. 28, March 3, 2014, No. 48, pp. 1)
Pub: American City Business Journals
Released: March 3, 2014. **Description:** The U.S. Treasury Department is investigating whether Rhode Island violated Federal rules when it used funds from the State Small Business Credit Initiative (SSBCI) to invest in Betaspring, a startup accelerator program for technology and design entrepreneurs ready to launch their businesses. The Lyon Park audit claims that Rhode Island violated SSBCI rules because a large portion of the money went to the business accelerator's operating expenses and not to the startups themselves.

38807 ■ *"Slow-Down Startups Hot"* in Austin Business JournalInc. (Vol. 28, September 12, 2008, No. 26, pp. 1)
Pub: American City Business Journals
Ed: Sandra Zaragoza. **Description:** A number of entrepreneurs from Austin, Texas are starting their own small business despite the economic slowdown. The Small Business Development Program in Austin has seen a 50 percent increase in the demand for its services in 2008 as compared to demand in 2007. Other details about the entrepreneurship trend are discussed.

ASSOCIATIONS AND OTHER ORGANIZATIONS

38808 ■ National Association of Government Guaranteed Lenders (NAGGL)
215 E 9th Ave.
Stillwater, OK 74074
Ph: (405)377-4022
Fax: (405)377-3931
URL: http://www.naggl.org
Contact: Anthony R. Wilkinson, President
Description: Aims to serve the needs and represents the interests of the small business lending community who utilize the Small Business Administrations and other government guaranteed loan programs. **Founded:** 1984. **Educational Activities:** National Association of Government Guaranteed Lenders Conference (Annual).

REFERENCE WORKS

38809 ■ *"3CDC's Biggest Year"* in Business Courier (Vol. 26, December 18, 2009, No. 34, pp. 1)
Ed: Lucy May. **Description:** Cincinnati Center City Development Corporation (3CDC) will make 2010 its biggest year with nearly $164 million projects in the works. Historic tax credits and continued help from the city have allowed the private nonprofit organization to finance mega projects such as the $43 million renovation and expansion of Washington Park. Other projects that 3CDC will start or complete in 2010 are presented.

38810 ■ *"$49M Defense Contract Hits Austin"* in *Austin Business JournalInc.* (Vol. 28, August 7, 2008, No. 21, pp. A1)
Pub: American City Business Journals
Ed: Laura Hipp. **Description:** BAE Systems PLC has landed a $49 million contract to build thermal cameras, which are expected to be installed on tanks in 2009 and 2010. BAE is expected to land other defense contracts and is likely to add employees in order to meet production demands.

38811 ■ *"$56M Coming to Cincinnati Children's Hospital, University of Cincinnati, from Stimulus Bill"* in *Business Courier* (Vol. 26, October 9, 2009, No. 24, pp. 1)
Pub: American City Business Journals, Inc.
Contact: Whitney Shaw, President
Ed: Dan Monk, James Ritchie. **Description:** Cincinnati's Children's Hospital Medical Center and the University of Cincinnati researchers are set to receive at least $56 million from the stimulus bill. The cash infusion has reenergized research scientists and enhances Cincinnati's national clout as a major research center.

38812 ■ *"$100 Million For Affordable Homes?"* in *Austin Business Journal* (Vol. 32, June 1, 2012, No. 13, pp. 1)
Pub: American City Business Journals, Inc.
Contact: Whitney Shaw, President
Ed: Sandra Zaragoza. **Released:** June 1, 2012. **Description:** Austin, Texas-based nonprofits seeking to provide affordable homes will push for $100 million in a coming bond election. The city is seen to need $13 billion to fix its housing problem.

38813 ■ *"$100 Million in Projects Jeopardized"* in *Business Courier* (Vol. 24, March 28, 2008, No. 51, pp. 1)
Pub: American City Business Journals, Inc.
Contact: Whitney Shaw, President
Ed: Dan Monk. **Description:** Ohio's historic preservation tax credit program may be reinstated after some companies planned to sue over its stoppage. The Ohio Department of Development said the program was halted because it exceeded the allocated budget for the credit. $34 million in credits are at stake for more than two dozen local projects if the program is reinstated.

38814 ■ *"Abroad, Not Overboard"* in *Entrepreneur* (Vol. 36, April 2008, No. 4, pp. 68)
Pub: Entrepreneur Press
Contact: Perlman Neil, President
Ed: Crystal Detamore-Rodman. **Description:** Export-Import Bank is an agency created by the U.S. government to help exporters get credit insurance and capital loans by providing them with loan guarantees. The bank, being criticized as supporting more the bigger exporters, has allotted to smaller businesses a bigger portion of the annual credit being approved.

38815 ■ *"Action: Huge Film Incentive Boost Eyed in Virginia"* in *Washington Business Journal* (Vol. 32, January 3, 2014, No. 38, pp. 5)
Pub: American City Business Journals
Released: January 3, 2014. **Description:** Senator John Watkins of Midlothian, Virginia is introducing a bill that would increase the film incentive program of the state from the existing 15 percent level to 20-25 percent and boost the credit fund from $5 million to $25 million every two years. The 15.7 percent increase in film industry employment in 2013 was credited by Governor Bob McDonnell to the government incentive program.

38816 ■ *"Advantage Capital Partners Awarded $60 Million Allocation in New Markets Tax Credit Program"* in *Economics & Business Week* (June 28, 2014, pp. 7)
Pub: NewsRX
Contact: Susan E. Hasty, Publisher
Released: June 28, 2014. **Description:** Leading venture capital and small business finance firm, Advantage Capital Partners, was awarded a $60 million allocation in competitive federal New Markets Tax Credit (NMTC) program. This allocation brings

the firm's total awards since the program's start in 2002 to $659 million, and maintains the investment firm's leadership role as a top program participant across the nation.

38817 ■ *"Affordable Financing for Acquisitions"* in *Franchising World* (Vol. 42, September 2010, No. 9, pp. 47)
Pub: International Franchise Association
Contact: Stephen J. Caldeira, President
E-mail: scaldeira@franchise.org
Ed: Gene Cerrotti. **Description:** Acquisition pricing is reasonable and interest rates are low and quality franchised resale opportunities are priced 4.5 times EBITDA. Information about Small Business Administration loans is also included.

38818 ■ *"Affordable Housing on Rise"* in *Philadelphia Business Journal* (Vol. 28, October 23, 2009, No. 36, pp. 1)
Pub: American City Business Journals Inc.
Ed: Natalie Kostelni. **Description:** Philadelphia, Pennsylvania led an affordable housing boom with more than 800 new affordable housing units in the works in spite of the recession. The converging of developers and federal stimulus money has driven the sudden increase with the launching of several projects across the city.

38819 ■ *"AIG Fixed; Is Michigan Next?"* in *Crain's Detroit Business* (Vol. 24, September 22, 2008, No. 38, pp. 1)
Pub: Crain Communications Inc.
Contact: Rance E. Crain, President
Ed: Jay Greene. **Description:** Michigan's economic future is examined as is the mortgage buyout plan and American International Group Inc.'s takeover by the U.S. government.

38820 ■ *"Airlines Mount PR Push to Win Public Support Against Big Oil"* in *Advertising Age* (Vol. 79, July 14, 2008, No. 7, pp. 1)
Pub: Crain Communications Inc.
Contact: Rance Crain, President
Ed: Michael Bush. **Description:** Top airline executives from competing companies have banded together in a public relations plan in which they are sending e-mails to their frequent fliers asking for aid in lobbying legislators to put a restriction on oil speculation.

38821 ■ *"All Indicators in Michigan Innovation Index Drop in 4Q"* in *Crain's Detroit Business* (Vol. 25, June 22, 2009, No. 25, pp. 9)
Pub: Crain Communications Inc. - Detroit
Contact: Keith Crain, Chairman
Ed: Ryan Beene. **Description:** Economic indicators that rate Michigan's innovation fell in the fourth quarter of 2008. The index of trademark applications, SBA loans, venture capital funding, new incorporations and other indicators traced dropped 12.6 points.

38822 ■ *"Amount Md. Pays to Unemployed Dips to Lowest Level Since '08"* in *Baltimore Business Journal* (Vol. 28, November 12, 2010, No. 27)
Pub: Baltimore Business Journal
Ed: Scott Dance. **Description:** Maryland paid out $50 million for unemployment benefits in September 2010 for its lowest payout since 2008. The drop in unemployment payout could mean lower taxes for employers who pay for the benefits. The unemployment rate in Maryland, however, increased to 7.5 percent.

38823 ■ *"Analysis of the U.S. Residential Solar Power Market"* in *PR Newswire* (September 19, 2012)
Pub: PR Newswire Association L.L.C.
Contact: David B. Armon, President
Description: Analysis of the residential solar power market in the United States is presented. Solar PV is the fastest growing technology in the energy sector for the nation during the last three years due to rising energy prices, volatile fuel costs, and government incentives for renewable energy.

38824 ■ *"The Annual Entitlement Lecture Medicare Elephantiasis"* in *Barron's* (March 31, 2008)
Pub: Dow Jones & Co., Inc.
Contact: Clare Hart, President
Ed: Thomas G. Donlan. **Description:** Expenditures on Medicare hospital insurance and the revenues available to pay for it have led to a gap of capital valued at $38.6 trillion. Slashing the benefits or raising taxes will not solve the gap which exists unless the government saves the money and invests it in private markets.

38825 ■ *"Are There Material Benefits To Social Diversity?"* in *Hispanic Business* (Vol. 30, September 2008, No. 9, pp. 10)
Ed: Brigida Benitez. **Description:** Diversity in American colleges and universities, where students view and appreciate their peers as individuals and do not judge them on the basis of race, gender, or ethnicity is discussed. The benefits of diversity in higher education are also acknowledged by the U.S. Supreme Court and by leading American corporations.

38826 ■ *"ATI Now Ready to Pounce on Biotech"* in *Austin Business JournalInc.* (Vol. 28, August 21, 2008, No. 23, pp. 1)
Pub: American City Business Journals
Ed: Laura Hipp. **Description:** Austin Technology Incubator has entered the biotechnology sector through a program of the University of Texas incubator. The company's bioscience program was set off by a grant from the City of Austin worth $125,000. The growth of Austin's biotechnology sector is examined.

38827 ■ *"Auto Bailout: Car Trouble"* in *Canadian Business* (Vol. 82, April 27, 2009, No. 7, pp. 11)
Pub: Rogers Media Inc.
Contact: Tony Viner, President
Ed: Thomas Watson. **Description:** The likely effects of a possible bailout of the U.S. automotive industry are examined. Some experts believe that a bailout will be good for the automotive industry and on the U.S. economy. Others argue however, that the nationalization may have a negative impact on the industry and on the economy.

38828 ■ *"Auto Supplier Stock Battered In Wake Of Wall Street Woes"* in *Crain's Detroit Business* (Vol. 24, September 29, 2008, No. 39, pp. 4)
Pub: Crain Communications Inc.
Contact: Rance E. Crain, President
Ed: Ryan Beene. **Description:** Due to the volatility of the stock market and public perception of the $700 billion banking bailout, auto suppliers are now facing a dramatic drop in their shares. Statistical data included.

38829 ■ *"Auxis Introduces Services for Government Contracting"* in *Entertainment Close-Up* (December 22, 2010)
Description: Profile of Auxis Inc., a management consulting and outsourcing company has launched a new service for companies involved in or bidding for government contracts. Details of the program are provided.

38830 ■ *"BABs in Bond Land"* in *Barron's* (Vol. 89, July 6, 2009, No. 27, pp. 14)
Pub: Dow Jones & Co., Inc.
Contact: Clare Hart, President
Ed: Jim McTague. **Description:** American Recovery and Reinvestment Act has created taxable Build America Bonds (BAB) to finance new construction projects. The issuance of the two varieties of taxable BABs is expected to benefit the municipal bond market.

38831 ■ *"Back on Track-Or Off the Rails?"* in *Business Week* (September 22, 2008, No. 4100, pp. 22)
Pub: Bloomberg L.P.
Contact: Matthew Winkler, Manager
Ed: Peter Coy, Tara Kalwarski. **Description:** Discusses the possible scenarios the American economy may undergo due to the takeover of Fannie Mae and Freddie Mac. Statistical data included.

38832 ■ *"Bailout Forgets the 'Little Guys'" in The Business Journal-Milwaukee (Vol. 25, September 26, 2008, No. 53, pp. A1)*
Pub: American City Business Journals, Inc.
Contact: Whitney Shaw, President
Ed: Rich Kirchen. **Description:** Community Bankers of Wisconsin and the Wisconsin Bankers Association are urging members to approach congressional representatives and remind them to include local banks in building the $700 billion bailout plan. WBA president and CEO Kurt Bauer thinks that it is only fair to include smaller institutions in the bailout. The initial bailout plan and its benefit for the smaller banks are examined.

38833 ■ *"Bailout May Force Cutbacks, Job Losses" in The Business Journal - Serving Phoenix and the Valley of the Sun (Vol. 29, September 26, 2008, No. 4, pp. 1)*
Ed: Mike Sunnucks. **Description:** Economists say the proposed $700 billion bank bailout could affect Arizona businesses as banks could be forced to reduce the amount and number of loans it has thereby forcing businesses to shrink capital expenditures and then jobs. However, the plan could also stimulate the economy by taking bad loans off banks balance sheets according to another economist.

38834 ■ *"Baltimore's Businesses: Equipment Tax Breaks Help, But Money Still Tight: Weighing the Write-Off" in Baltimore Business Journal (Vol. 28, September 10, 2010, No. 18, pp. 1)*
Pub: Baltimore Business Journal
Ed: Daniel J. Sernovitz. **Description:** President Barrack Obama has proposed to let business write off their investments in plant and equipment upgrades under a plan aimed at getting the economy going. The plan would allow a company to write off 100 percent of the depreciation for their new investments at one time instead of over several years.

38835 ■ *"Banking Bailout: Boost or Bust? Economic Insiders Mixed on Impact to State" in Crain's Detroit Business (Vol. 24, September 29, 2008, No. 39, pp. 1)*
Pub: Crain Communications Inc.
Contact: Rance E. Crain, President
Ed: Amy Lane. **Description:** Economic insiders discuss the banking bailout and how it might impact the state of Michigan.

38836 ■ *"Bankruptcies Shoot Up 68 Percent" in Sacramento Business Journal (Vol. 25, July 18, 2008, No. 20, pp. 1)*
Pub: American City Business Journals, Inc.
Contact: Whitney Shaw, President
Ed: Kathy Robertson. **Description:** Personal bankruptcy in the Sacramento area rose by 88 percent for the first half of 2008 while business bankruptcies rose by 50 percent for the same period. The numbers of consumer bankruptcy reflects the effect of high debt, rising mortgage costs, and declining home values on U.S. households.

38837 ■ *"Bankruptcy Blowback" in Business Week (September 22, 2008, No. 4100, pp. 36)*
Pub: Bloomberg L.P.
Contact: Matthew Winkler, Manager
Ed: Jessica Silver-Greenberg. **Description:** Changes to bankruptcy laws which were enacted in 2005 after banks and other financial institutions lobbied hard for them are now suffering the consequences of the laws which force more troubled borrowers to let their homes go into foreclosure; lenders suffer financially every time they have to take on a foreclosure and the laws in which they lobbied so hard to see enacted are now becoming a problem for these lending institutions. Details of the changes in the laws are outlined as are the affects on the consumer, the economy and the lenders.

38838 ■ *"Banks Fret About Gist Of Bailout" in The Business Journal-Serving Metropolitan Kansas City (Vol. 27, September 26, 2008, No. 2)*
Pub: American City Business Journals, Inc.
Contact: Whitney Shaw, President
Ed: James Dornbrook. **Description:** Banks from the Kansas City area hope that the proposed $700 billion bailout will not send the wrong message. UMB

Financial Corp. chairman says that he hopes that the bailout would benefit companies that were more risk restrained and punish those that took outsized risk. Other bank executives' perceptions on the planned bailout are given.

38839 ■ *"Barshop Leading 'Paradigm Shift' In Aging Research" in San Antonio Business Journal (Vol. 28, September 12, 2014, No. 31, pp. 4)*
Pub: American City Business Journals
Released: September 12, 2014. **Description:** The National Institute of Health has given a $7.5 million five-year grant to University of Texas Health Science at San Antonio's Barshop Insitute for Longevity and Aging Studies. The funding was awarded to help researchers accelerate the discoveries of commercial drugs that slow the aging process.

38840 ■ *"BETC Backers Plot Future" in Business Journal Portland (Vol. 27, December 10, 2010, No. 41, pp. 1)*
Pub: Portland Business Journal
Ed: Erik Siemers. **Description:** A coalition of clean energy groups and industrial manufacturers have spearheaded a campaign aimed at persuading Oregon legislators that the state's Business Energy Tax Credit (BETC) is vital in job creation. Oregon's BETC grants tax credits for 50 percent of an eligible renewable or clean energy project's cost. However, some legislators propose BETC's abolition.

38841 ■ *"Bigger TIF Makes Development Inroads near Kansas City International Airport" in The Business Journal-Serving Metropolitan Kansas City (Vol. 26, July 11, 2008, No. 44)*
Pub: American City Business Journals, Inc.
Contact: Whitney Shaw, President
Ed: Rob Roberts. **Description:** On July 9, 2008 the Tax Increment Financing Commission voted to expand a TIF district to Tiffany Springs Road. The plan for the TIF district close to Kansas City International Airport is to include a-half mile of the road. The impacts of the expansion on construction projects and on the road network are analyzed.

38842 ■ *"Birmingham's Turf War" in Birmingham Business Journal (Vol. 31, January 24, 2014, No. 4, pp. 4)*
Pub: American City Business Journals, Inc.
Contact: Whitney Shaw, President
Released: January 24, 2014. **Description:** Metropolitan Birmingham, Alabama area incentive battles have been a mainstay for years and smaller cities were forced to compete against cities with larger cash reserves. The fight often means paying up to protect their turf and tax revenue. The rising trend among local municipalities to use incentives to lure companies is discussed.

38843 ■ *"Boeing Partnership to Preserve Thousands of Acres of Threatened Wetlands in South Carolina" in Ecology, Environment & Conservation Business (August 2, 2014, pp. 3)*
Pub: NewsRX
Contact: Susan E. Hasty, Publisher
Released: August 2, 2014. **Description:** U.S. Army Corps of Engineers approved Boeing's comprehensive wetlands mitigation plan to preserve about 4,000 acres of land, including more than 2,000 acres of wetlands near the Francis Marion National Forest in South Carolina Lowcountry. Boeing worked in partnership with federal, state and local agencies and conservation organizations to identify the tracts for preservation in order to achieve conservation goals of regional and national significance.

38844 ■ *"Boeing Scores $21.7 Billion Order in Indonesia" in Wall Street Journal Eastern Edition (November 18 , 2011, pp. B6)*
Pub: Dow Jones & Co., Inc.
Contact: Clare Hart, President
Ed: David Kesmodel, Laura Meckler. **Description:** Boeing has garnered a large contract to deliver Boeing 737 jets to Indonesia's Lion Air. There are those

who are lobbying against the US government's practice of subsidizing foreign companies that make contracts with American aerospace companies.

38845 ■ *Bold Endeavors: How Our Government Built America, and Why It Must Rebuild Now*
Pub: Simon and Schuster Inc.
Contact: Carolyn Reidy, President
E-mail: carolyn.reidy@simonandschuster.com
Ed: Felix G. Rohatyn. **Released:** 2009. **Price:** $17.99, Paperback; $13.11. **Description:** The federal government built the nation by investing in initiatives like the Erie Canal and the G.I. Bill and why it should do the same at this point in history is examined. **Availability:** E-book.

38846 ■ *"Budget Woes Endanger E-Prep Progress" in Crain's Cleveland Business (Vol. 30, June 22, 2009, No. 24, pp. 6)*
Pub: Crain Communications Inc.
Ed: Brian Tucker. **Description:** The future of the Entrepreneurship Preparatory School located in Cleveland is being threatened by State budget concerns. The charter school requires all students to wear uniforms, respect discipline, and attend for longer hours and more weeks.

38847 ■ *"Building a Workforce" in Business Journal Milwaukee (Vol. 29, July 27, 2012, No. 44, pp. 1)*
Pub: American City Business Journals, Inc.
Contact: Whitney Shaw, President
Ed: Rich Kirchen. **Released:** July 27, 2012. **Description:** Governor Scott Walker's 'Wisconsin Working' initiative head Tim Sullivan announced that he will recommend the encouragement of immigration to meet current and future employment needs of the state. Sullivan believes immigration could help address the worker skills shortage that affected many southeaster Wisconsin businesses.

38848 ■ *"Business Looks for Results in Congress" in Baltimore Business Journal (Vol. 28, November 5, 2010, No. 26, pp. 1)*
Pub: Baltimore Business Journal
Ed: Kent Hoover. **Description:** Republican candidates in the 2010 Congressional elections were overwhelmingly supported by the business community. Republican John Boehner, who will be the next Speaker of the House, says that the party's victory would end economic uncertainty and would assist small businesses to rehire workers.

38849 ■ *"Buyer Sought for Clipper Windpower" in Gazette (March 16, 2012)*
Pub: McClatchy Tribune Information Services
Ed: Dave DeWitte. **Description:** United Technologies is seeking a buy for its Clipper Windpower, the wind turbine manufacturer located in Cedar Rapids, Iowa. Economic slowdown, tighter credit conditions, and uncertainty over renewal of federal wind energy tax credits are all contributors to the move by UT.

38850 ■ *"Cabela's Repays Incentives as Sales Lag" in Business Journal-Milwaukee (Vol. 28, November 19, 2010, No. 7, pp. A1)*
Pub: Milwaukee Business Journal
Ed: Stacy Vogel Davis. **Description:** Cabela's has given back $266,000 to the government of Wisconsin owing to its failure to meet projected revenue goals for its Richfield, Wisconsin store. It has also failed to meet sales tax and hiring projection. The company received $4 million in incentives from Washington County.

38851 ■ *"Cal-ISO Plans $125 Million Facility" in Sacramento Business Journal (Vol. 25, August 2, 2008, No. 22, pp. 1)*
Pub: American City Business Journals, Inc.
Contact: Whitney Shaw, President
Ed: Celia Lamb, Michael Shaw. **Description:** Sacramento, California-based nonprofit organization California Independent System Operator (ISO) is planning to build a new headquarters in Folsom. The new building would double its current leased space to 227,000 square feet. The ISO will seek tax-exempt bond financing for the project.

38852 ■ *"Can Avenue be Fashionable Again? Livernois Merchants, City Want Revival"* in *Crain's Detroit Business (March 10, 2008)*
Pub: Crain Communications Inc.
Contact: Rance E. Crain, President
Ed: Nancy Kaffer. **Description:** Once a busy retail district, the Avenue of Fashion, a Livernois Avenue strip between Six Mile and Eight Mile roads, is facing a community business effort being backed by city support whose aim is to restore the area to its former glory.

38853 ■ *"Cash for Appliances Targets HVAC Products, Water Heaters"* in *Contractor (Vol. 56, October 2009, No. 10, pp. 1)*
Pub: Penton Media, Inc.
Ed: Candace Roulo. **Description:** States and territories would need to submit a full application that specifies their implementation plans if they are interested in joining the Cash for Appliances program funded by the American Recovery and Reinvestment Act. The Department of Energy urges states to focus on heating and cooling equipment, appliances and water heaters since these offer the greatest energy savings potential.

38854 ■ *"Charlie Winburn's Big Idea"* in *Business Courier (Vol. 27, October 8, 2010, No. 23, pp. 1)*
Pub: Business Courier
Ed: Dan Monk, Lucy May. **Description:** Cincinnati Councilman Charlie Winburn proposed the creation of Cincinnati Competitive Edge Division and to remake a small-business division of the city in order to start a job-creation program. The new division will monitor compliance to the city's small business inclusion regulations, as well as to help small business owners grow.

38855 ■ *"Cincinnati Hospitals Wage War on 'Bounce-Backs"* in *Business Courier (Vol. 27, July 30, 2010, No. 13, pp. 1)*
Pub: Business Courier
Ed: James Ritchie. **Description:** Health care organizations in Greater Cincinnati area have tried a number of care and follow up programs, primarily focused on congestive heart failure to prevent readmissions to hospitals. Hospital administrators have made the averting of bounce-backs a priority due to new federal government plans on reimbursement.

38856 ■ *"Cincinnati's Freedom Center May have New Path"* in *Business Courier (Vol. 26, October 30, 2009, No. 27, pp. 1)*
Pub: American City Business Journals, Inc.
Contact: Whitney Shaw, President
Ed: Dan Monk, Lucy May. **Description:** National Underground Railroad Freedom Center in Price Hill, Cincinnati is in negotiations with US Rep. John Conyers for its possible classification as an independent establishment within the US federal government. If this happens, funding for the museum might be possibly augmented and the rights to use national archives might be furnished.

38857 ■ *"City Council Committee Votes Against Establishing Small and Minority Business Fund"* in *Commercial Appeal (November 10, 2010)*
Pub: Memphis Publishing Co.
Contact: Michael Erskine, Director
Ed: Amos Maki. **Description:** Memphis, Tennessee City Council decided against the establishment of a $1 million small and minority business fund until criteria can be set in place for disbursing the money.

38858 ■ *"City Eyeing Tax Breaks for Arena"* in *Boston Business Journal (Vol. 29, June 3, 2011, No. 4, pp. 1)*
Pub: American City Business Journals, Inc.
Ed: Daniel J. Sernovitz. **Description:** Baltimore City is opting to give millions of dollars in tax breaks and construction loans to a group of private investors led by William Hackerman who is proposing to build a new arena and hotel at the Baltimore Convention Center. The project will cost $500 million with the state putting up another $400 million for the center's expansion.

38859 ■ *"City Plans Downtown Congestion Fees"* in *Crain's Chicago Business (Vol. 31, May 5, 2008, No. 18, pp. 12)*
Pub: Crain Communications Inc.
Contact: Todd Johnson, Publisher
Description: By penalizing downtown drivers and rewarding public-transit users, Chicago officials plan to unclog Loop streets. The $153 million federal grant would establish a pilot network of express bus routes and set up a peak-period pricing system for city, street and private garage parking and for building loading zones.

38860 ■ *"City Sets Yamhill Makeover"* in *The Business Journal-Portland (Vol. 25, July 4, 2008, No. 17, pp. 1)*
Pub: American City Business Journals, Inc.
Contact: Whitney Shaw, President
Ed: Andy Giegerich. **Description:** City government is scheduled to redevelop Peterson's property on Yamhill Street in Portland. The redevelopment is seen as a way to better developing commercial properties in the area. Problems associated with the project, which include cost and developer selection, are also discussed.

38861 ■ *"City's Streetcar Utility Estimate Way Off Mark"* in *Business Courier (Vol27, November 19, 2010, No. 29. , pp. 1)*
Pub: Business Courier
Ed: Dan Monk, Lucy May. **Description:** Duke Energy Corporation has released new estimates that show moving electric and gas lines alone for Cincinnati, Ohio's proposed streetcar project could cost more than $20 million. However, the city has only estimated the relocation to cost $5 million in federal grant applications.

38862 ■ *"Cleaner and Greener"* in *Canadian Business (Vol. 80, February 12, 2007, No. 4, pp. 45)*
Pub: Rogers Media Inc.
Contact: Tony Viner, President
Ed: Zena Olijnyk. **Description:** Canadian research and government investments in clean coal technology are discussed.

38863 ■ *"Cleanup to Polish Plating Company's Bottom Line"* in *Crain's Cleveland Business (Vol. 28, October 29, 2007, No. 43, pp. 4)*
Pub: Crain Communications Inc.
Ed: Jay Miller. **Description:** Barker Products Co, a manufacturer of nuts and bolts, is upgrading its aging facility which will allow them to operate at capacity and will save the company several hundred thousand dollars a year in operating costs. The new owners secured a construction loan from the county's new Commercial Redevelopment Fund which will allow them to upgrade the building which was hampered by years of neglect.

38864 ■ *"Clock Ticking for Hotel Berry"* in *Sacramento Business Journal (Vol. 25, July 30, 2008, No. 21, pp. 1)*
Pub: American City Business Journals, Inc.
Contact: Whitney Shaw, President
Ed: Michael Shaw. **Description:** Federal tax credits worth $13.6 million have been awarded to boost the renovation project for the aging Hotel Berry in downtown Sacramento, California. The owners of the hotel have five months before the expiration of the tax credits to raise the remaining funding for the $20 million renovation.

38865 ■ *Code of Federal Regulations: Title 13: Business Credit and Assistance*
Pub: U. S. Government Printing Office
Contact: Veronica Meter, Director
E-mail: tpriebe@gpo.gov
Ed: Department of Commerce Staff. **Released:** January 2014. **Price:** $61. **Description:** Title 13 covers regulations governing the activities of the Small Business Administration and the Department of Commerce. Book covers information on business credit, finance, and economic development. **Availability:** Print.

38866 ■ *"Colorado Companies Adjust as Drought Boosts Food Prices"* in *Denver Business Journal (Vol. 64, August 17, 2012, No. 13, pp. 1)*
Pub: American City Business Journal
Description: The drought engulfing most of the US has led some Colorado companies to modify product offerings and declare that food prices will be raised by four percent next year. The federal government has already declared all of Colorado and half of the nation's counties as disaster areas, making them accessible for federal aid.

38867 ■ *"Colorado's Hollywood Wager"* in *Denver Business Journal (Vol. 65, April 25, 2014, No. 50, pp. A4)*
Pub: American City Business Journals
Released: April 25, 2014. **Description:** The successes and controversies surrounding the film incentives program of Colorado are explored. Some critics question the incentive have been directed to people who paid for the lobbying of House Bill 1286, while others ask if incentives are a proper use of public funds.

38868 ■ *"Coming Soon: Bailouts of Fannie and Freddie"* in *Barron's (Vol. 88, July 14, 2008, No. 28, pp. 14)*
Pub: Dow Jones & Co., Inc.
Contact: Clare Hart, President
Ed: Jonathan R. Laing. **Description:** Assurances from the government that Fannie Mae and Freddie Mac are adequately capitalized and able to carry on their duties as guarantors or owners of over $5 trillion of U.S. home mortgages are designed to keep both entities afloat until they attempt to raise $10 billion in new equity. The government would assume any losses in a bailout and owners of the banks' papers would profit as yields drop.

38869 ■ *"Companies Press Ottawa to End CN Labor Dispute"* in *Globe & Mail (April 16, 2007, pp. B1)*
Ed: Brent Jang. **Description:** The plea of several industries to the Canadian parliament to end the labor dispute at the Canadian National Railway Co. is discussed.

38870 ■ *"Condos Becoming FHA No-Lending Zones"* in *Providence Business News (Vol. 29, June 2, 2014, No. 9, pp. 7)*
Pub: American City Business Journals
Released: June 2, 2014. **Description:** Federal policy changes and decisions by condominium boards of directors have made the condominium development ineligible for Federal Housing Administration (FHA) loans, making several communities prohibited lending zones. As a result, the number of condo developments approved for FHA funding has fallen by more than half, presenting a growing problem for first-time buyers, those with modest down payment cash, and senior citizens using a reverse mortgage.

38871 ■ *"Congress Ponders Annuity Trusts"* in *National Underwriter Life & Health (Vol. 114, June 21, 2010, No. 12, pp. 10)*
Pub: Summit Professional Networks
Contact: Steve Weitzner, President
Ed: Arthur D. Postal. **Description:** Congress is looking over several bills, including the Small Business Jobs Tax Relief Act that would significantly narrow the advantages of using grantor-retained annuity trusts (GRATs) to avoid estate and gift taxes.

38872 ■ *"Cordish Seeks Tax Break for Project"* in *Baltimore Business Journal (Vol. 30, June 15, 2012, No. 6, pp. 1)*
Pub: American City Business Journals, Inc.
Contact: Whitney Shaw, President
Ed: James Briggs. **Released:** June 15, 2012. **Description:** Real estate developer David Cordish is seeking tax credit from the government of Baltimore for a mixed-use project. The company has requested a Payment in Lieu of Taxes as part of its project proposal. Meanwhile, the city has faced criticism for doling out tax breaks to developers.

38873 ■ *"Corporate Responsibility" in Professional Services Close-Up (July 2, 2010)* **Description:** List of firms awarded the inaugural Best Corporate Citizens in Government Contracting by the Corporate Responsibility Magazine is presented. The list is based on the methodology of the Magazine's Best Corporate Citizen's List, with 324 data points of publicly-available information in seven categories which include: environment, climate change, human rights, philanthropy, employee relations, financial performance, and governance.

38874 ■ *"Countywide Tax Could Fund Cincinnati's Metro" in Business Courier (Vol. 26, January 15, 2010, No. 39, pp. 1)* **Pub:** American City Business Journals, Inc. **Contact:** Whitney Shaw, President **Ed:** Lucy May, Dan Monk. **Description:** Cincinnati officials are considering a new countywide tax to fund the Metro bus system and extend healthcare to the poor.

38875 ■ *"CR Magazine Taps ITT As a 'Best Corporate Citizen' in Government Contracting" in Profesisonal Services Close-Up (July 30, 2010)* **Description:** ITT Corporation was named by Corporate Responsibility Magazine as a Best Corporate Citizen in Government Contracting. The list recognizes publicly-traded companies that exemplify transparency and accountability while serving the U.S. government.

38876 ■ *"Crowdsourcing Solutions to Prepare Our Communities" in The America's Intelligence Wire (November 2, 2010)* **Pub:** Highbeam Research **Contact:** Patrick Spain, Chief Executive Officer **Description:** The 2010 TEDMED conference in San Diego, California, held in October 2010, challenged leaders from government and the public sector to offer ideas to help communities prepare for disasters.

38877 ■ *"CUBRC Needs Funds For Its Testing Facilities" in Business First of Buffalo (Vol. 30, May 16, 2014, No. 35, pp. 7)* **Pub:** American City Business Journals, Inc. **Contact:** Whitney Shaw, President **Released:** May 16, 2014. **Description:** The Calspan-University of Buffalo Research Center (CUBRC) is seeking to raise Federal funding for its hypersonics tunnel systems. US Senator, Charles Shummer, has been pushing to restore funding for the Test and Evaluation/Science and Technology program. The CUBRC will need $10 million annually to maintain the hypersonic tunnels.

38878 ■ *"The Cudgel of Samson: How the Government Once Used 'Jawboning' to Fight Inflation" in Barron's (Vol. 88, March 24, 2008, No. 12, pp. 62)* **Pub:** Dow Jones & Co., Inc. **Contact:** Clare Hart, President **Ed:** Thomas G. Donlan. **Description:** Discusses the Federal Reserve is jawboning businesses against inflation while inflation is starting to rise because of the abundance of cheap money. The practice of jawboning has been used by the administrations of past US presidents with limited effect.

38879 ■ *"Daley's Efforts to Ease Traffic Woes Fall Short" in Crain's Chicago Business (Vol. 31, May 5, 2008, No. 18, pp. 18)* **Pub:** Crain Communications Inc. **Contact:** Todd Johnson, Publisher **Description:** Discusses some of the inherent problems of Mayor Daley's plan to reduce traffic congestion by creating a tax on drivers who park their cars downtown during peak traffic periods and putting articulated buses on new bus-only lanes on major arterial streets leading into the Loop.

38880 ■ *"Deer Springs Assisted Living: a Case Study" in Real Estate Review (Vol. 41, Summer 2012, No. 2, pp. 63)* **Released:** Summer 2012. **Description:** The development of the Silver Sky assisted living facility in Deer Springs, Nevada is discussed. The facility is a joint venture between the Nevada Housing and Neighborhood Development and the City of Las Vegas.

38881 ■ *"Defense Budget Ax May Not Come Down So Hard on Maryland" in Baltimore Business Journal (Vol. 28, August 20, 2010, No. 15, pp. 1)* **Pub:** Baltimore Business Journal **Ed:** Daniel J. Sernovitz. **Description:** U.S. Defense Secretary Robert M. Gates' planned budget cuts are having little effect on Maryland's defense industry. Gates will reduce spending on intelligence service contracts by 10 percent.

38882 ■ *"Delaware Diaper Maker Wanting To Expand Less Than a Year After Move" in Business First-Columbus (December 10, 2007, pp. A6)* **Pub:** American City Business Journals, Inc. **Ed:** Dan Eaton. **Description:** Duluth, Georgia-based Associated Hygienic Products LLC is planning to expand its production operations by 20 percent and hire new workers. The diaper maker was awarded state incentives to facilitate its transfer from Marion to Delaware. Details are included.

38883 ■ *"Detroit Residential Market Slows; Bright Spots Emerge" in Crain's Detroit Business (Vol. 24, October 6, 2008, No. 40, pp. 11)* **Pub:** Crain Communications Inc. **Contact:** Rance E. Crain, President **Ed:** Daniel Duggan. **Description:** Discusses the state of the residential real estate market in Detroit; although condominium projects receive the most attention, deals for single-family homes are taking place in greater numbers due to financing issues. Buyers can purchase a single family home with a 3.5 percent down payment compared to 20 percent for some condo deals because of the number of first-time homebuyer programs under the Federal Housing Administration.

38884 ■ *"Developers Tout Benefits of Federal Tax Breaks" in Business First of Buffalo (Vol. 30, March 14, 2014, No. 26, pp. 4)* **Pub:** American City Business Journals, Inc. **Contact:** Whitney Shaw, President **Released:** March 14, 2014. **Description:** President Obama has included a Federal tax credit program in the 2015 Federal budget that provides some relief to the local development community. Congressman Mark Higgins promised to support the program that offers tax breaks to urban developers who rehabilitate older buildings with new investments. The tax credit's economic benefits are also discussed.

38885 ■ *"The Display Group Is Super-Sized" in Michigan Vue (Vol. 13, July-August 2008, No. 4, pp. 34)* **Description:** Profile of the Display Group, located in downtown Detroit, this company provides custom designed mobile marketing displays as well as special event production services for trade show displays. The rental house and design service is also beginning to see more business due to the film initiative, which provides incentives for films that are shooting in Michigan.

38886 ■ *"Doctors Warn of Problems" in Austin Business JournalInc. (Vol. 29, December 4, 2009, No. 39, pp. 1)* **Pub:** American City Business Journals **Ed:** Sandra Zaragoza. **Description:** Texas physicians have voiced their concern regarding the potential cuts in Medicare reimbursement rates due to the 21 percent cut imposed by Centers for Medicare and Medicaid at the start of 2010. Experts believe the large cuts would result in the closure of some physician practices. Details of the Texas Medical Association's stand on the health reform bill are examined.

38887 ■ *"Dodge Pushes Reform Agenda" in Globe & Mail (February 6, 2006, pp. B1)* **Ed:** Heather Scoffield. **Description:** The impact of variations in global economy, on Canadian economy, is discussed. The recommendations of Governor David Dodge of Bank of Canada to resolve the issue are presented.

38888 ■ *"Doing the Right Thing: Enterpreneurs Make Social Responsibility Part of their Business" in Black Enterprise (Vol. 38, July 2008, No. 12, pp. 50)* **Pub:** Earl G. Graves Publishing Co. Inc. **Contact:** Earl G. Graves, Jr., President **Ed:** Tamara E. Holmes. **Description:** More business owners are trying to become more environmentally friendly, either due to their belief in social responsibility or for financial incentives or for both reasons. Tips for making one's business more environmentally responsible are included as well as a listing of resources that may be available to help owners in their efforts.

38889 ■ *"Don't Expect Quick Fix" in The Business Journal-Serving Metropolitan Kansas City (Vol. 27, October 3, 2008, No. 3, pp. 1)* **Pub:** American City Business Journals, Inc. **Contact:** Whitney Shaw, President **Ed:** James Dornbrook. **Description:** United States governmental entities cannot provide a quick fix solution to the current financial crisis. The economy requires a systemic change in the way people think about credit. The financial services industry should also focus on core lending principles.

38890 ■ *"Down the Tracks, a Whistle Is a-Blowin'" in Barron's (Vol. 89, July 27, 2009, No. 30, pp. 36)* **Pub:** Dow Jones & Co., Inc. **Contact:** Clare Hart, President **Ed:** Jim McTague. **Description:** Higher numbers of freight-rail carloads are a sign that the economy is improving and it is no stretch to imagine that this is aided by the American Recovery and Reinvestment Act. It is also predicted that 2009 municipal bond issuance will be above $373 billion with at least $55 billion of it made up of Buy America Bonds that are subsidized by the federal government.

38891 ■ *"Dox Choice Joins Growing Medical Records Industry" in Memphis Business Journal (Vol. 34, April 13, 2012, No. 53, pp. 1)* **Pub:** American City Business Journal **Description:** A profile of electronic health records provider Dox Choice LLC is presented. The company has received an incentive from the Center for Medicare and Medicaid Services.

38892 ■ *"Dream On" in Barron's (Vol. 89, July 27, 2009, No. 30, pp. 21)* **Pub:** Dow Jones & Co., Inc. **Contact:** Clare Hart, President **Ed:** Jonathan R. Laing. **Description:** California's budget agreement which purports to eliminate a $26 billion deficit is discussed. The frequent budgetary dustups in the state calls for several reforms including a rainy day fund of 15 percent of any budget and a constitutional convention. Other reform suggestions are discussed.

38893 ■ *"Economic Incentives - It's Not Just About City's Money" in Austin Business Journal (Vol. 34, June 20, 2014, No. 18, pp. 8)* **Pub:** American City Business Journals, Inc. **Contact:** Whitney Shaw, President **Released:** June 20, 2014. **Description:** The author opines that the decision by Dropbox Inc., U.S. Farathane Corporation, and National Instruments Corporation to cancel their incentive deals to expand within Austin highlights the agreements' excessively strict standards. Austin Mayor Lee Leffingwell is concerned that the City's rules would mean that a firm would meet the state standards, receive a sum from the Texas Enterprise Fund, and them moves jobs out of Austin.

38894 ■ *"Editor's Note" in Canadian Business (Vol. 81, March 17, 2008, No. 4, pp. 7)* **Pub:** Rogers Media Inc. **Contact:** Tony Viner, President **Ed:** Joe Chidley. **Description:** Canadian Consolidated government expenditures increased by an average of 4.5 percent annually from 2003 to 2007. Health care, housing, and the environment were some of the areas which experienced higher spending. However, government spending in labor, employment, and immigration dropped 6.6 percent.

38895 ■ "Education Path to Economic Growth in R.I." in Providence Business News (Vol. 29, June 23, 2014, No. 12, pp. 1)
Pub: American City Business Journals
Released: June 23, 2014. **Description:** A gubernatorial candidate in Rhode Island is offering an education-related initiative that involves the creation of a statewide internship program, managed by each local school district and offering high school students the chance to participate in an internship at a local company. The state would provide $2.5 million to set up the "Hope Internships" with the help of nonprofits and to provide tax incentives for participating firms. Human resource department interest of local firms is also discussed.

38896 ■ "Emerging Tech Fund Strong in 2009" in Austin Business JournalInc. (Vol. 29, December 25, 2009, No. 42, pp. 1)
Pub: American City Business Journals
Ed: Christopher Calnan. **Description:** Texas' Emerging Technology Fund (ETF) has seen an increase in applications from the state's technology companies in 2009. ETF received 87 applications in 2009 from Central Texas companies versus 50 during 2008 while $10.5 million was given to seven Texas companies compared with $10.6 million to ten companies in 2008.

38897 ■ "Employer Jobless Tax Could Rise" in Sacramento Business Journal (Vol. 28, May 27, 2011, No. 13, pp. 1)
Pub: Sacramento Business Journal
Ed: Kathy Robertson. **Description:** The government of California is facing an estimated $16 billion deficit in its unemployment insurance fund. Unemployment insurance spending has exceeded employer contributions to the fund. Statistics on unemployment insurance is included.

38898 ■ "Encouraging Study in Critical Languages" in Occupational Outlook Quarterly (Vol. 55, Summer 2011, No. 2, pp. 23)
Pub: U.S. Department of Labor Bureau of Labor Statistics
Contact: Philip L. Rones, Manager
E-mail: rones.philip@bls.gov
Description: Proficiency in particular foreign languages is vital to the defense, diplomacy, and security of the United States. Several federal programs provide scholarships and other funding to encourage high school and college students to learn languages of the Middle East, China, and Russia.

38899 ■ "ETF Process May be Tweaked" in Austin Business JournalInc. (Vol. 28, December 26, 2008, No. 41, pp. 3)
Ed: Christopher Calnan. **Description:** Some government officials are proposing for an adjustment of the Texas Emerging Technology Fund's (ETF) policies. The ETF was created to get startup companies capital to get off the ground. Reports show that the global recession had made it more difficult for startup companies to garner investment.

38900 ■ "Evolve Bank Ramps Up Staff for SBA Lending" in Memphis Business Journal (Vol. 33, February 24, 2012, No. 46, pp. 1)
Pub: American City Business Journal
Ed: Christopher Sheffield. **Description:** Memphis, Tennessee-based Evolve Bank has hired Marty Ferguson and Tre Luckett to handle its national and local Small Business Administration (SBA) lending operations. The two are long-time leaders in SBA lending.

38901 ■ "Exit Strategy" in Barron's (Vol. 89, July 6, 2009, No. 27, pp. 3)
Pub: Dow Jones & Co., Inc.
Contact: Clare Hart, President
Ed: Alan Abelson. **Description:** US Federal Reserve is not likely to change its easy-money strategy in the short term. States such as California are suffering

from spiraling costs and declining revenues and are struggling to balance their budgets. The US unemployment rate climbed to 9.5 percent in June 2009.

38902 ■ "Experts Take the Temp of Obama Plan" in The Business Journal-Serving Metropolitan Kansas City (Vol. 27, November 14, 2008, No. 10)
Pub: American City Business Journals, Inc.
Contact: Whitney Shaw, President
Ed: Rob Roberts. **Description:** Kansas City, Missouri-based employee benefits experts say president-elect Barack Obama's health care reform plan is on track. Insurance for children and capitalization for health information technology are seen as priority areas. The plan is aimed at reducing the number of uninsured people in the United States.

38903 ■ "Fannie and Freddie: How They'll Change" in Business Week (September 22, 2008, No. 4100, pp. 30)
Ed: Jane Sasseen. **Description:** Three possible outcomes of the fate of struggling mortgage giants Freddie Mac and Fannie Mae after the government bailout are outlined.

38904 ■ "Farm Aid" in Canadian Business (Vol. 80, November 5, 2007, No. 22, pp. 123)
Pub: Rogers Media Inc.
Contact: Tony Viner, President
Ed: Calvin Leung. **Description:** Canadian farmers experiencing difficulties with increasing their earning as the price of production is greater than the amount they earn from produce. Government assistance programs, including the Canadian Agricultural Income Stabilization, are aimed at helping farmers mitigate the impacts of the high prices of production. The effectiveness of Canadian farm policies are evaluated.

38905 ■ "Fast Release Calcium Could Help Control Club Root" in Farmer's Weekly (March 26, 2008, No. 320)
Pub: Reed Elsevier Group plc Reed Business Information
Contact: Mark Kelsey, Chief Executive Officer
Ed: Mike Abram. **Description:** According to initial observations from a new HGCA club root research study, applications of fertilizers that rapidly release calcium may help improve performance of both susceptible and resistant oilseed rape varieties.

38906 ■ "The Fed Still Has Ammunition" in Barron's (Vol. 90, August 30, 2010, No. 35, pp. M9)
Pub: Barron's Editorial & Corporate Headquarters
Ed: Randall W. Forsyth. **Description:** Federal Reserve chairman Ben Bernanke said the agency still has tools to combat deflation and a second downturn but these strategies are not needed at this time. The prospects of the Federal Open Market Committee's purchasing of treasuries are also discussed.

38907 ■ "Fed Tackles Bear of a Crisis" in Barron's (Vol. 88, March 17, 2008, No. 11, pp. M10)
Pub: Dow Jones & Co., Inc.
Contact: Clare Hart, President
Ed: Randall W. Forsyth. **Description:** Emergency funding package for Bear Stearns from the Federal Reserve Bank of New York through JPMorgan Chase is one of the steps taken by the central bank shore up bank liquidity. Prior to the emergency funding, the central bank announced the Term Securities Lending Facility to allow dealers to borrow easily saleable Treasuries in exchange for less-liquid issues.

38908 ■ "Federal Bailout, Three Years Later" in Business Owner (Vol. 35, September-October 2011, No. 5, pp. 6)
Pub: DL Perkins Company
Description: State of the economy and small business sector three years after the government stimulus and bailout programs were instituted.

38909 ■ "Federal Fund Valuable Tool For Small-Biz Innovators" in Crain's Detroit

Business (Vol. 24, September 29, 2008, No. 39, pp. 42)**
Pub: Crain Communications Inc.
Contact: Rance E. Crain, President
Ed: Nancy Kaffer. **Description:** Grants from the Small Business Innovation Research Program, or SBIR grants, are federal funds that are set aside for 11 federal agencies to allocate to tech-oriented small-business owners. Firms such as Biotechnology Business Consultants help these companies apply for SBIR grants.

38910 ■ "Feds to Pay University Hospital $20M" in Business Courier (Vol. 27, July 23, 2010, No. 12, pp. 3)
Pub: Business Courier
Ed: James Ritchie. **Description:** The U.S. government is set to pay University Hospital and medical residents who trained there $20 million as part of a tax dispute settlement. Around 1,000 former residents are to receive tax refunds. But the hospital must provide the U.S. Internal Revenue Service with extensive documentation.

38911 ■ "A Few Points of Contention" in Barron's (Vol. 88, July 14, 2008, No. 28, pp. 3)
Pub: Dow Jones & Co., Inc.
Contact: Clare Hart, President
Ed: Michael Santoli. **Description:** Headline inflation tends to revert to the lower core inflation, which excludes food and energy in its calculation over long periods. Prominent private equity figures believe that regulators should allow more than the de facto 10 percent to 25 percent limit of commercial banks to hasten the refunding of the financial sector.

38912 ■ "Fifth Third CEO Kabat: A World of Difference" in Business Courier (Vol. 26, January 1, 2010, No. 37, pp. 1)
Pub: American City Business Journals, Inc.
Contact: Whitney Shaw, President
Ed: Steve Watkins. **Description:** CEO Kevin Kabat of Cincinnati-based Fifth Third Bancorp believes that the bank's assets of $111 billion and stock value of more than $10 indicate the recovery from the low stock prices posted in February 2009. He attributes the recovery from the federal government's stress test finding in May 2009 that Fifth Third needs to generate $1.1 billion.

38913 ■ "Fight Against Fake" in The Business Journal-Portland (Vol. 25, July 18, 2008, No. 19, pp. 1)
Ed: Erik Siemers. **Description:** Companies, such as Columbia Sportswear Co. and Nike Inc., are fighting the counterfeiting of their sportswear and footwear products through the legal process of coordinating with law enforcement agencies to raid factories. Most of the counterfeiting factories are in China and India. Other details on the issue are discussed.

38914 ■ "Film Incentives: A Hit or a Flop?" in Michigan Vue (Vol. 13, July-August 2008, No. 4, pp. 10)
Description: Michigan's new film incentive legislation is fulfilling its core purpose, according to Lisa Dancsok of the Michigan Economic Development Corp. (MEDC), by kickstarting the state's entry into the multi-billion dollar industry; the initiative is considered to be very competitive with other states and countries and is thought to be a way in which to help revitalize Michigan's struggling economy.

38915 ■ "Final State Budget Is a Mixed Bag of Key Industries" in The Business Journal - Serving Phoenix and the Valley of the Sun (Vol. 28, July 4, 2008, No. 44, pp. 3)
Pub: American City Business Journals, Inc.
Contact: Whitney Shaw, President
Ed: Mike Sunnucks, Patrick O'Grady. **Description:** Approved by Governor Janet Napolitano and passed by the Arizona Legislature, the $9.9 billion state budget is beneficial to some industries in the business community. The tax cap for on Arizona Lottery has been removed which is beneficial to the industry, while the solar energy industry and real estate developers stand to lose from the spending bill. Other details of the finance budget are presented.

38916 ■ *"Finding Room for Financing" in The Business Journal-Serving Metropolitan Kansas City (Vol. 26, August 1, 2008, No. 47, pp. 1)*

Ed: Rob Roberts. **Description:** Kansas City officials are expecting to receive financing recommendations for a new 1,000-room convention headquarters hotel. The $300-million project could be financed either through private ownership with public subsidies, or through public ownership with tax-exempt bond financing. Other views and information on the project and its expected economic impact, are presented.

38917 ■ *"First-Time Homebuyer Credit May Add Some Momentum to Market" in Crain's Cleveland Business (Vol. 30, May 18, 2009, No. 20)*

Pub: Crain Communications Inc.

Ed: Stan Bullard. **Description:** Federal tax credits for first-time homebuyers have increased the number of homes being sold. Details of the tax credit are defined.

38918 ■ *"Five Area Businesses Win State Tax Breaks" in Crain's Detroit Business (Vol. 25, June 22, 2009, No. 25, pp. 9)*

Pub: Crain Communications Inc. - Detroit

Contact: Keith Crain, Chairman

Ed: Amy Lane. **Description:** Michigan Economic Growth Authority approved tax breaks for five area businesses among 15 across the state. Details of the tax credits are provided.

38919 ■ *"Five New Scientists Bring Danforth Center $16 Million" in Saint Louis Business Journal (Vol. 32, October 7, 2011, No. 6, pp. 1)*

Pub: Saint Louis Business Journal

Ed: E.B. Solomont. **Description:** Donald Danforth Plant Science Center's appointment of five new lead scientists has increased its federal funding by $16 million. Cornell University scientist Tom Brutnell is one of the five new appointees.

38920 ■ *"Free File Alliance & IRS Launch 10th Year of Free Online Tax Preparation Services for Millions of Americans" in Economics Week (February 3, 2012, pp. 82)*

Pub: NewsRX

Contact: Susan E. Hasty, Publisher

Released: February 3, 2012. **Description:** A coalition of tax software companies have partnered with the Internal Revenue Service to offer the 212 IRS Free File progam. The Free File Alliance offers low-to-moderate income taxpayers free access to online commercial tax preparation software. Details of the program are included.

38921 ■ *"Free 'Green Business' Workshops Set for Boynton Beach and Lake Worth" in Palm Beach Post (April 14, 2012)*

Pub: McClatchy Tribune Information Services

Ed: Eliot Kleinberg. **Description:** Florida Green Energy workshops will be held to assist companies to become certified as a green business and to also receive public money for energy-saving projects. The workshops will be held in Boynton Beach and Lake Worth, Florida.

38922 ■ *"From Buyout to Busted" in Business Week (September 22, 2008, No. 4100, pp. 18)*

Pub: Bloomberg L.P.

Contact: Matthew Winkler, Manager

Ed: Emily Thornton, Deborah Stead. **Description:** Bankruptcy filings by private equity-backed companies are at a record high with 134 American firms taken private (or invested in) by buyout firms that have filed for protection this year under Chapter 11; this is 91 percent higher than the previous year, which had set a record when 70 of such companies filed for protection under Chapter 11.

38923 ■ *"Geico and the USO of Metropolitan Washington Have Teamed Up to Provide Military Troops with a New 'Home Away From Home" in Best's Review (Vol. 113, September 2012, No. 5, pp. 13)*

Description: Geico and the USO of Metropolitan Washington have partnered to provide military troops and their families an area in the USO airport lounge at Ronald Reagan Washington National Airport with wireless Internet access, seating area with large-screen TV, assistance with travel-related questions, and a snack bar.

38924 ■ *"Georgia Looking to Expand Film Industry Tax Credits" in Atlanta Business Chronicle (June 27, 2014, pp. 3A)*

Pub: American City Business Journals, Inc.

Contact: Whitney Shaw, President

Released: June 27, 2014. **Description:** The lawmakers of the State of Georgia are looking to expand film tax incentives at a time when many states are eliminating or scaling back their film industry tax credits. A recently created legislative study committee will begin meeting to consider proposals to expand Georgia's film tax credit program to encourage an already rapidly growing industry.

38925 ■ *"Getting Creative With Cash" in Austin Business Journal (Vol. 34, May 9, 2014, No. 12, pp. 4)*

Pub: American City Business Journals, Inc.

Contact: Whitney Shaw, President

Released: May 9, 2014. **Description:** The economic development staff of Austin, Texas proposed the Creative Content Incentive Program, which adds city-funded film incentives of up to 0.75 percent of all wages paid to local workers to boost the filmmaking industry. The state of Texas offers cash grants of 22.5 percent on film and television projects.

38926 ■ *"Glendale Pumping $29 Million Into Redevelopment" in The Business Journal - Serving Phoenix and the Valley of the Sun (Vol. 28, August 1, 2008, No. 48, pp. 1)*

Pub: American City Business Journals, Inc.

Ed: Mike Sunnucks. **Description:** Glendale City is planning to invest $29 million to improve city infrastructure like roadways and water and sewer lines over the next five years. Glendale's city council is also planning to hold a workshop on the redevelopment projects in September 2008. Other views and information on the redevelopment project, are presented.

38927 ■ *"A Good Step, But There's a Long Way to Go" in Business Week (September 22, 2008, No. 4100, pp. 10)*

Ed: James C. Cooper. **Description:** Despite the historic action by the U.S. government to nationalize the mortgage giants Freddie Mac and Fannie Mae, rising unemployment rates may prove to be an even bigger roadblock to bringing back the economy from its downward spiral. The takeover is meant to restore confidence in the credit markets and help with the mortgage crisis but the rising rate in unemployment may make many households unable to take advantage of any benefits which arise from the bailout. Statistical data included.

38928 ■ *"Grant Could Help Schools Harness Wind" in Dallas Business Journal (Vol. 37, April 11, 2014, No. 31, pp. 8)*

Pub: American City Business Journals

Released: April 11, 2014. **Description:** Five universities led by Texas A&M have received a $2.2 million grant from the Texas Emerging Technologies Fund for use in wind technology research. The research will focus on turbines that feature bigger blades to capture more wind. Technology developed by the universities will eventually be handed to the state.

38929 ■ *"Gray Moves to Close Two Curious Tech Incentive Loopholes" in Washington Business Journal (Vol. 33, May 23, 2014, No. 5, pp. 12)*

Pub: American City Business Journals

Released: May 23, 2014. **Description:** District of Columbia Mayor Vincent Gray, has included in his budge recommendations small changes to definitions of a 'Qualified High Technology Company'. The proposals would expand the excluded industries into an online or brick-and-mortar retail store and a construction company from eligibility to claim the government tech incentives. The current incentive loopholes are outlined.

38930 ■ *"Green Light on Transit? Walker to Seek Funds for Rapid Bus Lines" in The Business Journal-Milwaukee (Vol. 25, July 25, 2008, No. 44, pp. A1)*

Pub: American City Business Journals, Inc.

Contact: Whitney Shaw, President

Ed: David Doege. **Description:** $50 million in federal funding is being sought by Wisconsin's Milwaukee County Executive Scott Walker for the creation of two bus rapid transit lines, and is to be added to the unspent Milwaukee area federal funds worth $91.5 million. The new transit line will have new higher-speed buses and fewer stops than the traditional line.

38931 ■ *"Green Rules To Drive Innovation: Charging for Carbon Can Inspire Conservation, Fuel Competition, and Enhance Competitiveness" in Harvard Business Review (Vol. 90, March 2012, No. 3, pp. 120)*

Pub: Harvard Business Review Press

Contact: Peter E. Walsh, Director

Ed: Daniel C. Esty, Steve Charnovitz. **Released:** March 2012. **Description:** Along with carbon emissions charges, other green policy recommendations include expanding domestic renewable power and the use of natural gas, increasing federal funding of clean-energy research, utilizing incentive-based approaches to encourage the adoption of renewable energy, and implementing the World Trade Organization's Doha negotiations on sustainable development.

38932 ■ *"Grocers Fight Food Stamp Plan" in Philadelphia Business Journal (Vol. 30, January 20, 2012, No. 49, pp. 1)*

Pub: American City Business Journal

Description: Grocers in Philadelphia, Pennsylvania have opposed the state's plan to eliminate food stamps for individuals and families with more than $2,000 in savings and other assets. About one-third of Philadelphia's population is eligible for food stamps.

38933 ■ *"Group To Urge Change For Use of Hotel Taxes" in Business Journal Milwaukee (Vol. 29, June 29, 2012, No. 40, pp. 1)*

Pub: American City Business Journals, Inc.

Contact: Whitney Shaw, President

Ed: Stacy Vogel Davis. **Released:** June 29, 2012. **Description:** Wisconsin Hotel & Lodging Association is looking at the state policy on hotel taxes. Group president, Trisha Pugal, says that hotel taxes are aimed at promoting overnight tourism, but many communities misuse the revenue as the state inadequately monitors the usage of such taxes. The association has proposed a requirement for more accountability and clarification on what can be considered as tourism promotion.

38934 ■ *"Growing Field" in Crain's Detroit Business (Vol. 26, January 11, 2010, No. 2, pp. 3)*

Pub: Crain Communications Inc.

Contact: Rance E. Crain, President

Description: Detroit's TechTown was awarded a combination loan and grant of $4.1 million from the U.S. Department of Housing and Urban Development to build a 15,000-square-foot stem cell center, a collection of laboratories that will be available to both for-profit companies and university researchers.

38935 ■ *"Half a World Away" in Tampa Bay Business Journal (Vol. 30, December 4, 2009, No. 50, pp. 1)*

Ed: Jane Meinhardt. **Description:** Enterprise Florida has offered four trade grants for Florida's marine industry businesses to give them a chance to tap into the Middle East market at the Dubai International Boat Show on March 9 to 13, 2010. The grants pay for 50 percent of the exhibition costs for the qualifying business.

38936 ■ *"Hank Paulson On the Housing Bailout and What's Ahead" in Business Week*

(September 22, 2008, No. 4100, pp. 19)
Ed: Maria Bartiromo. **Description:** Interview with Treasury Secretary Henry Paulson in which he discusses the bailout of Fannie Mae and Freddie Mac as well as the potential impact on the American economy and foreign interests and investments in the country. Paulson has faith that the government's actions will help to stabilize the housing market.

38937 ■ *"A Happier Ending for Uncle Sam and AIG" in Barron's (Vol. 92, September 17, 2012, No. 38, pp. 19)*
Description: The US Treasury Department sold 637 million shares of American International Group (AIG) for $20.7 billion. The shares were sold at $32.50 each and reduced the government's stake in the company by 53.4 percent.

38938 ■ *"Hastily Enacted Regulation Will Not Cure Economic Crisis" in Crain's Chicago Business (Vol. 31, May 5, 2008, No. 18, pp. 18)*
Pub: Crain Communications Inc.
Contact: Todd Johnson, Publisher
Ed: Stephen P. D'Arcy. **Description:** Policymakers are looking for ways to respond to what is possibly the greatest financial crisis of a generation due to the collapse of the housing market, the credit crisis and the volatility of Wall Street.

38939 ■ *"Health Care Braces for Federal Cuts" in Boston Business Journal (Vol. 29, August 19, 2011, No. 15, pp. 1)*
Pub: American City Business Journals, Inc.
Ed: Scott Dance. **Description:** The healthcare industry in Baltimore is expecting negative effects from the federal debt ceiling on Medicare and Medicaid spending. Medicare funds are expected to be slashed and could impact hospitals and doctors.

38940 ■ *"Health Care of the Future" in Business Journal Serving Greater Tampa Bay (Vol. 30, November 19, 2010, No. 48, pp. 1)*
Pub: Tampa Bay Business Journal
Ed: Margie Manning. **Description:** Information about accountable care organizations (ACO), which are integrated care systems with doctors and hospitals working closely together to handle patient care, is provided. The Patient Protection and Affordable Care Act paved the way for ACOs as Medicare demonstration projects.

38941 ■ *"Health Centers Plan Expansion: $3M from D.C. Expected; Uninsured a Target" in Crain's Detroit Business (Vol. 25, June 15, 2009, No. 24, pp. 3)*
Pub: Crain Communications Inc. - Detroit
Contact: Keith Crain, Chairman
Ed: Jay Greene. **Description:** Detroit has five federally qualified health centers that plan to receive over $3 million in federal stimulus money that will be used to expand projects that will care for uninsured patients.

38942 ■ *"Heart Hospitals Analyzed" in Philadelphia Business Journal (Vol. 30, September 2, 2011, No. 29, pp. 1)*
Pub: American City Business Journals Inc.
Ed: John George. **Description:** Centers for Medicare and Medicaid Services (CMS) released updated data on mortality rates for heart attack patients as hospitals in Pennsylvania. Doylestown Hospital posted the lowest mortality rates with 10.9 percent, tying the fourth best in the entire nation. Other details on the CMS data are presented.

38943 ■ *"Help, For Some" in Canadian Business (Vol. 81, December 8, 2008, No. 21, pp. 10)*
Ed: Joe Castaldo. **Description:** Over 80 percent of Canadian chief executives believe that government bailouts merely reward mediocre management and encourages companies to take risks because they know the government will help prevent their bankruptcy. Respondents to a COMPAS online survey believe bailouts are unfair for properly managed companies.

38944 ■ *"Help Wanted: 100 Hospital IT Workers" in Business Courier (Vol. 27, October 8, 2010, No. 23, pp. 1)*
Pub: Business Courier
Ed: James Ritchie. **Description:** Hospitals in the Greater Cincinnati area are expected to hire more than 100 information technology (IT) workers to help digitize medical records. Financial incentives from the health care reform bill encouraged investments in electronic medical record systems, increasing the demand for IT workers that would help make information exchange across the healthcare system easier.

38945 ■ *"Help in Wings for Aviation, Defense" in Globe & Mail (March 12, 2007, pp. B1)*
Ed: Simon Tuck. **Description:** The creation of a corporate subsidy fund by the Canadian government, to facilitate the growth of the aerospace and defense industries, is described.

38946 ■ *"Helping Small Businesses Create Jobs" in America's Intelligence Wire (August 27, 2010)*
Ed: Ross Raihala. **Description:** Ways the Small Business Jobs Tax Relief Act will help small businesses create jobs are investigated.

38947 ■ *"His Record, Not Polls, Is What Matters" in Bangor Daily News (October 13, 2010)*
Pub: Bangor Daily News
Ed: Nick Sambides, Jr. **Description:** The Small Business Jobs Tax Relief Act could spur investment in small businesses by increasing capital gains tax cuts for investors in small business in 2010 and increase to $20,000 from $5,000 the deduction for start-up businesses.

38948 ■ *"Hopkins, UMd Worry Reduced NIH Budget Will Impact Research" in Boston Business Journal (Vol. 29, August 19, 2011, No. 15, pp. 1)*
Pub: American City Business Journals, Inc.
Ed: Scott Dance. **Description:** The budget for the National Institutes of Health (NIH) is slated to be cut by at least 7.9 percent to $2.5 billion in 2013. This will have a big negative effect on medical and biotech research in Maryland, especially Johns Hopkins University and University of Maryland, Baltimore which could face stiffer completion for grants from the NIH.

38949 ■ *"Hospital Fighting for Its Life" in Crain's Chicago Business (April 28, 2008)*
Pub: Crain Communications Inc.
Contact: Todd Johnson, Publisher
Ed: Mike Colias. **Description:** Chicago's Catholic health chain was looking to sell the money-losing hospital St. Anthony Hospital on the West Side but with the financial picture improving and no merger offers in the works the investment bank hired to shop the hospital is hoping to operate the 111-year-old facility as an independent entity. St. Anthony serves as a 'safety net' for the region since an increasing number of its patients are uninsured or on public aid, which pays far less than commercial insurers.

38950 ■ *"Hot-Button Ordinances May Go Up for Review" in Crain's Detroit Business (Vol. 26, January 18, 2010, No. 3, pp. 1)*
Pub: Crain Communications Inc.
Contact: Rance E. Crain, President
Ed: Nancy Kaffer. **Description:** Detroit's economic fate may be tied to the city's anti-privatization ordinance and its policy of giving contract preference to Detroit-based businesses. The new administration feels that it is time to put everything on the table in an attempt to look for ways in which to save the city money.

38951 ■ *"House Committee on Small Business Calls for Sweeping Changes to SBIR Program" in Hispanic Business (March 2008, pp. 44)*
Description: Changes in the Small Business Innovation and Research Program would allow greater flexibility for firms participating in the program to leverage venture capital funds.

38952 ■ *"How Baltimore's Largest Private Companies Weathered the Recession's Punch; Top Private Companies" in Baltimore Business Journal (Vol. 28, August 27, 2010, No. 16, pp. 1)*
Pub: Baltimore Business Journal
Ed: Gary Haber. **Description:** The combined revenue of the 100 largest private firms in Maryland's Baltimore region dropped from about $22.7 billion in 2008 to $21 billion in 2009, an annual decrease of more than 7 percent. To survive the recession's impact, these firms resorted to strategies such as government contracting and overseas expansion. How these strategies affected the revenue of some firms is described.

38953 ■ *"How Bloated Is Social Spending In Europe?" in Canadian Business (Vol. 85, August 13, 2012, No. 13, pp. 66)*
Pub: George Media Inc.
Ed: James Cowan. **Released:** August 13, 2012. **Description:** A study conducted by the World Bank found that social spending in Europe is higher than the rest of the world combined. A chart is presented which illustrates government spending on social protection in European countries and in other countries.

38954 ■ *"How Green Is The Valley?" in Barron's (Vol. 88, July 4, 2008, No. 28, pp. 13)*
Description: San Jose, California has made a good start towards becoming a leader in alternative energy technology through the establishment of United Laboratories' own lab in the city. The certification process for photovoltaic cells will be dramatically shortened with this endeavor.

38955 ■ *"Illinois Bets On Recycling Programs" in Chicago Tribune (November 29, 2008)*
Pub: McClatchy-Tribune Information Services
Ed: Joel Hood. **Description:** Traditionally the holiday gift-giving season is one of the most wasteful times of year and the state of Illinois is granting $760,000 to small businesses and cities in an attempt to expand curbside recycling programs and hire additional workers to address electronic waste.

38956 ■ *In Fed We Trust: Ben Bernanke's Ware on the Great Panic*
Pub: Crown Business
Ed: David Wessel. **Released:** 2009. **Price:** $16. **Description:** A look at the central bank's reaction to the crisis and Ben Bernanke has been forced to play the crisis by ear in order to keep the economy from imploding.

38957 ■ *"In the SBA's Face" in American Small Business League (December 2010)*
Pub: Hispanic Business Inc.
Contact: Jesus Chavarria, President
Ed: Richard Larsen. **Description:** Lloyd Chapman uses the American Small Business League to champion small business. Statistical data included.

38958 ■ *"Incentives In Play for Astronautics" in Business Journal-Milwaukee (Vol. 28, November 5, 2010, No. 5, pp. A1)*
Pub: Milwaukee Business Journal
Ed: Sean Ryan. **Description:** Astronautics Corporation was offered incentives by local government officials in Milwaukee, Wisconsin and by Brewery Project LLC to move into a building in The Brewery in the city. The company's officials remain indecisive over the offers and incentives.

38959 ■ *"Income Tax Credit for Business Pushes the Job Creation Button" in Idaho Business Review (August 27, 2014)*
Pub: Dolan Co.
Contact: James P. Dolan, President
Released: August 27, 2014. **Description:** Idaho's new Reimbursement Incentive Act program creates a tax credit for businesses with a qualifying project that will add new jobs that are paid at or above the average wage for work performed. Legislation and technical requirements for small businesses to quality are outlined.

38960 ■ "Intel: Tax Breaks Key" in Business Journal Portland (Vol. 27, October 22, 2010, No. 34, pp. 1)
Pub: Portland Business Journal
Ed: Erik Siemers. Description: Intel Corporation believes that state tax incentives will be critical, especially in the purchase of manufacturing equipment, as they build a new chip factory in Hillsboro, Oregon. The tax breaks would help Intel avoid paying 10 times more in property taxes compared to average Washington County firms. Critics argue that Intel has about $15 billion in cash assets, and can afford the factory without the tax breaks.

38961 ■ "Is Fannie Mae the Next Government Bailout?" in Barron's (Vol. 88, March 10, 2008, No. 10, pp. 21)
Pub: Dow Jones & Co., Inc.
Contact: Clare Hart, President
Ed: Jonathan R. Laing. Description: Fannie Mae may need a government bailout as it faces huge hits brought about by the effects of the housing crisis. The shares of the government-sponsored enterprise have dropped 65 percent since the housing crisis began.

38962 ■ "Is Mulcair Good for Business?" in Canadian Business (Vol. 85, June 11, 2012, No. 10, pp. 20)
Pub: George Media Inc.
Ed: Sarah Barmak. Released: June 11, 2012. Description: Some of the pronouncements made by New Democratic Party leader Thomas Mulcair suggest that he may be both a friend and an enemy of the Canadian business community. He expressed support to the energy sector and endorsed lower taxes but also commented on the negative effect of oilsands development.

38963 ■ "It's Good to be Goldman" in Barron's (Vol. 89, July 20, 2009, No. 29, pp. 5)
Pub: Dow Jones & Co., Inc.
Contact: Clare Hart, President
Ed: Randall W. Forsyth. Description: Profits of Goldman Sachs rose to $3.44 billion in the second quarter of 2009, aided by federal financial stimulus programs. CIT Group is facing bankruptcy and may need up to $6 billion to survive. The federal economic stimulus programs are benefiting Wall Street more than the US economy itself.

38964 ■ "It's Not Easy Being Small" in Baltimore Business Journal (Vol. 27, October 9, 2009, No. 22, pp. 1)
Pub: American City Business Journals
Ed: Scott Dance. Description: A look at how small businesses were left out of the stimulus-funded federal contracts in Maryland. Small contractors were not listed in the federal contracts database USAspending.gov and none were hired for work in the state.

38965 ■ "It's Time To Swim" in Canadian Business (Vol. 81, March 3, 2008, No. 3, pp. 37)
Ed: Megan Harman. Description: Canadian manufacturers should consider Asian markets such as India and the United Arab Emirates as the U.S. economic downturn continues. Canada's shortage in skilled labor is also expected to negatively affect manufacturing industries. Ontario's plans to assist manufacturers are also presented.

38966 ■ K-21 Small Business Loan Program
Pub: International Wealth Success, Inc.
Ed: Tyler G. Hicks. Price: $100. Description: Guide to the Small Business Loan Program that offers loans to small and minority-owned companies doing work for government agencies, large corporations, hospitals, universities, and similar organizations.

38967 ■ "KC Incentives Debate Rages on Unabated" in The Business Journal-Serving Metropolitan Kansas City (Vol. 26, September 5, 2008, No. 52)
Pub: American City Business Journals, Inc.
Contact: Whitney Shaw, President
Ed: Rob Roberts. Description: Debate on the new economic development and incentives policy adopted by the Kansas City Council is still on. The city's

Planned Industrial Expansion Authority has rejected a standard property tax abatement proposal. The real estate development community has opposed the rejection of proposed the tax incentives policy.

38968 ■ "KC Sewer Solutions May Overflow With Green Ideas" in The Business Journal-Serving Metropolitan Kansas City (August 22, 2008)
Pub: American City Business Journals, Inc.
Contact: Whitney Shaw, President
Ed: Suzanna Stagemeyer. Description: Adding green solutions such as small, dispersed basins to catch runoffs and the use of deep rooted natural plants to fix the sewer system of Kansas could probably justify the $2.3 billion worth of funds needed for the project. The city has been ordered by the EPA and the Missouri Department of Natural Resources to fix their sewer systems that are overwhelmed by significant rains.

38969 ■ "Lawmakers, Execs Launch Effort to Save Rural Hospitals" in Atlanta Business Chronicle (June 13, 2014, pp. 7A)
Pub: American City Business Journals, Inc.
Contact: Whitney Shaw, President
Released: June 13, 2014. Description: Governor Nathan Deal has appointed a committee of Georgia lawmakers and healthcare executives to launch an effort to save the state's financially burdened rural hospitals. In addition, he plans to allow rural hospitals that have closed or are on the verge of closing, to scale back their operations, under a new rule approved by the Georgia Board of Community Health.

38970 ■ "Leaders Weigh In On Fannie Mae, Freddie Mac Failure, Fed Bailout" in The Business Journal - Serving Phoenix and the Valley of the Sun (Vol. 28, September 14, 2008, No. 53, pp. 1)
Pub: American City Business Journals, Inc.
Contact: Whitney Shaw, President
Ed: Chris Casacchia, Mike Sunnucks, Jan Buchholz. Description: Fannie Mae and Freddie Mac's federal takeover was a move to help stabilize the financial market and it helped bring down interest rates in the past week. Local executives from Arizona's Phoenix area share their thoughts on the immediate effect of the takeover and its upside and downside.

38971 ■ "Lending Act Touted by Michaud" in Morning Sentinel (June 21, 2010)
Ed: Doug Harlow. Description: If passed, the Small Business Jobs Tax Relief Act will leverage up to $300 billion in loans for small businesses through a $30 billion lending fund for small and medium-sized community banks, which focus on lending to small firms.

38972 ■ "A Limited Sphere of Influence?" in Mergers & Acquisitions: The Dealmaker's Journal (March 1, 2008)
Pub: SourceMedia Inc.
Contact: James M. Malkin, Chief Executive Officer
Ed: Ken MacFadyen. Description: Changes to the interest rate has had little impact on the mergers and acquisitions market since the federal funds rate does not link directly to the liquidity available to the M&A market; lenders are looking at cash flows and are likely to remain cautious due to other factors impacting the market.

38973 ■ "Local Film Industry Stands To Lose Jobs, Millions of Dollars Unless Florida Expands" in Orlando Business Journal (Vol. 30, March 14, 2014, No. 38, pp. 4)
Pub: American City Business Journals
Released: March 14, 2014. Description: Central Florida's motion picture and TV production industries are in need of more government incentives. Many TV programs have been cancelled due to lack of this funding. Meanwhile, members of the sectors are set to lobby legislature to pass a $1.2 billion incentive package.

38974 ■ "Lords Should Get Real About Food" in Farmer's Weekly (March 28, 2008, No. 320)
Description: Discusses the reasons why farming needs subsidies and suggests that the House of Lords should look at the way that grocery stores are operating.

38975 ■ "Major Renovation Planned for Southridge" in Business Journal-Milwaukee (Vol. 28, November 12, 2010, No. 6, pp. A1)
Pub: Milwaukee Business Journal
Ed: Stacy Vogel Davis. Description: Simon Property Group plans to invest more than $20 million in upgrading and renovating Southridge Mall in Milwaukee County, Wisconsin. The project, which is partially financed by a $10 million grant from the Village of Greendale, could boost the property's value by $52.5 million.

38976 ■ "Making It Stick" in Business Courier (Vol. 24, November 14, 2007, No. 30, pp. 1)
Pub: American City Business Journals, Inc.
Contact: Whitney Shaw, President
Ed: Lucy May. Description: Discusses a report by the Brookings Institution which shows the need for the U.S. government to offer greater support to the country's metro areas in order to excel globally. Ohio, which has seven of the country's 100 largest metropolitan areas, does not receive enough funds, due to the need to finance less populated areas. Because of this, Ohio politicians have to spread less funding in order to cover more constituents.

38977 ■ "M&I Execs May Get Golden Parachutes" in Business Journal-Milwaukee (Vol. 28, December 31, 2010, No. 14, pp. A3)
Pub: Milwaukee Business Journal
Ed: Rich Kirchen. Description: Marshall and Isley Corporation's top executives have a chance to receive golden-parachute payments it its buyer, BMO Financial Group, repays the Troubled Asset Relief Program (TARP) loan on behalf of the company. One TARP rule prevents golden-parachute payments to them and the next five most highly paid employees of TARP recipients.

38978 ■ "Manufacturers Urged to Adapt to Defense" in Crain's Cleveland Business (Vol. 30, June 22, 2009, No. 24, pp. 3)
Pub: Crain Communications Inc.
Ed: Dan Shingler. Description: Manufacturers in Northeast Ohio are making products for the military from steel, polymers or composite materials. The U.S. Department of Defense is teaching companies to work with titanium and other advanced metals in order to further manufacture for the military.

38979 ■ "Market Watch" in Barron's (Vol. 88, March 24, 2008, No. 12, pp. M18)
Pub: Dow Jones & Co., Inc.
Contact: Clare Hart, President
Ed: Ashraf Laidi, Marc Pado, David Kotok. Description: Latest measures implemented by the Federal Reserve to address the credit crisis did not benefit the US dollar, with the Japanese yen and the euro recouping earlier losses against the dollar. Goldman Sachs reported earnings of $3.23 per share, claiming a stronger liquidity position. The US markets bottomed early on 22 January 2007, according to evidence.

38980 ■ "Maryland Legislature to Tackle Crisis in Jobless Fund" in Baltimore Business Journal (Vol. 27, December 18, 2009, No. 32, pp. 1)
Pub: American City Business Journals
Ed: Scott Dance. Description: Maryland's General Assembly is set to finalize changes to the state's unemployment insurance system as soon as it convenes for the 2010 session. The move was aimed to draw $127 million in stimulus money that can support the nearly depleted fund of unemployment benefits within 45 days.

38981 ■ "Mayor Unveils Business Plan" in Boston Business Journal (Vol. 29, September 16, 2011, No. 19, pp. 1)
Pub: American City Business Journals, Inc.
Ed: Gary Haber. Description: Mayor Stephanie Rawlings-Blake of Baltimore, Maryland unveiled her plan to push the economy forward. Her key objectives include giving more support for the city's technology companies and refocusing the Baltimore Development Corporation on job creation and retention.

38982 ■ *"Md. Bankers Say 'Devil Is In the Details' of New $30B Loan Fund" in Baltimore Business Journal (Vol. 28, October 8, 2010, No. 22)*
Pub: Baltimore Business Journal
Ed: Gary Haber. **Description:** Maryland community bankers have expressed doubts over a new federal loan program for small business. The new law will also earmark $80 billion for community banks. Comments from executives also given.

38983 ■ *"Md. Housing Leaders Race to Stem Rising Tide of Foreclosures: Neighborhood Watch" in Baltimore Business Journal (Vol. 28, July 23, 2010, No. 11, pp. 1)*
Pub: Baltimore Business Journal
Ed: Daniel J. Sernovitz. **Description:** Maryland government and housing leaders are set to spend $100 million in federal funding to stem the increase in foreclosures in the area. The federal funding is seen as inadequate to resolve the problem of foreclosures.

38984 ■ *"Md. May Avoid Congress on Medicare Waiver" in Baltimore Business Journal (Vol. 30, June 15, 2012, No. 6, pp. 1)*
Pub: American City Business Journals, Inc.
Contact: Whitney Shaw, President
Ed: Sarah Gantz. **Released:** June 15, 2012. **Description:** Maryland leaders may not seek the US Congress' help to avoid losing a Medicare waiver. The waiver has standardized Medicare reimbursement rates for all hospitals. Comments from officials included.

38985 ■ *"Md.'s Film Industry Professionals have to Leave the State to Find Work: Exiting Stage Left" in Baltimore Business Journal (Vol. 28, June 18, 2010, No. 6, pp. 1)*
Pub: Baltimore Business Journal
Ed: Scott Dance. **Description:** Film professionals including crew members and actors have been leaving Maryland to find work in other states such as Michigan, Louisiana, and Georgia where bigger budgets and film production incentives are given. Other consequences of this trend in local TV and film production are discussed.

38986 ■ *"Md.'s Historic Tax Credit Plan Gains Support" in Baltimore Business Journal (Vol. 27, January 8, 2010, No. 36, pp. 1)*
Pub: American City Business Journals
Ed: Heather Harlan Warnack. **Description:** Maryland Governor Martin O'Malley plans to push legislation in the General Assembly to extend for three more years the tax credit program for rehabilitation of obsolete buildings. The Maryland Heritage Structure Rehabilitation Tax Credit Program has declined from almost $75 million in expenses in 2001 to roughly $5 million in 2010 fiscal year. Details on the projects that benefited from the program are explored.

38987 ■ *"Loan Dollars Sit Idle for Energy Plan" in Baltimore Business Journal (Vol. 28, September 10, 2010, No. 18, pp. 1)*
Pub: Baltimore Business Journal
Ed: Scott Dance. **Description:** The Maryland Energy Administration has millions of dollars in Federal stimulus and state energy efficiency cash sitting idle and might be lost once the window for stimulus spending is gone. However, businesses have no interest in betting on renewable energy because some cannot afford to take out more loans. Other challenges faced by these businesses are presented.

38988 ■ *"MEDC: Put Venture Funds to Work" in Crain's Detroit Business (Vol. 25, June 22, 2009, No. 25, pp. 1)*
Pub: Crain Communications Inc. - Detroit
Contact: Keith Crain, Chairman
Ed: Tom Henderson. **Description:** Michigan Strategic Fund board will finalize approval for ESP Holdings II LLC, Peninsula Capital Partners LLC, Triathlon Medical Ventures LLC and Arsenal Venture Partners Inc. are expected to share $35.5 million from the fund.

38989 ■ *"Medicaid Expansion Could Prompt New Taxes, Program Cuts in Maryland" in Baltimore Business Journal (Vol. 27, October 23, 2009, No. 24, pp. 1)*
Pub: American City Business Journals
Ed: Julekha Dash. **Description:** Effects of the expected federal expansion of Medicaid under federal health care reform on Maryland tax policy are presented. Health care executives believe new taxes are necessary for the state to pay for an expansion that could cost over $400 million to $600 million.

38990 ■ *"Mercy Parent Nets Almost $1B in 2011" in Sacramento Business Journal (Vol. 28, September 30, 2011, No. 31, pp. 1)*
Pub: Sacramento Business Journal
Ed: Kathy Robertson. **Description:** Catholic Healthcare West has reported almost $1 billion in profits for 2010. The company has reported a profit margin of 8.7 percent. It also absorbed more than $1 billion in costs from charity care and government programs.

38991 ■ *"Michaud Touts Small-Business Credentials" in Bangor Daily News (September 10, 2010)*
Pub: Bangor Daily News
Ed: Nick Sambides, Jr. **Description:** Mike Michaud, Democrat, is running against a Republican challenger in the 2nd District and states he will support the Small Business Jobs Tax Relief Act if reelected.

38992 ■ *"Michigan Means Growth: Sustaining Growth Through Thick and Thin: Michigan Companies Sustain Growth with Well-Timed Access to Capital" in Inc. (Vol. 36, September 2014, No. 7, pp. 164)*
Pub: Mansueto Ventures L.L.C.
Contact: John Koten, Chief Executive Officer
Released: September 2014. **Description:** Successful companies possess flexibility, foresight and resources to turn adversity into opportunity. The small businesses in Michigan who have sustained experienced sales growth despite the recession of 2007. The Michigan Economic Development Corporation has introduced three initiatives to help Michigan businesses grow, including venture capital, collateral support and loan participation through the State Small Business Credit Initiative, and cash incentives for businesses looking to invest in urban communities or grow jobs.

38993 ■ *"Microlending Seen as Having a Major Impact" in Business Journal Serving Greater Tampa Bay (Vol. 30, November 26, 2010, No. 49, pp. 1)*
Pub: Tampa Bay Business Journal
Ed: Margie Manning. **Description:** There are several organizations that are planning to offer microlending services in Tampa Bay, Florida. These include the Children's Board of Hillsborough County, and OUR Microlending Florida LLC. Organizations that are already offering these services in the area include the Small Business Administration and the Tampa Bay Black Business Investment Corp.

38994 ■ *"Millions More For Health Care?" in Austin Business Journal (Vol. 32, June 29, 2012, No. 17, pp. 3)*
Pub: American City Business Journals, Inc.
Contact: Whitney Shaw, President
Ed: Sandra Zaragoza. **Released:** June 29, 2012. **Description:** Central Health, Seton Healthcare Family and other government and health entities have been working on a plan that may result in millions more in federal funding for healthcare in Texas. The health care plan is part of the 1115 Waiver program under the Social Security Act. Insights on the waiver are also given.

38995 ■ *"Minnesota ABC Event Looks at Government Contracting" in Finance and Commerce Daily Newspaper (November 23, 2010)*
Pub: Dolan Media Newswires
Contact: Sylvia Dolan, Director
Ed: Brian Johnson. **Description:** Minnesota Associated Builders and Contractors hosted an event focusing on doing business with government agencies. Topics included bidding work, awarding jobs, paperwork, guidelines, certifications and upcoming projects.

38996 ■ *"Minority Auto Suppliers Get Help Diversifying" in Crain's Detroit Business (Vol. 26, January 11, 2010, No. 2, pp. 3)*
Pub: Crain Communications Inc.
Contact: Rance E. Crain, President
Ed: Sherri Welch. **Description:** Displaced minority auto suppliers are being given assistance by the Kauffman's Foundation Urban Entrepreneur Partnership Detroit program, a three-year effort to assist 150 of the region's suppliers into more diversified businesses.

38997 ■ *"Mission: Recruitment" in HRMagazine (Vol. 54, January 2009, No. 1, pp. 42)*
Pub: Society for Human Resource Management
Contact: Henry G. Jackson, President
E-mail: hjackson@shrm.org
Ed: Theresa Minton-Eversole. **Description:** Due to the hiring challenges faced by Army recruiters, they are partnering with employers in order to establish connections to high quality, Army-trained individuals when they separate from active duty.

38998 ■ *"MN Effort To Privatize Coverage Struggles" in Business Journal (Vol. 30, July 6, 2012, No. 6, pp. 1)*
Pub: American City Business Journals, Inc.
Contact: Whitney Shaw, President
Ed: Katharine Grayson. **Released:** July 6, 2012. **Description:** The Health Minnesota Contribution Program will move MinnesotaCare members to the private market. Health insurance brokers have supported passage of the law. MinnesotaCare members have received state-subsidized insurance premiums.

38999 ■ *"More Aid, Please: Letting the Sunshine In" in Barron's (Vol. 89, July 6, 2009, No. 27, pp. 11)*
Pub: Dow Jones & Co., Inc.
Contact: Clare Hart, President
Ed: Katherine Cheng. **Description:** Solar energy industry leaders believe the industry needs aid from the US government regarding the funding of its research efforts and lowering solar energy costs. The climate change bill passed by the US House of Representatives signifies the US government's desire to significantly reduce carbon dioxide emissions.

39000 ■ *"More Corporate Welfare?" in Canadian Business (Vol. 80, February 12, 2007, No. 4, pp. 96)*
Description: The burden on Canadian taxpayers by governmental efforts to finance loss-making companies in the name of corporate welfare is discussed.

39001 ■ *"More Jobs Heading to Suburb" in Austin Business JournalInc. (Vol. 29, November 20, 2009, No. 37, pp. 1)*
Pub: American City Business Journals
Ed: Kate Harrington. **Description:** Site of Advanced Integration Technologies (AIT) in Pflugerville, Texas might increase its workforce to 80 employees in the next six months due to the creation of an incentive package. Funds from the Pflugerville Community Development Corporation have been helping AIT's initiative to hire more workers. The firm receives $2,000 from the plan for every new employee it hires.

39002 ■ *"Multifamily Banks on Fannie, Freddie" in Memphis Business Journal (Vol. 33, February 24, 2012, No. 46, pp. 1)*
Pub: American City Business Journal
Ed: Andy Ashby. **Description:** The possible demise of Fannie Mae and Freddie Mac is seen to adversely impact the multifamily apartment market of Memphis, Tennessee. The apartment market relies on federal loans for funding.

39003 ■ *"Nampa Police Department: Electronic Systems Just One Tool in Business Security Toolbox" in Idaho Business Review (October 29, 2010)*
Pub: Dolan Media Newswires
Ed: Brad Carlson. **Description:** Police departments and private security firms can help small businesses with hard security and business consultants can assist with internal audit security and fraud prevention.

39004 ■ *Navigating Your Way to Business Success: An Entrepreneur's Journey*
Pub: FreeBridge Publishing, Inc.
Ed: Kathryn B. Freeland. Price: $24.95. Description: Learn first-hand from a successful entrepreneur about assessing skills and talent, envisioning your company, planning a path to success, and then tapping into available government agencies to make your business become a reality.

39005 ■ *"NAWBO Takes the Stage at Press Conference for Small Business Jobs, Credit and Tax Relief Acts" in Marketwired (June 17, 2010)*
Pub: COMTEX
Contact: Chip Brian, President
Description: A survey of the National Association of Women Business Owners reported optimism returning and women business owners are ready to invest in job creation. The Small Business Jobs Tax Relief Act will aid in their progress.

39006 ■ *"New Apartments To Rise Downtown" in Memphis Business Journal (Vol. 33, January 27, 2012, No. 42, pp. 1)*
Pub: American City Business Journal
Ed: Andy Ashby. Description: TOV Virginia LP is planning to build an apartment complex in Memphis, Tennessee. The construction project is estimated to cost around $10.5 million. The development wll be focused on affordable housing and will use local and federal incentives.

39007 ■ *"A New Kid on the Block" in Barron's (Vol. 88, March 17, 2008, No. 11, pp. 58)*
Pub: Dow Jones & Co., Inc.
Contact: Clare Hart, President
Ed: Thomas G. Donlan. Description: Discusses the Federal Reserve which has offered to lend $100 billion in cash to banks and $200 billion in Treasuries to Wall Street investment banks that have problems with liquidity. The reluctance of the banks to lend money to meet a margin call on securities that could still depreciate is the reason why the agency is going into the direct loan business.

39008 ■ *"New Minority Business Development Agency Office Opens in Memphis" in Commercial Appeal (July 13, 2012)*
Description: Memphis, Tennessee announces the opening of the Minority Business Development Agency. The federally funded program will help to expand minority entrepreneurship in the region. Details of the program and funding are also included.

39009 ■ *"New Ways to Finance Solar Power Projects Expected to Lower Cost of Capital, Cut Electricity Rates, Boost Profits, and Expand Investor Pool" in PR Newswire (September 28, 2012)*
Pub: PR Newswire Association L.L.C.
Contact: David B. Armon, President
Description: Renewable energy companies are examining new ways to finance solar power projects. One such strategy includes the use of the REIT structure as a means to lowering costs of capital, lower the cost of generating solar power by nearly 20 percent. Investors would be more interested in the easy and liquid means in which to own a part of the fast growing solar market. Statistical details included.

39010 ■ *"Newly Minted Rep. Tom Graves Hits the Ground Running" in Atlanta Journal-Constitution (June 20, 2010, pp. A6)*
Pub: Atlanta Journal-Constitution
Contact: Michael Joseph, Publisher
Ed: Bob Keefe. Description: Newly elected Republican Representative Tom Graves of Ranger supports the Small Business Jobs Tax Relief Act.

39011 ■ *"N.J. Tries to Push Stimulus Funds to Minorities" in Philadelphia Business Journal (Vol. 28, September 25, 2009, No. 32, pp. 1)*
Pub: American City Business Journals Inc.
Ed: Athena D. Merritt. Description: New Jersey Governor Jon S. Corzine signed an executive order that seeks to ease the way for minority and women-owned business to take on federal stimulus-funded work. New Jersey has also forged new relations with different organizations to reduce the time and cost of certifications for businesses.

39012 ■ *"No End to the Nightmare; America's Car Industry" in The Economist (Vol. 390, January 3, 2009, No. 8612, pp. 46)*
Description: Detroit's struggling auto industry and the government loan package is discussed as well as the United Auto Worker union, which is loathed by Senate Republicans.

39013 ■ *"Not Enough: Most First Place Creditors Left Holding the Bag" in The Business Journal-Milwaukee (Vol. 25, August 15, 2008, No. 47, pp. A1)*
Pub: American City Business Journals, Inc.
Contact: Whitney Shaw, President
Ed: David Doege. Description: Most of the creditors of bankrupt real estate developer Scott Fergus are likely to remain unpaid as he only has an estimated $30,000 available for paying debts. Creditors, as of the 13 August 2008 deadline for filing claims, have filed a total of $79.1 million in claims.

39014 ■ *"Now Entering A Secure Area" in Women Entrepreneur (January 14, 2009)*
Ed: Aliza Sherman. Description: Despite the fact that the field of government intelligence and security is dominated by males, many women entrepreneurs are finding opportunities for their products and services in homeland security. Profiles of several women who have found such opportunities are included.

39015 ■ *"Numbers Game" in Baltimore Business Journal (Vol. 27, February 6, 2010, No. 40, pp. 1)*
Pub: American City Business Journals
Ed: Scott Dance. Description: Doubts are being raised regarding the impact of the federal stimulus spending in addressing unemployment in Maryland, which has experienced 1,800 jobs created so far. Details on the view of companies and the insufficient amount of contracts that lead to the fewer number of workers being hired are discussed.

39016 ■ *"NYPA Grants Aid Area Companies" in Business First of Buffalo (Vol. 30, January 10, 2014, No. 17, pp. 6)*
Pub: American City Business Journals, Inc.
Contact: Whitney Shaw, President
Released: January 10, 2014. Description: New York Power Authority (NYPA) trustees have approved more than $3.5 million in financial aid to Western New York enterprises. The NYPA and Empire State Development have also funded a package that includes low cost hydropower and $7 million in capital grants and tax credits. The Western New York area manufacturers that were granted aid are also presented.

39017 ■ *"On Growth Path of Rising Star" in Boston Business Journal (Vol. 31, June 24, 2011, No. 22, pp. 3)*
Pub: Boston Business Journal
Ed: Kyle Alspach. Description: 1366 Technologies Inc. of Lexington, Massachusetts is considered a rising solar power technology company. The firm secured $150 million loan guarantee from the US Department of Energy that could go to the construction of a 1,000 megawatt solar power plant.

39018 ■ *"OPSEU: Developmental Service Workers Picketing Across Ontario to Raise Community Awareness" in Canadian Corporate News (May 16, 2007)*
Description: Across Ontario staff who support people with developmental disabilities are picketing local MPP offices and other community hubs to highlight the Ontario government's inadequate response to the crisis in developmental services.

39019 ■ *"Organic Food Industry Goes to College" in USA Today (April 9, 2012)*
Pub: Gannett Company Inc.
Contact: Craig A. Dubow, President
Ed: Chuck Raasch. Description: With the organic food industry growing the US Department of Agriculture is has pumped $117 million into organic research in the last three years. According to a recent report by the Organic Farming Research Foundation (OFRF), the number of states committing land for organic research has nearly doubled from 2003 to 2011. Universities offering academic programs in organic farming rose from none to nine. The OFRF supports organic farmers and producers.

39020 ■ *"Outlook 2008 (9 Sectors to Watch): Biotech" in Canadian Business (Vol. 81, December 19, 2007, No. 1, pp. 48)*
Pub: Rogers Media Inc.
Contact: Tony Viner, President
Ed: Calvin Leung. Description: Forecasts on the Canadian biotechnology sector for 2008 are presented. Details on the increase in the number of biotechnology companies and prediction on the government's plan for business incentives are discussed.

39021 ■ *"Pain Ahead as Profit Pressure Increases" in Crain's Chicago Business (Vol. 31, May 5, 2008, No. 18, pp. 4)*
Pub: Crain Communications Inc.
Contact: Todd Johnson, Publisher
Ed: Daniel Rome Levine. Description: Interview with David Klaskin, the chairman and chief investment officer at Oak Ridge Investments LLC, who discusses the outlook for the economy and corporate earnings, particularly in the housing and auto industries, the impact of economic stimulus checks, the weakness of the dollar and recommendations of stocks that individual investors may find helpful.

39022 ■ *"Past Promises Haunt Project" in The Business Journal-Portland (Vol. 25, August 1, 2008, No. 21, pp. 1)*
Pub: American City Business Journals, Inc.
Contact: Whitney Shaw, President
Ed: Aliza Earnshaw. Description: Oregon University System and Oregon Health and Science University will face the state Legislature to defend their request for a $250 million in state bonds to fund a life-sciences collaborative research building. The project is meant to help grow the Oregon bioscience industry. Comments from industry observers and legislators are also presented.

39023 ■ *"Pennsylvania DEP To Conduct Natural Gas Vehicle Seminar" in Travel & Leisure Close-Up (October 8, 2012)*
Description: Pennsylvania Department of Environmental Protection is holding a Natural Gas Vehicle seminar at the Bayfront Convention Center in Erie, PA, as well as other locations throughout the state. The seminars will help municipal and commercial fleet owners make better informed decisions when converting fleets from compressed natural gas and liquefied natural gas.

39024 ■ *"The People Puzzle; Re-Training America's Workers" in The Economist (Vol. 390, January 3, 2009, No. 8612, pp. 32)*
Description: With thousands of workers losing their jobs, America is now facing the task of getting them back to work. With an overall unemployment rate of 6.7 percent, the federal government has three main ways for leading workers back to employment: training them for new jobs, providing unemployment insurance in order to replace lost wages during the period of job-hunting; and matching employers who desire a skill with workers who have that skill. Specialized staffing agencies provide employers and potential employees with the help necessary to find a job in some of the more niche markets.

39025 ■ *"Photo Release - Affordable Housing Grant Helps Elderly Couple Regain Stability" in Benzinga.com (August 6, 2012)*
Pub: Benzinga.com
Contact: Kyle Bazzy, President
Released: August 6, 2012. Description: Martin and Darlene Desmond moved into their new Habitat for Humanity home, made possible by an Affordable Housing Program grant. Details about the Federal Home Loan Bank of Dallas, one of 12 district banks in the FHLBanki Syhstem that supports housing and comunity development providing low priced loans and other credit products to help low income people afford a home.

39026 ■ *A Piece of the Pie*
Pub: Outskirts Press Inc.
Contact: Brent Sampson, President
Released: July 2005. **Description:** Examination of the U.S. Small Business Administration's program 8(a), designed to help disadvantaged individuals grow their small businesses.

39027 ■ *"Pitch for SPX Expansion was Full of Energy"* in *Charlotte Business Journal* (Vol. 25, November 19, 2010, No. 35, pp. 1)
Pub: Charlotte Business Journal
Ed: John Downey. **Description:** SPX Corporation announced that it will expand their headquarters in Ballantyne after Charlotte and North Carolina leaders made an aggressive push to retain the company. SPX Corporation is expected to invest $70 million for the expansion, which would mean 180 new jobs in Charlotte.

39028 ■ *"Plan Targets Small Banks"* in *Business Journal Portland* (Vol. 26, December 11, 2009, No. 40, pp. 1)
Pub: American City Business Journals, Inc.
Ed: Courtney Sherwood. **Description:** Senator Jeff Merkley of Oregon has proposed an expansion of the Troubled Assets Relief Program to accommodate banks with capital levels of less than 10 percent. In his proposal, affected banks would be mandated on a stress test to evaluate capital requirements.

39029 ■ *"Polanco Fellows: A Capital Program that Changes Lives"* in *Hispanic Business* (Vol. 30, September 2008, No. 9, pp. 82)
Pub: Hispanic Business Inc.
Contact: Jesus Chavarria, President
Ed: John Schumacher. **Description:** Launched in 2003, the Polanco fellows program is named after former state Senator Richard Polanco, a founder and chairman of the California Latino Caucus Institute. The program offers young Hispanics a chance to experience public policy and the functioning of the California Capitol through a 12-month, on-the-job Capitol training.

39030 ■ *"Political Environments and Business Strategy: Implications for Managers"* in *Business Horizons* (Vol. 51, January-February 2008)
Pub: Elsevier Advanced Technology Publications
Ed: Gerald D. Keim, Amy J. Hillman. **Description:** Various government bodies and business organizations work together in shaping new business opportunities and policies that arise from globalization. Presented is framework of public policy considerations for business managers. The framework is based on Nobel laureate Douglas North's work.

39031 ■ *"The Power of Innovation"* in *Canadian Business* (Vol. 81, February 26, 2008, No. 4, pp. 57)
Pub: Rogers Media Inc.
Contact: Tony Viner, President
Ed: Andrew Wahl. **Description:** Canada ranks badly in terms innovation yardsticks that directly translate to economic growth such as business R&D as a percentage of GDP and R&D per capita. Canada's reliance on natural resources does not provide incentives to innovate unlike smaller countries with little natural resources. Canada could spur innovation through regulations that encourage industrial research.

39032 ■ *"The Price of Citizenship"* in *Canadian Business* (Vol. 79, August 14, 2006, No. 16-17, pp. 13)
Ed: Jack Mintz. **Description:** Safety and insurance benefits provided by the Canadian government to Canadian passport holders returning from Lebanon, is discussed.

39033 ■ *"Program To Steer Mexican Business Here"* in *Austin Business Journal* (Vol. 32, June 8, 2012, No. 14, pp. 1)
Pub: American City Business Journals, Inc.
Contact: Whitney Shaw, President
Ed: Vicky Garza. **Released:** June 8, 2012. **Description:** The Greater Austin Hispanic Chamber of Commerce has co-launched the Instituto de Empresas

de Austin (IDEA) to attract Mexican entrepreneurs to Austin. IDEA is a monthlong program that aims to provide Mexican entrepreneurs with necessary information and make it easy for them to invest in the city. The program was formed through a partnership with the University of Texas IC(super 2) Institute.

39034 ■ *"Providers Ride First Wave of eHealth Dollars"* in *Boston Business Journal* (Vol. 31, June 10, 2011, No. 20, pp. 1)
Pub: Boston Business Journal
Ed: Julie M. Donnelly. **Description:** Health care providers in Massachusetts implementing electronic medical records technology started receiving federal stimulus funds. Beth Israel Deaconess Medical Center was the first hospital to qualify for the funds.

39035 ■ *"Public Health Care Funding and the Montana Economy"* in *Montana Business Quarterly* (Vol. 49, Spring 2011, No. 1, pp. 23)
Pub: University of Montana Bureau of Business and Economic Research
Contact: Patrick Barkey, Director
E-mail: patrick.barkey@business.umt.edu
Ed: Gregg Davis. **Description:** Montana has more baby boomers and veterans per capita than any other state in the nation. The role of public health in the state is a crucial part of the state's economy.

39036 ■ *"Q&A: Saskatchewan Premier Brad Wall"* in *Canadian Business* (Vol. 82, April 27, 2009, No. 7, pp. 9)
Pub: Rogers Media Inc.
Contact: Tony Viner, President
Ed: Joe Castaldo. **Description:** Saskatchewan Premier Brad Wall believes that the mood in the province is positive, as its economy is one of the few that is expected to post growth in 2009. Wall actively promotes the province in job fairs, offering $20,000 in tuition for recent college and university graduates that relocate in the province for seven years. Wall's views on the province's economy and challenges are presented.

39037 ■ *"The Quest for the Smart Prosthetic"* in *Canadian Business* (Vol. 83, October 12, 2010, No. 17, pp. 26)
Pub: Rogers Media Inc.
Contact: Tony Viner, President
Ed: Jacqueline Nelson. **Description:** Information about a two-year research project led by Southern Methodist University (SMU) and funded by the Defense Advance Research Projects Agency (DARPA) is provided. The agency aims to create a 'smart prosthetic' which will improve the lives of military amputees. The planned prosthetic will use a sensor that can carry nerve signals through synthetic channels.

39038 ■ *"Ready for Our Ships to Come In"* in *Philadelphia Business Journal* (Vol. 33, April 11, 2014, No. 9, pp. 4)
Pub: American City Business Journals
Released: April 11, 2014. **Description:** Philadelphia Regional Port Authority planned the construction of the Southport Marine Terminal in South Philadelphia at a cost of $300 million to capitalize on changes in the shipping industry. The Tioga Marine Terminal in Port Richmond is also being improved using a mix of public and private money. The growing competition among the East Coast ports is also discussed.

39039 ■ *"Real Estate Vets Take Times In Stride"* in *The Business Journal-Serving Metropolitan Kansas City* (Vol. 26, July 25, 2008, No. 46)
Ed: Rob Roberts. **Description:** Kansas City, Missouri's real estate industry veterans like Allen Block believe that the challenges faced by the industry in the 1980s, when the Federal Reserve Board controlled the money supply to slow down inflation, were worse than the challenges faced today. Other views, trends and information on the real estate industry of the city, are presented.

39040 ■ *"Recession Fears Power Gold"* in *Barron's* (Vol. 88, March 17, 2008, No. 11, pp. M14)
Pub: Dow Jones & Co., Inc.
Contact: Clare Hart, President
Ed: Melanie Burton. **Description:** Gold prices have been more attractive as the U.S. dollar weakens and

the Dow Jones Industrial Average has slipped almost 10 percent in 2008. The rate cuts from the Federal Reserve Board has also spurred inflation fears adding upward pressure to the price of the metal.

39041 ■ *"Red Tape Ties Detroit Housing Rehab Plan"* in *Crain's Detroit Business* (Vol. 24, September 22, 2008, No. 38, pp. 1)
Pub: Crain Communications Inc.
Contact: Rance E. Crain, President
Ed: Ryan Beene. **Description:** Venture-capital firm Wilherst Oxford LLC is a Florida-based company that has purchased 300 inner-city homes which were in foreclosure in Detroit. Wilherst Oxford is asking the city to forgive the existing tax and utility liens so the firm can utilize the money for home improvements. The city, however, is reluctant but has stated that they are willing to negotiate.

39042 ■ *"Region to Be Named Innovation Hub"* in *Business Courier* (Vol. 27, July 2, 2010, No. 9, pp. 1)
Pub: Business Courier
Ed: Dan Monk. **Description:** The selection of Cincinnati's consumer-marketing cluster as a 'Hub of Innovation' by the Ohio Department of Development could boost Cincinnati's chances of receiving $100 million in grants from Ohio's Third Frontier program and other funding sources. Implications of the University of Cincinnati's designation as a Center of Excellence in Advanced Transportation and Aerospace are also discussed.

39043 ■ *"Region Ready to Dig Deeper into Tech Fund"* in *Business Courier* (Vol. 26, October 30, 2009, No. 27, pp. 1)
Pub: American City Business Journals, Inc.
Contact: Whitney Shaw, President
Ed: James Ritchie. **Description:** Southwest Ohio region aims for a bigger share in the planned renewal of Ohio's Third Frontier technology funding program. Meanwhile, University of Cincinnati vice president Sarah Degen will be appointed to the program's advisory board if the renewal proceeds.

39044 ■ *"R.I. Lags in Solar Incentives"* in *Providence Business News* (Vol. 29, May 26, 2014, No. 8, pp. 1)
Pub: American City Business Journals
Released: May 26, 2014. **Description:** The state of Rhode Island has offered less in government renewable energy incentives than its neighboring states and has yet to experience the growth of residential solar energy projects. The Rhode Island Renewable Energy Fund allocated $800,000 to the small scale solar program in 2014.

39045 ■ *"Rich or Poor, Hospitals Must Work Together"* in *Crain's Chicago Business* (Vol. 31, April 28, 2008, No. 17, pp. 22)
Pub: Crain Communications Inc.
Contact: Todd Johnson, Publisher
Description: Chicago-area safety-net hospitals that serve the poor, uninsured and underinsured are struggling to stay open while wealthier areas compete to build advanced facilities for the expensive surgical procedures their privately insured patients can afford. If these safety-net hospitals close, their patients, many of them in ambulances, will show up at the remaining hospitals resulting in a strain that will test the ability of hospitals across the region to care for all of their patients. Hospitals need to address the threats to the local health care system before it slips into crisis since the current every-hospital-for-itself approach that pays off big for some will eventually make losers of everyone.

39046 ■ *"Ride-Share Programs Seem to Fit City's Future"* in *San Antonio Business Journal* (Vol. 28, May 9, 2014, No. 13, pp. 6)
Pub: American City Business Journals
Released: May 9, 2014. **Description:** San Antonio, Texas Mayor Julian Castro has been promoting the SA2020 plan that calls for an increase in downtown living and expanded public transit options. Castro made positive comments regarding the ride sharing services, even if they include a few disqualifications. The potential benefits of the ride sharing services into the city's plan are examined.

39047 ■ *"RIM Reinforces Claim as Top Dog by Expanding BlackBerry Service"* in Globe & Mail (March 11, 2006, pp. B3)
Ed: Simon Avery. **Description:** The plans of Research In Motion Ltd. to enhance the features of BlackBerry, through acquisition of Ascendent Systems, are presented.

39048 ■ *"Rosewood Site Faces Big Cleanup Before Stevenson Can Expand"* in Baltimore Business Journal (Vol. 27, February 6, 2010, No. 40, pp. 1)
Pub: American City Business Journals
Ed: Daniel J. Sernovitz. **Description:** Environmental assessment report states that Maryland's Rosewood Center for the Developmentally Disabled has significant amounts of toxic chemicals, which could impact Stevenson University's decision to purchase the property. Senator Robert A. Zirkin believes that the state should pay for the cleanup, which is expected to cost millions.

39049 ■ *"RT Seeking Ways to Finance Expansion"* in Sacramento Business Journal (Vol. 28, July 29, 2011, No. 22, pp. 1)
Pub: Sacramento Business Journal
Ed: Melanie Turner. **Description:** Sacramento Regional Transit District is considering ways to finance all its capital projects outlined in a 30-year transit master plan which would cost more than $7 billion to complete. Current funding sources include developer fees and state and federal assistance and fares. Part of the master plan is a light-rail line to Sacramento International Airport.

39050 ■ *"Rural Hospitals a Dying Breed"* in Memphis Business Journal (No. 35, April 11, 2014, No. 53, pp. 4)
Pub: American City Business Journals
Released: April 11, 2014. **Description:** Crittenden Regional Hospital in West Memphis, Tennessee has joined a growing number of rural hospitals across the country that is in jeopardy. Rural hospitals care for a patient population that is getting smaller and poorer and more dependent on government programs like Medicare and Medicaid. The hospital's challenges are addressed.

39051 ■ *"Ryan Gilbert Wants SBA To Mean Speedy Business Administration"* in Philadelphia Business Journal (Vol. 33, May 9, 2014, No. 13, pp. 8)
Pub: American City Business Journals
Released: May 9, 2014. **Description:** Ryan Gilbert, CEO of San Francisco, California-based Better Finance explains that his company uses its financial technology, SmartBiz, to help banks expedite Small Business Administration (SBA) loans. Better Finance, formerly known as BillFloat, helps small business owners receive SBA 7(a) loans between $5,000 and $150,000 within five business days instead of several week, offering easy online access to SBA loans at low interest rates.

39052 ■ *"S3 Entertainment Group Partners with WFW International for Film Services in Michigan"* in Michigan Vue (July-August 2008)
Description: William F. White (WFW), one of North America's largest production equipment providers has partnered with S3 Entertainment Group (S3EG), a Michigan-based full-service film production services company due to the new incentives package which currently offers the highest incentives in the United States, up to 42 percent. S3EG will actively store, lease, manage, distribute and sell WFW's equipment to the growing number of production teams that are filming in the state.

39053 ■ *"A Safety Net in Need of Repair"* in The Economist (Vol. 390, January 3, 2009, No. 8612, pp. 33)
Description: America's unemployment-insurance scheme is outdated and skimpy compared to other industrialized countries despite the fact that Americans tend to work harder at returning to the job market; the benefits are lower and available for a smaller amount of time and less unemployed workers are even able to collect these benefits. Statistical data included.

39054 ■ *"Salmon's Gem Air Wants Grant For Year-round Boise Flight"* in Idaho Business Review (September 3, 2014)
Pub: Dolan Co.
Contact: James P. Dolan, President
Released: September 3, 2014. **Description:** Gem Air offers four flights between Salmon and Boise, for both tourists and businesspeople including doctors and architects. The airline is requesting a $250,000 federal grant in order to compete with larger airlines and hopes to attract more business travelers with a direct flight between Boise and Atlanta.

39055 ■ *"Samsung 'Holding Breath"* in Austin Business JournalInc. (Vol. 29, January 29, 2010, No. 47, pp. 1)
Pub: American City Business Journals
Ed: Jacob Dirr. **Description:** Samsung Austin Semiconductor LLC entered into an incentives agreement with the State of Texas in 2005, which involved $230 million in tax breaks and public financing. Terms of the agreement have been met, but some are questioning whether the company will be able to meet its goals for the Austin operations in 2010.

39056 ■ *"San Antonio's Clean-Energy Push May Need More Peddle Power"* in San Antonio Business Journal (Vol. 26, February 10, 2012, No. 2, pp. 1)
Pub: American City Business Journal
Ed: Sanford Nowlin, W. Scott Bailey, Tamarind Phinisee. **Description:** CPS Energy said the government of San Antonio, Texas should form a green-energy coalition to ensure the success of its push for the use of renewable energy. Prospective coalition members include utility, research and industry officials.

39057 ■ *"SBA Can Improve Your Cash Flow"* in Business Owner (Vol. 35, September-October 2011, No. 5, pp. 3)
Pub: DL Perkins Company
Description: Federal assistance available to small business is examined. The Small Business Administration loan guarantee program is designed to improve availability and attractiveness of small business loans.

39058 ■ *"SBA Intervenes to Keep Cash Flowing"* in Business First Columbus (Vol. 25, November 21, 2008, No. 14, pp. A1)
Pub: American City Business Journals
Ed: Adrian Burns. **Description:** U.S. Small Business Administration's loan volumes fell as it tried to cushion the impact of the economic crisis on small businesses. Large investors have pulled back buying SBA loans due to declining profits, but demand for SBA loans are seen to resurge due to low risk.

39059 ■ *"SBA Lauds Anchorage DQ Franchise"* in Alaska Business Monthly (Vol. 27, October 2011, No. 10, pp. 9)
Pub: Alaska Business Publishing Company Inc.
Contact: Jim Martin, President
Ed: Nancy Pounds. **Description:** US Small Business Administration (SBA) honored Greg Todd, operator of four DQ Grill and Chill eateries in Anchorage, Alaska. The firm has created 100 jobs since receiving SBA assistance.

39060 ■ *"SBA Lending Hits Record"* in Saint Louis Business Journal (Vol. 32, September 30, 2011, No. 5, pp. 1)
Pub: Saint Louis Business Journal
Ed: Rick Desloge. **Description:** US Small Business Administration loans have reached a record high of $200 million in 2011. The agency decreased the usual loan fees.

39061 ■ *"SBA Lending Jumps in May: Loan Guarantee Raised, Fee Axed"* in Crain's Detroit Business (Vol. 25, June 8, 2009, No. 23, pp. 1)
Pub: Crain Communications Inc. - Detroit
Contact: Keith Crain, Chairman
Ed: Nancy Kaffer. **Description:** U.S. Small Business Administration backed 102 loans through its 7(a) program in May. Statistical data included.

39062 ■ *"SBA Reinvigorates Loan Program"* in Crain's Cleveland Business (Vol. 30, June 29, 2009, No. 25, pp. 1)
Pub: Crain Communications Inc.
Ed: Arielle Kass. **Description:** U.S. Small Business Administration has changed its loan programs that encourage banks to lend and businesses to borrow. Details of the program are discussed.

39063 ■ *"Science Museum, Theater Seeking State Loans"* in Sacramento Business Journal (Vol. 31, May 30, 2014, No. 14, pp. 4)
Pub: American City Business Journals
Released: May 30, 2014. **Description:** The Powerhouse Science Center and B Street Theatre in Sacramento, California are hoping to secure loans from the California Infrastructure and Economic Development Bank. Both nonprofit organizations are planning to start their own construction projects as soon as loans are received.

39064 ■ *"A Second Chance at Road Dollars"* in Orlando Business Journal (Vol. 26, February 5, 2010, No. 36, pp. 1)
Pub: American City Business Journals
Description: Nearly $10 million worth of construction projects in Central Florida would give construction companies that missed the initial round of federal stimulus-funded local road building projects another opportunity. Cost savings in the initial round of road projects enabled Orange, Osceola, and Seminole Counties to secure additional projects.

39065 ■ *"Second to None"* in Crain's Detroit Business (Vol. 26, January 18, 2010, No. 3, pp. 9)
Pub: Crain Communications Inc.
Contact: Rance E. Crain, President
Ed: Nancy Kaffer. **Description:** Second-stage companies are beginning to attract more attention from government entities and the business community alike, due in part to their ability to create jobs more rapidly than their counterparts both smaller and larger. Second-stage companies have between 10-99 employees and consistently have supplied the most jobs, despite overall job declines in recent years.

39066 ■ *"Seeking SBA Loan in Cincinnati? Good Luck"* in Business Courier (Vol. 26, October 16, 2009, No. 25, pp. 1)
Pub: American City Business Journals, Inc.
Contact: Whitney Shaw, President
Ed: Steve Watkins. **Description:** The largest banks in Greater Cincinnati reduced Small Business Administration (SBA) lending by 41 percent for the fiscal year ended September 2009. For the year, local SBA loans from all banks in the area declined 25 percent. The importance of SBA loans for growth of small business is examined.

39067 ■ *"Sen. Mark Warner Holds a Hearing on Government Contracting Modernization"* in Political/Congressional Transcript Wire (July 20, 2010)
Description: Senate Committee on the Budget, Task Force on Government Performance held a hearing on modernizing the business of government. Details of that hearing are included.

39068 ■ *"Sharp Restarts Toner Manufacturing: Production Moved from Japan to Serve China Market"* in Memphis Business Journal (Vol. 34, May 11, 2012, No. 4, pp. 1)
Pub: American City Business Journal
Ed: Michael Sheffield. **Description:** Sharp Manufacturing Company of America has decided to reopen its ink toner production plant in Memphis, Tennessee because of cheapter material, labor and freight costs. The company's move was also attributed to local economic growth and the government support they received after a 2008 tornado hit the area surrounding the area.

39069 ■ *"Shining a Light on Entrepreneurial Opportunities"* in San Antonio Business Journal (Vol. 28, July 11, 2014, No. 22, pp. 4)
Pub: American City Business Journals
Released: July 11, 2014. **Description:** Café Commerce is a small business and entrepreneurship development program launched by the City of San

Antonio in partnership with microlender Accion Texas. The goal of the new resource center is to make entrepreneurship easier by complementing existing programs and serving as a platform to introduce new ones to the business community.

39070 ■ "Should the Fed Regulate Wall Street?" in Barron's (Vol. 88, March 24, 2008, No. 12, pp. M15)
Pub: Dow Jones & Co., Inc.
Contact: Clare Hart, President
Ed: Randall W. Forsyth. **Description:** Greater regulation of the financial sector by the Federal Reserve is essential for it to survive the crisis it is experiencing. The resulting regulation could be in complete contrast with the deregulation the sector previously experienced.

39071 ■ "Sky Harvest Windpower Corp. - Operational Update" in Benzinga.com (October 5, 2012)
Pub: Benzinga.com
Contact: Kyle Bazzy, President
Released: October 5, 2012. **Description:** Solar power is the fastest growing technology in the nation's energy industry and US utility-scale solar power market has grown over the last three years due to rising energy prices, volatility of fuel costs, and government incentives for renewable energy.

39072 ■ "Small Bank Has Big Lending Plans, New Hire" in Silicon Valley/San Jose Business Journal (Vol. 30, September 21, 2012, No. 26, pp. 1)
Pub: American City Business Journal
Description: Santa Cruz County Bank has hired government-backed loans specialist Sat Kanwar in addition to Susan Chandler, Jorge Reguerin and Daljit Bains to boost the bank's Small Business Administration lending department. According to Chandler, the bank will take on loans ranging from $25,000 to several million dollars.

39073 ■ "Small-Business Agenda: Increase Capital, Education, Tax Breaks" in Crain's Detroit Business (Vol. 24, March 30, 2008)
Pub: Crain Communications Inc.
Contact: Rance E. Crain, President
Ed: Nancy Kaffer. **Description:** Discusses the policy suggestions detailed in the Small Business Association of Michigan's entrepreneurial agenda which include five main categories of focus: making entrepreneurial education a higher state priority; increasing capital available to entrepreneurs; using the state's tax structure as an incentive for entrepreneurial growth; getting university research from the lab to the market; and limiting government regulation that's burdensome to small businesses and getting legislative support of entrepreneurial assistance efforts.

39074 ■ The Small Business Guide to HSAs
Pub: Brick Tower Press
Contact: Linda Goetz Holmes, Editor
Ed: JoAnn Mills Laing. **Released:** August 31, 2004. **Price:** $14.95. **Description:** Government-assisted Health Savings Accounts (HSAs) offer employees a tax-free way to accumulate savings to be used for qualified medical expenses, they can be rolled over without penalty for future spending, or invested to accumulate savings to pay for health needs after retirement. Employers offering HSAs can save up to two-thirds of business expenses on health insurance costs.

39075 ■ "Small Wind Power Market to Double by 2015 at $634 Million" in Western Farm Press (September 30, 2011)
Pub: Penton Media, Inc.
Description: Small wind power provides cost-effective electricity on a highly localized level, in both remote settings as well as in conjunction with power from the utility grid. Government incentives are spurring new growth in the industry.

39076 ■ "SNAP Grant and Rebuilding Together-Houston Provide New Roof for Elderly Homeowner" in Benzinga.com

(September 21, 2012)
Pub: Benzinga.com
Contact: Kyle Bazzy, President
Released: September 21, 2012. **Description:** Green Bank and the Federal Home Loan Bank of Dallas (FHLB Dallas), Rebuilding Together-Houston replaced an elderly woman's roof in order to keep her in her home. She qualified for a grant program that helps low-income seniors make repairs to their homes.

39077 ■ "Soldiering On to Remake the SBA" in Inc. (February 2008, pp. 21)
Description: Steven Preston discusses efforts to improve the Small Business Administration's processes to improve services to small businesses. Topics covered include customer service issues, loans, and fraud.

39078 ■ "South Lake Hospital Starting $47M Patient Tower" in Orlando Business Journal (Vol. 26, December 4, 2009, No. 26, pp. 1)
Pub: American City Business Journals
Ed: Melanie Stawicki Azam. **Description:** Clermont, Florida's South Lake Hospital has divulged intentions to issue $50.9 million in bonds in order to fund construction of the $47 million patient tower. The three-story, 124,000 square foot tower would add eighteen inpatient rooms, a new lobby and expanded pharmacy, diagnostic and lab services, and treatment areas.

39079 ■ "Southwest Key Programs Preps for Growth, Building $3.6M Center" in Austin Business JournalInc. (Vol. 29, January 22, 2010, No. 46, pp. 1)
Pub: American City Business Journals
Ed: Sandra Zaragoza. **Description:** Southwest Key Programs Inc. received a $2.1 million grant from the U.S. Economic Development Administration to help finance the building of a $3.6 million 'Social Enterprise Complex'. The complex is expected to create at least 100 jobs in East Austin, Texas. Details of the plan for the complex are presented.

39080 ■ "Spending the Stimulus" in Crain's Cleveland Business (Vol. 30, June 29, 2009, No. 25, pp. 3)
Pub: Crain Communications Inc.
Ed: Dan Shingler. **Description:** Three of northeast Ohio's industrial firms will receive funding from the President's economic stimulus package. Eaton Corporation, Cleveland, Ohio; Parker Hannifin Corporation and Timken Company are expected to see higher revenues from the government spending plans.

39081 ■ "Spin Zone: Where Hawaii's Leaders Face Off, Have High-Tech Tax Credits Helped or Hurt Hawaii?" in Hawaii Business (Vol. 53, December 2007, No. 6, pp. 28)
Pub: PacificBasin Communications
Description: Presents the opinons of Channel Capital LLC's Walter R. Roth and Hawaii Venture Capital Association's Bill Spencer concerning the impacts of tax credits. Roth thinks that Act 221 appeals to investors who can earn despite business failure while Spencer thinks that the legislation promotes investments in innovative technology firms. The need to support tax credits is also discussed.

39082 ■ "Spin Zone: Where Hawaii's Leaders Face Off, What Are Your Party's Legislative Priorities for 2008??" in Hawaii Business (Vol. 53, January 2008, No. 7, pp. 22)
Pub: PacificBasin Communications
Description: Discusses the Democratic Party of Hawaii which will prioritize giving more opportunities to earn a living wage in 2008, according to the party chairwoman Jeani Withington. The Republican Party chairman Willes K. Lee, meanwhile, states that his party will seek to enhance the local business climate. The political parties' plans for Hawaii for the year 2008 are presented in detail.

39083 ■ "Stains Still Set After SBA Scrub" in Black Enterprise (March 1, 2008)
Pub: Earl G. Graves Publishing Co. Inc.
Contact: Earl G. Graves, Jr., President
Ed: Marcia A. Wade. **Description:** Small Business Administration's attempt to ensure that federal contracts were legitimately rewarded to small businesses, however the report filed showed that $4.6 billion in incorrectly coded contracts were removed from the SBA database. Critics contend the report is filled with inaccuracies. Statistical data included.

39084 ■ "State Budget Woes Hurt Many Vendors, Senior Services" in Sacramento Business Journal (Vol. 25, August 15, 2008, No. 24, pp. 1)
Pub: American City Business Journals, Inc.
Contact: Whitney Shaw, President
Ed: Melanie Turner. **Description:** Delays in the passage of the California state budget have adversely affected the health care industry. The Robertson Adult Day Health Care had taken out loans to keep the business afloat. The state Legislature has reduced Medi-Cal reimbursement to health care providers by 10 percent.

39085 ■ "State Cuts Could Affect Senior Care Programs" in Journal Star (May 10, 2012)
Pub: McClatchy Tribune Information Services
Ed: Justin Glawe. **Description:** Medicaid reforms in Illinois have helped senior citizens in the state because of improvements in community care programs.

39086 ■ "State Expects Increase of $50 Million from Film Bills; Come Back, Al Roker" in Crain's Detroit Business (March 24, 2008)
Pub: Crain Communications Inc.
Contact: Rance E. Crain, President
Ed: Bill Shea. **Description:** Overview of the new film initiative and its incentives designed to entice more film work to Michigan; the measures could bring $50 million to $100 million in movie production work for the rest of this year compared to the $4 million total the state saw last year. Also discusses the show 'DEA' which was filmed in Detroit and stars Al Roker.

39087 ■ "State Investment Goes Sour" in Business Journal Portland (Vol. 26, December 4, 2009, No. 39, pp. 1)
Pub: American City Business Journals, Inc.
Ed: Erik Siemers. **Description:** Oregon might recoup only $500,000 of a $20 million loan to Vancouver-based Cascade Grain Products LLC. Cascade Grain's ethanol plant in Clatskanie, OR will be put into auction under the supervision of a bankruptcy court.

39088 ■ "State Moves to Improve Child Care" in Providence Business News (Vol. 29, April 7, 2014, No. 1, pp. 1)
Pub: American City Business Journals
Released: April 7, 2014. **Description:** Rhode Island Department of Human Services has been helping to administer BrightStars contracts to child care centers, home-based providers and educational programs to help ensure the availability of high quality child care to the workforce. Part of the BrightStars funding came from the $50 million Race to the Top grant. Insights on BrightStars rating systems are also given.

39089 ■ "Stimulus Effect Slow in Greater Baltimore" in Baltimore Business Journal (Vol. 27, October 23, 2009, No. 24, pp. 1)
Pub: American City Business Journals
Ed: Scott Dance. **Description:** Companies in Maryland have reported only 154 new jobs being created or saved in Greater Baltimore and 965 jobs overall in the state because of stimulus cash. The federal stimulus program was expected to create thousands of new jobs but statistics show its failure to reduce unemployment in the state.

39090 ■ "Stimulus 'Loser' Won't Build Plant in Mass." in Boston Business Journal (Vol. 30, November 5, 2010, No. 41, pp. 1)
Pub: Boston Business Journal
Ed: Kyle Alspach. **Description:** Boston-Power Inc. no longer plans to build an electric vehicle battery plant in Massachusetts after it failed to obtain stimulus funds from the federal government. The company is instead looking to build a lithium-ion battery plant in China and possibly Europe.

39091 ■ "Struggling Community Banks Find Little Help In Wall Street Bailout" in Crain's Detroit Business (Vol. 24, September 29,

2008, pp. 48)
Pub: Crain Communications Inc.
Contact: Rance E. Crain, President
Ed: Tom Henderson. **Description:** Both public and private Michigan bands have been hit hard by poorly performing loan portfolios and although their problems were not caused by high-risk securities but by a longtime statewide recession and a housing slump, these community banks have little hope of seeing any of the bailout money that has been allotted for the larger institutions.

39092 ■ *"Struggling States Slashing Health Care For Poor" in Chicago Tribune (January 15, 2009)*
Pub: McClatchy-Tribune Information Services
Ed: Noam N. Levey. **Description:** Health officials warn that even the huge federal rescue plan may not be enough to restore health services being eliminated due to the economic crisis.

39093 ■ *"Sunwest Vies To Stave Off Bankruptcy" in The Business Journal-Portland (Vol. 25, August 15, 2008, No. 23, pp. 1)*
Pub: American City Business Journals, Inc.
Contact: Whitney Shaw, President
Ed: Robin J. Moody. **Description:** Sunwest Management Inc. is teetering on the edge of bankruptcy as creditors start foreclosure on nine of their properties. This could potentially displace residents of the assisted living operator. Sunwest is trying to sell smaller packages of properties to get a $100 million bridge loan to maintain operations.

39094 ■ *"The Surplus Shell Game" in Canadian Business (Vol. 80, March 12, 2007, No. 6, pp. 72)*
Description: The effort of successive federal governments in Canada to ensure budget surpluses and its impact on the economy are discussed.

39095 ■ *"Survey: Don't Expect Big Results From Stimulus" in Crain's Detroit Business (Vol. 25, June 1, 2009, No. 22)*
Pub: Crain Communications Inc. - Detroit
Contact: Keith Crain, Chairman
Ed: Nancy Kaffer, Chad Halcom. **Description:** In a recent survey, Michigan business owners, operators or managers showed that 48 percent of respondents oppose the President's stimulus package and believe it will have little or no effect on the economy.

39096 ■ *"Suspense Hangs Over Fledgling Film Industry" in Crain's Detroit Business (Vol. 26, January 18, 2010, No. 3, pp. 3)*
Pub: Crain Communications Inc.
Contact: Rance E. Crain, President
Ed: Bill Shea. **Description:** Overview of the film incentive package which has fostered a growth in the industry with 52 productions completed in 2009, bringing in $223.6 million in gross in-state production expenditures of which the state will refund $87.2 million. Opposition to the incentives has been growing among legislatures who believe that the initiatives cost more than they ultimately bring into the state. Experts believe that the initiatives will remain since they have already fostered economic growth and are good for the state's image.

39097 ■ *"Tackling Tuition Increases Head On" in Pittsburgh Business Times (Vol. 34, July 25, 2014, No. 1, pp. 6)*
Pub: American City Business Journals
Released: July 25, 2014. **Description:** The University of Pittsburgh has tried to contain tuition increases after the state cut funding by about $70 million in the 2012 budget year. The measures include a one-time-only early retirement program offered in 2012, greater focus on sustainability and cutting energy costs, and streamlining operations and sharing services.

39098 ■ *"TARP Lending Idea Gets Mixed Reviews" in Tampa Bay Business Journal (Vol. 29, October 30, 2009, No. 45, pp. 1)*
Pub: American City Business Journals
Ed: Kent Hoover, Margie Manning. **Description:** Tampa Bay area, Florida's community banks have expressed disapproval to the proposal of President

Obama to increase lending to small business, wherein the government will provide cheap capital through US Treasury Troubled Asset Relief Program (TARP). The banks were hesitant on the plan because of the strings attached to TARP.

39099 ■ *"Tattooed Bellwethers of Economic Development" in Austin Business Journal (Vol. 34, May 2, 2014, No. 11, pp. A4)*
Pub: American City Business Journals, Inc.
Contact: Whitney Shaw, President
Released: May 2, 2014. **Description:** The creative community's art-centered business have helped Austin, Texas' growth by moving into transitional areas with low rents. Their kind of pioneering spirit primes the area for later commercial and residential development. The city's assistance programs for creative enterprises are also presented.

39100 ■ *"Tax Breaks Favor Outsiders, Business Owners Object" in Business Review Albany (Vol. 41, August 22, 2014, No. 22, pp. 7)*
Pub: American City Business Journals, Inc.
Contact: Whitney Shaw, President
Released: August 22, 2014. **Description:** New York business owners have criticized Governor Andrew Cuomo's Start-Up NY tax-break program. They argue that the existing companies are essentially ignored and they are concerned whether the companies receiving the tax breaks stay longer than ten years. Insights on the Start-Up NY program are included.

39101 ■ *"Tax Credit Crunch" in Miami Daily Business Review (March 26, 2008)*
Ed: Paula Iuspa-Abbott. **Description:** Uncertainty is growing over the future of the low-income housing project in South Florida and the tax credit program that helps fuel the projects.

39102 ■ *"Taxpayers' Banks Share Even Higher" in Business Courier (Vol. 24, October 25, 2007, No. 28, pp. 1)*
Pub: American City Business Journals, Inc.
Contact: Whitney Shaw, President
Ed: Dan Monk, Lucy May. **Description:** Banks Working Group originally announced that it needs $106 million in public funds to build the Banks riverfront development but then declared it needs $45 million more from Cincinnati and Hamilton County after it approved a deal for the project. It would not be easy for the city and the county to come up with the money but many decision-makers think it's worth it.

39103 ■ *"Taylor Tests Land Grant Program" in Austin Business Journal (Vol. 31, June 3, 2011, No. 13, pp. 1)*
Pub: American City Business Journals
Ed: Vicky Garza. **Description:** Taylor Economic Development Corporation implemented a land grant program called Build On Our Lot to lure businesses to Taylor City, Austin, Texas. They are targeting small businesses, especially those in the renewable energy, advanced manufacturing, technical services and food products. Program details are included.

39104 ■ *"Tempel Steel To Expand Its Chicago Plant" in Chicago Tribune (August 22, 2008)*
Pub: McClatchy-Tribune Information Services
Ed: James P. Miller. **Description:** Tempel Steel Co. is no longer considering transferring a Libertyville factory's production to Mexico; the company has responded to government incentives and will instead shift that work to its plant on Chicago's North Side.

39105 ■ *"Testing Firm to Add Jobs" in Business Courier (Vol. 26, December 11, 2009, No. 33, pp. 1)*
Ed: Dan Monk. **Description:** Cincinnati-based Q Laboratories announced plans to add dozens of jobs with the $1.6 million stimulus assisted expansion. The company hired Michael Lichtenberg & Sons Construction Co. to build a new 9,000 square foot laboratory building.

39106 ■ *"This Just In" in Crain's Detroit Business (Vol. 25, June 1, 2009, No. 22, pp. 1)*
Pub: Crain Communications Inc. - Detroit
Contact: Keith Crain, Chairman
Ed: Daniel Duggan. **Description:** Three veterans of the auto industry have partnered to create, Revital-

izing Michigan, a nonprofit dedicated to help manufacturers improve their processes. The firm is seeking federal, state and private grants to fund the mission.

39107 ■ *"This Just In. State House Introduces Film-Industry Stimulus Bills" in Crain's Detroit Business (Vol. 24, March 3, 2008, No. 9)*
Pub: Crain Communications Inc. - Detroit
Contact: Keith Crain, Chairman
Description: House Bills 5841-5856 would give Michigan the most competitive incentives in the U.S. to encourage projects by film industry. Provisions of the bill are outlined.

39108 ■ *"Tied to Home: Female Owned Businesses Export Less, And It's Not Just Because They're Smaller" in Canadian Business (April 14, 2008)*
Pub: Rogers Media Inc.
Contact: Tony Viner, President
Ed: Lauren McKeon. **Description:** Only 12 percent of small and midsized enterprises that are run by women export their products and services. Government agencies can be more proactive in promoting the benefits of exporting by including women in case studies and recruiting women as mentors. Exporting provides great growth potential especially for the service sector where women have an advantage.

39109 ■ *"TMC Development Closes $1.1 Million Real Estate Purchase for Mansa, LLC Using SBA 504 Real Estate Financing" in Marketwired (September 17, 2009)*
Pub: COMTEX News Network Inc.
Contact: Chip Brian, President
Description: TMC Development announced the closing of a $1.1 million real estate purchase for Mansa, LLC dba Kwikee Mart, a Napa-based convenience store; TMC helped the company secure a Small Business Administration 504 loan in order to purchase the acquisition of a 3,464 square foot building. SBA created the 504 loan program to provide financing for growing small and medium-sized businesses.

39110 ■ *"Today's Business Sale Climate" in Business Owner (Vol. 35, September-October 2011, No. 5, pp. 10)*
Pub: DL Perkins Company
Description: Despite the weak economy, there is a surplus of individuals wanting to purchase a small business. The Small Business Administration loan guarantees program helps with its loans for purchase/sale of business assistance.

39111 ■ *"Triad, Fortune Dump TARP Cut Costs, Boost Lending" in Saint Louis Business Journal (Vol. 32, October 7, 2011, No. 6, pp. 1)*
Pub: Saint Louis Business Journal
Ed: Greg Edwards. **Description:** St. Louis, Missouri-based Triad Bank and Fortune Bank have been using an alternative federal loan program to pay back financing from the Troubled Asset Relief Program. Triad got a $5 million loan at one percent interest rate from the US Small Business Lending Fund.

39112 ■ *"Turbulent Skies" in The Business Journal-Portland (Vol. 25, August 29, 2008, No. 25, pp. 1)*
Pub: American City Business Journals, Inc.
Contact: Whitney Shaw, President
Ed: Erik Siemers. **Description:** Small airlines are struggling to keep their commercial services amid the troubled commercial airline sector. Small communities, for example, were expected to pony up about $650,000 in revenue guarantees each in order to convince SkyWest Airlines to offer two direct flights to Portland daily beginning October 12, 2008. The trends in the commercial airline industry are analyzed.

39113 ■ *"U-Swirl Added to SBA's Franchise Registry" in Ice Cream Reporter (Vol. 23, September 20, 2010, No. 10, pp. 1)*
Description: Healthy Fast Food Inc., parent to the U-SWIRL Frozen Yogurt cafe chain announced that the U.S. Small Business Administration listed

U-SWIRL Frozen Yogurt on its official franchise registry. This move will allow U-SWIRL the benefits of a streamlined review process for SBA financing.

39114 ■ *"Union, Heal Thyself"* in Canadian Business (Vol. 81, July 21, 2008, No. 11, pp. 9)
Description: General Motors Corp. was offered by the federal government a $250 million fund after the company plans to close its facility in Ontario. The government move is geared towards supporting the workers who have refused to support the automotive company. Details of the labor contract between General Motors and the Canadian Auto Workers are presented.

39115 ■ *"Unions Pony Up $1 Million for McBride Stimulus"* in Saint Louis Business Journal (Vol. 31, July 29, 2011, No. 49, pp. 1)
Pub: Saint Louis Business Journal
Ed: Evan Binns. **Description:** Carpenters District Council of Greater St. Louis and International Brotherhood of Electrical Workers Local 1 were among the nine unions that agreed to split the cost of nearly $1 million in incentives for homebuyers who purchase homes in McBride communities. McBride & Son has spent over $100,000 to promote the incentive program.

39116 ■ *"U.S. Attorney Post the Latest Twist in A. Brian Albritton's Odyssey"* in The Business Journal-Serving Greater Tampa Bay (Vol. 28, July 28, 2008, No. 31, pp. 1)
Pub: American City Business Journals, Inc.
Contact: Whitney Shaw, President
Ed: Jane Meinhardt. **Description:** Tampa, Florida-based lawyer A. Brian Albritton has been nominated to be the U.S. Attorney for the Middle District of Florida. He is an expert in cases involving white-collar crime, secret theft, noncompete agreements, and other agreements.

39117 ■ *"University of Cincinnati Lobbies for Big Chunk of New Funds"* in Business Courier (Vol. 24, February 21, 2008, No. 46, pp. 1)
Pub: American City Business Journals, Inc.
Contact: Whitney Shaw, President
Ed: Laura Baverman. **Description:** Discusses the University of Cincinnati (UC) which has requested $192 million funding from the Ohio Innovation Partnership. The program was launched by governor Strickland in an attempt to drive research and innovation in the studies of biotechnology, aeronautics, and other fields that reflects Ohio's strengths. Details of UC's grant proposals are supplied.

39118 ■ *"US Cavalry Store"* in Retail Merchandiser (Vol. 51, September-October 2011, No. 5, pp. 70)
Pub: Phoenix Media Corporation
Description: US Cavalry Store serves enlisted military members. The store has launched a newly upgraded Website and has expanded its distribution center.

39119 ■ *"UTSA Entrepreneur Program Receives Federal Designation"* in San Antonio Business Journal (Vol. 28, June 6, 2014, No. 17, pp. 7)
Pub: American City Business Journals
Released: June 6, 2014. **Description:** The National Science Foundation has designated the University of Texas at San Antonio (UTSA) as an Innovation Corps Site because of its strong entrepreneurial system through the Center for Innovation and Technology Entrepreneurship. The UTSA expects to see an increase in entrepreneurial activity and successful technology commercialization with such designation.

39120 ■ *"VA Exceeds Government-Wide Goal for Veteran-Owned Business Procurement"* in Benzinga.com (July 3, 2012)
Pub: Benzinga.com
Contact: Kyle Bazzy, President
Ed: Aaron Wise. **Description:** Department of Veterans Affairs has surpassed its goal of government procurements of the Small Business Adminstration by more than six times. The VA's committment to the success of veteran-owned small businesses is covered.

39121 ■ *"Valenti: Roots of Financial Crisis Go Back to 1998"* in Crain's Detroit Business (Vol. 24, October 6, 2008, No. 40, pp. 25)
Pub: Crain Communications Inc.
Contact: Rance E. Crain, President
Ed: Tom Henderson, Nathan Skid. **Description:** Interview with Sam Valenti III who is the chairman and CEO of Valenti Capital L.L.C., a wealth-management firm; Valenti discusses in detail the history that led up to the current economic crisis as well as his prediction for the future of the country.

39122 ■ *"Vanity Plates"* in Canadian Business (Vol. 82, April 27, 2009, No. 7, pp. 26)
Ed: Andy Holloway. **Description:** Politicians in the U.S. called for the review of firms that availed of the bailout money but are under deals for naming rights of sports stadiums. Angus Reid's Corporate Reputation and Sponsorship Index found for example, that there is little correlation between sponsoring arenas on having a better brand image. It is suggested that firms who enter these deals build closer to people's homes.

39123 ■ *"The Venture Capital Infusions: Federal Incentives Mean More Money for VC Firms"* in Entrepreneur (August 2009)
Pub: Entrepreneur Press
Contact: Perlman Neil, President
Ed: Carol Tice. **Description:** American Recovery and Reinvestment Act of 2009 changed the rules for the Small Business Investment Corporations (SBIC) program under the Small Business Authority. The rule changes are meant to put more money from the program into circulation and it increases funding to existing SBICs.

39124 ■ *"The Venture Capital Infusions: Federal Incentives Mean More Money for VC Firms"* in Entrepreneur (Vol. 37, August 2009)
Pub: Entrepreneur Press
Contact: Perlman Neil, President
Ed: Carol Tice. **Description:** American Recovery and Reinvestment Act of 2009 changed the rules for the Small Business Investment Corporations (SBIC) program under the Small Business Authority. The rule changes are meant to put more money from the program into circulation and it increases funding to existing SBICs.

39125 ■ *"Verizon Reaffirms Long-Standing Commitment to Minority Business Enterprises in Maryland"* in Benzinga.com (July 17, 2012)
Pub: Benzinga.com
Contact: Kyle Bazzy, President
Description: Maryland Public Service Commission met with Verizon and other companies to discuss the state's supplier diversity initiatives. Verizon's response and their commitment to the program is presented.

39126 ■ *"VPA to Pay $9.5 Million to Settle Whistle-Blower Lawsuits"* in Crain's Detroit Business (Vol. 26, January 11, 2010, No. 2, pp. 13)
Pub: Crain Communications Inc.
Contact: Rance E. Crain, President
Ed: Jay Greene. **Description:** According to Terrence Berg, first assistant with the U.S. Attorney's Office in Detroit, Voluntary Physicians Association, a local home health care company, has agreed to pay $9.5 million to settle four whistle-blower lawsuits; the agreement settles allegations that VPA submitted claims to TriCare, the Michigan Medicaid program and Medicare for unnecessary home visits, tests and procedures.

39127 ■ *"Walker Seeks More Business Participation"* in Business Journal-Milwaukee (Vol. 28, December 10, 2010, No. 10, pp. A1)
Pub: Milwaukee Business Journal
Ed: Rich Kirchen. **Description:** Wisconsin governor Scott Walker is seeking the aid of Milwaukee business leaders to participate in resolving the challenges posed by the economic crisis. Walker is aiming to create 250,000 jobs. He is also planning to call a special session of the legislature to enact strategies to jumpstart the economy.

39128 ■ *"WEDC Credits Could Create 400 Area Jobs"* in Business Journal Milwaukee (Vol. 29, July 27, 2012, No. 44, pp. 1)
Pub: American City Business Journals, Inc.
Contact: Whitney Shaw, President
Ed: Rich Kirchen. Released: July 27, 2012. **Description:** Wisconsin Development Corporation (WEDC) has provided $2.2 million in tax credits to six southeastern Wisconsin employers that are expected to add nearly 400 jobs. The companies are Unico Inc., Spee-Dee Packaging Machinery, All Tool Sales Inc., Echo Lake Foods Inc., Novation Companies Inc., and Trico Corporation.

39129 ■ *"What's Ahead for Fannie and Fred?"* in Barron's (Vol. 90, August 30, 2010, No. 35, pp. 26)
Pub: Barron's Editorial & Corporate Headquarters
Ed: Jonathan R. Laing. **Description:** A meeting presided by Treasury Secretary Timothy Geithner discussed the future of Fannie Mae and Freddie Mac. The two government sponsored enterprises were mismanaged and reforming these two agencies is critical.

39130 ■ *"Whistling in the Dark"* in Canadian Business (Vol. 79, September 25, 2006, No. 19, pp. 17)
Ed: Jack Mintz. **Description:** Increasing subsidies for research projects in Canada is discussed.

39131 ■ *"Whistling Past the Graveyard? Higher Quality Stocks Beckon to Investors?"* in Barron's (Vol. 88, March 17, 2008, No. 11, pp. 15)
Pub: Dow Jones & Co., Inc.
Contact: Clare Hart, President
Ed: Michael Santoli. **Description:** Discusses the Federal Reserve's move to provide $200 billion to the system which can be seen as an effort to avoid the liquidity problems that Bear Stearns suffered. The Federal Reserve's move seems to frighten investors rather than reassure them.

39132 ■ *"Will Business be Stimulated?"* in Entrepreneur (Vol. 37, July 2009, No. 7, pp. 18)
Pub: Entrepreneur Press
Contact: Perlman Neil, President
Ed: Jennifer Wang. **Description:** Steven Strauss, Alberto G. Alvarado, Jeff Rosenweig, Al Gordon, and Theresa Alfaro Daytner share their views on how the American Recovery and Reinvestment Act of 2009, also known as the economic stimulus, will affect small businesses. Their backgrounds are also provided.

39133 ■ *"Will Focus on Maryland Businesses Continue?"* in Baltimore Business Journal (Vol. 28, November 5, 2010, No. 26, pp. 1)
Pub: Baltimore Business Journal
Ed: Scott Dance. **Description:** The 2010 election may call for new efforts to teach new lawmakers to assure that the viewpoints of businesses are considered and accurately delivered. The Greater Baltimore Committee and similar groups have gathered reports on the competitiveness of Maryland and are planning to use them to make a case of keeping business a top priority.

39134 ■ *"WindPower Innovations Releases Statement to Their Stockholders"* in Internet Wire (July 2, 2012)
Released: July 2, 2012. **Description:** WindPower Innovations Inc. released a letter stating corporate growth and strategy. WindPower, a small wind farm, was granted a special energy credit by the federal government. Statistical data included.

39135 ■ *"Young-Kee Kim: Deputy Director, Fermi National Accelerator Laboratory"* in Crain's Chicago Business (Vol. 31, May 5, 2008, No. 18)
Pub: Crain Communications Inc.
Contact: Todd Johnson, Publisher
Ed: Phuong Ly. **Description:** Profile of Young-Kee Kim who is the deputy director of Fermilab, a physics lab where scientists study the smallest particles in

the universe; Ms. Kim was a researcher at Fermilab before becoming deputy director two years ago; Fermilab is currently home to the most powerful particle accelerator in the world and is struggling to compete with other countries despite cuts in federal funding.

RESEARCH CENTERS

39136 ■ Center for International Private Enterprise (CIPE) [Centre International pour l'Entreprise Privée]
1155 15th St. NW, Ste. 700
Washington, DC 20005
Ph: (202)721-9200

Fax: (202)721-9250
Co. E-mail: info@cipe.org
URL: http://www.cipe.org
Contact: Thomas J. Donohue, President
Description: Encourages the growth of voluntary business organizations and private enterprise systems abroad, such as chambers of commerce, trade associations, employers' organizations, and business-oriented research groups, particularly in developing countries. Helps business communities abroad strengthen their organizational capabilities; creates exchanges among business leaders and institutions to strengthen the international private enterprise system; encourages development of active business participation in the political process. Activities include: developing leadership training for association executives and their voluntary leadership to strengthen business institutions; developing communications programs and educational materials for youth, employees, women's groups, academic institutions, government officials, political leaders, and other audiences to encourage entrepreneurship. **Scope:** Worldwide democracy through the promotion of private enterprise, market-oriented reform, and legal, regulatory and business institutions, including supporting strategies and techniques that address market-based democratic development and working with indigenous organizations in emerging democracies. Provides matching funds to a variety of developing country institutions for political and economic development. **Founded:** 1983. **Publications:** *Economic Reform Feature Service*. **Educational Activities:** Strengthening Women's Business Organizations; Training program for Business Association Management.

START-UP INFORMATION

39137 ■ *"Business With Brains" in Canadian Business (Vol. 85, September 17, 2012, No. 14, pp. 41)*
Pub: George Media Inc.
Ed: Richard Warnica. **Released:** September 17, 2012. **Description:** The Ontario Brain Institute launched the Entrepreneurs Program to provide funding, business training, and connections to Canadian medical researchers who believe they have great ideas for business. The program aims to close the gap between neuroscience publications and viable projects.

39138 ■ *"No. 407: What I Learned in the Military, and What I Had to Unlearn" in Inc. (Vol. 36, September 2014, No. 7, pp. 80)*
Pub: Mansueto Ventures L.L.C.
Contact: John Koten, Chief Executive Officer
Released: September 2014. **Description:** Profile of William Bailey, who served in the U.S. Army as information manager at the U.S. Military Academy at West Point. Bailey discusses his startup firm, Rapier Solutions, a government contractor providing IT, logistics, and social-work expertise. The firm has developed a new survivor outreach system for the U.S. Army.

39139 ■ *"Should State Invest in Startups?" in Providence Business News (Vol. 28, March 3, 2014, No. 48, pp. 1)*
Pub: American City Business Journals
Released: March 3, 2014. **Description:** The U.S. Treasury Department is investigating whether Rhode Island violated Federal rules when it used funds from the State Small Business Credit Initiative (SSBCI) to invest in Betaspring, a startup accelerator program for technology and design entrepreneurs ready to launch their businesses. The Lyon Park audit claims that Rhode Island violated SSBCI rules because a large portion of the money went to the business accelerator's operating expenses and not to the startups themselves.

ASSOCIATIONS AND OTHER ORGANIZATIONS

39140 ■ **Coalition for Government Procurement (CGP)**
1990 M St. NW, Ste. 450
Washington, DC 20036-3466
Ph: (202)331-0975
URL: http://thecgp.org/
Contact: Roger Waldron, President
E-mail: rwaldron@thecgp.org
Description: Represents large and small businesses interested in commercial product procurement issues. Works to help protect the interests of federal government commercial product suppliers; to monitor commercial product legislation, policies, regulations and procurement trends of federal agencies. Provides members with current information, changes and developments in procurement policies and their

impact. Conducts phone consultations. **Founded:** 1979. **Publications:** *Off the Shelf* (Monthly). **Awards:** Excellence in Partnership Award (Annual).

39141 ■ **National Contract Management Association**
21740 Beaumeade Cir., Ste. 125
Ashburn, VA 20147
Ph: (571)382-0082
Free: 800-344-8096
Fax: (703)448-0939
Co. E-mail: wearelistening@ncmahq.org
URL: http://www.ncmahq.org
Contact: Larry Trowel, President
E-mail: lmtrowel@gmail.com
Description: Professional individuals concerned with administration, procurement, acquisition, negotiation and management of contracts and subcontracts. Works for the education, improvement and professional development of members and nonmembers through national and chapter programs, symposia and educational materials. Offers certification in Contract Management (CPCM, CFCM, and CCCM) designations as well as a credential program. Operates speakers' bureau. **Publications:** *National Contract Management Journal* (Annual); *Contract Management* (Monthly); *Journal of Contract Management* (Annual). **Awards:** National Achievement Award (Annual); James E. Cravens Membership Award (Annual); NCMA Outstanding Fellow Award (Annual).

EDUCATIONAL PROGRAMS

39142 ■ **Advanced Writing and Editing for Government Proposals**
EEI Communications
8945 Guilford Rd., Ste. 145
Columbia, MD 21046
Ph: (410)309-8200
Free: 888-253-2762
Fax: (410)630-3980
Co. E-mail: train@eeicom.com
URL: http://www.eeicom.com/eei-training-services
Description: Developed for anyone who regularly writes, edits, or manages government proposals to explore proposal-specific writing and editing challenges, including how to ensure consistent voice no matter how many writers are involved. **Audience:** Industry professionals.

39143 ■ **Basics of Government Contract Administration (Onsite)**
Seminar Information Service Inc.
20 Executive Park, Ste. 120
Irvine, CA 92614
Ph: (949)261-9104
Free: 877-SEM-INFO
Fax: (949)261-1963
Co. E-mail: info@seminarinformation.com
URL: http://www.seminarinformation.com
URL(s): www.seminarinformation.com/qqbmwg/basics-of-government-contract-administration. **Description:** Designed to show you how to fill out the most common standard forms, where the forms are

found, and how proper forms preparation avoids administration pitfalls. **Audience:** General public. **Telecommunication Services:** info@seminarinformation.com.

39144 ■ **Government Contract Accounting (Onsite)**
Seminar Information Service Inc.
20 Executive Park, Ste. 120
Irvine, CA 92614
Ph: (949)261-9104
Free: 877-SEM-INFO
Fax: (949)261-1963
Co. E-mail: info@seminarinformation.com
URL: http://www.seminarinformation.com
Description: Accounting principles as they relate to procurement activities with the Federal Government, with focus on Government forms and formats, direct and indirect cost rate submissions, cost principles, dealing with Government auditors, changes and delay claims and terminations. **Audience:** Purchasing professionals.

39145 ■ **Government Proposal Writing Basics**
EEI Communications
8945 Guilford Rd., Ste. 145
Columbia, MD 21046
Ph: (410)309-8200
Free: 888-253-2762
Fax: (410)630-3980
Co. E-mail: train@eeicom.com
URL: http://www.eeicom.com/eei-training-services
Description: Designed for proposal novices at any level of writing ability, this course explains the unique features of government proposals and the government procurement process. **Audience:** Industry professionals.

REFERENCE WORKS

39146 ■ *"$161.9M 'Pit Stop' Fix-Up Will Create About 1,600 Jobs" in Orlando Business Journal (Vol. 26, January 22, 2010, No. 34, pp. 1)*
Pub: American City Business Journals
Ed: Anjali Fluker. **Description:** State of Florida will be providing $161.9 million to renovate eight service plazas starting November 2010. The project is expected to create 1,600 jobs across the state and is expected to be completed by 2012. Details on bid advertisements and facilities slated for improvement are discussed.

39147 ■ *"2012 Department of Homeland Security Small Business Achievement Award Given to Compass for Outstanding Performance" in Information Technology Business (May 1, 2012, pp. 16)*
Pub: NewsRX
Contact: Susan E. Hasty, Publisher
Released: May 1, 2012. **Description:** Compass Systems Consulting Inc. was presented with the 2012 Department of Homeland Security (DHS) Small Business Achievement Award for outstanding work in sup-

port of the DHS mission. Compass is a management consulting company specializing in Performance Improvement, Program & Project Management, Acquisition Management and Audit, and Freedom of InformationACT (FOIA).

39148 ■ *"AG Warns Slots MBE Plan Risky" in Boston Business Journal (Vol. 29, May 27, 2011, No. 3, pp. 1)*
Pub: American City Business Journals, Inc.
Ed: Scott Dance. **Description:** Attorney General Doug Gansler states that the law extending the minority business program on slots parlors contracting through 2018 could be open to lawsuits. He recommended that the state should conduct a study proving that minority- and women-owned businesses do not get a fair share in the gaming industry before it signs the bill to avoid lawsuits from majority-owned firms.

39149 ■ *"Airmall Mulls I-95 Travel Plazas Bid" in Boston Business Journal (Vol. 29, September 2, 2011, No. 17, pp. 3)*
Pub: American City Business Journals, Inc.
Ed: Alexander Jackson. **Description:** Airmall USA is planning to move its food courts from the Baltimore/ Washington International Thurgood Marshall Airport to the new travel plazas on Interstate 95. The plazas are up for bid.

39150 ■ *"Altron" in Business Journal (Vol. 31, May 16, 2014, No. 51, pp. 10)*
Pub: American City Business Journals
Released: May 16, 2014. **Description:** Altron, Inc. makes mechanical boxes and electronic assemblies and is owned by U.S. Air Force veteran, Alan Phillips. Marketing manager, Jim Merritt, shares that the business' veteran-owned status is important for defense contractors. One of the company's shift managers is also a veteran.

39151 ■ *"Annapolis Seeks City Market Vendors" in Boston Business Journal (Vol. 29, June 10, 2011, No. 5, pp. 3)*
Pub: American City Business Journals, Inc.
Ed: Daniel J. Sernovitz. **Description:** The city of Annapolis, Maryland is planning to revive the historical landmark Market House and it is now accepting bids from vendors until June 10, 2011. The city hopes to reopen the facility by July 2011 for a six-month period after which it will undergo renovations.

39152 ■ *"App Maker Thinks He Has the Ticket: But Denver Is Balking At Alternative To Parking Fines" in Denver Business Journal (Vol. 65, April 25, 2014, No. 50, pp. A10)*
Pub: American City Business Journals
Released: April 25, 2014. **Description:** Taylor Linnell started Ticket Cricket LLC with partner, Jeff Valdez, to make parking tickets obsolete in Denver, Colorado by using two smartphone applications, One, Ticket Cricket and 5 for 5. The Department of Public Works rejected Linnell's proposal; he was encouraged to try it with the city's parking system technology vendor, Xerox.

39153 ■ *"Apples, Decoded: WSU Scientist Unraveling the Fruit's Genetics" in Puget Sound Business Journal (Vol. 29, September 5, 2008, No. 20)*
Ed: Clay Holtzman. **Description:** Washington State University researcher is working to map the apple's genome in order to gain information about how the fruit grows, looks and tastes. His work, funded by a research grant from the US Department of Agriculture and the Washington Apple Commission is crucial to improving the state's position as an apple-producing region.

39154 ■ *Are Government Purchasing Policies Failing Small Business?: Roundtable Before the Committee on Small Business & Entrepreneurship, U.S. Senate*
Pub: DIANE Publishing Co.
Contact: Dorothy J. Perkins, Manager
E-mail: dorothyjperkins@hotmail.com
Released: September 2002. **Price:** $35, Paperback.
Description: Covers Congressional hearing: Steven App, Treasury Department; Fred Armendariz and

Major Clark, Small Business Administration; Susan Allen, Pan Asian American Chamber of Commerce; Stephen Denlinger, Latin American Management Association; Charles Henry, National Veteran's Business Development Corporation; Morris Hudson, MO Procurement Technology Assistance Centers; Bar Kasoff, Women Impact, Public Policy; Pam Mazza, Piliero, Massa and Pargament; Ron Newlan, Hub-Zone Contract National Council; Pat Parker, Native American Management Service; Joann Payne, Women First National Legislative Commission; Mike Robinson, MA Small Business Development Centers; Ramon Rodriguez, Hispanic Chamber of Commerce; Angela Styles, Office of Management and Budget; Ralph Thomas, NASA; John Turner, MN Business Enterprise Legal Defense Fund; James Turpin, American Subcontractor's Association, Inc.; and Henry Wilfong, National Association of Small Disadvantaged Business.

39155 ■ *"Auto Bankruptcies Could Weaken Defense" in Crain's Detroit Business (Vol. 25, June 8, 2009, No. 23, pp. 1)*
Pub: Crain Communications Inc. - Detroit
Contact: Keith Crain, Chairman
Ed: Chad Halcom. **Description:** Bankruptcy and supplier consolidation of General Motors Corporation and Chrysler LLC could interfere with the supply chains of some defense contractors, particularly makers of trucks and smaller vehicles.

39156 ■ *"Aviat Networks Partners With AT&T Government Solutions for Department of Homeland Security Business" in Entertainment Close-Up August 13, 2012*
Pub: Close-Up Media
Released: August 13, 2012. **Description:** Aviat Networks Inc. will provide US Department of Homeland Security and other federal agencies withh the capability to acquire microwave radio communication equipment, engineering, design, installation and maintenace services. Aviat is a subcontractor on the AT&T Government Solutions' team. Aviat has a history of partnerships in federal technology space.

39157 ■ *"Behind the Scenes: Companies at the Heart of Everyday Life" in Inc. (March 2008, pp. 34-35)*
Pub: Mansueto Ventures L.L.C.
Contact: John Koten, Chief Executive Officer
Ed: Athena Schindelheim. **Description:** Profiles of companies used to improve road conditions at the Bedford, New Hampshire Toll Plaza are presented. General Traffic Equipment provides LED traffic lights; TRMI, provided 8-foot strips treadles that count the number of axles that drive over them; E-Z Pass system is an antenna from Mark IV Industries that uses radio-frequency identification (RFID) technology to scan a small device attached to a car's windshield; and Transport Data Systems installed cameras that snap photos of passengers and license plates in order to catch individuals who try to dodge fees.

39158 ■ *"Bloomington Police to Buy 24-Hour Electronic Kiosk With Federal Grant" in Herald-Times (September 5, 2012)*
Pub: Hoosier Times Inc.
Released: September 5, 2012. **Description:** Bloomington, Indiana police department will purchase two electronic kiosks with money from a federal grant. The kiosks will operate 24 hours a day and provide the public with the ability to communicate with the police, obtain forms and permits, as well as other police-related activities.

39159 ■ *"Bombardier Deja Vu" in Canadian Business (Vol. 83, August 17, 2010, No. 13-14, pp. 28)*
Pub: Rogers Media Inc.
Contact: Tony Viner, President
Ed: Laura Cameron. **Description:** Foreign competitors have accused the Quebec government and the Societe de transport de Montreal of giving Bombardier preferential treatment when it bids for contract to replace Montreal metro's rail cars. Bombardier was in a similar situation in 1974 when it won the contract to build the metro's second generation rail cars.

39160 ■ *"Canada Seeks Collection Agency To Pursue $129M In Fines" in PaymentsSource (August 21, 2012)*
Pub: SourceMedia Inc.
Contact: James M. Malkin, Chief Executive Officer
Released: August 21, 2012. **Description:** Canada's federal government has posted a letter of interest seeking a collection agency to recover about $129 million in unpaid fines. Details of the program are covered.

39161 ■ *"Capital Metro May Soon Seek Contractor to Replace Star Tran" in Austin Business Journal (Vol. 31, June 10, 2011, No. 14, pp. 1)*
Pub: American City Business Journals
Ed: Vicky Garza. **Description:** Capital Metropolitan Transportation Authority may be forced to contract out its bus services provided by StarTran Inc. as early as September 2012 following legislation approved by the Texas legislature. The bill originates in a report by the Sunset Advisory Commission. Details are included.

39162 ■ *"Centerra Caught in Kyrgyzstan Dispute" in Globe & Mail (April 19, 2007, pp. B5)*
Ed: Andy Hoffman. **Description:** The details of the demonstrations carried against government proposal to nationalize Centerra Gold Inc.'s assets are presented.

39163 ■ *"CEO Forecast: With Cloudy Economy, Executives Turn to Government Contracting" in Hispanic Business (January-February 2009, pp. 34, 36)*
Pub: Hispanic Business Inc.
Contact: Jesus Chavarria, President
Ed: Jessica Haro, Richard Kaplan. **Description:** As economic uncertainty fogs the future, executives turn to government contracts in order to boost business. Revenue sources, health care challenges, environmental consulting and remediation services, as well as technological strides are discussed.

39164 ■ *"Chesapeake Firm Regains Veteran-Owned Status" in Virginian-Pilot (August 21, 2012)*
Pub: McClatchy Tribune Information Services
Ed: Philip Walzer. **Description:** Syncon LLC has regained status as a "veteran-owned" business. Mark Lilly, the president of Syncon is a retired Navy SEAL master chief who was wounded in combat in Afghanistan. Over-regulation by the US Department of Vetrans Affairs in order to stop fraud in the veteran certification program was responsible for the mistake.

39165 ■ *"Cincinnati Hospitals Face Big Whammy From State Fees" in Business Courier (Vol. 26, October 2, 2009, No. 23, pp. 1)*
Pub: American City Business Journals, Inc.
Contact: Whitney Shaw, President
Ed: James Ritchie. **Description:** Ohio hospitals are facing losses of nearly $145 million in franchise fees which are set to be levied by the state. Ohio hospitals will be responsible for a total of $718 million franchise fees as required by 2010-2011 state budget but will recover only 80 percent of the amount in increased Medicaid fees. Possible effects of anticipated losses to Ohio hospitals are examined.

39166 ■ *"City Seeks More Minorities" in Austin Business JournalInc. (Vol. 28, November 7, 2008, No. 34, pp. A1)*
Pub: American City Business Journals
Ed: Jean Kwon. **Description:** Austin, Texas is planning to increase the participation of minority- and women-owned businesses in government contracts. Contractors are required to show 'good faith' to comply with the specified goals. The city is planning to effect the changes in the construction and professional services sector.

39167 ■ *"A Civilian Cybersecurity Center for D.C.?" in Washington Business Journal (Vol. 32, March 7, 2014, No. 47, pp. 5)*
Pub: American City Business Journals
Released: March 7, 2014. **Description:** The U.S. General Services Administration (GSA) is investigating the possibility for a civilian cybersecurity center in

Washington DC to encourage further collaboration between government agencies. The GSA is seeking $35 million in the proposed 2015 federal budget for the project's design.

39168 ■ "Communications and Power Industries Awarded $6 Million to Support Apache Helicopter" in Defense & Aerospace Business (August 13, 2014, pp. 11)

Pub: NewsRX

Contact: Susan E. Hasty, Publisher

Released: August 13, 2014. Description: Communications and Power Industries LLC procured an order totaling $6 million from Lockheed Martin Missiles and Fire Control for manufacturing tactical common data links. These links will be installed on the AH-64E Guardian variant of the Apache helicopter used to support U.S. warfighters.

39169 ■ "Complete Discovery Source, Inc. (CDS) Receives Minority Owned Business Certification" in Marketwired (December 14, 2010)

Pub: COMTEX

Contact: Chip Brian, President

Description: Complete Discovery Source Inc. (CDS) was granted Minority-Owned Business Enterprise status by the New York State Department of Economic Development. The certification provides CDS, an end-to-end eDiscovery services provider, with access to contracting opportunities with 130 government agencies throughout New York state.

39170 ■ "Construction Firms Support Cincinnati NAACP Plan" in Business Courier (Vol. 27, September 24, 2010, No. 21, pp. 1)

Pub: Business Courier

Ed: Lucy May. Description: Executives of Turner Construction Company and Messer Construction Company expressed their support for the Cincinnati National Association for the Advancement of Colored People Construction Partnership Agreement. The agreement involves the setting of rules for the involvement of firms owned by African Americans in major projects in Cincinnati.

39171 ■ "Contractor Backlog Dip Signals New Uncertainty" in Washington Business Journal (Vol. 31, August 3, 2012, No. 15, pp. 1)

Pub: American City Business Journal

Description: Expected revenue from government awarded contracts may decline, US government contractors have reported. Budget uncertainties are seen to drive the development.

39172 ■ Contractor's Directory (Government contractors with +small business obligations)

Pub: Government Data Publications Inc.

Contact: Siegfried Lobel, President

URL(s): www.govdata.com. Released: Annual; February. Price: $49.50, Diskette edition; $15; $49.50, CD-ROM. Covers: Contractors who have received government contract under Public Law 95-507, which requires preferential treatment of small business for subcontracts. Entries include: Contractor name and address. Supplementary to 'Small Business Preferential Subcontracts Opportunities Monthly,' which lists companies with government contracts over $500,000 ($1,000,000 for construction) (see separate entry). Arrangement: Same information given alphabetically and by ZIP code.

39173 ■ "Contractors Scramble for Jobs" in Business Journal Portland (Vol. 26, December 18, 2009, No. 41, pp. 1)

Pub: American City Business Journals, Inc.

Ed: Andy Giegerich. Description: Contractors in Portland area are expected to bid for capital construction projects that will be funded by municipalities in the said area. Contracts for companies that work on materials handling, road improvement, and public safety structure projects will be issued.

39174 ■ "Corner Office" in Hispanic Business (December 2010)

Pub: Hispanic Business Inc.

Contact: Jesus Chavarria, President

Ed: Jesus Chavarria. Description: The gap opens up between government contracts and small busi-

nesses. The state of minority enterprise development in federal markets as well as other levels of government throughout the U.S. is examined.

39175 ■ "County Limited in Awarding Contracts" in Crain's Cleveland Business (Vol. 30, June 15, 2009, No. 23, pp. 8)

Pub: Crain Communications Inc.

Ed: Brian Tucker. Description: Cuyahoga County government has been accused of not offering fair levels of county-issued contracts to minority-owned companies.

39176 ■ "DCAA-Compliant Accounting Solution Provider Intros Redesign of Website at sympaq.com" in Entertainment Close-Up (April 18, 2011)

Pub: Close-Up Media

Description: Aldebaron Inc., developer of DCAA-compliant accounting solution SYMPAQ SQL, launched a new Website that will assist government contractors access information about their products and services.

39177 ■ "Decorated Marine Sues Contractor" in Wall Street Journal Eastern Edition (November 29, 2011, pp. A4)

Pub: Dow Jones & Co., Inc.

Contact: Clare Hart, President

Ed: Julian E. Barnes. Description: Marine Devon Maylie, who was awarded the Congressional Medal of Honor for bravery, has filed a lawsuit against defense contractor BAE Systems PLC claiming that the company prevented his hiring by another firm by saying he has a mental condition and a drinking problem. Maylie says that this was in retaliation for his objections to the company's plan to sell the Pakistani military high-tech sniper scopes.

39178 ■ "DEM Says River Needs Cleanup" in Providence Business News (Vol. 28, January 6, 2014, No. 40, pp. 1)

Pub: American City Business Journals

Released: January 6, 2014. Description: Rhode Island's Department of Environmental Management (DEM) called a meeting to gather information for its Ten Mile River water-quality-restoration plan. DEM announced the failure of the Ten Mile River and its impoundments to meet state water quality standards. The government grant received by Attleboro for the cleanup efforts is examined.

39179 ■ "DIA Contract Sets a Record for Denver Minority, Woman-Owned Business" in Denver Business Journal (Vol. 65, February 21, 2014, No. 41)

Pub: American City Business Journals

Released: February 21, 2014. Description: The City of Denver, Colorado has awarded a $39.6 million contract to Burgess Services Inc. to construct a transit and hotel project near the Denver International Airport. Burgess Services is owned by Denise Burgess. This is the largest public contract awarded to a woman0 or minority-owned business in the city's history.

39180 ■ "Disabled Veterans National Foundation Calls for Immediate Action to Correct Mismanagement of Program that Awards Contracts to Disabled Veteran-Owned Companies" in Benzinga.com (March 22, 2012)

Pub: Benzinga.com

Contact: Kyle Bazzy, President

Ed: Aaron Wise. Description: Veteran Owned Small Business program was launched in 2003 in order to provide opportunities to companies with at least 51 percent control by veterans who were disabled while in the military. The veteran must have responsibility for long-term decision-making and day-to-day management. The Disabled Veterans National Foundation is asking the Department of Defense to correct mismanagement of the program because contracts from 2010 show that $340.3 million in work was awarded to contractors who 'misstated' their company's eligibility. Details of the allegations are provided.

39181 ■ "The Diversity Q: Procurement Benefits" in Black Enterprise (Vol. 38, February 2008, No. 7, pp. 72)

Pub: Earl G. Graves Publishing Co. Inc.

Contact: Earl G. Graves, Jr., President

Ed: Aisha Sylvester. Description: Nearly 18 percent of all U.S. firms are minority-owned, according to the recent report called Minorities in Business: A Demographic Review of Minority Business Ownership produced by the Small Business Administration. Issues for working with diversity suppliers are addressed.

39182 ■ "DynCorp Honored for Commitment to Veteran-Owned Businesses" in Manufacturing Close-Up (April 3, 2012)

Description: The National Veteran-Owned Business Association recognized DynCorp International for its commitment to engaging veteran owned businesses as suppliers for the sixth consecutive year. Sixty-five percent of DynCorp's workforce consists of veterans and holds a strong tie with the veteran community. DynCorp is an international government services provider in support of US national security, foreign policy objectives, delivering support solutions for defense, diplomacy, and international development.

39183 ■ e-Business, e-Government and Small and Medium-Size Enterprises: Opportunities and Challenges

Pub: IGI Global

Contact: Dr. Mehdi Khosrow-Pour, President

Released: July 2003. Price: $79.95. Description: Electronic commerce and information technology research in small and medium-sized enterprises (SMEs). Policymakers, legislators, researchers and professionals address significant issues of importance to the small business sector. Availability: Print.

39184 ■ "El Paso Firm VEMAC Rides Boom to the Top: Spotlight on This Year's Fastest-Growing Company" in Hispanic Business (Vol. 30, July-August 2008, No. 7-8, pp. 28)

Pub: Hispanic Business Inc.

Contact: Jesus Chavarria, President

Ed: Jeremy Nisen. Description: VEMAC, a commercial construction management and general contracting firm that is experiencing success despite the plummeting construction market is discussed. VEMAC's success is attributed to the Pentagons' $5 billion investment in construction for the benefit of new personnel and their families to be transferred to Fort Bliss, a U.S. army base adjacent to El Paso.

39185 ■ Electronic Commerce: Technical, Business, and Legal Issues

Ed: Oktay Dogramaci; Aryya Gangopadhyay; Yelena Yesha; Nabil R. Adam. Released: August 1998. Description: Provides insight into the goals of using the Internet to grow a business in the areas of networking and telecommunication, security, and storage and retrieval; business areas such as marketing, procurement and purchasing, billing and payment, and supply chain management; and legal aspects such as privacy, intellectual property, taxation, contractual and legal settlements.

39186 ■ "Eminent Domain Fight Looks Imminent" in The Business Journal-Serving Metropolitan Kansas City (Vol. 26, August 1, 2008, No. 47)

Pub: American City Business Journals, Inc.

Contact: Whitney Shaw, President

Ed: Rob Roberts. Description: Views and information on the proposed constitutional amendments that will limit the use of eminent domain in Missouri, are presented. The proposals are expected to largely ban the taking of private property for private development. It may be included in a November 4,2008 statewide vote for approval.

39187 ■ "Energy Alliance Formed" in Austin Business Journal (Vol. 32, Jun 29, 2012, No. 17, pp. 1)

Pub: American City Business Journals, Inc.

Contact: Whitney Shaw, President

Ed: Christopher Calnan. Released: June 29, 2012. Description: Texas Battery and Energy Storage Consortium has held an organizational meeting at the Austin Chamber of Commerce in a bid to compete for a $120 million U.S. Department of Energy Hub grant. The grant would team university and industry leaders with the Oak Ridge National Research Laboratory to develop battery and energy storage technology. Insights on the hub are also given.

39188 ▪ *"EOTech Product Improves Holographic Gun Sights" in Crain's Detroit Business (Vol. 24, February 4, 2008, No. 5, pp. 9)*
Pub: Crain Communications Inc. - Detroit
Contact: Keith Crain, Chairman
Ed: Chad Halcom. **Description:** L-3 Communications EOTech Inc. procured new business contracts to fulfill military and law enforcement's demand for improved holographic sites used on handheld weapons.

39189 ▪ *"Flu is a Booster for Firms Here" in Philadelphia Business Journal (Vol. 28, September 25, 2009, No. 32, pp. 1)*
Pub: American City Business Journals Inc.
Ed: John George. **Description:** GlaxoSmithKline, AstraZeneca, CSL Biotherapies, and Sanofi Aventis were awarded contract by the US Government to supply swine flu vaccines. It is estimated that global sales of the vaccine could reach billions of dollars.

39190 ▪ *"General Dynamics Secures U.S. Navy Contract" in Travel & Leisure Close-Up (October 8, 2012)*
Description: General Dynamics Electric Boat was awarded a $100.4 million contract modification by the U.S. Navy. Electric Boat will provide lead-yard services for Virginia-class nuclear-powered attack submarines. Details of the government procured contract are included.

39191 ▪ *"Getting Out of an IRS Mess" in Black Enterprise (Vol. 37, December 2006, No. 5, pp. 53)*
Pub: Earl G. Graves Publishing Co. Inc.
Contact: Earl G. Graves, Jr., President
Ed: Carolyn M. Brown. **Description:** Owing back taxes to the IRS can lead to huge penalties and interest. Here are some tips on how to handle paying the IRS what you owe them.

39192 ▪ *Getting Started in Federal Contracting: A Guide through the Federal Procurement Maze*
Pub: Panoptic Enterprises
Contact: Vivina H. McVay, President
URL(s): www.fedgovcontracts.com. **Released:** Irregular; Latest edition 5th, 2009. **Price:** $49.95, Individuals. **Publication includes:** Lists of 26 offices of small and disadvantaged business utilization; 10 Department of Labor regional offices, 11 General Services Administration business service centers, and 11 Small Business Administration regional offices, plus 14 Government resource offices; 35 commercial resources; training; books; newsletters; and associations. These agencies are of use to those privately-owned businesses wishing to sell their products and services to the federal government. Plus 26 Federal Acquisition Computer Network (FAC-NET) Certified Value Added Networks (VANS). **Entries include:** Agency name, address, phone, geographical territory covered. Principal content is discussion of current procurement regulations and information on how to submit proposals. **Arrangement:** Classified by agency represented; type of resource. **Indexes:** Organization name.

39193 ▪ *"Goldbelt Inc.: Targeting Shareholder Development" in Alaska Business Monthly (Vol. 27, October 2011, No. 10, pp. 108)*
Pub: Alaska Business Publishing Company Inc.
Contact: Jim Martin, President
Ed: Tracy Kalytiak. **Description:** Profile of Goldbelt Inc., the company that has changed its original focus of timber to real estate to tourism and then to government contracting opportunities.

39194 ▪ *Government Prime Contractors Directory*
Pub: Government Data Publications Inc.
Contact: Siegfried Lobel, President
Released: Annual; July. **Price:** $15, Individuals; $49.95, Individuals diskettes; $49.95, Individuals CD-ROM. **Covers:** Organizations that received govern-

ment prime contracts during the previous two years. **Entries include:** Contractor name and address, product/service; contractors with contracts of more than $500,000 are marked. **Arrangement:** In two parts; Part 1 is alphabetical by company name and Part 2 is classified by zip code.

39195 ▪ *"Grant Program Boosting Biomedical Research" in Providence Business News (Vol. 28, February 24, 2014, No. 47, pp. 3)*
Pub: American City Business Journals
Released: February 24, 2014. **Description:** The role played by the Institutional Development Award Network of Biomedical Research Excellence (INBRE) is boosting biomedical research in Rhode Island. According to researcher, Niall G. Howlett, procuring startup funding through INBRE led to receiving other grants and working with graduate students who have the potential to become part of the biomedical workforce.

39196 ▪ *"Green Shift Sees Red' in Canadian Business (Vol. 81, September 29, 2008, No. 16)*
Ed: Jeff Sanford. **Description:** Green Shift Inc. is suing the Liberal Party of Canada in an $8.5 million lawsuit for using the phrase 'green shift' when they rolled out their carbon tax and climate change policy. The company has come to be recognized as a consultant and provider of green products such as non-toxic, biodegradable cups, plates, and utensils for events.

39197 ▪ *"Half a World Away" in Tampa Bay Business Journal (Vol. 30, December 4, 2009, No. 50, pp. 1)*
Ed: Jane Meinhardt. **Description:** Enterprise Florida has offered four trade grants for Florida's marine industry businesses to give them a chance to tap into the Middle East market at the Dubai International Boat Show on March 9 to 13, 2010. The grants pay for 50 percent of the exhibition costs for the qualifying business.

39198 ▪ *"HBMG Targets Federal Contracts from Under Raytheon's Wing" in Austin Business JournalInc. (Vol. 29, January 15, 2010, No. 45, pp. 1)*
Pub: American City Business Journals
Ed: Christopher Calnan. **Description:** Information Technology firm HBMG Inc. of Austin Texas has been chosen by Massachusetts-based subcontractor Raytheon Company and the US Department of Defense (DoD) to join DoD's Mentor-Protege program. HBMG will be allowed to vie for government contracts through the said program, potentially increasing business with the DoD by at least 700 percent.

39199 ▪ *"High-Tech Job-Apalooza!' in Orlando Business Journal (Vol. 26, January 15, 2010, No. 33, pp. 1)*
Pub: American City Business Journals
Ed: Christopher Boyd. **Description:** Science Applications International Corporation, Saab Training USA LLC, CAE USA, and Pelliconi &C.SPA attempt to obtain $939,000 in tax incentives to generate 222 technology and defense-related jobs in Orange County, Florida. Each job will provide an average salary of $67,000. Future plans of each technology and defense firm are also presented.

39200 ▪ *"Hilliard Scans Horizon, Finds Defense Contractor" in Business First Columbus (Vol. 25, October 17, 2008, No. 8, pp. A1)*
Pub: American City Business Journals
Ed: Brian R. Ball. **Description:** An incentive package being offered by Hilliard may prompt a Powell defense contractor to relocate in 2009. The package offered to Star Dynamics Corporation incorporates incentives that return a sizeable amount of income taxes to the company.

39201 ▪ *"How to Keep a US Naval Destroyer Warm" in Indoor Comfort Marketing (Vol. 70, April 2011, No. 4, pp. 34)*
Pub: Industry Publications Inc.
Contact: Shirleen Dorman, Editor
Ed: George R. Carey. **Description:** Boiler facts regarding US Naval destroyers are discussed.

39202 ▪ *"How to Pay Zero Taxes 2014: Your Guide to Every Tax Break the IRS Allows"*
Pub: The McGraw-Hill Book Co.
Released: December 3, 2013. **Price:** , $20.00 paperback. **Description:** Simple strategies to save your small business money in taxes, while following the government's tax regulations are covered, for this year and years beyond. The guide covers deductions organized into six categories: exclusions, general deductions, below the line deductions, traditional tax shelters, and super tax shelters.

39203 ▪ *"Indiana Town Reports Success With Collection Agency" in PaymentsSource (August 20, 2012)*
Pub: SourceMedia Inc.
Contact: James M. Malkin, Chief Executive Officer
Released: August 20, 2012. **Description:** Capital Recovery Systems has collected nearly $80,000 in unpaid parking fines in Bloomington, Indiana. The city's agreement with the collection agency allows them to pursue an unlimited amount of unpaid parking tickets at least 30 days late.

39204 ▪ *"Infusion Device Gets $1.47 Million Army Grant" in Memphis Business Journal (Vol. 33, January 20, 2012, No. 41, pp. 1)*
Pub: American City Business Journal
Ed: Michael Sheffield. **Description:** Infusense has procured a $1.47 million grant from the US Army to develop an automated delivery system for the anesthesia Propofol. The drug is used in more than 70 million surgeries and procedures in the country. The medical device would allow for the administration of the anesthesia to wounded soldiers by medics in the field.

39205 ▪ *"iRobot Appoints Former BAE Systems Vice President, Frank Wilson to Lead Defense & Security Business Unit" in News Bites US (August 9, 2012)*
Pub: Financial Times Ltd.
Contact: John Ridding, Chief Executive Officer
Released: August 9, 2012. **Description:** Frank Wilson will serve as senior vice president and general manager of iRobot's Defense & Security business unit. He will focus on strategic business development and product development in order for the firm to meet military, civil defense, and security needs. Tim Trainer, previous acting interim general manager, will remain vice president of programs.

39206 ▪ *"It's Not Easy Being Small' in Baltimore Business Journal (Vol. 27, October 9, 2009, No. 22, pp. 1)*
Pub: American City Business Journals
Ed: Scott Dance. **Description:** A look at how small businesses were left out of the stimulus-funded federal contracts in Maryland. Small contractors were not listed in the federal contracts database USAspending.gov and none were hired for work in the state.

39207 ▪ *"Job Corps Center Remains Vacant After Operator is Booted' in Tampa Bay Business Journal (Vol. 30, January 15, 2010, No. 4, pp. 1)*
Pub: American City Business Journals
Ed: Jane Meinhardt. **Description:** Pinellas County, Florida Job Corps Center has remained vacant due to a conflict over the $16 million contract awarded to Res-Care Inc. by the US Department of Labor (DOL) The DOL has ordered Res-Care to stop operation at the center and it is uncertain when it will open or what company will operate it.

39208 ▪ *"Lancaster Firm Helps Tidy Navy Aircraft Carriers" in Business First of Buffalol> (Vol. 30, February 7, 2014, No. 21, pp. 4)*
Pub: American City Business Journals, Inc.
Contact: Whitney Shaw, President
Released: February 7, 2014. **Description:** Performance Advantage Company sells aluminum took racking systems for use by fire trucks, SWAT teams and departments of public works. The Lancaster, New York-based firm also manufactures clamps and racks for the U.S. Navy, which uses them in aircraft carriers.

39209 ■ *"Local Companies Land Federal Securities Pacts" in Sacramento Business Journal (Vol. 31, March 7, 2014, No. 2, pp. 6)*
Pub: American City Business Journals
Released: March 7, 2014. **Description:** Three companies in Sacramento, California have received Federal security contracts in 2014. Capitol Digital Document Solutions has a five-year contract with the U.S. Department of Homeland Security, while Hewlett-Packard signed a deal with the same government agency. Stratovan Corporation secured two contracts from the U.S. Transportation Security Board.

39210 ■ *"Local Company Seeks Patent For Armored Trucks" in Crain's Detroit Business (Vol. 24, February 4, 2008, No. 5, pp. 10)*
Pub: Crain Communications Inc. - Detroit
Contact: Keith Crain, Chairman
Description: Profile of James LeBlanc Sr., mechanical engineer and defense contractor, discusses his eleven utility patents pending for a set of vehicles and subsystems that would work as countermeasures to explosively formed projectiles.

39211 ■ *"Maryland Ready to Defend Slots Minority Policy" in Boston Business Journal (Vol. 29, July 8, 2011, No. 9, pp. 3)*
Pub: American City Business Journals, Inc.
Ed: Scott Dance. **Description:** The legality of Maryland's minority inclusion policy may be put under scrutiny once the lawsuit filed by rejected slots developer Baltimore City Entertainment Group on July 5, 2011 is heard in court. The lawsuit aims to stop the bidding process on a proposed casino in Baltimore because the minority policy amounts to reverse discrimination.

39212 ■ *"Military Center Near Austin-Bergstrom International Airport a Go" in Austin Business JournalInc. (Vol. 29, December 11, 2009, No. 40, pp. 1)*
Pub: American City Business Journals
Ed: Kate Harrington. **Description:** The $40 million Armed Forces Guard and Reserve Center project at Austin-Bergstrom International Airport has resumed work after a delay of several years. The project is in both the House and Senate versions of the fiscal 2010 Military Construction and Veterans Appropriations Bill that would earmark $16.5 million for the center and $5.7 million for the maintenance facility. Details of construction plans are covered.

39213 ■ *"The Minitel (1978-2012)" in Canadian Business (Vol. 85, August 13, 2012, No. 13, pp. 12)*
Pub: George Media Inc.
Ed: Matthew McClearn. **Released:** August 13, 2012. **Description:** The Minitel online service was developed to reduce the costs of printing phone directories in the French postal and telecommunications ministry in 1978 and became popular in Paris in 1982. With its user-based halved annually and services declining in its waning years, France Telecom opted to terminate the service on June 30, 2012.

39214 ■ *"Montgomery & Barnes: a Service-Disabled, Veteran-Owned Small Business" in Underground Construction (Vol. 65, October 2010, No. 10)*
Pub: Oildom Publishing Company of Texas Inc.
Contact: Oliver C. Klinger, President
Description: Gary Montgomery, chairman of Montgomery and Barnes announced that President Wendell (Buddy) Barnes is now majority owner, thus making the Houston-based civil engineering and consulting services firm, eligible to quality as a Service-Disabled Veteran-Owned Small Business (SDVOSB).

39215 ■ *"Move HQ to Area? Not Now DRC Says" in Washington Business Journal (Vol. 31, July 13, 2012, No. 12, pp. 2)*
Pub: American City Business Journals, Inc.
Contact: Whitney Shaw, President
Ed: Jill R. Aitoro. **Released:** July 13, 2012. **Description:** Government contractor Dynamic Research Corporation (DRC) will stay in Andover, Massachusetts after considering a relocation of its headquarters to Arlington, Virginia. High priced labor along with the

upfront cost of transferring back-office operations are among the factors stopping DRC from relocating to the Washington Metropolitan area.

39216 ■ *"NASA and Partners Complete Unmanned Aircraft Testing" in Travel & Leisure Close-Up (October 8, 2012)*
Description: A partnership between the government, a not-for-profit research and development organization, and academia tested an unmanned aircraft for 'sense and avoid' technology in order to better integrate unmanned aircraft into the national air technology system.

39217 ■ *"N.E.'s Largest Solar Site Set for Scituate Landfill" in Boston Business Journal (Vol. 30, December 17, 2010, No. 47, pp. 1)*
Pub: Boston Business Journal
Ed: Kyle Alspach. **Description:** A closed 12-acre landfill in Scituate, Massachusetts is the proposed site for a 2.4-megawatt solar power plant. The town government will buy the power at a discounted rate, saving it $200,000 annually.

39218 ■ *"New Minority Business Development Agency Office Opens in Memphis" in Commercial Appeal (July 13, 2012)*
Description: Memphis, Tennessee announces the opening of the Minority Business Development Agency. The federally funded program will help to expand minority entrepreneurship in the region. Details of the program and funding are also included.

39219 ■ *"New Veteran Owned Company Helping Service Members Secure Affordable Home Loans While Helping Veteran Focused Charities" in Marketwired (February 21, 2012)*
Pub: COMTEX
Contact: Chip Brian, President
Description: VA Loan Captain Inc. was launched in 2012 at the first Veterans Affairs home loan sourcing company that partners with affiliate lenders that are commited to making a $200 charitable contribution to a participating veteran non-profit with every VA loan closed. Grant Moon, founder and president of VA Loan Captain, is a veteran of Operation Iraqi Freedom.

39220 ■ *"N.J. Tries to Push Stimulus Funds to Minorities" in Philadelphia Business Journal (Vol. 28, September 25, 2009, No. 32, pp. 1)*
Pub: American City Business Journals Inc.
Ed: Athena D. Merritt. **Description:** New Jersey Governor Jon S. Corzine signed an executive order that seeks to ease the way for minority and women-owned business to take on federal stimulus-funded work. New Jersey has also forged new relations with different organizations to reduce the time and cost of certifications for businesses.

39221 ■ *"Nonprofits May Lose MBE Status in MD" in Boston Business Journal (Vol. 29, September 2, 2011, No. 17, pp. 1)*
Pub: American City Business Journals, Inc.
Ed: Scott Dance. **Description:** A business group has been pushing to bar nonprofits from Maryland's Minority Business program. Nonprofits have been found to take a large portion of state contracts intended for women- and minority-owned businesses. The group is also crafting proposed legislation to remove nonprofits from the program.

39222 ■ *"North Carolina Town Hires Collection Agency" in PaymentsSource (April 24, 2012)*
Pub: SourceMedia Inc.
Contact: James M. Malkin, Chief Executive Officer
Released: April 24, 2012. **Description:** Selma, North Carolina hired TekCollect to collect about $500,000 in unpaid utility bills. The collection agency will be paid $13,000 up frnt for guaranteed collections on 500 of the 1,200 acccounts.

39223 ■ *"Not in Your Backyard?" in Canadian Business (Vol. 80, March 12, 2007, No. 6, pp. 44)*
Ed: John Gray. **Description:** The threat of losing residential property rights of persons whose land has rightful stakes from miners due to availability of minerals at the place is discussed.

39224 ■ *"Numbers Game" in Baltimore Business Journal (Vol. 27, February 6, 2010, No. 40, pp. 1)*
Pub: American City Business Journals
Ed: Scott Dance. **Description:** Doubts are being raised regarding the impact of the federal stimulus spending in addressing unemployment in Maryland, which has experienced 1,800 jobs created so far. Details on the view of companies and the insufficient amount of contracts that lead to the fewer number of workers being hired are discussed.

39225 ■ *"Outlook In Other Industries" in Crain's Detroit Business (Vol. 30, January 6, 2014, No. 1, pp. 3)*
Pub: Crain Communications Inc. - Detroit
Contact: Keith Crain, Chairman
Released: January 6, 2014. **Description:** Outlook for industries in the Detroit area are listed, including small business growth, restaurants, defense contracts, nonprofits, transportation, auto suppliers, healthcare, bankruptcy, and government.

39226 ■ *"PennDOT Invites Bidders to Heavy Equipment Auction" in Travel & Leisure Close-Up (October 8, 2012)*
Description: Pennsylvania Department of Transportation (PennDOT) is offering 161 items up for bid during the PennDOT Online Heavy Equipment Auction. The auction allows companies the ability to purchase heavy equipment such as snow plow trucks, anti-icing trucks, motor graders, excavators, wheel and backhoe loaders, asphalt equipment, dump trucks, spreaders, skid steers, generators and more.

39227 ■ *"Pentagon Awards $17.6B Contract for EB-Built Subs Through 2018" in Providence Business News (Vol. 29, April 28, 2014, No. 4)*
Pub: American City Business Journals
Released: April 28, 2014. **Description:** The U.S. Navy has signed a $17.6 billion contract with Newport News Shipbuilding and General Dynamics Corporation for construction of 10 new naval submarines. The deal will help employment at General Dynamics' Quonset Business Park Electric Boat production site. The submarines are scheduled to be built between 2014-2018. Electric Boat expects to hire 650 additional workers.

39228 ■ *"Post-Prison Center Idea Rankles Cincinnati's Over-the-Rhine" in Business Courier (Vol. 26, November 27, 2009, No. 31, pp. 1)*
Pub: American City Business Journals, Inc.
Contact: Whitney Shaw, President
Ed: Lucy May. **Description:** Cincinnati officials and community leaders oppose Firetree Ltd.'s plan to launch a residential program for federal offenders near the School for the Creative and Performing Arts in Over-the-Rhine. Firetree, a Pennsylvania-based reentry center services firm, proposed a five-year contract with the Federal Bureau of Prisons based on a letter to Cincinnati Police Chief Thomas Streicher.

39229 ■ *"Private Care's Next Phase: Serious Money Is Going Into Health Clinics" in Canadian Business (Vol. 85, June 11, 2012, No. 10, pp. 10)*
Pub: George Media Inc.
Ed: Laura Cameron. **Released:** June 11, 2012. **Description:** Some public-private partnerships in Canada include the acquisition of clinics by Centric Health Corporation and the partnership between Westbank First National and Johns Hopkins Hospital. Private healthcare providers have operated by dividing their funding among government contracts, clients not covered by Medicare and patients paying out of pocket and non-insured services.

39230 ■ *"Proposed Law Would Stop REIS Bid for Annexation by Livonia" in Crain's Detroit Business (Vol. 24, March 10, 2008, No. 10, pp. 2)*
Pub: Crain Communications Inc.
Contact: Rance E. Crain, President
Ed: Chad Halcom. **Description:** REIS Northville L.L. C., a joint venture made up of Real Estate Interests Group Inc. and Schostak Bros. & Co., has proposed

an $800 million project called Highwood at the former Northville Psychiatric Hospital site but has been stalled due to a disagreement with Northville Township on several terms including: the amount of retail at the site and the paying for cleanup of environmental and medical waste.

39231 ▪ "The Quest for the Smart Prosthetic" in Canadian Business (Vol. 83, October 12, 2010, No. 17, pp. 26)
Pub: Rogers Media Inc.
Contact: Tony Viner, President
Ed: Jacqueline Nelson. **Description:** Information about a two-year research project led by Southern Methodist University (SMU) and funded by the Defense Advance Research Projects Agency (DARPA) is provided. The agency aims to create a 'smart prosthetic' which will improve the lives of military amputees. The planned prosthetic will use a sensor that can carry nerve signals through synthetic channels. ▪

39232 ▪ "Rebuffed, BAE Systems Fights Army Contract Decision" in Business Courier (Vol. 26, September 25, 2009)
Pub: American City Business Journals, Inc.
Contact: Whitney Shaw, President
Ed: Jon Newberry. **Description:** BAE Systems filed a complaint with the US Government Accountability Office after the US Army issued an order to BAE's competitor for armoured trucks which is potentially worth over $3 billion. Hundreds of jobs in Butler County, Ohio hinge on the success of the contract protest.

39233 ▪ "The Return of the War Dividend" in Canadian Business (Vol. 87, July 2014, No. 7, pp. 25)
Pub: George Media Inc.
Released: July 2014. **Description:** Investors interested in defense industry stocks are advised to avoid any company with large ties to a single big-ticket project. The stability and good dividends generated by large defense companies are recommended for buy-and-hold investors.

39234 ▪ "A Safe Bet" in Entrepreneur (Vol. 35, October 2007, No. 10, pp. 26)
Pub: Entrepreneur Press
Contact: Perlman Neil, President
Ed: Carol Tice. **Description:** U.S. Department of Defense has developed a program, called the Defense Venture Catalyst Initiative or DeVenCI, that will match defense officials to the products that they need. DeVenCI uses conferences to showcase the defense contractors and their technologies to defense managers. Details of how this program helps both contractors and defense officials are overviewed.

39235 ▪ "SAIC To Be Honored For Supporting Veteran-Owned Businesses" in News Bites US (June 13, 2012)
Description: Science Applications International Corporation (SAIC) was recognized by the National Veteran Small Business Coalition at the Veteran Entrepreneur Training Symposium (VETS2012) 'Champions of Veteran Enterprise' luncheon held in Reno, Nevada in June. SAIC is honored for its work with veteran-owned and service-disabled veteran owned small businesses. Statistical data included.

39236 ▪ "SBA Makes Reforms To Federal Government Contracting" in Black Enterprise (Vol. 38, January 2008, No. 6, pp. 26)
Pub: Earl G. Graves Publishing Co. Inc.
Contact: Earl G. Graves, Jr., President
Ed: Alexis McCombs. **Description:** The U.S. Small Business Administration enacted a new requirement that small businesses recertify size status in order to remain eligible for federal contracts lasting more than five years. Prior regulations allowed companies declared small in earlier contracts may have grown through acquisitions, making them ineligible. This move may impact black businesses.

39237 ▪ "A Second Chance at Road Dollars" in Orlando Business Journal (Vol. 26, February 5, 2010, No. 36, pp. 1)
Pub: American City Business Journals
Description: Nearly $10 million worth of construction projects in Central Florida would give construction companies that missed the initial round of federal

stimulus-funded local road building projects another opportunity. Cost savings in the initial round of road projects enabled Orange, Osceola, and Seminole Counties to secure additional projects.

39238 ▪ "Six Arkansas Construction Projects Get LEED Certification" in Arkansas Business (Vol. 29, July 23, 2012, No. 30, pp. 19)
Pub: Arkansas Business Publishing Group
Ed: Lance Turner. **Description:** State of Arkansas has bestowed its Leadership in Energy and Environmental Design certification on 55 projects throughout the state. Six projects are identified and described. A list of all projects is included.

39239 ▪ "Slater Progress Stalled" in Providence Business News (Vol. 28, March 10, 2014, No. 49, pp. 1)
Pub: American City Business Journals
Released: March 10, 2014. **Description:** Slater Technology Fund has received only $1.9 million of the $9 million in expected federal funds. However, the venture capital firm decided to invest in some promising technology companies in Providence, Rhode Island. Slater senior managing director, Richard Horan, reveals that uncertainties with respect to grants have delayed private fundraising.

39240 ▪ "Southern California Edison Issues $400 Million in Bonds Utilizing Five Minority-, Woman- and Service-Disabled Veteran-Owned Underwriters" in Benzinga.com (March 20, 2012)
Pub: Benzinga.com
Contact: Kyle Bazzy, President
Ed: Aaron Wise. **Description:** Southern California Edison Company's sale of $400 million of 30-year first and refunding mortgage bonds will be used to repay short-term debt incurred to fund investment in its electric utility facilities. The bonds were sold through a group that includes minority-, woman-, and service-disabled veteran-owned firms. Details of the transaction are included.

39241 ▪ "Special Events Pro Mary Tribble Reveals Secrets of Winning Bids for Political Convention Business" in Special Events Magazine (May 30, 2012)
Ed: Lisa Hurley. **Released:** May 30, 2012. **Description:** Mary Tribble, successful event planner, offers tips for winning bids for political conventions. Tribble serves as chief of event planning for the "Charlotte in 2012" convention for the Democratic National Convention.

39242 ▪ "State Efforts to Boost Contract Efficiency Hurt Smaller Firms" in Boston Business Journal (Vol. 27, November 9, 2007, No. 41, pp. 1)
Ed: Lisa van der Pool. **Description:** Massachusetts Operational Services Division, which provides statewide telecommunications and data infrastructure contracts, announced that it is cutting the list of companies on the new contract from twelve to six. The cost-cutting efforts began in 2005, after a review by an independent consultant advised the state to adopt strategies that would save millions of dollars.

39243 ▪ "Stimulus Effect Slow in Greater Baltimore" in Baltimore Business Journal (Vol. 27, October 23, 2009, No. 24, pp. 1)
Pub: American City Business Journals
Ed: Scott Dance. **Description:** Companies in Maryland have reported only 154 new jobs being created or saved in Greater Baltimore and 965 jobs overall in the state because of stimulus cash. The federal stimulus program was expected to create thousands of new jobs but statistics show its failure to reduce unemployment in the state.

39244 ▪ "Taking Off" in Puget Sound Business Journal (Vol. 34, January 31, 2014, No. 42, pp. 4)
Pub: American City Business Journals
Released: January 31, 2014. **Description:** Washington State is at the forefront of the U.S. space flight industry, as the federal government shrinks its role and entrepreneurs are filling the gap. The region is

becoming a leader in the space sector because of its high-tech aerospace skills, software intellectuals, and investors willing to fund these enterprises.

39245 ▪ "Tax Committee To Appoint New Tax Collection" in Republican and Herald (June 27, 2012)
Pub: McClatchy Tribune Information Services
Released: June 27, 2012. **Description:** Schuylill County Tax Collection Committee hired Berkheimer Associates, Bangor, Northampton County as its 'provisional tax collector' after firing an Allegheny County firm that failed to process earned income tax bills in a timely fashion.

39246 ▪ "TIA Wrestles with Procurement Issues" in Business Journal Serving Greater Tampa Bay (Vol. 30, November 12, 2010, No. 47, pp. 1)
Pub: Tampa Bay Business Journal
Ed: Mark Holan. **Description:** Tampa International Airport (TIA) has been caught in conflict of interest and procurement policy issues after the Hillsborough County Aviation Authority learned of the spousal relationship of an employee with his wife's firm, Gresham Smith and Partners. Gresham already won contracts with TIA and was ahead of other firms in a new contract.

39247 ▪ "Training the Troops: Battlefield Simulations Bring Growth to UNITECH" in Black Enterprise (Vol. 38, February 2008, No. 7, pp. 30)
Pub: Earl G. Graves Publishing Co. Inc.
Contact: Earl G. Graves, Jr., President
Ed: Cliff Hocker. **Description:** Universal Systems and Technology (UNITECH) received a total of over $45 million U.S. Department of Defense orders during September and October 2007. UNITECH designs and manufactures battlefield simulation devices used to train troops in the Army and Marine Corps.

39248 ▪ "U-Swirl Added to SBA's Franchise Registry" in Ice Cream Reporter (Vol. 23, September 20, 2010, No. 10, pp. 1)
Description: Healthy Fast Food Inc., parent to the U-SWIRL Frozen Yogurt cafe chain announced that the U.S. Small Business Administration listed U-SWIRL Frozen Yogurt on its official franchise registry. This move will allow U-SWIRL the benefits of a streamlined review process for SBA financing.

39249 ▪ "U.S. Widens Rocket Field" in Wall Street Journal Eastern Edition (October 17, 2011, pp. B4)
Pub: Dow Jones & Co., Inc.
Contact: Clare Hart, President
Ed: Andy Pasztor. **Description:** An agreement has been reached between National Aeronautics and Space Administration, the Department of Defense and the Air Force that will assist small commercial space ventures in bidding for profitable contracts for government launching. The program will give those companies a chance to compete against larger corporations.

39250 ▪ "UW Wary of WSU's Wish for Spokane Medical School" in Puget Sound Business Journal (Vol. 35, May 9, 2014, No. 3, pp. 9)
Pub: American City Business Journals
Released: May 9, 2014. **Description:** University of Washington leaders believe that opening a medical school in Washington State University's (WSU) Spokane Campus will create more competition for state funding. However, WSU officials claim that the demand for new doctors demonstrates the need for a second school.

39251 ▪ "VA Exceeds Government-Wide Goal for Veteran-Owned Business Procurement" in Benzinga.com (July 3, 2012)
Pub: Benzinga.com
Contact: Kyle Bazzy, President
Ed: Aaron Wise. **Description:** Department of Veterans Affairs has surpassed its goal of government procurements of the Small Business Adminstration by more than six times. The VA's committment to the success of veteran-owned small businesses is covered.

39252 ■ *"Veteran-Owned Firm Enlists Street"*
in Traders (Vol. 25, May 1, 2012, No. 337)
Description: Academy Securities discusses its vision
to give US military veterans a chance at a career on
Wall Street. Academy is a veteran owned investment
brokerage firm and is pursuing Wall Street professionals willing to mentor veterans. The firm is
dedicated to giving back to the veterans who have
served the nation and is a certified Service Disabled
Veteran Owned Business.

39253 ■ *"Water Works Spinoff Could Make*
Big Splash" in Business Courier (Vol. 24,
October 18, 2007, No. 27, pp. 1)
Pub: American City Business Journals, Inc.
Contact: Whitney Shaw, President
Ed: Dan Monk. **Description:** Cincinnati, Ohio city
manager Milton Dohoney proposed to spin off the
city-owned Greater Cincinnati Water Works into a
regionally focused water district that could allow the
city to receive millions of dollars in annual dividends.
A feasibility study is to be conducted by a team of
outside consultants and city staffers and is expected
to be finished by summer of 2008.

39254 ■ *"Wi-Fi Finds Its Way Despite Nixed*
Plan for Free System" in Crain's Cleveland
Business (Vol. 28, November 12, 2007, No. 45,
pp. 3)
Pub: Crain Communications Inc.
Ed: Jay Miller. **Description:** Discusses the issues
facing Cleveland and Northeast Ohio concerning their
proposal to offer citizens wireless Internet services
for free or a small fee.

39255 ■ *Win Government Contracts for Your*
Small Business
Pub: Wolters Kluwer Law & Business CCH
Contact: Mike Sabbatis, President
Ed: John DiGiacomo. **Price:** $24.95. **Description:**
Techniques to help small companies negotiate and
win government contracts.

39256 ■ *"Your Next Big Customer" in*
Business Owner (Vol. 35,
November-December 2011, No. 6, pp. 7)
Pub: DL Perkins Company
Description: Learn how to sell goods and services
to the Federal Government. The Office of Govern-
ment Contracting is the agency responsible for
coordinating government purchases.

TRADE PERIODICALS

39257 ■ *Inside Missile Defense*
Pub: Inside Washington Publishers
Contact: Korila Malecha, Manager
URL(s): iwpnews.com/IWP-General/Inside-Washing-
ton-Publishers-General/products/menu-id-812.html.
Ed: Thomas Duffy, Editor. **Released:** Biweekly; every
other Wednesday. **Price:** $795, U.S. and Canada;
$845, Elsewhere. **Description:** Reports on U.S. mis-
sile defense programs, procurement, and policymaking.

CONSULTANTS

39258 ■ **Margiloff & Associates**
621 Royalview St.
Duarte, CA 91010-1346
Ph: (626)303-1266
Fax: (626)303-0127
Contact: Irwin B. Margiloff, Principal
E-mail: margiloff@compuserve.com
Scope: Energy and water conservation studies,
analysis of research and development, licensing,
economics and project management. Projects involve
development, training, utility review, cost analysis,
manufacturing system improvement, process modeling and expert witness services. Clients include in
the field of food, chemical, fermentation, energy,
financial and legal services, government and general
manufacturing fields. **Founded:** 1983.

COMPUTERIZED DATABASES

39259 ■ *Commerce Business Daily Online*
(CBD)
United Communications Group
9737 Washingtonian Blvd., Ste. 100
Gaithersburg, MD 20878-7364
Ph: (301)287-2700
Free: 800-824-1195
Fax: (301)287-2039
Co. E-mail: webmaster@ucg.com
URL: http://www.ucg.com
Availability: Online: U.S. Government Printing Office
- Federal Digital System. **Type:** Full-text; Directory.

39260 ■ *Federal Contracts Report™*
Bloomberg BNA
3 Bethesda Metro Center, Ste. 250
Bethesda, MD 20814-5377
Ph: (703)341-3000
Free: 800-372-1033
Fax: (800)253-0332
Co. E-mail: customercare@bna.com
URL: http://www.bna.com
Contact: Gregory McCaffrey, President
URL(s): www.bna.com/federal-contracts-report-
p6016. **Availability:** Online: Bloomberg BNA; Thom-
son Reuters - Westlaw. **Type:** Full-text.

LIBRARIES

39261 ■ **Georgia State University - Small**
Business Development Center (SBDC)
10 Park Place South SE, Ste. 450
Atlanta, GA 30303
Ph: (404)413-7830
Fax: (404)413-7832
Co. E-mail: atlanta@georgiasbdc.org
URL: http://sbdc.robinson.gsu.edu
Contact: Bernard J. Meineke, Director
URL(s): www.georgiasbdc.org. **Scope:** Small busi-
ness, marketing, finance, international business, and
government procurement. **Services:** Counseling;
Center open to the public for reference use only.

Founded: 1979. **Holdings:** Business directories;
government publications and journals, periodicals,
training manuals and videotapes. **Subscriptions:** 11
journals and other serials.

39262 ■ **NIGP: The Institute for Public**
Procurement - Library
151 Spring St.
Herndon, VA 20170
Ph: (703)736-8900
Free: 800-FOR-NIGP
Fax: (703)736-9639
Co. E-mail: customercare@nigp.org
URL: http://www.nigp.org/eweb/StartPage.aspx
Contact: Rick Grimm, Chief Executive Officer
E-mail: rgrimm@nigp.org
Description: Federal, state, provincial, county, and
local government buying agencies; hospital, school,
prison, and public utility purchasing agencies in the
U.S. and Canada. Also provides services to the
International procurement community. Develops
standards and specifications for governmental buy-
ing; promotes uniform purchasing laws and procedures; conducts specialized education and research
programs. Administers certification program for the
Universal Public Purchasing Certification Council
(UPPCC) for Certified Professional Public Buyer
(CPPB) and Certified Public Purchasing Officer
(CPPO); offers audit consulting services and cost-
saving programs and tools for governmental agencies, including product commodity code to online
specifications library. Maintains speakers' bureau;
compiles statistics, web-based products and services.
Scope: Federal, state, provincial, county, and local
government buying agencies; hospital, school, prison,
and public utility purchasing agencies in the U.S. and
Canada. Also provides services to the International
procurement community. Develops standards and
specifications for governmental buying; promotes
uniform purchasing laws and procedures; conducts
specialized education and research programs.
Administers certification program for the Universal
Public Purchasing Certification Council (UPPCC) for
Certified Professional Public Buyer (CPPB) and Certified Public Purchasing Officer (CPPO); offers audit
consulting services and cost-saving programs and
tools for governmental agencies, including product
commodity code to online specifications library.
Maintains speakers' bureau; compiles statistics, web-
based products and services. **Services:** Library open
to NIGP members. **Founded:** 1944. **Holdings:** Files
of specifications, government procurement (13,000),
searchable forms and documents (350). **Subscriptions:** 30060 reports. **Publications:** *NIGP Buy-
Weekly*; *The NIGP Source* (Quarterly); *The Procure-
ment Professional* (Bimonthly); *The Public Purchaser*
(Bimonthly). **Educational Activities:** NIGP Forum &
Products Exposition (Annual). **Awards:** NIGP Distin-
guished Service Awards (DSA) (Annual); Albert H.
Hall Memorial Award (Annual); NIGP Chapter of the
Year Award (Annual); NIGP Buyer of the Year Award
(Annual); NIGP Manager of the Year Award (Annual);
Best Practices Award (Annual); Innovative Practices
Award (Annual); Outstanding Agency Accreditation
Achievement (Annual).

START-UP INFORMATION

39263 ■ *"Are We There Yet?" in Entrepreneur (September 2014)*
Pub: Entrepreneur Media Inc.
Released: September 2014. **Description:** Entrepreneurs and small business advocates discuss the progress of Jumpstart Our Business Startups (JOBS) Act two years after it was signed into law in the U.S. in April 2012. The implementation of Title II in September 2013 allowed private companies to publicly advertise their fundraising efforts. Rewards-based crowdfunding also benefited from the publicity surrounding the JOBS Act. Crowdfunding advocates are looking forward to the finalization of Title III to address their concerns about red tape and compliance costs.

39264 ■ *"Breaking Barriers" in Baltimore Business Journal (Vol. 30, June 29, 2012, No. 8, pp. 1)*
Pub: American City Business Journals, Inc.
Contact: Whitney Shaw, President
Ed: Jack Lambert. **Released:** June 29, 2012. **Description:** Many Hispanic entrepreneurs have been struggling to start businesses in Baltimore, Maryland. Many necessary documents are available only in English. Hispanic businesses are seen to spark future economic growth in Baltimore.

39265 ■ *"Fundable.com, Crowdfunding for Startups, Chooses WePay's Marketplace API to Power Payments" in Internet Wire (June 20, 2012)*
Released: June 20, 2012. **Description:** Fundable.com has partnered with WePay to allow users to start accepting payments from funding sources immediately and does not require users to have a pre-existing merchant account. The Crowdfunding Bill creates a massive change or accessing capital for starting a new business venture.

39266 ■ *"JOBS Act Spurring Bio IPOs" in Philadelphia Business Journal (Vol. 33, May 2, 2014, No. 12, pp. 4)*
Pub: American City Business Journals
Released: May 2, 2014. **Description:** The Jumpstart Our Business Startups Act has important provisions that are helping many early-stage biotechnology companies in their initial public offerings. Trevena Inc. of King of Prussia, Pennsylvania benefited from the extra time to educate the investment community and from the exemptions on the regulatory requirements.

39267 ■ *The Small Business Start-Up Kit*
Pub: Nolo
Contact: Ralph Warner, Chief Executive Officer
Ed: Peri Pakroo. **Released:** February 2014. **Price:** $23.99; $20.99. **Description:** Entrepreneurial advice for launching a new business. Topics include compliance with state regulations, sole proprietorships, partnerships, corporations, limited liability companies, as well as accounting and tax information. **Availability:** PrintE-book.

39268 ■ *Small Business Survival Guide*
Ed: Cliff Ennico. **Price:** $12.95. **Description:** Small business expert provides strategies to start a company and survive in the 21st Century. He shows small business owners how to succeed despite challenges that can defeat any firm. His advice covers suppliers; customers and contractors; competitors and creditors; spouses, family and friends; as well as the ways lawyers, accountants and other can steal an entrepreneur's success. Ennico also describes how startups can comply with local regulations.

39269 ■ *"So What Is Crowdfunding Anyway? New Legislation by Obama and Congress Relaxes Solicitation by Startups" in Accounting Today (August 6, 2012)*
Pub: SourceMedia Inc.
Contact: James M. Malkin, Chief Executive Officer
Ed: Jim Brendel. **Released:** August 6, 2012. **Description:** An introduction to crowdfunding provides a concise description to the process in which a group of investors partner to fund small business and startups. Rules from the SEC regarding crowdfunding are expected to be in place by the end of the year.

39270 ■ *"StartX Med Prescribed for Innovation" in Silicon Valley/San Jose Business Journal (Vol. 30, June 8, 2012, No. 11, pp. 1)*
Pub: American City Business Journal
Description: StartX Med is a program started by entrepreneur Divya Nag along with Stanford student-led nonprofit StartX to help medical startups. Under the program, entrepreneurs will have access to wet and dry laboratory space, animal testing and information related to US Food and Drug Adminstration regulations.

ASSOCIATIONS AND OTHER ORGANIZATIONS

39271 ■ **American Senior Benefits Association (ASBA)**
PO Box 300777
Chicago, IL 60630-0777
Ph: (773)714-7990
Free: 877-906-2722
Co. E-mail: info@asbaonline.org
URL: http://www.asbaonline.org
Contact: Bill Hill, President
Description: Represents small business owners. Supports legislation favorable to the small business enterprise; organizes members to collectively oppose unfavorable legislation. Informs members of proposed legislation affecting small businesses; conducts business education programs. Operates scholarship program. **Founded:** 1975. **Publications:** *ASBA Today* (Quarterly); *ASBA Benefits Guide* (Annual); *ASBA Quarterly* (Quarterly). **Awards:** ASBA College Scholarship Program (Annual).

39272 ■ **Small Business Council of America (SBCA)**
1523 Concord Pike, Ste. 300
Brandywine E
Wilmington, DE 19803

Ph: (706)324-5435
URL: http://www.sbca.net
Contact: Leanne H. Redstone, Executive Director
E-mail: lredstone@shanlaw.com
Description: Small business and professional organizations. Goals are to keep federal tax and employee benefit legislation from becoming burdensome, and to support legislation creating economic incentives for small businesses. Lobbies Congress on behalf of members; alerts members to proposed legislation so that opposition or support can be mustered before a bill becomes law; operates ad hoc committees on specific legislation. Maintains speakers' bureau; compiles statistics. **Founded:** 1979. **Publications:** *Small Business Council of America--Alert*; *News Flashes*; *SBCA Member and Congressional Directory* (Annual); *Tax Report* (Monthly). **Educational Activities:** Congressional Awards Ceremony. **Awards:** Connie Murdoch Award (Annual); Small Business Person of the Year (Annual); Humanitarian of the Year (Annual).

39273 ■ **Small Business Legislative Council (SBLC)**
1100 H St. NW, Ste. 540
Washington, DC 20005
Ph: (202)639-8500
Co. E-mail: email@sblc.org
URL: http://www.sblc.org
Description: Serves as an independent coalition of trade and professional associations that share a common commitment to the future of small business. Represents the interests of small businesses in such diverse economic sectors as manufacturing, retailing, distribution, professional and technical services, construction, transportation, and agriculture. **Founded:** 1976.

EDUCATIONAL PROGRAMS

39274 ■ **Adobe Acrobat Section 508 Accessibility (Onsite)**
EEI Communications
8945 Guilford Rd., Ste. 145
Columbia, MD 21046
Ph: (410)309-8200
Free: 888-253-2762
Fax: (410)630-3980
Co. E-mail: train@eeicom.com
URL: http://www.eeicom.com/eei-training-services
URL(s): www.eeicom.com. **Description:** Covers the regulations by the Federal Government's Section 508 accessibility and the features of Adobe Acrobat software designed to meet the regulations, including definition of accessibility, authoring for accessibility, working with existing PDF files, forms, and scanned documents, using the accessibility checker, and tags palette, and testing your PDF files for accessibility. **Audience:** Professionals and public. **Telecommunication Services:** train@eeicom.com.

39275 ■ **ASTM Phase I & Phase II Environmental Site Assessment Processes (Onsite)**
Seminar Information Service Inc.
20 Executive Park, Ste. 120
Irvine, CA 92614

Ph: (949)261-9104
Free: 877-SEM-INFO
Fax: (949)261-1963
Co. E-mail: info@seminarinformation.com
URL: http://www.seminarinformation.com
Description: Gain an understanding how to use the standards and how the standards affect the way you do business. The 'Innocent Landowner Defense' under the Comprehensive Environmental Response, Compensation and Liability Act (CERCLA) and why due diligence is necessary will be covered. **Audience:** Industry professionals.

39276 ■ Automotive Glazing Materials (Onsite)
Seminar Information Service Inc.
20 Executive Park, Ste. 120
Irvine, CA 92614
Ph: (949)261-9104
Free: 877-SEM-INFO
Fax: (949)261-1963
Co. E-mail: info@seminarinformation.com
URL: http://www.seminarinformation.com
URL(s): www.seminarinformation.com. **Description:** An overview of the different automotive glazing materials, past, present and future, including the laws that govern their use, and manufacture, installation, usage, testing, safety aspects and how they affect automotive performance. Topics include the chemical, physical and design issues of annealed, laminated, tempered, glass-plastic and plastic glazing materials. **Audience:** Industry professionals. **Telecommunication Services:** info@seminarinformation.com.

39277 ■ Automotive Lighting (Onsite)
Seminar Information Service Inc.
20 Executive Park, Ste. 120
Irvine, CA 92614
Ph: (949)261-9104
Free: 877-SEM-INFO
Fax: (949)261-1963
Co. E-mail: info@seminarinformation.com
URL: http://www.seminarinformation.com
URL(s): www.seminarinformation.com. **Description:** Provides broad information about automotive lighting systems with emphasis on lighting functions, effectiveness, and technologies, including the legal aspects and implications related to automotive lighting and examine safety measurements used with lighting functions and human factors costs. **Audience:** Professionals. **Telecommunication Services:** info@seminarinformation.com.

39278 ■ Collections Law (Onsite)
Fred Pryor Seminars & CareerTrack
5700 Broadmoor St., Ste. 300
Mission, KS 66202
Ph: (800)780-8476
Free: 800-780-8476
Fax: (913)967-8849
Co. E-mail: customerservice@pryor.com
URL: http://www.pryor.com
Contact: Phil Love, Chief Executive Officer
Price: $139, for groups of 5 or more. **Description:** Ensure your organization is legally compliant, including strategies and techniques to gain quicker results in collecting money. **Audience:** Industry professionals. **Dates and Locations:** Cities throughout the United States.

39279 ■ DOT Hazardous Materials Training (Onsite)
Seminar Information Service Inc.
20 Executive Park, Ste. 120
Irvine, CA 92614
Ph: (949)261-9104
Free: 877-SEM-INFO
Fax: (949)261-1963
Co. E-mail: info@seminarinformation.com
URL: http://www.seminarinformation.com
URL(s): www.seminarinformation.com/qqaubm/dot-hazardous-materials-training. **Price:** $449. **Description:** DOT is changing virtually all of the rules for hazardous materials containers, labeling, shipping papers, placards, and shipping names. Learn how to comply with the regulations. **Audience:** Shipping

supervisors, purchasing managers, traffic managers, plant managers, shipping clerks, dispatchers, purchasing agents, drivers, and compliance managers .

39280 ■ Environmental, Health, and Safety Laws and Regulations
Description: Common sense approach to compliance with environmental, health, and safety laws and regulations.

39281 ■ Environmental Regulations Seminars
Description: 2-day seminar on how to comply with federal environmental regulations.

39282 ■ Hazardous Waste Management: The Complete Course
Seminar Information Service Inc.
20 Executive Park, Ste. 120
Irvine, CA 92614
Ph: (949)261-9104
Free: 877-SEM-INFO
Fax: (949)261-1963
Co. E-mail: info@seminarinformation.com
URL: http://www.seminarinformation.com
Description: Covers how to meet your annual training requirement and learn a systematic approach to understanding and complying with the latest state and federal regulations. **Audience:** Environmental coordinators, hazardous waste managers and plant managers .

39283 ■ Hazardous Waste Management: The Complete Course (Onsite)
Seminar Information Service Inc.
20 Executive Park, Ste. 120
Irvine, CA 92614
Ph: (949)261-9104
Free: 877-SEM-INFO
Fax: (949)261-1963
Co. E-mail: info@seminarinformation.com
URL: http://www.seminarinformation.com
URL(s): www.seminarinformation.com/qqajxq/hazardous-waste-management-the-complete-course. **Price:** $795. **Description:** Learn a systematic approach to understanding and complying with the latest state and federal regulations. **Audience:** Environmental coordinators, hazardous waste managers and plant managers.

39284 ■ Records Retention and Destruction (Onsite)
Fred Pryor Seminars & CareerTrack
5700 Broadmoor St., Ste. 300
Mission, KS 66202
Ph: (800)780-8476
Free: 800-780-8476
Fax: (913)967-8849
Co. E-mail: customerservice@pryor.com
URL: http://www.pryor.com
Contact: Phil Love, Chief Executive Officer
Price: $149.00; $139.00 for groups of 5 or more. **Description:** Gain valuable information for successfully organizing, storing, archiving and destroying your organization's critical business documents while eliminating risk and ensuring compliance with the latest legal requirements.

39285 ■ SARA Title III Workshop (Onsite)
Seminar Information Service Inc.
20 Executive Park, Ste. 120
Irvine, CA 92614
Ph: (949)261-9104
Free: 877-SEM-INFO
Fax: (949)261-1963
Co. E-mail: info@seminarinformation.com
URL: http://www.seminarinformation.com
URL(s): www.seminarinformation.com/qqakcg/sara-title-iii-workshop. **Price:** $399. **Description:** Step-by-step procedures for compliance with Title III of the Superfund Amendments. **Audience:** Safety coordinators, plant managers and training directors.

39286 ■ Storm Water Management: How to Comply with Federal and State Regulations (Onsite)
Seminar Information Service Inc.
20 Executive Park, Ste. 120
Irvine, CA 92614

Ph: (949)261-9104
Free: 877-SEM-INFO
Fax: (949)261-1963
Co. E-mail: info@seminarinformation.com
URL: http://www.seminarinformation.com
URL(s): www.seminarinformation.com/details.cfm?qc=qqakep. **Price:** $499. **Description:** Learn what discharges must be permitted, how to apply for a permit, and requirements for maintaining permit compliance. **Audience:** Environmental coordinators, safety coordinators, plant managers, and hazardous waste managers .

39287 ■ Workers' Compensation (Onsite)
Fred Pryor Seminars & CareerTrack
5700 Broadmoor St., Ste. 300
Mission, KS 66202
Ph: (800)780-8476
Free: 800-780-8476
Fax: (913)967-8849
Co. E-mail: customerservice@pryor.com
URL: http://www.pryor.com
Contact: Phil Love, Chief Executive Officer
URL(s): www.pryor.com/mkt_info/seminars/desc/wq.asp. **Price:** $299. **Description:** Learn strategies, insider tips, tools, and more to help manage entire workers' compensation plan more effectively, including how workers' compensation, FMLA, and ADA regulations can overlap. **Audience:** Professionals.

DIRECTORIES OF EDUCATIONAL PROGRAMS

39288 ■ *Neal-Schuman Guide to Finding Legal and Regulatory Information on the Internet*
Pub: Neal-Schuman Publishers Inc.
Contact: Patricia Glass Schuman, President
E-mail: pgs@neal-schuman.com
URL(s): www.neal-schuman.com. **Ed:** Yvonne J. Chandler. **Released:** new edition expected 2005. **Price:** $135, Individuals. **Covers:** 900 Internet sites offering local, state, and federal legal and government information. **Entries include:** Title, publishing agency, URL, brief description of the site.

REFERENCE WORKS

39289 ■ *"11th Circuit: Don't Break the Law to Comply with It"* in Miami Daily Business Review (October 21, 2009)
Pub: Incisive Media Inc.
Contact: Lee Feldman, Manager
E-mail: lee.feldman@incisivemedia.com
Ed: Janet L. Conley. **Description:** Niagara Credit Solutions argued with a three-judge panel that the company broke the rule saying debt collectors must identify themselves so that they could comply with a rule barring debt collectors from communicating about a debt with third parties.

39290 ■ *"$100 Million in Projects Jeopardized"* in Business Courier (Vol. 24, March 28, 2008, No. 51, pp. 1)
Pub: American City Business Journals, Inc.
Contact: Whitney Shaw, President
Ed: Dan Monk. **Description:** Ohio's historic preservation tax credit program may be reinstated after some companies planned to sue over its stoppage. The Ohio Department of Development said the program was halted because it exceeded the allocated budget for the credit. $34 million in credits are at stake for more than two dozen local projects if the program is reinstated.

39291 ■ *"401(k) Keys to Stable Value"* in Barron's (Vol. 88, March 10, 2008, No. 10, pp. 40)
Pub: Dow Jones & Co., Inc.
Contact: Clare Hart, President
Ed: Tom Sullivan. **Description:** Stable-value funds offer investors stability in a period of volatility in financial markets, attracting $888 million in funds. The Securities and Exchange Commission approved the launch of actively managed exchange-traded funds.

39292 ■ *"2015 Corporate Counsel Legal Pricing Guide - Mergers & Acquisitions" in Economics & Business Week (August 16, 2014, pp. 3)*
Pub: NewsRX
Contact: Susan E. Hasty, Publisher
Released: August 16, 2014. **Description:** Research and Markets has added the 2015 Corporate Counsel Legal Pricing Guide - Mergers & Acquisitions to its report. The guide details how the mergers and acquisitions market for law firms has increased since the downturn in 2008-2009 due mostly to an improved economy, increased corporate liquidity and some-times corporate tax policies of certain countries.

39293 ■ *"AAAFCO Unveils Pet Food Resource" in Feedstuffs (Vol. 83, August 29, 2011, No. 35, pp. 15)*
Pub: Miller Publishing Company
Description: The Association of American Feed Control Officials has launched a Website called The Business of Pet Food, which will address frequently asked questions about U.S. regulatory requirements for pet food. The site serves as an initial reference for anyone wishing to start a pet food business because it provides information and guidance.

39294 ■ *Access to Finance*
Ed: Barr. **Released:** December 2006. **Price:** , $39.95. **Description:** Challenges to help make financial systems more inclusive to promote successful venture in new markets while utilizing new technolo-gies and government policies to expand financial ac-cess to smaller companies.

39295 ■ *"Advocates Take Steps to Put $15 On Ballot" in Puget Sound Business Journal (Vol. 35, April 18, 2014, No. 53, pp. 3)*
Pub: American City Business Journals
Released: April 18, 2014. **Description:** Labor advocates within the group 15 Now have filed for a charter amendment to take the first step towards placing the $15 minimum wage debate to a public vote. 15 Now is preparing a backup plan in case the Seattle City Council fails to pass minimum wage regulation that does not meet their demands.

39296 ■ *"After Ruling, Rush Is On To Comply With ACA" in Austin Business Journal (Vol. 32, July 6, 2012, No. 18, pp. 1)*
Pub: American City Business Journals, Inc.
Contact: Whitney Shaw, President
Ed: Sandra Zaragoza. **Released:** July 6, 2012. **De-scription:** The U.S. Supreme Court ruling upholding the majority of the Patient Protection and Affordable Care Act has prompted employers to ramp up efforts to prepare for 2013 and 2014. Employers with 50 or more employees are required by the health care law to provide health care insurance or be penalized by about $2,000 per full-time employee in 2014. Insights on the rush are also given.

39297 ■ *"AG Warns Slots MBE Plan Risky" in Boston Business Journal (Vol. 29, May 27, 2011, No. 3, pp. 1)*
Pub: American City Business Journals, Inc.
Ed: Scott Dance. **Description:** Attorney General Doug Gansler states that the law extending the minority business program on slots parlors contract-ing through 2018 could be open to lawsuits. He recommended that the state should conduct a study proving that minority- and women-owned businesses do not get a fair share in the gaming industry before it signs the bill to avoid lawsuits from majority-owned firms.

39298 ■ *"Air Emissions Plunge in Birmingham" in Birmingham Business Journal (Vol. 29, June 15, 2012, No. 25, pp. 1)*
Pub: American City Business Journals, Inc.
Contact: Whitney Shaw, President
Ed: Nick Bowman. **Released:** June 15, 2012. **De-scription:** Air emissions in Birmingham, Alabama have declined in 2012. Birmingham has been strug-gling with air pollution owing its topography and steel production. But US Environmental Protection Agency standards have been accused of limiting industrial growth in the area.

39299 ■ *"Airlines Mount PR Push to Win Public Support Against Big Oil" in Advertising Age (Vol. 79, July 14, 2008, No. 7, pp. 1)*
Pub: Crain Communications Inc.
Contact: Rance Crain, President
Ed: Michael Bush. **Description:** Top airline execu-tives from competing companies have banded together in a public relations plan in which they are sending e-mails to their frequent fliers asking for aid in lobbying legislators to put a restriction on oil speculation.

39300 ■ *"Alabama Braces for Enrollment in Medicaid to Soar" in Birmingham Business Journal (Vol. 29, June 1, 2012, No. 23, pp. 1)*
Pub: American City Business Journals, Inc.
Contact: Whitney Shaw, President
Ed: Evan Belanger. **Released:** June 1, 2012. **De-scription:** Alabama has been preparing for the huge influx of Medicaid patients who would qualify in 2014 if the US Supreme Court upheld the new healthcare laws. The University of Alabama at Birmingham's study has shown nearly 471,000 additional state residents could qualify for the program under the new laws.

39301 ■ *"Alabama Lags as Online Sales Tax Law Gains Steam" in Birmingham Business Journal (Vol. 29, August 3, 2012, No. 32, pp. 1)*
Pub: American City Business Journals, Inc.
Contact: Whitney Shaw, President
Ed: Evan Belanger. **Released:** August 3, 2012. **De-scription:** A tax that would allow Alabama to collect around $347 million in uncollected sales and online taxes is brewing in the US Congress. Experts state that Alabama is lagging with the legislation needed for it to be able to collect taxes from online retailers and other businesses.

39302 ■ *"Alberta Star Begins Phase 2 Drilling On Its Eldorado & Contact Lake IOCG & Uranium Projects" in Canadian Corporate News (May 16, 2007)*
Description: Profile of Alberta Star Development Corp., a Canadian mineral exploration company that identifies, acquires, and finances advanced stage exploration projects in Canada, and its current undertaking of its 2007 drill program in which the company intends to begin accelerating its uranium and poly-metallic exploration and drilling activities on all of its drill targets for 2007 now that it has been granted its permits.

39303 ■ *"Alcan Statement on Water Rights Could Encourgage Bid" in Globe & Mail (April 25, 2007, pp. B5)*
Ed: Andy Hoffman. **Description:** The possibility for a foreign firm to bid for Alcan Inc. in the light of its agreement with Canadian government over water rights is discussed.

39304 ■ *"All Bubbles Must Burst" in Canadian Business (Vol. 83, August 17, 2010, No. 13-14, pp. 12)*
Pub: Rogers Media Inc.
Contact: Tony Viner, President
Ed: Matthew McClearn. **Description:** Canada's housing markets is showing signs of cooling down as home and condo sales both fell for the first time in 16 years. The Canadian government has fueled the market over an extended period through Canada Mortgage and Housing Corporation's role in insuring mortgage lenders against risk of defaults.

39305 ■ *"All Eyes On Iris" in Canadian Business (Vol. 81, July 22, 2008, No. 12-13, pp. 20)*
Ed: Jack Mintz. **Description:** Provincial governments in Canada are believed to be awaiting Alberta Finance Minister Iris Evans' financial and investment policies as well as Evans' development of a new sav-ing strategy. Alberta is the only Canadian province that is in position to invest in sovereign wealth funds after it eliminated its debt in 2005.

39306 ■ *"All For One, None for All?" in Canadian Business (Vol. 83, October 12, 2010, No. 17, pp. 60)*
Pub: Rogers Media Inc.
Contact: Tony Viner, President
Ed: Michael McCullogh. **Description:** The effect of the growth of Canada's overseas provincial trade offices on Canadian trade is discussed. Economic development commissions in the country have devised a single 'Consider Canada' campaign to pitch foreign investors. It is hoped that large cities will gain from banding together rather than competing against one another.

39307 ■ *"All-Star Execs: Top CEO: Gordon Nixon" in Canadian Business (Vol. 80, November 24, 2008, No. 22, pp. 9)*
Pub: Rogers Media Inc.
Contact: Tony Viner, President
Ed: Jeff Sanford. **Description:** Royal Bank of Canada (RBC) CEO, Gordon Nixon, believes the Canadian financial services segment is heavily regulated. Nixon also feels that it has become difficult for local banks to enter the market since foreign banks can easily come in and compete with them. His views on RBC's success are provided.

39308 ■ *"Alpharetta Seeding Startups To Encourage Job Growth" in Atlanta Business Chronicle(June 20, 2014, pp. 3A)*
Pub: American City Business Journals, Inc.
Contact: Whitney Shaw, President
Released: June 20, 2014. **Description:** The City of Alpharetta is witnessing several incubators and ac-celerators that will create the physical and educational infrastructure to convert ideas into sustainable busi-nesses. This will help startups develop a go-to-market strategy, prepare for FDA certification and insurance reimbursement as well as see that the company reaches a point where it can attract private equity or venture capital.

39309 ■ *"American Chemistry Council Launches Flagship Blog" in Ecology,Environment & Conservation Business (October 29, 2011, pp. 5)*
Pub: Highbeam Research
Contact: Patrick Spain, Chief Executive Officer
Description: American Chemistry Council (ACC) launched its blog, American Chemistry Matters, where interactive space allows bloggers to respond to news coverage and to discuss policy issues and their impact on innovation, competitiveness, job creation and safety.

39310 ■ *"Analysts: More Mergers for the Region's Hospitals" in Boston Business Journal (Vol. 30, October 15, 2010, No. 36, pp. 1)*
Pub: Boston Business Journal
Ed: Julie M. Donnelly. **Description:** A number of hospitals in Boston, Massachusetts are engaging in mergers and acquisitions. Caritas Christi Health Care is set to be purchased by Cerberus Capital Manage-ment. The U.S. healthcare reform law is seen to drive the development.

39311 ■ *"Ann Alexander: Senior Attorney, Natural Resources Defense Council" in Crain's Chicago Business (Vol. 31, May 5, 2008, No. 18)*
Pub: Crain Communications Inc.
Contact: Todd Johnson, Publisher
Ed: Emily Stone. **Description:** Profile of Ann Alex-ander who is the senior attorney at the Natural Resources Defense Council and is known for her dedication to the environment and a career spent battling oil companies, steelmakers and the govern-ment to change federal regulations. One recent project aims to improve the Bush administration's fuel economy standards for SUVs. Past battles include her work to prevent permits from slipping through the cracks such as the proposal by London-based BP PLC to dump 54 percent more ammonia and 35 percent more suspended solids from its Whit-ing, Indiana refinery into Lake Michigan-the source of drinking water for Chicago and its surrounding com-munities.

39312 ■ *"Another Baby Step"* in Canadian
Business *(Vol. 81, March 31, 2008, No. 5, pp.*
32)
Pub: Rogers Media Inc.
Contact: Tony Viner, President
Ed: Andrew Wahl. **Description:** Discusses the
Canadian government's federal budget which makes
it easier to tap into tax credits for corporate research
and development. However, these steps do not really
go far enough to boost industrial research levels in
Canada. Making these incentives at least partially
refundable could help during tough economic times.

39313 ■ *"Are EO Programs Right for Your*
Business?" in Contractor *(Vol. 56, October*
2009, No. 10, pp. 49)
Pub: Penton Media, Inc.
Ed: Susan Linden McGreevy. **Description:** Some of
the laws regarding equal opportunity programs are
discussed. Suggestions for mechanical contractors
who are considering certification to qualify for these
programs are presented.

39314 ■ *Are Government Purchasing Policies*
Failing Small Business?: Roundtable Before
the Committee on Small Business &
Entrepreneurship, U.S. Senate
Pub: DIANE Publishing Co.
Contact: Dorothy J. Perkins, Manager
E-mail: dorothyjperkins@hotmail.com
Released: September 2002. **Price:** $35, Paperback.
Description: Covers Congressional hearing: Steven
App, Treasury Department; Fred Armendariz and
Major Clark, Small Business Administration; Susan
Allen, Pan Asian American Chamber of Commerce;
Stephen Denlinger, Latin American Management As-
sociation; Charles Henry, National Veteran's Busi-
ness Development Corporation; Morris Hudson, MO
Procurement Technology Assistance Centers; Bar
Kasoff, Women Impact, Public Policy; Pam Mazza,
Piliero, Massa and Pargament; Ron Newlan, Hub-
Zone Contract National Council; Pat Parker, Native
American Management Service; Joann Payne,
Women First National Legislative Commission; Mike
Robinson, MA Small Business Development Centers;
Ramon Rodriguez, Hispanic Chamber of Commerce;
Angela Styles, Office of Management and Budget;
Ralph Thomas, NASA; John Turner, MN Business
Enterprise Legal Defense Fund; James Turpin,
American Subcontractor's Association, Inc.; and
Henry Wilfong, National Association of Small Disad-
vantaged Business.

39315 ■ *"Arkansas Attorney General Sues*
Collection Agency" in PaymentsSource *(July*
18, 2012)
Pub: SourceMedia Inc.
Contact: James M. Malkin, Chief Executive Officer
Released: July 18, 2012. **Description:** National
Credit Adjusters is being sued by Arkansas Attorney
General Dustin McDaniel's office. The lawsuit alleges
that the collection agency violated the Arkansas
Deceptive Trade Practices Act while attempting to
collect debts from payday and high-interest install-
ment loan debts.

39316 ■ *"The Art of Disclosure: Function*
Over Forms?" in Barron's *(Vol. 88, June 30,*
2008, No. 26, pp. 17)
Pub: Dow Jones & Co., Inc.
Contact: Clare Hart, President
Ed: Eric Savitz. **Description:** Securities and Exchange Commission (SEC) chairman Christopher
Cox wants the SEC to consider an overhaul of the
forms used to meet the agency's disclosure requirements. Cox also said that the U.S. Generally Accepted Accounting Standards has too many rules
with exceptions and alternative interpretations.

39317 ■ *"Asked and Answered:*
Crowdfunding" in Investment Advisor *(Vol.*
32, August 2012, No. 8, pp. 14)
Pub: Summit Professional Networks
Contact: Steve Weitzner, President
Released: August 2012. **Description:** Questions are
answered in detail regarding crowdfunding and
implementation of the Title II provisions within the
JOBS Act.

39318 ■ *"Attend To Your Corporate*
Housekeeping" in Women Entrepreneur
(December 4, 2008)
Ed: Nina Kaufman. **Description:** Business owners
can lose all the benefits and privileges of the corporate form if they do not follow proper corporate
formalities such as holding an annual meeting, electing officers and directors and adopting or passing
corporate resolutions. Creditors are able to take from
one's personal assets if such formalities have not
been followed.

39319 ■ *"Au Revoir Or Goodbye?"* in
Barron's *(Vol. 88, July 14, 2008, No. 28, pp. 5)*
Pub: Dow Jones & Co., Inc.
Contact: Clare Hart, President
Ed: Alan Abelson. **Description:** Former Senator Phil
Gramm's opinion that the U.S. is a 'nation of whin-
ers' as they moan about recession is another ex-
ample of the disconnection between Washington and
Wall Street on one hand and the real world on the
other. It would be a catastrophe for most of the world
if Fannie Mae and Freddie Mac were to go under and
take their trillions of mortgage debt with them.

39320 ■ *"Auditing the Auditors"* in Barron's
(Vol. 92, September 17, 2012, No. 38, pp. 16)
Description: The Public Company Accounting
Oversight Board banned Michael T. Studer, president
of the accounting firm Studer Group, because he
failed to comply with auditing standards in his audits
involving hinese reverse mergers.

39321 ■ *"Austin to Make it Easier for Stores*
to Just Pop In" in Austin Business Journal
(Vol. 31, August 19, 2011, No. 24, pp. A1)
Pub: American City Business Journals
Ed: Vicky Garza. **Description:** Temporary retail
stores may soon become common in Austin as City
Council has urged the city manager to look into the
possibility of amending the city codes to permit businesses to temporarily fill the vacant spaces downtown.

39322 ■ *"Austin Ponders Annexing FI*
Racetrack" in Austin Business Journal *(Vol.*
31, July 8, 2011, No. 18, pp. 1)
Pub: American City Business Journals
Ed: Vicky Garza. **Description:** City planners in
Austin, Texas are studying the feasibility of annexing
the land under and around the Circuit of the Americas
Formula One Racetrack being constructed east of
the city. The annexation could generate at least $13
million in financial gain over 25 years from property
taxes alone.

39323 ■ *"Austin Ventures: Is It a VC Firm?"* in
Austin Business Journal *(Vol. 31, June 17,*
2011, No. 15, pp. 1)
Pub: American City Business Journals
Ed: Christopher Calnan. **Description:** Investment
firm Austin Ventures could lose its classification as a
venture capital firm under a new definition of venture
capital by the Securities and Exchange Commission.
The reclassification could result in additional expenses for Austin Ventures, which has two-thirds of
its investments in growth equity transactions.

39324 ■ *"Austin on Verge of Losing 7,500*
Jobs" in Austin Business Journal *(Vol. 31,*
May 6, 2011, No. 9, pp. 1)
Pub: American City Business Journals
Ed: Jacob Dirr. **Description:** Proposed state budget
cuts are seen to result in the loss of as many as 7,500
public and private sector jobs in Austin, Texas, with
the private sector losing the majority of workers.
Comments from analysts are included.

39325 ■ *"Auto Bailout: Car Trouble"* in
Canadian Business *(Vol. 82, April 27, 2009,*
No. 7, pp. 11)
Pub: Rogers Media Inc.
Contact: Tony Viner, President
Ed: Thomas Watson. **Description:** The likely effects
of a possible bailout of the U.S. automotive industry
are examined. Some experts believe that a bailout
will be good for the automotive industry and on the

U.S. economy. Others argue however, that the
nationalization may have a negative impact on the
industry and on the economy.

39326 ■ *"Auto Supplier Stock Battered In*
Wake Of Wall Street Woes" in Crain's Detroit
Business *(Vol. 24, September 29, 2008, No.*
39, pp. 4)
Pub: Crain Communications Inc.
Contact: Rance E. Crain, President
Ed: Ryan Beene. **Description:** Due to the volatility
of the stock market and public perception of the $700
billion banking bailout, auto suppliers are now facing
a dramatic drop in their shares. Statistical data
included.

39327 ■ *"Azaya Therapeutics Taking Big*
Steps" in San Antonio Business Journal *(Vol.*
28, March 28, 2014, No. 7, pp. 8)
Pub: American City Business Journals
Released: March 28, 2014. **Description:** Azaya
Therapeutics believes that its $5 million funding round
will be completed in 2014. The convertible-note
bridge funding was initiated in October 2013. The
company, which plans to pursue regulatory approval
for its cancer medications, is also focusing on
expanding the business.

39328 ■ *"Back to Business for Bishop*
Museum" in Hawaii Business *(Vol. 54, August*
2008, No. 2, pp. 53)
Ed: Shara Enay. **Description:** Bishop Museum,
ranked 224 in Hawaii Business' top 250 companies
for 2008, had $29.5 million in gross sales for 2007,
up 52.8 percent from the $19.3 million gross sales in
2006. The company has cut 24 positions in a restructuring effort for the museum's sustainability. Grants,
artifacts and plans for sustainable operations are
discussed.

39329 ■ *"Back Off on ABM Legislation,*
Banks Warn MPs" in Globe & Mail *(April 20,*
2007, pp. B1)
Ed: Steven Chase. **Description:** The efforts of banks
to prevent legislation by the Canadian government
on the automated banking machine levies charged
from customers of other institutions are described.

39330 ■ *"Back on Track-Or Off the Rails?"* in
Business Week *(September 22, 2008, No.*
4100, pp. 22)
Pub: Bloomberg L.P.
Contact: Matthew Winkler, Manager
Ed: Peter Coy, Tara Kalwarski. **Description:** Dis-
cusses the possible scenarios the American economy
may undergo due to the takeover of Fannie Mae and
Freddie Mac. Statistical data included.

39331 ■ *Bad Money*
Ed: Kevin Phillips. **Released:** April 15, 2008. **De-**
scription: How the financial sector has hijacked the
American economy, aided by Washington's ruinous
faith in the efficiency of markets.

39332 ■ *"Bad Paper"* in Canadian Business
(Vol. 80, November 19, 2007, No. 23, pp. 34)
Ed: Al Rosen. **Description:** The Canadian government froze the market for non-bank asset-backed
commercial paper (ABCP) August 2007, which means
holders will be unable to withdraw investments. The
crisis and value of ABCP are discussed.

39333 ■ *Bad Samaritans: The Myth of Free*
Trade and the Secret History of Capitalism
Pub: Bloomsbury USA
Ed: Ha-Joon Chang. **Released:** August 09, 2010.
Price: $11.99; $17, paperback; $26.95, hardback.
Description: Economist challenges open-market
proponents and believes that free trade would do
more harm than good. **Availability:** E-bookPrint.

39334 ■ *"Bailout Forgets the 'Little Guys"* in
The Business Journal-Milwaukee *(Vol. 25,*
September 26, 2008, No. 53, pp. A1)
Pub: American City Business Journals, Inc.
Contact: Whitney Shaw, President
Ed: Rich Kirchen. **Description:** Community Bankers
of Wisconsin and the Wisconsin Bankers Association
are urging members to approach congressional
representatives and remind them to include local

banks in building the $700 billion bailout plan. WBA president and CEO Kurt Bauer thinks that it is only fair to include smaller institutions in the bailout. The initial bailout plan and its benefit for the smaller banks are examined.

39335 ■ *"Ballpark Sales Tax Extension Could Fund New Arena" in Milwaukee Business Journal (Vol. 27, January 29, 2010, No. 18, pp. A1)*

Pub: American City Business Journals

Ed: Mark Kass. **Description:** Milwaukee, Wisconsin-area business executives believe the extension of the Miller Park 0.1 percent sales tax could help fund a new basketball arena to replace the 21-year-old Bradley Center in downtown Milwaukee. However, any sales tax expansion that includes the new basketball arena would need approval by Wisconsin's legislature.

39336 ■ *"Baltimore Businesses Put Cash Behind Bernstein" in Baltimore Business Journal (Vol. 28, August 20, 2010, No. 15, pp. 1)*

Pub: Baltimore Business Journal

Ed: Scott Dance. **Description:** Baltimore, Maryland-based businesses have invested $40,000 to support lawyer Gregg L. Bernstein in the 2010 State Attorney election. The election campaign is being fueled by fear of a crime surge. Many businesses have been dealing with crimes such as muggings, shootings, and car break-ins.

39337 ■ *"Baltimore Car Dealers Have One More Shot to Get Their Franchises Back: Fighting Detroit" in Baltimore Business Journal (Vol. 27, January 22, 2010, No. 38, pp. 1)*

Pub: American City Business Journals

Ed: Daniel J. Sernovitz. **Description:** Baltimore, Maryland-based car dealers could retrieve their franchises from car manufacturers, Chrysler LLC and General Motors Corporation, through a forced arbitration. A provision in a federal budget mandates the arbitration. The revoking of franchises has been attributed to the car manufacturers' filing of bankruptcy protection.

39338 ■ *"Baltimore Councilman May Revive Labor Bill" in Baltimore Business Journal (Vol. 28, August 13, 2010, No. 14, pp. 1)*

Pub: Baltimore Business Journal

Ed: Daniel J. Sernovitz. **Description:** Baltimore, Maryland Councilman Bill Henry has started reviving controversial legislation that would force developers and contractors to give preference to union labor. The legislation requires contractors to give preference to city workers in order to lower Baltimore's unemployment rate.

39339 ■ *"Baltimore 'Living Wage' Bill Draws City, Retailers to Clash" in Baltimore Business Journal (Vol. 28, July 9, 2010, No. 9, pp. 1)*

Pub: Baltimore Business Journal

Ed: Daniel J. Sernovitz. **Description:** A bill pending before the City Council of Baltimore, Maryland would mandate the city's major retailers to pay their employees at least $10.57 per hour, $3 higher than was state law requires. Major retailers, as defined in the said bill by Councilwoman Mary Pat Clarke, have gross sales of at least $10 million. Reactions of the retailers affected are presented.

39340 ■ *"Baltimore's Tourism Bureau Seeks Hotel Tax Hike" in Baltimore Business Journal (Vol. 27, December 18, 2009, No. 32, pp. 1)*

Pub: American City Business Journals

Ed: Rachel Bernstein. **Description:** Baltimore, Maryland's tourism agency, Visit Baltimore, has proposed a new hotel tax that could produce $2 million annually for its marketing budget, fund improvements to the city's 30-year-old convention center and help it compete for World Cup soccer games. Baltimore hotel leaders discuss the new tax.

39341 ■ *"Ban Threatens Soda Fountain: Mayor's Size Limit Could Crimp Sales, Change Bottling" in Crain's New York Business (Vol. 28, July 30, 2012, No. 31, pp. 6)*

Pub: Crain Communications Inc.

Contact: Rance Crain, President

Ed: Lisa Fickenscher. **Released:** July 30, 2012. **Description:** New York City's Mayor is threatening to limit bottles and cups of soda and other sweetened beverages to 16 ounces. That means that the 20 ounce and 32 ounce drinks will be banned from the city. Details and the ban and responses from soft drink companies are included.

39342 ■ *"Bank Expects Profit After Rough Start" in Austin Business Journal (Vol. 32, April 20, 2012, No. 7, pp. 1)*

Pub: American City Business Journals, Inc.

Contact: Whitney Shaw, President

Ed: Christopher Calnan. **Released:** April 20, 2012. **Description:** Libertad Bank SSB has projected profitabilty in 2012 after it was fined by federal regulators for poor financial performance. The bank is being monitored for its compliance management plans.

39343 ■ *"Banking Bailout: Boost or Bust? Economic Insiders Mixed on Impact to State" in Crain's Detroit Business (Vol. 24, September 29, 2008, No. 39, pp. 1)*

Pub: Crain Communications Inc.

Contact: Rance E. Crain, President

Ed: Amy Lane. **Description:** Economic insiders discuss the banking bailout and how it might impact the state of Michigan.

39344 ■ *"Bankruptcy Blowback" in Business Week (September 22, 2008, No. 4100, pp. 36)*

Pub: Bloomberg L.P.

Contact: Matthew Winkler, Manager

Ed: Jessica Silver-Greenberg. **Description:** Changes to bankruptcy laws which were enacted in 2005 after banks and other financial institutions lobbied hard for them are now suffering the consequences of the laws which force more troubled borrowers to let their homes go into foreclosure; lenders suffer financially every time they have to take on a foreclosure and the laws in which they lobbied so hard to see enacted are now becoming a problem for these lending institutions. Details of the changes in the laws are outlined as are the affects on the consumer, the economy and the lenders.

39345 ■ *"Banks Lower Rates on CDs, Deposits" in Baltimore Business Journal (Vol. 27, January 1, 2010, No. 35, pp. 1)*

Pub: American City Business Journals

Ed: Gary Haber. **Description:** Greater Baltimore area banks in Maryland have lowered their rates on certificates of deposits (CDs) and money market accounts, which could indicate the incoming trend for the first half of 2010. A banking industry forecast shows that lower Federal Funds rate, low inflation, and a new Federal Deposit Insurance Corporation (FDIC) rule might cause the rates to drop even further. Details on the FDIC rule are given.

39346 ■ *"Banks, Retailers Squabble Over Fees" in Baltimore Business Journal (Vol. 28, June 18, 2010, No. 6, pp. 1)*

Pub: Baltimore Business Journal

Ed: Gary Haber. **Description:** How an amendment to the financial regulatory reform bill would affect the bankers' and retailers' conflict over interchange fees is discussed. Interchange fees are paid for by retailers every time consumers make purchases through debit cards. Industry estimates indicate that approximately $50 million in such fees are paid by retailers.

39347 ■ *"Bark and Bite" in Canadian Business (Vol. 81, March 31, 2008, No. 5, pp. 20)*

Pub: Rogers Media Inc.

Contact: Tony Viner, President

Ed: Rachel Pulfer. **Description:** Hillary Clinton and Barack Obama both want to renegotiate NAFTA but the most job losses in the American manufacturing industry is caused by technological change and Asian competition than with NAFTA. The risk of protectionist trade policies has increased given the political atmosphere.

39348 ■ *"Barred Collection Agency Sued by Colorado AG" in Collections & Credit Risk (Vol. 15, August 1, 2010, No. 7, pp. 7)*

Pub: SourceMedia Inc.

Contact: James M. Malkin, Chief Executive Officer

Description: Collection agency run by Chad Lee received notice that it is barred from collecting in the State of Colorado by Attorney General John Suther's office. A ruling cited that the firm engages in harassment or abuse and/or threats of violence, made false representations as to its legal status of debts, made false and misleading representations of nonpayment of debts that would result in arrest, and that Lee failed to disclose his previous felony conviction.

39349 ■ *"Basel3 Quick Fix Actually Neither" in Canadian Business (Vol. 83, October 12, 2010, No. 17, pp. 19)*

Pub: Rogers Media Inc.

Contact: Tony Viner, President

Ed: Thomas Watson. **Description:** Information about the so-called Basel 3 standards, which will require banks to hold top-quality capital totaling at least 7 percent of their risk-bearing assets is provided. The rules' supporters believe that a good balance has been reached between improving the Basel 2 framework and maintaining enough lending capital to stimulate an economic growth.

39350 ■ *"Battle of the Titans" in Canadian Business (Vol. 81, March 17, 2008, No. 4, pp. 15)*

Pub: Rogers Media Inc.

Contact: Tony Viner, President

Ed: Rachel Pulfer. **Description:** Regulatory authorities in Canada gave Thomson Corp and Reuters Group PLC the permission to go ahead with their merger. The merged companies could eclipse Bloomberg LP's market share of 33 percent. Authorities also required Thomson and Reuters to sell some of their databases to competitors.

39351 ■ *"BBVA Compass To Open Loan Office In Chicago" in Birmingham Business Journal (Vol. 29, July 20, 2012, No. 30, pp. 1)*

Pub: American City Business Journals, Inc.

Contact: Whitney Shaw, President

Ed: Antrenise Cole. **Released:** July 20, 2012. **Description:** Birmingham, Alabama-based BBVA Compass plans to open a commercial loan production office in Chicago, Illinois and has filed an application with the State of Alabama Banking Department. The company intends to serve companies of all sizes but plans to focus on firms with $500 million to $2 billion in revenue.

39352 ■ *"Belmont Annexation Approved" in Charlotte Observer (February 7, 2007)*

Ed: Jefferson George. **Description:** Belmont, North Carolina City Council approved annexation of nearly 64 acres. The land will be used to develop a residential community.

39353 ■ *"Beltway Monitor" in Mergers & Acquisitions: The Dealmaker's Journal (March 1, 2008)*

Pub: SourceMedia Inc.

Contact: James M. Malkin, Chief Executive Officer

Description: Discusses in detail The Foreign Investment and National Security Act of 2007 which was put into legislation due to the initially approved acquisition of certain U.S. ports by Dubai Ports World which set off a firestorm of controversy.

39354 ■ *"Bernier Open to Telecom Changes" in Globe & Mail (March 22, 2006, pp. B1)*

Ed: Simon Tuck. **Description:** Federal Industry Minister Maxime Bernier of Canada says that he is open to scrapping restrictions on foreign ownership in telecommunications. His views on telecom industry are detailed.

39355 ■ *"BETC Backers Plot Future"* in *Business Journal Portland (Vol. 27, December 10, 2010, No. 41, pp. 1)*
Pub: Portland Business Journal
Ed: Erik Siemers. **Description:** A coalition of clean energy groups and industrial manufacturers have spearheaded a campaign aimed at persuading Oregon legislators that the state's Business Energy Tax Credit (BETC) is vital in job creation. Oregon's BETC grants tax credits for 50 percent of an eligible renewable or clean energy project's cost. However, some legislators propose BETC's abolition.

39356 ■ *"Bethesda Inc. Stepping Out"* in *Business Courier (Vol. 27, October 15, 2010, No. 24, pp. 1)*
Pub: Business Courier
Ed: James Ritchie. **Description:** Nonprofit organization Bethesda Inc. is planning to donate $5 million a year for the next three years to Greater Cincinnati health care reforms. Bethesda revealed that it announced its donations to pressure other organizations to help.

39357 ■ *"Beware, Complacent Bankers"* in *Canadian Business (Vol. 85, September 17, 2012, No. 14, pp. 9)*
Pub: George Media Inc.
Ed: Sarah Barmak. **Released:** September 17, 2012. **Description:** Canadian Finance Minister Jim Flaherty has released draft rules that would allow credit unions to go national and compete with major banks. Approval of the rules would see a fianancial services mix that includes a few credit unions with coast-to-coast ATM networks.

39358 ■ *"Beware of E15"* in *Rental Product News (Vol. 33, October 2011)*
Pub: Cygnus Business Media
Contact: Paul Mackler, Chief Executive Officer
Ed: Curt Bennink. **Description:** Environmental Protection Agency (EPA) set a new regulation that grants partial waivers to allow gasoline containing up to 15 percent ethanol (E15) to be introduced into commerce for use in model year 2001 and newer light-duty motor vehicles, subject to certain conditions.

39359 ■ *"Beware of Rotting Money"* in *Barron's (Vol. 89, July 13, 2009, No. 28, pp. 31)*
Pub: Dow Jones & Co., Inc.
Contact: Clare Hart, President
Ed: Thomas G. Donlan. **Description:** Inflation can take hold of a country and do it great harm; it is caused by people, most particularly central bankers in charge of the world's reserve currency. Arrogant economists pushed the belief that the government can engineer the economy and it is argued that there is trouble ahead when the government tries to control the economy.

39360 ■ *"Bigger TIF Makes Development Inroads near Kansas City International Airport"* in *The Business Journal-Serving Metropolitan Kansas City (Vol. 26, July 11, 2008, No. 44)*
Pub: American City Business Journals, Inc.
Contact: Whitney Shaw, President
Ed: Rob Roberts. **Description:** On July 9, 2008 the Tax Increment Financing Commission voted to expand a TIF district to Tiffany Springs Road. The plan for the TIF district close to Kansas City International Airport is to include a-half mile of the road. The impacts of the expansion on construction projects and on the road network are analyzed.

39361 ■ *"Bill Kaneko, President and CEO of the Hawaii Institute for Public Affairs (HIPA)"* in *Hawaii Business (Vol. 53, December 2007, No. 6, pp. 32)*
Pub: PacificBasin Communications
Ed: David K. Choo. **Description:** Hawaii Institute for Public Affairs chief executive officer and president Bill Kaneko believes that the Hawaiian economy is booming, however, he also asserts that the economy is too focused on tourism and real estate. Kaneko has also realized the that the will of the people is strong while

he was helping with the Hawaiian 2050 Sustainability Plan. The difficulties of making a sustainable Hawaii are discussed.

39362 ■ *"Bill to Roll Back Banking Regulations Faces Tough Odds"* in *San Antonio Business Journal (Vol. 28, April 18, 2014, No. 10, pp. 6)*
Pub: American City Business Journals
Released: April 18, 2014. **Description:** U.S. Representative Henry Cuellar is co-sponsoring legislation that will ease some of the regulations governing community banks. The Community Lending Enhancement and Regulatory Relief Act has 129 co-sponsors in the House of Representatives.

39363 ■ *"Bill Targets Insurance Contract Pay Changes"* in *Memphis Business Journal (No. 35, February 14, 2014, No. 45, pp. 8)*
Pub: American City Business Journals
Released: February 14, 2014. **Description:** Lawmakers are pushing a new measure in the Tennessee General Assembly, tentatively dubbed the Payer Accountability Act. the bill would prohibit commercial health insurance companies from making mid-contract changes.

39364 ■ *"Billboard Co.'s HQ In Limbo"* in *Austin Business Journal (Vol. 32, April 6, 2012, No. 5, pp. A1)*
Pub: American City Business Journals, Inc.
Contact: Whitney Shaw, President
Ed: Vicky Garza. **Released:** April 6, 2012. **Description:** Reagan National Advertising has been awaiting the Austin City Council decision on whether it would be allowed to build a new headquarters that was on the drawing board for more than five years. However, approval of Reagan's plan would cut down several trees and that would violate the Heritage tree ordinance.

39365 ■ *"Bills Raise Blues Debate: An Unfair Edge or Level Playing Field?"* in *Crain's Detroit Business (Vol. 24, January 21, 2008, No. 3)*
Pub: Crain Communications Inc. - Detroit
Contact: Keith Crain, Chairman
Ed: Sherri Begin. **Description:** Changes in Michigan state law would change the way health insurance can be sold to individuals. Michigan Blue Cross Blue Shield is working to keep its tax-exempt status while staying competitive against for-profit insurers and nonprofit HMOs.

39366 ■ *"Bills Would Regulate Mortgage Loan Officers"* in *Crain's Detroit Business (Vol. 24, February 25, 2008, No. 8, pp. 9)*
Pub: Crain Communications Inc. - Detroit
Contact: Keith Crain, Chairman
Ed: Amy Lane. **Description:** New legislation in Michigan, if passed, would create a registration process for mortgage loan officers in the state in order to address the mortgage loan crisis.

39367 ■ *"Bloomington Police to Buy 24-Hour Electronic Kiosk With Federal Grant"* in *Herald-Times (September 5, 2012)*
Pub: Hoosier Times Inc.
Released: September 5, 2012. **Description:** Bloomington, Indiana police department will purchase two electronic kiosks with money from a federal grant. The kiosks will operate 24 hours a day and provide the public with the ability to communicate with the police, obtain forms and permits, as well as other police-related activities.

39368 ■ *"Blues at the Toy Fair: Industry Reeling From Recalls, Lower Sales Volumes"* in *Crain's New York Business (February 17, 2008)*
Pub: Crain Communications Inc.
Contact: Rance Crain, President
Ed: Elisabeth Cordova. **Description:** Over 1,500 toy developers and vendors will attend the American International Toy Fair, expected to be low-key due to recent recalls of toys not meeting American safety standards. Toy retailers and manufacturers, as well as the Chinese government, are promoting product testing to prevent toxic metals in toys.

39369 ■ *"Boatyard Expansion 8-Year Odyssey"* in *Providence Business News (Vol. 28, March 31, 2014, No. 52, p. 1)*
Pub: American City Business Journals
Released: March 31, 2014. **Description:** Bristol Marine owner, Andy Tyska, has found it challenging to operate and improve the boatyard due to lack of available coastal land and restrictive environmental regulations. Tyska made a large investment in plans for expanding the property he purchased in 1998. Tyska discusses the challenges faced while trying to improve his boatyard.

39370 ■ *Bold Endeavors: How Our Government Built America, and Why It Must Rebuild Now*
Pub: Simon and Schuster Inc.
Contact: Carolyn Reidy, President
E-mail: carolyn.reidy@simonandschuster.com
Ed: Felix G. Rohatyn. **Released:** 2009. **Price:** $17.99, Paperback; $13.11. **Description:** The federal government built the nation by investing in initiatives like the Erie Canal and the G.I. Bill and why it should do the same at this point in history is examined. **Availability:** E-book.

39371 ■ *"Boston Globe"* in *Ice Cream Reporter (Vol. 21, August 20, 2008, No. 9, pp. 7)*
Description: Boston City Council approved an ordinance that will limit when ice cream vendors can announce their presence with music over loud speakers. The rules are simple: when the wheels stop moving, the jingles stop playing.

39372 ■ *"Both Eyes on the Prize"* in *Canadian Business (Vol. 83, September 14, 2010, No. 15, pp. 42)*
Pub: Rogers Media Inc.
Contact: Tony Viner, President
Ed: Jacqueline Nelson. **Description:** North American executive compensation has fundamentally shifted partly due to pressure from the US government and recent adjustments in the way CEO pay packages are structured. The changes have also become common practice in Canada and helped in scrutinizing the executive pay.

39373 ■ *"Brace for the Bill"* in *Boston Business Journal (Vol. 27, December 28, 2007, No. 48, pp. 1)*
Ed: Mark Hollmer. **Description:** Historic 2006 Massachusetts Health Care Reform Law seems successful because many people have signed up for health insurance within one year of its implementation. However, rising premiums and other factors are threatening the health industry.

39374 ■ *"BRIEF: Mayor Signs Food Truck Regulations Into Law"* in *Buffalo News (February 6, 2012)*
Pub: McClatchy-Tribune Information Services
Ed: Aaron Besecker. **Released:** February 6, 2012. **Description:** Mayor Byron W. Brown set into law regulations governing food trucks in the city. Under the new rules, food trucks must be at least 100 feet from hot dog vendors and buildings with open kitchen restaurants. Food truck operating fee is set at $1,000. Both permit and entire law expire in April 2013 in order to give city officials time to analyze it befor making a longer commitment.

39375 ■ *"Bringing Manufacturing Concerns to Springfield"* in *Crain's Chicago Business (Vol. 31, March 31, 2008, No. 13, pp. 6)*
Pub: Crain Communications Inc.
Contact: Todd Johnson, Publisher
Ed: Paul Merrion. **Description:** Profile of the new executive vice-president of Tooling & Manufacturing Assn., Paul Merrion, a man who plans to grow TMA's membership with an aggressive legislative agenda in Springfield.

39376 ■ *"Brown At Center of Local CleanTech Lobbying Efforts"* in *Boston Business Journal (Vol. 30, October 15, 2010,*

No. 36, pp. 1)
Pub: Boston Business Journal
Ed: Kyle Alspach. **Description:** U.S. Senator Scott Brown has been active in lobbying for energy reform in Massachusetts. Brown has been meeting with business groups seeking the reforms.

39377 ■ *"Brownies Are Only for Medicine: Regulations Raise Pot Questions" in Puget Sound Business Journal (Vol. 35, July 4, 2014, No. 11, pp. 10)*
Pub: American City Business Journals
Released: July 4, 2014. **Description:** Washington Governor Jay Inslee announced that the future of edible marijuana products is in limbo because the rules and regulations to handle the unique challenges created are not in place. Magical Butter opened its marijuana-infused food truck and started selling pot browning to card-carrying medical marijuana patients from the truck. Impact of the vague law is examined.

39378 ■ *"Builders Aim to Cut Costs: Pushing Changes to Regain Share of Residential Market; Seek Council's Help" in Crain's New York Business*
Pub: Crain Communications Inc.
Contact: Rance Crain, President
Ed: Erik Engquist. **Description:** Union contractors and workers are worried about a decline in their market share for housing so they intend to ask the City Council to impose new safety and benefit standards on all contractors to avoid being undercut by nonunion competitors.

39379 ■ *"Building Targeted for Marriott in Violation" in Business Journal-Milwaukee (Vol. 28, December 24, 2010, No. 12, pp. A1)*
Pub: Milwaukee Business Journal
Ed: Sean Ryan. **Description:** Milwaukee, Wisconsin's Department of Neighborhood Services has ordered structural improvements and safeguards for the Pioneer Building after three violations from structural failures were found. Pioneer was among the five buildings wanted by Jackson Street Management LLC to demolish for the new Marriott Hotel.

39380 ■ *"Bullied Into Legislation" in Philadelphia Business Journal (Vol. 33, February 21, 2014, No. 2, pp. 4)*
Pub: American City Business Journals
Released: February 21, 2014. **Description:** The results of a study indicate that 35 percent of workers in the U.S. experience bullying firsthand. Because of this, Pennsylvania and other states have considered enacting anti-workplace bullying legislation. Many of these states use some version of the Healthy Workplace Act for their bills.

39381 ■ *"Bull's Eye: Canton Gets Its Target" in Baltimore Business Journal (Vol. 30, July 6, 2012, No. 9. pp. 1)*
Pub: American City Business Journals, Inc.
Contact: Whitney Shaw, President
Ed: James Briggs. **Released:** July 6, 2012. **Description:** Target Corporation and Harris Teeter Supermarkets Inc. are planning to open stores in Baltimore, Maryland. The city's Urban Design and Architecture Review Panel approved lans for the Target Store.

39382 ■ *"Business Looks for Results in Congress" in Baltimore Business Journal (Vol. 28, November 5, 2010, No. 26, pp. 1)*
Pub: Baltimore Business Journal
Ed: Kent Hoover. **Description:** Republican candidates in the 2010 Congressional elections were overwhelmingly supported by the business community. Republican John Boehner, who will be the next Speaker of the House, says that the party's victory would end economic uncertainty and would assist small businesses to rehire workers.

39383 ■ *"The Business of Medicine: Maintaining a Healthy Bottom Line" in Black Enterprise (Vol. 41, October 2010, No. 3, pp. 60)*
Ed: Marcia A. Reed-Woodard. **Description:** Sustainable government reform requires reconstruction in the areas of financing and delivery of services in the field of medicine.

39384 ■ *"Business Sidestepped Trouble" in Denver Business Journal (Vol. 65, May 9, 2014, No. 52, pp. A8)*
Pub: American City Business Journals
Released: May 9, 2014. **Description:** A number of business-friendly laws were adopted during the 2014 legislative session Colorado. the legislators passed 11 tax breaks, including the personal property tax break proposal.

39385 ■ *"Business Tax Complaints Prompt Action" in Sacramento Business Journal (Vol. 28, July 29, 2011, No. 22, pp. 1)*
Pub: Sacramento Business Journal
Ed: Michael Shaw. **Description:** California's Board of Equalization has amended a program to collect taxes from businesses for out-of-state purchases due to a flood of complaints from owners who find the paperwork costly and time consuming. The program was created in 2009 and fell short of expectations as it only brought in $56 million in the first two years against the projected $264 million.

39386 ■ *"Businesses Delayed Hiring As They Waited for Health Care Law Ruling" in Baltimore Business Journal (Vol. 30, June 29, 2012, No. 8, pp. 1)*
Pub: American City Business Journals, Inc.
Contact: Whitney Shaw, President
Ed: Sarah Gantz. **Released:** June 29, 2012. **Description:** Small businesses in Baltimore, Maryland have been putting off expansion plans pending the Supreme Court's ruling on the health care reform law. Workforce expansion would require businesses to provide employee health insurance.

39387 ■ *"Businesses Keep a Watchful Eye on Workers' Comp" in The Business Journal-Serving Greater Tampa Bay (September 5, 2008)*
Pub: American City Business Journals, Inc.
Contact: Whitney Shaw, President
Ed: Jane Meinhardt. **Description:** Pending a ruling from the Florida Supreme Court that could uphold the 2003 changes on workers' compensation law, the outcome would include restrictions on claimant attorneys' fees and allow the competitive workers' compensation insurance rates to remain low. However, insurance rates are expected to go up if the court overturns the changes.

39388 ■ *"By Land, Air, and Sea: New Passport Rules in Effect" in Black Enterprise (Vol. 37, January 2007, No. 6., pp. 101)*
Pub: Earl G. Graves Publishing Co. Inc.
Contact: Earl G. Graves, Jr., President
Ed: Stephanie Young. **Description:** As part of a new security measure by the Western Hemisphere Travel Initiative, a passport will now be required for U.S. citizens traveling by air between Mexico, Canada, South and Central America, and the Caribbean. This initiative, designed to easily identify travelers and enforce border security, will most likely extend to land or sea travel no later than January 1, 2008.

39389 ■ *"California Collection Agency Agrees To Refund $1.7M" in PaymentsSource (July 3, 2012)*
Pub: SourceMedia Inc.
Contact: James M. Malkin, Chief Executive Officer
Released: July 3, 2012. **Description:** DP and Associates agreed to return $1.7 million in refunds and cancelled debts to consumers in West Virginia. The California-based collection agency was engaged in 'unlawful and threatening' debt collection practices. DP did not have a license to practice.

39390 ■ *"California Redevelopment Update: the State Supreme Court's Ruling" in Real Estate Review (Vol. 41, Spring 2012, No. 1, pp. 99)*
Released: Spring 2012. **Description:** The California Supreme Court's ruling restricting redevelopment agencies from securing funding from school districts and property tax revenues is seen to adversely impact the state's redevelopment efforts. The ruling is part of the state's effort to address its budgeting deficit. The court also froze all redevelopment agency activities prior to its ruling.

39391 ■ *"Call for Jobs Tie-In Lacks City Backing" in Baltimore Business Journal (Vol. 30, June 1, 2012, No. 4, pp. 1)*
Pub: American City Business Journals, Inc.
Contact: Whitney Shaw, President
Ed: James Briggs. **Released:** June 1, 2012. **Description:** Officials of Baltimore, Maryland are seen to turn down the proposal to mandate local hiring rules for Lexington Square Partners. The plan is in line with the company's push for tax breaks on its superblock project.

39392 ■ *"A Call to Make SOX More Elastic" in Canadian Business (Vol. 80, February 12, 2007, No. 4, pp. 14)*
Ed: Rachel Pulfer. **Description:** The suggestion of New York City Governor Eliot Spitzer to relax the Sarbanes-Oxley Act of 2002 due to its 'excessive' regulation is discussed.

39393 ■ *"Can Turfway Park Stay in the Race?" in Business Courier (Vol. 26, January 8, 2010, No. 38, pp. 1)*
Pub: American City Business Journals, Inc.
Contact: Whitney Shaw, President
Ed: Jon Newberry. **Description:** Legalization of slot machine gambling in Kentucky could affect raceway Turfway Park and the state's thoroughbred industry. Thousands of farms and jobs in the industry could be lost if slot machine gambling is approved.

39394 ■ *"Canada Nears European Trade Treaty" in Globe & Mail (February 5, 2007, pp. B1)*
Ed: Steven Chase. **Description:** The probable establishment of a treaty by Canada with Norway, Switzerland and Iceland for free-trade is discussed. The treaty will allow an annual business of $11 billion to take place in Canada.

39395 ■ *"Canada Seeks Collection Agency To Pursue $129M In Fines" in PaymentsSource (August 21, 2012)*
Pub: SourceMedia Inc.
Contact: James M. Malkin, Chief Executive Officer
Released: August 21, 2012. **Description:** Canada's federal government has posted a letter of interest seeking a collection agency to recover about $129 million in unpaid fines. Details of the program are covered.

39396 ■ *"Canada Wins Second NAFTA Decision on Softwood Tariffs" in Globe & Mail (March 18, 2006, pp. B2)*
Ed: Steven Chase, Peter Kennedy. **Description:** Canada has won a second major North American Free Trade Agreement (NAFTA) victory in five years of legal battles over U.S. tariffs on softwood. Details of the controversy and ruling are presented.

39397 ■ *"Canada's Clean Energy Advantages Offer a Bright Future" in Canadian Business (Vol. 83, August 17, 2010, No. 13-14, pp. 38)*
Ed: Don McKinnon. **Description:** Canada has clean energy advantages in the greenhouse gas emission-free CANada Deuterium Uranium reactor technology and carbon neutral biomass fuels that were continuously ignored by policy makers. Both are proven to significantly reduce emissions while providing reliable, affordable and secure electricity.

39398 ■ *"Canada's New Government Introduces Amendments to Deny Work Permits to Foreign Strippers" in Marketwired (May 16, 2007)*
Pub: Comtex News Network Inc.
Description: Honourable Diane Finley, Minister of Citizenship and Immigration, introduced amendments to the Immigration and Refugee Protection Act (IRPA) to help prevent the exploitation and abuse of vulnerable foreign workers, such as strippers.

39399 ■ *"Canadian Hydropower Firm Places Its Bets On Massachusetts Market" in Boston Business Journal (Vol. 34, May 9, 2014, No. 14, pp. 3)*
Pub: American City Business Journals, Inc.
Contact: Whitney Shaw, President
Released: May 9, 2014. **Description:** Nalcor Energy has started work on its 824-megawatt Muskrat Falls hydroelectric plant that would supply the Provinces of

Newfoundland and Labrador with electricity from renewable sources by the end of 2017. Nalcor is interested in getting longer-term contracts in Massachusetts as part of the state's clean energy legislation.

39400 ■ "Candidates Differ On State's Green Streak" in Business Journal Portland (Vol. 27, October 22, 2010, No. 34, pp. 1)
Pub: Portland Business Journal

Ed: Andy Giegerich. Description: The views of Oregon gubernatorial candidates Chris Dudley and John Kitzhaber on the state's economy and on environmental policies are presented. Both Dudley, who is a Republican, and his Democratic challenger believe that biomass could help drive the state's economy. Both candidates also pledged changes in Oregon's business energy tax credit (BETC) program.

39401 ■ "Candidates Won't Bash Fed; Rate Cuts Bash Savers" in Barron's (Vol. 88, March 24, 2008, No. 12, pp. 31)
Pub: Dow Jones & Co., Inc.
Contact: Clare Hart, President

Ed: Jim McTague. Description: Candidates in the 2008 US presidential election, like the current administration, do not and will not bash the Federal Reserve. The Federal Reserve's aggressive interest rate cuts hurt the incomes of people depending on their savings accounts.

39402 ■ "CanWEA Unveils WindVision for BC: 5,250 MW of Wind Energy by 2025" in CNW Group (October 4, 2011)
Pub: CNW Group Ltd.
Contact: Carolyn McGill-Davidson, President

Description: Wind industry leaders are asking British Columbia, Canada policy makers to created conditions to further develop and integrate wind energy in accordance with greenhouse gas emission targets and projected economic growth. Statistical data included.

39403 ■ "Capital Metro May Soon Seek Contractor to Replace Star Tran" in Austin Business Journal (Vol. 31, June 10, 2011, No. 14, pp. 1)
Pub: American City Business Journals

Ed: Vicky Garza. Description: Capital Metropolitan Transportation Authority may be forced to contract out its bus services provided by StarTran Inc. as early as September 2012 following legislation approved by the Texas legislature. The bill originates in a report by the Sunset Advisory Commission. Details are included.

39404 ■ "Capitol Ideas: Regions to Lansing: Focus on Taxes, Reform, Keeping Talent" in Crain's Detroit Business (Vol. 24, October 6, 2008)
Pub: Crain Communications Inc.
Contact: Rance E. Crain, President

Ed: Amy Lane. Description: Michigan must make bold and dramatic changes in public policy regarding business legislation. The tax structure, unemployment issues and attracting and retaining talent are among the issues the state must confront, especially in this tough economic climate.

39405 ■ "Carbon Capture Hits a Wall: Alberta's Favoured Emissions-Control Plan is Falling Apart" in Canadian Business (Vol. 85, June 11, 2012, No. 10, pp. 13)
Pub: George Media Inc.

Ed: Matthew McClearn. Released: June 11, 2012. Description: The emissions-control plan of Alberta suffered a major setback following cancellations of major carbon capture and storage (CCS) pilot projects. Project Pioneer was cancelled because the saving did not justify the operating costs while discontinuation of Heartland Area Redwater Project was due to the uncertainty surrounding the province's changing CCS rules.

39406 ■ "Carbon Capture and Storage: Grave Concerns" in Canadian Business (Vol. 81,

July 21 2008, No. 11, pp. 25)
Pub: Rogers Media Inc.
Contact: Tony Viner, President

Ed: Andrew Nikiforuk. Description: Air pollution control regulations to reduce greenhouse gasses have been implemented by the Canadian government. The federal government is planning to construct a carbon funeral industry that will store the global warming gases, however the expenditure for the project will be shifted to the taxpayers. Details of the Bruce Peachy's initiative on how to reduce GHGs are presented.

39407 ■ "Carbon Trading: Current Schemes and Future Developments" in Energy Policy (Vol. 39, October 2011, No. 10, pp. 6040-6054)
Pub: Reed Elsevier Reference Publishing

Ed: Slobodan Perdan, Adisa Azapagic. Description: Current and future developments regarding carbon trading is highlighted.

39408 ■ "Case IH Announces Strategy to Meet 2014 Clean Air Standards" in Farm Industry News (September 15, 2011)
Pub: Penton Business Media Inc.
Contact: David Kieselstein, Chief Executive Officer

Ed: Jodie Wehrspann. Description: Case IH will meet EPA's stringent engine emissions limits imposed in 2014, called Tier 4. The limits call for a 90 percent reduction in particulate matter and nitrogen oxides (NOx) over the Tier 3 requirements from a few years ago.

39409 ■ "The Case for Treating the Sex Trade as an Industry" in Canadian Business (Vol. 83, October 12, 2010, No. 17, pp. 9)
Pub: Rogers Media Inc.
Contact: Tony Viner, President

Ed: Steve Maich. Description: It is believed that the worst aspects of prostitution in Canada are exacerbated by the fact that it must take place in secret. The laws that deal with the market for sex have led to an unsafe working environment. Prostitutes believe their industry needs to be sanctioned and regulated rather than ignored and reviled.

39410 ■ "Casino Mogul Explains Why He's Betting on Boston" in Boston Business Journal (Vol. 34, February 7, 2014, No. 1, pp. 4)
Pub: American City Business Journals, Inc.
Contact: Whitney Shaw, President

Released: February 7, 2014. Description: Investor Steve Wynn has cited Boston, Massachusetts' reputation as an international destination as the reason for his plan to open a casino in the city. Wynn has been pushing for changes in the state's casino rules and regulations. He states that his casino would be of higher quality than those of his competitors in the area.

39411 ■ "Cat Cafe Draws More Claws Than Purring in S.F." in San Francisco Business Times (Vol. 28, January 31, 2014, No. 28, pp. 3)
Pub: American City Business Journals

Released: January 31, 2014. Description: Courtney Hatt and co-founder David Braginsky have been planning to open KitTea Café, a place where people can buy tea and hang out with cats at the same time in San Francisco, California. However, they will need at least $100,000 to open the cat café as well address the health regulation concerns about mixing cats and food. Hatt's plan for funding the project are also presented.

39412 ■ "Cell Tower Potential" in Black Enterprise (Vol. 37, October 2006, No. 3, pp. 86)
Pub: Earl G. Graves Publishing Co. Inc.
Contact: Earl G. Graves, Jr., President

Ed: James C. Johnson. Description: Discusses the leasing of property for cell phone towers to wireless carriers. Only certain properties are eligible, due to such criteria as proximity to existing towers.

39413 ■ "The CEO Poll: And The Winner Is ..." in Canadian Business (Vol. 81, February 12, 2008, No. 3, pp. 21)
Pub: Rogers Media Inc.
Contact: Tony Viner, President

Ed: Joe Castaldo. Description: Thirty out of 141 Canadian chief executive officers think that Hilary Clinton would be best for U.S.-Canada relations if elected as U.S. president. Findings also revealed that 60 respondents believe that presidential candidate John McCain would be best on handling issues of international military-security. Views on the candidates' performance and their ability to deal with the declining U.S. economy as well as international trade issues are also given.

39414 ■ "The CEO Poll: Fuel for Thought II Canadian Business Leaders on Energy Policy" in Canadian Business (Vol. 81, September 15, 2008, No. 14-15, pp. 12)
Pub: Rogers Media Inc.
Contact: Tony Viner, President

Ed: Joe Castaldo. Description: Most Canadian business leaders worry about the unreliability of the oil supply but feel that Canada is in a better position to benefit from the energy supply crisis than other countries. Many respondents also highlighted the need to invest in renewable energy sources.

39415 ■ "The CEO Poll: Hot Air" in Canadian Business (Vol. 81, July 22, 2008, No. 12-13, pp. 16)
Pub: Rogers Media Inc.
Contact: Tony Viner, President

Ed: Joe Castaldo. Description: Over half of 101 business leaders who were recently surveyed oppose Liberal leader Stephane Dion's carbon-tax proposal, saying that manufacturers in Canada are likely to suffer from the plan. Additional key results of the survey are presented.

39416 ■ "CEOs Divided About Census" in Canadian Business (Vol. 83, August 17, 2010, No. 13-14, pp. 20)
Pub: Rogers Media Inc.
Contact: Tony Viner, President

Ed: Jacqueline Nelson. Description: A Compass poll of Canadian CEOs on what the government should do with controversial long-form census is presented. The poll results show that 30 percent believe the government should remove any threat of punishment for failure to complete the survey. The CEOs also believe the law must be enforced by the government to encourage participation.

39417 ■ "The CEO's New Armor" in Conde Nast Portfolio (Vol. 2, June 2008, No. 6, pp. 56)
Ed: John Cassidy. Description: Due to a new breed in C.E.O.'s contracts it is nearly impossible to fire them regardless of their performance. Despite the Sarbanes-Oxley Act in which attempted to codify C.E.O. responsibilities, corporate bosses responded by quietly demanding individual contracts, which, in many cases, were drawn up by their own lawyers and accepted by company boards with no outside oversight or review.

39418 ■ "CEOs Split on Migrant Workers" in Canadian Business (Vol. 83, September 14, 2010, No. 15, pp. 23)
Pub: Rogers Media Inc.
Contact: Tony Viner, President

Ed: Jacqueline Nelson. Description: A survey of Canadian CEOs shows that 49 percent of the respondents believe it was wrong to suspend the immigration programs and companies should be allowed to hire the most skilled workers regardless of citizenship. However, 42 percent believe the suspension was right because employment of Canadians must take precedence.

39419 ■ "Chafee Eyes Tax On Travel Sites" in Providence Business News (Vol. 28, March 24, 2014, No. 51, pp. 1)
Pub: American City Business Journals

Released: March 24, 2014. Description: Rhode Island Governor, Lincoln D. Chafee's 2015 budget will include new tax rules for travel Websites. State officials claim the new regulations will deal with a loophole that has allowed travel Websites to pay less in taxes. Many hotels enter into partnerships with travel Websites in order to sell rooms in bulk.

39420 ■ "Changes Sought to Health Law" in Baltimore Business Journal (Vol. 28, July 30, 2010, No. 12, pp. 1)

Pub: Baltimore Business Journal

Ed: Kent Hoover. **Description:** Business groups that opposed health care reform are working to undo parts of the new laws even before they go into effect. Business groups are gaining support for one legislative fix, which is repealing the law's provision that requires all businesses to file 1099 forms with the IRS any time they pay more than $600 a year to another business.

39421 ■ "Changes on Tap" in Washington Business Journal (Vol. 32, April 4, 2014, No. 51, pp. 6)

Pub: American City Business Journals

Released: April 4, 2014. **Description:** Breweries in Maryland could benefit from proposed changes in government regulations regarding the selling of beer. The new rules would allow them to sell pints without operating as a restaurant and sell beer directly to restaurants and bars.

39422 ■ "Changing the Rules of the Accounting Game" in Canadian Business (Vol. 81, December 8, 2008, No. 21, pp. 19)

Ed: Al Rosen. **Description:** Interference from world politicians in developing accounting standards is believed to have resulted in untested rules that are inferior to current standards. European lawmakers have recently asked to change International Financial Reporting Standards.

39423 ■ "Charlie Winburn's Big Idea" in Business Courier (Vol. 27, October 8, 2010, No. 23, pp. 1)

Pub: Business Courier

Ed: Dan Monk, Lucy May. **Description:** Cincinnati Councilman Charlie Winburn proposed the creation of Cincinnati Competitive Edge Division and to remake a small-business division of the city in order to start a job-creation program. The new division will monitor compliance to the city's small business inclusion regulations, as well as to help small business owners grow.

39424 ■ "Cheap Tubing Risk to Local Jobs, Execs Caution" in Pittsburgh Business Times (Vol. 33, May 23, 2014, No. 45, pp. 4)

Pub: American City Business Journals

Released: May 23, 2014. **Description:** U.S. Steel Corporation requests the U.S. Department of Commerce to take action against unfairly traded steel imports in the market because thousands of jobs are at risk. At least 26,400 jobs in Pennsylvania may be affected by the unfair trading practices of foreign exporters according to the office of Governor Tom Corbett.

39425 ■ "Chesapeake Firm Regains Veteran-Owned Status" in Virginian-Pilot (August 21, 2012)

Pub: McClatchy Tribune Information Services

Ed: Philip Walzer. **Description:** Syncon LLC has regained status as a "veteran-owned" business. Mark Lilly, the president of Syncon is a retired Navy SEAL master chief who was wounded in combat in Afghanistan. Over-regulation by the US Department of Vetrans Affairs in order to stop fraud in the veteran certification program was responsible for the mistake.

39426 ■ "China Vs the World: Whose Technology Is It?" in Harvard Business Review (Vol. 88, December 2010, No. 12, pp. 94)

Pub: Harvard Business School Publishing

Ed: Thomas M. Hout, Pankaj Ghemawat. **Description:** Examination of the regulation the Chinese government is implementing that require foreign corporations wishing to do business in the country to give up their new technologies. These regulations

avoid World Trade Organization technology transfer provisions and complicate the convergence of socialism and capitalism.

39427 ■ "China's Transition to Green Energy Systems" in Energy Policy (Vol. 39, October 2011, No. 10, pp. 5909-5919)

Pub: Reed Elsevier Reference Publishing

Ed: Wei Li, Guojun Song, Melanie Beresford, Ben Ma. **Description:** The economics of home solar water heaters and their growing popularity in Dezhous City, China is discussed.

39428 ■ Chinese Ethnic Business: Global and Local Perspectives

Pub: Routledge

Contact: Kevin Bradley, President

E-mail: kbradley@taylorandfrancis.com

Ed: Eric Fong, Chiu Luk. **Released:** May 2009. **Price:** $54.95, paperback; $180, hardback. **Description:** Globalization impacts on the development of Chinese businesses are analyzed, focusing on economic globalization of the United States, Australia, and Canada. Information is focused on economic globalization and Chinese community development, transnational linkages, local urban structures, homogenization and place attachment, as well as methodology such as ethnographic studies, historical analysis, geographic studies and statistical analysis. **Availability:** Print.

39429 ■ "Christmas Trees Keep Giving in St. Louis Area" in St. Louis Post-Dispatch (January 11, 2012)

Pub: McClatchy-Tribune Information Services

Released: January 11, 2012. **Description:** Missouri state law prohibiting disposing of Christmas trees into area lakes has forced citizens to find new ways to use their old trees. Saint Louis and other municipalities offers ways to recycle Christmas trees while creating a good habitat for fish. Cities have sunk a portion of the trees, then created mulch and is offered free to residents.

39430 ■ "Cincinnati Business Committee's Tom Williams: Future is Now" in Business Courier (Vol. 27, August 13, 2010, No. 15, pp. 1)

Pub: Business Courier

Ed: Lucy May. **Description:** Tom Williams, chairman of the Cincinnati Business Committee (CBC), maintains that politicians and business leaders must cooperate to ensure the competitiveness of the city for the 21st Century. Under Williams' leadership, the CBC has put emphasis on initiatives related to government efficiency, economic development, and public education. Williams' views on a proposed inland port are given.

39431 ■ "Cincinnati City Council Power Shift Could Benefit Business" in Business Courier (Vol. 26, November 6, 2009, No. 28, pp. 1)

Pub: American City Business Journals, Inc.

Contact: Whitney Shaw, President

Ed: Lucy May, Dan Monk. **Description:** A majority in the Cincinnati City Council, which is comprised of reelected members, might be created by Charlie Winburn's impending return to the council. It would be empowered to decide on public safety, stock options taxes, and environmental justice. How the presumed majority would affect the city's economic progress is discussed.

39432 ■ "Cincinnati Consults Executives on Police Chief Hire" in Business Courier (Vol. 27, August 27, 2010, No. 17, pp. 1)

Pub: Business Courier

Ed: Dan Monk, Lucy May. **Description:** The City of Cincinnati, Ohio has begun a selection process for the new police chief by consulting the city's business executives. The city charter amendment known as Issue 5 has removed civil service protection from the chief's post and enables City Manager Milton Dohoney to hire a chief from outside the department.

39433 ■ "Cincinnati Entrepreneur's DotLoop Software Being Tested by Realtors" in Business Courier (Vol. 26, September 11,

2009, No. 20, pp. 1)

Pub: American City Business Journals, Inc.

Contact: Whitney Shaw, President

Ed: Dan Monk. **Description:** DotLoop Company, owned by entrepreneur Austin Allison, is developing the DotLoop software, which eliminates paperwork in the processing of real estate contracts. The software allows realtors to take control of the negotiation process and is adaptable to the rules of different US states.

39434 ■ "Cincinnati Hospitals Wage War on 'Bounce-Backs" in Business Courier (Vol. 27, July 30, 2010, No. 13, pp. 1)

Pub: Business Courier

Ed: James Ritchie. **Description:** Health care organizations in Greater Cincinnati area have tried a number of care and follow up programs, primarily focused on congestive heart failure to prevent readmissions to hospitals. Hospital administrators have made the averting of bounce-backs a priority due to new federal government plans on reimbursement.

39435 ■ "Cincinnati's Broadway Casino Climbing Hills to Get to Gambling" in Business Courier (Vol. 26, January 1, 2010, No. 37, pp. 1)

Pub: American City Business Journals, Inc.

Contact: Whitney Shaw, President

Ed: Dan Monk. **Description:** Rock Ventures LLC, operators of the Broadway Commons Casino, needs approval from the Ohio General Assembly and the to-be-created Ohio Casino Control Commission to commence operations.

39436 ■ "Cincinnati's Freedom Center May have New Path" in Business Courier (Vol. 26, October 30, 2009, No. 27, pp. 1)

Pub: American City Business Journals, Inc.

Contact: Whitney Shaw, President

Ed: Dan Monk, Lucy May. **Description:** National Underground Railroad Freedom Center in Price Hill, Cincinnati is in negotiations with US Rep. John Conyers for its possible classification as an independent establishment within the US federal government. If this happens, funding for the museum might be possibly augmented and the rights to use national archives might be furnished.

39437 ■ Cities from the Arabian Desert: The Building of Jubail and Yambu in Saudi Arabia

Pub: Turnaround Associates

Contact: Andrea H. Pampanini, Founder

Ed: Andrea H. Pampanini. **Description:** An overview of Saudi Arabia's government to take control of the nation's natural resources and change the government, educational system, and its culture by evolving into a modern industrial society.

39438 ■ "City Board Tweaks Internet Cafe Ordinance" in Ocala Star-Banner (July 19, 2011)

Pub: Ocala Star-Banner

Contact: Allen Parsons, Publisher

Ed: Susan Latham Carr. **Description:** Ocala Planning and Zoning Commission revised the proposed draft of the Internet Cafe ordinance by eliminating the cap on the number of locations allowed, but keeping fees and number of devices the same.

39439 ■ "City Likely To Sell Sites Near Downtown" in Austin Business Journal (Vol. 32, June 15, 2012, No. 15, pp. 1)

Pub: American City Business Journals, Inc.

Contact: Whitney Shaw, President

Ed: Vicky Garza. **Released:** June 15, 2012. **Description:** Austin, Texas is required to sell four sites owned by the city along East 12th Street near downtown. The land was bought in 1999 using federal funds, but is still undeveloped. Real estate manager Regina Copic believes that the city needs to complete the projects in order to obtain federal entitlement in the future.

39440 ■ "City Rejects Plans for Waxter Site" in Baltimore Business Journal (Vol. 30, May

25, 2012, No. 3, pp. 1)
Pub: American City Business Journals, Inc.
Contact: Whitney Shaw, President
Ed: James Briggs. Released: May 25, 2012. Description: The City of Baltimore, Maryland has turned down a proposal for a mixed-use development project at the Waxter Center in Mount Vernon. The project is estimated to cost up to $70 million.

39441 ■ "CityLink Project On Hold" in Business Courier (Vol. 24, November 8, 2007, No. 30, pp. 3)
Pub: American City Business Journals, Inc.
Contact: Whitney Shaw, President
Ed: Dan Monk. Description: Developers of the CityLink project have indicated that it will be at least a year before they start the planned social services mall at 800 Bank West End. According to Tim Senff, Citylink CEO, the company wants to build bridges before constructing the buildings. The project's critics are still considering whether to appeal a court ruling regarding the facility's compliance with the city's zoning code.

39442 ■ "City's New Energy Audits to Spawn 'Fantastic' Market" in Austin Business JournalInc. (Vol. 28, November 14, 2008, No. 35, pp. 1)
Pub: American City Business Journals
Ed: Jean Kwon. Description: A new law requiring older homes to undergo energy use audits is seen to provide new business for some companies in the Austin, Texas area. The new law is seen to create a new industry of performance testers. Details of the new ordinance are also given.

39443 ■ "Clarence Firm Gets OK To Make Tobacco Products" in Business First of Buffalo (Vol. 30, March 14, 2014, No. 26, pp. 3)
Pub: American City Business Journals, Inc.
Contact: Whitney Shaw, President
Released: March 14, 2014. Description: Clarence, New York-based 22nd Century Group Inc.'s subsidiary Goodrich Tobacco Company, has received approval from the Alcohol and Tobacco Tax and Trade Bureau to produce tobacco products. The approval came after 22nd Century purchased the assets of North Carolina-based Nasco Products LLC, which holds a similar permit. Details of the deal are included.

39444 ■ "The Clash of the Cultures: Investment vs. Speculation"
Pub: John Wiley & Sons Inc.
Contact: Stephen M. Smith, President
Released: July 5, 2012. Price: , $29.95. Description: Founder of Vanguard Group urges a return to the common sense principles of long-term investing. John C. Bogle draws on his sixty-years of experience in the mutual fund industry to discuss his views on the changing culture in mutual fund investing, how speculation has invaded our national retirement system, the failure of institutional money managers to effectively participate in corporate governance, and the need for a federal standard of fiduciary duty. Bogle also discusses the history of the index mutual fund and how he created it.

39445 ■ "Climate Law Could Dig into our Coal-Dusted Pockets" in Business Courier (Vol. 26, November 20, 2009, No. 30, pp. 1)
Pub: American City Business Journals, Inc.
Contact: Whitney Shaw, President
Ed: Lucy May. Description: Passage of federal climate legislation into law is set to increase household cost for Greater Cincinnati, according to the calculation by the Brookings Institute. The increase for residents of the area will amount to $244 in 2020 and the city was ranked the sixth-highest rate in the nation, behind Indianapolis.

39446 ■ "Clusters Last Stand?" in Canadian Electronics (Vol. 23, February 2008, No. 1, pp. 6)
Description: Survival of technology clusters was the focus of Strategic Microelectronics Council's conference entitled, 'The Power of Community: Building Technology Clusters in Canada'. Clusters can help foster growth in the microelectronics sector, and it was recognized that government intervention is needed to maintain these clusters.

39447 ■ "CO2 Emissions Embodied in China-US Trade" in Energy Policy (Vol. 39, October 2011, No. 10, pp. 5980-5987)
Pub: Reed Elsevier Reference Publishing
Ed: Huibin Du, Guozhu Mao, Alexander M. Smith, Xuxu Wang, Yuan Wang, Jianghong Guo. Description: Input and output analysis based on the energy per dollar ratio for carbon dioxide emissions involved in China-United States trade is outlined.

39448 ■ Code of Federal Regulations: Title 13: Business Credit and Assistance
Pub: U. S. Government Printing Office
Contact: Veronica Meter, Director
E-mail: tpriebe@gpo.gov
Ed: Department of Commerce Staff. Released: January 2014. Price: $61. Description: Title 13 covers regulations governing the activities of the Small Business Administration and the Department of Commerce. Book covers information on business credit, finance, and economic development. Availability: Print.

39449 ■ "Collateral Damage" in Business Courier (Vol. 26, October 16, 2009, No. 25, pp. 1)
Pub: American City Business Journals, Inc.
Contact: Whitney Shaw, President
Ed: Jon Newberry. Description: Non-union construction firms representing Ohio Valley Associated Builders and Contractors Inc. have filed cases against unionized shops claiming violations of wage law in Ohio. Defendants say the violations are minor, however, they believe they are caught in the middle of the group's campaign to change the state's wage law.

39450 ■ "Collection Agency Issues Whitepaper on Legal and Ethical Methods of Collecting on Overdue Accounts" in Marketwired (July 20, 2009)
Pub: COMTEX News Network Inc.
Contact: Chip Brian, President
Description: American Profit Recovery, a collection agency based in Massachusetts and Michigan, has updated and reissued a whitepaper on what businesses can and cannot do regarding conversing with their customers in an attempt to collect on overdue accounts and payments. A detailed summary on the federal laws associated with collecting on overdue accounts is outlined in such a way that any business owner, manager, or responsible party can easily understand.

39451 ■ "Collection Agency To Chase Unpaid Fees From Former Inmates" in PaymentsSource (May 17, 2012)
Pub: SourceMedia Inc.
Contact: James M. Malkin, Chief Executive Officer
Released: May 17, 2012. Description: Houston County, Minnesota has contracted Grand American Resources Inc. to collect unpaid fees from former inmate of the County jail. Details of the plan are included.

39452 ■ "Colorado Could Set Record for Oil Production" in Denver Business Journal (Vol. 64, August 24, 2012, No. 14, pp. 1)
Pub: American City Business Journal
Description: Colorado's oil production is expected to set a record for 2012. This is due to the robust investment and drilling activities at the Niobrara rock formation. On the other hand, the efforts of several counties and city governments to introduce new regulations on drilling locations and processes threaten to limit the steady rise of oil production and investments in the area.

39453 ■ "Colorado Statehouse Races Key for Business" in Denver Business Journal (Vol. 64, August 31, 2012, No. 15, pp. 1)
Pub: American City Business Journal
Description: The elections for Colorado's Senate and House of Representatives can have a great impact on the state's economy. Republicans are focusing on regulatory-reform measures, while Democrats are pushing for bidding priorities given to companies that buy and hire locally. Experts state that Republican and Democratic candidates seem to agree on job-creation proposals.

39454 ■ "Column: Want People to Save? Force Them" in Harvard Business Review (Vol. 88, September 2010, No. 9, pp. 36)
Pub: Harvard Business School Publishing
Ed: Dan Ariely. Description: Contrasts in U.S. attitudes towards savings and government regulation with those of Chile, where all employees are required to save 11 percent of their salary in a retirement account, are highlighted.

39455 ■ "Column: Wealth and Jobs: the Broken Link" in Harvard Business Review (Vol. 88, November 2010, No. 11, pp. 44)
Pub: Harvard Business School Publishing
Ed: Nitin Nohria. Description: Rebuilding the link between business and job creation to shore up the middle class is advocated. A blend of government policies and business strategies that foster entrepreneurship and innovation are essential.

39456 ■ "Coming Soon: Bailouts of Fannie and Freddie" in Barron's (Vol. 88, July 14, 2008, No. 28, pp. 14)
Pub: Dow Jones & Co., Inc.
Contact: Clare Hart, President
Ed: Jonathan R. Laing. Description: Assurances from the government that Fannie Mae and Freddie Mac are adequately capitalized and able to carry on their duties as guarantors or owners of over $5 trillion of U.S. home mortgages are designed to keep both entities afloat until they attempt to raise $10 billion in new equity. The government would assume any losses in a bailout and owners of the banks' papers would profit as yields drop.

39457 ■ "Commentary" in Small Business Economic Trends (September 2010, pp. 3)
Pub: National Federation of Independent Business
Contact: Caitlin McDevitt, Program Manager
Ed: William C. Dunkelberg, Holly Wade. Description: A commentary on the economic trends for small businesses in the U.S. is presented. An analysis of the unemployment rate and inflation is given. Economic growth is also expected to remain sub-par for some time, unless new policies are introduced.

39458 ■ "Commentary. Small Business Economic Trends" in Small Business Economic Trends (March 2008, pp. 3)
Pub: National Federation of Independent Business
Contact: Caitlin McDevitt, Program Manager
Ed: William C. Dunkelberg, Holly Wade. Description: Commentary on the economic trends for small businesses in the U.S. is presented. Analysis of the labor market and low interest rates is given. The effect of the Federal Reserve's policy announcement on small business owner optimism is also discussed.

39459 ■ "Commentary. Small Business Economic Trends" in Small Business Economic Trends (February 2008, pp. 3)
Pub: National Federation of Independent Business
Contact: Caitlin McDevitt, Program Manager
Ed: William C. Dunkelberg, Holly Wade. Description: Commentary on the economic trends for small businesses in the U.S. is presented. Analysis of the U.S. Federal Reserve Board's efforts to prevent a recession is given. Reduction in business inventories is also discussed.

39460 ■ "Commentary. Small Business Economic Trends" in Small Business Economic Trends (January 2008, pp. 3)
Pub: National Federation of Independent Business
Contact: Caitlin McDevitt, Program Manager
Description: Federal Reserve cut interest rates and announced its economic outlook on September 18, 2007 to stimulate spending. The cut in interest rates, however, may not help in supporting consumer spending because savers may lose interest income. The expected economic impact of the interest rate cuts and the U.S. economic outlook are also discussed.

39461 ■ *"Commentary: US Economic Recovery and Policy" in Small Business Economic Trends (July 2010, pp. 3)*
Pub: National Federation of Independent Business
Contact: Caitlin McDevitt, Program Manager
Ed: William C. Dunkelberg, Holly Wade. **Description:** U.S. Government is making economic recovery difficult, with one of the largest tax increases in history arriving in six months. Meanwhile, Congress is looking into taxing successful businesses, which will potentially hamper growth and real investment. Other insights on the government's role in the country's economic growth are presented.

39462 ■ *"Commodity Speculation: Over the Top?" in Barron's (Vol. 89, July 13, 2009, No. 28, pp. 22)*
Pub: Dow Jones & Co., Inc.
Contact: Clare Hart, President
Ed: Gene Epstein. **Description:** Commodity Futures Trading Commission is planning to impose position limits on speculators of oil and other commodities as energy costs rebound from their lows. These regulations make much sense and these position limits would greatly diminish the cash commitment of the commodity index traders if these were imposed on speculators and swaps dealers properly.

39463 ■ *"Commotion Pictures; Bill C-10: Is It Censorship or Merely Inept?" in Canadian Business (Vol. 81, March 31, 2008, No. 5, pp. 10)*
Pub: Rogers Media Inc.
Contact: Tony Viner, President
Ed: Denis Seguin. **Description:** Filmmakers are claiming that Bill C-10 amounts to censorship as it could retract a production's eligibility for a tax credit if it is deemed offensive. However, the bill's backers say that the bill protects against tax dollars being directed at productions that run contrary to public policy.

39464 ■ *"Company Goes High-Tech To Attack Some Sore Spots" in Boston Business Journal (Vol. 27, December 7, 2007, No. 45, pp. 10)*
Ed: Mark Hollmer. **Description:** Transport Pharmaceuticals Inc. hopes to raise $35 million to fund a drug and a treatment device for treating cold sores, and seek federal regulatory approval. Dennis Goldberg, the company's CEO, believes that existing treatments that use acyclovir cream are relatively weak. Transport's drug uses a soluble gel cartridge with a higher concentration of acyclovir.

39465 ■ *"Complete Discovery Source, Inc. (CDS) Receives Minority Owned Business Certification" in Marketwired (December 14, 2010)*
Pub: COMTEX
Contact: Chip Brian, President
Description: Complete Discovery Source Inc. (CDS) was granted Minority-Owned Business Enterprise status by the New York State Department of Economic Development. The certification provides CDS, an end-to-end eDiscovery services provider, with access to contracting opportunities with 130 government agencies throughout New York state.

39466 ■ *"Computer Forensics Firms Get Boost From New Evidence Rules" in Crain's Detroit Business (Vol. 24, March 24, 2008, No. 12, pp. 28)*
Pub: Crain Communications Inc.
Contact: Rance E. Crain, President
Ed: Chad Halcom. **Description:** Computer forensics is a growing niche for firms such as the Center for Computer Forensics in Southfield; driving some of the growth are new amendments to the Federal Rules of Civil Procedure, which took effect about a year ago and address standards of evidence for electronic records, or 'e-discovery,' that are admissible for civil cases in federal courts.

39467 ■ *"Condos Becoming FHA No-Lending Zones" in Providence Business News (Vol. 29, June 2, 2014, No. 9, pp. 7)*
Pub: American City Business Journals
Released: June 2, 2014. **Description:** Federal policy changes and decisions by condominium boards of directors have made the condominium development

ineligible for Federal Housing Administration (FHA) loans, making several communities prohibited lending zones. As a result, the number of condo developments approved for FHA funding has fallen by more than half, presenting a growing problem for first-time buyers, those with modest down payment cash, and senior citizens using a reverse mortgage.

39468 ■ *"Congress Targets Ad Tracking" in Inc. (Vol. 33, November 2011, No. 9, pp. 30)*
Pub: Inc. Magazine
Ed: Issie Lapowsky. **Description:** Congressional bills dealing with behavioral tracking whereby advertising networks monitor people's online behavior and use the date to tailor ads to people's interest propose Do Not Track measures which would allow consumers to turn off online behavior tracking by clicking a button.

39469 ■ *"Contractors Must be Lead Certified" in Contractor (Vol. 57, February 2010, No. 2, pp. 3)*
Pub: Penton Media, Inc.
Description: Contractors should be trained and certified to comply with the U.S. Environmental Protection Agency's Lead Renovation, Repair, and Painting regulation if they work on housing built before 1978 by April 2010. Contractors with previous lead abatement training must be trained and certified under this new program.

39470 ■ *"Contractors Should Expand Their Services" in Contractor (Vol. 56, July 2009, No. 7, pp. 34)*
Pub: Intertec Publishing
Contact: John French, President
Ed: Steve Scandaliato. **Description:** All single family homes will be required to have fire sprinkler systems installed when the 2009 International Residential Code arrives. This presents an opportunity for plumbing contractors and they can be competitively priced against a fire protection contractor if they train their workforce to install sprinklers.

39471 ■ *"Controversial Bill Could Raise Rates for Homeowners" in Orlando Business Journal (Vol. 26, January 22, 2010, No. 34, pp. 1)*
Pub: American City Business Journals
Ed: Oscar Pedro Musibay, Christopher Boyd. **Description:** Florida Senate Bill 876 and its companion House Bill 447 are pushing for the deregulation of rates in the state's home insurance market. The bill is being opposed by consumer advocates as it could mean higher rates for homeowner insurance policies.

39472 ■ *"Convergence Collaboration: Revising Revenue Recognition" in Management Accounting Quarterly (Vol. 12, Spring 2011, No. 3, pp. 18)*
Pub: Management Accounting Quarterly
Ed: Jack T. Ciesielski, Thomas R. Weirich. **Description:** While revenue recognition is critical, regulations have been developed on an ad hoc basis until now. The joint FASB/IASB proposed accounting standard on revenue recognition is a meaningful convergence of standards that will require a major adjustment for financial statement preparers. The proposal is a radical departure from the way revenue has been recognized by the U.S. GAAP. For industries such as consulting, engineering, construction, and technology, it could dramatically change revenue recognition, impacting the top line. The new proposed standard, its potential impact, and the critical role that contracts play is examined thoroughly.

39473 ■ *"A Conversation With Money Manager William Vellon" in Crain's Chicago Business (Vol. 31, November 17, 2008, No. 46, pp. 4)*
Ed: Mike Colias. **Description:** Interview with William Vellon, the executive vice-president of Kingsbury Capital Investment Advisors; Vellon discusses ways in which the government can help the financial sector, his client base and bargains that investors should consider.

39474 ■ *"Convictions Under the Fisheries Act" in Marketwired (May 16, 2007)*
Pub: Comtex News Network Inc.
Description: Fisheries and Oceans Canada is mandated to protect and conserve marine resources

and thus released a list of fishers fined for various offences under the Fisheries Act in March and April.

39475 ■ *"Countdown" in Canadian Business (Vol. 81, March 3, 2008, No. 3, pp. 27)*
Ed: Al Rosen. **Description:** According to a recent poll only 42 percent of portfolio managers in Canada are aware that the country is planning to adopt the International Financial Reporting Standards beginning 2011. The shift to the new standards will have significant impacts on investment values and will be the biggest revolution in Canadian financial reporting. The effects of the transition on portfolio managers and investors are analyzed.

39476 ■ *"Credit Card Crackdown" in Business Journal-Portland (Vol. 24, November 23, 2007, No. 38, pp. 1)*
Pub: American City Business Journals, Inc.
Ed: Andy Giegerich. **Description:** Oregon's U.S. Senator Ron Wyden is sponsoring Credit Card Safety Act of 2007, a bill that requires credit card companies to reduce the jargon of credit card agreements and require the Federal Reserve Board to launch a public education campaign among credit card users. The legislation will also impose a rating system for credit card contracts with five being the safest for consumers to use.

39477 ■ *"Credit Unions Cast Wary Eye at Paulson Plan, But Not Panicking Yet" in The Business Review Albany (Vol. 35, April 11, 2008, No. 1)*
Pub: The Business Review
Ed: Barbara Pinckney. **Description:** Credit unions are suspicious of US Treasury Secretary Henry Paulson's plan to establish a single federally insured depository institution charter for all institutions covered by federal deposit insurance. The charter would replace national banks, federal savings associations, and federal credit union charters.

39478 ■ *"Credit Unions Seek to Raise Lending for Small Business" in Denver Business Journal (Vol. 64, September 28, 2012, No. 64, pp. 1)*
Pub: American City Business Journal
Description: United States Senator Mark Udall has introduced the Small Business Lending Enhancement Act, which aims to increase the commercial lending authority of credit unions. The bill's supporters claim that small business owners are still experiencing problems getting credit, and that the legislation will increase small business lending by $13 milliion within its first year of enactment.

39479 ■ *"Crowd Control" in Washington Business Journal (Vol. 33, August 15, 2014, No. 17, pp. 8)*
Pub: American City Business Journals
Released: August 15, 2014. **Description:** Washington DC's Department of Insurance, Securities and Banking issued a proposal that would create the legal framework by which companies can raise cash through crowdfunding. The DC proposal would allow District-based businesses to crowdfund from District-based backers. The advantages and drawbacks to the plan are examined.

39480 ■ *"CrowdFunding Made Simple Conference at University of Utah Ignites Ecosystem of Entrepreneurs and Investors" in Economics Week (June 29, 2012)*
Pub: NewsRX
Contact: Susan E. Hasty, Publisher
Released: June 29, 2012. **Description:** The first national conference on crowdfunding was held at the University of Utah Guest House and Conference Center May 31 through June 1, 2012. The event, CrowdFunding Made Simple, gathered entrepreneurs, business owners, professional service providers, investors, government officials and students to provide understanding and potential of crowdfunding, including information on the Jumpstart Our Business Startups (JOBS) Act.

39481 ■ *"A Crucial Step Toward Freer Trade" in Canadian Business (Vol. 85, August 13,*

2012, No. 13, pp. 7)
Pub: George Media Inc.
Ed: Tim Shufelt. **Released:** August 13, 2012. **Description:** The decision of the Canadian government to join the Trans-Pacific Partnership (TPP) has potential economic benefits in terms of trading with China and the U.S.Failure of the World Trade Ogranization's Doha Round and the admission of the U.S. to the TPP prompted Canada to join the trade agreement.

39482 ■ *"CTV's CHUM Proposal Gets Chilly Reception"* in Globe & Mail (May 1, 2007, pp. B1)
Ed: Grant Robertson. **Description:** The possible violation of broadcast regulations in case of acquisition of CHUM Ltd. by CTV Inc. for $1.4 billion is discussed.

39483 ■ *"The Cudgel of Samson: How the Government Once Used 'Jawboning' to Fight Inflation"* in Barron's (Vol. 88, March 24, 2008, No. 12, pp. 62)
Pub: Dow Jones & Co., Inc.
Contact: Clare Hart, President
Ed: Thomas G. Donlan. **Description:** Discusses the Federal Reserve is jawboning businesses against inflation while inflation is starting to rise because of the abundance of cheap money. The practice of jawboning has been used by the administrations of past US presidents with limited effect.

39484 ■ *"Curbing the Debt Collector"* in Business Journal-Portland (Vol. 24, October 5, 2007, No. 32, pp. 1)
Pub: American City Business Journals, Inc.
Ed: Andy Giergerich. **Description:** Republican representative Sal Esquivel, who had a bad personal experience with a Houston collector, is developing legislation that would give the state attorney general's office enforcement powers over debt collecting agencies. The existing Oregon legislation concerning the debt collection industry is also discussed.

39485 ■ *"Currency: I'm Outta Here"* in Entrepreneur (Vol. 35, October 2007, No. 10, pp. 72)
Pub: Entrepreneur Press
Contact: Perlman Neil, President
Ed: C.J. Prince. **Description:** Liberum Research revealed that 193 chief financial officers (CFOs) at small companies have either resigned or retired during the first half of 2007. A survey conducted by Tatum found that unreasonable expectations from the management and compliance to regulations are the main reasons why CFOs are leaving small firms. The chief executive officer's role in making CFOs stay is also discussed.

39486 ■ *"Daley's Efforts to Ease Traffic Woes Fall Short"* in Crain's Chicago Business (Vol. 31, May 5, 2008, No. 18, pp. 18)
Pub: Crain Communications Inc.
Contact: Todd Johnson, Publisher
Description: Discusses some of the inherent problems of Mayor Daley's plan to reduce traffic congestion by creating a tax on drivers who park their cars downtown during peak traffic periods and putting articulated buses on new bus-only lanes on major arterial streets leading into the Loop.

39487 ■ *"The Danger of Doing Nothing"* in Harvard Business Review (Vol. 90, April 2012, No. 4, pp. 38)
Pub: Harvard Business Review Press
Contact: Peter E. Walsh, Director
Ed: Erskine Bowles. **Released:** March 2012. **Description:** Solving the US economic crisis will require a blend of revenue increases, spending cuts, and bipartisan cooperation in Congress. The National Commission on Fiscal Responsibility and Reform, also known as Simpson-Bowles, has proposed a plan intended to make America competitive again.

39488 ■ *"The Data Drivers"* in Canadian Business (Vol. 81, September 15, 2008, No. 14-15, pp. 1)
Ed: Andrew Wahl. **Description:** Canadian regulators hope that an auction of telecommunications companies will inject more competition into the industry;

however, newcomers may not be able to rely on lower prices in order to gain market share from the three major telecommunications companies that already have a stronghold on the market. Analysts feel that providing additional data service is the key to surviving market disruptions.

39489 ■ *Dead on Arrival: How the Anti-Business Backlash is Destroying Entrepreneurship in America and What We Can Still Do About It!*
Ed: Bernie Marcus; Steve Gottry. **Released:** November 2006. **Price:** , $23.95. **Description:** Bernie Marcus, Home Depot leader, addresses regulations hurting small businesses in America.

39490 ■ *"Deal With Tribes Revives Revenue Stream"* in Crain's Detroit Business (Vol. 24, March 24, 2008, No. 12, pp. 6)
Pub: Crain Communications Inc.
Contact: Rance E. Crain, President
Ed: Amy Lane. **Description:** Michigan Bureau of State Lottery's 2003 launch of its Club Keno game caused the Little River Band of Ottawa Indians and the Little Traverse Bay Bands of Odawa Indians to halt payments of shared casino revenue with the state. The federal lawsuit that resulted has now been settled and tribal revenue sharing will resume as well as $26 million in previous payments to the state of Michigan that the tribes had put into escrow.

39491 ■ *"Dealing With Dangers Abroad"* in Financial Executive (Vol. 23, December 2007, No. 10, pp. 32)
Ed: Jeffrey Marshall. **Description:** Clear processes and responsibilities for risk management for all companies going global are essential. U.S. toy manufacturer, Matel was put into crisis mode after its Chinese-made toys were recalled due to the use of lead-based paint or tiny magnets in its products.

39492 ■ *"Death Spiral"* in Business Journal Serving Greater Tampa Bay (Vol. 30, October 29, 2010, No. 45, pp. 1)
Pub: Tampa Bay Business Journal
Ed: Margie Manning. **Description:** Bay Cities Bank has started working on the loan portfolio of its acquisition, Progress Bank of Florida. Regulators closed Progress Bank in October 2010 after capital collapsed due to charge-offs and increases in the provision for future loan losses.

39493 ■ *"Defend Your Research: People Often Trust Eloquence More Than Honesty"* in Harvard Business Review (Vol. 88, November 2010, No. 11, pp. 36)
Pub: Harvard Business School Publishing
Ed: Todd Rogers, Michael I. Norton. **Description:** The article shows how deftly side-stepping a question in an eloquent manner generates a more positive response in an audience than does a direct answer that is ineffectively delivered. Implications for both politics and business are discussed.

39494 ■ *"Defense Budget Ax May Not Come Down So Hard on Maryland"* in Baltimore Business Journal (Vol. 28, August 20, 2010, No. 15, pp. 1)
Pub: Baltimore Business Journal
Ed: Daniel J. Sernovitz. **Description:** U.S. Defense Secretary Robert M. Gates' planned budget cuts are having little effect on Maryland's defense industry. Gates will reduce spending on intelligence service contracts by 10 percent.

39495 ■ *"Defense Decision a Big Victory For New Balance"* in Boston Business Journal (Vol. 34, May 2, 2014, No. 13, pp. 3)
Pub: American City Business Journals, Inc.
Contact: Whitney Shaw, President
Released: May 2, 2014. **Description:** The Department of Defense announced that it will require recruits to buy American-made running shoes in compliance with the Berry Amendment. The decision is a huge boost for Boston, Massachusetts-base New Balance and its suppliers after the company's lobbying efforts in Congress. New Balance's investment to make a Berry-compliant shoe is also discussed.

39496 ■ *"Defenshield Takes Aim at New Gun-Friendly Location"* in Orlando Business Journal (Vol. 30, June 27, 2014, No. 53, pp. 9)
Pub: American City Business Journals
Released: June 27, 2014. **Description:** Coverage of Defenshield's move to St. Augustine, Florida, a gun-friendly location is discussed. The relocation occurred after New York's declaration of the SAFE Act, a new governmental gun control law. Defenshield manufactures military-grade bulletproof shields and barriers, which need heavy weaponry to test the products.

39497 ■ *"DEM Says River Needs Cleanup"* in Providence Business News (Vol. 28, January 6, 2014, No. 40, pp. 1)
Pub: American City Business Journals
Released: January 6, 2014. **Description:** Rhode Island's Department of Environmental Management (DEM) called a meeting to gather information for its Ten Mile River water-quality-restoration plan. DEM announced the failure of the Ten Mile River and its impoundments to meet state water quality standards. The government grant received by Attleboro for the cleanup efforts is examined.

39498 ■ *Democratization Without Representation: The Politics of Small Industry in Mexico*
Pub: Pennsylvania State University Press
Contact: Patrick H. Alexander, Director
E-mail: pha3@psu.edu
Ed: Kenneth C. Shalden. **Released:** March 2006. **Price:** $39.95, paperback; $94.95, hardcover. **Description:** Opportunities for individuals to participate in Mexico's democracy and how it is affecting the way industries do business. **Availability:** Print.

39499 ■ *A Demon of Our Own Design: Markets, Hedge Funds, and the Perils of Financial Innovation*
Pub: John Wiley & Sons Inc.
Contact: Stephen M. Smith, President
Ed: Richard Bookstaber. **Released:** November 2008. **Price:** $16.95, paperback; $27.95, hardcover; $11.99. **Description:** Longtime hedge-fund manager offers his take on a market and investment system that he believes is needlessly complex owing to investment banks, hedge funds, innovation, regulation, and safeguards and further compounded by investor and market instabilities. These complexities could create a large-scale disaster. **Availability:** PrintE-book.

39500 ■ *"Department of Agriculture"* in Ice Cream Reporter (Vol. 23, November 20, 2010, No. 12, pp. 8)
Description: Department of Agriculture notes that food price inflation for 2010 will be at its lowest since 1992.

39501 ■ *Department of Labor's Overtime Regulations Effect on Small Business: Hearing before the Committee on Small Business, U.S. House of Representatives*
Pub: DIANE Publishing Co.
Contact: Dorothy J. Perkins, Manager
E-mail: dorothyjperkins@hotmail.com
Released: 2004. **Price:** $20, paperback. **Description:** An overview of the Congressional hearing regarding the Department of Labor's regulations governing overtime and how they impact small business.

39502 ■ *"Despite Hot Toys, Holiday Sales Predicted To Be Ho-Ho-Hum"* in Drug Store News (Vol. 29, November 12, 2007, No. 14, pp. 78)
Ed: Doug Desjardins. **Description:** Summer toy recalls have retailers worried about holiday sales in 2007. Mattel was heavily impacted from the recall of millions of toys manufactured in China.

39503 ■ *"Diary of a Short-Seller"* in Conde Nast Portfolio (Vol. 2, June 2008, No. 6, pp. 44)
Ed: Jesse Eisinger. **Description:** Profile of David Einhorn who is a fund manager that spoke out against finance company Allied Capital whose stock fell nearly 20 percent the day after Einhorn's critique; Einhorn subsequently had to contend with attacks

against his credibility as well as investigations by the S.E.C.; Einhorn's experience illuminates our current economic crisis.

39504 ■ "A Different Kind of Waiting List" in Canadian Business (Vol. 80, April 9, 2007, No. 8, pp. 17)
Ed: Erin Pooley. **Description:** The adverse impact on drug companies' profitability due to regulatory delays in approving drugs is discussed.

39505 ■ "Director Elections Campaign Pays Off" in Globe & Mail (March 9, 2006, pp. B1)
Ed: Janet McFarland. **Description:** The details pertaining to the introduction of new voting standards by electing company directors by 20 major Canadian companies, after the Canadian Coalition for Good Governance campaigned for it, are presented.

39506 ■ "Directors May Revise HCA Collection Agency Regulations" in Standard-Speaker (May 20, 2012)
Pub: McClatchy Tribune Information Services
Released: May 20, 2012. **Description:** Hazelton, Pennsylvania authorities are thinking about changing ts 42-year-old regulations, thus having a collection agency pursue payment of outstanding water and trash fees. Details of the plan are included.

39507 ■ "Dispensaries In Dispute" in Puget Sound Business Journal (Vol. 34, January 24, 2014, No. 41, pp. 3)
Pub: American City Business Journals
Released: January 24, 2014. **Description:** Washington-based medical marijuana dispensary owners are expressing concern over government regulations that propose to merge the medical marijuana market with Initiative 502-created recreational pot shops. The decision could spell the end of their businesses because the total number of vendors in the I-502 system are capped. Owner reactions to the issues are presented.

39508 ■ "The Display Group Is Super-Sized" in Michigan Vue (Vol. 13, July-August 2008, No. 4, pp. 34)
Description: Profile of the Display Group, located in downtown Detroit, this company provides custom designed mobile marketing displays as well as special event production services for trade show displays. The rental house and design service is also beginning to see more business due to the film initiative, which provides incentives for films that are shooting in Michigan.

39509 ■ The Diversity Code: Unlock the Secrets to Making Differences Work in the Real World
Pub: AMACOM
Contact: Edward T. Reilly, Manager
Ed: Michelle T. Johnson. **Released:** September 2010. **Price:** $19.95. **Description:** The most diligent compliance with laws and regulations can't foster true work place diversity. The best organizations have become genuine cross-cultural communities that believe equality in reconciling difference and valuing them. The book promotes understanding by answering many of the toughest questions that professionals and their employers are afraid to ask. **Availability:** Print.

39510 ■ "Do the Math" in Canadian Business (Vol. 79, October 9, 2006, No. 20, pp. 17)
Ed: Al Rosen. **Description:** Faulty practices followed by regulators in Canadian stock market are discussed. The need for authorities to protect investors against these frauds are emphasized.

39511 ■ "Do We Need Human Drivers?" in Sacramento Business Journal (Vol. 31, August 29, 2014, No. 27, pp. 3)
Pub: American City Business Journals
Released: August 29, 2014. **Description:** The California Department of Motor Vehicles (DMV) issued new regulations on autonomous vehicles, effective September 16, 2014, as Google prepares to test a new generation of self-driving cars. The DMV requires test drivers to take immediate physical control of an autonomous vehicle that may involve installation of a manual override feature.

39512 ■ "Doctor: J and J Alerted in '06 to Procedure Risks" in Pittsburgh Business Times (Vol. 33, June 6, 2014, No. 47, pp. 4)
Pub: American City Business Journals
Released: June 6, 2014. **Description:** Dr. Robert Lamparter, then pathologist at Lewisburg's Evangelical Community Hospital, states that he had alerted Johnson and Johnson (J and J) in 2006 of the potential risk of spreading undetected cancer following the use of its power morcellator during hysterectomy procedures. J and J suspended worldwide sales of the device in April 2014 after the laboratory warning, and days after a US Food and Drug Administration advisory discouraging doctors from using it, but doctors are still divided over the morcellation procedure.

39513 ■ "Doctor Shortage Continues to Plague Region" in Business First of Buffalo (Vol. 30, April 11, 2014, No. 30, pp. 6)
Pub: American City Business Journals, Inc.
Contact: Whitney Shaw, President
Released: April 11, 2014. **Description:** New York hospitals need at least 1,000 additional physicians, particularly primary care doctors, as they try to meet the criteria set by Federal health reform's Affordable Care Act. The Western New York region gained only 421 new physicians, while losing 544 in 2013.

39514 ■ "Does it Add Up?" in Canadian Business (Vol. 81, October 13, 2008, No. 17, pp. 18)
Ed: Jack Mintz. **Description:** Views on Canada's tax policy, as well as on tax reforms planned by major parties and their expected economic impact are discussed. The Tories' proposal to cut federal diesel fuel tax is seen as politically smart, but reforms on other taxes could help generate economic growth. High income tax rates are believed to discourage talented individuals from working in Canada.

39515 ■ "Dog Days and Stimulus Fatigue" in Barron's (Vol. 92, August 25, 2012, No. 38, pp. M10)
Pub: Dow Jones & Co., Inc.
Contact: Clare Hart, President
Ed: Michael Aneiro. **Description:** Credit market movements in August 2012 have been influenced by small news and speculation. US Federal Reserve Chairman Ben Bernanke has been more transparent, yet this transparency can also confound investors.

39516 ■ Doing Business Anywhere: The Essential Guide to Going Global
Pub: John Wiley & Sons Inc.
Contact: Stephen M. Smith, President
Ed: Tom Travis. **Description:** Plans are given for new or existing businesses to organize, plan, operate and execute a business on a global basis. Trade agreements, brand protection and patents, ethics, security as well as cultural issues are among the issues addressed. **Availability:** E-book.

39517 ■ "DOL Stiffens Child Labor Penalties" in HR Specialist (Vol. 8, September 2010, No. 9, pp. 2)
Pub: Capitol Information Group Inc.
Description: U.S. Department of Labor (DOL) will impose new penalties for employers that violate U.S. child labor laws. Details of the new law are included.

39518 ■ "Domestic Workers Organize!" in WorkingUSA (Vol. 11, December 2008, No. 4, pp. 413)
Ed: Eileen Boris, Premilla Nadasen. **Description:** History of domestic workers in the U.S. is examined. The article challenges the long-standing assumption that these, primarily women of color cleaners, nannies, and elder care providers are unable to organize and assesses the possibilities and limitations of recent organizing efforts. The nature of the occupation, its location in the home, the isolated character of the work, informal arrangements with employers, and exclusions from labor law protection, has fostered community-based, social movement organizing to build coalitions, reform legislation and draw public attention to the plight of domestic workers.

39519 ■ "Don't Expect Quick Fix" in The Business Journal-Serving Metropolitan Kansas City (Vol. 27, October 3, 2008, No. 3, pp. 1)
Pub: American City Business Journals, Inc.
Contact: Whitney Shaw, President
Ed: James Dornbrook. **Description:** United States governmental entities cannot provide a quick fix solution to the current financial crisis. The economy requires a systemic change in the way people think about credit. The financial services industry should also focus on core lending principles.

39520 ■ "Don't Fall Foul of Farming's Workplace Killer" in Farmer's Weekly (March 28, 2008, No. 320)
Description: Discusses the Work at Height Regulations that were introduced to reduce the risk of injury and death caused by accidental falls in the workplace.

39521 ■ "Down the Tracks, a Whistle Is a-Blowin'" in Barron's (Vol. 89, July 27, 2009, No. 30, pp. 36)
Pub: Dow Jones & Co., Inc.
Contact: Clare Hart, President
Ed: Jim McTague. **Description:** Higher numbers of freight-rail carloads are a sign that the economy is improving and it is no stretch to imagine that this is aided by the American Recovery and Reinvestment Act. It is also predicted that 2009 municipal bond issuance will be above $373 billion with at least $55 billion of it made up of Buy America Bonds that are subsidized by the federal government.

39522 ■ "Duro Bag to Expand, Add 130 Jobs" in Business Courier (Vol. 27, August 6, 2010, No. 14, pp. 1)
Pub: Business Courier
Ed: Jon Newberry. **Description:** Duro Bag Manufacturing Company will expand capacity at its Florence, Kentucky plant and will add around 130 jobs over the next few years. The state of Kentucky has given preliminary approval for up to $1 million in tax incentives over 10 years, tied to the creation of new jobs. The company's investment will include new production and packaging equipment and building improvements.

39523 ■ E-Commerce in Regional Small to Medium Enterprises
Pub: IGI Global
Contact: Dr. Mehdi Khosrow-Pour, President
Ed: Robert MacGregor, Lejla Vrazalic. **Released:** June 2007. **Price:** $99.95. **Description:** Strategies small to medium enterprises (SMEs) need to implement in order to compete with larger, global businesses and the role electronic commerce plays in this process are outlined. Studies of e-commerce in multiple regional areas, focusing on the role of business size, business sector, market focus, gender of CEO, and education level of the CEO are discussed. **Availability:** Print; E-book.

39524 ■ "Economists Warn Against Smart Cap" in Orlando Business Journal (Vol. 29, September 21, 2012, No. 14, pp. 1)
Pub: American City Business Journal
Ed: Abraham Aboraya, Richard Bilbao. **Description:** Opponents to the proposed amendment to the Florida State Revenue Limitations warn about the economic impact of the plan to cap state government spending. Under the proposal, the amount of taxes that the state should spend each year will be capped and a rainy day fund will be created where excess revenue collected will be placed.

39525 ■ "Editorial: Competition At Last?" in Canadian Business (Vol. 81, July 22, 2008, No. 12-13, pp. 7)
Pub: Rogers Media Inc.
Contact: Tony Viner, President
Description: Competition Policy Review Panel's 'Compete to Win' report revealed that Canada is being 'hollowed-out' by foreign acquisitions. The panel investigated competition and foreign investment policies in Canada. Key information on the report, as well as views on the Investment Canada Act and the Competition Act, is presented.

39526 ■ *"EEOC Issues Enforcement Guidance Addressing Pregnancy-Related Disabilities" in Idaho Business Review (August 18, 2014)*

Pub: Dolan Co.

Contact: James P. Dolan, President

Released: August 18, 2014. **Description:** An overview of the Pregnancy Discrimination Act (PDA) is presented. The EEOC is finally addressing this prohibited form of discrimination again pregnant women in the workplace. Requirements that link pregnancy-related disabilities with duties imposed by the Americans With Disabilities Act are covered.

39527 ■ *Effect of the Overvalued Dollar on Small Exporters: Hearing Before the Committee on Small Business, U.S. House of Representatives*

Pub: DIANE Publishing Co.

Contact: Dorothy J. Perkins, Manager

E-mail: dorothyjperkins@hotmail.com

Released: September 2002. **Price:** $30. **Description:** Congressional hearing: Witnesses: Dr. Lawrence Chimerine, Economist; Tony Raimondo, President and CEO, Behlen Manufacturing Company; Robert J. Weskamp, President, Wes-Tech, Inc.; Wayne Dollar, President, Georgia Farm Bureau; and Vargese George, President and CEO, Westex International, Inc. Appendix includes correspondence sent to committee on the overvalued dollar. **Availability:** Print.

39528 ■ *"Elanco Challenges Bayer's Advantage, K9 Advantix Ad Claims" in Pet Product News (Vol. 64, November 2010, No. 11, pp. 11)*

Pub: Bowtie Inc.

Description: Elanco Animal Health has disputed Bayer Animal Health's print and Web advertising claims involving its flea, tick, and mosquito control products Advantage and K9 Advantix. The National Advertising Division of the Council of Better Business Bureaus recommended the discontinuation of ads, while Bayer Animal Health reiterated its commitment to self-regulation.

39529 ■ *"Elder Care: New Law Can Disrupt Home: State Rules Can Send Assisted Living Residents Packing. Families, Advocates Fear Consequences" in Atlanta Journal-Constitution (February 20, 2012, pp. D1)*

Description: Debra Ben-Dor, newly appointed executive director of Atria Johnson Ferry in Marietta, Georgia, sent letters to families of loved ones residing in the assisted living facility. Under new Georgia rules for assisted living communities, such facilities can discharge a resident if he or she develops a physical or mental condition that requires continual medical or nursing care. Details of this new law are examined.

39530 ■ *"Elder Care, Rx Drug Reforms Top Zoeller's Agenda" in Times (December 21, 2010)*

Pub: The Times

Ed: Sarah Tompkins. **Description:** Indiana Attorney General Greg Zoeller is hoping to develop a program in the state that will help regulate care for the elderly; freeze medical licenses for doctors involved in criminal investigations; address illegal drug use; and to establish a program to help individuals dispose of old prescription medications easily at pharmacies.

39531 ■ *"Election Could Undo Renewable Energy Quotas" in The Business Journal - Serving Phoenix and the Valley of the Sun (Vol. 28, July 11, 2008, No. 45, pp. 1)*

Pub: American City Business Journals, Inc.

Contact: Whitney Shaw, President

Ed: Patrick O'Grady. **Description:** Competition for the three open seats in the Arizona Corporation Commission is intense, with 12 candidates contesting for the three slots. The commission's mandates for renewable energy and infrastructure investment will also be at stake.

39532 ■ *"Election Futures are a Smart Idea" in Canadian Business (Vol. 85, June 11, 2012, No. 10, pp. 18)*

Pub: George Media Inc.

Ed: Mike Moffatt. **Released:** June 11, 2012. **Description:** The decision of the U.S. Commodity Futures Trading Commission to ban political-event derivatives contracts was criticized along with the idea that such products could cause a systemic financial collapse. Political derivatives can be used as tools to help reduce risk and predict future political events.

39533 ■ *Electronic Commerce: Technical, Business, and Legal Issues*

Ed: Oktay Dogramaci; Aryya Gangopadhyay; Yelena Yesha; Nabil R. Adam. **Released:** August 1998. **Description:** Provides insight into the goals of using the Internet to grow a business in the areas of networking and telecommunication, security, and storage and retrieval; business areas such as marketing, procurement and purchasing, billing and payment, and supply chain management; and legal aspects such as privacy, intellectual property, taxation, contractual and legal settlements.

39534 ■ *"Eminent Domain Fight Looks Imminent" in The Business Journal-Serving Metropolitan Kansas City (Vol. 26, August 1, 2008, No. 47)*

Pub: American City Business Journals, Inc.

Contact: Whitney Shaw, President

Ed: Rob Roberts. **Description:** Views and information on the proposed constitutional amendments that will limit the use of eminent domain in Missouri, are presented. The proposals are expected to largely ban the taking of private property for private development. It may be included in a November 4,2008 statewide vote for approval.

39535 ■ *"Emissions: Cloudy Skies" in Canadian Business (Vol. 81, October 27, 2008, No. 18, pp. 101)*

Pub: Rogers Media Inc.

Contact: Tony Viner, President

Ed: Andrew Wahl. **Description:** Canada's federal government is expected to implement its regulations on greenhouse-gas emissions by January 1, 2010, but companies are worried because the plan took so long and some details are yet to be revealed. Corporate Canada wants a firm, long-range plan similar to the European Union Emissions Trading Scheme in dealing with greenhouse-gas emissions.

39536 ■ *The Employer's Legal Advisor*

Pub: AMACOM

Contact: Edward T. Reilly, Manager

Ed: Thomas M. Hanna. **Released:** April 2007. **Price:** $24; C$30. **Description:** Attorney provides tips for reducing the possibility of a lawsuit and winning a case if one does go to court. **Availability:** Print.

39537 ■ *"Employers Tied in Knots" in Sacramento Business Journal (Vol. 25, August 15, 2008, No. 24, pp. 1)*

Pub: American City Business Journals, Inc.

Contact: Whitney Shaw, President

Ed: Kathy Robertson. **Description:** Conflicting laws on same sex marriage have been posing problems for companies, and insurers in California. The court ruling that allowed gay marriages has created differences between state and federal laws. Federal laws on same-sex spouse taxation are also seen to complicate the issue.

39538 ■ *"Empty Lots Could Be Full of Promise" in San Francisco Business Times (Vol. 28, March 14, 2014, No. 34, pp. 4)*

Pub: American City Business Journals

Released: March 14, 2014. **Description:** San Francisco, California officials are looking at the city's own landholdings in order to start constructing new homes. However, the use of city-owned land does not ensure that the home permit process will be trouble-free.

39539 ■ *Enabling Environments for Jobs and Entrepreneurship: The Role of Policy and Law in Small Enterprise Employment*

Ed: Gerhard Reinecke. **Released:** February 2004. **Price:** , $83.25. **Description:** National policies, laws and regulations governing workplace safety.

39540 ■ *"End of the Beginning" in Canadian Business (Vol. 81, November 10, 2008, No. 19, pp. 17)*

Pub: Rogers Media Inc.

Contact: Tony Viner, President

Ed: David Wolf. **Description:** The freeze in the money markets and historic decline in equity markets around the world finally forced governments into aggressive coordinated action. The asset price inflation brought on by cheap credit will now work in reverse and the tightening of credit will be difficult economically. Canada is exposed to the fallout everywhere, given that the U.S, the U.K. and Japan buy 30 percent of Canada's output.

39541 ■ *"The End of Clock-Punching" in Canadian Business (Vol. 83, September 14, 2010, No. 15, pp. 96)*

Pub: Rogers Media Inc.

Contact: Tony Viner, President

Ed: Lyndsie Bourgon. **Description:** Workplace consultant Peter Hadwen is pushing for the transformation of Canada's government departments into results-only work environments (ROWE). ROWE does not require employees to show up to work at a certain time as long as they are meeting goals and achieving results in their jobs. Details of studies regarding ROWE in US companies are examined.

39542 ■ *"Ending the Ebola Death Sentence" in Canadian Business (Vol. 83, August 17, 2010, No. 13-14, pp. 22)*

Ed: Michael McCullough. **Description:** US Army Medical Research Institute of Infectious Diseases made a $140 million agreement with Tekmira Pharmaceuticals Corporation to develop both a drug delivery system and delivery technology for curing the Ebola virus. Tekmira's delivery technology, which has been shown to halt Ebola in laboratory animals, might be the key to finding a cure.

39543 ■ *"Energy Efficiency Ordinance Softened" in Austin Business JournalInc. (Vol. 28, October 3, 2008, No. 29)*

Pub: American City Business Journals

Ed: Jean Kwon. **Description:** City of Austin has eliminated mandatory energy efficiency upgrades to single-family housing as a condition for selling or renting homes or buildings. The new law proposes that an energy performance audit be conducted on single-family homes before being sold and the results of the audit disclosed to perspectives buyers.

39544 ■ *"Energy Firms Face Stricter Definitions" in Globe & Mail (March 26, 2007, pp. B3)*

Pub: CTVglobemedia Publishing Inc.

Ed: David Ebner. **Description:** The Alberta Securities Commission has imposed strict securities regulations on oil and gas industries. Energy industries will have to submit revenue details to stake holders.

39545 ■ *"Enforcer In Fantasyland" in Crain's New York Business (Vol. 24, February 25, 2008, No. 8, pp. 10)*

Ed: Hilary Potkewitz. **Description:** Patent law, particularly in the toy and game industry, is recession-proof according to Barry Negrin, partner at Pryor Cashman. Negrin co-founded his patent practice group. Despite massive recalls of toys and the concern over toxic toys, legal measures are in place in this industry.

39546 ■ *Entrepreneurship and Technology Policy*

Pub: Edward Elgar Publishing Inc.

Contact: Richard Henning, Vice President

E-mail: kwight@e-elgar.com

Released: 2006. **Price:** £108. **Description:** Journal articles focusing how and the ways small businesses' technical contributions are affecting business. The book is divided into four parts: Government's Direct Support of R&D, Government's Leveraging of R&D, Government's Infrastructure Policies; and Knowledge Flows from Universities and Laboratories. **Availability:** Print.

39547 ■ *"EPA Grants E15 Waiver for 2001-2006 Vehicles" in Farm Industry News (January 21, 2011)*
Pub: Penton Business Media Inc.
Contact: David Kieselstein, Chief Executive Officer
Ed: Lynn Grooms. **Description:** U.S. Environmental Protection Agency waived a limitation on selling gasoline that contains more than 10 percent ethanol for model year 2001-2006 cars and light trucks, allowing fuel to contain up to 15 percent ethanol (E15) for these vehicles.

39548 ■ *"Equity 'Crowdfunding' Platform, RelayFund, Launched by Michigan Investor Group" in Economics Week (July 20, 2012)*
Pub: NewsRX
Contact: Susan E. Hasty, Publisher
Released: July 20, 2012. **Description:** RelayFund was launched by a group of Michigan venture capitalists, entrepreneurs, and investment bankers to link small investors with startup firms under the new JOBS (Jumpstart Our Business Startups) Act. Crowdfunding is money raised for charities, projects or pre-selling products or services and allows online micro investments for startup companies.

39549 ■ *"Errors in Tax Preparation by Mo' Money Taxes Cited" in Commerical Appeal (March 30, 2012)*
Pub: McClatchy-Tribune Information Services
Ed: Ted Evanoff. Released: March 30, 2012. **Description:** Mo' Money LLC is facing fraud and excessive fee charges by Attorney Generals in both Illinois and Missouri along with its sister firm MoneyCo USA LLC. Details of complaints filed against the company that is claiming software problems as the culprit.

39550 ■ *"Evaluating the 1996-2006 Employment Projections" in Montly Labor Review (Vol. 133, September 2010, No. 9, pp. 33)*
Pub: U.S. Department of Labor Bureau of Labor Statistics
Contact: Philip L. Rones, Manager
E-mail: rones.philip@bls.gov
Description: Bureau of Labor Statistics employment projections outperformed alternative naive models, but not projecting the housing bubble or the rise in oil prices caused some inaccuracies in the projects. These projections are used by policymakers, economists, and students.

39551 ■ *"Executives Exit at Wal-Mart in China" in Wall Street Journal Eastern Edition (October 17 , 2011, pp. B3)*
Pub: Dow Jones & Co., Inc.
Contact: Clare Hart, President
Ed: Laurie Burkitt. **Description:** Woes for Wal-Mart Inc.'s subsidiary in China are adding up as Wal-Mart China president and chief executive Ed Chan stepped down, as well as the company's senior vice president for human resources, Clara Wong. The company has been charged by regulators with mislabeling pork products, the result which has forced stores to close. Sales in China have been slow at the retail stores.

39552 ■ *"Expect Action on Health Care and the Economy" in Contractor (Vol. 57, January 2010, No. 1, pp. 30)*
Pub: Penton Media, Inc.
Ed: Kevin Schwalb. **Description:** The Plumbing-Heating-Cooling Contractors National Association is working to solidify its standing in the public policy arena as the legislative agenda will focus on health care reform, estate tax and immigration reform, all of which will impact the industries.

39553 ■ *"Expert Sees No Radical Reform of 401(K) System" in Workforce Management (Vol. 88, November 16, 2009, No. 12, pp. 12)*
Ed: Ed Frauenheim. **Description:** Although many would like to see an overhaul of the 401(k) retirement system, it is unlikely to occur anytime soon; however, the drastic stock market drop of 2008 has raised pointed questions about the 401(k) system and if it enables a secure retirement for American workers.

39554 ■ *"Experts Take the Temp of Obama Plan" in The Business Journal-Serving Metropolitan Kansas City (Vol. 27, November 14, 2008, No. 10)*
Pub: American City Business Journals, Inc.
Contact: Rob Roberts. **Description:** Kansas City, Missouri-based employee benefits experts say president-elect Barack Obama's health care reform plan is on track. Insurance for children and capitalization for health information technology are seen as priority areas. The plan is aimed at reducing the number of uninsured people in the United States.

39555 ■ *"Extortion: How Politicians Extract Your Money, Buy Votes, and Line Their Own Pockets"*
Pub: Mariner Books
Contact: Barry O'Callaghan, Chief Executive Officer
Released: October 7, 2014. **Price:** , $14.95 paperback. **Description:** Politicians and lawmakers have developed a new set of legislative tactics designed to extort wealthy industries and donors into huge contributions. This money is then funneled into the pockets of their friends and family members. Schweizer reveals the secret 'fees' each political party charges politicians for top committee assignments; how fourteen members of Congress received hundreds of thousands of dollars using a self-loan loophole; how PAC money is used to bankroll their lavish lifestyles; and more. The first time these unethical issues have been reported to the public.

39556 ■ *"Fair Play? China Cheats, Carney Talks and Rankin Walks; Here's the Latest" in Canadian Business (Vol. 81, March 17, 2008, No. 4)*
Pub: Rogers Media Inc.
Contact: Tony Viner, President
Description: Discusses the World Trade Organization which says that China is breaking trade rules by taxing imports of auto parts at the same rate as foreign-made finished cars. Mark Carney first speech as the governor of the Bank of Canada made economists suspect a rate cut on overnight loans. Andre Rankin was ordered by the Ontario Securities Commission to pay $250,000 in investigation costs.

39557 ■ *"Fair Tax Backers Hope MBT Anger Will Bring Votes" in Crain's Detroit Business (Vol. 24, March 31, 2008, No. 13, pp. 32)*
Pub: Crain Communications Inc.
Contact: Rance E. Crain, President
Ed: Amy Lane. **Description:** Discusses the Michigan Fair Tax Proposal which would eliminate Michigan's business taxes and income tax, raise the state sales tax to 9.75 percent and expand it to services.

39558 ■ *"Familiar Fun" in Crain's Cleveland Business (Vol. 28, October 22, 2007, No. 42, pp. 3)*
Ed: John Booth. **Description:** Marketing for the 2007 holiday season has toy retailers focusing on American-made products because of recent recalls of toys produced in China that do not meet U.S. safety standards.

39559 ■ *"Family Child Care Record-Keeping Guide, Ninth Edition (Redleaf Business Series)"*
Pub: Redleaf Press
Contact: Linda Hein, Director
E-mail: lhein@redleafpress.org
Released: October 28,, 2014. **Price:** , $17.95 paperback. **Description:** Writer, trainer, lawyer, and consultant provides concise information for home-based family child care (day care) providers. The book covers tracking expenses, being profitable, filing taxes, and meeting government regulations. This resources covers the process of accurate bookkeeping and recordkeeping to take advantage of all allowable tax deductions. Changes in depreciation rules, adjustments to food and mileage rates, and clarifications on how to calculate the Time-Space percentage are defined.

39560 ■ *"Fannie and Freddie: How They'll Change" in Business Week (September 22, 2008, No. 4100, pp. 30)*
Ed: Jane Sasseen. **Description:** Three possible outcomes of the fate of struggling mortgage giants Freddie Mac and Fannie Mae after the government bailout are outlined.

39561 ■ *Fast-Track Business Start-Up Kit: California*
Pub: Kaplan Books
Ed: Carolyn Usinger. **Released:** 2006. **Price:** $22.95; C$29. **Description:** Step-by-step guide for starting and running a business in California, including information on sole proprietors, partnerships, limited liability companies, S and C corporations, as well as details concerning business entities, sales taxes, environmental issues, human resources, and more.

39562 ■ *"The Favorite In the Casino, Racino Race" in Business Review Albany (Vol. 41, July 25, 2014, No. 18, pp. 7)*
Pub: The Business Journals
Released: July 25, 2014. **Description:** The New York Government's plan to license four casinos could adversely impact the earnings of racinos. Racinos combine harness racing with video slot machines. The planned casinos are expected to attract racino customers creating competition.

39563 ■ *"FCC Adopts New Media Ownership Rules" in Black Enterprise (Vol. 38, March 1, 2008, No. 8, pp. 26)*
Pub: Earl G. Graves Publishing Co. Inc.
Contact: Earl G. Graves, Jr., President
Ed: Joyce Jones. **Description:** Federal Communications Commission approved a ruling that lifts a ban on newspaper and/or broadcast cross ownership. Because of declining sales in newspaper advertising and readership the ban will allow companies to share local news gathering costs across multiple media platforms.

39564 ■ *"Fed May Ban Amphibian Trade" in Pet Product News (Vol. 64, November 2010, No. 11, pp. 13)*
Pub: Bowtie Inc.
Description: U.S. Fish and Wildlife Service is seeking public input on a petition submitted by the conservation activist group Defenders of Wildlife. The petition involves possible classification of chytrid fungus-infected amphibians and amphibian eggs as 'injurious wildlife' under the Lacey Act. Interstate trading or importation of injurious wildlife into the U.S. is not allowed.

39565 ■ *"Feds Finalize I-9 Form Rules Allowing Electronic Storage" in HR Specialist (Vol. 8, September 2010, No. 9, pp. 5)*
Pub: Capitol Information Group Inc.
Description: U.S. Department of Homeland Security issued regulations that give employers more flexibility to electronically sing and store I-9 employee verification forms.

39566 ■ *"Feds, Not City, Will Pick GSA Office Site" in Business Journal-Serving Metropolitan Kansas City (Vol. 26, November 30, 2007, No. 12)*
Pub: American City Business Journals, Inc.
Contact: Whitney Shaw, President
Ed: Jim Davis. **Description:** Mark Funkhouser wants the federal government to decide the location of the General Services Administration building site. The act of the Mayor enraged the executive director of Kansas City Port Authority, Vincent Gauthier. Details of the GSAs building location plans are discussed.

39567 ■ *"A Few Points of Contention" in Barron's (Vol. 88, July 14, 2008, No. 28, pp. 3)*
Pub: Dow Jones & Co., Inc.
Contact: Clare Hart, President
Ed: Michael Santoli. **Description:** Headline inflation tends to revert to the lower core inflation, which excludes food and energy in its calculation over long periods. Prominent private equity figures believe that regulators should allow more than the de facto 10 percent to 25 percent limit of commercial banks to hasten the refunding of the financial sector.

39568 ■ "Film Incentives: A Hit or a Flop?" in Michigan Vue (Vol. 13, July-August 2008, No. 4, pp. 10)
Description: Michigan's new film incentive legislation is fulfilling its core purpose, according to Lisa Dancsok of the Michigan Economic Development Corp. (MEDC), by kickstarting the state's entry into the multi-billion dollar industry; the initiative is considered to be very competitive with other states and countries and is thought to be a way in which to help revitalize Michigan's struggling economy.

39569 ■ "Final State Budget Is a Mixed Bag of Key Industries" in The Business Journal - Serving Phoenix and the Valley of the Sun (Vol. 28, July 4, 2008, No. 44, pp. 3)
Pub: American City Business Journals, Inc.
Contact: Whitney Shaw, President
Ed: Mike Sunnucks, Patrick O'Grady. **Description:** Approved by Governor Janet Napolitano and passed by the Arizona Legislature, the $9.9 billion state budget is beneficial to some industries in the business community. The tax cap for on Arizona Lottery has been removed which is beneficial to the industry, while the solar energy industry and real estate developers stand to lose from the spending bill. Other details of the finance budget are presented.

39570 ■ "Finally! Windsor Gets a New Bridge" in Canadian Business (Vol. 85, September 17, 2012, No. 14, pp. 20)
Pub: George Media Inc.
Ed: Tim Shufelt. **Released:** September 17, 2012.
Description: Canadian Prime Minister Stephen Harper agreed to loan Michigan $550 million to build its new highway interchange and customs plaza linking Windsor, Ontario and Detroit, Michigan. Billionaire Manuel Maroun, owner of the Ambassador Bridge, has initiated a signature campaign for a referendum on any new border crossings.

39571 ■ "Financing for NNSA Plant Is a Work in Progress" in The Business Journal-Serving Metropolitan Kansas City (October 24, 2008)
Ed: Rob Roberts. **Description:** The Kansas City Council approved a development plan for a $500 million nuclear weapons parts plant in south Kansas City. The US Congress approved a $59 million annual lease payment to the plant's developer. Financing for the construction of the plant remains in question as the plant's developers have to shoulder construction costs.

39572 ■ "Firm Restricts Cellphone Use While Driving" in Globe & Mail (January 30, 2006, pp. B3)
Ed: Catherine McLean. **Description:** The details on AMEC Plc, which adopted cellphone-free driving policy, are presented.

39573 ■ "First Sustainability Standard for Household Portable and Floor Care Appliances Developed to Identify Environmentally Responsible Products" in Ecology, Environment & Conservation Business (September 13, 2014, pp. 39)
Pub: NewsRX
Contact: Susan E. Hasty, Publisher
Released: September 13, 2014. **Description:** the Association of Home Appliance Manufacturers (AHAM), CSA Group, and the UL Environment released the AHAM 7002-2014/CSA SPE-7002-14/UL 7002, Sustainability Standard for Household Portable and Floor Care Appliances. This is the first voluntary sustainability standards for these appliances and is the third in a unit of product sustainability standards under development by the group. These standards are intended for use by manufacturers, governments, retailers, and others to identify products conforming to these standards in six key areas: materials, manufacturing and operations, energy consumption during use, end-of-life, consumables, and innovation.

39574 ■ "First-Time Landlord: Your Guide to Renting Out a Single-Family Home"
Pub: Nolo
Contact: Ralph Warner, Chief Executive Officer
Released: September 30, 2014. **Price:** , $24.99 paperback. **Description:** The basics for becoming an landlord for anyone wishing to start an entrepreneurial pursuit in home rentals are outlined. Concise information for renting out a single-family home includes, how to determine whether the property will turn a profit, landlord business basics, finding the right tenants, preparing and signing a lead, handling repairs, complying with state rental laws, dealing with problem tenants, and preparing for the sale of the property.

39575 ■ "5 Things You Should Know If Your Bank Fails" in Black Enterprise (Vol. 41, December 2010, No. 5, pp. 29)
Pub: Earl G. Graves Publishing Co. Inc.
Contact: Earl G. Graves, Jr., President
Ed: John Simons. **Description:** The Federal Deposit Insurance Corporation announced that the number of banks in trouble has reached the highest level since March 1993. Advice from the FDIC is cited. Statistical data included.

39576 ■ The Flaw of Averages: Why We Underestimate Risk in the Face of Uncertainty
Pub: John Wiley & Sons Inc.
Contact: Stephen M. Smith, President
Ed: Sam L. Savage. **Released:** March 2012. **Price:** $19.95, paperback; $12.99. **Description:** Personal and business plans are based on uncertainties on a daily basis. The common avoidable mistake individuals make in assessing risk in the face of uncertainty is defined. The explains why plans based on average assumptions are wrong, on average, in areas as diverse as finance, healthcare, accounting, the war on terror, and climate change. **Availability:** PrintEbook.

39577 ■ "'Focusing On the Moment" in Dallas Business Journal (Vol. 37, June 27, 2014, No. 42, pp. 4)
Pub: American City Business Journals
Released: June 27, 2014. **Description:** Southwest Airlines chairman, president, and CEO Gary Kelly, believes the key to the carrier's growth in 2014 will be to 'focus on the moment' and ensure that new projects are launched and strategies implemented successfully. Kelly discusses the potential impact of the repeal of the Wright Amendment on October 13, as well as Southwest's merger with AirTran and the launch of nonstop flights from New York and Washington DC.

39578 ■ "Food Truck Group Backs Proposed Regulations" in Buffalo News (January 18, 2012)
Pub: McClatchy-Tribune Information Services
Ed: Aaron Besecker. **Released:** January 18, 2012.
Description: Food truck operators in the city of Buffalo, New York have accepted the newly created rules governing their operations in the city, despite the higher-than-expected $1,000 permit fee. An attorney for the Western New York Food Truck Association stated that the proposed rules would be acceptable to the membership.

39579 ■ "For All It's Worth" in Entrepreneur (Vol. 36, April 2008, No. 4, pp. 46)
Pub: Entrepreneur Press
Contact: Perlman Neil, President
Ed: Farnoosh Torabi. **Description:** Discusses the federal estate tax system requires that 45 percent of the money beyond $2 million be given to the government. Ways on how to minimize the effects of estate tax on assets include: creating bypass trusts for married couples; setting up an irrevocable life insurance trust to avoid taxation of estate for insurance benefactors; and having annual gift tax exclusion.

39580 ■ "For Yung, Lady Luck a Fickle Mistress" in Business Courier (Vol. 24, November 29, 2007, No. 33, pp. 1)
Pub: American City Business Journals, Inc.
Contact: Whitney Shaw, President
Ed: Dan Monk. **Description:** Bill Yung's Columbia Sussex Corp. won the bid for the parent company of Tropicana casinos in November 2006, and a year after, the company is facing regulatory and labor issues.

39581 ■ "Former Prov. Mayor Sees Potential in Newport Grand" in Providence Business News (Vol. 29, July 21, 2014, No. 16, pp. 4)
Pub: American City Business Journals
Released: July 21, 2014. **Description:** Joseph R. Paolino, Jr., managing partner at Paolino Properties and former Providence Mayor, believes introducing table games to Newport Grand can help the gambling casino generate needed revenues. Paolino notes that if voters approve a ballot referendum to authorize table games in November, he and his partners will acquire and renovate Newport Grand as an entertainment center.

39582 ■ "Former Synthes Officers Receive Prison Sentences" in Wall Street Journal Eastern Edition (November 22 , 2011, pp. B4)
Pub: Dow Jones & Co., Inc.
Contact: Clare Hart, President
Ed: Peter Loftus. **Description:** Michael D. Huggins, formerly chief operating officer of medical-device maker Synthes Ltd., and Thomas B. Higgins, formerly the president of Synthes spine unit, were given prison sentences of nine months while a third executive, John J. Walsh, formerly director of regulatory and clinical affairs in the spine division, was given a five-month sentence for their involvement in the promotion of the unauthorized use of a bone cement produced by the company.

39583 ■ "Forsys Metals Corporation Goes "Live" With Q4's On-Demand Disclosure Management Software" in Canadian Corporate News (May 16, 2007)
Description: Forsys Metals Corp. selected Q4 Web Systems to automate its corporate website disclosure with Q4's software platform which also automates and simplifies many of the administrative tasks that Forsys was doing manually, allowing them to focus their internal resources on the business.

39584 ■ "Four Ways to Fix Banks: a Wall Street Veteran Suggests How To Cut Through the Industry's Complexity" in (Vol. 90, June 2012, No. 6, pp. 106)
Pub: Harvard Business Review Press
Contact: Peter E. Walsh, Director
Ed: Sallie Krawcheck. **Released:** June 2012. **Description:** Despite new regulations in the post-global economic crisis of 2008, banks are sill too complex for effective management of their boards. Recommendations for improving governance include incorporating bank debt in executive compensation to increase their sensitivity to risk, and paying dividends as a percentage of company earnings to maintain capital.

39585 ■ "Free Speech Vs. Privacy in Data Mining" in Information Today (Vol. 28, September 2011, No. 8, pp. 22)
Pub: Information Today, Inc.
Contact: Thomas H. Hogan, President
E-mail: ctuthill@infotoday.com
Ed: George H. Pike. **Description:** The U.S. Constitution does not explicitly guarantee the right of privacy. Organizations and businesses that require obtaining and disseminating information can be caught in the middle of privacy rights. The long-term impact on data mining, Internet marketing, and Internet privacy issues are examined.

39586 ■ "A Baby Step to the South" in Canadian Business (Vol. 81, July 22, 2008, No. 12-13, pp. 21)
Pub: Rogers Media Inc.
Contact: Tony Viner, President
Ed: Jane Bao. **Description:** Canada's free trade agreement (FTA) with Colombia is seen as Canada's re-engagement with Latin America. Some politicians believe that the FTA is more of a political agreement than a trade agreement with Colombia. Key information on Canada's trade agreements, as well as trade with Colombia and Latin American countries, is presented.

39587 ■ "Freeing the Wheels of Commerce" in Hispanic Business (July-August 2007, pp. 50, 52, 54)
Pub: Hispanic Business Inc.
Contact: Jesus Chavarria, President
Ed: Keith Rosenblum. **Description:** SecureOrigins, a border-based partnership with high-tech innovators is working to move goods faster, more efficiently, and securely.

39588 ■ *"Fresh Direct's Crisis" in Crain's New York Business (Vol. 24, January 14, 2008, No. 2, pp. 3)*
Ed: Lisa Fickenscher. **Description:** Freshdirect, an Internet grocery delivery service, finds itself under siege from federal immigration authorities, customers and labor organizations due to its employment practice of hiring illegals. At stake is the grocer's reputation as well as its ambitious growth plans, including an initial public offering of its stock.

39589 ■ *"Fresh Off its IPO, HomeStreet Bank is Now the No. 2 Mortgage Lender in King County" in Puget Sound Business Journal (Vol. 33, June 15, 2012, No. 8, pp. 3)*
Pub: American City Business Journal
Ed: Greg Lamm. **Description:** HomeStreet Bank has hired 300 new workers to work in its mortgage lending business and plans to open 13 new loan centers. Such moves has positioned the bank as King County's top two mortgage lenders. Federal regulators ordered HomeStreet Banki three years ago to raise additional capital of tens of millions.

39590 ■ *"Fruit Juice Ads and Sour Grapes" in Canadian Business (Vol. 85, July 16, 2012, No. 11-12, pp. 17)*
Pub: George Media Inc.
Ed: Chris MacDonald. **Released:** July 16, 2012. **Description:** The U.S. Federal Trade Commission (FTC) ruled on May 21, 2012 that at least some of the advertisements by Pom Wonderful pomegranate juice made false and misleading claims about the beneficial health effects of their product. The company issued a set of advertisements implying that the FTC judge support their health claims, a move which appears to undermine the market itself.

39591 ■ *"FTC Issues Final Version of Green Guides: Revision Target Broad Claims, Force More Proof On Smaller Ones" in Advertising Age (Vol. 83, October 1, 2012, No. 36, pp. 5)*
Pub: Crain Communications Inc.
Contact: Rance E. Crain, President
Ed: Jack Neff. **Description:** Federal Trade Commission issued its final version of its Green Guides regulations to eliminate unclear, unsubstantiated or misleading environmental claims. The final Green Guides do not address two common words used in green marketing: sustainable and natural. However, the words green and eco-friendly qualified as specific claims.

39592 ■ *"FTC Takes Aim At Foreclosure 'Rescue' Firm" in The Business Journal-Serving Greater Tampa Bay (Vol. 28, September 19, 2008, No. 39)*
Pub: American City Business Journals, Inc.
Contact: Whitney Shaw, President
Ed: Michael Hinman. **Description:** United Home Savers LLP has been ordered to halt its mortgage foreclosure rescue services after the Federal Trade Commission accused it of deceptive advertising. The company is alleged to have charged customers $1,200 in exchange for unfulfilled promises to keep them in their homes.

39593 ■ *Fugitive Denim: A Moving Story of People and Pants in the Borderless World of Global Trade*
Pub: W.W. Norton and Company Inc.
Contact: A Malmud, President
Ed: Rachel Louise Snyder. **Released:** April 2009. **Price:** $26.95, hardcover; $16.95, paperback. **Description:** In-depth study of the global production and processes of how jeans are designed, sewn, and transported as well as how the cotton for denim is grown, regulated, purchased and processed. **Availability:** Print.

39594 ■ *"Full Speed Ahead?" in San Antonio Business Journal (Vol. 28, May 9, 2014, No. 13, pp. 4)*
Pub: American City Business Journals
Released: May 9, 2014. **Description:** Lyft and Uber Technologies Inc. have launched ride-sharing services in San Antonio, Texas without the city's permission and the objections of taxi and limousine industries. The ride-sharing service issues were brought

into court and to the City Council, while the San Antonio Police Department issued a cease-and-desist order to the ride-sharing companies. The complaints against Lyft and Uber are outlined.

39595 ■ *"Funders Fuel Explosion of Biotech Activity" in Puget Sound Business Journal (Vol. 35, July 11, 2014, No. 12, pp. 3A)*
Pub: American City Business Journals
Released: July 11, 2014. **Description:** Washington's life sciences industry is experiencing problems due to a lack of support from state lawmakers, but the industry is receiving capital through initial public offerings, partnerships and venture equity. Joel Marcus of Alexandria Real Estate Equities claims that capital flows are at their highest levels since the dot-com bubble.

39596 ■ *"Funds "Friend" Facebook" in Barron's (Vol. 89, July 27, 2009, No. 30, pp. 30)*
Pub: Dow Jones & Co., Inc.
Contact: Clare Hart, President
Ed: Leslie P. Norton. **Description:** Mutual-fund companies are the latest entrants to the 'social media' space and several companies have already set up Facebook and Twitter pages. The use of this technology pose special challenges for compliance and regulators especially since the Financial Industry Regulatory Authority reminds companies that advertising, sales and literature are governed by regulations.

39597 ■ *"Future Fuzzy at Former Pemco Plant" in Baltimore Business Journal (Vol. 32, July 25, 2014, No. 12, pp. 10)*
Pub: American City Business Journals, Inc.
Contact: Whitney Shaw, President
Released: July 25, 2014. **Description:** The abandoned Pemco Corporation site on Eastern Avenue in Southeast Baltimore faces an uncertain future as new owner, MCB Real Estate LLC, fails to specify its prospective development plans for the property. City Councilman, James B. Kraft, wants to restrict the amount of retail space to be built at the Pemco and might even delay filing legislation on the space until MCB provides more details for the 20-acre property.

39598 ■ *"Futures Shock for the CME" in Crain's Chicago Business (Vol. 31, November 10, 2008, No. 45, pp. 8)*
Pub: Crain Communications Inc.
Contact: Todd Johnson, Publisher
Ed: Ann Saphir. **Description:** Chicago-based CME Group Inc., the largest futures exchange operator in the U.S., is facing a potentially radically altered regulatory landscape as Congress weighs sweeping reform of financial oversight. The possible merger of the CFTC and the Securities and Exchange Commission are among CME's concerns. Other details of possible regulatory measures are provided.

39599 ■ *"Georgia Collection Agency Settles Allegations" in PaymentsSource (March 2, 2012)*
Pub: SourceMedia Inc.
Contact: James M. Malkin, Chief Executive Officer
Released: March 2, 2012. **Description:** Wyteria Dorsey and Michael Thornton of Dorsey Thornton & Associates LLC collection agency have agreed to pay a $15.5 million settlement with Georgia's Governor's Office of Consumer Protection in order to resolve allegations that the agency harrassed and deceived consumers.

39600 ■ *"German Win Through Sharing" in Canadian Business (Vol. 83, September 14, 2010, No. 15, pp. 16)*
Pub: Rogers Media Inc.
Contact: Tony Viner, President
Ed: Jordan Timm. **Description:** German economic historian Eckhard Hoffner has a two-volume work showing how German's relaxed attitude toward copyright and intellectual property helped it catch up to industrialized United Kingdom. Hoffner's research was in response to his interest in the usefulness of software patents. Information on the debate regarding Canada's copyright laws is given.

39601 ■ *"Get Prepared for New Employee Free Choice Act" in HRMagazine (Vol. 53, December 2008, No. 12, pp. 22)*
Ed: Allen Smith. **Description:** According to the director of global labor and employee relations with Ingersoll Rand Company, unions may have started having employees signing authorization cards in anticipation of the Employee Free Choice Act. Once signed, the cards are good for one year and employers would have only ten days in which to prepare for bargaining with unions over the first labor contract. The Act also requires these negotiations be subject to mandatory arbitration if a contract is not reached within 120 days of negotiations with unions, resulting in employers' wage rates, health insurance, retirement benefits and key language about flexibility would be determined by an arbitrator with no vested interest in the success of the company.

39602 ■ *"Getting NORA reauthorized is high priority" in Indoor Comfort Marketing (Vol. 70, February 2011, No. 2, pp. 14)*
Pub: Industry Publications Inc.
Contact: Shirleen Dorman, Editor
Description: The importance of reauthorizing the National Oilheat Research Alliance is stressed.

39603 ■ *"Getting Out of an IRS Mess" in Black Enterprise (Vol. 37, December 2006, No. 5, pp. 53)*
Pub: Earl G. Graves Publishing Co. Inc.
Contact: Earl G. Graves, Jr., President
Ed: Carolyn M. Brown. **Description:** Owing back taxes to the IRS can lead to huge penalties and interest. Here are some tips on how to handle paying the IRS what you owe them.

39604 ■ *"Getting Rid of Global Glitches: Choosing Software For Trade Compliance" in Black Enterprise (Vol. 41, September 2010, No. 2, pp. 48)*
Pub: Earl G. Graves Publishing Co. Inc.
Contact: Earl G. Graves, Jr., President
Ed: Marcia Wade Talbert. **Description:** Compliance software for trading with foreign companies must be compatible with the U.S. Census Bureau's Automated Export System (www.aesdirect.gov). It has to be current with regulatory requirements for any country in the world. Whether owners handle their own compliance or hire a logistics company, they need to be familiar with this software in order to access reports and improve transparency and efficiency of theft supply chain.

39605 ■ *"The GHG Quandary: Whose Problem Is It Anyway?" in Canadian Business (Vol. 81, September 15, 2008, No. 14-15, pp. 72)*
Ed: Matthew McClearn. **Description:** Nongovernmental organizations were able to revoke the permit for Imperial Oil Ltd's Kearl oilsands project on the grounds of its expected greenhouse gas emission but the court's ruling was rendered irrelevant by bureaucratic paper-shuffling shortly after. The idea of an environmental impact assessment as a guide to identify the consequences of a project is also discussed.

39606 ■ *"A Gift For Banking Reformers: JPMorgan's Bungle Reopens the Door to Tighter Regulation" in Canadian Business (Vol. 85, June 11, 2012, No. 10, pp. 12)*
Pub: George Media Inc.
Ed: Joe Castaldo. **Released:** June 11, 2012. **Description:** The trading strategy of JPMorgan Chase is being questioned on whether it violated the Volcker rule, which prohibits banks with government-insured deposits from proprietary trading. The U.S. bank reported loss of more than $2 billion in April 2012 and claimed that their trading strategy was a legitimate hedge, not speculation.

39607 ■ *"GM's Volt Woes Cast Shadow on E-Cars" in Wall Street Journal Eastern Edition (November 28, 2011, pp. B1)*
Pub: Dow Jones & Co., Inc.
Contact: Clare Hart, President
Ed: Sharon Terlep. **Description:** The future of electric cars is darkened with the government investigation by the National Highway Traffic Safety Administration

into General Motor Company's Chevy Volt after two instances of the car's battery packs catching fire during crash tests conducted by the Agency.

39608 ■ "The Good Guys of ABWA" in Women In Business (Vol. 63, Fall 2011, No. 3, pp. 9)

Pub: American Business Women's Association
Contact: Lorie Burch, President
Ed: Rene Street. Description: The American Business Women's Association (ABWA) was an all-woman group since its founding in 1949. However, a Supreme Court ruling in 1987 opened all-male and all-female organizations of the opposite sex. Some of the male members of the ABWA are Bill Hense, James Drager, and John Lester.

39609 ■ "A Good Step, But There's a Long Way to Go" in Business Week (September 22, 2008, No. 4100, pp. 10)

Ed: James C. Cooper. Description: Despite the historic action by the U.S. government to nationalize the mortgage giants Freddie Mac and Fannie Mae, rising unemployment rates may prove to be an even bigger roadblock to bringing back the economy from its downward spiral. The takeover is meant to restore confidence in the credit markets and help with the mortgage crisis but the rising rate in unemployment may make many households unable to take advantage of any benefits which arise from the bailout. Statistical data included.

39610 ■ "Government Says Self-Regulation of Online Privacy is Coming Up Short" in Advertising Age (Vol. 81, December 6, 2010, No. 43, pp. 1)

Pub: Crain Communications Inc.
Contact: Rance Crain, President
Ed: Edmund Lee. Description: U.S. Federal Trade Commission and the Department of Commerce are concerned about the current state of digital privacy and stated that self-regulation has not been sufficient to date.

39611 ■ "Gray Moves to Close Two Curious Tech Incentive Loopholes" in Washington Business Journal (Vol. 33, May 23, 2014, No. 5, pp. 12)

Pub: American City Business Journals
Released: May 23, 2014. Description: District of Columbia Mayor Vincent Gray, has included in his budge recommendations small changes to definitions of a 'Qualified High Technology Company'. The proposals would expand the excluded industries into an online or brick-and-mortar retail store and a construction company from eligibility to claim the government tech incentives. The current incentive loopholes are outlined.

39612 ■ "The Great Cleanup" in Canadian Business (Vol. 81, April 14, 2008, No. 6, pp. 50)

Pub: Rogers Media Inc.
Contact: Tony Viner, President
Ed: Graham Silnicki. Description: China's rectification program includes the licensing of 100 percent of food producers and monitoring of 100 percent of raw materials for exports between August and December, 2007. There is a lot of money to be made for those who are willing to help China win its quality battle. PharmEng International Inc. is one of the companies that helps Chinese companies meet international quality standards.

39613 ■ "The Great Deformation: The Corruption of Capitalism in America"

Pub: PublicAffairs
Released: April 2, 2013. Price: , $35.00. Description: Washington's response to the recent financial crises and fiscal mismanagement is covered. The author provides a catalogue of economic corrupters and defenders of sound money, fiscal rectitude, and free markets. The book covers the history of political statesmen who championed balanced budgets and financial market discipline. The threat to free market prosperity and American political democracy are examined.

39614 ■ "Green Acres" in Hawaii Business (Vol. 54, September 2008, No. 3, pp. 48)

Pub: PacificBasin Communications
Ed: Jan Tenbruggencate. Description: Bill Cowern's Hawaiian Mahogany is a forestry business that processes low-value trees to be sold as wood chips, which can be burned to create biodiesel. Cowern is planning to obtain certification to market carbon credits and is also working with Green Energy Hawaii for the permit of a biomass-fueled power plant. Other details about Cowern's business are discussed.

39615 ■ "Green Energy Exec Hits State Policy" in Boston Business Journal (Vol. 30, December 3, 2010, No. 45, pp. 1)

Pub: Boston Business Journal
Ed: Kyle Alspach. Description: American Superconductor Corporation President Dan McGahn believes that the state government of Massachusetts is not proactive enough to develop the state into a manufacturing hub for wind power technology. McGahn believes that while Governor Deval Patrick campaigned for wind turbines in the state, his administration does not have the focus required to build the turbines in the state.

39616 ■ "Green Rules To Drive Innovation: Charging for Carbon Can Inspire Conservation, Fuel Competition, and Enhance Competitiveness" in Harvard Business Review (Vol. 90, March 2012, No. 3, pp. 120)

Pub: Harvard Business Review Press
Contact: Peter E. Walsh, Director
Ed: Daniel C. Esty, Steve Charnovitz. Released: March 2012. Description: Along with carbon emissions charges, other green policy recommendations include expanding domestic renewable power and the use of natural gas, increasing federal funding of clean-energy research, utilizing incentive-based approaches to encourage the adoption of renewable energy, and implementing the World Trade Organization's Doha negotiations on sustainable development.

39617 ■ "Green Shift Sees Red" in Canadian Business (Vol. 81, September 29, 2008, No. 16)

Ed: Jeff Sanford. Description: Green Shift Inc. is suing the Liberal Party of Canada in an $8.5 million lawsuit for using the phrase 'green shift' when they rolled out their carbon tax and climate change policy. The company has come to be recognized as a consultant and provider of green products such as non-toxic, biodegradable cups, plates, and utensils for events.

39618 ■ "Greenberg Sues U.S. Over AIG Rescue" in Wall Street Journal Eastern Edition (November 22 , 2011, pp. C3)

Pub: Dow Jones & Co., Inc.
Contact: Clare Hart, President
Ed: Liam Pleven, Serena Ng. Description: Former Chief Executive Officer of American International Group Inc., Maurice R. 'Hank' Greenberg, has filed a lawsuit against the United States and the Federal Reserve Bank of New York on behalf of shareholders and his company, Starr International Company Inc., claiming that the government was wrong in taking control of the insurance giant and used it to move tens of millions of dollars to the trading partners of AIG.

39619 ■ "Group To Urge Change For Use of Hotel Taxes" in Business Journal Milwaukee (Vol. 29, June 29, 2012, No. 40, pp. 1)

Pub: American City Business Journals, Inc.
Contact: Whitney Shaw, President
Ed: Stacy Vogel Davis. Released: June 29, 2012. Description: Wisconsin Hotel & Lodging Association is looking at the state policy on hotel taxes. Group president, Trisha Pugal, says that hotel taxes are aimed at promoting overnight tourism, but many communities misuse the revenue as the state inadequately monitors the usage of such taxes. The association has proposed a requirement for more accountability and clarification on what can be considered as tourism promotion.

39620 ■ "Gun Retailers Firing On All Cylinders Due To Economic, Political Uncertainty" in Birmingham Business Journal (Vol. 29, June 29, 2012, No. 27, pp. 1)

Pub: American City Business Journals, Inc.
Contact: Whitney Shaw, President
Ed: Nick Bowman. Released: June 29, 2012. Description: Birmingham, Alabama-based gun dealers have been expanding. Gun dealers have also reported strong sales despite the recession.

39621 ■ "Hank Paulson On the Housing Bailout and What's Ahead" in Business Week (September 22, 2008, No. 4100, pp. 19)

Ed: Maria Bartiromo. Description: Interview with Treasury Secretary Henry Paulson in which he discusses the bailout of Fannie Mae and Freddie Mac as well as the potential impact on the American economy and foreign interests and investments in the country. Paulson has faith that the government's actions will help to stabilize the housing market.

39622 ■ "Has Daylight Savings Time Fuelled Gasoline Consumption?" in Globe & Mail (April 18, 2007, pp. B1)

Ed: Shawn McCarthy. Description: The prospects of the acquisition of BCE Inc, by Canadian pension funds are discussed. The effect of the growth of these pension funds on the Canadian economy is described.

39623 ■ "Hastily Enacted Regulation Will Not Cure Economic Crisis" in Crain's Chicago Business (Vol. 31, May 5, 2008, No. 18, pp. 18)

Pub: Crain Communications Inc.
Contact: Todd Johnson, Publisher
Ed: Stephen P. D'Arcy. Description: Policymakers are looking for ways to respond to what is possibly the greatest financial crisis of a generation due to the collapse of the housing market, the credit crisis and the volatility of Wall Street.

39624 ■ "Hawaii Aquarium Legislation Dead...Or Is It?" in Pet Product News (Vol. 66, September 2012, No. 9, pp. 76)

Pub: Bowtie Inc.
Ed: John Dawes. Description: SB 580 is deemed as one of the Hawaii Senate bills that would lead to prohibition of, or heavy restrictions to, the collection of marine reef fish for home aquaria. Implications of these Senate bill on marine life conservation and stakeholder submissions are discussed.

39625 ■ "HBR Case Study: Setting Up Shop in a Political Hot Spot" in Harvard Business Review (Vol. 88, October 2010, No. 10, pp. 141)

Pub: Harvard Business School Publishing
Ed: Patrick Chun, John Coleman, Nabil El-Hage. Description: A fictitious foreign operations scenario is presented, with contributors providing comments and advice. The scenario involves a politically charged North Korean-South Korean business venture; suggestions range from ensuring financial flexibility in case of adverse events to avoiding any business venture until political stability is achieved.

39626 ■ "Health Care Changes Loom" in Business Journal Milwaukee (Vol. 29, July 13, 2012, No. 42, pp. 1)

Pub: American City Business Journals, Inc.
Contact: Whitney Shaw, President
Ed: Jon Olson. Released: July 13, 2012. Description: Business owners are worried about mandated health care coverage, which will start in 2014. Boyd Miller, president of Wisconsin Thermoset Molding, Inc., believes that eight Supreme Court justices voted purely on political grounds when they decided on President Obama's health care plan.

39627 ■ "Health Care of the Future" in Business Journal Serving Greater Tampa Bay (Vol. 30, November 19, 2010, No. 48, pp. 1)

Pub: Tampa Bay Business Journal
Ed: Margie Manning. Description: Information about accountable care organizations (ACO), which are integrated care systems with doctors and hospitals

working closely together to handle patient care, is provided. The Patient Protection and Affordable Care Act paved the way for ACOs as Medicare demonstration projects.

39628 ■ *"Health IT Regulations Generate Static Among Providers"* in *Philadelphia Business Journal (Vol. 28, January 29, 2010, No. 50, pp. 1)*
Pub: American City Business Journals Inc.
Ed: John George. **Description:** US Centers for Medicaid and Medicare Services and the Office of the National Coordinator for Health Information Technology have proposed rules regarding the meaningful use of electronic health records. The rules must be complied with by hospitals and physicians to qualify for federal stimulus funds.

39629 ■ *"Health Job Shift Looms"* in *Boston Business Journal (Vol. 31, June 3, 2011, No. 19, pp. 3)*
Pub: Boston Business Journal
Ed: Julie M. Donnelly. **Description:** Pending health care payment reform in Massachusetts is seen to adversely impact hospital staff. Hospitals are also seen to serve more patients once the bill is approved.

39630 ■ *"Health Reform Could Expand HSA-Based Plans"* in *Workforce Management (Vol. 88, December 14, 2009, No. 13, pp. 6)*
Ed: Jeremy Smerd. **Description:** HSA-qualified plans are the cheapest insurance plans on the market as they have a higher deductible but cost less upfront. If health care reform passes, HSA-qualified plans should benefit greatly.

39631 ■ *"Health Reform How-To"* in *Business Courier (Vol. 26, December 11, 2009, No. 33, pp. 1)*
Ed: James Ritchie. **Description:** Greater Cincinnati health care leaders shared views about the health care reform bill. Respondents included the Cincinnati Visiting Nurse's Wallen Falberg, healthcare consultant Hirsch Cohen, Greater Cincinnati Health Council's Coleen O'Toole, Employer Health Care Alliance's Sharron DiMario, Legal Aid Society of Greater Cincinnati's Col Owens, Christ Hospital's Susan Croushore, and Humana of Ohio's Tim Cappel.

39632 ■ *"Here's How Ride Services Will Roll Under New Seattle Law"* in *Puget Sound Business Journal (Vol. 35, July 18, 2014, No. 13, pp. 8)*
Pub: American City Business Journals
Released: July 18, 2014. **Description:** Members of the City Council of Seattle, Washington voted to approve the operation of Uber, Lyft and other ride-sharing services. Mayor Ed Murray negotiated a deal between taxi and limousine companies and ride services to find a compromise and create regulations.

39633 ■ *"Higher-Ed Finally in Session"* in *Business Journal Portland (Vol. 30, February 7, 2014, No. 49, pp. 4)*
Pub: American City Business Journals
Released: February 7, 2014. **Description:** Oregon lawmakers and voters are set to consider several proposals on how higher education is funded, including free community college and free college for a percentage of future earnings. State Treasurer, Ted Wheeler, is proposing a large endowment that would pay for scholarships and vocational training.

39634 ■ *"Hike in Md.'s Alcohol Tax May Be Hard For Lawmakers to Swallow"* in *Baltimore Business Journal (Vol. 28, November 19, 2010, No. 28)*
Pub: Baltimore Business Journal
Ed: Emily Mullin. **Description:** Maryland's General Assembly has been reluctant to support a dime-per-drink increase in alcohol tax that was drafted in the 2009 bill if the tax revenue goes into a separate fund. The alcohol tax increase is considered unnecessary by some lawmakers and business leaders due to impending federal spending boosts.

39635 ■ *"Hiring Unpaid Interns: Failing To Comply With Labor Laws Can Lead to Legal Trouble"* in *Black Enterprise (Vol. 44, June 2014, No. 10, pp. 22)*
Pub: Earl G. Graves Publishing Co. Inc.
Contact: Earl G. Graves, Jr., President
Released: June 2014. **Description:** Before hiring an intern for a small business it is critical to study the Department of Labor's legal criteria, determine whether the internship should be paid or unpaid, weigh the pros and cons, focus on the training aspect, and work with local colleges.

39636 ■ *"His Way"* in *Inc. (February 2008, pp. 90-97)*
Ed: Stephanie Clifford. **Description:** Profile of Chris Reed, founder of a natural soda company, who undertook an initial public offering (IPO). Reed discusses the challenges he faced mediating with the Securities Exchange Commission regarding his firm's IPO.

39637 ■ *"Hispanic Business 100 Influentials"* in *Hispanic Business (October 2009, pp. 22)*
Pub: Hispanic Business Inc.
Contact: Jesus Chavarria, President
Description: Profiles of the top one hundred influential Hispanics in business and government are presented.

39638 ■ *"Hispanic Business 100 Influentials: Profiles of the Top 100 Influentials"* in *Hispanic Business (October 2009, pp. 22)*
Pub: Hispanic Business Inc.
Contact: Jesus Chavarria, President
Description: Profiles of the top one hundred influential Hispanics in business and government are presented.

39639 ■ *"Historic Is Hot, But Challenging, in Bham"* in *Birmingham Business Journal (Vol. 31, August 1, 2014, No. 31, pp. 10)*
Pub: American City Business Journals, Inc.
Contact: Whitney Shaw, President
Released: August 1, 2014. **Description:** Birmingham, Alabama is witnessing a growing trend of restoring old and historic buildings for modern office spaces, driven by the new state credit for the projects. However, developers state that renovation projects present numerous challenges, including complying with current building codes and the use of energy-efficient innovation.

39640 ■ *"A History of Neglect"* in *Canadian Business (Vol. 79, September 11, 2006, No. 18, pp. 21)*
Ed: Al Rosen. **Description:** Faulty practices being followed by auditors and regulators of Canada are discussed. The need for appropriate steps to protect investors against these frauds are emphasized.

39641 ■ *"Hitting Bottom? Several Banks and Brokerages Are Ready to Pop Up for Air"* in *Barron's (Vol. 88, March 24, 2008, No. 12, pp. 21)*
Pub: Dow Jones & Co., Inc.
Contact: Clare Hart, President
Ed: Jacqueline Doherty. **Description:** Brokerage houses and banks may stabilize in 2008 as a result of regulatory responses brought about by the near-collapse of Bear Stearns. Some of their shares may rise by as much as 20 percent from 2008 to 2009.

39642 ■ *"The Hollow Debate"* in *Canadian Business (Vol. 81, March 3, 2008, No. 3, pp. 26)*
Ed: Thomas Watson. **Description:** According to a report conducted by the Conference Board of Canada, the Canadian business community is not being hollowed out by acquisitions made by foreign companies. Findings further showed that local businesses are protected by dual shares and that the economy can benefit more from foreign acquisitions than local mergers. The need to relax foreign ownership restrictions and other recommendations are presented.

39643 ■ *"Home Sprinklers Blocked in Texas, Long Beach, Calif."* in *Contractor (Vol. 56, July 2009, No. 7, pp. 1)*
Pub: Intertec Publishing
Contact: John French, President
Ed: Robert P. Mader. **Description:** Long Beach, California has exempted older residential high rises and large apartment complexes from a rule to install fire sprinkler systems. Texas has also prohibited municipalities from enacting residential sprinkler ordinances.

39644 ■ *"Home, Sweet Shipping Container"* in *Washington Business Journal (Vol. 33, July 18, 2014, No. 13, pp. 4)*
Pub: American City Business Journals
Released: July 18, 2014. **Description:** Brookland Equity Group LLC is converting a single-family home in Brookland into a three-story, four-unit shipping container apartment building in Washington DC. According to the Department of Consumer Regulatory Affairs, the application was reviewed for lighting, ventilation, insulation, and other construction standards. Discussion on the new micro small living spaces trend is presented.

39645 ■ *"Horse Racing Industry Cries Foul Over Budget Switch"* in *Philadelphia Business Journal (Vol. 31, March 23, 2012, No. 6, pp. 1)*
Pub: American City Business Journal
Description: Pennsylvania Governor Tom Corbett's proposal to slash $72 million from the Horse Racing Development Fund is seen to adversely impact the sector. The plan has been criticized by track operators, trainers, owners and horse breeders.

39646 ■ *"Hospitals Say Medicaid Expansion is Critical"* in *Dallas Business Journal (Vol. 35, August 3, 2012, No. 47, pp. 1)*
Pub: American City Business Journal
Ed: Bill Hethcock, Matt Joyce. **Description:** Governor Rick Perry's rejection of the Texas expansion of Medicaid is met with disapproval by health organizations such as the Methodist Health System. The federal government has extended $70 billion in financing to help more Texans become eligible for primary health care. Expansion supporters argue that Medicaid is critical in lowering insurance osts for those who need it.

39647 ■ *"Hot Air: On Global Warming and Carbon Tax"* in *Canadian Business (Vol. 81, October 13, 2008, No. 17, pp. 12)*
Ed: Joe Castaldo. **Description:** Survey of Canadian business leaders revealed that the environment is a key issue in Canada's federal elections. Respondents believe that Prime Minister Stephen Harper's views on global warming and climate change are closer to their own views. Other key information on the survey is presented.

39648 ■ *"House Committee on Small Business Calls for Sweeping Changes to SBIR Program"* in *Hispanic Business (Vol. 30, March 2008, No. 3)*
Description: Proposals suggested by the House Committee on small business to revamp the Small Business Innovation and Research Program (SBIR) are reported. These include allowing participating firms greater flexibility to use venture capital funds, increasing SBIR grants and faster processing of applications.

39649 ■ *"House Speaker Prepares To Move Major Biz Bills In Coming Months"* in *Boston Business Journal (Vol. 34, February 7, 2014, No. 1, pp. 3)*
Pub: American City Business Journals, Inc.
Contact: Whitney Shaw, President
Released: February 7, 2014. **Description:** Massachusetts House Speaker, Robert DeLeo, is set to push for the passage of a number of business bills, one being the minimum wage bill. His is also working on a bill aimed at stimulating economic growth in the state.

39650 ■ *"How Many Bottles Make a Case Against Prohibition? Online Wine and*

Virginia's Direct Shipment Ban"
Pub: CreateSpace
Contact: Daren Giles, President
Released: October 7, 2014. Price: , $12.95 paperback. Description: The impact of the Commonwealth of Virginia's ban on direct wine shipments from out-of-state sellers on wine prices and the variety of wine available to consumer in the Greater McLean, Virginia area is investigated. Virginia's direct shipment regulations ban reduces the varieties of wine to consumers and prevents them from purchase some premium wines at lower prices online. Statistical data included.

39651 ■ "How To: Manage Your Cash Better"
in Inc. (Volume 32, December 2010, No. 10,
pp. 69)
Pub: Inc. Magazine
Description: A monthly guide to policies, procedures and practices for managing cash for a small business.

39652 ■ "How To Reduce the Risk of
Discrimination" in Idaho Business Review
(September 11, 2014)
Pub: Dolan Co.
Contact: James P. Dolan, President
Released: September 11, 2014. Description: Human resource departments in small businesses in Boise are aware of the city's discrimination ordinance making it unlawful to use sexual orientation and gender identity/expression in any consideration of hiring or terminating an employee, or for any other issue. The impact of the ordinance is yet to be determined.

39653 ■ "How To Spark Up a Medical
Marijuana Firm in Florida - and Not Get
Burned in the Process" in Orlando Business
Journal (Vol. 30, March 21, 2014, No. 39, pp.
6)
Pub: American City Business Journals
Released: March 21, 2014. Description: Colorado business owners and experts offer tips on starting a medical marijuana business in Florida. Andy Williams recalls that he was filled with fear he would wake up in Federal prison and not see his family again when he started Medicine Man. Jerald Bovine of GreenZip-p.com advises those interested in entering the medical marijuana field to know the details of regulation of facilities and labs.

39654 ■ "How To Win the Fed's New Game"
in Barron's (Vol. 92, September 17, 2012, No.
38, pp. M10)
Description: Options trading strategies designed to take advantage of the US Federal Reserve's third quantitative easing program are discussed. Options traders are advised to invest in short-term options to maximize gains.

39655 ■ "The HST Hornet's Nest" in Canadian
Business (Vol. 83, September 14, 2010, No.
15, pp. 17)
Pub: Rogers Media Inc.
Contact: Tony Viner, President
Ed: Michael McCullough. Description: Canadian Premier Gordon Campbell's Harmonized Sales Tax (HST) initiative has left British Columbia's economic and political future stuck in uncertainty. The petition of a coalition group forced a bill to abolish the HST through legislation or referendum. How the HST's abolition will affect British Columbia's revenues is also discussed.

39656 ■ "Huge Fight Over Tiny Apartments"
in Puget Sound Business Journal (Vol. 35,
September 12, 2014, No. 21, pp. 8)
Pub: American City Business Journals
Released: September 12, 2014. Description: Smart Growth Seattle director, Roger Valdez and Seattle City Council member, Mike O'Brien, share their views about the proposed new rules and regulations governing micro-apartment buildings. Valdes says O'Brien's proposal would eliminate a choice for many people and force them to pay more or live elsewhere. O'Brien says the bill aims to apply existing construction rules to micro-housing in a fair way.

39657 ■ "The Human Factor" in Canadian
Business (Vol. 80, October 8, 2007, No. 20,
pp. 22)
Ed: Alex Mynek. Description: David Foot, a demographer and an economics professor at the University of Toronto, talks about Canada's future, including economic and demographic trends. He discusses activities that should be done by businessmen in order to prepare for the future. He also addresses the role of the Canadian government in economic development.

39658 ■ "I-5 Bridge Funding Unclear" in The
Business Journal-Portland (Vol. 25, July 11,
2008, No. 18, pp. 1)
Pub: American City Business Journals, Inc.
Contact: Whitney Shaw, President
Ed: Andy Giegerich. Description: Financing for a new Interstate 5 bridge is unclear as Washington lawmakers identify two priority projects other than the planned bridge, which is shared with Oregon. An estimate says that the two states could pay between $487.6 million and $1.5 billion for the new bridge. Other details on the financing of the project are discussed.

39659 ■ "I Just Love a Challenge" in South
Florida Business Journal (Vol. 34, July 18,
2014, No. 52, pp. 11)
Pub: American City Business Journals
Released: July 18, 2014. Description: Gregory Cunningham, president and CEO of Farm Credit of Florida, shares the lessons he learned from his military background that he applies to managing a company. He explains why he decided to take on the challenge of helping the agricultural credit group deal with its regulatory order.

39660 ■ "If Just One Person Applies, Are You
Required to Hire Him?" in HR Specialist (Vol.
8, September 2010, No. 9, pp. 7)
Description: It is legal to decline hiring an applicant, or even promoting a current employee, if they are the only applicant for a particular position. It may be good choice to wait for more applicants or to change recruiting strategy.

39661 ■ "IFRS Monopoly: the Pied Piper of
Financial Reporting" in Accounting and
Business Research (Vol. 41, Summer 2011,
No. 3, pp. 291)
Pub: American Institute of Certified Public
  Accountants
Contact: Barry C. Melancon, President
E-mail: bmelancon@aicpa.org
Ed: Shyam Sunder. Description: The disadvantages of granting monopoly to the international financial reporting standards (IFRS) are examined. Results indicate that an IFRS monopoly removes the chances for comparing alternative practices and learning from them. An IFRS monopoly also eliminates customization of financial reporting to fit local differences in governance, business, economic, and legal conditions.

39662 ■ "Ill. Residential Building Legislation
Includes New HVAC Requirements" in
Contractor (Vol. 56, July 2009, No. 7, pp. 3)
Pub: Intertec Publishing
Contact: John French, President
Ed: Candace Roulo. Description: Illinois' Energy Efficient Building Act will require all new buildings and houses to conform to the International Energy Conservation Code. The code includes a duct leakage requirement followed by a post-construction test to verify leakage rates and requires programmable thermostats on all houses.

39663 ■ "Illinois Regulators Revoke
Collection Agency's License" in Collections &
Credit Risk (Vol. 15, August 1, 2010, No. 7,
pp. 13)
Pub: SourceMedia Inc.
Contact: James M. Malkin, Chief Executive Officer
Description: Creditors Service Bureau of Springfield, Illinois had its license revoked by a state regulatory agency and was fined $55,000 because the owner and president, Craig W. Lewis, did not turn over portions of collected funds to clients.

39664 ■ "Immigration: Give Us Your Skilled"
in Canadian Business (Vol. 80, October 8,
2007, No. 20, pp. 78)
Pub: Rogers Media Inc.
Contact: Tony Viner, President
Ed: Zena Olijnyk. Description: Demand for skilled workers in Canada is discussed. Despite a strong demand, as evidenced by shortages in both skilled and unskilled labor, the country's immigration policy is affecting the recruitment process. Peter Veress, founder and president of Vermax Group, believes the country is wasting opportunities to take advantage of its attractiveness as a destination for foreign workers.

39665 ■ "Immigration Issues Frustrate
Owners From Overseas" in The Business
Journal-Serving Greater Tampa Bay (Vol. 28,
August 18, 2008)
Pub: American City Business Journals, Inc.
Contact: Whitney Shaw, President
Ed: Margie Manning. Description: Investors who availed the E-2 visa program believe that the tightened restrictions on the visa program has trapped them in the United States. The E-2 investor visa program was designed to attract investors into the U.S., but restrictions were tightened after the September 11, 2001 attacks. Other views and information on E-2 and its impact on investors are presented.

39666 ■ "Importers Share Safety Liability" in
Feedstuffs (Vol. 80, January 21, 2008, No. 3,
pp. 19)
Description: Pet food and toys containing lead paint are among products from China being recalled due to safety concerns. American Society for Quality's list of measures that outsourcing companies can take to help ensure safer products being imported to the U.S.

39667 ■ In Fed We Trust: Ben Bernanke's
Ware on the Great Panic
Pub: Crown Business
Ed: David Wessel. Released: 2009. Price: $16. Description: A look at the central bank's reaction to the crisis and Ben Bernanke has been forced to play the crisis by ear in order to keep the economy from imploding.

39668 ■ "In the SBA's Face" in American
Small Business League (December 2010)
Pub: Hispanic Business Inc.
Contact: Jesus Chavarria, President
Ed: Richard Larsen. Description: Lloyd Chapman uses the American Small Business League to champion small business. Statistical data included.

39669 ■ "In With the Good" in Canadian
Business (Vol. 80, November 5, 2007, No. 22,
pp. 22)
Ed: Jack Mintz. Description: Restriction on foreign direct investment in Canada is unlikely to materialize despite Minister of Industry Jim Prentice's opinion that new rules be set in Ottawa regarding foreign state-owned businesses. Reasons why governments would not unreasonably regulate foreign investments are investigated.

39670 ■ "Inco Takeover Faces Foreign
Hurdles" in Globe & Mail (February 13, 2006,
pp. B1)
Ed: Paul Waldie. Description: The issues that impact Inco Ltd.'s acquisition of Falconbridge Ltd., for $12.5 billion, are presented. Inco Ltd. is awaiting foreign regulatory approval in the United States and Europe.

39671 ■ Incorporate Your Business: A Legal
Guide to Forming a Corporation in Your State
Pub: Nolo
Contact: Ralph Warner, Chief Executive Officer
Ed: Anthony Mancuso. Released: May 2013. Price: $39.99; $34.99. Description: Legal guide to incorporating a business in the U.S., covering all 50 states. Availability: PrintE-book.

39672 ■ "Inco's Takeover Offer Extended
Four Months" in Globe & Mail (February 22,
2006, pp. B1)
Ed: Wendy Stueck. Description: United States and Europe competition authorities wanted more time to investigate Inco Ltd.'s takeover of Falconbridge Ltd. and compelling Inco to extend its $12.5 billion offer for the third time.

39673 ■ *"Indiana Town Reports Success With Collection Agency" in PaymentsSource (August 20, 2012)*
Pub: SourceMedia Inc.
Contact: James M. Malkin, Chief Executive Officer
Released: August 20, 2012. **Description:** Capital Recovery Systems has collected nearly $80,000 in unpaid parking fines in Bloomington, Indiana. The city's agreement with the collection agency allows them to pursue an unlimited amount of unpaid parking tickets at least 30 days late.

39674 ■ *"Industry Associations Seek Clarity of CFPB's Large Collection Agency Definition" in PaymentsSource (May 24, 2012)*
Pub: SourceMedia Inc.
Contact: James M. Malkin, Chief Executive Officer
Released: May 24, 2012. **Description:** ACA International and DBA International are questioning the Consumer Financial Protection Bureau's definition of a large collection agency. The ACA has filed comments arguing that the threshold needs to be raised to $250 million, rather than the $10 million or more in annual receipts or money recovered as its definition. Details are provided.

39675 ■ *"Industry Escalates Lobbying Efforts For Loan Program" in Crain's Detroit Business (Vol. 24, September 22, 2008, No. 38, pp. 22)*
Pub: Crain Communications Inc.
Contact: Rance E. Crain, President
Ed: Jay Greene, Ryan Beene, Harry Stoffer. **Description:** Auto suppliers such as Lear Corp., which is best known for vehicle seating, also supplies high-voltage wiring for Ford hybrids and is developing other hybrid components. These suppliers are joining automakers in lobbying for the loan program which would promote the accelerated development of fuel-efficient vehicles.

39676 ■ *"Infrastructure: Things Fall Apart" in Canadian Business (Vol. 80, October 8, 2007, No. 20, pp. 187)*
Pub: Rogers Media Inc.
Contact: Tony Viner, President
Ed: Jeff Sanford. **Description:** Infrastructure crisis in Canada and in other countries in North America is examined. Incidents that demonstrate this crisis, such as the collapse of a bridge in Minneapolis and the collapse of an overpass in Quebec, Canada are presented. It is estimated that the reconstruction in the country will cost between C$44 billion and C$200 billion.

39677 ■ *"Infrastructure: Borrow For Tomorrow" in Canadian Business (Vol. 80, October 8, 2007, No. 20, pp. 193)*
Pub: Rogers Media Inc.
Contact: Tony Viner, President
Ed: David Wolf. **Description:** The possibility of running deficits in order to finance infrastructures in Canada is discussed. Statistics show that the country's net government debt is below 25 percent of GDP as of 2007, and that the government is spending less on public infrastructure. Based on these figures, it is expected that an increase in government debt could help in making infrastructure investments.

39678 ■ *"Injured Workers Caught in the Middle" in Sacramento Business Journal (Vol. 28, June 10, 2011, No. 15, pp. 1)*
Pub: Sacramento Business Journal
Ed: Kelly Johnson. **Description:** A bill that would extend the cap on disability payments to nearly five years is in the works, but employers and insurance companies fear it would increase their costs. Proponents of the bill say, however, that it would correct unfairness suffered by the employees. Features of the bill are discussed as well as its effects on both parties and the State of California.

39679 ■ *"Innovation Central: Tech, Tweets, and Trolls" in Inc. (Vol. 36, September 2014, No. 7, pp. 102)*
Pub: Mansueto Ventures L.L.C.
Contact: John Koten, Chief Executive Officer
Released: September 2014. **Description:** Results of a survey regarding the ways small business is using technology to grow their businesses is presented.

Information covers social media applications, government software patents, trends impacting small business, and the most innovative technology companies.

39680 ■ *"Insurance Roars Back Into Style" in Barron's (Vol. 92, September 17, 2012, No. 38, pp. 11)*
Description: The US Federal Reserve's decision to implement a mortgage-buying policy is seen by the stock market as an insurance policy. The Federal Reserve will buy mortgage-backed securities worth $40 billion each month, a move which could bolster stock prices.

39681 ■ *"Insurers Enter Ridesharing Dispute" in Sacramento Business Journal (Vol. 31, June 6, 2014, No. 15, pp. 8)*
Pub: American City Business Journals
Released: June 6, 2014. **Description:** Insurance companies have been lobbying the California Assembly to pass legislation requiring ridesharing drivers to carry commercial liability insurance. Ridesharing companies provide drivers with liability coverage as a backup when an accident is not covered by personal insurance. The passage of such a bill would boost ridesharing companies' revenues.

39682 ■ *"Internet Cafe Logging in to Chardon Plaza?" in News-Herald (July 16, 2011)*
Pub: Journal Register Ohio
Ed: Betsy Scott. **Description:** Pearl's High Rollers Inc. applied for an Internet sweepstakes cafe license that would reside in a vacant space in Chardon Plaza. City officials have created regulations for such businesses and Pearl's applied for a license and is awaiting approval.

39683 ■ *"Internet Cafe Regulations Head to City Council Vote" in Vindicator (April 13, 2011)*
Pub: Vindicator
Ed: David Skolnick. **Description:** Youngstown City Council's safety committee agrees with proposed changes to the policy regulating Internet gaming cafes and sweepstakes businesses. The new amendments allow Internet cafe customers to buy Internet time and go to Websites and play sweepstakes games of change.

39684 ■ *"Investigation Hints at Workers' Comp Trouble" in Sacramento Business Journal (Vol. 25, July 4, 2008, No. 18, pp. 1)*
Pub: American City Business Journals, Inc.
Contact: Whitney Shaw, President
Ed: Kelly Johnson. **Description:** In 500 California firms, a survey of worker compensation revealed that 38 percent of the companies had problems with required coverage. Government investigators are bothered that 107 companies did not respond to the official inquiry. Other views and information on the survey and on the expected economic implications of the findings are presented.

39685 ■ *"Investment In Israel Is Investment in the Future of Georgia" in Atlanta Business Chronicle (May 30, 2014, pp. 22A)*
Pub: American City Business Journals, Inc.
Contact: Whitney Shaw, President
Released: May 30, 2014. **Description:** Georgia Governor Nathan Deal will travel to Israel to lead an economic and trade mission and consolidate Georgia's trade ties with Israel. Israel and the State of Georgia are already collaborating in the fields of health information technology, agrotechnology, homeland security, defense, aerospace and cybersecurity, and microelectronics and nanotechnology. The proposed visit by the Governor will build on this particular partnership from which both parties will benefit.

39686 ■ *"IP Transition Is Unlikely To Make Waves In R.I." in Providence Business News (Vol. 28, January 13, 2014, No. 41, pp. 1)*
Pub: American City Business Journals
Released: January 13, 2014. **Description:** The transition from copper and circuit switches to fiber and Internet Protocol is changing the telecommunications landscape across the U.S. The Rhode Island General Assembly passed a bill that deregulates wire-

less communications systems, which means that the growth of wireless in the area previously held by landlines will not change its status for now.

39687 ■ *"IPOs: Can You Keep a Secret?" in Silicon Valley/San Jose Business Journal (Vol. 30, August 31, 2012, No. 23, pp. 1)*
Pub: American City Business Journal
Description: Many business enterprises have been keeping their initial public offering (IPO) filings confidential through a new rule under the JOBS Act. The rule permits companies with less than $1 billion in revenue to keep their IPO filings confidential until 21 days before going public. As keeping IPO filings secret offer many advantages, drawbacks of this action are also discussed.

39688 ■ *"IRS Announces New Standards for Tax Preparers" in Bellingham Business Journal (Vol. February 2010, pp. 9)*
Pub: Sound Publishing Inc.
Contact: Gloria G. Fletcher, President
Ed: Isaac Bonnell. **Description:** A new oversight plan was announced by the Internal Revenue Services (IRS) that will require tax professionals to pass a competency test and register with the government in order to ensure greater accountability in the industry.

39689 ■ *"Is 5th Time the Charm? Discover Labs Awaits FDA Ruling" in Philadelphia Business Journal (Vol. 31, March 2, 2012, No. 3, pp. 1)*
Pub: American City Business Journal
Description: The US Food and Drug Administration is set to approve Discovery Laboratories' drug Surfaxin for use in the prevention of respiratory distress syndromes in premature newborns. The new drug is a synthetic surfactant designed to mimic the function of natural human surfactants. It is a lower-cost alternative to animal-derived surfactant products.

39690 ■ *"Is Hawaii Ready for Universal Health Care?" in Hawaii Business (Vol. 53, February 2008, No. 8, pp. 26)*
Pub: PacificBasin Communications
Description: Representative Lyn Finnegan does not believe that a universal health is good for Hawaii as health insurance for everyone will be difficult to achieve. Representative John M. Mizuno says that House Bill 1008 introduced in the state was a landmark for Hawaii as it will provide the people with health care insurance. Other details about their opinion on the topic are presented.

39691 ■ *"It's All in the Details" in Canadian Business (Vol. 80, December 25, 2006, No. 1, pp. 11)*
Pub: Rogers Media Inc.
Contact: Tony Viner, President
Ed: Andy Holloway. **Description:** The failure of several Canadian clothing retailers to disclose their labor practices is discussed.

39692 ■ *"Ivernia Mine Closing Could Boost Lead" in Globe & Mail (April 4, 2007, pp. B5)*
Ed: Andy Hoffman. **Description:** The closing of Ivernia Inc.'s mine in view of government investigation into alleged lead contamination at the port of Esperance is discussed. The likely increase in the price of lead is also discussed.

39693 ■ *"Jennifer Hernandez Helps Developers Transform Contaminated Properties" in Hispanic Business (Vol. 30, April 2008, No. 4, pp. 32)*
Pub: Hispanic Business Inc.
Contact: Jesus Chavarria, President
Ed: Hildy Medina. **Description:** Jennifer Hernandez is a partner and head of the law firm of Holland & Knight's environmental practice which specializes in the restoration of polluted land where former industrial and commercial buildings once stood, known as brownfields. Brownfield redevelopment can be lucrative but costly due to the cleaning up of contaminated land and challenging because of federal and state environmental laws.

39694 ■ *"Job Losses and Budget Shortfall Adding to Economic Woes" in Sacramento Business Journal (Vol. 25, July 14, 2008, No. 19, pp. 1)*
Pub: American City Business Journals, Inc.
Contact: Whitney Shaw, President
Ed: Kathy Robertson. **Description:** Budget cuts in California have been approved amid rising unemployment in a slowing economy. Statistics show that total industry employment in the Sacramento region decreased by 3,700 jobs from May 2007 to May 2008. Governor Arnold Schwarzenegger has ordered a 10 percent budget cut for state departments, but this cut will likely mean few layoffs.

39695 ■ *"Judge Refuses To Dismiss Claim Against Former Collection Agency Chief" in PaymentsSource (May 24, 2012)*
Pub: SourceMedia Inc.
Contact: James M. Malkin, Chief Executive Officer
Released: May 24, 2012. **Description:** Pennsylvania Attorney General's Office filed a lawsuit against Michael J. Covatto, former president of Unicredit America Inc. Covatto filed a complaint because his firm is now defunct and he feels he should not be responsible to pay the damages or claims that might arise from the suit filed against him. The Attorney General's office is seeking damages and restitution to Unicredit's clients.

39696 ■ *"Jump Ship On Your Wireless Contract: Leave Your Cell Phone Carrier Without Paying a Fee" in Black Enterprise (Vol. 38, January 2008, No. 6, pp. 87)*
Pub: Earl G. Graves Publishing Co. Inc.
Contact: Earl G. Graves, Jr., President
Ed: Nicole Norfleet. **Description:** Better Business Bureau reported it received more than 28,000 complaints in 2007. Four situations that allow consumers to be released from a long-term service contract with a carrier without paying penalty fees are addressed.

39697 ■ *"Kaboom!" in Canadian Business (Vol. 81, November 10, 2008, No. 19, pp. 18)*
Ed: Al Rosen, Mark Rosen. **Description:** International Financial Reporting Standards (IFRS) is a good idea in theory but was implemented in a hurry and had poor quality standards from the beginning.

39698 ■ *"KC Incentives Debate Rages on Unabated" in The Business Journal-Serving Metropolitan Kansas City (Vol. 26, September 5, 2008, No. 52)*
Pub: American City Business Journals, Inc.
Contact: Whitney Shaw, President
Ed: Rob Roberts. **Description:** Debate on the new economic development and incentives policy adopted by the Kansas City Council is still on. The city's Planned Industrial Expansion Authority has rejected a standard property tax abatement proposal. The real estate development community has opposed the rejection of proposed the tax incentives policy.

39699 ■ *"KC Sewer Solutions May Overflow With Green Ideas" in The Business Journal-Serving Metropolitan Kansas City (August 22, 2008)*
Pub: American City Business Journals, Inc.
Contact: Whitney Shaw, President
Ed: Suzanna Stagemeyer. **Description:** Adding green solutions such as small, dispersed basins to catch runoffs and the use of deep rooted natural plants to fix the sewer system of Kansas could probably justify the $2.3 billion worth of funds needed for the project. The city has been ordered by the EPA and the Missouri Department of Natural Resources to fix their sewer systems that are overwhelmed by significant rains.

39700 ■ *"Keith Crain: Business Must Stand Up And Be Counted" in Crain's Detroit Business (Vol. 24, October 6, 2008, No. 40, pp. 6)*
Pub: Crain Communications Inc.
Contact: Rance E. Crain, President
Description: Discusses the challenges that the new mayor of Detroit faces concerning business, the state of the economy and the exceptionally tight budget

the city is running on, which includes a lot of red ink. It is very likely that the city is going to see tax revenues fall substantially in the next few months and business leaders may find it in their favor to lend their support to the new mayor as well as provide him with the executive talent necessary to overcome some of these crucial issues.

39701 ■ *"Keltic Gets Nod to Build N.S. Petrochemical Plant" in Globe & Mail (March 15, 2007, pp. B9)*
Pub: CTVglobemedia Publishing Inc.
Ed: Shawn McCarthy. **Description:** The government of Nova Scotia has awarded clearance to Keltic Inc. for the construction of new petrochemical plant in Goldboro region. Complete details in this context are discussed.

39702 ■ *"Key Challenges Dog International Banking in South Florida" in South Florida Business Journal (Vol. 35, August 1, 2014, No. 1, pp. 4)*
Pub: American City Business Journals
Released: August 1, 2014. **Description:** Florida International Bankers Association president, Roberto R. Munoz, discusses the challenges and opportunities in the South Florida international banking market. He explains the impact on international banks with the loss of the Export-Import Bank of the United States charter and the Base1 III rules and regulations regarding higher capital requirements.

39703 ■ *"Key FDA Approval Yanked for Avastin" in Wall Street Journal Eastern Edition (November 19 , 2011, pp. B1)*
Pub: Dow Jones & Co., Inc.
Contact: Clare Hart, President
Ed: Thomas M. Burton, Jennifer Corbett Dooren. **Description:** Avastin, a drug manufactured by Genetech Inc. and used in the treatment of metastatic breast cancer in women, has had its approval by the US Food and Drug Administration withdrawn by the agency, which says there is no evidence the widely-used drug is successful in increasing the longevity of breast cancer patients.

39704 ■ *"Kiosks On Wheels: City, Boardwalk Business Owners Respond to FEMA Guidelines" in Destin Log (April 7, 2012)*
Ed: Matt Algarin. **Released:** April 7, 2012. **Description:** Federal Emergency Management Agency (FEMA) is developing guidelines for the kiosks and ticket booths located along the Destin, Florida harbor-front in terms of compliance with the floodplain standards it sets.

39705 ■ *"LA Passes HET Ordinance, California Greens Code" in Contractor (Vol. 56, September 2009, No. 9, pp. 1)*
Pub: Penton Media, Inc.
Ed: Candace Roulo. **Description:** Los Angeles City Council has passed a Water Efficiency Requirements ordinance. The law mandates lower low-flow plumbing requirements for plumbing fixtures installed in new buildings and retrofits. Under the ordinance, a toilet's maximum flush volume may not exceed 1.28-gpf.

39706 ■ *"Land Swap Key to Ending Royal Oak Project Impasse" in Crain's Detroit Business (Vol. 25, June 8, 2009, No. 23, pp. 20)*
Pub: Crain Communications Inc. - Detroit
Contact: Keith Crain, Chairman
Ed: Chad Halcom. **Description:** Details of the new construction of the LA Fitness health club near Woodward and Washington Avenues in Royal Oak, Michigan are discussed.

39707 ■ *"The Latest on E-Verify" in Contractor (Vol. 56, September 2009, No. 9, pp. 58)*
Pub: Penton Media, Inc.
Ed: Susan McGreevy. **Description:** United States government has required federal contractors to use its E-Verify program to verify the eligibility of incoming and existent employees. The use of the program is seen to eliminate Social Security mismatches.

39708 ■ *"Latest Volley Tries to Press Port Group" in Business Courier (Vol. 26, November 20, 2009, No. 30, pp. 1)*
Pub: American City Business Journals, Inc.
Contact: Whitney Shaw, President
Ed: Dan Monk. **Description:** Subcontractors filed a new legal argument to force the Port of Greater Cincinnati Development Authority to pursue default claim against Bank of America. The bank issued letters of credit to guarantee bond payments in addition to holding the mortgage of the Kenwood Towne Place. Details of the claim are discussed.

39709 ■ *"Law Allows Captive Insurance Companies to Form in State" in Crain's Detroit Business (Vol. 24, March 31, 2008, No. 13, pp. 29)*
Pub: Crain Communications Inc.
Contact: Rance E. Crain, President
Ed: Jerry Geisel. **Description:** Discusses new legislation allowing the formation of captive insurance companies in the state of Michigan; these companies are subsidiaries of non-insurers that are formed primarily to insure some or all of the risks of its parent company.

39710 ■ *"Law Reform, Collective Bargaining, and the Balance of Power: Results of an Empirical Study" in WorkingUSA (June 2008)*
Ed: Ellen Dannin, Michelle Dean, Gangaram Singh. **Description:** Despite Congress' having made clear policy statements in the National Labor Relations Act that the law was intended to promote equality of bargaining power between employers and employees, to promote the practice and procedure of collective bargaining as the method of setting workplace terms and conditions of employment, and forbidding construing the law 'so as to either interfere with or impede or diminish in any way the right to strike,' by early 1940, the courts had given employers the right to permanently replace strikers and implement their final offer at impasse. Judges have often justified these doctrines as promoting balance in bargaining. Critics contend that the doctrines have the capacity to destroy the right to strike, unbalance bargaining power, and divert parties from the process of bargaining collectively. Some have proposed allowing temporary but not permanent striker replacement. The article uses a bargaining simulation followed by a survey and debriefing comments to test these opposing claims.

39711 ■ *"Law Targets Unemployment Fraud That Cost State $15M" in Birmingham Business Journal (Vol. 29, June 22, 2012, No. 26, pp. 1)*
Pub: American City Business Journals, Inc.
Contact: Whitney Shaw, President
Ed: Evan Belanger. **Released:** June 22, 2012. **Description:** The government of Alabama has passed a law that will curb unemployment fraud. Around 12,000 people have fraudulently claimed unemployment benefits in 2011.

39712 ■ *"Lawmakers, Execs Launch Effort to Save Rural Hospitals" in Atlanta Business Chronicle (June 13, 2014, pp. 7A)*
Pub: American City Business Journals, Inc.
Contact: Whitney Shaw, President
Released: June 13, 2014. **Description:** Governor Nathan Deal has appointed a committee of Georgia lawmakers and healthcare executives to launch an effort to save the state's financially burdened rural hospitals. In addition, he plans to allow rural hospitals that have closed or are on the verge of closing, to scale back their operations, under a new rule approved by the Georgia Board of Community Health.

39713 ■ *"Lawsuit Seeks To Shut Down Illinois Collection Agency" in PaymentsSource (January 12, 2012)*
Pub: SourceMedia Inc.
Contact: James M. Malkin, Chief Executive Officer
Released: January 12, 2012. **Description:** PN Financial is facing charges by the Illinois State Attorney General's Office, alleging that the company used abusive and threatening actions against consumers. Details of the lawsuit are covered.

39714 ■ *"Lawsuits Claim Coke Sent Illegal Ad Texts"* in *Atlanta Business Chronicle (June 13, 2014, pp. 4A)*

Pub: American City Business Journals, Inc.

Contact: Whitney Shaw, President

Released: June 13, 2014. **Description:** Coca-Cola Company is facing lawsuits in San Diego and California from consumers who claim to have received unsolicited ads (short message service (SMS)) to their wireless phones, thus putting Coke in violation of the Federal law, called the Telephone Consumer Protection Act. The plaintiff of the California lawsuit is seeking damages amounting to $1,500 for each text message sent.

39715 ■ *"Lawyer Wants at Facebook"* in *Austin Business Journal (Vol. 32, June 15, 2012, No. 15, pp. 1)*

Pub: American City Business Journals, Inc.

Contact: Whitney Shaw, President

Ed: Christopher Calnan. **Released:** June 15, 2012. **Description:** Bogdan Rentea, a Facebook Inc. investor in Austin, Texas, was not allowed to access the company's pre-initial public offering (IPO) records. Rentea filed a petition for discovery with the US District Court for the Western District, but his petition was denied. The court believed that there was a lack of urgency for depositions.

39716 ■ *"Lawyers Cash In On Alcohol"* in *Business Journal Portland (Vol. 27, November 19, 2010, No. 38, pp. 1)*

Pub: Portland Business Journal

Ed: Andy Giegerich. **Description:** Oregon-based law firms have continued to corner big business on the state's growing alcohol industry as demand for their services increased. Lawyers, who represent wine, beer and liquor distillery interests, have seen their workload increased by 20 to 30 percent in 2009.

39717 ■ *"LCB Puts a Cork in Kiosk Wine Sales"* in *Times Leader (December 22, 2010)*

Pub: Wilkes-Barre Publishing Company

Ed: Andrew M. Seder. **Description:** The Pennsylvania Liquor Control Board closed down thirty Pronto Wine Kiosks located in supermarkets throughout the state. The Board cited mechanical and technological issues such as products not dispensing.

39718 ■ *"Lead-Free Products must Meet Requirements"* in *Contractor (Vol. 56, September 2009, No. 9, pp. 30)*

Pub: Penton Media, Inc.

Ed: Robert Gottermeier. **Description:** United States Environmental Protection Agency's adoption of the Safe Drinking Water Act is aimed at lowering lead extraction levels from plumbing products. Manufacturers have since deleaded brass and bronze potable water products. Meanwhile, California and Vermont have passed a law limiting lead content for potable water conveying plumbing products.

39719 ■ *"Legislating the Cloud"* in *Information Today (Vol. 28, October 2011, No. 9, pp. 1)*

Pub: Information Today, Inc.

Contact: Thomas H. Hogan, President

E-mail: ctuthill@infotoday.com

Description: Internet and telecommunications industry leaders are asking for legislation to address the emerging market in cloud computing. Existing communications laws do not adequately govern the modern Internet.

39720 ■ *"Legislation Introduced"* in *Indoor Comfort Marketing (Vol. 70, July 2011, No. 7, pp. 6)*

Pub: Industry Publications Inc.

Contact: Shirleen Dorman, Editor

Description: New industry legislation is examined by the National Oilheat Research Alliance.

39721 ■ *"Legislative Changes Providing Boost to San Antonio Distillers"* in *San Antonio Business Journal (Vol. 28, March 7,*

2014, No. 4, pp. 4)

Pub: American City Business Journals

Released: March 7, 2014. **Description:** Lawmakers in Texas have implemented legislative changes that will provide financial flexibility to brew pubs and breweries. Distilleries in the state are now allowed to sell their products directly to food companies. The growth in San Antonio, Texas' craft spirits industry is also discussed.

39722 ■ *"Legislators Must Cut Cost of Government"* in *Crain's Detroit Business (Vol. 24, October 6, 2008, No. 40, pp. 6)*

Pub: Crain Communications Inc.

Contact: Rance E. Crain, President

Description: Southeast and West Michigan business leaders are setting aside their differences and have proposed clear agendas, ranging from eliminating the Michigan Business Tax to overhauling public employee and retiree benefits and pensions. Lawmakers must also come together to find solutions for the state's economy and discover an entirely new vision for the future of Michigan business.

39723 ■ *"Legislature Passes Increased Tax Credit for Urban Brownfield Projects"* in *Crain's Detroit Business (Vol. 24, March 31, 2008, No. 13)*

Pub: Crain Communications Inc.

Contact: Rance E. Crain, President

Ed: Amy Lane. **Description:** Discusses the bill passed by the Legislature that creates a tax credit of up to 20 percent for projects in urban development areas.

39724 ■ *"Legoland Plans Could Tumble After State's Modesa Denial"* in *Business Journal-Serving Metropolitan Kansas City (November 16, 2007)*

Pub: American City Business Journals, Inc.

Ed: Jim Davis. **Description:** RED Development LLC's officials are not giving up after the Missouri Department of Economic Development said RED could not exploit the Missouri Downtown and Rural Economic Stimulus Act (Modesa) for the Legoland theme park development in Lee's Summit. Legoland's proposed site southeast of Interstate 470 and U.S. Highway 50 does not fit the Modesa because it is outside Lee's Summit.

39725 ■ *"Less Malaise in Malaysia"* in *Barron's (Vol. 88, March 17, 2008, No. 11, pp. M12)*

Pub: Dow Jones & Co., Inc.

Contact: Clare Hart, President

Ed: Assif Shameen. **Description:** Shares of Malaysia's Bursa have been in freefall while the Malaysia government prolongs its pitch to sell a 10 percent stake of the exchange to NYSE Euronext. Asian bourses had produced very good returns for five years and charge some of the highest fees for exchanges. A key growth driver for Asian bourses could be the derivatives markets and exchange-traded funds.

39726 ■ *"Less Than Zero"* in *Canadian Business (Vol. 80, November 5, 2007, No. 22, pp. 36)*

Ed: Andy Holloway. **Description:** Zero-tolerance policy with regards to discrimination and harassment at the workplace has been adopted by many companies. However, employers must exercise caution in terminating employees based on zero-tolerance policies since there are laws governing illegal dismissals. Important considerations employers should make in dismissing workers, such as proof of willful misconduct, are discussed.

39727 ■ *"Lessons Burma Taught Me"* in *Canadian Business (Vol. 85, July 16, 2012, No. 11-12, pp. 17)*

Pub: George Media Inc.

Ed: Michael Lavergne. **Released:** July 16, 2012. **Description:** The decision of the Canadian government to allow trade with Burma presents Canadian firms with the challenge of ensuring that their projects

benefit its people and its economy. Companies are advised to follow international monitoring agreements related to labor, ethnic rights, and environmental protection.

39728 ■ *"Let Markets Decide?"* in *Canadian Business (Vol. 80, October 8, 2007, No. 20, pp. 67)*

Ed: James Gillies. **Description:** Need to protect Canadian companies that could help boost the country's economy is discussed. It is expected that free markets alone will solve economic problems. Suggested policies that will discourage the takeover of major companies in the country, such as the organization of capitalization with multiple voting shares, are also presented.

39729 ■ *"Let the Wine Flow Freely: Feds To Allow Shipments Inside Canada"* in *Canadian Business (Vol. 85, August 13, 2012, No. 13, pp. 8)*

Pub: George Media Inc.

Ed: Sarah Barmak. **Released:** August 13, 2012. **Description:** The passage of federal Bill C-311 is anticipated to remove restriction on interprovincial wine trade imposed under the Importation of Intoxicating Liquors Act of 1928. There are claims that legalizing direct-to-consumer selling will not affect liquor store sales.

39730 ■ *"Let's Make a Deal"* in *Pittsburgh Business Times (Vol. 33, July 18, 2014, No. 53, pp. 10)*

Pub: American City Business Journals

Released: July 18, 2014. **Description:** The low interest rate, combined with regulation have reduced fixed income trading for banks, thus reducing their profits and increasing the volatility of quarterly earnings. Banks are being forced to consider new ways to make money as the low rates are a function of a Federally-structured government yield curve, reflecting lower economic growth and inflation expectations.

39731 ■ *"The Letter of the Law"* in *Collections and Credit Risk (Vol. 14, November 1, 2009, No. 9, pp. 40)*

Ed: Michelle Dunn. **Description:** Analyzes the regulatory landscape regarding debt collection and the ways in which those in the field are dealing with a tough economy, unclear laws and the newest regulations.

39732 ■ *"Levy Boards: From Unity Comes Farming's Strength"* in *Farmer's Weekly (March 28, 2008, No. 320)*

Description: Discusses the amalgamation of five farming levy boards to create the Agriculture and Horticulture Development Board.

39733 ■ *"Lindbergh Receives Kiosks to Expedite Travel Through Customs: Vetting Process 'Pre-Screens' Low-Risk Travelers"* in *San Diego Business Journal (Vol. 33, August 20, 2012, No. 34, pp. 8)*

Pub: CBJ, L.P.

Ed: Mike Allen. **Released:** August 20, 2012. **Description:** Lindbergh Field airport in California installed two automated kiosks to help international travelers pass through customs in minutes. Global Entry verifies identification and allows declaration of items and is used for low risk passsengers.

39734 ■ *"Liquor-Sales Issue in Kansas Creates Strange Bedfellows"* in *Wichita Business Journal (Vol. 27, February 10, 2012, No. 6, pp. 1)*

Pub: American City Business Journal

Description: How the business community in Kansas has reacted to House Bill 2532, a legislation that would alter the way liquor is sold in the state, is presented. Under the legislation, groceries and convenience stores would be allowed to get licenses to sell liquor, wine and full-strength beer. On the other hand, liquor stores would be permitted to sell other products on the premises.

39735 ■ *"A Little Less Hot Air"* in *Canadian Business (Vol. 81, March 17, 2008, No. 4, pp. 9)*

Pub: Rogers Media Inc.

Contact: Tony Viner, President

Description: British Columbia will levy an extra tax on all carbon-emitting fuels starting July 1, 2008. The tax will raise $1.8 billion in three years and in effect, the province will reduce general corporate income tax from 12 percent to 11 percent. The tax on small businesses and personal income will also be reduced.

39736 ■ "Live & Learn: Thomas D'Aquino" in Canadian Business (Vol. 80, November 19, 2007, No. 23, pp. 92)
Pub: Rogers Media Inc.
Contact: Tony Viner, President
Ed: Calvin Leung. Description: Thomas D'Aquino is the CEO and president of the Canadian Council of Chief Executives since 1981. D'Aquino thinks he has the best job in Canada because he can change the way policies are made and the way people think. Details of his career as a lawyer and CEO and his views on Canada's economy are provided.

39737 ■ "Living in a 'Goldfish Bowl'" in WorkingUSA (Vol. 11, June 2008, No. 2, pp. 277)
Ed: John Lund. Description: Recent changes in laws, regulations and even the reporting format of labor organization annual financial reports in both the U.S. and Australia have received surprisingly little attention, yet they have significantly increased the amount of information available both to union members and the public in general, as reports in both countries are available via government Websites. While such financial reporting laws are extremely rare in European countries, with the exception of the UK and Ireland, the U.S. and Australian reporting systems have become among the most detailed in the world. After reviewing these changes in financial reporting and the availability of these reports, as well as comparing and contrasting the specific reporting requirements of each country, this paper then examines the cost-benefit impact of more detailed financial reporting.

39738 ■ "Lobbying Begins to Save Tax Credits" in Business First of Buffalo (Vol. 30, June 13, 2014, No. 39, pp. 8)
Pub: American City Business Journals, Inc.
Contact: Whitney Shaw, President
Released: June 13, 2014. Description: The Brownfield Cleanup Program has been used effectively across Upstate New York as an economic development tool may be terminated unless New York lawmakers agree to extend the initiative beyond the 2015 end date. The program helps make old industrial sites viable for private sector-fueled projects and adds to municipal tax rolls. Groups like the Buffalo Niagara Partnership and Unshackle Upstate are working to get the program extended.

39739 ■ "Local Manufacturers See Tax Proposal Hurting Global Operations" in Crain's Cleveland Business (Vol. 30, May 18, 2009, No. 20)
Pub: Crain Communications Inc.
Ed: Dan Shingler. Description: New tax laws proposed by the Obama Administration could hinder the efforts of some Northeast Ohio industrial companies from expanding their overseas markets. The law is designed to prevent companies from moving jobs overseas.

39740 ■ "Locals Eager for $785M Medical Marijuana Business" in Orlando Business Journal (Vol. 30, March 21, 2014, No. 39, pp. 4)
Pub: American City Business Journals
Released: March 21, 2014. Description: A number of local companies in Central Florida are preparing for a ballot initiative to legalize medical marijuana in November 2014. The National Cannabis Association estimates the medical marijuana market in Florida at $785 million, with about 260,000 patients, while Orlando's share is estimated at $89.1 million, with 29,518 potential patients.

39741 ■ "Lofty Ambitions" in Canadian Business (Vol. 80, October 22, 2007, No. 21, pp. 26)
Ed: Thomas Watson. Description: Canada has made its first trade deal in six years through the European Free Trade Agreement. This is a boost to the Canadian economy, but focus must be made on taking out internal barriers to inter-provincial trade and from third-party trade liberalization.

39742 ■ "Lone Star Paralysis Foundation Readies to Find a Cure" in Austin Business JournalInc. (Vol. 29, December 11, 2009, No. 40, pp. 1)
Pub: American City Business Journals
Ed: Sandra Zaragoza. Description: Lone Star Paralysis Foundation revealed plans to launch a fundraising effort for the advancement of cures for spinal cord injuries via adult stem cells and also fund a new spinal injury rehabilitation center. Efforts to raise about $3 million will begin as soon as the adult stem cell research study by Dr. Wise Young receives Food and Drug Administration approval.

39743 ■ "A Long Dry Spell" in Barron's (Vol. 92, August 25, 2012, No. 35, pp. 47)
Pub: Dow Jones & Co., Inc.
Contact: Clare Hart, President
Ed: Thomas G. Donlan. Description: Farmers in the United States Farm Belt need relief from government policies that have artificially reduced water prices. The federal government should refrain from too much management of the nation's water supply, particularly in a time of intense drought.

39744 ■ "A Long Road to Recovery" in Barron's (Vol. 89, July 27, 2009, No. 30, pp. 37)
Pub: Dow Jones & Co., Inc.
Contact: Clare Hart, President
Ed: Henry Kaufman. Description: United States' economy remains hobbled by some underlying constraint and real recovery remains ephemeral. Much of the financial problems could have been avoided if t he Federal Reserve was effectively guarding the financial system.

39745 ■ "Looking To Hire Young? Be Careful" in Boston Business Journal (Vol. 30, November 19, 2010, No. 43, pp. 1)
Pub: Boston Business Journal
Ed: Lisa van der Pool. Description: The Massachusetts Commission Against Discrimination (MCAD) has been using undercover job applicants to expose discrimination. Cabot's Ice Cream and Restaurant has been accused of denying older workers equal employment opportunities. MCAD has discovered unfair hiring practices such as hiring high school and college students.

39746 ■ "Lower Prices No Shoo-In as Telcos Near Deregulation" in Globe & Mail (March 28, 2007, pp. B1)
Pub: CTVglobemedia Publishing Inc.
Ed: Catherine McLean. Description: The fall in market share and low quality of service among other issues that may disallow telecommunication industries in Canada from setting their phone rates is discussed.

39747 ■ "Make a Resolution: ADA Training" in HRMagazine (Vol. 54, January 2009, No. 1, pp. 81)
Pub: Society for Human Resource Management
Contact: Henry G. Jackson, President
E-mail: hjackson@shrm.org
Ed: Victoria Zellers. Description: Americans with Disabilities Act (ADA) Amendments Act took effect January 1, 2009. The ADA Amendments Act means that more applicants and employees are eligible for reasonable accommodations and that employers need to develop a new ADA compliance strategy.

39748 ■ "Managerial Ties with Local Firms and Governments: an Analysis of Japanese Firms In China" in International Journal of Business and Emerging Markets (Vol. 4, July 11, 2012, No. 3, pp. 181)
Released: July 11, 2012. Description: This study explores how managerial ties between foreign firms and local firms and those between foreign firms and local government officials affect the performance of firms operating in transition economies. Using survey data collected from Japanese firms operating in China, this study finds that managerial ties between foreign firms and local firms and local government officials are positively associated with the performance of Japanese firms in China.

39749 ■ "Managing the Federal HOME Program: Past and Future" in Real Estate Review (Vol. 41, Spring 2012, No. 1, pp. 29)
Released: Spring 2012. Description: The US Department of Housing and Urban Development's Home Investment Partnerships Program (HOME) is discussed. The program is allocated to eligible state and local governments, with the goal of increasing affordable housing. HOME has been criticized for idling home construction projects.

39750 ■ "M&I Execs May Get Golden Parachutes" in Business Journal-Milwaukee (Vol. 28, December 31, 2010, No. 14, pp. A3)
Pub: Milwaukee Business Journal
Ed: Rich Kirchen. Description: Marshall and Isley Corporation's top executives have a chance to receive golden-parachute payments it its buyer, BMO Financial Group, repays the Troubled Asset Relief Program (TARP) loan on behalf of the company. One TARP rule prevents golden-parachute payments to them and the next five most highly paid employees of TARP recipients.

39751 ■ "The Many Hats and Faces of NAOHSM" in Indoor Comfort Marketing (Vol. 70, May 2011, No. 5, pp. 8)
Pub: Industry Publications Inc.
Contact: Shirleen Dorman, Editor
Description: Profile of the National Association of Oil Heating Service Managers, and its role in the industry, is presented.

39752 ■ "Marine Act Amendments Gain Parliamentary Approval" in Canadian Sailings (July 7, 2008)
Ed: Alex Binkley. Description: Changes to the Canada Marine Act provides better borrowing deals as well as an ability to tap into federal infrastructure funding for environmental protection measures, security improvements and other site enhancements.

39753 ■ "Market Takes Shape for Emissions Credits" in Globe & Mail (April 16, 2007, pp. B3)
Ed: Shawn McCarthy. Description: The effort of Canadian companies to prepare for emissions trading after the government imposes climate change regulations is discussed.

39754 ■ "Market Watch" in Barron's (Vol. 88, March 24, 2008, No. 12, pp. M18)
Pub: Dow Jones & Co., Inc.
Contact: Clare Hart, President
Ed: Ashraf Laidi, Marc Pado, David Kotok. Description: Latest measures implemented by the Federal Reserve to address the credit crisis did not benefit the US dollar, with the Japanese yen and the euro recouping earlier losses against the dollar. Goldman Sachs reported earnings of $3.23 per share, claiming a stronger liquidity position. The US markets bottomed early on 22 January 2007, according to evidence.

39755 ■ "Martin Marietta Expands Rock Solid Port Manatee Presence" in Tampa Bay Business Journal (Vol. 30, January 8, 2010, No. 3, pp. 1)
Pub: American City Business Journals
Ed: Jane Meinhardt. Description: Raleigh, North Carolina-based Martin Marietta Materials Inc. has been granted by Florida's Manatee County Port Authority with a 30-year, $42 million contract. Through the contract, an aggregate terminal will be built by Martin Marietta at the port. Construction work is anticipated to start in earl 2010 with terminal operations commencing by late summer 2010.

39756 ■ "Maryland Businesses Balk at 1099 Provision in Health Reform Law" in Baltimore Business Journal (Vol. 28, August 13, 2010, No. 14, pp. 1)
Pub: Baltimore Business Journal
Ed: Scott Dance. Description: Small business advocates and accountants have criticized the Internal Revenue Service Form 1099 provision in the

health care reform law as not worth the cost of time and money. Critics believe the policy would create a deluge of the documents that is too much for the companies or the IRS to handle. Details of the provision are also discussed.

39757 ■ *"Maryland Doctors, Health Insurers Squabble Over Who Sends Patients the Bill'* in *Baltimore Business Journal (Vol. 27, February 6, 2010)*
Pub: American City Business Journals
Ed: Scott Graham. **Description:** Issue of allowing patients to send reimbursement checks to physicians who are not part of their health insurer's provider network is being debated in Maryland. Details on the proposed Maryland bill and the arguments presented by doctors and insurers are outlined.

39758 ■ *"Maryland Legislature to Tackle Crisis in Jobless Fund'* in *Baltimore Business Journal (Vol. 27, December 18, 2009, No. 32, pp. 1)*
Pub: American City Business Journals
Ed: Scott Dance. **Description:** Maryland's General Assembly is set to finalize changes to the state's unemployment insurance system as soon as it convenes for the 2010 session. The move was aimed to draw $127 million in stimulus money that can support the nearly depleted fund of unemployment benefits within 45 days.

39759 ■ *"Maryland Ready to Defend Slots Minority Policy'* in *Boston Business Journal (Vol. 29, July 8, 2011, No. 9, pp. 3)*
Pub: American City Business Journals, Inc.
Ed: Scott Dance. **Description:** The legality of Maryland's minority inclusion policy may be put under scrutiny once the lawsuit filed by rejected slots developer Baltimore City Entertainment Group on July 5, 2011 is heard in court. The lawsuit aims to stop the bidding process on a proposed casino in Baltimore because the minority policy amounts to reverse discrimination.

39760 ■ *"Mass-Transit Backers: Change in State Funding Needed'* in *Crain's Detroit Business (Vol. 24, October 6, 2008, No. 40, pp. 19)*
Ed: Bill Shea. **Description:** Options to reform transportation and infrastructure funding in the state of Michigan are examined. Transit revitalization investment zones are also discussed.

39761 ■ *"A Matter of Perspective'* in *Business Journal-Portland (Vol. 24, November 2, 2007, No. 35, pp. 1)*
Pub: American City Business Journals, Inc.
Ed: Andy Giegerich. **Description:** Oregon Governor Ted Kulongoski assembled the Mortgage Lending Work Group, made up of members of the mortgage industry and consumer groups, to recommend possible bills for the Oregon Senate and House to consider. How its members try to balance philosophical differences in mortgage lending rules is discussed.

39762 ■ *"MBT Add-On: Gone by 2012?'* in *Crain's Detroit Business (Vol. 24, October 6, 2008, No. 40, pp. 1)*
Pub: Crain Communications Inc.
Contact: Rance E. Crain, President
Ed: Amy Lane. **Description:** Discusses the Michigan Business Tax (MBT), which has angered many businesses in the state due to the addition of a 21.99 percent surcharge. Although the tax policy will cut taxes on 63 percent of businesses in the state and represent no tax liability change for another nine percent of firms, other businesses will see increases of 100 percent or more. This increase means that many business owners will be forced to relocate or close their establishment and others will have to eliminate jobs. Lawmakers are attempting to find a solution to this problem.

39763 ■ *"Md. Hospitals 'Worried' About Cost of Adapting to Health Care Law'* in *Baltimore Business Journal (Vol. 30, July 6, 2012, No. 9, pp. 1)*
Pub: American City Business Journals, Inc.
Contact: Whitney Shaw, President
Ed: Sarah Gantz. **Released:** July 6, 2012. **Description:** Baltimore, Maryland-based hospitals have expressed concern over the cost of complying with

health care reforms. Hospitals have been planning to update information technology systems and care centers. Comments from executives included.

39764 ■ *"Md.'s Historic Tax Credit Plan Gains Support'* in *Baltimore Business Journal (Vol. 27, January 8, 2010, No. 36, pp. 1)*
Pub: American City Business Journals
Ed: Heather Harlan Warnack. **Description:** Maryland Governor Martin O'Malley plans to push legislation in the General Assembly to extend for three more years the tax credit program for rehabilitation of obsolete buildings. The Maryland Heritage Structure Rehabilitation Tax Credit Program has declined from almost $75 million in expenses in 2001 to roughly $5 million in 2010 fiscal year. Details on the projects that benefited from the program are explored.

39765 ■ *"Meals on Wheels; Chicago Puts the Brakes on Upwardly Mobile Food Truck Operators'* in *Wall Street Journal (August 7, 2012, pp. A12)*
Pub: Dow Jones & Co., Inc.
Contact: Clare Hart, President
Released: August 7, 2012. **Description:** Details on the City of Chicago's move to regulate mobile food truck operators is presented.

39766 ■ *"Medicaid Expansion Could Prompt New Taxes, Program Cuts in Maryland'* in *Baltimore Business Journal (Vol. 27, October 23, 2009, No. 24, pp. 1)*
Pub: American City Business Journals
Ed: Julekha Dash. **Description:** Effects of the expected federal expansion of Medicaid under federal health care reform on Maryland tax policy are presented. Health care executives believe new taxes are necessary for the state to pay for an expansion that could cost over $400 million to $600 million.

39767 ■ *"Medical Collection Agency Refutes Allegations In AG's Report'* in *PaymentsSource (May 1, 2012)*
Pub: SourceMedia Inc.
Contact: James M. Malkin, Chief Executive Officer
Released: May 1, 2012. **Description:** Accretive Health Inc. denies allegations by the Minnesota State Attorney General's Office that the firm used heavy-handed tactics pressuring patients to pay for services before receiving treatment. The medical collection agency's report states 'inaccuracies, innuendo and unfounded speculation' in the charges.

39768 ■ *"Medical Pot Backers Say Industry Will Survive'* in *Sacramento Business Journal (Vol. 28, October 14, 2011, No. 33, pp. 1)*
Pub: Sacramento Business Journal
Ed: Melanie Turner. **Description:** Medical marijuana supporters have expected the industry to decline but will survive the federal restriction on growers and dispensaries across California. California Cannabis Association and National Cannabis Industry Association believe that some of the dispensaries will remain and the shakeout will lead to stronger state regulations.

39769 ■ *"Medicare Fraudsters Turn to Pharmacies'* in *South Florida Business Journal (Vol. 32, June 15, 2012, No. 47, pp. 1)*
Pub: American City Business Journal
Description: U.S. Department of Health and Human Services, Office of Inspector General reports indicate that 2,637 retail pharmacies, or 4.4 percent of all pharmacies, had dubious Part D practices in 2009. However, the Miami area led the nation with 19.4 percent of its retail pharmacies submitting dubious claims as unethical frauds turn them in.

39770 ■ *"Memos to the Prime Minister: What Canada Could Be in the 21st Century*
Ed: Harvey Schacter. **Released:** April 11, 2003. **Price:** , $16.95. **Description:** A look into the business future of Canada. Topics include business, healthcare, think tanks, policy groups, education, the arts, economy, and social issues.

39771 ■ *"Merger Expected to Bring New Player to TV Market'* in *Providence Business News (Vol. 28, March 31, 2014, No. 52, pp. 1)*
Pub: American City Business Journals
Released: March 31, 2014. **Description:** The proposed merger of Media General and Providence, Rhode Island-based LIN Media LLC has the potential to change the TV landscape in the state. The two media companies' TV stations overlap in five markets and ownership at one of the stations is expected to change due to federal regulations regarding TV station ownership. The two TV stations are outlined.

39772 ■ *"Miami Valley Hospital To Close Senior Day Care Center'* in *Dayton Daily News (March 27, 2012)*
Pub: McClatchy Tribune Information Services
Ed: Ben Sutherly. **Description:** Miami Valley Hospital is closing its day care center for senior citizens because it needs to shift resources to other areas of the hospital as it prepares for Obamacare.

39773 ■ *"Minimizing Import Risks'* in *Canadian Sailings (July 7, 2008)*
Ed: Jack Kohane. **Description:** New food and product safety laws may be enacted by Canada's Parliament; importers, retailers and manufacturers could face huge fines if the new laws are passed.

39774 ■ *"Misguided'* in *Canadian Business (Vol. 81, July 22, 2008, No. 12-13, pp. 30)*
Ed: Al Rosen. **Description:** Canada's securities regulations are discussed; differing views on using principles-based and rules-based securities regulations are also presented.

39775 ■ *"Missouri Public Service Commission Chooses APX'* in *Wireless News (January 22, 2010)*
Description: Missouri Public Service Commission, with the help of APX Inc., an infrastructure provider for environmental and energy markets, has selected the North American Registry as the renewable energy certificate management system for Missouri Renewable Energy Standard compliance. APX will continue to support the state's renewable energy programs and manage their environmental assets.

39776 ■ *"Mobile Hot Spots: Trucks On a Roll'* in *Philadelphia Business Journal (Vol. 33, August 15, 2014, No. 27, pp. 4)*
Pub: American City Business Journals
Released: August 15, 2014. **Description:** Food trucks are becoming increasingly popular in Philadelphia, Pennsylvania, offering a range of foods, from tacos to gourmet cuisine. However, food vendors face various obstacles in their business due to the city's outdated regulations on mobile food vending and large corporate restaurant chains exploiting the popularity of food trucks.

39777 ■ *"Modular Home Center Opens in Arcadia'* in *Charlotte Observer (February 1, 2007)*
Ed: John Lawhorne. **Description:** Arcadia Home Center features modular homes constructed on a steel frame; regulations regarding the manufacture and moving of these homes are included.

39778 ■ *"Monopoly Money Madness'* in *Canadian Business (Vol. 81, March 17, 2008, No. 4, pp. 9)*
Pub: Rogers Media Inc.
Contact: Tony Viner, President
Description: Enbridge was given permission by the Ontario Energy Board to collect $22 million it spent on an out-of-court settlement for charging unfair fees from 1994 to 2002. Customers are essentially being gouged twice in this scenario. The monopoly of Enbridge should end and the consumers should not have to pay for the system's faults.

39779 ■ *"Monsanto's Next Single-Bag Refuge Product Approved'* in *Farm Industry News (December 5, 2011)*
Pub: Penton Business Media Inc.
Contact: David Kieselstein, Chief Executive Officer
Description: Monsanto's refuge-in-a-bag (RIB) product was approved for commercialization in 2012. The Genuity VT Double Pro RIB Complete is a blend

of 95 percent Genuity VT Double Pro and 5 percent refuge (non-Bt) seed and provides above-ground pest control and not corn rootworm protection.

39780 ■ "More Aid, Please: Letting the Sunshine In" in Barron's (Vol. 89, July 6, 2009, No. 27, pp. 11)
Pub: Dow Jones & Co., Inc.
Contact: Clare Hart, President
Ed: Katherine Cheng. **Description:** Solar energy industry leaders believe the industry needs aid from the US government regarding the funding of its research efforts and lowering solar energy costs. The climate change bill passed by the US House of Representatives signifies the US government's desire to significantly reduce carbon dioxide emissions.

39781 ■ "More SouthPark Shopping" in Charlotte Business Journal (Vol. 25, July 16, 2010, No. 17, pp. 1)
Pub: Charlotte Business Journal
Ed: Will Boye. **Description:** Charlotte, North Carolina-based Bissel Companies has announced plans to expand its retail presence at the Siskey and Sharon properties in SouthPark. Bissel Companies has requested a rezoning to a mixed-use development classification so that it can utilize the entire ground floor of the Siskey building for restaurant and retail uses.

39782 ■ "MorphoTrust to Supply Delaware DMV With Self-Service Kiosks" in Entertainment Close-Up (September 19, 2012)
Pub: Close-Up Media
Released: September 19, 2012. **Description:** In a move to make driver license renewal and replacement easier, the state of Delaware has installed driver license and personal identification kiosks in Dover, Wilmington, and Georgetown. These kiosks incorporate digital cameras, scanners and other technology to maintain security during the process.

39783 ■ "Mortgage Mess Continues To Trigger Bids To Ease Crisis" in Business First-Columbus (December 13, 2007, pp. A1)
Pub: American City Business Journals, Inc.
Ed: Adrian Burns. **Description:** Measures to prevent foreclosures in Ohio are presented. On December 6, 2007, the Bush Administration started a national incentive that will establish a streamlined process for modifying loans. Some have questioned the proposal, since it is expected the plan will only help about 90,000 of the 1.8 million borrowers. According to Ohio Treasurer, Richard Cordray, one of the state's objectives is to calm the markets on Wall Street.

39784 ■ "Mortgage Servicers Back National Effort" in Business First-Columbus (October 22, 2007, pp. A1)
Pub: American City Business Journals, Inc.
Ed: Adrian Burns. **Description:** Ohio is having difficulty convincing mortgage companies to sign a compact containing guidelines when working with troubled borrowers. Many of Ohio's mortgage companies are supporting a national initiative to respond to the mortgage crisis instead.

39785 ■ "Mulroney on the Record" in Canadian Business (Vol. 79, September 11, 2006, No. 18, pp. 43)
Pub: Rogers Media Inc.
Contact: Tony Viner, President
Ed: Joe Chidley. **Description:** Canada's former prime minister and senior partner at the law firm Ogilvy Renault, Brain Mulroney speaks about the major policies and initiatives of the current government and its impact on the country's economy.

39786 ■ "MyWireless.org Commends Arizona Congressman Trent Franks for Committing to Wireless Tax Relief for American Consumers and Businesses" in PR Newswire (September 21, 2012)
Pub: PR Newswire Association L.L.C.
Contact: David B. Armon, President
Description: MyWireless.org presented Congressman Trent Franks from Arizona with the 2012 Wireless Consumer Hero Award for his work on wireless tax relief for American consumers and businesses.

Franks' 'Wireless Tax Fairness Act' (HR 1002) promotes access to wireless networks as a key ingredient of millions of Americans' livelihoods, whether phone, broadband Internet necessary to run a small business.

39787 ■ "National Crowdfunding Association Enters Into Deal with SCORE" in Professional Services Close-Up (August 7, 2012)
Pub: Close-Up Media
Released: August 7, 2012. **Description:** National Crowdfunding Association (NLCFA) will produce a series of educational webinars teaching the basics of crowdfunding for SCORE's 13,000 volunteers. Investment crowdfunding is a process designed to finance small businesses in the US. The JOBS Act allows small and startup businesses to raise up to $1 annually by issuing equity or debt security to groups of small investors through the Internet. Details of crowdfuding and the JOBS Act are outlined.

39788 ■ "N.C. Foreclosure Regulation Papered Over" in Charlotte Business Journal (Vol. 25, November 5, 2010, No. 33, pp.)
Pub: Charlotte Business Journal
Ed: Adam O'Daniel. **Description:** County courts in North Carolina are having challenges coping with its oversight and regulation duties as it becomes too busy with foreclosure cases. Clerks in some county courts have presided over foreclosure hearings because of the flooding of foreclosure cases.

39789 ■ "A New Era for Raiders" in Harvard Business Review (Vol. 88, November 2010, No. 11, pp. 34)
Pub: Harvard Business School Publishing
Ed: Guhan Subramanian. **Description:** The article presents evidence that Section 203 is vulnerable, and a new wave of corporate takeovers may develop. The authors suggest that since no bidders have able to use the 85 percent stipulation over the last 19 years, it does not present a meaningful opportunity for success.

39790 ■ "New Health Law, Lack of Docs Collide on Cape Cod" in Boston Business Journal (Vol. 27, October 12, 2007, No. 37, pp. 1)
Ed: Mark Hollmer. **Description:** There is a shortage of primary care providers at Outer Cape Health Services in Massachusetts, with the isolation of the area and as physicians look for higher paying careers in specialty positions. The Commonwealth Health Insurance Connector Authority is pushing for a new health insurance law and is working with Cape Cod Chamber of Commerce to conduct outreach programs.

39791 ■ "New Law Lets Shareholders Play Hardball With Firms" in Globe & Mail (January 2, 2006, pp. B1)
Pub: CTVglobemedia Publishing Inc.
Ed: Janet McFarland. **Description:** Business lawyer Wes Voorheis discusses about the launching of Bill 198 by plaintiffs' lawyers on behalf of ordinary retail investors.

39792 ■ "New Lawsuit Filed Against Defunct Collection Agency" in PaymentsSource (January 9, 2012)
Pub: SourceMedia Inc.
Contact: James M. Malkin, Chief Executive Officer
Released: January 9, 2012. **Description:** Unicredit America Inc. hopes to hold former company president, Michael J. Covatto and former vice president Anthony D. Covatto, personally responsible for the violations against consumer protection laws. Pennsylvania State Attorney General's Office has renewed its lawsuit against the firm.

39793 ■ "New Northern Kentucky Chamber Chief Walking the Talk" in Business Courier (Vol. 27, August 27, 2010, No. 17, pp. 1)
Pub: Business Courier
Ed: Lucy May. **Description:** National Brand & Tag Company president, Eric Haas, has vowed to put his various work experiences when he assumes the presidency of North Kentucky Chamber of Com-

merce. Haas wants to help the Chamber influence government policies that could help various businesses through the economic depression.

39794 ■ "New Rule Rankles In Jersey" in Philadelphia Business Journal (Vol. 30, September 16, 2011, No. 31, pp. 1)
Pub: American City Business Journals Inc.
Ed: Jeff Blumenthal. **Description:** A new rule in New Jersey which taxes out-of-state companies that conduct business in the state earned the ire of several banks, mortgage lenders and credit card companies and prompted opponents to threaten to file lawsuits. The new rule is an amendment to New Jersey Division of Taxation's corporate business tax regulation and is retroactive to 2002. Details are given.

39795 ■ "New State Rules Require Cranes and Operators to be Certified" in Bellingham Business Journal (Vol. February 2010, pp. 11)
Pub: Sound Publishing Inc.
Contact: Gloria G. Fletcher, President
Ed: Isaac Bonnell. **Description:** All construction cranes in Washington state must be inspected annually to be certified for use. The move is part of a larger L&I crane safety program that also requires crane operators to pass a written exam and a skill test.

39796 ■ New Technology-Based Firms in the New Millennium, Volume 6
Ed: Ray Oakey. **Released:** May 2008. **Price:** , $149.00. **Description:** Collection of papers from the Annual International High Technology Firms (HTSFs) Conference cover issues of importance to governments as they develop technological program. Papers are grouped into three sections: theory, strategy and clustering, and spin-off firms.

39797 ■ "New Wildcard On the Table" in Orlando Business Journal (Vol. 30, January 10, 2014, No. 29, pp. 4)
Pub: American City Business Journals
Released: January 10, 2014. **Description:** Florida's legislature is discussing the idea of a statewide vote to decide the expansion of gambling in the state beyond limited locations. The move to take the decision from lawmakers and business interests was done three times before the measure failed the referendum.

39798 ■ "New York Collection Agency's Bribery Case Resolved" in PaymentsSource (Vol. 15, August 1, 2010, No. 7, pp. 19)
Pub: SourceMedia Inc.
Contact: James M. Malkin, Chief Executive Officer
Description: Criminal conviction and civil settlement in a bribery case and Medicaid scam involving H.I.S. Holdings Inc. and owner Deborah Kantor is examined.

39799 ■ "The Next Step in Patent Reform" in Information Today (Vol. 28, November 2011, No. 10, pp. 1)
Pub: Information Today, Inc.
Contact: Thomas H. Hogan, President
E-mail: ctuthill@infotoday.com
Ed: George H. Pike. **Description:** The Leahy-Smith America Invents Act was signed into law in September 2011. The new act reformed the previous US patent system. Information involving the new patent law process is discussed.

39800 ■ "The Next Waive" in Hawaii Business (Vol. 53, January 2008, No. 7, pp. 27)
Pub: PacificBasin Communications
Ed: Cathy S. Cruz-George. **Description:** Only 40,000 Koreans took a visit to Hawaii in 2007, a decline from the pre-September averages of 123,000 visits. The number of Korean visitors in Hawaii could increase if the visa waiver proposal is passed. Efforts to improve Hawaiian tourism are presented.

39801 ■ "Nixon Assails Insurance Rules" in Globe & Mail (March 4, 2006, pp. B5)
Ed: Sinclair Stewart. **Description:** The opinions of chief executive officer Gordon Nixon of Royal Bank of Canada on the need to amend banking regulations, in order to provide insurance services, are presented.

39802 ■ *"No End to the Nightmare; America's Car Industry"* in *The Economist (Vol. 390, January 3, 2009, No. 8612, pp. 46)*

Description: Detroit's struggling auto industry and the government loan package is discussed as well as the United Auto Worker union, which is loathed by Senate Republicans.

39803 ■ *"No Shortage of Challenges for Cross-Border Trade"* in *Canadian Sailings (June 30, 2008)*

Ed: Kathlyn Horibe. **Description:** Pros and cons of the North American Free Trade Agreement are examined. The agreement between the U.S. and Canada concerning trade was an essential step toward securing economic growth for Canadian citizens. Two-way trade between the counties has tripled since the agreement and accounts for 7.1 million American and 3 million Canadian jobs.

39804 ■ *"Non-Daily Papers Eye Public Notice Revenue"* in *Birmingham Business Journal (Vol 29, June 8, 2012, No. 24, pp. 1)*

Pub: American City Business Journals, Inc.

Contact: Whitney Shaw, President

Ed: Ryan Poe. **Released:** June 8, 2012. **Description:** Alabama's local governments have expressed worry over their public notices requirement with the plan of Birmingham News to publish only three days a week. However, Senator Linda Coleman found provision in the state constitution that allows government to publish in any paper if there is no daily.

39805 ■ *Non-Standard Employment under Globalization: Flexible Work and Social Security in the Newly Industrializing Countries*

Pub: Palgrave Macmillan

Contact: Lisa Dunn, Manager

E-mail: l.dunn@palgrave.com

Ed: Koichi Usami. **Released:** December 2009. **Price:** £84, hardcover; $115. **Description:** Expansion of non-standard employment under globalization is being recognized in all of the newly industrialized countries. The book examines deregulation of labor markets, social protection for nonstandard workers, and social security reforms in accordance with the transformation of employment. **Availability:** PrintE-book.

39806 ■ *"Nonprofits May Lose MBE Status in MD"* in *Boston Business Journal (Vol. 29, September 2, 2011, No. 17, pp. 1)*

Pub: American City Business Journals, Inc.

Ed: Scott Dance. **Description:** A business group has been pushing to bar nonprofits from Maryland's Minority Business program. Nonprofits have been found to take a large portion of state contracts intended for women- and minority-owned businesses. The group is also crafting proposed legislation to remove nonprofits from the program.

39807 ■ *"Not In Our Backyard"* in *Canadian Business (Vol. 80, October 22, 2007, No. 21, pp. 76)*

Ed: Anrew Nikiforuk. **Description:** Alberta Energy and Utilities Board's proposed construction of electric transmission line has let to protests by landowners. The electric utility was also accused of spying on ordinary citizens and violating impartiality rules. Details of the case between Lavesta Area Group and the Board are discussed.

39808 ■ *"A Novel Fix for the Credit Mess"* in *Barron's (Vol. 88, March 31, 2008, No. 13, pp. 10)*

Pub: Dow Jones & Co., Inc.

Contact: Clare Hart, President

Ed: Michael Santoli. **Description:** Due to the common bank-leverage factor of 10, the $250 billion of lost bank capital would have supported $2.5 trillion in lending capacity. Jeffrey Lewis suggests onerous regulations on bank-holding companies that own 10 to 25 percent, as they are partly to blame. Statistical data included.

39809 ■ *"Now the Real Work Begins"* in *Baltimore Business Journal (Vol. 28, October 15, 2010, No. 23, pp. 1)*

Pub: Baltimore Business Journal

Ed: Emily Mullin. **Description:** The Henry J. Kaiser Family Foundation's survey shows nearly 53 percent of Americans remain confused about health care reform and it was up to the states to educate the people. However, Maryland is still trying to figure out how to conduct the campaign without guidance or funding from the Federal government.

39810 ■ *"Nude Maid Service Could Face Fines"* in *UPI NewsTrack (April 10, 2012)*

Pub: United Press International

Contact: Nicholas Chiaia, President

E-mail: president@upi.com

Released: April 10, 2012. **Description:** Lubbock Fantasy Maid Service, located in Texas, is facing fines because it is operating without a permit. The cleaning service provides maids dresses in lingerie, topless or nude. Without the permit, the firm could face fines of $2,000 daily. The company reports it is doing nothing illegally.

39811 ■ *"Numbers Game"* in *Baltimore Business Journal (Vol. 27, February 6, 2010, No. 40, pp. 1)*

Pub: American City Business Journals

Ed: Scott Dance. **Description:** Doubts are being raised regarding the impact of the federal stimulus spending in addressing unemployment in Maryland, which has experienced 1,800 jobs created so far. Details on the view of companies and the insufficient amount of contracts that lead to the fewer number of workers being hired are discussed.

39812 ■ *"Obama Orders Contractors To Raise Minimum Wage"* in *Atlanta Business Chronicle (June 20, 2014, pp. 9A)*

Pub: American City Business Journals, Inc.

Contact: Whitney Shaw, President

Released: June 20, 2014. **Description:** Discussion of the new rules set out by President Obama, which includes the minimum wage of employees and discrimination against employees doing business with the Federal government is presented. The minimum wage law will increase to $10 per hour from $7.25 per hour; and discrimination against employees on the basis of sexual orientation or gender identity will not be tolerated.

39813 ■ *"Obama Plan May Boost Maryland Cyber Security"* in *Boston Business Journal (Vol. 29, May 20, 2011, No. 2, pp. 1)*

Pub: American City Business Journals, Inc.

Ed: Scott Dance. **Description:** May 12, 2011 outline of the cyber security policies of President Obama may improve the cyber security industry in Maryland as the state is home to large defense and intelligence activities. Details of the proposed policies are discusses as well as their advantages to companies that deal in developing cyber security plans for other companies.

39814 ■ *"Observers See Different Messages if Voters Reject Ambassador Tax Rebate"* in *Wichita Business Journal (Vol. 27, February 17, 2012, No. 7, pp. 1)*

Pub: American City Business Journal

Description: Ambassador Hotel's room tax rebate has been put on a referendum in Wichita,Kansas and the rejection is expected to affect future downtown projects. However, the observers differ on the messages of a no vote would send to real estate investors. Insights on the ongoing debate on economic development policy are also given.

39815 ■ *"Ohio Collection Agency Settles Second Lawsuit"* in *Collections & Credit Risk (Vol. 15, July 1, 2010, No. 6, pp. 9)*

Pub: SourceMedia Inc.

Contact: James M. Malkin, Chief Executive Officer

Description: National Enterprise Systems, will pay $75,000 for illegal and abusive collection charged in a lawsuit filed by West Virginia's Attorney General's office. Money will be used to reimburse students and consumers who paid the illegal fees to the company.

39816 ■ *"Ohio Regulator Sues Collection Agency"* in *PaymentsSource (September 21, 2012)*

Pub: SourceMedia Inc.

Contact: James M. Malkin, Chief Executive Officer

Released: September 21, 2012. **Description:** Mike DeWine, Ohio Attorney General, is suing Royal Oak Financial Services, a collection agency doing business as Collection and Recovery Bureau. The suit alleges that the firm used collection tactics banned by federal law and also attempting to collect unverified debts.

39817 ■ *"Oil Prices Go Up In Flames"* in *Barron's (Vol. 92, September 17, 2012, No. 38, pp. M11)*

Description: Petroleum prices appear to be headed higher over the fall of 2012 due to continuing political tension in the Middle East. Demand for petroleum products is kept up by slow global economic growth.

39818 ■ *"O'Malley, Ehrlich Court Business Vote"* in *Baltimore Business Journal (Vol. 28, October 1, 2010, No. 21, pp. 1)*

Pub: Baltimore Business Journal

Ed: Scott Dance. **Description:** Maryland Governor Martin O'Malley and former Governor Robert Ehrlich reveal their business plans and platforms as they court business-minded votes in the state. Ehrlich, a Republican and O'Malley, a Democrat have both initiated programs that helped small businesses, but both have also introduced programs that made it more expensive and difficult to do business in the state.

39819 ■ *"Omniplex on the Case"* in *Black Enterprise (Vol. 37, December 2006, No. 5, pp. 38)*

Pub: Earl G. Graves Publishing Co. Inc.

Contact: Earl G. Graves, Jr., President

Ed: Glenn Townes. **Description:** Office of Personnel Management in Washington D.C. recently awarded a service contract to Omniplex World Services Corp. This Virginia-based company will perform security investigations and background checks on current and prospective federal employees and military personnel and contractors.

39820 ■ *"On the Horizon"* in *Advertising Age (Vol. 83, October 1, 2012, No. 35, pp. 5)*

Description: Federal Trade Commission is revising rules regarding online marketing aimed at children due to the growth of the Web and innovations like mobile applications. The current Children's Online Privacy Protection Act went into effect in 1998.

39821 ■ *"On Policy: Where Talk is Cheap"* in *Canadian Business (Vol. 80, January 29, 2007, No. 3, pp. 19)*

Ed: Jack Mintz. **Description:** The comparative analysis of the telecommunications policy of Canada and the United States of America is presented. The methods of improving Canada's telecommunications policy are discussed.

39822 ■ *"On tap: More Could Get MEGA Credits: Need to Look Outside State May Be Cut"* in *Crain's Detroit Business (April 7, 2008)*

Pub: Crain Communications Inc.

Contact: Rance E. Crain, President

Ed: Amy Lane. **Description:** In order to qualify for Michigan Economic Growth Authority tax credits Michigan businesses may no longer have to shop outside the state due to a new bill which has already passed the state Senate and will move on to the House; the bill, along with further changes to the MEGA program, is designed to provide incentives for investments that would add relevance and make Michigan more competitive.

39823 ■ *"On Thin Ice"* in *South Florida Business Journal (Vol. 34, July 11, 2014, No. 51, pp. 16)*

Pub: American City Business Journals

Released: July 11, 2014. **Description:** Local exporters in South Florida expressed concerns about the looming expiration of the authorization of Export-Import Bank of the United States on September 30,

2014. Failure to obtain the reauthorization would place at risk the $885 million in export sales that local companies made in 2013.

39824 ■ *"On the U.S. Election: Shaky on Free Trade" in Canadian Business (Vol. 81, December 19, 2007, No. 1, pp. 29)*
Pub: Rogers Media Inc.
Contact: Tony Viner, President
Ed: Rachel Pulfer. **Description:** Rhetoric at the U.S. presidential elections seems to be pointing toward a weaker free trade consensus, with Democratic candidates being against the renewal of free trade deals, while Republican candidates seem to be for free trade.

39825 ■ *"Open the Telecom Market" in Canadian Business (Vol. 80, April 23, 2007, No. 9, pp. 80)*
Description: The effects of federal telecommunication law on foreign investments in telecommunication industry are presented.

39826 ■ *"Oracle and Tauri Group Honored by Homeland Security and Defense Business Council" in Wireless News (December 15, 2009)*
Description: Selected as members of the year by the Homeland Security and Defense Business Council were Oracle, a software company that has provided thought leadership and strategic insights as well as The Tauri Group, an analytical consultancy, that has demonstrated a unique understanding of the role of small business and its vital contribution to the success of the country's security.

39827 ■ *"Orange County's Paid Sick Leave Initiative Draws Ire of Businesses" in Orlando Business Journal (Vol. 29, August 24, 2012, No. 10, pp. 1)*
Pub: American City Business Journal
Ed: Anjali Fluker. **Description:** A proposed sick leave initiative has been opposed by businesses in Orange County, Florida. The regulation will require businesses with more than than 15 employees to provide workers with paid sick leave benefits.

39828 ■ *"OSC Eyes New Tack on Litigation" in Globe & Mail (April 9, 2007, pp. B1)*
Ed: Janet McFarland. **Description:** The efforts of the Ontario Securities Commission to set up a tribunal for the investigation and control of securities fraud are described. The rate of the conviction of corporate officials in cases heard by the courts is discussed.

39829 ■ *"OSHA Proposes Historic Safety Penalty on BP" in Workforce Management (Vol. 88, November 16, 2009, No. 12, pp. 8)*
Pub: Crain Communications Inc.
Contact: Rance E. Crain, President
Ed: Mark Schoeff Jr. **Description:** Labor Secretary Hilda Solis has warned that she aims to toughen the enforcement of workplace laws; OSHA, the Occupational Safety and Health Administration, an agency within the Department of Labor, is penalizing BP Products North America Inc. for their failure to improve workplace safety.

39830 ■ *"Ottawa Advised to Underwrite Carbon Technology" in Globe & Mail (March 10, 2007, pp. B3)*
Ed: Shawn McCarthy. **Description:** A federal panel's suggestion that carbon tax in Canada was not adequate to encourage oil companies and utilities to take up costly technologies to reduce carbon emissions is discussed.

39831 ■ *"Ottawa Attacks!" in Canadian Business (Vol. 79, November 6, 2006, No. 22, pp. 21)*
Ed: Jeff Sanford. **Description:** The effects of new tax policy developed by Jim Flaherty, Finance Minister of Canada, on income trusts are presented.

39832 ■ *Overcoming Barriers to Entrepreneurship in the United States*
Pub: Lexington Books
Contact: Serena Leigh Kromback, Director
Ed: Diana Furchtgott-Roth. **Released:** March 28, 2008. **Price:** $32.99, Paperback; £19.95, Paperback. **Description:** Real and perceived barriers to the

founding and running of small businesses in America are discussed. Each chapter outlines how policy and economic environments can hinder business owners and offers tips to overcome these obstacles. Starting with venture capital access in Silicon Valley during the Internet bubble, the book goes on to question the link between personal wealth and entrepreneurship, examines how federal tax rates affect small business creation and destruction, explains the low rate of self-employment among Mexican immigrants, and suggests ways pension coverage can be increased in small businesses.

39833 ■ *"The Overlicensed Society" in Harvard Business Review (Vol. 90, April 2012, No. 4, pp. 38)*
Pub: Harvard Business Review Press
Contact: Peter E. Walsh, Director
Ed: Robert E. Litan. **Released:** April 2012. **Description:** The author argues that certification and licensing requirements are hindering professionals who might otherwise be able to find positions and provide services inexpensively. To key areas are healthcare and law. Federal mutual recognition agreements may be one method of addressing both practice and consumer protection issues.

39834 ■ *"An Overview of Energy Consumption of the Globalized World Economy" in Energy Policy (Vol. 39, October 2011, No. 10, pp. 5920-2928)*
Pub: Reed Elsevier Reference Publishing
Ed: Z.M. Chen, G.Q. Chen. **Description:** Energy consumption and its impact on the global world economy is examined.

39835 ■ *"Pa. Pushes for Collection of Online Sales Tax" in Philadelphia Business Journal (Vol. 31, March 2, 2012, No. 3, pp. 1)*
Pub: American City Business Journal
Description: The government of Pennsylvania is seeking to increase taxes from e-sales. The government estimates that it could lose $380 million in uncollected online sales and use tax to the e-commerce retail sector in 2012. It has also introduced tax forms that instruct taxpayers to report and remit use tax.

39836 ■ *"Panel to Call for Reduced Restraints on Telecom Sector" in Globe & Mail (March 17, 2006, pp. B1)*
Ed: Simon Tuck. **Description:** A federal panel called to adopt a more market-friendly approach to the lucrative telecommunications sector in Canada. Details of the report are presented.

39837 ■ *"Panel Calls for 'Fundamental' Change to Telecom Regulation" in Globe & Mail (March 23, 2006, pp. B1)*
Ed: Catherine McLean. **Description:** A federal panel review at Ottawa called for a shakeup of regulations and policies that govern telecommunications companies to contend with sweeping technological changes. Details of the panel review are presented.

39838 ■ *"Papal Permit Trumps Plumbing Code" in Contractor (Vol. 57, February 2010, No. 2, pp. 20)*
Pub: Penton Media, Inc.
Ed: Dave Yates. **Description:** Despite the plumbing code, a plumbing contractor was able to convince the inspector to approve his application to install a sacristy sink which drains into the ground instead of the sewer system. Details of the church's system are presented.

39839 ■ *"Past Promises Haunt Project" in The Business Journal-Portland (Vol. 25, August 1, 2008, No. 21, pp. 1)*
Pub: American City Business Journals, Inc.
Contact: Whitney Shaw, President
Ed: Aliza Earnshaw. **Description:** Oregon University System and Oregon Health and Science University will face the state Legislature to defend their request for a $250 million in state bonds to fund a life-sciences collaborative research building. The project is meant to help grow the Oregon bioscience industry. Comments from industry observers and legislators are also presented.

39840 ■ *"Pay Heed to 'Smack Stack" in Puget Sound Business Journal (Vol. 35, May 16, 2014, No. 4, pp. 6)*
Pub: American City Business Journals
Released: May 16, 2014. **Description:** Technology consultant, Geoffrey Moore, discloses the topics he plans to discuss at the annual State of Technology Luncheon held in Washington on May 19, 2014. He will explore the impact of technology and business trends on public-policy making and regulations.

39841 ■ *"Paying for the Recession: Rebalancing Economic Growth" in Montana Business Quarterly (Vol. 49, Spring 2011, No. 1, pp. 2)*
Pub: University of Montana Bureau of Business and Economic Research
Contact: Patrick Barkey, Director
E-mail: patrick.barkey@business.umt.edu
Ed: Patrick M. Barkey. **Description:** Four key issues required to address in order to rebalance economic growth in America are examined. They include: savings rates, global trade imbalances, government budgets and most importantly, housing price correction.

39842 ■ *"PCH Gets Trauma Center Status" in The Business Journal - Serving Phoenix and the Valley of the Sun (Vol. 28, July 11, 2008, No. 45)*
Ed: Angela Gonzales. **Description:** Phoenix Children's Hospital has been allowed by the Arizona Department of Health Services to launch the state's first trauma center for children. The trauma center is expected to cost the hospital $7 million a year.

39843 ■ *"Permit Reviews To Speed Up In Few Months" in Austin Business Journal (Vol. 33, June 22, 2012, No. 15, pp. A1)*
Pub: American City Business Journals, Inc.
Contact: Whitney Shaw, President
Ed: Vicky Garza. **Released:** June 22, 2012. **Description:** Austin, Texas is hiring 14 more staffers to help with the backlog of permits at the Planning and Developmet Review department. The additional employees will be paid for by the 25 percent increase in 421 development-related fees that will take effect July 1. Insights into the delay in getting a permit for new construction or renovation are also given.

39844 ■ *"Perspective: Borderline Issues" in Entrepreneur (Vol. 35, October 2007, No. 10, pp. 48)*
Pub: Entrepreneur Press
Contact: Perlman Neil, President
Ed: Joshua Kurlantzick. **Description:** Failure of the immigration reform bill is expected to result in increased difficulty in finding workers that would take on the dirty and perilous jobs, which are usually taken by immigrants. Regularizing immigration on the other hand will cost business owners money by making them spend for the legality of their employees' stay in the U.S. Other effects of immigration laws on entrepreneurs are discussed.

39845 ■ *"Peter Gilgan" in Canadian Business (Vol. 82, April 27, 2009, No. 7, pp. 58)*
Pub: Rogers Media Inc.
Contact: Tony Viner, President
Ed: Calvin Leung. **Description:** Mattamy Homes Ltd. president and chief executive officer Peter Gilgan believes that their business model of building communities in an organized way brings advantages to the firm and for their customers. He also believes in adopting their product prices to new market realities. Gilgan considers the approvals regime in Ontario his biggest challenge in the last 20 years.

39846 ■ *"Philadelphia's Largest Employers Will Fill 6,000 Jobs Within 6 Months" in Philadelphia Business Journal (Vol. 28, February 5, 2010, No. 51, pp. 1)*
Pub: American City Business Journals Inc.
Ed: Peter Van Allen. **Description:** Philadelphia, Pennsylvania's largest employers have openings for at least 6,000 jobs. But businesses remain cautious and are selective in hiring or waiting to see what happens to federal policy changes.

39847 ■ *"Piece of Health Law 'A Goner"' in Baltimore Business Journal (Vol. 28, November 19, 2010, No. 28, pp. 1)*
Pub: Baltimore Business Journal
Ed: Kent Hoover. **Description:** Montana Senator Max Baucus, a Democrat who heads the Senate Finance Committee, has revealed his plan to push legislation that would repeal the 1099 IRS provision that was created by the health care reform law and will result in more paperwork for small businesses when it goes into effect in 2012.

39848 ■ *"Pipeline Dreams" in Canadian Business (Vol. 80, October 22, 2007, No. 21, pp. 19)*
Ed: Rachel Pulfer. **Description:** Northwest Mackenzie Valley Pipeline has been under review by the National Energy Board since 2004. Hearings on the construction of the gas pipeline will wrap up in 2008. Pius Rolheiser, the spokesman of Imperial Oil Company Inc. believes the change of government in the area will not affect the negotiations on the pipeline construction.

39849 ■ *"Planned CO2 Regulations Could Hit Region Hard" in Pittsburgh Business Times (Vol. 33, June 6, 2014, No. 47, pp. 9)*
Pub: American City Business Journals
Released: June 6, 2014. **Description:** The U.S. Environmental Protection Agency's (EPA's) proposed rules to cut carbon dioxide (CO2) emissions by 30 percent over 16 years could have an adverse impact on southwestern Pennsylvania. The draft regulations, announced June 2, 2014, will affect the Pennsylvania region's power-generation sector as well as its coal industry, thereby impacting the regional economy.

39850 ■ *"Play It Safe" in Entrepreneur (Vol. 35, November 2007, No. 11, pp. 26)*
Pub: Entrepreneur Press
Contact: Perlman Neil, President
Ed: Gwen Moran. **Description:** U.S.-based toy manufacturers find opportunity from concerns regarding the recent recalls of toys that are made in China. The situation can provide better probability of parents buying toys made in the U.S. or Europe, where manufacturing standards are stricter.

39851 ■ *"Playfair Receives Drill Permit for Risby, Yukon Tungsten Deposit" in Marketwired (May 16, 2007)*
Pub: Comtex News Network Inc.
Description: Playfair Mining announced that it has received a 5 year Class III land use permit from the Mineral Resources Branch, Yukon which will allow the company to carry out a drill program during the upcoming drill season on the company-owned Risby, Yukon tungsten deposit. Statistical data included.

39852 ■ *"Polanco Fellows: A Capital Program that Changes Lives" in Hispanic Business (Vol. 30, September 2008, No. 9, pp. 82)*
Pub: Hispanic Business Inc.
Contact: Jesus Chavarria, President
Ed: John Schumacher. **Description:** Launched in 2003, the Polanco fellows program is named after former state Senator Richard Polanco, a founder and chairman of the California Latino Caucus Institute. The program offers young Hispanics a chance to experience public policy and the functioning of the California Capitol through a 12-month, on-the-job Capitol training.

39853 ■ *"Political Environments and Business Strategy: Implications for Managers" in Business Horizons (Vol. 51, January-February 2008)*
Pub: Elsevier Advanced Technology Publications
Ed: Gerald D. Keim, Amy J. Hillman. **Description:** Various government bodies and business organizations work together in shaping new business opportunities and policies that arise from globalization. Presented is framework of public policy considerations for business managers. The framework is based on Nobel laureate Douglas North's work.

39854 ■ *"Port of Greater Cincinnati Development Authority Taking Heat in Kenwood Mess" in Business Courier (Vol. 26,*

September 18, 2009, No. 21, pp. 1)
Pub: American City Business Journals, Inc.
Contact: Whitney Shaw, President
Ed: Dan Monk. **Description:** Port of Greater Cincinnati Development Authority is being criticized for not requiring payment and performance bonds to ensure that contractors would be paid. The criticism occurred after the general contractor for the project to build a parking garage at Kenwood Towne Plaza stopped paying its subcontractors.

39855 ■ *"Potash Sale Must Be Blocked' in Canadian Business (Vol. 83, October 12, 2010, No. 17, pp. 24)*
Pub: Rogers Media Inc.
Contact: Tony Viner, President
Ed: Kasey Coholan. **Description:** Chief executive officers (CEOs) and corporate leaders in Canada are concerned about the possible sale of Potash Corporation to foreign buyers. A Compas Inc. poll recently asked CEOs whether the Canadian Government should step in to block the sale of the country's largest fertilizer firm.

39856 ■ *"The Power Brokers" in Crain's Chicago Business (Vol. 31, April 28, 2008, No. 17, pp. 41)*
Pub: Crain Communications Inc.
Contact: Todd Johnson, Publisher
Ed: Samantha Stainburn. **Description:** Profile of BlueStar Energy Services Inc., one of the first suppliers to cash in on the deregulation f the electricity market by the Illinois Legislature; last year BlueStar's revenue was $171.1 million, up from $600,000 in 2002, the year the company was founded.

39857 ■ *"The Power of Innovation" in Canadian Business (Vol. 81, February 26, 2008, No. 4, pp. 57)*
Pub: Rogers Media Inc.
Contact: Tony Viner, President
Ed: Andrew Wahl. **Description:** Canada ranks badly in terms innovation yardsticks that directly translate to economic growth such as business R&D as a percentage of GDP and R&D per capita. Canada's reliance on natural resources does not provide incentives to innovate unlike smaller countries with little natural resources. Canada could spur innovation through regulations that encourage industrial research.

39858 ■ *"President Obama Appoints Record Number of Hispanics to High Office" in Hispanic Business (October 2009, pp. 12-13)*
Pub: Hispanic Business Inc.
Contact: Jesus Chavarria, President
Ed: Rob Kuznia. **Description:** Fourteen percent, or 43 of the Senate-approved appointees by President Obama are Hispanic; President George W. Bush appointed 34 Hispanics, Bill Clinton, 30 Hispanics.

39859 ■ *"Prime Site Lands Retirement Center" in Business Courier (Vol. 24, November 1, 2007, No. 29, pp. 1)*
Pub: American City Business Journals, Inc.
Contact: Whitney Shaw, President
Ed: Laura Baverman. **Description:** Erickson Retirement Communities plans to build a $220 milllion campus on 65 acres of land between Evendale and Glendale. The project will depend on votes casted by village councils in Evendale and Glendale, expected to take place in December 2007. Both areas must sign on and alter zoning rules before the development can proceed.

39860 ■ *"Prison Farms are Closing, but the Manure Remains" in Canadian Business (Vol. 83, August 17, 2010, No. 13-14, pp. 9)*
Pub: Rogers Media Inc.
Contact: Tony Viner, President
Ed: Steve Maich. **Description:** The explanation given by Canada's government ministers on planned closure of the prison farms and scrapping of the long form census are designed by mixing of spin, argument and transparent justification. The defense should have been plausible but the ministers could not handle the simple questions about statistics and prison job training with pretense.

39861 ■ *"Privacy Concern: Are 'Group' Time Sheets Legal?' in HR Specialist (Vol. 8, September 2010, No. 9, pp. 4)*
Pub: Capitol Information Group Inc.
Description: Under the Fair Labor Standards Act (FLSA) employers are required to maintain and preserve payroll or other records, including the number of hours worked, but it does not prescribe a particular order or form in which these records must be kept.

39862 ■ *"Prognosis: Uncertain" in Entrepreneur (May 2014)*
Pub: Entrepreneur Media Inc.
Released: May 2014. **Description:** The passage of the Patient Protection and Affordable Care Act has resulted in uncertainty for small business owners. The law has required health insurance coverage for companies with 50 or more full-time employees, placing additional costs on small businesses. It has also imposed additional administrative burdens such as reporting the scope of health insurance coverage for employees and tracking their actual number. Some businesses that are already paying for health insurance coverage opted to give their employees money to purchase their own insurance coverage plans.

39863 ■ *"Proposal Ruffles Builders" in Austin Business JournalInc. (Vol. 29, November 20, 2009, No. 37, pp. 1)*
Pub: American City Business Journals
Ed: Jacob Dirr. **Description:** A proposal that requires heating, ventilation and cooling equipment checking for a new commercial building having an area of at least 10,000 square feet might cost 25 cents to 50 cents per square foot for the owners. This may lead to higher housing costs. Both the Building and Fire Code Board of Appeals and the Mechanical Plumbing and Solar Board have recommended the plan.

39864 ■ *"Proposed Law Would Stop REIS Bid for Annexation by Livonia" in Crain's Detroit Business (Vol. 24, March 10, 2008, No. 10, pp. 2)*
Pub: Crain Communications Inc.
Contact: Rance E. Crain, President
Ed: Chad Halcom. **Description:** REIS Northville L.L.C., a joint venture made up of Real Estate Interests Group Inc. and Schostak Bros. & Co., has proposed an $800 million project called Highwood at the former Northville Psychiatric Hospital site but has been stalled due to a disagreement with Northville Township on several terms including: the amount of retail at the site and the paying for cleanup of environmental and medical waste.

39865 ■ *"Proposed Transit Legislation" in Crain's Detroit Business (Vol. 24, October 6, 2008, No. 40, pp. 19)*
Description: Breakdown of state Representative Marie Donigan's proposed transit legislation includes tax increment financing. Other pieces of the proposed legislation are examined.

39866 ■ *"Protection, Flexibility Make Single-Member LLCs Attractive" in Crain's Cleveland Business (Vol. 28, November 12, 2007, No. 45)*
Pub: Crain Communications Inc.
Ed: Peter A. Demarco. **Description:** Discusses the reasons why single-member limited liability companies are gaining popularity; LLC structure allows a great deal of flexibility and protects the owner from liability.

39867 ■ *"Provinces Tackle E-Waste Problem" in Canadian Electronics (Vol. 23, June-July 2008, No. 4, pp. 1)*
Pub: Action Communication Inc.
Ed: Ken Manchen. **Description:** Canadian provinces are implementing measures concerning the safe and environmentally friendly disposal of electronic waste. Alberta, British Columbia, Nova Scotia, and Saskatchewan impose an e-waste recycling fee on electronic equipment purchases.

39868 ■ *"PSC Approves $130M TECO Solar Project" in Tampa Bay Business Journal (Vol.*

30, December 18, 2009, No. 52, pp. 1)
Pub: American City Business Journals
Ed: Michael Hinman. **Description:** Florida's Public Service Commission has endorsed Tampa Electric Company's plan to add 25 megawatts of solar energy to its portfolio. TECO's plan needed the approval by PSC to defray additional costs for the project through ratepayers.

39869 ■ *"Publisher Steve Forbes: Small Business Can Flourish in Boise"* in Idaho Business Review (August 19, 2014)
Pub: Dolan Co.
Contact: James P. Dolan, President
Released: August 19, 2014. **Description:** Steve Forbes spoke at the Zions Bank Small Business Conference in Boise, Idaho. He explored the opportunities for small firms in the area in regards to the global economy. Forbes also addressed taxation and government regulations.

39870 ■ *"Putting Down Roots"* in Entrepreneur (August 2014)
Pub: Entrepreneur Media Inc.
Released: August 2014. **Description:** Entrepreneur Justin Hartfield and partner Doug Francis created Weedmaps.com, an online portal for marijuana dispensaries, after California legalized the sale of medical marijuana. Hartfield is looking forward to a billion-dollar business once the federal prohibition of marijuana is ended. Local dispensaries pay a monthly subscription of $420 to appear on the site while doctors pay $295 to be featured on the site. Harfield is seeking partnerships with lboratories that will provide marijuana testing and other services.

39871 ■ *"Q&A: RBC's Gordon Nixon"* in Canadian Business (Vol. 80, May 31, 2011, No. 22, pp. 9)
Pub: Rogers Media Inc.
Contact: Tony Viner, President
Ed: Rachel Pulfer. **Description:** Royal Bank of Canada (RBC) chief executive officer Gordon Nixon believes that the Canadian financial services segment is heavily regulated. Nixon also feels that it has become difficult for local banks to enter the market since foreign banks can easily come in and compete with Canadian banks. His views on RBC's success are provided.

39872 ■ *"Q&A: Take a Load Off Your HR"* in Entrepreneur (May 2014)
Pub: Entrepreneur Media Inc.
Released: May 2014. **Description:** A Professional Employer Organization (PEO) manages all the human resource (HR) needs of a small business. The PEO can help the business save money by purchasing insurance and benefit plans at significant savings, assist with employment-regulatory compliance and ensure effective management and access to personnel records, among other things. Business owners should consider hiring PEOs who are financially responsible and stable. A business needs a PEO when the accounting department asks for a dedicated HR person to handle all the paperwork.

39873 ■ *"Q&A: The CAPP's Greg Stringham"* in Canadian Business (Vol. 81, February 12, 2008, No. 3, pp. 8)
Pub: Rogers Media Inc.
Contact: Tony Viner, President
Ed: Michelle Magnan. **Description:** Canadian Association of Petroleum Producers' Greg Stringham thinks that the new royalty plan will result in companies pulling out their investments for Alberta's conventional oil and gas sector. Stringham adds that Alberta is losing its competitive advantage and companies must study their cost profiles to retrieve that advantage. The effects of the royalty system on Alberta's economy are examined further.

39874 ■ *"Qualified Mortgage Law Puts Some Home Loans Out of Reach"* in Memphis Business Journal (Vol. 35, February 21, 2014, No. 46, pp. 4)
Pub: American City Business Journals
Released: February 21, 2014. **Description:** The 2010 Dodd-Frank financial reform's qualified mortgages (QM) and ability to pay rules have pushed

some smaller Southeastern banks out of the home lending business, while others are changing business models. The legal protection reduced the incentive for lenders to loan to borrowers with terms that do not follow the QM standards. The affected loans are also discussed.

39875 ■ *"Que Pasa? A Canadian-Cuban Credit Card Crisis"* in Canadian Business (Vol. 81, March 31, 2008, No. 5, pp. 10)
Pub: Rogers Media Inc.
Contact: Tony Viner, President
Ed: Geoff Kirbyson. **Description:** Discusses the acquisition of CUETS Financial Ltd. by the Bank of America which means that CUETS-issued credit cards in Cuba are worthless since U.S. laws prohibit transactions from Cuba and other sanctioned countries. CUETS members are advised to take multiple payment methods to Cuba.

39876 ■ *"Queens' Neighbors Fighting Growth"* in Charlotte Business Journal (Vol. 27, July 20, 2012, No. 18, pp. 1)
Pub: American City Business Journals, Inc.
Contact: Whitney Shaw, President
Ed: Susan Stabley. **Released:** July 20, 2012. **Description:** Queens University of Charlotte has been experiencing a rapid growth and has several construction project under way. However, Myers Park Homeowners Association has filed a legal action against the school and the City of Charlotte, North Carolina for changes to the zoning code that allowed the Queens' current expansion.

39877 ■ *"Questions Abound in Voluminous Health Care Reform Law"* in Memphis Business Journal (Vol. 34, July 6, 2012, No. 12, pp. 1)
Pub: American City Business Journal
Ed: Cole Epley. **Description:** US Supreme Court has upheld the health care reform legislation, also known as Obamacare, as thelaw of the land. However, key questions remain and conjecture surrounding which direction states and insurance providers will pursue abounds. Insights on possible impact of health care providers of TennCare are also given.

39878 ■ *"Quicksilver Resources Receives Favorable Judgement"* in Canadian Corporate News (May 16, 2007)
Description: The 236th Judicial District Court of Texas ruled in favor of Quicksilver Resources Inc., a crude oil and natural gas exploration and production company, in the litigation between Quicksilver and CMS Marketing Services and Trading Company regarding the sale and purchase of 10,000 million British thermal units of natural gas per day at a minimum price of $2.47 per MMbtu, with the condition that the parties share any upside equally. The Court has rescinded the contract, rendering it void.

39879 ■ *"The Rabbi Trust: How to Earn It Now, But Defer the Tax to the Future"* in Barron's (Vol. 88, March 24, 2008, No. 12, pp. 55)
Pub: Dow Jones & Co., Inc.
Contact: Clare Hart, President
Ed: Joseph F. Gelband. **Description:** Discusses a rabbi trust which is a method of deferring taxes on compensation allowed by the Internal Revenue Service. Funding of the trust is not considered taxable. Other regulations concerning tax deferment are also discussed.

39880 ■ *"The Race Is On For High-Stakes Casino Gambling in Florida"* in South Florida Business Journal (Vol. 34, January 10, 2014, No. 25, pp. 12)
Pub: American City Business Journals
Released: January 10, 2014. **Description:** The Florida Senate is considering the possibility of expanding the limits of gambling in the state by establishing destination casinos. However, Professor Bob Jarvis believes that placing limits on the gambling sector could hinder economic development.

39881 ■ *"Raising Money: The Bond that Lasts"* in Entrepreneur (Vol. 35, October 2007,

No. 10, pp. 73)
Pub: Entrepreneur Press
Contact: Perlman Neil, President
Ed: Crystal Detamore-Rodman. **Description:** Tax-exempt bonds can be the solution to long-term financing needs of entrepreneurs. However, high initial costs may discourage some entrepreneurs to apply for these bonds, with transactions usually costing $3 mor more. How tax-exempt bonds work, and how rules vary with different states are discussed.

39882 ■ *Reading Financial Reports for Dummies*
Pub: John Wiley & Sons Inc.
Contact: Stephen M. Smith, President
Ed: Lita Epstein. **Released:** 3rd Edition. **Price:** $22.95, paperback; $14.99. **Description:** This second edition contains more new and updated information, including new information on the separate accounting and financial reporting standards for private/small businesses versus public/large businesses; updated information reflecting 2007 laws on international financial reporting standards; new content to match SEC and other governmental regulatory changes over the last three years; new information about how the analyst-corporate connection has changed the playing field; the impact of corporate communications and new technologies; new examples that reflect the current trends; and updated Websites and resources. **Availability:** PrintE-book.

39883 ■ *"Realtors Signing Out"* in The Business Journal-Serving Metropolitan Kansas City (Vol. 27, November 21, 2008, No. 11, pp. 1)
Pub: American City Business Journals, Inc.
Contact: Whitney Shaw, President
Ed: Rob Roberts. **Description:** The Kansas City Regional Association of Realtors has lost 1,000 of its members due to the downturn in the housing market. Applications for realtor licenses have dropped by 159 percent. Changes in Missouri's licensing requirements are seen as additional reasons for the declines.

39884 ■ *"Rebuffed, BAE Systems Fights Army Contract Decision"* in Business Courier (Vol. 26, September 25, 2009)
Pub: American City Business Journals, Inc.
Contact: Whitney Shaw, President
Ed: Jon Newberry. **Description:** BAE Systems filed a complaint with the US Government Accountability Office after the US Army issued an order to BAE's competitor for armoured trucks which is potentially worth over $3 billion. Hundreds of jobs in Butler County, Ohio hinge on the success of the contract protest.

39885 ■ *"Recession Fears Power Gold"* in Barron's (Vol. 88, March 17, 2008, No. 11, pp. M14)
Pub: Dow Jones & Co., Inc.
Contact: Clare Hart, President
Ed: Melanie Burton. **Description:** Gold prices have been more attractive as the U.S. dollar weakens and the Dow Jones Industrial Average has slipped almost 10 percent in 2008. The rate cuts from the Federal Reserve Board has also spurred inflation fears adding upward pressure to the price of the metal.

39886 ■ *"Reduce or Repay"* in Canadian Business (Vol. 80, November 5, 2007, No. 22, pp. 35)
Ed: Regan Ray. **Description:** The new greenhouse gas (GHG) policy of Alberta, Canada requires about 100 industrial facilities that emit over 100,000 tons of GHG per year to reduce emissions by 12 percent by the end of 2007. Facilities that fail to comply will pay $15 per ton of GHG emission beyond target. The economic impacts of the regulation are evaluated.

39887 ■ *"Refiners, Producers are at Odds in Debate Over U.S. Oil Exports"* in San Antonio Business Journal (Vol. 27, January 17, 2014, No. 50, pp. 4)
Pub: American City Business Journals
Released: January 17, 2014. **Description:** The American Petroleum Institute has been lobbying for the elimination of the decades-old ban on oil exports to open new markets for U.S. crude. Refiners such

as San Antonio-based Valero Energy Corporation and Tesoro Corporation are against lifting the ban because it would drive the price of crude and tighten margins. Insights into the debate over U.S. oil exports are provided.

39888 ■ *"Reform Law Spares Community Banks from FDIC Fee Hike"* in *Baltimore Business Journal (Vol. 28, July 23, 2010, No. 11, pp. 1)*
Pub: Baltimore Business Journal
Ed: Gary Haber. **Description:** A new financial regulator bill has exempted community banks from increased Federal Insurance Deposit Corporation fees. Large banks with assets of $10 billion and above will be required to pay the higher fee in 2010. Small banks are seen to hold bank fees at bay owing to the exemption.

39889 ■ *"Reform or Perish"* in *Canadian Business (Vol. 82, April 27, 2009, No. 7, pp. 20)*
Ed: Al Rosen. **Description:** It is believed that Canada needs to fix its financial regulatory framework in order to provide more oversight on accounting procedures that is often left up to auditors. While the U.S. has constantly rebuilt its regulatory framework, Canada has not instituted reforms on its regulations. Canada entered the recession with a strong system but needs to build more substance into it.

39890 ■ *"Reforms Equal Smaller 401(k)s"* in *Employee Benefit News (Vol. 25, December 1, 2011, No. 15, pp. 19)*
Pub: SourceMedia Inc.
Contact: James M. Malkin, Chief Executive Officer
Ed: Lisa V. Gillespie. **Description:** According to a new analysis by the Employee Benefit Research Institute, two recent proposals to change existing tax treatment of 401(k) retirement plans could cost workers because they would lower their account balances towards retirement.

39891 ■ *"Regulator Issues Warning On Reverse Mortgage Loans"* in *Retirement Advisor (Vol. 13, October 2012, No. 10, pp. 28)*
Pub: Summit Professional Networks
Contact: Steve Weitzner, President
Description: Reverse mortgages were first introduced in 1961 and are becoming popular now with aging baby boomers. The new Consumer Financial Protection Bureau warns the public to look closing before entering a reverse mortgage contract. The National Ethics Association encourages financial advisors to use the same caution and offers advise for advisors to help educate their clients about reverse mortgages.

39892 ■ *"Regulators Revoke Mann Bracken's Collection Agency Licenses"* in *Collections & Credit Risk (Vol. 15, September 1, 2010, No. 8, pp. 19)*
Pub: SourceMedia Inc.
Contact: James M. Malkin, Chief Executive Officer
Description: Maryland regulators have revoked the collections licenses of defunct law firm Mann Bracken LLP.

39893 ■ *"Rehab Centers Flourish Under Obamacare"* in *Puget Sound Business Journal (Vol. 35, August 1, 2014, No. 15, pp. 8)*
Pub: American City Business Journals
Released: August 1, 2014. **Description:** Hospitals are looking to partner with long-term care and rehabilitation facilities that can continue care with discharged patients in compliance with the Affordable Care Act. The government regulated insurance coverage could mean better follow-up care and less spending and waste in the health care system.

39894 ■ *"REITs Decry Foreign Limits on Investment"* in *Globe & Mail (March 29, 2007, pp. B4)*
Pub: CTVglobemedia Publishing Inc.
Ed: Elizabeth Church. **Description:** The planned legislation by Canadian government for regulation foreign investments by real estate investment trusts is discussed.

39895 ■ *"Rempant Phone Theft Drives Kill-Switch Law"* in *San Francisco Business Times (Vol. 28, February 14, 2014, No. 30, pp. 6)*
Pub: American City Business Journals
Released: February 14, 2014. **Description:** New legislation in San Francisco, California will focus on implementing mandatory 'kill switches' for cellular phones. Figures show that more than 50 percent of robberies in the city involve theft of a mobile phone and police believe about 113 smartphones are stolen each minute nationwide. The new regulation should help curb this trend.

39896 ■ *"Renewable Energy Adoption in an Aging Population"* in *Energy Policy (Vol. 39, October 2011, No. 10, pp. 6021-6029)*
Pub: Reed Elsevier Reference Publishing
Ed: Ken Willis, Riccardo Scarpa, Rose Gilroy, Neveen Hamza. **Description:** Attitudes and impacts of renewable energy adoption on an aging population is examined.

39897 ■ *"Rep. Loretta Sanchez Holds a Hearing on Small Business Cyber Security"* in *Political/Congressional Transcript Wire (July 29, 2010)*
Pub: CQ Roll Call
Description: U.S. House Committee on Armed Services, Subcommittee on Terrorism, Unconventional Threats and Capabilities held a hearing on small business cyber security innovation.

39898 ■ *"Research Reports: How Analysts Size Up Companies"* in *Barron's (Vol. 88, March 31, 2008, No. 13, pp. M13)*
Pub: Dow Jones & Co., Inc.
Contact: Clare Hart, President
Ed: Anita Peltonen. **Description:** Sirius Satellite's shares are ranked Outperform as it awaits approval from the Federal Communications Commission in its merger with XM. TiVo's shares are ranked Avoid as the company is in a sector that's being commoditized. Verizon Communications' rising dividend yield earns it a Focus List ranking. The shares of Bear Stearns, Churchill Downs, Corning, and Deerfield Triarc Capital are also reviewed. Statistical data included.

39899 ■ *"Restaurants Brace for New Era Prohibiting Bare Hands on Food"* in *Sacramento Business Journal (Vol. 30, January 24, 2014, No. 48, pp. 5)*
Pub: American City Business Journals
Released: January 24, 2014. **Description:** California's Retail Food Code has officially banned barehands contact with ready-to-eat foods, garnishes and beverage ingredients, effective January 1, 2014. Food service workers must wear gloves or use tongs or food-safe prophylactic tissues when handling food that is not heated to 165 degrees. The reactions to the enforcement of the new law are also explored.

39900 ■ *"Retirement Plan Disclosures: Prepare Now for Fiduciary Rules"* in *Employee Benefit News (Vol. 25, November 1, 2011, No. 14, pp. 24)*
Pub: SourceMedia Inc.
Contact: James M. Malkin, Chief Executive Officer
Ed: Brian M. Pinheiro, Kurt R. Anderson. **Description:** Department of Labor has delayed the deadlines on new affirmative obligations for fiduciaries of retirement plans subject to the Employee Retirement Income Security Act. Details included.

39901 ■ *"Retirement Plans in a Quandary"* in *Employee Benefit News (Vol. 25, December 1, 2011, No. 15, pp. 18)*
Pub: SourceMedia Inc.
Contact: James M. Malkin, Chief Executive Officer
Ed: Terry Dunne. **Description:** Complex issues arise when employees don't cash their 401(k) balance checks. The US Department of Labor permits plans to cash out accounts of former employees with less than $1,000 to reduce the cost and time required to manage them.

39902 ■ *"ReVenture Plan Appears Close to Landing Key Legislative Deal"* in *Charlotte Business Journal (Vol. 25, July 9, 2010, No. 16, pp. 1)*
Pub: Charlotte Business Journal
Ed: John Downey. **Description:** North Carolina lawmakers acted on special legislation that would boost development of Forsite Development 667-acre ReVenture Energy Park. The legislation could also improve chances that Duke Energy Carolinas will contract to purchase the power from the planned 50-megawatt biomass power plant located at the park. How utilities would benefit from the legislation is also discussed.

39903 ■ *"Reversal of Fortune"* in *Canadian Business (Vol. 85, June 11, 2012, No. 10, pp. 32)*
Pub: George Media Inc.
Ed: Matthew McClearn. **Released:** June 11, 2012. **Description:** First Quantum Minerals of Vancouver, British Columbia contested the decisio of the Democratic Republic of Congo to revoke their mining license in the Kolwezi Tailings by means of political pressure and international law. Eurasian National Resources Corporation agreed to pay First Quantum $1.25 billion in return for uncontested title to Congo mines and a ceasefire in January 2012.

39904 ■ *"Reviving Entrepreneurship: Policy Decisions in 12 Areas Could Nurture - Or Cripple - America's Greatest Asset"* in *Harvard Business Review (Vol. 90, March 2012, No. 3, pp. 116)*
Pub: Harvard Business Review Press
Contact: Peter E. Walsh, Director
Ed: Josh Lerner, William Sahlman. **Released:** March 2012. **Description:** Government policies should address entrepreneurship as a process, rather than an act. Several key areas for policymaking include basic and translational science, supply and quality of human capital, information availability, tax treatment of rewards and risks, intellectual property rights, workforce healthcare, and mobility of financial and human capital.

39905 ■ *The RFA at 25: Needed Improvements for Small Business Regulatory Relief*
Pub: U. S. Government Printing Office
Contact: Veronica Meter, Director
E-mail: tpriebe@gpo.gov
Description: Information regarding the hearing on needed improvements for small business regulatory relief before the Committee on Small Business, House of Representatives, One Hundred Ninth Congress, First Session, Washington, DC, March 16, 2005 is provided.

39906 ■ *"Ride-Share Field Has New Player"* in *Providence Business News (Vol. 29, April 21, 2014, No. 3, pp. 1)*
Pub: American City Business Journals
Released: April 21, 2014. **Description:** Lyft is Providence, Rhode Island's newest ride-sharing service. State officials continue to look for ways to regulate Internet vehicle services, taxis and limousines. Nearly all of Lyft's drivers are part-time employees using their own personal vehicles.

39907 ■ *"Riding the Export Wave: How To Find a Good Distributor Overseas"* in *Inc. (January 2008, pp. 49)*
Pub: Gruner and Jahr USA Publishing Co.
Contact: J. Russell Denson, President
Ed: Sarah Goldstein. **Description:** Small companies should contact the U.S. embassy in foreign companies in order to connect with the U.S. Commercial Service's Gold Key program that is designed to work with small and midsize exporters.

39908 ■ *"Riding Herd on Health Care"* in *Business Journal Portland (Vol. 30, February 7, 2014, No. 49, pp. 8)*
Pub: American City Business Journals
Released: February 7, 2014. **Description:** Singing rancher and aspiring gubernatorial candidate, Jon Justesen, explains his views on universal healthcare.

He expresses support for health care reform and Cover Oregon and he is looking at his options after dropping his Republican primary bid.

39909 ■ "Rising Above Flood-Insurance Costs" in Providence Business News (Vol. 28, February 3, 2014, No. 44, pp. 1)
Pub: American City Business Journals

Released: February 3, 2014. Description: Businesses are advised to examine flood insurance costs when rebuilding or expanding their facilities. Some firms choose to elevate their buildings in response to the redrawing of Federal Emergency Management Agency flood maps and regulations. The process for getting a flood-elevation survey is also explored.

39910 ■ "River Plan in Disarray" in Business Journal Portland (Vol. 26, December 4, 2009, No. 39, pp. 1)
Pub: American City Business Journals, Inc.

Ed: Andy Giegerich. Description: Portland's proposed rules on a waterfront development plan for the Willamette River calls for fees intended for river bank preservation, a move that could drive industrial manufacturers away. The manufacturers, under the Working Waterfront Coalition, claim that the proposals could increase riverfront building costs by 15 percent.

39911 ■ "Rogue's Gallery" in Canadian Business (Vol. 81, November 10, 2008, No. 19, pp. 44)
Pub: Rogers Media Inc.

Contact: Tony Viner, President

Ed: Rachel Pulfer. Description: Laissez-faire capitalism or poor oversight of Fannie Mae and Freddie Mac are causes for the financial crisis in the U.S., depending or Democrat or Republican viewpoint. Events leading up to the 2008 financial crisis are covered.

39912 ■ "Russia: Uncle Volodya's Flagging Christmas Spirit" in The Economist (Vol. 390, January 3, 2009, No. 8612, pp. 22)
Description: Overview of Russia's struggling economy as well as unpopular government decisions such as raising import duties on used foreign vehicles so as to protect Russian carmakers.

39913 ■ "S3 Entertainment Group Partners with WFW International for Film Services in Michigan" in Michigan Vue (July-August 2008)
Description: William F. White (WFW), one of North America's largest production equipment providers has partnered with S3 Entertainment Group (S3EG), a Michigan-based full-service film production services company due to the new incentives package which currently offers the highest incentives in the United States, up to 42 percent. S3EG will actively store, lease, manage, distribute and sell WFW's equipment to the growing number of production teams that are filming in the state.

39914 ■ "S.A. Officials Hunting for Prospects in California" in San Antonio Business Journal (Vol. 26, August 17, 2012, No. 29, pp. 1)
Released: August 17, 2012. Description: Officials of the San Antonio Economic Development Foundation in Texas will meet with 15 or more companies in Los Angeles, California in a bid to convince these businesses to relocated some of their operations to Alamo City. Officials are hoping the companies will recognize the advantages of San Antonio as they face pressures due to increased taxes and added government regulations in California.

39915 ■ "Sacramento Businesses Must Cut Water Use 20 Percent" in Sacramento Business Journal (Vol. 30, January 17, 2014, No. 47, pp. 5)
Pub: American City Business Journals

Released: January 17, 2014. Description: The Sacramento, California City, California Council's decision to reduce water use by 20 percent could have a big impact on businesses. Hotels and restaurants are among the biggest commercial users of water, while golf courses generally use well water. The need for businesses to purchase more efficient fixtures is also discussed.

39916 ■ "Sales of Pension Income Targeted by Senator" in Wall Street Journal Eastern Edition (November 21, 2011, pp. C7)
Pub: Dow Jones & Co., Inc.

Contact: Clare Hart, President

Ed: Leslie Scism. Description: Senator Tom Harkin is concerned about a widening business in which retirees and veterans sell pension income to investors in the secondary market. The business provides major profits for middlemen. Harkin wants those who are considering such a sale to have adequate information provided and knowledge in order to avoid unscrupulous dealings.

39917 ■ "San Marcos May Ban Smoking" in Austin Business Journal (Vol. 31, June 17, 2011, No. 15, pp. 1)
Pub: American City Business Journals

Ed: Vicky Garza. Description: The City Council of San Marcos, Texas will hold a public hearing regarding a proposed citywide smoking ban. The city is moving towards the smoking ban because it appears a statewide ban may be enacted.

39918 ■ "Sandi Jackson: Alderman, 7th Ward, City of Chicago" in Crain's Chicago Business (Vol. 31, May 5, 2008, No. 18, pp. 31)
Pub: Crain Communications Inc.

Contact: Todd Johnson, Publisher

Ed: Sarah A. Klein. Description: Profile of Sandi Jackson who is an alderman of the 7th ward of the city of Chicago and is addressing issues such as poverty and crime as well as counting on a plan to develop the former USX Corp. steel mill to revitalize the area's economic climate.

39919 ■ "Santa Clara Wineries at Odds with County Over Regulations" in Silicon Valley/San Jose Business Journal (Vol. 30, September 7, 2012, No. 24, pp. 1)
Pub: American City Business Journal

Description: A proposed ordinance in Santa Clara County, California will change existing winery regulations and implement a sliding fee system for event permits. Officials believe that the government ordinance will improve agricultural tourism, but winery owners claim that it would force them to choose between canceling events and footing the bill for certain costs.

39920 ■ "Santander 'Redlining' Suit is a Crass and Opportunistic Shakedown" in Boston Business Journal (Vol. 34, June 6, 2014, No. 18, pp. 7)
Pub: American City Business Journals, Inc.

Contact: Whitney Shaw, President

Released: June 6, 2014. Description: Santander Bank's residential mortgage lending to minorities in Providence, Massachusetts has declined by 34 percent in recent years. The development is a violation of the US Fair Housing Act and the Equal Credit Opportunity Act. The city has sued Santander over the issue.

39921 ■ Sarbanes-Oxley for Dummies
Pub: John Wiley & Sons Inc.

Contact: Stephen M. Smith, President

Ed: Jill Gilbert Welytok. Released: 2nd Edition. Price: $21.95, paperback; $14.99. Description: Provides the latest Sarbanes-Oxley (SOX) legislation with procedures to safely and effectively reduce compliance costs. Topics include way to: establish SOX standards for IT professionals, minimize compliances costs for every aspect of a business, survive a Section 404 audit, avoid litigation under SOX, anticipate future rules and trends, create a post-SOX paper trail, increase a company's standing and reputation, work with SOX in a small business, meet new SOX standards, build a board that can't be bought, and to comply with all SOX management mandates. Availability: PrintE-book.

39922 ■ "SBA Makes Reforms To Federal Government Contracting" in Black Enterprise (Vol. 38, January 2008, No. 6, pp. 26)
Pub: Earl G. Graves Publishing Co. Inc.

Contact: Earl G. Graves, Jr., President

Ed: Alexis McCombs. Description: The U.S. Small Business Administration enacted a new requirement that small businesses recertify size status in order to remain eligible for federal contracts lasting more than five years. Prior regulations allowed companies declared small in earlier contracts may have grown through acquisitions, making them ineligible. This move may impact black businesses.

39923 ■ "SCPA Members Seek Senate Support for H.R. 872" in Farm Industry News (May 26, 2011)
Pub: Penton Business Media Inc.

Contact: David Kieselstein, Chief Executive Officer

Ed: Forrest Laws. Description: U.S. House of Representatives passed legislation, H.R. 872 the Reducing Regulatory Burdens Act that frees pesticide applicators from having to obtain NPDES permits for applications over or near water.

39924 ■ "Seattle Slams Brakes on UberX, Lyft, Sidecar" in San Francisco Business Times (Vol. 28, March 21, 2014, No. 35, pp. 6)
Pub: American City Business Journals

Released: March 21, 2014. Description: Seattle, Washington's City Council decided to implement a 150-vehicle limit on the number of cars that can be active in an individual ride-sharing service. Observers believe that this regulation cap will affect the business of ride-ordering services such as UberX and Lyft. UberX wants Mayor Ed Murray to veto the ordinance and send it back to the City Council.

39925 ■ "SEC Extends Small Business Deadline for SOX Audit Requirement" in HRMagazine (Vol. 53, August 2008, No. 8, pp. 20)
Description: Securities and Exchange Commission has approved a one-year extension of the compliance date for smaller public companies to meet the Section 404(b) auditor attestation requirement of the Sarbanes-Oxley Act.

39926 ■ "SEC FAQs About Crowdfunding Intermediaries" in Mondaq Business Briefing (June 11, 2012)
Pub: Mondaq Ltd.

Ed: Yelena Barychev, Christin R. Cerullo, Francis E. Dehel, Melissa Palat Murawsky, Michael E. Plunkett. Description: Guide for implementing crowdfunding intermediary provisions of Title III of the JOBS Act is provided. Operating restrictions and legal obligations are outlined.

39927 ■ "SEC, NASAA Tell Small Businesses: Wait To Join the 'Crowd': Crowdfunding Is 'Not Yet Legal Until the Commission Appoints Rules', Says SEC's Kim" in Investment Advisor (Vol. 3, August 2012, No. 8, pp. 13)
Pub: Summit Professional Networks

Contact: Steve Weitzner, President

Ed: Melanie Waddell. Released: August 2012. Description: Securities and Exchange Commission along with state regulators have advised small businesses and entrepreneurs to wait until the SEC has produced rules governing crowdfunding practices. Until that happens, federal and state securities laws prohibit publicly accessible Internet securities offerings. An overview of crowdfunding and the JOBS Act is included.

39928 ■ "SEC Report On Rating Agencies Falls Short" in Barron's (Vol. 88, July 14, 2008, No. 28, pp. 35)
Pub: Dow Jones & Co., Inc.

Contact: Clare Hart, President

Ed: Jack Willoughby. Description: The Securities and Exchange Commissions report on credit-rating firms should have drawn attention to the slipshod practices in the offerings of collateralized debt obligations. The report fell short of prescribing correctives for the flawed system of these agencies' relationship with their clients.

39929 ■ *"Seed-Count Labeling" in Farm Industry News (October 20, 2010)*
Pub: Penton Business Media Inc.
Contact: David Kieselstein, Chief Executive Officer
Ed: Mark Moore. **Description:** National Conference on Weights and Measures voted to standardize testing methods and procedures that will verify seed-count labeling.

39930 ■ *"Seen and Noted: Pipe Show Finds a Way for Smokers to Light Up" in Crain's Chicago Business (Vol. 31, April 28, 2008, No. 17, pp. 57)*
Pub: Crain Communications Inc.
Contact: Todd Johnson, Publisher
Ed: H. Lee Murphy. **Description:** With the help of attorneys within its local membership of 150 pipe collectors, the Chicagoland Pipe Collectors Club will be allowed to smoke at its 13th International Pipe & Tobacciana Show at Pheasant Run Resort. The event is expected to draw 4,000 pipe enthusiasts from as far as China and Russia.

39931 ■ *"Selling Pressures Rise in China" in Barron's (Vol. 88, March 10, 2008, No. 10, pp. M9)*
Pub: Dow Jones & Co., Inc.
Contact: Clare Hart, President
Ed: Mohammed Hadi. **Description:** There are about 1.6 trillion yuan worth of shares up for sale in Chinese stock markets in 2008, adding to the selling pressures in these markets. The Chinese government has imposed restrictions to prevent a rapid rise in selling stocks.

39932 ■ *"Seminar on Crowdfunding Set for Aug. 1" in Gazette (July 25, 2012)*
Pub: Freedom Communications Inc.
Contact: Mitchell Stern, President
Released: July 25, 2012. **Description:** Senator Michael Bennet is co-hosting a seminar with Epicentral Coworking on crowdfunding featuring two panels with local entrepreneurs and business owners, legal experts, and representatives from investment firms. The seminar will be held August 1, 2012.

39933 ■ *"Sen. Mark Warner Holds a Hearing on Government Contracting Modernization" in Political/Congressional Transcript Wire (July 20, 2010)*
Description: Senate Committee on the Budget, Task Force on Government Performance held a hearing on modernizing the business of government. Details of that hearing are included.

39934 ■ *"Senate Approval Adds Steam to Port of Savannah Project" in Atlanta Business Chronicle (May 30, 2014, pp. 18A)*
Pub: American City Business Journals, Inc.
Contact: Whitney Shaw, President
Released: May 30, 2014. **Description:** U.S. Senate approved a budget for the long pending Savannah Harbor dredging project. The Senate approved $652 million for the dredging of the Savannah Harbor from 42 feet to 47 feet to enhance the port's ability to serve the new generation of supersized containerized cargo ships.

39935 ■ *"Senate Bill Would Eliminate MBT Surcharge in 2011" in Crain's Detroit Business (Vol. 24, April 7, 2008, No. 14, pp. 33)*
Pub: Crain Communications Inc.
Contact: Rance E. Crain, President
Ed: Amy Lane. **Description:** Discusses possible changes to the new Michigan Business Tax, including a proposed bill which would phase out a 21.99 percent surcharge on the tax.

39936 ■ *"Senate OKs Funds for Promoting Tourism" in Crain's Detroit Business (Vol. 24, March 31, 2008, No. 13, pp. 6)*
Pub: Crain Communications Inc.
Contact: Rance E. Crain, President
Ed: Amy Lane. **Description:** Discusses the Senate proposal which allocates funds for Michigan tourism and business promotion as well as Michigan's No

Worker Left Behind initiative, a program that provides free tuition at community colleges and other venues to train displaced workers for high-demand occupations.

39937 ■ *"Senate's Effort to Reform Immigration Policies Fizzles Out" in Hispanic Business (July-August 2007, pp. 62)*
Description: Legislators predict no further work towards comprehensive immigration reform is likely to occur until a new administration is in place in Washington, DC.

39938 ■ *"Senator Grills Collection Agency, Health System Executives" in PaymentsSource (May 31, 2012)*
Pub: SourceMedia Inc.
Contact: James M. Malkin, Chief Executive Officer
Released: May 31, 2012. **Description:** Accretive Health Inc. and Fairview Health Services executives were questioned by Senator Al Franken about its debt collection practices. The suit was initiated after unencrypted private information on 23,500 patients was stolen from an Acrretive employee's vehicle. Details of the lawsuit are outlined.

39939 ■ *"Senators Predict Online School Changes" in Puget Sound Business Journal (Vol. 29, September 19, 2008, No. 22, pp. 1)*
Pub: American City Business Journals
Ed: Clay Holtzman. **Description:** State senators promise to create new legislation that would tighten the monitoring and oversight of online public schools. The officials are concerned about the lack of oversight of the programs as well as lack of knowledge about content of the lessons.

39940 ■ *"Shattering the Myths About U.S. Trade Policy: Stop Blaming China and India. A More Active Trade Policy Can Lead to a Stronger U.S. Economy" in Harvard Business Review (Vol. 90, March 2012, No. 3, pp. 149)*
Pub: Harvard Business Review Press
Contact: Peter E. Walsh, Director
Ed: Robert Z. Lawrence, Lawrence Edwards. **Released:** March 2012. **Description:** Myths debunked include the belief that the US open trade policy has caused job losses, and that living standards are falling due to export market competition. American must leverage China's need for global economic engagement and secure an open domestic market in China. It must also persuade the World Trade Organization to improve market access.

39941 ■ *"Shopping Around for New Ideas" in Canadian Business (Vol. 79, July 17, 2006, No. 14-15, pp. 76)*
Description: Pensions should be a win-win situation for both the employer and the employee. The perspective of both parties concerning pension plans is explored as well as the need to amend laws in order to make sure that one class of merchant does not suffer at the cost of another.

39942 ■ *"Should the Fed Regulate Wall Street?" in Barron's (Vol. 88, March 24, 2008, No. 12, pp. M15)*
Pub: Dow Jones & Co., Inc.
Contact: Clare Hart, President
Ed: Randall W. Forsyth. **Description:** Greater regulation of the financial sector by the Federal Reserve is essential for it to survive the crisis it is experiencing. The resulting regulation could be in complete contrast with the deregulation the sector previously experienced.

39943 ■ *"Should State Invest in Startups?" in Providence Business News (Vol. 28, March 3, 2014, No. 48, pp. 1)*
Pub: American City Business Journals
Released: March 3, 2014. **Description:** The U.S. Treasury Department is investigating whether Rhode Island violated Federal rules when it used funds from the State Small Business Credit Initiative (SSBCI) to invest in Betaspring, a startup accelerator program for technology and design entrepreneurs ready to launch their businesses. The Lyon Park audit claims that Rhode Island violated SSBCI rules because a

large portion of the money went to the business accelerator's operating expenses and not to the startups themselves.

39944 ■ *"Signs of Light" in Puget Sound Business Journal (Vol. 33, August 10, 2012, No. 16, pp. 1)*
Description: Clear Channel Communications is set to deploy an electronic billboard in Tukwila, Washington. Outdoor advertising has been hampered by regulatory roadblocks.

39945 ■ *"A Simple Old Reg that Needs Dusting Off" in Barron's (Vol. 88, June 30, 2008, No. 26, pp. 35)*
Pub: Dow Jones & Co., Inc.
Contact: Clare Hart, President
Ed: Gene Epstein. **Description:** Senator Joe Lieberman has a point when he accused speculators of inflating the prices of food and fuel futures but introducing legislation to address speculation has an alternative. The senator's committee should instead demand that the Commodity Futures Trading Commission enforce position limits on the maximum number of contracts in a given market per speculative entity.

39946 ■ *"Single Most Important Problem" in Small Business Economic Trends (July 2010, pp. 18)*
Pub: National Federation of Independent Business
Contact: Caitlin McDevitt, Program Manager
Description: A table showing the single most important problem among small businesses surveyed in the U.S. for June 2010 is presented. Poor sales was selected by 30 percent of firms as the single most important problem, followed by taxes and government requirements and red tape. Graphs comparing selected single most important problem from January 1986 to June 2010 are also given.

39947 ■ *"Single Most Important Problem" in Small Business Economic Trends (July 2014, pp. 18)*
Pub: National Federation of Independent Business
Contact: Caitlin McDevitt, Program Manager
Released: July 2014. **Description:** A table of the single most important problem among small businesses surveyed in the U.S. in June 2014 is presented. Taxes was selected by 22 percent of firms as the single most important problem, followed by government requirements and red tape at 20 percent. Graphs comparing selected single most important problem from January 1986 to June 2014 are also given.

39948 ■ *Small Business Access to Health Care: Hearing Before the Committee on Small Business, U.S. House of Representatives*
Pub: DIANE Publishing Co.
Contact: Dorothy J. Perkins, Manager
E-mail: dorothyjperkins@hotmail.com
Released: 2002. **Price:** $25, paperback. **Description:** Congressional hearing held at Crystal Lake, Illinois. Witnesses: Mary Blankenbaker, Co-Owner, Benjamin's Restaurant; Ryan Brauns, Senior Vice President, Rockford Consulting and Brokerage; Scott Shalek, RHU, Shalek Financial Services; Brad Close, National Federation of Independent Businesses; Ken Koehler, Flowerwood, Inc.; Brad Buxton, Vice President of Networks and Medical Management, Blue Cross and Blue Shield of Illinois; Isabella Wilson, Chief Financial Office, Illinois Blower, Inc.; and James Milam, Illinois State Medical Society. **Availability:** Print.

39949 ■ *"Small Businesses Gain Health Exchange Access" in Puget Sound Business Journal (Vol. 35, September 5, 2014, No. 20, pp. 6)*
Pub: American City Business Journals
Released: September 5, 2014. **Description:** The government of Washington is planning to offer small businesses employee health coverage through the state's health exchange. Kaiser Health Plan of the Northwest and Moda Health Plan Inc. have received approval to sell 23 health plans inside the health exchange. Small businesses qualify for tax breaks by providing employee health plans.

39950 ■ "Small, But Mighty" in Employee Benefit News (Vol. 25, November 1, 2011, No. 14, pp. 32)
Pub: SourceMedia Inc.
Contact: James M. Malkin, Chief Executive Officer
Ed: Andrea Davis. Description: Three consulting firms are facing the challenge of helping clients understand the new health care reform in a tight economy.

39951 ■ "Small Firms Punch Ticket for Growth" in Houston Business Journal (Vol. 40, January 29, 2010, No. 38, pp. 1)
Pub: American City Business Journals
Ed: Allison Wollam. Description: Independent ticket agencies anticipate growth as American and Canadian authorities approved a merger between Ticketmaster and concert promoter Live Nation. Expansion of service offerings and acquisition of venues have also been done by independent ticket agencies in light of the merger. Details of the merger are included.

39952 ■ "Small Fortunes: How are Cincinnati's Small Banks Faring?" in Business Courier (Vol. 27, July 23, 2010, No. 12, pp. 1)
Pub: Business Courier
Ed: Steve Watkins. Description: Small banks in Cincinnati, Ohio have been faring well despite the economic crisis, a survey has revealed. Sixty percent of local small banks have capital levels above 15.8 percent median. But regulators are seen to close more banks in 2010 than since the financial crises began.

39953 ■ "A Smarter Kind of Taxes" in Canadian Business (Vol. 80, October 8, 2007, No. 20, pp. 203)
Ed: Jack Mintz. Description: Forecasts on Canada's tax system by 2020 are analyzed. It is expected that the country's aging society will place great demands on elderly-related spending such as pensions and healthcare. And, since the elderly pay fewer taxes, the revenue available to the government will be reduced. Other trends also show that several factors will cause significant change to the country's tax system.

39954 ■ "SolarWorld's Ongoing China Syndrome" in Business Journal Portland (Vol. 30, January 24, 2014, No. 47, pp. 16)
Pub: American City Business Journals
Released: January 24, 2014. Description: The Coalition for American Solar Manufacturing is working to stop China's imposing of duties on U.S. and Korean polysilicon suppliers. A trade loophole enables Chinese manufacturers to subsidize an export-intensive strategy that U.S. companies believe has allowed them to sell solar panels and other solar-related goods below cost in the U.S.

39955 ■ "Soldiers as Consumers: Predatory and Unfair Business Practices Harming the Military Community"
Pub: CreateSpace
Contact: Daren Giles, President
Released: October 5, 2014. Price: , $15.95 paperback. Description: Soldiers, airmen, sailors, and marines are young consumers and are appealing targets for unscrupulous businesses. There are lending organizations that prey upon their military offering products to help them bridge financial problems. Unethical elements of these loans includes higher interest rates and/or high fees or waivers of certain rights in fine print of contracts. A Federal Law called the Military Lending Act is supposed to protect service members from this kind of abuse, but the law only covers loans with terms of six months or less.

39956 ■ "Some Atlantic Beach Leaders Leery About Convenience Store Safety Measure" in Florida Times-Union (November 3, 2010)
Pub: Florida Times-Union
Ed: Drew Dixon. Description: Jacksonville, Florida authorities are proposing a new ordinance that would require convenience stores to upgrade safety measures to protect store workers and customers from robbery and other crimes.

39957 ■ "Some Homeowners Caught in Tax-Code Limbo" in Providence Business News (Vol. 29, June 23, 2014, No. 12, pp. 9)
Pub: American City Business Journals
Released: June 23, 2014. Description: The Mortgage Forgiveness Debt Relief Act expired on December 31, 2013 and Congress delayed reauthorizing the tax code, thus impacting homeowners looking for short sales in 2014. Short sellers are unsure whether they will avoid taxation on their forgiven mortgage debt or if the lack of reauthorization by Congress, retroactive to January 1, will lead to large income tax payouts in 2015.

39958 ■ "Some More Equal Than Others" in Canadian Business (Vol. 80, April 23, 2007, No. 9, pp. 23)
Ed: Jack Mintz. Description: The details of the equalization program to be started by United States to improve economic conditions of Canada are presented.

39959 ■ "Something Different in the Air? The Collapse of the Schwarzenegger Health Plan in California" in WorkingUSA (June 2008)
Ed: Daniel J.B. Mitchell. Description: In January 2007, California Governor Arnold Schwarzenegger proposed a state universal health care plan modeled after the Massachusetts individual mandate program. A year later, the plan was dead. Although some key interest groups eventually backed the plan, it was overwhelmed by a looming state budget crisis and a lack of gubernatorial focus. Although much acclaimed for his stance on greenhouse gases, stem cells, hydrogen highways, and other Big Ideas, diffused gubernatorial priorities and a failure to resolve California's chronic fiscal difficulties let the clock run out on universal health care.

39960 ■ "Sour Grapes: Georgian Wine Banned" in Canadian Business (Vol. 79, November 20, 2006, No. 23, pp. 28)
Pub: Rogers Media Inc.
Contact: Tony Viner, President
Ed: Michael Mainville. Description: The impact of the sanctions imposed by Russia on the Georgian wine exports to Russia is discussed.

39961 ■ "Soured Relationship Plays Out in Courts" in The Business Journal-Serving Greater Tampa Bay (Vol. 28, September 19, 2008, No. 39)
Pub: American City Business Journals, Inc.
Contact: Whitney Shaw, President
Ed: Janet Leiser. Description: Heirs of developer Julian Hawthorne Lifset won a court battle to end a 50-year lease with Specialty Restaurants Corp. in Rocky Point. The decision opens the Tampa Bay prime waterfront property for new development.

39962 ■ "Spin Zone: Where Hawaii's Leaders Face Off, Have High-Tech Tax Credits Helped or Hurt Hawaii?" in Hawaii Business (Vol. 53, December 2007, No. 6, pp. 28)
Pub: PacificBasin Communications
Description: Presents the opinons of Channel Capital LLC's Walter R. Roth and Hawaii Venture Capital Association's Bill Spencer concerning the impacts of tax credits. Roth thinks that Act 221 appeals to investors who can earn despite business failure while Spencer thinks that the legislation promotes investments in innovative technology firms. The need to support tax credits is also discussed.

39963 ■ "Spin Zone: Where Hawaii's Leaders Face Off, What Are Your Party's Legislative Priorities for 2008??" in Hawaii Business (Vol. 53, January 2008, No. 7, pp. 22)
Pub: PacificBasin Communications
Description: Discusses the Democratic Party of Hawaii which will prioritize giving more opportunities to earn a living a wage in 2008, according to the party chairwoman Jeani Withington. The Republican Party chairman Willes K. Lee, meanwhile, states that his party will seek to enhance the local business climate. The political parties' plans for Hawaii for the year 2008 are presented in detail.

39964 ■ "Stains Still Set After SBA Scrub" in Black Enterprise (March 1, 2008)
Pub: Earl G. Graves Publishing Co. Inc.
Contact: Earl G. Graves, Jr., President
Ed: Marcia A. Wade. Description: Small Business Administration's attempt to ensure that federal contracts were legitimately rewarded to small businesses, however the report filed showed that $4.6 billion in incorrectly coded contracts were removed from the SBA database. Critics contend the report is filled with inaccuracies. Statistical data included.

39965 ■ "Stakes Rising on Business Cyber Security" in Denver Business Journal (Vol. 63, May 18, 2012, No. 52, pp. A1)
Pub: American City Business Journal
Ed: Greg Avery. Released: May 18, 2012. Description: Congress and federal regulators are seeking to tighten rules for companies in infrastructure industries amid a series of high profile cyber attacks. The federal legislation might give the US Department of Homeland Security a role in ensuring they are not left vulnerable to cyber warfare and foreign Internet spies.

39966 ■ "Stan Chesley Fighting Kentucky Disbarment" in Business Courier (Vol. 27, September 10, 2010, No. 19, pp. 1)
Pub: Business Courier
Ed: Jon Newberry. Description: Stan Chesley, a Cincinnati attorney, has been accused of making false statements to the courts and bar officials, self-dealing in violation of the bar's conflict of interest rules, and failing to adequately inform clients. Kentucky Bar Association officials will seek to have Chesley permanently disbarred.

39967 ■ "State Barks at Mortgage Servicers Over Reluctance to Back Compact" in Business First-Columbus (2007, pp.)
Pub: American City Business Journals, Inc.
Ed: Adrian Burns. Description: State of Ohio asked members of the mortgage industry to back a compact as a way to prevent foreclosures. Mortgage services denied the state's request. Other measures to help borrowers avoid foreclosure are investigated.

39968 ■ "State Cuts Could Affect Senior Care Programs" in Journal Star (May 10, 2012)
Pub: McClatchy Tribune Information Services
Ed: Justin Glawe. Description: Medicaid reforms in Illinois have helped senior citizens in the state because of improvements in community care programs.

39969 ■ "State Defines Hot Dogs, Enacts Other Food Laws Beginning January 1" in Sacramento Business Journal (Vol. 30, January 3, 2014, No. 45, pp. 4)
Pub: American City Business Journals
Released: January 3, 2014. Description: California will implement new laws about food on January 1, 2014. One of these laws requires food companies to use gloves, utensils and deli tissue when handling ready-to-eat foods. However, many health departments have not yet presented compliance guidelines to restaurant operators.

39970 ■ "State Democrats Push for Changes to Plant Security Law" in Chemical Week (Vol. 172, July 19, 2010, No. 17, pp. 8)
Pub: Access Intelligence L.L.C.
Contact: Donald Pazour, President
Ed: Kara Sissell. Description: Legislation has been introduced to revise the existing U.S. Chemical Facility Anti-Terrorism Standards (CFATS) that would include a requirement for facilities to use inherently safer technology (IST). The bill would eliminate the current law's exemption of water treatment plants and certain port facilities and preserve the states' authority to establish stronger security standards.

39971 ■ "State Film Business Tops $1.3 Billion" in The Business Journal-Portland (Vol. 25, August 22, 2008, No. 24, pp. 1)
Pub: American City Business Journals, Inc.
Contact: Whitney Shaw, President
Ed: Andy Giegerich. Description: Oregon's film industry has generated $1.39 billion in direct and indirect economic impact in 2007, a 55 percent rise

from 2005 levels. The growth of the industry is attributed to tax incentives issued in 2007, which attracted film production companies from other states.

39972 ■ *"State Lawmakers Should Try Raising Jobs, Not Taxes" in Crain's Chicago Business (Vol. 31, March 24, 2008, No. 12, pp. 20)*
Pub: Crain Communications Inc.
Contact: Todd Johnson, Publisher
Ed: Doug Whitley. **Description:** According to U.S. Department of Labor figures through December 2007, Illinois has ranked 45th in the nation in job growth for seven straight months. Many feel that the state would not need to raise taxes if they spent more time working to keep and attract employers that create jobs.

39973 ■ *"State Pressure Keeps Rates Low" in Sacramento Business Journal (Vol. 31, August 8, 2014, No. 24, pp. 4)*
Pub: American City Business Journals
Released: August 8, 2014. **Description:** The proposed California Covered rate increases are likely to hit an average 4.2 percent in 2015, with the average increase in Sacramento expected at 3.7 percent. The health insurance exchange was set up to be an active purchaser so that it differs with the proposed exchange in other states, which range from 8 percent to 20 percent. Insights on the advantages of Covered California are presented.

39974 ■ *"State Printing Plant on the Move" in Sacramento Business Journal (Vol. 25, August 29, 2008, No. 26, pp. 1)*
Pub: American City Business Journals, Inc.
Contact: Whitney Shaw, President
Ed: Michael Shaw, Celia Lamb. **Description:** California is planning to replace its printing plant on Richards Boulevard and 7th Street with a newly built or leased facility in the Sacramento area. It was revealed that the project will meet the state's standards for new buildings. It is believed that the new site will require 15 acres or more depending on requirements.

39975 ■ *"State Reverses Food Truck Order" in Cape Cod Times (May 15, 2012)*
Pub: McClatchy-Tribune Information Services
Ed: Patrick Cassidy. **Released:** May 15, 2012. **Description:** Massachusetts Department of Transportation is developing a plan that will allow food truck owners to operate under a new pilot program. Owners must obtain a license to operate through the Transportation Department's legal division. License requirements will be modeled on present license applications and some modifications may be necessary. Insurance issues must be addressed.

39976 ■ *"State Targets Credit Fixers" in Business Journal-Portland (Vol. 24, October 12, 2007, No. 33, pp. 1)*
Pub: American City Business Journals, Inc.
Ed: Andy Giergerich, Justin Matlick. **Description:** Number of companies that offer quick fix to consumers is growing; the State of Oregon is considering rules to target them. A group working on a study in the state's mortgage lending regulations could craft bills to be examined for legislative session in February 2008.

39977 ■ *"State VC Fund To Get At Least $7.5 Million" in Crain's Detroit Business (Vol. 24, February 25, 2008, No. 8, pp. 14)*
Pub: Crain Communications Inc. - Detroit
Contact: Keith Crain, Chairman
Ed: Tom Henderson. **Description:** Michigan's 21st Century Investment Fund is expected to receive $7.5 million, financed by tobacco-settlement money. The Michigan Strategic Fund Board will determine which firms will receive venture capital, which is mandated by legislation to invest the fund within three years.

39978 ■ *"State Wants to Add Escape Clause to Leases" in Sacramento Business Journal (Vol. 28, October 14, 2011, No. 33, pp. 1)*
Pub: Sacramento Business Journal
Ed: Michael Shaw. **Description:** California Governor Jerry Brown's administration has decided to add escape clauses to new lease agreements, which created new worry for building owners and brokers in

Sacramento, California. Real estate brokers believe the appropriation of funds clauses have been making the lenders nervous and would result in less competition.

39979 ■ *Stay Out of Court: The Small Business Owners Guide to Prevent or Resolve Disputes and Avoid Lawsuit Hell*
Ed: Andrew A. Caffey. **Released:** January 24, 2005. **Price:** , $17.95. **Description:** Business law attorney offers tools to help small company owners to solve disputes without going to court.

39980 ■ *"Stelco Investors Told Their Stock Now Worthless" in Globe & Mail (January 23, 2006, pp. B4)*
Ed: Greg Keenan. **Description:** The reasons behind Ontario Superior Court's approval of Stelco Inc.'s restructuring proposal are presented.

39981 ■ *"Strathmore Receives Permit to Drill Roca Honda Project in New Mexico" in Marketwired (May 14, 2007)*
Pub: Comtex News Network Inc.
Description: New Mexico's Mining and Minerals Division approved a permit to allow Strathmore Minerals Corp. to conduct drilling at its Roca Honda Project located in McKinley County, New Mexico.

39982 ■ *Structuring Your Business*
Pub: Adams Media Corp.
Contact: Scott Watrous, President
E-mail: bobadams@adamsmedia.com
Ed: Michele Cagan. **Released:** 2004. **Price:** , $19.95. **Description:** Accountant and author shares insight into starting a new company. The guide assists entrepreneurs through the process, whether it is a corporation, an LLC, a sole proprietorship, or a partnership. Tax codes, accounting practices and legislation affecting every business as well as tips on managing finances are among the topics covered.

39983 ■ *"Struggling Turfway Pares Schedule in Hopes of Drawing More Horses, Bets" in Business Courier (Vol. 26, November 6, 2009, No. 28, pp. 1)*
Pub: American City Business Journals, Inc.
Contact: Whitney Shaw, President
Ed: Jon Newberry. **Description:** Kentucky's Turfway Park will be decreasing its weekly race schedule from five days to three days in the first two months of 2010, and to four days in March 2010. The decision to make reductions in the schedule is attributed to the relocation of thoroughbred racing to states that allow casino gambling. As a result, Turfway Park's resources and purse money would be focused on less days.

39984 ■ *Studies in Entrepreneurship, Business and Government in Hong Kong: The Economic Development of a Small Open Economy*
Pub: Edwin Mellen Press
Contact: Kazimierz Braun, Director
Ed: Fu-Lai Tony Yu. **Released:** November 2006. **Price:** $139.95; £94.95. **Description:** Institutional and Austrian theories are used to analyze the transformation taking place in Hong Kong's economy.

39985 ■ *"Sumitomo Invests in Desert Sunlight Solar Farm, the Largest PV Project Approved for Federal Land" in PR Newswire (October 2, 2012)*
Pub: PR Newswire Association L.L.C.
Contact: David B. Armon, President
Description: The Desert Sunlight Solar Farm, 550MW solar power project being constructed in the California desert area east of Palm Springs, is the largest solar photovoltaic (PV) facility approved for US public land. Sumitomo Corporation of America is investing in the project and plans to expand its renewable energy portfolio across the US.

39986 ■ *"The Sunday Newspaper (est. 1891): the Death of Three Postmedia Sunday Papers Leaves Few Remaining" in Canadian*

Business (Vol. 85, July 16, 2012, No. 11-12, pp. 14)
Pub: George Media Inc.
Ed: Conan Tobias. **Released:** July 16, 2012. **Description:** Postmedia Network Canada Corporation announced the cancellation of the Sunday editions of three of its newspapers, namely 'Calgary Herald', Edmonton Journal', and 'Ottawa Citizen', in order to focus on digital distribution. The first newspaper in Canada to publish a Sunday edition was 'The World' on May 24, 1891 but law required it to be delivered on Saturday.

39987 ■ *"A Supply-Side Solution for Health Care" in (Vol. 92, July 23, 2012, No. 30, pp. 30)*
Pub: Dow Jones & Co., Inc.
Contact: Clare Hart, President
Ed: H. Woody Brock. **Released:** July 23, 2012. **Description:** The United States should increase the supply of new doctors, nurses and other health care professionals to improve the American health care system by increasing supply. Health care reform proposals in the US Congress fail to address the supply side of the problem.

39988 ■ *"Taiwan Technology Initiatives Foster Growth" in Canadian Electronics (Vol. 23, February 2008, No. 1, pp. 28)*
Description: A study conducted by the Market Intelligence Center shows that currently, Taiwan is the world's larges producer of information technology products such as motherboards, servers, and LCD monitors. In 2006, Taiwan's LED industry reached a production value of NTD 21 billion. This push into the LED sector shows the Ministry of Economic Affairs' plan to target industries that are environmentally friendly.

39989 ■ *"Take the Wheel: the Pension Protection Act Doesn't Mean You Can Sit Back and Relax" In Black Enterprise (October 1, 2007)*
Pub: Earl G. Graves Publishing Co. Inc.
Contact: Earl G. Graves, Jr., President
Ed: Mellody Hobson. **Description:** Pension Protection Act provides multiple benefits and tax advantages for retirement, however the investment options and contribution rates are very conservative.

39990 ■ *"Taking the 'Comprehensive' Out of Immigration Reform" in Hispanic Business (September 2007, pp. 8)*
Ed: Patricia Guadalupe. **Description:** Information about the AgJOBS bill, legislation that would grant legal residency to migrant agricultural workers is discussed.

39991 ■ *"Taking the Jump Off the Fiscal Cliff" in Barron's (Vol. 92, August 25, 2012, No. 35, pp. 47)*
Pub: Dow Jones & Co., Inc.
Contact: Clare Hart, President
Ed: Thomas G. Donlan. **Description:** The arrival of tax increases and spending cuts by the end of 2012 should help the United States reduce its budget deficit. Policy prescriptions advocating looser monetary and fiscal policies are not going to help the country solve its budget problems.

39992 ■ *"Tao of Downfall" in International Journal of Entrepreneurship and Small Business (Vol. 11, August 31, 2010, No. 2, pp. 121)*
Pub: Publishers Communication Group
Contact: Doug Wright, Director
Ed: Wenxian Zhang, Ilan Alon. **Description:** Through historical reviews and case studies, this research seeks to understand why some initially successful entrepreneurs failed in the economic boom of past decades. Among various factors contributing to their downfall are a unique political and business environment, fragile financial systems, traditional cultural influences and personal characteristics.

39993 ■ *"TARP Lending Idea Gets Mixed Reviews" in Tampa Bay Business Journal*

(Vol. 29, October 30, 2009, No. 45, pp. 1)
Pub: American City Business Journals
Ed: Kent Hoover, Margie Manning. **Description:** Tampa Bay area, Florida's community banks have expressed disapproval to the proposal of President Obama to increase lending to small business, wherein the government will provide cheap capital through US Treasury Troubled Asset Relief Program (TARP). The banks were hesitant on the plan because of the strings attached to TARP.

39994 ■ *"Tauri Group Partner Joining Homeland Security and Defense"* in Wireless News (December 15, 2009)
Description: Managing partner Cosmo DiMaggio III of the Tauri Group, a provider of analytic consulting for homeland security, defense and space clients, has been elected to the Board of Directors at Homeland Security and Defense Business Council.

39995 ■ *"Tax Breaks Favor Outsiders, Business Owners Object"* in Business Review Albany (Vol. 41, August 22, 2014, No. 22, pp. 7)
Pub: American City Business Journals, Inc.
Contact: Whitney Shaw, President
Released: August 22, 2014. **Description:** New York business owners have criticized Governor Andrew Cuomo's Start-Up NY tax-break program. They argue that the existing companies are essentially ignored and they are concerned whether the companies receiving the tax breaks stay longer than ten years. Insights on the Start-Up NY program are included.

39996 ■ *"Tax Talk"* in Crain's Chicago Business (March 24, 2008)
Pub: Crain Communications Inc.
Contact: Todd Johnson, Publisher
Ed: Greg Hinz. **Description:** Discusses the possible raising of the state's income tax; The latest version of the income tax hike bill, sponsored by Senator James Meeks, D-Chicago, would boost individual rates to 5 percent from 3 percent, with the corporate rate rising to a total of 8 percent from 4.8 percent; about $3 billion of the projected $8 billion that would be brought in would be used to cut local property taxes and experts believe the business community overall would benefit.

39997 ■ *"Tax Tip: Affordable Health Care and Taxes"* in Pet Product News (Vol. 66, September 2012, No. 9, pp. 39)
Pub: Bowtie Inc.
Ed: Mark E. Battersby. **Description:** Implications of the US Supreme Court's ruling that the Affordable Care Act is now part of the Tax Code on small retail businesses, business owners, and self-employed persons are described. The ruling requires every individual to have health insurance to avoid tax penalties.

39998 ■ *"Taxes, Right-To-Work Top West Michigan Concerns"* in Crain's Detroit Business (Vol. 24, September 22, 2008, No. 38, pp. 6)
Pub: Crain Communications Inc.
Contact: Rance E. Crain, President
Ed: Amy Lane. **Description:** Two of the top priorities of business leaders in Western Michigan are the new business tax which they want to end as well as making the state a 'right-to-work' one through laws to prohibit unions from requiring workers to pay dues and membership as a condition of their employment.

39999 ■ *"Technology and Returnable Asset Management"* in Canadian Electronics (Vol. 23, February 2008, No. 1, pp. 6)
Ed: Mark Borkowski. **Description:** Peter Kastner, president of Vestigo Corporation, believes that public companies without an asset track, trace, and control system in place could face Sarbanes-Oakley liability if error-prone processes result to misstatements of asset inventory positions. He also thinks that the system can improve return on assets by increasing the utilization of returnables.

40000 ■ *"Tenacious Trailblazer: Sandra Hernandez, Public Health Pioneer, is Hispanic Business Woman of the Year®"* in Hispanic Business (Vol. 30, April 2008, No. 4, pp. 26)
Pub: Hispanic Business Inc.
Contact: Jesus Chavarria, President
Ed: Melinda Burns. **Description:** Dr. Sandra Hernandez has been named as Hispanic Business Woman of the Year for her pioneering work in health care reform. Dr. Hernandez is the first Hispanic and the first woman to serve as public health director for the city and county of San Francisco.

40001 ■ *"Texas Fold 'Em"* in Canadian Business (Vol. 79, October 9, 2006, No. 20, pp. 44)
Pub: Rogers Media Inc.
Contact: Tony Viner, President
Ed: John Gray. **Description:** New policies of the United States law makers for the online casino industries that could force many of them out of business are discussed.

40002 ■ *"They're Hopping Mad"* in Canadian Business (Vol. 80, October 22, 2007, No. 21, pp. 20)
Description: Alberta Review Panel is calling for a 20 percent increase in oil and gas development taxes. SABMiller and Molson Coors Brewing Company combined its U.S. and Puerto Rican operations, though the deal is still subject to regulatory approvals. Montreal Exchange Inc. filed for approval of the trade of Montreal Climate Exchange futures contracts.

40003 ■ *"Thomas and His Washington Friends"* in CFO (Vol. 23, October 2007, No. 10, pp. 18)
Ed: Alix Stuart. **Description:** Reliance on Chinese suppliers to America's toymakers may become quite costly as Congress considers legislation that would increase fines to as high as $50 million for companies selling tainted products. The legislation would also require independent mandatory testing for makers of products for children.

40004 ■ *"Thousands Balk at Health Law Sign-Up Mandate"* in Boston Business Journal (Vol. 27, November 9, 2007, No. 41, pp. 1)
Ed: Mark Hollmer. **Description:** About 100,000 Massachusetts residents have not signed up for insurance plans created as part of the state's health care reform law. Insurers have underestimated the number of new customers signing up for insurance and come close to risking penalties if they do not get insurance by the end of 2007. The Commonwealth Health Insurance Connector Authority's deadline to buy insurance before penalties kick in is November 15, 2007.

40005 ■ *"Three Alabama Insurers Will Owe $4M In Rebates"* in Birmingham Business Journal (Vol. 29, July 6, 2012, No. 28, pp. 1)
Pub: American City Business Journals, Inc.
Contact: Whitney Shaw, President
Ed: Evan Belanger. **Released:** July 6, 2012. **Description:** US Supreme Court's ruling on the health care reform has resulted in the mandatory payment of rebates by three health insurance firms. Golden Rule Insurance Company owes $2.58 million in rebates. Blue Cross and Blue Shield of Alabama, on the other had, is not slated to pay rebates in 2012.

40006 ■ The Three Secrets of Green Business: Unlocking Competitive Advantage in a Low Carbon Economy
Pub: Earthscan
Ed: Gareth Kane. **Released:** December 08, 2009. **Price:** $33.95, paperback; $135, hardback. **Description:** Small business is coming under increasing pressure from government, customers and campaigning groups to improve environmental performance. Soaring utility and compliance costs are critical financial burdens on small companies. **Availability:** Print.

40007 ■ *"Three Trails Blazes Tax Credit Deal"* in The Business Journal-Serving Metropolitan Kansas City (Vol. 27, November 7, 2008, No. 9)
Ed: Rob Roberts. **Description:** Three Trails Redevelopment LLC plans to redevelop the Bannister Mall area. The Missouri Development Finance Board is expected to approve $30 million in tax credits for the project. A verbal agreement on the terms and conditions has already been reached according to the agency's executive director.

40008 ■ *"TIA Wrestles with Procurement Issues"* in Business Journal Serving Greater Tampa Bay (Vol. 30, November 12, 2010, No. 47, pp. 1)
Pub: Tampa Bay Business Journal
Ed: Mark Holan. **Description:** Tampa International Airport (TIA) has been caught in conflict of interest and procurement policy issues after the Hillsborough County Aviation Authority learned of the spousal relationship of an employee with his wife's firm, Gresham Smith and Partners. Gresham already won contracts with TIA and was ahead of other firms in a new contract.

40009 ■ *"Time to Fight Back"* in Green Industry Pro (Vol. 23, March 2011, No. 3, pp. 8)
Pub: Cygnus Business Media
Contact: Paul Mackler, Chief Executive Officer
Ed: Rod Dickens. **Description:** Lawn care operators in the United States must learn from Canada that a shift to socialism will impact their industry in a negative way. Government regulation over the application of control products regarding environmental health in Canada has been a death sentence for small lawn care businesses.

40010 ■ *"Time is Right for Fiscal Authority"* in Canadian Business (Vol. 83, July 20, 2010, No. 11-12, pp. 24)
Ed: Jacqueline Nelson. **Description:** A survey of Canadian CEOs show that only 5 percent of them believe that the world is in a severe recession. Almost 80 percent of them believe that economic recessions and depressions are caused by failures of the free market and the government.

40011 ■ *"Time for State Tax Restructure?"* in Crain's Detroit Business (Vol. 26, January 18, 2010, No. 3, pp. 3)
Pub: Crain Communications Inc.
Contact: Rance E. Crain, President
Ed: Amy Lane. **Description:** Business Leaders for Michigan, a statewide CEO group, launched a proposal to cut the Michigan Business Tax by about $1.1 billion and replace the revenue by taxing services. Statistical data included.

40012 ■ *"Tory Green?"* in Canadian Business (Vol. 80, January 15, 2007, No. 2, pp. 72)
Ed: Joe Chidley. **Description:** The need for the government to participate actively in protecting the environment through proper enforcement of the Tories Clean Air Act, is discussed.

40013 ■ *"Tougher Securities Rules on the Way"* in Globe & Mail (February 21, 2007, pp. B1)
Ed: Janet McFarland. **Description:** The Canadian Securities Administration will implement new regulation for the securities industry by early next year. Securities companies will now have to register its employee details and earnings according to this new rule.

40014 ■ *"Toy Scares Drive Business"* in Boston Business Journal (Vol. 27, November 23, 2007, No. 43, pp. 1)
Ed: Joan Goodchild. **Description:** Several Boston businesses have tapped into the lead content scare in toys and other products manufactured in China. ConRoy Corporation LLC launched Toy Recall Alert!, an online tool to alert consumers about new recalls while Hybrivet Systems introduced screening test kit, LeadCheck. Other new products pertaining to toy safety are discussed.

40015 ■ *"Toy Story"* in Forbes (Vol. 180, October 15, 2007, No. 8, pp. 102)
Pub: Forbes Inc.
Contact: Malcolm S. Forbes, Jr., President
Ed: Tatiana Serafin. **Description:** Three voluntary recalls of Chinese-made toys were announced by American toymakers, sending Mattel stocks plummeting.

40016 ■ *"Toy Story: U.S.-Made a Hot Seller"* in Crain's Detroit Business (Vol. 23, December 17, 2007, No. 51, pp. 3)

Ed: Chad Halcom. **Description:** American Plastic Toys, located in Walled Lake, Michigan reports all its toys are made in the U.S. and have passed all U.S. safety standards. Revenue for American Plastic Toys reached nearly $33 million in 2005, and the company expects to exceed that because of recent toy safety recalls of products produced in China.

40017 ■ *"Trade Groups Push for Delay In Minimum Wage Hike"* in Boston Business Journal (Vol. 34, June 13, 2014, No. 19, pp. 6)

Pub: American City Business Journals, Inc.

Contact: Whitney Shaw, President

Released: June 13, 2014. **Description:** Trade groups from Massachusetts, the Retailers Association of Massachusetts and Associated Industries of Massachusetts, have requested legislatures to delay the proposed hike to the state minimum wage. They have asked the process be delayed until January 1, 2015. The House Bill that would bring the minimum wage up from $8 an hour to $10.50 an hour over three years, and the Senate Bill, which would bring the floor up to $11 an hour, would take effect with an increase to $9 an hour on July 1, 2014.

40018 ■ *"Trailing Indicator: This Issue: EI Form Reform"* in Canadian Business (Vol. 85, July 16, 2012, No. 11-12, pp. 73)

Pub: George Media Inc.

Ed: James Cowan. **Released:** July 16, 2012. **Description:** An employment questionnaire designed to ensure that Canadians are aware of the improvements made by the federal government to the Employment Insurance (EI) system is presented. Questions related to the Temporary Foreign Worker program is also included.

40019 ■ *"Training Center Wants to be College"* in Austin Business JournalInc. (Vol. 29, November 13, 2009, No. 36, pp. A1)

Pub: American City Business Journals

Ed: Sandra Zaragoza. **Description:** Texas-based CyberTex Institute, a job training center, has established technical careers in an effort to obtain federal accreditation as a college. A college status would allow CyperTex to extend financial assistance to students. Aside from potentially having an enlarged student body and expanded campus, CyberTex would be allowed to engage in various training programs.

40020 ■ *"Transborder Short-Sea Shipping: Hurdles Remain"* in Canadian Sailings (June 30, 2008)

Ed: Kathlyn Horibe. **Description:** Legislation that would exempt non-bulk commercial cargo by water in the Great Lakes region from U.S. taxation is discussed.

40021 ■ *"Trillium Turmoil"* in Canadian Business (Vol. 81, December 8, 2008, No. 21, pp. 16)

Pub: Rogers Media Inc.

Contact: Tony Viner, President

Ed: Jeff Sanford. **Description:** Ontario's manufacturing success in the past was believed to have been built by the 1965 Canada-U.S. automotive pact and by advantages such as low-cost energy. The loss of these advantages along with the challenging economic times has hurt Ontario's manufacturing industry.

40022 ■ *"Trinity To Move Forward on 280, Despite Setback"* in Birmingham Business Journal (Vol. 29, July 20, 2012, No. 30, pp. 1)

Pub: American City Business Journals, Inc.

Contact: Whitney Shaw, President

Ed: Evan Belanger. **Released:** July 20, 2012. **Description:** The construction of the HealthSouth digital hospital could resume in 2013 as the Alabama Civil Appeals Court could decide on applications by the Trinity Medical Center to move to the planned hospital. The city hospital has filed cases to allow it to relocate to the building but has been blocked by a ruling from the Montgomery County District Court.

40023 ■ *"Trust But Verify: FMLA Software Isn't Foolproof"* in HR Specialist (Vol. 8, September 2010, No. 9, pp. 3)

Pub: Capitol Information Group Inc.

Description: Employers are using software to track FMLA information, however, it is important for employers to review reasons for eligibility requirements, particularly when an employee is reportedly overstepping the bounds within leave regulations due to software error.

40024 ■ *"UEDs Would Light Up Street with News, Ads"* in Philadelphia Business Journal (Vol. 33, April 11, 2014, No. 9, pp. 8)

Pub: American City Business Journals

Released: April 11, 2014. **Description:** Catalyst Outdoor head, Thaddeus Bartkowski, has been working on legislation to create a digital district that would permit urban experiential displays (UEDs) in a well-defined area in Center City. UEDs, which would communicate advertising and news, are being considered as a potential revenue stream for the city. The challenges in the installation of UEDs are also presented.

40025 ■ *"Understanding the Fed: Get a Handle on How Ben Bernanke's Decisions Affect Your Wallet"* in Black Enterprise (Vol. 38, December 2007, No. 5, pp. 66)

Pub: Earl G. Graves Publishing Co. Inc.

Contact: Earl G. Graves, Jr., President

Ed: Steve Garmhausen. **Description:** The Federal Reserve System along with twelve regional banks regulates the value of money through the law of supply and demand. The Feds increase or decrease the supply of dollars in circulation which makes them cheap or expensive.

40026 ■ *"Union, Heal Thyself"* in Canadian Business (Vol. 81, July 21, 2008, No. 11, pp. 9)

Description: General Motors Corp. was offered by the federal government a $250 million fund after the company declared plans to close its facility in Ontario. The government move is geared towards supporting the workers who have refused to support the automotive company. Details of the labor contract between General Motors and the Canadian Auto Workers are presented.

40027 ■ *"Union Questions Patrick Cudahy Layoffs"* in Business Journal-Milwaukee (Vol. 28, December 3, 2010, No. 9, pp. A1)

Pub: Milwaukee Business Journal

Ed: Rich Rovito. **Description:** United Food and Commercial Workers Local 1473 is investigating Patrick Cudahy Inc.'s termination of 340 jobs. The union said the company has violated the law for failing to issue proper notice of a mass layoff.

40028 ■ *"Unions Prep For Right-To-Work Law"* in Business Journal Milwaukee (Vol. 29, June 15, 2012, No. 38, pp. 1)

Pub: American City Business Journals, Inc.

Contact: Whitney Shaw, President

Ed: Rich Rovito. **Released:** June 15, 2012. **Description:** Milwaukee, Wisconsin-based labor unions have started preparing for the passage of a right-to-work law. Badger Meter Inc. chief executive officer, Rich Meeusen, has expressed support for the bill.

40029 ■ *"U.S. Enters BlackBerry Dispute Compromise Sought Over Security Issues"* in Houston Chronicle (August 6, 2010)

Pub: Houston Chronicle

Contact: Sherry Adams, Director, Library Services

Ed: Matthew Lee. **Description:** U.S. State Department is working for a compromise with Research in Motion, manufacturer of the BlackBerry, over security issues. The Canadian company makes the smartphones and foreign governments believe they pose a security risk.

40030 ■ *"U.S. Primaries: An Amazing Race"* in Canadian Business (Vol. 81, February 12, 2008, No. 3, pp. 25)

Pub: Rogers Media Inc.

Contact: Tony Viner, President

Ed: Rachel Pulfer. **Description:** U.S. presidential candidates Barack Obama and Hilary Clinton lead the Democratic Part primaries while John McCain is a frontrunner at the Republican Party. These leading candidates have different plans for the U.S. economy which will affect Canada's own economy particularly concerning trade policies. The presidential candidates' proposals and the impacts of U.S. economic downturn on Canada are examined.

40031 ■ *United States Taxes and Tax Policy*

Pub: Cambridge University Press

Contact: Richard Ziemacki, President

E-mail: rziemacki@cambridge.org

Ed: David G. Davies. **Released:** April 2011. **Price:** $32. **Description:** This book expands the information on taxes found in public finance texts by using a combination of institutional, factual, theoretical and empirical information. It also stresses the economic effects of taxes and tax policy. **Availability:** E-book.

40032 ■ *"United's Next Hurdle: Costly Repairs"* in Crain's Chicago Business (Vol. 31, April 14, 2008, No. 15, pp. 1)

Pub: Crain Communications Inc.

Contact: Todd Johnson, Publisher

Ed: John Pletz. **Description:** Discusses the recent crackdown by aviation regulators concerning airline safety at United Airlines as well as other carriers. Maintenance costs at United for the upkeep on the company's older planes is severely affecting its bottom line which is already sagging under heavy fuel costs.

40033 ■ *"Univest Charter Switch Signals Banking Trend"* in Philadelphia Business Journal (Vol. 30, September 2, 2011, No. 29, pp. 1)

Pub: American City Business Journals Inc.

Ed: Jeff Blumenthal. **Description:** Univest Corporation of Pennsylvania changed from a federal to state charter because of cost savings and state agency has greater understanding of the intricacies of the local economy. The Pennsylvania Department of Banking has also received inquiries from seven other banks about doing the same this year.

40034 ■ *"Unlicensed Utah Collection Agency Settles with State Finance Department"* in Idaho Business Review, Boise (July 15, 2010)

Pub: Idaho Business Review

Description: Federal Recovery Acceptance Inc., doing business as Paramount Acceptance in Utah, agreed to pay penalties and expenses after the firm was investigated by the state for improprieties. The firm was charged with conducting unlicensed collection activity.

40035 ■ *"Up on the Farm"* in Canadian Business (Vol. 81, October 27, 2008, No. 18, pp. 119)

Ed: Sean Silcoff. **Description:** Investing in Saskatchewan's agricultural land is explored. Calvert government's lifting of restrictions on ownership of land have enabled Doug Emsley and Brad Farquhar to invest in farmlands in the area. Emsley and Farquhar lease the farmlands they own, enabling farmers to buy equipment and improve crop yields.

40036 ■ *"Up To Code? Website Eases Compliance Burden for Entrepreneurs"* in Black Enterprise (Vol. 38, March 1, 2008, No. 8, pp. 48)

Pub: Earl G. Graves Publishing Co. Inc.

Contact: Earl G. Graves, Jr., President

Ed: Robin White-Goode. **Description:** Business.gov is a presidential E-government project created to help small businesses easily find, understand, and comply with laws and regulations pertaining to a particular industry.

40037 ■ *"Utah Collection Agency Settles File-Sharing Charges"* inPaymentsSource (June 11, 2012)

Pub: SourceMedia Inc.

Contact: James M. Malkin, Chief Executive Officer

Released: June 11, 2012. **Description:** EPN Inc., doing business as Checknet Inc., settled charges filed by the Federal Trade Commission that it exposed sensitive information on its computers and networks creating a potential security risk to the consumer information it stored. Details of the suit are provided.

40038 ■ *"Va. Stalls on Health Exchange" in Washington Business Journal (Vol. 31, July 6, 2012, No. 11, pp. 2)*
Pub: American City Business Journals, Inc.
Contact: Whitney Shaw, President
Ed: Ben Fischer. **Released:** July 6, 2012. **Description:** Political leaders and health insurance companies in Virginia are at odds over the creation of a health benefits exchange in the state. Industry leaders want a swift creation of an online health benefits exchange, while conservative politicians in the state resist the creation of such an exchange.

40039 ■ *"Valenti: Roots of Financial Crisis Go Back to 1998" in Crain's Detroit Business (Vol. 24, October 6, 2008, No. 40, pp. 25)*
Pub: Crain Communications Inc.
Contact: Rance E. Crain, President
Ed: Tom Henderson, Nathan Skid. **Description:** Interview with Sam Valenti III who is the chairman and CEO of Valenti Capital L.L.C., a wealth-management firm; Valenti discusses in detail the history that led up to the current economic crisis as well as his prediction for the future of the country.

40040 ■ *"Vanity Plates" in Canadian Business (Vol. 82, April 27, 2009, No. 7, pp. 26)*
Ed: Andy Holloway. **Description:** Politicians in the U.S. called for the review of firms that availed of the bailout money but are under deals for naming rights of sports stadiums. Angus Reid's Corporate Reputation and Sponsorship Index found for example, that there is little correlation between sponsoring arenas on having a better brand image. It is suggested that firms who enter these deals build closer to people's homes.

40041 ■ *"VC Boosts WorkForce: Livonia Software Company to Add Sales, Marketing Staff" in Crain's Detroit Business (March 24, 2008)*
Pub: Crain Communications Inc.
Contact: Rance E. Crain, President
Ed: Tom Henderson. **Description:** WorkForce Software Inc., a company that provides software to manage payroll processes and oversee compliance with state and federal regulations and with union rules, plans to use an investment of $5.5 million in venture capital to hire more sales and marketing staff.

40042 ■ *"The View from the Field: Six Leaders Offer Their Perspectives On Sales Success" in (Vol. 90, July-August 2012, No. 7-8, pp. 101)*
Pub: Harvard Business Review Press
Contact: Peter E. Walsh, Director
Ed: Jim Koch, James Farley, Susan Silbermann, Duncan MacNaughton, Phil Guido, Suresh Goklaney. **Released:** July-August 2012. **Description:** Six business leaders provide their perspectives on successful selling. Common themes include engaging customers and seeking their input, personalizing their services, ensuring accountability, implementing community outreach, being mindful of cultural and regulatory issues, providing unique offerings, incorporating experiential learning, and properly identifying a customer's needs.

40043 ■ *"Volunteers Needed" in Canadian Business (Vol. 81, October 27, 2008, No. 18, pp. 60)*
Ed: Megan Harman. **Description:** Emissions-targeting regulations focus on the biggest polluters, missing out on other companies that leave carbon footprints in things such as shipping and travel. Some companies in Canada have initiated programs to offset their carbon emissions. Critics claim that offsetting does not reduce emissions and the programs merely justify pollution.

40044 ■ *"Waiting for the Sunset on Taxes" in Memphis Business Journal (Vol. 34, September 28, 2012, No. 24, pp. 1)*
Pub: American City Business Journal
Description: The implementation of the Tax Relief, Unemployment Reauthorization and Job Creation Act of 2010 will end on December 31, 2012. The exemption threshold will fall to $1 million, and the tax rate

on transfers above that limit will be at 55 percent. The effect of political uncertainty on tax planning is also discussed.

40045 ■ *"Walker Seeks More Business Participation" in Business Journal-Milwaukee (Vol. 28, December 10, 2010, No. 10, pp. A1)*
Pub: Milwaukee Business Journal
Ed: Rich Kirchen. **Description:** Wisconsin governor Scott Walker is seeking the aid of Milwaukee business leaders to participate in resolving the challenges posed by the economic crisis. Walker is aiming to create 250,000 jobs. He is also planning to call a special session of the legislature to enact strategies to jumpstart the economy.

40046 ■ *"Warning Signs As NY Makes One Big Bet" in Business Review Albany (Vol. 41, July 25, 2014, No. 18, pp. 4)*
Pub: The Business Journals
Released: July 25, 2014. **Description:** The debate over some New York county governments' plans to legalize gambling is discussed. Members of the Greenbrush Borad have opposed the plan to build a $300 million resort casino in the area. Meanwhile, supporters have cited the economic benefits of legalizing gambling as a reason for the plan.

40047 ■ *"Was Mandating Solar Power Water Heaters For New Homes Good Policy?" in Hawaii Business (Vol. 54, August 2008, No. 2, pp. 28)*
Pub: PacificBasin Communications
Description: Senator Gary L. Kooser of District 7 Kauai-Niihau believes that the mandating of energy-efficient water heaters for new single-family homes starting in 2010 will help cut Hawaii's oil consumption. Ron Richmond of the Hawaii Solar Energy Association says that the content of SB 644 has negative consequences as it allows for choice of energy and not just solar, and it also eliminates tax credits for new homebuyers.

40048 ■ *"Watchdogs for Health Care" in Money (Vol. 41, October 2012, No. 9, pp. 63)*
Pub: Time Inc.
Contact: Wayne Powers, President
Description: Bonnie Burns, California Health Advocates' policy specialist, discusses issues facity seniors regarding their health care.

40049 ■ *"Water Efficiency Bills Move Through Congress" in Contractor (Vol. 56, July 2009, No. 7, pp. 20)*
Pub: Penton Media, Inc.
Ed: Kevin Schwalb. **Description:** National Association, a plumbing-heating-cooling contractor, was instrumental in drafting the Water Advanced Technologies for Efficient Resource Use Act of 2009 and they are also backing the Water Accountability Tax Efficiency Reinvestment Act. The first bill promotes WaterSense-labeled products while the other promotes water conservation through tax credits.

40050 ■ *"Weaving a Stronger Fabric: Organizing a Global Sweat-Free Apparel Production Agreement" in WorkingUSA (Vol. 11, June 2008, No. 2)*
Ed: Eric Dirnbach. **Description:** Tens of millions of workers working under terrible sweatshop conditions in the global apparel industry. Workers are employed at apparel contractors and have been largely unsuccessful in organizing and improving their working conditions. The major apparel manufacturers and retailers have the most power in this industry, and they have adopted corporate social responsibility programs as a false solution to the sweatshop problem. The major North American apparel unions dealt with similar sweatshop conditions a century ago by organizing the contractors and brands into joint association contracts that significantly raised standards. Taking inspiration from their example, workers and their anti-sweatshop allies need to work together to coordinate a global organizing effort that builds worker power and establishes a global production agreement that negotiates with both contractors and the brands for improved wages, benefits, and working conditions.

40051 ■ *"Wellington to Vote On Increasing Size of Elder-Care Facility" in Palm Beach Post (September 11, 2012)*
Pub: Cox Media Group Inc.
Ed: Mitra Malek. **Description:** Wellington Elder Care plans to expand from 14 to 21 residents at its Lily Court locations in Palm Beach, Florida area. The village council approved zoning changes for a congregate-living facility to have up to 21 beds if the facility is specifically for senior housing with residents at least 65 years of age.

40052 ■ *"We're Drowning In Fine Print" in Canadian Business (Vol. 87, July 2014, No. 7, pp. 30)*
Pub: George Media Inc.
Released: July 2014. **Description:** The implications of mandatory disclosure rules for Canadian businesses and consumers are discussed. Businesses are advised to pay more attention to costs and benefits rather than force their customers to claim they have read and agree with the terms and conditions of lengthy and complex disclosures and privacy agreements.

40053 ■ *"What Can Michael Brown Do For Biz?" in Washington Business Journal (Vol. 31, June 15, 2012, No. 8, pp. 1)*
Pub: American City Business Journal
Description: Michael Brown, Washington DC's new economic development point man, aims to ease business regulation, speed up retail development, and create opportunities for local contractors. He is also expected to deal with oversight of all housing and economic development issues and agencies within the state.

40054 ■ *"What Do Your ISO Procedures Say?" in Modern Machine Shop (Vol. 84, September 2011, No. 4, pp. 34)*
Pub: Gardner Business Media, Inc.
Contact: Richard G. Kline, President
E-mail: rkline@gardnerweb.com
Ed: Wayne S. Chaneski. **Description:** ISO 9000 certification can be time-consuming and costly, but it is a necessary step in developing a quality management system that meets both current and potential customer needs.

40055 ■ *"What Enforcement?" in Canadian Business (Vol. 81, December 24, 2007, No. 1, pp. 26)*
Ed: Al Rosen. **Description:** Securities enforcement in Canada needs to be improved in order to tackle white collar crimes that influence investors' opinion of the country. There have been high-profile cases where investigations have not been initiated. Details on the responsibilities of the securities commissions and the need for enforcement mandate in a separate agency are discussed.

40056 ■ *"What the Future Holds for Consumers" in Black Enterprise (Vol. 41, August 2010, No. 1, pp. 47)*
Pub: Earl G. Graves Publishing Co. Inc.
Contact: Earl G. Graves, Jr., President
Ed: Sheiresa Ngo. **Description:** The way people purchase goods and service has changed with technology. With an increased focus on security (as well as privacy and fairness) the U.S. Congress began regulating the credit card industry with the Fair Credit Reporting Act of 1970 and the Credit Card Accountability, Responsibility, and Disclosure (CARD) Act of 2009.

40057 ■ *"What Happens in Vegas Could Happen in Baltimore, Too" in Boston Business Journal (Vol. 29, June 17, 2011, No. 6, pp. 1)*
Pub: American City Business Journals, Inc.
Ed: Daniel J. Sernovitz. **Description:** At least 36 companies expressed their interest in developing a casino in South Baltimore following the state commission's announcement for bids. Developers have until July 28, 2011 to submit their proposals. Baltimore's strong economy is the major factor for the interest, yet the fact that blackjack and poker are outlawed in Maryland could be a drawback.

40058 ■ *"What Keeps Global Leaders Up at Night"* in *Harvard Business Review (Vol. 90, April 2012, No. 4, pp. 32)*
Pub: Harvard Business Review Press
Contact: Peter E. Walsh, Director
Released: April 2012. **Description:** A chart uses colored squares to portray economic, environmental, geopolitical, societal, and technological concerns of industry leaders, and ranks them according to likelihood and impact.

40059 ■ *"What Most Banks Fail to See; New and Complex Financial Regulations Can be Daunting"* in *Gallup Management Journal (March 10, 2011)*
Pub: Gallup Inc.
Contact: Jim Clifton, Chief Executive Officer
Ed: Sean Williams, Daniel Porcelli. **Description:** New financial regulations are complicated and politically charged. But banks that move beyond the fear of those regulations will find a new opportunity to engage customers.

40060 ■ *"What Will Green Power Cost? Surcharge, Spending Cap Considered"* in *Crain's Detroit Business (Vol. 24, March 10, 2008, No. 10, pp. 1)*
Pub: Crain Communications Inc.
Ed: Amy Lane. **Description:** Due to a proposed mandate, which states that 10 percent of power will have to come from renewable sources by 2015 in the state of Michigan, concern is being raised about the higher electricity prices this legislation will undoubtedly cause to business and residential customers.

40061 ■ *"What's Ahead for Fannie and Fred?"* in *Barron's (Vol. 90, August 30, 2010, No. 35, pp. 26)*
Pub: Barron's Editorial & Corporate Headquarters
Ed: Jonathan R. Laing. **Description:** A meeting presided by Treasury Secretary Timothy Geithner discussed the future of Fannie Mae and Freddie Mac. The two government sponsored enterprises were mismanaged and reforming these two agencies is critical.

40062 ■ *"What's At Stake In Ex-Im Fight"* in *Puget Sound Business Journal (Vol. 35, July 4, 2014, No. 11, pp. 8)*
Pub: American City Business Journals
Released: July 4, 2014. **Description:** Boeing claims that it is at risk for being placed at a competitive disadvantage against rival Airbus if Congress declines to reauthorize the Export-Import Bank. The possibility of this scenario has increased since House Majority Leader, Eric Cantor, was replaced by Kevin McCarthy. The issue of the government's regulations is addressed.

40063 ■ *"What's In a Name? Fed's Latest Move Should Be Called 'Bankers and Brokers Relief Program"* in *Barron's (Vol. 88, March 17, 2008, No. 11, pp. 7)*
Pub: Dow Jones & Co., Inc.
Contact: Clare Hart, President
Ed: Alan Abelson. **Description:** Eliot Spitzer's resignation incidentally caused the stock market to go up by 400 points. The Federal Reserve Board's new Term Securities Lending Facility provides liquidity to the big lenders by funneling $200 billion in the form of 28-day loans of Treasuries. The analysis of Paul Brodsky and Lee Quaintance of QB Partners on the demand for commodities is also discussed.

40064 ■ *"What's More Important: Stag or Flation?"* in *Barron's (Vol. 88, July 14, 2008, No. 28, pp. M8)*
Pub: Dow Jones & Co., Inc.
Contact: Clare Hart, President
Ed: Randall W. Forsyth. **Description:** Economists are divided on which part of stagflation, an economic situation in which inflation and economic stagnation occur simultaneously and remain unchecked for a period of time, is more important. Some economists say that the Federal government is focusing on controlling inflation while others see the central bank as extending its liquidity facilities to the financial sector.

40065 ■ *"Where Canada Meets the World"* in *Canadian Business (Vol. 80, October 8, 2007, No. 20, pp. 86)*
Ed: Zena Olijnyk. **Description:** An overview of facilities within Canada's borders that contributes to the country's economy is presented. The facilities include fishing vessels and seaports. Agencies that regulate the borders such as the Canada Border Services Agency and the Department of Fisheries and Oceans are also presented.

40066 ■ *"Whistling Past the Graveyard? Higher Quality Stocks Beckon to Investors?"* in *Barron's (Vol. 88, March 17, 2008, No. 11, pp. 15)*
Pub: Dow Jones & Co., Inc.
Contact: Clare Hart, President
Ed: Michael Santoli. **Description:** Discusses the Federal Reserve's move to provide $200 billion to the system which can be seen as an effort to avoid the liquidity problems that Bear Stearns suffered. The Federal Reserve's move seems to frighten investors rather than reassure them.

40067 ■ *"Why Change?"* in *Canadian Business (Vol. 80, October 8, 2007, No. 20, pp. 9)*
Ed: Joe Chidley. **Description:** The need for economic change in Canada is discussed. Despite the country's economic growth and low unemployment rate, economic reform is needed in order to maximize its economic potential in the future. Other reasons for the need to further develop its economy, such as the rise of manufacturing and service industries in Asia and the emergence of regional trade pacts in South America are also tackled.

40068 ■ *"Why Japan Is So Interested In Alabama"* in *Birmingham Business Journal (Vol. 31, August 1, 2014, No. 31, pp. 11)*
Pub: American City Business Journals, Inc.
Contact: Whitney Shaw, President
Released: August 1, 2014. **Description:** Kazuo Sunaga, Consul General of Japan in Atlanta, Georgia lists several reasons why Alabama presents several opportunities for Japanese companies, including fewer labor laws, low tax rates and the availability of trained workers. The state's relationship with Japan will be further enhanced when Birmingham hosts the Southeast U.S./Japan Association meeting in 2015, which will be attended by leaders from the business, political, and nonprofit sectors.

40069 ■ *"Why Optimism Over Europe Won't Last"* in *Barron's (Vol. 92, August 25, 2012, No. 38, pp. M6)*
Pub: Dow Jones & Co., Inc.
Contact: Clare Hart, President
Ed: Jonathan Buck. **Description:** European markets could experience losses in the second half of 2012 as uncertainty over political events could wipe out market gains. Greece has to abide by the terms of ts agreements with creditors to receive bailout funds. The stock prices of BG Group could gain as much as 20 percent in 2013 due to its strong liqufied natural gas business.

40070 ■ *"Why the Rally Should Keep Rolling..for Now"* in *Barron's (Vol. 89, July 27, 2009, No. 30, pp. M3)*
Pub: Dow Jones & Co., Inc.
Contact: Clare Hart, President
Ed: Kopin Tan. **Description:** Stocks rallied for the second straight week as of July 24, 2009 and more companies reported better than expected earnings but the caveat is that companies are beating estimates chiefly by slashing expenses and firing workers. The regulatory risks faced by CME Group and the IntercontinentalExchange as well as the shares of KKR Private Equity Investors LP.

40071 ■ *"Why Seattle Children's Appealed"* in *Puget Sound Business Journal (Vol. 35, May 30, 2014, No. 6, pp. 6)*
Pub: American City Business Journals
Released: May 30, 2014. **Description:** Seattle Children's Hospital filed an appeal against the Washing State Office of the Insurance Commissioner for approving several health exchange plans that excluded the hospital. Children's argues that it offers unique services and treatments only available through their medical facility and health insurance plans excluding them is putting children at risk.

40072 ■ *"The Wild West"* in *Canadian Business (Vol. 80, January 15, 2007, No. 2, pp. 57)*
Ed: David Baines. **Description:** The impact of the introduction of regulations by the British Columbia Securities Commission on trading of securities by investors is discussed.

40073 ■ *"Will Baltimore's Role as Race Track Hurt or Help Business?: Squeeze Play"* in *Baltimore Business Journal (Vol. 28, September 3, 2010, No. 17, pp. 1)*
Pub: Baltimore Business Journal
Ed: Daniel J. Sornovitz. **Description:** The Baltimore Grand Prix is seen to benefit businesses in Baltimore, Maryland's Inner Harbor. It is also seen to create a rift between the city government and some office workers.

40074 ■ *"Will Bush Cuts Survive? Tax Thriller in D.C."* in *Barron's (Vol. 90, August 30, 2010, No. 35, pp. 17)*
Pub: Barron's Editorial & Corporate Headquarters
Ed: Jim McTague. **Description:** There are speculations on how Senator Harry Reid can push his bill to raise taxes on the wealthy while retaining the George W. Bush tax rates for the rest. Reid's challenge is to get the 60 votes needed to pass the bill.

40075 ■ *"Will Focus on Maryland Businesses Continue?"* in *Baltimore Business Journal (Vol. 28, November 5, 2010, No. 26, pp. 1)*
Pub: Baltimore Business Journal
Ed: Scott Dance. **Description:** The 2010 election may call for new efforts to teach new lawmakers to assure that the viewpoints of businesses are considered and accurately delivered. The Greater Baltimore Committee and similar groups have gathered reports on the competitiveness of Maryland and are planning to use them to make a case of keeping business a top priority.

40076 ■ *"Will Other Insurers Follow United's Lead?"* in *Birmingham Business Journal (Vol. 29, June 22, 2012, No. 26, pp. 1)*
Pub: American City Business Journals, Inc.
Contact: Whitney Shaw, President
Ed: Evan Belanger. **Released:** June 22, 2012. **Description:** UnitedHealtcare will continue offering patient protections as required by US health reform law. But United controls five percent of Alabama's health insurance market. Provisions of patient protections being offered by the company are also discussed.

40077 ■ *Winner Take All: How Competitiveness Shapes the Fate of Nations*
Pub: Basic Books
Contact: Elizabeth Maguire, Publisher
Ed: Richard J. Elkus, Jr. **Released:** June 16, 2009. **Price:** $27; C$34; £17.99. **Description:** American government and misguided business practices have allowed the U.S. to fall behind other countries in various market sectors such as cameras and televisions, as well as information technologies. It will take a national strategy for America to regain its lead in crucial industries. **Availability:** E-book.

40078 ■ *"Wins and Losses for Business, Tax Reform Progress in New Pa. Budget"* in *Philadelphia Business Journal (Vol. 28, October 16, 2009, No. 35, pp. 1)*
Pub: American City Business Journals Inc.
Ed: Athena D. Merritt. **Description:** It was reported that Pennsylvania's $27.8 billion budget arrived 101 days late, but business groups are encouraged that progress continues to be made on long-called-for tax reforms. The Research and Development Tax Credit, currently at $40 million, will drop to $20 million in 2009-2010.

40079 ■ *"With Mine Approval, Crystallex's Value as Target Seen on Rise"* in *Globe & Mail (March 28, 2006, pp. B3)*
Ed: Wendy Stueck. **Description:** Crystallex International Corp. obtains Venezuelan Ministry of Basic Industry and Mining's authorization on Las Cristinas mining project. The impact of the approval, which posted rise in shares by 21 percent for the company, is discussed.

40080 ■ *"Wood Increasingly Used in School Construction"* in *Arkansas Business (Vol. 29, July 23, 2012, No. 30, pp. 11)*
Pub: Arkansas Business Publishing Group
Ed: Jan Cottingham. **Description:** Arkansas state guidelines have increased the use of wood in school building construction. Wood is believed to provide strength and durability along with cost effectiveness and environmental benefits.

40081 ■ *"A Word With Connie Runia of Collection Bureau"* in *Idaho Business Review (September 8, 2014)*
Pub: Dolan Co.
Contact: James P. Dolan, President
Released: September 8, 2014. **Description:** Connie Runia, attorney and general counsel for Collection Bureau, located in Nampa, Idaho, joined the firm four years ago. These collection bureaus are licensed by the Department of Finance and regulated by the Federal Trade Commission. The Consumer Financial Protection Bureau is developing new rules for collection agencies. Statistical data included.

40082 ■ *"Workers' Comp May Pose Double Trouble for Companies in 2013"* in *Orlando Business Journal (Vol. 29, August 31, 2012, No. 11, pp. 1)*
Pub: American City Business Journal
Description: Companies are in for some difficulties with two waves of workers' compensation increases by 2013. In addition to a 20 percent increase of all workers' compensation premiums in Florida that was approved in July, the Florida Office of Insurance Regulation will consider a 6.1 percent increase in October. Bases for the proposed salary increase are discussed.

40083 ■ *"Workers' Comp System Cuts Through Paper"* in *Sacramento Business Journal (Vol. 25, July 11, 2008, No. 19, pp. 1)*
Pub: American City Business Journals, Inc.
Contact: Whitney Shaw, President
Ed: Kelly Johnson. **Description:** California has started testing a new paperless system for handling disputed workers' compensation claims. It is believed that the shift will affect people both inside and outside of the state Division of Workers' Compensation and the state Workers' Compensation Appeals Board. The other details of the planned system are also presented.

40084 ■ *"WQA Develops Certification Program"* in *Contractor (Vol. 57, January 2010, No. 1, pp. 56)*
Pub: Penton Media, Inc.
Ed: Dennis Sowards. **Description:** Water Quality Association is now offering a new certification program for companies that may be affected by California's law that prohibits any products intended to convey or dispense water for human consumption that is not lead-free. All pipe or plumbing fixtures must be certified by a third party certification body.

40085 ■ *"WQA's Leadership Conference Tackles Industry Issues"* in *Contractor (Vol. 56, October 2009, No. 10, pp. 3)*
Pub: Penton Media, Inc.
Ed: Candace Roulo. **Description:** Water Quality Association's Mid-Year Leadership Conference held in Bloomingdale, Illinois in September 2009 tackled lead regulation, water softeners, and product efficiency. The possibility of a WQA green seal was discussed by the Water Sciences Committee and the Government Relations Committee meeting.

40086 ■ *"Yield Vanishes, Inflation Lurks"* in *Barron's (Vol. 92, September 17, 2012, No. 38, pp. M12)*
Description: The US Federal Reserve's announcement of a third round of quantitative easing resulted in lower yields for bonds. Investors are becoming concerned with the probability of a rise in inflation after th quantitative easing program expires.

40087 ■ *"You Won't Go Broke Filling Up On The Stock"* in *Barron's (Vol. 88, July 14, 2008, No. 28, pp. 38)*
Pub: Dow Jones & Co., Inc.
Contact: Clare Hart, President
Ed: Assif Shameen. **Description:** Due to high economic growth, pro-business policies and a consumption boom, the Middle East is a good place to look for equities. The best ways in which to gain exposure to this market include investing in the real estate industry and telecommunications markets as well as large banks that serve corporations and consumers.

STATISTICAL SOURCES

40088 ■ *Regulatory Spending Soars: An Analysis of the US Budget for 2003*
Weidenbaum Center
Contact: Steven Smith, Director
Price: Free. **Description:** Provides information on government regulation, covering 2004 overall cost, barriers to economic growth, and benefits of deregulation, Includes graphs, charts, and statistics.

TRADE PERIODICALS

40089 ■ *Compliance Action*
Pub: Compliance Action
Contact: George B. Milner, Jr., Publisher
URL(s): www.bankersonline.com/bin/cahome.html. **Ed:** Lucy Griffin, Editor. **Released:** 16/year. **Price:** $339, Individuals /year. **Description:** Covers issues pertaining to regulatory compliance in financial institutions.

40090 ■ *Dickinson's FDA Review*
Pub: Ferdic Inc.
Contact: James Dickinson, Secretary
URL(s): www.fdareview.com. **Ed:** James G. Dickinson, Editor. **Released:** Monthly. **Price:** $1,195, Individuals; $1,295, Other countries. **Description:** Recurring features include interviews, news of research, a calendar of events, reports of meetings, and notices of publications available.

40091 ■ *Document Center--Update*
Pub: Document Center Inc.
Contact: Claudia Bach, President
URL(s): www.document-center.com. **Description:** Informs of the Center's specifications and standards services available to customers.

40092 ■ *FDA Week*
Pub: Inside Washington Publishers
Contact: Korila Malecha, Manager
URL(s): iwpnews.com/IWP-General/Inside-Washington-Publishers-Health/fda-week/menu-id-845.html. **Ed:** Donna Haseley, Editor. **Released:** Weekly (Fri.) **Price:** $685, U.S. and Canada; $735, Elsewhere. **Description:** Reports on Food and Drug Administration policy, regulation, and enforcement.

40093 ■ *Legislative Watch*
Pub: American Tort Reform Association
Contact: Sherman Joyce, President
E-mail: sjoyce@atra.org
Released: Weekly. **Price:** Included in membership. **Description:** Membership newsletter of the American Tort Reform Association.

40094 ■ *Ottawa Letter*
Pub: CCH Canadian Ltd.
Contact: Rick Lewis, Manager
URL(s): www.cch.ca/product.aspx?WebID=1637. **Released:** Biweekly **Price:** $1,350, Individuals. **Description:** Reports on current events and topics of Canada,

such as free trade, human rights, employment, and defense. Also provides statistics, lending, and foreign exchange rates.

40095 ■ *Russian Telecom Newsletter*
Pub: Information Gatekeepers Inc.
Contact: Roland King, President
URL(s): www.igigroup.com/nl/pages/russia.htm. **Ed:** Prof. Sergei L. Galkin, Editor. **Released:** Monthly **Price:** $555, U.S. and Canada; $595, Other countries. **Description:** Covers the telecommunications industry in Russia, including competition, government regulations, international business and ventures, cellular, satellites, and market intelligence. Also features new products and conference reports.

40096 ■ *The Small Business Advocate*
Pub: U.S. Small Business Administration - Office of Advocacy
Contact: Kathryn Tobias, Senior Editor
URL(s): www.sba.gov/category/advocacy-navigation-structure/newsroom/advocacy-newsletter. **Ed:** Rebecca Krafft, Editor. **Released:** Monthly or Bimonthly. **Price:** Free. **Description:** Provides updates on activities and issues of the Office of Advocacy, which examines the impact of legislative proposals and other public policy issues on small businesses.

40097 ■ *The Tan Sheet*
Pub: Elsevier Business Intelligence
Contact: Edie Mead, Director
URL(s): www.pharmamedtechbi.com/publications/the-tan-sheet. **Ed:** Christopher Walker, Editor. **Released:** Weekly, 50/year. **Price:** $2,230, Individuals print and web. **Description:** Provides "in-depth coverage of nonprescription pharmaceuticals and dietary supplement/nutritionals." Topics include congressional hearings and legislation, business and marketing news, FDA recalls and seizures, regular listing of product trademarks, and activities of FTC, CPSC, and FDA.

40098 ■ *Utilities Telecommunications News*
Pub: Information Gatekeepers Inc.
Contact: Roland King, President
URL(s): www.igigroup.com/nl/pages/utitelecom.html. **Released:** Monthly **Price:** $695, U.S. and Canada; $745, Other countries; $695, Individuals online. **Description:** Focuses on the role of utilities in telecommunications. Topics include government and regulations, business, and the Internet. Also features new products and conferences.

40099 ■ *Water Policy Report*
Pub: Inside Washington Publishers
Contact: Korila Malecha, Manager
URL(s): iwpnews.com/IWP-General/Inside-Washington-Publishers-General/products/menu-id-812.html. **Released:** Biweekly; every other Monday. **Price:** $700, U.S. and Canada; $750, Elsewhere. **Description:** Reports on federal water quality programs and policies. Covers topics such as drinking water, toxics, enforcement, monitoring, and state/EPA relations.

CONSULTANTS

40100 ■ *ARDITO Information & Research Inc.*
1019 Sedwick Dr., Ste. G
Wilmington, DE 19803
Ph: (302)479-5373
Free: 800-836-9068
Fax: (302)479-5375
Co. E-mail: sardito@ardito.com
URL: http://www.ardito.com
Contact: Stephanie C. Ardito, President
E-mail: sardito@ardito.com
Scope: A full-service information and research firm. Provides information in areas of financial data, published research, demographic data, industry-specific publications, competitor data, marketing and sales trends, new product developments, government relations, bibliographies. Industries served are pharmaceutical, health, publishing and environment and business. **Founded:** 1990. **Publications:** "The Swine flu pandemic: Authoritative information versus community gossip," Searcher, Oct, 2009; "The Medical blogosphere: How social networking platforms are changing medical searching," Searcher, May, 2009; "Social Networking and Video Web Sites: MyS-

pace and YouTube Meet the Copyright Cops," Searcher, May, 2007; "Copyright Clearance Center raises transactional fees," Information Today, Jul, 2004.

40101 ■ Daniel Bloom and Associates Inc. (DBAI)
11517 128th Ave. N
Largo, FL 33778
Ph: (727)581-6216
Fax: (727)216-8532
Co. E-mail: dan@dbaiconsulting.com
URL: http://www.dbaiconsulting.com
Contact: Sharon Megiel, Consultant
Scope: Human resources management consultant with a specialization in corporate relocation. Offers clients a turn key service aimed at meeting the unique relocation needs of their employees. Develops and implements training programs within the relocation industry. **Founded:** 1980. **Publications:** "Where Have All the Elders Gone," Aug, 2002; "Recoup Your Hiring Investment," Brainbuzz.com, Aug, 2000; "Managing Your Lump Sum Program," Brainbuzz. com, Jun, 2000; "Buyer Value Options," Brainbuzz. com, Apr, 2000; "Just Get Me There". **Seminars:** Chaos in the Workplace: Multiple Generational Interactions; Training Effectiveness: Is the Cost Justified?; Human Capital Resource Management: A Six-Sigma Based Approach to Paving Your Way to the Table; Welcome to My World.

40102 ■ Compliance Consultants [C2]
1151 Hope St.
Stamford, CT 06907
Ph: (203)329-2700
Fax: (203)329-2345
Co. E-mail: rkeen@fda-complianceconsultants.com
URL: http://www.fda-complianceconsultants.com
Contact: Lou Kale, Principal
Scope: A consultancy with expertise in regulatory engineering, product development and medical devices. Firm advises manufacturers of regulatory requirements and submits detailed engineering facts and marketing reports to obtain market approval from Federal Drug Administration. Serves domestic and foreign clients who wish to market products in the United States. **Founded:** 1988.

40103 ■ Envar Services Inc.
505 Milltown Rd.
North Brunswick, NJ 08902-3326
Ph: (732)296-9601
Fax: (732)296-9602
Co. E-mail: mail@envarservices.com
URL: http://www.envarservices.com
Contact: John F. Shultis, President
Scope: Provider of consultation services in the following areas: Engineering design and construction; environmental compliance; plant and process appraisals and upgrades; environmental audits and impact statements; air/oil pollution control and test analyses; feasibility studies; spill prevention; underground storage tank upgrades, removals, and remediation; waste-water treatment studies; and groundwater remediation. Industries served include chemical, petrochemical, pharmaceutical, and manufacturing. Serves eastern United States and Texas. **Founded:** 1960. **Publications:** "Method of Detoxification and Stabilization of Soils Contaminated with Chromium Ore Waste".

40104 ■ Environmental Affairs Management Inc. (EAM)
455 Dan St.
Akron, OH 44310
Ph: (330)384-9150
Free: 888-878-3664
Fax: (330)384-9169
Contact: John W. Brasnell, President
E-mail: envafsmgt@aol.com
Scope: Company provides facilities support services and Phase I and Phase II site assessment, regulatory compliance management and training programs, including OSHA HAZ-COM training, remedial operations and maintenance of underground storage tanks throughout the United States, Eastern sea board and southern states. Also facility decontamination and demolition services. **Founded:** 1988. **Seminars:** Hazard communication.

40105 ■ Environmental Assessment Services Inc.
124 S Main St.
Middletown, OH 45044
Ph: (513)424-3400
Fax: (513)424-2020
Contact: David W. Armentrout, Owner
Scope: Offers environmental and health and safety services in compliance auditing, program management and implementation, field services (monitoring/ testing) and real estate assessment. **Founded:** 1988.

40106 ■ Environmental Management Consultants Inc. (EMC)
427 Main St.
Evansville, IN 47708
Ph: (812)424-7768
Free: 800-280-7768
Fax: (812)424-7797
Co. E-mail: info2010@emcevv.com
URL: http://www.emcevv.com
Contact: Richard L. Reising, Principal
Scope: Offers environmental consulting in the following areas: Asbestos related services; air and water quality monitoring; environmental site assessments; training; underground and above-ground storage tanks; industrial regulatory compliance; and hazardous materials cleanups. Serves private sector and government environmental organizations, industry, financial, educational, hospitals, judicial, school systems, developers, petro-chemical and insurance agents and adjusters in Indiana, Kentucky and Illinois areas. **Founded:** 1988.

40107 ■ Environmental Monitoring Inc. (EMI)
5730 Industrial Park Rd.
Norton, VA 24273-4047
Ph: (276)679-6544
Free: 888-236-4522
Fax: (276)679-6549
Co. E-mail: rjporter@emilab.com
URL: http://www.emilab.com
Contact: Randall J. Porter, President
E-mail: rjporter@emilab.com
Scope: Designer of environmental inspection solutions. It offers groundwater monitoring, industrial waste characterization, visible emissions evaluations, municipal and industrial waste sampling, and analysis services. Provide sampling and analytical services as well as interpretative consultation services. **Founded:** 1983.

40108 ■ Environmental Solutions Inc.
1129 Woodmere Ave., Ste. I
Traverse City, MI 49686
Ph: (231)941-2025
Free: 800-968-0400
Fax: (231)941-8752
Contact: David E. Cooper, Principal
Scope: Full service environmental consulting firm providing environmental management systems, auditing, hydro geological, regulatory, waste minimization, site redevelopment and remediation services. It serves all industries. **Founded:** 1989.

40109 ■ Environmental Support Network Inc.
5376 Fulton Dr. NW
Canton, OH 44718-1808
Ph: (330)494-0905
Co. E-mail: esn@sssnet.com
URL: http://www.environmental-support.com
Contact: William P. Racine, President
Scope: Provides environmental, health and safety consulting and project management services. These include compliance auditing and remediation specifications concerning air, groundwater and soil quality. Also offers health and safety reviews, asbestos and lead-based paint handling, noise sampling, industrial permitting and UST management. Industries served: education, finance, industry and government. **Founded:** 1989. **Seminars:** Environmental Health and Safety Management in Ohio; Managing Compliance in Ohio; Environmental Site Remediation in Ohio and Surrounding States; Conducting ESAs by ASTM Standards; Health and Safety Management in the Medical Setting; Exposure Monitoring in Schools and Public Buildings.

40110 ■ Safety Management Services
4012 Santa Nella Pl.
San Diego, CA 92130-2291
Ph: (858)259-0591
Fax: (858)792-2350
Contact: J. Robert Harrell, President
E-mail: bharrell1@san.rr.com
Scope: Offers safety consulting services: Evaluates safety policies and procedures to determine degree of effectiveness; advises on compliance with OSHA standards; and provides safety programs for managers, supervisors and workers. Industries served: general contractors in new construction, renovation and demolition; and tenant improvement companies which hire general contractors to perform construction activities on their premises. Also assists litigation as construction safety expert witness. Safety training programs customized to meet clients needs. **Founded:** 1978. **Publications:** "What Can Go Wrong?," International Cranes magazine, Apr, 1994. **Seminars:** Federal OSHA Construction Safety and Health Course for Trainers, University of California, San Diego; OSHA 10-Hour Construction Safety Course; 90-Hour Construction Safety Management Certificate Course - 1991 to 1993; Fall Protection; Confined Space Standards; Cranes and Rigging; Scaffold or Trenching and Excavation; and Safe Construction Work Practices.

COMPUTERIZED DATABASES

40111 ■ *CCH Tax Protos™*
CCH Canadian Ltd.
90 Sheppard Ave. E, Ste. 300
Toronto, ON, Canada M2N 6X1
Ph: (416)224-2224
Free: 800-268-4522
Fax: (416)224-2243
Co. E-mail: cservice@cch.ca
URL: http://www.cch.ca
Contact: Rick Lewis, Manager
Availability: Online: CCH Canadian Ltd. **Type:** Bulletin board.

40112 ■ *KeyCite®*
Thomson Reuters Westlaw
610 Opperman Dr.
Eagan, MN 55123
Ph: (651)687-7000
Free: 800-344-5008
Fax: (651)687-5827
Co. E-mail: west.customer.service@thomson.com
Availability: Online: Thomson Reuters - Westlaw. **Type:** Bibliographic; Full-text.

40113 ■ *Product Safety & Liability Reporter™*
Bloomberg BNA
3 Bethesda Metro Center, Ste. 250
Bethesda, MD 20814-5377
Ph: (703)341-3000
Free: 800-372-1033
Fax: (800)253-0332
Co. E-mail: customercare@bna.com
URL: http://www.bna.com
Contact: Gregory McCaffrey, President
Type: Full-text.

40114 ■ *The Tax Directory®*
Tax Analysts
400 S Maple Ave., Ste. 400
Falls Church, VA 22046
Ph: (703)533-4400
Free: 800-955-2444
Fax: (703)533-4444
Co. E-mail: cservice@tax.org
URL: http://www.tax.org
Contact: Christopher E. Bergin, President
Availability: Online: LexisNexis. CD-ROM: Tax Analysts. **Type:** Directory.

LIBRARIES

40115 ■ Bryan Cave LLP Law Library
1155 F St., NW, Ste. 500
Washington, DC 20004
Ph: (202)508-6000

Fax: (202)508-6200
URL: http://www.bryancave.com
Contact: John Peirce
E-mail: john.peirce@bryancave.com
Scope: Government and politics; law - commercial, corporate, environmental, intellectual property, taxation. **Services:** Interlibrary loan; copying; faxing; library open to the public with restrictions. **Founded:** 1978. **Holdings:** 11,000 volumes. **Subscriptions:** 200 journals and other serials.

RESEARCH CENTERS

40116 ■ AEI Press [American Enterprise Institute (AEI)]
1150 17th St. NW

Washington, DC 20036
Ph: (202)862-5800
Free: 800-862-5801
Fax: (202)862-7177
Co. E-mail: custserv@nbnbooks.com
URL: http://www.aei.org
Contact: Arthur C. Brooks, President
Description: Description: Publishes books and periodicals. Nonpartisan and nonprofit research and educational organization. Sponsors research, conducts seminars and conferences. Offers a bimonthly magazine. Accepts unsolicited manuscripts. **Scope:** Economic policy, including domestic taxing, spending, and regulatory programs, and international trade and competitiveness; foreign and defense policy, including the spread of democracy and free enterprise, and the development of stable international security arrangements; social and political studies, including U.S. politics and public opinion, the Constitution and legal policy, and social welfare, educational and cultural issues. **Founded:** 1943. **Publications:** *AEI Newsletter* (Monthly); *The American Enterprise* (Bimonthly); *The American Enterprise: A National Magazine of Politics, Business, and Culture.* **Educational Activities:** AEI Debates and meetings, featuring discussions among experts on major public policy issues. **Awards:** American Enterprise Institute National Research Initiative Fellowships (NRI).

START-UP INFORMATION

40117 ■ *"Business With Brains" in Canadian Business (Vol. 85, September 17, 2012, No. 14, pp. 41)*

Pub: George Media Inc.

Ed: Richard Warnica. **Released:** September 17, 2012. **Description:** The Ontario Brain Institute launched the Entrepreneurs Program to provide funding, business training, and connections to Canadian medical researchers who believe they have great ideas for business. The program aims to close the gap between neuroscience publications and viable projects.

40118 ■ *"Former Ky. Gov. Fletcher Starts Blue Ash Firm" in Business Courier (Vol. 26, October 9, 2009, No. 24, pp. 1)*

Pub: American City Business Journals, Inc.

Contact: Whitney Shaw, President

Ed: Lucy May. **Description:** Former Kentucky Governor Ernie Fletcher partnered with Belcan Corporation founder Ralph Anderson to purchase Blue Ash, Ohio-based Virtual Medical Network and form Alton Healthcare LLC. The company's goal is to increase practice revenues by adapting technology to reinvent clinical practices and deliver best possible care to more patients.

40119 ■ *"An Insurer Stretches Out" in Business Journal Portland (Vol. 30, February 21, 2014, No. 51, pp. 4)*

Pub: American City Business Journals

Released: February 21, 2014. **Description:** The diversification strategy of Cambia Health Solutions has led to investments in several health care startups. The company earned $5.8 billion in revenue from insurance premiums in 2012 and posted a profit margin of about 2 percent for its net income of $173 million.

40120 ■ *"John Brownlee, Vidscrip.com" in Business Journal (Vol. 32, June 27, 2014, No. 5, pp. 6)*

Pub: American City Business Journals

Released: June 27, 2014. **Description:** John Brownlee, CEO of vidscrip.com, discusses the Minneapolis, Minnesota startup's deal with Partners HealthCare and what it means for the business. Partners Health-Care is using the vidscrip technology to create educational videos for patients.

40121 ■ *"The Knee Bone's Connected to the Smartphone" in Entrepreneur (June 2014)*

Pub: Entrepreneur Media Inc.

Released: June 2014. **Description:** French consumer electronics startup, Withings, has developed health care devices that integrate with applications and products using its application programming interface. Withings developed Wi-Fi Body Scale, an Internet-enabled bathroom scale that allows users to track and visualize their weight. Connecting it to the Internet has improved its processing power and storage capacity. Withings spent about a year creating the Body Scale and tailored it to work with the Apple

iPhone. The company is also developing Aura, a sleep system monitor to monitor a user's vital signs and environmental factors.

40122 ■ *"Made@Mayo" in Business Journal (Vol. 32, June 6, 2014, No. 2, pp. 10)*

Pub: American City Business Journals

Released: June 6, 2014. **Description:** Rochester, Minnesota-based Mayo Clinic Ventures has managed the licensing of Mayo Clinic technologies and invests in startups. Mayo Clinic Ventures has a $100 million growth fund for investing in startups and two smaller funds worth about $500,000 combined. Insights on the stories of Mayo researchers leading startups are also provided.

40123 ■ *"No. 173: Innovate: Ideas, Breakthroughs, Disruption Management of Pathway Genomics" in Inc. (Vol. 36, September 2014, No. 7, pp. 128)*

Pub: Mansueto Ventures L.L.C.

Contact: John Koten, Chief Executive Officer

Released: September 2014. **Description:** James Plante founded Pathway Genomic after his father died from cancer. His firm provides DNA collections kits and screening for genetic risk factors for illness. After a doctor orders, patients take home a kit, which comes with a vial to fill with saliva and findings come back in about two weeks. Pathway recently launched a new One-for-One program, that donates one breast cancer test to a patient in need for every kit purchased.

40124 ■ *"No. 407: What I Learned in the Military, and What I Had to Unlearn" in Inc. (Vol. 36, September 2014, No. 7, pp. 80)*

Pub: Mansueto Ventures L.L.C.

Contact: John Koten, Chief Executive Officer

Released: September 2014. **Description:** Profile of William Bailey, who served in the U.S. Army as information manager at the U.S. Military Academy at West Point. Bailey discusses his startup firm, Rapier Solutions, a government contractor providing IT, logistics, and social-work expertise. The firm has developed a new survivor outreach system for the U.S. Army.

40125 ■ *"One of the Best Ways to Build Wealth...Is to Take Equity In a Company" in Business Journal (Vol. 31, May 2, 2014, No. 49, pp. 9)*

Pub: American City Business Journals

Released: May 2, 2014. **Description:** Entrepreneur Abir Sen reveals that he was not planning to start a business after selling Bloom Health, but he soon discovered that he wanted to do something productive. He believes that the traditional model of employer-paid health care insurance is dying. His opinion on health care entrepreneurial activity in Minnesota is also examined.

40126 ■ *"Pot Watch" in Puget Sound Business Journal (Vol. 35, May 30, 2014, No. 6, pp. 10)*

Pub: American City Business Journals

Released: May 30, 2014. **Description:** Magical Butter is a startup in Seattle, Washington that sells a botanical extractor for infusing herbs into food

ingredients like the active ingredient in marijuana known as THC into butter or oil. Career chef, Jeremy Cooper, has perfected the peanut butter and jelly sandwich with THC and sells them from the company's food truck business in Denver, Colorado.

40127 ■ *Up and Running: Opening a Chiropractic Office*

Pub: PageFree Publishing, Incorporated

Ed: John L. Reizer. **Released:** March 2002. **Price:** , $30.00. **Description:** Tips for starting a chiropractic business.

ASSOCIATIONS AND OTHER ORGANIZATIONS

40128 ■ **AcademyHealth**
1150 17th St. NW, Ste. 600
Washington, DC 20036
Ph: (202)292-6700
Fax: (202)292-6800
URL: http://www.academyhealth.org
Contact: Paul Wallace, Chairman
Description: Promotes interaction across the health research and policy arenas by bringing together a broad spectrum of players to share their perspectives, learn from each other and strengthen their working relationships. Convenes national scientific and health policy conferences; helps public and private policymakers transform research and policy into workable programs; educates policymakers, researchers, government officials, and business leaders; disseminates vital information through research syntheses, special report findings, newsletters and website; and conducts major programs that serve the research community, health policy leaders, and business and government decision-makers. **Founded:** 1981. **Publications:** *AcademyHealth Reports* (Quarterly); *AcademyHealth Health Services Research*. **Educational Activities:** National Health Policy Conference (Annual). **Awards:** Article of the Year (Annual); Distinguished Investigator (Annual); Alice S. Hersh New Investigator Award (Annual).

40129 ■ **American Health Care Association (AHCA) - Mark A. Jerstad Information Resource Center**
1201 L St. NW
Washington, DC 20005
Ph: (202)842-4444
Fax: (202)842-3860
URL: http://www.ahcancal.org/Pages/Default.aspx
Description: Federation of state associations of long-term health care facilities. Promotes standards for professionals in long-term health care delivery and quality care for patients and residents in a safe environment. Focuses on issues of availability, quality, affordability, and fair payment. Operates as liaison with governmental agencies, Congress, and professional associations. Compiles statistics. **Scope:** long-term care, nursing facilities, assisted living, subacute care. **Services:** Interlibrary loan; copying; Library open to the public with restrictions by appointment. **Founded:** 1949. **Holdings:** 5000 volumes. **Subscriptions:** audiovisuals books clippings monographs

periodicals; 100 journals and other serials. **Publications:** *Assessing Your Needs: Consumer Guides to Nursing and Assisted Living Facilities; Caring for Someone with Alzheimer's Fact Sheet; Living in a Nursing Home: Myths and Realities Fact Sheet; Tips on Visiting Friends and Relatives Fact Sheet; Family Questions: The First Thirty Days Fact Sheet; Moving Into an Assisted Living Residence: Making a Successful Transition Fact Sheet; Making the Transition to Nursing Facility Life Fact Sheet; Paying for Long Term Care Pamphlet; Glossary of Terms Pamphlet; Advice for Families Pamphlet; Advance Preparation: Having the Conversation About Long Term Care Pamphlet; Coping with the Transition Pamphlet; Talking To Your Loved Ones About Their Care Pamphlet; Capitol Connection Newsletter, NCAL Focus Newsletter, AHCA Notes* (Monthly); *Provider: For Long Term Care Professionals* (Monthly); *Focus* (Monthly); *Provider--LTC Buyers' Guide Issue* (Annual); *American Health Care Association: Provider; Choosing a Nursing Home Pamphlet; Choosing An Assisted Living Residence: A Consumer's Guide; Having Your Say: Advance Directives Fact Sheet; Understanding Long Term Care Insurance Fact Sheet; Assisted Living State Regulatory Review* (Annual); *NCAL Connections; Resident Assistant Newsletter.* **Educational Activities:** American Health Care Association Annual Convention and Exposition (Annual). **Awards:** Adult Volunteer of the Year (Annual); Group Volunteer of the Year; Young Adult Volunteer of the Year Award (Annual); AHCA/NCAL Quality Award (Annual).

40130 ■ Associated Medical Services (AMS)
162 Cumberland St., Ste. 228
Toronto, ON, Canada M5R 3N5
Ph: (416)924-3368
Fax: (416)323-3338
Co. E-mail: info@ams-inc.on.ca
URL: http://php.ams-inc.on.ca
Contact: Dorothy Pringle, President
Description: Health services. Promotes increased availability of quality health care. Facilitates communication and cooperation among members; represents members' interests before government agencies, professional medical organizations, and the public. **Founded:** 1937. **Publications:** *Corporate Report* (Biennial). **Awards:** Hannah Independent Scholar Grant (Annual); Hannah Junior General Scholarship (Annual); Hannah Post Doctoral Fellowship (Annual); Jason A. Hannah Medal (Annual); Hannah Junior General Scholarships; Hannah Senior General Scholarships.

40131 ■ Association for Behavioral Health and Wellness (ABHW)
1325 G St. NW, Ste. 500
Washington, DC 20005
Ph: (202)449-7660
Fax: (202)449-7659
Co. E-mail: info@abhw.org
URL: http://www.abhw.org
Contact: Pamela Greenberg, President
Description: Managed behavioral healthcare organizations. Works to advance the value of managed behavioral healthcare and promotes the inclusion of mental illnesses and addiction disorders in benefit coverage. **Founded:** 1994. **Publications:** *Catalog of Special Reports.*

40132 ■ Association canadienne de la medecine du travail et de l'environnement (OEMAC) [Occupational and Environmental Medical Association of Canada]
503,386 Bdwy.
Winnipeg, MB, Canada R3C 3R6
Ph: (888)223-3808
Co. E-mail: info@oemac.org
URL: http://www.oemac.org
Contact: Oscar Howell, President
Description: Health care professionals with an active interest in occupational and environmental medicine. Promotes improved standards of education and practice in the field. Serves as a unified voice for Canadian occupational and environmental medicine; acts as a forum for exchange of scientific and professional information. Conducts continuing professional education programs. **Scope:** occupational medicine, environmental medicine. **Founded:** 1985. **Subscriptions:** periodicals. **Publications:** *Liaison Newsletter*

(Quarterly); *Liaison* (Quarterly); *Occupational Medicine.* **Awards:** Meritorious Service Award (Annual); Meritorious Service Award.

40133 ■ *CAG Newsletter*
263 McCaul St., Ste. 328
Toronto, ON, Canada M5T 1W7
Free: 855-224-2240
Co. E-mail: contact@cagacg.ca
URL: http://www.cagacg.ca
Contact: Maggie Gibson, President
Released: Quarterly **Price:** free for members; C$32. 10, for nonmembers.

40134 ■ Canadian Academy of Periodontology (CAP) [Academie Canadienne de Parodontologie]
1815 Alta Vista Dr., No. 201
Ottawa, ON, Canada K1G 3Y6
Ph: (613)523-9800
Fax: (613)523-1968
Co. E-mail: info@cap-acp.ca
URL: http://www.cap-acp.ca
Contact: Dr. Todd Jones, President
Description: Periodontologists, educators, and students. Promotes advancement in the practice and teaching of periodontology. Conducts continuing professional education courses for members. Maintains speakers' bureau. **Founded:** 1955. **Publications:** *CAPsule* (3/year).

40135 ■ Canadian Association of Gerontology (CAG) [Association canadienne de gerontologie]
263 McCaul St., Ste. 328
Toronto, ON, Canada M5T 1W7
Free: 855-224-2240
Co. E-mail: contact@cagacg.ca
URL: http://www.cagacg.ca
Contact: Maggie Gibson, President
Description: Focuses on the problems and process of aging. **Founded:** 1971. **Publications:** *CAG Newsletter, CAG Newsletter* (Quarterly); *Canadian Journal on Aging* (Quarterly). **Educational Activities:** Canadian Association of Gerontology Conference (Annual). **Awards:** Evelyn Shapiro Mentoring Award (Biennial); Betty Havens Award (Biennial); Award For Contribution to Gerontology; Distinguished Member Award; Donald Menzies Bursary Award; Honorary Member; Margery Boyce Bursary Awards; CAG Award for Contribution to Gerontology (Annual); CAG Distinguished Member Award (Annual); CAG Donald Menzies Bursary Awards (Annual); CAG Honorary Member (Annual); Margery Boyce Bursary (Annual).

40136 ■ Canadian Association for School Health (CASH)
16629 62A Ave.
Surrey, BC, Canada V3S 9L5
Ph: (604)575-3199
Co. E-mail: info@cash-aces.ca
URL: http://www.cash-aces.ca
Description: School health services. Promotes increased availability and quality of school health programs. Serves as a clearinghouse on school health services; facilitates communication and cooperation among members.

40137 ■ Canadian Cancer Society (CCS) [Societe Canadienne du Cancer]
55 St. Clair Ave. W, Ste. 300
Toronto, ON, Canada M4V 2Y7
Ph: (416)961-7223
Fax: (416)961-4189
Co. E-mail: ccs@cancer.ca
URL: http://www.cancer.ca/en/?region=on
Contact: Marc Genereux, Chairman
Description: Community-based volunteers. Promotes research into the causes, detection, and cure of cancer; seeks to improve the quality of life of people with cancer. Conducts fundraising activities benefiting cancer research; sponsors volunteer training programs; makes available educational courses. **Scope:** cancer. **Founded:** 1938. **Subscriptions:** archival material books clippings periodicals.

40138 ■ Canadian Cardiovascular Society (CCS) [Societe Canadienne de Cardiologie]
222 Queen St., Ste. 1403
Ottawa, ON, Canada K1P 5V9
Ph: (613)569-3407
Free: 877-569-3407
Fax: (613)569-6574
Co. E-mail: info@ccs.ca
URL: http://www.ccs.ca
Contact: Dr. Mario Talajic, President
Description: Physicians, surgeons, and scientists practicing or conducting research in cardiology and related fields. Works to advance the cardiovascular health and care of Canadians through leadership on professional development, advocacy, and the promotion, dissemination of research. **Founded:** 1946. **Publications:** *The Canadian Journal of Cardiology* (Monthly); *CCS News* (Biweekly). **Educational Activities:** Canadian Cardiovascular Congress (Annual). **Awards:** Achievement Award (Annual); Research Achievement (Annual); Young Investigator Award (Annual); Distinguished Teacher Award (Annual); Dr. Harold N. Segall Award of Merit (Annual); Dr. Robert E. Beamish Award (Annual); Trainee Research Award (TRA) (Annual); Trainee Excellence in Education Award (Annual); Research Achievement Award (Annual); Achievement Award (Annual); Distinguished Teacher Award (Annual); Harold N. Segall Award of Merit; Trainee Research Award (Annual); Trainee Excellence in Education Award (Annual); Young Investigator Award (Annual).

40139 ■ Canadian College of Health Leaders (CCHL) - Professional Development Library [College Canadien des Leaders en Sante]
292 Somerset St. W
Ottawa, ON, Canada K2P 0J6
Ph: (613)235-7218
Fax: (613)235-5451
Co. E-mail: info@cchl-ccls.ca
URL: http://www.learninglibrary.com/cchl-ccls
Contact: Ray J. Racette, President
Description: Serves health service executives in Canada. Offers a forum for the exchange of ideas and information, a career network, and professional development opportunities. **Scope:** Healthcare management. **Services:** Not open to the public. **Founded:** 1970. **Publications:** *Healthcare Management Forum* (Quarterly); *Healthcare Management FORUM* (Quarterly). **Educational Activities:** Provincial Health Conference & Exhibition; BC Health Leaders Conference (Annual); Scientific Basis of Health Services. **Awards:** Robert Zed Young Health Leader Award (Annual); Quality of Life Award (Annual); Robert Wood Johnson Award (Annual); 3M Health Care Quality Team Awards (Annual).

40140 ■ Canadian Dermatology Association (CDA) [Association Canadienne de Dermatologie (ACD)]
1385 Bank St., Ste. 425
Ottawa, ON, Canada K1H 8N4
Ph: (613)738-1748
Free: 800-267-3376
Fax: (613)738-4695
Co. E-mail: info@dermatology.ca
URL: http://www.dermatology.ca
Contact: Ms. Chantal Courchesne, Executive Director
Description: Certified dermatologists and related professionals interested in the professional advancement of dermatology. Promotes continuing education programs in dermatology. Provides public education program on skin cancer prevention. Holds an annual National Sun Awareness Week. Recognizes sun protection products. **Scope:** Dermatology. **Founded:** 1925. **Holdings:** 80 books; archival materials. **Publications:** *Journal of Cutaneous Medicine and Surgery* (Bimonthly); *Membership and Corporate Directory* (Annual). **Educational Activities:** Canadian Dermatology Association Annual Conference (Annual). **Awards:** Award of Merit; Barney Usher Research Award in Dermatology (Annual); President's Cup (Annual); Young Dermatologists' Volunteer Award (Annual); Award of Honour; Public Education Awards; Young Dermatologists' Volunteer Award (Annual);

Award of Honour (Annual); Barney Usher Award (Annual); CDA Public Education Award (Annual); President's Cup (Annual).

40141 ■ *Canadian Family Physician*
2360 Skymark Ave.
Mississauga, ON, Canada L4W 5A4
Ph: (905)629-0900
Free: 800-387-6197
Co. E-mail: info@cfpc.ca
URL: http://www.cfpc.ca
Contact: Dr. David Tannenbaum, Director
Released: Monthly Price: C$8.56, /issue.

40142 ■ Canadian Health Coalition (CHC) [Coalition Canadienne de la Sante]
251 Bank St., Ste. 212
Ottawa, ON, Canada K2P 1X3
Co. E-mail: info@healthcoalition.ca
URL: http://healthcoalition.ca
Contact: Pauline Worsfold, Chairperson
Description: Individuals and organizations with an interest in health care. Promotes increased availability and quality of health services. Monitors the performance of health care facilities and services and makes recommendations for their improvement. Founded: 1979.

40143 ■ *Canadian Journal on Aging*
263 McCaul St., Ste. 328
Toronto, ON, Canada M5T 1W7
Free: 855-224-2240
Co. E-mail: contact@cagacg.ca
URL: http://www.cagacg.ca
Contact: Maggie Gibson, President
URL(s): cagacg.ca/cja. Released: Quarterly Price: free for members; C$52.50, individual, plus GST; C$80.25, institution, plus GST.

40144 ■ *The Canadian Journal of Cardiology*
222 Queen St., Ste. 1403
Ottawa, ON, Canada K1P 5V9
Ph: (613)569-3407
Free: 877-569-3407
Fax: (613)569-6574
Co. E-mail: info@ccs.ca
URL: http://www.ccs.ca
Contact: Dr. Mario Talajic, President
URL(s): www.onlinecjc.ca/. Released: Monthly Price: $296, Individuals prine and online; $229, Students prine and online; $254, Canada prine and online; $300, Other countries prine and online.

40145 ■ *Canadian Journal of Infection Control*
PO Box 46125
Winnipeg, MB, Canada R3R 3S3
Ph: (204)897-5990
Free: 866-999-7111
Fax: (204)895-9595
URL: http://www.chica.org
Contact: Bruce Gamage, President
Released: Quarterly Price: C$36.

40146 ■ *The Canadian Journal of Psychiatry*
141 Laurier Ave. W, Ste. 701
Ottawa, ON, Canada K1P 5J3
Ph: (613)234-2815
Fax: (613)234-9857
Co. E-mail: cpa@cpa-apc.org
URL: http://www.cpa-apc.org
Contact: Donald Addington, Chairman of the Board
URL(s): publications.cpa-apc.org/browse/sections/0.
Released: Monthly; 12/yr. Price: $215, Canada print only; $320, Other countries print only; $215, Individuals online only; $260, Canada print and online; $385, Other countries print and online.

40147 ■ Canadian Medical Association (CMA)
1867 Alta Vista Dr.
Ottawa, ON, Canada K1G 5W8
Free: 888-855-2555
Fax: (613)236-8864
Co. E-mail: cmamsc@cma.ca
URL: http://www.cma.ca
Contact: Louis Hugo Francescutti, President
Description: Seeks to improve medical care for persons living in Canada. Works to maintain high standards of hospital care and health related services.

Encourages constant improvement in the medical profession. Founded: 1867. Publications: *CMA News* (Biweekly); *Canadian Association of Radiologists Journal*; *Strategy: The Financial Digest for Physicians* (Monthly); *Humane Medicine* (Quarterly); *Mediscan*; *Clinical and Investigative Medicine* (Bimonthly); *Canadian Medical Association Journal (CMAJ)* (Biweekly); *Journal of Psychiatry and Neuroscience* (Bimonthly).

40148 ■ Canadian Medical Protective Association (CMPA) [Association Canadienne de Protection Medicale]
875 Carling Ave.
Ottawa, ON, Canada K1S 5P1
Ph: (613)725-2000
Free: 877-763-1300
Fax: (613)725-1300
Co. E-mail: inquiries@cmpa.org
URL: http://www.cmpa-acpm.ca
Contact: John E. Gray, Chief Executive Officer
Description: Defense organization for physicians practicing in Canada. Founded: 1901.

40149 ■ Canadian Mental Health Association (CMHA) [Association Canadienne pour la Sante Mentale]
1110-151 Slater St.
Ottawa, ON, Canada K1P 5H3
Fax: (613)745-5522
Co. E-mail: webmaster@cmha.ca
URL: http://www.cmha.ca
Contact: Peter Coleridge, Chief Executive Officer
Description: Mental health professionals and other individuals with an interest in community mental health. Works to enable individuals, groups and communities to increase control over and enhance their mental health. Serves as a social advocate to encourage public action to strengthen community mental health services; conducts lobbying activities. Promotes mental health research; organizes and operates grass roots programs to help people whose mental health is at risk make use of the services available to them. Sponsors educational programs. Founded: 1918. Publications: *Mental Health Promotion-Train the Trainer*. Awards: Aleck Trawick Q.C. Award (Annual); Media Award (Periodic); Outstanding Volunteer Service Award (Periodic); Marjorie Hiscott Keyes Award (Annual); Consumer Involvement Award (Annual); National Distinguished Service Award (Annual); Mental Health in the Workplace Award (Annual); Media Award (Annual); C. M. Hincks Award (Annual).

40150 ■ Canadian Paediatric Society (CPS) - Library [Societe canadienne de pediatrie]
2305 Saint Laurent Blvd.
Ottawa, ON, Canada K1G 4J8
Ph: (613)526-9397
Fax: (613)526-3332
URL: http://www.cps.ca
Contact: Robert Moriartey, President
Description: Professional organization of pediatricians serving on committees and sections focusing on adolescent medicine, bioethics, drug therapy, hazardous substances, fetus and newborns, Indian and Inuit health, infectious disease and immunization, injury prevention, pediatric practice, nutrition, and psychological pediatrics. Provides services to Canadian children and to its membership. Serves as an advocate on issues relating to child health and welfare. Provides continuing education for the maintenance of competence of its members. Establishes Canadian standards/guidelines for pediatric care and practice, and promotes the interest of pediatricians. Scope: Infancy; childhood; adolescence. Services: Copying; library open to the public. Founded: 1922. Holdings: 230 books; 420 reports; 47 audio/visual materials. Publications: *CPS News* (5/year); *Clinical Practice Guidelines* (Periodic); *CPS News* (5/year); *Pediatrics & Child Health* (10/year). Awards: Ross Award (Annual); Geoffrey C. Robinson Award (Biennial); Noni MacDonald Award (Annual); Canadian Pediatric Society Career Research Award (Biennial); Alan Ross Award.

40151 ■ Canadian Pain Society (CPS) [La Societe Canadienne De La Douleur]
250 Consumers Rd., Ste. 301
Toronto, ON, Canada M2J 4V6
Ph: (416)642-6379
Fax: (416)495-8723
Co. E-mail: office@canadianpainsociety.ca
URL: http://www.canadianpainsociety.ca
Contact: Judy Watt-Watson, President
Description: Health care professionals and medical and pharmaceutical researchers with an interest in pain and its alleviation. Fosters research on the causes of pain; seeks improved methods of pain management. Facilitates communication and cooperation among pain researchers and clinicians; sponsors educational and research programs. Founded: 1982. Publications: *CPS Newsletter* (Quarterly); *Pain Research and Management* (Quarterly). Awards: Canadian Pain Society Post-Doctoral Fellowship Awards; Clinical Pain Management Fellowship Awards; CPS Excellence in Interprofessional Pain Education Awards (Annual); CPS Interprofessional Nursing Project Awards (Annual); CPS Knowledge Translation Research Awards (Annual); CPS Nursing Excellence in Pain Management Awards (Annual); CPS Nursing Research and Education Awards (Annual); CPS Outstanding Pain Mentorship Awards (Annual); CPS Trainee Research Awards (Annual).

40152 ■ Canadian Psychiatric Association (CPA) [Association des Psychiatres du Canada]
141 Laurier Ave. W, Ste. 701
Ottawa, ON, Canada K1P 5J3
Ph: (613)234-2815
Fax: (613)234-9857
Co. E-mail: cpa@cpa-apc.org
URL: http://www.cpa-apc.org
Contact: Donald Addington, Chairman of the Board
Description: Works to improve mental health and psychiatric care delivery systems in Canada. Fosters high standards among Canadian psychiatrists; promotes continuing education of members; encourages and participates in educational programs for patient care providers; promotes research into psychiatric disorders; advocates for mental health system reforms and on related issues affecting the practice of psychiatry. Founded: 1951. Publications: *The Canadian Journal of Psychiatry* (Monthly); *Canadian Psychology* (Quarterly). Educational Activities: Canadian Psychiatric Association Annual Conference (Annual). Awards: C.A. Roberts Award for Clinical Leadership (Annual); J.M. Cleghorn Award for Excellence and Leadership in Clinical Research (Annual); Paul Patterson Innovation in Education Leadership Award (Annual); President's Commendation (Periodic); Special Recognition Award (Periodic); Honorary Members (Periodic); Fellow of the CPA (Periodic); Alex Leighton Award in Psychiatric Epidemiology (Annual); Award for the Most Outstanding Continuing Education Activity in Psychiatry in Canada (Annual); R.O. Jones Awards for Best Papers (Annual); Awards for Best Posters (Annual); Paul Patterson Education Leadership Award (Annual).

40153 ■ Canadian Public Health Association (CPHA) [Association Canadienne De Sante Publique]
404-1525 Carling Ave.
Ottawa, ON, Canada K1Z 8R9
Ph: (613)725-3769
Fax: (613)725-9826
Co. E-mail: info@cpha.ca
URL: http://www.cpha.ca
Contact: Debra Lynkowski, Chief Executive Officer
Description: Works to mobilize national charitable and volunteer resources to address public health concerns worldwide. Conducts immunization, maternal and child health, and HIV/AIDS programs in at-risk areas. Founded: 1910. Publications: *Canadian Journal of Public Health* (Bimonthly); *CPHA Health Digest* (Quarterly). Educational Activities: Canadian Public Health Association Conference (Annual). Awards: R. D. Defries Award (Annual); Honorary Life Member (Annual); Certificate of Merit (Annual); Ron Draper Health Promotion Award (Annual); CPHA International Award (Annual); Dr. John Hastings Student Award (Annual); CPHA International Award

(Annual); Population and Public Health Student Awards (Annual); Public Health Human Resources Awards (Annual); R.D. Defries Award (Annual); Ron Draper Health Promotion Award (Annual).

40154 ■ Canadian Society for Clinical Investigation (CSCI) [Societe canadienne de recherches cliniques]
114 Cheyenne Way
Ottawa, ON, Canada K2J 0E9
Free: 877-968-9449
Fax: (613)491-0073
Co. E-mail: info@csci-scrc.ca
URL: http://www.csci-scrc.ca
Contact: Dr. Norman D. Rosenblum, President
Description: Canadian clinical investigators working in the field of human health. Represents members' interests. **Founded:** 1951. **Publications:** *Clinical and Investigative Medicine* (Bimonthly); *Clinical and Investigative Medicine* (Periodic). **Awards:** Distinguished Scientist Lecture and Award (Annual); Dr. Mel Silverman Distinguished Service Award (Annual); CSCI Distinguished Scientist Lectures and Awards; Henry Friesen Awards and Lectures.

40155 ■ Canadian Society for International Health [La Societe Canadienne de Sante Internationale (SCSI)]
1 Nicholas St., Ste. 1105
Ottawa, ON, Canada K1N 7B7
Ph: (613)241-5785
Co. E-mail: csih@csih.org
URL: http://www.csih.org
Contact: Kate Dickson, Co-Chairperson
Description: Health care services and individuals and organizations with an interest in global public health. Promotes increased availability and quality of health services in previously underserved areas worldwide. Advocates for health policy and programming that contributes to global objectives of health for all; equity, social justice through partnership building with Canadian and other institutions and organizations. **Founded:** 1977. **Publications:** *Online Synergy* (Weekly); *PAHO News* (Weekly). **Awards:** Lifetime Achievement Award; CSIH Lifetime Achievement Award for International Health (Annual).

40156 ■ CAPsule
1815 Alta Vista Dr., No. 201
Ottawa, ON, Canada K1G 3Y6
Ph: (613)523-9800
Fax: (613)523-1968
Co. E-mail: info@cap-acp.ca
URL: http://www.cap-acp.ca
Contact: Dr. Todd Jones, President
Released: 3/year

40157 ■ Catholic Health Alliance
Annex C, Saint-Vincent Hospital
60 Cambridge St. N
Ottawa, ON, Canada K1R 7A5
Ph: (613)562-6262
Fax: (613)782-2857
URL: http://www.chac.ca
Contact: Michael Shea, President
E-mail: shea.chac@gmail.com
Description: Represents the interests of Catholic Hospitals and nursing homes in Canada. Works to administer Christian principles within the Canadian healthcare system. Fosters competent and efficient health care services. **Scope:** healthcare, ethics, medicine, pastoral care. **Subscriptions:** 6000 articles books periodicals. **Publications:** *Catholic Health Association of Canada--Membership Directory*; *CHAC Info Newsletter*.

40158 ■ CCS News
222 Queen St., Ste. 1403
Ottawa, ON, Canada K1P 5V9
Ph: (613)569-3407
Free: 877-569-3407
Fax: (613)569-6574
Co. E-mail: info@ccs.ca
URL: http://www.ccs.ca
Contact: Dr. Mario Talajic, President
Released: Biweekly

40159 ■ CHA Guide to Canadian Healthcare Facilities
17 York St.
Ottawa, ON, Canada K1N 9J6
Ph: (613)241-8005
Free: 855-236-0213
Fax: (613)241-5055
Co. E-mail: chapress@cha.ca
URL: http://www.cha.ca
Contact: Pamela C. Fralick, President
URL(s): www.cha.ca/product/2013-guide-to-canadian-healthcare-facilities-vol-20/. **Released:** Annual **Price:** C$249.95, /year for individuals.

40160 ■ Chapter Press (CHA) [Canadian Healthcare Association (CHA)Association canadienne des soins de sante;]
17 York St.
Ottawa, ON, Canada K1N 9J6
Ph: (613)241-8005
Free: 855-236-0213
Fax: (613)241-5055
Co. E-mail: chapress@cha.ca
URL: http://www.cha.ca
Contact: Pamela C. Fralick, President
Description: Promotes a humane, effective, and efficient health system of the highest quality. **Founded:** 1989. **Publications:** *Guide to Canadian Healthcare Facilities* (Annual); *CHA Guide to Canadian Healthcare Facilities* (Annual); *Leadership in Health Services* (Bimonthly). **Educational Activities:** Navigating the Health System Data, Dollars and Decision. **Awards:** Marion Stephenson Award (Annual); Award for Distinguished Service (Annual).

40161 ■ Clinical and Investigative Medicine
114 Cheyenne Way
Ottawa, ON, Canada K2J 0E9
Free: 877-968-9449
Fax: (613)491-0073
Co. E-mail: info@csci-scrc.ca
URL: http://www.csci-scrc.ca
Contact: Dr. Norman D. Rosenblum, President
Released: Periodic

40162 ■ Clinical Practice Guidelines
2305 Saint Laurent Blvd.
Ottawa, ON, Canada K1G 4J8
Ph: (613)526-9397
Fax: (613)526-3332
URL: http://www.cps.ca
Contact: Robert Moriartey, President
Released: Periodic

40163 ■ College of Family Physicians of Canada - Ontario Chapter (CFPC) [College des Medecins de Famille du Canada]
2360 Skymark Ave.
Mississauga, ON, Canada L4W 5A4
Ph: (905)629-0900
Free: 800-387-6197
Co. E-mail: info@cfpc.ca
URL: http://www.cfpc.ca
Contact: Dr. David Tannenbaum, Director
URL(s): www.ocfp.on.ca. **Description:** National medical association of family physicians and general practitioners. Members must maintain a minimum of 50 hours of continuing medical education credits annually. Works to maintain standards of family medicine training in the 16 Canadian medical schools through support of the Departments of Family Medicine and the accreditation of family practice residency programs. Administers certification examinations in emergency medicine and family medicine. Runs practice assessment program. Offers public education programs on family medicine topics. **Scope:** Canadian library of family medicine. **Founded:** 1954. **Publications:** *Canadian Family Physician* (Monthly); *CFPC-Liaison Newsletter* (Quarterly); *Self-Evaluation*.

40164 ■ Community Health Nurses Association of Canada (CHNC) [Association canadienne des infirmieres et infirmiers en sante communantaire]
75 New Cove Rd.
Saint John's, NL, Canada A1A 2C2

Ph: (709)738-3541
Co. E-mail: info@chnc.ca
URL: http://www.chnc.ca
Contact: Anne Clarotto, President
E-mail: anne.clarotto@interiorhealth.ca
Description: Community health nurses and provincial organizations. Seeks to advance the practice of community health nursing and enhance members' professional status. Represents members' interests before government agencies and medical associations; provides support, services, and assistance to members. **Scope:** community health nursing. **Founded:** 1989. **Subscriptions:** archival material business records. **Publications:** *Electronic Newsletters* (3/year).

40165 ■ Community and Hospital Infection Control Association - Canada (CHICA) [Association Pour La Prevention Des Infections A l'hopital et dans La Communaute]
PO Box 46125
Winnipeg, MB, Canada R3R 3S3
Ph: (204)897-5990
Free: 866-999-7111
Fax: (204)895-9595
URL: http://www.chica.org
Contact: Bruce Gamage, President
Description: Health care professionals engaged in the prevention and control of infections. Seeks to improve the health of Canadians by promoting excellence in the practice of infection prevention and control. Serves as a clearinghouse on infection control standards and practices; facilitates communication and exchange of information among members; conducts continuing professional education programs for members. Collaborates with government agencies responsible for public health in the formulation and enforcement of certification standards and in the development of public policies. Provides advice and assistance to organizations and agencies concerned with specific diseases, including AIDS. Maintains speakers' bureau. **Founded:** 1971. **Publications:** *Canadian Journal of Infection Control* (Quarterly). **Educational Activities:** National Education Conference.

40166 ■ Corporate Report
162 Cumberland St., Ste. 228
Toronto, ON, Canada M5R 3N5
Ph: (416)924-3368
Fax: (416)323-3338
Co. E-mail: info@ams-inc.on.ca
URL: http://php.ams-inc.on.ca
Contact: Dorothy Pringle, President
Released: Biennial

40167 ■ CPS News
2305 Saint Laurent Blvd.
Ottawa, ON, Canada K1G 4J8
Ph: (613)526-9397
Fax: (613)526-3332
URL: http://www.cps.ca
Contact: Robert Moriartey, President
Released: 5/year

40168 ■ CPS Newsletter
250 Consumers Rd., Ste. 301
Toronto, ON, Canada M2J 4V6
Ph: (416)642-6379
Fax: (416)495-8723
Co. E-mail: office@canadianpainsociety.ca
URL: http://www.canadianpainsociety.ca
Contact: Judy Watt-Watson, President
Released: Quarterly **Price:** free for members.

40169 ■ Electronic Newsletters
75 New Cove Rd.
Saint John's, NL, Canada A1A 2C2
Ph: (709)738-3541
Co. E-mail: info@chnc.ca
URL: http://www.chnc.ca
Contact: Anne Clarotto, President
E-mail: anne.clarotto@interiorhealth.ca
URL(s): www.chnc.ca/community-health-nurse-newsletters.cfm. **Released:** 3/year

40170 ■ Epilepsy Canada (EC) [Epilepsie Canada]
2255B Queen St. E, Ste. 336
Toronto, ON, Canada M4E1G3
Free: 877-734-0873
Fax: (905)752-2298
URL: http://www.epilepsy.ca
Contact: Jacques Brunelle, President
E-mail: jbrunelle@tennistremblant.com
Description: People with epilepsy and their families; health care professionals with an interest in epilepsy and related disorders. Seeks to improve the quality of life of people affected by epilepsy through promotion and support of research. Offers education and awareness initiatives that build understanding and acceptance of epilepsy. **Scope:** epilepsy. **Founded:** 1966. **Subscriptions:** archival material. **Publications:** Lumina Newsletter; Lumina (Semiannual). **Awards:** Epilepsy Canada Research Program (Annual).

40171 ■ Heads Up
36 Eglinton W, Ste. 704
Toronto, ON, Canada M4R 1A1
Ph: (416)596-2700
Fax: (416)596-2721
Co. E-mail: info@smartrisk.ca
URL: http://www.smartrisknoregrets.ca
Contact: Philip Groff, President
Released: Monthly

40172 ■ Health Information Resource Center (HIRC)
328 W Lincoln Ave., Ste. 10
Libertyville, IL 60048-2725
Free: 800-828-8225
Fax: (847)816-8662
Co. E-mail: info@healthprograms.com
URL: http://www.healthawards.com
Description: Clearinghouse for consumer health information. Provides information and referral services to many organizations that use or produce consumer health information materials. Conducts market research. **Scope:** consumer health. **Founded:** 1993. **Subscriptions:** articles audiovisuals books clippings monographs periodicals. **Publications:** Health and Medical Media: The Comprehensive Sourcebook of Media Contacts for Healthcare Professionals (Biennial). **Awards:** National Health Information Awards (Annual); Web Health Awards (Annual).

40173 ■ Healthcare Management FORUM
292 Somerset St. W
Ottawa, ON, Canada K2P 0J6
Ph: (613)235-7218
Fax: (613)235-5451
Co. E-mail: info@cchl-ccls.ca
URL: http://www.cchl-ccls.ca
Contact: Ray J. Racette, President
URL(s): www.cchl-ccls.ca/site/publicationswww.healthcaremanagementforum.org/. **Released:** Quarterly; always March, June, September, and December. **Price:** C$85, individual in Canada; C$170, institution in Canada; C$115, international.

40174 ■ International Institute of Concern for Public Health (IICPH)
PO Box 40017
Toronto, ON, Canada M5R 0A2
Ph: (416)786-6128
Fax: (905)906-6128
Co. E-mail: info@iicph.org
URL: http://www.iicph.org
Contact: Dr. Marion Odell, President
Description: Promotes dissemination of information on public health and related topics including environmental and occupational health and human rights. Serves as a clearinghouse on international public health and related issues; assists in the development of model health-related human rights legislation. Conducts research and educational programs; compiles statistics; maintains speakers' bureau. Provides support and assistance to communities wishing to maintain their own public health databases. **Scope:** Improvement in environmental health status in communities in the areas of pesticides, nuclear industries and other commercial, military, and industrial products, and environmental disasters. **Founded:**

1984. **Subscriptions:** 4000 articles audio recordings audiovisuals books business records periodicals. **Publications:** International Perspectives in Public Health (Annual).

40175 ■ International Perspectives in Public Health
PO Box 40017
Toronto, ON, Canada M5R 0A2
Ph: (416)786-6128
Fax: (905)906-6128
Co. E-mail: info@iicph.org
URL: http://www.iicph.org
Contact: Dr. Marion Odell, President
Released: Annual

40176 ■ Journal of Cutaneous Medicine and Surgery
1385 Bank St., Ste. 425
Ottawa, ON, Canada K1I1 0N4
Ph: (613)738-1748
Free: 800-267-3376
Fax: (613)738-4695
Co. E-mail: info@dermatology.ca
URL: http://www.dermatology.ca
Contact: Ms. Chantal Courchesne, Executive Director
Released: Bimonthly **Price:** $230.35, /year for individuals in U.S.; C$242.55, /year for individuals in Canada.

40177 ■ Let's Face It USA
72 Victoria Ave.
Westgate on Sea CT8 8BH, United Kingdom
Ph: 44 1843 833724
URL: http://www.lets-face-it.org.uk
Contact: Christine Piff, Chief Executive Officer
E-mail: chrisletsfaceit@aol.com
Description: Provides information and support for people who have or who care for those with facial disfigurement. Website and annual publication with over 150 resources for professionals and families. Links to all related networks for specific conditions i.e. Genetic Disorders, Burns, Cancer, etc. **Founded:** 1987. **Publications:** Resources for People with Facial Difference (Semiannual).

40178 ■ Liaison
503,386 Bdwy.
Winnipeg, MB, Canada R3C 3R6
Ph: (888)223-3808
Co. E-mail: info@oemac.org
URL: http://www.oemac.org
Contact: Oscar Howell, President
Released: Quarterly **Price:** included in membership dues.

40179 ■ Membership and Corporate Directory
1385 Bank St., Ste. 425
Ottawa, ON, Canada K1H 8N4
Ph: (613)738-1748
Free: 800-267-3376
Fax: (613)738-4695
Co. E-mail: info@dermatology.ca
URL: http://www.dermatology.ca
Contact: Ms. Chantal Courchesne, Executive Director
Released: Annual

40180 ■ Mental Health Promotion-Train the Trainer
1110-151 Slater St.
Ottawa, ON, Canada K1P 5H3
Fax: (613)745-5522
Co. E-mail: webmaster@cmha.ca
URL: http://www.cmha.ca
Contact: Peter Coleridge, Chief Executive Officer
URL(s): www.cmha.ca/public_policy/mental-health-promotion-train-the-trainers-manual/#.U_ge1MU2a2w. **Price:** C$15.

40181 ■ National Council Against Health Fraud (NCAHF) [Quackwatch]
11312 US 15 501 N, Ste. 107/108
Chapel Hill, NC 27517-6377

Ph: (919)533-6009
Co. E-mail: sbinfo@quackwatch.org
URL: http://www.ncahf.org
Contact: Stephen Barrett, Board Member Editor
Description: Health professionals, researchers, legal professionals, and other interested individuals. Seeks to educate the public on fraud and quackery in health care. Offers advice to consumers. Provides witnesses for health fraud trials. Assists law enforcement officials with health fraud cases. Sponsors speaker's bureau and research programs. Offers aid to victims in the form of free legal screening. **Founded:** 1977.

40182 ■ National Health Policy Forum (NHPF)
George Washington University
2131 K St. NW, Ste. 500
Washington, DC 20037-1882
Ph: (202)872-1390
Fax: (202)862-9837
Co. E-mail: nhpf@gwu.edu
URL: http://www.nhpf.org
Contact: Judith Miller Jones, Director
E-mail: jmjones@gwu.edu
Description: Nonpartisan education program serving primarily senior federal legislative and executive branch health staff but also addressing the interests of state officials and their Washington representatives. Seeks to foster more informed government decision-making. Helps decision makers forge the personal acquaintances and understanding necessary for cooperation among government agencies and between government and the private sector. **Scope:** Health and welfare. **Founded:** 1971. **Publications:** NHPF Annual report; Online background papers (Occasionally); Online site visit reports (Occasionally); Online issue briefs (Occasionally); Site Visit Reports (Periodic).

40183 ■ Occupational Medicine
503,386 Bdwy.
Winnipeg, MB, Canada R3C 3R6
Ph: (888)223-3808
Co. E-mail: info@oemac.org
URL: http://www.oemac.org
Contact: Oscar Howell, President
Price: C$75, hard copy; C$250, /year.

40184 ■ Online Synergy
1 Nicholas St., Ste. 1105
Ottawa, ON, Canada K1N 7B7
Ph: (613)241-5785
Co. E-mail: csih@csih.org
URL: http://www.csih.org
Contact: Kate Dickson, Co-Chairperson
Released: Weekly **Price:** included in membership dues.

40185 ■ Operation Eyesight Universal (OEU)
4 Parkdale Crescent NW, Ste. 200
Calgary, AB, Canada T2N 3T8
Ph: (403)283-6323
Free: 800-585-8265
Fax: (403)270-1899
Co. E-mail: info@operationeyesight.com
URL: http://www.operationeyesight.com
Contact: Brian Foster, Executive Director
Description: Individuals, firms, churches, schools, service clubs, and other organizations united to promote sight restoration and blindness prevention through programs in developing countries. Provides medical and educational assistance to needy individuals. Assists in the establishment of: special programs to combat blindness due to malnutrition; eye care hospitals; eye care departments in health care institutions; rural mobile eye programs. Works with local blindness prevention societies. Operates training programs. **Founded:** 1963. **Publications:** Sightlines (3/year); Sightlines Newsletter. **Educational Activities:** Operation Eyesight Universal General Assembly (Annual).

40186 ■ Osteoporosis Canada - Library [Osteoporose Canada]
1090 Don Mills Rd., Ste. 301
Toronto, ON, Canada M3C 3R6
Ph: (416)696-2663
Free: 800-463-6842

Fax: (416)696-2673
Co. E-mail: info@osteoporosis.ca
URL: http://www.osteoporosis.ca
Contact: Dr. Famida Jiwa, President
Description: Individuals and organizations interested in the prevention, diagnosis, and treatment of osteoporosis. Supports research programs that seek to improve the quality of life for women with osteoporosis. Promotes education about osteoporosis among professional health practitioners. Disseminates informational materials to individuals with osteoporosis, physicians, and the public. **Founded:** 1982. **Publications:** *Osteoblast Newsletter; Osteoblast* (Quarterly); *Osteoporosis Update* (Quarterly).

40187 ■ *PAHO News*
1 Nicholas St., Ste. 1105
Ottawa, ON, Canada K1N 7B7
Ph: (613)241-5785
Co. E-mail: csih@csih.org
URL: http://www.csih.org
Contact: Kate Dickson, Co-Chairperson
Released: Weekly **Price:** included in membership dues.

40188 ■ *Pain Research and Management*
250 Consumers Rd., Ste. 301
Toronto, ON, Canada M2J 4V6
Ph: (416)642-6379
Fax: (416)495-8723
Co. E-mail: office@canadianpainsociety.ca
URL: http://www.canadianpainsociety.ca
Contact: Judy Watt-Watson, President
URL(s): www.canadianpainsociety.ca/en/journal.html-www.pulsus.com/journals/journalHome.jsp?sCurrPg=journal&jnlKy=7&fold=Home. **Released:** Quarterly **Price:** $220, Individuals print only; $175, Individuals online only; $275, Individuals print and online; C$205, Individuals print only; C$175, Individuals online only; C$260, Individuals print and online; $235, Other countries print only; $290, Other countries print and online.

40189 ■ *Pediatrics & Child Health*
2305 Saint Laurent Blvd.
Ottawa, ON, Canada K1G 4J8
Ph: (613)526-9397
Fax: (613)526-3332
URL: http://www.cps.ca
Contact: Robert Moriartey, President
URL(s): www.cps.ca/en/pch. **Released:** 10/year

40190 ■ Physicians Committee for Responsible Medicine (PCRM)
5100 Wisconsin Ave. NW, Ste. 400
Washington, DC 20016-4131
Ph: (202)686-2210
Fax: (202)686-2216
Co. E-mail: pcrm@pcrm.org
URL: http://www.pcrm.org
Contact: Neal D. Barnard, President
Description: Physicians, scientists, healthcare professionals, and interested others. Increases public awareness about the importance of preventive medicine and nutrition, and raises scientific and ethical questions pertaining to the use of humans and animals in medical research. Supports research into U.S. agricultural and public health policies. Promotes the New Four Food Groups, a no-cholesterol, low-fat alternative to U.S.D.A. dietary recommendations. Maintains the Gold Plan program, which includes information on low-fat, cholesterol-free entrees and nutrition for institutional food services. Offers fact sheets on nutrition, preventive medicine, and non-animal research topics. Maintains speakers' bureau. **Founded:** 1985. **Publications:** *Good Medicine Magazine* (Quarterly); *Good Medicine* (Quarterly).

40191 ■ *Sightlines*
4 Parkdale Crescent NW, Ste. 200
Calgary, AB, Canada T2N 3T8
Ph: (403)283-6323
Free: 800-585-8265

Fax: (403)270-1899
Co. E-mail: info@operationeyesight.com
URL: http://www.operationeyesight.com
Contact: Brian Foster, Executive Director
URL(s): www.operationeyesight.com/page.aspx?pid=246. **Released:** 3/year; Winter, Spring and Fall. **Price:** Free.

40192 ■ SMARTRISK
36 Eglinton W, Ste. 704
Toronto, ON, Canada M4R 1A1
Ph: (416)596-2700
Fax: (416)596-2721
Co. E-mail: info@smartrisk.ca
URL: http://www.smartrisknoregrets.ca
Contact: Philip Groff, President
Description: Works to reduce the number of injuries in Canada. Sponsors campaigns to raise public awareness of preventable causes of injury in all aspects of daily life. **Subscriptions:** 1000. **Publications:** *Heads Up* (Monthly); *Will It Float.*

40193 ■ Society for the Psychological Study of Social Issues (SPSSI)
208 I St. NE
Washington, DC 20002-4340
Ph: (202)675-6956
Free: 877-310-7778
Fax: (202)675-6902
Co. E-mail: spssi@spssi.org
URL: http://www.spssi.org
Contact: Dr. Susan Dudley, Executive Director
E-mail: sdudley@spssi.org
Description: Psychologists, sociologists, anthropologists, psychiatrists, political scientists, and social workers. Works to: obtain and disseminate to the public scientific knowledge about social change and other social processes; promote psychological research on significant theoretical and practical questions of social issues; encourage application of findings to problems of society. **Scope:** Psychological study of social issues, focusing on theoretical and practical questions about social life and change. **Founded:** 1936. **Subscriptions:** 100 books. **Publications:** *Journal of Social Issues* (Quarterly); *Analyses of Social Issues and Public Policy* (Annual); *Research Methods in Social Relations; SPSSI Newsletter, Forward* (3/year); *Analysis of Social Issues and Public Policy Newsletter (ASAP); Analysis of Social Issues and Public Policy* (Annual); *Journal of Social Issues* (Quarterly); *Forward* (3/year); *SPSSI Newsletter* (3/year); *The Compleat Academic: A Career Guide.* **Educational Activities:** SPSSI International conferences; Social Justice: Research, Action & Policy. **Awards:** Grants-In-Aid Program (Semiannual); Louise Kidder Early Career Award (Annual); Otto Klineberg Intercultural and International Relations Award (Annual); Outstanding Teaching and Mentoring Awards (Annual); SAGES Grant Program (Annual); Social Issues Dissertation Award (Annual); Gordon Allport Prize (Annual); Social Issues Dissertation Award; Otto Klineberg Award (Annual); Louise Kidder Early Career Award; Michele Alexander Early Career Award (Annual); Awards for Outstanding Teaching and Mentoring (Annual); Kurt Lewin Memorial Award (Annual); Applied Social Issues Internship Program (Annual); Dalmas A. Taylor Summer Minority Policy Fellowship (Annual); James Marshall Public Policy Scholar (Biennial); Louise Kidder Early Career Award (Annual); The Michele Alexander Early Career Award for Scholarship and Service (Annual); Otto Klineberg Intercultural and International Relations Award (Annual); Social Issues Dissertation Award (Annual); SPSSI Action Grants for Experienced Scholars (Annual); Clara Mayo Grants Program (Annual); Dalmas A. Taylor Summer Minority Fellow (Annual); Gordon Allport Intergroup Relations Prize (Annual); Kurt Lewin Memorial Award (Annual); Michele Alexander Early Career Award (Annual); Louise Kidder Early Career Award; Michele Alexander Early Career Award (Annual); Otto Klineberg Intercultural and International Relations Award (Annual); Social Issues Dissertation Award (Annual); Grants-in-aid (Semiannual); SPSSI Action Grants for Experienced Scholars (Annual).

40194 ■ Society for the Study of Social Problems (SSSP)
University of Tennessee
901 McClung Tower
Knoxville, TN 37996-0490

Ph: (865)689-1531
Fax: (865)689-1534
URL: http://www.sssp1.org
Contact: Anna Maria Santiago, President
Description: An interdisciplinary community of scholars, activists, practitioners, and students endeavoring to create greater social justice through social research. Members are often social scientists working in colleges and universities, in non-profit organizations and in other applied and policy settings. **Scope:** Global problems; institutional ethnography; community research and development; crime and juvenile delinquency; drinking and drugs; racial and ethnic minorities; conflict, social action, and change; family; poverty, class, and inequality; social problems theory; mental health; teaching social problems; sociology and social welfare; youth, aging, and the life course; educational problems; environment and technology; labor studies; sexual behavior, politics and communities; law and society; health, health policy and health services; disabilities; sport, leisure, and the body. **Founded:** 1951. **Publications:** *SSSP Newsletters* (3/year); *Social Problems* (Quarterly); *SSSP Social Problems* (Quarterly). **Educational Activities:** Society for the Study of Social Problems Annual Meeting (Annual); SSSP Symposia; Society for the Study of Social Problems Convention (Annual). **Awards:** Joseph B. Gittler (Annual); Social Action Award (Annual); Lee Student Support Fund (Annual); Erwin O. Smigel Award (Annual); Lee Scholar Support Fund (Annual); C. Wright Mills Award (Annual); Lee Founders Award (Annual); Thomas C. Hood Social Action Award (Annual); Racial/Ethnic Minority Graduate Scholarship (Annual).

40195 ■ Society for Women's Health Research (SWHR)
1025 Connecticut Ave. NW, Ste. 601
Washington, DC 20036
Ph: (202)223-8224
Fax: (202)833-3472
Co. E-mail: info@swhr.org
URL: http://www.womenshealthresearch.org
Contact: Phyllis Greenberger, President
Description: Seeks to improve the health of women by promoting equity in research. Advocates policies which promotes the inclusion of women in clinical trials; informs government agencies and private industry of issues affecting women's health and sex-based biology; educates women consumers on conditions that affect women; promotes funding for women's health research. **Founded:** 1990. **Publications:** *SWHR Journal of Women's Health* (Monthly); *Sexx Matters* (Quarterly); *Hearing Fact Sheet; Menopause/Hormone Therapy Fact Sheet, Mental Health, WHR Fact Sheet; Musculoskeletal Health Fact Sheet; Oral Health, WHR Fact Sheet; Pain, WHR Fact Sheet; Pharmaceuticals Fact Sheet; Preventing Birth Defects Fact Sheet; Sleep Fact Sheet; STDs and HIV/AIDS Fact Sheet; Urinary Tract Health/Incontinence Fact Sheet; Artherosclerosis Newsletter; Sex Differences in Autoimmune Disease Fact Sheet; Sex Differences in the Brain Fact Sheet; Sex Differences in Cancer Fact Sheet; Sex Differences in Cardio/Cerebrovascular Diseases Fact Sheet; Sex Differences in Diabetes Fact Sheet; Sex Differences in Response to Pharmaceuticals, Tobacco, Alcohol and Illicit Drugs Fact Sheet; Sex Differences in HIV/AIDS Fact Sheet; Sex Differences in Mental Health Fact Sheet; Sex Differences in Musculoskeletal Health Fact Sheet; Sex Differences in Obesity Fact Sheet; Asthma and Allergies Fact Sheet; Autoimmune Diseases Fact Sheet; Brain and Degenerative Disorders Fact Sheet; Cancer Fact Sheet, WHR; Cardiovascular Disease Fact Sheet; Diabetes, WHR Fact Sheet; Diet, Obesity and Eating Disorders Fact Sheet; Eye Health Fact Sheet.* **Educational Activities:** Scientific Advisory Meeting; Scientific Advisory Meeting: Update on Women's Health.

40196 ■ United Methodist Association of Health and Welfare Ministries
2800 W Main St.
Tupelo, MS 38801
Ph: (662)269-2955
Free: 800-411-9901
Fax: (662)269-2956
Co. E-mail: uma@umassociation.org
URL: http://umassociation.org
Contact: Mr. Stephen L. Vinson, President
Description: Offers communications and church relations guidance. Provides leadership development

training for health and human service professionals in United Methodist-related organizations and agencies. Develops ethical and theological statements on institutional care. Operates Educational Assessment Guidelines Leading Toward Excellence(EAGLE), a self-assessment and peer review accreditation program. Operates a Field Consultation Program; members may access skilled professionals to assist with governance questions. Offers audiovisual services to members. Administers the Order of Good Shepherds program designed to recognize ministry in the workplace by employees at member organizations. Maintains speakers' bureau; compiles statistics. **Founded:** 1940. **Publications:** *National Directory of Healthcare and Human Service Ministries* (Annual); *National Directory of all United Methodist Related Health and Welfare Ministries* (Annual).

40197 ■ *Will It Float*
36 Eglinton W, Ste. 704
Toronto, ON, Canada M4R 1A1
Ph: (416)596-2700
Fax: (416)596-2721
Co. E-mail: info@smartrisk.ca
URL: http://www.smartrisknoregrets.ca
Contact: Philip Groff, President

SCORE OFFICES

40198 ■ *"What New Federal Health Care Model Means to Florida Businesses"* in *Orlando Business Journal (Vol. 28, May 18, 2012, No. 50, pp. 1)*
American City Business Journal
111 Market Place, Ste. 720
Baltimore, MD 21202
Ph: (410)576-1161
Fax: (410)752-3112
URL: http://www.bizjournals.com/baltimore/
Description: Central Florida now has a total of three approved accountable care organizations (ACOs) that are responsible for coordinating the care of 13,500 Medicare patients. The ACO is an organization formed between health care providers and accepts bundled payment for managing the health of a population. Insights on the impact of ACOs addition to the health market are also provided.

REFERENCE WORKS

40199 ■ *"13D Filings"* in *Barron's (Vol. 88, March 24, 2008, No. 12, pp. M13)*
Pub: Dow Jones & Co., Inc.
Contact: Clare Hart, President
Description: HealthCor Management called as problematic the plan of Magellan Health Services to use its high cash balances for acquisitions. Carlson Capital discussed with Energy Partners possible changes in the latter's board. Investor Carl Icahn suggested that Enzon Pharmaceuticals consider selling itself or divest some of its assets.

40200 ■ *"26 Things Holding Canadians Back"* in *Canadian Business (Vol. 85, August 13, 2012, No. 13, pp. 27)*
Pub: George Media Inc.
Released: August 13, 2012. **Description:** A list of the problems that Canada needs to address in order to succeed as an economic superpower is presented. Some of these barriers include declining fertility rate, rising percentage of overweight and obese, and obsolete copyright laws.

40201 ■ *"$55M Bioscience Building at Health Village 40 Percent Pre-Leased"* in *Orlando Business Journal (Vol. 29, July 13, 2012, No. 4, pp. 1)*
Pub: American City Business Journal
Description: Around 40 percent of Windsor Healthcare Equities LLC's planned $55 million bioscience building was pre-leased by the company. The five-story building will become Central Florida's largest commercially available wet laboratory space. The city will also add heft to Central Florida's bioscience industry.

40202 ■ *"$56M Coming to Cincinnati Children's Hospital, University of Cincinnati, from Stimulus Bill"* in *Business Courier (Vol. 26, October 9, 2009, No. 24, pp. 1)*
Pub: American City Business Journals, Inc.
Contact: Whitney Shaw, President
Ed: Dan Monk, James Ritchie. **Description:** Cincinnati's Children's Hospital Medical Center and the University of Cincinnati researchers are set to receive at least $56 million from the stimulus bill. The cash infusion has reenergized research scientists and enhances Cincinnati's national clout as a major research center.

40203 ■ *"2010 Book of Lists"* in *Austin Business JournalInc. (Vol. 29, December 25, 2009, No. 42, pp. 1)*
Description: Rankings of companies and organizations within the business services, finance, healthcare, hospitality and travel, insurance, marketing and media, professional services, real estate, education and technology industries in Austin, Texas are presented. Rankings are based on sales, business size, and other statistics.

40204 ■ *"2010 Book of Lists"* in *Business Courier (Vol. 26, December 26, 2009, No. 36, pp. 1)*
Description: Rankings of companies and organizations within the business services, education, finance, health care, hospitality and tourism, real estate, and technology industries in the Cincinnati, Ohio-Northern Kentucky area are presented. Rankings are based on sales, business size, or other statistics.

40205 ■ *"2010 Book of Lists"* in *Tampa Bay Business Journal (Vol. 30, December 22, 2009, No. 53, pp. 1)*
Description: Rankings of companies and organizations within the human resources, banking and finance, business services, healthcare, real estate, technology, hospitality and travel, and education industries in the Greater Tampa Bay area are presented. Rankings are based on sales, business size, and more.

40206 ■ *"2012 Crain's Health Care Directory; Senior and Long-Term Care Services"* in *Crain's Cleveland Business (Vol. 33, September 17, 2012, No. 36, p. H8)*
Pub: Crain Communications Inc.
Description: Alphabetical listing of senior and long-term care services in Ohio is presented.

40207 ■ *"Abraxis Bets On Biotech Hub"* in *Business Journal-Serving Phoenix and the Valley of the Sun (Vol. 10, November 9, 2007, No. 28)*
Ed: Angela Gonzales. **Description:** Abraxis Bio-Science Inc. purchased a 200,000 square foot manufacturing facility in Phoenix, Arizona from Watson Pharmaceuticals Inc. The company has the technology to allow chemotherapy drugs to be injected directly into tumor cell membranes. A human protein, albumin is used to deliver the chemotherapy.

40208 ■ *"Achieve Tampa Bay Thrown a Lifeline in Proposed Merger"* in *Tampa Bay Business Journal (Vol. 30, January 22, 2010, No. 5, pp. 1)*
Pub: American City Business Journals
Ed: Margie Manning. **Description:** Mental Health Care Inc. proposed a merger with Achieve Tampa Bay Inc. The former proposes to administer the latter's operations and take over its assets while paying its debts.

40209 ■ *Achieving Planned Innovation: A Proven System for Creating Successful New Products and Services*
Pub: Simon & Schuster Higher Education Group
Contact: Larry Norton, President
Ed: Frank R. Bacon. **Released:** August 2007. **Price:** $16.95. **Description:** Planned innovation is a disciplined and practical step-by-step sequence of procedures for reaching the intended destination point: successful products. This easy-to-read book explains the system along with an action-oriented program for continuous success in new-product innovations. Five

steps outlined include: a disciplined reasoning process; lasting market orientation; proper selection criteria that reflect both strategic and tactical business objectives and goals along with dynamic matching of resources to present and future opportunities, and positive and negative requirements before making major expenditures; and proper organizational staffing. The author explains what to do and evaluating the potential of any new product or service, ranging from ventures in retail distribution to the manufacture of goods as diverse as bicycles, motorcycles, aerospace communication and navigation equipment, small business computers, food packaging, and medical products. **Availability:** Print.

40210 ■ *"Acsys Interactive Announces Crowdsourcing Comes to the Hospital Industry"* in *Marketwired (August 23, 2010)*
Pub: COMTEX
Contact: Chip Brian, President
Description: Hospital marketers are obtaining data through crowdsourcing as strategy to gain ideas and feedback. The Hospital Industry Crowdsourced Survey of Digital, Integrated and Emerging Marketing is the first initiative among hospitals.

40211 ■ *"Active Duty"* in *Crain's Cleveland Business (Vol. 28, November 26, 2007, No. 47, pp. 3)*
Pub: Crain Communications Inc.
Ed: David Bennett. **Description:** Discusses the Veteran Workforce Training Program, sponsored by the Volunteers of America - Greater Ohio; the program is meant to provide employment training for military veterans and to assist them in transitioning back into the work force.

40212 ■ *Adoption Resource Book*
Pub: HarperCollins Publishers Inc.
Contact: Jane Friedman, President
E-mail: jfriedman@harpercollins.com
URL(s): www.harpercollins.com/9780062733610/the-adoption-resource-book-4th-edition. **Released:** Irregular; Latest edition 4th. **Price:** $16.95, Individuals paperback. **Publication includes:** List of public and private adoption agencies, support groups, and services. **Entries include:** Agency name, address, phone, special requirements. Principal content of the publication is a discussion of adoption procedures and requirements, including adoption of foreign children and open adoption. **Arrangement:** Geographical.

40213 ■ *"After Ruling, Rush Is On To Comply With ACA"* in *Austin Business Journal (Vol. 32, July 6, 2012, No. 18, pp. 1)*
Pub: American City Business Journals, Inc.
Contact: Whitney Shaw, President
Ed: Sandra Zaragoza. **Released:** July 6, 2012. **Description:** The U.S. Supreme Court ruling upholding the majority of the Patient Protection and Affordable Care Act has prompted employers to ramp up efforts to prepare for 2013 and 2014. Employers with 50 or more employees are required by the health care law to provide health care insurance or be penalized by about $2,000 per full-time employee in 2014. Insights on the rush are also given.

40214 ■ *"Agennix Completes Merger with German Giant"* in *Houston Business Journal (Vol. 40, December 25, 2009, No. 33, pp. 2)*
Pub: American City Business Journals
Ed: Mary Ann Azevedo. **Description:** Agennix Inc. has completed its transformation into a German company after Germany-based GPC Biotech merged into the former publicly traded Agennix AG. One quarter of Agennix's 60 employees will remain in Houston. Details on Agennix's drug trials are examined.

40215 ■ *"Al Neyer Inc. Wants to Redevelop Cincinnati's Historic Vernon Manor Hotel"* in *Business Courier (Vol. 26, October 9, 2009, No. 24, pp. 1)*
Pub: American City Business Journals, Inc.
Contact: Whitney Shaw, President
Ed: Dan Monk. **Description:** Al Neyer Inc. will redevelop the Vernon Manor Hotel as an office building for the Cincinnati Children's Hospital Medical

Center. The project will cost $35 million and would generate a new investment vehicle for black investors who plan to raise $2.7 million in private offerings to claim majority ownership of the property after its renovations.

40216 ■ *"Alabama Braces for Enrollment in Medicaid to Soar" in Birmingham Business Journal (Vol. 29, June 1, 2012, No. 23, pp. 1)*
Pub: American City Business Journals, Inc.
Contact: Whitney Shaw, President
Ed: Evan Belanger. **Released:** June 1, 2012. **Description:** Alabama has been preparing for the huge influx of Medicaid patients who would qualify in 2014 if the US Supreme Court upheld the new healthcare laws. The University of Alabama at Birmingham's study has shown nearly 471,000 additional state residents could qualify for the program under the new laws.

40217 ■ *"Albany Molecular on Hiring Spree as Big Pharma Slashes Work Force" in Business Review, Albany New York (December 31, 2007)*
Pub: American City Business Journals, Inc.
Ed: Barbara Pinckney. **Description:** Albany Molecular Research Inc. (AMRI) is an outsourcing company that provides work forces for pharmaceutical companies due to large numbers of downsizings in the year 2007. In 2008, AMRI plans to hire several workers.

40218 ■ *"Ambitious Horse Center Is In the Works for Southeastern Idaho" in Idaho Business Review (August 25, 2014)*
Pub: Dolan Co.
Contact: James P. Dolan, President
Released: August 25, 2014. **Description:** Ernest Bleinberger is planning to develop a 167-acre mixed-use project called Horse Station and will be located in Cache Valley, Idaho. Horse Station will include stables for about 250 horses and an arena, along with medical facilities, a hotel, retail shopping center, and a farmers market.

40219 ■ *"Analysts: More Mergers for the Region's Hospitals" in Boston Business Journal (Vol. 30, October 15, 2010, No. 36, pp. 1)*
Pub: Boston Business Journal
Ed: Julie M. Donnelly. **Description:** A number of hospitals in Boston, Massachusetts are engaging in mergers and acquisitions. Caritas Christi Health Care is set to be purchased by Cerberus Capital Management. The U.S. healthcare reform law is seen to drive the development.

40220 ■ *"The Annual Entitlement Lecture Medicare Elephantiasis" in Barron's (March 31, 2008)*
Pub: Dow Jones & Co., Inc.
Contact: Clare Hart, President
Ed: Thomas G. Donlan. **Description:** Expenditures on Medicare hospital insurance and the revenues available to pay for it have led to a gap of capital valued at $38.6 trillion. Slashing the benefits or raising taxes will not solve the gap which exists unless the government saves the money and invests it in private markets.

40221 ■ *"Anthem Becomes First to Penalize Small-Business Employees for Smoking" in Denver Business Journal (Vol. 64, August 17, 2012, No. 13, pp. 1)*
Pub: American City Business Journal
Description: Health insurance companies Anthem Blue Cross and Blue Shield of Colorado are first to impose higher premiums on employee smokers who are under their small-group policies. The premiums may increase up to 15 percent starting September, to be paid by the smoking employees or the company. The law aims to help reduce tobacco-related health problems, as well as health care costs.

40222 ■ *"An Apple a Day" in Entrepreneur (Vol. 36, February 2008, No. 2, pp. 19)*
Pub: Entrepreneur Press
Contact: Perlman Neil, President
Ed: Mark Henricks. **Description:** Businesses are handling rising health coverage costs by providing employees with wellness programs, which include

smoking-cessation programs, consumer-directed plans for savings on premiums, and limited medical care plans. Details on the growing trend regarding employee health coverage are discussed.

40223 ■ *"Are You Ernest? How One Man Sincerely Grew His Business"*
Pub: Amazon Digital Services
Released: October 2, 2014. **Price:** , $0.99 Kindle. **Description:** Dr. Ernest Lee profiles his career in healthcare and shares his desire to make his life count. He discusses seven effective tools for growing a business, despite opposition, which are universal to business, charity, or relationship; a must read for anyone involved in public relations or sales.

40224 ■ *"Area Hurt By Doctor Deficiency" in The Business Journal-Serving Metropolitan Kansas City (Vol. 27, October 17, 2008, No. 5, pp. 1)*
Ed: Rob Roberts. **Description:** Kansas City, Missouri may face a shortage of doctors, according to the Metropolitan Medical Society of Greater Kansas City. Over the next ten years the city needs to recruit more doctors in order to address the problem. Practicing physicians are having difficulties recruiting.

40225 ■ *"Attorney Guides Biotech Company in $6 Million Initial Public Offering" in Miami Daily Business Review (March 26, 2008)*
Description: In order to raise capital to engage in a full-scale trial of MyoCell to receive clinical approval, Bioheart Inc., launched an initial public offering. Bioheart researches and develops cell therapies to treat heart damage.

40226 ■ *"Avoid the Stress of Traffic and Pollution with House Call Doctor Los Angeles" in Ecology, Environment & Conservation Business (May 24, 2014)*
Pub: NewsRX
Contact: Susan E. Hasty, Publisher
Released: May 24, 2014. **Description:** Record levels of air pollution in the Los Angeles, California area pose serious risks to those suffering from illness or injury. Michael Farzam and his team at House Call Doctor Los Angeles provides telephone medicine for those unable or unwilling to visit a physician in person. The mobile doctor in Los Angeles offers individuals throughout the area with concierge care without leaving home.

40227 ■ *"Baby Business Goes Green" in Northwest Florida Daily News (April 21, 2012)*
Description: Cindi Denbow combined her two companies, child birthing center Gentle Birth Options and mom and baby-focused retail store called Growing Green Bums in Niceville, Florida. Denbow is commited to the environment and running a green business.

40228 ■ *"Backtalk with Terrie M. Williams" in Black Enterprise (Vol. 38, December 2007, No. 5, pp. 204)*
Pub: Earl G. Graves Publishing Co. Inc.
Contact: Earl G. Graves, Jr., President
Ed: Tennille M. Robinson. **Description:** Profile of Terrie M. Williams, president of a public relations agency as well as founder of a youth empowerment organization called Stay Strong Foundation. Williams reflects on her bouts with depression and how the disease impacts sufferers and talks about her book that will inspire others dealing with depression.

40229 ■ *"Baltimore-Area Hospital Tower Projects Could Add Hundreds of New Jobs" in Baltimore Business Journal (Vol. 28, June 25, 2010, No. 7, pp. 1)*
Pub: Baltimore Business Journal
Ed: Scott Graham. **Description:** Greater Baltimore, Maryland has four hospitals that are in the middle of transforming their campuses with new facilities for treating various patients. Construction at Mercy Medical Center, Johns Hopkins Hospital, Franklin Square Hospital and Anne Rundle Hospital has helped bring the construction industry back to life. Insights into the hiring plans of these hospitals are also included.

40230 ■ *"Banking on Cord Blood" in Business Journal-Serving Phoenix & the Valley of the Sun (Vol. 31, September 10, 2010, No. 1, pp. 1)*
Pub: Phoenix Business Journal
Ed: Angela Gonzales. **Description:** Celebration Stem Cell Centre obtained contracts from Mercy Gilbert Medical Center and its two sister hospitals, St. Joseph Hospital and Medical Center in Phoenix, Arizona and Chandler Regional Medical Center. The contract will facilitate the donation of unused umbilical cord blood for research.

40231 ■ *"Bankruptcies" in Crain's Detroit Business (Vol. 24, March 24, 2008, No. 12, pp. 6)*
Pub: Crain Communications Inc.
Contact: Rance E. Crain, President
Description: Current list of business that filed for Chapter 7 or 11 protection in U.S. Bankruptcy Court in Detroit include a construction company, a medical care company, a physical therapy firm and a communications firm.

40232 ■ *"Baptist Hatching Health Care Plan" in Memphis Business Journal (Vol. 34, June 15, 2012, No. 9, pp. 1)*
Pub: American City Business Journal
Ed: Cole Epley. **Description:** Baptist Memorial Health Care Corporation is planning to launch its Select Health Alliance initiative. The program will focus on the improvement of care quality and efficiency through the measurement and tracking of quality standards.

40233 ■ *"Baptist Health System Plans to Expand Stone Oak-Area Hospital: $32 Million Project Will Add Two Floors, 100 Beds" in San Antonio Business Journal (Vol. 26, May 25, 2012, No. 17, pp. 1)*
Pub: American City Business Journal
Description: Baptist Health System is planning to start the $32 million expansion of the North Central Baptist Hospital in San Antonio, Texas that will include the addition of two floors and 100 beds. An estimate of hiring 200 new health care workers will be created by the expansion.

40234 ■ *"Barbara West" in Crain's Cleveland Business (Vol. 30, June 29, 2009, No. 25, pp. 14)*
Pub: Crain Communications Inc.
Ed: Shannon Mortland. **Description:** Profile of Barbara West, administrative director of emergency medicine at MetroHealth Medical Center in Ohio. Ms. West manages Metro Life Flight that uses helicopters to transport patients to MetroHealth. She discusses the challenges of taking care of patients when big emergencies occur.

40235 ■ *"Baylor Turns Around Carrollton Hospital" in Dallas Business Journal (Vol. 35, June 15, 2012, No. 40, pp. 1)*
Pub: American City Business Journal
Ed: Bill Hethcock. **Description:** Baylor Health Care System has boosted the service performance of Trinity Medical Center in Carrollton, Texas. Trinity was the worst performing hospital in the area in terms of mortality rates and patient satisfaction.

40236 ■ *"BBVA Offers Medical Practices help that Floats on a Cloud" in Dallas Business Journal (Vol. 37, May 30, 2014, No. 38, pp. 6)*
Pub: American City Business Journals
Released: May 30, 2014. **Description:** BBVA Compass is offering a package of bank services and health care technology for medical practices in Dallas-Fort Worth, Texas in partnership with technology platform provider CareCloud. The innovative cloud-based technology platform will allow the Birmingham, Alabama-based bank to help medical practices affected by the demands of technology and government regulations.

40237 ■ *"Bethesda Inc. Stepping Out" in Business Courier (Vol. 27, October 15, 2010,*

No. 24, pp. 1)
Pub: Business Courier
Ed: James Ritchie. **Description:** Nonprofit organization Bethesda Inc. is planning to donate $5 million a year for the next three years to Greater Cincinnati health care reforms. Bethesda revealed that it announced its donations to pressure other organizations to help.

40238 ■ *"Beyond Repair" in Business First Buffalo (Vol. 28, March 23, 2012, No. 27, pp. 1)*
Pub: American City Business Journals, Inc.
Contact: Whitney Shaw, President
Description: Episcopal Church Home and Affiliates once ran a thriving senior care community on a Rhode Island Street property located nearthe Peace Bridge entrance in Buffalo, New York. However, a proposed bridge expansion that would run across the campus has led to the phased shutdown that began seven years ago. Insights on the $14 million liens on the property are also given.

40239 ■ *"Big Losses Mount for Baltimore's Hospitals" in Baltimore Business Journal (Vol. 27, October 23, 2009, No. 24, pp. 1)*
Pub: American City Business Journals
Ed: Scott Graham. **Description:** Reported losses by nine of the 22 hospitals in the Greater Baltimore area during fiscal 2009 have proven that the health care industry is not immune to the recession. The rising costs of doing business and losses in the stock market have strongly affected the financial status of hospitals.

40240 ■ *"Big Paychecks for Hospital CEOs" in Sacramento Business Journal (Vol. 28, April 8, 2011, No. 6, pp. 1)*
Pub: Sacramento Business Journal
Ed: Kathy Robertson. **Description:** Hospital chief executives in Sacramento, California have been receiving large salaries, tax records show. The huge salaries reflect the high demand for successful hospital chief executives. Statistical data included.

40241 ■ *"Biotechnology Wants a Lead Role" in Business North Carolina (Vol. 28, March 2008, No. 3, pp. 14)*
Description: According to experts, North Carolina is poised as a leader in the biotechnology sector. Highlights of a recent roundtable discussion sponsored by the North Carolina Biotechnology Center in Research Triangle Park are presented.

40242 ■ *"Blue Cross Confronts Baby Blues" in Marketing to Women (Vol. 21, March 2008, No. 3, pp. 3)*
Description: Blue Cross of California has launched a Maternity Depression Program aimed at educating mothers suffering from postpartum depression.

40243 ■ *"Blue Cross to Put Kiosk in Mall" in News & Observer (November 9, 2010)*
Pub: News & Observer
Ed: Alan M. Wolf. **Description:** Blue Cross and Blue Shield of North Carolina has placed a kiosk in Durham's Streets of Southpoint in order to market its health insurance.

40244 ■ *"Board This Powertrain" in Barron's (Vol. 89, July 27, 2009, No. 30, pp. 30)*
Ed: Naureen S. Malik. **Description:** Siemens' American Depositary Receipts have risen 60 percent from their March 2009 low and they should continue heading higher. The company has solid earnings and revenue growth since they lead in growing markets such as alternative energy and health-care infrastructure. Their shares also look cheap at 1.9 times book value.

40245 ■ *"Book of Lists 2010" in Philadelphia Business Journal (Vol. 28, December 25, 2009, No. 45, pp. 1)*
Pub: American City Business Journals Inc.
Description: Rankings of companies and organizations within the banking, biotechnology, economic development, healthcare, hospitality, law and accounting, marketing and media, real estate, and

technology industries in the Philadelphia, Pennsylvania area are presented. Rankings are based on sales, business size, and more.

40246 ■ *"Brace for the Bill" in Boston Business Journal (Vol. 27, December 28, 2007, No. 48, pp. 1)*
Ed: Mark Hollmer. **Description:** Historic 2006 Massachusetts Health Care Reform Law seems successful because many people have signed up for health insurance within one year of its implementation. However, rising premiums and other factors are threatening the health industry.

40247 ■ *"Breast Surgery Breakthrough Propels Palo Alto Startup AirXpanders" in Silicon Valley/San Jose Business Journal (Vol. 30, June 22, 2012, No. 13, pp. 1)*
Pub: American City Business Journal
Description: Palo Alto, California-based AirXpanders Inc. has designed and started the testing of the Aero-Form tissue expander, a medical device to help women undergoing reconstructive surgery. The device helps in expanding tissue to accommodate reconstruction of a woman's breast following a mastectomy. The extent to which this device would succeed in the market is discussed.

40248 ■ *"BRIEF: District Using Bilingual Kiosks to Promote Health Literacy Among Hispanic Families" in Palm Beach Post (August 24, 2012)*
Pub: McClatchy Tribune Information Services
Released: August 24, 2012. **Description:** A partnership between the Palm Beach County School District and United Healthcare provides access to health information, in both English and Spanish in order to promote health literacy.

40249 ■ *"Brisk Activity in North Fulton Office Market" in Atlanta Business Chronicle (July 11, 2014, pp. 2B)*
Released: July 11, 2014. **Description:** Activity appears to have pickup up briskly in the North Fulton office market during the first six months of 2014, mainly due to the high profile deals involving major players in the technology and health care sectors.

40250 ■ *"Brownies Are Only for Medicine: Regulations Raise Pot Questions" in Puget Sound Business Journal (Vol. 35, July 4, 2014, No. 11, pp. 10)*
Pub: American City Business Journals
Released: July 4, 2014. **Description:** Washington Governor Jay Inslee announced that the future of edible marijuana products is in limbo because the rules and regulations to handle the unique challenges created are not in place. Magical Butter opened its marijuana-infused food truck and started selling pot browning to card-carrying medical marijuana patients from the truck. Impact of the vague law is examined.

40251 ■ *"Bryan's House Retools for New Funds: Dallas Nonprofit Expands Mission as Money Related to HIV/AIDS Plummets" in Dallas Business Journal (Vol. 35, April 20, 2012, No. 32, pp. 1)*
Description: Nonprofit organization Bryan's House in Dallas, Texas is expanding its HIV/AIDS services to include early childhood education services and other child care programs. New funding includes $315,000 for the early childhood program, $450,000 for an Early Head Start Program for special-needs children and $125,000 for the '"Wisdom's Hope Project for homeless special-needs children.

40252 ■ *"Budget Cuts Afflict Health Department" in Business Courier (Vol. 24, November 21, 2007, No. 32, pp. 1)*
Pub: American City Business Journals, Inc.
Contact: Whitney Shaw, President
Ed: Lucy May, James Ritchie. **Description:** Cincinnati must cut $25 million to balance its budget for 2008. As a result, the city will be cutting $704,000 from its Health Department's budget of $42 million, and will eliminate 31.6 positions by the end of 2007.

40253 ■ *"Building Alexian Brothers' Clinical Reputation" in Crain's Chicago Business (Vol. 31, May 5, 2008, No. 18, pp. 6)*
Pub: Crain Communications Inc.
Contact: Todd Johnson, Publisher
Ed: Mike Colias. **Description:** Profile of the CEO of Alexian Brothers Medical Center in Elk Grove Village who plans to stabilize Alexian Brothers' financial performance in part by eliminating $20 million in annual costs.

40254 ■ *"The Business of Medicine: Maintaining a Healthy Bottom Line" in Black Enterprise (Vol. 41, October 2010, No. 3, pp. 60)*
Ed: Marcia A. Reed-Woodard. **Description:** Sustainable government reform requires reconstruction in the areas of financing and delivery of services in the field of medicine.

40255 ■ *"A Business That Cares: Dale and Diana Bevington Purchased Their Home Instead Senior Care Franchise in 2007 and Have Seen It Grow From Strength to Strength" in Business Franchise (Vol. 213, May 2012, pp. 98)*
Pub: Circle Publishing
Contact: Robert Perry, President
Description: Dale and Diana Bevington have run their Home Instead Senior Care franchise since 2007. The Bevington's launched their company after watching Dale's father, who lived in Canada, was diagnosed with vascular dementia. They feel their franchise business offers everything they needed while caring for Dale's father.

40256 ■ *"Businesses Delayed Hiring As They Waited for Health Care Law Ruling" in Baltimore Business Journal (Vol. 30, June 29, 2012, No. 8, pp. 1)*
Pub: American City Business Journals, Inc.
Contact: Whitney Shaw, President
Ed: Sarah Gantz. Released: June 29, 2012. **Description:** Small businesses in Baltimore, Maryland have been putting off expansion plans pending the Supreme Court's ruling on the health care reform law. Workforce expansion would require businesses to provide employee health insurance.

40257 ■ *"California Company Suing City's Lupin Over its Generic Diabetes Drug" in Baltimore Business Journal (Vol. 27, January 1, 2010)*
Ed: Gary Haber. **Description:** California-based Depomed Inc. is suing Baltimore, Maryland-based Lupin Pharmaceuticals Inc. and its parent company in India over the patents to a diabetes drug. Lupin allegedly infringed on Depomed's four patents for Glumetza when it filed for permission to sell its own version of the drug with the US Food and Drug Administration. Details on generic pharmaceutical manufacturer tactics are discussed.

40258 ■ *"California has a Plan B for Enacting Health Care Reform" in Sacramento Business Journal (Vol. 29, May 18, 2012, No. 12, pp. 1)*
Pub: American City Business Journal
Description: California lawmakers are pushing for a bill that would implement health care reform in the state. The bill is in anticipation of the US Supreme Court's ruling on the Federal Affordable Healthcare Act.

40259 ■ *"Campbell Clinic in Expansion Mode: Plans to Triple Size of Surgery Center, Add Employees" in Memphis Business Journal (Vol. 34, August 24, 2012, No. 19, pp. 1)*
Pub: American City Business Journal
Description: The Campbell Clinic Inc. is pushing forward with its plan to expand and hire new employees. The clinic has filed a Certificate of Need with the Tennessee Health Services Development Agency worth $13 million. Expansion projects include the enlargement of the surgery center, which handles 700 cases a month, a figure which is expected to rise to 750 in August 2012.

40260 ■ *"Canadian Patients Give Detroit Hospitals a Boost" in Crain's Detroit Business (Vol. 24, April 14, 2008, No. 15, pp. 10)*
Pub: Crain Communications Inc.
Contact: Rance E. Crain, President
Ed: Jay Greene. **Description:** Each year thousands of Canadians travel to Detroit area hospitals seeking quicker solutions to medical problems or access to services that are limited or unavailable in Canada.

40261 ■ *"Canadian Wind Farm Sued Due to Negative Health Effects" in PC Magazine Online (September 22, 2011)*
Pub: PC Magazine
Description: Suncor Energy is being sued by a family in Ontario, Canada. The family claims that Suncor's wind turbines have created health problems for them, ranging from vertigo and sleep disturbance to depression and suicidal thoughts. The family's home is over 1,000 meters from the eight wind turbines, and according to Ontario officials, wind turbines must be a minimum of 550 meters from existing homes.

40262 ■ *"Cancer Genome Project Will Put San Antonio In Research Spotlight" in San Antonio Business Journal (Vol. 25, January 27, 2012, No. 53, pp. 1)*
Pub: American City Business Journal
Description: San Antonio, Texas-based South Texas Accelerated Research Therapeutics has been spearheading the development of a new cancer research effort. The San Antonio 1000 Cancer Genome Project will use the genome sequencing process to examine and compare the difference between normal tissue and tissue from some 1,000 tumors.

40263 ■ *"Cancer Therapy Raises Debate Over Shared Technology" in Crain's Detroit Business (Vol. 24, March 10, 2008, No. 10, pp. 1)*
Pub: Crain Communications Inc.
Contact: Rance E. Crain, President
Ed: Jay Greene. **Description:** Overview of a proposed collaborative approach among select hospitals that would allow the consortium to utilize proton-beam accelerators in order to treat cancer patients; this expensive new technology is possibly a better way to destroy cancers by using the proton beams to direct high dosages of radiation to destroy small tumors.

40264 ■ *"Cannabis Science Signs Exclusive and Non-Exclusive Agreement with Prescription Vending Machines" in Benzinga.com (October 29, 2011)*
Pub: Benzinga.com
Contact: Kyle Bazzy, President
Ed: Benzinga Staff. **Description:** Cannabis Science Inc., a biotech company developing pharmaceutical cannabis products has partnered with Prescription Vending Machines Inc. and its principal Vincent Meddizadeh to provide industry specific consulting and advisory services to Cannabis Science.

40265 ■ *"Capital Campaign Will Boost Local Research" in San Antonio Business Journal (Vol. 28, March 14, 2014, No. 5, pp. 8)*
Pub: American City Business Journals
Released: March 14, 2014. **Description:** The University of Texas Health Science Center at San Antonio's Campaign for the Future of fundraising project has been completed. The Health Science Center is expected to use the money to support research at the South Texas Medical Center. The capital campaign will allow the Health Science Center to become one of the most prominent universities in the U.S.

40266 ■ *"CareFirst To Reward Doctors for Reducing Costs, Improving Care" in Baltimore Business Journal (Vol. 28, June 4, 2010, No. 4, pp. 1)*
Pub: Baltimore Business Journal
Ed: Scott Graham. **Description:** CareFirst Blue Cross Blue Shield plans to introduce a program that dangles big financial rewards to physicians who change the way they deliver primary care by improving the health of their sickest patients while reducing

costs. The company will soon begin recruiting primary care physicians in Maryland, Washington DC, and Northern Virginia.

40267 ■ *"CARES Directory: Social and Health Services in the Greater New York Area*
URL(s): www.unitedwaynyc.org/?id=65. **Released:** Biennial **Covers:** Over 2,469 nonprofit social service agencies in the greater New York area. **Entries include:** Name, address, phone, names and titles of key personnel, agency mission, programs offered, eligibility requirements, fees, application procedure, geographic area served, other locations, site director name and title, accessibility to the handicapped, hours open, languages spoken, transportation facilities. **Arrangement:** Alphabetical by agency name. **Indexes:** Program, Keyword/Target Group.

40268 ■ *"Carilion Clinic's Collection Agency Gets Wrong Data" in Roanoke Times (May 26, 2012)*
Pub: McClatchy Tribune Information Services
Released: May 26, 2012. **Description:** Patients of the New River Valley Radiology group were sent collections letters for bills that had already been paid. SCA Credit Service put all accounts on hold while is addresses the mistake.

40269 ■ *"Celebrate Innovation, No Matter Where It Occurs" in Harvard Business Review (Vol. 90, April 2012, No. 4, pp. 36)*
Pub: Harvard Business Review Press
Contact: Peter E. Walsh, Director
Ed: Nitin Nohria. **Released:** April 2012. **Description:** Yoga is used to illustrate the global success of a given concept not originally construed as a product or service. Although yoga emerged in ancient India, it is now practiced worldwide and is at the center of many businesses and disciplines, from the health care industry to clothing and accessories.

40270 ■ *"Centerpoint Nurses Unionize Despite Change In Hospital CEO" in Business Journal-Serving Metropolitan Kansas City (November 16, 2007)*
Pub: American City Business Journals, Inc.
Ed: Rob Roberts. **Description:** The change in Centerpoint Medical Center's CEO did not stop the hospital's 336 registered nurses from joining Nurses United for Improved Patient Care. Carolyn Caldwell was named CEO of Centerpoint on October 8, 2007, one week after Dan Jones announced his resignation. Poor communications are pointed out as the reason why the nurses joined the union.

40271 ■ *"CEO Forecast: With Cloudy Economy, Executives Turn to Government Contracting" in Hispanic Business (January-February 2009, pp. 34, 36)*
Pub: Hispanic Business Inc.
Contact: Jesus Chavarria, President
Ed: Jessica Haro, Richard Kaplan. **Description:** As economic uncertainty fogs the future, executives turn to government contracts in order to boost business. Revenue sources, health care challenges, environmental consulting and remediation services, as well as technological strides are discussed.

40272 ■ *"Cerner Works the Business Circuit" in Business Journal-Serving Metropolitan Kansas City (Vol. 26, October 5, 2007, No. 4, pp. 1)*
Pub: American City Business Journals, Inc.
Ed: Rob Roberts. **Description:** Cerner Corporation is embracing the coming of the electronic medical record exchange by creating a regional health information organization (RHIO) called the CareEntrust. The RHIO convinced health insurers to share claims data with patients and clinicians. At the Center Health Conference, held October 7 to 10, Cerner will demonstrate the software it developed for CareEntrust to the 40,000 healthcare and information technology professionals.

40273 ■ *"The Change Foundation Awards Northumberland Community Partnership $3 Million Project To Improve Seniors' Healthcare Transitions and Use Patient Input*

to Drive Redesign" in CNW Group (June 5, 2012)
Released: June 5, 2012. **Description:** The Change Foundation has awarded the Northumberland Community Partnership with its $3 million project PATH-Partners Advancing Transitions in Healthcare for Ontario patients. The program brings together 12 health and social care organizations with patients and caregivers to identify healthcare transition issues in Central East Ontario, Canada. It will work with service providers to redesign care and to improve experiences.

40274 ■ *"Changes Sought to Health Law" in Baltimore Business Journal (Vol. 28, July 30, 2010, No. 12, pp. 1)*
Pub: Baltimore Business Journal
Ed: Kent Hoover. **Description:** Business groups that opposed health care reform are working to undo parts of the new laws even before they go into effect. Business groups are gaining support for one legislative fix, which is repealing the law's provision that requires all businesses to file 1099 forms with the IRS any time they pay more than $600 a year to another business.

40275 ■ *"Chelsea Community Hospital to Merge with St. Joseph Mercy Health" in Crain's Detroit Business (Vol. 24, March 27, 2008, No. 12)*
Pub: Crain Communications Inc.
Contact: Rance E. Crain, President
Ed: Jay Greene. **Description:** Chelsea Community Hospital has signed a letter of intent to merge with St. Joseph Mercy Health System and will negotiate merger terms, including a plan to fund an unspecified amount of facility improvements and equipment purchases at Chelsea.

40276 ■ *"Chemed Corp.'s Vitas Unit Aims to Acquire" in Business Courier (Vol. 27, July 9, 2010, No. 10, pp. 1)*
Pub: Business Courier
Ed: James Ritchie. **Description:** Chemed Corporation's Vitas Healthcare Corporation is looking for smaller nonprofit hospices as it looks to become more streamlined in a tougher reimbursement environment. CFO David Williams syas they want to acquire these hospices as fast as they can integrate them.

40277 ■ *"Chicago Senior Care Acquires The Clare at Water Tower" in Investment Weekly News (April 29, 2012, pp. 168)*
Pub: NewsRX
Contact: Susan E. Hasty, Publisher
Description: Senior Care Development LLC, Fundamental Advisors LP, and Life Care Companies LLC partnered to create Chicago Senior Care LLC (CSC) and won the bid for purchasing The Clare at Water Tower, a senior housing community.

40278 ■ *"Chief Boo Boo Officer" in Marketing to Women (Vol. 21, February 2008, No. 2, pp. 1)*
Ed: Ellen Neuborne. **Description:** Pharmaceutical companies are reaching out to women through innovative marketing techniques.

40279 ■ *"Children's Hospital to Grow" in Austin Business Journal (Vol. 31, July 22, 2011, No. 20, pp. A1)*
Pub: American City Business Journals
Ed: Sandra Zaragoza. **Description:** Austin, Texas-based Dell Children's Medical Center is set to embark on a tower expansion. The plan will accommodate more patients and make room for the hospital's growing specialty program.

40280 ■ *"Christ Hospital to Expand" in Business Courier (Vol. 27, June 25, 2010, No. 8, pp. 3)*
Pub: Business Courier
Ed: Dan Monk, James Ritchie. **Description:** Christ Hospital intends to invest more than $300 million and generate 200 jobs in an expansion of its Mount Auburn campus in Cincinnati, Ohio. About $22 million in retail activity can be created by the hospital expansion, which will also include a replacement garage and new surgery facilities.

40281 ■ *"Christ Hospital Moves Toward Self-Rule"* in Business Courier (Vol. 24, December 7, 2007, No. 34, pp. 1)
Pub: American City Business Journals, Inc.
Contact: Whitney Shaw, President

Ed: James Ritchie. **Description:** Christ Hospital is planning on hiring 100 employees that will work on its newly leased facility located in Eden Park Drive.

40282 ■ *"Cincinnati Hospitals Face Big Whammy From State Fees"* in Business Courier (Vol. 26, October 2, 2009, No. 23, pp. 1)
Pub: American City Business Journals, Inc.
Contact: Whitney Shaw, President

Ed: James Ritchie. **Description:** Ohio hospitals are facing losses of nearly $145 million in franchise fees which are set to be levied by the state. Ohio hospitals will be responsible for a total of $718 million franchise fees as required by 2010-2011 state budget but will recover only 80 percent of the amount in increased Medicaid fees. Possible effects of anticipated losses to Ohio hospitals are examined.

40283 ■ *"Cincinnati Hospitals Feel Pain from Slow Economy"* in Business Courier (Vol. 27, September 3, 2010, No. 18, pp. 1)
Pub: Business Courier

Ed: James Ritchie. **Description:** Hospitals in Cincinnati, Ohio have suffered from decreased revenues owing to the economic crises. Declining patient volumes and bad debt have also adversely impacted hospitals.

40284 ■ *"Cincinnati Hospitals Mandate Flu Shots"* in Business Courier (Vol. 27, November 19, 2010, No. 29, pp. 1)
Pub: Business Courier

Ed: James Ritchie. **Description:** TriHealth has mandated that employees who refuse to get the vaccination shot for 2010 could be penalized with unpaid administrative leave. Other hospital employers, such as University Hospital and Cincinnati Children's Hospital and Medical Center have fired employees for forgoing flu shots. Vaccination rates among hospital employees are given.

40285 ■ *"Cincinnati Hospitals Wage War on 'Bounce-Backs'"* in Business Courier (Vol. 27, July 30, 2010, No. 13, pp. 1)
Pub: Business Courier

Ed: James Ritchie. **Description:** Health care organizations in Greater Cincinnati area have tried a number of care and follow up programs, primarily focused on congestive heart failure to prevent readmissions to hospitals. Hospital administrators have made the averting of bounce-backs a priority due to new federal government plans on reimbursement.

40286 ■ *"Cincinnati's Chuck Kubicki Juggles Lineup at Vianda"* in Business Courier (Vol. 26, December 11, 2009, No. 33, pp. 1)
Pub: American City Business Journals, Inc.
Contact: Whitney Shaw, President

Ed: Dan Monk. **Description:** Cincinnati real estate developer Chuck Kubicki replaced the management team of Vianda LLC and cancelled contracts with two vendors that caused a surge of customer complaints. Vianda is a direct-response marketing firm that sells and distributes dietary supplements for wellness and sexual performance.

40287 ■ *"Clash of the Titans"* in San Francisco Business Times (Vol. 28, February 7, 2014, No. 29, pp. 4)
Pub: American City Business Journals

Released: February 7, 2014. **Description:** University of California, San Francisco (UCSF) Medical Center and Stanford Hospital and Clinics have been competing for dominance for San Francisco Bay Area's health care. Both medical centers are competing to affiliate with more doctors, gain more patients, and accomplish more fundraising. Ways the UCSF and Stanford plan to pursue their expansion and integration are also discussed.

40288 ■ *"Clinic to Use Medical Summit to Pump Up Cardiology Center"* in Crain's Cleveland Business (Vol. 28, October 1, 2007, No. 39, pp. 6)
Pub: Crain Communications Inc.

Ed: Chuck Soder. **Description:** Overview of the Medical Innovation Summit, sponsored by the Cleveland Clinic and regional business recruitment group Team NEO, whose theme was cardiology. The goal for this year's summit went beyond finding companies for the cardiovascular center, it also looked to market the region to other industries with growth potential.

40289 ■ *"Columbia Sale Narrowed To Two Developers"* in The Business Journal-Milwaukee (Vol. 25, July 18, 2008, No. 43, pp. A1)
Pub: American City Business Journals, Inc.
Contact: Whitney Shaw, President

Ed: Corrinne Hess. **Description:** Officials of Columbia St. Mary's Inc plan to pick one of two real-estate developers who will buy the 8-acre property of the Columbia Hospital which the company will move away from when their new hospital has been constructed. The hospital on Newport Ave. has been on the market since 2001.

40290 ■ *"Commercial Builders Take It on the Chin"* in Crain's Chicago Business (Vol. 31, April 28, 2008, No. 17, pp. 16)
Pub: Crain Communications Inc.
Contact: Todd Johnson, Publisher

Ed: Alby Gallun. **Description:** Although the health care development sector has seen growth, the rest of Chicago's local commercial building industry has seen steep declines in the first quarter of this year. According to McGraw-Hill Construction, Chicago-area non-residential construction starts totaled $731 million in the quarter, a 60 percent drop from the year-earlier period. Volume in the retail, office and hotel markets fell by nearly 70 percent.

40291 ■ *"Company Goes High-Tech To Attack Some Sore Spots"* in Boston Business Journal (Vol. 27, December 7, 2007, No. 45, pp. 10)
Ed: Mark Hollmer. **Description:** Transport Pharmaceuticals Inc. hopes to raise $35 million to fund a drug and a treatment device for treating cold sores, and seek federal regulatory approval. Dennis Goldberg, the company's CEO, believes that existing treatments that use acyclovir cream are relatively weak. Transport's drug uses a soluble gel cartridge with a higher concentration of acyclovir.

40292 ■ *"Competition Is Fierce For Hospital Rankings"* in Dallas Business Journal (Vol. 35, July 20, 2012, No. 45, pp. 1)
Pub: American City Business Journal

Ed: Bill Hethcock. **Description:** U.S. News and World Report has released its ranking of Best Hospitals and triggering press releases in the highly competitive North Texas health care market. The press releases are being taken seriously by the hospitals since they learn from each other.

40293 ■ *"Complementary Strengths Fuel Research Duo's Success"* in Providence Business News (Vol. 29, June 2, 2014, No. 9, pp. 22)
Pub: American City Business Journals

Released: June 2, 2014. **Description:** Johnna A. Pezzullo and Lynne A. Haughey achieved success with Omega Medical Research through their complementary strengths. The company has been successful and works with pharmaceutical companies like Pfizer and GlaxoSmithKline.

40294 ■ *"Complicated Medicals Confuse Houstonians"* in Houston Business Journal (Vol. 45, June 27, 2014, No. 7, pp. 14A)
Pub: American City Business Journals

Released: June 27, 2014. **Description:** A study by TransUnion Healthcare on the transparency of the medical billing process reveals that 50 percent of Houstonians are confused by their medical bills. Dave Wojczynski, senior vice president of TransUnion Healthcare, believes consumers' demands to address complex billing practices will change the system.

40295 ■ *"Connecting the Dots Between Wellness and Elder Care"* in Benefits and Compensation Digest (Vol. 47, August 2010, No. 8, pp. 18)
Pub: International Foundation of Employee Benefit Plans
Contact: Kenneth R. Boyd, President

Ed: Sandra Timmermann. **Description:** Employees caring for aged and infirm parents deal with time and financial issues and other stresses. The connection between health status of caregivers and employers' health care costs could be aided by linking programs and benefits with wellness and caregiving.

40296 ■ *"Consulting Firm Goes Shopping"* in Crain's Chicago Business (Vol. 31, April 28, 2008, No. 17, pp. 45)
Pub: Crain Communications Inc.
Contact: Todd Johnson, Publisher

Ed: Phuong Ly. **Description:** Clark & Wamberg LLC was created last year after the merger of Clark Inc. to a Dutch insurance conglomerate. Clark Inc. was a life insurance and benefits consultancy which had been on a downslide, returning just 5.6 percent a year to shareholders. In contrast Clark & Wamberg posted first-year revenue of $106.8 million, fueled by business from its executive compensation and health care clients.

40297 ■ *"Consumer Health Plan to be Launched in Memphis"* in Memphis Business Journal (Vol. 34, September 21, 2012, No. 23, pp. 1)
Pub: American City Business Journal

Ed: Cole Epley. **Description:** The Community Health Alliance, a Knoxville, Tennessee-based Consumer Oriented and Operated Plan (CO-OP), is an offspring of the Affordable Care Act. It is believed that this service will provide small businesses and individuals with an additional option when it comes to purchasing health insurance.

40298 ■ *"Contracting Firm Sees Timing Right for Expansion"* in Tampa Bay Business Journal (Vol. 29, November 13, 2009, No. 47, pp. 1)
Pub: American City Business Journals

Ed: Janet Leiser. **Description:** Construction management company Moss & Associates LLC of Fort Lauderdale, Florida has launched its expansion to Tampa Bay. Moss & Associates has started the construction of the Marlins stadium in Miami, Florida's Little Havana section. It also plans to diversify by embarking on other government development, such as health care facilities and airports.

40299 ■ *"Conversation Starters for the Holiday"* in Barron's (Vol. 89, July 6, 2009, No. 27, pp. 7)
Pub: Dow Jones & Co., Inc.
Contact: Clare Hart, President

Ed: Michael Santoli. **Description:** Investors are concerned that the US will experience high inflation due to low interest rates and improved money supply. US consumer spending has increased to 70 percent of gross domestic product, brought by health-care spending increases, while savings rates have risen to 6.9 percent.

40300 ■ *"Corporate Canada Eyes Retiree Health Benefit Cuts"* in Globe & Mail (March 8, 2006, pp. B3)
Ed: Virginia Galt. **Description:** A survey on Canadian companies reveals that due to rising health care costs and increasing number of baby boomer retirements, these companies are to cut down on health benefits they are providing to these retired employees.

40301 ■ *"Corrales Site of New Senior Living/Care Complex"* in America's Intelligence Wire (August 13, 2012)
Description: David Dronet, developer of Corrales Senior Living LLC, has chosen Corrales, New Mexico as its newest site to construct a continuum of care for senior citizens. The project entails a $60 million complex of private homes and health care units with amenities like a restaurant, fitness areas, and gardens.

40302 ■ "COSE: More Small Companies Offering Wellness Plans" in Crain's Cleveland Business (Vol. 28, December 3, 2007, No. 48, pp. 22)
Pub: Crain Communications Inc.
Ed: Shannon Mortland. Description: Discusses the Council of Smaller Enterprises (COSE) which is offering incentives to companies who implement wellness programs and can show that their employees are living healthier lives.

40303 ■ "Cost of Creating Health Insurance Exchange in Md. 'Largely Unknown'" in Baltimore Business Journal (Vol. 28, September 3, 2010, No. 17, pp. 1)
Pub: Baltimore Business Journal
Ed: Emily Mullin. Description: United States health reform is seen to result in increased health insurance prices in Maryland. However, health care reform advocates claim a new marketplace and increased competition will help keep costs down.

40304 ■ "Could UNCC Be Home to Future Med School Here?" in Charlotte Business Journal (Vol. 25, July 23, 2010, No. 18, pp. 1)
Pub: Charlotte Business Journal
Ed: Jennifer Thomas. Description: University of North Carolina, Charlotte chancellor Phil Dubois is proposing that a medical school be established at the campus. The idea began in 2007 and Dubois' plan is for students to spend all four years in Charlotte and train at the Carolinas Medical Center.

40305 ■ "Countywide Tax Could Fund Cincinnati's Metro" in Business Courier (Vol. 26, January 15, 2010, No. 39, pp. 1)
Pub: American City Business Journals, Inc.
Contact: Whitney Shaw, President
Ed: Lucy May, Dan Monk. Description: Cincinnati officials are considering a new countywide tax to fund the Metro bus system and extend healthcare to the poor.

40306 ■ "Covered California Adds Dental Benefits" in Sacramento Business Journal (Vol. 31, August 29, 2014, No. 27, pp. 8)
Pub: American City Business Journals
Released: August 29, 2014. Description: Health benefit exchange, Covered California, is introducing stand-alone family dental benefits for consumers who enroll in health insurance coverage for 2015. The Governor has yet to sign a bill that would establish a separate vision care marketplace linked to Covered California's Website.

40307 ■ "CPRIT May Dole Out Funds Differently" in Austin Business Journal (Vol. 32, July 20, 2012, No. 20, pp. 1)
Pub: American City Business Journals, Inc.
Contact: Whitney Shaw, President
Ed: Sandra Zaragoza. Released: July 20, 2012. Description: The Cancer Preventin Research Institute of Texas is involved in a series of workgroups and town hall meetings to help set the direction or the organization for the next seven years. The Institute could increase its spending in commercialization, prevention, and prevention research.

40308 ■ "Creating Health-Tech Opportunity" in Providence Business News (Vol. 29, April 14, 2014, No. 2, pp. 1)
Pub: American City Business Journals
Released: April 14, 2014. Description: MedMates has officially launched, in April 2013, as Rhode Island's first group for networking and advocacy in health technology. MedMates now have 410 members that span every sector of health technology and its membership is not exclusive to the private sector. Insights into MedMates' first year success are also presented.

40309 ■ "Criticare Sees Rapid Expansion" in Business Journal-Milwaukee (Vol. 28, December 31, 2010, No. 14, pp. A1)
Pub: Milwaukee Business Journal
Ed: Rich Rovito. Description: Criticare Systems Inc. expanded its distribution network, added customers, launched two new products and transferred into a new building in Pewaukee, Wisconsin at the start of their fiscal year. Criticare expanded its workforce and now has nearly 140 full time employees.

40310 ■ "David Low" in Hawaii Business (Vol. 53, October 2007, No. 4, pp. 38)
Pub: PacificBasin Communications
Ed: Cathy S. Cruz-George. Description: Hawaii Capital Management managing director David Low ranked first in the 2007 competition for fittest male executives in Hawaii. This 5-foot-9 executive, who weighed 225 lbs. in 2003, weighs 150 lbs. in 2007. The activities that improved Low's fitness, such as weight training, swimming, biking, and running, are discussed.

40311 ■ "Deals Dip In Florida Amid Squabbles Over Price" in South Florida Business Journal (Vol. 34, May 30, 2014, No. 45, pp. 4)
Pub: American City Business Journals
Released: May 30, 2014. Description: Private equity firm investments in local companies in Florida dropped from 146 in 2012 to 135 in 2013. James Cassel of Cassel, Salpeter and Company, says companies in the information technology and health care sectors have been acquired because of strong multiples of their book value.

40312 ■ "Design Challenge Seeks to Expand Access" in Philadelphia Business Journal (Vol. 33, April 25, 2014, No. 11, pp. 7)
Pub: American City Business Journals
Released: April 25, 2014. Description: The Thomas Scattergood Behavioral Health Foundation sponsored the 2014 design challenge on making mental health-care education, access and services available at retail clinics. The winner was the mental health screening tool, 'Wellness at Your Fingertips', submitted by the Philadelphia Department of Behavioral Health and Intellectual Disability Services in Pennsylvania.

40313 ■ "Developer To Use New Owasso Senior Care Center as Template for More Services, Expansion" in Journal Record (May 23, 2012)
Description: A new $7.5 million senior care and rehabilitation center will be built in Owasso, Oklahoma. The builder, Steve Cox, is using his Senior Suites of Owasso as his model. JRJ Construction of Weatherford, Texas will complete the 105-bed private-suite facility by spring 2013.

40314 ■ "Diana Bonta -- Keeping People Healthy and Thriving" in Hispanic Business (Vol. 30, April 2008, No. 4, pp. 30)
Pub: Hispanic Business Inc.
Contact: Jesus Chavarria, President
Ed: Leanndra Martinez. Description: Diana Bonta serves as vice president of public affairs for Kaiser Permanente and is a strong advocate for health reform and improving access to health care. In order to better serve the underinsured and uninsured, she directs Kaiser's Community Benefit division that devoted $369 million last year to this cause.

40315 ■ Directory of Human Services and Self Help Support Groups--Maricopa County (Arizona)
Pub: Community Information & Referral Inc.
Contact: Roberto Armijo, President
URL(s): www.cirs.orgwww.211arizona.org/maricopa.
Released: Annual; Latest edition 2014. Price: $40, plus 5 for shipping. Covers: More than 2,300 governmental and private non-profit human service organizations in Maricopa County, Arizona. Entries include: Organization name, address, phone, fax, e-mail, URL, Name and title of contact, affiliations, location, geographical area served, eligibility requirements, description of services, days and hours of operation, complete program and service descriptions. Arrangement: Alphabetical. Indexes: Subject, alphabetical.

40316 ■ "Discovery Communications" in Workforce Management (Vol. 88, December 14, 2009, No. 13, pp. 17)
Pub: Crain Communications Inc.
Contact: Rance E. Crain, President
Ed: Jeremy Smerd. Description: Discovery Communications provides its employees a wealth of free health services via a comprehensive work-site medical clinic that is available to its employees and their dependents. Overview of the company's innovative approach to healthcare is presented.??.

40317 ■ "Dispelling Rocky Mountain Myths Key to Wellness" in Employee Benefit News (Vol. 25, November 1, 2011, No. 14, pp. 12)
Pub: SourceMedia Inc.
Contact: James M. Malkin, Chief Executive Officer
Ed: Andrea Davis. Description: Andrew Sykes, chairman of Health at Work Wellness Actuaries, states that it is a myth that Colorado is ranked as the healthiest state in America. Sykes helped implement a wellness programs at Brighton School District in the Denver area.

40318 ■ "Docs Might Hold Cure for Baltimore-Area Real Estate, Banks" in Baltimore Business Journal (Vol. 28, November 5, 2010, No. 26, pp. 1)
Pub: Baltimore Business Journal
Ed: Gary Haber. Description: Health care providers, including physicians are purchasing their office space instead of renting it as banks lower interest rates to 6 percent on mortgages for medical offices. The rise in demand offers relief to the commercial real estate market. It has also resulted in a boom in building new medical offices.

40319 ■ "Docs Prop Up Health Insurer" in Business First-Columbus (December 14, 2007, pp. A1)
Ed: Carrie Ghose. Description: Doctors and executives supporting Physicians Assurance Corporation, a startup health insurer in Central Ohio, were required to raise $2.5 million before they could apply for a license from the state Department of Insurance. The company, which hopes to acquire its license by January 2007, will focus on doctor's offices and businesses with two to ninety-nine employees.

40320 ■ "Doctor: J and J Alerted in '06 to Procedure Risks" in Pittsburgh Business Times (Vol. 33, June 6, 2014, No. 47, pp. 4)
Pub: American City Business Journals
Released: June 6, 2014. Description: Dr. Robert Lamparter, then pathologist at Lewisburg's Evangelical Community Hospital, states that he had alerted Johnson and Johnson (J and J) in 2006 of the potential risk of spreading undetected cancer following the use of its power morcellator during hysterectomy procedures. J and J suspended worldwide sales of the device in April 2014 after the laboratory warning, and days after a US Food and Drug Administration advisory discouraging doctors from using it, but doctors are still divided over the morcellation procedure.

40321 ■ "Doctor On the Go: Concessions International Founder Opens Airport Clinic" in Black Enterprise (Vol. 38, October 1, 2007, No. 3, pp. 34)
Pub: Earl G. Graves Publishing Co. Inc.
Contact: Earl G. Graves, Jr., President
Ed: Tara C. Walker. Description: Aero Clinic is an onsite healthcare facility designed to care for travelers. Located at Atlanta's Hartsfield-Jackson International Airport, the clinic is the first of its kind.

40322 ■ "Doctor Shortage Continues to Plague Region" in Business First of Buffalo (Vol. 30, April 11, 2014, No. 30, pp. 6)
Pub: American City Business Journals, Inc.
Contact: Whitney Shaw, President
Released: April 11, 2014. Description: New York hospitals need at least 1,000 additional physicians, particularly primary care doctors, as they try to meet the criteria set by Federal health reform's Affordable Care Act. The Western New York region gained only 421 new physicians, while losing 544 in 2013.

40323 ■ "Doctors Eye Rating Plan With Caution" in The Business Journal-Portland (Vol. 25, July 4, 2008, No. 17, pp. 1)
Pub: American City Business Journals, Inc.
Contact: Whitney Shaw, President
Ed: Robin J. Moody. Description: Doctors in Portland, Oregon are wary of a new Providence Health Plan system that rates their performance on patients

with certain medical conditions. The system is expected to discourage wasteful procedures, thereby, saving employers' money. Other mechanics of the rating system are also discussed.

40324 ■ "Doctor's Orders" in Canadian Business (Vol. 79, November 20, 2006, No. 23, pp. 73)
Ed: Jeff Sanford. **Description:** George Cohon, the founder of McDonald's in Canada and Russia, speaks about the Canadian market and the experience of starting McDonald's in Canada.

40325 ■ "Doctors Warn of Problems" in Austin Business JournalInc. (Vol. 29, December 4, 2009, No. 39, pp. 1)
Pub: American City Business Journals
Ed: Sandra Zaragoza. **Description:** Texas physicians have voiced their concern regarding the potential cuts in Medicare reimbursement rates due to the 21 percent cut imposed by Centers for Medicare and Medicaid at the start of 2010. Experts believe the large cuts would result in the closure of some physician practices. Details of the Texas Medical Association's stand on the health reform bill are examined.

40326 ■ "DT Interpreting VideoHub Service Expanding" in Internet Wire (March 26, 2012)
Released: March 26, 2012. **Description:** Profile of the Deaf-Talk Inc. has launched its new DTViedeoHub, to improve and expand its interpreting services to healthcare facilities. Details of the new program are included.

40327 ■ "Ducking the New Health-Care Taxes" in Barron's (Vol. 92, September 15, 2012, No. 38, pp. 34)
Pub: Dow Jones & Co., Inc.
Contact: Clare Hart, President
Ed: Elizabeth Ody. **Description:** Strategies that investors can use to avoid paying higher taxes starting January 2013 are discussed. These include selling assets by December 2012, distributing dividends, purchasing private-placement life insurance and converting individual retirement accounts.

40328 ■ "E-Medical Records Save Money, Time in Ann Arbor" in Crain's Detroit Business (Vol. 24, January 21, 2008, No. 3, pp. 6)
Pub: Crain Communications Inc. - Detroit
Contact: Keith Crain, Chairman
Ed: Jay Greene. **Description:** Ann Arbor Area Health Information Exchange is improving patient outcomes by sharing clinical and administrative data in electronic medical record systems.

40329 ■ "Easing the Global (and Costly) Problem of Workplace Stress; Stress Is Reportedly the Leading Cause of Long-Term Sickness for Workers Around the World. But Relief Is In Sight" in Gallup Business Journal (March 27, 2014)
Pub: Gallup Press
Released: March 27, 2014. **Description:** Stress is considered the leading cause of long-term illness for workers globally. According to an employee engagement survey, workplace stress can be reduced through engagement.

40330 ■ "Editor's Note" in Canadian Business (Vol. 81, March 17, 2008, No. 4, pp. 7)
Pub: Rogers Media Inc.
Contact: Tony Viner, President
Ed: Joe Chidley. **Description:** Canadian Consolidated government expenditures increased by an average of 4.5 percent annually from 2003 to 2007. Health care, housing, and the environment were some of the areas which experienced higher spending. However, government spending in labor, employment, and immigration dropped 6.6 percent.

40331 ■ "Elder Care At Work" in HRMagazine (Vol. 53, September 2008, No. 9, pp. 111)
Pub: Society for Human Resource Management
Contact: Henry G. Jackson, President
E-mail: hjackson@shrm.org
Ed: Pamela Babcock. **Description:** Many employers are helping workers who face sudden, short-term elder care needs.

40332 ■ "Elements For Success" in Small Business Opportunities (November 2008)
Pub: Entrepreneur Press
Contact: Perlman Neil, President
Description: Profile of Elements, a physical fitness club that approach a healthy lifestyle for women, which includes the components of body, beauty and mind; the network of upscale, boutique style health clubs differ from other providers in its 'balanced lifestyle' approach to a healthy lifestyle. This unique niche is gaining in popularity despite the faltering economy.

40333 ■ "Elevated Status" in Business Courier (Vol. 24, March 21, 2008, No. 50, pp. 1)
Pub: American City Business Journals, Inc.
Contact: Whitney Shaw, President
Ed: James Ritchie. **Description:** Overview of Tri-Health Inc.'s growth is presented. Currently, the company's revenue is estimated to be around $1 billion. Since 2004, the company was able to build patient towers, an outpatient facility in Lebanon, and was able to acquire the Group Health Associates physician practice. TriHealth recently hired 500 nurses in order to meet its needs.

40334 ■ "Employers See Workers' Comp Rates Rising" in Sacramento Business Journal (Vol. 28, April 8, 2011, No. 6, pp. 1)
Pub: Sacramento Business Journal
Ed: Kelly Johnson. **Description:** Employers in California are facing higher workers compensation costs. Increased medical costs and litigation are seen to drive the trend.

40335 ■ "Employers Waking Up to Effects of Workers' Sleep Problems" in Crain's Cleveland Business (Vol. 28, December 3, 2007, No. 48, pp. 18)
Pub: Crain Communications Inc.
Ed: Jennifer Keirn. **Description:** Employers are beginning to realize that poor sleep quality can impact their bottom lines with higher health care costs and more lost-time accidents. The National Institutes of Health estimates that sleep deprivation, sleep disorders and excessive daytime sleepiness add about $15 billion to our national health care bill and cost employers $50 billion in lost productivity.

40336 ■ "Ending the Ebola Death Sentence" in Canadian Business (Vol. 83, August 17, 2010, No. 13-14, pp. 22)
Ed: Michael McCullough. **Description:** US Army Medical Research Institute of Infectious Diseases made a $140 million agreement with Tekmira Pharmaceuticals Corporation to develop both a drug delivery system and delivery technology for curing the Ebola virus. Tekmira's delivery technology, which has been shown to halt Ebola in laboratory animals, might be the key to finding a cure.

40337 ■ Episcopal Church Annual
Pub: The Morehouse Group
Contact: Laury Poland, Director
E-mail: lpoland@cpg.org
URL(s): www.churchpublishing.org/products/index. cfm?fuseaction=productDetail&productID=9912. **Released:** Annual; Latest Edition; May 2014. **Price:** $45, Individuals list price - hardcover. **Covers:** The churches and clergy of the Episcopal Church; seminaries, training schools, retreat centers, and social service agencies; dioceses, and provinces of Anglican Communion. **Entries include:** Name, address, phone of churches; name and address of clergy members; staff size, membership; the organizations, officers, and other information for the Episcopal Church in the United States of America with contacts, addresses, and phone numbers. **Database includes:** Information and statistics on dioceses, the structure of the church, and its institutions; biographies, with photographs, of recently consecrated bishops. **Arrangement:** Clergy list is alphabetical; diocesan list is alphabetical. **Indexes:** Alphabetical by categories; Classified Buyers' Guide classified by subject; alphabetical by advertisers.

40338 ■ "Ethics and the End of Life" in Crain's Chicago Business (Vol. 34, October 24, 2011, No. 42, pp. 31)
Pub: Crain Communications Inc.
Contact: Todd Johnson, Publisher
Ed: Lisa Bertagnoli. **Description:** Technology has enabled doctors to provide more and better methods for helping patients, however end of life issues faced by medical ethicists are discussed.

40339 ■ "Everett Hospice Planned" in Puget Sound Business Journal (Vol. 29, September 26, 2008, No. 23, pp. 1)
Ed: Peter Neurath. **Description:** Providence Senior and Community Services is pursuing a purchase-and-sales agreement for land in Everett to build a $9.7 million 20-bed hospice facility. The organization plans to break ground on the new facility in 2009.

40340 ■ "Executive Summary: Codeines and Coding" in Business Strategy Review (Vol. 23, Spring 2012, No. 1, pp. 82)
Released: Spring 2012. **Description:** Adam Powell, Sergei Savin, and Nicos Savva, 'Physician Workload and Hospital Reimbursement: Overworked Servers Generate Lower Income', working paper, August 2011 is examined.

40341 ■ "Expect Action on Health Care and the Economy" in Contractor (Vol. 57, January 2010, No. 1, pp. 30)
Pub: Penton Media, Inc.
Ed: Kevin Schwalb. **Description:** The Plumbing-Heating-Cooling Contractors National Association is working to solidify its standing in the public policy arena as the legislative agenda will focus on health care reform, estate tax and immigration reform, all of which will impact the industries.

40342 ■ "Experts Sound Off On Top Legal Trends" in Birmingham Business Journal (Vol. 31, January 17, 2014, No. 3, pp. 4)
Pub: American City Business Journals, Inc.
Contact: Whitney Shaw, President
Released: January 17, 2014. **Description:** Lawyers' views on potential legal trends in Birmingham, Alabama for 2014 are presented, with the Affordable Care Act leading the agenda. One attorney addressed the challenges associated with the use of social media.

40343 ■ "Experts Take the Temp of Obama Plan" in The Business Journal-Serving Metropolitan Kansas City (Vol. 27, November 14, 2008, No. 10)
Pub: American City Business Journals, Inc.
Contact: Whitney Shaw, President
Ed: Rob Roberts. **Description:** Kansas City, Missouri-based employee benefits experts say president-elect Barack Obama's health care reform plan is on track. Insurance for children and capitalization for health information technology are seen as priority areas. The plan is aimed at reducing the number of uninsured people in the United States.

40344 ■ "Family Takes Wind Turbine Companies to Court Over Gag Clauses on Health Effects of Turbines" in CNW Group (September 12, 2011)
Pub: CNW Group Ltd.
Contact: Carolyn McGill-Davidson, President
Description: Shawn and Trisha Drennan are concerned about the negative experiences other have had with wind turbines close to their homes, including adverse health effects. The couple's home will be approximately 650 meters from the Kingsbridge II wind farm project in Ontario, Canada.

40345 ■ "Faster To Dissolve, Faster To Work" in Philadelphia Business Journal (Vol. 33, March 14, 2014, No. 5, pp. 8)
Pub: American City Business Journals
Released: March 14, 2014. **Description:** The U.S. Food and Drug Administration approved Iroko Pharmaceutical's anti-inflammatory drug Tivorbex. The company's technology reformulates a braded drug's active ingredient as submicron particles 20 times smaller than their original size. Iroko also applies the technology to drugs used in oncology.

40346 ■ *"Feds to Pay University Hospital $20M"* **in** *Business Courier (Vol. 27, July 23, 2010, No. 12, pp. 3)*
Pub: Business Courier
Ed: James Ritchie. **Description:** The U.S. government is set to pay University Hospital and medical residents who trained there $20 million as part of a tax dispute settlement. Around 1,000 former residents are to receive tax refunds. But the hospital must provide the U.S. Internal Revenue Service with extensive documentation.

40347 ■ *"Finding Heart Help In the Skyway"* **in** *Business Journal (Vol. 30, August 10, 2012, No. 11, pp. 3)*
Pub: American City Business Journals, Inc.
Contact: Whitney Shaw, President
Ed: Katharine Grayson. **Released:** August 10, 2012. **Description:** The 2,000 square foot HeartSavers Clinic will start offering heart screening at the Baker Center in Minneapolis, Minnesota in September 2012. CardioVascular Centers chief executive officer, Maury Taylor, has licensed the Cohn Index for the tests and is funding his business through his medical device firm Hypertension Diagnostics.

40348 ■ *"Firms Bet On Games To Hike Wellness"* **in** *Business Journal (Vol. 30, June 1, 2012, No. 1, pp. 1)*
Pub: American City Business Journals, Inc.
Contact: Whitney Shaw, President
Ed: Katharine Grayson. **Released:** June 1, 2012. **Description:** Twin Cities-based firms providing corporate wellness services are integrating games into these programs. These games include friendly competitions between work teams or high-tech smartphone applications.

40349 ■ *"Five-Ring Circus"* **in** *Entrepreneur (Vol. 35, November 2007, No. 11, pp. 76)*
Pub: Entrepreneur Press
Contact: Perlman Neil, President
Ed: Scott Bernard Nelson. **Description:** China's economy is growing and is expected to do well even after the 2008 Olympics, but growth could slow from eleven percent to eight or nine percent. Chinese portfolio concerns with regard to health and environmental records and bureaucratic fraud are discussed.

40350 ■ *The Flaw of Averages: Why We Underestimate Risk in the Face of Uncertainty*
Pub: John Wiley & Sons Inc.
Contact: Stephen M. Smith, President
Ed: Sam L. Savage. **Released:** March 2012. **Price:** $19.95, paperback; $12.99. **Description:** Personal and business plans are based on uncertainties on a daily basis. The common avoidable mistake individuals make in assessing risk in the face of uncertainty is defined. The explains why plans based on average assumptions are wrong, on average, in areas as diverse as finance, healthcare, accounting, the war on terror, and climate change. **Availability:** PrintE-book.

40351 ■ *"Florida Hospital Planning $104.1M In Expansions"* **in** *Orlando Business Journal (Vol. 29, June 8, 2012, No. 53, pp. 1)*
Pub: American City Business Journal
Description: Florida Hospital is planning $104.1 million in expansion projects that will create about 140 new permanent health care jobs and 576 temporary contruction jobs. The projects include an emergency department and medical office space in Winter Garden, an expanded emergency department at Florida Hospital East Orlando and additional floors in Ginsburg Tower at Florida Hospital Orlando.

40352 ■ *"Florida Hospital, UCF Affiliation in Danger?"* **in** *Orlando Business Journal (Vol. 29, September 21, 2012, No. 29, pp. 1)*
Pub: American City Business Journal
Description: Florida Hospital is said to be considering the possibility of terminating its affiliation agreement with the University of Central Florida's (UCF) College of Medicine that ends June 30, 2018. Two of the reasons for the move include UCF's plans for a

teaching hospital and a new graduate medical education program that could place Florida Hospital into competition with UCF.

40353 ■ *"Flue Vaccines are Going Green"* **in** *Canadian Business (Vol. 83, September 14, 2010, No. 15, pp. 24)*
Pub: Rogers Media Inc.
Contact: Tony Viner, President
Ed: Angelia Chapman. **Description:** Quebec-based Medicago has found a solution to the bottleneck in the production of influenza vaccines by using plant-based processes instead of egg-based systems. Medicago's US Department of Defense funded research has produced the technology that speeds up the production time for vaccines by almost two-thirds. Insights into Medicago's patented process are also given.

40354 ■ *"For Gilead, Growth Beyond AIDS"* **in** *Barron's (Vol. 88, June 30, 2008, No. 26, pp. 18)*
Pub: Dow Jones & Co., Inc.
Contact: Clare Hart, President
Ed: Jay Palmer. **Description:** First-quarter 2008 revenue for Gilead Sciences grew by 22 percent and an earnings gain of 19 percent thanks to their HIV-treatment drugs that comprised over two-thirds of the company's sales in 2007. An analyst has a 12-month target from June, 2008 of 65 per share. The factors behind the company's prospects are also discussed.

40355 ■ *"For Hospitals, a Dating Game"* **in** *Business Courier (Vol. 26, December 4, 2009, No. 32, pp. 1)*
Ed: James Ritchie. **Description:** Drake Center, Fort Hamilton Hospital, and West Chester Medical Center are among the members of Cincinnati's Health Alliance looking for potential buyers or partners. Meanwhile, Jewish Hospital, another member of the Alliance, will be bought by Mercy Health Partners by January 7, 2010.

40356 ■ *"For-Profit Medical School Ramping Up for Business"* **in** *Sacramento Business Journal (Vol. 30, February 21, 2014, No. 52, pp. 6)*
Pub: American City Business Journals
Released: February 21, 2014. **Description:** California Northstate University got full accreditation for the College of Pharmacy at Elk Grove in summer 2013 and hopes to start classes in August or September 2014. The university is in talks to acquire a second building in the area worth $15 million.

40357 ■ *"Forest Park Medical Center to Double Operations"* **in** *Dallas Business Journal (Vol. 35, April 13, 2012, No. 31, pp. 1)*
Pub: American City Business Journal
Description: Dallas, Texas-based Neal Richards Group launched a growth plan for the Forest Park Medical Center System called '12 by 12' that will more than double its hospital count in the next two years. The group wants to have 12 Forest Park facilities open or in various levels of development by the end of 2012. Forest Park is a physician-owned system.

40358 ■ *"Former Synthes Officers Receive Prison Sentences"* **in** *Wall Street Journal Eastern Edition (November 22 , 2011, pp. B4)*
Pub: Dow Jones & Co., Inc.
Contact: Clare Hart, President
Ed: Peter Loftus. **Description:** Michael D. Huggins, formerly chief operating officer of medical-device maker Synthes Ltd., and Thomas B. Higgins, formerly the president of Synthes spine unit, were given prison sentences of nine months while a third executive, John J. Walsh, formerly director of regulatory and clinical affairs in the spine division, was given a five-month sentence for their involvement in the promotion of the unauthorized use of a bone cement produced by the company.

40359 ■ *"Fort Collins Senior Care Services Company, Seniors Helping Seniors, Partners With Pagel for SEO"* **in** *Internet Wire (June 27, 2012)*
Description: Seniors Helping Seniors has partnered with Page1 Online Marketing to help seniors and their families access elder care serves easier on the Inter-

net. Fort Collins offers senior care services for the elderly who are seeking independent senior living and requires no minimum weekly hours, no contracts or deposits and does not charge more for weekend home care hours. Page1 is a full service online marketing firm that specializes in Website marketing, including search engine optimization (SEO), Web design and maintenance, social medial marketing, public relations and more.

40360 ■ *"Fortis College Opens on St. Luke's Medical Center Site"* **in** *The Business Journal - Serving Phoenix and the Valley of the Sun (Vol. 28, September 7, 2008)*
Pub: American City Business Journals, Inc.
Contact: Whitney Shaw, President
Ed: Angela Gonzales. **Description:** Fortis College is planning to offer classes in Phoenix, Arizona. It has made its home at the St. Luke's Medical Center. Courses to be offered by the college are also provided.

40361 ■ *"Four Ways Hospitals Can Reduce Patient Readmissions; Hospitals Have a Powerful Financial Incentive to Reduce Readmissions. Here Are the Most Effective Strategies"* **in** *Gallup Business Journal (July 2, 2014)*
Pub: Gallup Press
Released: July 2, 2014. **Description:** The Centers for Medicare and Medicaid Services (CMS) report readmissions as hospitalizations that occur within 30 days of discharge. Hospitals need to identify and implement the right strategies to reduce readmissions.

40362 ■ *"From OTC Sellers to Surgeons, Healthcare Marketers Target Women to Achieve Growth"* **in** *Marketing to Women (February 2008)*
Description: Healthcare companies are targeting women with ad campaigns, new product development and new technology in order to reach and develop brand loyalty.

40363 ■ *"Generation Y: Engaging the Invincibles"* **in** *Employee Benefit News (Vol. 25, November 1, 2011, No. 14, pp. 22)*
Pub: SourceMedia Inc.
Contact: James M. Malkin, Chief Executive Officer
Ed: Brenna Shebel, Dannel Dan. **Description:** Employers will need to engage younger workers about healthcare decisions and lifestyle improvement as they become the majority worker as boomers retire.

40364 ■ *"Genetic Counselor"* **in** *Occupational Outlook Quarterly (Vol. 55, Summer 2011, No. 2, pp. 34)*
Pub: U.S. Department of Labor Bureau of Labor Statistics
Contact: Philip L. Rones, Manager
E-mail: rones.philip@bls.gov
Ed: John Mullins. **Description:** Genetic counseling involves the practice of informing clients about genetic disorders and to help them understand and manage a disorder. There are approximately 2,400 certified genetic counselors in the U.S. and earn a median annual salary of about $63,000, according to the American Board of Genetic Counseling. The US Bureau of Labor Statistics does not have data on employment or wages for genetic counselors.

40365 ■ *"Giving Biotech Startups a Hand"* **in** *Philadelphia Business Journal (Vol. 28, January 8, 2010, No. 47, pp. 1)*
Pub: American City Business Journals Inc.
Ed: John George. **Description:** Elkins Park, Pennsylvania-based BioStrategy Partners is a virtual life sciences incubator that is seeking to improve the dull ranking of Philadelphia in the small business vitality index of life sciences. BioStrategy provides technology and business development services to startup life sciences companies and university-based research projects.

40366 ■ *Global Health Directory*
Pub: Global Health Council
Contact: Dr. Christine Sow, Executive Director
URL(s): www.globalhealth.org. Ed: Annmarie Christensen. Released: Irregular; latest edition 2003-2004. Covers: Over 500 private voluntary organizations, universities, civic groups, professional associations, and other groups involved with global health. Entries include: Organization name, address, e-mail, website, contact name, number of employees, mission, services, regions served, publications, internships available, and volunteer information. Arrangement: Classified by title of organization.

40367 ■ *"Glossary of Health Benefit Terms"*
in HRMagazine (Vol. 53, August 2008, No. 8,
pp. 78)
Pub: Society for Human Resource Management
Contact: Henry G. Jackson, President
E-mail: hjackson@shrm.org
Description: Glossary of health benefit terms is presented to help when choosing a health benefits package.

40368 ■ *"Good for Business: Houston is a*
Hot Spot for Economic Growth" in Black
Enterprise (Vol. 37, October 2006, No. 3, pp.
216)
Pub: Earl G. Graves Publishing Co. Inc.
Contact: Earl G. Graves, Jr., President
Ed: Jeanette Valentine. Description: Fast-growing sectors in the biotechnology and healthcare industries are among the driving forces of Houston's economic growth. More than 76,000 small businesses in the area employ about one in four area workers, according to the Small Business Administration. Housing and business costs are 26 and 11 percent below the national average, respectively, garnering the attention of corporate giants.

40369 ■ *"Grants Focus on Taking Research*
From Lab Into Marketplace" in Puget Sound
Business Journal (Vol. 35, April 25, 2014, No.
1, pp. 9)
Pub: American City Business Journals
Released: April 25, 2014. Description: The Life Sciences Discovery Fund awarded a total of $1.25 million in grants to promising biotechnology firms. The grants went to projects focusing research into the treatment of age-related macular degeneration of the eye, leukemia and Parkinson's Disease. The fund has narrowly avoided dissolution from a bill that would have taken money away from the fund.

40370 ■ *"Growth In West Leads To Jobs*
Here" in Business First of Buffalo (Vol. 36,
May 23, 2014, No. 36, pp. 4)
Pub: American City Business Journals, Inc.
Contact: Whitney Shaw, President
Released: May 23, 2014. Description: The growth of business in California and other western states has the potential to boost employment at HealthNow NY Inc. in Buffalo. The company plans to shift more than 36 jobs from its HealthNow Administrative Services division in Blue Bell, Pennsylvania to company headquarters in downtown Buffalo.

40371 ■ *"Halls Give Hospital Drive $11 Million*
Infusion" in The Business Journal-Serving
Metropolitan Kansas City (Vol. 26, July 18,
2008)
Ed: Rob Roberts. Description: Don Hall, chairman of Hallmark Cards Inc., and eight family members have announced that they will give $11 million to Children's Mercy Hospitals and Clinics for its $800 million expansion plan. Hall Family Foundation president Bill Hall that contributions such as that for Children's Mercy reflect the charitable interests of the foundation's board and founders. The possible impacts of the Hall's donation are analyzed.

40372 ■ *"Handling New Health Insurance*
Regulations" in Baltimore Business Journal
(Vol. 31, April 25, 2014, No. 52, pp. 25)
Pub: American City Business Journals, Inc.
Contact: Whitney Shaw, President
Released: April 25, 2014. Description: Research and consulting firm, Mercer, surveyed businesses in January 2014 to examine their employer-sponsored

health plans following enrollment in the Affordable Care Act-created exchanges. The survey found employers were taking advantage of a delay to a key regulation in the Act on offering insurance to employees who work at least 30 hours a week.

40373 ■ *"Healing Power from Medical Waste"*
in Memphis Business Journal (Vol. 33, March
30, 2012, No. 51, pp. 1)
Pub: American City Business Journal
Description: Tennessee-based BioD LLC has been using amniotic fluid in placenta from cesarian section births, which was considered as biomedical waste, to make various compounds that are used to develop stem cell-based healing products. BioD has sales of $3 million in 2011 and it expects sales of $6 million in 2012.

40374 ■ *"Health Alliance Could Sell GCAP" in*
Business Courier (Vol. 27, June 18, 2010, No.
7, pp. 1)
Pub: Business Courier
Ed: James Ritchie. Description: Health Alliance could sell the 31-doctor Greater Cincinnati Associated Physicians Group. The group has seen several members withdraw ever since the group filed a complaint asking to be released from services to Health Alliance.

40375 ■ *"Health Care Braces for Federal*
Cuts" in Boston Business Journal (Vol. 29,
August 19, 2011, No. 15, pp. 1)
Pub: American City Business Journals, Inc.
Ed: Scott Dance. Description: The healthcare industry in Baltimore is expecting negative effects from the federal debt ceiling on Medicare and Medicaid spending. Medicare funds are expected to be slashed and could impact hospitals and doctors.

40376 ■ *"Health Care Changes Loom" in*
Business Journal Milwaukee (Vol. 29, July 13,
2012, No. 42, pp. 1)
Pub: American City Business Journals, Inc.
Contact: Whitney Shaw, President
Ed: Jon Olson. Released: July 13, 2012. Description: Business owners are worried about mandated health care coverage, which will start in 2014. Boyd Miller, president of Wisconsin Thermoset Molding, Inc., believes that eight Supreme Court justices voted purely on political grounds when they decided on President Obama's health care plan.

40377 ■ *"Health Care Checkup" in Business*
Courier (Vol. 24, November 14, 2007, No. 31,
pp. 1)
Pub: American City Business Journals, Inc.
Contact: Whitney Shaw, President
Ed: James Ritchie. Description: Discusses a survey of 300 Greater Cincinnati residents about the quality of local health care and access to doctors indicates that there were improvements from five years ago. About 65 percent of those surveyed said the quality of their health care is good or excellent, a 12 percent improvement from a similar survey conducted five years ago. The other findings of the survey are also presented.

40378 ■ *"Health Care of the Future" in*
Business Journal Serving Greater Tampa Bay
(Vol. 30, November 19, 2010, No. 48, pp. 1)
Pub: Tampa Bay Business Journal
Ed: Margie Manning. Description: Information about accountable care organizations (ACO), which are integrated care systems with doctors and hospitals working closely together to handle patient care, is provided. The Patient Protection and Affordable Care Act paved the way for ACOs as Medicare demonstration projects.

40379 ■ *"Health-Care Highway" in Saint Louis*
Business Journal (Vol. 32, October 14, 2011,
No. 7, pp. 1)
Pub: Saint Louis Business Journal
Ed: Angela Mueller. Description: Around $2.6 billion will be invested in health care facilities along the Highway 64/40 corridor in St. Louis, Missouri. Mercy Hospital is planning to invest $19 million in a virtual care center. St. Elizabeth's Hospital on the other hand, will purchase 105 acres in the corridor.

40380 ■ *"Health Care Leads Sectors*
Attracting Capital" in Hispanic Business
(March 2008, pp. 14-16, 18)
Pub: Hispanic Business Inc.
Contact: Jesus Chavarria, President
Ed: Scott Williams. Description: U. S. Hispanic healthcare, media, and food were the key industries in the U.S. gaining investors in 2007.

40381 ■ *"Health Care Leads Sectors*
Attracting Capital; Health Care, Media, and
Food Were Key Industries Gaining Investors
in the 2007 U.S. Hispanic Market" in Hispanic
Business (Vol. 30, March 2008, No. 3, pp. 14)
Pub: Hispanic Business Inc.
Contact: Jesus Chavarria, President
Ed: Scott Williams. Description: Discusses the capital gains of Hispanic-owned companies and other Hispanic leaders in the investment and retail fields in the year 2007. Sectors like health care, media, food and technology saw a healthy flow of capital due to successful mergers, acquisitions and increased private equity investments.

40382 ■ *"Health care: Medicare Inc." in*
Canadian Business (Vol. 80, October 8, 2007,
No. 20, pp. 160)
Pub: Rogers Media Inc.
Contact: Tony Viner, President
Ed: Erin Pooley. Description: State of Canada's health care system is discussed. A report by the Fraser Institute in Vancouver predicts that public health spending in six of ten provinces in the country will use more than half the revenues from all sources by 2020. Experts believe competition in the health care industry will help solve the current problems in the sector.

40383 ■ *"Health Center Offers BMW Financial*
Services On-Site Medical Care" in Travel &
Leisure Close-Up (October 8, 2012)
Description: BMW Group Financial Services is providing on-site medical care for its associates and their covered dependents through the BMW Medical Plan. A nurse practitioner and medical assistant will be available at a newly created health center located at BMW's operations center. Acute/episodic services provided are listed.

40384 ■ *"Health Centers Plan Expansion:*
$3M from D.C. Expected; Uninsured a Target"
in Crain's Detroit Business (Vol. 25, June 15,
2009, No. 24, pp. 3)
Pub: Crain Communications Inc. - Detroit
Contact: Keith Crain, Chairman
Ed: Jay Greene. Description: Detroit has five federally qualified health centers that plan to receive over $3 million in federal stimulus money that will be used to expand projects that will care for uninsured patients.

40385 ■ *"Health Clinic Expansion Fuels*
Debate Over Care In Massachusetts" in
Boston Business Journal (Vol. 34, June 27,
2014, No. 21, pp. 9)
Pub: American City Business Journals, Inc.
Contact: Whitney Shaw, President
Released: June 27, 2014. Description: The announcement of expansion by several retail health clinics has fueled debate over their quality and competiveness. AFC Doctors Express, a fast-growing chain of retail health clinics, announced its plan to open two new locations in Massachusetts in 2014 and CVS's MinuteClinic announced its intention to open nine additional locations. Concerns are being raised about the cost and quality of this type of healthcare, with a medical society expressing concern that this is fragmented care, not comprehensive care.

40386 ■ *"Health Giants Throw Support*
Behind Sports Centers" in Pittsburgh
Business Times (Vol. 34, July 25, 2014, No. 1,
pp. 8)
Pub: American City Business Journals
Released: July 25, 2014. Description: Allegheny Health Network will provide health services for the $19 million Cool Springs Sports Complex being constructed in two phases in Bethel Park. Meanwhile, UPMC is developing the $70 UPMC Lemieux Sports

Complex in Cranberry Township, which will include a center for sports medicine together with two ice rinks that will be used as a practice facility for the Pittsburgh Penguins as well as by high school teams and figure skaters.

40387 ■ Health Groups in Washington: A Directory (District of Columbia)
Pub: National Health Council
Contact: Myrl Weinberg, Chief Executive Officer
URL(s): www.nationalhealthcouncil.org/pages/page-content.php?pageid=82. Released: Biennial; August of odd years; Latest edition 2009. Price: $40, Members; $60, Nonmembers. Covers: Over 900 professional, voluntary, consumer, insurance, union, business, and academic organizations with some impact on the development of federal health policies. Entries include: Name of organization, address, phone, e-mail address, website address, names of Washington representatives. Arrangement: Alphabetical. Indexes: Subject index; personnel index.

40388 ■ "Health IT Regulations Generate Static Among Providers" in Philadelphia Business Journal (Vol. 28, January 29, 2010, No. 50, pp. 1)
Pub: American City Business Journals Inc.
Ed: John George. Description: US Centers for Medicaid and Medicare Services and the Office of the National Coordinator for Health Information Technology have proposed rules regarding the meaningful use of electronic health records. The rules must be complied with by hospitals and physicians to qualify for federal stimulus funds.

40389 ■ "Health Job Shift Looms" in Boston Business Journal (Vol. 31, June 3, 2011, No. 19, pp. 3)
Pub: Boston Business Journal
Ed: Julie M. Donnelly. Description: Pending health care payment reform in Massachusetts is seen to adversely impact hospital staff. Hospitals are also seen to serve more patients once the bill is approved.

40390 ■ "Health Nuts and Bolts" in Entrepreneur (Vol. 36, April 2008, No. 4, pp. 24)
Pub: Entrepreneur Press
Contact: Perlman Neil, President
Ed: Jacquelyn Lynn. Description: Encouraging employees to develop good eating habits can promote productivity at work. Ways on how to improve employee eating habits include employers setting a good example themselves and offering employees healthy options. Other details about the topic are discussed.

40391 ■ "Health Providers Throw Lifeline to Clinics" in Sacramento Business Journal (Vol. 25, July 30, 2008, No. 21, pp. 1)
Pub: American City Business Journals, Inc.
Contact: Whitney Shaw, President
Ed: Kathy Robertson. Description: Health Net of California Inc., Catholic Healthcare West and Sutter Health are each providing up to $5 million in no-interest and low-interest loans to clinics in California, while the Sisters of Mercy of the Americas Burlingame Regional Community is offering $300,000. Other details on the short term loans are discussed.

40392 ■ "Health Reform Could Expand HSA-Based Plans" in Workforce Management (Vol. 88, December 14, 2009, No. 13, pp. 6)
Ed: Jeremy Smerd. Description: HSA-qualified plans are the cheapest insurance plans on the market as they have a higher deductible but cost less upfront. If health care reform passes, HSA-qualified plans should benefit greatly.

40393 ■ "Health Reform How-To" in Business Courier (Vol. 26, December 11, 2009, No. 33, pp. 1)
Ed: James Ritchie. Description: Greater Cincinnati health care leaders shared views about the health care reform bill. Respondents included the Cincinnati Visiting Nurse's Wallen Falberg, healthcare consultant Hirsch Cohen, Greater Cincinnati Health Council's Coleen O'Toole, Employer Health Care Alliance's

Sharron DiMario, Legal Aid Society of Greater Cincinnati's Col Owens, Christ Hospital's Susan Croushore, and Humana of Ohio's Tim Cappel.

40394 ■ "The 'Health' of a Senior's Retirement Plan" in Senior Market Advisor (Vol. 13, October 2012, No. 10, pp. 48)
Description: Seniors are the fastest growing demographic, accounting for 16 percent of the population. Medicare changes taking place with the implementation of Obamacare make it essential for Americans 62 years of age and older to understand how to navigate the system. Medicare recipients will experience a reduction of access to doctors, hospitals, diagnostic facilities and other medical centers.

40395 ■ "Healthcare Facilities Increasingly Embracing Dynamic Glass to Benefit Patients" in Ecology, Environment & Conservation Business (May 24, 2014)
Pub: NewsRX
Contact: Susan E. Hasty, Publisher
Released: May 24, 2014. Description: According to research, optimizing natural daylight and outdoor views in healthcare helps to improve outcomes and shorter recovery times for patients. Therefore, a growing number of healthcare facilities are incorporating SageGlass(R) dynamic glass, a product of Saint-Gobain, into their new construction and remodeling/renovation designs.

40396 ■ "HealthTronics Eager to Buy" in Austin Business JournalInc. (Vol. 28, September 12, 2008, No. 26, pp. 1)
Pub: American City Business Journals
Ed: Laura Hipp. Description: HealthTronics Inc., an Austin, Texas urology equipment company has repeated its offer to buy Endocare Inc., an Irvine, California tumor technology firm for $26.9 million. The proposal has been revised to allow Endocare shareholders to choose between HealthTronics cash or shares. Endocare has not commented on the offer.

40397 ■ "Healthy Dose of New Vitality" in Business Courier (Vol. 24, February 28, 2008, No. 47, pp. 1)
Pub: American City Business Journals, Inc.
Contact: Whitney Shaw, President
Ed: Dan Monk. Description: Healthy Advice plans to become a leading consumer brand and expand to pharmacies and hospitals. The growth opportunities for healthy Advice are discussed.

40398 ■ "Healthy Start for Medical Kiosks; Lions Kick in $20K" in Crain's Detroit Business" (Vol. 28, June 11, 2012, No. 24, pp. 18)
Pub: Crain Communications Inc.
Contact: Rance E. Crain, President
Released: June 11, 2012. Description: Detroit Lions Charities has given Henry Ford Health System's school-based and community health program money to purchase nine interactive health kiosks. These kiosks will be provided by Medical Imagineering LLC, a spinoff of Henry Ford's Innovation Institute and installed in elementary and middle schools in Detroit.

40399 ■ "Hearing Damage Leads to Settlement" in Register-Guard (August 13, 2011)
Pub: Register-Guard
Ed: Karen McCowan. Description: Cynergy Pest Control lost a court battle when a rural Cottage Grove man was granted a $37,000 settlement after his hearing was damaged by the pest control companies method to eradicate gophers, using blasts in his neighbor's yard.

40400 ■ "The Heart of Health Village" in Orlando Business Journal (Vol. 30, May 16, 2014, No. 47, pp. 4)
Pub: American City Business Journals
Released: May 16, 2014. Description: The economic impact of Florida Hospital's planned Health Village in downtown Orlando is explored. The 172-acre development aims to bring together business people, scientists for research, and early and mid-stage companies to combine co-working activities in its Medical Innovation Laboratory.

40401 ■ "Heart Hospitals Analyzed" in Philadelphia Business Journal (Vol. 30, September 2, 2011, No. 29, pp. 1)
Pub: American City Business Journals Inc.
Ed: John George. Description: Centers for Medicare and Medicaid Services (CMS) released updated data on mortality rates for heart attack patients as hospitals in Pennsylvania. Doylestown Hospital posted the lowest mortality rates with 10.9 percent, tying the fourth best in the entire nation. Other details on the CMS data are presented.

40402 ■ "Heart Test No Boom for BG Medical" in Boston Business Journal (Vol. 31, June 17, 2011, No. 21, pp. 1)
Pub: Boston Business Journal
Ed: Julie M. Donnelly. Description: The Galectin-3 test failed to boost stock prices of its manufacturer, BG Medicine, which has fallen to $6.06/share. The company hopes that its revenue will be boosted by widespread adoption of an automated and faster version of the test, which diagnoses for heart failure.

40403 ■ "Help Wanted: 100 Hospital IT Workers" in Business Courier (Vol. 27, October 8, 2010, No. 23, pp. 1)
Pub: Business Courier
Ed: James Ritchie. Description: Hospitals in the Greater Cincinnati area are expected to hire more than 100 information technology (IT) workers to help digitize medical records. Financial incentives from the health care reform bill encouraged investments in electronic medical record systems, increasing the demand for IT workers that would help make information exchange across the healthcare system easier.

40404 ■ "Henry Ford Health Leases Lab Space at TechTown" in Crain's Detroit Business (Vol. 24, April 1, 2008, No. 13, pp. 5)
Pub: Crain Communications Inc.
Contact: Rance E. Crain, President
Ed: Tom Henderson. Description: Henry Ford Health System has signed a seven-year lease at TechTown, the high-tech incubator and research park affiliated with Wayne State University, to take over 14,000 square feet of space for four research groups and laboratories. Construction has already begun and Henry Ford officials hope to take occupancy as early as June 1.

40405 ■ "HER's: the Future is Free" in Benzinga.com (October 29, 2011)
Pub: Benzinga.com
Contact: Kyle Bazzy, President
Ed: Benzinga Staff. Description: In order to create and maintain electronic health records that connects every physician and hospital it is essential to create a reliable, easy-to-use, certified Web-based ambulatory ERH using an ad-supported model. eBay seems to be the company showing the most potential for improving services to physicians and consumers, but requires sellers to pay fees based upon sales price.

40406 ■ "His Banking Industry Software Never Caught On, so Bill Randle is Now Targeting the Health Care Market" in Inc. (March 2008)
Pub: Mansueto Ventures L.L.C.
Contact: John Koten, Chief Executive Officer
Ed: Alex Salkever. Description: Profile of Bill Randle, bank executive turned entrepreneur; Randle tells how he changed his focus for his company from banking software to healthcare software. The firm employs ten people who secure online billing and recordkeeping systems for hospitals and insurers. Randle discusses critical decisions that will impact his firm in the coming year. Three experts offer advice.

40407 ■ "Home Instead Senior Care Debuts Free Online Alzheimer's Training Program for Family Caregivers" in Internet Wire (May 15, 2012)
Released: May 15, 2012. Description: Home Instead Senior Care is launching an online Alzheimer's training program called Alzheimer's CARE. The free program is for caregivers and families of person's with this disease. The program helps encourage mental engagement to help relatives remain safely at home and in familiar surroundings.

40408 ■ *"Home Instead Senior Care Debuts Senior Fraud Awareness Campaign" in Entertainment Close-Up (August 2, 2012)*
Description: Home Instead Senior Care has created a program to help older Americans and their families protect themselves from unethical scammers targeting seniors. Home Instead provides in-home companion care services and calls the program Protect Seniors from Fraud. Details of the program and the available protection kit are described.

40409 ■ *"Home Instead Senior Care Introduces Post-Discharge Care Initiative; Aims to Reduce Hospital Readmissions Among Seniors" in Benzinga.com (September 18, 2012)*
Pub: Benzinga.com
Contact: Kyle Bazzy, President
Description: Home Instead Senior Care(R) launched its new, much-needed health program that provides care and support services, mostly for seniors, after being discharged from the hospital. The service is aimed at reducing the number of unnecessary hospital readmissions.

40410 ■ *"Home Instead Senior Care of Seacoast and Southern New Hampshire" inNew Hampshire Business Review (Vol. 34, April 6, 2012, No. 7, pp. 45)*
Pub: Business Publications Corp.
Contact: Connie Wimer, President
Released: April 6, 2012. **Description:** Portsmouth, New Hampshire-based Home Instead Senior Care of Seacoast and Southern New Hampshire launched a specialized training program for professional and family caregivers designed to help them improve the quality of life for those living with dementia and the families who support them.

40411 ■ *"Hopkins, UMd Worry Reduced NIH Budget Will Impact Research" in Boston Business Journal (Vol. 29, August 19, 2011, No. 15, pp. 1)*
Pub: American City Business Journals, Inc.
Ed: Scott Dance. **Description:** The budget for the National Institutes of Health (NIH) is slated to be cut by at least 7.9 percent to $2.5 billion in 2013. This will have a big negative effect on medical and biotech research in Maryland, especially Johns Hopkins University and University of Maryland, Baltimore which could face stiffer completion for grants from the NIH.

40412 ■ *"Hospital Communication Goes Mobile" in Providence Business News (Vol. 29, July 7, 2014, No. 14, pp. 12)*
Pub: American City Business Journals
Released: July 7, 2014. **Description:** Software company, Care Thread, has designed a mobile health records application that allows providers to share patient e-medical records over a secure network. Care Thread signed a contract for the system with Eastern Connecticut Health Network and Boston's Brigham and Women's Hospital as well as a deal with health care management firm Beacon Partners Inc. to sell and implement the app across the U.S.

40413 ■ *"Hospital Errors Made Public" in Sacramento Business Journal (Vol. 25, August 10, 2008, No. 23, pp. 1)*
Pub: American City Business Journals, Inc.
Contact: Whitney Shaw, President
Ed: Kathy Robertson. **Description:** California hospitals reported 1,224 serious and preventable errors for the fiscal year ended June 30, 2008. Consumer groups have expressed concerns at the number and level of violations. Views and information on the errors, as well as a table detailing the number of hospital errors classified by error type, are presented.

40414 ■ *"Hospital Fighting for Its Life" in Crain's Chicago Business (April 28, 2008)*
Pub: Crain Communications Inc.
Contact: Todd Johnson, Publisher
Ed: Mike Colias. **Description:** Chicago's Catholic health chain was looking to sell the money-losing hospital St. Anthony Hospital on the West Side but with the financial picture improving and no merger offers in the works the investment bank hired to shop

the hospital is hoping to operate the 111-year-old facility as an independent entity. St. Anthony serves as a 'safety net' for the region since an increasing number of its patients are uninsured or on public aid, which pays far less than commercial insurers.

40415 ■ *"Hospital Pegged for Lakeway" in Austin Business JournalInc. (Vol. 28, August 7, 2008, No. 21, pp. A1)*
Pub: American City Business Journals
Ed: Kate Harrington. **Description:** Views and information on the development of the Lakeway Regional Medical Center in Texas, are presented. The hospital, which is expected to cost more than $250 million, will include 244,000 square feet of medical space. Shops, offices, hike-and-bike trails are also planned around hospital.

40416 ■ *"Hospital Revenue Healthier in 2009" in Orlando Business Journal (Vol. 26, February 5, 2010, No. 36, pp. 1)*
Pub: American City Business Journals
Ed: Melanie Stawicki Azam. **Description:** Orlando Health, Health Central and Adventist Health System are Florida-based hospital systems that generated the most profits in 2009. Orlando Health had the highest profit in 2009 at $73.3 million, contrary to about $31 million in losses in 2008. The increased profits are attributed to stock market recovery, cost-cutting initiatives, and rising patient volumes.

40417 ■ *"Hospital Tax Could Be a Separate Bill" in Business Journal-Milwaukee (Vol. 25, October 26, 2007, No. 4, pp. A1)*
Pub: American City Business Journals
Ed: Elizabeth Sanders. **Description:** Hospital officials are working on reintroducing a hospital tax proposal that would increase Medicaid reimbursement, thereby generating millions of dollars of revenue for the Milwaukee-area hospitals. The bill sponsored by Governor Jim Doyle was supported by the Wisconsin Hospital Association. Details of the proposed hospital tax are presented.

40418 ■ *"Hospitals Say Medicaid Expansion is Critical" in Dallas Business Journal (Vol. 35, August 3, 2012, No. 47, pp. 1)*
Pub: American City Business Journal
Ed: Bill Hethcock, Matt Joyce. **Description:** Governor Rick Perry's rejection of the Texas expansion of Medicaid is met with disapproval by health organizations such as the Methodist Health System. The federal government has extended $70 billion in financing to help more Texans become eligible for primary health care. Expansion supporters argue that Medicaid is critical in lowering insurance osts for those who need it.

40419 ■ *"Hospitals See Major Shift To Outpatient Care" in The Business Journal-Milwaukee (Vol. 25, September 12, 2008, No. 51, pp. A1)*
Pub: American City Business Journals, Inc.
Contact: Whitney Shaw, President
Ed: Corrinne Hess. **Description:** Statistics show that the revenue of Wisconsin hospitals from outpatient medical care is about to surpass revenue from hospital patients who stay overnight. This revenue increase is attributed to new technology and less-invasive surgery. Trends show that the shift toward outpatient care actually started in the late 1980s and early 1990s.

40420 ■ *"Hospitals Singing OB Blues" in Philadelphia Business Journal (Vol. 31, April 6, 2012, No. 8, pp. 1)*
Pub: American City Business Journal
Description: Pennsylvania hospitals are seen to receive lower payments for normal born births involving women covered by medical assistance. The Pennsylvania Department of Welfare has proposed to eliminate separate payments for infant care for normal deliveries.

40421 ■ *"Hospitals Try to Buy Smarter" in Crain's Detroit Business (Vol. 25, June 1,*

2009, No. 22, pp. M025)
Pub: Crain Communications Inc. - Detroit
Contact: Keith Crain, Chairman
Ed: Jay Greene. **Description:** Hospitals in southeast Michigan are using bulk discount purchasing of medical and non-medical supplies through group purchasing organizations in order to cut costs.

40422 ■ *"Hospitals Vying to Buy Physician Associates LLC" in Orlando Business Journal (Vol. 29, August 31, 2012, No. 11, pp. 1)*
Pub: American City Business Journal
Description: Hospitals are battling it out on who gets to buy Physician Associates LLC, the largest multi-specialty practice in Central Florida. The most likely candidates to purchase the practice are Orlando Health and Florida Hospital. The deal could be worth $20 million to $60 million and it could also hike health care costs since Physician Asociates serves 19 percent of Central Florida's uninsured population.

40423 ■ *"Houston Doctors Buy In to Medical Timeshares" in Houston Business Journal (Vol. 40, December 11, 2009, No. 31, pp. 1)*
Pub: American City Business Journals
Ed: Mary Ann Azevedo. **Description:** Memorial Hermann Hospital System has leased to doctors three examination rooms and medical office space in the Memorial Hermann Medical Plaza in line with its new timeshare concept. The concept was designed to bring primary care physicians to its Texas Medical Center campus.

40424 ■ *"How Bloated Is Social Spending In Europe?" in Canadian Business (Vol. 85, August 13, 2012, No. 13, pp. 66)*
Pub: George Media Inc.
Ed: James Cowan. **Released:** August 13, 2012. **Description:** A study conducted by the World Bank found that social spending in Europe is higher than the rest of the world combined. A chart is presented which illustrates government spending on social protection in European countries and in other countries.

40425 ■ *"How to Conduct a Functional Magnetic Resonance (fMRI) Study in Social Science Research" in MIS Quarterly (Vol. 36, September 2012, No. 3, pp. 811)*
Pub: MIS Research Center, Carlson School of Management
Ed: Angelika Dimoka. **Price:** $10. **Description:** A set of guidelines for conducting functional magnetic resonance imaging studies in social sciences and information systems research is provided.

40426 ■ *"How Healthcare Managers Can Improve Outcomes and Patient Care; They Can Start With These Five Steps for Turning their Organization's Employee Engagement Results Into Clinical Improvements" in Gallup Business Journal (August 7, 2014)*
Pub: Gallup Press
Released: August 7, 2014. **Description:** Health care managers can improve outcomes and patient care by following the five steps outlined in this article.

40427 ■ *"How Healthcare Organizations Can Improve This Year; Three Strategies for 2014 That Will Help Leaders Achieve Goals Related to Patient Satisfaction Employee Onboarding Time, and Medical Supply Availability, Among Others' in Gallup Business Journal (February 13, 2014)*
Pub: Gallup Press
Released: February 13, 2014. **Description:** Three strategies to enable healthcare organizations to increase their management's success in achieving goals and visions related to patient satisfaction, employee onboarding time, and medical supply availability are outlined to help improve 2014 performance.

40428 ■ *How to Start a Home-Based Senior Care Business*
Pub: Globe Pequot Press Inc.
Contact: Robert Irwin, Manager
E-mail: robert.irwin@globepequot.com
Ed: James L. Ferry. **Released:** January 06, 2010. **Price:** $18.95, paperback. **Description:** Information is provided to start a home-based senior care business. **Availability:** Print.

40429 ■ *"How To Make a Deal in Three Days"* *in San Antonio Business Journal (Vol. 28, June 20, 2014, No. 19, pp. 11)*
Pub: American City Business Journals
Released: June 20, 2014. **Description:** Nexus Medical Consulting, provider of medical quality of care reviews to healthcare companies and law firms, signed a long-term lease with R.L. Worth & Associates for 35,000-square-feet of space within the Heritage Business Center in New Braunfels, Texas. Nexus president, Ed Bolton, comments on the ease and speed at which the lease was done.

40430 ■ *"How To Spark Up a Medical Marijuana Firm in Florida - and Not Get Burned in the Process" in Orlando Business Journal (Vol. 30, March 21, 2014, No. 39, pp. 6)*
Pub: American City Business Journals
Released: March 21, 2014. **Description:** Colorado business owners and experts offer tips on starting a medical marijuana business in Florida. Andy Williams recalls that he was filled with fear he would wake up in Federal prison and not see his family again when he started Medicine Man. Jerald Bovine of GreenZip-p.com advises those interested in entering the medical marijuana field to know the details of regulation of facilities and labs.

40431 ■ *"Humana Seeks Higher Stake in Memphis Market" in Memphis Business Journal (Vol. 33, February 17, 2012, No. 45, pp. 1)*
Pub: American City Business Journal
Ed: Christopher Sheffield. **Description:** Humana of Tennessee has been hoping to get a bigger share of the West Tennessee insurance market through its new three-year contract with Baptist Memorial Health Care Corporation. Louisville, Kentucky-based Humana Inc. has a business relationship with Baptist that stretches back more than two decades.

40432 ■ *"Humana: Take Pay Cut or Get Out" in Business Courier (Vol. 24, January 31, 2008, No. 43, pp. 1)*
Pub: American City Business Journals, Inc.
Contact: Whitney Shaw, President
Ed: James Ritchie. **Description:** Insurer Humana Inc. is removing some surgery centers from its network for refusing to welcome the new payment system. Evendale Surgery Center and the Surgery Center of Cincinnati will be removed from the network because they resist the newly imposed lower rates. Speculations over Humana's decision are discussed.

40433 ■ *"Hunhu Healthcare Gets Some Mayo Help" in Business Journal (Vol. 32, August 29, 2014, No. 14, pp. 4)*
Pub: American City Business Journals
Released: August 29, 2014. **Description:** Hunhu Healthcare Inc. has signed a licensing agreement with Mayo Clinic to develop mobile and Web applications that will enable patients to communicate with the company's network using social networking tools. The firm is expected to charge a monthly fee for the service.

40434 ■ *"IBC Reverses Member Slide" in Philadelphia Business Journal (Vol. 30, September 23, 2011, No. 32, pp. 1)*
Pub: American City Business Journals Inc.
Ed: John George. **Description:** Health insurer Independence Blue Cross (IBC) added more than 40,000 members across all product lines since the start of 2011. It has 2.2 million members in Pennsylvania's Philadelphia region and 3.1 million members across the U.S. Services and other growth-related plans of IBC are covered.

40435 ■ *"Impressive Numbers: Companies Experience Substantial Increases in Dollars, Employment" in Hispanic Business (July-August 2007)*
Pub: Hispanic Business Inc.
Contact: Jesus Chavarria, President
Ed: Derek Reveron. **Description:** Profiles of five fastest growing Hispanic companies reporting increases in revenue and employment include Brightstar, distributor of wireless products; Greenway Ford Inc.,

a car dealership; Fred Loya Insurance, auto insurance carrier; and Group O, packaging company; and Diverse Staffing, Inc., an employment and staffing firm.

40436 ■ *"Improving Women's Health" in Entrepreneur (May 2014)*
Pub: Entrepreneur Media Inc.
Released: May 2014. **Description:** Surbhi Sarna, a graduate of molecular and cellular biology at the University of California, Berkeley, founded nVision Medical with $500,000 seed funding in 2012. The medial device company closed a $4.5 million investment round led by Catalyst Health Ventures in April 2013. The company is developing two catheter-based diagnostic tools, one for the early detection of ovarian cancer and the other for use by gynecologists to detect blockage of fallopian tubes. The company was awarded with office and laboratory space at the Fogarty Institute for Innovation in January 2014.

40437 ■ *"IMRA's Ultrafast Lasers Bring Precision, profits; Ann Arbor Company Eyes Expansion" in Crain's Detroit Business (March 10, 2008)*
Pub: Crain Communications Inc.
Contact: Rance E. Crain, President
Ed: Tom Henderson. **Description:** IMRA America Inc. plans to expand its headquarters and has applied for permits to build a fourth building that will house research and development facilities and allow the company more room for manufacturing; the company plans to add about 20 more employees that would include research scientists, manufacturing and assembly workers, engineers and salespeople. The growth is due mainly to a new technology of ultrafast fiber lasers that reduce side effects for those getting eye surgeries and help manufacturers of computer chips to reduce their size and cost.

40438 ■ *"In Chesterfield: Paletta's Operations Raise Competitors' Blood Pressure" in St. Louis Business Journal (Vol. 33, August 17, 2012, No. 52, pp. 1)*
Pub: American City Business Journal
Description: The proposed relocation of Doctor George Paletta Jr.'s Orthopedic Center of Saint Louis to a new 62,000-square-foot facility was met with opposition by local hospital officials and the Missouri Hospital Association. Officials state the facility must be licensed as a hospital in order to provide overnight post-operative care as planned by Paletta.

40439 ■ *"In It For the Long Run" in Business Journal-Serving Phoenix & the Valley of the Sun (Vol. 30, August 20, 2010, No. 50, pp. 1)*
Pub: Phoenix Business Journal
Ed: Angela Gonzales. **Description:** Cancer survivor Helene Neville has finished a record-breaking 2,520-mile run in 93 days and then celebrated her 50th birthday despite being diagnosed with Hodgkins' lymphoma in 1991. Neveille, who is also a Phoenix area registered nurse, made stops along the way to promote her book, 'Nurses in Shape'. Neville also discusses how she fought her cancer through running.

40440 ■ *"In the Raw: Karyn Calabrese Brings Healthy Dining to a New Sophisticated Level" in Black Enterprise (Vol. 41, September 2010)*
Pub: Earl G. Graves Publishing Co. Inc.
Contact: Earl G. Graves, Jr., President
Ed: Sonia Alleyne. **Description:** Profile of Karyn Calabrese whose businesses are based in Chicago, Illinois. Calabrese has launched a complete line of products (vitamins and beauty items), services (spa, chiropractic, and acupuncture treatments), and restaurants to bring health dining and lifestyles to a better level.

40441 ■ *"Infusion Device Gets $1.47 Million Army Grant" in Memphis Business Journal (Vol. 33, January 20, 2012, No. 41, pp. 1)*
Pub: American City Business Journal
Ed: Michael Sheffield. **Description:** Infusense has procured a $1.47 million grant from the US Army to develop an automated delivery system for the anesthesia Propofol. The drug is used in more than

70 million surgeries and procedures in the country. The medical device would allow for the administration of the anesthesia to wounded soldiers by medics in the field.

40442 ■ *"Initiative Offers Many Paths Down Wellness Road" in Pittsburgh Business Times (Vol. 33, June 6, 2014, No. 47, pp. 12)*
Pub: American City Business Journals
Released: June 6, 2014. **Description:** Oberg Industries, Category Winner in the 500 to 1,999 employee group in Healthiest Employers of Western Pennsylvania 2014, offers several awareness programs to help employees adopt a healthier lifestyle. Initiatives to increase employee participation in wellness programs include the National Walk at Lunch Day and providing free blood work services.

40443 ■ *"Injury and Illness Data" in Montly Labor Review (Vol. 133, September 2010, No. 9, pp. 147)*
Pub: U.S. Department of Labor Bureau of Labor Statistics
Contact: Philip L. Rones, Manager
E-mail: rones.philip@bls.gov
Description: Occupational injury and illness rates by industry in the U.S. are presented.

40444 ■ *"Innovative Trauma Care Sets Up U.S. HQ in San Antonio" in San Antonio Business Journal (Vol. 26, August 31, 2012, No. 31, pp. 1)*
Pub: American City Business Journal
Description: Canadian biotech firm Innovative Trauma Care (ITC) has selected San Antonio, Texas as the location of its new US headquarters. The selection could boost the reputation of San Antonio region as a hub for medical technology and trauma-related expertise.

40445 ■ *"Insurers Warn Brokers" in Sacramento Business Journal (Vol. 25, August 24, 2008, No. 25, pp. 1)*
Pub: American City Business Journals, Inc.
Contact: Whitney Shaw, President
Ed: Kathy Robertson. **Description:** Sacramento, California-based health plans have warned insurance brokers not to combine two different kinds of insurance products or they will be stricken from the sales network. The health plans also asked employers to promise not to combine plans with self-insurance. Such schemes are seen to destroy lower-premium health products.

40446 ■ *"Internet Translation Service Helps Burmese" in News-Sentinel (May 10, 2011)*
Pub: New-Sentinel
Ed: Ellie Bogue. **Description:** Catherine Kasper Place, Parkview Health Community Outreach, Allen County-Fort Wayne Department of Health and Advantage Health have partnered to help the Burmese Community in the area by providing an online service that links doctors' offices with translators in order to provide better healthcare.

40447 ■ *"Inventive Doctor New Venture Partner" in Houston Business Journal (Vol. 40, January 29, 2010, No. 38, pp. A2)*
Pub: American City Business Journals
Ed: Ford Gunter. **Description:** Dr. Billy Cohn, a surgeon from Houston, Texas has been named as venture partner for venture firm Sante Ventures LLC of Austin, Texas. Cohn will be responsible for seeing marketable developing technologies in the medical industry. The motivation for Cohn's naming as venture partner is his development of a minimally invasive therapy for end-stage renal disease.

40448 ■ *"Investigation Hints at Workers' Comp Trouble" in Sacramento Business Journal (Vol. 25, July 4, 2008, No. 18, pp. 1)*
Pub: American City Business Journals, Inc.
Contact: Whitney Shaw, President
Ed: Kelly Johnson. **Description:** In 500 California firms, a survey of worker compensation revealed that 38 percent of the companies had problems with required coverage. Government investigators are bothered that 107 companies did not respond to the

official inquiry. Other views and information on the survey and on the expected economic implications of the findings are presented.

40449 ■ *"Investing In Employee Health, Wellness"* in *South Florida Business Journal (Vol. 34, June 6, 2014, No. 46, pp. 28)*
Pub: American City Business Journals
Released: June 6, 2014. **Description:** Companies are investing in employee wellness programs as an employee benefit because health issues within the organization can lead to absenteeism and unproductive employees. The results of a study indicate that losses from absenteeism across all professions could reach $84 billion.

40450 ■ *"Investment In Israel Is Investment in the Future of Georgia"* in *Atlanta Business Chronicle (May 30, 2014, pp. 22A)*
Pub: American City Business Journals, Inc.
Contact: Whitney Shaw, President
Released: May 30, 2014. **Description:** Georgia Governor Nathan Deal will travel to Israel to lead an economic and trade mission and consolidate Georgia's trade ties with Israel. Israel and the State of Georgia are already collaborating in the fields of health information technology, agrotechnology, homeland security, defense, aerospace and cybersecurity, and microelectronics and nanotechnology. The proposed visit by the Governor will build on this particular partnership from which both parties will benefit.

40451 ■ *"Is 5th Time the Charm? Discover Labs Awaits FDA Ruling"* in *Philadelphia Business Journal (Vol. 31, March 2, 2012, No. 3, pp. 1)*
Pub: American City Business Journal
Description: The US Food and Drug Administration is set to approve Discovery Laboratories' drug Surfaxin for use in the prevention of respiratory distress syndromes in premature newborns. The new drug is a synthetic surfactant designed to mimic the function of natural human surfactants. It is a lower-cost alternative to animal-derived surfactant products.

40452 ■ *"Is Hawaii Ready for Universal Health Care?"* in *Hawaii Business (Vol. 53, February 2008, No. 8, pp. 26)*
Pub: PacificBasin Communications
Description: Representative Lyn Finnegan does not believe that a universal health is good for Hawaii as health insurance for everyone will be difficult to achieve. Representative John M. Mizuno says that House Bill 1008 introduced in the state was a landmark for Hawaii as it will provide the people with health care insurance. Other details about their opinion on the topic are presented.

40453 ■ *"Is Your Employees' BMI Your Business?"* in *Canadian Business (Vol. 83, September 14, 2010, No. 15, pp. 98)*
Pub: Rogers Media Inc.
Contact: Tony Viner, President
Ed: Jacqueline Nelson. **Description:** Canada's Public Health Agency's research shows that there is a solid business case for companies to promote active living to their employees. However, employers must toe the line between being helpful and being invasive. Insights into the issues faces by companies when introducing health programs are discussed.

40454 ■ *It's Your Life!: A Gynecologist's Guide for Taking Control of It (Gynecology)*
Pub: Blue Dolphin Publishing Inc.
Contact: Paul M. Clemens, President
URL(s): www.bluedolphinpublishing.com/itsyour.htm.
Price: $16.95, Individuals Paperback; $24.95, Individuals Cloth. **Publication includes:** Resources covering health care for women. **Entries include:** Publication name, address. Principal content of publication is articles and suggestions on health care and social and emotional issues for women. **Indexes:** Yes.

40455 ■ *"I've Always Been an Entrepreneur"* in *South Florida Business Journal (Vol. 34, June 13, 2014, No. 47, pp. 11)*
Pub: American City Business Journals
Released: June 13, 2014. **Description:** Modernizing Medicine CEO, Daniel Cane, says he started doing business at age six when he opened a lemonade

stand. His firm helps physicians increase efficiencies in their practices while improving both business and treatment outcomes. He surrounds himself with talented people, which is what he likes most about his job. Cane added that dividing time between work and family is difficult for entrepreneurs.

40456 ■ *"Kaiser Permanente's Innovation on the Front Lines"* in *Harvard Business Review (Vol. 88, September 2010, No. 9, pp. 92)*
Pub: Harvard Business School Publishing
Ed: Lew McCreary. **Description:** Kaiser Permanente's human-centered model for organizational effectiveness emphasizes the roles of patients and providers as collaborators driving quality improvement and innovation.

40457 ■ *"Kaiser Says Hospital Room Service Saves Money"* in *Pacific Business News (Vol. 26, August 22, 2014, No. 26, pp. 10)*
Pub: American City Business Journals
Released: August 22, 2014. **Description:** Kaiser Permanente Hawaii's Moanalua Medical Center reveals that it has save nearly $1.5 million annually in food costs since it introduced in-house meal preparation and room service for patients two years ago. The hospital, which previous outsourced meal preparation to Aramark, finds that the new policy avoids waste by allowing patients to choose their own food as well as their mealtime.

40458 ■ *"Kari Leong"* in *Hawaii Business (Vol. 53, October 2007, No. 4, pp. 39)*
Pub: PacificBasin Communications
Ed: Cathy S. Cruz-George. **Description:** Greater Good Inc. president Kari Leong is the number 1 fittest female executive in Hawaii for 2007. Leong exercises at the gym and at her home, and carries her two children for strength training. The physical activities she had undergone during her college life at the Gonzaga University are discussed.

40459 ■ *"KCET Takes On Elder-Care With Robust Your Turn To Care Website"* in *PR Newswire (July 31, 2012)*
Pub: PR Newswire Association L.L.C.
Contact: David B. Armon, President
Description: Your Turn To Care is a new Website created by KCET, the nation's largest independent public television station. The network, serving southern and central California, offers the Website to serve as a resource for families, caregivers and seniors in te US facing the challenges of caring for an ailing or aging loved one. The Website also covers issues involved in aging.

40460 ■ *"The Keeper of Records"* in *Black Enterprise (Vol. 41, December 2010, No. 5, pp. 54)*
Pub: Earl G. Graves Publishing Co. Inc.
Contact: Earl G. Graves, Jr., President
Ed: Denise A. Campbell. **Description:** Medical billing and coding, submission of claims to health insurance companies and Medicare or Medicaid for payment is one of the fastest growing disciplines in healthcare.

40461 ■ *"Kids in Crisis"* in *Employee Benefit News (Vol. 25, November 1, 2011, No. 14, pp. 26)*
Pub: SourceMedia Inc.
Contact: James M. Malkin, Chief Executive Officer
Ed: Lisa V. Gillespie. **Description:** Employers and vendor are taking more aggressive steps to help battle childhood obesity.

40462 ■ *"King of the Crib: How Good Samaritan Became Ohio's Baby HQ"* in *Business Courier (Vol. 27, June 18, 2010, No. 7, pp. 1)*
Pub: Business Courier
Ed: James Ritchie. **Description:** Cincinnati's Good Samaritan hospital had 6,875 live births in 2009, which is more than any other hospital in Ohio. They specialize in the highest-risk pregnancies and deliveries and other hospitals are trying to grab Good Samaritan's share in this niche.

40463 ■ *"Know Your Bones: Take Your Bone Health Seriously"* in *Women In Business (Vol. 62, June 2010, No. 2, pp. 40)*
Pub: American Business Women's Association
Contact: Lorie Burch, President
Description: Bone health for women with postmenopausal osteoporosis is encouraged to help create an appropriate health plan that includes exercise, diet and medication. Questions to consider when discussing possible plans with health care providers are presented.

40464 ■ *"A Late Night Run: After-Hours Pediatric Practice Fills Void for Affordable Urgent Care"* in *Black Enterprise (February 2008)*
Pub: Earl G. Graves Publishing Co. Inc.
Contact: Earl G. Graves, Jr., President
Ed: Erinn R. Johnson. **Description:** Practicing pediatricians in Texas founded the Night Light After Hours Pediatrics facility in order to provide urgent care to children without the trauma witnessed in emergency rooms at hospitals.

40465 ■ *"Lawmakers, Execs Launch Effort to Save Rural Hospitals"* in *Atlanta Business Chronicle (June 13, 2014, pp. 7A)*
Pub: American City Business Journals, Inc.
Contact: Whitney Shaw, President
Released: June 13, 2014. **Description:** Governor Nathan Deal has appointed a committee of Georgia lawmakers and healthcare executives to launch an effort to save the state's financially burdened rural hospitals. In addition, he plans to allow rural hospitals that have closed or are on the verge of closing, to scale back their operations, under a new rule approved by the Georgia Board of Community Health.

40466 ■ *"Lawrence: Larger than Life Sciences"* in *Business Journal-Serving Metropolitan Kansas City (Vol. 26, November 2, 2007, No. 8, pp. 1)*
Pub: American City Business Journals, Inc.
Ed: Rob Roberts. **Description:** Greater Kansas City Community Foundation has more than $1 billion to spend on life sciences initiatives and chairwoman Sandra Lawrence will unveil a multimillion-dollar master plan for Children's Mercy Hospitals and Clinics. Details regarding Lawrence's dedication to the foundation are discussed.

40467 ■ *"Lean Machine: Health Care Follows Auto's Lead, Gears Up for Efficiency"* in *Crain's Detroit Business (Vol. 26, Jan. 11, 2010)*
Pub: Crain Communications Inc.
Contact: Rance E. Crain, President
Ed: Jay Greene. **Description:** Reducing waste and becoming more efficient is a goal of many businesses involved in the health care industry. These firms are looking to the local manufacturing sector, comparing themselves in specifically to the auto industry, for ways in which to become more efficient.

40468 ■ *"Lean Machine; Health Care Follows Auto's Lead, Gears Up for Efficiency"* in *Crain's Detroit Business (Vol. 26, January 11, 2010)*
Pub: Crain Communications Inc.
Contact: Rance E. Crain, President
Ed: Jay Greene. **Description:** Reducing waste and becoming more efficient is a goal of many businesses involved in the health care industry. These firms are looking to the local manufacturing sector, comparing themselves in specifically to the auto industry, for ways in which to become more efficient.

40469 ■ *"Lee Jones, Rebiotix Inc."* in *Business Journal (Vol. 32, August 8, 2014, No. 11, pp. 6)*
Pub: American City Business Journals
Released: August 8, 2014. **Description:** Rebiotix Inc. CEO, Lee Jones, says the company has secured fresh capital mostly from venture capitalists. She also said that the potential of the company's development of C.defficile treatment has attracted investors. Jones added that Rebiotix is the first company to develop a drug to treat digestive tract infections.

40470 ■ *"Leisureworld Announces August Dividend"* in *Internet Wire (August 15, 2012)*
Description: Profile of Leisureworld Senior Care Corporation, Canada's fifth largest senior housing operator and third largest provider of LTC senior homes in Ontario. The firm owns and operates six retirement residences and one independent living residence in Ontario and British Columbia. Preferred Health Care Services are one of their subsidiaries and offers professional nursing and supports services as is Ontario Long Term Care which provides services, dietary, social work, and other regulated health professional services.

40471 ■ *"Life's Work: Oliver Sacks"* in *Harvard Business Review (Vol. 88, November 2010, No. 11, pp. 152)*
Pub: Harvard Business School Publishing
Ed: Lisa Burrell. **Description:** Neurologist and author Oliver Sacks discusses whether different types of minds tend toward certain skills, physician-patient communication, and his own perspectives from being a patient himself.

40472 ■ *"Lifesavers"* in *Black Enterprise (Vol. 41, December 2010, No. 5, pp. 38)*
Pub: Earl G. Graves Publishing Co. Inc.
Contact: Earl G. Graves, Jr., President
Ed: Tamara E. Holmes. **Description:** Profile of Interventional Nephrology Specialists Access Center and founders Dr. Omar Davis and Dr. Natarsha Grant; the center generated $5.5 million in revenue for 2009. Details on how they run their successful center are included.

40473 ■ *"Like Pulling Teeth: Companies Use Creative Amenities to Lure Workers"* in *Houston Business Journal (Vol. 44, April 4, 2014, No. 48, pp. 8)*
Pub: American City Business Journals
Released: April 4, 2014. **Description:** Houston, Texas-based Online Dental Solutions has converted a conference room at Phillips 66 interim headquarters when the oil company added the in-house dentist to its amenities to recruit and retain talent. The dental office also plans to put another one at Phillips 66 new corporate campus in the Westchase district. Insights on Online Dental Solutions' practice are also presented.

40474 ■ *"The Little Biotech that Could"* in *Barron's (Vol. 89, July 27, 2009, No. 30, pp. 19)*
Pub: Dow Jones & Co., Inc.
Contact: Clare Hart, President
Ed: Christopher C. Williams. **Description:** OSI Pharmaceuticals' shares is a compelling investment bet among small biotech firms due to its Tarceva anticancer drug which has a 23 percent market share as well as their strong balance sheet. OSI is planning to expand the use of Tarceva which could re-ignite sales and one analyst expects the shares to trade in the 40s one year from July 2009.

40475 ■ *"Locals Eager for $785M Medical Marijuana Business"* in *Orlando Business Journal (Vol. 30, March 21, 2014, No. 39, pp. 4)*
Pub: American City Business Journals
Released: March 21, 2014. **Description:** A number of local companies in Central Florida are preparing for a ballot initiative to legalize medical marijuana in November 2014. The National Cannabis Association estimates the medical marijuana market in Florida at $785 million, with about 260,000 patients, while Orlando's share is estimated at $89.1 million, with 29,518 potential patients.

40476 ■ *"Lone Star Paralysis Foundation Readies to Find a Cure"* in *Austin Business JournalInc. (Vol. 29, December 11, 2009, No. 40, pp. 1)*
Pub: American City Business Journals
Ed: Sandra Zaragoza. **Description:** Lone Star Paralysis Foundation revealed plans to launch a fundraising effort for the advancement of cures for spinal cord injuries via adult stem cells and also fund a new spinal injury rehabilitation center. Efforts to raise

about $3 million will begin as soon as the adult stem cell research study by Dr. Wise Young receives Food and Drug Administration approval.

40477 ■ *"Los Angeles Jewish Home to Expand to Westside With New Senior Care Community and In-Home Services"* in *PR Newswire (September 12, 2012)*
Pub: PR Newswire Association L.L.C.
Contact: David B. Armon, President
Description: Los Angeles Jewish Home plans to develop a senior care community at The Village at Playa Vista on the west side of Los Angeles, California. They will serve residential, healthcare and in-home care for seniors living on the west side of LA. Gonda Healthy Aging Westside Campus, donated by Leslie and Susan Gonda (Goldschmied) Foundation, will be part of the Jewish Home's mission to serve seniors in the area. Statistical data included.

40478 ■ *"Losses Threaten Comp Care's Future Viability"* in *The Business Journal-Serving Greater Tampa Bay (Vol. 28, August 15, 2008, No. 34)*
Pub: American City Business Journals, Inc.
Contact: Whitney Shaw, President
Ed: Margie Manning. **Description:** Comprehensive Care Corp. expressed that it may have to cease or drastically curtail its operations if it won't be able to raise additional funding in the next two or three months. The firm, which provides managed behavioral health care services, is also believed to be exploring a sale. Other views and information on Comprehensive Care's finances and plans are presented.

40479 ■ *"Lower Unemployment Hasn't Offset Total Losses"* in *Sacramento Business Journal (Vol. 31, May 23, 2014, No. 13, pp. 6)*
Pub: American City Business Journals
Released: May 23, 2014. **Description:** The decline in Sacramento, California's unemployment rate has not reduced the city's economic losses. Unemployment in the area has decreased by 7.5 percent in April 2014. Meanwhile, educational and health services are expected to be the job growth sectors in the next 12 months.

40480 ■ *"Macroeconomic Policy and U.S. Competitiveness: A Reformed Fiscal Policy Is Vital To Renewing America's Productivity"* in *Harvard Business Review (Vol. 90, March 2012, No. 3, pp. 112)*
Pub: Harvard Business Review Press
Contact: Peter E. Walsh, Director
Ed: Richard H.K. Vietor, Matthew Weinzierl. **Released:** March 2012. **Description:** Improving productivity requires increasing physical capital (such as equipment or technology), raising human capital, or using both of these types of capital more efficiently. The authors promote a plan that blends cuts in defense and health care spending, adjustments to Social Security, and carbon and gas taxes.

40481 ■ *"Making Sure the Doctor Is Always In"* in *Austin Business Journal (Vol. 34, June 6, 2014, No. 16, pp. B12)*
Pub: American City Business Journals, Inc.
Contact: Whitney Shaw, President
Released: June 6, 2014. **Description:** John Erwin, CEO of Carenet feels that the investment his company has made in finding the best talent in high-performing professionals who share a passion for and dedication to positively impacting the country's health care system is the reason behind the company's success. He believes that failure is a big part of success and that one learns from the mistakes more than one learns from doing things right.

40482 ■ *Management Lessons from Mayo Clinic*
Pub: McGraw-Hill
Ed: Leonard L. Berry, Kent D. Seltman. **Released:** June 06, 2008. **Price:** $27.95. **Description:** Management practices employed by the Mayo Clinic are examined to show why it is one of the world's most successful health care facilities.

40483 ■ *Managing Health Benefits in Small and Mid-Sized Organizations*
Ed: Patricia Halo. **Released:** July 1999. **Description:** Comprehensive guide for developing health care plans for companies employing between 50 and 5,000 employees in order to provide employees with better health care at lower prices.

40484 ■ *"Mapping the Gender Gap"* in *Business Journal Portland (Vol. 31, April 25, 2014, No. 8, pp. 4)*
Pub: American City Business Journals
Released: April 25, 2014. **Description:** The level of gender equality in the health care, banking, technology and commercial real estate industries of Oregon is examined. Gender bias in the workplace is one significant reason behind the wage gap and the lack of women in leadership positions.

40485 ■ *"Maryland Businesses Balk at 1099 Provision in Health Reform Law"* in *Baltimore Business Journal (Vol. 28, August 13, 2010, No. 14, pp. 1)*
Pub: Baltimore Business Journal
Ed: Scott Dance. **Description:** Small business advocates and accountants have criticized the Internal Revenue Service Form 1099 provision in the health care reform law as not worth the cost of time and money. Critics believe the policy would create a deluge of the documents that is too much for the companies or the IRS to handle. Details of the provision are also discussed.

40486 ■ *"Maryland Hospitals Cope with Rare Drop in Patient Admissions"* in *Boston Business Journal (Vol. 29, September 23, 2011, No. 20, pp. 1)*
Pub: American City Business Journals, Inc.
Ed: Scott Dance. **Description:** Admissions to Maryland hospitals have dropped to less than 700,000 in fiscal year 2010 and initial figures for fiscal 2011 show in-patient admissions are now nearing 660,000. The decline can be partly attributed to new ways health insurers are paying hospitals for care and to the financial reward hospitals get for cutting back on admissions.

40487 ■ *"The Massachusetts Mess"* in *Barron's (Vol. 89, July 27, 2009, No. 30, pp. 39)*
Pub: Dow Jones & Co., Inc.
Contact: Clare Hart, President
Ed: Thomas G. Donlan. **Description:** Massachusetts' mandatory health insurance has produced the highest rate of insurance coverage among the states but the state is now unable to afford its dream of universal coverage just three years after they enacted it. This supposed model for federal health-care reform is turning out to be a joke.

40488 ■ *"mChip: Claros Diagnostics"* in *Inc. (Vol. 33, November 2011, No. 9, pp. 42)*
Pub: Inc. Magazine
Ed: Christine Lagorio. **Description:** Harvard University researchers have developed a device called the mChip that produces accurate blood tests in about 10 minutes. Plans to apply for FDA approval for the mChip in the US should happen in 2012.

40489 ■ *"Md. Hospitals 'Worried' About Cost of Adapting to Health Care Law"* in *Baltimore Business Journal (Vol. 30, July 6, 2012, No. 9, pp. 1)*
Pub: American City Business Journals, Inc.
Contact: Whitney Shaw, President
Ed: Sarah Gantz. **Released:** July 6, 2012. **Description:** Baltimore, Maryland-based hospitals have expressed concern over the cost of complying with health care reforms. Hospitals have been planning to update information technology systems and care centers. Comments from executives included.

40490 ■ *"Md. May Avoid Congress on Medicare Waiver"* in *Baltimore Business Journal (Vol. 30, June 15, 2012, No. 6, pp. 1)*
Pub: American City Business Journals, Inc.
Contact: Whitney Shaw, President
Ed: Sarah Gantz. **Released:** June 15, 2012. **Description:** Maryland leaders may not seek the US Con-

gress' help to avoid losing a Medicare waiver. The waiver has standardized Medicare reimbursement rates for all hospitals. Comments from officials included.

40491 ■ "Medicaid Expansion Could Prompt New Taxes, Program Cuts in Maryland" in Baltimore Business Journal (Vol. 27, October 23, 2009, No. 24, pp. 1)
Pub: American City Business Journals
Ed: Julekha Dash. **Description:** Effects of the expected federal expansion of Medicaid under federal health care reform on Maryland tax policy are presented. Health care executives believe new taxes are necessary for the state to pay for an expansion that could cost over $400 million to $600 million.

40492 ■ "Medical Collection Agency Refutes Allegations In AG's Report" in PaymentsSource (May 1, 2012)
Pub: SourceMedia Inc.
Contact: James M. Malkin, Chief Executive Officer
Released: May 1, 2012. **Description:** Accretive Health Inc. denies allegations by the Minnesota State Attorney General's Office that the firm used heavy-handed tactics pressuring patients to pay for services before receiving treatment. The medical collection agency's report states 'inaccuracies, innuendo and unfounded speculation' in the charges.

40493 ■ "Medical Connectors: Meeting the Demands of Reliability, Portability, Size and Cost" in Canadian Electronics (February 2008)
Ed: Murtaza Fidaali, Ted Worroll. **Description:** Component manufacturers who serve the medical industry need to ensure component reliability in order to maintain patient safety. Because of this, connectors in medical equipment are becoming more versatile. It is concluded that these manufacturers are facing challenges meeting the medical industry standards or reliability, miniaturization, portability, and cost.

40494 ■ "Medical Pot Backers Say Industry Will Survive" in Sacramento Business Journal (Vol. 28, October 14, 2011, No. 33, pp. 1)
Pub: Sacramento Business Journal
Ed: Melanie Turner. **Description:** Medical marijuana supporters have expected the industry to decline but will survive the federal restriction on growers and dispensaries across California. California Cannabis Association and National Cannabis Industry Association believe that some of the dispensaries will remain and the shakeout will lead to stronger state regulations.

40495 ■ "Medical Tech Jobs Take More Than a Month To Fill" in Austin Business Journal (Vol. 34, July 11, 2014, No. 21, pp. 10)
Pub: American City Business Journals, Inc.
Contact: Whitney Shaw, President
Released: July 11, 2014. **Description:** A report by Brookings Institute has revealed that nearly half of Austin's jobs require STEM - science, technology, engineering and mathematical skills. However, these jobs generally take more than a month to fill.

40496 ■ "Medical Tourism: The World Is Your Hospital" in Canadian Business (Vol. 81, July 22, 2008, No. 12-13, pp. 62)
Pub: Rogers Media Inc.
Contact: Tony Viner, President
Ed: Sharda Prashad. **Description:** Medical tourism is seen as a booming industry around the world and is expected to grow to around $40 billion in 2010. Key information regarding medical tourism and services are presented. Views on the possible impact of medical tourism on Canada's health care industry, as well as medical tourism opportunities in Canada, are also given.

40497 ■ "Medicare Plans Step Up Battle for Subscribers" in Sacramento Business Journal (Vol. 28, October 21, 2011, No. 34, pp. 1)
Pub: Sacramento Business Journal
Ed: Kathy Robertson. **Description:** California's market for health plans have become increasingly competitive as more than 313,000 seniors try to figure

out the best plans to meet their needs for 2012. Health plans are rated on Medicare materials to help consumers distinguish among the Medicare health maintenance organizations (HMOs).

40498 ■ Medicare & You Handbook
Pub: Health Care Financing Administration U.S. Department of Health & Human Service
URL(s): www.cms.gov/Newsroom/MediaReleaseDatabase/Press-releases/2014-Press-releases-items/2014-10-15-2.html. **Released:** Irregular; Latest Edition 2015. **Price:** Free. **Publication includes:** Lists of Medicare carriers in individual states. Principal content includes discussion of what Medicare is, what its various options are, and what new benefits have been added recently.

40499 ■ "Medtronic In Talks for Local Heart-Monitor Firm" in Business Journal (Vol. 32, May 30, 2014, No. 1, pp. 6)
Pub: American City Business Journals
Released: May 30, 2014. **Description:** Medtronic Inc. is negotiations to buy St. Paul, Minnesota-based Corventis Inc., maker of waterproof Band-Aid-like patch that patients wear on their chests to monitor their hearts. Corventis technology would likely fit into the patient monitoring business of Medtronic's latest acquisition, Cardiocom. The function of the Corventis patch is also described.

40500 ■ Memos to the Prime Minister: What Canada Could Be in the 21st Century
Ed: Harvey Schacter. **Released:** April 11, 2003. **Price:** , $16.95. **Description:** A look into the business future of Canada. Topics include business, healthcare, think tanks, policy groups, education, the arts, economy, and social issues.

40501 ■ "Mercy Parent Nets Almost $1B in 2011" in Sacramento Business Journal (Vol. 28, September 30, 2011, No. 31, pp. 1)
Pub: Sacramento Business Journal
Ed: Kathy Robertson. **Description:** Catholic Healthcare West has reported almost $1 billion in profits for 2010. The company has reported a profit margin of 8.7 percent. It also absorbed more than $1 billion in costs from charity care and government programs.

40502 ■ "Methodist Plans Richardson Hospital" in Dallas Business Journal (Vol. 35, June 29, 2012, No. 42, pp. 1)
Pub: American City Business Journal
Ed: Bill Hethcock. **Description:** Methodist Health System is planning to build a hospital in Richardson, Texas. The hospital will have a capacity of 125 beds and employ around 900 people. Comments from executives are included.

40503 ■ "Methodist Sees Dwindling Transplant Organs" in Memphis Business Journal (Vol. 34, June 29, 2012, No. 11, pp. 1)
Pub: American City Business Journal
Ed: Cole Epley. **Description:** The Methodist University Hospital Transplant Institute opposes the national organ policies established by the United Network for Organ Sharing as it would impact their liver transplant program negatively. Mid-South Transplant Foundation refuses to go forward with a merger with Tennessee Donor Services as favored by the Methodist program.

40504 ■ "Miami Valley Hospital To Close Senior Day Care Center" in Dayton Daily News (March 27, 2012)
Pub: McClatchy Tribune Information Services
Ed: Ben Sutherly. **Description:** Miami Valley Hospital is closing its day care center for senior citizens because it needs to shift resources to other areas of the hospital as it prepares for Obamacare.

40505 ■ "Michigan Institute of Urology Grows in Expertise, Services" in Crain's Detroit Business (Vol. 24, April 7, 2008, No. 14, pp. 13)
Pub: Crain Communications Inc.
Contact: Rance E. Crain, President
Ed: Jay Greene. **Description:** One of the nation's largest urology groups, the Michigan Institute of Urology, plans to continue its growth by adding doctors and offering new treatment options. The growth is

financially beneficial to the group, but it also cuts down on health care costs since the group can perform procedures for a lesser rate than at a hospital.

40506 ■ Microtrends: The Small Forces Behind Tomorrow's Big Changes
Ed: Mark J. Penn. **Released:** 2007. **Price:** , $25.99. **Description:** Political pollster and lead presidential campaign strategist for Hillary Clinton, identifies seventy-five microtrends he believes are changing the social and cultural landscape in the U.S. and globally. The book covers the areas of health and wellness, technology, education and more.

40507 ■ "Millions More For Health Care?" in Austin Business Journal (Vol. 32, June 29, 2012, No. 17, pp. 3)
Pub: American City Business Journals, Inc.
Contact: Whitney Shaw, President
Ed: Sandra Zaragoza. **Released:** June 29, 2012. **Description:** Central Health, Seton Healthcare Family and other government and health entities have been working on a plan that may result in millions more in federal funding for healthcare in Texas. The health care plan is part of the 1115 Waiver program under the Social Security Act. Insights on the waiver are also given.

40508 ■ "MMRGlobal Home Health and Senior Care Programs to Be Showcased at Visiting Nurse Associations of America's Annual Meeting" in Marketwired (April 12, 2012)
Pub: COMTEX
Contact: Chip Brian, President
Description: MMR Global Inc. will highlight its storage and solutions and electronic document management and imaging systems for healthcare professionals at the Visiting Nurse Associations of America (VNAA) 30th Annual Meeting in Phoenix, Arizona. Personal Health Records (PHRs), MyEsafeDeposit-Box and other programs are profiled.

40509 ■ "MN Effort To Privatize Coverage Struggles" in Business Journal (Vol. 30, July 6, 2012, No. 6, pp. 1)
Pub: American City Business Journals, Inc.
Contact: Whitney Shaw, President
Ed: Katharine Grayson. **Released:** July 6, 2012. **Description:** The Health Minnesota Contribution Program will move MinnesotaCare members to the private market. Health insurance brokers have supported passage of the law. MinnesotaCare members have received state-subsidized insurance premiums.

40510 ■ "The Moody Blues" in Entrepreneur (Vol. 36, April 2008, No. 4, pp. 87)
Pub: Entrepreneur Press
Contact: Perlman Neil, President
Ed: Mark Henricks. **Description:** Depression among employees can affect their productivity and cost the company. Businesses with a workforce that is likely to have depression should inform their employees about the health benefits covered by insurance. Other details on how to address depression concerns among employees are discussed.

40511 ■ "More Businesses Will Shift Health Costs to Workers" in Business Review, Albany New York (Vol. 34, November 16, 2007, No. 33, pp. 1)
Pub: American City Business Journals, Inc.
Ed: Barbara Pinckney. **Description:** Survey conducted by consulting firm Benetech Inc. showed that sixty percent of employers are planning to increase payroll deductions to pay for health insurance premiums. More than ninety percent of the employers prefer HMO plans, followed by Preferred Provider Organizations. Other details of the survey are discussed.

40512 ■ "More Small Businesses in Baltimore Willing to Fund Employees' Health Benefits" in Baltimore Business Journal (Vol. 28, June 18, 2010, No. 6, pp. 1)
Pub: Baltimore Business Journal
Ed: Scott Graham. **Description:** An increasing number of small businesses in Maryland are tapping into potentially cheaper self-funded health plans

instead of providing fully insured benefits to employees through traditional health plans. Self-funded health plans charge employers for health care up to a specified level. Economic implications of self-funded plans to small businesses are discussed.

40513 ■ "Most States Have High-Risk Health Insurance Pools" in Crain's Detroit Business (Vol. 24, March 24, 2008, No. 12, pp. 31)
Pub: Crain Communications Inc.
Contact: Rance E. Crain, President
Ed: Jay Greene. **Description:** High-risk health insurance pools, designed to cover individuals with medical conditions that essentially make them otherwise uninsurable, are being debated by the Senate Health Policy Committee; the pool concept is supported by Blue Cross Blue Shield of Michigan and contested by a number of consumer groups and competing health insurers.

40514 ■ National Wellness Institute--Member Directory (Online only)
Pub: National Wellness Institute
Contact: Judd Allen, Director
E-mail: judda@healthyculture.com
URL(s): www.nationalwellness.org/ ?page=MemberBenefits. **Released:** updated daily. **Covers:** more than 1,600 health and wellness promotion professionals in corporations, hospitals, colleges, government agencies, universities, community organizations, schools (K-12), and consulting firms, and managed care. **Entries include:** Member name, address, and phone, fax, email. **Arrangement:** Same information given in alphabetical, and geographical and work setting arrangements.

40515 ■ "Neurosciences, Orthopedics Push Mease Dunedin Plan" in Tampa Bay Business Journal (Vol. 29, October 30, 2009, No. 45, pp. 1)
Pub: American City Business Journals
Ed: Margie Manning. **Description:** Mease Dunedin Hospital has pushed with a $19 million renovation and expansion plan that would triple the space in its operating suites, in line with its effort to become a center of excellence focused on neurosciences, orthopedics and the spine. The hospital expects these kinds of specialties will help offset the cost of less profitable services.

40516 ■ "New Book Takes Alternate View on Ontario's Wind Industry" in CNW Group (September 19, 2011)
Pub: CNW Group Ltd.
Contact: Carolyn McGill-Davidson, President
Description: Dirty Business: The Reality Behind Ontario's Rush to Wind Power, was written by editor and health care writer Jane Wilson of Ottawa, Ontario, Canada along with contributing editor Parker Gallant. The book contains articles and papers on the wind business, including information on illnesses caused from the environmental noise.

40517 ■ "A New Cloud-Based Phone System Is Installed Remotely for North Carolina Senior Care Council" in Information Technology Business (June 19, 2012)
Description: North Carolina Senior Care Council (NcSCC) has partnered with VoxNet to provide long-term care for Cloud-based PBX to help NcSCC manage their system that assists seniors.

40518 ■ "New Database Brings Cincinnati Doctors Out of the Dark" in Business Courier (Vol. 26, October 23, 2009, No. 26, pp. 1)
Pub: American City Business Journals, Inc.
Contact: Whitney Shaw, President
Ed: James Ritchie. **Description:** A database created by managed care consulting firm Praesentia allows doctors in Cincinnati to compare average reimbursements from health insurance companies in different areas. Specialist doctors in the city are paid an average of $172.25 for every office consultation.

40519 ■ "New Drug Could Revitalize Amgen" in Barron's (Vol. 88, July 7, 2008, No. 27, pp. 23)
Ed: Johanna Bennett. **Description:** Shares of the biotechnology company Amgen could receive a boost from the release of the anti-osteoporosis drug denos-

umab. The shares, priced at $48.84 each, are trading at 11 times expected earnings for 2008 and could also be boosted by cost cutting measures.

40520 ■ "New Health Care Payment Model Coming to Boise" in Idaho Business Review (August 20, 2014)
Pub: Dolan Co.
Contact: James P. Dolan, President
Released: August 20, 2014. **Description:** Direct primary care is coming to the Boise, Idaho area. The process offers patients a range of treatment options, including most wellness and acute care but not hospital visits or some pharmaceuticals, for a monthly membership fee. This trend does not allow health insurance or health savings accounts to pay the monthly fees. Proponents believe direct primary care benefits doctors, patients and the overall health system in many ways.

40521 ■ "New Health Care Sector" in Hispanic Business (July-August 2009, pp. 10-12)
Pub: Hispanic Business Inc.
Contact: Jesus Chavarria, President
Description: Despite the recession and reform, the health care sector continues to grow at a fast rate. The top ten health care organizations are outlined.

40522 ■ "New Health Law, Lack of Docs Collide on Cape Cod" in Boston Business Journal (Vol. 27, October 12, 2007, No. 37, pp. 1)
Ed: Mark Hollmer. **Description:** There is a shortage of primary care providers at Outer Cape Health Services in Massachusetts, with the isolation of the area and as physicians look for higher paying careers in specialty positions. The Commonwealth Health Insurance Connector Authority is pushing for a new health insurance law and is working with Cape Cod Chamber of Commerce to conduct outreach programs.

40523 ■ "New Practice Offers High-End, On-Call Care" in Dallas Business Journal (Vol. 35, March 23, 2012, No. 28, pp. 1)
Description: MD2 International is set to open an office in Dallas, Texas. The company provides around-the-clock access to medical care with more personalized care to patients.

40524 ■ "A New Set of Health Codes" in Washington Business Journal (Vol. 33, July 11, 2014, No. 12, pp. 6)
Pub: American City Business Journals
Released: July 11, 2014. **Description:** Restaurants in Washington DC are preparing for the implementation of the Health Care Reform Act.

40525 ■ The New Wellness Revolution: How to Make a Fortune in the Next Trillion Dollar Industry
Pub: John Wiley & Sons Inc.
Contact: Stephen M. Smith, President
Ed: Paul Zane Pilzer. **Released:** January 2007. **Price:** $34.95; $22.99. **Description:** Tips for starting and running a healthcare business. **Availability:** PrintE-book.

40526 ■ "Newton Robotics Company Bets On Rehab Robots for Growth" in Boston Business Journal (Vol. 34, April 4, 2014, No. 9, pp. 6)
Pub: American City Business Journals, Inc.
Contact: Whitney Shaw, President
Released: April 4, 2014. **Description:** Robotics firm Barrett Technology is transforming into a health care company by developing rehabilitation robots. The business is expected to generate 80 percent of its revenue from its health care clients over the next five years. The possibility of hiring new employees is also discussed.

40527 ■ The No Asshole Rule
Ed: Robert I. Sutton PhD. **Released:** February 22, 2007. **Price:** $22.99. **Description:** Problem employees are more than just a nuisance they are a serious and costly threat to corporate success and employee health.

40528 ■ "Non-Users Still Inhale Nicotine From E-Cigarettes" in Business First of Buffalo (Vol. 30, February 7, 2014, No. 21, pp. 6)
Pub: American City Business Journals, Inc.
Contact: Whitney Shaw, President
Released: February 7, 2014. **Description:** A group of researchers at Roswell Park Cancer Institute's Department of Health Behavior, led by Maciej Goniewicz, found traces of some potentially dangerous chemical in the vapor of electronic cigarettes. Although smoking e-cigarettes is less harmful than regular cigarettes, non-users are still exposed to nicotine in the same way as secondhand smoke.

40529 ■ "Not Just for Kids: ADHD can be Debilitating for an Employee, and Frustrating for Bosses" in Canadian Business (April 14, 2008)
Pub: Rogers Media Inc.
Contact: Tony Viner, President
Ed: Andy Holloway. **Description:** Up to four percent of North American adults continue to feel the effects of Attention Deficit Hyperactivity Disorder or Attention Deficit Disorder. Explaining the value of the task at hand to people who are afflicted with these conditions is one way to keep them engaged in the workplace. Giving them opportunities to create their own working structure is another strategy to manage these people.

40530 ■ "Notes on Current Labor Statistics" in Montly Labor Review (Vol. 133, September 2010, No. 9, pp. 75)
Pub: U.S. Department of Labor Bureau of Labor Statistics
Contact: Philip L. Rones, Manager
E-mail: rones.philip@bls.gov
Description: Principal statistics and calculated by the Bureau of Labor Statistics are presented. The series includes statistics on labor force; employment; unemployment; labor compensation; consumer, producer, and international prices; productivity; international comparisons; and injury and illness statistics.

40531 ■ "Novi Eyed for $11 Million, 100-Bed Medilodge" in Crain's Detroit Business (Vol. 25, June 1, 2009, No. 22, pp. M032)
Pub: Crain Communications Inc. - Detroit
Contact: Keith Crain, Chairman
Description: Novi, Michigan is one of the cities being considered for construction of a new 110-bed skilled nursing facility. Details of the project are included.

40532 ■ "NOW: Ideas at the Speed of Business: Cancer Care's Quantum Leap" in Hawaii Business (Vol. 53, October 2007, No. 4, pp. 17)
Pub: PacificBasin Communications
Ed: Cathy S. Cruz-George. **Description:** TomoTherapy is an innovative device for cancer treatment that gives high-intensity radiation to more accurate parts of the body compared to conventional treatments. Hawaii has one of the 70 TomoTherapy machines in the nation, and it is expected to help advance cancer care in the area. Details on how the machine works are provided.

40533 ■ "Now the Real Work Begins" in Baltimore Business Journal (Vol. 28, October 15, 2010, No. 23, pp. 1)
Pub: Baltimore Business Journal
Ed: Emily Mullin. **Description:** The Henry J. Kaiser Family Foundation's survey shows nearly 53 percent of Americans remain confused about health care reform and it was up to the states to educate the people. However, Maryland is still trying to figure out how to conduct the campaign without guidance or funding from the Federal government.

40534 ■ "Number-Cruncher Gets 'Pushback" in Philadelphia Business Journal (Vol. 33, August 22, 2014, No. 28, pp. 10)
Pub: American City Business Journals
Released: August 22, 2014. **Description:** Bryan Wellen, senior director of clinical informatics for Continuum Health Alliance (CHA), asserts that while some physicians are receptive to patient information,

others respond with an element of 'pushback' and criticism of the data. CHA and Horizon Blue Cross Blue Shield of New Jersey are using data analysis to create strategies that improve health care and reduce costs.

40535 ■ *"Nurse Next Door Home Health Care Franchise Meets Growing Challenges of Senior Care"* in Benzinga.com (September 11, 2012)
Pub: Benzinga.com
Contact: Kyle Bazzy, President
Description: The need for home health care services in the United States is revealed through federal data. Responding to the lack of services, Nurse Next Door, a Canadian home health care franchise, has begun a program to aggressively expand services in the US market. Statistical data included.

40536 ■ *Nurses Come To Fore as Care Landscape Shifts*
Pub: American City Business Journals, Inc.
Contact: Whitney Shaw, President
Ed: Sarah Gantz. **Released:** July 20, 2012. **Description:** Maryland's healthcare industry is looking to increase the supply of nursesto meet an anticipated growth in demand for primary care services. The industry is working with nursing schools and colleges to increase enrollment and improve the education of existing nurses.

40537 ■ *"Oakland County Hopes Auto Suppliers Can Drive Medical Industry Growth"* in Crain's Detroit Business (March 10, 2008)
Pub: Crain Communications Inc.
Contact: Rance E. Crain, President
Ed: Chad Halcom. **Description:** Oakland County officials are hoping to create further economic development for the region by pairing health care companies and medical device makers with automotive suppliers in an attempt to discover additional crossover technology.

40538 ■ *"Obamacare Is Here, But Primary Docs Await New Patients"* in Baltimore Business Journal (Vol. 32, June 6, 2014, No. 5, pp. 9)
Pub: American City Business Journals, Inc.
Released: June 6, 2014. **Description:** Health care reform under the Affordable Care Act, sometimes referred to as Obamacare, has enabled millions of Americans to have health insurance. However, primary care doctors in the Baltimore area and elsewhere have not seen the surge of patients many were expecting as a result of the Federal health reform. Those who have signed up for the health insurance are older and sicker than expected, with few young adults signing up, thus creating costly healthcare expenses.

40539 ■ *"Of Paper Towels and Health Insurance"* in Philadelphia Business Journal (Vol. 28, May 11, 2012, No. 13, pp. 1)
Pub: American City Business Journal
Description: Health insurance companies are using different strategies to take advantage of the demand growth in health coverage in markets such as Philadelphia. Horizon Blue Cross lue Shield of New Jersey, for example, is creating a retail center where customers can get information from specially trained staff about insurance, health and wellness. IBC, on the other hand, has partnered with AAA Mid-Atlantic to market its plan option to AAA members.

40540 ■ *"On Their Own"* in Crain's Cleveland Business (Vol. 28, November 12, 2007, No. 45, pp. 19)
Pub: Crain Communications Inc.
Ed: Eileen Beal. **Description:** Discusses the reasons more physicians with entrepreneurial spirit are opening their own practices as well as the added challenges and responsibilities that comes with owning one's own practice.

40541 ■ *"On the Use of Neurophysiological Tools In IS Research: Developing a Research Agenda for NeuroIS"* in MIS Quarterly (Vol.

36, September 2012, No. 3, pp. 679)
Pub: MIS Research Center, Carlson School of Management
Ed: Angelika Dimoka. **Price:** $10. **Description:** The role of neurophysiological tools and neuroimaging tools in information systems research is discussed. Promising application areas and research questions regarding the use of neurophysiological data to benefit information systems researchers are identified.

40542 ■ *"One Personal Trainer's Fitness Goal: Help Cancer Patients Feel Better During and After Treatment"* in America's Intelligence Wire (February 1, 2012)
Description: Laura Rosencrantz quit her job as a fitness instructor to develop a specialized training program to help cancer patients remain stronger while in treatment, stronger in recovery, or to help them feel better in their final months. She watched her grandfather grow weak during his cancer treatment and she knew she could help others during this time.

40543 ■ *"The One Thing That's Holding Back Your Wellness Program"* in Employee Benefit News (Vol. 25, December 1, 2011, No. 15, pp. 8)
Pub: SourceMedia Inc.
Contact: James M. Malkin, Chief Executive Officer
Description: A 13-year study shows that women who sat for more than six hours a day were 94 percent more likely to die during the study period. Most women sit at their desks an average of 7.7 hours while at work.

40544 ■ *"'Only Way To Go Is Up"* in Pittsburgh Business Times (Vol. 33, May 30, 2014, No. 46, pp. 6)
Pub: American City Business Journals
Released: May 30, 2014. **Description:** The United Steelworkers (USW) are leading efforts to unionize adjunct professors across the U.S. in the hopes of improving their working conditions. USW organizers claim that low pay, lack of healthcare benefits, and no job security are the largest issues facing local adjuncts in Pittsburgh, Pennsylvania and nationally.

40545 ■ *"Open Enrollment: Staying Healthy During Enrollment Season"* in Employee Benefit News (Vol. 25, November 1, 2011, No. 14, pp. 41)
Pub: SourceMedia Inc.
Contact: James M. Malkin, Chief Executive Officer
Ed: Shana Sweeney. **Description:** Tips for staying healthy during your benefit open enrollment period are outlined.

40546 ■ *"Orlando Health to Build $24M Proton Therapy Facility"* in Orlando Business Journal (Vol. 26, January 22, 2010, No. 34, pp. 1)
Pub: American City Business Journals
Ed: Melanie Stawicki Azam. **Description:** Orlando Health is planning to construct a $24 million proton therapy facility at its MD Anderson Cancer Center Orlando in Florida. The facility, which aims for a 2011 opening, will be using radiation for more accurate targeting of tumors and avoiding the damage to surrounding tissues and organs.

40547 ■ *"Other Players Want In On Ellis-St. Peter's Deal"* in Business Review Albany (Vol. 41, July 4, 2014, No. 15, pp. 9)
Pub: American City Business Journals, Inc.
Contact: Whitney Shaw, President
Released: July 4, 2014. **Description:** Other hospital systems and smaller health care providers expressed interest in joining the partnership between Ellis Medicine and St. Peter's Health Partners in Albany, New York. The partnership aims to transform a scattered health care industry into regional networks while allowing companies to maintain independent operations.

40548 ■ *"Outlook In Other Industries"* in Crain's Detroit Business (Vol. 30, January 6,

2014, No. 1, pp. 3)
Pub: Crain Communications Inc. - Detroit
Contact: Keith Crain, Chairman
Released: January 6, 2014. **Description:** Outlook for industries in the Detroit area are listed, including small business growth, restaurants, defense contracts, nonprofits, transportation, auto suppliers, healthcare, bankruptcy, and government.

40549 ■ *"Over and Out"* in Entrepreneur (Vol. 36, February 2008, No. 2, pp. 25)
Pub: Entrepreneur Press
Contact: Perlman Neil, President
Ed: Chris Penttila. **Description:** Ben Wolin, owner of Waterfront Media that operates wellness and health Websites, had employed the services of human resource consulting firm to advise him in regard to overtime pay. Guidelines on how to avoid overtime pay violations are presented.

40550 ■ *"The Overlicensed Society"* in Harvard Business Review (Vol. 90, April 2012, No. 4, pp. 38)
Pub: Harvard Business Review Press
Contact: Peter E. Walsh, Director
Ed: Robert E. Litan. **Released:** April 2012. **Description:** The author argues that certification and licensing requirements are hindering professionals who might otherwise be able to find positions and provide services inexpensively. To key areas are healthcare and law. Federal mutual recognition agreements may be one method of addressing both practice and consumer protection issues.

40551 ■ *"Park Nicollet Warms Up to Maple Grove"* in Business Journal (Vol. 30, June 29, 2012, No. 5, pp. 1)
Pub: American City Business Journals, Inc.
Contact: Whitney Shaw, President
Ed: Katharine Grayson. **Released:** June 29, 2012. **Description:** Park Nicollet Health Services has decided to move a group of OB/GYN specialists to the Maple Grove Hospital campus. Park Nicollet has also leased 12,000 square feet of space near the baby labor and delivery suites at Maple Grove. The popularity of Maple Grove among expectant mothers is also discussed.

40552 ■ *"Patients to Elect to Cut Care"* in The Business Journal-Serving Metropolitan Kansas City (Vol. 27, November 21, 2008, No. 11, pp. 1)
Pub: American City Business Journals, Inc.
Contact: Whitney Shaw, President
Ed: Rob Roberts. **Description:** Patients in Kansas City, Missouri are cutting down on health care services due to the economic crisis. A decline in diagnostic procedures has been observed at Northland Cardiology. Elective reconstructive procedures have also been reduced by 25 percent. Additional information and statistics regarding the healthcare sector is included.

40553 ■ *"Patients: Make Mine a Single"* in Business Courier (Vol. 24, March 28, 2008, No. 51, pp. 1)
Pub: American City Business Journals, Inc.
Contact: Whitney Shaw, President
Ed: James Ritchie. **Description:** Hospitals in the Tri-State area are switching from double to private rooms since patients heal better in private rooms and also they provide peace and quiet to patients. Private rooms also contribute to the reduction of medical errors and hospital acquired infection rates.

40554 ■ *"Patricia Hemingway Hall: President, Chief Operating Officer, Health Care Service Corp."* in Crain's Chicago Business (May 5, 2008)
Pub: Crain Communications Inc.
Contact: Todd Johnson, Publisher
Ed: Mike Colias. **Description:** Profile of Patricia Hemingway Hall who is the president and chief operating officer of Health Care Service Corp., a new strategy launched by Blue Cross & Blue Shield of Illinois; the new endeavor will emphasize wellness rather than just treatment across its four health plans.

40555 ■ "PCH Gets Trauma Center Status" in The Business Journal - Serving Phoenix and the Valley of the Sun (Vol. 28, July 11, 2008, No. 45)

Ed: Angela Gonzales. **Description:** Phoenix Children's Hospital has been allowed by the Arizona Department of Health Services to launch the state's first trauma center for children. The trauma center is expected to cost the hospital $7 million a year.

40556 ■ "Peduto Widens Reach with UPMC Mediation" in Pittsburgh Business Times (Vol. 33, March 14, 2014, No. 35, pp.4)

Pub: American City Business Journals

Released: March 14, 2014. **Description:** Pittsburgh, Pennsylvania Mayor Bill Peduto is working to settle the contract dispute between University of Pittsburgh Medical Center and Highmark Inc. Peduto met with UPMC president, Jeffrey Romoff, to discuss the issue that has spilled over to some city officials. Peduto said the dispute is hampering the city's economic growth.

40557 ■ "Pet Store Fish Provide Clue to How Alzheimer's Disease May Start" in Internet Wire (July 9, 2012)

Released: July 9, 2012. **Description:** Western University of Health Sciences in Pomona, California researchers report that studies with zebrafish provided an important clue to understanding how Alzheimer's disease starts. Details of the study are included.

40558 ■ "PetCareRx.com Makes Donations to Service-Dog Charity" in Pet Product News (Vol. 66, September 2012, No. 9, pp. 18)

Description: Lynbrook, New York-based online pet pharmacy PetCareRx.com has persuaded its customers via email to buy products. Five percent of the purchased products' proceeds would be donated to help the Educated Canines Assisting with Disabilities (ECAD), a nonprofit dedicated to matching assistance dogs with persons with disabilities.

40559 ■ "Physicians Development Groupn Kicks Off $13M Skilled Nursing Facility in NE Wichita" in Wichita Business Journal (Vol. 27, January 20, 2012, No. 3, pp. 1)

Pub: American City Business Journal

Description: Physicians Development Group has started construction of a skilled nursing facility in Wichita, Kansas. The 80-bed nursing facility is estimated to cost around $13 million.

40560 ■ "Physics for Females" in Occupational Outlook Quarterly (Vol. 55, Summer 2011, No. 2, pp. 22)

Pub: U.S. Department of Labor Bureau of Labor Statistics

Contact: Philip L. Rones, Manager

E-mail: rones.philip@bls.gov

Description: Free resources to help females investigate careers in medical physics and health physics are available from the American Physical Society. The booklet is designed for girls in middle and high school and describes the work of 15 women who use physics to solve medical mysteries, discover planets, research new materials, and more.

40561 ■ "Piece of Health Law 'A Goner'" in Baltimore Business Journal (Vol. 28, November 19, 2010, No. 28, pp. 1)

Pub: Baltimore Business Journal

Ed: Kent Hoover. **Description:** Montana Senator Max Baucus, a Democrat who heads the Senate Finance Committee, has revealed his plan to push legislation that would repeal the 1099 IRS provision that was created by the health care reform law and will result in more paperwork for small businesses when it goes into effect in 2012.

40562 ■ "Pioneers Get All The Perks" in Canadian Business (Vol. 81, March 3, 2008, No. 3, pp. 18)

Description: Suncor Energy Inc. will face royalty payments from 25% to 30% of net profits as it signs a new deal with Alberta. Biovail Corp., meanwhile, is under a U.S. grand jury investigation for supposed improprieties in Cardizem LA heart drug launch. The Conference Board of Canada's proposal to impose taxes on greenhouse gas emissions and other developments in the business community are discussed.

40563 ■ "Plan: Put Health Centers in ERs" in Crain's Detroit Business (Vol. 25, June 22, 2009, No. 25, pp. 1)

Pub: Crain Communications Inc. - Detroit

Contact: Keith Crain, Chairman

Ed: Jay Greene. **Description:** It has been suggested by top CEOs in the Detroit, Michigan area to put satellites of federally qualified health centers within emergency room departments. The plan would have the health centers pay a monthly fee for each patient treated.

40564 ■ "Positive Social Interactions and the Human Body at Work: Linking Organizations and Physiology" in Academy of Management Review (January 2008, pp. 137)

Pub: ScholarOne Inc.

Contact: William T. Carden, Jr., President

Ed: Emily D. Heaphy, Jane E. Dutton. **Description:** Research is recommended for the manner in which positive social interactions in organizational contexts can influence employees' health and physiological resourcefulness.

40565 ■ "Prescription for Health: Choosing the Best Healthcare Plan for your workforce and your Bottom Line" in Black Enterprise (Vol. 38, July 2008, No. 12, pp. 48)

Pub: Earl G. Graves Publishing Co. Inc.

Contact: Earl G. Graves, Jr., President

Ed: Tamara E. Holmes. **Description:** According to a survey of small-business owners conducted by Sure-Payroll Inc., 20 percent of respondents have had a prospective employee refuse a job offer because healthcare benefits did not come with it. Cost is not the only reason many small-business owners do not offer these benefits. Guidelines to help take some of the confusion out of the guesswork that comes with trying to find the proper fit concerning healthcare benefits are outlined.

40566 ■ "Presidential Address: Innovation in Retrospect and Prospect" in Canadian Journal of Electronics (Vol. 43, November 2010, No. 4)

Pub: Journal of the Canadian Economics Association

Ed: James A. Brander. **Description:** Has innovation slowed in recent decades? While there has been progress in information and communications technology, the recent record of innovation in agriculture, energy, transportation and healthcare sectors is cause for concern.

40567 ■ "Priority: Business For Sale" in Inc. (January 2008, pp. 28)

Pub: Gruner and Jahr USA Publishing Co.

Contact: J. Russell Denson, President

Ed: Elaine Appleton Grant. **Description:** Profile of an employment agency providing registered nurses to hospitals and nursing homes. The company began as an temporary placement agency for IT professionals and is now for sale at the asking price of $4.2 million.

40568 ■ "Private Care's Next Phase: Serious Money Is Going Into Health Clinics" in Canadian Business (Vol. 85, June 11, 2012, No. 10, pp. 10)

Pub: George Media Inc.

Ed: Laura Cameron. **Released:** June 11, 2012. **Description:** Some public-private partnerships in Canada include the acquisition of clinics by Centric Health Corporation and the partnership between Westbank First National and Johns Hopkins Hospital. Private healthcare providers have operated by dividing their funding among government contracts, clients not covered by Medicare and patients paying out of pocket and non-insured services.

40569 ■ "Proactive Elder-Care Workshop Scheduled" in News-Sentinel (February 15, 2012)

Description: Proactive Elder Care has partnered with IPFW to provide an educational workshop open to caregivers, seniors, family members, employed caregivers and employers. Breakout sessions cover when to begin care, finances, law, healthcare, housing, community services, and bioethics.

40570 ■ "Professor: More Will Follow CVS Ban on Tobacco" in Philadelphia Business Journal (Vol. 33, February 14, 2014, No. 1, pp. 6)

Pub: American City Business Journals

Released: February 14, 2014. **Description:** Professor Daniel A. Hussar believes that CVS Caremark's decision to discontinue the sale of tobacco products reflects the company's concern for the health of consumers. He thinks that other drugstores will follow suit. The need for CVS Caremark to emphasize the importance of pharmacists' services is also examined.

40571 ■ "Prognosis: Uncertain" in Entrepreneur (May 2014)

Pub: Entrepreneur Media Inc.

Released: May 2014. **Description:** The passage of the Patient Protection and Affordable Care Act has resulted in uncertainty for small business owners. The law has required health insurance coverage for companies with 50 or more full-time employees, placing additional costs on small businesses. It has also imposed additional administrative burdens such as reporting the scope of health insurance coverage for employees and tracking their actual number. Some businesses that are already paying for health insurance coverage opted to give their employees money to purchase their own insurance coverage plans.

40572 ■ "Providence Exec Explains Why the Deal with Boeing is the Way of the Future" in Puget Sound Business Journal (Vol. 35, June 27, 2014, No. 10, pp. 6)

Pub: American City Business Journals

Released: June 27, 2014. **Description:** Providence-Swedish Accountable Care Organization CEO, Joe Gifford, shares his views on the deal to provide health care to Boeing employees. Gifford says there is opportunity to grow the business if public image spreads showing they offer great quality and service in providing unique healthcare and benefits at a lower cost. Gifford believes meeting directly with the employer customer they create a direct loop of process improvement.

40573 ■ "Providers Ride First Wave of eHealth Dollars" in Boston Business Journal (Vol. 31, June 10, 2011, No. 20, pp. 1)

Pub: Boston Business Journal

Ed: Julie M. Donnelly. **Description:** Health care providers in Massachusetts implementing electronic medical records technology started receiving federal stimulus funds. Beth Israel Deaconess Medical Center was the first hospital to qualify for the funds.

40574 ■ "Public Health Care Funding and the Montana Economy" in Montana Business Quarterly (Vol. 49, Spring 2011, No. 1, pp. 23)

Pub: University of Montana Bureau of Business and Economic Research

Contact: Patrick Barkey, Director

E-mail: patrick.barkey@business.umt.edu

Ed: Gregg Davis. **Description:** Montana has more baby boomers and veterans per capita than any other state in the nation. The role of public health in the state is a crucial part of the state's economy.

40575 ■ Public Human Services Directory

Pub: American Public Human Services Association

Contact: Susan Dreyfus, President

URL(s): www.aphsa.org. **Ed:** Sybil Walker Barnes. **Released:** Annual; Latest edition 2009. **Price:** $225, Individuals; $200, Members; $350, Institutions. **Covers:** Federal, state, territorial, county, and major municipal public human service agencies. **Entries include:** Agency name, address, phone, fax, e-mail address, web site address, names of key personnel, program area. **Database includes:** Information on all major human service programs, such as child welfare, child support enforcement, Medicaid eligibility and claims, interstate compacts, and other programs. **Arrangement:** Geographical.

40576 ■ *""Put the Good, the Bad and the Ugly on the Table""* in South Florida Business Journal (Vol. 35, September 19, 2014, No. 8, pp. 13)
Pub: American City Business Journals
Released: September 19, 2014. **Description:** United Way of Broward County chief executive, Kathleen Cannon, says the creation of a macropractice for social work is the most rewarding part of her job. She also said teaching people how to give back is the most challenging part of her role.

40577 ■ *"Putting Down Roots"* in Entrepreneur (August 2014)
Pub: Entrepreneur Media Inc.
Released: August 2014. **Description:** Entrepreneur Justin Hartfield and partner Doug Francis created Weedmaps.com, an online portal for marijuana dispensaries, after California legalized the sale of medical marijuana. Hartfield is looking forward to a billion-dollar business once the federal prohibition of marijuana is ended. Local dispensaries pay a monthly subscription of $420 to appear on the site while doctors pay $295 to be featured on the site. Harfield is seeking partnerships with lboratories that will provide marijuana testing and other services.

40578 ■ *"Q&A With Devin Ringling: Franchise's Services Go Beyond Elder Care"* in Gazette (October 2, 2010)
Pub: The Gazette
Ed: Bill Radford. **Description:** Profile of franchise, Interim HealthCare, in Colorado Springs, Colorado; the company offers home care services that include wound care and specialized feedings to shopping and light housekeeping. It also runs a medical staffing company that provides nurses, therapists and other health care workers to hospitals, prisons, schools and other facilities.

40579 ■ *"The Quest for the Smart Prosthetic"* in Canadian Business (Vol. 83, October 12, 2010, No. 17, pp. 26)
Pub: Rogers Media Inc.
Contact: Tony Viner, President
Ed: Jacqueline Nelson. **Description:** Information about a two-year research project led by Southern Methodist University (SMU) and funded by the Defense Advance Research Projects Agency (DARPA) is provided. The agency aims to create a 'smart prosthetic' which will improve the lives of military amputees. The planned prosthetic will use a sensor that can carry nerve signals through synthetic channels.

40580 ■ *"Questions Abound in Voluminous Health Care Reform Law"* in Memphis Business Journal (Vol. 34, July 6, 2012, No. 12, pp. 1)
Pub: American City Business Journal
Ed: Cole Epley. **Description:** US Supreme Court has upheld the health care reform legislation, also known as Obamacare, as thelaw of the land. However, key questions remain and conjecture surrounding which direction states and insurance providers will pursue abounds. Insights on possible impact of health care providers of TennCare are also given.

40581 ■ *"Quincy Veterinarian Advises That Pets as 'Young' as Seven Years Need Senior Care"* in Benzinga.com (September 9, 2012)
Pub: Benzinga.com
Contact: Kyle Bazzy, President
Description: Veterinarian advises pet owners to have their pets over seven years of age seen for regular senior office visits. That age in animals is equal to middle age of humans. At age 10, a pet is considered geriatric. Health conditions after age seven can include arthritis, heart disease, liver or kidney problems, and thyroid problems.

40582 ■ *"Rebels' Cause: Adult Stem Cell"* in Austin Business Journal (Vol. 31, June 3, 2011, No. 13, pp. 1)
Pub: American City Business Journals
Ed: Sandra Zaragoza. **Description:** MedRebels Foundation was launched in February 2011 with the goal of providing millions of dollars for research funding, education and advocacy for adult stem cell-

focused medicine. The foundation, whose major contributor is SpineSmith LP, is a collaboration of other adult stem cell-related companies and nonprofit partners. It hopes to raise $200,000 by the end of 2011.

40583 ■ *"Recovery on Tap for 2010?"* in Orlando Business Journal (Vol. 26, January 1, 2010, No. 31, pp. 1)
Pub: American City Business Journals
Ed: Melanie Stawicki Azam, Richard Bilbao, Christopher Boyd, Anjali Fluker. **Description:** Economic forecasts for Central Florida's leading business sectors in 2010 are presented. These sectors include housing, film and TV, sports business, law, restaurants, aviation, tourism and hospitality, banking and finance, commercial real estate, retail, health care, insurance, higher education, and manufacturing. According to some local executives, Central Florida's economy will slowly recover in 2010.

40584 ■ *"Red Tape: A Business Opportunity"* in Business Journal (Vol. 30, July 20, 2012, No. 8, pp. 1)
Pub: American City Business Journals, Inc.
Contact: Whitney Shaw, President
Ed: Katharine Grayson. **Released:** July 20, 2012.
Description: The transition from the International Statistical Classification of Diseases and Related Health Problems (ICD)-9 coding system to ICD-10 creates business opportunities for software and professional services companies in Minneapolis, Minnesota. Coding-related products and services are being offered to help healthcare providers and insurers comply with the 2014 federal mandate.

40585 ■ *"Region Wins as GE Puts Plants Close to R&D"* in Business Review Albany (Vol. 41, July 4, 2014, No. 15, pp. 8)
Pub: American City Business Journals, Inc.
Contact: Whitney Shaw, President
Released: July 4, 2014. **Description:** General Electric Company (GE) invested over $400 million into the expansion of its health care, battery and renewable energy businesses in the Albany, New York region. The company's local growth secured about 7,000 private-sector jobs in the area and strengthened the relationship between GE research and manufacturing.

40586 ■ *"Rehab Centers Flourish Under Obamacare"* in Puget Sound Business Journal (Vol. 35, August 1, 2014, No. 15, pp. 8)
Pub: American City Business Journals
Released: August 1, 2014. **Description:** Hospitals are looking to partner with long-term care and rehabilitation facilities that can continue care with discharged patients in compliance with the Affordable Care Act. The government regulated insurance coverage could mean better follow-up care and less spending and waste in the health care system.

40587 ■ *"Renal Solutions Move Not a Sign of the Times"* in l>Pittsburgh Business Times (Vol. 33, February 14, 2014, No. 31, pp. 5)
Pub: American City Business Journals
Released: February 14, 2014. **Description:** Renal Solutions, a Pittsburgh, Pennsylvania-based company, has decided to relocate to California. Company founder, Pete DeComo, believes that the firm's move should not be a cause for concern within the city's business community. Renal Solutions was acquired by Fresenius Medical Care North America in 2007.

40588 ■ *"Renewed Vision"* in Hawaii Business (Vol. 54, August 2008, No. 2, pp. 49)
Ed: Jason Ubay. **Description:** Saint Francis Healthcare System of Hawaii, ranked 81 in Hawaii's top 250 companies for 2008, has been rebranding to focus on senior community healthcare and sold some of its operations, which explains the decline in gross sales from $219.5M in 2006 to $122.7M in 2007. The system's senior services and home hospice service expansion are provided.

40589 ■ *"Report Card Gives Employees Health Grade"* in Pittsburgh Business Times

(Vol. 33, June 6, 2014, No. 47, pp. 7)
Pub: American City Business Journals
Released: June 6, 2014. **Description:** Excela Health, Category Winner in the 1,200 to 4,999 employees group in Healthiest Employers of Western Pennsylvania 2014, offered employees a report card giving a letter grade summary of their biometric screening results and forwarded same to primary care doctors within 30 minutes of the test. The initiative was extended to spouses and partners and also carried a financial incentive to participate.

40590 ■ *"Research Reports: How Analysts Size Up Companies"* in Barron's (Vol. 88, June 30, 2008, No. 26, pp. M11)
Pub: Dow Jones & Co., Inc.
Contact: Clare Hart, President
Ed: Anita Peltonen. **Description:** Shares of Developers Diversified Realty Corp. get a 'Long-Term Buy' rating while the shares of HealthSouth Corp. and Onyx Pharmaceutical get a rating of 'Underperform' and a 'Buy' rating respectively. The shares of American Capital Agency, American Public Education, Bankrate, and Werner Enterprises are also ranked.

40591 ■ *"Research, Treatment to Expand"* in Philadelphia Business Journal (Vol. 28, June 22, 2012, No. 19, pp. 1)
Pub: American City Business Journal
Description: Fox Chase Cancer Center and Temple University Health System have been planning several projects once their merger is completed. Their plans include the construction of a unit for cancer patients on the third floor of the Founder's Building at Jeanes Hospital and a granting mechanism to fund research collaborations.

40592 ■ *"Retail Clinic Chain Moves Into Capitol Region"* in Sacramento Business Journal (Vol. 31, August 15, 2014, No. 25, pp. 4)
Pub: American City Business Journals
Released: August 15, 2014. **Description:** Minute-Clinic is planning to open a third clinic in Fair Oaks, California. Minuteclinics are open seven days a week and do not require appointments. The new clinic is part of the company's aggressive expansion plan.

40593 ■ *"Retail Health Clinics Sprout in Area; Doctors Feel Threat, Have Concerns"* in Crain's Detroit Business (April 7, 2008)
Pub: Crain Communications Inc.
Contact: Rance E. Crain, President
Ed: Mike Scott. **Description:** Competing with doctors' offices for routine patient visits are the retail health clinics which have made their way into the metro Detroit area. Physicians are concerned about the limited doctor supervision on site.

40594 ■ *"Retailers, Your Will, and More"* in Agency Sales Magazine (Vol. 39, July 2009, No. 7, pp. 46)
Ed: Melvin H. Daskal. **Description:** IRS audit guide for small retail businesses is presented. Tips on how to make a will with multiple beneficiaries are discussed together with medical expenses that can not be deducted.

40595 ■ *"Reviving Entrepreneurship: Policy Decisions in 12 Areas Could Nurture - Or Cripple - America's Greatest Asset"* in Harvard Business Review (Vol. 90, March 2012, No. 3, pp. 116)
Pub: Harvard Business Review Press
Contact: Peter E. Walsh, Director
Ed: Josh Lerner, William Sahlman. **Released:** March 2012. **Description:** Government policies should address entrepreneurship as a process, rather than an act. Several key areas for policymaking include basic and translational science, supply and quality of human capital, information availability, tax treatment of rewards and risks, intellectual property rights, workforce healthcare, and mobility of financial and human capital.

40596 ■ *"ReWalk Robotics Aims for IPO"* in Boston Business Journal (Vol. 34, July 18,

2014, No. 24, pp. 7)
Pub: American City Business Journals, Inc.
Contact: Whitney Shaw, President
Released: July 18, 2014. **Description:** ReWalk Robotics, an Israeli firm that manufactures wearable robotics exoskeletons for paraplegics, wants to launch an initial public offering (IPO) to raise US$57.5 million. In a July 2014 filing, ReWalk cited an accumulated debt of US$27 million at the end of 2013, justifying the need to go public and raise additional funds.

40597 ▪ *"RF Technologies Celebrates 25th Anniversary of Keeping Patients and Senior Care Residents Safe and Secure"* in PR Newswire (August 1, 2012)
Pub: PR Newswire Association L.L.C.
Contact: David B. Armon, President
Description: RF Technologies has entered into the senior care market by offering wireless wandering managemnt systems and transmitters to help reduce the risk of resident elopements. RF is a leading provider of customized radio frequency identification (RFID) healthcare safety and security solutions for the healthcare sector.

40598 ▪ *"Rich or Poor, Hospitals Must Work Together"* in Crain's Chicago Business (Vol. 31, April 28, 2008, No. 17, pp. 22)
Pub: Crain Communications Inc.
Contact: Todd Johnson, Publisher
Description: Chicago-area safety-net hospitals that serve the poor, uninsured and underinsured are struggling to stay open while wealthier areas compete to build advanced facilities for the expensive surgical procedures their privately insured patients can afford. If these safety-net hospitals close, their patients, many of them in ambulances, will show up at the remaining hospitals resulting in a strain that will test the ability of hospitals across the region to care for all of their patients. Hospitals need to address the threats to the local health care system before it slips into crisis since the current every-hospital-for-itself approach that pays off big for some will eventually will make losers of everyone.

40599 ▪ *"Riding Herd on Health Care"* in Business Journal Portland (Vol. 30, February 7, 2014, No. 49, pp. 8)
Pub: American City Business Journals
Released: February 7, 2014. **Description:** Singing rancher and aspiring gubernatorial candidate, Jon Justesen, explains his views on universal healthcare. He expresses support for health care reform and Cover Oregon and he is looking at his options after dropping his Republican primary bid.

40600 ▪ *"Riding the Wave: Past Trends and Future Directions for Health IT Research"* in MIS Quarterly (Vol. 36, September 2012, No. 3, pp. III)
Pub: MIS Research Center, Carlson School of
    Management
Description: Trends in healthcare information technologies, also known as health informatics, are discussed.

40601 ▪ *"The Right Remedy: Entrepreneur's Success Is a Matter of Life and Death"* in Black Enterprise (Vol. 38, February 2008, No. 7, pp. 46)
Pub: Earl G. Graves Publishing Co. Inc.
Contact: Earl G. Graves, Jr., President
Ed: Tamara E. Holmes. **Description:** Profile of Leah Brown, whose company conducts clinical trials to determine if specific drugs will relieve particular symptoms. Her company will also visit physician's offices to make certain doctors are following proper protocol for a clinical trial or will collect data from patients.

40602 ▪ *"Roseville Ob-Gyn Group Grows With Patient Focus, Diverse Services"* in Crain's Detroit Business (Vol. 24, April 7, 2008, No. 14)
Pub: Crain Communications Inc.
Contact: Rance E. Crain, President
Ed: Christine Snyder. **Description:** According to the American Medical Association, the number of medical groups of 10 or more physicians has been grow-

ing. Eastside Gynecology Obstetrics is one such group which has seen its yearly revenue grow due to a good business plan and a diversity of services and doctors.

40603 ▪ *"Roswell Supports New Rochester Institute"* in Business First of Buffalo (Vol. 30, May 16, 2014, No. 35, pp. 6)
Pub: American City Business Journals, Inc.
Contact: Whitney Shaw, President
Released: May 16, 2014. **Description:** The Roswell Park Cancer Institute said the University of Roswell in Rochester's new Wilmot Cancer Institute will benefit patients in the area. The organization will also launch a $30 million campaign to support cancer research. The center is also planning to purchase Batavia Radiation Oncology Associates.

40604 ▪ *"Rural Hospitals a Dying Breed"* in Memphis Business Journal (No. 35, April 11, 2014, No. 53, pp. 4)
Pub: American City Business Journals
Released: April 11, 2014. **Description:** Crittenden Regional Hospital in West Memphis, Tennessee has joined a growing number of rural hospitals across the country that is in jeopardy. Rural hospitals care for a patient population that is getting smaller and poorer and more dependent on government programs like Medicare and Medicaid. The hospital's challenges are addressed.

40605 ▪ *"St. David's South Austin Hospital to Get $72M Makeover"* in Austin Business JournalInc. (Vol. 29, January 15, 2010, No. 45, pp. 1)
Pub: American City Business Journals
Ed: Sandra Zaragoza. **Description:** St. David's South Austin Medical Center, formerly St. David's South Austin Hospital, is undertaking an expansion and renovation project worth $72 million. Meanwhile, CEO Erol Akdamar has resigned to serve as CEO of Medical City Hospital in Dallas, Texas. A new CEO and a general contractor for the project are yet to be chosen by the hospital.

40606 ▪ *"St. Elizabeth Healthcare Fights for Share at St. Lukes"* in Business Courier (Vol. 27, November 12, 2010, No. 28, pp. 1)
Pub: Business Courier
Ed: James Ritchie. **Description:** Key information on how St. Elizabeth Healthcare helps partner St. Luke's Hospitals increase market share in the healthcare industry are presented. Some of St. Luke's hospitals, such as the St. Elizabeth Fort Thomas in Kentucky, are struggling with low occupancy rates, prompting St. Elizabeth to invest about $24 million to help St. Luke's increase its market share.

40607 ▪ *"St. Luke's Gets Shot in the Arm From Outpatient Services"* in Saint Louis Business Journal (Vol. 31, August 19, 2011, No. 52, pp. 1)
Pub: Saint Louis Business Journal
Ed: Angela Mueller, E.B. Solomont. **Description:** St. Louis, Missouri-based St. Luke's Hospital benefited from investing in outpatient services as contained in its latest bond offering. Fitch Ratings gave the bond issuance an A rating.

40608 ▪ *"San Antonlo Researchers Develop New Laser-Based Imaging System"* in San Antonio Business Journal (Vol. 26, August 24, 2012, No. 30, pp. 1)
Pub: American City Business Journal
Description: Researchers at the University of Texas Health Science Center at San Antonio in Texas have developed an optical sensor-dependent medical imaging system, which is ready for commercialization. The laser-based imaging system is expected to improve non-invasive imaging for medical diagnostics.

40609 ▪ *"Scottsdale Business Bank Plans 4Q Opening"* in The Business Journal - Serving Phoenix and the Valley of the Sun (Vol. 28, August 15, 2008, No. 50)
Pub: American City Business Journals, Inc.
Contact: Whitney Shaw, President
Ed: Chris Casacchia. **Description:** Arizona's Department of Financial Institutions has approved Scottsdale Business Bank, a community bank which plans

to open in the fourth quarter of 2008. The bank, which is to be located near McCormick Ranch in Scottsdale, Arizona, will cater to small business owners in the professional sector, such as accountants and doctors.

40610 ▪ *Selling the Invisible: A Field Guide to Modern Marketing*
Pub: Business Plus
Ed: Harry Beckwith. **Released:** March 20, 2012. **Price:** $15.99; C$17.50; $9.99; $10.99. **Description:** Tips for marketing and selling intangibles such as health care, entertainment, tourism, legal services, and more are provided. **Availability:** PrintElectronic publishing.

40611 ▪ *"Senator Grills Collection Agency, Health System Executives"* in PaymentsSource (May 31, 2012)
Pub: SourceMedia Inc.
Contact: James M. Malkin, Chief Executive Officer
Released: May 31, 2012. **Description:** Accretive Health Inc. and Fairview Health Services executives were questioned by Senator Al Franken about its debt collection practices. The suit was initiated after unencrypted private information on 23,500 patients was stolen from an Acrretive employee's vehicle. Details of the lawsuit are outlined.

40612 ▪ *"Senior Care Provider AdCare Health Systems Enters Tulsa Market"* in Journal Record (August 28, 2012)
Pub: Dolan Media Inc.
Ed: Kirby Lee Davis. **Description:** AdCare Health Systems has expanded to the Tulsa, Oklahoma area with a $5.7 million purchase of the 121-bed Companions Specialized Care Center. Details of the deal are disclosed.

40613 ▪ *"Seton Grows Heart Institute"* in Austin Business Journal (Vol. 31, July 15, 2011, No. 19, pp. A1)
Pub: American City Business Journals
Ed: Sandra Zaragoza. **Description:** Seton Heart Institute experienced significant growth in the last six months. The organization added physicians, specialists and outreach offices across Central Texas.

40614 ▪ *"Seven Things Great Employers Do (That Others Don't); Unusual, Innovative, and Proven Tactics To Create Productive and Profitable Working Environments"* in Gallup Business Journal (April 15, 2014)
Pub: Gallup Press
Released: April 15, 2014. **Description:** Seven unusual, innovative, and proven tactics that create productive and profitable working environments are examined through researching 32 companies. These firms represented many industries, including healthcare, financial services, hospitality, manufacturing, and retail throughout the world.

40615 ▪ *"Shape Up! Jamal Williams Develops KIDFIT App to Combat Childhood Obesity"* in Black Enterprise (Vol. 41, August 2010, No. 1, pp. 62)
Pub: Earl G. Graves Publishing Co. Inc.
Contact: Earl G. Graves, Jr., President
Ed: Sonya A. Donaldson. **Description:** Profile of Jamal Williams who developed KIDFIT, an app that helps to combat childhood obesity by offering 150 various exercises for children, with an emphasis on training, conditioning, coordination, and flexibility.

40616 ▪ *"Shop Happy: Harvesting Happiness Announces Grassroots Crowdfunding Site for HH4Heroes"* in Internet Wire (July 2, 2012)
Released: July 12, 2012. **Description:** Shop Happy online store has created a fundraising aspect to their customers' shopping experience. Shoppers can assist in helping to heal post combat veterans suffering from PTSD, TBI, MST, andMSA who have served as combat warriors in Operations Iraqi and Enduring Freedom. Lisa Cypers Kamen, founder of Harvesting Happiness believes this program will help both veterans and customers to empower themselves and our veterans in a positive way (HH4Heroes.org).

40617 ■ *"Sinai Doctor's Research May Lead to Rival Plavix Drug"* in *Baltimore Business Journal (Vol. 28, July 16, 2010, No. 10, pp. 1)*
Pub: Baltimore Business Journal

Ed: Emily Mullin. **Description:** Paul Gurbel, Sinai Hospital Center for Thrombosis Research director, is seeking an FDA approval of Brilinta, a drug which he helped create and test. Gurbel says that the approval could bring the drug to market as early as December 2010. The drug is expected to rival Bristol-Myers' Plavix, which generated almost $6.2 billion in 2009.

40618 ■ *"Six Things You Can Do To Ride Out A Turbulent Market"* in *Hispanic Business (Vol. 30, March 2008, No. 3, pp. 20)*
Pub: Hispanic Business Inc.
Contact: Jesus Chavarria, President

Ed: Hildy Medina, Michael Bowker. **Description:** Top financial experts' views on managing investment portfolios during turbulent periods in the stock market are reported. Experts prefer investing in health care, short term investments, international bonds and preferred stocks or just maintain cash until such times as the market settles.

40619 ■ *"Sixty-Acre Vision for North Suburbs"* in *Business Courier (Vol. 24, April 4, 2008, No. 52, pp. 1)*
Pub: American City Business Journals, Inc.
Contact: Whitney Shaw, President

Ed: Laura Baverman. **Description:** Al Neyer Inc. plans for a mixed-use development at the 60-acre site it has recently purchased. The mixed-use project could cost up to $100 million, and will include medical offices, residential buildings, and corporate offices. Details of Al Neyer's plans for the site are given.

40620 ■ *"Sleep Apnea Pill Nears Human Tests"* in *Philadelphia Business Journal (Vol. 33, May 9, 2014, No. 13, pp. 8)*
Pub: American City Business Journals

Released: May 9, 2014. **Description:** Galleon Pharmaceuticals is set to begin human testing of its experimental therapy GAL-160, an oral medicine for sleep apnea, and has already started human testing of GAL-021, an intravenous drug to treat respiratory complications in patients receiving anesthetics and opiate pain medication. Galleon CEO, James C. Mannion, hopes that both drugs pass the proof-of-concept stage and move to mid-stage clinical testing in humans by mid-2015.

40621 ■ *"SLU, Des Peres Hospitals Face Unions"* in *St. Louis Business Journal (Vol. 32, June 1, 2012, No. 41, pp. 1)*
Pub: American City Business Journal

Description: Executives at St. Louis University (SLU) Hospital and Des Peres Hospital are watching efforts by labor unions to organize workers at the hospitals. The simultaneous campaigns are being led by the California Nurses Association/National Nurses Organizing Committee and SEIU Healthcare. SLU Hospital nurses will vote on union representation on June 7, 2012.

40622 ■ *"Sluggish Market Gives Hospitals the Financial Chills"* in *The Business Journal-Serving Greater Tampa Bay (Vol. 28, August 4, 2008)*
Pub: American City Business Journals, Inc.
Contact: Whitney Shaw, President

Ed: Margie Manning. **Description:** Operating margins for hospitals in the Tampa Bay, Florida area have been reduced from 2 percent in 2006 to 0.8 percent in 2007 due to a weaker US economy. Total margins, on the other hand, rose from 2.9 percent to 3.3 percent in the same period.

40623 ■ *"Small Biz Owners Are Tapping Into Health Savings Plans"* in *Small Business Opportunities (Fall 2007)*

Ed: Michael L. Corne. **Description:** Health savings accounts were developed by Golden Rule, a United Healthcare company. Today, more than 40 percent of the company's customers are covered by health savings account plans.

40624 ■ *Small Business Access and Alternatives to Health Care: Hearing before the Committee on Small Business, U.S. House of Representatives*
Pub: DIANE Publishing Co.
Contact: Dorothy J. Perkins, Manager
E-mail: dorothyjperkins@hotmail.com
Released: 2003. **Price:** $35, paperback. **Description:** Congressional hearings regarding the health care crisis facing America's small businesses is discussed.

40625 ■ *Small Business Access to Health Care: Hearing Before the Committee on Small Business, U.S. House of Representatives*
Pub: DIANE Publishing Co.
Contact: Dorothy J. Perkins, Manager
E-mail: dorothyjperkins@hotmail.com
Released: 2002. **Price:** $25, paperback. **Description:** Congressional hearing held at Crystal Lake, Illinois. Witnesses: Mary Blankenbaker, Co-Owner, Benjamin's Restaurant; Ryan Brauns, Senior Vice President, Rockford Consulting and Brokerage; Scott Shalek, RHU, Shalek Financial Services; Brad Close, National Federation of Independent Businesses; Ken Koehler, Flowerwood, Inc.; Brad Buxton, Vice President of Networks and Medical Management, Blue Cross and Blue Shield of Illinois; Isabella Wilson, Chief Financial Office, Illinois Blower, Inc.; and James Milam, Illinois State Medical Society. **Availability:** Print.

40626 ■ *The Small Business Guide to HSAs*
Pub: Brick Tower Press
Contact: Linda Goetz Holmes, Editor
Ed: JoAnn Mills Laing. **Released:** August 31, 2004. **Price:** $14.95. **Description:** Government-assisted Health Savings Accounts (HSAs) offer employees a tax-free way to accumulate savings to be used for qualified medical expenses, they can be rolled over without penalty for future spending, or invested to accumulate savings to pay for health needs after retirement. Employers offering HSAs can save up to two-thirds of business expenses on health insurance costs.

40627 ■ *"Small Businesses Changing Their Health Plan Preferences"* in *Boston Business Journal (Vol. 29, June 24, 2011, No. 7, pp. 1)*
Pub: American City Business Journals, Inc.
Ed: Scott Dance. **Description:** Small businesses in Maryland are shifting from traditional health plans to the consumer-oriented health savings accounts or HSAs. Health insurance industry experts say the change is indicative of the insurance buyers' desire to be more thrifty and discerning in their health care purchases.

40628 ■ *"Small, But Mighty"* in *Employee Benefit News (Vol. 25, November 1, 2011, No. 14, pp. 32)*
Pub: SourceMedia Inc.
Contact: James M. Malkin, Chief Executive Officer
Ed: Andrea Davis. **Description:** Three consulting firms are facing the challenge of helping clients understand the new health care reform in a tight economy.

40629 ■ *"'Smart' Google Contacts on the Way"* in *Dallas Business Journal (Vol. 37, July 18, 2014, No. 45, pp. 11)*
Pub: American City Business Journals
Released: July 18, 2014. **Description:** Efforts are being undertaken by Alcon Labs, the Fort Worth-based company along with Google Inc. to develop smart contact lenses with embedded electronics to monitor health and improve vision. Some of the applications of the lenses include monitoring the wearer's blood sugar, correct vision, as well as other ocular capabilities.

40630 ■ *"Smart Questions: Health Care: How to Get a Better Deal"* in *Inc. (November 2007, pp. 34)*
Pub: Mansueto Ventures L.L.C.
Contact: John Koten, Chief Executive Officer
Ed: Sarah Goldstein. **Description:** Things to consider when choosing an insurance carrier for your employees are explored.

40631 ■ *"A Smarter Kind of Taxes"* in *Canadian Business (Vol. 80, October 8, 2007, No. 20, pp. 203)*
Ed: Jack Mintz. **Description:** Forecasts on Canada's tax system by 2020 are analyzed. It is expected that the country's aging society will place great demands on elderly-related spending such as pensions and healthcare. And, since the elderly pay fewer taxes, the revenue available to the government will be reduced. Other trends also show that several factors will cause significant change to the country's tax system.

40632 ■ *"The Smell of Fear: Is a Bottom Near?"* in *Barron's (Vol. 88, March 17, 2008, No. 11, pp. M3)*
Pub: Dow Jones & Co., Inc.
Contact: Clare Hart, President
Ed: Kopin Tan. **Description:** Liquidity problems at Bear Stearns frightened investors in markets around the world due to the fear of the prospects of a big bank's failure. Shares of health maintenance organizations got battered led by WellPoint, and Humana but longer-term investors who could weather short-term volatility may find value here. The value of J. Crew shares is also discussed.

40633 ■ *"A Social Context Model of Envy and Social Undermining"* in *Academy of Management Journal (Vol. 55, June 1, 2012, No. 3, pp. 643)*
Pub: Academy of Management
Contact: Ming-Jer Chen, President
Ed: Michelle K. Duffy, Kristin L. Scott, Jason D. Shaw, Bennett J. Tepper, Karl Aquino. **Description:** The relationship between envy and social undermining is investigated using the case of hospital employees. Results show that the impact of envy on social undermining through moral disengagement is higher when social identification ith coworkers is low. The indirect effect of envy is also greater in teams with high team undermining norms and low team identification.

40634 ■ *"Something Different in the Air? The Collapse of the Schwarzenegger Health Plan in Calfornia"* in *WorkingUSA (June 2008)*
Ed: Daniel J.B. Mitchell. **Description:** In January 2007, California Governor Arnold Schwarzenegger proposed a state universal health care plan modeled after the Massachusetts individual mandate program. A year later, the plan was dead. Although some key interest groups eventually backed the plan, it was overwhelmed by a looming state budget crisis and a lack of gubernatorial focus. Although much acclaimed for his stance on greenhouse gases, stem cells, hydrogen highways, and other Big Ideas, diffused gubernatorial priorities and a failure to resolve California's chronic fiscal difficulties let the clock run out on universal health care.

40635 ■ *"Sorry: Good Defense for Mal Offense"* in *The Business Journal-Serving Metropolitan Kansas City (Vol. 26, July 4, 2008, No. 43, pp. 1)*
Ed: Rob Roberts. **Description:** According to a survey conducted by the Kansas City Business Journal, ten hospitals in Kansas City showed that they have adopted disclosure policies that include prompt apologies and settlement offers. The policy is effective in minimizing medical malpractice lawsuits. Other details of the survey are presented.

40636 ■ *"South Lake Hospital Starting $47M Patient Tower"* in *Orlando Business Journal (Vol. 26, December 4, 2009, No. 26, pp. 1)*
Pub: American City Business Journals
Ed: Melanie Stawicki Azam. **Description:** Clermont, Florida's South Lake Hospital has divulged intentions to issue $50.9 million in bonds in order to fund construction of the $47 million patient tower. The three-story, 124,000 square foot tower would add eighteen inpatient rooms, a new lobby and expanded pharmacy, diagnostic and lab services, and treatment areas.

40637 ■ *"SpineThera Raises $750K for Steroid Alternative"* in *Business Journal (Vol.*

32, June 13, 2014, No. 3, pp. 6)

Pub: American City Business Journals

Released: June 13, 2014. **Description:** SpineThera Inc. received $750,000 from angel investors for the development of its new injectable drug for the treatment of lower back pain. The new drug would serve as an alternative to steroid injections for back and neck pain. The effect of the drug is also expected to last longer than steroid injections.

40638 ■ *"Spinout Success: New Leadership Steps In At UW's C4C" in Puget Sound Business Journal (Vol. 35, June 27, 2014, No. 10, pp. 11)*

Pub: American City Business Journals

Released: June 27, 2014. **Description:** University of Washington's Center for Commercialization vice provost, Vikram Jandhyala, talks about his new position with the school. Jandhyala says he plans to build more synergy between the medical school and engineering and between social sciences and computer science. He also says the medical and software industry need to grow to accommodate the volume of data crossing and stored within the Internet.

40639 ■ *"Spouses, Health Coaching Added to Mix" in Pittsburgh Business Times (Vol. 33, June 6, 2014, No. 47, pp. 5)*

Pub: American City Business Journals

Released: June 6, 2014. **Description:** Hospital giant, UPMC, was the Category Winner in the 5,000+ employees group of Healthiest Employers in Western Pennsylvania, for its initiative in expanding its health assessment and wellness programs to the spouses and partners of all its employees, regardless of their health insurance carrier. In addition, UPMC Health Plan expanded its individual health coaching option for members as well as corporate clients.

40640 ■ *"Spouses Plan for the Return of the Company Doctor" in Philadelphia Business Journal (Vol. 33, May 2, 2014, No. 12, pp. 4)*

Pub: American City Business Journals

Released: May 2, 2014. **Description:** Nephrologist, Scott Bralow and primary care physician, Vick Bralow, started a company called Affordable Care Options in Philadelphia, Pennsylvania. The couple's company will provide physicians to the workplace to monitor the health of employees for a monthly fee.

40641 ■ *"Startup Osteosphere Formed to Develop Laboratory Discovery" in Houston Business Journal (Vol. 40, January 8, 2010, No. 35, pp. 1)*

Pub: American City Business Journals

Ed: Casey Wooten. **Description:** Biotech startup company Osteosphere in Houston, Texas aims to market a technology in which laboratory-grown bone tissues can be processed to appear like a real human bone tissue. The technology was developed by a co-founder of the startup and it can be applied to bone disease and injury treatment. Osteophere's future plans, such as the search for possible investors, is also outlined.

40642 ■ *"State Budget Woes Hurt Many Vendors, Senior Services" in Sacramento Business Journal (Vol. 25, August 15, 2008, No. 24, pp. 1)*

Pub: American City Business Journals, Inc.

Contact: Whitney Shaw, President

Ed: Melanie Turner. **Description:** Delays in the passage of the California state budget have adversely affected the health care industry. The Robertson Adult Day Health Care had taken out loans to keep the business afloat. The state Legislature has reduced Medi-Cal reimbursement to health care providers by 10 percent.

40643 ■ *"State Cuts Could Affect Senior Care Programs" in Journal Star (May 10, 2012)*

Pub: McClatchy Tribune Information Services

Ed: Justin Glawe. **Description:** Medicaid reforms in Illinois have helped senior citizens in the state because of improvements in community care programs.

40644 ■ *"The Stem Cell Revolution" in Canadian Business (Vol. 79, November 20, 2006, No. 23, pp. 31)*

Pub: Rogers Media Inc.

Contact: Tony Viner, President

Ed: Erin Pooley. **Description:** The commercial prospects and the future of stem cell therapeutics are presented. The use of stem cell therapy to heal the chronic conditions of patients is also discussed.

40645 ■ *"Stent Cases at Md. Hospitals Falling" in Baltimore Business Journal (Vol. 28, November 12, 2010, No. 27, pp. 1)*

Pub: Baltimore Business Journal

Ed: Emily Mullin. **Description:** Cardiologists believe that the recent drop in cardiac stent procedures in Maryland can be associated with the ongoing investigation of Dr. Mark G. Midei and St. Joseph Medical Center. Midei is accused of performing unnecessary stent procedures on patients and was let go from the clinical practice in St. Joseph in 2009.

40646 ■ *"Strategic Issue Management as Change Catalyst" in Strategy and Leadership (Vol. 39, September-October 2011, No. 5, pp. 20-29)*

Pub: Emerald Group Publishing Inc.

Ed: Bruce E. Perrott. **Description:** A study analyzes the case of a well-known Australian healthcare organization to examine how a company's periodic planning cycle is supplemented with a dynamic, real-time, strategic-issue-management system under high turbulence conditions. Findings highlight the eight steps that a company's management can use in its strategic issue management (SIM) process to track, monitor and manage strategic issues so as to ensure that the corporate, strategy, and capability are aligned with one another in turbulent times.

40647 ■ *"Struggling States Slashing Health Care For Poor" in Chicago Tribune (January 15, 2009)*

Pub: McClatchy-Tribune Information Services

Ed: Noam N. Levey. **Description:** Health officials warn that even the huge federal rescue plan may not be enough to restore health services being eliminated due to the economic crisis.

40648 ■ *"SunLink Health Systems Subsidiaries Open Senior Behavioral Care Units in Dahlonega, GA and Fulton, MO" in Mental Health Weekly Digest (July 16, 2012, pp. 326)*

Pub: NewsRX

Contact: Susan E. Hasty, Publisher

Description: SunLink Health Systems Inc. opened Changing Seasons, a 10-bed geriatric psychiatric unit in Dahlonega, Georgia and Kingdom Senior Solutions opened a 19-bed geriatric psychiatric unit in Fulton, Georgia. Details of the new facilities are defined.

40649 ■ *"Surgical Center Relocating to St. Joseph Campus" in Business First of Buffalo (Vol. 30, January 24, 2014, No. 19, pp. 3)*

Pub: American City Business Journals, Inc.

Contact: Whitney Shaw, President

Released: January 24, 2014. **Description:** The Sisters of Charity Hospital is relocating its off-site ambulatory surgery center to its St. Joseph campus in Buffalo, New York. the moves makes better use of available space, reduces costs and allows for ongoing redevelopment of the Cheektowaga campus, according to vice president of operations, Marty Boryszak.

40650 ■ *"Survey: Most Approve of Donating Used Pacemakers to Medically Underserved" in Crain's Detroit Business (Vol. 25, June 1, 2009)*

Pub: Crain Communications Inc. - Detroit

Contact: Keith Crain, Chairman

Description: According to a survey conducted by University of Michigan Cardiovascular Center, 87 percent of those with pacemakers and 71 percent of the general population would donate the device to patients in underserved nations.

40651 ■ *"Sutter, CHW Reject Blue Cross Deal" in Sacramento Business Journal (Vol. 25, August 15, 2008, No. 24, pp. 1)*

Pub: American City Business Journals, Inc.

Contact: Whitney Shaw, President

Ed: Kathy Robertson. **Description:** California-based Sutter Health and Catholic Healthcare West have rejected the $11.8 million class action settlement in connection with contract rescissions between California hospitals and Anthem Blue Cross. Blue Cross can halt the settlement if not enough hospitals accept it. The deal covers all hospitals that owe money due to rescinded Blue Cross coverage.

40652 ■ *"Sutter Court Win is Part of Trend" in Sacramento Business Journal (Vol. 31, July 25, 2014, No. 22, pp. 3)*

Pub: American City Business Journals

Released: July 25, 2014. **Description:** The Third District Court of Appeals dismissed 13 coordinated data-breach lawsuits filed against Sutter Health of Sacramento, California. The plaintiffs claim $4 billion in damages over theft of patient data from a local Sutter Health office in October 2011.

40653 ■ *"The Swedish Solution" in San Francisco Business Times (Vol. 28, May 2, 2014, No. 41, pp. 4)*

Pub: American City Business Journals

Released: May 2, 2014. **Description:** Seattle, Washington's Swedish Health Services decided to cut prices for outpatient procedures by about 35 percent. Some patients are hoping that the San Francisco Bay Area in California will see Swedish Health do the same, but observers think the region will have a hard time implementing price reductions.

40654 ■ *"Swift Shift" in Crain's Cleveland Business (Vol. 28, November 12, 2007, No. 45, pp. 1)*

Pub: Crain Communications Inc.

Ed: Shannon Mortland. **Description:** Discusses the ways in which Southwest General Health Center is working to stay competitive in a region that is highly saturated with health care providers.

40655 ■ *"Taking the Right Road" in Entrepreneur (Vol. 37, October 2009, No. 10, pp. 104)*

Pub: Entrepreneur Press

Contact: Perlman Neil, President

Ed: Jason Daley. **Description:** Joe Grubb's franchise of BrightStar Healthcare, a home health care provider, in Knoxville, Tennessee has grown into a $1 million business. Grubb, a former sales agent, experienced slow growth for his franchise and had to deal with cash flow issues during its first few months.

40656 ■ *"Targeting Back Pain, With a Big Backer" in Business Journal (Vol. 31, May 2, 2014, No. 49, pp. 6)*

Pub: American City Business Journals

Released: May 2, 2014. **Description:** Orthology, a startup chain of orthopedic-pain clinics, plans to open new facilities. The company's clinics allow patients to schedule appointments online. Pat Tarnowski, Orthology's director of operations, believes that the company's focus on patient experience will allow the business to differentiate itself from competition.

40657 ■ *"Tax Tip: Affordable Health Care and Taxes" in Pet Product News (Vol. 66, September 2012, No. 9, pp. 39)*

Pub: Bowtie Inc.

Ed: Mark E. Battersby. **Description:** Implications of the US Supreme Court's ruling that the Affordable Care Act is now part of the Tax Code on small retail businesses, business owners, and self-employed persons are described. The ruling requires every individual to have health insurance to avoid tax penalties.

40658 ■ *"TECHNOLOGY: Elder Care Enters the Digital Age: Wireless Companies Devise Ways to Aid Home Health, Let People Stay in Homes" in Atlanta Journal-Constitution (April*

29, 2012, pp. D1)
Description: Mobile phone industry is actually helping families keep aging loved one in their homes. The home healthcare industry is adding technology, telecommunications, smartphone applications and other devices to make it easier for seniors to remain in their homes. Details on this growing industry are included along with statistical data.

40659 ■ *"Tenacious Trailblazer: Sandra Hernandez, Public Health Pioneer, is Hispanic Business Woman of the Year®"* in *Hispanic Business* (Vol. 30, April 2008, No. 4, pp. 26)
Pub: Hispanic Business Inc.
Contact: Jesus Chavarria, President
Ed: Melinda Burns. **Description:** Dr. Sandra Hernandez has been named as Hispanic Business Woman of the Year for her pioneering work in health care reform. Dr. Hernandez is the first Hispanic and the first woman to serve as public health director for the city and county of San Francisco.

40660 ■ *"Tenant Demands Broaden Medical Office Landscape"* in *San Antonio Business Journal* (Vol. 28, September 12, 2014, No. 31, pp. 8)
Pub: American City Business Journals
Released: September 12, 2014. **Description:** The NAI REOC San Antonio report has shown a demand among health care firms for real estate in San Antonio, Texas. However, the slight decline in absorption of space in the medical office market highlight the changing demand among medical users to facilities other than medical office buildings. The thriving healthcare industry in San Antonio is also discussed.

40661 ■ *"Thousands Balk at Health Law Sign-Up Mandate"* in *Boston Business Journal* (Vol. 27, November 9, 2007, No. 41, pp. 1)
Ed: Mark Hollmer. **Description:** About 100,000 Massachusetts residents have not signed up for insurance plans created as part of the state's health care reform law. Insurers have underestimated the number of new customers signing up for insurance and come close to risking penalties if they do not get insurance by the end of 2007. The Commonwealth Health Insurance Connector Authority's deadline to buy insurance before penalties kick in is November 15, 2007.

40662 ■ *"Ticketmaster Unveils Pink Tickets to Support Breast Cancer Awareness Month"* in *Travel & Leisure Close-Up* (October 8, 2012)
Description: National Football League is helping to raise awareness for the National Breast Cancer Awareness Month by issuing all tickets purchased through Ticketmaster be pink. A portion of every NFL ticket sold on Ticketmaster and on NFL Ticket Exchange will go toward the American Cancer Society's fight against breast cancer.

40663 ■ *"To Help Maintain an Adequate Blood Supply During the Summer Months"* in *Ice Cream Reporter* (Vol. 21, August 20, 2008, No. 9, pp. 8)
Description: Friendly's and the American Red Cross have partnered to offer blood donors a coupon for one free carton of Friendly's ice cream in order to maintain an adequate supply during summer months.

40664 ■ *"Today's Rx: Solo Physician Practice Loses Appeal"* in *Dallas Business Journal* (Vol. 35, July 13, 2012, No. 44, pp. 1)
Pub: American City Business Journal
Ed: Bill Hethcock. **Description:** The national statistics has shown a trend toward doctors increasingly choosing to work for hospitals, clinics and physician groups. Irving, Texas-based Merritt Hawkins has found in a survey that solo physicians accounted for just one percent of all the firm's searches. Survey details are included.

40665 ■ *"Top 10 Retirement Mistakes and How to Avoid Them"* in *Canadian Business* (Vol. 83, July 20, 2010, No. 11-12, pp. 39)
Pub: Rogers Media Inc.
Contact: Tony Viner, President
Ed: Jacqueline Nelson, Angelina Chapin. **Description:** Some of the top retirement mistakes is relying on selling one's house to find a retirement. Other

mistakes are paying too much for investments and planning to work in retirement since no one can be sure that they will be healthy enough to accomplish this. Suggestions to avoid these pitfalls are discussed.

40666 ■ *"Top 100 Consolidate Gains"* in *Hispanic Business* (Vol. 30, July-August 2008, No. 7-8, pp. 30)
Ed: Richard Kaplan. **Description:** Data developed by HispanTelligence on the increase in revenue posted by the top 100 fastest-growing U.S. Hispanic firms over the last five years is reported. Despite the economic downturn, the service sector, IT and health suppliers showed an increase in revenue whereas construction companies showed a marginal slump in revenue growth.

40667 ■ *"Top Male and Female Fittest CEO"* in *Hawaii Business* (Vol. 53, October 2007, No. 4, pp. 40)
Pub: PacificBasin Communications
Ed: Cathy S. Cruz-George. **Description:** Discusses the outcome of the fittest chief executive officers in Hawaii competition for 2007. Hawaii Capital Management's David Low leads the list while Group Pacific (Hawaii) Inc.'s Chip Doyle and Greater Good Inc.'s Kari Leong placed second and third, respectively. The CEO's routines, eating habits, and inspirations for staying fit are provided.

40668 ■ *"Top South Florida Diagnostic Centers"* in *South Florida Business Journal* (Vol. 34, April 18, 2014, No. 39, pp. 12)
Pub: American City Business Journals
Released: April 18, 2014. **Description:** Rankings of medical diagnostic centers in South Florida are presented. Rankings were based on the number of patients each laboratory or medical facility saw in 2013.

40669 ■ *"Trinity To Move Forward on 280, Despite Setback"* in *Birmingham Business Journal* (Vol. 29, July 20, 2012, No. 30, pp. 1)
Pub: American City Business Journals, Inc.
Contact: Whitney Shaw, President
Ed: Evan Belanger. **Released:** July 20, 2012. **Description:** The construction of the HealthSouth digital hospital could resume in 2013 as the Alabama Civil Appeals Court could decide on applications by the Trinity Medical Center to move to the planned hospital. The city hospital has filed cases to allow it to relocate to the building but has been blocked by a ruling from the Montgomery County District Court.

40670 ■ *"Trisun Healthcare Eager to Add Centers"* in *Austin Business JournalInc.* (Vol. 28, August 21, 2008, No. 23, pp. 1)
Pub: American City Business Journals
Ed: Kate Harrington. **Description:** Austin-based nursing and rehabilitation centers operator Trisun Healthcare plans to build more facilities as part of a growth strategy that can expand beyond Texas. Trisun has 16 facilities along the corridor from San Antonio to Temple, and projects to have three more in Texas in 2008.

40671 ■ *"Types of Health Plans"* in *HRMagazine* (Vol. 53, August 2008, No. 8, pp. 72)
Pub: Society for Human Resource Management
Contact: Henry G. Jackson, President
E-mail: hjackson@shrm.org
Description: Definitions are given for various types of health care coverage available. Fee-for-service (FFS), health maintenance organization (HMO), preferred provider organization (PPO), point of service (POS) and consumer-directed health plan (CDHP) are outlined.

40672 ■ *"The Ultimate Cure"* in *Conde Nast Portfolio* (Vol. 2, June 2008, No. 6, pp. 110)
Ed: David Ewing Duncan. **Description:** Small upstarts as well as pharmaceutical giants are developing drugs for the neurotechnology industry; these firms are attempting to adapt groundbreaking research into the basic workings of the brain to new drugs for ailments ranging from multiple sclerosis to dementia to insomnia.

40673 ■ *"Union-Hospital Deal Offers Few Details"* in *Sacramento Business Journal* (Vol. 31, May 9, 2014, No. 11, pp. 4)
Pub: American City Business Journals
Released: May 9, 2014. **Description:** The California Hospital Association and Service Employees International Union (SEIU)-United Healthcare Workers West agreed on a deal to create $100 million joint advocacy fund to address issues in health care costs, efficiency, and quality of care. The SEIU agreed to drop two ballot measures that target CEO pay and hospital prices in exchange for the deal.

40674 ■ *"U.S. Combined Life and Health Writers--Industry's Reported Admitted Assets of $5.7 Trillion"* in *Best's Review* (Vol. 113, September 2012, No. 5, pp. 33)
Description: U.S. Combined Life and Health Writers--Industry's Reported Admitted Assets of $5.7 Trillion report is presented. Companies/Groups are ranked in 2011 by admitted assets.

40675 ■ *"UnitedHealthcare Resists Prognosis"* in *The Business Journal-Serving Metropolitan Kansas City* (Vol. 26, August 29, 2008, No. 51)
Ed: Rob Roberts. **Description:** Saint Luke's Hospital Systems terminated UnitedHealthcare from its insurance provider network on July 25, 2008. Negotiators with both parties have stopped speaking, and employees under UnitedHealthcare plans will have to pay higher bills unless Saint Luke's reconsiders its decision. The parties' previous negotiations are discussed.

40676 ■ *"Unwanted News for Hospitals"* in *Business Courier* (Vol. 24, October 25, 2007, No. 28, pp. 1)
Pub: American City Business Journals, Inc.
Contact: Whitney Shaw, President
Ed: James Ritchie. **Description:** Christ and St. Luke Hospital might be sharing responsibility costs on the $207 million hospital being built by Health Alliance, the group they are parting with. Christ and St. Lu ke hospitals will be paying $60 million and $25 miilion for partial liability res pectively because the plans for the said project were already underway before they decided to withdraw. Christ Hospital is involved in a whistleblower case that might cause $424 million in liability across the group.

40677 ■ *"UPMC Aims to Profit From Billing Angst"* in *Pittsburgh Business Times* (Vol. 33, Jun3 27, 2014, No. 50, pp. 8)
Pub: American City Business Journals
Released: June 27, 2014. **Description:** Hospital network UPMC has created a wholly owned, for-profit subsidiary named Ovation Revenue Cycle Solutions that helps medical providers with the complex new Medicare billing codes that take effect October 2015. The service provides revenue-cycle tools designed to help medical groups enhance efficiency, cut rejection rates and reduce time between billing and payment.

40678 ■ *"UPMC Develops Own Billing Solutions"* in *Pittsburgh Business Times* (Vol. 33, January 17, 2014, No. 27, pp. 6)
Pub: American City Business Journals
Released: January 17, 2014. **Description:** How University of Pittsburgh Medical Center (UPMC) Health System transformed its accounts payable department by passing its process to a subsidiary, Prodigo Solutions, is discussed. UPMC moved suppliers and purchasers to a shared electronic platform and created a digital marketplace. The system's no purchase order, no pay policy has reduced the number of rogue purchases.

40679 ■ *"UW Wary of WSU's Wish for Spokane Medical School"* in *Puget Sound Business Journal* (Vol. 35, May 9, 2014, No. 3, pp. 9)
Pub: American City Business Journals
Released: May 9, 2014. **Description:** University of Washington leaders believe that opening a medical school in Washington State University's (WSU) Spokane Campus will create more competition for

state funding. However, WSU officials claim that the demand for new doctors demonstrates the need for a second school.

40680 ■ "VA Seeking Bidders for Fort Howard" in Baltimore Business Journal (Vol. 28, June 25, 2010, No. 7, pp. 1)
Pub: Baltimore Business Journal
Ed: Daniel J. Servnoitz. **Description:** The Veterans Affairs Maryland Health Care Systems has requested proposals from developers to build a retirement community at Fort Howard in Baltimore County. The historic site, which has about 36 mostly vacant buildings, could become the home to hundreds of war veterans. Details of the proposed development are discussed.

40681 ■ "Va. Stalls on Health Exchange" in Washington Business Journal (Vol. 31, July 6, 2012, No. 11, pp. 2)
Pub: American City Business Journals, Inc.
Contact: Whitney Shaw, President
Ed: Ben Fischer. **Released:** July 6, 2012. **Description:** Political leaders and health insurance companies in Virginia are at odds over the creation of a health benefits exchange in the state. Industry leaders want a swift creation of an online health benefits exchange, while conservative politicians in the state resist the creation of such an exchange.

40682 ■ "VC Round Will Pay for 'Sham' Surgery Trial" in Business Journal (Vol. 31, April 11, 2014, No. 46, pp. 6)
Pub: American City Business Journals
Released: April 11, 2014. **Description:** Holaira Inc. is preparing for a clinical trial of its technology for treating lung disease after raising $42 million in venture capital. The clinical trial will take place in Europe and will involve about 170 patients.

40683 ■ "Victory Healthcare Moves Into Dallas-Fort Worth Market" in Dallas Business Journal (Vol. 35, May 18, 2012, No. 36, pp. 1)
Pub: American City Business Journal
Ed: Bill Hethcock. **Description:** Victory Healthcare Holdings is to open Victory Medical Center in Plano, Texas. The company is also planning two more health facilities in the Dallas-Fort Worth area. Victory Medical will provide rehabilitative care as well as spinal and orthopedic surgery, which both have high demands.

40684 ■ "VPA to Pay $9.5 Million to Settle Whistle-Blower Lawsuits" in Crain's Detroit Business (Vol. 26, January 11, 2010, No. 2, pp. 13)
Pub: Crain Communications Inc.
Contact: Rance E. Crain, President
Ed: Jay Greene. **Description:** According to Terrence Berg, first assistant with the U.S. Attorney's Office in Detroit, Voluntary Physicians Association, a local home health care company, has agreed to pay $9.5 million to settle four whistle-blower lawsuits; the agreement settles allegations that VPA submitted claims to TriCare, the Michigan Medicaid program and Medicare for unnecessary home visits, tests and procedures.

40685 ■ "Walgreen Takes Up Doctoring" in Crain's Chicago Business (Vol. 31, March 31, 2008, No. 13, pp. 18)
Pub: Crain Communications Inc.
Contact: Todd Johnson, Publisher
Ed: Mark Bruno. **Description:** Walgreen Co. has agreed to acquire two firms that provide on-site medical and pharmaceutical services to large companies. Walgreen feels that these facilities mark the future of health care for a number of large corporations.

40686 ■ "Walgreens May Help Solve U.S. Healthcare Crisis; Walgreens' Healthcare Clinics Can Treat Dozens of Minor Medical Problems Before They Turn Into Major Health Issues" in Gallup Business Journal (April 1, 2014)
Pub: Gallup Press
Released: April 1, 2014. **Description:** Walgreens Healthcare Clinics are attracting patients at a very fast pace by treating minor medical issues before

they become major illnesses. The average patient wait is around 20 minutes and most services are available for less than $100. The article addresses the challenges being faced by the healthcare industry today.

40687 ■ "Walk-In Retail Clinics Enjoying Robust Health" in Memphis Business Journal (Vol. 34, April 27, 2012, No. 2, pp. 1)
Pub: American City Business Journal
Description: Walk-in clinics in Memphis, Tennessee have reported increased profits in 2012. Such clinics offer consumers immediate care while retail shopping.

40688 ■ "Want To Increase Hospital Revenues? Engage Your Physicians. When Doctors Are Frustrated, Patient Care and Hospital Revenues Suffer. Here's How to Boost Physicians' Engagement -- and the Bottom Line" in Gallup Business Journal (June 5, 2014)
Pub: Gallup Press
Released: June 5, 2014. **Description:** Hospitals need to engage their doctors in order to be successful for both patient care and the bottom line. Four key practices to drive physician engagement are outlined.

40689 ■ "Watchdogs for Health Care" in Money (Vol. 41, October 2012, No. 9, pp. 63)
Pub: Time Inc.
Contact: Wayne Powers, President
Description: Bonnie Burns, California Health Advocates' policy specialist, discusses issues facity seniors regarding their health care.

40690 ■ "Waukesha Firm Hit for $8.9M for Junk Faxes" in Business Journal Milwaukee (Vol. 29, August 3, 2012, No. 45, pp. 1)
Pub: American City Business Journals, Inc.
Contact: Whitney Shaw, President
Ed: Stacy Vogel Davis. **Released:** August 3, 2012. **Description:** Waukesha County, Wisconsin-based Easy PC Solutions LLC has been facing an $8.9 million settlement for sending unsolicited faxes to 7,000 health care providers. However, the company won't have to pay since the plaintiffs are expected to go after its insurance company.

40691 ■ "Wayne, Oakland Counties Create Own 'Medical Corridor'" in Crain's Detroit Business (Vol. 24, October 6, 2008, No. 40, pp. 8)
Pub: Crain Communications Inc.
Contact: Rance E. Crain, President
Ed: Jay Greene. **Description:** Woodward Medical Corridor that runs along Woodward Avenue and currently encompasses twelve hospitals and is rapidly growing with additional physician offices, advanced oncology centers and new hospitals. Beaumont Hospital is building a $160 million proton-beam therapy cancer center on its Royal Oak campus in a joint venture with Procure Treatment Centers of Bloomington Ind. That is expected to open in 2010 and will employ approximately 145 new workers.

40692 ■ "'We Are Not a Marketing Company'" in Boston Business Journal (Vol. 31, June 10, 2011, No. 20, pp. 1)
Pub: Boston Business Journal
Ed: Julie M. Donnelly. **Description:** Vertex Pharmaceuticals Inc. is marketing its new Hepatitis C treatment, Incivek. The company hired people to connect patients to the drug. Vertex is also set to move to a new facility in Boston, Massachusetts.

40693 ■ "Week on the Web" in Crain's Detroit Business (Vol. 25, June 22, 2009, No. 25, pp. 19)
Pub: Crain Communications Inc. - Detroit
Contact: Keith Crain, Chairman
Description: Blue Cross Blue Shield of Michigan, in a class-action lawsuit, will pay about 100 families whose children were either denied coverage for autism treatment or paid for treatment out of pocket. The settlement is worth about $ million.

40694 ■ "A Well-Crafted Employee Handbook Can Make Work Run More Smoothly" in Idaho Business Review (September 17, 2014)
Pub: Dolan Co.
Contact: James P. Dolan, President
Released: September 17, 2014. **Description:** An employee handbook will provide a complaint process, provide company management flexibility and clarity and keep a company out of legal problems. Training, compensation, benefits, security, health, performance appraisals, and safety issues must be covered. Human resource managers and other mangers should cover basics to help communicate with workers.

40695 ■ "What Business Schools Can Learn From the Medical Profession" in Harvard Business Review (Vol. 90, January-February 2012, No.1-2, pp. 38)
Pub: Harvard Business Review Press
Contact: Peter E. Walsh, Director
Ed: Nitin Nohria. **Released:** January-February 2012. **Description:** The author recommends closing the knowing-doing gap by applying health care feedback methods to business school instruction. Hospital residents receive feedback after making their rounds; so too should business school students and faculty assemble on a regular basis so that they can discuss what they are learning.

40696 ■ "What Choice Did I Have?" in Entrepreneur (Vol. 37, October 2009, No. 10, pp. 88)
Pub: Entrepreneur Press
Contact: Perlman Neil, President
Ed: Craig Matsuda. **Description:** Profile of a worker at a financial services company who acquired first hand knowledge concerning the relationship between health insurance costs and coverage. The worker's son got severely ill, forcing the worker to spend above what is covered by health insurance.

40697 ■ "What Your Workplace Wellness Programs are Missing; Companies Can Benefit From Taking a Holistic Approach To Their Employees. Here's How" in Gallup Business Journal (July 7, 2014)
Pub: Gallup Press
Released: July 7, 2014. **Description:** Companies should take a holistic approach to their employees' well being when addressing physical wellness in their workforce. Although employers are working to improve the physical wellness of workers, including weight loss, smoking cessation, and stress management, five essential elements: purpose, social, financial, community and physical issues would round out a good program.

40698 ■ "Wheel Genius" in Entrepreneur (June 2014)
Pub: Entrepreneur Media Inc.
Released: June 2014. **Description:** Electric car startup, Kenguru, has developed a hatchback that aims to improve mobility for wheelchair users, who enter the vehicle using a rear-opening tailgate and automatic ramp. The Kenguru, which is Hungarian for kangaroo, uses motorcycle-style handlebars instead of steering wheels. The 1,000-pound car has an estimated range of 60 miles and can travel up to 35 miles per hour. The Kenguru could sell for about $25,000. Founder Stacy Zoern partnered with Budapest, Hungary-based Istvan Kissaroslaki in developing the new car.

40699 ■ "Where the Money Is" in Conde Nast Portfolio (Vol. 2, June 2008, No. 6, pp. 113)
Description: Revenue generated from treatments for common brain disorders that are currently on the market are listed.

40700 ■ "Why Seattle Children's Appealed" in Puget Sound Business Journal (Vol. 35, May 30, 2014, No. 6, pp. 6)
Pub: American City Business Journals
Released: May 30, 2014. **Description:** Seattle Children's Hospital filed an appeal against the Washing State Office of the Insurance Commissioner for approving several health exchange plans that excluded the hospital. Children's argues that it offers

unique services and treatments only available through their medical facility and health insurance plans excluding them is putting children at risk.

40701 ■ *"Will Other Insurers Follow United's Lead?" in Birmingham Business Journal (Vol. 29, June 22, 2012, No. 26, pp. 1)*
Pub: American City Business Journals, Inc.
Contact: Whitney Shaw, President
Ed: Evan Belanger. **Released:** June 22, 2012. **Description:** UnitedHealtcare will continue offering patient protections as required by US health reform law. But United controls five percent of Alabama's health insurance market. Provisions of patient protections being offered by the company are also discussed.

40702 ■ *"Winner Nonprofit, Hospitals" in Crain's Detroit Business (Vol. 25, June 22, 2009, No. 25, pp. E002)*
Pub: Crain Communications Inc. - Detroit
Contact: Keith Crain, Chairman
Ed: Jay Greene. **Description:** James Connelly, CFO for Henry Ford Health System, discusses the financial status of the system. Statistical data included.

40703 ■ *Wisconsin Medical Directory*
Pub: Jola Publications
URL(s): www.jolapub.com/index_med_order_t.html. **Released:** Annual; Latest Edition July, 2014-2015. **Price:** $25, Individuals. **Covers:** Approximately 15,000 doctors, hospitals, clinics, nursing homes, and other selected health care providers in Wisconsin. **Entries include:** Doctor or facility name, address, phone, fax, doctors' UPINS. **Arrangement:** Classified by type of facility or care provided. **Indexes:** Name, product/service, subject.

40704 ■ *Women's Health Concerns Sourcebook*
Pub: Omnigraphics Inc.
Contact: Frederick G. Ruffner, Jr., President
URL(s): omnigraphics.com/shop/womens-health-concerns-sourcebook-4th-ed/#description. **Ed:** Sandra J. Judd. **Released:** Irregular; latest edition 4th; 2013. **Price:** $85, Individuals Hardcover; $95, Individuals List price. **Publication includes:** Resources on women's health issues. **Entries include:** Publication name, address. Principal content of publication is articles on specific health issues, definitions, symptoms, risks, treatment, and answers to frequently asked questions. **Arrangement:** Topic. **Indexes:** subject index/alpha.

40705 ■ *"Work At It!" in Hawaii Business (Vol. 53, October 2007, No. 4, pp. 44)*
Pub: PacificBasin Communications
Ed: Cathy S. Cruz-George. **Description:** Employers in Hawaii are mitigating the effects of rising healthcare costs by giving their employees health insurance and offering wellness programs. Employer-based health insurance has increases by 87 percent in the United States over the 2000-2006 period. Wellness programs that address different aspects of employees' health, such as food consumption, drug compliance and smoking habits, are discussed.

40706 ■ *"Workers' Comp System Cuts Through Paper" in Sacramento Business Journal (Vol. 25, July 11, 2008, No. 19, pp. 1)*
Pub: American City Business Journals, Inc.
Contact: Whitney Shaw, President
Ed: Kelly Johnson. **Description:** California has started testing a new paperless system for handling disputed workers' compensation claims. It is believed that the shift will affect people both inside and outside of the state Division of Workers' Compensation and the state Workers' Compensation Appeals Board. The other details of the planned system are also presented.

40707 ■ *"Workplace Wellness" in Entrepreneurs (June 2014)*
Pub: Entrepreneur Media Inc.
Released: June 2014. **Description:** Workplace wellness programs can be started by checking with insurers who may provide program and activity suggestions promotional materials or other resources. Teaming up with others is encouraged. For instance, employees from various departments or nearby

companies can get flu shots or blood pressure screening. Management should also get involved in these programs, because it will then be known among employees that wellness is taken seriously. It is also important that workplace wellness programs are kept safe and legally sound.

40708 ■ *"The Worst-Run Industry in Canada: Health Care" in Canadian Business (Vol. 83, October 12, 2010, No. 17, pp. 39)*
Pub: Rogers Media Inc.
Contact: Tony Viner, President
Ed: Rachel Mendleson. **Description:** Most Canadians believe that the problem of the country's health care system is rooted in insufficient funding, demographic overload, or corporate profiteering. However, health economists and policy analysts think the real issues is mismanagement, as the pervasive inefficiency is affecting the system's structure.

TRADE PERIODICALS

40709 ■ *The AARP Pharmacy Service Enjoying Good Health Newsletter*
Pub: Retired Persons Services Inc.
URL(s): www.rpspharmacy.com/nl. **Ed:** Joan M. Zimmermann, Editor, jzimmermann@rpsrx.com. **Released:** Bimonthly. **Description:** Offers health information and medical tips on topics relevant for the elderly. Recurring features include notices of publications available.

40710 ■ *Abbeyfield Houses Society of Canada Newsletter*
Pub: Abbeyfield Houses Society of Canada
URL(s): www.abbeyfield.ca/pages/06news.html. **Ed:** Robert McMullan, Editor. **Released:** Quarterly. **Description:** Reports on news of Abbeyfield Houses Society of Canada, a provider of care and companionship for the elderly. Also features articles related to aging, housing, and lifestyle in Canada and internationally. Recurring features include letters to the editor, and columns titled News of Local Societies and Bits 'n Bites.

40711 ■ *Academic Emergency Medicine: Official Journal of the Society for Academic Emergency Medicine*
Pub: Blackwell Publishing Inc.
Contact: Gordon Tibbitts, III, President
URL(s): www.wiley.com/WileyCDA/WileyTitle/productCd-ACEM.htmlonlinelibrary.wiley.com/journal/10.1111/(ISSN)1553-2712. **Ed:** Carey D. Chisholm. **Released:** Monthly **Price:** $190, Individuals print + online, The americas; €144, Individuals print + online; £95, Other countries print + online, individuals; $373, Institutions print + online; £197, Institutions print + online; $326, Institutions online, The Americas; £173, Institutions online; $103, Members print + online; €78, Members print + online; £53, Members print + online.

40712 ■ *Advances*
Pub: Robert Wood Johnson Foundation
Contact: Risa Lavizzo-Mourey, President
URL(s): www.rwjf.org. **Ed:** Larry Blumenthal, Editor, lblumen@rwjf.org. **Released:** Monthly. **Price:** Included in membership. **Description:** The National Newsletter of The Robert Wood Johnson Foundation. Reports on issues related to the Foundations grantmaking. Recurring features include interviews, news of research, and columns titled Profile, Abridge, Grants, and People.

40713 ■ *AHA News: American Hospital Association News*
Pub: Health Forum L.L.C.
Contact: Michael Springer, President
URL(s): www.ahanews.com/. **Released:** Biweekly **Price:** $75, Members 2 years; 2nd class mail; $125, Members 2 years; 1st class mail; $195, Members 2 years; other countries (prepaid); $375, Members 2 years; international air (prepaid); $160, Nonmembers 2 years; 2nd class mail; $210, Nonmembers 2 years; 1st class mail; $280, Nonmembers 2 years; other countries (prepaid); $460, Nonmembers international air (prepaid).

40714 ■ *Air Medical Journal*
Pub: Mosby Inc.
URL(s): journals.elsevierhealth.com/periodicals/ymam. **Ed:** Jacqueline C. Stocking, Eric R. Swanson. **Released:** Bimonthly **Price:** $140, Individuals online and print; $197, Canada and Mexico online and print; $197, Other countries online and print.

40715 ■ *Alcohol Research and Health*
Pub: U. S. Government Printing Office
Contact: Veronica Meter, Director
E-mail: tpriebe@gpo.gov
URL(s): bookstore.gpo.gov/products/sku/717-004-00000-1?ctid=. **Released:** Quarterly **Price:** $33, Individuals; $12, Single issue; $16.80, Single issue in other countries; $33, Other countries.

40716 ■ *Alive*
Pub: Alive Publishing Group Inc.
Contact: Vic LoBouthillier, Chief Executive Officer
URL(s): www.alive.com/. **Released:** Monthly **Price:** C$42.30, Individuals; C$71.10, Two years.

40717 ■ *American Journal of Infection Control (AJIC)*
Pub: Mosby Inc.
URL(s): www.ajicjournal.orgwww.elsevier.com. **Ed:** Elaine L. Larson. **Released:** Monthly **Price:** $211, Individuals online only; $253, Individuals print and online; $325, Canada print and online.

40718 ■ *The Arc News*
Pub: The Arc of Carroll County Inc.
Price: Included in membership. **Description:** Spotlights issues concerning the mentally and physically disabled. Discusses rehabilitation, safety, housing, and centers.

40719 ■ *Archives of Environmental & Occupational Health: An International Journal*
Pub: Taylor & Francis Group Journals
Contact: Kevin J. Bradley, President
URL(s): www.tandfonline.com/toc/vaeh20/current. **Released:** 4/yr. **Price:** $677, Institutions print & online; $471, Individuals print & online; $592, Institutions online only.

40720 ■ *Bulletin of Experimental Treatments for AIDS (BETA)*
Pub: San Francisco AIDS Foundation
Contact: Neil Giuliano, Chief Executive Officer
URL(s): www.sfaf.org/hiv-info/hot-topics/beta/. **Ed:** Reilly O'Neal. **Released:** Biennial **Price:** Free.

40721 ■ *Business Insurance*
Pub: Crain Communications Inc.
Contact: Rance E. Crain, President
URL(s): www.businessinsurance.com. **Released:** Weekly **Price:** $799, Individuals data + print and digital; $149, Individuals print & digital; $125, Individuals digital edition. **Availability:** Online: LexisNexis; Crain Communications Inc. **Type:** Full-text.

40722 ■ *Cambridge Quarterly of Healthcare Ethics*
Pub: Cambridge University Press
Contact: Richard Ziemacki, President
E-mail: rziemacki@cambridge.org
URL(s): journals.cambridge.org/action/displayJournal?jid=CQH. **Ed:** Steve Heilig, Dr. Thomasine Kushner. **Released:** Quarterly **Price:** $360, Institutions online & print; $300, Institutions online; $45, Single issue article; £225, Institutions online & print; £188, Institutions online.

40723 ■ *Canadian Journal of Dietetic Practice and Research*
Pub: Dietitians of Canada
Contact: Marsha Sharp, Chief Executive Officer
URL(s): dcjournal.metapress.com/home/main.mpx. **Released:** Quarterly **Price:** $90, Individuals outside Canada; $250, Institutions outside Canada.

40724 ■ *Canadian Journal of Public Health*
Pub: Canadian Public Health Association
Contact: Debra Lynkowski, Chief Executive Officer
URL(s): www.cpha.ca/en/cjph.aspx. **Ed:** Dr. Gilles Paradis. **Released:** Bimonthly **Price:** C$160, Individuals online only; C$480, Institutions online only.

40725 ■ *Canadian Journal of Respiratory Therapy: Leadership through Advocacy, Service and Unity for Respiratory Therapists in Canada*

Pub: Canadian Society of Respiratory Therapists
Contact: Christiane Menard, Executive Director
URL(s): www.csrt.com/en/publications/journal.asp.
Released: 4/yr. **Price:** C$100, Canada; $110, U.S.; $120, Other countries.

40726 ■ *Canadian Respiratory Journal: The Official Journal of the Canadian Thorasic Society*

Pub: Pulsus Group Inc.
URL(s): www.pulsus.com/journals/journalHome.
jsp?jnlKy=4&/home2.htm. **Released:** 8/year **Price:** $275, Individuals print and online; C$260, Individuals print and online; $290, Other countries print and online.

40727 ■ *Care Management Journals: "Journal of Case Management" and "The Journal of Long Term Home Health Care"*

Pub: Springer Publishing Co.
Contact: Ursula Springer, President
URL(s): www.springerpub.com/product/15210987#.
UB8RbPbiZIR. **Ed:** Joan Quinn. **Released:** Quarterly **Price:** $105, Individuals print; $265, Institutions print; $95, Individuals online; $255, Institutions online.

40728 ■ *Child and Youth Services*

Pub: Routledge Journals Taylor & Francis Group
URL(s): www.tandfonline.com/toc/wcys20/current.
Ed: Doug Magnuson, Jerome Beker. **Released:** Quarterly **Price:** $138, Individuals online ; $148, Individuals print + online; $701, Institutions online; $801, Institutions print + online.

40729 ■ *Children's Voice*

Pub: Child Welfare League of America
Contact: Chris James-Brown, President
E-mail: cjamesbrown@cwla.org
URL(s): www.cwla.org/pubs/welcome.htm. **Released:** Bimonthly **Price:** $140, Nonmembers; $255, Nonmembers 2 years.

40730 ■ *Clinical Laboratory News*

Pub: American Association for Clinical Chemistry
Contact: Steven H. Wong, President
URL(s): www.aacc.org/publications/cln/2014/
november/Pages/default.aspx#. **Released:** Monthly **Price:** Free to qualified subscribers; Included in membership.

40731 ■ *Clinical Leadership and Management Review: CLMR*

Pub: Clinical Laboratory Management Association
Contact: Paul L. Epner, President
URL(s): www.clma.org/?page=Publications_Overvie.
Ed: Tony Kurec. **Released:** Bimonthly

40732 ■ *The CMA Today: Professional Medical Assistant*

Pub: American Association of Medical Assistants
Contact: Nina Watson, President
E-mail: President@aama-ntl.org
URL(s): www.aama-ntl.org/cmatoday/about.aspx. **Released:** Bimonthly **Price:** Included in membership; $60, Nonmembers.

40733 ■ *The Counselor*

Pub: The Counselor
Ed: Steve Erickson, Editor. **Released:** 6/year. **Description:** Reports on membership news and other public relations topics.

40734 ■ *EHS Today: The Magazine of Safety, Health and Loss Prevention*

Pub: Intertec Publishing
Contact: John French, President
URL(s): ehstoday.com. **Ed:** Sandy Smith. **Released:** Monthly

40735 ■ *Encounters*

Pub: Venice Family Clinic
Contact: Elizabeth Benson Forer, Chief Executive Officer
URL(s): www.venicefamilyclinic.org/index.
php?view=publication. **Released:** Biennial. **Price:** Free. **Description:** Reports on news, events, pro-

grams, and activities of the Venice Family Clinic in Los Angeles, California whose mission is "to provide comprehensive primary health care that is affordable, accessible and compassionable for people with no other access to such care.".

40736 ■ *Evaluation & the Health Professions*

Pub: Pine Forge Press
Contact: Blaise R. Simqu, President
URL(s): www.sagepub.com/journalsProdDesc.
nav?prodId=Journal200787&. **Ed:** R. Barker Bausell, Carolyn F. Waltz. **Released:** Quarterly **Price:** $842, Institutions combined (print & e-access); $926, Institutions current volume (print & all online content); $758, Institutions e-access; $842, Institutions backfile lease, e-access plus backfile; $1,351, Institutions backfile purchase, e-access (content through 1998); $825, Institutions print only; $161, Individuals print only; $227, Institutions single print; $52, Individuals single print.

40737 ■ *FDA Week*

Pub: Inside Washington Publishers
Contact: Korila Malecha, Manager
URL(s): iwpnews.com/IWP-General/Inside-Washington-Publishers-Health/fda-week/menu-id-845.html.
Ed: Donna Haseley, Editor. **Released:** Weekly (Fri.) **Price:** $685, U.S. and Canada; $735, Elsewhere. **Description:** Reports on Food and Drug Administration policy, regulation, and enforcement.

40738 ■ *Fertility Weekly*

Pub: Keith Key
Contact: Keith Key, Publisher
E-mail: keithkey@mindspring.com
URL(s): www.fertilityweekly.com. **Released:** Weekly **Price:** $659, U.S. and other countries online; $699, Individuals print; $739, Individuals print and online; $799, Other countries print; $839, Other countries print and online. **Description:** Discusses information pertaining to fertility. Recurring features include news of research, a calendar of events, reports of meetings, and a column titled Periodical Review.

40739 ■ *Focus on Autism and Other Developmental Disabilities*

Pub: Pine Forge Press
Contact: Blaise R. Simqu, President
URL(s): www.sagepub.com/journalsProdDesc.
nav?ct_p=boards&prodId=Journal201875. **Ed:** Richard Simpson, Joel Arick, Diane Adreon. **Released:** Quarterly **Price:** $67, Individuals print & e-access; $212, Institutions print & e-access; $191, Institutions e-access; $208, Institutions print only; $57, Institutions Single Print Issue; $22, Individuals Single Print Issue.

40740 ■ *Forensic Drug Abuse Advisor*

Pub: Forensic Drug Abuse Advisor Inc.
URL(s): www.fdaa.com/. **Ed:** Steven B. Karch, M.D., Editor. **Released:** 10/year. **Price:** $197, individuals. **Description:** Acts as a drug information source. Emphasizes the latest scientific discoveries in drug abuse, workplace drug testing, federal drug law, and forensic pathology. An absolute necessity in drug related litigation. Recurring features include letters to the editor, news of research, a calendar of events, reports of meetings, news of educational opportunities, book reviews, and notices of publications available. Continuing medical education available.

40741 ■ *Frontiers of Health Services Management*

Pub: Health Administration Press
Contact: Alyson Pitman Giles, Director
E-mail: agiles@ache.org
URL(s): www.ache.org/pubs/frontiers.cfmache.org/
pubs/Frontiers/frontiers_index.cfm. **Ed:** Margaret F. Schulte. **Released:** Quarterly; Latest Edition; Volume 30, Number 3, Spring 2014. **Price:** $130, Individuals U.S; $140, Individuals Canada and all other countries; $35, Single issue.

40742 ■ *Good Health Bulletin*

Pub: Harvey W. Watt & Company Inc.
URL(s): www.harveywatt.com/. **Released:** Monthly. **Price:** $19.95, U.S. and Canada. **Description:** Contains up-to-date helpful medical and related information concerning health, fitness, and longevity. Recurring features include news of research.

40743 ■ *Government Recreation and Fitness*

Pub: Executive Business Media Inc.
UHL(s): www.ebmpubs.com/GRF/Index.asp. **Released:** 9/year **Price:** $40, Individuals; $70, Two years; $5, Single issue.

40744 ■ *Health Affairs: The Policy Journal of the Health Sphere*

Pub: Project HOPE
Contact: Dr. John Howe, III, President
URL(s): www.healthaffairs.org. **Ed:** John K. Iglehart. **Released:** Bimonthly **Price:** $578, Institutions print & online; $697, Institutions, Canada print & online; $668, Institutions, other countries print & online; $526, Institutions online only; $603, Institutions all digital; $173, U.S. print and online; $272, Canada print and online; $263, Other countries print and online; $185, U.S. premium; $284, Canada premium; $275, Other countries premium (print, online, mobile, iPad app); $144, Individuals digital (online, mobile, iPad app).

40745 ■ *Health Care for Women International: Official Journal of the International Council on Women's Health Issues*

Pub: Routledge
Contact: Kevin Bradley, President
E-mail: kbradley@taylorandfrancis.com
URL(s): www.tandfonline.com/toc/uhcw20/current.
Ed: Carole Anne McKenzie. **Released:** Monthly **Price:** $365, Individuals print only; $1,358, Institutions online only; $1,552, Institutions print and online.

40746 ■ *Health Progress: Official Journal of the Catholic Health Association of the United States*

Pub: Catholic Health Association of the United States
Contact: Sr. Carol Keehan, President
URL(s): www.chausa.org/publications/health-progress. **Ed:** Pamela Schaeffer. **Released:** Bimonthly **Price:** $55, Members CHA; $65, Other countries; $65, Nonmembers; $10, Nonmembers single copy; Free to members, single copy.

40747 ■ *Health and Safety Science Abstracts*

Pub: Cambridge Information Group
Contact: David Levy, President
URL(s): www.csa.com/www.csa.com/factsheets/
health-safety-set-c.php. **Released:** Monthly

40748 ■ *Health Science: Living Well Into the Future*

Pub: National Health Association
Contact: Mark Huberman, President
URL(s): www.healthscience.org/education/health-science-magazine. **Released:** Quarterly **Price:** $35, U.S. and Canada; $55, Other countries; $65, Two years; $95, Other countries 2 years.

40749 ■ *Healthcare Corporate Finance News*

Pub: Irving Levin Associates Inc.
Contact: Stephen M. Monroe, Managing Editor
URL(s): www.levinassociates.com. **Ed:** Gretchen S. Swanson, Editor. **Released:** Monthly. **Price:** $495. **Description:** Reports on the growth strategies of managed care providers, hospitals, drug companies, medical device manufacturers, and other healthcare organizations. Also reports on the latest deals in the healthcare sector, and how healthcare companies are doing on Wall Street.

40750 ■ *Healthcare Executive*

Pub: American College of Healthcare Executives
Contact: Deborah J. Bowen, President
URL(s): www.ache.org/HEOnline/digital/heonline_
index.cfm. **Released:** Bimonthly **Price:** $110, Individuals in the U.S.

40751 ■ *Healthcare Purchasing News: Business News and Analysis for Purchasing Decision-Makers*

Pub: Nelson Publishing Inc.
Contact: Bob West, Associate Publisher
E-mail: bwest@nelsonpub.com
URL(s): www.hpnonline.com. **Ed:** Susan Cantrell. **Released:** Monthly **Price:** $72, Individuals; $110, Canada; $130, Other countries.

40752 ■ *Heart and Lung: The Journal of Acute and Critical Care*
Pub: Mosby An Imprint of Elsevier Science Inc. Elsevier Inc. Health Sciences
URL(s): www.elsevier.comwww.heartandlung.org.
Ed: Nancy S. Redeker. **Released:** Bimonthly; Jan, Mar, May, July, Sept, Nov. **Price:** $181, Other countries print and online; $127, Individuals print and online; $127, Students print and online.

40753 ■ *Hemophilia Ontario News*
Pub: Hemophilia Ontario
URL(s): www.hemophilia.on.ca/Support/newsletter_downloads.htm. **Released:** Quarterly, 3-4/yr. **Price:** $15, individuals in Canada; $20, institutions in Canada. **Description:** Hemophilia Ontario is committed to improve the quality of life of people affected by hemophilia and related blood conditions, and to work towards a cure. Publishes on current events, new treatments, volunteer update, and advocacy news. Recurring features include news of research, a calendar of events, and job listings.

40754 ■ *Home Health Care Management and Practice*
Pub: Pine Forge Press
Contact: Blaise R. Simqu, President
URL(s): www.sagepub.com/journalsProdDesc.nav?prodId=Journal201504. **Released:** Bimonthly **Price:** $583, Institutions print & e-access; $641, Institutions current volume print & all online content; $525, Institutions e-access; $583, Institutions all online content; $554, Institutions content through 1998; $571, Institutions print only; $180, Individuals print only; $157, Institutions single print; $59, Individuals single print.

40755 ■ *Home Health Care Services Quarterly*
Pub: Routledge Journals Taylor & Francis Group
URL(s): www.tandfonline.com/toc/whhc20/current#.U3L4rtIW2qY. **Ed:** Maria Aranda. **Released:** Quarterly **Price:** $141, Individuals online; $152, Individuals print & online.

40756 ■ *Homecare Administrative HORIZONS*
Pub: Beacon Health Corp.
Contact: Diane J. Omdahl, Editor-in-Chief
URL(s): www.beaconhealth.org/. **Released:** Monthly. **Price:** $347, individuals. **Description:** Provides homecare agency management information on all kinds of business and personnel topics. Incorporates comprehensive how-to information, current regulatory requirements, and documentation strategies. Runs a series of articles, including how to move into managed care, how to manage and measure outcomes, how to survive scrutiny by medicare's fraud squad, strengthening agency/physician relationships, and personnel issues. Recurring features include columns titled Peaks & Valleys, Fine-tuning the Fundamentals, Clearing the Fog, and Higher Ground.

40757 ■ *Hospital News Canada*
Pub: Trader Media Corp.
URL(s): hospitalnews.com. **Released:** Monthly **Price:** $39, Canada; $144, Individuals bulk subscriptions; 25 copies per month; $220, Individuals bulk subscriptions; 50 copies per month; $380, Individuals bulk subscriptions; 100 copies per month; $660, Individuals bulk subscriptions; 150 copies per month; $750, Individuals bulk subscriptions; 200 copies per month; $69, Two years; $75, Other countries; $45, Individuals in U.S.

40758 ■ *Hospital Topics*
Pub: Routledge
Contact: Kevin Bradley, President
E-mail: kbradley@taylorandfrancis.com
URL(s): www.tandf.co.uk/journals/titles/00185868.asp. **Released:** Quarterly **Price:** $179, Institutions online only; $73, Individuals print and online; $205, Institutions print and online.

40759 ■ *Industrial Hygiene News*
Pub: Rimbach Publishing Inc.
URL(s): www.rimbach.com. **Released:** Bimonthly

40760 ■ *International Journal of Health Planning and Management*
Pub: John Wiley & Sons Inc.
Contact: Stephen M. Smith, President
URL(s): onlinelibrary.wiley.com/journal/10.1002/(-ISSN)1099-1751. **Ed:** Prof. Kenneth Lee, Dr. Ruby Barrow. **Released:** Quarterly **Price:** $3,153, Institutions print and online; £1,608, Institutions print and online; €2,033, Institutions print and online; $1,849, Individuals print and online.

40761 ■ *International Journal of Health Services*
Pub: Baywood Publishing Company Inc.
Contact: Stuart Cohen, President
URL(s): www.baywood.com/journals/PreviewJournals.asp?Id=0020-7314. **Ed:** Linda Strange. **Released:** Quarterly **Price:** $486, Institutions; $462, Institutions online.

40762 ■ *International Journal of Technology Assessment in Health Care*
Pub: Cambridge University Press
Contact: Richard Ziemacki, President
E-mail: rziemacki@cambridge.org
URL(s): journals.cambridge.org/action/displayJournal?jid=THC. **Ed:** Prof. Egon Jonsson. **Released:** Quarterly **Price:** $616, Institutions online only; £353, Institutions online only.

40763 ■ *The Joint Commission Journal on Quality and Patient Safety*
Pub: The Joint Commission Journal on Quality Improvement
URL(s): www.jcrinc.com/the-joint-commission-journal-on-quality-and-patient-safety/. **Released:** Monthly **Price:** $995, Institutions site license - 1 year; $299, Individuals online only - single user; $319, Individuals print and online.

40764 ■ *Journal of Agromedicine*
Pub: Taylor & Francis
Contact: William Germanno, Manager
E-mail: williamgermano@gmail.com
URL(s): www.tandfonline.com/toc/wagr20/current. **Ed:** Matthew C. Keifer. **Released:** Quarterly **Price:** $154, Individuals online; $170, Individuals print & online; $335, Institutions online; $383, Institutions print & online.

40765 ■ *Journal of American College Health*
Pub: Routledge
Contact: Kevin Bradley, President
E-mail: kbradley@taylorandfrancis.com
URL(s): www.tandf.co.uk/journals/titles/07448481.asp. **Released:** 8/year **Price:** $396, Institutions online only; $154, Individuals print and online; $453, Institutions print and online.

40766 ■ *Journal of the Association of Nurses in AIDS Care*
Pub: Elsevier Inc.
URL(s): www.journals.elsevier.com/journal-of-the-association-of-nurses-in-aids-care/. **Ed:** Lucy Bradley-Springer. **Released:** Bimonthly **Price:** $634, Institutions, other countries; $128, Individuals; $574, Institutions; $180, Other countries.

40767 ■ *Journal of Behavioral Health Services & Research*
Pub: Springer-Verlag New York Inc.
Contact: Ruediger Gebauer, President
URL(s): jbhsr.fmhi.usf.eduwww.springer.com/public+health/journal/11414, link.springer.com/journal/11414. **Released:** Quarterly **Price:** €337, Institutions print or online; €404, Institutions print & enchanced access.

40768 ■ *Journal of Ethnic & Cultural Diversity in Social Work: Innovations in Theory, Research & Practice*
Pub: Routledge Journals Taylor & Francis Group
URL(s): www.tandfonline.com/toc/wecd20/current. **Ed:** Mo Yee Lee. **Released:** Quarterly **Price:** $148, Individuals online only; $160, Individuals print + online; $524, Institutions online only; $658, Institutions print + online.

40769 ■ *Journal of Health Care Chaplaincy*
Pub: Routledge Journals Taylor & Francis Group
URL(s): www.tandfonline.com/toc/whcc20/current. **Released:** Quarterly **Price:** $63, Individuals online only; $69, Individuals print + online; $331, Institutions online only; $378, Institutions print + online.

40770 ■ *Journal of Health Care Finance*
Pub: Wolters Kluwer Law and Business
Contact: Mark Dorman, President
Released: Quarterly **Price:** $319, Individuals.

40771 ■ *Journal of Health Care for the Poor and Underserved (JHCPU)*
Pub: Johns Hopkins University Press
Contact: Wendy Harris, Director
E-mail: wharris@press.jhu.edu
URL(s): www.press.jhu.edu/journals/journal_of_health_care_for_the_poor_and_underserved. **Ed:** Virginia Brennan. **Released:** Quarterly; Latest edition: 2014, Volume 25. **Price:** $705, Individuals print; $395, Institutions print; $790, Institutions print, 2 years; $75, Individuals print; $135, Two years individual.

40772 ■ *Journal of Health & Social Behavior*
Pub: American Sociological Association
Contact: Roberta Spalter-Roth, Director
E-mail: spalter-roth@asanet.org
URL(s): www.asanet.org/journals/jhsb/jhsb.cfmwww.sagepub.com/journals/Journal201971/manuscriptSubmission#tabview=title. **Ed:** Gilbert C. Gee. **Released:** Quarterly; March, June, September, December. **Price:** $425, Institutions Combined (Print & E-access); $335, Institutions E-access; $417, Institutions Print Only.

40773 ■ *Journal for Healthcare Quality: The Official Journal of the National Association for Healthcare Quality*
Pub: National Association for Healthcare Quality
Contact: Stephanie Mercado, Executive Director
URL(s): onlinelibrary.wiley.com/journal/10.1111/(-ISSN)1945-1474. **Released:** Bimonthly **Price:** $193, Individuals print and online; $252, Institutions print and online.

40774 ■ *Journal of Intensive Care Medicine*
Pub: Springer-Verlag GmbH & Company KG
URL(s): www.sagepub.com/journals/Journal201630. **Ed:** Nicholas Smyrnios, James M. Rippe, Yuka-Marie Vinagre, James M. Rippe. **Released:** Bimonthly; January, March, May, July, September, November. **Price:** $1,076, Institutions Combined (Print & E-access); $1,184, Institutions Current Volume Print & All Online Content; $968, Institutions E-access; $1,076, Institutions All Online Content; $982, Institutions E-access (Content through 1998); $1,054, Institutions Print Only; $145, Institutions Single Print Issue; $54, Individuals Single Print Issue; $626, Institutions print & e-access; $657, Institutions current volume print & all online content; $563, Institutions e-access; $594, Institutions e-access plus backfile (all online content); $622, Institutions e-access (content through 1999); $613, Institutions print only; $264, Individuals print only; $113, Institutions single print issue; $57, Individuals single print issue. **Telecommunication Services:** Email: journal.icm@hmn.ap.hop-paris.fr .

40775 ■ *Journal of Nuclear Cardiology: Official Journal of the American Society of Nuclear Cardiology*
Pub: Springer-Verlag New York Inc.
Contact: Ruediger Gebauer, President
URL(s): www.springer.com/medicine/cardiology/journal/12350. **Ed:** Barry L. Zaret. **Released:** Bimonthly **Price:** €461, Institutions print + online; €553, Institutions print + enhanced access.

40776 ■ *Journal of Social Service Research*
Pub: Routledge Journals Taylor & Francis Group
URL(s): www.tandfonline.com/toc/wssr20/current. **Ed:** Sophia F. Dziegielewski. **Released:** 5/year **Price:** $132, Individuals online only; $143, Individuals print + online; $948, Institutions online only; $1,083, Institutions print + online.

40777 ■ *Leaven*
Pub: La Leche League International
Contact: Viola Lennon, Director
URL(s): www.llli.org/llleaderweb/lv/index.htmlwww.llli.org/lvdate. **Released:** Quarterly **Price:** $30, Members box of back issues; $35, Individuals box of back issues; online; $35, Individuals box of back issues.

40778 ■ *Managed Healthcare Executive: The News Magazine for Health Care Costs and Quality*
Pub: Advanstar Communications Inc.
Contact: Mr. Joseph Loggia, Chief Executive Officer
E-mail: jloggia@advanstar.com
URL(s): managedhealthcareexecutive.modernmedicine.com. **Released:** Monthly **Price:** $89.25, Individuals; $131.25, Two years; $7.35, Single issue prepaid; $173.25, Canada and Mexico; $267.25, Canada and Mexico two years; $19.95, Single issue Canada & Mexico.

40779 ■ *Marketing Health Services*
Pub: American Marketing Association
Contact: Lucille Pointer, President
URL(s): www.marketingpower.comwww.ama.org/publications/MarketingHealthServices/Pages/About.aspx. **Ed:** Rhoda Weiss. **Released:** Quarterly **Price:** $140, Individuals print only; $140, Institutions print only; $110.25, Canada print only; $147, Institutions, Canada print only; $175, Institutions, other countries print only; $105, Other countries print only; $95, Other countries print only.

40780 ■ *Massage Therapy Journal (mtj)*
Pub: American Massage Therapy Association
Contact: Bill Brown, Executive Director
URL(s): www.amtamassage.org/. **Ed:** Michael Schwanz. **Released:** Quarterly **Price:** $25, Individuals /year.

40781 ■ *Medicine on the Net*
Pub: COR Healthcare Resources
URL(s): www.hcpro.com/services/corhealth/. **Ed:** Bridget Meaney, Editor. **Released:** Monthly **Price:** $229, Individuals. **Description:** Spotlights developing issues in the use of the Internet by medical professionals. Recurring features include letters to the editor, interviews, news of research, and book reviews.

40782 ■ *Modern Healthcare: The Weekly Healthcare Business News Magazine*
Pub: Crain Communications Inc.
Contact: Todd Johnson, Publisher
URL(s): www.modernhealthcare.com. **Ed:** Merrill Goozner. **Released:** Weekly **Price:** $164, Individuals print; $215, Individuals digital and print; $399, Individuals premium digital.

40783 ■ *Morbidity and Mortality Weekly Report: Morbidity and Mortality Weekly Report*
Pub: Centers for Disease Control and Prevention Office of Scientific and Health Communications
Contact: Dr. Ileana Arias, Director
URL(s): www.cdc.gov/mmwr. **Released:** Weekly (Fri.) **Price:** Free electronic copy; $4.25, Single issue domestic; $5.95, Single issue foreign.

40784 ■ *The Nation's Health*
Pub: American Public Health Association
Contact: Joyce R. Gaufin, President
URL(s): thenationshealth.aphapublications.org. **Released:** 10/year; with combined issues in May/June and November/December. **Price:** $75, U.S. and Canada print only; $105, U.S. and Canada print + online; $155, Institutions print + online, u.s/canada; $95, Individuals online only; $125, Institutions online only; $120, Individuals print + online, international; 170, Institutions print + online, international.

40785 ■ *NCPD National Update*
Pub: National Catholic Partnership on Disability
Contact: Janice Benton, Executive Director
URL(s): www.ncpd.org. **Released:** Quarterly. **Price:** Free. **Description:** Focuses on disabled persons with a Catholic slant.

40786 ■ *The Neurodiagnostic Journal*
Pub: American Society of Electroneurodiagnostic Technologists
Contact: Arlen Reimnitz, Executive Director
E-mail: arlen@aset.org
URL(s): www.aset.org/i4a/pages/index.cfm?pageid=3314. **Released:** Quarterly **Price:** $110, Individuals; $130, Other countries individual; $150, Institutions; $180, Institutions, other countries; $150, Other countries Airmail Delivery; $200, Institutions, other countries Airmail Delivery.

40787 ■ *New Beginnings*
Pub: La Leche League International
Contact: Viola Lennon, Director
URL(s): www.llli.org/nbdate.html. **Released:** Bimonthly

40788 ■ *New Horizons*
Pub: San Fernando Valley Association for the Retarded
Ed: Nancy Banks, Editor. **Released:** 3/year. **Price:** Included in membership. **Description:** Reports on membership news of the San Fernando Valley Association for the Retarded. Spotlights volunteers, activities, and events. Recurring features include columns titled Legislative Corner and President's Corner.

40789 ■ *Nursing Education Perspectives*
Pub: National League for Nursing
Contact: Judith A. Halstead, President
URL(s): www.nln.org/nlnjournal/index.htm. **Ed:** Joyce Fitzpatrick. **Released:** Bimonthly; January, March, May, July, September, and November. **Price:** $45, Individuals; $95, Nonmembers; $115, Canada nonmembers; $125, Other countries non-member; C$177, Libraries; $187, Other countries libraries.

40790 ■ *Nutrition & Foodservice Edge Magazine*
Pub: Dietary Managers Association
Contact: Ricky Clark, Chairman of the Board
URL(s): www.anfponline.org/Publications/Dietary_Manager.shtml. **Ed:** Diane Everett. **Released:** 10/year **Price:** $40, Individuals.

40791 ■ *Nutrition & Mental Health*
Pub: International Schizophrenia Foundation
Contact: Gregory Schilhab, Editor
E-mail: gschil@orthomed.org
URL(s): www.healthy.net. **Released:** Quarterly. **Price:** $30, U.S. and Canada. **Description:** Acquaints readers with the effects of nutrition on mental health, with on emphasis on schizophrenia.

40792 ■ *Nutrition Today*
Pub: Lippincott Williams & Wilkins
Contact: J. W. Lippincott, President
URL(s): journals.lww.com/nutritiontodayonline/pages/default.aspx. **Ed:** Johanna Dwyer. **Released:** Bimonthly **Price:** $109, Individuals; $430, Institutions; $62, Individuals in-training; $219, Other countries; $586, Institutions, other countries.

40793 ■ *Occupational Therapy in Health Care: A Journal of Contemporary Practice*
Pub: Informa Healthcare
URL(s): informahealthcare.com/loi/ohc. **Ed:** Anne Elizabeth Dickerson. **Released:** Quarterly **Price:** $775, Institutions; €577, Institutions; £432, Institutions.

40794 ■ *Osteoporosis International*
Pub: Springer-Verlag New York Inc.
Contact: Ruediger Gebauer, President
URL(s): www.springer.com/medicine/orthopedics/journal/198link.springer.com/journal/198. **Released:** Monthly **Price:** €2,275, Institutions print + online; €2,730, Institutions print + enhanced access.

40795 ■ *Peritoneal Dialysis International*
Pub: Multimed Inc.
URL(s): www.pdiconnect.comwww.multi-med.com. **Ed:** D.G. Oreopoulos, Nicholas Topley. **Released:** Bimonthly **Price:** $570, U.S. and Canada libraries & institutions; print; $720, Other countries libraries & institutions; print; $770, Other countries libraries & institutions; online; $850, U.S. and Canada libraries & institutions; print & online; $1,000, Other countries libraries/institutions-print & online; $345, Individuals Medical Doctor/PhD; print; $410, Individuals Medical Doctor/PhD; print & online.

40796 ■ *Physical and Occupational Therapy in Pediatrics: A Quarterly Journal of Developmental Therapy*
Pub: Informa Healthcare
URL(s): informahealthcare.com/loi/pop. **Ed:** Robert J. Palisano, Doreen Bartlett. **Released:** Quarterly **Price:** $1,146, Institutions; €849, Institutions; £641, Institutions.

40797 ■ *Physician Executive*
Pub: American College of Physician Executives
Contact: Peter Angood, Chief Executive Officer
URL(s): www.physicianleaders.org. **Ed:** Bill Steiger. **Released:** Bimonthly **Price:** $100, Individuals; $120, Other countries.

40798 ■ *Provider: For Long Term Care Professionals*
Pub: American Health Care Association
URL(s): www.providermagazine.com. **Released:** Monthly **Price:** Free to qualified long-term and post-acute care professionals.; $48, /year for nonmembers and libraries; $61, Canada and Mexico; $85, Other countries.

40799 ■ *Psychoanalytic Social Work*
Pub: Routledge Journals Taylor & Francis Group
URL(s): www.tandfonline.com/toc/wpsw20/current. **Ed:** Morton Chethik, Max Bruck, William Borden, Shoshana Ringel, Linda A. Chernus, Naomi Abramowitz, Eda Goldstein. **Released:** Semiannual **Price:** $126, Individuals online only; $138, Individuals print + online; $587, Institutions online only; $671, Institutions print + online.

40800 ■ *PT in Motion*
Pub: American Physical Therapy Association
Contact: Paul Rockar, Jr., President
URL(s): www.apta.org/PTinMotion. **Ed:** Eric Ries, Donald Tepper. **Released:** Monthly **Price:** $104, Individuals; $124, Other countries; $184, Other countries Airmail; $134, Institutions; $154, Institutions, other countries; $214, Institutions, other countries Airmail; $45, Members life.

40801 ■ *Qualitative Health Research*
Pub: Pine Forge Press
Contact: Blaise R. Simqu, President
URL(s): www.sagepub.com/journalsProdDesc.nav?prodId=Journal200926. **Ed:** Janice M. Morse. **Released:** Monthly **Price:** $1,542, Institutions combined (print & e-access); $1,696, Institutions backfile lease, combined plus backfile; $1,388, Institutions e-access; $1,542, Institutions backfile lease, e-access plus backfile; $1,388, Institutions backfile, e-access (content through 1998); $1,511, Institutions print only; $250, Individuals print only; $139, Institutions single print; $27, Individuals single print.

40802 ■ *Revista Panamericana de Salud Publica*
Pub: Pan American Health Organization
Contact: Dr. Carissa Etienne, Director
URL(s): journal.paho.org/www.scielosp.org/scielo.php?script=sci_serial&pid=1020-4989&lng=en&nrm=iso. **Released:** Monthly **Price:** $44, Individuals electronic; $81, Two years electronic; $72, Institutions electronic; $133, Institutions two years, electronic; Free print.

40803 ■ *Seizure: European Journal of Epilepsy*
Pub: British Horn Society
URL(s): www.journals.elsevier.com/seizure-european-journal-of-epilepsy/www.harcourt-international.com, intl.elsevierhealth.com/journals/seiz/. **Ed:** T. Betts. **Released:** Monthly; 8/yr. **Price:** $1,248, Institutions; $574, Individuals.

40804 ■ *Share*
Pub: SHARE
Contact: Alice Yaker, Executive Director
URL(s): www.sharecancersupport.org. **Released:** Semiannual. **Description:** Acts as a forum for information, meetings, resources, and support groups for women with breast or ovarian cancer.

40805 ■ *Sleep*
Contact: Jerome A. Barrett, Executive Director
URL(s): www.journalsleep.org/. **Released:** Monthly
Price: $425, Nonmembers institution - online only;
Free member - online only; $225, Members individual
- online only.

40806 ■ *Social Work with Groups: A Journal of Community and Clinical Practice*
Pub: Routledge Journals Taylor & Francis Group
URL(s): www.tandfonline.com/toc/wswg20/current.
Released: Quarterly **Price:** $148, Individuals online
only; $160, Individuals print + online; $831, Institutions online only; $950, Institutions print + online.

40807 ■ *Social Work in Health Care: A Quarterly Journal Adopted by the Society for Social Work Leadership in Health Care*
Pub: Routledge Journals Taylor & Francis Group
URL(s): www.tandf.co.uk/journals/WSHC. **Ed:** Toba
Schwaber Kerson, Gary Rosenberg. **Released:** 10/
year **Price:** $357, Individuals online only; $396,
Individuals print + online; $1,420, Institutions online
only; $1,623, Institutions print + online.

40808 ■ *Social Work in Public Health*
Pub: Routledge Journals Taylor & Francis Group
URL(s): www.tandfonline.com/toc/whsp20/current.
Ed: Marvin D. Feit, Stanley F. Battle. **Released:**
7/year **Price:** $154, Individuals online only; $170,
Individuals print + online; $951, Institutions online
only; $1,087, Institutions print + online.

40809 ■ *Therapeutic Recreation Journal*
Pub: National Recreation and Park Association
Contact: Barbara Tulipane, President
URL(s): www.nrpa.org/trj/. **Ed:** Dr. Marcia Jean
Carter. **Released:** Quarterly **Price:** $100, Individuals
print and online; $120, Other countries print and online; $340, Institutions print and online; $380, Other
countries print and online; $80, Individuals online
only; $300, Institutions online only; $64, Members
online only; $80, Members print and online.

40810 ■ *Topics in Clinical Nutrition (TICN)*
Pub: Lippincott Williams & Wilkins
URL(s): journals.lww.com/topicsinclinicalnutrition/
pages/default.aspx. **Ed:** Prof. Judith A. Gilbride, Judith A. Gilbride. **Released:** Quarterly **Price:** $123,
Individuals Canada & Mexico; $129, Canada and
Mexico; $238, Other countries; $503, Institutions;
$528, Institutions, Canada and Mexico; $623, Institutions, other countries; $117, Individuals U.S.; $460,
Institutions U.S.; $483, Institutions Canada & Mexico;
$145, Individuals UK/Australia; $570, Institutions UK/
Australia; $226, Individuals other countries; $570,
Institutions other countries.

40811 ■ *Trustee: The Magazine for Hospital Governing Boards*
Pub: Health Forum L.L.C.
Contact: Michael Springer, President
URL(s): www.trusteemag.com. **Ed:** Jane Jeffries. **Released:** Monthly **Price:** $52, Individuals; $120,
Canada; $200, Other countries; $10, Single issue
domestic; $16, Single issue other countries.

40812 ■ *Women and Health: A Multi Disciplinary Journal of Women's Health Issues*
Pub: Routledge Journals Taylor & Francis Group
URL(s): www.tandfonline.com/toc/wwah20/current.
Released: 8/year **Price:** $297, Individuals online
only; $337, Individuals print + online; $1,739, Institutions online only; $1,987, Institutions print + online.

40813 ■ *Worksight*
Pub: Mississippi State University Rehabilitation
Research and Training Center on Blindness and
Low Vision
Contact: Michele Capella McDonnall, Director (Acting)
URL(s): www.blind.msstate.edu. **Released:** Annual.
Price: Free. **Description:** Discusses news, activities,
research, and training programs of the Rehabilitation
Research and Training Center on Blindness and Low
Vision. **Remarks:** TDD available at (662)325-8693.

VIDEOCASSETTES/ AUDIOCASSETTES

40814 ■ *Confidentiality: Ethical and Legal Considerations*
Channing Bete Company Inc.
1 Community Pl.
South Deerfield, MA 01373-0200
Ph: (413)665-7611
Free: 800-477-4776
Fax: (800)499-6464
Co. E-mail: custsvcs@channing-bete.com
URL: http://www.channing-bete.com
Contact: Mike Bete, President
E-mail: mikebete@channing-bete.com
Released: 1994. **Price:** $295. **Description:** Discusses privacy issues, defamation, instances when
information must be shared, patient and family access to information, and the impact of computers on
confidentiality. Program approved for 1 hour of CEU
credits. **Availability:** VHS.

40815 ■ *Continuous Quality Improvement in Health Care*
Channing Bete Company Inc.
1 Community Pl.
South Deerfield, MA 01373-0200
Ph: (413)665-7611
Free: 800-477-4776
Fax: (800)499-6464
Co. E-mail: custsvcs@channing-bete.com
URL: http://www.channing-bete.com
Contact: Mike Bete, President
E-mail: mikebete@channing-bete.com
Released: 1993. **Price:** $199. **Description:** Discusses leadership, training, empowerment, data collection, and tools for interpreting data. Program approved for 3 hours of CEU credits. **Availability:** VHS.

40816 ■ *Continuous Quality Improvement in Long-Term Care*
Channing Bete Company Inc.
1 Community Pl.
South Deerfield, MA 01373-0200
Ph: (413)665-7611
Free: 800-477-4776
Fax: (800)499-6464
Co. E-mail: custsvcs@channing-bete.com
URL: http://www.channing-bete.com
Contact: Mike Bete, President
E-mail: mikebete@channing-bete.com
Released: 1993. **Price:** $99. **Description:** Discusses
leadership, training, empowerment, data collection,
and tools for interpreting data. Program approved for
2 hours of CEU credits. **Availability:** VHS.

40817 ■ *Controlling Violence in Health Care*
Channing Bete Company Inc.
1 Community Pl.
South Deerfield, MA 01373-0200
Ph: (413)665-7611
Free: 800-477-4776
Fax: (800)499-6464
Co. E-mail: custsvcs@channing-bete.com
URL: http://www.channing-bete.com
Contact: Mike Bete, President
E-mail: mikebete@channing-bete.com
Released: 1994. **Price:** $199. **Description:** Covers
verbal de-escalation, limit setting, pharmacological
intervention, and physical containment. Program approved for 1 hour of CEU credit. **Availability:** VHS.

40818 ■ *Coronary Artery Disease*
Concept Media
PO Box 6904
Florence, KY 41022-6904
Free: 800-354-9706
Fax: (800)487-8488
Co. E-mail: cpgcs@cengage.com
URL: http://www.conceptmedia.com
Contact: Myrtle Ewing, Supervisor
Released: 1997. **Description:** Four-volume series
discusses nursing assessment, diagnosis, intervention and evaluation of patients with this condition.
Availability: VHS.

40819 ■ *Health Care for the Homeless*
National Film Board of Canada (NFB)
PO Box 6100
Montreal, QC, Canada H3C 3H5
Ph: (514)283-9000
Free: 800-267-7710
Fax: (514)283-7564
Co. E-mail: webmaster@nfb.ca
URL: http://www.nfb.ca
Contact: Claude Joli-Coeur, Manager
E-mail: c.jolicoeur@nfb.ca
Released: 1989. **Price:** $295. **Description:** This
program examines the nexus of poverty and ill health
in its extremes, and asks questions about the
responsibility of physicians to treat any and all ill
people that come to them. **Availability:** VHS; 3/4 U.

40820 ■ *Issues in Homecare Nursing*
Concept Media
PO Box 6904
Florence, KY 41022-6904
Free: 800-354-9706
Fax: (800)487-8488
Co. E-mail: cpgcs@cengage.com
URL: http://www.conceptmedia.com
Contact: Myrtle Ewing, Supervisor
Released: 1997. **Description:** Four-volume series
that helps healthcare professionals, experienced
practitioners and students address aspects of care in
the home. **Availability:** VHS.

40821 ■ *Patient Rights: The Art of Caring*
Channing Bete Company Inc.
1 Community Pl.
South Deerfield, MA 01373-0200
Ph: (413)665-7611
Free: 800-477-4776
Fax: (800)499-6464
Co. E-mail: custsvcs@channing-bete.com
URL: http://www.channing-bete.com
Contact: Mike Bete, President
E-mail: mikebete@channing-bete.com
Released: 1990. **Price:** $199. **Description:** Explains
patients rights to information, self-determination, communication, privacy, personal property, and freedom
from abuse and restraint. Program approved for 2
hours of CEU credits. **Availability:** VHS.

40822 ■ *S.O.S. Kids: Infant/Child Emergency Life Saving Video*
Tapeworm Video Distributors Inc.
25876 The Old Rd., Ste. 141
Stevenson Ranch, CA 91381
Ph: (661)257-4904
Fax: (661)257-4820
Contact: Connie Figgins, President
E-mail: connief@tapeworm.com
Released: 1997. **Price:** $19.95. **Description:** EMT
Paramedic Richard Hardman describes and demonstrates what to do in various medical emergencies.
Availability: VHS.

40823 ■ *What Tadoo*
Tapeworm Video Distributors Inc.
25876 The Old Rd., Ste. 141
Stevenson Ranch, CA 91381
Ph: (661)257-4904
Fax: (661)257-4820
Contact: Connie Figgins, President
E-mail: connief@tapeworm.com
Released: 1997. **Price:** $14.95. **Description:** Puppet
frogs, What and Tadoo help children deal with issues
of child abuse and prevention. **Availability:** VHS.

TRADE SHOWS AND CONVENTIONS

40824 ■ *American Public Health Association Public Health Expo*
American Public Health Association (APHA)
800 I St. NW
Washington, DC 20001-3710
Ph: (202)777-2742

Fax: (202)777-2534
Co. E-mail: comments@apha.org
URL: http://www.apha.org
Contact: Joyce R. Gaufin, President
URL(s): www.apha.org. **Frequency:** Annual. **Audience:** Public health professionals, physicians, nurses, and health administrators. **Principal Exhibits:** Medical, products-related and pharmaceutical, health services, publishers, computer/software, educational, government, schools of public health. **Dates and Locations:** 2015 Nov 07-11; venue not reported. **Telecommunication Services:** comments@apha.org.

40825 ■ American School Health Association National School Health Conference
American School Health Association (ASHA)
1760 Old Meadow Rd., Ste. 500
McLean, VA 22102
Ph: (703)506-7675
Fax: (703)506-3266
Co. E-mail: info@ashaweb.org
URL: http://www.ashaweb.org
Contact: Susan F. Wooley, Director
E-mail: swooley@ashaweb.org
URL(s): www.ashaweb.org. **Price:** $195, Members; $290, Non-members; $215, Onsite registered, members; $310, Onsite registered, non-members. **Frequency:** Annual. **Audience:** School nurses, health educators, physicians, teachers, school administrators, dentists, school counselors, physical educators, and school health coordinators. **Principal Exhibits:** Publications, pharmaceuticals, clinical and medical equipment and supplies, information on health organizations, and health education methods and materials. **Telecommunication Services:** mbramsier@ashaweb.org.

40826 ■ Association for Research on Nonprofit Organizations and Voluntary Action Conference (ACNOVA)
Association for Research on Nonprofit Organizations and Voluntary Action (ARNOVA)
550 W North St., Ste. 301
Indianapolis, IN 46202
Ph: (317)684-2120
Fax: (317)684-2128
URL: http://www.arnova.org
Contact: Francie Ostrower, President
E-mail: fostrower@austin.utexas.edu
URL(s): www.arnova.org. **Frequency:** Annual. **Principal Exhibits:** Exhibits for citizen participation and voluntary action, including social movements, interest groups, consumer groups, political participation, community development, and religious organizations. **Telecommunication Services:** conference@arnova.org.

40827 ■ Virginia Health Care Association Annual Convention and Trade Show
Virginia Health Care Association (VHCA)
2112 W Laburnum Ave., Ste. 206
Richmond, VA 23227
Ph: (804)353-9101
Fax: (804)353-3098
URL: http://www.vhca.org
Contact: Stephen Morrisette, President
URL(s): www.vhca.org. **Frequency:** Annual. **Audience:** Health care professionals. **Principal Exhibits:** Equipment, supplies, and services for nursing home operations, including food, medical supplies, furniture, computer systems, linen, medical equipment, insurance, pharmaceuticals, optometrists, psychologists, and transportation.

CONSULTANTS

40828 ■ Alternative Services Inc.
32625 7 Mile Rd., Ste. 10
Livonia, MI 48152
Ph: (248)471-4880
Fax: (248)471-5230
URL: http://www.asi-mi.org
Contact: Arthur Mack, President
Scope: Services: Developmental disabilities training. **Founded:** 1978.

40829 ■ BioSciCon Inc. [Biomedical Science Consulting Co.]
14905 Forest Landing Cir.
Rockville, MD 20850
Ph: (301)610-9130
Fax: (301)610-7662
Co. E-mail: info@bioscicon.com
URL: http://www.bioscicon.com
Contact: Nenad Markovic, President
Scope: Sponsoring development of the technology of the Pap test accuracy via introduction of a new bio-marker that enhances visibility of abnormal cells on Pap smears or mono-layers of cervical cells obtained in solution. Conducts clinical trials for assessment of the test efficacy and safety, manufactures research tools for conduct of trials, and markets IP to license manufacturing, marketing, sales and distribution rights of the new technology line of products. **Founded:** 1996. **Publications:** "Cervical Acid Phosphates: A Biomarker of Cervical Dysplasia and Potential Surrogate Endpoint for Colposcopy," 2004; "Enhancing Pap test with a new biological marker of cervical dysplasia," 2004; "A cytoplasmic biomarker for liquid-based Pap," The FACEB Journal Experimental Biology, 2004; "Pap test and new biomarker-based technology for enhancing visibility of abnormal cells," 2004. **Special Services:** MarkPap®; PreservCyt®.

40830 ■ Center for Lifestyle Enhancement - Columbia Medical Center of Plano
3901 W 15th St.
Plano, TX 75075
Ph: (972)596-6800
Fax: (972)519-1299
Co. E-mail: mcp.cle@hcahealthcare.com
URL: http://www.medicalcenterofplano.com
Contact: Mary Jo Steallano, Principal
Scope: Provides professional health counseling in the areas of general nutrition for weight management, eating disorders, diabetic education, cholesterol reduction and adolescent weight management. Offers work site health promotion and preventive services. Also coordinates speaker's bureau, cooking classes and physician referrals. Industries served: education, insurance, healthcare, retail or wholesale, data processing and manufacturing throughout Texas. **Founded:** 1975. **Seminars:** Rx Diet and Exercise; Smoking Cessation; Stress Management; Health Fairs; Fitness Screenings; Body Composition; Nutrition Analysis; Exercise Classes; Prenatal Nutrition; SHAPEDOWN; Successfully Managing Diabetes; Gourmet Foods for Your Heart; The Aging Heart; Heart Smart Saturday featuring Day of Dance; Weight-Loss Management Seminars; The Right Stroke for Men; Peripheral Artery Disease Screening; Menstruation: The Cycle Begins; Boot Camp for New Dads; Grand parenting 101: Caring for Kids Today; Teddy Bear Camp; New Baby Day Camp; Safe Sitter Baby-Sitting Class.

40831 ■ The Children's Psychological Trauma Center
2105 Divisadero St.
San Francisco, CA 94115
Ph: (415)292-7119
Fax: (415)749-2802
Co. E-mail: gil.kliman@cphc-sf.org
URL: http://www.cphc-sf.org
Contact: Joe Herzberg
Scope: Treats those with psychological trauma claimed from stressors including institutional negligence, vehicular and aviation accidents, wrongful death in the family, rape, molestation, fire, explosion, flood, earthquake, loss of parents, terrorism, kidnapping, disfiguring events, emotional damage from social work, medical malpractice or defective products. Provides evaluation and reports to referring professionals. Experienced in forensic consultation and testimony. **Founded:** 1992. **Publications:** "My Personal Story About Tropical Storm Stan," Feb, 2006; "My Personal Story About Hurricanes Katrina and Rita: A guided activity workbook to help coping, learning and Healthy expression," Sep, 2005; "Helping Patients and their Families Cope in a National Disaster," Jan, 2002; "The practice of behavioral treatment in the acute rehabilitation setting".

40832 ■ Diversified Health Resources Inc.
875 N Michigan Ave., Ste. 3250
Chicago, IL 60611-1901
Ph: (312)266-0466
Fax: (312)266-0715
Contact: Andrea R. Rozran, President
Scope: Offers health care consulting for hospitals, nursing homes including homes for the aged and other health related facilities and companies. Specializes in planning and marketing. Also conducts executive searches for top level health care administrative positions. Serves private industries as well as government agencies. **Founded:** 1979. **Publications:** "City Finance".

40833 ■ Environmental Health Science Inc.
418 Wall St.
Princeton, NJ 08540
Ph: (609)924-7616
Free: 800-841-8923
Fax: (609)924-0793
Co. E-mail: healthscience@comcast.net
URL: http://www.speechgeneratingdevices.com
Contact: David Goldberg, President
E-mail: davidg@patmedia.net
Scope: Specialists in rehabilitation technology for speech disorder and physically disabled persons. Offers demonstrations, evaluations and sales of the following types of equipment: augmentative speech communication systems, adaptive switches and specialty controls, and computer access devices. Industries served: hospitals and rehabilitation centers, schools, and special service organizations such as United Cerebral Palsy Association, Department of Human Services, etc. **Founded:** 1984. **Publications:** "Play & Learn"; "Bookworm Literacy Tool"; "Meville to Weville". **Seminars:** Augmentative Communication and Assistive Devices. **Special Services:** Boardmaker®; Dynamically Pro®.

40834 ■ Family Resource Center on Disabilities (FRCD)
11 E Adams St., Ste. 1002
Chicago, IL 60603
Ph: (312)939-3513
Fax: (312)854-8980
Co. E-mail: info@frcd.org
URL: http://frcd.org
Contact: Michelle Phillips, Executive Director
Description: Parents, professionals, and volunteers seeking to improve services for all children with disabilities. Originally organized as a result of the 1969 Illinois law mandating the education of all children with disabilities and operates as a coalition to inform and activate parents. Provides information and referral services, individualized support services for low-income Chicago families, transition services, and special education rights training. **Scope:** Provider of consulting services to advocacy groups and individuals seeking support for children with disabilities. **Founded:** 1969. **Publications:** "How to Get Services By Being Assertive"; "How to Organize an Effective Parent/Advocacy Group and Move Bureaucracies"; "Main roads Travel to Tomorrow - a Road Map for the Future"; "Does Your Child Have Special Education Needs"; "How to Prepare for a Successful Due Process Hearing"; "How to Participate Effectively in Your Child's IEP Meeting"; "Tax Guide for Parents". **Seminars:** How to Support Parents as Effective Advocates; How to Get Services by Being Assertive; How to Develop an Awareness Program for Nondisabled Children; How to Organize a Parent Support Group; How to Move Bureaucratic Mountains; How to Raise Money Painlessly through Publishing; How to Use Humor in Public Presentations.

40835 ■ Grief Counseling & Support Services
8600 W Chester Pke., Ste. 304
Upper Darby, PA 19082
Ph: (610)789-7707
Fax: (610)469-9499
Contact: Jeffrey Kauffman, President
E-mail: jkharry@voicenet.com
Scope: Specializing in consulting and training services for organizations dealing with loss, trauma and grief issues. These services may include management consultations, crisis intervention, educational programming, policy development, program design, group process work, individual counseling or

other support services. Training and support services also provided for loss issues for mental retardation service providers. Serves private industries as well as government agencies. **Founded:** 1984.

40836 ■ Jest for the Health of It Services
PO Box 8484
Santa Cruz, CA 95061-8484
Ph: (831)425-8436
Fax: (831)425-8437
Co. E-mail: pwooten@jesthealth.com
URL: http://www.jesthealth.com
Contact: Shirley Trout, Manager
E-mail: strout@nurseswhostay.com
Scope: Develops and presents seminars, keynotes and skill shops about the power of humor. Provides consulting services for development of humor rooms and comedy carts in hospitals. Conducts training for clowns to make visits in hospitals and nursing homes. Industries served: health professionals and businesses wishing to educate staff about healthy lifestyle choices. **Publications:** "Heart Humor and Healing"; "Compassionate Laughter: Jest for Your Health"; "The Hospital Clown: A Closer Look"; "Humor: An Antidote for Stress"; "Humor, Laughter and Play: Maintaining Balance in a Serious World"; "You've Got to Be Kidding: Humor Skills for Surviving Managed Care"; "Laughter as Therapy for Patient and Caregiver"; "Patty Wooten: Nurse Healer"; "Humor: An antidote for stress".

40837 ■ Kanata Intercultural Consulting Inc.
82 Douglas Woods Close SE
Calgary, AB, Canada T2Z 1Z5
Ph: (403)807-9200
Fax: (403)207-9405
Co. E-mail: info@kanataint.ca
Contact: Cam Stewart, Owner
E-mail: cam.stewart@hotmail.com
Scope: Firm helps organizations reach their diversity objectives by creating and implementing custom solutions that address inter cultural issues. Consulting services include diversity assessments; diversity initiative creation and execution; an on-site diversity consultant in house to eliminate the need to hire additional staff to address issues of diversity; and diversity training workshops tailored to address specific issues facing a business. **Seminars:** Diverse Staff Hiring/Retention; Building A Culture of Diversity In Your Business; Problem solving and conflict resolution; How to effectively reach intercultural communities.

40838 ■ Occupational & Environmental Health Consulting Services Inc.
635 Harding Rd.
Hinsdale, IL 60521-4814
Ph: (630)325-2083
Fax: (630)325-2098
Co. E-mail: bobb@safety-epa.com
URL: http://www.oehcs.com
Contact: Robert C. Brandys, President
E-mail: bobb@safety-epa.com
Scope: Provider of consulting to industry on safety program development and implementation, industrial hygiene monitoring programs, occupational health nursing, wellness programs, medical monitoring, accident trending and statistics, emergency response planning, multilingual training, right-to-know compliance and training, hazardous waste management, random monitoring and mitigation, asbestos school inspection, and project management. Also offers indoor air quality, expert witnessing service. **Founded:** 1984. **Publications:** "Worldwide Exposure Standards for Mold and Bacteria"; "Global Occupational Exposure Limits for Over 5000 Specific Chemicals"; "Post-Remediation Verification and Clearance Testing for Mold and Bacteria Risk Based Levels of Cleanliness". **Seminars:** Right-To-Know Compliance; Setting Internal Exposure Standards; Hospital Right-to-Know and Contingency Response; Ethylene Oxide Control; Industrial Hygiene Training; Asbestos Worker Training; Biosafety; Asbestos Operations and Maintenance. **Special Services:** Safety Software Program, Audiogram Analysis, First Report of Injury Form, Human Resources Database; Material Safety Data Sheet (MSDS); NPDES Monthly Reports; Lockout/Tagout (LOTO) Procedure Software; VOC Usage Tracking and Reporting Software, Medi-

cal Department Patient Records Database, Pictorial Labels for Chemical Containers, TIER II Hazardous Material Inventory Form & Database.

40839 ■ Pathways To Wellness
617 Everhart Rd.
Corpus Christi, TX 78411
Ph: (361)985-9642
Fax: (361)949-4627
Co. E-mail: path2wellness@earthlink.net
URL: http://www.path2wellness.com
Contact: Evy Coppola, Owner
Scope: Offer natural holistic health counseling, yoga and hatha yoga classes, teachers training and cookery classes for individuals and companies. Health counseling includes nutritional guidance, kinesiology, iridology, reflexology, energy healing, massage therapy, herbal and vitamin therapy, creative visualization and meditation. Provides supplements which bring about the same effects as that of natural sunshine. **Founded:** 1988. **Seminars:** Is It You Holding You Back?; The Balancing Act Career Family and Self; Learning the Art of Friendly Persuasion; Stop Accepting What You Are Getting and Start Asking for What You Want!; Introduction to Natural Health and Healthy Living; Learn Why One Size Approaches to the Answers on Health Do Not Work; Introduction to Yoga. What is it? Who can do it? What can it do for you.

40840 ■ Professional Counseling Centers Inc.
543 Coventry Way
Noblesville, IN 46062-9024
Ph: (317)877-3111
Contact: Margie Hanrahan, Owner
Scope: Business counselors offering services in the following areas: employee assistance, managed care, alcohol and drug treatment, labor and union consultation and industrial mental health.

FRANCHISES AND BUSINESS OPPORTUNITIES

40841 ■ Boston Bartenders School of America
Boston Bartenders School Associates, Inc.
64 Enterprise Rd.
Hyannis, MA 02601
Free: 800-357-3210
Fax: (508)771-1165
Contact: William Green, Chief Executive Officer
Description: Program in mixology and alcohol awareness. **No. of Franchise Units:** 10. **No. of Company-Owned Units:** 3. **Founded:** 1968. **Franchised:** 1994. **Equity Capital Needed:** $50,000. **Franchise Fee:** $10,000. **Financial Assistance:** Yes. **Training:** Yes.

40842 ■ ComForcare Senior Services
ComForcare Healthcare Holdings Inc.
2510 Telegraph Rd., Ste. 100
Bloomfield Hills, MI 48302
Ph: (248)745-9700
Free: 800-886-4044
Fax: (248)745-9763
Co. E-mail: info@comforcare.com
URL: http://www.comforcare.com
Description: Franchise provides home health care for seniors. **No. of Franchise Units:** 150. **No. of Company-Owned Units:** 1. **Founded:** 1996. **Franchised:** 2001. **Equity Capital Needed:** $105,000-$155,000 includes franchise fee. **Franchise Fee:** $39,500. **Training:** Yes.

40843 ■ CPR Services, Inc.
158 Pond St., Ste. A
Ashland, MA 01721
Ph: (508)881-5107
Free: 800-547-5107
Fax: (508)881-4718
Description: CPR and First Aid Training. **No. of Franchise Units:** 1. **No. of Company-Owned Units:** 1. **Founded:** 1985. **Franchised:** 1998. **Equity Capital Needed:** $13,500-$16,500. **Franchise Fee:** $7,500. **Financial Assistance:** No. **Training:** Yes.

40844 ■ The Dentist Choice, Inc.
Choice Corporation, Inc.
33971 Selva Rd., Ste. 200
Dana Point, CA 92629
Free: 888-757-1333
Fax: (949)443-2074
Description: Dental health services. **No. of Franchise Units:** 120. **No. of Company-Owned Units:** 1. **Founded:** 1994. **Franchised:** 1994. **Equity Capital Needed:** $60,000. **Franchise Fee:** $45,000. **Financial Assistance:** Yes. **Training:** Provides 1 week at headquarters and ongoing support.

40845 ■ Interim Health Care
1601 Sawgrass Corporate Pkwy., Ste. 100
Sunrise, FL 33323
Free: 800-338-7786
URL: http://www.interimhealthcare.com
Contact: Kathleen Gilmartin, President
Description: Franchises nursing and home health care personnel services. **No. of Franchise Units:** 267. **No. of Company-Owned Units:** 20. **Founded:** 1966. **Franchised:** 1966. **Equity Capital Needed:** Medical staffing $100,000-$125,000; home health care $250,000-$400,000. **Franchise Fee:** $5,000; $20,000-$30,000. **Training:** Yes.

40846 ■ Superior Senior Care
Superior Senior Care Franchises, L.L.C.
PO Box 505
Hot Springs, AR 71902
Ph: (479)783-1206
Fax: (479)783-1232
Co. E-mail: Franchise@SuperiorSeniorCare.com
URL: http://www.SuperiorSeniorCare.com
Description: Provider of light housekeeping and home management, meal preparation, shopping, transportation and companionship. **No. of Franchise Units:** 7. **No. of Company-Owned Units:** 7. **Founded:** 1985. **Franchised:** 2000. **Equity Capital Needed:** $18,771. **Franchise Fee:** $15,000. **Training:** Yes.

PUBLISHERS

40847 ■ "A Supply-Side Solution for Health Care" in (Vol. 92, July 23, 2012, No. 30, pp. 30)
Dow Jones & Co., Inc.
1211 Avenue of the Americas
New York, NY 10036
Free: 800-369-5663
Co. E-mail: service@dowjones.com
URL: http://new.dowjones.com
Contact: Clare Hart, President
Ed: H. Woody Brock. **Released:** July 23, 2012. **Description:** The United States should increase the supply of new doctors, nurses and other health care professionals to improve the American health care system by increasing supply. Health care reform proposals in the US Congress fail to address the supply side of the problem.

COMPUTERIZED DATABASES

40848 ■ GrantSelect™
Schoolhouse Partners L.L.C.
Kurz Purdue Technology Ctr.
1281 Win Hintschel Blvd.
West Lafayette, IN 47906
Ph: (765)237-3390
Fax: (765)594-4302
Co. E-mail: info@schoolhousepartners.net
URL: http://www.schoolhousepartners.net
Availability: Online: Schoolhouse Partners L.L.C. **Type:** Directory; Numeric.

40849 ■ Health Care Daily Report™
Bloomberg BNA
3 Bethesda Metro Center, Ste. 250
Bethesda, MD 20814-5377
Ph: (703)341-3000
Free: 800-372-1033

Fax: (800)253-0332
Co. E-mail: customercare@bna.com
URL: http://www.bna.com
Contact: Gregory McCaffrey, President
URL(s): www.bna.com/health-care-daily-p6781.
Availability: Online: Bloomberg BNA; Thomson Reuters - Westlaw. **Type:** Full-text.

40850 ■ *Health Care Policy Report*
Bloomberg BNA
3 Bethesda Metro Center, Ste. 250
Bethesda, MD 20814-5377
Ph: (703)341-3000
Free: 800-372-1033
Fax: (800)253-0332
Co. E-mail: customercare@bna.com
URL: http://www.bna.com
Contact: Gregory McCaffrey, President
URL(s): www.bna.com/health-care-policy-p6782.
Availability: Online: Bloomberg BNA; Thomson Reuters - Westlaw. **Type:** Full-text.

LIBRARIES

40851 ■ Association of Gospel Rescue Missions (AGRM) - Wooley Library
7222 Commerce Center Dr., Ste. 120
Colorado Springs, CO 80919
Ph: (719)266-8300
Free: 800-4RE-SCUE
Fax: (719)266-8600
Co. E-mail: info@agrm.org
URL: http://www.agrm.org/agrm/default.asp
Contact: John Ashmen, President
E-mail: jashmen@agrm.org
Description: Rescue ministry executives and staff, and concerned individuals in 6 countries. Promotes rescue mission work for all persons experiencing crisis. Aims to sponsor coffee-houses for youths, emergency shelters for men and women, women with children, and families, day camps, resident camps, and wilderness camps for inner-city children, cafeterias for low-income persons. Serves meals and provide sleeping space to individuals in need. Sponsors long-term residential programs offering addiction recovery, education and employment services, and assistance to the elderly and mentally ill. Maintains speakers' bureau; offers placement service; compiles statistics. Rescue College is the accredited online distance learning program of the organization. **Scope:** Homelessness, urban ministry, alcohol and drug assistance, history of Christian efforts to inner city poor. **Services:** Library open to the public for reference use only. **Founded:** 1913. **Holdings:** 2118 periodicals, books, clippings, audio/visuals, and archival material. **Publications:** *How to Have a Better Board of Directors*; *Membership and Resource Directory*; *RESCUE Happenings* (Bimonthly); *RESCUE Magazine* (Bimonthly); *Rescue Mission Salary Survey* (Annual); *Sample Staff Policy Manual*; *Association of Gospel Rescue Missions Directory and Resource Book* (Biennial). **Educational Activities:** Association of Gospel Rescue Missions (Annual). **Awards:** President Citation of Merit (Periodic); Rescuer Award (Periodic).

40852 ■ National Families in Action (NFIA) - Library
PO Box 133136
Atlanta, GA 30333-3136
Ph: (404)248-9676
Co. E-mail: nfia@nationalfamilies.org
URL: http://www.nationalfamilies.org
Contact: Sue Rusche, President
E-mail: srusche@nationalfamilies.org
Description: Parents and other adults concerned about preventing drug abuse. Seeks to: educate parents, children, and the community about the use of drugs; counteract social pressures that condone and promote drug use; stop drug use. Worked for passage of statewide drug paraphernalia statutes. Collects and disseminates information about the effects of drugs. Maintains Drug Information Center, which contains more than 500,000 documents, studies, books, brochures, and films and videos relating to drug abuse. Operates after-school program for parents and youth. **Scope:** Drug use, drug legalization, drug usage prevention. **Services:** Library open

to the public for reference use only. **Founded:** 1977.
Holdings: 1 million books, periodicals, clippings, audio/visuals, monographs, and archival material.
Publications: *Drug Abuse Update* (Quarterly); *Crack Update*; *A Step Backward*; *False Messengers: How Addictive Drugs Change the Brain*; *Guide to the Drug Legalization Movement and How You Can Stop It*; *Twelve Reasons Not to Legalize Drugs*; *Twelve Tips for Helping Your Children Stay Drug-Free*. **Educational Activities:** Parent Leader Certification.

40853 ■ Wisconsin HIV/STD/Hepatitis Information & Referral Center
PO Box 510498
Milwaukee, WI 53203
Free: 800-334-2437
Co. E-mail: irc-wisconsin@arcw.org
URL: http://www.irc-wisconsin.org
Contact: Angie Clark, Manager
Scope: AIDS, HIV, STDs, hepatitis. **Services:** Library open to the public. **Founded:** 1985.

RESEARCH CENTERS

40854 ■ African Medical and Research Foundation, U.S.A. (AMREF USA)
4 W 43rd St., 2nd Fl.
New York, NY 10036
Ph: (212)768-2440
Fax: (212)768-4230
Co. E-mail: info@amrefusa.org
URL: http://www.amrefusa.org
Contact: Lisa K. Meadowcraft, Executive Director
Scope: The spread and prevention of AIDS, malaria, and hydatid disease. Also creates health care and training models used by developing countries worldwide. **Services:** Health education courses. **Founded:** 1957.

40855 ■ American College of Apothecaries Research and Education Foundation - Research and Education Resource Center
2830 Summer Oaks Dr.
Bartlett, TN 38184-3811
Ph: (901)383-8119
Fax: (901)383-8882
Co. E-mail: refinfo@acainfo.org
URL: http://ref.acainfo.org/resource-center
Contact: Edward J. Hesterlee, Executive Vice President
Scope: Three-fold objective of the Foundation is to promote public welfare through development of services in institutions providing health care, encourage and conduct research to improve health care and education, and encourage health care practitioners to improve the quality and availability of their services. **Founded:** 1978. **Educational Activities:** Research and Education Resource Center Community education program; Research and Education Resource Center Conferences.

40856 ■ Baylor College of Medicine - Center for Medical Ethics and Health Policy
1 Baylor Plz., MS BCM420
Houston, TX 77030
Ph: (713)798-6290
Fax: (713)798-5678
Co. E-mail: amcguire@bcm.edu
URL: http://www.bcm.edu/centers/research/medical-ethics
Contact: Amy L. McGuire, Director
Scope: Priorities for health care services, methods of funding health care services, and social controls on health care service, including studies on ethics in clinical decision making and value issues in controlling the cost of medicine. **Services:** Consultation Services. **Founded:** 1982. **Publications:** *News Bulletin* (Semimonthly). **Educational Activities:** Center for Medical Ethics and Health Policy Clinical Instruction; Center for Medical Ethics and Health Policy Continuing Education Programs; Center for Medical Ethics and Health Policy Education Courses, in medical ethics; Center for Medical Ethics and Health Policy Lectures, visiting scholars.

40857 ■ Benaroya Research Institute at Virginia Mason (BRI)
1201 9th Ave.
Seattle, WA 98101-2795
Ph: (206)583-6500
Fax: (206)223-7543
Co. E-mail: info@benaroyaresearch.org
URL: http://www.benaroyaresearch.org
Contact: Dr. Gerald T. Nepom, Director
Scope: Immunology, diabetes and clinical research. **Services:** Educational opportunities through high school programs and postdoctoral training. **Founded:** 1956. **Publications:** *Bulletin of the Virginia Mason Clinic*.

40858 ■ Blanton-Peale Institute and Counseling Center
7 W 30th St., 9th Fl.
New York, NY 10001
Ph: (212)725-7850
Fax: (212)967-4919
Co. E-mail: info@blantonpeale.org
URL: http://www.blantonpeale.org
Contact: Rev. Paul W. Bradley, President
Scope: Policy studies related to psychoanalysis, marriage and family therapy, pastoral care, and the dialogue between theology and psychology. **Founded:** 1937. **Publications:** *Journal of Religion and Health* (Quarterly); *Labyrinth Newsletter* (Semiannual). **Educational Activities:** Blanton-Peale Institute Lectures; Marriage and Family Therapy Residency; Pastoral Care Studies Program; Psychoanalytic Residency.

40859 ■ Brandeis University - Schneider Institutes for Health Policy (SIHP)
Heller School for Social Policy & Management, MS 035
415 S St.
Waltham, MA 02454-9110
Ph: (781)736-3901
Fax: (781)736-3905
Co. E-mail: wallack@brandeis.edu
URL: http://sihp.brandeis.edu
Contact: Stanley S. Wallack, Executive Director
Scope: Health care, focusing on the intersection of health behavior and systems of care, including policy studies in the areas of financing organization, value of health services, quality, high cost and high risk populations, and technology. **Founded:** 1978. **Publications:** *Background Reports*; *Heller Highlights* (3/year); *Major Issue Papers*; *Program Analyses*; *Publication Catalogue*. **Educational Activities:** AHRQ Training Program (3/year); NIAAA Training Program (3/year).

40860 ■ Brown University - Watson Institute for International Studies
111 Thayer St., Box 1970
Providence, RI 02912-1970
Ph: (401)863-2809
Fax: (401)863-1270
Co. E-mail: watson_institute@brown.edu
URL: http://watson.brown.edu
Contact: Richard M. Locke, Director
E-mail: richard_locke@brown.edu
Scope: Contemporary global problems and challenges in security, economy, ecology, identity and culture. **Services:** Extensive outreach activities: for community and policy makers. **Founded:** 1986. **Publications:** *Watson Institute for International Studies Annual Report*; *Blogs*; *Conference Reports*; *Documentaries*; *Watson Institute for International Studies Newsletters* (Semiannual); *Streaming video*; *Studies in Comparative International Development*. **Educational Activities:** Choices for the 21st Century Education program; Development studies undergraduate major; Faculty and student foreign exchange programs; International relations undergraduate major; Watson Institute for International Studies Lectures; Watson Institute for International Studies Seminars; Watson Institute for International Studies Conferences.

40861 ■ California State University, Los Angeles - Edmund G. "Pat" Brown Institute of Public Affairs
5151 State University Dr.
Los Angeles, CA 90032-8261
Ph: (323)343-3770
Fax: (323)343-3774
Co. E-mail: raphael.sonenshein@calstatela.edu
URL: http://www.patbrowninstitute.org/
Contact: Raphael J. Sonenshein, Executive Director
Scope: Applied research and analysis of public policy issues of California and greater Los Angeles area, including ethnic community participation in politics, futures planning, the environment, mental health, law and justice, water, the homeless, history, infrastructure, the judicial system, health care, education, transportation, and emergency disaster management. **Services:** Technical assistance and consulting: on policy issues. **Founded:** 1980. **Educational Activities:** Pat Brown Institute of Public Affairs Conferences and forums. **Awards:** Edmund G. "Pat" Brown Institute of Public Affairs.

40862 ■ Center for the Study of Social Policy (CSSP)
1575 Eye St. NW, Ste. 500
Washington, DC 20005
Ph: (202)371-1565
Fax: (202)371-1472
Co. E-mail: info@cssp.org
URL: http://www.cssp.org
Contact: Frank Farrow, Director
Description: Serves as research organization that provides analyses on the effects of contemporary policy issues on states, communities, families, and individuals for federal, state, and local decision makers, as well as employers, voluntary agencies, and informal care systems. Seeks to anticipate long-term problems. Analyzes problems using interdisciplinary research techniques. Informs the government and private sector of research findings. Includes issues of concern: poverty and income support programs; long-term care for the elderly and disabled; healthcare for the disadvantaged; children and youth services; disability policy. Seeks to identify policy directions to finance and deliver human services more effectively. **Scope:** Social policy, including studies on children and youth, income support, long-term care, health, disability, and minorities. Focus on children and family services and policy. **Founded:** 1979. **Publications:** *Building Community Ownership in Neighborhood Revitalization.*

40863 ■ Dalhousie University - Population Health Research Unit (PHRU)
Department of Community Health & Epidemiology
Faculty of Medicine
5790 University Ave.
Halifax, NS, Canada B3H 1V7
Ph: (902)494-1785
Fax: (902)494-1597
Co. E-mail: upal@dal.ca
URL: http://www.phru.dal.ca
Contact: Upal Nath, Director
Scope: Health and social sciences, particularly population health, health services utilization and their interrelationships. **Founded:** 1993.

40864 ■ Dartmouth College - Geisel School of Medicine - Dartmouth Institute for Health Policy and Clinical Practice
35 Centerra Pky.
Lebanon, NH 03766
Ph: (603)653-0800
Fax: (603)653-0820
Co. E-mail: the.dartmouth.institute@dartmouth.edu
URL: http://tdi.dartmouth.edu
Contact: Elliott Fisher, Director
Scope: Evaluative clinical science and health care delivery, including medical care epidemiology, health policy, health behavior, efficacy of medical procedures, quality of medical and surgical care, distribution of health care resources, medical interventions and consequences for patients, care at the end of life, distribution of health care resources across hospital market areas, geriatric health, and sociology of medical organizations. **Services:** Fellowships to physicians, administrators, and health policy makers.

Founded: 1989. **Publications:** *The Dartmouth Atlas of Health Care.* **Educational Activities:** Dartmouth Institute for Health Policy and Clinical Practice Graduate programs in evaluative clinical science.

40865 ■ Forum for State Health Policy Leadership
444 N Capital St. NW, Ste. 515
Washington, DC 20001
Ph: (202)624-5400
Fax: (202)737-1069
Co. E-mail: ncslnet-admin@ncsl.org
URL: http://www.ncsl.org/Default.
    aspx?tabid=160#NCSL_programs
Contact: Donna Folkemer, Director
Scope: Health laws and programs of the states, including research in such areas as alternatives to institutional care, state health care reform, managing and funding health care programs, preventive health services for children, state Medicaid programs, state comprehensive and catastrophic health insurance programs, Medicaid cost containment, state health promotion and disease prevention initiatives, AIDS, and private health insurance benefits for alcoholism, drug abuse, and mental illness. **Services:** Assistance: on particular issues and research projects; Legislative and state clearinghouses; Maintains a network of health policy correspondents: in each of the 50 states who keep the project abreast of significant developments in the states; State legislative tracking service. **Founded:** 1977. **Publications:** *Primary Care News*; *Reports on long-term care, primary care, and children's health*; *State Health Notes* (Semimonthly); *State Health Notes Newsletter.* **Educational Activities:** Health Policy Conference.

40866 ■ Freedom Foundation
PO Box 552
Olympia, WA 98507
Ph: (360)956-3482
Fax: (360)352-1874
Co. E-mail: info@myfreedomfoundation.org
URL: http://www.myfreedomfoundation.com
Contact: Tom McCabe, Chief Executive Officer
Description: Works to advance individual liberty, free enterprise and limited, accountable government. **Scope:** Health care, budget, taxes, education, welfare reform, citizenship and governance issues, with emphasis on limited, accountable, representative government, and working partnerships between governing bodies and the private sector. **Services:** Briefings,: during legislative session when requested. **Founded:** 1991. **Publications:** *In-Briefs*; *Policy Highlighters*; *EFF Newsletter* (Monthly). **Educational Activities:** EFF Speaking engagements, at service clubs and community organizations.

40867 ■ Georgia State University - Center for Risk Management and Insurance Research
PO Box 4036
Atlanta, GA 30302-4036
Ph: (404)413-7515
Fax: (404)413-7516
Co. E-mail: rwklein@gsu.edu
URL: http://rmictr.gsu.edu
Contact: Robert W. Klein, Director
URL(s): www.rmi.gsu.edu. **Scope:** Insurance, finance, and economics. Provides technical materials and policy research in the areas of health care financing, international issues, law and regulation, corporate finance, retirement financing, risk, risk management, insurance, finance, economics. Research focuses on risk management and insurance including insurance markets, catastrophe risk, financial instruments, social insurance, health care financing, retirement, law, public policy, and regulation. **Services:** Consultation; Develops technical and professional materials; Issues working papers; Responds to proposal requests. **Founded:** 1969. **Publications:** *Reprint series*; *Research report series*; *Working paper series.* **Educational Activities:** Research and analysis; Center for Risk Management and Insurance Research Seminars and workshops, on risk management and insurance industry financial, actuarial and regulatory topics.

40868 ■ Health Research and Educational Trust (HRET)
155 N Wacker, Ste. 400
Chicago, IL 60606
Ph: (312)422-2600
Fax: (312)422-4568
URL: http://www.hret.org
Contact: Rhonda Anderson, Chief Executive Officer
Description: Advances ideas and practices beneficial to health care practitioners, institutions, consumers and society at large. Principal activities focus on identifying, exploring, demonstrating and evaluating key strategic health care issues affecting innovative health care delivery systems, educating the field about the implications of changing health policies and developing strategies for community health improvement. **Scope:** Improvement in the delivery of hospital and health care. **Founded:** 1944. **Publications:** *HSR: Impacting Health Practice and policy through state-of-the-art Research and Thinking* (Bimonthly); *Health Services Research* (Bimonthly). **Educational Activities:** HRET Conference (Annual). **Awards:** Trust Award (Annual).

40869 ■ Health Research and Educational Trust of New Jersey
760 Alexander Rd.
Princeton, NJ 08543-0001
Ph: (609)275-4000
Fax: (609)275-4271
Co. E-mail: eryan@njha.com
URL: http://www.njha.com/community-health
Contact: Elizabeth A. Ryan, President
Scope: Health services in New Jersey. Topics explored include access to primary healthcare, parenting education, breast cancer, newborn screening. **Services:** Continuing education courses. **Founded:** 1964. **Publications:** *Shaping Healthier Tomorrows.* **Educational Activities:** HRET Annual Meeting. **Awards:** Community Outreach Awards; Health Careers Scholarships.

40870 ■ Heartland Institute (HI)
1 S Wacker Dr., No. 2740
Chicago, IL 60606
Ph: (312)377-4000
Fax: (312)377-5000
Co. E-mail: think@heartland.org
URL: http://www.heartland.org
Contact: Joseph L. Bast, President
E-mail: jbast@heartland.org
Description: Seeks to discover, develop, and promote free-market solutions to social and economic problems such as parental choice in education, choice and personal responsibility in health care, market-based approaches to environmental protection, privatization of public services, and deregulation in areas where property rights and markets do a better job than government bureaucracies. **Scope:** The firm sponsors, distributes and publicizes research on free-market solutions to state and local government problems. Also serves as are source center for academics, journalists and government officials who seek information on privatization, deregulation and tax reform. **Services:** Library open to the public by appointment. **Founded:** 1984. **Holdings:** 2500 books; 300 reports; 200 audiocassettes; 100 videotapes. **Subscriptions:** 200 journals and other serials. **Publications:** "Abraham Lincoln: Friend or Foe of Freedom," Sep, 2008; "Booker T. Washington: A Re-Examination," Jun, 2008; "Why We Spend Too Much on Health Care"; "More Choices, Better Health," May, 2007; "Scientific Consensus on Global Warming," Apr, 2007; "Energy Policy for America," Jan, 2007; "Please Don't Poop in My Salad," Jul, 2006; "Emerging Issues 2006," Jan, 2006; "Destroying Insurance Markets," Oct, 2005; "Emerging Issues 2005," Aug, 2005; "Antitrust after Microsoft: The Obsolescence of Antitrust in the Digital Era". **Educational Activities:** Heartland Institute Book tours; Heartland Institute Mealtime conferences and seminars, open to the public. **Awards:** Heartland Liberty Prize.

40871 ■ Indiana University-Purdue University at Indianapolis - William S. and Christine S.

Hall Center for Law and Health
Lawrence W Inlow Hall
IU Robert H. McKinney School of Law
530 W New York St.
Indianapolis, IN 46202-3225
Ph: (317)274-8945
Fax: (317)274-0455
Co. E-mail: centerclh@iupui.edu
URL: http://mckinneylaw.iu.edu/health-law
Contact: Prof. David Orentlicher, Director
Scope: All issues related to health law and policy.
Founded: 1987. **Publications:** *Hall Centre Newsletter* (Semiannual). **Awards:** Research, Scholarships, Health Law Policy and Law School Courses (Annual).

40872 ■ Institute for SocioEconomic Studies (ISES) - Library
10 New King St.
White Plains, NY 10604-1204
Ph: (914)686-7112
Fax: (914)686-0581
Co. E-mail: mail@socioeconomic.org
URL: http://www.socioeconomic.org
Contact: Thomas M. Cassidy, Manager
Description: Works with broad research interests on the quality of life, economic development, health care, social motivation, poverty, urban regeneration, and the problems of the elderly. **Scope:** Quality of life, economic development, social motivation, poverty, urban regeneration, problems of the elderly, health care and other related socioeconomic issues. **Services:** Library not open to the public. **Founded:** 1974. **Holdings:** 5500 volumes. **Publications:** *Socioeconomic Bulletin* (Bimonthly).

40873 ■ Institute for Women's Policy Research (IWPR)
1200 18th St. NW, Ste. 301
Washington, DC 20036
Ph: (202)785-5100
Fax: (202)833-4362
Co. E-mail: iwpr@iwpr.org
URL: http://www.iwpr.org
Contact: Heidi I. Hartmann, President
Description: Individuals and organizations concerned with economic and social justice for women and families. Designs, executes, and disseminates research findings that illuminate policy issues affecting women and families. Works to addressing complex issues engendered by race, ethnicity, and class. Focuses on survival issues such as welfare reform, family and medical leave, childcare, pay equity and the wage gap, the glass ceiling, labor law reform, and equal opportunity for women of all race and ethnic backgrounds. Builds a network of individuals and organizations that conduct and use women-oriented policy research. **Scope:** Causes and consequences of women's poverty, particularly of minority women; costs and benefits of family and work policies; pay equity; wages and employment opportunities; impact of tax policy on women and families; and access to and costs of health care. Specific issues include the impact of the Pregnancy Discrimination Act, the costs and benefits of family and medical leave, pay equity in 20 state civil service systems, the wage gap between women of color and white women, low-wage work, welfare reform, microenterprise, women and labor unions (labor law reform), and women's economic agendas. **Services:** First Friday Forums: a discussion series. **Founded:** 1987. **Publications:** *Research News Reporter* (Monthly). **Educational Activities:** IWPR Conferences; IWPR Workshops. **Awards:** Mariam K. Chamberlain Fellowships in Women and Public Policy (Annual); Research action minigrants; IWPR Summer Internships.

40874 ■ International Development Research Centre (IDRC) [Le Centre de Recherches pour le Developpement InternationalInternational Development Research Centre Books; Centre de Recherches pour le Développement International (CRDI);]
150 Kent St.
Ottawa, ON, Canada K1P 0B2
Ph: (613)236-6163
Fax: (613)238-7230
Co. E-mail: info@idrc.ca
URL: http://www.idrc.ca
Contact: Naser Faruqui, Director
E-mail: nfaruqui@idrc.ca
Description: Supports and promotes research on international development and related issues. Gathers and disseminates information on research activities in developing countries; conducts fundraising activities; sponsors research programs in developing countries. **Scope:** Supports scientific and technical research projects identified and carried out by research institutions in developing countries. IDRC maintains the following program initiative areas: strategies and policies for healthy societies; sustainable employment; equity in natural resources management; biodiversity conservation; food security; information and communication; peace building and reconstruction. Research activities focus on integrating environmental, social, and economic policies; technology and the environment; information and communication for development; health and the environment; and biodiversity. Supports research that is essential to sustainable and equitable development through three areas of enquiry: social and economic equity; environmental and natural resource management; and information and communication technologies for development. Research activities focus areas include water resource management, ecosystem management, biodiversity control, governance, delivery of public services (health, education, social security), small enterprise and livelihoods, information access, information capacity-building, macroeconomic policy, regional integration, and global threats to health (social instability, AIDS, malnutrition, tobacco use). **Founded:** 1970. **Publications:** *IDRC Annual Report* (Annual); *IDRC Reports* (Quarterly); *Searching Series*. **Awards:** Centre Sabbatical Award (Periodic); Awards International Development Journalism (Periodic); Young Canadian Researchers Award; The Bentley Cropping Systems Fellowship (Biennial); Gemini and Periscoop internships (Annual); John Bene Fellowship in Social Forestry (Annual); Pearson Fellowship; Training fellowships.

40875 ■ Jacobs Institute of Women's Health (JIWH)
School of Public Health & Health Services
George Washington University
2021 K St. NW, Ste. 800
Washington, DC 20006
Ph: (202)994-4184
Fax: (202)994-4040
Co. E-mail: whieditor@gwu.edu
URL: http://www.jiwh.org
Contact: Susan Wood, Executive Director
Scope: Women's health care services and policy issues, focusing on the interaction of medical and social systems. **Founded:** 1990. **Publications:** *Women's Health Issues* (Bimonthly). **Educational Activities:** JIWH Seminars; JIWH Symposia. **Awards:** Charles E. Gibbs MD Leadership Prize (Annual).

40876 ■ Johns Hopkins University Bloomberg School of Public Health - Center for Health Services and Outcomes Research (CHSOR)
Hampton House, 6th Fl.
Department of Health Policy & Management
624 N Broadway
Baltimore, MD 21205-1901
Ph: (410)955-6567
Fax: (410)955-0470
Co. E-mail: awu@jhsph.edu
URL: http://www.jhsph.edu/research/centers-and-institutes/health-services-outcomes-research/index.html
Contact: Dr. Albert Wu, Director
Scope: Health services, including determinants of health outcomes; the impacts of alternative health care systems on cost and quality; effective strategies for health promotion and disease prevention; and methods of meeting the needs of high risk populations such as the poor, elderly, mentally ill, disabled, and children. **Services:** Technical assistance: for local and national groups. **Founded:** 1969.

40877 ■ Johns Hopkins University - Center for Hospital Finance and Management
624 N Broadway, Rm. 493
Baltimore, MD 21205
Ph: (410)955-3241
Fax: (410)955-2301
Co. E-mail: ganderso@jhsph.edu
URL: http://www.jhsph.edu/departments/health-policy-and-management/_archive/research-and-centers/index.html
Contact: Prof. Gerard Anderson, Director
Scope: Hospital finance and management, technology assessment, reform of cost containment and payment, policies, clinical education, managed care, and medical effectiveness. **Services:** Offers Congressional testimony. **Founded:** 1979. **Educational Activities:** Training to pre- and postdoctoral fellows.

40878 ■ Kaiser Permanente Center for Health Research (CHR)
3800 N Interstate Ave.
Portland, OR 97227-1098
Ph: (503)335-2400
Fax: (503)335-6311
Co. E-mail: information@kpchr.org
URL: http://www.kpchr.org/research/public/default.aspx
Contact: Don Freel, Executive Director
Scope: Organization, financing, costs and quality of medical care in an HMO; mental health; medical informatics; patient safety; health behavior interventions; epidemiology; effectiveness of alternative therapies and services; nutrition; genetics; dental research; and biometry and research methods. **Founded:** 1964. **Educational Activities:** CHR Residence program, in public health; CHR Saward Lecture (Annual).

40879 ■ Kaiser Permanente Medical Care Program - Division of Research (DOR)
2000 Broadway
Oakland, CA 94612
Ph: (510)891-3400
Co. E-mail: alan.s.go@kp.org
URL: http://www.dor.kaiser.org/external/dorexternal/index.aspx
Contact: Dr. Alan S. Go, Director, Science
Scope: Epidemiology, biometrics and biostatistics, technology assessment, health services research, and health education research and evaluation. Supports clinical research in medical centers. **Services:** Staff teaches at local universities and performs editorial and review services for scientific and medical journals. **Founded:** 1961. **Educational Activities:** In-house seminars and conferences. **Awards:** Kaiser Permanente Northern California Delivery Science Fellowships Program.

40880 ■ La Rabida Children's Hospital and Research Center
E 65th St. at Lake Michigan
Chicago, IL 60649
Ph: (773)363-6700
Fax: (773)363-7160
Co. E-mail: info@larabida.org
URL: http://www.larabida.org
Contact: Dr. Brenda J. Wolf, President
Scope: Economic, educational, cultural, and medical effects of childhood chronic illness and disability on families and society. Areas of research include patterns of health care financing, medically complex children, community-based service systems, and the nature of family constellations, including the tracking of child development in family contexts, and intervention studies. **Services:** Technical assistance and consulting for the community. **Founded:** 1989. **Educational Activities:** La Rabida Children's Hospital and Research Center Informal mentoring program; La Rabida Children's Hospital and Research Center Professional symposium, at pediatricians, therapists, social workers, psychologists and other health care professionals; La Rabida Children's Hospital and Research Center Seminars and workshops.

40881 ■ Marshall University Research Corp. (MURC)
Coal Exchange Bldg., Ste. 1400
401 11th St.
Huntington, WV 25701

Ph: (304)696-6598
Fax: (304)697-2770
Co. E-mail: maherj@marshall.edu
URL: http://www.marshall.edu/murc
Contact: John Maher, Executive Director
Scope: Provides technical and research assistance to West Virginia businesses and governments, focusing on business and industry, including business and job development, marketing research, and feasibility studies; community and government, including housing, zoning, recreation, criminology, traffic safety, transportation, personnel administration, and finance; education, including basic teaching skills, educational financing, and extended training for primary and secondary instructors; arts and culture, including developing, coordinating, and promoting cultural activities, and assisting local arts and cultural organizations in obtaining funding; health, including basic and applied research, and mechanisms for continuing growth of health care services and education; family and consumer, including problems of families in transition, support of displaced workers, housing norms, retirement preparation and adjustment, and consumer issues. **Services:** Counseling and referral services; Technical and research assistance. **Founded:** 1984. **Educational Activities:** MURC Educational seminars, workshops, and lectures; MURC Graduate cooperative education programs.

40882 ■ Medical Technology and Practice Patterns Institute, Inc. (MTPPI)
4733 Bethesda Ave., Ste. 510
Bethesda, MD 20814
Ph: (301)652-4005
Fax: (301)652-8335
Co. E-mail: info@mtppi.org
URL: http://www.mtppi.org
Contact: Dennis J. Cotter, President
Scope: New and emerging health-care technologies and their implications for local, national, and international policy. Research efforts fall into three broad areas: Health Services Research, encompassing patient outcomes, pharmacoeconomics, quality-of-life assessments, and cost-effectiveness analyses; International Activities, including conducting surveys of health technology assessment activities worldwide technology assessment modeling, and sponsorship of workshops and seminars on health policy issues; and Special Programs, encompassing health-facility planning, vaccine research and development, and educational outreach. Technologies studied include magnetic resonance imaging, extracorporeal shock-wave lithotripsy, endocardial electrical stimulation, implantable cardiac defibrillators, percutaneous transluminal coronary angioplasty, percutaneous lithotripsy, heart transplantation, ambulatory blood pressure monitoring, total parenteral nutrition, liver transplantation, bone marrow transplantation, and dialysis treatment for end-stage renal disease. **Services:** Consulting for public and private organizations. **Founded:** 1986. **Publications:** *Diagnostic Imaging and Child Abuse*; *Direct and Indirect Costs of Diabetes* (Occasionally); *Implications of NAFTA for Trade in Health Care Technology*; *Rational Use of Health Technologies*; *Reports on various health technologies*. **Educational Activities:** Senior Resident Scholar Program.

40883 ■ Methodist Research Institute (MRI)
1812 N Capitol Ave.
Indianapolis, IN 46202
Ph: (317)962-8613
Free: 800-297-5961
Fax: (317)962-5961
Co. E-mail: methresearchinst@iuhealth.org
URL: http://iuhealth.org/researchers/research-centers/iu-health-methodist-research-institute
Scope: Pharmaceutical and device clinical trials, experimental cell research, cell signaling, ion channel physiology, immunology, nutrition angiogenesis, cancer, shock. Other research involves heart, kidney, lung, pancreas, and liver transplants; biliary and renal extracorporeal shock wave lithotripsy; and clot lysis programs. **Services:** Statistical analysis, abstract and manuscript preparation, and grant proposal writing. **Founded:** 1956. **Educational Activities:** MRI

Seminars; Educational seminars on research topics; Staff physician training in surgical techniques; Summer Student Research Program.

40884 ■ Michigan Family Forum (MFF)
PO Box 15216
Lansing, MI 48901-5216
Ph: (517)374-1171
Fax: (517)374-6112
Co. E-mail: info@michiganfamily.org
URL: http://www.michiganfamily.org
Contact: Brad Snavely, Executive Director
Description: Research and education organization that focuses on family issues in the Michigan Legislature. **Scope:** Public policy issues and responsible citizenship, focusing on strengthening families. Areas of study include education, sex education, educational choice, educational curriculum, divorce, adoption, euthanasia, marriage and marriage protection, welfare reform, and health care. **Founded:** 1990. **Publications:** *The Forum* (Quarterly); *Forum Online* (Weekly); *Voter Guides*; *Forum* (Semiannual); *Forum* (Bimonthly; Weekly (Wed.); Semiannual; Monthly; Quarterly; Annual; Biweekly; 3/year). **Educational Activities:** MFF Special events; MFF Choose Freedom Peer Abstinence Network.

40885 ■ Mount Sinai School of Medicine of City University of New York - International Longevity Center-USA (ILC)
60 E 86th St.
New York, NY 10028
Ph: (212)288-1468
Fax: (212)288-3132
Co. E-mail: info@ilcusa.org
URL: http://www.ilcusa.org
Contact: Dr. Robert N. Butler, President
Scope: Health, long-term care, and productive aging, emphasizing policy implications for future generations and institutions. **Services:** Consulting services: for policymakers, the general public, and the media. **Founded:** 1990. **Publications:** *ILC Annual report*; *ILC Newsletter*. **Educational Activities:** ILC Exchange program, for scholars and students.

40886 ■ New Mexico Clinical Research and Osteoporosis Center
300 Oak St. NE
Albuquerque, NM 87106
Ph: (505)855-5525
Fax: (505)884-4006
URL: http://www.nmbonecare.com
Contact: Dr. Lance A. Rudolph, Director, Research
Scope: Health care quality, health promotion, clinical research, and continuing medical education. **Founded:** 1987. **Publications:** *New Mexico Clinical Research and Osteoporosis Center Newsletter* (Quarterly).

40887 ■ New School University - Center for New York City Affairs
72 5th Ave., 6th Fl.
New York, NY 10011
Ph: (212)229-5418
Fax: (212)229-5335
Co. E-mail: centernyc@newschool.edu
URL: http://www.newschool.edu/milano/nycaffairs/
Contact: Andrew White, Director
Scope: Applied research and journalism on public policy in urban centers, including children and families, immigrant communities, poverty and politics. **Services:** Conferences, lectures, short courses, and seminars. **Founded:** 1964. **Publications:** *Child Welfare Watch* (Semiannual); *Developmental Disabilities Watch* (Annual); *Center for New York City Affairs Working papers* (Occasionally).

40888 ■ Pacific Health Research and Education Institute (PHREI)
3375 Koapaka St., Ste. I-540
Honolulu, HI 96819
Ph: (808)524-4411
Fax: (808)524-5559
Co. E-mail: info@phrei.org
URL: http://www.phrihawaii.org
Contact: Vicki L. Shambaugh, Executive Director (Acting)
E-mail: vlshambaugh@phrihawaii.org
Scope: Health services and clinical research, including breast cancer, hypertension, osteoporosis,

diabetes, heart attacks, drug studies, effects of chemical exposure, and cost-effectiveness analysis. Specific studies focus on risk factors associated with breast cancer, methods of delaying or preventing postmenopausal osteoporosis, isolated systolic hypertension among the elderly, outcomes research, leprosy, interactive videodiscs, geriatrics, and prostate, lung, colorectal, and ovarian cancer screening. Participates in a statewide consortium of hospitals to address quality and cost of care. Hawaii MEDTEP (Medical Treatment Effectiveness Program) Research Center, outcomes research with a focus on minority populations. **Founded:** 1960.

40889 ■ Pacific Research Institute (PRI)
1 Embarcadero Ctr., Ste. 350
San Francisco, CA 94111-3631
Ph: (415)989-0833
Fax: (415)989-2411
Co. E-mail: info@pacificresearch.org
URL: http://www.pacificresearch.org
Contact: Sally C. Pipes, President
E-mail: spipes@pacificresearch.org
Description: Aims to inform the public about issues that affect the free enterprise system and the rights of individuals. Studies public policy issues, including education, environment, technology, economics, health and welfare. Maintains speakers' bureau. Conducts educational programs. **Scope:** Public policy issues. Administers a publishing program focusing on health care, environment, education, technology, and privatization, with an outreach program of breakfasts, luncheons, conferences, briefings, and opinion editorials. **Founded:** 1979. **Publications:** *Capital Ideas*; *The Contrarian*; *PRI Newsletter* (Quarterly); *Policy Briefings*; *Studies*. **Educational Activities:** Issues Luncheons; Privatization Competition (Annual).

40890 ■ Portland VA Research Foundation, Inc. (PVARF)
Bldg. 104, Rm. G218 & 219
3710 SW US Veterans Hospital Rd.
Portland, OR 97239
Ph: (503)273-5228
Fax: (503)402-2866
Co. E-mail: linda.ganzini@va.gov
URL: http://www.pvarf.org
Contact: Dr. Linda Ganzini, President
Scope: Medicine and medical research. **Founded:** 1989.

40891 ■ Public Citizen Health Research Group (PCHRG)
1600 20th St. NW
Washington, DC 20009
Ph: (202)588-1000
Co. E-mail: member@citizen.org
URL: http://www.citizen.org
Contact: Sidney M. Wolfe, Founder Advisor
Description: Works on issues of health care delivery, workplace safety and health, drug regulation, food additives, medical device safety, and environmental influences on health. Petitions or sues federal agencies on consumers' behalf, testifies before Congress on health matters, and monitors the enforcement of health and safety legislation. Publicizes important health findings; makes available to the public a broad spectrum of research and consumer action materials in the form of books and reports. **Scope:** Health care delivery, workplace safety and health, drug regulation, food additives, medical device safety, and environmental influences on health. Conducts consumer advocacy and lobbying on health matters and monitors the enforcement of health and safety legislation. **Founded:** 1971. **Publications:** *PCHRG Health Letter* (Monthly); *Worst Pills, Best Pills News* (Monthly); *Health Letter* (Monthly); *Health Research Group List of Publications* (Annual); *Worst Pills, Best Bills*.

40892 ■ Regenstrief Institute, Inc.
410 W 10th St., Ste. 2000
Indianapolis, IN 46202-3012
Ph: (317)423-5500
Co. E-mail: wtierney@iupui.edu
URL: http://www.regenstrief.org
Contact: William M. Tierney, President
Scope: Health care, including use of computers in health care delivery, and use of engineering and

computer techniques to improve medical diagnosis and therapy. **Founded:** 1969.

40893 ■ RTI International - Library and Information Services
3040 E Cornwallis Rd.
Research Triangle Park, NC 27709-2194
Ph: (919)541-6000
Fax: (919)541-5985
Co. E-mail: listen@rti.org
URL: http://www.rti.org
Contact: E. Wayne Holden, President
E-mail: wholden@rti.org
Scope: Performs interdisciplinary research and development and provides technical services in social and economic systems and human resources, statistical sciences and survey research, chemistry and life sciences and toxicology, energy and environmental sciences, and electronics and engineered systems. Industries served health care products, electronics, chemicals, oil and gas, manufacturing, government agencies, and electric utilities. **Services:** Library not open to the public. **Founded:** 1958. **Holdings:** 100 books; 50 videotapes. **Publications:** "Differences in contraceptive use across generations of migration among women of Mexican origin," Sep, 2009; "Peer effects in adolescent overweight," Sep, 2008; "South Africa: Access Before Quality, and What to Do Now," 2006; "Assistive Technology Data Collection Project," Oct, 2003; "Automated Testing of the Census Cfu Instrument"; "Challenges of Designing and Implementing Multi mode Instruments: Fedcasic"; "Research and Development in Audio-Recorded Interviewing"; "Web-Based Meta data Tracking System Designed for the National Survey on Drug Use and Health". **Seminars:** Whither SA's education investment? A rights and skills agenda, Investment Choices for Education In Africa, Sep, 2006; Family and early childhood; Elementary and secondary education; Postsecondary education; International education policy and systems; Disability policy and programs. **Special Services:** SUDAAN, ExhibitAR, AVATALK-Survey, Geode.

40894 ■ Rush University - Center for Health Management Studies
1700 W Van Burren St., Rm. 126-B
Chicago, IL 60612
Ph: (312)942-5402
Fax: (312)942-4957
Co. E-mail: rush_hsm@rush.edu
URL: http://www.rushu.rush.edu/hsm/
Contact: Andy Garman, Associate
Scope: Health care organizations, including studies in organization and administration, organizational behavior, research design and statistics, cost containment, health economics, health care financial management, quantitative methods and epidemiology, long-term care, and information systems. **Services:** Methodological and statistical assistance to health care clinicians, managers, and students for developing research projects. **Founded:** 1978. **Publications:** *Center for Health Management Studies Annual report*; *Center for Health Management Studies Working papers* (Semiannual). **Educational Activities:** Annual Symposium of Health Affairs, on current topics in healthcare management research and policy; Faculty Development Program; Journal Club; Symposia, seminars, continuing education/executive development programs, and other special programs (Weekly).

40895 ■ Rutgers University - Institute for Health, Health Care Policy, and Aging Research
112 Paterson St.
New Brunswick, NJ 08901-1293
Ph: (848)932-8413
Fax: (732)932-1253
Co. E-mail: ihhcpar_webmaster@ifh.rutgers.edu
URL: http://www.ihhcpar.rutgers.edu
Contact: Allan Victor Herwitz, Director (Acting)
Scope: Research divisions include and focus on the following activities: the Division of Health studies the impact of stress on emotional states and health and risk behaviors and how these latter factors influence the immune system and morbidity and mortality, and studies how stress and emotional states affect symptom appraisal and the decision to use health care; the Division of Health Care Policy analyzes the

health and cost outcomes of the current allocation of health resources, with emphasis on preventive care and chronic illnesses; analyzes the evolution of managed care and its impact on patient outcomes, medical professions and utilization of services; examines trust relationships among consumers and physicians and managed care organizations; the Division on Aging measures income inequality, investigates the role of instrumental and social support as buffers against stress and chronic illness, and identifies predictors of poor self-assessments of health among the elderly and assesses treatments and outcomes in long term care; the AIDS Policy Research Group measures health care utilization and cost among patients with HIV illness; the Center for Mental Health Services and Criminal Justice Research Division conducts research on improving care and treatment of persons with mental illness in the criminal justice systems; the Center for the Study of Health Beliefs and Behavior targets the relationships among cognitions, emotions, personality, social relationships and health and health behavior. Investigators are developing models to improve communications among practitioners, clients and families to facilitate quality health outcomes; the Center for Obesity Research and Intervention investigates the treatment of obesity; the Center for Health Services Research on Pharmacotherapy, Chronic Disease Management and Outcomes fosters collaborative research on pharmacotherapy for persons with chronic illness, including more effective use of drugs, the impact of policy changes and sociocultural influences on utilization; the Center for State Health Policy analyzes and researches state health policy; the Center for Education and Research in Therapeutics studies the use of antidepressant and antipsychotic medications among children and adolescents, psychotropic drug use among adults and the frail elderly, and the outcomes of pharmaceutical care. **Founded:** 1986. **Publications:** *Peer-reviewed articles*. **Educational Activities:** Brown Bag luncheon seminars (Weekly), on health, mental health and health policy; Research training, for undergraduates from minority backgrounds; Institute for Health, Health Care Policy, and Aging Research Seminars (Occasionally), open to the public.

40896 ■ Rutgers University - Institute for Health, Health Care Policy, and Aging Research - Division on Aging - AIDS Policy Research Group (ARG)
112 Paterson St.
New Brunswick, NJ 08901
Ph: (732)932-8413
Co. E-mail: caboyer@rci.rutgers.edu
URL: http://www.ihhcpar.rutgers.edu/org_units/default.asp?v=2&o=6
Contact: Dr. Carol A. Boyer, Associate Director
Scope: AIDS, and gerontology, focusing on policy issues and applying social science methodology to the planning and evaluation of programs and policies designed to meet public health objectives. Specific areas of research include HIV health services, long-term care, social networks, mental health programs, the social context of health-related behavior in Hispanic and black subcultures, health cognition and health belief systems, legal aspects of serving endangered and high-risk populations, and cost of care and services utilization studies. Special areas of emphasis include quality of life and long-term care for the elderly, intervention-focused behavioral science research, increasing patientprovider communication, furthering methods of research in the health services field, adherence and access to prescription drugs and medical care, social and behavioral AIDS research, and mental health issues in relation to previous areas listed. **Founded:** 1987. **Publications:** *ARG Annual report*; *State health policy reports*; *White papers*. **Educational Activities:** ARG Major talks and presentations; ARG Seminars; ARG Training programs for undergraduate, graduate and postdoctoral students; ARG Group meetings.

40897 ■ Seton Hall University - College of Arts and Sciences - Center for Public Service
Jubilee Hall
400 S Orange Ave.
South Orange, NJ 07079
Ph: (973)761-9501

Fax: (973)275-2463
Co. E-mail: wishnaom@shu.edu
URL: http://www.shu.edu/academics/artsci/publicservice
Contact: Naomi B. Wish, Director
Scope: Nonprofit management education; health policy issues, finance, and management; nonprofit information technology; service learning; strategic planning; etc. **Services:** Technical assistance and training. **Founded:** 1986. **Educational Activities:** Distinguished Lecture Series in Philanthropy; Center for Public Service Graduate certificates, in Health Care Administration and Nonprofit Organization Management; Center for Public Service Master's program, in public and healthcare administration. **Awards:** Center for Public Service Scholarships.

40898 ■ Society for the Study of Social Problems (SSSP)
University of Tennessee
901 McClung Tower
Knoxville, TN 37996-0490
Ph: (865)689-1531
Fax: (865)689-1534
URL: http://www.sssp1.org
Contact: Anna Maria Santiago, President
Description: An interdisciplinary community of scholars, activists, practitioners, and students endeavoring to create greater social justice through social research. Members are often social scientists working in colleges and universities, in non-profit organizations and in other applied and policy settings. **Scope:** Global problems; institutional ethnography; community research and development; crime and juvenile delinquency; drinking and drugs; racial and ethnic minorities; conflict, social action, and change; family; poverty, class, and inequality; social problems theory; mental health; teaching social problems; sociology and social welfare; youth, aging, and the life course; educational problems; environment and technology; labor studies; sexual behavior, politics and communities; law and society; health, health policy and health services; disabilities; sport, leisure, and the body. **Founded:** 1951. **Publications:** *SSSP Newsletters* (3/year); *Social Problems* (Quarterly); *SSSP Social Problems* (Quarterly). **Educational Activities:** Society for the Study of Social Problems Annual Meeting (Annual); SSSP Symposia; Society for the Study of Social Problems Convention (Annual). **Awards:** Joseph B. Gittler (Annual); Social Action Award (Annual); Lee Student Support Fund (Annual); Erwin O. Smigel Award (Annual); Lee Scholar Support Fund (Annual); C. Wright Mills Award (Annual); Lee Founders Award (Annual); Thomas C. Hood Social Action Award (Annual); Racial/Ethnic Minority Graduate Scholarship (Annual).

40899 ■ Southern Illinois University at Carbondale - Center for Rural Health and Social Service Development (CRHSSD)
1745 Innovation Dr., Ste. C
Carbondale, IL 62903
Ph: (618)453-1262
Fax: (618)453-0252
Co. E-mail: ksanders@rural.siu.edu
URL: http://crhssd.siuc.edu
Contact: Dr. Kimberly J. (Kim) Sanders, Director
Scope: Health care and social service issues that impact the lives and productivity of the citizens in Illinois and the nation, including alternative service delivery systems and policy alternatives. Studies include rural health care, rural safety, rural medical transportation mental, health and substance use, violence prevention, tobacco initiatives, and obesity prevention. **Services:** Community needs assessments; Project development and management. **Founded:** 1989. **Publications:** *Center Briefs* (Quarterly). **Educational Activities:** Research projects, program evaluations; Training, curriculum development.

40900 ■ Texas A&M University - Bush School of Government and Public Service - Institute for Science, Technology and Public Policy (ISTPP)
1112 Allen Bldg.
4350 TAMU
College Station, TX 77843-4350

Ph: (979)862-8855
Fax: (979)862-8856
Co. E-mail: avedlitz@tamu.edu
URL: http://bush.tamu.edu/istpp
Contact: Arnold Vedlitz, Director
Scope: Social and policy implications of emerging science and technology research. Specific research areas include public policy issues related to the environment and natural resources, emerging technologies such as nanotechnology and biotechnology, infrastructure and the built environment, and health. **Founded:** 1993. **Publications:** *Articles in scholarly, peer-reviewed journals; ISTPP Reports* (Occasionally). **Educational Activities:** ISTPP Conferences, workshops; ISTPP Scholarship (Annual).

40901 ■ Texas Tech University - Center for Healthcare Innovation, Education and Research (CHIER)
Rawls College of Business Administration
Lubbock, TX 79409
Ph: (806)742-1236
Fax: (806)742-3434
Co. E-mail: tim.huerta@ttu.edu
URL: http://chier.ba.ttu.edu/index.asp
Contact: Timothy R. Huerta, Director
Scope: Interdisciplinary approaches to studying healthcare safety issues and addition of electronic medical records. **Founded:** 1997. **Publications:** *Advances in Health Care Management* (Annual). **Educational Activities:** CHIER Graduate programs, on health organization management; John A. Buesseler Lecture Series; CHIER Management education and development series; CHIER Professional development programming, related to healthcare organizations.

40902 ■ Texas Tech University - Institute for Leadership Research (ILR)
Rawls College of Business Administration
Lubbock, TX 79409-2101
Ph: (806)742-3175
Fax: (806)742-3848
Co. E-mail: ilr@ttu.edu
URL: http://www.ilr.ba.ttu.edu
Contact: Prof. Michael Ryan, Executive Director
Scope: Develops and tests state of the art leadership theory. Applies theory to leaders at all organizational levels. Incorporates effective existing and emerging leadership practice into the development of new theory for managerial leaders. **Founded:** 1988. **Publications:** *Journal of Management Inquiry* (Quarterly); *ILR Monographs.* **Educational Activities:** ILR Distinguished lecturer and panel discussions; ILR Forums for chief executive officers; ILR Leadership Development Series, series of workshop offered to the regional business community to enhance leadership development in the business and community sectors.

40903 ■ Thomas Jefferson University - Center for Research in Medical Education and Health Care (CRMEHC)
College Bldg., Ste. 119
Jefferson Medical College
1025 Walnut St.
Philadelphia, PA 19107
Ph: (215)955-8907
Fax: (215)923-6939
Co. E-mail: joseph.gonnella@jefferson.edu
URL: http://www.tju.edu/jmc/crmehc
Contact: Joseph S. Gonnella, Director
Scope: Medical education process and factors affecting the quality of cost of health care. Medical education research focuses on the following areas: measurement of physician competence; long-term follow-up study of graduates; program evaluation; specialty choice; and refinement of evaluation methods. Health services research focuses on the concept and system of disease staging for classification of severity of illness, cost, and quality of care. **Services:** Consultation and technical services. **Founded:** 1983. **Publications:** *ABSTRACTS: Longitudinal Study of Medical Students and Graduates; Center for Research in Medical Education and Health Care Annual report* (Annual). **Educational Activities:** Provides abstracts of graduating students'

performance to graduate program coordinators; Center for Research in Medical Education and Health Care Seminars.

40904 ■ University of Alabama at Birmingham - Lister Hill Center for Health Policy
Ryals Public Health Bldg.
1665 University Blvd.
Birmingham, AL 35294-0022
Ph: (205)975-9007
Fax: (205)934-3347
Co. E-mail: morrisey@uab.edu
URL: http://www.soph.uab.edu/index.php?q=listerhill
Contact: Michael A. Morrisey, Director
Scope: Health policy research, focusing on health care markets and managed care, maternal and child health, management in public health organizations, aging policy, and outcomes research. **Founded:** 1987. **Publications:** *Health Policy Abstract* (Monthly). **Educational Activities:** Methods workshops; Lister Hill Center for Health Policy Research seminars (Monthly). **Awards:** Intramural Grant Program (Annual); Health Policy Fellowship (Annual).

40905 ■ University of Arizona - Native American Research and Training Center (NARTC)
1642 E Helen St.
Tucson, AZ 85719
Ph: (520)621-5920
Fax: (520)621-9802
Co. E-mail: solomont@email.arizona.edu
URL: http://nartc.fcm.arizona.edu
Contact: Teshia G. Arambula Solomon, Director
Scope: Health and rehabilitation of disabled and chronically ill Native Americans. Core areas include the following: needs assessment, service delivery, and evaluation as determined by or in cooperation with the tribal community and empowerment that is sensitive to Indian values and needs. Also studies the impact of government policy on the delivery of health care. Promotes self determination and parity among Native Americans in health and rehabilitation. Serve as a national resource for all North American tribes and Alaska natives. **Founded:** 1983. **Publications:** *NARTC Books; Dual track videotapes; NARTC Reports.* **Educational Activities:** NARTC Conferences and workshops; Training programs for indigenous trainers and direct-service providers.

40906 ■ University of California, Berkeley - Center for Labor Research and Education [The Labor Center - Institute for Research on Labor and Employment]
2521 Channing Way, No. 5555
Berkeley, CA 94720-5555
Ph: (510)642-0323
Fax: (510)642-6432
Co. E-mail: kjacobs9@berkeley.edu
URL: http://laborcenter.berkeley.edu
Contact: Ken Jacobs, Chairperson Chairman of the Board
Description: Works to develop educational programs to meet the needs of unions. Conducts research concerning organized labor and the workforce; offers management training courses; holds computer training workshops; sponsors multi-union conferences on labor issues. Maintains speakers' bureau. **Scope:** Labor standards: job quality, living wages, healthcare. Organizing models: human services, immigrant workers, young workers, Black workers, workers in the global economy. **Founded:** 1964. **Publications:** *Labor Center Reporter; California Workers Rights, and various pamphlets; Eyes on the Fries; Falling Apart: Declining Job-Based Health Coverage for Working Families in California and the United States; Hidden Costs of Wal-Mart Jobs; Hidden Public Costs of Low Wage Work; Kids at Risk: Declining Employer-Based Health Coverage in California and the U.S.; Organize to Improve the Quality of Jobs in the Black Community; The State of Labor Education in the U.S.; Trade Secrets; The Weingarten Decision and the Right to Representation on the Job; Winning at Work; Hey, The Boss Just Called Me into the Office.* **Educational Activities:** California Lead Organizers Institute; California Union Leadership School; China labor rights curriculum; C.L. Dellums African American

Leadership School; Export processing zone workers organizing curriculum; Financial Skills Workshop; Labor summer internships, in unions and community organizations; Latino American Leadership School; Media Skills Workshop; Strategic Campaigns Workshop; Strategic Research Workshop; Center for Labor Research and Education Board meeting.

40907 ■ University of California, San Francisco - Institute for Health Policy Studies
3333 California St., Ste. 265
San Francisco, CA 94118
Ph: (415)476-5255
Fax: (415)476-0705
Co. E-mail: claire.brindis@ucsf.edu
URL: http://healthpolicy.ucsf.edu
Contact: Claire Brindis, Director
Scope: Health policy and health services research. **Founded:** 1972. **Awards:** Institute for Health Policy Studies Postdoctoral Fellowships.

40908 ■ University of Colorado at Denver - Center for Health Services Research
Division of Health Care Policy & Research
13611 E Colfax Ave., Ste. 100
Aurora, CO 80045-5701
Ph: (303)724-2400
Fax: (303)724-2530
Contact: Dr. Andrew Kramer, Director
Scope: Health services and health policies at the federal and state levels, emphasizing Medicare and Medicaid quality assurance and reimbursement for long-term care providers, including home health agencies, subacute care facilities, swing-bed hospitals, and traditional nursing homes. **Founded:** 1977.

40909 ■ University of Connecticut - School of Medicine - Department of Community Medicine and Health Care - Center for International Community Health Studies (CICHS)
MC 6325
263 Farmington Ave.
Farmington, CT 06030-6325
Ph: (860)679-1570
Fax: (860)679-5464
Co. E-mail: schensul@nso2.uchc.edu
URL: http://www.commed.uchc.edu/cichs
Contact: Stephen L. Schensul, Director
Scope: The health of underprivileged people in the U.S. and abroad, emphasizing international primary health care and community health, including international health policy, urban health in developing and developed countries, maternal and child health, health programs and problems in Peru, Sri Lanka, Kenya, Mauritius, and Connecticut, effects of economic development on health, and the role of the hospital in the developing world. Facilitates international health research for faculty and graduate students through consultation on grant proposals, networking with international contacts, advocating for researchers within international agencies, and establishing foreign research and educational placements. **Founded:** 1981. **Publications:** *Annual Training Program Catalogue; CICHS Connections Newsletter.* **Educational Activities:** Develops curricula in the medical, dental, and other health professional schools; Language training programs, short-term research, evaluation, curriculum design, and management training programs (Annual), for health professionals from Africa, Asia, the Middle East, Latin America, and The New Independent States (NIS); Conference on International Community Health (Annual).

40910 ■ University of Illinois at Chicago - Institute for Health Research and Policy - Center for Health Services Research (CHSR)
Westside Research Office Bldg., Rm. 560 CU3
1747 W Roosevelt Rd., MC 275
Chicago, IL 60608
Ph: (312)996-1062
Fax: (312)996-5356
Co. E-mail: jzwanzig@uic.edu
URL: http://ihrp.uic.edu/center/center-health-services-research
Contact: Jack Zwanziger, Director
Scope: New health care technologies, medical informatics, health manpower, observation unit medicine in the hospital emergency room, and performance of

preventive through tertiary healthcare delivery at the systems, program, and specific intervention levels. Studies focus on access, appropriateness, acceptability, cost, safety, availability, effectiveness, benefits, and overall quality of healthcare. Specific topics include clinical decision-making, health information management, psychological and social sciences, and public health policy analysis. **Services:** Internships and independent studies. **Founded:** 1972.

40911 ■ University of Illinois - Health Systems Research (HSR)
College of Medicine
1601 Parkview Ave.
Rockford, IL 61107
Ph: (815)395-5639
Fax: (815)395-5602
Co. E-mail: joelc@uic.edu
URL: http://www.rockford.medicine.uic.edu
Scope: Community health, primary care, public health, geriatrics, substance abuse, evaluation of delivery of health services, mental health services, demographic studies, health care planning, program evaluation. **Founded:** 1972. **Publications:** *Information Service Letter* (Quarterly).

40912 ■ University of Manitoba - Manitoba Centre for Nursing and Health Research (MCNHR) [University of Manitoba - Manitoba Nursing Research Institute (MNRI)]
Helen Glass Ctr. for Nursing
Ft. Garry Campus
89 Curry Pl.
Winnipeg, MB, Canada R3T 2N2
Ph: (204)474-9080
Free: 800-432-1960
Fax: (204)474-7683
Co. E-mail: mcnhr@cc.umanitoba.ca
URL: http://umanitoba.ca/nursing/mcnhr/index.html
Contact: Diana Clarke, Director
Scope: Quality assurance for nursing education & nursing and health care research. **Services:** Consultation: for faculty, graduate students and community nurses; Research support: for research grant applications and knowledge translation activities. **Founded:** 1985. **Publications:** *MCNHR Annual reports* (Annual); *Research activity reports* (Semiannual). **Educational Activities:** Dr. Helen P. Glass Researcher in Residence Program (Annual); Research seminars, workshops and training (Monthly). **Awards:** Fort Garry Legion Poppy Trust Fund Research Grant (Annual); Kathleen and Winnifred Ruane Graduate Student Research Grant for Nurses (Annual); Manitoba Centre for Nursing and Health Research Research Grants.

40913 ■ University of Maryland at College Park - Center on Aging
2367 SPH Bldg.
College Park, MD 20742-2611
Ph: (301)405-2469
Fax: (301)405-2542
Co. E-mail: lwilson@umd.edu
URL: http://www.sph.umd.edu/hlsa/aging/index.cfm
Contact: Dr. Laura B. Wilson, Director
Scope: Gerontology, including senior service and volunteerism, long-term care financing, service credit banking, informal caregiving, aging and disabilities, productive aging, lifelong learning and engagement, health care delivery systems and cost containment. Conducts health assessment and longitudinal data base projects on aging, lifelong learning and civil engagement. **Services:** Curriculum development. **Founded:** 1974. **Publications:** *Community Gerontology.* **Educational Activities:** Graduate Gerontology Certificate Program; Legacy Leadership Institutes.

40914 ■ University of Michigan - Health Management Research Center (UM-HMRC)
1015 E Huron St.
Ann Arbor, MI 48104-1688
Ph: (734)763-2462
Fax: (734)763-2206
Co. E-mail: hmrc-contact@umich.edu
URL: http://www.hmrc.umich.edu
Contact: Dr. Michael O'Donnell, Director
Scope: Examines the relationships between lifestyle behaviors, quality of life, organizational productivity, and health care costs. **Services:** Consultation on

wellness programs. **Founded:** 1977. **Publications:** *Cost Benefit Analysis* (Annual). **Educational Activities:** Wellness in the Workplace Seminar.

40915 ■ University of Minnesota - Division of Health Policy and Management (HPM)
School of Public Health, MMC 729
420 Delaware St. SE
Minneapolis, MN 55455-0392
Ph: (612)624-6151
Fax: (612)624-2196
Co. E-mail: mosco001@umn.edu
URL: http://www.sph.umn.edu/hpm
Contact: Ira Moscovice, Director
Scope: Long-term care, health insurance, managed health care, patient care outcomes, rural health services, and health policy analysis. **Founded:** 1978. **Publications:** *Institute News* (3/year); *Research brief* (Monthly). **Educational Activities:** Minnesota Health Services Research Conference (Annual); HPM Postdoctoral training program.

40916 ■ University of Pennsylvania - Leonard Davis Institute of Health Economics (LDI)
Colonial Penn Ctr.
3641 Locust Walk
Philadelphia, PA 19104-6218
Ph: (215)898-5611
Fax: (215)898-0229
Co. E-mail: polsky@mail.med.upenn.edu
URL: http://ldi.upenn.edu
Contact: Daniel Polsky, Executive Director
E-mail: polsky@mail.med.upenn.edu
URL(s): www.upenn.edu. **Scope:** Health economics; health care financing; systems design, organization, and management; evaluation of medical practices; and related policy issues that address the efficient allocation of health resources, the appropriate use of health services, the development of innovative health care delivery systems, and changing patient and provider behavior. Areas of concern include evaluation and optimization of clinical care and new technologies; access to health care; payment/reimbursement mechanisms and insurance; and institutional structure, management, and governance. **Founded:** 1967. **Publications:** *LDI Brochures*; *Issue briefs* (Occasionally). **Educational Activities:** LDI Advanced management education programs, to senior health care executives and other health care professionals; LDI Health Policy Seminar Series; LDI Research conference (Semimonthly); LDI Research Seminar Series; Summer Undergraduate Minority Research Program.

40917 ■ University of South Florida - Louis de la Parte Florida Mental Health Institute - College of Behavioral and Community Sciences - Center for HIV Education and Research
13301 Bruce B. Downs Blvd., MHC 1715
Tampa, FL 33612
Ph: (813)974-4430
Free: 866-352-2382
Fax: (813)974-8451
Co. E-mail: knox@usf.edu
URL: http://usfcenter.org
Contact: Kimberly Molnar, Director
Scope: Diagnosis, treatment, and care of persons infected with HIV, study of HIV risk factors, and HIV/AIDS prevention. **Services:** Consulting: to hospitals, clinics, public health centers, community health centers, and substance abuse centers. **Founded:** 1988. **Publications:** *HIV/AIDS Primary Care Guide*; *HIV Carelink Newsletter*; *Pocket Treatment Cards.* **Educational Activities:** Educational events, on HIV and AIDS for physicians and other primary care clinicians; Florida/Caribbean AIDS Education and Training Center (Annual); HIV Conference, designed to increase the knowledge and skills of HIV healthcare providers; Perinatal Transmission Prevention Program; Center for HIV Education and Research Workshops, on topics related to and on clinical management for public health and correctional medical personnel specifically addressing HIV/AIDS.

40918 ■ University of Wisconsin—Madison - Center for Health System Research and Analysis (CHSRA)
WARF Bldg., 11th Fl.
610 Walnut St.
Madison, WI 53726-2397
Ph: (608)263-5722
Fax: (608)263-4523
Co. E-mail: jim_robinson@chsra.wisc.edu
URL: http://www.chsra.wisc.edu
Contact: James M. Robinson, Director
Scope: Five major research areas: quality assessment and improvement, long term care, public health policy and program evaluation, consumer decision making, and patient education and support. **Founded:** 1973.

40919 ■ Vanderbilt University - Center for Health Policy
1207 18th Ave. S
Nashville, TN 37212
Ph: (615)322-0045
Fax: (615)322-8081
URL: http://www.vanderbilt.edu/VIPPS/HPC/HPChome.html
Contact: James F. Blumstein, Director
Scope: Health care reform, hospital competition, effects of medicaid policy on long term care decisions, hospital investment behavior, and choice of physicians.

40920 ■ Vanderbilt University - Vanderbilt Institute for Public Policy Studies (VIPPS)
Department of Sociology
Nashville, TN 37235-1811
Ph: (615)322-7536
Fax: (615)322-7505
Co. E-mail: daniel.b.cornfield@vanderbilt.edu
URL: http://www.vanderbilt.edu/VIPPS/
Contact: Dr. Daniel B. Cornfield, Director (Acting)
Scope: Strives to provide a bridge between academic research on child and family policy options and the worlds of state and local policy makers. Fosters collaboration among faculty members at the University by operating research centers. **Founded:** 1975. **Publications:** *VIPPS Annual Report*; *Semiannual Newsletter.* **Educational Activities:** VIPPS Conferences; VIPPS Faculty discussion groups; Freshman Tennessee Legislator Issue Workshop; VIPPS Orientation and budget workshops; VIPPS Technical and general interest seminars.

40921 ■ Walther Cancer Institute, Inc. - Mary Margaret Walther Program for Cancer Care Research
Indiana University School of Nursing
1033 E 3rd St., NU 340 G
Bloomington, IN 47405-7005
Ph: (317)274-7563
Fax: (317)278-2021
Co. E-mail: vchampio@iupui.edu
URL: http://nursing.iupui.edu/research/mmw
Contact: Dr. Victoria L. Champion, Director, Science
Scope: Cancer prevention/control, survivorship, and cancer care delivery, focusing on developing an interdisciplinary effort to conduct behavioral research improving the quality of life for cancer patients and their families. Research addresses the psychological, economic, sociological and spiritual needs of those going through the cancer experience; increasing early detection of cancer and decreasing the occurrence of cancer through individual, family, and community behaviors; and improving the delivery of cost-effective cancer care by health professionals to cancer patients and their families. **Founded:** 1985. **Publications:** *Mary Margaret Walther Program for Cancer Care Research Brochures* (Annual). **Awards:** Postdoctoral and predoctoral fellowships.

40922 ■ Welfare Research, Inc. (WRI)
14 Columbia Cir., Ste. 104
Albany, NY 12203
Ph: (518)713-4726

Fax: (518)608-5435
Co. E-mail: info@welfareresearch.org
URL: http://www.welfareresearch.org
Contact: Lee Lounsbury, Executive Director
Description: A consulting organization aimed at improving social service agencies operations and services. Provides research, evaluation, training, and technical and management assistance to the human services community. Conducts policy studies in child welfare, adolescent health, teen pregnancy, employment for welfare recipients, and service needs of refugees. Emphasis is on training needs of minority community agencies and staff of mental health and long term care facilities. Operates orientation program for public employees. **Scope:** Child welfare, AIDS, human services, health services, mental hygiene, nutrition assistance, public housing, employment and training, and nonprofit organization management. **Services:** Management assistance; Program evaluation projects: health and human services and public administration. **Founded:** 1967. **Publications:** *Adoption Recruitment Brochure*; *Congregate Care Health Services Manual*; *Foster Care Team Manual for Niagara County*; *New York State Foster Parent Manual*; *When Your Child is in Foster Care: A Handbook for Parents*; *WRI Annual Report*. **Educational Activities:** WRI Communication and public information programs.

START-UP INFORMATION

40923 ■ *"46 Cents of Every VC Dollar Went to Tech In Q1" in Austin Business Journal (Vol. 34, April 25, 2014, No. 10, pp. A8)*
Pub: American City Business Journals, Inc.
Contact: Whitney Shaw, President
Released: April 25, 2014. **Description:** Austin, Texas-based technology startups have accounted for 46 percent, or $99 million of the total $213.8 million raised from venture capital activity during the first quarter of 2014. The median funding round amount increased from $3.8 million during 2013's Q1 to $4.8 million in the same period in 2014. The largest recipients of financing are also presented.

40924 ■ *"Adventure Capital" in Austin Business Journal (Vol. 34, June 20, 2014, No. 18, pp. 4)*
Pub: American City Business Journals, Inc.
Contact: Whitney Shaw, President
Released: June 20, 2014. **Description:** Several startup companies in the Austin, Texas area have raised millions of dollars from venture capital firms over several years, without reaching profitability or becoming self-funded. However, while this strategy has been successful for startups such as hologram technology developer Zebra Imaging Inc., others like solar panel maker Helio Volt Corporation and low-power chip maker Calxeda Inc. have been forced to shut down despite receiving substantial amounts of investment capital.

40925 ■ *"After $4M Funding, ThisClicks CEO Talks What's Next" in Business Journal (Vol. 31, January 10, 2014, No. 33, pp. 7)*
Pub: American City Business Journals
Released: January 10, 2014. **Description:** Chad Halvorson, CEO of technology startup ThisClicks, describes the fundraising process for the Roseville, Minnesota-based company. He discusses the factors driving the startup's growth and the firm's new products.

40926 ■ *"Ailing Economy Nibbling at Tech-Sector Jobs" in Puget Sound Business Journal (Vol. 29, November 7, 2008, No. 29, pp. 1)*
Ed: Eric Engleman, John Cook. **Description:** Seattle-area tech start-up companies including Redfin, Zillow, WildTangent, Daptiv, Avelle, and Intrepid Learning Solutions have cut staff as the nation's economy staggers. The layoffs are reminiscent of the tech bubble era, but most startups these days have been more prudent about spending and hiring as compared to that period.

40927 ■ *"ATI Now Ready to Pounce on Biotech" in Austin Business JournalInc. (Vol. 28, August 21, 2008, No. 23, pp. 1)*
Pub: American City Business Journals
Ed: Laura Hipp. **Description:** Austin Technology Incubator has entered the biotechnology sector through a program of the University of Texas incuba-
tor. The company's bioscience program was set off by a grant from the City of Austin worth $125,000. The growth of Austin's biotechnology sector is examined.

40928 ■ *"Collective Wisdom" in Entrepreneur (July 2014)*
Pub: Entrepreneur Media Inc.
Released: July 2014. **Description:** Several entrepreneurs share advice they have received to succeed in business. Foursquare CEO, Dennis Crowley, adheres to his mother's advice to follow his heart in very decision he makes. Skullcandy founder, Rick Alden, says he learned everything he needs to know about startups from the book, "The Art of the Start", by Guy Kawasaki. Peter Relan, founder of technology incubator, 9+, explains how a great entrepreneur can take a bad idea and turn it into something good.

40929 ■ *"Creating Cultural Commerce" in Entrepreneur (June 2014)*
Pub: Entrepreneur Media Inc.
Released: June 2014. **Description:** The nonprofit business incubator, New Inc, could practice the scientific finding that the so-called left/right brain divide, or the difference between analytical and creative thinking, is non-existent. New Inc will seek ways that a museum can support new cross-disciplinary modes of cultural production. Moreover, New Inc could fill gaps in traditional artist residencies and tech incubators. New Inc will not take equity in the companies it fosters. Aside from giving technology creative breathing room for exploration, New Inc will relieve some of the revenue pressures of a startup.

40930 ■ *"Do Cool Sh*t: Quit Your Day Job, Start Your Own Business, and Live Happily Ever After"*
Pub: Harper Business
Released: August 6, 2013. **Price:** , $24.99. **Description:** Serial social entrepreneur, angel investor, and woman business leader, Miki Agrawal, teaches how to start and run a successful new business. She covers all issues from brainstorming, to raising money to getting press without any connections, and still have time to enjoy life. She created WILD, a farm-to-table pizzeria in New York City and Las Vegas; partnered in a children's multimedia company called Super Sprowtz,, a story-driven nutrition program for children; and launched a patented high-tech underware business called THINX. Agrawal also discusses the growth in her businesses.

40931 ■ *"EDCO Doling Out Capital Along Border" in Austin Business JournalInc. (Vol. 28, August 1, 2008, No. 20, pp. 1)*
Pub: American City Business Journals
Ed: Sandra Zaragoza. **Description:** Non-profit business incubator Economic Development Catalyst Organization Ventures is searching for promising startup companies. The company is targeting startups in green energy, technology and consumer markets. EDCO has partnered with consumer electronics repair company CherryFusion and technology firm MiniDonations.

40932 ■ *"ETF Process May be Tweaked" in Austin Business JournalInc. (Vol. 28, December 26, 2008, No. 41, pp. 3)*
Ed: Christopher Calnan. **Description:** Some government officials are proposing for an adjustment of the Texas Emerging Technology Fund's (ETF) policies. The ETF was created to get startup companies capital to get off the ground. Reports show that the global recession had made it more difficult for startup companies to garner investment.

40933 ■ *"'Find a Customer To Validate Your Idea" in South Florida Business Journal (Vol. 34, May 2, 2014, No. 41, pp. 15)*
Pub: American City Business Journals
Released: May 2, 2014. **Description:** Venture Hive founder, Susan Amat, share her views on her mission to nurture the entrepreneurial ecosystem from South Florida to the Americas. Amat says Venture Hive is a safe space where world-class technologists can learn to scale their businesses. Amat is a 40 Under 40 honoree, a White House Champion of Change, chair of Startup Florida, an Emerging Leader and a Woman to Watch.

40934 ■ *"Former Ky. Gov. Fletcher Starts Blue Ash Firm" in Business Courier (Vol. 26, October 9, 2009, No. 24, pp. 1)*
Pub: American City Business Journals, Inc.
Contact: Whitney Shaw, President
Ed: Lucy May. **Description:** Former Kentucky Governor Ernie Fletcher partnered with Belcan Corporation founder Ralph Anderson to purchase Blue Ash, Ohio-based Virtual Medical Network and form Alton Healthcare LLC. The company's goal is to increase practice revenues by adapting technology to reinvent clinical practices and deliver best possible care to more patients.

40935 ■ *"GeoEye CEO Sees Investors In His Future: Matt O'Connell Eyeing Intel Startup Post-Sale" in Washington Business Journal (Vol. 31, September 14, 2012, No. 21, pp. 1)*
Pub: American City Business Journal
Description: GeoEye Inc. chief executive officer, Matt O'Connell, plans to start a new technology venture in Northern Virginia like the one that supports intelligence gathering once DigitalGlobe Inc. has completed the acquisition of his company in 2013. He will work in an advisory role for DigitalGlobal following the acquisition and will not be involved in satellite imagery security for competitive reasons.

40936 ■ *"Giving Biotech Startups a Hand" in Philadelphia Business Journal (Vol. 28, January 8, 2010, No. 47, pp. 1)*
Pub: American City Business Journals Inc.
Ed: John George. **Description:** Elkins Park, Pennsylvania-based BioStrategy Partners is a virtual life sciences incubator that is seeking to improve the dull ranking of Philadelphia in the small business vitality index of life sciences. BioStrategy provides technology and business development services to startup life sciences companies and university-based research projects.

40937 ■ *"Go West, Young Startup?" in Boston Business Journal (Vol. 30, October 22, 2010, No. 39, pp. 1)*

Pub: Boston Business Journal

Ed: Galen Moore. **Description:** Startup companies Lark Technologies, Baydin and E la Cart Inc. are planning to leave Boston, Massachusetts for Silicon Valley. Lark has developed a vibrating wrist strap that syncs with a mobile phone's alarm clock.

40938 ■ *"Gotta Go!" in Entrepreneur (September 2014)*

Pub: Entrepreneur Media Inc.

Released: September 2014. **Description:** Tooshlights is an LED lighting system for public bathrooms developed by entrepreneurs, Allen Klevens and Todd Bermann. The Los Angeles, California-based firm uses a wireless, infrared-based color scheme that allows bathroom users to determine which stalls are unoccupied. The partners funded the company with their own money and are looking for potential investors. The firm is also working on a new product application that will allow spectators to see how many stalls are available at any given time during a concert of sports event.

40939 ■ *High Tech Start Up*

Pub: Simon and Schuster Inc.

Contact: Carolyn Reidy, President

E-mail: carolyn.reidy@simonandschuster.com

Ed: John L. Nesheim. **Released:** September 2000. **Price:** $34.61. **Availability:** E-book.

40940 ■ *"Home Is Where Your Startup Is" in Dallas Business Journal (Vol. 37, January 31, 2014, No. 21, pp. 6)*

Pub: American City Business Journals

Released: January 31, 2014. **Description:** Business accelerator Tech Wildcatters is planning to open a startup house in Dallas, Texas. The facility will bring together entrepreneurs, artists, and other creative individuals. A brief description of the facility is also included.

40941 ■ *"JOBS Act Spurring Bio IPOs" in Philadelphia Business Journal (Vol. 33, May 2, 2014, No. 12, pp. 4)*

Pub: American City Business Journals

Released: May 2, 2014. **Description:** The Jumpstart Our Business Startups Act has important provisions that are helping many early-stage biotechnology companies in their initial public offerings. Trevena Inc. of King of Prussia, Pennsylvania benefited from the extra time to educate the investment community and from the exemptions on the regulatory requirements.

40942 ■ *"Leading Digital: Turning Technology into Business Transformation"*

Pub: Harvard Business Review Press

Contact: Peter E. Walsh, Director

Released: October 14, 2014. **Price:** , $30.00. **Description:** Mobile technology, analytics, social media, sensors, and cloud computing have changed the entire business environment in every industry. A guide to help any small startup business in any industry gain strategic advantage using digital, including where to invest in digital technologies and how to lead the transformation. The guide teaches how to engage better with customers, digitally enhance operations, create a digital vision, and govern digital activities.

40943 ■ *"The Little Festival That Grew" in Austin Business Journal (Vol. 34, June 6, 2014, No. 16, pp. B4)*

Pub: American City Business Journals, Inc.

Contact: Whitney Shaw, President

Released: June 6, 2014. **Description:** The annual March event held in Austin, Texas, known as SXSW Interactive, has seen ten straight years of steady growth through 2014. The startup- and social-media-focused component of SXSW is the biggest attraction of the festival as it serves as a launching pad for digitally focused startups from all over the world. The festival was co-founded by Hugh Forrest Louis Black, Roland Swenson and Nick Barbaro.

40944 ■ *"Made@Mayo" in Business Journal (Vol. 32, June 6, 2014, No. 2, pp. 10)*

Pub: American City Business Journals

Released: June 6, 2014. **Description:** Rochester, Minnesota-based Mayo Clinic Ventures has managed the licensing of Mayo Clinic technologies and invests in startups. Mayo Clinic Ventures has a $100 million growth fund for investing in startups and two smaller funds worth about $500,000 combined. Insights on the stories of Mayo researchers leading startups are also provided.

40945 ■ *"Martek's Former Top Execs Start Company to Advise Startups" in Baltimore Business Journal (Vol. 29, May 4, 2012, No. 53, pp. 1)*

Pub: American City Business Journals, Inc.

Contact: Whitney Shaw, President

Ed: Gary Haber. **Released:** May 4, 2012. **Description:** Steve Dubin and David Abramson, former executives of Martek Biosciences Corporation, have started the consulting firm SDA Ventures. The firm advises early-stage companies on topics such as mergers and acquisitions, corporate development and customer relations.

40946 ■ *The Mousedriver Chronicles: The True-Life Adventures Of Two First-time Entrepreneurs*

Pub: The Perseus Books Group

Contact: David Steinberger, President

E-mail: david.steinberger@perseusbooks.com

Ed: John Lusk, Kyle Harrison. **Released:** April 29, 2009. **Price:** $16.95; C$21.50. **Description:** Entrepreneurial voyage through the startup business of two ivy-league business school graduates and the lessons they learned while developing their idea of a computer mouse that looks like a golf driver into the marketplace. The book is an inspiration for those looking to turn an idea into a company. **Availability:** E-book.

40947 ■ *"No. 407: What I Learned in the Military, and What I Had to Unlearn" in Inc. (Vol. 36, September 2014, No. 7, pp. 80)*

Pub: Mansueto Ventures L.L.C.

Contact: John Koten, Chief Executive Officer

Released: September 2014. **Description:** Profile of William Bailey, who served in the U.S. Army as information manager at the U.S. Military Academy at West Point. Bailey discusses his startup firm, Rapier Solutions, a government contractor providing IT, logistics, and social-work expertise. The firm has developed a new survivor outreach system for the U.S. Army.

40948 ■ *"Online Fortunes" in Small Business Opportunities (Fall 2008)*

Description: Fifty hot, e-commerce enterprises for the aspiring entrepreneur to consider are featured; virtual assistants, marketing services, party planning, travel services, researching, web design and development, importing as well as creating an online store are among the businesses featured.

40949 ■ *"Red McCombs, Partner Rolling Out New Venture Capital Fund" in San Antonio Business Journal (Vol. 26, April 20, 2012, No. 12, pp. 1)*

Pub: American City Business Journal

Description: Entrepreneur Red McCombs has partnered with businessman Chase Fraser to create a new venture capital fund. This new fund will focus on technology startups in the automotive sector.

40950 ■ *"SBA Program Helped New Company Survive As It Built Company Base" in Philadelphia Business Journal (Vol. 33, May 9, 2014, No. 13, pp. 4)*

Pub: American City Business Journals

Released: May 9, 2014. **Description:** The Small Business Administration (SBA) Indiana District Business Office helped Netwise Resources set up its information technology (IT) consulting business with a six-month SBA-backed loan and the 8(a) Business Development Program for small disadvantaged businesses. Owner, Mark Gibson, attributes Netwise

Resources' success to its focus on branding, recruiting skilled staff, and establishing relationships with clients within the target market.

40951 ■ *Seed-Stage Venture Investing: An Insider's Guide to Start-Ups for Scientists, Engineers, and Investors*

Ed: William L. Robbins, Jonathan Lasch. **Released:** November 01, 2011. **Price:** $39.96. **Description:** Ideas for starting, funding, and managing technology-based firms, also known as, venture capitalists, are featured. **Availability:** Print.

40952 ■ *"Should State Invest in Startups?" in Providence Business News (Vol. 28, March 3, 2014, No. 48, pp. 1)*

Pub: American City Business Journals

Released: March 3, 2014. **Description:** The U.S. Treasury Department is investigating whether Rhode Island violated Federal rules when it used funds from the State Small Business Credit Initiative (SSBCI) to invest in Betaspring, a startup accelerator program for technology and design entrepreneurs ready to launch their businesses. The Lyon Park audit claims that Rhode Island violated SSBCI rules because a large portion of the money went to the business accelerator's operating expenses and not to the startups themselves.

40953 ■ *"Start-Up! So You Want to Be an Entrepreneur. So You Want to Be Rich"*

Pub: Amazon Digital Services

Released: October 10, 2014. **Price:** , $14.99 Kindle. **Description:** Entrepreneur offers a guide for startups. Jim Lewis shares the innovative thinking that helped him launch, grow and sell two successful high-tech companies.

40954 ■ *"Starting Up All Over Again: Alex Bogusky Backs Bootcamp for Advertising Startup" in Denver Business Journal (Vol. 65, February 7, 2014, No. 39, pp. 8)*

Pub: American City Business Journals

Released: February 7, 2014. **Description:** Once called the Elvis of advertising, Alex Bogusky is now launching a new startup named 'Boomtown' with an aim to cultivate a new generation of advertising, marketing, design, and media related tech companies. The end goal of boomtown will be to figure out the trend in which media as well as the relationship between brands and people is going.

40955 ■ *"Startup to Serve Bar Scene" in Austin Business JournalInc. (Vol. 29, December 18, 2009, No. 41, pp. 1)*

Ed: Christopher Calnan. **Description:** Startup ATX Innovation Inc. of Austin, Texas has developed a test version of TabbedOut, a Web-based tool that would facilitate mobile phone-based restaurant and bar bill payment. TabbedOut has been tested by six businesses in Austin and will be available to restaurant and bar owners for free. Income would be generated by ATX through a 99-cent convenience charge per transaction.

40956 ■ *"Tale of Two Tech Facilities" in Business Journal Portland (Vol. 30, January 3, 2014, No. 44, pp. 12)*

Pub: American City Business Journals

Released: January 3, 2014. **Description:** The cities of Pittsburgh, Pennsylvania and Portland, Oregon share similarities when it comes to supporting technology startups. Both have been collaborating with the startup community. Portland has the capability to build strong companies due to its local talent pool.

40957 ■ *"TDP Inc. Aims to Cut Out Coupon Clipping" in The Business Journal-Serving Metropolitan Kansas City (Vol. 26, August 15, 2008, No. 49)*

Pub: American City Business Journals, Inc.

Contact: Whitney Shaw, President

Ed: Suzanna Stagemeyer. **Description:** TDP Inc., who started operations 18 months ago, aims to transform stale coupon promotions using technology by digitizing the entire coupon process. The process is expected to enable consumers to hunt coupons online where they will be automatically linked to loyalty cards. Other views and information on TDP and its services are presented.

40958 ■ *Technology Ventures: From Idea to Enterprise*
Pub: McGraw-Hill Higher Education
Contact: Edward Stanford, President
E-mail: ed_stanford@mcgraw-hill.com
Ed: Richard C. Dorf, Thomas H. Byers. **Price:** $181.67, retail; $136.25, wholesale. **Description:** Textbook examining technology entrepreneurship on a global basis; technology management theories are explored. **Availability:** Print.

40959 ■ *Technology Ventures: From Idea to Enterprise*
Pub: McGraw-Hill Higher Education
Contact: Edward Stanford, President
E-mail: ed_stanford@mcgraw-hill.com
Ed: Richard C. Dorf, Thomas H. Byers, Andrew Nelson. **Released:** 2nd Edition. **Description:** An action-approached through the use of examples, exercises, cases, sample business plans, and recommended sources helps entrepreneurs start and run a technology-base small business.

40960 ■ *"Texas State Building a Home for Startups" in Austin Business Journal (Vol. 32, April 20, 2012, No. 7, pp. 1)*
Pub: American City Business Journals, Inc.
Contact: Whitney Shaw, President
Ed: Sandra Zaragoza. **Released:** April 20, 2012. **Description:** Texas State University is set to open a new business incubator for technology startups. The incubator will have secure wet labs, clean rooms and office space.

40961 ■ *"Troy Patent Law Firm Launches Rent-Free Tech Incubator" in Crain's Detroit Business (Vol. 25, June 8, 2009, No. 23, pp. 4)*
Pub: Crain Communications Inc. - Detroit
Contact: Keith Crain, Chairman
Ed: Tom Henderson. **Description:** Young Basile Hanlon MacFarlane & Helmholdt PC, a patent law firm located in Troy, Michigan has created a small, rent-free technology incubator on site. The incubator will be called North Woodward Tech Incubator and has room for four or five startups. The incubator is for the earliest or pre-seed stage for entrepreneurs who have not yet gotten significant investment capital.

40962 ■ *"Wanted: Angels in the Country" in Austin Business JournalInc. (Vol. 28, July 18, 2008, No. 18, pp. 1)*
Pub: American City Business Journals
Ed: Laura Hipp. **Description:** A proposal is being pushed forward by managers of Texas' Emerging Technology Fund to create an angel investors' network. The proposal is asking that tax credits for those who invest in research and development projects be granted in order to boost the number of technology companies in the state.

40963 ■ *"Where the Next Big Thing Lives In Our Nation's Research Labs. Hard Part: Turning Scientists Into Entrepreneurs" in Inc. (Vol. 34, September 2012, No. 7, pp. 43)*
Pub: Mansueto Ventures L.L.C.
Contact: John Koten, Chief Executive Officer
Ed: Steve Blank. **Released:** September 2012. **Description:** Steve Blank, former entrepreneur, was invited to speak to the National Science Foundation's new rogram called Innovation Corps. The program is designed to help identify and commercialize research projects and involves mentoring from entrepreneurs, venture capitalists and technology developers.

40964 ■ *"The Y Factor" in Entrepreneur (Vol. 35, November 2007, No. 11, pp. 58)*
Pub: Entrepreneur Press
Contact: Perlman Neil, President
Ed: Sara Wilson. **Description:** Venture capital company Y Combinator hosts a three-month program wherein the firm's founders select technology entrepreneurs from across the U.S. to help and to mentor them on starting a business.

EDUCATIONAL PROGRAMS

40965 ■ Application Systems Development Audit and Security
Seminar Information Service Inc.
20 Executive Park, Ste. 120
Irvine, CA 92614
Ph: (949)261-9104
Free: 877-SEM-INFO
Fax: (949)261-1963
Co. E-mail: info@seminarinformation.com
URL: http://www.seminarinformation.com
Price: $2,150. **Description:** Learn an end-to-end approach for ensuring the design, security, integrity, and performance of your application system. **Audience:** Financial, Operational, Business Applications, Information Technology, and External Auditors. **Dates and Locations:** San Francisco, CA; New York, NY; and Atlanta, GA.

40966 ■ Auditing Business Application Systems (Onsite)
Seminar Information Service Inc.
20 Executive Park, Ste. 120
Irvine, CA 92614
Ph: (949)261-9104
Free: 877-SEM-INFO
Fax: (949)261-1963
Co. E-mail: info@seminarinformation.com
URL: http://www.seminarinformation.com
Description: Three-day seminar attendees will learn how to audit and how to develop controls for complex automated applications which use online/real-time, distributed processing, and/or database technologies, including an opportunity to actually prepare an audit plan for a complex application system. **Audience:** Information technology, financial, operations, and business applications auditors and audit managers .

40967 ■ Auditing Networked Computers (Onsite)
Seminar Information Service Inc.
20 Executive Park, Ste. 120
Irvine, CA 92614
Ph: (949)261-9104
Free: 877-SEM-INFO
Fax: (949)261-1963
Co. E-mail: info@seminarinformation.com
URL: http://www.seminarinformation.com
Price: $1,950.00. **Description:** Seminar designed as a first look at LANs, WANs, workstations, and servers where you will focus on understanding the technology, evaluating the risks, and establishing n audit approach.

40968 ■ Auditing and Securing Oracle Databases (Onsite)
Seminar Information Service Inc.
20 Executive Park, Ste. 120
Irvine, CA 92614
Ph: (949)261-9104
Free: 877-SEM-INFO
Fax: (949)261-1963
Co. E-mail: info@seminarinformation.com
URL: http://www.seminarinformation.com
Price: $2,595. **Description:** Learn Oracle's database facilities and terminology along with the commands you need to know to provide security, audit and query controls for Oracle and Oracle-controlled data. **Audience:** Experienced IT auditors.

40969 ■ BGP - Configuring BGP on Cisco Routers (Onsite)
Seminar Information Service Inc.
20 Executive Park, Ste. 120
Irvine, CA 92614
Ph: (949)261-9104
Free: 877-SEM-INFO
Fax: (949)261-1963
Co. E-mail: info@seminarinformation.com
URL: http://www.seminarinformation.com
Price: $3,295. **Description:** Comprehensive five-day course explores the theory of BGP, configuration of BGP on Cisco IOS routers, and detailed troubleshooting information. **Audience:** Internet service providers, and networking professionals. **Dates and Locations:** Dallas, TX; and New York, NY.

40970 ■ Computer Forensics and Incident Response: Hands-On - Analyzing Windows-Based Systems (Onsite)
Seminar Information Service Inc.
20 Executive Park, Ste. 120
Irvine, CA 92614
Ph: (949)261-9104
Free: 877-SEM-INFO
Fax: (949)261-1963
Co. E-mail: info@seminarinformation.com
URL: http://www.seminarinformation.com
URL(s): www.seminarinformation.com. **Description:** Learn how to: Implement a computer forensics incident-response strategy; Lead a successful investigation from the initial response to completion; Conduct disk-based analysis and recover deleted files; Identify information-hiding techniques; Reconstruct user activity from e-mail, temporary Internet files and cached data; Assess the integrity of system memory and process architecture to reveal malicious code. **Audience:** Industry professionals. **Telecommunication Services:** info@seminarinformation.com.

40971 ■ Deploying Intrusion Detection Systems: Hands-On (Onsite)
Seminar Information Service Inc.
20 Executive Park, Ste. 120
Irvine, CA 92614
Ph: (949)261-9104
Free: 877-SEM-INFO
Fax: (949)261-1963
Co. E-mail: info@seminarinformation.com
URL: http://www.seminarinformation.com
URL(s): www.seminarinformation.com. **Description:** Learn how to: Detect and respond to network- and host-based intruder attacks; Integrate intrusion detection systems (IDS) into your current network topology; Analyze IDS alerts using the latest tools and techniques; Identify methods hackers use to attack systems; Recognize detection avoidance schemes; Stop attackers with Intrusion Prevention Systems (IPSs). **Audience:** Industry professionals. **Telecommunication Services:** info@seminarinformation.com.

40972 ■ Deterring Social Engineering Attacks: Resisting Human Deception (Onsite)
Seminar Information Service Inc.
20 Executive Park, Ste. 120
Irvine, CA 92614
Ph: (949)261-9104
Free: 877-SEM-INFO
Fax: (949)261-1963
Co. E-mail: info@seminarinformation.com
URL: http://www.seminarinformation.com
URL(s): www.seminarinformation.com. **Description:** Learn how to: Help prevent social engineering exploits by heightening your security awareness; Decode the art of human deception; Identify the social engineering attack cycle; Define and help protect corporate and personal assets; Assess and quantify the impact of social engineering attacks; Integrate your corporate security policy into your professional responsibilities; Apply an employee social engineering defense checklist. **Audience:** Industry professionals and general public. **Telecommunication Services:** info@seminarinformation.com.

40973 ■ Developing High-Performance SQL Server Databases: Hands-On Onsite Meeting
Seminar Information Service Inc.
20 Executive Park, Ste. 120
Irvine, CA 92614
Ph: (949)261-9104
Free: 877-SEM-INFO
Fax: (949)261-1963
Co. E-mail: info@seminarinformation.com
URL: http://www.seminarinformation.com
Price: $2,950. **Description:** Learn how to design and implement high-performance databases for SQL Server 2005 and 2000; Create indexes that optimize different types of queries; Design transactions that maximize concurrency and minimize contention; Interpret the data access plans produced by the query optimizer; Minimize I/O by designing efficient physical data structures; Improve response time by

introducing controlled redundancy; and analyze and cure performance problems using SQL Server's tools. **Audience:** Industry professionals. **Dates and Locations:** Rockville, MD; Toronto, CN; New York, NY; and Reston, VA.

40974 ■ Disaster Recovery Planning: Ensuring Business Continuity (Onsite)
Seminar Information Service Inc.
20 Executive Park, Ste. 120
Irvine, CA 92614
Ph: (949)261-9104
Free: 877-SEM-INFO
Fax: (949)261-1963
Co. E-mail: info@seminarinformation.com
URL: http://www.seminarinformation.com
Price: $2,990. **Description:** Learn how to: Create, document and test continuity arrangements for your organization; Perform a risk assessment and Business Impact Assessment (BIA) to identify vulnerabilities; Select and deploy an alternate site for continuity of mission-critical activities; Identify appropriate strategies to recover the infrastructure and processes; Organize and manage recovery teams; Test and maintain an effective recovery plan in a rapidly changing technology environment. **Audience:** Industry professionals. **Dates and Locations:** 2015 Mar 10-13; venue not reported.

40975 ■ DSP: Digital Signal Processing (Onsite)
Seminar Information Service Inc.
20 Executive Park, Ste. 120
Irvine, CA 92614
Ph: (949)261-9104
Free: 877-SEM-INFO
Fax: (949)261-1963
Co. E-mail: info@seminarinformation.com
URL: http://www.seminarinformation.com
URL(s): www.seminarinformation.com/details. cfm?qc=qqbftd. **Price:** $1,895. **Description:** Introduction to DSP concepts and implementation, including a complete model of a DSP system from the input transducer through all the stages. **Audience:** Technicians and engineers.

40976 ■ Ethical Hacking and Countermeasures: Hands-On - Preventing Network and System Breaches (Onsite)
Seminar Information Service Inc.
20 Executive Park, Ste. 120
Irvine, CA 92614
Ph: (949)261-9104
Free: 877-SEM-INFO
Fax: (949)261-1963
Co. E-mail: info@seminarinformation.com
URL: http://www.seminarinformation.com
Description: Learn how to deploy ethical hacking to expose weaknesses in your organization and select countermeasures; Gather intelligence by employing social engineering, published data and scanning tools; Probe and compromise your network using hacking tools to improve your security; Discover how malicious hackers exploit weaknesses to 'own' the network; Protect against privilege escalation to prevent intrusions; Defend against evasions of antivirus, firewalls and IDS. **Audience:** Industry professionals.

40977 ■ Fundamentals of Information Security (Onsite)
Seminar Information Service Inc.
20 Executive Park, Ste. 120
Irvine, CA 92614
Ph: (949)261-9104
Free: 877-SEM-INFO
Fax: (949)261-1963
Co. E-mail: info@seminarinformation.com
URL: http://www.seminarinformation.com
Description: Three-day seminar will guide you through the basics of information security in today's high-tech, business environment, including external threats, establishing effective security policies, contingency planning, and employee privacy rights. **Audience:** Industry professionals.

40978 ■ Introduction to Soundtrack Pro
EEI Communications
8945 Guilford Rd., Ste. 145
Columbia, MD 21046
Ph: (410)309-8200
Free: 888-253-2762
Fax: (410)630-3980
Co. E-mail: train@eeicom.com
URL: http://www.eeicom.com/eei-training-services
Price: $745.00. **Description:** Course includes an introduction to Soundtrack Pro Interface, basic audio editing, importing audio, post-production techniques with audio and video, producing podcasts with Soundtrack Pro, and exporting your audio projects.

40979 ■ IT Auditing and Controls (Onsite)
Seminar Information Service Inc.
20 Executive Park, Ste. 120
Irvine, CA 92614
Ph: (949)261-9104
Free: 877-SEM-INFO
Fax: (949)261-1963
Co. E-mail: info@seminarinformation.com
URL: http://www.seminarinformation.com
Description: Three-day seminar outlines the concepts of information systems you need to know in order to understand the audit concerns in the IS environment. You will learn the necessary controls for application systems- the session pinpoints specific controls to evaluate when auditing currently installed system, new systems under development, and the various activities within the information systems department, as well as techniques for auditing automated systems. **Audience:** Financial, operational, business applications and external auditors.

40980 ■ A Practical Guide to Controls for IT Professionals (Onsite)
Seminar Information Service Inc.
20 Executive Park, Ste. 120
Irvine, CA 92614
Ph: (949)261-9104
Free: 877-SEM-INFO
Fax: (949)261-1963
Co. E-mail: info@seminarinformation.com
URL: http://www.seminarinformation.com
Description: Designed to provide all levels of IT personnel with an understanding of what controls are and why they are critical to safeguarding information assets. Discover why it is important to have a business-process view of IT controls and review the critical role they play in providing for a smooth running, efficiently manager IT environment. **Audience:** IT management and staff, other IT personnel and IT auditors.

REFERENCE WORKS

40981 ■ "2nd Watch Rides AWS Market Maturity to 400% Growth" in Computer Business Week (August 28, 2014, pp. 21)
Released: August 28, 2014. **Description:** 2nd Watch reports record earnings for the second quarter of 2014. The firm helps companies develop and implement IT strategies that are based on Amazon Web Services (AWS). Details of the companies business strategies are outlined.

40982 ■ The 7 Irrefutable Rules of Small Business Growth
Pub: John Wiley & Sons Inc.
Contact: Stephen M. Smith, President
Ed: Steven S. Little. **Released:** February 2005. **Price:** $18.95. **Description:** Proven strategies to maintain small business growth are outlined, covering topics such as technology, business plans, hiring, and more. **Availability:** Print.

40983 ■ "7 Trends Affecting the Security Technology Business" in IP SecurityWatch.com (March 2012)
Pub: Cygnus Business Media
Contact: Paul Mackler, Chief Executive Officer
Released: March 2012. **Description:** Scott Harkins, president of Honeywell Security Products for the Americas, outlines the seven trends affecting the security technology business. He covers smart phones and tablets, home automation, interctive services, integration beyond security systems, cloud services, standards, and apps.

40984 ■ "2010 Book of Lists" in Austin Business JournalInc. (Vol. 29, December 25, 2009, No. 42, pp. 1)
Description: Rankings of companies and organizations within the business services, finance, healthcare, hospitality and travel, insurance, marketing and media, professional services, real estate, education and technology industries in Austin, Texas are presented. Rankings are based on sales, business size, and other statistics.

40985 ■ "2010 Book of Lists" in Business Courier (Vol. 26, December 26, 2009, No. 36, pp. 1)
Description: Rankings of companies and organizations within the business services, education, finance, health care, hospitality and tourism, real estate, and technology industries in the Cincinnati, Ohio-Northern Kentucky area are presented. Rankings are based on sales, business size, or other statistics.

40986 ■ "2010 Book of Lists" in Tampa Bay Business Journal (Vol. 30, December 22, 2009, No. 53, pp. 1)
Description: Rankings of companies and organizations within the human resources, banking and finance, business services, healthcare, real estate, technology, hospitality and travel, and education industries in the Greater Tampa Bay area are presented. Rankings are based on sales, business size, and more.

40987 ■ "2014 Promises Tech IPO Frenzy" in San Francisco Business Times (Vol. 28, January 3, 2014, No. 24, pp. 6)
Pub: American City Business Journals
Released: January 3, 2014. **Description:** Bay Area-based venture-backed technology companies are expected to fill 2014 with initial public offerings (IPOs) and fuel more venture capital funding in the region. The U.S. IPO market has recorded more than 220 pricings and was the strongest since the dot-com bubble of 2000. California-based technology companies that valued at $1 billion or more are also profiled.

40988 ■ "Abraxis Bets On Biotech Hub" in Business Journal-Serving Phoenix and the Valley of the Sun (Vol. 10, November 9, 2007, No. 28)
Ed: Angela Gonzales. **Description:** Abraxis Bio-Science Inc. purchased a 200,000 square foot manufacturing facility in Phoenix, Arizona from Watson Pharmaceuticals Inc. The company has the technology to allow chemotherapy drugs to be injected directly into tumor cell membranes. A human protein, albumin is used to deliver the chemotherapy.

40989 ■ "Achieving Greatness" in Black Enterprise (Vol. 38, January 2008, No. 6, pp. 50)
Pub: Earl G. Graves Publishing Co. Inc.
Contact: Earl G. Graves, Jr., President
Ed: Marcia A. Reed-Woodard. **Description:** Randall Pinkett, winner of a reality show on television and chairman of BCT Partners, insists that a business cannot survive by doing just enough or more of the same. Pinkett's New Jersey company provides management, technology and consulting to other firms.

40990 ■ Achieving Planned Innovation: A Proven System for Creating Successful New Products and Services
Pub: Simon & Schuster Higher Education Group
Contact: Larry Norton, President
Ed: Frank R. Bacon. **Released:** August 2007. **Price:** $16.95. **Description:** Planned innovation is a disciplined and practical step-by-step sequence of procedures for reaching the intended destination point: successful products. This easy-to-read book explains the system along with an action-oriented program for continuous success in new-product innovations. Five steps outlined include: a disciplined reasoning process; lasting market orientation; proper selection criteria that reflect both strategic and tactical busi-

ness objectives and goals along with dynamic matching of resources to present and future opportunities, and positive and negative requirements before making major expenditures; and proper organizational staffing. The author explains what to do and evaluating the potential of any new product or service, ranging from ventures in retail distribution to the manufacture of goods as diverse as bicycles, motorcycles, aerospace communication and navigation equipment, small business computers, food packaging, and medical products. **Availability:** Print.

40991 ■ *Advanced Manufacturing Technology*
Pub: John Wiley & Sons Inc. Scientific, Technical, Medical, and Scholarly Div. (Wiley-Blackwell)
Contact: William J. Pesce, Manager
E-mail: wpesce@wiley.com
URL(s): www.apnf.org/frostbody.htm. **Ed:** Leo O'Connor. **Released:** Monthly **Publication includes:** List of companies involved in developing advanced manufacturing technologies such as robotics, artificial intelligence in computers, ultrasonics, lasers, and waterjet cutters; also lists sources of information and education on high-technology. **Entries include:** Company or organization name, address, phone, name of contact; description of process, product, or service. Principal content is articles and analysis of advanced manufacturing technology. **Arrangement:** Classified by subject.

40992 ■ *"After Price Cuts, Competition GPS Makers Lose Direction" in Brandweek (Vol. 49, April 21, 2008, No. 16, pp. 16)*
Pub: Nielsen Business Media Inc.
Contact: Howard Appelbaum, President
Ed: Steve Miller. **Description:** Garmin and TomTom, two of the leaders in portable navigation devices, have seen lowering revenues due to dramatic price cuts and unexpected competition from the broadening availability of personal navigation on mobile phones. TomTom has trimmed its sales outlook for its first quarter while Garmin's stock dropped 40 percent since February.

40993 ■ *Aging and Working in the New Economy: Changing Career Structures in Small IT Firms*
Pub: Edward Elgar Publishing Inc.
Contact: Richard Henning, Vice President
E-mail: kwight@e-elgar.com
Ed: Juliie Ann McMullin, Victor W. Marshall. **Released:** March 01, 2010. **Price:** £67.50. **Description:** Case studies and analyses provide insight into the structural features of small- and medium-sized firms in the information technology sector, and the implications of these features for the careers of people employed by them.

40994 ■ *"Agricharts Launches New Mobile App for Ag Market" in Farm Industry News (December 1, 2011)*
Pub: Penton Business Media Inc.
Contact: David Kieselstein, Chief Executive Officer
Description: AgriCharts provides market data, agribusiness Website hosting and technology solutions for the agricultural industry. AgriCharts is a division of Barchart.com Inc. and announced the release of a new mobile applications that offers real-time or delayed platform for viewing quotes, charts and analysis of grains, livestock and other commodity markets.

40995 ■ *"Airlines Mount PR Push to Win Public Support Against Big Oil" in Advertising Age (Vol. 79, July 14, 2008, No. 7, pp. 1)*
Pub: Crain Communications Inc.
Contact: Rance Crain, President
Ed: Michael Bush. **Description:** Top airline executives from competing companies have banded together in a public relations plan in which they are sending e-mails to their frequent fliers asking for aid in lobbying legislators to put a restriction on oil speculation.

40996 ■ *"All About The Benjamins" in Canadian Business (Vol. 81, September 29,*
2008, No. 16, pp. 92)
Ed: David Baines. **Description:** Discusses real estate developer Royal Indian Raj International Corp., a company that planned to build a $3 billion 'smart city' near the Bangalore airport; to this day nothing has ever been built. The company was incorporated in 1999 by Manoj C. Benjamin one investor, Bill Zack, has been sued by the developer for libel due to his website that calls the company a scam. Benjamin has had a previous case of fraud issued against him as well as a string of liabilities and lawsuits.

40997 ■ *"All Those Applications, and Phone Users Just Want to Talk" in Advertising Age (Vol. 79, August 11, 2008, No. 31, pp. 18)*
Pub: Crain Communications Inc.
Contact: Rance Crain, President
Ed: Mike Vorhaus. **Description:** Although consumers are slowly coming to text messaging and other data applications, a majority of those Americans surveyed stated that they simply want to use their cell phones to talk and do not care about other activities. Statistical data included.

40998 ■ *Alpha Dogs: How Your Small Business Can Become a Leader of the Pack*
Pub: HarperCollins Publishers Inc.
Contact: Jane Friedman, President
E-mail: jfriedman@harpercollins.com
Ed: Donna Fenn. **Released:** May 08, 2007. **Price:** $14.95, paperback; $9.99; C$11.99. **Description:** Profiles of eight successful entrepreneurs along with information for developing customer service, technology and competition. **Availability:** PrintE-book.

40999 ■ *"Alternative Energy: The Lithium Deficit" in Canadian Business (Vol. 82, April 27, 2009, No. 7, pp. 17)*
Pub: Rogers Media Inc.
Contact: Tony Viner, President
Ed: Joe Castaldo. **Description:** Experts are concerned that there may not be enough lithium available to support the expected rise in demand for the natural resource. Lithium is used in lithium ion batteries, the standard power source for electric and hybrid vehicles. Experts believe that the demand for lithium can only be measured once the technology is out in the market.

41000 ■ *"Analysts: Intel Site May Be Last Major U.S.-Built Fab" in Business Journal-Serving Phoenix and the Valley of the Sun (October 18, 2007)*
Pub: American City Business Journals, Inc.
Ed: Ty Young. **Description:** Intel's million-square-foot manufacturing facility, called Fab 32, is expected to open in 2007. The plant will mass-produce the 45-nanometer microchip. Industry analysts believe Fab 32 may be the last of its kind to be built in the U.S., as construction costs are higher in America than in other countries. Intel's future in Chandler is examined.

41001 ■ *"Ann Arbor Google's Growth Dips" in Crain's Detroit Business (Vol. 25, June 8, 2009, No. 23, pp. 3)*
Pub: Crain Communications Inc. - Detroit
Contact: Keith Crain, Chairman
Ed: Bill Shea. **Description:** Global recession has slowed the growth of Google Inc. Three years ago, when Google moved to Ann Arbor, Michigan it estimated it would provide 1,000 new jobs within five years, so far the firm employs 250.

41002 ■ *"Anything Could Happen" in Inc. (March 2008, pp. 116-123)*
Pub: Mansueto Ventures L.L.C.
Contact: John Koten, Chief Executive Officer
Ed: Max Chafkin. **Description:** Profile of Evan Williams, founder of Blogger and Twitter, a new type of technology idea; Williams answers ten questions and share insight into growing both of his companies.

41003 ■ *"Anytime Access" in Crain's Cleveland Business (Vol. 28, October 22, 2007, No. 42, pp. 17)*
Ed: Brad Dicken. **Description:** Technology continues to evolve in the competitive world of mobile communications in which the phone has become a sleek multitool that can take a call, send and e-mail, calculate the tip after dinner and snap a photograph.

41004 ■ *"App Brings Real-Time Personal Security, Company Says" in Philadelphia Business Journal (Vol. 33, July 4, 2014, No. 21, pp. 11)*
Pub: American City Business Journals
Released: July 4, 2014. **Description:** EmergenSee, which is a mobile technology that transforms smartphones or tablets into personal security systems by downloading the app. It has the ability to stream live video and audio.

41005 ■ *"App Maker Thinks He Has the Ticket: But Denver Is Balking At Alternative To Parking Fines" in Denver Business Journal (Vol. 65, April 25, 2014, No. 50, pp. A10)*
Pub: American City Business Journals
Released: April 25, 2014. **Description:** Taylor Linnell started Ticket Cricket LLC with partner, Jeff Valdez, to make parking tickets obsolete in Denver, Colorado by using two smartphone applications, One, Ticket Cricket and 5 for 5. The Department of Public Works rejected Linnell's proposal; he was encouraged to try it with the city's parking system technology vendor, Xerox.

41006 ■ *"App Time: Smartphone Applications Aren't Just for Fun and Games Anymore" in Inc. (Volume 32, December 2010, No. 10, pp. 116)*
Pub: Inc. Magazine
Ed: Jason Del Rey. **Description:** Smart phone technology can help any small business market their products and services.

41007 ■ *"Apple's iPhone 3G: A Marketing 50 Case Study" in Advertising Age (Vol. 79, November 17, 2008, No. 43, pp. 15)*
Pub: Crain Communications Inc.
Contact: Rance Crain, President
Ed: Beth Snyder Bulik. **Description:** Review of Apple's new iPhone 3G which includes the addition of smart-phone applications as well as a price drop; the new functionalities as well as the lower price seems to be paying off for Apple who reported sales of 6.9 million iPhones in its most recent quarter, in which the 3G hit store shelves.

41008 ■ *"Apps For Anybody With an Idea" in Advertising Age (Vol. 79, October 17, 2008, No. 39, pp. 29)*
Pub: Crain Communications Inc.
Contact: Rance Crain, President
Ed: Beth Snyder Bulik. **Description:** Apple's new online App Store is open to anyone with an idea and the ability to write code and many of these developers are not only finding a sense of community through this venue but are also making money since the sales are split with Apple, 30/70 in the developer's favor.

41009 ■ *"ART Announces New Distribution Arrangement with GE Healthcare for eXplore Optix" in Marketwired (May 14, 2007)*
Pub: Comtex News Network Inc.
Description: ART Advanced Research Technologies Inc., a medical device company and a leader in optical molecular imaging products for the pharmaceutical and healthcare industries, announced that it signed an agreement with GE Healthcare regarding worldwide distribution of its eXplore Optix preclinical optical molecular imaging system.

41010 ■ *"As Technology Changes, So Must African American Business" in Black Enterprise (Vol. 41, August 2010, No. 1, pp. 61)*
Pub: Earl G. Graves Publishing Co. Inc.
Contact: Earl G. Graves, Jr., President
Ed: Sonya A. Donaldson. **Description:** Social media is essential to compete in today's business environment, especially for African American firms.

41011 ■ *"As Windows 8 Looms, Tech Investors Hold Their Breath" in (Vol. 92, July 23, 2012, No. 30, pp. 22)*
Pub: Dow Jones & Co., Inc.
Contact: Clare Hart, President
Ed: Tiernan Ray. **Released:** July 23, 2012. **Description:** Launch of the Microsoft Windows 8 operating

system could affect the stock prices of Microsoft and Intel. The effects of the software's introduction on the market share of personal computers remains uncertain.

41012 ■ "Asterand Eyes Jump to Ann Arbor" in Crain's Detroit Business (Vol. 25, June 22, 2009)
Pub: Crain Communications Inc. - Detroit
Contact: Keith Crain, Chairman
Ed: Tom Henderson. **Description:** Asterand PLC is considering a move to Ann Arbor from its current location as anchor tenant at TechTown, an incubator and technology park associated with Wayne State University. The university believes the Ann Arbor location's rent is too expensive for the tissue bank company.

41013 ■ "Astral Fine-Tunes Details of Standard Purchase" in Globe & Mail (February 26, 2007, pp. B1)
Ed: Grant Robertson. **Description:** The proposed acquisition of Standard Radio Inc. by Astral Media Inc. for $1.2 billion is discussed.

41014 ■ "Attention, Please" in Entrepreneur (Vol. 36, April 2008, No. 4, pp. 52)
Pub: Entrepreneur Press
Contact: Perlman Neil, President
Ed: Andrea Cooper. **Description:** Gurbaksh Chahal created his own company ClickAgents at the age of 16, and sold it two years later for $40 million to Value-Click. He then founded BlueLithium, an online advertising network on behavioral targeting, which Yahoo! Inc. bought in 2007 for $300 million. Chahal, now 25, talks about his next plans and describes how BlueLithium caught Yahoo's attention.

41015 ■ "Attivio Brings Order to Data" in Information Today (Vol. 26, February 2009, No. 2, pp. 14)
Pub: Information Today, Inc.
Contact: Thomas H. Hogan, President
E-mail: ctuthill@infotoday.com
Ed: Marji McClure. **Description:** Profile of Attivio, the high tech firm offering next-generation software that helps businesses to consolidate data and eliminate enterprise silos.

41016 ■ "Auction-Rate Cash Frees Up" in The Business Journal-Portland (Vol. 25, August 15, 2008, No. 23, pp. 1)
Pub: American City Business Journals, Inc.
Contact: Whitney Shaw, President
Ed: Aliza Earnshaw. **Description:** FEI Co. and Radi-Sys Corp. have received notices that UBS AG will buy back the auction-rate securities that were sold to them in around two years from 2008. FEI had $110.1 million invested in auction-rate securities while Radi-Sys holds $62.8 million of these securities.

41017 ■ "Aviat Networks Partners With AT&T Government Solutions for Department of Homeland Security Business" in Entertainment Close-Up August 13, 2012
Pub: Close-Up Media
Released: August 13, 2012. **Description:** Aviat Networks Inc. will provide US Department of Homeland Security and other federal agencies withh the capability to acquire microwave radio communication equipment, engineering, design, installation and maintenace services. Aviat is a subcontractor on the AT&T Government Solutions' team. Aviat has a history of partnerships in federal technology space.

41018 ■ "Back Off on ABM Legislation, Banks Warn MPs" in Globe & Mail (April 20, 2007, pp. B1)
Ed: Steven Chase. **Description:** The efforts of banks to prevent legislation by the Canadian government on the automated banking machine levies charged from customers of other institutions are described.

41019 ■ "Baker Building A Snapshot Of Corridor's Future; Long-Empty Euclid Avenue Site Already Houses Two Tech Tenants, with

Developer Eyeing More" in Crain's Cleveland Business
Pub: Crain Communications Inc.
Ed: Stan Bullard. **Description:** Due to a new transit line and the redevelopment of the old Baker Electric Building, the Euclid Ave. area of Cleveland is transforming from a known drug activity area to a new area for high-tech ventures.

41020 ■ "Banks Fall Short in Online Services for Savvy Traders" in Barron's (Vol. 88, March 17, 2008, No. 11, pp. 35)
Pub: Dow Jones & Co., Inc.
Contact: Clare Hart, President
Ed: Theresa W. Carey. **Description:** Banc of America Investment Services, WellsTrade, and ShareBuilder are at the bottom of the list of online brokerages because they offer less trading technologies and product range. Financial shoppers miss out on a lot of customized tools and analytics when using these services.

41021 ■ "Bark and Bite" in Canadian Business (Vol. 81, March 31, 2008, No. 5, pp. 20)
Pub: Rogers Media Inc.
Contact: Tony Viner, President
Ed: Rachel Pulfer. **Description:** Hillary Clinton and Barack Obama both want to renegotiate NAFTA but the most job losses in the American manufacturing industry is caused by technological change and Asian competition than with NAFTA. The risk of protectionist trade policies has increased given the political atmosphere.

41022 ■ "BBVA Offers Medical Practices help that Floats on a Cloud" in Dallas Business Journal (Vol. 37, May 30, 2014, No. 38, pp. 6)
Pub: American City Business Journals
Released: May 30, 2014. **Description:** BBVA Compass is offering a package of bank services and health care technology for medical practices in Dallas-Fort Worth, Texas in partnership with technology platform provider CareCloud. The innovative cloud-based technology platform will allow the Birmingham, Alabama-based bank to help medical practices affected by the demands of technology and government regulations.

41023 ■ "BCE Wireless Growth Flags in Fourth Quarter" in Globe & Mail (February 8, 2007, pp. B5)
Ed: Catherine McLean. **Description:** BCE Inc., the largest telecommunications provider in Canada, reported $699 million profit in the final quarter of 2006. The company signed up 169,000 wireless customers in the important holiday season.

41024 ■ "Bearish Ken Rosen Growls About Tech" in San Francisco Business Times (Vol. 28, May 2, 2014, No. 41, pp. 3)
Pub: American City Business Journals
Released: May 2, 2014. **Description:** Ken Rose, chairman of the University of California Berkeley's Fisher Center, believes that 50 percent of technology companies will fail. He thinks that these firms will not be able to use all the office space they are taking. However, real estate developers are optimistic about office demand in the technology sector.

41025 ■ Behind the Cloud
Pub: Jossey-Bass
Contact: William J. Pesce, President
Ed: Marc R. Benioff, Carlye Adler. **Released:** 2010. **Price:** $27.95, Hardcover. **Description:** Salesforce.com is the world's most successful business-to-business cloud-computing company that sells an online service that helps businesses manage sales, customer service, and marketing functions.

41026 ■ "The Bell Tolls for Thee" in Canadian Business (Vol. 81, March 3, 2008, No. 3, pp. 36)
Ed: Andrew Wahl. **Description:** Bell Canada has formed the Canadian Coalition for Tomorrow's IT Skills to solve the shortage of technology talent in the country. Canada's total workforce has only around 4%, or 600,000 people employed in information

technology-related fields. The aims of the Bell-led coalition, which is supported by different industry associations and 30 corporations, are investigated.

41027 ■ "Bernier Open to Telecom Changes" in Globe & Mail (March 22, 2006, pp. B1)
Ed: Simon Tuck. **Description:** Federal Industry Minister Maxime Bernier of Canada says that he is open to scrapping restrictions on foreign ownership in telecommunications. His views on telecom industry are detailed.

41028 ■ "Beyond Microsoft and Yahoo!: Some M&A Prospects" in Barron's (Vol. 88, March 17, 2008, No. 11, pp. 39)
Pub: Dow Jones & Co., Inc.
Contact: Clare Hart, President
Ed: Eric J. Savitz. **Description:** Weak quarterly earnings report for Yahoo! could pressure the company's board to cut a deal with Microsoft. Electronic Arts is expected to win its hostile $26-a-share bid for Take-Two Interactive Software. Potential targets and buyers for mergers and acquisitions are mentioned.

41029 ■ "Beyond the RAZR's Edge" in Canadian Business (Vol. 79, November 6, 2006, No. 22, pp. 15)
Ed: Andrew Wahl. **Description:** Features of Motorola RAZR, such as low weight and camera accessibility, are presented.

41030 ■ "The Big Picture" in Canadian Business (Vol. 79, December 4, 2006, No. 24, pp. 142)
Pub: Rogers Media Inc.
Contact: Tony Viner, President
Ed: Andy Holloway. **Description:** The features of the new range of high-definition television sets released by Matushita Electric Corporation of America are described. The pricing of the television sets is discussed.

41031 ■ The Big Switch
Ed: Nicholas Carr. **Released:** January 19, 2009. **Price:** $16.95, paperback. **Description:** Today companies are dismantling private computer systems and tapping into services provided via the Internet. This shift is remaking the computer industry, bringing competitors such as Google to the forefront ant threatening traditional companies like Microsoft and Dell. The book weaves together history, economics, and technology to explain why computing is changing and what it means for the future.

41032 ■ The Big Switch: Rewiring the World, From Edison to Google
Pub: W.W. Norton and Company Inc.
Contact: A Malmud, President
Ed: Nicholas Carr. **Released:** June 2013. **Price:** $16.95, paperback. **Description:** Companies such as Google, Microsoft, and Amazon.com are building huge centers in order to create massive data centers. Together these centers form a giant computing grid that will deliver the digital universe to scientific labs, companies and homes in the future. This trend could bring about a new, darker phase for the Internet, one where these networks could operate as a fearsome entity that will dominate the lives of individuals worldwide. **Availability:** Print.

41033 ■ "BioPark Eyes New Anchor" in Baltimore Business Journal (Vol. 30, June 22, 2012, No. 7, pp. 1)
Pub: American City Business Journals, Inc.
Contact: Whitney Shaw, President
Ed: Sarah Gantz. **Released:** June 22, 2012. **Description:** University of Maryland BioPark leaders are wooing a biotechnology firm in Boston to become the anchor tenant of the park's third office building. Getting an anchor tenant would start construction of the BioPark's new 200,000 square-foot building. The 12-acre park's recovery from the struggling economy is described.

41034 ■ "Biotech Reels In $120M for 1Q" in Philadelphia Business Journal (Vol. 31, March 30, 2012, No. 7, pp. 1)
Pub: American City Business Journal
Description: Philadelphia, Pennsylvania-based biotechnology firms have raised over $120 million in

2012 by selling stocks and debts. Discovery Laboratories has accounted for more than a third of the total funding.

41035 ■ *"Biotechnology Wants a Lead Role"* **in Business North Carolina (Vol. 28, March 2008, No. 3, pp. 14)**

Description: According to experts, North Carolina is poised as a leader in the biotechnology sector. Highlights of a recent roundtable discussion sponsored by the North Carolina Biotechnology Center in Research Triangle Park are presented.

41036 ■ *"Biotechs Are Using Back Door to Go Public"* **in Boston Business Journal (Vol. 31, May 27, 2011, No. 18, pp. 1)**

Pub: Boston Business Journal

Ed: Julie M. Donnelly. **Description:** Members of Massachusetts' biotechnology sector have been engaging in reverse mergers as an alternative to initial public offerings. Reverse mergers provide access to institutional investors and hedge funds.

41037 ■ *"Birmingham Tech Firms Eye Growth in 2014"* **in Birmingham Business Journal (Vol. 31, January 10, 2014, No. 2, pp. 4)**

Pub: American City Business Journals, Inc.

Contact: Whitney Shaw, President

Released: January 10, 2014. **Description:** Birmingham, Alabama-based high-tech firms, ProctorU and Chronicle Studio are planning to expand their work forces in 2014. ProctorU will add more than 50 employees, while Chronicle will add three more positions to their staff.

41038 ■ *"Bitcoin 'Killer App' Or the Currency of the Future?"* **in Providence Business News (Vol. 28, January 6, 2014, No. 40, pp. 1)**

Pub: American City Business Journals

Released: January 6, 2014. **Description:** The Providence Bitcoin Meetup has gathered several technology experts to discuss Bitcoin, the popular digital currency. However, software developers, engineers and entrepreneurs see Bitcoin as the next killer app for the Internet and is changing how information and data is stored, shared and verified. The Bitcoin's impact in Rhode Island is examined.

41039 ■ *"Biz Assesses 'Textgate' Fallout: Conventions, Smaller Deals Affected"* **in Crain's Detroit Business (Vol. 24, March 31, 2008)**

Pub: Crain Communications Inc.

Contact: Rance E. Crain, President

Ed: Tom Henderson. **Description:** Businesspeople who were trying to measure the amount of economic damage is likely to be caused due to Mayor Kwame Kilpatrick's indictment on eight charges and found that: automotive and other large global deals are less likely to be affected than location decisions by smaller companies and convention site decisions. Also being affected are negotiations in which Mexican startup companies were planning a partnership with the TechTown incubator to pursue opportunities in the auto sector; those plans are being put on hold while they look at other sites.

41040 ■ *"Biz U: Cool for School"* **in Entrepreneur (Vol. 35, October 2007, No. 10, pp. 144)**

Pub: Entrepreneur Press

Contact: Perlman Neil, President

Ed: Nichole L. Torres. **Description:** Forming a high technology business while still in college has its advantages such as having information resources nearby and having students from various fields to ask for help and advice. School business competitions are also helpful in building networks with investors. Ways that the college environment can be useful to aspiring entrepreneurs, particularly to those who are into high technology business, are discussed.

41041 ■ *"Blacks Go Broadband: High-Speed Internet Adoption Grows Among African Americans"* **in Black Enterprise (Vol. 38, February 2008)**

Pub: Earl G. Graves Publishing Co. Inc.

Contact: Earl G. Graves, Jr., President

Ed: Cliff Hocker. **Description:** Number of black households using broadband Internet services tripled since 2005 according to a survey conducted by Pew Internet and American Life Project.

41042 ■ *"Blockbuster Launches Internet Movie Downloads to Compete Against Netflix, Others"* **in Chicago Tribune (December 3, 2008)**

Pub: McClatchy-Tribune Information Services

Ed: Eric Benderoff. **Description:** Blockbuster Inc., the DVD rental giant, has launched a new service that delivers movies to their customer's homes via the Internet in an attempt to compete against Netflix and other competitors.

41043 ■ *"Blog Buzz Heralds Arrival of IPhone 2.0"* **in Advertising Age (Vol. 79, June 9, 2008, No. 40, pp. 8)**

Pub: Crain Communications Inc.

Contact: Rance Crain, President

Ed: Abbey Klaassen. **Description:** Predictions concerning the next version of the iPhone include a global-positioning-system technology as well as a configuration to run on a faster, 3G network.

41044 ■ *"BofA Cutting 70 Charlotte Tech Jobs"* **in Charlotte Observer (January 31, 2007)**

Ed: Rick Rothacker. **Description:** Bank of America announced the elimination of 70 technology positions at their Charlotte, North Carolina facility. The move is part of the company's effort to increase efficiency.

41045 ■ *"Bon Voyager"* **in Entrepreneur (Vol. 36, April 2008, No. 4, pp. 58)**

Pub: Entrepreneur Press

Contact: Perlman Neil, President

Ed: Heather Clancy. **Description:** LG Voyager, especially made for Verizon Wireless, is a smart phone that is being compared to Apple iPhone. The Voyager has a 2.8-inch external touchscreen and has a clamshell design, which features an internal keyboard. It does not have Wi-Fi support like iPhone, but it has 3G support. Other differences between the two phones are discussed.

41046 ■ *"Book of Lists 2010"* **in Philadelphia Business Journal (Vol. 28, December 25, 2009, No. 45, pp. 1)**

Pub: American City Business Journals Inc.

Description: Rankings of companies and organizations within the banking, biotechnology, economic development, healthcare, hospitality, law and accounting, marketing and media, real estate, and technology industries in the Philadelphia, Pennsylvania area are presented. Rankings are based on sales, business size, and more.

41047 ■ *"Boom has Tech Grads Mulling Their Options"* **in Globe & Mail (March 14, 2006, pp. B1)**

Ed: Grant Robertson. **Description:** Internet giant Google Inc. has stepped up its efforts to hire the talented people, in Canada, at Waterloo University in southern Ontario, to expand its operations. The details of the job market and increasing salaries are analyzed.

41048 ■ *"Boosting Your Merchant Management Services With Wireless Technology"* **In Franchising World (Vol. 42, August 2010, No. 8, pp. 27)**

Pub: International Franchise Association

Contact: Stephen J. Caldeira, President

E-mail: scaldeira@franchise.org

Ed: Michael S. Slominski. **Description:** Franchises should have the capability to accept credit cards away from their businesses. This technology will increase sales.

41049 ■ *"Boots Treat Street Rolls Out Trolley Dash App on Androis and iPhone OS"* **in Entertainment Close-Up (October 24, 2011)**

Pub: Close-Up Media

Description: Shoppers using Boots Treat Street can now download the Trolley Dash app game, available from the Apple Store and the Android Market, and enjoy the pastel colored street featuring favorite retailers such as eBay, New Look and Play.com collecting prizes while avoiding hazards.

41050 ■ *"Border Boletin: UA to Take Lie-Detector Kiosk to Poland"* **in Arizona Daily Star (September 14, 2010)**

Pub: Arizona Daily Star

Contact: John Humenik, President

E-mail: jhumenik@azstarnet.com

Ed: Brady McCombs. **Description:** University of Arizona's National Center for Border Security and Immigration Research will send a team to Warsaw, Poland to show border guards from 27 European Union countries the center's Avatar Kiosk. The Avatar technology is designed for use at border ports and airports to assist Customs officers detect individuals who are lying.

41051 ■ *"Boxing, Tech Giants Team to Help Teens"* **in Hispanic Business (January-February 2009, pp. 44)**

Ed: Daniel Soussa. **Description:** Microsoft and Oscar de la Hoya are providing teens a head start for careers in the sciences by offering a competition in the categories of photography, short films or Web-based games.

41052 ■ *"Branding Your Way"* **in Canadian Business (Vol. 80, February 12, 2007, No. 4, pp. 31)**

Ed: Erin Pooley. **Description:** The trend in involving consumers in brand marketing by seeking their views through contests or inviting them to produce and submit commercials through Internet is discussed.

41053 ■ *"Breaking From Tradition Techstyle"* **in Providence Business News (Vol. 28, March 17, 2014, No. 50, pp. 1)**

Pub: American City Business Journals

Released: March 17, 2014. **Description:** Providence, Rhode Island's Techstyle Haus is being constructed by a group of students from Brown University. The textile house features a flexible exterior that uses high-performance materials and solar cells. Techstyle Haus is one of two entries from the U.S. competing in the Solar Decathlon Europe 2014.

41054 ■ *"Brisk Activity in North Fulton Office Market"* **in Atlanta Business Chronicle (July 11, 2014, pp. 2B)**

Released: July 11, 2014. **Description:** Activity appears to have pickup up briskly in the North Fulton office market during the first six months of 2014, mainly due to the high profile deals involving major players in the technology and health care sectors.

41055 ■ *"Broadband Reaches Access Limits in Europe"* **in Information Today (Vol. 26, February 2009, No. 2, pp. 22)**

Pub: Information Today, Inc.

Contact: Thomas H. Hogan, President

E-mail: ctuthill@infotoday.com

Ed: Jim Ashling. **Description:** Eurostat (the Statistical Office of the European communities) reports results from is survey regarding Internet use by businesses throughout its 27-member states. Iceland, Finland and the Netherlands provide the most access at broadband speeds, followed by Belgium, Spain and France.

41056 ■ *"Brown At Center of Local CleanTech Lobbying Efforts"* **in Boston Business Journal (Vol. 30, October 15, 2010, No. 36, pp. 1)**

Pub: Boston Business Journal

Ed: Kyle Alspach. **Description:** U.S. Senator Scott Brown has been active in lobbying for energy reform in Massachusetts. Brown has been meeting with business groups seeking the reforms.

41057 ■ *"Building His Dream"* **in Business Courier (Vol. 24, January 24, 2008, No. 42, pp. 1)**

Pub: American City Business Journals, Inc.

Contact: Whitney Shaw, President

Ed: Laura Baverman. **Description:** Technology entrepreneur Mahendra Vora plans to build a more than $100 million local IT headquarters for VTech Holdings Ltd by 2010. Acquisition of four $5 million companies within 2008 are part of the owner's plan to expand the office equipment company. Other plans for the IT company are discussed.

41058 ■ *"The Business Case for Mobile Content Acceleration" in Streaming Media (November 2011, pp. 78)*
Pub: Information Today, Inc.
Contact: Thomas H. Hogan, President
E-mail: ctuthill@infotoday.com
Ed: Dan Rayburn. **Description:** Last holiday season, eBay became a mobile commerce (m-commerce) giant when sales rose by 134 percent, as most online retailers offered customers the ability to purchase items using their mobile devices.

41059 ■ *"Business Still Expected to Take Hit in 2008" in Business Journal-Serving Phoenix and the Valley of the Sun (December 28, 2007)*
Ed: Ty Young. **Description:** Semiconductor industry is forecasting a slow first quarter for 2008 and industry analysts believe there will be decreased growth for the rest of the year. The impending recession in the U.S. will lead to a fall in consumer spending, which will in turn drive down the demand for electronics. The semiconductor revenue forecast for 2010 is also discussed.

41060 ■ *"Buyer's Guide: Room for Improvement" in Entrepreneur (Vol. 35, October 2007, No. 10, pp. 62)*
Pub: Entrepreneur Press
Contact: Perlman Neil, President
Ed: Amanda C. Kooser. **Description:** Buyers guide for wireless routers is presented. Price, features and availability of the Belkin N1 Vision, Buffalo Wireless-N Nfinit Router, D-Link Xtreme Gigabit Router DIR 655, Linksys Wireless-N Gigabit Security Router, Netgear RangeMax Next Wireless-N Router and Zyxel NBG-460N are provided.

41061 ■ *"The Buzz About HD Radio" in Black Enterprise (Vol. 37, February 2007, No. 7, pp. 58)*
Pub: Earl G. Graves Publishing Co. Inc.
Contact: Earl G. Graves, Jr., President
Ed: James C. Johnson. **Description:** HD radio broadcasting will send CD quality sound and extra information to more radio stations using the same amount of bandwidth.

41062 ■ *"Call Them Gorgeous" in Entrepreneur (Vol. 35, October 2007, No. 10, pp. 54)*
Pub: Entrepreneur Press
Contact: Perlman Neil, President
Ed: Amanda C. Kooser. **Description:** Smart phones are known for their high technology features, unique names and extraordinary design. Features of the Apple iPhone, Helio Ocean, Blackberry Curve, T-Mobile Wing and Motorola Razr2 V9 are described.

41063 ■ *"Can America Invent Its Way Back?" in Business Week (September 22, 2008, No. 4100, pp. 52)*
Pub: Bloomberg L.P.
Contact: Matthew Winkler, Manager
Ed: Michael Mandel. **Description:** Business leaders as well as economists agree that innovative new products, services and ways of doing business may be the only way in which America can survive the downward spiral of the economy; innovation economics may be the answer and may even provide enough growth to enable Americans to prosper in the years to come.

41064 ■ *"Can Slow and Steady Win the Eco-Devo Race?" in Birmingham Business Journal (Vol. 31, June 6, 2014, No. 23, pp. 8)*
Pub: American City Business Journals, Inc.
Contact: Whitney Shaw, President
Released: June 6, 2014. **Description:** Evonik Corporation's expansion in Birmingham, Alabama reflects the city's economic development strategy. The company's creation of 25 jobs may be replicated by other companies. Birmingham is serious about becoming a biotechnology hub.

41065 ■ *"Can Tech Industry Share Wealth?" in Puget Sound Business Journal (Vol. 35,*

May 23, 2014, No. 5, pp. 10)
Pub: American City Business Journals
Released: May 23, 2014. **Description:** Nearly 700 local technology leaders gathered at the annual State of Technology event organized by Tech Alliance in Washington in May 2014. Trade show speaker, Geoffrey Moore, emphasized the role of the technology industry as a driver of local economies.

41066 ■ *"Can You Hear Them Now?" in Hawaii Business (Vol. 54, August 2008, No. 2, pp. 48)*
Ed: Jason Ubay. **Description:** Coral Wireless LLC (dba Mobi PCS) is ranked 237 in Hawaii Business' list of the state's top 250 companies for 2008. The company is a local wireless phone provider, which has expanded its market to Oahu, Maui and the Big Island since opening in 2006, offering 13 phones and unlimited texts and calls. Details on the company's sales are provided.

41067 ■ *"Canada Tomorrow" in Canadian Business (Vol. 80, October 8, 2007, No. 20, pp. 14)*
Ed: Donald J. Johnston. **Description:** An assessment of Canada's future in terms of its educational, social, and economic environment is presented. Concerns regarding the country's educational system such as the declining interest in science and technology and the possible lack of teachers in the future are discussed. In terms of its social and economic aspects, the need to support entrepreneurs and other qualified people is explained.

41068 ■ *"Canada's Clean Energy Advantages Offer a Bright Future" in Canadian Business (Vol. 83, August 17, 2010, No. 13-14, pp. 38)*
Ed: Don McKinnon. **Description:** Canada has clean energy advantages in the greenhouse gas emission-free CANada Deuterium Uranium reactor technology and carbon neutral biomass fuels that were continuously ignored by policy makers. Both are proven to significantly reduce emissions while providing reliable, affordable and secure electricity.

41069 ■ *"Canadians Keep Memories in 'Inboxes' Instead of Shoe Boxes; MSN Canada" in Marketwired (May 14, 2007)*
Pub: Comtex News Network Inc.
Description: According to an MSN Canada online poll, 76 percent of Canadians are creating 'virtual shoeboxes' with their email inboxes and archiving important messages, photos, and documents.

41070 ■ *"Capital Coming Into City, but Local Money Lags" in Pittsburgh Business Times (Vol. 33, March 21, 2014, No. 36, pp. 4)*
Pub: American City Business Journals
Released: March 21, 2014. **Description:** The strong investment market in Pittsburgh, Pennsylvania is fueled by capital from a combination of angel, venture, corporate and other sources, attracting $338 million in capital to finance 148 deals in 2013, but local money is lagging behind. Lynette Horrell of Ernst & Young notes that local money is not keeping up with the growth of technology companies in Pittsburgh.

41071 ■ *"Catch the Wind Announces Filing of Injunction Against Air Data Systems LLC and Philip Rogers" in CNW Group (September 30, 2011)*
Pub: CNW Group Ltd.
Contact: Carolyn McGill-Davidson, President
Description: Catch the Wind, providers of laser-based wind sensor products and technology, filed an injunction against Optical Air Data Systems (OADS) LLC and its former President and CEO Philip L. Rogers. The complaint seeks to have OADS and Rogers return tangible and intangible property owned by Catch the Wind, which the firm believes to be critical to the operations of their business.

41072 ■ *"Catch the Wind to Hold Investor Update Conference Call on October 18, 2011" in CNW Group (October 4, 2011)*
Pub: CNW Group Ltd.
Contact: Carolyn McGill-Davidson, President
Description: Catch the Wind Ltd., providers of laser-based wind sensor products and technology, held a

conference call for analysts and institutional investors. The high-growth technology firm is headquartered in Manassas, Virginia.

41073 ■ *"CBC Eyes Partners for TV Downloads" in Globe & Mail (February 9, 2006, pp. B1)*
Ed: Grant Robertson. **Description:** The details on Canadian Broadcasting Corp.'s distribution agreement with Google Inc. and Apple Computer Inc. are presented.

41074 ■ *"Cell Phone the Ticket on American Airlines" in Chicago Tribune (November 14, 2008)*
Pub: McClatchy-Tribune Information Services
Ed: Julie Johnsson. **Description:** American Airlines is testing a new mobile boarding pass at O'Hare International Airport. Travelers on American can board flights and get through security checkpoints by flashing a bar code on their phones. Passengers must have an Internet-enabled mobile device and an active e-mail address in order to utilize this service.

41075 ■ *"Cell Tower Potential" in Black Enterprise (Vol. 37, October 2006, No. 3, pp. 86)*
Pub: Earl G. Graves Publishing Co. Inc.
Contact: Earl G. Graves, Jr., President
Ed: James C. Johnson. **Description:** Discusses the leasing of property for cell phone towers to wireless carriers. Only certain properties are eligible, due to such criteria as proximity to existing towers.

41076 ■ *"CEO Forecast: With Cloudy Economy, Executives Turn to Government Contracting" in Hispanic Business (January-February 2009, pp. 34, 36)*
Pub: Hispanic Business Inc.
Contact: Jesus Chavarria, President
Ed: Jessica Haro, Richard Kaplan. **Description:** As economic uncertainty fogs the future, executives turn to government contracts in order to boost business. Revenue sources, health care challenges, environmental consulting and remediation services, as well as technological strides are discussed.

41077 ■ *"Certification Experts Germanischer Lloyd Wind Energy Assist NaiKun's Offshore Wind Project" in Marketwired (May 14, 2007)*
Pub: Comtex News Network Inc.
Description: Germanischer Lloyd Wind Energy (GL Wind) will examine, inspect, and provide quality management services for the engineering, design, and construction of the offshore wind project planned by NaiKun Wind Development Inc. in northwest British Columbia.

41078 ■ *"Charlotte Becoming a Tech Hub?" in Charlotte Business Journal (Vol. 27, June 29, 2012, No. 15, pp. 1)*
Pub: American City Business Journals, Inc.
Contact: Whitney Shaw, President
Ed: Adam O'Daniel. **Released:** June 29, 2012. **Description:** North Carolina Technology Association opened a branch office in Charlotte. The development is seen as a first step towards the city becoming a technology hub. Executive comments included.

41079 ■ *"China Vs the World: Whose Technology Is It?" in Harvard Business Review (Vol. 88, December 2010, No. 12, pp. 94)*
Pub: Harvard Business School Publishing
Ed: Thomas M. Hout, Pankaj Ghemawat. **Description:** Examination of the regulation the Chinese government is implementing that require foreign corporations wishing to do business in the country to give up their new technologies. These regulations avoid World Trade Organization technology transfer provisions and complicate the convergence of socialism and capitalism.

41080 ■ *"Chinese Outbound Tourists' Destination Image of America: Part I" in Journal of Travel Research (Vol. 51, May*

2012, No. 3, pp. 250)
Pub: Pine Forge Press
Contact: Blaise R. Simqu, President
Ed: Xiang (Robert) Li, Svetlana Stepchenkova. **Description:** Several studies are conducted to examine the mental picture of the United States as a travel destination as observed in the Chinese long-haul outbound travelers. These Chinese tourists often foresee America as a highly urban country with high technology and big cities.

41081 ■ *"The Chips Are In"* in Business Journal-Portland (Vol. 24, November 2, 2007, No. 35, pp. 1)
Ed: Aliza Earnshaw. **Description:** The $30 million funding round of Ambric Inc., which brings a total investment of $51 million, is about to close, and its clients are releasing over half-dozen products containing Ambric chips in January 2008. The features of Ambric's semiconductors, its market sectors and market positioning, as well as its investor relations, are discussed.

41082 ■ *"Clash of the Titans"* in Canadian Business (Vol. 80, March 12, 2007, No. 6, pp. 27)
Ed: Andrew Wahl. **Description:** The frequent allegations of Google Inc. and Microsoft Corp. against each other over copyright and other legal issues, with a view to taking away other's market share, is discussed.

41083 ■ *"Cloud City"* in Puget Sound Business Journal (Vol. 34, February 28, 2014, No. 46, pp. 4)
Pub: American City Business Journals
Released: February 28, 2014. **Description:** Seattle, Washington is experiencing an influx of the world's most innovative cloud companies. Businesses are shifting their applications from in-house servers or private data center into public cloud infrastructure, which is less expensive than buying the servers and managing the data systems. Seattle software companies are taking advantage of this trend and developing products.

41084 ■ *"Clusters Last Stand?"* in Canadian Electronics (Vol. 23, February 2008, No. 1, pp. 6)
Description: Survival of technology clusters was the focus of Strategic Microelectronics Council's conference entitled, 'The Power of Community: Building Technology Clusters in Canada'. Clusters can help foster growth in the microelectronics sector, and it was recognized that government intervention is needed to maintain these clusters.

41085 ■ *"CN to Webcast 2007 Analyst Meeting in Toronto May 23-24"* in Canadian Corporate News (May 16, 2007)
Description: Canadian National Railway Company (CN) broadcast its analyst meeting in Toronto with a webcast which focused on CN's opportunities, strategies, and financial outlook through the year 2010.

41086 ■ *"CommScope and Comsearch to Showcase Innovative Wind Power Solutions at WINDPOWER 2012 in Atlanta"* in Benzinga.com (May 31, 2012)
Pub: Benzinga.com
Contact: Kyle Bazzy, President
Ed: Aaron Wise. **Description:** CommScope Inc. and its subsidiary CommScope will highlight their complete wind power solution products during the WINDPOWER 2012 Conference and Exhibition in Atlanta, Georgia this year. CommScope's wind power products include fiber optic cabling solutions, while Comsearch offers wind energy services that address the siting challenges resulting from complex telecommunications issues.

41087 ■ *"Company Goes High-Tech To Attack Some Sore Spots"* in Boston Business Journal (Vol. 27, December 7, 2007, No. 45, pp. 10)
Ed: Mark Hollmer. **Description:** Transport Pharmaceuticals Inc. hopes to raise $35 million to fund a drug and a treatment device for treating cold sores, and seek federal regulatory approval. Dennis Gold-

berg, the company's CEO, believes that existing treatments that use acyclovir cream are relatively weak. Transport's drug uses a soluble gel cartridge with a higher concentration of acyclovir.

41088 ■ *"Computer Forensics Firms Get Boost From New Evidence Rules"* in Crain's Detroit Business (Vol. 24, March 24, 2008, No. 12, pp. 28)
Pub: Crain Communications Inc.
Contact: Rance E. Crain, President
Ed: Chad Halcom. **Description:** Computer forensics is a growing niche for firms such as the Center for Computer Forensics in Southfield; driving some of the growth are new amendments to the Federal Rules of Civil Procedure, which took effect about a year ago and address standards of evidence for electronic records, or 'e-discovery,' that are admissible for civil cases in federal courts.

41089 ■ *"Conferencing Takes on High-Tech Futuristic Feel"* in Crain's Cleveland Business (Vol. 28, October 29, 2007, No. 43, pp. 17)
Pub: Crain Communications Inc.
Ed: Chuck Soder. **Description:** Overview of the newest technologies which are making local company's meetings more effective including: tele-presence, a videoconferencing technology, as well as virtual flip charts.

41090 ■ *"Congestion Relief"* in Canadian Business (Vol. 80, February 12, 2007, No. 4, pp. 31)
Ed: Andrea Jezovit. **Description:** The development of a satellite-based system for traffic management including paying for parking fees by Skymeter Corp. is discussed.

41091 ■ *"Connections: United We Gab"* in Entrepreneur (Vol. 35, October 2007, No. 10, pp. 60)
Pub: Entrepreneur Press
Contact: Perlman Neil, President
Ed: Mike Hogan. **Description:** T-Mobile and AT&T introduced dual-mode service to consumers, helping them to switch between cellular and Wi-Fi networks easily. These services, such as Hotspot@Home, reduces the cost of long distance calls by routing them over the Internet with the use of WiFi. Benefits of dual mode service, such as lower hardware price and better call coverage are given.

41092 ■ *"Connectors for Space, Mil/Aero and Medical Applications"* in Canadian Electronics (Vol. 23, June-July 2008, No. 4, pp. 13)
Ed: Gilles Parguey. **Description:** Product information on electrical connectors for use in space, military, aeronautics, and medical applications is provided. These connectors are built to withstand the extreme conditions offered by the harsh working environments in those applications.

41093 ■ *"Consumers Turned Off? Not at Best Buy"* in Barron's (Vol. 88, March 24, 2008, No. 12, pp. 29)
Pub: Dow Jones & Co., Inc.
Contact: Clare Hart, President
Ed: Sandra Ward. **Description:** Shares of Best Buy, trading at $42.41 each, are expected to rise to an average of $52 a share due to the company's solid fundamentals. The company's shares have fallen 20 percent from their 52-week high and are attractive given the company's bright prospects in the video game sector and high-definition video.

41094 ■ *"Contec Innovations Inc.: MovieSet.com First to Mobilize Content Using BUZmob"* in Canadian Corporate News (May 16, 2007)
Description: Contec Innovations Inc., a provider of mobile infrastructure software, announced that MovieSet.com is the first Internet portal to mobilize their content using BUZmob, the company's new mobile publishing service that allows content publishers to enable mobile access to their feed-based content on any mobile device or network in real-time.

41095 ■ *"Controlling Costs: Update Your Information Technology Program"* in Franchising World (Vol. 42, August 2010, No. 8, pp. 18)
Pub: International Franchise Association
Contact: Stephen J. Caldeira, President
E-mail: scaldeira@franchise.org
Ed: Jeff Dumont. **Description:** It is imperative for any franchise to understand its technology needs in order to control costs. Needs analysis; creating a Request for Proposal; and information regarding the choices between renting, buying or building technology are covered. Relationship contingency in franchised organizations is also covered.

41096 ■ *"Conversations Need to Yield Actions Measured in Dollars"* in Advertising Age (Vol. 79, July 7, 2008, No. 26, pp. 18)
Pub: Crain Communications Inc.
Contact: Rance Crain, President
Ed: Jonathan Salem Baskin. **Description:** New ways in which to market to consumers are discussed.

41097 ■ *"Covington-Based Valley Forge Ready to Meet Stepped-Up Airport Security Needs: Scanning the Field"* in Business Courier (Vol. 26, January 8, 2010, No. 38, pp. 1)
Pub: American City Business Journals, Inc.
Contact: Whitney Shaw, President
Ed: Jon Newberry. **Description:** Anti-terror detection systems developer Valley Force Composite Technologies Inc. of Kentucky plans to enter the market with its high-resolution ODIN and Thor-LVX screening systems. These systems are expected to meet the increasing demand for airport security equipment.

41098 ■ *"CradlePoint Is Adding Workers, Seeking More Space"* in Idaho Business Review (September 3, 2014)
Pub: Dolan Co.
Contact: James P. Dolan, President
Released: September 3, 2014. **Description:** CradlePoint makes networking routers and software, focusing on security for businesses. The firm is hiring new workers at a rate higher than predicted and is seeking new office space in downtown Boise, Idaho. CradlePoint is a major player in the growing wireless service and cloud platform market and is growing faster than its competitors.

41099 ■ *"Creating Health-Tech Opportunity"* in Providence Business News (Vol. 29, April 14, 2014, No. 2, pp. 1)
Pub: American City Business Journals
Released: April 14, 2014. **Description:** MedMates has officially launched, in April 2013, as Rhode Island's first group for networking and advocacy in health technology. MedMates now have 410 members that span every sector of health technology and its membership is not exclusive to the private sector. Insights into MedMates' first year success are also presented.

41100 ■ *"Credit Crunch Gives, Takes Away"* in The Business Journal-Serving Metropolitan Kansas City (Vol. 27, October 17, 2008, No. 5, pp. 1)
Ed: Suzanna Stagemeyer. **Description:** Although many Kansas City business enterprises have been adversely affected by the U.S. credit crunch, others have remained relatively unscathed. Examples of how local businesses are being impacted by the crisis are provided including: American Trailer & Storage Inc., which declared bankruptcy after failing to pay a long-term loan; and NetStandard, a technology firm who, on the other hand, is being pursued by prospective lenders.

41101 ■ *Crossing the Chasm: Marketing and Selling Disruptive Products to Mainstream Customers*
Pub: HarperCollins Publishers Inc.
Contact: Jane Friedman, President
E-mail: jfriedman@harpercollins.com
Ed: Geoffrey A. Moore. **Price:** $17.99, paperback; 12.99; C$11.99. **Description:** A guide for marketing in high-technology industries, focusing on the Internet. **Availability:** PrintE-book.

41102 ■ *"Cyberwise"* in Black Enterprise (Vol. 41, December 2010, No. 5, pp. 50)
Ed: Marica Wade Talbert. **Description:** Information is given regarding single platforms that can be used to develop applications for iPhone, Android, Blackberry, and Nokia.

41103 ■ *"Danaher to Acquire Tectronix"* in Canadian Electronics (Vol. 22, November-December 2007, No. 7, pp. 1)
Description: Leading supplier of measurement, test and monitoring equipment Tektronix will be acquired by Danaher Corporation for $2.8 billion. Tektronix products are expected to complement Danaher's test equipment sector. The impacts of the deal on Tektronix shareholders and Danaher's operations are discussed.

41104 ■ *"The Data Drivers"* in Canadian Business (Vol. 81, September 15, 2008, No. 14-15, pp. 1)
Ed: Andrew Wahl. **Description:** Canadian regulators hope that an auction of telecommunications companies will inject more competition into the industry; however, newcomers may not be able to rely on lower prices in order to gain market share from the three major telecommunications companies that already have a stronghold on the market. Analysts feel that providing additional data service is the key to surviving market disruptions.

41105 ■ *"Deals Dip In Florida Amid Squabbles Over Price"* in South Florida Business Journal (Vol. 34, May 30, 2014, No. 45, pp. 4)
Pub: American City Business Journals
Released: May 30, 2014. **Description:** Private equity firm investments in local companies in Florida dropped from 146 in 2012 to 135 in 2013. James Cassel of Cassel, Salpeter and Company, says companies in the information technology and health care sectors have been acquired because of strong multiples of their book value.

41106 ■ *"Dear Diary, Arbitron is Dumping You"* in Business Courier (Vol. 26, September 25, 2009, No. 22, pp. 1)
Pub: American City Business Journals, Inc.
Contact: Whitney Shaw, President
Ed: Dan Monk. **Description:** Arbitron Inc. is replacing hand-written ratings diaries with Portable People Meters or electronic sensors that measure local radio audiences. The technology counts all exposure to radio and stations; those that penetrate the workplace will see success, while the more 'niche' oriented formats will have a more difficult time.

41107 ■ *"Dell OEM Solutions Helps Gratifon S.A. Power VoIP Kiosks and Prepare for Future Growth"* in Benzinga.com (March 7, 2012)
Pub: Benzinga.com
Contact: Kyle Bazzy, President
Released: March 7, 2012. **Description:** Gratifon S.A. is working to obtain Dell OEM Solutions' ptiPlex XE PCs and cloud services for 50 kiosks providing sponsored phone calls free to residents and tourists in Panama. Details of the plan are outlined.

41108 ■ *"Design Programs for HVAC Sizing Solutions"* in Contractor (Vol. 57, January 2010, No. 1, pp. 44)
Pub: Intertec Publishing
Contact: John French, President
Ed: William Feldman, Patti Feldman. **Description:** Rhvac 8 is an HVAC design program that lets users calculate peak heating and cooling load requirements for rooms, zones, systems, and entire buildings. The HVAC Pipe Sizer software for the iPhone enables quick sizing of a simple piping system.

41109 ■ *"Detroit Hosts Conferences on Green Building, IT, Finance"* in Crain's Detroit Business (Vol. 25, June 1, 2009, No. 22, pp. 9)
Pub: Crain Communications Inc. - Detroit
Contact: Keith Crain, Chairman
Ed: Tom Henderson. **Description:** Detroit will host three conferences in June 2009, one features green technology, one information technology and the third will gather black bankers and financial experts from across the nation.

41110 ■ *"Digital Duplication"* in Crain's Cleveland Business (Vol. 28, October 1, 2007, No. 39, pp. 3)
Pub: Crain Communications Inc.
Ed: David Bennett. **Description:** Profile of the business plan of eBlueprint Holdings LLC, a reprographics company that found success by converting customers' paper blueprints to an electronic format; the company plans to expand into other geographic markets by acquiring solid reprographics companies and converting their computer systems so that customers' blueprints can be managed electronically.

41111 ■ *"Digital Edge: Stay Tuned"* in Entrepreneur (Vol. 35, October 2007, No. 10, pp. 56)
Pub: Entrepreneur Press
Contact: Perlman Neil, President
Ed: Mike Hogan. **Description:** Future of set-top boxes, particularly the digital video recorders is promising. TiVo HD, for example, already receives content from Websites, while companies such as Diego and Microsoft are soon to release similar devices. The potential applications of television and computer convergence are provided.

41112 ■ *"Digital Marketing: Integrating Strategy and Tactics with Values, A Guidebook for Executives, Managers, and Students"*
Pub: Routledge
Contact: Kevin Bradley, President
E-mail: kbradley@taylorandfrancis.com
Released: October 22, 2014. **Price:** , $38.95 paperback. **Description:** Guidebook filled with information on the latest digital marketing tactics and strategic insights to help small businesses generate sustainable growth and achieve competitive advantage through digital integration. A five-step program: mindset, model, strategy, implementation, and sustainability is explained.

41113 ■ *"Digital Power Management and the PMBus"* in Canadian Electronics (Vol. 23, June-July 2008, No. 4, pp. 8)
Ed: Torbjorn Hohnberg. **Description:** PMBus is an interface that can be applied to a variety of devices including power management devices. Information on digital power management products using this interface are also provided.

41114 ■ *"The Digital Revolution is Over. Long Live the Digital Revolution!"* in Business Strategy Review (Vol. 21, Spring 2010, No. 1, pp. 74)
Pub: John Wiley & Sons Inc. Scientific, Technical, Medical, and Scholarly Div. (Wiley-Blackwell)
Contact: William J. Pesce, Manager
E-mail: wpesce@wiley.com
Ed: Gianvito Lanzolla, Jamie Anderson. **Description:** Many businesses are now involved in the digital marketplace. The authors argue that the new reality of numerous companies offering overlapping products means that it is critical for managers to understand digital convergence and to observe the imperatives for remaining competitive.

41115 ■ *"Do We Need Human Drivers?"* in Sacramento Business Journal (Vol. 31, August 29, 2014, No. 27, pp. 3)
Pub: American City Business Journals
Released: August 29, 2014. **Description:** The California Department of Motor Vehicles (DMV) issued new regulations on autonomous vehicles, effective September 16, 2014, as Google prepares to test a new generation of self-driving cars. The DMV requires test drivers to take immediate physical control of an autonomous vehicle that may involve installation of a manual override feature.

41116 ■ *"Dr. Melanie Brown"* in Women in Business (Vol. 65, Winter 2013, No. 3, pp. 40)
Pub: Women In Business
Released: Winter 2013. **Description:** Milestones in the career of Melanie Brown, PhD, are highlighted in light of her selection as the 2014 American Business Woman of American Business Women's Association

(ABWA). An ABWA member since 2007, Dr. Brown is also the Information Technology Strategic and Analytics Manager at CenterPoint Energy.

41117 ■ *"The Dominance of Doubt"* in Barron's (Vol. 89, July 13, 2009, No. 28, pp. M3)
Pub: Dow Jones & Co., Inc.
Contact: Clare Hart, President
Ed: Jay Palmer. **Description:** Five straight down days leading up to July 10, 2009 in the U.S. stock market reminds one strategist of 1982 when there was a feeling that things could never be the same again. One analyst is bullish on the stocks of Apple Inc. and sees the stocks rising to at least 180 in 12 months. The prospects of the shares of GM and Ford are also discussed.

41118 ■ *"Don't Touch My Laptop, If You Please Mr. Customs Man"* in Canadian Electronics (Vol. 23, June-July 2008, No. 4, pp. 6)
Ed: Mark Borkowski. **Description:** Canadian businessmen bringing electronic devices to the US can protect the contents of their laptops by hiding their data from US border agents. They can also choose to clean up the contents of their laptop using file erasure programs.

41119 ■ *"Dougherty: AuthenTec Embedded Security Business Building Momentum"* in Benzinga.com (March 5, 2012)
Pub: Benzinga.com
Contact: Kyle Bazzy, President
Released: March 5, 2012. **Description:** According to research conducted by Dougherty & Company, AuthenTec Inc.'s embedded security business is waiting for the fingerprint sensor businesss is completely developed.

41120 ■ *"Downturn Tests HCL's Pledge to Employees"* in Workforce Management (Vol. 88, November 16, 2009, No. 12, pp. 23)
Pub: Crain Communications Inc.
Contact: Rance E. Crain, President
Ed: Ed Frauenheim. **Description:** HCL Technologies has kept its promise to keep from laying any employees off during the recession which served as a test for the tech firm's Employee First program, which seeks to give workers greater income security as well as a stronger voice in the firm.

41121 ■ *"Drive Traffic To Your Blog"* in Women Entrepreneur (January 13, 2009)
Ed: Lesley Spencer Pyle. **Description:** Internet social networking has become a vital component to marketing one's business. Tips are provided on how to establish a blog that will attract attention to one's business and keep one's customers coming back for more.

41122 ■ *"Dropped Calls"* in Canadian Business (Vol. 80, November 5, 2007, No. 22, pp. 34)
Ed: Andrew Wahl. **Description:** Control over Canada's telecommunications market by Telus, Rogers and Bell Canada has resulted in a small number of innovations. The pricing regimes of these carriers have also stifled innovations in the telecommunications industry. The status of Canada's telecommunications industry is further analyzed.

41123 ■ *"DST Turns to Banks for Credit"* in The Business Journal-Serving Metropolitan Kansas City (Vol. 27, October 3, 2008, No. 3, pp. 1)
Pub: American City Business Journals, Inc.
Contact: Whitney Shaw, President
Ed: Rob Roberts. **Description:** Kansas City, Missouri-based DST Systems Inc., a company that provides sophisticated information processing, computer software services and business solutions, has secured a new five-year, $120 million credit facility from Enterprise Bank and Bank of the West. The deal is seen to reflect that the region and community-banking model remain stable. Comments from executives are also provided.

41124 ■ *"The Easy Route" in Entrepreneur (Vol. 36, April 2008, No. 4, pp. 60)*
Pub: Entrepreneur Press
Contact: Perlman Neil, President
Ed: Amanda C. Kooser. **Description:** Buyer's guide of wireless office routers is presented. All products included in the list use the latest draft-n technology. Price and availability of the products are provided.

41125 ■ *"eBay Introduces Open Commerce Ecosystem" in Entertainment Close-Up (October 24, 2011)*
Pub: Close-Up Media
Description: eBay's new X.commerce is an open commerce ecosystem that will arm developers and merchants with the technology tools required to keep pace with the ever-changing industry. X.commerce brings together the technology assets and developer communities of eBay, PayPal, Magento and partners to expand on eBays vision for enabling commerce.

41126 ■ *"Economy: The Case for a Bright Future" in Canadian Business (Vol. 83, July 20, 2010, No. 11-12, pp. 58)*
Pub: Rogers Media Inc.
Contact: Tony Viner, President
Ed: Andrew Potter. **Description:** Writer Matt Ridley argues that trade is the determinant of development and that it is the reason why humans got rich. Ridley believes that the important innovations are often low-tech and is often processes rather than products.

41127 ■ *Electronic Commerce*
Pub: Course Technology
Contact: Manuel Guzman, President (Acting)
Ed: Gary P. Schneider, Bryant Chrzan, Charles McCormick. **Released:** May 01, 2010. **Price:** $149.99. **Description:** E-commerce can open the door to more opportunities than ever before for small business. Packed with real-world examples and cases, the book delivers comprehensive coverage of emerging online technologies and trends and their influence on the electronic marketplace. It details how the landscape of online commerce is evolving, reflecting changes in the economy and how business and society are responding to those changes. Balancing technological issues with the strategic business aspects of successful e-commerce, the new edition includes expanded coverage of international issues, social networking, mobile commerce, Web 2.0 technologies, and updates on spam, phishing, and identity theft. **Availability:** Print.

41128 ■ *"Electronics Assembly" in Canadian Electronics (Vol. 23, February 2008, No. 1, pp. 12)*
Description: I&J Fisnar Inc. has launched a new system of bench top dispensing robots while Vitronics Soltec and KIC have introduced a new reflow soldering machine. Teknek, on the other hand, has announced a new product, called the CM10, which an be used in cleaning large format substrates. Other new products and their description are presented.

41129 ■ *"Elemental Nabs $5.5 Million" in The Business Journal-Portland (Vol. 25, July 18, 2008, No. 19, pp. 1)*
Pub: American City Business Journals, Inc.
Contact: Whitney Shaw, President
Ed: Aliza Earnshaw. **Description:** Elemental Technologies Inc., a Portland, Oregon-based software company got $5.5 million in new funding, bringing its total invested capital to $7.1 million in nine months since October 2008. The company plans to launch Badaboom, software for converting video into various formats, later in 2008.

41130 ■ *Elsewhere, U.S.A.: How We Got From the Company Man, Family Dinners, and the Affluent Society to the Home Office, Blackberry Moms, and Economic Anxiety*
Pub: Pantheon Books Inc.
Contact: Dan Frank, Director
Ed: Dalton Conley. **Released:** 2009. **Description:** The alienation of the working middle class in America and the downturned economy is examined. **Availability:** E-book; Print.

41131 ■ *"Emerging Tech Fund Strong in 2009" in Austin Business JournalInc. (Vol. 29, December 25, 2009, No. 42, pp. 1)*
Pub: American City Business Journals
Ed: Christopher Calnan. **Description:** Texas' Emerging Technology Fund (ETF) has seen an increase in applications from the state's technology companies in 2009. ETF received 87 applications in 2009 from Central Texas companies versus 50 during 2008 while $10.5 million was given to seven Texas companies compared with $10.6 million to ten companies in 2008.

41132 ■ *"The End of RIM" in Canadian Business (Vol. 85, August 13, 2012, No. 13, pp. 22)*
Pub: George Media Inc.
Ed: Joe Castaldo. **Released:** August 13, 2012. **Description:** The potential implications of the collapse of Research in Motion (RIM) on the Canadian technology sector are examined. The country is expected to lose its biggest training ground for technology talent without RIM, but the company's decline will not stop Canadians from trying to build and sustain multinational technolgy companies.

41133 ■ *"End of Wristband Era?' in Austin Business Journal (Vol. 34, July 25, 2014, No. 23, pp. 7)*
Pub: American City Business Journals, Inc.
Contact: Whitney Shaw, President
Released: July 25, 2014. **Description:** Front Gate Tickets plans to unveil RFID radio chip technology at Chicago's Lollapalooza festival. This technology will be incorporated into wristbands and allow the patrons to make purchases by swiping them instead of using cash or cards. Front Gate Tickets president, Maura Gibson, shares his views on RFID technology's implementation into Smartphone apps, next generation innovations in ticketing and future plans of the company.

41134 ■ *"Ending the Ebola Death Sentence" in Canadian Business (Vol. 83, August 17, 2010, No. 13-14, pp. 22)*
Ed: Michael McCullough. **Description:** US Army Medical Research Institute of Infectious Diseases made a $140 million agreement with Tekmira Pharmaceuticals Corporation to develop both a drug delivery system and delivery technology for curing the Ebola virus. Tekmira's delivery technology, which has been shown to halt Ebola in laboratory animals, might be the key to finding a cure.

41135 ■ *"Energy Boom Spurring Manufacturing Growth" in Pittsburgh Business Times (Vol. 33, May 2, 2014, No. 42, pp. 7)*
Pub: American City Business Journals
Released: May 2, 2014. **Description:** The manufacturing and energy technology sectors both showed strong growth, according to the Pittsburgh Technology Council in Pennsylvania. Data shows that the sectors added about 7,000 jobs as a result of the growth in the Marcellus Shale from 2010 to 2012.

41136 ■ *"Engineering Services Supplier Launches 'Robotic Renaissance" in Modern Machine Shop (Vol. 84, September 2011, No. 4, pp. 46)*
Pub: Gardner Business Media, Inc.
Contact: Richard G. Kline, President
E-mail: rkline@gardnerweb.com
Description: Profile of Applied Manufacturing Technologies (AMT) new hiring initiative that supports continuing growth in the robotics industry. AMT is located in Orion, Michigan and supplies factory automation design, engineering and process consulting services.

41137 ■ *Entrepreneurial Finance: A Casebook*
Pub: John Wiley & Sons Inc.
Contact: Stephen M. Smith, President
Ed: Paul A. Gompers, William Sahlman. **Released:** December 2001. **Price:** $142.95, paperback. **Description:** Investment analysis, entrepreneurial financing, harvesting, and renewal in the entrepreneurial firm are among the topics discussed. **Availability:** Print.

41138 ■ *Entrepreneurial Strategies: New Technologies and Emerging Markets*
Pub: Blackwell Publishing Inc.
Contact: Gordon Tibbitts, III, President
Released: August 2006. **Price:** $100; $80.99. **Description:** Ideas to help a small business expand into emerging market economies (EMEs) are discussed. Despite the high failure rate, this book helps a small firm develop a successful plan. **Availability:** PrintE-book.

41139 ■ *Entrepreneurship and Technology Policy*
Pub: Edward Elgar Publishing Inc.
Contact: Richard Henning, Vice President
E-mail: kwight@e-elgar.com
Released: 2006. **Price:** £108. **Description:** Journal articles focusing how and the ways small businesses' technical contributions are affecting business. The book is divided into four parts: Government's Direct Support of R&D, Government's Leveraging of R&D, Government's Infrastructure Policies; and Knowledge Flows from Universities and Laboratories. **Availability:** Print.

41140 ■ *"EOTech Product Improves Holographic Gun Sights" in Crain's Detroit Business (Vol. 24, February 4, 2008, No. 5, pp. 9)*
Pub: Crain Communications Inc. - Detroit
Contact: Keith Crain, Chairman
Ed: Chad Halcom. **Description:** L-3 Communications EOTech Inc. procured new business contracts to fulfill military and law enforcement's demand for improved holographic sites used on handheld weapons.

41141 ■ *"Ethics and the End of Life" in Crain's Chicago Business (Vol. 34, October 24, 2011, No. 42, pp. 31)*
Pub: Crain Communications Inc.
Contact: Todd Johnson, Publisher
Ed: Lisa Bertagnoli. **Description:** Technology has enabled doctors to provide more and better methods for helping patients, however end of life issues faced by medical ethicists are discussed.

41142 ■ *"Etiquette, Common Sense Often Lag Behind Smarter Devices" in Crain's Cleveland Business (Vol. 28, October 22, 2007, No. 42, pp. 21)*
Pub: Crain Communications Inc.
Ed: Chrissy Kadleck. **Description:** Discusses the importance of good etiquette in regards to electronic communication both within as well as outside the business world.

41143 ■ *"The Evolution of the Mobile Entrepreneur" in Entrepreneur (Vol. 37, August 2009, No. 8, pp. 31)*
Pub: Entrepreneur Press
Contact: Perlman Neil, President
Ed: Dan O'Shea. **Description:** Covers the timeline of important events that led to the mobile businessperson today; includes the first cell phone call made by Martin Cooper in 1973 and the invention of Apple and the Newton in 1989. The first BlackBerry appeared in 1999 and the iPod was launched in 2001.

41144 ■ *"Executive Decision: How to Plug in to the Wireless Revolution" in Globe & Mail (March 11, 2006, pp. B3)*
Ed: Catherine McLean. **Description:** The plans of president David Dobbin of Toronto Hydro Telecom Inc., to establish WiFi service, are presented.

41145 ■ *"Executive Decision: XM Mulls Betting the Bank in Competitive Game of Subscriber Growth" in Globe & Mail (March 18, 2006, pp. B3)*
Ed: Grant Robertson. **Description:** Canadian Satellite Radio Inc., XM Canada, president and Chief Operating Officer Stephen Tapp feel that establishing a profile in satellite radio to attract subscribers is a very big challenge. His views on the Canadian radio market are detailed.

41146 ■ *"Experts Take the Temp of Obama Plan" in The Business Journal-Serving Metropolitan Kansas City (Vol. 27, November 14, 2008, No. 10)*
Pub: American City Business Journals, Inc.
Contact: Whitney Shaw, President
Ed: Rob Roberts. **Description:** Kansas City, Missouri-based employee benefits experts say president-elect Barack Obama's health care reform plan is on track. Insurance for children and capitalization for health information technology are seen as priority areas. The plan is aimed at reducing the number of uninsured people in the United States.

41147 ■ *"F-Secure Mobile Security for Business V5" in SC Magazine (Vol. 20, August 2009, No. 8, pp. 55)*
Pub: Haymarket Media, Inc.
Description: Review of F-Secure's Mobile Security for Business v5 which offers protection for business smartphones that can be centralized for protection monitoring by IT administrators.

41148 ■ *"Facebook, Adobe, Kenshoo, Outright and Cignex Datamatics Sign On to X.commerce" in Entertainment Close-Up (October 24, 2011)*
Pub: Close-Up Media
Description: Facebook, Adobe, Kenshoo, Outright and Cignex Datamatics have all partnered with X.commerce's ecosystem, where developers build and merchants can come to shop for new technologies and services.

41149 ■ *"Far Out: Satellite Radio Finds New Way to Tally Listeners" in Globe & Mail (March 14, 2007, pp. B14)*
Ed: Grant Robertson. **Description:** The marketing strategy adopted by satellite radio broadcasting firm XM Satellite Radio Inc. in Canada for increasing its subscriber based is discussed.

41150 ■ *"Fast Revival Unlikely For Indian 'Net Stocks" in Barron's (Vol. 88, July 7, 2008, No. 27, pp. 12)*
Pub: Dow Jones & Co., Inc.
Contact: Clare Hart, President
Ed: Leslie P. Norton. **Description:** Shares of Indian Internet companies Rediff.com and Sify are not likely to stage a rebound due to weak financial results. Rediff.com shares have declined 39.2 percent in 2008, while Sify shares are down 35.8 percent.

41151 ■ *"Federal Fund Valuable Tool For Small-Biz Innovators" in Crain's Detroit Business (Vol. 24, September 29, 2008, No. 39, pp. 42)*
Pub: Crain Communications Inc.
Contact: Rance E. Crain, President
Ed: Nancy Kaffer. **Description:** Grants from the Small Business Innovation Research Program, or SBIR grants, are federal funds that are set aside for 11 federal agencies to allocate to tech-oriented small-business owners. Firms such as Biotechnology Business Consultants help these companies apply for SBIR grants.

41152 ■ *"Finalist: Private Company, Less Than $100M" in Crain's Detroit Business (Vol. 25, June 22, 2009, No. 25)*
Pub: Crain Communications Inc. - Detroit
Contact: Keith Crain, Chairman
Ed: Nancy Kaffer. **Description:** Profile of W3R Consulting and CFO Patrick Tomina. The company offers information technology consulting. Tomina discusses the company's 505 strategy: to grow its annual revenue to $50 million in five years.

41153 ■ *"Firm Raises City's Largest VC Fund In 3 Years" in Dallas Business Journal (Vol. 35, July 20, 2012, No. 45, pp. 1)*
Pub: American City Business Journal
Ed: Jeff Bounds. **Description:** Trailblazer Capital has raised $25 million in commitments for its second fund, the largest fund raised by a Dallas-Fort Worth Metropolitan Area-based ventury company since at least 2009. VC funding has been uncommon in the area since the technology and telecom bubble burst in 2000 and 2001. Insights into Trailblazer's approach to investing is provided.

41154 ■ *"First Impressions of Robotic Farming Systems" in Farm Industry News (September 30, 2011)*
Pub: Penton Business Media Inc.
Contact: David Kieselstein, Chief Executive Officer
Ed: Jodie Wehrspann. **Description:** Farm Science Review featured tillage tools and land rollers, including John Deere's GPS system where a cart tractor is automatically controlled as well as a new line of Kinze's carts and a video of their robotic system for a driver-less cart tractor.

41155 ■ *"FIS-Metavante Deal Paying Off for Many" in Business Journal-Milwaukee (Vol. 28, December 17, 2010, No. 11, pp. A1)*
Pub: Milwaukee Business Journal
Ed: Rich Kirchen. **Description:** Jacksonville, Florida-based Fidelity National Information Services Inc., also known as FIS, has remained committed to Milwaukee, Wisconsin more than a year after purchasing Metavante Technologies Inc. FIS has transferred several operations into Metropolitan Milwaukee and has continued its contribution to charitable organizations in the area.

41156 ■ *"Five Things: For Photo Fun" in Hawaii Business (Vol. 53, October 2007, No. 4, pp. 20)*
Pub: PacificBasin Communications
Ed: Cathy S. Cruz-George. **Description:** Featured is a buyers guide of products used for capturing or displaying digital photos; products featured include the Digital Photo Wallet and Light Affection.

41157 ■ *"For Apple, It's Showtime Again" in Barron's (Vol. 90, August 30, 2010, No. 35, pp. 29)*
Pub: Barron's Editorial & Corporate Headquarters
Ed: Eric J. Savitz. **Description:** Speculations on what Apple Inc. will unveil at its product launch event are presented. These products include a possible new iPhone Nano, a new update to its Apple TV, and possibly a deal with the Beatles to distribute their songs over iTunes.

41158 ■ *"Forsys Metals Corporation Goes "Live" With Q4's On-Demand Disclosure Management Software" in Canadian Corporate News (May 16, 2007)*
Description: Forsys Metals Corp. selected Q4 Web Systems to automate its corporate website disclosure with Q4's software platform which also automates and simplifies many of the administrative tasks that Forsys was doing manually, allowing them to focus their internal resources on the business.

41159 ■ *"The Fort" in Hawaii Business (Vol. 53, November 2007, No. 5, pp. 19)*
Ed: Jason Ubay. **Description:** DRFortress' flagship data center The Fort located at Honolulu's Airport Industrial Park provides companies a place to store their servers in an ultra-secure environment. Anything stored in here that requires power has a back up and in case of an outage generators can supply power up to 80 hrs. The Fort caters to major carriers and Internet service providers.

41160 ■ *Founders at Work: Stories of Startups' Early Days*
Pub: Apress L.P.
Contact: Dominic Shakeshaft, Director
E-mail: dominic.shakeshaft@apress.com
Ed: Jessica Livingston. **Released:** September 18, 2008. **Price:** $17.99; $12.99. **Description:** Through interviews with founders of companies such as Apple, Flickr and PayPal, the book shows the qualities required to be a successful entrepreneur. **Availability:** PrintE-book.

41161 ■ *"Free Your Mind" in Entrepreneur (Vol. 37, October 2009, No. 10, pp. 24)*
Pub: Entrepreneur Press
Contact: Perlman Neil, President
Description: Writer Chris Anderson believes that firms in the digital age should allow products and services to initially be sold for free. These companies could then charge for premium versions of these products and services after the free versions have gained attention.

41162 ■ *"Freeing the Wheels of Commerce" in Hispanic Business (July-August 2007, pp. 50, 52, 54)*
Pub: Hispanic Business Inc.
Contact: Jesus Chavarria, President
Ed: Keith Rosenblum. **Description:** SecureOrigins, a border-based partnership with high-tech innovators is working to move goods faster, more efficiently, and securely.

41163 ■ *"'Frozen' Assets: Refrigeration Goes High Tech as Hussmann Invests $7 Million in Global Hub" in St. Louis Business Journal (Vol. 33, September 21, 2012, No. 4, pp. 1)*
Pub: American City Business Journal
Description: Hussmann Corporation is spending $7 million to create a high-tech innovation and clients collaboration center that will be called Global Hub, a venue for grocery food retailers, industry trend setters and through leaders. The company is also focusing on tapping the potential of convenience marts and dollar-store retailers.

41164 ■ *"Full-Court Press for Apple" in Barron's (Vol. 88, March 24, 2008, No. 12, pp. 47)*
Pub: Dow Jones & Co., Inc.
Contact: Clare Hart, President
Ed: Mark Veverka. **Description:** Apple Inc. is facing more intellectual property lawsuits in 2008, with 30 patent lawsuits filed compared to 15 in 2007 and nine in 2006. The lawsuits, which involve products such as the iPod and the iPhone, present some concern for Apple's shareholders.

41165 ■ *"Funbrain Launches Preschool Content" in Marketing to Women (Vol. 21, March 2008, No. 3, pp. 3)*
Description: Funbrain.com launches The Moms and Kids Playground, a section of the website devoted to activities and games for moms and kids aged 2 to 6; content aims at building early computer skills and to teach basic concepts such as counting and colors.

41166 ■ *"Funders Fuel Explosion of Biotech Activity" in Puget Sound Business Journal (Vol. 35, July 11, 2014, No. 12, pp. 3A)*
Pub: American City Business Journals
Released: July 11, 2014. **Description:** Washington's life sciences industry is experiencing problems due to a lack of support from state lawmakers, but the industry is receiving capital through initial public offerings, partnerships and venture equity. Joel Marcus of Alexandria Real Estate Equities claims that capital flows are at their highest levels since the dot-com bubble.

41167 ■ *"Funds "Friend" Facebook" in Barron's (Vol. 89, July 27, 2009, No. 30, pp. 30)*
Pub: Dow Jones & Co., Inc.
Contact: Clare Hart, President
Ed: Leslie P. Norton. **Description:** Mutual-fund companies are the latest entrants to the 'social media' space and several companies have already set up Facebook and Twitter pages. The use of this technology pose special challenges for compliance and regulators especially since the Financial Industry Regulatory Authority reminds companies that advertising, sales and literature are governed by regulations.

41168 ■ *"The Future of Work" in Black Enterprise (Vol. 41, August 2010, No. 1, pp. 65)*
Pub: Earl G. Graves Publishing Co. Inc.
Contact: Earl G. Graves, Jr., President
Ed: Annya M. Lott. **Description:** Technology, globalization, and outsourcing will continue to shape the future of work. Social media is a means for small companies to market goods and services.

41169 ■ *"The Future of Work" in Business Strategy Review (Vol. 21, Autumn 2010, No. 3, pp. 16)*
Pub: Blackwell Publishers Ltd.
Ed: Lynda Gratton. **Description:** Work is universal. But how, why, where and when we work has never been so open to individual interpretation. The certainties of the past have been replaced by ambiguity, questions and the steady hum of technology. Now, in a groundbreaking research project covering 21 global companies and more than 200 executives, the author is making sense of the future of work.

41170 ■ *"The Future of Work" in Business Strategy Review (Vol. 21, Autumn 2010, No. 3, pp. 16)*
Pub: John Wiley & Sons Inc. Scientific, Technical, Medical, and Scholarly Div. (Wiley-Blackwell)
Contact: William J. Pesce, Manager
E-mail: wpesce@wiley.com
Ed: Lynda Gratton. **Description:** Work is universal. Buy, how, why, where and when we work has never been so open to individual interpretation. The certainties of the past have been replaced by ambiguity, questions and the steady hum of technology. Research covering 21 global companies and more than 200 executives covers the future of work.

41171 ■ *"Gadget Makers Aim for New Chapter in Reading" in Crain's Cleveland Business (Vol. 28, October 22, 2007, No. 42, pp. 20)*
Pub: Crain Communications Inc.
Ed: Jennifer McKevitt. **Description:** Although e-books and e-audiobooks are becoming more popular, e-readers, devices that display digital books, still haven't caught on with the public. Experts feel that consumers, many of whom have to look at a computer screen all day for work, still like the feel of a real book in their hands.

41172 ■ *"Galvanizing the Scientific Community" in Information Today (Vol. 26, February 2009, No. 2, pp. 20)*
Pub: Information Today, Inc.
Contact: Thomas H. Hogan, President
E-mail: ctuthill@infotoday.com
Ed: Barbara Brynko. **Description:** Profile of John Haynes, newly appointed vice president of publishing for the American Institute of Physics; the Institute consists of ten organizations specializing in STM publishing as well as providing publishing services for over 170 science and engineering journals.

41173 ■ *"Game On" in Canadian Business (Vol. 80, February 12, 2007, No. 4, pp. 15)*
Ed: Calvin Leung. **Description:** The plan of president of TransGaming Vikas Gupta to create innovative software programs for games that can be played in different operating systems is discussed.

41174 ■ *"Game On! African Americans Get a Shot at $17.9 Billion Video Game Industry" in Black Enterprise (Vol. 38, July 2008, No. 12, pp. 56)*
Pub: Earl G. Graves Publishing Co. Inc.
Contact: Earl G. Graves, Jr., President
Ed: Carolyn M. Brown. **Description:** Despite the economic crisis, consumers are still purchasing the hottest video games and hardware. Tips for African American developers who want to become a part of this industry that lacks content targeting this demographic are offered.

41175 ■ *"Game Plan" in Canadian Business (Vol. 79, September 11, 2006, No. 18, pp. 50)*
Pub: Rogers Media Inc.
Contact: Tony Viner, President
Ed: Joe Castaldo. **Description:** Strategies adopted by gaming companies to revitalize their business and give a stimulus to their falling resources are presented.

41176 ■ *"gdgt: The New Online Home for Gadget Fans" in Hispanic Business (July-August 2009, pp. 15)*
Pub: Hispanic Business Inc.
Contact: Jesus Chavarria, President
Ed: Jeremy Nisen. **Description:** Profile of the new online Website for gadget lovers. The site combines a leek interface, gadget database, and social networking-type features which highlights devices for the consumer.

41177 ■ *"GeckoSystems Reduces Sensor Fusion Costs Due to Elder Care Robot Trials" in Marketwired (December 14, 2010)*
Pub: COMTEX
Contact: Chip Brian, President
Description: GeckoSystems International Corporation has been able to reduce the cost of its sensor fusion system while maintaining reliability and performance. The firm's ongoing first in-home elder care robot trials have sparked interest regarding its business model, technologies available for licensing, and joint domestic and international ventures.

41178 ■ *"The Genius Below the Surface" in Canadian Business (Vol. 85, August 13, 2012, No. 13, pp. 15)*
Pub: George Media Inc.
Ed: Navneet Alang. **Released:** August 13, 2012. **Description:** The launch of the Surface Windows 8 Tablet enables Microsoft to achieve two significant goals: to encourage competition from partners like HP and Dell and for Surface to serve as a proving ground for the software company's stake in Windows 8. Microsoft's move to control the hardware, software, and applications market promotes new competitiveness against Apple.

41179 ■ *"Gennum: Being Big By Design" in Canadian Business (Vol. 82, April 27, 2009, No. 7, pp. 39)*
Pub: Rogers Media Inc.
Contact: Tony Viner, President
Ed: Andrew Wahl. **Description:** Gennum expects that its planned acquisition of Tundra Semiconductor will expand its market presence and leverage its research and development better than working alone. The proposed friendly acquisition could challenge Zarlink Semiconductor as the largest Canadian semiconductor firm in terms of revenue. The merger could expand Gennum's addressable market to about $2 billion.

41180 ■ *"Genzyme: Underrated Oversold" in Barron's (Vol. 88, March 24, 2008, No. 12, pp. 58)*
Ed: Johanna Bennett. **Description:** Shares of biotechnology company Genzyme appear oversold and underrated at their $71.86 level. The company's finances are on a solid foundation, with revenues over $3.8 billion in 2007 and forecasts of $4.5-4.7 billion in revenue for 2008.

41181 ■ *The Geography of Small Firm Innovation*
Pub: Springer-Verlag New York Inc.
Contact: Ruediger Gebauer, President
Ed: Grant Black. **Released:** January 2005. **Price:** $179; $139. **Description:** Concentration of high-tech innovation across metropolitan areas in the U.S. during the 1990s and the role geography plays in innovation. **Availability:** PrintE-book.

41182 ■ *"Get Online or Be Left Behind" in Women In Business (Vol. 61, August-September 2009, No. 4, pp. 33)*
Pub: American Business Women's Association
Contact: Lorie Burch, President
Ed: Diane Stafford. **Description:** Technology's significance for the connectivity purposes among business people is discussed. Details on the use of wireless tools and online social media to boost technology IQ are presented.

41183 ■ *"Get Paid and Get Moving" in Entrepreneur (Vol. 37, October 2009, No. 10, pp. 38)*
Description: GoPayments application from Intuit allows mobile telephones to process payments like credit card terminals. The application costs $19.95 a month and can be used on the Internet browsers of mobile telephones.

41184 ■ *"Get Personal" in Entrepreneur (Vol. 36, April 2008, No. 4)*
Pub: Entrepreneur Press
Contact: Perlman Neil, President
Ed: Romanus Wolter. **Description:** Customers appreciate personal contact, and communicating with them can help business owners' customer relations. Some ways on how to keep a personal touch with customers and improve business dealings include blending technology with personal interaction and knowing what the customers want. Other tips are provided.

41185 ■ *"Getting a Grip on the Saddle: Chasms or Cycles?" in Journal of Marketing (Vol. 75, July 2011, No. 4, pp. 21)*
Pub: American Marketing Association
Contact: Lucille Pointer, President
Ed: Deepa Chandrasekaran, Gerald J. Tellis. **Description:** A study of the saddle's generality across products and countries is presented. The saddle is fairly pervasive based on empirical analysis of historical sales data from ten products across 19 countries. The results indicate chasms and technological cycles for information/entertainment products while business cycles and technological cycles affect kitchen/laundry products.

41186 ■ *"Giants Now Admit They Roam Planet Earth; Time To Buy?" in Barron's (Vol. 88, March 31, 2008, No. 13, pp. 39)*
Pub: Dow Jones & Co., Inc.
Contact: Clare Hart, President
Ed: Eric J. Savitz. **Description:** Oracle's third-quarter results showed that top-line growth fell short of expectations but the company is expected to fare better than most applications companies in the downturn. Google had a flat growth in the number of people who click their online ads. The time for investors in the tech sector with a long-term horizon has arrived.

41187 ■ *"The Globe: Singapore Airlines' Balancing Act" in Harvard Business Review (Vol. 88, July-August 2010, No. 7-8, pp. 145)*
Pub: Harvard Business School Publishing
Ed: Loizos Heracleous, Jochen Wirtz. **Description:** Singapore Airlines is used as an illustration of organizational effectiveness. The article includes the firm's 4-3-3 rule of spending, its promotion of centralized as well as decentralized innovation, use of technology, and strategic planning.

41188 ■ *"Go Beyond Local Search With Hyper-Local" in Women Entrepreneur (October 30, 2008)*
Ed: Lena West. **Description:** According to Forrester Research, as much as $500 billion in local spending in 2007 was influenced by the Internet and industry analysts report that consumers spend approximately 80 percent of their income within 50 miles of their home. Discussion of ways in which to capitalize on the hyper-local trend that is being driven by greater Internet connectivity and use of the web to find information is provided.

41189 ■ *"Google Edges into Wireless E-Mail" in Globe & Mail (February 19, 2007, pp. B5)*
Ed: Simon Avery. **Description:** Google Inc. has introduced a free mobile e-mail service in Canada. The mobile users can read, send, and search messages using the new software.

41190 ■ *"Google, MySpace Deal Hits Snag" in Globe & Mail (February 7, 2007, pp. B11)*
Ed: Julia Angwin; Kevin J. Delaney. **Description:** MySpace's intention to partner with eBay which is delaying the finalization of its $900 million online advertising deal signed with Google Inc. is discussed.

41191 ■ *"Google Places a Call to Bargain Hunters" in Advertising Age (Vol. 79, September 29, 2008, No. 36, pp. 13)*
Pub: Crain Communications Inc.
Contact: Rance Crain, President
Ed: Abbey Klaassen. **Description:** Google highlighted application developers who have created tools for its Android mobile phone in the device's unveiling; applications such as ShopSavvy and CompareEvery-

where help shoppers to find bargains by allowing them to compare prices in their local areas and across the web.

41192 ■ The Google Story: Inside the Hottest Business, Media, and Technology Success of Our Time
Pub: Random Housing Publishing Group
Ed: David A. Vise, Mark Malseed. **Released:** September 23, 2008. **Price:** $16. **Availability:** Print.

41193 ■ "Google's Next Stop: Below 350?" in Barron's (Vol. 88, March 10, 2008, No. 10, pp. 17)
Pub: Dow Jones & Co., Inc.
Contact: Clare Hart, President
Ed: Jacqueline Doherty. **Description:** Share prices of Google Inc. are expected to drop from their level of $433 each to below $350 per share. The company is expected to miss its earnings forecast for the first quarter of 2008, and its continued aggressive spending on non-core areas will eventually bring down earnings.

41194 ■ "Grant Could Help Schools Harness Wind" in Dallas Business Journal (Vol. 37, April 11, 2014, No. 31, pp. 8)
Pub: American City Business Journals
Released: April 11, 2014. **Description:** Five universities led by Texas A&M have received a $2.2 million grant from the Texas Emerging Technologies Fund for use in wind technology research. The research will focus on turbines that feature bigger blades to capture more wind. Technology developed by the universities will eventually be handed to the state.

41195 ■ "Gray Moves to Close Two Curious Tech Incentive Loopholes" in Washington Business Journal (Vol. 33, May 23, 2014, No. 5, pp. 12)
Pub: American City Business Journals
Released: May 23, 2014. **Description:** District of Columbia Mayor Vincent Gray, has included in his budge recommendations small changes to definitions of a 'Qualified High Technology Company'. The proposals would expand the excluded industries into an online or brick-and-mortar retail store and a construction company from eligibility to claim the government tech incentives. The current incentive loopholes are outlined.

41196 ■ "Green Energy Exec Hits State Policy" in Boston Business Journal (Vol. 30, December 3, 2010, No. 45, pp. 1)
Pub: Boston Business Journal
Ed: Kyle Alspach. **Description:** American Superconductor Corporation President Dan McGahn believes that the state government of Massachusetts is not proactive enough to develop the state into a manufacturing hub for wind power technology. McGahn believes that while Governor Deval Patrick campaigned for wind turbines in the state, his administration does not have the focus required to build the turbines in the state.

41197 ■ "Greg Lueck: Glass Blowing" in Inc. (Volume 32, December 2010, No. 10, pp. 36)
Pub: Inc. Magazine
Ed: April Joyner. **Description:** Profile of Greg Lueck, partner and COO of Centerstance, a tech consulting firm in Portland, Oregon. Lueck opened Firehouse Glass, a studio that provides workspace and equipment for glass blowers. He says glass blowing serves as a welcome counterbalance to the cerebral work he does at the office.

41198 ■ Groundswell: Winning in a World Transformed by Social Technologies
Pub: Harvard Business Review Press
Contact: Peter E. Walsh, Director
Ed: Charlene Li, Josh Bernoff. **Released:** June 09, 2011. **Price:** $14.95. **Description:** Individuals are using online social technologies such as blogs, social networking sites, YouTube, and podcasts to discuss products and companies, write their own news, and find their own deals. When consumers you've never met are rating your company's products in public forums with which you have no experience or influ-

ence, your company is vulnerable. This book teaches the tools and data necessary to turn this treat into an opportunity. **Availability:** Print; E-book.

41199 ■ Grown Up Digital: How the Net Generation Is Changing Your World
Pub: The McGraw-Hill Companies
Ed: Don Tapscott. **Released:** October 24, 2008. **Price:** $27.95. **Description:** As baby boomers retire, business needs to understand what makes the Internet work for business.

41200 ■ "Happy New Year, Celestica?" in Canadian Business (Vol. 80, January 15, 2007, No. 2, pp. 25)
Ed: Andrew Wahl. **Description:** Speculations on the performance of the electronics manufacturing company Celestica Inc. in 2007, which has been labelled as a 'sick' company in recent times, are presented.

41201 ■ "The Hard Thing About Hard Things: Building a Business When There Are No Easy Answers"
Pub: HarperCollins Publishers
Released: March 4, 2014. **Price:** , $29.99. **Description:** Cofounder of Andreessen Horowitz and well-respected Silicon Valley entrepreneur, offers advice for building and running a startup small business. Horowitz analyzes issues confronting leaders daily and shares insights he gained from managing, selling, buying investing in, and supervising technology firms.

41202 ■ "Hardware Stores Get Some Love" in Business Journal Portland (Vol. 31, May 9, 2014, No. 10, pp. 8)
Pub: American City Business Journals
Released: May 9, 2014. **Description:** Contract manufacturer Axiom Electronics launched an incubator called Electr0n. Axiom believes the incubator will help deliver innovation and insight. Axiom president, Robert Toppel, thinks that open hardware is coming and it will affect the company and its customers. Axiom delivers mission critical flight hardware, spacecraft components, medical products, test systems, and other high performance systems.

41203 ■ "Harlequin Leads the Way" in Marketing to Women (Vol. 22, July 2009, No. 7, pp. 1)
Pub: EPM Communications Inc.
Contact: Ira Mayer, President
E-mail: imayer@epmcom.com
Description: Although the publishing industry has been slow to embrace new media options, the Internet is now a primary source for reaching women readers. Harlequin has been eager to court their female consumers over the Internet and often uses women bloggers in their campaigns strategies.

41204 ■ "Has Microsoft Found a Way to Get at Yahoo?" in Advertising Age (Vol. 79, July 7, 2008, No. 26, pp. 4)
Pub: Crain Communications Inc.
Contact: Rance Crain, President
Ed: Abbey Klaassen. **Description:** Microsoft's attempt to acquire Yahoo's search business is discussed as is Yahoo's plans for the future at a time when the company's shares have fallen dangerously low.

41205 ■ "HBMG Targets Federal Contracts from Under Raytheon's Wing" in Austin Business JournalInc. (Vol. 29, January 15, 2010, No. 45, pp. 1)
Pub: American City Business Journals
Ed: Christopher Calnan. **Description:** Information Technology firm HBMG Inc. of Austin Texas has been chosen by Massachusetts-based subcontractor Raytheon Company and the US Department of Defense (DoD) to join DoD's Mentor-Protege program. HBMG will be allowed to vie for government contracts through the said program, potentially increasing business with the DoD by at least 700 percent.

41206 ■ "Health Care Leads Sectors Attracting Capital; Health Care, Media, and Food Were Key Industries Gaining Investors in the 2007 U.S. Hispanic Market" in Hispanic

Business (Vol. 30, March 2008, No. 3, pp. 14)
Pub: Hispanic Business Inc.
Contact: Jesus Chavarria, President
Ed: Scott Williams. **Description:** Discusses the capital gains of Hispanic-owned companies and other Hispanic leaders in the investment and retail fields in the year 2007. Sectors like health care, media, food and technology saw a healthy flow of capital due to successful mergers, acquisitions and increased private equity investments.

41207 ■ "HealthTronics Eager to Buy" in Austin Business JournalInc. (Vol. 28, September 12, 2008, No. 26, pp. 1)
Pub: American City Business Journals
Ed: Laura Hipp. **Description:** HealthTronics Inc., an Austin, Texas urology equipment company has repeated its offer to buy Endocare Inc., an Irvine, California tumor technology firm for $26.9 million. The proposal has been revised to allow Endocare shareholders to choose between HealthTronics cash or shares. Endocare has not commented on the offer.

41208 ■ High-Tech Entrepreneurship: Managing Innovation, Variety and Uncertainty
Pub: Routledge
Contact: Kevin Bradley, President
E-mail: kbradley@taylorandfrancis.com
Ed: Michel Bernasconi, Simon Harris, Mette Moensted. **Released:** August 02, 2006. **Price:** $57.95, paperback; $190, hardback. **Description:** Profiles of successful high tech companies is included; high tech companies are driving innovation globally. **Availability:** Print.

41209 ■ "High-Tech Job-Apalooza!" in Orlando Business Journal (Vol. 26, January 15, 2010, No. 33, pp. 1)
Pub: American City Business Journals
Ed: Christopher Boyd. **Description:** Science Applications International Corporation, Saab Training USA LLC, CAE USA, and Pelliconi &C.SPA attempt to obtain $939,000 in tax incentives to generate 222 technology and defense-related jobs in Orange County, Florida. Each job will provide an average salary of $67,000. Future plans of each technology and defense firm are also presented.

41210 ■ "High-Tech Machines Show a New Age of Vending" in Wisconsin State Journal (October 14, 2011)
Pub: Wisconsin State Journal
Ed: Barry Adams. **Description:** Vending machines are looking more like an iPad than the machines of the past. These high tech machines are seeing sharp rises in use.

41211 ■ "High-Tech, Niche Options Change Sports Marketing" in Crain's Detroit Business (Vol. 24, March 17, 2008, No. 11, pp. 14)
Pub: Crain Communications Inc.
Contact: Rance E. Crain, President
Ed: Leah Boyd. **Description:** Sports advertisers have an ever-increasing menu of high-tech or niche marketing options such as interactive campaigns through cell phones and electronic banners which can span arenas.

41212 ■ "High-Tech Security Stands Guard Over Arkansas Scholarship Lottery" in Arkansas Business (Vol. 26, September 28, 2009, No. 39, pp. 1)
Pub: Arkansas Business Publishing Group
Ed: George Waldon. **Description:** Arkansas Lottery Commission was initially criticized for what was seen as a major breach in security protocol by revealing the exact location of 26 million lottery tickets during a publicity stunt in which the media was invited to the main distribution center; however, due to the high-tech security that has been implemented the tickets are worthless until their status is changed after passing through multiple security scans.

41213 ■ "His Banking Industry Software Never Caught On, so Bill Randle is Now Targeting the Health Care Market" in Inc.

(March 2008)
Pub: Mansueto Ventures L.L.C.
Contact: John Koten, Chief Executive Officer
Ed: Alex Salkever. **Description:** Profile of Bill Randle, bank executive turned entrepreneur; Randle tells how he changed his focus for his company from banking software to healthcare software. The firm employs ten people who secure online billing and recordkeeping systems for hospitals and insurers. Randle discusses critical decisions that will impact his firm in the coming year. Three experts offer advice.

41214 ■ *"Home Security In a Smartphone"* in Denver Business Journal (Vol. 65, March 21, 2014, No. 55, pp. A12)
Pub: American City Business Journals
Released: March 21, 2014. **Description:** Denver, Colorado-based startup Rentbits developed a home automation application (app) called Remotely that allows people to lock doors, switch the lights on and off, adjust thermostat and monitor home security through a smartphone. The app was built for the security of a 40-million household rental market and for vacation rentals in the U.S.

41215 ■ *"Homing In On the Future"* in Black Enterprise (Vol. 38, October 1, 2007, No. 3, pp. 61)
Pub: Earl G. Graves Publishing Co. Inc.
Contact: Earl G. Graves, Jr., President
Ed: Sean Drakes. **Description:** More and more people are wanting new homes wired automated systems that integrate multiple home devices such as computers, audio/visual entertainment, security, communications, utilities, and lighting and environmental controls.

41216 ■ *"Hope Grows for a Muscular Dystrophy Drug"* in Barron's (Vol. 92, August 25, 2012, No. 35, pp. 35)
Pub: Dow Jones & Co., Inc.
Contact: Clare Hart, President
Ed: Andrew Bary. **Description:** The stocks of biotechnology firm Sarepta Therapeutics could gain value if trials for eterpirsen, a drug being developed for Duchenne muscular dystrophy, are successful. The company's stock prices could rise from $10/share to as high as $26/share.

41217 ■ *"Horse Race: Putting the App in Apple"* in Inc. (Vol. 30, November 2008, No. 11, pp.)
Pub: Mansueto Ventures L.L.C.
Contact: John Koten, Chief Executive Officer
Ed: Nitasha Tiku. **Description:** Aftermarket companies are scrambling to develop games and widgets for Apple's iPhone. Apple launched a kit for developers interested in creating iPhone-specific software along with the App Store, and an iTunes spinoff. Profiles of various software programs that may be used on the iPhone are given.

41218 ■ *"Houston Tech Company Eyes California for HQ Move"* in Houston Business Journal (Vol. 45, July 18, 2014, No. 10, pp. 10A)
Pub: American City Business Journals
Released: July 18, 2014. **Description:** Ed Chipul, CEO of Tendenci, a longtime Houston technology company, has stated that they are looking for a headquarters move to California. The decision to move to Silicon Valley is mainly due to a lack of synergy within the venture capital community in Houston.

41219 ■ *"How to Beat Jet Lag for $550,000"* in Globe & Mail (January 3, 2006, pp. B1)
Pub: CTVglobemedia Publishing Inc.
Ed: Simon Avery. **Description:** The details on DreamWorks Animation SKG Inc., which developed videoconferencing software 'Halo' in association with Hewlett-Packard Co., are presented.

41220 ■ *"How Church Street Exchange May Bring Retail, 350 Jobs"* in Orlando Business Journal (Vol. 30, February 28, 2014, No. 36, pp. 10)
Pub: American City Business Journals
Released: February 28, 2014. **Description:** Nonprofit organization, Canvs, is finalizing a lease for 14,069 square feet of technology-focused co-working space at Church Street Exchange in downtown Orlando, Florida. Jones Lang LaSalle is negotiating for more space than the 87,000-square-foot building has that could bring 300 to 350 high-tech jobs to the area.

41221 ■ *"How Dell Will Dial for Dollars"* in Austin Business JournalInc. (Vol. 29, December 4, 2009, No. 39, pp. 1)
Pub: American City Business Journals
Ed: Christopher Calnan. **Description:** Dell Inc. revealed plans to launch a Mini3i smartphone in China which could enable revenue sharing by bundling with wireless service subscription. Dell's smartphone plan is similar to the netbook business, which Dell sold with service provided by AT&T Inc.

41222 ■ *"How Not to Build a Website"* in Women Entrepreneur (December 24, 2008)
Ed: Erica Ruback; Joanie Reisen. **Description:** Tips for producing a unique and functional Website are given as well as a number of lessons a pair of entrepreneurs learned while trying to launch their networking website, MomSpace.com.

41223 ■ *"How to Play the Tech Mergers"* in Barron's (Vol. 90, August 30, 2010, No. 35, pp. 18)
Pub: Barron's Editorial & Corporate Headquarters
Ed: Tiernan Ray. **Description:** The intense bidding by Hewlett-Packard and Dell for 3Par was foreseen in a previous Barron's cover story and 3Par's stock has nearly tripled since reported. Other possible acquisition targets in the tech industry include Brocade Communication Systems, NetApp, Xyratex, and Isilon Systems.

41224 ■ *"How Technology has Changed the Way People Lead"* in Pittsburgh Business Times (Vol. 33, April 25, 2014, No. 41, pp. 8)
Pub: American City Business Journals
Released: April 25, 2014. **Description:** Members of the Pittsburgh chapter of the Young Presidents' Organization (YPO) in Pennsylvania discuss how technology has influenced the way they lead their companies and organizations as part of a roundtable discussion on leadership. They note how technology has improved connection with employees, accessibility to clients, multitasking, among other things.

41225 ■ *"How To Fill Birmingham's Tech Talent Pool"* in Birmingham Business Journal (Vol. 31, March 7, 2014, No. 10, pp. 4)
Pub: American City Business Journals, Inc.
Contact: Whitney Shaw, President
Released: March 7, 2014. **Description:** Discussion on ways the City of Birmingham, Alabama could increase the number of technology workers in the area is presented. The sector should allow more work off-site to attract technology workers. Meanwhile, local schools have been expanding their offerings to cater to the technology sector needs.

41226 ■ *"HP Eats Into Rival Dell Sales as Profits Soar"* in Globe & Mail (February 21, 2007, pp. B15)
Ed: Connie Guglielmo. **Description:** The world's largest personal computer maker Hewlett Packard Co. has reported increased profits by 26 percent to $1.55 billion during the first quarter. The company has outpaced its competitor Dell Inc. by offering low priced personal computers during this period.

41227 ■ *"HR Tech on the Go"* in Workforce Management (Vol. 88, November 16, 2009, No. 12, pp. 1)
Pub: Crain Communications Inc.
Contact: Rance E. Crain, President
Ed: Ed Frauenheim. **Description:** Examination of the necessity of mobile access of human resources software applications that allow managers to recruit, schedule and train employees via their mobile devices; some industry leaders believe that mobile HR applications are vital while others see this new technology as hype.

41228 ■ *"HR Technology: Meetings Go Virtual"* in HRMagazine (Vol. 54, January 2009, No. 1, pp. 74)
Pub: Society for Human Resource Management
Contact: Henry G. Jackson, President
E-mail: hjackson@shrm.org
Ed: Elizabeth Agnvall. **Description:** Microsoft Office Live Meeting conferencing software allows companies to schedule meetings from various company locations, thus saving travel costs.

41229 ■ *IBM on Demand Technology for the Growing Business: How to Optimize Your Computing Environment for Today and Tomorrow*
Ed: Jim Hoskins. **Released:** June 2005. **Price:** , $29.95. **Description:** IBM is offering computer solutions to small companies entering the On Demand trend in business.

41230 ■ *"IBM's Best-Kept Secret"* in Canadian Business (Vol. 79, September 25, 2006, No. 19, pp. 19)
Ed: Andrew Wahl. **Description:** The contribution of IBM vice-president Steve Mills in company's development is discussed.

41231 ■ *"Image Consultants"* in Entrepreneur (June 2014)
Pub: Entrepreneur Media Inc.
Released: June 2014. **Description:** The ASAP54 mobile application, created by a company of the same name, uses visual recognition technology to help users determine the name of the designer or retailer of a clothing item using photographs. The company has compiled a database consisting of more than 1 million products from its retail partners. It claims an average of 5 percent commission on purchases completed through the application. Other useful wearable gadgets include Nymi, which authenticates identities based on cardiac rhythms, and Netatmo, a bracelet that measures daily sun exposure.

41232 ■ *Imagining India: The Idea of a Renewed Nation*
Pub: Dutton Children's Books
Contact: Lauri Hornik, President
Ed: Nandan Nilekani. **Released:** 2009. **Price:** $17, Paperback. **Description:** National technology leader, Nandan Nilekan warns of pitfalls, obstacles and the danger of letting down the people of India.

41233 ■ *"The Impact of Acquisitions On the Productivity of Inventors at Semiconductor Firms: A Synthesis of Knowledge-Based and Incentive-Based Perspective"* in Academy of Management Journal (Vol. 50, No. 5, October 1, 2007, pp. 1133)
Pub: Academy of Management
Contact: Ming-Jer Chen, President
Ed: Rahul Kapoor, Kwanghui Lim. **Description:** Study examined the relation between knowledge-based and incentive-based outlook in explaining the impact of acquisitions on the productivity of inventors at acquired semiconductor firms. Results showed a definite relation between the two perspectives.

41234 ■ *"Impressive Numbers: Companies Experience Substantial Increases in Dollars, Employment"* in Hispanic Business (July-August 2007)
Pub: Hispanic Business Inc.
Contact: Jesus Chavarria, President
Ed: Derek Reveron. **Description:** Profiles of five fastest growing Hispanic companies reporting increases in revenue and employment include Brightstar, distributor of wireless products; Greenway Ford Inc., a car dealership; Fred Loya Insurance, auto insurance carrier; and Group O, packaging company; and Diverse Staffing, Inc., an employment and staffing firm.

41235 ■ *"In the Bag?"* in Canadian Business (Vol. 81, March 3, 2008, No. 3, pp. 57)
Ed: Calvin Leung. **Description:** American stocks are beginning to appear cheap amidst the threat of a worldwide economic slowdown, United States economic crisis and declining stock portfolios. Investors

looking for bargain stocks should study the shares of Apple and Oshkosh Corp. Evaluation of other cheap-looking stocks such as the shares of Coach and 3M is also given.

41236 ■ "In the Fast Lane" in Chain Store Age (Vol. 85, November 2009, No. 11, pp. 44)
Pub: Lebhar-Friedman Inc.
Contact: Roger Friedman, President
Ed: Samantha Murphy. **Description:** Quick Chek, which operates some 120 convenience stores in New Jersey and southern New York, is testing a new self-checkout system in order to examine how speed affects its in-store experience.

41237 ■ "Incentives In Play for Astronautics" in Business Journal-Milwaukee (Vol. 28, November 5, 2010, No. 5, pp. A1)
Pub: Milwaukee Business Journal
Ed: Sean Ryan. **Description:** Astronautics Corporation was offered incentives by local government officials in Milwaukee, Wisconsin and by Brewery Project LLC to move into a building in The Brewery in the city. The company's officials remain indecisive over the offers and incentives.

41238 ■ Information Technology And Small Businesses: Antecedents and Consequences of Technology Adoption
Pub: Edward Elgar Publishing Inc.
Contact: Richard Henning, Vice President
E-mail: kwight@e-elgar.com
Ed: Andrea Ordanini. **Released:** 2006. **Price:** £66.60, hardback. **Description:** Issues involving information communication technology adoption among small and medium-sized firms are discussed. **Availability:** Print.

41239 ■ "Information Technology Changes Roles, Highlights Hiring Needs" in South Florida Business Journal (Vol. 34, February 14, 2014, No. 30, pp. 3)
Pub: American City Business Journals
Released: February 14, 2014. **Description:** Results of the Steven Douglas Associates survey of 218 senior and mid-level information technology executives in South Florida are presented. About 75 percent of the respondents cited cloud services, mobile technologies, big data and enterprise reporting planning as having the most profound impact on their roles. The challenges they face with the expected hiring growth are also examined.

41240 ■ Information Technology for the Small Business: How to Make IT Work For Your Company
Ed: T.J. Benoit. **Released:** June 2006. **Price:** , $17.95. **Description:** Basics of information technology to help small companies maximize benefits are covered. Topics include pitfalls to avoid, email and Internet use, data backup, recovery and overall IT organization.

41241 ■ "Ingrian and Channel Management International Sign Distribution Agreement" in Canadian Corporate News (May 16, 2007)
Description: Channel Management International (CMI), a Canadian channel management and distribution company, and Ingrian Networks, Inc., the leading provider of data privacy solutions, announced a Canadian distribution agreement to resell Ingrian encryption solutions to the Canadian market.

41242 ■ "Innovation in 3D: NextFab" in Philadelphia Business Journal (Vol. 28, January 22, 2010, No. 49, pp. 1)
Pub: American City Business Journals Inc.
Ed: Peter Key. **Description:** NextFab Studio LLC is set to offer product development services using 3D technology. The company has developed a three-dimensional printer which fabricates objects usually made of plastic.

41243 ■ Innovation And Entrepreneurship In Biotechnology: An International Perspective
Pub: Edward Elgar Publishing Inc.
Contact: Richard Henning, Vice President
E-mail: kwight@e-elgar.com
Ed: Damian Hine, John Kapeleris. **Price:** £72, hardback; £33.60, paperback. **Description:** Innova-tion processes underlying successful entrepreneurship in the biotechnology sector are explored. **Availability:** Print.

41244 ■ "Innovation & Inspiration" in Dallas Business Journal (Vol. 37, May 30, 2014, No. 38, pp. 4)
Pub: American City Business Journals
Released: May 30, 2014. **Description:** The honorees in the 2014 class of North Texas Women in Technology Awards reached the top technology positions in their companies, started their own firms and have supported other women in the industry. Some of the honorees emphasize the need for more women to enter the technology sector.

41245 ■ Innovation Nation: Canadian Leadership from Java to Jurassic Park
Pub: John Wiley & Sons Inc.
Contact: Stephen M. Smith, President
Ed: Leonard Brody, Wendy Cukier, Ken Grant, Matt Holland, Catherine Middleton, Denise Shortt. **Released:** October 2002. **Price:** $38, paperback; $24.99. **Description:** Canadian's have risen to the top of the largest technology firms, from development of the Java and the Blackberry to defining specifications for XML. **Availability:** PrintE-book.

41246 ■ "Innovation Station" in Canadian Business (Vol. 80, October 8, 2007, No. 20, pp. 42)
Ed: Andrew Wahl. **Description:** Study and teaching of entrepreneurship at the University of Waterloo is discussed. Research projects in the university are expected to be influential in Canada's economic development. In spite of the success of these studies, financing is still a problem for the university, especially in technological innovations.

41247 ■ "Innovative Trauma Care Sets Up U.S. HQ in San Antonio" in San Antonio Business Journal (Vol. 26, August 31, 2012, No. 31, pp. 1)
Pub: American City Business Journal
Description: Canadian biotech firm Innovative Trauma Care (ITC) has selected San Antonio, Texas as the location of its new US headquarters. The selection could boost the reputation of San Antonio region as a hub for medical technology and trauma-related expertise.

41248 ■ "Innovators Critical in Technical Economy" in Crain's Cleveland Business (Vol. 28, November 5, 2007, No. 44, pp. 10)
Pub: Crain Communications Inc.
Ed: Peter Rea. **Description:** Discusses the importance to attract, develop and retain talented innovators on Ohio's economy. Also breaks down the four fronts on which the international battle for talent is being waged.

41249 ■ "Inside the New Nortel" in Canadian Business (Vol. 79, November 6, 2006, No. 22, pp. 93)
Pub: Rogers Media Inc.
Contact: Tony Viner, President
Ed: Andrew Wahl. **Description:** The plans of Nortel Networks to improve its technology market by appointing new teams are analyzed.

41250 ■ "Intel Forges New Strategy With Chinese Fabrication Plant" in Globe & Mail (March 26, 2007, pp. B6)
Ed: Don Clark. **Description:** World's largest semiconductor manufacturing giant Intel Corp. is planning to construct a new chip fabrication plant in China. It will be investing an estimated $2.5 billion for this purpose.

41251 ■ "The Intel Trinity: How Robert Noyce, Gordon Moore, and Andy Grove Built the World's Most Important Company"
Pub: Harper Business
Released: July 15, 2014. **Price:** , $34.99. **Description:** A complete history of Intel Corporation, the essential company of the digital age, is presented. After over four decades Intel remains the most important company in the world, a defining company of the global digital economy. The inventors of the microprocessor that powers nearly every intelligent electronic device worldwide are profiled. These entrepreneurs made the personal computer, Internet, telecommunications, and personal electronics all possible. The challenges and successes of the company and its ability to maintain its dominance, its culture and its legacy are examined.

41252 ■ "Interactive Stores a Big Part of Borders' Turnaround Plan" in Crain's Detroit Business (Vol. 24, February 18, 2008, No. 7, pp. 4)
Pub: Crain Communications Inc. - Detroit
Contact: Keith Crain, Chairman
Ed: Nathan Skid. **Description:** Borders Group Inc. is using digital technology and interactive media as a part of the firm's turnaround plan. The digital store will allow shoppers to create CDs, download audio books, publish their own works, print photos and search family genealogy.

41253 ■ "The Internet Of You" in Canadian Business (Vol. 87, July 2014, No. 7, pp. 43)
Pub: George Media Inc.
Released: July 2014. **Description:** Wearable computers like smart watches, fitness trackers, and bracelets like Nymi are starting to break down the barrier between human beings and the digital world. The Nymi is a wrist-worn device developed by Bionym that allows the wearer to be instantly recognizable to any wireless device.

41254 ■ "Into the Groove: Fine-Tune Your Biz By Getting Into the Good Habit Groove" in Small Business Opportunities (Spring 2008)
Description: Profile of Ty Freyvogel and his consulting firm Freyvogel Communications. Freyvogel serves the telecommunications need of Fortune 500 and mid-sized businesses.

41255 ■ "Investing in the IT that Makes a Competitive Difference" in Harvard Business Review (Vol. 86, July-August 2008, No. 8, pp. 98)
Pub: Harvard Business Review Press
Contact: Peter E. Walsh, Director
Ed: Andrew McAfee, Erik Brynjolfsson. **Description:** Components of a successful information technology management strategy are examined. These techniques are broad in spectrum, produce immediate results, are consistent and precise, facilitate monitoring, and promote enforceability.

41256 ■ "Investment In Israel Is Investment in the Future of Georgia" in Atlanta Business Chronicle (May 30, 2014, pp. 22A)
Pub: American City Business Journals, Inc.
Contact: Whitney Shaw, President
Released: May 30, 2014. **Description:** Georgia Governor Nathan Deal will travel to Israel to lead an economic and trade mission and consolidate Georgia's trade ties with Israel. Israel and the State of Georgia are already collaborating in the fields of health information technology, agrotechnology, homeland security, defense, aerospace and cybersecurity, and microelectronics and nanotechnology. The proposed visit by the Governor will build on this particular partnership from which both parties will benefit.

41257 ■ "iPhone Apps Big Business" in Austin Business JournalInc. (Vol. 28, November 14, 2008, No. 35, pp. 1)
Pub: American City Business Journals
Ed: Christopher Calnan. **Description:** Members of the computer software industry in Austin, Texas have benefited from developing applications for Apple Inc.'s iPhone. Pangea Software Inc.'s revenues have grown by developing iPhone applications. Lexcycle LLC, on the other hand, has created an application that enables users to read books on the iPhone.

41258 ■ "IPO: To Go, Or Not To Go?" in San Francisco Business Times (Vol. 28, March 7, 2014, No. 33, pp. 4)
Pub: American City Business Journals
Released: March 7, 2014. **Description:** Analysts believe that funding rounds could either influence technology companies to file initial public offerings (IPOs) or move away from the public fray. However,

some observers claim that these companies needn't jump into the IPO window because of the availability of other funding.

41259 ■ "iPod Killers?" in Canadian Business (Vol. 79, November 20, 2006, No. 23, pp. 68)
Pub: Rogers Media Inc.
Contact: Tony Viner, President

Ed: Gerry Blackwell. **Description:** The features of Apple iPod that distinguishes it from other MP3 players available in the market are discussed.

41260 ■ "iSymmetry's Technological Makeover: Or, How a Tech Company Finally Grew Up and Discovered the World Wide Web" in Inc. (October 2007)
Pub: Mansueto Ventures L.L.C.
Contact: John Koten, Chief Executive Officer

Ed: Elizabeth S. Bennett. **Description:** Profile of iSymmetry, an Atlanta, Georgia-based IT recruiting firm, covering the issues the company faces keeping its technology equipment up-to-date. The firm has devised a program that will replace its old server-based software systems with on-demand software delivered via the Internet, known as software-as-a-service. Statistical information included.

41261 ■ "It's Not About the G1; Google Just Wants You to Use the Mobile Web" in Advertising Age (Vol. 79, September 29, 2008, No. 36, pp. 32)
Ed: Abbey Klaassen. **Description:** Google's Android is the first serious competitor to Apple's iPhone; the company says that its goal is to simplify the mobile market and get wireless subscribers to use the mobile Internet and purchase smartphones.

41262 ■ "Jack, Be Nimble" in Business Courier (Vol. 24, October 25, 2007, No. 28, pp. 1)
Pub: American City Business Journals, Inc.
Contact: Whitney Shaw, President

Ed: Laura Baverman. **Description:** Cincinnati Bell is losing around 47,000 phone lines a year due to the advent of wireless technology and increased competition from cable companies.

41263 ■ "Jacksonville Doing Well In Growing Economy" in Orlando Business Journal (Vol. 30, June 27, 2014, No. 53, pp. 8)
Pub: American City Business Journals

Released: June 27, 2014. **Description:** Jerry Mallot is the president of JaxUSA Partnership, the economic development arm of the Jax Chambers. According to Mallot, Northeast Florida's strongest selling points for business site or relocation there include advanced manufacturing, financial services, aviation and aerospace technology, life sciences, logistics and information technology.

41264 ■ "Java Computing: Second Cup?" in Canadian Business (Vol. 81, June 11, 2008, No. 11, pp. 50)
Pub: Rogers Media Inc.
Contact: Tony Viner, President

Ed: Calvin Leung. **Description:** Profile of James Gosling who is credited as the inventor of the Java programming language; however, the 53-year-old software developer feels ambivalent for being credited as inventor since many people contributed to the language. Netscape and Sun Microsystems incorporation of the programming language into Java is presented.

41265 ■ "The Joy of Overseas Calling" in Canadian Business (Vol. 85, August 13, 2012, No. 13, pp. 49)
Pub: George Media Inc.

Ed: Bryan Borzykowski. **Released:** August 13, 2012. **Description:** Investors should consider growth prospects, regulation and wireless penetration when investing in foreign telecommunications companies. Investment opportunities are available in Europe, Asia, and Latin America and investors should look into dividends, debt and the mix of product offerings.

41266 ■ "JumpTV to Hold Conference Call to Discuss Q1 Results and Annual General Meeting" in Canadian Corporate News (May 16, 2007)
Description: Profile of JumpTv, the world's leading broadcaster of ethnic television over the Internet, and the results of a conference that discussed their first quarter 2007 financial report as well as the company's business goals. Statistical data included.

41267 ■ "Just Following Directions" in Entrepreneur (Vol. 36, February 2008, No. 2, pp. 56)
Pub: Entrepreneur Press
Contact: Perlman Neil, President

Ed: Amanda C. Kooser. **Description:** Buyer's guide for purchasing Global Positioning System units is presented.

41268 ■ "Keeping Up With the Joneses: Outfitting Your Company With Up-To-Date Technology is Vital" in Black Enterprise (November 2007)
Ed: Sonya A. Donaldson. **Description:** Small businesses, whether home-based or not, need to keep up with new technological developments including hardware, software, and the Internet.

41269 ■ "Keeping the Vehicle On the Road -- a Survey On On-Road Lane Detection Systems" in ACM Computing Surveys (Vol. 46, Spring 2014, No. 1, pp. 2)
Pub: Association for Computing Machinery - High Plains Chapter
Contact: Stewart Jenkins, Chairman

Released: Spring 2014. **Description:** The development of wireless sensor networks, such as researchers Advanced Driver Assistance Systems (ADAS) requires the ability to analyze the road scene in the same as a human. Road scene analysis is an essential, complex, and challenging task and it consists of: road detection and obstacle detection. The detection of the road borders, the estimation of the road geometry, and the localization of the vehicle are essential tasks in this context since they are required for the lateral and longitudinal control of the vehicle. A comprehensive review of vision-based road detection systems vision in automobiles and trucks is examined.

41270 ■ "Kenyans Embrace Moving Money By Text Message" in Chicago Tribune (October 7, 2008)
Pub: McClatchy-Tribune Information Services

Ed: Laurie Goering. **Description:** Cell phone banking services are becoming more common, especially for foreign residents; customers are able to establish a virtual cell phone bank account through companies such as M-Pesa which allows their customers to pay bills, withdraw cash, pay merchants or text money to relatives.

41271 ■ "Kineta Helps Grow Start Group of 5 Biotech Partners" in Puget Sound Business Journal (Vol. 35, June 13, 2014, No. 8, pp. 6)
Pub: American City Business Journals

Released: June 13, 2014. **Description:** Kineta Inc is seeking new funding through its KPI Therapeutics. Kineta offers investors a return on their investments after three to five years. KPI Therapeutics is a new collaborative initiative between drug development firms and private investors. KPI's vision is to create a better way to develop early- and mid-stage therapies for patients and will act as an investment group and a strategic research hub.

41272 ■ "Kodak Cuts Deep in Effort to Change Focus" in Globe & Mail (February 9, 2007, pp. B8)
Ed: Gillian Wee. **Description:** Eastman Kodak Co., the world's largest photography company, is eliminating 5,000 more jobs than the originally planned 28,000 jobs. The job cuts are being driven by the sale of Kodak's health-imaging unit.

41273 ■ "Kodiak Assembly Solutions Bucks Bear Market" in Austin Business JournalInc.

(Vol. 29, December 18, 2009, No. 41, pp. 1)
Pub: American City Business Journals

Ed: Kate Harrington. **Description:** Austin, Texas-based Kodiak Assembly Solutions LLC, a company that installs components into printed circuit boards for product or evaluation tool kit prototyping purposes, will expand despite the recession. It will relocate from a 28,000 square foot space to a 42,000 square foot space in North Austin. The firm will also increase its workforce by 20 employees.

41274 ■ "A League of Their Own" in St. Louis Business Journal (Vol. 32, May 4, 2012, No. 37, pp. 1)
Pub: American City Business Journal

Description: Entrepreneurs Brian and Carol Matthews, Jim McKelvey and Rick Holton Jr. have partnered to create Cultivation Capital. The venture capital fund will target technology firms.

41275 ■ "LED Screen Technology Takes Centre Stage" in Canadian Electronics (Vol. 23, June-July 2008, No. 4, pp. 17)
Ed: Ed Whitaker. **Description:** Display technologies based on light emitting diodes are becoming more popular due to their flexibility, versatility and reproducibility of displays. These are being increasingly used in different applications, such as advertising and concerts.

41276 ■ "Legislators Must Cut Cost of Government" in Crain's Detroit Business (Vol. 24, October 6, 2008, No. 40, pp. 6)
Pub: Crain Communications Inc.
Contact: Rance E. Crain, President

Description: Southeast and West Michigan business leaders are setting aside their differences and have proposed clear agendas, ranging from eliminating the Michigan Business Tax to overhauling public employee and retiree benefits and pensions. Lawmakers must also come together to find solutions for the state's economy and discover an entirely new vision for the future of Michigan business.

41277 ■ "Let the Online Games Begin" in Canadian Business (Vol. 80, January 29, 2007, No. 3, pp. 23)
Ed: Andy Holloway. **Description:** The trends pertaining to the promotion of the products and services of different Canadian companies on the internet are discussed.

41278 ■ "Like Being There" in Canadian Business (Vol. 79, August 14, 2006, No. 16-17, pp. 77)
Pub: Rogers Media Inc.
Contact: Tony Viner, President

Ed: Gerry Blackwell. **Description:** Latest video conferencing facilities at the Halo Collaboration Studio, are discussed.

41279 ■ "The Little Insect" in Canadian Electronics (Vol. 23, June-July 2008, No. 4, pp. 6)
Ed: Tim Gouldson. **Description:** Electronics designers should not be underestimated because they can manufacture technologies vital to saving lives and bringing peace. They have designed robots and other electronic equipment that are as small as insects.

41280 ■ "A Look Ahead Into 2007" in Canadian Business (Vol. 80, December 25, 2006, No. 1, pp. 40)
Description: The 2007 forecasts for various industrial sectors like telecom, information technology, manufacturing, retail, financial and energy among others is discussed.

41281 ■ "Looking Out for the Little Guys" in Black Enterprise (Vol. 38, October 1, 2007, No. 3, pp. 58)
Pub: Earl G. Graves Publishing Co. Inc.
Contact: Earl G. Graves, Jr., President

Description: Biz Tech-Connect is a Web portal that offers free online and social networking, along with four modules that help small businesses with marketing and advertising, communications and mobility, financial management, and customer relationship management.

41282 ■ *"Looks Life We Made It (In Philadelphia)" in Philadelphia Business Journal (Vol. 32, January 24, 2014, No. 50, pp. 4)*
Pub: American City Business Journals
Released: January 24, 2014. Description: Philadelphia, Pennsylvania was once viewed as a manufacturing city, and its manufacturing workforce reached 365,000 in the early 1950s. The city is now focusing on advanced manufacturing that requires scientific and technical expertise. The decrease in the number of manufacturing jobs is also examined.

41283 ■ *"Loyalty Pays" in Entrepreneur (Vol. 36, February 2008, No. 2, pp. 63)*
Pub: Entrepreneur Press
Contact: Perlman Neil, President
Description: Michael Vadini, chief executive officer of Titan Technology Partners looks after his stockholders and investors by making sure that they are protected from risk. Having been affected by the downturn in the technology industry between 2001 and 2004, Vadini granted his investors a liquidity preference. Details regarding his actions to retain investor loyalty are discussed.

41284 ■ *"Made In Canada" in Canadian Business (Vol. 80, March 12, 2007, No. 6, pp. 11)*
Ed: Ian Harvey. Description: The devision of Christie Digital Systems Canada Inc. to increase production of its DLP projectors, in view of high demand from the United States, is discussed.

41285 ■ *"Major Tech Employers Pulling Out" in Sacramento Business Journal (Vol. 25, August 1, 2008, No. 22, pp. 1)*
Pub: American City Business Journals, Inc.
Contact: Whitney Shaw, President
Ed: Celia Lamb. Description: Biotechnology company Affymetrix Inc. is planning to close its West Sacramento, California plant and lay off 110 employees. The company said it will expand a corporate restructuring plan. Affymetrix also plans to lease out or sell its building at Riverside Parkway.

41286 ■ *"Make It Easy" in Entrepreneur (Vol. 36, May 2008, No. 5, pp. 49)*
Pub: Entrepreneur Press
Contact: Perlman Neil, President
Ed: Mike Hogan. Description: Zoho has a Planner that keep contacts, notes and reminders and a DB & Reports feature for reports, data analysis and pricing comparisons. WebEx WebOffice Workgroup supports document management and templates for contacts lists, time sheets and sales tracking. Other online data manages are presented.

41287 ■ *"Making Visitors Out Of Listeners" in Hawaii Business (Vol. 54, July 2008, No. 1, pp. 18)*
Pub: PacificBasin Communications
Ed: Casey Chin. Description: Japanese workers are subscribing to the Official Hawaii Podcast in iTunes, which offers a free 20-minute, Japanese-language audio content on different topics, such as dining reviews and music from local artists. The concept is a way to attract Japanese travelers to come to Hawaii.

41288 ■ *"Making Waves" in Business Journal Portland (Vol. 27, November 26, 2010, No. 39, pp. 1)*
Pub: Portland Business Journal
Ed: Erik Siemers. Description: Corvallis, Oregon-based Columbia Power Technologies LLC is about to close a $2 million Series A round of investment initiated by $750,000 from Oregon Angel Fund. The wave energy startup company was formed to commercialize the wave buoy technology developed by Oregon State University researchers.

41289 ■ *"Managing the Facebookers; Business" in The Economist (Vol. 390, January 3, 2009, No. 8612, pp. 10)*
Pub: Economist Newspaper Ltd.
Description: According to a report from PricewaterhouseCoopers, a business consultancy, workers from Generation Y, also known as the Net Generation, are more difficult to recruit and integrate into companies that practice traditional business acumen. 61 percent of chief executive managers say that they have trouble with younger employees who tend to be more narcissistic and more interested in personal fulfillment with a need for frequent feedback and an over-precise set of objectives on the path to promotion which can be hard for managers who are used to a different relationship with their subordinates. Older bosses should prepare to make some concessions to their younger talent since some of the issues that make them happy include cheaper online ways to communicate and additional coaching, both of which are good for business.

41290 ■ *"Mapping the Gender Gap" in Business Journal Portland (Vol. 31, April 25, 2014, No. 8, pp. 4)*
Pub: American City Business Journals
Released: April 25, 2014. Description: The level of gender equality in the health care, banking, technology and commercial real estate industries of Oregon is examined. Gender bias in the workplace is one significant reason behind the wage gap and the lack of women in leadership positions.

41291 ■ *"Market and Technology Orientations for Service Delivery Innovation: the Link of Innovative Competence" in Journal of Business & Industrial Marketing (Vol. 29, July 2014, No. 6)*
Pub: Emerald Group Publishing Inc.
Released: July 2014. Description: A study to formulate an alternative method of predicting service delivery innovation based on market and technology orientations and innovative competence is examined. Five hypotheses were proposed and tested using the Partial Least Square (PLS) analysis. It was observed that proactive market orientation and technology orientation regulate exploratory and exploitative innovative competences, while exploitative competence influences service delivery innovation.

41292 ■ *"Marketers Push for Mobile Tuesday as the New Black Friday" in Advertising Age (Vol. 79, December 1, 2008, No. 44, pp. 21)*
Pub: Crain Communications Inc.
Contact: Rance Crain, President
Ed: Natalie Zmuda. Description: Marketers are using an innovative approach in an attempt to stimulate business on the Tuesday following Thanksgiving by utilizing consumer's cell phones to alert them of sales or present them with coupons for this typically slow retail business day; with this campaign both advertisers and retailers are hoping to start Mobile Tuesday, another profitable shopping day in line with Black Friday and Cyber Monday.

41293 ■ *"Marketing On Location" in Denver Business Journal (Vol. 65, April 4, 2014, No. 47, pp. A4)*
Pub: American City Business Journals
Released: April 4, 2014. Description: A growing number of local software companies in Denver, Colorado are working to make location-based technology useful for consumers, brands and retailers. Roximity is expanding its location-based app initially installed in Ford, Honda, and Subaru cars into mobile phones. PlaceWise Media combines in-store and on-line marketing for clients like malls and grocery stores.

41294 ■ *"Maryland Tech Tax Heroes Go from Political Neophytes to Savvy Fundraisers" in Baltimore Business Journal (Vol. 27, November 20, 2009, No. 28)*
Pub: American City Business Journals
Ed: Scott Dance. Description: A group of computer services and information technology executives in Maryland have arranged a private dinner that will function as a fundraiser for Governor Martin O'Malley and Lieutenant Governor Anthony Brown. The event is seen as an effort to ensure the industry's involvement in the state after fighting for the repeal of the tech tax in 2007.

41295 ■ *"Mass. STEM Approach and R.I. Model?" in Providence Business News (Vol. 28, March 10, 2014, No. 49, pp. 1)*
Pub: American City Business Journals
Released: March 10, 2014. Description: Rhode Island is in the process of developing an educational system that prepares students to excel in science, technology, engineering and math (STEM). Educational services in the state are examining the Massachusetts educational program in order to generate ideas.

41296 ■ *"Matchmakers Anticipating Tech Valley Boom" in Business Review, Albany New York (Vol. 34, November 2, 2007, No. 31, pp. 1)*
Pub: American City Business Journals, Inc.
Ed: Adam Sichko. Description: Qualified candidates are coming to permanent placement companies after being downsized elsewhere. The top five projected fastest-growing and top five projected fasted-decreasing jobs in the Capital Region are presented.

41297 ■ *"Mayor Unveils Business Plan" in Boston Business Journal (Vol. 29, September 16, 2011, No. 19, pp. 1)*
Pub: American City Business Journals, Inc.
Ed: Gary Haber. Description: Mayor Stephanie Rawlings-Blake of Baltimore, Maryland unveiled her plan to push the economy forward. Her key objectives include giving more support for the city's technology companies and refocusing the Baltimore Development Corporation on job creation and retention.

41298 ■ *"MBlox, Which Sends Coupons to Phones and Tables, Raises $43.5M" in Atlanta Business Chronicle (July 11, 2014, pp. 12A)*
Pub: American City Business Journals, Inc.
Contact: Whitney Shaw, President
Released: July 11, 2014. Description: mBlox, the mobile technology firm that sends coupons to hphones and tablets has managed to successfully raise $43.5 million to undertake global expansion.

41299 ■ *"Me First! Putting Others' Needs Before Your Own Can Be Hazardous to Your Career and Your Health" in Black Enterprise (Vol. 38, December 2007, No. 5, pp. 107)*
Pub: Earl G. Graves Publishing Co. Inc.
Contact: Earl G. Graves, Jr., President
Ed: Tamara E. Holmes. Description: Profile of Andrew J. Milisits Jr., entrepreneur and operating manager of an information technology firm; Milisits shares his experiences when taking on increasing responsibilities and his inability to balance the conflicting demands of career and family.

41300 ■ *"Med-Tech Vet's Trip From Heart to Sleeve" in Business Journal (Vol. 31, February 14, 2014, No. 38, pp. 8)*
Pub: American City Business Journals
Released: February 14, 2014. Description: Conventus Orthopaedics CEO, Paul Buckman, describes the device which repairs wrist fractures. Buckman reveals plans to use the $17 million venture capital to continue research and development and to conduct clinical studies to justify use of the technology.

41301 ■ *"Medical Connectors: Meeting the Demands of Reliability, Portability, Size and Cost" in Canadian Electronics (February 2008)*
Ed: Murtaza Fidaali, Ted Worroll. Description: Component manufacturers who serve the medical industry need to ensure component reliability in order to maintain patient safety. Because of this, connectors in medical equipment are becoming more versatile. It is concluded that these manufacturers are facing challenges meeting the medical industry standards or reliability, miniaturization, portability, and cost.

41302 ■ *"Medtronic In Talks for Local Heart-Monitor Firm" in Business Journal (Vol. 32, May 30, 2014, No. 1, pp. 6)*
Pub: American City Business Journals
Released: May 30, 2014. Description: Medtronic Inc. is negotiations to buy St. Paul, Minnesota-based Corventis Inc., maker of waterproof Band-Aid-like patch that patients wear on their chests to monitor

their hearts. Corventis technology would likely fit into the patient monitoring business of Medtronic's latest acquisition, Cardiocom. The function of the Corventis patch is also presented.

41303 ■ *"Meet the Golden 100 List's Youngest Firm: Kavaliro"* **in Orlando Business Journal (Vol. 29, September 21, 2012, No. 14, pp. 1)**
Pub: American City Business Journal
Description: Technology and information technology staffing firm Kavaliro is the youngest company in the 2012 Golden 100 list of top privately held cmpanies in Central Florida ranked by the 'Orlando Business Journal'. Kavaliro provides 5-10 percent of the local staffing market and has 373 employees, with about 16 working in Central Florida.

41304 ■ *"Meet the White-Label Cash Kings"* **in Globe & Mail (April 23, 2007, pp. B1)**
Ed: Tara Perkins, Tavia Grant. **Description:** The services provided by the independent Canadian companies managing automated banking machines are described. The trends of ownership of automated banking machines in Canada are discussed.

41305 ■ *"Merkle Lands $75M Private-Equity Investment"* **in Baltimore Business Journal (Vol. 28, October 15, 2010, No. 23, pp. 1)**
Pub: Baltimore Business Journal
Ed: Gary Haber. **Description:** Baltimore, Maryland-based Merkle has received a $75 million investment from Silicon Valley-based Technology Crossover Ventures. The private equity firm's cash infusion was considered the biggest stake made in a company in the region and provides a healthy sign for Greater Baltimore's company.

41306 ■ *"Microsoft Goes Macrosoft"* **in Barron's (Vol. 89, July 27, 2009, No. 30, pp. 25)**
Pub: Dow Jones & Co., Inc.
Contact: Clare Hart, President
Ed: Mark Veverka. **Description:** Microsoft reported a weak quarter on the heels of a tech rally which suggests the economy has not turned around. Marc Andreesen describes his new venture-capital fund as focused on 'classic tech' and that historical reference places him in the annals of the last millennium.

41307 ■ *"Microsoft's Big Gamble"* **in Canadian Business (Vol. 81, March 3, 2008, No. 3, pp. 13)**
Ed: Andrew Wahl. **Description:** Microsoft Corp. is taking a big risk in buying Yahoo, as it is expected to pay more than $31 a share to finalize the acquisition. The deal would be seven and a half times bigger than any other that Microsoft has entered before, an execution of such deal is also anticipated to become a challenge for Microsoft. Recommendations on how Microsoft should handle the integration of the two businesses are given.

41308 ■ *"Microsoft's Diversity Program Clicks into High Speed"* **in Hispanic Business (Vol. 30, July-August 2008, No. 7-8, pp. 54)**
Pub: Hispanic Business Inc.
Contact: Jesus Chavarria, President
Ed: Derek Reveron. **Description:** Microsoft's diversity hiring and vendor diversity program to capture more Hispanic consumer and business-to-business market is described. One of the main goals of these programs is to hire more Hispanic executives and managers who will help the company develop and market products and services that will appeal and benefit Hispanic consumers.

41309 ■ *"MicroTech: No. 1 Fastest-Growing Company"* **in Hispanic Business (July-August 2009, pp. 20, 22)**
Pub: Hispanic Business Inc.
Contact: Jesus Chavarria, President
Ed: Suzanne Heibel. **Description:** Profile of Tony Jimenez, former lieutenant colonel in the Army and CEO and founder of Virginia-based information technology firm, Micro Tech LLC. Jimenez was named Latinos in Information Science and Technology Association's CEO of the Year for 2008.

41310 ■ *"Microtrends: The Small Forces Behind Tomorrow's Big Changes"*
Ed: Mark J. Penn. **Released:** 2007. **Price:** , $25.99.
Description: Political pollster and lead presidential campaign strategist for Hillary Clinton, identifies seventy-five microtrends he believes are changing the social and cultural landscape in the U.S. and globally. The book covers the areas of health and wellness, technology, education and more.

41311 ■ *"Miller's Crossroad"* **in Canadian Business (Vol. 83, September 14, 2010, No. 15, pp. 58)**
Pub: Rogers Media Inc.
Contact: Tony Viner, President
Ed: Joe Castaldo. **Description:** Future Electronics founder and billionaire Robert Miller shares the secret of Future's unique operating model, which is based on inventory and market research. Miller attributes much of the company's success to its privately held status that enables quick movement against competitors.

41312 ■ *"Mobile Marketing Grows With Size of Cell Phone Screens"* **in Crain's Detroit Business (Vol. 24, January 14, 2008, No. 2, pp. 13)**
Pub: Crain Communications Inc. - Detroit
Contact: Keith Crain, Chairman
Ed: Bill Shea. **Description:** Experts are predicting increased marketing for cell phones with the inception of larger screens and improved technology.

41313 ■ *"Mobile Office: The Essential Small Business Guide to Office Technology"*
Pub: Double Storey Books
Ed: Arthur Goldstruck, Steven Ambrose. **Released:** September 1, 2009. **Price:** , $6.95. **Description:** Essential pocket guide for startup businesses and entrepreneurs which provides information to create a mobile office in order to maximize business potential while using current technologies.

41314 ■ *"Mobility: So Happy Together"* **in Entrepreneur (Vol. 35, October 2007, No. 10, pp. 64)**
Pub: Entrepreneur Press
Contact: Perlman Neil, President
Ed: Heather Clancy. **Description:** Joshua Burnett, CEO and founder of 9ci, uses index cards to keep track of what he needs to do despite the fact that he has a notebook computer, cell phone and PDA. Kim Hahn, a media entrepreneur, prefers jotting her ideas down in a spiral notebook, has a team that would organize her records for her, and a personal assistant that would keep track of changes to her schedule. Reasons why these entrepreneurs use old-fashioned methods along with new technology are given.

41315 ■ *"A Model Development"* **in Crain's Cleveland Business (Vol. 28, October 1, 2007, No. 39, pp. 12)**
Pub: Crain Communications Inc.
Ed: Scott Suttell. **Description:** Profile a Forest City Enterprises Inc., a firm that is developing a project in New Mexico called Mesa del Sol. The Albuquerque development is being seen as the vanguard of master-planned communities with its high-tech economic development center which is expected to become the site of 60,000 jobs, 38,000 homes and a town center.

41316 ■ *"Molycorp Funds Wind Energy Technology Company"* **in Manufacturing Close-Up (September 19, 2011)**
Pub: Close-Up Media
Description: Molycorp Inc., producer of rare earth oxides (REO) and a REO producer outside of China, announced it will invest in Boulder Wind Power, which has designed a rare earth magnet powered wind turbine generator. This new generator can produce electricity as low as $0.04 per Kilowatt Hour. Boulder Wind Power's patented wind turbine technology allows for use of rare earth permanent magnets that do not require dysprosium, which is relatively scarce.

41317 ■ *"Moosylvania Releases Latest XL Marketing Trends Report"* **in Wireless News (October 6, 2009)**
Description: Moosylvania, a digital promotion and branding agency that also has an on-site research facility, has released its 2nd XL Marketing Trends Report which focuses on digital video; the study defines the top digital video trends marketers must focus on now and well into the future and notes that in 2010, Mobile Web Devices, such as smart phones will outnumber computers in this country. Statistical data included.

41318 ■ *"More Jobs Heading to Suburb"* **in Austin Business JournalInc. (Vol. 29, November 20, 2009, No. 37, pp. 1)**
Pub: American City Business Journals
Ed: Kate Harrington. **Description:** Site of Advanced Integration Technologies (AIT) in Pflugerville, Texas might increase its workforce to 80 employees in the next six months due to the creation of an incentive package. Funds from the Pflugerville Community Development Corporation have been helping AIT's initiative to hire more workers. The firm receives $2,000 from the plan for every new employee it hires.

41319 ■ *"Mosaid Grants First Wireless Parent License To Matsushita"* **in Canadian Electronics (Vol. 23, June-July 2008, No. 5, pp. 1)**
Description: Matsushita Electric Industrial Co. Ltd. has been granted a six-and-a-half-year license by Mosaid Technologies Inc. to manufacture the latter's products. The patent portfolio license agreement covers Mosaid's Wi-Fi, Wi-Max, CDMA-enabled notebook computers and other products.

41320 ■ *"A Motorola Spinoff Is No Panacea"* **in Barron's (Vol. 88, March 31, 2008, No. 13, pp. 19)**
Pub: Dow Jones & Co., Inc.
Contact: Clare Hart, President
Ed: Mark Veverka. **Description:** Motorola's plan to try and spinoff their handset division is bereft of details as to how or specifically when in 2009 the spinoff would occur. There's no reason to buy the shares since there's a lot of execution risk to the plan. Motorola needs to hire a proven cellphone executive and develop a compelling new cellphone platform.

41321 ■ *"Motors and Motion Control"* **in Canadian Electronics (Vol. 23, February 2008, No. 1, pp. 23)**
Description: A new version of MicroMo Electronics Inc.'s Smoovy Series 0303..B has been added to MicroMo's DC motor product line. United Electronic Industries, on the other hand, has introduced the new UEIPAC series of programmable automation controllers that can offer solutions to various applications such as unmanned vehicle controllers. Features and functions of other new motors and motion control devices are given.

41322 ■ *"A Muted Money Hunt"* **in Washington Business Journal (Vol. 33, July 11, 2014, No. 12, pp. 8)**
Pub: American City Business Journals
Released: July 11, 2014. **Description:** Columbia Capital is planning to raise $425 million for a new fund. The company is forming a parallel offshore fund. Columbia specializes in enterprise information technology, infrastructure and other high-dollar technology investments.

41323 ■ *"My Start-Up Life: What a (Very) Young CEO Learned on His Journey Through Silicon Valley"*
Pub: Jossey-Bass Publishers
Contact: Matthew Hoover, Manager
E-mail: fwelsch@jbp.com
Ed: Ben Casnocha. **Released:** May 2007. **Price:** $24.95, hardcover; $16.99. **Description:** Profile of Ben Casnocha, a young entrepreneur who shares insight into starting a running a new business. **Availability:** PrintE-book.

41324 ■ *"Naked Ambitions Put Telus on the Spot"* in Globe & Mail (February 6, 2007, pp. B3)
Ed: Catherine McLean. **Description:** The offering of pornographic content on mobile phones by the telecommunications company Telus Corp., is discussed.

41325 ■ *"Nanoready?"* in Entrepreneur (Vol. 36, May 2008, No. 5, pp. 20)
Ed: Andrea Cooper. **Description:** Experts predict that the medicine and energy sectors are among those that will see nanotechnology innovations in the coming years, and that nanotechnology will produce significant commercial value in new products. Some entrepreneurs are investing in nanotech and are partnering with universities. Details on nanotech funding concerns are discussed.

41326 ■ *"Nanotech Impact is Smaller Than Hoped For"* in Boston Business Journal (Vol. 27, October 26, 2007, No. 39, pp. 1)
Ed: Jackie Noblett. **Description:** Survey by the Massachusetts Technology Collaborative showed that nanotechnology firms are within the early stages of operations and need funding to make them profitable. Details on some nanotech companies and their operations and difficulties in developing or mass producing their products are discussed.

41327 ■ *"National Automatic Merchandising Association Takes Vending on the Road"* in Food and Beverage Close-Up (September 6, 2011)
Pub: Close-Up Media
Description: National Automatic Merchandising Association launched the new age of vending and is taking its machines, products and technology on the road to say thank you to loyal users of vending machines.

41328 ■ *"National Instruments Connects with Lego"* in Austin Business JournalInc. (Vol. 28, August 25, 2008, No. 23, pp. 1)
Pub: American City Business Journals
Ed: Laura Hipp. **Description:** Austin-based National Instruments Corporation has teamed with Lego Group from Denmark to create a robot that can be built by children and can be used to perform tasks. Lego WeDo, their latest product, uses computer connection to power its movements. The educational benefits of the new product are discussed.

41329 ■ *"Need Grub? Start Texting at Kroger"* in Business Courier (Vol. 24, December 20, 2007, No. 36, pp. 1)
Pub: American City Business Journals, Inc.
Contact: Whitney Shaw, President
Ed: Laura Baverman. **Description:** Discusses the University of Cincinnati which is teaming up to release a technology platform called Macopay that would link a cell phone to a bank account and allow a person to make payments at participating retailers by sending a text message. Details with regard to the new service and its growth potential are discussed.

41330 ■ *"Nerd Alert on 3rd"* in Philadelphia Business Journal (Vol. 28, August 17, 2012, No. 27, pp. 1)
Pub: American City Business Journal
Description: The transformation of North 3rd Street in the neighborhood of Old City in Philadelphia, Pennsylvania into a cluster of technology businesses and workers, dubbed at N3rd (pronounced 'nerd'), is described. Some of the firms located in the area include the Web engineering company Jarv.us Innovations and the collaborative workspace Devnuts. Prospects of the cluster's growth are also discussed.

41331 ■ *Nerds on Wall Street: Math, Machines and Wired Markets*
Pub: John Wiley & Sons Inc.
Contact: Stephen M. Smith, President
Ed: David J. Leinweber. **Released:** May 2009. **Price:** $39.95, hardcover; $25.99. **Description:** The history of technology and how it will transform investing and trading on Wall Street is outlined. **Availability:** PrintE-book.

41332 ■ *"NETGEAR Upgrades Small Business Security Line With Multiple Industry Firsts"* in Benzinga.com (March 1, 2012)
Pub: Benzinga.com
Contact: Kyle Bazzy, President
Released: March 1, 2012. **Description:** Netgear's launched its new firmware that delivers affordable application firewall and redundant connectivity as well as extending virtually unlimited logging capacity.

41333 ■ *"Network TV"* in Canadian Business (Vol. 79, September 11, 2006, No. 18, pp. 136)
Pub: Rogers Media Inc.
Contact: Tony Viner, President
Ed: Gerry Blackwell. **Description:** The functions and features of the new Mediasmart LCD TV offered by Hewlett-Packard are discussed.

41334 ■ *"New Giants CEO Goes to Bat for Sponsorships"* in Silicon Valley/San Jose Business Journal (Vol. 29, February 3, 2012, No. 45, pp. 1)
Pub: American City Business Journal
Description: New San Jose Giants baseball team, chief executive Dan Orum, is planning to increase the team's sponsorship, advertising, and ticket revenue. Orum will target technology companies and other firms as prospective sponsors. Orum's career background and achievements are also outlined.

41335 ■ *The New Innovators: How Canadians are Shaping the Knowledge-Based Economy*
Pub: James Lorimer & Company Ltd.
Ed: Roger Voyer, Patti Ryan. **Released:** January 01, 1994. **Price:** C$29.95. **Description:** Details are examined showing how the innovation process works and how ideas are successfully translated into marketable products. **Availability:** Print.

41336 ■ *"New IPhone Also Brings New Way of Mobile Marketing"* in Advertising Age (Vol. 79, June 16, 2008, No. 24, pp. 23)
Pub: Crain Communications Inc.
Contact: Rance Crain, President
Ed: Abbey Klaassen. **Description:** Currently there are two kinds of applications for the iPhone and other mobile devices: native applications that allow for richer experiences and take advantage of features that are built into a phone and web applications, those that allow access to the web through specific platforms. Marketers are interested in creating useful experiences for customers and opening up the platforms which will allow them to do this.

41337 ■ *"New Jersey Bio Grows Despite Turbulent Times"* in Philadelphia Business Journal (Vol. 28, August 17, 2012, No. 27, pp. 1)
Pub: American City Business Journal
Description: The number of biotechnology firms with operations in New Jersey increased from about 300 to more than 340, while the number of employees working at those grew 9.3 percent from 15,000 in July 2012 to 16,400 in 2012. The growth has been realized despite issues that are said to affect the national and international economic situation. Calls to develop economic incentives are also examined.

41338 ■ *"New Sony HD Ads Tout Digital"* in Brandweek (Vol. 49, April 21, 2008, No. 16, pp. 5)
Description: Looking to promote Sony Electronics' digital imaging products, the company has launched another campaign effort known as HDNA, a play on the words high-definition and DNA; originally Sony focused the HDNA campaign on their televisions, the new ads will include still and video cameras as well and marketing efforts will consist of advertising in print, Online, television spots and publicity at various venues across the country.

41339 ■ *"New Sprint Phone Whets Appetite for Applications"* in The Business Journal-Serving Metropolitan Kansas City (Vol. 26, July 25, 2008)
Ed: Suzanna Stagemeyer. **Description:** Firms supporting the applications of the new Samsung Instinct, which was introduced by Sprint Nextel Corp. in June 2008, have reported usage rates increase for their

products. Handmark, whose mobile services Pocket Express comes loaded with Instinct, has redirected employees to meet the rising demand for the services. Other views and information on Instinct, are presented.

41340 ■ *New Technology-Based Firms in the New Millennium, Volume 5*
Ed: Ray Oakey; Saleema Kauser; Aard Groen; Peter van der Sijde. **Released:** November 2006. **Price:** , $145.00. **Description:** Papers from the Annual High Technology Smal Firms conference are presented. Experts address strategic growth for these small firms.

41341 ■ *New Technology-Based Firms in the New Millennium, Volume 6*
Ed: Ray Oakey. **Released:** May 2008. **Price:** , $149.00. **Description:** Collection of papers from the Annual International High Technology Firms (HTSFs) Conference cover issues of importance to governments as they develop technological program. Papers are grouped into three sections: theory, strategy and clustering, and spin-off firms.

41342 ■ *"A New Way to Tell When to Fold 'Em"* in Barron's (Vol. 88, July 7, 2008, No. 27, pp. 27)
Pub: Dow Jones & Co., Inc.
Contact: Clare Hart, President
Ed: Theresa W. Carey. **Description:** Overview of the Online trading company SmartStops, a firm that aims to tell investors when to sell the shares of a particular company. The company's Web site categorizes stocks as moving up, down, or sideways, and calculates exit points for individual stocks based on an overall market trend.

41343 ■ *"New Work Order"* in Black Enterprise (Vol. 38, March 1, 2008, No. 8, pp. 60)
Pub: Earl G. Graves Publishing Co. Inc.
Contact: Earl G. Graves, Jr., President
Ed: Marcia A. Reed-Woodward. **Description:** Today's management challenges includes issues of more competition, globalization, outsourcing and technological advances. Suggestions to help create progressive leadership in small business that sustains a competitive edge are listed.

41344 ■ *"Newton Robotics Company Bets On Rehab Robots for Growth"* in Boston Business Journal (Vol. 34, April 4, 2014, No. 9, pp. 6)
Pub: American City Business Journals, Inc.
Contact: Whitney Shaw, President
Released: April 4, 2014. **Description:** Robotics firm Barrett Technology is transforming into a health care company by developing rehabilitation robots. The business is expected to generate 80 percent of its revenue from its health care clients over the next five years. The possibility of hiring new employees is also discussed.

41345 ■ *"The Next Big Thing"* in Farm Industry News (Vol. 42, January 1, 2009, No. 1)
Pub: Intertec Publishing
Contact: John French, President
Ed: David Hest. **Description:** Communication technology that allows farmers to detect equipment location, travel speed and real-time fuel and sprayer/combine tank levels will pay off with better machine use efficiency, improved maintenance and reduced downtime. These telemetry systems will be widely available in the next few years.

41346 ■ *"The Next Dimension"* in Entrepreneur (Vol. 35, November 2007, No. 11, pp. 62)
Pub: Entrepreneur Press
Contact: Perlman Neil, President
Ed: Heather Clancy. **Description:** Entrepreneurs can make use of virtual worlds like Second Life to promote their products or services. Details and cautions on the use of virtual worlds are discussed.

41347 ■ *"No More Ivory Towers: Local Colleges and Universities are Here to Help Your Business"* in Orlando Business Journal

(Vol. 30, February 28, 2014, No. 36, pp. 4)
Pub: American City Business Journals
Released: February 28, 2014. **Description:** A number of school leaders in Central Florida share their views on partnering with the business community, boosting science and technology graduates, benefits of a private college, economic development efforts and fixing the higher education construction gridlock. Local universities and colleges have a combined economic impact of $15 billion each year.

41348 ■ *"Noise Busters: The Next Generation of Bluetooth Headsets"* in *Inc.* (Vol. 31, January-February 2009, No. 1, pp. 41)
Pub: Mansueto Ventures L.L.C.
Contact: John Koten, Chief Executive Officer
Ed: Mark Spoonauer. **Description:** Information on the latest Bluetooth headsets that allow users to talk hands-free and the new technology that blocks ambient sounds is given. Aliph Jawbone, Plantronics Voyager Jabra BT530, and Motorola Motopure H15 are profiled.

41349 ■ *The Nokia Revolution: The Story of an Extraordinary Company That Transformed an Industry*
Ed: Dan Steinbock. **Released:** May 31, 2001. **Description:** Profile of Nokia, the world's largest wireless communications company. Nokia started in 1865 in rural Finland and merged its rubber company and a cabling firm to form the corporation around 1965. The firm's corporate strategy in the mobile communications industry is highlighted.

41350 ■ *"Nonprofit Ready to Get More Girls into 'STEM' Jobs"* in *Austin Business JournalInc.* (Vol. 29, December 25, 2009, No. 42, pp. 1)
Pub: American City Business Journals
Ed: Sandra Zaragoza. **Description:** Girlstart has completed its $1.5 million capital campaign to buy the building it will care the Girlstart Tech Center. Girlstart is a nonprofit organization that prepares girls for science, technology, engineering and mathematics or STEM careers. Details of the program are highlighted.

41351 ■ *"Nortel Makes Customers Stars in New Campaign"* in *Brandweek* (Vol. 49, April 21, 2008, No. 16, pp. 8)
Pub: Nielsen Business Media Inc.
Contact: Howard Appelbaum, President
Ed: Mike Beirne. **Description:** Nortel has launched a new television advertising campaign in which the business-to-business communications technology provider cast senior executives in 30-second TV case studies that show how Nortel's technology helped their businesses innovate.

41352 ■ *"Nortel Romances Chinese Rival Huawei"* in *Globe & Mail* (February 2, 2006, pp. B1)
Ed: Simon Avery. **Description:** The reasons behind Nortel Networks Corp.'s joint venture with Huawei Technologies Company Ltd. are presented.

41353 ■ *"Not Your Father's Whiteboard"* in *Inc.* (Vol. 33, November 2011, No. 9, pp. 50)
Pub: Inc. Magazine
Ed: Adam Baer. **Description:** Sharp's new interactive whiteboard is really a 70-inch touch screen monitor with software for importing presentations from any Windows 7 computer.

41354 ■ *"NovAtel Inc. Licensed to Sell Galileo Receivers"* in *Marketwired* (May 14, 2007)
Pub: Comtex News Network Inc.
Description: NovAtel Inc., a leading provider of precision Global Navigation Satellite System (GNSS) components and subsystems that afford its customers rapid integration of precise positioning technology, has received a license valid for ten years that allows NovAtel to sell receivers that track Galileo signals.

41355 ■ *"NOW: Ideas at the Speed of Business: Cancer Care's Quantum Leap"* in

Hawaii Business (Vol. 53, October 2007, No. 4, pp. 17)
Pub: PacificBasin Communications
Ed: Cathy S. Cruz-George. **Description:** TomoTherapy is an innovative device for cancer treatment that gives high-intensity radiation to more accurate parts of the body compared to conventional treatments. Hawaii has one of the 70 TomoTherapy machines in the nation, and it is expected to help advance cancer care in the area. Details on how the machine works are provided.

41356 ■ *"Now See This"* in *Entrepreneur* (Vol. 36, April 2008, No. 4, pp. 53)
Pub: Entrepreneur Press
Contact: Perlman Neil, President
Ed: Mike Hogan. **Description:** New high definition (HD) products are to be introduced in 2008 at the Consumer Electronics Show and the Macworld Conference & Expo. HD lineup from companies such as Dell Inc. and Hewlett-Packard Co. are discussed.

41357 ■ *"No. 82: a Few Good Apps"* in *Inc.* (Vol. 36, September 2014, No. 7, pp. 103)
Pub: Mansueto Ventures L.L.C.
Contact: John Koten, Chief Executive Officer
Released: September 2014. **Description:** Alan S. Knitowski, former U.S. Army Captain, and his Austin, Texas-based mobile-focused development company is profiled. Phunware, creates apps for clients like ESPN, Cisco, Noscar, WWE, and NBC Sports. The firm won awards for its MythBusters app.

41358 ■ *"Nvidia Shares Clobbered After Gloomy Warning"* in *Barron's* (Vol. 88, July 7, 2008, No. 27, pp. 25)
Pub: Dow Jones & Co., Inc.
Contact: Clare Hart, President
Ed: Eric J. Savitz. **Description:** Shares of graphics chip manufacturer Nvidia suffered a 30 percent drop in its share price after the company warned that revenue and gross margin forecasts for the quarter ending July 27, 2008 will be below expectations. Stan Glasgow, chief operating officer of Sony Electronics, believes the US economic slowdown will not affect demand for the company's products. Statistical data included.

41359 ■ *"Nvidia's Picture Brighter Than Stock Price Indicates"* in *Barron's* (Vol. 88, March 24, 2008, No. 12, pp. 46)
Pub: Dow Jones & Co., Inc.
Contact: Clare Hart, President
Ed: Eric J. Savitz. **Description:** Shares of graphics chip maker Nvidia, priced at $18.52 each, do not indicate the company's strong position in the graphics chip market. The company's shares have dropped due to fears of slower demand for PCs, but the company is not as exposed to broader economic forces.

41360 ■ *"NYC Tops Hub in Tech VC Dollars"* in *Boston Business Journal* (Vol. 31, August 5, 2011, No. 28, pp. 1)
Pub: Boston Business Journal
Ed: Kyle Alspach. **Description:** New York City has been outdoing Boston in terms of venture capital for technology firms since second quarter 2010. New York tech firms raised $865 million during the first two quarters of 2011 against Boston techs' $682 million. Boston has the edge, though, when it comes to hiring engineering talent as it is home to the Massachusetts Institute of Technology.

41361 ■ *"Obama Plan May Boost Maryland Cyber Security"* in *Boston Business Journal* (Vol. 29, May 20, 2011, No. 2, pp. 1)
Pub: American City Business Journals, Inc.
Ed: Scott Dance. **Description:** May 12, 2011 outline of the cyber security policies of President Obama may improve the cyber security industry in Maryland as the state is home to large defense and intelligence activities. Details of the proposed policies are discusses as well as their advantages to companies that deal in developing cyber security plans for other companies.

41362 ■ *"Office Retooled"* in *Canadian Business* (Vol. 80, March 26, 2007, No. 7, pp. 67)
Ed: Andrew Wahl. **Description:** The merits and demerits of using new Google Apps Premier Edition are presented.

41363 ■ *"On Technology: The Web Gets Real"* in *Canadian Business* (Vol. 79, July 17, 2006, No. 14-15, pp. 19)
Pub: Rogers Media Inc.
Contact: Tony Viner, President
Ed: Andrew Wahl. **Description:** Ron Lake's efforts of bringing the virtual and physical worlds more closely together by using Geographic Markup Language (GML) are presented.

41364 ■ *"Online Training Requires Tools, Accessories"* in *Contractor* (Vol. 56, September 2009, No. 9, pp. 67)
Pub: Penton Media, Inc.
Ed: Larry Drake. **Description:** Importance of the right equipment and tools to members of the United States plumbing industry undergoing online training is discussed. Portable devices such as Blackberrys and I-phones could be used for online training. The use of headphones makes listening easier for the trainee.

41365 ■ *"Optimal Awarded US $256 Thousand Contract to Conduct LiDAR Survey for a Major Electric Utility in the Southwest"* in *Canadian Corporate News*
Description: Optimal Geomatics, a company specializing in the science and technology of analyzing, gathering, interpreting, distributing, and using geographic information, was awarded a new contract from a long-standing electric utility customer in the Southwest to conduct a LiDAR survey for a part of the utility's overhead transmission line system.

41366 ■ *"Oracle: No Profit of Doom"* in *Barron's* (Vol. 88, March 31, 2008, No. 13, pp. 40)
Pub: Dow Jones & Co., Inc.
Contact: Clare Hart, President
Ed: Mark Veverka. **Description:** Oracle's revenues grew by 21 percent but fell short of expectation and their profits came in at the low-end of expectations. The company's shares dropped 8 percent but investors are advised to pay more attention to the company's earnings expansion rather than revenue growth in a slow economy. Nokia's Rick Simonson points out that their markets in Asia and particularly India is growing so they are not as affected by the U.S. economic conditions.

41367 ■ *"Ordering Pizza Hut From Your Facebook Page? It's on the Way"* in *Advertising Age* (Vol. 79, November 10, 2008, No. 42, pp. 50)
Pub: Crain Communications Inc.
Contact: Rance Crain, President
Ed: Emily Bryson York. **Description:** Fast-food chains are experimenting with delivery/takeout services via social networks such as Facebook and iPhone applications. This also allows the chains to build valuable databases of their customers.

41368 ■ *"Orlando Patents Forecast Biz Diversity and Growth"* in *Orlando Business Journal* (Vol. 30, April 18, 2014, No. 43, pp. 4)
Pub: American City Business Journals
Released: April 18, 2014. **Description:** Orlando, Florida ranked among cities in the state in terms of number of patents filed. Around 275 patents were issued to Orlando-based inventors and businesses in 2013. The increase in the number of high technology companies entering the city has contributed to this trend.

41369 ■ *"Our Gadget of the Week"* in *Barron's* (Vol. 89, July 27, 2009, No. 30, pp. 26)
Ed: Jay Palmer. **Description:** Zeo Sleep Coach has a lightweight headband with built-in sensors which measures the user's brain waves and records their sleep patterns. The device details the time the users spends in deep sleep, light sleep and the restorative

REM (rapid eye movement) sleep mode. Users can get lifestyle change recommendations from a website to improve their sleep.

41370 ■ *"Our Gadget of the Week: Balancing Act" in Barron's (Vol. 88, March 31, 2008, No. 13, pp. 40)*
Pub: Dow Jones & Co., Inc.
Contact: Clare Hart, President
Ed: Naureen S. Malik. **Description:** Wii Fit gives users the experience of a virtual personal trainer and workouts that become progressively harder. The device turns the typical fitness regimes into fun exercises and users can choose workouts in four categories including yoga, balance, strength-training and, low impact aerobics.

41371 ■ *"Our Gadget of the Week: Business Buddy" in Barron's (Vol. 88, July 7, 2008, No. 27, pp. 26)*
Pub: Dow Jones & Co., Inc.
Contact: Clare Hart, President
Ed: Jay Palmer. **Description:** Review and evaluation of the Lenovo X300 laptop computer which offers executives a variety of features despite its smaller size and weight. The laptop is about 0.73 inch thick, comes with a 64-gigabyte solid-state drive from Samsung, and weighs less than three pounds.

41372 ■ *"Our Gadget of the Week: Mostly, I Liked It" in Barron's (Vol. 88, July 14, 2008, No. 28, pp. 31)*
Ed: Jay Palmer. **Description:** Review of the Apple iPhone 3G, which costs $199, has better audio and is slightly thicker than its predecessor; using the 3G wireless connection makes going online faster but drains the battery faster too.

41373 ■ *"Our Gadget of the Week: Screen Star" in Barron's (Vol. 88, March 10, 2008, No. 10, pp. 36)*
Pub: Dow Jones & Co., Inc.
Contact: Clare Hart, President
Ed: Jay Palmer. **Description:** Review of the $1,599 Fujitsu Lifebook T2010 tablet notebook which is a lightweight notebook offering a comfortable keyboard and a 12-inch screen illuminated by light emitting diodes. The notebook, however, also offers limited capability with its low-end processor and the lack of a built-in optical drive and a touchpad.

41374 ■ *"Our Gadget of the Week: Your Back Pages" in Barron's (Vol. 88, March 24, 2008, No. 12, pp. 47)*
Pub: Dow Jones & Co., Inc.
Contact: Clare Hart, President
Ed: Tiernan Ray. **Description:** Review of the $299 Apple Time Capsule, which is a 500-megabyte hard disk drive and a Wi-Fi router, rolled into one device. The device allows users to create backup files without the need for sophisticated file management software.

41375 ■ *Out of the Comfort Zone: Learning to Expect the Unexpected*
Ed: Lisbeth Borbye. **Released:** May 10, 2010. **Price:** $35. **Description:** A collection of lectures covering technology, management and entrepreneurship.

41376 ■ *"Outlook 2008 (9 Sectors to Watch): Biotech" in Canadian Business (Vol. 81, December 19, 2007, No. 1, pp. 48)*
Pub: Rogers Media Inc.
Contact: Tony Viner, President
Ed: Calvin Leung. **Description:** Forecasts on the Canadian biotechnology sector for 2008 are presented. Details on the increase in the number of biotechnology companies and prediction on the government's plan for business incentives are discussed.

41377 ■ *"Outlook 2008 (9 Sectors to Watch): Telecom" in Canadian Business (Vol. 81, December 19, 2007, No. 1, pp. 44)*
Pub: Rogers Media Inc.
Contact: Tony Viner, President
Ed: Andrew Wahl. **Description:** Forecasts on the Canadian telecommunications industry for 2008 are presented. Details on consumer spending growth, the popularity of broadband, and activities in the wireless sector are also discussed.

41378 ■ *Outsourcing: Information Technology, Original Equipment Manufacturer, Leo, Oursourcing, Offshoring Research Network, Crowdsourcing*
Released: May 01, 2010. **Price:** $14.14. **Description:** Chapters include information for outsourcing firms and how to maintain an outsourcing business.

41379 ■ *Overcoming Barriers to Entrepreneurship in the United States*
Pub: Lexington Books
Contact: Serena Leigh Kromback, Director
Ed: Diana Furchtgott-Roth. **Released:** March 28, 2008. **Price:** $32.99, Paperback; £19.95, Paperback. **Description:** Real and perceived barriers to the founding and running of small businesses in America are discussed. Each chapter outlines how policy and economic environments can hinder business owners and offers tips to overcome these obstacles. Starting with venture capital access in Silicon Valley during the Internet bubble, the book goes on to question the link between personal wealth and entrepreneurship, examines how federal tax rates affect small business creation and destruction, explains the low rate of self-employment among Mexican immigrants, and suggests ways pension coverage can be increased in small businesses.

41380 ■ *"Paging Dr. Phil" in Canadian Business (Vol. 79, September 25, 2006, No. 19, pp. 21)*
Ed: John Gray. **Description:** Increasing corporate crimes in software industry is discussed by focusing on recent case of Hewlett and Packard.

41381 ■ *"Panasonic UF-5500 Enhanced Security Business-Class Fax Named BERTL Best" in Internet Wire (February 16, 2012)*
Released: February 16, 2012. **Description:** Panasonic System Communications Company of North America received a 2011 Business Equipment Research and Test Laboratories Inc. BERTL's Best Award for the PanaFax UF-550 multifunction laser fax/scanner, high-speed, high-output unit for small to mid-sized healthcare, corporate and public service offices.

41382 ■ *"Panel to Call for Reduced Restraints on Telecom Sector" in Globe & Mail (March 17, 2006, pp. B1)*
Ed: Simon Tuck. **Description:** A federal panel called to adopt a more market-friendly approach to the lucrative telecommunications sector in Canada. Details of the report are presented.

41383 ■ *"Panel Calls for 'Fundamental' Change to Telecom Regulation" in Globe & Mail (March 23, 2006, pp. B1)*
Ed: Catherine McLean. **Description:** A federal panel review at Ottawa called for a shakeup of regulations and policies that govern telecommunications companies to contend with sweeping technological changes. Details of the panel review are presented.

41384 ■ *"Paterson Plots Comeback With Internet IPO" in Globe & Mail (February 20, 2006, pp. B1)*
Ed: Grant Robertson. **Description:** The initial public offering plans of chief executive officer Scott Paterson of JumpTV.com are presented.

41385 ■ *"Paul Hawken and Other Top Lumnaries to Participate in Green Business BASE CAMP in Los Angeles" in Benzinga.com (April 19, 2012)*
Pub: Benzinga.com
Contact: Kyle Bazzy, President
Ed: Aaron Wise. **Description:** Paul Hawken, environmentalist, entrepreneur and author, is one of many people participating in the Green Business BASE CAMP, a four-day workshop for green business and cleantech entrepreneurs. The event will be held in Los Angeles, California from May 31 through June 3, 2012. Insider guidance will be offered to early-stage entrepreneurs seeking to compete within this sector.

41386 ■ *"Pay Heed to 'Smack Stack" in Puget Sound Business Journal (Vol. 35, May*

16, 2014, No. 4, pp. 6)
Pub: American City Business Journals
Released: May 16, 2014. **Description:** Technology consultant, Geoffrey Moore, discloses the topics he plans to discuss at the annual State of Technology Luncheon held in Washington on May 19, 2014. He will explore the impact of technology and business trends on public-policy making and regulations.

41387 ■ *"PC Connection Acquires Cloud Software Provider" in New Hampshire Business Review (Vol. 33, March 25, 2011, No. 6, pp. 8)*
Pub: Business Publications Inc.
Description: Merrimack-based PC Connection Inc. acquired ValCom Technology, a provider of cloud-based IT service management software. Details of the deal are included.

41388 ■ *"Auto Asphyxiation" in Canadian Business (Vol. 85, August 13, 2012, No. 13, pp. 42)*
Pub: George Media Inc.
Ed: Peter Shawn Taylor. **Released:** August 13, 2012. **Description:** The reality behind economist Jeff Rubin's claim that oil is the single most important factor in global economics is explored. Rubin is advised to follow the example of technology watcher Don Tapscott who avoids delivering a negative message and make concreted predictions that will eventually prove wrong if he is looking for a long and lucrative career in the guru business.

41389 ■ *"Personal Tech: Ring Ka-Ching" in Canadian Business (Vol. 79, November 6, 2006, No. 22, pp. 106)*
Pub: Rogers Media Inc.
Contact: Tony Viner, President
Ed: Gerry Blackwell. **Description:** A brief profile of Jajah including its web activated telephone services is presented.

41390 ■ *"Philanthropy Good For Business" in Crain's Detroit Business (Vol. 24, February 18, 2008, No. 7, pp. 14)*
Pub: Crain Communications Inc. - Detroit
Contact: Keith Crain, Chairman
Ed: Sheena Harrison. **Description:** Profile of Burce McCully, founder of Dynamic Edge Inc., and his views on philanthropy as a key to any small company's success. The Ann Arbor, Michigan information technology firm has volunteered and raised funds for many causes since 1999 when the company was founded.

41391 ■ *"Pioneers Get All The Perks" in Canadian Business (Vol. 81, March 3, 2008, No. 3, pp. 18)*
Description: Suncor Energy Inc. will face royalty payments from 25% to 30% of net profits as it signs a new deal with Alberta. Biovail Corp., meanwhile, is under a U.S. grand jury investigation for supposed improprieties in Cardizem LA heart drug launch. The Conference Board of Canada's proposal to impose taxes on greenhouse gas emissions and other developments in the business community are discussed.

41392 ■ *Power Up Your Small-Medium Business: A Guide to Enabling Network Technologies*
Pub: Cisco Press
Ed: Robyn Aber. **Released:** March 05, 2004. **Price:** $25.57, Members; $31.96, Nonmembers. **Description:** Network technologies geared to small and medium-size business, focusing on access, IP telephony, wireless technologies, security, and computer network management. **Availability:** E-book.

41393 ■ *Practical Tech for Your Business*
Ed: Michael J. Martinez. **Released:** 2002. **Description:** Advice is offered to help small business owners choose the right technology for their company. The guide tells how to get started, network via the Internet, create an office network, use database software, and conduct business using mobile technology.

41394 ■ *"Prepaid Phones Surge in Bad Economy"* in Advertising Age (Vol. 79, November 17, 2008, No. 43, pp. 6)
Pub: Crain Communications Inc.
Contact: Rance Crain, President
Ed: Rita Chang. **Description:** Prepay cell phone offerings are becoming increasingly competitive amid a greater choice of plans and handsets. In an economic environment in which many consumers are unable to pass the credit checks required for traditional cell phone plans, the prepay market is surging.

41395 ■ *"Presidential Address: Innovation in Retrospect and Prospect"* in Canadian Journal of Electronics (Vol. 43, November 2010, No. 4)
Pub: Journal of the Canadian Economics Association
Ed: James A. Brander. **Description:** Has innovation slowed in recent decades? While there has been progress in information and communications technology, the recent record of innovation in agriculture, energy, transportation and healthcare sectors is cause for concern.

41396 ■ *"Pressed for Time"* in Marketing to Women (Vol. 21, March 2008, No. 3, pp. 1)
Description: Statistical data concerning the tools women use for time management which include gadgets as well as traditional media such as calendars.

41397 ■ *"Products and Services"* in Canadian Electronics (Vol. 23, August 2008, No. 5, pp. 46)
Description: Directory of companies under the alphabetical listing of electronic equipment and allied components that they offer is presented.

41398 ■ *"The Promised Land"* in San Francisco Business Times (Vol. 28, January 3, 2014, No. 24, pp. 4)
Pub: American City Business Journals
Released: January 3, 2014. **Description:** San Francisco Bay Area in California has become the site selection for investment, technology and talent. The financing finding its way to the Bay Area has led to robust job creation, drawing people and increasing the population by 2.6 percent to 805,000. The impact of the Bay Area's technology boon in rents and home prices are also presented.

41399 ■ *"Providing Expertise Required to Develop Microsystems"* in Canadian Electronics (Vol. 23, February 2008, No. 1, pp. 6)
Ed: Ian McWalter. **Description:** CMC Microsystems, formerly Canadian Microelectronics Corporation, is focused on empowering microelectronics and Microsystems research in Canada. Microsystems offers the basis for innovations in the fields of science, environment, technology, automotives, energy, aerospace and communications technology. CMC's strategy in developing Microsystems in Canada is described.

41400 ■ *"Punta Gorda Interested in Wi-Fi Internet"* in Charlotte Observer (February 1, 2007)
Ed: Steve Reilly. **Description:** Punta Gorda officials are developing plans to provide free wireless Internet services to businesses and residents.

41401 ■ *"Put a Projector in Your Pocket"* in Inc. (Vol. 31, January-February 2009, No. 1, pp. 42)
Pub: Mansueto Ventures L.L.C.
Contact: John Koten, Chief Executive Officer
Description: PowerPoint presentations can be given using the Optoma Pico Pocket Projector. The device can be connected to laptops, cell phones, digital cameras, and iPods.

41402 ■ *"Put Your Data to Work in the Marketplace"* in Harvard Business Review (Vol. 86, September 2008, No. 9, pp. 34)
Pub: Harvard Business Review Press
Contact: Peter E. Walsh, Director
Ed: Thomas C. Redman. **Description:** Nine strategies are presented for data asset marketing including exploiting asymmetries, unbundling, repackaging, and offering new content.

41403 ■ *"Qualcomm Could Win Big as the IPhone 3G Calls"* in Barron's (Vol. 88, July 4, 2008, No. 28, pp. 30)
Pub: Dow Jones & Co., Inc.
Contact: Clare Hart, President
Ed: Eric J. Savitz. **Description:** Apple iPhone 3G's introduction could widen the smartphone market thereby benefiting handset chipmaker Qualcomm in the process. Qualcomm Senior V.P., Bill Davidson sees huge potential for his company's future beyond phones with their Snapdragon processor. The prospects of Sun Microsystems' shares are also discussed.

41404 ■ *"Quantivo Empowers Online Media Companies to Immediately Expand Audiences and Grow Online Profits"* in Marketwired (November 18, 2009)
Pub: COMTEX News Network Inc.
Contact: Chip Brian, President
Description: Quantivo, the leader in on-demand Behavioral Analytics, has launched a new solution that includes 22 of the most critical Internet audience behavior insights as out-of-the-box reports; Internet marketers need to understand their audience, what they want and how often to offer it to them in order to gain successful branding and campaigns online.

41405 ■ *The Race for a New Game Machine: Creating the Chips Inside the Xbox 360 and the PlayStation 3*
Pub: Citadel Press
Contact: Steven Zacharius, President
E-mail: szacharius@kensingtonbooks.com
Ed: David Shippy, Mickie Phipps. **Released:** 2009. **Price:** $11.75. **Description:** The story of Microsoft and Sony's race to deliver the goods for the Xbox 360 and Playstation 3 is explored. **Availability:** Electronic publishing.

41406 ■ *"Racing to Beam Electricity to Devices Wirelessly"* in San Francisco Business Times (Vol. 28, April 11, 2014, No. 38, pp. 6)
Pub: American City Business Journals
Released: April 11, 2014. **Description:** Pleasanton, California-based Energous Corporation has developed a technology that safely converts radio waves into electrical current. The innovation makes it possible to charge multiple/cellular mobile phones or other electrical devices from a distance of 15 feet. The prototype of Energous founder, Michael Leabman's invention is also outlined.

41407 ■ *"Radiant Commences In-Lab Testing for US Air Mobility Command"* in Canadian Corporate News (May 16, 2007)
Description: The Boeing Company will be conducting in-lab infrared material testing for the Radiant Energy Corporation, developer and marketer of InfraTek, the environmentally friendly, patented infrared pre-flight aircraft deicing system.

41408 ■ *"Radio Feels Heat from iPod Generation"* in Globe & Mail (March 16, 2006, pp. B1)
Ed: Simon Tuck, Grant Robertson. **Description:** Conventional radio stations are losing the younger generation listeners to new technology such as MP3 players, satellite radio and music-playing cell phones. The report of Canadian Association of Broadcasters (CAB) is detailed.

41409 ■ *"Raptor Opens Consultancy"* in Austin Business Journal (Vol. 31, July 8, 2011, No. 18, pp. 1)
Pub: American City Business Journals
Ed: Christopher Calnan. **Description:** Boston hedge fund operator Raptor Group launched Raptor Accelerator, a consulting business providing sales and advisory services to early-stage companies in Central Texas. Aside from getting involved with the startups in which the Raptor Group invests, Raptor Accelerator will target firms operating in the sports, media, entertainment, and content technology sectors.

41410 ■ *"RavenBrick Ready to Manufacture Its High-Tech Windows"* in Denver Business Journal (Vol. 64, September 7, 2012, No. 16, pp. 1)
Pub: American City Business Journal
Description: RavenBrick LLC is set to build a new manufacturing plant in Denver, Colorado. The company manufactures auto-darkening window films. RavenBrick has raised a total of $13.5 million in new investment capital.

41411 ■ *"Raytheon Stock Up, Will Pay New Quarterly Dividend"* in Barron's (Vol. 88, March 31, 2008, No. 13)
Pub: Dow Jones & Co., Inc.
Contact: Clare Hart, President
Ed: Shirley A. Lazo. **Description:** Raytheon hiked their quarterly dividend to 28 cents per share from 25.5 cents. Aircastle slashed their quarterly common dividend by 64 percent for them to retain additional capital that can be used to increase their liquidity position.

41412 ■ *Reading Financial Reports for Dummies*
Pub: John Wiley & Sons Inc.
Contact: Stephen M. Smith, President
Ed: Lita Epstein. **Released:** 3rd Edition. **Price:** $22.95, paperback; $14.99. **Description:** This second edition contains more new and updated information, including new information on the separate accounting and financial reporting standards for private/small businesses versus public/large businesses; updated information reflecting 2007 laws on international financial reporting standards; new content to match SEC and other governmental regulatory changes over the last three years; new information about how the analyst-corporate connection has changed the playing field; the impact of corporate communications and new technologies; new examples that reflect the current trends; and updated Websites and resources. **Availability:** PrintE-book.

41413 ■ *"Rebuffed, BAE Systems Fights Army Contract Decision"* in Business Courier (Vol. 26, September 25, 2009)
Pub: American City Business Journals, Inc.
Contact: Whitney Shaw, President
Ed: Jon Newberry. **Description:** BAE Systems filed a complaint with the US Government Accountability Office after the US Army issued an order to BAE's competitor for armoured trucks which is potentially worth over $3 billion. Hundreds of jobs in Butler County, Ohio hinge on the success of the contract protest.

41414 ■ *"Recent Austin Deals Signal an M&A Resurgence"* in Austin Business JournalInc. (Vol. 29, January 22, 2010, No. 46, pp. 1)
Pub: American City Business Journals
Ed: Jacob Dirr. **Description:** The acquisition of at least six Austin, Texas technology companies reflects the growing acquisition activity in the US. Corporations have bought 86 companies and spent $7.3 billion during the fourth quarter of 2009. Insights into the impact of the acquisition activity to Austin's entrepreneurial energy are also given.

41415 ■ *"Recession Management"* in Canadian Business (Vol. 81, March 3, 2008, No. 3, pp. 62)
Ed: Joe Castaldo. **Description:** Some companies such as Capital One Financial Corp. are managing their finances as if a recession has already taken place to prepare themselves for the looming economic downturn. Intel Corp., meanwhile shows how increasing its investments during a recession could be advantageous. Tips on how companies can survive a recession are provided.

41416 ■ *"Red One and The Rain Chronicles"* in Michigan Vue (Vol. 13, July-August 2008, No. 4, pp. 30)
Ed: Evan Cornish. **Description:** Troy-based film school the Motion Picture Institute (MPI) implemented the latest technology by shooting the second of their trilogy, 'The Rain Chronicles', on the Red One camera. This is the first feature film in Michigan to utilize this exciting new camera, which includes

proprietary software for rendering and color correction. Brian K. Johnson heads up the visual effects team as visual effects supervisor and lead CG artist. His company, Dream Conduit Studios, had to tackle the task of employing the new work flow through a post-production pipeline that would allow him to attack complex visual effects shots, many of which were shot with a moving camera, a technique rarely seen in films at this budgetary level where the camera is traditionally locked off.

41417 ■ *"Region to Be Named Innovation Hub" in Business Courier (Vol. 27, July 2, 2010, No. 9, pp. 1)*
Pub: Business Courier

Ed: Dan Monk. **Description:** The selection of Cincinnati's consumer-marketing cluster as a 'Hub of Innovation' by the Ohio Department of Development could boost Cincinnati's chances of receiving $100 million in grants from Ohio's Third Frontier program and other funding sources. Implications of the University of Cincinnati's designation as a Center of Excellence in Advanced Transportation and Aerospace are also discussed.

41418 ■ *"Region Ready to Dig Deeper into Tech Fund" in Business Courier (Vol. 26, October 30, 2009, No. 27, pp. 1)*
Pub: American City Business Journals, Inc.
Contact: Whitney Shaw, President

Ed: James Ritchie. **Description:** Southwest Ohio region aims for a bigger share in the planned renewal of Ohio's Third Frontier technology funding program. Meanwhile, University of Cincinnati vice president Sarah Degen will be appointed to the program's advisory board if the renewal proceeds.

41419 ■ *Remix: Making Art and Commerce Thrive in the Hybrid Economy*
Pub: Dutton Children's Books
Contact: Lauri Hornik, President

Ed: Lawrence Lessig. **Released:** September 29, 2009. **Price:** $17, paperback. **Description:** An examination of copyright laws in the digital age. **Availability:** Print.

41420 ■ *"Remote Control: Working From Wherever" in Inc. (February 2008, pp. 46-47)*
Ed: Ryan Underwood. **Description:** New technology allows workers to perform tasks from anywhere via the Internet. Profiles of products to help connect to your office from afar include, LogMein Pro, a Web-based service that allowsaccess to a computer from anywhere; Xdrive, an online service that allows users to store and swap files; Basecamp, a Web-based tools that works like a secure version of MySpace; MojoPac Freedom, is software that allows users to copy their computer's desktop to a removable hard drive and plug into any PC; WatchGuard Firebox X Core e-Series UTM Bundle, hardware that blocks hackers and viruses while allowing employees to work remotely; TightVNC, a free open-source software that lets you control another computer via the Internet.

41421 ■ *"Reportlinker.com Adds Report: GeoWeb and Local Internet Markets: 2008 Edition" in Entertainment Close-Up (September 11, 2009)*
Description: Reportlinker.com is adding a new market research report that is available in its catalogue: GeoWeb and Local Internet Markets - 2008 Edition; highlights include the outlook for consumer mapping services and an examination of monetizing services and an analysis the development outlook for geospacial Internet market, also referred to as the Geoweb.

41422 ■ *"Research and Market Adds Report: Endpoint Security for Business" in Wireless News (October 26, 2009)*
Description: Summarizes Research and Markets Adds Report: Endpoint Security for Business: Desktops, Laptops & Mobile Devices 2009-2014; highlights include a detailed analysis of where the industry is at present and forecasts regarding how it will develop over the next five years.

41423 ■ *"Research and Markets Adds Report: The U.S. Mobile Web Market" in Entertainment Close-Up (December 10, 2009)*
Description: Highlights of the new Research and Markets report 'The U.S. Mobile Web Market: Taking Advantage of the iPhone Phenomenon' include: mobile Internet marketing strategies; the growth of mobile web usage; the growth of revenue in the mobile web market; and a look at Internet business communications, social media and networking.

41424 ■ *"Research Reports: How Analysts Size Up Companies" in Barron's (Vol. 88, March 31, 2008, No. 13, pp. M13)*
Pub: Dow Jones & Co., Inc.
Contact: Clare Hart, President

Ed: Anita Peltonen. **Description:** Sirius Satellite's shares are ranked Outperform as it awaits approval from the Federal Communications Commission in its merger with XM. TiVo's shares are ranked Avoid as the company is in a sector that's being commoditized. Verizon Communications' rising dividend yield earns it a Focus List ranking. The shares of Bear Stearns, Churchill Downs, Corning, and Deerfield Triarc Capital are also reviewed. Statistical data included.

41425 ■ *"Research Reports: How Analysts Size Up Companies" in Barron's (Vol. 88, March 17, 2008, No. 11, pp. M13)*
Pub: Dow Jones & Co., Inc.
Contact: Clare Hart, President

Ed: Anita Peltonen. **Description:** Shares of Applied Industrial Technologies are ranked Market Perform while the shares of Google get a buy rating. Salix Pharmaceuticals gets a Sell/Above-Average risk rating. The shares of Dune Energy, Franklin Resources, Internet Brands, Piper Jaffray, and Texas Instruments are also rated.

41426 ■ *"ReWalk Robotics Aims for IPO" in Boston Business Journal (Vol. 34, July 18, 2014, No. 24, pp. 7)*
Pub: American City Business Journals, Inc.
Contact: Whitney Shaw, President

Released: July 18, 2014. **Description:** ReWalk Robotics, an Israeli firm that manufactures wearable robotics exoskeletons for paraplegics, wants to launch an initial public offering (IPO) to raise US$57.5 million. In a July 2014 filing, ReWalk cited an accumulated debt of US$27 million at the end of 2013, justifying the need to go public and raise additional funds.

41427 ■ *"Riding the Wave: Past Trends and Future Directions for Health IT Research" in MIS Quarterly (Vol. 36, September 2012, No. 3, pp. III)*
Pub: MIS Research Center, Carlson School of Management
Description: Trends in healthcare information technologies, also known as health informatics, are discussed.

41428 ■ *"RIM: A Torch in the Darkness" in Canadian Business (Vol. 83, August 17, 2010, No. 13-14, pp. 66)*
Pub: Rogers Media Inc.
Contact: Tony Viner, President

Ed: Joe Castaldo. **Description:** Research In Motion (RIM) unveiled the BlackBerry Touch, featuring a touch screen as well as a physical keyboard, in an attempt to repel competitors and expand share in the consumer smart phone market. RIM shares have fallen 43 percent from its peak in 2009.

41429 ■ *"RIM Reinforces Claim as Top Dog by Expanding BlackBerry Service" in Globe & Mail (March 11, 2006, pp. B3)*
Ed: Simon Avery. **Description:** The plans of Research In Motion Ltd. to enhance the features of BlackBerry, through acquisition of Ascendent Systems, are presented.

41430 ■ *"Ripple Effect From Solar Frontier May Be Big" in Business First of Buffalo (Vol. 30, April 25, 2014, No. 32, pp. 4)*
Pub: American City Business Journals, Inc.
Contact: Whitney Shaw, President

Released: April 25, 2014. **Description:** A memorandum of understanding was signed by Japanese solar technology manufacturer Solar Frontier K.K. with the

State University of New York, College of Nanoscale Science and Engineering in Albany. The agreement is expected to create about 1,000 new jobs in the U.S. and at least $700 million in investments.

41431 ■ *"Rising in the East; Research and Development" in The Economist (Vol. 390, January 3, 2009, No. 8612, pp. 47)*
Description: Impressive growth of the technological research and development in Asian countries is discussed. Statistical data included.

41432 ■ *Risk Takers and Innovators, Great Canadian Business Ventures Since 1950*
Pub: Altitude Publishing

Ed: Sandra Phinney. **Released:** June 15, 2004. **Price:** , $7.95. **Description:** Successful business leaders share their creativity, technology skills, and entrepreneurship.

41433 ■ *"The Road to Newness" in Entrepreneur (June 2014)*
Pub: Entrepreneur Media Inc.

Released: June 2014. **Description:** A number of business experts share their thoughts on science, invention and innovation and how they are shaping the development of new products, technologies and commodities. Only nonprofit organizations, universities and few rich companies invest in scientific research because it is the riskiest form of investment. Some corporations are spending money on invention rather than science but spending is carefully controlled. People who want to see a quick return on their investment should choose innovation.

41434 ■ *"Roku: Connecting TV Sets to the Vast World of Online Video" in Inc. (Vol. 34, September 2012, No. 7, pp. 28)*
Pub: Mansueto Ventures L.L.C.
Contact: John Koten, Chief Executive Officer

Ed: April Joyner. **Released:** September 2012. **Description:** Profile of Anthony Wood and his firm Roku that developed the new Streaming Stick that brings the Internet to any television. The small device allows users to stream online movies and shows to their TV set.

41435 ■ *"RS Information Systems Signs Buyout Deal" in Black Enterprise (Vol. 38, February 2008, No. 7, pp. 27)*
Pub: Earl G. Graves Publishing Co. Inc.
Contact: Earl G. Graves, Jr., President

Ed: Alan Hughes. **Description:** Details of the RS Information Systems buyout by Wyle, a privately held provider of high-tech aerospace engineering, testing, and research services.

41436 ■ *"Rule of Thumb" in Entrepreneur (Vol. 36, May 2008, No. 5, pp. 44)*
Pub: Entrepreneur Press
Contact: Perlman Neil, President

Ed: Guy Kawasaki. **Description:** Business presentations using PowerPoint are recommended to have no more than 10 slides, last no longer than 20 minutes and have font no smaller than 30 points. Topics covered should include problem, solution, business model, underlying technology, and projections among others.

41437 ■ *"The Rypple Effect; Performance Management" in The Economist (Vol. 390, January 3, 2009, No. 8612, pp. 48)*
Description: New companies such as Rypple, a new, web-based service, claim that they can satisfy the Net Generation's need for frequent assessments while easing the burden this creates for management.

41438 ■ *"Sales Communications in a Mobile World: Using the Latest Technology and Retaining the Personal Touch" in Business Communication Quarterly (December 2007, pp. 492)*
Pub: Pine Forge Press
Contact: Blaise R. Simqu, President

Ed: Daniel T. Norris. **Description:** Salespeople can take advantage of the latest mobile technologies while maintaining a personal touch with clients and customers through innovation, formality in interactions, client interactions, and protection and security of mobile data.

41439 ■ *"Sales Strategy: Funny Business" in Canadian Business (Vol. 82, April 27, 2009, No. 7, pp. 27)*
Pub: Rogers Media Inc.
Contact: Tony Viner, President
Ed: Rachel Pulfer. **Description:** Companies are advised to use humor in marketing to drive more revenue. IBM Canada, for example, commissioned Second City Communications for a marketing campaign that involved humor. While IBM Canada declined to give sales or traffic figures, firm executives rank the marketing campaign as an overall success.

41440 ■ *"Samsung 'Holding Breath" in Austin Business JournalInc. (Vol. 29, January 29, 2010, No. 47, pp. 1)*
Pub: American City Business Journals
Ed: Jacob Dirr. **Description:** Samsung Austin Semiconductor LLC entered into an incentives agreement with the State of Texas in 2005, which involved $230 million in tax breaks and public financing. Terms of the agreement have been met, but some are questioning whether the company will be able to meet its goals for the Austin operations in 2010.

41441 ■ *"Samsung's Metamorphosis" in Austin Business Journal (Vol. 31, May 20, 2011, No. 11, pp. 1)*
Pub: American City Business Journals
Ed: Christopher Calnan. **Description:** Samsung Austin Semiconductor LP, a developer of semiconductors for smartphones and tablet computers, plans to diversify its offerings to include niche products: flash memory devices and microprocessing devices. In light of this strategy, Samsung Austin will be hiring 300 engineers as part of a $3.6 billion expansion of its plant.

41442 ■ *"San Francisco Technology Employers" in San Francisco Business Times (Vol. 28, February 21, 2014, No. 31, pp. 7)*
Pub: American City Business Journals
Released: February 21, 2014. **Description:** Rankings of companies within the computer and information technology services industries in the San Francisco, California area are presented. Rankings are based on the number of San Francisco-based employees.

41443 ■ *"San Jose Hopes to Build on Uptick in Manufacturing" in Silicon Valley/San Jose Business Journal (Vol. 30, July 13, 2012, No. 16, pp. 1)*
Pub: American City Business Journal
Description: San Jose, California-based manufacturing companies that cater to high-technology companies and startups have been experiencing an uptick in business. The San Jose metropolitan area is the country's second-largest specialized manufacturing market and the city has rolled out its efforts to help support this growth.

41444 ■ *"Say Goodbye to Voicemail" in Agency Sales Magazine (Vol. 39, November 2009, No. 10, pp. 3)*
Description: Salespeople should think twice before leaving a voicemail. The emerging modern etiquette is to send a text message or to e-mail the customer or client. Communication suggestions for both salespeople and their principals are presented.

41445 ■ *Science Lessons: What the Business of Biotech Taught Me About Management*
Pub: Harvard Business Review Press
Contact: Peter E. Walsh, Director
Ed: Gordon Binder, Philip Bashe. **Released:** April 15, 2008. **Price:** $35, hardcover. **Description:** Former CFO of biotechnology startup Amgen and veteran of Ford Motor Company provides a universal guide to management based on some of the same scientific principles used to create new drugs. **Availability:** Print.

41446 ■ *"Scientific American Builds Novel Blog Network" in Information Today (Vol. 28, September 2011, No. 8, pp. 12)*
Pub: Information Today, Inc.
Contact: Thomas H. Hogan, President
E-mail: ctuthill@infotoday.com
Ed: Kurt Schiller. **Description:** Scientific American launched a new blog network that joins a diverse lineup of bloggers cover various scientific topics under one banner. The blog network includes 60 bloggers providing insights into the ever-changing world of science and technology.

41447 ■ *"Search Engines: Image Conscious" in Canadian Business (Vol. 81, February 26, 2008, No. 4, pp. 36)*
Pub: Rogers Media Inc.
Contact: Tony Viner, President
Ed: Andrew Wahl. **Description:** Idee Inc. is testing an Internet search engine for images that does not rely on tags but compares its visual data to a database of other images. The company was founded and managed by Leila Boujnane as an off-shoot of their risk-management software firm. Their software has already been used by image companies to track copyrighted images and to find images within their own archives.

41448 ■ *"The Second Machine Age: Work, Progress, and Prosperity in a Time of Brilliant Technologies"*
Pub: W.W. Norton and Co.
Released: January 20, 2014. **Price:** , $26.95. **Description:** Insights into ways digital technologies are transforming our economy in order to develop new business models, new technologies, and new policies to enhance human capabilities are provided.

41449 ■ *"Security Alert: Data Server" in Entrepreneur (Vol. 36, February 2008, No. 2, pp. 28)*
Ed: Amanda C. Kooser. **Description:** Michael Kogon is the founder of Definition 6, a technology consulting and interactive marking firm. He believes in the philosophy that the best way to keep sensitive data safe is not to store it. Details on the security policies of his firm are discussed.

41450 ■ *"Seen & Noted: PDAs Are Great - As Long As You Can Find Them" in Crain's Chicago Business (Vol. 31, May 5, 2008, No. 18, pp. 41)*
Pub: Crain Communications Inc.
Contact: Todd Johnson, Publisher
Ed: Jennifer Olvera. **Description:** Discusses a new service from Global Lost & Found Inc. in which after paying a one-time fee, customers receive a label with an identification number and a toll free phone number so if they lose a gadget such as a cell phone, PDA or laptop the finder can return the device and are rewarded with a gift card.

41451 ■ *"Seven Ways to Fail Big" in Harvard Business Review (Vol. 86, September 2008, No. 9, pp. 82)*
Pub: Harvard Business Review Press
Contact: Peter E. Walsh, Director
Ed: Paul B. Carroll, Chunka Mui. **Description:** Seven factors involved in business failures are identified, and ways to avoid them are described. These factors include flawed financial engineering, hurrying into consolidation, and investing in technology that is not a good fit.

41452 ■ *"Sherwin-Williams Workers Forgo Travel for Virtual Trade Show" in Crain's Cleveland Business (Vol. 28, October 15, 2007, No. 41, pp. 4)*
Pub: Crain Communications Inc.
Ed: John Booth. **Description:** Overview of Cyber-Coating 2007, a cutting-edge virtual three-dimensional trade show that exhibitors such as Sherwin-Williams Co.'s Chemical Coatings Division will take part in by chatting verbally or via text messages in order to exchange information and listen to pitches just like they would on an actual trade show floor.

41453 ■ *"Show and Tell" in Entrepreneur (Vol. 36, May 2008, No. 5, pp. 54)*
Pub: Entrepreneur Press
Contact: Perlman Neil, President
Ed: Heather Clancy. **Description:** FreshStart Telephone uses recorded video testimonials of customers, by using Pure Digital Flip Video that downloads content directly to the computer, and uploads it in the company's website to promote their wireless phone service.

41454 ■ *"Silicon Valley's Economic Recovery Picking Up Pace" in Globe & Mail (January 29, 2007, pp. B13)*
Ed: Pui-Wing Tam. **Description:** The addition of 30,000 new jobs, rise in average annual wages and household income, along with other factors that have contributed to Silicon Valley's economic recovery are discussed.

41455 ■ *"The Skype's the Limit" in Canadian Business (Vol. 80, February 12, 2007, No. 4, pp. 70)*
Ed: Gerry Blackwell. **Description:** The increase in the market share of Skype Technologies S.A.'s Internet phone service to 171 million users is discussed.

41456 ■ *"Slater Progress Stalled" in Providence Business News (Vol. 28, March 10, 2014, No. 49, pp. 1)*
Pub: American City Business Journals
Released: March 10, 2014. **Description:** Slater Technology Fund has received only $1.9 million of the $9 million in expected federal funds. However, the venture capital firm decided to invest in some promising technology companies in Providence, Rhode Island. Slater senior managing director, Richard Horan, reveals that uncertainties with respect to grants have delayed private fundraising.

41457 ■ *"Slow but Steady into the Future" in Barron's (Vol. 88, July 7, 2008, No. 27, pp. M)*
Pub: Dow Jones & Co., Inc.
Contact: Clare Hart, President
Ed: Mark Veverka. **Description:** Investors are advised to maintain their watch on the shares of business software company NetSuite. The company's chief executive officer, Zach Nelson, claims that the company has a 10-year lead on its competitors with the development of software-as-a service.

41458 ■ *Small Business Clustering Technologies: Applications in Marketing, Management, IT and Economics*
Pub: IGI Global
Contact: Dr. Mehdi Khosrow-Pour, President
Ed: Robert C. MacGregor, Ann T. Hodgkinson. **Released:** September 2006. **Price:** 94.95, hardcover; $145, Institutions. **Description:** An overview of the development and role of small business clusters in disciplines that include economics, marketing, management and information systems. **Availability:** PrintE-book.

41459 ■ *SMEs and New Technologies: Learning E-Business and Development*
Pub: Palgrave Macmillan
Contact: Lisa Dunn, Manager
E-mail: l.dunn@palgrave.com
Ed: Banji Oyelaran-Oyeyinka, Kaushalesh Lal. **Released:** July 2006. **Price:** £84, hardcover; $125. **Description:** Adoption and learning of new information technologies in developing nations is covered. New technologies are opening opportunities for small companies in these countries. **Availability:** Print; E-book.

41460 ■ *"Social Media Conference NW 2010" in Bellingham Business Journal (Vol. February 2010, pp. 3)*
Pub: Sound Publishing Inc.
Contact: Gloria G. Fletcher, President
Ed: Lance Henderson. **Description:** Center for Economic Vitality (CEV) and the Technology Alliance Group (TAG) will host the 2010 Social Media Conference at the McIntyre Hall Performing Arts & Conference Center in Mt. Vernon, Washington. The event will provide networking opportunities for attendees.

41461 ■ *"Social Networking Site for Moms"* in *Marketing to Women (Vol. 21, March 2008, No. 3, pp. 3)*
Description: The Cradle is a social networking site devoted to pregnancy and new parenthood.

41462 ■ *"The Solution"* in *Entrepreneur (Vol. 37, October 2009, No. 10, pp. 71)*
Pub: Entrepreneur Press
Contact: Perlman Neil, President
Ed: Jennifer Wang. **Description:** Ford's 2010 Transit Connect is a compact commercial van developed specifically for small business owners. The compact van offers an integrated in-dash computer system providing a cellular broadband connection.

41463 ■ *"Some Big Biotechs Buying Own Stock"* in *Boston Business Journal (Vol. 30, November 5, 2010, No. 41, pp. 1)*
Ed: Julie M. Donnelly. **Description:** Biotechnology companies such as Biogen Idec and Genzyme Corporation are conducting stock buybacks as they look to invest their cash holdings. Other analysts see the buybacks as reluctance in committing to longer-term investments.

41464 ■ *"Sources"* in *Canadian Electronics (Vol. 23, August 2008, No. 5, pp. 12)*
Description: Directory of electronic manufacturers, distributors and representatives in Canada is provided. The list presents distributors and representatives under each manufacturer.

41465 ■ *"The Spark's Back in Sanyo"* in *Barron's (Vol. 88, March 31, 2008, No. 13, pp. M9)*
Pub: Dow Jones & Co., Inc.
Contact: Clare Hart, President
Ed: Jay Alabaster. **Description:** Things are looking up for Sanyo Electric after its string of calamities that range from major losses brought on by earthquake damage to its semiconductor operations and its near collapse and bailout. The company looks poised for a rebound as they are on track for their first net profit since 2003 and could beat its earnings forecast for 2008.

41466 ■ *"Spell It Out"* in *Entrepreneur (Vol. 36, April 2008, No. 4, pp. 123)*
Pub: Entrepreneur Press
Contact: Perlman Neil, President
Ed: Emily Weisberg. **Description:** IM:It is an apparel and accessories company that markets products with instant messaging (IM) acronyms and emoticons. Examples of these are 'LOL' and 'GTG'. Other details on IM:It products are discussed.

41467 ■ *"Spin Zone: Where Hawaii's Leaders Face Off, Have High-Tech Tax Credits Helped or Hurt Hawaii?"* in *Hawaii Business (Vol. 53, December 2007, No. 6, pp. 28)*
Pub: PacificBasin Communications
Description: Presents the opinons of Channel Capital LLC's Walter R. Roth and Hawaii Venture Capital Association's Bill Spencer concerning the impacts of tax credits. Roth thinks that Act 221 appeals to investors who can earn despite business failure while Spencer thinks that the legislation promotes investments in innovative technology firms. The need to support tax credits is also discussed.

41468 ■ *"A Sports Extravaganza - To Go"* in *Canadian Business (Vol. 79, June 19, 2006, No. 13, pp. 21)*
Ed: Andy Holloway. **Description:** Television broadcasting industry in Canada utilizing advanced technologies like mobile television and internet protocol television in broadcasting major sports events. Large number of new technologies are being invented to support increasing demand.

41469 ■ *"Staffing Firm Grows by Following Own Advice-Hire a Headhunter"* in *Crain's Detroit Business (Vol. 24, October 6, 2008, No. 40, pp. 1)*
Pub: Crain Communications Inc.
Contact: Rance E. Crain, President
Ed: Sherri Begin. **Description:** Profile of Venator Holdings L.L.C., a staffing firm that provides searches for companies in need of financial-accounting and technical employees; the firm's revenue has increased from $1.1 million in 2003 to a projected $11.5 million this year due to a climate in which more people are exiting the workforce than are coming in with those particular specialized skills and the need for a temporary, flexible workforce for contract placements at companies that do not want to take on the legacy costs associated with permanent employees. The hiring of an external headhunter to find the right out-of-state manager for Venator is also discussed.

41470 ■ *"STAR TEC Incubator's Latest Resident Shows Promise"* in *The Business Journal-Serving Greater Tampa Bay (August 11, 2008)*
Pub: American City Business Journals, Inc.
Contact: Whitney Shaw, President
Ed: Jane Meinhardt. **Description:** Field Forensics Inc., a resident of the STAR Technology Enterprise Center, has grown after being admitted into the business accelerator. The producer of defense and security devices and equipment has doubled 2007 sales as of 2008.

41471 ■ *"Startup Osteosphere Formed to Develop Laboratory Discovery"* in *Houston Business Journal (Vol. 40, January 8, 2010, No. 35, pp. 1)*
Pub: American City Business Journals
Ed: Casey Wooten. **Description:** Biotech startup company Osteosphere in Houston, Texas aims to market a technology in which laboratory-grown bone tissues can be processed to appear like a real human bone tissue. The technology was developed by a co-founder of the startup and it can be applied to bone disease and injury treatment. Osteophere's future plans, such as the search for possible investors, is also outlined.

41472 ■ *"State Efforts to Boost Contract Efficiency Hurt Smaller Firms"* in *Boston Business Journal (Vol. 27, November 9, 2007, No. 41, pp. 1)*
Ed: Lisa van der Pool. **Description:** Massachusetts Operational Services Division, which provides state-wide telecommunications and data infrastructure contracts, announced that it is cutting the list of companies on the new contract from twelve to six. The cost-cutting efforts began in 2005, after a review by an independent consultant advised the state to adopt strategies that would save millions of dollars.

41473 ■ *"State of Play"* in *Canadian Business (Vol. 79, June 19, 2006, No. 13, pp. 25)*
Ed: Andrew Wahl; Zena Olijnyk; Jeff Sanford. **Description:** Top 100 information technology companies in Canada are ranked by their market capitalization as of June 1. The statistics that show the revenues of these companies are also presented.

41474 ■ *"Steelhead Makes High-Tech Tanks"* in *Denver Business Journal (Vol. 65, March 28, 2014, No. 46, pp. A7)*
Pub: American City Business Journals
Released: March 28, 2014. **Description:** Steelhead Composites LLC is known for its high-technology tanks that hold pressurized gases. The company, which was founded in October 2012, aimed to tackle problems associated with long delivery times. Reports show that the firm's supporters have invested more than $5 million into the business.

41475 ■ *"Sticking to Stories: Harvey Ovshinksy Changes Method, Keeps the Mission"* in *Crain's Detroit Business (Vol. 24, March 31, 2008)*
Pub: Crain Communications Inc.
Contact: Rance E. Crain, President
Ed: Daniel Duggan. **Description:** Profile of Harvey Ovshinsky, an award-winning documentary filmmaker who has reinvented his work with corporations who want to market themselves with the transition to digital media. His company, HKO Media, takes Ovshinsky's art of storytelling and enhances it through multimedia operations on the Internet through a joint venture with a man he once mentored, Bob Kernen.

41476 ■ *"STMicroelectronics"* in *Canadian Electronics (Vol. 23, February 2008, No. 1, pp. 1)*
Description: STMicroelectronics, a semiconductor maker, revealed that it plans to acquire Genesis Microchip Inc. Genesis develops image and video processing systems. It was reported that the acquisition has been approved by Genesis' Board of Directors. It is expected that Genesis will enhance STMicroelectronics' technological capabilities.

41477 ■ *"The Story Of Diane Greene"* in *Barron's (Vol. 88, July 14, 2008, No. 28, pp. 31)*
Pub: Dow Jones & Co., Inc.
Contact: Clare Hart, President
Ed: Mark Veverka. **Description:** Discusses the ousting of Diane Greene as a chief executive of VMWare, a developer of virtualization software, after the firm went public; in this case Greene, a brilliant engineer, should not be negatively impacted by the decision because it is common for companies to bring in new executive leadership that is more operations oriented after the company goes public.

41478 ■ *"Study Puts Hub On Top of the Tech Heap"* in *Boston Business Journal (Vol. 30, November 26, 2010, No. 44, pp. 1)*
Pub: Boston Business Journal
Ed: Galen Moore. **Description:** The Ewing Marion Kauffman Foundation ranked Massachusetts at the top in its evaluations of states' innovative industries, government leadership, and education. Meanwhile, research blog formDs.com also ranked Massachusetts number one in terms of venture-capital financings per capita.

41479 ■ *"Stuff that Works for You: In the Mobikey of Life"* in *Canadian Business (Vol. 81, June 11, 2008, No. 11, pp. 42)*
Pub: Rogers Media Inc.
Contact: Tony Viner, President
Ed: John Gray. **Description:** Toronto-based Route1 has created a data security software system that allows employees to access files and programs stored in the head office without permanently transferring data to the actual computer being used. Mobikey technology is useful in protecting laptops of chief executive officers, which contain confidential financial and customer data.

41480 ■ *"Stuff that Works for You: Touching the Future"* in *Canadian Business (Vol. 81, June 11, 2008, No. 11, pp. 41)*
Pub: Rogers Media Inc.
Contact: Tony Viner, President
Ed: Matt McClearn. **Description:** Microsoft Corp. has launched a multi-touch product which is both a software and hardware technology called Microsoft Surface. The innovative product allows people to use it at the same time, however touch-based computers are reported to be around $100,000. Other features and benefits of the product are presented.

41481 ■ *"Suited for Success"* in *Retail Merchandiser (Vol. 51, July-August 2011, No. 4, pp. 6)*
Pub: Phoenix Media Corporation
Description: MyBestFit is a size-matching body scanner that helps consumers find the perfect size clothing for themselves, giving brick and mortar retailers an edge on ecommerce competitors.

41482 ■ *"The Superfluous Position"* in *Entrepreneur (Vol. 37, July 2009, No. 7, pp. 62)*
Pub: Entrepreneur Press
Contact: Perlman Neil, President
Description: Profile of an anonymous editor at a multimedia company that publishes tourism guides who shares his experiences in dealing with an office-mate who was promoted as creative manager of content. Everyone was irritated by this person, who would constantly do something to justify his new title. The biggest problem was the fact that this person didn't have a clear job description.

41483 ■ *"The Superpower Dilemma" in Canadian Business (Vol. 83, August 17, 2010, No. 13-14, pp. 42)*
Description: Canada has been an energy superpower partly because it controls the energy source and the production means, particularly of fossil fuels. However, Canada's status as superpower could diminish if it replaces petroleum exports with renewable technology for using sources of energy available globally.

41484 ■ *"The Sweet Sound of Download Revenues: Mobile: Juanes Fans Sing for Sprint" in Advertising Age (Vol. 79, November 3, 2008, No. 41, pp. 22)*
Pub: Crain Communications Inc.
Contact: Rance Crain, President
Ed: Laurel Wentz. **Description:** Marketers are appealing to the Hispanic market since they are more prone to use their cell phones to respond to contests, download videos, ringtones, or other data activity. Sprint recently sponsored a contest inviting people to sing like Colombian megastar Juanes; the participants filmed and sent their videos using their cell phones rather than laptops or camcorders illustrating the Hispanic overindex on mobile-phone technology. The contest generated hundreds of thousands of dollars in additional fee revenue, as monthly downloads increased 63 percent.

41485 ■ *"A Swifter, Better Marketplace" in Barron's (Vol. 89, July 13, 2009, No. 28, pp. M13)*
Pub: Dow Jones & Co., Inc.
Contact: Clare Hart, President
Ed: Eric W. Noll. **Description:** Listed-derivatives market is moving towards greater trading through computerized systems with an emphasis on speed and innovation. The market for listed options is also being changed by new techniques from other markets such as algorithmic trading, dark pools, and new-order priority systems.

41486 ■ *"Symbility Solutions Joins Motion Computing Partner Program" in Marketwired (May 14, 2007)*
Pub: Comtex News Network Inc.
Description: Symbility Solutions Inc., a wholly owned subsidiary of Automated Benefits Corp., announced an agreement with Alliance Partner of Motion Computing, a leader in wireless communications and mobile computing, in which both companies will invest in a sales and marketing strategy that focuses specifically on the insurance market.

41487 ■ *"Tabular Dreams" in Canadian Business (Vol. 80, February 12, 2007, No. 4, pp. 36)*
Ed: Christina Campbell. **Description:** The research of Raymor Industries in developing carbon nanotubes by bonding carbon atoms using high technology is discussed.

41488 ■ *"Taiwan Technology Initiatives Foster Growth" in Canadian Electronics (Vol. 23, February 2008, No. 1, pp. 28)*
Description: A study conducted by the Market Intelligence Center shows that currently, Taiwan is the world's larges producer of information technology products such as motherboards, servers, and LCD monitors. In 2006, Taiwan's LED industry reached a production value of NTD 21 billion. This push into the LED sector shows the Ministry of Economic Affairs' plan to target industries that are environmentally friendly.

41489 ■ *"Taking on 911 - and Making a New Tech Biz In the Process" in Orlando Business Journal (Vol. 30, January 24, 2014, No. 31, pp. 3)*
Pub: American City Business Journals
Released: January 24, 2014. **Description:** Central Florida-based TapShield LLC is on the path to growth. The firm has developed a mobile application that enables University of Florida students to coordinate with police. Meanwhile, TapShield is in negotiations with large companies for similar deals.

41490 ■ *"Taking on Intel: AMD Faces Off" in Canadian Business (Vol. 79, October 23, 2006, No. 21, pp. 27)*
Pub: Rogers Media Inc.
Contact: Tony Viner, President
Ed: Andrew Wahl. **Description:** The decision of ATI Technologies Inc., a Canadian computer peripherals company to acquire cash and stocks worth US$5.4-billion from American microprocessor maker Advanced Micro Devices Inc., is discussed.

41491 ■ *"Taking a Leap With Mobile Wi-Fi" in Austin Business Journal (Vol. 34, July 25, 2014, No. 23, pp. 10)*
Pub: American City Business Journals, Inc.
Contact: Whitney Shaw, President
Released: July 25, 2014. **Description:** Austin-based semi-conductor design company Nitero Inc.'s recent release of its Wi-Fi chip, Nietero's key rival Wilocity Ltd.'s acquisition by a tech giant, pushing demand for semiconductors; thus spurring growth for Nitero. It's Wi-Fi's system for mobile platforms will enable users to do more things on their Smartphones, thus converging more devices into one.

41492 ■ *"Taking Off" in Puget Sound Business Journal (Vol. 34, January 31, 2014, No. 42, pp. 4)*
Pub: American City Business Journals
Released: January 31, 2014. **Description:** Washington State is at the forefront of the U.S. space flight industry, as the federal government shrinks its role and entrepreneurs are filling the gap. The region is becoming a leader in the space sector because of its high-tech aerospace skills, software intellectuals, and investors willing to fund these enterprises.

41493 ■ *"Taking the Steps Into the Clouds" in New Hampshire Business Review (Vol. 33, March 25, 2011, No. 6, pp. 19)*
Pub: Business Publications Inc.
Ed: Tim Wessels. **Description:** Cloud services include Internet and Web security, spam filtering, message archiving, work group collaboration, IT asset management, help desk and disaster recovery backup.

41494 ■ *"Tale of a Gun" in Canadian Business (Vol. 80, February 26, 2007, No. 5, pp. 37)*
Ed: Matthew McClearn. **Description:** The technology behind automated ballistic identification systems, which can be used to analyze fired ammunition components and link them to crime guns and suspects, developed by Canadian companies is presented.

41495 ■ *"Tale of the Tape: IPhone Vs. G1" in Advertising Age (Vol. 79, October 27, 2008, No. 40, pp. 6)*
Pub: Crain Communications Inc.
Contact: Rance Crain, President
Ed: Rita Chang. **Description:** T-Mobile's G1 has been positioned as the first serious competitor to Apple's iPhone. G1 is the first mobile phone to run on the Google-backed, open-source platform Android.

41496 ■ *"Targeted Technology Raises More Than $40 Million" in San Antonio Business Journal (Vol. 28, September 5, 2014, No. 30, pp. 8)*
Pub: American City Business Journals
Released: September 5, 2014. **Description:** Targeted Technology has raised more than $40 million in venture capital funding for early-stage biotechnology companies in San Antonio, Texas through its Targeted Technology Fund II. Senior managing partner, Paul Castella, recognizes the lack of venture capital funds in the area and the role played by his organization to help these firms.

41497 ■ *"Taylor Tests Land Grant Program" in Austin Business Journal (Vol. 31, June 3, 2011, No. 13, pp. 1)*
Pub: American City Business Journals
Ed: Vicky Garza. **Description:** Taylor Economic Development Corporation implemented a land grant program called Build On Our Lot to lure businesses to Taylor City, Austin, Texas. They are targeting small

businesses, especially those in the renewable energy, advanced manufacturing, technical services and food products. Program details are included.

41498 ■ *"The Tech 100" in Canadian Business (Vol. 81, July 21, 2008, No. 11, pp. 48)*
Ed: Calvin Leung. **Description:** Absolute Software Corp. Day4 Energy Inc., Sandvine Corp., Norsat International Inc. and Call Genie Inc. are the five technology firms included in the annual ranking of top companies in Canada by market capitalization. The services and the one-year total return potential of the companies are presented.

41499 ■ *"Tech Coalition Warns Takeover Spree is Nigh" in Globe & Mail (February 6, 2007, pp. B1)*
Ed: Steven Chase. **Description:** The declaration by an alliance of technology-rich companies, that the huge credits that these companies have to endure due to research and development activities may lead to company takeovers, is discussed.

41500 ■ *"Tech Data Launches Unified Communications and Network Security Specialized Business Units" in Wireless News (October 22,2009)*
Description: Responding to the growing demand for unified communications and network security, Tech Data announced the formation of two new Specialized Business Units.

41501 ■ *"Tech Giving 2.0" in Boston Business Journal (Vol. 31, August 5, 2011, No. 28, pp. 1)*
Pub: Boston Business Journal
Ed: Mary Moore. **Description:** Entrepreneurs and venture capitalists in Boston have launched Technology Underwriting Greater Good, the tech industry's answer to the criticism that they are not charitable. The foundation finances nonprofits that aid young people through entrepreneurship, education and life experience. Other tech firms in Boston doing charitable works are discussed.

41502 ■ *"Tech Godfather Steve Walker Winding Down Howard Venture Fund" in Baltimore Business Journal (Vol. 27, December 11, 2009, No. 31)*
Pub: American City Business Journals
Ed: Scott Dance. **Description:** Steve Walker, president of venture capital fund firm Walker Ventures, will be closing the Howard County, Maryland-based firm as the economic situation is finding it difficult to recover investor's money. According to Walker, the economy also constrained investors from financing venture funds. Despite the closure, Walker will continue his work in the local angel investing community.

41503 ■ *"Tech Investing: March's Long Road" in Canadian Business (Vol. 80, January 29, 2007, No. 3, pp. 67)*
Ed: Calvin Leung. **Description:** The efforts of March Networks, a manufacturer of digital surveillance equipment, from the decline in the price of its shares at the beginning of the year 2007 are described.

41504 ■ *"Tech Jobs Rebound from Downturn" in Denver Business Journal (Vol. 65, March 7, 2014, No. 43, pp. A9)*
Pub: American City Business Journals
Released: March 7, 2014. **Description:** Denver, Colorado's employment in core technology industries has returned from pre-Great Recession figures. The computer software industry's surging job growth and the slight increase in the broadcasts and telecommunications industry offset the job losses in biotechnology and private aerospace industry from 2008 through 2013. The growth in specific industries is also discussed.

41505 ■ *"TechLift Strives to Fill in Gaps in Entrepreneurial Support Efforts" in Crain's Cleveland Business (November 12, 2007)*
Pub: Crain Communications Inc.
Ed: Marsha Powers. **Description:** Profile of the program, TechLift, a new business model launched by NorTech, that is aiming to provide assistance to technology-based companies that may not be a good fit for other entrepreneurial support venues.

41506 ■ *"Technically Speaking" in Black Enterprise (Vol. 38, February 2008, No. 7, pp. 64)*
Ed: Sonia Alleyne. **Description:** Marketing manager for Texas Instruments discusses the Strategic Marketing of Technology Products course offered at the California Institute of Technology. The course helps turn products into profits.

41507 ■ *Technological Entrepreneurship*
Pub: Edward Elgar Publishing Inc.
Contact: Richard Henning, Vice President
E-mail: kwight@e-elgar.com
Released: October 2006. **Price:** $238.50, hardback. **Description:** Technological entrepreneurship at universities is discussed. The book covers four related topics: university licensing and patenting; science parks and incubators; university-based startups; and the role of academic science in entrepreneurship. **Availability:** Print.

41508 ■ *"Technology Companies are Increasing Their Hiring" in Philadelphia Business Journal (Vol. 31, March 16, 2012, No. 5, pp. 1)*
Pub: American City Business Journal
Description: Technology firms in Pennsylvania have been expanding their work force. Online advertisements for computer and math science hiring have increased.

41509 ■ *"Technology Drivers to Boost Your Bottom Line" in Franchising World (Vol. 42, August 2010, No. 8, pp. 15)*
Pub: International Franchise Association
Contact: Stephen J. Caldeira, President
E-mail: scaldeira@franchise.org
Ed: Dan Dugal. **Description:** Technological capabilities are expanding quickly and smart franchises should stay updated on all the new developments, including smart phones, global positioning systems, and social media networks.

41510 ■ *"TECHNOLOGY: Elder Care Enters the Digital Age: Wireless Companies Devise Ways to Aid Home Health, Let People Stay in Homes" in Atlanta Journal-Constitution (April 29, 2012, pp. D1)*
Description: Mobile phone industry is actually helping families keep aging loved one in their homes. The home healthcare industry is adding technology, telecommunications, smartphone applications and other devices to make it easier for seniors to remain in their homes. Details on this growing industry are included along with statistical data.

41511 ■ *"Technology-Market Combinations and the Identification of Entrepreneurial Opportunities: an Investigation of the Opportunity-Individual Nexus" in Academy of Management Journal (Vol. 55, August 1, 2012, No. 4, pp. 753)*
Pub: Academy of Management
Contact: Ming-Jer Chen, President
Ed: Denis A. Gregoire, Dean A. Shepherd. **Description:** The effects of differences among opportunity ideas on entrepreneurs' opportunity beliefs are investigated. Results indicate that the formation of opportunity beliefs is influenced by the superficial and structural similarities of technology-market combinations and individual differences pay a significant role in moderating these relationships.

41512 ■ *"Technology and Returnable Asset Management" in Canadian Electronics (Vol. 23, February 2008, No. 1, pp. 6)*
Ed: Mark Borkowski. **Description:** Peter Kastner, president of Vestigo Corporation, believes that public companies without an asset track, trace, and control system in place could face Sarbanes-Oakley liability if error-prone processes result to misstatements of asset inventory positions. He also thinks that the system can improve return on assets by increasing the utilization of returnables.

41513 ■ *"Tech's Payout Problem" in Barron's (Vol. 90, September 13, 2010, No. 37, pp. 19)*
Pub: Barron's Editorial & Corporate Headquarters
Ed: Andrew Bary. **Description:** Big tech companies have the potential to be good dividend payers, but instead just hoard their cash for acquisitions and

share buybacks. If these companies offered more dividends, they could boost their shares and attract more income-oriented investors.

41514 ■ *"TELUS Drawing More Power From Its Wireless Operations" in Globe & Mail (February 17, 2007, pp. B3)*
Ed: Catherine McLean. **Description:** TELUS Corp., the fast-growing wireless business company, posted tripled profits in the fourth quarter of 2006. The revenues of the company increased 8 percent in the same period.

41515 ■ *"Texas Fold 'Em" in Canadian Business (Vol. 79, October 9, 2006, No. 20, pp. 44)*
Pub: Rogers Media Inc.
Contact: Tony Viner, President
Ed: John Gray. **Description:** New policies of the United States law makers for the online casino industries that could force many of them out of business are discussed.

41516 ■ *"They Like It Cold" in Business Journal Portland (Vol. 27, October 15, 2010, No. 33, pp. 1)*
Pub: Portland Business Journal
Ed: Erik Siemers. **Description:** Ajinomoto Frozen Foods USA Inc. has been investing in its Portland, Oregon facility. The company has completed a new rice production line. It has also spent $1.2 million on a new packaging technology.

41517 ■ *"Thinking Strategically About Technology" in Franchising World (Vol. 42, August 2010, No. 8, pp. 9)*
Pub: International Franchise Association
Contact: Stephen J. Caldeira, President
E-mail: scaldeira@franchise.org
Ed: Bruce Franson. **Description:** Nearly 25 percent of companies waste money from their technology budget. Most of the budget is spent on non-strategic software. Ways to spend money on technology for any franchise are examined.

41518 ■ *"This Is Marc Benioff's Time" in San Francisco Business Times (Vol. 28, April 18, 2014, No. 39, pp. 4)*
Pub: American City Business Journals
Released: April 18, 2014. **Description:** Salesforce CEO, Marc Benioff, has adopted the role as the conscience of the technology industry in San Francisco, California. Benioff's spreading reputation and public image as a leading edge in philanthropy is shaping up his defining moment in trying to push back the city's tech companies to be involved in civic engagement. Insights into Benioff's social responsibility and companies giving back is discussed.

41519 ■ *"Thumbing Around: U3 Flash Drive" in Canadian Business (Vol. 79, October 9, 2006, No. 20, pp. 143)*
Pub: Rogers Media Inc.
Contact: Tony Viner, President
Ed: Gerry Blackwell. **Description:** The features, functions of Cruzer Titanium, a serial bus standard to interface device developed by SanDisk Corporation are discussed.

41520 ■ *"Tim Armstrong" in Canadian Business (Vol. 81, July 21, 2008, No. 11, pp. 10)*
Ed: Calvin Leung. **Description:** Interview with Tim Armstrong who is the president of advertising and commerce department of Google Inc. for North America; the information technology company executive talked about the emerging trends and changes to YouTube made by the company since its acquisition in 2006.

41521 ■ *"A Timely Boon for Small Investors" in Barron's (Vol. 88, March 24, 2008, No. 12, pp. 48)*
Pub: Dow Jones & Co., Inc.
Contact: Clare Hart, President
Ed: Theresa W. Carey. **Description:** Nasdaq Data Store's new program called Market Replay allows investors to accurately track stock price movements.

The replay can be as long as a day of market time and allows investors to determine whether they executed stock trades at the best possible price.

41522 ■ *"TiVo, Domino's Team to Offer Pizza Ordering by DVR" in Advertising Age (Vol. 79, November 17, 2008, No. 43, pp. 48)*
Pub: Crain Communications Inc.
Contact: Rance Crain, President
Ed: Brian Steinberg. **Description:** Domino's Pizza and TiVo are teaming up to make it possible for customers to order from the restaurant straight from their DVR. The companies see that this kind of interactive television and consumer experience will only serve to generate more sales as the customer can be exposed to a fuller range of menu selections and will not have to interrupt their viewing, while workers can spend more time making the product.

41523 ■ *"To Build for the Future, Reach Beyond the Skies" in Canadian Business (Vol. 83, June 15, 2010, No. 10, pp. 11)*
Pub: Rogers Media Inc.
Contact: Tony Viner, President
Ed: Richard Branson. **Description:** Richard Branson says that tackling an engineering challenge or a scientific venture is a real adventure for an entrepreneur. Branson discusses Virgin's foray into the aviation business and states that at Virgin, they build for the future.

41524 ■ *"TomTom GO910: On the Road Again" in Black Enterprise (Vol. 37, January 2007, No. 6, pp. 52)*
Pub: Earl G. Graves Publishing Co. Inc.
Contact: Earl G. Graves, Jr., President
Ed: Stephanie Young. **Description:** TomTom GO 910 is a GPS navigator that offers detailed maps of the U.S., Canada, and Europe. Consumers view their routes by a customizable LCD screen showing everything from the quickest to the shortest routes available or how to avoid toll roads. Business travelers may find this product invaluable as it also functions as a cell phone and connects to a variety of other multi-media devices.

41525 ■ *"Too Much of a Good Thing" in San Francisco Business Times (Vol. 28, February 21, 2014, No. 31, pp. 4)*
Pub: American City Business Journals
Released: February 21, 2014. **Description:** San Francisco, California is experiencing an increase of technology workers grow by more than 13,000 since 2010 to reach nearly 50,000 in 2014. However, a portion of the city's population feels the tech industry becomes influential in city affairs and negatively affects housing affordability and neighborhoods. San Francisco's overreliance on the technology industry is also discussed.

41526 ■ *"Too Much Precaution About Biotech Corn" in Barron's (Vol. 88, March 17, 2008, No. 11, pp. 54)*
Pub: Dow Jones & Co., Inc.
Contact: Clare Hart, President
Ed: Mark I. Schwartz. **Description:** In the U.S., 90 percent of cultivated soybeans are biotech varietals as well as 60 percent of the corn. Farmers have significantly reduced their reliance on pesticides in the growing of biotech corn. Biotech cotton cultivation has brought hundreds of millions of dollars in net financial gains to farmers. The European Union has precluded the cultivation or sale of biotech crops within its border.

41527 ■ *"Top 100 Consolidate Gains" in Hispanic Business (Vol. 30, July-August 2008, No. 7-8, pp. 30)*
Ed: Richard Kaplan. **Description:** Data developed by HispanTelligence on the increase in revenue posted by the top 100 fastest-growing U.S. Hispanic firms over the last five years is reported. Despite the economic downturn, the service sector, IT and health suppliers showed an increase in revenue whereas construction companies showed a marginal slump in revenue growth.

41528 ■ *"Top Architecture Firms"* in *South Florida Business Journal (Vol. 34, June 13, 2014, No. 47, pp. 13)*
Pub: American City Business Journals
Released: June 13, 2014. **Description:** The top architectural firms in South Florida, as of June 13, 2014, ranked by gross billings are listed. AECOM Technology Corporation got the top spot, ADD Inc. ranked third.

41529 ■ *"Top IPhone Apps"* in *Advertising Age (Vol. 79, December 15, 2008, No. 46, pp. 17)*
Pub: Crain Communications Inc.
Contact: Rance Crain, President
Ed: Marissa Miley. **Description:** Free and low cost applications for the iPhone are described including Evernote, an application that allows users to outsource their memory to keep track of events, notes, ides and more; Handshake, a way for users to exchange business cards and pictures across Wi-Fi and 3G; CityTransit, an interactive map of the New York subway system that uses GPS technology to find nearby stations and also tells the user if a train is out of commission that day; and Stage Hand which allows users to deliver a presentation, control timing and slide order on the spot.

41530 ■ *"Top Women In Tech: Whether It's Mobile or Engineering, These Mavens Are Making an Impact on Today's Tech Scene"* in *Black Enterprise (Vol. 44, February 2014, No. 6, pp. 29)*
Pub: Earl G. Graves Publishing Co. Inc.
Contact: Earl G. Graves, Jr., President
Released: February 2014. **Description:** There are fewer women than men in technology, science, engineering, and mathematics professions. As part of the magazine's Women of Power coverage, three successful minority women in their fields are profiled.

41531 ■ *"The Total Cost of Ignorance: Avoiding Top Tech Mistakes"* in *Black Enterprise (Vol. 38, October 1, 2007, No. 3, pp. 64)*
Pub: Earl G. Graves Publishing Co. Inc.
Contact: Earl G. Graves, Jr., President
Ed: Alwin A.D. Jones. **Description:** Cost of data loss for any small business can be devastating; lack of security is another mistake companies make when it comes to technology.

41532 ■ *"Toward a Better Future"* in *Canadian Business (Vol. 83, August 17, 2010, No. 13-14, pp. 51)*
Description: A look at certain realities in order to build a better future for Canada's energy industry is presented. Canada must focus on making the oil cleaner, instead of replacing it with another source since dependency on oil will remain in this lifetime. Canada must also develop solutions toward clean technology power sources.

41533 ■ *"Training Center Wants to be College"* in *Austin Business JournalInc. (Vol. 29, November 13, 2009, No. 36, pp. A1)*
Pub: American City Business Journals
Ed: Sandra Zaragoza. **Description:** Texas-based CyberTex Institute, a job training center, has established technical careers in an effort to obtain federal accreditation as a college. A college status would allow CyperTex to extend financial assistance to students. Aside from potentially having an enlarged student body and expanded campus, CyberTex would be allowed to engage in various training programs.

41534 ■ *"Training the Troops: Battlefield Simulations Bring Growth to UNITECH"* in *Black Enterprise (Vol. 38, February 2008, No. 7, pp. 30)*
Pub: Earl G. Graves Publishing Co. Inc.
Contact: Earl G. Graves, Jr., President
Ed: Cliff Hocker. **Description:** Universal Systems and Technology (UNITECH) received a total of over $45 million U.S. Department of Defense orders during September and October 2007. UNITECH designs and manufactures battlefield simulation devices used to train troops in the Army and Marine Corps.

41535 ■ *"Transfusion"* in *Puget Sound Business Journal (Vol. 33, August 31, 2012, No. 19, pp. 1)*
Description: Seattle, Washington-based nonprofit biotechnology companies have been hiring people with fundraising and scientific skills. The development is part of efforts to find new funding resources.

41536 ■ *"The Transparent Supply Chain"* in *Harvard Business Review (Vol. 88, October 2010, No. 10, pp. 76)*
Pub: Harvard Business School Publishing
Ed: Steve New. **Description:** Examination of the use of new technologies to create a transparent supply chain, such as next-generation 2D bar codes in clothing labels that can provide data on a garment's provenance.

41537 ■ *"The Traveler's Traveler"* in *Entrepreneur (Vol. 37, September 2009, No. 9, pp. 22)*
Pub: Entrepreneur Press
Contact: Perlman Neil, President
Ed: Kim Orr. **Description:** Business travel columnist Joe Sharkey says technology may someday replace business travel. Airlines are realizing that a part of the business travel market has disappeared. Sharkey also says airlines can never get those customers back.

41538 ■ *"Tripwire Aligns Information Security With Business Objectives and Goals With New Versions of Tripwire(R) Enterprise, Tripwire Log Center(R) and VIA(TM) Data Mart"* in *Internet Wire September 5, 2012*
Pub: COMTEX
Contact: Chip Brian, President
Released: September 5, 2012. **Description:** Tripwire Inc. launched three new coordinated product enhancements that enable companies to connect their IT security to the businesses and missions it serves. Details of each product are included. Tripwire is a worldwide provider of security solutions for business.

41539 ■ *"Turnaround Plays: The Return of Wi-LAN"* in *Canadian Business (Vol. 80, January 29, 2007, No. 3, pp. 68)*
Ed: Joe Castaldo. **Description:** The recovery of the wireless equipment manufacturing firm Wi-LAN from near-bankruptcy, under the leadership of Jim Skippen, is described.

41540 ■ *"Turning Drivers Into Geeks; Auto Dealers Debate Need for Technology Specialists to Bring Buyers Up to Speed"* in *Crain's Detroit Business (Vol. 30, January 6, 2014, No. 1, pp. 3)*
Pub: Crain Communications Inc. - Detroit
Contact: Keith Crain, Chairman
Released: January 6, 2014. **Description:** Dealers at the 2014 North American International Auto Show discuss the need for technology specialists to educate sales staff as well as customers on the new high-tech items manufactured on today's automobiles and trucks.

41541 ■ *"Twice the Innovation, Half the Tears"* in *Business Courier (Vol. 24, March 7, 2008, No. 48, pp. 1)*
Pub: American City Business Journals, Inc.
Contact: Whitney Shaw, President
Ed: Lisa Biank Fasig. **Description:** Procter & Gamble was able to develop a pant-style diaper called Pampers First Pants by creating a virtual, three-dimensional baby. The company was able to reduce the number of real mock-ups that it had to make by putting the diapers on the virtual baby first. Specifics about product designs were not revealed by the company.

41542 ■ *"Two Local Firms Make Inc. List: Minority Business"* in *Indianapolis Business Journal (Vol. 31, August 30, 2010, No. 26, pp. 13A)*
Description: Smart IT staffing agency and Entap Inc., an IT outsourcing firm were among the top ten fastest growing black-owned businesses in the U.S. by Inc. magazine.

41543 ■ *"Unbreakable: Computer Software"* in *Canadian Business (Vol. 79, October 9, 2006, No. 20, pp. 111)*
Pub: Rogers Media Inc.
Contact: Tony Viner, President
Ed: Robert Hercz. **Description:** The features and functions of Neutrino, an embedded operating system developed by QNX Software Systems are discussed.

41544 ■ *"Understanding Geeks: A Field Guide To Your Tech Staff"* in *Inc. (December 2007, pp. 62-63)*
Pub: Gruner and Jahr USA Publishing Co.
Contact: J. Russell Denson, President
Ed: Adam Bluestein. **Description:** Guide to demystify managing the information technology staff of any small business is presented, including a list of do's and don'ts and a glossary of technical terms.

41545 ■ *"UTM Appliances Protect Small Businesses/Hotspots/Branch Offices"* in *Product News Network (March 7, 2012)*
Pub: Thomas Publishing Company L.L.C.
Contact: C. T. Holst-Knudsen, President
E-mail: hholstknudsen@thomaspublishing.com
Released: March 7, 2012. **Description:** Five 1GbE ports, WatchGuard(R) XTM 25 and XTM 26 are profiled. All deliver intrusion prevention, spam-blocking, and gateway anti-virus functionality. Borth models profiled integrate VPN, HTTPS inspection and VoIP support along with options for Application Control and other WatchGuard security services already available. Details are included.

41546 ■ *"UTSA Entrepreneur Program Receives Federal Designation"* in *San Antonio Business Journal (Vol. 28, June 6, 2014, No. 17, pp. 7)*
Pub: American City Business Journals
Released: June 6, 2014. **Description:** The National Science Foundation has designated the University of Texas at San Antonio (UTSA) as an Innovation Corps Site because of its strong entrepreneurial system through the Center for Innovation and Technology Entrepreneurship. The UTSA expects to see an increase in entrepreneurial activity and successful technology commercialization with such designation.

41547 ■ *"Valenti: Roots of Financial Crisis Go Back to 1998"* in *Crain's Detroit Business (Vol. 24, October 6, 2008, No. 40, pp. 25)*
Pub: Crain Communications Inc.
Contact: Rance E. Crain, President
Ed: Tom Henderson, Nathan Skid. **Description:** Interview with Sam Valenti III who is the chairman and CEO of Valenti Capital L.L.C., a wealth-management firm; Valenti discusses in detail the history that led up to the current economic crisis as well as his prediction for the future of the country.

41548 ■ *"VC Boosts WorkForce: Livonia Software Company to Add Sales, Marketing Staff"* in *Crain's Detroit Business (March 24, 2008)*
Pub: Crain Communications Inc.
Contact: Rance E. Crain, President
Ed: Tom Henderson. **Description:** WorkForce Software Inc., a company that provides software to manage payroll processes and oversee compliance with state and federal regulations and with union rules, plans to use an investment of $5.5 million in venture capital to hire more sales and marketing staff.

41549 ■ *The Venture Cafe: Secrets, Strategies, and Stories from America's High-Tech Entrepreneurs*
Pub: Business Plus
Ed: Teresa Esser. **Released:** March 2002. **Price:** $24.95, hardcover. **Description:** Research covering the types of entrepreneurs who build new, high-technology ventures from the ground up. Author interviewed over 150 high-tech professionals in order to gather information to help others start high-tech companies. **Availability:** Print.

41550 ■ *"Venturing Into New Territory: Career Experiences of Corporate Venture Capital Managers and Practice Variation"* in *Academy of Management Journal (Vol. 55, June 1,*

2012, No. 3, pp. 563)
Pub: Academy of Management
Contact: Ming-Jer Chen, President
Ed: Gina Dokko, Vibha Gaba. **Description:** The role of venture capital managers' experiences in information technology firms' practice variation is investigated. Findings reveal that firms with managers who have practice-specific experience invest more in diverse industries and early-stage startups. The firm's goal orientation also tend to change from financial to strategic when venture capital managers have firm-specific experience and engineering experience.

41551 ■ *"VeriFone Announces Global Security Solutions Business" in Marketing Weekly News (October 3, 2009)*
Pub: Investment Weekly News
Description: Focused on delivering innovative security solutions, VeriFone Holdings, Inc. announced the formation of its Global Security Solutions Business Unit, including VeriShield Protect, an end-to-end encryption to protect cardholder data throughout the merchant and processor systems. The business will focus on consulting, sales and implementation of these new products in order to help retailers and processors protect customer data.

41552 ■ *"Verizon Small Business Awards Give Companies a Technology Edge" in Hispanic Business (July-August 2009, pp. 32)*
Ed: Patricia Marroquin. **Description:** Verizon Wireless awards grants to twenty-four companies in California. The winning businesses ranged from barbershop to coffee shop, tattoo parlor to florist.

41553 ■ *"Verizon's Big Gamble Comes Down to the Wire" in Globe & Mail (February 3, 2007, pp. B1)*
Ed: Catherine McLean. **Description:** The launch of a new broadband service by Verizon Communications Inc. based on fiber optic cable technology is discussed. The company has spent $23 billion for introducing the new service.

41554 ■ *"Video Surveillance Enters Digital Era, Makes Giant Strides" in Arkansas Business (Vol. 26, September 28, 2009, No. 39, pp. 1)*
Ed: Jamie Walden. **Description:** Arkansas business owners are finding that the newest technology in video surveillance is leading to swift apprehension of thieves due to the high-quality digital imagery now being captured on surveillance equipment. Motion detection software for these systems is enhancing the capabilities of these systems and providing opportunities for businesses that would normally have problems integrating these systems.

41555 ■ *"Virgin Mobile has Big Plans for Year Two" in Globe & Mail (March 6, 2006, pp. B5)*
Ed: Catherine McLean. **Description:** The business growth plans of Virgin Mobile Canada are presented.

41556 ■ *"The Virtual Office" in Canadian Business (Vol. 80, April 9, 2007, No. 8, pp. 64)*
Ed: Andrew Wahl. **Description:** The business operation of Eloqua which runs all its IT systems using its own online software is discussed.

41557 ■ *"Virtual Offices: Anybody Out There?" in Canadian Business (Vol. 81, July 21 2008, No. 11, pp. 31)*
Pub: Rogers Media Inc.
Contact: Tony Viner, President
Ed: Andrew Wahl. **Description:** Virtual offices or shared office services provide solutions to companies that can no longer accommodate additional workspaces. The alternative working arrangement allows the company to have a kind of distributed work system. The disadvantages of employing virtual offices are presented.

41558 ■ *"Vonage V-Phone: Use Your Laptop to Make Calls Via the Internet" in Black Enterprise (Vol. 37, January 2007, No. 6, pp. 52)*
Pub: Earl G. Graves Publishing Co. Inc.
Contact: Earl G. Graves, Jr., President
Ed: James C. Johnson. **Description:** Overview of the Vonage V-Phone, which is small flash drive device that lets you make phone calls through a high-

speed Internet connection and plugs into any computer's USB port. Business travels may find this product to be a wonderful solution as it includes 250MB of memory and can store files, digital photos, MP3s, and more.

41559 ■ *"Vornado Rebrands 555 Cal." in San Francisco Business Times (Vol. 28, May 2, 2014, No. 41, pp. 6)*
Pub: American City Business Journals
Released: May 2, 2014. **Description:** Vornado Realty Trust, the majority owner of the Bank of America Building on California Street, will redevelop and rebrand the facility in order to appeal to technology companies. Supercell and Microsoft Corporation have already signed leases in the building.

41560 ■ *"VTech Targets Tots With a Wee Wii" in Advertising Age (Vol. 79, September 8, 2008, No. 33, pp. 14)*
Pub: Crain Communications Inc.
Contact: Rance Crain, President
Ed: Beth Snyder Bulik. **Description:** V-Motion is a video-game console targeting 3-to-7-year-olds and is manufactured by educational toy company VTech. The company is marketing the product as a kind of Wii for preschoolers and hopes to build a formidable brand presence in the kids' electronics market.

41561 ■ *"Waterloo's Quiet Tech Titan" in Canadian Business (Vol. 87, July 2014, No. 7, pp. 39)*
Pub: George Media Inc.
Released: July 2014. **Description:** OpenText chief executive officer Mark Barrenechea feels confident about the financial health of the Waterloo, Ontario-based software company. He adds that the company is exploring opportunities by the big data phenomenon.

41562 ■ *"Watson May Study New Field" in Business Review Albany (Vol. 41, July 18, 2014, No. 17, pp. 10)*
Pub: The Business Journals
Released: July 18, 2014. **Description:** IBM Corporation has extended its Watson computer system's cognitive capacities to the Cloud. Rensselaer Polytechnic Institute has been training Watson to be a data advisor. It is also using the system to study human thought and cognition.

41563 ■ *"Wear Your App" in Puget Sound Business Journal (Vol. 34, January 24, 2014, No. 41, pp. 4)*
Pub: American City Business Journals
Released: January 24, 2014. **Description:** Seattle, Washington companies are well represented in the fast growing $1.4 billion a year wearable technology industry that turns apparel into computers. The sensors embedded in a wearable item collect information and the wireless connection transfers the data, which will be managed by a smartphone application via the cloud. Wearable technology products are profiled.

41564 ■ *"Weathering the BlackBerry Storm" in Hispanic Business (January-February 2009, pp. 52)*
Pub: Hispanic Business Inc.
Contact: Jesus Chavarria, President
Description: Profile of BlackBerry Storm, the smartphone from Research in Motion.

41565 ■ *"Web Biz Brulant Surfing for Acquisition Candidates" in Crain's Cleveland Business (Vol. 28, December 3, 2007, No. 48, pp. 6)*
Ed: Chuck Soder. **Description:** Brulant Inc., a provider of web development and marketing services, is looking to acquire other companies after growing for five years straight. The company is one of the largest technology firms in Northeast Ohio.

41566 ■ *"What Keeps Global Leaders Up at Night" in Harvard Business Review (Vol. 90, April 2012, No. 4, pp. 32)*
Pub: Harvard Business Review Press
Contact: Peter E. Walsh, Director
Released: April 2012. **Description:** A chart uses colored squares to portray economic, environmental, geopolitical, societal, and technological concerns of industry leaders, and ranks them according to likelihood and impact.

41567 ■ *"What Online Brokers Are Doing To Keep Their Customers' Accounts Safe" in Barron's (Vol. 88, March 10, 2008, No. 10, pp. 37)*
Pub: Dow Jones & Co., Inc.
Contact: Clare Hart, President
Ed: Theresa W. Carey. **Description:** Online brokerage firms employ different methods to protect the accounts of their customers from theft. These methods include secure Internet connections, momentary passwords, and proprietary algorithms.

41568 ■ *"What We Know - And What We Don't - About Apple TV" in Barron's (Vol. 92, August 25, 2012, No. 38, pp. 27)*
Pub: Dow Jones & Co., Inc.
Contact: Clare Hart, President
Ed: Alexander Eule. **Description:** Apple Inc.'s entry into the television market is not likely to involve an introduction of disruptive technologies. Cable companies are the most likely partners of Apple as it seeks to enter the television broadcasting market.

41569 ■ *"What Will Be the Biggest Telecommunication and Technology Issue In 2014? Executives Weigh In" in Dallas Business Journal (Vol. 37, January 3, 2014, No. 17, pp. 8)*
Pub: American City Business Journals
Released: January 3, 2014 . **Description:** The executives' views on the biggest issue in telecommunications and technology in 2014 are presented. Genband chief marketing officer Brad Bush sees embedded communications, the Internet of everything, and virtual reality becoming real with products as three trends that will finally take off in 2014.

41570 ■ *"What's the Latest?" in Entrepreneur (July 2014)*
Pub: Entrepreneur Media Inc.
Released: July 2014. **Description:** Entrepreneur magazine selects the top 15 new and 15 established franchises in the U.S. to show that franchising and innovation can be a successful combination. The selection includes companies with services that have never been franchised before or with surprise twists on old ideas. Established franchisors like Arby's Restaurants Group are taking risks with unusual menu items, new technologies and creative marketing strategies. New franchises on the list include Baby Bodyguards, Bio-One and Chocolate Works.

41571 ■ *"What's Working Now: In Providing Jobs for North Carolinians" in Business North Carolina (Vol. 28, February 2008, No. 2, pp. 16)*
Pub: Business North Carolina
Ed: Edward Martin, Frank Maley. **Description:** Individuals previously employed in the furniture, tobacco, or textile manufacturing sectors have gone back to school to be trained in new sectors in the area such as life sciences, finances and other emerging sectors.

41572 ■ *"When Will Next Biotech Blockbuster Emerge?" in Puget Sound Business Journal (Vol. 35, August 1, 2014, No. 15, pp. 8)*
Pub: American City Business Journals
Released: August 1, 2014. **Description:** Amgen is closing its facilities in Puget Sound, Washington by the end of 2014. The closing will cause the layoff of 660 workers in Seattle and Bothell offices. The biotechnology firm is also closing facilities in Colorado, resulting to 2,400 and 2,900 lost jobs.

41573 ■ *"When Worlds Collide" in Entrepreneur (September 2014)*
Pub: Entrepreneur Media Inc.
Released: September 2014. **Description:** A growing number of startups are connecting the real world with its digital counterpart by leveraging next-generation software, robotics and artificial intelligence to revolutionize traditional entertainment. Anki introduces toy race cars with virtual steering wheels that can be controlled by human gamers or an artificial intelligence. Tiggly, creator of learning games and products for toddlers, manufactured thermoplastic rubber toys with silicon touch points that interact with a tablet screen.

41574 ■ "Who's Next?" in Boston Business Journal (Vol. 27, November 16, 2007, No. 42, pp. 1)
Ed: Lisa van der Pool. Description: Boston, Massachusetts' burgeoning technology and biotech industries along with rising billing rates make it a unique legal market. Law firms cross the threshold either by merging with or acquiring a smaller law firm. Boston as a unique legal market is discussed.

41575 ■ "Why Alabama's Aerospace Is Still Sitting Pretty After 777X" in Birmingham Business Journal (Vol. 31, January 10, 2014, No. 2, pp. 3)
Pub: American City Business Journals, Inc.
Contact: Whitney Shaw, President
Released: January 10, 2014. Description: Alabama's aerospace sector can still benefit from Boeing despite the state's failure to attract the company's 777X project. Boeing is planning to do some of the project's engineering work in Huntsville, Alabama. The company plans to move about 400 engineering jobs to the state.

41576 ■ "Why Intel Should Dump Its Flash-Memory Business" in Barron's (Vol. 88, March 10, 2008, No. 10, pp. 35)
Pub: Dow Jones & Co., Inc.
Contact: Clare Hart, President
Ed: Eric J. Savitz. Description: Intel Corp. must sell its NAND flash-memory business as soon as it possibly can to the highest bidder to focus on its PC processor business and take advantage of other business opportunities. Apple should consider a buyback of 10 percent of the company's shares to lift its stock.

41577 ■ "Why Life Science Needs Its Own Silicon Valley: Human Genomics Won't Reach Its Full Potential Until It Has a Sizable Industry Cluster" in (Vol. 90, July-August 2012, No. 7-8, pp. 25)
Pub: Harvard Business Review Press
Contact: Peter E. Walsh, Director
Ed: Fariborz Ghadar, John Sviokla, Dietrich A. Stephan. Released: July-August 2012. Description: The creation of an industry cluster will be key to advancing human genomics research. High degrees of specialization via multiple contributors will be needed to generate significant innovations; an accessible, coherent data source will also be necessary.

41578 ■ "Why-Max?" in Canadian Business (Vol. 81, July 22, 2008, No. 12-13, pp. 19)
Ed: Andrew Wahl. Description: Nascent technology known as LTE (Long Term Evolution) is expected to challenge Intel's WiMax wireless technology as the wireless broadband standard. LTE, which is believed to be at least two years behind WiMax in development, is likely to be supported by wireless and mobile-phone carriers. Views and information on WiMax and LTE are presented.

41579 ■ "Why Some Get Shafted By Google Pricing" in Advertising Age (Vol. 79, July 14, 2008, No. 7, pp. 3)
Pub: Crain Communications Inc.
Contact: Rance Crain, President
Ed: Abbey Klaassen. Description: Google's search advertising is discussed as well as the company's pricing structure for these ads.

41580 ■ "Wi-Fi Finds Its Way Despite Nixed Plan for Free System" in Crain's Cleveland Business (Vol. 28, November 12, 2007, No. 45, pp. 3)
Pub: Crain Communications Inc.
Ed: Jay Miller. Description: Discusses the issues facing Cleveland and Northeast Ohio concerning their proposal to offer citizens wireless Internet services for free or a small fee.

41581 ■ "Wi-Fi On Steroids: Will WiMAX Provide the Juice For Souped-Up Connections?" in Black Enterprise (November 2007)
Pub: Earl G. Graves Publishing Co. Inc.
Contact: Earl G. Graves, Jr., President
Ed: Fiona Haley. Description: WiMAX, Worldwide Interoperability for Microwave Access in the U.S. WiMax is technology that moves data and connects faster and at greater distances than before.

41582 ■ "The Wiki-Powered Workplace" in Workforce Management (Vol. 88, November 16, 2009, No. 12, pp. 8)
Pub: Crain Communications Inc.
Contact: Rance E. Crain, President
Description: Many organizations are successfully using wikis inside the corporate structure for business communications and knowledge sharing. Wikis can be a very powerful tool due to the inherent transparency that comes with allowing everything to be edited with the accountability of seeing who is doing the editing. A brilliant employee may be noticed sooner because they are doing work in the wiki and the work is being judged on its own merit.

41583 ■ "Will Work for Equity" in Inc. (March 2008, pp. 50, 52)
Pub: Mansueto Ventures L.L.C.
Contact: John Koten, Chief Executive Officer
Ed: Ryan McCarthy. Description: Profile of Dave Graham and his information technology company; Graham built his business by taking equity in client firms rather than charging fees. Four tips to consider before signing a work-for-equity business deal are outlined.

41584 ■ Winner Take All: How Competitiveness Shapes the Fate of Nations
Pub: Basic Books
Contact: Elizabeth Maguire, Publisher
Ed: Richard J. Elkus, Jr. Released: June 16, 2009. Price: $27; C$34; £17.99. Description: American government and misguided business practices have allowed the U.S. to fall behind other countries in various market sectors such as cameras and televisions, as well as information technologies. It will take a national strategy for America to regain its lead in crucial industries. Availability: E-book.

41585 ■ "Winners & Losers" in Canadian Business (Vol. 85, July 16, 2012, No. 11-12, pp. 22)
Pub: George Media Inc.
Released: July 16, 2012. Description: Canadian Pacific Railway's 4,800 locomotive engineers and conductors walked out in protest of the proposed work rules and pension cuts. Shareholders rejected a $25-million bonus and retention payout to Astral Media chief executive officer Ian Greenburg. The Dragon spacecraft of Space Exploration Technologies delivered supplies and experiments to the International Space Station.

41586 ■ "Wireless: Full Service" in Entrepreneur (Vol. 35, October 2007, No. 10, pp. 60)
Ed: Amanda C. Kooser. Description: Palm Foleo, the $599 smart phone enables users to access and compose email, browse the Internet, view documents and play Powerpoint files. It weighs 2.5 pounds and has a 10-inch screen. Other features, such as built-in WiFi are presented.

41587 ■ "Wireless Provider's Star Grows $283 Million Brighter" in Hispanic Business (July-August 2007, pp. 60)
Description: Profile of Brightstar Corporation, the world's largest wireless phone distribution and supply chain reported record growth in 2007.

41588 ■ "Women Losing IT Ground" in Marketing to Women (Vol. 21, February 2008, No. 2, pp. 6)
Description: According to a study conducted by The National Center for Women & Information Technology, women in technology are losing ground. Statistical data included.

41589 ■ "Woodlands Tech Company Grapples With a Rapidly Changing Market" in Houston Business Journal (Vol. 44, January 10, 2014, No. 36, pp. 6)
Pub: American City Business Journals
Released: January 10, 2014. Description: Woodlands, Texas-based UniPixel Inc. has experienced some significant changes in 2013 that cause the company to experience rapid rises and falls. The resignation of the company's CEO, Reed Killion, from his position resulted in a drop in UniPixel shares from

$11.80 on December 30 to $10.08 on December 31. The story behind the rise and fall of UniPixel's share prices is also presented.

41590 ■ "Work Naked" in Canadian Business (Vol. 80, March 12, 2007, No. 6, pp. 33)
Ed: Andrew Wahl. Description: The disadvantages of teleworking for both employees and the company, in view of lack of an office environment and self-discipline on the part of workers, are discussed.

41591 ■ "Work Smarter" in Entrepreneur (Vol. 36, April 2008, No. 4, pp. 70)
Pub: Entrepreneur Press
Contact: Perlman Neil, President
Ed: Amanda C. Kooser. Description: Online applications that address a business' particular needs are presented. These web applications offer email services, collaboration services of sharing and editing documents and presentations, and tie-ups with online social networking sites. Details on various web applications are provided.

41592 ■ "A World of Investors" in Entrepreneur (Vol. 35, November 2007, No. 11, pp. 72)
Pub: Entrepreneur Press
Contact: Perlman Neil, President
Ed: Gail Dutton. Description: Information technology services company mPortal Inc. raised nearly $15 million in financing from venture capital company Friedli Corporate Finance. The biggest international investors are European companies, while the venture capital market is growing in Asia.

41593 ■ "World Wide Technology Expands" in Black Enterprise (Vol. 37, December 2006, No. 5, pp. 34)
Pub: Earl G. Graves Publishing Co. Inc.
Contact: Earl G. Graves, Jr., President
Ed: Marcia Wade Talbert. Description: World Wide Technology Inc. opened a streamlined, higher capacity 12,000-square-foot Integration Technology Center near its corporate headquarters in St. Louis. The new venture will transfer lower costs to customers.

41594 ■ "XM Burning Through Cash to Catch Sirius" in Globe & Mail (April 17, 2007, pp. B5)
Ed: Grant Robertson. Description: The effort of XM Satellite Radio Holdings Inc. to spend about $45 million to increase sale of its radio in Canada is discussed.

41595 ■ "XM and Sirius Satellite Radio Face Up to Their Losses and Decide to Get Hitched" in Globe & Mail (February 20, 2007, pp. B17)
Ed: Grant Robertson. Description: XM Satellite Radio and Sirius Satellite Radio are planning to merge operations, after years of losses. The possible merger could create a $13 billion company.

41596 ■ "The Yahoo Family Tree" in Conde Nast Portfolio (Vol. 2, June 2008, No. 6, pp. 34)
Pub: Conde Nast Publications
Contact: Charles T. Townsend, President
Ed: Blaise Zerega. Description: Yahoo, founded in 1994 by Stanford students Jerry Yang and David Filo, is still an Internet powerhouse. The company's history is also outlined as well as the reasons in which Microsoft desperately wants to acquire the firm.

41597 ■ "Yahoo! - Microsoft Pact: Alive Again?" in Barron's (Vol. 89, July 27, 2009, No. 30, pp. 8)
Pub: Dow Jones & Co., Inc.
Contact: Clare Hart, President
Ed: Mark Veverka. Description: Yahoo! reported higher than expected earnings in the second quarter of 2009 under CEO Carol Bartz who has yet to articulate her long-term vision and strategy for turning around the company. The media reported that Yahoo! and Microsoft are discussing an advertising-search partnership which should benefit both companies.

41598 ■ *"Young-Kee Kim: Deputy Director, Fermi National Accelerator Laboratory" in Crain's Chicago Business (Vol. 31, May 5, 2008, No. 18)*

Pub: Crain Communications Inc.
Contact: Todd Johnson, Publisher
Ed: Phuong Ly. **Description:** Profile of Young-Kee Kim who is the deputy director of Fermilab, a physics lab where scientists study the smallest particles in the universe; Ms. Kim was a researcher at Fermilab before becoming deputy director two years ago; Fermilab is currently home to the most powerful particle accelerator in the world and is struggling to compete with other countries despite cuts in federal funding.

41599 ■ *"Zebra's Changing Stripes" in Crain's Chicago Business (Vol. 31, November 17, 2008, No. 46, pp. 4)*

Pub: Crain Communications Inc.
Contact: Todd Johnson, Publisher
Ed: John Pletz. **Description:** Zebra Technologies Corp., the world's largest manufacturer of bar-code printers is profiled; the company's stock has plunged with shares declining 40 percent in the past three months grinding the firm's growth to a halt. Zebra's plans to regain revenue growth are also discussed.

TRADE PERIODICALS

41600 ■ *Optics & Photonics News*

Pub: Optical Society of America
Contact: Elizabeth A. Rogan, Chief Executive Officer
E-mail: erogan@osa.org
URL(s): www.osa-opn.org/. **Released:** Monthly. **Price:** Free. **Description:** Concerned with optical research, instruction, applications, manufacturing, and equipment. Supplies information on developments in all branches of optics, such as space optics, medical optics, fiber optics, lasers, color optics, and optical communications. Recurring features include reports on Society activities, news of members, and a calendar of events.

41601 ■ *Robotics Online E-Newsletter*

Pub: Robotic Industries Association
Contact: Jeff Burnstein, President
URL(s): www.robotics.org/newsletters.cfm. **Ed:** Mary Kay Morel, Editor. **Released:** Quarterly **Price:** Included in membership. **Description:** Promotes the use and acceptance of robotic technology through the exchange of technical and trade-related information. Provides news of the Association and its affiliate organization, the Automated Imaging Association.

41602 ■ *Sensor Technology*

Pub: Technical Insights
URL(s): www.insights.com. **Ed:** Leo O'Connor, Editor. **Released:** Monthly. **Price:** $650, U.S. and Canada year; $710, elsewhere year. **Description:** Informs readers of the latest scientific and technological developments in the field of sensors. Focuses on process and machine control, including robotics; also covers environmental and medical uses. Recurring features include a calendar of events, news of research, book reviews, and columns titled Key Patents and Keep an Eye On.

CONSULTANTS

41603 ■ **I.H.R. Solutions**

3333 E Bayaud Ave., Ste. 219
Denver, CO 80209
Ph: (303)588-4243

Fax: (303)978-0473
Contact: Deborah Hollands, Owner
E-mail: dhollands@ihrsolutions.com
Scope: Provides joint-venture and start-up human resource consulting services as well as advice on organization development for international human capital. Industries served: high-tech and telecommunications. **Founded:** 1997.

41604 ■ **ProActive English**

4355 SE 29th Ave.
Portland, OR 97202
Ph: (503)231-2906
Co. E-mail: infopae@proactive-english.com
URL: http://www.proactive-english.com
Contact: Margaret Lyman, Manager
E-mail: mlyman@proactive-english.com
Scope: Offers on-site individual and small group language and communication training. Sets up learning plans tailored to the needs and schedules of managers and executives who are non-native English speakers. Serves all industries. **Founded:** 1997. **Seminars:** Communicating in Business Situations; Presentations and Pronunciation; Tailored Curriculum; One-on-One Programs.

RESEARCH CENTERS

41605 ■ **Georgia Institute of Technology - Advanced Technology Development Center (ATDC)**

75 5th St. NW, Ste. 200
Atlanta, GA 30308
Ph: (404)894-3575
Fax: (404)894-4545
Co. E-mail: info@atdc.org
URL: http://www.atdc.org
Contact: Stephen Fleming
Description: A start-up accelerator helping technology entrepreneurs in Georgia. **Scope:** Promotes the development of advanced technology-based companies throughout Georgia. including firms involved in advanced structural materials, electronic equipment, biotechnology, health and medical products, artificial intelligence, environmental sciences, telecommunications, aerospace systems, instrumentation and test equipment, robotics, and related technologies. **Services:** Business assistance: to start-up technology companies; General management consulting; Technical and business management services: to entrepreneurs. **Founded:** 1979. **Publications:** *Technology Partners* (Quarterly).

41606 ■ **National Center for Technology Planning (NCTP)**

PO Box 2393
Tupelo, MS 38803-2393
Ph: (662)844-9630
Fax: (662)844-9630
Co. E-mail: larry@nctp.com
URL: http://www.nctp.com
Contact: Dr. Larry S. Anderson, President
Scope: Technology planning, with dissemination looking to guide those developing technology plans, working on unfinished technology plans, implementing new technology plans, or evaluating current plans. **Services:** Consulting. **Founded:** 1992. **Educational Activities:** NCTP Speeches and presentations; NCTP Workshops.

41607 ■ **Progress Corporate Park**

FrontStreet Realty Group, LLC
Progress Blvd.
Alachua, FL 32615

Ph: (386)418-1001
URL: http://progresscorporatepark.com
Scope: 200-acre research and technology park open to both public and private research and manufacturing organizations emphasizing high-technology development, including electronics, biotechnology, advanced materials, pharmacology, and agriculture. Center provides a link between University researchers and industry and transfers new technologies from the laboratory to the marketplace. **Services:** Assistance: in entrepreneurial development, commercialization of scientific and technological innovations, and international marketing. **Founded:** 1984.

41608 ■ **University of California, Berkeley - Berkeley Roundtable on International Economy (BRIE)**

2234 Piedmont Ave., MC 2322
Berkeley, CA 94720-2322
Ph: (510)642-1705
Fax: (510)643-6617
Co. E-mail: juliana.brie@gmail.com
URL: http://brie.berkeley.edu
Contact: Prof. Stephen S. Cohen, Director
Scope: Policy studies of the interaction of high technology development and the international economy. **Founded:** 1982. **Publications:** *BRIE Working Paper Series*.

41609 ■ **University of Illinois at Urbana-Champaign - Technology Commercialization Laboratory (TCL)**

2004 S Wright St.
Urbana, IL 61802
Ph: (217)244-7742
Fax: (217)333-4050
Co. E-mail: kybrown@uiuc.edu
URL: http://www.researchpark.uiuc.edu
Scope: Assists new and growing business by providing affordable space, shared services, and access to University of Illinois expertise, entrepreneurs, and students. Spaces are occupied by start-up firms and satellite units of established corporations. **Services:** Assistance in identifying specialists in the areas of accounting, business start-up, planning and budgeting, and financial management; Provides specialists in industrial relations, manufacturing operations, organizational development, and strategic planning; Provides specialists in management of marketing and sales, human resources, and personnel areas.

41610 ■ **Washington Technology Center (WTC)**

300 Fluke Hall
University of Washington Campus
Seattle, WA 98195-2140
Ph: (206)685-1920
Fax: (206)543-3059
Co. E-mail: info@watechcenter.org
URL: http://www.watechcenter.org
Contact: Chris Coleman, Executive Director
Description: A joint industry/state/university enterprise engaged in commercially promising research and technology development. **Scope:** Commercially viable technologies, particularly advanced materials and manufacturing systems technology, biotechnology/biomedical devices, microelectronics technology, and computer systems and software technology. **Services:** Statewide Technology Assistance Program. **Founded:** 1983. **Publications:** *At-A-Glance Newsletter* (Quarterly); *Index of Innovation* (Annual); *WTC Annual Report*. **Educational Activities:** SBIR training; WTC Workshops and seminars, on future research projects.

START-UP INFORMATION

41611 ■ *The Art of the Start: The Time-Tested, Battle-Hardened Guide for Anyone Starting Anything*
Pub: Penguin Books USA Inc.
Ed: Guy Kawasaki. **Released:** September 09, 2004. **Price:** $27.95, hardcover. **Description:** Advice for someone starting a new business covering topics such as hiring employees, building a brand, business competition, and management.

41612 ■ *The Complete Idiot's Guide to Starting and Running a Thrift Store*
Pub: Alpha Publishing House
Ed: Ravel Buckley, Carol Costa. **Released:** January 05, 2010. **Price:** $13.26, paperback. **Description:** Thrift stores saw a 35 percent increase in sales during the falling economy in 2008. Despite the low startup costs, launching and running a thrift store is complicated. Two experts cover the entire process, including setting up a store on a nonprofit basis, choosing a location, funding, donations for saleable items, recruiting and managing staff, sorting items, pricing, and recycling donations. **Availability:** Print.

41613 ■ *"Motus Motorcycles To Take Old Barber Sport in Lakeview" in Birmingham Business Journal (Vol. 29, July 20, 2012, No. 30, pp. 1)*
Pub: American City Business Journals, Inc.
Contact: Whitney Shaw, President
Ed: Ryan Poe. **Released:** July 20, 2012. **Description:** Startup luxury motorcycle maker Motus Motorcycles plans to lease the former Barber Vintage Motorsports Museum in Birmingham, Alabama. The startup is expected to get $75,000 in city tax rebates over four years as it stays in Birmingham and plans to create 15 new jobs.

41614 ■ *"The Toughest Sell" in Inc. (Vol. 36, September 2014, No. 7, pp. 69)*
Pub: Mansueto Ventures L.L.C.
Contact: John Koten, Chief Executive Officer
Released: September 2014. **Description:** Finding top talent for a new startup company is challenging. It is suggested that entrepreneurs should sell the challenges faced by the new firm when hiring new workers. Startup recruiting is examined.

ASSOCIATIONS AND OTHER ORGANIZATIONS

41615 ■ **International Association of Corporate and Professional Recruitment (IACPR)**
327 N Palm Dr., Ste. 201
Beverly Hills, CA 90210
Ph: (310)550-0304
Fax: (206)202-4838
Co. E-mail: office@iacpr.org
URL: http://www.iacpr.org
Contact: Pat Hicks, Executive Director
Description: Human resources executives and executive search professionals who are leaders in executive recruitment and retention. Serves as a communications network for sharing information and solving problems within the corporate recruiting industry. **Founded:** 1978. **Publications:** *Quick Takes* (Bimonthly). **Awards:** Professional Recruiters Ovation Award (Annual).

41616 ■ **National Association of Executive Recruiters (NAER)**
1 E Wacker Dr., Ste. 2600
Chicago, IL 60601
Ph: (618)398-6027
Co. E-mail: lisom@hhisearch.com
URL: http://www.naer.org
Contact: Jim Schneider, President
Description: Executive recruitment and search specialist firms providing counsel and assistance in identifying and hiring candidates for middle- and senior-level management positions. Promotes and enhances the public image, awareness, and understanding of the executive search profession. Serves as a forum for exchange of ideas among members; conducts educational programs and owners' roundtable. Maintains code of ethics and professional practice guidelines. **Founded:** 1984. **Educational Activities:** National Association of Executive Recruiters Conference (Annual).

REFERENCE WORKS

41617 ■ *"4 Common Habits of Bad Bosses" in Inc. (Vol. 36, September 2014, No. 7, pp. 18)*
Pub: Mansueto Ventures L.L.C.
Contact: John Koten, Chief Executive Officer
Released: September 2014. **Description:** Four common habits of managers include: waiting to perform background checks after employee is hired; refusing to put employee appraisals in writing; paying higher wages to new hires; and being nice when letting a worker go.

41618 ■ *The 7 Irrefutable Rules of Small Business Growth*
Pub: John Wiley & Sons Inc.
Contact: Stephen M. Smith, President
Ed: Steven S. Little. **Released:** February 2005. **Price:** $18.95. **Description:** Proven strategies to maintain small business growth are outlined, covering topics such as technology, business plans, hiring, and more. **Availability:** Print.

41619 ■ *"$49M Defense Contract Hits Austin" in Austin Business JournalInc. (Vol. 28, August 7, 2008, No. 21, pp. A1)*
Pub: American City Business Journals
Ed: Laura Hipp. **Description:** BAE Systems PLC has landed a $49 million contract to build thermal cameras, which are expected to be installed on tanks in 2009 and 2010. BAE is expected to land other defense contracts and is likely to add employees in order to meet production demands.

41620 ■ *"$50 Million Project for West Chester" in Business Courier (Vol. 24,*
December 13, 2007, No. 35, pp. 1)
Pub: American City Business Journals, Inc.
Contact: Whitney Shaw, President
Ed: Laura Baverman. **Description:** Commercial developer Scott Street Partners is planning to invest $50 million for the development of a site south of the Streets of West Chester retail center. The 31-acre project will generate 1,200 jobs, and will bring in offices, restaurants and a hotel. The development plans and the features of the site are discussed as well.

41621 ■ *"$161.9M 'Pit Stop' Fix-Up Will Create About 1,600 Jobs" in Orlando Business Journal (Vol. 26, January 22, 2010, No. 34, pp. 1)*
Pub: American City Business Journals
Ed: Anjali Fluker. **Description:** State of Florida will be providing $161.9 million to renovate eight service plazas starting November 2010. The project is expected to create 1,600 jobs across the state and is expected to be completed by 2012. Details on bid advertisements and facilities slated for improvement are discussed.

41622 ■ *"A123-Fisker Deal May Mean 540 Jobs" in Crain's Detroit Business (Vol. 26, January 18, 2010, No. 3, pp. 4)*
Pub: Crain Communications Inc.
Contact: Rance E. Crain, President
Ed: Dustin Walsh. **Description:** Manufacturing plants in Livonia and Romulus may be hiring up to 540 skilled workers due to a contract that was won by A123 Systems Inc. that will result in the company supplying lithium-ion batteries to Fisker Automotive Inc. to be used in their Karma plug-in hybrid electric vehicle.

41623 ■ *"Active Duty" in Crain's Cleveland Business (Vol. 28, November 26, 2007, No. 47, pp. 3)*
Pub: Crain Communications Inc.
Ed: David Bennett. **Description:** Discusses the Veteran Workforce Training Program, sponsored by the Volunteers of America - Greater Ohio; the program is meant to provide employment training for military veterans and to assist them in transitioning back into the work force.

41624 ■ *"AdvancePierre Heats Up" in Business Courier (Vol. 27, October 29, 2010, No. 26, pp. 1)*
Pub: Business Courier
Ed: Jon Newberry. **Description:** Bill Toler, chief executive officer of AdvancePierre Foods, is aiming for more growth and more jobs. The company was formed after the merger of Pierre Foods with two Oklahoma-based food processing companies. Toler wants to expand production and is set to start adding employees in the next 6-12 months.

41625 ■ *"Advancing the Ball" in Inside Healthcare (Vol. 6, December 2010, No. 7, pp. 31)*
Ed: Michelle McNickle. **Description:** Profile of Medicalodges an elder-care specialty company that provides both patient care and technology develop-

ment. President and CEO of the firm believes that hiring good employees is key to growth for any small business.

41626 ■ *"After Recession, Texas Cities Lead National Recovery" in Dallas Business Journal (Vol. 37, June 27, 2014, No. 42, pp. 28)*
Pub: American City Business Journals
Released: June 27, 2014. **Description:** A study of 510 U.S. cities by NeredWallet finds that 11 Texas cities are among those showing the fastest recovery since the recession began. NerdWallet analyst Sreekar Jasthi attributes this to growing business investment, rising employment, and an increase in median home values in cities such as Richardson and Gran Prairie.

41627 ■ *"Airport Projects to Provide Billion-Dollar Shot in the Arm" in Orlando Business Journal (Vol. 29, August 24, 2012, No. 10, pp. 1)*
Pub: American City Business Journal
Ed: Bill Orben. **Description:** Proposed projects at the Orlando International Airport is seen to create up to 11,000 new hire jobs. The projects include renovation and extension of the airport's people mover system and a parking garage. The construction projects are also expected to inject $1.1 billion into the local economy.

41628 ■ *"Akron Community Foundation Hires Help for CEO Search" in Crain's Cleveland Business (Vol. 28, October 29, 2007, No. 43, pp. 6)*
Ed: Shannon Mortland. **Description:** Waverly Partners LLC, an executive search firm, has been hired by the Akron Community Foundation to search for its next president and CEO as Jody Bacon, the company's current CEO, will retire on July 31, 2008.

41629 ■ *"Albany Molecular on Hiring Spree as Big Pharma Slashes Work Force" in Business Review, Albany New York (December 31, 2007)*
Pub: American City Business Journals, Inc.
Ed: Barbara Pinckney. **Description:** Albany Molecular Research Inc. (AMRI) is an outsourcing company that provides work forces for pharmaceutical companies due to large numbers of downsizings in the year 2007. In 2008, AMRI plans to hire several workers.

41630 ■ *""All We've Done is Hire People That Believe In the Direction We're Going"" in Business Journal (Vol. 31, January 31, 2014, No. 36, pp. 9)*
Pub: American City Business Journals
Released: January 31, 2014. **Description:** Fastenal founder, Bob Kierline, keeps hiring standards high in order to promote his firm's growth. He also said Fastenal's School of Business employs 40 licensed teachers. Their CEO, Will Oberton, said the company has done a better job in customer relations than its competitors.

41631 ■ *"Apprenticeship: Earn While You Learn" in Occupational Outlook Quarterly (Vol. 54, Fall 2010, No. 3, pp. 24)*
Pub: U.S. Department of Labor Bureau of Labor Statistics
Contact: Philip L. Rones, Manager
E-mail: rones.philip@bls.gov
Description: Paid training, or apprenticeships, are examined. Registered apprenticeship programs conform to certain guidelines and industry-established training standards and may be run by businesses, trade or professional associations, or partnerships with business and unions.

41632 ■ *"Are There Material Benefits To Social Diversity?" in Hispanic Business (Vol. 30, September 2008, No. 9, pp. 10)*
Ed: Brigida Benitez. **Description:** Diversity in American colleges and universities, where students view and appreciate their peers as individuals and do not judge them on the basis of race, gender, or ethnicity is discussed. The benefits of diversity in higher education are also acknowledged by the U.S. Supreme Court and by leading American corporations.

41633 ■ *"Area Hurt By Doctor Deficiency" in The Business Journal-Serving Metropolitan Kansas City (Vol. 27, October 17, 2008, No. 5, pp. 1)*
Ed: Rob Roberts. **Description:** Kansas City, Missouri may face a shortage of doctors, according to the Metropolitan Medical Society of Greater Kansas City. Over the next ten years the city needs to recruit more doctors in order to address the problem. Practicing physicians are having difficulties recruiting.

41634 ■ *"The Art of Persuasion: How You Can Get the Edge You Need To Reach Every Goal" in Small Business Opportunities (November 2007)*
Ed: Paul Endress. **Description:** Expert in the field of psychology to business in the areas of communication, hiring and retention discusses a unique approach to solving business problems.

41635 ■ *"Ask Inc.: Managing and Real Estate" in Inc. (December 2007, pp. 83-84)*
Pub: Gruner and Jahr USA Publishing Co.
Contact: J. Russell Denson, President
Ed: Ari Weinzweig. **Description:** Questions regarding knowledge management in the case of a retiring CFO, issues involved in opening a satellite office for a New York realtor, and information for hiring a multicultural workforce are all discussed.

41636 ■ *"At the Drugstore, the Nurse Will See You Now" in Globe & Mail (April 13, 2007, pp. B1)*
Ed: Marina Strauss. **Description:** The appointment of several health professionals including nurse, podiatrists, etc. by Rexall Co. at its drugstores to face competition from rivals, is discussed.

41637 ■ *"At This Bakery, Interns' Hope Rises Along With the Bread" in Chicago Tribune (October 31, 2008)*
Pub: McClatchy-Tribune Information Services
Ed: Mary Schmich. **Description:** Profile of Sweet Miss Givings Bakery and its diverse founder, interns and employees; the bakery was founded by Stan Sloan, an Episcopal priest who started the business to help fund his ministry; Sloan saw a need for jobs for those living with HIV and other disabilities and through the bakery the interns learn the skills needed to eventually find work elsewhere.

41638 ■ *"At Your Career Crossroads" in Women In Business (Vol. 61, December 2009, No. 6, pp. 26)*
Pub: American Business Women's Association
Contact: Lorie Burch, President
Ed: Diane Stafford. **Description:** Guidelines for employees who are considering a job or career change are presented. Among the reasons for lead employees to make these changes are downsizing, job loss, environments that are not conducive to work or unfavorable work relationships with bosses.

41639 ■ *"Auto Suppliers Bringing Blue-Collar Jobs: US Farathane, American Tire Take Larger Sites" in Austin Business Journal (Vol. 32, May 4, 2012, No. 9, pp. 1)*
Pub: American City Business Journals, Inc.
Contact: Whitney Shaw, President
Ed: Jan Buccholz. **Released:** May 4, 2012. **Description:** Deals involving automobile suppliers have improved the industrial real estate and job markets in Austin, Texas. US Frathane Corporation is relocating to a new manufacturing facility and is hiring for manufacturing posts, customer service staff and a warehouse supervisor. The new distribution center of American Tire Distributors Inc. will open in August 2012 and will also hire workers.

41640 ■ *"Baltimore-Area Hospital Tower Projects Could Add Hundreds of New Jobs" in Baltimore Business Journal (Vol. 28, June 25, 2010, No. 7, pp. 1)*
Pub: Baltimore Business Journal
Ed: Scott Graham. **Description:** Greater Baltimore, Maryland has four hospitals that are in the middle of transforming their campuses with new facilities for treating various patients. Construction at Mercy Medical Center, Johns Hopkins Hospital, Franklin Square

Hospital and Anne Rundle Hospital has helped bring the construction industry back to life. Insights into the hiring plans of these hospitals are also included.

41641 ■ *"Bank on It: Scouting and Keeping Good Talent in the Workplace" in Hawaii Business (Vol. 53, January 2008, No. 7, pp. 50)*
Pub: PacificBasin Communications
Ed: Christine Dermengian. **Description:** Tips on improving employee selection and retention are presented. The strategies in choosing and keeping the right employees include identifying which type of people the company needs and improving the workplace environment.

41642 ■ *"Baptist Health System Plans to Expand Stone Oak-Area Hospital: $32 Million Project Will Add Two Floors, 100 Beds" in San Antonio Business Journal (Vol. 26, May 25, 2012, No. 17, pp. 1)*
Pub: American City Business Journal
Description: Baptist Health System is planning to start the $32 million expansion of the North Central Baptist Hospital in San Antonio, Texas that will include the addition of two floors and 100 beds. An estimate of hiring 200 new health care workers will be created by the expansion.

41643 ■ *"Bar Bailout" in Puget Sound Business Journal (Vol. 33, August 24, 2012, No. 18, pp. 1)*
Description: Some large law firms in Washington are recruiting prospective senior leaders while smaller firms are expanding searches nationwide in preparation for a broad-based succession crisis. A Washington State Bar Association revealed that 7,200 of its members are leaving the profession, while the number of state bar admissions decreased by 13 percent between 2007 and 2011.

41644 ■ *"The Bell Tolls for Thee" in Canadian Business (Vol. 81, March 3, 2008, No. 3, pp. 36)*
Ed: Andrew Wahl. **Description:** Bell Canada has formed the Canadian Coalition for Tomorrow's IT Skills to solve the shortage of technology talent in the country. Canada's total workforce has only around 4%, or 600,000 people employed in information technology-related fields. The aims of the Bell-led coalition, which is supported by different industry associations and 30 corporations, are investigated.

41645 ■ *"Best Companies for Diversity" in Black Enterprise (Vol. 38, July 2008, No. 12, pp. 12)*
Pub: Earl G. Graves Publishing Co. Inc.
Contact: Earl G. Graves, Jr., President
Description: Maintaining excellence in a company's diversity efforts requires critical challenges such as recruiting, retaining and developing talent in the executive pipeline. Top young and diverse emerging executives in corporate America are featured.

41646 ■ *"Best (Professional) Foot Forward: Effective Marketing Strategies for any Phase of Your Career" in Black Enterprisel> (Vol. 44, June 2014, No. 10, pp. 44)*
Pub: Earl G. Graves Publishing Co. Inc.
Contact: Earl G. Graves, Jr., President
Released: June 2014. **Description:** Because hiring managers face long-term vacancies and skills gaps, the importance of creating a professional marketing strategy when applying for a professional position is stressed. Advice is given to help guide applicants through the entire application, interviewing, and hiring process.

41647 ■ *"BETC Backers Plot Future" in Business Journal Portland (Vol. 27, December 10, 2010, No. 41, pp. 1)*
Pub: Portland Business Journal
Ed: Erik Siemers. **Description:** A coalition of clean energy groups and industrial manufacturers have spearheaded a campaign aimed at persuading Oregon legislators that the state's Business Energy Tax Credit (BETC) is vital in job creation. Oregon's

BETC grants tax credits for 50 percent of an eligible renewable or clean energy project's cost. However, some legislators propose BETC's abolition.

41648 ■ "Better than Advertised: Chip Plant Beats Expectations" in Business Review Albany (Vol. 41, June 27, 2014, No. 14, pp. 4)

Pub: American City Business Journals, Inc.

Contact: Whitney Shaw, President

Released: June 27, 2014. **Description:** The $8.5 billion computer chip manufacturing plant and research center of GlobalFoundries in Malta, New York has strengthened the local economy in Saratoga County and helped the local manufacturing and construction industries recover from the recession. The Malta Plant construction project created more than 2,000 direct new construction jobs and over 10,000 indirect positions.

41649 ■ "BioRASI Aims to Fill Larger HQ With More Jobs" in South Florida Business Journal (Vol. 34, April 11, 2014, N. 38, pp. 4)

Pub: American City Business Journals

Released: April 11, 2014. **Description:** BioRASI has announced plans to hire an additional 20 or 30 workers in Florida in 2014 after moving into a larger headquarters in Aventura. The contract research organization added 40 employees during 2013 and now has 80 working in Florida. Other insights on BioRASI's growing presence in Florida are given.

41650 ■ "Bioscience Hiring Flat in Florida" in South Florida Business Journal (Vol. 34, July 4, 2014, No. 50, pp. 8)

Pub: American City Business Journals

Released: July 4, 2014. **Description:** The bioscience industry in Florida showed little growth in job creation since 2007, despite heavy state investments. The bioscience sector lost 1 percent of its jobs from 2007 to 2010, while the following two years only recovered the losses of previous years.

41651 ■ "Birmingham: Losing the Mid Game" in Birmingham Business Journal (Vol. 31, February 28, 2014, No. 9, pp. 4)

Pub: American City Business Journals, Inc.

Contact: Whitney Shaw, President

Released: February 28, 2014. **Description:** Birmingham, Alabama's short supply of college graduates has resulted in economic loss for the city. The city has ranked 77th in a study conducted by American City Business Journals. Economic effects include lost potential income.

41652 ■ "Birmingham Tech Firms Eye Growth in 2014" in Birmingham Business Journal (Vol. 31, January 10, 2014, No. 2, pp. 4)

Pub: American City Business Journals, Inc.

Contact: Whitney Shaw, President

Released: January 10, 2014. **Description:** Birmingham, Alabama-based high-tech firms, ProctorU and Chronicle Studio are planning to expand their work forces in 2014. ProctorU will add more than 50 employees, while Chronicle will add three more positions to their staff.

41653 ■ "Black Gold: Jobs Aplenty" in Canadian Business (Vol. 79, August 14, 2006, No. 16-17, pp. 57)

Pub: Rogers Media Inc.

Contact: Tony Viner, President

Ed: Erin Pooley. **Description:** A list of the top ten jobs in the petroleum industry in Canada along with pay and nature of jobs, is presented.

41654 ■ "The Board Shorts Executive" in Hawaii Business (Vol. 53, January 2008, No. 7, pp. 33)

Pub: PacificBasin Communications

Ed: Mike Markrich. **Description:** Vans Triple Crown of Surfing executive director Randy Rarick believes that the surfing business requires knowledge of the sport and integity to the game's lifestyle and spirit. His organization manages surfing events, and has generated jobs for the locals. Plans for Vans Triple Crown are supplied.

41655 ■ "Bob's Discount Furniture Moving Into Harford County, Region" in Baltimore Business Journal (Vol. 27, January 22, 2010, No. 38, pp. 1)

Pub: American City Business Journals

Ed: Daniel J. Sernovitz. **Description:** Manchester, Connecticut-based Bob's Discount Furniture signed a lease for 672,000 square feet of space in Harford County, Maryland. The site will become the discount furniture retailer's distribution center in mid-Atlantic US. As many as 200 jobs could be generated when the center opens.

41656 ■ "Boom has Tech Grads Mulling Their Options" in Globe & Mail (March 14, 2006, pp. B1)

Ed: Grant Robertson. **Description:** Internet giant Google Inc. has stepped up its efforts to hire the talented people, in Canada, at Waterloo University in southern Ontario, to expand its operations. The details of the job market and increasing salaries are analyzed.

41657 ■ "Building a Workforce" in Business Journal Milwaukee (Vol. 29, July 27, 2012, No. 44, pp. 1)

Pub: American City Business Journals, Inc.

Contact: Whitney Shaw, President

Ed: Rich Kirchen. **Released:** July 27, 2012. **Description:** Governor Scott Walker's 'Wisconsin Working' initiative head Tim Sullivan announced that he will recommend the encouragement of immigration to meet current and future employment needs of the state. Sullivan believes immigration could help address the worker skills shortage that affected many southeaster Wisconsin businesses.

41658 ■ "Business Looks for Results in Congress" in Baltimore Business Journal (Vol. 28, November 5, 2010, No. 26, pp. 1)

Pub: Baltimore Business Journal

Ed: Kent Hoover. **Description:** Republican candidates in the 2010 Congressional elections were overwhelmingly supported by the business community. Republican John Boehner, who will be the next Speaker of the House, says that the party's victory would end economic uncertainty and would assist small businesses to rehire workers.

41659 ■ "Businesses Delayed Hiring As They Waited for Health Care Law Ruling" in Baltimore Business Journal (Vol. 30, June 29, 2012, No. 8, pp. 1)

Pub: American City Business Journals, Inc.

Contact: Whitney Shaw, President

Ed: Sarah Gantz. **Released:** June 29, 2012. **Description:** Small businesses in Baltimore, Maryland have been putting off expansion plans pending the Supreme Court's ruling on the health care reform law. Workforce expansion would require businesses to provide employee health insurance.

41660 ■ "Businesses Need to Know State, Federal Laws for Employing Minors" in Crain's Detroit Business (Vol. 25, June 15, 2009, No. 24)

Pub: Crain Communications Inc. - Detroit

Contact: Keith Crain, Chairman

Ed: Nancy Kaffer. **Description:** Small business owners must know the law before employing minors. According to Steven Fishman, partner with Bodman LLP, who practices workplace law, most small business owners are not aware of laws regarding employment of minors.

41661 ■ "Cabela's Repays Incentives as Sales Lag" in Business Journal-Milwaukee (Vol. 28, November 19, 2010, No. 7, pp. A1)

Pub: Milwaukee Business Journal

Ed: Stacy Vogel Davis. **Description:** Cabela's has given back $266,000 to the government of Wisconsin owing to its failure to meet projected revenue goals for its Richfield, Wisconsin store. It has also failed to meet sales tax and hiring projection. The company received $4 million in incentives from Washington County.

41662 ■ "Call for Jobs Tie-In Lacks City Backing" in Baltimore Business Journal (Vol. 30, June 1, 2012, No. 4, pp. 1)

Pub: American City Business Journals, Inc.

Contact: Whitney Shaw, President

Ed: James Briggs. **Released:** June 1, 2012. **Description:** Officials of Baltimore, Maryland are seen to turn down the proposal to mandate local hiring rules for Lexington Square Partners. The plan is in line with the company's push for tax breaks on its superblock project.

41663 ■ "Campbell Clinic in Expansion Mode: Plans to Triple Size of Surgery Center, Add Employees" in Memphis Business Journal (Vol. 34, August 24, 2012, No. 19, pp. 1)

Pub: American City Business Journal

Description: The Campbell Clinic Inc. is pushing forward with its plan to expand and hire new employees. The clinic has filed a Certificate of Need with the Tennessee Health Services Development Agency worth $13 million. Expansion projects include the enlargement of the surgery center, which handles 700 cases a month, a figure which is expected to rise to 750 in August 2012.

41664 ■ "Cancer-Fighting Entrepreneurs" in Austin Business Journal (Vol. 31, August 5, 2011, No. 22, pp. 1)

Pub: American City Business Journals

Ed: Sandra Zaragoza. **Description:** Cancer Prevention and Research Institute of Texas has invested $10 million in recruiting known faculty to the University of Texas. The move is seen to bolster Austin's position as a major cancer research market. The institute has awarded grants to researchers Jonghwan Kim, Guangbin Dong and Kyle Miller.

41665 ■ "Capital One Expanding Campus in Plano" in Dallas Business Journal (Vol. 35, April 20, 2012, No. 2, pp. 1)

Pub: American City Business Journal

Ed: Candace Carlisle. **Description:** The financial services division of Capital One Financial Corporation in Plano, Texas will hire an additional 300 employees and start construction of two office buildings and 2,600-space parking garage in summer 2012. Cost of the 400,000-square-foot office space is estimated at $76 million and $19.5 million for the garage.

41666 ■ "Capital Position: M&I Acquisition Opens the Door for Rivals to Gain Market Share" in Business Journal-Milwaukee (Vol. 28, December 24, 2010, No. 12, pp. A1)

Pub: Milwaukee Business Journal

Ed: Rich Kirchen. **Description:** Canada-based BMO Financial Group has purchased Marshall and Isley Corporation (M and I), which dominated lending among Wisconsin businesses for decades. The sale of M and I will enable other banks to recruit M and I's customers but BMO Financial remains a stronger competitor since it possesses a more potent capital position.

41667 ■ "Capitol Ideas: Regions to Lansing: Focus on Taxes, Reform, Keeping Talent" in Crain's Detroit Business (Vol. 24, October 6, 2008)

Pub: Crain Communications Inc.

Contact: Rance E. Crain, President

Ed: Amy Lane. **Description:** Michigan must make bold and dramatic changes in public policy regarding business legislation. The tax structure, unemployment issues and attracting and retaining talent are among the issues the state must confront, especially in this tough economic climate.

41668 ■ "Cashing in Before You Join: Negotiating a Signing Bonus" in Black Enterprise (Vol. 37, October 2006, No. 3, pp. 90)

Pub: Earl G. Graves Publishing Co. Inc.

Contact: Earl G. Graves, Jr., President

Ed: Chauntelle Folds. **Description:** Information on how to research and negotiate a signing deal, including how to avoid a tax hit.

41669 ■ *"Casinos See College as Job Jackpot" in The Business Journal-Serving Metropolitan Kansas City (Vol. 26, August 1, 2008, No. 47)*
Ed: Suzanna Stagemeyer. **Description:** Wyandotte County casino managers revealed plans to develop partnerships with Kansas City Kansas Community College. The planned partnership is expected to include curriculum development and degree programs that would help train employees for the planned casinos. Other views and information on the project are presented.

41670 ■ *"Catching Creatives; Detroit Group Gets Grant to Attract 1,000 Design Pros" in Crain's Detroit Business (March 23, 2008)*
Pub: Crain Communications Inc.
Contact: Rance E. Crain, President
Ed: Sherri Begin. **Description:** Design Detroit was given a $200,000 planning grant by the Knight Foundation, an organization that strives to back initiatives that leverage talent and resources in each of the 26 U.S. cities it funds, to inspire strategies to attract up to 1,000 creative professionals to live in Detroit.

41671 ■ *"Cautious Hiring in January Report" in Charlotte Observer (February 3, 2007)*
Ed: Kerry Hall. **Description:** U.S. Labor Department released a report that shows 111,000 new positions in January 2007, compared to 206,000 in December 2006. Employers remain cautious about hiring.

41672 ■ *"CEOs Split on Migrant Workers" in Canadian Business (Vol. 83, September 14, 2010, No. 15, pp. 23)*
Pub: Rogers Media Inc.
Contact: Tony Viner, President
Ed: Jacqueline Nelson. **Description:** A survey of Canadian CEOs shows that 49 percent of the respondents believe it was wrong to suspend the immigration programs and companies should be allowed to hire the most skilled workers regardless of citizenship. However, 42 percent believe the suspension was right because employment of Canadians must take precedence.

41673 ■ *"Channeling for Growth: HSN's Independence a Windfall for Local Professional Service Practitioners" in The Business Journal-Serving Greater Tampa Bay (Vol. 28, July 11, 2008, No. 29, pp. 1)*
Pub: American City Business Journals, Inc.
Contact: Whitney Shaw, President
Ed: Margie Manning. **Description:** HSN Inc., one of the largest employers in Tampa Bay, Florida, is expected to spend an additional $9.7 million annually as it plans to hire more accounting, internal audit, legal, treasury and tax personnel after its spin-off to a public company. Details on the company's sales growth are provided.

41674 ■ *"Charged Up for Sales" in Charlotte Business Journal (Vol. 25, October 15, 2010, No. 30, pp. 1)*
Pub: Charlotte Business Journal
Ed: Susan Stabley. **Description:** Li-Ion Motors Corporation is set to expand its production lines of electric cars in Sacramento, California. The plan is seen to create up to 600 jobs. The company's total investment is seen to reach $500 million.

41675 ■ *"Charlie Winburn's Big Idea" in Business Courier (Vol. 27, October 8, 2010, No. 23, pp. 1)*
Pub: Business Courier
Ed: Dan Monk, Lucy May. **Description:** Cincinnati Councilman Charlie Winburn proposed the creation of Cincinnati Competitive Edge Division and to remake a small-business division of the city in order to start a job-creation program. The new division will monitor compliance to the city's small business inclusion regulations, as well as to help small business owners grow.

41676 ■ *"Christ Hospital to Expand" in Business Courier (Vol. 27, June 25, 2010, No. 8, pp. 3)*
Pub: Business Courier
Ed: Dan Monk, James Ritchie. **Description:** Christ Hospital intends to invest more than $300 million and generate 200 jobs in an expansion of its Mount Auburn campus in Cincinnati, Ohio. About $22 million in retail activity can be created by the hospital expansion, which will also include a replacement garage and new surgery facilities.

41677 ■ *"Christ Hospital Moves Toward Self-Rule" in Business Courier (Vol. 24, December 7, 2007, No. 34, pp. 1)*
Pub: American City Business Journals, Inc.
Contact: Whitney Shaw, President
Ed: James Ritchie. **Description:** Christ Hospital is planning on hiring 100 employees that will work on its newly leased facility located in Eden Park Drive.

41678 ■ *"Cincinnati Consults Executives on Police Chief Hire" in Business Courier (Vol. 27, August 27, 2010, No. 17, pp. 1)*
Pub: Business Courier
Ed: Dan Monk, Lucy May. **Description:** The City of Cincinnati, Ohio, has begun a selection process for the new police chief by consulting the city's business executives. The city charter amendment known as Issue 5 has removed civil service protection from the chief's post and enables City Manager Milton Dohoney to hire a chief from outside the department.

41679 ■ *"Citadel Hires Three Lehman Execs" in Chicago Tribune (October 2, 2008)*
Ed: James P. Miller. **Description:** Citadel Investment Group LLC, Chicago hedge-fund operator, has hired three former senior executives of bankrupt investment banker Lehman Brothers Holding Inc. Citadel believes that the company's hiring spree will help them to further expand the firm's capabilities in the global fixed income business.

41680 ■ *"CitiMortgage to Hire Hundreds in Dallas-Fort Worth" in Dallas Business Journal (Vol. 35, April 20, 2012, No. 32, pp. 1)*
Pub: American City Business Journal
Ed: Jeff Bounds. **Description:** Citibank NA mortgage lending and servicing arm of CitMortgage is hiring at least 750 employees to work with borrowers in relation to a $2.2 billion settlement of alleged questionable foreclosure practices. Most of the staff will work in Dallas-Fort Worth, Texas in areas such as default servicing, refinancing an single points of contact as required under the settlement.

41681 ■ *"ClearEdge Hums Along" in Business Journal Portland (Vol. 26, December 18, 2009, No. 41, pp. 1)*
Pub: American City Business Journals, Inc.
Ed: Erik Siemers. **Description:** Hillsboro-based ClearEdge Power Inc. expanded its workforce and facilities with $15M capital from investors. Since May 2009, the number of employees increased from 40 to 150 and headquarters expanded from 5,000 to 80,000 square feet.

41682 ■ *"Colorado Statehouse Races Key for Business" in Denver Business Journal (Vol. 64, August 31, 2012, No. 15, pp. 1)*
Pub: American City Business Journal
Description: The elections for Colorado's Senate and House of Representatives can have a great impact on the state's economy. Republicans are focusing on regulatory-reform measures, while Democrats are pushing for bidding priorities given to companies that buy and hire locally. Experts state that Republican and Democratic candidates seem to agree on job-creation proposals.

41683 ■ *"Column: Wealth and Jobs: the Broken Link" in Harvard Business Review (Vol. 88, November 2010, No. 11, pp. 44)*
Pub: Harvard Business School Publishing
Ed: Nitin Nohria. **Description:** Rebuilding the link between business and job creation to shore up the middle class is advocated. A blend of government policies and business strategies that foster entrepreneurship and innovation are essential.

41684 ■ *"Comcast Garners Recognition as a Top 10 Company for Its Work with Veteran-Owned Businesses" in Entertainment Close-Up (April 16, 2012)*
Description: Comcast Corporation was honored for the sixth consecutive year as one of the top US companies working with veteran owned businesses. The National Veteran-Owned Business Association recognizes large corporations that engage the three million veteran-owned small businesses as suppliers. NBCUniversal, another honoree, and Comcast have committed to hiring 1,000 US veterans over the next three years as part of their 'Hiring Our Heroes' program.

41685 ■ *"Commentary. Small Business Economic Trends" in Small Business Economic Trends (March 2008, pp. 3)*
Pub: National Federation of Independent Business
Contact: Caitlin McDevitt, Program Manager
Ed: William C. Dunkelberg, Holly Wade. **Description:** Commentary on the economic trends for small businesses in the U.S. Is presented. Analysis of the labor market and low interest rates is given. The effect of the Federal Reserve's policy announcement on small business owner optimism is also discussed.

41686 ■ *"Commentary. Small Business Economic Trends" in Small Business Economic Trends (February 2008, pp. 3)*
Pub: National Federation of Independent Business
Contact: Caitlin McDevitt, Program Manager
Ed: William C. Dunkelberg, Holly Wade. **Description:** Commentary on the economic trends for small businesses in the U.S. is presented. Analysis of the U.S. Federal Reserve Board's efforts to prevent a recession is given. Reduction in business inventories is also discussed.

41687 ■ *"Commentary. Small Business Economic Trends" in Small Business Economic Trends (January 2008, pp. 3)*
Pub: National Federation of Independent Business
Contact: Caitlin McDevitt, Program Manager
Description: Federal Reserve cut interest rates and announced its economic outlook on September 18, 2007 to stimulate spending. The cut in interest rates, however, may not help in supporting consumer spending because savers may lose interest income. The expected economic impact of the interest rate cuts and the U.S. economic outlook are also discussed.

41688 ■ *"Comparative Indicators" in Montly Labor Review (Vol. 133, September 2010, No. 9, pp. 87)*
Pub: U.S. Department of Labor Bureau of Labor Statistics
Contact: Philip L. Rones, Manager
E-mail: rones.philip@bls.gov
Description: Labor market indicators for years 2008 and 2009 are given. Statistical data included.

41689 ■ *"Competing for Jobs" in Women In Business (Vol. 63, Summer 2011, No. 2, pp. 37)*
Pub: American Business Women's Association
Contact: Lorie Burch, President
Ed: Leigh Elmore. **Description:** Job hunting tips for women in the US in relation to generation demographic groups are presented. Effective communications and positive interactions are essential to career development. Generation groups' strengths and weaknesses as job seekers are also given.

41690 ■ *"Contractors Scramble for Jobs" in Business Journal Portland (Vol. 26, December 18, 2009, No. 41, pp. 1)*
Pub: American City Business Journals, Inc.
Ed: Andy Giegerich. **Description:** Contractors in Portland area are expected to bid for capital construction projects that will be funded by municipalities in the said area. Contracts for companies that work on materials handling, road improvement, and public safety structure projects will be issued.

41691 ■ *"Cool Jobs in Hot Markets" in Canadian Business (Vol. 80, March 26, 2007, No. 7, pp. 66)*
Pub: Rogers Media Inc.
Contact: Tony Viner, President
Ed: Marlene Rego. **Description:** The growth in employment opportunities in various parts of the Canada is analyzed.

41692 ■ *"Corporate Diversity Driving Profits"* in Hispanic Business (Vol. 30, September 2008, No. 9, pp. 12)

Ed: Michael Bowker. **Description:** U.S. businesses are beginning to appreciate the importance of diversity and are developing strategies to introduce a diverse workforce that reflects the cultural composition of their customers. The realization that diversity increases profits and the use of professional networks to recruit and retain skilled minority employees are two other new trends impacting corporate diversity in the U.S.

41693 ■ *"CradlePoint Is Adding Workers, Seeking More Space"* in Idaho Business Review (September 3, 2014)

Pub: Dolan Co.

Contact: James P. Dolan, President

Released: September 3, 2014. **Description:** Cradle-Point makes networking routers and software, focusing on security for businesses. The firm is hiring new workers at a rate higher than predicted and is seeking new office space in downtown Boise, Idaho. CradlePoint is a major player in the growing wireless service and cloud platform market and is growing faster than its competitors.

41694 ■ *"Crain's Makes Ad Sales, Custom Marketing Appointments"* in Crain's Chicago Business (Vol. 34, October 24, 2011, No. 42, pp. 13)

Pub: Crain Communications Inc.

Contact: Todd Johnson, Publisher

Description: Crain's Chicago Business announced key appointments in its sales department: David Denor has been named first director of custom marketing services and Kate Van Etten will succeed Denor as advertising director.

41695 ■ *"Craning for Workers"* in Puget Sound Business Journal (Vol. 35, August 15, 2014, No. 17, pp. 4)

Pub: American City Business Journals

Released: August 15, 2014. **Description:** The U.S. Department of Labor statistics show that Washington State has 15, 510 laborers in 2013. However, construction companies are having difficulty hiring skilled workers, particularly as apprentices. The Associated General Contractors of Washington's expansion of training slots for crane and other heave equipment operators is discussed.

41696 ■ *"Criticare Sees Rapid Expansion"* in Business Journal-Milwaukee (Vol. 28, December 31, 2010, No. 14, pp. A1)

Pub: Milwaukee Business Journal

Ed: Rich Rovito. **Description:** Criticare Systems Inc. expanded its distribution network, added customers, launched two new products and transferred into a new building in Pewaukee, Wisconsin at the start of their fiscal year. Criticare expanded its workforce and now has nearly 140 full time employees.

41697 ■ *"Crucible: Battling Back from Betrayal"* in Harvard Business Review (Vol. 88, December 2010, No. 12, pp. 130)

Pub: Harvard Business School Publishing

Ed: Daniel McGinn. **Description:** Stephen Greer's scrap metal firm, Hartwell Pacific, lost several million dollars due to a lack of efficient and appropriate inventory audits, accounting procedures, and new-hire reference checks for his foreign operations. Greer believes that balancing growth with control is a key component of success.

41698 ■ *"Crucible: Losing the Top Job - And Winning It Back"* in Harvard Business Review (Vol. 88, October 2010, No. 10, pp. 136)

Pub: Harvard Business School Publishing

Ed: Alison Beard. **Description:** Michael Mack chronicles the changes in perspectives that occurred when he was fired from Garden Fresh, a restaurant firm he co-owned. Once again at the company helm, he is now more receptive to outside input and acknowledges the importance of work-life balance.

41699 ■ *"CSX Transportation: Supplier Diversity on the Right Track"* in Hispanic Business (July-August 2009, pp. 34)

Pub: Hispanic Business Inc.

Contact: Jesus Chavarria, President

Description: CSX Transportation is a leader in delivering essential products, operating as many as 1,200 trains and a fleet of more than 100,000 freight cars. CSX attributes its success by valuing diversity in both hiring and supplier contracts.

41700 ■ *"Cultural Due Diligence"* in Canadian Business (Vol. 80, April 23, 2007, No. 9, pp. 60)

Ed: Graham Lowe. **Description:** The factors to be considered by job seekers during judging good workplace with relation to corporate culture are presented.

41701 ■ *"Custom Fit"* in Canadian Business (Vol. 80, November 19, 2007, No. 23, pp. 42)

Ed: Andy Holloway. **Description:** Proper employee selection will help ensure a company has the people with the skills it really needs. Employee development is integral in coping with changes in the company. The importance of hiring the right employee and developing his skills is examined.

41702 ■ *"Dallas Top-Performing City for Small Business Growth"* in Dallas Business Journal (Vol. 37, July 11, 2014, No. 44, pp. 13)

Pub: American City Business Journals

Released: July 11, 2014. **Description:** Dallas has been ranked as Texas' top-performing metropolitan area for small business job growth in 2014. The 1.07 percent growth rate spike placed Dallas at 104.02 on the index, and it was observed that the market conditions and economy of Dallas made it easier to start a new business. It is reported that though the index indicated a drop, small business job growth in Dallas remained at a record high.

41703 ■ *"Datebook"* in Crain's Chicago Business (Vol. 31, March 24, 2008, No. 12, pp. 18)

Pub: Crain Communications Inc.

Contact: Todd Johnson, Publisher

Description: Listing of events in the Chicago area, including conferences addressing entrepreneurialism, economic development, secrets of getting hired, and women business ownership.

41704 ■ *"Datebook"* in Crain's Chicago Business (Vol. 31, March 31, 2008, No. 13, pp. 1)

Pub: Crain Communications Inc.

Contact: Todd Johnson, Publisher

Description: Listing of events in the Detroit area include conferences addressing entrepreneurialism, economic development, secrets of getting hired, and women business ownership.

41705 ■ *"David Maus Debuting New Dealership"* in Orlando Business Journal (Vol. 26, February 5, 2010, No. 36, pp. 1)

Pub: American City Business Journals

Ed: Anjali Fluker. **Description:** Automotive dealers David Maus Automotive Group and Van Tuyl Automotive Investment Group will launch David Maus Chevrolet in Sanford, Florida in fall 2010. The 12-acre site of the Chevy dealership will be located adjacent to the David Maus Toyota dealership. The new store is expected to generate nearly 125 new jobs.

41706 ■ *"Dealer Gets a Lift with Acquisitions at Year's End"* in Crain's Detroit Business (Vol. 26, January 11, 2010, No. 2, pp. 3)

Pub: Crain Communications Inc.

Contact: Rance E. Crain, President

Ed: Ryan Beene. **Description:** Alta Equipment Co., a forklift dealer, closed 2009 with a string of acquisitions expecting to double the firm's employee head-count and triple its annual revenue. Alta Lift Truck Services, Inc., as the company was known before the acquisitions, was founded in 1984 as Michigan's dealer for forklift manufacturer Yale Materials Handling Corp.

41707 ■ *"Debt-Collection Agency to Lay Off 368 in Hampton Center"* in Virginian-Pilot (December 4, 2010)

Pub: Virginian-Pilot

Ed: Tom Shean. **Description:** NCO Financial Systems Inc., provider of debt-collection and outsourcing services will permanently lay off 368 workers at its Hampton call center in 2011.

41708 ■ *"Decorated Marine Sues Contractor"* in Wall Street Journal Eastern Edition (November 29, 2011, pp. A4)

Pub: Dow Jones & Co., Inc.

Contact: Clare Hart, President

Ed: Julian E. Barnes. **Description:** Marine Devon Maylie, who was awarded the Congressional Medal of Honor for bravery, has filed a lawsuit against defense contractor BAE Systems PLC claiming that the company prevented his hiring by another firm by saying he has a mental condition and a drinking problem. Maylie says that this was in retaliation for his objections to the company's plan to sell the Pakistani military high-tech sniper scopes.

41709 ■ *"Delaware Diaper Maker Wanting To Expand Less Than a Year After Move"* in Business First-Columbus (December 10, 2007, pp. A6)

Pub: American City Business Journals, Inc.

Ed: Dan Eaton. **Description:** Duluth, Georgia-based Associated Hygienic Products LLC is planning to expand its production operations by 20 percent and hire new workers. The diaper maker was awarded state incentives to facilitate its transfer from Marion to Delaware. Details are included.

41710 ■ *"Delta Air Lines Looks at Downtown Departure"* in Business Courier (Vol. 27, October 1, 2010, No. 22, pp. 1)

Pub: Business Courier

Ed: Dan Monk. **Description:** Delta Air Lines Inc. has been looking for a smaller office for its reservations center in downtown Cincinnati, Ohio. Delta has informed the city of its plan to seek proposals on office space alternatives in advance of the 2011 lease expiration. Insights on the current employment status at the reservations center are also given.

41711 ■ *"Dexter Gauntlett Gauges the Wind"* in Business Journal Portland (Vol. 30, January 31, 2014, No. 48, pp. 6)

Pub: American City Business Journals

Released: January 31, 2014. **Description:** Navigant Research senior research analyst, Dexter Gauntlett says Vestas-American Wind Systems could boost its revenues. He added that the company has being hiring employees at its manufacturing plants. Gauntlett also said that wind energy will greatly boost state renewable portfolios.

41712 ■ *"Disunion in the House: the Steep Price We Pay"* in Philadelphia Business Journal (Vol. 33, March 28, 2014, No. 7, pp. 4)

Pub: American City Business Journals

Released: March 28, 2014. **Description:** Some members of the Ironworkers Local 401 Union in Philadelphia, Pennsylvania face federal indictment on charges of participating in an alleged conspiracy to commit extortion, arson, assault and destruction of property. The alleged motive of their actions was to force construction contractors to hire union ironworkers.

41713 ■ *"Do You Have A Retirement Parachute?"* in Barron's (Vol. 88, July 7, 2008, No. 27, pp. 32)

Pub: Dow Jones & Co., Inc.

Contact: Clare Hart, President

Ed: Jane White. **Description:** The idea that American companies should emulate the Australian retirement system which implements a forced contribution rate for all employers regarding an adequate retirement plan for their employees is discussed.

41714 ■ *"Downtowns Must Court Young, CEOs for Cities President Says"* in Crain's Detroit Business (Vol. 24, October 6, 2008,

No. 40, pp. 18)

Ed: Amy Lane. **Description:** It is important to produce more college graduates, and keep them in Michigan, according to CEOs for Cities President Carol Coletta when she spoke to a session at the West Michigan Regional Policy Conference which was held in September in Grand Rapids. Ways in which city leaders can connect students to communities, resulting in employees who have vested interest in the region, are also discussed.

41715 ■ *"Dreyer's Grand Ice Cream" in Ice Cream Reporter (Vol. 23, September 20, 2010, No. 10, pp. 8)*

Description: Dreyer's Grand Ice Cream will add one hundred new manufacturing jobs at its plant in Laurel, Maryland and another 65 new hires before the end of 2010 and another 35 in 2011.

41716 ■ *"Duro Bag to Expand, Add 130 Jobs" in Business Courier (Vol. 27, August 6, 2010, No. 14, pp. 1)*

Pub: Business Courier

Ed: Jon Newberry. **Description:** Duro Bag Manufacturing Company will expand capacity at its Florence, Kentucky plant and will add around 130 jobs over the next few years. The state of Kentucky has given preliminary approval for up to $1 million in tax incentives over 10 years, tied to the creation of new jobs. The company's investment will include new production and packaging equipment and building improvements.

41717 ■ *"Eclipse to Hire 50 for Airp;ort Hangar" in Business Review, Albany New York (Vol. 34, November 9, 2007, No. 32, pp. 3)*

Pub: American City Business Journals, Inc.

Ed: Robin K. Cooper. **Description:** Eclipse Aviation, a jet manufacturer will hire fifty workers who will operate its new maintenance hangar at Albany International Airport. The company was expected to hire around twenty-five employees after it announced its plan to open one of the seven U.S. Factory Service Centers in 2005. Denise Zieske, the airport Economic Development Manager, expects the hangar construction to be completed by December 2007.

41718 ■ *"Electrolux Nears Product Testing" in Memphis Business Journal (Vol. 34, September 21, 2012, No. 23, pp. 1)*

Pub: American City Business Journal

Ed: Michael Sheffield. **Description:** Electrolux Home Products Inc.'s new manufacturing facility is expected to be ready for use by the end of September 2012. The company will start producing 'pilot' products once the testing of manufacturing systems is completed. Electrolux will also hire 200 employees who will assemble the first products ready for shipmenht in the first quarter of 2013.

41719 ■ *"Elon Musk's Solar Firm Is Nearly Doubling Its Massachusetts Workforce" in Boston Business Journal (Vol. 34, May 30, 2014, No. 17, pp. 3)*

Pub: American City Business Journals, Inc.

Contact: Whitney Shaw, President

Released: May 30, 2014. **Description:** SolarCity is planning to add 100 jobs to its Massachusetts operations. The solar panel firm opened a second operations center in the state. State business incentives have enabled the company to expand presence in the area.

41720 ■ *"Empathy: An Entrepreneur's Killer App" in Women Entrepreneur (February 3, 2009)*

Ed: Kristi Hedges. **Description:** It is just as important to treat employees with courtesy and respect during bad economic times as it is in a good economy. Employers sometimes take advantage of such bad economic times since they realize that employees are grateful to have a job and cannot just quit and easily find work elsewhere. The importance of empathy in a company's leadership personnel is discussed.

41721 ■ *"End of an Era" in Barron's (Vol. 88, July 7, 2008, No. 27, pp. 3)*

Pub: Dow Jones & Co., Inc.

Contact: Clare Hart, President

Ed: Alan Abelson. **Description:** June 2008 was a very bad month for US stocks, with investors losing as much as 41.9 percent in the first half of 2008 signaling an end to the financial environment that prevailed around the world since the 1980's. The US job market lost 62,000 jobs in June 2008.

41722 ■ *"Energy Sparks Job Growth" in The Business Journal-Serving Greater Tampa Bay (Vol. 28, August 11, 2008, No. 33, pp. 1)*

Pub: American City Business Journals, Inc.

Contact: Whitney Shaw, President

Ed: Margie Manning. **Description:** Energy infrastructure projects in Tampa Bay, Florida, are increasing the demand for labor in the area. Energy projects requiring an increase in labor include TECO Energy Inc.'s plan for a natural gas pipeline in the area and the installation of energy management system in Bank of America's branches in the area.

41723 ■ *"Enriching the Ecosystem: A Four-Point Plan for Linking Innovation, Enterprises, and Jobs" in Harvard Business Review (Vol. 90, March 2012, No. 3, pp. 140)*

Pub: Harvard Business Review Press

Contact: Peter E. Walsh, Director

Ed: Rosabeth Moss Kanter. **Released:** March 2012. **Description:** The four goals for enriching the ecosystem include: linking venture creation and knowledge creation to speed up the idea-to-enterprise transition; revitalizing small-, medium-, and large-sized firms via partnerships; improving matches between education and employment opportunities; and bringing together leaders across different sectors to create regional strategies.

41724 ■ *"Entrepreneur Thorkil Sonne on What You Can Learn from Employees with Autism" in Harvard Business Review (Vol. 86, September 2008, No. 9, pp. 32)*

Pub: Harvard Business Review Press

Contact: Peter E. Walsh, Director

Ed: Susan Donovan. **Description:** Danish software entrepreneur Thorkil Sonne has helped improve employment for individuals with autism after discovering the perception of detail and remarkable memory skills in his own son, who has autism. His company, Specialisterne, was built via focusing on these strengths.

41725 ■ *The Entrepreneur's Guide to Managing Growth and Handling Crises*

Pub: Greenwood Publishing Group Inc.

Contact: Janann Sherman, Manager

Ed: Theo J. Van Dijk. **Released:** December 2007. **Price:** $39.95, hardcover. **Description:** The author explains how entrepreneurs can overcome crisis by changing the way they handle customers, by putting new processes and procedures in place, and managing employees in a professional manner. The book includes appendices with tips for hiring consultants, creating job descriptions, and setting up systems to chart cash flow as well as worksheets, tables and figures and a listing of resources. **Availability:** Print.

41726 ■ *"Essex Leases Space for Largest Retail Store" in Memphis Business Journal (Vol. 34, September 28, 2012, No. 24, pp. 1)*

Pub: American City Business Journal

Description: Essex Technology Group Inc. will build its third Memphis, Tennessee-area store in DeSoto County. The company signed a five-year, 69,342-square-foot lease at Stateline Square in Southaven. The new facility, which could open by January 2013, is expected to hire 30-35 employees.

41727 ■ *"Evaluating the 1996-2006 Employment Projections" in Montly Labor Review (Vol. 133, September 2010, No. 9, pp. 33)*

Pub: U.S. Department of Labor Bureau of Labor Statistics

Contact: Philip L. Rones, Manager

E-mail: rones.philip@bls.gov

Description: Bureau of Labor Statistics employment projections outperformed alternative naive models, but not projecting the housing bubble or the rise in oil

prices caused some inaccuracies in the projects. These projections are used by policymakers, economists, and students.

41728 ■ *"Even Money on Recession" in Barron's (Vol. 88, March 10, 2008, No. 10, pp. M9)*

Pub: Dow Jones & Co., Inc.

Contact: Clare Hart, President

Ed: Gene Epstein. **Description:** Discusses the US unemployment rate which was steady in February 2008 at 4.8 percent, while nonfarm payroll employment decreased by 63,000 in the same month, with the private sector losing 101,000 jobs. The economic indicators showed mixed signals on whether or not the US economy is in a recession.

41729 ■ *"Every Resume Tells a Story" in Women In Business (Vol. 62, September 2010, No. 3, pp. 26)*

Pub: American Business Women's Association

Contact: Lorie Burch, President

Ed: Kathleen Leighton. **Description:** Ways in which job applicants can write a good resume and promote themselves are discussed. It is believed that applicants should be proud of their accomplishments and they need to add details that will make them stand out. The importance of including a professional narrative in the resume is also explained.

41730 ■ *"Exit Strategy" in Barron's (Vol. 89, July 6, 2009, No. 27, pp. 3)*

Pub: Dow Jones & Co., Inc.

Contact: Clare Hart, President

Ed: Alan Abelson. **Description:** US Federal Reserve is not likely to change its easy-money strategy in the short term. States such as California are suffering from spiraling costs and declining revenues and are struggling to balance their budgets. The US unemployment rate climbed to 9.5 percent in June 2009.

41731 ■ *"Face Issues if Elder Care, Unemployment Collide" In Atlanta Journal-Constitution (December 26, 2010, pp. G1)*

Ed: Amy Lindgren. **Description:** More issues arise during holiday for families with older members requiring care, including the issue of employment for those doing the caregiving.

41732 ■ *The Facebook Era: Tapping Online Social Networks to Build Better Products, Reach New Audiences, and Sell More Stuff*

Ed: Clara Shih. **Price:** , $24.99. **Description:** The '90s were about the World Wide Web of information and the power of linking Web pages. Today it's about the World Wide Web of people and the power of the social graph. Online social networks are fundamentally changing the way we live, work, and interact. They offer businesses immense opportunities to transform customer relationships for profit: opportunities that touch virtually every business function, from sales and marketing to recruiting, collaboration to executive decision-making, product development to innovation.

41733 ■ *"Falcons' Blank Kicking Off 'Westside Works' Job Training Program" in Atlanta Business Chronicle (May 30, 2014, pp. 6A)*

Pub: American City Business Journals, Inc.

Contact: Whitney Shaw, President

Released: May 30, 2014. **Description:** Arthur Blank, owner of the Atlanta Falcons, is kicking off 'Westside Works', an initiative to build a world-class football/soccer stadium in Atlanta and transform the adjacent communities. Westside Works, a partnership between The Arthur M. Blank Family Foundation, the Construction Education Foundation of Georgia, and Integrity CDC will provide construction jobs for at least 100 men and women from the Westside neighborhoods in the next 12 months. The program will also provide job training, skills assessment, adult education programs, interview preparedness, and job placement.

41734 ■ *"Filling the Business Gap" in Hispanic Business (December 2010)*

Ed: Richard Larsen. **Description:** New York group seeks to increase state diversity supplier spending to help create jobs and boost the economy. According to a recent study, six out of 10 small business owners will increase capital spending but delay hiring in 2011. However, potential job creation is good among businesses owned by women and minorities.

41735 ■ "Firms Upbeat About Future, Survey Shows" in Globe & Mail (January 17, 2006, pp. B4)

Ed: Heather Scoffield. **Description:** The issue of labor shortage for manufacturing sector, in Canada, is discussed. The survey results of Bank of Canada are presented.

41736 ■ "FirstMerit's Top Executive Turns Around Credit Quality" in Crain's Cleveland Business (Vol. 28, October 15, 2007, No. 41, pp. 3)

Pub: Crain Communications Inc.

Ed: Shawn A. Turner. **Description:** Discusses the ways in which chairman and CEO Paul Greig has been able to improve FirstMerit Corp.'s credit quality and profit margin. Strategies included selling more than $70 million in bad loans, hiring a new chief credit officer and redirecting its focus on cross-selling its wealth and investment services to its commercial customers. Statistical data included.

41737 ■ "Five Great Business Tools" in Black Enterprise (Vol. 44, June 2014, No. 10, pp. 24)

Pub: Earl G. Graves Publishing Co. Inc.

Contact: Earl G. Graves, Jr., President

Released: June 2014. **Description:** Five products to help run a small business are listed: Legal Zoom Business Plan Attorney, provides attorney reviews of contracts and other legal documents; Shopify.com, is a fully hosted and customizable online shopping cart; SurveyMonkey.com, builds free surveys to conduct market research; Expensify.com handles credit card transactions, receipts, and invoices; and Intelius.com which allows companies to browse criminal records and other information for hiring purposes.

41738 ■ "Fresh Direct's Crisis" in Crain's New York Business (Vol. 24, January 14, 2008, No. 2, pp. 3)

Ed: Lisa Fickenscher. **Description:** Freshdirect, an Internet grocery delivery service, finds itself under siege from federal immigration authorities, customers and labor organizations due to its employment practice of hiring illegals. At stake is the grocer's reputation as well as its ambitious growth plans, including an initial public offering of its stock.

41739 ■ "Frontage Labs Moves, Plans to Hire 100" in Philadelphia Business Journal (Vol. 28, July 13, 2012, No. 22, pp. 1)

Pub: American City Business Journal

Ed: Natalie Kostelni, John George. **Description:** Frontage Pharmaceuticals will relocate its headquarters from the Valley Creek Corporate Center in Exton, Pennsylvania after signing a long-term lease on 80,000 square feet of space at the Eagleview Corporate Center. The relocation came as the company intended to consolidate its offices. Frontage Pharmaceuticals will also hire up to 100 new employees.

41740 ■ "Fuller Warns: Don't Be Fooled By All the Cranes" in Washington Business Journal (Vol. 33, August 22, 2014, No. 18, pp. 4)

Pub: American City Business Journals

Released: August 22, 2014. **Description:** The Greater Washington economy has been damaged worse than previously reported, according to George Mason University economist, Stephen Fuller. He emphasizes the need for business investment that supports added value jobs and to attract companies with higher paying wages when hiring.

41741 ■ "The Future Is Another Country; Higher Education" in The Economist (Vol. 390, January 3, 2009, No. 8612, pp. 43)

Description: Due to the growth of the global corporation, more ambitious students are studying at universities abroad; the impact of this trend is discussed.

41742 ■ The Game-Changer: How You Can Drive Revenue and Profit Growth with Innovation

Pub: Crown Business

Ed: A.G Lafley, Ram Charan. **Price:** $27.50, Hardcover. **Description:** Management guru Charan and Proctor & Gamble CEO Lafley provide lessons to encourage innovation at all levels, including how to hire for and encourage an environment of communication and tangible work processes.

41743 ■ "Generation Y Goes To Work; Management" in The Economist (Vol. 390, January 3, 2009, No. 8612, pp. 48)

Description: Unemployment rates among people in their 20s has increased significantly and there is a lower turnover in crisis-hit firms, which has made it more difficult to simply find another job if one is unsatisfied with the management style of his or her company. Managers are adopting a more command-and-control approach which is the antithesis of the open, collaborative style that younger employees prefer.

41744 ■ "Get Hired Now! A 28-Day Program for Landing the Job You Want" in Black Enterprise (Vol. 37, October 2006, No. 3, pp. 119)

Pub: Earl G. Graves Publishing Co. Inc.

Contact: Earl G. Graves, Jr., President

Ed: C.J. Hayden, Frank Traditi. **Description:** Finding a job can be a challenge. Surveys estimate that 74 to 85 percent of those available are never advertised. Tips for searching out employment opportunities and landing the job you desire are explored.

41745 ■ "Getting Going on Going Green" in HRMagazine (Vol. 53, August 2008, No. 8, pp. 8)

Pub: Society for Human Resource Management

Contact: Henry G. Jackson, President

E-mail: hjackson@shrm.org

Ed: Rita Zeidner. **Description:** Being eco-friendly can help recruit and retain workers. Resources to help firms create green initiatives are presented.

41746 ■ "Gilt Groupe's CEO On Building a Team of A Players" in Harvard Business Review (Vol. 90, January-February 2012, No.1-2, pp. 43)

Pub: Harvard Business Review Press

Contact: Peter E. Walsh, Director

Ed: Kevin Ryan. Released: January-February 2012. **Description:** The author stresses the role of human capital in a firm's success, and the importance of employment references in determining a candidate's talents. Key questions include whether the reference would hire the person, whether people enjoy working with him or her, and what areas could use improvements.

41747 ■ "Give 'Em a Break" in Entrepreneur (Vol. 35, November 2007, No. 11, pp. 32)

Pub: Entrepreneur Press

Contact: Perlman Neil, President

Ed: J.J. Ramberg. **Description:** Andy Walter and Peer Pedersen founded Blue Orchid Capital, a fund of hedge funds, and Steamboat Foundation a foundation that helps college students find high-profile summer internships. Details on the fund and the foundation are presented.

41748 ■ "The Globe Goes Birmingham" in Birmingham Business Journal (Vol. 31, July 4, 2014, No. 27, pp. 4)

Pub: American City Business Journals, Inc.

Contact: Whitney Shaw, President

Released: July 4, 2014. **Description:** Foreign-owned firms are investing heavily in the city of Birmingham, Alabama and are creating jobs. The number of employees in Birmingham at foreign-owned firms continues to rise and it is a trend not expected to slow in the near future. This is helping the area economy that has struggled with job creation during the low economic times. Low taxes, lower wage requirements and labor laws, and Birmingham's location and proximity to key manufacturers are factors attracting multi-million dollar investments in the city.

41749 ■ "Grace Puma: Senior Vice-President of Strategic Sourcing, United Airlines" in Crain's Chicago Business (May 5, 2008)

Pub: Crain Communications Inc.

Contact: Todd Johnson, Publisher

Ed: John Rosenthal. **Description:** Profile of Grace Puma who is the senior vice-president of strategic sourcing at United Airlines and is responsible for cutting costs at the company in a number of ways including scheduling safety inspections at the same time as routine maintenance, thereby reducing the downtime of each aircraft by five days as well as replacing a third of her staff with outside talent.

41750 ■ "The Great Fall: Here Comes The Humpty Dumpty Economy" in Barron's (Vol. 88, March 10, 2008, No. 10, pp. 5)

Pub: Dow Jones & Co., Inc.

Contact: Clare Hart, President

Ed: Alan Abelson. **Description:** Discusses the US economy is considered to be in a recession, with the effects of the credit crisis expected to intensify as a result. Inflation is estimated at 4.3 percent in January 2008, while 63,000 jobs were lost in February 2008.

41751 ■ "The Green Industry Jobs Gap" in Green Industry Pro (Vol. 23, October 2011)

Pub: Cygnus Business Media

Contact: Paul Mackler, Chief Executive Officer

Ed: Gregg Wartgow. **Description:** According to the U.S. Bureau of Labor Statistics, the landscaping industry employs over 829,000 workers. According to another private study, the industry would employ more if they were able to find more people interested in performing the required work.

41752 ■ "Green Light" in The Business Journal-Portland (Vol. 25, July 11, 2008, No. 18, pp. 1)

Ed: Erik Siemers. **Description:** Ecos Consulting, a sustainability consulting company based in Portland, Oregon, is seeing a boost in revenue as more businesses turn to sustainable practices. The company's revenue rose by 50 percent in 2007 and employees increased from 57 to 150. Other details about Ecos' growth are discussed.

41753 ■ "Growing Encryptics Trades Frisco for Austin" in Austin Business Journal (Vol. 34, April 25, 2014, No. 10, pp. A8)

Pub: American City Business Journals, Inc.

Contact: Whitney Shaw, President

Released: April 25, 2014. **Description:** Frisco, Texas-based Encryptics Inc. has announced plans to relocate its headquarters with its 21 employees and negotiating for office space in West Austin's Loop 360 area. Encryptics also plans to increase the number of its employees to about 80 next year. Insights into Encryptics' email security softward area also given.

41754 ■ "Guidance On Career Guidance for Offender Reentry" in Occupational Outlook Quarterly (Vol. 54, Fall 2010, No. 3, pp. 24)

Pub: U.S. Department of Labor Bureau of Labor Statistics

Contact: Philip L. Rones, Manager

E-mail: rones.philip@bls.gov

Description: Stable employment is a key factor in the successful rehabilitation of law offenders. The National Institute of Corrections hopes to improve offenders' long-term employment prospects.

41755 ■ "Hello, and Goodbye" in Entrepreneur (June 2014)

Pub: Entrepreneur Media Inc.

Released: June 2014. **Description:** Companies must implement strategies to ensure the creation of an ethical workplace. They must be able to deal with clients that experience problems and try to bully their counterparts as a result. Executive search firms must be responsible for compensating new executive hires by helping them find new jobs. Businesses must communicate to their employees about their importance as a way of making them feel appreciated and, thus, contribute to ethical behavior.

41756 ■ *"Help for Job Seekers"* in Crain's Detroit Business (Vol. 26, January 4, 2010, No. 1, pp. 14)
Pub: Crain Communications Inc.
Contact: Rance E. Crain, President
Description: CareerWorks is weekly paper targeting readers who are in a career transition or are looking for new employment.

41757 ■ *"Help for Job Seekers"* in Crain's Detroit Business (Vol. 26, January 18, 2010, No. 3, pp. 14)
Pub: Crain Communications Inc.
Contact: Rance E. Crain, President
Description: CareerWorks is aimed at helping those who are in career transition or are looking for new jobs; this weekly collection of news, advertising and information includes weekly stories, events and the highlighting of a person who has successfully made the transition from one profession to another. On the Website, readers are welcome to post an anonymous resume in order to attract employers.

41758 ■ *"'Help Wanted' Meets 'Buy It Now': Why More Companies Are Integrating Marketing and Recruiting"* in Inc. (November 2007, pp. 50-52)
Pub: Mansueto Ventures L.L.C.
Contact: John Koten, Chief Executive Officer
Ed: Ryan McCarthy. **Description:** Five tips to merge marketing and recruiting together, including: thinking of every help-wanted ad as a marketing opportunity, treating every job candidate as a potential customer, involving the youngest employees in the interview process, looking for way to promote recruiting events, and sponsoring community-oriented events.

41759 ■ *"Help Wanted: Only the Best Need Apply"* in Pet Product News (Vol. 66, April 2012, No. 4, pp. 24)
Description: Simi Valley, California-based pet supplies store, Theresa's Country Feed and Pet is said to have achieved success by hiring quality customer-oriented employees. In view of its receipt of the Pet Product News International's 2011-2012 Retailer of the Year Award for Outstanding General Pet Store, Theresa's approach to recruitment and customer relations are discussed.

41760 ■ *"Hickory Unemployment Stays Steady"* in Charlotte Observer (February 2, 2007)
Ed: Jen Aronoff. **Description:** Unemployment rates remained unchanged in Hickory, North Carolina area; the region reported 6.1 percent unemployment.

41761 ■ *"High-Tech Job-Apalooza!"* in Orlando Business Journal (Vol. 26, January 15, 2010, No. 33, pp. 1)
Pub: American City Business Journals
Ed: Christopher Boyd. **Description:** Science Applications International Corporation, Saab Training USA LLC, CAE USA, and Pelliconi &C.SPA attempt to obtain $939,000 in tax incentives to generate 222 technology and defense-related jobs in Orange County, Florida. Each job will provide an average salary of $67,000. Future plans of each technology and defense firm are also presented.

41762 ■ *"Highmark-Owned Glasses Chain Eyeing Phila. Expansion"* in Philadelphia Business Journal (Vol. 28, May 18, 2012, No. 14, pp. 1)
Pub: American City Business Journal
Description: Pittsburgh, Pennsylvania-based Highmark's subsidiary, Visionworks, has outlined its plan to open 25 stores in the Philadelphia region. The retail eyeglasses store chain has also been trying to recruit opticians to hire in the area.

41763 ■ *"Hire Education"* in Canadian Business (Vol. 79, September 11, 2006, No. 18, pp. 114)
Pub: Rogers Media Inc.
Contact: Tony Viner, President
Ed: Erin Pooley. **Description:** Study results showing the perceptions of students while considering full-time employment and the attributes they look for in their future employers are presented.

41764 ■ *"HireDiversity: Some Companies Developing Affinity for Employee Groups"* in Hispanic Business (October 2007, pp. 86-87)
Ed: Hildy Medina. **Description:** Affinity groups, also known as employee resource networks, help companies identify and recruit candidates.

41765 ■ *"The Hiring Handbook: Tips & Tactics to Attract Top Tier Talent"*
Pub: CreateSpace
Contact: Daren Giles, President
Released: October 22, 2014. **Price:** , $11.95 paperback. **Description:** All the information needed to recruit and hire the best talent for any small business is presented. While intended for hiring managers, the information is useful for any human resources executives as well as job seekers.

41766 ■ *"Hiring Unpaid Interns: Failing To Comply With Labor Laws Can Lead to Legal Trouble"* in Black Enterprise (Vol. 44, June 2014, No. 10, pp. 22)
Pub: Earl G. Graves Publishing Co. Inc.
Contact: Earl G. Graves, Jr., President
Released: June 2014. **Description:** Before hiring an intern for a small business it is critical to study the Department of Labor's legal criteria, determine whether the internship should be paid or unpaid, weigh the pros and cons, focus on the training aspect, and work with local colleges.

41767 ■ *"Hold the McJobs: Canada's High-End Employment Boom"* in Globe & Mail (February 17, 2006, pp. B1)
Ed: Heather Scoffield. **Description:** A focus the increasing rate of high-end or professional jobs Canada and its negative influence on low-end and middle level jobs is presented.

41768 ■ *"How to Attract Big-City Talent to Small Towns"* in Advertising Age (Vol. 79, July 7, 2008, No. 26, pp. 24)
Pub: Crain Communications Inc.
Contact: Rance Crain, President
Ed: Joe Erwin. **Description:** Advice concerning ways in which to attract talent to mid-market agencies is given and innovative techniques that have worked for some firms are discussed.

41769 ■ *How to Become a Great Boss: The Rules for Getting and Keeping the Best Employees*
Pub: Hyperion
Ed: Jeffrey J. Fox. **Released:** May 15, 2002. **Price:** $17, hardcover; C$19, hardcover. **Description:** The book offers valuable advice to any manager or entrepreneur to improve leadership and management skills. Topics covered include: hiring, managing, firing, partnership and competition, self and organization, employee performance, attitude, and priorities. **Availability:** Print.

41770 ■ *"How to Heal a Broken Legg"* in Barron's (Vol. 92, September 17, 2012, No. 38, pp. 18)
Description: Legg Mason is looking for a new chief executive officer after Mark Fetting announced his resignation effective October 1, 2012. Fetting is credited with saving the company by reducing operating expenses, but had a tense relationship with the firm's affiliates. The company has limited options in finding a replacement and undertaking reorganization.

41771 ■ *How to Hire, Train and Keep the Best Employees for Your Small Business*
Pub: Atlantic Publishing Co.
Contact: Amanda Miller, Manager
E-mail: amiller@atlantic-pub.com
Ed: Dianna Podmoroff. **Released:** June 2004. **Price:** $29.95, with companion CD-ROM. **Description:** Costs of hiring, training, and lost productivity costs related to losing employees. **Availability:** Print.

41772 ■ *How to Make Money While You Look for a Job: Start a Very Small Service Business on a Shoestring, A Step-by-step Workbook*
Pub: Booklocker.com Inc.
Contact: Angela Adair-Hoy, Publisher
Ed: Donna Boyette. **Released:** March 2005. **Description:** Six steps to make money while searching for employment are outlined, from setting up a home-based office to selling a service.

41773 ■ *"How to Pick an All-Star"* in Canadian Business (Vol. 79, October 9, 2006, No. 20, pp. 15)
Ed: Andy Holloway. **Description:** Factors that determine the competency levels o f individuals are discussed. The need for firms to take into consideration the right selection factors while hiring an employee is presented.

41774 ■ *"How to Protect Your Job in a Recession"* in Harvard Business Review (Vol. 86, September 2008, No. 9, pp. 113)
Pub: Harvard Business Review Press
Contact: Peter E. Walsh, Director
Ed: Janet Banks, Diane Coutu. **Description:** Strategies are presented for enhancing one's job security. These include being a team player, empathizing with management, preserving optimism, and concentrating on the customer.

41775 ■ *"How to Secure U.S. Jobs"* in Gallup Management Journal (October 27, 2011)
Pub: Gallup Inc.
Contact: Jim Clifton, Chief Executive Officer
Ed: Jim Clifton. **Description:** If America doubled its number of engaged customers globally, it could triple exports, which would create more good jobs and put the US economy back on track.

41776 ■ *How to Start a Home-Based Senior Care Business: Develop a Winning Business Plan*
Pub: Globe Pequot Press Inc.
Contact: Robert Irwin, Manager
E-mail: robert.irwin@globepequot.com
Ed: James L. Ferry. **Released:** January 06, 2010. **Price:** $18.95, paperback. **Description:** Everything needed to know in order to start and run a profitable, ethical, and satisfying senior care business from your home. Information covers writing a good business plan, marketing services to families, creating a fee structure, and developing a network of trusted caregivers and service providers. **Availability:** Print.

41777 ■ *"How To Reduce the Risk of Discrimination"* in Idaho Business Review (September 11, 2014)
Pub: Dolan Co.
Contact: James P. Dolan, President
Released: September 11, 2014. **Description:** Human resource departments in small businesses in Boise are aware of the city's discrimination ordinance making it unlawful to use sexual orientation and gender identity/expression in any consideration of hiring or terminating an employee, or for any other issue. The impact of the ordinance is yet to be determined.

41778 ■ *Hug Your Customers: The Proven Way to Personalize Sales and Achieve Astounding Results*
Pub: Hyperion Books
Contact: Ellen Archer, President
Ed: Jack Mitchell. **Released:** June 09, 2003. **Price:** $19.95; C$29.95. **Description:** The CEO of Mitchells/Roberts, two very successful clothing stores, professes his belief in showering customers with attention. His secrets for long-term business success include advice about attracting a good staff, lowering marketing costs, and maintaining higher gross margins and revenues.

41779 ■ *"'Huge Contract' Means 299 New Jobs, $96M Expansion for ZF Steering Systems"* in Business Courier (Vol. 26, November 6, 2009, No. 28, pp. 1)
Pub: American City Business Journals, Inc.
Contact: Whitney Shaw, President
Ed: Jon Newberry. **Description:** Proposed $96 million expansion of German-owned automotive supplier ZF Steering systems LLC is anticipated to generate

299 jobs in Boone County, Kentucky. ZF might invest $90 million in equipment, while the rest will go to building and improvements.

41780 ■ "If Just One Person Applies, Are You Required to Hire Him?" in HR Specialist (Vol. 8, September 2010, No. 9, pp. 7)
Description: It is legal to decline hiring an applicant, or even promoting a current employee, if they are the only applicant for a particular position. It may be good choice to wait for more applicants or to change recruiting strategy.

41781 ■ "Illinois Bets On Recycling Programs" in Chicago Tribune (November 29, 2008)
Pub: McClatchy-Tribune Information Services

Ed: Joel Hood. **Description:** Traditionally the holiday gift-giving season is one of the most wasteful times of year and the state of Illinois is granting $760,000 to small businesses and cities in an attempt to expand curbside recycling programs and hire additional workers to address electronic waste.

41782 ■ "Immigration: Give Us Your Skilled" in Canadian Business (Vol. 80, October 8, 2007, No. 20, pp. 78)
Pub: Rogers Media Inc.

Contact: Tony Viner, President

Ed: Zena Olijnyk. **Description:** Demand for skilled workers in Canada is discussed. Despite a strong demand, as evidenced by shortages in both skilled and unskilled labor, the country's immigration policy is affecting the recruitment process. Peter Veress, founder and president of Vermax Group, believes the country is wasting opportunities to take advantage of its attractiveness as a destination for foreign workers.

41783 ■ "IMRA's Ultrafast Lasers Bring Precision, profits; Ann Arbor Company Eyes Expansion" in Crain's Detroit Business (March 10, 2008)
Pub: Crain Communications Inc.

Contact: Rance E. Crain, President

Ed: Tom Henderson. **Description:** IMRA America Inc. plans to expand its headquarters and has applied for permits to build a fourth building that will house research and development facilities and allow the company more room for manufacturing; the company plans to add about 20 more employees that would include research scientists, manufacturing and assembly workers, engineers and salespeople. The growth is due mainly to a new technology of ultrafast fiber lasers that reduce side effects for those getting eye surgeries and help manufacturers of computer chips to reduce their size and cost.

41784 ■ "Incapital Set to Add Jobs, Expand Space" in South Florida Business Journal (Vol. 33, August 3, 2012, No. 1, pp. 1)
Pub: American City Business Journal

Description: Chicago, Illinois-based Incapital has announced plans to hire 25 to 30 more financial professionals over the next 12 months. Incapital is also planning to expand its Boca Raton, Florida with construction totalling 5,000 additional square feet to accommodate future growth.

41785 ■ "Income Tax Credit for Business Pushes the Job Creation Button" in Idaho Business Review (August 27, 2014)
Pub: Dolan Co.

Contact: James P. Dolan, President

Released: August 27, 2014. **Description:** Idaho's new Reimbursement Incentive Act program creates a tax credit for businesses with a qualifying project that will add new jobs that are paid at or above the average wage for work performed. Legislation and technical requirements for small businesses to quality are outlined.

41786 ■ "Indiana Collection Agency Announces Expansion Plans" in PaymentsSource (March 23, 2012)
Pub: SourceMedia Inc.

Contact: James M. Malkin, Chief Executive Officer

Released: March 23, 2012. **Description:** DECA Financial Services plans to buy a vacant building in Fishers, Indiana and renovate the property. The

agency specializes in collection consumer and tax debts for both companies and government agencies. The company plans to hire 140 new employees over the next 3 years.

41787 ■ "Information Technology Changes Roles, Highlights Hiring Needs" in South Florida Business Journal (Vol. 34, February 14, 2014, No. 30, pp. 3)
Pub: American City Business Journals

Released: February 14, 2014. **Description:** Results of the Steven Douglas Associates survey of 218 senior and mid-level information technology executives in South Florida are presented. About 75 percent of the respondents cited cloud services, mobile technologies, big data and enterprise reporting planning as having the most profound impact on their roles. The challenges they face with the expected hiring growth are also examined.

41788 ■ "The Ins and Outs of Unemployment in Canada, 1976-2008" in Canadian Journal of Economics (Vol. 44, November 2011, No. 4, pp. 1331)
Pub: Wiley-Blackwell

Contact: Gordon Tibbitts, President

Ed: Michele Campolieti. **Description:** Flows into and out of unemployment in Canada at an aggregate and a number of disaggregated levels are studied.

41789 ■ "Inside the New Nortel" in Canadian Business (Vol. 79, November 6, 2006, No. 22, pp. 93)
Pub: Rogers Media Inc.

Contact: Tony Viner, President

Ed: Andrew Wahl. **Description:** The plans of Nortel Networks to improve its technology market by appointing new teams are analyzed.

41790 ■ "Insurance Jobs" in Best's Review (Vol. 113, September 2012, No. 5, pp. 10)
Description: Jobs report from the US Bureau of Labor Statistics is presented, reporting only 100 new jobs in July 2012. Statistical data included.

41791 ■ "Insuraprise Growing Fast" in Austin Business Journal (Vol. 31, April 22, 2011, No. 7, pp. 1)
Pub: American City Business Journals

Ed: Sandra Zaragoza. **Description:** Austin, Texas-based Insuraprise Inc. is finalizing the purchase of a 24,000-square-foot office at 12116 Jekel Circle. The firm, with 23 salespeople and sales that are growing nearly 300 percent over the past 18 months, will now have room to grow. Insuraprise plans to hire 35 new salespersons for its call center.

41792 ■ "Interbrand's Creative Recruiting Keeps Top Talent in Cincinnati" in Business Courier (Vol. 27, November 12, 2010, No. 28, pp. 1)
Pub: Business Courier

Ed: Dan Monk. **Description:** Global brand consulting firm Interbrand uses a creative recruitment agency to attract new employees into the company. Interbrand uses themed parties to attract prospective employees. The 'Alice In Wonderland' tea party for example, allowed the company to hire five new employees.

41793 ■ "Interest in 'Encore Careers' is Growing" In HRMagazine (Vol. 53, November 2008, No. 11, pp. 22)
Pub: Society for Human Resource Management

Contact: Henry G. Jackson, President

E-mail: hjackson@shrm.org

Ed: Kathy Gurchiek. **Description:** Unexpectedly large numbers of baby boomers are looking for jobs that can provide them with 'means and meaning', according to a survey by MetLife and Civic Ventures. They can find those jobs in encore careers, an opportunity to do work that has a social impact and personal meaning.

41794 ■ "Job Losses and Budget Shortfall Adding to Economic Woes" in Sacramento Business Journal (Vol. 25, July 14, 2008, No. 19, pp. 1)
Pub: American City Business Journals, Inc.

Contact: Whitney Shaw, President

Ed: Kathy Robertson. **Description:** Budget cuts in California have been approved amid rising unemployment in a slowing economy. Statistics show that total

industry employment in the Sacramento region decreased by 3,700 jobs from May 2007 to May 2008. Governor Arnold Schwarzenegger has ordered a 10 percent budget cut for state departments, but this cut will likely mean few layoffs.

41795 ■ "Job Seeker's Readiness Guide: Unemployment's High and Competition is Tough" in Black Enterprise (Vol. 40, July 2010, No. 12, pp. 83)
Pub: Earl G. Graves Publishing Co. Inc.

Contact: Earl G. Graves, Jr., President

Description: Five key areas to help someone seeking employment gain the competitive edge are listed.

41796 ■ "A Jobs Compact for America's Future: Badly Needed Investments In Human Capital Are Not Being Made. What We Can Do - Together - To Jump-Start the Process?" in Harvard Business Review (Vol. 90, March 2012, No. 3, pp. 64)
Pub: Harvard Business Review Press

Contact: Peter E. Walsh, Director

Ed: Thomas A. Kochan. **Released:** March 2012. **Description:** Obstacles to strengthening US human capital are a lack of focus on obtaining both high wages and high productivity, and a lack of value placed on human capital as a competitive advantage. Business schools are well positioned to address these obstacles via curricula, programs, and partnerships.

41797 ■ "Jobs Data Show A Slow Leak" in Barron's (Vol. 88, July 7, 2008, No. 27, pp. 34)
Pub: Dow Jones & Co., Inc.

Contact: Clare Hart, President

Ed: Gene Epstein. **Description:** In June 2008, the United States manufacturing sector showed an expansion, with the purchasing managers' index rising to 50.2 from 49.6; the unemployment rate in the US, which stayed steady at 5.5 percent in June 2008 is also discussed. Statistical data included.

41798 ■ "Jobs Data Show Wild Card" in Barron's (Vol. 90, September 6, 2010, No. 36, pp. M12)
Pub: Barron's Editorial & Corporate Headquarters

Ed: Gene Epstein. **Description:** August 2010 jobs report revealed a 54,000 decline in non-farm payrolls and that the unemployment rate remains unchanged at 9.6 percent. The report also shows a welcome rise of 848,999 in the household-data category. The unemployment rate shows a reversed trend where men's 10.6 percent unemployment is higher than women's 8.6 percent rate.

41799 ■ "Jobs Gain Cast Shadow On Recovery" in Providence Business News (Vol. 29, April 7, 2014, No. 1, pp. 1)
Pub: American City Business Journals

Released: April 7, 2014. **Description:** Rhode Island Department of Labor and Training data has indicated the creation of nearly 21,000 jobs in the state since summer of 2009. However, the 503,300 state's residents working in February 2014, was 45,586 fewer than pre-recession peak in December 2006, despite the job gains. The factors separating job growth from resident employment and the economic impact is discussed.

41800 ■ "The Jobs Man: Working with Cincinnati's Unemployed" in Business Courier (Vol. 26, December 25, 2009, No. 35, pp. 1)
Pub: American City Business Journals, Inc.

Contact: Whitney Shaw, President

Ed: Lucy May. **Description:** Entrepreneur Bob Messer, a volunteer for Jobs Plus Employment Network in Cincinnati's Over-the-Rhine neighborhood, regularly conducts a seminar that aims to help attendees prepare for employment. Jobs Plus founder Burr Robinson asked Messer to create the seminar in order to help unemployed jobseekers. So far, the program has helped 144 individuals with full time jobs in 2009.

41801 ■ *"Jobs: On the Clock" in Canadian Business (Vol. 82, April 27, 2009, No. 7, pp. 28)*

Pub: Rogers Media Inc.

Contact: Tony Viner, President

Ed: Sarka Halas. **Description:** Survey of 100 Canadian executives found that senior managers can be out of a job for about nine months before their careers are adversely affected. The nine month mark can be avoided if job seekers build networks even before they lose their jobs. Job seekers should also take volunteer work and training opportunities to increase their changes of landing a job.

41802 ■ *"Kinnser: Sales In Overdrive" in Austin Business Journal (Vol. 32, March 30, 2012, No. 4, pp. 1)*

Pub: American City Business Journals, Inc.

Contact: Whitney Shaw, President

Ed: Christopher Calnan. **Released:** March 30, 2012. **Description:** Kinnser Software Inc.'s receipt of fresh capitalization is seen to enable the company to pursue its acquisition strategy. The company is planning to grow organically. It is also planning to double the number of its employees.

41803 ■ *"Know It All Finds Applicants are Stretching the Truth" in Philadelphia Business Journal (Vol. 28, September 11, 2009, No. 30, pp. 1)*

Pub: American City Business Journals Inc.

Ed: Athena D. Merritt. **Description:** Know It All Background Research Services has reported that discrepancies in background checks reached 19.8 percent in 2009. Reports show that 42 percent of the discrepancies involve lying about previous employment, and 37 percent involve education information. Marc Bourne, the company's vice president, believes that employers have cause to be concerned.

41804 ■ *"Kodiak Assembly Solutions Bucks Bear Market" in Austin Business JournalInc. (Vol. 29, December 18, 2009, No. 41, pp. 1)*

Pub: American City Business Journals

Ed: Kate Harrington. **Description:** Austin, Texas-based Kodiak Assembly Solutions LLC, a company that installs components into printed circuit boards for product or evaluation tool kit prototyping purposes, will expand despite the recession. It will relocate from a 28,000 square foot space to a 42,000 square foot space in North Austin. The firm will also increase its workforce by 20 employees.

41805 ■ *"The Labor Crunch is Coming" in Canadian Business (Vol. 80, December 25, 2006, No. 1, pp. 74)*

Description: The need for skilled and educated workforce to meet labor shortage in future in Canada is discussed.

41806 ■ *"Labor Force Data" in Montly Labor Review (Vol. 133, September 2010, No. 9, pp. 89)*

Pub: U.S. Department of Labor Bureau of Labor Statistics

Contact: Philip L. Rones, Manager

E-mail: rones.philip@bls.gov

Description: Employment status of the population of the U.S. by sex, age, race and origin is presented.

41807 ■ *"Labor Pains" in Canadian Business (Vol. 79, August 14, 2006, No. 16-17, pp. 80)*

Description: Canada's employment insurance is analyzed in view of the growing shortage of labor.

41808 ■ *"LaSalle St. Firms Cherry-Pick Talent As Wall St. Tanks" in Crain's Chicago Business (Vol. 31, November 17, 2008, No. 46)*

Pub: Crain Communications Inc.

Contact: Todd Johnson, Publisher

Ed: H. Lee Murphy. **Description:** Many local businesses are taking advantage of the lay offs that many major Wall Street firms are undergoing in their workforces; these companies see the opportunity to woo talent and expand their staff with quality executives.

41809 ■ *"Last Founder Standing" in Conde Nast Portfolio (Vol. 2, June 2008, No. 6, pp. 124)*

Ed: Kevin Maney. **Description:** Interview with Amazon CEO Jeff Bezos in which he discusses the economy, the company's new distribution center and the hiring of employees for it, e-books, and the overall vision for the future of the firm.

41810 ■ *"Laying the Groundwork: In Developing Personnel, the Work Takes Place Beforehand" in Black Enterprise (February 2008)*

Pub: Earl G. Graves Publishing Co. Inc.

Contact: Earl G. Graves, Jr., President

Ed: Tamara E. Holmes. **Description:** Small business owners know the devastation of hiring the wrong employee for a position. Steps to improve hiring using a long-term plan are outlined.

41811 ■ *"Leading Ohio Internet Marketing Firm Announces Growth in September" in Marketing Weekly News (September 26, 2009, pp. 24)*

Pub: Investment Weekly News

Description: Despite a poor economy, Webbed Marketing, a leading social media marketing and search engine optimization firm in the Midwest, has added five additional professionals to its fast-growing team. The company continues to win new business, provide more services and hire talented employees.

41812 ■ *"Legalities of Diversity" in Hispanic Business (September 2007, pp. 26)*

Ed: Francisco Ramos Jr., Bill Krutzen. **Description:** Most companies in America have diversity programs, however, critics believe diversity can be used as reverse discrimination because minorities are getting preferential treatment in hiring, promotion, and admissions.

41813 ■ *The Logic of Life: The Rational Economics of an Irrational World*

Pub: Ballantine/ Del Rey/Fawcett/Ivy Books

Contact: Gilbert Perlman, President

Ed: Tim Harford. **Released:** February 10, 2009. **Price:** $15, paperback; $11.99. **Description:** Harford excels at making economists' studies palatable for discerning but non-expert readers. The uses hard data to show why promiscuous teens are actually health-conscious, divorce hasn't gotten a fair shake, corporate bosses will always be overpaid and job prospects for minorities continue to be grim. **Availability:** PrintE-book.

41814 ■ *"Looking To Hire Young? Be Careful" in Boston Business Journal (Vol. 30, November 19, 2010, No. 43, pp. 1)*

Pub: Boston Business Journal

Ed: Lisa van der Pool. **Description:** The Massachusetts Commission Against Discrimination (MCAD) has been using undercover job applicants to expose discrimination. Cabot's Ice Cream and Restaurant has been accused of denying older workers equal employment opportunities. MCAD has discovered unfair hiring practices such as hiring high school and college students.

41815 ■ *"Looming Labor Crunch Already Pushing Up Construction Prices" in Business Journal (Vol. 32, August 8, 2014, No. 11, pp. 10)*

Pub: American City Business Journals

Released: August 8, 2014. **Description:** Minneapolis, Minnesota's construction sector is expected to suffer from a worker shortage. An increase in the demand for construction labor will result in higher wages. Meanwhile, higher wages are expected to drive up construction costs.

41816 ■ *"Managing the Facebookers; Business" in The Economist (Vol. 390, January 3, 2009, No. 8612, pp. 10)*

Pub: Economist Newspaper Ltd.

Description: According to a report from PricewaterhouseCoopers, a business consultancy, workers from Generation Y, also known as the Net Generation, are more difficult to recruit and integrate into companies that practice traditional business acumen. 61 percent of chief executive managers say that they have trouble with younger employees who tend to be more narcissistic and more interested in personal fulfillment with a need for frequent feedback and an overprecise set of objectives on the path to promotion which can be hard for managers who are used to a different relationship with their subordinates. Older bosses should prepare to make some concessions to their younger talent since some of the issues that make them happy include cheaper online ways to communicate and additional coaching, both of which are good for business.

41817 ■ *Managing the Older Worker: How to Prepare for the New Organizational Order*

Pub: Harvard Business Press

Ed: Peter Cappelli, Bill Novelli. **Released:** August 17, 2010. **Price:** $29.95, hardcover. **Description:** Your organization needs older workers more than ever: They transfer knowledge between generations, transmit your company's values to new hires, make excellent mentors for younger employees, and provide a 'just in time' workforce for special projects. **Availability:** Print.

41818 ■ *"Managing Yourself: Job-Hopping to the Top and Other Career Fallacies" in Harvard Business Review (Vol. 88, July-August 2010, No. 7-8, pp. 154)*

Pub: Harvard Business School Publishing

Ed: Monika Hamori. **Description:** Fallacies identified and discussed include the belief that a career move should always be a move up, that industry and career switches are penalized, and that large corporations are the only loci for reaping large rewards.

41819 ■ *"M&A Weakness Takes Toll on Phila. Law Firms" in Philadelphia Business Journal (Vol. 28, August 10, 2012, No. 26, pp. 1)*

Pub: American City Business Journal

Description: Slowdown in mergers and acquisitions impact law firms in Philadelphia, Pennsylvania. Data show that M&A activity involving the US has decreased by 35 percent int he first half of 2012. With the number of deals decreasing, local firms have become cautious about hiring transactional lawyers in terms of selecting those from high revenue areas such as intellectual property.

41820 ■ *"A Manufacturing Revival" in Boston Business Journal (Vol. 31, May 27, 2011, No. 18, pp. 1)*

Pub: Boston Business Journal

Ed: Kyle Alspach. **Description:** Massachusetts' manufacturing sector has grown despite the high cost of labor, real estate and electricity. Manufacturing jobs in the state have increased to 2,800 in April 2011.

41821 ■ *"Market Resource Set for Expansion: Supply Chain Firm to Add Up to 700 Employees" in Memphis Business Journal (Vol. 34, May 11, 2012, No. 4, pp. 1)*

Pub: American City Business Journal

Description: Market Resource Packaging LLC is planning to expand its operation in Memphis, Tennessee under the new ownership of IAM Acquisition. The supply chain services company plans to increase its distribution space from 260,000 square feet to 1 million square feet in three years and to grow its employees from 300 to 1,000 in 18 months.

41822 ■ *"MBAs by the Hour" in Entrepreneur (August 2014)*

Pub: Entrepreneur Media Inc.

Released: August 2014. **Description:** HourlyNerd started from a classroom project by Pat Petitti and Rob Biederman at Harvard Business School in Boston, Massachusetts in 2003. the temporary-staffing firm recruits business students to act as consultants to small businesses that hire them. Consultants must come from one of the top 40 Master of Business Administration Programs in the U.S. in order to bid on a project. The firm receives 15 percent of the project fee from the hiring company while the business consultants pay 5 percent to the company.

41823 ■ *"Medical Tech Jobs Take More Than a Month To Fill"* in Austin Business Journal (Vol. 34, July 11, 2014, No. 21, pp. 10)
Pub: American City Business Journals, Inc.
Contact: Whitney Shaw, President
Released: July 11, 2014. **Description:** A report by Brookings Institute has revealed that nearly half of Austin's jobs require STEM - science, technology, engineering and mathematical skills. However, these jobs generally take more than a month to fill.

41824 ■ *"Meet the Gatekeepers"* in Crain's Chicago Business (Vol. 30, February 2007, No. 6, pp. 40)
Ed: Kate Ryan. **Description:** Recruiters at big investment banking firms agree that the way to get your foot in the door requires common sense issues such as not answering your phone in the middle of an interview, proofreading your cover letter, and research. Interviews with three top executives give more insight and advice.

41825 ■ *"Memphis Pays Healthy Price To Compete for Jobs, Investment"* in Memphis Business Journal (Vol. 35, January 3, 2014, No. 39, pp. 4)
Pub: American City Business Journals
Released: January 3, 2014. **Description:** Memphis, Tennessee Mayor A.C. Wharton announced that Economic Development Growth Engine (EDGE) had a solid year and he thinks 2014 will be even better. EDGE has committed $103,718 in pilot-lieu-of-tax property tax reductions for every job created in 2013. The economic development projects in Memphis and in peer cities are also presented.

41826 ■ *"Michigan Means Growth: Sustaining Growth Through Thick and Thin: Michigan Companies Sustain Growth with Well-Timed Access to Capital"* in Inc. (Vol. 36, September 2014, No. 7, pp. 164)
Pub: Mansueto Ventures L.L.C.
Contact: John Koten, Chief Executive Officer
Released: September 2014. **Description:** Successful companies possess flexibility, foresight and resources to turn adversity into opportunity. The small businesses in Michigan who have sustained experienced sales growth despite the recession of 2007. The Michigan Economic Development Corporation has introduced three initiatives to help Michigan businesses grow, including venture capital, collateral support and loan participation through the State Small Business Credit Initiative, and cash incentives for businesses looking to invest in urban communities or grow jobs.

41827 ■ *"Microsoft's Diversity Program Clicks into High Speed"* in Hispanic Business (Vol. 30, July-August 2008, No. 7-8, pp. 54)
Pub: Hispanic Business Inc.
Contact: Jesus Chavarria, President
Ed: Derek Reveron. **Description:** Microsoft's diversity hiring and vendor diversity program to capture more Hispanic consumer and business-to-business market is described. One of the main goals of these programs is to hire more Hispanic executives and managers who will help the company develop and market products and services that will appeal and benefit Hispanic consumers.

41828 ■ *"Mill Creek Greenway Project Could Forge Path to Jobs, Growth"* in Business Courier (Vol. 26, September 11, 2009, No. 20, pp. 1)
Pub: American City Business Journals, Inc.
Contact: Whitney Shaw, President
Ed: Lucy May. **Description:** The planned 13.5 mile Mill Creek Greenway Trail extension could create 445 jobs and bring $52 million to the economy of Cincinnati, Ohio. The trail extension would cost $24 million and would be used for recreational purposes.

41829 ■ *"Mission: Recruitment"* in HRMagazine (Vol. 54, January 2009, No. 1, pp. 42)
Pub: Society for Human Resource Management
Contact: Henry G. Jackson, President
E-mail: hjackson@shrm.org
Ed: Theresa Minton-Eversole. **Description:** Due to the hiring challenges faced by Army recruiters, they are partnering with employers in order to establish connections to high quality, Army-trained individuals when they separate from active duty.

41830 ■ *"Mobile Tech Firm Revs Hiring, Spins Off Startup"* in Business Journal (Vol. 30, August 17, 2012, No. 12, pp. 1)
Pub: American City Business Journals, Inc.
Contact: Whitney Shaw, President
Ed: Katharine Grayson. **Released:** August 17, 2012. **Description:** Minneapolis, Minnesota-based Mentor-Mate has grown rapidly to about 150 employees and the company expects to hire about 50 more people within the year. MentorMate, a software development firm focusing on mobile technology, has also spun off one of its products called iQPaak into a separate company. This move enables MentorMate to focus on its fast-growing services business.

41831 ■ *"Mobis to Set Up Lancaster Distribution Center"* in Dallas Business Journal (Vol. 35, April 6, 2012, No. 30, pp. 1)
Pub: American City Business Journal
Description: Irvine, California-based Mobis Parts America bought a 442,000-square-foot Saint Pointe Building in Lancaster, Texas from KTR Capital Partners for an undisclosed price. Mobisplans to make the building a distribution center for regional Hyundai and Kia dealerships, creating more than 30 jobs to start.

41832 ■ *"A Model Development"* in Crain's Cleveland Business (Vol. 28, October 1, 2007, No. 39, pp. 12)
Pub: Crain Communications Inc.
Ed: Scott Suttell. **Description:** Profile a Forest City Enterprises Inc., a firm that is developing a project in New Mexico called Mesa del Sol. The Albuquerque development is being seen as the vanguard of master-planned communities with its high-tech economic development center which is expected to become the site of 60,000 jobs, 38,000 homes and a town center.

41833 ■ *"The Money Train: How Public Projects Shape Our Economic Future"* in Hawaii Business (Vol. 54, September 2008, No. 3, pp. 31)
Ed: Jason Ubay. **Description:** Public projects impact the construction industry as such projects create jobs and new infrastructure that can lead to private developments. Details on the government contracts and construction projects in Hawaii and their rising costs and impact on the state's economy are discussed.

41834 ■ *"Monogram Foods Eyes Acquisition: Midwest Manufacturer Target of Latest Expansion"* in Memphis Business Journal (Vol. 34, August 10, 2012, No. 17, pp. 1)
Pub: American City Business Journal
Description: Monogram Food Solutions, a Memphis-based food company is raising $12.5 million for the acquisition of an undisclosed company or companies. The acquistion is expected to generate $50 million revenue, add 200 new employees for Monogram, and strengthen its manufacturing arm.

41835 ■ *"Montana Collection Agency Will Move HQ To Florida"* in PaymentsSource (January 2, 2012)
Pub: SourceMedia Inc.
Contact: James M. Malkin, Chief Executive Officer
Released: January 2, 2012. **Description:** Stellar Recovery collection agency is moving its headquarters from Kalispell, Montana to Jacksonville, Florida. The move will create up to 100 new jobs.

41836 ■ *"More than Able"* in Entrepreneur (Vol. 36, March 2008, No. 3, pp. 81)
Pub: Entrepreneur Press
Contact: Perlman Neil, President
Ed: Mark Henricks. **Description:** Disabled workers are motivated employees and work longer hours. A study shows that accommodating disabled workers is very low cost and provides benefits to employers, such as improved employee retention and increased customer base. Other details about hiring disabled workers are discussed.

41837 ■ *"More Jobs Heading to Suburb"* in Austin Business JournalInc. (Vol. 29, November 20, 2009, No. 37, pp. 1)
Pub: American City Business Journals
Ed: Kate Harrington. **Description:** Site of Advanced Integration Technologies (AIT) in Pflugerville, Texas might increase its workforce to 80 employees in the next six months due to the creation of an incentive package. Funds from the Pflugerville Community Development Corporation have been helping AIT's initiative to hire more workers. The firm receives $2,000 from the plan for every new employee it hires.

41838 ■ *"More Mexican Labor Needed in Oil Patch, Executives Say"* in Globe & Mail (February 23, 2007, pp. B1)
Ed: Steven Chase. **Description:** The plans of top North American chief executive officers to recommend the employment of temporary workers from Mexico for the development of oil sands in Alberta, Canada, are discussed.

41839 ■ *"Morgan Keegan Feeds Wunderlich"* in Memphis Business Journal (Vol. 34, May 18, 2012, No. 5, pp. 1)
Pub: American City Business Journal
Ed: Cole Epley. **Description:** Wunderlich Securities Inc. has augmented its equity markets group with a dozen former Morgan Keegan & Company Inc. professionals. Wunderlich assigned ten of the new hires in Memphis, Tennessee while the two joined its institutional sales department in New York.

41840 ■ *"Mortgage Companies are Adding Staff"* in Sacramento Business Journal (Vol. 29, September 14, 2012, No. 29, pp. 1)
Pub: American City Business Journal
Ed: Sanford Nax. **Description:** Mortgage companies have been increasing their hiring as a result of persistently low interest rates and tough new government regulations. The mortgage industry has gained 1,335 jobs in the second quarter nationally, while the number of applications to receive a mortgage loan originator license is rising in California.

41841 ■ *"Mortgage Servicer Wingspan Portfolio Advisors Makes Mark in Frisco"* in Dallas Business Journal (Vol. 35, September 7, 2012, No. 52, pp. 1)
Pub: American City Business Journal
Ed: Candace Carlisle. **Description:** Carrollton, Texas-based Wingspan Portfolio Advisors LLC has seen rapid growth in its business and the company plans to hire another 500 employees. Wingspan has subleased a 125,000-square-foot building in Firsco, Texa to accommodate the expansion and making it the company's third site in North Texas.

41842 ■ *"A Motorola Spinoff Is No Panacea"* in Barron's (Vol. 88, March 31, 2008, No. 13, pp. 19)
Pub: Dow Jones & Co., Inc.
Contact: Clare Hart, President
Ed: Mark Veverka. **Description:** Motorola's plan to try and spinoff their handset division is bereft of details as to how or specifically when in 2009 the spinoff would occur. There's no reason to buy the shares since there's a lot of execution risk to the plan. Motorola needs to hire a proven cellphone executive and develop a compelling new cellphone platform.

41843 ■ *"The Myth of the Overqualified Worker"* in Harvard Business Review (Vol. 88, December 2010, No. 12, pp. 30)
Pub: Harvard Business School Publishing
Ed: Andrew O'Connell. **Description:** It is recommended to seriously consider job candidates with qualifications exceeding the position being recruited because research shows these individuals work harder, but do not quit any sooner than those whose qualifications more closely match the position.

41844 ■ *"NASA Taps Younger Talent Pool to Supplement Aging Work Force"* in Crain's Cleveland Business (Vol. 30, June 22, 2009,

No. 24, pp. 1)
Pub: Crain Communications Inc.
Ed: Chuck Soder. **Description:** NASA's Glenn Research Center has reversed the trend towards hiring older workers with more experience by recruiting for entry-level positions as part of a pilot program to attract younger talent.

41845 ■ *"NEMRA Announces Headquarters Move"* in *Agency Sales Magazine (Vol. 39, September-October 2009, No. 9, pp. 53)*
Description: NEMRA, the National Electrical Manufacturers' Representatives Association is moving their headquarters to 28 Deer Street, Suite 302, Portsmouth, New Hampshire. The association has also added Michelle Rivers-Jameson as their manager of operations and Kirsty Stebbins as their manager of marketing and member services.

41846 ■ *"Networking Web Sites: a Two-Edge Sword"* in *Contractor (Vol. 56, October 2009, No. 10, pp. 52)*
Pub: Penton Media, Inc.
Ed: H. Kent Craig. **Description:** People need to be careful about the information that they share on social networking Web sites. They should realize that future bosses, coworkers, and those that might want to hire them might read those information. Posting on these sites can cost career opportunities and respect.

41847 ■ *"Never Boring: Cincinnati Ad Agencies' Big Changes"* in *Business Courier (Vol. 24, February 7, 2008, No. 44, pp. 1)*
Pub: American City Business Journals, Inc.
Contact: Whitney Shaw, President
Ed: Dan Monk. **Description:** Many changes are occurring in Cincinnati's advertising industry, including new clients, acquisitions, and market leaders, and an increase in employment. Bridge Worldwide passed Northlich LLC as the city's largest advertising agency.

41848 ■ *"New Boss at Nortel Mines GE for New Executives"* in *Globe & Mail (February 6, 2006, pp. B1)*
Ed: Catherine McLean. **Description:** Chief executive officer Mike Zafirovski of Nortel Networks Corp. appoints executives Dennis Carey, Joel Hackney and Don McKenn of GE Electric Co. The managerial abilities of Mike are discussed.

41849 ■ *"A New Breed of Entrepreneurs"* in *Black Enterprise (Vol. 37, November 2006, No. 4, pp. 16)*
Description: Black entrepreneurs are an important part of the chain for providing economic opportunities within the community. Many black business owners are more likely to hire black employees and apply innovative strategies in building their businesses rather than taking the traditional route.

41850 ■ *The New Job Security: The 5 Best Strategies for Taking Control of Your Career*
Ed: Pam Lassiter. **Released:** September 07, 2010.
Price: $14.99. **Description:** This book will help individuals to uncover interesting alternative jobs, generate multiple income streams, shape their job to reflect values and goals, move successfully through the company, and plan for career transitions to keep them in control. Online resources, real-life examples, practical exercises and a no-nonsense approach will aid in job stability.

41851 ■ *"New Jobless Claims Filed in December Soar in Maryland"* in *Baltimore Business Journal (Vol. 27, January 29, 2010, No. 39, pp. 1)*
Pub: American City Business Journals
Ed: Scott Dance. **Description:** Maryland received 48,693 new claims for unemployment benefits in December 2009, reaching its highest monthly total since 1974. The number of claims was up 49 percent from November and 13 percent from the same period in 2008. Labor officials and economists discuss this trend.

41852 ■ *"New Jobs Coming From New Breed"* in *Memphis Business Journal (Vol. 34, September 21, 2012, No. 23, pp. 1)*
Pub: American City Business Journal
Ed: Andy Ashby. **Description:** New Breed Logistics has opened a new distribution center in Southeast Memphis, Tennessee. It is believed that this new

service will create hundreds of new jobs over the next two years. The company may become the largest-third party logistics company operating in Memphis.

41853 ■ *"Newton Company Becomes One of Region's Fastest-Growing PR Firms"* in *Boston Business Journal (Vol. 34, March 21, 2014, No. 7, pp. 4)*
Pub: American City Business Journals, Inc.
Contact: Whitney Shaw, President
Released: March 21, 2014. **Description:** HB Agency's acquisition of Winans Creative has made the company one of the fastest growing public relations firms in Boston, Massachusetts. The purchase has expanded the company's digital expertise in database management and research engine optimization. The company plans to hire additional staff.

41854 ■ *"Niagara Bottling Co. Eyeing Region for a New Plant"* in *Charlotte Business Journal (Vol. 25, December 10, 2010, No. 38, pp. 1)*
Pub: Charlotte Business Journal
Ed: Ken Elkins. **Description:** California-based Niagara Bottling Company is hoping to find a site in Charlotte, North Carolina where it can build a water bottling plant that would employ 70 workers. The investment is expected to cost about $25 million to $40 million.

41855 ■ *"No Fluff: My Pillow Soars After Infomercial"* in *Business Journal (Vol. 30, June 22, 2012, No. 4, pp. 1)*
Pub: American City Business Journals, Inc.
Contact: Whitney Shaw, President
Ed: John Vomhof Jr. **Released:** June 22, 2012. **Description:** The growth of Chanhassen, Minnesota-based open-cell, poly-foam pillow manufacturer My Pillow Inc. in terms of sales and workforce happened following the launch of a 30-minute infomercial in October 2011. Aside from increasing its workforce from 40 to more than 400 since then, sales could reach $150 million in 2012.

41856 ■ *"No Time to Grieve"* in *Women In Business (Vol. 63, Fall 2011, No. 3, pp. 22)*
Pub: American Business Women's Association
Contact: Lorie Burch, President
Ed: Diane Stafford. **Description:** Individuals who have experienced job loss must go through the emotional stages related to this event in order to gain the best re-employment opportunities. The first step towards re-employment is to make the job search public. Tips for improving one's online footprint are also given.

41857 ■ *"Northern Kentucky Adds 1,355 Jobs in '07"* in *Business Courier (Vol. 24, February 14, 2008, No. 45, pp. 3)*
Pub: American City Business Journals, Inc.
Contact: Whitney Shaw, President
Ed: Lucy May. **Description:** Jobs generated by new and expanding businesses in Northern Kentucky in 2007 totaled to 1,355, which boosted total business sales to $410 million. The ripple effects of the businesses are expected to create 5,432 new jobs and increase business sales to more than $888 million.

41858 ■ *"Numbers Game"* in *Baltimore Business Journal (Vol. 27, February 6, 2010, No. 40, pp. 1)*
Pub: American City Business Journals
Ed: Scott Dance. **Description:** Doubts are being raised regarding the impact of the federal stimulus spending in addressing unemployment in Maryland, which has experienced 1,800 jobs created so far. Details on the view of companies and the insufficient amount of contracts that lead to the fewer number of workers being hired are discussed.

41859 ■ *"NYC Tops Hub in Tech VC Dollars"* in *Boston Business Journal (Vol. 31, August 5, 2011, No. 28, pp. 1)*
Pub: Boston Business Journal
Ed: Kyle Alspach. **Description:** New York City has been outdoing Boston in terms of venture capital for technology firms since second quarter 2010. New York tech firms raised $865 million during the first

two quarters of 2011 against Boston techs' $682 million. Boston has the edge, though, when it comes to hiring engineering talent as it is home to the Massachusetts Institute of Technology.

41860 ■ *"Oakland County to Survey Employers on Needed Skills"* in *Crain's Detroit Business (Vol. 24, April 14, 2008, No. 15, pp. 30)*
Pub: Crain Communications Inc.
Contact: Rance E. Crain, President
Ed: Chad Halcom. **Description:** In an attempt to aid educators and attract talent, Oakland County plans to collect data from 1,000 local employers on workforce skills they need now or will need soon.

41861 ■ *"Old Ford Plant to Sign New Tenants"* in *Business Courier (Vol. 27, August 13, 2010, No. 15, pp. 1)*
Pub: Business Courier
Ed: Dan Monk. **Description:** Ohio Realty Advisors LLC, a company handling the marketing of the 1.9 million-square-foot former Ford Batavia plant is on the brink of landing one distribution and three manufacturing firms as tenants. These tenants are slated to occupy about 20 percent of the facility and generate as many as 250 jobs in Ohio.

41862 ■ *"OmniSYS Plans Big Richardson Expansion"* in *Dallas Business Journal (Vol. 35, June 8, 2012, No. 39, pp. 1)*
Pub: American City Business Journal
Ed: Bill Hethcock. **Description:** OmniSYS LLC will hire about 250 more people in the next two years and open a 50,000-square-foot office in Richardson, Texas in October 2012. The Medicare claims processing company posted revenue growth of more than 30 percent in 2011 primarily in the Medicare audit and compliance area.

41863 ■ *"On Hire Ground"* In *Entrepreneur (Vol. 36, February 2008, No. 2, pp. 19)*
Pub: Entrepreneur Press
Contact: Perlman Neil, President
Ed: Mark Henricks. **Description:** ADP Small Business Services, an economic consulting firm, showed that small businesses had increased employment rates in 2007 and added 77,000 jobs in November 2007. Entrepreneurial employment and data showing the contribution of small businesses to job growth are presented.

41864 ■ *"Online Tools for Jobseekers"* in *Occupational Outlook Quarterly (Vol. 55, Fall 2011, No. 3, pp. 20)*
Pub: U.S. Department of Labor Bureau of Labor Statistics
Contact: Philip L. Rones, Manager
E-mail: rones.philip@bls.gov
Description: U.S. Department of Labor's CareerOneStop provides a collection of Web-based tools serving students, jobseekers, employers, and the workforce. The top six categories for job listings nationwide include general job boards, niche job boards, career planning tools, career explorations sites, social media job search sites, and other tools which include interview preparation tools and training grants.

41865 ■ *"Orders Up; Jobs Below Forecast"* in *Charlotte Observer (February 2, 2007)*
Ed: Kerry Hall. **Description:** U.S. Labor Department reported unemployment rates at 4.6 percent, up one-tenth of a percent. Economists had predicted 170,000 new jobs, but only 111,000 were created.

41866 ■ *"Out to Draw Work, Talent: Animation-Graphics Studio Hires Locally and Thinks Globally"* in *Crain's Detroit Business (Vol. 24, April 14, 2008, No. 15, pp. 3)*
Pub: Crain Communications Inc.
Contact: Rance E. Crain, President
Ed: Bill Shea. **Description:** Profile of Southfield-based Kinetic Post Inc., a growing post-production house that offers video, audio, animation, print, online and related services to corporations and advertising agencies.

41867 ■ *"Outlook 2007: The Global Picture"* in Canadian Business (Vol. 80, December 25, 2006, No. 1, pp.)
Pub: Rogers Media Inc.
Contact: Tony Viner, President
Ed: David Wolf. **Description:** Economists' 2007 forecast on global economy, particularly about Canada's housing and labor market among other sectors, is discussed.

41868 ■ *"Overqualified. Underemployed"* in Philadelphia Business Journal (Vol. 33, August 1, 2104, No. 25, pp. 14)
Pub: American City Business Journals
Released: August 1, 2014. **Description:** Overqualified workers often find themselves in employment situations where their education, experience and skills are beyond the requirements of the job. The implications of underemployment for the worker, the organization and the overall U.S. economy are discussed.

41869 ■ *"Overseas Overtures"* in Business Journal-Portland (Vol. 24, October 26, 2007, No. 35, pp. 1)
Pub: American City Business Journals, Inc.
Ed: Robin J. Mood. **Description:** Oregon has a workforce shortage, specifically for the health care industry. Recruiting agencies, such as the International Recruiting Network Inc., answers the high demand for workforce by recruiting foreign employees. The difficulties recruiting companies experience with regards to foreign labor laws are investigated.

41870 ■ *"Part-Time Assignments"* in Black Enterprise (Vol. 37, December 2006, No. 5, pp. 70)
Description: During critical change initiatives interim management, an employment model which uses senior-level executives to manage a special project or specific business function on a temporary basis, can have many benefits.

41871 ■ *"Pay Me! How to Get the Money You're Owed When No One Seems to Have Any"* in Entrepreneur (Vol. 37, July 2009, No. 7, pp. 49)
Pub: Entrepreneur Press
Contact: Perlman Neil, President
Ed: Randy B. Hecht. **Description:** How certain collections scenarios with clients, who have already fallen behind on their payments, should be handled is discussed. During a down economy, business owners should properly manage collection and billing because this can actually strengthen client relationships. Insights on hiring a collections agency are also presented.

41872 ■ *"Pentagon Awards $17.6B Contract for EB-Built Subs Through 2018"* in Providence Business News (Vol. 29, April 28, 2014, No. 4)
Pub: American City Business Journals
Released: April 28, 2014. **Description:** The U.S. Navy has signed a $17.6 billion contract with Newport News Shipbuilding and General Dynamics Corporation for construction of 10 new naval submarines. The deal will help employment at General Dynamics' Quonset Business Park Electric Boat production site. The submarines are scheduled to be built between 2014-2018. Electric Boat expects to hire 650 additional workers.

41873 ■ *"The People Puzzle; Re-Training America's Workers"* in The Economist (Vol. 390, January 3, 2009, No. 8612, pp. 32)
Description: With thousands of workers losing their jobs, America is now facing the task of getting them back to work. With an overall unemployment rate of 6.7 percent, the federal government has three main ways for leading workers back to employment: training them for new jobs, providing unemployment insurance in order to replace lost wages during the period of job-hunting; and matching employers who desire a skill with workers who have that skill. Specialized staffing agencies provide employers and potential employees with the help necessary to find a job in some of the more niche markets.

41874 ■ *"Permit Reviews To Speed Up In Few Months"* in Austin Business Journal (Vol. 33, June 22, 2012, No. 15, pp. A1)
Pub: American City Business Journals, Inc.
Contact: Whitney Shaw, President
Ed: Vicky Garza. **Released:** June 22, 2012. **Description:** Austin, Texas is hiring 14 more staffers to help with the backlog of permits at the Planning and Developmet Review department. The additional employees will be paid for by the 25 percent increase in 421 development-related fees that will take effect July 1. Insights into the delay in getting a permit for new construction or renovation are also given.

41875 ■ *"Perspective: Borderline Issues"* in Entrepreneur (Vol. 35, October 2007, No. 10, pp. 48)
Pub: Entrepreneur Press
Contact: Perlman Neil, President
Ed: Joshua Kurlantzick. **Description:** Failure of the immigration reform bill is expected to result in increased difficulty in finding workers that would take on the dirty and perilous jobs, which are usually taken by immigrants. Regularizing immigration on the other hand will cost business owners money by making them spend for the legality of their employees' stay in the U.S. Other effects of immigration laws on entrepreneurs are discussed.

41876 ■ *"PG&E Buys New Employee-Designed Gas Trucks"* in Travel & Leisure Close-Up (October 8, 2012)
Description: Pacific Gas and Electric Company has ordered trucks designed by a crew of their gas workers in Stockton, California. A truck assembly plant in Tracy, California has added 50 new workers to help assemble the utility's next-generation of gas maintenance and construction trucks. These trucks will be built to exact specifications and will help the economic vitality of the communities PG&E serve.

41877 ■ *"Philadelphia's Largest Employers Will Fill 6,000 Jobs Within 6 Months"* in Philadelphia Business Journal (Vol. 28, February 5, 2010, No. 51, pp. 1)
Pub: American City Business Journals Inc.
Ed: Peter Van Allen. **Description:** Philadelphia, Pennsylvania's largest employers have openings for at least 6,000 jobs. But businesses remain cautious and are selective in hiring or waiting to see what happens to federal policy changes.

41878 ■ *"A Piece of the Action: To Attract Top Chefs to His Sushi Restaurant, This Entrepreneur Used Equity as an Incentive"* in Black Enterprise (Vol. 38, January 2008, No. 6, pp. 42)
Pub: Earl G. Graves Publishing Co. Inc.
Contact: Earl G. Graves, Jr., President
Ed: Alan Hughes. **Description:** Andre Williams, owner of Kaze Sushi restaurant, offered generous incentive plan-equity in the business in order to acquire Chef Kaze Chan and Chef Hari Chan. Williams' entrepreneurial pursuits are discussed.

41879 ■ *"Pitch for SPX Expansion was Full of Energy"* in Charlotte Business Journal (Vol. 25, November 19, 2010, No. 35, pp. 1)
Pub: Charlotte Business Journal
Ed: John Downey. **Description:** SPX Corporation announced that it will expand their headquarters in Ballantyne after Charlotte and North Carolina leaders made an aggressive push to retain the company. SPX Corporation is expected to invest $70 million for the expansion, which would mean 180 new jobs in Charlotte.

41880 ■ *"Plan Your Future with My Next Move"* in Occupational Outlook Quarterly (Vol. 55, Summer 2011, No. 2, pp. 22)
Pub: U.S. Department of Labor Bureau of Labor Statistics
Contact: Philip L. Rones, Manager
E-mail: rones.philip@bls.gov
Description: My Next Move, an online tool offering a variety of user-friendly ways to browse more than 900 occupations was created by the National Center for O NET Development for the US Department of

Labor's Employment and Training Administration. Clicking on an occupation presents a one-page profile summarizing key information for specific careers.

41881 ■ *"Plenty of Jobs, Will Workers Follow?"* in Providence Business News (Vol. 28, January 27, 2014, No. 43, pp. 1)
Pub: American City Business Journals
Released: January 27, 2014. **Description:** Electric Boat announced a plan to hire 650 employees in 2014 for its facility at Quonset Business Park in North Kingstown, Rhode Island. However, meeting the hiring goals will be a challenge because of smaller educational pipeline for welders, electricians, shipfitters, and pipefitters. Rhode Island's internship programs to fill the skills gap are also discussed.

41882 ■ *"Polanco Fellows: A Capital Program that Changes Lives"* in Hispanic Business (Vol. 30, September 2008, No. 9, pp. 82)
Pub: Hispanic Business Inc.
Contact: Jesus Chavarria, President
Ed: John Schumacher. **Description:** Launched in 2003, the Polanco fellows program is named after former state Senator Richard Polanco, a founder and chairman of the California Latino Caucus Institute. The program offers young Hispanics a chance to experience public policy and the functioning of the California Capitol through a 12-month, on-the-job Capitol training.

41883 ■ *"Predicting Success: Evidence-Based Strategies to Hire the Right People and Build the Best Team"*
Pub: John Wiley & Sons Inc.
Contact: Stephen M. Smith, President
Released: September 22, 2014. **Price:** , $25.00. **Description:** Guide for human resource management teams choose the right employee when hiring. It teaches how to apply the principles and tools of human analytics to the work place to avoid bad culture fits, mismatched skillsets, entitled workers, and other hiring mistakes that hurt employee motivation and morale. The Predictive Index TM, behavior analytics, hiring assessments, and other resources for better outcomes are presented.

41884 ■ *"Prescription for Health: Choosing the Best Healthcare Plan for your workforce and your Bottom Line"* in Black Enterprise (Vol. 38, July 2008, No. 12, pp. 48)
Pub: Earl G. Graves Publishing Co. Inc.
Contact: Earl G. Graves, Jr., President
Ed: Tamara E. Holmes. **Description:** According to a survey of small-business owners conducted by Sure-Payroll Inc., 20 percent of respondents have had a prospective employee refuse a job offer because healthcare benefits did not come with it. Cost is not the only reason many small-business owners do not offer these benefits. Guidelines to help take some of the confusion out of the guesswork that comes with trying to find the proper fit concerning healthcare benefits are outlined.

41885 ■ *"Prichard the Third"* in Canadian Business (Vol. 83, October 12, 2010, No. 17, pp. 34)
Pub: Rogers Media Inc.
Contact: Tony Viner, President
Ed: Thomas Watson. **Description:** Robert Prichard, the new chair of international business law firm Torys, talks about his current role; his job involved advising clients, representing the firm, being part of the leadership team, and recruiting talent. He considers 'Seven Days in Tibet' as the first book to have an influence on his world view.

41886 ■ *"Private-Sector Is Back, Roadblocks Be Damned"* in Business Review Albany (Vol. 41, July 4, 2014, No. 15, pp. 4)
Pub: American City Business Journals, Inc.
Contact: Whitney Shaw, President
Released: July 4, 2014. **Description:** Private sector jobs in New York experienced significant growth, reaching an all-time high of almost 7.6 million jobs in May 2014, as government jobs suffered a decline. Large international corporations, including General Electric, are tapping into cash reserves, adding jobs and expanding operations after years of cutting staff.

41887 ■ *"The Profitability of Mobility"* in *Entrepreneur (Vol. 37, September 2009, No. 9, pp. 98)*
Pub: Entrepreneur Press
Contact: Perlman Neil, President

Ed: John Daley. **Description:** Wireless Zone franchisee Jonah Engler says he manages the business by hiring managers that could do the job. He has given his employees small equity ownership in the company. He also says great service and referrals have contributed to his business' growth.

41888 ■ *"A Proper Welcome"* in *Canadian Business (Vol. 79, July 17, 2006, No. 14-15, pp. 67)*
Pub: Rogers Media Inc.
Contact: Tony Viner, President

Ed: Graham Lowe. **Description:** New-employee orientation programs of various companies are highlighted. Useful practices to create a comfortable ambiance for new recruits are elucidated as well.

41889 ■ *"Protecting Company Secrets"* in *Inc. (February 2008, pp. 38-39)*
Ed: Scott Westcott. **Description:** A legal guide for noncompete clauses when hiring new employees is outlined, stressing how each state has its own set of laws.

41890 ■ *"Prudential Courts Hispanics"* in *Hispanic Business (March 2008, pp. 38, 40)*
Ed: Melinda Burns. **Description:** Prudential Financial Inc. is reaching out to Hispanic Chambers of Commerce in an effort to hire and do business with the Hispanic community in the U.S.

41891 ■ *"Putting Vets to Work"* in *Business Week (September 22, 2008, No. 4100, pp. 18)*
Pub: Bloomberg L.P.
Contact: Matthew Winkler, Manager

Ed: Deborah Stead. **Description:** Advice is provided by former Marine Sal Cepeda, a consultant who advises employers on hiring veterans, for former military personnel coming back into the workforce.

41892 ■ *"PwC to Add 400 Workers in North Texas"* in *Dallas Business Journal (Vol. 35, April 6, 2012, No. 30, pp. 1)*
Pub: American City Business Journal

Description: London, England-headquartered PwC, formerly known as PricewaterhouseCoopers LLP, announced plans to hire 400 employees for its North Texas operations during the next 12 months. The firm provides auditing, consulting, and tax services to public, private and government clients.

41893 ■ *"Q&A: Saskatchewan Premier Brad Wall"* in *Canadian Business (Vol. 82, April 27, 2009, No. 7, pp. 9)*
Pub: Rogers Media Inc.
Contact: Tony Viner, President

Ed: Joe Castaldo. **Description:** Saskatchewan Premier Brad Wall believes that the mood in the province is positive, as its economy is one of the few that is expected to post growth in 2009. Wall actively promotes the province in job fairs, offering $20,000 in tuition for recent college and university graduates that relocate in the province for seven years. Wall's views on the province's economy and challenges are presented.

41894 ■ *"Questioning Authority"* in *Entrepreneur (June 2014)*
Pub: Entrepreneur Media Inc.

Released: June 2014. **Description:** Smarterer is a platform that facilitates the evaluation of prospective hires through crowdsourced assessment tests quantifying their professional skills and strengths. The platform has more than 900 multiple-choice tests covering a variety of professions. It uses an adaptive machine-learning algorithm that ensures the uniqueness of every test. Users can choose to make their test results public and can perform do-overs on some tests. The platform was launched in 2010 as a way of identifying potential talent and identifying skill inventories among existing employees.

41895 ■ *"Quick Earnings Revival Unlikely"* in *Barron's (Vol. 88, June 30, 2008, No. 26, pp. 31)*
Pub: Dow Jones & Co., Inc.
Contact: Clare Hart, President

Ed: Johanna Bennett. **Description:** Analysts are pushing back their prediction of a U.S. economy turnaround to 2009. A recession in the first half of 2008 may not have happened but unemployment is rising and house prices continue to fall.

41896 ■ *"Quits Versus Layoffs"* in *Occupational Outlook Quarterly (Vol. 55, Fall 2011, No. 3, pp. 36)*
Pub: U.S. Department of Labor Bureau of Labor Statistics
Contact: Philip L. Rones, Manager
E-mail: rones.philip@bls.gov

Description: Data from the U.S. Bureau of Labor Statistics provides data from the Job Openings and Labor Turnover Survey regarding quits and layoffs.

41897 ■ *"Race and Gender Diversity: A Discussion of Recent Findings"* in *Business Horizons (November-December 2007, pp. 445)*
Pub: Elsevier Technology Publications

Ed: James C. Wimbush. **Price:** $35.95. **Description:** Research conducted on diversity building, employee recruitment, gender issues in management, and pay inequality from 2006 through present are discussed. Diversity conditions and attitudes toward it are slowly improving based on these findings. **Availability:** PDF.

41898 ■ *"Recruiters Look Beyond Backyard to Find Gen Y Workers"* in *HRMagazine (Vol. 53, November 2008, No. 11, pp. 22)*
Description: More than two-thirds of recent college graduates would relocate for a job, and 70 percent would be willing to move for an employer, according to the 2008 Hot Cities Survey; New York, Washington DC, and Chicago top the list of most desirable cities for relocation.

41899 ■ *"Recruiting 2.0"* in *Entrepreneur (Vol. 35, November 2007, No. 11, pp. 100)*
Pub: Entrepreneur Press
Contact: Perlman Neil, President

Ed: Andrea Cooper. **Description:** Technology is becoming a tool to help small companies find the best employees. Firms can look into social networking sites to see recommendations from the applicants' colleagues. Tips on how to select the employees online are listed.

41900 ■ *"Region Wins as GE Puts Plants Close to R&D"* in *Business Review Albany (Vol. 41, July 4, 2014, No. 15, pp. 8)*
Pub: American City Business Journals, Inc.
Contact: Whitney Shaw, President

Released: July 4, 2014. **Description:** General Electric Company (GE) invested over $400 million into the expansion of its health care, battery and renewable energy businesses in the Albany, New York region. The company's local growth secured about 7,000 private-sector jobs in the area and strengthened the relationship between GE research and manufacturing.

41901 ■ *"Regional Talent Network Unveils Employment Web Site"* in *Crain's Cleveland Business (Vol. 30, June 1, 2009, No. 21, pp. 11)*
Pub: Crain Communications Inc.

Ed: Chuck Soder. **Description:** Regional Talent Network launched WhereToFindHelp.org, a Website designed to act as a directory of all Northeast Ohio resources that can help employers recruit and job seekers look for positions. The site also lists organizations offering employment and training services.

41902 ■ *"Reps Have Needs Too!"* in *Agency Sales Magazine (Vol. 39, December 2009, No. 11, pp. 16)*
Ed: Bill Heyden. **Description:** There is common information that a sales representatives needs to know prior to choosing a manufacturer to represent. Both parties must keep promises made to customers and prospects. Reps also need the support from the

manufacturers and to clear matters regarding their commission. Interviewing tips for representatives to get this vital information are presented.

41903 ■ *"Reps Vs. Factory Direct Sales Force..Which Way to Go?"* in *Agency Sales Magazine (Vol. 39, September-October 2009, No. 9, pp. 28)*
Ed: Eric P. Johnson. **Description:** Hiring independent manufacturers' sales representative is a cost-effective alternative to a direct sales force. Sales reps have predictable sales costs that go up and down with sales, stronger local relationships and better market intelligence.

41904 ■ *"Reps Vs. Factory Direct Sales Force..Which Way to Go?"* in *Agency Sales Magazine (Vol. 39, September-October 2009, No. 9, pp. 28)*
Ed: Eric P. Johnson. **Description:** Hiring independent manufacturers' sales representative is a cost-effective alternative to a direct sales force. Sales reps have predictable sales costs that go up and down with sales, stronger local relationships and better market intelligence.

41905 ■ *The Restaurant Manager's Handbook: How to Set Up, Operate, and Manage a Financially Successful Food Service Operation*
Pub: Atlantic Publishing Co.
Contact: Amanda Miller, Manager
E-mail: amiller@atlantic-pub.com

Ed: Douglas R. Brown. **Released:** September 25, 2007. **Price:** $79.95. **Description:** Insight is offered on running a successful food service business. Nine new chapters detail restaurant layout, new equipment, principles for creating a safer work environment, and new effective techniques to interview, hire, train, and manage employees.

41906 ■ *"'Resume Mining' Services Can Save Time, Money"* in *HR Specialist (Vol. 8, September 2010, No. 9, pp. 7)*
Pub: Capitol Information Group Inc.

Description: Low-cost resume mining services can help human resource departments save time and money by searching online resume databases for candidates matching specific job qualifications.

41907 ■ *"Retiring Baby Boomers and Dissatisfied Gen-Xers Cause..Brain Drain"* in *Agency Sales Magazine (Vol. 39, November 2009, No. 10)*
Ed: Denise Kelly. **Description:** Due to the impending retirement of the baby boomers a critical loss of knowledge and experience in businesses will result. Creating a plan to address this loss of talent centered on the development of the younger generation is discussed.

41908 ■ *"Ringing Up New Sales"* in *Baltimore Business Journal (Vol. 29, February 24, 2012, No. 43, pp. 1)*
Pub: American City Business Journals, Inc.
Contact: Whitney Shaw, President

Ed: Gary Haber. **Released:** February 24, 2012. **Description:** Micros Systems is planning to enter into the corporate cyber security business. The company is also set to hire 100 additional workers.

41909 ■ *"Ripple Effect From Solar Frontier May Be Big"* in *Business First of Buffalo (Vol. 30, April 25, 2014, No. 32, pp. 4)*
Pub: American City Business Journals, Inc.
Contact: Whitney Shaw, President

Released: April 25, 2014. **Description:** A memorandum of understanding was signed by Japanese solar technology manufacturer Solar Frontier K.K. with the State University of New York, College of Nanoscale Science and Engineering in Albany. The agreement is expected to create about 1,000 new jobs in the U.S. and at least $700 million in investments.

41910 ■ *"Ronald Taketa"* in *Hawaii Business (Vol. 54, September 2008, No. 3, pp. 28)*
Ed: Shara Enay. **Description:** Interview with Ronald Taketa of the Hawaii Carpenters Union who states that the economic downturn has affected the con-

struction industry as 20 percent of the union's 7,800 members are unemployed. He shares his thoughts about the industry's economic situation, the union's advertisements, and his role as a leader of the union.

41911 ■ "Rudy's Tortillas Wraps Up Expansion Plan in Carrollton" in Dallas Business Journal (Vol. 35, August 31, 2012, No. 51, pp. 1)
Pub: American City Business Journal
Ed: Candace Carlisle. **Description:** Rudy's Tortillas Corporation, a 67-year old family business based in Dallas, Texas, is moving into a new plant on Belt Line Road, Carrollton. The expansion will also involve the hiring of 150 new workers and enable the company to expand its operations. Rudy's will spend $14 million dollars on construction and equipment on the new tortilla plant.

41912 ■ "The Rypple Effect; Performance Management" in The Economist (Vol. 390, January 3, 2009, No. 8612, pp. 48)
Description: New companies such as Rypple, a new, web-based service, claim that they can satisfy the Net Generation's need for frequent assessments while easing the burden this creates for management.

41913 ■ "A Safety Net in Need of Repair" in The Economist (Vol. 390, January 3, 2009, No. 8612, pp. 33)
Description: America's unemployment-insurance scheme is outdated and skimpy compared to other industrialized countries despite the fact that Americans tend to work harder at returning to the job market; the benefits are lower and available for a smaller amount of time and less unemployed workers are even able to collect these benefits. Statistical data included.

41914 ■ "Safety Products Firm Expanding" in Memphis Business Journal (Vol. 33, March 16, 2012, No. 49, pp. 1)
Pub: American City Business Journal
Description: Safety products importer and supplier International Sourcing Company Inc., the parent firm of Cordova Safety Products and Cordova Consumer Products, has purchased the 1 million-square-foot Cleo property in southeast Memphis, Tennessee. Aside from relocating its warehouse and office operations to the facility, the firm will add 20 new jobs as part of its growth initiative.

41915 ■ "Samsung's Metamorphosis" in Austin Business Journal (Vol. 31, May 20, 2011, No. 11, pp. 1)
Pub: American City Business Journals
Ed: Christopher Calnan. **Description:** Samsung Austin Semiconductor LP, a developer of semiconductors for smartphones and tablet computers, plans to diversify its offerings to include niche products: flash memory devices and microprocessing devices. In light of this strategy, Samsung Austin will be hiring 300 engineers as part of a $3.6 billion expansion of its plant.

41916 ■ "San Jose Cuts Fees, Red Tape On Office R and D" in Silicon Valley/San Jose Business Journal (Vol. 29, February 3, 2012, No. 45, pp. 1)
Description: The San Jose, California City Council has approved measures to reduce construction taxes on tenant improvements. It has also cut fees developers must pay for traffic improvements in North San Jose. The Council is also set to speed up permit processing by hiring additional personnel.

41917 ■ "Screening-Oriented Recruitment Messages: Antecedents and Relationships with Applicant Pool Quality" in Human Resource Management (Vol. 51, May- June 2012, No. 3, pp. 343-360)
Pub: John Wiley & Sons Inc.
Contact: Stephen M. Smith, President
Ed: Brian R. Dineen, Ian O. Williamson. **Description:** Factors associated with the use of screening-oriented messages for recruitment are investigated. Results indicate that labor supply perceptions, the reputation of recruiting firms and quality-based

compensation incentives are associated with the use of screening-oriented messages, which are associated with the quality of the applicant pool.

41918 ■ "A Second Chance to Make a Living" in The Business Journal-Milwaukee (Vol. 25, September 19, 2008, No. 52, pp. A1)
Description: Unemployed workers and baby boomers are driving interest in purchasing small businesses. BizBuySell general manager Mike Handelsman reveals that the supply of small businesses for sale is decreasing due to the increased demand. The trends in the small business market are analyzed.

41919 ■ "Second to None" in Crain's Detroit Business (Vol. 26, January 18, 2010, No. 3, pp. 9)
Pub: Crain Communications Inc.
Contact: Rance E. Crain, President
Ed: Nancy Kaffer. **Description:** Second-stage companies are beginning to attract more attention from government entities and the business community alike, due in part to their ability to create jobs more rapidly than their counterparts both smaller and larger. Second-stage companies have between 10-99 employees and consistently have supplied the most jobs, despite overall job declines in recent years.

41920 ■ "Sign of the Times: Temp-To-Perm Attorneys" in HRMagazine (Vol. 54, January 2009, No. 1, pp. 24)
Ed: Bill Leonard. **Description:** A growing number of law firms are hiring professional staff on a temp-to-perm basis according to the president of Professional Placement Services in Florida. Firms can save money while testing potential employees on a temporary basis.

41921 ■ "Sign Up To Grow Your Business, Generate Jobs" in Women Entrepreneur (November 25, 2008)
Ed: Eve Gumpel. **Description:** Nell Merlino has announced the new Make Mine A Million-Dollar Race, which aims to encourage hundreds of thousands of women entrepreneurs to grow their business to revenue goals of $250,00, $500,000 or $1 million and more as well as create 800,000 new jobs in an attempt to stimulate the nation's economy.

41922 ■ "Six Ways Employees on LinkedIn Benefit the Boss" in South Florida Business Journal (Vol. 34, April 25, 2014, No. 40)
Pub: American City Business Journals
Released: April 25, 2014. **Description:** LinkedIn can be a useful tool for executives. In addition to finding staff when hiring, the information service can give U.S.-based users a more global perspective. It can also be a way to share recent company accomplishment.

41923 ■ "Size Matters" in Entrepreneur (Vol. 36, April 2008, No. 4, pp. 44)
Pub: Entrepreneur Press
Contact: Perlman Neil, President
Ed: Robert Kiyosaki. **Description:** Entrepreneurs planning to expand their business face challenges when it comes to employing more people and addressing internal relationships, communications and procedures. People skills, organizational skills and leadership skills are some of the things to consider before adding employees.

41924 ■ "Skill Seekers" in South Florida Business Journal (Vol. 34, February 7, 2014, No. 29, pp. 15)
Pub: American City Business Journals
Released: February 7, 2014. **Description:** Executives talk about the need for schools to help businesses find talent to hire. Robin Sandler of Charter School USA reveals that the organization's 'Leading Edge' program allows teachers to participate in leadership opportunities, while Mason Jackson of WorkForce One Employment Solutions believes that schools need to customize the curriculum in order to support internships.

41925 ■ "Small Bank Has Big Lending Plans, New Hire" in Silicon Valley/San Jose Business Journal (Vol. 30, September 21,

2012, No. 26, pp. 1)
Pub: American City Business Journal
Description: Santa Cruz County Bank has hired government-backed loans specialist Sat Kanwar in addition to Susan Chandler, Jorge Reguerin and Daljit Bains to boost the bank's Small Business Administration lending department. According to Chandler, the bank will take on loans ranging from $25,000 to several million dollars.

41926 ■ "Small Business Employment" in Small Business Economic Trends (April 2008, pp. 9)
Pub: National Federation of Independent Business
Contact: Caitlin McDevitt, Program Manager
Ed: William C. Dunkelberg, Holly Wade. **Description:** Four tables and a graph representing employment rates of small businesses in the U.S. are presented. The tables include figures on employment changes, number of qualified applicants, job openings, and hiring plans.

41927 ■ "Small Business Employment" in Small Business Economic Trends (March 2008, pp. 9)
Pub: National Federation of Independent Business
Contact: Caitlin McDevitt, Program Manager
Ed: William C. Dunkelberg, Holly Wade. **Description:** Four tables and a graph that present employment rates of small businesses in the U.S. are provided. The tables include figures on employment changes, number of qualified applicants, job openings and hiring plans.

41928 ■ "Small Business Employment" in Small Business Economic Trends (February 2008, pp. 9)
Pub: National Federation of Independent Business
Contact: Caitlin McDevitt, Program Manager
Ed: William C. Dunkelberg, Holly Wade. **Description:** Four tables and a graph that present employment rates of small businesses in the U.S. are provided. The tables include figures on employment changes, number of qualified applicants, job openings and hiring plans.

41929 ■ "Small Business Employment" in Small Business Economic Trends (January 2008, pp. 9)
Pub: National Federation of Independent Business
Contact: Caitlin McDevitt, Program Manager
Ed: William C. Dunkelberg, Holly Wade. **Description:** Table from a survey of small businesses in the U.S. is given, representing actual employment changes from January 2002 to December 2007. A graph comparing planned employment and current job openings from January 1986 to December 2007 is also supplied. Tables showing job opening, hiring plans, and qualified applicants for job openings are also presented.

41930 ■ "Small Business Employment" in Small Business Economic Trends (September 2010, pp. 9)
Pub: National Federation of Independent Business
Contact: Caitlin McDevitt, Program Manager
Description: A table from a survey of small businesses in the U.S. is given, representing actual employment changes from January 2005 to August 2010. A graph comparing planned employment and current job openings from January 1986 to August 2010 is also supplied. Tables showing job openings, hiring plans, and qualified applicants for job openings are also presented.

41931 ■ "Small Business Employment" in Small Business Economic Trends (July 2010, pp. 9)
Pub: National Federation of Independent Business
Contact: Caitlin McDevitt, Program Manager
Ed: William C. Dunkelberg, Holly Wade. **Description:** A table from a survey of small businesses in the U.S. is given representing actual employment changes from January 2005 to June 2010. A graph comparing planned employment and current job openings from January 1986 to June 2010 is also supplied. Tables showing job openings, hiring plans, and qualified applicants for job openings are also presented.

41932 ■ *"Small Business Employment" in Small Business Economic Trends (July 2014, pp. 9)*
Pub: National Federation of Independent Business
Contact: Caitlin McDevitt, Program Manager
Released: July 2014. **Description:** A table from a survey of small businesses in the U.S. is given, representing actual employment changes from January 1986 to June 2014. A graph comparing planned employment and current job openings from January 1986 to June 2014 is supplied. Tables showing job openings, hiring plans, and qualified applicants for job openings are also presented.

41933 ■ *The Small Business Owner's Manual: Everything You Need to Know to Start Up and Run Your Business*
Pub: Career Press Inc.
Contact: Ron Fry, President
Ed: Joe Kennedy. **Released:** June 2005. **Price:** $19.99. **Description:** Comprehensive guide for starting a small business, focusing on twelve ways to obtain financing, business plans, selling and advertising products and services, hiring and firing employees, setting up a Web site, business law, accounting issues, insurance, equipment, computers, banks, financing, customer credit and collection, leasing, and more. **Availability:** Print.

41934 ■ *"Soft Skills, Hard Success: Employers Seek Leaders Who Offer More than Just Education and Credentials" in Black Enterprise (Vol. 45, July-August 2014, No. 1, pp. 44)*
Pub: Earl G. Graves Publishing Co. Inc.
Contact: Earl G. Graves, Jr., President
Released: July-August 2014. **Description:** The top ten soft skills employer look for include: strong work ethic, dependability, positive attitude, self-motivation, team oriented, organizational skills, works well under pressure, effective communication, flexibility, and confidence.

41935 ■ *"Southwest Key Programs Preps for Growth, Building $3.6M Center" in Austin Business JournalInc. (Vol. 29, January 22, 2010, No. 46, pp. 1)*
Pub: American City Business Journals
Ed: Sandra Zaragoza. **Description:** Southwest Key Programs Inc. received a $2.1 million grant from the U.S. Economic Development Administration to help finance the building of a $3.6 million 'Social Enterprise Complex'. The complex is expected to create at least 100 jobs in East Austin, Texas. Details of the plan for the complex are presented.

41936 ■ *"Staffing Firm Grows by Following Own Advice-Hire a Headhunter" in Crain's Detroit Business (Vol. 24, October 6, 2008, No. 40, pp. 1)*
Pub: Crain Communications Inc.
Contact: Rance E. Crain, President
Ed: Sherri Begin. **Description:** Profile of Venator Holdings L.L.C., a staffing firm that provides searches for companies in need of financial-accounting and technical employees; the firm's revenue has increased from $1.1 million in 2003 to a projected $11.5 million this year due to a climate in which more people are exiting the workforce than are coming in with those particular specialized skills and the need for a temporary, flexible workforce for contract placements at companies that do not want to take on the legacy costs associated with permanent employees. The hiring of an external headhunter to find the right out-of-state manager for Venator is also discussed.

41937 ■ *"Star Power" in Small Business Opportunities (September 2008)*
Pub: Entrepreneur Press
Contact: Perlman Neil, President
Description: Employee retention is an important factor for corporate executives to consider because the impact of excessive turnovers can be devastating to a company causing poor morale, unemployment claims, hiring costs, lost production and customer loss. Although there is no specific formula for retaining employees, there are several things every organization can do to keep their workers happy and increase the chances that they will stay loyal and keep working for the company for years to come; tips aimed at management regarding good employee relationships are included.

41938 ■ *"Start Filling Your Talent Gap - Now" in Business Strategy Review (Vol. 21, Spring 2010, No. 1, pp. 56)*
Pub: John Wiley & Sons Inc. Scientific, Technical, Medical, and Scholarly Div. (Wiley-Blackwell)
Contact: William J. Pesce, Manager
E-mail: wpesce@wiley.com
Ed: Alan Bird, Lori Flees, Paul Di Paola. **Description:** As businesses steer their way out of turbulence, they have a unique opportunity to identify their leadership supply and demand and then to close the talent gap in their organization. Authors explain how to take immediate steps to build the right team now and lay the groundwork for a long-term approach for nurturing talent within the organization.

41939 ■ *"Startup Activity Among Jobless Execs is the Highest Since 2009, Survey Says" in South Florida Business Journal (Vol. 34, February 21, 2014, No. 31, pp. 3)*
Pub: American City Business Journals
Released: February 21, 2014. **Description:** The percentage of startup activity among former managers and executives in the U.S. increased 31 percent in 2013 according to consulting firm Challenger, Gray & Christmas. According to the survey, 5.5 percent of job-seeking executive launched their own business during each quarter in 2013, compared with 4.2 percent in 2012 and 3.2 percent in 2011.

41940 ■ *"Steeling Themselves" in Baltimore Business Journal (Vol. 30, July 6, 2012, No. 9, pp. 1)*
Pub: American City Business Journals, Inc.
Contact: Whitney Shaw, President
Ed: James Bach. **Released:** July 6, 2012. **Description:** Members of Maryland's steel sector have been seeking to revive the Sparrows Point steel plant. The plan also involves saving 2,000 jobs. Comments from executives included.

41941 ■ *"Stimulus Effect Slow in Greater Baltimore" in Baltimore Business Journal (Vol. 27, October 23, 2009, No. 24, pp. 1)*
Pub: American City Business Journals
Ed: Scott Dance. **Description:** Companies in Maryland have reported only 154 new jobs being created or saved in Greater Baltimore and 965 jobs overall in the state because of stimulus cash. The federal stimulus program was expected to create thousands of new jobs but statistics show its failure to reduce unemployment in the state.

41942 ■ *"The Story Of Diane Greene" in Barron's (Vol. 88, July 14, 2008, No. 28, pp. 31)*
Pub: Dow Jones & Co., Inc.
Contact: Clare Hart, President
Ed: Mark Veverka. **Description:** Discusses the ousting of Diane Greene as a chief executive of VMWare, a developer of virtualization software, after the firm went public; in this case Greene, a brilliant engineer, should not be negatively impacted by the decision because it is common for companies to bring in new executive leadership that is more operations oriented after the company goes public.

41943 ■ *"Succeed at a New Job" in Canadian Business (Vol. 79, November 20, 2006, No. 23, pp. 65)*
Pub: Rogers Media Inc.
Contact: Tony Viner, President
Ed: Claire Gagne. **Description:** Collections of questions that job-seekers can ask the interviewer during employment interviews are presented.

41944 ■ *"SunBank Plans Expansion Via Wal-Mart" in Business Journal-Serving Phoenix and the Valley of the Sun (Vol. 10, November 8, 2007)*
Pub: American City Business Journals, Inc.
Ed: Chris Casacchia. **Description:** SunBank plans to install 12 to 14 branches in Wal-Mart stores in Arizona and hire 100 bankers by the end of 2008. Wal-Mart also offers financial products at other stores through partnerships with other banks.

41945 ■ *"SunTrust Builds a New Team" in Charlotte Business Journal (Vol. 27, July 13, 2012, No. 17, pp. 1)*
Pub: American City Business Journals, Inc.
Contact: Whitney Shaw, President
Ed: Adam O'Daniel. **Released:** July 13, 2012. **Description:** SunTrust Banks Inc. hired new bankers from competing banks as part of its continued effort to grow its market share in Charlotte, North Carolina. Regional president Bill Peele, is focused on serving commercial accounts and he believes professional services have the most promising prospects for growth.

41946 ■ *"A Supply-Side Solution for Health Care" in (Vol. 92, July 23, 2012, No. 30, pp. 30)*
Pub: Dow Jones & Co., Inc.
Contact: Clare Hart, President
Ed: H. Woody Brock. **Released:** July 23, 2012. **Description:** The United States should increase the supply of new doctors, nurses and other health care professionals to improve the American health care system by increasing supply. Health care reform proposals in the US Congress fail to address the supply side of the problem.

41947 ■ *"Talent Shows" in Canadian Business (Vol. 81, December 24, 2007, No. 1, pp. 14)*
Ed: Megan Harman. **Description:** Canadian companies are increasingly turning to marketing to promote themselves as employers, as concerns on employee recruitment increase with the nearing retirement age of the baby boomers. Details on skills shortage, the potential advantage for the immigrant workforce, and employee retention are discussed.

41948 ■ *"Tata's Novi Unit Looks to Hire 200 Engineers" in Crain's Detroit Business (Vol. 26, January 18, 2010, No. 3, pp. 4)*
Pub: Crain Communications Inc.
Contact: Rance E. Crain, President
Ed: Lindsay Chappell. **Description:** Indian conglomerate Tata Sons Ltd.'s Novi-based engineering subsidiary is expected to hire around 200 engineers in the next three months or so, in part due to a more sophisticated attitude about outsourcing vehicle engineering to other companies.

41949 ■ *"Technology Companies are Increasing Their Hiring" in Philadelphia Business Journal (Vol. 31, March 16, 2012, No. 5, pp. 1)*
Pub: American City Business Journal
Description: Technology firms in Pennsylvania have been expanding their work force. Online advertisements for computer and math science hiring have increased.

41950 ■ *"Testing Firm to Add Jobs" in Business Courier (Vol. 26, December 11, 2009, No. 33, pp. 1)*
Ed: Dan Monk. **Description:** Cincinnati-based Q Laboratories announced plans to add dozens of jobs with the $1.6 million stimulus assisted expansion. The company hired Michael Lichtenberg & Sons Construction Co. to build a new 9,000 square foot laboratory building.

41951 ■ *"Three Steps to Follow when Job Hunting" in Contractor (Vol. 56, September 2009, No. 9, pp. 62)*
Pub: Penton Media, Inc.
Ed: H. Kent Craig. **Description:** Advice on how project managers in the United States plumbing industry should look for jobs in view of the economic crisis. Job seekers should consider relocating to places where there are an abundance of project management jobs. Resumes should also be revised to make an applicant stand out.

41952 ■ *"Tough Sell" in Black Enterprise (Vol. 37, October 2006, No. 3, pp. 92)*
Pub: Earl G. Graves Publishing Co. Inc.
Contact: Earl G. Graves, Jr., President
Ed: Sonia Alleyne. **Description:** Career coaches can evaluate your talents and skills. In an era where more companies are downsizing, a coach can help you decide if you are suited for your industry or should try switching careers.

41953 ▪ *"Toyota Revs Up Plans for Ontario Plant"* in Globe & Mail (February 7, 2006, pp. B1)

Ed: Greg Keenan. **Description:** The production output and workforce addition proposals of Toyota Motor Corp., at Ontario plant, are presented.

41954 ▪ *"Trade Craft: Take Pride in Your Trade, Demand Excellence"* in Contractor (Vol. 56, October 2009, No. 10, pp. 24)

Pub: Penton Media, Inc.

Ed: Al Schwartz. **Description:** There is a need for teaching, developing, and encouraging trade craft. An apprentice plumber is not only versed in the mechanical aspects of the trade but he also has a working knowledge of algebra, trigonometry, chemistry, and thermal dynamics. Contractors should be demanding on their personnel regarding their trade craft and should only keep and train the very best people they can hire.

41955 ▪ *"Tri-State Lags Peer Cities in Jobs, Human Capital, Study Says"* in Business Courier (Vol. 27, September 24, 2010, No. 21, pp. 1)

Pub: Business Courier

Ed: Dan Monk, Lucy May. **Description:** Greater Cincinnati, Ohio has ranked tenth overall in the 'Agenda 360/Vision 2015 Regional Indicators Project' report. The study ranked 12-city-peer groups in categories such as job indicators standing and people indicators standing. The ranking of jobs and human capital study is topped by Minneapolis, followed by Denver, Raleigh, and Austin.

41956 ▪ *"Tuesday Morning's Corporate Clearance Rack"* in Dallas Business Journal (Vol. 37, February 28, 2014, No. 25, pp. 4)

Pub: American City Business Journals

Released: February 28, 2014. **Description:** Tuesday Morning CEO, Michael Rouleau, has been working to help the company recover from its financial problems. Rouleau has improved the shopping experience from garage sale to discount showroom. The company has also been hiring different executives in the past few years.

41957 ▪ *"Uncertain Labor Pool Troubles Businesses"* in Business First-Columbus (October 22, 2007, pp. A1)

Pub: American City Business Journals, Inc.

Ed: Kevin Kemper. **Description:** Businesses in Columbus, Ohio are having difficulty finding skilled workers and expect this trend to continue through 2010-2020. They are trying to recruit young workers to address the shortage in skilled labor.

41958 ▪ *"Under Pressure"* in Canadian Business (Vol. 81, July 21, 2008, No. 11, pp. 18)

Ed: Joe Castaldo. **Description:** According to a survey conducted by COMPASS Inc., meeting revenue targets is the main cause of job stress for chief executive officers. Staffing and keeping expenditures lower also contribute to the workplace stress experienced by business executives. Other results of the survey are presented.

41959 ▪ *"Unemployment Rates"* in The Economist (Vol. 390, January 3, 2009, No. 8612, pp. 75)

Description: Countries that are being impacted the worst by rising unemployment rates are those that have also been suffering from the housing market crisis. Spain has been the hardest hit followed by Ireland. America and Britain are also seeing levels of unemployment that indicate too much slack in the economy.

41960 ▪ *"Union Questions Patrick Cudahy Layoffs"* in Business Journal-Milwaukee (Vol. 28, December 3, 2010, No. 9, pp. A1)

Pub: Milwaukee Business Journal

Ed: Rich Rovito. **Description:** United Food and Commercial Workers Local 1473 is investigating Patrick Cudahy Inc.'s termination of 340 jobs. The union said the company has violated the law for failing to issue proper notice of a mass layoff.

41961 ▪ *"U.S. Economy's Underlying Strengths Limit Recession Threat"* in Hispanic Business (Vol. 30, April 2008, No. 4, pp. 14)

Pub: Hispanic Business Inc.

Contact: Jesus Chavarria, President

Ed: Dr. Juan B. Solana. **Description:** Large and small businesses as well as consumers and policymakers are attempting to identify the areas of risk and loss created by the economic crisis; analysts are now estimating that U.S. mortgage losses could reach the $380 to $400 billion mark. Also discusses the falling of wages and the rising of unemployment. Statistical data included.

41962 ▪ *"Urban League Training Program Finds Jobs for Cincinnati's 'Hard to Serve"* in Business Courier (Vol. 27, July 2, 2010, No. 9, pp. 1)

Pub: Business Courier

Ed: Lucy May. **Description:** Stephen Tucker, director of workforce development for the Urban League of Greater Cincinnati, is an example of how ex-offenders can be given chances for employment after service jail sentences. How the Urban Leagues' Solid Opportunities for Advancement job training program helped Tucker and other ex-offenders is discussed.

41963 ▪ *"Use Benefits Checklist to Smooth New-Hire Onboarding"* in HR Specialist (Vol. 8, September 2010, No. 9, pp. 4)

Pub: Capitol Information Group Inc.

Description: Checklist to help employees enroll in a company's benefit offerings is provided, courtesy of Wayne State University in Detroit, Michigan.

41964 ▪ *"VC Boosts WorkForce: Livonia Software Company to Add Sales, Marketing Staff"* in Crain's Detroit Business (March 24, 2008)

Pub: Crain Communications Inc.

Contact: Rance E. Crain, President

Ed: Tom Henderson. **Description:** WorkForce Software Inc., a company that provides software to manage payroll processes and oversee compliance with state and federal regulations and with union rules, plans to use an investment of $5.5 million in venture capital to hire more sales and marketing staff.

41965 ▪ *"Verizon Comes Calling With 500 Jobs"* in Business First Columbus (Vol. 25, September 15, 2008, No. 4, pp. 1)

Pub: American City Business Journals

Ed: Brian R. Ball. **Description:** Hilliard, Ohio offered Verizon Wireless a 15-year incentive package worth $3.4 million for the company to move 300 customer financial services jobs to the city in addition to the 200 jobs from their facility in Dublin, Ohio. The incentives include a return of 15 percent of the income tax generated by the jobs.

41966 ▪ *"Veteran-Owned Business Energizes Employees To Give Back"* in Investment Weekly News (June 23, 2012, pp. 768)

Description: Service Disabled Veteran-Owned Small Business (SDVOSB) and Certified (AITC) are commited to American veterans. AITC's staff is composed of 50 percent veterans and sees this model as a means of giving back to the soldiers, a cause they proudly support. Details of programs that support wounded warriors and their families, and are supported by AITC, are described.

41967 ▪ *"Veterans Train to Use Military Skills In Civilian Workforce"* in South Florida Business Journal (Vol. 34, April 18, 2014, No. 39, pp. 10)

Pub: American City Business Journals

Released: April 18, 2014. **Description:** United Way of Broward County has launched the Mission United program that offers a one-stop shop of information and resources to meet the needs of military veterans. Mission United aims to reduce the jobless rate among veterans by creating two programs to help veterans and connect them with potential employers who are hiring. Details of the job training program is explored.

41968 ▪ *"Village at Waugh Chapel $275M Expansion Begins"* in Baltimore Business Journal (Vol. 28, August 27, 2010, No. 16, pp. 1)

Pub: Baltimore Business Journal

Ed: Daniel J. Sernovitz. **Description:** Developer Greenberg Gibbons Corporation has broken ground on a $275 million, 1.2 million-square-foot addition to its Village at the Waugh Chapel mixed-use complex. Aside from creating 2,600 permanent jobs, the addition, named Village South, is expected to lure Target and Wegmans Food Markets to Crofton, Maryland. Funding for this project is discussed.

41969 ▪ *"Wal-Mart Sharpens Focus on Roxbury"* in Boston Business Journal (Vol. 31, July 8, 2011, No. 24, pp. 1)

Pub: Boston Business Journal

Ed: Mary Moore. **Description:** Wal-Mart Stores is boosting its search for a possible location in the Roxbury section of Boston, Massachusetts. The search is focused on underserved communities in terms of jobs and access to reasonably-priced merchandise. The extent Boston's African American community has clashed with Mayor Thomas M. Menino over the accommodations of the retailer in Roxbury is discussed.

41970 ▪ *"Walker Seeks More Business Participation"* in Business Journal-Milwaukee (Vol. 28, December 10, 2010, No. 10, pp. A1)

Pub: Milwaukee Business Journal

Ed: Rich Kirchen. **Description:** Wisconsin governor Scott Walker is seeking the aid of Milwaukee business leaders to participate in resolving the challenges posed by the economic crisis. Walker is aiming to create 250,000 jobs. He is also planning to call a special session of the legislature to enact strategies to jumpstart the economy.

41971 ▪ *The Wall Street Journal. Complete Small Business Guidebook*

Pub: Three Rivers Press

Contact: Caroline Sincerbeaux, Editor

E-mail: csincerbeaux@randomhouse.com

Ed: Colleen DeBaise. **Released:** December 29, 2009. **Price:** $15. **Description:** The mechanics of building, running and growing a profitable business are outlined, teaching how to write a business plan, ways to finding money during lean years, how to keep stress in check, time management, investment in technology, hiring, marketing, management basics, angel investing and venture capital, as well as an exit strategy.

41972 ▪ *"Wanted: African American Professional for Hire"* in Black Enterprise (Vol. 37, November 2006, No. 4, pp. 93)

Pub: Earl G. Graves Publishing Co. Inc.

Contact: Earl G. Graves, Jr., President

Ed: Joe Watson. **Description:** Excerpt from the book, Without Excuses: Unleash the Power of Diversity to Build Your Business, speaks to the lack of diversity in the corporate arena and why executives, recruiters, and HR professionals claim they are unable to find qualified individuals of different races when hiring.

41973 ▪ *"The War for Good Jobs; The World Will IBe Led with Economic Force"* in Gallup Management Journal (September 7, 2011)

Pub: Gallup Inc.

Contact: Jim Clifton, Chief Executive Officer

Ed: Jim Clifton. **Description:** Gallup's chairman believes the next world war will be for good jobs and the winner will triumph with economic force, driven primarily by job creation and quality GDP growth.

41974 ▪ *"The War for Talent"* in Canadian Business (Vol. 80, January 29, 2007, No. 3, pp. 60)

Ed: Erin Pooley. **Description:** The recruitment policies of Canadian businesses are described. The trends pertaining to the growth of executive salaries in Canada are discussed.

41975 ▪ *"Wattles Plugs Back Into State"* in Business Journal Portland (Vol. 27, November 19, 2010, No. 38, pp. 1)

Pub: Portland Business Journal

Ed: Wendy Culverwell. **Description:** Denver, Colorado-based Ultimate Electronics Inc.'s first store in Oregon was opened in Portland and the 46th store in the chain of electronic superstores is expected to employ 70-80 workers. The venture is the latest for Mark Wattles, one of Oregon's most successful entrepreneurs, who acquired Ultimate from bankruptcy.

41976 ■ *"Wayne, Oakland Counties Create Own 'Medical Corridor" in Crain's Detroit Business (Vol. 24, October 6, 2008, No. 40, pp. 8)*

Pub: Crain Communications Inc.

Contact: Rance E. Crain, President

Ed: Jay Greene. **Description:** Woodward Medical Corridor that runs along Woodward Avenue and currently encompasses twelve hospitals and is rapidly growing with additional physician offices, advanced oncology centers and new hospitals. Beaumont Hospital is building a $160 million proton-beam therapy cancer center on its Royal Oak campus in a joint venture with Procure Treatment Centers of Bloomington Ind. That is expected to open in 2010 and will employ approximately 145 new workers.

41977 ■ *"Web Site Design, Content Can Boost Diversity" in HRMagazine (Vol. 53, August 2008, No. 8, pp. 20)*

Description: Design and content of an employer's Website influences prospective young job candidates, especially young black job seekers, a new academic study has found. The findings appear in Black and White and Read All Over: Race Differences in Reactions To Recruitment Web Sites, published in the summer 2008 issue of the Human Resource Management Journal.

41978 ■ *"Web Site Focuses on Helping People Find Jobs, Internships with Area Businesses" in Crain's Detroit Business (Vol. 26, Jan. 4, 2010)*

Pub: Crain Communications Inc.

Contact: Rance E. Crain, President

Ed: Dustin Walsh. **Description:** DetroitIntern.com, LLC is helping metro Detroit college students and young professionals find career-advancing internships or jobs with local businesses.

41979 ■ *"Website Drives British Travel Firm To Open In Boston" in Boston Business Journal (Vol. 34, February 28, 2014, No. 4, pp. 4)*

Pub: American City Business Journals, Inc.

Contact: Whitney Shaw, President

Released: February 28, 2014. **Description:** United Kingdom-based Audley Travel is planning to open an office in Boston, Massachusetts. The company has hired 27 people for the new office. Audley's earnings have increased $120 million 2013.

41980 ■ *"WEDC Credits Could Create 400 Area Jobs" in Business Journal Milwaukee (Vol. 29, July 27, 2012, No. 44, pp. 1)*

Pub: American City Business Journals, Inc.

Contact: Whitney Shaw, President

Ed: Rich Kirchen. **Released:** July 27, 2012. **Description:** Wisconsin Development Corporation (WEDC) has provided $2.2 million in tax credits to six southeastern Wisconsin employers that are expected to add nearly 400 jobs. The companies are Unico Inc., Spee-Dee Packaging Machinery, All Tool Sales Inc., Echo Lake Foods Inc., Novation Companies Inc., and Trico Corporation.

41981 ■ *"Wegmans Adding 1,600-Plus Jobs Here Over the Next Year" in Boston Business Journal (Vol. 34, February 14, 2014, No. 2, pp. 3)*

Pub: American City Business Journals, Inc.

Contact: Whitney Shaw, President

Released: February 14, 2014. **Description:** Wegmans, a family-owned grocery chain, is planning to add the most jobs of any firm in Massachusetts in 2014. The company will create more than 1,600 full-and part-time positions by opening three stores. Bill Congdon, Wegmans' New England division manager, reveals that the company is also planning to open a store in the city of Boston.

41982 ■ *The Well-Timed Strategy: Managing Business Cycle for Competitive Advantage*

Pub: Wharton School Publishing

Ed: Peter Navarro. **Released:** January 13, 2006. **Price:** $39.99, Nonmembers; $31.99, Members. **Description:** An overview of business cycles and risks is presented. Recession is a good time to find key personnel for a small business. Other issues addressed include investment, production, and marketing in order to maintain a competitive edge. **Availability:** Print; E-book.

41983 ■ *"We're Falling Behind the Rest of the Country" in Canadian Business (Vol. 85, August 13, 2012, No. 13, pp. 46)*

Pub: George Media Inc.

Ed: Joe Castaldo. **Released:** August 13, 2012. **Description:** Clearwater Seafoods cofounder John Risley is concerned about the future of the Canadian economy, particularly the Atlantic Provinces, with high unemployment rates and demographic shift. He believes that Atlantic Canadians are great entrepreneurs and workers.

41984 ■ *"What Businesses Can Do: Growing the Supply of Highly Skilled Graduates" in Canadian Business (Vol. 81, October 27, 2008, No. 18)*

Description: Employers in Canada have expressed concerns over the findings of various studies that revealed current and projected labor shortages in the country. A low birthrate and an aging population is contributing to the problem. Ways businesses can increase the supply of highly skilled workers in Canada is presented.

41985 ■ *"What You Look Like Online" in Black Enterprise (Vol. 37, January 2007, No. 6, pp. 56)*

Ed: Marcia A. Reed-Woodard. **Description:** Of 100 executive recruiters 77 percent stated that they use search engines to check the backgrounds of potential job candidates, according to a survey conducted by ExecuNet. Of those surveyed 35 percent stated that they eliminate potential candidates based on information they find online so it is important to create a positive Web presence which highlights professional image qualities.

41986 ■ *"What's More Important: Talent or Engagement? A Study With Retailer ANN INC. Seeks To Find the Essential Ingredients To High-Performing Managers and Employees" in Gallup Business Journal (April 22, 2014)*

Pub: Gallup Press

Released: April 22, 2014. **Description:** ANN INC. is a leading women's clothing retailer that is exploring the necessary steps to achieving both high-performing managers and employees. The firm found that hiring people with the right talent and engaging them will maximize performance.

41987 ■ *"What's Working Now: In Providing Jobs for North Carolinians" in Business North Carolina (Vol. 28, February 2008, No. 2, pp. 16)*

Pub: Business North Carolina

Ed: Edward Martin, Frank Maley. **Description:** Individuals previously employed in the furniture, tobacco, or textile manufacturing sectors have gone back to school to be trained in new sectors in the area such as life sciences, finances and other emerging sectors.

41988 ■ *"When To Make Private News Public: Should a Job Candidate Reveal That She's Pregnant?" in Harvard Business Review (Vol. 90, March 2012, No. 3, pp. 161)*

Pub: Harvard Business Review Press

Contact: Peter E. Walsh, Director

Ed: Tiziana Casciaro, Victoria W. Winston. **Released:** March 2012. **Description:** A fictitious hiring scenario is presented, with contributors providing advice on whether a candidate for a position involving extensive business travel should inform her manager that she is expecting. Contributors agree the employee should inform her manager, but not necessarily before she is

offered the position, and that the conversation remains focused on how she will perform the job and address challenges.

41989 ■ *"When You Need Strong Millennials in Your Workplace" in Agency Sales Magazine (Vol. 39, November 2009, No. 10, pp. 22)*

Ed: Joanne G. Sujansky. **Description:** Millennials are bringing a new set of skills and a different kind of work ethics to the workplace. This generation is used to receiving a great deal of positive feedback and they expect to continue receiving this on the job. Expectations should be made clear to this generation and long-term career plans and goals should also be discussed with them.

41990 ■ *"Why Does Firm Reputation In Human Resource Policies Influence College Students? The Mechanisms Underlying Job Pursuit Intentions" in Human Resource Management (Vol. 51, January-February 2012, No. 1, pp. 121-142)*

Pub: John Wiley & Sons Inc.

Contact: Stephen M. Smith, President

Ed: Julie Holliday Wayne, Wendy J. Casper. **Description:** The effects of reputational information about human resource practices of companies on college students seeking employment are examined. The reputation of firms in compensation, work-family, and diversity efforts are found to increase intentions to pursue employment in these firms.

41991 ■ *"Why Entrepreneurs Matter More Than Innovators" in Gallup Management Journal (November 22, 2011)*

Pub: Gallup Inc.

Contact: Jim Clifton, Chief Executive Officer

Ed: Jim Clifton. **Description:** In the race to create good jobs, leaders are not paying enough attention to cultivating talented entrepreneurs, rather they invest too much attention on innovation.

41992 ■ *"Why Great Managers Are So Rare; Companies Fail To Choose the Candidate With the Right Talent For the Job 82 Percent of the Time, Gallup Finds" in Gallup Business Journal (March 25, 2014)*

Pub: Gallup Press

Released: March 25, 2014. **Description:** Gallup research suggests that companies hire the wrong person to manage their firm about 82 percent of the time. Many times management talent already exists within the company, but for some reason, companies look elsewhere for that talent. Bad managers cost billions of dollars to businesses annually.

41993 ■ *"Why I Stopped Firing Everyone and Started Being a Better Boss" in Inc. (Vol. 34, September 2012, No. 7, pp. 86)*

Pub: Mansueto Ventures L.L.C.

Contact: John Koten, Chief Executive Officer

Ed: April Joyner. **Released:** September 2012. **Description:** Indigo Johnson, former Marine, discusses her management style when starting her business. She fired employees regularly. Johnson enrolled in a PhD program in leadership and established a better hiring program and learned to utilize her workers' strengths.

41994 ■ *"Why Is It So Hard To Find Good People? The Problem Might Be You" in Inc. (Vol. 33, November 2011, No. 9, pp. 100)*

Pub: Inc. Magazine

Ed: April Joyner. **Description:** Entrepreneurs sometimes struggle to find good workers. A recent survey shows hiring as their top concern. Four common mistakes that can occur during the hiring process our outlined.

41995 ■ *"Work/Life Balance" in Dallas Business Journal (Vol. 37, June 20, 2014, No. 41, pp. 4)*

Pub: American City Business Journals

Released: June 20, 2014. **Description:** Younger generations of corporate employees are increasingly looking for a more engaged workplace community. Research firm, Quantum Workplace, identifies several trends that help to attract and retain employees, including jobs that align with the workers' own values, growth opportunities within the firm, social interactions with co-workers, and employee health benefits.

41996 ■ "Work To Do" in Canadian Business (Vol. 81, July 22, 2008, No. 12-13, pp. 22)
Ed: Jane Bao. **Description:** Recruiting firm Manpower revealed that 36 percent of Canadian employers had trouble filling positions in 2007, highlighting the labor shortage and the need to bring in more workers. Underemployment of immigrants costs up to $6 billion to Canada's economy every year. Other views regarding Canada's labor shortage and on its economic impact are presented.

41997 ■ The Worst-Case Scenario Business Survival Guide: How to Survive the Recession, Handle Layoffs, Raise Emergency Cash, Thwart an Employee Coup, and Avoid Other Potential Disasters
Pub: John Wiley & Sons Inc.
Contact: Stephen M. Smith, President
Ed: David Borgenicht, Mark Joyner. **Released:** September 28, 2009. **Price:** $17.95. **Description:** Since 1999, the Worst-Case Scenario survival handbooks have provided readers with real answers for the most extreme situations. Now, in a time of economic crisis, the series returns with a new, real-world guide to avoiding the worst business cataclysms.

41998 ■ "WPC Announces Executive Leadership Team Hires to Grow Business and Security & Compliance Practice" in Internet Wire (February 13, 2012)
Released: February 13, 2012. **Description:** Ray Guzman was appointed senior vice president of sales and business development and Brad Hutson was named chief security officer a WPC. The firm offers full service healthcare business process consulting. The move expands WPC's security and compliance consulting team.

41999 ■ "Xymogen Poised for Huge Growth, Hiring" in Orlando Business Journal (Vol. 29, September 14, 2012, No. 13, pp. 1)
Pub: American City Business Journal
Description: Xymogen has made changes to its business model. The company is planning to hire at least 50 new workers in 2013. Xymogen posted $39.3 million in profits in 2011.

42000 ■ "Yodle To Hire Hundreds Here" in Austin Business Journal (Vol. 32, July 20, 2012, No. 20, pp. 1)
Pub: American City Business Journals, Inc.
Contact: Whitney Shaw, President
Ed: Jan Buchholz. **Released:** July 20, 2012. **Description:** Internet marketing firm Yodle Inc. plans to employ more than 800 people in the Austin, Texas area as part of its expansion plan. The company, which already employs nearly 400 people, leased nearly 100,000 square feet at Plaza 35 in North Austin.

42001 ■ "You Are What They Click" in Entrepreneur (Vol. 37, July 2009, No. 7, pp. 43)
Pub: Entrepreneur Press
Contact: Perlman Neil, President
Ed: Mikal E. Belicove. **Description:** Hiring the right website design firm is the first stage in building an online business, and this involves various factors such as price, technical expertise, and talent. Writing a request for proposal (RFP) detailing the website's details, which include purpose, budget and audience, is the first step the process. Other tips in finding the right web designer are given.

42002 ■ "Your First 100 Days on Your New Job" in Women In Business (Vol. 63, Spring 2011, No. 1, pp. 28)
Pub: American Business Women's Association
Contact: Lorie Burch, President
Ed: Diane Stafford. **Description:** The first 100 days on the job are crucial if the person's permanent hiring is conditional on surviving a probationary period. The new hire must do more than just master the job's

technical details to maximize the chance of success. Details of some basic tips to fit into the corporate culture and get along with coworkers are also discussed.

42003 ■ "Your Web Brand Counts" in Black Enterprise (Vol. 44, June 2014, No. 10, pp. 46)
Pub: Earl G. Graves Publishing Co. Inc.
Contact: Earl G. Graves, Jr., President
Released: June 2014. **Description:** Forty-eight percent of employers use Google or other search engines to find information about job applicants and 25 percent of executives hired were originally identified or contacted through social media, thus the importance of a good Web presence is outlined.

42004 ■ "Youth Employment in the Summer of 2010" in Montly Labor Review (Vol. 133, September 2010, No. 9, pp. 2)
Pub: U.S. Department of Labor Bureau of Labor Statistics
Contact: Philip L. Rones, Manager
E-mail: rones.philip@bls.gov
Description: The number of youth 16 to 24 years old rose by 1.8 million from April to July 2010. Statistical data included.

TRADE PERIODICALS

42005 ■ Insight into Diversity: The EEO Recruitment Publication
Pub: INSIGHT Into Diversity
URL(s): www.insightintodiversity.comwww.aarjobs.com. **Released:** Monthly **Price:** $9.95, Individuals subscription per/year; Free online. **Covers:** In each issue, about 300 positions at a professional level (most requiring advanced study) available to women, minorities, veterans, and the handicapped; listings are advertisements placed by employers with affirmative action programs. **Entries include:** Company or organization name, address, contact name; description of position including title, requirements, duties, application procedure, salary, etc. **Arrangement:** Classified by profession.

VIDEOCASSETTES/ AUDIOCASSETTES

42006 ■ Brief Encounters
Excellence in Training Corp.
c/o ICON Training
804 Roosevelt St.
Polk City, IA 50226
Free: 800-609-0479
Co. E-mail: info@icontraining.com
URL: http://www.icontraining.com
Contact: Linda Russell, Vice President
Released: 1991. **Price:** $695. **Description:** A presentation on 10 techniques to help interviewers select the best-qualified job applicant. **Availability:** VHS; 3/4 U; Special order formats.

42007 ■ Chinese for Affirmative Action
Chinese for Affirmative Action (CAA)
17 Walter U. Lum Pl.
San Francisco, CA 94108
Ph: (415)274-6750
Fax: (415)397-8770
Co. E-mail: info@caasf.org
URL: http://www.caasf.org
Contact: Andy Wong, Director
Released: 1974. **Description:** "Chinese for Affirmative Action" is a promotional program about the civil rights organization based in San Francisco's Chinatown. **Availability:** 3/4 U.

42008 ■ Communication Series: Interviewing
Michigan State University
201 Morrill Hall
East Lansing, MI 48824
Ph: (517)355-9571
Fax: (517)353-3755
Co. E-mail: jowett@msu.edu
URL: http://www.msu.edu
Contact: Steven Jowett, Manager
E-mail: jowett@msu.edu
Released: 1981. **Description:** Mike Wallace, George Gallup and John Shingleton are interviewed about the techniques they use for interviewing. **Availability:** VHS; 3/4 U.

42009 ■ The Effective Manager
Nightingale-Conant Corp.
1400 South Wolf Rd., Bldg. 300, Ste. 103
Wheeling, IL 60090
Ph: (847)647-0300
Free: 800-557-1660
Fax: (847)647-7145
Co. E-mail: sales@nightingale.com
URL: http://www.nightingale.com
Contact: L. Victor Conant, President
Released: 19??. **Price:** $95. **Description:** A series of award-winning programs designed to promote effective management and help increase sales. Audio tapes and booklets are included, and the series can be purchased individually or as a set. **Availability:** VHS.

42010 ■ Equal Treatment/Equal Opportunity
Gulf Publishing Co.
2 Greenway Plz., Ste. 1020
Houston, TX 77046-0208
Ph: (713)529-4301
Free: 800-231-6275
Fax: (713)520-4433
Co. E-mail: customerservices@gulfpub.com
URL: http://www.gulfpub.com
Contact: John D. Meador, President
Released: 1984. **Price:** $375. **Description:** This program is designed to help the workforce to understand what comprises discrimination. **Availability:** VHS; 3/4 U.

42011 ■ Man Hunt
Video Arts, Inc.
c/o Aim Learning Group
8238-40 Lehigh
Morton Grove, IL 60053-2615
Free: 877-444-2230
Fax: (416)252-2155
Co. E-mail: service@aimlearninggroup.com
URL: http://www.aimlearninggroup.com
Released: 1974. **Price:** $790. **Description:** Often, managers feels that they know the person they want for a job just by seeing them. The purpose of this program is to make managers realize this is not so. It shows where and how the principal faults occur: failure to prepare for the interview, failure to draw the candidate out and get him to talk freely, and failure to come out with direct, probing questions. **Availability:** VHS; 8 mm; 3/4 U; Special order formats.

42012 ■ Managing Frontline Service
Video Arts, Inc.
c/o Aim Learning Group
8238-40 Lehigh
Morton Grove, IL 60053-2615
Free: 877-444-2230
Fax: (416)252-2155
Co. E-mail: service@aimlearninggroup.com
URL: http://www.aimlearninggroup.com
Released: 1989. **Price:** $730. **Description:** Through case studies in two highly successful corporations, this video shows how to improve performance by selecting, training, and motivating the right people. **Availability:** VHS; 8 mm; 3/4 U; Special order formats.

42013 ■ More Than a Gut Feeling 2
Excellence in Training Corp.
c/o ICON Training
804 Roosevelt St.
Polk City, IA 50226
Free: 800-609-0479
Co. E-mail: info@icontraining.com
URL: http://www.icontraining.com
Contact: Linda Russell, Vice President
Released: 1991. **Price:** $695. **Description:** This follow-up to "More Than a Gut Feeling" shows how to gauge a job candidate's future performance by getting her or him talk about past job experience. A leader's guide, desk reminder card, and charts of legal and illegal questions are included. **Availability:** VHS; 3/4 U; Special order formats.

CONSULTANTS

42014 ■ Barada Associates Inc.
130 E 2nd St.
Rushville, IN 46173
Ph: (765)932-5917
Fax: (765)932-2938
Co. E-mail: info@baradainc.com
URL: http://www.baradainc.com
Contact: William C. Barada, President
E-mail: will@baradainc.com
Scope: Professional employment screening services provides client companies within dependent and objective reference reports on candidates for salaried and hourly employment. **Founded:** 1979. **Publications:** "Reference Checking for Everyone," 2004; "Reference Checking is More Than Ever," Human Resource Magazine, 1996; "The Paper Chase," Indianapolis Monthly, 1995; "Check it Out-Hiring? What You Don't Know Could Hurt You," the American School Board Journal, 1994; "Reference Checking: Increased Necessity to Exercise Reasonable Care," Kin cannon & Reed, 1994; "Reference Checking

More Critical Than Ever," Association of Executive Search Consultants Inc, Dec, 1993; "Honest References," Human Resource Executive, Sep, 1993; "Check References with Care," Nation's Business, May, 1993; "Don't Overlook Reference Checks," the School Administrator, May, 1992.

42015 ■ Gately Consulting
115 Dutcher St.
Hopedale, MA 01747-1006
Ph: (508)473-0955
Co. E-mail: bob@gatelyconsulting.com
URL: http://www.gatelyconsulting.com
Contact: Robert F. Gately, President
E-mail: bob@gatelyconsulting.com
Scope: Provides the PofileXT assessment, an innovative assessment technology, for personnel and pre-employment evaluations and ensuring success in matching people to jobs and 360's. **Founded:** 1992. **Publications:** "The Employer's Advantage Newsletter". **Seminars:** The New Art of Hiring Smart.

42016 ■ Edward M. Hepner & Associates
4667 Macarthur Blvd., Ste. 405
Newport Beach, CA 92660

Ph: (714)250-0818
Fax: (714)553-8437
Scope: An immigration consultant and labor certification specialist. Assists in obtaining visa for work, immigration and business development within the United States and Canada.

COMPUTERIZED DATABASES

42017 ■ *ABI/INFORM®*
ProQuest L.L.C.
789 E Eisenhower Pkwy.
Ann Arbor, MI 48106-1346
Ph: (734)761-4700
Free: 800-521-0600
Fax: (734)662-4554
Co. E-mail: info@proquest.com
URL: http://www.proquest.com
Contact: Matt Dunie, President
Availability: Online: ProQuest L.L.C.; ProQuest LLC; LexisNexis. **Type:** Full-text; Bibliographic; Image.

START-UP INFORMATION

42018 ■ *101 Businesses You Can Start at With Less Than One Thousand Dollars: For Retirees*
Pub: Atlantic Publishing Co.
Contact: Amanda Miller, Manager
E-mail: amiller@atlantic-pub.com
Ed: Christina Bultinck. **Price:** $21.95. **Description:** Business ideas to help retirees start a home-based business on a low budget.

42019 ■ *101 Businesses You Can Start at With Less Than One Thousand Dollars: For Stay-at-Home Moms & Dads*
Pub: Atlantic Publishing Co.
Contact: Amanda Miller, Manager
E-mail: amiller@atlantic-pub.com
Ed: Christina Bultinck. **Price:** $21.95. **Description:** Business ideas to help stay-at-home moms and dads start a home-based business on a low budget.

42020 ■ *101 Internet Businesses You Can Start from Home: How to Choose and Build Your Own Successful E-Business*
Pub: Maximum Press
Contact: James W. Hoskins, President
Ed: Susan Sweeney. **Released:** August 31, 2010. **Price:** $23.31, paperback. **Description:** Guide for starting and growing an Internet business; information for developing a business plan, risk levels, and promotional techniques are included. **Availability:** Print.

42021 ■ *Breaking Free: How to Work at Home with the Perfect Small Business Opportunity*
Pub: Lulu.com
Ed: Brian Armstrong. **Released:** June 21, 2008. **Price:** $24.95, Perfect-bound Paperback; $12.95. **Description:** Three ways to smooth the transition from working for someone else to starting your own business are outlined. Seven exercises to help discover the type of business you should start, how to incorporate, get important tax benefits, and start accepting payments immediately are examined. **Availability:** PrintE-book; PDF.

42022 ■ *"Breakthrough: How to Build a Million Dollar Business by Helping Others Succeed"*
Pub: CreateSpace
Contact: Daren Giles, President
Released: October 23, 2014. **Price:** , $14.95 paperback. **Description:** Instruction for starting and growing a thriving business from home is provided. The book teaches how to listing to the small voice within, follow your instincts, deliver effective presentations, attract customers who require your products or services, host home meetings, develop leadership skills, discover purpose, and clarify your entrepreneurial visions and goals.

42023 ■ *"Caring Concern" in Small Business Opportunities (September 2010)*
Pub: Harris Publications Inc.
Description: Profile of Joshua Hoffman, founder and CEO of HomeWell Senior Care, Inc., provider of non-medical live-in and hourly personal care, companionship and homemaker services for seniors so they can remain in their own homes.

42024 ■ *The Complete Guide to Making Money at Home: Everything You Need to Know to Earn Riches at Home*
Ed: Gary J. Fuller. **Released:** January 2006. **Price:** , $19.95. **Description:** Guide for starting and running an at-home business.

42025 ■ *The Crafts Business Answer Book: Starting, Managing, and Marketing a Homebased Arts, Crafts, or Design Business*
Pub: M. Evans and Company, Incorporated
Ed: Barbara Brabec. **Released:** July 2006. **Price:** $16.95. **Description:** Expert advice for starting a home-based art or crafts business is offered. **Availability:** Print.

42026 ■ *Earn Cash Crafting at Home: An MBA At-Home Mom Explains Step-by-Step Her Fun, Proven, Money-Making, Own-Your-Own Business Formula*
Ed: Maria Colman. **Released:** March 2006. **Price:** , $10.00. **Description:** Manual offering advice to start and run an at-home craft business.

42027 ■ *"Etsy: Etsy Business for Beginners! Master Etsy and Build a Profitable Business In No Time"*
Pub: Amazon Digital Services
Released: October 18, 2014. **Price:** , $2.99 Kindle. **Description:** Craft artisans take note: information is offered to start an online business through Etsy. Whether handmade home accessories, clothing, or knick-knacks, Etsy is the perfect option for artists and crafters to start a home-based, online retail operation.

42028 ■ *"The Fashion Designer Survival Guide, Revised and Expanded Edition: Start and Run Your Own Fashion Business"*
Pub: Kaplan Publishing
Released: March 10, 2009. **Price:** , $22.95 paperback. **Description:** Author, industry authority, and fashion designer consultant offers insights and critical business information for starting and maintaining a successful independent clothing designer business. Fabric and material needs; loans or investments for the startup; challenges for working from a home-based venture as well as internationally; marketing, branding, and selecting retail stores to display your designs; creating an image and getting public attention.

42029 ■ *"Fast-Forward Fortune" in Small Business Opportunities (July 2010)*
Pub: Harris Publications Inc.
Description: Profile of Steve Dalbec and his home-based Home Video Studio where he earns income by offering a wide variety of video services to clients from duplicating CDs, video to DVD transfer, sports videos and more. Dalbec believes this is the perfect home-based business.

42030 ■ *"Five Low-Cost Home Based Startups" in Women Entrepreneur (December 16, 2008)*
Ed: Lesley Spencer Pyle. **Description:** During tough economic times, small businesses have an advantage over large companies because they can adjust to economic conditions more easily and without having to go through corporate red tape that can slow the implementation process. A budding entrepreneur may find success by taking inventory of his or her skills, experience, expertise and passions and utilizing those qualities to start a business. Five low-cost home-based startups are profiled. These include starting an online store, a virtual assistant service, web designer, sales representative and a home staging counselor.

42031 ■ *Getting Rich In Your Underwear: How To Start and Run a Profitable Home-Based Business*
Pub: HCM Publishing
Price: $17.95. **Description:** Book offers insight into starting a home-based business. Entrepreneurs will learn about business models and the home business; distribution and fulfillment of product or service; marketing and sales; how to overcome the fear of starting a business; personal success characteristics; naming a business; zoning and insurance; intellectual capital; copyrights, trademarks, and patents; limited liability companies and S-corporations; business expenses and accounting; taxes; fifteen basic steps for starting a home-based business, state resources for starting a home company; and seven home-based business ideas.

42032 ■ *Going Solo: Developing a Home-Based Consulting Business from the Ground Up*
Ed: William J. Bond. **Released:** January 1997. **Description:** Ways to turn specialized knowledge into a home-based successful consulting firm, focusing on targeting client needs, business plans, and growth.

42033 ■ *"Green Clean Machine" in Small Business Opportunities (Winter 2010)*
Pub: Harris Publications Inc.
Description: Eco-friendly maid franchise plans to grow its $62 million sales base. Profile of Maid Brigade, a green-cleaning franchise is planning to expand across the country.

42034 ■ *Home-Based Business for Dummies*
Pub: John Wiley & Sons Inc.
Contact: Stephen M. Smith, President
Ed: Paul Edwards, Sarah Edwards, Peter Economy. **Released:** 3rd Edition. **Price:** $19.95, paperback; $12.99. **Description:** Provides all the information needed to start and run a home-based business. Topics include: selecting the right business; setting up a home office; managing money, credit, and financing; marketing; and ways to avoid distractions while working at home. **Availability:** PrintE-book.

42035 ■ *Home-Based Travel Agent, 5th Edition*
Ed: Kelly Monaghan. **Released:** March 2006. **Price:** , $59.95. **Description:** Advice for starting and running a home-based travel agency is given.

42036 ■ *"Home Work" in Black Enterprise (Vol. 37, October 2006, No. 3, pp. 78)*
Pub: Earl G. Graves Publishing Co. Inc.
Contact: Earl G. Graves, Jr., President
Ed: James C. Johnson. **Description:** Information on starting a resume-writing service is profiled.

42037 ■ *How to Make Money While You Look for a Job: Start a Very Small Service Business on a Shoestring, A Step-by-step Workbook*
Pub: Booklocker.com Inc.
Contact: Angela Adair-Hoy, Publisher
Ed: Donna Boyette. **Released:** March 2005. **Description:** Six steps to make money while searching for employment are outlined, from setting up a home-based office to selling a service.

42038 ■ *How to Open & Operate a Financially Successful Landscaping, Nursery, or Lawn Service Business: With Companion CD-ROM*
Pub: Atlantic Publishing Co.
Contact: Amanda Miller, Manager
E-mail: amiller@atlantic-pub.com
Ed: Lynn Wasnak. **Price:** $39.95. **Description:** Guide provides understanding of the basic concepts of starting and running a service business, focusing on the operation of a small nursery, landscaping, or lawn service or combining the three operations. It also offers tips for running the business from the home.

42039 ■ *How to Start a Home-Based Consulting Business: Define Your Specialty Build a Client Base Make Yourself Indispensable*
Pub: Globe Pequot Press Inc.
Contact: Robert Irwin, Manager
E-mail: robert.irwin@globepequot.com
Ed: Bert Holtje. **Released:** January 06, 2010. **Price:** $18.95, paperback. **Description:** Everything needed for starting and running a successful consulting business from home. **Availability:** Print.

42040 ■ *How to Start a Home-based Craft Business*
Pub: Globe Pequot Press Inc.
Contact: Robert Irwin, Manager
E-mail: robert.irwin@globepequot.com
Ed: Kenn Oberrecht, Patrice Lewis. **Released:** 6th Edition. **Price:** $19.95, paperback. **Description:** Step-by-step guide for starting and growing a home-based craft business. **Availability:** Print.

42041 ■ *How to Start a Home-Based Craft Business*
Pub: Globe Pequot Press Inc.
Contact: Robert Irwin, Manager
E-mail: robert.irwin@globepequot.com
Ed: Kenn Oberrecht, Patrice Lewis. **Released:** Sixth Edition. **Price:** $19.95, Paperback. **Description:** Advice for starting a home-based craft business is given, including sources for finding supplies on the Internet, writing a business plan, publicity, zoning ordinances, and more. **Availability:** Print.

42042 ■ *How to Start a Home-Based Event Planning Business*
Pub: Globe Pequot Press Inc.
Contact: Robert Irwin, Manager
E-mail: robert.irwin@globepequot.com
Ed: Jill Moran. **Released:** 3rd Edition. **Price:** $19.95, paperback. **Description:** Guide to starting and growing a business planning events from a home-based firm.

42043 ■ *How to Start a Home-Based Interior Design Business*
Pub: Globe Pequot Press Inc.
Contact: Robert Irwin, Manager
E-mail: robert.irwin@globepequot.com
Ed: Nita B. Phillips. **Released:** 5th Edition. **Price:** $18.95, paperback. **Description:** Tips for starting and running a home-based interior design business are given. **Availability:** Print.

42044 ■ *How to Start a Home-Based Interior Design Business*
Pub: Globe Pequot Press Inc.
Contact: Robert Irwin, Manager
E-mail: robert.irwin@globepequot.com
Ed: Nita Phillips. **Released:** 5th Edition. **Price:** $18.95, paperback. **Availability:** Print.

42045 ■ *How to Start a Home-Based Landscaping Business*
Pub: Globe Pequot Press Inc.
Contact: Robert Irwin, Manager
E-mail: robert.irwin@globepequot.com
Ed: Owen E. Dell. **Released:** January 06, 2010. **Price:** $18.95, paperback. **Description:** Guide to starting and running a home-based landscaping business. **Availability:** Print.

42046 ■ *How to Start a Home-Based Landscaping Business*
Pub: Globe Pequot Press Inc.
Contact: Robert Irwin, Manager
E-mail: robert.irwin@globepequot.com
Ed: Owen E. Dell. **Released:** January 06, 2010. **Price:** $18.95. **Description:** Guide to starting and running a successful home-based landscaping business, including tips for marketing on the Internet. **Availability:** Print.

42047 ■ *How to Start a Home-Based Mail Order Business*
Pub: Globe Pequot Press Inc.
Contact: Robert Irwin, Manager
E-mail: robert.irwin@globepequot.com
Ed: Georganne Fiumara. **Released:** June 01, 2011. **Price:** $18.95, paperback. **Description:** Step-by-step guide for starting and growing a home-based mail order business. Information about equipment, pricing, online marketing, are included along with worksheets and checklists for planning. **Availability:** Print.

42048 ■ *How to Start a Home-Based Online Retail Business*
Pub: Globe Pequot Press Inc.
Contact: Robert Irwin, Manager
E-mail: robert.irwin@globepequot.com
Ed: Jeremy Shepherd. **Released:** Second Edition. **Price:** $19.95, Paperback. **Description:** Information for starting an online retail, home-based business is shared. **Availability:** Print.

42049 ■ *How to Start a Home-Based Personal Chef Business*
Pub: Globe Pequot Press Inc.
Contact: Robert Irwin, Manager
E-mail: robert.irwin@globepequot.com
Ed: Denise Vivaldo. **Released:** 2nd Edition. **Price:** $18.95, paperback. **Description:** Everything needed to know to start a personal chef business is featured. **Availability:** Print.

42050 ■ *How to Start a Home-Based Professional Organizing Business*
Pub: Globe Pequot Press Inc.
Contact: Robert Irwin, Manager
E-mail: robert.irwin@globepequot.com
Ed: Dawn Noble. **Released:** Second Edition. **Price:** $18.95, Paperback. **Description:** Tips for starting a home-based professional organizing business are presented. **Availability:** Print.

42051 ■ *How to Start a Home-Based Senior Care Business: Develop a Winning Business Plan*
Pub: Globe Pequot Press Inc.
Contact: Robert Irwin, Manager
E-mail: robert.irwin@globepequot.com
Ed: James L. Ferry. **Released:** January 06, 2010. **Price:** $18.95, paperback. **Description:** Everything needed to know in order to start and run a profitable, ethical, and satisfying senior care business from your home. Information covers writing a good business plan, marketing services to families, creating a fee structure, and developing a network of trusted caregivers and service providers. **Availability:** Print.

42052 ■ *How to Start a Home-Based Web Design Business*
Pub: Globe Pequot Press Inc.
Contact: Robert Irwin, Manager
E-mail: robert.irwin@globepequot.com
Ed: Jim Smith. **Released:** July 13, 2010. **Price:** $18.95, Paperback. **Description:** Information for starting a home-based Web design firm is given. **Availability:** Print.

42053 ■ *How to Start a Home-Based Web Design Business, 4th Edition*
Pub: Globe Pequot Press Inc.
Contact: Robert Irwin, Manager
E-mail: robert.irwin@globepequot.com
Ed: Jim Smith. **Released:** July 13, 2010. **Price:** $18.95, Paperback. **Description:** Comprehensive guide contains all the necessary tools and strategies required to successfully launch and grow a Web design business.

42054 ■ *"Legendary Success" in Small Business Opportunities (November 2010)*
Pub: Harris Publications Inc.
Description: Von Schrader is famous in the cleaning industry and more than 50,000 individuals have started their own professional cleaning service businesses using the company's air cell technology cleaning systems along with their proven business systems. This is a perfect business for anyone wishing to start and run it from their home.

42055 ■ *"Moms Mean Business: A Guide to Creating a Successful Company and Happy Life as a Mom Entrepreneur"*
Pub: Career Press Inc.
Contact: Ron Fry, President
Released: October 20, 2014. **Price:** , $15.99. **Description:** Currently, more women are starting new businesses than men and there are 9 million women-owned businesses in the United States; most of these women are also moms. A guide to help women start and run a successful home-based business is presented.

42056 ■ *101 Businesses You Can Start at With Less Than One Thousand Dollars: For Stay-at-Home Moms & Dads*
Pub: Atlantic Publishing Co.
Contact: Amanda Miller, Manager
E-mail: amiller@atlantic-pub.com
Ed: Heather Lee Shepherd. **Released:** August 2007. **Price:** $21.95. **Description:** Over 100 business ideas are detailed to help stay-at-home parents earn extra money to add to the family income. These businesses can be started with minimum training and investment and most can be easily operated by one person and eventually be sold for an additional profit; many are started with less than one hundred dollars and can be run from home. **Availability:** Print.

42057 ■ *"Road Map To Riches" in Small Business Opportunities (September 2010)*
Pub: Harris Publications Inc.
Description: Profile of Philip Nenadov who launched The Transportation Network Group during the recession. This franchise is low cost and can earn six figures while working from home by becoming a trucking agent.

42058 ■ *Scrapbooking for Profit: Cashing in on Retail, Home-Based and Internet Opportunities*
Pub: Allworth Press
Contact: Tad Crawford, Author
Ed: Rebecca Pittman. **Released:** January 02, 2014. **Price:** $16.95, paperback. **Description:** Eleven strategies for starting a scrapbooking business, including brick-and-mortar stores, home-based businesses, and online retail and wholesale outlets. **Availability:** Print.

42059 ■ *"Selling Groceries & More on Amazon: The Ultimate Home Based Business for Families"*
Pub: Amazon Digital Services
Released: October 16, 2014. **Price:** , $7.99 Kindle. **Description:** Tips for starting an online grocery store from your home are shared. Grocery inventory,

coupons and store promotions, setting up a seller account, application and approval for the grocery category, shipping information, sales techniques and private labeling are all addressed for this family owned type of business.

42060 ■ *"Social Media Bootcamp: How Not To Suck At Social Media"*

Pub: Amazon Digital Services

Released: September 29, 2014. **Price:** , $0.99 Kindle. **Description:** Seven steps to build a social media presence are presented in boot camp style. Whether direct sales, multi-level marketing, online store, or another type of online, home-based startup business, this book give tips for would-be entrepreneurs.

42061 ■ *Start and Run a Home-Based Food Business*

Pub: Self-Counsel Press Inc.

Ed: Mimi Shortland Fix. **Released:** January 10, 2010. **Price:** C$23.95. **Description:** Information is shared to help start and run a home-based food business, selling your own homemade foods.

42062 ■ *Start Your Own Fashion Accessories Business*

Pub: Entrepreneur Press

Contact: Perlman Neil, President

Ed: Eileen Figure Sandlin. **Released:** Second Edition. **Price:** $19.95, paperback. **Description:** Entrepreneurs wishing to start a fashion accessories business will find important information for setting up a home workshop and office, exploring the market, managing finances, publicizing and advertising the business and more. **Availability:** Print.

42063 ■ *"T-Shirt Business: How To Work From Home Starting your Own Online Business In A Popular Teespring Niche!"*

Pub: Amazon Digital Services

Released: September 12, 2014. **Price:** , $5.99. **Description:** Advice is given to launch a T-shirt business without investing a lot of money. Profile of Teespring T-shirts, a company that helps entrepreneurs start a home-based online store, is provided. It teaches how to sell, entice a niche, copyright infringement information, competition, social media marketing and advertising, and more.

42064 ■ *"This Biz Is Booming" in Small Business Opportunities (Winter 2010)*

Pub: Harris Publications Inc.

Description: Non-medical home care is a $52 billion industry. Advice to start a non-medical home care business is provided, focusing on franchise FirstLight HomeCare, but showing that independent home care agencies are also successful.

42065 ■ *Ultimate Homebased Business Handbook: How to Start, Run, and Grow Your Own Profitable Business*

Pub: Entrepreneur Press

Contact: Perlman Neil, President

Ed: James Stephenson. **Released:** June 2008. **Description:** Detailed information for anyone wanting to start a home-based business. Topics include how-to tips, ideas, tools, and print and online resources.

42066 ■ *Work at Home Now: The No-Nonsense Guide to Finding Your Perfect Home-Based Job, Avoiding Scams, and Making a Great Living*

Pub: Career Press Inc.

Contact: Ron Fry, President

Ed: Christine Durst, Michael Haaren. **Released:** November 20, 2009. **Price:** $14.99. **Description:** There are legitimate home-based jobs and projects that can be found on the Internet, but trustworthy guidance is scarce. There is a 58 to 1 scam ratio in work at-home advertising filled with fraud.

42067 ■ *Work@home: A Practical Guide for Women Who Want to Work from Home*

Ed: Glynnis Whitwer. **Released:** March 2007. **Price:** , $15.99. **Description:** Fifty-three percent of all small business are home-based. The book provides tips to women for starting a home-based business.

42068 ■ *"Working From Home: A Guide to Setting Up You Own Work From Home Income: On Your Own Terms with Real Companies"*

Pub: CreateSpace

Contact: Daren Giles, President

Released: October 19, 2014. **Price:** , $8.99 paperback. **Description:** A guide for starting and running a home business is provided.

ASSOCIATIONS AND OTHER ORGANIZATIONS

42069 ■ **American Home Business Association (AHBA)**

53 W 9000 S

Sandy, UT 84070

Ph: (801)273-2350

Free: 866-396-7773

Fax: (866)396-7773

Co. E-mail: info@homebusinessworks.com

URL: http://www.homebusinessworks.com

Description: Offers benefits and services dedicated to supporting the needs of home business, small business and entrepreneurs. Benefits include health-auto-home insurance, legal, low long distance and 800 numbers, business line of credit, merchant accounts, tax programs, office supply and travel discounts and more. Seeks to provide members access to the best traditional benefits and timely information that is critical to conduct a successful home, small or Internet business. **Founded:** 1994. **Publications:** *AHBA Hotline Newsletter* (Bimonthly).

42070 ■ **Canadian Federation of Independent Business (CFIB) [Federation Canadienne de l'Entreprise Independante]**

401-4141 Yonge St.

Toronto, ON, Canada M2P 2A6

Ph: (416)222-8022

Free: 888-234-2232

Fax: (416)222-6103

Co. E-mail: cfib@cfib.ca

URL: http://www.cfib-fcei.ca/english/index.html

Contact: Danny Kelly, President

Description: Independent businesses. Promotes economic well-being of members and seeks to maintain a healthy domestic business climate. Represents members' interests before government agencies, labor and industrial organizations, and the public. **Scope:** entrepreneurship, economic policy, small business, public policy. **Founded:** 1971. **Subscriptions:** 4000 books periodicals reports. **Publications:** *Mandate* (Quarterly); *Quarterly Business Barometer* (3/year).

42071 ■ *Mandate*

401-4141 Yonge St.

Toronto, ON, Canada M2P 2A6

Ph: (416)222-8022

Free: 888-234-2232

Fax: (416)222-6103

Co. E-mail: cfib@cfib.ca

URL: http://www.cfib-fcei.ca/english/index.html

Contact: Danny Kelly, President

Released: Quarterly

42072 ■ **National Association for Business Organizations (NAFBO)**

5432 Price Ave.

Baltimore, MD 21215

Ph: (410)367-5309

Co. E-mail: nahbb@msn.com

URL: http://www.ameribizs.com/global

Contact: Rudolph Lewis, President

Description: Business organizations that develop and support small businesses that have the capability to provide their products or services on a national level. Promotes small business in a free market system; represents the interests of small businesses to government and community organizations on small business affairs; monitors and reviews laws that affect small businesses; promotes a business code of ethics. Supplies members with marketing and management assistance; encourages joint marketing services between members. Operates a Home Based Business Television Network that provides an affordable audio/visual media for small and home based businesses. **Founded:** 1986. **Awards:** Entrepreneur Certificate.

42073 ■ **National Association of Home Based Businesses (NAHBB)**

5432 Price Ave.

Baltimore, MD 21215

Ph: (410)367-5308

Co. E-mail: nahbb@msn.com

URL: http://www.usahomebusiness.com

Contact: Rudolph Lewis, President

Description: Provides support and development services to home-based businesses. Offers business models and franchise development and marketing services. **Founded:** 1984. **Publications:** *National Register of U.S. Home Based Business* (Annual). **Educational Activities:** National Association of Home Based Businesses Convention (Annual); National Home Based Business Convention.

42074 ■ *Quarterly Business Barometer*

401-4141 Yonge St.

Toronto, ON, Canada M2P 2A6

Ph: (416)222-8022

Free: 888-234-2232

Fax: (416)222-6103

Co. E-mail: cfib@cfib.ca

URL: http://www.cfib-fcei.ca/english/index.html

Contact: Danny Kelly, President

URL(s): www.cfib-fcei.ca/english/research/canada/34-business-barometer.html. **Released:** 3/year

REFERENCE WORKS

42075 ■ *The 30-Second Commute*

Pub: McGraw-Hill

Ed: Beverley Williams, Donald Cooper. **Released:** June 22, 2004. **Price:** Rs 1,072.93, Softcover. **Description:** Home-based business owners explain how entrepreneurs can avoid long commutes and high costs of working outside the home by starting a home-based company. Essential steps for launching a successful home-based business are covered, including type of business, legal issues, and writing a business plan. **Availability:** Print.

42076 ■ *"As Traditional Web Site Adoption Slows, Facebook and Other Social Networks Become Key Platforms for Home-Based Business Promotional and Commercial Activity Online"* in Marketing Weekly News (June 16, 2012)

Description: Websites have provided an inexpensive means for businesses to market their products and services. However, home-based businesses are using social networking, email marketing, search engine optimization,, search engine marketing, Website optimization for mobile devices, banner advertisements, and the use of ecommerce platforms such as eBay, Craigs list, and Amazon.

42077 ■ *Being Self-Employed: How to Run a Business Out of Your Home, Claim Travel and Depreciation and Earn a Good Income Well into Your 70s or 80s*

Pub: Allyear Tax Guides

Ed: Holmes F. Crouch, Irma Jean Crouch, Barbara J. MacRae. **Released:** September 2004. **Price:** , $24.95 (US), $37.95 (Canadian). **Description:** Guide for small business to keep accurate tax records.

42078 ■ *Business Know-How: An Operational Guide for Home-Based and Micro-Sized Businesses with Limited Budgets*

Ed: Janet Attard. **Price:** , $17.95.

42079 ■ *Careers for Homebodies & Other Independent Souls*

Pub: McGraw-Hill

Ed: Jan Goldberg. **Released:** August 23, 2010. **Price:** Rs 883.03. **Description:** The books offers insight into choosing the right career for individuals. Jobs range from office to outdoors, job markets, and levels of education requirements. **Availability:** Print.

42080 ■ *"Daddy's Home! Fathers Stay Home To Watch the Kids and Build Businesses To Suit Their Values" in Black Enterprise (October 1, 2007)*
Pub: Earl G. Graves Publishing Co. Inc.
Contact: Earl G. Graves, Jr., President
Ed: George Alexander. **Description:** Fathers are staying home and running home-based businesses in order to spend more time with their families.

42081 ■ *"Family Child Care Record-Keeping Guide, Ninth Edition (Redleaf Business Series)"*
Pub: Redleaf Press
Contact: Linda Hein, Director
E-mail: lhein@redleafpress.org
Released: October 28,, 2014. **Price:** , $17.95 paperback. **Description:** Writer, trainer, lawyer, and consultant provides concise information for home-based family child care (day care) providers. The book covers tracking expenses, being profitable, filing taxes, and meeting government regulations. This resources covers the process of accurate bookkeeping and recordkeeping to take advantage of all allowable tax deductions. Changes in depreciation rules, adjustments to food and mileage rates, and clarifications on how to calculate the Time-Space percentage are defined.

42082 ■ *"Floral-Design Kiosk Business in Colorado Springs Blossoming" in Colorado Springs Business Journal (September 24, 2010)*
Pub: Dolan Media Newswires
Ed: Monica Mendoza. **Description:** Profile of Shellie Greto and her mother Jackie Martin who started a wholesale flower business in their garage. The do-it-yourself floral arrangement firm started a kiosk business in supermarkets called Complete Design.

42083 ■ *Great Tips for Your Small Business: Increase Your Profit and Joy in Your Work*
Pub: Dundurn Press Ltd.
Contact: Kirk Howard, President
Ed: Julie V. Watson. **Released:** September 2006. **Price:** $24.99, paperback; $11.99. **Description:** Tips and hints for home-based, micro, and small businesses are presented. **Availability:** PrintE-book.

42084 ■ *Greater Phoenix Chamber Membership List--Home-Based Businesses*
Pub: Greater Phoenix Chamber of Commerce
Contact: Todd Sanders, President
E-mail: tsanders@phoenixchamber.com
URL(s): www.phoenixchamber.com/. **Price:** $295, Members; $500, Nonmembers. **Covers:** 67 home-based businesses in the greater Phoenix, Arizona area. **Entries include:** Contact details.

42085 ■ *Home Business Tax Deductions: Keep What You Earn*
Pub: Nolo
Contact: Ralph Warner, Chief Executive Officer
Ed: Stephen Fishman. **Released:** November 2013. **Price:** $27.99; $20.99. **Description:** Home business tax deductions are outlined. Basic information on the ways various business structures are taxed and how deductions work is included. **Availability:** PrintE-book.

42086 ■ *Homemade Money: How to Select, Start, Manage, Market and Multiply the Profits of a Business at Home (Home-based +businesses)*
Pub: Rowman and Littlefield Publishers Inc.
Contact: Jason Aronson, President
URL(s): www.rlpgtrade.com. **Released:** Published in two volumes. **Price:** $24.95, Individuals book 1 and 2. **Publication includes:** A special 76 page, updated "A-Z Crash Course" on business basics and a directory of 300 listings. **Entries include:** Supplier name, address, description of information, price, order information. Principal content of the book is editorial matter on beginning and developing a home-based business. **Arrangement:** Classified by subject. **Indexes:** Alphabetical.

42087 ■ *Housecleaning Business: Organize Your Business - Get Clients and Referrals - Set Rates and Services*
Pub: Globe Pequot Press Inc.
Contact: Robert Irwin, Manager
E-mail: robert.irwin@globepequot.com
Ed: Laura Jorstad, Melinda Morse. **Released:** June 24, 2009. **Price:** $18.95, paperback. **Description:** This book shares insight into starting a housecleaning business. It shows how to develop a service manual, screen clients, serve customers, select cleaning products, competition, how to up a home office, using the Internet to grow the business and offering green cleaning options to clients. **Availability:** Print.

42088 ■ *How to Create an Unlimited Income Sitting at Home in Your Pajamas*
Pub: PublishAmerica, Incorporated
Contact: Willem Meiners, Chief Executive Officer
Ed: Michael Klisouris. **Price:** $24.95, Softcover. **Description:** Step-by-step guide for starting, operating and expanding a home-based business is featured. **Availability:** Print.

42089 ■ *"How to Set Up an Effective Home Office" in Women Entrepreneur (August 22, 2008)*
Ed: Laura Stack. **Description:** Checklist provides ways in which one can arrange their home office to provide the greatest efficiency which will allow maximum productivity and as a result the greater the chance of success.

42090 ■ *How to Start a Home-Based Senior Care Business*
Pub: Globe Pequot Press Inc.
Contact: Robert Irwin, Manager
E-mail: robert.irwin@globepequot.com
Ed: James L. Ferry. **Released:** January 06, 2010. **Price:** $18.95, paperback. **Description:** Information is provided to start a home-based senior care business. **Availability:** Print.

42091 ■ *How to Start a Home-Based Writing Business*
Pub: Globe Pequot Press Inc.
Contact: Robert Irwin, Manager
E-mail: robert.irwin@globepequot.com
Ed: Lucy V. Parker. **Released:** Fifth Edition. **Price:** $18.95, Paperback. **Description:** Guide for starting and running a home-based writing business. **Availability:** Print.

42092 ■ *"Independent Contractor, Sole Proprietor, and LLC Taxes Explained in 100 Pages or Less"*
Pub: Simple Subjects LLC
Released: July 28, 2014. **Price:** , $15.00 paperback. **Description:** A small business tax primer which includes information of home office deduction, estimated tax payments, self-employment tax, business retirement plans, numerous business deductions, and audit protection.

42093 ■ *"Is It Time to Move to a Real Office?" in Women Entrepreneur (December 30, 2008)*
Ed: Aliza Sherman. **Description:** Before moving a company from a home-office to a real office it is important to make sure that the additional overhead that will be incurred by the move is comfortably covered and that the move is being done for the right reasons. Several women entrepreneurs who have moved their businesses from their homes to an actual rental space are profiled.

42094 ■ *Make Your Business Survive and Thrive!: 100+ Proven Marketing Methods to Help You Beat the Odds and Build a Successful Small or Home-Based Enterprise*
Pub: John Wiley & Sons Inc.
Contact: Stephen M. Smith, President
Ed: Priscilla Y. Huff. **Released:** November 2006. **Price:** $19.95, paperback; 12.99. **Description:** One hundred proven methods to successfully run a small home-based business are outlined. **Availability:** PrintE-book.

42095 ■ *Make Your Business Survive and Thrive!: 100+ Proven Marketing Methods to Help You Beat the Odds and Build a Successful Small or Home-Based Enterprise*
Pub: John Wiley & Sons Inc.
Contact: Stephen M. Smith, President
Ed: Priscilla Y. Huff. **Released:** November 2006. **Price:** $19.95, paperback; $12.99. **Description:** Small business and entrepreneurial expert gives information to help small and home-based businesses grow. **Availability:** PrintE-book.

42096 ■ *More Than a Pink Cadillac*
Pub: McGraw-Hill
Ed: Jim Underwood. **Released:** January 08, 2003. **Price:** Rs 1,389.43, softcover. **Description:** Profile of Mary Kay Ash who turned her $5,000 investment into a billion-dollar corporation. Ash's nine principles that form the foundation of her company's global success are outlined. Stories from her sales force leaders share ideas for motivating employees, impressing customers and building a successful company. The book emphasizes the leadership skills required to drive performance in any successful enterprise. **Availability:** Print.

42097 ■ *My So-Called Freelance Life: How to Survive and Thrive as a Creative Professional for Hire*
Pub: Seal Press
Contact: Christina Henry de Tessan, Editor
E-mail: christina@avalonpub.com
Ed: Michelle Goodman. **Released:** October 2008. **Price:** $15.95. **Description:** Guidebook for women wishing to start a freelancing business; tips, advice, how-to's and all the information needed to survive working from home are included.

42098 ■ *"A New Single Mom Solution - Women's Home Based Business Training From Industry Leader Rod Stinson" in Investment Weekly News (March 24, 2012, pp. 65)*
Description: The economic downturn has led many women to start their own home based businesses in order to supplement or replace a second income. Issues faced by women wishing to start their own company are given a resource in this article from a 27-year veteran of the home based business industry.

42099 ■ *No Place Like Home: Organizing Home-Based Labor in the Era of Structural Adjustment*
Pub: Routledge
Contact: Kevin Bradley, President
E-mail: kbradley@taylorandfrancis.com
Ed: David Staples. **Released:** 2006. **Price:** $48.95, paperback; $145, hardback. **Description:** The book examines the role of home-based women workers in contemporary capitalism. **Availability:** Print.

42100 ■ *101 Best Home-Based Success Secrets for Women*
Ed: Priscilla Y. Huff. **Released:** 1999.

42101 ■ *"Opportunity Knocks" in Small Business Opportunities (September 2008)*
Description: Profile of YourOffice USA, a franchise that provides home-based and small businesses cost-effective and efficient support through 'virtual' offices that are available as much or as little as the client needs it; they also supply necessary tools such as a professional business address, private mailbox service, personalized telephone answering and more that supports clients who want to look, act and operate with an advanced business image.

42102 ■ *"Remote: Office Not Required"*
Pub: Crown Business
Released: October 31, 2013. **Price:** , $23.00. **Description:** The growing trend in working from home, or anywhere else, and the challenges and benefits from working from home are explored. Technology has enabled one in five global workers to telecommute and about ten percent of employees work from home. Some of the advantages in remote jobs is an increase in the talent pool, reduces turnover, lessens a firm's real estate footprint, and improves the ability to conduct business across time zones.

42103 ■ *"Right at Home China Celebrates 1 Year Anniversary as U.S. In-Home Senior Care Master Franchise" in Professional Service Close-Up (June 24, 2012)*
Description: Franchisor, Right at Home International Inc., provides in-home senior care and assistance and has experienced a one year franchise license agreement in China. Right at Home China predicts growth because China has 200 million adults over 65 years of age.

42104 ■ *Save $2000 to $8000 in Taxes with a Home-Based Business*
Pub: TKG Publishing
Ed: Greco Garcia. **Released:** February 2007. **Price:** , $16.99. **Description:** Tax advice for a home-based business is given.

42105 ■ *Shedworking: The Alternative Workplace Revolution*
Pub: Frances Lincoln Limited
Ed: Alex Johnson. **Released:** June 03, 2010. **Price:** £16.99, paperback. **Description:** Shedworking is an alternative office space for those working at home. The book features shedworkers and shedbuilders from around the world who are leading this alternative workplace revolution and why this trend is working. **Availability:** Print.

42106 ■ *Smart Tax Write-Offs*
Pub: Rayve Productions Inc.
Contact: Norm Ray, President
Ed: Norm Ray. **Released:** Fifth Edition. **Price:** $15. 95, Softcover. **Description:** Guidebook to help small business owners take advantage of legitimate tax deductions for home-based and other entrepreneurial businesses. **Availability:** Print.

42107 ■ *"Teleworkers Confess Biggest At-Home Distractions" in Employee Benefit News (Vol. 25, November 1, 2011, No. 14, pp. 7)*
Pub: SourceMedia Inc.
Contact: James M. Malkin, Chief Executive Officer
Ed: Kelley M. Butler. **Description:** Telecommuting can actually make some workers more efficient and productive versus working inside the office.

42108 ■ *"Tips for Marketing your Business From Home"*
Pub: Amazon Digital Services
Released: October 13, 2014. **Price:** , $2.99 Kindle. **Description:** Steps for marketing a business from home are addressed. This guide offers marketing strategies for home-based businesses.

42109 ■ *The Travel Agent's Complete Desk Reference, 5th Edition*
Pub: Intrepid Traveler
Contact: Kelly Monaghan, Publisher
Ed: Kelly Monaghan. **Released:** August 25, 2009. **Price:** , $39.95. **Description:** Reference book that provides essential information to the home-based travel agent.

42110 ■ *"TW Trade Shows to Offer Seminars On Niche Selling, Social Media" in Travel Weekly (Vol. 69, October 4, 2010, No. 40, pp. 9)*
Pub: NorthStar Travel Media LLC
Contact: Tom Kemp, Chief Executive Officer
Description: Travel Weekly's Leisure World 2010 and Fall Home Based Travel Agent Show focused on niche selling, with emphasis on all-inclusives, young consumers, groups, incentives, culinary vacations, and honeymoon or romance travel.

42111 ■ *"The Ultimate Home Shopping Network" in Austin Business JournalInc. (Vol. 28, October 17, 2008, No. 31, pp. A1)*
Pub: American City Business Journals
Ed: Sandra Zaragoza. **Description:** New York-based Etcetera sells their clothing through more than 850 fashion consultants in the U.S. Central Texas is one of the company's top markets and the company is looking to increase its fashion consultants in the area from five to about 20 since they believe there is plenty of room to expand their customer base in the area.

42112 ■ *"Want to Showoff Your Nonprofit or Home-Based Business? Showcase Offers Opportunity" in America's Intelligence Wire (January 15, 2012)*
Description: Nonprofits and home-based business owners can set up a booth to market their organizations at the Las Cruces Showcase in New Mexico. Details of the convention are given.

42113 ■ *What Losing Taught Me about Winning: The Ultimate Guide for Success in Small and Home-Based Business*
Pub: Simon & Schuster Adult Publishing Group
Contact: Carolyn Reidy, President
E-mail: carolyn.reidy@simonandschuster.com
Ed: Fran Tarkenton, Wes Smith. **Released:** April 1999. **Price:** $17.95, paperback. **Description:** Provides insight into running a successful small business.

42114 ■ *Work From Home Jobs Directory*
Pub: Lulu.com
Ed: Debra Mundell. **Released:** September 30, 2011. **Price:** $7; $23.10, paperback. **Description:** Resources for starting and growing a home-based business are listed. **Availability:** E-book; PDFPrint.

42115 ■ *Working for Yourself: Law & Taxes for Independent Contractors, Freelancers & Consultants*
Pub: NOLO Publications
Ed: Stephen Fishman. **Released:** February 2014. **Price:** $34.99; $27.99. **Description:** In-depth information is shared for contractors, freelancers and consultants involving business law and small business taxes. **Availability:** PrintE-book.

TRADE PERIODICALS

42116 ■ *At-Home Dad*
Pub: Peter Baylies
Contact: Peter Baylies, Editor
URL(s): www.angelfire.com/zine2/athomedad/index. blog. **Released:** Monthly. **Price:** $14.95 U.S.; $18, Canada; $24, elsewhere. **Description:** Promotes the concept of fathers staying home to raise the children. Includes stories from at-home-dads, home business stories, recipes, lists of resources, and playgroups to join. Recurring features include letters to the editor, interviews, news of research, book reviews, notices of publications available, and a column titled Dr. Bob.

42117 ■ *Home-Based Working Moms*
Pub: Home-Based Working Moms
Contact: Lesley Spencer Pyle, President
E-mail: lesley.pyle@hbwm.com
Ed: Lesley Spencer, Editor, lesley@hbwm.com. **Released:** Monthly. **Price:** $49; $54, Canada; $65, other countries. **Description:** Directed toward parents working at home and those interested in doing so. Designed to provide support, networking, and information related to working at home with children. Recurring features include interviews, job listings, marketing tips, and a column titled Home Business Ideas.

42118 ■ *Our Place*
Pub: Home-Based Working Moms
Contact: Lesley Spencer Pyle, President
E-mail: lesley.pyle@hbwm.com
Ed: Lesley Spencer, Editor, lesley@hbwm.com. **Released:** 10/year; Biweekly, 10/year. **Price:** $49, U.S.; $54, Canada; $65, elsewhere. **Description:** Advocates home employment and home businesses to allow parents more time with their children. Offers ideas, marketing tips, member profiles to promote successful employment at home. Recurring features include interviews, job listings, and book reviews.

VIDEOCASSETTES/ AUDIOCASSETTES

42119 ■ *Alternate Work Sites: At Home, at Work*
Encyclopedia Britannica
331 N La Salle St.
Chicago, IL 60654

Ph: (312)347-7000
Free: 800-323-1229
Fax: (312)294-2104
URL: http://www.corporate.britannica.com
Contact: Jacob E. Safra
Released: 1988. **Price:** $395. **Description:** This film features Control Data Corporation of Minneapolis and workers in an Alpine Swiss village showing how to create a work site. **Availability:** VHS; 3/4 U.

42120 ■ *American Institute of Small Business: Setting Up a Home-Based Business*
American Institute of Small Business (AISB)
23075 Hwy. 7, Ste. 200
Shorewood, MN 55331-3168
Ph: (952)545-7001
Free: 800-328-2906
Fax: (952)545-7020
Co. E-mail: info@aisb.biz
URL: http://www.aisb.biz
Contact: Kris Solie-Johnson, President
E-mail: kris@aisb.biz
Released: 199?. **Price:** $69.95. **Description:** Step-by-step guide to operating a business out of your home. **Availability:** VHS.

42121 ■ *Inc. Magazine Business Success Programs*
Films Media Group of Cos.
132 W 31st St., 17th Fl.
New York, NY 10001-3406
Ph: (609)671-1000
Free: 800-257-5126
Fax: (609)671-0266
Co. E-mail: custserv@films.com
URL: http://www.cambridgeeducational.com
Contact: David Waldherr, President
Released: 1987. **Price:** $99.95. **Description:** These four programs contain a step-by-step explanation of what must be done to succeed in business. **Availability:** VHS; CC.

TRADE SHOWS AND CONVENTIONS

42122 ■ *National Association of Home Based Businesses Convention*
National Association of Home Based Businesses (NAHBB)
5432 Price Ave.
Baltimore, MD 21215
Ph: (410)367-5308
Co. E-mail: nahbb@msn.com
URL: http://www.usahomebusiness.com
Contact: Rudolph Lewis, President
URL(s): www.usahomebusiness.com. **Frequency:** Annual. **Audience:** Industry professionals. **Principal Exhibits:** Home based business products and services, support associations, trade supplies, and related equipment. **Dates and Locations:** 2015; venue not reported.

CONSULTANTS

42123 ■ *Joanne H. Pratt Associates*
3520 Routh St.
Dallas, TX 75219-4730
Ph: (214)528-6540
Fax: (214)528-5730
Co. E-mail: joannepratt@post.harvard.edu
Contact: John A. Davis, Manager
Scope: Performs market research and advising on the virtual office, including telecommuting and home based businesses. Helps organizations implement teleworking and telecommuting. Recent emphasis on related topics such as e commerce and personnel productivity. Also helps employees obtain permission to telework. Serves private industries as well as government agencies worldwide. **Founded:** 1981. **Publications:** "The Impact of Location on Net Income: A Comparison of Home based and Non-home based Sole Proprietors," 2006; "Telework: The Latest Figures and what they Mean," 2005; "Teleworking Comes of Age with Broadband," Apr, 2003; "Telework Trends in the United States," 2003; "Strate-

gies for Small Business Success," 2002; "Teleworkers, Trips and Telecommunications: Technology drives telework-but does it reduce trips?," 2002; "Telework and Society-Implications for Corporate and Societal Cultures, in Telework: The New Workplace of the 21st Century," Oct, 2000. **Seminars:** The Connected Home: Paradise or Poison; Equipping for Telework Success; Myths and Realities of Working at Home; Using Telemanagement to Increase Staff Productivity; Meet Your Home Office Customers; Telecommuting: What is it? Will it Work for Me?; Telemanaging a Remote Workforce.

FRANCHISES AND BUSINESS OPPORTUNITIES

42124 ■ CMIT Solutions
500 N Capital of TX Hwy., Bldg. 6, Ste. 200
Austin, TX 78746
Free: 800-710-2648
URL: http://www.cmitsolutions.com
Description: Offers IT service and computer support to small businesses. Franchise can be home-based, as we service the client at their place of business. **No. of Franchise Units:** 137. **Founded:** 1994. **Franchised:** 1998. **Equity Capital Needed:** $124,800-$150,950 total investment. **Franchise Fee:** $49,500. **Royalty Fee:** 6%. **Financial Assistance:** Limited third party financing available. **Training:** Offers 3 weeks training at headquarters, 1 week onsite with ongoing support.

42125 ■ Crock A Doodle
299 Wayne Gretzy Pkwy.
Brantford, ON, Canada N3R 8A5
Ph: (519)752-8080
URL: http://www.imaginelovingwhatyoudo.com
Description: Provides a variety of pottery painting events and activities for groups of all kinds. For women, we offer a calendar full of pottery-painting workshops and classes, as well as creative activities for girls' nights, bridal showers and special occasions. For children, we offer birthday parties, seasonal events and pottery-painting classes, as well as creative programming for camps, schools, teams and groups. The opportunity extends throughout the community to corporate team builders, fundraisers and community events of all kinds. **No. of Franchise Units:** 10. **No. of Company-Owned Units:** 2. **Founded:** 2002. **Franchised:** 2004. **Equity Capital Needed:** Total investment from $75,000. **Franchise Fee:** $20,000. **Training:** Provides 2 weeks plus ongoing support.

42126 ■ DEI Sales Ltd.
PO Box 30169
Cincinnati, OH 45230
Ph: (212)581-7390
Free: 800-224-2140
Co. E-mail: info@dei-sales.com
URL: http://www.dei-sales.com
Description: Sales training industry. **No. of Franchise Units:** 32. **No. of Company-Owned Units:** 1. **Founded:** 1979. **Franchised:** 2003. **Equity Capital Needed:** $60,000-$75,000. **Franchise Fee:** $50,000. **Royalty Fee:** 7%. **Training:** Offers 2 weeks home-based training and 2 weeks at headquarters with ongoing support.

42127 ■ DNA Services of America
130 Fifth Ave., 10th Fl.
New York, NY 10011-4399
Ph: (212)242-4399
Description: Own a high-demand, innovative business that serves the growing needs of Americans by offering members of your community peace of mind through evidence provided by DNA identification test results for paternity, family relationship establishment, infidelity testing and forensic DNA. **Equity Capital Needed:** $49,175-$97,100 total investment. **Training:** Offers a complete, proven business system, ongoing support, and thorough training.

42128 ■ Home Video Studio
118 N Salem St.
Apex, NC 27502

Free: 866-831-0436
Co. E-mail: peter.g@homevideostudio.com
URL: http://www.homevideostudio.com
Description: Home based video studio. **No. of Franchise Units:** 70. **No. of Company-Owned Units:** 2. **No. of Operating Units:** 75. **Founded:** 1991. **Franchised:** 2006. **Equity Capital Needed:** $69,050-$97,300. **Franchise Fee:** $25,000. **Royalty Fee:** 7%. **Financial Assistance:** Limited third party financing available. **Training:** Yes.

42129 ■ Interiors by Decorating Den
8659 Commerce Dr.
Easton, MD 21601
Free: 800-332-3367
URL: http://www.decoratingden.com
Description: Interiors by Decorating is one of the oldest, international, shop-at-home interior decorating franchises in the world. Our company-trained interior decorators bring 1000's of samples including window coverings, wall coverings, floor coverings, furniture and accessories to their customer's home in our uniquely equipped ColorVan. Special business features include: home-based, marketing systems, business systems, training, support, and complete sampling. **No. of Franchise Units:** 501. **Founded:** 1969. **Franchised:** 1970. **Equity Capital Needed:** $25,000. **Franchise Fee:** $29,900. **Training:** Training combines classroom work, home study, meetings, seminars and on-the-job experience including working with an experienced interior decorator. Secondary, advanced and graduate certification training continue throughout the franchise owner's career with Interiors by Decorating Den.

42130 ■ The LiceSquad Inc.
Lice Squad Canada Inc.
3A King St.
Cookstown, ON, Canada L0L 1L0
Free: 888-542-3778
Fax: (705)458-8887
URL: http://www.licesquad.com
Description: Join Canada's leading head lice removal and Education Company. Low start up costs and proven potential. Perfect for those in the nursing, hairdressing and child care fields. Our clients include schools, families, camps and other child care organizations. Our home-based business model allows flexibility. Enjoy both family and career. 15 successful LiceSquad franchises operating in Ontario with master franchises available. **No. of Franchise Units:** 9. **No. of Company-Owned Units:** 20. **Founded:** 2001. **Franchised:** 2002. **Equity Capital Needed:** $42,000-$85,000 investment required; start-up capital required $25,000-$35,000. **Franchise Fee:** $20,000. **Training:** Provides training (excluding travel/hotel costs).

42131 ■ Liquid Capital Canada Corp.
5734 Yonge St., Ste. 400
Toronto, ON, Canada M2M 4E7
Ph: (416)222-5599
Free: 877-228-0800
Fax: (416)222-0166
URL: http://www.lcfranchise.com
URL(s): liquidcapitalcorp.com. **Description:** Operation of home-based B2B providing account receivable financing to small business. **No. of Franchise Units:** 27. **No. of Company-Owned Units:** 1. **Founded:** 1999. **Franchised:** 2000. **Equity Capital Needed:** $200,000. **Franchise Fee:** $50,000. **Training:** Yes.

42132 ■ On Track Power Window Repair
On Track Franchising, LLC
4616 Popular Level Rd.
Louisville, KY 40213
Ph: (502)777-0114
Fax: (502)962-6250
Co. E-mail: john@ontrackrepair.com
URL: http://www.OnTrackRepair.com
Description: Power window repair. This is virtually an untapped multi-billion dollar market. There is a continuous supply of window systems to repair. **No. of Company-Owned Units:** 1. **Founded:** 2002. **Franchised:** 2007. **Equity Capital Needed:** $64,200-$77,900. **Franchise Fee:** $32,000. **Royalty Fee:** 7%.

Training: Provides 2 weeks hands on training and in depth technical instruction as it relates to power and manual window, door locks, mirrors, latches and door handles.

42133 ■ The Original Basket Boutique
363 Sioux Rd., Ste. 140
Sherwood Park, AB, Canada T8A 4W7
Ph: (780)416-2530
Free: 877-622-8008
Co. E-mail: info@originalbasketboutique.com
URL: http://www.originalbasketboutique.com
Description: The Original Basket Boutique, Canada's exclusive custom gift basket franchise. **No. of Franchise Units:** 26. **No. of Operating Units:** 38. **Founded:** 1989. **Franchised:** 1989. **Equity Capital Needed:** $47,500-$59,000. **Franchise Fee:** $35,000. **Royalty Fee:** $225/month. **Financial Assistance:** Financial assistance available with franchise fee. **Training:** Offers 3-4 days training at headquarters with ongoing support.

42134 ■ Padgett Business Services
3100 boul le Carrefour, Ste. 554
Laval, QC, Canada H7T 2K7
Ph: (888)723-4388
Fax: (877)231-4911
URL: http://www.padgetfranchises.ca
Description: Supplier of small business services including accounting, tax preparation and consultation, payroll services and business advice. **No. of Franchise Units:** 120. **Founded:** 1966. **Franchised:** 1975. **Equity Capital Needed:** $40,000-$48,000 investment required; $30,000-$50,000 start-up capital required. **Franchise Fee:** $25,000. **Training:** Complete program of training and support.

42135 ■ Par-T-Perfect Party Planners
T-20 Bowen Bay Rd.
Bowen Island, BC, Canada V0N 1G0
Ph: (604)947-0274
Co. E-mail: info@par-t-perfect.com
URL: http://www.par-t-perfect.com
Contact: Michelle Gibson, Founder
Description: Par-T-Perfect is a unique children's party and event service. A great home-based business opportunity!. **No. of Franchise Units:** 21. **No. of Company-Owned Units:** 2. **Founded:** 1988. **Franchised:** 2001. **Equity Capital Needed:** $10,000-$20,000 including franchise fee. **Franchise Fee:** $15,000-$24,500. **Training:** 2 weeks and ongoing.

42136 ■ Suburban Cylinder Express
Suburban Franchising, Inc.
240 Rte. 10 W
Whippany, NJ 07981
Free: 866-218-7026
URL: http://www.suburbancylinderexpress.com
Description: The franchise is a home-based business opportunity center. It provides propane cylinders to residential and commercial customers. **No. of Company-Owned Units:** 21. **Founded:** 2001. **Franchised:** 2002. **Equity Capital Needed:** $63,450-$123,200. **Franchise Fee:** $34,900. **Training:** Provides initial start-up training, ongoing business consultation, customized business software, scheduling and route optimization software, national phone customer sales center, technology help desk, a consumer website, brochures, flyers, coupons and other direct mail and mass marketing tools and materials.

42137 ■ Travel Lines Express Franchise Group
9858 Glades Rd.
Boca Raton, FL 33434
Ph: (561)482-9557
Description: Full service home based travel agency. **No. of Franchise Units:** 50. **No. of Company-Owned Units:** 1. **Founded:** 1980. **Franchised:** 2003. **Equity Capital Needed:** $1,000-$3,000. **Franchise Fee:** $300. **Training:** Yes.

42138 ■ Two Blonds & A Brunette Gift Co.
201 Park Pl. E
Winnipeg, MB, Canada R3P 2E4
Ph: (204)488-2779
URL: http://www.twobandb.com
Contact: Alana Gunn, Contact
E-mail: alanagunn@twobandb.com

Description: Initial home-based gift-giving business. **No. of Franchise Units:** 10. **Founded:** 2002. **Franchised:** 2006. **Equity Capital Needed:** Franchise fee plus $1,000 set-up fee. **Franchise Fee:** $15,000 plus, includes inventory, training, and materials. **Training:** 3 days; airfare and hotel paid.

ASSOCIATIONS AND OTHER ORGANIZATIONS

42139 ■ ASTD - Information Center [American Society for Training and Development]
1640 King St.
Alexandria, VA 22314-2746
Ph: (703)683-8100
Free: 800-628-2783
Fax: (703)683-1523
Co. E-mail: customercare@astd.org
URL: http://www.astd.org
Contact: Tony Bingham, President
E-mail: tbingham@astd.org
Description: Represents workplace learning and performance professionals. **Scope:** training and development, workplace performance. **Services:** Library open to national members of the Society. **Founded:** 1943. **Holdings:** 3000 bound volumes. **Publications:** *ASTD Buyer's Guide* (Annual); *ASTD Buyer's Guide* (Annual); *Member Information Exchange (MIX)*; *TRAINET*; *ATD Buyer's Guide* (Annual); *Buyer's Guide & Consultant Directory*; *American Society for Training and Development--Training Video Directory*; *ASTD Buyer's Guide and Consultants Directory*; *Who's Who in Training and Development* (Annual); *ASTD Buyer's Guide and Consultants Directory*; *American Society Training and Development Buyer's Guide and Consultant Directory* (Annual); *Technical Training: Learning Technology for Performance Improvement*; *ASTD Buyer's Guide & Consultant Directory* (Annual); *TD at Work* (Monthly); *Learning Circuits* (Monthly); *T and D Magazine*; *TD Magazine* (Monthly). **Educational Activities:** International Exposition (Annual); American Society for Training and Development Conference (Annual); TechKnowledge Conference and Exposition (Annual). **Awards:** ASTD BEST Award; Excellence in Practice; Awards in the Advancing Workplace Learning and Performance; Gordon M. Bliss Memorial Award; Dissertation Award; Distinguished Contribution Award; Torch Award.

42140 ■ *Canadian Learning Journal*
720 Spadina Ave., Ste. 315
Toronto, ON, Canada M5S 2T9
Ph: (416)367-5900
Free: 866-257-4275
Fax: (416)367-1642
URL: http://www.cstd.ca
Contact: Isabel Feher Watters, Vice President
E-mail: ifeher-watters@cstd.ca
Released: Semiannual **Price:** included in membership dues.

42141 ■ Canadian Society for Training and Development (CSTD) [Societe Canadienne pour la Formation et le Perfectionnement]
720 Spadina Ave., Ste. 315
Toronto, ON, Canada M5S 2T9
Ph: (416)367-5900
Free: 866-257-4275

Fax: (416)367-1642
URL: http://www.cstd.ca
Contact: Isabel Feher Watters, Vice President
E-mail: ifeher-watters@cstd.ca
Description: Works for the profession of training, workplace learning and human resources development. **Founded:** 2003. **Publications:** *Canadian Learning Journal* (Semiannual). **Awards:** President's Award; Volunteer Recognition Award (Annual); President's Award (Annual); Volunteer Award (Annual).

42142 ■ HR People and Strategy (HRPS)
1800 Duke St.
Alexandria, VA 22314
Free: 888-602-3270
Fax: (703)535-6490
Co. E-mail: info@hrps.org
URL: http://www.hrps.org
Contact: Kevin Rubens, Director
Description: Human resource planning professionals representing 160 corporations and 3,000 individual members, including strategic human resources planning and development specialists, staffing analysts, business planners, line managers, and others who function as business partners in the application of strategic human resource management practices. Seeks to increase the impact of human resource planning and management on business and organizational performance. Sponsors program of professional development in human resource planning concepts, techniques, and practices. Offers networking opportunities. **Founded:** 1977. **Publications:** *Human Resource Planning*; *People and Strategy* (Quarterly); *Human Resource Planning Society--Membership Directory* (Annual); *People & Strategy* (Quarterly).

42143 ■ Human Resources Research Organization (HumRRO) - Van Evera Library [HumRRO]
66 Canal Center Plz., Ste. 700
Alexandria, VA 22314-1578
Ph: (703)549-3611
Fax: (703)548-5574
URL: http://www.humrro.org
Contact: William J. Strickland, President
Description: Behavioral and social science researchers seeking to improve human performance, particularly in organizational settings, through behavioral and social science research, development, consultation and instruction. Promotes research and development to solve specific problems in: training and education; development, refinement, and instruction in the technology of training and education; studies and development of techniques to improve the motivation of personnel in training and on the job; research of leadership and management, and development of leadership programs; criterion development, individual assessment, and program evaluation in training and operating systems; measurement and evaluation of human performance under varying circumstances; organizational development studies, including performance counseling, group decision-making, and factors that affect organizational competence; development of manpower information systems and the application of management science on

personnel systems. Encourages use of high technology for instructional purposes by means of computer assisted instruction, interactive video, and computer literacy. Offers technical publication services including data analysis and editorial, word processing, production, and printing services. **Scope:** An independent, nonprofit corporation which strives to improve human performance (primarily in organizational settings) through behavioral and social science research, product development, consultation, and instruction. Active in the fields of education and training, testing and assessment, survey research, program evaluation, and human factors engineering. **Services:** Interlibrary loan; copying (limited); Library open to the public by appointment. **Founded:** 1951. **Holdings:** 1500 books; 220 bound periodical volumes; 5000 technical reports. **Subscriptions:** 25 journals and other serials. **Awards:** Meredith P. Crawford Fellowships in I/O Psychology; Meredith P. Crawford Fellowship in I/O Psychology (Annual); Meredith Crawford Fellowship for Industrial and Organizational Psychology (Annual), Scholarship to graduate students in Industrial and Organizational Psychology for completing dissertations. **Seminars:** An examination of the properties of local dependence measures when applied to adaptive data, Computing and communicating test accuracy for high-stakes decisions, Development of cross-cultural perspective taking skills, Developing, implementing, and scoring valid job simulations, Executive and senior leader development: A best practices review, Integrating reliability and validity based perspectives on error in performance ratings, Job incumbent perceptions of faking on noncognitive inventories, Modeling the psychometric properties of multisource ratings: CFA vs. GLMM, Performance level descriptions: Similarities and differences among select states, Reducing bias through propensity scoring: A study of SAT coaching, Retaining personality measures after failure: Changes in scores and strategies, Review of information and communication technology literacy measures, Self-presentation on personality measures: A meta-analysis, Using cases as a proxy for experience in leadership development, Using patterns to understand the dynamics of leader behavior, Verification testing in unproctored internet testing programs, A cross-cultural look at items of logic-based reasoning, An overlooked problem with standard practices for analyzing ratings data from ill-structured measurement designs, Context effects in internet testing: A literature review, Differentiating in the Upper Tail: Selecting Among High-Scoring Applicants, Gaining insight into situational judgment test functioning via spline regression, Ill-Structured measurement designs and reliability: The tale of a HumRRO IR&D project, Influence of subject matter expert (SME) personality on job analysis ratings, Modeling intraindividual change in soldiers attitudes and values during the first term of enlistment SES and admissions test validity: Within race analyses, The Feasibility of using O NET to study skill changes, Validation of a person organization personality hybrid measure, Validating psychological screening examinations and background investigations for applicant screening.

42144 ■ International Personnel Management Association - Canada (IPMA) [L'Association

internationale de la gestion du personnel - Canada]
20 Edwards Pl.
Mount Pearl, NL, Canada A1N 3V5
Free: 888-226-5002
Co. E-mail: national@ipma-aigp.ca
URL: http://ipma-aigp.ca
Contact: Carol Hopkins, Executive Director
Description: Human resources professionals employed by public agencies. Seeks to advance the practice of personnel management. Facilitates ongoing professional development of members; sponsors research and educational programs. **Awards:** Gold Star Agency Award (Annual).

42145 ■ Public Risk Management Association (PRIMA) - Library
700 S Washington St., Ste. 218
Alexandria, VA 22314
Ph: (703)528-7701
Fax: (703)739-0200
Co. E-mail: info@primacentral.org
URL: http://www.primacentral.org
Contact: Marshall Davies, Executive Director
Description: Public agency risk, insurance, human resources, attorneys, and/or safety managers from cities, counties, villages, towns, school boards, and other related areas. Provides an information clearinghouse and communications network for public risk managers to share resources, ideas, and experiences. Offers information on risk, insurance, and safety management. Monitors state and federal legislative actions and court decisions that deal with immunity, tort liability, and intergovernmental risk pools. Maintains library containing current reports from governmental units on their insurance procedures, self-insurance plans, and loss control and safety programs; and copies of policy statements, job descriptions, contractual arrangements, and indemnification clauses. **Scope:** risk management, public health and safety, varied RFPs, job descriptions. **Founded:** 1978. **Holdings:** 3000 business records, papers, reports, and video recordings. **Publications:** *Public Risk* (Monthly); *PRIMA Public Risk* (10/year). **Educational Activities:** Annual Conference for Public Agencies (Annual); Government Risk Management Seminar (Annual). **Awards:** Outstanding Achievement Awards (Annual); Public Risk Manager of the Year Award (Annual); Public Sector Risk Manager of the Year (Annual).

EDUCATIONAL PROGRAMS

42146 ■ Advanced Diversity Strategies (Onsite)
Seminar Information Service Inc.
20 Executive Park, Ste. 120
Irvine, CA 92614
Ph: (949)261-9104
Free: 877-SEM-INFO
Fax: (949)261-1963
Co. E-mail: info@seminarinformation.com
URL: http://www.seminarinformation.com
Price: $1,495. **Description:** Covers the fundamentals of carrying out an evaluation and the acknowledging and rewarding progress, including best practices for senior managers, line managers, and employees. **Audience:** HR and EEO/AA, diversity managers.

42147 ■ Advanced Employee Complaint Handling (Onsite)
Seminar Information Service Inc.
20 Executive Park, Ste. 120
Irvine, CA 92614
Ph: (949)261-9104
Free: 877-SEM-INFO
Fax: (949)261-1963
Co. E-mail: info@seminarinformation.com
URL: http://www.seminarinformation.com
URL(s): www.seminarinformation.com/details. cfm?qc=qqayrp. **Price:** $1,595. **Description:** Advanced skills needed to handle complex employee internal complaints and investigations. **Audience:** Professionals.

42148 ■ Advanced Issues in EEO Law
Seminar Information Service Inc.
20 Executive Park, Ste. 120
Irvine, CA 92614
Ph: (949)261-9104
Free: 877-SEM-INFO
Fax: (949)261-1963
Co. E-mail: info@seminarinformation.com
URL: http://www.seminarinformation.com
URL(s): www.seminarinformation.com/qqanjm/human-resources-and-the-law. **Price:** $1,195. **Description:** Interactive workshop provides advanced skills needed to identify and address more complex issues in Equal Opportunity Law and procedure. **Audience:** HR managers and professionals.

42149 ■ Affirmative Action Plan Workshop (Onsite)
Seminar Information Service Inc.
20 Executive Park, Ste. 120
Irvine, CA 92614
Ph: (949)261-9104
Free: 877-SEM-INFO
Fax: (949)261-1963
Co. E-mail: info@seminarinformation.com
URL: http://www.seminarinformation.com
URL(s): www.seminarinformation.com/details. cfm?qc=qqblfb. **Price:** $1,050. **Description:** Learn how to write an affirmative action plan, including the preparation statistical analysis. **Audience:** Industry professionals.

42150 ■ Applying Diversity Management to Innovation, Decision Making, Complex Problem Solving and Business Results (Onsite)
Seminar Information Service Inc.
20 Executive Park, Ste. 120
Irvine, CA 92614
Ph: (949)261-9104
Free: 877-SEM-INFO
Fax: (949)261-1963
Co. E-mail: info@seminarinformation.com
URL: http://www.seminarinformation.com
Price: $995.00. **Description:** Learn to look at diversity to create value and results versus recruiting and retention, including how to determine "true diversity" based on perspectives, interpretations, and predictive models, how to use diversity as a trigger for innovation, and examples of how diversity produces performance, productivity, creativity, quality decisions, and commercial value.

42151 ■ Bob Pike's Train-the-Trainer Boot Camp (Onsite)
Seminar Information Service Inc.
20 Executive Park, Ste. 120
Irvine, CA 92614
Ph: (949)261-9104
Free: 877-SEM-INFO
Fax: (949)261-1963
Co. E-mail: info@seminarinformation.com
URL: http://www.seminarinformation.com
URL(s): www.seminarinformation.com/details. cfm?qc=qqadlf. **Price:** $1,495. **Description:** Gives you the powerful high content, high involvement skills you'll need to add new energy and excitement to your own training sessions. **Audience:** Human resource development/organizational development personnel, private sector suppliers and presenters of seminars, conferences, and workshops.

42152 ■ The Complete Course on Interviewing People (Onsite)
Padgett-Thompson Seminars
Rockhurst University CEC
14502 W 105th St.
Lenexa, KS 66215
Free: 800-349-1935
URL: http://www.findaseminar.com/tpd/Padgett-Thompson-Seminars.asp
URL(s): www.findaseminar.com/event1.asp?eventID=8234. **Description:** A one-day seminar that teaches insider techniques for going beyond the basics to master the art of interviewing people. **Audience:** Professional.

42153 ■ Creative Problem Solving and Strategic Thinking (Onsite)
Fred Pryor Seminars & CareerTrack
5700 Broadmoor St., Ste. 300
Mission, KS 66202
Ph: (800)780-8476
Free: 800-780-8476
Fax: (913)967-8849
Co. E-mail: customerservice@pryor.com
URL: http://www.pryor.com
Contact: Phil Love, Chief Executive Officer
URL(s): www.pryor.com/mkt_info/seminars/desc/PU. asp. **Price:** $149, 139 for five or more. **Description:** Learn to think beyond traditional thinking patterns and behaviors gaining a new set of skills for developing strategies that generate results. **Audience:** Professionals.

42154 ■ The Essentials of HR Law
Fred Pryor Seminars & CareerTrack
5700 Broadmoor St., Ste. 300
Mission, KS 66202
Ph: (800)780-8476
Free: 800-780-8476
Fax: (913)967-8849
Co. E-mail: customerservice@pryor.com
URL: http://www.pryor.com
Contact: Phil Love, Chief Executive Officer
URL(s): www.pryor.com/mkt_info/seminars/desc/HL. asp. **Price:** $249. **Description:** Learn what you need to know to handle the legal issues and gray areas you face every day keeping your organization compliant. **Audience:** HR professionals.

42155 ■ The Essentials of Human Resources Law (Onsite)
Fred Pryor Seminars & CareerTrack
5700 Broadmoor St., Ste. 300
Mission, KS 66202
Ph: (800)780-8476
Free: 800-780-8476
Fax: (913)967-8849
Co. E-mail: customerservice@pryor.com
URL: http://www.pryor.com
Contact: Phil Love, Chief Executive Officer
Description: How to keep your organization legally sound and compliant while learning how to think like a lawyer, so you can anticipate problems before they arise. **Audience:** Industry professionals.

42156 ■ Essentials for Personnel and HR Assistants (Onsite)
Padgett-Thompson Seminars
Rockhurst University CEC
14502 W 105th St.
Lenexa, KS 66215
Free: 800-349-1935
URL: http://www.findaseminar.com/tpd/Padgett-Thompson-Seminars.asp
URL(s): www.findaseminar.com/event1.asp?eventID=1750. **Description:** A one-day seminar that covers the important trends and changes facing HR professionals today. **Audience:** Human resource personnel.

42157 ■ FMLA Compliance (Onsite)
Padgett-Thompson Seminars
Rockhurst University CEC
14502 W 105th St.
Lenexa, KS 66215
Free: 800-349-1935
URL: http://www.findaseminar.com/tpd/Padgett-Thompson-Seminars.asp
URL(s): www.findaseminar.com/HUMAN-RESOURCES-MANAGEMENT-Training/FMLA-Compliance-Update-Seminar-by-National-Seminars-Train ing-Group/7604.html?filter=ON&city=TOPEKA&state=KS&category=HUMAN-RESOURCES-MANAGEMENT. **Price:** $249. **Description:** Seminar covers the top five issues that land companies in the courtroom over FMLA disputes. **Audience:** Human resource and benefits professionals, business managers, office managers, administrators, directors, payroll professionals, attorneys, supervisors, and managers.

42158 ■ Fundamentals of Employee Benefits (Onsite)
Seminar Information Service Inc.
20 Executive Park, Ste. 120
Irvine, CA 92614
Ph: (949)261-9104
Free: 877-SEM-INFO
Fax: (949)261-1963
Co. E-mail: info@seminarinformation.com
URL: http://www.seminarinformation.com
Price: $1,395.00. **Description:** Course will provide a comprehensive overview of the full-range of benefits responsibilities, as well as an in-depth look at the key aspects of benefits, alternatives for your organization and approaches for containing costs.

42159 ■ Fundamentals of Human Resources Management
Canadian Management Centre (CMC)
150 York St., 5th Fl.
Toronto, ON, Canada M5H 3S5
Free: 877-262-2519
Fax: (416)214-6047
Co. E-mail: cmcinfo@cmcoutperform.com
URL: http://cmcoutperform.com
Contact: John Wright, President
URL(s): www.cmctraining.org/fundamentals-human-resource-management. **Price:** C$2,195, Members; C$2,395, Non-members. **Description:** Covers HR planning and administration, staffing, training, technology, compensation, and legal issues. **Audience:** Non-human resource professionals,, managers and hr specialists. **Dates and Locations:** 2015 Mar 11-13; venue not reported. **Telecommunication Services:** cmcinfo@cmctraining.org.

42160 ■ HR Administration and the Law (Onsite)
Seminar Information Service Inc.
20 Executive Park, Ste. 120
Irvine, CA 92614
Ph: (949)261-9104
Free: 877-SEM-INFO
Fax: (949)261-1963
Co. E-mail: info@seminarinformation.com
URL: http://www.seminarinformation.com
Price: $370, Non-members; $275, Members MRA. **Description:** Offers practical compliance suggestions for the most common employment law-related issues faced today. **Audience:** Professionals responsible for the HR function. **Dates and Locations:** Waukesha, WI; and Palatine, IL.

42161 ■ Human Resources for Anyone with Newly Assigned HR Responsibilities (Onsite)
Fred Pryor Seminars & CareerTrack
5700 Broadmoor St., Ste. 300
Mission, KS 66202
Ph: (800)780-8476
Free: 800-780-8476
Fax: (913)967-8849
Co. E-mail: customerservice@pryor.com
URL: http://www.pryor.com
Contact: Phil Love, Chief Executive Officer
URL(s): www.pryor.com/mkt_info/seminars/desc/hn.asp. **Price:** $149. **Description:** A comprehensive primer on all the issues including recordkeeping, hiring, firing, discrimination, and more. **Audience:** HR professionals.

42162 ■ Human Resources and the Law (Onsite)
Seminar Information Service Inc.
20 Executive Park, Ste. 120
Irvine, CA 92614
Ph: (949)261-9104
Free: 877-SEM-INFO
Fax: (949)261-1963
Co. E-mail: info@seminarinformation.com
URL: http://www.seminarinformation.com
Price: $1,995. **Description:** Provides the human resources professional with an understanding of the laws that obligate employers, recent legislation and court cases defining employer/employee rights and obligations, legal and business considerations bearing on employer decisions, practical implications of the laws in day-to-day human resources operations, impact of the laws on the development of policies

and procedures, and alternatives for minimizing the company's exposure to employee lawsuits and administrative charges. **Audience:** Human resources professionals. **Dates and Locations:** 2015 Mar 02-04; venue not reported.

42163 ■ Human Resources for Professionals who've Recently Assumed HR Responsibilities (Onsite)
Seminar Information Service Inc.
20 Executive Park, Ste. 120
Irvine, CA 92614
Ph: (949)261-9104
Free: 877-SEM-INFO
Fax: (949)261-1963
Co. E-mail: info@seminarinformation.com
URL: http://www.seminarinformation.com
Price: $199.00. **Description:** Fast-paced and information-rich, this program condenses the most important of the most important HR basics into clear, concise, easy-to-understand training.

42164 ■ Human Resources for Professionals Who've Recently Assumed HR Responsibilities (Onsite)
Padgett-Thompson Seminars
Rockhurst University CEC
14502 W 105th St.
Lenexa, KS 66215
Free: 800-349-1935
URL: http://www.findaseminar.com/tpd/Padgett-Thompson-Seminars.asp
URL(s): www.nationalseminarstraining.com/onsite/SpeakerBio.cfm?SNO=64289. **Description:** Workshop provides the information and confidence needed to meet tough HR challenges. **Audience:** HR assistants, HR specialists, office managers, executive assistants, and administrative assistants.

42165 ■ Instructional Design for Participant-Centered Training (Onsite)
Seminar Information Service Inc.
20 Executive Park, Ste. 120
Irvine, CA 92614
Ph: (949)261-9104
Free: 877-SEM-INFO
Fax: (949)261-1963
Co. E-mail: info@seminarinformation.com
URL: http://www.seminarinformation.com
URL(s): www.seminarinformation.com/details.cfm?qc=qqbmbv. **Price:** $1,795. **Description:** Learn to apply the eight step design process to create a training course from nothing or enhance an existing program. **Audience:** Trainers.

42166 ■ Instructional Design for Trainers (Onsite)
Seminar Information Service Inc.
20 Executive Park, Ste. 120
Irvine, CA 92614
Ph: (949)261-9104
Free: 877-SEM-INFO
Fax: (949)261-1963
Co. E-mail: info@seminarinformation.com
URL: http://www.seminarinformation.com
URL(s): www.seminarinformation.com/details.cfm?qc=qqargh. **Price:** $2,345. **Description:** Applications-based workshop where you will prepare a training plan designed to meet your company's every need. **Audience:** Trainers.

42167 ■ Introduction to Human Resources Law
Price: $995.00. **Description:** Overview of the legal issues associated with day-to-day employment-related decisions and actions.

42168 ■ Recruiting, Interviewing and Selecting Employees (Onsite)
American Management Association (AMA)
1601 Broadway
New York, NY 10019-7420
Ph: (212)586-8100
Free: 877-566-9441

Fax: (212)903-8168
Co. E-mail: customerservice@amanet.org
URL: http://www.amanet.org
Contact: Edward T. Reilly, President
URL(s): www.amaseminars.org/training/seminars/Recruiting-Interviewing-and-Selecting-Employees.aspx. **Price:** $2,345.00 for non-members; $2,095.00 for AMA members; and $1,794.00 for General Services Administration (GSA) members. **Frequency:** Monthly. **Description:** Covers recruitment sources, filtering applicants, interview techniques and questions, and EEO and affirmative action guidelines. **Audience:** human resource professionals and human resource practitioners. **Dates and Locations:** Chicago, IL; Los Angeles, CA; and New York, NY. **Telecommunication Services:** customerservice@amanet.org.

42169 ■ Succession Planning: Developing Leaders from Within (Onsite)
American Management Association (AMA)
1601 Broadway
New York, NY 10019-7420
Ph: (212)586-8100
Free: 877-566-9441
Fax: (212)903-8168
Co. E-mail: customerservice@amanet.org
URL: http://www.amanet.org
Contact: Edward T. Reilly, President
URL(s): www.amanet.org/training/seminars/Succession-Planning-Developing-Leaders-from-Within.aspx. **Price:** $2,195, Non-members; $1,995, Members AMA; $1,708, Members GSA. **Description:** Learn to implement a succession plan to minimize gaps in leadership. **Audience:** Mid to senior level managers, business unit heads, human resources personnel and organizational development professionals.

42170 ■ Train the Trainer: Facilitation Skills Workshop Onsite
Canadian Management Centre (CMC)
150 York St., 5th Fl.
Toronto, ON, Canada M5H 3S5
Free: 877-262-2519
Fax: (416)214-6047
Co. E-mail: cmcinfo@cmcoutperform.com
URL: http://cmcoutperform.com
Contact: John Wright, President
URL(s): cmcoutperform.com/train-the-trainer. **Price:** $1,995, Members; $2,195, Non-members. **Description:** Gain practical, proven techniques and strategies for facilitating high impact learning experiences. **Audience:** Facilitators.

42171 ■ Training for Impact
Seminar Information Service Inc.
20 Executive Park, Ste. 120
Irvine, CA 92614
Ph: (949)261-9104
Free: 877-SEM-INFO
Fax: (949)261-1963
Co. E-mail: info@seminarinformation.com
URL: http://www.seminarinformation.com
URL(s): www.seminarinformation.com/details.cfm?qc=qqasgk. **Description:** Designed for those accountable for delivering face-to-face training programs. **Audience:** Personnel officers, training managers and coordinators.

42172 ■ The Workshop for Personnel/HR Assistants (Onsite)
Seminar Information Service Inc.
20 Executive Park, Ste. 120
Irvine, CA 92614
Ph: (949)261-9104
Free: 877-SEM-INFO
Fax: (949)261-1963
Co. E-mail: info@seminarinformation.com
URL: http://www.seminarinformation.com
Price: $399.00. **Description:** Learn the essentials of accepted human resources procedures, as well as a clear understanding of current employment law, rules and regulations. **Audience:** Personnel, and Human Resource staff . **Dates and Locations:** Cities throughout the United States.

REFERENCE WORKS

42173 ■ The 4-Hour Workweek
Pub: Crown Publishing/Random House
Ed: Timothy Ferriss. **Released:** April 24, 2007. **Price:** $22, Hardcover. **Description:** Examination of ways to cut the hours you work and find more enjoyment in your life.

42174 ■ "The 7 Deadly Toxins of Employee Engagement: How They Decimate Your Performance, Your Effectiveness & Your Bottom Line"
Pub: Bookshaker
Released: $10.00. **Price:** , $10.00 paperback. **Description:** Human resources managers, and all business leaders, need to recognize the importance of employee engagement. They also need to understand the seven deadly toxins that are destructive and are built into every solution that addresses problems.

42175 ■ 365 Answers about Human Resources for the Small Business Owner: What Every Manager Needs to Know about Work Place Law
Pub: Atlantic Publishing Co.
Contact: Amanda Miller, Manager
E-mail: amiller@atlantic-pub.com
Ed: Mary Holihan. **Price:** $21.95. **Description:** Common questions employers ask about employees and the law are answered.

42176 ■ "2010 Book of Lists" in Tampa Bay Business Journal (Vol. 30, December 22, 2009, No. 53, pp. 1)
Description: Rankings of companies and organizations within the human resources, banking and finance, business services, healthcare, real estate, technology, hospitality and travel, and education industries in the Greater Tampa Bay area are presented. Rankings are based on sales, business size, and more.

42177 ■ Achieving Planned Innovation: A Proven System for Creating Successful New Products and Services
Pub: Simon & Schuster Higher Education Group
Contact: Larry Norton, President
Ed: Frank R. Bacon. **Released:** August 2007. **Price:** $16.95. **Description:** Planned innovation is a disciplined and practical step-by-step sequence of procedures for reaching the intended destination point: successful products. This easy-to-read book explains the system along with an action-oriented program for continuous success in new-product innovations. Five steps outlined include: a disciplined reasoning process; lasting market orientation; proper selection criteria that reflect both strategic and tactical business objectives and goals along with dynamic matching of resources to present and future opportunities, and positive and negative requirements before making major expenditures; and proper organizational staffing. The author explains what to do and evaluating the potential of any new product or service, ranging from ventures in retail distribution to the manufacture of goods as diverse as bicycles, motorcycles, aerospace communication and navigation equipment, small business computers, food packaging, and medical products. **Availability:** Print.

42178 ■ "Advancing the Ball" in Inside Healthcare (Vol. 6, December 2010, No. 7, pp. 31)
Ed: Michelle McNickle. **Description:** Profile of Medicalodges an elder-care specialty company that provides both patient care and technology development. President and CEO of the firm believes that hiring good employees is key to growth for any small business.

42179 ■ Aging and Working in the New Economy: Changing Career Structures in Small IT Firms
Pub: Edward Elgar Publishing Inc.
Contact: Richard Henning, Vice President
E-mail: kwight@e-elgar.com
Ed: Juliie Ann McMullin, Victor W. Marshall. **Released:** March 01, 2010. **Price:** £67.50. **Description:** Case studies and analyses provide insight into the structural features of small- and medium-sized firms in the information technology sector, and the implications of these features for the careers of people employed by them.

42180 ■ American Bar Association Legal Guide for Small Business: Everything You Need to Know About Small Business
Ed: American Bar Association. **Released:** June 10, 2010. **Description:** The American Bar Association provides insight into financial, health and family issues affecting small business, including start up issues, employment laws, financing a business, and selling a business.

42181 ■ "American Chemistry Council Launches Flagship Blog" in Ecology, Environment & Conservation Business (October 29, 2011, pp. 5)
Pub: Highbeam Research
Contact: Patrick Spain, Chief Executive Officer
Description: American Chemistry Council (ACC) launched its blog, American Chemistry Matters, where interactive space allows bloggers to respond to news coverage and to discuss policy issues and their impact on innovation, competitiveness, job creation and safety.

42182 ■ "Amount Md. Pays to Unemployed Dips to Lowest Level Since '08" in Baltimore Business Journal (Vol. 28, November 12, 2010, No. 27)
Pub: Baltimore Business Journal
Ed: Scott Dance. **Description:** Maryland paid out $50 million for unemployment benefits in September 2010 for its lowest payout since 2008. The drop in unemployment payout could mean lower taxes for employers who pay for the benefits. The unemployment rate in Maryland, however, increased to 7.5 percent.

42183 ■ "The Anatomy of a High Potential" in Business Strategy Review (Vol. 21, Autumn 2010, No. 3, pp. 52)
Pub: Blackwell Publishers Ltd.
Ed: Doug Ready, Jay Conger, Linda Hill, Emily Stecker. **Description:** Companies have long been interested in identifying high potential employees, but few firms know how to convert top talent into game changers, or people who can shape the future of the business. The authors have found the 'x factors' that can make a high-potential list into a strong competitive advantage.

42184 ■ "The Anatomy of a High Potential" in Business Strategy Review (Vol. 21, Autumn 2010, No. 3, pp. 52)
Pub: John Wiley & Sons Inc. Scientific, Technical, Medical, and Scholarly Div. (Wiley-Blackwell)
Contact: William J. Pesce, Manager
E-mail: wpesce@wiley.com
Ed: Doug Ready, Jay Conger, Linda Hill, Emily Stecker. **Description:** Companies have long been interested in identifying high-potential employees, but few firms know how to convert top talent into game changers - people who can shape the future of the business. The authors have found the x-factors that can make the high-potential list into a strong competitive advantage.

42185 ■ "Apprenticeship: Earn While You Learn" in Occupational Outlook Quarterly (Vol. 54, Fall 2010, No. 3, pp. 24)
Pub: U.S. Department of Labor Bureau of Labor Statistics
Contact: Philip L. Rones, Manager
E-mail: rones.philip@bls.gov
Description: Paid training, or apprenticeships, are examined. Registered apprenticeship programs conform to certain guidelines and industry-established training standards and may be run by businesses, trade or professional associations, or partnerships with business and unions.

42186 ■ "Ask Inc." in Inc. (November 2007, pp. 69)
Description: The best time to terminate an employee is discussed.

42187 ■ "At Your Service: Corporate Concierges Come in Three Varieties" in Incentive (August 25, 2008)
Ed: Nathan Adkisson. **Description:** Companies are offering corporate concierge services to handle tasks for new employees as a sign-on benefit. Concierge of Boston has six employees that focus on fulfilling the needs of individuals.

42188 ■ Atiyah's Accidents, Compensation and the Law
Pub: Cambridge University Press
Contact: Richard Ziemacki, President
E-mail: rziemacki@cambridge.org
Ed: Peter Cane. **Released:** Eighth Edition. **Price:** $56, paperback; $45. **Description:** Leading authority on the law of personal injuries compensation and the social, political and economic issues surrounding it. **Availability:** PrintE-book.

42189 ■ "Austin Startup on Cusp of Trend" in Austin Business JournalInc. (Vol. 29, January 8, 2010, No. 44, pp. 1)
Pub: American City Business Journals
Ed: Christopher Calnan. **Description:** Austin-based Socialware Inc. introduced a new business called social middleware, which is a software that is layered between the company network and social networking Website used by workers. The software was designed to give employers a measure of control over content while allowing workers to continue using online social networks.

42190 ■ "Austin on Verge of Losing 7,500 Jobs" in Austin Business Journal (Vol. 31, May 6, 2011, No. 9, pp. 1)
Pub: American City Business Journals
Ed: Jacob Dirr. **Description:** Proposed state budget cuts are seen to result in the loss of as many as 7,500 public and private sector jobs in Austin, Texas, with the private sector losing the majority of workers. Comments from analysts are included.

42191 ■ "Baltimore-Area Hospital Tower Projects Could Add Hundreds of New Jobs" in Baltimore Business Journal (Vol. 28, June 25, 2010, No. 7, pp. 1)
Pub: Baltimore Business Journal
Ed: Scott Graham. **Description:** Greater Baltimore, Maryland has four hospitals that are in the middle of transforming their campuses with new facilities for treating various patients. Construction at Mercy Medical Center, Johns Hopkins Hospital, Franklin Square Hospital and Anne Rundle Hospital has helped bring the construction industry back to life. Insights into the hiring plans of these hospitals are also included.

42192 ■ "Baltimore 'Living Wage' Bill Draws City, Retailers to Clash" in Baltimore Business Journal (Vol. 28, July 9, 2010, No. 9, pp. 1)
Pub: Baltimore Business Journal
Ed: Daniel J. Sernovitz. **Description:** A bill pending before the City Council of Baltimore, Maryland would mandate the city's major retailers to pay their employees at least $10.57 per hour, $3 higher than was state law requires. Major retailers, as defined in the said bill by Councilwoman Mary Pat Clarke, have gross sales of at least $10 million. Reactions of the retailers affected are presented.

42193 ■ "Bar Hopping: Your Numbers At a Glance" in Inc. (January 2008, pp. 44-45)
Pub: Gruner and Jahr USA Publishing Co.
Contact: J. Russell Denson, President
Ed: Michael Fitzgerald. **Description:** Software that helps any company analyze data include Crystal Xcelsius, a program that takes data from Excel documents and turns them into animated gauges, charts and graphs; CashView, a Web-based application that tracks receivables and payables; iDashboards, a Web-based programs that produces animated gauges, maps, pie charts and graphs; Corda Human Capital Management, that transforms stats like head count, productivity, and attrition into graphs and dials; NetSuite, a Web-based application that tracks key indicators; and Cognos Now, that gauges, dials, and graphs data.

42194 ■ *"Best (Professional) Foot Forward: Effective Marketing Strategies for any Phase of Your Career" in Black Enterprisel> (Vol. 44, June 2014, No. 10, pp. 44)*
Pub: Earl G. Graves Publishing Co. Inc.
Contact: Earl G. Graves, Jr., President
Released: June 2014. **Description:** Because hiring managers face long-term vacancies and skills gaps, the importance of creating a professional marketing strategy when applying for a professional position is stressed. Advice is given to help guide applicants through the entire application, interviewing, and hiring process.

42195 ■ *"BETC Backers Plot Future" in Business Journal Portland (Vol. 27, December 10, 2010, No. 41, pp. 1)*
Pub: Portland Business Journal
Ed: Erik Siemers. **Description:** A coalition of clean energy groups and industrial manufacturers have spearheaded a campaign aimed at persuading Oregon legislators that the state's Business Energy Tax Credit (BETC) is vital in job creation. Oregon's BETC grants tax credits for 50 percent of an eligible renewable or clean energy project's cost. However, some legislators propose BETC's abolition.

42196 ■ *"Beyond Auto; Staffing Firm Malace Grabs Revenue Jump" in Crain's Detroit Business (Vol. 26, January 18, 2010, No. 3, pp. 3)*
Pub: Crain Communications Inc.
Contact: Rance E. Crain, President
Ed: Sherri Welch. **Description:** Malace & Associates Inc., the Troy-based human resources management company, expects its diversification into nonautomotive industries to help double its revenues this year. Due to the automotive downturn, between October 2008 and March 2009 the company lost approximately 48 percent of its business.

42197 ■ *"Big Paychecks for Hospital CEOs" in Sacramento Business Journal (Vol. 28, April 8, 2011, No. 6, pp. 1)*
Pub: Sacramento Business Journal
Ed: Kathy Robertson. **Description:** Hospital chief executives in Sacramento, California have been receiving large salaries, tax records show. The huge salaries reflect the high demand for successful hospital chief executives. Statistical data included.

42198 ■ *"BofA Cutting 70 Charlotte Tech Jobs" in Charlotte Observer (January 31, 2007)*
Ed: Rick Rothacker. **Description:** Bank of America announced the elimination of 70 technology positions at their Charlotte, North Carolina facility. The move is part of the company's effort to increase efficiency.

42199 ■ *Boosting Corporate Entrepreneurship Through HRM Practices: Evidence from German SMEs" in Human Resource Management (Vol. 49, July-August 2010, No. 4)*
Pub: John Wiley
Ed: Ralf Schmelter, Rene Mauer, Christiane Borsch, Malte Brettel. **Description:** A study was conducted to determine which human resource management (HRM) practices promote corporate entrepreneurship (CE) in small and medium-sized enterprises (SMEs). Findings indicate that staff selection, staff development, training, and staff rewards on CE have a strong impact on SMEs.

42200 ■ *"Boosting Strategy With An Online Community" in Business Strategy Review (Vol. 21, Spring 2010, No. 1, pp. 40)*
Pub: John Wiley & Sons Inc. Scientific, Technical, Medical, and Scholarly Div. (Wiley-Blackwell)
Contact: William J. Pesce, Manager
E-mail: wpesce@wiley.com
Ed: Lynda Gratton, Joel Casse. **Description:** A program that merged online communities with strategic development and implementation at Nokia has provided valuable lessons about new ways employees are able to engage and interact.

42201 ■ *"Both Eyes on the Prize" in Canadian Business (Vol. 83, September 14, 2010, No. 15, pp. 42)*
Pub: Rogers Media Inc.
Contact: Tony Viner, President
Ed: Jacqueline Nelson. **Description:** North American executive compensation has fundamentally shifted partly due to pressure from the US government and recent adjustments in the way CEO pay packages are structured. The changes have also become common practice in Canada and helped in scrutinizing the executive pay.

42202 ■ *"Bracing for More Layoffs" in Sacramento Business Journal (Vol. 28, September 30, 2011, No. 31, pp. 1)*
Pub: Sacramento Business Journal
Ed: Melanie Turner. **Description:** Sacramento, California workers are preparing for a fresh wave of layoffs. The weak economy is seen to drive the development.

42203 ■ *"Breaking Bad: Rid Yourself of Negative Habits" in Black Enterprise (Vol. 40, July 2010, No. 12, pp. 104)*
Pub: Earl G. Graves Publishing Co. Inc.
Contact: Earl G. Graves, Jr., President
Ed: Renita Burns. **Description:** Tardiness, procrastination, chronic complaining are among the bad habits that can make people bad employees; tips for breaking these habits are outlined.

42204 ■ *"Bridging the Worlds" in Academy of Management Journal (Vol. 50, No. 5, October 1, 2007, pp. 1043)*
Pub: Academy of Management
Contact: Ming-Jer Chen, President
Ed: Lise Saari. **Description:** Need to transfer human resource research information published in journals to practitioners and organizations is investigated, along with suggestions on ways of achieving this goal.

42205 ■ *"Brief: Janitorial Company Must Pay Back Wages" in Buffalo News (September 24, 2011)*
Pub: The Buffalo News
Contact: Warren T. Colville, President
Ed: Jonathan D. Epstein. **Description:** Knights Facilities Management, located in Michigan, provides grounds maintenance and janitorial services at the Ralph Wilson Stadium in Buffalo, New York. The US Department of Labor ordered the firm to pay $22,000 in back wages and damages to 26 employees for overtime and minimum wage compensation. Details of the company's violation of the Fair Labor Standards Act are included.

42206 ■ *Business Black Belt: Develop the Strength, Flexibility and Agility to Run Your Company*
Ed: Burke Franklin. **Released:** November 1, 2010. **Price:** $15.99. **Description:** Manual offering insights that will enable anyone to become successful in small business. Seventy short chapters included topics such as attitude, management, marketing, selling, employees, money, MBAs, lawyers, consultants, and investors.

42207 ■ *"Business Guide and Employment Role"*
Pub: AuthorHouse
Contact: Bryan Smith, President
Released: October 10, 2014. **Price:** , $15.18 paperback. **Description:** Financial expert discusses the importance of economic and business and their role in employment. The business and finance manager is crucial to any small business. The guide is an essential tool for any entrepreneur, the investor in business enterprise, the individual businessman, the human resources manager, and the business and finance professional to learn the merits to do business and play a role in employment.

42208 ■ *Business Warrior: Strategy for Entrepreneurs*
Ed: Sun Tzu. **Released:** September 2006. **Price:** , $19.95. **Description:** Advice to help entrepreneurs understand competitive strategies in order to succeed, focusing on sales, marketing, and personnel management.

42209 ■ *"Businesses Need to Know State, Federal Laws for Employing Minors" in Crain's Detroit Business (Vol. 25, June 15, 2009, No. 24)*
Pub: Crain Communications Inc. - Detroit
Contact: Keith Crain, Chairman
Ed: Nancy Kaffer. **Description:** Small business owners must know the law before employing minors. According to Steven Fishman, partner with Bodman LLP, who practices workplace law, most small business owners are not aware of laws regarding employment of minors.

42210 ■ *"Calling All Recruiters: Agent HR Puts Staffing Agents In Charge" in Black Enterprise (Vol. 38, December 2007, No. 5, pp. 72)*
Pub: Earl G. Graves Publishing Co. Inc.
Contact: Earl G. Graves, Jr., President
Ed: Chana Garcia. **Description:** Recruiting and staffing agencies are seeing a drop in services due to slow economic growth. AgentHR partners with full-service recruiters who have three to five year's experience-specialists soliciting their own clients, provide staffing services, and manage their own accounts, thus combining the roles of recruiter and salesperson.

42211 ■ *"Capital Position: M&I Acquisition Opens the Door for Rivals to Gain Market Share" in Business Journal-Milwaukee (Vol. 28, December 24, 2010, No. 12, pp. A1)*
Pub: Milwaukee Business Journal
Ed: Rich Kirchen. **Description:** Canada-based BMO Financial Group has purchased Marshall and Isley Corporation (M and I), which dominated lending among Wisconsin businesses for decades. The sale of M and I will enable other banks to recruit M and I's customers but BMO Financial remains a stronger competitor since it possesses a more potent capital position.

42212 ■ *"Cautious Hiring in January Report" in Charlotte Observer (February 3, 2007)*
Ed: Kerry Hall. **Description:** U.S. Labor Department released a report that shows 111,000 new positions in January 2007, compared to 206,000 in December 2006. Employers remain cautious about hiring.

42213 ■ *"The CEO of General Electric On Sparking an American Manufacturing Renewal" in Harvard Business Review (Vol. 90, March 2012, No. 3, pp. 43)*
Pub: Harvard Business Review Press
Contact: Peter E. Walsh, Director
Ed: Jeffrey R. Immelt. **Released:** March 2012. **Description:** General Electric Company utilized human innovation and lean manufactring to improve the firm's competitiveness. By engaging the firm's entire workforce, utilizing technology and improving labor-management relations, GE boosted efficiency and reduced cost and waste.

42214 ■ *"CEO Pay: Best Bang for Buck" in Philadelphia Business Journal (Vol. 30, September 30, 2011, No. 33, pp. 1)*
Pub: American City Business Journals Inc.
Ed: Jeff Blumenthal. **Description:** A study by Strategic Research Solutions on the compensation of chief executive officers in Philadelphia, Pennsylvania-based public companies reveals that only a few of them performed according to expectations. These include Brian Roberts of Comcast, John Conway of Crown Holdings, and Frank Hermance of Ametek Inc.

42215 ■ *"CEO Pay: The Details" in Crain's Detroit Business (Vol. 25, June 22, 2009, No. 25, pp.)*
Pub: Crain Communications Inc. - Detroit
Contact: Keith Crain, Chairman
Description: Total compensation packages for CEOs at area companies our outlined. These packages include salary, bonuses, stock awards, and options.

42216 ■ *"The CEO Poll: A Say on Pay" in Canadian Business (Vol. 82, April 27, 2009,*

No. 7, pp. 14)
Pub: Rogers Media Inc.
Contact: Tony Viner, President
Ed: Joe Castaldo. **Description:** A COMPAS Inc. survey of 134 Canadian chief executive officers found that 44 percent agree that CEO compensation should be subject to a non-binding vote. The respondents were also divided on whether to allow shareholders to exercise retroactive clawbacks on executive compensation if firm performance turns out to be worse than projected.

42217 ■ *"CEOs Split on Migrant Workers"* in *Canadian Business (Vol. 83, September 14, 2010, No. 15, pp. 23)*
Pub: Rogers Media Inc.
Contact: Tony Viner, President
Ed: Jacqueline Nelson. **Description:** A survey of Canadian CEOs shows that 49 percent of the respondents believe it was wrong to suspend the immigration programs and companies should be allowed to hire the most skilled workers regardless of citizenship. However, 42 percent believe the suspension was right because employment of Canadians must take precedence.

42218 ■ *"CEOs With a Functional Background in Operations"* in *Human Resource Management (Vol. 49, September-October 2010, No. 5)*
Pub: John Wiley
Ed: Burak Koyuncu, Shainaz Firfiray, Bjorn Claes, Monika Hamori. **Description:** A study was conducted to determine whether companies that appoint chief executive officers (CEOs) with an operations background exhibit better post-succession financial performance relative to organizations that appoint CEOs with other functional backgrounds. A total of 437 CEOs from U.S. firms in eight industries were included in the study.

42219 ■ *"Charlie Winburn's Big Idea"* in *Business Courier (Vol. 27, October 8, 2010, No. 23, pp. 1)*
Pub: Business Courier
Ed: Dan Monk, Lucy May. **Description:** Cincinnati Councilman Charlie Winburn proposed the creation of Cincinnati Competitive Edge Division and to remake a small-business division of the city in order to start a job-creation program. The new division will monitor compliance to the city's small business inclusion regulations, as well as to help small business owners grow.

42220 ■ *"Cincinnati Consults Executives on Police Chief Hire"* in *Business Courier (Vol. 27, August 27, 2010, No. 17, pp. 1)*
Pub: Business Courier
Ed: Dan Monk, Lucy May. **Description:** The City of Cincinnati, Ohio has begun a selection process for the new police chief by consulting the city's business executives. The city charter amendment known as Issue 5 has removed civil service protection from the chief's post and enables City Manager Milton Dohoney to hire a chief from outside the department.

42221 ■ *"Cincinnati Hospitals Mandate Flu Shots"* in *Business Courier (Vol. 27, November 19, 2010, No. 29, pp. 1)*
Pub: Business Courier
Ed: James Ritchie. **Description:** TriHealth has mandated that employees who refuse to get the vaccination shot for 2010 could be penalized with unpaid administrative leave. Other hospital employers, such as University Hospital and Cincinnati Children's Hospital and Medical Center have fired employees for forgoing flu shots. Vaccination rates among hospital employees are given.

42222 ■ *"The Classless Workplace: The Digerati and the New Spirit of Technocapitalism"* in *WorkingUSA (Vol. 11, June 2008, No. 2, pp. 181)*
Ed: Eran Fisher. **Description:** Article argues the formation of a new type of economic actor at the intersection of a new capitalism and a new technology: The Dierati. The discourse in based on the analysis of the popular magazine Wired, which registers the culture of contemporary technocapital-

ism. The suggestion that the new persona of the digerati is constructed as a rejection of the ethics, which dominated the Fordist workplace and Fordist society: Hierarchy and differentiation between workers, on the one hand and capitalists and managers, on the other hand. The transformation of these two categories, workers and capitalists into the digerati worker and the digerati entrepreneur, is described. Set within the context of the structural transformations of capitalism from Fordism to post-Fordism, the article shows the ideological fit of the new ethics of the digerati to the new working arrangements of post-Fordist capitalism, characterized by more privatizes, flexible, and precarious working arrangements.

42223 ■ *"Cloud Computing for a Crowd"* in *CIO (Vol. 24, October 2, 2010, No. 1, pp. 16)*
Pub: CIO
Ed: Stephanie Overby. **Description:** Information about a project which aimed to implement a cloud-based crowdsourcing platform and innovation-management process is provided. Chubb Group of Insurance Companies wanted to mine revenue-generating ideas from its 10,400 employees and hundreds of thousands of external agents. The company hosted its first innovation event using its new system in October 2008.

42224 ■ *"Coffee Breaks Don't Boost Productivity After All"* in *Harvard Business Review (Vol. 90, May 2012, No. 5, pp. 34)*
Pub: Harvard Business Review Press
Contact: Peter E. Walsh, Director
Ed: Charlotte Fritz. **Released:** May 2012. **Description:** Research shows no statistical correlation between taking a short break at work and one's fatigue and vitality levels. However, a link was found between personal productivity and assisting a co-worker. Employees detach from work more successfully during long breaks rather than short ones.

42225 ■ *"Collateral Damage"* in *Business Courier (Vol. 26, October 16, 2009, No. 25, pp. 1)*
Pub: American City Business Journals, Inc.
Contact: Whitney Shaw, President
Ed: Jon Newberry. **Description:** Non-union construction firms representing Ohio Valley Associated Builders and Contractors Inc. have filed cases against unionized shops claiming violations of wage law in Ohio. Defendants say the violations are minor, however, they believe they are caught in the middle of the group's campaign to change the state's wage law.

42226 ■ *"Column: Wealth and Jobs: the Broken Link"* in *Harvard Business Review (Vol. 88, November 2010, No. 11, pp. 44)*
Pub: Harvard Business School Publishing
Ed: Nitin Nohria. **Description:** Rebuilding the link between business and job creation to shore up the middle class is advocated. A blend of government policies and business strategies that foster entrepreneurship and innovation are essential.

42227 ■ *"Column: What 17th-Century Pirates Can Teach Us About Job Design"* in *Harvard Business Review (Vol. 88, October 2010, No. 10, pp. 44)*
Pub: Harvard Business School Publishing
Ed: Hayagreeva Rao. **Description:** Ways in which pirates typify the importance of separating star tasks, or strategic work, from guardian tasks, or the operational work are outlined.

42228 ■ *"Commentary"* in *Small Business Economic Trends (September 2010, pp. 3)*
Pub: National Federation of Independent Business
Contact: Caitlin McDevitt, Program Manager
Ed: William C. Dunkelberg, Holly Wade. **Description:** A commentary on the economic trends for small businesses in the U.S. is presented. An analysis of the unemployment rate and inflation is given. Economic growth is also expected to remain sub-par for some time, unless new policies are introduced.

42229 ■ *"Commentary. Small Business Economic Trends"* in *Small Business*

Economic Trends (March 2008, pp. 3)
Pub: National Federation of Independent Business
Contact: Caitlin McDevitt, Program Manager
Ed: William C. Dunkelberg, Holly Wade. **Description:** Commentary on the economic trends for small businesses in the U.S. is presented. Analysis of the labor market and low interest rates is given. The effect of the Federal Reserve's policy announcement on small business owner optimism is also discussed.

42230 ■ *"Commentary. Small Business Economic Trends"* in *Small Business Economic Trends (February 2008, pp. 3)*
Pub: National Federation of Independent Business
Contact: Caitlin McDevitt, Program Manager
Ed: William C. Dunkelberg, Holly Wade. **Description:** Commentary on the economic trends for small businesses in the U.S. is presented. Analysis of the U.S. Federal Reserve Board's efforts to prevent a recession is given. Reduction in business inventories is also discussed.

42231 ■ *"Commentary. Small Business Economic Trends"* in *Small Business Economic Trends (January 2008, pp. 3)*
Pub: National Federation of Independent Business
Contact: Caitlin McDevitt, Program Manager
Description: Federal Reserve cut interest rates and announced its economic outlook on September 18, 2007 to stimulate spending. The cut in interest rates, however, may not help in supporting consumer spending because savers may lose interest income. The expected economic impact of the interest rate cuts and the U.S. economic outlook are also discussed.

42232 ■ *"Comparative Indicators"* in *Montly Labor Review (Vol. 133, September 2010, No. 9, pp. 87)*
Pub: U.S. Department of Labor Bureau of Labor Statistics
Contact: Philip L. Rones, Manager
E-mail: rones.philip@bls.gov
Description: Labor market indicators for years 2008 and 2009 are given. Statistical data included.

42233 ■ *"A Comparison of Adverse Impact Levels Based on Top-Down, Multisource, and Assessment Center Data: Promoting Diversity and Reducing Legal Challenges"* in *Human Resource Management (Vol. 51, May-June 2012, No. 3, pp. 313-341)*
Pub: John Wiley & Sons Inc.
Contact: Stephen M. Smith, President
Ed: H. John Bernardin, Robert Konopaske, Christine M. Hagan. **Description:** Levels of adverse impact against minorities and women were compared based on promotional decision methods. Results indicate significant effects for race and minority status in favor of white people but not for gender.

42234 ■ *"Competing for Jobs"* in *Women In Business (Vol. 63, Summer 2011, No. 2, pp. 37)*
Pub: American Business Women's Association
Contact: Lorie Burch, President
Ed: Leigh Elmore. **Description:** Job hunting tips for women in the US in relation to generation demographic groups are presented. Effective communications and positive interactions are essential to career development. Generation groups' strengths and weaknesses as job seekers are also given.

42235 ■ *"Competing on Talent Analytics"* in *Harvard Business Review (Vol. 88, October 2010, No. 10, pp. 52)*
Pub: Harvard Business School Publishing
Ed: Thomas H. Davenport, Jeanne Harris, Jeremy Shapiro. **Description:** Six ways to use talent analytics to obtain the highest level of value from employees are listed. These include human-capital investment analysis, talent value models, workforce forecasts, and talent supply chains.

42236 ■ *"Complaints, Workforce Composition, Productivity, Organizational Values"* in *HRMagazine (Vol. 54, January*

2009, No. 1, pp. 29)
Pub: Society for Human Resource Management
Contact: Henry G. Jackson, President
E-mail: hjackson@shrm.org
Ed: Amy Maingault, Regan Halvorsen, Rue Dooley, Liz Petersen. **Description:** Workforce composition trends that management should monitor are outlined. A goal-development process is discussed.

42237 ■ Complete Employee Handbook: A Step-by-Step Guide to Create a Custom Handbook That Protects Both the Employer and the Employee
Ed: Michael A. Holzschu. **Released:** August 2007. **Price:** , $39.95. **Description:** Comprehensive guide for employers deal with personnel issues; CD-ROM contains sample employee handbooks, federal regulations and laws, forms for complying with government programs and worksheets for assessing personnel needs and goals.

42238 ■ "Compulsory Proportional Representation: Allaying Potential Concerns" in WorkingUSA (Vol. 11, September 2008, No. 3, pp. 349)
Ed: Mark Harcourt, Helen Lam. **Description:** Present union certification system has many faults, the most important of which is its failure to deliver employee representation to all but a small and declining minority of workers. As an alternative, compulsory proportional representation (CPR) would have many advantages, particularly when compared with other reform proposals, most of which are designed to only reinvigorate, modify, or supplement the existing system.

42239 ■ "Condensed Capitalism: Campbell Soup and the Pursuit of Cheap Production in the Twentieth Century" in Human Resource Management (Vol. 49, September-October 2010, No. 5, pp. 965-968)
Pub: John Wiley
Ed: Matthew M. Bodah. **Description:** Review of the book, 'Condensed Capitalism: Campbell Soup and the Pursuit of Cheap Production in the Twentieth Century'.

42240 ■ "Connecting the Dots Between Wellness and Elder Care" in Benefits and Compensation Digest (Vol. 47, August 2010, No. 8, pp. 18)
Pub: International Foundation of Employee Benefit Plans
Contact: Kenneth R. Boyd, President
Ed: Sandra Timmermann. **Description:** Employees caring for aged and infirm parents deal with time and financial issues and other stresses. The connection between health status of caregivers and employers' health care costs could be aided by linking programs and benefits with wellness and caregiving.

42241 ■ "The Consequences of Tardiness" in Modern Machine Shop (Vol. 84, August 2011, No. 3, pp. 34)
Pub: Gardner Business Media, Inc.
Contact: Richard G. Kline, President
E-mail: rkline@gardnerweb.com
Ed: Wayne S. Chaneski. **Description:** Five point addressing motivating factors behind employees who are tardy and those who choose to be on time in the workplace are shared.

42242 ■ "A Conversation with: Renea Butler" in Crain's Detroit Business (Vol. 25, June 8, 2009, No. 23, pp. 12)
Pub: Crain Communications Inc. - Detroit
Contact: Keith Crain, Chairman
Ed: Ryan Beene. **Description:** Renea Butler, vice president of administration and human resources for Real Estate One Inc. in Southfield as well as vice president for public relations for the Human Resource Association of Greater Detroit, talks about how the economy has affected human resource services.

42243 ■ "Corporate Responsibility" in Professional Services Close-Up (July 2, 2010)
Description: List of firms awarded the inaugural Best Corporate Citizens in Government Contracting by the Corporate Responsibility Magazine is presented. The

list is based on the methodology of the Magazine's Best Corporate Citizen's List, with 324 data points of publicly-available information in seven categories which include: environment, climate change, human rights, philanthropy, employee relations, financial performance, and governance.

42244 ■ Create Your Own Employee Handbook: A Legal & Practical Guide for Employers
Pub: Nolo
Contact: Ralph Warner, Chief Executive Officer
Ed: Amy DelPo, Lisa Guerin. **Released:** May 2013. **Price:** $39.99; $34.99. **Description:** Information for business owners to develop an employee handbook that covers company benefits, policies, procedures, and more. **Availability:** PrintE-book.

42245 ■ "Creating Your Personal Succession Plan" in Black Enterprise (Vol. 38, December 2007, No. 5, pp. 86)
Pub: Earl G. Graves Publishing Co. Inc.
Contact: Earl G. Graves, Jr., President
Ed: Marcia A. Reed-Woodard. **Description:** Society for Human Resource Management's Succession Planning Survey Report shows that over 58 percent of companies surveyed use succession plans for employees preparing to transition to higher-level positions.

42246 ■ The Creative Business Guide to Running a Graphic Design Business
Pub: W. W. Norton & Company, Inc.
Contact: Rachel Comerford, Manager
Ed: Cameron S. Foote. **Released:** September 2009. **Price:** $35. **Description:** Advice for running a graphic design firm, focusing on organizations, marketing, personnel and operations. **Availability:** Print.

42247 ■ "Creative In-Sourcing Boosts Franchisee Performance" in Franchising World (Vol. 42, September 2010, No. 9, pp. 16)
Pub: International Franchise Association
Contact: Stephen J. Caldeira, President
E-mail: scaldeira@franchise.org
Ed: Daniel M. Murphy. **Description:** Operational training and support is usually provided by franchisors. To be successful in this process it is important to balance the reality of limited financial and human resources.

42248 ■ "Crucible: Battling Back from Betrayal" in Harvard Business Review (Vol. 88, December 2010, No. 12, pp. 130)
Pub: Harvard Business School Publishing
Ed: Daniel McGinn. **Description:** Stephen Greer's scrap metal firm, Hartwell Pacific, lost several million dollars due to a lack of efficient and appropriate inventory audits, accounting procedures, and new-hire reference checks for his foreign operations. Greer believes that balancing growth with control is a key component of success.

42249 ■ "Crucible: Losing the Top Job - And Winning It Back" in Harvard Business Review (Vol. 88, October 2010, No. 10, pp. 136)
Pub: Harvard Business School Publishing
Ed: Alison Beard. **Description:** Michael Mack chronicles the changes in perspectives that occurred when he was fired from Garden Fresh, a restaurant firm he co-owned. Once again at the company helm, he is now more receptive to outside input and acknowledges the importance of work-life balance.

42250 ■ "CSX Transportation: Supplier Diversity on the Right Track" in Hispanic Business (July-August 2009, pp. 34)
Pub: Hispanic Business Inc.
Contact: Jesus Chavarria, President
Description: CSX Transportation is a leader in delivering essential products, operating as many as 1,200 trains and a fleet of more than 100,000 freight cars. CSX attributes its success by valuing diversity in both hiring and supplier contracts.

42251 ■ "Custom Fit" in Canadian Business (Vol. 80, November 19, 2007, No. 23, pp. 42)
Ed: Andy Holloway. **Description:** Proper employee selection will help ensure a company has the people with the skills it really needs. Employee development

is integral in coping with changes in the company. The importance of hiring the right employee and developing his skills is examined.

42252 ■ "Cutting Health Care Costs: the 3-Legged Stool" in HR Specialist (Vol. 8, September 2010, No. 9, pp. 1)
Pub: Capitol Information Group Inc.
Description: Employer spending on health insurance benefits to employees is investigated.

42253 ■ "Debt-Collection Agency to Lay Off 368 in Hampton Center" in Virginian-Pilot (December 4, 2010)
Pub: Virginian-Pilot
Ed: Tom Shean. **Description:** NCO Financial Systems Inc., provider of debt-collection and outsourcing services will permanently lay off 368 workers at its Hampton call center in 2011.

42254 ■ "Delta Air Lines Looks at Downtown Departure" in Business Courier (Vol. 27, October 1, 2010, No. 22, pp. 1)
Pub: Business Courier
Ed: Dan Monk. **Description:** Delta Air Lines Inc. has been looking for a smaller office for its reservations center in downtown Cincinnati, Ohio. Delta has informed the city of its plan to seek proposals on office space alternatives in advance of the 2011 lease expiration. Insights on the current employment status at the reservations center are also given.

42255 ■ Department of Labor's Overtime Regulations Effect on Small Business: Hearing before the Committee on Small Business, U.S. House of Representatives
Pub: DIANE Publishing Co.
Contact: Dorothy J. Perkins, Manager
E-mail: dorothyjperkins@hotmail.com
Released: 2004. **Price:** $20, paperback. **Description:** An overview of the Congressional hearing regarding the Department of Labor's regulations governing overtime and how they impact small business.

42256 ■ "Developing the Next Generation of Rosies" in Employee Benefit News (Vol. 25, November 1, 2011, No. 14, pp. 36)
Pub: SourceMedia Inc.
Contact: James M. Malkin, Chief Executive Officer
Ed: Kathleen Koster. **Description:** According to the research group Catalyst, women made up 46.7 percent of the American workforce in 2010, however only 14.4 percent were Fortune 500 executive officers and 15.7 percent held Fortune 500 board seats. Statistical data included.

42257 ■ "Dispelling Rocky Mountain Myths Key to Wellness" in Employee Benefit News (Vol. 25, November 1, 2011, No. 14, pp. 12)
Pub: SourceMedia Inc.
Contact: James M. Malkin, Chief Executive Officer
Ed: Andrea Davis. **Description:** Andrew Sykes, chairman of Health at Work Wellness Actuaries, states that it is a myth that Colorado is ranked as the healthiest state in America. Sykes helped implement a wellness programs at Brighton School District in the Denver area.

42258 ■ The Diversity Code: Unlock the Secrets to Making Differences Work in the Real World
Pub: AMACOM
Contact: Edward T. Reilly, Manager
Ed: Michelle T. Johnson. **Released:** September 2010. **Price:** $19.95. **Description:** The most diligent compliance with laws and regulations can't foster true work place diversity. The best organizations have become genuine cross-cultural communities that believe equality in reconciling difference and valuing them. The book promotes understanding by answering many of the toughest questions that professionals and their employers are afraid to ask. **Availability:** Print.

42259 ■ "DOL Stiffens Child Labor Penalties" in HR Specialist (Vol. 8, September 2010, No. 9, pp. 2)
Pub: Capitol Information Group Inc.
Description: U.S. Department of Labor (DOL) will impose new penalties for employers that violate U.S. child labor laws. Details of the new law are included.

42260 ■ *"Downturn Tests HCL's Pledge to Employees"* in *Workforce Management (Vol. 88, November 16, 2009, No. 12, pp. 23)*
Pub: Crain Communications Inc.
Contact: Rance E. Crain, President
Ed: Ed Frauenheim. **Description:** HCL Technologies has kept its promise to keep from laying any employees off during the recession which served as a test for the tech firm's Employee First program, which seeks to give workers greater income security as well as a stronger voice in the firm.

42261 ■ *"Dynamic Supply Chain Alignment: A New Business Model for Peak Performance in Enterprise Supply Chains Across All Geographies"* in *Human Resource Management (Vol. 49, September-October 2010, No. 5, pp. 969-973)*
Pub: John Wiley
Ed: Kim Sundtoft Hald. **Description:** Review of the book, 'Dynamic Supply Chain Alignment: A New Business Model for Peak Performance in Enterprise Supply Chains Across All Geographies'.

42262 ■ *"Education Path to Economic Growth in R.I."* in *Providence Business News (Vol. 29, June 23, 2014, No. 12, pp. 1)*
Pub: American City Business Journals
Released: June 23, 2014. **Description:** A gubernatorial candidate in Rhode Island is offering an education-related initiative that involves the creation of a statewide internship program, managed by each local school district and offering high school students the chance to participate in an internship at a local company. The state would provide $2.5 million to set up the "Hope Internships" with the help of nonprofits and to provide tax incentives for participating firms. Human resource department interest of local firms is also discussed.

42263 ■ *"Elder Care At Work"* in *HRMagazine (Vol. 53, September 2008, No. 9, pp. 111)*
Pub: Society for Human Resource Management
Contact: Henry G. Jackson, President
E-mail: hjackson@shrm.org
Ed: Pamela Babcock. **Description:** Many employers are helping workers who face sudden, short-term elder care needs.

42264 ■ *"Employee Called for Jury Duty"* in *Business Owner (Vol. 35, March-April 2011, No. 2, pp. 14)*
Pub: DL Perkins Company
Description: State laws govern small business rights and obligations regarding employee jury duty obligations. All states do require that employers allow employees to fulfill their jury duty obligations and retaliation, demotion, discipline or termination resulting from jury duty is illegal.

42265 ■ *Employee Management for Small Business*
Pub: Self-Counsel Press Inc.
Ed: Lin Grensing-Pophal. **Released:** October 15, 2009. **Price:** $20.95. **Description:** Management tools to help entrepreneurs maintain an effective human resources plan for a small company. **Availability:** Print.

42266 ■ *"Employees Can't Be Punished for Refusing to Work Due to Safety Concerns"* in *HR Specialist (Vol. 8, September 2010, No. 9, pp. 1)*
Description: Whistle-blower provisions in several federal laws make it illegal for employers to retaliate against employees who raise safety concerns to their employer or the government.

42267 ■ *"Employees Change Clothes at Work? Heed New Pay Rules"* in *HR Specialist (Vol. 8, September 2010, No. 9, pp. 1)*
Pub: Capitol Information Group Inc.
Description: U.S. Department of Labor issued a new interpretation letter that states times spent changing in and out of 'protective clothing' (e.g., helmets, smocks, aprons, gloves, etc.) is considered paid time. It also says time spent changing 'ordinary clothes' (i.e., uniform) may not be compensable itself, but could start the clock on the workday, meaning all

activities after - such as walking to the workstation - would be paid time. More details and a link to the DOL are included.

42268 ■ *Employer Legal Forms Simplified*
Ed: Daniel Sitarz. **Released:** August 2007. **Price:** , $24.95. **Description:** Business reference containing the following forms needed to handle employees in any small business environment: application, notice, confidentiality, absence, federal employer forms and notices, and many payroll forms. All forms are included on a CD that comes in both PDF and text formats. Adobe Acrobat Reader software is also included on the CD. The forms are valid in all fifty states and Washington, DC.

42269 ■ *"Encouraging Study in Critical Languages"* in *Occupational Outlook Quarterly (Vol. 55, Summer 2011, No. 2, pp. 23)*
Pub: U.S. Department of Labor Bureau of Labor Statistics
Contact: Philip L. Rones, Manager
E-mail: rones.philip@bls.gov
Description: Proficiency in particular foreign languages is vital to the defense, diplomacy, and security of the United States. Several federal programs provide scholarships and other funding to encourage high school and college students to learn languages of the Middle East, China, and Russia.

42270 ■ *"The End of Clock-Punching"* in *Canadian Business (Vol. 83, September 14, 2010, No. 15, pp. 96)*
Pub: Rogers Media Inc.
Contact: Tony Viner, President
Ed: Lyndsie Bourgon. **Description:** Workplace consultant Peter Hadwen is pushing for the transformation of Canada's government departments into results-only work environments (ROWE). ROWE does not require employees to show up to work at a certain time as long as they are meeting goals and achieving results in their jobs. Details of studies regarding ROWE in US companies are examined.

42271 ■ *"Entrepreneurial Human Resource Leadership: A Conversation with Dwight Carlson"* in *Human Resource Management (Vol. 49, July-August 2010, No. 4, pp. 793-804)*
Pub: John Wiley
Ed: David C. Strubler, Benjamin W. Redekop. **Description:** Dwight Carlson, a visionary entrepreneur, talks about his main role as a leader. He believes that experience can help in making choices between difficult alternatives. He also thinks that leaders do not really motivate people, they actually create an environment where they motivate themselves.

42272 ■ *The Entrepreneur's Guide to Managing Growth and Handling Crises*
Pub: Greenwood Publishing Group Inc.
Contact: Janann Sherman, Manager
Ed: Theo J. Van Dijk. **Released:** December 2007. **Price:** $39.95, hardcover. **Description:** The author explains how entrepreneurs can overcome crisis by changing the way they handle customers, by putting new processes and procedures in place, and managing employees in a professional manner. The book includes appendices with tips for hiring consultants, creating job descriptions, and setting up systems to chart cash flow as well as worksheets, tables and figures and a listing of resources. **Availability:** Print.

42273 ■ *"Evaluating the 1996-2006 Employment Projections"* in *Monthly Labor Review (Vol. 133, September 2010, No. 9, pp. 33)*
Pub: U.S. Department of Labor Bureau of Labor Statistics
Contact: Philip L. Rones, Manager
E-mail: rones.philip@bls.gov
Description: Bureau of Labor Statistics employment projections outperformed alternative naive models, but not projecting the housing bubble or the rise in oil prices caused some inaccuracies in the projects. These projections are used by policymakers, economists, and students.

42274 ■ *"Every Resume Tells a Story"* in *Women In Business (Vol. 62, September 2010, No. 3, pp. 26)*
Pub: American Business Women's Association
Contact: Lorie Burch, President
Ed: Kathleen Leighton. **Description:** Ways in which job applicants can write a good resume and promote themselves are discussed. It is believed that applicants should be proud of their accomplishments and they need to add details that will make them stand out. The importance of including a professional narrative in the resume is also explained.

42275 ■ *"Evidence-Based Management and the Marketplace For Ideas"* in *Academy of Management Journal (Vol. 50, No. 5, October 2007, pp. 1009)*
Pub: Academy of Management
Contact: Ming-Jer Chen, President
Ed: Wayne F. Cascio. **Description:** Study examines the relevance of material to actual usage in human resource management. Results reveal that it is important to design modules with execution in mind in seeking advice from professionals in relevant organizations.

42276 ■ *"Executives Exit at Wal-Mart in China"* in *Wall Street Journal Eastern Edition (October 17 , 2011, pp. B3)*
Pub: Dow Jones & Co., Inc.
Contact: Clare Hart, President
Ed: Laurie Burkitt. **Description:** Woes for Wal-Mart Inc.'s subsidiary in China are adding up as Wal-Mart China president and chief executive Ed Chan stepped down, as well as the company's senior vice president for human resources, Clara Wong. The company has been charged by regulators with mislabeling pork products, the result which has forced stores to close. Sales in China have been slow at the retail stores.

42277 ■ *"Explaining Organizational Responsiveness to Work-Life Balance Issues: the Role of Business Strategy and High-Performance Work Systems"* in *Human Resource Management (Vol. 51, May- June 2012, No. 3, pp. 407-432)*
Pub: John Wiley & Sons Inc.
Contact: Stephen M. Smith, President
Ed: Jing Wang, Anil Verma. **Description:** The effects of business strategies and high-performance work systems on the adoption of work-life balance programs are examined. Results indicate a mediating role of high-performance work systems in the relationship between business strategies and the adoption of work-life balance programs.

42278 ■ *"Exploring Supportive and Developmental Career Management Through Business Strategies and Coaching"* in *Human Resource Management (Vol. 51, January-February 2012, No. 1, pp. 99-120)*
Pub: John Wiley & Sons Inc.
Contact: Stephen M. Smith, President
Ed: Jesse Segers, Ilke Inceoglu. **Description:** Coaching and other career practices that are part of supportive and developmental career management are examined. Such practices are found to be most present in organizations with a prospector strategy.

42279 ■ *"Face Issues if Elder Care, Unemployment Collide"* in *Atlanta Journal-Constitution (December 26, 2010, pp. G1)*
Ed: Amy Lindgren. **Description:** More issues arise during holiday for families with older members requiring care, including the issue of employment for those doing the caregiving.

42280 ■ *The Facebook Era: Tapping Online Social Networks to Build Better Products, Reach New Audiences, and Sell More Stuff*
Ed: Clara Shih. **Price:** , $24.99. **Description:** The '90s were about the World Wide Web of information and the power of linking Web pages. Today it's about the World Wide Web of people and the power of the social graph. Online social networks are fundamentally changing the way we live, work, and interact. They offer businesses immense opportunities to transform customer relationships for profit: opportuni-

ties that touch virtually every business function, from sales and marketing to recruiting, collaboration to executive decision-making, product development to innovation.

42281 ■ "Falling Local Executive Pay Could Suggest a Trend" in Tampa Bay Business Journal (Vol. 30, January 15, 2010, No. 4, pp. 1)
Pub: American City Business Journals
Ed: Margie Manning. **Description:** Tampa Bay, Florida-based Raymond James Financial Inc. and MarineMax Inc.'s proxy statements have shown the decreasing compensation of the companies' highest paid executives. The falling trend in executive compensation was a result of intensified shareholder scrutiny and the economy.

42282 ■ Fast-Track Business Start-Up Kit: California
Pub: Kaplan Books
Ed: Carolyn Usinger. **Released:** 2006. **Price:** $22.95; C$29. **Description:** Step-by-step guide for starting and running a business in California, including information on sole proprietors, partnerships, limited liability companies, S and C corporations, as well as details concerning business entities, sales taxes, environmental issues, human resources, and more.

42283 ■ "Feds Finalize I-9 Form Rules Allowing Electronic Storage" in HR Specialist (Vol. 8, September 2010, No. 9, pp. 5)
Pub: Capitol Information Group Inc.
Description: U.S. Department of Homeland Security issued regulations that give employers more flexibility to electronically sing and store I-9 employee verification forms.

42284 ■ "Filling the Business Gap" in Hispanic Business (December 2010)
Ed: Richard Larsen. **Description:** New York group seeks to increase state diversity supplier spending to help create jobs and boost the economy. According to a recent study, six out of 10 small business owners will increase capital spending but delay hiring in 2011. However, potential job creation is good among businesses owned by women and minorities.

42285 ■ "First Franchising Census Report Highlights Industry's Economic Role" in Franchising World (Vol. 42, November 2010, No. 11, pp. 41)
Pub: International Franchise Association
Contact: Stephen J. Caldeira, President
E-mail: scaldeira@franchise.org
Ed: John Reynolds. **Description:** Franchise businesses accounted for 10.5 percent of businesses with paid employees in the year 2007.

42286 ■ "Future Autoworkers will Need Broader Skills" in Crain's Detroit Business (Vol. 25, June 8, 2009, No. 23, pp. 13)
Pub: Crain Communications Inc. - Detroit
Contact: Keith Crain, Chairman
Ed: Ryan Beene. **Description:** Auto industry observers report that new workers in the industry will need advanced skills and educational backgrounds in engineering and technical fields because jobs in the factories will become more technology-based and multidisciplinary.

42287 ■ "The Future of Work" in Black Enterprise (Vol. 41, August 2010, No. 1, pp. 65)
Pub: Earl G. Graves Publishing Co. Inc.
Contact: Earl G. Graves, Jr., President
Ed: Annya M. Lott. **Description:** Technology, globalization, and outsourcing will continue to shape the future of work. Social media is a means for small companies to market goods and services.

42288 ■ "The Future of Work" in Business Strategy Review (Vol. 21, Autumn 2010, No. 3, pp. 16)
Pub: John Wiley & Sons Inc. Scientific, Technical, Medical, and Scholarly Div. (Wiley-Blackwell)
Contact: William J. Pesce, Manager
E-mail: wpesce@wiley.com
Ed: Lynda Gratton. **Description:** Work is universal. Buy, how, why, where and when we work has never been so open to individual interpretation. The certain-

ties of the past have been replaced by ambiguity, questions and the steady hum of technology. Research covering 21 global companies and more than 200 executives covers the future of work.

42289 ■ "Generation Y: Engaging the Invincibles" in Employee Benefit News (Vol. 25, November 1, 2011, No. 14, pp. 22)
Pub: SourceMedia Inc.
Contact: James M. Malkin, Chief Executive Officer
Ed: Brenna Shebel, Dannel Dan. **Description:** Employers will need to engage younger workers about healthcare decisions and lifestyle improvement as they become the majority worker as boomers retire.

42290 ■ "Get Prepared for New Employee Free Choice Act" in HRMagazine (Vol. 53, December 2008, No. 12, pp. 22)
Ed: Allen Smith. **Description:** According to the director of global labor and employee relations with Ingersoll Rand Company, unions may have started having employees signing authorization cards in anticipation of the Employee Free Choice Act. Once signed, the cards are good for one year and employers would have only ten days in which to prepare for bargaining with unions over the first labor contract. The Act also requires these negotiations be subject to mandatory arbitration if a contract is not reached within 120 days of negotiations with unions, resulting in employers' wage rates, health insurance, retirement benefits and key language about flexibility would be determined by an arbitrator with no vested interest in the success of the company.

42291 ■ "Getting Going on Going Green" in HRMagazine (Vol. 53, August 2008, No. 8, pp. 8)
Pub: Society for Human Resource Management
Contact: Henry G. Jackson, President
E-mail: hjackson@shrm.org
Ed: Rita Zeidner. **Description:** Being eco-friendly can help recruit and retain workers. Resources to help firms create green initiatives are presented.

42292 ■ "Gilt Groupe's CEO On Building a Team of A Players" in Harvard Business Review (Vol. 90, January-February 2012, No.1-2, pp. 43)
Pub: Harvard Business Review Press
Contact: Peter E. Walsh, Director
Ed: Kevin Ryan. **Released:** January-February 2012. **Description:** The author stresses the role of human capital in a firm's success, and the importance of employment references in determining a candidate's talents. Key questions include whether the reference would hire the person, whether people enjoy working with him or her, and what areas could use improvements.

42293 ■ "Give 'Em a Break" in Entrepreneur (Vol. 35, November 2007, No. 11, pp. 32)
Pub: Entrepreneur Press
Contact: Perlman Neil, President
Ed: J.J. Ramberg. **Description:** Andy Walter and Peer Pedersen founded Blue Orchid Capital, a fund of hedge funds, and Steamboat Foundation a foundation that helps college students find high-profile summer internships. Details on the fund and the foundation are presented.

42294 ■ "The Global Talent Hunt" in Business Strategy Review (Vol. 21, Spring 2010, No. 1, pp. 78)
Pub: John Wiley & Sons Inc. Scientific, Technical, Medical, and Scholarly Div. (Wiley-Blackwell)
Contact: William J. Pesce, Manager
E-mail: wpesce@wiley.com
Ed: Richard Emerton. **Description:** Richard Emerton explains how the new 'triple context' of economy, environment and society will have profound implications for human resource practices. He suggests that viewing talent as abundant is the right perspective for a manager.

42295 ■ "Glossary of Health Benefit Terms" in HRMagazine (Vol. 53, August 2008, No. 8, pp. 78)
Pub: Society for Human Resource Management
Contact: Henry G. Jackson, President
E-mail: hjackson@shrm.org
Description: Glossary of health benefit terms is presented to help when choosing a health benefits package.

42296 ■ The Green Collar Economy: How One Solution Can Fix Our Two Biggest Problems
Pub: HarperCollins Publishers Inc.
Contact: Jane Friedman, President
E-mail: jfriedman@harpercollins.com
Ed: Van Jones. **Released:** September 29, 2009. **Price:** $14.99, paperack; $10.99; C$11.99. **Description:** This book offers insight into rebuilding the nation's infrastructure and creating alternative energy sources that could boost the economy through increased employment and higher wages while decreasing our dependence on fossil fuels. **Availability:** PrintE-book.

42297 ■ "The Green Industry Jobs Gap" in Green Industry Pro (Vol. 23, October 2011)
Pub: Cygnus Business Media
Contact: Paul Mackler, Chief Executive Officer
Ed: Gregg Wartgow. **Description:** According to the U.S. Bureau of Labor Statistics, the landscaping industry employs over 829,000 workers. According to another private study, the industry would employ more if they were able to find more people interested in performing the required work.

42298 ■ "Grooming Your Online Persona" in Women In Business (Vol. 62, June 2010, No. 2, pp. 36)
Pub: American Business Women's Association
Contact: Lorie Burch, President
Ed: Diane Stafford. **Description:** Employees' use of online social networks could become a basis on how their employers, clients, or business partners would judge them. Personal details, pictures and other online data should be filtered to avoid inappropriate or uncomfortable situations and distinguish personal from professional or work life.

42299 ■ "Guidance On Career Guidance for Offender Reentry" in Occupational Outlook Quarterly (Vol. 54, Fall 2010, No. 3, pp. 24)
Pub: U.S. Department of Labor Bureau of Labor Statistics
Contact: Philip L. Rones, Manager
E-mail: rones.philip@bls.gov
Description: Stable employment is a key factor in the successful rehabilitation of law offenders. The National Institute of Corrections hopes to improve offenders' long-term employment prospects.

42300 ■ "Health Job Shift Looms" in Boston Business Journal (Vol. 31, June 3, 2011, No. 19, pp. 3)
Pub: Boston Business Journal
Ed: Julie M. Donnelly. **Description:** Pending health care payment reform in Massachusetts is seen to adversely impact hospital staff. Hospitals are also seen to serve more patients once the bill is approved.

42301 ■ "Hickory Unemployment Stays Steady" in Charlotte Observer (February 2, 2007)
Ed: Jen Aronoff. **Description:** Unemployment rates remained unchanged in Hickory, North Carolina area; the region reported 6.1 percent unemployment.

42302 ■ "High-Tech Job-Apalooza!" in Orlando Business Journal (Vol. 26, January 15, 2010, No. 33, pp. 1)
Pub: American City Business Journals
Ed: Christopher Boyd. **Description:** Science Applications International Corporation, Saab Training USA LLC, CAE USA, and Pelliconi &C.SPA attempt to obtain $939,000 in tax incentives to generate 222 technology and defense-related jobs in Orange County, Florida. Each job will provide an average salary of $67,000. Future plans of each technology and defense firm are also presented.

42303 ■ "Hire Power" in Entrepreneur (Vol. 35, November 2007, No. 11, pp. 105)
Pub: Entrepreneur Press
Contact: Perlman Neil, President
Ed: Mark Henricks. **Description:** Companies with big resources may hire human resource (HR) consultants to help with writing manuals, drafting policies

and designing benefits for employees. HR consultants may also be hired to assist with specific functions or other strategic aspects.

42304 ■ "HireDiversity: Some Companies Developing Affinity for Employee Groups" in Hispanic Business (October 2007, pp. 86-87)
Ed: Hildy Medina. **Description:** Affinity groups, also known as employee resource networks, help companies identify and recruit candidates.

42305 ■ "The Hiring Handbook: Tips & Tactics to Attract Top Tier Talent"
Pub: CreateSpace
Contact: Daren Giles, President
Released: October 22, 2014. **Price:** , $11.95 paperback. **Description:** All the information needed to recruit and hire the best talent for any small business is presented. While intended for hiring managers, the information is useful for any human resources executives as well as job seekers.

42306 ■ "Holiday Cheer" in Business Journal-Serving Phoenix & the Valley of the Sun (Vol. 31, December 3, 2010, No. 13, pp. 1)
Pub: Phoenix Business Journal
Ed: Lynn Ducey, Mike Sunnucks. **Description:** Results of a study conducted by Challenger, Gray & Christmas Inc., shows that 68 percent of companies are planning holiday parties in 2010, up slightly from 62 percent in 2009. About 53 percent of those having holiday parties are holding them on company premises.

42307 ■ "Host"
Pub: Solutions Business Publishing
Released: October 1, 2014. **Price:** , $15.99 paperback. **Description:** Great engagement is the key to any successful business leadership. Host leadership involves six new roles in employee engagement: adopt the four positions for a Host Leader; understand how to step into and out of the six new roles of engagement; achieve greater agility, flexibility, and responsiveness; become a leader with a highly tuned sense of relationship building and engagement.

42308 ■ "Hourly Payment and Volunteering: The Effect of Organizational Practices on Decisions About Time Use" in Academy of Management Journal (Vol. 50, No. 4, August 1, 2007, pp. 783)
Pub: Academy of Management
Contact: Ming-Jer Chen, President
Ed: Sanford E. DeVoe, Jeffrey Pfeffer. **Description:** Brief description about theoretically important class of work, which is freely undertaken without remuneration, is presented.

42309 ■ "How to Avoid Leave-Related Lawsuits" in Employee Benefit News (Vol. 25, December 1, 2011, No. 15, pp. 12)
Pub: SourceMedia Inc.
Contact: James M. Malkin, Chief Executive Officer
Ed: John F. Galvin. **Description:** Tips for employers when adding disability and maternity leave benefits to workers are outlined, with focus on ways to avoid leave-related lawsuits.

42310 ■ How to Become a Great Boss: The Rules for Getting and Keeping the Best Employees
Pub: Hyperion
Ed: Jeffrey J. Fox. **Released:** May 15, 2002. **Price:** $17, hardcover; C$19, hardcover. **Description:** The book offers valuable advice to any manager or entrepreneur to improve leadership and management skills. Topics covered include: hiring, managing, firing, partnership and competition, self and organization, employee performance, attitude, and priorities. **Availability:** Print.

42311 ■ "How Hard Could It Be? The Four Pillars of Organic Growth" in Inc. (January 2008, pp. 69-70)
Pub: Gruner and Jahr USA Publishing Co.
Contact: J. Russell Denson, President
Ed: Joel Spolsky. **Description:** Revenue, head count, public relations, and quality are the four most important aspects of any growing business.

42312 ■ How to Start and Run Your Own Corporation: S-Corporations For Small Business Owners
Pub: HCM Publishing
Ed: Peter I. Hupalo. **Released:** Second Edition. **Price:** $22.46, paperback. **Description:** Basics of corporate business structure are explained. Topics include discovering the best business structure for your company; how to decided between an S-Corporation and LLC; choosing the state in which to incorporate, how to form a corporation, angel investing, special issues for one-person corporations, the role of bylaws and corporate minutes, board of directors, taxes, workers' compensation issues, retirement plans, and more. **Availability:** Print.

42313 ■ "How To Reduce the Risk of Discrimination" in Idaho Business Review (September 11, 2014)
Pub: Dolan Co.
Contact: James P. Dolan, President
Released: September 11, 2014. **Description:** Human resource departments in small businesses in Boise are aware of the city's discrimination ordinance making it unlawful to use sexual orientation and gender identity/expression in any consideration of hiring or terminating an employee, or for any other issue. The impact of the ordinance is yet to be determined.

42314 ■ "How to Turn Employee Conflict Into a Positive, Productive Force" in HR Specialist (Vol. 8, September 2010, No. 9, pp. 6)
Pub: Capitol Information Group Inc.
Description: Ways to help manage a team of workers are presented, focusing on ways to avoid conflict within the group are discussed.

42315 ■ "HR Technology: Meetings Go Virtual" in HRMagazine (Vol. 54, January 2009, No. 1, pp. 74)
Pub: Society for Human Resource Management
Contact: Henry G. Jackson, President
E-mail: hjackson@shrm.org
Ed: Elizabeth Agnvall. **Description:** Microsoft Office Live Meeting conferencing software allows companies to schedule meetings from various company locations, thus saving travel costs.

42316 ■ HRD in Small Organizations: Research and Practice
Pub: Routledge
Contact: Kevin Bradley, President
E-mail: kbradley@taylorandfrancis.com
Released: March 26, 2007. **Price:** $54.95, paperback. **Description:** Approaches to human resource development in small organizations are evaluated. **Availability:** Print.

42317 ■ "Human Capital: When Change Means Terminating an Employee" in Black Enterprise (Vol. 41, November 2010, No. 4, pp. 40)
Pub: Earl G. Graves Publishing Co. Inc.
Contact: Earl G. Graves, Jr., President
Ed: Tamara E. Holmes. **Description:** Covering successful business change strategies, this article focuses on how the law and nondiscrimination policies can affect this aspect of the workplace.

42318 ■ "The Human Element" in Canadian Business (Vol. 80, April 23, 2007, No. 9, pp. 78)
Ed: Jeff Sanford. **Description:** The effects of human resource programs on stocks and investor relations are presented.

42319 ■ Human Resource Executive's Market Resource (Human resources)
Pub: LRP Publications Library
Contact: Kenneth Kahn, President
E-mail: kKahn@lrp.com
URL(s): www.lrp.com. **Released:** Annual; November. **Covers:** Approximately 100 vendor companies and associations serving all aspects of human resources administration, including benefits, consulting and information services, software, employee assistance programs, health care, meeting and conference facilities, out placement and recruitment services, pension

and retirement, recognition awards and incentives, relocation services, safety and security, temporary services, testing and assessment, training and development, and other services. **Entries include:** Company name, address, phone, product/service, company philosophy, facilities, literature available, etc. **Database includes:** Human resources calendar of events; new literature review. **Arrangement:** Classified by product/service. **Indexes:** Name.

42320 ■ "Human Resource Management: Challenges for Graduate Education" in Business Horizons (Vol. 51, March-April 2008, No. 2, pp. 151)
Pub: Elsevier Advanced Technology Publications
Ed: James C. Wimbush. **Description:** Human resource management education at the master's and doctoral degree levels is discussed. There is an ever-increasing need to produce human resource managers who understand the value of human resource management as a strategic business contributor. uman.

42321 ■ "Human Resources or was it Human Remains? True Stories from a Career in HR"
Pub: CreateSpace
Contact: Daren Giles, President
Released: October 20, 2014. **Price:** , $12.85 paperback. **Description:** True stories covering a twenty year career in Human Resources and the challenges faced by these managers is presented.

42322 ■ Human Resources for Small Business Made Easy
Ed: Ruth Zimmerman. **Released:** November 2006. **Description:** Guide for human resource development for small businesses.

42323 ■ "I Quit...Six Months From Now" in Canadian Business (Vol. 85, July 16, 2012, No. 11-12, pp. 71)
Pub: George Media Inc.
Ed: Matthew McClearn. **Released:** July 16, 2012. **Description:** Employees who are planning to resign should consider the notice period, the time it will take for employers to find a replacement and the reason for leaving. Departing employees can use their knowledge and skills to compete directly with their former employer, but they should be wary of unfair competition.

42324 ■ "If Just One Person Applies, Are You Required to Hire Him?" in HR Specialist (Vol. 8, September 2010, No. 9, pp. 7)
Description: It is legal to decline hiring an applicant, or even promoting a current employee, if they are the only applicant for a particular position. It may be good choice to wait for more applicants or to change recruiting strategy.

42325 ■ "Immigration: Give Us Your Skilled" in Canadian Business (Vol. 80, October 8, 2007, No. 20, pp. 78)
Pub: Rogers Media Inc.
Contact: Tony Viner, President
Ed: Zena Olijnyk. **Description:** Demand for skilled workers in Canada is discussed. Despite a strong demand, as evidenced by shortages in both skilled and unskilled labor, the country's immigration policy is affecting the recruitment process. Peter Veress, founder and president of Vermax Group, believes the country is wasting opportunities to take advantage of its attractiveness as a destination for foreign workers.

42326 ■ "The Incentive Bubble: Outsourcing Pay Decisions To Financial Markets Has Skewed Compensation and, With It, American Capitalism" in Harvard Business Review (Vol. 90, March 2012, No. 3, pp. 124)
Pub: Harvard Business Review Press
Contact: Peter E. Walsh, Director
Ed: Mihir Desai. **Released:** March 2012. **Description:** Basing incentive contracts and executive compensation on financial markets actually rewards luck rather than performance, and can promote dangerous risk taking. This has led to America's two main crises of capitalism: growing income inequality and governance failures. Boards of directors must

focus on performance rather than stocks, and endowments and foundations must focus on incentives for long-term growth.

42327 ■ "Inch by Inch, Employees Lose Ground" in Business Courier (Vol. 26, November 13, 2009, No. 29, pp. 1)
Pub: American City Business Journals, Inc.
Contact: Whitney Shaw, President
Ed: James Ritchie. **Description:** Employees in Ohio who retained their jobs have suffered losses in salary and other benefits, as companies exert efforts to save money. Thirty-four percent of employees experienced pay cuts. Statistical data included.

42328 ■ "Increasing HR's Strategic Participation: the Effect of HR Service Quality and Contribution Expectations" in Human Resource Management (Vol. 51, January-February 2012, No. 1, pp. 3-23)
Pub: John Wiley & Sons Inc.
Contact: Stephen M. Smith, President
Ed: Jin Feng Uen, David Ahlstrom, Shu-Yuan Chen, Pai-Wei Tseng. **Description:** The impact of human resources service quality and human resources contribution expectations on the strategic participation of human resources in organizations is examined. Human resource professionals are found to increase the organizational value of human resources through improving quality and addressing the needs of potential internal customers.

42329 ■ "Injury and Illness Data" in Montly Labor Review (Vol. 133, September 2010, No. 9, pp. 147)
Pub: U.S. Department of Labor Bureau of Labor Statistics
Contact: Philip L. Rones, Manager
E-mail: rones.philip@bls.gov
Description: Occupational injury and illness rates by industry in the U.S. are presented.

42330 ■ "The Ins and Outs of Unemployment in Canada, 1976-2008" in Canadian Journal of Economics (Vol. 44, November 2011, No. 4, pp. 1331)
Pub: Wiley-Blackwell
Contact: Gordon Tibbitts, President
Ed: Michele Campolieti. **Description:** Flows into and out of unemployment in Canada at an aggregate and a number of disaggregated levels are studied.

42331 ■ "Interbrand's Creative Recruiting Keeps Top Talent in Cincinnati" in Business Courier (Vol. 27, November 12, 2010, No. 28, pp. 1)
Pub: Business Courier
Ed: Dan Monk. **Description:** Global brand consulting firm Interbrand uses a creative recruitment agency to attract new employees into the company. Interbrand uses themed parties to attract prospective employees. The 'Alice In Wonderland' tea party for example, allowed the company to hire five new employees.

42332 ■ "Interest in 'Encore Careers' is Growing" in HRMagazine (Vol. 53, November 2008, No. 11, pp. 22)
Pub: Society for Human Resource Management
Contact: Henry G. Jackson, President
E-mail: hjackson@shrm.org
Ed: Kathy Gurchiek. **Description:** Unexpectedly large numbers of baby boomers are looking for jobs that can provide them with 'means and meaning', according to a survey by MetLife and Civic Ventures. They can find those jobs in encore careers, an opportunity to do work that has a social impact and personal meaning.

42333 ■ "International Benefits Roundup" in Employee Benefit News (Vol. 25, December 1, 2011, No. 15)
Pub: SourceMedia Inc.
Contact: James M. Malkin, Chief Executive Officer
Description: Employee contributions to an employer-sponsored defined contribution plan in Japan will allowed on a tax-deductible basis; however, currently employee contributions are not allowed. The defined contribution plan is outlined for better understanding.

42334 ■ "International Comparisons Data" in Montly Labor Review (Vol. 133, September 2010, No. 9, pp. 143)
Pub: U.S. Department of Labor Bureau of Labor Statistics
Contact: Philip L. Rones, Manager
E-mail: rones.philip@bls.gov
Description: Unemployment rates adjusted to U.S. concepts and ten countries are presented.

42335 ■ International Handbook of Entrepreneurship and HRM
Pub: Edward Elgar Publishing Inc.
Contact: Richard Henning, Vice President
E-mail: kwight@e-elgar.com
Ed: Rowena Barrett, Susan Mayson. **Released:** 2010. **Price:** £31.20, paperback. **Description:** Conceived on the basis that there is a growing recognition of the interplay between human resource management and entrepreneurship, this volume offers insights into the role of HRM and entrepreneurial firms. **Availability:** Print.

42336 ■ "Interning Your Way to the Right Career" in Business Review Albany (Vol. 41, June 20, 2014, No. 12, pp. 9)
Pub: American City Business Journals, Inc.
Contact: Whitney Shaw, President
Released: June 20, 2014. **Description:** The degree boom has made it increasingly important for students to participate in internship programs in order to stand out. Internship programs also provide companies with several benefits.

42337 ■ "Is It Time to Ban Swearing in the Workplace?" in HR Specialist (Vol. 8, September 2010, No. 9, pp. 2)
Pub: Capitol Information Group Inc.
Description: Screening software has been developed to identify profanity used in business correspondence.

42338 ■ "Is Your Employees' BMI Your Business?" in Canadian Business (Vol. 83, September 14, 2010, No. 15, pp. 98)
Pub: Rogers Media Inc.
Contact: Tony Viner, President
Ed: Jacqueline Nelson. **Description:** Canada's Public Health Agency's research shows that there is a solid business case for companies to promote active living to their employees. However, employers must toe the line between being helpful and being invasive. Insights into the issues faces by companies when introducing health programs are discussed.

42339 ■ "Job Corps Center Remains Vacant After Operator is Booted" in Tampa Bay Business Journal (Vol. 30, January 15, 2010, No. 4, pp. 1)
Pub: American City Business Journals
Ed: Jane Meinhardt. **Description:** Pinellas County, Florida Job Corps Center has remained vacant due to a conflict over the $16 million contract awarded to Res-Care Inc. by the US Department of Labor (DOL) The DOL has ordered Res-Care to stop operation at the center and it is uncertain when it will open or what company will operate it.

42340 ■ "Job Reviews: Annual Assessments Still the Norm" in HR Specialist (Vol. 8, September 2010, No. 9, pp. 1)
Description: An OfficeTeam survey of 500 HR professionals asked how their organizations conduct formal performance appraisals. Responses to the questions are examined.

42341 ■ "Job Seeker's Readiness Guide: Unemployment's High and Competition is Tough" in Black Enterprise (Vol. 40, July 2010, No. 12, pp. 83)
Pub: Earl G. Graves Publishing Co. Inc.
Contact: Earl G. Graves, Jr., President
Description: Five key areas to help someone seeking employment gain the competitive edge are listed.

42342 ■ "A Jobs Compact for America's Future: Badly Needed Investments In Human Capital Are Not Being Made. What We Can Do - Together - To Jump-Start the Process?" in

Harvard Business Review (Vol. 90, March 2012, No. 3, pp. 64)
Pub: Harvard Business Review Press
Contact: Peter E. Walsh, Director
Ed: Thomas A. Kochan. **Released:** March 2012. **Description:** Obstacles to strengthening US human capital are a lack of focus on obtaining both high wages and high productivity, and a lack of value placed on human capital as a competitive advantage. Business schools are well positioned to address these obstacles via curricula, programs, and partnerships.

42343 ■ "Jobs Data Show Wild Card" in Barron's (Vol. 90, September 6, 2010, No. 36, pp. M12)
Pub: Barron's Editorial & Corporate Headquarters
Ed: Gene Epstein. **Description:** August 2010 jobs report revealed a 54,000 decline in non-farm payrolls and that the unemployment rate remains unchanged at 9.6 percent. The report also shows a welcome rise of 848,999 in the household-data category. The unemployment rate shows a reversed trend where men's 10.6 percent unemployment is higher than women's 8.6 percent rate.

42344 ■ "The Jobs Man: Working with Cincinnati's Unemployed" in Business Courier (Vol. 26, December 25, 2009, No. 35, pp. 1)
Pub: American City Business Journals, Inc.
Contact: Whitney Shaw, President
Ed: Lucy May. **Description:** Entrepreneur Bob Messer, a volunteer for Jobs Plus Employment Network in Cincinnati's Over-the-Rhine neighborhood, regularly conducts a seminar that aims to help attendees prepare for employment. Jobs Plus founder Burr Robinson asked Messer to create the seminar in order to help unemployed jobseekers. So far, the program has helped 144 individuals with full time jobs in 2009.

42345 ■ "Jobs: On the Clock" in Canadian Business (Vol. 82, April 27, 2009, No. 7, pp. 28)
Pub: Rogers Media Inc.
Contact: Tony Viner, President
Ed: Sarka Halas. **Description:** Survey of 100 Canadian executives found that senior managers can be out of a job for about nine months before their careers are adversely affected. The nine month mark can be avoided if job seekers build networks even before they lose their jobs. Job seekers should also take volunteer work and training opportunities to increase their changes of landing a job.

42346 ■ "Know It All Finds Applicants are Stretching the Truth" in Philadelphia Business Journal (Vol. 28, September 11, 2009, No. 30, pp. 1)
Pub: American City Business Journals Inc.
Ed: Athena D. Merritt. **Description:** Know It All Background Research Services has reported that discrepancies in background checks reached 19.8 percent in 2009. Reports show that 42 percent of the discrepancies involve lying about previous employment, and 37 percent involve education information. Marc Bourne, the company's vice president, believes that employers have cause to be concerned.

42347 ■ "Labor Force Data" in Montly Labor Review (Vol. 133, September 2010, No. 9, pp. 89)
Pub: U.S. Department of Labor Bureau of Labor Statistics
Contact: Philip L. Rones, Manager
E-mail: rones.philip@bls.gov
Description: Employment status of the population of the U.S. by sex, age, race and origin is presented.

42348 ■ "Laying the Groundwork: In Developing Personnel, the Work Takes Place Beforehand" in Black Enterprise (February 2008)
Pub: Earl G. Graves Publishing Co. Inc.
Contact: Earl G. Graves, Jr., President
Ed: Tamara E. Holmes. **Description:** Small business owners know the devastation of hiring the wrong employee for a position. Steps to improve hiring using a long-term plan are outlined.

42349 ■ "Layoffs Continue to Be a Drag on Region's Recovery" in Philadelphia Business Journal (Vol. 28, January 22, 2010, No. 49, pp. 1)
Pub: American City Business Journals Inc.
Ed: Athena D. Merritt. Description: Mass layoffs continue to hamper Pennsylvania's economic recovery. Job losses are predicted to decline in 2010.

42350 ■ "The Leadership Equation: 10 Practices That Build Trust, Spark Innovation, and Create High-Performing Organizations"
Pub: Greenleaf Book Group Press
Released: September 30, 2014. Price: , $18.95 paperback. Description: Entrepreneur and business consultant draws upon his work with corporations, government agencies, and nonprofit organizations and their human resource departments to explain the workings of high-performing organizations with his equation: Trust + Spark = Leadership Culture. He describes the ten more important practices for building trust and spark that improves team performance, the business unit, and the entire organization.

42351 ■ "Legalities of Diversity" in Hispanic Business (September 2007, pp. 26)
Ed: Francisco Ramos Jr., Bill Krutzen. Description: Most companies in America have diversity programs, however, critics believe diversity can be used as reverse discrimination because minorities are getting preferential treatment in hiring, promotion, and admissions.

42352 ■ "Less Than Zero" in Canadian Business (Vol. 80, November 5, 2007, No. 22, pp. 36)
Ed: Andy Holloway. Description: Zero-tolerance policy with regards to discrimination and harassment at the workplace has been adopted by many companies. However, employers must exercise caution in terminating employees based on zero-tolerance policies since there are laws governing illegal dismissals. Important considerations employers should make in dismissing workers, such as proof of willful misconduct, are discussed.

42353 ■ "Linking HRM and Knowledge Transfer Via Individual-Level Mechanisms" in Human Resource Management (Vol. 51,May-June 2012, No. 3, pp. 387-405)
Pub: John Wiley & Sons Inc.
Contact: Stephen M. Smith, President
Ed: Dana B. Minbaeva, Kristina Makela, Larissa Rabbiosi. Description: The relationship between human resource management and knowledge transfer and the role of individual-level mechanisms in this relationship are examined. Results indicate that individual-level perceptions of organizational commitment to knowledge sharing and extrinsic motivation affect internal knowledge exchange among employees.

42354 ■ "Linking Human Capital to Competitive Advantages: Flexibility in a Manufacturing Firm's Supply Chain" in Human Resource Management (Vol. 49, September-October 2010, No. 5)
Pub: John Wiley
Ed: Yan Jin, Margaret M. Hopkins, Jenell L.S. Wittmer. Description: A study was conducted to confirm the links among human capital, firm flexibility, and firm performance. The study also examines the emerging role of flexibility for a company's performance. A total of 201 senior supply chain management professionals from several manufacturing companies were included in the study.

42355 ■ "Looking To Hire Young? Be Careful" in Boston Business Journal (Vol. 30, November 19, 2010, No. 43, pp. 1)
Pub: Boston Business Journal
Ed: Lisa van der Pool. Description: The Massachusetts Commission Against Discrimination (MCAD) has been using undercover job applicants to expose discrimination. Cabot's Ice Cream and Restaurant has been accused of denying older workers equal employment opportunities. MCAD has discovered unfair hiring practices such as hiring high school and college students.

42356 ■ "Lowering Retirement System Barriers for Women" in Employee Benefit News (Vol. 25, December 1, 2011, No. 15)
Pub: SourceMedia Inc.
Contact: James M. Malkin, Chief Executive Officer
Ed: Mary Nell Billings. Description: Challenges faced by small business for lowering retirement benefits barriers for women and minorities, which is difficult to put into practice, is discussed.

42357 ■ "Macroeconomic Policy and U.S. Competitiveness: A Reformed Fiscal Policy Is Vital To Renewing America's Productivity" in Harvard Business Review (Vol. 90, March 2012, No. 3, pp. 112)
Pub: Harvard Business Review Press
Contact: Peter E. Walsh, Director
Ed: Richard H.K. Vietor, Matthew Weinzierl. Released: March 2012. Description: Improving productivity requires increasing physical capital (such as equipment or technology), raising human capital, or using both of these types of capital more efficiently. The authors promote a plan that blends cuts in defense and health care spending, adjustments to Social Security, and carbon and gas taxes.

42358 ■ "Make a Resolution: ADA Training" in HRMagazine (Vol. 54, January 2009, No. 1, pp. 81)
Pub: Society for Human Resource Management
Contact: Henry G. Jackson, President
E-mail: hjackson@shrm.org
Ed: Victoria Zellers. Description: Americans with Disabilities Act (ADA) Amendments Act took effect January 1, 2009. The ADA Amendments Act means that more applicants and employees are eligible for reasonable accommodations and that employers need to develop a new ADA compliance strategy.

42359 ■ Managing the Older Worker: How to Prepare for the New Organizational Order
Pub: Harvard Business Press
Ed: Peter Cappelli, Bill Novelli. Released: August 17, 2010. Price: $29.95, hardcover. Description: Your organization needs older workers more than ever: They transfer knowledge between generations, transmit your company's values to new hires, make excellent mentors for younger employees, and provide a 'just in time' workforce for special projects. Availability: Print.

42360 ■ "Managing Risks: A New Framework: Smart Companies Match Their Approach to the Nature of the Threats They Face" in (Vol. 90, June 2012, No. 6, pp. 48)
Pub: Harvard Business Review Press
Contact: Peter E. Walsh, Director
Ed: Robert S. Kaplan, Anette Mikes. Released: June 2012. Description: The importance of strategic planning in effect risk management practices is stressed. Discussion includes preventable risks, strategy risks, and external risks and provides objectives, control models, staff functions, and the business-unit interrelationships of each.

42361 ■ "Managing Yourself: Job-Hopping to the Top and Other Career Fallacies" in Harvard Business Review (Vol. 88, July-August 2010, No. 7-8, pp. 154)
Pub: Harvard Business School Publishing
Ed: Monika Hamori. Description: Fallacies identified and discussed include the belief that a career move should always be a move up, that industry and career switches are penalized, and that large corporations are the only loci for reaping large rewards.

42362 ■ "M&I Execs May Get Golden Parachutes" in Business Journal-Milwaukee (Vol. 28, December 31, 2010, No. 14, pp. A3)
Pub: Milwaukee Business Journal
Ed: Rich Kirchen. Description: Marshall and Isley Corporation's top executives have a chance to receive golden-parachute payments it its buyer, BMO Financial Group, repays the Troubled Asset Relief Program (TARP) loan on behalf of the company. One TARP rule prevents golden-parachute payments to them and the next five most highly paid employees of TARP recipients.

42363 ■ "A Manufacturing Revival" in Boston Business Journal (Vol. 31, May 27, 2011, No. 18, pp. 1)
Pub: Boston Business Journal
Ed: Kyle Alspach. Description: Massachusetts' manufacturing sector has grown despite the high cost of labor, real estate and electricity. Manufacturing jobs in the state have increased to 2,800 in April 2011.

42364 ■ "Mapping Out a Career" in Occupational Outlook Quarterly (Vol. 54, Fall 2010, No. 3, pp. 12)
Pub: U.S. Department of Labor Bureau of Labor Statistics
Contact: Philip L. Rones, Manager
E-mail: rones.philip@bls.gov
Ed: Audrey Watson. Description: Geographic distribution of occupations is studied, along with lifestyle considerations when choosing a career.

42365 ■ "Market Recoups Its Losses - And Its Optimism" in Barron's (Vol. 89, July 20, 2009, No. 29, pp. M3)
Pub: Dow Jones & Co., Inc.
Contact: Clare Hart, President
Ed: Kopin Tan. Description: US stock markets gained heavily in the third week of July 2009, rising by about 7 percent during the week. The shares of human resource management companies could be overpriced as they are trading at very high price-earnings multiples. Baxter International faces a class-action suit due to its alleged conspiracy with CSL to fix blood-plasma product prices.

42366 ■ "Maryland Legislature to Tackle Crisis in Jobless Fund" in Baltimore Business Journal (Vol. 27, December 18, 2009, No. 32, pp. 1)
Pub: American City Business Journals
Ed: Scott Dance. Description: Maryland's General Assembly is set to finalize changes to the state's unemployment insurance system as soon as it convenes for the 2010 session. The move was aimed to draw $127 million in stimulus money that can support the nearly depleted fund of unemployment benefits within 45 days.

42367 ■ "May I Handle That For You?" in Inc. (March 2008, pp. 40, 42)
Pub: Mansueto Ventures L.L.C.
Contact: John Koten, Chief Executive Officer
Ed: Taylor Mallory. Description: According to a recent survey, 53 percent of all companies outsource a portion of their human resources responsibilities. Ceridian, Administaff, Taleo, KnowledgeBank, and CheckPoint HR are among the companies profiled.

42368 ■ "Mayor Unveils Business Plan" in Boston Business Journal (Vol. 29, September 16, 2011, No. 19, pp. 1)
Pub: American City Business Journals, Inc.
Ed: Gary Haber. Description: Mayor Stephanie Rawlings-Blake of Baltimore, Maryland unveiled her plan to push the economy forward. Her key objectives include giving more support for the city's technology companies and refocusing the Baltimore Development Corporation on job creation and retention.

42369 ■ MBA In A Day: What You Would Learn At Top-Tier Business Schools (If You Only Had The Time!)
Pub: John Wiley & Sons Inc.
Contact: Stephen M. Smith, President
Ed: Steven Stralser. Released: September 2004. Price: $34.95, hardcover; $22.99. Description: Management professor presents important concepts, business topics and strategies that can be used by anyone to manage a small business or professional practice. Topics covered include: human resources and personal interaction, ethics and leadership skills, fair negotiation tactics, basic business accounting practices, project management, and the fundamentals of economics and marketing. Availability: PrintE-book.

42370 ■ *"Meet Rebecca. She's Here to Fire You"* in *Inc. (November 2007, pp. 25-26)*
Pub: Mansueto Ventures L.L.C.
Contact: John Koten, Chief Executive Officer
Ed: Max Chafkin. **Description:** Amid liability concerns as well as CEO guilt, more and more firms are using consulting companies to fire workers. These outsourced firms help small companies structure severance and document information in order to limit legal liability when firing an employee.

42371 ■ *"Mill Creek Greenway Project Could Forge Path to Jobs, Growth"* in *Business Courier (Vol. 26, September 11, 2009, No. 20, pp. 1)*
Pub: American City Business Journals, Inc.
Contact: Whitney Shaw, President
Ed: Lucy May. **Description:** The planned 13.5 mile Mill Creek Greenway Trail extension could create 445 jobs and bring $52 million to the economy of Cincinnati, Ohio. The trail extension would cost $24 million and would be used for recreational purposes.

42372 ■ *"Mind the Gap"* in *Canadian Business (Vol. 80, November 5, 2007, No. 22, pp. 21)*
Ed: Matthew McCleam. **Description:** The average difference in median wages between men and women who have full-time jobs, according to the Organization Co-operation and Development is over 15 percent and that number is above 20 percent in Canada. The difference in earnings has become smaller since the 1960s, as more women have joined the labor market. The reasons for the wage gap are examined.

42373 ■ *"Mismanaging Pay and Performance"* in *Business Strategy Review (Vol. 21, Summer 2010, No. 2, pp. 54)*
Pub: John Wiley & Sons Inc. Scientific, Technical, Medical, and Scholarly Div. (Wiley-Blackwell)
Contact: William J. Pesce, Manager
E-mail: wpesce@wiley.com
Ed: Rupert Merson. **Description:** Understanding the relationship between performance measurement and desired behaviors is an important element of a company's talent management.

42374 ■ *"Miss Manners Minds Your Business"*
Pub: W.W. Norton and Co.
Released: October 20, 2014. **Price:** , $16.95 paperback. **Description:** Office etiquette is outlined. Practical, pertinent and correct advice is given covering office manners for anyone from convening a focus group to Human Resources management.

42375 ■ *"Mission: Recruitment"* in *HRMagazine (Vol. 54, January 2009, No. 1, pp. 42)*
Pub: Society for Human Resource Management
Contact: Henry G. Jackson, President
E-mail: hjackson@shrm.org
Ed: Theresa Minton-Eversole. **Description:** Due to the hiring challenges faced by Army recruiters, they are partnering with employers in order to establish connections to high quality, Army-trained individuals when they separate from active duty.

42376 ■ *"The Moderating Effects of Organizational Context On the Relationship Between Voluntary Turnover and Organizational Performance: Evidence from Korea"* in *Human Resource Management (Vol. 51, January-February 2012, No. 1, pp. 47-70)*
Pub: John Wiley & Sons Inc.
Contact: Stephen M. Smith, President
Ed: Kiwook Kwon, Kweontaek Chung, Hyuntak Roh, Clint Chadwick, John J. Lawler. **Description:** The ability of organizational context to moderate the relationship between voluntary employee turnover and organizational performance is examined using data from South Korean firms. The effects of employee involvement practices, investment in employee training and development, and the availability of potential workers on this relationship are studied.

42377 ■ *"The Moment You Can't Ignore: When Big Trouble Leads to a Great Future"*
Pub: PublicAffairs
Released: October 7, 2014. **Price:** , $25.99. **Description:** New forms of work, communication, and technology are exposing the ways in which an organization's culture conflicts with new competitive demands. Questions for small companies to ask about identity, leadership, and capacity for innovation are addressed.

42378 ■ *"Monitor Work Productivity"* in *Business Owner (Vol. 35, July-August 2011, No. 4, pp. 4)*
Pub: DL Perkins Company
Description: Tips for tracking employee productivity are explained.

42379 ■ *"More than Able"* in *Entrepreneur (Vol. 36, March 2008, No. 3, pp. 81)*
Pub: Entrepreneur Press
Contact: Perlman Neil, President
Ed: Mark Henricks. **Description:** Disabled workers are motivated employees and work longer hours. A study shows that accommodating disabled workers is very low cost and provides benefits to employers, such as improved employee retention and increased customer base. Other details about hiring disabled workers are discussed.

42380 ■ *"More Jobs Heading to Suburb"* in *Austin Business JournalInc. (Vol. 29, November 20, 2009, No. 37, pp. 1)*
Pub: American City Business Journals
Ed: Kate Harrington. **Description:** Site of Advanced Integration Technologies (AIT) in Pflugerville, Texas might increase its workforce to 80 employees in the next six months due to the creation of an incentive package. Funds from the Pflugerville Community Development Corporation have been helping AIT's initiative to hire more workers. The firm receives $2,000 from the plan for every new employee it hires.

42381 ■ *"More Small Businesses in Baltimore Willing to Fund Employees' Health Benefits"* in *Baltimore Business Journal (Vol. 28, June 18, 2010, No. 6, pp. 1)*
Pub: Baltimore Business Journal
Ed: Scott Graham. **Description:** An increasing number of small businesses in Maryland are tapping into potentially cheaper self-funded health plans instead of providing fully insured benefits to employees through traditional health plans. Self-funded health plans charge employers for health care up to a specified level. Economic implications of self-funded plans to small businesses are discussed.

42382 ■ *"The Myth of the Overqualified Worker"* in *Harvard Business Review (Vol. 88, December 2010, No. 12, pp. 30)*
Pub: Harvard Business School Publishing
Ed: Andrew O'Connell. **Description:** It is recommended to seriously consider job candidates with qualifications exceeding the position being recruited because research shows these individuals work harder, but do not quit any sooner than those whose qualifications more closely match the position.

42383 ■ *"NASA Taps Younger Talent Pool to Supplement Aging Work Force"* in *Crain's Cleveland Business (Vol. 30, June 22, 2009, No. 24, pp. 1)*
Pub: Crain Communications Inc.
Ed: Chuck Soder. **Description:** NASA's Glenn Research Center has reversed the trend towards hiring older workers with more experience by recruiting for entry-level positions as part of a pilot program to attract younger talent.

42384 ■ *"New Career Center Opens at Right Time: Laid-Off Freightliner Workers Will Need Help"* in *Charlotte Observer (February 1, 2007)*
Ed: Gail Smith-Arrants. **Description:** Rowan-Cabarrus Community College announced the opening of its new career development center that will help area workers train for new careers.

42385 ■ *The New Job Security: The 5 Best Strategies for Taking Control of Your Career*
Ed: Pam Lassiter. **Released:** September 07, 2010. **Price:** $14.99. **Description:** This book will help individuals to uncover interesting alternative jobs, generate multiple income streams, shape their job to reflect values and goals, move successfully through the company, and plan for career transitions to keep them in control. Online resources, real-life examples, practical exercises and a no-nonsense approach will aid in job stability.

42386 ■ *"New Jobless Claims Filed in December Soar in Maryland"* in *Baltimore Business Journal (Vol. 27, January 29, 2010, No. 39, pp. 1)*
Pub: American City Business Journals
Ed: Scott Dance. **Description:** Maryland received 48,693 new claims for unemployment benefits in December 2009, reaching its highest monthly total since 1974. The number of claims was up 49 percent from November and 13 percent from the same period in 2008. Labor officials and economists discuss this trend.

42387 ■ *The No Asshole Rule*
Ed: Robert I. Sutton PhD. **Released:** February 22, 2007. **Price:** $22.99. **Description:** Problem employees are more than just a nuisance they are a serious and costly threat to corporate success and employee health.

42388 ■ *"No Time to Grieve"* in *Women In Business (Vol. 63, Fall 2011, No. 3, pp. 22)*
Pub: American Business Women's Association
Contact: Lorie Burch, President
Ed: Diane Stafford. **Description:** Individuals who have experienced job loss must go through the emotional stages related to this event in order to gain the best re-employment opportunities. The first step towards re-employment is to make the job search public. Tips for improving one's online footprint are also given.

42389 ■ *Non-Standard Employment under Globalization: Flexible Work and Social Security in the Newly Industrializing Countries*
Pub: Palgrave Macmillan
Contact: Lisa Dunn, Manager
E-mail: l.dunn@palgrave.com
Ed: Koichi Usami. **Released:** December 2009. **Price:** £84, hardcover; $115. **Description:** Expansion of non-standard employment under globalization is being recognized in all of the newly industrialized countries. The book examines deregulation of labor markets, social protection for nonstandard workers, and social security reforms in accordance with the transformation of employment. **Availability:** PrintE-book.

42390 ■ *"Notes on Current Labor Statistics"* in *Montly Labor Review (Vol. 133, September 2010, No. 9, pp. 75)*
Pub: U.S. Department of Labor Bureau of Labor Statistics
Contact: Philip L. Rones, Manager
E-mail: rones.philip@bls.gov
Description: Principal statistics and calculated by the Bureau of Labor Statistics are presented. The series includes statistics on labor force; employment; unemployment; labor compensation; consumer, producer, and international prices; productivity; international comparisons; and injury and illness statistics.

42391 ■ *"Numbers Game"* in *Baltimore Business Journal (Vol. 27, February 6, 2010, No. 40, pp. 1)*
Pub: American City Business Journals
Ed: Scott Dance. **Description:** Doubts are being raised regarding the impact of the federal stimulus spending in addressing unemployment in Maryland, which has experienced 1,800 jobs created so far. Details on the view of companies and the insufficient amount of contracts that lead to the fewer number of workers being hired are discussed.

42392 ■ Off-Ramps and On-Ramps: Keeping Talented Women on the Road to Success
Pub: Harvard Business Review Press
Contact: Peter E. Walsh, Director
Ed: Sylvia Ann Hewlett. Released: May 15, 2007. Price: $29.95, hardcover. Description: Hewlett (founding president for the Center for Work-Life Policy) examines why many women exit their careers, taking 'off-ramps' (leaving altogether) or 'scenic routes' (opting to work part-time), often during critical, competitive times. She also provides valuable suggestions for companies hoping to retain talented employees of any gender. Availability: Print.

42393 ■ "Olympus is Urged to Revise Board" in Wall Street Journal Eastern Edition (November 28, 2011, pp. B3)
Pub: Dow Jones & Co., Inc.
Contact: Clare Hart, President
Ed: Phred Dvorak. Description: Koji Miyata, once a director on the board of troubled Japanese photographic equipment company, is urging the company to reorganize its board, saying the present group should resign their board seats but keep their management positions. The company has come under scrutiny for its accounting practices and costly acquisitions.

42394 ■ "On Hire Ground" in Entrepreneur (Vol. 36, February 2008, No. 2, pp. 19)
Pub: Entrepreneur Press
Contact: Perlman Neil, President
Ed: Mark Henricks. Description: ADP Small Business Services, an economic consulting firm, showed that small businesses had increased employment rates in 2007 and added 77,000 jobs in November 2007. Entrepreneurial employment and data showing the contribution of small businesses to job growth are presented.

42395 ■ One Foot Out the Door: How to Combat the Psychological Recession That's Alienating Employees and Hurting American Business
Pub: AMACOM
Contact: Edward T. Reilly, Manager
Ed: Judith M. Bardwick. Released: October 31, 2007. Price: $24.95; C$32.95. Description: Drawing on research that indicates Generation X and younger baby boomers feel disconnected from their jobs, the author explores the causes (bad management) of that disengagement. Her pragmatic suggestions about how companies can prove their commitment to employees is beneficial.

42396 ■ "One Workforce - Many Languages" in HRMagazine (Vol. 54, January 2009, No. 1, pp. 32)
Pub: Society for Human Resource Management
Contact: Henry G. Jackson, President
E-mail: hjackson@shrm.org
Ed: Rita Zeidner. Description: Many U.S. employers are investing in English classes to upgrade their immigrant workers' skills on the job.

42397 ■ "Online Tools for Jobseekers" in Occupational Outlook Quarterly (Vol. 55, Fall 2011, No. 3, pp. 20)
Pub: U.S. Department of Labor Bureau of Labor Statistics
Contact: Philip L. Rones, Manager
E-mail: rones.philip@bls.gov
Description: U.S. Department of Labor's CareerOneStop provides a collection of Web-based tools serving students, jobseekers, employers, and the workforce. The top six categories for job listings nationwide include general job boards, niche job boards, career planning tools, career explorations sites, social media job search sites, and other tools which include interview preparation tools and training grants.

42398 ■ "Open Enrollment: Staying Healthy During Enrollment Season" in Employee Benefit News (Vol. 25, November 1, 2011, No. 14, pp. 41)
Pub: SourceMedia Inc.
Contact: James M. Malkin, Chief Executive Officer
Ed: Shana Sweeney. Description: Tips for staying healthy during your benefit open enrollment period are outlined.

42399 ■ "Optimism Index" in Black Enterprise (Vol. 41, September 2010, No. 2, pp. 24)
Pub: Earl G. Graves Publishing Co. Inc.
Contact: Earl G. Graves, Jr., President
Description: According to a Pew Research Center report, 81 percent of African Americans expect to improve their finances in 2011. Blacks have carried a disproportionate share of job losses and housing foreclosures in the recession that began in 2007.

42400 ■ "Orders Up; Jobs Below Forecast" in Charlotte Observer (February 2, 2007)
Ed: Kerry Hall. Description: U.S. Labor Department reported unemployment rates at 4.6 percent, up one-tenth of a percent. Economists had predicted 170,000 new jobs, but only 111,000 were created.

42401 ■ "Organization Redesign and Innovative HRM" in Human Resource Management (Vol. 49, July-August 2010, No. 4, pp. 809-811)
Pub: John Wiley
Ed: Pat Lynch. Description: An overview of the book, 'Organization Redesign and Innovative HRM' is presented.

42402 ■ Organizations Alive!: Six Things That Challenge - Seven That Bring Success
Pub: Yuill & Associates
Ed: Jan Yuill. Price: C$18.95, paperback. Description: New insight into understanding how organizations function as individuals is presented by an international consultant. Customer service, resource management, outsourcing, and management are among the issues covered.

42403 ■ "Outplacement Services" in Black Enterprise (Vol. 38, March 1, 2008, No. 8, pp. 60)
Pub: Earl G. Graves Publishing Co. Inc.
Contact: Earl G. Graves, Jr., President
Ed: Marcia A. Reed-Woodard. Description: Tips to use while in career-transition are offered. Many times outplacement services are provided as part of a severance package to employees.

42404 ■ "Over and Out" in Entrepreneur (Vol. 36, February 2008, No. 2, pp. 25)
Pub: Entrepreneur Press
Contact: Perlman Neil, President
Ed: Chris Penttila. Description: Ben Wolin, owner of Waterfront Media that operates wellness and health Websites, had employed the services of human resource consulting firm to advise him in regard to overtime pay. Guidelines on how to avoid overtime pay violations are presented.

42405 ■ "Overqualified. Underemployed" in Philadelphia Business Journal (Vol. 33, August 1, 2104, No. 25, pp. 14)
Pub: American City Business Journals
Released: August 1, 2014. Description: Overqualified workers often find themselves in employment situations where their education, experience and skills are beyond the requirements of the job. The implications of underemployment for the worker, the organization and the overall U.S. economy are discussed.

42406 ■ "Pack Mentality: Why Black Can Be Slimming" in Crain's Chicago Business (Vol. 31, April 21, 2008, No. 16, pp. 31)
Pub: Crain Communications Inc.
Contact: Todd Johnson, Publisher
Ed: Sarah A. Klein. Description: Jill Smart, the head of human resources for a company with 170,000 employees worldwide, frequently travels to India, London and Singapore; Ms. Smart provides advice concerning efficiency, time management and avoiding jet-lag.

42407 ■ "Paid to Persuade: Careers in Sales" in Occupational Outlook Quarterly (Vol. 55, Summer 2011, No. 2, pp. 24)
Pub: U.S. Department of Labor Bureau of Labor Statistics
Contact: Philip L. Rones, Manager
E-mail: rones.philip@bls.gov
Ed: Ilka Maria Torpey. Description: Sales workers are paid to persuade others to buy goods and services. There were over 13 million wage and salary sales workers in the US in 2010. Wages in sales careers can vary and some become lucrative, lifelong career positions. Seven sales occupations with annual wages higher than $33,000 are profiled.

42408 ■ "Pay Fell for Many Baltimore Execs in '09" in Baltimore Business Journal (Vol. 28, July 2, 2010, No. 8, pp. 1)
Pub: Baltimore Business Journal
Ed: Gary Haber. Description: Compensation for the 100 highest-paid executives in the Baltimore, Maryland area decreased in 2009, compared with 2008. At least $1 million were received by 59 out of 100 executives in 2009, while 75 earned the said amount in 2008. Factors that contributed to the executives' decisions to take pay cuts are discussed.

42409 ■ "Paychecks of Some Bank CEOs Have a Pre-Recession Look" in Boston Business Journal (Vol. 29, May 13, 2011, No. 1, pp. 1)
Pub: American City Business Journals, Inc.
Ed: Gary Haber. Description: The salaries of United States-based bank chief executive officers have increased to pre-recession levels. Wells Fargo and Company's John G. Stumpf received $17.6 million in 2010. Community bank executives, on the other hand, have seen minimal increases.

42410 ■ "People Tools for Business: 50 Strategies for Building Success, Creating Wealth, and Finding Happiness"
Pub: Select Books
Contact: Rose Perl, Owner
Released: September 29, 2014. Price: , $16.95 paperback. Description: Tools required to enjoy success in both career and life are given. People Tools are help to develop self-confidence, improve management skills, and find constructive ways for Human Resource managers to fire workers and ways for workers to respond. Each people tool is concise and provides a straightforward strategy to produce positive results.

42411 ■ "Perks Still Popular: Jets May be Out, but CEO Benefits Abound" in Crain's Detroit Business (Vol. 25, June 22, 2009)
Pub: Crain Communications Inc. - Detroit
Contact: Keith Crain, Chairman
Ed: Ryan Beene. Description: Benefits packages of local CEOs are outlined. Statistical data included.

42412 ■ "Perspective: Borderline Issues" in Entrepreneur (Vol. 35, October 2007, No. 10, pp. 48)
Pub: Entrepreneur Press
Contact: Perlman Neil, President
Ed: Joshua Kurlantzick. Description: Failure of the immigration reform bill is expected to result in increased difficulty in finding workers that would take on the dirty and perilous jobs, which are usually taken by immigrants. Regularizing immigration on the other hand will cost business owners money by making them spend for the legality of their employees' stay in the U.S. Other effects of immigration laws on entrepreneurs are discussed.

42413 ■ Pink Slip Power!: Recover and Succeed It's Up To You!
Pub: Infinity Publishing
Contact: Tom Gregory, President
Ed: Wade J. Wnuk. Released: 2004. Price: $9.95. Description: Advice is given to those facing loss of employment. The book discusses issues such as: restraining emotions before reacting to a severance package ceasing to brood on the past, focusing on the future, networking and looking for hidden job opportunities, preparing resumes, and gearing up for interviews. Four chapters cover ideas for facing reality, formulating a plan, promoting one's self, and persisting in the face of adversity.

42414 ■ "Plan Your Future with My Next Move" in Occupational Outlook Quarterly (Vol. 55, Summer 2011, No. 2, pp. 22)
Pub: U.S. Department of Labor Bureau of Labor Statistics
Contact: Philip L. Rones, Manager
E-mail: rones.philip@bls.gov
Description: My Next Move, an online tool offering a variety of user-friendly ways to browse more than 900 occupations was created by the National Center

for O NET Development for the US Department of Labor's Employment and Training Administration. Clicking on an occupation presents a one-page profile summarizing key information for specific careers.

42415 ■ *"Plays Well With Others: How To Work With People You Can't Stand"*
Pub: CreateSpace
Contact: Daren Giles, President
Released: October 19, 2014. **Price:** , $6.97 paperback. **Description:** Human resource managers, as well as coworkers, will benefit from this book that helps employees deal with difficult people at work.

42416 ■ *"Predicting Success: Evidence-Based Strategies to Hire the Right People and Build the Best Team"*
Pub: John Wiley & Sons Inc.
Contact: Stephen M. Smith, President
Released: September 22, 2014. **Price:** , $25.00. **Description:** Guide for human resource management teams choose the right employee when hiring. It teaches how to apply the principles and tools of human analytics to the work place to avoid bad culture fits, mismatched skillsets, entitled workers, and other hiring mistakes that hurt employee motivation and morale. The Predictive Index TM, behavior analytics, hiring assessments, and other resources for better outcomes are presented.

42417 ■ *Prepare for the Worst, Plan for the Best: Disaster Preparedness and Recovery for Small Businesses*
Pub: John Wiley & Sons Inc.
Contact: Stephen M. Smith, President
Ed: Donna R. Childs. **Released:** 2nd Edition. **Price:** $24.95, paperback; $44.95, hardcover. **Description:** Guide to help small businesses protect themselves from disasters. New information is presented on Redundant Arrays of Independent Disk (RAID) hardware backups, calling trees and the Internet, power outages and suppliers, as well as wireless networks. **Availability:** Print.

42418 ■ *"Privacy Concern: Are 'Group' Time Sheets Legal?" in HR Specialist (Vol. 8, September 2010, No. 9, pp. 4)*
Pub: Capitol Information Group Inc.
Description: Under the Fair Labor Standards Act (FLSA) employers are required to maintain and preserve payroll or other records, including the number of hours worked, but it does not prescribe a particular order or form in which these records must be kept.

42419 ■ *"Productivity Data" in Montly Labor Review (Vol. 133, September 2010, No. 9, pp. 137)*
Pub: U.S. Department of Labor Bureau of Labor Statistics
Contact: Philip L. Rones, Manager
E-mail: rones.philip@bls.gov
Description: Productivity data is presented through indexes of productivity, hourly compensation and unit costs in 2007.

42420 ■ *"Protecting Company Secrets" in Inc. (February 2008, pp. 38-39)*
Ed: Scott Westcott. **Description:** A legal guide for noncompete clauses when hiring new employees is outlined, stressing how each state has its own set of laws.

42421 ■ *"Prudential Courts Hispanics" in Hispanic Business (March 2008, pp. 38, 40)*
Ed: Melinda Burns. **Description:** Prudential Financial Inc. is reaching out to Hispanic Chambers of Commerce in an effort to hire and do business with the Hispanic community in the U.S.

42422 ■ *"Putting an End to End-of-Year Reviews" in Inc. (December 2007, pp. 58, 61)*
Pub: Gruner and Jahr USA Publishing Co.
Contact: J. Russell Denson, President
Ed: Scott Westcott. **Description:** Performance assessments can be used in place of blunt employee reviews in order to create effective annual reviews.

42423 ■ *"Q&A: Saskatchewan Premier Brad Wall" in Canadian Business (Vol. 82, April 27, 2009, No. 7, pp. 9)*
Pub: Rogers Media Inc.
Contact: Tony Viner, President
Ed: Joe Castaldo. **Description:** Saskatchewan Premier Brad Wall believes that the mood in the province is positive, as its economy is one of the few that is expected to post growth in 2009. Wall actively promotes the province in job fairs, offering $20,000 in tuition for recent college and university graduates that relocate in the province for seven years. Wall's views on the province's economy and challenges are presented.

42424 ■ *"Q&A: Take a Load Off Your HR" in Entrepreneur (May 2014)*
Pub: Entrepreneur Media Inc.
Released: May 2014. **Description:** A Professional Employer Organization (PEO) manages all the human resource (HR) needs of a small business. The PEO can help the business save money by purchasing insurance and benefit plans at significant savings, assist with employment-regulatory compliance and ensure effective management and access to personnel records, among other things. Business owners should consider hiring PEOs who are financially responsible and stable. A business needs a PEO when the accounting department asks for a dedicated HR person to handle all the paperwork.

42425 ■ *"Questioning Authority" in Entrepreneur (June 2014)*
Pub: Entrepreneur Media Inc.
Released: June 2014. **Description:** Smarterer is a platform that facilitates the evaluation of prospective hires through crowdsourced assessment tests quantifying their professional skills and strengths. The platform has more than 900 multiple-choice tests covering a variety of professions. It uses an adaptive machine-learning algorithm that ensures the uniqueness of every test. Users can choose to make their test results public and can perform do-overs on some tests. The platform was launched in 2010 as a way of identifying potential talent and identifying skill inventories among existing employees.

42426 ■ *"Quits Versus Layoffs" in Occupational Outlook Quarterly (Vol. 55, Fall 2011, No. 3, pp. 36)*
Pub: U.S. Department of Labor Bureau of Labor Statistics
Contact: Philip L. Rones, Manager
E-mail: rones.philip@bls.gov
Description: Data from the U.S. Bureau of Labor Statistics provides data from the Job Openings and Labor Turnover Survey regarding quits and layoffs.

42427 ■ *Race and Entrepreneurial Success: Black-, Asian-, and White-Owned Businesses in the United States*
Pub: The MIT Press
Contact: Ellen W. Faran, Director
E-mail: ewfaran@mit.edu
Ed: Robert W. Fairlie, Alicia M. Robb. **Released:** August 2010. **Price:** $19, paperback; £13.95. **Description:** Trends in minority small business ownership are explored, focusing on the importance of human capital, financial capital, and family business background in successful business ownership.

42428 ■ *"Race and Gender Diversity: A Discussion of Recent Findings" in Business Horizons (November-December 2007, pp. 445)*
Pub: Elsevier Technology Publications
Ed: James C. Wimbush. **Price:** $35.95. **Description:** Research conducted on diversity building, employee recruitment, gender issues in management, and pay inequality from 2006 through present are discussed. Diversity conditions and attitudes toward it are slowly improving based on these findings. **Availability:** PDF.

42429 ■ *Reality-Based Leadership: Ditch the Drama, Restore Sanity to the Workplace, & Turn Excuses into Results*
Pub: Jossey-Bass
Ed: Cy Wakeman. **Released:** August 2010. **Price:** $27.95, hardcover; $18.99. **Description:** Recent polls show that 71 percent of workers think about quitting

their jobs every day. That number would be shocking if people actually were quitting. Worse, they go to work, punching time clocks and collecting pay checks, while checked out emotionally. Cy Wakeman reveals how to be the kind of leader who changes the way people think about and perceive their circumstances, one who deals with the facts, clarifies roles, gives clear and direct feedback, and insists that everyone do the same without drama or defensiveness. **Availability:** PrintE-book.

42430 ■ *"Rebuffed, BAE Systems Fights Army Contract Decision" in Business Courier (Vol. 26, September 25, 2009)*
Pub: American City Business Journals, Inc.
Contact: Whitney Shaw, President
Ed: Jon Newberry. **Description:** BAE Systems filed a complaint with the US Government Accountability Office after the US Army issued an order to BAE's competitor for armoured trucks which is potentially worth over $3 billion. Hundreds of jobs in Butler County, Ohio hinge on the success of the contract protest.

42431 ■ *"Recession Drags Down CEO Pay: Full Impact May Not Have Played Out" in Crain's Detroit Business (Vol. 25, June 22, 2009, No. 25)*
Pub: Crain Communications Inc. - Detroit
Contact: Keith Crain, Chairman
Ed: Ryan Beene. **Description:** Median overall compensation package for Detroit's top-compensated 50 CEOs was down 10.67 percent from $2.3 million in 2007 to $2.06 million in 2008. Statistical data included.

42432 ■ *"Recruiters Look Beyond Backyard to Find Gen Y Workers" in HRMagazine (Vol. 53, November 2008, No. 11, pp. 22)*
Description: More than two-thirds of recent college graduates would relocate for a job, and 70 percent would be willing to move for an employer, according to the 2008 Hot Cities Survey; New York, Washington DC, and Chicago top the list of most desirable cities for relocation.

42433 ■ *"Recruiting 2.0" in Entrepreneur (Vol. 35, November 2007, No. 11, pp. 100)*
Pub: Entrepreneur Press
Contact: Perlman Neil, President
Ed: Andrea Cooper. **Description:** Technology is becoming a tool to help small companies find the best employees. Firms can look into social networking sites to see recommendations from the applicants' colleagues. Tips on how to select the employees online are listed.

42434 ■ *"Recruiting Diversifies" in Advertising Age (Vol. 83, October 8, 2012, No. 36, pp. 25)*
Description: Heidrick & Struggles launches a data and analytics practice that filles the void as marketing becomes more data-riven. H&S specializes in recruiting and filling CEO and other senior-level positions for human resource departments of large firms.

42435 ■ *"Regional Talent Network Unveils Employment Web Site" in Crain's Cleveland Business (Vol. 30, June 1, 2009, No. 21, pp. 11)*
Pub: Crain Communications Inc.
Ed: Chuck Soder. **Description:** Regional Talent Network launched WhereToFindHelp.org, a Website designed to act as a directory of all Northeast Ohio resources that can help employers recruit and job seekers look for positions. The site also lists organizations offering employment and training services.

42436 ■ *"Remind Managers to Avoid Talk of Employee Longevity" in HR Specialist (Vol. 8, September 2010, No. 9, pp. 3)*
Description: Supervisors need to understand that casual conversations can be used against an organization in law suits.

42437 ■ *"Renren Partnership With Recruit to Launch Social Wedding Services" in*

Benzinga.com (June 7, 2011)
Pub: Benzinga.com
Contact: Kyle Bazzy, President
Ed: Benzinga Staff. **Description:** Renren Inc., the leading real name social networking Internet platform in China has partnered with Recruit Company Limited, Japan's largest human resource and classified media group to form a joint venture to build a wedding social media catering to the needs of engaged couples and newlyweds in China.

42438 ■ *"Research in Personnel and Human Resources Management, Vol. 28" in Human Resource Management (Vol. 49, July-August 2010, No. 4)*
Pub: John Wiley
Ed: Mukta Kulkarni. **Description:** An overview of the book, 'Research in Personnel and Human Resources Management', Vol. 28 is presented.

42439 ■ *"'Resume Mining' Services Can Save Time, Money" in HR Specialist (Vol. 8, September 2010, No. 9, pp. 7)*
Pub: Capitol Information Group Inc.
Description: Low-cost resume mining services can help human resource departments save time and money by searching online resume databases for candidates matching specific job qualifications.

42440 ■ *"Retirement Plan Disclosures: Prepare Now for Fiduciary Rules" in Employee Benefit News (Vol. 25, November 1, 2011, No. 14, pp. 24)*
Pub: SourceMedia Inc.
Contact: James M. Malkin, Chief Executive Officer
Ed: Brian M. Pinheiro, Kurt R. Anderson. **Description:** Department of Labor has delayed the deadlines on new affirmative obligations for fiduciaries of retirement plans subject to the Employee Retirement Income Security Act. Details included.

42441 ■ *"Retirement Plans in a Quandary" in Employee Benefit News (Vol. 25, December 1, 2011, No. 15, pp. 18)*
Pub: SourceMedia Inc.
Contact: James M. Malkin, Chief Executive Officer
Ed: Terry Dunne. **Description:** Complex issues arise when employees don't cash their 401(k) balance checks. The US Department of Labor permits plans to cash out accounts of former employees with less than $1,000 to reduce the cost and time required to manage them.

42442 ■ *"Reviving Entrepreneurship: Policy Decisions in 12 Areas Could Nurture - Or Cripple - America's Greatest Asset" in Harvard Business Review (Vol. 90, March 2012, No. 3, pp. 116)*
Pub: Harvard Business Review Press
Contact: Peter E. Walsh, Director
Ed: Josh Lerner, William Sahlman. **Released:** March 2012. **Description:** Government policies should address entrepreneurship as a process, rather than an act. Several key areas for policymaking include basic and translational science, supply and quality of human capital, information availability, tax treatment of rewards and risks, intellectual property rights, workforce healthcare, and mobility of financial and human capital.

42443 ■ *"The Rise of the Supertemp: The Best Executive and Professional Jobs May No Longer Be Full-Time Gigs" in Harvard Business Review (Vol. 90, May 2012, No. 5, pp. 50)*
Pub: Harvard Business Review Press
Contact: Peter E. Walsh, Director
Ed: Jody Greenstone Miller, Matt Miller. **Released:** May 2012. **Description:** Supertemps are independent contractors who perform mission-critical work on a project basis. Supertemps enjoy a high degree of flexibility and freedom, and offer companies new opportunities for innovation and growth.

42444 ■ *"Risk Management Starts at the Top" in Business Strategy Review (Vol. 21, Spring 2010, No. 1, pp. 18)*
Pub: John Wiley & Sons Inc. Scientific, Technical, Medical, and Scholarly Div. (Wiley-Blackwell)
Contact: William J. Pesce, Manager
E-mail: wpesce@wiley.com
Ed: Paul Strebel, Hongze Lu. **Description:** Authors question why, at the end of 2008, Citigroup, Merrill Lynch and UBS had well over $40 billion in sub-prime write-downs and credit losses, while some of their competitors were much less exposed. Their research into the situation revealed correlations of great import to today's firms.

42445 ■ *"The Role of Leadership In Successful International Mergers and Acquisitions: Why Renault-Nissan Succeeded and DaimlerChrysler-Mitsubishi Failed" in Human Resource Management (Vol. 51,May-June 2012, No. 3, pp. 433-456)*
Pub: John Wiley & Sons Inc.
Contact: Stephen M. Smith, President
Ed: Carol Gill. **Description:** The effects of national and organizational culture on the performance of Nissan and Mitsubishi after their mergers with Renault and DaimlerChrysler respectively are examined. Japanese national culture was found to influence organizational culture and human resource management practices, while leadership affected the success of their turnaround efforts.

42446 ■ *"Screening-Oriented Recruitment Messages: Antecedents and Relationships with Applicant Pool Quality" in Human Resource Management (Vol. 51,May- June 2012, No. 3, pp. 343-360)*
Pub: John Wiley & Sons Inc.
Contact: Stephen M. Smith, President
Ed: Brian R. Dineen, Ian O. Williamson. **Description:** Factors associated with the use of screening-oriented messages for recruitment are investigated. Results indicate that labor supply perceptions, the reputation of recruiting firms and quality-based compensation incentives are associated with the use of screening-oriented messages, which are associated with the quality of the applicant pool.

42447 ■ *"Several Europe-Based Employers Cut MN Jobs" in Business Journal (Vol. 30, July 6, 2012, No. 6, pp. 1)*
Pub: American City Business Journals, Inc.
Contact: Whitney Shaw, President
Ed: Jim Hammerand. **Released:** July 6, 2012. **Description:** A number of Europe-based employers have cut jobs in Minnesota. Allianz SE has reduced its workforce by 380. Executive comments included.

42448 ■ *"Shocks and Final Straws: Using Exit-Interview Data to Examine the Unfolding Model's Decision Paths" in Human Resource Management (Vol. 51, January-February 2012, No. 1, pp. 25-46)*
Pub: John Wiley & Sons Inc.
Contact: Stephen M. Smith, President
Ed: Carol T. Kulik, Gerry Treuren, Prashant Bordia. **Description:** Employees leaving their organizations are examined according to the unfolding model using data from exit interviews. Results indicate that employees along the same exit path may experience different kinds and combinations of shocks, while some experience shock-like events.

42449 ■ *"Six SIGMA for Small Business*
Pub: Entrepreneur Press
Contact: Perlman Neil, President
Ed: Greg Brue. **Description:** Jack Welch's Six SIGMA approach to business covers accounting, finance, sales and marketing, buying a business, human resource development, and new product development.

42450 ■ *"16 Creative and Cheap Ways to Say 'Thank You" in HR Specialist (Vol. 8, September 2010, No. 9, pp. 8)*
Pub: Capitol Information Group Inc.
Description: Tips for starting an employee appreciation program for a small company are presented.

42451 ■ *"Small is Beautiful: Implications of Reliability and Statistical Power for Testing the Efficacy of HR Interventions" in Human Resource Management (Vol. 51, January-February 2012, No. 1, pp. 143-160)*
Pub: John Wiley & Sons Inc.
Contact: Stephen M. Smith, President
Ed: Sujin K. Horwitz, Irwin B. Horwitz. **Description:** The use of measurement procedures to increase statistical power for detecting human resource intervention effects is studied. These increase statistical power beyond sample size and can be implemented by human resources professionals.

42452 ■ *"Small Business Employment" in Small Business Economic Trends (April 2008, pp. 9)*
Pub: National Federation of Independent Business
Contact: Caitlin McDevitt, Program Manager
Ed: William C. Dunkelberg, Holly Wade. **Description:** Four tables and a graph representing employment rates of small businesses in the U.S. are presented. The tables include figures on employment changes, number of qualified applicants, job openings, and hiring plans.

42453 ■ *"Small Business Employment" in Small Business Economic Trends (March 2008, pp. 9)*
Pub: National Federation of Independent Business
Contact: Caitlin McDevitt, Program Manager
Ed: William C. Dunkelberg, Holly Wade. **Description:** Four tables and a graph that present employment rates of small businesses in the U.S. are provided. The tables include figures on employment changes, number of qualified applicants, job openings and hiring plans.

42454 ■ *"Small Business Employment" in Small Business Economic Trends (February 2008, pp. 9)*
Pub: National Federation of Independent Business
Contact: Caitlin McDevitt, Program Manager
Ed: William C. Dunkelberg, Holly Wade. **Description:** Four tables and a graph that present employment rates of small businesses in the U.S. are provided. The tables include figures on employment changes, number of qualified applicants, job openings and hiring plans.

42455 ■ *"Small Business Employment" in Small Business Economic Trends (January 2008, pp. 9)*
Pub: National Federation of Independent Business
Contact: Caitlin McDevitt, Program Manager
Ed: William C. Dunkelberg, Holly Wade. **Description:** Table from a survey of small businesses in the U.S. is given, representing actual employment changes from January 2002 to December 2007. A graph comparing planned employment and current job openings from January 1986 to December 2007 is also supplied. Tables showing job opening, hiring plans, and qualified applicants for job openings are also presented.

42456 ■ *"Small Business Employment" in Small Business Economic Trends (September 2010, pp. 9)*
Pub: National Federation of Independent Business
Contact: Caitlin McDevitt, Program Manager
Description: A table from a survey of small businesses in the U.S. is given, representing actual employment changes from January 2005 to August 2010. A graph comparing planned employment and current job openings from January 1986 to August 2010 is also supplied. Tables showing job openings, hiring plans, and qualified applicants for job openings are also presented.

42457 ■ *"Small Business Employment" in Small Business Economic Trends (July 2010, pp. 9)*
Pub: National Federation of Independent Business
Contact: Caitlin McDevitt, Program Manager
Ed: William C. Dunkelberg, Holly Wade. **Description:** A table from a survey of small businesses in the U.S. is given representing actual employment changes from January 2005 to June 2010. A graph comparing planned employment and current job

openings from January 1986 to June 2010 is also supplied. Tables showing job openings, hiring plans, and qualified applicants for job openings are also presented.

42458 ■ "Small Business Employment" in Small Business Economic Trends (July 2014, pp. 9)
Pub: National Federation of Independent Business
Contact: Caitlin McDevitt, Program Manager
Released: July 2014. **Description:** A table from a survey of small businesses in the U.S. is given, representing actual employment changes from January 1986 to June 2014. A graph comparing planned employment and current job openings from January 1986 to June 2014 is supplied. Tables showing job openings, hiring plans, and qualified applicants for job openings are also presented.

42459 ■ "Something Different in the Air? The Collapse of the Schwarzenegger Health Plan in Calfornia" in WorkingUSA (June 2008)
Ed: Daniel J.B. Mitchell. **Description:** In January 2007, California Governor Arnold Schwarzenegger proposed a state universal health care plan modeled after the Massachusetts individual mandate program. A year later, the plan was dead. Although some key interest groups eventually backed the plan, it was overwhelmed by a looming state budget crisis and a lack of gubernatorial focus. Although much acclaimed for his stance on greenhouse gases, stem cells, hydrogen highways, and other Big Ideas, diffused gubernatorial priorities and a failure to resolve California's chronic fiscal difficulties let the clock run out on universal health care.

42460 ■ "Sometimes You Have to Ignore the Rule Book" in Canadian Business (Vol. 83, September 14, 2010, No. 15, pp. 13)
Pub: Rogers Media Inc.
Contact: Tony Viner, President
Ed: Richard Branson. **Description:** The rule book has provided a clear framework for employees particularly when cash and accounting are at issue. However, sometimes rules were made to be broken and the rule book should not become an excuse for poor customer service or hinder great service. How Virgin Atlantic practices this type of corporate culture is discussed.

42461 ■ "A Stakeholder--Human Capital Perspective On the Link Between Social Performance and Executive Compensation" in Business Ethics Quarterly (Vol. 24, January 2014, No. 1, pp. 1)
Pub: Business Ethics Quarterly
Released: January 2014. **Description:** The link between firm corporate social performance (CSP) and executive compensation could be driven by a sorting effect (a firm's CSP is related to the initial levels of compensation of newly hired executives), or by an incentive effect (incumbent executives are rewarded for past firm CSP). An exploration of the sorting effect of firm CSP on the initial compensation of newly hired executives is discussed.

42462 ■ "Stand Out Via Service: How Volunteering Can Boost Your Professional Bottom Line" in Black Enterprise (Vol. 44, June 2014, No. 10, pp. 42)
Pub: Earl G. Graves Publishing Co. Inc.
Contact: Earl G. Graves, Jr., President
Released: June 2014. **Description:** According to the 2013 Deloitte Volunteer IMPACT Survey, more than three of every four human resource executives volunteer. This strategy can lead to career satisfaction and help a business advance and fuel growth for individuals and the firm. Tips for finding the right volunteer opportunity are included.

42463 ■ "Start Filling Your Talent Gap - Now" in Business Strategy Review (Vol. 21, Spring 2010, No. 1, pp. 56)
Pub: John Wiley & Sons Inc. Scientific, Technical, Medical, and Scholarly Div. (Wiley-Blackwell)
Contact: William J. Pesce, Manager
E-mail: wpesce@wiley.com
Ed: Alan Bird, Lori Flees, Paul Di Paola. **Description:** As businesses steer their way out of turbulence, they have a unique opportunity to identify their leader-

ship supply and demand and then to close the talent gap in their organization. Authors explain how to take immediate steps to build the right team now and lay the groundwork for a long-term approach for nurturing talent within the organization.

42464 ■ "Streaming Hot Currie" in Canadian Business (Vol. 80, April 23, 2007, No. 9, pp. 10)
Ed: Paul Brent. **Description:** The views of Richard Currie, former president of Loblow Cos. Ltd., on the human resource policy of the company are presented.

42465 ■ "Stung by Recession, Hemmer Regroups with New Strategy" in Business Courier (Vol. 27, June 4, 2010, No. 5, pp. 1)
Pub: Business Courier
Ed: Lucy May. **Description:** Paul Hemmer Companies reduced its work force and outsourced operations such as marketing and architecture, in order for the commercial and construction firm to survive the recession. Hammer's total core revenue in 2009 dropped to less than $30 million forcing the closure of its Chicago office.

42466 ■ "Surprise Package" in Business Courier (Vol. 27, June 25, 2010, No. 8, pp. 1)
Pub: Business Courier
Ed: Dan Monk, Jon Newberry, Steve Watkins. **Description:** More than 60 percent of the chief executive officers (CEOs) in Greater Cincinnati's 35 public companies took a salary cut in 2009, but stock grants resulted in large paper gains for the CEOs. The salary cuts show efforts of boards of directors to observe austerity. Statistics on increased values of stock awards for CEOs, median pay for CEOs, and median shareholder return are also presented.

42467 ■ "Survey Profile" in Small Business Economic Trends (September 2010, pp. 19)
Pub: National Federation of Independent Business
Contact: Caitlin McDevitt, Program Manager
Ed: William C. Dunkelberg, Holly Wade. **Description:** Two graphs and a table presenting the profile of small businesses that participated in the National Federation of Independent Business (NFIB) survey are provided. The actual number of firms, their industry types, and the number of full and part-time employees are presented.

42468 ■ "Swimming Against the Tide: Outward Staffing Flows from Multinational Subsidiaries" in Human Resource Management (Vol. 49, July-August 2010, No. 4, pp. 575-598)
Pub: John Wiley
Ed: David G. Collings, Anthony McDonnell, Patrick Gunnigle, Jonathan Lavelle. **Description:** A study was conducted to provide a benchmark of outward flows of international assignees from the Irish subsidiaries of foreign-owned multinational enterprises (MNEs) to corporate headquarters and other worldwide operations. Findings indicate that almost half of all MNEs use some form of outward staffing flows.

42469 ■ "Swinging For the Fences: The Effects of Ceo Stock Options on Company Risk Taking and Performance" in Academy of Management Journal (Vol. 50, No. 5, October 1, 2007, pp. 1055)
Pub: Academy of Management
Contact: Ming-Jer Chen, President
Ed: Gerard Sanders, Donald C. Hambrick. **Description:** Study examines managerial risk-taking vis-a-vis stock options of the company; results reveal that stock options instigate CEOs to take unwise risks that could bring huge losses to the company.

42470 ■ Tactical Entrepreneur: The Entrepreneur's Game Plan
Pub: Sortis Publishing
Ed: Brian J. Hazelgren. **Price:** $24.95, plus $3.99 for shipping and handling. **Description:** A smart, realistic business plan is essential for any successful entrepreneur. Besides offering products or services, small business owners must possess skills in accounting, planning, human resources management, marketing, and information technology.

42471 ■ The Talent Masters: Why Smart Leaders Put People Before Numbers
Ed: Bill Conaty, Ram Charan. **Released:** November 09, 2010. **Price:** $27.50. **Description:** This book helps leaders recognize talent in their employees, and to put that talent to work to help achieve business success.

42472 ■ "Talent Shows" in Canadian Business (Vol. 81, December 24, 2007, No. 1, pp. 14)
Ed: Megan Harman. **Description:** Canadian companies are increasingly turning to marketing to promote themselves as employers, as concerns on employee recruitment increase with the nearing retirement age of the baby boomers. Details on skills shortage, the potential advantage for the immigrant workforce, and employee retention are discussed.

42473 ■ "Teleworkers Confess Biggest At-Home Distractions" in Employee Benefit News (Vol. 25, November 1, 2011, No. 14, pp. 7)
Pub: SourceMedia Inc.
Contact: James M. Malkin, Chief Executive Officer
Ed: Kelley M. Butler. **Description:** Telecommuting can actually make some workers more efficient and productive versus working inside the office.

42474 ■ "The Ten Commandments of Legal Risk Management" in Business Horizons (Vol. 51, January-February 2008, No. 1, pp. 13)
Pub: Elsevier Advanced Technology Publications
Ed: Michael B. Metzger. **Description:** Effective legal risk management is tightly linked with ethical and good management, and managers' behaviors have to be professional and based on ethically defensible principles of action. Basic human tendencies cannot be used in justifying questionable decisions in court. Guidelines for legal risk management are presented.

42475 ■ 30 Reasons Employees Hate Their Managers: What Your People May Be Thinking and What You Can Do About It
Pub: AMACOM
Contact: Edward T. Reilly, Manager
Ed: Bruce L. Katcher, Adam Snyder. **Released:** March 07, 2007. **Price:** $18.95, Paper or Softback. **Description:** Thirty reasons why American employees are unhappy in their jobs are outlined. Each chapter is opened with a reason, an examination of how it creates work difficulties, and makes suggestions to managers on how to best address each issue. **Availability:** Print.

42476 ■ "This Just In" in Crain's Detroit Business (Vol. 25, June 22, 2009, No. 25, pp. 1)
Pub: Crain Communications Inc. - Detroit
Contact: Keith Crain, Chairman
Ed: Chad Halcom. **Description:** Yamasaki Associates, an architectural firm has been sued for non payment of wages to four employees. Yamasaki spokesperson stated the economy has affected the company and it is focusing marketing efforts on areas encouraged by recovery funding.

42477 ■ "To Win With Natural Talent, Go For Additive Effects; Four Human Capital Strategies Combine to Drive Up to 59 Percent More Growth In Revenue Per Employee" in Gallup Business Journal (June 3, 2014)
Pub: Gallup Press
Released: June 3, 2014. **Description:** Four human capital strategies, when used together, can drive growth in revenue per employee by as much as 59 percent. The strategies for selecting and implementing the right managers are explored.

42478 ■ "'Tone-Deaf' Suitor or True Harasser: How to Tell" in HR Specialist (Vol. 8, September 2010, No. 9, pp. 1)
Pub: Capitol Information Group Inc.
Description: Details are critical to any harassment charge in the workplace. Courts now list factors employers should consider when trying to determine whether an employee has been sexually harassed at work.

42479 ■ *"TrendHR Changes Rockwall Landscape with $25M Office Tower"* in Dallas Business Journal (Vol. 35, May 25, 2012, No. 37, pp. 1)

Pub: American City Business Journal

Ed: Candace Carlisle. **Description:** TrendHR Services is planning to build an executive tower in Rockwall, Texas. The company provides human resource outsourcing, employee benefits, and consulting services.

42480 ■ *"Tri-State Lags Peer Cities in Jobs, Human Capital, Study Says"* in Business Courier (Vol. 27, September 24, 2010, No. 21, pp. 1)

Pub: Business Courier

Ed: Dan Monk, Lucy May. **Description:** Greater Cincinnati, Ohio has ranked tenth overall in the 'Agenda 360/Vision 2015 Regional Indicators Project' report. The study ranked 12-city-peer groups in categories such as job indicators standing and people indicators standing. The ranking of jobs and human capital study is topped by Minneapolis, followed by Denver, Raleigh, and Austin.

42481 ■ *"Trust But Verify: FMLA Software Isn't Foolproof"* in HR Specialist (Vol. 8, September 2010, No. 9, pp. 3)

Pub: Capitol Information Group Inc.

Description: Employers are using software to track FMLA information, however, it is important for employers to review reasons for eligibility requirements, particularly when an employee is reportedly overstepping the bounds within leave regulations due to software error.

42482 ■ *"Types of Health Plans"* in HRMagazine (Vol. 53, August 2008, No. 8, pp. 72)

Pub: Society for Human Resource Management

Contact: Henry G. Jackson, President

E-mail: hjackson@shrm.org

Description: Definitions are given for various types of health care coverage available. Fee-for-service (FFS), health maintenance organization (HMO), preferred provider organization (PPO), point of service (POS) and consumer-directed health plan (CDHP) are outlined.

42483 ■ *"Uncertain Labor Pool Troubles Businesses"* in Business First-Columbus (October 22, 2007, pp. A1)

Pub: American City Business Journals, Inc.

Ed: Kevin Kemper. **Description:** Businesses in Columbus, Ohio are having difficulty finding skilled workers and expect this trend to continue through 2010-2020. They are trying to recruit young workers to address the shortage in skilled labor.

42484 ■ *"Unfair Distraction of Employees"* in Business Owner (Vol. 35, March-April 2011, No. 2, pp. 8)

Pub: DL Perkins Company

Description: Fair Credit Collection Practices Act makes it illegal for collectors to contact a debtor at his or her place of employment if the collector is made aware that it is against personnel policy of the employer for the worker to take such a call.

42485 ■ *"Union Ethics Training: Building the Legitimacy and Effectiveness of Organized Labor"* in WorkingUSA (Vol. 11, September 2008, No. 3)

Ed: Maggie Cohen. **Description:** Arguments are presented for the implementation of serious ethics training at all levels of labor unions and their contribution to union effectiveness by enhancing union legitimacy-understood as an amalgam of legal, pragmatic, and moral legitimacy and by paving the way to stable recognition of the labor movement as an integral part of American society, necessary to economic prosperity and the realization of fundamental American moral and social values.

42486 ■ *"Union Questions Patrick Cudahy Layoffs"* in Business Journal-Milwaukee (Vol.

28, December 3, 2010, No. 9, pp. A1)

Pub: Milwaukee Business Journal

Ed: Rich Rovito. **Description:** United Food and Commercial Workers Local 1473 is investigating Patrick Cudahy Inc.'s termination of 340 jobs. The union said the company has violated the law for failing to issue proper notice of a mass layoff.

42487 ■ *"Urban League Training Program Finds Jobs for Cincinnati's 'Hard to Serve'"* in Business Courier (Vol. 27, July 2, 2010, No. 9, pp. 1)

Pub: Business Courier

Ed: Lucy May. **Description:** Stephen Tucker, director of workforce development for the Urban League of Greater Cincinnati, is an example of how ex-offenders can be given chances for employment after service jail sentences. How the Urban Leagues' Solid Opportunities for Advancement job training program helped Tucker and other ex-offenders is discussed.

42488 ■ *"URI Centre Seen as Bridge From Campus to Employment"* in Providence Business News (Vol. 29, June 30, 2014, No. 13, pp. 4)

Pub: American City Business Journals

Released: June 30, 2014. **Description:** Kimberly S. Washor is the first director of University of Rhode Island's (URIs) new Centre for Career and Experiential Education that combines the missions of Experiential Learning and Community Engagement along with Career Services and Employer Relations. By joining the two offices, URI is implementing a new database that will meet the needs of both career and internship advising, where adviser will be able to track industry human resource partners.

42489 ■ *"Use Benefits Checklist to Smooth New-Hire Onboarding"* in HR Specialist (Vol. 8, September 2010, No. 9, pp. 4)

Pub: Capitol Information Group Inc.

Description: Checklist to help employees enroll in a company's benefit offerings is provided, courtesy of Wayne State University in Detroit, Michigan.

42490 ■ *"The Value of Human Resource Management for Organizational Performance"* in Business Horizons (November-December 2007, pp. 503)

Pub: Elsevier Technology Publications

Ed: Yongmei Liu, James G. Combs, David J. Ketchen, Jr., R. Duane Ireland. **Price:** $35.95. **Description:** Benefits of human resource management for business are studied using date from 19,000 organizations. Human resource management adds value to business, especially when it is integrated with business strategy and when human resource systems are emphasized. **Availability:** PDF.

42491 ■ *"Village at Waugh Chapel $275M Expansion Begins"* in Baltimore Business Journal (Vol. 28, August 27, 2010, No. 16, pp. 1)

Pub: Baltimore Business Journal

Ed: Daniel J. Sernovitz. **Description:** Developer Greenberg Gibbons Corporation has broken ground on a $275 million, 1.2 million-square-foot addition to its Village at the Waugh Chapel mixed-use complex. Aside from creating 2,600 permanent jobs, the addition, named Village South, is expected to lure Target and Wegmans Food Markets to Crofton, Maryland. Funding for this project is discussed.

42492 ■ *"Voices From the Front Lines: Four Leaders on the Cross-Border Challenges They've Faced"* in Harvard Business Review (Vol. 92, September 2014, No. 9, pp. 77)

Pub: Harvard Business Publishing

Released: September 2014. **Description:** Points presented include building cultural sensitivity into organizations, employing varying talent to respond to market specifics, creating standard human resource practices worldwide, and emphasizing the importance of emerging markets.

42493 ■ *"Walker Seeks More Business Participation"* in Business Journal-Milwaukee

(Vol. 28, December 10, 2010, No. 10, pp. A1)

Pub: Milwaukee Business Journal

Ed: Rich Kirchen. **Description:** Wisconsin governor Scott Walker is seeking the aid of Milwaukee business leaders to participate in resolving the challenges posed by the economic crisis. Walker is aiming to create 250,000 jobs. He is also planning to call a special session of the legislature to enact strategies to jumpstart the economy.

42494 ■ *"Wanted: African American Professional for Hire"* in Black Enterprise (Vol. 37, November 2006, No. 4, pp. 93)

Pub: Earl G. Graves Publishing Co. Inc.

Contact: Earl G. Graves, Jr., President

Ed: Joe Watson. **Description:** Excerpt from the book, Without Excuses: Unleash the Power of Diversity to Build Your Business, speaks to the lack of diversity in the corporate arena and why executives, recruiters, and HR professionals claim they are unable to find qualified individuals of different races when hiring.

42495 ■ *"The War for Good Jobs; The World Will IBe Led with Economic Force"* in Gallup Management Journal (September 7, 2011)

Pub: Gallup Inc.

Contact: Jim Clifton, Chief Executive Officer

Ed: Jim Clifton. **Description:** Gallup's chairman believes the next world war will be for good jobs and the winner will triumph with economic force, driven primarily by job creation and quality GDP growth.

42496 ■ *"We Have a Budget, Too"* in Entrepreneur (Vol. 37, October 2009, No. 10, pp. 89)

Pub: Entrepreneur Press

Contact: Perlman Neil, President

Ed: Craig Matsuda. **Description:** One human resources executive at a financial services company claims that health care issues are as costly and irritating for companies as they are for the employees. Health care vendors and insurers try as much as possible to maximize profits, while companies exert much effort to maximize benefits for their workers.

42497 ■ *"Web Site Design, Content Can Boost Diversity"* in HRMagazine (Vol. 53, August 2008, No. 8, pp. 20)

Description: Design and content of an employer's Website influences prospective young job candidates, especially young black job seekers, a new academic study has found. The findings appear in Black and White and Read All Over: Race Differences in Reactions To Recruitment Web Sites, published in the summer 2008 issue of the Human Resource Management Journal.

42498 ■ *"A Well-Crafted Employee Handbook Can Make Work Run More Smoothly"* in Idaho Business Review (September 17, 2014)

Pub: Dolan Co.

Contact: James P. Dolan, President

Released: September 17, 2014. **Description:** An employee handbook will provide a complaint process, provide company management flexibility and clarity and keep a company out of legal problems. Training, compensation, benefits, security, health, performance appraisals, and safety issues must be covered. Human resource managers and other mangers should cover basics to help communicate with workers.

42499 ■ *"Well Done!"* in Canadian Business (Vol. 80, April 23, 2007, No. 9, pp. 47)

Ed: Joe Castaldo. **Description:** The human resource management methods applied by different companies like Deloitte & Touche LLP are presented.

42500 ■ *The Well-Timed Strategy: Managing Business Cycle for Competitive Advantage*

Pub: Wharton School Publishing

Ed: Peter Navarro. **Released:** January 13, 2006. **Price:** $39.99, Nonmembers; $31.99, Members. **Description:** An overview of business cycles and risks is presented. Recession is a good time to find key personnel for a small business. Other issues addressed include investment, production, and marketing in order to maintain a competitive edge. **Availability:** Print; E-book.

42501 ■ *"We're Falling Behind the Rest of the Country"* in Canadian Business (Vol. 85, August 13, 2012, No. 13, pp. 46)
Pub: George Media Inc.
Ed: Joe Castaldo. **Released:** August 13, 2012. **Description:** Clearwater Seafoods cofounder John Risley is concerned about the future of the Canadian economy, particularly the Atlantic Provinces, with high unemployment rates and demographic shift. He believes that Atlantic Canadians are great entrepreneurs and workers.

42502 ■ *"What Businesses Can Do: Growing the Supply of Highly Skilled Graduates"* in Canadian Business (Vol. 81, October 27, 2008, No. 18)
Description: Employers in Canada have expressed concerns over the findings of various studies that revealed current and projected labor shortages in the country. A low birthrate and an aging population is contributing to the problem. Ways businesses can increase the supply of highly skilled workers in Canada is presented.

42503 ■ *"What Employees Worldwide Have in Common"* in Gallup Management Journal (September 22, 2011)
Pub: Gallup Inc.
Contact: Jim Clifton, Chief Executive Officer
Ed: Steve Crabtree. **Description:** According to a Gallup study, workplace conditions are strongly tied to personal wellbeing, regardless of geographic region. The employee study covered 116 countries.

42504 ■ *"What to Pay Your Top Team"* in Inc. (March 2008, pp. 108-112, 114)
Pub: Mansueto Ventures L.L.C.
Contact: John Koten, Chief Executive Officer
Ed: Jennifer Gill. **Description:** In-depth examination to help business owners decide if they paying their executives properly. A guide to executive salaries at private companies is presented. Statistical data included.

42505 ■ *"What Recovery?"* in Canadian Business (Vol. 82, April 27, 2009, No. 7, pp. 18)
Ed: Rachel Pulfer. **Description:** U.S. markets have rallied on the end of March 2009 but experts and analysts believe that it could be short-lived. Market rallies were found to be common during recessions and are not indicative of economic recovery. Meanwhile, it is believed that employment will be a key factor that will determine the U.S. economic recovery.

42506 ■ *"What's Working Now: In Providing Jobs for North Carolinians"* in Business North Carolina (Vol. 28, February 2008, No. 2, pp. 16)
Pub: Business North Carolina
Ed: Edward Martin, Frank Maley. **Description:** Individuals previously employed in the furniture, tobacco, or textile manufacturing sectors have gone back to school to be trained in new sectors in the area such as life sciences, finances and other emerging sectors.

42507 ■ *"When R&D Spending Is Not Enough: The Critical Role of Culture When You Really Want to Innovate"* in Human Resource Management (Vol. 49, July-August 2010, No. 4, pp. 767-792)
Pub: John Wiley
Ed: Sheng Wang, Rebecca M. Guidice, Judith W. Tansky, Zhong-Ming Wang. **Description:** A study was conducted to examine the effect of contextual contingencies on innovation. Findings indicate that Chinese manufacturers with cultures emphasizing innovation and teamwork more effectively utilize financial resources in the innovation process. Results also show that a culture emphasizing outcomes and stability leads to lower levels innovation irrespective of investments.

42508 ■ *"When To Make Private News Public: Should a Job Candidate Reveal That She's Pregnant?"* in Harvard Business Review (Vol.

90, March 2012, No. 3, pp. 161)
Pub: Harvard Business Review Press
Contact: Peter E. Walsh, Director
Ed: Tiziana Casciaro, Victoria W. Winston. **Released:** March 2012. **Description:** A fictitious hiring scenario is presented, with contributors providing advice on whether a candidate for a position involving extensive business travel should inform her manager that she is expecting. Contributors agree the employee should inform her manager, but not necessarily before she is offered the position, and that the conversation remains focused on how she will perform the job and address challenges.

42509 ■ *"Why Did We Ever Go Into HR?"* in Harvard Business Review (Vol. 86, July-August 2008, No. 8, pp. 39)
Pub: Harvard Business Review Press
Contact: Peter E. Walsh, Director
Ed: Matthew D. Breitfelder, Daisy Wademan Dowling. **Description:** Examines the role of human resource directors and how their jobs foster new ideas and generate optimism.

42510 ■ *"Why Does Firm Reputation In Human Resource Policies Influence College Students? The Mechanisms Underlying Job Pursuit Intentions"* in Human Resource Management (Vol. 51, January-February 2012, No. 1, pp. 121-142)
Pub: John Wiley & Sons Inc.
Contact: Stephen M. Smith, President
Ed: Julie Holliday Wayne, Wendy J. Casper. **Description:** The effects of reputational information about human resource practices of companies on college students seeking employment are examined. The reputation of firms in compensation, work-family, and diversity efforts are found to increase intentions to pursue employment in these firms.

42511 ■ *"Why His Merit Raise Is Bigger Than Hers"* in Harvard Business Review (Vol. 90, April 2012, No. 4, pp. 26)
Pub: Harvard Business Review Press
Contact: Peter E. Walsh, Director
Ed: Stephen Benard. **Released:** April 2012. **Description:** Research indicates that companies that utilize meritocracy as their pay-for-performance system are paradoxically more likely to award pay on biases, and specifically, to give smaller increases to women. Tranparency and accountability are therefore key in the implementation of merit pay.

42512 ■ *"Why HR Practices Are Not Evidence-Based"* in Academy of Management Journal (Vol. 50, No. 5, October 1, 2007, pp. 1033)
Pub: Academy of Management
Contact: Ming-Jer Chen, President
Ed: Edward E. Lawler. **Description:** A suggestion that an Evidence-Based Management Collaboration (EBMC) can be established to facilitate effective transfer of ideas between science and practice is presented.

42513 ■ *"Why Is It So Hard To Find Good People? The Problem Might Be You"* in Inc. (Vol. 33, November 2011, No. 9, pp. 100)
Pub: Inc. Magazine
Ed: April Joyner. **Description:** Entrepreneurs sometimes struggle to find good workers. A recent survey shows hiring as their top concern. Four common mistakes that can occur during the hiring process our outlined.

42514 ■ *"Why Make Diversity So Hard to Achieve?"* in (Vol. 90, June 2012, No. 6, pp. 40)
Pub: Harvard Business Review Press
Contact: Peter E. Walsh, Director
Ed: John Rice. **Released:** June 2012. **Description:** Four obstacles to workplace diversity are identified: distributing the responsibility for improving diversity; managing activities rather than outcomes; focusing on correcting the culture rather than on promotion rates; and prioritizing minority candidates for diversity department positions without enabling them to transcend problems they themselves may be facing.

42515 ■ *"Why Men Still Get More Promotions Than Women"* in Harvard Business Review (Vol. 88, September 2010, No. 9, pp. 80)
Pub: Harvard Business School Publishing
Ed: Herminia Ibarra, Nancy M. Carter, Christine Silva. **Description:** Sponsorship, rather than mentoring, is identified as the main difference in why men still receive more promotions than women. Active executive sponsorship is key to fostering career advancement.

42516 ■ *"Why Motivating People Doesn't Work...and What Does: The New Science of Leading, Energizing, and Engaging"*
Pub: Berrett-Koehler Communications Inc.
Contact: Steve Piersanti, President
E-mail: spiersanti@bkpub.com
Released: September 30, 2014. **Price:** , $24.95. **Description:** Leadership researcher, consultant, and business coach, Susan Fowler, shares the latest research on the nature of human motivation to present a tested model and course of action to help Human Resource leaders and managers guide workers towards motivation that will not only increase productivity and engagement but will provide employees with a sense of purpose and fulfillment.

42517 ■ *"Why Top Young Managers Are In a Nonstop Job Hunt"* in (Vol. 90, July-August 2012, No. 7-8, pp. 28)
Pub: Harvard Business Review Press
Contact: Peter E. Walsh, Director
Ed: Monika Hamori, Jie Cao, Burak Koyuncu. **Released:** July-August 2012. **Description:** Managers are moving from firm to firm in part because companies are not addressing formal training, coaching, and mentoring needs. While these are costly, companies might benefit from the investment, as managers may tend to stay longer in firms where they are provided.

42518 ■ *"Will Workers Be Left To Build It Here?"* in Boston Business Journal (Vol. 31, June 3, 2011, No. 19, pp. 1)
Pub: Boston Business Journal
Ed: Kyle Alspach. **Description:** Lack of skilled workers has resulted in delayed expansion of local manufacturing operations in Massachusetts. Acme Packet Inc. expects to add only 10 jobs by the end of 2011.

42519 ■ *"Work Force: In the Mix"* in Entrepreneur (Vol. 35, October 2007, No. 10, pp. 109)
Pub: Entrepreneur Press
Contact: Perlman Neil, President
Ed: Mark Henricks. **Description:** A study of 708 companies' diversity programs shows that diversity training alone is not the most effective way of increasing diversity in management. It was found that one effective way of putting minorities and women in management teams is to give a team or a person the task of improving diversity in the company. The reason why accountability succeeds in diversifying the workforce is discussed.

42520 ■ *"Working For Pennies? Huge Pay Gap Between Top Executives and Black Employees"* in Black Enterprise (Vol. 38, March 2008, No. 8)
Pub: Earl G. Graves Publishing Co. Inc.
Contact: Earl G. Graves, Jr., President
Ed: Cliff Hocker. **Description:** CEO pay is out of control because most board members approving high salaries and compensation packages are often executives at other firms. According to a study conducted by the Institute for Policy Studies, CEOs earn more than 1,085 times the average full-time black worker's median earnings.

42521 ■ *"The Workplace Generation Gaps"* in Women In Business (Vol. 62, June 2010, No. 2, pp. 8)
Pub: American Business Women's Association
Contact: Lorie Burch, President
Ed: Leigh Elmore. **Description:** Generation gaps among baby boomers, Generation X and Generation Y in the workplace are attributed to technological divides and differences in opinions. These factors

could lead to workplace misunderstandings, employee turnover and communication difficulties. Details on managing such workplace gaps are discussed.

42522 ■ The Worst-Case Scenario Business Survival Guide: How to Survive the Recession, Handle Layoffs, Raise Emergency Cash, Thwart an Employee Coup, and Avoid Other Potential Disasters
Pub: John Wiley & Sons Inc.
Contact: Stephen M. Smith, President
Ed: David Borgenicht, Mark Joyner. Released: September 28, 2009. Price: $17.95. Description: Since 1999, the Worst-Case Scenario survival handbooks have provided readers with real answers for the most extreme situations. Now, in a time of economic crisis, the series returns with a new, real-world guide to avoiding the worst business cataclysms.

42523 ■ "Your First 100 Days on Your New Job" in Women In Business (Vol. 63, Spring 2011, No. 1, pp. 28)
Pub: American Business Women's Association
Contact: Lorie Burch, President
Ed: Diane Stafford. Description: The first 100 days on the job are crucial if the person's permanent hiring is conditional on surviving a probationary period. The new hire must do more than just master the job's technical details to maximize the chance of success. Details of some basic tips to fit into the corporate culture and get along with coworkers are also discussed.

42524 ■ "Youth Employment in the Summer of 2010" in Montly Labor Review (Vol. 133, September 2010, No. 9, pp. 2)
Pub: U.S. Department of Labor Bureau of Labor Statistics
Contact: Philip L. Rones, Manager
E-mail: rones.philip@bls.gov
Description: The number of youth 16 to 24 years old rose by 1.8 million from April to July 2010. Statistical data included.

TRADE PERIODICALS

42525 ■ Employee Benefit Plan Review
Pub: Aspen Publishers, Inc.
Contact: Robert Becker, President
URL(s): www.aspenpublishers.com/Product.asp?catalog_name=Aspen&product_id=SS00136808.
Released: Monthly Price: $395, Individuals.

42526 ■ Employee Terminations Law Bulletin
Pub: Quinlan Publishing Co.
Released: Monthly. Price: $170.82, full set.

42527 ■ FERA--Focus
Pub: Formative Evaluation Research Associates
URL(s): www.feraonline.com/. Ed: John A. Seeley, Editor. Released: 3/year. Price: Free. Description: Discusses consulting work and research on evaluation of corporate training, human resource development programs, community-based social services, and educational programs.

42528 ■ HRMagazine: On Human Resource Management
Pub: Society for Human Resource Management
Contact: Henry G. Jackson, President
E-mail: hjackson@shrm.org
URL(s): www.shrm.org/Publications/hrmagazine/Pages/default.aspx. Ed: Nancy M. Davis. Released: 10/year Price: $70, Individuals 1 year - 12 issues; $100, Two years; $90, Canada; $125, Other countries; $34.99, Individuals digital issue; $2.99, Single issue.

42529 ■ Journal of Workplace Rights
Pub: Baywood Publishing Company Inc.
Contact: Stuart Cohen, President
URL(s): baywood.com/journals/previewjournals.asp?id=jwr. Ed: Joel Rudin. Released: Quarterly Price: $422, Institutions print and online; $401, Institutions online only.

42530 ■ What's Working in Human Resources
Pub: American Future Systems Inc.
Contact: Tom Schubert, Manager
E-mail: tschubert@pbp.com
URL(s): www.pbp.com; www.pbp.com. Released: Semimonthly. Price: $299, individuals. Description: Reports on the latest trends in Human Resources, including the latest employment law rulings. Recurring features include interviews, news of research, a calendar of events, news of educational opportunities, and a column titlted Sharpen Your Judgment.

VIDEOCASSETTES/ AUDIOCASSETTES

42531 ■ Conducting an Effective Job Interview
Phoenix Learning Group
2349 Chaffee Dr.
Saint Louis, MO 63146-3306
Ph: (314)569-0211
Free: 800-221-1274
Fax: (314)569-2834
URL: http://www.phoenixlearninggroup.com
Released: 1988. Price: $450. Description: This video teaches you how to interview effectively. Availability: VHS; 8 mm; 3/4 U.

42532 ■ Conflicts, Conflicts!
University of Washington Educational Media Collection
Kane Hall, Rm. 35
Campus Box 353095
Seattle, WA 98195
Ph: (206)543-9907
Fax: (206)616-6501
URL: http://www.css.washington.edu/emc
Released: 1985. Description: This is a management training film demonstrating techniques for avoiding conflicts. Availability: VHS; 3/4 U.

42533 ■ Creating Effective Workshops: The Design Doctor Is In
ASTD
1640 King St.
Alexandria, VA 22314-2746
Ph: (703)683-8100
Free: 800-628-2783
Fax: (703)683-1523
Co. E-mail: customercare@astd.org
URL: http://www.astd.org
Contact: Tony Bingham, President
E-mail: tbingham@astd.org
Released: 1989. Description: The successes and failures of others can help you plan your next training sessions. From start to finish, expert trainer and Human Resource Development manager Susan Warshauer shows how to control fears associated with learning new skills, how to ensure new skills make it back to the workplace, and how to move smoothly through a variety of topics. Availability: VHS; 3/4 U.

42534 ■ Fair & Effective Discipline
Business & Legal Resources, Inc. (BLR)
141 Mill Rock Rd., E
Old Saybrook, CT 06475
Ph: (860)510-0100
Free: 800-454-0404
Fax: (860)510-7220
Co. E-mail: service@blr.com
URL: http://www.blr.com
Contact: Dan Oswald, Chief Executive Officer
Released: 1986. Description: A training film for managers in handling employee problems-absenteeism, poor performance, etc. Availability: VHS; 3/4 U.

42535 ■ Flexible Working Time: More Time to Live
Encyclopedia Britannica
331 N La Salle St.
Chicago, IL 60654
Ph: (312)347-7000
Free: 800-323-1229

Fax: (312)294-2104
URL: http://www.corporate.britannica.com
Contact: Jacob E. Safra
Released: 1988. Price: $395. Description: A look at the Dutch postal service and a German department store, two places where the employees have flexible working hours. Availability: VHS; 3/4 U.

42536 ■ Hiring and Firing
Aspen Publishers, Inc.
7201 McKinney Cir.
Frederick, MD 21704
Ph: (301)698-7100
Free: 800-234-1660
Fax: (800)901-9075
Co. E-mail: customerservice@aspenpublisher.com
URL: http://www.aspenpublishers.com
Contact: Robert Becker, President
Released: 1985. Description: For business supervisors, a film on how to decide when to terminate and hire personnel. Availability: VHS; 3/4 U; Special order formats.

42537 ■ How to Interview Clients Effectively
American Law Institute - Committee on Continuing Professional Education (ALI CLE)
4025 Chestnut St.
Philadelphia, PA 19104
Ph: (215)243-1600
Free: 800-253-6397
Fax: (215)243-1636
Co. E-mail: in-house@ali-aba.org
URL: http://www.ali.org
Contact: Julene Franki, Executive Director
E-mail: jfranki@ali-aba.org
Released: 1993. Price: $95. Description: Studies the interviewing process, offering advice on opening the interview, probing for details, testing theories, and closing the interview. Includes study guide. Availability: VHS.

42538 ■ The Power of Positive and Effective Communication
Aspen Publishers, Inc.
7201 McKinney Cir.
Frederick, MD 21704
Ph: (301)698-7100
Free: 800-234-1660
Fax: (800)901-9075
Co. E-mail: customerservice@aspenpublisher.com
URL: http://www.aspenpublishers.com
Contact: Robert Becker, President
Released: 1987. Price: $495. Description: A program which teaches supervisors how to be sure to give clear instructions to their subordinates. Availability: VHS; 3/4 U; Special order formats.

42539 ■ The Trouble with Words
National Safety Council, California Chapter Film Library
4553 Glencoe Ave., Ste. 150
Marina Del Rey, CA 90292
Ph: (310)827-9781
Free: 800-421-9585
Fax: (310)827-9861
Co. E-mail: california@nsc.org
URL: http://www.nsc.org/nsc_near_you/FindYourLocalChapter/Pages/California.aspx
Contact: Joseph M. Kaplan, President
Released: 198?. Description: Provides some suggestions for creating better communication and higher productivity among employees. Availability: VHS; 3/4 U.

42540 ■ Understanding EEOC, Part 1-3
RMI Media
1365 N. Winchester St.
Olathe, KS 66061-5880
Ph: (913)768-1696
Free: 800-745-5480
Fax: (800)755-6910
Co. E-mail: actmedia@act.org
URL: http://www.actmedia.com
Released: 1987. Price: $80. Description: In this three-part series, equal employment opportunity laws are explained and followed by suggestions for companies seeking to develop practices, policies, and procedures in this area. Availability: VHS; 3/4 U.

42541 ■ *Who Wants to Play God?*
National Safety Council, California Chapter Film
  Library
4553 Glencoe Ave., Ste. 150
Marina Del Rey, CA 90292
Ph: (310)827-9781
Free: 800-421-9585
Fax: (310)827-9861
Co. E-mail: california@nsc.org
URL: http://www.nsc.org/nsc_near_you/FindYourLo-
  calChapter/Pages/California.aspx
Contact: Joseph M. Kaplan, President
Released: 198?. **Description:** This is an examina-
tion of why many performance reviews fail to increase
employee effectiveness. **Availability:** VHS; 3/4 U.

CONSULTANTS

**42542 ■ Advanced Benefits & Human
Resources**
9350-F Snowden River Pky., Ste. 222
Columbia, MD 21045
Ph: (410)290-9037
Contact: Linda B. Polacek, President
Scope: Provides human resource consulting to high
technology businesses. Offers services in the areas
of human resources, benefits and training. Creates,
maintains, or updates current human resource functions. **Founded:** 1996.

42543 ■ Arnold Consulting Group Inc. (ACG)
7839 Main St., Ste. 683
Fishers, NY 14453-9800
Ph: (585)507-4259
Co. E-mail: acg4u@aol.com
URL: http://www.arnoldconsultinggroup.com
Contact: Brian C. Arnold, President
Scope: It is a management consulting firm dedicated
to partnering with companies to create, design, and
implement leadership and organizational solutions
aligned with their business strategies. Given the
changing organizational dynamics, new technology,
government scrutiny, and global competition, the
challenges facing business leaders are daunting.
ACG understands leaders of effective organizations
need continuously updated skills, keener insight and
increased creativity to compete effectively in the
global marketplace. **Seminars:** Negotiation Strategies; Leadership Development; Competency Design;
High Performance Teams Development; Management
of Conflict; Employee Empowerment; Team Building;
Job Search.

42544 ■ Barker & Associates
1974 Wexford Cir.
Wheaton, IL 60187-6166
Ph: (630)260-9927
Contact: John Donald Porter, President
Scope: Consulting, training and coaching firm
specializing in providing human resource assessment, selection and development services focused
primarily on people skills. Serves small, mid and
large-size organizations in both private industry and
not-for-profit associations. **Founded:** 1982. **Semi-
nars:** Strategic Marketing; Consultative Selling and
Customer Service; From Hiring to Appraising -
Developing Your Employees; Increased Productivity
Through Managed Stress; Producing People Results
Through Team building; Conflict Management; Communications, Managing Transition and Change;
Creative Problem Solving.

42545 ■ BeamPines Inc.
232 Madison Ave., 10th Fl.
New York, NY 10016
Ph: (212)476-4100
Fax: (212)986-7798
Co. E-mail: leadership@beampines.com
URL: http://www.beampines.com
Contact: Jonathan B. Santamaria, President
E-mail: jsantamaria@beampines.com
Scope: A human resource consultancy with expertise
in employment and employee development. Serves
businesses in the United States Provides comprehen-
sive talent management services to help organiza-
tions attract, retain and continuously develop the best
people. **Founded:** 1981. **Publications:** "Ontarios
Green Energy and Green Economy Act," 2009;

"Citizens Guide to Pollution Prevention,"; "Le Guide
du citoyen pour la prevention de la pollution," Mar,
2005; "Ontarios Industrial Emissions Reduction Plan,"
2005; "Ensuring Green Power Supplies in Ontario
Responding to Perverse Subsidies and Other Market
Inequities," Oct, 2003; "A Municipal Guide to Wind
Power Development in Ontario," Apr, 2003; "Green
Power Opportunities for Ontario," 2002; "Third Annual
Green Power Trade Show," 2002; "Sixth Annual
Report on Ontarios Environment" 2002; "Ontarios
Environment and the Common Sense Revolution: A
Fifth Year Report," 2000; "The Quality of Air," Mar,
1999. **Seminars:** Executive Development Counsel-
ing.

42546 ■ Benefit Partners Inc.
2140 Regent St., Ste. 1
Sudbury, ON, Canada P3E 5S8
Ph: (705)524-1559
Free: 800-461-6326
Fax: (705)524-5553
Co. E-mail: info@benefitpartners.com
URL: http://www.benefitpartners.com
Contact: Bruce Frick, Managing Director
E-mail: bruce.frick@benefitpartners.com
Scope: Services include employee benefits, pension,
executive compensation, human resources and
financial management. Industries served: Corporate
and personal insurance planning and private wealth
management.

42547 ■ Benefits Dynamics Inc. (BDI)
89 N Haddon Ave., Ste. D
Haddonfield, NJ 08033-2473
Ph: (856)616-1400
Fax: (856)616-1401
Co. E-mail: benefit@benefitdynamics.com
Contact: Carmen Laverghetta, Vice President
Scope: A full service employee benefit, record keeping consultant and outsourcing organization. Provides
pension consulting, administration and actuarial
services, cafeteria and flexible benefit plans, human
resource systems outsourcing, interactive voice-
response systems, electronic employee benefit enrollment and transportation plans. **Founded:** 1979.

42548 ■ Bijan International Inc.
11776 Jollyville Rd., Ste. 250
Austin, TX 78759-3900
Ph: (512)923-6932
Fax: (512)219-0383
Co. E-mail: info@bijanintl.com
URL: http://www.bijanintl.com
Contact: Bijan Afkami, Principal
Scope: A leadership development consulting and
training firm. Offers leadership training workshops,
seminars and programs, corporate training, and
executive coaching. Consultants interact with senior
management to conduct assessment processes;
facilitate motivation within groups to accelerate the
learning process; implement customized and exciting
training programs; design long range initiatives and
incentive programs; and create improvements in
individual and team performance. **Founded:** 1993.
Publications: "Coaching firm Rallies Businesses,"
Jan, 2003; "A Journey of 1000 Miles". **Seminars:**
Emotional Intelligence; Discovering Diversity; Empowered Women; High-Velocity Change; The Positive
Power of Feed back; Team work; Customer Service;
Sexual Harassment; Leaders In Sales; Body Therapy;
Personal Effectiveness; Teamwork Skills; Leadership
Abilities.

42549 ■ Blankinship & Associates Inc.
322 C St.
Davis, CA 95616
Ph: (530)757-0941
Fax: (530)757-0940
Co. E-mail: blankinship@envtox.com
URL: http://www.h2osci.com
Contact: Michael Blankinship, President
E-mail: mike@envtox.com
Scope: Specializes in assisting water resource and
conveyance, golf and production, protection and
enhancement of natural resources. **Founded:** 2000.
Publications: "Air Blast Sprayer Calibration and
Chlorpyrifos Irrigation Study," Oct, 2007; "How Green
is your golf course," Prosper Magazine, 2007. **Semi-
nars:** CDFG Wildlands IPM Seminar, Oct, 2009.

42550 ■ Brown Associates Inc.
65 Birch Hill Rd.
Belmont, MA 02478-1730
Ph: (617)489-2500
Contact: George Vaccaro, Vice President
Scope: Provider of outsourced human resources
consulting and training services to business, educational and municipal clients. It is also engaged in
staffing, manpower planning, compensation and
performance evaluation solutions. **Founded:** 1967.
Publications: "The Legal Evolution of Sexual Harassment"; "Top 10 Human Resource Mistakes and How
to Avoid Them"; "Do You Need a Consultant?". **Seminars:** Preventing Sexual Harassment in the Workplace; Employment Law: All You Need to Know From
A to Z; Selecting and Preparing Employees for
International Assignments; Outplacement-How to
Humanely Handle a Reduction in Force.

42551 ■ Carelli & Associates
17 Reid Pl.
Delmar, NY 12054
Ph: (518)439-0233
Fax: (518)439-3006
Co. E-mail: truthaboutsupervision@yahoo.com
URL: http://www.carelli.com
Contact: Anne O Brien Carelli, Owner
E-mail: anneobriencarelli@yahoo.com
Scope: Provider of writing and editing services to
industry and businesses, health care and educational
institutions, and government agencies. Also provides
program management in creating and disseminating
publications and in implementing related training. Assists organizations in designing and implementing
team-based management. Offers supervisory skills
training and problem-solving work sessions for
managers. Individual Consultation are provided for
managers, CEOs, potential supervisors including 360
degree assessments. **Founded:** 1988. **Publications:**
"The Truth About Supervision: Coaching, Teamwork,
Interviewing, Appraisals, 360 degree Assessments,
and Recognition". **Seminars:** Supervisory Skills
Training Series; Problem-Solving Work Sessions for
Managers; Effective Leadership.

**42552 ■ Center for Organizational Excellence
(COE)**
15204 Omega Dr., Ste. 300
Rockville, MD 20850
Ph: (301)948-1922
Free: 877-ORG-EXCEL
Fax: (301)948-2158
Co. E-mail: results@center4oe.com
URL: http://www.center4oe.com
Contact: Steve Goodrich, President
Scope: An organizational effectiveness consulting
firm specializing in helping organizations achieve
results through people, process and performance.
Service areas include organizational performance
systems, leadership systems, customer systems and
learning systems. **Founded:** 1984.

**42553 ■ CFI Group USA L.L.C. [Claes Fornell
International]**
625 Avis Dr.
Ann Arbor, MI 48108
Ph: (734)930-9090
Free: 800-930-0933
Fax: (734)930-0911
Co. E-mail: askcfi@cfigroup.com
URL: http://www.cfigroup.com
Contact: Sheri Petras, Chief Executive Officer
E-mail: steodoru@mail.cfigroup.com
Scope: Management consulting firm that helps its
clients worldwide to maximize shareholder value by
optimizing customer and employee satisfaction.
Clients span a variety of industries, including manu-
facturing, telecommunications, retail and government.
Founded: 1988. **Publications:** "Customer Satisfac-
tion and Stock Prices: High Returns, Low Risk,"
American Marketing Association, Jan, 2006; "Cus-
tomer Satisfaction Index Climbs," The Wall Street
Journal, Feb, 2004; "What's Next? Customer Service
is Key to Post-Boom Success," The Bottom Line, Mar,
2003; "Boost Stock Performance, Nation's Economy,"
Quality Progress, Feb, 2003.

42554 ■ Cole Financial Service Inc.
3170 E, Lafayette Blvd.
Detroit, MI 48207-4378
Ph: (313)962-7055
Free: 877-972-7055
Fax: (313)962-7815
Co. E-mail: jason.a.cole@colefinancial1.net
URL: http://www.colefinancial1.net
Contact: Patricia Allen Cole, President
E-mail: patricia.a.cole@colefinancial1.net
Scope: A full service human capital development firm providing services in recruiting, coaching, retaining, developing and retiring. Works with front line staff, managers and executive level decision makers that set strategy. Industries served: Engineering, construction, government and other business entities. **Founded:** 1983. **Seminars:** How to Run Your Own Business; 25Ways to stay in Business 25Years; How to Tap Your Potential and Discover Your GENIUS; The Job Ladder Steps to SUCCESS; Making and Keeping a Budget; Records Retention and Disposal; Take Control of Your Life; Time and Priority Management; TQM - Total Quality Management; Leadership 101; Leadership 201; Diversity Agent or Opponent A Personal Development Workshop; Coaching in a Diverse Workplace.

42555 ■ Consulting & Conciliation Service (CCS)
2219 H St., Ste. 1
Sacramento, CA 95816
Ph: (916)396-0480
Free: 888-898-9780
Fax: (916)441-2828
Co. E-mail: service@azurewings.net
Contact: Jane A. McCluskey, Principal
E-mail: service@azurewings.net
Scope: Offers consulting and conciliation services. Provides pre-mediation counseling, training and research on preparing for a peaceful society, mediation and facilitation and preparation for shifts in structure, policy and personnel. Offers sliding scale business rates and free individual consultation. **Publications:** "Native America and Tracking Shifts in US Policy"; "Biogenesis: A Discussion of Basic Social Needs and the Significance of Hope". **Seminars:** Positive Approaches to Violence Prevention: Peace building in Schools and Communities.

42556 ■ Controlled Resources
1021 E 1st Ave., Apt. 822
Broomfield, CO 80020
Ph: (708)798-2978
Fax: (727)532-3955
Scope: Firm offers business and management consultancy services.

42557 ■ CoStaff Services L.L.C.
29100 NW Highway, Ste. 240
Southfield, MI 48034
Ph: (248)671-1400
Free: 866-426-7823
Fax: (248)692-0816
Co. E-mail: sales@costaffservices.com
URL: http://www.costaffservices.com
Contact: Diane Bonk, Director
Scope: Services: Human resource. **Founded:** 2000.

42558 ■ The Devine Group Inc.
7755 Montgomery Rd., Ste. 180
Cincinnati, OH 45236
Ph: (513)792-7500
Free: 866-792-7500
Fax: (513)793-8535
Co. E-mail: sales@devinegroup.com
URL: http://www.devinegroup.com
Contact: Joe Koczwara, Chief Information Officer
Scope: A human resource consulting company devoted to providing reliable and responsive information focusing on performance issues and answers. Dedicated to analyzing and enhancing job performance. Custom design and implement programs and workshops that will result in demonstrable behavior change on the job. Assist clients enhance their productivity via behavior analysis. **Founded:** 1970. **Publications:** "Leveraging Assessments for Enterprise Improvement," Oct, 2006; "Evaluation of Assessment Tools: The Five Criteria," Oct, 2006;

"People Improvement Using Behavior Assessment," Aug, 2005; "Measuring Personality: The Good, the Bad and the Ugly". **Special Services:** The Devine Inventory®.

42559 ■ DiversityWorks
800 Heinz Ave., Ste. 14
Berkeley, CA 94710
Ph: (510)540-7008
Fax: (510)540-6976
Co. E-mail: mail@diversityworks.org
URL: http://www.diversityworks.org
Contact: Moses J. Ceaser, Director
E-mail: moses@diversityworks.org
Scope: Offers diversity consulting to businesses, schools, youth groups and a variety of organizations. Designs programs to suit to individual clients' needs. Areas of expertise include: Community-building (and team-building), consciousness-raising, skill building (leadership development, popular education, facilitation) and taking action. **Founded:** 1998. **Publications:** "Diversity Words"; "A Woman's Beauty"; "Youth Violence"; "Modern Day Minstrels"; "Love Makes the World Go Round"; "Glorification of White Supremacy through Movies".

42560 ■ DJT Consulting Group L.L.C.
PO Box 8595
San Jose, CA 95155
Ph: (408)280-1153
Co. E-mail: sherry@djtconsulting.com
URL: http://www.djtconsulting.com
Contact: Sherry V. Bruning, Principal
Scope: Offers a range of grant management services including contract monitoring, research, grant writing, evaluation and project management. Specializes in grant proposal writing, project management and program development. Assists enhance financial resources, programs and services. **Founded:** 2000. **Seminars:** Finding and Winning Government Grants.

42561 ■ Dorn & Associates Inc.
8506 Bass Lake Rd.
Minneapolis, MN 55428-5304
Ph: (763)533-7689
Contact: John L. Dorn, President
Scope: Services include accounting, marketing, employment partnership, new doctor agreements, personnel issues and human resources assessment, practice management, practice merger acquisition sale and liquidation, practice surveys and valuation, staff development and training.

42562 ■ Eastern Point Consulting Group Inc.
36 Glen Ave.
Newton, MA 02464
Ph: (617)965-4141
Fax: (617)965-4172
Co. E-mail: info@eastpt.com
URL: http://www.eastpt.com
Contact: Katherine A. Herzog, President
E-mail: kherzog@eastpt.com
Scope: Specializes in bringing practical solutions to complex challenges. Provides consulting and training in managing diversity; comprehensive sexual-harassment policies and programs; organizational development; benchmarks 360 skills assessment; executive coaching; strategic human resource planning; team building; leadership development for women; mentoring programs; and gender issues in the workplace. **Founded:** 1995. **Seminars:** Leadership Development for Women.

42563 ■ Effective Compensation Inc. (ECI)
30792 Southview Dr., Ste. 101
Evergreen, CO 80439
Ph: (303)854-1000
Free: 877-746-4324
Fax: (303)854-1030
Co. E-mail: eci@effectivecompensation.com
URL: http://www.effectivecompensation.com
Contact: Kathleen Piper, Vice President, Technical Services
Scope: Independent compensation consulting firm specializing in working with clients on a collaborative basis to improve their organization's efficiency through competitive, focused total compensation processes. Helps organizations determine how to competitively pay their employees. Provides quality,

culture sensitive, compensation consulting assistance to all types of employers. Specializes in surveys like drilling industry compensation surveys, environmental industry compensation surveys, liquid pipeline round table compensation surveys; and oil and gas E and P industry compensation surveys. **Founded:** 1991. **Publications:** "Alternative Job Evaluation Approaches"; "Broad Banding: A Management Overview"; "Job Evaluation: Understanding the Issues"; "Industry Compensation Surveys"; "Skill Based Pay"; "Four Levels of Team Membership"; "Factors in Designing an Incentive Plan"; "Key Stock Allocation Issues"; "Stock Plans Primer". **Seminars:** Alternative Job Evaluation Approaches; Broad Banding: A Management Overview; Skill Based Pay; Job Evaluation: Understanding the Issues; Designing Compensation Programs that Motivate Employees; Master the Compensation Maze; Base Salary Administration Manual.

42564 ■ Effective Resources Inc. (ERI)
118 N Peters Rd., Ste. 171
Knoxville, TN 37923
Free: 800-288-6044
Fax: (800)409-2812
Co. E-mail: customerservice@effectiveresources.com
URL: http://www.effectiveresources.com
Contact: Barry L. Brown, President
E-mail: barry@effectiveresources.com
Scope: Human resource consulting firm helping clients in all aspects of planning and implementation, to assure the program meets their objectives and budget considerations. Can work with clients on an interim basis or as consultants on short term assignment. Products and services include salary and benefits surveys, employee satisfaction surveys, performance management, compensation administration, compliance assistance and personality profile testing. Specializes in compensation and incentive plans, performance appraisals, team building and personnel policies and procedures, affirmative action plan preparation. **Founded:** 1988. **Special Services:** DiSC® Personality Profile.

42565 ■ Executive Directions International Inc.
1536 NW 97th St.
Clive, IA 50325-6402
Ph: (515)457-9300
Co. E-mail: culp@workwise.net
URL: http://www.workwise.net
Contact: Dr. Mildred L. Culp, President
E-mail: culp@workwise.net
Scope: Developer of customized contents. It also addresses the needs of print and online editors in newspaper groups and their independent counterparts. **Founded:** 1981. **Publications:** "Be Work Wise: Re-tooling your work for the 21st century," Executive Directions International, 1994; "After belief," 1976. **Seminars:** Getting the Right Media Attention. **Special Services:** WorkWise; WorkWise Interactive™; WorkWise Advice™.

42566 ■ The Executive Group
1645 Parkhill Dr., Ste. 4
Billings, MT 59102
Ph: (406)252-7770
Free: 800-755-5161
Fax: (406)255-7478
Co. E-mail: exgzinfo@wtp.net
URL: http://www.executivegroup.biz
Contact: Jamie Mathis, Manager
Scope: Services: Recruitment and executive placement. **Founded:** 1985.

42567 ■ Fox Lawson & Associates L.L.C.
1335 County Road D, Cir. E
Saint Paul, MN 55109-5260
Ph: (651)635-0976
Free: 800-383-0976
Fax: (651)635-0980
Co. E-mail: jfox@foxlawson.com
URL: http://www.foxlawson.com
Contact: James C. Fox, Managing Director
E-mail: jfox@foxlawson.com
Scope: A compensation and human resources consulting firm, provides services to businesses of all sizes including finance, manufacturing, high tech,

software development, food, retail, wholesale trade, communications, transportation, service, not-for-profit and education. **Founded:** 1995. **Seminars:** Compensation Strategies - Not Having a Plan Could Break the Bank.

42568 ■ Stephen J. Gill Consulting
3051 Geddes Ave.
Ann Arbor, MI 48104
Ph: (734)665-7728
Fax: (734)665-7864
Co. E-mail: sjgill@stephenjgill.com
URL: http://www.stephenjgill.com
Contact: Dr. Stephen J. Gill, Owner
E-mail: sjgill@stephenjgill.com
Scope: A consultant for human performance improvement, provides needs analysis, program evaluation and impact assessment services. Assists companies in planning effective learning programs. Industries served: Automobile manufacturing, furniture manufacturing, software development, healthcare, utilities, colleges, universities, nonprofits and philanthropic foundations. **Founded:** 1993. **Publications:** "Communication in High Performance Organizations: Principles and Best Practices," Kindle, 2011; "Developing a Learning Culture in Nonprofit Organizations," Sage, 2010; "The 5As Framework," RealTime Performance, 2009; "Myth and Reality of E-Learning," Nov, 2003; "The Manager's Pocket Guide to Organizational Learning," HRD Press, Sep, 2000; "The Learning Alliance: Systems Thinking in Human Resource Development," Jossey-Bass, Aug, 1994; "Developing a Learning Culture in Non profit Organizations". **Seminars:** Organizational Learning; High Impact Training; Training Evaluation; Survey Design; Outcomes and Impact Assessment.

42569 ■ Global Business Consultants (GBC)
200 Lake Hills Rd.
Pinehurst, NC 28374-0776
Ph: (910)295-5991
Co. E-mail: gbc@pinehurst.net
Contact: Nan S. Leaptrott, President
E-mail: nan@yourculturecoach.com
Scope: Firm specializes in human resources management; project management; software development; and international trade. Offers litigation support. **Founded:** 1987. **Publications:** "Culture to Culture: Mission Trip Do's and Don'ts," Jul, 2005; "Rules of the Game: Global Business Protocol". **Seminars:** Cross-Cultural Training.

42570 ■ Goren & Associates Inc.
32000 Northwestern Hwy., Ste. 128
Farmington Hills, MI 48334-1565
Ph: (248)851-0824
Free: 800-851-0824
Fax: (248)851-8751
Co. E-mail: info@gorentrain.com
URL: http://www.gorentrain.com
Contact: Dr. Keith Levick, Chief Executive Officer
Scope: Services: Organizational and workforce education and training. **Founded:** 1981. **Publications:** "The healthy child cookbook: 146 healthy snacks, meals, and desserts," The wellness institute; "Why is my child so overweight". **Seminars:** Instituting Change; Adjusting to Stress and Change; Initiating and Managing Change For Leaders; Deterring Sexual Harassment; Deterring Workplace Violence; Diversity in the Workplace; Collaborative Negotiation; Customizing our Service, Servicing our Customers; Dealing with Difficult Customers; Stress Management; Conducting Successful Meetings; How to Deliver a Dynamic Presentation; Creating a Motivating Team; Coaching Skills for Leaders.

42571 ■ Pamela K. Henry & Associates
13329 Kingman Dr., Ste. B
Austin, TX 78729-4908
Ph: (512)335-1237
Fax: (512)335-1237
Co. E-mail: info@pamelakhenry.com
URL: http://www.pamelakhenry.com
Contact: Pamela K. Henry, Principal
Scope: Specializes in career transition skills consulting. Services in resume development and interview coaching. Also offers consulting in workplace diversity and sexual harassment prevention. **Publications:** "Diversity and the Bottom Line: Prospering in the

Global Economy". **Seminars:** Competency-based Interviewing; Executive Interviewing; Selection Best Practices; Career Transitioning; Effectively Recruiting a Diverse Workforce; Creating Cultural Competence & Inclusion on Teams; Preventing Sexual Harassment.

42572 ■ Edward M. Hepner & Associates
4667 Macarthur Blvd., Ste. 405
Newport Beach, CA 92660
Ph: (714)250-0818
Fax: (714)553-8437
Scope: An immigration consultant and labor certification specialist. Assists in obtaining visa for work, immigration and business development within the United States and Canada.

42573 ■ C. W. Hines and Associates Inc.
[C&W Associates Inc.]
344 Churchill Cir., Sanctuary Bay
White Stone, VA 22578
Ph: (804)435-8844
Fax: (804)435-8855
Co. E-mail: turtlecwh@aol.com
URL: http://www.cwhinesassociates.org
Contact: William A. Hines, Jr., Vice President
Scope: Management consultants with expertise in the following categories: advertising and public relations; health and human resources; management sciences; organizational development; computer sciences; financial management; behavioral sciences; environmental design; technology transfer; project management; facility management; program evaluation; and business therapy. Also included are complementary areas such as sampling procedures; job training; managerial effectiveness; corporate seminars; gender harassment; training for trainers and leadership and management skills development. **Founded:** 1979. **Publications:** "Money Muscle, 120 Exercises To Build Spiritual And Financial Strength," 2004; "Inside Track: Executives Coaching Executives"; "Money Muscle: 122 Exercises to Build Financial Strength"; "Nuts and Bolts of Work Force Diversity"; "Legal Issues, published in the Controllers Business Advisor"; "Identifying Racism: Specific Examples"; "BOSS Spelled Backwards is double SSOB! Or is it?"; "A No-Nonsense Guide to Being Stressed". **Seminars:** Career Development; Coaching and Counseling for Work Success; Communicating More Effectively in a Diverse Work Environment; Communications 600: Advanced Skills for Relationship Building; Customer Service: Building a Caring Culture.

42574 ■ HR Advice.com
PO Box 313
Mountain Lakes, NJ 07046
Free: 877-854-0469
Co. E-mail: hrpro@hradvice.com
URL: http://www.hradvice.com
Contact: Susan Gordon, Manager
Scope: Specializes in the areas of employee relations, business planning and strategy, recruiting, human resources policy, compensation and benefits, training, development and performance systems. Provides services including human resources and business planning, resolves challenging workplace issues, defines organizational culture and creates or modifies human resources policies and programs. Also provides guidance to salary, benefits and incentive in the workplace.

42575 ■ HR Answers Inc.
7659 SW Mohawk St.
Tualatin, OR 97062
Ph: (503)885-9815
Free: 877-287-4476
Fax: (503)885-8614
Co. E-mail: info@hranswers.com
URL: http://www.hranswers.com
Contact: Judith Clark, President
E-mail: jclark@hranswers.com
Scope: Provider of all types of human resource management consulting services, either on a retained or project basis. Services include compensation program design or support, benefit plan assessment, policy and procedure manuals, AAP and EEO/OFCCP compliance, human resource function audits, supervisory, managerial and employee training,

employee relation issues/assistance, employment law compliance, employee handbooks, risk management, performance management design and information and organizational development and transition strategies. **Founded:** 1985. **Seminars:** Creating Your Safety Committee, Oct, 2006; Top Ten Best Practicesforl-9's, Oct, 2006; Sailing the Rough C's - Communication, Counseling & Conflict Resolution; Breaking the Secret Codes of Communication; Can We Talk; Coach or Discipline - What Action is Appropriate; Catch Your Employees Doing Something Right; The Future of Human Resources.

42576 ■ The HR Dept.
22 W Pennsylvania Ave.
Bel Air, MD 21014
Ph: (410)893-0901
Fax: (410)893-0901
Co. E-mail: ghr@hrdept.com
URL: http://www.hrdept.com
Contact: Gerald H. Reynolds, Jr., President
E-mail: ghr@hrdept.com
Scope: Provides human resources management support to small business employers on a part-time basis. Standard support services include the review of the human resources functions, compliance issues, performance appraisal programs, handbooks and policy manuals, annual human resources calendar, quarterly human resources reports, formal compensation structure, benefit plans analysis, manager training, human resources training, day to day employee issues and human resources advice and augmenting HR departments. **Founded:** 1998.

42577 ■ Human Networks Inc.
210 Crest St.
Ann Arbor, MI 48103-4316
Contact: Michael Murphy, Principal Owner
E-mail: mbmurphy-aa@excite.com
Scope: Provider of the following consulting services: training in the areas of stress management, team building, supervisory skills and leadership skills; and consultation regarding organizational climate assessment and improvement. Industries served include automotive, banking, small business, school, universities and human service agencies. **Founded:** 1983. **Publications:** "Grassroot Development: Establishing Successful Microenterprises". **Seminars:** Mind Over Matter; How Things Work at Work; The Internal Consultant: Special Skills; The External Consultant: Skills.

42578 ■ Human Resource Specialties Inc.
3 Monroe Pky., Ste. 900
Lake Oswego, OR 97035
Ph: (503)697-3329
Free: 800-354-3512
Fax: (503)636-1594
URL: http://www.hrspecialties.com
Contact: Sandy Henderson, President
E-mail: sandyh@hrspecialties.com
Scope: Provider of human resources assistance to organizations. Offers preparation of affirmative action plans, support documents, and adverse impact studies of personnel activities. Also offers customized consultations in small business services, diversity and discrimination, and investigations, complaints and grievances. Provides investigations, including allegations of unfair treatment, equal employment opportunity (EEO) and racial or sexual harassment. Offers customized web-based training (webinars) on a variety of HR, EEO and AAP-related topics. **Founded:** 1984.

42579 ■ I.H.R. Solutions
3333 E Bayaud Ave., Ste. 219
Denver, CO 80209
Ph: (303)588-4243
Fax: (303)978-0473
Contact: Deborah Hollands, Owner
E-mail: dhollands@ihrsolutions.com
Scope: Provides joint-venture and start-up human resource consulting services as well as advice on organization development for international human capital. Industries served: high-tech and telecommunications. **Founded:** 1997.

42580 ■ In Plain English [R.H. Wohl & Associates Inc.]

14501 Antigone Dr.
Gaithersburg, MD 20885-3300
Ph: (301)340-2821
Free: 800-274-9645
Fax: (301)279-0115
Co. E-mail: rwohl@inplainenglish.com
URL: http://www.inplainenglish.com
Contact: Ronald H. Wohl, President
E-mail: rwohl@inplainenglish.com
Scope: Management consultants helping government and businesses research, design, write and produce user oriented management information for human resources, employee benefits, business process, corporate and marketing needs. Services include: GSA mob is schedule for consulting to the government; employee benefit communications, plain English business writing workshops for print and electronic media; communicating strategy and tactics; marketing research, business planning and communications; readability testing; usability testing and monitoring strategy. **Founded:** 1977. **Publications:** "The Benefits Communication"; "The Employee Benefits Communication ToolKit," Commerce Clearinghouse; "Benefits Communication," Business and Legal Reports. **Seminars:** Plain English Writing Training; Summary Plan Description Compliance workshops; Re-Humanizing the Corporation, Human Resources and Employee Benefits Communication Workshop; 21 Writing Tips for the 21st Century; Make the Write Impression; Writing to Inform and Instruct; The Dreaded Nuts and Bolts; Writing to Persuade; Writing Policy and Procedure Manuals In Plain English; Writing for Accountants and Auditors In Plain English. **Special Services:** In Plain English®.

42581 ■ Incentive Solutions Inc. (ISI)

2337 Perimeter Park Dr., Ste. 220
Atlanta, GA 30341
Ph: (770)457-4597
Free: 800-463-5836
Fax: (770)457-4994
Co. E-mail: info@incentivesolutions.com
URL: http://www.incentivesolutions.com
Contact: Mark Herbert, President
E-mail: mherbert@incentivesolutions.com
Scope: Corporate incentive and motivation programs from group travel to incentive debit cards and merchandise gift certificates. Specializes in business meeting planning, audio/visual services, and Internet development to support business communications. **Founded:** 1994. **Special Services:** RewardTrax®.

42582 ■ KEYGroup

1800 St. Claire Plz., 1121 Boyce Rd.
Pittsburgh, PA 15241-3918
Ph: (724)942-7900
Free: 800-456-5790
Fax: (724)942-4648
URL: http://www.keygroupconsulting.com
Contact: Jan Ferri-Reed, President
Scope: A management consulting and training firm providing expertise in the areas of creativity, influencing skills, leadership, teambuilding, assessment and organizational effectiveness. Industries served: Fortune 500executives, healthcare administrators, manufacturing managers, government/military supervisors, insurance, financial and service industry managers, educational administrators, small business owners and community leaders. **Founded:** 1980. **Publications:** "Keeping the Millennials"; "Leading a Multi-Generational Workforce"; "Keys That Open Doors to Success - Key Words for Leaders"; "The Power of Partnering"; "The Keys to Conquering Change: 100 Tales of Success"; "The Keys to Putting Change in Your Pocket"; "The Keys to Mastering Leadership"; "Training Games for Managing Change"; "Private Sector: We Get You! Make Work Cultures Fit the Needs and Aspirations of Young Adults, and They Will Stay Here," Sep, 2005. **Seminars:** Performance Management, Enhancing Creativity Leading Others; Coaching for Improved Performance; Team-Building; Supervisory Development; Train-the-Trainer; Stress Management; Presentation Skills; Think-on-Your-Feet; Communicating Your BEST; leadership training team building. **Special Services:** KEYGroup®.

42583 ■ William E. Kuhn & Associates

234 Cook St.
Denver, CO 80206-5305
Ph: (303)322-8233
Fax: (303)331-9032
Scope: Firm specializes in strategic planning; profit enhancement; small business management; mergers and acquisitions; joint ventures; divestitures; human resources management; performance appraisals; team building; sales management; appraisals and valuations. **Founded:** 1980. **Publications:** "Creating a High-Performance Dealership," Office SOLUTIONS and Office DEALER, Jul-Aug, 2006.

42584 ■ LRP Publications - Library

lrp.com Technology Contacts
747 Dresher Rd., Ste. 500
Horsham, PA 19044
Ph: (215)784-0860
Free: 800-341-7874
Fax: (215)784-9639
Co. E-mail: techsup@lrp.com
URL: http://www.lrp.com
Contact: Kenneth Kahn, President
E-mail: kKahn@lrp.com
URL(s): www.dartnellcorp.com. **Description:** Description: Publishes legal loose-leaf and information in the areas of workers 'compensation, federal government employee relations, labor arbitration, bankruptcy and education law and state and local employment law. Offers online employment litigation tracking service and arbitration searches. Accepts unsolicited manuscripts. Reaches market through direct mail and telephone sales. **Scope:** Multi-faceted publisher of business-to-business newsletters, magazines, loose-leaf publications, videos, software and on-line services covering various professional markets, such as human resources, education, employment law, federal-sector employment, bankruptcy, health, disability, elder care, workers' compensation and personal injury verdicts and settlements. Offers training and professional development in national conferences and trade shows. **Founded:** 1977. **Holdings:** 5000 books; 1000 bound periodical volumes. **Publications:** *Risk and Insurance* (Monthly); *CTD News*; *Workers' Compensation Monitor*; *Human Resource Executive's Market Resource* (Annual); *Instant Computer Arbitration Search*; *Human Resource Executive*; *Counterpoint* (Quarterly); *Disability Compliance Bulletin* (Biweekly); *AIDS Policy and Law*; *Workplace Substance Abuse Advisor*; *Risk & Insurance Magazine* (Monthly); *The AIDS Directory*; *Pennsylvania Workers' Compensation Law Reporter* (Semimonthly); *Missouri Workers' Compensation Law Reporter* (Monthly); *Federal Equal Opportunity Reporter* (Semimonthly); *New York Workers' Compensation Law Reporter* (Semimonthly); *Michigan Workers' Compensation Law Reporter* (Semimonthly); *Current Award Trends in Personal Injury* (Annual); *Early Childhood Law and Policy Reporter* (Monthly); *Today's School Psychologist Newsletter*; *Risk & Insurance* (Monthly); *Federal Human Resources Week: News, Strategies and Best Practices for the HR Professional*; *AIDS Policy and Law: The Biweekly Newsletter on Legislation, Regulation, and Litigation Concerning AIDS* (11/year); *Team Leader*.

42585 ■ Lubin Schwartz & Goldman Inc.

2369 Franklin Rd.
Bloomfield Hills, MI 48302
Ph: (248)332-3100
Fax: (248)332-6396
Co. E-mail: info@lsgip.com
Contact: Sheldon Goldman, Principal
Scope: Firm specializes in property and casualty insurance, employee health and welfare programs and financial services. Offers strategic consulting services. **Founded:** 1967.

42586 ■ JG Manley and Associates

1403 Sneed Rd. W
Franklin, TN 37069-6932
Ph: (615)309-6999
Fax: (615)309-8874
Contact: John G. Manley, President
E-mail: manleyjg@aol.com
Scope: Consulting firm whose services include labor relations and law, collective bargaining, employment law, benefits and compensation and training for businesses. Specializes in labor relations, employment law, organizational planning, administration, healthcare and employee benefit plans, compensation, training, safety and human resources.

42587 ■ McCreight & Company Inc.

36 Grove St.
New Canaan, CT 06840
Ph: (203)801-5000
Fax: (866)646-8339
Co. E-mail: roc@implementstrategy.com
URL: http://www.implementstrategy.com
Contact: Sharon E. Carrigan, Vice President, Communications
E-mail: sec@implementstrategy.com
Scope: Assist the global clients with strategy implementation involving large scale change, including mergers, divestitures, alliances and new business launches. **Founded:** 1983. **Publications:** "The Board's Role in Strengthening M and A Success," Boardroom Briefing, 2008; "Creating the Future," Ask Magazine, 2007; "Strategy Implementation Insights," Mccreight and Company Inc, Oct, 2007; "Sustaining Growth," Deloitte and Ct Technology Council, Jul, 2006; "A Four Phase Approach to Succession Planning," Southern Connecticut Newspapers Inc, 2005. **Seminars:** Successful Mergers and Acquisitions-An Implementation Guide; Global 100One-Face-to-the-Customer; Implementation of Strategic Change.

42588 ■ Harvey A. Meier Co. (HAM)

410 W Nevada St.
Ashland, OR 97520-1043
Ph: (509)458-3210
Fax: (541)488-7905
Co. E-mail: harvey@harveymeier.com
URL: http://www.harveymeier.com
Contact: Dr. Harvey A. Meier, President
E-mail: harvey@harveymeier.com
Scope: Services: Management consulting. **Publications:** "The D'Artagnan Way".

42589 ■ Michigan CFO Associates Inc.

12900 Hall Rd., Ste. 455
Sterling Heights, MI 48313
Ph: (586)580-3285
Fax: (586)580-3287
Co. E-mail: info@michigancfoservices.com
URL: http://www.michiganCFOservices.com
Contact: Erica Johnson, Analyst
Scope: Firm that provides part-time Chief Financial Officer expertise on a long-term basis. **Publications:** "Is the Flight Attendant Flying the Plane? Mismatching Skills Causes Many Businesses to Crash"; "Are You Worth $15/per hour? Getting Maximum Value Out of YOUR Time"; "CFO Insider Tools: Flexible Budgets". **Seminars:** 10 Keys to a Healthy Business.

42590 ■ Dawn Miller and Associates

1486 Bonniebrook Heights Rd.
Gibsons, BC, Canada V0N 1V5
Ph: (604)886-8278
Fax: (604)886-5313
Contact: Bob Miller, Principal
E-mail: bobmmiller@home.com
Scope: Provides human resources development, planning, consulting and training for small businesses. **Publications:** "10 Keys to Thriving in Changing Times".

42591 ■ R.E. Moulton Inc.

50 Doaks Ln.
Marblehead, MA 1945
Ph: (781)631-1325
Fax: (781)631-2165
URL: http://www.oneamerica.com/wps/wcm/connect/REMoulton
Contact: Willard A. Knarr, Jr., President
Scope: Offers underwriting services, marketing solutions, claims administration and adjudication; policy and commission administration; and risk management solutions to clients. Supplementary service s include risk management and employee assistance. Clients include individuals, business men, employers and finance professionals. **Founded:** 1976.

42592 ■ The Murdock Group Holding Corp.

4084 S 300 W
Salt Lake City, UT 84107

Ph: (801)268-3232
Free: 888-888-0892
Contact: K. C. Holmes, President
Scope: Specializes in providing full service career services and seminars for individuals and companies, including out-placements, 'The Hiring Series' and career expos. **Founded:** 1997. **Publications:** "The Job Seekers Bible". **Seminars:** Networking; Interviewing, Negotiating; Marketing Yourself, Effective Hiring Fundamentals On-site Training Topics.

42593 ▪ New England Human Resource Group
36 Cedar Pond Dr.
Warwick, RI 02886
Ph: (401)826-2137
Scope: Firm specializes in compensation systems, benefits, legal compliance, personnel policies, resources, employee relations law, safety and risk management, training and development, continuous improvement, career management, organizational change, strategic planning, human resource audits, ISO 9000 and QS 9000, professional development, financial planning, staffing and executive development. **Founded:** 1985.

42594 ▪ Nightingale Associates
7445 Setting Sun Way
Columbia, MD 21046
Ph: (410)381-4280
Co. E-mail: fredericknightingale@nightingaleassociates.net
URL: http://www.nightingaleassociates.net
Contact: Frederick C. Nightingale, Managing Director
E-mail: fredericknightingale@nightingaleassociates.net
Scope: Management training and consulting firm offering the following skills: productivity and accomplishment; leadership skills for the experienced manager; management skills for the new manager; leadership and teambuilding; supervisory development; creative problem solving; real strategic planning; providing superior customer service; international purchasing and supply chain management; negotiation skills development and fundamentals of purchasing. **Founded:** 1984. **Seminars:** Productivity and Accomplishment Management Skills for the New Manager; Leadership and Team building; Advanced Management; Business Process Re engineering; Strategic Thinking; Creative Problem Solving; Customer Service; International Purchasing and Materials Management; Fundamentals of Purchasing; Negotiation Skills Development; Providing superior customer service; Leadership skills for the experienced manager.

42595 ▪ Organizational Synergies
10497 Town & Country Way, Ste. 950
Houston, TX 77024-1117
Ph: (713)461-2203
Fax: (713)461-5024
Contact: Darlene Underwood, President
Scope: Offers services in organizational effectiveness, outplacement and outsourcing. Specific services include employee development, business effectiveness analysis, business plans, climate analysis, corporate culture, departmental effectiveness analysis, management assessment, organizational effectiveness, organizational planning/design, strategic planning/direction, succession planning, work process analysis, visioning, measuring employee and management perceptions, management planning for shared vision and purpose, strategic planning/business unit planning, structure and work flow process analysis, management assessment and support services, skill and competency assessment, staff selection, alternative work arrangements, culture analysis compensation and employee benefit plan analysis.

42596 ▪ Palmetto Business Group Inc. (PBG)
1531 Blanding St., Ste. 2
Columbia, SC 29201
Ph: (803)252-4411
Fax: (803)252-3080
URL: http://www.palmettobusinessgroup.com
Contact: Toby Chaffin, President
Scope: Provides human resources consulting services; specializes in the areas: Accident prevention, affirmative action plans, drug free workplace, EEOC compliance, employee training, interviewing, leadership, search, management recruiting, outplacement, performance appraisals, safety and health administration, strategic planning, teambuilding and wage and benefit administration. **Seminars:** Excelling as a supervisor, Mar, 2012; Becoming a more effective leader, Feb, 2012.

42597 ▪ Papa and Associates Inc.
200 Consumers Rd., Ste. 305
Toronto, ON, Canada M2J 4R4
Ph: (416)512-7272
Fax: (416)512-2016
Co. E-mail: ppapa@papa-associates.com
Contact: Peter Papakostantinu, President
E-mail: ppapa@papa-associates.com
Scope: Provider of broad based management consulting services in the areas of quality assurance, environmental, health and safety and integrated management systems. **Founded:** 1989.

42598 ▪ PATH Associates
19 Coldwater Ct., Ruxton Crossing
Towson, MD 21204
Ph: (410)821-0538
Co. E-mail: pathassoc@aol.com
URL: http://www.pathassociatesonline.com
Contact: Robert Younglove, President
E-mail: robert_younglove@pathassociatesonline.com
Scope: Provider of keynote talks and workshops to associations, corporations, high growth industries, hospitals and government agencies. Emphasis is on effective programs to prevent stress and develop mental potential to increase effectiveness on the job and in life management. Also active in the areas of management training, health education, human energy and power and youth leadership development. Offers individual consultation and coaching sessions on motivation, career goals and stress management. **Founded:** 1974. **Publications:** "Speaking of Success," Volume 5, Insight Publishing, 2007; "Self-Confidence on the Job Survey," 2007; "Prioritize Your Values"; "Don't Let Kids Push Your Hot Button"; "When will you get a Round Tuit?"; "Sponsor Success, A Workbook for Turning Good Intentions Into Positive Results". **Seminars:** Staying Healthy in Times of Change; Dealing with People in Difficult Situations; Coaching for Performance Improvement and Influence Management; Sharpen Your Skills at Positively Influencing Children and Teens.

42599 ▪ Norman Peterson & Associates (NPA) [OUR System]
526 Washington St., Ste. 1
Ashland, OR 97520
Ph: (541)488-0162
Free: 800-497-1368
Fax: (541)488-5408
Co. E-mail: info@returntowork.com
URL: http://www.returntowork.com
Contact: Shelly Riley, Manager
E-mail: sriley@returntowork.com
Scope: A workers' compensation consulting firm that assists organizations in addressing workers compensation and ADA issues. Primary service is implementation of a copyrighted transitional work program, which documents productive temporary assignments for injured employees. Industries served: Governmental units, hospitals, school districts, manufacturers, food and beverage distribution, construction, printing and others. **Founded:** 1985. **Publications:** "Planning Pays Off in Back to Work Programs," Ohio Association of School Business Officials Chronicle; "Diving into a pool Return-to-Work program," Public Risk Magazine. **Special Services:** OUR®; Bridglt.

42600 ▪ Pitts - Aldrich Associates (PAA)
1501 Oxford Rd.
Grosse Pointe Woods, MI 48236-1848
Ph: (313)881-3433
Co. E-mail: christina@pittsaldrichassociates.com
URL: http://www.pittsaldrichassociates.com
Contact: Christina Pitts, President
E-mail: christina@pittsaldrichassociates.com
Scope: Firm offers consulting, facilitations, coaching, and training in strategic planning, change and transitions, culture and diversity, performance goals, project management, leader development, team effectiveness, retention/succession, coaching, board

governance, fund development and corporate citizenship. **Founded:** 1990. **Publications:** "At the Podium/In the Press: Optimize 5"; "Leadership Basics"; "Managing Change"; "A Gift of the Four-Legs: Presence, Trust, Vulnerability and...; "Leadership Has Gone to the Horses'; "Brown Paper Bag"; "The Phoenix Challenge: Rising to Fulfillment"; "Navigating the Badlands- Leadership in the New Century," 2009; "Color Me Purple- Embracing Differences to Optimize Performance"; "The End of Work & Rise of the Nonprofit Sector"; "Building Mentoring Inside Your Organization". **Seminars:** Journey to Authencity; Optimize5-From the World of Horses - Practical Wisdom for Success; The Phoenix Challenge: Rising to Fulfillment; Optimizing Relationship, Partnership & Teamwork; Change: Your Ally For Success.

42601 ▪ The Plotkin Group
5650 El Camino Real, Ste. 223
Carlsbad, CA 92008-7146
Ph: (760)603-8791
Free: 800-877-5685
Fax: (760)603-8570
Co. E-mail: info@plotkingroup.com
URL: http://www.plotkingroup.com
Contact: James Plotkin, President
E-mail: jim@plotkingroup.com
Scope: Employee testing and training organization offering pre-employment honesty, altitude, aptitude and skills tests; and past employment, 360degree assessments, behavior, style and communication tests by phone, paper and pencil, computers, the web, employee attitude surveys, customer service, sales and management training. **Founded:** 1968. **Publications:** "Building a Winning Team"; "Achieving Above and Beyond Service"; "American Businesses Face Mountain of Problems"; "Appreciating the Richness of Cultural Diversity"; "Attitude is Everything"; "Club members spems are Driving Us All Crazy"; "Credibility and Trust"; "Crime Prevention: The Integrity Business"; "Employee Theft: Hidden Enemy"; "Empowering Employees Without Losing Control"; "How to Build Customer Loyalty"; "Hr Issues of the Millennium"; "Just the Facts (Honesty Testing)"; "Nation's Jobless Must Be Retrained, Put to Work"; "Phone Answering Systems: A Blessing Or a Curse?"; "Strive to Convert Poor Service Into Good Service"; "Tests are Best for Picking Best Worker for the Job"; "The Pre-Interview Hiring Process"; "Time Management"; "What Do Members Want"; "Who to Promote"; "You Can't Turn a Frog Into a Prince"; "Club members speak out about their dining room"; "Companies should stress attitudes over skills (SUN)"; "Companies will always need honest and dependable workers (SUN)"; "Dealing with the angry member"; "Employee selection: A key to member retention"; "Good customer service is the best route to profits (SUN)"; "Hiring, the key to profitability (SUN)"; "Honesty tests are legitimate tool for finding good employees (SUN)"; "How not to handle a crisis"; "How not to open a theater"; "How to determine an applicant's attitude"; "How to identify and develop leadership traits in employees"; "How to introduce pre-employment testing into an organization"; "Integrity among youth is on decline (SUN)"; "Issues of concern for owners"; "Issues of concern for golf companies"; "Ownership and empowerment"; "Road to success paved with customer satisfaction (SUN)"; "Screen applicants to weed out thieves (SUN)"; "When the going gets tough". **Seminars:** Building a Winning Team; Above and Beyond Customer Service Training; Taking the Guess Work Out of Hiring and Promoting.

42602 ▪ Shannon Staffing Inc.
636 Chestnut St.
Coshocton, OH 43812
Ph: (740)622-2600
Fax: (740)622-9638
Co. E-mail: coshocton@shannonstaffing.com
URL: http://www.shannonstaffing.com
Contact: Edward A. Seitz, Chief Executive Officer
E-mail: eseitz@shannonstaffing.com
Scope: Serving broad range of industries and public sector organizations and foundations. Specializing in human resources recruiting and outplacement counseling on international scale for businesses of all sizes. Offers expertise in human resources policies and procedures, supervisor development, manager leadership style development, interview training, etc.

Provides consulting to small business in human resources, advertising, marketing, sales, public relations and community relations. **Founded:** 1985. **Publications:** "Powells Rules for Picking People". **Seminars:** Time Management workshop.

42603 ■ Siebrand-Wilton Associates Inc.
PO Box 369
Marlboro, NJ 07746-0369
Ph: (732)917-0239
Fax: (732)972-0214
Co. E-mail: clientsvcs@s-wa.com
URL: http://www.s-wa.com
Contact: John S. Sturges, President
E-mail: bencomp@s-wa.com
Scope: Assesses, plans and implements human resources aspects of mergers and acquisitions. Offers human resources consulting in compensation and benefit plan design, mergers and acquisitions (HR aspects), business ethics assessment and development, editing, writing and association management services, and contract professionals and interim executives. **Founded:** 1986. **Publications:** "Should Government or Business Try to Save Medicare," HR News; "Executive Temping," HR Horizons; "When is an Employee Truly an Employee," HR Magazine; "Examining Your Insurance Carrier," HR Magazine.

42604 ■ Ted Smith Associates (TSA)
PO Box 4217
Austin, TX 78765-4217
Ph: (512)627-0951
Fax: (512)453-4551
Scope: Business and technical communication training consultant. Consulting services include curriculum development and editing, technical writing and editing, business writing and editing and voice over talent. Also provides writing coaching, executive writing coaching and presentation coaching. **Founded:** 1985. **Publications:** "Writing at Work: Professional Writing Skills for People on the Job". **Seminars:** Business Communication and Technical Communication Training.

42605 ■ Speech Coach for Executives
2186 Mountain Grove Ave., Ste. 171
Burlington, ON, Canada L7R 1L2
Ph: (905)335-1997
Free: 800-304-1861
Fax: (905)335-2176
Co. E-mail: coach@torok.com
URL: http://www.SpeechCoachforExecutives.com
Contact: George Torok, Principal
E-mail: george@torok.com
Scope: Consultant provides speaking and presentation skills coaching and training for executives, business professionals and sales leaders. **Publications:** "Too much information: not enough time"; "Establish Your Believability"; "Smile: say cheese"; "Master the pause: it will make you a master"; "Presentation Power does not come from PowerPoint"; "Boardroom Presentations: Sweat Like a Horse"; "Presentation Skills Success"; "How to write your speech in five minutes"; "10 Power Tips for Presentations with Computer Projection". **Special Services:** Power Presentations™.

42606 ■ STAR Associates Inc. [Strategies, Tactics and Results Associates Inc.]
The BeuMar Bldg., 12 W Montgomery St.
Baltimore, MD 21230
Ph: (410)727-1558
Free: 877-708-7827
Fax: (410)752-2579
Co. E-mail: barbara@starassociatesinc.com
URL: http://www.starassociatesinc.com
Contact: Barbara A. Robinson, President
E-mail: barbara@starassociates.com
Scope: Provide in-home aide health care to the senior population. Also provide transportation services for the department of aging. Provide training for all related health care industry needs. Provide residential group homes for youth between the ages of 13 and 18 years. Diversity and leadership training and development programs for women. **Founded:** 1985. **Publications:** "Eyes of the Beholder," Jun, 2000; "And Still, I Cry," 1993; "Yes You Can". **Seminars:** Supervisory or Management Practices; Team

Playing and Group Dynamics; Time and Stress Management; Effective Communication: One Minute Management; Progressive Discipline; Project Management; Creative Decision Making and Problem Solving; Leadership Development; Absenteeism Reduction; Sales Training; Marketing Strategies; Making the leap from worker to supervisor; How to make things happen-boosting worker productivity, enthusiasm and commitment; Personal self-leadership as an essential ingredient; Who am I.

42607 ■ Stier Associates
4 Dunellen
Cromwell, CT 06416-2702
Ph: (860)635-1590
Contact: Dr. Suzanne Stier, President
Scope: Offers personal development consulting. Services include: succession planning, executive coaching, strategic management, team building and board development. Consulting services for public companies include: process consulting, team building, executive coaching, diversity management, strategic management and religious institutions. **Founded:** 1981.

42608 ■ Sylvia M. Sultenfuss
3317 Alden Pl. Dr.
Atlanta, GA 30319
Ph: (404)237-7130
Co. E-mail: sylvia@joyofadulthood.com
URL: http://www.joyofadulthood.com
Contact: Sylvia M. Sultenfuss, Manager
Scope: Offers organizational consultation and programs such as specialized management training, excellence in productivity, stress management program, teambuilding, working together with different styles of communication, stress reduction program, leadership effectiveness, conflict resolution, corporate wellness programs, and employee assistance programs. The focus is on small businesses or divisions where personnel issues and development are the target need. Serves private industries as well as government agencies. **Founded:** 1980. **Publications:** "Take the time to make time for yourself," AJC Pulse, May, 2005; "The Joy of Adulthood: A Crash Course in Designing the Life You Want," Palladium Productions, 2004; "Wake Up and Live the Life You Love: Finding Your Life's Passion," Little Seed Publishing, 2004; "Going Home for the Holidays," Labrys Atlanta, Dec, 2004; "Strategies to help resolve conflicts that arise," AJC Pulse, Feb, 2003; "On forgiveness," AJC Pulse, May, 2002; "The healer's grief: Learning to let go, say goodbye," AJC Pulse, Dec, 2001; "A way toward healing of the nation's post-traumatic grief," AJC Pulse, Dec, 2001; "The Joy Of Adulthood: A Crash Course In Designing The Life You Want". **Seminars:** Leadership: What it Is and Isn't; Bringing Passion and Spirit to Leadership; Mentoring for Success; Gender Communication in the Workplace: The Hormones Do Make a Difference; Designing and Sustaining a Conscious Adult Being; Communicating with Difficult People; Having What You Want Without Controlling Life; Sustaining Balance in the Midst of Chaos; Who's Speaking? Who's Listening Bring Power to Your Communication; Breaking the Love Patterns that Bind; Discovering, Sustaining and Building your Spiritual Relationships; Healing Significant Woundings of Life; Living Life Like it Matters; Love and Honor; Trust and Forgiveness; The Next Step.

42609 ■ Vaccari & Associates Inc.
17 Cypress St. 1
Marblehead, MA 01945-1925
Ph: (781)639-0946
Fax: (781)639-0946
Contact: Ralph J. Vaccari, President
Scope: A provider of appraisals for primary and secondary mortgages, mortgage refinancing, employee relocation, private mortgage insurance removal, estate planning and divorce settlement. **Founded:** 1996.

42610 ■ Verbit & Co.
19 Bala Ave.
Bala Cynwyd, PA 19004-3202

Ph: (610)668-9840
Co. E-mail: verbitcompany@earthlink.net
Contact: Alan C. Verbit, President
Scope: Management consulting firm to assist executives and managers fulfill their mission and to assure that adequate planning of day-to-day operations occurs; that controls sufficient to safeguard valuable resources; and that results of decisions reviewed in sufficient time to effect continuing action. Financial planning and control-to develop accounting, budgeting, forecasting and other information systems for the management of resources and evaluation of strategies. Services also include: Evaluation of desk-top computer systems for small firms; CAD/CAM implementation plan and orderly introduction of CAD/CAM. Industries served: manufacturing, distribution, metals casting, equipment and components, professional services, health care, retail, nonprofit and government. **Founded:** 1981. **Seminars:** Integrating Manufacturing Management Systems with Business Systems; Negotiating Information Systems Agreements with Suppliers.

42611 ■ Wheeler & Associates
13902 N Dale Mabry Hwy.
Tampa, FL 33618
Ph: (813)264-4977
Contact: S. Earl Wheeler, Business Manager
Scope: Provider of services in career and vocational counseling, human resource development and training and managerial development assistance for all levels of management. Offers organizational effectiveness studies and organizational design assistance for private and public enterprises. Industries served include educational institutions and training schools, small businesses and engineering firms. **Founded:** 1985.

42612 ■ Workplace Dimensions Inc.
7004 Lakewood Dr.
Richmond, VA 23229-6934
Ph: (804)673-8777
Fax: (804)673-8178
URL: http://www.workplacedimensions.com
Contact: Carol R. Losee, Principal
Scope: Offers human resources services including designing salary programs and performance management systems, customizing employee handbooks and personnel policy manuals, conducting employee and management training on harassment prevention and other relevant topics, and reviewing business practices for compliance. **Founded:** 1995. **Special Services:** Interviewer's Toolkit; Employer's Toolkit.

COMPUTERIZED DATABASES

42613 ■ *Human Resources Report*
Bloomberg BNA
3 Bethesda Metro Center, Ste. 250
Bethesda, MD 20814-5377
Ph: (703)341-3000
Free: 800-372-1033
Fax: (800)253-0332
Co. E-mail: customercare@bna.com
URL: http://www.bna.com
Contact: Gregory McCaffrey, President
URL(s): www.bna.com/human-resources-report-p4458. **Availability:** Online: Bloomberg BNA. **Type:** Full-text.

LIBRARIES

42614 ■ ASTD - Information Center [American Society for Training and Development]
1640 King St.
Alexandria, VA 22314-2746
Ph: (703)683-8100
Free: 800-628-2783
Fax: (703)683-1523
Co. E-mail: customercare@astd.org
URL: http://www.astd.org
Contact: Tony Bingham, President
E-mail: tbingham@astd.org
Description: Represents workplace learning and performance professionals. **Scope:** training and development, workplace performance. **Services:**

Library open to national members of the Society. **Founded:** 1943. **Holdings:** 3000 bound volumes. **Publications:** *ASTD Buyer's Guide* (Annual); *ASTD Buyer's Guide* (Annual); *Member Information Exchange (MIX)*; *TRAINET*; *ATD Buyer's Guide* (Annual); *Buyer's Guide & Consultant Directory*; *American Society for Training and Development--Training Video Directory*; *ASTD Buyer's Guide and Consultants Directory*; *Who's Who in Training and Development* (Annual); *ASTD Buyer's Guide and Consultants Directory*; *American Society Training and Development Buyer's Guide and Consultant Directory* (Annual); *Technical Training: Learning Technology for Performance Improvement*; *ASTD Buyer's Guide & Consultant Directory* (Annual); *TD at Work* (Monthly); *Learning Circuits* (Monthly); *T and D Magazine*; *TD Magazine* (Monthly). **Educational Activities:** International Exposition (Annual); American Society for Training and Development Conference (Annual); TechKnowledge Conference and Exposition (Annual). **Awards:** ASTD BEST Award; Excellence in Practice; Awards in the Advancing Workplace Learning and Performance; Gordon M. Bliss Memorial Award; Dissertation Award; Distinguished Contribution Award; Torch Award.

42615 ■ Walt Disney World - Global Business Technology Strategy Library
PO Box 10000
Lake Buena Vista, FL 32830-1000
Ph: (407)939-5277
URL: http://disneyworld.disney.go.com
Contact: David W. Hartman, Librarian Researcher
Scope: Computer science, human resources, general business. **Services:** Center not open to the public. **Founded:** 1986. **Holdings:** 4000 books, videos, DVDs, and CDs; 100 AV equipment. **Subscriptions:** 200 journals and other serials; 3 newspapers.

42616 ■ Towers Perrin - Western Canada Information Centre
3700, 150 - 6 Ave., SW
Calgary, AB, Canada T2P 3Y7
Ph: (403)261-1432
Fax: (403)237-6733
Co. E-mail: val.ward@towers.com
Contact: Val Ward
Scope: Human resource management, total rewards, pensions, employee benefits, executive compensation, employee communications, pension and benefits administration services, pension fund asset management. **Services:** Interlibrary loan. **Founded:** 1984. **Holdings:** 1000 books. **Subscriptions:** 100 journals and other serials; 4 newspapers.

42617 ■ Towers Watson Information Centre
1100 Melville St., Ste. 1600
Vancouver, BC, Canada V6E 4A6
Ph: (604)691-1000
Fax: (604)691-1062
URL: http://www.towerswatson.com
Scope: Actuarial science, employee benefits, compensation, human resources. **Holdings:** Figures not available.

42618 ■ Walgreen Performance Development Library
200 Wilmot Rd.
Deerfield, IL 60015
Ph: (847)914-2500
Free: 877-250-5823
URL: http://www.walgreens.com
Scope: Human resources, performance technology. **Services:** Library not open to the public. **Holdings:** 1000 books; 200 archival items. **Subscriptions:** 80 journals and other serials.

RESEARCH CENTERS

42619 ■ University of British Columbia - Bureau for Research on Applications of Information Technology (BRITE)
2053 Main Mall
Faculty of Commerce & Business Administration
Vancouver, BC, Canada V6T 1Z2
Ph: (604)822-8390
Fax: (604)822-0045
Co. E-mail: carson.woo@ubc.ca
URL: http://www.sauder.ubc.ca/Faculty/Research_
 Centres/Bureau_for_Research_on_Applications_
 of_IT
Contact: Prof. Carson Woo, Director
Scope: Corporate information systems development and human issues.

REFERENCE WORKS

42620 ■ *Choosing the Right Legal Form of Business: The Complete Guide to Becoming a Sole Proprietor, Partnership, LLC, or Corporation*
Pub: Atlantic Publishing Co.
Contact: Amanda Miller, Manager
E-mail: amiller@atlantic-pub.com

Ed: Pat Mitchell. **Released:** January 01, 2009. **Price:** $24.95. **Description:** According to the U.S. Small Business Administration, nearly 250,000 new businesses start up annually; currently there are over nine million small companies in the nation. The importance of choosing the proper legal form of business is stressed. **Availability:** Print.

42621 ■ *"Coca-Cola Bottler Up for Sale: CEO J. Bruce Llewellyn Seeks Retirement"* in *Black Enterprise (Vol. 37, December 2006, No. 5, pp. 31)*
Pub: Earl G. Graves Publishing Co. Inc.
Contact: Earl G. Graves, Jr., President
Ed: Marcia A. Wade. **Description:** J. Bruce Llewellyn of Brucephil Inc., the parent company of the Philadelphia Coca-Cola Bottling Co. has agreed to sell its remaining shares to Coca-Cola Co., which previously owned 31 percent of Philly Coke. Analysts believe that Coca-Cola will eventually sell its shares to another bottler.

42622 ■ *"Protect Your Assets"* in *Black Enterprise (Vol. 38, January 2008, No. 6, pp. 38)*
Pub: Earl G. Graves Publishing Co. Inc.
Contact: Earl G. Graves, Jr., President
Ed: Trevor Delaney. **Description:** The owner of rental properties seeks advice for incorporating versus getting an LLC for a business.

42623 ■ *"SoBran Partners with U.S. Navy"* in *Black Enterprise (Vol. 37, October 2006, No. 3, pp. 38)*
Pub: Earl G. Graves Publishing Co. Inc.
Contact: Earl G. Graves, Jr., President
Ed: Glenn Townes. **Description:** SoBran Inc. partnered with Lockheed Martin and signed a three-year production service contract with the Naval Aviation Depot in Jacksonville, Florida. The $44 million contract will allow SoBran to transport and warehouse materials for Navy facilities.

42624 ■ *"World Wide Technology Expands"* in *Black Enterprise (Vol. 37, December 2006, No. 5, pp. 34)*
Pub: Earl G. Graves Publishing Co. Inc.
Contact: Earl G. Graves, Jr., President
Ed: Marcia Wade Talbert. **Description:** World Wide Technology Inc. opened a streamlined, higher capacity 12,000-square-foot Integration Technology Center near its corporate headquarters in St. Louis. The new venture will transfer lower costs to customers.

START-UP INFORMATION

42625 ■ *"Alpharetta Seeding Startups To Encourage Job Growth"* in *Atlanta Business Chronicle* (June 20, 2014, pp. 3A)
Pub: American City Business Journals, Inc.
Contact: Whitney Shaw, President
Released: June 20, 2014. **Description:** The City of Alpharetta is witnessing several incubators and accelerators that will create the physical and educational infrastructure to convert ideas into sustainable businesses. This will help startups develop a go-to-market strategy, prepare for FDA certification and insurance reimbursement as well as see that the company reaches a point where it can attract private equity or venture capital.

42626 ■ *"Consumer Startup Hub Set for Downtown"* in *Atlanta Business Chronicle* (June 13, 2014, pp. 3A)
Pub: American City Business Journals, Inc.
Contact: Whitney Shaw, President
Released: June 13, 2014. **Description:** Michael Tavani, co-founder of Scoutmob, believes that Atlanta is fast becoming the hub for consumer- and design-focused startups. He is planning to locate his consumer-focused startup, Switchyards, in a 1920s building downtown, which will become a hive for mobile app, media, and ecommerce startups.

42627 ■ *"Creating Cultural Commerce"* in *Entrepreneur (June 2014)*
Pub: Entrepreneur Media Inc.
Released: June 2014. **Description:** The nonprofit business incubator, New Inc, could practice the scientific finding that the so-called left/right brain divide, or the difference between analytical and creative thinking, is non-existent. New Inc will seek ways that a museum can support new cross-disciplinary modes of cultural production. Moreover, New Inc could fill gaps in traditional artist residencies and tech incubators. New Inc will not take equity in the companies it fosters. Aside from giving technology creative breathing room for exploration, New Inc will relieve some of the revenue pressures of a startup.

42628 ■ *"Home Is Where Your Startup Is"* in *Dallas Business Journal (Vol. 37, January 31, 2014, No. 21, pp. 6)*
Pub: American City Business Journals
Released: January 31, 2014. **Description:** Business accelerator Tech Wildcatters is planning to open a startup house in Dallas, Texas. The facility will bring together entrepreneurs, artists, and other creative individuals. A brief description of the facility is also included.

42629 ■ *"A Messy Job"* in *Washington Business Journal (Vol. 33, May 30, 2014, No. 6, pp. 6)*
Pub: American City Business Journals
Released: May 30, 2014. **Description:** Mess Hall founder, Al Goldberg, shares his views on business incubators for culinary entrepreneurs in District of Columbia. Goldberg says he expects to accommodate up to 100 members in the space of the former warehouse turned culinary center for entrepreneurs wishing to start restaurants, bakeries or bars.

42630 ■ *"The New Orleans Saints"* in *Entrepreneur (Vol. 37, August 2009, No. 8, pp. 40)*
Pub: Entrepreneur Press
Contact: Perlman Neil, President
Ed: Jason Meyers. **Description:** Idea Village is a nonprofit group that fosters entrepreneurship in New Orleans, Louisiana. Entrepreneurship is indeed growing in the city during a time when the city is still recovering from the damage of hurricane Katrina.

42631 ■ *"The New Orleans Saints"* in *Entrepreneur (Vol. 37, August 2009, No. 8, pp. 40)*
Pub: Entrepreneur Press
Contact: Perlman Nell, President
Ed: Jason Meyers. **Description:** Idea Village is a nonprofit group that fosters entrepreneurship in New Orleans, Louisiana. Entrepreneurship is indeed growing in the city during a time when the city is still recovering from the damage of hurricane Katrina.

42632 ■ *"A Piece of the Action"* in *Entrepreneur (May 2014)*
Pub: Entrepreneur Media Inc.
Released: May 2014. **Description:** Franchisor, Mandy Calara of Forever Yogurt explains how his online crowdfunding platform called CrowdFranchise can help potential franchisees find investors. He details the successful opening of their first Forever Yogurt store at Wicker Park in Chicago, Illinois through the CrowdFranchise. He explains the incubator program called Velocity and the use of Crowd-Franchise to measure support. He believes that emerging franchisors and startups with fewer than 20 units will be interested in their concept.

42633 ■ *"Rehab Will Turn Hospital Into Incubator"* in *The Business Journal-Serving Metropolitan Kansas City (Vol. 26, September 12, 2008)*
Ed: Rob Roberts. **Description:** Independence Regional Health Center will be purchased by CEAH Realtors and be converted into the Independence Regional Entrepreneurial Center, a business incubator that will house startups and other tenants. Other details about the planned entrepreneurial center are provided.

42634 ■ *"Victoria Colligan; Co-Founder, Ladies Who Launch Inc., 38"* in *Crain's Cleveland Business (Vol. 28, November 19, 2007, No. 46)*
Pub: Crain Communications Inc.
Ed: Jay Miller. **Description:** Profile of Victoria Colligan who is the co-founder of Ladies Who Launch Inc., an organization with franchises in nearly 50 cities; the company offers women entrepreneurs workshops and a newsletter to help women balance their businesses with other aspects of their lives. Ms. Colligan found that women were learning about being business owners differently than men and she felt that there was a need to create opportunities for networking for women launching businesses that had more of a lifestyle purpose.

REFERENCE WORKS

42635 ■ *"Ballston Bout Has Surprise Ending"* in *Washington Business Journal (Vol. 33, June 6, 2014, No. 7, pp. 7)*
Pub: American City Business Journals
Released: June 6, 2014. **Description:** One of the finalists in the restaurant incubator challenge of the Ballston Business Improvement District pulled out of the competition and the other finalist was declared the winner of a restaurant space in Washington DC. Chefs, Victor Albisu and Christiana Campos, were supposed to compete in a Top Chef Restaurant Wars-style competition when Albisu made his decision to drop out.

42636 ■ *"Biz Assesses 'Textgate' Fallout: Conventions, Smaller Deals Affected"* in *Crain's Detroit Business (Vol. 24, March 31, 2008)*
Pub: Crain Communications Inc.
Contact: Rance E. Crain, President
Ed: Tom Henderson. **Description:** Businesspeople who were trying to measure the amount of economic damage is likely to be caused due to Mayor Kwame Kilpatrick's indictment on eight charges and found that: automotive and other large global deals are less likely to be affected than location decisions by smaller companies and convention site decisions. Also being affected are negotiations in which Mexican startup companies were planning a partnership with the TechTown incubator to pursue opportunities in the auto sector; those plans are being put on hold while they look at other sites.

42637 ■ *"The Business of Activism"* in *Entrepreneur (Vol. 37, September 2009, No. 9, pp. 43)*
Pub: Entrepreneur Press
Contact: Perlman Neil, President
Ed: Mary Catherine O'Connor. **Description:** San Francisco, California-based business incubator Virgance has been promoting sustainable projects by partnering with businesses. The company has launched campaigns which include organizing homeowners in negotiating with solar installers. The company is also planning to expand its workforce.

42638 ■ *"Henry Ford Health Leases Lab Space at TechTown"* in *Crain's Detroit Business (Vol. 24, April 1, 2008, No. 13, pp. 5)*
Pub: Crain Communications Inc.
Contact: Rance E. Crain, President
Ed: Tom Henderson. **Description:** Henry Ford Health System has signed a seven-year lease at TechTown, the high-tech incubator and research park affiliated with Wayne State University, to take over 14,000 square feet of space for four research groups and laboratories. Construction has already begun and Henry Ford officials hope to take occupancy as early as June 1.

42639 ■ *"Incubators Experiencing a Baby Boom"* in *Philadelphia Business Journal (Vol. 31, March 23, 2012, No. 6, pp. 1)*

Pub: American City Business Journal

Description: At least seven business incubators have opened in Philadelphia, Pennsylvania since November 2011. Five of the seven incubators are nonprofit organizations.

42640 ■ *"Life Science Companies in I-35 Corridor Get New Booster"* in *Dallas Business Journal (Vol. 35, March 16, 2012, No. 2, pp. 1)*

Pub: American City Business Journal

Description: The Texas Bio Corridor Alliance intends to promote the development of life science firms along the Interstate 35 corridor. It comprises business incubators, cities, economic development organizations and companies in Texas.

42641 ■ *"Mexican Companies to Rent Space in TechTown, Chinese Negotiating"* in *Crain's Detroit Business (Vol. 24, September 29, 2008, No. 39)*

Pub: Crain Communications Inc.

Contact: Rance E. Crain, President

Ed: Tom Henderson. **Description:** Wayne State University's TechTown, the business incubator and research park, has signed an agreement with the Mexican government that will provide temporary office space to 25 Mexican companies looking to find customers or establish partnerships in Michigan. TechTown's executive director is negotiating with economic development officials from China. To accommodate foreign visitors the incubator is equipping offices with additional equipment and resources.

42642 ■ *"Spread Your Wings"* in *Canadian Business (Vol. 81, March 17, 2008, No. 4, pp. 31)*

Ed: Megan Harman. **Description:** Financing from angel investors is one avenue that should be explored by startups. Angel investors are typically affluent individuals who invest their own money. Angel investors usually want at least 10 times their initial investment within eight years but they benefit the businesses through their help in decision-making and the industry expertise they provide.

42643 ■ *"STAR TEC Incubator's Latest Resident Shows Promise"* in *The Business Journal-Serving Greater Tampa Bay (August 11, 2008)*

Pub: American City Business Journals, Inc.

Contact: Whitney Shaw, President

Ed: Jane Meinhardt. **Description:** Field Forensics Inc., a resident of the STAR Technology Enterprise Center, has grown after being admitted into the business accelerator. The producer of defense and security devices and equipment has doubled 2007 sales as of 2008.

42644 ■ *"TechLift Strives to Fill in Gaps in Entrepreneurial Support Efforts"* in *Crain's Cleveland Business (November 12, 2007)*

Pub: Crain Communications Inc.

Ed: Marsha Powers. **Description:** Profile of the program, TechLift, a new business model launched by NorTech, that is aiming to provide assistance to technology-based companies that may not be a good fit for other entrepreneurial support venues.

42645 ■ *"The Union of Town and Gown"* in *Entrepreneur (Vol. 37, October 2009, No. 10, pp. 47)*

Pub: Entrepreneur Press

Contact: Perlman Neil, President

Ed: Jason Daley. **Description:** Ten of the best entrepreneurial initiatives involving cities and local universities in the US are described. Cities and universities are joining up for these efforts to strengthen local economies and stop brain drain.

START-UP INFORMATION

42646 ■ *"Docs Prop Up Health Insurer"* in *Business First-Columbus (December 14, 2007, pp. A1)*
Ed: Carrie Ghose. **Description:** Doctors and executives supporting Physicians Assurance Corporation, a startup health insurer in Central Ohio, were required to raise $2.5 million before they could apply for a license from the state Department of Insurance. The company, which hopes to acquire its license by January 2007, will focus on doctor's offices and businesses with two to ninety-nine employees.

42647 ■ *"An Insurer Stretches Out"* in *Business Journal Portland (Vol. 30, February 21, 2014, No. 51, pp. 4)*
Pub: American City Business Journals
Released: February 21, 2014. **Description:** The diversification strategy of Cambia Health Solutions has led to investments in several health care startups. The company earned $5.8 billion in revenue from insurance premiums in 2012 and posted a profit margin of about 2 percent for its net income of $173 million.

42648 ■ *"'One of the Best Ways to Build Wealth...Is to Take Equity In a Company"* in *Business Journal (Vol. 31, May 2, 2014, No. 49, pp. 9)*
Pub: American City Business Journals
Released: May 2, 2014. **Description:** Entrepreneur Abir Sen reveals that he was not planning to start a business after selling Bloom Health, but he soon discovered that he wanted to do something productive. He believes that the traditional model of employer-paid health care insurance is dying. His opinion on health care entrepreneurial activity in Minnesota is also examined.

42649 ■ *"Startup ETMG LLC Makes Attempt to 'Reform' Health Insurance"* in *Austin Business JournalInc. (Vol. 29, January 15, 2010, No. 45, pp. 1)*
Pub: American City Business Journals
Ed: Sandra Zaragoza. **Description:** Health insurance provider ETMG LLC of Austin, Texas plans to act as a managing general agent and a third-party administrator that can facilitate customized plans for small businesses and sole proprietors. According to CEO Mark Adams, profitability is expected for ETMG, which have also clinched $1.5 million worth of investments. Entities that have agreed to do business with ETMG are presented.

ASSOCIATIONS AND OTHER ORGANIZATIONS

42650 ■ National Council of Self-Insurers (NCSI)
1253 Springfield Ave.
PMB 345
New Providence, NJ 07974
Ph: (908)665-2152
Fax: (908)665-4020
Co. E-mail: natcouncil@aol.com
URL: http://www.natcouncil.com
Description: State associations, individual companies, associate members, and professional members concerned with self-insurance under the workmen's compensation laws. Promotes and protects, at all governmental levels, the interests of self-insurers or legally non-insured employers and their employees in matters of legislative and administrative activity affecting workmen's compensation; assists, advises, and uses its resources in developing and implementing common objectives among self-insurers. Current goals are: a workmen's compensation program that is just, both to the individual and to the employer; equitable distribution of the compensation dollar; strong vocational rehabilitation incentives for the injured employee. **Founded:** 1946. **Publications:** *Self-Insurance Requirements of the States* (Periodic). **Educational Activities:** National Council of Self-Insurers Meeting (Annual).

EDUCATIONAL PROGRAMS

42651 ■ AMA's Insurance and Risk Management Workshop (Onsite)
American Management Association (AMA)
1601 Broadway
New York, NY 10019-7420
Ph: (212)586-8100
Free: 877-566-9441
Fax: (212)903-8168
Co. E-mail: customerservice@amanet.org
URL: http://www.amanet.org
Contact: Edward T. Reilly, President
URL(s): www.amanet.org/training/seminars/finance-and-accounting-training.aspx. **Description:** Covers everything from coverage and cost to liability limits, retention and broker services. **Audience:** Insurance and risk management professionals .

REFERENCE WORKS

42652 ■ *"2010 Book of Lists"* in *Austin Business JournalInc. (Vol. 29, December 25, 2009, No. 42, pp. 1)*
Description: Rankings of companies and organizations within the business services, finance, healthcare, hospitality and travel, insurance, marketing and media, professional services, real estate, education and technology industries in Austin, Texas are presented. Rankings are based on sales, business size, and other statistics.

42653 ■ *"Abroad, Not Overboard"* in *Entrepreneur (Vol. 36, April 2008, No. 4, pp. 68)*
Pub: Entrepreneur Press
Contact: Perlman Neil, President
Ed: Crystal Detamore-Rodman. **Description:** Export-Import Bank is an agency created by the U.S. government to help exporters get credit insurance and capital loans by providing them with loan guarantees.

The bank, being criticized as supporting more the bigger exporters, has allotted to smaller businesses a bigger portion of the annual credit being approved.

42654 ■ *"ACE Expands M&A Practice"* in *Economics & Business Week (March 22, 2014, pp. 2)*
Pub: NewsRX
Contact: Susan E. Hasty, Publisher
Released: March 22, 2014. **Description:** ACE Group announced an expansion of its mergers and acquisitions practice focusing on insurance solutions for private equity firms, their portfolio companies as well as their M&A transactions.

42655 ■ *"Affordable Housing Meets God and the City: a Primer on Catastrophic Loss When You Can Lease Bear It"* in *Real Estate Review (Vol. 41, Summer 2012, No. 2, pp. 21)*
Released: Summer 2012. **Description:** A case study on how a real estate development company should deal with catastrophic property loss is presented. The event involved a fire that damaged an apartment building in Houston, Texas. Issues involved include multiple insurance claims, deteriorating infrastructure, and marketing problems.

42656 ■ *"After Ruling, Rush Is On To Comply With ACA"* in *Austin Business Journal (Vol. 32, July 6, 2012, No. 18, pp. 1)*
Pub: American City Business Journals, Inc.
Contact: Whitney Shaw, President
Ed: Sandra Zaragoza. **Released:** July 6, 2012. **Description:** The U.S. Supreme Court ruling upholding the majority of the Patient Protection and Affordable Care Act has prompted employers to ramp up efforts to prepare for 2013 and 2014. Employers with 50 or more employees are required by the health care law to provide health care insurance or be penalized by about $2,000 per full-time employee in 2014. Insights on the rush are also given.

42657 ■ *"All-Star Advice 2010"* in *Black Enterprise (Vol. 41, October 2010, No. 3, pp. 97)*
Pub: Earl G. Graves Publishing Co. Inc.
Contact: Earl G. Graves, Jr., President
Ed: Renita Burns, Sheiresa Ngo, Marcia Wade Talbert. **Description:** Financial experts share tips on real estate, investing, taxes, insurance and debt management.

42658 ■ *"Alpharetta Seeding Startups To Encourage Job Growth"* in *Atlanta Business Chronicle(June 20, 2014, pp. 3A)*
Pub: American City Business Journals, Inc.
Contact: Whitney Shaw, President
Released: June 20, 2014. **Description:** The City of Alpharetta is witnessing several incubators and accelerators that will create the physical and educational infrastructure to convert ideas into sustainable businesses. This will help startups develop a go-to-market strategy, prepare for FDA certification and insurance reimbursement as well as see that the company reaches a point where it can attract private equity or venture capital.

42659 ■ *"The Annual Entitlement Lecture Medicare Elephantiasis"* in *Barron's (March 31, 2008)*
Pub: Dow Jones & Co., Inc.
Contact: Clare Hart, President
Ed: Thomas G. Donlan. Description: Expenditures on Medicare hospital insurance and the revenues available to pay for it have led to a gap of capital valued at $38.6 trillion. Slashing the benefits or raising taxes will not solve the gap which exists unless the government saves the money and invests it in private markets.

42660 ■ *"Anthem Becomes First to Penalize Small-Business Employees for Smoking"* in *Denver Business Journal (Vol. 64, August 17, 2012, No. 13, pp. 1)*
Pub: American City Business Journal
Description: Health insurance companies Anthem Blue Cross and Blue Shield of Colorado are first to impose higher premiums on employee smokers who are under their small-group policies. The premiums may increase up to 15 percent starting September, to be paid by the smoking employees or the company. The law aims to help reduce tobacco-related health problems, as well as health care costs.

42661 ■ *"Anthem Leading the Way in Social Tech Revolution"* in *Inside Business (Vol. 13, September-October 2011, No. 5, pp. 1B3)*
Pub: Great Lakes Publishing Co.
Ed: Ryan Clark. Description: Anthem Blue Cross and Blue Shield is leading the way in social technology. The firm's social media initiatives to promote itself are outlined.

42662 ■ *"An Apple a Day"* in *Entrepreneur (Vol. 36, February 2008, No. 2, pp. 19)*
Pub: Entrepreneur Press
Contact: Perlman Neil, President
Ed: Mark Henricks. Description: Businesses are handling rising health coverage costs by providing employees with wellness programs, which include smoking-cessation programs, consumer-directed plans for savings on premiums, and limited medical care plans. Details on the growing trend regarding employee health coverage are discussed.

42663 ■ *"Are Prepaid Legal Services Worthwhile?"* in *Contractor (Vol. 56, December 2009, No. 12, pp. 31)*
Pub: Penton Media, Inc.
Ed: Susan Linden McGreevy. Description: Companies' provision of legal insurance as an employee benefit in the United States is discussed. Stoppage of premium payment halts employee coverage. It also does not cover all kinds of personal issues.

42664 ■ *"Are You Overinsured? Some Policies May Not Offer Much Additional Benefit"* in *Black Enterprise (Vol. 38, March 1, 2008, No. 8, pp. 126)*
Pub: Earl G. Graves Publishing Co. Inc.
Contact: Earl G. Graves, Jr., President
Ed: Tamara E. Holmes. Description: Travel insurance, identity-theft insurance, specific disease or health condition insurance policies are described. Advice is given to help determine if you are over-insured.

42665 ■ *"At risk: Young Adults Go Without Health Insurance"* in *Business Review, Albany New York (Vol. 34, December 3, 2007, No. 35, pp. 1)*
Pub: American City Business Journals, Inc.
Ed: Barbara Pinckney. Description: U.S. Census Bureau revealed that in 2006, 19 million people between the ages of 18 and 34 were without health insurance, or 40 percent of the uninsured individuals in the country. College graduation usually means the end of health coverage, since most fresh graduates opt to not get any health insurance plan. Solutions to this growing issue are also addressed.

42666 ■ *"Baldwin Connelly Partnership Splits"* in *Business Journal Serving Greater*

Tampa Bay (Vol. 30, November 19, 2010, No. 48, pp. 1)
Pub: Tampa Bay Business Journal
Ed: Alexis Muellner. Description: The fast-growing insurance brokerage Baldwin Connelly is now breaking up after five years. Two different entrepreneurial visions have developed within the organization and founders Lowry Baldwin and John Connell will not take separate tracks. Staffing levels in the firm are expected to remain the same.

42667 ■ *"Bank Forces Brooke Founder To Sell His Holdings"* in *The Business Journal-Serving Metropolitan Kansas City (October 10, 2008)*
Pub: American City Business Journals, Inc.
Contact: Whitney Shaw, President
Ed: James Dornbrook. Description: Robert Orr who is the founder of Brooke Corp., a franchise of insurance agencies, says that he was forced to sell virtually all of his stocks in the company by creditors. First United Bank held the founder's stock as collateral for two loans worth $5 million and $7.9 million, which were declared in default in September 2008. Details of the selling of the company's stocks are provided.

42668 ■ *"Bank On It: Year-End Tax Tips"* in *Hawaii Business (Vol. 53, December 2007, No. 6, pp. 136)*
Pub: PacificBasin Communications
Ed: Kathleen Bryan. Description: Tax planning tips for the end of 2007, in relation to the tax breaks that are scheduled to expire, are presented. Among the tax breaks that will be expiring at the 2007 year-end are sales tax deduction in the state and local level, premiums on mortgage insurance, and deduction on tuition. The impacts of these changes are discussed.

42669 ■ *"Bill Targets Insurance Contract Pay Changes"* in *Memphis Business Journal (No. 35, February 14, 2014, No. 45, pp. 8)*
Pub: American City Business Journals
Released: February 14, 2014. Description: Lawmakers are pushing a new measure in the Tennessee General Assembly, tentatively dubbed the Payer Accountability Act. the bill would prohibit commercial health insurance companies from making mid-contract changes.

42670 ■ *"Bills Raise Blues Debate: An Unfair Edge or Level Playing Field?"* in *Crain's Detroit Business (Vol. 24, January 21, 2008, No. 3)*
Pub: Crain Communications Inc. - Detroit
Contact: Keith Crain, Chairman
Ed: Sherri Begin. Description: Changes in Michigan state law would change the way health insurance can be sold to individuals. Michigan Blue Cross Blue Shield is working to keep its tax-exempt status while staying competitive against for-profit insurers and nonprofit HMOs.

42671 ■ *"Blue Cross Confronts Baby Blues"* in *Marketing to Women (Vol. 21, March 2008, No. 3, pp. 3)*
Description: Blue Cross of California has launched a Maternity Depression Program aimed at educating mothers suffering from postpartum depression.

42672 ■ *" Blue Cross Loses Market Share, Not Dominance"* in *Birmingham Business Journal (Vol. 29, June 8, 2012, No. 24, pp. 1)*
Pub: American City Business Journals, Inc.
Contact: Whitney Shaw, President
Ed: Evan Belanger. Released: June 8, 2012. Description: American Medical Association has reported that Blue Cross and Blue Shield of Alabama's share of the health insurance market has fallen from 93 percent to 90 percent during the recession of 2008 and 2009. However, the losses did not make a dent in its dominance.

42673 ■ *"Blue Cross to Put Kiosk in Mall"* in *News & Observer (November 9, 2010)*
Pub: News & Observer
Ed: Alan M. Wolf. Description: Blue Cross and Blue Shield of North Carolina has placed a kiosk in Durham's Streets of Southpoint in order to market its health insurance.

42674 ■ *"Branding Diverse Markets"* in *Best's Review (Vol. 113, September 2012, No. 5, pp. 13)*
Description: Five tips to help insurance agencies promote their brands in diverse markets include developing strategic priorities through building trust, knwo the market/sector, set quantifiable/trackable goals, the team should reflect its market, and keeping it real.

42675 ■ *"BRIEF: District Using Bilingual Kiosks to Promote Health Literacy Among Hispanic Families"* in *Palm Beach Post (August 24, 2012)*
Pub: McClatchy Tribune Information Services
Released: August 24, 2012. Description: A partnership between the Palm Beach County School District and United Healthcare provides access to health information, in both English and Spanish in order to promote health literacy.

42676 ■ *Business Insurance--Agent/Broker Profiles Issue*
Pub: Crain Communications Inc.
Contact: Todd Johnson, Publisher
URL(s): www.businessinsurance.com. Released: Annual; Latest edition 2014. Publication includes: List of top 10 insurance agents/brokers worldwide specializing in commercial insurance. Entries include: Firm name, address, phone, fax, branch office locations, year established, names of subsidiaries, gross revenues, premium volume, number of employees, principal officers, percent of revenue generated by commercial retail brokerage, acquisitions. Arrangement: Alphabetical by company. Indexes: Geographical.

42677 ■ *"Businesses Delayed Hiring As They Waited for Health Care Law Ruling"* in *Baltimore Business Journal (Vol. 30, June 29, 2012, No. 8, pp. 1)*
Pub: American City Business Journals, Inc.
Contact: Whitney Shaw, President
Ed: Sarah Gantz. Released: June 29, 2012. Description: Small businesses in Baltimore, Maryland have been putting off expansion plans pending the Supreme Court's ruling on the health care reform law. Workforce expansion would require businesses to provide employee health insurance.

42678 ■ *"Businesses Keep a Watchful Eye on Workers' Comp"* in *The Business Journal-Serving Greater Tampa Bay (September 5, 2008)*
Pub: American City Business Journals, Inc.
Contact: Whitney Shaw, President
Ed: Jane Meinhardt. Description: Pending a ruling from the Florida Supreme Court that could uphold the 2003 changes on workers' compensation law, the outcome would include restrictions on claimant attorneys' fees and allow the competitive workers' compensation insurance rates to remain low. However, insurance rates are expected to go up if the court overturns the changes.

42679 ■ *"CareFirst To Reward Doctors for Reducing Costs, Improving Care"* in *Baltimore Business Journal (Vol. 28, June 4, 2010, No. 4, pp. 1)*
Pub: Baltimore Business Journal
Ed: Scott Graham. Description: CareFirst Blue Cross Blue Shield plans to introduce a program that dangles big financial rewards to physicians who change the way they deliver primary care by improving the health of their sickest patients while reducing costs. The company will soon begin recruiting primary care physicians in Maryland, Washington DC, and Northern Virginia.

42680 ■ *"The New Janus CEO of Battle-Hardened Money Manager Plots Comeback"* in *Denver Business Journal (Vol. 64, August 31, 2012, No. 15, pp. 1)*
Pub: American City Business Journal
Description: Richard Well, chief executive officer of Janus Capital Group Inc., discusses the strategic plans of the mutual fund company. He touches on

the firm's alliance with Dai-chi Life Insurance Company Ltd., the future of equity markets, and the company's intelligent diversification strategy.

42681 ■ *"Cerner Works the Business Circuit"* in Business Journal-Serving Metropolitan Kansas City (Vol. 26, October 5, 2007, No. 4, pp. 1)

Pub: American City Business Journals, Inc.

Ed: Rob Roberts. **Description:** Cerner Corporation is embracing the coming of the electronic medical record exchange by creating a regional health information organization (RHIO) called the CareEntrust. The RHIO convinced health insurers to share claims data with patients and clinicians. At the Center Health Conference, held October 7 to 10, Cerner will demonstrate the software it developed for CareEntrust to the 40,000 healthcare and information technology professionals.

42682 ■ *"Changes Sought to Health Law"* in Baltimore Business Journal (Vol. 28, July 30, 2010, No. 12, pp. 1)

Pub: Baltimore Business Journal

Ed: Kent Hoover. **Description:** Business groups that opposed health care reform are working to undo parts of the new laws even before they go into effect. Business groups are gaining support for one legislative fix, which is repealing the law's provision that requires all businesses to file 1099 forms with the IRS any time they pay more than $600 a year to another business.

42683 ■ *"Cincinnati Hospitals Wage War on 'Bounce-Backs"* in Business Courier (Vol. 27, July 30, 2010, No. 13, pp. 1)

Pub: Business Courier

Ed: James Ritchie. **Description:** Health care organizations in Greater Cincinnati area have tried a number of care and follow up programs, primarily focused on congestive heart failure to prevent readmissions to hospitals. Hospital administrators have made the averting of bounce-backs a priority due to new federal government plans on reimbursement.

42684 ■ *"CNinsure Offers Safety in Numbers"* in Barron's (Vol. 90, September 13, 2010, No. 37, pp. 29)

Ed: Teresa Rivas. **Description:** China's insurance holding company CNinsure has a long growth future due to the nascent insurance market in the country. It has also been diversifying its offerings and it has a broad network in the nation. The shares of the company are trading cheaply at nearly 14 times its 2011 earnings, and is considered a good point for investors.

42685 ■ *"Collision Centers See Business Boom"* in Atlanta Business Chronicle (February 7, 2014, pp. 3A)

Pub: American City Business Journals, Inc.

Contact: Whitney Shaw, President

Released: February 7, 2014. **Description:** Collision repair shops in Atlanta, Georgia are benefitting from the recent snow storm. The storm resulted in $10 million insured losses to homes and automobiles. Meanwhile, collision centers have also extended business hours to accommodate more customers.

42686 ■ *"Commissioner Wants to Expand Private Market for Insurance"* in South Florida Business Journal (Vol. 32, June 8, 2012, No. 46, pp. 1)

Pub: American City Business Journal

Description: Florida insurance commissioner Keven McCarty shares his views about the major risks to the state's property insurance system. McCarty believes the bigger issue is what might happen to the market in the aftermath of a catastrophe. He also shared their activities in bringing more private property insurers into Florida.

42687 ■ *"Connecting the Dots Between Wellness and Elder Care"* in Benefits and Compensation Digest (Vol. 47, August 2010,

No. 8, pp. 18)

Pub: International Foundation of Employee Benefit Plans

Contact: Kenneth R. Boyd, President

Ed: Sandra Timmermann. **Description:** Employees caring for aged and infirm parents deal with time and financial issues and other stresses. The connection between health status of caregivers and employers' health care costs could be aided by linking programs and benefits with wellness and caregiving.

42688 ■ *"Consulting Firm Goes Shopping"* in Crain's Chicago Business (Vol. 31, April 28, 2008, No. 17, pp. 45)

Pub: Crain Communications Inc.

Contact: Todd Johnson, Publisher

Ed: Phuong Ly. **Description:** Clark & Wamberg LLC was created last year after the merger of Clark Inc. to a Dutch insurance conglomerate. Clark Inc. was a life insurance and benefits consultancy which had been on a downslide, returning just 5.6 percent a year to shareholders. In contrast Clark & Wamberg posted first-year revenue of $106.8 million, fueled by business from its executive compensation and health care clients.

42689 ■ *"Consumer Health Plan to be Launched in Memphis"* in Memphis Business Journal (Vol. 34, September 21, 2012, No. 23, pp. 1)

Pub: American City Business Journal

Ed: Cole Epley. **Description:** The Community Health Alliance, a Knoxville, Tennessee-based Consumer Oriented and Operated Plan (CO-OP), is an offspring of the Affordable Care Act. It is believed that this service will provide small businesses and individuals with an additional option when it comes to purchasing health insurance.

42690 ■ *"Continuously Monitoring Workers' Comp Can Limit Costs"* in Crain's Cleveland Business (Vol. 28, October 8, 2007, No. 40, pp. 21)

Pub: Crain Communications Inc.

Ed: Michael Agnoni. **Description:** When operating without a plan for managing its workers' compensation program, a company risks losing money. For most companies workers' compensation insurance premiums are often reduced to an annual budget entry but employers who are actively involved in the management of their programs are more likely to experience reductions in premiums and limit indirect costs associated with claims.

42691 ■ *"Controversial Bill Could Raise Rates for Homeowners"* in Orlando Business Journal (Vol. 26, January 22, 2010, No. 34, pp. 1)

Pub: American City Business Journals

Ed: Oscar Pedro Musibay, Christopher Boyd. **Description:** Florida Senate Bill 876 and its companion House Bill 447 are pushing for the deregulation of rates in the state's home insurance market. The bill is being opposed by consumer advocates as it could mean higher rates for homeowner insurance policies.

42692 ■ *"Cost of Creating Health Insurance Exchange in Md. 'Largely Unknown"* in Baltimore Business Journal (Vol. 28, September 3, 2010, No. 17, pp. 1)

Pub: Baltimore Business Journal

Ed: Emily Mullin. **Description:** United States health reform is seen to result in increased health insurance prices in Maryland. However, health care reform advocates claim a new marketplace and increased competition will help keep costs down.

42693 ■ *"Courting Canadian Customers Confounds Car Dealers"* in Business First Buffalo (November 12, 2007, pp. 1)

Pub: American City Business Journals, Inc.

Ed: James Fink. **Description:** Strength of the Canadian dollar has led to an influx of potential customers for the Western New York automobile industry, but franchising restrictions and licensing as well as insurance issues have limited the potential of having larger sales figures. Border and trade issues that affect the car industry in WNY are also discussed.

42694 ■ *"Covered California Adds Dental Benefits"* in Sacramento Business Journal (Vol. 31, August 29, 2014, No. 27, pp. 8)

Pub: American City Business Journals

Released: August 29, 2014. **Description:** Health benefit exchange, Covered California, is introducing stand-alone family dental benefits for consumers who enroll in health insurance coverage for 2015. The Governor has yet to sign a bill that would establish a separate vision care marketplace linked to Covered California's Website.

42695 ■ *"Crop Insurance Harvest Prices in 2011"* in Farm Industry News (November 9, 2011)

Pub: Penton Business Media Inc.

Contact: David Kieselstein, Chief Executive Officer

Ed: Gary Schnitkey. **Description:** Risk Management Agency (RMA) reported harvest prices for corn and soybean grown in the Midwest with corn at $6.32 per bushel, 31 cents higher than the project $6.01; soybeans were at $12.14 per bushel, down $1.35 from the projected price of $13.49.

42696 ■ *"Cutting Health Care Costs: the 3-Legged Stool"* in HR Specialist (Vol. 8, September 2010, No. 9, pp. 1)

Pub: Capitol Information Group Inc.

Description: Employer spending on health insurance benefits to employees is investigated.

42697 ■ *"Dallas-Foth Worth Banks Debate Need to Grow Branches"* in Dallas Business Journal (Vol. 35, April 13, 2012, No. 31, pp. 1)

Pub: American City Business Journal

Description: Dallas-Fort Worth Metropolitan Area (DFW)-based banks have been debating whether to add more branches as more customers go online to handle their finances. The Federal Deposit Insurance Corporation (FDIC) has reported the number of bank and thrift branches in DFW fell 5 percent to 1.717 in June 2011 from 1,809 in June 2009. Details of the FDIC report are also discussed.

42698 ■ *"Diana Bonta -- Keeping People Healthy and Thriving"* in Hispanic Business (Vol. 30, April 2008, No. 4, pp. 30)

Pub: Hispanic Business Inc.

Contact: Jesus Chavarria, President

Ed: Leanndra Martinez. **Description:** Diana Bonta serves as vice president of public affairs for Kaiser Permanente and is a strong advocate for health reform and improving access to health care. In order to better serve the underinsured and uninsured, she directs Kaiser's Community Benefit division that devoted $369 million last year to this cause.

42699 ■ *Dictionary of Real Estate Terms*

Pub: Barron's Educational Series Inc.

Contact: Ellen Sibley, President

E-mail: ellen@barronseduc.com

Ed: Jack P. Friedman, Jack C. Harris, J. Bruce Lindeman. **Released:** 8th Edition. **Price:** $14.99, Paperback. **Description:** More than 2,500 real estate terms relating to mortgages and financing, brokerage law, architecture, rentals and leases, property insurance, and more.

42700 ■ *"Discovery Communications"* in Workforce Management (Vol. 88, December 14, 2009, No. 13, pp. 17)

Pub: Crain Communications Inc.

Contact: Rance E. Crain, President

Ed: Jeremy Smerd. **Description:** Discovery Communications provides its employees a wealth of free health services via a comprehensive work-site medical clinic that is available to its employees and their dependents. Overview of the company's innovative approach to healthcare is presented.??.

42701 ■ *"Distribution Dilemma"* in Best's Review (Vol. 113, September 2012, No. 5, pp. 15)

Description: Life insurance companies are addressing the obstacles prohibiting them from increasing sales.

42702 ■ *"Doctor Shortage Continues to Plague Region" in Business First of Buffalo (Vol. 30, April 11, 2014, No. 30, pp. 6)*
Pub: American City Business Journals, Inc.
Contact: Whitney Shaw, President
Released: April 11, 2014. Description: New York hospitals need at least 1,000 additional physicians, particularly primary care doctors, as they try to meet the criteria set by Federal health reform's Affordable Care Act. The Western New York region gained only 421 new physicians, while losing 544 in 2013.

42703 ■ *"Doctors Eye Rating Plan With Caution" in The Business Journal-Portland (Vol. 25, July 4, 2008, No. 17, pp. 1)*
Pub: American City Business Journals, Inc.
Contact: Whitney Shaw, President
Ed: Robin J. Moody. Description: Doctors in Portland, Oregon are wary of a new Providence Health Plan system that rates their performance on patients with certain medical conditions. The system is expected to discourage wasteful procedures, thereby, saving employers' money. Other mechanics of the rating system are also discussed.

42704 ■ *"Doctor's Orders" in Canadian Business (Vol. 79, November 20, 2006, No. 23, pp. 73)*
Ed: Jeff Sanford. Description: George Cohon, the founder of McDonald's in Canada and Russia, speaks about the Canadian market and the experience of starting McDonald's in Canada.

42705 ■ *"Doctors Warn of Problems" in Austin Business JournalInc. (Vol. 29, December 4, 2009, No. 39, pp. 1)*
Pub: American City Business Journals
Ed: Sandra Zaragoza. Description: Texas physicians have voiced their concern regarding the potential cuts in Medicare reimbursement rates due to the 21 percent cut imposed by Centers for Medicare and Medicaid at the start of 2010. Experts believe the large cuts would result in the closure of some physician practices. Details of the Texas Medical Association's stand on the health reform bill are examined.

42706 ■ *"Ducking the New Health-Care Taxes" in Barron's (Vol. 92, September 15, 2012, No. 38, pp. 34)*
Pub: Dow Jones & Co., Inc.
Contact: Clare Hart, President
Ed: Elizabeth Ody. Description: Strategies that investors can use to avoid paying higher taxes starting January 2013 are discussed. These include selling assets by December 2012, distributing dividends, purchasing private-placement life insurance and converting individual retirement accounts.

42707 ■ *"E-Medical Records Save Money, Time in Ann Arbor" in Crain's Detroit Business (Vol. 24, January 21, 2008, No. 3, pp. 6)*
Pub: Crain Communications Inc. - Detroit
Contact: Keith Crain, Chairman
Ed: Jay Greene. Description: Ann Arbor Area Health Information Exchange is improving patient outcomes by sharing clinical and administrative data in electronic medical record systems.

42708 ■ *"Elder Care Costs Surge" in National Underwriter Life & Health (Vol. 114, November 8, 2020, No. 21, pp. 25)*
Pub: Summit Professional Networks
Contact: Steve Weitzner, President
Ed: Trevor Thomas. Description: Nursing home and assisted living rates rose from 2009 to 2010, according to MetLife Mature Market Institute. Statistical data included.

42709 ■ *"Employer Jobless Tax Could Rise" in Sacramento Business Journal (Vol. 28, May 27, 2011, No. 13, pp. 1)*
Pub: Sacramento Business Journal
Ed: Kathy Robertson. Description: The government of California is facing an estimated $16 billion deficit in its unemployment insurance fund. Unemployment insurance spending has exceeded employer contributions to the fund. Statistics on unemployment insurance is included.

42710 ■ *"Employers Tied in Knots" in Sacramento Business Journal (Vol. 25, August 15, 2008, No. 24, pp. 1)*
Pub: American City Business Journals, Inc.
Contact: Whitney Shaw, President
Ed: Kathy Robertson. Description: Conflicting laws on same sex marriage have been posing problems for companies, and insurers in California. The court ruling that allowed gay marriages has created differences between state and federal laws. Federal laws on same-sex spouse taxation are also seen to complicate the issue.

42711 ■ *"Employers Waking Up to Effects of Workers' Sleep Problems" in Crain's Cleveland Business (Vol. 28, December 3, 2007, No. 48, pp. 18)*
Pub: Crain Communications Inc.
Ed: Jennifer Keirn. Description: Employers are beginning to realize that poor sleep quality can impact their bottom lines with higher health care costs and more lost-time accidents. The National Institutes of Health estimates that sleep deprivation, sleep disorders and excessive daytime sleepiness add about $15 billion to our national health care bill and cost employers $50 billion in lost productivity.

42712 ■ *"Experts Take the Temp of Obama Plan" in The Business Journal-Serving Metropolitan Kansas City (Vol. 27, November 14, 2008, No. 10)*
Pub: American City Business Journals, Inc.
Contact: Whitney Shaw, President
Ed: Rob Roberts. Description: Kansas City, Missouri-based employee benefits experts say president-elect Barack Obama's health care reform plan is on track. Insurance for children and capitalization for health information technology are seen as priority areas. The plan is aimed at reducing the number of uninsured people in the United States.

42713 ■ *"Export Initiative Launched" in Philadelphia Business Journal (Vol. 28, December 11, 2009, No. 43, pp. 1)*
Pub: American City Business Journals Inc.
Ed: Athena D. Merritt. Description: The first initiative that came out of the partnership between the Export-Import Bank of the US, the city of Philadelphia, and the World Trade Center of Greater Philadelphia is presented. A series of export finance workshops have featured Ex-Im Bank resources that can provide Philadelphia businesses with working capital, insurance protection and buyer financing.

42714 ■ *"Fewer Small Employers in Maryland Offering Health Care" in Baltimore Business Journal (Vol. 28, June 11, 2010, No. 5, pp. 1)*
Pub: Baltimore Business Journal
Ed: Scott Graham. Description: Maryland Health Care Commission report figures have shown only 47,661 small businesses provided some level of health coverage to 381,517 employees in 2009. These numbers are down from 51,283 employers who offered benefits to 407,983 employees in 2008 to highlight a disturbing trend in Maryland's small-group insurance market. Reasons for the drop are discussed.

42715 ■ *"Firms Sue Doracon to Recoup More Than $1M in Unpaid Bills" in Baltimore Business Journal (Vol. 28, July 9, 2010, No. 9, pp. 1)*
Pub: Baltimore Business Journal
Ed: Scott Dance. Description: Concrete supplier Paul J. Rach Inc., Selective Insurance Company, and equipment leasing firm Colonial Pacific Leasing Corporation intend to sue Baltimore, Maryland-based Doracon Contracting Inc. for $1 million in unpaid bills. Doracon owed Colonial Pacific $794,000 and the equipment is still in Doracon's possession. Selective Insurance and Paul J. Rach respectively seek $132,000 and $88,000.

42716 ■ *"For All It's Worth" in Entrepreneur (Vol. 36, April 2008, No. 4, pp. 46)*
Pub: Entrepreneur Press
Contact: Perlman Neil, President
Ed: Farnoosh Torabi. Description: Discusses the federal estate tax system requires that 45 percent of the money beyond $2 million be given to the government. Ways on how to minimize the effects of estate tax on assets include: creating bypass trusts for married couples; setting up an irrevocable life insurance trust to avoid taxation of estate for insurance benefactors; and having annual gift tax exclusion.

42717 ■ *"Generational Savvy" in Hawaii Business (Vol. 54, August 2008, No. 2, pp. 135)*
Pub: PacificBasin Communications
Ed: Jolyn Okimoto Rosa. Description: Lawrence Takeo Kagawa founded Security Insurance Agency, later renamed Occidental Underwriters of Hawaii Ltd., in 1933 to provide insurance to Asian-Americans in Hawaii at lower premiums. Details on the company's history, growth investment products and Transamerica Life products and 75 years of family-run business are discussed.

42718 ■ *Green Your Small Business: Profitable Ways to Become an Ecopreneur*
Pub: McGraw-Hill
Ed: Scott Cooney. Released: November 2008. Price: A$29.95; NZ$35. Description: Advice and guidance is given to help any entrepreneur start, build or grow a green business, focusing on green business basics, market research and financing, as well as handling legal and insurance issues.

42719 ■ *"Greenberg Sues U.S. Over AIG Rescue" in Wall Street Journal Eastern Edition (November 22 , 2011, pp. C3)*
Pub: Dow Jones & Co., Inc.
Contact: Clare Hart, President
Ed: Liam Pleven, Serena Ng. Description: Former Chief Executive Officer of American International Group Inc., Maurice R. 'Hank' Greenberg, has filed a lawsuit against the United States and the Federal Reserve Bank of New York on behalf of shareholders and his company, Starr International Company Inc., claiming that the government was wrong in taking control of the insurance giant and used it to move tens of millions of dollars to the trading partners of AIG.

42720 ■ *"Ground Forces: Insurance Companies Should Help Agents to Build the Skills and Relationships that Translate Into More Business" in Best's Review (Vol. 113, September 2012, No. 5, pp. 25)*
Description: The economic challenges of the past few years required insurance agents and financial professionals to better trained. Insurance companies should help their agents build skills and relationships in order to grow.

42721 ■ *"Growth In West Leads To Jobs Here" in Business First of Buffalo (Vol. 36, May 23, 2014, No. 36, pp. 4)*
Pub: American City Business Journals, Inc.
Contact: Whitney Shaw, President
Released: May 23, 2014. Description: The growth of business in California and other western states has the potential to boost employment at HealthNow NY Inc. in Buffalo. The company plans to shift more than 36 jobs from its HealthNow Administrative Services division in Blue Bell, Pennsylvania to company headquarters in downtown Buffalo.

42722 ■ *"Handling New Health Insurance Regulations" in Baltimore Business Journal (Vol. 31, April 25, 2014, No. 52, pp. 25)*
Pub: American City Business Journals, Inc.
Contact: Whitney Shaw, President
Released: April 25, 2014. Description: Research and consulting firm, Mercer, surveyed businesses in January 2014 to examine their employer-sponsored health plans following enrollment in the Affordable Care Act-created exchanges. The survey found employers were taking advantage of a delay to a key regulation in the Act on offering insurance to employees who work at least 30 hours a week.

42723 ■ *"Harleysville Eyes Growth After Nationwide Deal' in Philadelphia Business Journal (Vol. 30, October 7, 2011, No. 34, pp. 1)*
Pub: American City Business Journals Inc.
Ed: Jeff Blumenthal. **Description:** Harleysville Group announced growth plans after the company was sold to Columbus, Ohio-based Nationwide Mutual Insurance Company for about $1.63 billion. Nationwide gained an independent agency platform in 32 states with the Harleysville deal.

42724 ■ *"Health Alliance Could Sell GCAP' in Business Courier (Vol. 27, June 18, 2010, No. 7, pp. 1)*
Pub: Business Courier
Ed: James Ritchie. **Description:** Health Alliance could sell the 31-doctor Greater Cincinnati Associated Physicians Group. The group has seen several members withdraw ever since the group filed a complaint asking to be released from services to Health Alliance.

42725 ■ *"Health Care Braces for Federal Cuts" in Boston Business Journal (Vol. 29, August 19, 2011, No. 15, pp. 1)*
Pub: American City Business Journals, Inc.
Ed: Scott Dance. **Description:** The healthcare industry in Baltimore is expecting negative effects from the federal debt ceiling on Medicare and Medicaid spending. Medicare funds are expected to be slashed and could impact hospitals and doctors.

42726 ■ *"Health Care Changes Loom" in Business Journal Milwaukee (Vol. 29, July 13, 2012, No. 42, pp. 1)*
Pub: American City Business Journals, Inc.
Contact: Whitney Shaw, President
Ed: Jon Olson. **Released:** July 13, 2012. **Description:** Business owners are worried about mandated health care coverage, which will start in 2014. Boyd Miller, president of Wisconsin Thermoset Molding, Inc., believes that eight Supreme Court justices voted purely on political grounds when they decided on President Obama's health care plan.

42727 ■ *"Health Care of the Future" in Business Journal Serving Greater Tampa Bay (Vol. 30, November 19, 2010, No. 48, pp. 1)*
Pub: Tampa Bay Business Journal
Ed: Margie Manning. **Description:** Information about accountable care organizations (ACO), which are integrated care systems with doctors and hospitals working closely together to handle patient care, is provided. The Patient Protection and Affordable Care Act paved the way for ACOs as Medicare demonstration projects.

42728 ■ *"Health Centers Plan Expansion: $3M from D.C. Expected; Uninsured a Target' in Crain's Detroit Business (Vol. 25, June 15, 2009, No. 24, pp. 3)*
Pub: Crain Communications Inc. - Detroit
Contact: Keith Crain, Chairman
Ed: Jay Greene. **Description:** Detroit has five federally qualified health centers that plan to receive over $3 million in federal stimulus money that will be used to expand projects that will care for uninsured patients.

42729 ■ *"Health Insurance Dilemmas" in Hispanic Business (January-February 2008, pp. 58)*
Pub: Hispanic Business Inc.
Contact: Jesus Chavarria, President
Ed: Anna Davison. **Description:** Small business owners discussed the challenges they face providing health insurance to employees.

42730 ■ *"Health IT Regulations Generate Static Among Providers" in Philadelphia Business Journal (Vol. 28, January 29, 2010, No. 50, pp. 1)*
Pub: American City Business Journals Inc.
Ed: John George. **Description:** US Centers for Medicaid and Medicare Services and the Office of the National Coordinator for Health Information Technology have proposed rules regarding the meaningful use of electronic health records. The rules must be complied with by hospitals and physicians to qualify for federal stimulus funds.

42731 ■ *"Health Reform Could Expand HSA-Based Plans" in Workforce Management (Vol. 88, December 14, 2009, No. 13, pp. 6)*
Ed: Jeremy Smerd. **Description:** HSA-qualified plans are the cheapest insurance plans on the market as they have a higher deductible but cost less upfront. If health care reform passes, HSA-qualified plans should benefit greatly.

42732 ■ *"Health Reform How-To" in Business Courier (Vol. 26, December 11, 2009, No. 33, pp. 1)*
Ed: James Ritchie. **Description:** Greater Cincinnati health care leaders shared views about the health care reform bill. Respondents included the Cincinnati Visiting Nurse's Wallen Falberg, healthcare consultant Hirsch Cohen, Greater Cincinnati Health Council's Coleen O'Toole, Employer Health Care Alliance's Sharron DiMario, Legal Aid Society of Greater Cincinnati's Col Owens, Christ Hospital's Susan Croushore, and Humana of Ohio's Tim Cappel.

42733 ■ *"Here's How Buffett Spent 2007' in Barron's (Vol. 88, March 10, 2008, No. 10, pp. 48)*
Ed: Andrew Bary. **Description:** Earnings of Berkshire Hathaway may decline in 2008 due to a tighter insurance market, but its portfolio is expected to continue growing. Warren Buffett purchased $19.1 billion worth of stocks in 2007.

42734 ■ *"Home Sweet Home" in Canadian Business (Vol. 79, October 9, 2006, No. 20, pp. 22)*
Pub: Rogers Media Inc.
Contact: Tony Viner, President
Ed: Peter Shawn Taylor. **Description:** Changes being made in the management of mortgage insurance business in Canada are critically analyzed.

42735 ■ *"Hospital Fighting for Its Life" in Crain's Chicago Business (April 28, 2008)*
Pub: Crain Communications Inc.
Contact: Todd Johnson, Publisher
Ed: Mike Colias. **Description:** Chicago's Catholic health chain was looking to sell the money-losing hospital St. Anthony Hospital on the West Side but with the financial picture improving and no merger offers in the works the investment bank hired to shop the hospital is hoping to operate the 111-year-old facility as an independent entity. St. Anthony serves as a 'safety net' for the region since an increasing number of its patients are uninsured or on public aid, which pays far less than commercial insurers.

42736 ■ *"Hospitals Say Medicaid Expansion is Critical" in Dallas Business Journal (Vol. 35, August 3, 2012, No. 47, pp. 1)*
Pub: American City Business Journal
Ed: Bill Hethcock, Matt Joyce. **Description:** Governor Rick Perry's rejection of the Texas expansion of Medicaid is met with disapproval by health organizations such as the Methodist Health System. The federal government has extended $70 billion in financing to help more Texans become eligible for primary health care. Expansion supporters argue that Medicaid is critical in lowering insurance osts for those who need it.

42737 ■ *"Hospitals See Major Shift To Outpatient Care" in The Business Journal-Milwaukee (Vol. 25, September 12, 2008, No. 51, pp. A1)*
Pub: American City Business Journals, Inc.
Contact: Whitney Shaw, President
Ed: Corrinne Hess. **Description:** Statistics show that the revenue of Wisconsin hospitals from outpatient medical care is about to surpass revenue from hospital patients who stay overnight. This revenue increase is attributed to new technology and less-invasive surgery. Trends show that the shift toward outpatient care actually started in the late 1980s and early 1990s.

42738 ■ *"Hospitals Vying to Buy Physician Associates LLC" in Orlando Business Journal (Vol. 29, August 31, 2012, No. 11, pp. 1)*
Pub: American City Business Journal
Description: Hospitals are battling it out on who gets to buy Physician Associates LLC, the largest multi-specialty practice in Central Florida. The most likely candidates to purchase the practice are Orlando Health and Florida Hospital. The deal could be worth $20 million to $60 million and it could also hike health care costs since Physician Asociates serves 19 percent of Central Florida's uninsured population.

42739 ■ *"How to Avoid Leave-Related Lawsuits" in Employee Benefit News (Vol. 25, December 1, 2011, No. 15, pp. 12)*
Pub: SourceMedia Inc.
Contact: James M. Malkin, Chief Executive Officer
Ed: John F. Galvin. **Description:** Tips for employers when adding disability and maternity leave benefits to workers are outlined, with focus on ways to avoid leave-related lawsuits.

42740 ■ *"How to Maximize Your Investment Income" in Contractor (Vol. 56, December 2009, No. 12, pp. 33)*
Pub: Penton Media, Inc.
Ed: Irving L. Blackman. **Description:** Private placement life insurance (PPLI) can minimize taxes and protect assets. PPLI is a form of variable universal insurance that is offered privately. Risk of insurance company illiquidity is avoided as investments are placed in separate accounts.

42741 ■ *How to Start a Home-Based Senior Care Business*
Pub: Globe Pequot Press Inc.
Contact: Robert Irwin, Manager
E-mail: robert.irwin@globepequot.com
Ed: James L. Ferry. **Released:** January 06, 2010. **Price:** $18.95, paperback. **Description:** Information is provided to start a home-based senior care business. **Availability:** Print.

42742 ■ *"How a Unique Culture Proposition Became a USP' in Business Strategy Review (Vol. 21, Spring 2010, No. 1, pp. 52)*
Pub: John Wiley & Sons Inc. Scientific, Technical, Medical, and Scholarly Div. (Wiley-Blackwell)
Contact: William J. Pesce, Manager
E-mail: wpesce@wiley.com
Ed: Adam Kingl. **Description:** How can you transform the way you do things into a compelling sales proposition? Zurich Insurance has created a Unique Culture Proposition which may be its Unique Selling Point.

42743 ■ *"Humana Planning Pa. HMO' in Philadelphia Business Journal (Vol. 28, August 10, 2012, No. 26, pp. 1)*
Pub: American City Business Journal
Description: Humana plans to establish an HMO in Philadelphia and other areas of Pennsylvania. Along with this plan is an insurance offering in the Medicare Advantage market focused on senior citizens. The new offering would complement the company's existing preferred provider organization product.

42744 ■ *"Humana Seeks Higher Stake in Memphis Market' in Memphis Business Journal (Vol. 33, February 17, 2012, No. 45, pp. 1)*
Pub: American City Business Journal
Ed: Christopher Sheffield. **Description:** Humana of Tennessee has been hoping to get a bigger share of the West Tennessee insurance market through its new three-year contract with Baptist Memorial Health Care Corporation. Louisville, Kentucky-based Humana Inc. has a business relationship with Baptist that stretches back more than two decades.

42745 ■ *"Humana: Take Pay Cut or Get Out' in Business Courier (Vol. 24, January 31, 2008, No. 43, pp. 1)*
Pub: American City Business Journals, Inc.
Contact: Whitney Shaw, President
Ed: James Ritchie. **Description:** Insurer Humana Inc. is removing some surgery centers from its network for refusing to welcome the new payment

system. Evendale Surgery Center and the Surgery Center of Cincinnati will be removed from the network because they resist the newly imposed lower rates. Speculations over Humana's decision are discussed.

42746 ■ "IBC Reverses Member Slide" in Philadelphia Business Journal (Vol. 30, September 23, 2011, No. 32, pp. 1)

Pub: American City Business Journals Inc.

Ed: John George. **Description:** Health insurer Independence Blue Cross (IBC) added more than 40,000 members across all product lines since the start of 2011. It has 2.2 million members in Pennsylvania's Philadelphia region and 3.1 million members across the U.S. Services and other growth-related plans of IBC are covered.

42747 ■ "Impressive Numbers: Companies Experience Substantial Increases in Dollars, Employment" in Hispanic Business (July-August 2007)

Pub: Hispanic Business Inc.

Contact: Jesus Chavarria, President

Ed: Derek Reveron. **Description:** Profiles of five fastest growing Hispanic companies reporting increases in revenue and employment include Brightstar, distributor of wireless products; Greenway Ford Inc., a car dealership; Fred Loya Insurance, auto insurance carrier; and Group O, packaging company; and Diverse Staffing, Inc., an employment and staffing firm.

42748 ■ "Injured Workers Caught in the Middle" in Sacramento Business Journal (Vol. 28, June 10, 2011, No. 15, pp. 1)

Pub: Sacramento Business Journal

Ed: Kelly Johnson. **Description:** A bill that would extend the cap on disability payments to nearly five years is in the works, but employers and insurance companies fear it would increase their costs. Proponents of the bill say, however, that it would correct unfairness suffered by the employees. Features of the bill are discussed as well as its effects on both parties and the State of California.

42749 ■ "Insurance Firm Consolidates Offices: Integro Finds the Right Price Downtown" in Crain's New York Business (January 13, 2008)

Pub: Crain Communications Inc.

Contact: Rance Crain, President

Description: Integro insurance brokers is relocating its headquarters to 1 State Street Plaza, where it will consolidate its operations in March. The firm feels that the upscale design will provide an appropriate setting for entertaining clients and an engaging work environment for employees.

42750 ■ "Insurance Jobs" in Best's Review (Vol. 113, September 2012, No. 5, pp. 10)

Description: Jobs report from the US Bureau of Labor Statistics is presented, reporting only 100 new jobs in July 2012. Statistical data included.

42751 ■ "Insurance: Marathon Effort" in Canadian Business (Vol. 80, January 29, 2007, No. 3, pp. 11)

Ed: Jeff Sanford. **Description:** The efforts of the insurance firm ING Canada Inc. to manage its relations with its customers are described. The enhancement of the insurance services provided by the company is discussed.

42752 ■ "An Insurance Roll-Up In Danger of Unraveling" in Barron's (Vol. 88, March 17, 2008, No. 11, pp. 51)

Pub: Dow Jones & Co., Inc.

Contact: Clare Hart, President

Ed: Bill Alpert. **Description:** Shares of National Financial Partners have fallen below their initial offering price as sputtering sales and management turnover leave many investors wondering. One of the company's star brokers is being sued for their 'life settlement' contracts while another broker is being pursued by the IRS for unpaid taxes.

42753 ■ "Insuraprise Growing Fast" in Austin Business Journal (Vol. 31, April 22, 2011, No. 7, pp. 1)

Pub: American City Business Journals

Ed: Sandra Zaragoza. **Description:** Austin, Texas-based Insuraprise Inc. is finalizing the purchase of a 24,000-square-foot office at 12116 Jekel Circle. The firm, with 23 salespeople and sales that are growing nearly 300 percent over the past 18 months, will now have room to grow. Insuraprise plans to hire 35 new salespersons for its call center.

42754 ■ "Insurers Enter Ridesharing Dispute" in Sacramento Business Journal (Vol. 31, June 6, 2014, No. 15, pp. 8)

Pub: American City Business Journals

Released: June 6, 2014. **Description:** Insurance companies have been lobbying the California Assembly to pass legislation requiring ridesharing drivers to carry commercial liability insurance. Ridesharing companies provide drivers with liability coverage as a backup when an accident is not covered by personal insurance. The passage of such a bill would boost ridesharing companies' revenues.

42755 ■ "Insurers No Longer Paying Premium for Advertising" in Brandweek (Vol. 49, April 21, 2008, No. 16, pp. SR3)

Pub: Nielsen Business Media Inc.

Contact: Howard Appelbaum, President

Ed: Eric Newman. **Description:** Insurance companies are cutting their advertising budgets after years of accelerated double-digit growth in spending due to the economic downturn, five years of record-breaking ad spend and a need to cut expenditures as claims costs rise and a competitive market keeps premiums in place. Statistical data included.

42756 ■ "Insurers Warn Brokers" in Sacramento Business Journal (Vol. 25, August 24, 2008, No. 25, pp. 1)

Pub: American City Business Journals, Inc.

Contact: Whitney Shaw, President

Ed: Kathy Robertson. **Description:** Sacramento, California-based health plans have warned insurance brokers not to combine two different kinds of insurance products or they will be stricken from the sales network. The health plans also asked employers to promise not to combine plans with self-insurance. Such schemes are seen to destroy lower-premium health products.

42757 ■ "Internet Marketing 2.0: Closing the Online Chat Gap" in Agent's Sales Journal (November 2009, pp. 14)

Pub: Summit Professional Networks

Contact: Steve Weitzner, President

Ed: Jeff Denenholz. **Description:** Advice regarding the implementation of an Internet marketing strategy for insurance agencies includes how and why to incorporate a chat feature in which a sales agent can communicate in real-time with potential or existing customers. It is important to understand if appropriate response mechanisms are in place to convert leads into actual sales.

42758 ■ "Is Hawaii Ready for Universal Health Care?" in Hawaii Business (Vol. 53, February 2008, No. 8, pp. 26)

Pub: PacificBasin Communications

Description: Representative Lyn Finnegan does not believe that a universal health is good for Hawaii as health insurance for everyone will be difficult to achieve. Representative John M. Mizuno says that House Bill 1008 introduced in the state was a landmark for Hawaii as it will provide the people with health care insurance. Other details about their opinion on the topic are presented.

42759 ■ "Is the Insurance Sector at Risk?" in Business Strategy Review (Vol. 25, Summer 2014, No. 2, pp. 30)

Pub: Blackwell Publishing Professional

Contact: Stephen M. Smith, President

Released: Summer 2014. **Description:** In the wake of the financial crisis, the insurance sector has been overlooked. New light is shed on the rise of shadow insurance and the increasing risk levels in American life insurance markets.

42760 ■ "Is There a Doctor In the House?" in Black Enterprise (Vol. 41, December 2010, No. 5, pp. 42)

Pub: Earl G. Graves Publishing Co. Inc.

Contact: Earl G. Graves, Jr., President

Ed: Renita Burns. **Description:** Health insurance premiums have increased between 15 percent and 20 percent for small business owners, making it one of the most expensive costs. Ways to evaluate a health plan's costs and effectiveness are examined.

42761 ■ "Is Your Business Disaster Proof? How To Keep Your Company Up and Running Even After an Emergency" in Black Enterprise (Vol. 44, March 2014, No. 7, pp. 15)

Pub: Earl G. Graves Publishing Co. Inc.

Contact: Earl G. Graves, Jr., President

Released: March 2014. **Description:** Nearly 40 percent of all small businesses never reopen following a disaster. Floods are the most common event causing thousands of dollars in damages and shutting down companies. Commercial property insurance rarely covers flood damage. It usually covers physical assets such as buildings, equipment, inventory, computers, and records damaged by the event. Flood insurance must be purchased separately.

42762 ■ "It's Time for Insurance Carriers To Win More Customers; About One-Third of Insurance Customers are Engaged. This Means the Industry Has a Massive Opportunity to Gain More Business" in Gallup Business Journal (May 28, 2014)

Pub: Gallup Press

Released: May 28, 2014. **Description:** The insurance industry has the opportunity to engage and increase business and profits. Only one-third of insurance customers are engaged. Tips to help engage customers are offered.

42763 ■ "JK Lasser's New Rules for Estate, Retirement, and Tax Planning"

Pub: John Wiley & Sons Inc.

Contact: Stephen M. Smith, President

Released: October 20, 2014. **Price:** , $24.95 paperback. **Description:** The authoritative guide to estate, retirement and tax planning is fully updated and reflects the new changes and legal updates. Estate planning section covers: planning, taxation, investing, wills, executors, trusts, life insurance, retirement planning, Social Security, business planning, succession, asset protection and family limited partnerships.

42764 ■ "The Keeper of Records" in Black Enterprise (Vol. 41, December 2010, No. 5, pp. 54)

Pub: Earl G. Graves Publishing Co. Inc.

Contact: Earl G. Graves, Jr., President

Ed: Denise A. Campbell. **Description:** Medical billing and coding, submission of claims to health insurance companies and Medicare or Medicaid for payment is one of the fastest growing disciplines in healthcare.

42765 ■ King of Capital: Sandy Weill and the Making of Citigroup

Pub: John Wiley & Sons Inc.

Contact: Stephen M. Smith, President

Ed: Amey Stone, Mike Brewster. **Released:** March 2004. **Price:** $16.95, paperback. **Description:** Biography of Sandy Weill describes how he became a billionaire business giant by creating successful companies from smaller, sometimes failing firms; creating successful new products where none previously existed; and making deals no one thought possible. He is also responsible for changing the landscape of the banking industry and insurance business when he created Citigroup in 1998, the world's largest financial services firm. **Availability:** Print.

42766 ■ "Labor Pains" in Canadian Business (Vol. 79, August 14, 2006, No. 16-17, pp. 80)

Description: Canada's employment insurance is analyzed in view of the growing shortage of labor.

42767 ■ "Law Allows Captive Insurance Companies to Form in State" in Crain's

Detroit Business (Vol. 24, March 31, 2008, No. 13, pp. 29)
Pub: Crain Communications Inc.
Contact: Rance E. Crain, President
Ed: Jerry Geisel. **Description:** Discusses new legislation allowing the formation of captive insurance companies in the state of Michigan; these companies are subsidiaries of non-insurers that are formed primarily to insure some or all of the risks of its parent company.

42768 ■ "Life Insurance Issued Rose 2.3 Percent in 2011" in Best's Review (Vol. 113, September 2012, No. 5, pp. 18)
Description: The number of life insurance policies issued during 2011 rose 2.3 percent. The industry sustained only modest investment impairments and it maintained strong regulatory capital and favorable operating earnings. Statistical data included.

42769 ■ "Lifetime Planning with a Twist" in Contractor (Vol. 56, July 2009, No. 7, pp. 40)
Pub: Intertec Publishing
Contact: John French, President
Ed: Irving L. Blackman. **Description:** Private Placement Life Insurance lets wealthy investors make their investment gains tax-free and can be set up so investors can make tax-free loans from the policy. This can be used on a younger member of the family as a wealth-building strategy if the investor is uninsurable.

42770 ■ Managing Health Benefits in Small and Mid-Sized Organizations
Ed: Patricia Halo. **Released:** July 1999. **Description:** Comprehensive guide for developing health care plans for companies employing between 50 and 5,000 employees in order to provide employees with better health care at lower prices.

42771 ■ "Manulife Posts Billion-Dollar Profit" in Globe & Mail (February 14, 2007, pp. B7)
Ed: Andrew Willis. **Description:** Manulife Financial Corp., Canada's largest insurer, reported $1.1 billion profit in the fourth quarter of 2006. The financial results of Manulife reflected a 39 percent rise in quarterly profit at the nation's wealth management division.

42772 ■ "Markel American Insurance Company Announces Wedding and Special Event Insurance for Consumers" in Benzinga.com (February 16, 2011)
Pub: Benzinga.com
Contact: Kyle Bazzy, President
Ed: Benzinga Staff. **Description:** Markel American Insurance Company, headquartered in Waukesha, Wisconsin has launched its new special event insurance and wedding insurance to protect both liabilities and cancellations associated with these events.

42773 ■ "Maryland Businesses Balk at 1099 Provision in Health Reform Law" in Baltimore Business Journal (Vol. 28, August 13, 2010, No. 14, pp. 1)
Pub: Baltimore Business Journal
Ed: Scott Dance. **Description:** Small business advocates and accountants have criticized the Internal Revenue Service Form 1099 provision in the health care reform law as not worth the cost of time and money. Critics believe the policy would create a deluge of the documents that is too much for the companies or the IRS to handle. Details of the provision are also discussed.

42774 ■ "Maryland Doctors, Health Insurers Squabble Over Who Sends Patients the Bill" in Baltimore Business Journal (Vol. 27, February 6, 2010)
Pub: American City Business Journals
Ed: Scott Graham. **Description:** Issue of allowing patients to send reimbursement checks to physicians who are not part of their health insurer's provider network is being debated in Maryland. Details on the proposed Maryland bill and the arguments presented by doctors and insurers are outlined.

42775 ■ "Maryland Hospitals Cope with Rare Drop in Patient Admissions" in Boston Business Journal (Vol. 29, September 23,
2011, No. 20, pp. 1)
Pub: American City Business Journals, Inc.
Ed: Scott Dance. **Description:** Admissions to Maryland hospitals have dropped to less than 700,000 in fiscal year 2010 and initial figures for fiscal 2011 show in-patient admissions are now nearing 660,000. The decline can be partly attributed to new ways health insurers are paying hospitals for care and to the financial reward hospitals get for cutting back on admissions.

42776 ■ "The Massachusetts Mess" in Barron's (Vol. 89, July 27, 2009, No. 30, pp. 39)
Pub: Dow Jones & Co., Inc.
Contact: Clare Hart, President
Ed: Thomas G. Donlan. **Description:** Massachusetts' mandatory health insurance has produced the highest rate of insurance coverage among the states but the state is now unable to afford its dream of universal coverage just three years after they enacted it. This supposed model for federal health-care reform is turning out to be a joke.

42777 ■ "MCM Bulks Up by Merging With Maritime Insurer" in Puget Sound Business Journal (Vol. 33, June 1, 2012, No. 6, pp. 1)
Pub: American City Business Journal
Ed: Peter Neurath. **Description:** Seattle, Washington-based brokerage and benefits company MCM has formed a merger with Global Insurance Specialists that would strengthen its property-casualty insurance brokerage division. MCM has 2012 premium volume of $794.7 million, a total of 75 employees and provides service in areas such as employee benefits, executive benefits, and retirement plans.

42778 ■ "Meadowbrook CEO Sees 20 Percent Growth With New Acquisition" in Crain's Detroit Business (Vol. 24, March 11, 2008, No. 10, pp. 4)
Pub: Crain Communications Inc.
Contact: Rance E. Crain, President
Ed: Jay Greene. **Description:** Discusses the major turnaround of Meadowbrook Insurance Group after Robert Cubbin became CEO and implemented a new business strategy.

42779 ■ "Meadowbrook To Acquire ProCentury in $272.6 Million Deal" in Crain's Detroit Business (Vol. 24, February 21, 2008, No. 8, pp. 4)
Pub: Crain Communications Inc. - Detroit
Contact: Keith Crain, Chairman
Ed: Jay Greene. **Description:** Meadowbrook Insurance Group, based in Southfield, Michigan reports its proposed acquisition of ProCentury Corporation based in Columbus, Ohio. Meadowbrook provides risk-management to agencies, professional and trade associations and small-to-midsize businesses.

42780 ■ "Medicaid Insurers See Growth in Small Business Market" in Boston Business Journal (Vol. 31, July 15, 2011, No. 25, pp. 1)
Pub: Boston Business Journal
Ed: Julie M. Donnelly. **Description:** BMC HealthNet Plan announced plans to launch small business products to serve small businesses that are priced out of rising premium rates at large Massachusetts insurers. BMC joined competitors CeltiCare Health Plan and Neighborhood Health Plan in augmenting its core business.

42781 ■ "Medicare Plans Step Up Battle for Subscribers" in Sacramento Business Journal (Vol. 28, October 21, 2011, No. 34, pp. 1)
Pub: Sacramento Business Journal
Ed: Kathy Robertson. **Description:** California's market for health plans have become increasingly competitive as more than 313,000 seniors try to figure out the best plans to meet their needs for 2012. Health plans are rated on Medicare materials to help consumers distinguish among the Medicare health maintenance organizations (HMOs).

42782 ■ "MN Effort To Privatize Coverage Struggles" in Business Journal (Vol. 30, July 6, 2012, No. 6, pp. 1)
Pub: American City Business Journals, Inc.
Contact: Whitney Shaw, President
Ed: Katharine Grayson. **Released:** July 6, 2012. **Description:** The Health Minnesota Contribution Program will move MinnesotaCare members to the private market. Health insurance brokers have supported passage of the law. MinnesotaCare members have received state-subsidized insurance premiums.

42783 ■ "The Moody Blues" in Entrepreneur (Vol. 36, April 2008, No. 4, pp. 87)
Pub: Entrepreneur Press
Contact: Perlman Neil, President
Ed: Mark Henricks. **Description:** Depression among employees can affect their productivity and cost the company. Businesses with a workforce that is likely to have depression should inform their employees about the health benefits covered by insurance. Other details on how to address depression concerns among employees are discussed.

42784 ■ "More Businesses Will Shift Health Costs to Workers" in Business Review, Albany New York (Vol. 34, November 16, 2007, No. 33, pp. 1)
Pub: American City Business Journals, Inc.
Ed: Barbara Pinckney. **Description:** Survey conducted by consulting firm Benetech Inc. showed that sixty percent of employers are planning to increase payroll deductions to pay for health insurance premiums. More than ninety percent of the employers prefer HMO plans, followed by Preferred Provider Organizations. Other details of the survey are discussed.

42785 ■ "More Small Businesses in Baltimore Willing to Fund Employees' Health Benefits" in Baltimore Business Journal (Vol. 28, June 18, 2010, No. 6, pp. 1)
Pub: Baltimore Business Journal
Ed: Scott Graham. **Description:** An increasing number of small businesses in Maryland are tapping into potentially cheaper self-funded health plans instead of providing fully insured benefits to employees through traditional health plans. Self-funded health plans charge employers for health care up to a specified level. Economic implications of self-funded plans to small businesses are discussed.

42786 ■ "Most States Have High-Risk Health Insurance Pools" in Crain's Detroit Business (Vol. 24, March 24, 2008, No. 12, pp. 31)
Pub: Crain Communications Inc.
Contact: Rance E. Crain, President
Ed: Jay Greene. **Description:** High-risk health insurance pools, designed to cover individuals with medical conditions that essentially make them otherwise uninsurable, are being debated by the Senate Health Policy Committee; the pool concept is supported by Blue Cross Blue Shield of Michigan and contested by a number of consumer groups and competing health insurers.

42787 ■ "Nationwide Bank Ready for December Conversion" in Business First-Columbus (October 15, 2007, pp. A1)
Pub: American City Business Journals, Inc.
Ed: Adrian Burns. **Description:** Nationwide Bank will increase marketing to its customers, including the 45,000 that came from the acquisition of Nationwide Federal Credit Union in December 2006. Upgrading its online banking system and Website will bring the company and its services closer to clients. The influence of the insurance industry on the bank's marketing strategy is also examined.

42788 ■ "New Database Brings Cincinnati Doctors Out of the Dark" in Business Courier (Vol. 26, October 23, 2009, No. 26, pp. 1)
Pub: American City Business Journals, Inc.
Contact: Whitney Shaw, President
Ed: James Ritchie. **Description:** A database created by managed care consulting firm Praesentia allows doctors in Cincinnati to compare average reimburse-

ments from health insurance companies to doctors in different areas. Specialist doctors in the city are paid an average of $172.25 for every office consultation.

42789 ■ "New Health Law, Lack of Docs Collide on Cape Cod" in Boston Business Journal (Vol. 27, October 12, 2007, No. 37, pp. 1)
Ed: Mark Hollmer. **Description:** There is a shortage of primary care providers at Outer Cape Health Services in Massachusetts, with the isolation of the area and as physicians look for higher paying careers in specialty positions. The Commonwealth Health Insurance Connector Authority is pushing for a new health insurance law and is working with Cape Cod Chamber of Commerce to conduct outreach programs.

42790 ■ "Nixon Assails Insurance Rules" in Globe & Mail (March 4, 2006, pp. B5)
Ed: Sinclair Stewart. **Description:** The opinions of chief executive officer Gordon Nixon of Royal Bank of Canada on the need to amend banking regulations, in order to provide insurance services, are presented.

42791 ■ "North American Pet Health Insurance Market Poised for Growth" in Pet Product News (Vol. 64, December 2010, No. 12, pp. 4)
Pub: Bowtie Inc.
Ed: David Lummis. **Description:** The pet health insurance market is expected to further grow after posting about $350 million in sales in 2009, a gain of more than $40 million. Pet insurance firms have offered strategies such as product humanization in response to this growth forecast. Meanwhile, pet insurance shoppers have been provided more by insurance firms with wider choices.

42792 ■ "Norvax University Health Insurance Sales Training and Online Marketing Conference" in Marketwired (January 27, 2010)
Pub: COMTEX News Network Inc.
Contact: Chip Brian, President
Description: Overview of the Norvax University Marketing and Sales Success Conference Tour which includes insurance sales training seminars, proven and innovative online marketing techniques and a host of additional information and networking opportunities.

42793 ■ "Now the Real Work Begins" in Baltimore Business Journal (Vol. 28, October 15, 2010, No. 23, pp. 1)
Pub: Baltimore Business Journal
Ed: Emily Mullin. **Description:** The Henry J. Kaiser Family Foundation's survey shows nearly 53 percent of Americans remain confused about health care reform and it was up to the states to educate the people. However, Maryland is still trying to figure out how to conduct the campaign without guidance or funding from the Federal government.

42794 ■ "Number-Cruncher Gets 'Pushback" in Philadelphia Business Journal (Vol. 33, August 22, 2014, No. 28, pp. 10)
Pub: American City Business Journals
Released: August 22, 2014. **Description:** Bryan Wellen, senior director of clinical informatics for Continuum Health Alliance (CHA), asserts that while some physicians are receptive to patient information, others respond with an element of 'pushback' and criticism of the data. CHA and Horizon Blue Cross Blue Shield of New Jersey are using data analysis to create strategies that improve health care and reduce costs.

42795 ■ "Obamacare Is Here, But Primary Docs Await New Patients" in Baltimore Business Journal (Vol. 32, June 6, 2014, No. 5, pp. 9)
Pub: American City Business Journals, Inc.
Contact: Whitney Shaw, President
Released: June 6, 2014. **Description:** Health care reform under the Affordable Care Act, sometimes referred to as Obamacare, has enabled millions of Americans to have health insurance. However,

primary care doctors in the Baltimore area and elsewhere have not seen the surge of patients many were expecting as a result of the Federal health reform. Those who have signed up for the health insurance are older and sicker than expected, with few young adults signing up, thus creating costly healthcare expenses.

42796 ■ "Of Paper Towels and Health Insurance" in Philadelphia Business Journal (Vol. 28, May 11, 2012, No. 13, pp. 1)
Pub: American City Business Journal
Description: Health insurance companies are using different strategies to take advantage of the demand growth in health coverage in markets such as Philadelphia. Horizon Blue Cross lue Shield of New Jersey, for example, is creating a retail center where customers can get information from specially trained staff about insurance, health and wellness. IBC, on the other hand, has partnered with AAA Mid-Atlantic to market its plan option to AAA members.

42797 ■ "Open Enrollment: Staying Healthy During Enrollment Season" in Employee Benefit News (Vol. 25, November 1, 2011, No. 14, pp. 41)
Pub: SourceMedia Inc.
Contact: James M. Malkin, Chief Executive Officer
Ed: Shana Sweeney. **Description:** Tips for staying healthy during your benefit open enrollment period are outlined.

42798 ■ "Passing It On: Using Life Insurance as an Estate Planning Tool" in Inc. (October 2007, pp. 47-49)
Pub: Mansueto Ventures L.L.C.
Contact: John Koten, Chief Executive Officer
Ed: Elaine Appleton Grant. **Description:** Permanent life insurance policies can be used to cover estate taxes for heirs inheriting large estates, while allowing them time to sell any small business. Six tips are included to assist in choosing the right policy.

42799 ■ "Patients to Elect to Cut Care" in The Business Journal-Serving Metropolitan Kansas City (Vol. 27, November 21, 2008, No. 11, pp. 1)
Pub: American City Business Journals, Inc.
Contact: Whitney Shaw, President
Ed: Rob Roberts. **Description:** Patients in Kansas City, Missouri are cutting down on health care services due to the economic crisis. A decline in diagnostic procedures has been observed at North-land Cardiology. Elective reconstructive procedures have also been reduced by 25 percent. Additional information and statistics regarding the healthcare sector is included.

42800 ■ "Patricia Hemingway Hall: President, Chief Operating Officer, Health Care Service Corp." in Crain's Chicago Business (May 5, 2008)
Pub: Crain Communications Inc.
Contact: Todd Johnson, Publisher
Ed: Mike Colias. **Description:** Profile of Patricia Hemingway Hall who is the president and chief operating officer of Health Care Service Corp., a new strategy launched by Blue Cross & Blue Shield of Illinois; the new endeavor will emphasize wellness rather than just treatment across its four health plans.

42801 ■ "PCH Gets Trauma Center Status" in The Business Journal - Serving Phoenix and the Valley of the Sun (Vol. 28, July 11, 2008, No. 45)
Ed: Angela Gonzales. **Description:** Phoenix Children's Hospital has been allowed by the Arizona Department of Health Services to launch the state's first trauma center for children. The trauma center is expected to cost the hospital $7 million a year.

42802 ■ "The People Puzzle; Re-Training America's Workers" in The Economist (Vol. 390, January 3, 2009, No. 8612, pp. 32)
Description: With thousands of workers losing their jobs, America is now facing the task of getting them back to work. With an overall unemployment rate of 6.7 percent, the federal government has three main ways for leading workers back to employment: train-

ing them for new jobs, providing unemployment insurance in order to replace lost wages during the period of job-hunting; and matching employers who desire a skill with workers who have that skill. Specialized staffing agencies provide employers and potential employees with the help necessary to find a job in some of the more niche markets.

42803 ■ "Planning a Wedding Fit for a Royal? Read This First, Urge Legal and General" in Benzinga.com (April 21, 2011)
Pub: Benzinga.com
Contact: Kyle Bazzy, President
Ed: Benzinga Staff. **Description:** When planning a wedding, the author suggests checking life insurance to be sure you are covered for any situations that may arise.

42804 ■ "Prairie States Enterprises Adds Senior Health Care Executive To Lead Sales to Self-Insured Organizations" in Benzinga.com (March 19, 2012)
Pub: Benzinga.com
Contact: Kyle Bazzy, President
Ed: Aaron Wise. **Description:** Prairie States Enterprises (PSE) is a third party administrator of self-funded employee group health benefits. PSE founded by registered nurse, Felicia Wilhelm and is headquartered in Chicago, Illinois.

42805 ■ "Prescription for Health: Choosing the Best Healthcare Plan for your workforce and your Bottom Line" in Black Enterprise (Vol. 38, July 2008, No. 12, pp. 48)
Pub: Earl G. Graves Publishing Co. Inc.
Contact: Earl G. Graves, Jr., President
Ed: Tamara E. Holmes. **Description:** According to a survey of small-business owners conducted by Sure-Payroll Inc., 20 percent of respondents have had a prospective employee refuse a job offer because healthcare benefits did not come with it. Cost is not the only reason many small-business owners do not offer these benefits. Guidelines to help take some of the confusion out of the guesswork that comes with trying to find the proper fit concerning healthcare benefits are outlined.

42806 ■ "The Price of Citizenship" in Canadian Business (Vol. 79, August 14, 2006, No. 16-17, pp. 13)
Ed: Jack Mintz. **Description:** Safety and insurance benefits provided by the Canadian government to Canadian passport holders returning from Lebanon, is discussed.

42807 ■ "Private Care's Next Phase: Serious Money Is Going Into Health Clinics" in Canadian Business (Vol. 85, June 11, 2012, No. 10, pp. 10)
Pub: George Media Inc.
Ed: Laura Cameron. **Released:** June 11, 2012. **Description:** Some public-private partnerships in Canada include the acquisition of clinics by Centric Health Corporation and the partnership between Westbank First National and Johns Hopkins Hospital. Private healthcare providers have operated by dividing their funding among government contracts, clients not covered by Medicare and patients paying out of pocket and non-insured services.

42808 ■ "Prognosis: Uncertain" in Entrepreneur (May 2014)
Pub: Entrepreneur Media Inc.
Released: May 2014. **Description:** The passage of the Patient Protection and Affordable Care Act has resulted in uncertainty for small business owners. The law has required health insurance coverage for companies with 50 or more full-time employees, placing additional costs on small businesses. It has also imposed additional administrative burdens such as reporting the scope of health insurance coverage for employees and tracking their actual number. Some businesses that are already paying for health insurance coverage opted to give their employees money to purchase their own insurance coverage plans.

42809 ■ "Public Health Care Funding and the Montana Economy" in Montana Business

Quarterly (Vol. 49, Spring 2011, No. 1, pp. 23)
Pub: University of Montana Bureau of Business and Economic Research
Contact: Patrick Barkey, Director
E-mail: patrick.barkey@business.umt.edu
Ed: Gregg Davis. **Description:** Montana has more baby boomers and veterans per capita than any other state in the nation. The role of public health in the state is a crucial part of the state's economy.

42810 ■ "Q&A: Take a Load Off Your HR" in Entrepreneur (May 2014)
Pub: Entrepreneur Media Inc.
Released: May 2014. **Description:** A Professional Employer Organization (PEO) manages all the human resource (HR) needs of a small business. The PEO can help the business save money by purchasing insurance and benefit plans at significant savings, assist with employment-regulatory compliance and ensure effective management and access to personnel records, among other things. Business owners should consider hiring PEOs who are financially responsible and stable. A business needs a PEO when the accounting department asks for a dedicated HR person to handle all the paperwork.

42811 ■ "Questions Abound in Voluminous Health Care Reform Law" in Memphis Business Journal (Vol. 34, July 6, 2012, No. 12, pp. 1)
Pub: American City Business Journal
Ed: Cole Epley. **Description:** US Supreme Court has upheld the health care reform legislation, also known as Obamacare, as the law of the land. However, key questions remain and conjecture surrounding which direction states and insurance providers will pursue abounds. Insights on possible impact of health care providers of TennCare are also given.

42812 ■ "Reaching Out: the LIFE Foundation Provides Free Tools and Resources to Help Agents Boost Their Life Insurance Sales" in Best's Review (Vol. 113, September 2012, No. 5, pp. 26)
Description: The LIFE Foundation's LIFE program is profiled. The program offers free tools and resources for life insurance agents.

42813 ■ "Recovery on Tap for 2010?" in Orlando Business Journal (Vol. 26, January 1, 2010, No. 31, pp. 1)
Pub: American City Business Journals
Ed: Melanie Stawicki Azam, Richard Bilbao, Christopher Boyd, Anjali Fluker. **Description:** Economic forecasts for Central Florida's leading business sectors in 2010 are presented. These sectors include housing, film and TV, sports business, law, restaurants, aviation, tourism and hospitality, banking and finance, commercial real estate, retail, health care, insurance, higher education, and manufacturing. According to some local executives, Central Florida's economy will slowly recover in 2010.

42814 ■ "Red Tape: A Business Opportunity" in Business Journal (Vol. 30, July 20, 2012, No. 8, pp. 1)
Pub: American City Business Journals, Inc.
Contact: Whitney Shaw, President
Ed: Katharine Grayson. **Released:** July 20, 2012. **Description:** The transition from the International Statistical Classification of Diseases and Related Health Problems (ICD)-9 coding system to ICD-10 creates business opportunities for software and professional services companies in Minneapolis, Minnesota. Coding-related products and services are being offered to help healthcare providers and insurers comply with the 2014 federal mandate.

42815 ■ "Rehab Centers Flourish Under Obamacare" in Puget Sound Business Journal (Vol. 35, August 1, 2014, No. 15, pp. 8)
Pub: American City Business Journals
Released: August 1, 2014. **Description:** Hospitals are looking to partner with long-term care and rehabilitation facilities that can continue care with discharged patients in compliance with the Affordable

Care Act. The government regulated insurance coverage could mean better follow-up care and less spending and waste in the health care system.

42816 ■ "Rich or Poor, Hospitals Must Work Together" in Crain's Chicago Business (Vol. 31, April 28, 2008, No. 17, pp. 22)
Pub: Crain Communications Inc.
Contact: Todd Johnson, Publisher
Description: Chicago-area safety-net hospitals that serve the poor, uninsured and underinsured are struggling to stay open while wealthier areas compete to build advanced facilities for the expensive surgical procedures their privately insured patients can afford. If these safety-net hospitals close, their patients, many of them in ambulances, will show up at the remaining hospitals resulting in a strain that will test the ability of hospitals across the region to care for all of their patients. Hospitals need to address the threats to the local health care system before it slips into crisis since the current every-hospital-for-itself approach that pays off big for some will eventually will make losers of everyone.

42817 ■ "Ride Apps Uber, Lyft, Sidecar Hit Speed Bumps" in San Francisco Business Times (Vol. 28, January 24, 2014, No. 27, pp. 4)
Pub: American City Business Journals
Released: January 24, 2014. **Description:** California's Public Utilities Commission (PUC) has reversed its earlier prohibition and allowed mobile app ride services, while imposing insurance and safety regulations on these alternatives to taxicabs and limousine services. However, the PUC did not take action when the issue of liability and insurance were raised due to the death of Sofia Liu, who was hit by an Uber driver. The lawsuits against Uber are discussed.

42818 ■ "Riding Herd on Health Care" in Business Journal Portland (Vol. 30, February 7, 2014, No. 49, pp. 8)
Pub: American City Business Journals
Released: February 7, 2014. **Description:** Singing rancher and aspiring gubernatorial candidate, Jon Justesen, explains his views on universal healthcare. He expresses support for health care reform and Cover Oregon and he is looking at his options after dropping his Republican primary bid.

42819 ■ "Rising Above Flood-Insurance Costs" in Providence Business News (Vol. 28, February 3, 2014, No. 44, pp. 1)
Pub: American City Business Journals
Released: February 3, 2014. **Description:** Businesses are advised to examine flood insurance costs when rebuilding or expanding their facilities. Some firms choose to elevate their buildings in response to the redrawing of Federal Emergency Management Agency flood maps and regulations. The process for getting a flood-elevation survey is also explored.

42820 ■ "RPA Preps for Building Radiant Conference, Show" in Contractor (Vol. 57, January 2010, No. 1, pp. 5)
Pub: Penton Media, Inc.
Description: Radiant Panel Association is accepting registrations for its Building Radiant 2010 Conference and Trade Show. The conference will discuss radiant heating as well as insurance and other legal matters for mechanical contractors.

42821 ■ "Sacramento-Based Dental Insurer Agrees to Sale" in Sacramento Business Journal (Vol. 31, April 11, 2014, No. 7, pp. 4)
Pub: American City Business Journals
Released: April 11, 2014. **Description:** New York-based Guardian Life Insurance Company of American agreed to acquire Sacramento, California-based Premier Access Insurance Company that provides dental insurance to more than 634,000 members in five states and Mexico. Guardian's existing dental network in several states will be strengthened by the proposed deal. The potential layoff in Sacramento is also discussed.

42822 ■ "A Safety Net in Need of Repair" in The Economist (Vol. 390, January 3, 2009, No. 8612, pp. 33)
Description: America's unemployment-insurance scheme is outdated and skimpy compared to other industrialized countries despite the fact that Ameri-

cans tend to work harder at returning to the job market; the benefits are lower and available for a smaller amount of time and less unemployed workers are even able to collect these benefits. Statistical data included.

42823 ■ "Sam Zell In Talks To Buy Normandale Office Park" in Business Journal (Vol. 30, June 8, 2012, No. 2, pp. 1)
Pub: American City Business Journals, Inc.
Contact: Whitney Shaw, President
Ed: Sam Black. **Released:** June 8, 2012. **Description:** Chicago billionaire real estate investor, Sam Zell, has been in negotiation to purchase Normandale Lake Office Park in Bloomington, Minnesota. New York-based Teachers Insurance and Annuity Association-College Retirement Fund has hired Cushman & Wakefield/NorthMarq to sell the multitenant office park.

42824 ■ "Sluggish Market Gives Hospitals the Financial Chills" in The Business Journal-Serving Greater Tampa Bay (Vol. 28, August 4, 2008)
Pub: American City Business Journals, Inc.
Contact: Whitney Shaw, President
Ed: Margie Manning. **Description:** Operating margins for hospitals in the Tampa Bay, Florida area have been reduced from 2 percent in 2006 to 0.8 percent in 2007 due to a weaker US economy. Total margins, on the other hand, rose from 2.9 percent to 3.3 percent in the same period.

42825 ■ "Small Biz Owners Are Tapping Into Health Savings Plans" in Small Business Opportunities (Fall 2007)
Ed: Michael L. Corne. **Description:** Health savings accounts were developed by Golden Rule, a United Healthcare company. Today, more than 40 percent of the company's customers are covered by health savings account plans.

42826 ■ Small Business Access and Alternatives to Health Care: Hearing before the Committee on Small Business, U.S. House of Representatives
Pub: DIANE Publishing Co.
Contact: Dorothy J. Perkins, Manager
E-mail: dorothyjperkins@hotmail.com
Released: 2003. **Price:** $35, paperback. **Description:** Congressional hearings regarding the health care crisis facing America's small businesses is discussed.

42827 ■ Small Business Desk Reference
Pub: Penguin Books USA Inc.
Released: December 2004. **Price:** $29.95. **Description:** Comprehensive guide for starting or running a successful small business, focusing on buying a business or franchise, writing a business plan, financial management, accounting, legal issues, human resources management, operations, marketing, sales, customer service, taxes, insurance, and ethics. Information for launching a restaurant, property management firm, retail outlet, consulting firm, and service business is included.

42828 ■ "Small Businesses Changing Their Health Plan Preferences" in Boston Business Journal (Vol. 29, June 24, 2011, No. 7, pp. 1)
Pub: American City Business Journals, Inc.
Ed: Scott Dance. **Description:** Small businesses in Maryland are shifting from traditional health plans to the consumer-oriented health savings accounts or HSAs. Health insurance industry experts say the change is indicative of the insurance buyers' desire to be more thrifty and discerning in their health care purchases.

42829 ■ "Small Businesses Gain Health Exchange Access" in Puget Sound Business Journal (Vol. 35, September 5, 2014, No. 20, pp. 6)
Pub: American City Business Journals
Released: September 5, 2014. **Description:** The government of Washington is planning to offer small businesses employee health coverage through the state's health exchange. Kaiser Health Plan of the Northwest and Moda Health Plan Inc. have received

approval to sell 23 health plans inside the health exchange. Small businesses qualify for tax breaks by providing employee health plans.

42830 ■ "Small, But Mighty" in Employee Benefit News (Vol. 25, November 1, 2011, No. 14, pp. 32)
Pub: SourceMedia Inc.
Contact: James M. Malkin, Chief Executive Officer
Ed: Andrea Davis. Description: Three consulting firms are facing the challenge of helping clients understand the new health care reform in a tight economy.

42831 ■ "Smart Questions: Health Care: How to Get a Better Deal" in Inc. (November 2007, pp. 34)
Pub: Mansueto Ventures L.L.C.
Contact: John Koten, Chief Executive Officer
Ed: Sarah Goldstein. Description: Things to consider when choosing an insurance carrier for your employees are explored.

42832 ■ "The Smell of Fear: Is a Bottom Near?" in Barron's (Vol. 88, March 17, 2008, No. 11, pp. M3)
Pub: Dow Jones & Co., Inc.
Contact: Clare Hart, President
Ed: Kopin Tan. Description: Liquidity problems at Bear Stearns frightened investors in markets around the world due to the fear of the prospects of a big bank's failure. Shares of health maintenance organizations got battered led by WellPoint, and Humana but longer-term investors who could weather short-term volatility may find value here. The value of J. Crew shares is also discussed.

42833 ■ "Spouses, Health Coaching Added to Mix" in Pittsburgh Business Times (Vol. 33, June 6, 2014, No. 47, pp. 5)
Pub: American City Business Journals
Released: June 6, 2014. Description: Hospital giant, UPMC, was the Category Winner in the 5,000+ employees group of Healthiest Employers in Western Pennsylvania, for its initiative in expanding its health assessment and wellness programs to the spouses and partners of all its employees, regardless of their health insurance carrier. In addition, UPMC Health Plan expanded its individual health coaching option for members as well as corporate clients.

42834 ■ Starting & Running Your Own Horse Business
Pub: Storey Publishing, LLC
Contact: Pam Art, President
Ed: Mary Ashby McDonald. Released: November 04, 2009. Price: $19.95, paperback. Description: Insight into starting and running a successful equestrian business is given. The book covers safety, tips for operating a riding school or horse camp, strategies for launching a carriage business, along with tax and insurance advice. Availability: Print.

42835 ■ "State Pressure Keeps Rates Low" in Sacramento Business Journal (Vol. 31, August 8, 2014, No. 24, pp. 4)
Pub: American City Business Journals
Released: August 8, 2014. Description: The proposed California Covered rate increases are likely to hit an average 4.2 percent in 2015, with the average increase in Sacramento expected at 3.7 percent. The health insurance exchange was set up to be an active purchaser so that it differs with the proposed exchange in other states, which range from 8 percent to 20 percent. Insights on the advantages of Covered California are presented.

42836 ■ "Steeling for Battle" in Crain's Chicago Business (Vol. 31, April 21, 2008, No. 16, pp. 3)
Pub: Crain Communications Inc.
Contact: Todd Johnson, Publisher
Ed: Bob Tita. Description: Discusses contract negotiations between the United Steelworkers union and ArcelorMittal USA Inc., the nation's largest steelmaker, and U.S. Steel Corp., the third-largest; the union sees these negotiations as the best chance in two decades to regain lost ground but industry experts predict the companies will try to reduce

benefits, demand a separate, lower wage scale for new hires and look for relief from the rising costs for retirees' health insurance coverage.

42837 ■ "Struggling States Slashing Health Care For Poor" in Chicago Tribune (January 15, 2009)
Pub: McClatchy-Tribune Information Services
Ed: Noam N. Levey. Description: Health officials warn that even the huge federal rescue plan may not be enough to restore health services being eliminated due to the economic crisis.

42838 ■ "Survivorship Policies: Planning a Policy for Two" in Employee Benefit News (Vol. 25, November 1, 2011, No. 14, pp. 20)
Pub: SourceMedia Inc.
Contact: James M. Malkin, Chief Executive Officer
Ed: Marli D. Riggs. Description: Survivorship insurance is becoming an added benefit high net worth individuals and executives should consider when evaluating life insurance policies.

42839 ■ "Sutter, CHW Reject Blue Cross Deal" in Sacramento Business Journal (Vol. 25, August 15, 2008, No. 24, pp. 1)
Pub: American City Business Journals, Inc.
Contact: Whitney Shaw, President
Ed: Kathy Robertson. Description: California-based Sutter Health and Catholic Healthcare West have rejected the $11.8 million class action settlement in connection with contract rescissions between California hospitals and Anthem Blue Cross. Blue Cross can halt the settlement if not enough hospitals accept it. The deal covers all hospitals that owe money due to rescinded Blue Cross coverage.

42840 ■ "Symbility Solutions Joins Motion Computing Partner Program" in Marketwired (May 14, 2007)
Pub: Comtex News Network Inc.
Description: Symbility Solutions Inc., a wholly owned subsidiary of Automated Benefits Corp., announced an agreement with Alliance Partner of Motion Computing, a leader in wireless communications and mobile computing, in which both companies will invest in a sales and marketing strategy that focuses specifically on the insurance market.

42841 ■ "Synergy Coverage Solutions Buys Foundation For The Carolinas' Building" in Charlotte Business Journal (Vol. 25, December 17, 2010, No. 39, pp. 1)
Pub: Charlotte Business Journal
Ed: Will Boye. Description: Charlotte, North Carolina-based Synergy Coverage Solutions has purchased the three-story building owned by Foundations For the Carolinas for slightly more than $3 million. Synergy plans to relocate its operation in the uptown building by August 2011.

42842 ■ "Taking Full Advantage: What You Need To Know During Open-Enrollment Season" in Black Enterprise (Vol. 38, November 2007, No. 4)
Pub: Earl G. Graves Publishing Co. Inc.
Contact: Earl G. Graves, Jr., President
Ed: Donald Jay Korn. Description: Employees can change or enroll in new insurance benefits during the fall season. It is important to assess each plan offered and to determine your deductible. Statistical data included.

42843 ■ "Tax Tip: Affordable Health Care and Taxes" in Pet Product News (Vol. 66, September 2012, No. 9, pp. 39)
Pub: Bowtie Inc.
Ed: Mark E. Battersby. Description: Implications of the US Supreme Court's ruling that the Affordable Care Act is now part of the Tax Code on small retail businesses, business owners, and self-employed persons are described. The ruling requires every individual to have health insurance to avoid tax penalties.

42844 ■ "Tenacious Trailblazer: Sandra Hernandez, Public Health Pioneer, is Hispanic Business Woman of the Year®" in Hispanic

Business (Vol. 30, April 2008, No. 4, pp. 26)
Pub: Hispanic Business Inc.
Contact: Jesus Chavarria, President
Ed: Melinda Burns. Description: Dr. Sandra Hernandez has been named as Hispanic Business Woman of the Year for her pioneering work in health care reform. Dr. Hernandez is the first Hispanic and the first woman to serve as public health director for the city and county of San Francisco.

42845 ■ "Thousands Balk at Health Law Sign-Up Mandate" in Boston Business Journal (Vol. 27, November 9, 2007, No. 41, pp. 1)
Ed: Mark Hollmer. Description: About 100,000 Massachusetts residents have not signed up for insurance plans created as part of the state's health care reform law. Insurers have underestimated the number of new customers signing up for insurance and come close to risking penalties if they do not get insurance by the end of 2007. The Commonwealth Health Insurance Connector Authority's deadline to buy insurance before penalties kick in is November 15, 2007.

42846 ■ "Three Alabama Insurers Will Owe $4M In Rebates" in Birmingham Business Journal (Vol. 29, July 6, 2012, No. 28, pp. 1)
Pub: American City Business Journals, Inc.
Contact: Whitney Shaw, President
Ed: Evan Belanger. Released: July 6, 2012. Description: US Supreme Court's ruling on the health care reform has resulted in the mandatory payment of rebates by three health insurance firms. Golden Rule Insurance Company owes $2.58 million in rebates. Blue Cross and Blue Shield of Alabama, on the other had, is not slated to pay rebates in 2012.

42847 ■ "Top 50 In Total Revenue" in Canadian Business (Vol. 81, Summer 2008, No. 9, pp. 119)
Description: Table showing the top 50 Canadian companies in terms of total revenue is presented. Manulife Financial Corp. topped the list with revenue of 34.5 billion. The financial services firm is the 6th largest provider of life insurance in the world and the second largest in North America.

42848 ■ "Top Insurance Agencies" in South Florida Business Journal (Vol. 34, May 2, 2014, No. 41, pp. 10)
Pub: American City Business Journals
Released: May 2, 2014. Description: Rankings of insurance agencies in the South Florida area are presented. Rankings were based on the 2013 premium volume.

42849 ■ "Trailing Indicator: This Issue: EI Form Reform" in Canadian Business (Vol. 85, July 16, 2012, No. 11-12, pp. 73)
Pub: George Media Inc.
Ed: James Cowan. Released: July 16, 2012. Description: An employment questionnaire designed to ensure that Canadians are aware of the improvements made by the federal government to the Employment Insurance (EI) system is presented. Questions related to the Temporary Foreign Worker program is also included.

42850 ■ "Tropeano Takes Charge" in Philadelphia Business Journal (Vol. 33, August 22, 2014, No. 28, pp. 11)
Pub: American City Business Journals
Released: August 22, 2014. Description: Dan Tropeano will serve as the new head of United Healthcare of Pennsylvania, while continuing in his position as executive director of United Healthcare's Pennsylvania and Delaware health plans. Tropeano discusses his new role and notes that the medical insurance market has become increasingly competitive as consumers seek cheaper and more flexible products.

42851 ■ "Trusted Choice: Mobile App" in Best's Review (Vol. 113, September 2012, No. 5, pp. 14)
Description: Profile of Trusted Choice, the new mobile app launched in March 2012 for use on smartphones and tablet computers. The app helps clients contact their independent insurance agent. Consumers can keep an inventory of insured personal pos-

sessions, document a car accident with photos, read insurance tips, communicate with Trusted Choice agent and ask insurance-related questions.

42852 ■ *"United Insurance To Grow St. Pete's Corporate Base" in The Business Journal-Serving Greater Tampa Bay (August 29, 2008)*
Pub: American City Business Journals, Inc.
Contact: Whitney Shaw, President

Ed: Margie Manning. **Description:** United Insurance Holdings LC is on its way to becoming a public company by agreeing in a reverse merger with FMG Acquisition Corp. The $104.3 million agreement will provide the company's St. Petersburg operations the opportunity to grow. The other impacts of the proposed reverse merger are examined.

42853 ■ *"U.S. Combined Life and Health Writers--Industry's Reported Admitted Assets of $5.7 Trillion" in Best's Review (Vol. 113, September 2012, No. 5, pp. 33)*
Description: U.S. Combined Life and Health Writers--Industry's Reported Admitted Assets of $5.7 Trillion report is presented. Companies/Groups are ranked in 2011 by admitted assets.

42854 ■ *"UnitedHealthcare Resists Prognosis" in The Business Journal-Serving Metropolitan Kansas City (Vol. 26, August 29, 2008, No. 51)*
Ed: Rob Roberts. **Description:** Saint Luke's Hospital Systems terminated UnitedHealthcare from its insurance provider network on July 25, 2008. Negotiators with both parties have stopped speaking, and employees under UnitedHealthcare plans will have to pay higher bills unless Saint Luke's reconsiders its decision. The parties' previous negotiations are discussed.

42855 ■ *"Va. Stalls on Health Exchange" in Washington Business Journal (Vol. 31, July 6, 2012, No. 11, pp. 2)*
Pub: American City Business Journals, Inc.
Contact: Whitney Shaw, President

Ed: Ben Fischer. **Released:** July 6, 2012. **Description:** Political leaders and health insurance companies in Virginia are at odds over the creation of a health benefits exchange in the state. Industry leaders want a swift creation of an online health benefits exchange, while conservative politicians in the state resist the creation of such an exchange.

42856 ■ *"Virtually Secure" in Rough Notes (Vol. 155, February 2012, No. 2, pp. 46)*
Pub: The Rough Notes Company Inc.
Contact: Walter J. Gdowski, President
Released: February 2012.

42857 ■ *"VPA to Pay $9.5 Million to Settle Whistle-Blower Lawsuits" in Crain's Detroit Business (Vol. 26, January 11, 2010, No. 2, pp. 13)*
Pub: Crain Communications Inc.
Contact: Rance E. Crain, President

Ed: Jay Greene. **Description:** According to Terrence Berg, first assistant with the U.S. Attorney's Office in Detroit, Voluntary Physicians Association, a local home health care company, has agreed to pay $9.5 million to settle four whistle-blower lawsuits; the agreement settles allegations that VPA submitted claims to TriCare, the Michigan Medicaid program and Medicare for unnecessary home visits, tests and procedures.

42858 ■ *"We Have a Budget, Too" in Entrepreneur (Vol. 37, October 2009, No. 10, pp. 89)*
Pub: Entrepreneur Press
Contact: Perlman Neil, President

Ed: Craig Matsuda. **Description:** One human resources executive at a financial services company claims that health care issues are as costly and irritating for companies as they are for the employees. Health care vendors and insurers try as much as possible to maximize profits, while companies exert much effort to maximize benefits for their workers.

42859 ■ *"Week on the Web" in Crain's Detroit Business (Vol. 25, June 22, 2009, No. 25, pp. 19)*
Pub: Crain Communications Inc. - Detroit
Contact: Keith Crain, Chairman
Description: Blue Cross Blue Shield of Michigan, in a class-action lawsuit, will pay about 100 families whose children were either denied coverage for autism treatment or paid for treatment out of pocket. The settlement is worth about $ million.

42860 ■ *"Western & Southern to Trim Rich Retirement Plan" in Business Courier (Vol. 27, October 15, 2010, No. 24, pp. 1)*
Pub: Business Courier

Ed: Dan Monk. **Description:** Insurance firm Western & Southern Financial Group announced that it will reduce the pension benefits of its 4,000 associates by more than 30 percent starting January 1, 2011. The move is expected to reduce annual retirement payments by several thousand dollars per associate. Western is a Fortune 500 company and has $34 billion in total assets.

42861 ■ *"What Choice Did I Have?" in Entrepreneur (Vol. 37, October 2009, No. 10, pp. 88)*
Pub: Entrepreneur Press
Contact: Perlman Neil, President

Ed: Craig Matsuda. **Description:** Profile of a worker at a financial services company who acquired first hand knowledge concerning the relationship between health insurance costs and coverage. The worker's son got severely ill, forcing the worker to spend above what is covered by health insurance.

42862 ■ *"Why Seattle Children's Appealed" in Puget Sound Business Journal (Vol. 35, May 30, 2014, No. 6, pp. 6)*
Pub: American City Business Journals
Released: May 30, 2014. **Description:** Seattle Children's Hospital filed an appeal against the Washing State Office of the Insurance Commissioner for approving several health exchange plans that excluded the hospital. Children's argues that it offers unique services and treatments only available through their medical facility and health insurance plans excluding them is putting children at risk.

42863 ■ *"Will Other Insurers Follow United's Lead?" in Birmingham Business Journal (Vol. 29, June 22, 2012, No. 26, pp. 1)*
Pub: American City Business Journals, Inc.
Contact: Whitney Shaw, President

Ed: Evan Belanger. **Released:** June 22, 2012. **Description:** UnitedHealtcare will continue offering patient protections as required by US health reform law. But United controls five percent of Alabama's health insurance market. Provisions of patient protections being offered by the company are also discussed.

42864 ■ *"Work At It!" in Hawaii Business (Vol. 53, October 2007, No. 4, pp. 44)*
Pub: PacificBasin Communications

Ed: Cathy S. Cruz-George. **Description:** Employers in Hawaii are mitigating the effects of rising healthcare costs by giving their employees health insurance and offering wellness programs. Employer-based health insurance has increases by 87 percent in the United States over the 2000-2006 period. Wellness programs that address different aspects of employees' health, such as food consumption, drug compliance and smoking habits, are discussed.

42865 ■ *"Work/Life Balance" in Dallas Business Journal (Vol. 37, June 20, 2014, No. 41, pp. 4)*
Pub: American City Business Journals
Released: June 20, 2014. **Description:** Younger generations of corporate employees are increasingly looking for a more engaged workplace community. Research firm, Quantum Workplace, identifies several trends that help to attract and retain employees, including jobs that align with the workers' own values, growth opportunities within the firm, social interactions with co-workers, and employee health benefits.

42866 ■ *"Workers' Comp May Pose Double Trouble for Companies in 2013" in Orlando Business Journal (Vol. 29, August 31, 2012, No. 11, pp. 1)*
Pub: American City Business Journal
Description: Companies are in for some difficulties with two waves of workers' compensation increases by 2013. In addition to a 20 percent increase of all workers' compensation premiums in Florida that was approved in July, the Florida Office of Insurance Regulation will consider a 6.1 percent increase in October. Bases for the proposed salary increase are discussed.

42867 ■ *"Workplace Wellness" in Entrepreneurs (June 2014)*
Pub: Entrepreneur Media Inc.
Released: June 2014. **Description:** Workplace wellness programs can be started by checking with insurers who may provide program and activity suggestions promotional materials or other resources. Teaming up with others is encouraged. For instance, employees from various departments or nearby companies can get flu shots or blood pressure screening. Management should also get involved in these programs, because it will then be known among employees that wellness is taken seriously. It is also important that workplace wellness programs are kept safe and legally sound.

42868 ■ *"The Worst-Run Industry in Canada: Health Care" in Canadian Business (Vol. 83, October 12, 2010, No. 17, pp. 39)*
Pub: Rogers Media Inc.
Contact: Tony Viner, President

Ed: Rachel Mendleson. **Description:** Most Canadians believe that the problem of the country's health care system is rooted in insufficient funding, demographic overload, or corporate profiteering. However, health economists and policy analysts think the real issues is mismanagement, as the pervasive inefficiency is affecting the system's structure.

TRADE PERIODICALS

42869 ■ *The John Liner Letter*
Pub: Standard Publishing Corp.
Contact: John C. Cross, President
E-mail: j.cross@spcpub.com
Ed: Robert Montgomery, Editor. **Released:** Monthly. **Price:** $262, U.S.; $340.60, elsewhere. **Description:** Provides risk management and technical insurance advice for business firms, such as broadening coverage, cutting costs, and anticipating special insurance problems.

42870 ■ *Risk & Insurance Magazine*
Pub: LRP Publications Library
Contact: Kenneth Kahn, President
E-mail: kKahn@lrp.com
URL(s): www.riskandinsurance.com/. Ed: Cyril Tuohy, Managing Editor. **Released:** Monthly; semi-monthly in April, September and October. **Description:** Provides business executives and insurance professionals with the insight, information and strategies they need to mitigate challenging business risks. Discusses a wide variety of business risks and mitigation strategies from insurance, employee benefits and alternative risk transfer to emerging risks and the strategies for addressing them.

VIDEOCASSETTES/ AUDIOCASSETTES

42871 ■ *Going Bare: Crisis in Insurance*
New Jersey Network (NJN)
25 S Stockton St.
Trenton, NJ 08608
Ph: (609)777-5273
Free: 800-792-8645
Fax: (609)643-4004
Co. E-mail: productioncenter@njn.org
Contact: Janice Selinger, Director
Released: 1988. **Description:** Examines the history of the insurance industry, price wars between insurance companies, and small businesses who are without liability insurance because of extremely high premiums. **Availability:** VHS; 3/4 U.

CONSULTANTS

42872 ■ A.E. Roberts Co.
11490 Xeon St. NW, Ste. 200
Coon Rapids, MN 55448-3111
Ph: (763)757-5119
Free: 800-486-4585
Fax: (413)215-6877
Contact: Mark Mosiman, Owner
Scope: Specializes in compliance training, focusing on regulatory compliance and human resource management issues. **Founded:** 1989. **Seminars:** ADA Seminar; COBRA Seminar; FMLA Seminar; HIPAA Privacy Seminar; HIPAA Portability Seminar; Section 125 Cafeteria Plans Seminar.

42873 ■ Leonard R. Friedman Risk Management Inc. (LRF/RM)
170 Great Neck Rd., Ste. 140
Great Neck, NY 11021-3337
Ph: (516)466-0750
Fax: (516)466-0997
Co. E-mail: info@lrfrm.com
URL: http://www.lrfrm.com
Contact: Alice B. Weiss, Vice President
Scope: Provider of risk and insurance management and safety and claims managements services to corporations across the country. Analyzes exposure to loss, audits insurance contracts, structures competitive bidding, reviews contracts and leases, implements and monitors safety and claims management programs and recommends risk transfer programs to reduce exposure to loss. Industries served: profit and nonprofit companies engaged in retail, manufacturing, distributing, hospitality, real estate and service.

42874 ■ Health Insurance Specialists Inc. (HISI)
17620-B Redland Rd.
Rockville, MD 20855
Ph: (301)590-0006
Fax: (301)590-0661
Co. E-mail: info@his-inc.com
URL: http://www.his-inc.com
Scope: Services: Insurance and financial planning solutions. **Founded:** 1982.

42875 ■ Siver Insurance Consultants [E W Siver & Associates Inc.]
805 Executive Center Dr. W, Ste. 110
Saint Petersburg, FL 33702
Ph: (727)577-2780
Fax: (727)579-8692
Co. E-mail: gerickson@siver.com
URL: http://www.siver.com
Contact: Theresa Conley, Consultant
Scope: Services: Insurance advice and consultancy. **Founded:** 1970. **Seminars:** Third Party Administrators Performance Audit: Self Funded Group Medical Programs; Self Funded Workers Compensation Programs.

42876 ■ United Insurance Consultants Inc. [UIC Inc.]
1 Park Way, 3rd Fl.
Upper Saddle River, NJ 07458
Ph: (201)661-5010
Fax: (201)221-7529
Co. E-mail: tpalmer@uici.com
URL: http://www.uici.com
Contact: Thomas A. Kovatch, President
Scope: An independent insurance consulting firm that informs and educates clients of the importance of properly protecting the value of their business.

Helps companies understand their insurance contracts, costs involved in properly protecting their assets and liability exposures. **Founded:** 1978.

FRANCHISES AND BUSINESS OPPORTUNITIES

42877 ■ Paul Davis Restoration Inc.
1 Independent Dr., Ste. 2300
Jacksonville, FL 32202-5020
Ph: (904)737-2779
Free: 800-722-1818
Fax: (904)737-4204
Co. E-mail: info@pdrestoration.com
URL: http://www.pdrestoration.com
Contact: Scott Baker, President
E-mail: sbaker@pdrestoration.com
Description: Computerized contracting and cleaning services to the insurance industry. **No. of Franchise Units:** 230. **Founded:** 1966. **Franchised:** 1971. **Equity Capital Needed:** $45,000-$144,000 emergency service; $180,000-$240,000 restoration. **Franchise Fee:** $29,000 or $75,000. **Financial Assistance:** Yes. **Training:** 4 week training at corporate headquarters, followed by 1 week of onsite training at new franchise location.

42878 ■ Paul's Professional Window Washing Franchise Inc.
Paul's Prof. Window Washing Inc.
2707 Foothill Blvd.
La Cresenta, CA 91214
Ph: (818)249-7917
Fax: (818)249-7806
Description: Residential window cleaning company. **No. of Company-Owned Units:** 1. **Founded:** 1981. **Franchised:** 2004. **Equity Capital Needed:** $42,500-$76,000 initial investment. **Franchise Fee:** $17,500. **Training:** Yes.

42879 ■ Puroclean - The Paramedics of Property Damage
PuroSystems, Inc.
6001 Hiatus Rd., Ste. 13
Tamarac, FL 33321
Free: 800-775-PURO
Fax: (800)995-8527
Co. E-mail: sales@puroclean.com
URL: http://www.puroclean.com
Description: Property damage restoration. **No. of Franchise Units:** 275. **Founded:** 1989. **Franchised:** 1990. **Equity Capital Needed:** $74,710-$99,825. **Franchise Fee:** $45,000. **Financial Assistance:** Yes. **Training:** Provides 3 weeks at corporate training center & 1 week field training covering customer service, marketing/advertising, computer software, product knowledge, management, & hands-on application with ongoing 24 hour support.

COMPUTERIZED DATABASES

42880 ■ *Business Insurance*
Crain Communications Inc.
1155 Gratiot Ave.
Detroit, MI 48207-2732
Ph: (313)446-6000
Co. E-mail: info@crain.com
URL: http://www.crain.com
Contact: Rance E. Crain, President
URL(s): www.businessinsurance.com. **Released:** Weekly **Price:** $799, Individuals data + print and digital; $149, Individuals print & digital; $125, Individuals digital edition. **Availability:** Online: LexisNexis; Crain Communications Inc. **Type:** Full-text.

LIBRARIES

42881 ■ Anderson Kill P.C. - Library
1717 Pennsylvania Ave. NW, Ste. 200
Washington, DC 20006
Ph: (202)416-6500
Fax: (202)416-6555
Co. E-mail: akodc@andersonkill.com
URL: http://www.andersonkill.com
Scope: Insurance - property, fire, medical disability, casualty; law - civil, insurance. **Services:** Interlibrary loan; library not open to the public. **Holdings:** Books and periodicals. **Subscriptions:** 15 journals and other serials; 4 newspapers.

42882 ■ Buffalo & Erie County Public Library - Business, Science & Technology
1 Lafayette Sq.
Buffalo, NY 14203-1823
Ph: (716)858-8900
Fax: (716)858-6211
URL: http://www.buffalolib.org
Contact: Nancy Mueller, Division Manager
Scope: Investments, real estate, economics, marketing, engineering, computer science, technology, medical information for laymen, consumer information, automotive repair. **Services:** Interlibrary loan; copying; library open to the public. **Founded:** 1952. **Holdings:** 312,916 books; 60,516 bound periodical volumes; 600 periodical. **Subscriptions:** 2908 journals and other serials; 4 newspapers.

42883 ■ Long & Levit Library
465 California St., 5th Fl.
San Francisco, CA 94104
Ph: (415)397-2222
Fax: (415)397-6392
Co. E-mail: info@longlevit.com
URL: http://www.longlevit.com
Scope: Insurance; environment; professional liability; construction. **Services:** Interlibrary loan; copying; library open to the public at librarian's discretion. **Founded:** 1927. **Holdings:** 10,000 books. **Subscriptions:** 75 journals and other serials; 4 newspapers.

42884 ■ National Association of Professional Insurance Agents (PIA) - Library
400 N Washington St.
Alexandria, VA 22314
Ph: (703)836-9340
Fax: (703)836-1279
Co. E-mail: web@pianet.org
URL: http://www.pianet.com
Contact: Mike Becker, Chief Executive Officer
E-mail: mikebe@pianet.org
Description: Represents independent agents in all fifty states, Puerto Rico and the District of Columbia. Represents members' interests in government and industry; provides educational programs; compiles statistics; conducts research programs; develops products/services unique to independent agencies; provides information and networking opportunities. **Scope:** Anti-Semitism, insurance, insurance law. **Services:** Library not open to the public. **Founded:** 1931. **Holdings:** 1400 volumes. **Publications:** *Consumer Brochures for Your Clients*; *PIA Connection* (10/year); *Professional Agent* (Monthly). **Awards:** Agent of the Year (Annual); Company Representative of the Year (Annual); PIA National Company Award of Excellence (Annual); National Company Representative of the Year (Annual); PIA National Professional Agent of the Year (Annual); CSR of the Year (Annual).

FARM CREDIT ADMINISTRATION

42885 ■ *"Transforming the Business Portfolio: How Multinationals Reinvent Themselves" in Journal of Business Strategy (Vol. 35, May-June 2014, No. 3, pp. 4-17)*
Emerald Group Publishing Inc.
Brickyard Office Park
84 Sherman St.
Cambridge, MA 02140
Ph: (617)945-9130
Fax: (617)945-9136
Co. E-mail: america@emeraldinsight.com
URL: http://www.emeraldinsight.com
Released: May-June 2014. **Description:** Study on the process of business portfolio transformations to investigate its precursors, practices, and outcomes, including repositioning, refocusing, and diversifying of portfolio restructurings is presented. It is observed that poor performance and over-diversification induce portfolio restructuring. The results also revealed that diversifying or repositioning transformations feature a low success rate, whereas refocusing transformations generally happen to be more successful.

TENNESSEE VALLEY AUTHORITY

42886 ■ *"Six Ways Employees on LinkedIn Benefit the Boss" in South Florida Business Journal (Vol. 34, April 25, 2014, No. 40)*
American City Business Journals (ACBJ)
Released: April 25, 2014. **Description:** LinkedIn can be a useful tool for executives. In addition to finding staff when hiring, the information service can give U.S.-based users a more global perspective. It can also be a way to share recent company accomplishment.

START-UP INFORMATION

42887 ■ *Canadian Small Business Kit for Dummies*
Pub: CDG Books Canada Inc.
Contact: Tom Best, President
E-mail: tbest@cdgbooks.com
Ed: Margaret Kerr, JoAnn Kurtz. **Released:** March 2007. **Price:** , $37.99 (Canadian). **Description:** Entrepreneurial guide to starting and running a small business in Canada.

42888 ■ *The Canadian Small Business Survival Guide: How to Start and Operate Your Own Successful Business*
Pub: Dundurn Group
Contact: Kirk Howard, President
E-mail: khoward@dundurn.com
Ed: Benj Gallander. **Released:** April 2002. **Price:** $26.99, paperback; $12.99. **Description:** Ideas for starting and running a successful small business.

Topics include selecting a business, financing, government assistance, locations, franchises, and marketing ideas. **Availability:** PrintE-book.

42889 ■ *"CrowdFunding Platform, START.ac, Announces It Is Expanding Its International Scope From the US, Canada and the UK to 36 Countries Including Australia, India, Israel, Italy and Africa" in Benzinga.com (July 11, 2012)*
Pub: Benzinga.com
Contact: Kyle Bazzy, President
Released: July 11, 2012. **Description:** START.ac is expanding its CrowdFunding site to include 36 countries and increasing its scope to include business startups, teen projects, as well as medical products. START.ac projects are in the fundraising stage at this point, with 23 percent located outside the United States.

42890 ■ *"The Fashion Designer Survival Guide, Revised and Expanded Edition: Start and Run Your Own Fashion Business"*
Pub: Kaplan Publishing
Released: March 10, 2009. **Price:** , $22.95 paperback. **Description:** Author, industry authority, and fashion designer consultant offers insights and critical business information for starting and maintaining a successful independent clothing designer business. Fabric and material needs; loans or investments for the startup; challenges for working from a home-based venture as well as internationally; marketing, branding, and selecting retail stores to display your designs; creating an image and getting public attention.

42891 ■ *International Entrepreneurship: Starting, Developing, and Managing a Global Venture*
Pub: Pine Forge Press
Contact: Blaise R. Simqu, President
Ed: Robert D. Hisrich. **Released:** Second Edition. **Price:** $79, paperback. **Description:** International entrepreneurship combines the aspects of domestic entrepreneurship along with other disciplines, including anthropology, economics, geography, history, jurisprudence, and language. **Availability:** Print.

42892 ■ *"Savvy Solutions" in Black Enterprise (Vol. 41, September 2010, No. 2, pp. 46)*
Pub: Earl G. Graves Publishing Co. Inc.
Contact: Earl G. Graves, Jr., President
Ed: Tennille M. Robinson. **Description:** Insight is given to help start an import and export business.

ASSOCIATIONS AND OTHER ORGANIZATIONS

42893 ■ **American Association of Exporters and Importers (AAEI) - Library**
1050 17th St. NW, Ste. 810
Washington, DC 20036
Ph: (202)857-8009

Fax: (202)857-7843
Co. E-mail: hq@aaei.org
URL: http://www.aaei.org
Contact: Kate Terricciano, Chairperson
Description: Exporters and importers of goods, products, and raw materials; wholesalers and retailers; customs brokers and forwarders; banks; insurance underwriters; steamship companies; customs attorneys and others engaged directly or indirectly in dealing with exports and imports. Seeks fair and equitable conditions for world trade. Anticipates problems of interpretation of laws and regulations affecting members' businesses; gathers and disseminates data on world trade; supports and creates legislation promoting balanced international trade; works for fair administration of policy. Maintains liaison with government committees, agencies, and other trade policy groups. Studies problems concerning export and import. **Scope:** Importing, exporting, wholesaling, retailing, banking, insurance. **Founded:** 1921. **Publications:** *International Trade Alert* (Weekly).

42894 ■ **American Hellenic Institute (AHI)**
1220 16th St. NW
Washington, DC 20036
Ph: (202)785-8430
Fax: (202)785-5178
Co. E-mail: nlarigakis@ahiworld.org
URL: http://www.ahiworld.org
Contact: Nick Larigakis, President
Description: Seeks to strengthen political, cultural, trade, commerce, and related matters between the U.S. and Greece, Cyprus, and the American Hellenic community. Conducts research on issues such as Turkish threats to the Aegean, Cyprus, the rule of law, and human rights. Sponsors internship program and seminars. **Founded:** 1974. **Publications:** *AHI Report* (3/year); *American Hellenic Who's Who*; *General News*; *Handbook on United States Relations with Greece and Cyprus*; *Rule of Law and Conditions on Foreign Aid to Turkey.* **Educational Activities:** Hellenic Heritage and National Public Service Awards Dinner (Annual).

42895 ■ **American Indonesian Chamber of Commerce (AICC)**
317 Madison Ave., Ste. 1619
New York, NY 10017
Ph: (212)687-4505
Fax: (212)867-5844
Co. E-mail: wayne@aiccusa.org
URL: http://www.aiccusa.org
Contact: Wayne Forrest, President
Description: Holds briefings on new trade policies in Indonesia and offers orientation workshops to company personnel traveling to Indonesia. **Founded:** 1949. **Publications:** *American Business Directory for Indonesia* (Periodic); *Executive Diary*; *Members Bulletin* (Periodic); *Outlook Indonesia* (Quarterly); *Sourcing Products in Indonesia: A Guide for Importers.*

42896 ■ **American Israel Chamber of Commerce - Southeast Region (AICC)**
400 Northridge Rd., Ste. 250
Sandy Springs, GA 30350

Ph: (404)843-9426
Fax: (404)843-1416
Co. E-mail: aiccse@aiccse.org
URL: http://www.aiccse.org
Contact: Tom Glaser, President
Description: American and Israeli companies. Promotes increased trade between Israel and the United States, with emphasis on increasing Israeli-American trade involving companies in the southeastern U.S. Facilitates networking and contact development involving Israeli and U.S. corporations; makes available trade mentoring and matchmaking services; sponsors educational programs. **Founded:** 1992. **Publications:** *Latest Southeast-Israel Business News* (Monthly).

42897 ■ American-Uzbekistan Chamber of Commerce (AUCC)
1300 Connecticut Ave. NW, Ste. 501
Washington, DC 20036
Ph: (202)223-1770
Co. E-mail: info@aucconline.com
URL: http://www.aucconline.com
Contact: Carolyn B. Lamm, Chairman of the Board
Description: Brings together companies and individual professionals interested in promoting trade and investment between Uzbekistan and the United States. Represents business and industry to promote growth in interest of the U.S. business community in Uzbekistan. **Founded:** 1993.

42898 ■ Australian Trade Commission (AUSTRADE)
150 E 42nd St., 34th Fl.
New York, NY 10017-5612
Ph: (646)344-8111
Fax: (212)867-7710
Co. E-mail: info@austrade.gov.au
URL: http://www.austrade.gov.au
Contact: Bruce Gosper, Chief Executive Officer
Description: Works in the promotion of Australian products and investments in the U.S. **Publications:** *Export Update* (Monthly).

42899 ■ Austrian Trade Commission (ATC)
120 W 45th St., 9th Fl.
New York, NY 10036
Ph: (212)421-5250
Fax: (212)421-5251
Co. E-mail: newyork@advantageaustria.org
Description: Promotes U.S.-Austrian trade with particular emphasis on Austrian exports to the U.S.; identifies Austrian trade sources to meet U.S. commercial demand. Handles inquiries related to trade between the two nations and deals with issues such as customs duties, trade laws, and licensing. Compiles statistics. Sponsors trade exhibits. **Founded:** 1950.

42900 ■ Austrian Trade Commissions in the United States (ATCUSC)
11601 Wilshire Blvd., Ste. 2420
Los Angeles, CA 90025
Ph: (310)477-9988
Fax: (310)477-1643
Co. E-mail: losangeles@advantageaustria.org
URL: http://www.advantageaustria.org/us
Contact: Rudolf Thaler, Commissioner
Description: Corporations in Austria, Canada and the United States. Promotes increased trade between the U.S., Canada, and Austria. Works to remove legislative barriers to international trade; represents members before international trade organizations and agencies; facilitates establishment of joint ventures and other international business connections involving members.

42901 ■ Brazilian-American Chamber of Commerce (BACC)
509 Madison Ave., Ste. 304
New York, NY 10022
Ph: (212)751-4691
Fax: (212)751-7692
URL: http://www.brazilcham.com
Contact: Vicente J. Bonnard, President
Description: Corporations, partnerships, financial institutions, and individuals either in the U.S. or Brazil interested in fostering two-way trade and investment between the countries. Compiles statistics and

provides special mailings, press releases, information, and business contacts. Maintains files on business and trade information. Sponsors breakfast briefings, luncheons, seminars and gala dinners. **Founded:** 1968. **Publications:** *Brazilian-American Who's Who* (Irregular); *Brazilian-American Business Review/Directory* (Annual). **Awards:** Person of the Year (Annual).

42902 ■ Brazilian Government Trade Bureau of the Consulate General of Brazil in New York (BGTB)
220 E 42nd St.
New York, NY 10017-5806
Ph: (917)777-7777
Fax: (212)827-0225
Co. E-mail: cg.novayork@itamaraty.gov.br
URL: http://novayork.itamaraty.gov.br/en-us
Description: Commercial Office of the Brazil Consulate in New York. Offers online match between Brazilian exporters of goods and services and U.S. importers. **Founded:** 1936.

42903 ■ British Trade Office at Consulate-General
845 3rd Ave.
New York, NY 10022
Ph: (212)745-0200
Fax: (212)745-0456
URL: http://www.gov.uk/government/world/organisations/british-consulate-general-new-york
URL(s): www.projectvisa.com/embassydetail.asp?seednum=3008. **Description:** British government office that promotes trade with the U.S.; assists British companies selling in the U.S.; aids American companies that wish to import goods from or invest in Britain.

42904 ■ BritishAmerican Business Inc. of New York and London
52 Vanderbilt Ave., 20th Fl.
New York, NY 10017
Ph: (212)661-4060
Fax: (212)661-4074
Co. E-mail: nyinfo@babinc.org
URL: http://www.babinc.org
Contact: Richard Fursland, Chief Executive Officer
E-mail: nrosier@babinc.org
Description: Works to increase the trade and investment between the U.S. and the U.K. by offering member companies a full range of transatlantic business services, information, and contacts. **Publications:** *American British Business Handbook* (Annual); *British American Business Handbook* (Annual); *BritishAmerican Business Inc. - Membership Directory* (Annual); *Investment News* (Monthly); *Issue Insight* (Quarterly); *Network London* (Quarterly); *Network New York* (Quarterly); *British American Business Inc.--Membership Directory* (Annual); *British-American Chamber of Commerce--UK and US Investment Directory* (Biennial); *The UK/USA Investment Directory & Business Resource* (Biennial); *UK & USA* (Quarterly); *UK and USA Directory of Investment* (Semimonthly).

42905 ■ Canada-United States Business Association (CUSBA)
2000 Town Center Ste. 1800
Southfield, MI 48075
Co. E-mail: info@cusbaonline.com
URL: http://www.canadainternational.gc.ca/detroit/commerce_can/ba-ab.aspx?lang=eng
Contact: Mark R. High, President
Description: Consists of supporters of business such as labor, banking, consulting, government, and academia. Promotes stronger business and trading lineages between the U.S. and Canada by providing a forum to exchange information and ideas and to build relationships. Conducts educational programs; maintains speakers' bureau, panels, and special events. **Founded:** 1992.

42906 ■ Canadian-American Business Council (CABC)
1900 K St. NW, Ste. 100
Washington, DC 20006
Ph: (202)496-7906

Fax: (202)496-7756
Co. E-mail: info@cabc.co
URL: http://cabc.co
Contact: Ms. Emma Rigby, Executive Director
Description: Individuals, corporations, institutions and organizations with an interest in trade between the United States and Canada. Promotes free trade. Gathers and disseminates information; maintains speakers' bureau. **Founded:** 1987. **Educational Activities:** Pharmaceuticals Conference. **Awards:** Canadian-American Business Achievement Award (Annual).

42907 ■ Colombian American Association (CAA)
641 Lexington Ave., Ste. 1430
New York, NY 10022
Ph: (212)233-7776
Fax: (212)233-7779
Co. E-mail: info@andean-us.com
URL: http://www.colombianamerican.org
Contact: Christian Murrle, President
Description: Facilitates commerce and trade between the Republic of Colombia and the U.S. Fosters and advances cultural relations and goodwill between the two nations. Encourages sound investments in Colombia by Americans and in the U.S. by Colombians. Disseminates information in the U.S. concerning Colombia. **Founded:** 1927.

42908 ■ Council of the Americas (CoA)
680 Park Ave.
New York, NY 10065
Ph: (212)249-8950
Fax: (212)249-5868
Co. E-mail: communications@as-coa.org
URL: http://www.as-coa.org
Contact: Susan L. Segal, President
Description: Promotes on behalf of its members, policies and practices favoring free trade and investment, market economies and the rule of law in West Hemisphere. Provides a forum for its members to discuss economic, political and social issues relevant to the Hemisphere with public and private sector leaders. Represents the membership in public policy discussions. Assists members in the achievement of their business objectives in the region. **Founded:** 1965.

42909 ■ Danish American Chamber of Commerce (DACC)
1 Dag Hammarskjold Plz.
885 2nd Ave., 18th Fl.
New York, NY 10017-2201
Ph: (646)790-7169
Co. E-mail: daccny@daccny.com
URL: http://www.daccny.com
Contact: Daniel Skaven Ruben, General Manager
Description: Danish and American business leaders; firms and institutions. Functions as an advisory board to support and promote commercial relations between the United States and Denmark, in both directions; makes itself available for consultation with the Danish diplomatic representatives in the U.S. and to the U.S. Department of Commerce, as well as to trade groups and members in Denmark and the U.S. Attempts to avoid duplication of governmental activities. **Founded:** 1974.

42910 ■ Federation of International Trade Associations (FITA)
172 5th Ave., No. 118
Brooklyn, NY 11217
Ph: (703)634-3482
Free: 888-491-8833
Co. E-mail: info@fita.org
URL: http://www.fita.org
Contact: Kimberly Park, President
Description: Fosters international trade by strengthening the role of local, regional, and national associations throughout the United States, Mexico, and Canada that have an international mission; affiliates are 450 independent international associations. **Founded:** 1984. **Publications:** *Directory of North American Trade Association* (Annual); *FITA's Really Useful Sites* (Biweekly). **Awards:** Really Useful Sites Award (Biweekly).

42911 ■ Finnish American Chamber of Commerce (FACC)

20 W 20 St., Ste. 212
New York, NY 10011
Ph: (212)821-0225
Fax: (212)750-4418
Co. E-mail: faccnyc@verizon.net
URL: http://facc-ny.com
Contact: Jorma Sahlstedt, President
E-mail: jorma.sahlstedt@metsagroup.com
Description: Maintains liaison with similar groups abroad; conducts seminars; arranges meetings with speakers. **Founded:** 1958.

42912 ■ French-American Chamber of Commerce (FACC)

1350 Broadway, Ste. 2101
New York, NY 10018
Ph: (212)867-0123
Fax: (212)867-9050
Co. E-mail: info@faccnyc.org
URL: http://www.faccnyc.org
Contact: Elsa Berry, President
Description: Promotes trade between the U.S. and France and fosters economic, commercial and financial relations between the two countries. Functions in an advisory and informative capacity and assists in organizing business contacts for its members. Holds roundtable discussions, business card exchanges and other events. Sponsors educational programs. **Founded:** 1896. **Publications:** *French-American Chamber of Commerce-- Membership Directory* (Annual); *National Membership Directory of the French-American Chamber of Commerce* (Annual).

42913 ■ Global Offset and Countertrade Association (GOCA)

818 Connecticut Ave. NW, 12th Fl.
Washington, DC 20006
Ph: (202)887-9011
Fax: (202)872-8324
Co. E-mail: goca@globaloffset.org
URL: http://www.globaloffset.org
Contact: Mary O. Fromyer, Executive Director
Description: Promotes trade and commerce between companies and their foreign customers who engage in reciprocal trade, including offset and countertrade, as a form of doing business. **Founded:** 1986.

42914 ■ Guam Chamber of Commerce

173 Aspinall Ave., Ste. 101, Ada Plaza Ctr.
Hagatna, GU 96910
Ph: (671)472-6311
URL: http://www.guamchamber.com.gu
Contact: Peter R. Sgro, Jr., President
E-mail: psgros@ite.net
Description: Businesses and trade organizations. Promotes increased international trade and tourism. Gathers and disseminates information; conducts promotional activities; represents members' interests. **Founded:** 1924. **Publications:** *Directory of Members* (Annual); *President's Report* (Monthly); *Small Business Focus* (Quarterly); *Guam Chamber of Commerce--Directory of Members*; *The President's Report* (Monthly). **Educational Activities:** Guam Chamber of Commerce Meeting (Monthly). **Awards:** Commerce Scholarship Award (Annual); Small Business Awards (Annual).

42915 ■ Hellenic-American Chamber of Commerce

370 Lexington Ave., 27th Fl.
New York, NY 10017
Ph: (212)629-6380
Fax: (212)564-9281
Co. E-mail: hellenicchamber-nyc@att.net
URL: http://www.hellenicamerican.cc
Contact: John C. Stratakis, Director
Description: Promotes commerce and trade; represents members' interests. **Founded:** 1947.

42916 ■ Hong Kong Trade Development Council (HKTDC)

219 E 46th St.
New York, NY 10017
Ph: (212)838-8688

Fax: (212)838-8941
Co. E-mail: new.york.office@hktdc.org
URL: http://www.hktdc.com
Description: Quasi-governmental body responsible for promoting Hong Kong trade with the rest of the world and creating a favorable image for Hong Kong as a trading partner and international trade center. Sponsors trade missions and participates in major trade shows around the world. Maintains library of trade publications in both Hong Kong and its North American offices. Compiles statistics. **Founded:** 1966. **Publications:** *Hong Kong Apparel* (Quarterly); *Hong Kong Electronics* (Semiannual); *Hong Kong Enterprise* (Monthly); *Hong Kong for the Business Visitor* (Annual); *Hong Kong Gifts and Premiums* (Annual). **Educational Activities:** Hong Kong Electronics Fair (Annual); Hong Kong Fashion Week for Fall/Winter (Annual); Hong Kong Toys and Games Fair (Annual); Hong Kong Watch and Clock Fair (Annual).

42917 ■ Innovation Norway - United States [Norwegian Trade CouncilExport Council of Norway;]

655 3rd Ave., Ste. 1810
New York, NY 10017-9111
Ph: (212)885-9700
Fax: (212)885-9710
Co. E-mail: newyork@innovationnorway.no
URL: http://www.innovasjonnorge.no/Kontorer-i-utlan- det/usa-newyork/
Description: U.S. branch of the Export Council of Norway. Assists Norwegian companies in marketing their goods and services in the U.S. Provides information to Norwegian exporters on U.S. markets, tariffs and statistics, trade constraints, and distribution channels. Establishes contacts with U.S. authorities, marketing and manufacturing firms, local lawyers, accountants, banks, patent offices, advertising and public relations agencies, consultants, and credit and debt collection agencies. Aids in establishing Norwegian subsidiaries in the U.S. **Founded:** 1945.

42918 ■ Italian-American Chamber of Commerce (IACC)

500 N Michigan Ave., Ste. 506
Chicago, IL 60611
Ph: (312)553-9137
Fax: (312)553-9142
Co. E-mail: info@iacc-chicago.com
URL: http://www.iacc-chicago.com
Contact: Fulvio Calcinardi, Executive Director
Description: Promotes trade between Italy and the U.S. and aids Italian organizations and companies to promote their products and/or services in the U.S. Organizes trade missions to Italian trade shows and trade delegations of U.S. businesses in Italy to meet with companies and organizations. Represents CASIC-BIC Sardinia to promote foreign investments in the industrial area of Cagliari, Sardinia. **Founded:** 1907. **Publications:** *Italian American Chamber of Commerce of Chicago Bulletin* (Bimonthly).

42919 ■ Italy-America Chamber of Commerce (IACC)

730 5th Ave., Ste. 502
New York, NY 10019
Ph: (212)459-0044
Fax: (212)459-0090
Co. E-mail: info@italchamber.org
URL: http://www.italchamber.org
Contact: Alberto Comini, President
Description: Brings together businesses ranging from individual entrepreneurs to large corporations. Advances the interests of its members through contacts and interaction with government agencies, trade associations and leading international organizations. **Founded:** 1887. **Publications:** *Trade with Italy* (Bimonthly); *IACC Newsletter* (Monthly); *Trade With Italy* (Bimonthly); *United States - Italy Trade Directory* (Annual); *Trade with Italy* (Biennial). **Educational Activities:** Mifur - International Fur and Leather Exhibition (Annual). **Awards:** Business and Culture Award (Annual).

42920 ■ Japan External Trade Organization (JETRO)

1221 Ave. of the Americas
McGraw Hill Bldg., 42nd Fl.
New York, NY 10020

Ph: (212)997-0400
Fax: (212)997-0464
URL: http://www.jetro.org
Contact: Masaki Fujihara, Director
Description: Supports foreign companies in export and/or investment to Japan-related business ventures. Disseminates comprehensive information on the Japanese economy and market through surveys, reports, publications, and newsletters. Conducts trade and investment promotion seminars and symposia. Sponsors trade shows and exhibitions. Provides professional business consultation services and handles trade-related inquiries and provides opportunities for international exchange. **Founded:** 1958.

42921 ■ Japanese Chamber of Commerce and Industry of New York (JCCINY)

145 W 57th St.
New York, NY 10019
Ph: (212)246-8001
Fax: (212)246-8002
Co. E-mail: info@jcciny.org
URL: http://www.jcciny.org
Contact: Kazuhiro Takeuchi, President
Description: Japanese and non-Japanese corporations. Fosters improved trade relations between the U.S. and Japan. Conducts seminars and surveys. **Founded:** 1932. **Publications:** *Japan's Industries and Trade: Profiles and Interrelationships with the United States*; *Joining In! A Handbook for Better Corporate Citizenship in the U.S.*.

42922 ■ Joint Industry Group (JIG)

111 Rockville Pike, Ste. 410
Rockville, MD 20850
Ph: (202)466-5490
Fax: (202)559-0131
Co. E-mail: jig@moinc.com
URL: http://www.jig.org
Contact: Megan Giblin, Chairperson
Description: Trade associations and business and professional firms engaged in international trade. Seeks to influence administration of customs and related trade laws to facilitate trade and encourage compliance. **Founded:** 1976.

42923 ■ Latin Chamber of Commerce of U.S.A. [Camara de Comercio Latina de los EEUU]

1417 W Flagler St.
Miami, FL 33135
Ph: (305)642-3870
Fax: (305)642-0653
Co. E-mail: patricia@camacol.org
URL: http://www.camacol.org
Contact: Patricia Arias, Managing Director
Description: Provides placement services; compiles statistics. Maintains information and referral service. **Founded:** 1965. **Educational Activities:** Hemispheric Congress (Annual); CAMACOL Hemispheric Congress (Annual).

42924 ■ Moroccan American Business Council (MABC)

1085 Commonwealth Ave., Ste. 194
Boston, MA 02215-1002
Ph: (508)230-9943
Co. E-mail: moulay@usa-morocco.org
URL: http://www.usa-morocco.org
Contact: Moulay M. Alaoui, Chairman
Description: Promotes commerce and business between Morocco and the United States. **Founded:** 1995.

42925 ■ National Association of Export Companies (NEXCO)

Grand Central Station
New York, NY 10163
Free: 877-291-4901
Fax: (646)349-9628
Co. E-mail: director@nexco.org
URL: http://www.nexco.org
Contact: Barney Lehrer, President
Description: Established independent international trade firms, bilateral chambers of commerce, banks, law firms, accounting firms, trade associations, insurance companies, and product/service providers;

export trading companies; export management companies. Promotes expansion of U.S. trade. Promotes the participation of members in international trade. Conducts educational programs. **Founded:** 1963.

42926 ■ National Association of Foreign-Trade Zones (NAFTZ)
1001 Connecticut Ave. NW, Ste. 350
Washington, DC 20036
Ph: (202)331-1950
Fax: (202)331-1994
URL: http://www.naftz.org
Contact: Jan Frantz, Chairman of the Board
Description: Foreign-trade zone grantees, operators, and users; law firms, automobile manufacturers, port authorities, customs brokers, industrial firms, chambers of commerce, magazine and newspaper firms, development corporations, and concerned individuals. Aims to promote, stimulate, and improve foreign-trade zones and their utilization as integral and valuable tools in the international commerce of the U.S.; to encourage the establishment of foreign-trade zones to foster investment and the creation of jobs in the US. Sponsors seminars. **Founded:** 1973. **Publications:** *The Impact of Foreign Trade Zones on the 50 States and Puerto Rico*; *U.S. Foreign Trade Zones*; *Zones Report* (Monthly).

42927 ■ Netherlands Chamber of Commerce in the United States (NLCOC)
267 5th Ave., Ste. 910
New York, NY 10016-7503
Ph: (212)265-6460
URL: http://www.netherlands.org
Description: Aims to maintain and expand business relations between The Netherlands and the United States. **Founded:** 1903.

42928 ■ Norwegian-American Chamber of Commerce (NACC)
655 3rd Ave., Ste. 1810
New York, NY 10017
Ph: (212)885-9737
Co. E-mail: nacc@naccusa.org
URL: http://www.naccusa.org
Contact: Ole Schroder, President
Description: Promotes business and trade among members and between Norway and the United States. Provides networking opportunities and source information. **Founded:** 1915. **Publications:** *Norwegian American Commerce* (Quarterly); *Norwegian American Chamber of Commerce--Membership Directory* (Biennial). **Awards:** NACC Achievement Award (Annual); Trade Award (Annual).

42929 ■ Romanian-U.S. Business Council
620 8th Ave.
New York, NY 10018
Ph: (646)678-2905
Co. E-mail: info@usrobc.org
URL: http://usrobc.org
Description: Advocates American business interests with respect to U.S. Romanian trade and investments. Provides the American and Romanian business communities with a means of discussing bilateral trade and investment issues and the formulation of policy positions that will promote and expand economic relations between the two countries. Facilitates appropriate legislation and policies regarding trade between the U.S. and Romania. Has sponsored seminars on topics such as possibilities for cooperative commercial efforts in other countries and cooperation in energy development. **Founded:** 1974.

42930 ■ Society of International Business Fellows (SIBF)
Peachtree Center
South Tower
225 Peachtree St. NE, Ste. 1410
Atlanta, GA 30303
Ph: (404)525-7423
Fax: (404)525-5331
Co. E-mail: susan.folds@sibf.org
URL: http://www.sibf.org
Contact: Nancy Haselden, Executive Director
Description: Businesspeople active or with an interest in international trade. Promotes "enhancement of the international competitiveness and prosperity of its

members and the growth of the South as a vital region for global business." Works to strengthen personal and professional relations among members; conducts educational programs in international business and trade. **Founded:** 1981.

42931 ■ Spain-United States Chamber of Commerce - Library [Camera de Comercio Espana - Estados Unidos]
Empire State Bldg.
350 5th Ave., Ste. 2600
New York, NY 10118
Ph: (212)967-2170
Fax: (212)564-1415
Co. E-mail: info@spainuscc.org
URL: http://www.spainuscc.org
Contact: Xavier Ruiz, Chairman
Description: Spanish and U.S. business persons dedicated to the expansion of Spanish-American trade and goodwill. **Scope:** Spanish-American relations - trade, economics, statistics. **Services:** Library not open to the public (information requests by fax). **Founded:** 1959. **Holdings:** 1600 volumes. **Publications:** *Business Directories*; *Visa and Work Permits for the USA*; *Spain-United States Chamber of Commerce--Membership Directory*. **Educational Activities:** Tapas and Tarjetas. **Awards:** Business Leader of the Year Award (Annual).

42932 ■ Swedish Trade Council
150 N Michigan Ave., Ste. 1950
Chicago, IL 60601
Ph: (312)781-6222
Fax: (312)276-8606
Co. E-mail: usa@swedishtrade.se
URL: http://www.swedishtrade.se/english
Contact: James Armstrong, Associate
Description: Promotes Swedish exports and assists American companies in contacting Swedish suppliers. Performs market developments studies and research, partner searches, and project management. **Founded:** 1972. **Publications:** *Swedish Export Directory* (Annual).

42933 ■ Trans-Atlantic Business Council (TABC)
919 18th St. NW, Ste. 220
Washington, DC 20006
Ph: (202)828-9104
Fax: (202)828-9106
URL: http://transatlanticbusiness.org
Contact: Tim Bennett, Chief Executive Officer
Description: Represents over 50 major European and North American companies with a focus on promoting trans-Atlantic growth, bilateral trade, and investment in order to foster prosperity and stability between the U.S. and Europe. Committed to fortifying EU-US economic integration, growth and competitiveness. **Founded:** 1989.

42934 ■ U.S. Austrian Chamber of Commerce
165 W 46th St., Ste. 1113
New York, NY 10036
Ph: (212)819-0117
Co. E-mail: office@usaustrianchamber.org
URL: http://usaustrianchamber.org
Contact: Johannes P. Hofer, President
Description: Hosts receptions and luncheons. Sponsors Viennese Opera Ball, panel discussions, and business assistance. **Founded:** 1946. **Educational Activities:** Viennese Opera Ball (Annual).

42935 ■ United States Council for International Business (USCIB)
1212 Avenue of the Americas
New York, NY 10036
Ph: (212)354-4480
Fax: (212)575-0327
Co. E-mail: info@uscib.org
URL: http://www.uscib.org
Contact: Mr. Peter M. Robinson, President
E-mail: probinson@uscib.org
Description: Serves as the U.S. National Committee of the International Chamber of Commerce. Enables multinational enterprises to operate effectively by representing their interests to intergovernmental and governmental bodies and by keeping enterprises advised of international developments having a major impact on their operations. Serves as: U.S. represen-

tative to the International Organization of Employers; national affiliate to the U.S.A. Business and Industry Advisory Committee to the BIAC. Operates ATA Carnet export service, which enables goods to be shipped overseas duty-free for demonstration and exhibition. Sponsors seminars and luncheon briefings. **Founded:** 1945. **Publications:** *United States Council Foundation: Occasional Paper*. **Awards:** International Leadership Award (Annual); International Leadership Award (Annual).

42936 ■ United States Mexico Chamber of Commerce (USMCOC)
PO Box 14414
Washington, DC 20044
Ph: (703)752-4751
Fax: (703)642-1088
Co. E-mail: news-hq@usmcoc.org
URL: http://www.usmc.org
Contact: Al Zapanta, President
Description: U.S. businessmen and chambers of commerce in Mexico representing 350,000 companies. Works to promote private sector trade and investment between the United States and Mexico. Offers advice on economic, legal, and trade issues; informs members of long-range advantages of alternative plant locations. Works with both governments on the executive, legislative, and federal levels. Monitors legislation and regulations concerning trade issues critical to business development in both countries. Conducts seminars and luncheons. **Founded:** 1973. **Publications:** *United States-Mexico Chamber of Commerce--Membership Directory and Resource Guide*; *Chamber News* (Quarterly); *United States-Mexico Chamber of Commerce--Regional Newsletters* (Periodic). **Educational Activities:** NFTA Update. **Awards:** Good Neighbor Award (Annual); Good Neighbor Award (Annual).

42937 ■ U.S. Pan Asian American Chamber of Commerce (USPAACC)
1329 18th St. NW
Washington, DC 20036
Ph: (202)296-5221
Fax: (202)296-5225
Co. E-mail: info@uspaacc.com
URL: http://www.uspaacc.com
Contact: Susan Au Allen, President
Description: Businesspersons and professionals united to promote contract, education and other opportunities for Asian American businesses and their partners in corporate America and government agencies. Promotes programs and activities to help members pursue owning and growing their business; enter mainstream society; and participate in procurement, commerce, trade, investment and employment opportunities in corporate America and government. Conducts educational and networking activities. Maintains scholarship fund. Holds business colloquies. Sponsors speakers' bureau. Conducts research and charitable programs. **Founded:** 1984. **Publications:** *East-West Report* (Quarterly); *East West Report* (Quarterly). **Educational Activities:** CelebrAsian Conference (Annual). **Awards:** Corporation of the Year (Annual); Government Agency of the Year (Annual); USPAACC Scholarships (Annual); USPAACC/Wells Fargo Asian Business Leadership Award (Annual); Paul Shearman Allen and Associate Scholarships; Asian American Scholarships; Bruce Lee Scholarships; Ruth Mu-Lan and James S.C. Chao Scholarships; Pepsico Scholarships; Philip Morris USA Scholarships; Drs. Poh Shien and Judy Young Scholarships; U.S. Pan Asian American Chamber of Commerce McDonald's Scholarships; U.S. Pan Asian American Chamber of Commerce UPS Scholarships.

42938 ■ U.S.-Russia Business Council (USRBC)
1110 Vermont Ave. NW, Ste. 350
Washington, DC 20005
Ph: (202)739-9180
Fax: (202)659-5920
Co. E-mail: info@usrbc.org
URL: http://www.usrbc.org
Contact: Daniel A. Russell, President
Description: U.S. corporations doing business in Russia. Promotes adoption of public policies conducive to international trade in both the United States

and Russia. Conducts lobbying activities; facilitates establishment of joint ventures involving U.S. and Russian companies; maintains bank of job listings; compiles trade statistics. Gathers and disseminates information on political, economic, and social issues affecting trade with Russia. **Scope:** Russia, international trade. **Founded:** 1993. **Subscriptions:** books periodicals. **Publications:** *Russia Business Watch* (Quarterly).

42939 ■ U.S.A. - Business and Industry Advisory Committee to the OECD (USA-BIAC)
13/15, Chaussee de la Muette
75016 Paris, France
Ph: 33 1 42300960
Fax: 33 1 42887838
Co. E-mail: biac@biac.org
URL: http://www.uscib.org
Contact: Phil O'Reilly, Chairman

URL(s): www.biac.org. **Description:** Sponsored by United States Council for International Business. Represents the United States on the Business and Industry Advisory Committee to the Organisation for Economic Co-Operation and Development. Acts as the official channel for conveying the views of the business community to the OECD in the fields of economics, finance, international trade, industrial relations, information and telecommunications policy investment, and taxation. **Founded:** 1962.

42940 ■ Venezuelan American Association of the United States (VAAUS)
641 Lexington Ave., Ste. 1430
New York, NY 10022
Ph: (212)233-7776
Fax: (212)233-7779
Co. E-mail: info@andean-us.com
URL: http://www.venezuelanamerican.org
Contact: Lourdes Jordan, President

Description: Financial institutions, businesses, organizations, and individuals interested in the expansion and improvement of trade and trade relations between Venezuela and the United States. Fosters cultural and commercial relations, facilitates investment between the U.S. and Venezuela, and promotes improved understanding between businesspersons of the two nations. Conducts informal meetings with speakers and discussions. **Founded:** 1936. **Publications:** *Venezuela News Bulletin* (Monthly).

EDUCATIONAL PROGRAMS

42941 ■ Creating a Positive, High-Energy Workplace (Onsite)
Padgett-Thompson Seminars
Rockhurst University CEC
14502 W 105th St.
Lenexa, KS 66215
Free: 800-349-1935
URL: http://www.findaseminar.com/tpd/Padgett-Thompson-Seminars.asp

URL(s): www.findaseminar.com/event1.asp?eventID=6680. **Description:** A seminar for those who want to gain crucial insights into increasing their bottom line by fostering an energized climate where anything is possible. **Audience:** Managers, supervisors, and team leaders .

42942 ■ Foreign Military Sales (Onsite)
Seminar Information Service Inc.
20 Executive Park, Ste. 120
Irvine, CA 92614
Ph: (949)261-9104
Free: 877-SEM-INFO
Fax: (949)261-1963
Co. E-mail: info@seminarinformation.com
URL: http://www.seminarinformation.com

URL(s): www.seminarinformation.com/qqbkmv/foreign-military-sales. **Price:** $1,260. **Description:** Contractors who want to engage in international contracting successfully and profitably must be able to navigate a complex web of statutes, regulations and policies governing FRMS, FMF and U.S. export controls. **Audience:** Manufacturers, exporters and advisors .

REFERENCE WORKS

42943 ■ "$600 Million, 270-Megawatt South Kent Wind Project Example of Investments Sought by Ontario Clean Technology Alliance at WINDPOWER 2012" in Investment Business Weekly (June 24, 2012, pp. 49)
Description: WINDPOWER 2012 will be held in Atlanta, Georgia. The event will announce news of the completed plans for a $600 million, 270-megawatt South Kent Wind joint venture between Pattern Energy Group LP and Samsung Renewable Energy Inc. A group of 11 regional and municipal partners called Ontario Clean Technology Alliance, partnered with federal and provincial trade and innovation ministries to attract more wind industry companies to the province.

42944 ■ "2015 Corporate Counsel Legal Pricing Guide - Mergers & Acquisitions" in Economics & Business Week (August 16, 2014, pp. 3)
Pub: NewsRX
Contact: Susan E. Hasty, Publisher

Released: August 16, 2014. **Description:** Research and Markets has added the 2015 Corporate Counsel Legal Pricing Guide - Mergers & Acquisitions to its report. The guide details how the mergers and acquisitions market for law firms has increased since the downturn in 2008-2009 due mostly to an improved economy, increased corporate liquidity and sometimes corporate tax policies of certain countries.

42945 ■ "ABB Could Still Engineer an Upside" in Barron's (Vol. 89, July 20, 2009, No. 29, pp. M6)
Pub: Dow Jones & Co., Inc.
Contact: Clare Hart, President

Ed: Goran Mijuk. **Description:** Swiss engineering company ABB can remain profitable as its power transmission and distribution activities continue to generate earnings. The company is also benefiting from increased exposure in emerging markets.

42946 ■ "Abroad, Not Overboard" in Entrepreneur (Vol. 36, April 2008, No. 4, pp. 68)
Pub: Entrepreneur Press
Contact: Perlman Neil, President

Ed: Crystal Detamore-Rodman. **Description:** Export-Import Bank is an agency created by the U.S. government to help exporters get credit insurance and capital loans by providing them with loan guarantees. The bank, being criticized as supporting more the bigger exporters, has allotted to smaller businesses a bigger portion of the annual credit being approved.

42947 ■ "According to the Chinese Zodiac, 2009 is the Year of the Ox" in Canadian Business (Vol. 81, December 8, 2008, No. 21, pp. 74)
Ed: Zarka Halas. **Description:** Forecasts for China in 2009 are presented. China is expected to maintain an 8 percent growth rate to keep the current labor market. A total of 68,000 companies have collapsed in China in the first half of 2008, while 2.5 million workers are likely to lose jobs in the Pearl River Delta by the end of 2008.

42948 ■ "Acquisition to Give Mylan Tax Benefits, Boost Sales" in Pittsburgh Business Times (Vol. 33, July 18, 2014, No. 53, pp. 3)
Pub: American City Business Journals

Released: July 18, 2014. **Description:** Mylan Inc.'s acquisition of Abbot's foreign specialty and branded generic drug business is a win situation for the company. The acquisition will help Mylan expand and diversify in the largest markets outside the U.S. as well as prove beneficial in growth through enhanced financial flexibility and a more competitive global tax structure.

42949 ■ "Actian, Data Transformed and Yellowfin BI Mashup Helps Kollaras Group Reap Big Data Rewards" in Computer

Business Week (August 28, 2014, pp. 22)
Pub: NewsRX
Contact: Susan E. Hasty, Publisher
Released: August 28, 2014. **Description:** Actian announced that Australian liquor, hospitality and property investment company, Kollaras Group can now access real-time analytics; fast, simple and accurate data warehousing; and Yellowfin's Business Intelligence (BI) platform is examined. The BI provides better insights and decision-making across diverse business units.

42950 ■ "Addition by Subtraction in Tokyo" in Barron's (Vol. 92, August 25, 2012, No. 38, pp. 20)
Pub: Dow Jones & Co., Inc.
Contact: Clare Hart, President
Ed: Kopin Tan. **Description:** Investors in Japan could benefit from the increase in management buyouts, particularly of small capitalization stocks. This increase would shrink the number of Japanese stocks, many of which are trading below book value.

42951 ■ "Adidas' Brand Ambitions" in Business Journal Portland (Vol. 27, December 10, 2010, No. 41, pp. 1)
Pub: Portland Business Journal
Ed: Erik Siemers. **Description:** Adidas AG, the second-largest sporting goods brand in the world, hopes to increase global revenue by 50 percent by 2015. The German company, which reported $14.5 billion sales, plans to improve its U.S. market. The U.S. is Adidas' largest, but also the most underperforming market for the firm.

42952 ■ "AF Expands in New Green Building in Gothenburg" in Ecology,Environment & Conservation Business (September 24, 2011, pp. 2)
Pub: Highbeam Research
Contact: Patrick Spain, Chief Executive Officer
Description: AF signed a ten-year tenancy contract with Skanska for the premises of its new green building in Gothenburg, Sweden. AF offers qualified services and solutions for industrial processes, infrastructure projects and the development of products and IT systems.

42953 ■ "Africa Rising" in Harvard Business Review (Vol. 86, September 2008, No. 9, pp. 36)
Pub: Harvard Business Review Press
Contact: Peter E. Walsh, Director
Ed: Vijay Mahajan. **Description:** Review of the book entitled, 'Africa Rising: How 900 Million African Consumers Offer More Than You Think' provides advice for marketing to those on the African continent.

42954 ■ "Agennix Completes Merger with German Giant" in Houston Business Journal (Vol. 40, December 25, 2009, No. 33, pp. 2)
Pub: American City Business Journals
Ed: Mary Ann Azevedo. **Description:** Agennix Inc. has completed its transformation into a German company after Germany-based GPC Biotech merged into the former publicly traded Agennix AG. One quarter of Agennix's 60 employees will remain in Houston. Details on Agennix's drug trials are examined.

42955 ■ "Airing It Out: Flanders Corp. Commits to Global Expansion" in The Business Journal-Serving Greater Tampa Bay (Vol. 28, July 14, 2008, No. 29, pp. 1)
Pub: American City Business Journals, Inc.
Contact: Whitney Shaw, President
Ed: Jane Meinhardt. **Description:** Flanders Corp. is planning to expand its business in Europe and Southeast Asia. The St. Petersburg, Florida-based company has about 2,800 employees and manufactures air filtration products for industrial and residential applications.

42956 ■ "All About The Benjamins" in Canadian Business (Vol. 81, September 29, 2008, No. 16, pp. 92)
Ed: David Baines. **Description:** Discusses real estate developer Royal Indian Raj International Corp., a company that planned to build a $3 billion 'smart

city' near the Bangalore airport; to this day nothing has ever been built. The company was incorporated in 1999 by Manoj C. Benjamin one investor, Bill Zack, has been sued by the developer for libel due to his website that calls the company a scam. Benjamin has had a previous case of fraud issued against him as well as a string of liabilities and lawsuits.

42957 ■ "All For One, None for All?" in Canadian Business (Vol. 83, October 12, 2010, No. 17, pp. 60)
Pub: Rogers Media Inc.
Contact: Tony Viner, President
Ed: Michael McCullogh. Description: The effect of the growth of Canada's overseas provincial trade offices on Canadian trade is discussed. Economic development commissions in the country have devised a single 'Consider Canada' campaign to pitch foreign investors. It is hoped that large cities will gain from banding together rather than competing against one another.

42958 ■ "All-Star Execs: Top CEO: Gordon Nixon" in Canadian Business (Vol. 80, November 24, 2008, No. 22, pp. 9)
Pub: Rogers Media Inc.
Contact: Tony Viner, President
Ed: Jeff Sanford. Description: Royal Bank of Canada (RBC) CEO, Gordon Nixon, believes the Canadian financial services segment is heavily regulated. Nixon also feels that it has become difficult for local banks to enter the market since foreign banks can easily come in and compete with them. His views on RBC's success are provided.

42959 ■ "Alliance Offers to Help Italian Workers Settle In" in Crain's Detroit Business (Vol. 25, June 15, 2009, No. 24, pp. 21)
Pub: Crain Communications Inc. - Detroit
Contact: Keith Crain, Chairman
Ed: Nancy Kaffer. Description: Italian American Alliance for Business and Technology will help workers arriving from Italy to transition to their new homes in the Detroit area.

42960 ■ "Allied Brands Loses Baskin-Robbins Franchise Down Under" in Ice Cream Reporter (Vol. 23, November 20, 2010, No. 12, pp. 2)
Description: Dunkin Brands, worldwide franchisor of Baskin-Robbins, terminated the master franchise agreement for Australia held by the food marketer Allied Brands Services.

42961 ■ "American Airlines Works to Keep Its Brand Aloft" in Dallas Business Journal (Vol. 35, May 18, 2012, No. 36, pp. 1)
Pub: American City Business Journal
Ed: Matt Joyce. Description: As American Airlines is undergoing restructuring, the company is planning to redesign its international aircraft as part of its marketing strategy. But the airline's efforts to improve its brand image present a challenge made difficult by labor relations. Labor unions representing American Airlines employees are fighting the company over their collective bargaining agreements.

42962 ■ American Chambers of Commerce Abroad
Pub: U.S. Chamber of Commerce
Contact: Thomas J. Donohue, President
E-mail: tdonohue@uschamber.com
URL(s): www.uschamber.comwww.uschamber.com/international/directory/default. Covers: 116 American chambers of commerce in 103 countries. Entries include: Name, address, phone, fax, title, telex, E-mail and web addresses, geographical area served, and subsidiary and branch names and locations. Arrangement: Geographical.

42963 ■ "The Americans Are Coming" in The Economist (Vol. 390, January 3, 2009, No. 8612, pp. 44)
Description: Student recruitment consultancies, which help place international students at universities in other countries and offer services such as interpreting or translating guidelines, are discussed; American universities who have shunned these agencies in the

past; the result has been that America underperforms in relation to its size with a mere 3.5 percent of students on its campuses that are from abroad.

42964 ■ "Ampm Focus Has BP Working Overtime" in Crain's Chicago Business (April 28, 2008)
Pub: Crain Communications Inc.
Contact: Todd Johnson, Publisher
Ed: John T. Slania. Description: Britian's oil giant BP PLC is opening its ampm convenience stores in the Chicago market and has already begun converting most of its 78 Chicago-area gas stations to ampms. The company has also started to franchise the stores to independent operators. BP is promoting the brand with both traditional and unconventional marketing techniques such s real or simulated 3D snacks embedded in bus shelter ads and an in-store Guitar Hero contest featuring finalists from a recent contest at the House of Blues.

42965 ■ Animal Spirits: How Human Psychology Drives the Economy, and Why it Matters for Global Capitalism
Pub: Princeton University Press
Contact: Shirley M. Tilghman, President
Ed: George A. Akerlof, Robert J. Shiller. Released: 2009. Price: $24.95; £16.95. Description: Psychological factors that led to the depressed economy and how it may impede a turnaround.

42966 ■ "Ann Alexander: Senior Attorney, Natural Resources Defense Council" in Crain's Chicago Business (Vol. 31, May 5, 2008, No. 18)
Pub: Crain Communications Inc.
Contact: Todd Johnson, Publisher
Ed: Emily Stone. Description: Profile of Ann Alexander who is the senior attorney at the Natural Resources Defense Council and is known for her dedication to the environment and a career spent battling oil companies, steelmakers and the government to change federal regulations. One recent project aims to improve the Bush administration's fuel economy standards for SUVs. Past battles include her work to prevent permits from slipping through the cracks such as the proposal by London-based BP PLC to dump 54 percent more ammonia and 35 percent more suspended solids from its Whiting, Indiana refinery into Lake Michigan-the source of drinking water for Chicago and its surrounding communities.

42967 ■ "Another Determinant of Entrepreneurship" in International Journal of Entrepreneurship and Small Business (Vol. 10, July 6, 2010)
Pub: Publishers Communication Group
Contact: Doug Wright, Director
Ed: Felix Pauligard Ntep, Wilton Wilton. Description: Interviews were carried out with entrepreneurs of Douala, Cameroon. These entrepreneurs believe that witchcraft existed and could bring harm to them or their enterprises.

42968 ■ "Arario Gallery Opens First American Space" in Art Business News (Vol. 34, November 2007, No. 11, pp. 14)
Description: Opening a new space in New York's Chelsea gallery district is Arario Gallery, a leader in the field of Asian contemporary art; the gallery will feature new works by Chinese artists at its opening.

42969 ■ "Areva Diversifies Further Into Wind" in Wall Street Journal Eastern Edition (November 29, 2011, pp. B7)
Pub: Dow Jones & Co., Inc.
Contact: Clare Hart, President
Ed: Max Colchester, Noemie Bisserbe. Description: French engineering company Areva SA is diversifying and moving away from nuclear energy projects. One sign of that is its recent discussion to construct 120 wind turbines to be located at two German wind farms. Such a deal, if signed, would be worth about US$1.59 billion.

42970 ■ "Arizona Firms In Chicago Go For Gold With '08 Games" in The Business Journal - Serving Phoenix and the Valley of

the Sun (Vol. 28, August 8, 2008, No. 49, pp. 1)
Ed: Patrick O'Grady. Description: More than 20 U.S. athletes will wear Arizona-based eSoles LLC's custom-made insoles to increase their performance at the 2008 Beijing Olympics making eSoles one of the beneficiaries of the commercialization of the games. Translation software maker Auralog Inc saw a 60 percent jump in sales from its Mandarin Chinese language applications.

42971 ■ "Around the World" in Entrepreneur (Vol. 36, March 2008, No. 3, pp. 82)
Pub: Entrepreneur Press
Contact: Perlman Neil, President
Ed: Gail Dutton. Description: Joining a global consortium can improve a business greater access to services and expertise from other members around the world. The goal is to develop the company to be able to reach to a wider customer base; other details on the benefits of joining a consortium are discussed.

42972 ■ "Around the World in a Day" in Agency Sales Magazine (Vol. 39, August 2009, No. 8, pp. 36)
Ed: Jack Foster. Description: Highlights of Manufacturer's Agents National Association (MANA) member Les Rapchak one-day visit to Basra, Iraq are presented. Rapchak completed the trip via Frankfurt, Germany and Kuwait with a stop afterwards in Istanbul, Turkey. His purpose for the trip was to take part in a seminar at the State Company for Petrochemical Industries.

42973 ■ "Asia Breathes a Sigh of Relief" in Business Week (September 22, 2008, No. 4100, pp. 32)
Ed: Bruce Einhorn; Theo Francis; Chi-Chu Tschang; Moon Ihlwan; Hiroko Tashiro. Description: Foreign bankers, such as those in Asia, that had been investing heavily in the United States began to worry as the housing crisis deepened and the impact on Freddie Mac and Fannie Mae became increasingly clear. Due to the government bailout, however, central banks will most likely continue to buy American debt.

42974 ■ "The Asian Decade" in Hawaii Business (Vol. 53, January 2008, No. 7, pp. 19)
Ed: Cathy S. Cruz-George. Description: Chaney Brooks, a Hawaiian real estate company, has affiliated with commercial real estate network NAI Global. The NAI partnership will improve Hawaii's international business, particularly its Asian investments. Hawaii's diverse workforce is evaluated, with regards to being an asset for international businesses.

42975 ■ Asian Godfathers: Money and Power in Hong Kong and Southeast Asia
Pub: Grove/Atlantic Inc.
Contact: Morgan Entrekin, President
E-mail: mentrekin@groveatlantic.com
Ed: Joe Studwell. Released: September 2008. Price: $15.95, paperback. Description: Expose of some of Southeast Asia's top business moguls is highlighted, along with a look into the region's economic and social cultures. Availability: Print.

42976 ■ "Au Revoir Or Goodbye?" in Barron's (Vol. 88, July 14, 2008, No. 28, pp. 5)
Pub: Dow Jones & Co., Inc.
Contact: Clare Hart, President
Ed: Alan Abelson. Description: Former Senator Phil Gramm's opinion that the U.S. is a 'nation of whiners' as they moan about recession is another example of the disconnection between Washington and Wall Street on one hand and the real world on the other. It would be a catastrophe for most of the world if Fannie Mae and Freddie Mac were to go under and take their trillions of mortgage debt with them.

42977 ■ "AV Concept Expands Into Green Energy Storage" in Wireless News (January 25, 2010)
Description: Electronics distributor and manufacturer AV Concept Holdings Limited announced a marketing partnership with Boston-Power, a provider of lithium-ion batteries, with a focus in the Chinese and Korean markets.

42978 ■ *"Awaiting a Call from Deutsche Telekom"* in Barron's (Vol. 90, September 6, 2010, No. 36, pp. M5)

Pub: Barron's Editorial & Corporate Headquarters

Ed: Vito J. Racanelli. **Description:** Deutsche Telekom's (DT) T-Mobile USA Unit has settled in the number four position in the market and the parent company will need to decide if it will hold onto the company in the next 12-18 months from September 2010. T-Mobile's rivals will make critical improvements during this time and DT has the option to upgrade T-Mobile at the cost of improvements to its other units.

42979 ■ *"B2B Commercial Collection Agency Accounts Fall"* in Managing Credit, Receivables & Collections (November 2010, No. 10-11, pp. 9)

Pub: Institute of Management & Administration Inc.

Contact: David L. Foster, President

E-mail: davidf@ioma.com

Description: A fall in the number of Business-To-Business collection accounts reflects the pace of the global economic recovery.

42980 ■ *"Back in the Race. New Fund Manager Has Whipped Sentinel International Equity Back into Shape"* in Barron's (Vol. 88, March 17, 2008, No. 11, pp. 43)

Pub: Dow Jones & Co., Inc.

Contact: Clare Hart, President

Ed: Leslie P. Norton. **Description:** Katherine Schapiro was able to get Sentinel International Equity's Morningstar classification to blended fund from a value fund rating after joining Sentinel from her former jobs at Strong Overseas Fund. Schapiro aims to benefit from the global rebalancing as the U.S.'s share of the world economy shrinks.

42981 ■ *"Back on Track-Or Off the Rails?"* in Business Week (September 22, 2008, No. 4100, pp. 22)

Pub: Bloomberg L.P.

Contact: Matthew Winkler, Manager

Ed: Peter Coy, Tara Kalwarski. **Description:** Discusses the possible scenarios the American economy may undergo due to the takeover of Fannie Mae and Freddie Mac. Statistical data included.

42982 ■ *Bad Samaritans: The Myth of Free Trade and the Secret History of Capitalism*

Pub: Bloomsbury USA

Ed: Ha-Joon Chang. **Released:** August 09, 2010. **Price:** $11.99; $17, paperback; $26.95, hardback. **Description:** Economist challenges open-market proponents and believes that free trade would do more harm than good. **Availability:** E-bookPrint.

42983 ■ *"Bank Takes Charge: Who Gets Last Laugh?"* in Barron's (Vol. 88, March 31, 2008, No. 13, pp. 17)

Pub: Dow Jones & Co., Inc.

Contact: Clare Hart, President

Ed: Leslie P. Norton. **Description:** Nord/LB will take a charge of 82.5 million euros to cover potential losses apparently related to Vatas' refusal to take the shares of Remote MDx Inc. after buying the shares. Remote MDx's main product is an ankle bracelet to monitor criminals; the firm has lost over half of its market cap due to the Nord/LB troubles and questions about its revenues.

42984 ■ *"Bargain Hunting In Vietnam"* in Barron's (Vol. 88, July 14, 2008, No. 28, pp. M6)

Pub: Dow Jones & Co., Inc.

Contact: Clare Hart, President

Ed: Elliot Wilson. **Description:** Vietnam's economy grew by just 6.5 percent for the first half of 2008 and its balance of payments ballooned to $14.4 billion. The falling stock prices in the country is a boon for bargain hunters and investing in the numerous domestic funds is one way of investing in the country. Some shares that investors are taking an interest in are also discussed.

42985 ■ *"Bark and Bite"* in Canadian Business (Vol. 81, March 31, 2008, No. 5, pp. 20)

Pub: Rogers Media Inc.

Contact: Tony Viner, President

Ed: Rachel Pulfer. **Description:** Hillary Clinton and Barack Obama both want to renegotiate NAFTA but the most job losses in the American manufacturing industry is caused by technological change and Asian competition than with NAFTA. The risk of protectionist trade policies has increased given the political atmosphere.

42986 ■ *"Baskin-Robbins Expanding in China and U.S."* in Ice Cream Reporter (Vol. 21, August 20, 2008, No. 9, pp. 1)

Description: Baskin-Robbins will open its first store in Shanghai, China along with plans for 100 more shops in that country. They will also be expanding their market in the Dallas/Fort Worth, Texas area as well as Greater Cincinnati/Northern Kentucky regions.

42987 ■ *"Baskin-Robbins: New in U.S., Old in Japan"* in Ice Cream Reporter (Vol. 23, August 20, 2010, No. 9, pp. 2)

Description: Baskin-Robbins is celebrating its first franchise in Japan.

42988 ■ *"BayTSP, NTT Data Corp. Enter Into Reseller Pact to Market Online IP Monitoring"* in Professional Services Close-Up (Sept. 11, 2009)

Description: Due to incredible interest from distributors and content owners across Asia, NTT Data Corp. will resell BayTSP's online intellectual property monitoring, enforcement, business intelligence and monetization services in Japan.

42989 ■ *"Be a Better Manager: Live Abroad"* in Harvard Business Review (Vol. 88, September 2010, No. 9, pp. 24)

Pub: Harvard Business School Publishing

Ed: William W. Maddux, Adam D. Galinsky, Carmit T. Tadmor. **Description:** Interrelationship between international experience and entrepreneurship is discussed. Individuals with international experience are likelier to be promoted and to develop new products and businesses.

42990 ■ *"Bedandbreakfast.eu: Bed & Breakfast Emerging in Europe"* in Travel & Leisure Close-Up (January 11, 2012)

Pub: Close-Up Media

Released: January 11, 2012. **Description:** According to experts, only 15 percent of all bed and breakfast operations in Europe were launched before the year 2000, with the majority opening after 2005. Reports show approximately 2,400 new operations opening on a monthly basis. Bedandbreakfast.eu offer current offerings for vacationers interested in staying at a bed and breakfast while visiting Europe.

42991 ■ *"Beltway Monitor"* in Mergers & Acquisitions: The Dealmaker's Journal (March 1, 2008)

Pub: SourceMedia Inc.

Contact: James M. Malkin, Chief Executive Officer

Description: Discusses in detail The Foreign Investment and National Security Act of 2007 which was put into legislation due to the initially approved acquisition of certain U.S. ports by Dubai Ports World which set off a firestorm of controversy.

42992 ■ *Benchmarking the Canadian Business Presence in East Asia*

Pub: University of Toronto Press Inc.

Contact: John Yates, President

E-mail: jyates@utpress.utoronto.ca

Ed: A.E. Safarian, Wendy Dobson. **Released:** October 1995. **Price:** $12.57. **Description:** Covers Canadian trade with East Asian economies. **Availability:** Print.

42993 ■ *"Best Growth Stocks"* in Canadian Business (Vol. 81, Summer 2008, No. 9, pp. 61)

Ed: Calvin Leung. **Description:** Table showing the one-year performance of growth stocks is presented. Edmonton-based Stantec Inc. expects to advance its

sales and profits by 15 percent to 20 percent per year through tapping international markets and acquisitions. Analysts forecast a 17.1 percent growth rate annually over the next 3 to 5 years.

42994 ■ *"Best Turnaround Stocks"* in Canadian Business (Vol. 82, Summer 2009, No. 8, pp. 32)

Pub: Rogers Media Inc.

Contact: Tony Viner, President

Ed: Calvin Leung. **Description:** Canadian companies that are believed to have the potential for the best turnaround stocks are presented. Suggested stocks include those of Migao Corporation, which is rated by most research firms as a Buy. Migao produces potash-based fertilizers for the Chinese market.

42995 ■ *"Bet on China"* in Canadian Business (Vol. 80, November 5, 2007, No. 22, pp. 30)

Ed: Thomas Watson. **Description:** Former U.S. Federal Reserve Board head, Alan Greenspan, warns that contraction will happen in the Chinese market. However, the economic success of China does not seem to be at the point of ending, as the country remains the largest market for mobile telecommunications. Forecasts for Chinese trading and investments are provided.

42996 ■ *"Bet on the Subcontinent"* in Canadian Business (Vol. 81, April 14, 2008, No. 6, pp. 27)

Pub: Rogers Media Inc.

Contact: Tony Viner, President

Ed: Calvin Leung. **Description:** Morgan Stanley Capital International India Index is down 28 percent for the first half of 2008 but this index rebounded 6 percent in 2002 then skyrocketed 65 percent in 2003. The economic reforms in the 1990's have created a growing middle class and households that can afford discretionary items will grow from eight million to 94 million by 2025. India's equity market could outperform developed markets if its economy grows at its current rate.

42997 ■ *"A Better Way to Tax U.S. Businesses"* in (Vol. 90, July-August 2012, No. 7-8, pp. 134)

Pub: Harvard Business Review Press

Contact: Peter E. Walsh, Director

Ed: Mihir A. Desai. **Released:** July-August 2012. **Description:** Correcting the US corporate tax code will require ending the disconnect between earnings stated to investors and taxable income, implementing rate reductions, eliminating the taxing of overseas income, and securing an agreement by business leaders to acknowledge taxes as a responsibility.

42998 ■ *"Betting On Volatile Materials"* in Barron's (Vol. 88, July 14, 2008, No. 28, pp. M11)

Pub: Dow Jones & Co., Inc.

Contact: Clare Hart, President

Ed: John Marshall. **Description:** Economic slowdowns in the U.S., Europe and China could cause sharp short-term declines in the materials sector. The S&P Materials sector is vulnerable to shifts in the flow of funds. Statistical data included.

42999 ■ *"Beware this Chinese Export"* in Barron's (Vol. 90, August 30, 2010, No. 35, pp. 21)

Pub: Barron's Editorial & Corporate Headquarters

Ed: Bill Alpert, Leslie P. Norton. **Description:** A look at 158 China reverse-merger stocks in the U.S. reveal that the median underperformed the index of U.S. listed Chinese companies by 75 percent in their first three years. These reverse merger stocks also lagged the Russell 2000 index of small cap stocks by 66 percent.

43000 ■ *"Beware, Complacent Bankers"* in Canadian Business (Vol. 85, September 17, 2012, No. 14, pp. 9)

Pub: George Media Inc.

Ed: Sarah Barmak. **Released:** September 17, 2012. **Description:** Canadian Finance Minister Jim Flaherty has released draft rules that would allow credit unions to go national and compete with major banks. Approval of the rules would see a fianancial services mix that includes a few credit unions with coast-to-coast ATM networks.

43001 ■ Billions of Entrepreneurs: How China and India Are Reshaping Their Futures and Yours
Pub: Harvard Business Review Press
Contact: Peter E. Walsh, Director
Ed: Tarun Khanna. Released: March 17, 2011. Price: $16.95, paperback. Description: Various success strategies for success in both China and India are examined. Implications of the concurrent economic booms in both countries are cited. Availability: Print.

43002 ■ "Biz Assesses 'Textgate' Fallout: Conventions, Smaller Deals Affected" in Crain's Detroit Business (Vol. 24, March 31, 2008)
Pub: Crain Communications Inc.
Contact: Rance E. Crain, President
Ed: Tom Henderson. Description: Businesspeople who were trying to measure the amount of economic damage is likely to be caused due to Mayor Kwame Kilpatrick's indictment on eight charges and found that: automotive and other large global deals are less likely to be affected than location decisions by smaller companies and convention site decisions. Also being affected are negotiations in which Mexican startup companies were planning a partnership with the TechTown incubator to pursue opportunities in the auto sector; those plans are being put on hold while they look at other sites.

43003 ■ "Black Diamond Holdings Corp. Receives SEC Approval" in Canadian Corporate News (May 16, 2007)
Description: Black Diamond Holdings, Corp., a British Columbia domiciled company and its two wholly owned subsidiaries are engaged in the bottling, importation, distribution, marketing, and brand creation of premium spirits and wines to worldwide consumers, announced that it has completed the SEC review process and has applied to list for trading in the United States on the OTC.BB.

43004 ■ "Blood Diamonds are Forever" in Canadian Business (Vol. 83, August 17, 2010, No. 13-14, pp. 59)
Ed: Matthew McClearn. Description: The failed case against Donald McKay who was found in possession of rough diamonds in a raid by Royal Canadian Mounted Police has raised doubts about Kimberley Process (KP) attempts to stop the illicit global trade in diamonds. KP has managed to reduce total global trade of blood diamonds by 1 percent in mid-2000.

43005 ■ "Blues at the Toy Fair: Industry Reeling From Recalls, Lower Sales Volumes" in Crain's New York Business (February 17, 2008)
Pub: Crain Communications Inc.
Contact: Rance Crain, President
Ed: Elisabeth Cordova. Description: Over 1,500 toy developers and vendors will attend the American International Toy Fair, expected to be low-key due to recent recalls of toys not meeting American safety standards. Toy retailers and manufacturers, as well as the Chinese government, are promoting product testing to prevent toxic metals in toys.

43006 ■ "BMW Makes Bet on Carbon Maker" in Wall Street Journal Eastern Edition (November 19 , 2011, pp. B3)
Pub: Dow Jones & Co., Inc.
Contact: Clare Hart, President
Ed: Christoph Rauwald. Description: Eight months ago, Volkswagen AG acquired a 10 percent holding in carbon-fiber maker SGL Carbon SE. Its rival BMW AG is catching up by acquiring 15.2 percent stake in SGL as it seeks alliances like the rest of the industry in order to share industrial costs of new product development.

43007 ■ "Bodovino Is a World Leader in Self-Service Wine Tasting" in Idaho Business Review (September 8, 2014)
Pub: Dolan Co.
Contact: James P. Dolan, President
Released: September 8, 2014. Description: Bodovino's wine bar and retail shop offers self-service wine tasting for its customers. It is the largest outlet

globally for the Italian wine dispenser manufacturer WineEmotion. Visitors to the shop can choose from 144 wines set up in the dispensing machines.

43008 ■ "Boeing Scores $21.7 Billion Order in Indonesia" in Wall Street Journal Eastern Edition (November 18 , 2011, pp. B6)
Pub: Dow Jones & Co., Inc.
Contact: Clare Hart, President
Ed: David Kesmodel, Laura Meckler. Description: Boeing has garnered a large contract to deliver Boeing 737 jets to Indonesia's Lion Air. There are those who are lobbying against the US government's practice of subsidizing foreign companies that make contracts with American aerospace companies.

43009 ■ "Boeing Updates On Air Cargo Market" in Travel & Leisure Close-Up (October 8, 2012)
Description: Boeing World Air Cargo Forecast 2012/2013 predicts that the global air cargo market will grow by a 5.2 percent annual rate over the next 20 years. Growth will be driven by world gross domestic product that is predicted to nearly double over the forecast period. Trade is expected to increase due to the liberalization of markets and more efficient aircraft and infrastructure improvements that will reduce the cost of air cargo.

43010 ■ "Bombardier Deja Vu" in Canadian Business (Vol. 83, August 17, 2010, No. 13-14, pp. 28)
Pub: Rogers Media Inc.
Contact: Tony Viner, President
Ed: Laura Cameron. Description: Foreign competitors have accused the Quebec government and the Societe de transport de Montreal of giving Bombardier preferential treatment when it bids for contract to replace Montreal metro's rail cars. Bombardier was in a similar situation in 1974 when it won the contract to build the metro's second generation rail cars.

43011 ■ Boosting Corporate Entrepreneurship Through HRM Practices: Evidence from German SMEs" in Human Resource Management (Vol. 49, July-August 2010, No. 4)
Pub: John Wiley
Ed: Ralf Schmelter, Rene Mauer, Christiane Borsch, Malte Brettel. Description: A study was conducted to determine which human resource management (HRM) practices promote corporate entrepreneurship (CE) in small and medium-sized enterprises (SMEs). Findings indicate that staff selection, staff development, training, and staff rewards on CE have a strong impact on SMEs.

43012 ■ "Border Boletin: UA to Take Lie-Detector Kiosk to Poland" in Arizona Daily Star (September 14, 2010)
Pub: Arizona Daily Star
Contact: John Humenik, President
E-mail: jhumenik@azstarnet.com
Ed: Brady McCombs. Description: University of Arizona's National Center for Border Security and Immigration Research will send a team to Warsaw, Poland to show border guards from 27 European Union countries the center's Avatar Kiosk. The Avatar technology is designed for use at border ports and airports to assist Customs officers detect individuals who are lying.

43013 ■ "Bottler Will Regain Its Pop" in Barron's (Vol. 88, March 17, 2008, No. 11, pp. 56)
Ed: Alexander Eule. Description: Discusses he 30 percent drop in the share price of PepsiAmericas Inc. from their 2007 high which presents an opportunity to buy into the company's dependable U.S. market and fast growing Eastern European business. The bottler's Eastern European operating profits in 2007 grew to $101 million from $21 million in 2006.

43014 ■ "Bottom-Fishing and Speed-Dating in India-How Investors Feel About the Indian Market" in Barron's (Vol. 88, March 24, 2008,

No. 12, pp. M12)
Pub: Dow Jones & Co., Inc.
Contact: Clare Hart, President
Ed: Elliot Wilson. Description: Indian stocks have fallen hard in 2008, with Mumbai's Sensex 30 down 30 percent from its January 2008 peak of 21,000 to 14,995 in March. The India Private Equity Fair 2008 attracted 140 of the world's largest private equity firms and about 24 of India's fastest-growing corporations. Statistical data included.

43015 ■ "Bountiful Barrels: Where to Find $140 Trillion" in Barron's (Vol. 88, July 14, 2008, No. 28, pp. 40)
Pub: Dow Jones & Co., Inc.
Contact: Clare Hart, President
Ed: Andrew Bary. Description: Surge in oil prices has caused a large transfer of wealth to oil-producing countries thereby reshaping the global economy. Oil reserves of oil exporting countries are now valued at $140 trillion. Economist Stephen Jen believes that this wealth will be transformed into paper assets as these countries invest in global stocks and bonds.

43016 ■ Brazilian-American Business Review/Directory
Pub: Brazilian-American Chamber of Commerce
Contact: Vicente J. Bonnard, President
URL(s): www.brazilcham.com. Released: Annual; Latest edition 2009. Price: $80, for nonmembers in U.S.; $100, for nonmembers outside U.S.; $150, CD-ROM in U.S.; $200, CD-ROM outside U.S. Covers: Brazilian and American businesses interested in developing trade and investment between the two countries. Entries include: Company name, address, phone, fax, key personnel, Standard Industrial Classification (SIC) code. Database includes: Economic and business statistics; U.S. -Brazil business information.

43017 ■ "Brazil's New King of Food" in Barron's (Vol. 89, July 13, 2009, No. 28, pp. 28)
Pub: Dow Jones & Co., Inc.
Contact: Clare Hart, President
Ed: Kenneth Rapoza. Description: Perdigao and Sadia's merger has resulted in the creation of Brasil Foods and the shares of Brasil Foods provides a play on both Brazil's newly energized consumer economy and its role as a major commodities exporter. Brasil Foods shares could climb as much as 36 percent.

43018 ■ "Brewing a Love-Haiti Relationship" in The Business Journal - Serving Phoenix and the Valley of the Sun (Vol. 28, July 4, 2008, No. 44)
Ed: Yvonne Zusel. Description: Jean and Alicia Marseille have ventured into a coffee distribution company called Ka Bel LLC which markets Marabou brand of coffee imported from Haiti. Part of the proceeds of the business is donated to entrepreneurs from Jean's country, Haiti. Details of the Marseille's startup business and personal mission to help are discussed.

43019 ■ "Brewing National Success" in Hawaii Business (Vol. 53, November 2007, No. 5, pp. 46)
Pub: PacificBasin Communications
Description: Kona Brewing Co. (KBC) is already selling its brews in four cities in Florida and 17 other states and Japan as well. KBC is currently forming a deal with Red Hook to produce Longboard Lager and other KBC brews at Red Hooks' brewery in New Hampshire. KBC's chief executive officer Mattson Davis shares KBC's practices for success.

43020 ■ "Broadband Reaches Access Limits in Europe" in Information Today (Vol. 26, February 2009, No. 2, pp. 22)
Pub: Information Today, Inc.
Contact: Thomas H. Hogan, President
E-mail: ctuthill@infotoday.com
Ed: Jim Ashling. Description: Eurostat (the Statistical Office of the European communities) reports results from is survey regarding Internet use by busi-

nesses throughout its 27-member states. Iceland, Finland and the Netherlands provide the most access at broadband speeds, followed by Belgium, Spain and France.

43021 ■ *"Bubble Trouble?" in Puget Sound Business Journal (Vol. 34, April 18, 2014, No. 53, pp. 4)*
Pub: American City Business Journals
Released: April 18, 2014. Description: Redfin disclosed that nearly one third of homes listed in the real estate market in King County, Washington were sold above the listing price in February 2014 and it is forecast that the housing market is headed into a new bubble. Statistics indicate that the trend in rising prices is slowing even in the face of a declining supply of available homes. The impact of international buyers is also discussed.

43022 ■ *"Buhler Versatile Launches Next Generation of Equipment" in Farm Industry News (November 23, 2011)*
Pub: Penton Business Media Inc.
Contact: David Kieselstein, Chief Executive Officer
Ed: Jodie Wehrspann. Description: Canadian owned Versatile is expanding its four-wheel drive tractor division with sprayers, tillage, and seeding equipment.

43023 ■ *"Building Inclusive Markets in Rural Bangladesh: How Intermediaries Work Institutional Voids" in Academy of Management Journal (Vol. 55, August 1, 2012, No. 4, pp. 819)*
Pub: Academy of Management
Contact: Ming-Jer Chen, President
Ed: Johanna Mair, Ignasi Marti, Marc J. Ventresca. Description: The process of building inclusive markets in rural Bangladesh through Building Resources Across Communities program is analyzed. Results identifying institutional voids as the source of market exclusion and that redefining market architecture and the effort to legitimate new market actors are critical to building inclusive markets.

43024 ■ *"Building a Portfolio, BRIC by BRIC" in Barron's (Vol. 92, August 25, 2012, No. 38, pp. M8)*
Pub: Dow Jones & Co., Inc.
Contact: Clare Hart, President
Ed: Reshma Kapadia.

43025 ■ *Building Wealth in China: 36 True Stories of Chinese Millionaires and How They Made Their Fortunes*
Ed: Ling, Zhu. Released: April 27, 2010. Price: $15. Description: Thirty-six of China's most successful and innovative entrepreneurs discuss valuable lessons for growing a business in China.

43026 ■ *Business Stripped Bare: Adventures of a Global Entrepreneur*
Pub: Virgin Books/Random House
Ed: Richard Branson. Released: January 22, 2010. Price: £20, Hardback; £9.99, Paperback. Description: Successful entrepreneur, Sir Richard Branson, shares the inside track on some of his greatest achievements in business and the lessons learned from setbacks.

43027 ■ *"Cabi to Develop Major Retail Project" in South Florida Business Journal (Vol. 32, July 6, 2012, No. 50, pp. 1)*
Pub: American City Business Journal
Description: Aventura, Florida-based Cabi Developers has received a bankruptcy court approval to begin construction of a major retail project called Capital Brickell Place in the Brickell neighborhood. Mexican real estate developer GICSA will finance the project and Cabi has been talking with retailers like Costco, Targt and Trader Joe's as potential tenants.

43028 ■ *"Calendar" in Crain's Detroit Business (Vol. 26, January 11, 2010, No. 2, pp. 16)*
Pub: Crain Communications Inc.
Contact: Rance E. Crain, President
Description: Listing of events includes seminars sponsored by the Detroit Economic Club as well as conferences dealing with globalization and graphic design.

43029 ■ *"Calendar" in Crain's Detroit Business (Vol. 26, January 18, 2010, No. 3, pp. 16)*
Pub: Crain Communications Inc.
Contact: Rance E. Crain, President
Description: Listing of events includes seminars sponsored by the Detroit Economic Club as well as conferences dealing with globalization and marketing.

43030 ■ *"California Company Suing City's Lupin Over its Generic Diabetes Drug" in Baltimore Business Journal (Vol. 27, January 1, 2010)*
Ed: Gary Haber. Description: California-based Depomed Inc. is suing Baltimore, Maryland-based Lupin Pharmaceuticals Inc. and its parent company in India over the patents to a diabetes drug. Lupin allegedly infringed on Depomed's four patents for Glumetza when it filed for permission to sell its own version of the drug with the US Food and Drug Administration. Details on generic pharmaceutical manufacturer tactics are discussed.

43031 ■ *"Cambodia Calls" in Barron's (Vol. 89, July 27, 2009, No. 30, pp. M7)*
Pub: Dow Jones & Co., Inc.
Contact: Clare Hart, President
Ed: Leslie P. Norton. Description: Interest in frontier markets could jump if enthusiasm about growth in the developed world gathers steam. Cambodia is the latest market to get attention where a handful of investors are trying to set up funds. One investor believes that Cambodia is back open for business but others are still cautious about investing in the country.

43032 ■ *"Can a Brazilian SUV Take On the Jeep Wrangler?" in Business Week (September 10, 2008, No. 4100, pp. 50)*
Pub: Bloomberg L.P.
Contact: Matthew Winkler, Manager
Ed: Helen Walters. Description: Profile of the Brazilian company TAC as well as the flourishing Brazilian car market; TAC has launched a new urban vehicle, the Stark, which has won prizes for innovation; the company uses local technology and manufacturing expertise.

43033 ■ *"Canada Nears European Trade Treaty" in Globe & Mail (February 5, 2007, pp. B1)*
Ed: Steven Chase. Description: The probable establishment of a treaty by Canada with Norway, Switzerland and Iceland for free-trade is discussed. The treaty will allow an annual business of $11 billion to take place in Canada.

43034 ■ *"Canada, Not China, Is Partner In Our Economic Prosperity" in Crain's Chicago Business (Vol. 31, April 14, 2008, No. 15, pp. 14)*
Pub: Crain Communications Inc.
Contact: Todd Johnson, Publisher
Ed: Paul O'Connor. Description: In 2005 more than $500 billion in two-way trade crossed the friendly border between the Great Lakes states and Canadian provinces and for decades Canada is every Great Lakes State's number one and growing export market.

43035 ■ *"Canada Wins Second NAFTA Decision on Softwood Tariffs" in Globe & Mail (March 18, 2006, pp. B2)*
Ed: Steven Chase, Peter Kennedy. Description: Canada has won a second major North American Free Trade Agreement (NAFTA) victory in five years of legal battles over U.S. tariffs on softwood. Details of the controversy and ruling are presented.

43036 ■ *Canadian Entrepreneurship and Small Business Management*
Pub: McGraw-Hill Ryerson Ltd.
Contact: Robert J. Bahash, President
Ed: D. Wesley Balderson. Price: C$104.36, Members; C$115.95, Nonmembers. Description: Successful entrepreneurship and small business management is shown through the use of individual Canadian small business experiences. Availability: Print.

43037 ■ *"Canadian Hydronics Businesses Promote 'Beautiful Heat" in Indoor Comfort Marketing (Vol. 70, September 2011, No. 9, pp. 20)*
Pub: Industry Publications Inc.
Contact: Shirleen Dorman, Editor
Description: Canadian hydronics companies are promoting their systems as beautiful heat. Hydronics is the use of water as the heat-transfer medium in heating and cooling system.

43038 ■ *Canadian Multinationals and International Finance*
Pub: Taylor & Francis Ltd.
Contact: Peter Rigby, Chief Executive Officer
Ed: Gregory P. Marchildon, Duncan McDowall. Released: September 30, 1992. Price: C$206, hardback. Description: Seven stories that explore the role of Canadian multinational enterprise in world finance, trade and direct investment. Availability: Print.

43039 ■ *"Canadian Patients Give Detroit Hospitals a Boost" in Crain's Detroit Business (Vol. 24, April 14, 2008, No. 15, pp. 10)*
Pub: Crain Communications Inc.
Contact: Rance E. Crain, President
Ed: Jay Greene. Description: Each year thousands of Canadians travel to Detroit area hospitals seeking quicker solutions to medical problems or access to services that are limited or unavailable in Canada.

43040 ■ *"Canadian Solar Expands Into Puerto Rico With Planned 26MW Solar Power Plant Installation" in Benzinga.com (October 2, 2012)*
Pub: Benzinga.com
Contact: Kyle Bazzy, President
Description: Canadian Solar Inc. is expanding into Puerto Rico with the delivery of 26mg of CS6P-P solar power modules for the San Fermin solar power plant. Canadian Solar is one of the world's largest solar firms. The solar power system is expected to be completed and connected to the national grid by December 2012.

43041 ■ *"The Canadians Are Coming!" in Canadian Business (Vol. 80, October 22, 2007, No. 21, pp. 15)*
Ed: Rachel Pulfer. Description: Toronto-Dominion Bank declared its acquisition of the New Jersey-based Commerce Bancorp for C$8.5 billion. Royal Bank of Canada has scooped up Trinidad-based Financial Group for C$2.2 billion. Details of the foreign acquisitions, as well as the impact of high Canadian dollars on the mergers are discussed.

43042 ■ *"Capitalizing On Our Intellectual Capital" in Harvard Business Review (Vol. 90, May 2012, No. 5, pp. 42)*
Pub: Harvard Business Review Press
Contact: Peter E. Walsh, Director
Ed: Iqbal Quadir. Released: May 2012. Description: By managing education as an export, the US can benefit not only from revenue received from tuition, but also from the relationships forged with foreign students. The students will import the networks and technologies they used while in the US and their education levels will help create global growth.

43043 ■ *"Caterpillar to Expand Research, Production in China" in Chicago Tribune (August 27, 2008)*
Ed: James P. Miller. Description: Caterpillar Inc., the Peoria-based heavy-equipment manufacturer, plans to establish a new research-and-development center at the site of its rapidly growing campus in Wuxi.

43044 ■ *"Cemex Paves a Global Road to Solid Growth" in Barron's (Vol. 88, March 10, 2008, No. 10, pp. 24)*
Pub: Dow Jones & Co., Inc.
Contact: Clare Hart, President
Ed: Sandra Ward. Description: Shares of Cemex are expected to perform well with the company's expected strong performance despite fears of a US recession. The company has a diverse geographical reach and benefits from a strong worldwide demand for cement.

43045 ■ *"Central Valley Local Fund II Has $110M to Invest" in Sacramento Business Journal (Vol. 29, May 25, 2012, No. 13, pp. 1)*
Pub: American City Business Journal
Description: CVF Capital Partners has raised $110 million to fund investments in mature companies. CVF's Central Valley Fund II is twice the size of the fund launched by the company in December 2005. The second hand, which was established by a total of 10 banks and a Mexican equity fund, is considered a vote of confidence in Central Valley industries.

43046 ■ *"Cents & Sensibility" in Playthings (Vol. 107, January 1, 2009, No. 1, pp. 19)*
Pub: Reed Elsevier Group plc Reed Business Information
Contact: Mark Kelsey, Chief Executive Officer
Ed: Pamela Brill, Gary Evans. **Description:** Recent concerns over safety, phthalate and lead paint and other toxic materials, as well as consumers going green, are issues discussed by toy manufacturers. Doll manufacturers also face increase labor and material costs and are working to design dolls that girls will love.

43047 ■ *"The CEO Poll: And The Winner Is ..." in Canadian Business (Vol. 81, February 12, 2008, No. 3, pp. 21)*
Pub: Rogers Media Inc.
Contact: Tony Viner, President
Ed: Joe Castaldo. **Description:** Thirty out of 141 Canadian chief executive officers think that Hilary Clinton would be best for U.S.-Canada relations if elected as U.S. president. Findings also revealed that 60 respondents believe that presidential candidate John McCain would be best on handling issues of international military-security. Views on the candidates' performance and their ability to deal with the declining U.S. economy as well as international trade issues are also given.

43048 ■ *"CEO Putting Rubber to Road at Lanxess Corporation" in Pittsburgh Business Times (Vol. 33, May 2, 2014, No. 42, pp. 4)*
Pub: American City Business Journals
Released: May 2, 2014. **Description:** Flemming Bjoernslev, CEO for the North American operations of Germany-based Lanxess Corporation, discusses their recovery efforts following their first financial loss in 2013. He is confident that the U.S. tire manufacturing industry will help their business further in North America.

43049 ■ *"CEOs Decry Budget Taxation Change" in Globe & Mail (April 2, 2007, pp. B1)*
Pub: CTVglobemedia Publishing Inc.
Ed: Steven Chase. **Description:** The views of the chief executive officers of Canadian firms, on the changes in the country's policy governing the taxation of foreign deals, are presented.

43050 ■ *"Champion Enterprises Buys UK Company" in Crain's Detroit Business (Vol. 24, March 10, 2008, No. 11, pp. 4)*
Pub: Crain Communications Inc.
Contact: Rance E. Crain, President
Ed: Daniel Duggan. **Description:** With the acquisition of ModularUK Building Systems Ltd., a steel-frame modular manufacturer, Champion Enterprises has continued its expansion outside the United States.

43051 ■ *Change in SMEs: The New European Capitalism*
Pub: Palgrave Macmillan
Contact: Lisa Dunn, Manager
E-mail: l.dunn@palgrave.com
Ed: Katharina Bluhm, Rudi Schmidt. **Released:** September 2008. **Price:** £77, hardcover. **Description:** Effects of global change on corporate governance, management, competitive strategies and labor relations in small-to-medium sized enterprises in various European countries are discussed. **Availability:** Print; E-book; Electronic publishing.

43052 ■ *"A Change Would Do You Good" in Canadian Business (Vol. 80, November 19, 2007, No. 23, pp. 15)*
Ed: Geoff Kirbyson. **Description:** Western Glove Works will be manufacturing clothing offshore, including Sheryl Crow's jeans collection, in countries such as China and the Philippines. The company decided to operate offshore after 86 years of existence due to the high price of manufacturing jeans in Canada. Western Glove's focus on producing celebrity-endorsed goods is discussed.

43053 ■ *"Changing the Rules of the Accounting Game" in Canadian Business (Vol. 81, December 8, 2008, No. 21, pp. 19)*
Ed: Al Rosen. **Description:** Interference from world politicians in developing accounting standards is believed to have resulted in untested rules that are inferior to current standards. European lawmakers have recently asked to change International Financial Reporting Standards.

43054 ■ *"Charlotte Pipe Launches Satirical Campaign" in Contractor (Vol. 57, January 2010, No. 1, pp. 6)*
Pub: Penton Media, Inc.
Description: Charlotte Pipe and Foundry Co. launched an advertising campaign that uses social media and humor to make a point about how it can be nearly impossible to determine if imported cast iron pipes and fittings meet the same quality standards as what is made in the U.S. The campaign features 'pipe whisperers' and also spoofs pipe sniffing dogs.

43055 ■ *"Cheap Tubing Risk to Local Jobs, Execs Caution" in Pittsburgh Business Times (Vol. 33, May 23, 2014, No. 45, pp. 4)*
Pub: American City Business Journals
Released: May 23, 2014. **Description:** U.S. Steel Corporation requests the U.S. Department of Commerce to take action against unfairly traded steel imports in the market because thousands of jobs are at risk. At least 26,400 jobs in Pennsylvania may be affected by the unfair trading practices of foreign exporters according to the office of Governor Tom Corbett.

43056 ■ *"Children's Place Retail Stores Put Call Ratio Increases 6.0 Percent, Stock Dips 0.2 Percent" in News Bites US (August 20, 2012)*
Pub: Financial Times Ltd.
Contact: John Ridding, Chief Executive Officer
Released: August 20, 2012. **Description:** Investment information regarding Children's Place Retail Stores Inc., the largest children's specialty apparel retailer in the United States, is provided. Thefirm has signed a 10-year franchise agreement with Apparel Group to open shops in the Arab Gulf States of the UAE, Kuwait, Qatar, Bahrain and Oman.

43057 ■ *"The China Connection" in Crain's Chicago Business (Vol. 31, March 24, 2008, No. 12, pp. 26)*
Pub: Crain Communications Inc.
Contact: Todd Johnson, Publisher
Ed: Samantha Stainburn. **Description:** Interview with Ben Munoz who studied abroad in Beijing, China for three months to study international economics, e-commerce and global leadership.

43058 ■ *"China Pegs Surplus at $101.9 Billion" in Globe & Mail (January 12, 2006, pp. B1)*
Pub: CTVglobemedia Publishing Inc.
Ed: Barrie McKenna. **Description:** The reasons behind the trade surplus of $101.9 billion, in China, are presented.

43059 ■ *"The China Tax" in Forbes (Vol. 180, October 1, 2007, No. 6, pp. 35)*
Ed: Robyn Meredith. **Description:** U.S. consumers can see a rise in prices for goods made in China due to growing pressure from Congress to ensure safe products from that country. Taxing products imported from China could be levied in five different forms listed.

43060 ■ *"China Trade Deficit Costs California Jobs" in Sacramento Business Journal (Vol. 25, August 10, 2008, No. 23, pp. 1)*
Pub: American City Business Journals, Inc.
Contact: Whitney Shaw, President
Ed: Melanie Turner. **Description:** California topped the ranking of states with job losses because of the rising trade deficit with China, losing 325,800 jobs between 2001-2007. The U.S. has lost 2.3 million workers within the period. Other views and information on the job loses because of the trade deficit with China, are presented.

43061 ■ *"China Vs the World: Whose Technology Is It?" in Harvard Business Review (Vol. 88, December 2010, No. 12, pp. 94)*
Pub: Harvard Business School Publishing
Ed: Thomas M. Hout, Pankaj Ghemawat. **Description:** Examination of the regulation the Chinese government is implementing that require foreign corporations wishing to do business in the country to give up their new technologies. These regulations avoid World Trade Organization technology transfer provisions and complicate the convergence of socialism and capitalism.

43062 ■ *"China's Dagong Show" in Canadian Business (Vol. 83, August 17, 2010, No. 13-14, pp. 15)*
Pub: Rogers Media Inc.
Contact: Tony Viner, President
Ed: Matthew McClearn. **Description:** Beijing, China-based Dagong Global Credit Rating has downgraded US credit ratings, as well as other developed countries such as Canada, while granting higher ratings to China, Russia and Brazil. However, there is a perceived disconnection between Dagong's ratings and its official pronouncements.

43063 ■ *China's Rational Entrepreneurs: The Development of the New Private Business Sector*
Pub: Routledge
Contact: Kevin Bradley, President
E-mail: kbradley@taylorandfrancis.com
Ed: Barbara Krug. **Released:** November 2012. **Price:** $54.95, paperback. **Description:** Difficulties faced by entrepreneurs in China are discussed, including analysis for understanding their behavior and relations with local governments in order to secure long-term business success. **Availability:** Print.

43064 ■ *"China's Slowing Growth Could Benefit the Global Economy; An Expert On China's Economy Says the Country Is Seeing an Upside to Slowing Down" in Gallup Business Journal (April 8, 2014)*
Pub: Gallup Press
Released: April 8, 2014. **Description:** An expert on China's economy reports that the country is acknowledging an upside to slowing down, and is creating opportunities for a market economy never seen before. Ways that China is looking to expand its economy, thus expand the global economy, is investigated.

43065 ■ *"China's Super Consumers: What 1 Billion Customers Want and How to Sell It to Them"*
Pub: John Wiley & Sons Inc.
Contact: Stephen M. Smith, President
Released: September 3, 2014. **Price:** , $25.00. **Description:** China has become the largest consumer market in the world. An exploration into the birth of consumerism in China and what the Chinese consumer buys, how they buy, and why they buy is presented. Advice for successfully entering this international market include a hands-on resource, real stories of companies making an impact in China, what the Chinese consumer wants and how to deliver the goods.

43066 ■ *"China's Transition to Green Energy Systems" in Energy Policy (Vol. 39, October 2011, No. 10, pp. 5909-5919)*
Pub: Reed Elsevier Reference Publishing
Ed: Wei Li, Guojun Song, Melanie Beresford, Ben Ma. **Description:** The economics of home solar water heaters and their growing popularity in Dezhous City, China is discussed.

43067 ■ *"Chinese Coal Giant Shifts Focus with ECA Pact" in Pittsburgh Business Times (Vol. 33, January 10, 2014, No. 26, pp. 3)*
Pub: American City Business Journals
Released: January 10, 2014. **Description:** China Shenhua Energy Company has signed a deal with Energy Corporation of America (ECA) for a joint venture with its U.S. subsidiary, Shenhua America Holdings Corporation, to drill 25 wells in Greene County, Pennsylvania. Shenhua will initially provide $90 million to cover the costs of drilling and production for the wells in ECA-owned land.

43068 ■ *Chinese Ethnic Business: Global and Local Perspectives*
Pub: Routledge
Contact: Kevin Bradley, President
E-mail: kbradley@taylorandfrancis.com
Ed: Eric Fong, Chiu Ming Luk. **Price:** $54.95, paperback; $180, hardback. **Description:** Impact of globalization on Chinese ethnic small businesses is covered, focusing on U.S., Australia, and Canada. **Availability:** Print.

43069 ■ *Chinese Ethnic Business: Global and Local Perspectives*
Pub: Routledge
Contact: Kevin Bradley, President
E-mail: kbradley@taylorandfrancis.com
Ed: Eric Fong, Chiu Luk. **Released:** May 2009. **Price:** $54.95, paperback; $180, hardback. **Description:** Globalization impacts on the development of Chinese businesses are analyzed, focusing on economic globalization of the United States, Australia, and Canada. Information is focused on economic globalization and Chinese community development, transnational linkages, local urban structures, homogenization and place attachment, as well as methodology such as ethnographic studies, historical analysis, geographic studies and statistical analysis. **Availability:** Print.

43070 ■ *"Chinese Fund Loans $33.5 Million to Prestolite" in Crain's Detroit Business (Vol. 26, January 18, 2010, No. 3, pp. 1)*
Pub: Crain Communications Inc.
Contact: Rance E. Crain, President
Ed: Ryan Beene. **Description:** Prestolite Electric Inc., a distributor of alternators and starter motors for commercial and heavy-duty vehicles, looked to China for fresh capital in order to fund new product launches.

43071 ■ *"Chinese Invasion" in Canadian Business, (Vol. 85, September 17, 2012, No. 14, pp. 24)*
Pub: George Media Inc.
Ed: Matthew McClearn. **Released:** September 17, 2012. **Description:** The economic implication for Canada of China National Offshore Oil Corp.Es bid for Nexen at 61 percent above the share price is discussed. Canadians are encouraged to view the Nexen bid as an invitation to China to form a deeper economic relationship.

43072 ■ *"Chinese Outbound Tourists' Destination Image of America: Part I" in Journal of Travel Research (Vol. 51, May 2012, No. 3, pp. 250)*
Pub: Pine Forge Press
Contact: Blaise R. Simqu, President
Ed: Xiang (Robert) Li, Svetlana Stepchenkova. **Description:** Several studies are conducted to examine the mental picture of the United States as a travel destination as observed in the Chinese long-haul outbound travelers. These Chinese tourists often foresee America as a highly urban country with high technology and big cities.

43073 ■ *"Chinese Solar Panel Manufacturer Scopes Out Austin" in Austin Business JournalInc. (Vol. 29, October 30, 2009, No. 34, pp. 1)*
Pub: American City Business Journals
Ed: Jacob Dirr. **Description:** China's Yingli Green Energy Holding Company Ltd. is looking for a site in order to construct a $20 million photovoltaic panel plant. Both Austin and San Antonio are vying to house the manufacturing hub. The project could create about 300 jobs and give Austin a chance to become

a player in the solar energy market. Other solar companies are also considering Central Texas as an option to set up shop.

43074 ■ *Cities from the Arabian Desert: The Building of Jubail and Yambu in Saudi Arabia*
Pub: Turnaround Associates
Contact: Andrea H. Pampanini, Founder
Ed: Andrea H. Pampanini. **Description:** An overview of Saudi Arabia's government to take control of the nation's natural resources and change the government, educational system, and its culture by evolving into a modern industrial society.

43075 ■ *"City Slickers" in Canadian Business (Vol. 81, March 31, 2008, No. 5, pp. 36)*
Pub: Rogers Media Inc.
Contact: Tony Viner, President
Ed: Joe Castaldo. **Description:** Richard Florida believes that the creative class drives the economy and the prosperity of countries depends on attracting and retaining these people. Florida has brought attention to developing livable and economically vibrant cities thanks in part to his promotional skills. However, he has also drawn critics who see his data on his theories as flimsy and inadequate.

43076 ■ *"Clicks From Round the World: Simplifying International E-Commerce" in Inc. (Volume 32, December 2010, No. 10, pp. 146)*
Pub: Inc. Magazine
Ed: Ryan Underwood. **Description:** By 2014, global e-commerce spending is expected to increase more than 90 percent, with much of that growth coming from Latin America.

43077 ■ *"Closed Minds and Open Skies" in Barron's (Vol. 88, March 10, 2008, No. 10, pp. 50)*
Pub: Dow Jones & Co., Inc.
Contact: Clare Hart, President
Ed: Thomas G. Donlan. **Description:** American politicians have closed minds when it comes to fair trade. The American government must not interfere with the country's manufacturing industries or worry about outsourcing defense contracts to European aerospace company Airbus.

43078 ■ *"CNinsure Offers Safety in Numbers" in Barron's (Vol. 90, September 13, 2010, No. 37, pp. 29)*
Ed: Teresa Rivas. **Description:** China's insurance holding company CNinsure has a long growth future due to the nascent insurance market in the country. It has also been diversifying its offerings and it has a broad network in the nation. The shares of the company are trading cheaply at nearly 14 times its 2011 earnings, and is considered a good point for investors.

43079 ■ *"CO2 Emissions Embodied in China-US Trade" in Energy Policy (Vol. 39, October 2011, No. 10, pp. 5980-5987)*
Pub: Reed Elsevier Reference Publishing
Ed: Huibin Du, Guozhu Mao, Alexander M. Smith, Xuxu Wang, Yuan Wang, Jianghong Guo. **Description:** Input and output analysis based on the energy per dollar ratio for carbon dioxide emissions involved in China-United States trade is outlined.

43080 ■ *"Cold Stone Creamery" in Ice Cream Reporter (Vol. 22, January 20, 2009, No. 2, pp. 8)*
Description: Franchise News reports that Cold Stone Creamery is looking for master franchisees to support its expansion into the North German market. The report notes that following its successful launch in Denmark, the firm is also preparing for expansion into France.

43081 ■ *"Column: Want People to Save? Force Them" in Harvard Business Review (Vol. 88, September 2010, No. 9, pp. 36)*
Pub: Harvard Business School Publishing
Ed: Dan Ariely. **Description:** Contrasts in U.S. attitudes towards savings and government regulation with those of Chile, where all employees are required to save 11 percent of their salary in a retirement account, are highlighted.

43082 ■ *"Coming: Cheaper Oil and a Stronger Buck" in Barron's (Vol. 88, March 24, 2008, No. 12, pp. 53)*
Pub: Dow Jones & Co., Inc.
Contact: Clare Hart, President
Ed: Lawrence C. Strauss. **Description:** Carl C. Weinberg, the chief economist of High Frequency Economics, forecasts that Chinese economic growth will slow down and that oil prices will drop to $80 a barrel in 2008. He also believes that the US dollar will start rising the moment the Federal Reserve stops cutting interest rates.

43083 ■ *"Coming: The End of Fiat Money" in (Vol. 92, July 23, 2012, No. 30, pp. 32)*
Pub: Dow Jones & Co., Inc.
Contact: Clare Hart, President
Ed: Leslie Norton. **Released:** July 23, 2012. **Description:** Stephanie Pomboy, founder of MicroMavens, discusses her views on the global financial system. She believes that the global fiat currency system may collapse within five years and be replaced by a gold-backed currency system.

43084 ■ *Competing in Emerging Markets*
Pub: Taylor & Francis Ltd.
Contact: Peter Rigby, Chief Executive Officer
Ed: Hemant Merchant. **Released:** October 2007. **Price:** $78.95, paperback; $245, hardback. **Description:** Understanding the perils and promises of emerging markets to the growth of companies is discussed. Readings and case studies focus on the strategic and operational challenges companies face while competing in emerging markets. **Availability:** Print.

43085 ■ *"Confidence High, But Lenders More Cautious" in Farmer's Weekly (March 28, 2008, No. 320)*
Description: Discusses the effect of the global credit crunch on farmers as well as recent auctions which were timed to beat changes to capital gains tax.

43086 ■ *"Coping With a Shrinking Planet" in Agency Sales Magazine (Vol. 39, December 2009, No. 11, pp. 46)*
Ed: Mark Young. **Description:** China and India are forcing big changes in the world and are posing a huge threat to U.S. manufacturers and their sales representatives. Reps may want to consider expanding into these territories. Helping sell American products out of the country presents an opportunity for economic expansion.

43087 ■ *"Copy Karachi?" in Barron's (Vol. 88, June 30, 2008, No. 26, pp. 5)*
Pub: Dow Jones & Co., Inc.
Contact: Clare Hart, President
Ed: Randall W. Forsyth. **Description:** Karachi bourse had a historic 8.6 percent one-day gain because the bourse banned short-selling for a month and announced a 30 billion rupee fund to stabilize the market. The shares of General Motors are trading within the same values that it had in 1974. The reasons for this decline are discussed.

43088 ■ *"Corporate Governance Reforms in China and India: Challenges and Opportunities" in Business Horizons (January-February 2008)*
Pub: Elsevier Advanced Technology Publications
Ed: Nandini Rajagopalan, Yan Zhang. **Description:** The evolution of corporate governance reforms and the role of privatization and globalization in India and China are studied. Shortage of qualified independent directors and lack of incentives were found to be two of the major challenges in governance. The implications of and solutions to these challenges are highlighted.

43089 ■ *"Corporate Social Responsibility and Trade Unions: Perspectives Across Europe"*
Pub: Routledge
Contact: Kevin Bradley, President
E-mail: kbradley@taylorandfrancis.com
Released: October 10, 2014. **Price:** , $140.76. **Description:** Although interest in corporate social responsibility (CSR) is focused on the relationship between business and key stakeholders such as

NGOs and local communities, the role of trade unions is rarely connected to CSR. Experts discuss the gap in the literature on both CSR and employment relations, namely trade union policies toward CSR as well as union engagement with particular CSR initiatives. The research covers eleven European countries which represent a sample of industrial relations structures across the continent.

43090 ■ *"Cost Remains Top Factor In Considering Green Technology"* **in Canadian Sailings (June 30, 2008)**
Ed: Julie Gedeon. **Description:** Improving its environmental performance remains a priority in the shipping industry; however, testing new technologies can prove difficult due to the harsh conditions that ships endure as well as installation which usually requires a dry dock.

43091 ■ *Country Studies in Entrepreneurship: A Historical Perspective*
Pub: Palgrave Macmillan
Contact: Lisa Dunn, Manager
E-mail: l.dunn@palgrave.com
Released: May 2006. **Price:** £90. **Description:** Comparison of eight national entrepreneurial ventures, covering three continents, is discussed. **Availability:** Print.

43092 ■ *"Courting Canadian Customers Confounds Car Dealers"* **in Business First Buffalo (November 12, 2007, pp. 1)**
Pub: American City Business Journals, Inc.
Ed: James Fink. **Description:** Strength of the Canadian dollar has led to an influx of potential customers for the Western New York automobile industry, but franchising restrictions and licensing as well as insurance issues have limited the potential of having larger sales figures. Border and trade issues that affect the car industry in WNY are also discussed.

43093 ■ *"CPR-CN Deal to Ease Vancouver Logjam"* **in Globe & Mail (January 27, 2006, pp. B4)**
Ed: Brent Jang. **Description:** In a bid to lessen West coast port grid lock Canadian Pacific Railway Ltd and Canadian National Railway Co. has agreed to share tracks in the Vancouver region. This will allow the trains to operate more efficiently from the Vancouver Port.

43094 ■ *"A Crash Course in Global Relations"* **in Canadian Business (Vol. 87, July 2014, No. 7, pp. 77)**
Pub: George Media Inc.
Released: July 2014. **Description:** Teach Away Inc. is a global education firm based in Toronto, Ontario that recruits English-speaking teachers to work abroad. The firm's revenues have grown by 1,621 percent from 2008 to 2013, placing it in the 37th spot on the 2014 Profit ranking of fastest growing companies in Canada.

43095 ■ *Creating Capitalism: Joint-Stock Enterprise in British Politics and Culture, 1800-1870*
Pub: Royal Historical Society
Contact: Prof. Peter Mandler, President
Ed: James Taylor. **Released:** 2006. **Description:** The growth of joint-stock business in Victorian Britain is discussed, particularly the resistance to it.

43096 ■ *"Creativity: A Key Link to Entrepreneurial Behavior"* **in Business Horizons (September-October 2007, pp. 365)**
Pub: Elsevier Technology Publications
Ed: Stephen Ko, John E. Butler. **Price:** $35.95. **Description:** Importance of creativity and its link to entrepreneurial behavior is examined. In a study of various entrepreneurs, studies concluded that a solid knowledge base, a well-developed social network, and a strong focus on identifying opportunities are relevant to entrepreneurial behavior.

43097 ■ *"Critics Target Bribery Law"* **in Wall Street Journal Eastern Edition (November 28, 2011, pp. B1)**
Pub: Dow Jones & Co., Inc.
Contact: Clare Hart, President
Ed: Joe Palazzuolo. **Description:** Concern about how the Foreign Corrupt Practices Act, the United States' anti-bribery law, is enforced has drawn the

focus of corporate lobbyists. Corporations have paid some $4 billion in penalties in cases involving the law, which prohibits companies from paying foreign officials bribes. The US Chamber of Commerce believes amending the act should be a priority.

43098 ■ *"A Crucial Step Toward Freer Trade"* **in Canadian Business (Vol. 85, August 13, 2012, No. 13, pp. 7)**
Pub: George Media Inc.
Ed: Tim Shufelt. **Released:** August 13, 2012. **Description:** The decision of the Canadian government to join the Trans-Pacific Partnership (TPP) has potential economic benefits in terms of trading with China and the U.S.Failure of the World Trade Ogranization's Doha Round and the admission of the U.S. to the TPP prompted Canada to join the trade agreement.

43099 ■ *"Crucible: Battling Back from Betrayal"* **in Harvard Business Review (Vol. 88, December 2010, No. 12, pp. 130)**
Pub: Harvard Business School Publishing
Ed: Daniel McGinn. **Description:** Stephen Greer's scrap metal firm, Hartwell Pacific, lost several million dollars due to a lack of efficient and appropriate inventory audits, accounting procedures, and new-hire reference checks for his foreign operations. Greer believes that balancing growth with control is a key component of success.

43100 ■ *Currency Internationalization: Global Experiences and Implications for the Renminbi*
Pub: Palgrave Macmillan
Contact: Lisa Dunn, Manager
E-mail: l.dunn@palgrave.com
Released: November 2009. **Price:** £79; $115. **Description:** A collection of academic studies relating to the potential internationalization of China's remninbi. It also discusses the increasing use of China's remninbi currency in international trade and finance. **Availability:** PrintE-book; PDF.

43101 ■ *D & B Principal International Businesses: The World Marketing Directory*
Pub: Dun & Bradstreet Inc.
Contact: Bob Carrigan, President
URL(s): dnb.com.au/Sales_and_Marketing/International_business_directories/Principal_International_Business_Directorywww.dnbla.com/pub.htm. **Released:** Annual **Price:** $595, commercial & library price. **Covers:** approximately 55,000 leading businesses in all lines, outside of the U.S., in 143 countries. **Entries include:** Company name, address, phone, fax, D&B number, telex, up to six Standard Industrial Classification (SIC) code, line of business, sales volume (in U.S. currency), number of employees, parent company and location, executive name and title, year established, and import/export designation. **Arrangement:** Geographical. **Indexes:** Geographical, cross-referenced alphabetical, industry classification.

43102 ■ *"Deal Snapshot: United Technologies Finalizes Clipper Windpower Sale"* **in M & A Navigator (August 30, 2012)**
Description: United TechnologiesCorporation (UTC) sold its subsidiary Clipper Windpower PLC, a wind turbine maker in the United Kingdom, to private equity firm Platinum Equity LLC.

43103 ■ *"Dealing With Dangers Abroad"* **in Financial Executive (Vol. 23, December 2007, No. 10, pp. 32)**
Ed: Jeffrey Marshall. **Description:** Clear processes and responsibilities for risk management for all companies going global are essential. U.S. toy manufacturer, Matel was put into crisis mode after its Chinese-made toys were recalled due to the use of lead-based paint or tiny magnets in its products.

43104 ■ *"Decline in Assets Is Costly for Advisers"* **in The Business Journal-Serving Metropolitan Kansas City (Vol. 27, October 24, 2008)**
Ed: James Dornbrook. **Description:** Financial advisers in the Kansas City, Missouri area are forced to cut costs as their assets have decreased sharply due

to the huge drop in stock prices. American Century Investments was forced to diversify into foreign assets and cut 90 jobs as its assets dropped to $84 billion. Diversification has softened the impact of the steep decline in stock prices for Waddell & Reed Financial Inc.

43105 ■ *"Deere to Open Technology Center in Germany"* **in Chicago Tribune (September 3, 2008)**
Ed: James P. Miller. **Description:** Deere & Co. plans to open a technology and innovation center in Germany; details of the company's expansion plans are discussed.

43106 ■ *"Delivering the Milk"* **in Barron's (Vol. 92, July 23, 2012, No. 30, pp. M7)**
Pub: Dow Jones & Co., Inc.
Contact: Clare Hart, President
Ed: Kopin Tan. **Released:** July 23, 2012. **Description:** The stocks of China Mengniu Dairy could continue losing value in the short term but could gain value in the long term. The company's revenue growth and profit margins face downward pressure due to aggressive pricing after food safety scandals.

43107 ■ *Democratization Without Representation: The Politics of Small Industry in Mexico*
Pub: Pennsylvania State University Press
Contact: Patrick H. Alexander, Director
E-mail: pha3@psu.edu
Ed: Kenneth C. Shalden. **Released:** March 2006. **Price:** $39.95, paperback; $94.95, hardcover. **Description:** Opportunities for individuals to participate in Mexico's democracy and how it is affecting the way industries do business. **Availability:** Print.

43108 ■ *"The Design of Tax Policy in Canada"* **in Canadian Journal of Economics (Vol. 44, November 2011, No. 4, pp. 1184)**
Pub: Wiley-Blackwell
Contact: Gordon Tibbitts, President
Ed: Kevin Milligan. **Description:** Empirical evidence and tax policy design are presented by Richard Blundell.

43109 ■ *"Despite Hot Toys, Holiday Sales Predicted To Be Ho-Ho-Hum"* **in Drug Store News (Vol. 29, November 12, 2007, No. 14, pp. 78)**
Ed: Doug Desjardins. **Description:** Summer toy recalls have retailers worried about holiday sales in 2007. Mattel was heavily impacted from the recall of millions of toys manufactured in China.

43110 ■ *"Destination Africa: A Look at How Tourism Could Change the Face and Economics of Africa"* **in Black Enterprise (February 2008)**
Pub: Earl G. Graves Publishing Co. Inc.
Contact: Earl G. Graves, Jr., President
Ed: Aisha Sylvester. **Description:** Countries in Africa are experiencing higher rates of growth in tourism than the worldwide average. Statistical data included.

43111 ■ *"Deutsche Bank Joins the Club Of Banks With Problems"* **in Barron's (Vol. 88, March 31, 2008, No. 13, pp. M6)**
Pub: Dow Jones & Co., Inc.
Contact: Clare Hart, President
Ed: Arindam Nag. **Description:** Deutsche Bank's tangible leverage has worsened sharply in the past year from 2.1 percent to 2.3 percent during 2002-2006 to only 1.6 percent. The bank has also been accumulating a lot of illiquid assets and its Level-3 assets are three times its tangible equity.

43112 ■ *"Developing Strategic Plan for Long-Term Growth"* **in Pittsburgh Business Times (Vol. 33, July 11, 2014, No. 52, pp. 10)**
Pub: American City Business Journals
Released: July 11, 2014. **Description:** Raymond Betler, new CEO of Wabtec Corporation, the only company with a 13-year streak of annual stock price increase on US exchanges is profiled. Betler attributes the company's growth to four corporate

strategies, including to grow internationally, focus on new product development, expand after-market opportunities, and pursue acquisitions.

43113 ■ Developmental Entrepreneurship: Adversity, Risk, and Isolation

Pub: Emerald Group Publishing Ltd.

Contact: Peter Shelley, Director

Released: July 05, 2006. Price: £67.95. Description: Volume five of the series, this book focuses on the fields of entrepreneurship, sociology, and economics. Fifteen articles related to entrepreneurship and small business development within a global environment are included. Availability: Print.

43114 ■ "DHL Receives Top Award for Corporate Responsibility Efforts" in Ecology, Environment & Conservation Business (April 26, 2014, pp. 6)

Pub: NewsHX

Contact: Susan E. Hasty, Publisher

Released: April 26, 2014. Description: DHL, freight forwarding company, is the only international express logistics provider recognized at the 4th Asian Excellence Recognition Awards for its outstanding Corporate Social Responsibility work. DHL Express Hong Kong is accredited as a '10 Years+ Caring Company' for its ten year contribution to the community.

43115 ■ Digital Divide: Civic Engagement, Information Poverty, and the Internet Worldwide

Pub: Cambridge University Press

Contact: Richard Ziemacki, President

E-mail: rziemacki@cambridge.org

Ed: Pippa Norris. Released: September 2001. Price: $32.99, paperback; $82, hardback. Description: The expansive growth of the Internet is intensifying existing inequalities between the information rich and poor. The book examines the evidence for access and use of the Internet in 179 countries and discusses the global divide that is evident between industrialized and developing societies. Availability: Print.

43116 ■ "Direct Recovery Associates Debt Collection Agency Beats Industry Record" in Internet Wire (June 24, 2010)

Pub: COMTEX

Contact: Chip Brian, President

Description: Direct Recovery Associates Inc. was named as one of the highest collection records in the industry, which has consistently improved over 18 years. The firm is an international attorney-based debt collection agency.

43117 ■ "Direct Recovery Associates, Inc. Debt Collection Agency Founder Featured in China Daily" in Marketwired (November 9, 2010)

Pub: COMTEX

Contact: Chip Brian, President

Description: Richard Hart, founder of Direct Recovery Associates, was featured in an article published in the China Daily. The article discussed the increased credit and debt collection demands involving the U.S. and China.

43118 ■ "Disney Has High Hopes for Duffy" in Canadian Business (Vol. 83, October 12, 2010, No. 17, pp. 14)

Pub: Rogers Media Inc.

Contact: Tony Viner, President

Ed: James Cowan. Description: The reintroduction of Duffy is expected to create a new, exclusive product line that distinguishes Disney's parks and stores from competitors. Duffy, a teddy bear, was first introduced at a Disney World store in Florida in 2002. The character was incorporated into the Disney mythology when its popularity grew in Japan.

43119 ■ "Diversity Knocks" in Canadian Business (Vol. 83, October 12, 2010, No. 17, pp. 62)

Pub: Rogers Media Inc.

Contact: Tony Viner, President

Ed: Angelina Chapin. Description: Canadian companies have a global edge because of their multicultural workforce. However, most of these organizations do not take advantage and avoid doing business abroad. Canadian firms could leverage their multicultural staff with language skills and knowledge of local customs.

43120 ■ "Dividing to Conquer" in Barron's (Vol. 88, March 31, 2008, No. 13, pp. 22)

Ed: Andrew Bary. Description: Altria's spin off of Philip Morris International could unlock substantial value for both domestic and international cigarette concerns. The strong brands and ample payouts from both companies will most likely impress investors.

43121 ■ "DocuSign Raises $85 Million for Electronic Signatures" in San Francisco Business Times (Vol. 28, March 7, 2014, No. 33, pp. 6)

Pub: American City Business Journals

Released: March 7, 2014. Description: DocuSign, the market leader in electronic signatures, reported that it was able to raise another $85 million in capital. The company is expected to file an initial public offering in 2014 or 2015. CFO, Mike Dinsdale, shares that the firm also wants to expand internationally.

43122 ■ Doing Business Anywhere: The Essential Guide to Going Global

Pub: John Wiley & Sons Inc.

Contact: Stephen M. Smith, President

Ed: Tom Travis. Description: Plans are given for new or existing businesses to organize, plan, operate and execute a business on a global basis. Trade agreements, brand protection and patents, ethics, security as well as cultural issues are among the issues addressed. Availability: E-book.

43123 ■ "Dollar Daze: Canadian Businesses Must Adjust to a New Reality" in Canadian Business (Vol. 80, Winter 2007, No. 24, pp. 11)

Ed: Jeff Sanford. Description: Several Canadian businessmen lost massive amounts in the Canadian value of their investments due to the volatility of the U.S. dollar. The factors that weighed down the value of the U.S. dollar include the announcement by China to diversify their currency reserves away from the U.S. dollar and concerns about the price of oil.

43124 ■ "Dollar Doldrums: How American Companies are Beating the Currency Crunch" in Inc. (March 2008, pp. 45-46)

Pub: Mansueto Ventures L.L.C.

Contact: John Koten, Chief Executive Officer

Ed: Sarah Goldstein. Description: Despite the low American dollar, some exporters are seeing a growth in their businesses, while other have had to relocate operations and switch to U.S. supplier. Four business owners tell how they are dealing with the current economic conditions.

43125 ■ "Don't Bet Against The House" in Barron's (Vol. 88, July 14, 2008, No. 28, pp. 20)

Pub: Dow Jones & Co., Inc.

Contact: Clare Hart, President

Ed: Sandra Ward. Description: Shares of Nasdaq OMX have lost more than 50 percent of their value from November 2007 to July 2008 but the value of these shares could climb 50 percent on the strength of world security exchanges. Only 15 percent of the company's revenues come from the U.S. and the shares are trading at 12.5 times the amount expected for 2008.

43126 ■ "Don't Tweak Your Supply Chain - Rethink It End to End" in Harvard Business Review (Vol. 88, October 2010, No. 10, pp. 62)

Pub: Harvard Business School Publishing

Ed: Hau L. Lee. Description: Hong Kong apparel firm Esquel Apparel Ltd. is used to illustrate supply chain reorganization to improve a firm's sustainability. Discussion focuses on taking a broad approach rather than addressing individual steps or processes.

43127 ■ "Dow Champions Innovative Energy Solutions for Auto Industry at NAIAS" in Business of Global Warming (January 25, 2010, pp. 7)

Description: This year's North American International Auto Show in Detroit will host the 'Electric Avenue' exhibit sponsored by the Dow Chemical Company. The display will showcase the latest in innovative energy solutions from Dow as well as electric vehicles and the technology supporting them. This marks the first time a non-automotive manufacturer is part of the main floor of the show.

43128 ■ "Down Mexico Way" in Canadian Business (Vol. 79, September 25, 2006, No. 19, pp. 27)

Description: Presidential election in Mexico and its effects on its economy is discussed.

43129 ■ "Downtown Living Gets Boost" in Dallas Business Journal (Vol. 35, March 9, 2012, No. 25, pp. 1)

Pub: American City Business Journal

Description: Turkey-based Polidev International LLC has anounced a plan to convert the 1401 Elm Street Tower in Dallas, Texas into 528 apartments or 39-stories of residential real estate. The real estate development company's plan would bring the largest block of apartments in a single tower within the central business district.

43130 ■ "Dragon, but.." in Canadian Business (Vol. 81, December 8, 2008, No. 21, pp. 45)

Pub: Rogers Media Inc.

Contact: Tony Viner, President

Ed: Matthew McClearn. Description: The greatest challenge in smooth trade relations between China and Canada is believed to be lukewarm relations with China over human rights issues. Australia on the other hand, has attracted huge Chinese outward direct investments because of strong trade relations.

43131 ■ "Dreaming in Macau" in Canadian Business (Vol. 81, December 8, 2008, No. 21, pp. 65)

Pub: Rogers Media Inc.

Contact: Tony Viner, President

Ed: Joe Chidley. Description: Key information, as well as views on the economic aspects of Macau are presented. Macau was once monopolized by Stanley Ho's Sociedad de Turismo e Diversoes de Macau, but the government transformed the area into a leisure-and-entertainment spot. Details about Cirque de Soleil are also presented.

43132 ■ "Drilling Deep and Flying High" in Barron's (Vol. 88, June 30, 2008, No. 26, pp. 34)

Pub: Dow Jones & Co., Inc.

Contact: Clare Hart, President

Ed: Kenneth Rapoza. Description: Shares of Petrobras could rise another 25 percent if the three deep-water wells that the company has found proves as lucrative as some expect. Petrobras will become an oil giant if the reserves are proven.

43133 ■ E-Commerce in Regional Small to Medium Enterprises

Pub: IGI Global

Contact: Dr. Mehdi Khosrow-Pour, President

Ed: Robert MacGregor, Lejla Vrazalic. Released: June 2007. Price: $99.95. Description: Strategies small to medium enterprises (SMEs) need to implement in order to compete with larger, global businesses and the role electronic commerce plays in this process are outlined. Studies of e-commerce in multiple regional areas, focusing on the role of business size, business sector, market focus, gender of CEO, and education level of the CEO are discussed. Availability: Print; E-book.

43134 ■ "EADS Consolidates Cyber Security Expertise" in Flight International (May 8, 2012, No. 789)

Pub: Reed Elsevier Group plc Reed Business Information

Contact: Mark Kelsey, Chief Executive Officer

Released: May 8, 2012. Description: Defence EADS' Caddidian Defense Division launched Cassidian Cyber Security to address markets located in

Europe, the Middle East. Initially EADS is focusing on Germany, the UK and France and is targeting sales to reach $657 million by 2017.

43135 ■ "Easy to be Queasy" in Canadian Business (Vol. 81, December 24, 2007, No. 1, pp. 25)

Ed: Jack Mintz. **Description:** Canada could be facing a slowdown in economic growth for 2008 as the country's economy depends on the U.S. economy, which is still facing recession in the subprime market. Details on Canada's economic growth, the impact of the weak U.S. dollar, increase in the unemployment rate, and decline in tax revenue are explored.

43136 ■ "easyhome Ltd. Discovers Employee Fraud at an Easyfinancial Kiosk Company" in Internet Wire (October 14, 2010)

Pub: COMTEX

Contact: Chip Brian, President

Description: Canada's leading merchandise leasing company and provider of financial services, easyhome Ltd., reported employee fraud totaling $3.4 million that was perpetrated against the firm's easyfinancial services business.

43137 ■ "EBay Finally Gaining Traction in China" in San Jose Mercury News (October 26, 2011)

Pub: San Jose Mercury News Inc.

Contact: Barbara Vroman, Manager

E-mail: bvroman@sjmercury.com

Ed: John Boudreau. **Description:** eBay has developed a new strategy in China that allows exporters of every type of merchandise to sell directly to eBays 97 million overseas users.

43138 ■ EBay Income: How ANYONE of Any Age, Location, and/or Background Can Build a Highly Profitable Online Business with eBay

Pub: Atlantic Publishing Co.

Contact: Amanda Miller, Manager

E-mail: amiller@atlantic-pub.com

Released: Revised Second Edition. **Price:** $24.95. **Description:** A complete overview of eBay is given and guides any small company through the entire process of creating the auction and auction strategies, photography, writing copy, text and formatting, multiple sales, programming tricks, PayPal, accounting, creating marketing, merchandising, managing email lists, advertising plans, taxes and sales tax, best time to list items and for how long, sniping programs, international customers, opening a storefront, electronic commerce, buy-it now pricing, keywords, Google marketing and eBay secrets.

43139 ■ "Economic Distance and the Survival of Foreign Direct Investments" in Academy of Management Journal (Vol. 50, No. 5, October 1, 2007, pp. 1156)

Pub: Academy of Management

Contact: Ming-Jer Chen, President

Ed: Eric W.K. Tsang, Paul S.L. Yip. **Description:** Study was undertaken to assess the relationship between economic disparities of various countries and foreign direct investments, focusing on Singapore. Results revealed that economic distance has a definite impact on foreign direct investment hazard rates.

43140 ■ The Economics and Management of Small Business: An International Perspective

Pub: Routledge

Contact: Kevin Bradley, President

E-mail: kbradley@taylorandfrancis.com

Ed: Graham Bannock. **Released:** January 20, 2005. **Price:** $200, hardback. **Description:** International perspectives on the economics and management of small business, featuring case studies and empirical research. **Availability:** Print.

43141 ■ "Economics: The User's Guide"

Pub: Bloomsbury Press

Released: August 26, 2014. **Price:** , $30.00. **Description:** Cambridge economist explains how the global economy is working. He provides a concise knowledge of history with a disregard for conventional economic traditions and offers insights into economic behavior.

43142 ■ "Edging Toward Disaster" in Canadian Business (Vol. 85, July 16, 2012, No. 12, pp. 9)

Pub: George Media Inc.

Ed: Graham F. Scott. **Released:** July 16, 2012. **Description:** The possibility that Green may default and exit from the Eurozone could trigger a series of bank runs in Europe and not even the solvenc of the European Central Bank is guaranteed, having already spent over trillion Euro in bailouts. Greek banks have lost 72 billion Euro in deposits since 2010 while clients withdrew 97 billion Euro from Spanish banks in the first quarter 2012.

43143 ■ "Editorial: Competition At Last?" in Canadian Business (Vol. 81, July 22, 2008, No. 12-13, pp. 7)

Pub: Rogers Media Inc.

Contact: Tony Viner, President

Description: Competition Policy Review Panel's 'Compete to Win' report revealed that Canada is being 'hollowed-out' by foreign acquisitions. The panel investigated competition and foreign investment policies in Canada. Key information on the report, as well as views on the Investment Canada Act and the Competition Act, is presented.

43144 ■ "An Educated Play on China" in Barron's (Vol. 88, June 30, 2008, No. 26, pp. M6)

Pub: Dow Jones & Co., Inc.

Contact: Clare Hart, President

Ed: Mohammed Hadi. **Description:** New Oriental Education & Technology Group sells English-language courses to an increasingly competitive Chinese workforce that values education. The shares in this company have been weighed down by worries on the impact of the Beijing Olympics on enrollment and the Sichuan earthquake. These shares could be a great way to get exposure to the long-term growth in China.

43145 ■ Effect of the Overvalued Dollar on Small Exporters: Hearing Before the Committee on Small Business, U.S. House of Representatives

Pub: DIANE Publishing Co.

Contact: Dorothy J. Perkins, Manager

E-mail: dorothyjperkins@hotmail.com

Released: September 2002. **Price:** $30. **Description:** Congressional hearing: Witnesses: Dr. Lawrence Chimerine, Economist; Tony Raimondo, President and CEO, Behlen Manufacturing Company; Robert J. Weskamp, President, Wes-Tech, Inc.; Wayne Dollar, President, Georgia Farm Bureau; and Vargese George, President and CEO, Westex International, Inc. Appendix includes correspondence sent to committee on the overvalued dollar. **Availability:** Print.

43146 ■ "Elastic Path Software Joins Canada in G20 Young Entrepreneur Summit" in Internet Wire (June 14, 2010)

Pub: COMTEX

Contact: Chip Brian, President

Description: The Canadian Youth Business Foundation hosted the G20 Young Entrepreneur Summit and announced that Harry Chemko of British Columbia's Elastic Path Software will be a member of the Canadian delegation at the G20 Young Entrepreneur Summit. Details are included.

43147 ■ Electronic Commerce

Pub: Course Technology

Contact: Manuel Guzman, President (Acting)

Ed: Gary P. Schneider, Bryant Chrzan, Charles McCormick. **Released:** May 01, 2010. **Price:** $149.99. **Description:** E-commerce can open the door to more opportunities than ever before for small business. Packed with real-world examples and cases, the book delivers comprehensive coverage of emerging online technologies and trends and their influence on the electronic marketplace. It details how the landscape of online commerce is evolving, reflecting changes in the economy and how business and society are responding to those changes. Balancing technological issues with the strategic business aspects of successful e-commerce, the new edition includes expanded coverage of international issues, social

networking, mobile commerce, Web 2.0 technologies, and updates on spam, phishing, and identity theft. **Availability:** Print.

43148 ■ The Elephant and the Dragon: The Rise of India and China and What It Means for All of Us

Pub: W.W. Norton and Company Inc.

Contact: A Malmud, President

Ed: Robyn Meredith. **Released:** June 2008. **Price:** $25.95, hardcover; $16.95, paperback. **Description:** The author illustrates how both China and India have followed their own economic path, and examines the countries' similarities and considers the repercussions of their growing involvement in the world market. **Availability:** Print.

43149 ■ Emerging Business Online: Global Markets and the Power of B2B Internet Marketing

Pub: FT Press

Contact: Timothy C. Moore, Vice President

Ed: Lara Fawzy, Lucas Dworski. **Released:** October 04, 2010. **Price:** $49.99. **Description:** An introduction into ebocube (emerging business online), a comprehensive proven business model for Internet B2B marketing in emerging markets.

43150 ■ "End of the Beginning" in Canadian Business (Vol. 81, November 10, 2008, No. 19, pp. 17)

Pub: Rogers Media Inc.

Contact: Tony Viner, President

Ed: David Wolf. **Description:** The freeze in the money markets and historic decline in equity markets around the world finally forced governments into aggressive coordinated action. The asset price inflation brought on by cheap credit will now work in reverse and the tightening of credit will be difficult economically. Canada is exposed to the fallout everywhere, given that the U.S, the U.K. and Japan buy 30 percent of Canada's output.

43151 ■ "The End of RIM" in Canadian Business (Vol. 85, August 13, 2012, No. 13, pp. 22)

Pub: George Media Inc.

Ed: Joe Castaldo. **Released:** August 13, 2012. **Description:** The potential implications of the collapse of Research in Motion (RIM) on the Canadian technology sector are examined. The country is expected to lose its biggest training ground for technology talent without RIM, but the company's decline will not stop Canadians from trying to build and sustain multinational technolgy companies.

43152 ■ "Enforcer In Fantasyland" in Crain's New York Business (Vol. 24, February 25, 2008, No. 8, pp. 10)

Ed: Hilary Potkewitz. **Description:** Patent law, particularly in the toy and game industry, is recession-proof according to Barry Negrin, partner at Pryor Cashman. Negrin co-founded his patent practice group. Despite massive recalls of toys and the concern over toxic toys, legal measures are in place in this industry.

43153 ■ Enterprising Women in Urban Zimbabwe: Gender, Microbusiness, and Globalization

Pub: Indiana University Press

Contact: Robert Sloan, Director

E-mail: rjsloan@indiana.edu

Ed: Mary Johnson Osirim. **Released:** May 01, 2009. **Price:** $23.97, cloth. **Description:** An investigation into the business and personal experiences of women entrepreneurs in the microenterprise sector in Zimbabwe. Many of these women work as market traders, crocheters, seamstresses, and hairdressers. **Availability:** Print.

43154 ■ The Entrepreneurial Culture: Network Advantage Within Chinese and Irish Software Firms

Pub: Edward Elgar Publishing Inc.

Contact: Richard Henning, Vice President

E-mail: kwight@e-elgar.com

Ed: Denise Tsang. **Released:** 2006. **Price:** £66.60. **Description:** Ways national cultural heritage influences entrepreneurial ventures are discussed. **Availability:** Print.

43155 ■ *Entrepreneurial Strategies: New Technologies and Emerging Markets*
Pub: Blackwell Publishing Inc.
Contact: Gordon Tibbitts, III, President
Released: August 2006. **Price:** $100; $80.99. **Description:** Ideas to help a small business expand into emerging market economies (EMEs) are discussed. Despite the high failure rate, this book helps a small firm develop a successful plan. **Availability:** PrintE-book.

43156 ■ *Entrepreneurship: Frameworks and Empirical Investigations from Forthcoming Leaders of European Research*
Pub: Emerald Group Publishing Ltd.
Contact: Peter Shelley, Director
Released: May 25, 2006. **Price:** £67.95. **Description:** Entrepreneurial research and theory cover the early growth of research-based startups and the role of learning in international entrepreneurship, focusing on Europe. **Availability:** Print.

43157 ■ *Entrepreneurship, Investment and Spatial Dynamics: Lessons and Implications for an Enlarged EU*
Pub: Edward Elgar Publishing Inc.
Contact: Richard Henning, Vice President
E-mail: kwight@e-elgar.com
Ed: Peter Nijkamp, Ronald L. Moomaw, Iulia Traistaru-Siedschlag. **Released:** 2006. **Price:** £67.50. **Description:** Understanding the impact and interaction between investment, knowledge and entrepreneurship with an expanding European Union. **Availability:** Print.

43158 ■ *Entrepreneurship and Small Business*
Pub: Palgrave Macmillan
Contact: Lisa Dunn, Manager
E-mail: l.dunn@palgrave.com
Ed: Paul Burns. **Released:** 3rd Edition . **Price:** $78, paperback; £44.99, paperback. **Description:** Entrepreneurial skills, focusing on good management practices are discussed. Topics include family businesses, corporate, international and social entrepreneurship.

43159 ■ *Entrepreneurship and Small Business Development in the Former Soviet Bloc*
Ed: David Smallbone, Friederike Welter. **Released:** January 10, 2010. **Price:** $140. **Description:** Examination of entrepreneurship and small business in Russia and other key countries of Eastern Europe, showing how far small businesses have developed in the region.

43160 ■ *Entrepreneurship and SMEs in the Euro-Zone*
Pub: Imperial College Press
Ed: Leo-Paul Dana. **Description:** Information regarding entrepreneurship and SMEs in Europe is presented.

43161 ■ *"ESolar Partners With Penglai on Landmark Solar Thermal Agreement for China"* in Business of Global Warming (January 25, 2010, pp. 8)
Description: Penglai Electric, a privately-owned Chinese electrical power equipment manufacturer, and eSolar, a global provider of cost-effective and reliable solar power plants, announced a master licensing agreement in which eSolar will build at least 2 gigawatts of solar thermal power plants in China over the next 10 years.

43162 ■ *"Espirito Santo Bank Mulls Potential Buyers"* in South Florida Business Journal (Vol. 35, August 22, 2014, No. 4, pp. 4)
Pub: American City Business Journals
Released: August 22, 2014. **Description:** G. Frederick Reinhardt is looking for potential buyers of his $735 million asset Espirito Santo Bank in Miami, Florida. Reinhardt says the bank would be a good franchise for buyers interested in international banking.

43163 ■ *"European Stocks on Deck"* in Barron's (Vol. 89, July 27, 2009, No. 30, pp. M7)
Pub: Dow Jones & Co., Inc.
Contact: Clare Hart, President
Ed: Vito J. Racanelli. **Description:** European stocks are cheap and these trade at a discount to U.S. equities rarely seen in the past 40 years. This represents an opportunity for Americans and trends show that Europe's stocks outperform when there is a discrepancy between the price to earnings ratio in European stocks versus U.S. stocks and when sentiment on European equities are downbeat.

43164 ■ *"Europe's Meltdown"* in Canadian Business (Vol. 83, June 15, 2010, No. 10, pp. 76)
Ed: Bryan Borzykowski. **Description:** As European countries such as Greece, Spain, and Portugal struggle with debt problems, it is worth noting that its equities trade at a 30 percent discount to the U.S. and that a 10 percent drop in the Euro translates to a 10 percent rise in profitability for exporters. Investors may also want to focus on business-to-business operations rather than consumer-focused ones.

43165 ■ *"Event Stresses Cross-Border Cooperation"* in Crain's Detroit Business (Vol. 24, March 30, 2008, No. 13, pp. 5)
Pub: Crain Communications Inc.
Contact: Rance E. Crain, President
Ed: Chad Halcom. **Description:** According to John Austin, a senior fellow of The Brookings Institution, open immigration policies, better transportation and trade across the border and a cleanup of the Great Lakes will bring economic resurgence to Midwestern states and Canadian provinces with manufacturing economies.

43166 ■ *"Everybody Wants To Save the World: But When You Start a Charity Overseas, Good Intentions Often Go Awry"* In Inc. (December 2007)
Pub: Gruner and Jahr USA Publishing Co.
Contact: J. Russell Denson, President
Ed: Dalia Fahmy. **Description:** Unique set of challenges faced by small businesses wanting to create a charity overseas. Five key issues to explore before starting a charity overseas are examined.

43167 ■ *"Ex-Im Bank Accepts $105 Million in Financing for Aquarium in Brazil"* in Travel & Leisure Close-Up (October 8, 2012)
Description: Export-Import Bank of the United States authorized a $105 million direct loan to the Brazilian state of Ceara to finance the export of American goods and services for the construction of an aquarium in Fortaleza, Brazil. This transaction will support 700 American jobs and at least 90 percent of the export contract value will be provided by U.S. small businesses.

43168 ■ *"Executive Session: Mike Bergey, Bergey Windpower"* in Journal Record (June 1, 2012)
Pub: Dolan Media Inc.
Ed: Sarah Terry-Cobo. **Description:** Cofounder and president of Bergey Windpower located in Norman, Oklahoma, is working to keep manufacturing going in the US. His firm manufactures small wind turbines for homes and businesses. He addresses aggressive government programs in the European Union that are increasing sales in the United Kingdom and other countries in the region. California, New York, Ohio and Vermont are the strongest markets in the United States.

43169 ■ *"Executives Exit at Wal-Mart in China"* in Wall Street Journal Eastern Edition (October 17 , 2011, pp. B3)
Pub: Dow Jones & Co., Inc.
Contact: Clare Hart, President
Ed: Laurie Burkitt. **Description:** Woes for Wal-Mart Inc.'s subsidiary in China are adding up as Wal-Mart China president and chief executive Ed Chan stepped down, as well as the company's senior vice president for human resources, Clara Wong. The company has been charged by regulators with mislabeling pork products, the result which has forced stores to close. Sales in China have been slow at the retail stores.

43170 ■ *"Export Opportunity"* in Business Journal-Portland (Vol. 24, October 12, 2007, No. 33, pp. 1)
Ed: Matthew Kish. **Description:** U.S. dollar is weak, hitting an all-time low against the Euro, while the Canadian dollar is also performing well it hit parity for the first time after more than thirty years. The weak U.S. dollar is making companies that sell overseas benefit as it makes their goods cheaper to buy.

43171 ■ *Export Sales and Marketing Manual*
Pub: Export Institute
Contact: Mr. John R. Jagoe, Director
Released: Annual; Latest edition 24th; 2011. **Price:** $295, Individuals print or CD; $395, Other countries print & CD. **Publication includes:** List of approximately 4,000 international trade contacts, including World Trade Centers, U.S. Department of Commerce Trade Specialists and Country Desk Officers, State International Trade offices, small business development centers, U.S. Customs services, U.S. Port Authorities, U.S. embassies, foreign trade associations in the U.S., and chambers of commerce in foreign countries, and foreign embassies and chambers of commerce in the U.S. **Entries include:** Name, address, phone, fax, name and title of contact, geographical area served, products covered, description of services, and 1,200 internet addresses of export-related sites. Principal content of publication is a step-by-step program showing U.S. companies and entrepreneurs how to begin exporting or increase their existing overseas sales. **Arrangement:** Classified by product/service and export marketing functions. **Indexes:** General, international trade or export/import. Worksheets, graphs, flow charts, pricing and budgeting formats, international price quotations, export contracts, international shipping documents, samples of international correspondence, glossaries, index and illustrations.

43172 ■ *"Face Values: Responsibility Inc"* in Business Strategy Review (Vol. 21, Summer 2010, No. 2, pp. 66)
Pub: John Wiley & Sons Inc. Scientific, Technical, Medical, and Scholarly Div. (Wiley-Blackwell)
Contact: William J. Pesce, Manager
E-mail: wpesce@wiley.com
Ed: John Connolly. **Description:** Investment and growth in emerging markets will bring new opportunities, but with them added responsibility. Will companies be able to rise to meet the new responsibility agenda?.

43173 ■ *"Face Values: Responsibility Inc."* in Business Strategy Review (Vol. 21, Summer 2010, No. 2, pp. 66)
Pub: Blackwell Publishers Ltd.
Ed: John Connolly. **Description:** Investment and growth in emerging markets will bring new opportunities, but added responsibility comes with it. Will companies be able to rise to meet the new responsibility agenda?.

43174 ■ *Facilitating Sustainable Innovation through Collaboration: A Multi-Stakeholder Perspective*
Pub: Springer-Verlag New York Inc.
Contact: Ruediger Gebauer, President
Ed: Joseph Sarkis, James J. Cordeiro, Diego Vazquez Brust. **Released:** March 10, 2010. **Price:** €95.19; €114.99, Hardcover. **Description:** An international perspective of sustainable innovation with contributions from Australia, Europe, and North America, by prominent policy makers, scientific researchers and others. **Availability:** E-book.

43175 ■ *"Facing the Future"* in Canadian Business (Vol. 81, March 31, 2008, No. 5, pp. 69)
Pub: Rogers Media Inc.
Contact: Tony Viner, President
Ed: John Gray. **Description:** Discusses a web poll of 122 Canadian CEOs which shows that these leaders are convinced that the U.S. economy is slowing but are split on the impact that this will have on the

Canadian economy. The aging and retiring workforce and the strong Canadian dollar are other concerns by these leaders.

43176 ■ *Factory Girls: From Village to City in a Changing China*
Pub: Spiegel & Grau
Ed: Leslie T. Chang. **Released:** August 04, 2009. **Price:** $16, paperback. **Description:** Young women who flee the rural villages in China find exhausting work and social mobility working in factories. **Availability:** Print.

43177 ■ *"Fair Play? China Cheats, Carney Talks and Rankin Walks; Here's the Latest"* in *Canadian Business (Vol. 81, March 17, 2008, No. 4)*
Pub: Rogers Media Inc.
Contact: Tony Viner, President
Description: Discusses the World Trade Organization which says that China is breaking trade rules by taxing imports of auto parts at the same rate as foreign-made finished cars. Mark Carney first speech as the governor of the Bank of Canada made economists suspect a rate cut on overnight loans. Andre Rankin was ordered by the Ontario Securities Commission to pay $250,000 in investigation costs.

43178 ■ *False Economy: A Surprising Economic History of the World*
Ed: Alan Beattie. **Released:** 2009. **Price:** $26.95. **Description:** History shows that the choices made by countries, not luck, determine its economic fate.

43179 ■ *"Familiar Fun"* in *Crain's Cleveland Business (Vol. 28, October 22, 2007, No. 42, pp. 3)*
Ed: John Booth. **Description:** Marketing for the 2007 holiday season has toy retailers focusing on American-made products because of recent recalls of toys produced in China that do not meet U.S. safety standards.

43180 ■ *"Fast Revival Unlikely For Indian 'Net Stocks"* in *Barron's (Vol. 88, July 7, 2008, No. 27, pp. 12)*
Pub: Dow Jones & Co., Inc.
Contact: Clare Hart, President
Ed: Leslie P. Norton. **Description:** Shares of Indian Internet companies Rediff.com and Sify are not likely to stage a rebound due to weak financial results. Rediff.com shares have declined 39.2 percent in 2008, while Sify shares are down 35.8 percent.

43181 ■ *Faster Cheaper Better*
Ed: Michael Hammer. **Released:** December 28, 2010. **Price:** $27.50. **Description:** Nine levels for transforming work in order to achieve business growth are outlined. The book helps small business compete against the low-wage countries.

43182 ■ *"Fed May Ban Amphibian Trade"* in *Pet Product News (Vol. 64, November 2010, No. 11, pp. 13)*
Pub: Bowtie Inc.
Description: U.S. Fish and Wildlife Service is seeking public input on a petition submitted by the conservation activist group Defenders of Wildlife. The petition involves possible classification of chytrid fungus-infected amphibians and amphibian eggs as 'injurious wildlife' under the Lacey Act. Interstate trading or importation of injurious wildlife into the U.S. is not allowed.

43183 ■ *Female Entrepreneurship in East and South-East Asia: Opportunities and Challenges*
Pub: Woodhead Publishing Ltd.
Ed: Philippe Debroux. **Released:** February 10, 2010. **Price:** $145. **Description:** A detailed study of female entrepreneurship in Asia, where public authorities are slowly realizing the importance of women as workers and entrepreneurs. **Availability:** Print; E-book.

43184 ■ *"Fertilizer for Growth"* in *Canadian Business (Vol. 83, September 14, 2010, No. 15, pp. 76)*
Pub: Rogers Media Inc.
Contact: Tony Viner, President
Ed: Bryan Borzykowski. **Description:** Australian-based BHP Billiton launches a C$38.5 billion hostile takeover bid for Saskatchewan-based Potash Corpo-

ration and some investors immediately bought Potash stock at C$130. However, Potash has resisted BHP's offer and announced a plan to try to stop the deal.

43185 ■ *"Fight Against Fake"* in *The Business Journal-Portland (Vol. 25, July 18, 2008, No. 19, pp. 1)*
Ed: Erik Siemers. **Description:** Companies, such as Columbia Sportswear Co. and Nike Inc., are fighting the counterfeiting of their sportswear and footwear products through the legal process of coordinating with law enforcement agencies to raid factories. Most of the counterfeiting factories are in China and India. Other details on the issue are discussed.

43186 ■ *"Finally! Windsor Gets a New Bridge"* in *Canadian Business (Vol. 85, September 17, 2012, No. 14, pp. 20)*
Pub: George Media Inc.
Ed: Tim Shufelt. **Released:** September 17, 2012. **Description:** Canadian Prime Minister Stephen Harper agreed to loan Michigan $550 million to build its new highway interchange and customs plaza linking Windsor, Ontario and Detroit, Michigan. Billionaire Manuel Maroun, owner of the Ambassador Bridge, has initiated a signature campaign for a referendum on any new border crossings.

43187 ■ *"The Finance Function In A Global Corporation"* in *Harvard Business Review (Vol. 86, July-August 2008, No. 8, pp. 108)*
Pub: Harvard Business Review Press
Contact: Peter E. Walsh, Director
Ed: Mihir A. Desai. **Description:** Designing and implementing a successful finance function in a global setting is discussed. Additional topics include the internal capital market, managing risk and budgeting capital internationally.

43188 ■ *"Finding A Higher Gear"* in *Harvard Business Review (Vol. 86, July-August 2008, No. 8, pp. 68)*
Pub: Harvard Business Review Press
Contact: Peter E. Walsh, Director
Ed: Thomas A. Stewart, Anand P. Raman. **Description:** Anand G. Mahindra, the chief executive officer of Mahindra and Mahindra Ltd., discusses how his company fosters innovation, drawn from customer centricity, and how this will grow the company beyond India's domestic market.

43189 ■ *"Finding a Bargain Amid China's Rubble"* in *Barron's (Vol. 92, August 25, 2012, No. 38, pp. M7)*
Pub: Dow Jones & Co., Inc.
Contact: Clare Hart, President
Ed: Kopin Tan. **Description:** Chinese stock prices have fallen due to uncertainty about the strength of the Chinese economy. The stock prices of China Communciations Construction could rise as the company continues to increase construction activity in China and overseas.

43190 ■ *"Finding Life Behind the Numbers"* in *Crain's Chicago Business (Vol. 31, March 24, 2008, No. 12, pp. 25)*
Pub: Crain Communications Inc.
Contact: Todd Johnson, Publisher
Ed: Samantha Stainburn. **Description:** Interview with Phillip Capodice who is a graduate student at DePaul University's Kellstadt Graduate School of Business and studied abroad in Lima, Peru where he visited a number of companies including some who are trade partners with the United States.

43191 ■ *"Finding the Right Resources to Get Started Overseas"* in *Pittsburgh Business Times (Vol. 33, January 3, 2014, No. 25, pp. 4)*
Pub: American City Business Journals
Released: January 3, 2014. **Description:** Pittsburgh, Pennsylvania-based companies can develop relationships abroad and take advantage of the market opportunity to expand. Companies are unaware of the many helpful agencies, organizations and Websites that help them become international. Tips for developing relationships overseas are presented.

43192 ■ *"Finding Your Place in the World: Global Diversity Has Become a Corporate Catchphrase"* in *Black Enterprise (November 2007)*
Pub: Earl G. Graves Publishing Co. Inc.
Contact: Earl G. Graves, Jr., President
Ed: Wendy Harris. **Description:** Does the inclusion of workers from other countries mean exclusion of African American workers in the U.S.?.

43193 ■ *"Firm Takes 'Local' Worldwide"* in *Hispanic Business (July-August 2007, pp. 48)*
Pub: Hispanic Business Inc.
Contact: Jesus Chavarria, President
Ed: Keith Rosenblum. **Description:** Willy A. Bermello tells how he has expanded his architectural, engineering and construction firm globally.

43194 ■ *"Five-Ring Circus"* in *Entrepreneur (Vol. 35, November 2007, No. 11, pp. 76)*
Pub: Entrepreneur Press
Contact: Perlman Neil, President
Ed: Scott Bernard Nelson. **Description:** China's economy is growing and is expected to do well even after the 2008 Olympics, but growth could slow from eleven percent to eight or nine percent. Chinese portfolio concerns with regard to health and environmental records and bureaucratic fraud are discussed.

43195 ■ *"Flying the Unfriendly Skies"* in *Crain's Chicago Business (Vol. 31, April 21, 2008, No. 16, pp. 26)*
Pub: Crain Communications Inc.
Contact: Todd Johnson, Publisher
Ed: Sarah A. Klein. **Description:** Due to the number of Chicago companies and entrepreneurs who are traveling overseas more frequently in order to strengthen ties with customers, companies and oftentimes even business partners, the number of flights leaving O'Hare International Airport for destinations abroad has surged; In 2007, international passengers departing O'Hare totaled 5.7 million, up from 2.4 million in 1990.

43196 ■ *"For Baxter, A Lingering PR Problem"* in *Crain's Chicago Business (April 21, 2008)*
Pub: Crain Communications Inc.
Contact: Todd Johnson, Publisher
Ed: Mike Colias. **Description:** Baxter International Inc.'s recall of the blood-thinning medication heparin has exposed the company to costly litigation and put the perils of overseas drug manufacturing in the spotlight. Wall Street investors predict that an indefinite halt in production of the drug should not hurt the company's bottom line since heparin represents a tiny sliver of the business. Since Baxter began recalling the drug in January its shares have continued to outpace most other medical stocks.

43197 ■ *Forces of Fortune: The Rise of the New Muslim Middle Class and What It Will Mean for Our World*
Ed: Vali Nasr. **Released:** September 10, 2009. **Price:** $26. **Description:** The author argues that entrepreneurial, religiously conservative contingents in such countries as Turkey, Pakistan, and Iran can propel the Middle East into democratic and prosperous times.

43198 ■ *"ForeSee Finds Satisfaction On Web Sites, Bottom Line"* in *Crain's Detroit Business (Vol. 24, February 25, 2008, No. 8, pp. 3)*
Pub: Crain Communications Inc. - Detroit
Contact: Keith Crain, Chairman
Ed: Tom Henderson. **Description:** Ann Arbor-based ForeSee Results Inc. evaluates user satisfaction on Web sites. The company expects to see an increase of 40 percent in revenue for 2008 with plans to expand to London, Germany, Italy and France by the end of 2009.

43199 ■ *"The Foundations of Supplier Engagement; Companies' Relationships With Their Suppliers Are Vital To Their Success. Here Are the Fundamental Ways Businesses Can Measure and Manage Those Relationships"* in *Gallup Business Journal*

(June 26, 2014)
Pub: Gallup Press
Released: June 26, 2014. **Description:** The global economy has changed the nature of supplier-customer relationships. A company's relationship with their suppliers is critical to success. Fundamental ways any business can measure and manage their relationships with suppliers and become a customer of choice are examined.

43200 ■ *"The Four Cheapest Plays in Emerging Markets"* in Barron's (Vol. 89, July 27, 2009, No. 30, pp. 34)
Pub: Dow Jones & Co., Inc.
Contact: Clare Hart, President
Ed: Lawrence C. Strauss. **Description:** Portfolio manager Arjun Divecha of the GMO Emerging Markets III Fund says that the main thing in investing in emerging markets is getting the country right since getting it wrong makes it harder to add value. Divecha says that the four countries that they are positive on are Turkey, Russia, South Korea, and Thailand.

43201 ■ *"Franchise Law in China: Law, Regulations, and Guidelines"* in Franchise Law Journal (Vol. 27, Summer 2007, No. 1, pp. 57)
Pub: American Bar Association
Contact: Carolyn Lamm, President
Ed: Paul Jones, Erik B. Wulff. **Description:** Issues faced by foreign franchising are discussed, with a focus on China.

43202 ■ *"A Baby Step to the South"* in Canadian Business (Vol. 81, July 22, 2008, No. 12-13, pp. 21)
Pub: Rogers Media Inc.
Contact: Tony Viner, President
Ed: Jane Bao. **Description:** Canada's free trade agreement (FTA) with Colombia is seen as Canada's re-engagement with Latin America. Some politicians believe that the FTA is more of a political agreement than a trade agreement with Colombia. Key information on Canada's trade agreements, as well as trade with Colombia and Latin American countries, is presented.

43203 ■ *"Freeing the Wheels of Commerce"* in Hispanic Business (July-August 2007, pp. 50, 52, 54)
Pub: Hispanic Business Inc.
Contact: Jesus Chavarria, President
Ed: Keith Rosenblum. **Description:** SecureOrigins, a border-based partnership with high-tech innovators is working to move goods faster, more efficiently, and securely.

43204 ■ *"Fries With That?"* in Canadian Business (Vol. 81, September 29, 2008, No. 16, pp. 33)
Ed: Calvin Leung. **Description:** Profile of Toronto-based New York Fries, which has four stores in South Korea, is planning to expand further as well as into Hong Kong and Macau; the company also has a licensee in the United Arab Emirates whom is also planning to expand.

43205 ■ *"From American Icon to Global Juggernaut"* in Automotive News (Vol. 86, October 31, 2011, No. 6488, pp. S003)
Pub: Crain Communications Inc.
Contact: Rance E. Crain, President
Ed: Peter Brown. **Description:** Chevrolet celebrates its 100th Anniversary. The brand revolutionized its market with affordable cars that bring technology to the masses. Chevys have been sold in 140 countries and the company is responding to a broader market.

43206 ■ *"From Malls to Steel Plants"* in Crain's Chicago Business (Vol. 31, April 28, 2008, No. 17, pp. 30)
Pub: Crain Communications Inc.
Contact: Todd Johnson, Publisher
Ed: Samantha Stainburn. **Description:** Profile of the company Graycor Inc. which started out as a sandblasting and concrete-breaking firm but has grown into four businesses due to innovation and acquisitions. Graycor's businesses include: Graycor Industrial Constructors Inc., which builds and renovates

power plants and steel mills; Graycor Construction Co., which erects stores, medical centers and office buildings; Graycor Blasting Co., which uses explosives and blasts tunnels for industrial cleaning, and Graycor International Inc., which provides construction services in Mexico.

43207 ■ *"From War Zone to Franchise Zone"* in Entrepreneur (Vol. 37, August 2009, No. 8, pp. 104)
Pub: Entrepreneur Press
Contact: Perlman Neil, President
Ed: Jason Daley. **Description:** Ross Paterson says that he realized that the material he used in the Growth Coach franchise could give the people of Afghanistan the systematic model they need. Paterson says that the Afghans are very business-oriented people but that they work in a different system than Americans.

43208 ■ *Fugitive Denim: A Moving Story of People and Pants in the Borderless World of Global Trade*
Pub: W.W. Norton and Company Inc.
Contact: A Malmud, President
Ed: Rachel Louise Snyder. **Released:** April 2009. **Price:** $26.95, hardcover; $16.95, paperback. **Description:** In-depth study of the global production and processes of how jeans are designed, sewn, and transported as well as how the cotton for denim is grown, regulated, purchased and processed. **Availability:** Print.

43209 ■ *"Furniture Making May Come Back--Literally"* in Business North Carolina (Vol. 28, March 2008, No. 3, pp. 32)
Pub: Business North Carolina
Description: Due to the weak U.S. dollar and the fact that lumber processors never left the country, foreign furniture manufacturers are becoming interested in moving manufacturing plants to the U.S.

43210 ■ *"Future of Diversity: Cultural Inclusion Is a Business Imperative"* in Black Enterprise (Vol. 41, August 2010, No. 1, pp. 75)
Pub: Earl G. Graves Publishing Co. Inc.
Contact: Earl G. Graves, Jr., President
Ed: Annya M. Lott. **Description:** As globalization continues to make the world a smaller place, workforce diversity will be imperative to any small company in order to be sustainable.

43211 ■ *"The Future Is Another Country; Higher Education"* in The Economist (Vol. 390, January 3, 2009, No. 8612, pp. 43)
Description: Due to the growth of the global corporation, more ambitious students are studying at universities abroad; the impact of this trend is discussed.

43212 ■ *"The Future of Work"* in Black Enterprise (Vol. 41, August 2010, No. 1, pp. 65)
Pub: Earl G. Graves Publishing Co. Inc.
Contact: Earl G. Graves, Jr., President
Ed: Annya M. Lott. **Description:** Technology, globalization, and outsourcing will continue to shape the future of work. Social media is a means for small companies to market goods and services.

43213 ■ *"The Future of Work"* in Business Strategy Review (Vol. 21, Autumn 2010, No. 3, pp. 16)
Pub: Blackwell Publishers Ltd.
Ed: Lynda Gratton. **Description:** Work is universal. But how, why, where and when we work has never been so open to individual interpretation. The certainties of the past have been replaced by ambiguity, questions and the steady hum of technology. Now, in a groundbreaking research project covering 21 global companies and more than 200 executives, the author is making sense of the future of work.

43214 ■ *"The Future of Work"* in Business Strategy Review (Vol. 21, Autumn 2010, No. 3, pp. 16)
Pub: John Wiley & Sons Inc. Scientific, Technical, Medical, and Scholarly Div. (Wiley-Blackwell)
Contact: William J. Pesce, Manager
E-mail: wpesce@wiley.com
Ed: Lynda Gratton. **Description:** Work is universal. Buy, how, why, where and when we work has never

been so open to individual interpretation. The certainties of the past have been replaced by ambiguity, questions and the steady hum of technology. Research covering 21 global companies and more than 200 executives covers the future of work.

43215 ■ *"G20 Young Entrepreneur Alliance Signs Charter Outlining Commitment to Entrepreneurship"* in Internet Wire (November 10, 2010)
Pub: COMTEX
Contact: Chip Brian, President
Description: G20 Young Entrepreneur Summit members created a charter document that outlines their support for the G20 process to include entrepreneurship on its agenda. Details of the Summit are included.

43216 ■ *"Gamesa Office Closing Part of Political Reality"* in Pittsburgh Business Times (Vol. 33, February 7, 2014, No. 30, pp. 6)
Pub: American City Business Journals
Released: February 7, 2014. **Description:** Due to political uncertainty surrounding the production tax credit for wind energy and changes in the supply chain needs in the North America wind market, a Spanish wind blade maker Gamesa will be shutting down its manufacturing unit in Ebesnburg March 31, 2014. The general counsel for Gamesa, Frank Fuselier, stated that optimizing the company's supply chain will help them survive in a market devoid of a production tax credit.

43217 ■ *"Gaming Infrastructure Paves Ready Path for Manufacturing"* in Memphis Business Journal (No. 35, February 14, 2014, No. 45, pp. 4)
Pub: American City Business Journals
Released: February 14, 2014. **Description:** The city of Tunica, Mississippi is trying to expand its reputation as a gaming destination into manufacturing in an effort seek new opportunities for economic development and revenue. German crankshaft manufacturer, Feurer Powertrain, is building a $140 million manufacturing facility that will open in late 2014.

43218 ■ *"German Win Through Sharing"* in Canadian Business (Vol. 83, September 14, 2010, No. 15, pp. 16)
Pub: Rogers Media Inc.
Contact: Tony Viner, President
Ed: Jordan Timm. **Description:** German economic historian Eckhard Hoffner has a two-volume work showing how German's relaxed attitude toward copyright and intellectual property helped it catch up to industrialized United Kingdom. Hoffner's research was in response to his interest in the usefulness of software patents. Information on the debate regarding Canada's copyright laws is given.

43219 ■ *"Getting a Grip on the Saddle: Chasms or Cycles?"* in Journal of Marketing (Vol. 75, July 2011, No. 4, pp. 21)
Pub: American Marketing Association
Contact: Lucille Pointer, President
Ed: Deepa Chandrasekaran, Gerald J. Tellis. **Description:** A study of the saddle's generality across products and countries is presented. The saddle is fairly pervasive based on empirical analysis of historical sales data from ten products across 19 countries. The results indicate chasms and technological cycles for information/entertainment products while business cycles and technological cycles affect kitchen/laundry products.

43220 ■ *"Getting Rid of Global Glitches: Choosing Software For Trade Compliance"* in Black Enterprise (Vol. 41, September 2010, No. 2, pp. 48)
Pub: Earl G. Graves Publishing Co. Inc.
Contact: Earl G. Graves, Jr., President
Ed: Marcia Wade Talbert. **Description:** Compliance software for trading with foreign companies must be compatible with the U.S. Census Bureau's Automated Export System (www.aesdirect.gov). It has to be current with regulatory requirements for any country in the world. Whether owners handle their own compli-

ance or hire a logistics company, they need to be familiar with this software in order to access reports and improve transparency and efficiency of theft supply chain.

43221 ■ "Global Business Speaks English: Why You Need a Language Strategy Now" in Harvard Business Review (Vol. 90, May 2012, No. 5, pp. 116)
Pub: Harvard Business Review Press
Contact: Peter E. Walsh, Director

Ed: Tsedal Neeley. **Released:** May 2012. **Description:** English is rapidly becoming the language of businesses regardless of where they are located. To improve efficiency, the author advocates implementing an English-only policy. However, this must be conducted with sufficient training and support, and appropriate cultural sensitivity.

43222 ■ Global E-Commerce: Impacts of National Environment and Policy
Pub: Cambridge University Press
Contact: Richard Ziemacki, President
E-mail: rziemacki@cambridge.org
Released: September 2011. **Price:** $59, paperback; $111, hardback; $47. **Description:** Global assessment of the impact of e-business on companies as well as countries. **Availability:** PrintE-book; PDF.

43223 ■ Global Economic Crisis: Impact on Small Business
Pub: Cengage South-Western
Released: March 01, 2009. **Description:** A discussion of the historical context of the global economic crisis is presented, along with a discussion on the impact of this crisis on small businesses. It also provides learning goals, questions, key terms, and digital access to the Global Economic Crisis Resource Center.

43224 ■ "The Global Economy, the Labor Force and Franchising's Future" in Franchising World (Vol. 42, September 2010, No. 9, pp. 35)
Pub: International Franchise Association
Contact: Stephen J. Caldeira, President
E-mail: scaldeira@franchise.org
Ed: Jeffrey A. Rosensweig. **Description:** Point forecasting and the methodology called scenario analysis are presented looking at the global economy and future of franchising in the U.S. and abroad.

43225 ■ "Global Economy: The World Tomorrow" in Canadian Business (Vol. 81, December 19, 2007, No. 1, pp. 35)
Pub: Rogers Media Inc.
Contact: Tony Viner, President

Ed: Zena Olijnyk. **Description:** Global economy is predicted to be in a difficult period as analysts expect a slowdown in economic growth. Germany's Deutsche Bank wrote in a report about 'growth recession' that the chances of the world growth falling below two percent being one in three. Forecasts on other global economic aspects are explored.

43226 ■ Global Electronic Business Research: Opportunities and Directions
Pub: IGI Global
Contact: Dr. Mehdi Khosrow-Pour, President

Ed: Nabeel A.Y. Al-Qirim. **Released:** December 2005. **Price:** $89.95. **Description:** Importance electronic commerce research plays in small to medium-sized enterprises in various countries. **Availability:** Print.

43227 ■ "The Global Environment Movement is Bjorn Again" in Canadian Business (Vol. 83, September 14, 2010, No. 15, pp. 11)
Pub: Rogers Media Inc.
Contact: Tony Viner, President

Ed: Steve Maich. **Description:** Danish academic Bjorn Lomborg is in favor of decisive action to combat climate change in his new book and was given front page treatment by a London newspaper. Environmentalist groups see this as a victory since Lomborg had not previously considered climate change an immediate issue.

43228 ■ "Global Imagery in Online Advertisements" in Business Communication Quarterly (December 2007, pp. 487)
Pub: Pine Forge Press
Contact: Blaise R. Simqu, President

Ed: Geraldine E. Hynes, Marius Janson. **Description:** Respondents from six countries were interviewed about their reactions to two online ads to determine cultural differences in understanding advertising elements. Universal appeals and cultural values determine the effectiveness of symbols in online advertising.

43229 ■ "Global Market Could Be Silver Lining" in Hispanic Business (January-February 2008, pp. 14, 16, 18)
Pub: Hispanic Business Inc.
Contact: Jesus Chavarria, President

Ed: Dr. Juan B. Solana. **Description:** Economic slowdown in the U.S. is expected to continue through 2008. However, the export sector should hold steady during the same period.

43230 ■ "Global-Preneuring: Tax Ramifications Can Make or Break a Worldwide Enterprise" in Small Business Opportunities (May 2008)
Description: It is imperative to consider the tax ramifications when starting or expanding a global enterprise.

43231 ■ "Global: Put It on Autopilot" in Entrepreneur (Vol. 35, October 2007, No. 10, pp. 110)
Pub: Entrepreneur Press
Contact: Perlman Neil, President

Ed: Laurel Delaney. **Description:** A business that aims to enter the global market must first streamline its global supply chain (GSC). A streamlined GSC can be achieved by laying out the company's processes and by automating it with supply chain management software. Advantages of GSC automation such as credibility are provided.

43232 ■ "The Global Talent Hunt" in Business Strategy Review (Vol. 21, Spring 2010, No. 1, pp. 78)
Pub: John Wiley & Sons Inc. Scientific, Technical, Medical, and Scholarly Div. (Wiley-Blackwell)
Contact: William J. Pesce, Manager
E-mail: wpesce@wiley.com

Ed: Richard Emerton. **Description:** Richard Emerton explains how the new 'triple context' of economy, environment and society will have profound implications for human resource practices. He suggests that viewing talent as abundant is the right perspective for a manager.

43233 ■ "The Globe: A Cautionary Tale for Emerging Market Giants" in Harvard Business Review (Vol. 88, September 2010, No. 9, pp. 99)
Pub: Harvard Business School Publishing

Ed: J. Stewart Black, Allen J. Morrison. **Description:** Key factors that negatively affected Japan corporate growth and organizational effectiveness include: devotion to established path, isolated domestic markets, homogenous executive teams, and a non-contentious labor force. Solutions include leadership development programs, multicultural input, and cross-cultural training.

43234 ■ "The Globe Goes Birmingham" in Birmingham Business Journal (Vol. 31, July 4, 2014, No. 27, pp. 4)
Pub: American City Business Journals, Inc.
Contact: Whitney Shaw, President
Released: July 4, 2014. **Description:** Foreign-owned firms are investing heavily in the city of Birmingham, Alabama and are creating jobs. The number of employees in Birmingham at foreign-owned firms continues to rise and it is a trend not expected to slow in the near future. This is helping the area economy that has struggled with job creation during the low economic times. Low taxes, lower wage requirements and labor laws, and Birmingham's location and proximity to key manufacturers are factors attracting multi-million dollar investments in the city.

43235 ■ "The Globe: How to Conquer New Markets With Old Skills" in Harvard Business Review (Vol. 88, November 2010, No. 11, pp. 118)
Pub: Harvard Business School Publishing

Ed: Mauro F. Guillen, Esteban Garcia-Canal. **Description:** Exploration of business-networking factors that have helped lead to the success of Spain's multinational companies is provided. These include development of political skills, access to capabilities and resources, globalization partnerships, and speed of implementation.

43236 ■ "The Globe: Let Emerging Market Customers Be Your Teachers" in Harvard Business Review (Vol. 88, December 2010, No. 12, pp. 115)
Pub: Harvard Business School Publishing

Ed: Guillermo D'Andrea, David Marcotte, Gwen Dixon Morrison. **Description:** Examination of effective strategies for emerging markets is presented. These include helping educate customers as well as selling to them, adapting to customers' habits, and focusing brands appropriately. Magazine Luiza, a chain store in Brazil, is used to illustrate these points.

43237 ■ "Going the Distance" in Hispanic Business (July-August 2007, pp. 38-40, 42-43)
Pub: Hispanic Business Inc.
Contact: Jesus Chavarria, President

Ed: Keith Rosenblum. **Description:** Top Hispanic export companies are discussed; charts with exporters by sector as well as a complete listing that includes company name, CEO, number of employees, revenue information, export sales, growth, products and services and destinations are included.

43238 ■ "Golden Spoon Accelerates Expansion Here and Abroad" in Ice Cream Reporter (Vol. 22, December 20, 2008, No. 1, pp. 2)
Description: Golden Spoon frozen yogurt franchise chain is developing 35 more locations in the Phoenix, Arizona area along with plans to open a store in Japan.

43239 ■ Grassroots NGOs by Women for Women: The Driving Force of Development in India
Pub: Pine Forge Press
Contact: Blaise R. Simqu, President

Ed: Femida Handy, Meenaz Kassam, Suzanne Feeney, Bhagyashree Ranade. **Released:** 2006. **Price:** $38, paperback. **Description:** Understanding the role of non-governmental organizations in women's development is offered through interviews with twenty women in India who have founded NGOs serving women. **Availability:** Print.

43240 ■ "The Great Cleanup" in Canadian Business (Vol. 81, April 14, 2008, No. 6, pp. 50)
Pub: Rogers Media Inc.
Contact: Tony Viner, President

Ed: Graham Silnicki. **Description:** China's rectification program includes the licensing of 100 percent of food producers and monitoring of 100 percent of raw materials for exports between August and December, 2007. There is a lot of money to be made for those who are willing to help China win its quality battle. PharmEng International Inc. is one of the companies that helps Chinese companies meet international quality standards.

43241 ■ "The Great Fall of China" in Canadian Business (Vol. 85, June 11, 2012, No. 10, pp. 26)
Pub: George Media Inc.

Ed: Michael McCullough. **Released:** June 11, 2012. **Description:** China has a growing influence over the future of Canada's economy as emerging economies and commodity prices recover from the recession. Among the problems unique to China which could impact the Canadian economy are the housing market, its demographic risk and the lack of transparency in the corporate and financial sector.

43242 ■ *"Grote Company Puts Final Wrap on Sandwich-Making Line" in Business First-Columbus (October 29, 2007, pp. A1)*
Pub: American City Business Journals, Inc.
Ed: Dan Eaton. Description: Grote Company acquired Oxfordshire, England-based Advanced Food Technology Ltd., giving the Ohio-based food cutting equipment company a manufacturing base in Europe. This is the company's second deal in four months. Details on Grote Company's plan to tap into the prepared fresh sandwich market are discussed.

43243 ■ *"The Growth Opportunity That Lies Next Door: How a Brazilian Cosmetics Giant Saw the Beauty In Neighboring Markets" in (Vol. 90, July-August 2012, No. 7-8, pp. 141)*
Pub: Harvard Business Review Press
Contact: Peter E. Walsh, Director
Ed: Geoffrey Jones. Released: July-August 2012. Description: Brazilian company Natura Cosmetics found that focusing on expanding into the emerging markets represented by neighboring countries, rather than on well-established markets in developed nations, offered more opportunities and greater rewards.

43244 ■ *Growth-Oriented Women Entrepreneurs and Their Businesses: A Global Research Perspective*
Pub: Edward Elgar Publishing Inc.
Contact: Richard Henning, Vice President
E-mail: kwight@e-elgar.com
Ed: Candida G. Brush, Nancy M. Carter, Elizabeth J. Gatewood, Patricia G. Greene, Myra M. Hart. Released: 2006. Price: £89.10. Description: Roles women play in entrepreneurship globally and their economic impact are examined. Availability: Print.

43245 ■ *"Guts Not Included" in Canadian Business (Vol. 81, March 31, 2008, No. 5, pp. 46)*
Pub: Rogers Media Inc.
Contact: Tony Viner, President
Ed: Andrew Wahl. Description: Executives need the vision to create a strategy that prepares for an uncertain future in light of growing global competition. Canadian business leaders have the right skills and education but do not have enough tolerance for risk.

43246 ■ *"A Hacker in India Hijacked His Website Design and Was Making Good Money Selling It" in Inc. (December 2007, pp. 77-78, 80)*
Ed: Darren Dahl. Description: John Anton, owner of an online custom T-shirt business and how a company in India was selling software Website templates identical to his firm's Website.

43247 ■ *"Half a World Away" in Tampa Bay Business Journal (Vol. 30, December 4, 2009, No. 50, pp. 1)*
Ed: Jane Meinhardt. Description: Enterprise Florida has offered four trade grants for Florida's marine industry businesses to give them a chance to tap into the Middle East market at the Dubai International Boat Show on March 9 to 13, 2010. The grants pay for 50 percent of the exhibition costs for the qualifying business.

43248 ■ *"H&M Offers a Dress for Less" in Canadian Business (Vol. 83, September 14, 2010, No. 15, pp. 20)*
Pub: Rogers Media Inc.
Contact: Tony Viner, President
Ed: Laura Cameron. Description: Swedish clothing company H&M has implemented loss leader strategy by pricing some dresses at extremely low prices. The economy has forced retailers to keep prices down despite the increasing cost of manufacturing, partly due to Chinese labor becoming more expensive. How the trend will affect apparel companies is discussed.

43249 ■ *"Hank Paulson On the Housing Bailout and What's Ahead" in Business Week (September 22, 2008, No. 4100, pp. 19)*
Ed: Maria Bartiromo. Description: Interview with Treasury Secretary Henry Paulson in which he discusses the bailout of Fannie Mae and Freddie Mac as well as the potential impact on the American

economy and foreign interests and investments in the country. Paulson has faith that the government's actions will help to stabilize the housing market.

43250 ■ *"HBR Case Study: Setting Up Shop in a Political Hot Spot" in Harvard Business Review (Vol. 88, October 2010, No. 10, pp. 141)*
Pub: Harvard Business School Publishing
Ed: Patrick Chun, John Coleman, Nabil El-Hage. Description: A fictitious foreign operations scenario is presented, with contributors providing comments and advice. The scenario involves a politically charged North Korean-South Korean business venture; suggestions range from ensuring financial flexibility in case of adverse events to avoiding any business venture until political stability is achieved.

43251 ■ *"The HBR Interview:"We Had to Own the Mistakes"" in Harvard Business Review (Vol. 88, July-August 2010, No. 7-8, pp. 108)*
Pub: Harvard Business School Publishing
Ed: Adi Ignatius. Description: Interview with Howard Schultz, CEO of Starbucks, covers topics that include investment in retraining, the impact of competition, premium quality, authenticity, customer services, strategy development, work-and-life issues, and international presence.

43252 ■ *"Headwinds From the New Sod Slow Aer Lingus" in Barron's (Vol. 88, March 10, 2008, No. 10, pp. M6)*
Pub: Dow Jones & Co., Inc.
Contact: Clare Hart, President
Ed: Sean Walters, Arindam Nag. Description: Aer Lingus faces a drop in its share prices with a falling US market, higher jet fuel prices, and lower long-haul passenger load factors. British media companies Johnston Press and Yell Group are suffering from weaker ad revenue and heavier debt payments due to the credit crunch.

43253 ■ *"Heavy Duty: The Case Against Packing Lightly" in Crain's Chicago Business (Vol. 31, April 21, 2008, No. 16, pp. 29)*
Pub: Crain Communications Inc.
Contact: Todd Johnson, Publisher
Ed: Sarah A. Klein. Description: Penelope Biggs, a Northern Trust executive who manages sales teams in North America, Europe and Asia gives advice on traveling abroad for business including time management skills, handling time-zone hops and avoiding jet-lag.

43254 ■ *"Helping Apple Go Wearable" in Austin Business Journal (Vol. 34, July 4, 2014, No. 20, pp. 13)*
Pub: American City Business Journals, Inc.
Contact: Whitney Shaw, President
Released: July 4, 2014. Description: Andrew Hamra, CEO and designer at Red Street Ventures will launch the Runnur Hands Free iPad Clip and Carry Case across the U.S. in July 2014 following the success of his flagship product the Hands Free Carry-All. Hamra builds and designs the products and controls startup costs by outsourcing most of the production to China's Xiamen Uptex Industrial Company Ltd.

43255 ■ *"The High-Intensity Entrepreneur" in Harvard Business Review (Vol. 88, September 2010, No. 9, pp. 74)*
Pub: Harvard Business School Publishing
Ed: Anne S. Habiby, Deirdre M. Coyle, Jr. Description: Examination of the role of small companies in promoting global economic growth is presented. Discussion includes identifying entrepreneurial capability.

43256 ■ *"HNM Global Logistics" in Orlando Business Journal (Vol. 30, June 27, 2014, No. 53, pp. 8)*
Pub: American City Business Journals
Released: June 27, 2014. Description: Tony L. McGee is the CEO of HNM Global Logistics, a full service freight forwarder that reduced its logistic spending by 22 percent in 2013. He believes that America will see a revival in manufacturing coupled with more free trade agreements.

43257 ■ *"Hola and Aloha" in Hawaii Business (Vol. 53, December 2007, No. 6, pp. 131)*
Pub: PacificBasin Communications
Ed: Jason Ubay. Description: Juan Carlos Bianchetti is the trilingual owner of Ole Tours Hawaii, a travel wholesaler that targets Portuguese and Spanish-speaking visitors. The competition for American and Japanese tourists is already tight, which is why Bianchetti opted to target a different segment of the Hawaii tourism market. Plans for the company's expansion in Kauai, Brazil, and Argentina, are mentioned.

43258 ■ *"The Hollow Debate" in Canadian Business (Vol. 81, March 3, 2008, No. 3, pp. 26)*
Ed: Thomas Watson. Description: According to a report conducted by the Conference Board of Canada, the Canadian business community is not being hollowed out by acquisitions made by foreign companies. Findings further showed that local businesses are protected by dual shares and that the economy can benefit more from foreign acquisitions than local mergers. The need to relax foreign ownership restrictions and other recommendations are presented.

43259 ■ *"Hong Kong's Boom in IPOs" in Barron's (Vol. 89, July 13, 2009, No. 28, pp. M7)*
Pub: Dow Jones & Co., Inc.
Contact: Clare Hart, President
Ed: Nick Lord. Description: Hong Kong's IPO (initial public offering) market is booming with 13 Chinese IPOs already on the market for the year as July 2009. One of them is Bawang International which raised $214 million after generating $9 billion in order which makes it 42 times oversubscribed.

43260 ■ *"Honolulu Cookie Company Looks to Las Vegas Japan and Korea for New Store Locations" in Pacific Business News (Vol. 52, February 14, 2014, No. 52, pp. 5)*
Pub: American City Business Journals
Released: February 14, 2014. Description: Honolulu Cookie Company is exploring the international market, particularly Japan and Korea for new store locations. The company is also planning to open its first store outside of Hawaii that will be located in the Grand Canal Shoppes at the Venetian and palazzo in Las Vegas, Nevada.

43261 ■ *"Hoop Culture Opens Showroom, Expands Reach Globally" in Orlando Business Journal (Vol. 30, February 28, 2014, No. 36, pp. 3)*
Pub: American City Business Journals
Released: February 28, 2014. Description: Hoop Culture Inc. president, Mike Brown, shares how the online basketball apparel retailer/wholesaler online store has expanded globally. He mentions that Orlando, Florida is one of their biggest markets.

43262 ■ *"Hot For All The Wrong Reasons" in Canadian Business (Vol. 81, March 31, 2008, No. 5, pp. 19)*
Pub: Rogers Media Inc.
Contact: Tony Viner, President
Ed: Andrea Jezovit. Description: Soaring platinum prices are due to South Africa's platinum mining industry's safety issues and power supply disruptions that exacerbate the metal's supply problems. South Africa supplies 80 percent of the world's platinum. South Africa's power utility has said that it cannot guarantee the industry's power needs until 2013.

43263 ■ *"How Bad Is It?" in Hawaii Business (Vol. 54, July 2008, No. 1, pp. 35)*
Pub: PacificBasin Communications
Ed: Jolyn Okimoto Rosa. Description: Donald G. Horner, chief executive officer of First Hawaiian Bank, says that the current Hawaiian economic situation is a cyclical slowdown. Maurice Kaya, an energy consultant, says the slowdown is due to overdependence on imported fuels. Other local leaders, such as Constance H. Lau, also discuss their view on the current economic situation in Hawaii.

43264 ■ *"How Baltimore's Largest Private Companies Weathered the Recession's Punch; Top Private Companies"* in *Baltimore Business Journal (Vol. 28, August 27, 2010, No. 16, pp. 1)*
Pub: Baltimore Business Journal
Ed: Gary Haber. **Description:** The combined revenue of the 100 largest private firms in Maryland's Baltimore region dropped from about $22.7 billion in 2008 to $21 billion in 2009, an annual decrease of more than 7 percent. To survive the recession's impact, these firms resorted to strategies such as government contracting and overseas expansion. How these strategies affected the revenue of some firms is described.

43265 ■ *"How Dell Will Dial for Dollars"* in *Austin Business JournalInc. (Vol. 29, December 4, 2009, No. 39, pp. 1)*
Pub: American City Business Journals
Ed: Christopher Calnan. **Description:** Dell Inc. revealed plans to launch a Mini3i smartphone in China which could enable revenue sharing by bundling with wireless service subscription. Dell's smartphone plan is similar to the netbook business, which Dell sold with service provided by AT&T Inc.

43266 ■ *"How Exports Could Save America"* in *Barron's (Vol. 89, July 20, 2009, No. 29, pp. 15)*
Pub: Dow Jones & Co., Inc.
Contact: Clare Hart, President
Ed: Jonathan R. Laing. **Description:** Increase in US exports should help drive up the nation's economic growth, according to Wells Capital Management strategist Jim Paulsen. He believes US gross domestic product could grow by 3-3.5 percent annually starting in 2010 due to a more favorable trade balance.

43267 ■ *"How Facebook Will Find Its Next Billion Users: With U.S. Saturated, Social Site Turns to Advertising in Select Countries to Find Friends"* in *Advertising Age (Vol. 83, October 8, 2012, No. 36, pp. 8)*
Pub: Crain Communications Inc.
Contact: Rance E. Crain, President
Ed: Cotton Delo. **Description:** With over a billion Facebook users in the United States, the company is advertising in other countries in the hopes of recruiting users there. Details of this marketing plan are outlined.

43268 ■ *"How Foreigners Could Disrupt U.S. Markets"* in *Barron's (Vol. 90, September 13, 2010, No. 37, pp. 30)*
Pub: Barron's Editorial & Corporate Headquarters
Ed: Jim McTague. **Description:** An informal meeting by the House Homeland Security Panel concluded that U.S. stock exchanges and related trading routes can be the subject of attacks from rogue overseas traders. A drop in funding for the U.S. Department of Defense is discussed.

43269 ■ *"How High Can Soybeans Fly?"* in *Barron's (Vol. 88, March 10, 2008, No. 10, pp. M14)*
Pub: Dow Jones & Co., Inc.
Contact: Clare Hart, President
Ed: Kenneth Rapoza. **Description:** Prices of soybeans have risen to $14.0875 a bushel, up 8.3 percent for the week. Increased demand, such as in China and in other developing economies, and the investment-driven commodities boom are boosting prices.

43270 ■ *"How Not to Raise Bank Capital"* in *Barron's (Vol. 88, June 30, 2008, No. 26, pp. M6)*
Pub: Dow Jones & Co., Inc.
Contact: Clare Hart, President
Ed: Sean Walters. **Description:** French bank Natixis wants to raise 1 billion euros from cash provided by their two major owners. Natixis will reimburse Banque Populaire and Caisses d'Epargne with hybrid securities so this move will not benefit Natixis' core Tier 1 ratio. This has also given the impression that the company is afraid of a full rights issue which could shake investors' faith in the bank.

43271 ■ *"How to Secure U.S. Jobs"* in *Gallup Management Journal (October 27, 2011)*
Pub: Gallup Inc.
Contact: Jim Clifton, Chief Executive Officer
Ed: Jim Clifton. **Description:** If America doubled its number of engaged customers globally, it could triple exports, which would create more good jobs and put the US economy back on track.

43272 ■ *"How To Win In Emerging Markets: Lessons From Japan"* in *Harvard Business Review (Vol. 90, May 2012, No. 5, pp. 126)*
Pub: Harvard Business Review Press
Contact: Peter E. Walsh, Director
Ed: Shigeki Ichii, Susumu Hattori, David Michael. **Released:** May 2012. **Description:** Corporate Japan's four challenges in engaging emerging markets are an aversion to mergers and acquisitions, an aversion to low- and middle-end segments, lack of organizational or financial commitments to emerging markets, and a shortage of executive talent placed in emerging markets. By addressing these weaknesses, Japan can succeed in global expansion.

43273 ■ *"How Two Flourishing Exporters Did It"* in *Hispanic Business (Vol. 30, July-August 2008, No. 7-8, pp. 46)*
Ed: Richard Kaplan. **Description:** Vigorous growth in export revenues posted by two Hispanic-owned export companies Compasa LLC and Ametza LLC is discussed; both firms have benefited from their closer locations to major Mexican markets, superior quality of their products, market knowledge and the relationships of trust developed with key business partners.

43274 ■ *"How Young Professionals Can Position Themselves for Board Membership: 4 Quick Tips to Get You Started"* in *Black Enterprise (Vol. 45, July-August 2014, No. 1, pp. 46)*
Pub: Earl G. Graves Publishing Co. Inc.
Contact: Earl G. Graves, Jr., President
Released: July-August 2014. **Description:** Four tips to help young professionals secure a position on a company's board focus on: starting with nonprofits, focus on key areas of interest, continue to growth through networking and training programs, and to gain global experience.

43275 ■ *"'Huge Contract' Means 299 New Jobs, $96M Expansion for ZF Steering Systems"* in *Business Courier (Vol. 26, November 6, 2009, No. 28, pp. 1)*
Pub: American City Business Journals, Inc.
Contact: Whitney Shaw, President
Ed: Jon Newberry. **Description:** Proposed $96 million expansion of German-owned automotive supplier ZF Steering systems LLC is anticipated to generate 299 jobs in Boone County, Kentucky. ZF might invest $90 million in equipment, while the rest will go to building and improvements.

43276 ■ *"Husband-Wife Team Opens Somali Interpreting Business in Willmar, Minn."* in *West Central Tribune (May 22, 2012)*
Pub: McClatchy-Tribune Regional News
Ed: Linda Vanderwerf. **Released:** May 22, 2012. **Description:** Profile of husband and wife team who launched an interpreting service in Somali. Details of the business are included.

43277 ■ *"Hyundai Reports Sales Figures"* in *Travel & Leisure Close-Up (October 8, 2012)*
Description: Hyundai Auto Canada Corporation reports 11,403 vehicles sold in September 2012, a 2.6 percent increase over September 2011. The company has shown increased sales for 45 consecutive months.

43278 ■ *"IBR Breakfast Series: Idaho's Dairy Industry Quietly Grows"* in *Idaho Business Review (August 15, 2014)*
Pub: Dolan Co.
Contact: James P. Dolan, President
Released: August 15, 2014. **Description:** Several dairy industry members were called to a breakfast to discuss the past, present and future of the Idaho dairy

farms and products. The impact of technology changes and rising foreign market demands as well as creating more and different products was addressed.

43279 ■ *"Ideas at Work: Sparkling Innovation"* in *Business Strategy Review (Vol. 21, Summer 2010, No. 2, pp. 7)*
Pub: Blackwell Publishers Ltd.
Ed: Julian Birkinshaw, Peter Robbins. **Description:** GlaxoSmithKline faced a situation common to large global organizations: how to allocate marketing resources to smaller, regional brands. A report on the company's inventive approach to worldwide marketing that led to the development of a unique and productive network are explored.

43280 ■ *"Ideas at Work: Sparkling Innovation"* in *Business Strategy Review (Vol. 21, Summer 2010, No. 2, pp. 07)*
Pub: John Wiley & Sons Inc. Scientific, Technical, Medical, and Scholarly Div. (Wiley-Blackwell)
Contact: William J. Pesce, Manager
E-mail: wpesce@wiley.com
Ed: Julian Birkinshaw, Peter Robbins. **Description:** GlaxoSmithKline faced a situation common to large global organizations: how to allocate marketing resources to smaller, regional brands. The company's approach to worldwide marketing that led to the development of a unique and productive network is outlined.

43281 ■ *"Ideas at Work: Total Communicator"* in *Business Strategy Review (Vol. 21, Autumn 2010, No. 3, pp. 10)*
Pub: Blackwell Publishers Ltd.
Ed: Stuart Crainer. **Description:** Vittorio Colao has been chief executive of Vodafone Group for two years. He brings to the company special experience as CEO of RCS MediaGroup in Milan, which publishes newspapers, magazines and books in Italy, Spain and France. Prior to RCS, he held other positions within Vodaphone. Colao shares his views on business, the global economy and leading Vodafone.

43282 ■ *"Ideas at Work: Total Communicator"* in *Business Strategy Review (Vol. 21, Autumn 2010, No. 3, pp. 10)*
Pub: John Wiley & Sons Inc. Scientific, Technical, Medical, and Scholarly Div. (Wiley-Blackwell)
Contact: William J. Pesce, Manager
E-mail: wpesce@wiley.com
Ed: Stuart Crainer. **Description:** Vittorio Colao has been chief executive of Vodafone Group for two years. He brings to the company some special experience: from 2004-2006 he was CEO of RCS MediaGroup in Milan, which publishes newspapers, magazines and books in Italy, Spain and France. Colao shares his views on business, the global economy and leading Vodafone.

43283 ■ *"IFRS Monopoly: the Pied Piper of Financial Reporting"* in *Accounting and Business Research (Vol. 41, Summer 2011, No. 3, pp. 291)*
Pub: American Institute of Certified Public Accountants
Contact: Barry C. Melancon, President
E-mail: bmelancon@aicpa.org
Ed: Shyam Sunder. **Description:** The disadvantages of granting monopoly to the international financial reporting standards (IFRS) are examined. Results indicate that an IFRS monopoly removes the chances for comparing alternative practices and learning from them. An IFRS monopoly also eliminates customization of financial reporting to fit local differences in governance, business, economic, and legal conditions.

43284 ■ *"An Ill Wind: Icelandic Bank Failures Chill Atlantic Canada"* in *Canadian Business (Vol. 81, November 10, 2008, No. 19, pp. 10)*
Pub: Rogers Media Inc.
Contact: Tony Viner, President
Ed: Charles Mandel. **Description:** Bank failures in Iceland have put a stop to flights ferrying Icelanders to Newfoundland to purchase Christmas gifts, thereby threatening Newfoundland's tourism industry. The

credit of Newfoundland's fisheries is also being squeezed since most of Atlantic Canadian seafood processors hold lines of credit from Icelandic banks.

43285 ■ *"Ill Winds; Cuba's Economy"* in *The Economist (Vol. 390, January 3, 2009, No. 8612, pp. 20)*
Description: Cuba's long-term economic prospects remain poor with the economy forecasted to grow only 4.3 percent for the year, about half of the original forecast, due in part to Hurricane Gustav which caused $10 billion in damage and disrupted the food-supply network and devastated farms across the region; President Raul Castro made raising agricultural production a national priority and the rise in global commodity prices hit the country hard. The only bright spot has been the rise in tourism which is up 9.3 percent over 2007.

43286 ■ *Imagining India: The Idea of a Renewed Nation*
Pub: Dutton Children's Books
Contact: Lauri Hornik, President
Ed: Nandan Nilekani. **Released:** 2009. **Price:** $17, Paperback. **Description:** National technology leader, Nandan Nilekan warns of pitfalls, obstacles and the danger of letting down the people of India.

43287 ■ *"Immigration Issues Frustrate Owners From Overseas"* in *The Business Journal-Serving Greater Tampa Bay (Vol. 28, August 18, 2008)*
Pub: American City Business Journals, Inc.
Contact: Whitney Shaw, President
Ed: Margie Manning. **Description:** Investors who availed the E-2 visa program believe that the tightened restrictions on the visa program has trapped them in the United States. The E-2 investor visa program was designed to attract investors into the U.S., but restrictions were tightened after the September 11, 2001 attacks. Other views and information on E-2 and its impact on investors are presented.

43288 ■ *"iMozi Integrates Esprida LiveControl for Advanced DVD Kiosk Hardware"* in *Wireless News (December 20, 2010)*
Pub: Close-Up Media
Description: Provider of self-service entertainment technology, iMozi Canada has partnered with Esprida to make its automated DVD Kiosk solutions Esprida-enabled. Esprida develops remote device management solutions and will offer enhanced capabilities and to improve customer experience for users.

43289 ■ *Import/Export Kit For Dummies*
Pub: John Wiley & Sons Inc.
Contact: Stephen M. Smith, President
Ed: John J. Capela. **Released:** 2nd Edition. **Price:** $34.95, paperback; $22.99. **Description:** Provides entrepreneurs and small- to medium-size businesses with information required to start exporting products globally and importing goods to the U.S. Topics covered include the ins and outs of developing or expanding operations to gain market share, with details on the top ten countries in which America trades, from Canada to Germany to China. **Availability:** PrintE-book.

43290 ■ *"Importers Share Safety Liability"* in *Feedstuffs (Vol. 80, January 21, 2008, No. 3, pp. 19)*
Description: Pet food and toys containing lead paint are among products from China being recalled due to safety concerns. American Society for Quality's list of measures that outsourcing companies can take to help ensure safer products being imported to the U.S.

43291 ■ *"In the Bag?"* in *Canadian Business (Vol. 81, March 3, 2008, No. 3, pp. 57)*
Ed: Calvin Leung. **Description:** American stocks are beginning to appear cheap amidst the threat of a worldwide economic slowdown, United States economic crisis and declining stock portfolios. Investors looking for bargain stocks should study the shares of Apple and Oshkosh Corp. Evaluation of other cheap-looking stocks such as the shares of Coach and 3M is also given.

43292 ■ *"In China, Railways to Riches"* in *Barron's (Vol. 88, July 7, 2008, No. 27, pp. M9)*
Pub: Dow Jones & Co., Inc.
Contact: Clare Hart, President
Ed: Assif Shameen. **Description:** Shares of Chinese railway companies look to benefit from multimillion-dollar investments aimed at upgrading the Chinese railway network. Investment in the sector is expected to reach $210 billion for the 2006-2010 period.

43293 ■ *"In India, A Gold-Price Threat?"* in *Barron's (Vol. 88, June 30, 2008, No. 26, pp. M12)*
Pub: Dow Jones & Co., Inc.
Contact: Clare Hart, President
Ed: Melanie Burton. **Description:** Gold purchases in India are falling as record prices take its toll on demand. Gold imports to India fell by 52 percent in May 2008 from the previous year and local prices are higher by one-third from the previous year to 12,540 rupees for 10 grams.

43294 ■ *"In Radical Change-Up, P&G Streamlines How it Promotes Brands"* in *Business Courier (Vol. 26, October 2, 2009, No. 23, pp. 1)*
Pub: American City Business Journals, Inc.
Contact: Whitney Shaw, President
Ed: Lisa Biank Fasig. **Description:** Procter & Gamble (P&G) revised the way it works with marketing, design and public relations firms. Creative discussions will be managed by only two representatives, the franchise leader and the brand agency leader in order for P&G to simplify operations as it grows larger and more global.

43295 ■ *"In the Wake of Pet-Food Crisis, Iams Sales Plummet Nearly 17 Percent"* in *Advertising Age (Vol. 78, May 14, 2007, No. 18, pp. 3)*
Pub: Crain Communications Inc.
Contact: Rance Crain, President
Ed: Jack Neff. **Description:** Although the massive U.S. pet-food recall impacted more than 100 brands, Procter & Gamble Co.'s Iams lost more sales and market share than any other industry player. According to Information Resources Inc. data, the brand's sales dropped 16.5 percent in the eight-week period ended April 22. Many analysts feel that the company could have handled the crisis in a better manner.

43296 ■ *"In With the Good"* in *Canadian Business (Vol. 80, November 5, 2007, No. 22, pp. 22)*
Ed: Jack Mintz. **Description:** Restriction on foreign direct investment in Canada is unlikely to materialize despite Minister of Industry Jim Prentice's opinion that new rules be set in Ottawa regarding foreign state-owned businesses. Reasons why governments would not unreasonably regulate foreign investments are investigated.

43297 ■ *"Indigenous Tourism Operators"* in *International Journal of Entrepreneurship and Small Business (Vol. 10, July 6, 2010, No. 4)*
Pub: Publishers Communication Group
Contact: Doug Wright, Director
Ed: Andrews Cardow, Peter Wiltshier. **Description:** Emergent enthusiasm for tourism as a savior for economic development in the Chatham Islands of New Zealand is highlighted.

43298 ■ *"The Influencers"* in *Entrepreneur (Vol. 36, February 2008, No. 3, pp. 66)*
Pub: Entrepreneur Press
Contact: Perlman Neil, President
Ed: Andrea Cooper. **Description:** Among the 25 people, events, and trends that will influence business in 2008 are: the 2008 U.S. presidential elections, climate change, China, weakening U.S. dollar, mortgage crisis, generational shift, Bill Drayton, and Bill Gates. Other 2008 influencers are presented.

43299 ■ *Innovate to Great: Re-Igniting Sustainable Innovation to Win in the Global Economy*
Pub: McGraw-Hill
Ed: Judy Estrin. **Released:** September 12, 2008. **Price:** , $27.95. **Description:** The author explores

innovation and creativity as a means for small companies to survive and expand in the global economy.

43300 ■ *"Innovating Globally"* in *Business Strategy Review (Vol. 21, Spring 2010, No. 1, pp. 24)*
Pub: John Wiley & Sons Inc. Scientific, Technical, Medical, and Scholarly Div. (Wiley-Blackwell)
Contact: William J. Pesce, Manager
E-mail: wpesce@wiley.com
Ed: Costas Markides, Stuart Crainer. **Description:** Costas Markides has spent over two decades studying business strategy and innovation. Recently, he has been focusing on the bigger picture of how people can address major social problems. Can the techniques used by managers to create innovation inside organizations work with global change?.

43301 ■ *"Innovating Low-Cost Business Models"* in *Strategy and Leadership (Vol. 39, March-April 2011, No. 2, pp. 43)*
Pub: Emerald Group Publishing Inc.
Ed: Nicholas Kachaner, Zhenya Lindgardt, David Michael. **Description:** A process that can be used to implement low-cost innovation is presented. The process can be used to address the competitive challenges presented by multinationals' practice of presenting applications and price points that are intended for developing markets into developed markets. The process involves targeting large, and low-income segments of the market.

43302 ■ *"Innovators Critical in Technical Economy"* in *Crain's Cleveland Business (Vol. 28, November 5, 2007, No. 44, pp. 10)*
Pub: Crain Communications Inc.
Ed: Peter Rea. **Description:** Discusses the importance to attract, develop and retain talented innovators on Ohio's economy. Also breaks down the four fronts on which the international battle for talent is being waged.

43303 ■ *"Insider"* in *Canadian Business (Vol. 81, March 3, 2008, No. 3, pp. 96)*
Description: History of gold usage and gold trading is presented in a timeline. Gold was a symbol of power and wealth in 2500 B.C., and in 1500 B.C., it became the first currency to be recognized internationally. Other remarkable events in the gold industry and laws that covered gold are discussed.

43304 ■ *"International Benefits Roundup"* in *Employee Benefit News (Vol. 25, December 1, 2011, No. 15)*
Pub: SourceMedia Inc.
Contact: James M. Malkin, Chief Executive Officer
Description: Employee contributions to an employer-sponsored defined contribution plan in Japan will allowed on a tax-deductible basis; however, currently employee contributions are not allowed. The defined contribution plan is outlined for better understanding.

43305 ■ *"International Business Law: Interpreting the Term 'Like Products"* in *Business Recorder (June 7, 2012)*
Pub: Highbeam Research
Contact: Patrick Spain, Chief Executive Officer
Ed: Zafar Azeem. **Released:** June 7, 2012. **Description:** The term 'like products' needs to be defined for international trade. The battle between the United States and Indonesia regarding this issue is discussed. A technical barrier clause being used by foreign countries is prohibiting imports and hurting competitiveness.

43306 ■ *"International Comparisons Data"* in *Montly Labor Review (Vol. 133, September 2010, No. 9, pp. 143)*
Pub: U.S. Department of Labor Bureau of Labor Statistics
Contact: Philip L. Rones, Manager
E-mail: rones.philip@bls.gov
Description: Unemployment rates adjusted to U.S. concepts and ten countries are presented.

43307 ■ *"International Dairy Queen" in Ice Cream Reporter (Vol. 23, October 20, 2010, No. 11, pp. 7)*
Description: International Dairy Queen will open more than 100 new outlets in China in 2011, adding to the current level of more than 300 outlets in that country.

43308 ■ *International Entrepreneurship*
Pub: Edward Elgar Publishing Inc.
Contact: Richard Henning, Vice President
E-mail: kwight@e-elgar.com
Ed: Benjamin M. Oviatt, Patricia Phillips McDougall.
Released: 2007. **Price:** £175.50, hardback. **Description:** Universities are focusing research efforts on international entrepreneurship. The book features critical articles on the topic. **Availability:** Print.

43309 ■ *International Entrepreneurship Education: Issues and Newness*
Pub: Edward Elgar Publishing Inc.
Contact: Richard Henning, Vice President
E-mail: kwight@e-elgar.com
Ed: Alain Fayolle, Heinz Klandt. **Released:** 2006.
Price: £76.50. **Description:** Entrepreneurial education, focusing on economic, political and social needs of a changing world; ideas for reassessing, redeveloping, and renewing curricula and methods for teaching entrepreneurship are offered. **Availability:** Print.

43310 ■ *International Entrepreneurship in Small and Medium Size Enterprises: Orientation, Environment and Strategy*
Pub: Edward Elgar Publishing Inc.
Contact: Richard Henning, Vice President
E-mail: kwight@e-elgar.com
Ed: Hamid Etemad. **Released:** October 2004. **Price:** $123.30, hardback. **Description:** Issues involved in internationalizing small and medium sized (SME) businesses. Topics include an investigation into the emerging patterns of SME growth and international expansion in response to the changing competitive environment, dynamics of competitive behavior, entrepreneurial processes and a formulation of strategy. **Availability:** Print.

43311 ■ *"International ETFs: Your Passport to the World" in Barron's (Vol. 89, July 13, 2009, No. 28, pp. L10)*
Pub: Dow Jones & Co., Inc.
Contact: Clare Hart, President
Ed: John Hintze. **Description:** International exchange traded funds give investors more choices in terms of investment plays and there are 174 U.S. ETF listings worth $141 billion as of July 2009. Suggestions on how to invest in these funds based on one's conviction on how the global economy will unfold are presented.

43312 ■ *"International Growth" in Black Enterprise (Vol. 38, July 2008, No. 12, pp. 64)*
Pub: Earl G. Graves Publishing Co. Inc.
Contact: Earl G. Graves, Jr., President
Ed: Marcia A. Reed-Woodard. **Description:** Becoming an increasingly smaller portion of the global business environment is the U.S. economy. Christopher Catlin, an associate with Booz Allen Hamilton, a technology management and strategy-consulting firm, shares what he has learned about the global market.

43313 ■ *International Growth of Small and Medium Enterprises*
Pub: Routledge
Contact: Kevin Bradley, President
E-mail: kbradley@taylorandfrancis.com
Released: February 10, 2010. **Price:** $54.95, Paperback; $160, Hardback. **Description:** This volume focuses on how companies expand their operations across borders through opportunity exploration and exploitation, and identification and development of innovations.

43314 ■ *International Handbook of Women and Small Business Entrepreneurship*
Pub: Edward Elgar Publishing Inc.
Contact: Richard Henning, Vice President
E-mail: kwight@e-elgar.com
Ed: Sandra L. Fielden, Marilyn J. Davidson. **Price:** £107.10, hardback; £28.80, paperback. **Description:** Practical initiatives and strategies for women entering small business entrepreneurial ventures are examined. **Availability:** Print.

43315 ■ *The Internationalization of Asset Ownership in Europe*
Pub: Cambridge University Press
Contact: Richard Ziemacki, President
E-mail: rziemacki@cambridge.org
Ed: Harry Huizinga, Lars Jonung. **Released:** November 2005. **Price:** $140, hardback. **Description:** Ten financial experts provide analysis of the growth and the implications of foreign ownership in Europe's financial markets. **Availability:** Print.

43316 ■ *"Investment In Israel Is Investment in the Future of Georgia" in Atlanta Business Chronicle (May 30, 2014, pp. 22A)*
Pub: American City Business Journals, Inc.
Contact: Whitney Shaw, President
Released: May 30, 2014. **Description:** Georgia Governor Nathan Deal will travel to Israel to lead an economic and trade mission and consolidate Georgia's trade ties with Israel. Israel and the State of Georgia are already collaborating in the fields of health information technology, agrotechnology, homeland security, defense, aerospace and cybersecurity, and microelectronics and nanotechnology. The proposed visit by the Governor will build on this particular partnership from which both parties will benefit.

43317 ■ *"IRS Rules Could Affect Foreign Bank Deposits" in Dallas Business Journal (Vol. 35, February 24, 2012, No. 24, pp. 1)*
Released: February 24, 2012. **Description:** IRS has proposed a rule that requires US banks to disclose foreign depositors' account information. However, bankers and trade groups believe the regulation could prompt deposit runs at banks across Texas since foreign nationals are afraid that information might be used against them.

43318 ■ *"Is Globalization Threatening U.S. Hispanic Progress?" in Hispanic Business (Vol. 30, September 2008, No. 9, pp. 16)*
Ed: Jessica Haro. **Description:** Talented Hispanic employees are making progress within the increasingly diverse American corporate scenario. However, while some experts believe the induction of foreign professionals through globalization will not impact this progress, others feel it could hamper opportunities for American Hispanics.

43319 ■ *"Is the Sun Setting on Oil Sector's Heydey?" in Globe & Mail (January 25, 2007, pp. B3)*
Ed: Shawn McCarthy. **Description:** The effects of fuel efficiency management policies of the United States on Canadian petroleum industry are discussed. Canada is the largest exporter of crude oil to America after the Middle East.

43320 ■ *"Is 'Tsunami' of Freight in our Future?" in Business Courier (Vol. 26, November 27, 2009, No. 31, pp. 1)*
Pub: American City Business Journals, Inc.
Contact: Whitney Shaw, President
Ed: Dan Monk. **Description:** Freight companies are planning for cargo-container shipping facilities on the riverfront of Cincinnati in light of the completion of the $5 billion Panama Canal expansion in 2015. The city's capability to utilize the growth in freight has been under investigation by authorities.

43321 ■ *"Islamic Banks Get a 'Libor' of Their Own" in Wall Street Journal Eastern Edition (November 25 , 2011, pp. C4)*
Pub: Dow Jones & Co., Inc.
Contact: Clare Hart, President
Ed: Katy Burne. **Description:** The London interbank offered rate, or Libor, has been used by banks internationally for years. It is the rate at which banks lend money to each other. The rate has not been used by Islamic banks, but now sixteen banks have come up with the Islamic Interbank Benchmark Rate.

43322 ■ *"It May Be Cheaper to Manufacture At Home" in Harvard Business Review (Vol. 88, October 2010, No. 10, pp. 84)*
Pub: Harvard Business School Publishing
Ed: Suzanne de Treville, Lenos Trigeorgis. **Description:** Using a real options framework rather than a discounted cash flow model to assess and value supply chain processes is examined. This enables companies to assess costs for a variety of situations, not just ideal or normal circumstances, which can make the difference between domestic and foreign manufacturing decisions.

43323 ■ *"Itochu Joins KKR in Samson Buyout" in Wall Street Journal Eastern Edition (November 25 , 2011, pp. B7)*
Pub: Dow Jones & Co., Inc.
Contact: Clare Hart, President
Description: Samson Investment Company is the target of a $7.2 billion leveraged buyout by a consortium led by US investment firm Kohlberg Kravis Roberts & Company and Tokyo-based Itochu Corporation, part of the consortium is coming in on the deal for a 25 percent holding, for which it will pay $1.04 billion.

43324 ■ *"It's Good To Be King" in South Florida Business Journal (Vol. 35, August 29, 2014, No. 5, pp. 12)*
Pub: American City Business Journals
Released: August 29, 2014. **Description:** The $11.4 billion deal that will create a new holding company for Burger King Worldwide and Tim Hortons will be based in Oakville, Ontario, Canada and was met with public outrage. Burger King declares that the merger with the Canadian coffee and doughnut franchise chain was about global growth, not a strategy to avoid millions of dollars in corporate income tax payments to the U.S. government.

43325 ■ *"It's Time To Swim" in Canadian Business (Vol. 81, March 3, 2008, No. 3, pp. 37)*
Ed: Megan Harman. **Description:** Canadian manufacturers should consider Asian markets such as India and the United Arab Emirates as the U.S. economic downturn continues. Canada's shortage in skilled labor is also expected to negatively affect manufacturing industries. Ontario's plans to assist manufacturers are also presented.

43326 ■ *"It's What You Know. It's Who You Know. It's China" in Inc. (Vol. 33, October 2011, No. 8, pp. 80)*
Pub: Inc. Magazine
Ed: David H. Freedman. **Description:** Michael Lee will be the first American entrepreneur to build big in China. The company is piloting two large commercial real estate developments, one in New York City the other in Nanjing, China.

43327 ■ *"Jobs, Export Surge Confirm Recovery" in Globe & Mail (March 10, 2007, pp. B5)*
Ed: Heather Scoffield. **Description:** The increase in the number of jobs and exports that is forecast to reverse the slowdown in the Canadian economy is discussed.

43328 ■ *"The Joy of Overseas Calling" in Canadian Business (Vol. 85, August 13, 2012, No. 13, pp. 49)*
Pub: George Media Inc.
Ed: Bryan Borzykowski. **Released:** August 13, 2012. **Description:** Investors should consider growth prospects, regulation and wireless penetration when investing in foreign telecommunications companies. Investment opportunities are available in Europe, Asia, and Latin America and investors should look into dividends, debt and the mix of product offerings.

43329 ■ *"Keeping Railcars 'Busy At All Times' At TTX" in Crain's Chicago Business (Vol. 31, April 28, 2008, No. 17, pp. 6)*
Pub: Crain Communications Inc.
Contact: Todd Johnson, Publisher
Ed: Bob Tita. **Description:** Profile of the president of Chicago railcar pool operator TTX Co. and his business plan for the company which includes improving fleet management and car purchasing through better use of data on railroad demand.

43330 ■ *"Kenyans Embrace Moving Money By Text Message" in Chicago Tribune (October 7, 2008)*
Pub: McClatchy-Tribune Information Services
Ed: Laurie Goering. **Description:** Cell phone banking services are becoming more common, especially for foreign residents; customers are able to establish

a virtual cell phone bank account through companies such as M-Pesa which allows their customers to pay bills, withdraw cash, pay merchants or text money to relatives.

43331 ■ *"Ketchup King Heinz Seeks to Boost Soy-Sauce Empire in China"* **in** *Advertising Age (Vol. 83, October 8, 2012, No. 36, pp. 3)*
Description: Heinz is buying up local soy sauce firms in China with a buy-and-build strategy to expand into other markets in the country. Soy sauce total sales are about $4 billion annually in China, while ketchup sales amount to $100 million to $200 million there.

43332 ■ *"Kids, Computers and the Social Networking Evolution"* **in** *Canadian Business (Vol. 81, October 27, 2008, No. 18, pp. 93)*
Ed: Penny Milton. **Description:** Social networking was found to help educate students in countries like the U.S., Canada and Mexico. Schools that embrace social networking teach students how to use computers safely and responsibility in order to counter threats to children on the Internet.

43333 ■ *"Kinetico Exec Going Global to Increase Growth Flow"* **in** *Crain's Cleveland Business (Vol. 28, October 1, 2007, No. 39, pp. 5)*
Pub: Crain Communications Inc.
Ed: David Bennett. **Description:** Shamus Hurley, the new CEO and president of Kinetico Inc., a manufacturer of water filtering and softening equipment for residential, commercial and municipal use, plans to expand the company to target markets overseas.

43334 ■ *Kocham Business Directory (Korea)*
Pub: Korean Chamber of Commerce and Industry in USA Inc.
URL(s): kocham.org/business-directory. **Released:** Annual **Covers:** About 700 offices of leading Korean companies operated by Korean nationals located throughout the United States. Other Korean service firms (banks, trade organizations, etc.) are also listed. **Entries include:** Firm name, address, phone, cable address, telex, name of United States representative or president. Exporter listings include above information for headquarters' address and product line. Importer listings include products. **Arrangement:** Exporters and importers are alphabetical; service firms are classified by type of service.

43335 ■ *"Kroger Girds for Invasion of U.K. Chain"* **in** *Business Courier (Vol. 24, November 1, 2007, No. 29, pp. 1)*
Pub: American City Business Journals, Inc.
Contact: Whitney Shaw, President
Ed: Jon Newberry. **Description:** Tesco PLC will be opening its first Fresh & Easy Neighborhood Markets in Southern California. The company has committed $500 million per year to get a share of the $500 billion US food retailing market and will be opening more stores in quick succession. Tesco's arrival can be difficult for Kroger because Kroger had obtained much of its success by using Tesco's UK model.

43336 ■ *"Land Agent Taken Over"* **in** *Farmer's Weekly (March 28, 2008, No. 320)*
Description: Property business Smiths Gore will take over Cluttons' rural division, one of the oldest names in land agency. Cluttons said it had decided to sell its rural business as part of a strategic repositioning that would refocus the business on commercial, residential and overseas opportunities.

43337 ■ *"The Last Ingredient?"* **in** *Canadian Business (Vol. 81, October 13, 2008, No. 17, pp. 88)*
Ed: Rachel Pulfer. **Description:** Views and information on Cookie Jar Group's plan to acquire rights for Strawberry Shortcake and the Care Bears are discussed. The move would make Cookie Jar a major player in the global children's entertainment market. Cookie Jar chief executive, Michael Hirsh is believed to be securing funds for the planned $195 million acquisition.

43338 ■ *"The Latin Beat Goes On"* **in** *Barron's (Vol. 88, July 7, 2008, No. 27, pp. L5)*
Pub: Dow Jones & Co., Inc.
Contact: Clare Hart, President
Ed: Tom Sullivan. **Description:** Latin American stocks have outperformed other regional markets due

to rising commodities prices and favorable economic climate. Countries such as Brazil, Mexico, Chile, and Peru provide investment opportunities, while Argentina and Venezuela are tougher places to invest.

43339 ■ *"Leaks in the Pipeline"* **in** *Hispanic Business (September 2007, pp. 18, 20, 22, 24)*
Pub: Hispanic Business Inc.
Contact: Jesus Chavarria, President
Ed: Holly Ocasio Rizzo. **Description:** Graduate schools need to focus on domestic diversity in order to attract Hispanic students in a growing global economy.

43340 ■ *"Learning to Love Our Trading Monopoly"* **in** *Canadian Business (Vol. 85, September 17, 2012, No. 14, pp. 11)*
Pub: George Media Inc.
Ed: Richard Warnica. **Released:** September 17, 2012. **Description:** The Maple Group has acquired the TMX Group for $50 a share along with competitor Alpha and the Canadian Depository for Securities, allowing the new TMX to control some 85 percent of equities traffic in Canada. Although the new TMX dominates the market, it will not be free from competition for Canadian business.

43341 ■ *"Leasing Midway"* **in** *Crain's Chicago Business (May 5, 2008)*
Pub: Crain Communications Inc.
Contact: Todd Johnson, Publisher
Ed: Paul Merrion. **Description:** According to experts, bids for the first privatization of a major U.S. airport could run as high as $3.5 billion. Information-gathering and negotiations will soon get under way with some or all of the six major international investor groups that recently expressed interest in running Midway.

43342 ■ *"Leisureworld Announces August Dividend"* **in** *Internet Wire (August 15, 2012)*
Description: Profile of Leisureworld Senior Care Corporation, Canada's fifth largest senior housing operator and third largest provider of LTC senior homes in Ontario. The firm owns and operates six retirement residences and one independent living residence in Ontario and British Columbia. Preferred Health Care Services are one of their subsidiaries and offers professional nursing and supports services as is Ontario Long Term Care which provides services, dietary, social work, and other regulated health professional services.

43343 ■ *"Lessons Burma Taught Me"* **in** *Canadian Business (Vol. 85, July 16, 2012, No. 11-12, pp. 17)*
Pub: George Media Inc.
Ed: Michael Lavergne. **Released:** July 16, 2012. **Description:** The decision of the Canadian government to allow trade with Burma presents Canadian firms with the challenge of ensuring that their projects benefit its people and its economy. Companies are advised to follow international monitoring agreements related to labor, ethnic rights, and environmental protection.

43344 ■ *"Lightening the Load"* **in** *Crain's Cleveland Business (Vol. 28, October 8, 2007, No. 40, pp. 3)*
Ed: Jay Miller. **Description:** Companies reliant on barge deliveries are running well below capacity due to both the building up of silt at the bottom of the Cuyahoga River as well as the lower water levels which are causing a number of problems for the barges and big boats that deliver goods to the region.

43345 ■ *"Li'l Guy Rolls Up Into Bigger Company"* **in** *The Business Journal-Serving Metropolitan Kansas City (Vol. 26, September 12, 2008)*
Pub: American City Business Journals, Inc.
Contact: Whitney Shaw, President
Ed: Suzanna Stagemeyer. **Description:** Li'l Guy Foods, a Mexican food company in Kansas City, Missouri, has merged with Tortilla King Inc. Li'l Guy's revenue in 2007 was $3.3 million, while a newspaper report said that Tortilla King's revenue in 2001 was $7.5 million. Growth opportunities for the combined companies and Li'l Guy's testing of the Wichita market are discussed.

43346 ■ *"Live & Learn: Maurice Strong"* **in** *Canadian Business (Vol. 81, December 8, 2008, No. 21, pp. 70)*
Pub: Rogers Media Inc.
Contact: Tony Viner, President
Ed: Andrew Wahl. **Description:** Peking University honorary professor Maurice Strong believes that a lot of Westerners, including Canadians, do not take time to understand the business culture in China.

43347 ■ *"Lobster Mania Hits China: They Just Had To Get Used To the Claws"* **in** *Canadian Business (Vol. 85, July 16, 2012, No. 11-12, pp. 10)*
Pub: George Media Inc.
Ed: Joe Castaldo. **Released:** July 16, 2012. **Description:** Canadian lobster exports to China have tripled to almost $30 million annually since 2010 as a result of marketing efforts by Maritimes governments including pitching lobster to cooking shows and organizing training sessions for Chinese chefs. Canadian exporters must decide whether their lobster is a premium product or a commodity product to solidify its image in China.

43348 ■ *Local Enterprises in the Global Economy: Issues of Governance and Upgrading*
Pub: Edward Elgar Publishing Inc.
Contact: Richard Henning, Vice President
E-mail: kwight@e-elgar.com
Released: November 2004. **Price:** $54.40, paperback; $146.70, hardback. **Description:** Examination of the relationships between globalization, corporate governance, and the economic performance of small businesses and local enterprises.

43349 ■ *"Local Manufacturers See Tax Proposal Hurting Global Operations"* **in** *Crain's Cleveland Business (Vol. 30, May 18, 2009, No. 20)*
Pub: Crain Communications Inc.
Ed: Dan Shingler. **Description:** New tax laws proposed by the Obama Administration could hinder the efforts of some Northeast Ohio industrial companies from expanding their overseas markets. The law is designed to prevent companies from moving jobs overseas.

43350 ■ *"Lofty Ambitions"* **in** *Canadian Business (Vol. 80, October 22, 2007, No. 21, pp. 26)*
Ed: Thomas Watson. **Description:** Canada has made its first trade deal in six years through the European Free Trade Agreement. This is a boost to the Canadian economy, but focus must be made on taking out internal barriers to inter-provincial trade and from third-party trade liberalization.

43351 ■ *"Look, Leap, and License"* **in** *Retail Merchandiser (Vol. 51, July-August 2011, No. 4, pp. 16)*
Pub: Phoenix Media Corporation
Description: Toys highlighting the Licensing International Expo 2011 included a life-sized Cookie Monster, Papa Smurf, Power Rangers, Transformer, and margarita wrestlers. Taking licensed properties international was a common theme at this year's show.

43352 ■ *"Loonie Tunes: When Will the Dollar Rise Again?"* **in** *Canadian Business (Vol. 81, November 10, 2008, No. 19, pp. 62)*
Pub: Rogers Media Inc.
Contact: Tony Viner, President
Ed: Joe Castaldo. **Description:** The Canadian dollar has weakened against the U.S. Dollar as the U.S. financial crisis rocked global markets. A currency strategist says that the strength of the U.S. dollar is not based on people's optimism on the U.S. economy but on a structural demand where U.S. non-financial corporations have been repatriating greenbacks from foreign subsidiaries.

43353 ■ *"Loonies Buy U.S. Cable"* **in** *Canadian Business (Vol. 85, September 17, 2012, No. 14, pp. 8)*
Pub: George Media Inc.
Ed: Jeff Beer. **Released:** September 17, 2012. **Description:** The move by two Canadian companies to invest in the U.S. cable industry get mixed reactions

from analyst and observers. Cogeco Cable purchased Atlantic Broadband for $1.36 billion while the Canada Pension Plan Investment Board announced its partnership with European private equity firm BC Partners to acquire Suddenlink Communications for $6.6 billion.

43354 ■ *"Lots of Explanations, Not Much Growth" in Barron's (Vol. 92, August 25, 2012, No. 35, pp. 38)*
Pub: Dow Jones & Co., Inc.
Contact: Clare Hart, President
Ed: Gene Epstein. **Description:** The slow growth of the US economy culd be due to the insufficiency of US fiscal and monetary policy. It could also be attributed to the effects of the recession in Europe, the banking and financial crises, and to the decline in economic freedom.

43355 ■ *Macrowikinomics: Rebooting Business and the World*
Pub: Portfolio Hardcover
Ed: Don Tapscott, Anthony D. Williams. **Released:** September 28, 2010. **Price:** $34, hardcover; $20, paperback; $12.99. **Description:** Wikinomics Don Tapscott and Anthony Williams showed how mass collaboration was changing the way businesses communicate, create value, and compete in the new global marketplace in 2007. Now, in the wake of the global financial crisis, the principles of wikinomics have become more powerful than ever. **Availability:** PrintE-book; Electronic publishing.

43356 ■ *Made in China: Secrets of China's Dynamic Entrepreneurs*
Pub: John Wiley & Sons Inc.
Contact: Stephen M. Smith, President
Ed: Winter Nie, Katherine Xin, Lily Zhang. **Released:** December 2008. **Price:** $24.95, paperback. **Description:** Insight and analysis of the strategies leading to China's rapidly growing economy are profiled. **Availability:** Print.

43357 ■ *"Magpower May Build Solar Panels Here" in Austin Business Journal (Vol. 31, May 13, 2011, No. 10, pp. A1)*
Pub: American City Business Journals
Ed: Christopher Calnan. **Description:** RRE Austin Solar LLC CEO Doven Mehta has revealed plans to partner with Portugal-based Magpower SA, only if Austin energy buys electricity from planned solar energy farm in Pflugerville. Austin Energy has received 100 bids from 35 companies to supply 200 megawatts of solar- and wind-generated electricity.

43358 ■ *"Major Advances in Heat Pump Technology - Part Two" in Contractor (Vol. 57, February 2010, No. 2, pp. 22)*
Pub: Penton Media, Inc.
Ed: Mark Eatherton. **Description:** Chinese and Japanese companies have come up with refrigerant based heat pump products that are air based which will significantly lower the installed cost of heat pump based systems. Some of these newer models have variable speed, soft start compressors and have the ability to perform high-efficiency heat pump operation on a modulating basis.

43359 ■ *"Making Factory Tours Count" in Playthings (Vol. 107, January 1, 2009, No. 1, pp. 14)*
Pub: Reed Elsevier Group plc Reed Business Information
Contact: Mark Kelsey, Chief Executive Officer
Ed: Malcolm Denniss. **Description:** The importance of touring an overseas toy supplier's manufacturing facility is stressed. Strategies for general factory visits are outlined in order to determine safety-related quality assurance issues in production.

43360 ■ *"Making It Stick" in Business Courier (Vol. 24, November 14, 2007, No. 30, pp. 1)*
Pub: American City Business Journals, Inc.
Contact: Whitney Shaw, President
Ed: Lucy May. **Description:** Discusses a report by the Brookings Institution which shows the need for the U.S. government to offer greater support to the country's metro areas in order to excel globally. Ohio, which has seven of the country's 100 largest metro-

politan areas, does not receive enough funds, due to the need to finance less populated areas. Because of this, Ohio politicians have to spread less funding in order to cover more constituents.

43361 ■ *"Managerial Ties with Local Firms and Governments: an Analysis of Japanese Firms In China" in International Journal of Business and Emerging Markets (Vol. 4, July 11, 2012, No. 3, pp. 181)*
Released: July 11, 2012. **Description:** This study explores how managerial ties between foreign firms and local firms and those between foreign firms and local government officials affect the performance of firms operating in transition economies. Using survey data collected from Japanese firms operating in China, this study finds that managerial ties between foreign firms and local firms and local government officials are positively associated with the performance of Japanese firms in China.

43362 ■ *Managing Complexity and Change in SMEs: Frontiers in European Research*
Pub: Edward Elgar Publishing Inc.
Contact: Richard Henning, Vice President
E-mail: kwight@e-elgar.com
Ed: Poul Rind Christensen, Flemming Poulfelt. **Released:** 2006. **Price:** £72. **Description:** Complexities faced by entrepreneurs in an expanding marketplace are discussed. **Availability:** Print.

43363 ■ *Managing Economies, Trade and International Business*
Pub: Palgrave Macmillan
Contact: Lisa Dunn, Manager
E-mail: l.dunn@palgrave.com
Released: January 19, 2010. **Price:** £77. **Description:** An in-depth look at the areas that affect and influence international business, exploring specific issues businesses face in terms of economic development, trade law, and international marketing and management. **Availability:** Print.

43364 ■ *Managing India's Small Industrial Economy: The Catalytic Role of Industrial Counselors and Policy Makers*
Pub: Pine Forge Press
Contact: Blaise R. Simqu, President
Released: June 2004. **Price:** $39, paperback. **Description:** Case studies and methodology are used to discuss the areas where industrial consultants are influencing sustainability and growth of small businesses in India's industrial economy.

43365 ■ *"Manufacturing Behind the Great Wall: What Works, What Doesn't" in Canadian Electronics (Vol. 23, February 2008, No. 1, pp. 6)*
Ed: Michel Jullian. **Description:** Electronic component producers are increasingly transitioning their manufacturing operations to China in order to take advantage of the growing Chinese manufacturing industry. It is believed that manufacturers have to carefully consider whether their run sizes are appropriate for Chinese manufacturing before moving their operations.

43366 ■ *"Manufacturing in the Middle Kingdom" in Inc. (December 2007, pp. 54-57)*
Pub: Gruner and Jahr USA Publishing Co.
Contact: J. Russell Denson, President
Ed: Alex Salkever. **Description:** Tips for manufacturing any new product in China as well as marketing said product is examined; five key steps for successfully managing Chinese contractors are listed.

43367 ■ *"Marine Act Amendments Gain Parliamentary Approval" in Canadian Sailings (July 7, 2008)*
Ed: Alex Binkley. **Description:** Changes to the Canada Marine Act provides better borrowing deals as well as an ability to tap into federal infrastructure funding for environmental protection measures, security improvements and other site enhancements.

43368 ■ *"Market Gamble" in Business Journal-Serving Phoenix and the Valley of the Sun (Vol. 5, October 5, 2007, No. 28, pp. 1)*
Ed: Mike Padgett. **Description:** Al-BSR LLC, an Israeli group believes the housing market will regain its strength within three years. The group plans to

build its $385 million project, called One Phoenix. The condominiums start at $500,000, with units ranging from 800 to 2,000 square feet.

43369 ■ *"Market Watch" in Barron's (Vol. 88, March 24, 2008, No. 12, pp. M18)*
Pub: Dow Jones & Co., Inc.
Contact: Clare Hart, President
Ed: Ashraf Laidi, Marc Pado, David Kotok. **Description:** Latest measures implemented by the Federal Reserve to address the credit crisis did not benefit the US dollar, with the Japanese yen and the euro recouping earlier losses against the dollar. Goldman Sachs reported earnings of $3.23 per share, claiming a stronger liquidity position. The US markets bottomed early on 22 January 2007, according to evidence.

43370 ■ *"Market Watch" in Barron's (Vol. 89, July 20, 2009, No. 29, pp. M10)*
Pub: Dow Jones & Co., Inc.
Contact: Clare Hart, President
Ed: Peter Greene, Michael Darda, Ian Wyatt, Stephanie Pomboy. **Description:** Concerns about a possible increase in US inflation rates are overblown as the country remains in a deflationary environment. Goldman Sachs's second quarter 2009 earnings have already been priced in as its shares rose. Germany's plans of a possible dollar bond sale are in anticipation of a rise in the euro's value.

43371 ■ *"Market Watch: A Sampling of Advisory Opinion US Stock Price Trends, Economic Effects of Global Trade, Chinese Economic Trends" in Barron's (Vol. 92, July 23, 2012, No. 30, pp. M14)*
Pub: Dow Jones & Co., Inc.
Contact: Clare Hart, President
Ed: Richard M. Salsman, Jack Ablin, Francois Sicart. **Released:** July 23, 2012. **Description:** US stocks are considered inexpensive due to their low price-earnings ratios compared to levels before the global financial crisis. The US economy is becoming more dependent on the rest of the worldas a result of global trade. The Chinese economy continues to have strong economic growth despite a slowdown.

43372 ■ *"Markets 2008: Grin and Bear It" in Canadian Business (Vol. 81, February 12, 2008, No. 3, pp. 53)*
Pub: Rogers Media Inc.
Contact: Tony Viner, President
Ed: Jeff Sanford. **Description:** Discusses the United States economic downturn, caused by the credit market crisis, which is expected to affect the Canadian economy, as Canada depend on the U.S. for 80 percent of its exports. Economist David Rosenberg thinks that in 2008, housing prices will decline by 15 percent and gross domestic product growth will slow to 0.8 percent. Other forecasts for Canadian economy are given.

43373 ■ *"Maryland Doctors, Health Insurers Squabble Over Who Sends Patients the Bill" in Baltimore Business Journal (Vol. 27, February 6, 2010)*
Pub: American City Business Journals
Ed: Scott Graham. **Description:** Issue of allowing patients to send reimbursement checks to physicians who are not part of their health insurer's provider network is being debated in Maryland. Details on the proposed Maryland bill and the arguments presented by doctors and insurers are outlined.

43374 ■ *"Massage Heights Chasing Big Expansion Opportunities" in San Antonio Business Journal (Vol. 28, April 25, 2014, No. 11, pp. 6)*
Pub: American City Business Journals
Released: April 25, 2014. **Description:** Massage Heights, offering deep tissue massage, hot stone massage and facials, has opened a second corporate-owned facility in Stone Oak, Texas. The company, founded in April 2004, is focusing on expansion plans due to investor interest in the firm's growth. Massage Heights currently has five facilities in Canada.

43375 ■ *"Masu Accelerates for Sushi Avenue"* in Business Journal (Vol. 30, June 1, 2012, No. 1, pp. 1)
Pub: American City Business Journals, Inc.
Contact: Whitney Shaw, President
Ed: John Vomhof Jr. **Released:** June 1, 2012. **Description:** Sushi Avenue Inc. plans to boost growth by opening 10 Masu Sushi & Robata restaurants by 2015, mostly outside the Twin Cities area. The company is also looking to expand into Southeast Asia by opening stores in Singapore.

43376 ■ *"Matthews-Schawk Deal Years in the Making"* in Pittsburgh Business Times (Vol. 33, March 21, 2014, No. 36, pp. 3)
Pub: American City Business Journals
Released: March 21, 2014. **Description:** Matthews International Corporation of Pittsburgh, Pennsylvania is acquiring Schawk Inc. of Des Plaines, Illinois in a cash and stock deal worth $577 million. The mergor would all Matthews and Schawk to offer a united global front for clients and to expand Matthews' marketing and brand deployment business.

43377 ■ *"Maybe We're Exploiting China"* in Canadian Business (Vol. 85, September 17, 2012, No. 14, pp. 4)
Pub: George Media Inc.
Ed: Duncan Hood. **Released:** September 17, 2012. **Description:** The proposed deal by China National Offshore Oil Corp. (CNOOC) to acquire Canada's Nexen for $27.50 a share is met with uncertainty by the public. The U.S. is believed to be opposing the deal because it would no longer have quite as much power to set oil prices in Canada.

43378 ■ The Mechanics of Modernity in Europe and East Asia: Institutional Origins of Social Change and Stagnation
Pub: Routledge
Contact: Kevin Bradley, President
E-mail: kbradley@taylorandfrancis.com
Ed: Erik Ringmar. **Released:** August 12, 2009. **Price:** $54.95, paperback; $180, hardback. **Description:** Discussion of reasons why certain countries embarked on a path of sustained economic growth while others declined in Europe and East Asia. **Availability:** Print.

43379 ■ *"Medical Tourism: The World Is Your Hospital"* in Canadian Business (Vol. 81, July 22, 2008, No. 12-13, pp. 62)
Pub: Rogers Media Inc.
Contact: Tony Viner, President
Ed: Sharda Prashad. **Description:** Medical tourism is seen as a booming industry around the world and is expected to grow to around $40 billion in 2010. Key information regarding medical tourism and services are presented. Views on the possible impact of medical tourism on Canada's health care industry, as well as medical tourism opportunities in Canada, are also given.

43380 ■ *"Medtronic Heading to Foreign Markets"* in Memphis Business Journal (Vol. 34, September 28, 2012, No. 24, pp. 1)
Pub: American City Business Journal
Description: Medtronics Inc.'s Spinal and Biologics Division will launch a new spinal surgery system in 2012. The spinal fusion procedure has not yet been approved by international surgical governing bodies, but the company is already rolling it out in different countries. The new service uses the company's various surgical systems and implants.

43381 ■ *"Melamine Analytical Methods Released"* in Feedstuffs (Vol. 80, October 6, 2008, No. 41, pp. 2)
Pub: Miller Publishing Company
Description: Romer Labs has released new validations for its AgraQuant Melamine enzyme-linked immunosorbent assay. The test kit screens for melamine in feed and diary products, including pet foods, milk and milk powder. Melamine by itself is nontoxic in low doses, but when combined with cyanuric acid it can cause fatal kidney stones. The Chinese dairy industry is in the midst of a huge melamine crisis; melamine-contaminated dairy and food products from China have been found in more than 20 countries.

43382 ■ *"Memphis Excels Among Tennessee Brands"* in Memphis Business Journal (No. 35, March 28, 2014, No. 51, pp. 7)
Pub: American City Business Journals
Released: March 28, 2014. **Description:** Global shipping and logistics company, FedEx Corporation has been named by Brand Finance as the most valuable brand in Tennessee. Three of the top four bands on the list of the top 500 most valuable brands in the U.S. are based in Memphis, Tennessee, including FedEx, AutoZone, and International Paper.

43383 ■ *"Merchant Cash-Advance Company Enters Canada"* in Cardline (Vol. 8, February 29, 2008, No. 9, pp. 1)
Description: Merchant cash-advance company is expanding operations into Canada.

43384 ■ *"Mexican Companies to Rent Space in TechTown, Chinese Negotiating"* in Crain's Detroit Business (Vol. 24, September 29, 2008, No. 39)
Pub: Crain Communications Inc.
Contact: Rance E. Crain, President
Ed: Tom Henderson. **Description:** Wayne State University's TechTown, the business incubator and research park, has signed an agreement with the Mexican government that will provide temporary office space to 25 Mexican companies looking to find customers or establish partnerships in Michigan. TechTown's executive director is negotiating with economic development officials from China. To accommodate foreign visitors the incubator is equipping offices with additional equipment and resources.

43385 ■ *"Micro-Finance Agencies and SMEs"* in International Journal of Entrepreneurship and Small Business (Vol. 11, August 3, 2010)
Pub: Publishers Communication Group
Contact: Doug Wright, Director
Ed: Patricia A. Rowe, Michael J. Christie, Frank Hoy. **Description:** Institutional preparedness of economic development agencies for developing small and medium-sized enterprises (SMEs) is discussed. The cases presented illustrate variations in the micro-finance lender agency-enterprise development of processes for sharing vision and interdependence.

43386 ■ *"Mine Woes Could Rouse Zinc"* in Barron's (Vol. 88, July 7, 2008, No. 27, pp. M12)
Pub: Dow Jones & Co., Inc.
Contact: Clare Hart, President
Ed: Andrea Hotter. **Description:** Prices of zinc could increase due to supply problems in producing countries such as Australia and China. London Metal Exchange prices for the metal have dropped about 36 percent in 2008.

43387 ■ *"Minimizing Import Risks"* in Canadian Sailings (July 7, 2008)
Ed: Jack Kohane. **Description:** New food and product safety laws may be enacted by Canada's Parliament; importers, retailers and manufacturers could face huge fines if the new laws are passed.

43388 ■ *"Mission to China"* in Canadian Business (Vol. 81, December 8, 2008, No. 21, pp. 28)
Pub: Rogers Media Inc.
Contact: Tony Viner, President
Ed: Andrew Wahl. **Description:** Canada China Business Council and the Council of the Federation visited China for a three-city trade mission. The trade mission aims to re-establish the strong relationship between China and Canada.

43389 ■ *"The Moderating Effects of Organizational Context On the Relationship Between Voluntary Turnover and Organizational Performance: Evidence from Korea"* in Human Resource Management (Vol. 51, January-February 2012, No. 1, pp. 47-70)
Pub: John Wiley & Sons Inc.
Contact: Stephen M. Smith, President
Ed: Kiwook Kwon, Kweontaek Chung, Hyuntak Roh, Clint Chadwick, John J. Lawler. **Description:** The ability of organizational context to moderate the relationship between voluntary employee turnover and organizational performance is examined using data from South Korean firms. The effects of employee involvement practices, investment in employee training and development, and the availability of potential workers on this relationship are studied.

43390 ■ *"Montreal Port Head Lands CP Ships Deal"* in Globe & Mail (January 5, 2006, pp. B4)
Description: The opinions of president Dominic Taddeo, on the positive impact of TUI AG's acquisition of CP Ships Ltd. on operations at Port of Montreal, are presented.

43391 ■ *"The Mood of a Nation"* in Canadian Business (Vol. 81, April 14, 2008, No. 6, pp. 56)
Pub: Rogers Media Inc.
Contact: Tony Viner, President
Ed: Joe Castaldo. **Description:** Independent Fish Harvesters Inc. processes more kilograms a year and has had to hire more workers but its managers worry about how a slowdown in the U.S. economy will affect his business. A planned shopping complex in Mirabel Quebec, the manufacturing industry in Kitchener, Ontario, and a cattle farming business in Sarnia, Ontario are discussed to provide a snapshot of the challenges that business in Canada are facing as recession looms.

43392 ■ More Than a Pink Cadillac
Pub: McGraw-Hill
Ed: Jim Underwood. **Released:** January 08, 2003. **Price:** Rs 1,389.43, softcover. **Description:** Profile of Mary Kay Ash who turned her $5,000 investment into a billion-dollar corporation. Ash's nine principles that form the foundation of her company's global success are outlined. Stories from her sales force leaders share ideas for motivating employees, impressing customers and building a successful company. The book emphasizes the leadership skills required to drive performance in any successful enterprise. **Availability:** Print.

43393 ■ *"Mover and Sheika"* in Conde Nast Portfolio (Vol. 2, June 2008, No. 6, pp. 104)
Ed: John Arlidge. **Description:** Profile of Princess Sheika Lubna who is the first female foreign trade minister in the Middle East, the United Arab Emirates biggest business envoy, paving the way for billions in new investment, and also a manufacturer of her own perfume line.

43394 ■ *"A Muddle at Marks & Spencer"* in Barron's (Vol. 88, July 7, 2008, No. 27, pp. M7)
Pub: Dow Jones & Co., Inc.
Contact: Clare Hart, President
Ed: Molly Neal. **Description:** British retail outfit Marks & Spencer is encountering turbulent financial conditions but remains confident in spending 900 million pounds sterling. The company has not made a profit forecast for the first half of 2008 and is suffering from a shrinking cash flow.

43395 ■ The Multinational Enterprise Revisited: The Essential Buckley and Casson
Pub: Palgrave Macmillan
Contact: Lisa Dunn, Manager
E-mail: l.dunn@palgrave.com
Ed: Peter J. Buckley, Mark Casson. **Released:** November 2009. **Price:** £69, hardcover; £56.65; $110. **Description:** A compilation of essays gathered from over thirty years discussing the future of the multinational enterprise, and includes a new introduction and conclusion to bond the pieces together in a comprehensive overview of the theory of the multinational enterprise. **Availability:** PrintE-book; Electronic publishingE-book; PDF.

43396 ■ *"A Muted Money Hunt"* in Washington Business Journal (Vol. 33, July 11, 2014, No. 12, pp. 8)
Pub: American City Business Journals
Released: July 11, 2014. **Description:** Columbia Capital is planning to raise $425 million for a new fund. The company is forming a parallel offshore fund. Columbia specializes in enterprise information technology, infrastructure and other high-dollar technology investments.

43397 ■ *"MyReviewsNow.net Announces New Affiliate Partner Gift Baskets Overseas" in M2 EquityBites (EQB) (June 22, 2012)*
Pub: Normans Media Ltd.
Released: June 22, 2012. **Description:** MyReviews-Now.net has partnered with Gift Baskets Overseas in order to offer gift baskets to be shipped overseas. Gift Baskets Oversease works with local florists and shippers worldwide. No financial details were disclosed.

43398 ■ *"National Instruments Connects with Lego" in Austin Business JournalInc. (Vol. 28, August 25, 2008, No. 23, pp. 1)*
Pub: American City Business Journals
Ed: Laura Hipp. **Description:** Austin-based National Instruments Corporation has teamed with Lego Group from Denmark to create a robot that can be built by children and can be used to perform tasks. Lego WeDo, their latest product, uses computer connection to power its movements. The educational benefits of the new product are discussed.

43399 ■ *"Native Wisdom" in Canadian Business (Vol. 80, October 8, 2007, No. 20, pp. 121)*
Ed: Bernd Christmas. **Description:** Roles of Canadian indigenous peoples in the country's economic development are discussed. It is believed that empowering Canadian natives to contribute to the country's economy will positively affect the country's future. The need for education in preparing natives for the global economy is also tackled.

43400 ■ *"Needed: A Strategy; Banking In China" in The Economist (Vol. 390, January 3, 2009, No. 8612, pp. 54)*
Description: International banks are competing for a role in China but are finding obstacles in their paths such as a reduction in the credit their operations may receive from Chinese banks and the role they can play in the public capital markets which remain limited.

43401 ■ *"Nestle Acquires Waggin' Train Dog Treat Company" in Pet Product News (Vol. 64, November 2010, No. 11, pp. 7)*
Pub: Bowtie Inc.
Description: Vevey, Switzerland-based Nestle has acquired South Carolina-based dog treat firm Waggin' Train LLC from private equity firm VMG Partners in September 2010. Waggin' Train LLC, which will be operated as a wholly owned subsidiary, is expected to fill a gap in Nestle's dog treat product portfolio.

43402 ■ *"A New Alliance For Global Change" in Harvard Business Review (Vol. 88, September 2010, No. 9, pp. 56)*
Pub: Harvard Business School Publishing
Ed: Bill Drayton, Valeria Budinich. **Description:** Collaboration between social organizations and for-profit firms through the development of hybrid value chains to target complex global issues is promoted. While social organizations offer links to communities and consumers, firms provide financing and scale expertise.

43403 ■ *"New Argentine Investment Taps Real Estate" in South Florida Business Journal (Vol. 32, June 22, 2012, No. 48, pp. 1)*
Pub: American City Business Journal
Description: Industry experts believe that Miami, Florida is becoming the go-to-investment destination of Argentines looking for real estate development opportunities. For example, Consultatio paid $220 million for 5.5 acres in Bal Harbour where it plans to construct condominiums. It appears Argentines are selecting sites in Miami as investments.

43404 ■ *"New Game Plan to Grow Trade?" in Providence Business News (Vol. 29, May 19, 2014, No. 7, pp. 1)*
Pub: American City Business Journals
Released: May 19, 2014. **Description:** The state of Rhode Island is trying a new approach for expanding its foreign trade connections by offering its location to foreign businesses instead of taking local companies abroad. The four-member Rhode Island delegation visited companies and their leadership teams in Ireland and Italy.

43405 ■ *"New Generation Deans Lead Atlanta Area Business Schools Into the Future" in Atlanta Business Chronicle (July 25, 2014, pp. 3A)*
Pub: American City Business Journals, Inc.
Contact: Whitney Shaw, President
Released: July 25, 2014. **Description:** An interview with five business school deans from Georgia share their views on the future of business education, changing business education needs, and other issues affecting the Atlanta area business schools. The growing demands for greater global competences, good communication skills across various cultures, and other challenges faced by the students and employers are discussed. Other topics include the role of women in the corporate world.

43406 ■ *"New Global Hot Spots: Look Beyond Shanghai for the Next Big Thing" in Inc. (October 2007, pp. 40-41)*
Pub: Mansueto Ventures L.L.C.
Contact: John Koten, Chief Executive Officer
Ed: Nitasha Tiku. **Description:** The Chinese government is investing money to lure U.S. companies to start doing business in Chengdu, China. The government is upgrading Chengdu's infrastructure and establishing free trade zones in a less polluted environment. Other cities profiled in the article include: Yekaterinburg, Russia; Poznan, Poland; Ahmadabad and Kolkata, India; Suzhou, China; Belo Horizonte, Brazil; Ras Al Khaimah, United Arab Emirates; and Aguascalientes, Mexico.

43407 ■ *"New Institutional Accounting and IFRS" in Accounting and Business Research (Vol. 41, Summer 2011, No. 3, pp. 309)*
Pub: American Institute of Certified Public Accountants
Contact: Barry C. Melancon, President
E-mail: bmelancon@aicpa.org
Ed: Peter Wysocki. **Description:** A new framework for institutional accounting research is presented. It has five fundamental components — efficient versus inefficient results, interdependencies, causation, level of analysis, and institutional structure. The use of the framework for evaluation accounting institutions such as the international financial reporting standards is discussed.

43408 ■ *"New Institutional Accounting and IFRS" in Accounting and Business Research (Vol. 41, Summer 2011, No. 3, pp. 309)*
Pub: Routledge
Contact: Kevin Bradley, President
E-mail: kbradley@taylorandfrancis.com
Ed: Peter Wysocki. **Description:** A new framework for institutional accounting research is presented. It has five fundamental components: efficient versus inefficient results, interdependencies, causation, level of analysis, and institutional structure. The use of the framework for evaluation accounting institutions such as the international financial reports standards (IFRS) is discussed.

43409 ■ *"New King Tops the Charts" in The Business Journal-Portland (Vol. 25, August 8, 2008, No. 22, pp. 1)*
Pub: American City Business Journals, Inc.
Contact: Whitney Shaw, President
Ed: Andy Giegerich. **Description:** Spanish-language KRYP-FM station's spring 2008 ratings soared to 6.4 from 2.8 for the previous year. The station timing is flawless given the fact that one of every three new Portland-area residents between 2002 and 2007 were Latino.

43410 ■ *The New Role of Regional Management*
Pub: Palgrave Macmillan
Contact: Lisa Dunn, Manager
E-mail: l.dunn@palgrave.com
Ed: Bjorn Ambos, Bodo B. Schlegelmilch. **Released:** December 2009. **Price:** £69, hardcover; £56.65; $110. **Description:** Regional management is becoming more important to companies as they expand globally. This book explores the challenges of European, United States and Asian companies and outlines how regional headquarters can develop into Dynamic Competence Relay centers to master these issues. **Availability:** PrintE-book; Electronic publishingE-book; PDF.

43411 ■ *New Technology-Based Firms in the New Millennium, Volume 6*
Ed: Ray Oakey. **Released:** May 2008. **Price:** , $149.00. **Description:** Collection of papers from the Annual International High Technology Firms (HTSFs) Conference cover issues of importance to governments as they develop technological program. Papers are grouped into three sections: theory, strategy and clustering, and spin-off firms.

43412 ■ *"New Texas South-International Alliance Seeking to Net Foreign Firms for South Texas" in San Antonio Business Journal (Vol. 26, June 22, 2012, No. 21, pp. 1)*
Pub: American City Business Journal
Description: The city of San Antonio, Texas is partnering with Brownsville, Corpus Christi, Edinburg, Laredo, and San Marcos, to form the Texas South-International Alliance. The alliance is aimed at attracting more international economic development opportunities and investment to South Texas.

43413 ■ *"New Thinking for a New Financial Order" in Harvard Business Review (Vol. 86, September 2008, No. 9, pp. 26)*
Pub: Harvard Business Review Press
Contact: Peter E. Walsh, Director
Ed: Diana Farrell. **Description:** Factors driving the current global economy are analyzed with a focus on the influence of new public and private sectors and the impact of unregulated markets.

43414 ■ *"New Work Order" in Black Enterprise (Vol. 38, March 1, 2008, No. 8, pp. 60)*
Pub: Earl G. Graves Publishing Co. Inc.
Contact: Earl G. Graves, Jr., President
Ed: Marcia A. Reed-Woodward. **Description:** Today's management challenges includes issues of more competition, globalization, outsourcing and technological advances. Suggestions to help create progressive leadership in small business that sustains a competitive edge are listed.

43415 ■ *"New Zealand Natural Co-Branding with Mrs. Fields" in Ice Cream Reporter (Vol. 23, November 20, 2010, No. 12, pp. 2)*
Description: Mrs. Fields has partnered with a New Zealand firm to co-brand ice cream and cookies in Australian markets.

43416 ■ *"New Zealand Natural Ice Cream is Opening a Second U.S. Scoop Shop" in Ice Cream Reporter (Vol. 21, October 20, 2008, No. 11, pp. 7)*
Description: New Zealand Natural Ice Cream is opening a second store in California. The company is a market leader in New Zealand and has gained distribution through 300 outlets in California.

43417 ■ *"The Next Waive" in Hawaii Business (Vol. 53, January 2008, No. 7, pp. 27)*
Pub: PacificBasin Communications
Ed: Cathy S. Cruz-George. **Description:** Only 40,000 Koreans took a visit to Hawaii in 2007, a decline from the pre-September averages of 123,000 visits. The number of Korean visitors in Hawaii could increase if the visa waiver proposal is passed. Efforts to improve Hawaiian tourism are presented.

43418 ■ *"No Shortage of Challenges for Cross-Border Trade" in Canadian Sailings (June 30, 2008)*
Ed: Kathlyn Horibe. **Description:** Pros and cons of the North American Free Trade Agreement are examined. The agreement between the U.S. and Canada concerning trade was an essential step toward securing economic growth for Canadian citizens. Two-way trade between the counties has tripled since the agreement and accounts for 7.1 million American and 3 million Canadian jobs.

43419 ■ *Non-Standard Employment under Globalization: Flexible Work and Social Security in the Newly Industrializing Countries*
Pub: Palgrave Macmillan
Contact: Lisa Dunn, Manager
E-mail: l.dunn@palgrave.com
Ed: Koichi Usami. **Released:** December 2009. **Price:** £84, hardcover; $115. **Description:** Expansion of non-standard employment under globalization is being recognized in all of the newly industrialized countries. The book examines deregulation of labor markets, social protection for nonstandard workers, and social security reforms in accordance with the transformation of employment. **Availability:** PrintEbook.

43420 ■ *"Not In My Backyard" in Entrepreneur (Vol. 36, May 2008, No. 5, pp. 42)*
Pub: Entrepreneur Press
Contact: Perlman Neil, President
Ed: Farnoosh Torabi. **Description:** More investors are turning to overseas real estate investments as the U.S. market sees a slowdown. Analysts say that risk-averse investors opt for funds with record of strong returns and U.S. real estate investment trusts that partner with foreign businesses for transparency purposes. Other details about foreign real estate investments are discussed.

43421 ■ *"Now You See It.." in Canadian Business (Vol. 81, November 10, 2008, No. 19, pp. 20)*
Pub: Rogers Media Inc.
Contact: Tony Viner, President
Ed: Sharda Prashad. **Description:** Total return swaps were offered by Deutsche Bank AG and UBS AG to foreign investors for them to avoid paying taxes on the proceeds of their shares of Fording Canadian Coal Trust when Teck Cominco offered to buy the company. This means that the Canadian government is losing tax revenue from foreigners and it is argued that a simpler tax system would avoid this practice.

43422 ■ *"No. 381: Metallica and Other Forms of Hardware" in Inc. (Vol. 36, September 2014, No. 7, pp. 107)*
Pub: Mansueto Ventures L.L.C.
Contact: John Koten, Chief Executive Officer
Released: September 2014. **Description:** Profile of Mikhail Orlov, who stayed in American instead of fighting a war he did not believe in while living in Chechnya, Russia. Orlov discovered his entrepreneurial spirit when he began importing Russian army surplus gear. He operates his startup online store selling guns, ammo, and hunting accessories.

43423 ■ *"Nurse Next Door Home Health Care Franchise Meets Growing Challenges of Senior Care" in Benzinga.com (September 11, 2012)*
Pub: Benzinga.com
Contact: Kyle Bazzy, President
Description: The need for home health care services in the United States is revealed through federal data. Responding to the lack of services, Nurse Next Door, a Canadian home health care franchise, has begun a program to aggressively expand services in the US market. Statistical data included.

43424 ■ *"Olympus is Urged to Revise Board" in Wall Street Journal Eastern Edition (November 28, 2011, pp. B3)*
Pub: Dow Jones & Co., Inc.
Contact: Clare Hart, President
Ed: Phred Dvorak. **Description:** Koji Miyata, once a director on the board of troubled Japanese photographic equipment company, is urging the company to reorganize its board, saying the present group should resign their board seats but keep their management positions. The company has come under scrutiny for its accounting practices and costly acquisitions.

43425 ■ *"OMERS Joins Bid for U.K. Port Giant" in Globe & Mail (March 28, 2006, pp. B1)*
Ed: Paul Waldie. **Description:** The plans of Ontario Municipal Employees Retirement Board to partner with Goldman Sachs Group Inc., in order to acquire Associated British Ports PLC, are presented.

43426 ■ *"On the Itinerary: Your Future" in Entrepreneur (Vol. 37, October 2009, No. 10, pp. 92)*
Pub: Entrepreneur Press
Contact: Perlman Neil, President
Ed: Joel Holland. **Description:** Josh Hackler's Spanish Vines imports and distributes wines from Spain while using Spanish culture to help market the wines. The business was hatched after Hackler signed up for a study-abroad program in Spain.

43427 ■ *"On the U.S. Election: Shaky on Free Trade" in Canadian Business (Vol. 81, December 19, 2007, No. 1, pp. 29)*
Pub: Rogers Media Inc.
Contact: Tony Viner, President
Ed: Rachel Pulfer. **Description:** Rhetoric at the U.S. presidential elections seems to be pointing toward a weaker free trade consensus, with Democratic candidates being against the renewal of free trade deals, while Republican candidates seem to be for free trade.

43428 ■ *On the Wealth of Nations: Books That Changed the World*
Pub: Grove/Atlantic Inc.
Contact: Morgan Entrekin, President
E-mail: mentrekin@groveatlantic.com
Ed: P.J. O'Rourke. **Released:** January 2008. **Price:** $13, paperback. **Description:** Author defends the tenets of freedom of trade, the healthy pursuit of self-interest, and the importance of being a person who 'adheres, on all occasions, steadily and resolutely to his maxims.'. **Availability:** Print.

43429 ■ *"OPEC Exposed" in Hawaii Business (Vol. 54, September 2008, No. 3, pp. 2)*
Ed: Serena Lim. **Description:** Organization of the Petroleum Exporting Countries (OPEC) has said that their effort in developing an alternative energy source has driven prices up. The biofuel sector is criticizing the statement, saying that a research study found that biofuels push petroleum prices down by 15 percent. Details on the effect of rising petroleum prices are discussed.

43430 ■ *"Open Skies: Opportunity, Challenge for Airlines" in Crain's Chicago Business (April 21, 2008)*
Pub: Crain Communications Inc.
Contact: Todd Johnson, Publisher
Ed: Paul Merrion. **Description:** Discusses the new aviation agreement between Europe and the United States known as Open Skies; the pact creates opportunities for U.S. carriers to fly to new destinations in Europe from more U.S. cities; it also allows carriers to fly between European cities, something they have not been able to do until now.

43431 ■ *"Oracle: No Profit of Doom" in Barron's (Vol. 88, March 31, 2008, No. 13, pp. 40)*
Pub: Dow Jones & Co., Inc.
Contact: Clare Hart, President
Ed: Mark Veverka. **Description:** Oracle's revenues grew by 21 percent but fell short of expectation and their profits came in at the low-end of expectations. The company's shares dropped 8 percent but investors are advised to pay more attention to the company's earnings expansion rather than revenue growth in a slow economy. Nokia's Rick Simonson points out that their markets in Asia and particularly India is growing so they are not as affected by the U.S. economic conditions.

43432 ■ *"Ottawa to Push for Gas Deal Between Petrocan, Gazprom" in Globe & Mail (February 13, 2006, pp. B1)*
Ed: Greame Smith. **Description:** Jim Flaherty, finance minister of Canada is negotiating a 1.3 billion dollar deal between state owned Petro-Canada and Russia's OAO Gazprom. This once again highlighted the country's increasing dependence on Russia for its energy requirements.

43433 ■ *Outsourcing: Information Technology, Original Equipment Manufacturer, Leo, Oursourcing, Offshoring Research Network, Crowdsourcing*
Released: May 01, 2010. **Price:** $14.14. **Description:** Chapters include information for outsourcing firms and how to maintain an outsourcing business.

43434 ■ *"Overseas Marketing Key to Success of Chicago Spire" in Commercial Property News (March 17, 2008)*
Description: New construction of the Chicago Spire, a condominium project located on Lake Michigan's shore, is being marketed to would-be clients in Asia where Chicago is viewed as an emerging world city.

43435 ■ *"Overseas Overtures" in Business Journal-Portland (Vol. 24, October 26, 2007, No. 35, pp. 1)*
Pub: American City Business Journals, Inc.
Ed: Robin J. Mood. **Description:** Oregon has a workforce shortage, specifically for the health care industry. Recruiting agencies, such as the International Recruiting Network Inc., answers the high demand for workforce by recruiting foreign employees. The difficulties recruiting companies experience with regards to foreign labor laws are investigated.

43436 ■ *"An Overview of Energy Consumption of the Globalized World Economy" in Energy Policy (Vol. 39, October 2011, No. 10, pp. 5920-2928)*
Pub: Reed Elsevier Reference Publishing
Ed: Z.M. Chen, G.Q. Chen. **Description:** Energy consumption and its impact on the global world economy is examined.

43437 ■ *"Ownership Form, Managerial Incentives, and the Intensity of Rivalry" in Academy of Management Journal (Vol. 50, No. 4, August 1, 2007, pp. 901)*
Pub: Academy of Management
Contact: Ming-Jer Chen, President
Ed: Govert Vroom, Javier Gimeo. **Description:** Ways in which differences in ownership form between franchised and company-owned units alter managerial incentives and competitive pricing in different oligopolistic contexts, or following competitors into foreign markets, is presented.

43438 ■ *"Pacific Place Makes History" in Puget Sound Business Journal (Vol. 35, July 18, 2014, No. 13, pp. 10)*
Pub: American City Business Journals
Released: July 18, 2014. **Description:** The 15-year-old Pacific Place retail shopping mall in Seattle, Washington was sold to a private company, Madison Marquette and other foreign investors for $271 million. The deal did not include the city-owned 1,200-stall parking garage.

43439 ■ *"Pack Mentality: Why Black Can Be Slimming" in Crain's Chicago Business (Vol. 31, April 21, 2008, No. 16, pp. 31)*
Pub: Crain Communications Inc.
Contact: Todd Johnson, Publisher
Ed: Sarah A. Klein. **Description:** Jill Smart, the head of human resources for a company with 170,000 employees worldwide, frequently travels to India, London and Singapore; Ms. Smart provides advice concerning efficiency, time management and avoiding jet-lag.

43440 ■ *"Parent Firm's Global Reach, Stricter Air Quality Rules Have Stock Smiling" in Crain's Cleveland Business (October 15, 2007)*
Pub: Crain Communications Inc.
Ed: David Bennett. **Description:** Since Stock Equipment Co., a firm that makes industrial pollution control equipment, was acquired by Schenck Process Group, a diversified global manufacturer based in Germany, the company's orders from abroad have been on the rise. The purchase has opened the doors to regions such as Eastern and Central Europe, Latin America and Australia.

43441 ■ *"Patience Will Pay Off in Africa"* in *Barron's (Vol. 92, September 17, 2012, No. 38, pp. M8)*
Description: The stocks of African companies present long-term capital appreciation opportunities for investors. This is due to a commodities boom, economic reform and relative political stability in many African countries.

43442 ■ *"Paying for the Recession: Rebalancing Economic Growth"* in *Montana Business Quarterly (Vol. 49, Spring 2011, No. 1, pp. 2)*
Pub: University of Montana Bureau of Business and Economic Research
Contact: Patrick Barkey, Director
E-mail: patrick.barkey@business.umt.edu
Ed: Patrick M. Barkey. **Description:** Four key issues required to address in order to rebalance economic growth in America are examined. They include: savings rates, global trade imbalances, government budgets and most importantly, housing price correction.

43443 ■ *"PBSJ Launches Internal Probe"* in *Tampa Bay Business Journal (Vol. 30, January 8, 2010, No. 3, pp. 1)*
Pub: American City Business Journals
Ed: Margie Manning. **Description:** Florida-based engineering firm PBSJ Corporation has started an internal investigation into possible violations of any laws, including the Foreign Corrupt Practices Act. Projects handled by subsidiary PBS&J International in foreign countries are the focus of the investigation.

43444 ■ *"Auto Asphyxiation"* in *Canadian Business (Vol. 85, August 13, 2012, No. 13, pp. 42)*
Pub: George Media Inc.
Ed: Peter Shawn Taylor. **Released:** August 13, 2012. **Description:** The reality behind economist Jeff Rubin's claim that oil is the single most important factor in global economics is explored. Rubin is advised to follow the example of technology watcher Don Tapscott who avoids delivering a negative message and make concreted predictions that will eventually prove wrong if he is looking for a long and lucrative career in the guru business.

43445 ■ *The Perfect Scent: A Year Inside the Perfume Industry in Paris and New York*
Pub: Henry Holt and Co.
Contact: Michael Naumann, President
Ed: Chandler Burr. **Released:** January 2009. **Price:** $17, paperback. **Description:** An insider's glimpse at the development of two new fragrances from Hermes and Coty. **Availability:** Print.

43446 ■ *"The Perils of Partnering in Developing Markets: How a Health Care Provider Addresses the Risks That Come With Globalization"* in *Harvard Business Review (Vol. 90, No. 6, June 2012, pp. 23)*
Pub: Harvard Business Review Press
Contact: Peter E. Walsh, Director
Ed: Steven J. Thompson. **Description:** Effective evaluation of international risk includes assessing the opportunity; ramping up processes, operations, and metrics; and establishing long-term functionality. Warning signs for each stage are also presented.

43447 ■ *"Pet-Food Industry Too Slow: Crisis-PR Gurus"* in *Advertising Age (Vol. 78, March 23, 2007, No. 13, pp. 29)*
Pub: Crain Communications Inc.
Contact: Rance Crain, President
Ed: Jack Neff. **Description:** Many crisis-communications experts believe that the pet-food industry mishandled the problem by waiting almost a month to recall the 60 million 'wet-food' products after numerous consumer complaints. Experts site that the first 24 to 49 hours are the most important in dealing with a crisis of this nature.

43448 ■ *Petty Capitalists and Globalization: Flexibility, Entrepreneurship, and Economic Development*
Pub: State University of New York Press
Contact: James Peltz, Director
E-mail: james.peltz@sunypress.edu
Price: $29.95, paperback; $70, hardcover. **Description:** Investigation into ways small businesses in Europe, Asia, and Latin America are required to operate and compete in the fast-growing transnational economy. **Availability:** Print.

43449 ■ *"Phoenix Company, Dreambrands Inc., Realizing Dream of Global Growth"* in *The Business Journal - Serving Phoenix and the Valley of the Sun (Vol. 28, July 18, 2008, No. 46, pp. 1)*
Pub: American City Business Journals, Inc.
Contact: Whitney Shaw, President
Ed: Chris Casacchia. **Description:** Phoenix, Arizona-based lubricant maker DreamBrands Inc. is realizing global growth. The company, which has been generating interest from institutional investors, is seeking a second round of funding. Details of the company's products and marketing plans are also discussed.

43450 ■ *"A Place in the Sun"* in *Canadian Business (Vol. 81, July 22, 2008, No. 12-13, pp. 56)*
Description: Experts believe that it is the best time for Canadians to own a retirement home in the U.S., where real estate prices are up to 50 percent below their peak. Other views concerning the economic conditions occurring in the United States, as well as on the implications for Canadians planning to invest in the country are presented.

43451 ■ *"Play It Safe"* in *Entrepreneur (Vol. 35, November 2007, No. 11, pp. 26)*
Pub: Entrepreneur Press
Contact: Perlman Neil, President
Ed: Gwen Moran. **Description:** U.S.-based toy manufacturers find opportunity from concerns regarding the recent recalls of toys that are made in China. The situation can provide better probability of parents buying toys made in the U.S. or Europe, where manufacturing standards are stricter.

43452 ■ *"Play It Safe At Home, Or Take a Risk Abroad? A US Lease-To-Own Chain Considers Whether To Test Its Business In Mexico"* in *Harvard Business Review (Vol. 90, January-February 2012, No.1-2, pp. 145)*
Pub: Harvard Business Review Press
Contact: Peter E. Walsh, Director
Ed: Michael Chu. **Released:** January-February 2012. **Description:** A fictitious foreign-market entry scenario is presented, with contributors providing advice. Recommendations include ensuring that expansion will not compromise the firm's core business, and that expansion, while necessary to growth, must be done carefully.

43453 ■ *"Political Environments and Business Strategy: Implications for Managers"* in *Business Horizons (Vol. 51, January-February 2008)*
Pub: Elsevier Advanced Technology Publications
Ed: Gerald D. Keim, Amy J. Hillman. **Description:** Various government bodies and business organizations work together in shaping new business opportunities and policies that arise from globalization. Presented is framework of public policy considerations for business managers. The framework is based on Nobel laureate Douglas North's work.

43454 ■ *"Port May Put Supersize New Cranes to Work"* in *Puget Sound Business Journal (Vol. 35, May 23, 2014, No. 5, pp. 4)*
Pub: American City Business Journals
Released: May 23, 2014. **Description:** The Port of Seattle, Washington is investing millions of dollar in the new large cranes in a bid to attract a new breed of megaships for freight forwarding. Port commissioners are hoping that by installing 12 or more of these cranes, it will attract operators to bring large cargo ship to Terminal 5 for importing and exporting of goods.

43455 ■ *"Port Metro Vancouver Unveiled"* in *Canadian Sailings (July 7, 2008)*
Description: Vancouver Fraser Port Authority is marketing the port as Port Metro Vancouver; Along with the new name the port has announced additional strategies for continued growth and launched a new logo.

43456 ■ *"Port in the Storm"* in *Canadian Business (Vol. 81, October 13, 2008, No. 17, pp. 101)*
Ed: Calvin Leung. **Description:** Interport Inc.'s state-of-the-art studio complex in Toronto is discussed. The strong Canadian dollar, along with disputes within the movie industry, are creating challenges for the studio to secure Hollywood projects. Interport plans to compete for Hollywood projects based on quality.

43457 ■ *"Potash Sale Must Be Blocked"* in *Canadian Business (Vol. 83, October 12, 2010, No. 17, pp. 24)*
Pub: Rogers Media Inc.
Contact: Tony Viner, President
Ed: Kasey Coholan. **Description:** Chief executive officers (CEOs) and corporate leaders in Canada are concerned about the possible sale of Potash Corporation to foreign buyers. A Compas Inc. poll recently asked CEOs whether the Canadian Government should step in to block the sale of the country's largest fertilizer firm.

43458 ■ *"Pressure Growing on Processors"* in *Farmer's Weekly (March 28, 2008, No. 320)*
Description: Increasing milk prices may be inevitable in order to stop more farmers from leaving the industry and encourage them to produce more milk.

43459 ■ *"Private Equity Firms Shopping Valley For Deals"* in *The Business Journal - Serving Phoenix and the Valley of the Sun (Vol. 29, September 21, 2008, No. 3, pp. 1)*
Pub: American City Business Journals, Inc.
Contact: Whitney Shaw, President
Ed: Mike Sunnucks. **Description:** Private equity firms from California, Boston, New York, and overseas are expected to invest in growth-oriented real estate markets that include Phoenix. Real estate experts revealed that privately held investment and acquisition firms are looking to invest in real estate markets hit by the housing crisis. Views and information on private equity firms' real estate investments are presented.

43460 ■ *"Procter & Gamble Boosts Bet on Exclusive Brands"* in *Business Courier (Vol. 27, July 9, 2010, No. 10, pp. 1)*
Pub: Business Courier
Ed: Jon Newberry. **Description:** Procter & Gamble is creating more special versions of its brands such as Pringles and Pampers exclusively for retail partners such as Tesco in the U.K. The greater push towards this direction is seen as a way to regain market share.

43461 ■ *"Public Media Works to Launch DVD Kiosk Operations in Toronto, Canada"* in *Internet Wire (November 15, 2010)*
Pub: COMTEX
Contact: Chip Brian, President
Description: Public Media Works Inc. along with its EntertainmentXpress Inc., have partnered with Spot Venture Distribution Inc. and Signifi Solutions Inc., both headquartered in Toronto, Canada, to manage and expand the Spot DVD movie and game kiosk business in greater Toronto and other Canadian locations.

43462 ■ *"Pulque with Flavor"* in *Canadian Business (Vol. , pp.)*
Ed: Augusta Dwyer. **Description:** Mexico-based Pulque Poliqhui, which has exported 20,000 bottles of Pulque into Canada in March 2008, plans to distribute in Ontario and Quebec. Pulque Poliqhui is introducing Cool Passion, a fruit-flavored version of pulque in Canada.

43463 ■ "Putting the World at Your Fingertips" in Barron's (Vol. 88, July 7, 2008, No. 27, pp. L13)
Pub: Dow Jones & Co., Inc.
Contact: Clare Hart, President
Ed: Neil A. Martin. **Description:** Currency-traded exchange funds allow investors to diversify their assets and take advantage of investment opportunities such as speculation and hedging. Investors can use these funds to build positions in favor of or against the US dollar.

43464 ■ "Q&A: Bolder Investment Partners' Ian Gordon" in Canadian Business (Vol. 81, May 22, 2008, No. 9, pp. 10)
Pub: Rogers Media Inc.
Contact: Tony Viner, President
Ed: Matthew McClearn. **Description:** Bolder Investment Partners' Ian Gordon discussed the economic theory promulgated by Russian economist Nikolai Kondratieff. The cycle begins with a rising economy then followed by deflationary depression. Details of his views on the Kondratieff cycle and its application to the current economy are presented.

43465 ■ "Q&A: RBC's Gordon Nixon" in Canadian Business (Vol. 80, May 31, 2011, No. 22, pp. 9)
Pub: Rogers Media Inc.
Contact: Tony Viner, President
Ed: Rachel Pulfer. **Description:** Royal Bank of Canada (RBC) chief executive officer Gordon Nixon believes that the Canadian financial services segment is heavily regulated. Nixon also feels that it has become difficult for local banks to enter the market since foreign banks can easily come in and compete with Canadian banks. His views on RBC's success are provided.

43466 ■ "Qorvis Communications Gets Sabre Award for Search Engine Optimization" in Entertainment Close-Up (May 29, 2012)
Pub: Close-Up Media
Released: May 29, 2012. **Description:** Qorvis Communications received the Gold Sabre Award by the Holmes Report for Search Engine Optimization for its work on the Marca Paid Imagen de Mexico on the MexicoToday campaign. MexicoToday.org is a next-generation Website and external branding initiative which focuses on digital and social media. The site hopes to change the world's perception of Mexico, particularly Europeans and Americans.

43467 ■ "Quality Performance of SMEs in a Developing Economy: Direct and Indirect Effects of Service Innovation and Entrepreneurial Orientation" in Journal of Business & Industrial Marketing (Vol. 29, July 2014, No. 6)
Pub: Emerald Group Publishing Inc.
Released: July 2014. **Description:** A study was conducted to investigate the effects of innovation and EO (entrepreneurial orientation) on organizational performance in Asian small enterprise context. Strategic management literature and the relationship between EO, innovation, and quality performance was tested. The results indicated that a noteworthy direct and indirect positive relationship exists between EO dimensions, innovation, and quality performance.

43468 ■ "Que Pasa? A Canadian-Cuban Credit Card Crisis" in Canadian Business (Vol. 81, March 31, 2008, No. 5, pp. 10)
Pub: Rogers Media Inc.
Contact: Tony Viner, President
Ed: Geoff Kirbyson. **Description:** Discusses the acquisition of CUETS Financial Ltd. by the Bank of America which means that CUETS-issued credit cards in Cuba are worthless since U.S. laws prohibit transactions from Cuba and other sanctioned countries. CUETS members are advised to take multiple payment methods to Cuba.

43469 ■ "Raising Game" in Birmingham Business Journal (Vol. 31, May 2, 2014, No. 18, pp. 4)
Pub: American City Business Journals, Inc.
Contact: Whitney Shaw, President
Released: May 2, 2014. **Description:** Birmingham, Alabama has grown its reputation in the sports world in recent years by hosting global events that draw

tourists and overage from around the world. However, the Metro needs a facilities upgrade to further elevate its game. The long-debated project to replace the Birmingham-Jefferson Convention Complex and Legion Field is also examined.

43470 ■ "R&R Launches Upscale Spoony's and Low Fat Dragon's Den" in Ice Cream Reporter (Vol. 23, August 20, 2010, No. 9, pp. 3)
Description: European ice cream manufacturer R&R has acquired French ice cream maker Rolland and will position itself as an upscale challenger to brands like Ben & Jerry's.

43471 ■ Reading Financial Reports for Dummies
Pub: John Wiley & Sons Inc.
Contact: Stephen M. Smith, President
Ed: Lita Epstein. **Released:** 3rd Edition. **Price:** $22. 95, paperback; $14.99. **Description:** This second edition contains more new and updated information, including new information on the separate accounting and financial reporting standards for private/small businesses versus public/large businesses; updated information reflecting 2007 laws on international financial reporting standards; new content to match SEC and other governmental regulatory changes over the last three years; new information about how the analyst-corporate connection has changed the playing field; the impact of corporate communications and new technologies; new examples that reflect the current trends; and updated Websites and resources. **Availability:** PrintE-book.

43472 ■ "Ready To Take Your Business Global?" in Black Enterprise (Vol. 41, August 2010, No. 1, pp. 89)
Pub: Earl G. Graves Publishing Co. Inc.
Contact: Earl G. Graves, Jr., President
Ed: Alan Hughes. **Description:** The 2010 Black Enterprise Entrepreneurs Conference held in May stressed the need for all small firms to promote a global agenda in order to stay competitive.

43473 ■ "Recalls Cause Consumers to Put More Stock in Online Reviews" in Crain's Cleveland Business (Vol. 28, November 12, 2007, No. 45)
Ed: Jack Neff. **Description:** Due to the string of product recalls over the last year, consumers are looking at online product reviews to help them make purchasing decisions which could reshape marketing for a wide range of products.

43474 ■ "Red October" in Canadian Business (Vol. 81, December 8, 2008, No. 21, pp. 61)
Pub: Rogers Media Inc.
Contact: Tony Viner, President
Ed: Mitch Moxley. **Description:** Analysts predict that Chinese stock market traders practice prudence amidst the challenging financial conditions in stock markets. The Chinese stock markets imploded in the last 12 months, losing two-thirds of its value.

43475 ■ "Religious Revival" in Canadian Business (Vol. 81, December 8, 2008, No. 21, pp. 57)
Pub: Rogers Media Inc.
Contact: Tony Viner, President
Ed: Paul Webster. **Description:** Canada-based lawyer Cyndee Todgham Cherniak believes that Canadians wishing to do business in China should have professional competence, as well as cultural and spiritual sensitivity. Chinese government officials also acknowledge the role of religion in China's economy.

43476 ■ "Renren Partners With Recruit to Launch Social Wedding Services" in Benzinga.com (June 7, 2011)
Pub: Benzinga.com
Contact: Kyle Bazzy, President
Ed: Benzinga Staff. **Description:** Renren Inc. and Recruit Company Ltd. partnered to build a wedding social media catering to engaged couples and newlyweds in China. The platform will integrate online wedding related social content and offline media such as magazine and wedding exhibitions.

43477 ■ "Renren Partnership With Recruit to Launch Social Wedding Services" in Benzinga.com (June 7, 2011)
Pub: Benzinga.com
Contact: Kyle Bazzy, President
Ed: Benzinga Staff. **Description:** Renren Inc., the leading real name social networking Internet platform in China has partnered with Recruit Company Limited, Japan's largest human resource and classified media group to form a joint venture to build a wedding social media catering to the needs of engaged couples and newlyweds in China.

43478 ■ "Reportlinker Adds Report: Social Networks: Five Consumer Trends for 2009" in Wireless News (October 23, 2009)
Description: 'Social Networks: Five Consumer Trends for 2009,' a new market research report by Reportlinker.com found that in the countries of Italy and Spain lag behind their European neighbors in Internet development. Since large numbers of consumers in these two countries remain offline, only a minimal portion of total advertising spending goes into Internet marketing, and those advertising campaigns are directed at the relatively young, affluent users. Statistical data included.

43479 ■ "Reps Continue to Move to International Trade" in Agency Sales Magazine (Vol. 39, September-October 2009, No. 9, pp. 24)
Ed: Jack Foster. **Description:** Sales representatives should get involved and look into international trade if they want to be successful in the future. The weak U.S. dollar, labor costs, and the low cost of transportation are factors that drive the trend towards international trade.

43480 ■ "RES Stakes Its Claim in Area" in Philadelphia Business Journal (Vol. 28, January 29, 2010, No. 50, pp. 1)
Pub: American City Business Journals Inc.
Ed: Peter Key. **Description:** RES Software Company Inc. of Amsterdam, Netherlands appointed Jim Kirby as president for the Americas and Klaus Besier as chairman in an effort to boost the firm's presence in the US. Brief career profiles of Kirby and Besier are included. RES develops software that allows management of information flow between an organization and its employees regardless of location.

43481 ■ "Research and Markets Adds Report: Asian - Internet Market" in Health and Beauty Close-Up (January 19, 2010)
Description: Overview of Research and Markets new report regarding Internet marketing and e-commerce in the Asian region; statistical data included.

43482 ■ "Research and Markets Adds Report: Cyprus: Convergence, Broadband and Internet Market" in Wireless News (September 4, 2009)
Description: Overview of a new report by Research and Markets entitled, 'Cyprus Convergence, Broadband and Internet Market - Overview, Statistics and Forecasts.' Highlights include information regarding broadband accounts which now account for the majority of household Internet connections.

43483 ■ "Research and Markets Adds Report: Ghana: Convergence, Broadband and Internet Market" in Wireless News (September 4, 2009)
Description: Overview of a new report by Research and Markets entitled, 'Ghana Convergence, Broadband and Internet Market - Overview, Statistics and Forecasts.' Ghana was among the first countries in Africa connected to the Internet and to introduce ADSL broadband services; however, only 30 of the 140 licensed ISP's are operational making the sector highly competitive.

43484 ■ "Research and Markets Offers Report: Global Interactive Kiosks Market" in Entertainment Close-Up (May 5, 2012)
Pub: Close-Up Media
Released: May 5, 2012. **Description:** Frost & Sullivan's report, 'Global Interactive Kiosks Market' reports that global interactive kiosks increase sales and save costs. Detailed revenue and forecasts are included in the report.

43485 ■ *"Retail Doesn't Cross Borders: Here's Why and What To Do About It"* in *Harvard Business Review (Vol. 90, April 2012, No. 4, pp. 104)*

Pub: Harvard Business Review Press

Contact: Peter E. Walsh, Director

Ed: Marcel Corstijens, Rajiv Lal. **Released:** April 2012. **Description:** Globalization poses challenges for retailers, such as competing directly with well established local businesses. To succeed, retailers should enter markets at the right time, focus not on synergies but on differentiation, and introduce new and innovative products and services.

43486 ■ *"Reversal of Fortune"* in *Canadian Business (Vol. 85, June 11, 2012, No. 10, pp. 32)*

Pub: George Media Inc.

Ed: Matthew McClearn. **Released:** June 11, 2012. **Description:** First Quantum Minerals of Vancouver, British Columbia contested the decisio of the Democratic Republic of Congo to revoke their mining license in the Kolwezi Tailings by means of political pressure and international law. Eurasian National Resources Corporation agreed to pay First Quantum $1.25 billion in return for uncontested title to Congo mines and a ceasefire in January 2012.

43487 ■ *"A Reverse-Innovation Playbook: Insights From a Company That Developed Products For Emerging Markets and Then Brought Them Back Home"* in *Harvard Business Review (Vol. 90, April 2012, No. 4, pp. 120)*

Pub: Harvard Business Review Press

Contact: Peter E. Walsh, Director

Ed: Vijay Govindarajan. **Released:** April 2012. **Description:** An overview is presented on the organizational change implemented by Harman International Industries Inc. to create products for emerging markets and ensure that they would be accepted in already established middle markets. Components include setting radical goals, selecting team leaders with no competing interests, and leveraging global resources.

43488 ■ *"ReWalk Robotics Aims for IPO"* in *Boston Business Journal (Vol. 34, July 18, 2014, No. 24, pp. 7)*

Pub: American City Business Journals, Inc.

Contact: Whitney Shaw, President

Released: July 18, 2014. **Description:** ReWalk Robotics, an Israeli firm that manufactures wearable robotics exoskeletons for paraplegics, wants to launch an initial public offering (IPO) to raise US$57.5 million. In a July 2014 filing, ReWalk cited an accumulated debt of US$27 million at the end of 2013, justifying the need to go public and raise additional funds.

43489 ■ *"RIAC: Green Air Link to Ireland No Flight of Fancy"* in *Providence Business News (Vol. 29, May 26, 2014, No. 8, pp. 1)*

Pub: American City Business Journals

Released: May 26, 2014. **Description:** Rhode Island Airport Corporation president and CEO, Kelly Fredericks, joined the European trade mission led by the state government to pitch nonstop flights from T.F. Green Airport in Warwick, RI to Ireland. Fredericks is in discussions with Shannon Airport and Ireland West Airport Knock about cargo/freight forwarding and passenger services.

43490 ■ *"Rice & Roll Onigiri Food Truck to Tour Los Angeles Area"* in *Entertainment Close-Up (July 30, 2012)*

Pub: Close-Up Media

Released: July 30, 2012. **Description:** Rice & Roll Onigiri food truck service is entering the US market, offering Japanese stuffed rice balls in a variety of flavors and fillings. Asian cuisine is popular in restaurants and markets. The ten locations to visit Rice & Roll in California are listed.

43491 ■ *"Riding the Export Wave: How To Find a Good Distributor Overseas"* in *Inc.*

(January 2008, pp. 49)

Pub: Gruner and Jahr USA Publishing Co.

Contact: J. Russell Denson, President

Ed: Sarah Goldstein. **Description:** Small companies should contact the U.S. embassy in foreign companies in order to connect with the U.S. Commercial Service's Gold Key program that is designed to work with small and midsize exporters.

43492 ■ *"Right at Home China Celebrates 1 Year Anniversary as U.S. In-Home Senior Care Master Franchise"* in *Professional Service Close-Up (June 24, 2012)*

Description: Franchisor, Right at Home International Inc., provides in-home senior care and assistance and has experienced a one year franchise license agreement in China. Right at Home China predicts growth because China has 200 million adults over 65 years of age.

43493 ■ *"Ripple Effect From Solar Frontier May Be Big"* in *Business First of Buffalo (Vol. 30, April 25, 2014, No. 32, pp. 4)*

Pub: American City Business Journals, Inc.

Contact: Whitney Shaw, President

Released: April 25, 2014. **Description:** A memorandum of understanding was signed by Japanese solar technology manufacturer Solar Frontier K.K. with the State University of New York, College of Nanoscale Science and Engineering in Albany. The agreement is expected to create about 1,000 new jobs in the U.S. and at least $700 million in investments.

43494 ■ *"Rising in the East; Research and Development"* in *The Economist (Vol. 390, January 3, 2009, No. 8612, pp. 47)*

Description: Impressive growth of the technological research and development in Asian countries is discussed. Statistical data included.

43495 ■ *"Risk and Reward"* in *Canadian Business (Vol. 81, October 13, 2008, No. 17, pp. 21)*

Ed: Calvin Leung. **Description:** Macro-economist and currency analyst Mark Venezia believes that stable financial institutions, free-market reforms, and the role of central banks in keeping inflation and exchange rates stable could make emerging-market bonds strong performers for better future returns. Venezia's other views on emerging-market bonds are discussed.

43496 ■ *"Rough Trade: the Canada-Chile Free Trade Agreement"* in *Canadian Business (Vol. 79, September 11, 2006, No. 18, pp. 31)*

Pub: Rogers Media Inc.

Contact: Tony Viner, President

Ed: Christina Campbell. **Description:** The divergence between trade policy agreements entered into by Chile and the Canadian government are highlighted. Canada-Chile Free Trade Agreement and the myth around the big benefits to be reaped by bilateral trade policy agreements are discussed.

43497 ■ *"Russia: Uncle Volodya's Flagging Christmas Spirit"* in *The Economist (Vol. 390, January 3, 2009, No. 8612, pp. 22)*

Description: Overview of Russia's struggling economy as well as unpopular government decisions such as raising import duties on used foreign vehicles so as to protect Russian carmakers.

43498 ■ *"Russian Renaissance"* in *Chicago Tribune (September 22, 2008)*

Pub: McClatchy-Tribune Information Services

Ed: Alex Rodriguez. **Description:** Winemakers from Russia are returning to the craft and quality of winemaking now that they are free from Soviet restraints.

43499 ■ *"SABMiller Deal Hit by Tax Ruling"* in *Wall Street Journal Eastern Edition (November 21 , 2011, pp. B9)*

Pub: Dow Jones & Co., Inc.

Contact: Clare Hart, President

Ed: David Fickling, Simon Zekaria. **Description:** SABMiller PLC, the giant brewer in the United Kingdom, is acquiring Australian beer icon Foster's Group Ltd. for US$9.9 billion, but will have to come

up with another A$582 million following a tax ruling by the Australian Taxation Office in order that shareholders of Foster's don't lose.

43500 ■ *Saudi Arabia: Moving Towards a Privatized Economy*

Ed: Andrea H. Pampanini. **Released:** April 2005. **Price:** $30. **Description:** An overview of how Saudi Arabia took control of its natural resources and created change in the government, education, and culture of the country. Production of oil and natural gas is control entirely by the Saudi Government; however, the book discusses the trend towards privatizing particular sectors of the nation in order to compete globally.

43501 ■ *"Saudi Overtures"* in *The Business Journal-Portland (Vol. 25, August 15, 2008, No. 23, pp. 1)*

Pub: American City Business Journals, Inc.

Contact: Whitney Shaw, President

Ed: Aliza Earnshaw. **Description:** Saudi Arabia's huge revenue from oil is creating opportunities for Oregon companies as the country develops new cities, industrial zones, and tourism centers. Oregon exported only $46.8 million worth of goods to Saudi Arabia in 2007 but the kingdom is interested in green building materials and methods, renewable energy and water quality control, and nanotechnology all of which Oregon has expertise in.

43502 ■ *"Saving Face Time"* in *Canadian Business (Vol. 81, December 8, 2008, No. 21, pp. 21)*

Pub: Rogers Media Inc.

Contact: Tony Viner, President

Ed: Calvin Leung. **Description:** Landing business deals in China requires fostering informal relationships as well as avoiding offensive gestures. Canadians planning to do business in China should be aware of the Chinese concept of 'face'. Other tips for doing business in China are listed.

43503 ■ *"Say What?"* in *Entrepreneur (Vol. 35, November 2007, No. 11, pp. 106)*

Pub: Entrepreneur Press

Contact: Perlman Neil, President

Ed: Gail Dutton. **Description:** Business enterprises with units and employees in different parts of the world may encounter problems with culture clashes. The employees' different cultural backgrounds can cause misunderstanding that can affect a company's operations. So before doing business in a particular region, it is important to study the history and culture of the area.

43504 ■ *"Scorched Earth: Will Environmental Risks in China Overwhelm Its Opportunities?"* in *Harvard Business Review (Vol. 85, June 2007, No. 6)*

Pub: Harvard Business School Publishing

Ed: Elizabeth Economy, Kenneth Lieberthal. **Price:** $6.93. **Description:** Environmental risks for business in China include water supply access, energy needs, pollution, and soil erosion. However, the nation's government is investing money to develop green technology and alternative energy sources. **Availability:** PDF.

43505 ■ *"Scripps' Dinner Bell"* in *Business Courier (Vol. 24, October 18, 2007, No. 27, pp. 1)*

Pub: American City Business Journals, Inc.

Contact: Whitney Shaw, President

Ed: Dan Monk. **Description:** Discusses the split of E.W. Scripps Co.'s Food Network into a separate publicly traded company Scripps Networks Interactive could produce expansion into Asia and Europe.

43506 ■ *"Sedo Keeps Trucking in Good Times and Bad"* in *Crain's Chicago Business (Vol. 31, April 28, 2008, No. 17, pp. 35)*

Ed: Samantha Stainburn. **Description:** Discusses Seko Worldwide Inc., an Itasca-based freight forwarder, and its complicated road to growth and expansion on a global scale.

43507 ■ *"Seen and Noted: Pipe Show Finds a Way for Smokers to Light Up" in Crain's Chicago Business (Vol. 31, April 28, 2008, No. 17, pp. 57)*
Pub: Crain Communications Inc.
Contact: Todd Johnson, Publisher
Ed: H. Lee Murphy. **Description:** With the help of attorneys within its local membership of 150 pipe collectors, the Chicagoland Pipe Collectors Club will be allowed to smoke at its 13th International Pipe & Tobacciana Show at Pheasant Run Resort. The event is expected to draw 4,000 pipe enthusiasts from as far as China and Russia.

43508 ■ *"Selling Michigan; R&D Pushed as Reason For Chinese To Locate In State" in Crain's Detroit Business (Vol. 24, January 14, 2008)*
Pub: Crain Communications Inc. - Detroit
Contact: Keith Crain, Chairman
Ed: Marti Benedetti. **Description:** Southeast Michigan Economic Development organizations are working to develop relationships with Chinese manufacturers so they will locate their automotive research and development operations in the state.

43509 ■ *"Selling Pressures Rise in China" in Barron's (Vol. 88, March 10, 2008, No. 10, pp. M9)*
Pub: Dow Jones & Co., Inc.
Contact: Clare Hart, President
Ed: Mohammed Hadi. **Description:** There are about 1.6 trillion yuan worth of shares up for sale in Chinese stock markets in 2008, adding to the selling pressures in these markets. The Chinese government has imposed restrictions to prevent a rapid rise in selling stocks.

43510 ■ *"Sense and Consensus" in Canadian Business (Vol. 81, October 13, 2008, No. 17, pp. 22)*
Ed: David Wolf. **Description:** Stock analysts' agree that earning estimates are seen to be optimistic in relation to their global economic outlook. Analysts are expected to cut earnings projections by fall because it may negatively affect the Canadian stock market. Other view on market analysis are presented.

43511 ■ *"The Service Imperative" in Business Horizons (Vol. 51, January-February 2008, No. 1, pp. 39)*
Pub: Elsevier Advanced Technology Publications
Ed: Mary Jo Bitner, Stephen W. Brown. **Description:** The importance of services is growing in developing countries like India and China, but little attention is given to service research, education and innovation. The 'service imperative' seeks to promote the advancement of services. The scope, objectives and philosophy of the service imperative platform are outlined.

43512 ■ *"Several Europe-Based Employers Cut MN Jobs" in Business Journal (Vol. 30, July 6, 2012, No. 6, pp. 1)*
Pub: American City Business Journals, Inc.
Contact: Whitney Shaw, President
Ed: Jim Hammerand. **Released:** July 6, 2012. **Description:** A number of Europe-based employers have cut jobs in Minnesota. Allianz SE has reduced its workforce by 380. Executive comments included.

43513 ■ *"Sharp To Halt Panel Production In Face of Foreign Competition" in Memphis Business Journal (Vol. 35, January 31, 2014, No. 43, pp. 7)*
Pub: American City Business Journals
Released: January 31, 2014. **Description:** Sharp Manufacturing Company of America will no longer produce solar panels in Memphis, Tennessee because of increased competition in the solar industry. The company, which benefited from the Solar Investment Tax Credit, reveals that its solar business is changing with new technology.

43514 ■ *"Shattering the Myths About U.S. Trade Policy: Stop Blaming China and India. A More Active Trade Policy Can Lead to a Stronger U.S. Economy" in Harvard Business Review (Vol. 90, March 2012, No. 3, pp. 149)*
Pub: Harvard Business Review Press
Contact: Peter E. Walsh, Director
Ed: Robert Z. Lawrence, Lawrence Edwards. **Released:** March 2012. **Description:** Myths debunked include the belief that the US open trade policy has caused job losses, and that living standards are falling due to export market competition. American must leverage China's need for global economic engagement and secure an open domestic market in China. It must also persuade the World Trade Organization to improve market access.

43515 ■ *"Shire Seeking New Digs for Headquarters" in Philadelphia Business Journal (Vol. 30, September 2, 2011, No. 29, pp. 1)*
Pub: American City Business Journals Inc.
Ed: Natalie Kostelni. **Description:** Dublin, Ireland-based Shire PLC announced plans to relocate its North American headquarters from Chesterbrook Corporate Center in Wayne, Pennsylvania and currently evaluating their options. The specialty biopharmaceutical firm is also considering a move to New Jersey or Delaware.

43516 ■ *"Shopped Out; Retailing Gloom" in The Economist (Vol. 390, January 3, 2009, No. 8612, pp. 26)*
Description: Economic volatility in the retail sector is having an impact on a number of countries around the globe. Europe is experiencing hard economic times as well and unless businesses have a strong business plan banks feel unable to lend the money necessary to tide the retailers over. The falling pound has increased the cost of imported goods and small to midsize retail chains may not be able to weather such an unforgiving economic climate.

43517 ■ *"Short Alert: Darkness Falling.." in Barron's (Vol. 89, July 20, 2009, No. 29, pp. 13)*
Pub: Dow Jones & Co., Inc.
Contact: Clare Hart, President
Ed: Robin Goldwyn Blumenthal. **Description:** Newsletter writer Arch Crawford believes that market indicators signal a possible downturn in US stock markets. High risk areas also include China and Japan.

43518 ■ *"Sign of Progress" in Playthings (Vol. 106, October 1, 2008, No. 9, pp. 4)*
Pub: Reed Elsevier Group plc Reed Business Information
Contact: Mark Kelsey, Chief Executive Officer
Ed: Cliff Annicelli. **Description:** The ramifications of the toy recalls in 2007 are discussed. Mandates for lead-free toys and other safety issues are having an impact on the American toy industry.

43519 ■ *"Six Leading Economists on What to Expect in the Year Ahead: David Wolf" in Canadian Business (Dec. 24, 2007)*
Ed: David Wolf. **Description:** The Canadian dollar recently hit parity with the U.S. dollar, and the exchange rate is going fast and overvaluation of the Canadian dollar could bring in competition from U.S. products. Details on the impact of the slowdown of the U.S. economy on the exchange rate speed are discussed.

43520 ■ *"Six Things You Can Do To Ride Out A Turbulent Market" in Hispanic Business (Vol. 30, March 2008, No. 3, pp. 20)*
Pub: Hispanic Business Inc.
Contact: Jesus Chavarria, President
Ed: Hildy Medina, Michael Bowker. **Description:** Top financial experts' views on managing investment portfolios during turbulent periods in the stock market are reported. Experts prefer investing in health care, short term investments, international bonds and preferred stocks or just maintain cash until such times as the market settles.

43521 ■ *"Size Does Matter" in International Journal of Globalisation and Small Business (Vol. 4, September 21, 2010, No. 1, pp. 61)*
Pub: Publishers Communication Group
Contact: Doug Wright, Director
Ed: Julia Cornnell, Ranjit Voola. **Description:** Examination of how members of an Australian-based manufacturing and engineering cluster share knowledge through networking as a means to improve competitive advantage.

43522 ■ *"Sky Harvest Windpower Corp. - Operational Update" in Investment Weekly News (March 10, 2012, pp. 744)*
Pub: NewsRX
Contact: Susan E. Hasty, Publisher
Released: March 10, 2012. **Description:** Sky Harvest Windpower Corporation is rebranding its focus on gas and power activities both nationally and internationally. The firm's Canadian projects are outlined as well as its commitment to purse the Green Options Partners Program in 2012.

43523 ■ *"A Slice of Danish; Fixing Finance" in The Economist (Vol. 390, January 3, 2009, No. 8612, pp. 55)*
Description: Denmark's mortgage-holders and the county's lending system is presented.

43524 ■ *"Slimmed-Down Supplier TI Automotive Relaunches" in Crain's Detroit Business (Vol. 26, January 11, 2010, No. 2, pp. 14)*
Pub: Crain Communications Inc.
Contact: Rance E. Crain, President
Ed: Robert Sherefkin. **Description:** TI Automotive Ltd., one of the world's largest suppliers of fuel storage and delivery systems, has reorganized the company by splitting it into five global divisions and is relaunching its brand which is now more focused on new technology.

43525 ■ *"Small Firms Punch Ticket for Growth" in Houston Business Journal (Vol. 40, January 29, 2010, No. 38, pp. 1)*
Pub: American City Business Journals
Ed: Allison Wollam. **Description:** Independent ticket agencies anticipate growth as American and Canadian authorities approved a merger between Ticketmaster and concert promoter Live Nation. Expansion of service offerings and acquisition of venues have also been done by independent ticket agencies in light of the merger. Details of the merger are included.

43526 ■ *The Small-Mart Revolution: How Local Businesses Are Beating the Global Competition*
Pub: Berrett-Koehler Communications Inc.
Contact: Steve Piersanti, President
E-mail: spiersanti@bkpub.com
Ed: Michael H. Shuman. **Price:** $16.95, paperback; $24, hardcover; $16.95. **Description:** Advice is given to help small businesses compete in a global environment. **Availability:** PrintPDF.

43527 ■ *Small and Medium-Sized Enterprises in Countries in Transition*
Released: January 2005. **Price:** , $18.00. **Description:** Characteristics of small and medium enterprise (SME) sector in transition countries and emerging market economies.

43528 ■ *SME Cluster Development: A Dynamic View on Survival Clusters in Developing Countries*
Pub: Palgrave Macmillan
Contact: Lisa Dunn, Manager
E-mail: l.dunn@palgrave.com
Ed: Mario Davide Parrilli. **Released:** February 2007. **Price:** £84, hardcover. **Description:** Survival clustering in developing countries is discussed in order to increase effectiveness of policy-making and development operations in local contexts. **Availability:** Print; E-book; Electronic publishing.

43529 ■ *Social Enterprise in Europe*
Ed: Marthe Nyssens. **Released:** August 2006. **Price:** , $145.00 hardcopy; $46.95 paperback. **Description:** Social enterprises in Europe are examined through three ideas: that they have a complex mixture of

goals, that they mobilize various kinds of markets and non-market resources, and that they are embedded in the political context.

43530 ■ *"Solar Credit Lapse Spur Late Demand" in The Business Journal - Serving Phoenix and the Valley of the Sun (Vol. 28, July 18, 2008)*

Pub: American City Business Journals, Inc.

Contact: Whitney Shaw, President

Ed: Patrick O'Grady. Description: Businesses looking to engage in the solar energy industry are facing the problems of taxation and limited solar panel supply. Solar panels manufacturers are focusing more on the European market. Political issues surrounding the federal tax credit policy on solar energy users are also discussed.

43531 ■ *"SolarBridge Technologies Introduces Global Microinverter Platform at Solar Power International" in Benzinga.com (September 10, 2012)*

Pub: Benzinga.com

Contact: Kyle Bazzy, President

Description: SolarBridge Technologies provides integrated microinverters for certified AC modules. They will introduce their new global Pantheon(TM) II microinverter platform at the Solor Power International conference. These nw 50-Hz/203-volt versions will first be introduced to the Australian and United Kingdom market, while the current 60-Hz product line for the United States, Canada, Mexico, Taiwan and the Phillipines is in use.

43532 ■ *"SolarWorld's Ongoing China Syndrome" in Business Journal Portland (Vol. 30, January 24, 2014, No. 47, pp. 16)*

Pub: American City Business Journals

Released: January 24, 2014. Description: The Coalition for American Solar Manufacturing is working to stop China's imposing of duties on U.S. and Korean polysilicon suppliers. A trade loophole enables Chinese manufacturers to subsidize an export-intensive strategy that U.S. companies believe has allowed them to sell solar panels and other solar-related goods below cost in the U.S.

43533 ■ *"Some Relief Possible Following Painful Week" in Barron's (Vol. 88, July 14, 2008, No. 28, pp. M3)*

Pub: Dow Jones & Co., Inc.

Contact: Clare Hart, President

Ed: Kopin Tan. Description: Dow Chemical is offering a 74 percent premium to acquire Rohm & Haas' coatings and electronics materials operations. Frontline amassed a 5.6 percent stake in rival Overseas Shipholding Group and a merger between the two would create a giant global fleet with pricing power. Highlights of the U.S. stock market during the week that ended in July 11, 2008 are discussed. Statistical data included.

43534 ■ *"Sound Advice From Dr. Sleep" in Crain's Chicago Business (Vol. 31, April 21, 2008, No. 16, pp. 30)*

Pub: Crain Communications Inc.

Contact: Todd Johnson, Publisher

Ed: Sarah A. Klein. Description: James K. Wyatt, the director of the Sleep Disorders Centers at Rush University Medical Center in Chicago, gives advice to business executives concerning what to eat, how to nap and which drugs to take or avoid in order to ease the strain of air travel, particularly on overseas flights.

43535 ■ *"South African Connections: Small Business Owners Work Toward Forming Strategic Alliances" in Black Enterprise (March 1, 2008)*

Pub: Earl G. Graves Publishing Co. Inc.

Contact: Earl G. Graves, Jr., President

Ed: Aisha Sylvester. Description: National Minority Supplier Development Council Inc. is working to create business partnerships between African American businesses and black-owned South African companies within the country's pharmaceutical supply industry.

43536 ■ *"Speaking In Tongues: Rosetta Stone's TOTALE Adds 'Social' To Language Learning" in Black Enterprise (Vol. 41, September 2010, No. 2)*

Pub: Earl G. Graves Publishing Co. Inc.

Contact: Earl G. Graves, Jr., President

Ed: Sonya A. Donaldson. Description: As small businesses become more globalized, it is necessary to learn new languages in order to compete. Rosetta Stone's TOTALe is profiled.

43537 ■ *A Splendid Exchange: How Trade Shaped the World*

Pub: Atlantic Monthly Press

Ed: William J. Bernstein. Released: May 2009. Price: $18, paperback. Description: Chronicle of how commerce defined cultures and shaped history. Availability: Print.

43538 ■ *Start-Up Nation*

Ed: Dan Senor, Paul Singer. Released: 2009. Price: $26.99. Description: Amid the turmoil in the Middle East, Israel's economy continues to thrive.

43539 ■ *"Stimulus 'Loser' Won't Build Plant in Mass." in Boston Business Journal (Vol. 30, November 5, 2010, No. 41, pp. 1)*

Pub: Boston Business Journal

Ed: Kyle Alspach. Description: Boston-Power Inc. no longer plans to build an electric vehicle battery plant in Massachusetts after it failed to obtain stimulus funds from the federal government. The company is instead looking to build a lithium-ion battery plant in China and possibly Europe.

43540 ■ *Stop Working: Start a Business, Globalize It, and Generate Enough Cash Flow to Get Out of the Rat Race*

Pub: Eye Contact Media Inc.

Contact: Rohan Hall, Chief Executive Officer

Ed: Rohan Hall. Released: November 2004. Price: , $15.99. Description: Advice is given to small companies to compete in the global marketplace by entrepreneur using the same strategy for his own business.

43541 ■ *"StubHub Launches in the UK" in Entertainment Close-Up (March 25, 2012)*

Description: StubHub, an eBay company, is expanding to the United Kingdom. The firm sells tickets, third party, to music, sport, and entertainment events by connecting buyers and sellers. Details of the service and expansion are explored.

43542 ■ *Studies in Entrepreneurship, Business and Government in Hong Kong: The Economic Development of a Small Open Economy*

Pub: Edwin Mellen Press

Contact: Kazimierz Braun, Director

Ed: Fu-Lai Tony Yu. Released: November 2006. Price: $139.95; £94.95. Description: Institutional and Austrian theories are used to analyze the transformation taking place in Hong Kong's economy.

43543 ■ *The Subprime Solution: How Today's Global Financial Crisis Happened, and What to Do About It*

Pub: Princeton University Press

Contact: Shirley M. Tilghman, President

Ed: Robert J. Shiller. Released: 2012. Price: $14.95, paperback; £10.95, paperback. Description: Yale economist discusses the worldwide financial crisis and offers plans to reform the system. Availability: Print.

43544 ■ *"Suit: Bank Bypassing Minorities" in Providence Business News (Vol. 29, June 9, 2014, No. 10, pp. 1)*

Pub: American City Business Journals

Released: June 9, 2014. Description: The City of Providence, Rhode Island filed a lawsuit against the U.S. operations of Santander Bank for purposely bypassing minority neighborhoods in prime mortgage lending. The lawsuit alleges the Madrid, Spain-based bank of violating the Fair Housing Act by not lending into the minority communities of the city.

43545 ■ *"The Superpower Dilemma" in Canadian Business (Vol. 83, August 17, 2010, No. 13-14, pp. 42)*

Description: Canada has been an energy superpower partly because it controls the energy source and the production means, particularly of fossil fuels. However, Canada's status as superpower could diminish if it replaces petroleum exports with renewable technology for using sources of energy available globally.

43546 ■ *"Suppliers May Follow Fiat: Local Group Says Italian Firms are Inquiring" in Crain's Detroit Business (Vol. 25, June 15, 2009, No. 24, pp. 1)*

Pub: Crain Communications Inc. - Detroit

Contact: Keith Crain, Chairman

Ed: Ryan Beene. Description: Italian suppliers to Fiat SpA are looking toward Detroit after the formation of Chrysler Group LLC, the Chrysler-Fiat partnership created from Chrysler's bankruptcy. The Italian American Alliance for Business and Technology is aware of two Italy-based powertrain component suppliers that are considering a move to Detroit.

43547 ■ *"Supply Chain Visibility A Two-Way Street" in Canadian Sailings (July 7, 2008)*

Ed: Jack Kohane. Description: Canada is experiencing unprecedented market pressures due to globalization. Competition from foreign countries, demand for better and faster service from customers and shorter innovation cycles are some of the problems the country is facing regarding trade and the importing and exporting industry.

43548 ■ *"Surge in the South" in Canadian Business (Vol. 85, June 11, 2012, No. 10, pp. 48)*

Pub: George Media Inc.

Ed: Jeff Beer. Released: June 11, 2012. Description: Canada should get involved as a trading partner in the emerging markets as South-South trade, which is between these markets, is projected to grow between 2012 and 2030 from 13 percent of global trade to 26 percent. Canadian firms can join the South-South trade by setting up operations in an emeging market and use it as a base for trade or by acting as facilitator between trade partners.

43549 ■ *"Survey Distorts Cost of Capitals" in Canadian Business (Vol. 83, October 12, 2010, No. 17, pp. 22)*

Pub: Rogers Media Inc.

Contact: Tony Viner, President

Ed: Matthew McClearn. Description: Swiss bank UBS publishes a study comparing the costs of goods and services in megalopolises every three years. The study ranked Toronto and Montreal outside the Top 30 in 2009, but the two cities jumped to eighth and ninth in a recent update. This change can be contributed to the conversion of prices into Euros before making comparisons.

43550 ■ *"A Survival Guide for Crazy Times" in Canadian Business (Vol. 81, March 3, 2008, No. 3, pp. 61)*

Ed: David Wolf. Description: Investors should ensure that their portfolios are positioned defensively more than the average as the U.S. and Canadian markets face turbulent times. They should not assume that U.S. residential property is a good place to invest only because prices have dropped and the Canadian dollar is showing strength. Other tips that investors can use during unstable periods are supplied.

43551 ■ *"Sustainability On the Subcontinent: Efficiency Lessons from India's Greenest Buildings" in Real Estate Review (Vol. 41, Spring 2012, No. 1, pp. 67)*

Released: Spring 2012. Description: India's adoption of green design in building construction is examined. The country's CLL Godrej Green Building Centre was the first building to earn LEED's highest rating outside the United States. Several buildings in the country return more water to the local aquifer than they use.

43552 ■ *Swedish-American Chamber of Commerce of the United States--Membership Directory*

Pub: Swedish-American Chamber of Commerce

Contact: Renee Lundholm, President

E-mail: renee.lundholm@saccny.org

URL(s): www.saccny.org/publications/membership-directory. Released: Annual; Latest edition 2013. Price: only available to members. Covers: About 1,800 United States and 200 Swedish members of the chamber, concerned with promoting commercial relations between the two countries. Entries include: Company name, address, phone, fax. Arrangement: Separate alphabetical lists by country. Indexes: Classified.

43553 ■ *"Swimming Against the Tide: Outward Staffing Flows from Multinational Subsidiaries" in Human Resource Management (Vol. 49, July-August 2010, No. 4, pp. 575-598)*

Pub: John Wiley

Ed: David G. Collings, Anthony McDonnell, Patrick Gunnigle, Jonathan Lavelle. Description: A study was conducted to provide a benchmark of outward flows of international assignees from the Irish subsidiaries of foreign-owned multinational enterprises (MNEs) to corporate headquarters and other worldwide operations. Findings indicate that almost half of all MNEs use some form of outward staffing flows.

43554 ■ *"Taiwan Technology Initiatives Foster Growth" in Canadian Electronics (Vol. 23, February 2008, No. 1, pp. 28)*

Description: A study conducted by the Market Intelligence Center shows that currently, Taiwan is the world's larges producer of information technology products such as motherboards, servers, and LCD monitors. In 2006, Taiwan's LED industry reached a production value of NTD 21 billion. This push into the LED sector shows the Ministry of Economic Affairs' plan to target industries that are environmentally friendly.

43555 ■ *"Taking the Over-the-Counter Route to U.S." in Barron's (Vol. 88, July 7, 2008, No. 27, pp. 24)*

Pub: Dow Jones & Co., Inc.

Contact: Clare Hart, President

Ed: Eric Uhlfelder. Description: Many multinational companies have left the New York Stock Exchange and allowed their shares to trade over-the-counter. The companies have taken advantage of a 2007 SEC rule allowing publicly listed foreign companies to change trading venues if less than 5 percent of global trading volume in the past 12 months occurred in the US.

43556 ■ *"Talent Shows" in Canadian Business (Vol. 81, December 24, 2007, No. 1, pp. 14)*

Ed: Megan Harman. Description: Canadian companies are increasingly turning to marketing to promote themselves as employers, as concerns on employee recruitment increase with the nearing retirement age of the baby boomers. Details on skills shortage, the potential advantage for the immigrant workforce, and employee retention are discussed.

43557 ■ *"Tales of the City" in Canadian Business (Vol. 81, December 8, 2008, No. 21, pp. 37)*

Ed: Joe Chidley. Description: Key information on doing business in Hong Kong are shared by an entrepreneur, a consultant, an exporter, and a financier who were from Canada. Hong Kong hosts about 3,900 regional headquarters or offices of international companies.

43558 ■ *"Tao of Downfall" in International Journal of Entrepreneurship and Small Business (Vol. 11, August 31, 2010, No. 2, pp. 121)*

Pub: Publishers Communication Group

Contact: Doug Wright, Director

Ed: Wenxian Zhang, Ilan Alon. Description: Through historical reviews and case studies, this research seeks to understand why some initially successful entrepreneurs failed in the economic boom of past decades. Among various factors contributing to their downfall are a unique political and business environment, fragile financial systems, traditional cultural influences and personal characteristics.

43559 ■ *"Tasti D-Lite Has Franchise Agreement for Australia" in Ice Cream Reporter (Vol. 23, November 20, 2010, No. 12, pp. 3)*

Description: Tasti D-Lite signed an international master franchise agreement with Friezer Australia Pty. Ltd. and will open 30 units throughout Australia over the next five years.

43560 ■ *"The Tata Way" in Business Strategy Review (Vol. 21, Summer 2010, No. 2, pp. 14)*

Pub: John Wiley & Sons Inc. Scientific, Technical, Medical, and Scholarly Div. (Wiley-Blackwell)

Contact: William J. Pesce, Manager

E-mail: wpesce@wiley.com

Ed: Stuart Crainer. Description: Tata Motors is one of the world's most talked-about companies. Its new ultra-low-cost Nano car is being heralded as the people's car. Vice chairman, Ravi Kant, talks about India and its emerging markets.

43561 ■ *"Tax Planning for Royalties"*

Pub: CreateSpace

Contact: Daren Giles, President

Released: October 19, 2014. Price: , $15.99 paperback. Description: Tax planning and copyright royalty issues are defined for entrepreneurs living in the United Kingdom. Topics covered include: electronic book and copyright royalties, how IP holding companies work, transferring royalties to offshore business, double tax treaties to reduce withholding taxes, patents, and more.

43562 ■ *"Tax Services Firm Ryan Prepares for Growth" in Dallas Business Journal (Vol. 35, June 29, 2012, No. 42, pp. 1)*

Pub: American City Business Journal

Ed: Candace Carlisle. Description: Ryan LLC is seen to grow with three pending acquisitions. The tax services firm has opened offices in Australia and Singapore.

43563 ■ *"Teacher's Pet" in Entrepreneur (September 2014)*

Pub: Entrepreneur Media Inc.

Released: September 2014. Description: Entrepreneur, Andrew Geant, partnered with software developer, Michael Weishuhn, to launch WyzAnt, an online tutoring service based in Chicago, Illinois. Tutors can boost their ranking on the platform by earning positive reviews, their ability to accept electronic payments or use the service's cloud-based schedule system. A tutor's hourly fee ranges from $30 to $60. Geant and Weishuhn are planning for an international expansion of WyzAnt and support development of a series of mobile applications for tutors, students, and parents.

43564 ■ *"Tempel Steel To Expand Its Chicago Plant" in Chicago Tribune (August 22, 2008)*

Pub: McClatchy-Tribune Information Services

Ed: James P. Miller. Description: Tempel Steel Co. is no longer considering transferring a Libertyville factory's production to Mexico; the company has responded to government incentives and will instead shift that work to its plant on Chicago's North Side.

43565 ■ *"10 Trends That Are Shaping Global Media Consumption" in Advertising Age (Vol. 81, December 6, 2010, No. 43, pp. 3)*

Pub: Crain Communications Inc.

Contact: Rance Crain, President

Ed: Ann Marie Kerwin. Description: Ad Age offers the statistics from the TV penetration rate in Kenya to the number of World Cup watchers and more.

43566 ■ *"Thai Ice Cream Cremo Expanding to Middle East" in Ice Cream Reporter (Vol. 23, September 20, 2010, No. 10, pp. 3)*

Description: Thai-based frozen dessert manufacturer Chomthana, maker of Cremo brand ice cream, is expanding into the Middle East.

43567 ■ *"There's More Upside in Germany" in Barron's (Vol. 90, September 6, 2010, No. 36, pp. M7)*

Pub: Barron's Editorial & Corporate Headquarters

Ed: Jonathan Buck. Description: Germany's stocks have gone up since the beginning of 2010, and investors can still benefit. These stocks will benefit from Germany's stellar economic performance and the relative weakness of the Euro. The prospects of the shares of Daimler and Hochtief are discussed.

43568 ■ *"TheStreet.com: Study Abroad" in Entrepreneur (Vol. 35, October 2007, No. 10, pp. 44)*

Pub: Entrepreneur Press

Contact: Perlman Neil, President

Ed: Farnoosh Torabi. Description: Businessmen who wish to pursue foreign investments should study the country in which they will operate. Some investors do their research by completely exposing themselves to their prospective country, while others prefer studying the market home-based. Details of how investors pick their country and the different ways of investing in foreign land are presented.

43569 ■ *"Things Will Improve, or Not: A Chartered Financial Analyst Explains It All" in Canadian Business (Vol. 81, November 10, 2008)*

Pub: Rogers Media Inc.

Contact: Tony Viner, President

Ed: Jeff Sanford. Description: Myles Zyblock expects the global economic slowdown to deepen over the next six to nine months. Zyblock addressed the Toronto CFA Society at their annual dinner in October 2008. He stressed a tight correlation between the credit ratio and asset prices and predicts the S&P 500 to be up by 11 percent by October 2009.

43570 ■ *"35-Year-Old Downtown Fabric Store Closes Doors" in The Times and Democrat (September 29, 2009)*

Pub: The Times and Democrat

Description: Warren's Fashion Fabrics Inc., a 35-year-old retail fabric, decor and sewing store, officially closed its doors due, in part, to the changing tide of the industry in which fewer women sew and products from countries such as China are so cheap.

43571 ■ *"Thomas and His Washington Friends" in CFO (Vol. 23, October 2007, No. 10, pp. 18)*

Ed: Alix Stuart. Description: Reliance on Chinese suppliers to America's toymakers may become quite costly as Congress considers legislation that would increase fines to as high as $50 million for companies selling tainted products. The legislation would also require independent mandatory testing for makers of products for children.

43572 ■ *"The Three Amigos" in Canadian Business (Vol. 81, March 17, 2008, No. 4, pp. 19)*

Ed: Rachel Pulfer. Description: Mexican president Felipe Calderon said that Mexico exported 30 percent more to Europe and 25 percent more to other countries in Latin America in 2006 in light of the downturn in the U.S. economy. Calderon made this announcement in a speech at Harvard University while protestors marched outside protesting against NAFTA.

43573 ■ *"Three Ways Columbia's Stock Can Keep Rising" in Business Journal Portland (Vol. 30, February 21, 2014, No. 51, pp. 8)*

Pub: American City Business Journals

Released: February 21, 2014. Description: The shares of Columbia Sportswear Company reached a record high of $88.25 in February 2014. The company's cold-weather gear, its TurboDown technology and its new joint venture with China are expected to contribute significantly in keeping stock prices high.

43574 ■ *"Tied to Home: Female Owned Businesses Export Less, And It's Not Just Because They're Smaller" in Canadian

Business (April 14, 2008)
Pub: Rogers Media Inc.
Contact: Tony Viner, President
Ed: Lauren McKeon. **Description:** Only 12 percent of small and midsized enterprises that are run by women export their products and services. Government agencies can be more proactive in promoting the benefits of exporting by including women in case studies and recruiting women as mentors. Exporting provides great growth potential especially for the service sector where women have an advantage.

43575 ■ *"Time to Engage Europe"* in Canadian Business (Vol. 79, June 19, 2006, No. 13, pp. 19)
Pub: Rogers Media Inc.
Contact: Tony Viner, President
Ed: Jack Mintz. **Description:** European and Canadian governments improved their trade and investment relations with the March 18, 2004 frame work to develop a Trade and Investment Enhancement Agreement. Still there is lot of opportunities to solve tax and trade issues.

43576 ■ *"Time For a Change at Canon?"* in Barron's (Vol. 92, July 23, 2012, No. 30, pp. 17)
Pub: Dow Jones & Co., Inc.
Contact: Clare Hart, President
Ed: Neil A. Martin. **Released:** July 23, 2012. **Description:** Stocks of Japanese imaging equipment maker Canon could lose value unless the company undergoes changes in operations and governance. Prices of the company's American Depositary Receipts could fall 20 percent from $37.22 per share within 12 months.

43577 ■ *"Timken's Bearings Rolling in China, India"* in Crain's Cleveland Business (Vol. 28, October 29, 2007, No. 43, pp. 14)
Pub: Crain Communications Inc.
Ed: David Bennett. **Description:** Canton-based Timken Co., a manufacturer of bearings and specialty metals, is seeing growing demand for its line of tapered roller bearings, which allow rail users to carry heavy car loads. The company is finding significant growth in China and India due to their rapidly growing rail markets.

43578 ■ *"To Keep Freight Rolling, Ill. Has to Grease the Hub"* in Crain's Chicago Business (Vol. 31, April 21, 2008, No. 16, pp. 22)
Pub: Crain Communications Inc.
Contact: Todd Johnson, Publisher
Ed: Paul O'Connor. **Description:** Discusses the importance of upgrading Chicago's continental-hub freight rail system which is integral to moving international products as well as domestic ones. Global tonnage is expected to double by 2020 and unless more money is designated to upgrade the infrastructure the local and national economy will suffer.

43579 ■ *"To Offshore Or Not To Offshore?"* in Converting (Vol. 25, October 1, 2007, No. 10, pp. 10)
Ed: Mark Spaulding. **Description:** Offshore manufacturing and the issue of buying raw materials from foreign suppliers by American companies is discussed. Results of a study conducted by Cap Gemini and Pro Logis regarding offshore manufacturing, especially to China, are presented.

43580 ■ *"Too Much Precaution About Biotech Corn"* in Barron's (Vol. 88, March 17, 2008, No. 11, pp. 54)
Pub: Dow Jones & Co., Inc.
Contact: Clare Hart, President
Ed: Mark I. Schwartz. **Description:** In the U.S., 90 percent of cultivated soybeans are biotech varietals as well as 60 percent of the corn. Farmers have significantly reduced their reliance on pesticides in the growing of biotech corn. Biotech cotton cultivation has brought hundreds of millions of dollars in net financial gains to farmers. The European Union has precluded the cultivation or sale of biotech crops within its border.

43581 ■ *"Top 50 Exporters: In Volatile Market, Food and Green Companies Lead the List"* in Hispanic Business (Vol. 30, July-August 2008, No. 7-8, pp. 42)
Pub: Hispanic Business Inc.
Contact: Jesus Chavarria, President
Ed: Hildy Medina. **Description:** Increases in exports revenues reported by food exporters and green companies in a time of economic slowdown in the U.S are described. Food exporters have benefited from the growth of high-volume grocery stores in underdeveloped countries and the German governments' promotion of solar energy has benefited the U.S. solar heating equipment and solar panel manufactures.

43582 ■ *"Toward a Political Conception of Corporate Responsibility: Business and Society Seen from a Habermasian Perspective"* in Academy of Management Review (October 2007, pp. 1096)
Pub: ScholarOne Inc.
Contact: William T. Carden, Jr., President
Ed: Andreas Georg Scherer, Guido Palazzo. **Description:** The limitations of studies on corporate social responsibility and a new theory based on Jurgen Habermas theory of democracy are highlighted. The key role played by the business firm in globalization of society is presented.

43583 ■ *"Toy Scares Drive Business"* in Boston Business Journal (Vol. 27, November 23, 2007, No. 43, pp. 1)
Ed: Joan Goodchild. **Description:** Several Boston businesses have tapped into the lead content scare in toys and other products manufactured in China. ConRoy Corporation LLC launched Toy Recall Alert!, an online tool to alert consumers about new recalls while Hybrivet Systems introduced screening test kit, LeadCheck. Other new products pertaining to toy safety are discussed.

43584 ■ *"Toy Story"* in Forbes (Vol. 180, October 15, 2007, No. 8, pp. 102)
Pub: Forbes Inc.
Contact: Malcolm S. Forbes, Jr., President
Ed: Tatiana Serafin. **Description:** Three voluntary recalls of Chinese-made toys were announced by American toymakers, sending Mattel stocks plummeting.

43585 ■ *"Toy Story: U.S.-Made a Hot Seller"* in Crain's Detroit Business (Vol. 23, December 17, 2007, No. 51, pp. 3)
Ed: Chad Halcom. **Description:** American Plastic Toys, located in Walled Lake, Michigan reports all its toys are made in the U.S. and have passed all U.S. safety standards. Revenue for American Plastic Toys reached nearly $33 million in 2005, and the company expects to exceed that because of recent toy safety recalls of products produced in China.

43586 ■ *"Trade Mission Provides Global Entry Point"* in Pittsburgh Business Times (Vol. 33, January 3, 2014, No. 25, pp. 4)
Pub: American City Business Journals
Released: January 3, 2014. **Description:** Carnegie, Pennsylvania-based Neural Ware CEO, Jack Cooper, claims trade missions can give companies a focal point when they trade overseas. Neural Ware uses the high respect for mayors in China and builds trust with potential customers. Insights into Cooper's advice for visiting target countries are discussed.

43587 ■ *"Trade Winds"* in Canadian Sailings (June 30, 2008)
Ed: Peter Malkovsky. **Description:** Trade between Canada and the United States is discussed as well as legislation concerning foreign trade and the future of this trade relationship.

43588 ■ Trading Places - Smes In The Global Economy: A Critical Research Handbook
Pub: Edward Elgar Publishing Inc.
Contact: Richard Henning, Vice President
E-mail: kwight@e-elgar.com
Ed: Lester Lloyd-Reason, Leigh Sear. **Released:** 2007. **Price:** £88.20, hardback. **Description:** An overview of international research for small and medium-sized companies wishing to expand in the global economy. **Availability:** Print; E-book.

43589 ■ *"Transborder Short-Sea Shipping: Hurdles Remain"* in Canadian Sailings (June 30, 2008)
Ed: Kathlyn Horibe. **Description:** Legislation that would exempt non-bulk commercial cargo by water in the Great Lakes region from U.S. taxation is discussed.

43590 ■ *"The Transparent Supply Chain"* in Harvard Business Review (Vol. 88, October 2010, No. 10, pp. 76)
Pub: Harvard Business School Publishing
Ed: Steve New. **Description:** Examination of the use of new technologies to create a transparent supply chain, such as next-generation 2D bar codes in clothing labels that can provide data on a garment's provenance.

43591 ■ *"Tri-State to Get New Headquarters"* in Business Courier (Vol. 27, October 22, 2010, No. 25, pp. 1)
Ed: James Ritchie. **Description:** Hong Kong-based corn processing firm Global Bio-Chem Technology is set to choose Greater Cincinnati, Ohio as a location of its North American headquarters. The interstate access, central location, and low labor and property costs might have enticed Global Bio-Chem to invest in the region. Statistics on Chinese direct investment in U.S. are also presented.

43592 ■ *"Trillium Turmoil"* in Canadian Business (Vol. 81, December 8, 2008, No. 21, pp. 16)
Pub: Rogers Media Inc.
Contact: Tony Viner, President
Ed: Jeff Sanford. **Description:** Ontario's manufacturing success in the past was believed to have been built in the 1965 Canada-U.S. automotive pact and by advantages such as low-cost energy. The loss of these advantages along with the challenging economic times has hurt Ontario's manufacturing industry.

43593 ■ *"Tweaking On-Board Activities, Equipment Saves Fuel, Reduces CO2"* in Canadian Sailings (June 30, 2008)
Description: Optimizing ship activities and equipment uses less fuel and therefore reduces greenhouse gas emissions. Ways in which companies are implementing research and development techniques in order to monitor ship performance and analyze data in an attempt to become more efficient are examined.

43594 ■ *"Twitter Hack: Made in Japan? User Says Attack Showed Security Flaw"* in Houston Chronicle (September 24, 2010, pp. 3)
Pub: Houston Chronicle
Contact: Sherry Adams, Director, Library Services
Ed: Tomoko A. Hosaka. **Description:** Details of the attack on Twitter caused by a Japanese computer hacker are revealed.

43595 ■ *"Two Countries, Two Tour Boat Operators"* in Business First of Buffalo (Vol. 30, May 9, 2014, No. 34, pp. 3)
Pub: American City Business Journals, Inc.
Contact: Whitney Shaw, President
Released: May 9, 2014. **Description:** Maid of the Mist Steamboat Company will start its operation as Niagara Falls exclusive tour boat operator in the U.S. while Hornblower Niagara Cruises will commence its tour operation from Canada. Maid of the Mist lost its Canadian rights to Hornblower in a competitive bidding process undertaken by the Niagara Parks Commission of New York in 2012.

43596 ■ *"2008: Year of the Rat Race"* in Mergers & Acquisitions: The Dealmaker's Journal (March 1, 2008)
Pub: SourceMedia Inc.
Contact: James M. Malkin, Chief Executive Officer
Ed: Danelle Fugazy. **Description:** Although China still presents opportunities to Western investors, many are discovering that much more research needs to be done concerning doing business in that country before investing there becomes truly mainstream. According to one source, there are at least

300,000 small state-owned enterprises in China and millions of middle-market privately owned companies; the Chinese stock market can only handle about 50 to 70 IPOs a year and lists about 1,500 companies at a time.

43597 ■ *"Uncovering Offshoring's Invisible Costs"* in HRMagazine (Vol. 54, January 2009, No. 1, pp. 1)
Pub: Society for Human Resource Management
Contact: Henry G. Jackson, President
E-mail: hjackson@shrm.org
Ed: Rita Zeidner. **Description:** Nearly half of all offshore service work fails, often due to the invisible costs of communication and cultural friction according to researchers. The challenges of offshore services are discussed.

43598 ■ *Understanding Exporting in the Small and Micro Enterprise*
Pub: Nova Science Publishers Inc.
Contact: Frank Columbus, President
Ed: Densil A. Williams. **Released:** 2009. **Price:** $99, hardcover. **Description:** An examination into the reasons why some small and micro locally-owned businesses choose to sell a portion of their goods abroad while others facing similar market conditions remain focused on the domestic market. **Availability:** Print.

43599 ■ *"Unemployment Rates"* in The Economist (Vol. 390, January 3, 2009, No. 8612, pp. 75)
Description: Countries that are being impacted the worst by rising unemployment rates are those that have also been suffering from the housing market crisis. Spain has been the hardest hit followed by Ireland. America and Britain are also seeing levels of unemployment that indicate too much slack in the economy.

43600 ■ *"Unilever Acquiring EVGA's Ice Cream Brands in Greece"* in Ice Cream Reporter (Vol. 23, October 20, 2010, No. 11, pp. 1)
Pub: Ice Cream Reporter
Description: Unilever will acquire the ice cream brands and distribution network of the Greek frozen dessert manufacturer EVGA.

43601 ■ *"U.S. Competitiveness and the Chinese Challenge"* in Harvard Business Review (Vol. 90, March 2012, No. 3, pp. 40)
Pub: Harvard Business Review Press
Contact: Peter E. Walsh, Director
Ed: Xu Xiaonian. **Released:** March 2012. **Description:** Although China's shift from cntral planningto market-oriented policies has boosted innovation, intellectual property rights and original research are still insufficiently valued. The U.S. has the edge on China in this respect; it remains for the U.S. to restore confidence in its innovation and creativity.

43602 ■ *"U.S. Enters BlackBerry Dispute Compromise Sought Over Security Issues"* in Houston Chronicle (August 6, 2010)
Pub: Houston Chronicle
Contact: Sherry Adams, Director, Library Services
Ed: Matthew Lee. **Description:** U.S. State Department is working for a compromise with Research in Motion, manufacturer of the BlackBerry, over security issues. The Canadian company makes the smartphones and foreign governments believe they pose a security risk.

43603 ■ *"U.S. Primaries: An Amazing Race"* in Canadian Business (Vol. 81, February 12, 2008, No. 3, pp. 25)
Pub: Rogers Media Inc.
Contact: Tony Viner, President
Ed: Rachel Pulfer. **Description:** U.S. presidential candidates Barack Obama and Hilary Clinton lead the Democratic Part primaries while John McCain is a frontrunner at the Republican Party. These leading candidates have different plans for the U.S. economy which will affect Canada's own economy particularly concerning trade policies. The presidential candidates' proposals and the impacts of U.S. economic downturn on Canada are examined.

43604 ■ *"U.S. Targets China's Exported Paper"* in Globe & Mail (March 31, 2007, pp. B5)
Pub: CTVglobemedia Publishing Inc.
Ed: Barrie McKenna. **Description:** The prospects of the rise in duties on goods imported into the United States, due to the levy of duties on imports of Chinese paper, are discussed.

43605 ■ *"U.S. Trade Body Clears Apple in Patent Case"* in Wall Street Journal Eastern Edition (November 23 , 2011, pp. C1)
Pub: Dow Jones & Co., Inc.
Contact: Clare Hart, President
Ed: Matt Jarzemsky, Paul Mozur. **Description:** HTC Corporation alleged in its patent-infringement case against Apple Inc. that Apple violated patents of S3 Graphics Inc., a company which was acquired by HTC Corporation. Now the International Trade Commission has issued a ruling saying that Apple did not violate the patents.

43606 ■ *"Up On The Farm"* in Canadian Business (Vol. 81, March 31, 2008, No. 5, pp. 23)
Pub: Rogers Media Inc.
Contact: Tony Viner, President
Ed: John Gray. **Description:** Agricultural products have outperformed both energy and metal and even the prospect of a global economic slowdown does not seem to hinder its prospects. The Organization for Economic Cooperation and Development sees prices above historic equilibrium levels during the next ten years given that fuel and fertilizers remain high and greater demand from India and China remain steady.

43607 ■ *"Upsurge"* in Puget Sound Business Journal (Vol. 33, July 13, 2012, No. 12, pp. 1)
Description: Kent, Washington-based Flow International Corporation posted a record of $254 million in annual sales for fiscal 2012 and it is expected to reach about $300 million by 2014. Flow is being lifted by a global manufacturing revival and by its machines' ability to handle the carbon-fiber composites used in aerospace. Insights on Flow's water jet cutting tools are also given.

43608 ■ *"V&J Scores Partnership with Shaq"* in Business Journal-Milwaukee (Vol. 25, October 12, 2007, No. 2, pp. A1)
Pub: American City Business Journals
Ed: Rich Kirchen. **Description:** O'Neal Franchise Group has agreed to a partnership with V&J Foods of Milwaukee to handle Auntie Anne's shops in New York, South Africa, Michigan, and the Caribbean. V&J O'Neal Enterprises will open six Auntie Anne's soft pretzel shops in Detroit towards the end of 2007. Planned international ventures of the partnership are presented.

43609 ■ *"VASCO DIGIPASS GO3 in Combination With IDENTIKEY Enhances the Security of Business Intelligence Solution Developed by CDS for General Motors Brazil"* in News Bites US (March 29, 2012)
Pub: Financial Times Ltd.
Contact: John Ridding, Chief Executive Officer
Released: March 29, 2012. **Description:** VASCO Data Security International Inc. will provide Condominio de Corporativas, a vendor and business solutions integrator, its DIGIPASS GO 3 authentication solution along with IDENTIKEY Authentacation Server to provide security to the BI Retail Program developed for General Motors Brazil. VASCO is a leading software security firm specializing in authentication products.

43610 ■ *"Vicki Avril: Senior Vice-President of Tubular Division, Ipsco Inc."* in Crain's Chicago Business (Vol. 31, May 5, 2008, No. 18)
Pub: Crain Communications Inc.
Contact: Todd Johnson, Publisher
Ed: Miriam Gottfried. **Description:** Profile of Vicki Avril who is the senior vice-president of the tubular division at Ipsco Inc. where she supervises 2,800 employees and 13 mills throughout the United States and Canada.

43611 ■ *"Vision Statement: Mapping the Social Internet"* in Harvard Business Review (Vol. 88, July-August 2010, No. 7-8, pp. 32)
Pub: Harvard Business School Publishing
Ed: Mikolaj Jan Piskorski, Tommy McCall. **Description:** Chart compares and contrasts online social networks in selected countries.

43612 ■ *"Vision Statement: Why Mumbai at 1 PM is the Center of the Business World"* in Harvard Business Review (Vol. 88, October 2010, No. 10, pp. 38)
Pub: Harvard Business School Publishing
Ed: Michael Segalla. **Description:** A time zone chart is presented for assisting in the planning of international conference calls.

43613 ■ *"Viva Brazil"* in Business Strategy Review (Vol. 21, Autumn 2010, No. 3, pp. 24)
Pub: John Wiley & Sons Inc. Scientific, Technical, Medical, and Scholarly Div. (Wiley-Blackwell)
Contact: William J. Pesce, Manager
E-mail: wpesce@wiley.com
Ed: Georgina Peters. **Description:** Brazil's current status as a major emerging market with a boundless economic horizon is a radical shift from its place in the world in the late 1960s to the mid 1990s. Lessons Brazil can teach other countries are outlined.

43614 ■ *"Viva La Evolucion"* in Canadian Business (Vol. 80, February 12, 2007, No. 4, pp. 63)
Pub: Rogers Media Inc.
Contact: Tony Viner, President
Ed: Denis Seguin. **Description:** The rise of Cuba as an importance source of oil and its significance for the Canadian economy is discussed.

43615 ■ *"Voices From the Front Lines: Four Leaders on the Cross-Border Challenges They've Faced"* in Harvard Business Review (Vol. 92, September 2014, No. 9, pp. 77)
Pub: Harvard Business Publishing
Released: September 2014. **Description:** Points presented include building cultural sensitivity into organizations, employing varying talent to respond to market specifics, creating standard human resource practices worldwide, and emphasizing the importance of emerging markets.

43616 ■ *"Wake-Up Call"* in Canadian Business (Vol. 80, October 8, 2007, No. 20, pp. 58)
Ed: Andrea Mandel-Campbell. **Description:** The need for Canadian companies to develop global marketing strategies is discussed. Thomas Caldwell, chairman of Caldwell Securities, believes the country's average performance in global markets should be a cause for alarm. The factors affecting the country's current economic state is also presented.

43617 ■ *"Wanted: Nuclear Warheads, Gently Used: Why Cameco Coveted Germany's Nukem Energy"* in Canadian Business (Vol. 85, August 13, 2012, No. 13, pp. 10)
Pub: George Media Inc.
Ed: Richard Warnica. **Released:** August 13, 2012. **Description:** Cameco Corporation has acquired Nukem Energy gmbH from private equity firm Advent International for $136 million as part of the Canadian mining company's plan to double annual uranium production to 40 million pounds by 2018. Such agreement gives Cameco access to some of the last of the uranium supply in the Megatons to Megawatt deal between Russia and the U.S. which expires in 2013.

43618 ■ *"A Warning Sign From Global Companies"* in Harvard Business Review (Vol. 90, March 2012, No. 3, pp. 74)
Pub: Harvard Business Review Press
Contact: Peter E. Walsh, Director
Ed: Matthew J. Slaughter, Laura D'Andrea Tyson. **Released:** March 2012. **Description:** Multiple charts demonstrate the importance of the multinational corporation to the American economy, and that the US needs to become more attractive to these types of firms.

43619 ■ *"Weaving a Stronger Fabric: Organizing a Global Sweat-Free Apparel Production Agreement"* in WorkingUSA (Vol. 11, June 2008, No. 2)
Ed: Eric Dirnbach. Description: Tens of millions of workers working under terrible sweatshop conditions in the global apparel industry. Workers are employed at apparel contractors and have been largely unsuccessful in organizing and improving their working conditions. The major apparel manufacturers and retailers have the most power in this industry, and they have adopted corporate social responsibility programs as a false solution to the sweatshop problem. The major North American apparel unions dealt with similar sweatshop conditions a century ago by organizing the contractors and brands into joint association contracts that significantly raised standards. Taking inspiration from their example, workers and their anti-sweatshop allies need to work together to coordinate a global organizing effort that builds worker power and establishes a global production agreement that negotiates with both contractors and the brands for improved wages, benefits, and working conditions.

43620 ■ *"Website Drives British Travel Firm To Open In Boston"* in Boston Business Journal (Vol. 34, February 28, 2014, No. 4, pp. 4)
Pub: American City Business Journals, Inc.
Contact: Whitney Shaw, President
Released: February 28, 2014. Description: United Kingdom-based Audley Travel is planning to open an office in Boston, Massachusetts. The company has hired 27 people for the new office. Audley's earnings have increased $120 million 2013.

43621 ■ *"Wegmans Uses Database for Recall"* in Supermarket News (Vol. 56, September 22, 2008, No. 38)
Pub: Penton Business Media Inc.
Ed: Carol Angrisani. Description: Wegmans used data obtained through its loyalty card that, in turn, sent automated telephone calls to every customer who had purchased tainted pet food when Mars Petcare recalled dog food products.

43622 ■ *"Welsh Meat Sales on the Rise in 2008 According to Hybu Cig Cymru"* in Farmer's Weekly (March 29, 2008, No. 320)
Pub: Reed Elsevier Group plc Reed Business Information
Contact: Mark Kelsey, Chief Executive Officer
Ed: Bob Davies. Description: Due, in part, to marketing efforts, retail sales of Welsh lamb and beef rose significantly in the first two months of 2008.

43623 ■ *"What Keeps Global Leaders Up at Night"* in Harvard Business Review (Vol. 90, April 2012, No. 4, pp. 32)
Pub: Harvard Business Review Press
Contact: Peter E. Walsh, Director
Released: April 2012. Description: A chart uses colored squares to portray economic, environmental, geopolitical, societal, and technological concerns of industry leaders, and ranks them according to likelihood and impact.

43624 ■ *What Works: Success in Stressful Times*
Pub: Harper Press
Ed: Hamish McRae. Released: November 30, 2001. Price: $14.95, paperback. Description: Exploration of success stories from across the glove, and what Michelle Obama referred to as 'the flimsy difference between success and failure.' Why do some initiatives take off while others flounder? How have communities managed to achieve so much while others struggle? What distinguishes the good companies from the bad? What lessons can be learned from the well-ordered Mumbai community made famous by 'Slumdog Millionaire'? Why have Canadian manners helped Whistler become the most popular ski resort in North America?. Availability: Print.

43625 ■ *"What'll You Have Tonight?"* in Barron's (Vol. 88, July 4, 2008, No. 28, pp. 22)
Pub: Dow Jones & Co., Inc.
Contact: Clare Hart, President
Ed: Neil A. Martin. Description: Shares of Diageo could rise by 30 percent a year from June 2008 after

it slipped due to U.S. sales worries. The company also benefits from the trend toward more premium alcoholic beverage brands worldwide especially in emerging markets.

43626 ■ *"Wheatfield First Choice for Canadian Manufacturer"* in Business First Buffalo (November 26, 2007, pp. 1)
Pub: American City Business Journals, Inc.
Ed: James Fink. Description: Niagara County Industrial Development Agency is preparing an enticement program that would lure automotive parts manufacturer Pop & Lock Corporation to shift manufacturing operations to Wheatfield, Niagara County, New York. The package includes job-training grants and assistance for acquiring new machinery. Details of the plan are included.

43627 ■ *"Where Canada Meets the World"* in Canadian Business (Vol. 80, October 8, 2007, No. 20, pp. 86)
Ed: Zena Olijnyk. Description: An overview of facilities within Canada's borders that contributes to the country's economy is presented. The facilities include fishing vessels and seaports. Agencies that regulate the borders such as the Canada Border Services Agency and the Department of Fisheries and Oceans are also presented.

43628 ■ *"Where Michigan Does Business; Canada"* in Crain's Detroit Business (Vol. 30, October 13, 2014, No. 41, pp. 22)
Pub: Crain Communications Inc. - Detroit
Contact: Keith Crain, Chairman
Released: October 13, 2014. Description: Canada is Michigan's closest trading partner. Canada's most significant industries include chemicals, minerals, wood/paper products, food products, transportation equipment, petroleum and natural gas. Canada is also the largest energy supplier to the United States, thus helping Canada's petroleum sector grow. Major export partners of Canada include: U.S. (74.5 percent), China (4.3 percent) and the United Kingdom (4.1 percent). Major exports include motor vehicles and parts, aircraft, telecommunication equipment, chemicals, crude petroleum and natural gas.

43629 ■ *"Where Next?"* in Business Strategy Review (Vol. 21, Summer 2010, No. 2, pp. 20)
Pub: John Wiley & Sons Inc. Scientific, Technical, Medical, and Scholarly Div. (Wiley-Blackwell)
Contact: William J. Pesce, Manager
E-mail: wpesce@wiley.com
Ed: Stuart Crainer. Description: The emergence of large, vibrant and seemingly unstoppable new markets has been the good news story of the past decade. Brazil, Russia, India and China (BRIC) are among those who have emerged blinking into the new economy.

43630 ■ *"Where Oil-Rich Nations Are Placing Their Bets"* in Harvard Business Review (Vol. 86, September 2008, No. 9, pp. 119)
Pub: Harvard Business Review Press
Contact: Peter E. Walsh, Director
Ed: Rawi Abdelal, Ayesha Khan, Tarun Khanna. Description: Investment strategies of the Gulf Cooperation Council nations are examined in addition to how these have impacted the global economy and capitalism.

43631 ■ *"Who Produces for Whom in the World Economy?"* in Canadian Journal of Economics (Vol. 44, November 2011, No. 4, pp. 1403)
Pub: Wiley-Blackwell
Contact: Gordon Tibbitts, President
Ed: Guillaume Daudin, Christine Rifflart, Danielle Schweisguth. Description: For two decades, the share of trade in inputs, also called vertical trade, has been dramatically increasing. In reallocating trade flows to their original input-producing industries and countries, the article suggests a new measure of international trade: 'value-added trade' and makes it possible to answer the question, 'who produces for whom?'.

43632 ■ *Who's Your City? How the Creative Economy is Making Where to Live the Most Important Decision of Your Life*
Pub: Basic Books
Contact: Elizabeth Maguire, Publisher
Ed: Richard Florida. Released: June 30, 2009. Price: $16.99, paperback; £9.99; C$16.99; £11.99. Description: Richard Florida disagrees with the notion that under globalization, a leveling has taken away the economic advantages of any place in particular. Florida believes that globalization has also created higher-level economic activities such as innovation, design, finance, and media to cluster in a smaller number of locations. Availability: PrintE-book.

43633 ■ *"Why Change?"* in Canadian Business (Vol. 80, October 8, 2007, No. 20, pp. 9)
Ed: Joe Chidley. Description: The need for economic change in Canada is discussed. Despite the country's economic growth and low unemployment rate, economic reform is needed in order to maximize its economic potential in the future. Other reasons for the need to further develop its economy, such as the rise of manufacturing and service industries in Asia and the emergence of regional trade pacts in South America are also tackled.

43634 ■ *"Why 'I'm Sorry' Doesn't Always Translate"* in (Vol. 90, June 2012, No. 6, pp. 26)
Pub: Harvard Business Review Press
Contact: Peter E. Walsh, Director
Ed: William W. Maddux, Peter H. Kim, Tetsushi Okumura, Jeanne M. Brett. Released: July 2012. Description: Studies indicate that Americans associate an apology with culpability and personal responsibility, while Japan and other countries with group-oriented cultures view an apology as an acknowledgement that a transgression has occurred and that it is unfortunate. Implications for the role of the apology in negotiations and establishing trust are presented.

43635 ■ *"Why Japan Is So Interested In Alabama"* in Birmingham Business Journal (Vol. 31, August 1, 2014, No. 31, pp. 11)
Pub: American City Business Journals, Inc.
Contact: Whitney Shaw, President
Released: August 1, 2014. Description: Kazuo Sunaga, Consul General of Japan in Atlanta, Georgia lists several reasons why Alabama presents several opportunities for Japanese companies, including fewer labor laws, low tax rates and the availability of trained workers. The state's relationship with Japan will be further enhanced when Birmingham hosts the Southeast U.S./Japan Association meeting in 2015, which will be attended by leaders from the business, political, and nonprofit sectors.

43636 ■ *"Why Optimism Over Europe Won't Last"* in Barron's (Vol. 92, August 25, 2012, No. 38, pp. M6)
Pub: Dow Jones & Co., Inc.
Contact: Clare Hart, President
Ed: Jonathan Buck. Description: European markets could experience losses in the second half of 2012 as uncertainty over political events could wipe out market gains. Greece has to abide by the terms of ts agreements with creditors to receive bailout funds. The stock prices of BG Group could gain as much as 20 percent in 2013 due to its strong lifquified natural gas business.

43637 ■ *"Why U.S. Competitiveness Matters To All Of Us: The World Wants America to Regain It s Vibrancy. Let's Stop Assigning Blame and Instead Focus On Solutions"* in Harvard Business Review (Vol. 90, March 2012, No. 3, pp. 49)
Pub: Harvard Business Review Press
Contact: Peter E. Walsh, Director
Ed: Nitin Nohria. Released: March 2012. Description: The introduction to this special issue presents perspectives on the US economy from citizens of other nations. While they realize globalization means countries are interdependent and that a strong

America provides an international boost, they feel US leaders are concerned more with politics than economic growth. Action is needed instead.

43638 ■ *"Why You Aren't Buying Venezuelan Chocolate" in Harvard Business Review (Vol. 88, December 2010, No. 12, pp. 25)*
Pub: Harvard Business School Publishing
Ed: Rohit Deshpande. **Description:** The concept of provenance paradox is defined as the preconceived notions consumers have about the country of origin of a given product, which can pose significant difficulties for emerging markets. Five strategies are presented for combating this problem, including building on historic events that have informed cultural perspectives.

43639 ■ *"The Wine Spectator" in Business Courier (Vol. 27, November 26, 2010, No. 30, pp. 1)*
Pub: Business Courier
Ed: Dan Monk. **Description:** Vintner Select, a wine distributor, will introduce an internationally known portfolio of more than 50 German and Austrian wines. The company now distributes about 900 different wine labels from 220 producers in 10 countries to smaller, independent retailers in Indiana, Kentucky and Ohio.

43640 ■ *"Winner: Caparo Group Plc" in Crain's Detroit Business (Vol. 24, March 24, 2008, No. 12, pp. 12)*
Pub: Crain Communications Inc.
Contact: Rance E. Crain, President
Ed: Brent Snavely. **Description:** London-based Caparo Group plc saw its acquisition of Voestalpine Polynorm as an opportunity to gain a foothold in the North American automotive industry. Caparo was impressed with the company's breadth of manufacturing capabilities and quality systems as well as with the management team.

43641 ■ *Winner Take All: How Competitiveness Shapes the Fate of Nations*
Pub: Basic Books
Contact: Elizabeth Maguire, Publisher
Ed: Richard J. Elkus, Jr. **Released:** June 16, 2009. **Price:** $27; C$34; £17.99. **Description:** American government and misguided business practices have allowed the U.S. to fall behind other countries in various market sectors such as cameras and televisions, as well as information technologies. It will take a national strategy for America to regain its lead in crucial industries. **Availability:** E-book.

43642 ■ *"Winning Gold" in The Business Journal-Milwaukee (Vol. 25, August 8, 2008, No. 46, pp. A1)*
Pub: American City Business Journals, Inc.
Contact: Whitney Shaw, President
Ed: Rich Rovito. **Description:** Johnson Controls Inc. of Milwaukee, Wisconsin is taking part in the 2008 Beijing Olympics with the installation of its sustainable control equipment and technology that monitor over 58,000 points in 18 Olympic venues. Details of Johnson Controls' green products and sustainable operations in China are discussed.

43643 ■ *"With Whom Do You Trade? Defensive Innovation and the Skill-Bias" in Canadian Journal of Electronics (Vol. 43, November 2010)*
Pub: Journal of the Canadian Economics Association
Ed: Pushan Dutt, Daniel Traca. **Description:** Examination into whether increased trade with ineffective protection of intellectual property has contributed to the skill-deepening of the 1980s. An index of effective protection of intellectual property at the country level, combining data on protection of patents and rule of law are presented. An industry-specific index of this index is given using as weights each country's trade share in the total trade of the industry. A decline is seen in this trade-weighted index, owing to a rise in trade with countries with low effective protection of intellectual property, which explains 29 percent of the rise within-industry skill-intensity.

43644 ■ *"WNY Cashing In On Loonie's Climb" in Business First Buffalo (November 26, 2007, pp. 1)*
Pub: American City Business Journals, Inc.
Ed: G. Scott Thomas. **Description:** Economy of Western New York has rebounded since the 9/11 recession and the rise of the Canadian dollar, which has contributed to the areas economic growth. Canadian shoppers are frequenting markets in the area due to the parity of the U.S. and Canadian dollar. Details of the cross-border shopping and its impact in WNY are discussed.

43645 ■ *"A World of Investors" in Entrepreneur (Vol. 35, November 2007, No. 11, pp. 72)*
Pub: Entrepreneur Press
Contact: Perlman Neil, President
Ed: Gail Dutton. **Description:** Information technology services company mPortal Inc. raised nearly $15 million in financing from venture capital company Friedli Corporate Finance. The biggest international investors are European companies, while the venture capital market is growing in Asia.

43646 ■ *"The World Is Your Oyster" in Canadian Business (Vol. 80, October 22, 2007, No. 21, pp. 140)*
Ed: Regan Ray. **Description:** Business graduates are not that keen on working abroad. Fortune 500 companies are requiring executives to have a multi-country focus. The skill required for jobs abroad, as well as employment opportunities are discussed.

43647 ■ *"A World of Opportunity: Foreign Markets Offer Diversity to Keen Investors" in Canadian Business (Vol. 81, Summer 2008, No. 9)*
Ed: Andrew Wahl. **Description:** International Monetary Fund projected in its 'World Economy Outlook' that there is a 25 percent chance that a global recession will occur in 2008 and 2009. Global growth rate is forecasted at 3.7 percent in 2008. Inflation in Asia emerging markets and forecasts on stock price indexes are presented.

43648 ■ *"The World is Their Classroom" in Crain's Chicago Business (Vol. 31, March 24, 2008, No. 12, pp. 24)*
Pub: Crain Communications Inc.
Contact: Todd Johnson, Publisher
Ed: Samantha Stainburn. **Description:** Due to globalization more business students are studying abroad; 89 percent of eligible students in its executive MBA program went overseas in 2007 compared to 15 percent ten years ago.

43649 ■ *"Wrigley's Newest Taste: Wolfberry" in Crain's Chicago Business (Vol. 31, March 31, 2008, No. 13, pp. 1)*
Pub: Crain Communications Inc.
Contact: Todd Johnson, Publisher
Ed: David Sterrett. **Description:** Wm. Wrigley Jr. Co. has introduced a gum line in China that touts the medicinal advantages of aloe vera to improve skin and wolfberry to boost energy in an attempt to keep the company positioned as the top candy firm in China.

43650 ■ *"Yao Ming Courts China's Wine Boom" in Wall Street Journal Eastern Edition (November 28, 2011, pp. B4)*
Pub: Dow Jones & Co., Inc.
Contact: Clare Hart, President
Ed: Jason Chow. **Description:** Yao Ming, the former NBA 7-foot 6-inch Chinese basketball star, is set to cash in on the market potential for wine in China. He has created his own winery in California, Yao Family Wines, which will produce wines solely for the Chinese market.

43651 ■ *"You Won't Go Broke Filling Up On The Stock" in Barron's (Vol. 88, July 14, 2008, No. 28, pp. 38)*
Pub: Dow Jones & Co., Inc.
Contact: Clare Hart, President
Ed: Assif Shameen. **Description:** Due to high economic growth, pro-business policies and a consumption boom, the Middle East is a good place to look for equities. The best ways in which to gain exposure to this market include investing in the real estate industry and telecommunications markets as well as large banks that serve corporations and consumers.

SOURCES OF SUPPLY

43652 ■ *Importers Manual USA: The Single Source Reference Encyclopedia for Importing to the United States*
World Trade Press
Contact: Roy Hinkelman, Manager
E-mail: roy@worldtradepress.com
URL(s): store.worldtradepress.com/Importers_Manual_USA.php. **Released:** Biennial; latest edition 4, 2003. **Price:** $145, Individuals Hardcover; $108.75, Individuals Sale Price. **Publication includes:** Lists of trade fairs, embassies, chambers of commerce, banks, and other sources of information on various aspects of international trade. **Entries include:** Source name, address, phone, telex, description. Principal content of publication is information on importing to the U.S. , including coverage of U.S. Customs, banking, laws, shipping, and insurance. **Indexes:** Product/service, geographical, source name.

TRADE PERIODICALS

43653 ■ *The International Trade Journal: Western Hemispheric Studies*
Pub: Routledge Journals Taylor & Francis Group
URL(s): www.tandfonline.com/toc/uitj20/current#.UzJ9iqiSxWU. **Ed:** Antonio J. Rodriguez. **Released:** 5/year **Price:** $377, Individuals print only; $582, Institutions online only; $665, Individuals print and online.

43654 ■ *International Trade Reporter*
Pub: Bureau of National Affairs
Contact: James D. Crowne, Managing Editor
URL(s): www.bna.com/international-trade-reporter-p6101/. **Released:** Weekly **Price:** $1,159, Individuals. **Description:** Covers current international trade policies of the U.S. and of major U.S. trading partners. Topics include bilateral negotiations, customs, export/import policy, foreign investment, standards, taxation, and other related issues. Recurring features include a calendar of events, reports of meetings, and notices of publications available.

43655 ■ *International Trade Reporter Decisions*
Pub: Bureau of National Affairs
Contact: James D. Crowne, Managing Editor
URL(s): www.bna.com/international-trade-decisions-p6710/. **Ed:** Linda G. Botsford, Editor, lbotsford@bna.com. **Released:** Biweekly **Description:** Carries digested, classified, and indexed judicial and administrative decisions dealing with legal issues arising from U.S. trade law.

43656 ■ *Journal of Asia-Pacific Business*
Pub: Routledge Journals Taylor & Francis Group
URL(s): www.tandfonline.com/toc/wapb20/current. **Ed:** Riad A. Ajami. **Released:** Quarterly **Price:** $373, Institutions online only; $130, Individuals online only; $415, Institutions print & online; $144, Individuals print & online.

43657 ■ *Journal of East-West Business*
Pub: Routledge Journals Taylor & Francis Group
URL(s): www.tandfonline.com/loi/wjeb20. **Ed:** Erdener Kaynak. **Released:** Quarterly **Price:** $530, Institutions online only; $152, Individuals online only; $606, Institutions print + online; $168, Individuals print + online.

43658 ■ *Ottawa Letter*
Pub: CCH Canadian Ltd.
Contact: Rick Lewis, Manager
URL(s): www.cch.ca/product.aspx?WebID=1637. **Released:** Biweekly **Price:** $1,350, Individuals. **Description:** Reports on current events and topics of Canada, such as free trade, human rights, employment, and defense. Also provides statistics, lending, and foreign exchange rates.

43659 ■ Political Risk Letter
Pub: The PRS Group Inc.
Contact: Mary Lou O. Walsh, Chief Executive Officer
E-mail: mlw@prsgroup.com
URL(s): https://www.prsgroup.com/. Released: Monthly, 12/year. Price: $415, U.S. and Canada. Description: Offers concise political and economic forecasts for both 18 month and 5 year time spans. Provides country risk forecasts and analysis on 100 countries around the world and provides indepth coverage on 20 countries.

43660 ■ SACC In New York
Pub: Swedish-American Chamber of Commerce
Contact: Renee Lundholm, President
E-mail: renee.lundholm@saccny.org
URL(s): saccny.org. Released: Monthly. Price: Included in membership. Description: Concerned with developments in the Swedish and U.S. business communities: unemployment rates, industry plans and investments, exports, government measures to stimulate the economy, and similar subjects. Covers the membership activities of the SACC. Recurring features include interviews with Swedish and U.S. executives.

43661 ■ Washington Tariff & Trade Letter
Pub: Gilston Communications Group
Contact: Samuel M. Gilston, Chief Executive Officer
E-mail: sgilston@comcast.net
URL(s): www.wttlonline.com. Ed: Samuel M. Gilston, Editor. Released: Weekly Price: $597, Individuals print or electronic. Description: Reports on U.S. trade policies, negotiations, regulations, and legislation.

VIDEOCASSETTES/ AUDIOCASSETTES

43662 ■ Building the Trans-National Team
Learning Communications L.L.C.
5520 Trabuco Rd.
Irvine, CA 92620
Free: 800-622-3610
Fax: (949)727-4323
Co. E-mail: sales@learncom.com
URL: http://www.learncom.com
Contact: Lloyd W. Singer, President
Released: 1994. Price: $495. Description: Underlines the difficulties of doing business with people of various nationalities including French, Spanish, German, and British. Focusses on cultural differences. Comes with guide. Availability: VHS.

43663 ■ The Dollars and Sense of Exporting: How to Navigate the Global Market
PBS Home Video
2100 Crystal Dr.
Arlington, VA 22202-3784
URL: http://www.pbs.org
Contact: Pat Mitchell, President
Released: 1989. Price: $300. Description: Helpful information for companies that wish to enter or expand in the international marketplace. Includes tips on assistance offered by various levels of government. Availability: VHS; 3/4 U.

CONSULTANTS

43664 ■ 2010 Fund 5
24351 Spartan St.
Mission Viejo, CA 92691-3920
Ph: (949)583-1992
Fax: (949)583-0474
Contact: Wally Eater, Principal
Scope: Funds in formation that will invest in technologies licensed from 30 universities. Founded: 1982.

43665 ■ Americas Consulting Group Inc.
[Americas Project Management Services]
741 Riversville Rd.
Greenwich, CT 06831-2626
Ph: (203)863-9168

Fax: (203)863-9161
Co. E-mail: contact@americaspms.com
Contact: Laurent Martinez, Managing Director
E-mail: l.martinez@americaspms.com
Scope: A consultant whose expertise is in assisting companies in developing growth strategies within the western hemisphere. Also expertise's in international business with a special focus on marketing, information acquisition and investigations. Founded: 1998.

43666 ■ Cohen & Associates
1625 Holly Ln.
Munster, IN 46321
Ph: (219)923-3133
Fax: (219)923-2622
Contact: Chaim J. Cohen, Owner
Scope: Domestic and international business development. Counsels companies from the start-up stage through the opening of foreign markets. Import/Export strategies, general management consulting, marketing planning and business development. Founded: 1990.

43667 ■ First Washington Associates Ltd.
1501 Lee Hwy., Ste. 102
Arlington, VA 22209-1047
Ph: (703)525-0966
Contact: Delio E. Gianturco, President
Scope: Provider of technical assistance in all aspects of international trade finance, small business development and related disciplines, including feasibility studies, market research, design and implementation of export credit, guarantee and insurance programs, formulation of policies, procedures and programs for public and private sector clients. Founded: 1977.

43668 ■ Global Business Consultants (GBC)
200 Lake Hills Rd.
Pinehurst, NC 28374 0776
Ph: (910)295-5991
Co. E-mail: gbc@pinehurst.net
Contact: Nan S. Leaptrott, President
E-mail: nan@yourculturecoach.com
Scope: Firm specializes in human resources management; project management; software development; and international trade. Offers litigation support. Founded: 1987. Publications: "Culture to Culture: Mission Trip Do's and Don'ts," Jul, 2005; "Rules of the Game: Global Business Protocol". Seminars: Cross-Cultural Training.

43669 ■ Great Lakes Consulting Group Inc.
54722 Little Flower Trl.
Mishawaka, IN 46545
Ph: (574)287-4500
Contact: James E. Schrager, President
Scope: Provides consulting services in the areas of strategic planning; feasibility studies; start-up businesses; small business management; mergers and acquisitions; joint ventures; divestitures; interim management; crisis management; turnarounds; business process re-engineering; venture capital; and international trade. Founded: 1989.

43670 ■ Intex Exhibit Systems L.L.C.
1846 Sequoia Ave.
Orange, CA 92868
Ph: (714)940-0369
Free: 800-331-6633
Fax: (714)935-0223
Co. E-mail: info@intexexhibits.com
URL: http://www.intexexhibits.com
Contact: Matthias D. Kemeny, President
E-mail: mdk@intexexhibits.com
Scope: Specializes in the design and production of exhibits, displays and pavilions for world fairs, tradeshows and similar events. Services include product design, industrial and engineering design for educational exhibits, museum exhibits and science and technology museology. Serves private industry as well as government agencies. Founded: 1979. Publications: "Trade Show Marketing," Sep, 2000; "Exhibitor Times," 1998. Special Services: Fastpack™; Panelflo™; affordable-1™; thegraphic arm™; Expression™; TigerMark™.

43671 ■ Nightingale Associates
7445 Setting Sun Way
Columbia, MD 21046

Ph: (410)381-4280
Co. E-mail: fredericknightingale@nightingaleassociates.net
URL: http://www.nightingaleassociates.net
Contact: Frederick C. Nightingale, Managing Director
E-mail: fredericknightingale@nightingaleassociates.net
Scope: Management training and consulting firm offering the following skills: productivity and accomplishment; leadership skills for the experienced manager; management skills for the new manager; leadership and teambuilding; supervisory development; creative problem solving; real strategic planning; providing superior customer service; international purchasing and supply chain management; negotiation skills development and fundamentals of purchasing. Founded: 1984. Seminars: Productivity and Accomplishment Management Skills for the New Manager; Leadership and Team building; Advanced Management; Business Process Re engineering; Strategic Thinking; Creative Problem Solving; Customer Service; International Purchasing and Materials Management; Fundamentals of Purchasing; Negotiation Skills Development; Providing superior customer service; Leadership skills for the experienced manager.

43672 ■ Plans and Solutions Inc.
7823 Mistic View Ct.
Derwood, MD 20855
Ph: (301)947-8150
Fax: (240)525-5601
Co. E-mail: info@plansandsolutions.com
URL: http://www.plansandsolutions.com
Contact: Kenneth D. Weiss, President
E-mail: kw@plansandsolutions.com
Scope: Market research and competitive analysis; marketing and promotion planning, and executing promotion plans. Specializes in registration and problem solving services that include food canning establishment and process registration, registration under the terrorism act, assistance in case of detention of shipments, and on-site inspection of processing plants and records. Most clients are minority-owned businesses in the USA and companies overseas that want to begin or increase exports to the United States and Canada. Founded: 1996. Publications: "Building an Import/Export Business," John Wiley & Sons, 2002; "How to Conquer the U.S. Market"; "Going Global (Getting Started in International Trade)". Seminars: U.S. Import Regulations on Food Products.

43673 ■ Ralph J. Sigona Associates
1575 Center Ave.
Fort Lee, NJ 07024-4644
Ph: (201)461-3067
Contact: Ralph J. Sigona, President
Scope: International business consultants offering these services: Formulation and execution of commercial and marketing programs for imported and/or exported products in the United States, in Europe and in other major world markets; search for and selection of importers and distributors for the introduction of manufactured products in foreign markets; market research and market intelligence services; evaluation and implementation of business and product opportunities on behalf of qualified clients. Serves private industries as well as government agencies. Founded: 1981. Seminars: How to Sell Overseas, International Marketing Procedures and Practices.

COMPUTERIZED DATABASES

43674 ■ Antitrust & Trade Regulation Report
Bloomberg BNA
3 Bethesda Metro Center, Ste. 250
Bethesda, MD 20814-5377
Ph: (703)341-3000
Free: 800-372-1033
Fax: (800)253-0332
Co. E-mail: customercare@bna.com
URL: http://www.bna.com
Contact: Gregory McCaffrey, President
Availability: Online: LexisNexis; Bloomberg BNA; Thomson Reuters - Westlaw. Type: Full-text.

43675 ■ _Business Browser North America_
OneSource Information Services Inc.
300 Baker Ave.
Concord, MA 01742-2131
Ph: (978)318-4300
Free: 800-554-5501
Fax: (978)318-4690
Co. E-mail: Support@onesource.com
URL: http://www.onesource.com
Contact: Philip J. Garlick, President
Availability: Online: OneSource Information Services
Inc. **Type:** Directory; Numeric; Statistical; Full-text.

43676 ■ _EIU ViewsWire_
The Economist Intelligence Unit Ltd.
26 Red Lion Sq.
London WC1R 4HQ, United Kingdom
Ph: 44 020 7576 8181
Fax: 44 020 7576 8476
Co. E-mail: emea@eiu.com
URL: http://www.eiu.com
Contact: Andrew Rashbass, Director
Availability: Online: LexisNexis; The Economist Intel-
ligence Unit Ltd. **Type:** Full-text; Numeric.

43677 ■ _Global Business Browser_
OneSource Information Services Inc.
300 Baker Ave.
Concord, MA 01742-2131
Ph: (978)318-4300
Free: 800-554-5501
Fax: (978)318-4690
Co. E-mail: Support@onesource.com
URL: http://www.onesource.com
Contact: Philip J. Garlick, President
Availability: Online: OneSource Information Services
Inc. **Type:** Directory; Numeric; Statistical; Full-text.

43678 ■ _International Trade Reporter™_
Bloomberg BNA
3 Bethesda Metro Center, Ste. 250
Bethesda, MD 20814-5377
Ph: (703)341-3000
Free: 800-372-1033
Fax: (800)253-0332
Co. E-mail: customercare@bna.com
URL: http://www.bna.com
Contact: Gregory McCaffrey, President
URL(s): www.bna.com/international-trade-reporter-
p6101. **Availability:** Online: Bloomberg BNA; Thom-
son Reuters - Westlaw. **Type:** Full-text.

**43679 ■ _United States International Trade in
Goods and Services_**
U.S. Census Bureau Foreign Trade Division
4600 Silver Hill Rd.
Washington, DC 20233-0001
Free: 800-549-0595
Co. E-mail: ftdwebmaster@census.gov
URL: http://www.census.gov/foreign-trade
Contact: Robert Groves, Director
Availability: Online: U.S. Census Bureau - Foreign
Trade Division. **Type:** Statistical.

**43680 ■ _Ward's Business Directory of U.S.
Private and Public Companies_**
Cengage Learning Inc.
20 Channel Center St.
Boston, MA 02210
Ph: (617)289-7700
Free: 800-487-8488
Fax: (617)289-7844
Co. E-mail: investors@cengage.com
URL: http://www.cengage.com
Contact: Michael Hansen, Chief Executive Officer
URL(s): www.cengage.com/search/productOverview.
do?Ntt=2677896851550767518288621891942626
816&N=197+4294904996&Ntk=P_EPI. **Released:**
Annual; 56th edition. **Price:** Edition 56, 8-vol. set,
$4,485.00 (includes inter-edition supplement). Some
individual volumes also sold separately.; $3,627,
Individuals five-volume set; $3,205, Individuals four-
volume set; $1,697, Individuals volumes 5, 6, or 7;

$1,149, Individuals volume 8. **Covers:** Approximately
112,000 companies, 90% of which are privately
owned, representing all industries. **Entries include:**
Company name, address, phone, fax, toll-free, e-mail,
URL, names and titles of up to five officers, up to four
Standard Industrial Classification (SIC) codes, NAICS
code, revenue figure, number of employees, year
founded, ticker symbol, stock exchange, immediate
parent, fiscal year end, import/export, type of company (public, private, subsidiary, etc.). In Vol. 4, lists
of top 1,000 privately held companies ranked by sales
vol., top 1,000 publicly held companies ranked by
sales volume, and top 1,000 employers ranked by
number of employees; analyses of public and private
companies by state, revenue per employee for top
1,000 companies, public and private companies by
SIC code and NAICS code. In volume 5, national
Standard Industrial Classification (SIC) code rankings
are listed, while volumes 6 and 7 lists Standard
Industrial Classification (SIC) code rankings by state.
In all volumes, guide to abbreviations, codes, and
symbols; explanation of classification system; numerical and alphabetical listings of SIC and NAICS codes.
In volume 8, NAICS rankings. In the supplement,
10,000 new listings not contained in the main edition
are included. **Arrangement:** Volumes 1, 2, and 3,
alphabetical; volume 4 is geographical by state, then
ascending zip; volume 5 is classified by 4-digit SIC
code, then ranked by sales; volumes 6 and 7 are
classified by Standard Industrial Classification (SIC)
code within state; volume 8 classified by NAICS, then
ranked; supplement arranged alphabetical and
Standard Industrial Classification (SIC) code. **Indexes:** Company name index in volumes 5, 7, and 8.
Availability: Online: Cengage Learning Inc. CD-
ROM: Cengage Learning Inc. **Type:** Directory;
Numeric.

LIBRARIES

**43681 ■ Canada Department of Foreign
Affairs and International Trade - Main Library
[Affaires Etrangeres et Commerce
International Canada - Bibliotheque]**
Lester B. Pearson Bldg.
125 Sussex Dr.
Ottawa, ON, Canada K1A 0G2
Ph: (613)992-6150
Fax: (613)944-0222
Co. E-mail: library-biblio.aiml@international.gc.ca
URL: http://www.international.gc.ca/library-
bibliotheque
Contact: Jo-Anne Valentine, Librarian
Scope: International relations, International law,
International economics, trade, investment, Interna-
tional organizations. **Services:** Interlibrary loan; copy-
ing; library open to the public with restrictions.
Founded: 1909. **Holdings:** 50,000 books; 30,000
bound periodical volumes; 550,000 documents;
200,000 microforms; 800 maps.

**43682 ■ Canadian International Trade
Tribunal Library [Tribunal Canadien du
Commerce Exterieur]**
333 Laurier Ave. W, 15th Fl.
Ottawa, ON, Canada K1A 0G7
Ph: (613)990-2452
Fax: (613)990-2439
Co. E-mail: secretary-secretaire@citt-tcce.gc.ca
URL: http://www.citt.gc.ca
Contact: Ursula Schultz, Librarian
Scope: Trade, tariffs, customs and excise, Canadian
law, commerce, economics. **Services:** Interlibrary
loan; copying; library open to the public by appoint-
ment. **Founded:** 1989. **Holdings:** 6000 books; 1000
bound periodical volumes. **Subscriptions:** 300
journals and other serials; 12 newspapers.

**43683 ■ Ontario Ministry of Economic
Development and Trade - InfoSource**
900 Bay St.
Hearst Block, 8th Fl.
Toronto, ON, Canada M7A 2E1

Ph: (416)325-6666
Fax: (416)325-6688
Co. E-mail: info@edt.gov.on.ca
Scope: Trade, industry, small business, manage-
ment, company information, economic development.
Services: Copying; scanning. **Founded:** 1994. **Hold-
ings:** 200 books; microfiche; 20 CD-ROMs.

43684 ■ Woodbury University Library
7500 Glenoaks Blvd.
Burbank, CA 91504-1052
Ph: (818)252-5201
Fax: (818)767-4534
Co. E-mail: jennifer.rosenfeld@woodbury.edu
URL: http://library.woodbury.edu
Contact: Nedra Peterson, Director
Scope: Business and management, International
business, art, architecture, interior design, fashion
marketing and design, psychology, animation. **Services:** Interlibrary loan; copying; Library open to the
public for reference use only. **Founded:** 1884. **Holdings:** 65,000 books; 3070 bound periodical volumes;
17,401 slides; 2000 DVD/VHS. **Subscriptions:** 300
journals and other serials; 5 newspapers.

RESEARCH CENTERS

**43685 ■ Georgia Institute of Technology -
Enterprise Innovation Institute**
75 5th St.
Atlanta, GA 30308
Ph: (404)894-6986
Fax: (404)894-1192
Co. E-mail: stephen.fleming@innovate.gatech.edu
URL: http://innovate.gatech.edu
Contact: Stephen Fleming, Vice President
Scope: International standards and quality, particu-
larly exporting to European Community and Asian
markets. Provides information, training and technical
assistance and conducts research for southeastern
firms interested in exporting. **Services:** Market
Analysis; Product Analysis; Quality Assessments; Re-
engineering and Design Services; Standards Interpre-
tation; Standards Updating Service. **Founded:** 1991.
Publications: _European Market Bulletin_; _European
Standards Directory_ (Annual); _Standards Newsletter_.
Educational Activities: Seminars and workshops on
standards-related topics; Training Seminars and
Workshops.

**43686 ■ University of Maryland at College
Park - Center for Global Business Education
(CGBE)**
2410 Van Munching Hall
Robert H. Smith School of Business
College Park, MD 20742-1815
Ph: (301)405-0200
Fax: (301)314-9526
Co. E-mail: lbarnard@rhsmith.umd.edu
URL: http://www.rhsmith.umd.edu/global
Contact: Lisa Barnard, Director
Scope: Global business and management. **Founded:**
1990. **Educational Activities:** CGBE Conferences
and workshops.

**43687 ■ University of Maryland at College
Park - International Communications and
Negotiations Simulations (ICONS)**
0145 Tydings Hall
Department of Government & Politics
College Park, MD 20742
Ph: (301)405-4172
Fax: (301)314-9301
Co. E-mail: dfridl@umd.edu
URL: http://www.icons.umd.edu
Contact: Daniella Fridl, Director
Scope: Focuses on the critical connections between
international issues and the perspectives that differ-
ent cultures bring to negotiations. Also teaches cross
cultural negotiation and develops international
economic, environmental, and political scenarios/cur-
riculum materials for university and high school
students. **Founded:** 1982.

Intrapreneurship

REFERENCE WORKS

43688 ■ *"Black Gold: Jobs Aplenty"* in *Canadian Business (Vol. 79, August 14, 2006, No. 16-17, pp. 57)*
Pub: Rogers Media Inc.
Contact: Tony Viner, President
Ed: Erin Pooley. **Description:** A list of the top ten jobs in the petroleum industry in Canada along with pay and nature of jobs, is presented.

43689 ■ *"Diana Bonta -- Keeping People Healthy and Thriving"* In *Hispanic Business (Vol. 30, April 2008, No. 4, pp. 30)*
Pub: Hispanic Business Inc.
Contact: Jesus Chavarria, President
Ed: Leanndra Martinez. **Description:** Diana Bonta serves as vice president of public affairs for Kaiser Permanente and is a strong advocate for health reform and improving access to health care. In order to better serve the underinsured and uninsured, she directs Kaiser's Community Benefit division that devoted $369 million last year to this cause.

43690 ■ *"Female Hispanic Professionals by the Number"* in *Hispanic Business (Vol. 30, April 2008, No. 4, pp. 8)*
Description: More executive opportunities are presenting themselves for future generations of Hispanic women who are more frequently being found in high-level positions. Statistical data included.

43691 ■ *"The Ten Worst Leadership Habits"* in *Canadian Business (Vol. 81, March 31, 2008, No. 5, pp. 63)*
Pub: Rogers Media Inc.
Contact: Tony Viner, President
Ed: Michael Stern. **Description:** Ten leadership behaviors that aspiring leaders need to avoid are presented. These include expecting colleagues and subordinates to be like themselves, attending too many meetings, being miserly when it comes to recognition and praise, and giving an opinion often.

43692 ■ *"The Trusty Sidekick"* in *Canadian Business (Vol. 81, March 31, 2008, No. 5, pp. 33)*
Pub: Rogers Media Inc.
Contact: Tony Viner, President
Ed: John Gray. **Description:** Being second-in-command is a good opportunity to be mentored by the boss and puts the executive in the position to see the whole organization and have influence to make changes. However, the chief operating officer has the unenviable task of trying to achieve unattainable goals. Executives who want to become the right hand man must go beyond their job description.

43693 ■ *"The Winner's Circle: Hispanic Business Magazine's Elite Women"* in *Hispanic Business (Vol. 30, April 2008, No. 4, pp. 20)*
Pub: Hispanic Business Inc.
Contact: Jesus Chavarria, President
Ed: Hildy Medina. **Description:** Although there has been progress concerning Hispanic women profes-sionals who are growing in numbers in the upper echelons of the corporate arena, many still find that they face discrimination when it comes to pay and promotions. Statistical data included.

43694 ■ *"Young Giants"* in *Canadian Business (Vol. 79, August 14, 2006, No. 16-17, pp. 47)*
Ed: Brad Purdy. **Description:** New generations of young chiefs of oil and gas companies in Canada, are featured.

VIDEOCASSETTES/ AUDIOCASSETTES

43695 ■ *Inspiring Innovation*
American Management Association (AMA)
1601 Broadway
New York, NY 10019-7420
Ph: (212)586-8100
Free: 877-566-9441
Fax: (212)903-8168
Co. E-mail: customerservice@amanet.org
URL: http://www.amanet.org
Contact: Edward T. Reilly, President
Released: 19??. **Price:** $545. **Description:** Contains information on how to get started with the idea of innovation. **Availability:** VHS; CC.

EARLY STAGE FINANCING

43696 ■ *"Acacia Subsidiary Acquires Patents Related to Shared Memory for Multimedia Processing from a Major Corporation" in Economics & Business Week (April 26, 2014, pp. 5)*
NewsRX
2727 Paces Ferry Rd. SE, Ste. 2-440
Atlanta, GA 30339
Ph: (770)507-7777
Free: 800-726-4550
Fax: (770)435-6800
Co. E-mail: techsupport@newsrx.com
URL: http://www.newsrx.com
Contact: Susan E. Hasty, Publisher
Released: April 26, 2014. **Description:** Acacia Research Corporation that a subsidiary has acquired U.S. patents and foreign counterparts related to the use of shared memory in multimedia processing systems such as mobile phones, tablets and other consumer electronic devices.

START-UP INFORMATION

43697 ■ *"Brand Storytelling Becomes a Booming Business" in Entrepreneur (April 2012)*
Pub: Entrepreneur Press
Contact: Perlman Neil, President
Released: April 2012. **Description:** San Francisco-based Story House Creative engages in helping small businesses connect with their audience in communicating their brand identity. Web content, bios and tag lines are some of the marketing materials Story House Creative creates for its clients. The company also does search engine optimization, video, design, and copywriting. The Brandery, another brand-building company, helps startups promote their business. Eight to ten Brandery mentors are assigned to assist each startup client. Meanwhile, Brand Journalists is a Tennessee-based company focusing on corporate storytelling. It offers Web and blog content, human stories reporting and ghostwriting services.

43698 ■ *"Do Cool Sh*t: Quit Your Day Job, Start Your Own Business, and Live Happily Ever After"*
Pub: Harper Business
Released: August 6, 2013. **Price:** , $24.99. **Description:** Serial social entrepreneur, angel investor, and woman business leader, Miki Agrawal, teaches how to start and run a successful new business. She covers all issues from brainstorming, to raising money to getting press without any connections, and still have time to enjoy life. She created WILD, a farm-to-table pizzeria in New York City and Las Vegas; partnered in a children's multimedia company called Super Sprowtz,, a story-driven nutrition program for children; and launched a patented high-tech underware business called THINX. Agrawal also discusses the growth in her businesses.

43699 ■ *"Eat 'em If You Got 'em" in Entrepreneur (June 2014)*
Pub: Entrepreneur Media Inc.
Released: June 2014. **Description:** Dixie Elixirs and Edibles developed cannabis-infused products for the adult retail marijuana market in Colorado. The startup uses a variety of delivery systems for THC, the active ingredient in cannabis, including carbonated beverages, mints, capsules, and oils. The company, founded by Tripp Keber, is looking to build its own brand and eventually expand outside the state by licensing the brand and its recipes.

43700 ■ *Entrepreneurship Strategy: Changing Patterns in New Venture Creation, Growth, and Reinvention*
Pub: Pine Forge Press
Contact: Blaise R. Simqu, President
Ed: Lisa K. Gundry, Jill R. Kickul. **Released:** 2007. **Price:** $122. **Description:** Entrepreneurial strategies that incorporate new venture emergence, early growth, and reinvention and innovation are examined. **Availability:** Print.

43701 ■ *"Firefighter Wins ABC's American Inventor" in Hispanic Business (August 2, 2007, pp. 94)*
Pub: Hispanic Business Inc.
Contact: Jesus Chavarria, President
Description: Greg Chavez, firefighter, won ABC televisions American Inventor award of $1 million for his Guardian Angel invention. The device makes Christmas trees safer.

43702 ■ *"The Innovator's Method: Bringing the Lean Start-up into Your Organization"*
Pub: Harvard Business Review Press
Contact: Peter E. Walsh, Director
Released: August 19, 2014. **Price:** , $30.00. **Description:** The innovator's method was developed using research inside corporations and successful startups to create, refine, and bring ideas and inventions to the marketplace. Advice is provided to test, validate and commercialize ideas with the lean, design, and agile techniques used by successful startups.

43703 ■ *"Made@Mayo" in Business Journal (Vol. 32, June 6, 2014, No. 2, pp. 10)*
Pub: American City Business Journals
Released: June 6, 2014. **Description:** Rochester, Minnesota-based Mayo Clinic Ventures has managed the licensing of Mayo Clinic technologies and invests in startups. Mayo Clinic Ventures has a $100 million growth fund for investing in startups and two smaller funds worth about $500,000 combined. Insights on the stories of Mayo researchers leading startups are also provided.

43704 ■ *"Making 'Freemium' Work: Many Start-Ups Fail to Recgonize the Challenges of This Popular Business Model" in Harvard Business Review (Vol. 92, May 2014, No. 5, pp. 27)*
Pub: Harvard Business Publishing
Released: May 2014. **Description:** The key to successful 'freemium' business model is identifying which features to offer free of charge, and how to price the remaining features. Target conversion rates conversion life cycle preparation, and commitment to innovation are also discussed.

43705 ■ *Mommy Millionaire: How I Turned My Kitchen Table Idea Into a Million Dollars and How You Can, Too!*
Pub: Palgrave Macmillan
Contact: Lisa Dunn, Manager
E-mail: l.dunn@palgrave.com
Ed: Kim Lavine. **Released:** February 2008. **Price:** $17.99, paperback; $7.99. **Description:** Advice, secrets and lessons for making a million dollars from a mom who turned her kitchen into a successful business; tools cover developing and patenting an idea, cold calling, trade shows, QVC, big retailers, manufacturing, and raising venture capital. **Availability:** PrintE-book.

43706 ■ *The Mousedriver Chronicles: The True-Life Adventures Of Two First-time Entrepreneurs*
Pub: The Perseus Books Group
Contact: David Steinberger, President
E-mail: david.steinberger@perseusbooks.com
Ed: John Lusk, Kyle Harrison. **Released:** April 29, 2009. **Price:** $16.95; C$21.50. **Description:** Entrepreneurial voyage through the startup business of two ivy-league business school graduates and the lessons they learned while developing their idea of a computer mouse that looks like a golf driver into the marketplace. The book is an inspiration for those looking to turn an idea into a company. **Availability:** E-book.

43707 ■ *"The Self Starting Entrepreneurs Handbook"*
Pub: CreateSpace
Contact: Daren Giles, President
Released: September 24, 2014. **Price:** , $17.95 paperback. **Description:** Information for starting a business is provided. Advice is given for writing a business plan, naming your new business, obtaining a business license if required, and building a marketing strategy for entrepreneurs.

43708 ■ *"So You Want To Be a Food Truck Vendor?" in Philadelphia Business Journal (Vol. 33, August 15, 2014, No. 27, pp. 7)*
Pub: American City Business Journals
Released: August 15, 2014. **Description:** Food truck vendors assert that the most challenging part of starting a food truck business is acquiring a license as well as the price and number of licenses and permits required. Other costs include additional fees to vend in prime locations, maintenance, and inventory.

43709 ■ *"Steal Your Success" in Canadian Business (Vol. 87, July 2014, No. 7, pp. 64)*
Pub: George Media Inc.
Released: July 2014. **Description:** The act of borrowing an idea to start a business can be critical to success when its done effectively. Imitation is as important as innovation and entrepreneurs need to realize that great ideas are often borrowed.

43710 ■ *"Troy Patent Law Firm Launches Rent-Free Tech Incubator"* in *Crain's Detroit Business (Vol. 25, June 8, 2009, No. 23, pp. 4)*
Pub: Crain Communications Inc. - Detroit
Contact: Keith Crain, Chairman
Ed: Tom Henderson. **Description:** Young Basile Hanlon MacFarlane & Helmholdt PC, a patent law firm located in Troy, Michigan has created a small, rent-free technology incubator on site. The incubator will be called North Woodward Tech Incubator and has room for four or five startups. The incubator is for the earliest or pre-seed stage for entrepreneurs who have not yet gotten significant investment capital.

ASSOCIATIONS AND OTHER ORGANIZATIONS

43711 ■ **American Society of Inventors (ASI)**
PO Box 354
Feasterville, PA 19053
Ph: (215)546-6601
Co. E-mail: info@asoi.org
URL: http://asoi.org
Description: Engineers, scientists, businessmen, and others who are interested in a cooperative effort to serve both the short- and long-term needs of the inventor and society. Works with government and industry to improve the environment for the inventor. Aims to encourage invention and innovation; help the independent inventor become self-sufficient. Establishes a networking system for inventors and businessmen to solve problems. Sponsors educational programs. **Founded:** 1953. **Publications:** *Inventors Digest* (Annual).

43712 ■ **International Licensing Industry Merchandisers' Association (LIMA)**
350 5th Ave., Ste. 4019
New York, NY 10118
Ph: (212)244-1944
Fax: (212)563-6552
Co. E-mail: info@licensing.org
URL: http://www.licensing.org
Contact: Charles M. Riotto, President
Description: Companies and individuals engaged in the marketing and servicing of licensed properties, both as agents and as property owners; manufacturers and retailers in the licensing business; supporters of the licensing industry. Professional association for the licensing industry worldwide. Objectives are to establish a standard reflecting a professional and ethical management approach to the marketing of licensed properties; to become the leading source of information in the industry; to communicate this information to members and others in the industry through publishing, public speaking, seminars, and an open line; to represent the industry in trade and consumer media and in relationships with the government, retailers, manufacturers, other trade associations, and the public. Conducts research programs. Compiles statistics; maintains hall of fame and placement service. **Founded:** 1985. **Publications:** *LIMA BottomLine* (Quarterly); *LIMA Worldwide Licensing Resource Directory* (Annual). **Educational Activities:** Licensing International and Licensing University (Annual). **Awards:** LIMA International Licensing Award (Annual).

43713 ■ **International Trademark Association (INTA) - Library**
655 3rd Ave., 10th Fl.
New York, NY 10017-5617
Ph: (212)642-1700
Fax: (212)768-7796
Co. E-mail: info@inta.org
URL: http://www.inta.org
Contact: Gregg Marrazzo, President
URL(s): www.inta.org/cle. **Description:** Trademark owners; associate members are lawyers, law firms, advertising agencies, designers, market researchers, and others in the trademark industries. Seeks to: protect the interests of the public in the use of trademarks and trade names; promote the interests of members and of trademark owners generally in the use of their trademarks and trade names; disseminate information concerning the use, registration, and protection of trademarks in the United States, its territories, and in foreign countries. Maintains job bank and speakers' bureau. **Scope:** trademarks. **Services:** Limited services to the public. **Founded:** 1878. **Holdings:** 2000 books; 80 bound periodical volumes. **Publications:** *The Trademarker Reporter* (Bimonthly); *International Trademark Association--Membership Directory; INTA Bulletin* (Biweekly); *The Trademark Reporter* (Bimonthly). **Educational Activities:** International Trademark Association Meeting (Annual). **Awards:** International Trademark Association-Ladas Memorial Awards (Annual).

43714 ■ **Inventors Assistance League (IAL)**
1053 Colorado Blvd., Ste. G1
Los Angeles, CA 90041
Ph: (818)246-6542
Free: 877-433-2246
Fax: (818)246-6546
URL: http://www.inventions.org
Contact: Rusty Ruscetta, Chief Executive Officer
Description: Inventors and manufacturers. Helps inventors get their products into the marketplace and assists manufacturers in finding new products to make and market. Brings together inventors and manufacturers for mutual benefit. Maintains speakers' bureau, small museum, and hall of fame. **Founded:** 1963. **Publications:** *Inventor's Advisory.*

43715 ■ **National Inventors Foundation (NIF)**
Inventors Assistance League
1053 Colorado Blvd., Ste. G1
Los Angeles, CA 90041
Ph: (818)246-6542
Free: 877-433-2246
Fax: (818)246-6546
Co. E-mail: rustyr@earthlink.net
URL: http://www.inventions.org
Description: Independent inventors united to educate individuals regarding the protection and promotion of inventions and new products. Instructs potential inventors on patent laws and how to protect their inventions through methods developed by the foundation. Teaches advertising, sales and marketing techniques to get ideas into the marketplace to determine their commercial value. Assists individuals throughout the U.S. and in 44 other countries. Maintains speakers' bureau, hall of fame, and museum. **Scope:** patents, copyrights, trademarks, sales, advertising and marketing. **Founded:** 1963. **Subscriptions:** 1800.

REFERENCE WORKS

43716 ■ *"26 Things Holding Canadians Back"* in *Canadian Business (Vol. 85, August 13, 2012, No. 13, pp. 27)*
Pub: George Media Inc.
Released: August 13, 2012. **Description:** A list of the problems that Canada needs to address in order to succeed as an economic superpower is presented. Some of these barriers include declining fertility rate, rising percentage of overweight and obese, and obsolete copyright laws.

43717 ■ *"100 Brilliant Companies"* in *Entrepreneur (May 2014)*
Pub: Entrepreneur Media Inc.
Released: May 2014. **Description:** Entrepreneur magazine annually selects 100 companies, ideas, innovations and applications which the editors feel offer unique, simple and high-tech solutions to various everyday problems. These may include design developments, innovations in wearable gadgets, travel applications and other new ideas which represent 21st Century breakthroughs and thinking outside the box. The list is divided into ten categories, including Fashion, The Human Factor, and Travel and Transportation.

43718 ■ *"ABM Janitorial Services Receives Service Excellence Award from Jones Lang LaSalle"* in *Investment Weekly News (July 16, 2011, pp. 75)*
Pub: NewsRX
Contact: Susan E. Hasty, Publisher
Description: ABM Janitorial Services was awarded the 2010 Jones Lang LaSalle Distinction award in the category of Service Excellence. LaSalle is a leading financial and professional services firm that specializes in real estate services and investment management. The program recognizes supplier partners who play a vital role in LaSalle's aim to provide the highest quality of services, value and innovation to clients.

43719 ■ *The Accidental Entrepreneur: The 50 Things I Wish Someone Had Told Me About Starting a Business*
Pub: AMACOM
Contact: Edward T. Reilly, Manager
Ed: Susan Urquhart-Brown. **Released:** May 2008. **Price:** $17.95, Paper or Softback. **Description:** Advice is offered to any would-be entrepreneur, including eight questions to ask before launching a new business, ten traits of a successful entrepreneur, how to obtain licenses and selling permits, best way to create a business plan, ten ways to get referrals, six secrets of marketing, investment and financial information, ways to avoid burnout, and the seven biggest pitfalls to avoid. **Availability:** Print.

43720 ■ *Achieving Planned Innovation: A Proven System for Creating Successful New Products and Services*
Pub: Simon & Schuster Higher Education Group
Contact: Larry Norton, President
Ed: Frank R. Bacon. **Released:** August 2007. **Price:** $16.95. **Description:** Planned innovation is a disciplined and practical step-by-step sequence of procedures for reaching the intended destination point: successful products. This easy-to-read book explains the system along with an action-oriented program for continuous success in new-product innovations. Five steps outlined include: a disciplined reasoning process; lasting market orientation; proper selection criteria that reflect both strategic and tactical business objectives and goals along with dynamic matching of resources to present and future opportunities, and positive and negative requirements before making major expenditures; and proper organizational staffing. The author explains what to do and evaluating the potential of any new product or service, ranging from ventures in retail distribution to the manufacture of goods as diverse as bicycles, motorcycles, aerospace communication and navigation equipment, small business computers, food packaging, and medical products. **Availability:** Print.

43721 ■ *"Adams Morgan Moratorium Lifts on Eatery Liquor Licenses"* in *Washington Business Journal (Vol. 33, July 11, 2014, No. 12, pp. 6)*
Pub: American City Business Journals
Released: July 11, 2014. **Description:** The Washington DC Alcoholic Beverage Control Board has lifted its moratorium on restaurant liquor licenses in Adams Morgan. The move will allow new restaurants to apply for Class C Licenses. However, the board has retained its ban on new tavern or nightclub licenses.

43722 ■ *"All Indicators in Michigan Innovation Index Drop in 4Q"* in *Crain's Detroit Business (Vol. 25, June 22, 2009, No. 25, pp. 9)*
Pub: Crain Communications Inc. - Detroit
Contact: Keith Crain, Chairman
Ed: Ryan Beene. **Description:** Economic indicators that rate Michigan's innovation fell in the fourth quarter of 2008. The index of trademark applications, SBA loans, venture capital funding, new incorporations and other indicators traced dropped 12.6 points.

43723 ■ *"American Chemistry Council Launches Flagship Blog"* in *Ecology,Environment & Conservation Business (October 29, 2011, pp. 5)*
Pub: Highbeam Research
Contact: Patrick Spain, Chief Executive Officer
Description: American Chemistry Council (ACC) launched its blog, American Chemistry Matters, where interactive space allows bloggers to respond to news coverage and to discuss policy issues and their impact on innovation, competitiveness, job creation and safety.

43724 ■ *"Are You a Young Canadian Entrepreneur Looking for Recognition?"* in

CNW Group (November 10, 2010)
Pub: COMTEX
Contact: Chip Brian, President
Description: Business Development Bank of Canada is looking for young Canadian entrepreneurs ages 19 to 35 for its 2011 Young Entrepreneur Awards. The awards pay tribute to remarkable young Canadian entrepreneurs for their creativity, innovative spirit and community development, as well as business success.

43725 ■ "The Art of Rapid, Hands-On Execution Innovation" in Strategy and Leadership (Vol. 39, March-April 2011, No. 2, pp. 28)
Pub: Emerald Group Publishing Inc.
Ed: Anssi Tuulenmaki, Liisa Valikangas. **Description:** A model of 'rapid execution innovation' that can be used to increase the chances of achieving innovations that develop into successful new business models is introduced. The model involves company experiments that inspire the radical rethinking business opportunities, and by continuing these experiments until the idea evolves into a product.

43726 ■ "Auto Show Aims to Electrify" in Crain's Detroit Business (Vol. 26, January 11, 2010, No. 2, pp. 1)
Pub: Crain Communications Inc.
Contact: Rance E. Crain, President
Ed: Ryan Beene. **Description:** Overview of the North American International Auto show include sixteen production and concept vehicles including eight from the Detroit 3. High-tech battery suppliers as well as hybrid and electric vehicles will highlight the show.

43727 ■ "Auxilium Drug's New Use: Putting Squeeze On Cellulite" in Philadelphia Business Journal (Vol. 30, September 16, 2011, No. 31, pp. 1)
Pub: American City Business Journals Inc.
Ed: John George. **Description:** Auxilium Pharmaceuticals and BioSpecifics Technologies are getting on with their plans of finding new uses for their drug Xiaflex, a possible treatment for cellulite. The two firms have dismissed their pending litigations and mapped out an amended licensing agreement for their search for the potential uses of the drug.

43728 ■ "Avoiding Invention Scams" in Black Enterprise (Vol. 37, January 2007, No. 6, pp. 46)
Pub: Earl G. Graves Publishing Co. Inc.
Contact: Earl G. Graves, Jr., President
Ed: James C. Johnson. **Description:** Invention promotion firms provide inventors assistance in developing a prototype for product development. It is important to research these companies before making a commitment to work with them because there are a number of these firms that are not legitimate and have caused independent inventors to lose thousands of dollars by making false claims as to the market potential of the inventions.

43729 ■ "Baltimore Vendors Brave Heat, Red Tape to Eke Out a Living: Working the Streets" in Baltimore Business Journal (Vol. 28, July 30, 2010, No. 12, pp. 1)
Pub: Baltimore Business Journal
Ed: Amanda Pino. **Description:** Reports show that street vendors are popping up on new corners in Baltimore, Maryland, with city-inspected stainless steel food carts in tow. Applications for street vending licenses shot up at the end of 2009 and into this summer. It is believed that pinning down the exact number of vendors operating at any one point is difficult.

43730 ■ "Bankruptcy Claims Brooke, Gives Franchisees Hope" in The Business Journal-Serving Metropolitan Kansas City (October 31, 2008)
Pub: American City Business Journals, Inc.
Contact: Whitney Shaw, President
Ed: James Dornbrook, Steve Vockrodt. **Description:** Insurer Brooke Corp. was required to file for Chapter 11 bankruptcy for a deal to sell all of its assets to businessmen Terry Nelson and Lysle Davidson. The

new Brooke plans to share contingency fees with franchisees. The impacts of the bankruptcy case on Brooke franchisees are discussed.

43731 ■ "Be Innovative In Other Ways" in Green Industry Pro (Vol. 23, March 2011, No. 3, pp. 4)
Pub: Cygnus Business Media
Contact: Paul Mackler, Chief Executive Officer
Ed: Rod Dickens. **Description:** Emphasis is put on the importance of putting the customer first in order to successfully market any product or service. Six marketing ideas are presented to promote a landscaping business.

43732 ■ "Best Growth Stocks" in Canadian Business (Vol. 82, Summer 2009, No. 8, pp. 28)
Pub: Rogers Media Inc.
Contact: Tony Viner, President
Ed: Calvin Leung. **Description:** Canadian stocks that are considered as the best growth stocks, and whose price-earnings ratio is less than their earnings growth rate, are suggested. Suggestions include pharmaceutical firm Paladin Labs, which was found to have 13 consecutive years of revenue growth. Paladin Labs acquires or licenses niche drugs and markets them in Canada.

43733 ■ "Bitumen Oilsands: Slick Science" in Canadian Business (Vol. 81, September 15, 2008, No. 14-15, pp. 55)
Pub: Rogers Media Inc.
Contact: Tony Viner, President
Ed: Andrew Nikiforuk. **Description:** N-Solv Corp's John Nenniger has discovered a better alternative to steam-assisted gravity drainage methods for extracting bitumen. Nenniger's technique also relies on gravity but replaces steam with propane, which leaves behind impurities like asphaltenes and heavy metals that are too dirty to burn.

43734 ■ "Blast from the Past" in Entrepreneur (Vol. 35, November 2007, No. 11, pp. 48)
Pub: Entrepreneur Press
Contact: Perlman Neil, President
Ed: Robert Kiyosaki. **Description:** Entrepreneurs of today face the challenge of creating new ideas. Collaborating with younger employees provides new perspective, but it also has to be a partnership with old ideas and sharing experiences between the older and the younger to forecast the future.

43735 ■ "Bloomberg Law Upgraded Its Online Legal Research Platform" in Information Today (Vol. 28, September 2011, No. 8, pp. 28)
Pub: Information Today, Inc.
Contact: Thomas H. Hogan, President
E-mail: ctuthill@infotoday.com
Description: Bloomberg Law upgraded its online legal research platform for law practices. The new services includes a redesigned interface, improved search capabilities, and expanded collaboration and workflow features, while maintaining it comprehensive law resources such as mergers and acquisitions, antitrust, and securities.

43736 ■ "Born of Culture of Innovation" in Canadian Business (Vol. 81, October 27, 2008, No. 18, pp. 98)
Description: MaRS, an independent nonprofit organization, aims to better capture the relevant commercial potential of Ontario's research and to connect the worlds of science, business, and capital as well as to stimulate a culture of innovation. Profile of MaRS and its 'MaRS Innovation' program is included.

43737 ■ Borrowing Brilliance: The Six Steps to Business Innovation by Building on the Ideas of Others
Ed: David Kord Murray. **Price:** $26. **Description:** The author builds the case that cherry-picking the ideas of others is a vital part of the research and development process for any small firm.

43738 ■ "Bridging the Talent Gap Through Partnership and Innovation" in Canadian Business (Vol. 81, October 27, 2008, No. 18, pp. 88)
Description: Research revealed that North America is short by more than 60,000 qualified networking professionals. Businesses, educators and communities are collaborating in order to address the shortfall.

43739 ■ "Brooke Agents Claim Mistreatment" in The Business Journal-Serving Metropolitan Kansas City (Vol. 27, October 24, 2008, No. 7, pp. 1)
Pub: American City Business Journals, Inc.
Contact: Whitney Shaw, President
Ed: James Dornbrook. **Description:** Franchisees of Brooke Corp., an insurance franchise, face uncertainty as their bills remain unpaid and banks threaten to destroy their credit. The company bundled and sold franchisee loans to different banks, but the credit crunch left the company with massive debts and legal disputes.

43740 ■ "A Burning Issue: Lives Are at Stake Every Day" in Contractor (Vol. 56, October 2009, No. 10, pp. 29)
Ed: Julius A. Ballanco; Stanley Wolfson. **Description:** American Society of Plumbing Engineers has been accused of being biased for supporting rules that require residential fire sprinklers although the society's members will not receive any benefit from their installation. The organization trains and certifies plumbing engineers who design life-saving fire protection systems.

43741 ■ "California Company Suing City's Lupin Over its Generic Diabetes Drug" in Baltimore Business Journal (Vol. 27, January 1, 2010)
Ed: Gary Haber. **Description:** California-based Depomed Inc. is suing Baltimore, Maryland-based Lupin Pharmaceuticals Inc. and its parent company in India over the patents to a diabetes drug. Lupin allegedly infringed on Depomed's four patents for Glumetza when it filed for permission to sell its own version of the drug with the US Food and Drug Administration. Details on generic pharmaceutical manufacturer tactics are discussed.

43742 ■ "The Call of the City" in Puget Sound Business Journal (Vol. 35, September 5, 2014, No. 20, pp. 16)
Pub: American City Business Journals
Released: September 5, 2014. **Description:** A number of large companies have moved their headquarters to Seattle, Washington. The area is known to be transit-accessible with mixed-use offices and retail space, making it a great site selection. Seattle also embraces innovations and inventions in area districts that bring a diverse workforce.

43743 ■ "Calling All Creatives, Innovators, 'Expats': Detroit Is Hopping In September" in Crain's Detroit Business (Vol. 30, September 1, 2014, No. 35, pp. 6)
Pub: Crain Communications Inc. - Detroit
Contact: Keith Crain, Chairman
Released: September 1, 2014. **Description:** Wayne State University is hosting a seminar September 16, 2014 which will focus on Detroit, Michigan as a center for innovation. Six other such seminars seeking investment in the city will be held in September.

43744 ■ "Can America Invent Its Way Back?" in Business Week (September 22, 2008, No. 4100, pp. 52)
Pub: Bloomberg L.P.
Contact: Matthew Winkler, Manager
Ed: Michael Mandel. **Description:** Business leaders as well as economists agree that innovative new products, services and ways of doing business may be the only way in which America can survive the downward spiral of the economy; innovation economics may be the answer and may even provide enough growth to enable Americans to prosper in the years to come.

43745 ■ *"Can He Win the Patent Game?" in Globe & Mail (February 20, 2006, pp. B1)*
Ed: Simon Avery, Paul Waldie. **Description:** A profile on managerial abilities of chief executive officer Jim Balsillie of Research In Motion Ltd., who will face the patent case with NTP Inc., is presented.

43746 ■ *"Canadian Research Generates Innovation and Prosperity" in Canadian Business (Vol. 81, October 27, 2008, No. 18, pp. 87)*
Description: Universities play a key role in helping Canadians achieve prosperity, competitiveness, and quality of life by conducting more than a third of Canada's research. Research in universities help train graduates to apply sophisticated knowledge to real problems.

43747 ■ *"A Chinese Approach to Management: A Generation of Entrepreneurs Is Writing Its Own Rules" in Harvard Business Review (Vol. 92, September 2014, No. 9, pp. 103)*
Pub: Harvard Business Publishing
Released: September 2014. **Description:** The Chinese approach to management include simple structures for organizations, quick development of products, responsiveness to local values and needs, and investment in source firms and vendors. Manufacturing and engineering operations are typically co-located.

43748 ■ *"Clash of the Titans" in Canadian Business (Vol. 80, March 12, 2007, No. 6, pp. 27)*
Ed: Andrew Wahl. **Description:** The frequent allegations of Google Inc. and Microsoft Corp. against each other over copyright and other legal issues, with a view to taking away other's market share, is discussed.

43749 ■ *Clicking Through: A Survival Guide for Bringing Your Company Online*
Ed: Jonathan I. Ezor. **Released:** October 1999. **Description:** Summary of legal compliance issues faced by small companies doing business on the Internet, including copyright and patent laws.

43750 ■ *"Clusters Last Stand?" in Canadian Electronics (Vol. 23, February 2008, No. 1, pp. 6)*
Description: Survival of technology clusters was the focus of Strategic Microelectronics Council's conference entitled, 'The Power of Community: Building Technology Clusters in Canada'. Clusters can help foster growth in the microelectronics sector, and it was recognized that government intervention is needed to maintain these clusters.

43751 ■ *"Code Name: Inventors: Go From Golden Idea to Agent of Invention" in Black Enterprise (Vol. 41, November 2010, No. 4, pp. 78)*
Pub: Earl G. Graves Publishing Co. Inc.
Contact: Earl G. Graves, Jr., President
Ed: Renita Burns. **Description:** Profile of Andre Woolery, inventor of a magnetic wristband that holds small nails, screws, drill bits, and small tools, allowing handymen to keep essential tools at hand while working.

43752 ■ *"Companies Must Innovate, Regardless of Economy" in Crain's Detroit Business (Vol. 25, June 1, 2009, No. 22, pp. M007)*
Pub: Crain Communications Inc. - Detroit
Contact: Keith Crain, Chairman
Ed: Sherri Begin Welch. **Description:** Despite the economy, leaders of Michigan's successful companies stress that small businesses must innovate in order to grow.

43753 ■ *"Connectors for Space, Mil/Aero and Medical Applications" in Canadian Electronics (Vol. 23, June-July 2008, No. 4, pp. 13)*
Ed: Gilles Parguey. **Description:** Product information on electrical connectors for use in space, military, aeronautics, and medical applications is provided.

These connectors are built to withstand the extreme conditions offered by the harsh working environments in those applications.

43754 ■ *Content Rich: Writing Your Way to Wealth on the Web*
Ed: Jon Wuebben. **Released:** April 2008. **Price:** , $19.95. **Description:** A definitive search engine optimization (SEO) copywriting guide for search engine rankings and sales conversion. It includes topics not covered in other books on the subject and targets the small to medium sized business looking for ways to maximize online marketing activities as well as designers and Web developers seeking to incorporate more SEO techniques into design and content.

43755 ■ *"Copyright Clearance Center (CCC) Partnered with cSubs" in Information Today (Vol. 28, November 2011, No. 10, pp. 14)*
Pub: Information Today, Inc.
Contact: Thomas H. Hogan, President
E-mail: ctuthill@infotoday.com
Description: Copyright Clearance Center (CCC) partnered with cSubs to integrate CCC's point-of-content licensing solution RightsLink Basic directly into cSubs workflow. The partnership will allow cSubs' customers a user-friendly process for obtaining permissions. Csubs is a corporate subscription management service for books, newspapers, and econtent.

43756 ■ *"The Copyright Evolution" in Information Today (Vol. 28, November 2011, No. 10, pp. 1)*
Pub: Information Today, Inc.
Contact: Thomas H. Hogan, President
E-mail: ctuthill@infotoday.com
Ed: Nancy Davis Kho. **Description:** For information professionals, issues surrounding copyright compliance have traditionally been on the consumption side. However, today, content consumption is only half the program because blogging, tweeting, and commenting is a vital part of more standard duties for workers as corporations aim to create authentic communications with customers.

43757 ■ *"Courting Canadian Customers Confounds Car Dealers" in Business First Buffalo (November 12, 2007, pp. 1)*
Pub: American City Business Journals, Inc.
Ed: James Fink. **Description:** Strength of the Canadian dollar has led to an influx of potential customers for the Western New York automobile industry, but franchising restrictions and licensing as well as insurance issues have limited the potential of having larger sales figures. Border and trade issues that affect the car industry in WNY are also discussed.

43758 ■ *Craft, Inc.*
Pub: Chronicle Books L.L.C.
Contact: Frank Vega, President
Ed: Meg Mateo Ilasco. **Released:** Revised Edition. **Price:** $16.95. **Description:** Business primer for entrepreneurial crafters wishing to turn their hobbies into a small business, including tips for developing products, naming the company, writing a business plan, applying for licenses, and paying taxes.

43759 ■ *"The Design of Things to Come" in Business Horizons (Vol. 51, January-February 2008, No. 1, pp. 74)*
Ed: Mimi Dollinger. **Description:** Review of the book that helps entrepreneurs develop and market new products, 'The Design of Things to Come: How Ordinary People Create Extraordinary Products'.

43760 ■ *"DFW Inventors Psyched for New, Local Patent Office" in Dallas Business Journal (Vol. 35, August 3, 2012, No. 47, pp. 1)*
Pub: American City Business Journal
Ed: Jeff Bounds. **Description:** The United States Patent & Trademark Office is planning to expand by adding three satellite offices, including one in Dallas-Fort Worth, Texas. Inventors look forward to the planned expansion as it is expected to make the process of patent licensing more effective.

43761 ■ *Doing Business Anywhere: The Essential Guide to Going Global*
Pub: John Wiley & Sons Inc.
Contact: Stephen M. Smith, President
Ed: Tom Travis. **Description:** Plans are given for new or existing businesses to organize, plan, operate and execute a business on a global basis. Trade agreements, brand protection and patents, ethics, security as well as cultural issues are among the issues addressed. **Availability:** E-book.

43762 ■ *"Dropped Calls" in Canadian Business (Vol. 80, November 5, 2007, No. 22, pp. 34)*
Ed: Andrew Wahl. **Description:** Control over Canada's telecommunications market by Telus, Rogers and Bell Canada has resulted in a small number of innovations. The pricing regimes of these carriers have also stifled innovations in the telecommunications industry. The status of Canada's telecommunications industry is further analyzed.

43763 ■ *"Economy: The Case for a Bright Future" in Canadian Business (Vol. 83, July 20, 2010, No. 11-12, pp. 58)*
Pub: Rogers Media Inc.
Contact: Tony Viner, President
Ed: Andrew Potter. **Description:** Writer Matt Ridley argues that trade is the determinant of development and that it is the reason why humans got rich. Ridley believes that the important innovations are often low-tech and is often processes rather than products.

43764 ■ *Embedded Entrepreneurship: The Institutional Dynamics of Innovation*
Pub: Routledge
Contact: Kevin Bradley, President
E-mail: kbradley@taylorandfrancis.com
Ed: Alexander Ebner. **Released:** April 10, 2010. **Price:** $160, Hardback. **Description:** In this book, Alexander Ebner reconstructs the theory of entrepreneurship from an institutional perspective.

43765 ■ *"End of Wristband Era?" in Austin Business Journal (Vol. 34, July 25, 2014, No. 23, pp. 7)*
Pub: American City Business Journals, Inc.
Contact: Whitney Shaw, President
Released: July 25, 2014. **Description:** Front Gate Tickets plans to unveil RFID radio chip technology at Chicago's Lollapalooza festival. This technology will be incorporated into wristbands and allow the patrons to make purchases by swiping them instead of using cash or cards. Front Gate Tickets president, Maura Gibson, shares his views on RFID technology's implementation into Smartphone apps, next generation innovations in ticketing and future plans of the company.

43766 ■ *"Enforcer In Fantasyland" in Crain's New York Business (Vol. 24, February 25, 2008, No. 8, pp. 10)*
Ed: Hilary Potkewitz. **Description:** Patent law, particularly in the toy and game industry, is recession-proof according to Barry Negrin, partner at Pryor Cashman. Negrin co-founded his patent practice group. Despite massive recalls of toys and the concern over toxic toys, legal measures are in place in this industry.

43767 ■ *Enlightened Leadership: Best Practice Guidelines and Time Tools for Easily Implementing Learning Organizations*
Pub: Learning House Publishing, Inc.
Ed: Ralph LoVuolo; Alan G. Thomas. **Released:** May 2006. **Price:** , $79.99. **Description:** Innovation and creativity are essential for any successful small business. The book provides owners, managers, and team leaders with the tools necessary to produce 'disciplined innovation'.

43768 ■ *Enterprise, Entrepreneurship and Innovation: Concepts, Context and Commercialization*
Pub: Elsevier Science and Technology Books
Ed: Robin Lowe, Sue Marriott. **Released:** May 2006. **Description:** Application of enterprise, innovation and entrepreneurship are discussed to help companies grow.

43769 ■ *Enterprise Planning and Development: Small Business and Enterprise Start-Up Survival and Growth*
Pub: Elsevier Science and Technology Books
Ed: David Butler. **Released:** June 2006. **Description:** Innovation, intellectual property, and exit strategies are among the issues discussed in this book involving current entrepreneurship.

43770 ■ *"Entrepreneurial Orientation and Firm Performance" in Journal of Small Business and Entrepreneurship (Vol. 23, Winter 2010, No. 1)*
Pub: Canadian Council for Small Business and Entrepreneurship
Contact: Sandra Altner, President
Description: The article develops a theoretical model of the relationship between firm-level entrepreneurship and firm performance. This model is intended to further clarify the consequences of an 'entrepreneurial orientation', paying particular attention to the differential relationship that exists between the three sub-dimensions of entrepreneurial orientation and firm performance. Included in the theoretical model are other important variables (such as organizational structure and environmental characteristics) that may impact the EO-performance relationship. Propositions are developed regarding the various configurations of the sub-dimensions of EO and organizational structure that would be most appropriate in a given environmental context. Future research may also benefit from considering the important role that organizational strategy and life cycle stage play in this model. The implications of this model for both researchers and managers are discussed.

43771 ■ *Entrepreneurship, Innovation and Economic Growth*
Pub: Edward Elgar Publishing Inc.
Contact: Richard Henning, Vice President
E-mail: kwight@e-elgar.com
Ed: David B. Audretsch. **Released:** 2006. **Price:** £117. **Description:** Links between entrepreneurship, innovation and economic growth are examined. **Availability:** Print.

43772 ■ *"Entrepreneurship and Service Innovation" in Journal of Business & Industrial Marketing (Vol. 29, July 2014, No. 6)*
Pub: Emerald Group Publishing Inc.
Released: July 2014. **Description:** An overview of entrepreneurship and service innovation and the association between entrepreneurial orientation, innovation, and entrepreneurship or new entry. Analysis of secondary data was performed and observed that EO (entrepreneurial orientation), innovation, and entrepreneurship feature a triadic connect. EO supports innovation, innovation endorses new venture creation, and it in turn commercializes innovations.

43773 ■ *"Evolutionary Psychology in the Business Sciences"*
Pub: Springer Publishing Co.
Contact: Ursula Springer, President
Released: September 28, 2014. **Price:** , $150.93. **Description:** All individuals operating in the business sphere share a common biological heritage, including consumers, employers, employees, entrepreneurs, or financial traders, to name a few. The evolutionary behavioral sciences and specific business contexts including marketing, consumer behavior, advertising, innovation and creativity and invention, intertemporal choice, negotiations, competition and cooperation in organizational settings, sex differences in workplace patterns, executive leadership, business ethics, store and office design, behavioral decision making, and electronic communications and commerce are all addressed.

43774 ■ *The Facebook Era: Tapping Online Social Networks to Build Better Products, Reach New Audiences, and Sell More Stuff*
Ed: Clara Shih. **Price:** , $24.99. **Description:** The '90s were about the World Wide Web of information and the power of linking Web pages. Today it's about the World Wide Web of people and the power of the social graph. Online social networks are fundamentally changing the way we live, work, and interact. They offer businesses immense opportunities to transform customer relationships for profit: opportunities that touch virtually every business function, from sales and marketing to recruiting, collaboration to executive decision-making, product development to innovation.

43775 ■ *"Facebook, Google, LinkedIn Line Up In Patent Case Before Supreme Court" in San Francisco Business Times (Vol. 28, March 28, 2014, No. 36)*
Pub: American City Business Journals
Released: March 28, 2014. **Description:** The U.S. Supreme Court is set to hear a case involving Alice Corporation Pty. Ltd. and CLS Bank International in a dispute over a patented computer-implemented escrow service. The case has larger implications to tech companies concerning whether a business method can be patented if it is made electronic.

43776 ■ *"Facilitating and Rewarding Creativity During New Product Development" in Journal of Marketing (Vol. 75, July 2011, No. 4, pp. 53)*
Pub: American Marketing Association
Contact: Lucille Pointer, President
Ed: James E. Burroughs, Darren W. Dahl, C. Page Moreau, Amitava Chattopadhay, Gerald J. Gorn. **Description:** A study to determine the effects of rewards to creativity in the process of new product development is presented. The findings show that the effect of rewards can be made positive if combined with appropriate creativity training.

43777 ■ *Facilitating Sustainable Innovation through Collaboration: A Multi-Stakeholder Perspective*
Pub: Springer-Verlag New York Inc.
Contact: Ruediger Gebauer, President
Ed: Joseph Sarkis, James J. Cordeiro, Diego Vazquez Brust. **Released:** March 10, 2010. **Price:** €95.19; €114.99, Hardcover. **Description:** An international perspective of sustainable innovation with contributions from Australia, Europe, and North America, by prominent policy makers, scientific researchers and others. **Availability:** E-book.

43778 ■ *"Falling Behind in Ingenuity? Rhode Island Lags U.S. in New Patents" in Providence Business News (Vol. 28, February 24 , 2014, No. 47, pp. 1)*
Pub: American City Business Journals
Released: February 24, 2014. **Description:** Jennifer Bradley of the Brookings Institute reported Rhode Island's innovation problem during the annual meeting of the Providence Preservation Society. Bradley said there was divergence in the rate of annual patent growth in Providence from the national growth rate.

43779 ■ *Fast Company's Greatest Hits: 10 Years of the Most Innovative Ideas in Business*
Pub: Penguin Group USA
Contact: Phyllis Grann, President
Ed: Mark N. Vamosand, David Lidsky, Jim Collins. **Released:** July 2006. **Price:** $24.95. **Description:** Offering of Fast Company's best articles covering business ideas and profiles of successful firms and their leaders. **Availability:** Print.

43780 ■ *"Federal Fund Valuable Tool For Small-Biz Innovators" in Crain's Detroit Business (Vol. 24, September 29, 2008, No. 39, pp. 42)*
Pub: Crain Communications Inc.
Contact: Rance E. Crain, President
Ed: Nancy Kaffer. **Description:** Grants from the Small Business Innovation Research Program, or SBIR grants, are federal funds that are set aside for 11 federal agencies to allocate to tech-oriented small-business owners. Firms such as Biotechnology Business Consultants help these companies apply for SBIR grants.

43781 ■ *"The Fences of a Patent" in Information Today (Vol. 26, February 2009,* No. 2, pp. 13)
Pub: Information Today, Inc.
Contact: Thomas H. Hogan, President
E-mail: ctuthill@infotoday.com
Ed: George H. Pike. **Description:** Patent law is examined using the Blackboard course management software used by many colleges and universities as its example.

43782 ■ *"Fewer Inventions Patented in Alabama" in Birmingham Business Journal (Vol. 29, June 1, 2012, No. 23, pp. 1)*
Pub: American City Business Journals, Inc.
Contact: Whitney Shaw, President
Ed: Evan Belanger. **Released:** June 1, 2012. **Description:** U.S. Patent and Trademark Office issued only 352 invention patents across Alabama in 2011, 92 fewer than the year before. The decline could mark the first time the impact of national recession in annual patent reports since patent grants are a trailing economic indicator.

43783 ■ *"Finding Heart Help In the Skyway" in Business Journal (Vol. 30, August 10, 2012, No. 11, pp. 3)*
Pub: American City Business Journals, Inc.
Contact: Whitney Shaw, President
Ed: Katharine Grayson. **Released:** August 10, 2012. **Description:** The 2,000 square foot HeartSavers Clinic will start offering heart screening at the Baker Center in Minneapolis, Minnesota in September 2012. CardioVascular Centers chief executive officer, Maury Taylor, has licensed the Cohn Index for the tests and is funding his business through his medical device firm Hypertension Diagnostics.

43784 ■ *"FinOvation 2009" in Farm Industry News (Vol. 42, January 1, 2009, No. 1)*
Pub: Intertec Publishing
Contact: John French, President
Ed: Karen McMahon, Mark Moore, David Hest. **Description:** New and innovative products and technologies are presented.

43785 ■ *"Fledgling Brands May Take the Fall With Steve & Barry's" in Advertising Age (Vol. 79, July 7, 2008, No. 26, pp. 6)*
Pub: Crain Communications Inc.
Contact: Rance Crain, President
Ed: Natalie Zmuda. **Description:** Steve & Barry's, a retailer that holds licensing deals with a number of designers and celebrities, may have to declare bankruptcy; this leaves the fate of the retailer's hundreds of licensing deals and exclusive celebrity lines in question.

43786 ■ *"Flu is a Booster for Firms Here" in Philadelphia Business Journal (Vol. 28, September 25, 2009, No. 32, pp. 1)*
Pub: American City Business Journals Inc.
Ed: John George. **Description:** GlaxoSmithKline, AstraZeneca, CSL Biotherapies, and Sanofi Aventis were awarded contract by the US Government to supply swine flu vaccines. It is estimated that global sales of the vaccine could reach billions of dollars.

43787 ■ *"Flue Vaccines are Going Green" in Canadian Business (Vol. 83, September 14, 2010, No. 15, pp. 24)*
Pub: Rogers Media Inc.
Contact: Tony Viner, President
Ed: Angelia Chapman. **Description:** Quebec-based Medicago has found a solution to the bottleneck in the production of influenza vaccines by using plant-based processes instead of egg-based systems. Medicago's US Department of Defense funded research has produced the technology that speeds up the production time for vaccines by almost two-thirds. Insights into Medicago's patented process are also given.

43788 ■ *"For Tech Companies, Holding Onto Prized Patents Can Be Expensive" in Puget Sound Business Journal (Vol. 33, May 18, 2012, No. 4, pp. 1)*
Pub: American City Business Journal
Description: Patent lawsuits have been rising steadily over the past 20 years and the damage rewards are also growing. Microsoft is currently

engaged in more than 60 patent infringement lawsuits worldwide and the largest is a 2 year fight over a series of patents that Motorola holds and Microsoft uses.

43789 ■ *"Foreign Flavor of U.S. Innovation: Report Makes New Case for Immigration Reform"* **in Silicon Valley/San Jose Business Journal (Vol. 30, July 20, 2012, No. 17, pp. 1)**
Pub: American City Business Journal
Description: The results of a recent study show that 76 percent of the patents created at the top 10 patent-producing universities include at least one foreign-born invetor. Findings also indicate that immigrants are three times more likely and US-born individuals to file a patent. Information about H1-B Visas is also provided.

43790 ■ *"Freeing the Wheels of Commerce"* **in Hispanic Business (July-August 2007, pp. 50, 52, 54)**
Pub: Hispanic Business Inc.
Contact: Jesus Chavarria, President
Ed: Keith Rosenblum. **Description:** SecureOrigins, a border-based partnership with high-tech innovators is working to move goods faster, more efficiently, and securely.

43791 ■ *"Fries With That?"* **in Canadian Business (Vol. 81, September 29, 2008, No. 16, pp. 33)**
Ed: Calvin Leung. **Description:** Profile of Toronto-based New York Fries, which has four stores in South Korea, is planning to expand further as well as into Hong Kong and Macau; the company also has a licensee in the United Arab Emirates whom is also planning to expand.

43792 ■ *From Concept To Consumer: How to Turn Ideas Into Money*
Pub: Financial Times/Prentice Hall
Contact: Richard Stagg, Director
Ed: Phil Baker. **Released:** October 01, 2008. **Price:** £16. **Description:** Renowned product developer Phil Baker explains how a great idea accounts for only 5 percent of all the factors of success and why the majority of success is dependent upon a myriad of other factors, including the time it takes to get to market, price, marketing and distribution. By being their own best competition, a small company can stay one step ahead of competitors.

43793 ■ *"Fueling Change"* **in Entrepreneur (Vol. 35, November 2007, No. 11, pp. 46)**
Pub: Entrepreneur Press
Contact: Perlman Neil, President
Ed: Carol Tice. **Description:** Creativity guru John Kao says the United States is complacent when it comes to business. He talks about how entrepreneurs should think innovatively in terms of big changes.

43794 ■ *"Full-Court Press for Apple"* **in Barron's (Vol. 88, March 24, 2008, No. 12, pp. 47)**
Pub: Dow Jones & Co., Inc.
Contact: Clare Hart, President
Ed: Mark Veverka. **Description:** Apple Inc. is facing more intellectual property lawsuits in 2008, with 30 patent lawsuits filed compared to 15 in 2007 and nine in 2006. The lawsuits, which involve products such as the iPod and the iPhone, present some concern for Apple's shareholders.

43795 ■ *The Game-Changer: How You Can Drive Revenue and Profit Growth with Innovation*
Pub: Crown Business
Ed: A. G. Lafley, Ram Charan. **Released:** April 08, 2008. **Price:** $27.50, hardcover; $15.99. **Description:** Former Proctor and Gamble CEO A.G. Lafley outlines principles of innovation that turned the company around and shows how that strategy can work for any business. **Availability:** PrintE-book.

43796 ■ *The Game Makers*
Ed: Philip E. Orbanes. **Released:** November 2003. **Price:** , $29.95. **Description:** Profile of game expert and president of a specialty game company, author of books about games, Monopoly championship

judge, senior vice president of research and development at Parker Brothers, and inventor of board and card games in highlighted.

43797 ■ *"GeckoSystems Reduces Sensor Fusion Costs Due to Elder Care Robot Trials"* **in Marketwired (December 14, 2010)**
Pub: COMTEX
Contact: Chip Brian, President
Description: GeckoSystems International Corporation has been able to reduce the cost of its sensor fusion system while maintaining reliability and performance. The firm's ongoing first in-home elder care robot trials have sparked interest regarding its business model, technologies available for licensing, and joint domestic and international ventures.

43798 ■ *"German Win Through Sharing"* **in Canadian Business (Vol. 83, September 14, 2010, No. 15, pp. 16)**
Pub: Rogers Media Inc.
Contact: Tony Viner, President
Ed: Jordan Timm. **Description:** German economic historian Eckhard Hoffner has a two-volume work showing how German's relaxed attitude toward copyright and intellectual property helped it catch up to industrialized United Kingdom. Hoffner's research was in response to his interest in the usefulness of software patents. Information on the debate regarding Canada's copyright laws is given.

43799 ■ *"Getting Inventive With..Ed Spellman"* **in Crain's Cleveland Business (Vol. 28, October 22, 2007, No. 42, pp. 18)**
Pub: Crain Communications Inc.
Ed: Kimberly Bonvissuto. **Description:** Profile featuring Ed Spellman, a mechanical engineer who decided to quit his job at Invacare Corp., a medical equipment manufacturer and distributor, in order to devote his full attention to promoting his numerous inventions, including the DV-Grip, a vehicle mount for portable DVD players.

43800 ■ *"Getting Inventive With..John Nottingham and John Spirk"* **in Crain's Cleveland Business (Vol. 28, October 22, 2007, No. 42, pp. 19)**
Pub: Crain Communications Inc.
Ed: Kimberly Bonvissuto. **Description:** Profile featuring John Spirk and John Nottingham of the Cleveland-based firm, Nottingham-Spirk Design Associates; the company holds 486 issued and commercialized patents and has reported over $30 billion in new product sales.

43801 ■ *"Getting Inventive With..Richard Brindisi and Gregory Vittardi"* **in Crain's Cleveland Business (Vol. 28, October 22, 2007, No. 42)**
Pub: Crain Communications Inc.
Ed: Kimberly Bonvissuto. **Description:** Profile of the SmartShopper, a handheld, voice-recognition device for dictating shopping and errand lists, and its creators, Richard G. Brindisi and Gregory Vittardi.

43802 ■ *"Getting the Word Out"* **in Modern Machine Shop (Vol. 84, September 2011, No. 4, pp. 16)**
Pub: Gardner Business Media, Inc.
Contact: Richard G. Kline, President
E-mail: rkline@gardnerweb.com
Ed: Derek Korn. **Description:** Many times machine shops create devices to streamline their own machining processes and find these devices can be used by other shops, thus developing a marketable product. Tips for this process are outlined.

43803 ■ *"The Globe: Singapore Airlines' Balancing Act"* **in Harvard Business Review (Vol. 88, July-August 2010, No. 7-8, pp. 145)**
Pub: Harvard Business School Publishing
Ed: Loizos Heracleous, Jochen Wirtz. **Description:** Singapore Airlines is used as an illustration of organizational effectiveness. The article includes the firm's 4-3-3 rule of spending, its promotion of centralized as well as decentralized innovation, use of technology, and strategic planning.

43804 ■ *The Gridlock Economy: How Too Much Ownership Wrecks Markets, Stops Innovation, and Costs Lives*
Pub: Basic Books
Contact: Elizabeth Maguire, Publisher
Ed: Michael Heller. **Released:** February 23, 2010. **Price:** C$21.50, paperback; $16.95; C$27.95; £11.99. **Description:** While private ownership generally creates wealth, the author believes that economic gridlock results when too many people own pieces of one thing, which results in too many people being able to block each other from creating or using a scarce source. **Availability:** PrintE-book.

43805 ■ *"GTI Licenses TMC to Cannon Boiler Works"* **in Contractor (Vol. 56, December 2009, No. 12, pp. 6)**
Pub: Penton Media, Inc.
Description: Gas Technology Institute has licensed Cannon Boiler Works Inc. to use its transport membrane condenser technology. The technology can be applied to elevated-temperature industrial processes such as boilers. It allows the capture and beneficial use of latent waste heat and water vapor from exhaust/flue gas.

43806 ■ *"Harnessing the Wisdom of Crowd"* **in Entrepreneur (Vol. 37, September 2009, No. 9, pp. 74)**
Pub: Entrepreneur Press
Contact: Perlman Neil, President
Description: Online customer service business Get Satisfaction has registered growth. The business enables customers to search for answers to common product questions. Customers use the service to post questions, complaints, and even product ideas.

43807 ■ *"Help Yourself"* **in Entrepreneur (September 2014)**
Pub: Entrepreneurial Press
Released: September 2014. **Description:** Employers can create a workplace where mutual trust is possible by expressing clearly what they expect from their employees, giving feedback that reinforces positive behavior and mentoring them to improve customer service. A leader needs to talk to a pregnant worker about her job priorities, deadlines and communicate ways to help her meet expectations. The best way to approach a company for unsolicited ideas is to find out the contact person who would be responsible for inventors or potential collaborators.

43808 ■ *"Hispanic Executives Continue Their Rise to Power Amid a Shaky Economy"* **in Hispanic Business (January-February 2009, pp. 12-14)**
Pub: Hispanic Business Inc.
Contact: Jesus Chavarria, President
Ed: Michael Bowker. **Description:** Hispanic Business Media's 2009 Corporate Elite winners defied expectations and a tough economy and rose to the top of their industries; innovation being cited as key to growth of Hispanic-owned companies.

43809 ■ *"Honoring Creativity"* **in Playthings (Vol. 107, January 1, 2009, No. 1, pp. 28)**
Pub: Reed Elsevier Group plc Reed Business Information
Contact: Mark Kelsey, Chief Executive Officer
Ed: Cliff Annicelli. **Description:** Toy & Game Inventors Expo is held annually in conjunction with the Chicago Toy & Game Fair. The event honors toy inventors in the categories of Game Design, Toy Design and Rising Stars, plus a lifetime achievement award. Profile of the company, Toying With Games, founded by Joyce Johnson and Colleen McCarthy-Evans are included in the article.

43810 ■ *"How Hard Could It Be? Why the Most Important Innovations Are Often Those That Appear To Be Fatally Flawed"* **in Inc. (February 2008)**
Ed: Joel Spolsky. **Description:** Many times, things that seemed silly or impossible have become great innovations.

43811 ■ *"How Innovative Is Michigan? Index Aims To Keep Track" in Crain's Detroit Business (Vol. 24, February 4, 2008, No. 5, pp. 1)*
Pub: Crain Communications Inc. - Detroit
Contact: Keith Crain, Chairman
Ed: Chad Halcom. **Description:** Profile of the newly created 'Innovation Index', released by the University of Michigan-Dearborn. The report showed a combination of indicators that gauged innovation activity in the state slightly lower for second quarter 2007, but ahead of most levels for most of 2006. Statistical data included.

43812 ■ *"How Sharing Sent Record Sales Soaring" in Business Strategy Review (Vol. 25, Summer 2014, No. 2, pp. 7)*
Pub: Blackwell Publishing Inc.
Contact: Gordon Tibbitte, III, President
Released: Summer 2014. **Description:** Removing copy protection from songs actually increased music sales.

43813 ■ *How to Start an Internet Sales Business Without Making the Government Mad*
Pub: Lulu.com
Ed: Dan Davis. **Released:** September 30, 2011. **Price:** $14.38. **Description:** Small business guide for launching an Internet sales company. Topics include business structure, licenses, and taxes. **Availability:** PDF.

43814 ■ *How to Start and Run a Small Book Publishing Company: A Small Business Guide to Self-Publishing and Independent Publishing*
Pub: HCM Publishing
Ed: Peter I. Hupalo. **Released:** August 30, 2002. **Price:** $18.95. **Description:** The book teaches all aspects of starting and running a small book publishing company. Topics covered include: inventory accounting in the book trade, just-in-time inventory management, turnkey fulfillment solutions, tax deductible costs, basics of sales and use tax, book pricing, standards in terms of the book industry, working with distributors and wholesalers, cover design and book layout, book promotion and marketing, how to select profitable authors to publish, printing process, printing on demand, the power of a strong backlist, and how to value copyright.

43815 ■ *"Hunhu Healthcare Gets Some Mayo Help" in Business Journal (Vol. 32, August 29, 2014, No. 14, pp. 4)*
Pub: American City Business Journals
Released: August 29, 2014. **Description:** Hunhu Healthcare Inc. has signed a licensing agreement with Mayo Clinic to develop mobile and Web applications that will enable patients to communicate with the company's network using social networking tools. The firm is expected to charge a monthly fee for the service.

43816 ■ *"Idea-Generation Program Creates Winning Programs" in Business Journal-Serving Metropolitan Kansas City (October 19, 2007)*
Ed: James Dombrook. **Description:** Eureka Ranch has developed 'Eureka! Winning Ways', a program that helps companies create new ideas for their business. Brunson Instruments is the first Missouri manufacturer to engage in the program. The procedures in the new product idea generation program are supplied.

43817 ■ *"Ideas at Work: Sparkling Innovation" in Business Strategy Review (Vol. 21, Summer 2010, No. 2, pp. 7)*
Pub: Blackwell Publishers Ltd.
Ed: Julian Birkinshaw, Peter Robbins. **Description:** GlaxoSmithKline faced a situation common to large global organizations: how to allocate marketing resources to smaller, regional brands. A report on the company's inventive approach to worldwide marketing that led to the development of a unique and productive network are explored.

43818 ■ *"Ideas at Work: Sparkling Innovation" in Business Strategy Review (Vol. 21, Summer 2010, No. 2, pp. 07)*
Pub: John Wiley & Sons Inc. Scientific, Technical, Medical, and Scholarly Div. (Wiley-Blackwell)
Contact: William J. Pesce, Manager
E-mail: wpesce@wiley.com
Ed: Julian Birkinshaw, Peter Robbins. **Description:** GlaxoSmithKline faced a situation common to large global organizations: how to allocate marketing resources to smaller, regional brands. The company's approach to worldwide marketing that led to the development of a unique and productive network is outlined.

43819 ■ *"Illinois Regulators Revoke Collection Agency's License" in Collections & Credit Risk (Vol. 15, August 1, 2010, No. 7, pp. 13)*
Pub: SourceMedia Inc.
Contact: James M. Malkin, Chief Executive Officer
Description: Creditors Service Bureau of Springfield, Illinois had its license revoked by a state regulatory agency and was fined $55,000 because the owner and president, Craig W. Lewis, did not turn over portions of collected funds to clients.

43820 ■ *"The Impact of Acquisitions On the Productivity of Inventors at Semiconductor Firms: A Synthesis of Knowledge-Based and Incentive-Based Perspective" in Academy of Management Journal (Vol. 50, No. 5, October 1, 2007, pp. 1133)*
Pub: Academy of Management
Contact: Ming-Jer Chen, President
Ed: Rahul Kapoor, Kwanghui Lim. **Description:** Study examined the relation between knowledge-based and incentive-based outlook in explaining the impact of acquisitions on the productivity of inventors at acquired semiconductor firms. Results showed a definite relation between the two perspectives.

43821 ■ *"In Chesterfield: Paletta's Operations Raise Competitors' Blood Pressure" in St. Louis Business Journal (Vol. 33, August 17, 2012, No. 52, pp. 1)*
Pub: American City Business Journal
Description: The proposed relocation of Doctor George Paletta Jr.'s Orthopedic Center of Saint Louis to a new 62,000-square-foot facility was met with opposition by local hospital officials and the Missouri Hospital Association. Officials state the facility must be licensed as a hospital in order to provide overnight post-operative care as planned by Paletta.

43822 ■ *"In the Huddle: Expanding Business Opportunities for Players, Licensees and Retailers Is What NFL Players Inc. Is All About" in Retail Merchandiser (Vol. 54, July-August 2014, No. 4, pp. S8)*
Pub: S & R Media Corporation
Released: July-August 2014. **Description:** NFL Players Inc. is the licensing and marketing arm of the NFL Players Association(NFLPA) and NFLPA is a subsidiary of the union for professional football players in the National Football League (NFL). The NFLPI is responsible for generating revenue and contribute funds that benefit the players in the association. NFLPI works with online and traditional retail outlets for sale of athletic apparel, trading cards, video games, murals, figurines, photos, drinkware and more.

43823 ■ *"In Search of the Next Big Thing: It's Out There - Just Waiting For You To Find It" in Inc. (Volume 32, December 2010, No. 10, pp. 34)*
Pub: Inc. Magazine
Ed: April Joyner. **Description:** Innovation is the future for small business. A new book, Inside Real Innovation: How the Right Approach Can Move Ideas from R&D to Market - And Get the Economy Moving helps to break down the process by which innovation occurs.

43824 ■ *Innovate to Great: Re-Igniting Sustainable Innovation to Win in the Global Economy*
Pub: McGraw-Hill
Ed: Judy Estrin. **Released:** September 12, 2008. **Price:** , $27.95. **Description:** The author explores

innovation and creativity as a means for small companies to survive and expand in the global economy.

43825 ■ *"Innovate or Stagnate: How Doing Things Differently Helps Business" in South Florida Business Journal (Vol. 34, January 10, 2014, No. 25, pp. 10)*
Pub: American City Business Journals
Released: January 10, 2014. **Description:** Business enterprises can drive growth by focusing on innovations. Companies are advised to consider radical ideas, invent different ways of working and avoid bureaucracy. Peter Drucker, a management consultant, believes that business has two functions: marketing and innovation.

43826 ■ *"Innovating Globally" in Business Strategy Review (Vol. 21, Spring 2010, No. 1, pp, 24)*
Pub: John Wiley & Sons Inc. Scientific, Technical, Medical, and Scholarly Div. (Wiley-Blackwell)
Contact: William J. Pesce, Manager
E-mail: wpesce@wiley.com
Ed: Costas Markides, Stuart Crainer. **Description:** Costas Markides has spent over two decades studying business strategy and innovation. Recently, he has been focusing on the bigger picture of how people can address major social problems. Can the techniques used by managers to create innovation inside organizations work with global change?.

43827 ■ *"Innovating Low-Cost Business Models" in Strategy and Leadership (Vol. 39, March-April 2011, No. 2, pp. 43)*
Pub: Emerald Group Publishing Inc.
Ed: Nicholas Kachaner, Zhenya Lindgardt, David Michael. **Description:** A process that can be used to implement low-cost innovation is presented. The process can be used to address the competitive challenges presented by multinationals' practice of presenting applications and price points that are intended for developing markets into developed markets. The process involves targeting large, and low-income segments of the market.

43828 ■ *Innovation And Entrepreneurship In Biotechnology: An International Perspective*
Pub: Edward Elgar Publishing Inc.
Contact: Richard Henning, Vice President
E-mail: kwight@e-elgar.com
Ed: Damian Hine, John Kapeleris. **Price:** £72, hardback; £33.60, paperback. **Description:** Innovation processes underlying successful entrepreneurship in the biotechnology sector are explored. **Availability:** Print.

43829 ■ *"Innovation Central: Tech, Tweets, and Trolls" in Inc. (Vol. 36, September 2014, No. 7, pp. 102)*
Pub: Mansueto Ventures L.L.C.
Contact: John Koten, Chief Executive Officer
Released: September 2014. **Description:** Results of a survey regarding the ways small business is using technology to grow their businesses is presented. Information covers social media applications, government software patents, trends impacting small business, and the most innovative technology companies.

43830 ■ *Innovation and Entrepreneurship*
Ed: Peter F. Drucker. **Released:** May 2007. **Price:** , $27.95. **Description:** Profile of entrepreneurial innovation.

43831 ■ *Innovation and Entrepreneurship*
Pub: Harper Business
Ed: Peter F. Drucker. **Released:** May 09, 2006. **Price:** $16.99. **Description:** Innovation and entrepreneurship in America's new economy. **Availability:** Print.

43832 ■ *Innovation and Entrepreneurship*
Pub: HarperCollins Publishers Inc.
Contact: Jane Friedman, President
E-mail: jfriedman@harpercollins.com
Ed: Peter F. Drucker. **Released:** May 09, 2006. **Price:** $16.99; $12.49; C$11.99. **Description:** Presentation of entrepreneurship and innovation and a purposeful and systematic discipline and the challenges and opportunities of the American entrepreneurial economy. **Availability:** PrintE-book.

43833 ■ Innovation and Its Discontents: How Our Broken Patent System is Endangering Innovation and Progress, and What to Do About It
Pub: Princeton University Press
Contact: Shirley M. Tilghman, President
Ed: Josh Lerner, Adam B. Jaffe. **Released:** 2007.
Price: $26.95, U.S., hardcover/paperback orders in the Canada, Latin America, Asia, and Australia; £18.95, hardcover/paperback orders in Europe, Africa, the Middle East, and India. **Description:** According to the authors, America's patent system does not effectively serve as a generator and protector of patents and intellectual property. **Availability:** Print.

43834 ■ Innovation Methodologies in Enterprise Research
Pub: Edward Elgar Publishing Inc.
Contact: Richard Henning, Vice President
E-mail: kwight@e-elgar.com
Ed: Damian Hine. **Price:** £81, hardback; £33.60, paperback. **Description:** The importance of qualitative, interpretist research in the field of enterprise research is discussed. The book stresses how enterprise research is a new method and permits a wide scope for new and innovative research studies. **Availability:** Online.

43835 ■ Innovation Nation: How America Is Losing Its Innovation Edge, Why It Matters, and How We Can Get It Back
Pub: Free Press/Simon & Schuster Inc.
Ed: John Kao. **Released:** October 02, 2007. **Price:** $28, Hardcover. **Description:** Diagnoses of the lack of innovation being seen in the United States today is examined by a former Harvard Business School professor. He explains how innovation works and puts forth a strategy proposal in an attempt to help America regain its edge on innovation.

43836 ■ "Innovation Station" in Canadian Business (Vol. 80, October 8, 2007, No. 20, pp. 42)
Ed: Andrew Wahl. **Description:** Study and teaching of entrepreneurship at the University of Waterloo is discussed. Research projects in the university are expected to be influential in Canada's economic development. In spite of the success of these studies, financing is still a problem for the university, especially in technological innovations.

43837 ■ "Innovation's Holy Grail" in Harvard Business Review (Vol. 88, July-August 2010, No. 7-8, pp. 132)
Pub: Harvard Business School Publishing
Ed: C.K. Prahalad, R.A. Mashelkar. **Description:** Three forms of business innovation are presented, inspired by the tenets of Mahatma Gandhi. They are: changing organizational capabilities, sourcing or creating new capabilities, and disrupting conventional business models. Illustrations for these methods are also included.

43838 ■ "Innovative Ability and Entrepreneurial Activity: Two Factors to Enhance 'Quality of Life'" in Journal of Business & Industrial Marketing (Vol. 29, July 2014, No. 6)
Pub: Emerald Group Publishing Inc.
Released: July 2014. **Description:** Examination of how aspects of knowledge economy covered by the KEI (Knowledge Economy Index) and those of entrepreneurial activity covered by the GEI (Global Entrepreneurship Index) affect QOL (quality of Life) in a country. KEI, GEI, and QOL data gathered from different countries was analyzed using correlation and regression analyses. It was observed that KEI and GEI feature a momentous effect on QOL, while innovation index and total early stage entrepreneurship improve it.

43839 ■ The Innovators: How a Group of Hackers, Geniuses, and Geeks Created the Digital Revolution
Pub: Simon and Schuster Inc.
Contact: Carolyn Reidy, President
E-mail: carolyn.reidy@simonandschuster.com
Released: October 7, 2014. **Price:** , $35.00. **Description:** Profiles of the individuals who created the computer and the Internet are provided describing

the talents of certain inventors and entrepreneurs who are able to turn their business visions and goals into realities, while others have failed. The author begins with Ada Lovelace, Lord Byron's daughter, who pioneered computer programming back in the 1840s and continues by exploring the minds of Vannevar Bush, Alan Turing, John von Neumann, J.C.R. Licklider, Doug Englebart, Robert Noyce, Bill Gates, Steve Wozniak, Steve Jobs, Tim Berners-Lee and Larry Page.

43840 ■ "The Innovator's Solution: Creating and Sustaining Successful Growth"
Pub: Harvard Business Review Press
Contact: Peter E. Walsh, Director
Released: October 22, 2013. **Price:** , $30.00. **Description:** Even in today's hyper-accelerated business environment any small company can transform their business. Advice on business decisions crucial to achieving truly disruptive growth and purpose guidelines for developing their own disruptive growth engine is given. The forces that cause managers to make bad decisions as they plan new ideas for their company are identified and new frameworks to help develop the right conditions, at the right time, for a disruption to succeed. Managers and business leaders responsible for innovation and growth will benefit their business and their teams with this information.

43841 ■ "Inside Out" in Playthings (Vol. 107, January 1, 2009, No. 1, pp. 3)
Description: Mattel signed on as the global master toy licensee for Cartoon Network's The Secret Saturdays while Toy Island signed a deal for wooden toys based on several leading Nick Jr. properties.

43842 ■ "The Intel Trinity: How Robert Noyce, Gordon Moore, and Andy Grove Built the World's Most Important Company"
Pub: Harper Business
Released: July 15, 2014. **Price:** , $34.99. **Description:** A complete history of Intel Corporation, the essential company of the digital age, is presented. After over four decades Intel remains the most important company in the world, a defining company of the global digital economy. The inventors of the microprocessor that powers nearly every intelligent electronic device worldwide are profiled. These entrepreneurs made the personal computer, Internet, telecommunications, and personal electronics all possible. The challenges and successes of the company and its ability to maintain its dominance, its culture and its legacy are examined.

43843 ■ International Growth of Small and Medium Enterprises
Pub: Routledge
Contact: Kevin Bradley, President
E-mail: kbradley@taylorandfrancis.com
Released: February 10, 2010. **Price:** $54.95, Paperback; $160, Hardback. **Description:** This volume focuses on how companies expand their operations across borders through opportunity exploration and exploitation, and identification and development of innovations.

43844 ■ "Inventive Doctor New Venture Partner" in Houston Business Journal (Vol. 40, January 29, 2010, No. 38, pp. A2)
Pub: American City Business Journals
Ed: Ford Gunter. **Description:** Dr. Billy Cohn, a surgeon from Houston, Texas has been named as venture partner for venture firm Sante Ventures LLC of Austin, Texas. Cohn will be responsible for seeing marketable developing technologies in the medical industry. The motivation for Cohn's naming as venture partner is his development of a minimally invasive therapy for end-stage renal disease.

43845 ■ "Java Computing: Second Cup?" in Canadian Business (Vol. 81, June 11, 2008, No. 11, pp. 50)
Pub: Rogers Media Inc.
Contact: Tony Viner, President
Ed: Calvin Leung. **Description:** Profile of James Gosling who is credited as the inventor of the Java programming language; however, the 53-year-old software developer feels ambivalent for being credited

as inventor since many people contributed to the language. Netscape and Sun Microsystems incorporation of the programming language into Java is presented.

43846 ■ "Judge Gives RIM One Last Chance" in Globe & Mail (February 24, 2006, pp. B5)
Ed: Barrie McKenna, Paul Waldie. **Description:** United States District Court Judge James Spencer offers more time for Research In Motion Ltd. (RIM) to settle the patent infringement dispute with NTP Inc. RIM's shares increase by 6.2 percent following the decision.

43847 ■ Jump Start Your Business Brain: Ideas, Advice and Insights for Immediate Marketing and Innovation Success
Ed: Doug Hall. **Released:** April 2005. **Price:** , $23.99. **Description:** Strategies to improve sales, marketing, and business development.

43848 ■ Jump Start Your Business Brain: The Scientific Way To Make More Money
Pub: Brain Brew Books
Ed: Doug Hall, Tom Peters. **Released:** April 01, 2005.
Price: $12.36, paperback. **Description:** Author focuses on helping small business owners to become more successful using simple tools that help them discover, develop, and identify great ideas. **Availability:** Print.

43849 ■ "Kaiser Permanente's Innovation on the Front Lines" in Harvard Business Review (Vol. 88, September 2010, No. 9, pp. 92)
Pub: Harvard Business School Publishing
Ed: Lew McCreary. **Description:** Kaiser Permanente's human-centered model for organizational effectiveness emphasizes the roles of patients and providers as collaborators driving quality improvement and innovation.

43850 ■ "Lawyers Sued Over Lapsed Lacrosse Patent" in Crain's Detroit Business (Vol. 25, June 8, 2009, No. 23, pp. 5)
Pub: Crain Communications Inc. - Detroit
Contact: Keith Crain, Chairman
Ed: Chad Halcom. **Description:** Warrior Sports Inc., a manufacturer of lacrosse equipment located in Warren, Michigan is suing the law firm Dickinson Wright PLLC and two of its intellectual property lawyers over patent rights to lacrosse equipment.

43851 ■ Life Entrepreneurs: Ordinary People Creating Extraordinary Lives
Pub: Jossey-Bass
Ed: Christopher Gergen, Gregg Vanourek. **Released:** February 2008. **Price:** $24.95, hardcover; $16.99.
Description: Consultants Christopher Gergen and Gregg Vanourek present the basic principles for becoming a successful entrepreneur: recognizing opportunity, taking risks, and innovation. **Availability:** PrintE-book.

43852 ■ "Life's Work: James Dyson" in Harvard Business Review (Vol. 88, July-August 2010, No. 7-8, pp. 172)
Pub: Harvard Business School Publishing
Ed: Alison Beard. **Description:** The founder of appliance company Dyson Ltd. discusses the role of making mistakes in learning and innovation, and emphasizes the importance of hands-on involvement to make a company successful.

43853 ■ "The Little Insect" in Canadian Electronics (Vol. 23, June-July 2008, No. 4, pp. 6)
Ed: Tim Gouldson. **Description:** Electronics designers should not be underestimated because they can manufacture technologies vital to saving lives and bringing peace. They have designed robots and other electronic equipment that are as small as insects.

43854 ■ "Local Company Seeks Patent For Armored Trucks" in Crain's Detroit Business (Vol. 24, February 4, 2008, No. 5, pp. 10)
Pub: Crain Communications Inc. - Detroit
Contact: Keith Crain, Chairman
Description: Profile of James LeBlanc Sr., mechanical engineer and defense contractor, discusses his eleven utility patents pending for a set of vehicles and subsystems that would work as countermeasures to explosively formed projectiles.

43855 ■ *"Look, Leap, and License"* in *Retail Merchandiser (Vol. 51, July-August 2011, No. 4, pp. 16)*
Pub: Phoenix Media Corporation
Description: Toys highlighting the Licensing International Expo 2011 included a life-sized Cookie Monster, Papa Smurf, Power Rangers, Transformer, and margarita wrestlers. Taking licensed properties international was a common theme at this year's show.

43856 ■ *"Look Out, Barbie, Bratz are Back"* in *Canadian Business (Vol. 83, August 17, 2010, No. 13-14, pp. 18)*
Pub: Rogers Media Inc.
Contact: Tony Viner, President
Ed: Joe Castaldo. Description: California-based MGA Entertainment has wrestled back control over Bratz from Mattel after a six-year legal battle. However, MGA owner Isaac Larian could still face legal hurdles if Mattel pursues a retrial. He now has to revive the brand which virtually disappeared from stores when Mattel won the rights for Bratz.

43857 ■ *"MaggieMoo's Ice Cream and Treatery"* in *Ice Cream Reporter (Vol. 23, September 20, 2010, No. 10, pp. 7)*
Description: MaggieMoo's Ice Cream and Treatery has launched a new Website where visitors can learn about the brands newest ice cream innovations.

43858 ■ *"Managing Yourself: How to Save Good Ideas"* in *Harvard Business Review (Vol. 88, October 2010, No. 10, pp. 129)*
Pub: Harvard Business School Publishing
Ed: Jeff Kehoe. Description: Harvard Business School Professor John P. Kotter identifies situations that may hinder the development and implementation of ideas, and discusses effective ways to counter them.

43859 ■ *Market Rebels: How Activists Make or Break Radical Innovations*
Pub: Princeton University Press
Contact: Shirley M. Tilghman, President
Ed: Hayagreeva Rao. Released: 2009. Price: $24.95; £16.95. Description: Informal groups of enthusiasts could be the key to making a new product the next big thing to hit the marketplace.

43860 ■ *"Market and Technology Orientations for Service Delivery Innovation: the Link of Innovative Competence"* in *Journal of Business & Industrial Marketing (Vol. 29, July 2014, No. 6)*
Pub: Emerald Group Publishing Inc.
Released: July 2014. Description: A study to formulate an alternative method of predicting service delivery innovation based on market and technology orientations and innovative competence is examined. Five hypotheses were proposed and tested using the Partial Least Square (PLS) analysis. It was observed that proactive market orientation and technology orientation regulate exploratory and exploitative innovative competences, while exploitative competence influences service delivery innovation.

43861 ■ *Medici Effect*
Ed: Frans Johansson. Released: October 30, 2006. Price: $16. Description: Examples of how ideas can be turned into path-breaking innovations.

43862 ■ *"Mentor Medical Device Maker's Partnerships Open New Opportunities"* in *Crain's Cleveland Business (Vol. 30, June 22, 2009, No. 24)*
Pub: Crain Communications Inc.
Ed: Chuck Soder. Description: Frantz Medical Development Ltd. develops medical devices based on ideas from outside inventors. The company wants to manufacture the innovations at its Mentor campus.

43863 ■ *"Miracle Portfolio Cure!"* in *Canadian Business (Vol. 85, September 17, 2012, No. 14, pp. 65)*
Pub: George Media Inc.
Ed: Bryan Borzykowski. Released: September 17, 2012. Description: The pharmaceutical industry remains a strong investment in the volatile markets despite concerns over patent expirations of some

popular drugs. Investors are advised to choose brand name companies and to consider price-to-earnings in terms of valuation.

43864 ■ *"Molycorp Funds Wind Energy Technology Company"* in *Manufacturing Close-Up (September 19, 2011)*
Pub: Close-Up Media
Description: Molycorp Inc., producer of rare earth oxides (REO) and a REO producer outside of China, announced it will invest in Boulder Wind Power, which has designed a rare earth magnet powered wind turbine generator. This new generator can produce electricity as low as $0.04 per Kilowatt Hour. Boulder Wind Power's patented wind turbine technology allows for use of rare earth permanent magnets that do not require dysprosium, which is relatively scarce.

43865 ■ *"Monsanto Wins Patent Case Against DuPont"* in *Farm Journal (Vol. 136, September 2012, No. 8, pp. 8)*
Pub: Farm Journal Media Inc.
Description: Monsanto Company was awarded a $1 billion settlement by a federal jury for a patent infringement lawsuit the company filed againt DuPont regarding Roundup Ready seed technolgy. Details of the lawsuit are included.

43866 ■ *"Mortgage Companies are Adding Staff"* in *Sacramento Business Journal (Vol. 29, September 14, 2012, No. 29, pp. 1)*
Pub: American City Business Journal
Ed: Sanford Nax. Description: Mortgage companies have been increasing their hiring as a result of persistently low interest rates and tough new government regulations. The mortgage industry has gained 1,335 jobs in the second quarter nationally, while the number of applications to receive a mortgage loan originator license is rising in California.

43867 ■ *"Mosaid Grants First Wireless Parent License To Matsushita"* in *Canadian Electronics (Vol. 23, June-July 2008, No. 5, pp. 1)*
Description: Matsushita Electric Industrial Co. Ltd. has been granted a six-and-a-half-year license by Mosaid Technologies Inc. to manufacture the latter's products. The patent portfolio license agreement covers Mosaid's Wi-Fi, Wi-Max, CDMA-enabled notebook computers and other products.

43868 ■ *"Much Work Still To Be Done on Meadows Deal"* in *Pittsburgh Business Times (Vol. 33, May 16, 2014, No. 44, pp. 3)*
Pub: American City Business Journals
Released: May 16, 2014. Description: Real estate investment trust, Gaming and Leisure Properties Inc., is acquiring the Meadows Racetrack & Casino in Washington, Pennsylvania from Cannery Casino & Resorts LLC in a $465 million deal. The process of finding an operator and getting the license transfers approved will be the next critical step following the deal.

43869 ■ *"MultiLing Expands HQ to Provide Room for Translation, Business Development Teams"* in *Entertainment Close-Up (May 6, 2012)*
Pub: Close-Up Media
Released: May 6, 2012. Description: MultiLing has expanded to improve its standarization and centralized intellectual property translations around the world. MultiLing provides IP translation to patent attorneys and corporations globally.

43870 ■ *"The Natural Environment, Innovation, and Firm Performance"* in *Family Business Review (Vol. 19, December 2006, No. 4)*
Pub: Family Firm Institute
Contact: Judy L. Green, President
Ed: Justin Craig, Clay Dibrell. Description: Comparative study of the impact of firm-level natural environment-related policies on innovation and performance of family and non-family firms is presented.

43871 ■ *"Necessity Mother of This Startup"* in *Providence Business News (Vol. 28, January 6, 2014, No. 40, pp. 1)*
Pub: American City Business Journals
Released: January 6, 2014. Description: Kailas Narendran, founder of kiinde LLC, invented a device that can quickly thaw breast milk to precisely the right temperature for feeding a baby without losing nutrients. Innovative products for mothers and babies are now being sold by kiine throughout the U.S., Canada and South Korea. New product development is discussed by Narendran.

43872 ■ *"New Approach Could Boost Ivory Tower Innovation"* in *Business Journal-Portland (Vol. 24, November 16, 2007, No. 37, pp. 1)*
Pub: American City Business Journals, Inc.
Ed: Aliza Earnshaw. Description: New approach which aims to help universities move to a corporate structure, secure funds, and find professional managers is being explored. Accelerator Corporation was able to help six companies through its funding. Joe Tanous who is behind Oregon's State University's enhanced commercialization, would like to apply the same approach Accelerator used to help Oregon State University, the University of Oregon, Portland State University and Oregon Health and Science University.

43873 ■ *The New Innovators: How Canadians are Shaping the Knowledge-Based Economy*
Pub: James Lorimer & Company Ltd.
Ed: Roger Voyer, Patti Ryan. Released: January 01, 1994. Price: C$29.95. Description: Details are examined showing how the innovation process works and how ideas are successfully translated into marketable products. Availability: Print.

43874 ■ *"New Life for Old Chemistries"* in *Farm Industry News (Vol. 42, January 1, 2009, No. 1)*
Pub: Intertec Publishing
Contact: John French, President
Ed: Mark Moore. Description: To expand the uses of familiar crop protection products, chemical companies are utilizing biotechnology research and development tools; many off-patent products are being rejuvenated with small changes to make the product even better than it was when originally conceived.

43875 ■ *"The Next Great Canadian Idea: Peripiteia Generator"* in *Canadian Business (Vol. 81, July 21, 2008, No. 11, pp. 45)*
Pub: Rogers Media Inc.
Contact: Tony Viner, President
Ed: Sharda Prashad. Description: Thane Heins has invented a generator that produces energy in an isolated system which contradicts the law of conservation of energy. Perepiteia generator is referred to as a 'perpetual motion machine.' Other inventions slated for the Canadian invention competition include Rob Matthies' batteries and Frank Naumann's Smart Trap.

43876 ■ *"The Next Step in Patent Reform"* in *Information Today (Vol. 28, November 2011, No. 10, pp. 1)*
Pub: Information Today, Inc.
Contact: Thomas H. Hogan, President
E-mail: ctuthill@infotoday.com
Ed: George H. Pike. Description: The Leahy-Smith America Invents Act was signed into law in September 2011. The new act reformed the previous US patent system. Information involving the new patent law process is discussed.

43877 ■ *"Nike's Next Splash"* in *The Business Journal-Portland (Vol. 25, August 22, 2008, No. 24, pp. 1)*
Pub: American City Business Journals, Inc.
Contact: Whitney Shaw, President
Ed: Erik Siemers. Description: Business analysts expect Nike to bid for the endorsement services of swimmer Michael Phelps after the swimmer's contract with Speedo expires. The company, however, is a lightweight in the swimming apparel market and is not focusing on swimming as a growth sector.

43878 ■ *"No Lines, No Waiting: Voda LLC Is Where SRI-St. Petersburg Will Be" in The Business Journal-Serving Greater Tampa Bay (Vol. 28, August 18, 2008, No. 34, pp. 1)*
Pub: American City Business Journals, Inc.
Contact: Whitney Shaw, President
Ed: Jane Meinhardt. **Description:** Voda LLC, which was founded to commercialize developments by David Fries, develops outdoor sensor networks used for environmental monitoring by markets like research, the security industry, and the government. Fries already licensed 12 technologies for clients for about $130,000 per technology. Other information on Voda LLC is presented.

43879 ■ *"Of Marks and Men" in Canadian Business (Vol. 80, March 12, 2007, No. 6, pp. 59)*
Ed: Andy Holloway. **Description:** The importance on the part of business enterprises to register for trademarks to avoid any threat of litigation in future is discussed.

43880 ■ *"Organization Redesign and Innovative HRM" in Human Resource Management (Vol. 49, July-August 2010, No. 4, pp. 809-811)*
Pub: John Wiley
Ed: Pat Lynch. **Description:** An overview of the book, 'Organization Redesign and Innovative HRM' is presented.

43881 ■ *"Orlando Patents Forecast Biz Diversity and Growth" in Orlando Business Journal (Vol. 30, April 18, 2014, No. 43, pp. 4)*
Pub: American City Business Journals
Released: April 18, 2014. **Description:** Orlando, Florida ranked among cities in the state in terms of number of patents filed. Around 275 patents were issued to Orlando-based inventors and businesses in 2013. The increase in the number of high technology companies entering the city has contributed to this trend.

43882 ■ *"The Overlicensed Society" in Harvard Business Review (Vol. 90, April 2012, No. 4, pp. 38)*
Pub: Harvard Business Review Press
Contact: Peter E. Walsh, Director
Ed: Robert E. Litan. **Released:** April 2012. **Description:** The author argues that certification and licensing requirements are hindering professionals who might otherwise be able to find positions and provide services inexpensively. To key areas are healthcare and law. Federal mutual recognition agreements may be one method of addressing both practice and consumer protection issues.

43883 ■ *"Patent Pain" in Canadian Business (Vol. 80, November 19, 2007, No. 23, pp. 43)*
Pub: Rogers Media Inc.
Contact: Tony Viner, President
Ed: Andrew Wahl. **Description:** James McBride of World Standard Fitness has prepared a patent for his invention, a rubberized lifting strap. The patent helped raid interest for the product, however other similar products have already been available in the market. Benefits of having an invention patented are examined.

43884 ■ *"Patently Absurd" in Globe & Mail (January 28, 2006, pp. B4)*
Ed: Barrie McKenna; Paul Waldie; Simon Avery. **Description:** An overview of facts about patent dispute between Research In Motion Ltd. and NTP Inc. is presented.

43885 ■ *"Patently (Un)Clear" in Business Strategy Review (Vol. 21, Spring 2010, No. 1, pp. 28)*
Pub: John Wiley & Sons Inc. Scientific, Technical, Medical, and Scholarly Div. (Wiley-Blackwell)
Contact: William J. Pesce, Manager
E-mail: wpesce@wiley.com
Ed: Markus Reitzig, Stefan Wagner. **Description:** After developing a great product or process, it's important to protect it. The benefits of using internal patent lawyers versus outsourcing the task are examined.

43886 ■ *"Patent's Handbook: A Guide for Inventors and Researchers to Searching Patent Documents and Preparing and Making an Application*
Pub: McFarland & CPI, Publishers
Contact: Shelia Baldwin, Manager
E-mail: sbaldwin@mcfarlandpub.com
URL(s): www.mcfarlandpub.com/book-2.php?id=978-0-7864-4321-5. **Price:** $39.95, Individuals softcover. **Publication includes:** List of information sources for researching patents and inventorship. Principal content of publication is an overview of the patent system in the United States. **Database includes:** Diagrams, facsimiles, appendix. **Indexes:** Master.

43887 ■ *"Payback: Reaping the Rewards of Innovation*
Pub: Harvard Business School Publishing
Ed: James P. Andrew, Harold L. Sirkin, John Butman. **Released:** January 09, 2007. **Price:** $29.95, hardcover. **Description:** Three different business innovation models are presented: integration, orchestration, and serving as licensor.

43888 ■ *"Personal Trainer Fitness Certification Offers Secrets to Personal Training Business and Career Success" in Marketing Weekly News (January 14, 2012, pp. 56)*
Description: The National Exercise and Sports Trainers Association (NESTA) is offering an online NCCA accredited four-year training certification with cost savings over most other certification programs. The program is 100 percent online and self-paced.

43889 ■ *"PGA Tour: Course Management" in Retail Merchandiser (Vol. 51, September-October 2011, No. 5, pp. 38)*
Pub: Phoenix Media Corporation
Ed: Eric Slack. **Description:** PGA Tour must reach new customers and solidify relationships with its traditional base in order to continue its success. The PGA brand equity has translated into one of the largest retail licensing operations worldwide.

43890 ■ *"Phillip Frost: 'Technology Is the Future'" in South Florida Business Journal (Vol. 34, June 20, 2014, No. 48, pp. 16)*
Pub: American City Business Journals
Released: June 20, 2014. **Description:** Entrepreneur, Phillip Frost, shares his strategies and perspectives on the business climate of Miami, Florida. He describes investment strategy for the diverse holdings of Opko Health and his criteria for buying companies and licensing technologies.

43891 ■ *"Pick A Trademark You Can Protect" in Women Entrepreneur (November 3, 2008)*
Ed: Nina L. Kaufman. **Description:** Provides information regarding trademarks, how to choose a name that will win approval from the U.S. Patent and Trademark Office, and how to choose a trademark that one can protect.

43892 ■ *"Pioneering Strategies for Entrepreneurial Success" in Business Horizons (Vol. 51, January-February 2008, No. 1, pp. 21)*
Pub: Elsevier Advanced Technology Publications
Ed: Candida G. Brush. **Description:** Entrepreneurs are known for new products, services, processes, markets and industries. In order to achieve success, they have to develop a clear vision, creatively manage finances, and use social skills to persuade others to commit to the venture. Pioneering strategies and their implementation are examined.

43893 ■ *"Practical Approach to Addressing Holdover Ex-Franchisee Trademark Issues" in Franchise Law Journal (Vol. 27, Summer 2007, No. 1, pp. 30)*
Pub: American Bar Association
Contact: Carolyn Lamm, President
Ed: Christopher P. Bussert, William Bryner. **Description:** Franchisor-franchisee relationships can become legally complicated when they are terminated. Laws governing trademarks and other proprietary materials are examined.

43894 ■ *"Presidential Address: Innovation in Retrospect and Prospect" in Canadian Journal of Electronics (Vol. 43, November 2010, No. 4)*
Pub: Journal of the Canadian Economics Association
Ed: James A. Brander. **Description:** Has innovation slowed in recent decades? While there has been progress in information and communications technology, the recent record of innovation in agriculture, energy, transportation and healthcare sectors is cause for concern.

43895 ■ *"Probability Processing Chip: Lyric Semiconductor" in Inc. (Volume 32, December 2010, No. 10, pp. 52)*
Pub: Inc. Magazine
Ed: Christine Lagorio. **Description:** Lyric Semiconductor, a start up located in Cambridge, Massachusetts, has developed a computer chip that also uses values that fall between zero and one, resulting in a chip that can process information using probabilities, considering many possible answers that find the best fit.

43896 ■ *"Profile: Lynda Gratton" in Business Strategy Review (Vol. 21, Autumn 2010, No. 3, pp. 74)*
Pub: John Wiley & Sons Inc. Scientific, Technical, Medical, and Scholarly Div. (Wiley-Blackwell)
Contact: William J. Pesce, Manager
E-mail: wpesce@wiley.com
Ed: Stuart Crainer. **Description:** The early 20th Century marked the dawn of modern enterprise management, and no one influenced its practice more than Frederick W. Taylor, inventor of 'scientific management'. This radical transformation of management and among the few thinkers most influencing this transformation is Lynda Gratton, London Business School Professor of Management Practice.

43897 ■ *"Protect Your Domain Name From Cybersquatters" in Idaho Business Review (September 1, 2014)*
Pub: Dolan Co.
Contact: James P. Dolan, President
Released: September 1, 2014. **Description:** Cybersquatting is the practice of registering, trafficking in or using domain names with the intent to profit from the goodwill of recognizable trade names or trademarks of other companies. Companies can protect their Website domain by following these steps: register domain names, promptly renew registrations, maintain proper records, obtain additional top-level domains, and monitor your site for cybersquatters.

43898 ■ *"Providing Expertise Required to Develop Microsystems" in Canadian Electronics (Vol. 23, February 2008, No. 1, pp. 6)*
Ed: Ian McWalter. **Description:** CMC Microsystems, formerly Canadian Microelectronics Corporation, is focused on empowering microelectronics and Microsystems research in Canada. Microsystems offers the basis for innovations in the fields of science, environment, technology, automotives, energy, aerospace and communications technology. CMC's strategy in developing Microsystems in Canada is described.

43899 ■ *"Q&A: Celestica's Craig Muhlhauser" in Canadian Business (Vol. 81, September 15, 2008, No. 14-15, pp. 6)*
Pub: Rogers Media Inc.
Contact: Tony Viner, President
Ed: Andrew Wahl. **Description:** Interview with Craig Muhlhauser who is the CEO of Celestica, a manufacturing company that provides services for the electronics sector; Muhlhauser discusses the company's restructuring program, which he feels was the secret to their surprising first-quarter results. Muhlhauser states that the company is operating with more forward visibility and that understanding the opportunities during the current economic situation presents the biggest challenge.

43900 ■ *"Quality Performance of SMEs in a Developing Economy: Direct and Indirect Effects of Service Innovation and*

Entrepreneurial Orientation" in Journal of Business & Industrial Marketing (Vol. 29, July 2014, No. 6)

Pub: Emerald Group Publishing Inc.

Released: July 2014. **Description:** A study was conducted to investigate the effects of innovation and EO (entrepreneurial orientation) on organizational performance in Asian small enterprise context. Strategic management literature and the relationship between EO, innovation, and quality performance was tested. The results indicated that a noteworthy direct and indirect positive relationship exists between EO dimensions, innovation, and quality performance.

43901 ■ "The Quest for the Smart Prosthetic" in Canadian Business (Vol. 83, October 12, 2010, No. 17, pp. 26)

Pub: Rogers Media Inc.

Contact: Tony Viner, President

Ed: Jacqueline Nelson. **Description:** Information about a two-year research project led by Southern Methodist University (SMU) and funded by the Defense Advance Research Projects Agency (DARPA) is provided. The agency aims to create a 'smart prosthetic' which will improve the lives of military amputees. The planned prosthetic will use a sensor that can carry nerve signals through synthetic channels.

43902 ■ "Racing to Beam Electricity to Devices Wirelessly" in San Francisco Business Times (Vol. 28, April 11, 2014, No. 38, pp. 6)

Pub: American City Business Journals

Released: April 11, 2014. **Description:** Pleasanton, California-based Energous Corporation has developed a technology that safely converts radio waves into electrical current. The innovation makes it possible to charge multiple/cellular mobile phones or other electrical devices from a distance of 15 feet. The prototype of Energous founder, Michael Leabman's invention is also outlined.

43903 ■ "Radiant Commences In-Lab Testing for US Air Mobility Command" in Canadian Corporate News (May 16, 2007)

Description: The Boeing Company will be conducting in-lab infrared material testing for the Radiant Energy Corporation, developer and marketer of InfraTek, the environmentally friendly, patented infrared pre-flight aircraft deicing system.

43904 ■ "Realtors Signing Out" in The Business Journal-Serving Metropolitan Kansas City (Vol. 27, November 21, 2008, No. 11, pp. 1)

Pub: American City Business Journals, Inc.

Contact: Whitney Shaw, President

Ed: Rob Roberts. **Description:** The Kansas City Regional Association of Realtors has lost 1,000 of its members due to the downturn in the housing market. Applications for realtor licenses have dropped by 159 percent. Changes in Missouri's licensing requirements are seen as additional reasons for the declines.

43905 ■ "Region to Be Named Innovation Hub" in Business Courier (Vol. 27, July 2, 2010, No. 9, pp. 1)

Pub: Business Courier

Ed: Dan Monk. **Description:** The selection of Cincinnati's consumer-marketing cluster as a 'Hub of Innovation' by the Ohio Department of Development could boost Cincinnati's chances of receiving $100 million in grants from Ohio's Third Frontier program and other funding sources. Implications of the University of Cincinnati's designation as a Center of Excellence in Advanced Transportation and Aerospace are also discussed.

43906 ■ "Regulators Revoke Mann Bracken's Collection Agency Licenses" in Collections & Credit Risk (Vol. 15, September 1, 2010, No. 8, pp. 19)

Pub: SourceMedia Inc.

Contact: James M. Malkin, Chief Executive Officer

Description: Maryland regulators have revoked the collections licenses of defunct law firm Mann Bracken LLP.

43907 ■ "Remix: Making Art and Commerce Thrive in the Hybrid Economy

Pub: Dutton Children's Books

Contact: Lauri Hornik, President

Ed: Lawrence Lessig. **Released:** September 29, 2009. **Price:** $17, paperback. **Description:** An examination of copyright laws in the digital age. **Availability:** Print.

43908 ■ "Rep. Loretta Sanchez Holds a Hearing on Small Business Cyber Security" in Political/Congressional Transcript Wire (July 29, 2010)

Pub: CQ Roll Call

Description: U.S. House Committee on Armed Services, Subcommittee on Terrorism, Unconventional Threats and Capabilities held a hearing on small business cyber security innovation.

43909 ■ "Rethinking the Organization" in Strategy & Leadership (Vol. 38, September-October 2010, No. 5, pp. 13-19)

Pub: Emerald Inc.

Ed: Stephen Denning. **Description:** A study identifies the changes needed to be adopted by top managers to achieve game-changing innovation at an organization-wide level. Findings indicate that CEOs should practice pull management in order to nurture fruitful communication between employees and customers and achieve organizational involvement of customers.

43910 ■ "Reversal of Fortune" in Canadian Business (Vol. 85, June 11, 2012, No. 10, pp. 32)

Pub: George Media Inc.

Ed: Matthew McClearn. **Released:** June 11, 2012. **Description:** First Quantum Minerals of Vancouver, British Columbia contested the decisio of the Democratic Republic of Congo to revoke their mining license in the Kolwezi Tailings by means of political pressure and international law. Eurasian National Resources Corporation agreed to pay First Quantum $1.25 billion in return for uncontested title to Congo mines and a ceasefire in January 2012.

43911 ■ "Reviving Entrepreneurship: Policy Decisions in 12 Areas Could Nurture - Or Cripple - America's Greatest Asset" in Harvard Business Review (Vol. 90, March 2012, No. 3, pp. 116)

Pub: Harvard Business Review Press

Contact: Peter E. Walsh, Director

Ed: Josh Lerner, William Sahlman. **Released:** March 2012. **Description:** Government policies should address entrepreneurship as a process, rather than an act. Several key areas for policymaking include basic and translational science, supply and quality of human capital, information availability, tax treatment of rewards and risks, intellectual property rights, workforce healthcare, and mobility of financial and human capital.

43912 ■ "RIM Says It's Willing to Cut a Check" in Globe & Mail (February 24, 2006, pp. B1)

Ed: Simon Avery. **Description:** The settlement terms proposed by Research In Motion Ltd. in a patent infringement case with NTP Inc. are presented.

43913 ■ "RIM's Test of Faith" in Canadian Business (Vol. 80, April 9, 2007, No. 8, pp. 29)

Ed: Joe Castaldo. **Description:** The growth of Research In Motion Ltd. in terms of its sales and profits despite a patent suit on it and competition of rivals is discussed.

43914 ■ Risk Takers and Innovators, Great Canadian Business Ventures Since 1950

Pub: Altitude Publishing

Ed: Sandra Phinney. **Released:** June 15, 2004. **Price:** , $7.95. **Description:** Successful business leaders share their creativity, technology skills, and entrepreneurship.

43915 ■ "The Road to Newness" in Entrepreneur (June 2014)

Pub: Entrepreneur Media Inc.

Released: June 2014. **Description:** A number of business experts share their thoughts on science, invention and innovation and how they are shaping the development of new products, technologies and commodities. Only nonprofit organizations, universities and few rich companies invest in scientific research because it is the riskiest form of investment. Some corporations are spending money on invention rather than science but spending is carefully controlled. People who want to see a quick return on their investment should choose innovation.

43916 ■ "Safer Ammonium-Nitrate-Based Fertilizer" in Farm Industry News (Vol. 42, January 1, 2009, No. 1)

Pub: Intertec Publishing

Contact: John French, President

Description: Honeywell has patented a new technology which it will use to develop a highly effective, safer ammonium-nitrate-based fertilizer that has a significantly lower potential for explosion.

43917 ■ "San Jose Cuts Fees, Red Tape On Office R and D" in Silicon Valley/San Jose Business Journal (Vol. 29, February 3, 2012, No. 45, pp. 1)

Description: The San Jose, California City Council has approved measures to reduce construction taxes on tenant improvements. It has also cut fees developers must pay for traffic improvements in North San Jose. The Council is also set to speed up permit processing by hiring additional personnel.

43918 ■ "Serials Solutions Launches 360 Resource Manager Consortium Edition" in Information Today (Vol. 26, February 2009, No. 2, pp. 32)

Description: Serials Solutions new Serials Solutions 360 Resource Manager Consortium Edition helps consortia, groups and member libraries with their e-resource management services. The products allows users to consolidate e-resource metadata and acquisition information into one place, which enables groups to manage holdings, subscriptions, licensing, contacts, and cost information and to streamline delivery of information to members.

43919 ■ "The Service Imperative" in Business Horizons (Vol. 51, January-February 2008, No. 1, pp. 39)

Pub: Elsevier Advanced Technology Publications

Ed: Mary Jo Bitner, Stephen W. Brown. **Description:** The importance of services is growing in developing countries like India and China, but little attention is given to service research, education and innovation. The 'service imperative' seeks to promote the advancement of services. The scope, objectives and philosophy of the service imperative platform are outlined.

43920 ■ "Shedding Light on Innovation" in Rental Product News (Vol. 33, June 2011)

Pub: Cygnus Business Media

Contact: Paul Mackler, Chief Executive Officer

Ed: Rod Dickens. **Description:** Light tower manufacturers have introduced numerous new products that feature alternative power sources, LED lighting and a second generation of performance and value.

43921 ■ "Sinai Doctor's Research May Lead to Rival Plavix Drug" in Baltimore Business Journal (Vol. 28, July 16, 2010, No. 10, pp. 1)

Pub: Baltimore Business Journal

Ed: Emily Mullin. **Description:** Paul Gurbel, Sinai Hospital Center for Thrombosis Research director, is seeking an FDA approval of Brilinta, a drug which he helped create and test. Gurbel says that the approval could bring the drug to market as early as December 2010. The drug is expected to rival Bristol-Myers' Plavix, which generated almost $6.2 billion in 2009.

43922 ■ "The Sky's the Limit" in Retail Merchandiser (Vol. 51, July-August 2011, No. 4, pp. 64)

Pub: Phoenix Media Corporation

Ed: John Capizzi. **Description:** Mars Retail Group (MRG) is the licensing division handling M&M's Brand Candies. Since taking over the brand they have expanded from 12 licensees to 50 licensees with new offerings.

43923 ■ Small Business: Innovation, Problems and Strategy
Pub: Nova Science Publishers Inc.
Contact: Frank Columbus, President
Released: 2009. Price: $117, hardcover; $79. Description: Innovation is a fundamental determinant of value creation in businesses and can also be a key to successful economic growth. The innovative process and innovative effort of small companies are examined and evaluated, along with alternative strategies. Availability: PrintE-book.

43924 ■ Small Business Legal Tool Kit
Pub: Entrepreneur Press
Contact: Perlman Neil, President
Ed: Ira Nottonson, Theresa A. Pickner. Description: Legal expertise is provided by two leading entrepreneurial attorneys. Issues covered include forming and operating a business: taxes, contracts, leases, bylaws, trademarks, small claims court, etc.

43925 ■ "A Sports Extravaganza - To Go" in Canadian Business (Vol. 79, June 19, 2006, No. 13, pp. 21)
Ed: Andy Holloway. Description: Television broadcasting industry in Canada utilizing advanced technologies like mobile television and internet protocol television in broadcasting major sports events. Large number of new technologies are being invented to support increasing demand.

43926 ■ "Steve Meginniss Helped Reinvent the Toothbrush. Can He Do the Same Thing for Wheels?" in Inc. (February 2008, pp. 32)
Ed: Dalia Fahmy. Description: Profile of Steve Meginniss, co-inventor of Sonicare Toothbrush and inventor of a two-gear wheel for wheelchairs. Mgeinniss discusses his need to raid $1 million to promote and cut manufacturing costs for this new product that helps reduce pain for users.

43927 ■ "Stop the Innovation Wars" in Harvard Business Review (Vol. 88, July-August 2010, No. 7-8, pp. 76)
Pub: Harvard Business School Publishing
Ed: Vijay Govindarajan, Chris Trimble. Description: Methods for managing conflicts between partners during the innovation initiative process are highlighted. These include dividing the labor, assembling a dedicated team, and mitigating likelihood for any potential conflict.

43928 ■ "Street Beaters: How the Top Stock Earners on Our List Pulled It Off" in Canadian Business (Vol. 80, Winter 2007, No. 24, pp. 135)
Ed: Jeff Sanford. Description: Shares of Research in Motion Ltd. jumped 163 percent in 2007 after setting their dispute. ShawCor Ltd.'s stocks rose 99.6 percent while Onex Corporation's shares reached a high of $41.25 in 2007 from its $25 average in 2006.

43929 ■ "Study Puts Hub On Top of the Tech Heap" in Boston Business Journal (Vol. 30, November 26, 2010, No. 44, pp. 1)
Pub: Boston Business Journal
Ed: Galen Moore. Description: The Ewing Marion Kauffman Foundation ranked Massachusetts at the top in its evaluations of states' innovative industries, government leadership, and education. Meanwhile, research blog formDs.com also ranked Massachusetts number one in terms of venture-capital financings per capita.

43930 ■ "Successful Patent Troll Targets HomeAway" in Austin Business Journal (Vol. 32, July 6, 2012, No. 18, pp. 1)
Pub: American City Business Journals, Inc.
Contact: Whitney Shaw, President
Ed: Vicky Garza. Released: July 6, 2012. Description: Unified Messaging Solutions LLC, a subsidiary of Acacia Research Corporation, has made allegations that Austin, Texas-based HomeAway Inc. infringed on five patents related to online messaging. The company has sued about 100 prominent companies and could receive a settlement deal if its streak continues. Insights on Acacia's business model are also given.

43931 ■ SuperCorp: How Vanguard Companies Create Innovation, Profits, Growth, and Social Good
Pub: Crown Business
Ed: Rosabeth Moss Kanter. Released: 2009. Price: $15.99; $27.50, Hardcover. Description: Harvard professor makes a persuasive case showing how social good is good for any company's bottom line. Availability: E-bookPrint.

43932 ■ "The 'Supply Side' of the Auto Industry" in Montly Labor Review (Vol. 133, September 2010, No. 9, pp. 72)
Pub: U.S. Department of Labor Bureau of Labor Statistics
Contact: Philip L. Rones, Manager
E-mail: rones.philip@bls.gov
Description: Restructuring and geographic change in the automobile industry is discussed.

43933 ■ "T-Shirt Business: How To Work From Home Starting your Own Online Business In A Popular Teespring Niche!"
Pub: Amazon Digital Services
Released: September 12, 2014. Price: , $5.99. Description: Advice is given to launch a T-shirt business without investing a lot of money. Profile of Teespring T-shirts, a company that helps entrepreneurs start a home-based online store, is provided. It teaches how to sell, entice a niche, copyright infringement information, competition, social media marketing and advertising, and more.

43934 ■ "Tastee-Freez Celebrates 60th Anniversary" in Ice Cream Reporter (Vol. 23, July 20, 2010, No. 8, pp. 2)
Description: Tastee-Freez founders, Leo Moranz (inventor) and Harry Axene, an inventor partnered to market the soft-serve pump and freezer for serving frozen treats back in 1950.

43935 ■ "Tax Planning for Royalties"
Pub: CreateSpace
Contact: Daren Giles, President
Released: October 19, 2014. Price: , $15.99 paperback. Description: Tax planning and copyright royalty issues are defined for entrepreneurs living in the United Kingdom. Topics covered include: electronic book and copyright royalties, how IP holding companies work, transferring royalties to offshore business, double tax treaties to reduce withholding taxes, patents, and more.

43936 ■ Technological Entrepreneurship
Pub: Edward Elgar Publishing Inc.
Contact: Richard Henning, Vice President
E-mail: kwight@e-elgar.com
Released: October 2006. Price: $238.50, hardback. Description: Technological entrepreneurship at universities is discussed. The book covers four related topics: university licensing and patenting; science parks and incubators; university-based startups; and the role of academic science in entrepreneurship. Availability: Print.

43937 ■ "Think Disruptive! How to Manage In a New Era of Innovation" in Strategy & Leadership (Vol. 38, July-August 2010, No. 4, pp. 5-10)
Pub: Emerald Inc.
Ed: Brian Leavy, John Sterling. Description: The views expressed by Scott Anthony, president of an innovation consultancy Innosight, on the need for corporate leaders to apply disruptive innovation in a recessionary environment are presented. His suggestion that disruptive innovation is the only way to survive during the economic crisis is discussed.

43938 ■ "Time for a Leap Of Faith?" in Women Entrepreneur (November 18, 2008)
Ed: Cynthia McKay. Description: Starting a new business, despite the downturn in the economy, can prove to be a successful endeavor if one has the time, energy and most importantly a good idea.

43939 ■ The Tipping Point
Ed: Malcom Gladwell. Price: $14.95. Description: How and why certain products and ideas become fads.

43940 ■ The Tipping Point: How Little Things Can Make a Big Difference
Pub: Little, Brown and Company
Ed: Malcolm Gladwell. Released: January 07, 2002. Price: $16.99; C$19.99. Description: Correlation between societal changes and marketing and business trends. Availability: Print.

43941 ■ "Tool Time" in Entrepreneur (Vol. 36, March 2008, No. 3, pp. 90)
Pub: Entrepreneur Press
Contact: Perlman Neil, President
Ed: Nichole L. Torres. Description: DaVinci Institute holds an annual event in Colorado to display new products and inventions. Innovative Design Engineering Animation is a consulting company that helps inventors develop product through various stages. NineSigma Inc. has an online marketplace where inventors can post ideas for clients needing new products.

43942 ■ "Top 25 Engineering Firms" in South Florida Business Journal (Vol. 34, February 14, 2014, No. 30, pp. 12)
Pub: American City Business Journals
Released: February 14, 2014. Description: Rankings of the companies within the engineering services in South Florida are presented. Rankings are based on the number of licensed engineers in the region.

43943 ■ Trade-Off: The Ever-Present Tension Between Quality and Conscience
Ed: Kevin Maney. Released: August 17, 2010. Price: $15. Description: The tension between fidelity (the quality of a consumer's experience) and convenience (the ease of getting and paying for a product) are shown to be the forces that determine the success or failure of new products and services in the marketplace.

43944 ■ "Under Armour Wants to Equip Athletes, Too" in Boston Business Journal (Vol. 29, July 8, 2011, No. 9, pp. 1)
Pub: American City Business Journals, Inc.
Ed: Ryan Sharrow. Description: Baltimore sportswear maker Under Armour advances plans to enter into the equipment field, aiming to strengthen its hold on football, basketball and lacrosse markets where it already has a strong market share. The company is now cooking up licensing deals to bolster the firm's presence among athletes.

43945 ■ "U.S. Trade Body Clears Apple in Patent Case" in Wall Street Journal Eastern Edition (November 23 , 2011, pp. C1)
Pub: Dow Jones & Co., Inc.
Contact: Clare Hart, President
Ed: Matt Jarzemsky, Paul Mozur. Description: HTC Corporation alleged in its patent-infringement case against Apple Inc. that Apple violated patents of S3 Graphics Inc., a company which was acquired by HTC Corporation. Now the International Trade Commission has issued a ruling saying that Apple did not violate the patents.

43946 ■ "Universal Music Sues Grooveshark's Parent" in Wall Street Journal Eastern Edition (November 22 , 2011, pp. B5)
Pub: Dow Jones & Co., Inc.
Contact: Clare Hart, President
Ed: Ethan Smith. Description: Escape Media Group Inc., the parent company of online-music service Grooveshark, and seven of its executives have been sued by Universal Music Group, which alleges patent infringement involving its sound recordings. The executives are alleged to have uploaded thousands of songs onto Grooveshark.

43947 ■ "Unlicensed Utah Collection Agency Settles with State Finance Department" in Idaho Business Review, Boise (July 15, 2010)
Pub: Idaho Business Review
Description: Federal Recovery Acceptance Inc., doing business as Paramount Acceptance in Utah, agreed to pay penalties and expenses after the firm was investigated by the state for improprieties. The firm was charged with conducting unlicensed collection activity.

43948 ■ *"The Valuation of Players"* in *Canadian Business (Vol. 80, October 22, 2007, No. 21, pp. 39)*
Ed: Jeff Sanford. **Description:** Business professionals are supplementing their Masters in Business Administration degrees with CBV or chartered business valuator. CBVs are trained, not only in business tangibles, but also in business intangibles such as market position, reputation, intellectual property, and patent. Details of employment opportunities for chartered business valuators are discussed.

43949 ■ *"Viewing Ironman As Gold, R.I. Firm Buys Its Parent"* in *The Business Journal-Serving Greater Tampa Bay (Vol. 28, September 19, 2008)*
Pub: American City Business Journals, Inc.
Contact: Whitney Shaw, President
Ed: Pete Williams. **Description:** Providence Equity Partners purchased World Triathlon Corp., parent company of the Ironman Triathlon, for an undisclosed sum. The acquisition means that the World Triathlon Headquarters will move to Tampa, Florida, and allows Providence Equity Partners to stage or license rights to Ironman and half-Ironman distance events.

43950 ■ *"Voices: The Strategic Innovation Cube"* in *Business Strategy Review (Vol. 23, Spring 2012, No. 1, pp. 84)*
Released: Spring 2012. **Description:** Companies that innovate tend to prosper. Yet the process used by most innovative firms remains a mystery. Is there a way that any company can discern whether to commit resources to an innovation idea? Kiriti Rambhatla has blended the fields of science and management and offers a new way of thinking about innovation inside any company.

43951 ■ *"Wall Street Is No Friend to Radical Innovation"* in *Harvard Business Review (Vol. 88, July-August 2010, No. 7-8, pp. 28)*
Pub: Harvard Business School Publishing
Ed: Julia Kirby. **Price:** $6. **Description:** Research indicates that investors are skittish about backing a business that proposes significant changes to its product or service status quo. **Availability:** PDF.

43952 ■ *"Water Distiller"* in *Canadian Business (Vol. 81, September 29, 2008, No. 16, pp. 52)*
Ed: Matthew McClearn. **Description:** Les Fairn's invention of a water distiller called a Solarsphere was recognized in the Great Canadian Invention Competition. Fairn's invention resembles a buoy that uses the sun's energy to vaporize dirty water then leaves the impurities behind in a sump. The invention has an application for producing potable water in impoverished countries.

43953 ■ *"What Players in the Midmarket Are Talking About"* in *Mergers & Acquisitions: The Dealmaker's Journal (March 1, 2008)*
Description: Sports Properties Acquisition Corp. went public at the end of January; according to the company's prospectus, it is not limiting its focus to just teams, it is also considering deals for stadium construction companies, sports leagues, facilities, sports-related advertising and licensing of products, in addition to other related segments.

43954 ■ *"When and How to Innovate Your Business Model"* in *Strategy & Leadership (Vol. 38, July-August 2010, No. 4, pp. 17-26)*
Pub: Emerald Inc.
Ed: Edward Giesen, Eric Riddleberger, Richard Christner, Ragna Bell. **Description:** A study uses survey data to identify factors that are considered by corporate leaders regarding when and how they should innovate their business model. Findings identify a set of characteristics called the 'Three A's', Namely, Aligned, Analytical and Adaptable, which corporate leaders use consistently to successfully design and execute business-model innovation.

43955 ■ *"When R&D Spending Is Not Enough: The Critical Role of Culture When You Really Want to Innovate"* in *Human Resource Management (Vol. 49, July-August*

2010, No. 4, pp. 767-792)
Pub: John Wiley
Ed: Sheng Wang, Rebecca M. Guidice, Judith W. Tansky, Zhong-Ming Wang. **Description:** A study was conducted to examine the effect of contextual contingencies on innovation. Findings indicate that Chinese manufacturers with cultures emphasizing innovation and teamwork more effectively utilize financial resources in the innovation process. Results also show that a culture emphasizing outcomes and stability leads to lower levels innovation irrespective of investments.

43956 ■ *"Where Good Ideas Come From: The Natural History of Innovation"* in *Business Owner (Vol. 35, July-August 2011, No. 4, pp. 6)*
Pub: DL Perkins Company
Description: A history of ideas, concepts, innovations and technologies that have created a successful small business environment are explored.

43957 ■ *"Where New Economy Initiative Grants Have Gone"* in *Crain's Detroit Business (Vol. 25, June 1, 2009, No. 22, pp. M014)*
Pub: Crain Communications Inc. - Detroit
Contact: Keith Crain, Chairman
Ed: Sherri Begin Welch. **Description:** Listing of grants totaling $20.5 million focusing on talent development, attraction and retention; innovation and entrepreneurship; and shifting to a culture that values learning, work and innovation, is presented.

43958 ■ *"A Whiteboard that Peels and Sticks"* in *Inc. (Volume 32, December 2010, No. 10, pp. 58)*
Pub: Inc. Magazine
Ed: Issie Lapwosky. **Description:** Profile of an affordable adhesive whiteboard that can be restuck multiple times; the whiteboard was created by three college friends. The students share insight in the contacts they used in order to promote the sale of their invention.

43959 ■ *"Why Copyright Isn't Property"* in *Information Today (Vol. 26, February 2009, No. 2, pp. 18)*
Pub: Information Today, Inc.
Contact: Thomas H. Hogan, President
E-mail: ctuthill@infotoday.com
Ed: Matthew K. Dames. **Description:** An overview of intellectual property is presented. Intellectual property refers to 'creations of the mind: inventions, literary and artistic works, and symbols, names, and designs used in commerce', according to the World Intellectual Property Organization (WIPO). WIPO divides intellectual property into two categories: industrial property consisting of patents, trademarks, and industrial designs; and copyright: literary, artistic, creative, and aesthetic works.

43960 ■ *"Why Entrepreneurs Matter More Than Innovators"* in *Gallup Management Journal (November 22, 2011)*
Pub: Gallup Inc.
Contact: Jim Clifton, Chief Executive Officer
Ed: Jim Clifton. **Description:** In the race to create good jobs, leaders are not paying enough attention to cultivating talented entrepreneurs, rather they invest too much attention on innovation.

43961 ■ *"Why Life Science Needs Its Own Silicon Valley: Human Genomics Won't Reach Its Full Potential Until It Has a Sizable Industry Cluster"* in *(Vol. 90, July-August 2012, No. 7-8, pp. 25)*
Pub: Harvard Business Review Press
Contact: Peter E. Walsh, Director
Ed: Fariborz Ghadar, John Sviokla, Dietrich A. Stephan. **Released:** July-August 2012. **Description:** The creation of an industry cluster will be key to advancing human genomics research. High degrees of specialization via multiple contributors will be needed to generate significant innovations; an accessible, coherent data source will also be necessary.

43962 ■ *"With Whom Do You Trade? Defensive Innovation and the Skill-Bias"* in *Canadian Journal of Electronics (Vol. 43, November 2010)*
Pub: Journal of the Canadian Economics Association
Ed: Pushan Dutt, Daniel Traca. **Description:** Examination into whether increased trade with ineffective protection of intellectual property has contributed to the skill-deepening of the 1980s. An index of effective protection of intellectual property at the country level, combining data on protection of patents and rule of law are presented. An industry-specific version of this index is given using as weights each country's trade share in the total trade of the industry. A decline is seen in this trade-weighted index, owing to a rise in trade with countries with low effective protection of intellectual property, which explains 29 percent of the rise within-industry skill-intensity.

43963 ■ *"YourEncore's Corps of Scientists, Engineers Helps Cincinnati's P&G, Others Fight Fires"* in *Business Courier (Vol. 26, November 13, 2009, No. 29, pp. 1)*
Pub: American City Business Journals, Inc.
Contact: Whitney Shaw, President
Ed: Lisa Biank Fasig. **Description:** YourForce has nearly 6,000 retired scientists and researchers who work together in helping Procter & Gamble (P&G) and other companies in addressing various project needs. Operating as an online innovation community, YourEncore is a result of P&G's Connect Develop program.

TRADE PERIODICALS

43964 ■ *BNA's Patent, Trademark & Copyright Journal*
Pub: Bureau of National Affairs
Contact: James D. Crowne, Managing Editor
Released: Weekly. **Price:** $1,289. **Description:** Monitors developments in the intellectual property field, including patents, trademarks, and copyrights. Covers proposed and enacted legislation, litigation, Patent and Trademark Office decisions, Copyright Office practices, activities of professional associations, government contracting, and international developments.

43965 ■ *Eureka! The Canadian Invention & Innovation Newsletter*
Pub: Canadian Innovation Centre
Contact: Josie Graham, Chief Executive Officer
E-mail: jgraham@innovationcentre.ca
URL(s): www.innovationcentre.ca. **Ed:** Carolyn Parks, Editor. **Released:** Quarterly. **Price:** Free. **Description:** Serves as a forum for Canadian inventors and innovators.

43966 ■ *United States Patents Quarterly*
Pub: Bureau of National Affairs
Contact: James D. Crowne, Managing Editor
URL(s): www.bna.com/iprc_uspq. **Released:** Weekly. **Price:** $1,539. **Description:** Reports important decisions dealing with patents, trademarks, copyrights, unfair competition, trade secrets, and computer chip protection.

VIDEOCASSETTES/ AUDIOCASSETTES

43967 ■ *Entrepreneurs Series, Part 1: The Entrepreneurs*
Instructional Video
2219 C St.
Lincoln, NE 68502-1745
Ph: (402)475-6570
Free: 800-228-0164
Fax: (402)475-6500
Co. E-mail: orders@insvideo.com
URL: http://www.insvideo.com
Contact: Kathy Damkroger, President
Released: 19??. **Price:** $19.98. **Description:** Part one of the six-part Entrepreneurs Series. Profiles King Gillette, Wally Amos, John H. Johnson, Charles Darrow, Thomas Edison, and others. **Availability:** VHS.

43968 ■ *Entrepreneurs Series, Part 2: The Land & Its People*
Instructional Video
2219 C St.
Lincoln, NE 68502-1745
Ph: (402)475-6570
Free: 800-228-0164
Fax: (402)475-6500
Co. E-mail: orders@insvideo.com
URL: http://www.insvideo.com
Contact: Kathy Damkroger, President
Released: 19??. **Price:** $19.98. **Description:** Part 2 of the six-part Entrepreneurs Series. Profiles Cyrus McCormick, Harland Sanders, John D. Rockefeller, Gustavius Swift, and others. **Availability:** VHS.

43969 ■ *Entrepreneurs Series, Part 3: Expanding America*
Instructional Video
2219 C St.
Lincoln, NE 68502-1745
Ph: (402)475-6570
Free: 800-228-0164
Fax: (402)475-6500
Co. E-mail: orders@insvideo.com
URL: http://www.insvideo.com
Contact: Kathy Damkroger, President
Released: 19??. **Price:** $19.98. **Description:** Part three of the six-part Entrepreneurs Series. Profiles DeWitt Clinton, Henry Ford, Deke Slayton, James Hill, Charles Lindbergh, and others. **Availability:** VHS.

43970 ■ *Entrepreneurs Series, Part 4: Made in America*
Instructional Video
2219 C St.
Lincoln, NE 68502-1745
Ph: (402)475-6570
Free: 800-228-0164
Fax: (402)475-6500
Co. E-mail: orders@insvideo.com
URL: http://www.insvideo.com
Contact: Kathy Damkroger, President
Released: 19??. **Price:** $19.98. **Description:** Fourth part of the six-part Entrepreneurs Series. Profiles Andrew Carnegie, Eli Whitney, Samuel Colt, Henry Kaiser, and others. **Availability:** VHS.

43971 ■ *Entrepreneurs Series, Part 5: Giving 'Em What They Want*
Instructional Video
2219 C St.
Lincoln, NE 68502-1745
Ph: (402)475-6570
Free: 800-228-0164
Fax: (402)475-6500
Co. E-mail: orders@insvideo.com
URL: http://www.insvideo.com
Contact: Kathy Damkroger, President
Released: 19??. **Price:** $19.98. **Description:** Part five of the six-part Entrepreneurs Series. Profiles P.T. Barnum, Richard Sears, Lillian Vernon Katz, Victor Kiam, Lee Iacocca, and others. **Availability:** VHS.

43972 ■ *Entrepreneurs Series, Part 6: Instant America*
Instructional Video
2219 C St.
Lincoln, NE 68502-1745
Ph: (402)475-6570
Free: 800-228-0164
Fax: (402)475-6500
Co. E-mail: orders@insvideo.com
URL: http://www.insvideo.com
Contact: Kathy Damkroger, President
Released: 19??. **Price:** $19.98. **Description:** Part six of the six-part Entrepreneurs Series. Profiles Samuel Morse, Alexander Graham Bell, Adolph Zukor, David Sarnoff, George Eastman, and others. **Availability:** VHS.

43973 ■ *From Mind to Market: The Patent Process*
Instructional Video
2219 C St.
Lincoln, NE 68502-1745
Ph: (402)475-6570

Free: 800-228-0164
Fax: (402)475-6500
Co. E-mail: orders@insvideo.com
URL: http://www.insvideo.com
Contact: Kathy Damkroger, President
Released: 19??. **Price:** $34.95. **Description:** Outlines the patent process, covering ways to protect your ideas, innovation, disclosure documents, prototypes, patent types, patent searches, marketing, and inventor show information. **Availability:** VHS.

43974 ■ *Handling Trademark Registrations under the New Law*
American Law Institute - Committee on Continuing Professional Education (ALI CLE)
4025 Chestnut St.
Philadelphia, PA 19104
Ph: (215)243-1600
Free: 800-253-6397
Fax: (215)243-1636
Co. E-mail: in-house@ali-aba.org
URL: http://www.ali.org
Contact: Julene Franki, Executive Director
E-mail: jfranki@ali-aba.org
Released: 1989. **Price:** $95. **Description:** Discusses the result of the 1989 changes in the U.S. Trademark Law. Complete with study guide. **Availability:** VHS.

CONSULTANTS

43975 ■ Jordan Driks
284 Melrose Ave.
Merion Station, PA 19066
Ph: (610)664-0290
Fax: (610)664-0292
Contact: Jordan J. Driks, Principal
Scope: Extensive background in all phases of patent practice including negotiation and drafting of agreements, Preparation and prosecution of patent applications, negotiating with the government and designing licensing programs.

43976 ■ Invent Resources Inc. (IRI)
PO Box 548
Lexington, MA 02420-0005
Ph: (781)862-0200
Fax: (781)721-2300
Co. E-mail: pavelle@comcast.net
URL: http://www.weinvent.com
Contact: Dr. Richard Pavelle, President
E-mail: pavelle@comcast.net
Scope: Provider of consultancy services to provide support in developing and prototyping new, proprietary products. Offer inventory services on demand. Assist clients who need innovations in product lines, have hit technical bottlenecks, or need improvements in manufacturing processes. Provide assistance to individuals and clients in obtaining, reviewing, and strengthening patents. **Founded:** 1991.

43977 ■ Margiloff & Associates
621 Royalview St.
Duarte, CA 91010-1346
Ph: (626)303-1266
Fax: (626)303-0127
Contact: Irwin B. Margiloff, Principal
E-mail: margiloff@compuserve.com
Scope: Energy and water conservation studies, analysis of research and development, licensing, economics and project management. Projects involve development, training, utility review, cost analysis, manufacturing system improvement, process modeling and expert witness services. Clients include in the field of food, chemical, fermentation, energy, financial and legal services, government and general manufacturing fields. **Founded:** 1983.

43978 ■ Jerome W. McGee & Associates [Bruce W. McGee & Associates]
7826 Eastern Ave. NW, Ste. 300
Washington, DC 20012
Ph: (202)726-7272
Fax: (202)726-2946
Contact: Bruce W. McGee, President
Scope: Business consultants experienced in office automation, small business management, invention and patent counseling, technology commercialization, loan packaging and business plan development.

Founded: 1985. **Seminars:** Marketing Research for the High-Technology Business; Introduction to Microcomputers; Marketing Technological Products to Industry; How to Evaluate Your Technical Idea; Patenting Your Own Invention.

43979 ■ National Congress of Inventor Organizations (NCIO)
8306 Wilshire Blvd., Ste. 391
Beverly Hills, CA 90211
Ph: (323)278-4928
Co. E-mail: ncio@inventionconvention.com
URL: http://www.inventionconvention.com/ncio
Contact: Stephen Paul Gnass, Executive Director
E-mail: gnass@businessofinventing.com
Description: Represents inventors' groups. Coordinates information relating to inventor education and programs such as wanted and available inventions and credible organizations offering development and marketing assistance. Offers children's services and educational programs. Maintains speakers' bureau. **Scope:** Offers group and one-on-one consultations to independent inventors and small companies to guide them towards self reliance and responsibility in getting products into the marketplace. Customized evaluation and strategy along with matchmaking, networking and support services are personalized to help companies and individuals speed up the process of launching new products and technologies into the marketplace. Industries served: independent inventors, engineers, research and development labs, invent-to-order job shops, innovation and technology centers, universities, as well as small businesses, legal professions, manufacturing, distributors, sales and marketing professionals, inventor groups and government agencies. **Founded:** 1986. **Subscriptions:** books. **Publications:** "Inventors Idol"; "Invention Connections"; "Getting in the [VIPs] Door - Improving the Odds by Professionalizing Your Presentation"; "Are Licensing Agents Incognito?"; "OOOPS! Looks Like I Have a "Co-Inventor"!"; "Patented Inventors: Don't Lose Your Patent!!!"; "Too Many Cooks in the Kitchen Spoil the Broth". **Educational Activities:** National Innovation Workshop. **Seminars:** Exhibitor Excellence, Boothmanship - Maximizing Tradeshow Performances; Masters of the Invention Process. **Special Services:** Invention Connection®.

43980 ■ Patent Attornies & Agents
1601 Market St., Ste. 2400
Philadelphia, PA 19103-2301
Ph: (215)563-4100
Fax: (215)563-4044
Contact: John S. Child, Jr., Principal
Scope: Provide solutions in the area of patent trademark and copyright laws. Technical area of specialization is chemistry. Involved in legal matters relating to trade secrets. **Founded:** 1974.

COMPUTERIZED DATABASES

43981 ■ *Canadian Patent Reporter Plus (CPR)*
Canada Law Book Inc.
1 Corporate Plz.
2075 Kennedy Rd.
Toronto, ON, Canada M1T 3V4
Ph: (416)609-3800
Free: 800-387-5164
Fax: (416)298-5082
Co. E-mail: carswell.customerrelations@thomsonreuters.com
URL: http://www.canadalawbook.ca
Contact: Wendy Moffatt, Manager
Availability: Online: Canada Law Book Inc. CD-ROM: Canada Law Book Inc. **Type:** Full-text.

43982 ■ *CLAIMS® Citation Database*
IFI CLAIMS Patent Services
PO Box 1148
Madison, CT 06443-1148
Ph: (203)779-5301
Fax: (203)583-4521
Co. E-mail: info@ificlaims.com
URL: http://www.ificlaims.com
Contact: Mike Baycroft, Chief Executive Officer
Availability: Online: ProQuest LLC. **Type:** Bibliographic.

43983 ■ *Industrial Patent Activity in the United States Parts 1 and 2, 1974-1998 (IPA)*
U.S. Department of Commerce U.S. Patent and
    Trademark Office
Madison Bldgs. (East & West)
600 Dulany St.
Alexandria, VA 22314
Ph: (571)272-1000
Free: 800-786-9199
Co. E-mail: usptoinfo@uspto.gov
URL: http://www.uspto.gov
Contact: John Owens, II, Chief Information Officer
Availability: Online: ; U.S. Department of Commerce
-National Technical Information Service. CD-ROM:
U.S. Department of Commerce -National Technical
Information Service. **Type:** Full-text.

43984 ■ *LexisNexis Patent & Trademark File History Services*
LexisNexis
9443 Springboro Pke.
Dayton, OH 45342
Ph: (937)865-6800
Free: 800-227-4908
Fax: (937)865-1211
Co. E-mail: legalnotices@lexisnexis.com
URL: http://www.bender.com
Contact: Michael Walsh, President
Availability: Online: LexisNexis. CD-ROM: LexisN-
exis. **Type:** Full-text.

43985 ■ *Patent, Trademark & Copyright Journal®*
Bloomberg BNA
3 Bethesda Metro Center, Ste. 250
Bethesda, MD 20814-5377
Ph: (703)341-3000
Free: 800-372-1033
Fax: (800)253-0332
Co. E-mail: customercare@bna.com
URL: http://www.bna.com
Contact: Gregory McCaffrey, President
URL(s): www.bna.com/patent-trademark-copyright-
journal-p5942. **Availability:** Online: Bloomberg BNA;
Thomson Reuters - Westlaw. **Type:** Full-text.

LIBRARIES

43986 ■ Chicago Public Library Central Library - Business/Science/Technology Division
Harold Washington Library Center, 4th Fl.
400 S State St.
Chicago, IL 60605
Ph: (312)747-4300
URL: http://www.chipublib.org/resources/science-
technology
Contact: Linda Johnson Rice, President
Scope: Small business, marketing, technology,
corporate reports, investments, management, person-
nel, patents, physical and biological sciences,
medicine, health, computer science, careers, environmental information, gardening, cookbooks. **Services:**
Interlibrary loan; copying; division open to the public.
Founded: 1977. **Holdings:** 415,000 books; 52,100
bound periodical volumes; 33,000 reels of microfilm;
Securities and Exchange Commission (SEC) reports;
federal specifications and standards; American
National Standards Institute standards; corporate annual reports. **Subscriptions:** 4,000 journals and
other serials; 8 newspapers.

43987 ■ Finnegan, Henderson, Farabow, Garrett and Dunner Library
901 New York Ave. NW
Washington, DC 20001-4432
Ph: (202)408-4000
Fax: (202)408-4400
Co. E-mail: barbara.mccurdy@finnegan.com
URL: http://www.finnegan.com
Contact: Virginia McNitt, Director, Library Services
Scope: Patent law, trademark law, federal procedure.
Services: Interlibrary loan; library not open to the
public. **Founded:** 1966. **Holdings:** 11,000 books;
200 bound periodical volumes. **Subscriptions:** 700
journals and other serials; 6 newspapers.

43988 ■ O'Melveny & Myers LLP Library
2 Embarcadero Ctr., 28th Fl.
San Francisco, CA 94111-3823
Ph: (415)984-8700
Fax: (415)984-8701
URL: http://www.omm.com
Contact: Michael Tubach, Partner
Scope: Law. **Services:** Library not open to the public.
Founded: 1989. **Holdings:** 8000 books. **Subscrip-
tions:** 75 journals and other serials; 10 newspapers.

43989 ■ Sentron Medical Inc. - Senmed Medical Ventures Library
4445 Lake Forest Dr., No. 600
Cincinnati, OH 45242-3798
Ph: (513)563-3240
Fax: (513)563-3261
Contact: Rosanne Wohlwender
Scope: Biotechnology, medical devices and diagnostics, technology transfer, pharmaceuticals, venture
capital, licensing. **Services:** Library not open to the
public. **Founded:** 1987. **Holdings:** 800 books; 50
reports. **Subscriptions:** 100 journals and other serials; 2 newspapers.

RESEARCH CENTERS

43990 ■ Indiana State University - Office of Sponsored Programs (OSP)
Holmstedt Hall, Rm. 272
200 N 7th St.
Terre Haute, IN 47809-1902
Ph: (812)237-3088
Free: 800-468-6478
Fax: (812)237-3092
Co. E-mail: dawn.underwood@indstate.edu
URL: http://www.indstate.edu/research/osp.php
Contact: Dawn Underwood, Director
Scope: Coordinates pre-award activities associated
with external funding and supports research and
proposal development. Assists with patents, licens-
ing, and technology transfer. Also facilitates the
administrative review and approval of proposals. **Services:** Offers individual assistance: in the preparation
and submission of proposals. **Publications:** *Creating
a Grant Proposal Budget*; *Finding Money for Your
Project*; *Preparing a Winning Grant Proposal*. **Educational Activities:** OSP Seminars and workshops.

43991 ■ University of Wisconsin—Whitewater - Wisconsin Innovation Service Center (WISC)
1200 Hyland Hall
Whitewater, WI 53190
Ph: (262)472-1365
Fax: (262)472-1600
Co. E-mail: innovate@uww.edu
URL: http://www.uww.edu/wisc
Contact: Ronald (Bud) Gayhart, Director
Scope: Performs early-stage market research for
independent inventors and manufacturers. **Services:**
Market information to clients; Technical reviews.
Founded: 1980.

START-UP INFORMATION

43992 ■ *"Buried Under Orders" in Entrepreneur (May 2014)*
Pub: Entrepreneur Media Inc.
Released: May 2014. **Description:** Supply chain management expert, Hau Lee, provides tips for on ways startups can act fast and take advantage of sudden demand. He asserts that startups have to formulate a plan on how to scale up production and distribution in case the business becomes successful. He describes some early indications that can help entrepreneurs determine the possibility of a sales surge. He explains how to estimate the period of high volume for inventory. He offers suggestions on what to communicate to customers when the product is out of stock.

43993 ■ *"Selling Groceries & More on Amazon: The Ultimate Home Based Business for Families"*
Pub: Amazon Digital Services
Released: October 16, 2014. **Price:** , $7.99 Kindle. **Description:** Tips for starting an online grocery store from your home are shared. Grocery inventory, coupons and store promotions, setting up a seller account, application and approval for the grocery category, shipping information, sales techniques and private labeling are all addressed for this family owned type of business.

43994 ■ *"So You Want To Be a Food Truck Vendor?" in Philadelphia Business Journal (Vol. 33, August 15, 2014, No. 27, pp. 7)*
Pub: American City Business Journals
Released: August 15, 2014. **Description:** Food truck vendors assert that the most challenging part of starting a food truck business is acquiring a license as well as the price and number of licenses and permits required. Other costs include additional fees to vend in prime locations, maintenance, and inventory.

EDUCATIONAL PROGRAMS

43995 ■ **Best Practices for Managing Inventories and Cycle Counts (Onsite)**
Seminar Information Service Inc.
20 Executive Park, Ste. 120
Irvine, CA 92614
Ph: (949)261-9104
Free: 877-SEM-INFO
Fax: (949)261-1963
Co. E-mail: info@seminarinformation.com
URL: http://www.seminarinformation.com
Price: $199.00. **Description:** Learn how to use specific techniques that will actually improve speed and accuracy when counting inventory. **Dates and Locations:** Cities throughout the United States.

43996 ■ **How to Manage Inventories and Cycle Counts**
Fred Pryor Seminars & CareerTrack
5700 Broadmoor St., Ste. 300
Mission, KS 66202
Ph: (800)780-8476

Free: 800-780-8476
Fax: (913)967-8849
Co. E-mail: customerservice@pryor.com
URL: http://www.pryor.com
Contact: Phil Love, Chief Executive Officer
Price: $199.00; $189.00 for groups of 5 or more. **Description:** Cost saving methods and time saving techniques to ensure accurate counts and inventories. **Dates and Locations:** Cities throughout the United States.

43997 ■ **Inventory Management Techniques (Onsite)**
Seminar Information Service Inc.
20 Executive Park, Ste. 120
Irvine, CA 92614
Ph: (949)261-9104
Free: 877-SEM-INFO
Fax: (949)261-1963
Co. E-mail: info@seminarinformation.com
URL: http://www.seminarinformation.com
URL(s): www.seminarinformation.com/qqajau/inventory-management-techniques. **Price:** $2,345, Nonmembers; $2,095, Members AMA. **Description:** Learn how to assure less inventory where the product pipeline begins and greater customer satisfaction where it ends. **Audience:** Material inventory, control purchasing, logistics, and distribution professionals.

43998 ■ **Managing Inventories and Cycle Counts (Onsite)**
Padgett-Thompson Seminars
Rockhurst University CEC
14502 W 105th St.
Lenexa, KS 66215
Free: 800-349-1935
URL: http://www.findaseminar.com/tpd/Padgett-Thompson-Seminars.asp
URL(s): www.findaseminar.com/event1.asp?eventID=893. **Price:** $199. **Description:** One-day workshop focusing on methods to streamline processes and keep a warehouse running smoothly. **Audience:** Inventory, quality control or warehouse management professionals.

43999 ■ **Successful Inventory Management (Onsite)**
Fred Pryor Seminars & CareerTrack
5700 Broadmoor St., Ste. 300
Mission, KS 66202
Ph: (800)780-8476
Free: 800-780-8476
Fax: (913)967-8849
Co. E-mail: customerservice@pryor.com
URL: http://www.pryor.com
Contact: Phil Love, Chief Executive Officer
URL(s): www.pryor.com/mkt_info/seminars/desc/iv.asp. **Price:** $199. **Description:** Learn proven cost saving methods that improve inventory and cycle count accuracy. **Audience:** Professionals.

REFERENCE WORKS

44000 ■ *"Beyond Zipcar: Collaborative Consumption" in Harvard Business Review*

(Vol. 88, October 2010, No. 10, pp. 30)
Pub: Harvard Business School Publishing
Ed: Rachel Botsman, Roo Rogers. **Description:** Description of the rise of collaborative consumption, the sharing or redistributing of products, rather than the purchasing thereof is discussed.

44001 ■ *"The CEO of TJX On How To Train First-Class Buyers" in Harvard Business Review (Vol. 92, May 2014, No. 5, pp. 45)*
Pub: Harvard Business Press
Released: May 2014. **Description:** The CEO of clothing retailer TJX Companies Inc. emphasizes the importance of buyer training to ensure that store merchandise inventory optimizes consumer response. Buyers must be curious, knowledgeable about customers, and willing to take risks.

44002 ■ *"ChemSW Software Development Services Available for Outsourcing" in Information Today (Vol. 26, February 2009, No. 2, pp. 30)*
Description: ChemSW software development services include requirements analysis, specification development, design, development, testing, and system documentation as an IT outsourcing solution. The company can also develop software tracking systems for satellite stockrooms, provide asset management integration solutions and more.

44003 ■ *"Commentary. Small Business Economic Trends" in Small Business Economic Trends (February 2008, pp. 3)*
Pub: National Federation of Independent Business
Contact: Caitlin McDevitt, Program Manager
Ed: William C. Dunkelberg, Holly Wade. **Description:** Commentary on the economic trends for small businesses in the U.S. is presented. Analysis of the U.S. Federal Reserve Board's efforts to prevent a recession is given. Reduction in business inventories is also discussed.

44004 ■ *"Commentary. Small Business Economic Trends" in Small Business Economic Trends (January 2008, pp. 3)*
Pub: National Federation of Independent Business
Contact: Caitlin McDevitt, Program Manager
Description: Federal Reserve cut interest rates and announced its economic outlook on September 18, 2007 to stimulate spending. The cut in interest rates, however, may not help in supporting consumer spending because savers may lose interest income. The expected economic impact of the interest rate cuts and the U.S. economic outlook are also discussed.

44005 ■ *"Commercial Industry May Be Cooling While Residential Clamors To Meet Demands" in Houston Business Journal (Vol. 44, January 3, 2014, No. 35, pp. 6)*
Pub: American City Business Journals
Released: January 3, 2014. **Description:** Greater Houston Partnership has predicted that the real estate industry will remain active for the years ahead in Houston, Texas. However, commercial real estate

might cool down while residential sales are expected to remain hot with demand outpacing supply. Houston's construction boom in each sector is also discussed.

44006 ■ *"Crucible: Battling Back from Betrayal" in Harvard Business Review (Vol. 88, December 2010, No. 12, pp. 130)*
Pub: Harvard Business School Publishing
Ed: Daniel McGinn. **Description:** Stephen Greer's scrap metal firm, Hartwell Pacific, lost several million dollars due to a lack of efficient and appropriate inventory audits, accounting procedures, and new-hire reference checks for his foreign operations. Greer believes that balancing growth with control is a key component of success.

44007 ■ *"Dean Foods" in Ice Cream Reporter (Vol. 23, September 20, 2010, No. 10, pp. 8)*
Description: Dean Foods promoted Joseph Scalzo to President and Chief Operating Officer to oversee the firm's operational turnaround and near-term strategic initiatives as well as business units. Key functions will include worldwide supply chain and research and development.

44008 ■ *"Don't Tweak Your Supply Chain - Rethink It End to End" in Harvard Business Review (Vol. 88, October 2010, No. 10, pp. 62)*
Pub: Harvard Business School Publishing
Ed: Hau L. Lee. **Description:** Hong Kong apparel firm Esquel Apparel Ltd. is used to illustrate supply chain reorganization to improve a firm's sustainability. Discussion focuses on taking a broad approach rather than addressing individual steps or processes.

44009 ■ *"Dynamic Supply Chain Alignment: A New Business Model for Peak Performance in Enterprise Supply Chains Across All Geographies" in Human Resource Management (Vol. 49, September-October 2010, No. 5, pp. 969-973)*
Pub: John Wiley
Ed: Kim Sundtoft Hald. **Description:** Review of the book, 'Dynamic Supply Chain Alignment: A New Business Model for Peak Performance in Enterprise Supply Chains Across All Geographies'.

44010 ■ *eBay Business the Smart Way*
Ed: Joseph T. Sinclair. **Released:** June 6, 2007. **Price:** , $17.95. **Description:** eBay commands ninety percent of all online auction business. Computer and software expert and online entrepreneur shares information to help online sellers get started and move merchandise on eBay. Tips include the best ways to build credibility, find products to sell, manage inventory, create a storefront Website, and more.

44011 ■ *"Economic Trends for Small Business" in Small Business Economic Trends (April 2008, pp. 1)*
Ed: William C. Dunkelberg, Holly Wade. **Description:** Summary of economic trends for small businesses in the U.S. is presented. Economic indicators such as capital spending, inventories and sales, inflation, and profits are given. Analysis of credit markets is also provided.

44012 ■ *"Energy Outfitter Wings Into Houston" in Houston Business Journal (Vol. 40, December 4, 2009, No. 30, pp. 2A)*
Pub: American City Business Journals
Ed: Ford Gunter. **Description:** Red Wing Shoe Company Inc. has launched its personal protective equipment (PPE) line for oil and gas industry crewmen in North America by opening a 13,000 square foot distribution hub in Houston, Texas. The Houston facility was created to supply directly the oil and gas industry and to carry inventory for select distributors.

44013 ■ *"Global: Put It on Autopilot" in Entrepreneur (Vol. 35, October 2007, No. 10, pp. 110)*
Pub: Entrepreneur Press
Contact: Perlman Neil, President
Ed: Laurel Delaney. **Description:** A business that aims to enter the global market must first streamline its global supply chain (GSC). A streamlined GSC can be achieved by laying out the company's pro-

cesses and by automating it with supply chain management software. Advantages of GSC automation such as credibility are provided.

44014 ■ *"Hot Kicks, Cool Price" in Black Enterprise (Vol. 37, December 2006, No. 5, pp. 34)*
Pub: Earl G. Graves Publishing Co. Inc.
Contact: Earl G. Graves, Jr., President
Ed: Topher Sanders. **Description:** Stephon Marbury of the New York Nicks introduced a new basketball shoe, the Starbury One, costing $14.98. The shoes are an addition to the Starbury clothing line and although the privately owned company would not disclose figures; stores sold out of a month's worth of inventory in merely three days.

44015 ■ *Housecleaning Business: Organize Your Business - Get Clients and Referrals - Set Rates and Services*
Pub: Globe Pequot Press Inc.
Contact: Robert Irwin, Manager
E-mail: robert.irwin@globepequot.com
Ed: Laura Jorstad, Melinda Morse. **Released:** June 24, 2009. **Price:** $18.95, paperback. **Description:** This book shares insight into starting a housecleaning business. It shows how to develop a service manual, screen clients, serve customers, select cleaning products, competition, how to up a home office, using the Internet to grow the business and offering green cleaning options to clients. **Availability:** Print.

44016 ■ *How to Start and Run a Small Book Publishing Company: A Small Business Guide to Self-Publishing and Independent Publishing*
Pub: HCM Publishing
Ed: Peter I. Hupalo. **Released:** August 30, 2002. **Price:** $18.95. **Description:** The book teaches all aspects of starting and running a small book publishing company. Topics covered include: inventory accounting in the book trade, just-in-time inventory management, turnkey fulfillment solutions, tax deductible costs, basics of sales and use tax, book pricing, standards in terms of the book industry, working with distributors and wholesalers, cover design and book layout, book promotion and marketing, how to select profitable authors to publish, printing process, printing on demand, the power of a strong backlist, and how to value copyright.

44017 ■ *"Iconic Boise Skateboard Shop to Close" in Idaho Business Review (August 19, 2014)*
Pub: Dolan Co.
Contact: James P. Dolan, President
Released: August 19, 2014. **Description:** Lori Wright and Lori Ambur have owned Newt & Harold's for over 30 years. The partners are closing the firm that sold skateboards and snowboards. Wright focused on the marketing and inventory aspects of the retail shop, while Ambur ran the organizational and financial end. Wright and Ambur say they are leaving retail because the industry has faced so many changes since they first opened, particularly competing with online stores.

44018 ■ *"Inventory Glut" in Business Courier (Vol. 24, March 28, 2008, No. 51, pp. 1)*
Pub: American City Business Journals, Inc.
Contact: Whitney Shaw, President
Ed: Laura Baverman. **Description:** Indian Hill and the downtown area have the highest monthly absorption rate for housing on a list of 42 Greater Cincinnati and Northern Kentucky neighborhoods. The two neighborhoods have 19 and 27 months of housing inventory respectively, which means home sellers need to either lower their prices or be very patient.

44019 ■ *"Is Your Supply Chain Sustainable?" in Harvard Business Review (Vol. 88, October 2010, No. 10, pp. 74)*
Pub: Harvard Business School Publishing
Description: Charts and models are presented to help a firm assess its sustainability.

44020 ■ *"It May Be Cheaper to Manufacture At Home" in Harvard Business Review (Vol. 88, October 2010, No. 10, pp. 84)*
Pub: Harvard Business School Publishing
Ed: Suzanne de Treville, Lenos Trigeorgis. **Description:** Using a real options framework rather than a discounted cash flow model to assess and value supply chain processes is examined. This enables companies to assess costs for a variety of situations, not just ideal or normal circumstances, which can make the difference between domestic and foreign manufacturing decisions.

44021 ■ *"JoS. A. Bank Suits Look Better Than Its Shares" in Barron's (Vol. 88, March 31, 2008, No. 13, pp. 25)*
Pub: Dow Jones & Co., Inc.
Contact: Clare Hart, President
Ed: Bill Alpert. **Description:** Jos. A. Bank's inventory has increased sharply raising questions about the company's growth prospects. The company's shares have already dropped significantly from 46 to 23 and could still continue its slide. The company is also battling a class action suit where plaintiffs allege that the Bank inventories were bloated.

44022 ■ *"Miller's Crossroad" in Canadian Business (Vol. 83, September 14, 2010, No. 15, pp. 58)*
Pub: Rogers Media Inc.
Contact: Tony Viner, President
Ed: Joe Castaldo. **Description:** Future Electronics founder and billionaire Robert Miller shares the secret of Future's unique operating model, which is based on inventory and market research. Miller attributes much of the company's success to its privately held status that enables quick movement against competitors.

44023 ■ *"Monaco Pay Cut Draws Attention" in The Business Journal-Portland (Vol. 25, August 8, 2008, No. 22, pp. 1)*
Pub: American City Business Journals, Inc.
Contact: Whitney Shaw, President
Ed: Erik Siemers. **Description:** Monaco Coach Corp. cut the salaries of five top executives in an effort to reduce the company's $178 million worth of inventory. The executives can earn the lost salary back if the inventory is reduced by $58 million a year after August 2008.

44024 ■ *"Niche Discounters, Already Prospering, Step Up Products Sluggish Economy A Plus Dollar Stores Expanding Food, Beauty; TJX Focus on Fast, Lean Inventory" in Investor's Business Daily (August 16, 2012, pp. A1)*
Released: August 16, 2012. **Description:** Discount stores are working to increase profits and sales by upgrading store formats, expanding inventory, and making shopping more convenient. Statistical data included.

44025 ■ *"No. 252: H. Bloom: Floral Subscriptions" in Inc. (Vol. 36, September 2014, No. 7, pp. 132)*
Pub: Mansueto Ventures L.L.C.
Contact: John Koten, Chief Executive Officer
Released: September 2014. **Description:** Spoilage is the largest problem facing flower shops. H. Bloom provides custom floral designs to high-end hotels, spas, restaurants, retailers, and apartment and office buildings through their subscription service. The firm found that regular orders provides better inventory control and less waste. Weekly, biweekly, or monthly deliveries are available.

44026 ■ *"Online Reverse Auctions: Common Myths Versus Evolving Reality" in Business Horizons (September-October 2007, pp. 373)*
Pub: Elsevier Technology Publications
Ed: Tobias Schoenherr, Vincent A. Mabert. **Price:** $35.95. **Description:** Common misconceptions about online reverse auctions are examined based on the data obtained from 30 case study companies. Strategies for maintaining a good buyer-supplier relationship and implications for firms and supply managers are presented.

44027 ■ *"Oreos, Mercedes Join Super Bowl Ad Lineup; 90 Percent of Inventory Sold" in Advertising Age (Vol. 83, October 8, 2012, No. 36, pp. 3)*
Description: Mercedes-Benz and Oreo cookes, along with Coca-Cola and Best Buy, announced marketing plans to advertise during Super Bowl XLVII.

44028 ■ *"Perfecting Customer Services" in Pet Product News (Vol. 64, November 2010, No. 11, pp. 18)*
Pub: Bowtie Inc.
Description: Pet supply retailers are encouraged to emphasize customer experience and sales representatives' knowledge of the store's product offerings to foster repeat business. Employee protocols could be implemented to improve customer interaction. Other guidelines on developing a pet supply retail environment that advances repeat business are presented.

44029 ■ *"Sheets Makers Optimistic Amid Price, Delivery Issues" in Home Textiles Today (Vol. 31, May 24, 2011, No. 13, pp. 8)*
Pub: Reed Elsevier Group plc Reed Business Information
Contact: Mark Kelsey, Chief Executive Officer
Ed: Jill Rowen. **Description:** Retail sales of sheets and pillowcases dropped 4.7 percent in volume in 2009. Retailers pulled back inventory significantly in 2010. Statistical data included.

44030 ■ *"A Size Smaller, But a Better Fit" in Business Journal (Vol. 31, May 2, 2014, No. 49, pp. 12)*
Pub: American City Business Journals
Released: May 2, 2014. **Description:** LuAnn Via, Christopher & Banks Corporation's CEO, helped improve the company's financial results. She was responsible for closing hundreds of retail women's clothing stores and overhauling the business inventory. Via completed the organization's turnaround management strategy by walking away from the firm's core customer.

44031 ■ *"Small Business Inventories" in Small Business Economic Trends (April 2008, pp. 14)*
Pub: National Federation of Independent Business
Contact: Caitlin McDevitt, Program Manager
Ed: William C. Dunkelberg, Holly Wade. **Description:** Three tables and a graph presenting the inventories of small businesses in the U.S. are provided. The tables include figures on actual inventory changes, inventory satisfaction, and inventory plans.

44032 ■ *"Small Business Inventories" in Small Business Economic Trends (March 2008, pp. 14)*
Pub: National Federation of Independent Business
Contact: Caitlin McDevitt, Program Manager
Ed: William C. Dunkelberg, Holly Wade. **Description:** Three tables and a graph presenting the inventories of small businesses in the U.S. are given. The tables include figures on actual inventory changes, inventory satisfaction, and inventory plans.

44033 ■ *"Small Business Inventories" in Small Business Economic Trends (February 2008, pp. 14)*
Pub: National Federation of Independent Business
Contact: Caitlin McDevitt, Program Manager
Ed: William C. Dunkelberg, Holly Wade. **Description:** Three tables and a graph presenting the inventories of small businesses in the U.S. are given. The tables include figures on actual inventory changes, inventory satisfaction, and inventory plans.

44034 ■ *"Small Business Inventories" in Small Business Economic Trends (January 2008, pp. 14)*
Pub: National Federation of Independent Business
Contact: Caitlin McDevitt, Program Manager
Ed: William C. Dunkelberg, Holly Wade. **Description:** Graph representing actual and planned inventories among small businesses surveyed in the U.S. from January 1986 to December 2007 is presented. A graph comparing inventory satisfaction and inven-

tory plans over the same time period is also given. Tables showing actual inventory changes, inventory satisfaction, and inventory plans are also supplied.

44035 ■ *"Small Business Inventories" in Small Business Economic Trends (September 2010, pp. 15)*
Pub: National Federation of Independent Business
Contact: Caitlin McDevitt, Program Manager
Ed: William C. Dunkelberg, Holly Wade. **Description:** A graph representing actual and planned inventories among small businesses surveyed in the U.S. from January 1986 to August 2010 is presented. A graph comparing inventory satisfaction and inventory plans over the same time period is also given. Tables showing actual changes, inventory satisfaction and inventory plans are also supplied.

44036 ■ *"Small Business Inventories" in Small Business Economic Trends (July 2010, pp. 14)*
Pub: National Federation of Independent Business
Contact: Caitlin McDevitt, Program Manager
Description: A graph representing actual and planned inventories among small businesses surveyed in the U.S. from January 1986 to June 2010 is presented. A graph comparing inventory satisfaction and inventory plans over the same time period is also given. Tables showing actual inventory changes, inventory satisfaction, and inventory plans are also supplied.

44037 ■ *"Small Business Inventories" in Small Business Economic Trends (July 2014, pp. 14)*
Pub: National Federation of Independent Business
Contact: Caitlin McDevitt, Program Manager
Released: July 2014. **Description:** A graph representing actual and planned inventories among small businesses surveyed in the U.S. from January 1986 to June 2014 is presented. A graph comparing inventory satisfaction and inventory plans over the same time period is given. Tables showing actual inventory changes, inventory satisfaction and inventory plans are also supplied.

44038 ■ *Small Business Management*
Pub: John Wiley & Sons Inc.
Contact: Stephen M. Smith, President
Ed: Margaret Burlingame. **Released:** March 2007. **Price:** , $44.95. **Description:** Advice for starting and running a small business as well as information on the value and appeal of small businesses, is given. Topics include budgets, taxes, inventory, ethics, e-commerce, and current laws.

44039 ■ *"Summary. Economic Trends for Small Business" in Small Business Economic Trends (March 2008, pp. 1)*
Ed: William C. Dunkelberg, Holly Wade. **Description:** Summary of economic trends for small businesses in the U.S. is provided. Economic indicators such as capital spending, inventories and sales, inflation, and profits are given. Analysis of credit markets is also provided.

44040 ■ *"Summary. Economic Trends for Small Business" in Small Business Economic Trends (February 2008, pp. 1)*
Pub: National Federation of Independent Business
Contact: Caitlin McDevitt, Program Manager
Ed: William C. Dunkelberg, Holly Wade. **Description:** Summary of economic trends for small businesses in the U.S. is provided. Economic indicators such as capital spending, inventories and sales, inflation, and profits are given. Analysis of credit markets is also provided.

44041 ■ *"A Supply-Side Solution for Health Care" in (Vol. 92, July 23, 2012, No. 30, pp. 30)*
Pub: Dow Jones & Co., Inc.
Contact: Clare Hart, President
Ed: H. Woody Brock. **Released:** July 23, 2012. **Description:** The United States should increase the supply of new doctors, nurses and other health care professionals to improve the American health care

system by increasing supply. Health care reform proposals in the US Congress fail to address the supply side of the problem.

44042 ■ *"The Sustainable Supply Chain" in Harvard Business Review (Vol. 88, October 2010, No. 10, pp. 70)*
Pub: Harvard Business School Publishing
Ed: Steven Prokesch. **Description:** Peter Senge, founder of the Society for Organizational Learning, emphasizes the importance of assessing the system as a whole under which one is operating, and learning how to work with individuals with which one has not worked previously. He also points to nongovernmental organizations to provide assistance and legitimacy.

44043 ■ *"Swagelok Boss Doesn't Follow Conventional Path" in Crain's Cleveland Business (Vol. 30, June 29, 2009, No. 25, pp. 4)*
Pub: Crain Communications Inc.
Ed: Dan Shingler. **Description:** Swagelok Company president and CEO has not laid off an employee in its 65 years of existence and said at a recent convention that he plans to keep his 4,000 employees working and inventories at normal levels despite the recession.

44044 ■ *"Technology and Returnable Asset Management" in Canadian Electronics (Vol. 23, February 2008, No. 1, pp. 6)*
Ed: Mark Borkowski. **Description:** Peter Kastner, president of Vestigo Corporation, believes that public companies without an asset track, trace, and control system in place could face Sarbanes-Oakley liability if error-prone processes result to misstatements of asset inventory positions. He also thinks that the system can improve return on assets by increasing the utilization of returnables.

44045 ■ *"The Transparent Supply Chain" in Harvard Business Review (Vol. 88, October 2010, No. 10, pp. 76)*
Pub: Harvard Business School Publishing
Ed: Steve New. **Description:** Examination of the use of new technologies to create a transparent supply chain, such as next-generation 2D bar codes in clothing labels that can provide data on a garment's provenance.

44046 ■ *"An Unfair Knock on Nokia" in Barron's (Vol. 88, March 10, 2008, No. 10, pp. 36)*
Pub: Dow Jones & Co., Inc.
Contact: Clare Hart, President
Ed: Mark Veverka. **Description:** Discusses the decision by the brokerage house Exane to recommend a Sell on Nokia shares, presumably due to higher inventories, which is unfounded. The news that the company's inventories are rising is not an indicator of falling demand for its products. The company is also benefiting from solid management and rising market share.

44047 ■ *"Waterloo Gardens Files for Bankruptcy" in Philadelphia Business Journal (Vol. 28, July 20, 2012, No. 23, pp. 1)*
Pub: American City Business Journal
Description: Nursery and garden center Waterloo Gardens Inc. has voluntarily filed Chapter 11 bankruptcy protection in the Eastern District of Pennsylvania as it attempts to reorganize. Watrloos' Devon location will be closing, while its inventory will be relocated to its Exton location. Factors that might have contributed to the bankruptcy filing are also discussed.

44048 ■ *"Weathering the Economic Storm" in Playthings (Vol. 107, January 1, 2009, No. 1, pp. 10)*
Pub: Reed Elsevier Group plc Reed Business Information
Contact: Mark Kelsey, Chief Executive Officer
Ed: J. Tol Broome, Jr. **Description:** Six steps for toy companies to survive the economic turndown are outlined: Outline your business model; seek professional input; meet with your banker; cut your costs; manage your inventory; and use your trade credit.

44049 ■ *"Zacks Industry Outlook Highlights: Target, Cabela's and Family Dollar Stores" in Marketing Weekly News (April 28, 2012, pp. 351)*

Description: Zacks Industry Outlook focuses on retailers such as Target, Cabela's and Family Dollar Stores. An examination of ways retailers are working to improve sales and profits and productivity is given, including supply-chain management, cost containment, inventory management, and merchandise initiatives.

VIDEOCASSETTES/ AUDIOCASSETTES

44050 ■ *Inventory Observation and Valuation*
SmartPros Ltd.
12 Skyline Dr.
Hawthorne, NY 10532-2133
Ph: (914)345-2620
Co. E-mail: admin@smartpros.com
URL: http://www.smartpros.com
Contact: Jack Fingerhut, President
Released: 1991. **Description:** A review of inventory observation for staff accountants. **Availability:** VHS; 3/4 U.

CONSULTANTS

44051 ■ **R. J. Levulis & Associates**
601 Sequoia Trl.
Roselle, IL 60172
Ph: (630)924-9494
Fax: (630)924-9507
Scope: Aids manufacturing and distribution clients in securing lasting benefits through cost and investment containment, customer service improvement, cycle time reduction, factory and warehouse space layout and similar operations and distribution activities.
Founded: 1989. **Publications:** "Finite Scheduling";

"Warehouse Management Systems"; "Materials Handling an Overlooked Weapon"; "The Abc of Inventory Management". **Seminars:** World Class Manufacturing; Better Warehousing; Basic Principles of Commercial Activities.

44052 ■ **Williamson Imagineering**
621 NE 162nd Ave., Ste. 19
Portland, OR 97230-5750
Ph: (503)252-9891
Contact: Steve Williamson, Owner
Scope: Database developer specializing in retail quoting and inventory control applications in the PC environment. Provides system analysis of existing procedures and/or applications and offers consultation for efficiency recommendations. Provides user training on developed applications as well as off-the-shelf software and operating systems. Industries served: small business, municipal and light industrial.
Founded: 1994. **Publications:** "Saving Money on Backpacking Food".

FRANCHISES AND BUSINESS OPPORTUNITIES

44053 ■ **AccuTrak Inventory Specialists**
PO Box 14782
Surfside Beach, SC 29587
Ph: (843)293-8274
Fax: (843)293-5075
Description: Inventory consultants. **No. of Franchise Units:** 28. **No. of Company-Owned Units:** 1.
Founded: 1993. **Franchised:** 2000. **Equity Capital Needed:** $49,000-$58,000. **Franchise Fee:** $32,500.
Royalty Fee: 7%. **Training:** Provides 4 days at headquarters, 4 days at approved franchisee training site with ongoing support.

44054 ■ **Bevinco**
505 Consumers Rd., Ste. 510
Toronto, ON, Canada M2J 4V8
Ph: (416)490-6266

Fax: (416)490-6899
Co. E-mail: info@bevinco.com
URL: http://www.bevinco.com
Description: Liquor inventory control system for bars, restaurants, hotels, clubs, etc. **No. of Franchise Units:** 250. **No. of Company-Owned Units:** 1.
Founded: 1987. **Franchised:** 1991. **Equity Capital Needed:** $40,000. **Franchise Fee:** $40,000. **Financial Assistance:** Yes. **Training:** 7 days corporate training in Toronto, 5-10 days regional training with state master franchise.

COMPUTERIZED DATABASES

44055 ■ *Atlantic Provinces Reports (APR)*
Maritime Law Book Ltd.
PO Box 302
Fredericton, NB, Canada E3B 4Y9
Ph: (506)453-9921
Free: 800-561-0220
Fax: (506)453-9525
Co. E-mail: help@mlb.nb.ca
URL: http://www.mlb.nb.ca
Availability: Online: LexisNexis Canada Inc. **Type:** Bibliographic.

COMPUTER SYSTEMS/ SOFTWARE

44056 ■ *PCINV: Inventory Control*
Computer Related Services, Inc.
Pembroke 5, Ste. 108
Virginia Beach, VA 23462
Ph: (757)499-8911
Fax: (757)490-5932
Co. E-mail: crsweb@crsva.com
URL: http://www.crsva.com
Description: Available for IBM computers. System provides inventory data management for various businesses.

ASSOCIATIONS AND OTHER ORGANIZATIONS

44057 ■ Strategic and Competitive Intelligence Professionals (SCIP)
7550 IH 10 W, Ste. 400
San Antonio, TX 78229
Ph: (703)739-0696
Fax: (703)739-2524
Co. E-mail: info@scip.org
URL: http://www.scip.org
Contact: August Jackson, Chairman
Description: Acts as a forum for the exchange of news and ideas among professionals involved in competitive intelligence and analysis. Addresses legal and ethical concerns; provides opportunities for improving professional expertise. Conducts programs of interest to members. **Founded:** 1986. **Publications:** *Competitive Intelligence* (Bimonthly); *Journal of Competitive Intelligence and Management* (Quarterly); *SCIP Online* (Biweekly); *SCIP.ORG In-box* (Weekly). **Awards:** Catalyst Award (Annual); Faye Brill Award (Biennial); Fellows Award; Meritorious Award; Fellows Award (Annual); Meritorious Award (Annual).

REFERENCE WORKS

44058 ■ "Ask Inc.: Managing and Real Estate" in *Inc. (December 2007, pp. 83-84)*
Pub: Gruner and Jahr USA Publishing Co.
Contact: J. Russell Denson, President
Ed: Ari Weinzweig. **Description:** Questions regarding knowledge management in the case of a retiring CFO, issues involved in opening a satellite office for a New York realtor, and information for hiring a multi-cultural workforce are all discussed.

44059 ■ "Behind Frenemy Lines" in *Entrepreneur (May 2014)*
Pub: Entrepreneur Media Inc.
Released: May 2014. **Description:** Entrepreneurs have three options when it comes to socializing with competitors. One is to avoid them socially, another is to socialize with them as if they are not competitors, or they can take the occasionally awkward dance of the two competitors. The dance involves giving up some personal and business information, while protecting proprietary information at the same time. Entrepreneurs should view the competitor as a threat who should not be treated like a threat. They can turn a potentially awkward situation into a social and professional advantage by seeing threat as an opportunity.

44060 ■ "Bridging the Worlds" in *Academy of Management Journal (Vol. 50, No. 5, October 1, 2007, pp. 1043)*
Pub: Academy of Management
Contact: Ming-Jer Chen, President
Ed: Lise Saari. **Description:** Need to transfer human resource research information published in journals to practitioners and organizations is investigated, along with suggestions on ways of achieving this goal.

44061 ■ "Bring Out the Best in Your Team" in *Harvard Business Review Vol. 92, September 2014, No. 9, pp. 26)*
Pub: Harvard Business Publishing
Released: September 2014. **Description:** Social influence often impacts team decision making, as more outgoing members tend to dominate discussion. To replace social influence with informational influence, have team members state at the beginning what knowledge they have regarding the task at hand.

44062 ■ "The Business of Security Is the Business" in *Security Dealer & Integrator (Vol. 34, February 2012)*
Pub: Cygnus Business Media
Contact: Paul Mackler, Chief Executive Officer
Released: February 2012. **Description:** Details covering the annual ASG Summit in Seattle, held every March, are examined. The security industry requires trust and collective knowledge and skill within the industry will increase the value of security to customers.

44063 ■ "Capitalizing On Our Intellectual Capital" in *Harvard Business Review (Vol. 90, May 2012, No. 5, pp. 42)*
Pub: Harvard Business Review Press
Contact: Peter E. Walsh, Director
Ed: Iqbal Quadir. **Released:** May 2012. **Description:** By managing education as an export, the US can benefit not only from revenue received from tuition, but also from the relationships forged with foreign students. The students will import the networks and technologies they used while in the US and their education levels will help create global growth.

44064 ■ Conquering Information Chaos in the Growing Business: IBM Solutions for Managing Information in an On Demand World
Ed: Jim Hoskins. **Released:** April 2005. **Price:** , $29.95. **Description:** Information management is critical to any business.

44065 ■ "Contextual Intelligence: Despite 30 Years of Experimentation and Study, We are Only Starting to Understand that Some Managerial Knowledge is Universal and Some is Specific to a Market or a Culture" in *Harvard Business Review (Vol. 92, September 2014, No. 9, pp. 58)*
Pub: Harvard Business Publishing
Released: September 2014. **Description:** Contextual intelligence is defined as the ability to adapt knowledge to circumstances different from those under which the knowledge was initially developed. Firms should observe both employees and customers to understand local variations.

44066 ■ "Creativity: A Key Link to Entrepreneurial Behavior" in *Business Horizons (September-October 2007, pp. 365)*
Pub: Elsevier Technology Publications
Ed: Stephen Ko, John E. Butler. **Price:** $35.95. **Description:** Importance of creativity and its link to entrepreneurial behavior is examined. In a study of

various entrepreneurs, studies concluded that a solid knowledge base, a well-developed social network, and a strong focus on identifying opportunities are relevant to entrepreneurial behavior.

44067 ■ "Dynamically Integrating Knowledge in Teams: Transforming Resources Into Performance" in *Academy of Management Journal (Vol. 55, August 1, 2012, No. 4, pp. 998)*
Pub: Academy of Management
Contact: Ming-Jer Chen, President
Ed: Heidi K. Gardner, Francesca Gino, Bradley R. Staats. **Description:** A method for developing a knowledge-integration capability to dynamically integrate the resources of team members into higher performance is proposed. Results suggest that the development of this capability is aided by the use of relational, structural, and experiential resources while uncertainty plays a moderating role in these relationships.

44068 ■ Electronic Commerce: Technical, Business, and Legal Issues
Ed: Oktay Dogramaci; Aryya Gangopadhyay; Yelena Yesha; Nabil R. Adam. **Released:** August 1998. **Description:** Provides insight into the goals of using the Internet to grow a business in the areas of networking and telecommunication, security, and storage and retrieval; business areas such as marketing, procurement and purchasing, billing and payment, and supply chain management; and legal aspects such as privacy, intellectual property, taxation, contractual and legal settlements.

44069 ■ "Enriching the Ecosystem: A Four-Point Plan for Linking Innovation, Enterprises, and Jobs" in *Harvard Business Review (Vol. 90, March 2012, No. 3, pp. 140)*
Pub: Harvard Business Review Press
Contact: Peter E. Walsh, Director
Ed: Rosabeth Moss Kanter. **Released:** March 2012. **Description:** The four goals for enriching the ecosystem include: linking venture creation and knowledge creation to speed up the idea-to-enterprise transition; revitalizing small-, medium-, and large-sized firms via partnerships; improving matches between education and employment opportunities; and bringing together leaders across different sectors to create regional strategies.

44070 ■ Enterprise Planning and Development: Small Business and Enterprise Start-Up Survival and Growth
Pub: Elsevier Science and Technology Books
Ed: David Butler. **Released:** June 2006. **Description:** Innovation, intellectual property, and exit strategies are among the issues discussed in this book involving current entrepreneurship.

44071 ■ Entrepreneurship and Technology Policy
Pub: Edward Elgar Publishing Inc.
Contact: Richard Henning, Vice President
E-mail: kwight@e-elgar.com
Released: 2006. **Price:** £108. **Description:** Journal articles focusing how and the ways small businesses' technical contributions are affecting business. The

book is divided into four parts: Government's Direct Support of R&D, Government's Leveraging of R&D, Government's Infrastructure Policies; and Knowledge Flows from Universities and Laboratories. **Availability:** Print.

44072 ■ *"Expatriate Knowledge Transfer, Subsidiary Absorptive Capacity, and Subsidiary Performance" in Academy of Management Journal (Vol. 55, August 1, 2012, No. 4, pp. 927)*
Pub: Academy of Management
Contact: Ming-Jer Chen, President
Ed: Yi-Ying Chang, Yaping Gong, Mike W. Peng. **Description:** The influence of expatriate competencies in knowledge transfer on the performance of subsidiary companies is examined. Results suggest that the success of knowledge transfer and subsidiary performance rely on the expatriates' ability and motivation to transfer knowledge as well as on the action taken by multinational corporations to develop subsidiary absorptive capacity.

44073 ■ *"From the Battlefield to the Boardroom" in Business Horizons (Vol. 51, March-April 2008, No. 2, pp. 79)*
Pub: Elsevier Advanced Technology Publications
Ed: Catherine M. Dalton. **Description:** Effective intelligence gathering, a thorough understanding of the mission, efficient use of resources, and strategic leadership are vital to achieving success in business as well as in the battlefield. Examples of effective leadership in the battle of Gettysburg are cited.

44074 ■ *"From Common To Uncommon Knowledge: Foundations of Firm-Specific Use of Knowledge as a Resource" in Academy of Management Journal (Vol. 55, April 1, 2012, No. 2, pp. 421)*
Pub: Academy of Management
Contact: Ming-Jer Chen, President
Ed: Rajiv Nag. **Description:** A model of how top managers seek, use, and transform common knowledge into distinctive, uncommon knowledge as an approach to competitive advantage is developed. In this context, knowledge is not just regarded as a basis for strategy but also a strategic resource. Characteristics of knowledge adaptation and augmentation are also described as distinct forms of knowledge-use-in-practice.

44075 ■ *"German Win Through Sharing" in Canadian Business (Vol. 83, September 14, 2010, No. 15, pp. 16)*
Pub: Rogers Media Inc.
Contact: Tony Viner, President
Ed: Jordan Timm. **Description:** German economic historian Eckhard Hoffner has a two-volume work showing how German's relaxed attitude toward copyright and intellectual property helped it catch up to industrialized United Kingdom. Hoffner's research was in response to his interest in the usefulness of software patents. Information on the debate regarding Canada's copyright laws is given.

44076 ■ *Getting Rich In Your Underwear: How To Start and Run a Profitable Home-Based Business*
Pub: HCM Publishing
Price: $17.95. **Description:** Book offers insight into starting a home-based business. Entrepreneurs will learn about business models and the home business; distribution and fulfillment of product or service; marketing and sales; how to overcome the fear of starting a business; personal success characteristics; naming a business; zoning and insurance; intellectual capital; copyrights, trademarks, and patents; limited liability companies and S-corporations; business expenses and accounting; taxes; fifteen basic steps for starting a home-based business, state resources for starting a home company; and seven home-based business ideas.

44077 ■ *"How Business Intelligence Can Affect Bottomline" in Canadian Electronics (Vol. 23, February 2008, No. 1, pp. 6)*
Ed: Mark Borkowski. **Description:** Business intelligence has an important role in delivering the right information in a secured manner. However, coping with data volume, cost, workload, time, availability and compliance have been a problem for business intelligence projects. Ways to avoid problems in business intelligence projects and examples of business intelligence applications are provided.

44078 ■ *"I Quit...Six Months From Now" in Canadian Business (Vol. 85, July 16, 2012, No. 11-12, pp. 71)*
Pub: George Media Inc.
Ed: Matthew McClearn. **Released:** July 16, 2012. **Description:** Employees who are planning to resign should consider the notice period, the time it will take for employers to find a replacement and the reason for leaving. Departing employees can use their knowledge and skills to compete directly with their former employer, but they should be wary of unfair competition.

44079 ■ *"The Impact of Acquisitions On the Productivity of Inventors at Semiconductor Firms: A Synthesis of Knowledge-Based and Incentive-Based Perspective" in Academy of Management Journal (Vol. 50, No. 5, October 1, 2007, pp. 1133)*
Pub: Academy of Management
Contact: Ming-Jer Chen, President
Ed: Rahul Kapoor, Kwanghui Lim. **Description:** Study examined the relation between knowledge-based and incentive-based outlook in explaining the impact of acquisitions on the productivity of inventors at acquired semiconductor firms. Results showed a definite relation between the two perspectives.

44080 ■ *Innovation and Its Discontents: How Our Broken Patent System is Endangering Innovation and Progress, and What to Do About It*
Pub: Princeton University Press
Contact: Shirley M. Tilghman, President
Ed: Josh Lerner, Adam B. Jaffe. **Released:** 2007. **Price:** $26.95, U.S., hardcover/paperback orders in the Canada, Latin America, Asia, and Australia; £18.95, hardcover/paperback orders in Europe, Africa, the Middle East, and India. **Description:** According to the authors, America's patent system does not effectively serve as a generator and protector of patents and intellectual property. **Availability:** Print.

44081 ■ *"Innovative Ability and Entrepreneurial Activity: Two Factors to Enhance 'Quality of Life'" in Journal of Business & Industrial Marketing (Vol. 29, July 2014, No. 6)*
Pub: Emerald Group Publishing Inc.
Released: July 2014. **Description:** Examination of how aspects of knowledge economy covered by the KEI (Knowledge Economy Index) and those of entrepreneurial activity covered by the GEI (Global Entrepreneurship Index) affect QOL (quality of Life) in a country. KEI, GEI, and QOL data gathered from different countries was analyzed using correlation and regression analyses. It was observed that KEI and GEI feature a momentous effect on QOL, while innovation index and total early stage entrepreneurship improve it.

44082 ■ *"Integrating Business Core Knowledge through Upper Division Report Composition" in Business Communication Quarterly (December 2007)*
Pub: Pine Forge Press
Contact: Blaise R. Simqu, President
Ed: Joy Roach, Daniel Tracy, Kay Durden. **Description:** An assignment that integrates subjects and encourages the use of business communication report-writing skills is presented. This assignment is designed to complement business school curricula and help develop critical thinking and organizational skills.

44083 ■ *Know-Who Based Entrepreneurship: From Knowledge Creation to Business Implementation*
Pub: Edward Elgar Publishing Inc.
Contact: Richard Henning, Vice President
E-mail: kwight@e-elgar.com
Ed: Sigvald J. Harrysson. **Price:** £90.90, hardback; £33.60, paperback. **Description:** Analysis of the knowledge and interconnected areas of entrepreneurship and networking across various levels is presented. Best practice companies are profiled. **Availability:** Print.

44084 ■ *"Lawyers Sued Over Lapsed Lacrosse Patent" in Crain's Detroit Business (Vol. 25, June 8, 2009, No. 23, pp. 5)*
Pub: Crain Communications Inc. - Detroit
Contact: Keith Crain, Chairman
Ed: Chad Halcom. **Description:** Warrior Sports Inc., a manufacturer of lacrosse equipment located in Warren, Michigan is suing the law firm Dickinson Wright PLLC and two of its intellectual property lawyers over patent rights to lacrosse equipment.

44085 ■ *"Legislating the Cloud" in Information Today (Vol. 28, October 2011, No. 9, pp. 1)*
Pub: Information Today, Inc.
Contact: Thomas H. Hogan, President
E-mail: ctuthill@infotoday.com
Description: Internet and telecommunications industry leaders are asking for legislation to address the emerging market in cloud computing. Existing communications laws do not adequately govern the modern Internet.

44086 ■ *"LIBOR's Hidden Lesson: Instant Messages Are Deadly" in Canadian Business (Vol. 85, September 17, 2012, No. 14, pp. 75)*
Pub: George Media Inc.
Ed: Vanessa Farquharson. **Released:** September 17, 2012. **Description:** The appropriate use of instant messaging in the workplace is discussed. Employees involved in a business that deals with other people's finances or intellectual property are advised to keep all of their work and private email accounts separate.

44087 ■ *"Linking HRM and Knowledge Transfer Via Individual-Level Mechanisms" in Human Resource Management (Vol. 51, May-June 2012, No. 3, pp. 387-405)*
Pub: John Wiley & Sons Inc.
Contact: Stephen M. Smith, President
Ed: Dana B. Minbaeva, Kristina Makela, Larissa Rabbiosi. **Description:** The relationship between human resource management and knowledge transfer and the role of individual-level mechanisms in this relationship are examined. Results indicate that individual-level perceptions of organizational commitment to knowledge sharing and extrinsic motivation affect internal knowledge exchange among employees.

44088 ■ *Managing the Older Worker: How to Prepare for the New Organizational Order*
Pub: Harvard Business Press
Ed: Peter Cappelli, Bill Novelli. **Released:** August 17, 2010. **Price:** $29.95, hardcover. **Description:** Your organization needs older workers more than ever: They transfer knowledge between generations, transmit your company's values to new hires, make excellent mentors for younger employees, and provide a 'just in time' workforce for special projects. **Availability:** Print.

44089 ■ *"Managing Your Innovation Portfolio: People Throughout Your Organization Are Energetically Pursuing the New. But Does All That Add Up To a Strategy?" in Harvard Business Review (Vol. 90, May 2012, No. 5, pp. 66)*
Pub: Harvard Business Review Press
Contact: Peter E. Walsh, Director
Ed: Bansi Nagji, Geoff Tuff. **Released:** May 2012. **Description:** Returns on innovation are higher with transformational initiatives than with core or adjacent pursuits, but require unique management methods. These include establishing a diverse talent set, separating teams from daily operations, and obtaining funding from outside the regular budget cycle.

44090 ■ *"The Metrics of Knowledge: Mechanisms for Preserving the Value of Managerial Knowledge" in Business Horizons*

(November-December 2007)
Pub: Elsevier Technology Publications
Ed: Eliezer Geisler. **Price:** $35.95. **Description:** Mechanisms to reduce the loss of managerial knowledge, such as socialization, tutoring, mentoring, and continuous reporting are proposed. These informal mechanisms should become integral components of knowledge management or organizations. **Availability:** PDF.

44091 ■ "MultiLing Expands HQ to Provide Room for Translation, Business Development Teams" in Entertainment Close-Up (May 6, 2012)
Pub: Close-Up Media
Released: May 6, 2012. **Description:** MultiLing has expanded to improve its standarization and centralized intellectual property translations around the world. MultiLing provides IP translation to patent attorneys and corporations globally.

44092 ■ Organizations Alive!: Six Things That Challenge - Seven That Bring Success
Pub: Yuill & Associates
Ed: Jan Yuill. **Price:** C$18.95, paperback. **Description:** New insight into understanding how organizations function as individuals is presented by an international consultant. Customer service, resource management, outsourcing, and management are among the issues covered.

44093 ■ "Perfecting Customer Services" in Pet Product News (Vol. 64, November 2010, No. 11, pp. 18)
Pub: Bowtie Inc.
Description: Pet supply retailers are encouraged to emphasize customer experience and sales representatives' knowledge of the store's product offerings to foster repeat business. Employee protocols could be implemented to improve customer interaction. Other guidelines on developing a pet supply retail environment that advances repeat business are presented.

44094 ■ "Protect Your Trade Secrets" in Business Owner (Vol. 35, July-August 2011, No. 4, pp. 11)
Pub: DL Perkins Company
Description: Every business has secret information which can include customer lists and contracts or secret formulas and methods used in production of goods vital to the operation. A list of things every small business owner should do to protect these secrets is outlined.

44095 ■ "Protecting Company Secrets" in Inc. (February 2008, pp. 38-39)
Ed: Scott Westcott. **Description:** A legal guide for noncompete clauses when hiring new employees is outlined, stressing how each state has its own set of laws.

44096 ■ "Research Note" in International Journal of Globalisation and Small Business (Vol. 4, September 21, 2010, No. 1, pp. 92)
Pub: Publishers Communication Group
Contact: Doug Wright, Director
Ed: Alexander Bode, Tobias B. Talmon l'Armee, Simon Alig. **Description:** The cluster concept has steadily increased its importance during the past years both from practitioners' and reearchers' points of view. Simultaneously, many corporate networks are established. Researchers from different areas (business management, economic social and geographical science) are trying to explain both phenomena.

44097 ■ "Reviving Entrepreneurship: Policy Decisions in 12 Areas Could Nurture - Or Cripple - America's Greatest Asset" in Harvard Business Review (Vol. 90, March

2012, No. 3, pp. 116)
Pub: Harvard Business Review Press
Contact: Peter E. Walsh, Director
Ed: Josh Lerner, William Sahlman. **Released:** March 2012. **Description:** Government policies should address entrepreneurship as a process, rather than an act. Several key areas for policymaking include basic and translational science, supply and quality of human capital, information availability, tax treatment of rewards and risks, intellectual property rights, workforce healthcare, and mobility of financial and human capital.

44098 ■ "Seattle a Cybercrime Center" in Puget Sound Business Journal (Vol. 33, June 8, 2012, No. 7, pp. 1)
Description: Reports show that cybercrime is now a serious concern in Puget Sound, Washington. Organized criminals and international groups now steal personal medical information, private firms' intellectual property, and state secrets. Estimates show that the cybercrime industry is worth $1 trillion.

44099 ■ "Size Does Matter" in International Journal of Globalisation and Small Business (Vol. 4, September 21, 2010, No. 1, pp. 61)
Pub: Publishers Communication Group
Contact: Doug Wright, Director
Ed: Julia Cornnell, Ranjit Voola. **Description:** Examination of how members of an Australian-based manufacturing and engineering cluster share knowledge through networking as a means to improve competitive advantage.

44100 ■ "A Strategic Risk Approach to Knowledge Management" in Business Horizons (November-December 2007, pp. 523)
Pub: Elsevier Technology Publications
Ed: Bruce E. Perrott. **Price:** $35.95. **Description:** Knowledge management practices of Ramsay Health Care are studied to investigate the issues facing effective knowledge management. A knowledge process model is developed and presented. **Availability:** PDF.

44101 ■ Strategies for Growth in SMEs: The Role of Information and Information Systems
Pub: Elsevier Science and Technology Books
Released: November 29, 2004. **Price:** $77.95; $74.95. **Description:** Role of information and information systems in the growth of small and medium-sized enterprises in the U.S. **Availability:** PrintE-book.

44102 ■ Successful Proposal Strategies for Small Businesses: Using Knowledge Management to Win Government, Private-Sector, and International Contracts
Pub: Artech House Inc.
Contact: Joan Bazzy Egan, Director
Ed: Robert S. Frey. **Released:** 2012. **Price:** $139, CD-ROM Included. **Description:** Front-end proposal planning and storyboarding, focusing on the customer mission in proposals, along with the development of grant proposals. **Availability:** Print; E-book.

44103 ■ "U.S. Competitiveness and the Chinese Challenge" in Harvard Business Review (Vol. 90, March 2012, No. 3, pp. 40)
Pub: Harvard Business Review Press
Contact: Peter E. Walsh, Director
Ed: Xu Xiaonian. **Released:** March 2012. **Description:** Although China's shift from cntral planningto market-oriented policies has boosted innovation, intellectual property rights and original research are still insufficiently valued. The U.S. has the edge on China in this respect; it remains for the U.S. to restore confidence in its innovation and creativity.

44104 ■ "Valuation of Intangible Assets in Franchise Companies and Multinational Groups: A Current Issue" in Franchise Law

Journal (Vol. 27, No. 3, Winter 2008)
Pub: American Bar Association
Contact: Carolyn Lamm, President
Ed: Bruce D. Schaeffer, Susan J. Robins. **Description:** Intangible assets, also known as intellectual properties are the most valuable assets for companies today. Legal intellectual property issues faced by franchises firms are discussed.

44105 ■ "The Valuation of Players" in Canadian Business (Vol. 80, October 22, 2007, No. 21, pp. 39)
Ed: Jeff Sanford. **Description:** Business professionals are supplementing their Masters in Business Administration degrees with CBV or chartered business valuator. CBVs are trained, not only in business tangibles, but also in business intangibles such as market position, reputation, intellectual property, and patent. Details of employment opportunities for chartered business valuators are discussed.

44106 ■ "Why Copyright Isn't Property" in Information Today (Vol. 26, February 2009, No. 2, pp. 18)
Pub: Information Today, Inc.
Contact: Thomas H. Hogan, President
E-mail: ctuthill@infotoday.com
Ed: Matthew K. Dames. **Description:** An overview of intellectual property is presented. Intellectual property refers to 'creations of the mind: inventions, literary and artistic works, and symbols, names, and designs used in commerce', according to the World Intellectual Property Organization (WIPO). WIPO divides intellectual property into two categories: industrial property consisting of patents, trademarks, and industrial designs; and copyright: literary, artistic, creative, and aesthetic works.

44107 ■ "Why HR Practices Are Not Evidence-Based" in Academy of Management Journal (Vol. 50, No. 5, October 1, 2007, pp. 1033)
Pub: Academy of Management
Contact: Ming-Jer Chen, President
Ed: Edward E. Lawler. **Description:** A suggestion that an Evidence-Based Management Collaboration (EBMC) can be established to facilitate effective transfer of ideas between science and practice is presented.

44108 ■ "With Whom Do You Trade? Defensive Innovation and the Skill-Bias" in Canadian Journal of Electronics (Vol. 43, November 2010)
Pub: Journal of the Canadian Economics Association
Ed: Pushan Dutt, Daniel Traca. **Description:** Examination into whether increased trade with ineffective protection of intellectual property has contributed to the skill-deepening of the 1980s. An index of effective protection of intellectual property at the country level, combining data on protection of patents and rule of law are presented. An industry-specific version of this index is given using as weights each country's trade share in the total trade of the industry. A decline is seen in this trade-weighted index, owing to a rise in trade with countries with low effective protection of intellectual property, which explains 29 percent of the rise within-industry skill-intensity.

CONSULTANTS

44109 ■ VenturEdge Corp.
4711 Yonge St., Ste. 1105
Toronto, ON, Canada M2N 6K8
Ph: (416)224-2000
Fax: (416)224-2376
Contact: Mark Klingbaum, Manager
E-mail: klingbaum@venturedge.com
Scope: Provides services including strategy formulation; business planning; financial management; business coaching; performance improvement; information management; merger, acquisitions and divestitures; family succession planning; competitive intelligence. **Founded:** 1972. **Publications:** "Reputation," Harvard Business School Press, 1996; "Competing for the Future," Harvard Business School Press, 1994; "The Fifth Discipline," 1990.

START-UP INFORMATION

44110 ■ *"3rd Annual 'OneMedForum NY 2012', July 11th-12th, to Spotlight JOBS Act, Crowdfunding, and Promising Areas for Healthcare Investment" in Investment Weekly (June 23, 2012)*
Pub: NewsRX
Contact: Susan E. Hasty, Publisher
Released: June 23, 2012. **Description:** Third annual forum presented by OneMed provided sessions for understanding the changes in regulation due to the new JOBS Act, which will create opportunities for investors and entrepreneurs. Experts in healthcare and life science investments will be featured. Details of the event are covered.

44111 ■ *"Allied Brokers of Texas Looking to Fill Private Lending Gap" in San Antonio Business Journal (Vol. 26, March 23, 2012, No. 8, pp. 1)*
Pub: American City Business Journal
Description: San Antonio, Texas-based Allied Brokers of Texas has announced the expansion of its services to offer private lending. The move would provide direct private financing of $250,000 to $5 million to entrepreneurs looking to buy or sell a small business. Insights into the firm's new subsidiary, Allied Lending Services, are also offered.

44112 ■ *"Alpharetta Seeding Startups To Encourage Job Growth" in Atlanta Business Chronicle(June 20, 2014, pp. 3A)*
Pub: American City Business Journals, Inc.
Contact: Whitney Shaw, President
Released: June 20, 2014. **Description:** The City of Alpharetta is witnessing several incubators and accelerators that will create the physical and educational infrastructure to convert ideas into sustainable businesses. This will help startups develop a go-to-market strategy, prepare for FDA certification and insurance reimbursement as well as see that the company reaches a point where it can attract private equity or venture capital.

44113 ■ *Angel Financing: How to Find and Invest in Private Equity*
Pub: John Wiley & Sons Inc.
Contact: Stephen M. Smith, President
Ed: Gerald A. Benjamin, Joel B. Margulis. **Released:** October 1999. **Price:** $73.95, hardcover. **Description:** The book provides a proven strategy to help entrepreneurs find angel investors. Interviews with angel investors as well as information about investors' hedging strategies, risk assessments, syndication orientation, financial return expectations, deal structuring preferences, monitoring investments, harvesting returns, and realist exit strategies are covered. **Availability:** Print.

44114 ■ *The Art of the Start: The Time-Tested, Battle-Hardened Guide for Anyone Starting Anything*
Pub: Penguin Books USA Inc.
Ed: Guy Kawasaki. **Released:** September 09, 2004. **Price:** $27.95, hardcover. **Description:** Advice for

someone starting a new business covering topics such as hiring employees, building a brand, business competition, and management.

44115 ■ *"Asked and Answered: Crowdfunding" in Investment Advisor (Vol. 32, August 2012, No. 8, pp. 14)*
Pub: Summit Professional Networks
Contact: Steve Weitzner, President
Released: August 2012. **Description:** Questions are answered in detail regarding crowdfunding and implementation of the Title II provisions within the JOBS Act.

44116 ■ *The Beermat Entrepreneur: Turn Your Good Idea Into a Great Business*
Pub: Pearson Education Ltd.
Contact: Rod Bristow, President
Ed: Mike Southon, Chris West. **Released:** 2nd Edition. **Price:** £14.99, paperback; £9.99. **Description:** Information to help start, maintain and grow a small business is given, along with suggestions for working with a bank. **Availability:** PrintElectronic publishing.

44117 ■ *"Begslist.org Launches Crowdfunding On Its Website" in Computer Business Week (August 2, 2012)*
Pub: NewsRX
Contact: Susan E. Hasty, Publisher
Released: August 2, 2012. **Description:** Donation Website called Begslist has added crowdfunding to its site. Crowdfunding and begging are popular among small startups wishing to procure funding for their new companies.

44118 ■ *"Beyond Bootstrapping" in Inc. (Vol. 36, September 2014, No. 7, pp. 64)*
Pub: Mansueto Ventures L.L.C.
Contact: John Koten, Chief Executive Officer
Released: September 2014. **Description:** Dave Lerner, serial entrepreneur, angel investor, B-school professor, and author, explains the challenges entrepreneurs face when self-funding their startup business.

44119 ■ *Building a Dream: A Canadian Guide to Starting Your Own Business*
Pub: McGraw-Hill Ryerson Ltd.
Contact: Robert J. Bahash, President
Ed: Walter S. Good. **Released:** 9th Edition. **Price:** C$74. **Description:** Topics covered include evaluating business potential, new business ideas, starting or buying a business, franchise opportunities, business organization, protecting an idea, arranging financing, and developing a business plan. **Availability:** Print.

44120 ■ *The Canadian Small Business Survival Guide: How to Start and Operate Your Own Successful Business*
Pub: Dundurn Group
Contact: Kirk Howard, President
E-mail: khoward@dundurn.com
Ed: Benj Gallander. **Released:** April 2002. **Price:** $26.99, paperback; $12.99. **Description:** Ideas for starting and running a successful small business.

Topics include selecting a business, financing, government assistance, locations, franchises, and marketing ideas. **Availability:** PrintE-book.

44121 ■ *Cash In On Cash Flow*
Pub: Simon and Schuster Inc.
Contact: Carolyn Reidy, President
E-mail: carolyn.reidy@simonandschuster.com
Ed: Lawrence J. Pino. **Released:** July 2005. **Price:** $19.95. **Description:** Guide to assist entrepreneurs with starting a new business as a cash flow specialist. **Availability:** Print.

44122 ■ *The Complete Idiot's Guide to Starting and Running a Thrift Store*
Pub: Alpha Publishing House
Ed: Ravel Buckley, Carol Costa. **Released:** January 05, 2010. **Price:** $13.26, paperback. **Description:** Thrift stores saw a 35 percent increase in sales during the falling economy in 2008. Despite the low startup costs, launching and running a thrift store is complicated. Two experts cover the entire process, including setting up a store on a nonprofit basis, choosing a location, funding, donations for saleable items, recruiting and managing staff, sorting items, pricing, and recycling donations. **Availability:** Print.

44123 ■ *"Crowdfunding Becomes Relevant for Medical Start-Ups as TCB Medical Launches Campaign On Idiegogo to Bring Life-Saving Epinephrine Key to Market" in PR Newswire*
Pub: PR Newswire Association L.L.C.
Contact: David B. Armon, President
Released: July 31, 2012. **Description:** Startup company, TCB Medical Devices, is hoping to raise money through crowdfunding to launch its life-saving Epinephrine Key to the marketplace. According to allergist, Thomas C. Beller, MD, epinephrine provides safe and effective relief to allergy sufferers.

44124 ■ *"CrowdFunding Platform, START.ac, Announces It Is Expanding Its International Scope From the US, Canada and the UK to 36 Countries Including Australia, India, Israel, Italy and Africa" in Benzinga.com (July 11, 2012)*
Pub: Benzinga.com
Contact: Kyle Bazzy, President
Released: July 11, 2012. **Description:** START.ac is expanding its CrowdFunding site to include 36 countries and increasing its scope to include business startups, teen projects, as well as medical products. START.ac projects are in the fundraising stage at this point, with 23 percent located outside the United States.

44125 ■ *"Crowdfunding Roadshow Makes Memphis Stop, Pitching the Possibilities of the New JOBS Act" in Commercial Appeal (August 7, 2012)*
Pub: McClatchy-Tribune Information Services
Ed: James Dowd. **Released:** August 7, 2012. **Description:** EarlyShares founder, Maurice Lopes, is touring 24 cities across the US featuring his crowdfunding roadshow which meets with entrepreneurs

and investors. The Jumpstart Our Business Startups (JOBS) Act, a nonpartisan program should help small money investors pool resources in order to fund, or crowdfund, startup small businesses. Details of the roadshow are covered.

44126 ■ "Discover the Power of Many" in Pet Product News (Vol. 66, September 2012, No. 9, pp. 42)
Pub: Bowtie Inc.

Ed: Alison Bour. **Description:** Crowdsourcing, driven mainly by social media and online searchers, can help pet product startups to obtain quality marketing materials, feedback from target audiences, and funds. How some pet product retailers have employed crowdsourcing to propel their businesses towards success is presented.

44127 ■ The Entrepreneur and Small Business Problem Solver
Pub: John Wiley & Sons Inc.
Contact: Stephen M. Smith, President

Ed: William A. Cohen. **Released:** November 2005. **Price:** $31.95; C$26.99. **Description:** Revised edition of the resource for entrepreneurs and small business owners that covers everything from start-up financing and loans to new product promotion and more. **Availability:** Print.

44128 ■ "Entrepreneurs: Search Party" in Business Strategy Review (Vol. 21, Autumn 2010, No. 3, pp. 30)
Pub: John Wiley & Sons Inc. Scientific, Technical, Medical, and Scholarly Div. (Wiley-Blackwell)
Contact: William J. Pesce, Manager
E-mail: wpesce@wiley.com

Ed: Georgina Peters. **Description:** Entrepreneurs tend to be fixated on coming up with a foolproof idea for a new business and then raising money to start it. Raising startup funds is difficult, but it doesn't have to be that way. Search funds offers an innovative alternative, and the results are often impressive.

44129 ■ Entrepreneurship
Pub: John Wiley & Sons Inc.
Contact: Stephen M. Smith, President

Ed: William D. Bygrave, Andrew Zacharakis. **Released:** Third Edition. **Price:** $218.95, paperback; $52. **Description:** Information for starting a new business is shared, focusing on marketing and financing a product or service. **Availability:** PrintE-book.

44130 ■ "Equity 'Crowdfunding' Platform, RelayFund, Launched by Michigan Investor Group" in Economics Week (July 20, 2012)
Pub: NewsRX
Contact: Susan E. Hasty, Publisher

Released: July 20, 2012. **Description:** RelayFund was launched by a group of Michigan venture capitalists, entrepreneurs, and investment bankers to link small investors with startup firms under the new JOBS (Jumpstart Our Business Startups) Act. Crowdfunding is money raised for charities, projects or pre-selling products or services and allows online micro investments for startup companies.

44131 ■ "ETF Process May be Tweaked" in Austin Business JournalInc. (Vol. 28, December 26, 2008, No. 41, pp. 3)
Ed: Christopher Calnan. **Description:** Some government officials are proposing for an adjustment of the Texas Emerging Technology Fund's (ETF) policies. The ETF was created to get startup companies capital to get off the ground. Reports show that the global recession had made it more difficult for startup companies to garner investment.

44132 ■ "The Fashion Designer Survival Guide, Revised and Expanded Edition: Start and Run Your Own Fashion Business"
Pub: Kaplan Publishing

Released: March 10, 2009. **Price:** , $22.95 paperback. **Description:** Author, industry authority, and fashion designer consultant offers insights and critical business information for starting and maintaining a successful independent clothing designer business. Fabric and material needs; loans or investments for the startup; challenges for working from a home-

based venture as well as internationally; marketing, branding, and selecting retail stores to display your designs; creating an image and getting public attention.

44133 ■ "Home Grown" in Hawaii Business (Vol. 53, November 2007, No. 5, pp. 51)
Pub: PacificBasin Communications

Ed: Jolyn Okimoto Rosa. **Description:** Discusses a program that focuses on Native Hawaiian entrepreneurs and offers business training at the Kapiolani Community College; upon completion of the program, participants may apply for a loan provided by the Office of Hawaiian Affairs (OHA) to help them start their business. OHA plans to present the restructured loan program in November 2007, with aims of shortening the loan process.

44134 ■ How to Get the Financing for Your New Small Business: Innovative Solutions from the Experts Who Do It Every Day
Pub: Atlantic Publishing Co.
Contact: Amanda Miller, Manager
E-mail: amiller@atlantic-pub.com

Ed: Sharon L. Fullen. **Released:** May 2006. **Price:** $39.95, Includes companion CD-Rom. **Description:** Ready capital is essential for starting and expanding a small business. Topics include traditional financing methods, financial statements, and a good business plan. **Availability:** Print.

44135 ■ "iAM Scientist Launches To Provide a Crowdfunding Platform for Science, Technology, and Medicine" in Benzinga.com (July 31, 2012)
Pub: Benzinga.com
Contact: Kyle Bazzy, President

Released: July 31, 2012. **Description:** Medical, technology, and science researchers will be able to seach for funding through the newly launched iAMscientist platform. The sitewill provide a site with funding and shared research opportunities. The new tools, better models, and quicker data collection processes will help make research interdisciplinary, collaborative, data driven, and less predictable. Open Access Funding Platform (OAFP) can be used to solicit funding required to carry out research projects.

44136 ■ "Kickstarter Funds the Future; Crowdfunding Services Such as Kickstarter Have Been Hailed as a New Way To Get Started In Business and Cut Out the Traditional Money Men" in Telegraph Online (June 24, 2012)
Pub: Telegraph Media Group Ltd.
Contact: Murdoch MacLennan, Chief Executive Officer

Ed: Monty Munford. **Released:** June 24, 2012. **Description:** More than 530 crowdfunding services are expected to his the net by the end of the year. Crowdfunding helps companies raise money from investors for specific projects. A musician was able to raise over $1 million to fund a new record.

44137 ■ "Legal Matters: 'Crowdfunding' a Boon for Entrepreneurs, If They Clear Regulatory Hurdles" in Finance and Commerce (July 17, 2012)
Pub: Dolan Co.
Contact: James P. Dolan, President

Ed: Dan Heilman. **Released:** July 17, 2012. **Description:** Part of the Jumpstart Our Business Startups Act (JOBS) is crowdfunding, which allows the funding of a company by selling small parts of equity to a group of investors. Kickstarter, a Website for raising funds for business entitites, is primarily used for film and book projects. Most businesses cannot adopt Kickstarter's model because of the legality of receiving investor funds without offering security.

44138 ■ "MicroVentures: New Crowdfunding Game Makes Startups the Stars, Prepares Players for a New Kind of Investing" in Health & Beauty Close-Up (July 31, 2012)
Pub: Close-Up Media

Released: July 31, 2012. **Description:** MicroVentures created the MicroVentures Investor Challenge as a game on Facebook. The game features real startups such as AirBnB, Etsy, and Pinterest and

players invest in these firms. The game has real startups face off in six weekly rounds and the players act as venture capitalists. One startup and one investor will win the game.

44139 ■ "Military Vet Uses SBA Program to Help Fund His Business" in Philadelphia Business Journal (Vol. 33, May 9, 2014, No. 13, pp. 6)
Pub: American City Business Journals

Released: May 9, 2014. **Description:** Colonel Richard Elam and his wife Kimberly, both with the Florida Army National Guard, secured funding through the Small Business Administration's (SBA's) Veterans Advantage program to launch iPlay, which rents mobile entertainment equipment such as rock walls and laser-tag setups for group events. The capital access initiative, launched in January 2014, waives the origination fee for SBA Express loans to qualified veteran entrepreneurs.

44140 ■ "Money Matters: Using Sound Resources, You Can Find Capital For Your Business" in Black Enterprise (Vol. 38, November 2007, No. 4)
Ed: Carolyn M. Brown. **Description:** Profile of fashion designer Kara Saun who inspired an angel investor from Connecticut to help launch her Fall 2006 clothing line.

44141 ■ "National Crowdfunding Association Enters Into Deal with SCORE" in Professional Services Close-Up (August 7, 2012)
Pub: Close-Up Media

Released: August 7, 2012. **Description:** National Crowdfunding Association (NLCFA) will produce a series of educational webinars teaching the basics of crowdfunding for SCORE's 13,000 volunteers. Investment crowdfunding is a process designed to finance small businesses in the US. The JOBS Act allows small and startup businesses to raise up to $1 annually by issuing equity or debt security to groups of small investors through the Internet. Details of crowdfuding and the JOBS Act are outlined.

44142 ■ "No. 64: Scaling the Business Meant Rebuilding a Bridge" in Inc. (Vol. 36, September 2014, No. 7, pp. 48)
Pub: Mansueto Ventures L.L.C.
Contact: John Koten, Chief Executive Officer

Released: September 2014. **Description:** Profile of Susan Meitner, mortgage industry veteran who founded Centennial Lending Group, a mortgage lending institution. Meitner and her family helped raise the needed $2.5 million to launch the firm in order to provide loans to new customers.

44143 ■ Raising Capital
Ed: Andrew J. Sherman. **Price:** $34.95. **Description:** Corporate attorney provides a comprehensive guide using in-depth, practical advice on raising money to start and grow a business. A 115-page appendix contains samples of financing agreements, forms and questionnaires.

44144 ■ "SBA Program Helped New Company Survive As It Built Company Base" in Philadelphia Business Journal (Vol. 33, May 9, 2014, No. 13, pp. 4)
Pub: American City Business Journals

Released: May 9, 2014. **Description:** The Small Business Administration (SBA) Indiana District Business Office helped Netwise Resources set up its information technology (IT) consulting business with a six-month SBA-backed loan and the 8(a) Business Development Program for small disadvantaged businesses. Owner, Mark Gibson, attributes Netwise Resources' success to its focus on branding, recruiting skilled staff, and establishing relationships with clients within the target market.

44145 ■ "SBA Streamlines Loans and Ramps Up Web Presence" in Hispanic Business (January-February 2008, pp. 64)
Description: Federal government's Small Business Administration offers informational resources and tools to individuals wishing to start a new company as well as those managing existing firms. The site

consists of over 20,000 pages with information, advice and tips on starting, financing and managing any small business. Free online courses are also provided.

44146 ▪ *"SEC, NASAA Tell Small Businesses: Wait To Join the 'Crowd': Crowdfunding Is 'Not Yet Legal Until the Commission Appoints Rules', Says SEC's Kim" in Investment Advisor (Vol. 3, August 2012, No. 8, pp. 13)*
Pub: Summit Professional Networks
Contact: Steve Weitzner, President

Ed: Melanie Waddell. **Released:** August 2012. **Description:** Securities and Exchange Commission along with state regulators have advised small businesses and entrepreneurs to wait until the SEC has produced rules governing crowdfunding practices. Until that happens, federal and state securities laws prohibit publicly accessible Internet securities offerings. An overview of crowdfunding and the JOBS Act is included.

44147 ▪ *The Small Business Owner's Manual: Everything You Need to Know to Start Up and Run Your Business*
Pub: Career Press Inc.
Contact: Ron Fry, President

Ed: Joe Kennedy. **Released:** June 2005. **Price:** $19.99. **Description:** Comprehensive guide for starting a small business, focusing on twelve ways to obtain financing, business plans, selling and advertising products and services, hiring and firing employees, setting up a Web site, business law, accounting issues, insurance, equipment, computers, banks, financing, customer credit and collection, leasing, and more. **Availability:** Print.

44148 ▪ *"So What Is Crowdfunding Anyway? New Legislation by Obama and Congress Relaxes Solicitation by Startups" in Accounting Today (August 6, 2012)*
Pub: SourceMedia Inc.
Contact: James M. Malkin, Chief Executive Officer

Ed: Jim Brendel. **Released:** August 6, 2012. **Description:** An introduction to crowdfunding provides a concise description to the process in which a group of investors partner to fund small business and startups. Rules from the SEC regarding crowdfunding are expected to be in place by the end of the year.

44149 ▪ *"State Fund That Aids New Companies Likely To Wither" in Crain's Detroit Business (Vol. 24, February 25, 2008, No. 8, pp. 16)*
Pub: Crain Communications Inc. - Detroit
Contact: Keith Crain, Chairman

Ed: Tom Henderson. **Description:** Officials are committed to fighting to save funding for the statewide Strategic Economic Investment and Commercialization Board which provides pre-seed money to start-up firms.

44150 ▪ *"Three Common Computer Repair Franchise Funding Sources Revealed by SP Home Run Inc." in Investment Weekly News (May 12, 2012)*
Released: May 12, 2012. **Description:** SP Home Run discusses three popular sources for initial funding capital when starting a computer repair franchise: family, friends, and fools. It is advised that if money could become a problem within any relationship it is best to avoid that type of funding source.

44151 ▪ *The Toilet Paper Entrepreneur: The Tell-It-Like-It-Is Guide to Cleaning Up In Business, Even If You Are At the End of Your Roll*
Pub: Obsidian Launch LLC

Ed: Mike Michalowicz. **Price:** $24.95. **Description:** The founder of three multimillion-dollar companies, including Obsidian Launch, a company that partners with first-time entrepreneurs to grow their concepts into industry leaders.

44152 ▪ *"Want Capital? Avoid These 7 Mistakes" in Birmingham Business Journal*

(Vol. 31, March 7, 2014, No. 10, pp. 10)
Pub: American City Business Journals, Inc.
Contact: Whitney Shaw, President

Released: March 7, 2014. **Description:** Advice to entrepreneurs to help secure capital for their small business is given. Entrepreneurs should not approach investors prior to having a strong management team or great business potential. It is important to comply with all federal rules and regulations.

44153 ▪ *"What Portland Startups Need the Most: More Angels" in Business Journal Portland (Vol. 30, February 28, 2014, No. 52, pp. 4)*
Pub: American City Business Journals

Released: February 28, 2014. **Description:** Portland, Oregon-based startups are in need of more angel investors. Angel investors have helped launch some of the area's most prominent startups, which include Janrain and Puppet Labs. Meanwhile, Angel Oregon has been educating early-stage entrepreneurs on the benefits of investing in the area's startup companies.

44154 ▪ *Working for Yourself: An Entrepreneur's Guide to the Basics*
Pub: Kogan Page, Limited
Contact: Philip Kogan, Chairman of the Board

Ed: Jonathan Reuvid. **Released:** June 03, 2009. **Price:** £12.99. **Description:** Guide for starting a new business venture, focusing on raising financing, legal and tax issues, marketing, information technology, and site location. **Availability:** Print.

ASSOCIATIONS AND OTHER ORGANIZATIONS

44155 ▪ Commercial Finance Association (CFA)
370 7th Ave., Ste. 1801
New York, NY 10001
Ph: (212)792-9390
Fax: (212)564-6053
Co. E-mail: info@cfa.com
URL: http://www.cfa.com
Contact: Michael Haddad, Chairman of the Board

Description: Organizations engaged in asset-based financial services including commercial financing and factoring and lending money on a secured basis to small- and medium-sized business firms. Acts as a forum for information and consideration about ideas, opportunities and legislation concerning asset-based financial services. Seeks to improve the industry's legal and operational procedures. Offers job placement and reference services for members. Sponsors School for Field Examiners and other educational programs. Compiles statistics; conducts seminars and surveys; maintains speakers' bureau and 21 committees. **Founded:** 1944. **Publications:** *The Secured Lender* (Bimonthly). **Educational Activities:** Commercial Finance Association Convention (Annual).

44156 ▪ National Association of Development Companies (NADCO)
6764 Old McLean Village Dr.
McLean, VA 22101
Ph: (703)748-2575
Fax: (703)748-2582
Co. E-mail: info@nadco.org
URL: http://www.nadco.org
Contact: Christopher L. Crawford, President

Description: Small Business Administration Section 504 certified development companies. Provides long-term financing to small and medium-sized businesses. Represents membership in negotiations with the SBA, Congress, and congressional staff members; negotiates changes in legislation, regulations, operation procedures, and other matters such as prepayments problems, reporting requirements, and loan servicing procedures. Provides technical assistance and information regarding special training programs, marketing techniques, audit checklists, and loan closing and processing procedures. Compiles statistics. **Founded:** 1981. **Publications:** *NADCO News* (Monthly). **Educational Activities:** Winter Board Meeting (Annual).

44157 ▪ Risk Management Association (RMA)
1801 Market St., Ste. 300
Philadelphia, PA 19103-1613
Ph: (215)446-4000
Fax: (215)446-4101
Co. E-mail: rmaar@rmahq.org
URL: http://www.rmahq.org
Contact: Kevin M. Blakey, President

Description: Commercial and savings banks, and savings and loan, and other financial services companies. Conducts research and professional development activities in areas of loan administration, asset management, and commercial lending and credit to increase professionalism. **Scope:** commercial lending and credit. **Founded:** 1914. **Subscriptions:** archival material books monographs periodicals. **Publications:** *Compare2*; *Member Roster* (Annual); *RMA Annual Statement Studies* (Annual); *The RMA Journal* (10/year); *Annual Statement Studies* (Annual); *Annual Statement Studies: Industry Default Probabilities and Cash Flow Measures* (Annual). **Educational Activities:** Lending and Credit Risk Management; RMA, The Risk Management Association Annual Conference of Lending and Credit Risk Management (Annual); International Securities Lending; Loan Management Seminar. **Awards:** Award for Journalistic Excellence (Annual); National Paper Writing Competition Award (Annual).

REFERENCE WORKS

44158 ▪ *"5 Things You Should Know About Getting a Small Business Loan: Insights From a Banking Executive to Improve Your Odds" in Black Enterprise (Vol. 44, June 2014, No. 10, pp. 20)*
Pub: Earl G. Graves Publishing Co. Inc.
Contact: Earl G. Graves, Jr., President

Released: June 2014. **Description:** Five important tips for small businesses seeking a loan, include a credit profile, positive feedback from vendors and customers, presence on social media, bringing banker to business on a regular basis, and every six months to three times a year talk to banker about your industry.

44159 ▪ *"Abroad, Not Overboard" in Entrepreneur (Vol. 36, April 2008, No. 4, pp. 68)*
Pub: Entrepreneur Press
Contact: Perlman Neil, President

Ed: Crystal Detamore-Rodman. **Description:** Export-Import Bank is an agency created by the U.S. government to help exporters get credit insurance and capital loans by providing them with loan guarantees. The bank, being criticized as supporting more the bigger exporters, has allotted to smaller businesses a bigger portion of the annual credit being approved.

44160 ▪ *"Advance America Closing All Pa. Stores" in American Banker (Vol. 172, December 20, 2007, No. 244, pp. 11)*
Ed: William Launder. **Description:** Advance America Cash Advance Centers Inc. is closing its 66 locations in Pennsylvania while it awaits a state Supreme Court ruling about the excessively high fees it carries for loan products.

44161 ▪ *"Affordable Financing for Acquisitions" in Franchising World (Vol. 42, September 2010, No. 9, pp. 47)*
Pub: International Franchise Association
Contact: Stephen J. Caldeira, President
E-mail: scaldeira@franchise.org

Ed: Gene Cerrotti. **Description:** Acquisition pricing is reasonable and interest rates are low and quality franchised resale opportunities are priced 4.5 times EBITDA. Information about Small Business Administration loans is also included.

44162 ▪ *"All Indicators in Michigan Innovation Index Drop in 4Q" in Crain's Detroit Business (Vol. 25, June 22, 2009, No. 25, pp. 9)*
Pub: Crain Communications Inc. - Detroit
Contact: Keith Crain, Chairman

Ed: Ryan Beene. **Description:** Economic indicators that rate Michigan's innovation fell in the fourth quarter of 2008. The index of trademark applications, SBA loans, venture capital funding, new incorporations and other indicators traced dropped 12.6 points.

44163 ■ American Bar Association Legal Guide for Small Business: Everything You Need to Know About Small Business
Ed: American Bar Association. **Released:** June 10, 2010. **Description:** The American Bar Association provides insight into financial, health and family issues affecting small business, including start up issues, employment laws, financing a business, and selling a business.

44164 ■ "Angel Investing 2009" in Inc. (Vol. 31, January-February 2009, No. 1, pp. 83)
Pub: Mansueto Ventures L.L.C.
Contact: John Koten, Chief Executive Officer
Ed: Kasey Wehrum. **Description:** Tips for finding funding in tough economic times are presented, including secrets for closing second-round deals.

44165 ■ "Angel Investors Across State Collaborate" in Austin Business Journal (Vol. 31, May 20, 2011, No. 11, pp. 1)
Pub: American City Business Journals
Ed: Christopher Calnan. **Description:** Texas' twelve angel investing groups are going to launch the umbrella organization Alliance of Texas Angel Networks (ATAN) to support more syndicated deals and boost investments in Texas. In 2010, these investing groups infused more than $24 million to startups in 61 deals.

44166 ■ "Apartment Market Down, Not Out" in Crain's Detroit Business (Vol. 24, October 6, 2008, No. 40, pp. 9)
Pub: Crain Communications Inc.
Contact: Rance E. Crain, President
Ed: Daniel Duggan. **Description:** Detroit's apartment market is considered to have some of the strongest fundamentals of any apartment market in the country with relatively low vacancy rates and a relatively low supply of new units compared with demand. Investors continue to show interest in the buildings but the national lending market is making it difficult to invest in the city.

44167 ■ "Are We There Yet?" in Business Courier (Vol. 24, April 4, 2008, No. 52, pp. 1)
Pub: American City Business Journals, Inc.
Contact: Whitney Shaw, President
Ed: Lucy May; Dan Monk. **Description:** Groundbreaking for The Banks project happened in April 2, 2008, however, the future of the development remains uncertain due to some unresolved issues such as financing. Developers Harold A. Dawson Co. and Carter still have to pass final financing documents to Hamilton County and Cincinnati. The issue of financial commitment for the central riverfront project is examined.

44168 ■ "Area VCs Take Praise, Lumps, on Web site" in Boston Business Journal (Vol. 27, October 26, 2007, No. 39, pp. 1)
Ed: Jesse Noyes. **Description:** TheFunded.com is a social networking site that allows entrepreneurs to rate venture capitalists and post their comments. Information about venture capitalist firms such as size and the partners behind it are also provided.

44169 ■ The Art of the Start: The Time-Tested, Battle-Hardened Guide for Anyone Starting Anything
Pub: Portfolio Publishing
Contact: Adrian Zackheim, President
Ed: Guy Kawasaki. **Released:** September 09, 2004. **Price:** $27.95, hardcover; $19.99. **Description:** Apple's Guy Kawasaki offers information to help would-be entrepreneurs create new enterprises. As founder and CEO of Garage Technology Ventures, he has field-tested his ideas with newly hatched companies and he takes readers through every phase of creating a business, from the very basics of raising money and designing a business model through the many stages that eventually lead to success and thus giving back to society. **Availability:** PrintElectronic publishing.

44170 ■ "Asia Breathes a Sigh of Relief" in Business Week (September 22, 2008, No. 4100, pp. 32)
Ed: Bruce Einhorn; Theo Francis; Chi-Chu Tschang; Moon Ihlwan; Hiroko Tashiro. **Description:** Foreign bankers, such as those in Asia, that had been investing heavily in the United States began to worry as the housing crisis deepened and the impact on Freddie Mac and Fannie Mae became increasingly clear. Due to the government bailout, however, central banks will most likely continue to buy American debt.

44171 ■ "Au Revoir Or Goodbye?" in Barron's (Vol. 88, July 14, 2008, No. 28, pp. 5)
Pub: Dow Jones & Co., Inc.
Contact: Clare Hart, President
Ed: Alan Abelson. **Description:** Former Senator Phil Gramm's opinion that the U.S. is a 'nation of whiners' as they moan about recession is another example of the disconnection between Washington and Wall Street on one hand and the real world on the other. It would be a catastrophe for most of the world if Fannie Mae and Freddie Mac were to go under and take their trillions of mortgage debt with them.

44172 ■ "Auto Loan Company Revved for Growth" in Dallas Business Journal (Vol. 35, March 9, 2012, No. 25, pp. 1)
Released: March 9, 2012. **Description:** Irving, Texas-based Exeter Finance Corporation has filed plans to more than double its personnel, open 12 to 15 new branch offices and introduce a 76,061-square-foot customer service and collection center. The new center will have enough room to handle the company's growth in those departments for the next two to three years.

44173 ■ "Auto Loan Demand On the Upswing" in Memphis Business Journal (Vol. 34, May 25, 2012, No. 6, pp. 1)
Pub: American City Business Journal
Ed: Cole Epley. **Description:** Demand for auto loans in the US has increased in April 2012. Auto loans have surpassed consumerm loans during the first quarter of the year.

44174 ■ "Back on Track-Or Off the Rails?" in Business Week (September 22, 2008, No. 4100, pp. 22)
Pub: Bloomberg L.P.
Contact: Matthew Winkler, Manager
Ed: Peter Coy, Tara Kalwarski. **Description:** Discusses the possible scenarios the American economy may undergo due to the takeover of Fannie Mae and Freddie Mac. Statistical data included.

44175 ■ "Bad-Loan Bug Bites Mid-Tier Banks" in Crain's Chicago Business (May 5, 2008)
Pub: Crain Communications Inc.
Contact: Todd Johnson, Publisher
Ed: Steve Daniels. **Description:** Mid-sized commercial banks form the bedrock of Chicago's financial-services industry and they are now feeling the results of the credit crisis that has engulfed the nation's largest banks and brokerages. Commercial borrowers are seeing tighter terms on loans and higher interest rates while bank investors are unable to forecast lenders' earnings performance from quarter to quarter. Statistical data included.

44176 ■ "Bad Loans Start Piling Up" in Crain's New York Business (Vol. 24, January 6, 2008, No. 1, pp. 2)
Pub: Crain Communications Inc.
Contact: Rance Crain, President
Ed: Tom Fredrickson. **Description:** Problems in the subprime mortgage industry have extended to other lending activities as evidenced by bank charge-offs on bad commercial and industrial loans which have more than doubled in the third quarter.

44177 ■ "Bailout May Force Cutbacks, Job Losses" in The Business Journal - Serving Phoenix and the Valley of the Sun (Vol. 29, September 26, 2008, No. 4, pp. 1)
Ed: Mike Sunnucks. **Description:** Economists say the proposed $700 billion bank bailout could affect Arizona businesses as banks could be forced to

reduce the amount and number of loans it has thereby forcing businesses to shrink capital expenditures and then jobs. However, the plan could also stimulate the economy by taking bad loans off banks balance sheets according to another economist.

44178 ■ "Baltimore Commercial Real Estate Foreclosures Continue to Rise" in Baltimore Business Journal (Vol. 28, October 1, 2010, No. 21, pp. 1)
Pub: Baltimore Business Journal
Ed: Daniel J. Sernovitz. **Description:** Foreclosures of commercial real estate across the Greater Baltimore area have continued to rise. The region is now host to about $2 billion worth of commercial properties that carry a maturing debt or have been foreclosed. Commercial real estate owners are unable to finance their debts because banks have become stricter in passing out loans.

44179 ■ "Bane of Bad Debt on Downsizing" in Pittsburgh Business Times (Vol. 33, March 28, 2014, No. 37, pp. 4)
Pub: American City Business Journals
Released: March 28, 2014. **Description:** The Pittsburgh region in Pennsylvania saw a decline in bad loans and foreclosed property levels at eight of the ten largest banks, according to the latest BankTracker Report. Combined troubled assets across the U.S. were $151.8 billion by December 31, 2013.

44180 ■ "Bank Bullish on Austin" in Austin Business JournalInc. (Vol. 29, November 13, 2009, No. 36, pp. A1)
Pub: American City Business Journals
Ed: Kate Harrington. **Description:** American Bank's presence in Austin, Texas has been boosted by new management and a new 20,000 square foot building. This community bank intends to focus on building relationship with commercial banking customers. American Bank also plans to extend investment banking, treasury management, and commercial lending services.

44181 ■ "Bank Forces Brooke Founder To Sell His Holdings" in The Business Journal-Serving Metropolitan Kansas City (October 10, 2008)
Pub: American City Business Journals, Inc.
Contact: Whitney Shaw, President
Ed: James Dornbrook. **Description:** Robert Orr who is the founder of Brooke Corp., a franchise of insurance agencies, says that he was forced to sell virtually all of his stocks in the company by creditors. First United Bank held the founder's stock as collateral for two loans worth $5 million and $7.9 million, which were declared in default in September 2008. Details of the selling of the company's stocks are provided.

44182 ■ "A Banking Play Without Banking Plagues" in Barron's (Vol. 88, March 31, 2008, No. 13, pp. 26)
Ed: Jack Willoughby. **Description:** Fiserv's shares have been dragged down by about 20 percent which presents an appealing entry point since the shares could rise by 30 percent or more by 2009. The company enables banks to post and open new checks and keeps track of loans which are not discretionary processes of banks.

44183 ■ "Bankruptcies Shoot Up 68 Percent" in Sacramento Business Journal (Vol. 25, July 18, 2008, No. 20, pp. 1)
Pub: American City Business Journals, Inc.
Contact: Whitney Shaw, President
Ed: Kathy Robertson. **Description:** Personal bankruptcy in the Sacramento area rose by 88 percent for the first half of 2008 while business bankruptcies rose by 50 percent for the same period. The numbers of consumer bankruptcy reflects the effect of high debt, rising mortgage costs, and declining home values on U.S. households.

44184 ■ "Bankruptcies Swell" in The Business Journal-Portland (Vol. 25, July 4, 2008, No. 17, pp. 1)
Pub: American City Business Journals, Inc.
Contact: Whitney Shaw, President
Ed: Andy Giegerich. **Description:** Individual and business bankruptcy filings in Portland, Oregon had increased. The rising gas and food prices, mortgage

crisis and tightening lending standards are seen as causes of bankruptcies. Statistics on bankruptcy filings are also provided.

44185 ■ "Bankruptcy Blowback" in Business Week (September 22, 2008, No. 4100, pp. 36)

Pub: Bloomberg L.P.

Contact: Matthew Winkler, Manager

Ed: Jessica Silver-Greenberg. Description: Changes to bankruptcy laws which were enacted in 2005 after banks and other financial institutions lobbied hard for them are now suffering the consequences of the laws which force more troubled borrowers to let their homes go into foreclosure; lenders suffer financially every time they have to take on a foreclosure and the laws in which they lobbied so hard to see enacted are now becoming a problem for these lending institutions. Details of the changes in the laws are outlined as are the affects on the consumer, the economy and the lenders.

44186 ■ "Banks Continue March Out of Bad-Loan Numbers: Total Loans Up, Non-Performing Loans Decline" in Memphis Business Journal (Vol. 34, August 24, 2012, No. 19, pp. 1)

Pub: American City Business Journal

Description: Banks in Memphis, Tennessee continue to improve their capital status throughout the second quarter of 2012. The twenty-five banks observed showed improvements in total loan volume, as well as in non-performing loans and real estate. Total loans grew $723.26 million, while non-performing loans and real-estate-owned assets fell $322.4 million.

44187 ■ "Banks Find Borrowers Off the Beaten Path" in Boston Business Journal (Vol. 30, December 3, 2010, No. 45, pp. 1)

Pub: Boston Business Journal

Ed: Tim McLaughlin. Description: Banks in Boston have found unlikely applicants for bank loans in organizations such as the Dorchester Collegiate Academy. Dorchester is a charter school in its second year of operation, but qualified for $1.08 million to finance its own building. Other information, as well as views on the unexpected borrowers in Boston, is presented.

44188 ■ "Banks Looking to Lend, Compete to Make Small-Business Loans" in Puget Sound Business Journal (Vol. 33, August 17, 2012, No. 17, pp. 1)

Pub: American City Business Journal

Ed: Greg Lamm. Description: Mobile Tool Management has grown from four employees to 30 during the past five years, and its expansion was completed after owner Mike woogerd applied for a loan from Chase. Figures show that Chase lent $132 million in the second quarter of 2012 to businesses. A report by the Federal Reserve shows that large banks are owering their standatrds for lending to large and medium-sized companies.

44189 ■ "Banks Seeing Demand for Home Equity Loans Slowing" in Crain's Cleveland Business (Vol. 28, December 3, 2007, No. 48, pp. 1)

Pub: Crain Communications Inc.

Ed: Shawn A. Turner. Description: Discusses the reasons for the decline in demand for home equity loans and lines of credit. Statistical data included.

44190 ■ "BankUnited, Banco do Brasil Lead Local Lenders" in South Florida Business Journal (Vol. 35, September 12, 2014, No. 7, pp. 5)

Pub: American City Business Journals

Released: September 12, 2014. Description: South Florida banks have reported a $7.54 billion increase in loans in 2014. BankUnited registered the highest growth with a total of $3.75 billion in loans. National Bank of Florida came in second with $585 million.

44191 ■ "Basel3 Quick Fix Actually Neither" in Canadian Business (Vol. 83, October 12,

2010, No. 17, pp. 19)

Pub: Rogers Media Inc.

Contact: Tony Viner, President

Ed: Thomas Watson. Description: Information about the so-called Basel 3 standards, which will require banks to hold top-quality capital totaling at least 7 percent of their risk-bearing assets is provided. The rules' supporters believe that a good balance has been reached between improving the Basel 2 framework and maintaining enough lending capital to stimulate an economic growth.

44192 ■ "BBVA Compass To Open Loan Office In Chicago" in Birmingham Business Journal (Vol. 29, July 20, 2012, No. 30, pp. 1)

Pub: American City Business Journals, Inc.

Contact: Whitney Shaw, President

Ed: Antrenise Cole. Released: July 20, 2012. Description: Birmingham, Alabama-based BBVA Compass plans to open a commercial loan production office in Chicago, Illinois and has filed an application with the State of Alabama Banking Department. The company intends to serve companies of all sizes but plans to focus on firms with $500 million to $2 billion in revenue.

44193 ■ "The Bear Stearns-JPMorgan Deal - Rhymes with Steal - Of A Lifetime" in Barron's (Vol. 88, March 24, 2008, No. 12, pp. 24)

Pub: Dow Jones & Co., Inc.

Contact: Clare Hart, President

Ed: Andrew Bary. Description: JPMorgan Chase's impending acquisition of Bear Stearns for $2.50 a share is a huge steal for the former. JPMorgan is set to acquire a company with a potential annual earnings of $1 billion while the Federal Reserve funds Bear's illiquid assets by providing $30 billion in non-recourse loans.

44194 ■ "The Beauty of Banking's Big Ugly" in Barron's (Vol. 89, July 27, 2009, No. 30, pp. 31)

Pub: Dow Jones & Co., Inc.

Contact: Clare Hart, President

Ed: Andrew Bary. Description: Appeal of the shares of Citigroup comes from its sharp discount to its tangible book value and the company's positive attributes include a strong capital position, high loan-loss reserves, and their appealing global-consumer. The shares have the potential to generate nice profits and decent stock gains as the economy turns.

44195 ■ "Best Turnaround Stocks" in Canadian Business (Vol. 81, Summer 2008, No. 9, pp. 65)

Ed: Calvin Leung. Description: Share prices of Sierra Wireless Inc. and EXFO Electro Optical Engineering Inc. have fallen over the past year but have good chance at a rebound considering that the companies have free cash flow and no long-term debt. One-year stock performance analysis of the two companies is presented.

44196 ■ "Beware the Ides of March" in Canadian Business (Vol. 81, April 14, 2008, No. 6, pp. 13)

Pub: Rogers Media Inc.

Contact: Tony Viner, President

Ed: Jeff Sanford. Description: Financial troubles of Bear Stearns in March, 2008 was part of the credit crunch that started in the summer of 2007 in the U.S. when subprime mortgages that were written for people who could barely afford the payments started defaulting. The bankruptcy protection given to 20 asset backed commercial paper trusts is being fought by the investors in these securities who could stand to lose 40 percent of their money under the agreement.

44197 ■ "Big Deals With More To Come" in Business Journal Portland (Vol. 30, January 24, 2014, No. 47, pp. 14)

Pub: American City Business Journals

Released: January 24, 2014. Description: D.A. Davidson & Company investment banking head, Brad Gevurtz, describes the local mergers and acquisi-

tions (M&A) market in Portland, Oregon in 2013. Gevurtz says 2014 will be a good year for M&A because corporations have a lot of cash and lenders are lending.

44198 ■ "The Big Leap" in Entrepreneur (June 2014)

Pub: Entrepreneur Media Inc.

Released: June 2014. Description: Several franchises used their frontline experience and took advantage of the opportunities they saw to start their own franchises. Cory Wiedel's experience as a GNC nutritional supplement franchisee helped him run Complete Nutrition as a 100 percent franchised system. Michael Debenham of American Title Loans says he gained confidence to start his own franchise business by observing Liberty Tax Service as a franchisee. Ashley Morris thinks being a franchisee of Capriotti's Sandwich Shop gave him the advantage when he became the franchisor of the restaurant.

44199 ■ "BMO Harris Plans Boost In Local Biz Banking Unit" in Business Journal (Vol. 30, June 29, 2012, No. 5, pp. 1)

Pub: American City Business Journals, Inc.

Contact: Whitney Shaw, President

Ed: Jim Hammerand. Released: June 29, 2012. Description: BMO Harris Bank plans to bulk up its commercial banking group in Minnesota. The company, which is a subsidiary of Bank of Montreal, is assigning Todd Senger to oversee commercial banking operations and strategy. It is believed that BMO Harris' expansion will drive growth in other business lines.

44200 ■ "BofA Goes for Small Business" in Austin Business Journal (Vol. 31, July 22, 2011, No. 20, pp. A1)

Pub: American City Business Journals

Ed: Christopher Calnan. Description: Bank of America is planning to target small businesses as new customers. The bank lost its number one market share in Austin, Texas in 2010.

44201 ■ "Bouncing Back" in Orlando Business Journal (Vol. 29, September 7, 2012, No. 12, pp. 1)

Description: The Federal Financial Institutions Examination Council's data has shown the total value of small business loans originated in Central Florida by regional and national banks increased by 21.4 percent in 2011 after three years of decline. The total value reached $911 million compared to $750.7 million in 2010.

44202 ■ "Bracing for a Bear of a Week" in Barron's (Vol. 88, March 17, 2008, No. 11, pp. 24)

Pub: Dow Jones & Co., Inc.

Contact: Clare Hart, President

Ed: Jacqueline Doherty. Description: JPMorgan Chase and the Federal Reserve Bank of New York's opening of a line of credit to Bear Stearns cut the stock price of Bear Stearns by 47 percent to 30 followed by speculation of an imminent sale. JP Morgan may be the only potential buyer for the firm and some investors say Bears could be sold at $20 to $30. Bears prime assets include its enormous asset base worth $395 billion.

44203 ■ Bridging the Equity Gap for Innovative SMEs

Pub: Palgrave Macmillan

Contact: Lisa Dunn, Manager

E-mail: l.dunn@palgrave.com

Ed: Elisabetta Gualandri, Valeria Venturelli. Released: October 2008. Price: £90, hardcover. Description: This book addresses the evaluation of financial constraints faced by innovative and startup companies and explores ways for bridging the financing and equity gap faced by small to medium business enterprises. Availability: Print; E-book; Electronic publishing.

44204 ■ "Builders: Land Prices Up, Bank Lending Down" in Orlando Business Journal (Vol. 30, January 31, 2014, No. 32, pp. 5)

Pub: American City Business Journals

Released: January 31, 2014. Description: A look at the views of residential real estate executives on the rising land prices and financing of construction is presented. The limited supply of lots in great locations has resulted in landowners raising asking prices. The real estate downturn has also resulted in the reluctance of many banks to lend money to home builders to finance construction in Central Florida.

44205 ■ "Burdened by Debt, Borders Group Suspends Dividends, May Be Sold" in Crain's Detroit Business (Vol. 24, March 24, 2008, No. 12)

Pub: Crain Communications Inc.

Contact: Rance E. Crain, President

Ed: Nancy Kaffer. **Description:** Ann Arbor-based Borders Group Inc. is exploring its options and may put itself up for sale due to its declining stock price and mounting debt. The company's fiscal year was capped by poor holiday sales and Borders does not have the cash on hand to meet the 2009 goals set in its strategic plan.

44206 ■ "Cabela's Repays Incentives as Sales Lag" in Business Journal-Milwaukee (Vol. 28, November 19, 2010, No. 7, pp. A1)

Pub: Milwaukee Business Journal

Ed: Stacy Vogel Davis. **Description:** Cabela's has given back $266,000 to the government of Wisconsin owing to its failure to meet projected revenue goals for its Richfield, Wisconsin store. It has also failed to meet sales tax and hiring projection. The company received $4 million in incentives from Washington County.

44207 ■ "Can You Say $1 Million? A Language-Learning Start-Up Is Hoping That Investors Can" in Inc. (Vol. 33, November 2011, No. 9, pp. 116)

Pub: Inc. Magazine

Ed: April Joyner. **Description:** Startup, Verbling is a video platform that links language learners and native speakers around the world. The firm is working to raise money to hire engineers in order to build the product and redesign their Website.

44208 ■ "Can Your Business Still Land a Loan?" in Entrepreneur (Vol. 37, August 2009, No. 8, pp. 62)

Pub: Entrepreneur Press

Contact: Perlman Neil, President

Ed: Carol Tice. **Description:** Banks are now sticking to the rules before making business loans. A business's existing bank should be the first place they should go to for a loan but if this fails, they should then look to smaller community and regional banks.

44209 ■ "Capital Position: M&I Acquisition Opens the Door for Rivals to Gain Market Share" in Business Journal-Milwaukee (Vol. 28, December 24, 2010, No. 12, pp. A1)

Pub: Milwaukee Business Journal

Ed: Rich Kirchen. **Description:** Canada-based BMO Financial Group has purchased Marshall and Isley Corporation (M and I), which dominated lending among Wisconsin businesses for decades. The sale of M and I will enable other banks to recruit M and I's customers but BMO Financial remains a stronger competitor since it possesses a more potent capital position.

44210 ■ "Cautions On Loans With Your Business" in Business Owner (Vol. 35, July-August 2011, No. 4, pp. 5)

Pub: DL Perkins Company

Description: Caution must be used when borrowing from or lending to any small business. Tax guidelines for the borrowing and lending practice are also included.

44211 ■ "Centerpoint Funding In Limbo" in The Business Journal - Serving Phoenix and the Valley of the Sun (Vol. 28, August 1, 2008, No. 48)

Ed: Jan Buchholz. **Description:** Avenue Communities LLC has threatened to file a case against Mortgages Ltd. over the finance of the Centerpoint development project in Tempe, Arizona. Avenue Communities want Mortgages Ltd. to file a motion with the U.S. Bankruptcy Court so that it can secure financing for the project. Other views and information on the finance of Centerpoint, are presented.

44212 ■ "Central Texas Angel Network Investments Tripled in 2009" in Austin Business JournalInc. (Vol. 29, January 8, 2010, No. 44, pp. 1)

Pub: American City Business Journals

Ed: Christopher Calnan. **Description:** Central Texas Angel Network (CTAN) has invested $3.5 million in 12 ventures, which include 10 in Austin, Texas in 2009 to triple the amount it invested during 2008. The largest recipient of CTAN's investments is life sciences, which attracted 20 percent of the capital, while software investments fell to 18 percent. The new screening process that helps startups secure CTAN capital is explored.

44213 ■ "Centrue Sets Down New Roots in St. Louis" in Crain's Chicago Business (May 5, 2008)

Pub: Crain Communications Inc.

Contact: Todd Johnson, Publisher

Ed: H. Lee Murphy. **Description:** Centrue Financial Corp. has moved its headquarters from Ottawa to suburban St. Louis in search of higher-growth markets. The banks acquisitions and expansion plans are also discussed.

44214 ■ Chain of Blame: How Wall Street Caused the Mortgage and Credit Crisis

Pub: John Wiley & Sons Inc.

Contact: Stephen M. Smith, President

Ed: Paul Muolo, Mathew Padilla. **Released:** January 2010. **Price:** $14.95, paperback; $9.99. **Description:** The book describes how risky loans given irresponsibly put big investment banks at the center of the subprime crisis. **Availability:** PrintE-book.

44215 ■ "Channelside On the Blocks" in The Business Journal-Serving Greater Tampa Bay (Vol. 28, September 1, 2008, No. 36, pp. 1)

Pub: American City Business Journals, Inc.

Contact: Whitney Shaw, President

Ed: Michael Hinman. **Description:** In a bankruptcy auction for The Place, one of the more visible condominium projects at Channelside, the lowest bid is just below $73 a square foot. KeyBank National Association, the Key Developers Group LLC's lender, leads the auction planned for October 15, 2008. The reason behind the low minimum bid required to participate in the said action is discussed.

44216 ■ "Chasing Credit" in Canadian Business (Vol. 81, November 10, 2008, No. 19, pp. 59)

Pub: Rogers Media Inc.

Contact: Tony Viner, President

Ed: Joe Castaldo. **Description:** Small and medium sized companies are dealing with tightening credit because they appear riskier than usual. Some of these businesses are turning to private investors, but this is not easy since many have invested everything in the stock market. The sector is expected to weaken with the broader Canadian market in the next six months from October 2008.

44217 ■ "Chinese Fund Loans $33.5 Million to Prestolite" in Crain's Detroit Business (Vol. 26, January 18, 2010, No. 3, pp. 1)

Pub: Crain Communications Inc.

Contact: Rance E. Crain, President

Ed: Ryan Beene. **Description:** Prestolite Electric Inc., a distributor of alternators and starter motors for commercial and heavy-duty vehicles, looked to China for fresh capital in order to fund new product launches.

44218 ■ "Cincinnati Hospitals Feel Pain from Slow Economy" in Business Courier (Vol. 27, September 3, 2010, No. 18, pp. 1)

Pub: Business Courier

Ed: James Ritchie. **Description:** Hospitals in Cincinnati, Ohio have suffered from decreased revenues owing to the economic crises. Declining patient volumes and bad debt have also adversely impacted hospitals.

44219 ■ "City Eyeing Tax Breaks for Arena" in Boston Business Journal (Vol. 29, June 3,

2011, No. 4, pp. 1)

Pub: American City Business Journals, Inc.

Ed: Daniel J. Sernovitz. **Description:** Baltimore City is opting to give millions of dollars in tax breaks and construction loans to a group of private investors led by William Hackerman who is proposing to build a new arena and hotel at the Baltimore Convention Center. The project will cost $500 million with the state putting up another $400 million for the center's expansion.

44220 ■ "Cleanup to Polish Plating Company's Bottom Line" in Crain's Cleveland Business (Vol. 28, October 29, 2007, No. 43, pp. 4)

Pub: Crain Communications Inc.

Ed: Jay Miller. **Description:** Barker Products Co, a manufacturer of nuts and bolts, is upgrading its aging facility which will allow them to operate at capacity and will save the company several hundred thousand dollars a year in operating costs. The new owners secured a construction loan from the county's new Commercial Redevelopment Fund which will allow them to upgrade the building which was hampered by years of neglect.

44221 ■ "Clock Ticks On Columbia Sussex Debt" in Business Courier (Vol. 27, July 30, 2010, No. 13, pp. 1)

Pub: Business Courier

Ed: Dan Monk. **Description:** Cincinnati, Ohio-based Columbia Sussex Corporation has made plans to restructure a $1 billion loan bundle that was scheduled to mature in October 2010. The privately held hotel has strived in a weak hotel market to keep pace with its $3 billion debt load.

44222 ■ "Co-Op Launches Revolving Loan Program for Farmers" in Bellingham Business Journal (Vol. February 2010, pp. 3)

Pub: Sound Publishing Inc.

Contact: Gloria G. Fletcher, President

Ed: Lance Henderson. **Description:** Community Food Co-op's Farm Fund received a $12,000 matching grant from the Sustainable Whatcom Fund of the Whatcom Community Foundation. The Farm Fund will create a new revolving loan program for local farmers committed to using sustainable practices.

44223 ■ "Coming Soon: Bailouts of Fannie and Freddie" in Barron's (Vol. 88, July 14, 2008, No. 28, pp. 14)

Pub: Dow Jones & Co., Inc.

Contact: Clare Hart, President

Ed: Jonathan R. Laing. **Description:** Assurances from the government that Fannie Mae and Freddie Mac are adequately capitalized and able to carry on their duties as guarantors or owners of over $5 trillion of U.S. home mortgages are designed to keep both entities afloat until they attempt to raise $10 billion in new equity. The government would assume any losses in a bailout and owners of the banks' papers would profit as yields drop.

44224 ■ "Commercial Loans Ready for Refinance: High Number of Mortgages Creates Buying Opportunities" in Memphis Business Journal (Vol. 34, June 22, 2012, No. 10, pp. 1)

Pub: American City Business Journal

Ed: Cole Epley. **Description:** Commercial mortgage lending in Memphis, Tennessee improves as area volume loan increased from 2010 to 2011. The industry is projecting $600 billion in commercial mortgages held by banks coming to term over the next four to eight quarters.

44225 ■ The Commonsense Way to Build Wealth: One Entrepreneur Shares His Secrets

Ed: Jack Chou. **Released:** September 2004. **Price:** , $19.95. **Description:** Entrepreneurial tips to accumulate wealth, select the proper business or franchise, choose and manage rental property, and how to negotiate a good lease.

44226 ■ "Community Banks Fill Lending Gap For Homebuilders" in Birmingham Business

Journal (Vol. 29, July 13, 2012, No. 29, pp. 1)
Pub: American City Business Journals, Inc.
Contact: Whitney Shaw, President
Ed: Antrenise Cole. **Released:** July 13, 2012. **Description:** Alabama-based homebuilders have received financing from community banks for residential construction on developed lots as large banks continue to stay clear from the sector. However, homebuilders are still worried that the housing market's slow recovery might be halted by the lenders' unwillingness to finance developments of new lots.

44227 ■ The Complete Guide to Buying a Business
Pub: Nolo
Contact: Ralph Warner, Chief Executive Officer
Ed: Fred S. Steingold. **Released:** Third Edition. **Price:** $23.99; $20.99. **Description:** Key steps in buying a business are highlighted, focusing on legal issues, tax considerations, approaches for valuing a business, financing, structuring the deal, along with forms and documents for taking ownership are included. **Availability:** PrintE-book; Electronic publishing; PDF.

44228 ■ "Compounding Opportunity" in Hispanic Business (October 2007, pp. 72, 74-75)
Pub: Hispanic Business Inc.
Contact: Jesus Chavarria, President
Ed: Hildy Medina. **Description:** New banks are targeting Hispanic entrepreneurs.

44229 ■ "Condominium Sales Fall to a Seven-Year Low" in Crain's Chicago Business (Vol. 31, November 10, 2008, No. 45, pp. 2)
Pub: Crain Communications Inc.
Contact: Todd Johnson, Publisher
Ed: Alby Gallun. **Description:** Downtown Chicago condominium market is experiencing the lowest number of sales in years due to the tightening of the mortgage lending market, the Wall Street crisis and the downturn in the economy. The supply of new condos is soaring, the result of the building boom of 2005 and 2006; many developers are finding it difficult to pay off construction loans and fear foreclosure on their properties. Additional information and statistical data related to the downtown condominium market is provided.

44230 ■ "Condos Becoming FHA No-Lending Zones" in Providence Business News (Vol. 29, June 2, 2014, No. 9, pp. 7)
Pub: American City Business Journals
Released: June 2, 2014. **Description:** Federal policy changes and decisions by condominium boards of directors have made the condominium development ineligible for Federal Housing Administration (FHA) loans, making several communities prohibited lending zones. As a result, the number of condo developments approved for FHA funding has fallen by more than half, presenting a growing problem for first-time buyers, those with modest down payment cash, and senior citizens using a reverse mortgage.

44231 ■ "Consumers Finding It Harder to Get and Keep Credit" in Chicago Tribune (January 10, 2009)
Pub: McClatchy-Tribune Information Services
Ed: Susan Chandler. **Description:** Five tips to maintain a good credit rating in these economic times are outlined and discussed.

44232 ■ "A Conversation With; Ron Gantner, Jones Lang LaSalle" in Crain's Detroit Business (Vol. 24, October 6, 2008, No. 40, pp. 9)
Pub: Crain Communications Inc.
Contact: Rance E. Crain, President
Description: Interview with Ron Gantner who is a corporate real estate adviser with the real estate company Jones Lang LaSalle as well as the company's executive vice president and part of the tenant advisory team; Gantner speaks about the impact that the Wall Street crisis is having on the commercial real estate market in Detroit.

44233 ■ "Cornered by Credit: As $1B in Loans Come Due, Will Landlords Find Funds?" in Crain's Detroit Business (October 6, 2008)
Pub: Crain Communications Inc.
Contact: Rance E. Crain, President
Ed: Daniel Duggan. **Description:** Conduit loans are used by many real estate investors and are normally issued in 7- to 10-year terms with balloon payments due at the end, requiring the full balance to be paid upon maturity. Many building owners may find their properties going into foreclosure as these loans mature next year since these loans cannot be extended like typical loans and the credit crisis along with falling property values is making it more difficult to secure new sources of funding. Possible solutions to this problem are also explored.

44234 ■ "Corus Eases Off Ailing Condo Market" in Crain's Chicago Business (April 28, 2008)
Pub: Crain Communications Inc.
Contact: Todd Johnson, Publisher
Ed: H. Lee Murphy. **Description:** Corus Bankshares Inc., a specialist in lending for the condominium high-rise construction market, is diversifying its portfolio by making loans to office developers and expects to be investing in hotels through the rest of the year. Corus' $7.57 billion loan portfolio is also discussed in detail as well as the company's earnings and share price. Statistical data included.

44235 ■ "Crash Pads" in Business Courier (Vol. 24, November 2, 2007, No. 29, pp. 1)
Pub: American City Business Journals, Inc.
Contact: Whitney Shaw, President
Ed: Jon Newberry. **Description:** Francisca Webster accumulated $4 million in mortgage debt in about 2 months. She filed a lawsuit against her tax preparer and her mortgage broker contending that the defendants had breached their fiduciary duties to her and made fraudulent misrepresentations to her. The other details of the case are supplied.

44236 ■ "The Credit Crisis Continues" in Barron's (Vol. 88, March 10, 2008, No. 10, pp. M12)
Pub: Dow Jones & Co., Inc.
Contact: Clare Hart, President
Ed: Randall W. Forsyth. **Description:** Short-term Treasury yields dropped to new cyclical lows in early March 2008, with the yield for the two-year Treasury note falling to 1.532 percent. Spreads of the mortgage-backed securities of Fannie Mae and Freddie Mac rose on suspicion of collapses in financing.

44237 ■ "Credit Crisis Puts Market in Unprecedented Territory" in Crain's New York Business (Vol. 24, January 6, 2008, No. 1, pp. 14)
Pub: Crain Communications Inc.
Contact: Rance Crain, President
Ed: Aaron Elstein. **Description:** Banks are being forced to take enormous losses due to investors who are refusing to buy anything linked to subprime mortgages and associated securities.

44238 ■ "Credit Crunch Gives, Takes Away" in The Business Journal-Serving Metropolitan Kansas City (Vol. 27, October 17, 2008, No. 5, pp. 1)
Ed: Suzanna Stagemeyer. **Description:** Although many Kansas City business enterprises have been adversely affected by the U.S. credit crunch, others have remained relatively unscathed. Examples of how local businesses are being impacted by the crisis are provided including: American Trailer & Storage Inc., which declared bankruptcy after failing to pay a long-term loan; and NetStandard, a technology firm who, on the other hand, is being pursued by prospective lenders.

44239 ■ "Credit Crunch Takes Bite Out Of McDonald's" in Advertising Age (Vol. 79, September 29, 2008, No. 36, pp. 1)
Pub: Crain Communications Inc.
Contact: Rance Crain, President
Ed: Emily Bryson York. **Description:** McDonald's will delay its launch of coffee bars inside its restaurants due to the banking crisis which has prompted Bank of America to halt loans to the franchise chains.

44240 ■ "Credit-Market Crisis Batters Origen Financial's Bottom Line" in Crain's Detroit Business (Vol. 24, March 31, 2008, No. 13, pp. 4)
Pub: Crain Communications Inc.
Contact: Rance E. Crain, President
Ed: Tom Henderson. **Description:** Overview of the effect the credit-market crisis has had on Origen Financial Inc., a company that underwrites and services loans for manufactured housing. CEO Ronald Klein didn't think Origen would be affected by the collapse due to its sound operations but the company's share price dropped considerably causing its auditors to warn that the company's existence could be in jeopardy.

44241 ■ "Credit Unions Buck Trend, Lend Millions More" in Saint Louis Business Journal (Vol. 32, September 9, 2011, No. 2, pp. 1)
Pub: Saint Louis Business Journal
Ed: Greg Edwards. **Description:** St. Louis, Missouri-based credit unions have been making more loans despite the weak economy. Credit unions have made a total of $3.46 billion in outstanding loans as of June 30, 2011.

44242 ■ "Credit Unions Seek to Raise Lending for Small Business" in Denver Business Journal (Vol. 64, September 28, 2012, No. 64, pp. 1)
Pub: American City Business Journal
Description: United States Senator Mark Udall has introduced the Small Business Lending Enhancement Act, which aims to increase the commercial lending authority of credit unions. The bill's supporters claim that small business owners are still experiencing problems getting credit, and that the legislation will increase small business lending by $13 milliion within its first year of enactment.

44243 ■ "Critics: Efforts to Fix Loans Won't Stop Foreclosure Wave" in Business First Columbus (Vol. 25, November 14, 2008, No. 12, pp. A1)
Pub: American City Business Journals
Ed: Adrian Burns. **Description:** Efforts by U.S. banks to help homeowners pay mortgages are seen to have little if any impact on foreclosures. Banks have announced plans to identify and aid troubled borrowers. Statistical data included.

44244 ■ "Crowdfunding Author Thinks Google Will Beat Facebook to the Punch on InvestP2P Acquisition" in GlobeNewswire (July 17, 2012)
Released: July 17, 2012. **Description:** Author, Mark Kanter, explores the potentials of crowdfunding Websites, especially InvestP2P (aka: peer to peer lending) in his new book, "Street Smart CEO". Invest P2P has social networking tools built into its system. Kanter predicts Google to acquire InvestP2P.

44245 ■ "CrowdFunding Made Simple Conference at University of Utah Ignites Ecosystem of Entrepreneurs and Investors" in Economics Week (June 29, 2012)
Pub: NewsRX
Contact: Susan E. Hasty, Publisher
Released: June 29, 2012. **Description:** The first national conference on crowdfunding was held at the University of Utah Guest House and Conference Center May 31 through June 1, 2012. The event, CrowdFunding Made Simple, gathered entrepreneurs, business owners, professional service providers, investors, government officials and students to provide understanding and potential of crowdfunding, including information on the Jumpstart Our Business Startups (JOBS) Act.

44246 ■ "Culture, Community and Chicken Fingers" in Entrepreneur (Vol. 37, July 2009, No. 7, pp. 96)
Pub: Entrepreneur Press
Contact: Perlman Neil, President
Ed: Jason Daley. **Description:** Raising Cane's Chicken Fingers founder Todd Graves shares his experiences in running the company - from getting funding to plans for company. Graves believes that

the company wants franchisees to live and breathe the brand, and that the key to its success is doing one thing and doing it right. Cane's Pillar Program, a financial support program for franchisees, is also discussed.

44247 ■ "Dealers Fight To Steer Course" in The Business Journal-Serving Metropolitan Kansas City (Vol. 27, November 7, 2008, No. 9, pp. 1)
Pub: American City Business Journals, Inc.
Contact: Whitney Shaw, President
Ed: Steve Vockrodt. **Description:** One local automobile dealer says that their sales are down by 30 to 40 percent and that car financing is now in the low 60 percentile from 85 to 88 percent. The National Automobile Dealers Association says that 700 dealerships are likely to be lost for 2008.

44248 ■ "Death Spiral" in Business Journal Serving Greater Tampa Bay (Vol. 30, October 29, 2010, No. 45, pp. 1)
Pub: Tampa Bay Business Journal
Ed: Margie Manning. **Description:** Bay Cities Bank has started working on the loan portfolio of its acquisition, Progress Bank of Florida. Regulators closed Progress Bank in October 2010 after capital collapsed due to charge-offs and increases in the provision for future loan losses.

44249 ■ "Delinquent Properties in Greater Cincinnati on the Rise" in Business Courier (Vol. 27, June 11, 2010, No. 6, pp. 1)
Pub: Business Courier
Ed: Dan Monk. **Description:** Reports show that Cincinnati now ranks in the U.S. Top 20 for its delinquency rate on securitized commercial real estate loans. In December 2009, the region ranked 28th out of 50 cities studied by Trepp LLC. As of May 30, 2010, more than $378 million in commercial mortgage-backed security loans were more than 60 days past due.

44250 ■ "Developer Donald E. Phillips Wins Bout with Bank in Roundabout Way" in Tampa Bay Business Journal (Vol. 30, January 29, 2010, No. 6, pp. 1)
Pub: American City Business Journals
Ed: Janet Leiser. **Description:** Developer Donald E. Phillips of Phillips Development and Realty LLC won against the foreclosure filed by First Horizon National Corporation, which is demanding the company to fully pay its $2.9 million loan. Phillips requested that his company pay monthly mortgage and extend the loan's maturity date.

44251 ■ "Do-Gooder Finance: How a New Crop of Investors Is Helping Social Entrepreneurs" in Inc. (February 2008, pp. 29-30)
Ed: Nitasha Tiku. **Description:** Social venture firms are not seeking to sell companies as quickly as traditional venture companies. Four socially minded venture capital firms and banks profiled include, Underdog Venture, Island Pond, Vermont; Root Capital, Cambridge, Massachusetts; ShoreBank Pacific, Ilwaco, Washington; and TBL Capital, Sausalito, California.

44252 ■ "Don't Count Your Millions Yet" in Business Courier (Vol. 24, January 10, 2008, No. 40, pp. 1)
Pub: American City Business Journals, Inc.
Contact: Whitney Shaw, President
Ed: Steve Watkins. **Description:** Merger and acquisition deals have been difficult to complete since 2007 largely due to a weaker economy and the credit crunch. Buyers have become more cautious because of the state of the economy and capital has become tougher to obtain because of the credit market crisis. The trends in mergers and acquisitions are analyzed further.

44253 ■ "Don't Expect Quick Fix" in The Business Journal-Serving Metropolitan Kansas City (Vol. 27, October 3, 2008, No. 3, pp. 1)
Pub: American City Business Journals, Inc.
Contact: Whitney Shaw, President
Ed: James Dornbrook. **Description:** United States governmental entities cannot provide a quick fix solution to the current financial crisis. The economy requires a systemic change in the way people think about credit. The financial services industry should also focus on core lending principles.

44254 ■ "Economic Woes Portend Consumer Shift" in The Business Journal-Serving Metropolitan Kansas City (Vol. 27, September 26, 2008, No. 2, pp. 1)
Pub: American City Business Journals, Inc.
Contact: Whitney Shaw, President
Ed: Suzanna Stagemeyer. **Description:** Black Bamboo owner Tim Butt believes that prolonged tightening of the credit market will result in consumer spending becoming more cash-driven that credit card driven. The financial crisis has already constricted spending among consumers. Forecasts for the US economy are provided.

44255 ■ "EDF Ventures Dissolves Fund, Begins Anew On Investment" in Crain's Detroit Business (Vol. 24, February 25, 2008, No. 8, pp. 14)
Pub: Crain Communications Inc. - Detroit
Contact: Keith Crain, Chairman
Ed: Tom Henderson. **Description:** EDF Ventures is Michigan's oldest venture capital firm and was part of the second round of investments by the state's 21st Century Investment Fund and the Venture Michigan Fund.

44256 ■ "Emerging Tech Fund Strong in 2009" in Austin Business JournalInc. (Vol. 29, December 25, 2009, No. 42, pp. 1)
Pub: American City Business Journals
Ed: Christopher Calnan. **Description:** Texas' Emerging Technology Fund (ETF) has seen an increase in applications from the state's technology companies in 2009. ETF received 87 applications in 2009 from Central Texas companies versus 50 during 2008 while $10.5 million was given to seven Texas companies compared with $10.6 million to ten companies in 2008.

44257 ■ The Entrepreneur's Guide to Raising Capital
Pub: Greenwood Publishing Group, Inc.
Ed: David Nour. **Released:** March 2009. **Price:** $39.95, hardcover; £25; €32. **Description:** An overview to help entrepreneurs find capital for starting and maintaining a small business is presented. The author shows how to develop long-term relationships with financial partners and ways to attract financing to fund the startup and growth phases of any business. Entrepreneurs tell how they raised money from friends, family, angel investors, banks and venture capitalists and private equity firms. **Availability:** Print.

44258 ■ "Evolve Bank Ramps Up Staff for SBA Lending" in Memphis Business Journal (Vol. 33, February 24, 2012, No. 46, pp. 1)
Pub: American City Business Journal
Ed: Christopher Sheffield. **Description:** Memphis, Tennessee-based Evolve Bank has hired Marty Ferguson and Tre Luckett to handle its national and local Small Business Administration (SBA) lending operations. The two are long-time leaders in SBA lending.

44259 ■ "Ex-Im Bank Accepts $105 Million in Financing for Aquarium in Brazil" in Travel & Leisure Close-Up (October 8, 2012)
Description: Export-Import Bank of the United States authorized a $105 million direct loan to the Brazilian state of Ceara to finance the export of American goods and services for the construction of an aquarium in Fortaleza, Brazil. This transaction will support 700 American jobs and at least 90 percent of the export contract value will be provided by U.S. small businesses.

44260 ■ "Export Initiative Launched" in Philadelphia Business Journal (Vol. 28, December 11, 2009, No. 43, pp. 1)
Pub: American City Business Journals Inc.
Ed: Athena D. Merritt. **Description:** The first initiative that came out of the partnership between the Export-Import Bank of the US, the city of Philadelphia, and the World Trade Center of Greater Philadelphia is presented. A series of export finance workshops have featured Ex-Im Bank resources that can provide Philadelphia businesses with working capital, insurance protection and buyer financing.

44261 ■ "Extortion: How Politicians Extract Your Money, Buy Votes, and Line Their Own Pockets"
Pub: Mariner Books
Contact: Barry O'Callaghan, Chief Executive Officer
Released: October 7, 2014. **Price:** , $14.95 paperback. **Description:** Politicians and lawmakers have developed a new set of legislative tactics designed to extort wealthy industries and donors into huge contributions. This money is then funneled into the pockets of their friends and family members. Schweizer reveals the secret 'fees' each political party charges politicians for top committee assignments; how fourteen members of Congress received hundreds of thousands of dollars using a self-loan loophole; how PAC money is used to bankroll their lavish lifestyles; and more. The first time these unethical issues have been reported to the public.

44262 ■ "Fair Play? China Cheats, Carney Talks and Rankin Walks; Here's the Latest" in Canadian Business (Vol. 81, March 17, 2008, No. 4)
Pub: Rogers Media Inc.
Contact: Tony Viner, President
Description: Discusses the World Trade Organization which says that China is breaking trade rules by taxing imports of auto parts at the same rate as foreign-made finished cars. Mark Carney first speech as the governor of the Bank of Canada made economists suspect a rate cut on overnight loans. Andre Rankin was ordered by the Ontario Securities Commission to pay $250,000 in investigation costs.

44263 ■ Family Limited Partnership Deskbook
Pub: American Bar Association
Contact: Carolyn Lamm, President
Ed: David T. Lewis, Andrea C. Chomakos. **Released:** 2007. **Price:** $169.95, Paperback. **Description:** Forming and funding a family limited partnership or limited liability company is complicated. In-depth analysis of all facets of this business entity are examined using detailed guidance on the basic principles of drafting, forming, funding, and valuing an FLP or LLC and also covers tax concerns. Examples and extensive sample forms are included on a CD-ROM included with the book.

44264 ■ "Fannie and Freddie: How They'll Change" in Business Week (September 22, 2008, No. 4100, pp. 30)
Ed: Jane Sasseen. **Description:** Three possible outcomes of the fate of struggling mortgage giants Freddie Mac and Fannie Mae after the government bailout are outlined.

44265 ■ "Fight Ensues Over Irreplaceable Princess Diana Gowns" in Tampa Bay Business Journal (Vol. 30, January 15, 2010, No. 4, pp. 1)
Pub: American City Business Journals
Ed: Janet Leiser. **Description:** People's Princess Charitable Foundation Inc. founder Maureen Rorech Dunkel has sought Chapter 11 bankruptcy protection before a state court decides on the fate of the five of 13 Princess Diana Gowns. Dunkel and the nonprofit were sued by Patricia Sullivan of HRH Venture LLC who claimed they defaulted on $1.5 million in loans.

44266 ■ "Financing for NNSA Plant Is a Work in Progress" in The Business Journal-Serving Metropolitan Kansas City (October 24, 2008)
Ed: Rob Roberts. **Description:** The Kansas City Council approved a development plan for a $500 million nuclear weapons parts plant in south Kansas City. The US Congress approved a $59 million annual lease payment to the plant's developer. Financing for the construction of the plant remains in question as the plant's developers have to shoulder construction costs.

44267 ■ Financing Your Business: Get a Grip on Finding the Money
Pub: Self-Counsel Press Inc.
Ed: Angie Mohr. **Released:** 2005. **Description:** Recommendations to help raise capital for a new or expanding small company.

44268 ■ *Financing Your Small Business*

Ed: Robert Walter. **Released:** December 2003. **Description:** Tips for raising venture capital, dealing with bank officials, and initiating public offerings of stock shares for small business.

44269 ■ *"Find Private Money for FutureGen Plant" in Crain's Chicago Business (Vol. 34, September 12, 2011, No. 37, pp. 18)*

Pub: Crain Communications Inc.

Contact: Todd Johnson, Publisher

Description: FutureGen is a clean-coal power plant being developed in Southern Illinois. The need for further funding is discussed.

44270 ■ *"Florin Car Dealers Drive Plan" in Sacramento Business Journal (Vol. 25, August 24, 2008, No. 25, pp. 1)*

Pub: American City Business Journals, Inc.

Contact: Whitney Shaw, President

Ed: Melanie Turner. **Description:** Automobile dealers in Sacramento, California are working with the city and the business district in planning for future redevelopment in Florin Road. The move stemmed from pressure from the Elk Grove Auto Mall, high fuel prices and the credit crunch. The area has suffered business closures recently.

44271 ■ *"Former Mayor, Paul Johnson, Driving $500M Real Estate Equity Fund" in The Business Journal - Serving Phoenix and the Valley of the Sun (Vol. 28, August 15, 2008, No. 50, pp. 1)*

Pub: American City Business Journals, Inc.

Contact: Whitney Shaw, President

Ed: Jan Buchholz. **Description:** Paul John, the former mayor of Phoenix, is establishing a $500 million real estate asset management fund. The fund is dubbed Southwest Next Capital Management and has attracted three local partners, namely Joseph Meyer, Jay Michalowski, and James Mullany, who all have background in finance and construction.

44272 ■ *"Gateway Delays Start" in The Business Journal-Serving Metropolitan Kansas City (Vol. 27, October 31, 2008, No. 8, pp. 1)*

Ed: Rob Roberts. **Description:** Economic problems caused, in part, by the Wall Street crisis has resulted in the setback of a proposed mixed-use redevelopment project, The Gateway. The $307 million project, which includes the Kansas Aquarium, will be delayed due to financing problems. Details of the project are given.

44273 ■ *"Going to Bat" in Canadian Business (Vol. 80, February 26, 2007, No. 5, pp. S7)*

Description: Various strategies to make the business loan lending process simple and faster are presented.

44274 ■ *Golden States Financial Directory (Western United States)*

Pub: Accuity Inc.

Contact: Hugh M. Jones, IV, President

URL(s): store.accuitysolutions.com/order.html. **Released:** Semiannual; January and July. **Price:** $540, Individuals. **Covers:** Holding companies, head offices and branches of all commercial banks, savings and loans, and credit unions with assets over $5 million in Alaska, Arizona, California, Colorado, Hawaii, Idaho, Montana, New Mexico, Oregon, Utah, Washington, and Wyoming. **Entries include:** Name, address, phone, fax, key bank officers by functional title, directors, date established, detailed financial data, association's membership, correspondent banks, out-of-town branches, holding company affiliation, ABA Transit Number and Routing Symbol, MICR number with check digit, type of charter. **Arrangement:** Geographical. **Indexes:** Alphabetical.

44275 ■ *"A Good Step, But There's a Long Way to Go" in Business Week (September 22, 2008, No. 4100, pp. 10)*

Ed: James C. Cooper. **Description:** Despite the historic action by the U.S. government to nationalize the mortgage giants Freddie Mac and Fannie Mae, rising unemployment rates may prove to be an even bigger roadblock to bringing back the economy from

its downward spiral. The takeover is meant to restore confidence in the credit markets and help with the mortgage crisis but the rising rate in unemployment may make many households unable to take advantage of any benefits which arise from the bailout. Statistical data included.

44276 ■ *"Good Track Record Helps Developer Secure Construction Loan for Offices" in Miami Daily Business Review (March 26, 2008)*

Description: Luis Lamar, developer, has secured a $64.75 million construction loan to construct a Class A office building in Kendall, Florida. Details of the loan and proposed construction are presented.

44277 ■ *"Goodwill Haunts Local Companies" in Crain's Chicago Business (Apr. 28, 2008)*

Pub: Crain Communications Inc.

Contact: Todd Johnson, Publisher

Ed: Ann Saphir. **Description:** Many companies are having to face the reality that they overpaid for acquisitions made in better economic times; investors often dismiss such one-time charges as mere accounting adjustments but writeoffs related to past acquisitions can signal future problems because they mean the expected profits that justified the purchase have not materialized. Writeoffs are particularly worrisome for firms with a lot of debt and whose banks require them to have enough assets to back up their borrowings.

44278 ■ *"Grounded Condo Development Poised for Construction Takeoff" in Memphis Business Journal (Vol. 35, February 7, 2014, No. 44, pp. 4)*

Pub: American City Business Journals

Released: February 7, 2014. **Description:** Developers in Memphis, Tennessee are hoping that the economic recovery will help revive the condominium market. However, industry experts believe that inventory will have to all and prices will have to rise before the market recovers. The impact of loose lending practices on condominium developers is also discussed.

44279 ■ *"Growing Field" in Crain's Detroit Business (Vol. 26, January 11, 2010, No. 2, pp. 3)*

Pub: Crain Communications Inc.

Contact: Rance E. Crain, President

Description: Detroit's TechTown was awarded a combination loan and grant of $4.1 million from the U.S. Department of Housing and Urban Development to build a 15,000-square-foot stem cell center, a collection of laboratories that will be available to both for-profit companies and university researchers.

44280 ■ *"Hank Paulson On the Housing Bailout and What's Ahead" in Business Week (September 22, 2008, No. 4100, pp. 19)*

Ed: Maria Bartiromo. **Description:** Interview with Treasury Secretary Henry Paulson in which he discusses the bailout of Fannie Mae and Freddie Mac as well as the potential impact on the American economy and foreign interests and investments in the country. Paulson has faith that the government's actions will help to stabilize the housing market.

44281 ■ *"Hard Times for Hard Money" in Sacramento Business Journal (Vol. 25, July 18, 2008, No. 20, pp. 1)*

Pub: American City Business Journals, Inc.

Contact: Whitney Shaw, President

Ed: Michael Shaw. **Description:** Three private lenders who supplied $1 million sued VLD Realty, its associated companies and owners Volodymyr and Leonid Dubinsky accusing them of default after a plan to build two subdivisions fell through. Investigators are finding that borrowers and lenders ignored most rules on private investments on real estate.

44282 ■ *"Hayes Lemmerz Reports Some Good News Despite Losses" in Crain's Detroit Business (Vol. 24, April 14, 2008, No. 15, pp. 4)*

Pub: Crain Communications Inc.

Contact: Nancy Kaffer, President

Ed: Nancy Kaffer. **Description:** Hayes Lemmerz International Inc., a wheel manufacturer from Northville that has reported a positive free cash flow for

the first time in years, a narrowed net loss in the fourth quarter and significant restructuring of the company's debt.

44283 ■ *"Health Care Leads Sectors Attracting Capital" in Hispanic Business (March 2008, pp. 14-16, 18)*

Pub: Hispanic Business Inc.

Contact: Jesus Chavarria, President

Ed: Scott Williams. **Description:** U. S. Hispanic healthcare, media, and food were the key industries in the U.S. gaining investors in 2007.

44284 ■ *"Health Providers Throw Lifeline to Clinics" in Sacramento Business Journal (Vol. 25, July 30, 2008, No. 21, pp. 1)*

Pub: American City Business Journals, Inc.

Contact: Whitney Shaw, President

Ed: Kathy Robertson. **Description:** Health Net of California Inc., Catholic Healthcare West and Sutter Health are each providing up to $5 million in no-interest and low-interest loans to clinics in California, while the Sisters of Mercy of the Americas Burlingame Regional Community is offering $300,000. Other details on the short term loans are discussed.

44285 ■ *Home-Based Business for Dummies*

Pub: John Wiley & Sons Inc.

Contact: Stephen M. Smith, President

Ed: Paul Edwards, Sarah Edwards, Peter Economy. **Released:** 3rd Edition. **Price:** $19.95, paperback; $12.99. **Description:** Provides all the information needed to start and run a home-based business. Topics include: selecting the right business; setting up a home office; managing money, credit, and financing; marketing; and ways to avoid distractions while working at home. **Availability:** PrintE-book.

44286 ■ *"A Home of Her Own" in Hawaii Business (Vol. 53, October 2007, No. 4, pp. 51)*

Pub: PacificBasin Communications

Ed: Maria Torres-Kitamura. **Description:** It was observed that the number of single women in Hawaii purchasing their own home has increased, as that in the whole United States where the percentage has increased from 14 percent in 1995 to 22 percent in 2006. However, First Hawaiian Bank's Wendy Lum thinks that the trend will not continue in Hawaii due to lending restrictions. The factors that women consider in buying a home of their own are presented.

44287 ■ *"Homes Stall As Owners Resist Major Price Cuts" in Crain's Chicago Business (Vol. 31, April 21, 2008, No. 16, pp. 38)*

Pub: Crain Communications Inc.

Contact: Todd Johnson, Publisher

Ed: Kevin Davis. **Description:** Discusses the high-end housing market and the owners who are resisting major price cuts as well as the buyers who look at long market times as a sign that something is wrong with the property.

44288 ■ *How to Raise Capital: Techniques and Strategies for Financing and Valuing Your Small Business*

Ed: Jeffrey A. Timmons, Stephen Spinelli, Andrew Zacharakis. **Released:** May 2004. **Price:** , $16.95 (US), $24.95 (Canadian). **Description:** Small business financing process is examined. Tips for identifying the financial life cycle of new ventures, developing a framework for financial strategies, and understanding an investor's prospective.

44289 ■ *How to Start and Run Your Own Corporation: S-Corporations For Small Business Owners*

Pub: HCM Publishing

Ed: Peter I. Hupalo. **Released:** Second Edition. **Price:** $22.46, paperback. **Description:** Basics of corporate business structure are explained. Topics include discovering the best business structure for your company; how to decided between an S-Corporation and LLC; choosing the state in which to incorporate, how to form a corporation, angel investing, special issues for one-person corporations, the role of bylaws and corporate minutes, board of directors, taxes, workers' compensation issues, retirement plans, and more. **Availability:** Print.

44290 ■ *"How To Get a Loan the Web 2.0 Way"* in *Black Enterprise (Vol. 41, December 2010, No. 5, pp. 23)*
Pub: Earl G. Graves Publishing Co. Inc.
Contact: Earl G. Graves, Jr., President
Ed: John Simons. **Description:** People are turning to online peer-to-peer network for personal loans as banks are lending less money.

44291 ■ *"Identity Theft Can Have Long-Lasting Impact"* in *Providence Business News (Vol. 28, February 10, 2014, No. 45, pp. 7)*
Pub: American City Business Journals
Released: February 10, 2014. **Description:** According to mortgage credit experts, recently reported massive data breaches at Nieman Marcus, Target, and other merchants could have negative impacts on several real estate deals scheduled for the upcoming months. Although victims are not liable for the unlawful debts, their credit reports and scores can be damaged for months, thus endangering loan applications for mortgages on home sale transactions.

44292 ■ *"If You Go Into the Market Today.."* in *Canadian Business (Vol. 82, Summer 2009, No. 8, pp. 18)*
Ed: Jeff Sanford. **Description:** Opinions of experts and personalities who are known to have bear attitudes towards the economy were presented in the event 'A Night with the Bears' in Toronto in April 2009. Known bears that served as resource persons in the event were Nouriel Roubini, Eric Sprott, Ian Gordon, and Meredith Whitney. The bears were observed to have differences regarding consumer debt.

44293 ■ *"In 2011, Wichita-Area Banks Cleaned Up Books, Grew Earnings"* in *Wichita Business Journal (Vol. 27, February 17, 2012, No. 7, pp. 1)*
Pub: American City Business Journal
Description: Wichita, Kansas-based banks have reported smaller loan portfolios and higher loan-loss allowances at the end of 2011 compared to the previous year. The earnings of the 35 banks in the metro area also grew strongly both for the quarter and for the year, while their assets increased. How the banks managed to generate positive earnings results is also discussed.

44294 ■ *"In the SBA's Face"* in *American Small Business League (December 2010)*
Pub: Hispanic Business Inc.
Contact: Jesus Chavarria, President
Ed: Richard Larsen. **Description:** Lloyd Chapman uses the American Small Business League to champion small business. Statistical data included.

44295 ■ *"Industry Escalates Lobbying Efforts For Loan Program"* in *Crain's Detroit Business (Vol. 24, September 22, 2008, No. 38, pp. 22)*
Pub: Crain Communications Inc.
Contact: Rance E. Crain, President
Ed: Jay Greene, Ryan Beene, Harry Stoffer. **Description:** Auto suppliers such as Lear Corp., which is best known for vehicle seating, also supplies high-voltage wiring for Ford hybrids and is developing other hybrid components. These suppliers are joining automakers in lobbying for the loan program which would promote the accelerated development of fuel-efficient vehicles.

44296 ■ *"Inside the Mind of an Investor: Lessons from Bill Draper"* in *Inc. (Volume 32, December 2010, No. 10, pp. 140)*
Pub: Inc. Magazine
Ed: Leigh Buchanan. **Description:** Profile of the three-generation Draper family, the first venture capital firm west of the Mississippi.

44297 ■ *"Insider"* in *Canadian Business (Vol. 81, March 31, 2008, No. 5, pp. 76)*
Pub: Rogers Media Inc.
Contact: Tony Viner, President
Ed: John Gray. **Description:** Discusses a comparison of an average Canadian family's finances in 1990 with the data from 2007. The average family in 2007

has over $80,000 in debt compared to just under $52,000 in 1990. However, Canadians have also been accumulating solid assets such as homes and stocks. This means that Canadian debt load has fallen from 22 percent in 1990 to 20 percent in 2007 when taken as a percentage of total net worth.

44298 ■ *"Investment Bank Predicts Shakeup in Farm Equipment Industry"* in *Farm Industry News (November 16, 2011)*
Pub: Penton Business Media Inc.
Contact: David Kieselstein, Chief Executive Officer
Ed: Jodie Wehrspann. **Description:** Farming can expect to see more mergers and acquisitions in the agricultural equipment industry, as it appears to be in the early stages of growth over the next few years.

44299 ■ *"Is Fannie Mae the Next Government Bailout?"* in *Barron's (Vol. 88, March 10, 2008, No. 10, pp. 21)*
Pub: Dow Jones & Co., Inc.
Contact: Clare Hart, President
Ed: Jonathan R. Laing. **Description:** Fannie Mae may need a government bailout as it faces huge hits brought about by the effects of the housing crisis. The shares of the government-sponsored enterprise have dropped 65 percent since the housing crisis began.

44300 ■ *"Is Fierce Competition Loosening Standards?"* in *Birmingham Business Journal (Vol. 31, February 14, 2014, No. 7, pp. 6)*
Pub: American City Business Journals, Inc.
Contact: Whitney Shaw, President
Released: February 14, 2014. **Description:** Bankers have been seeing an intense competition for business loans in the Birmingham, Alabama market because of the limited number of qualified borrowers. However, some bankers expressed concerns that the trend signals a return to pre-recession habits for lenders.

44301 ■ *"Islamic Banks Get a 'Libor' of Their Own"* in *Wall Street Journal Eastern Edition (November 25 , 2011, pp. C4)*
Pub: Dow Jones & Co., Inc.
Contact: Clare Hart, President
Ed: Katy Burne. **Description:** The London interbank offered rate, or Libor, has been used by banks internationally for years. It is the rate at which banks lend money to each other. The rate has not been used by Islamic banks, but now sixteen banks have come up with the Islamic Interbank Benchmark Rate.

44302 ■ *K-21 Small Business Loan Program*
Pub: International Wealth Success, Inc.
Ed: Tyler G. Hicks. **Price:** $100. **Description:** Guide to the Small Business Loan Program that offers loans to small and minority-owned companies doing work for government agencies, large corporations, hospitals, universities, and similar organizations.

44303 ■ *"Karen Case: President of Commercial Real Estate Lending, Privatebancorp Inc."* in *Crain's Chicago Business (May 5, 2008)*
Pub: Crain Communications Inc.
Contact: Todd Johnson, Publisher
Ed: Dee Gill. **Description:** Profile of Karen Case who was hired by PrivateBancorp Inc. to turn its minor share of the city's commercial real estate lending market into a major one.

44304 ■ *"Kenosha 'Lifestyle Center' Delayed"* in *The Business Journal-Milwaukee (Vol. 25, August 8, 2008, No. 46, pp. A1)*
Pub: American City Business Journals, Inc.
Contact: Whitney Shaw, President
Ed: Rich Kirchen. **Description:** Quality Centers of Orlando, Florida has postponed construction plans for the Kenosha Town Center in Kenosha County, Wisconsin to 2009 due to the economic downturn and lending concerns. The $200-million, 750,000-square-foot retail and residential center will be located near the corner of Wisconsin Highway 50 and I-94.

44305 ■ *"Kerry Steel to Sell Inventory, Close Business After 30 Years"* in *Crain's Detroit Business (Vol. 24, March 30, 2008, No. 11, pp. 26)*
Pub: Crain Communications Inc.
Contact: Rance E. Crain, President
Ed: Brent Snavely. **Description:** Kerry Steel Inc. has confirmed that it is selling all of its inventory and equipment and is going out of business; the company, which was once one of the largest steel service centers in the Midwest, has sustained financial losses and is in violation of its loan agreements.

44306 ■ *"Kimball Hill Files for Chapter 11"* in *Crain's Chicago Business (Vol. 31, April 28, 2008, No. 17, pp. 12)*
Pub: Crain Communications Inc.
Contact: Todd Johnson, Publisher
Ed: Alby Gallun. **Description:** Homebuilder Kimball Hill filed for Chapter 11 bankruptcy protection after months of negotiations with lenders. The firm plans to continue operations as it restructures its debt.

44307 ■ *"Know Your Numbers"* in *Inc. (Volume 32, December 2010, No. 10, pp. 39)*
Pub: Inc. Magazine
Ed: Norm Brodsky. **Description:** Ways to maximize profit and minimize tax burden are presented.

44308 ■ *"Lack of Support Drives Scientists Away from Valley"* in *The Business Journal - Serving Phoenix and the Valley of the Sun (Vol. 28, August 1, 2008, No. 48, pp. 1)*
Pub: American City Business Journals, Inc.
Contact: Whitney Shaw, President
Ed: Angela Gonzales. **Description:** Lack of support for scientists has caused scientists like Dietrich Stephan to depart from the city. Stephan is expected to relocate to California where he has found funding for his company Navigenics. Other views and information on the rising rate of the departure of scientists are presented.

44309 ■ *"Laugh or Cry? How to Look at the Current State of the Market"* in *Barron's (Vol. 88, March 24, 2008, No. 12, pp. 7)*
Pub: Dow Jones & Co., Inc.
Contact: Clare Hart, President
Ed: Alan Abelson. **Description:** Discusses the American economy which is just starting to feel the effect of the credit and housing crises. JPMorgan Chase purchased Bear Stearns for $2 a share, much lower than its share price of $60, while quasi-government entities Fannie Mae and Freddie Mac are starting to run into trouble.

44310 ■ *"Law Firms See Improvement in Financing Climate"* in *Sacramento Business Journal (Vol. 28, October 14, 2011, No. 33, pp. 1)*
Pub: Sacramento Business Journal
Ed: Kathy Robertson. **Description:** Sacramento, California-based Weintraub Genshlea Chediak Law Corporation has helped close 26 financing deals worth more than $1.6 billion in 2010, providing indication of improvement in Sacramento's economy. Lawyers have taken advantage of low interest rates to make refinancing agreements and help clients get new funds.

44311 ■ *"Leaning Tower"* in *Business Courier (Vol. 27, June 4, 2010, No. 5, pp. 1)*
Pub: Business Courier
Ed: Jon Newberry. **Description:** New York-based developer Armand Lasky, owner of Tower Place Mall in downtown Cincinnati, Ohio has sued Birmingham, Alabama-based Regions Bank to prevent the bank's foreclosure on the property. Regions Bank claims Lasky was in default on an $18 million loan agreement. Details on the mall's leasing plan is also discussed.

44312 ■ *"Leasing: Welcome Back"* in *Canadian Business (Vol. 82, April 27, 2009, No. 7, pp. 25)*
Pub: Rogers Media Inc.
Contact: Tony Viner, President
Ed: Sarka Halas. **Description:** Some Canadian companies such as Gennum Corporation have taken advantage of corporate sale-leasebacks to raise

money at a time when credit is hard to acquire. Corporate sale-leasebacks allow companies to sell their property assets while remaining as tenants of the building. Sale-leasebacks allow firms to increase capital while avoiding the disruptions that may result with moving.

44313 ■ "Legal Barriers Keep 16-Story Horizon at Ground Level" in Memphis Business Journal (Vol. 34, August 24, 2012, No. 19, pp. 1)

Pub: American City Business Journal

Description: Construction on the Horizon building at 717 Riverside Drive remains unfinished as legal battles ensue among banks and construction firms involved in the project. The root of the legal proceedings is the Bryan Company's defaulting from a $58.6 million loan from four banks and the foreclosureof the property.

44314 ■ "Lehman's Hail Mary Pass" in Business Week (September 22, 2008, No. 4100, pp. 28)

Ed: Matthew Goldstein; David Henry; Ben Levison. **Description:** Overview of Lehman Brothers' CEO Richard Fuld's plan to keep the firm afloat and end the stock's plunge downward; Fuld's strategy calls for selling off a piece of the firm's investment management business.

44315 ■ "Lenders Get Boost from Low Rates" in Saint Louis Business Journal (Vol. 32, September 9, 2011, No. 2, pp. 1)

Pub: Saint Louis Business Journal

Ed: Greg Edwards. **Description:** St. Louis, Missouri-based lenders have benefitted from record low mortgage interest rates. Housing loan applications have increased in view of the development.

44316 ■ "Lenders: Private Equity Funding Most Commercial Real Estate Deals" in The Business Journal - Serving Phoenix and the Valley of the Sun (Vol. 28, July 25, 2008, No. 47, pp. 1)

Pub: American City Business Journals, Inc.

Contact: Whitney Shaw, President

Ed: Jan Buchholz. **Description:** Private equity lender Investor Mortgage Holdings Inc. has continued growing despite the crisis surrounding the real estate and financial industries and has accumulated a $700 million loan portfolio. Private lending has become increasingly important in financing real estate deals as commercial credit has dried up.

44317 ■ "Lending Door Slams" in Puget Sound Business Journal (Vol. 29, October 24, 2008, No. 27, pp. 1)

Ed: Jeanne Lang Jones, Kirsten Grind. **Description:** KeyBank's closure of its Puget Sound unit that services single-family homebuilders is part of a nationwide shutdown that includes similar closures in other cities. Bank of America is adopting more conservative terms for homebuilding loans while Union Bank of California is still offering credit for market rate housing.

44318 ■ "Lending Grows as Banks Make Moves" in Pittsburgh Business Times (Vol. 33, May 9, 2014, No. 43, pp. 4)

Pub: American City Business Journals

Released: May 9, 2014. **Description:** Pittsburgh, Pennsylvania-based biggest retail banks have bigger loan portfolios at the end of 2014s first quarter compared with the same period in 2013. Business lending has been driving activity and the surge also includes the impact of merger and acquisition strategies to capture customers in Ohio. The rising loan portfolio of the banks are examined.

44319 ■ "Lending Stays Down at Cincinnati Banks" in Business Courier (Vol. 27, October 1, 2010, No. 22, pp. 1)

Pub: Business Courier

Ed: Steve Watkins. **Description:** Greater Cincinnati's largest banks have experienced decreases in loans in the past year due to weak economy and sagging loan demands. Analysis of mid-year data has shown

that loans drop by a total of $3.6 billion or 4 percent at the ten largest banks as of June 30, 2010 compared to same period in 2009.

44320 ■ "A Limited Sphere of Influence?" in Mergers & Acquisitions: The Dealmaker's Journal (March 1, 2008)

Pub: SourceMedia Inc.

Contact: James M. Malkin, Chief Executive Officer

Ed: Ken MacFadyen. **Description:** Changes to the interest rate has had little impact on the mergers and acquisitions market since the federal funds rate does not link directly to the liquidity available to the M&A market; lenders are looking at cash flows and are likely to remain cautious due to other factors impacting the market.

44321 ■ "The Loan Arranger" in Canadian Business (Vol. 80, October 22, 2007, No. 21, pp. 15)

Ed: Rachel Pulfer. **Description:** Muhammad Yunus received the Nobel Prize in 2006 for the organization that he founded, the Grameen Bank. The bank has helped women in developing countries and has also begun helping millions of individuals to make loans in the U.S. through the Grameen Bank. An evaluation of the Grameen model is provided.

44322 ■ "Loans Aplenty From Local Banks in Q4" in South Florida Business Journal (Vol. 34, February 7, 2014, No. 29, pp. 4)

Pub: American City Business Journals

Released: February 7, 2014. **Description:** Figures show that eight of the 25 largest banks in South Florida increased loans by more than $50 million in the fourth quarter of 2013. Ocean Bank, Legacy Bank of Florida, Intercredit Bank and Anchor Commercial Bank regained well capitalized status. The decrease in Regent Bank's capital ratios is also discussed.

44323 ■ "Loans Are Plentiful for Small Businesses" in South Florida Business Journal (Vol. 35, September 12, 2014, No. 7, pp. 16)

Pub: American City Business Journals

Released: September 12, 2014. **Description:** Banks have relaxed requirements for small business loans in South Florida. Total bank loans increased by 11.4 percent in 2014. It has also become easier for small businesses to secure credit for acquisitions and mergers and growth.

44324 ■ "Local Firms Will Feel Impact Of Wall St. Woes" in The Business Journal-Milwaukee (Vol. 25, September 19, 2008, No. 52, pp. A1)

Pub: American City Business Journals, Inc.

Contact: Whitney Shaw, President

Ed: Rich Kirchen. **Description:** Wall Street's crisis is expected to affect businesses in Wisconsin, in terms of decreased demand for services and products and increased financing costs. Businesses in Milwaukee area may face higher interest rates and tougher loan standards. The potential impacts of the Wall Street crisis on local businesses are examined further.

44325 ■ "Local Lending Tumbles $10 Billion Since '08" in Saint Louis Business Journal (Vol. 31, August 26, 2011, No. 53, pp. 1)

Pub: Saint Louis Business Journal

Ed: Greg Edwards. **Description:** St. Louis, Missouri-based banks lending fell by more than 30 percent in less than three years, from about $30 billion in third and fourth quarters 2008 to about $20 billion in the most recent quarter. However, community banks revealed that they want to lend but there is no loan demand.

44326 ■ "Local M&A Activity Sputters in 1Q" in Crain's Chicago Business (Vol. 31, April 21, 2008, No. 16, pp. 20)

Pub: Crain Communications Inc.

Contact: Todd Johnson, Publisher

Ed: H. Lee Murphy. **Description:** Local mergers-and-acquisitions activity is down by 34 percent in the first quarter compared to the fourth quarter of last year due to the credit crisis making financing harder to obtain.

44327 ■ "Lotus Starts Slowly, Dodges Subprime Woes" in Crain's Detroit Business (Vol. 24, April 14, 2008, No. 15, pp. 3)

Pub: Crain Communications Inc.

Contact: Rance E. Crain, President

Ed: Tom Henderson. **Description:** Discusses Lotus Bancorp Inc. and their business plan, which although is not right on target due to the subprime mortgage meltdown, is in a much better position than its competitors due to the quality of their loans.

44328 ■ "Making Waves" in Business Journal Portland (Vol. 27, November 26, 2010, No. 39, pp. 1)

Pub: Portland Business Journal

Ed: Erik Siemers. **Description:** Corvallis, Oregon-based Columbia Power Technologies LLC is about to close a $2 million Series A round of investment initiated by $750,000 from Oregon Angel Fund. The wave energy startup company was formed to commercialize the wave buoy technology developed by Oregon State University researchers.

44329 ■ "M&I Execs May Get Golden Parachutes" in Business Journal-Milwaukee (Vol. 28, December 31, 2010, No. 14, pp. A3)

Pub: Milwaukee Business Journal

Ed: Rich Kirchen. **Description:** Marshall and Isley Corporation's top executives have a chance to receive golden-parachute payments it its buyer, BMO Financial Group, repays the Troubled Asset Relief Program (TARP) loan on behalf of the company. One TARP rule prevents golden-parachute payments to them and the next five most highly paid employees of TARP recipients.

44330 ■ "The Marathon Club: Building a Bridge to Wealth" in Hispanic Business (March 2008, pp. 24)

Pub: Hispanic Business Inc.

Contact: Jesus Chavarria, President

Ed: Hildy Medina. **Description:** Minority businesses find it more difficult to secure venture capital for entrepreneurial pursuits. Joe Watson, CEO of Without Excuses and Strategic Hire, suggests Hispanics and African Americans collaborate on issues of importance to minority entrepreneurs.

44331 ■ "Marine Act Amendments Gain Parliamentary Approval" in Canadian Sailings (July 7, 2008)

Ed: Alex Binkley. **Description:** Changes to the Canada Marine Act provides better borrowing deals as well as an ability to tap into federal infrastructure funding for environmental protection measures, security improvements and other site enhancements.

44332 ■ "Market Watch: A Sampling of Advisory Opinion" in Barron's (Vol. 88, March 17, 2008, No. 11, pp. M10)

Pub: Dow Jones & Co., Inc.

Contact: Clare Hart, President

Ed: Paul Schatz, William Gibson, Michael Darda. **Description:** S&P 500 bank stocks were down 46 percent from their 2007 peak while the peak to through fall in 1989-1990 was just over 50 percent. This suggests that the bottom on the bank stocks could be near. The Federal Reserve Board announced they will lend up to $200 billion to primary lenders in exchange other securities.

44333 ■ "Marketing is Everything, But Timing Helps" in Idaho Business Review (September 9, 2014)

Pub: Dolan Co.

Contact: James P. Dolan, President

Released: September 9, 2014. **Description:** Profile of Ladd Family Pharmacy, founded by husband and wife Kip and Elaine, who borrowed money from Idaho Banking Company to start their pharmacy. The firm has expanded from three workers in 2008 to 22 to date and reported $6.2 million in revenue for 2013.

44334 ■ "A Matter of Interest: Payday Loans" in Canadian Business (Vol. 79, July 17, 2006,

No. 14-15, pp. 21)
Pub: Rogers Media Inc.
Contact: Tony Viner, President
Ed: Jeff Sanford. **Description:** With the steady decrease in savings, the need for growth in Canada's payloan industry is discussed. Also emphasized are the challenges faced by payloan operators.

44335 ■ "Md. Bankers Say 'Devil Is In the Details' of New $30B Loan Fund" in Baltimore Business Journal (Vol. 28, October 8, 2010, No. 22)
Pub: Baltimore Business Journal
Ed: Gary Haber. **Description:** Maryland community bankers have expressed doubts over a new federal loan program for small business. The new law will also earmark $80 billion for community banks. Comments from executives also given.

44336 ■ "Md. Banks Beef Up Deposits, But Lending Lags" in Baltimore Business Journal (Vol. 28, October 29, 2010, No. 25, pp. 1)
Pub: Baltimore Business Journal
Ed: Gary Haber. **Description:** Bank deposits in the Greater Baltimore area have increased but commercial loans have not. Small business owners complain that banks do not help them expand their businesses, but banks argue that they want to lend but the borrowers have to meet standard qualifications.

44337 ■ "Md. Housing Leaders Race to Stem Rising Tide of Foreclosures: Neighborhood Watch" in Baltimore Business Journal (Vol. 28, July 23, 2010, No. 11, pp. 1)
Pub: Baltimore Business Journal
Ed: Daniel J. Sernovitz. **Description:** Maryland government and housing leaders are set to spend $100 million in federal funding to stem the increase in foreclosures in the area. The federal funding is seen as inadequate to resolve the problem of foreclosures.

44338 ■ "Loan Dollars Sit Idle for Energy Plan" in Baltimore Business Journal (Vol. 28, September 10, 2010, No. 18, pp. 1)
Pub: Baltimore Business Journal
Ed: Scott Dance. **Description:** The Maryland Energy Administration has millions of dollars in Federal stimulus and state energy efficiency cash sitting idle and might be lost once the window for stimulus spending is gone. However, businesses have no interest in betting on renewable energy because some cannot afford to take out more loans. Other challenges faced by these businesses are presented.

44339 ■ "Measuring the Impact" in Mergers & Acquisitions: The Dealmaker's Journal (March 1, 2008)
Pub: SourceMedia Inc.
Contact: James M. Malkin, Chief Executive Officer
Ed: Ken MacFadyen. **Description:** Discusses a new study out of Europe which contends that the private equity market does not have as much impact on the overall economy as critics contend.

44340 ■ "MEDC: Put Venture Funds to Work" in Crain's Detroit Business (Vol. 25, June 22, 2009, No. 25, pp. 1)
Pub: Crain Communications Inc. - Detroit
Contact: Keith Crain, Chairman
Ed: Tom Henderson. **Description:** Michigan Strategic Fund board will finalize approval for ESP Holdings II LLC, Peninsula Capital Partners LLC, Triathlon Medical Ventures LLC and Arsenal Venture Partners Inc. are expected to share $35.5 million from the fund.

44341 ■ "Merchant Cash-Advance Company Enters Canada" in Cardline (Vol. 8, February 29, 2008, No. 9, pp. 1)
Description: Merchant cash-advance company is expanding operations into Canada.

44342 ■ "Michigan Means Growth: Sustaining Growth Through Thick and Thin: Michigan Companies Sustain Growth with Well-Timed Access to Capital" in Inc. (Vol. 36, September

2014, No. 7, pp. 164)
Pub: Mansueto Ventures L.L.C.
Contact: John Koten, Chief Executive Officer
Released: September 2014. **Description:** Successful companies possess flexibility, foresight and resources to turn adversity into opportunity. The small businesses in Michigan who have sustained experienced sales growth despite the recession of 2007. The Michigan Economic Development Corporation has introduced three initiatives to help Michigan businesses grow, including venture capital, collateral support and loan participation through the State Small Business Credit Initiative, and cash incentives for businesses looking to invest in urban communities or grow jobs.

44343 ■ "Micro-Finance Agencies and SMEs" in International Journal of Entrepreneurship and Small Business (Vol. 11, August 3, 2010)
Pub: Publishers Communication Group
Contact: Doug Wright, Director
Ed: Patricia A. Rowe, Michael J. Christie, Frank Hoy. **Description:** Institutional preparedness of economic development agencies for developing small and medium-sized enterprises (SMEs) is discussed. The cases presented illustrate variations in the micro-finance lender agency-enterprise development of processes for sharing vision and interdependence.

44344 ■ "Microlending Seen as Having a Major Impact" in Business Journal Serving Greater Tampa Bay (Vol. 30, November 26, 2010, No. 49, pp. 1)
Pub: Tampa Bay Business Journal
Ed: Margie Manning. **Description:** There are several organizations that are planning to offer microlending services in Tampa Bay, Florida. These include the Children's Board of Hillsborough County, and OUR Microlending Florida LLC. Organizations that are already offering these services in the area include the Small Business Administration and the Tampa Bay Black Business Investment Corp.

44345 ■ "Midwest Seeks Concessions From Creditors" in The Business Journal-Milwaukee (Vol. 25, July 25, 2008, No. 44, pp. A1)
Pub: American City Business Journals, Inc.
Contact: Whitney Shaw, President
Ed: Rich Rovito. **Description:** Midwest Airlines Inc. is turning to creditors and lease holders for the financial aspect of its restructuring, which involves going back to serving popular business destinations. Chief executive officer Timothy believes that the company can survive in a niche market as long as it provides quality service. He discusses Midwest's restructuring plan.

44346 ■ "Millions Needed To Finish First Place" in The Business Journal-Milwaukee (Vol. 25, August 15, 2008, No. 47, pp. A1)
Pub: American City Business Journals, Inc.
Contact: Whitney Shaw, President
Ed: Rich Kirchen. **Description:** First Place on the River condominium project in Milwaukee, Wisconsin, needs $18.2 million before it can be completed. A total of $6.8 million have already been spent since the project went into receivership on 31 January 2008.

44347 ■ "MoneyGram In Pact With Payday Lender" in American Banker (Vol. 173, March 7, 2008, No. 46, pp. 6)
Ed: William Launder. **Description:** Details of pact between MoneyGram International Inc. and Advance America Cash Advance Centers are examined.

44348 ■ "More Contractors Unpaid" in Puget Sound Business Journal (Vol. 29, October 3, 2008, No. 24, pp. 1)
Ed: Brad Berton. **Description:** An 80 percent rise in the filing of mechanics' liens was reported in Seattle, Washington. It is believed that financial problems are spreading to construction companies and contractors as home sales slide and builders default on construction loans. Delinquencies of single-family construction homes has increased.

44349 ■ "Morgan Hill Attracts Manufacturing to South County" in Silicon Valley/San Jose Business Journal (Vol. 30, September 21, 2012, No. 26, pp. 1)
Pub: American City Business Journal
Description: The Grow Morgan Hill Fund offers $2 million in loans to qualifying businesses off of an initial $500,000 city investment. The fund is a way for the city of Morgan Hill, California to help local businesses expand int he absence of redevelopment agencies.

44350 ■ "Mortgage Securities Drop Hits Home" in The Business Journal-Serving Metropolitan Kansas City (Vol. 27, October 17, 2008, No. 5)
Pub: American City Business Journals, Inc.
Contact: Whitney Shaw, President
Ed: Rob Roberts. **Description:** Sale of commercial mortgage-backed securities (CMBS) in Kansas City, Missouri have declined. The area may avoid layoffs if the United States government succeeds in stabilizing the economy. Major CMBS players in the area include Midland Loan Services Inc. and KeyBank Real Estate Capital.

44351 ■ "Mr. Deeds" in Canadian Business (Vol. 81, March 31, 2008, No. 5, pp. 24)
Pub: Rogers Media Inc.
Contact: Tony Viner, President
Ed: Thomas Watson. **Description:** Ron Sandler has the right experience to save Northern Rock PLC get through its liquidity problems. Sandler is known for saving Lloyd's of London in the mid-90's and he is not afraid to make enemies. Ron Sandler's assignment to help Northern Rock comes at a time when the health of the U.K. housing is not great.

44352 ■ "Muddy Portfolio Raises a Question: Just What Is National City Worth?" in Crain's Detroit Business (Vol. 24, April 7, 2008, No. 14)
Pub: Crain Communications Inc.
Contact: Rance E. Crain, President
Ed: Jay Miller. **Description:** National City Bank is looking at strategies to help it deal with its credit and loan problems which are reflected in its falling stock price. One possible solution is a merger with another bank, however most national banks are facing their own home-loan portfolio issues and may be unable to tackle another company's unresolved problems. Statistical data included.

44353 ■ "Multifamily Banks on Fannie, Freddie" in Memphis Business Journal (Vol. 33, February 24, 2012, No. 46, pp. 1)
Pub: American City Business Journal
Ed: Andy Ashby. **Description:** The possible demise of Fannie Mae and Freddie Mac is seen to adversely impact the multifamily apartment market of Memphis, Tennessee. The apartment market relies on federal loans for funding.

44354 ■ "NetSpend, Payday Firm in Pact" in American Banker (Vol. 173, February 22, 2008, No. 7, pp. 7)
Ed: Daniel Wolfe. **Description:** NetSpend Corporation of Austin, Texas is providing its prepaid cards to Advance America Cash Advance Centers Inc., a Spartanburg, South Carolina payday lender.

44355 ■ "A New Kid on the Block" in Barron's (Vol. 88, March 17, 2008, No. 11, pp. 58)
Pub: Dow Jones & Co., Inc.
Contact: Clare Hart, President
Ed: Thomas G. Donlan. **Description:** Discusses the Federal Reserve which has offered to lend $100 billion in cash to banks and $200 billion in Treasuries to Wall Street investment banks that have problems with liquidity. The reluctance of the banks to lend money to meet a margin call on securities that could still depreciate is the reason why the agency is going into the direct loan business.

44356 ■ "New Veteran Owned Company Helping Service Members Secure Affordable Home Loans While Helping Veteran Focused

Charities" in Marketwired (February 21, 2012)
Pub: COMTEX
Contact: Chip Brian, President
Description: VA Loan Captain Inc. was launched in 2012 at the first Veterans Affairs home loan sourcing company that partners with affiliate lenders that are commited to making a $200 charitable contribution to a participating veteran non-profit with every VA loan closed. Grant Moon, founder and president of VA Loan Captain, is a veteran of Operation Iraqi Freedom.

44357 ■ "No End to the Nightmare; America's Car Industry" in The Economist (Vol. 390, January 3, 2009, No. 8612, pp. 46)
Description: Detroit's struggling auto industry and the government loan package is discussed as well as the United Auto Worker union, which is loathed by Senate Republicans.

44358 ■ "Not Enough: Most First Place Creditors Left Holding the Bag" in The Business Journal-Milwaukee (Vol. 25, August 15, 2008, No. 47, pp. A1)
Pub: American City Business Journals, Inc.
Contact: Whitney Shaw, President
Ed: David Doege. **Description:** Most of the creditors of bankrupt real estate developer Scott Fergus are likely to remain unpaid as he only has an estimated $30,000 available for paying debts. Creditors, as of the 13 August 2008 deadline for filing claims, have filed a total of $79.1 million in claims.

44359 ■ "A Novel Fix for the Credit Mess" in Barron's (Vol. 88, March 31, 2008, No. 13, pp. 10)
Pub: Dow Jones & Co., Inc.
Contact: Clare Hart, President
Ed: Michael Santoli. **Description:** Due to the common bank-leverage factor of 10, the $250 billion of lost bank capital would have supported $2.5 trillion in lending capacity. Jeffrey Lewis suggests onerous regulations on bank-holding companies that own 10 to 25 percent, as they are partly to blame. Statistical data included.

44360 ■ "Ohio Commerce Draws Closer to Profitability" in Crain's Cleveland Business (Vol. 28, October 29, 2007, No. 43, pp. 14)
Pub: Crain Communications Inc.
Ed: Shawn A. Turner. **Description:** Overview of the business plan of Ohio Commerce Bank, a de novo, or startup bank that is close to turning the corner to profitability. The bank opened in November 2006 and focuses on dealing with small businesses totaling $5 million or less in annual revenues.

44361 ■ "OK, Bring in the Lawyers" in Crain's Chicago Business (Vol. 31, November 17, 2008, No. 46, pp. 26)
Pub: Crain Communications Inc.
Contact: Todd Johnson, Publisher
Ed: Daniel Rome Levine. **Description:** Bankruptcy attorneys are finding the economic and credit crisis a benefit for their businesses due to the high number of business owners and mortgage holders that are need of their services. One Chicago firm is handling ten times the number of cases they did the previous year and of that about 80 percent of their new clients are related to the real estate sector.

44362 ■ "On Growth Path of Rising Star" in Boston Business Journal (Vol. 31, June 24, 2011, No. 22, pp. 3)
Pub: Boston Business Journal
Ed: Kyle Alspach. **Description:** 1366 Technologies Inc. of Lexington, Massachusetts is considered a rising solar power technology company. The firm secured $150 million loan guarantee from the US Department of Energy that could go to the construction of a 1,000 megawatt solar power plant.

44363 ■ "Past Due: $289 Million in Loans" in Saint Louis Business Journal (Vol. 32, September 23, 2011, No. 4, pp. 1)
Pub: Saint Louis Business Journal
Ed: Evans Binns. **Description:** New York-based Trepp LLC research found about $289 million in local commercial mortgage-backed securities loans on 20

properties delinquent in payments by 30 days or more as of August 31, 2011. The report also placed the delinquency rate for St. Louis at that time at 9.64 percent.

44364 ■ "Photo Release - Affordable Housing Grant Helps Elderly Couple Regain Stability" in Benzinga.com (August 6, 2012)
Pub: Benzinga.com
Contact: Kyle Bazzy, President
Released: August 6, 2012. **Description:** Martin and Darlene Desmond moved into their new Habitat for Humanity home, made possible by an Affordable Housing Program grant. Details about the Federal Home Loan Bank of Dallas, one of 12 district banks in the FHLBanki Syhstem that supports housing and comunity development providing low priced loans and other credit products to help low income people afford a home.

44365 ■ "Picture of Success" in Black Enterprise (Vol. 38, December 2007, No. 5, pp. 71)
Pub: Earl G. Graves Publishing Co. Inc.
Contact: Earl G. Graves, Jr., President
Ed: Sheiresa Ngo. **Description:** Profile of Kenya Cagle, president and CEO of Caglevision Inc., an independent motion picture production company. Cagle, former off-Broadway child actor, kept his company afloat with financial backing and support from friends, employees, and business colleagues.

44366 ■ "Placer Land Sells for $12 Million" in Sacramento Business Journal (Vol. 25, July 30, 2008, No. 21, pp. 1)
Pub: American City Business Journals, Inc.
Contact: Whitney Shaw, President
Ed: Michael Shaw, Celia Lamb. **Description:** Reynen & Bardis Communities Inc., a Sacramento, California-based homebuilder, has purchased the Antonio Mountain Ranch in Placer County, California shortly before the property's scheduled foreclosure on June 27, 2008. Placer County Recorder's data show that the purchase price of the 808-acre wetland-rich property is $12 million.

44367 ■ "'Pre-Sale' for Planned Could Mich Tower" in Crain's Chicago Business (Vol. 31, March 24, 2008, No. 12, pp. 14)
Ed: Eddie Baeb. **Description:** Condominium developer William Warman is planning to build a mixed-use tower at 300 North Michigan Avenue which would include a hotel, retail space, apartments and a parking garage. Mr. Warman is looking for investors to buy part or all of the space in order to make it easier to land financing.

44368 ■ Prepare to Be a Teen Millionaire
Pub: Health Communications, Inc.
Contact: Peter Vegso, President
Ed: Kimberly Spinks-Burleson, Robyn Collins. **Released:** March 03, 2008. **Price:** $13.56, Members, paperback; $16.95, Nonmembers, paperback. **Description:** Business reference for any teenager wishing to become a successful entrepreneur; advice is given from successful teenage millionaires. Topics covered include: choosing a business name, type, and location; use of the Internet; legal issues; branding, sales, and marketing; funding and financial management; return on investment; retirement; development of a sound business plan; and certification for minority or women-owned companies. **Availability:** Print.

44369 ■ "Private Equity Firms Shopping Valley For Deals" in The Business Journal - Serving Phoenix and the Valley of the Sun (Vol. 29, September 21, 2008, No. 3, pp. 1)
Pub: American City Business Journals, Inc.
Contact: Whitney Shaw, President
Ed: Mike Sunnucks. **Description:** Private equity firms from California, Boston, New York, and overseas are expected to invest in growth-oriented real estate markets that include Phoenix. Real estate experts revealed that privately held investment and acquisition firms are looking to invest in real estate markets hit by the housing crisis. Views and information on private equity firms' real estate investments are presented.

44370 ■ "Proposed Accounting Changes Could Complicate Tenants' Leases" in Baltimore Business Journal (Vol. 28, July 2, 2010, No. 8, pp. 1)
Pub: Baltimore Business Journal
Ed: Daniel J. Sernovitz. **Description:** The Financial Accounting Standards Board has proposed that companies must indicate the value of real estate leases as assets and liabilities on balance sheets instead of expenses. The proposals could cause some companies to document millions of dollars in charges on their books or find difficulty in getting loans.

44371 ■ "Qualified Mortgage Law Puts Some Home Loans Out of Reach" in Memphis Business Journal (Vol. 35, February 21, 2014, No. 46, pp. 4)
Pub: American City Business Journals
Released: February 21, 2014. **Description:** The 2010 Dodd-Frank financial reform's qualified mortgages (QM) and ability to pay rules have pushed some smaller Southeastern banks out of the home lending business, while others are changing business models. The legal protection reduced the incentive for lenders to loan to borrowers with terms that do not follow the QM standards. The affected loans are also discussed.

44372 ■ Race and Entrepreneurial Success: Black-, Asian-, and White-Owned Businesses in the United States
Pub: The MIT Press
Contact: Ellen W. Faran, Director
E-mail: ewfaran@mit.edu
Ed: Robert W. Fairlie, Alicia M. Robb. **Released:** August 2010. **Price:** $19, paperback; £13.95. **Description:** Trends in minority small business ownership are explored, focusing on the importance of human capital, financial capital, and family business background in successful business ownership.

44373 ■ "Race, Not Income, Played Role in Subprime Loans" in Black Enterprise (Vol. 40, July 2010, No. 12, pp. 26)
Pub: Earl G. Graves Publishing Co. Inc.
Contact: Earl G. Graves, Jr., President
Ed: Deborah Creighton Skinner. **Description:** African Americans were 80 percent more likely than whites to receive a subprime loan and were almost 20 percent more likely to go into foreclosure, according to a study done by the National Community Reinvestment Coalition. Statistical data included.

44374 ■ "Radisson Hotel San Jose Airport Headed Into Foreclosure" in Silicon Valley/San Jose Business Journal (Vol. 29, February 3, 2012, No. 45, pp. 1)
Pub: American City Business Journal
Description: The Radisson Hotel San Jose Airport is set to be foreclosed. Hotel owner, Silicon Valley Hwang LLC has yet to pay a $15.9 million loan.

44375 ■ Raising Capital
Pub: AMACOM
Contact: Edward T. Reilly, Manager
Ed: Andrew J. Sherman. **Released:** Third Edition. **Price:** $34.95, Hardback. **Availability:** Print.

44376 ■ Raising Venture Capital for the Serious Entrepreneur
Pub: McGraw Hill Financial Inc.
Contact: Douglas L. Peterson, President
Ed: Dermot Berkery. **Released:** October 2007. **Price:** £30.99, hardback. **Description:** Sourcebook to help entrepreneurs secure venture capital from investors.

44377 ■ "Ready for a Rally?" in The Economist (Vol. 390, January 3, 2009, No. 8612, pp. 54)
Description: Analysts predict that the recession could end by 2010. The current economic crisis is presented in detail.

44378 ■ "Real Estate Defaults Top $300M" in Business Courier (Vol. 26, January 15, 2010, No. 39, pp. 1)
Ed: Dan Monk. **Description:** Cincinnati commercial real estate owners defaulting in securitized loans

reached $306 million at the end of 2009. The trend has lifted the region's default rate to nearly 9 percent. National average for commercial real estate default is examined.

44379 ■ "Real Estate Woes Mount for State's Smaller Banks" in Boston Business Journal (Vol. 27, November 30, 2007, No. 44, pp. 1)
Ed: Craig M. Douglas. **Description:** Massachusetts banking industry is facing a steep increase on loan defaults such as in home mortgages and condominium projects, contrary to public belief that the local industry is safe from the real estate meltdown. The dollar value of local banks' nonperforming loans doubled in 2007, and is rising statewide. Other banking issues in the state are discussed.

44380 ■ "Recession-Proof Your Startup" in Crain's Chicago Business (Vol. 31, November 10, 2008, No. 45, pp. 24)
Description: Detailed information concerning ways in which to start a business during an economic crisis is provided. Ways in which to find financing, the importance of a solid business plan, customer service, problem-solving and finding the right niche for the region are also discussed.

44381 ■ "Refi Requests Soar, But New Rules May Mean Fewer Closings" in The Business Review Albany (Vol. 35, April 4, 2008, No. 53, pp. 1)
Pub: The Business Review
Ed: Barbara Pinckney. **Description:** National refinancing applications grew by 82 percent in the week that ended March 21, 2008, due to the depressed real estate market and lower interest rates. Refinancing applicants, however, may be surprised with new rules on loan applications such as the required credit score of at least 720 in avoiding payment of extra fees. The developments in application standards for home loans are also examined.

44382 ■ "Refinance: To Do Or Not To Do?" in Real Estate Review (Vol. 41, Spring 2012, No. 1, pp. 91)
Released: Spring 2012. **Description:** An author's experiences in home mortgage refinancing are presented. The author's encounter with home appraisers is mentioned. Special or streamlined loans can be secured by parties with existing conforming loans.

44383 ■ "Region's Small Business Lending Rises by $440M" in South Florida Business Journal (Vol. 33, September 7, 2012, No. 6, pp. 1)
Pub: American City Business Journal
Description: Reports show that small business lending in South Florida increased by $440 million in 2011. Figures also indicate that banks originated $3.24 billion in small business loans during the same period, up from $2.8 billion in the previous year. It is believed that the region's economy is slowly improving.

44384 ■ "Research Reports" in Barron's (Vol. 88, March 24, 2008, No. 12, pp. M10)
Pub: Dow Jones & Co., Inc.
Contact: Clare Hart, President
Ed: Anita Peltonen. **Description:** Investors are recommending purchasing shares of Ampco Pittsburgh due to an expected surge in earnings. Deteriorating credit quality presents problems for the shares of BankAtlantic Bancorp, whose price targets have been lowered from $7 to $5 each. Shares of Helicos Biosciences are expected to move sideways from their $6 level. Statistical data included.

44385 ■ "Restaurants Rewrite Menu to Get Financing" in Saint Louis Business Journal (Vol. 31, August 19, 2011, No. 52, pp. 1)
Pub: Saint Louis Business Journal
Ed: Peter Solomont. **Description:** St. Louis, Missouri-based restaurants are finding new ways to secure financing. The weak economy has made it difficult for restaurants to secure bank financing.

44386 ■ "Return to Wealth; Bank Strategy" in The Economist (Vol. 390, January 3, 2009, No. 8612, pp. 56)
Description: UBS' strategy to survive these trying economic times is presented. Statistical data included. UBS has a stronger balance-sheet than most of its investment-banking peers and has reduced its portfolio.

44387 ■ "Running the Franchise Numbers" in Entrepreneur (Vol. 37, July 2009, No. 7, pp. 87)
Pub: Entrepreneur Press
Contact: Perlman Neil, President
Ed: Carol Tice. **Description:** Ways in which entrepreneurs can assess if they are ready to be a multi-unit franchisee are presented. Choosing the right locations, knowing how much assistance they can get from the franchisor, and financing are the key considerations when planning additional franchise units. Examples of success in multi-unit operations and multi-unit terms are also presented.

44388 ■ "Ryan Gilbert Wants SBA To Mean Speedy Business Administration" in Philadelphia Business Journal (Vol. 33, May 9, 2014, No. 13, pp. 8)
Pub: American City Business Journals
Released: May 9, 2014. **Description:** Ryan Gilbert, CEO of San Francisco, California-based Better Finance explains that his company uses its financial technology, SmartBiz, to help banks expedite Small Business Administration (SBA) loans. Better Finance, formerly known as BillFloat, helps small business owners receive SBA 7(a) loans between $5,000 and $150,000 within five business days instead of several week, offering easy online access to SBA loans at low interest rates.

44389 ■ "Samsung 'Holding Breath'" in Austin Business JournalInc. (Vol. 29, January 29, 2010, No. 47, pp. 1)
Pub: American City Business Journals
Ed: Jacob Dirr. **Description:** Samsung Austin Semiconductor LLC entered into an incentives agreement with the State of Texas in 2005, which involved $230 million in tax breaks and public financing. Terms of the agreement have been met, but some are questioning whether the company will be able to meet its goals for the Austin operations in 2010.

44390 ■ "Savvy Solutions" in Black Enterprise (Vol. 41, December 2010, No. 5, pp. 42)
Pub: Earl G. Graves Publishing Co. Inc.
Contact: Earl G. Graves, Jr., President
Ed: Tennille M. Robinson. **Description:** Individual asks for advice in launching a graphic design business, particularly grants available in a slow economy.

44391 ■ "Savvy Solutions" in Black Enterprise (Vol. 41, October 2010, No. 3, pp. 52)
Pub: Earl G. Graves Publishing Co. Inc.
Contact: Earl G. Graves, Jr., President
Ed: Tennille M. Robinson. **Description:** Husband and wife team seek advice for expanding their catering business. They are also seeking funding resources.

44392 ■ "SBA-Backed Lending Slides; Economy, Close Scrutiny of Applications Cited" in Crain's Detroit Business (March 9, 2008)
Pub: Crain Communications Inc.
Contact: Rance E. Crain, President
Ed: Nancy Kaffer. **Description:** Due to the state of the economy and a closer scrutiny on applications, Small Business Administration-backed loans are down by a significant margin in one loan program and have decreased slightly across the board. Statistical data included.

44393 ■ "SBA Can Improve Your Cash Flow" in Business Owner (Vol. 35, September-October 2011, No. 5, pp. 3)
Pub: DL Perkins Company
Description: Federal assistance available to small business is examined. The Small Business Adminis-

tration loan guarantee program is designed to improve availability and attractiveness of small business loans.

44394 ■ "SBA Intervenes to Keep Cash Flowing" in Business First Columbus (Vol. 25, November 21, 2008, No. 14, pp. A1)
Pub: American City Business Journals
Ed: Adrian Burns. **Description:** U.S. Small Business Administration's loan volumes fell as it tried to cushion the impact of the economic crisis on small businesses. Large investors have pulled back buying SBA loans due to declining profits, but demand for SBA loans are seen to resurge due to low risk.

44395 ■ "SBA Lending Hits Record" in Saint Louis Business Journal (Vol. 32, September 30, 2011, No. 5, pp. 1)
Pub: Saint Louis Business Journal
Ed: Rick Desloge. **Description:** US Small Business Administration loans have reached a record high of $200 million in 2011. The agency decreased the usual loan fees.

44396 ■ "SBA Lending Jumps in May: Loan Guarantee Raised, Fee Axed" in Crain's Detroit Business (Vol. 25, June 8, 2009, No. 23, pp. 1)
Pub: Crain Communications Inc. - Detroit
Contact: Keith Crain, Chairman
Ed: Nancy Kaffer. **Description:** U.S. Small Business Administration backed 102 loans through its 7(a) program in May. Statistical data included.

44397 ■ SBA Loans: A Step-by-Step Guide
Pub: John Wiley & Sons Inc.
Contact: Stephen M. Smith, President
URL(s): as.wiley.com/WileyCDA/WileyTitle/productCd-0471207527.html. **Released:** Latest edition 4th; Published May, 2002. **Price:** $27.95, Individuals paperback. **Publication includes:** A directory of Small Business Association field offices and a directory of services offered by the SBA. Principal content of publication is Step-by-step information of locating and securing a small business loan, including developing a business plan, researching finance options, recent lending statistics, eligibility requirements and other details.

44398 ■ "SBA Reinvigorates Loan Program" in Crain's Cleveland Business (Vol. 30, June 29, 2009, No. 25, pp. 1)
Pub: Crain Communications Inc.
Ed: Arielle Kass. **Description:** U.S. Small Business Administration has changed its loan programs that encourage banks to lend and businesses to borrow. Details of the program are discussed.

44399 ■ "Science Museum, Theater Seeking State Loans" in Sacramento Business Journal (Vol. 31, May 30, 2014, No. 14, pp. 4)
Pub: American City Business Journals
Released: May 30, 2014. **Description:** The Powerhouse Science Center and B Street Theatre in Sacramento, California are hoping to secure loans from the California Infrastructure and Economic Development Bank. Both nonprofit organizations are planning to start their own construction projects as soon as loans are received.

44400 ■ "Seeking SBA Loan in Cincinnati? Good Luck" in Business Courier (Vol. 26, October 16, 2009, No. 25, pp. 1)
Pub: American City Business Journals, Inc.
Contact: Whitney Shaw, President
Ed: Steve Watkins. **Description:** The largest banks in Greater Cincinnati reduced Small Business Administration (SBA) lending by 41 percent for the fiscal year ended September 2009. For the year, local SBA loans from all banks in the area declined 25 percent. The importance of SBA loans for growth of small business is examined.

44401 ■ "Seminar on Crowdfunding Set for Aug. 1" in Gazette (July 25, 2012)
Pub: Freedom Communications Inc.
Contact: Mitchell Stern, President
Released: July 25, 2012. **Description:** Senator Michael Bennet is co-hosting a seminar with Epicentral Coworking on crowdfunding featuring two panels

with local entrepreneurs and business owners, legal experts, and representatives from investment firms. The seminar will be held August 1, 2012.

44402 ■ *"Sense of Discovery" in Business Journal Portland (Vol. 27, November 19, 2010, No. 38, pp. 1)*
Pub: Portland Business Journal
Ed: Erik Siemers. **Description:** Tigard, Oregon-based Exterro Inc. CEO Bobby Balachandran announced plans to go public without the help of an institutional investor. Balachandran believes Exterro could grow to a $100 million legal compliance software company in the span of three years. Insights on Exterro's growth as market leader in the $1 billion legal governance software market are also given.

44403 ■ *"Sentiment Split on Financials: Is the Worse Over or Still to Come?" in Barron's (Vol. 88, March 24, 2008, No. 12, pp. M14)*
Pub: Dow Jones & Co., Inc.
Contact: Clare Hart, President
Ed: Steven M. Sears. **Description:** Experts in the financial sector are split as to whether or not the worst of the financial crisis brought on by the credit crunch is over. Some options traders are trading on are defensive puts, expecting the worst, while investors buying calls are considered as bullish.

44404 ■ *"Sharing the Micro Wealth" in Entrepreneur (Vol. 37, July 2009, No. 7, pp. 46)*
Pub: Entrepreneur Press
Contact: Perlman Neil, President
Ed: Jennie Dorris. **Description:** Step-by-step guide is presented on how Kiva.org, a website which allows people to make microloans to entrepreneurs across the world, works. The website, founded by Matt Flannery, raises $1 million weekly and it will add U.S. entrepreneurs to its list of loan recipients in June 2010. Other features of Kiva.org are discussed.

44405 ■ *"Shining a Light on Entrepreneurial Opportunities" in San Antonio Business Journal (Vol. 28, July 11, 2014, No. 22, pp. 4)*
Pub: American City Business Journals
Released: July 11, 2014. **Description:** Café Commerce is a small business and entrepreneurship development program launched by the City of San Antonio in partnership with microlender Accion Texas. The goal of the new resource center is to make entrepreneurship easier by complementing existing programs and serving as a platform to introduce new ones to the business community.

44406 ■ *"Shopped Out; Retailing Gloom" in The Economist (Vol. 390, January 3, 2009, No. 8612, pp. 26)*
Description: Economic volatility in the retail sector is having an impact on a number of countries around the globe. Europe is experiencing hard economic times as well and unless businesses have a strong business plan banks feel unable to lend the money necessary to tide the retailers over. The falling pound has increased the cost of imported goods and small to midsize retail chains may not be able to weather such an unforgiving economic climate.

44407 ■ *"'Short Sales,' A Sign of Housing Troubles, Start Popping Up" in The Business Review Albany (Vol. 35, April 11, 2008, No. 1, pp. 1)*
Pub: The Business Review
Ed: Michael DeMasi. **Description:** Discusses the number of short sales, where homeowners ask banks to forgive part of their mortgages to sell the properties, which is starting to increase in the Albany, New York area. Real estate agents in the area are taking up crash courses in short selling.

44408 ■ *"A Slice of Danish; Fixing Finance" in The Economist (Vol. 390, January 3, 2009, No. 8612, pp. 55)*
Description: Denmark's mortgage-holders and the county's lending system is presented.

44409 ■ *"Small Bank Has Big Lending Plans, New Hire" in Silicon Valley/San Jose Business Journal (Vol. 30, September 21, 2012, No. 26, pp. 1)*
Pub: American City Business Journal
Description: Santa Cruz County Bank has hired government-backed loans specialist Sat Kanwar in addition to Susan Chandler, Jorge Reguerin and Daljit Bains to boost the bank's Small Business Administration lending department. According to Chandler, the bank will take on loans ranging from $25,000 to several million dollars.

44410 ■ *"Small Business Credit Conditions" in Small Business Economic Trends (April 2008, pp. 12)*
Pub: National Federation of Independent Business
Contact: Caitlin McDevitt, Program Manager
Ed: William C. Dunkelberg, Holly Wade. **Description:** Graphs and tables that present the credit conditions of small businesses in the U.S. are provided. The tables include figures on availability of loans, interest rates, and expected credit conditions.

44411 ■ *"Small Business Credit Conditions" in Small Business Economic Trends (February 2008, pp. 12)*
Pub: National Federation of Independent Business
Contact: Caitlin McDevitt, Program Manager
Ed: William C. Dunkelberg, Holly Wade. **Description:** Graphs and tables that present the credit conditions of small businesses in the U.S. are provided. The tables include figures on availability of loans, interest rates, and expected credit conditions.

44412 ■ *"Small Business Credit Conditions" in Small Business Economic Trends (January 2008, pp. 12)*
Pub: National Federation of Independent Business
Contact: Caitlin McDevitt, Program Manager
Ed: William C. Dunkelberg, Holly Wade. **Description:** Graphs representing loan availability and interest rates among U.S. small businesses surveyed from January 1986 to December 2007 are given. Tables showing regular borrowers, availability of loans, satisfied borrowing needs, expected credit conditions, relative interest rate paid by regular borrowers, and actual interest rate paid on short-term loans by borrowers are also presented.

44413 ■ *"Small Business Credit Conditions" in Small Business Economic Trends (September 2010, pp. 12)*
Pub: National Federation of Independent Business
Contact: Caitlin McDevitt, Program Manager
Ed: William C. Dunkelberg, Holly Wade. **Description:** Graphs representing loan availability and interest rates among U.S. small businesses surveyed from January 1986 to August 2010 are given. Tables showing regular borrowers, availability of loans, satisfied borrowing needs, expected credit conditions, relative interest rate paid by regular borrowers, and actual interest rate paid on short-term loans by borrowers are also presented.

44414 ■ *"Small Business Credit Conditions" in Small Business Economic Trends (July 2010, pp. 12)*
Pub: National Federation of Independent Business
Contact: Caitlin McDevitt, Program Manager
Description: Graphs representing loan availability and interest rates among U.S. small businesses surveyed from January 1986 to June 2010 are given. Tables showing regular borrowers, availability of loans, satisfied borrowing needs, expected credit conditions, relative interest rate paid by regular borrowers, and actual interest rate paid on short-term loans by borrowers are also presented.

44415 ■ *"Small Business Credit Conditions" in Small Business Economic Trends (July 2014, pp. 12)*
Pub: National Federation of Independent Business
Contact: Caitlin McDevitt, Program Manager
Released: July 2014. **Description:** Graphs representing loan availability and interest rates among U.S. small businesses surveyed from January 1986 to June 2014 are given. Tables showing regular borrowers, availability of loans, satisfied borrowing

needs, expected credit conditions, relative interest rate paid by regular borrowers, and actual interest rate paid on short-term loans by borrowers are also presented.

44416 ■ *"Small Business Lending Rebounds to 3-Year High" in Washington Business Journal (Vol. 31, August 31, 2012, No. 19, pp. 1)*
Pub: American City Business Journal
Description: Loans made to small companies in the Washington DC area rose to 83,522 in 2011, up 14 percent from 2010 levels. The amount lent in 2011 reached $3.3 billion, up 9 percent from 2010, but down 44 percent from 2007 levels.

44417 ■ *"Small Businesses Finding It Easier To Get Capital" in Birmingham Business Journal (Vol. 31, July 11, 2014, No. 28, pp. 10)*
Pub: American City Business Journals, Inc.
Contact: Whitney Shaw, President
Released: July 11, 2014. **Description:** According to the Federal Reserve Bank of Atlanta, small businesses that applied for credit received the financing requested, showing increased confidence among Birmingham businesses. With a robust lending environment, Birmingham is expecting the trend to continue in 2014 with more business plans for expansion and new capital spends.

44418 ■ *"Soldiering On to Remake the SBA" in Inc. (February 2008, pp. 21)*
Description: Steven Preston discusses efforts to improve the Small Business Administration's processes to improve services to small businesses. Topics covered include customer service issues, loans, and fraud.

44419 ■ *"Soldiers as Consumers: Predatory and Unfair Business Practices Harming the Military Community"*
Pub: CreateSpace
Contact: Daren Giles, President
Released: October 5, 2014. **Price:** , $15.95 paperback. **Description:** Soldiers, airmen, sailors, and marines are young consumers and are appealing targets for unscrupulous businesses. There are lending organizations that prey upon our military offering products to help them bridge financial problems. Unethical elements of these loans includes higher interest rates and/or high fees or waivers of certain rights in fine print of contracts. A Federal Law called the Military Lending Act is supposed to protect service members from this kind of abuse, but the law only covers loans with terms of six months or less.

44420 ■ *"Some Credit Unions Are Big on Business Loans" in South Florida Business Journal (Vol. 35, September 5, 2014, No. 6, pp. 4)*
Pub: American City Business Journals
Released: September 5, 2014. **Description:** Business loans provided by credit unions in Florida have increased in 2014. Business loans in the state have risen to $1.36 billion. Jetstream Federal Credit Union increased its business loans by 456 percent.

44421 ■ *"South Jersey Office Space in Doldrums" in Philadelphia Business Journal (Vol. 31, March 16, 2012, No. 5, pp. 1)*
Pub: American City Business Journal
Description: Morgage lenders have been trying to boost office building occupancies in preparation of eventual sales. They are also selling loans at discounted prices.

44422 ■ *Southwestern Financial Directory: 11th Fed, Dallas*
Pub: Accuity Inc.
Contact: Hugh M. Jones, IV, President
URL(s): store.accuitysolutions.com/order.html. **Released:** Semiannual; January and July. **Price:** $400, Individuals. **Covers:** Holding companies, head offices and branches of every commercial bank, Savings & Loan, and credit union over $5 million in the states of Arkansas, Louisiana, New Mexico, Oklahoma, and Texas. **Entries include:** Name, address, phone, fax, key bank officers by functional title, directors, date established, detailed financial data, association's

membership, correspondent banks, out-of-town branches, holding company affiliation, ABA Transit Number and Routing Symbol, MICR number with check digit, type of charter. **Arrangement:** Geographical. **Indexes:** Alphabetical.

44423 ■ *"State Budget Woes Hurt Many Vendors, Senior Services"* in *Sacramento Business Journal (Vol. 25, August 15, 2008, No. 24, pp. 1)*
Pub: American City Business Journals, Inc.
Contact: Whitney Shaw, President
Ed: Melanie Turner. **Description:** Delays in the passage of the California state budget have adversely affected the health care industry. The Robertson Adult Day Health Care had taken out loans to keep the business afloat. The state Legislature has reduced Medi-Cal reimbursement to health care providers by 10 percent.

44424 ■ *"State Investment Goes Sour"* in *Business Journal Portland (Vol. 26, December 4, 2009, No. 39, pp. 1)*
Pub: American City Business Journals, Inc.
Ed: Erik Siemers. **Description:** Oregon might recoup only $500,000 of a $20 million loan to Vancouver-based Cascade Grain Products LLC. Cascade Grain's ethanol plant in Clatskanie, OR will be put into auction under the supervision of a bankruptcy court.

44425 ■ *"State VC Fund To Get At Least $7.5 Million"* in *Crain's Detroit Business (Vol. 24, February 25, 2008, No. 8, pp. 14)*
Pub: Crain Communications Inc. - Detroit
Contact: Keith Crain, Chairman
Ed: Tom Henderson. **Description:** Michigan's 21st Century Investment Fund is expected to receive $7.5 million, financed by tobacco-settlement money. The Michigan Strategic Fund Board will determine which firms will receive venture capital, which is mandated by legislation to invest the fund within three years.

44426 ■ *"State Wants to Add Escape Clause to Leases"* in *Sacramento Business Journal (Vol. 28, October 14, 2011, No. 33, pp. 1)*
Pub: Sacramento Business Journal
Ed: Michael Shaw. **Description:** California Governor Jerry Brown's administration has decided to add escape clauses to new lease agreements, which created new worry for building owners and brokers in Sacramento, California. Real estate brokers believe the appropriation of funds clauses have been making the lenders nervous and would result in less competition.

44427 ■ *"Sterotaxis Needs $10 Million in 60 Days"* in *Saint Louis Business Journal (Vol. 32, October 7, 2011, No. 6, pp. 1)*
Pub: Saint Louis Business Journal
Ed: E.B. Solomont. **Description:** Medical device firm Stereotaxis signed a loan modification deal with Silicon Valley Bank. The company suffered massive losses during second quarter 2011. Under the deal, the company waived the minimum tangible net work covenant of the original loan in exchange for reduction in its credit line.

44428 ■ *"Still No Arena Financing Plan"* in *Sacramento Business Journal (Vol. 28, May 27, 2011, No. 13, pp. 1)*
Pub: Sacramento Business Journal
Ed: Kelly Johnson. **Description:** The government of Sacramento, California has yet to devise a plan to finance the construction of a proposed stadium. The arena is estimated to cost $387 million. A brief description of the facility is also included.

44429 ■ *"Struggling Community Banks Find Little Help In Wall Street Bailout"* in *Crain's Detroit Business (Vol. 24, September 29, 2008, pp. 48)*
Pub: Crain Communications Inc.
Contact: Rance E. Crain, President
Ed: Tom Henderson. **Description:** Both public and private Michigan bands have been hit hard by poorly performing loan portfolios and although their problems were not caused by high-risk securities but by a longtime statewide recession and a housing slump,

these community banks have little hope of seeing any of the bailout money that has been allotted for the larger institutions.

44430 ■ *"Stuck With Two Mortgages"* in *Crain's Chicago Business (Vol. 31, April 21, 2008, No. 16)*
Pub: Crain Communications Inc.
Contact: Todd Johnson, Publisher
Ed: Darci Smith. **Description:** Discusses the problem a number of people are facing due to the slump in the housing market: being stuck with two mortgages when they move because their former homes have not sold. Many thought they could afford to move to a larger home, anticipating significant equity appreciation that did not occur; now they are left with lowering their price and competing with the host of new developments.

44431 ■ *"Sunwest Vies To Stave Off Bankruptcy"* in *The Business Journal-Portland (Vol. 25, August 15, 2008, No. 23, pp. 1)*
Pub: American City Business Journals, Inc.
Contact: Whitney Shaw, President
Ed: Robin J. Moody. **Description:** Sunwest Management Inc. is teetering on the edge of bankruptcy as creditors start foreclosure on nine of their properties. This could potentially displace residents of the assisted living operator. Sunwest is trying to sell smaller packages of properties to get a $100 million bridge loan to maintain operations.

44432 ■ *"Survey: Ag Lenders Less Optimistic"* in *Idaho Business Review (June 27, 2014)*
Pub: Dolan Co.
Contact: James P. Dolan, President
Released: June 27, 2014. **Description:** According to a survey conducted by Kansas State University, agricultural lenders are showing less optimism than previously felt last fall. Lenders are expecting interest rates to rise, while the spread over cost of funds is expected to increase in the long term. Statistical data included.

44433 ■ *"Survival Guide: There Can Be an Upside to Managing a Downturn"* in *Canadian Business (Vol. 81, November 10, 2008, No. 19, pp. 54)*
Ed: Sharda Prashad. **Description:** Canada-based Foxy is already limiting its exposure to retailers who could be a credit problem in case of recession. Retirement Life Communities is entering into fixed-rate and fixed-term loans for them to have sufficient financing to grow. Business owners need to realize that customers want more for less.

44434 ■ *"TARP Lending Idea Gets Mixed Reviews"* in *Tampa Bay Business Journal (Vol. 29, October 30, 2009, No. 45, pp. 1)*
Pub: American City Business Journals
Ed: Kent Hoover, Margie Manning. **Description:** Tampa Bay area, Florida's community banks have expressed disapproval to the proposal of President Obama to increase lending to small business, wherein the government will provide cheap capital through US Treasury Troubled Asset Relief Program (TARP). The banks were hesitant on the plan because of the strings attached to TARP.

44435 ■ *"Tech Godfather Steve Walker Winding Down Howard Venture Fund"* in *Baltimore Business Journal (Vol. 27, December 11, 2009, No. 31)*
Pub: American City Business Journals
Ed: Scott Dance. **Description:** Steve Walker, president of venture capital fund firm Walker Ventures, will be closing the Howard County, Maryland-based firm as the economic situation is finding it difficult to recover investor's money. According to Walker, the economy also constrained investors from financing venture funds. Despite the closure, Walker will continue his work in the local angel investing community.

44436 ■ *"This Just In"* in *Crain's Detroit Business (Vol. 25, June 1, 2009, No. 22, pp. 1)*
Pub: Crain Communications Inc. - Detroit
Contact: Keith Crain, Chairman
Ed: Daniel Duggan. **Description:** Three veterans of the auto industry have partnered to create, Revital-

izing Michigan, a nonprofit dedicated to help manufacturers improve their processes. The firm is seeking federal, state and private grants to fund the mission.

44437 ■ *"THL Credit Is Hunting In Middle Market"* in *Boston Business Journal (Vol. 30, October 22, 2010, No. 39, pp. 1)*
Pub: Boston Business Journal
Ed: Tim McLaughlin. **Description:** THL Credit has been supplying capital to middle market companies in Massachusetts. The company has reported investment income of $2.44 million at the end of June 2010.

44438 ■ *"TMC Development Closes $1.1 Million Real Estate Purchase for Mansa, LLC Using SBA 504 Real Estate Financing"* in *Marketwired (September 17, 2009)*
Pub: COMTEX News Network Inc.
Contact: Chip Brian, President
Description: TMC Development announced the closing of a $1.1 million real estate purchase for Mansa, LLC dba Kwikee Mart, a Napa-based convenience store; TMC helped the company secure a Small Business Administration 504 loan in order to purchase the acquisition of a 3,464 square foot building. SBA created the 504 loan program to provide financing for growing small and medium-sized businesses.

44439 ■ *"Today's Business Sale Climate"* in *Business Owner (Vol. 35, September-October 2011, No. 5, pp. 10)*
Pub: DL Perkins Company
Description: Despite the weak economy, there is a surplus of individuals wanting to purchase a small business. The Small Business Administration loan guarantees program helps with its loans for purchase/ sale of business assistance.

44440 ■ *"Too Much Information?"* in *Black Enterprise (Vol. 37, December 2006, No. 5, pp. 59)*
Pub: Earl G. Graves Publishing Co. Inc.
Contact: Earl G. Graves, Jr., President
Ed: James C. Johnson. **Description:** African American business owners often face the dilemma of whether or not to divulge their minority status when soliciting new customers and financial institutions. The quality of the products or services is always the key factor and race should never define one's business; however, it is appropriate to market oneself as a minority- or women-owned business, especially if the company is in an industry where those clients are offered top-tier contracts.

44441 ■ *"Training Center Wants to be College"* in *Austin Business JournalInc. (Vol. 29, November 13, 2009, No. 36, pp. A1)*
Pub: American City Business Journals
Ed: Sandra Zaragoza. **Description:** Texas-based CyberTex Institute, a job training center, has established technical careers in an effort to obtain federal accreditation as a college. A college status would allow CyperTex to extend financial assistance to students. Aside from potentially having an enlarged student body and expanded campus, CyberTex would be allowed to engage in various training programs.

44442 ■ *"Triad, Fortune Dump TARP Cut Costs, Boost Lending"* in *Saint Louis Business Journal (Vol. 32, October 7, 2011, No. 6, pp. 1)*
Pub: Saint Louis Business Journal
Ed: Greg Edwards. **Description:** St. Louis, Missouri-based Triad Bank and Fortune Bank have been using an alternative federal loan program to pay back financing from the Troubled Asset Relief Program. Triad got a $5 million loan at one percent interest rate from the US Small Business Lending Fund.

44443 ■ *"Troubled Project In Court"* in *The Business Journal-Portland (Vol. 25, July 25, 2008, No. 20, pp. 1)*
Pub: American City Business Journals, Inc.
Contact: Whitney Shaw, President
Ed: Wendy Culverwell. **Description:** Views and information on Salpare Bay's Hayden Island project, as well as on financing problems and cases associated with the project, are presented. Construction of luxurious waterside condominiums stopped last fall,

after the discovery of financing problems and subcontractors and other parties started filing claims and counterclaims.

44444 ■ *"Try, Try Again"* in Baltimore Business Journal (Vol. 28, August 20, 2010, No. 15, pp. 1)
Ed: Gary Haber. **Description:** Customers' refinancing of mortgages has boosted Baltimore, Maryland mortgage banking business. The housing decline has resulted in a decrease in the number of people looking for new mortgages.

44445 ■ *"Turmoil Means Changes For Retailers"* in The Business Journal-Serving Metropolitan Kansas City (Vol. 27, October 10, 2008, No. 4)
Pub: American City Business Journals, Inc.
Contact: Whitney Shaw, President
Ed: Suzanna Stagemeyer. **Description:** Impacts of the financial crisis on Kansas Metropolitan Area retailers are varied. Rob Dalzell, for instance, found it difficult to secure a loan for his new self-serve yogurt store Yummo. The trends in retailing in the area are examined further as well as ways in which local businesses are changing in an attempt to stay solvent during the economic downturn.

44446 ■ *"U-Swirl Added to SBA's Franchise Registry"* in Ice Cream Reporter (Vol. 23, September 20, 2010, No. 10, pp. 1)
Description: Healthy Fast Food Inc., parent to the U-SWIRL Frozen Yogurt cafe chain announced that the U.S. Small Business Administration listed U-SWIRL Frozen Yogurt on its official franchise registry. This move will allow U-SWIRL the benefits of a streamlined review process for SBA financing.

44447 ■ *"U.S. Economy's Underlying Strengths Limit Recession Threat"* in Hispanic Business (Vol. 30, April 2008, No. 4, pp. 14)
Pub: Hispanic Business Inc.
Contact: Jesus Chavarria, President
Ed: Dr. Juan B. Solana. **Description:** Large and small businesses as well as consumers and policymakers are attempting to identify the areas of risk and loss created by the economic crisis; analysts are now estimating that U.S. mortgage losses could reach the $380 to $400 billion mark. Also discusses the falling of wages and the rising of unemployment. Statistical data included.

44448 ■ *"VA Exceeds Government-Wide Goal for Veteran-Owned Business Procurement"* in Benzinga.com (July 3, 2012)
Pub: Benzinga.com
Contact: Kyle Bazzy, President
Ed: Aaron Wise. **Description:** Department of Veterans Affairs has surpassed its goal of government procurements of the Small Business Adminstration by more than six times. The VA's committment to the success of veteran-owned small businesses is covered.

44449 ■ *"Valenti: Roots of Financial Crisis Go Back to 1998"* in Crain's Detroit Business (Vol. 24, October 6, 2008, No. 40, pp. 25)
Pub: Crain Communications Inc.
Contact: Rance E. Crain, President
Ed: Tom Henderson, Nathan Skid. **Description:** Interview with Sam Valenti III who is the chairman and CEO of Valenti Capital L.L.C., a wealth-management firm; Valenti discusses in detail the history that led up to the current economic crisis as well as his prediction for the future of the country.

44450 ■ *"VC Money Down In State, Number of Deals Up"* in Crain's Detroit Business (Vol. 24, January 28, 2008, No. 4, pp. 18)
Pub: Crain Communications Inc. - Detroit
Contact: Keith Crain, Chairman
Ed: Tom Henderson. **Description:** Despite the amount of money invested by venture capitalists in Michigan is down, the number of deals rose according to the annual Money Tree report. Venture capital firms invested a combined $105.4 million in 22 deals that involved 19 companies in the state.

44451 ■ *The Wall Street Journal. Complete Small Business Guidebook*
Pub: Three Rivers Press
Contact: Caroline Sincerbeaux, Editor
E-mail: csincerbeaux@randomhouse.com
Ed: Colleen DeBaise. **Released:** December 29, 2009. **Price:** $15. **Description:** The mechanics of building, running and growing a profitable business are outlined, teaching how to write a business plan, ways to finding money during lean years, how to keep stress in check, time management, investment in technology, hiring, marketing, management basics, angel investing and venture capital, as well as an exit strategy.

44452 ■ *"Wanted: Angels in the Country"* in Austin Business JournalInc. (Vol. 28, July 18, 2008, No. 18, pp. 1)
Pub: American City Business Journals
Ed: Laura Hipp. **Description:** A proposal is being pushed forward by managers of Texas' Emerging Technology Fund to create an angel investors' network. The proposal is asking that tax credits for those who invest in research and development projects be granted in order to boost the number of technology companies in the state.

44453 ■ *"What's In a Name? Fed's Latest Move Should Be Called 'Bankers and Brokers Relief Program"* in Barron's (Vol. 88, March 17, 2008, No. 11, pp. 7)
Pub: Dow Jones & Co., Inc.
Contact: Clare Hart, President
Ed: Alan Abelson. **Description:** Eliot Spitzer's resignation incidentally caused the stock market to go up by 400 points. The Federal Reserve Board's new Term Securities Lending Facility provides liquidity to the big lenders by funneling $200 billion in the form of 28-day loans of Treasuries. The analysis of Paul Brodsky and Lee Quaintance of QB Partners on the demand for commodities is also discussed.

44454 ■ *"What's In a Relationship? The Case of Commercial Lending"* in Business Horizons (Vol. 51, March-April 2008, No. 2, pp. 93)
Pub: Elsevier Advanced Technology Publications
Ed: Gregory F. Udell. **Description:** Academic literature on relationship lending and banking to small and medium enterprises is analyzed. This practice is best suited to some SME types but creates special challenges for bank managers. Relationship lending may also be better delivered by community banks.

44455 ■ *"Where the Loans Are"* in Boston Business Journal (Vol. 30, October 22, 2010, No. 39, pp. 1)
Pub: Boston Business Journal
Ed: Craig M. Douglas. **Description:** Massachusetts-based community banks have been investing in multi-family apartment projects. Lending has decline during the first half of 2010. A $264 million increase in multifamily loans has also been observed.

44456 ■ *"Where Small Biz Gets a 'Yes' More Often"* in Denver Business Journal (Vol. 65, February 28, 2014, No. 42, pp. A10)
Pub: American City Business Journals
Released: February 28, 2014. **Description:** The Biz2Credit Small Business Lending Index has found that alternative lenders granted 66.9 percent of funding requests in Colorado compared to the 15.1 percent approval of loans requests by big banks. The big banks' low approval rates were attributed to their less aggressive lending efforts and the state's fewer restrictions on alternative lending. Other findings from the study are discussed.

44457 ■ *"Where to Stash Your Cash"* in Barron's (Vol. 88, March 17, 2008, No. 11, pp. 41)
Pub: Dow Jones & Co., Inc.
Contact: Clare Hart, President
Ed: Mike Hogan. **Description:** Investors are putting their money in money-market mutual funds seeking fractionally better yields and a safe haven from the

uncertainties that was brought about by subprime lending. These funds, however, are hovering near 3.20 percent which is less than the 4 percent inflation rate.

44458 ■ *Wiley Pathways Small Business Management*
Pub: John Wiley & Sons Inc.
Contact: Stephen M. Smith, President
Ed: Richard M. Hodgetts, Donald F. Kuratko, Margaret Burlingame, Don Gulbrandsen. **Released:** March 2007. **Price:** $76.95, paperback; $42.50. **Description:** Tips for starting and running a successful small business are given, including advice on writing a business plan, financing, and the law. **Availability:** PrintE-book.

44459 ■ *"Wobbling Economy has a KC Wary"* in The Business Journal-Serving Metropolitan Kansas City (Vol. 27, September 26, 2008, No. 2, pp. 1)
Pub: American City Business Journals, Inc.
Contact: Whitney Shaw, President
Ed: Rob Roberts. **Description:** Real estate developers in Kansas City Metropolitan Area are worried of the possible impacts of the crisis at Wall Street. They expect tightening of the credit market, which will result in difficulty of financing their projects. The potential effects of the Wall Street crisis are examined further.

44460 ■ *Women Entrepreneurs in The Global Marketplace*
Pub: Edward Elgar Publishing Inc.
Contact: Richard Henning, Vice President
E-mail: kwight@e-elgar.com
Ed: Andrea E. Smith-Hunter. **Released:** 2013. **Price:** £85.50, hardback. **Description:** Focus is on women entrepreneurs; information includes human capital, network structures and financial capital, with comparative analysis across racial lines. **Availability:** Print.

44461 ■ *"Women: Send Me An Angel"* in Entrepreneur (Vol. 35, October 2007, No. 10, pp. 38)
Pub: Entrepreneur Press
Contact: Perlman Neil, President
Ed: Aliza Sherman. **Description:** Golden Seeds has invested in Enter Artemis Woman LLC when the latter decided to put its products into Wal-Mart. Golden Seeds was formed by angel investors who aim to help women build their own businesses. Tips on how to approach angel investors and getting angel funding are given.

44462 ■ *"The Worst Lies Ahead for Wall Street: More Losses Certain; More Expensive Capital to Be Needed"* in Crain's New York Business (Vol. 24, January 20, 2008, No. 3, pp. 1)
Pub: Crain Communications Inc.
Contact: Rance Crain, President
Ed: Aaron Elstein. **Description:** Due to the weakening economy, many financial institutions will face further massive losses forcing them to borrow more at higher interest rates and dragging down their earnings for years to come. The effects on commercial real estate and credit card loans are also discussed as well as the trend to investing in Asia and the Middle East.

44463 ■ *"The Wrong Tune"* in The Business Journal-Portland (Vol. 25, July 25, 2008, No. 20, pp. 1)
Pub: American City Business Journals, Inc.
Contact: Whitney Shaw, President
Ed: Robin J. Moody. **Description:** Views and information on turnaround management and recovery plans of the Oregon Symphony, are presented. The non-profit organization has lost a total of $5.1 million between 2002 and 2008, and $400,000 annual interest payments for a $7 million bank loan. Increased ticket sales, as well as cost cutting measures, are helping improve the finance of the organization.

44464 ■ *"You Better Shop Around: Four Steps to Getting the Best Deal On a Home Loan"* in Black Enterprise (Vol. 40, July 2010,

No. 12, pp. 78)
Pub: Earl G. Graves Publishing Co. Inc.
Contact: Earl G. Graves, Jr., President
Ed: Tara-Nicholle Nelson. **Description:** Four steps to help anyone seeking a mortgage for a home purchase are listed.

44465 ■ *"Your Exposure to Bear Stearns" in Barron's (Vol. 88, March 17, 2008, No. 11, pp. 45)*
Pub: Dow Jones & Co., Inc.
Contact: Clare Hart, President
Ed: Tom Sullivan, Jack Willoughby. **Description:** Bear Stearns makes up 5.5 percent of Pioneer Independence's portfolio, 1.4 percent of Vanguard Windsor II's portfolio, 1.2 percent of Legg Mason Value Trust, about 1 percent of Van Kampen Equity & Income, and 0.79 percent of Putnam Fund for Growth & Income. Ginnie Mae securities are now trading at 1.78 percentage points over treasuries due to the mortgage crises.

44466 ■ *Your Guide to Arranging Bank & Debt Financing for Your Own Business in Canada*
Pub: Productive Publications
Contact: Iain Williamson, Manager
Ed: Iain Williamson. **Released:** August 2013. **Price:** C$81.95, softcover. **Description:** Bank financing for small businesses in Canada is discussed. **Availability:** Print.

44467 ■ *Your Guide to Canadian Export Financing: Successful Techniques for Financing Your Exports from Canada*
Pub: Productive Publications
Contact: Iain Williamson, Manager
Ed: Iain Williamson. **Released:** August 2013. **Price:** C$59.95, softcover. **Description:** Canadian export financing is covered. **Availability:** Print.

44468 ■ *Your Guide to Preparing a Plan to Raise Money for Your Own Business*
Pub: Productive Publications
Contact: Iain Williamson, Manager
Ed: Iain Williamson. **Released:** August 2013. **Price:** C$46.95, softcover. **Description:** A good business plan is essential for raising money for any small business. **Availability:** Print.

44469 ■ *"Zions Offers Step-by-Step Small Business Guidance" in Idaho Business Review (September 1, 2014)*
Pub: Dolan Co.
Contact: James P. Dolan, President
Released: September 15, 2014. **Description:** Zions bank provides small business guidance to clients through its Zions Bank Idaho Business Resource Center. The program helps entrepreneurs learn the basic rules of running a small business. Free courses teach the essentials of finance, marketing and selling, .

TRADE PERIODICALS

44470 ■ *Mortgage Technology*
Pub: SourceMedia Inc.
Contact: James M. Malkin, Chief Executive Officer
URL(s): www.nationalmortgagenews.com/technology/. **Released:** Monthly **Price:** $88, U.S.; $108, Canada; $108, Other countries.

CONSULTANTS

44471 ■ Pioneer Business Consultants
9042 Garfield Ave., Ste. 211
Huntington Beach, CA 92646
Ph: (714)964-7600
Fax: (714)962-6585
Contact: Ron von Freyman, President
Scope: Offers general management consulting specializing in business acquisitions, tax and business planning, cash flow analyses, business valua-

tions and business sales and expert witness court testimony regarding business sales, valuations and accounting. **Founded:** 1980.

FRANCHISES AND BUSINESS OPPORTUNITIES

44472 ■ Stop 'N' Cash
Stop 'N' Cash 5000 Inc.
2880 King St. E, Ste. D
Kitchener, ON, Canada N2A 1A7
Ph: (519)895-2888
URL: http://www.stopncash.com
Description: The franchise provides a payday loan scheme and a solid investment return. **No. of Franchise Units:** 64. **No. of Company-Owned Units:** 9. **Founded:** 1998. **Franchised:** 1999. **Equity Capital Needed:** $150,000-$200,000. **Franchise Fee:** $30,000. **Training:** 1 week of in-house in Kitchener, and ongoing support.

RESEARCH CENTERS

44473 ■ University of Nebraska—Kearney - Nebraska Business Development Center (NBDC)
West Center Bldg., Rm. 127E
1917 W 24th St.
Kearney, NE 68849-4440
Ph: (308)865-8344
Fax: (308)865-8153
Co. E-mail: nbdcunk@unk.edu
URL: http://www.unk.edu/academics/nbdc.aspx?id=1936
Contact: Odee Ingersoll, Director
Scope: Management education, market research, business and marketing plans, strategic planning, financial planning, cash flow budgeting, capital budgeting and loan packaging. **Services:** Consulting. **Founded:** 1977. **Publications:** *NBDC Business Calendar* (Quarterly). **Educational Activities:** NBDC Continuing education programs.

TENNESSEE VALLEY AUTHORITY

44474 ■ *"What Direction Is Your Company Moving In?" in South Florida Business Journal (Vol. 35, August 29, 2014, No. 5, pp. 8)*
American City Business Journals (ACBJ)
Released: August 29, 2014. **Description:** Senior management should have a clear perspective about the direction of a company and work hard to effectively communicate such perspective to all stakeholders. Some ways on how corporate leaders can clarify the strategic plan of a company to its key stakeholders are suggested.

START-UP INFORMATION

44475 ■ *"'Entrepreneurial Spirit' Leads Executives to Form New Tower Company" in South Florida Business Journal (Vol. 34, February 21, 2014, No. 31, pp. 6)*
Pub: American City Business Journals
Released: February 21, 2014. **Description:** Phoenix Tower International is a new company in Boca Raton, Florida formed by the former executives of Global Tower Partners, a multibillion-dollar company that was sold in October 2013. Phoenix is self-funded and will focused on owning, leasing, and managing cellular phone service towers.

44476 ■ *Entrepreneurship and Effective Small Business Management*
Pub: Prentice Hall Higher Education
Ed: Norman M. Scarborough, Jeffrey R. Cornwall. **Released:** Eleventh Edition. **Price:** $217.40. **Description:** Provides undergraduate and graduate entrepreneurship and/or small business management courses with information to successfully launch a new company. The books offers entrepreneurs the tools required to develop staying power to succeed and grow their new business. **Availability:** Print.

44477 ■ *Essentials of Entrepreneurship and Small Business Management*
Pub: Prentice Hall PTR
Ed: Norman M. Scarborough, Thomas W. Zimmerer, Doug Wilson. **Released:** 7th Edition. **Price:** $199.80. **Description:** New venture creation and the knowledge required to start a new business are shared. The challenges of entrepreneurship, business plans, marketing, e-commerce, and financial considerations are explored.

44478 ■ *"From the Boardroom to the Drawing Board" in Dallas Business Journal (Vol. 37, July 18, 2014, No. 45, pp. 4)*
Pub: American City Business Journals
Released: July 18, 2014. **Description:** Several former North Texas Executive Directors resigned from their positions at top of the corporate ladder to start their own entrepreneurial ventures. Some of the challenges faced and how they overcame them to succeed are highlighted.

44479 ■ *"The Hard Thing About Hard Things: Building a Business When There Are No Easy Answers"*
Pub: HarperCollins Publishers
Released: March 4, 2014. **Price:** , $29.99. **Description:** Cofounder of Andreessen Horowitz and well-respected Silicon Valley entrepreneur, offers advice for building and running a startup small business. Horowitz analyzes issues confronting leaders daily and shares insights he gained from managing, selling, buying investing in, and supervising technology firms.

44480 ■ *"The Introvert's Guide to Entrepreneurship: How to Become a Successful Entrepreneur as an Introvert"*
Pub: CreateSpace
Contact: Daren Giles, President
Released: October 15, 2014. **Price:** , $9.99 paperback. **Description:** The five main strengths and the five harmful weaknesses for an introvert wishing to become an entrepreneur are listed. Three key strategies to help an introvert run his new company are examined. Five key attributes of a good business partner are considered. Management tips are also shared for introverted leaders.

44481 ■ *"The Responsible Entrepreneur: Four Game-Changing Archetypes for Founders, Leaders, and Impact Investors"*
Pub: Jossey-Bass
Contact: William J. Pesce, President
Released: July 14, 2014. **Price:** , $28.00. **Description:** Responsible entrepreneurs are special people who are able to transform industries as well as society. They challenge and refine cultural assumptions, laws, regulations, along with the processes of governance. They think beyond the status quo of entrepreneurship. Sanford provides the makings for this new type of business leadership, describing the ways in which any entrepreneur can achieve a higher level of work. Four archetypes are cover to help managers and entrepreneurs start and scale any business venture.

44482 ■ *Small Business Management*
Pub: John Wiley & Sons Inc.
Contact: Stephen M. Smith, President
Ed: Margaret Burlingame. **Released:** March 2007. **Price:** , $44.95. **Description:** Advice for starting and running a small business as well as information on the value and appeal of small businesses, is given. Topics include budgets, taxes, inventory, ethics, e-commerce, and current laws.

44483 ■ *Small Business Management: Launching and Growing New Ventures*
Pub: Nelson Education Ltd.
Contact: Greg Nordal, President
Ed: Justin G. Longenecker. **Released:** 5th Edition. **Price:** $136.95, paperback; $79.95. **Description:** Tips for starting and running a successful new company are provided. **Availability:** PrintE-book.

44484 ■ *Small Business Tool Kit*
Ed: Linda M. Magoon. **Released:** April 10, 2010. **Price:** $40. **Description:** When starting a business, new managers and entrepreneurs require many resources to get the company up and running successfully. This book covers a wide range of topics that are critical for any new business owner.

44485 ■ *"Startup Activity Among Jobless Execs is the Highest Since 2009, Survey Says" in South Florida Business Journal (Vol. 34, February 21, 2014, No. 31, pp. 3)*
Pub: American City Business Journals
Released: February 21, 2014. **Description:** The percentage of startup activity among former managers and executives in the U.S. increased 31 percent in 2013 according to consulting firm Challenger, Gray & Christmas. According to the survey, 5.5 percent of job-seeking executive launched their own business during each quarter in 2013, compared with 4.2 percent in 2012 and 3.2 percent in 2011.

ASSOCIATIONS AND OTHER ORGANIZATIONS

44486 ■ **American Management Association (AMA)**
1601 Broadway
New York, NY 10019-7420
Ph: (212)586-8100
Free: 877-566-9441
Fax: (212)903-8168
Co. E-mail: customerservice@amanet.org
URL: http://www.amanet.org
Contact: Edward T. Reilly, President
Description: Provides educational forums worldwide where members and their colleagues learn superior, practical business skills and explore best practices of world-class organizations through interaction with each other and expert faculty practitioners. Maintains a publishing program providing tools individuals use to extend learning beyond the classroom in a process of life-long professional growth and development through education. **Founded:** 1923. **Publications:** *HR Focus* (Monthly); *Organizational Dynamics: A Quarterly Review of Organizational Behavior for Management Executives; Small Business Reports: For Decision Makers in America's Small and Mid-Size Companies* (Monthly); *Organizational Dynamics: A Quarterly Review of Organizational Behavior for Professional Managers* (Quarterly); *AMA's Directory of Human Resource Products and Services; Management Review* (Monthly); *The Take-Charge Assistant* (Monthly); *Make Your Contacts Count.* **Educational Activities:** Writing for the Web; Principles of Professional Selling; Negotiating to Win; Successfully Managing People; Assertiveness Training (Onsite); Advanced Sales Management (Onsite); Effective Technical Writing (Onsite); Accounting's New Guidelines: From GAAP to IFRS (Onsite); Achieving Leadership Success Through People (Onsite); Essentials of Project Management for the Nonproject Manager; Conference for Executive Secretaries and Administrative Assistants; Management Skills for

Administrative Professionals; Fundamentals of Finance and Accounting for Administrative Professionals (Onsite); Project Management for Administrative Professionals (Onsite) (Monthly); Managing Chaos: Dynamic Time Management, Recall, Reading, and Stress Management Skills for Administrative Professionals (Onsite); How to Sharpen Your Business Writing Skills (Onsite); The Voice of Leadership: How Leaders Inspire, Influence, and Achieve Results (Onsite); Making the Transition to Management (Onsite); Making the Transition from Staff Member to Supervisor (Onsite); Master Organizational Politics, Influence and Alliances (Onsite); Territory and Time Management for Salespeople (Onsite); Technical Project Management (Onsite); Successful Meeting Planning (Onsite); Leading Virtual and Remote Teams; Managing a World-Class IT Department (Onsite); Successful Product Management (Onsite); AMA's Course on Mergers and Acquisitions (Onsite); Improving Your Project Management Skills: The Basics for Success; Partnering with Your Boss: Strategic Skills for Administrative Professionals; Greater Productivity Through Improved Work Processes: A Guide for Administrative Professionals (Onsite); Effective Technical Writing (Onsite); Strategies for Developing Effective Presentation Skills (Onsite); Projecting a Positive Professional Image; Customer Service Excellence: How to Win and Keep Customers; Fundamentals of Cost Accounting (Onsite) (Bimonthly); Fixed Asset Accounting (Onsite); AMA's Course on Financial Analysis; Export/Import Procedures and Documentation (Onsite); Recruiting, Interviewing and Selecting Employees (Onsite) (Monthly); Managing Emotions in the Workplace: Strategies for Success (Onsite); Responding to Conflict: Strategies for Improved Communication; Assertiveness Training for Women in Business; Leadership and Team Development for Managerial Success (Onsite); AMA's Leading with Emotional Intelligence (Onsite); AMA's 5-Day MBA Workshop (Onsite); Taking on Greater Responsibility: Step-up Skills for Nonmanagers (Onsite); How to Work Most Effectively with Your Boss (Onsite); Managing Chaos: How to set Priorities and Make Decisions Under Pressure; Moving Ahead: Breaking Behavior Patterns That Hold You Back (Onsite); The Effective Facilitator: Maximizing Involvement and Results; Confronting the Tough Stuff: Advanced Management Skills for Supervisors (Onsite); Coaching and Counseling for Outstanding Job Performance; Conference for Executive Secretaries and Administrative Assistants; Advanced Critical Thinking Applications Workshop (Onsite); Advanced Leadership Communication Strategies (Onsite); AMA's Advanced Course in Strategic Marketing (Onsite); AMA's Advanced Executive Leadership Program (Onsite); AMA's Budgeting Workshop (Onsite); AMA's Comprehensive Project Management Workshop (Onsite); AMA's Finance Workshop for Nonfinancial Executives (Onsite); AMA's Financial Modeling and Forecasting Workshop (Onsite); AMA's Insurance and Risk Management Workshop (Onsite); AMA's Myers-Briggs Type Indicator (MBTI) Certification Program; AMA's PMP Exam Prep Express (Onsite); Building Better Work Relationships: New Techniques for Results-oriented Communication ; Business Conversation Skills for the Multilingual Professional (Onsite); Assertiveness Training for Managers (Onsite); Managing Chaos: Tools to Set Priorities and Make Decisions Under Pressure (Onsite); Improve Your Analytical Skills: Making Information Work for You (Onsite); AMA's 2-Day Business Writing Workshop (Live Online); Business Writing for Administrative Professionals; Business Writing for the Multilingual Professional; Effective Executive Speaking (Onsite); Communication and Interpersonal Skills: A Seminar for IT and Technical Professionals (Onsite); Communication Boot Camp (Onsite); Developing Effective Business Conversation Skills (Onsite); Dynamic Listening Skills for Successful Communication (Onsite); Interpersonal Skills for Managers (Onsite); How to Present Online: A Skills-Based Workshop; Succession Planning: Developing Leaders from Within (Onsite); The 8th Habit: From Effectiveness to Greatness; Collaborative Leadership Skills for Managers (Onsite); How to Write a Killer Marketing Plan (Onsite); Fundamentals of Marketing: Your Action Plan for Success; Information Technology Project Management (Onsite); Best Practices for the Multi-project Manager (Onsite); Managerial and Team-building Skills for Project Managers; Fundamentals of Purchasing for the New Buyer (Onsite); Selling to Major Accounts: A Strategic Approach (Onsite); Strategic Sales Negotiations (Onsite).

44487 ■ Association for Corporate Growth - Toronto Chapter (ACG) [Canadian Angus Association]
720 Spadina Ave., Ste. 202
Toronto, ON, Canada M5S 2T9
Ph: (416)868-1881
Fax: (416)391-3633
Co. E-mail: acgtoronto@acg.org
URL: http://www.acg.org/toronto
Contact: Stephen B. Smith, President
Description: Professionals with a leadership role in strategic corporate growth. Seeks to facilitate the professional advancement of members, and the practice of corporate growth management. Fosters communication and cooperation among members; conducts continuing professional education programs. **Founded:** 1973. **Publications:** *Mergers & Acquisitions - The Dealmaker's Journal* (Monthly). **Educational Activities:** Association for Corporate Growth - Toronto Chapter Board meeting (Monthly); Capital Connection (Annual).

44488 ■ Business Modeling and Integration Domain Task Force (BMIDTF)
Object Management Group
109 Highland Ave.
Needham, MA 02494
Ph: (781)444-0404
Fax: (781)444-0320
Co. E-mail: info@omg.org
URL: http://bmi.omg.org
Contact: Mr. Fred A. Cummins, Co-Chairperson
Description: Aims to empower all companies, across all industries, to develop and operate business processes that span multiple applications and business partners, behind the firewall and over the Internet. **Scope:** business process management. **Founded:** 2000. **Subscriptions:** articles papers.

44489 ■ Canadian Institute of Management (CIM) [Institut Canadien de Gestion]
Lower Level
15 Collier St.
Barrie, ON, Canada L4M 1G5
Ph: (705)725-8926
Fax: (705)725-8196
Co. E-mail: office@cim.ca
URL: http://www.cim.ca
Contact: Dr. Matthew Jelavic, President
Description: Management personnel. Seeks to advance the practice of business management; promotes continuing professional development of members. Serves as a clearinghouse on management and related topics; facilitates exchange of information among members; makes available educational and training programs. **Founded:** 1942. **Publications:** *Canadian Manager* (Quarterly); *Canadian Manager: The Magazine for Managers* (Quarterly).

44490 ■ Canadian Management Centre (CMC)
150 York St., 5th Fl.
Toronto, ON, Canada M5H 3S5
Free: 877-262-2519
Fax: (416)214-6047
Co. E-mail: cmcinfo@cmcoutperform.com
URL: http://cmcoutperform.com
Contact: John Wright, President
Description: Managers of corporations and organizations. Promotes excellence in management. Conducts educational and training programs for management personnel. **Scope:** Provides courses in areas such as general management, communications, marketing, sales, project management and finance. Specialized services include customized on-site training and programs tailored for the government sector. **Founded:** 1963. **Publications:** "The Seven-Second Advantage"; "Stress and Coaching"; "Great Managers Attract (and Keep) Great Talent"; "Why Aren't There More Good Managers?"; "Don't Delegate More - Delegate More Effectively"; "Managing in Uncertain Times: Transforming Employees from "Comfeartable" to Courageous"; "Ten Obstacles to Successful Decision Making"; "How to Be a Super Supervisor"; "The Evolution of Diversity: From 'The Right Thing' to Business Strategy"; "Okay, Okay, We Get It About Talent Management, But Do We Really"; "What High-Performing Companies Are Doing Now to Retain Talent Later"; "How Do You Want To Be Treated"; "The Ethics Dilemma"; "Understanding And Coping With Difficult Managers"; "Great Managers Lead Differently"; "Time Management for the Hurried and the Harried Professional"; "Well-Trained People Are Priceless"; "What Should We Be Measuring-Satisfaction or Engagement". **Educational Activities:** Communicating Change; Strategic Planning; Strategic Agility and Resilience: Embracing Change to Drive Growth; Moving Ahead: Breaking Behaviour Patterns That Hold You Back; Financial Modeling and Forecasting; High-Impact Decision Making (Onsite); Making the Transition to Supervising and Managing Others; Management Skills for New Supervisors and Managers; PMP Exam Prep Workshop (Onsite); Project Cost Management: Estimating, Budgeting and Earned Value Analysis (Onsite); The Comprehensive Project Management Workshop (Onsite); Strategy Execution: Getting it Done (Onsite); Train the Trainer: Facilitation Skills Workshop Onsite; Confronting the Tough Stuff: Turning Managerial Challenges into Positive Results (Bimonthly); Process Management: Applying Process Mapping to Analyze and Improve Your Operation (Periodic); Developing Executive Leadership (Periodic); Leadership and Team Development for Managerial Success (Bimonthly); Canadian Management Centre's 5-Day "MBA"; Stepping Up to Leadership; The Project Planning Workshop; Negotiating to Win; High Performance Business Writing; Maximum Performance Leadership Canada; Fundamentals of Marketing: Your Action Plan for Success; Preparing for Leadership: What It Takes to Take the Lead; Assertiveness Training for Managers; Assertiveness Training for Women in Business Canada; Responding to Conflict: Strategies for Improved Communication; Communication and Interpersonal Skills for IT & Technical Professionals; Interpersonal Skills for Managers; Fundamentals of Purchasing; CMC's Course on Financial Analysis; Leadership Skills for Supervisors; Dealing with Competing Demands; Successfully Managing People; Improving Your Managerial Effectiveness; The Effective Facilitator; Getting Results Without Authority; Improving Your Project Management Skills: The Basics for Success; Senior Project Management; Technical Project Management; Fundamentals of Human Resources Management; Coaching: A Strategic Tool for Effective Leadership; Communicating Up, Down and Across the Organization (Bimonthly); How to Communicate with Diplomacy, Tact and Credibility (Bimonthly). **Seminars:** Skills Plus: Selling Different Clients Differently, Toronto, May, 2007; Management Skills for New Managers, Calgary, May, 2007; Time and Territory Management for Salespeople, Toronto, May, 2007; Developing Executive Leadership, Toronto, Apr, 2007; Building Business Acumen for Learning Professionals, Toronto, Apr, 2007; Communicating Up, Down and Across the Organization, Toronto, Mar, 2007; Managing Customer Conflict, Toronto, Feb, 2007; Negotiating to Win, Toronto, Jan, 2007.

44491 ■ *Canadian Manager*
Lower Level
15 Collier St.
Barrie, ON, Canada L4M 1G5
Ph: (705)725-8926
Fax: (705)725-8196
Co. E-mail: office@cim.ca
URL: http://www.cim.ca
Contact: Dr. Matthew Jelavic, President
Released: Quarterly **Price:** free for members.

44492 ■ International Council for Small Business (ICSB)
Funger Hall, Ste. 315
2201 G. St. NW
Washington, DC 20052
Ph: (202)994-0704
Fax: (202)994-4930
Co. E-mail: info@icsb.org
URL: http://www.icsb.org
Contact: Ruben Ascua, President
Description: Management educators, researchers, government officials and professionals in 80 countries. Fosters discussion of topics pertaining to the

development and improvement of small business management. **Founded:** 1955. **Publications:** *Journal of Small Business Management* (Quarterly).

44493 ■ **Machinery Information Management Open Systems Alliance (MIMOSA)**
204 Marina Dr., Ste. 100
Tuscaloosa, AL 35406
Ph: (949)625-8616
Fax: (949)625-8616
Co. E-mail: info@mimosa.org
URL: http://www.mimosa.org
Contact: Alan T. Johnston, President
Description: Develops and encourages the adoption of open information standards for Operations and Maintenance and Collaborative Asset Lifecycle Management in commercial and military applications. Provides a forum for the members, bringing together subject matter experts in cross disciplinary technologies, to enable complex solutions for Equipment Operators, Maintainers and Fleet Managers.

44494 ■ *Mergers & Acquisitions - The Dealmaker's Journal*
720 Spadina Ave., Ste. 202
Toronto, ON, Canada M5S 2T9
Ph: (416)868-1881
Fax: (416)391-3633
Co. E-mail: acgtoronto@acg.org
URL: http://www.acg.org/toronto
Contact: Stephen B. Smith, President
Released: Monthly **Price:** Included in membership.

44495 ■ **National Management Association (NMA)**
2210 Arbor Blvd.
Dayton, OH 45439
Ph: (937)294-0421
Co. E-mail: nma@nma1.org
URL: http://www.nma1.org
Contact: Steve Bailey, President
E-mail: steve@nma1.org
Description: Business and industrial management personnel; membership comes from supervisory level, with the remainder from middle management and above. Seeks to develop and recognize management as a profession and to promote the free enterprise system. Prepares chapter programs on basic management, management policy and practice, communications, human behavior, industrial relations, economics, political education, and liberal education. Maintains speakers' bureau and hall of fame. Maintains educational, charitable, and research programs. Sponsors charitable programs. **Founded:** 1925. **Publications:** *Manage* (Quarterly); *Manage* (Quarterly); *National Speakers' Directory* (Periodic). **Awards:** NMA Leadership Speech Contest Award (Annual); Executive of the Year Award (Annual).

44496 ■ **Organization Design Forum (ODF)**
5016 E Mulberry Dr.
Phoenix, AZ 85018-6525
Ph: (602)510-9105
Co. E-mail: info@organizationdesignforum.org
URL: http://organizationdesignforum.org
Contact: Tanya Spelts, Administrator
Description: Academics, practitioners, consultants, and human resource professionals. Works to promote the knowledge and practice of organizational design. Focuses on the effect organization structure and processes have on the performance of individuals, groups, and the organization itself. Offers basic and advanced training in organization design techniques. **Scope:** recipients of Crystal Apple Award presentation. **Founded:** 1989. **Subscriptions:** 3 video recordings. **Publications:** *Organization Design.*

44497 ■ **SCORE**
1175 Herndon Pkwy., Ste. 900
Herndon, VA 20170
Free: 800-634-0245
Co. E-mail: help@score.org
URL: http://www.score.org
Contact: Kenneth W. Yancey, Jr., Chief Executive Officer
Description: Serves as volunteer program sponsored by U.S. Small Business Administration in which working and retired business management professionals provide free business counseling to men and women

who are considering starting a small business, encountering problems with their business, or expanding their business. Offers free one-on-one counseling, online counseling and low cost workshops on a variety of business topics. **Scope:** business. **Founded:** 1964. **Subscriptions:** books clippings periodicals. **Publications:** *SCORE eNews* (Monthly); *SCORE Today* (Monthly). **Awards:** SCORE Chapter of the Year Award (Annual); Outstanding Woman-owned Small Business Award (Annual).

44498 ■ **Society for Advancement of Management (SAM)**
6300 Ocean Dr.
OCNR 330, Unit 5807
Corpus Christi, TX 78412
Ph: (361)825-3045
Free: 888-827-6077
Fax: (361)825-5609
Co. E-mail: moustafa.abdelsamad@tamucc.edu
URL: http://www.samnational.org
Contact: Dr. Moustafa H. Abdelsamad, President
Description: Represents management executives in industry commerce, government, and education. Fields of interest include management education, policy and strategy, MIS, international management, administration, budgeting, collective bargaining, distribution, incentives, materials handling, quality control, and training. **Founded:** 1912. **Publications:** *Advanced Management Journal* (Quarterly); *SAM Advanced Management Journal* (Quarterly); *SAM Management In Practice* (Quarterly); *The SAM News International* (Quarterly); *Society for Advancement of Management--International Business Conference Proceedings* (Annual). **Educational Activities:** Society for Advancement of Management Meeting (Annual); Society for Advancement of Management International Business Conference.

44499 ■ **Women in Management (WIM)**
PO Box 6690
Elgin, IL 60121-6690
Co. E-mail: wimfoxvalley@gmail.com
URL: http://www.wimonline.org
Contact: Dana Vierck, President
Description: Supports network of women in professional and management positions that facilitate the exchange of experience and ideas. Promotes self-growth in management; provides speakers who are successful in management; sponsors workshops and special interest groups to discuss problems and share job experiences. **Founded:** 1976. **Publications:** *Women in Management--National Directory* (Annual).

44500 ■ **World Confederation of Productivity Science (WCPS)**
c/o Linda Carbone, Executive Secretary
500 Sherbrooke St. W, Ste. 900
Montreal, QC, Canada H3A 3C6
Co. E-mail: secretariat@wcps.info
URL: http://www.wcps.info
Contact: John Heap, President
Description: Fraternal association of manufacturing and commercial enterprises and employees, government agencies, professional institutions, and researchers. Goals are to promote productivity science, advance management techniques, and improve the quality of working life and environment. **Founded:** 1969. **Subscriptions:** 3000. **Educational Activities:** World Productivity Congress (Biennial).

EDUCATIONAL PROGRAMS

44501 ■ **The 8th Habit: From Effectiveness to Greatness**
American Management Association (AMA)
1601 Broadway
New York, NY 10019-7420
Ph: (212)586-8100
Free: 877-566-9441
Fax: (212)903-8168
Co. E-mail: customerservice@amanet.org
URL: http://www.amanet.org
Contact: Edward T. Reilly, President
URL(s): www.amanet.org/training/seminars/The-8th-Habit-Unleashing-the-Greatness-in-Yourself-and-Others.aspx. **Price:** $2,195, Non-members; $1,995, Members AMA; $1,708, Members GSA. **Description:**

Learn to reach your full potential and inspire others through the teachings of Dr. Stephen R. Covey of FranklinCovey. **Audience:** Directors, VPs, team leaders, executives, department heads and experienced managers.

44502 ■ **Achieving Leadership Success Through People (Onsite)**
American Management Association (AMA)
1601 Broadway
New York, NY 10019-7420
Ph: (212)586-8100
Free: 877-566-9441
Fax: (212)903-8168
Co. E-mail: customerservice@amanet.org
URL: http://www.amanet.org
Contact: Edward T. Reilly, President
URL(s): www.amanet.org/training/seminars/Achieving-Leadership-Success-Through-People.aspx. **Price:** $2,645, Non-members; $2,395, Members AMA; $2,051, Members GSA. **Description:** Learn to lead more effectively by creating rapport, synergy, and two-way trust in this two-day course. **Audience:** Senior managers, directors, vice presidents and executives.

44503 ■ **Advanced Issues in Employee Relations**
Seminar Information Service Inc.
20 Executive Park, Ste. 120
Irvine, CA 92614
Ph: (949)261-9104
Free: 877-SEM-INFO
Fax: (949)261-1963
Co. E-mail: info@seminarinformation.com
URL: http://www.seminarinformation.com
Description: Key topics include coaching managers to more effectively manage high performing employees who consistently demonstrate one serious performance failing, collaborating with managers to assist them in focusing on performance issues without being influenced by employees' personal circumstances, working with managers on dealing more effectively with strong negative employee reactions to direction or feedback, and addressing managers' behavior that is inappropriate and potentially high risk. **Audience:** Professionals.

44504 ■ **Advanced IT Audit School (Onsite)**
Seminar Information Service Inc.
20 Executive Park, Ste. 120
Irvine, CA 92614
Ph: (949)261-9104
Free: 877-SEM-INFO
Fax: (949)261-1963
Co. E-mail: info@seminarinformation.com
URL: http://www.seminarinformation.com
Price: $3,095. **Description:** This advanced hands-on workshop will show you how to use software tools to identify and test key control points in your organization's network infrastructure. **Audience:** IT auditors managers and supervisors.

44505 ■ **AMA's 5-Day MBA Workshop (Onsite)**
American Management Association (AMA)
1601 Broadway
New York, NY 10019-7420
Ph: (212)586-8100
Free: 877-566-9441
Fax: (212)903-8168
Co. E-mail: customerservice@amanet.org
URL: http://www.amanet.org
Contact: Edward T. Reilly, President
URL(s): www.amaseminars.org/training/seminars/5-Day-MBA-Workshop.
aspx?state=Washington&city=Seattle. **Description:** Five-day seminar; covers a broad overview of business concepts typically covered in university-level MBA programs. **Audience:** Anyone interested in obtaining an effective, broad-based overview of the functional areas often covered in university-level MBA programs. **Telecommunication Services:** customerservice@amanet.org.

44506 ■ AMA's Advanced Executive Leadership Program (Onsite)
American Management Association (AMA)
1601 Broadway
New York, NY 10019-7420
Ph: (212)586-8100
Free: 877-566-9441
Fax: (212)903-8168
Co. E-mail: customerservice@amanet.org
URL: http://www.amanet.org
Contact: Edward T. Reilly, President
URL(s): www.amanet.org/training/seminars/Advanced-Executive-Leadership-Program.aspx.
Price: $2,645, Non-members; $2,395, Members AMA; $2,051, Members GSA. **Description:** An intensive three day seminar focusing on executive leadership. **Audience:** Executives, directors and managers.

44507 ■ AMA's Comprehensive Project Management Workshop (Onsite)
American Management Association (AMA)
1601 Broadway
New York, NY 10019-7420
Ph: (212)586-8100
Free: 877-566-9441
Fax: (212)903-8168
Co. E-mail: customerservice@amanet.org
URL: http://www.amanet.org
Contact: Edward T. Reilly, President
URL(s): www.amanet.org/training/seminars/Comprehensive-Project-Management-Workshop.aspx. **Price:** $3,095, Non-members; $2,795, Members AMA; $2,393, Members GSA. **Description:** Five-day seminar examining the framework, reviewing project management body of knowledge, initiating the project, planning the project, executing project plan, monitoring and controlling project and closing the project. **Audience:** Project managers, program managers, and project team leaders.

44508 ■ AMA's Leading with Emotional Intelligence (Onsite)
American Management Association (AMA)
1601 Broadway
New York, NY 10019-7420
Ph: (212)586-8100
Free: 877-566-9441
Fax: (212)903-8168
Co. E-mail: customerservice@amanet.org
URL: http://www.amanet.org
Contact: Edward T. Reilly, President
URL(s): www.amanet.org/. **Description:** Covers the importance of emotional intelligence in the workplace, and developing a style to effectively communicate and use emotions positively. **Audience:** Business professionals who want to maximize their performance by increasing emotion management and self-understanding through emotional intelligence training. **Telecommunication Services:** customerservice@amanet.org.

44509 ■ The Art of Coaching Employees to Excel (Onsite)
Padgett-Thompson Seminars
Rockhurst University CEC
14502 W 105th St.
Lenexa, KS 66215
Free: 800-349-1935
URL: http://www.findaseminar.com/tpd/Padgett-Thompson-Seminars.asp
URL(s): www.findaseminar.com/event1.asp?eventID=10000. **Description:** Teaches managers how to approach performance issues, set morale, and create self-esteem in the workplace. **Audience:** Professionals.

44510 ■ Assertive Management (Onsite)
Seminar Information Service Inc.
20 Executive Park, Ste. 120
Irvine, CA 92614
Ph: (949)261-9104
Free: 877-SEM-INFO

Fax: (949)261-1963
Co. E-mail: info@seminarinformation.com
URL: http://www.seminarinformation.com
URL(s): www.seminarinformation.com/qqbeah/positive-assertive. **Description:** Develop the qualities necessary for successful, assertive management. Participants gain confidence and skill in being 'proactive' in communicating with others, including how to use positive, win-win approaches and to defuse emotionally charged situations in order to work more effectively with their fellow workers, supervisors and subordinates. **Audience:** Supervisors and managers. **Telecommunication Services:** info@seminarinformation.com.

44511 ■ Assertiveness Skills: Communicating with Authority and Impact (Onsite)
Seminar Information Service Inc.
20 Executive Park, Ste. 120
Irvine, CA 92614
Ph: (949)261-9104
Free: 877-SEM-INFO
Fax: (949)261-1963
Co. E-mail: info@seminarinformation.com
URL: http://www.seminarinformation.com
Price: $1,890. **Description:** Learn how to develop a positive assertive style, including how to respond productively to challenging behavior patterns in others, react positively in demanding situations, and improve your relationships through a productive and powerful attitude. **Audience:** Industry professionals.

44512 ■ Assertiveness Skills for Managers and Supervisors (Onsite)
Padgett-Thompson Seminars
Rockhurst University CEC
14502 W 105th St.
Lenexa, KS 66215
Free: 800-349-1935
URL: http://www.findaseminar.com/tpd/Padgett-Thompson-Seminars.asp
URL(s): findaseminar.com/GENERAL-MANAGEMENT-Training/Assertiveness-Skills-for-Managers-and-Supervisors-Seminar-by-Padgett-Thompson-Seminars/859.html?filter=ON&city=Oakland&state=CA&category=GENERAL-MANAGEMENT. **Price:** $199. **Description:** Attendees will gain assertiveness skills they need to achieve the recognition they deserve. **Audience:** Professionals, managers and supervisors.

44513 ■ Assertiveness Training for Managers (Onsite)
American Management Association (AMA)
1601 Broadway
New York, NY 10019-7420
Ph: (212)586-8100
Free: 877-566-9441
Fax: (212)903-8168
Co. E-mail: customerservice@amanet.org
URL: http://www.amanet.org
Contact: Edward T. Reilly, President
URL(s): www.amanet.org/training/seminars/Assertiveness-Training-for-Managers.aspx. **Price:** $2,345, Non-members; $2,095, Members AMA; $1,794, Members GSA. **Description:** Learn how your behavior impacts your performance and how to take control without isolating others. **Audience:** Managers.

44514 ■ Become a World Class Assistant (Onsite)
Seminar Information Service Inc.
20 Executive Park, Ste. 120
Irvine, CA 92614
Ph: (949)261-9104
Free: 877-SEM-INFO
Fax: (949)261-1963
Co. E-mail: info@seminarinformation.com
URL: http://www.seminarinformation.com
URL(s): www.seminarinformation.com/details.cfm?qc=qqbqyw. **Price:** $2,295. **Description:** How to partner strategically for business success. **Audience:** Seasoned executive assistants and other high-caliber assistants.

44515 ■ Best Practices for the Multi-project Manager (Onsite)
American Management Association (AMA)
1601 Broadway
New York, NY 10019-7420
Ph: (212)586-8100
Free: 877-566-9441
Fax: (212)903-8168
Co. E-mail: customerservice@amanet.org
URL: http://www.amanet.org
Contact: Edward T. Reilly, President
URL(s): www.amaseminars.org/training/seminars/onsite/Best-Practices-for-the-Multi-Project-Manager.aspx. **Description:** Covers balancing work load, reducing risk and conflict, time management, prioritizing, and monitoring and reporting on multiple projects. **Audience:** Project managers who are working on multiple projects simultaneously and would like to learn tips and techniques to improve their effectiveness and efficiency. **Telecommunication Services:** customerservice@amanet.org.

44516 ■ Building a Positive, Motivated and Cooperative Team (Onsite)
Seminar Information Service Inc.
20 Executive Park, Ste. 120
Irvine, CA 92614
Ph: (949)261-9104
Free: 877-SEM-INFO
Fax: (949)261-1963
Co. E-mail: info@seminarinformation.com
URL: http://www.seminarinformation.com
URL(s): www.seminarinformation.com/qqbsmq/building-a-positive-motivated-and-cooperative-team. **Price:** $199. **Description:** Learn to create positive and productive results within the workplace utilizing real world examples. **Audience:** Professionals.

44517 ■ Building a Successful Business Analysis Work Plan
Learning Tree International Inc.
1805 Library St.
Reston, VA 20190-5660
Ph: (703)709-9119
Free: 800-843-8733
Fax: (703)709-6405
Co. E-mail: uscourses@learningtree.com
URL: http://www.learningtree.com
Contact: Nicholas R. Schacht, President
URL(s): www.learningtree.com/investor/releases/pr090507.htm. **Description:** Learn to develop and execute a work plan using practical project management tools, methods, and techniques. **Audience:** Business professionals.

44518 ■ Building a Successful Business Analysis Work Plan: Effective Project Management Skills for Business Analysts (Onsite)
Seminar Information Service Inc.
20 Executive Park, Ste. 120
Irvine, CA 92614
Ph: (949)261-9104
Free: 877-SEM-INFO
Fax: (949)261-1963
Co. E-mail: info@seminarinformation.com
URL: http://www.seminarinformation.com
Price: $2,490.00. **Description:** Learn practical project management methods, tools and techniques to adapt a work plan to the needs of the project and its stakeholders.

44519 ■ Business Analysis Essentials (Onsite)
Seminar Information Service Inc.
20 Executive Park, Ste. 120
Irvine, CA 92614
Ph: (949)261-9104
Free: 877-SEM-INFO
Fax: (949)261-1963
Co. E-mail: info@seminarinformation.com
URL: http://www.seminarinformation.com
Price: $2,195. **Description:** Learn to define the scope of work and master requirements-gathering techniques that will work for a variety of projects and audiences. **Audience:** Systems analysts, business

analysts, requirements analysts, developers, and software engineers. **Dates and Locations:** New York, NY; Dallas, TX; and Orlando, FL.

44520 ■ Business Process Analysis
Seminar Information Service Inc.
20 Executive Park, Ste. 120
Irvine, CA 92614
Ph: (949)261-9104
Free: 877-SEM-INFO
Fax: (949)261-1963
Co. E-mail: info@seminarinformation.com
URL: http://www.seminarinformation.com
Price: $2,495. **Description:** Learn to model business processes as they are currently enacted, assess the quality of those business processes, and collaborate with the stakeholders to identify improvements. **Audience:** Systems analysts, business analysts, IT project managers, project managers, project coordinators, and project analysts. **Dates and Locations:** Cities throughout Canada.

44521 ■ Canadian Management Centre's 5-Day "MBA"
Canadian Management Centre (CMC)
150 York St., 5th Fl.
Toronto, ON, Canada M5H 3S5
Free: 877-262-2519
Fax: (416)214-6047
Co. E-mail: cmcinfo@cmcoutperform.com
URL: http://cmcoutperform.com
Contact: John Wright, President
Price: $3,195.00 Canadian for non-members; $2,945.00 Canadian for CMC members. **Description:** Seminar that covers how the various components of a business must be linked, aligned and integrated into a successful business system, including business competencies, finance and accounting, marketing strategies, and leadership. Held in Toronto, ON; Ottawa, ON; and Calgary, AB. Also offers course on request.

44522 ■ Coaching: A Strategic Tool for Effective Leadership
Canadian Management Centre (CMC)
150 York St., 5th Fl.
Toronto, ON, Canada M5H 3S5
Free: 877-262-2519
Fax: (416)214-6047
Co. E-mail: cmcinfo@cmcoutperform.com
URL: http://cmcoutperform.com
Contact: John Wright, President
URL(s): www.cmctraining.org/coaching-effective-leadership. **Description:** Covers creating a successful environment, problem resolution, teamwork, soliciting valuable feedback, and models for successful coaching. **Audience:** Managers, supervisors, project managers and team leaders. **Telecommunication Services:** cmcinfo@cmctraining.org.

44523 ■ Coaching and Counseling for Outstanding Job Performance
American Management Association (AMA)
1601 Broadway
New York, NY 10019-7420
Ph: (212)586-8100
Free: 877-566-9441
Fax: (212)903-8168
Co. E-mail: customerservice@amanet.org
URL: http://www.amanet.org
Contact: Edward T. Reilly, President
URL(s): www.amaseminars.org/training/seminars/Coaching-and-Counseling-for-Outstanding-Job-Performance.aspx. **Price:** $2,195, Non-members; $1,995, Members; $1,708, Members General Services Administration (GSA). **Description:** Covers creating a successful environment, problem resolution, teamwork, soliciting valuable feedback, and models for successful coaching. Held in Arlington, VA; San Francisco, CA; and Washington, DC. Also available live online. **Audience:** Managers who want to improve results and get higher performance from their team. **Dates and Locations:** 2015 Mar 02-04; venue not reported. **Telecommunication Services:** customerservice@amanet.org.

44524 ■ Coaching, Mentoring & Team-Building Skills (Onsite)
Seminar Information Service Inc.
20 Executive Park, Ste. 120
Irvine, CA 92614
Ph: (949)261-9104
Free: 877-SEM-INFO
Fax: (949)261-1963
Co. E-mail: info@seminarinformation.com
URL: http://www.seminarinformation.com
URL(s): www.seminarinformation.com/details.cfm?qc=qqbvsr. **Price:** $299. **Description:** Learn how to motivate, inspire and guide people to success, including tools for improving cooperation, communication, and a high-energy environment that fosters teamwork. **Audience:** Managers, supervisors, team leaders and business owners.

44525 ■ Collaborative Leadership Skills for Managers (Onsite)
American Management Association (AMA)
1601 Broadway
New York, NY 10019-7420
Ph: (212)586-8100
Free: 877-566-9441
Fax: (212)903-8168
Co. E-mail: customerservice@amanet.org
URL: http://www.amanet.org
Contact: Edward T. Reilly, President
URL(s): www.amanet.org/training/seminars/Collaborative-Leadership-Skills-for-Managers.aspx. **Price:** $2,195, Non-members; $1,995, Members AMA; $1,708, Members GSA. **Description:** Learn to develop a collaborative style to build a mutual trust with your team and other departments. **Audience:** Managers.

44526 ■ The Comprehensive Project Management Workshop (Onsite)
Canadian Management Centre (CMC)
150 York St., 5th Fl.
Toronto, ON, Canada M5H 3S5
Free: 877-262-2519
Fax: (416)214-6047
Co. E-mail: cmcinfo@cmcoutperform.com
URL: http://cmcoutperform.com
Contact: John Wright, President
URL(s): cmcoutperform.com/comprehensive-project-management. **Price:** $2,995, Non-members; $2,745, Members AMA. **Description:** Promotes project management expertise and prepares participants for PMP certification in this five-day seminar. **Audience:** Project managers.

44527 ■ Conducting Employee Performance Evaluations (Onsite)
Padgett-Thompson Seminars
Rockhurst University CEC
14502 W 105th St.
Lenexa, KS 66215
Free: 800-349-1935
URL: http://www.findaseminar.com/tpd/Padgett-Thompson-Seminars.asp
URL(s): www.findaseminar.com/event1.asp?eventID=921. **Description:** For managers and supervisors who want to learn more about conducting fair, legal evaluations and make the review process an integral part of improving employee performance. **Audience:** Human resource professionals, managers, and supervisors.

44528 ■ Confronting the Tough Stuff: Advanced Management Skills for Supervisors (Onsite)
American Management Association (AMA)
1601 Broadway
New York, NY 10019-7420
Ph: (212)586-8100
Free: 877-566-9441
Fax: (212)903-8168
Co. E-mail: customerservice@amanet.org
URL: http://www.amanet.org
Contact: Edward T. Reilly, President
URL(s): www.amaseminars.org/training/seminars/onsite/Confronting-the-Tough-Stuff-Management-Skills-for-Supervisors.aspx. **Description:** Covers diffusing potential legal situations, dealing with challenges, writing performance evaluations, enhancing

productivity, and managing diversity. **Audience:** Managers and supervisors with three to five years of experience, process and production supervisors and graduates of AMA's Management Skills for New Managers, Management Skills for New Supervisors and Making the Transition from Staff Member to Supervisor. **Telecommunication Services:** customerservice@amanet.org.

44529 ■ Confronting the Tough Stuff: Turning Managerial Challenges into Positive Results
Canadian Management Centre (CMC)
150 York St., 5th Fl.
Toronto, ON, Canada M5H 3S5
Free: 877-262-2519
Fax: (416)214-6047
Co. E-mail: cmcinfo@cmcoutperform.com
URL: http://cmcoutperform.com
Contact: John Wright, President
URL(s): www.cmctraining.org/managerial-challenges-positive-results. **Price:** $1,995.00 Canadian for non-members; $1,845.00 Canadian for CMC members. **Frequency:** Bimonthly. **Description:** Seminar that covers the challenges and the problem-solving skills in the workplace, including coaching uncooperative employees, constructive and destructive conflict, techniques for using conflict to increase cohesion, four stages of mediation and techniques to mediate disputes between employees, and avoid potentially litigious situations. Held in Mississauga, ON and Toronto, ON. **Audience:** supervisors and managers. **Telecommunication Services:** cmcinfo@cmctraining.org.

44530 ■ Creative Leadership for Managers, Supervisors, and Team Leaders (Onsite)
Fred Pryor Seminars & CareerTrack
5700 Broadmoor St., Ste. 300
Mission, KS 66202
Ph: (800)780-8476
Free: 800-780-8476
Fax: (913)967-8849
Co. E-mail: customerservice@pryor.com
URL: http://www.pryor.com
Contact: Phil Love, Chief Executive Officer
Price: $179.00; $169.00 for groups of 5 or more. **Description:** Learn techniques that increase your leadership skills and get employees on track in performance and productivity including, why traditional management models just don't measure up in today's workplace and what to use instead. **Audience:** Industry professional. **Dates and Locations:** Cities throughout the United States.

44531 ■ Creative Leadership Workshop for Managers, Supervisors, and Team Leaders
Seminar Information Service Inc.
20 Executive Park, Ste. 120
Irvine, CA 92614
Ph: (949)261-9104
Free: 877-SEM-INFO
Fax: (949)261-1963
Co. E-mail: info@seminarinformation.com
URL: http://www.seminarinformation.com
URL(s): www.seminarinformation.com/details.cfm?qc=qqbqgb. **Price:** $348. **Description:** Learn a bold new approach to motivate employees for greater productivity, stronger teamwork and improved morale in today's complex workforce. **Audience:** Managers, supervisors and team leaders .

44532 ■ Creativity and Innovation (Onsite)
Seminar Information Service Inc.
20 Executive Park, Ste. 120
Irvine, CA 92614
Ph: (949)261-9104
Free: 877-SEM-INFO
Fax: (949)261-1963
Co. E-mail: info@seminarinformation.com
URL: http://www.seminarinformation.com
Price: $2,095, Non-members; $1,895, Members AMA. **Description:** Develop creative thinking methods to generate ideas and solutions and learn how to align your ideas with corporate needs to add value and increase recognition. **Audience:** Managers, team leaders, directors, project managers, and supervisors . **Dates and Locations:** New York, NY; and Arlington, VA.

44533 ■ Critical Thinking: A New Paradigm for Peak Performance (Onsite)
Seminar Information Service Inc.
20 Executive Park, Ste. 120
Irvine, CA 92614
Ph: (949)261-9104
Free: 877-SEM-INFO
Fax: (949)261-1963
Co. E-mail: info@seminarinformation.com
URL: http://www.seminarinformation.com
URL(s): www.seminarinformation.com/details.cfm?qc=qqbvpa. **Price:** $2,095, Non-members; $1,895, Members. **Description:** Learn different styles of thinking and identify your personal preferences, including how to challenge assumptions and expand perceptions about situations. **Audience:** Executives, directors, managers, team leaders and business professionals .

44534 ■ Criticism & Discipline Skills for Managers and Supervisors (Onsite)
Fred Pryor Seminars & CareerTrack
5700 Broadmoor St., Ste. 300
Mission, KS 66202
Ph: (800)780-8476
Free: 800-780-8476
Fax: (913)967-8849
Co. E-mail: customerservice@pryor.com
URL: http://www.pryor.com
Contact: Phil Love, Chief Executive Officer
Description: Learn proven techniques for managing difficult employees without incurring resentment, making enemies, or destroying relationships, including how to discipline employees who have a bad attitude, are chronically tardy, miss work often, refuse to take responsibility and challenge your authority. **Audience:** Industry professionals.

44535 ■ Developing Executive Leadership
Canadian Management Centre (CMC)
150 York St., 5th Fl.
Toronto, ON, Canada M5H 3S5
Free: 877-262-2519
Fax: (416)214-6047
Co. E-mail: cmcinfo@cmcoutperform.com
URL: http://cmcoutperform.com
Contact: John Wright, President
URL(s): www.cmctraining.org. **Price:** $2,195.00 Canadian for non-members; $1,995.00 Canadian for CMC members. **Frequency:** Periodic. **Description:** Seminar that covers leadership in today's business environment, including techniques to improve effectiveness, leading individuals and groups, keys to developing influence, and how to create your own leadership development plan. **Audience:** executive leaders. **Telecommunication Services:** cmcinfo@cmctraining.org.

44536 ■ Developing Into a Powerful Leader (Onsite)
Seminar Information Service Inc.
20 Executive Park, Ste. 120
Irvine, CA 92614
Ph: (949)261-9104
Free: 877-SEM-INFO
Fax: (949)261-1963
Co. E-mail: info@seminarinformation.com
URL: http://www.seminarinformation.com
URL(s): www.seminarinformation.com/details.cfm?qc=qqbeak. **Price:** $1,595. **Description:** Enhance your ability to lead others and have them feel good about the process. **Audience:** Managers.

44537 ■ Developing Your Emotional Intelligence (Onsite)
Padgett-Thompson Seminars
Rockhurst University CEC
14502 W 105th St.
Lenexa, KS 66215
Free: 800-349-1935
URL: http://www.findaseminar.com/tpd/Padgett-Thompson-Seminars.asp
URL(s): www.findaseminar.com/PERSONAL-DEVELOPMENT-Training/Developing-Your-Emotional-Intelligence-Seminar-by-American-Management-Association-Seminars/8018.html?filter=ON&city=ARLINGTON&state=VA. **Price:** $2,345, Non-members; $2,095, Members AMA

Member. **Description:** Seminar provides skills to the eliminate stress and frustration brought on by others in the workplace. **Audience:** Business professionals.

44538 ■ The Difference Between Good and Great Supervisors
Padgett-Thompson Seminars
Rockhurst University CEC
14502 W 105th St.
Lenexa, KS 66215
Free: 800-349-1935
URL: http://www.findaseminar.com/tpd/Padgett-Thompson-Seminars.asp
URL(s): www.findaseminar.com/event1.asp?eventID=9782. **Description:** Workshop presents positive solutions, real-world tips, and strategies for managers and supervisors. **Audience:** Supervisors and professionals.

44539 ■ Driving Innovation: Proven Processes, Tools and Strategies for Growth (Onsite)
Seminar Information Service Inc.
20 Executive Park, Ste. 120
Irvine, CA 92614
Ph: (949)261-9104
Free: 877-SEM-INFO
Fax: (949)261-1963
Co. E-mail: info@seminarinformation.com
URL: http://www.seminarinformation.com
Price: $1,495.00. **Description:** Learn to use proven processes and tools to imagine and execute new innovation opportunities, regardless of your creative disposition or your role in the organization.

44540 ■ Earned Value Management Systems (EVMS) for Project Managers
EEI Communications
500 Montgomery St., Ste. 400
Alexandria, VA 22314-5507
Ph: (410)309-8200
Free: 888-253-2762
Fax: (703)683-7310
Co. E-mail: info@eeicom.com
URL: http://www.eeicom.com
Contact: James T. DeGraffenreid, President
URL(s): www.eeicom.com/eei-training-services/classes/project-management/. **Price:** $745.00. **Description:** Seminar based on ANSI/EIA-748-A, Earned Value Management Systems, and the Project Management Institute's (PMI) Project Management Body of Knowledge (PMBOK) that covers resource planning and estimating, project budgeting, EVM (Earned Value Management) performance metrics, variance analyses, and EVMS reports. **Audience:** Newly assigned program managers, project managers and project administrators. **Dates and Locations:** Silver Spring, MD; Alexandria, VA; Hunt Valley, MD; and Columbia, MD. **Telecommunication Services:** info@eeicom.com.

44541 ■ Effective Meeting Management (Onsite)
Seminar Information Service Inc.
20 Executive Park, Ste. 120
Irvine, CA 92614
Ph: (949)261-9104
Free: 877-SEM-INFO
Fax: (949)261-1963
Co. E-mail: info@seminarinformation.com
URL: http://www.seminarinformation.com
URL(s): www.seminarinformation.com. **Price:** Contact for fees. **Description:** Learn how to keep control throughout the meeting, while creating a receptive, engaging, and energetic atmosphere. **Audience:** Individuals in lead worker or group leader positions who are not officially management employees. **Telecommunication Services:** info@seminarinformation.com.

44542 ■ Effective Negotiating
Karrass USA Ltd.
8370 Wilshire Blvd., Ste. 300
Beverly Hills, CA 90211-2333
Ph: (323)866-3800
Free: 800-232-8000

Fax: (800)232-8000
Co. E-mail: mail@karrass.com
URL: http://www.karrass.com
Contact: Dr. Chester L. Karrass, Founder
URL(s): www.karrass.com/effective-negotiating-two-day-seminar. **Description:** Seminar topics include, sticking to your own game plan, what people forget to do, you have more power than you think, and using hidden leverage. **Audience:** Business professionals .

44543 ■ Effective Project Communications, Negotiations and Conflict (Onsite)
EEI Communications
8945 Guilford Rd., Ste. 145
Columbia, MD 21046
Ph: (410)309-8200
Free: 888-253-2762
Fax: (410)630-3980
Co. E-mail: train@eeicom.com
URL: http://www.eeicom.com/eei-training-services
Description: Learn what you need to know to lead projects through their initiation, planning, execution, and control phases, including the skills needed to find common ground, overcome resistance, resolve disputes, and gain commitment to project management efforts. **Audience:** Industry professionals.

44544 ■ Effective Training Techniques for Group Leaders (Onsite)
Seminar Information Service Inc.
20 Executive Park, Ste. 120
Irvine, CA 92614
Ph: (949)261-9104
Free: 877-SEM-INFO
Fax: (949)261-1963
Co. E-mail: info@seminarinformation.com
URL: http://www.seminarinformation.com
URL(s): www.seminarinformation.com/qqadnm/effective-training-techniques-for-group-leaders. **Description:** Provides group leaders precise and practical methods to train their employees. Leaders also learn to spot worker training needs and provide effective on-the-job training. **Audience:** Team leaders. **Telecommunication Services:** info@seminarinformation.com.

44545 ■ Enhancing Your Management Skills (Onsite)
Seminar Information Service Inc.
20 Executive Park, Ste. 120
Irvine, CA 92614
Ph: (949)261-9104
Free: 877-SEM-INFO
Fax: (949)261-1963
Co. E-mail: info@seminarinformation.com
URL: http://www.seminarinformation.com
Description: Learn the critical success factors for driving results through goal alignment, coaching for performance, building trust, and driving committed action through stronger leadership. Receive practical, state-of-the-art tools and techniques for holding conversations that set clear expectations, provide focused feedback, create a motivational environment, and build commitment for needed change. **Audience:** Industry professionals.

44546 ■ Essential Coaching and Mentoring Skills for Managers, Supervisors and Team Leaders (Onsite)
Padgett-Thompson Seminars
Rockhurst University CEC
14502 W 105th St.
Lenexa, KS 66215
Free: 800-349-1935
URL: http://www.findaseminar.com/tpd/Padgett-Thompson-Seminars.asp
URL(s): www.findaseminar.com/event1.asp?eventID=3399. **Price:** $199. **Description:** Seminar provides solutions to the toughest leadership problems. **Audience:** Managers, supervisors, team leaders, and business owners.

44547 ■ Essential Facilitation
Interaction Associates
70 Fargo St., Ste. 908
Boston, MA 02210
Ph: (617)535-7000

Fax: (617)535-7099
URL: http://www.interactionassociates.com
URL(s): interactionassociates.com/public-workshops/
essential-facilitation. **Price:** $2,495. **Description:**
This seminar will show you how to effectively facilitate
meetings and group processes. Addresses content,
conflict, and context within meetings. Held in Luling,
LA; Arlington, VA; San Francisco CA;Boston, MA;
and Dallas, TX. Also available live online. **Audience:**
Professionals. **Dates and Locations:** 2015 Mar 03-
05; venue not reported.

44548 ■ Essentials of Project Management for the Nonproject Manager

American Management Association (AMA)
1601 Broadway
New York, NY 10019-7420
Ph: (212)586-8100
Free: 877-566-9441
Fax: (212)903-8168
Co. E-mail: customerservice@amanet.org
URL: http://www.amanet.org
Contact: Edward T. Reilly, President
URL(s): www.amanet.org/training/seminars/Es-
sentials-of-Project-Management-for-the-Nonproject-
Manager.aspx. **Price:** $2,095, Non-members; $1,895,
Members AMA; $1,623, Members GSA. **Description:**
Learn and apply basic elements of project manage-
ment to your job. Also available live online. **Audi-
ence:** Industry professionals.

44549 ■ Excelling as A Manager or Supervisor (Onsite)

Seminar Information Service Inc.
20 Executive Park, Ste. 120
Irvine, CA 92614
Ph: (949)261-9104
Free: 877-SEM-INFO
Fax: (949)261-1963
Co. E-mail: info@seminarinformation.com
URL: http://www.seminarinformation.com
URL(s): www.seminarinformation.com/details.
cfm?qc=qqbfmk. **Price:** $149. **Description:** Offers
solutions to help you fully achieve your potential as a
true leader. **Audience:** Newly appointed managers
and supervisors.

44550 ■ Excelling as a Highly Effective Team Leader (Onsite)

Seminar Information Service Inc.
20 Executive Park, Ste. 120
Irvine, CA 92614
Ph: (949)261-9104
Free: 877-SEM-INFO
Fax: (949)261-1963
Co. E-mail: info@seminarinformation.com
URL: http://www.seminarinformation.com
URL(s): www.seminarinformation.com/details.
cfm?qc=qqbjfh. **Price:** $399. **Description:** Learn the
personal leadership characteristics and skills that
create energy and enthusiasm increasing productivity
and performance. **Audience:** Leaders of teams and
potential leaders .

44551 ■ Exceptional Management Skills

Baker Communications Inc. (BCI)
10101 SW Fwy., Ste. 630
Houston, TX 77074
Ph: (713)627-7700
Fax: (713)587-2051
Co. E-mail: information@bakercommunications.com
URL: http://www.bakercommunications.com
Contact: Walter Rogers, President
URL(s): www.bakercommunications.com/Excep-
tional-Management-Skills.htm. **Description:** This
two-day interactive workshop will provide the tools to
make the most of interactions with subordinates.
Cloud-based training also available. **Audience:**
Managers.

44552 ■ Facilitation Skills (Onsite)

Seminar Information Service Inc.
20 Executive Park, Ste. 120
Irvine, CA 92614
Ph: (949)261-9104
Free: 877-SEM-INFO

Fax: (949)261-1963
Co. E-mail: info@seminarinformation.com
URL: http://www.seminarinformation.com
Price: $2,490.00. **Description:** Learn how to facilitate
goal-oriented results through planning, collaboration
and consensus; Maintain facilitative focus by adopting the right frame of mind; Create a targeted agenda
to make meetings productive; Start-up, manage and
close effective meetings; Resolve disagreement using
a range of consensus-building techniques; Develop
and implement a facilitative action plan. **Dates and
Locations:** Toronto and Ottawa, CN.

44553 ■ Facilitative Leadership

Interaction Associates
70 Fargo St., Ste. 908
Boston, MA 02210
Ph: (617)535-7000
Fax: (617)535-7099
URL: http://www.interactionassociates.com
URL(s): interactionassociates.com/public-workshops/
facilitative-leadership. **Price:** $1,950. **Description:**
Two-day seminar that offers seven principles to form
a strategic framework for leadership. **Audience:**
Project managers, department heads, team leaders
and supervisors.

44554 ■ Facilities Management (Onsite)

Fred Pryor Seminars & CareerTrack
5700 Broadmoor St., Ste. 300
Mission, KS 66202
Ph: (800)780-8476
Free: 800-780-8476
Fax: (913)967-8849
Co. E-mail: customerservice@pryor.com
URL: http://www.pryor.com
Contact: Phil Love, Chief Executive Officer
Description: Covers techniques used by leading
facilities managers to run a safe, cost-effective, and
employee friendly environment. **Audience:** Profes-
sionals.

44555 ■ Foundation for Leading Teams (Onsite)

Seminar Information Service Inc.
20 Executive Park, Ste. 120
Irvine, CA 92614
Ph: (949)261-9104
Free: 877-SEM-INFO
Fax: (949)261-1963
Co. E-mail: info@seminarinformation.com
URL: http://www.seminarinformation.com
URL(s): www.seminarinformation.com/details.
cfm?qc=qqazet. **Price:** $295, Members; $390, Non-
members. **Description:** learn to develop a clear
understanding of effective team behaviors. **Audi-
ence:** Team leaders .

44556 ■ Fundamentals of Project Management (Onsite)

Fred Pryor Seminars & CareerTrack
5700 Broadmoor St., Ste. 300
Mission, KS 66202
Ph: (800)780-8476
Free: 800-780-8476
Fax: (913)967-8849
Co. E-mail: customerservice@pryor.com
URL: http://www.pryor.com
Contact: Phil Love, Chief Executive Officer
URL(s): www.pryor.com/mkt_info/seminars/desc/p2.
asp. **Price:** $299. **Description:** Learn to plan, budget
and schedule project in on time and within a budget.
Audience: Project managers.

44557 ■ Fundamentals of Successful Project Management (Onsite)

Seminar Information Service Inc.
20 Executive Park, Ste. 120
Irvine, CA 92614
Ph: (949)261-9104
Free: 877-SEM-INFO
Fax: (949)261-1963
Co. E-mail: info@seminarinformation.com
URL: http://www.seminarinformation.com
URL(s): www.seminarinformation.com/details.
cfm?qc=qqbdrn. **Price:** $399. **Description:** How to
create a plan, implement it, monitor progress, correct
as necessary and deliver as promised. **Audience:**
Managers.

44558 ■ Getting Results Without Authority

Canadian Management Centre (CMC)
150 York St., 5th Fl.
Toronto, ON, Canada M5H 3S5
Free: 877-262-2519
Fax: (416)214-6047
Co. E-mail: cmcinfo@cmcoutperform.com
URL: http://cmcoutperform.com
Contact: John Wright, President
URL(s): www.cmctraining.com/results-without-author-
ity. **Price:** C$2,195, Members; C$2,395, Nonmembers. **Description:** Covers how to achieve
results via other employees despite not having direct
authority over them. Held in Vancouver, BC; Toronto,
ON; Edmonton, AB; Calgary, AB; and Mississauga,
ON. **Audience:** Professionals who need to improve
their influencing skills to achieve results through others. **Dates and Locations:** 2015 Feb 18-20; venue
not reported. **Telecommunication Services:** cm-
cinfo@cmctraining.org.

44559 ■ Global Competencies for Diversity Leaders (Onsite)

Seminar Information Service Inc.
20 Executive Park, Ste. 120
Irvine, CA 92614
Ph: (949)261-9104
Free: 877-SEM-INFO
Fax: (949)261-1963
Co. E-mail: info@seminarinformation.com
URL: http://www.seminarinformation.com
Price: $995.00. **Description:** Through the use of
case studies, exercises, discussion with peers, and
guidance from experts in the field, participants will
develop a toolkit of competencies to achieve success,
including why a global diversity strategy is essential,
differences between U.S. and multinational diversity
implementation, and key steps in creating a global
diversity strategy.

44560 ■ High-Impact Decision Making (Onsite)

Canadian Management Centre (CMC)
150 York St., 5th Fl.
Toronto, ON, Canada M5H 3S5
Free: 877-262-2519
Fax: (416)214-6047
Co. E-mail: cmcinfo@cmcoutperform.com
URL: http://cmcoutperform.com
Contact: John Wright, President
URL(s): cmcoutperform.com/high-impact-decision-
making. **Price:** $1,845, Members; $1,995, Non-
members. **Description:** Learn to make the best deci-
sion every time by reducing risks and maximizing
results. **Audience:** Managers and professionals.

44561 ■ How to Be a Highly Successful Team Leader (Onsite)

Seminar Information Service Inc.
20 Executive Park, Ste. 120
Irvine, CA 92614
Ph: (949)261-9104
Free: 877-SEM-INFO
Fax: (949)261-1963
Co. E-mail: info@seminarinformation.com
URL: http://www.seminarinformation.com
Price: $299. **Description:** Intensive two-day work-
shop that teaches the many dimensions of effective
leadership and develop the skills needed to lead your
team to maximum performance. **Audience:** New
team leader.

44562 ■ How to Be a Highly Successful Team Leader (Onsite)

Padgett-Thompson Seminars
Rockhurst University CEC
14502 W 105th St.
Lenexa, KS 66215
Free: 800-349-1935
URL: http://www.findaseminar.com/tpd/Padgett-
Thompson-Seminars.asp
URL(s): www.findaseminar.com/event1.asp?even-
tID=965. **Description:** Two-day workshop to help
explore the many dimensions of effective leadership
and develop the skills needed to lead a team to peak
performance. **Audience:** Team leaders and professionals.

44563 ■ How to Deal with Unacceptable Employee Behavior (Onsite)
Fred Pryor Seminars & CareerTrack
5700 Broadmoor St., Ste. 300
Mission, KS 66202
Ph: (800)780-8476
Free: 800-780-8476
Fax: (913)967-8849
Co. E-mail: customerservice@pryor.com
URL: http://www.pryor.com
Contact: Phil Love, Chief Executive Officer
Description: Learn effective management techniques for dealing with problem employees, and how to tailor an individual approach for each employee's situation. **Audience:** Industry professionals.

44564 ■ How to Effectively Manage Multiple Locations (Onsite)
Seminar Information Service Inc.
20 Executive Park, Ste. 120
Irvine, CA 92614
Ph: (949)261-9104
Free: 877-SEM-INFO
Fax: (949)261-1963
Co. E-mail: info@seminarinformation.com
URL: http://www.seminarinformation.com
URL(s): www.seminarinformation.com/details. cfm?qc=qqbsuu. **Price:** $399. **Description:** Gain critical know-how for realizing full potential as a manager and a leader in one of the most challenging situations any manager could find themselves in. **Audience:** Professionals.

44565 ■ How to Effectively Supervise People: Fundaments of Leading With Success! (Onsite)
Seminar Information Service Inc.
20 Executive Park, Ste. 120
Irvine, CA 92614
Ph: (949)261-9104
Free: 877-SEM-INFO
Fax: (949)261-1963
Co. E-mail: info@seminarinformation.com
URL: http://www.seminarinformation.com
URL(s): www.seminarinformation.com/details. cfm?qc=qqbvvb. **Price:** $199. **Description:** This seminar teaches the fundamentals of leading with success, including what's expected of you and how to deal with various personalities and problem employees. **Audience:** Supervisors.

44566 ■ How to Excel at Managing and Supervising People (Onsite)
Seminar Information Service Inc.
20 Executive Park, Ste. 120
Irvine, CA 92614
Ph: (949)261-9104
Free: 877-SEM-INFO
Fax: (949)261-1963
Co. E-mail: info@seminarinformation.com
URL: http://www.seminarinformation.com
URL(s): www.seminarinformation.com/qqbpmt/how-to-excel-at-managing-and-supervising-people. **Price:** $399, $349.00 for 4 or more. **Description:** Learn skills to manage change, motivate, discipline, delegate, including problem solving for success. **Audience:** Managers and supervisors.

44567 ■ How to Gather and Document User Requirements (Onsite)
Seminar Information Service Inc.
20 Executive Park, Ste. 120
Irvine, CA 92614
Ph: (949)261-9104
Free: 877-SEM-INFO
Fax: (949)261-1963
Co. E-mail: info@seminarinformation.com
URL: http://www.seminarinformation.com
URL(s): www.seminarinformation.com/details. cfrn?qc=qqbqak. **Price:** $2,295. **Description:** Introduces the roles of the business analyst as they relate to the analysis and documentation requirements. **Audience:** Business analysts.

44568 ■ How to Get More Organized (Onsite)
Padgett-Thompson Seminars
Rockhurst University CEC
14502 W 105th St.
Lenexa, KS 66215
Free: 800-349-1935
URL: http://www.findaseminar.com/tpd/Padgett-Thompson-Seminars.asp
URL(s): www.findaseminar.com/event1.asp?eventID=923. **Description:** Seminar will teach how to meet deadlines by getting more done in less time. **Audience:** Business professionals.

44569 ■ How to Handle Conflict and Confrontation (Onsite)
Padgett-Thompson Seminars
Rockhurst University CEC
14502 W 105th St.
Lenexa, KS 66215
Free: 800-349-1935
URL: http://www.findaseminar.com/tpd/Padgett-Thompson-Seminars.asp
URL(s): www.findaseminar.com/event1.asp?eventID=7032. **Price:** $199. **Description:** A change management seminar that shows participants how to find positive solutions to negative situations. **Audience:** People having to deal with conflict and confrontation .

44570 ■ How to Manage Emotions and Excel Under Pressure (Onsite)
Padgett-Thompson Seminars
Rockhurst University CEC
14502 W 105th St.
Lenexa, KS 66215
Free: 800-349-1935
URL: http://www.findaseminar.com/tpd/Padgett-Thompson-Seminars.asp
URL(s): www.findaseminar.com/event1.asp?eventID=7345. **Price:** $199. **Description:** Workshop teaches the skills required to maintain emotional control in the workplace. **Audience:** People having deal with conflict, anger, confrontation and stress.

44571 ■ How to Supervise People (Onsite)
Seminar Information Service Inc.
20 Executive Park, Ste. 120
Irvine, CA 92614
Ph: (949)261-9104
Free: 877-SEM-INFO
Fax: (949)261-1963
Co. E-mail: info@seminarinformation.com
URL: http://www.seminarinformation.com
URL(s): www.seminarinformation.com/details. cfm?qc=qqbwjn. **Price:** $149. **Description:** Participants learn how to rate performance, relate to former peers, maintain a positive motivational climate, and handle conflicts. **Audience:** Supervisors.

44572 ■ Improving Your Managerial Effectiveness
Canadian Management Centre (CMC)
150 York St., 5th Fl.
Toronto, ON, Canada M5H 3S5
Free: 877-262-2519
Fax: (416)214-6047
Co. E-mail: cmcinfo@cmcoutperform.com
URL: http://cmcoutperform.com
Contact: John Wright, President
URL(s): www.cmctraining.org/improving-managerial-effectiveness. **Price:** C$2,195, Members; C$2,395, Non-members. **Description:** Addresses issues faced by most management professionals, including personal, operational, organizational, and interpersonal effectiveness in today's workplace. Course on request. **Audience:** Managers and supervisors who want to make a positive impact on overall team performance. **Dates and Locations:** 2015 Mar 02-04; venue not reported. **Telecommunication Services:** cmcinfo@cmctraining.org.

44573 ■ Improving Your Project Management Skills: The Basics for Success
American Management Association (AMA)
1601 Broadway
New York, NY 10019-7420
Ph: (212)586-8100
Free: 877-566-9441

Fax: (212)903-8168
Co. E-mail: customerservice@amanet.org
URL: http://www.amanet.org
Contact: Edward T. Reilly, President
URL(s): www.amaseminars.org/training/seminars/ Improving-Your-Project-Management-Skills-The-Basics-for-Success.aspx?state=Illinois&city=Chicago. **Price:** $2,195.00 for non-members; $1,995.00 for AMA members; and $1,708.00 for General Services Administration (GSA) members. **Description:** Covers the basic principles of project management, including setting goals and schedules, managing a project plan, estimating, and budgeting. Also available live online. **Audience:** newly project managers. **Dates and Locations:** Cities throughout the United States. **Telecommunication Services:** customerservice@amanet. org.

44574 ■ Improving Your Project Management Skills: The Basics for Success
Canadian Management Centre (CMC)
150 York St., 5th Fl.
Toronto, ON, Canada M5H 3S5
Free: 877-262-2519
Fax: (416)214-6047
Co. E-mail: cmcinfo@cmcoutperform.com
URL: http://cmcoutperform.com
Contact: John Wright, President
URL(s): www.cmctraining.org/improving-project-management-skills-basics-online. **Price:** C$1,995, Members; C$2,195, Non-members. **Description:** Topics include understanding project management, project planning and scheduling, documentation and reporting, and quality control. Held in Edmonton, AB; Calgary, AB; Vaughan, ON; Ottawa, ON; Mississauga, ON; Vancouver, BC; and Toronto, ON. **Audience:** Individuals new to project management, experienced project managers looking to review current tools, techniques and processes, and all others who contribute to projects. **Dates and Locations:** 2015 Feb 02-05; venue not reported. **Telecommunication Services:** cmcinfo@cmctraining.org.

44575 ■ Information Technology Project Management (Onsite)
American Management Association (AMA)
1601 Broadway
New York, NY 10019-7420
Ph: (212)586-8100
Free: 877-566-9441
Fax: (212)903-8168
Co. E-mail: customerservice@amanet.org
URL: http://www.amanet.org
Contact: Edward T. Reilly, President
URL(s): www.amaseminars.org/training/seminars/ onsite/Information-Technology-Project-Management. aspx. **Description:** Covers the entire information systems process from start to finish, including budgeting, software tools, and scheduling. **Audience:** Directors and managers of IT, project managers and team leaders, programmers/analysts, systems analysts, project office staff members. **Telecommunication Services:** customerservice@amanet.org.

44576 ■ Interpersonal Skills for Managers (Onsite)
American Management Association (AMA)
1601 Broadway
New York, NY 10019-7420
Ph: (212)586-8100
Free: 877-566-9441
Fax: (212)903-8168
Co. E-mail: customerservice@amanet.org
URL: http://www.amanet.org
Contact: Edward T. Reilly, President
URL(s): www.amanet.org/training/seminars/ Interpersonal-Skills-for-Managers.aspx. **Price:** $2,345, Non-members; $2,095, Members AMA; $1,794, Members GSA. **Description:** Covers organizational change, diversity and electronic communication channels in the workplace. **Audience:** Managers, team leaders and supervisors.

44577 ■ Introduction to Project Management (Onsite)
EEI Communications
8945 Guilford Rd., Ste. 145
Columbia, MD 21046

Ph: (410)309-8200
Free: 888-253-2762
Fax: (410)630-3980
Co. E-mail: train@eeicom.com
URL: http://www.eeicom.com/eei-training-services
URL(s): www.eeicom.com/eei-training-services/
classes/project-management/. **Price:** $745.00. **Description:** Topics include understanding project
management, characteristics of an effective manager,
documentation, and quality control. **Audience:**
project managers. **Dates and Locations:** Silver
Spring, MD; Alexandria, VA; Hunt Valley, MD; and
Columbia, MD. **Telecommunication Services:**
train@eeicom.com.

**44578 ■ IT Relationship Management:
Aligning IT with the Business (Onsite)**
Seminar Information Service Inc.
20 Executive Park, Ste. 120
Irvine, CA 92614
Ph: (949)261-9104
Free: 877-SEM-INFO
Fax: (949)261-1963
Co. E-mail: info@seminarinformation.com
URL: http://www.seminarinformation.com
Price: $2,490, $2,490.00. **Description:** Learn the
best practices of an IT Relationship Manager (ITRM)
for facilitating IT solutions that provide value to the
business and satisfy the needs of business stakehold-
ers. **Audience:** Business analysts, project managers,
IT department managers, and IT executives. **Dates
and Locations:** Rockville, MD; New York, NY; Reston, VA; and Toronto, CN.

**44579 ■ Keys to Effectively Supervising
People (Onsite)**
Padgett-Thompson Seminars
Rockhurst University CEC
14502 W 105th St.
Lenexa, KS 66215
Free: 800-349-1935
URL: http://www.findaseminar.com/tpd/Padgett-
Thompson-Seminars.asp
URL(s): www.findaseminar.com/event1.asp?even-
tID=6692. **Description:** One-day seminar that im-
merses participants in the supervisory techniques,
tools, and solutions needed to be more effective.
Audience: Managers, supervisors, and team lead-
ers.

44580 ■ Leadership Development for Women
Seminar Information Service Inc.
20 Executive Park, Ste. 120
Irvine, CA 92614
Ph: (949)261-9104
Free: 877-SEM-INFO
Fax: (949)261-1963
Co. E-mail: info@seminarinformation.com
URL: http://www.seminarinformation.com
Description: Provides the knowledge, network, and
impetus necessary to thrive at work, at home, and
within your community. **Audience:** Women Business
Professionals.

**44581 ■ Leadership Skills: Building Success
Through Teamwork (Onsite)**
Seminar Information Service Inc.
20 Executive Park, Ste. 120
Irvine, CA 92614
Ph: (949)261-9104
Free: 877-SEM-INFO
Fax: (949)261-1963
Co. E-mail: info@seminarinformation.com
URL: http://www.seminarinformation.com
Description: Learn how to: Develop your teams to
maximize their strengths and enhance productivity;
Optimize organization and work design for success in
service delivery teams; Motivate your team with effec-
tive performance measurement; Integrate your role
as a leader into your management style; Leverage
the complementary skills and styles of your team;
Eliminate barriers and chokepoints that block teamwork; Apply a diverse and multilevel approach to
minimize communication breakdowns. **Audience:**
Industry professionals.

**44582 ■ Leadership Skills: Building Success
Through Teamwork (Onsite)**
Learning Tree International Inc.
1805 Library St.
Reston, VA 20190-5660
Ph: (703)709-9119
Free: 800-843-8733
Fax: (703)709-6405
Co. E-mail: uscourses@learningtree.com
URL: http://www.learningtree.com
Contact: Nicholas R. Schacht, President
URL(s): www.learningtree.com/info/pdfs/gsa-pricing1.
pdf. **Price:** $2,213. **Description:** Learn to develop
teams to maximize their strengths and enhance
productivity. **Audience:** Professionals.

44583 ■ Leadership Skills for Supervisors
Canadian Management Centre (CMC)
150 York St., 5th Fl.
Toronto, ON, Canada M5H 3S5
Free: 877-262-2519
Fax: (416)214-6047
Co. E-mail: cmcinfo@cmcoutperform.com
URL: http://cmcoutperform.com
Contact: John Wright, President
URL(s): www.cmctraining.org/management-skills-
supervisors-managers. **Price:** C$2,195, Members;
C$2,395, Non-members. **Description:** Covers em-
powering supervisors and staff; using flow chart
techniques as a means of assessing work flow and
streamlining processes; coaching, mentoring, and
providing feedback; organizing and leading productive meetings; and using brainstorming to cultivate
ideas. **Audience:** Supervisors and managers with
one to 3 years of experience supervising and managing others. **Dates and Locations:** 2015 Feb 09-11;
venue not reported. **Telecommunication Services:**
cmcinfo@cmctraining.org.

**44584 ■ Leadership Skills and Team
Development for IT and Technical
Professionals (Onsite)**
Seminar Information Service Inc.
20 Executive Park, Ste. 120
Irvine, CA 92614
Ph: (949)261-9104
Free: 877-SEM-INFO
Fax: (949)261-1963
Co. E-mail: info@seminarinformation.com
URL: http://www.seminarinformation.com
URL(s): www.seminarinformation.com/details.
cfm?qc=qqatpm. **Price:** $2,345. **Description:** Interac-
tive seminar provides hands-on exercises designed
to help technical professionals build and lead a team,
evaluate the team's performance, and develop an
action plan for leadership success. **Audience:** IT and
Technical team leaders, technical managers and
technical professionals .

**44585 ■ Leadership and Supervisory Skills
for Women (Onsite)**
Padgett-Thompson Seminars
Rockhurst University CEC
14502 W 105th St.
Lenexa, KS 66215
Free: 800-349-1935
URL: http://www.findaseminar.com/tpd/Padgett-
Thompson-Seminars.asp
URL(s): www.findaseminar.com/event1.asp?even-
tID=891. **Description:** A one-day workshop to learn
strategies for effective leadership at all levels. **Audi-
ence:** Women leaders and supervisors .

**44586 ■ Leadership and Team Development
for Managerial Success (Onsite)**
American Management Association (AMA)
1601 Broadway
New York, NY 10019-7420
Ph: (212)586-8100
Free: 877-566-9441
Fax: (212)903-8168
Co. E-mail: customerservice@amanet.org
URL: http://www.amanet.org
Contact: Edward T. Reilly, President
URL(s): www.amaseminars.org. **Description:** Cov-
ers the difference between managing and leading,
developing and communicating goals, motivating a
team, and various team concepts. **Audience:** New

managers, team leaders and business professionals
interested in acquiring effective leadership skills for
managers. **Telecommunication Services:** custom-
erservice@amanet.org.

**44587 ■ Leading Effective Teams II -
Communicating with Your Teammates
(Onsite)**
Seminar Information Service Inc.
20 Executive Park, Ste. 120
Irvine, CA 92614
Ph: (949)261-9104
Free: 877-SEM-INFO
Fax: (949)261-1963
Co. E-mail: info@seminarinformation.com
URL: http://www.seminarinformation.com
Price: $350.00 for non-members; $275.00 for MRA
members. **Description:** Leaders learn their com-
munication style and how it relates to their team
members, as well as how to motivate through com-
munication. **Dates and Locations:** Waukesha, WI.

**44588 ■ Leading High-Performance Project
Teams**
Seminar Information Service Inc.
20 Executive Park, Ste. 120
Irvine, CA 92614
Ph: (949)261-9104
Free: 877-SEM-INFO
Fax: (949)261-1963
Co. E-mail: info@seminarinformation.com
URL: http://www.seminarinformation.com
URL(s): www.seminarinformation.com/details.
cfm?qc=qqbmxs. **Price:** $1,995. **Description:** Fast-
paced, highly engaging workplace simulation enables
you to integrate and apply five practices of exemplary
leaders, and eight dimensions of high-performing
teams, becoming a confident and competent leader.
Audience: Managers with a thorough understanding
of basic project management including knowledge of
Gantt charts, resource leveling and general leadership principles.

44589 ■ Leading High Performance Teams
Seminar Information Service Inc.
20 Executive Park, Ste. 120
Irvine, CA 92614
Ph: (949)261-9104
Free: 877-SEM-INFO
Fax: (949)261-1963
Co. E-mail: info@seminarinformation.com
URL: http://www.seminarinformation.com
URL(s): www.seminarinformation.com/qqbtkk/project-
leadership-building-high-performance-teams. **Price:**
$2,990. **Description:** Builds awareness and skill in
the areas of team dynamics, group problem solving,
and group decision making. You will develop leadership skills applicable to many areas, but especially
suited to self-directed work teams, employee participation teams, interdepartmental task groups, and
other group situations where combined efforts are
needed to reach optimal performance levels. **Audience:** Team leaders and project managers. **Dates
and Locations:** 2015 Mar 17-20; venue not reported.
Telecommunication Services: info@seminarinfor-
mation.com.

**44590 ■ Leading Project Managers: A Guide
to Success (Onsite)**
Seminar Information Service Inc.
20 Executive Park, Ste. 120
Irvine, CA 92614
Ph: (949)261-9104
Free: 877-SEM-INFO
Fax: (949)261-1963
Co. E-mail: info@seminarinformation.com
URL: http://www.seminarinformation.com
URL(s): www.seminarinformation.com/details.
cfm?qc=qqbmxr. **Price:** $1,645. **Description:** Gain
perspectives and review best practices on issues
critical to those who manage project managers. **Audi-
ence:** Managers of project managers with a basic
understanding of project management.

44591 ■ Leading Virtual and Remote Teams
American Management Association (AMA)
1601 Broadway
New York, NY 10019-7420
Ph: (212)586-8100

Free: 877-566-9441
Fax: (212)903-8168
Co. E-mail: customerservice@amanet.org
URL: http://www.amanet.org
Contact: Edward T. Reilly, President
URL(s): www.amaseminars.org/training/seminars/
Leading-Virtual-and-Remote-Teams.aspx. **Price:**
$2,545.00 for non-members; $2,295.00 for AMA
members; and $1,965.00 for General Services
Administration (GSA) members. **Description:** Covers
leadership models, communication between teams,
virtual team development, measuring performance,
and utilizing technology effectively. Held in Chicago,
IL; Arlington, VA; Washington, DC; San Franciso, CA;
Dallas, TX; New York, NY; and Las Vegas, CA.. Also
available live online. **Audience:** managers, senior
managers, directors and project leaders . **Telecommunication Services:** customerservice@amanet.
org.

44592 ■ Legal Issues for Managers (Onsite)
Seminar Information Service Inc.
20 Executive Park, Ste. 120
Irvine, CA 92614
Ph: (949)261-9104
Free: 877-SEM-INFO
Fax: (949)261-1963
Co. E-mail: info@seminarinformation.com
URL: http://www.seminarinformation.com
Price: $1,990.00. **Description:** Using a case study,
practical examples, and discussions participants will
explore the law as it relates to making nondiscrimina-
tory employment decisions, compliance with wage
and hour laws, safety and health rights and responsibilities, required versus discretionary leaves of
absence, managing employees covered by labor
agreements, and individual rights and wrongful
discharge.

44593 ■ Making Successful Business Decisions: Getting it Right the First Time (Onsite)
Seminar Information Service Inc.
20 Executive Park, Ste. 120
Irvine, CA 92614
Ph: (949)261-9104
Free: 877-SEM-INFO
Fax: (949)261-1963
Co. E-mail: info@seminarinformation.com
URL: http://www.seminarinformation.com
Price: $2,490.00. **Description:** Learn how to make
intelligent decisions with limited time and information,
how to convert conflicting opinions into useful
insights, foster efficient and effective group decision
making, and ensure decisions are implemented by
the organization.

44594 ■ Making the Transition to Management (Onsite)
American Management Association (AMA)
1601 Broadway
New York, NY 10019-7420
Ph: (212)586-8100
Free: 877-566-9441
Fax: (212)903-8168
Co. E-mail: customerservice@amanet.org
URL: http://www.amanet.org
Contact: Edward T. Reilly, President
URL(s): www.amaseminars.org/training/seminars/
Making-the-Transition-to-Management.aspx. **Price:**
$1,995.00 for non-members; $1,795.00 for AMA
members; and $1,537.00 for General Services
Administration (GSA) members. **Description:** Covers
various aspects of the transition to manager, under-
standing what managers do, effective communication
and coaching skills, setting attainable goals, and
creating a positive atmosphere. **Audience:** Newly
promoted supervisors. **Dates and Locations:** Cities
throughout the United States. **Telecommunication
Services:** customerservice@amanet.org.

44595 ■ Making the Transition from Staff Member to Supervisor (Onsite)
American Management Association (AMA)
1601 Broadway
New York, NY 10019-7420
Ph: (212)586-8100
Free: 877-566-9441

Fax: (212)903-8168
Co. E-mail: customerservice@amanet.org
URL: http://www.amanet.org
Contact: Edward T. Reilly, President
URL(s): www.amaseminars.org/training/seminars/
Making-the-Transition-from-Staff-Member-to-Supervi-
sor.aspx?state=Illinois&city=Chicago. **Price:**
$1,895.00 for non-members; $1,695.00 for AMA
members; and $1,451.00 for General Services
Administration (GSA) members. **Description:** Covers
various aspects of taking on a management position,
setting goals, motivation, behavior styles, and time
management. **Audience:** newly promoted supervisors. **Dates and Locations:** Cities throughout the
United States. **Telecommunication Services:** cus-
tomerservice@amanet.org.

44596 ■ Making the Transition to Supervising and Managing Others
Canadian Management Centre (CMC)
150 York St., 5th Fl.
Toronto, ON, Canada M5H 3S5
Free: 877-262-2519
Fax: (416)214-6047
Co. E-mail: cmcinfo@cmcoutperform.com
URL: http://cmcoutperform.com
Contact: John Wright, President
URL(s): cmcoutperform.com/supervising-managing-
others. **Price:** $1,845, Members; $1,995, Non-
members. **Description:** This seminar prepares you
for a complete change of responsibilities and helps
eliminate the anxiety that can accompany it. Held in
Montreal, PQ; Ottawa, ON; Regina, SK; Toronto, ON;
Calgary, AB; Edmonton, AB; Vaughan, ON; Missis-
sauga, ON; and Vancouver, BC. **Audience:** Newly
appointed supervisors and managers.

44597 ■ Management and Leadership Skills for First-Time Supervisors and Managers (Onsite)
Padgett-Thompson Seminars
Rockhurst University CEC
14502 W 105th St.
Lenexa, KS 66215
Free: 800-349-1935
URL: http://www.findaseminar.com/tpd/Padgett-
Thompson-Seminars.asp
URL(s): www.findaseminar.com/event1.asp?even-
tID=895. **Description:** An intensive two-day workshop
for new supervisors who want to develop their
management skills quickly. **Audience:** Supervisors,
managers, team leaders and professionals.

44598 ■ Management Skills for Administrative Professionals
American Management Association (AMA)
1601 Broadway
New York, NY 10019-7420
Ph: (212)586-8100
Free: 877-566-9441
Fax: (212)903-8168
Co. E-mail: customerservice@amanet.org
URL: http://www.amanet.org
Contact: Edward T. Reilly, President
URL(s): www.amaseminars.org/training/seminars/
Management-Skills-for-Administrative-Professionals.
aspx. **Price:** $1,895.00 for non-members; $1,695.00
for AMA members; and $1,451.00 for General Ser-
vices Administration (GSA) members. **Description:**
Geared towards the experienced administrative
professional, this seminar covers effective com-
munication skills, conflict resolution, organizational
skills, partnering with your boss, and setting attainable goals. Held in Arlington, VA; Washington, DC;
Chicago, IL; San Francisco, CA; New York, NY; and
Dallas, TX. Also available live online. **Audience:**
administrative professionals. **Telecommunication
Services:** customerservice@amanet.org.

44599 ■ Management Skills: Building Performance and Productivity
Seminar Information Service Inc.
20 Executive Park, Ste. 120
Irvine, CA 92614
Ph: (949)261-9104
Free: 877-SEM-INFO

Fax: (949)261-1963
Co. E-mail: info@seminarinformation.com
URL: http://www.seminarinformation.com
Price: $2,990. **Description:** Learn how to: Develop
the vision and skills that result in real team commitment; Build and lead empowered and motivated
teams; Delegate tasks and authority while maintaining control; Communicate effectively at all levels; Create world-class team performance; Become a skilled
and effective leader. **Audience:** New and experienced managers. **Dates and Locations:** 2015 Feb
24-27; venue not reported.

44600 ■ Management Skills: Building Performance and Productivity (Onsite)
Learning Tree International Inc.
1805 Library St.
Reston, VA 20190-5660
Ph: (703)709-9119
Free: 800-843-8733
Fax: (703)709-6405
Co. E-mail: uscourses@learningtree.com
URL: http://www.learningtree.com
Contact: Nicholas R. Schacht, President
URL(s): www.learningtree.com/courses/290/manage-
ment-skills/. **Description:** The course is valuable for
both new and experienced managers. Provides
information on how to become a skilled and effective
leader. **Audience:** Managers and professionals.

44601 ■ Management Skills for First-Time Supervisors (Onsite)
Padgett-Thompson Seminars
Rockhurst University CEC
14502 W 105th St.
Lenexa, KS 66215
Free: 800-349-1935
URL: http://www.findaseminar.com/tpd/Padgett-
Thompson-Seminars.asp
URL(s): www.findaseminar.com/GENERAL-MAN-
AGEMENT-Training/Management-Skills-for-First-
Time-Supervisors-Seminar-by-National-Seminars-
Training-Group/901.html?filter=ON&city=Buffalo&
state=NY&category=GENERAL-MANAGEMENT.
Price: $179. **Description:** Through accelerated
learning techniques, teaches skills and supervisory
how-to's. **Audience:** Supervisors and managers.

44602 ■ Management Skills for an IT Environment (Onsite)
Seminar Information Service Inc.
20 Executive Park, Ste. 120
Irvine, CA 92614
Ph: (949)261-9104
Free: 877-SEM-INFO
Fax: (949)261-1963
Co. E-mail: info@seminarinformation.com
URL: http://www.seminarinformation.com
Price: $2,810. **Description:** Learn how to apply a
proven management model for leading technical staff
to excellence; identify key success criteria for leadership in an IT environment; leverage emotion to
optimize communication and performance; motivate
and empower technical professionals to achieve
results; delegate proactively to focus on strengths of
IT teams and build accountability. **Audience:** IT
managers. **Dates and Locations:** Heston, VA; Ottawa, CN; Schaumburg, IL; Los Angeles, CA; Philadelphia, PA; Toronto, CN; New York, NY; Alexandria,
VA; and Rockville, MD.

44603 ■ Management Skills for New Supervisors and Managers
Canadian Management Centre (CMC)
150 York St., 5th Fl.
Toronto, ON, Canada M5H 3S5
Free: 877-262-2519
Fax: (416)214-6047
Co. E-mail: cmcinfo@cmcoutperform.com
URL: http://cmcoutperform.com
Contact: John Wright, President
URL(s): cmcoutperform.com/management-skills-
supervisors-managers. **Price:** $2,195, Members;
$2,395, Non-members. **Description:** Learn the tools
to plan, organize, communicate, and monitor every
situation effectively. Held in Calgary, AB; Montreal,

PQ; Vancouver, BC; Halifax, NS; Regina, SK; Ottawa, ON; and Toronto, ON. Also offers course on request. **Audience:** Supervisors and managers.

44604 ■ **Management Skills for Secretaries, Administrative Assistants, and Support Staff (Onsite)**
Fred Pryor Seminars & CareerTrack
5700 Broadmoor St., Ste. 300
Mission, KS 66202
Ph: (800)780-8476
Free: 800-780-8476
Fax: (913)967-8849
Co. E-mail: customerservice@pryor.com
URL: http://www.pryor.com
Contact: Phil Love, Chief Executive Officer
URL(s): www.pryor.com/mkt_info/seminars/desc/SK. asp. **Price:** $199. **Description:** Learn how to make decisions, manage change, solve problems, and negotiate what you need. **Audience:** Secretaries, administrative assistants and support staff .

44605 ■ **Managerial Skills of the New Supervisors**
1601 Broadway
New York, NY 12983
Ph: (518)891-1500
Free: 800-262-9699
Fax: (518)891-0368
Co. E-mail: customerservice@amanet.org
URL: http://www.amanet.org
Description: Program topics include handling managerial responsibilities; utilizing leadership style; facilitating communication; motivating staff; coaching staff; delegating responsibilities; doing performance appraisals; and time management.

44606 ■ **Managerial and Team-building Skills for Project Managers**
American Management Association (AMA)
1601 Broadway
New York, NY 10019-7420
Ph: (212)586-8100
Free: 877-566-9441
Fax: (212)903-8168
Co. E-mail: customerservice@amanet.org
URL: http://www.amanet.org
Contact: Edward T. Reilly, President
URL(s): www.amaseminars.org. **Description:** Covers improving people skills in order to create a powerful, cooperative project team. **Audience:** Industry professionals.

44607 ■ **Managing Change: People and Process (Onsite)**
Seminar Information Service Inc.
20 Executive Park, Ste. 120
Irvine, CA 92614
Ph: (949)261-9104
Free: 877-SEM-INFO
Fax: (949)261-1963
Co. E-mail: info@seminarinformation.com
URL: http://www.seminarinformation.com
Price: $3,190.00. **Description:** Learn how to manage change through the total integration of people and process, design and implement a framework for managing change, evaluate best practice approaches to people and process for delivering successful change, reduce the impact of risk while maximizing the benefit of change, overcome resistance to change, and assemble a practical toolkit tailored to the needs of your organization. **Dates and Locations:** Toronto, CN.

44608 ■ **Managing Chaos: Dynamic Time Management, Recall, Reading, and Stress Management Skills for Administrative Professionals (Onsite)**
American Management Association (AMA)
1601 Broadway
New York, NY 10019-7420
Ph: (212)586-8100
Free: 877-566-9441

Fax: (212)903-8168
Co. E-mail: customerservice@amanet.org
URL: http://www.amanet.org
Contact: Edward T. Reilly, President
URL(s): www.amaseminars.org/training/seminars/ Managing-Chaos-Dynamic-Time-Management.aspx. **Price:** $1,645.00 for non-members; $1,495.00 for AMA members; and $1,280.00 for General Services Administration (GSA) members. **Description:** Covers learning techniques, productive planning, setting goals, and methods of controlling stress. **Audience:** executive secretaries, secretaries, administrative assistants, executive assistants and sales assistants. **Dates and Locations:** New York, NY; Arlington, VA; Washington, DC; and Atlanta, GA. **Telecommunication Services:** customerservice@amanet.org.

44609 ■ **Managing Chaos: How to set Priorities and Make Decisions Under Pressure**
American Management Association (AMA)
1601 Broadway
New York, NY 10019-7420
Ph: (212)586-8100
Free: 877-566-9441
Fax: (212)903-8168
Co. E-mail: customerservice@amanet.org
URL: http://www.amanet.org
Contact: Edward T. Reilly, President
URL(s): www.amanet.org. **Price:** $1,995, Non-members; $1,795, Members; $1,537, Members General Services Administration (GSA). **Description:** Covers practical tools to prepare for unpredictable demands and balance changing priorities. Also available live online. **Audience:** Anyone facing shifting priorities, expanding workloads, tight deadlines, organizational restructuring, multiple projects and increased uncertainty. **Dates and Locations:** 2015 Mar 16-25; venue not reported. **Telecommunication Services:** customerservice@amanet.org.

44610 ■ **Managing Chaos: Tools to Set Priorities and Make Decisions Under Pressure (Onsite)**
American Management Association (AMA)
1601 Broadway
New York, NY 10019-7420
Ph: (212)586-8100
Free: 877-566-9441
Fax: (212)903-8168
Co. E-mail: customerservice@amanet.org
URL: http://www.amanet.org
Contact: Edward T. Reilly, President
URL(s): www.amanet.org/training/articles/Managing-Chaos-Tools-to-Set-Priorities-and-Make-Decisions-Under-Pressure-Seminar.aspx. **Price:** $1,995, Non-members; $1,795, Members AMA; $1,537, Members GSA. **Description:** Two-day seminar where you will learn techniques to adjust to the shifting challenges and demands. **Audience:** Professionals.

44611 ■ **Managing Information Overload: Techniques for Working Smarter (Onsite)**
Seminar Information Service Inc.
20 Executive Park, Ste. 120
Irvine, CA 92614
Ph: (949)261-9104
Free: 877-SEM-INFO
Fax: (949)261-1963
Co. E-mail: info@seminarinformation.com
URL: http://www.seminarinformation.com
Price: $1,890.00. **Description:** Learn how to increase your productivity with effective information management skills, apply creative strategies, including mind maps, for processing information, adopt speed-reading techniques to quickly digest reports, and develop advanced memory skills to retain important information. **Dates and Locations:** Reston, VA; and Rockland MD.

44612 ■ **Managing Multiple Project, Competing Priorites and Tight Deadlines (Onsite)**
Padgett-Thompson Seminars
Rockhurst University CEC
14502 W 105th St.
Lenexa, KS 66215

Free: 800-349-1935
URL: http://www.findaseminar.com/tpd/Padgett-Thompson-Seminars.asp
URL(s): www.findaseminar.com/event1.asp?eventID=9520. **Description:** Seminar provides the skills needed to immediately and effectively deal with multiple projects. **Audience:** Project managers, administrators, administrative assistants, receptionists, secretaries and professionals.

44613 ■ **Managing Multiple Projects and Priorities (Onsite)**
Seminar Information Service Inc.
20 Executive Park, Ste. 120
Irvine, CA 92614
Ph: (949)261-9104
Free: 877-SEM-INFO
Fax: (949)261-1963
Co. E-mail: info@seminarinformation.com
URL: http://www.seminarinformation.com
URL(s): www.seminarinformation.com/details. cfm?qc=qqbpaj. **Price:** $199. **Description:** Learn to gain control of your time, your projects and your priorities. **Audience:** Professionals.

44614 ■ **Managing Organizational Transition (Onsite)**
Seminar Information Service Inc.
20 Executive Park, Ste. 120
Irvine, CA 92614
Ph: (949)261-9104
Free: 877-SEM-INFO
Fax: (949)261-1963
Co. E-mail: info@seminarinformation.com
URL: http://www.seminarinformation.com
URL(s): www.seminarinformation.com/details. cfm?qc=qqbqfl. **Description:** Learn the critical elements for driving successful change and develop coaching skills to create a change-ready culture. **Audience:** Managers.

44615 ■ **Managing People in Projects (Onsite)**
Seminar Information Service Inc.
20 Executive Park, Ste. 120
Irvine, CA 92614
Ph: (949)261-9104
Free: 877-SEM-INFO
Fax: (949)261-1963
Co. E-mail: info@seminarinformation.com
URL: http://www.seminarinformation.com
URL(s): www.seminarinformation.com/details. cfm?qc=qqbmug. **Price:** $1,400. **Description:** Learn how to have people want to work on your projects and how to improve your project results by applying a powerful approach to managing the people who work on them. **Audience:** Project managers and leaders .

44616 ■ **Managing Subcontracts (Onsite)**
Seminar Information Service Inc.
20 Executive Park, Ste. 120
Irvine, CA 92614
Ph: (949)261-9104
Free: 877-SEM-INFO
Fax: (949)261-1963
Co. E-mail: info@seminarinformation.com
URL: http://www.seminarinformation.com
Price: $1,445. **Description:** Examines effective management and administration of subcontracts and complex purchase orders, including tailoring of the terms and conditions. **Audience:** Subcontractors, prime contractors, and government representatives .

44617 ■ **Managing in Tough Times (Onsite)**
Seminar Information Service Inc.
20 Executive Park, Ste. 120
Irvine, CA 92614
Ph: (949)261-9104
Free: 877-SEM-INFO
Fax: (949)261-1963
Co. E-mail: info@seminarinformation.com
URL: http://www.seminarinformation.com
Price: $2,490.00. **Description:** Learn how to demonstrate authentic and strong leadership to create an atmosphere of confidence and trust in tough times, share your vision and display confidence that the

problems your team currently faces will be solved, and minimize stress and maximize productivity and performance during difficult times.

44618 ■ Managing a World-Class IT Department (Onsite)

American Management Association (AMA)
1601 Broadway
New York, NY 10019-7420
Ph: (212)586-8100
Free: 877-566-9441
Fax: (212)903-8168
Co. E-mail: customerservice@amanet.org
URL: http://www.amanet.org
Contact: Edward T. Reilly, President
URL(s): www.amaseminars.org. **Price:** $2,345.00 for non-members; $2,095.00 for AMA members; and $1,794.00 for General Services Administration (GSA) members. **Description:** Three-day seminar for new or prospective IT managers; covers leadership techniques, common challenges, budgeting, planning, testing, and decision making. **Dates and Locations:** New York, NY; and Atlanta, GA. **Telecommunication Services:** customerservice@amanet.org.

44619 ■ Master Organizational Politics, Influence and Alliances (Onsite)

American Management Association (AMA)
1601 Broadway
New York, NY 10019-7420
Ph: (212)586-8100
Free: 877-566-9441
Fax: (212)903-8168
Co. E-mail: customerservice@amanet.org
URL: http://www.amanet.org
Contact: Edward T. Reilly, President
URL(s): www.amaseminars.org. **Price:** $2,195.00 for non-members; $1,995.00 for AMA members; and $1,708.00 for General Services Administration (GSA) members. **Description:** Three-day seminar for experienced supervisors; covers driving high performance, relationship management, coaching, delegating, and your political image. **Dates and Locations:** Atlanta, GA; and San Francisco, CA. **Telecommunication Services:** customerservice@amanet.org.

44620 ■ Maximum Performance Leadership Canada

Canadian Management Centre (CMC)
150 York St., 5th Fl.
Toronto, ON, Canada M5H 3S5
Free: 877-262-2519
Fax: (416)214-6047
Co. E-mail: cmcinfo@cmcoutperform.com
URL: http://cmcoutperform.com
Contact: John Wright, President
URL(s): www.cmctraining.org. **Description:** Covers advanced leadership skills for managers with several years of experience. **Audience:** Industry professionals. **Telecommunication Services:** cmcinfo@cmctraining.org.

44621 ■ Motivation and Trust Building for Group Leaders (Onsite)

Seminar Information Service Inc.
20 Executive Park, Ste. 120
Irvine, CA 92614
Ph: (949)261-9104
Free: 877-SEM-INFO
Fax: (949)261-1963
Co. E-mail: info@seminarinformation.com
URL: http://www.seminarinformation.com
URL(s): www.seminarinformation.com/details.cfm?qc=qqaakg. **Price:** $390, Non-members; $295, Members. **Description:** A practical understanding of basic leadership skills, work values, and organizational responsibility. **Audience:** Professionals.

44622 ■ Moving Ahead: Breaking Behaviour Patterns That Hold You Back

Canadian Management Centre (CMC)
150 York St., 5th Fl.
Toronto, ON, Canada M5H 3S5
Free: 877-262-2519

Fax: (416)214-6047
Co. E-mail: cmcinfo@cmcoutperform.com
URL: http://cmcoutperform.com
Contact: John Wright, President
URL(s): cmcoutperform.com/breaking-behaviour-patterns. **Price:** $1,845, Members; $1,995, Non-members. **Description:** Change your professional image by overcoming destructive workplace behavior. **Audience:** Managers, supervisors and team leaders.

44623 ■ Performance Management, Leading Change, and Putting It All Together (Onsite)

Seminar Information Service Inc.
20 Executive Park, Ste. 120
Irvine, CA 92614
Ph: (949)261-9104
Free: 877-SEM-INFO
Fax: (949)261-1963
Co. E-mail: info@seminarinformation.com
URL: http://www.seminarinformation.com
Description: Participants will learn a performance management system including how to prepare for and conduct performance reviews, how to manage individual and group change and the manager's role in the organizational change process. **Audience:** General public.

44624 ■ Personal Skills for Professional Excellence (Onsite)

Seminar Information Service Inc.
20 Executive Park, Ste. 120
Irvine, CA 92614
Ph: (949)261-9104
Free: 877-SEM-INFO
Fax: (949)261-1963
Co. E-mail: info@seminarinformation.com
URL: http://www.seminarinformation.com
Price: $2,990. **Description:** Learn how to: Achieve maximum productivity and effectiveness in your organization; Build and leverage your professional reputation; Get results working with different and difficult personality types; Maintain focus in pressure situations; Work productively within the political environment of your organization; Build and present persuasive proposals; Make a balanced choice between professional and personal commitments. **Audience:** Industry professionals. **Dates and Locations:** 2015 Mar 24-27; venue not reported.

44625 ■ Persuasive Communications

EEI Communications
8945 Guilford Rd., Ste. 145
Columbia, MD 21046
Ph: (410)309-8200
Free: 888-253-2762
Fax: (410)630-3980
Co. E-mail: train@eeicom.com
URL: http://www.eeicom.com/eei-training-services
Price: $1,065. **Description:** Course designed for department heads and project managers, as well as mid-level communications professionals who want to expand their public relations and marketing skills. **Audience:** Industry professionals.

44626 ■ Persuasive Leadership: Storytelling that Inspires (Onsite)

Seminar Information Service Inc.
20 Executive Park, Ste. 120
Irvine, CA 92614
Ph: (949)261-9104
Free: 877-SEM-INFO
Fax: (949)261-1963
Co. E-mail: info@seminarinformation.com
URL: http://www.seminarinformation.com
URL(s): www.seminarinformation.com/details.cfm?qc=qqbfng. **Description:** Participants develop their storytelling abilities and learn how to use humor to persuade and motivate others, as well as polish their existing speaking skills and develop powerful new ones. **Audience:** Executives, managers, others in positions of influence and experienced speakers. **Telecommunication Services:** info@seminarinformation.com.

44627 ■ PMP Exam Prep Workshop (Onsite)

Canadian Management Centre (CMC)
150 York St., 5th Fl.
Toronto, ON, Canada M5H 3S5
Free: 877-262-2519

Fax: (416)214-6047
Co. E-mail: cmcinfo@cmcoutperform.com
URL: http://cmcoutperform.com
Contact: John Wright, President
URL(s): cmcoutperform.com/pmp-exam-prep. **Price:** $1,995, Members; $2,195, Non-members. **Description:** This three-day, PMP certification exam prep seminar covers the Guide to the Project Management Body of Knowledge on which the exam is based. **Audience:** Project management professionals.

44628 ■ Positive Assertive Management (Onsite)

Seminar Information Service Inc.
20 Executive Park, Ste. 120
Irvine, CA 92614
Ph: (949)261-9104
Free: 877-SEM-INFO
Fax: (949)261-1963
Co. E-mail: info@seminarinformation.com
URL: http://www.seminarinformation.com
URL(s): www.seminarinformation.com/details.cfm?qc=qqbeah. **Price:** $1,495. **Description:** Covers the meaning of assertiveness, how assertiveness can benefit you, using assertive behavior, constructive confrontation and assertive listening. **Audience:** Supervisors and managers .

44629 ■ A Practical Guide to Controls for IT Professionals (Onsite)

Seminar Information Service Inc.
20 Executive Park, Ste. 120
Irvine, CA 92614
Ph: (949)261-9104
Free: 877-SEM-INFO
Fax: (949)261-1963
Co. E-mail: info@seminarinformation.com
URL: http://www.seminarinformation.com
Description: Designed to provide all levels of IT personnel with an understanding of what controls are and why they are critical to safeguarding information assets. Discover why it is important to have a business-process view of IT controls and review the critical role they play in providing for a smooth running, efficiently manager IT environment. **Audience:** IT management and staff, other IT personnel and IT auditors.

44630 ■ Preparing for Leadership: What It Takes to Take the Lead

Canadian Management Centre (CMC)
150 York St., 5th Fl.
Toronto, ON, Canada M5H 3S5
Free: 877-262-2519
Fax: (416)214-6047
Co. E-mail: cmcinfo@cmcoutperform.com
URL: http://cmcoutperform.com
Contact: John Wright, President
URL(s): www.cmctraining.org/preparing-for-leadership. **Price:** C$1,845, Members; C$1,995, Non-members. **Description:** Covers leadership roles, the characteristics of leaders, dealing with organizational politics, and creating an action plan. Held in Ottawa, ON; Calgary, AB; Vancouver, BC; Regina, SK; and Toronto, ON. **Audience:** High potential individuals and managers who are candidates for a leadership role or those who are about to take on a new leadership responsibility. **Dates and Locations:** 2015 Feb 05-06; venue not reported. **Telecommunication Services:** cmcinfo@cmctraining.org.

44631 ■ The Proactive Leader I: Develop an Effective Agenda, Build Support, and Gain Traction

Seminar Information Service Inc.
20 Executive Park, Ste. 120
Irvine, CA 92614
Ph: (949)261-9104
Free: 877-SEM-INFO
Fax: (949)261-1963
Co. E-mail: info@seminarinformation.com
URL: http://www.seminarinformation.com
URL(s): www.seminarinformation.com. **Description:** Learn to identify and prioritize arenas where you can effect change in your organization, including the skills of political competence to take the next steps toward

building support and gaining traction for your idea. **Audience:** Industry professionals. **Telecommunication Services:** info@seminarinformation.com.

44632 ■ Problem Solving and Decision Making (Onsite)
Seminar Information Service Inc.
20 Executive Park, Ste. 120
Irvine, CA 92614
Ph: (949)261-9104
Free: 877-SEM-INFO
Fax: (949)261-1963
Co. E-mail: info@seminarinformation.com
URL: http://www.seminarinformation.com
Description: Based on the principles of rational process and a systematic approach to problem solving and decision making pioneered by Drs. Benjamin Tregoe and Charles Kepner. Participants develop an in-depth understanding of systematic process through case study practice, and apply these principles to urgent job-related concerns. Focus is on immediate, practical results. **Audience:** Managers and professionals .

44633 ■ Process Management: Applying Process Mapping to Analyze and Improve Your Operation
Canadian Management Centre (CMC)
150 York St., 5th Fl.
Toronto, ON, Canada M5H 3S5
Free: 877-262-2519
Fax: (416)214-6047
Co. E-mail: cmcinfo@cmcoutperform.com
URL: http://cmcoutperform.com
Contact: John Wright, President
URL(s): www.cmctraining.org/pmi-approved-courses. **Price:** $2,095.00 Canadian for non-members; $2,295.00 Canadian for CMC members. **Frequency:** Periodic. **Description:** Seminar that covers process mapping techniques, and application and documentation of standard operation procedures, including work simplification analysis and value added versus non-value added activity analysis. **Audience:** managers and supervisors. **Telecommunication Services:** cmcinfo@cmctraining.org.

44634 ■ Project Change Management (Onsite)
EEI Communications
8945 Guilford Rd., Ste. 145
Columbia, MD 21046
Ph: (410)309-8200
Free: 888-253-2762
Fax: (410)630-3980
Co. E-mail: train@eeicom.com
URL: http://www.eeicom.com/eei-training-services
URL(s): www.eeicom.com/. **Description:** Seminar based on the Project Management Institute's (PMI) Project Management Body of Knowledge (PMBOK) that covers the principles of change management as applied to project management and products, including change control system, configuration management, coordinating changes throughout the project, and change management and project closure. **Audience:** Negotiators, manager, supervisors and team leaders. **Telecommunication Services:** train@eeicom.com.

44635 ■ Project Leadership: Building High-Performance Teams (Onsite)
Seminar Information Service Inc.
20 Executive Park, Ste. 120
Irvine, CA 92614
Ph: (949)261-9104
Free: 877-SEM-INFO
Fax: (949)261-1963
Co. E-mail: info@seminarinformation.com
URL: http://www.seminarinformation.com
Price: $2,990. **Description:** Learn how to: Develop the leadership skills to build and sustain high-performing project teams; Develop effective team performance through the Leadership Services Model; Build a strong team identity through vision, purpose and commitment; Foster positive and productive team communication and define ground rules; Protect the team and convert conflicts into advantages that promote high performance; Maximize your leadership

abilities when you return to your organization. **Audience:** Team leaders and project managers. **Dates and Locations:** 2015 Mar 17-20; venue not reported.

44636 ■ Project Management for Administrative Professionals (Onsite)
American Management Association (AMA)
1601 Broadway
New York, NY 10019-7420
Ph: (212)586-8100
Free: 877-566-9441
Fax: (212)903-8168
Co. E-mail: customerservice@amanet.org
URL: http://www.amanet.org
Contact: Edward T. Reilly, President
URL(s): www.amaseminars.org/training/seminars/Project-Management-for-Administrative-Professionals.aspx. **Price:** $1,895.00 for non-members; $1,695.00 for AMA members; and $1,451.00 for General Services Administration (GSA) members. **Frequency:** Monthly. **Description:** Covers methods for planning, controlling, organizing, and tracking projects; problem solving techniques; and time management. **Audience:** Executive secretaries and assistants, administrative assistants and administrative support personnels, office managers and sales assistants. **Dates and Locations:** Boston, MA; Arlington, VA; New York, NY; and San Francisco, CA . **Telecommunication Services:** customerservice@amanet.org.

44637 ■ Project Management for Auditors (Onsite)
Seminar Information Service Inc.
20 Executive Park, Ste. 120
Irvine, CA 92614
Ph: (949)261-9104
Free: 877-SEM-INFO
Fax: (949)261-1963
Co. E-mail: info@seminarinformation.com
URL: http://www.seminarinformation.com
URL(s): www.seminarinformation.com/details.cfm?qc=qqbmll. **Price:** $2,050. **Description:** Learn improved cost control, resource utilization, and more timely conclusions with project management techniques that are applicable to internal audit. **Audience:** Financial, operational, information technology, and external auditors with two more years of audit experience .

44638 ■ Project Management: Skills for Success (Onsite)
Seminar Information Service Inc.
20 Executive Park, Ste. 120
Irvine, CA 92614
Ph: (949)261-9104
Free: 877-SEM-INFO
Fax: (949)261-1963
Co. E-mail: info@seminarinformation.com
URL: http://www.seminarinformation.com
Price: $2,810. **Description:** Learn how to: Produce a project plan for successful delivery; Plan and run projects using best practices in a 6-step project management process; Implement risk management techniques and mitigation strategies; Estimate and schedule task work and duration with confidence; Implement monitoring tools and controls to keep you fully in command of the project; Recognize and practice the leadership skills needed to run a motivated team. **Audience:** Industry professionals. **Dates and Locations:** Cities throughout the United States and Toronto and Ottawa, CN.

44639 ■ Project Management for Software Development - Planning and Managing Successful Projects (Onsite)
Seminar Information Service Inc.
20 Executive Park, Ste. 120
Irvine, CA 92614
Ph: (949)261-9104
Free: 877-SEM-INFO
Fax: (949)261-1963
Co. E-mail: info@seminarinformation.com
URL: http://www.seminarinformation.com
Price: $2,990. **Description:** Learn how to: Deliver successful software projects that support your organization's strategic goals; Match organizational needs to the most effective software development

model; Plan and manage projects at each stage of the software development life cycle (SDLC); Create project plans that address real-world management challenges; Develop the skills for tracking and controlling the project deliverables; Focus on key tasks for the everyday management of software projects; Build an effective and committed team and keep them motivated day to day. **Audience:** Industry professionals. **Dates and Locations:** 2015 Mar 03-06; venue not reported.

44640 ■ Project Management for Streaming DVD, and Multimedia
EEI Communications
500 Montgomery St., Ste. 400
Alexandria, VA 22314-5507
Ph: (410)309-8200
Free: 888-253-2762
Fax: (703)683-7310
Co. E-mail: info@eeicom.com
URL: http://www.eeicom.com
Contact: James T. DeGraffenreid, President
URL(s): www.eeicom.com/eei-training-services/classes/project-management/. **Price:** $425.00. **Description:** Covers an overview of the steps involved in bringing a multimedia or CD-ROM project to completion, including audience and purpose analysis, information and graphic design, planning and resources, managing the creative process, scheduling and budgeting, quality control, and video and sound options. **Audience:** project managers. **Dates and Locations:** Silver Spring, MD; Alexandria, VA; Hunt Valley, MD; and Columbia, MD. **Telecommunication Services:** info@eeicom.com.

44641 ■ Project Management: The Human and Technical View (Onsite)
Seminar Information Service Inc.
20 Executive Park, Ste. 120
Irvine, CA 92614
Ph: (949)261-9104
Free: 877-SEM-INFO
Fax: (949)261-1963
Co. E-mail: info@seminarinformation.com
URL: http://www.seminarinformation.com
URL(s): www.seminarinformation.com/details.cfm?qc=qqaucg. **Price:** $625. **Description:** A systematic, practical approach to successful project management, including skills to handle problems with members who won't commit, who resist change, or who won't cooperate. **Audience:** Functional managers and supervisors, and project leaders.

44642 ■ Project Management for Web Development (Onsite)
EEI Communications
8945 Guilford Rd., Ste. 145
Columbia, MD 21046
Ph: (410)309-8200
Free: 888-253-2762
Fax: (410)630-3980
Co. E-mail: train@eeicom.com
URL: http://www.eeicom.com/eei-training-services
URL(s): www.eeicom.com. **Description:** Covers the basics of managing and maintaining the development of a website. **Audience:** Web developers and general public. **Telecommunication Services:** train@eeicom.com.

44643 ■ Project Management Workshop (Onsite)
Fred Pryor Seminars & CareerTrack
5700 Broadmoor St., Ste. 300
Mission, KS 66202
Ph: (800)780-8476
Free: 800-780-8476
Fax: (913)967-8849
Co. E-mail: customerservice@pryor.com
URL: http://www.pryor.com
Contact: Phil Love, Chief Executive Officer
URL(s): www.pryor.com/mkt_info/seminars/desc/PM.asp. **Price:** $199. **Description:** One-day seminar guaranteed to help you complete projects in a timely manner within a budget. **Audience:** Project management professionals.

44644 ■ Project Scope and Requirements Management (Onsite)
Seminar Information Service Inc.
20 Executive Park, Ste. 120
Irvine, CA 92614
Ph: (949)261-9104
Free: 877-SEM-INFO
Fax: (949)261-1963
Co. E-mail: info@seminarinformation.com
URL: http://www.seminarinformation.com
URL(s): www.seminarinformation.com/details.cfm?qc=qqbssb. **Price:** $2,095, Non-members; $1,895, Members. **Description:** Learn how to achieve project success by mastering scope control. **Audience:** Project and program managers, directors, PMO managers, team leaders and business analysts.

44645 ■ Risk Management (Onsite)
Seminar Information Service Inc.
20 Executive Park, Ste. 120
Irvine, CA 92614
Ph: (949)261-9104
Free: 877-SEM-INFO
Fax: (949)261-1963
Co. E-mail: info@seminarinformation.com
URL: http://www.seminarinformation.com
URL(s): www.seminarinformation.com/details.cfm?qc=qqbebx. **Price:** $1,595. **Description:** Learn how to evaluate and respond to risk at the project and task levels. **Audience:** Executives, project managers and team members.

44646 ■ Sales and Use Tax 2013 Workshop (Onsite)
Seminar Information Service Inc.
20 Executive Park, Ste. 120
Irvine, CA 92614
Ph: (949)261-9104
Free: 877-SEM-INFO
Fax: (949)261-1963
Co. E-mail: info@seminarinformation.com
URL: http://www.seminarinformation.com
URL(s): www.seminarinformation.com/details.cfm?qc=qqcqns. **Price:** C$249. **Description:** Gain a better understanding of sales and use tax and how to apply it to keep your bottom line in check. **Audience:** Finance and tax professionals.

44647 ■ Senior Project Management
Canadian Management Centre (CMC)
150 York St., 5th Fl.
Toronto, ON, Canada M5H 3S5
Free: 877-262-2519
Fax: (416)214-6047
Co. E-mail: cmcinfo@cmcoutperform.com
URL: http://cmcoutperform.com
Contact: John Wright, President
URL(s): www.cmctraining.org. **Description:** Covers project management basics, measuring project accomplishments, trends, human factors, and automated and administrative project support. **Audience:** Industry professionals. **Telecommunication Services:** cmcinfo@cmctraining.org.

44648 ■ Situational Leadership II Workshop (Onsite)
Seminar Information Service Inc.
20 Executive Park, Ste. 120
Irvine, CA 92614
Ph: (949)261-9104
Free: 877-SEM-INFO
Fax: (949)261-1963
Co. E-mail: info@seminarinformation.com
URL: http://www.seminarinformation.com
URL(s): www.seminarinformation.com/qqbqnh/situational-leadership-ii-workshop. **Price:** $2,195, Non-members; $1,995, Members AMA. **Description:** Diagnose the needs of an individual at any particular point in time, then be able to apply the leadership style that is most responsive an productive for the situation at hand. **Audience:** Managers at all levels, project managers, team leaders and supervisors.

44649 ■ Stepping Up to Leadership
Canadian Management Centre (CMC)
150 York St., 5th Fl.
Toronto, ON, Canada M5H 3S5
Free: 877-262-2519

Fax: (416)214-6047
Co. E-mail: cmcinfo@cmcoutperform.com
URL: http://cmcoutperform.com
Contact: John Wright, President
Price: $2,195.00 Canadian for non-members; $1,995.00 Canadian for CMC members. **Description:** Seminar that covers the role of leadership, including attitudes and barriers that prevent you from taking a leadership role, create partnerships that get you the information you need, team leading without the authority, Emotional Intelligence (EI), and career development strategies.

44650 ■ Strategic Agility and Resilience: Embracing Change to Drive Growth
Canadian Management Centre (CMC)
150 York St., 5th Fl.
Toronto, ON, Canada M5H 3S5
Free: 877-262-2519
Fax: (416)214-6047
Co. E-mail: cmcinfo@cmcoutperform.com
URL: http://cmcoutperform.com
Contact: John Wright, President
URL(s): cmcoutperform.com/agility-and-resilience-global-study. **Description:** Master the competencies of agile leadership. **Audience:** Executives and managers.

44651 ■ Strategic Diversity Retention (Onsite)
Seminar Information Service Inc.
20 Executive Park, Ste. 120
Irvine, CA 92614
Ph: (949)261-9104
Free: 877-SEM-INFO
Fax: (949)261-1963
Co. E-mail: info@seminarinformation.com
URL: http://www.seminarinformation.com
URL(s): www.seminarinformation.com/details.cfm?qc=qqbppw. **Price:** $1,495. **Description:** Step-by-step approach to developing a diversity retention strategy and why it fails. **Audience:** Managers, recruiters and human resources.

44652 ■ Successfully Managing People
American Management Association (AMA)
1601 Broadway
New York, NY 10019-7420
Ph: (212)586-8100
Free: 877-566-9441
Fax: (212)903-8168
Co. E-mail: customerservice@amanet.org
URL: http://www.amanet.org
Contact: Edward T. Reilly, President
URL(s): www.amanet.org. **Price:** $2,345, Non-members; $2,095, Members; $1,794, Members General Services Administration (GSA). **Description:** Three day seminar covering negotiation, motivation, confidence, leadership skills, and dealing with various types of employees. Also available live online. **Audience:** Managers and individuals with management responsibilities whose success depends on managing people successfully through clear communication, a cooperative attitude and commitment to shared goals. **Dates and Locations:** 2015 Mar 02-04; venue not reported. **Telecommunication Services:** customerservice@amanet.org.

44653 ■ Successfully Managing People
Canadian Management Centre (CMC)
150 York St., 5th Fl.
Toronto, ON, Canada M5H 3S5
Free: 877-262-2519
Fax: (416)214-6047
Co. E-mail: cmcinfo@cmcoutperform.com
URL: http://cmcoutperform.com
Contact: John Wright, President
URL(s): www.cmctraining.org/successfully-managing-people. **Price:** C$2,195, Members; C$2,395, Non-members. **Description:** Covers negotiation, motivation, confidence, leadership skills, and dealing with various types of employees. Held in Toronto, ON; Calgary, AB; and Mississauga, ON. **Audience:** Supervisors, managers and others with management responsibilities looking to step-up their people management skills. **Dates and Locations:** 2015 Feb 09-11; venue not reported. **Telecommunication Services:** cmcinfo@cmctraining.org.

44654 ■ Supporting Multiple Bosses (Onsite)
Seminar Information Service Inc.
20 Executive Park, Ste. 120
Irvine, CA 92614
Ph: (949)261-9104
Free: 877-SEM-INFO
Fax: (949)261-1963
Co. E-mail: info@seminarinformation.com
URL: http://www.seminarinformation.com
URL(s): www.seminarinformation.com/details.cfm?qc=qqbtxe. **Price:** $1,545. **Description:** Learn to deal with multiple bosses with different agendas, priorities, styles, and expectations. **Audience:** Executive secretaries and assistants, administrative support staff, office managers, coordinators, team members and associates and office coordinators/supervisors/managers.

44655 ■ Systems Thinking (Onsite)
Seminar Information Service Inc.
20 Executive Park, Ste. 120
Irvine, CA 92614
Ph: (949)261-9104
Free: 877-SEM-INFO
Fax: (949)261-1963
Co. E-mail: info@seminarinformation.com
URL: http://www.seminarinformation.com
Price: $1,395. **Description:** Learn how to become a systems thinker so you can resolve complex, systematic business dilemmas in a practical manner. **Audience:** Industry professionals.

44656 ■ Taking on Greater Responsibility: Step-up Skills for Nonmanagers (Onsite)
American Management Association (AMA)
1601 Broadway
New York, NY 10019-7420
Ph: (212)586-8100
Free: 877-566-9441
Fax: (212)903-8168
Co. E-mail: customerservice@amanet.org
URL: http://www.amanet.org
Contact: Edward T. Reilly, President
URL(s): www.amaseminars.org. **Description:** Two-day seminar for new or prospective managers; covers management responsibilities, aligning with other managers, building respect with your team, coaching, motivating, and delegating. **Audience:** Those interested in greater career development and getting the skills to improve their performance and growth within their organization should attend this course. **Telecommunication Services:** customerservice@amanet.org.

44657 ■ Team Leadership Effectiveness Program 'Team Top Gun' (Onsite)
Seminar Information Service Inc.
20 Executive Park, Ste. 120
Irvine, CA 92614
Ph: (949)261-9104
Free: 877-SEM-INFO
Fax: (949)261-1963
Co. E-mail: info@seminarinformation.com
URL: http://www.seminarinformation.com
Price: $1,195, Onsite. **Description:** Three-day seminar using psychological profiles, 360 degree feedback, extensive experiential simulations, and state of the art content relating to success in team based organizations. **Audience:** Industry professionals. **Dates and Locations:** 2015 Feb 03-04; venue not reported.

44658 ■ Technical Project Management
Canadian Management Centre (CMC)
150 York St., 5th Fl.
Toronto, ON, Canada M5H 3S5
Free: 877-262-2519
Fax: (416)214-6047
Co. E-mail: cmcinfo@cmcoutperform.com
URL: http://cmcoutperform.com
Contact: John Wright, President
URL(s): www.cmctraining.org/pmi-approved-courses. **Description:** Covers defining cost, time, and scope; project leadership; utilizing status reports; and technical project control systems. **Audience:** Technical professionals. **Telecommunication Services:** cmcinfo@cmctraining.org.

44659 ■ Technical Project Management (Onsite)
American Management Association (AMA)
1601 Broadway
New York, NY 10019-7420
Ph: (212)586-8100
Free: 877-566-9441
Fax: (212)903-8168
Co. E-mail: customerservice@amanet.org
URL: http://www.amanet.org
Contact: Edward T. Reilly, President
URL(s): www.amaseminars.org/training/seminars/
Technical-Project-Management.aspx. **Price:**
$2,195.00 for non-members; $1,995.00 for AMA
members; and $1,708.00 for General Services
Administration (GSA) members. **Frequency:** 3 days
in a certain month. **Description:** Covers defining
cost, time, and scope; project leadership; utilizing
status reports; and scheduling with milestones. **Audience:** research and development professionals,
engineers, scientists and principal investigators,
project managers, facility engineers and plant managers. **Dates and Locations:** New York, NY; Washington, DC; Chicago, IL; and Arlington, VA. **Telecommunication Services:** customerservice@amanet.
org.

**44660 ■ Thinking Outside the Lines for
Managers and Supervisors (Onsite)**
Seminar Information Service Inc.
20 Executive Park, Ste. 120
Irvine, CA 92614
Ph: (949)261-9104
Free: 877-SEM-INFO
Fax: (949)261-1963
Co. E-mail: info@seminarinformation.com
URL: http://www.seminarinformation.com
URL(s): www.seminarinformation.com/qqbqjy/think-
ing-outside-the-lines-for-managers-and-supervisors.
Price: $199. **Description:** Techniques and solutions
for daily real world problems, including speedy deci-
sion making and motivating for results. **Audience:**
Executives, managers, and team leaders .

44661 ■ Thinking Outside the Lines (Onsite)
Padgett-Thompson Seminars
Rockhurst University CEC
14502 W 105th St.
Lenexa, KS 66215
Free: 800-349-1935
URL: http://www.findaseminar.com/tpd/Padgett-
Thompson-Seminars.asp
URL(s): www.findaseminar.com/event1.asp?even-
tID=1747. **Description:** For executives, managers,
and team leaders who do not want to follow the same
old way of doing things. **Audience:** Business leaders
and managers.

**44662 ■ The Ultimate Supervisor's Workshop
(Onsite)**
Padgett-Thompson Seminars
Rockhurst University CEC
14502 W 105th St.
Lenexa, KS 66215
Free: 800-349-1935
URL: http://www.findaseminar.com/tpd/Padgett-
Thompson-Seminars.asp
URL(s): www.nationalseminarstraining.com/Semi-
narSearchResults/The_Ultimate_Supervisor%92s_
Workshop/YSUP2/index.html. **Description:** A two-
day workshop where leaders come for fresh ideas
and proven strategies. **Audience:** Supervisors and
professionals.

**44663 ■ Uncovering Fraud in Core Business
Functions (Onsite)**
Seminar Information Service Inc.
20 Executive Park, Ste. 120
Irvine, CA 92614
Ph: (949)261-9104
Free: 877-SEM-INFO
Fax: (949)261-1963
Co. E-mail: info@seminarinformation.com
URL: http://www.seminarinformation.com
URL(s): www.seminarinformation.com/details.
cfm?qc=qqbnxq. **Price:** $2,050. **Description:** Pin-
point the areas most prone to internal fraud and

identify key indicators of potential crime. **Audience:**
Audit managers, corporate attorneys and information
security professionals .

**44664 ■ The Voice of Leadership: How
Leaders Inspire, Influence, and Achieve
Results (Onsite)**
American Management Association (AMA)
1601 Broadway
New York, NY 10019-7420
Ph: (212)586-8100
Free: 877-566-9441
Fax: (212)903-8168
Co. E-mail: customerservice@amanet.org
URL: http://www.amanet.org
Contact: Edward T. Reilly, President
URL(s): www.amaseminars.org/training/seminars/
The-Voice-of-Leadership-How-Leaders-Inspire-Influ-
ence-and-Achieve-Results.aspx?state=Texas&.
Price: $2,545.00 for non-members; $2,295.00 for
AMA members; and $1,965.00 for General Services
Administration (GSA) members. **Description:** Covers
managing change, how to inspire and influence, ef-
fective communication skills, coaching, and address-
ing conflict. **Audience:** managers and executives.
Dates and Locations: Cities throughout the United
States. **Telecommunication Services:** customerser-
vice@amanet.org.

44665 ■ Win-Win Negotiations Training
Baker Communications Inc. (BCI)
10101 SW Fwy., Ste. 630
Houston, TX 77074
Ph: (713)627-7700
Fax: (713)587-2051
Co. E-mail: information@bakercommunications.com
URL: http://www.bakercommunications.com
Contact: Walter Rogers, President
URL(s): www.bakercommunications.com/win_
negotiations.htm. **Description:** In this hands-on
workshop, participants learn through practice exer-
cises how to strengthen their negotiation skills. Cloud-
based training also available. **Audience:** Industry
professionals.

REFERENCE WORKS

**44666 ■ "4 Common Habits of Bad Bosses"
in Inc. (Vol. 36, September 2014, No. 7, pp.
18)**
Pub: Mansueto Ventures L.L.C.
Contact: John Koten, Chief Executive Officer
Released: September 2014. **Description:** Four common habits of managers include: waiting to perform
background checks after employee is hired; refusing
to put employee appraisals in writing; paying higher
wages to new hires; and being nice when letting a
worker go.

**44667 ■ The 4 Routes to Entrepreneurial
Success**
Pub: Berrett-Koehler Communications Inc.
Contact: Steve Piersanti, President
E-mail: spiersanti@bkpub.com
Ed: John B. Miner. **Price:** $18.95, paperback. **De-
scription:** After researching one hundred successful
entrepreneurs, the author discovered there are basi-
cally four personality types of entrepreneurs: the
personal achiever, the super salesperson, the real
manager, and the expert idea generator. **Availability:**
Print.

**44668 ■ "The 7 Deadly Toxins of Employee
Engagement: How They Decimate Your
Performance, Your Effectiveness & Your
Bottom Line"**
Pub: Bookshaker
Released: $10.00. **Price:** , $10.00 paperback. **Description:** Human resources managers, and all business leaders, need to recognize the importance of
employee engagement. They also need to understand
the seven deadly toxins that are destructive and are
built into every solution that addresses problems.

**44669 ■ "13D Filings" in Barron's (Vol. 88,
March 24, 2008, No. 12, pp. M13)**
Pub: Dow Jones & Co., Inc.
Contact: Clare Hart, President
Description: HealthCor Management called as
problematic the plan of Magellan Health Services to
use its high cash balances for acquisitions. Carlson
Capital discussed with Energy Partners possible
changes in the latter's board. Investor Carl Icahn
suggested that Enzon Pharmaceuticals consider selling itself or divest some of its assets.

**44670 ■ "13D Filings" in Barron's (Vol. 88,
March 10, 2008, No. 10, pp. M11)**
Pub: Dow Jones & Co., Inc.
Contact: Clare Hart, President
Description: Barington Capital and Clinton Group
sent a letter to Dillard's demanding a list of the
company's stockholders. Elliott Associates announced that it is prepared to take over Packeteer for
$5.50 a share. Strongbow capital suggested a
change in leadership in Duckwall-ALCO Stores.

**44671 ■ "13D Filings: Investors Report to the
SEC" in Barron's (Vol. 88, March 31, 2008, No.
13, pp. M10)**
Description: Obrem Capital Management wants Micrel to rescind Micrel's shareholder-rights plan and to
boost its board to six members from five. Patricia L.
Childress plans to nominate herself to the board of
Sierra Bancorp, and Luther King Capital Management may consider a competing acquisition proposal
for Industrial Distribution Group.

**44672 ■ "13D Filings: Investors Report to the
SEC" in Barron's (Vol. 88, July 4, 2008, No.
28, pp. M10)**
Description: Robino Stortini Holdings will seek
control of Investors Capital Holdings either alone or
with members of the company's management. Discovery Group I will withhold its votes at the nomina-
tion of directors for TESSCO Technologies while JMB
Capital Partners Master Fund plans to nominate a
slate of candidates to the board of Maguire Properties.

**44673 ■ 30 Reasons Employees Hate their
Managers**
Pub: AMACOM
Contact: Edward T. Reilly, Manager
Ed: Bruce L. Katcher, Adam Snyder. **Released:**
March 2007. **Price:** $18.95, Paper or Softback. **De-
scription:** Issues involved in employee negative feel-
ings towards managers are discussed; a survey of
more than 50,000 employees in 65 organizations of
all types and sizes cited 30 main causes for ill will.
Availability: Print; E-book.

**44674 ■ 32 Ways to Be a Champion in
Business**
Pub: Three Rivers Press
Contact: Caroline Sincerbeaux, Editor
E-mail: csincerbeaux@randomhouse.com
Ed: Earvin Magic Johnson. **Released:** December 29,
2009. **Price:** , $18.94. **Description:** Earvin Johnson
discusses his transition from athlete to entrepreneur
and discusses the importance of hard work in order
to pursue your dreams of starting and running a successful business.

**44675 ■ "105 CEOs Depart In July" in South
Florida Business Journal (Vol. 35, August 15,
2014, No. 3, pp. 5)**
Pub: American City Business Journals
Released: August 15, 2014. **Description:** Challenger, Gray & Christmas has reported 105 CEO
departures in July 2014 and these include seven in
Florida. US-based companies announced 766 CEO
changes in management during the first seven
months of 2014. CEO departure trend by industry are
given.

**44676 ■ 365 Answers about Human
Resources for the Small Business Owner:
What Every Manager Needs to Know about**

Work Place Law
Pub: Atlantic Publishing Co.
Contact: Amanda Miller, Manager
E-mail: amiller@atlantic-pub.com
Ed: Mary Holihan. **Price:** $21.95. **Description:** Common questions employers ask about employees and the law are answered.

44677 ■ "The 2007 Black Book" in Hawaii Business (Vol. 53, December 2007, No. 6, pp. 43)
Description: Brief biographies of 364 top executives in Hawaii are presented. Information on their educational achievement, membership in associations, hobbies, family, present position and the company they work for are supplied.

44678 ■ "2008 Woman of the Year Event Filled with Hope and Inspiration" in Hispanic Business (Vol. 30, July-August 2008, No. 7-8, pp. 58)
Pub: Hispanic Business Inc.
Contact: Jesus Chavarria, President
Ed: Brynne Chappell. **Description:** Brief report on the sixth annual Women of the Year Awards gala which was held at JW Marriott Desert Ridge Resort and Spa is given; 20 women were honored with these awards for their professional contribution, commitment to the advancement of the Hispanic community and involvement with charitable organizations.

44679 ■ "2009 Corporate Elite - The Complete List" in Hispanic Business (January-February 2009, pp. 16, 18, 20, 22)
Pub: Hispanic Business Inc.
Contact: Jesus Chavarria, President
Description: Profiles of Hispanic Business Media's 2009 Corporate Elite are presented.

44680 ■ "A&E Networks" in Brandweek (Vol. 49, April 21, 2008, No. 16, pp. SR9)
Pub: Nielsen Business Media Inc.
Contact: Howard Appelbaum, President
Ed: Anthony Crupi. **Description:** Provides contact information for sales and marketing personnel for the A&E Networks as well as a listing of the station's top programming and an analysis of the current season and the target audience for those programs running in the current season. A&E has reinvented itself as a premium entertainment brand over the last five years and with its $2.5 million per episode acquisition of The Sopranos, the station signaled that it was serious about getting back into the scripted programming business. The acquisition also helped the network compete against other cable networks and led to a 20 percent increase in prime-time viewers.

44681 ■ "ABC" in Brandweek (Vol. 49, April 21, 2008, No. 16, pp. SR6)
Ed: John Consoli. **Description:** Provides contact information for sales and marketing personnel for the ABC network as well as a listing of the station's top programming and an analysis of the current season and the target audience for those programs running in the current season.

44682 ■ "The Accountability Lens: A New Way to View Management Issues" in Business Horizons (September-October 2007, pp. 405)
Pub: Elsevier Technology Publications
Ed: Angela T. Hall, Michael G. Bowen, Gerald R. Ferris, M. Todd Royle, Dale E. Fitzgibbons. **Price:** $35.95. **Description:** Organizations are viewed through an accountability lens in terms of source, focus, salience, and intensity to explain issues on corporate governance and ethics. Accountability environment, the individual's immediate work environment that directly affects the subjective experience of felt accountability, and its four main aspects are discussed.
Availability: PDF.

44683 ■ "Achieving Greatness" in Black Enterprise (Vol. 38, January 2008, No. 6, pp. 50)
Pub: Earl G. Graves Publishing Co. Inc.
Contact: Earl G. Graves, Jr., President
Ed: Marcia A. Reed-Woodard. **Description:** Randall Pinkett, winner of a reality show on television and chairman of BCT Partners, insists that a business

cannot survive by doing just enough or more of the same. Pinkett's New Jersey company provides management, technology and consulting to other firms.

44684 ■ "Actions to Implement Three Potent Post-Crisis Strategies" in Strategy & Leadership (Vol. 38, September-October 2010, No. 5)
Pub: Emerald Inc.
Ed: Saul J. Berman, Richard Christner, Ragna Bell. **Description:** The need for organizations to design and implement strategies to cope with the possible situations in the post-economic crisis environment is emphasized. The plans that organizations should implement to successfully manage uncertainty and complexity and to foster their eventual growth are discussed.

44685 ■ "Adapt or Die" in Black Enterprise (Vol. 38, July 2008, No. 12, pp. 27)
Pub: Earl G. Graves Publishing Co. Inc.
Contact: Earl G. Graves, Jr., President
Ed: Rebecca Frances Rohan. **Description:** Turbulence in the domestic auto industry is hitting auto suppliers hard and black suppliers, the majority of whom contract with the Big Three, are just beginning to establish relationships with import car manufacturers. The more savvy CEOs are adopting new technologies in order to weather the downturn in the economy and in the industry as a whole.

44686 ■ "Addition by Subtraction in Tokyo" in Barron's (Vol. 92, August 25, 2012, No. 38, pp. 20)
Pub: Dow Jones & Co., Inc.
Contact: Clare Hart, President
Ed: Kopin Tan. **Description:** Investors in Japan could benefit from the increase in management buyouts, particularly of small capitalization stocks. This increase would shrink the number of Japanese stocks, many of which are trading below book value.

44687 ■ "Air Canada to Slash 600 Non-Union Jobs" in Globe & Mail (February 11, 2006, pp. B3)
Ed: Brent Jang. **Description:** The reasons behind workforce reduction by ACE Aviation Holdings Inc. at Air Canada are presented.

44688 ■ Airline Without a Pilot: Lessons in Leadership
Pub: Targetmark Books
Ed: Harry L. Nolan, Jr. **Released:** December 2005. **Price:** , $24.95. **Description:** The events that destroyed Delta Air Lines are used to define the failures when solid leadership is not at the helm of a company.

44689 ■ "Airlines Mount PR Push to Win Public Support Against Big Oil" in Advertising Age (Vol. 79, July 14, 2008, No. 7, pp. 1)
Pub: Crain Communications Inc.
Contact: Rance Crain, President
Ed: Michael Bush. **Description:** Top airline executives from competing companies have banded together in a public relations plan in which they are sending e-mails to their frequent fliers asking for aid in lobbying legislators to put a restriction on oil speculation.

44690 ■ "Akron Community Foundation Hires Help for CEO Search" in Crain's Cleveland Business (Vol. 28, October 29, 2007, No. 43, pp. 6)
Ed: Shannon Mortland. **Description:** Waverly Partners LLC, an executive search firm, has been hired by the Akron Community Foundation to search for its next president and CEO as Jody Bacon, the company's current CEO, will retire on July 31, 2008.

44691 ■ "All In Good Fun" in Entrepreneur (Vol. 36, May 2008, No. 5, pp. 22)
Pub: Entrepreneur Press
Contact: Perlman Neil, President
Ed: Christopher Percy Collier. **Description:** According to a study conducted in 2007, humor in the workplace helps people communicate effectively and

improves camaraderie. Company leaders and entrepreneurs can also tell humorous stories about themselves, but must also set lines that should not be crossed. The humorous atmosphere in the company YouSendIt is presented.

44692 ■ "The Alliance: Managing Talent in the Networked Age"
Pub: Harvard Business Review Press
Contact: Peter E. Walsh, Director
Released: July 8, 2014. **Price:** , $25.00. **Description:** It is suggested that management see their workers as allies instead of family or free agents in order to create a realistic loyalty pact between employer and employee. Both sides need to trust each other for the company to succeed and the employee to further their career with the firm.

44693 ■ "Always Striving" in Women In Business (Vol. 61, December 2009, No. 6, pp. 28)
Pub: American Business Women's Association
Contact: Lorie Burch, President
Ed: Kathleen Leighton. **Description:** Jennifer Mull discusses her responsibilities and how she attained success as CEO of Backwoods, a gear and clothing store founded by her father in 1973. She places importance on being true to one's words and beliefs, while emphasizing the capacity to tolerate risks in business. Mull defines success as an evolving concept and believes there must always be something to strive for.

44694 ■ The AMA Handbook of Project Management
Pub: AMACOM
Contact: Edward T. Reilly, Manager
Ed: Paul C. Dinsmore, Jeannette Cabanis-Brewin. **Released:** Third Edition. **Price:** $79.95, Hardback. **Description:** A comprehensive reference presenting the critical concepts and theories all project managers must master using essays and advice from the field's top professionals. **Availability:** Print.

44695 ■ "Amazing Apple Does It Again" in Barron's (Vol. 92, September 15, 2012, No. 38, pp. 26)
Pub: Dow Jones & Co., Inc.
Contact: Clare Hart, President
Ed: Tiernan Ray. **Description:** The introduction of the Apple iPhone 5 lacked the flair of previous product introductions by the company. New chief executive officer Tim Cook has been criticized for this lack of flair for marketing, although pre-orders for the iPhone 5 remain high.

44696 ■ "American Water's Ed Vallejo Chosen for 2012 Minority Business Leader Awards" in Manufacturing Close-Up (July 30, 2012)
Description: Ed Vallejo, vice presient of investor relations at American Water, has been awarded the 2012 Minority Business Leader Award from the Philadelphia Business Journal. Vallejo is responsible for developing investor relations strategies for the publicly traded water and wastewater utility firm. He also serves as the company's liaison with financial analyst and investor communities.

44697 ■ "Analysts Not Too Sad Over Joel Gemunder's Departure from Omnicare" in Business Courier (Vol. 27, August 6, 2010, No. 14, pp. 1)
Pub: Business Courier
Ed: James Ritchie. **Description:** Analysts and investors do not understand why Omnicare chief executive officer (CEO) Joel Gemunder suddenly retired after nearly thirty years with the Covington, Kentucky company. They believe that new leadership might invigorate the firm, which provides pharmacy and related services to the long-term care industry.

44698 ■ "The Anatomy of a High Potential" in Business Strategy Review (Vol. 21, Autumn 2010, No. 3, pp. 52)
Pub: Blackwell Publishers Ltd.
Ed: Doug Ready, Jay Conger, Linda Hill, Emily Stecker. **Description:** Companies have long been interested in identifying high potential employees, but

few firms know how to convert top talent into game changers, or people who can shape the future of the business. The authors have found the 'x factors' that can make a high-potential list into a strong competitive advantage.

44699 ■ *"Anatomy of a Rumor"* in *Entrepreneur (Vol. 37, September 2009, No. 9, pp. 18)*
Pub: Entrepreneur Press
Contact: Perlman Neil, President
Ed: Jason Daley. **Description:** Progression and adverse effect of office rumors on businesses are discussed. The quality of someone's work, tenure and personnel changes are the most prevalent categories of rumors. Workers can lose trust in management and one another as a result of rumors.

44700 ■ *"Anja Carroll; Media Director-McDonald's USA"* in *Advertising Age (Vol. 79, November 17, 2008, No. 34, pp. 6)*
Pub: Crain Communications Inc.
Contact: Rance Crain, President
Ed: Emily Bryson York. **Description:** Profile of Anja Carroll who is the media director for McDonald's USA and has the challenge of choosing the right mix of media for the corporation.

44701 ■ *"Ann Alexander: Senior Attorney, Natural Resources Defense Council"* in *Crain's Chicago Business (Vol. 31, May 5, 2008, No. 18)*
Pub: Crain Communications Inc.
Contact: Todd Johnson, Publisher
Ed: Emily Stone. **Description:** Profile of Ann Alexander who is the senior attorney at the Natural Resources Defense Council and is known for her dedication to the environment and a career spent battling oil companies, steelmakers and the government to change federal regulations. One recent project aims to improve the Bush administration's fuel economy standards for SUVs. Past battles include her work to prevent permits from slipping through the cracks such as the proposal by London-based BP PLC to dump 54 percent more ammonia and 35 percent more suspended solids from its Whiting, Indiana refinery into Lake Michigan-the source of drinking water for Chicago and its surrounding communities.

44702 ■ *"Applying Continuous Process Improvement for Managing Customer Loyalty"* in *Agency Sales Magazine (Vol. 39, November 2009, No. 10)*
Ed: Bob Cicerone; Aaron Hekele; Jason Morado. **Description:** Steps in effective process improvement that reveals where opportunities exist to improve management practices and control customer loyalty are discussed. The process consists of thirteen factors grouped into three sets.

44703 ■ *"Are There Material Benefits To Social Diversity?"* in *Hispanic Business (Vol. 30, September 2008, No. 9, pp. 10)*
Ed: Brigida Benitez. **Description:** Diversity in American colleges and universities, where students view and appreciate their peers as individuals and do not judge them on the basis of race, gender, or ethnicity is discussed. The benefits of diversity in higher education are also acknowledged by the U.S. Supreme Court and by leading American corporations.

44704 ■ *"Are Your Goals Hitting the Right Target?"* in *Business Strategy Review (Vol. 21, Autumn 2010, No. 3, pp. 46)*
Pub: Blackwell Publishers Ltd.
Ed: Alan Meekings, Steve Briault, Andy Neely. **Description:** Setting targets is normal in most organizations. The authors think such a practice can cause more harm than good and offer a better strategy.

44705 ■ *"The Art of Appreciation"* in *Business Horizons (November-December 2007, pp. 441)*
Pub: Elsevier Technology Publications
Ed: Catherine M. Dalton. **Price:** $35.95. **Description:** The art of appreciation is an art less and less practices by employees. Employers should lead by example and practice this art to inspire employees to do the same. **Availability:** PDF.

44706 ■ *"The Art of the Huddle: How To Run a Prompt, Productive, and Painless Morning Meeting"* in *Inc. (November 2007, pp. 40, 42-43)*
Pub: Mansueto Ventures L.L.C.
Contact: John Koten, Chief Executive Officer
Ed: Leigh Buchanan. **Description:** Five CEOs describe the ways they use meetings to improve their companies: team building, coordinating, efficiency, motivation, and strategic planning.

44707 ■ *"The Art of Persuasion: How You Can Get the Edge You Need To Reach Every Goal"* in *Small Business Opportunities (November 2007)*
Ed: Paul Endress. **Description:** Expert in the field of psychology to business in the areas of communication, hiring and retention discusses a unique approach to solving business problems.

44708 ■ *"The Art of War for Women"* in *Hawaii Business (Vol. 54, July 2008, No. 1, pp. 23)*
Pub: PacificBasin Communications
Ed: Chin-Ning Chu. **Description:** Business consultant Chi-Ning Chu talks about her new book 'The Art of War for Women: Sun Tzu's Ancient Strategies and Wisdom for Winning at Work', which discusses how women can more effectively win in business. She also shares her thoughts about the advantages that women have, which they can use in businesses decisions.

44709 ■ *"Ask Inc."* in *Inc. (November 2007, pp. 69)*
Description: The best time to terminate an employee is discussed.

44710 ■ *"Atlific Adds Management of 4 Hotels to Its Portfolio in Fort McMurray"* in *Canadian Corporate News (May 16, 2007)*
Description: Atlific Hotels & Resorts took over management for Merit Inn & Suites, The Merit Hotel, The Nomad Hotel and The Nomad Suites in Fort McMurray. The company feels that they will be able to increase the hotels' abilities to promote their services through their vast network of sales personnel and marketing and e-commerce team.

44711 ■ *"avVaa World Health Care Products Rolls Out Internet Marketing Program"* in *Health and Beauty Close-Up (September 18, 2009)*
Description: avVaa World Health Care Products, Inc., a biotechnology company, manufacturer and distributor of nationally branded therapeutic, natural health care and skin products, has signed an agreement with Online Performance Marketing to launch of an Internet marketing campaign in order to broaden its presence online. The impact of advertising on the Internet to generate an increase in sales is explored.

44712 ■ *"Back in the Race. New Fund Manager Has Whipped Sentinel International Equity Back into Shape"* in *Barron's (Vol. 88, March 17, 2008, No. 11, pp. 43)*
Pub: Dow Jones & Co., Inc.
Contact: Clare Hart, President
Ed: Leslie P. Norton. **Description:** Katherine Schapiro was able to get Sentinel International Equity's Morningstar classification to blended fund from a value fund rating after joining Sentinel from her former jobs at Strong Overseas Fund. Schapiro aims to benefit from the global rebalancing as the U.S.'s share of the world economy shrinks.

44713 ■ *"The Balanced Business"* in *Women In Business (Vol. 63, Spring 2011, No. 1, pp. 14)*
Pub: American Business Women's Association
Contact: Lorie Burch, President
Ed: Leigh Elmore. **Description:** The balance scoreboard has developed to a full strategic planning and management system from its early use as a simple performance measurement network. Executives are able to execute their strategies by using information from the balance scoreboard. Insights on Mayer Group Inc. executive Ken Mayer's view of the balance scorecard are also shared.

44714 ■ *Balls!: 6 Rules for Winning Today's Business Game*
Pub: John Wiley & Sons Inc.
Contact: Stephen M. Smith, President
Ed: Alexi Venneri. **Released:** January 2005. **Price:** $29.95. **Description:** In order to be successful business leaders must be brave, authentic, loud, lovable, and spunky and they need to lead their competition. **Availability:** Print.

44715 ■ *"B&B Hopes to Appeal to Fiat Execs"* in *Crain's Detroit Business (Vol. 25, June 15, 2009, No. 24, pp. 21)*
Pub: Crain Communications Inc. - Detroit
Contact: Keith Crain, Chairman
Ed: Daniel Duggan. **Description:** Cobblestone Manor, a ten-room bed and breakfast in Auburn Hills, Michigan is hoping to provide rooms for Fiat executives. The owners have been working with travel organizations to promote the castle-like bed and breakfast which appeals to European visitors.

44716 ■ *"Bank Bullish on Austin"* in *Austin Business JournalInc. (Vol. 29, November 13, 2009, No. 36, pp. A1)*
Pub: American City Business Journals
Ed: Kate Harrington. **Description:** American Bank's presence in Austin, Texas has been boosted by new management and a new 20,000 square foot building. This community bank intends to focus on building relationship with commercial banking customers. American Bank also plans to extend investment banking, treasury management, and commercial lending services.

44717 ■ *"Bank on It: Scouting and Keeping Good Talent in the Workplace"* in *Hawaii Business (Vol. 53, January 2008, No. 7, pp. 50)*
Pub: PacificBasin Communications
Ed: Christine Dermengian. **Description:** Tips on improving employee selection and retention are presented. The strategies in choosing and keeping the right employees include identifying which type of people the company needs and improving the workplace environment.

44718 ■ *"Bank On It: Handle With Care"* in *Hawaii Business (Vol. 53, October 2007, No. 5, pp. 66)*
Pub: PacificBasin Communications
Ed: Kenneth Sheffield. **Description:** Discusses a fiduciary, who may be a board member, business owner, or a trustee, and is someone who supervises and manages the affairs and the resources of a principal. Fiduciary duties, which include accounting, cost review and risk management, must be served with the benefit of the principal as the priority. Ways of breaching fiduciary duties and how to avoid them are discussed.

44719 ■ *"Banks Fret About Gist Of Bailout"* in *The Business Journal-Serving Metropolitan Kansas City (Vol. 27, September 26, 2008, No. 2)*
Pub: American City Business Journals, Inc.
Contact: Whitney Shaw, President
Ed: James Dornbrook. **Description:** Banks from the Kansas City area hope that the proposed $700 billion bailout will not send the wrong message. UMB Financial Corp. chairman says that he hopes that the bailout would benefit companies that were more risk restrained and punish those that took outsized risk. Other bank executives' perceptions on the planned bailout are given.

44720 ■ *"Barbara West"* in *Crain's Cleveland Business (Vol. 30, June 29, 2009, No. 25, pp. 14)*
Pub: Crain Communications Inc.
Ed: Shannon Mortland. **Description:** Profile of Barbara West, administrative director of emergency medicine at MetroHealth Medical Center in Ohio. Ms. West manages Metro Life Flight that uses helicopters to transport patients to MetroHealth. She discusses the challenges of taking care of patients when big emergencies occur.

44721 ■ *"Barnes Shakes Up Sara Lee Exec Suite"* in *Crain's Chicago Business* (Vol. 31, April 21, 2008, No. 16, pp. 1)
Pub: Crain Communications Inc.
Contact: Todd Johnson, Publisher
Ed: David Sterrett. Description: In an attempt to cut costs and boost profits, Sara Lee Corp.'s CEO Brenda Barnes is restructuring the company's management team.

44722 ■ *"BC Forest Safety Council Unveils Supervisor Course to Respond to Industry Demands"* in *Marketwired* (May 14, 2007)
Pub: Comtex News Network Inc.
Description: BC Forest Safety Council launched the sector's first supervisor training program that will lead to certification of forest supervisors in response to an industry-wide demand for standardized safety training for supervisors.

44723 ■ *"Be a Better Manager: Live Abroad"* in *Harvard Business Review* (Vol. 88, September 2010, No. 9, pp. 24)
Pub: Harvard Business School Publishing
Ed: William W. Maddux, Adam D. Galinsky, Carmit T. Tadmor. Description: Interrelationship between international experience and entrepreneurship is discussed. Individuals with international experience are likelier to be promoted and to develop new products and businesses.

44724 ■ *Be the Elephant: Build a Bigger, Better Business*
Pub: Workman Publishing Co.
Contact: Kristina Peterson, Director
E-mail: kristina@workman.com
Ed: Steve Kaplan. Price: $19.95. Description: Entrepreneur and author sets out an accessible, no-frills plan for business owners, managers, and other industrialists to grow their businesses into elephants: big and strong but also smart. Advice is given on fostering a growth mind-set, assessing risk, and creating unique selling propositions. Availability: E-book.

44725 ■ *Be the Hero: Three Powerful Ways to Overcome Challenges in Work and In Life*
Pub: Berrett-Koehler Communications Inc.
Contact: Steve Piersanti, President
E-mail: spiersanti@bkpub.com
Ed: Noah Blumenthal. Released: January 09, 2012. Price: $15.95, paperback; $19.95, hardcover. Description: Details are given to help individuals perform at their best when challenges are the greatest. It shows how to turn self-defeating thoughts and behavior into heroic actions. Availability: Print; PDF.

44726 ■ *"Before Happiness: The 5 Hidden Keys to Achieving Success, Spreading Happiness, and Sustaining Positive Change"*
Pub: Crown Business Books
Released: September 10, 2013. Price: , $26.00. Description: Harvard trained researcher explains proven strategies for changing attitudes to positive include, the most valuable reality to see a broader range of ideas and solutions; success mapping, setting goals around things that matter to you most; the x-spot, using success accelerants to propel you more quickly towards goals; noise-canceling, boost the signal pointing to opportunities and possibilities others miss; and positive inception, transferring your skills to your team, employees and everyone around you.

44727 ■ *"Being Emotional During Decision Making-Good or Bad? An Empirical Investigation"* in *Academy of Management Journal* (Vol. 50, No. 4, August 1, 2007, pp. 923)
Pub: Academy of Management
Contact: Ming-Jer Chen, President
Ed: Myeong-Gu Seo, Lisa Feldman Barrett. Description: Relationship between affective experience and decision-making performance is studied.

44728 ■ *"Best Companies for Diversity"* in *Black Enterprise* (Vol. 38, July 2008, No. 12, pp. 12)
Pub: Earl G. Graves Publishing Co. Inc.
Contact: Earl G. Graves, Jr., President
Description: Maintaining excellence in a company's diversity efforts requires critical challenges such as recruiting, retaining and developing talent in the executive pipeline. Top young and diverse emerging executives in corporate America are featured.

44729 ■ *"The Best Execs in Canada"* in *Canadian Business* (Vol. 79, October 9, 2006, No. 20, pp. 68)
Description: The annual list of the most outstanding and innovative business executives of Canada is presented.

44730 ■ *"Best Managed Companies"* in *Canadian Business* (Vol. 81, Summer 2008, No. 9, pp. 71)
Ed: Calvin Leung. Description: Table showing the five-year annualized growth rate and one-year stock performance of companies that have grown their cash flow per share at an annualized rate of 15 percent or more over the past five years. Analysts project that the cash flow trend will continue. Other details of the stock performance index are presented.

44731 ■ *"Best Managed Companies (Canada)"* in *Canadian Business* (Vol. 82, Summer 2009, No. 8, pp. 38)
Ed: Calvin Leung. Description: Agrium Inc. and Barrick Gold Corporation are among those that are found to be the best managed companies in Canada. Best managed companies also include software firm Open Text Corporation, which has grown annual sales by 75 percent and annual profits by 160 percent since 1995. Open Text markets software that allow firms to manage word-based data, and has 46,000 customers in 114 countries.

44732 ■ *"Best (Professional) Foot Forward: Effective Marketing Strategies for any Phase of Your Career"* in *Black Enterprise!>* (Vol. 44, June 2014, No. 10, pp. 44)
Pub: Earl G. Graves Publishing Co. Inc.
Contact: Earl G. Graves, Jr., President
Released: June 2014. Description: Because hiring managers face long-term vacancies and skills gaps, the importance of creating a professional marketing strategy when applying for a professional position is stressed. Advice is given to help guide applicants through the entire application, interviewing, and hiring process.

44733 ■ *"The Big Idea: No, Management Is Not a Profession"* in *Harvard Business Review* (Vol. 88, July-August 2010, No. 7-8, pp. 52)
Pub: Harvard Business School Publishing
Ed: Richard Barker. Description: An argument is presented that management is not a profession, as it is less focused on mastering a given body of knowledge than it is on obtaining integration and collaboration skills. Implications for teaching this new approach are also examined.

44734 ■ *"The Big Idea: The Case for Professional Boards"* in *Harvard Business Review* (Vol. 88, December 2010, No. 12, pp. 50)
Pub: Harvard Business School Publishing
Ed: Robert C. Pozen. Description: A professional directorship model can be applied to corporate governance. Suggestions for this include the reduction of board size to seven members in order to improve the effectiveness of decision making, along with the requirement that directors have industry expertise.

44735 ■ *"Big Paychecks for Hospital CEOs"* in *Sacramento Business Journal* (Vol. 28, April 8, 2011, No. 6, pp. 1)
Pub: Sacramento Business Journal
Ed: Kathy Robertson. Description: Hospital chief executives in Sacramento, California have been receiving large salaries, tax records show. The huge salaries reflect the high demand for successful hospital chief executives. Statistical data included.

44736 ■ *"Big Shoes to Fill for New United Way Chairman"* in *Business Courier* (Vol. 27, June 25, 2010, No. 8, pp. 4)
Ed: Lucy May. Description: David Dougherty, chairman of the nonprofit United Way of Greater Cincinnati, explains how he can surpass the nonprofit's 2009 campaign kickoff that raised $62 million. For 2010, Dougherty has prepared a $2 million matching grant from a group of local individuals, corporations, and foundations. Dougherty also discusses what he learned from participating in the 2009 campaign.

44737 ■ *"BIM and LPS Improve Project Management"* in *Contractor* (Vol. 57, January 2010, No. 1, pp. 56)
Pub: Intertec Publishing
Contact: John French, President
Ed: Dennis Sowards. Description: Building Information Modeling helps reduce workspace conflicts and construction problems that are not seen in typical design efforts for mechanical contractors. The Last Planner System in Lean Construction also helps improve productivity in project management.

44738 ■ *"BIM: What to Watch Out For"* in *Contractor* (Vol. 57, February 2010, No. 2, pp. 28)
Pub: Penton Media, Inc.
Ed: Susan Linden McGreevy. Description: Legal and risk management issues surrounding Building Information Modeling (BIM) can be divided into three categories namely; intellectual property, liability for content, and the responsibility for the inputs into the model. The agreement should be done in a way that protects the intellectual rights of the authors when using BIM.

44739 ■ *"Black Gold: Jobs Aplenty"* in *Canadian Business* (Vol. 79, August 14, 2006, No. 16-17, pp. 57)
Pub: Rogers Media Inc.
Contact: Tony Viner, President
Ed: Erin Pooley. Description: A list of the top ten jobs in the petroleum industry in Canada along with pay and nature of jobs, is presented.

44740 ■ *"Black's Truth: Will a Prison Stay Change the Way Conrad Black Operates?"* in *Canadian Business* (Vol. 81, March 31, 2008, No. 5)
Pub: Rogers Media Inc.
Contact: Tony Viner, President
Ed: Matthew McClearn. Description: Conrad Black will serve a 6 and a half years in prison but he asserts that his successors at Hollinger International and Hollinger Inc. grossly mismanaged and unjustly enriched themselves. Black also asserts that International violated the so-called November Agreement and that he is the aggrieved party. Black's assertions show a character flaw that cannot be corrected in prison.

44741 ■ *"The Blazers' Money Maker"* in *Business Journal Portland* (Vol. 31, April 18, 2014, No. 7, pp. 4)
Pub: American City Business Journals
Released: April 18, 2014. Description: The turnaround strategy used by CEO, Chris McGowan, to make the Portland Trail Blazers basketball team profitable by July 2016 is discussed. His personal restructuring effort was aimed at combining the Blazers' operations with day-to-day management of the Moda Center. The team also returned to selling tickets and sponsorship deals.

44742 ■ *"Blindspot: Hidden Biases of Good People"*
Pub: Ballantine/ Del Rey/Fawcett/Ivy Books
Contact: Gilbert Perlman, President
Released: February 12, 2013. Price: , $27.00. Description: Perceptions of social groups that shape our likes and dislikes and our judgments about people's character, abilities and potential include exposure to and attitudes about age, gender, race, ethnicity, religion, social class, sexuality, disability status, and nationality are examined. Hidden biases impact everyone, including business leaders, entrepreneurs and managers in decision making.

44743 ■ *"Block Plans Office Park Along K-10 Corridor"* in *The Business Journal-Serving Metropolitan Kansas City* (Vol. 27, October 3, 2008)
Pub: American City Business Journals, Inc.
Contact: Whitney Shaw, President
Ed: Rob Roberts. Description: Kansas City, Missouri-based Block and Co. is planning to build four office buildings at the corner of College Boule-

vard and Ridgeview Road in Olathe. Features of the planned development are provided. Comments from executives are also presented.

44744 ■ *The Board Book: An Insider's Guide for Directors and Trustees*
Pub: W.W. Norton and Company Inc.
Contact: A Malmud, President
Ed: William G. Bowen. **Released:** April 2012. **Price:** $16.95, paperback. **Description:** A primer for all directors and trustees that provides suggestions for getting back to good-governance basics in business. **Availability:** Print.

44745 ■ *"The Board Shorts Executive" in Hawaii Business (Vol. 53, January 2008, No. 7, pp. 33)*
Pub: PacificBasin Communications
Ed: Mike Markrich. **Description:** Vans Triple Crown of Surfing executive director Randy Rarick believes that the surfing business requires knowledge of the sport and integity to the game's lifestyle and spirit. His organization manages surfing events, and has generated jobs for the locals. Plans for Vans Triple Crown are supplied.

44746 ■ *"Boards That Lead: When to Take Charge, When to Partner, and When to Stay Out of the Way"*
Pub: Harvard Business Review Press
Contact: Peter E. Walsh, Director
Released: March 4, 2014. **Price:** , $26.00. **Description:** As boards take a more active role in decision making at companies, leadership at the top is being redefined. Boardroom veterans describe the successes and pitfalls of this new leadership style and explain how to define the central idea of the company, ensure that the right CEO is in place and potential successors are identified, recruit directors who add value, root out board dysfunction, select a board leader who bridges the divide between management and the board, and to set a high bar on ethics and risk.

44747 ■ *The Book of Hard Choices: How to Make the Right Decisions at Work and Keep Your Self-Respect*
Pub: Broadway Business
Contact: David Drake, Manager
E-mail: ddrake@randomhouse.com
Ed: Peter Roy, James A. Autry. **Released:** December 2006. **Price:** $13.99. **Availability:** E-book.

44748 ■ *"Book Smart" in Hawaii Business (Vol. 53, December 2007, No. 6, pp. 39)*
Ed: David K. Choo. **Description:** Different parts of a biography entry in the Black Book are examined in relation to their usage in starting a conversation with an executive. The second part, which is the educational background, is considered the most significant of all, due to the amount of information given. The importance of making connections in Hawaii is discussed.

44749 ■ *Bo's Lasting Lessons*
Ed: Bo Schembechler; John U. Bacon. **Price:** $13.99. **Description:** Leadership skills are taught.

44750 ■ *"Both Eyes on the Prize" in Canadian Business (Vol. 83, September 14, 2010, No. 15, pp. 42)*
Pub: Rogers Media Inc.
Contact: Tony Viner, President
Ed: Jacqueline Nelson. **Description:** North American executive compensation has fundamentally shifted partly due to pressure from the US government and recent adjustments in the way CEO pay packages are structured. The changes have also become common practice in Canada and helped in scrutinizing the executive pay.

44751 ■ *Bottom-Line Training: Performance-Based Results*
Pub: Training Education Management
Contact: Donald J. Ford, President
Ed: Donald J. Ford. **Released:** Second Edition. **Price:** $29. **Description:** Training is critical to any successful enterprise. The key to any successful training program involves defining and constantly focusing on the desired results of the program. The

author provides a training model based on five phases, known as ADDIE: analysis, design, development, implementation and evaluation.

44752 ■ *"Boundaries for Leaders (Enhanced Edition): Results, Relationships, and Being Ridiculously In Charge"*
Pub: Harper Business
Released: April 16, 2013. **Price:** , $28.99. **Description:** Clinical psychologist and author explains how the best business leaders set boundaries within their organizations, with their teams and themselves, to improve performance and increase customer and employee satisfaction. Practical advice is given to manage teams, coach direct reports, and create an organization with strong ethics and culture.

44753 ■ *"Box-Store Bosses Score a Win In Employer Rankings" in Puget Sound Business Journal (Vol. 34, March 28, 2014, No. 50, pp. 8)*
Pub: American City Business Journals
Released: March 28, 2014. **Description:** Glassdoor, an employer rating company, reveals that retail executives in Seattle, Washington are more popular with the staff than the city's technology, CEOs. Craif Jelinek of warehouse Costco was the fifth-highest in the CEO ratings, while Howard Schultz of Starbucks coffee took the eight spot. A table that presents information on the top ten rated CEOs of 2014 is presented.

44754 ■ *Bradford's International Directory of Marketing Research Agencies*
Pub: Business Research Services Inc.
Contact: Thomas D. Johnson, President
URL(s): www.bradfordsdirectory.comwww.sba8a.com/brs.htm. **Released:** Biennial; Latest edition 30th. **Price:** $95, Individuals in-print; $95, Individuals CD-ROM; $125, Individuals in print and CD-ROM. **Covers:** Over 2,300 marketing research agencies worldwide. Includes domestic and international demographic data and professional association contacts. **Entries include:** Company name, address, phone, name and title of contact, date founded, number of employees, description of products or services, e-mail, URL. **Arrangement:** Geographical. **Indexes:** Alphabetical by company. **Availability:** CD-ROM: Business Research Services Inc. **Type:** Directory.

44755 ■ *"Brief: Make a Bigger Impact by Saying Less"*
Pub: John Wiley & Sons Inc.
Contact: Stephen M. Smith, President
Released: February 10, 2014. **Price:** , $15.93. **Description:** Communication is key to any business success. Today, busy executives demand respect and manage their time more efficiently than ever. The author addresses the challenges of inattention, interruptions, and impatience faced by professionals and to help leaders gain the strength required to eliminate wasteful words and stand out from others when communicating.

44756 ■ *"Bringing Big Guns" in Business Courier (Vol. 24, January 22, 2008, No. 41, pp. 1)*
Pub: American City Business Journals, Inc.
Contact: Whitney Shaw, President
Ed: Lucy May. **Description:** Chief executive officer of Nidland Co. John Hayden was assigend as Cincinnati USA Partnership chairman. Hayden will bring his expertise to help the partnership drive economic development in the Greater Cincinnati area. Details of the parntership's plans are suplied.

44757 ■ *"Bringing Manufacturing Concerns to Springfield" in Crain's Chicago Business (Vol. 31, March 31, 2008, No. 13, pp. 6)*
Pub: Crain Communications Inc.
Contact: Todd Johnson, Publisher
Ed: Paul Merrion. **Description:** Profile of the new executive vice-president of Tooling & Manufacturing Assn., Paul Merrion, a man who plans to grow TMA's membership with an aggressive legislative agenda in Springfield.

44758 ■ *"Bringing Out the Best in Employees" in Business Strategy Review (Vol. 23, Spring 2012, No. 1, pp. 39)*
Released: Spring 2012. **Description:** Employees who find their work frustrating, boring and worthless have found their hero in Scott Adams' Dilbert, the nine-to-five man who lets us know just how bad managers can be at their jobs. Julian Birkinshaw, Vyla Rollins and Stefano Turconi believe that bad bosses can change to become true leaders.

44759 ■ *"The Buck Stops Here" in Canadian Business (Vol. 81, November 10, 2008, No. 19, pp. 25)*
Pub: Rogers Media Inc.
Contact: Tony Viner, President
Ed: Sarka Halas. **Description:** Reputation strategist Leslie Gaines-Ross says that minimizing the damage followed by the identification of what went wrong are the first steps that companies need to take when trying to salvage their reputation. Gaines-Ross states that it is up to the CEO to ensure the company's speedy recovery and they need to be at the forefront of the process.

44760 ■ *"Budget Strategically to Stay on Course" in Entrepreneur (August 28, 2008)*
Pub: Entrepreneur Press
Contact: Perlman Neil, President
Ed: Tim Berry. **Description:** Budgeting is one of the most valuable tools in a manager's arsenal. The importance of budgeting is discussed and tips for surviving an economic recession are provided.

44761 ■ *"Building Alexian Brothers' Clinical Reputation" in Crain's Chicago Business (Vol. 31, May 5, 2008, No. 18, pp. 6)*
Pub: Crain Communications Inc.
Contact: Todd Johnson, Publisher
Ed: Mike Colias. **Description:** Profile of the CEO of Alexian Brothers Medical Center in Elk Grove Village who plans to stabilize Alexian Brothers' financial performance in part by eliminating $20 million in annual costs.

44762 ■ *Business Black Belt: Develop the Strength, Flexibility and Agility to Run Your Company*
Ed: Burke Franklin. **Released:** November 1, 2010. **Price:** $15.99. **Description:** Manual offering insights that will enable anyone to become successful in small business. Seventy short chapters included topics such as attitude, management, marketing, selling, employees, money, MBAs, lawyers, consultants, and investors.

44763 ■ *Business Diagnostics*
Pub: Trafford Publishing
Contact: Steen Marcussen, Manager
Ed: Michael Thompson, Richard Mimick. **Released:** April 10, 2002. **Price:** C$70. **Description:** Business management skills are outlined. **Availability:** Print.

44764 ■ *"Business Ethics, Strategic Decision Making, and Firm Performance" in Business Horizons (September-October 2007, pp. 353)*
Pub: Elsevier Technology Publications
Ed: Michael A. Hitt, Jaime D. Collins. **Price:** $35.95. **Description:** Strategic management and decision-making process are linked to business ethics. The Strengths, Weakness, Opportunities, and Threats (SWOT) analysis model is employed to design an effective strategy for companies. **Availability:** PDF.

44765 ■ *"Business Forecast: Stormy and Successful" in Women In Business (Vol. 62, June 2010, No. 2, pp. 12)*
Pub: American Business Women's Association
Contact: Lorie Burch, President
Ed: Kathleen Leighton. **Description:** Stormy Simon, vice president of customer service at Overstock.com is a self-made career woman who started out as a temporary employee in the company in 2001. She was not able to attend college because she had two sons to care for after her divorce. Simon got involved in advertising and media buying and shares her love for business.

44766 ■ "Business Guide and Employment Role"
Pub: AuthorHouse
Contact: Bryan Smith, President
Released: October 10, 2014. **Price:** , $15.18 paperback. **Description:** Financial expert discusses the importance of economic and business and their role in employment. The business and finance manager is crucial to any small business. The guide is an essential tool for any entrepreneur, the investor in business enterprise, the individual businessman, the human resources manager, and the business and finance professional to learn the merits to do business and play a role in employment.

44767 ■ Business Management for Entrepreneurs
Pub: Double Storey Books
Ed: Cecile Nieuwenhuizen. **Released:** March 1, 2009. **Price:** , $35.95. **Description:** Lack of good management skills are usually the reason for any small company to fail. This book introduces entrepreneurs and managers of small to medium-sized firms to all functions required to manage successfully.

44768 ■ Business Management for Tropical Dairy Farmers
Pub: CSIRO Publishing
Contact: Megan Clark, Chief Executive Officer
Ed: John Moran. **Released:** 2009. **Price:** A$49.95, paperback. **Description:** Business management skills required for dairy farmers are addressed, focusing on financial management and ways to improve cattle housing and feeding systems. **Availability:** Print.

44769 ■ Business Stripped Bare: Adventures of a Global Entrepreneur
Pub: Virgin Books/Random House
Ed: Richard Branson. **Released:** January 22, 2010. **Price:** £20, Hardback; £9.99, Paperback. **Description:** Successful entrepreneur, Sir Richard Branson, shares the inside track on some of his greatest achievements in business and the lessons learned from setbacks.

44770 ■ "Business as Usual at RIM, Balsillie Says" in Globe & Mail (March 6, 2007, pp. B1)
Ed: Simon Avery. **Description:** The continuation of normal business at Research In Motion Ltd., after the resignation of Jim Balsillie from the chairman's post, is described. The investigation of securities fraud at Research In Motion Ltd. and the continuation of Jim Balsillie as the co-chief executive officer of the company are discussed.

44771 ■ Business Warrior: Strategy for Entrepreneurs
Ed: Sun Tzu. **Released:** September 2006. **Price:** , $19.95. **Description:** Advice to help entrepreneurs understand competitive strategies in order to succeed, focusing on sales, marketing, and personnel management.

44772 ■ Busting the Myth of the Heroic CEO
Ed: Michel Villette, Catherine Vuillermot. **Released:** 2010. **Price:** $24.95. **Description:** According to the authors, corporate leaders do not get ahead through productive risk-taking and innovation, but through ruthless exploitation of market imperfections and rivals.

44773 ■ "Bye-Bye, Ol' Boys" in Canadian Business (Vol. 80, January 15, 2007, No. 2, pp. 16)
Ed: Michelle Magnan. **Description:** A profile of Kathy Sendall, senior vice-president of Petro-Canada of the North American division and chairperson of the Canadian Association of Petroleum Producers, is presented.

44774 ■ "C. Andrew McCartney; President, Owner, Bowden Manufacturing Corp., 37" in Crain's Cleveland Business (November 19, 2007)
Pub: Crain Communications Inc.
Ed: David Bennett. **Description:** Profile of C. Andrew McCartney who was named president of Bowden Manufacturing Corp., a company that machines and fabricates metal and plastic parts for products rang-

ing from airplanes to medical equipment; Mr. McCartney has since purchased the company, which posted $8 million in sales last year. He feels that part of his success is due to adherence to such policies such as gaining the employees trust and to avoid making promises to customers that Bowden cannot keep.

44775 ■ "Can He Win the Patent Game?" in Globe & Mail (February 20, 2006, pp. B1)
Ed: Simon Avery, Paul Waldie. **Description:** A profile on managerial abilities of chief executive officer Jim Balsillie of Research In Motion Ltd., who will face the patent case with NTP Inc., is presented.

44776 ■ "Can You Hear Me Now?" in Harvard Business Review (Vol. 86, July-August 2008, No. 8, pp. 23)
Pub: Harvard Business Review Press
Contact: Peter E. Walsh, Director
Ed: Katharina Pick. **Description:** Tips for improving communication among boardroom members are presented. These include encouraging frankness via in-meeting leaders, and the ability of directors to meet without managers.

44777 ■ "Can You Really Manage Engagement Without Managers? Zappos May Soon Find Out, as the Online Retailer is Eliminating the Traditional Manager Role" in Gallup Business Journal (April 24, 2014)
Pub: Gallup Press
Released: April 24, 2014. **Description:** Online retailer, Zappos, will do away with the traditional manager role to lessen the chain of control within the organization. The concept of self-managed teams is explored.

44778 ■ Canadian Entrepreneurship and Small Business Management
Pub: McGraw-Hill Ryerson Ltd.
Contact: Robert J. Bahash, President
Ed: D. Wesley Balderson. **Price:** C$104.36, Members; C$115.95, Nonmembers. **Description:** Successful entrepreneurship and small business management is shown through the use of individual Canadian small business experiences. **Availability:** Print.

44779 ■ "Captain Planet" in (Vol. 90, June 2012, No. 6, pp. 112)
Pub: Harvard Business Review Press
Contact: Peter E. Walsh, Director
Ed: Adi Ignatius. **Released:** June 2012. **Description:** Paul Polman, chief executive officer of Unilever N.V., discusses his company's sustainable living plan, which integrates social responsibility with corporate objectives. Topics include sustainable sourcing, abolishing quarterly reporting in favor of long-term perspectives, the impact of the 2008 global economic crisis, and turning a company into a learning organization.

44780 ■ "The Carpenter: A Story About the Greatest Success Strategies of All"
Pub: John Wiley & Sons Inc.
Contact: Stephen M. Smith, President
Released: May 27, 2014. **Price:** , $23.00. **Description:** John Gordon draws upon his work with business leaders, sales people, professional and college sports teams, nonprofit organizations and schools to share a story that will inspire people to build a better life, career and team with successful business strategies.

44781 ■ The Carrot Principle: How the Best Managers Use Recognition to Engage Their People, Retain Talent, and Accelerate Performance
Pub: Simon and Schuster Inc.
Contact: Carolyn Reidy, President
E-mail: carolyn.reidy@simonandschuster.com
Released: April 2009. **Price:** $23.99. **Description:** Book show ways that managers can fail to acknowledge special achievements of employees thereby risking alienating the best workers or losing them to competing firms. **Availability:** Print.

44782 ■ "A Case Study: Real-Life Business Planning" in Entrepreneur (February 3, 2009)
Pub: Entrepreneur Press
Contact: Perlman Neil, President
Ed: Tim Berry. **Description:** Provides a case study of a two-day planning meeting for Palo Alto Software in which the executives of the company met for their annual planning cycle and discussed ways in which the company needed to change in order to stay viable in today's tough economic climate.

44783 ■ "CBS" in Brandweek (Vol. 49, April 21, 2008, No. 16, pp. SR6)
Ed: John Consoli. **Description:** Provides contact information for sales and marketing personnel for the CBS network as well as a listing of the station's top programming and an analysis of the current season and the target audience for those programs running in the current season.

44784 ■ "CBS Television Distribution" in Brandweek (Vol. 49, April 21, 2008, No. 16, pp. SR13)
Pub: Nielsen Business Media Inc.
Contact: Howard Appelbaum, President
Ed: Marc Berman. **Description:** Provides contact information for sales and marketing personnel for CBS Television Distribution as well as a listing of the station's top programming and an analysis of the current season and the target audience for those programs running in the current season. Due to the unprecedented, decade-plus advantage of first-run leaders such as Wheel of Fortune, Oprah, Judge Judy and Entertainment Tonight, CBS is poised to remain a leader among the syndicates.

44785 ■ "The Center of Success: Author Explores How Confidence Can Take You Further" in Black Enterprise (Vol. 38, March 1, 2008, No. 8)
Pub: Earl G. Graves Publishing Co. Inc.
Contact: Earl G. Graves, Jr., President
Ed: Ayana Dixon. **Description:** Motivational speaker and author, Valorie Burton, provides a 50-question confidence quotient assessment to help business owners and managers develop confidence in order to obtain goals.

44786 ■ "The CEO of Anglo American On Getting Serious About Safety" in (Vol. 90, June 2012, No. 6, pp. 43)
Pub: Harvard Business Review Press
Contact: Peter E. Walsh, Director
Ed: Cynthia Carroll. **Released:** June 2012. **Description:** The author discusses her decision to shut down Anglo American PLC's platinum mine, the world's largest, for a complete overhaul of the firm's safety procedures. This involved a thorough retraining of the mine's workforce, replacing nearly all of the managers, and promoting the changes throughout the rest of the industry.

44787 ■ "CEO Forecast: With Cloudy Economy, Executives Turn to Government Contracting" in Hispanic Business (January-February 2009, pp. 34, 36)
Pub: Hispanic Business Inc.
Contact: Jesus Chavarria, President
Ed: Jessica Haro, Richard Kaplan. **Description:** As economic uncertainty fogs the future, executives turn to government contracts in order to boost business. Revenue sources, health care challenges, environmental consulting and remediation services, as well as technological strides are discussed.

44788 ■ "CEO Pay: Best Bang for Buck" in Philadelphia Business Journal (Vol. 30, September 30, 2011, No. 33, pp. 1)
Pub: American City Business Journals Inc.
Ed: Jeff Blumenthal. **Description:** A study by Strategic Research Solutions on the compensation of chief executive officers in Philadelphia, Pennsylvania-based public companies reveals that only a few of them performed according to expectations. These include Brian Roberts of Comcast, John Conway of Crown Holdings, and Frank Hermance of Ametek Inc.

44789 ■ *"CEO Pay: The Details"* in Crain's Detroit Business (Vol. 25, June 22, 2009, No. 25, pp.)
Pub: Crain Communications Inc. - Detroit
Contact: Keith Crain, Chairman
Description: Total compensation packages for CEOs at area companies our outlined. These packages include salary, bonuses, stock awards, and options.

44790 ■ *"The CEO Poll: A Say on Pay"* in Canadian Business (Vol. 82, April 27, 2009, No. 7, pp. 14)
Pub: Rogers Media Inc.
Contact: Tony Viner, President
Ed: Joe Castaldo. **Description:** A COMPAS Inc. survey of 134 Canadian chief executive officers found that 44 percent agree that CEO compensation should be subject to a non-binding vote. The respondents were also divided on whether to allow shareholders to exercise retroactive clawbacks on executive compensation if firm performance turns out to be worse than projected.

44791 ■ *"CEO Tapped for Perrier, Poland Springs: John J. Harris Takes the Helm of Nestle Waters"* in Black Enterprise (Vol. 38, February 2008, No. 7, pp. 30)
Pub: Earl G. Graves Publishing Co. Inc.
Contact: Earl G. Graves, Jr., President
Ed: Brenda Porter. **Description:** John J. Harris, newly appointed CEO, is hoping to increase market share of Nestle's bottled water products.

44792 ■ *"CEOs Decry Budget Taxation Change"* in Globe & Mail (April 2, 2007, pp. B1)
Pub: CTVglobemedia Publishing Inc.
Ed: Steven Chase. **Description:** The views of the chief executive officers of Canadian firms, on the changes in the country's policy governing the taxation of foreign deals, are presented.

44793 ■ *"CEOs Divided About Census"* in Canadian Business (Vol. 83, August 17, 2010, No. 13-14, pp. 20)
Pub: Rogers Media Inc.
Contact: Tony Viner, President
Ed: Jacqueline Nelson. **Description:** A Compass poll of Canadian CEOs on what the government should do with controversial long-form census is presented. The poll results show that 30 percent believe the government should remove any threat of punishment for failure to complete the survey. The CEOs also believe the law must be enforced by the government to encourage participation.

44794 ■ *"CEOs Find Pay Tied to Performance"* in Baltimore Business Journal (Vol. 30, June 29, 2012, No. 8, pp. 1)
Pub: American City Business Journals, Inc.
Contact: Whitney Shaw, President
Ed: Gary Haber. **Released:** June 29, 2012. **Description:** Baltimore, Maryland chief executives' salaries have been linked to their respective companies' financial performance. The area's ten highest paid chief executives had a combined earning of $88 million in 2011. Statistics on CEO salaries are also included.

44795 ■ *"CEOs Gone Wild"* in Canadian Business (Vol. 79, August 14, 2006, No. 16-17, pp. 15)
Ed: Thomas Watson. **Description:** Stock investment decisions of chief executive officers of metal companies in Canada, are discussed.

44796 ■ *"CEOs Keep Bringing Home the Perks"* in Baltimore Business Journal (Vol. 30, May 18, 2012, No. 2, pp. 1)
Pub: American City Business Journals, Inc.
Contact: Whitney Shaw, President
Ed: Gary Haber. **Released:** May 18, 2012. **Description:** According to the annual proxy statement of Baltimore-based Stanley Black & Decker, executive chairman Nolan D. Archibald received a $12.3 million compensation package in 2011. According to the company, Archibald's perks are part of his employ-

ment agreement which was duly approved by the shareholders during the merger of Stanley Works and Black & Decker.

44797 ■ *"The CEO's New Armor"* in Conde Nast Portfolio (Vol. 2, June 2008, No. 6, pp. 56)
Ed: John Cassidy. **Description:** Due to a new breed in C.E.O.'s contracts it is nearly impossible to fire them regardless of their performance. Despite the Sarbanes-Oxley Act in which attempted to codify C.E.O. responsibilities, corporate bosses responded by quietly demanding individual contracts, which, in many cases, were drawn up by their own lawyers and accepted by company boards with no outside oversight or review.

44798 ■ *"CEOs Split on Migrant Workers"* in Canadian Business (Vol. 83, September 14, 2010, No. 15, pp. 23)
Pub: Rogers Media Inc.
Contact: Tony Viner, President
Ed: Jacqueline Nelson. **Description:** A survey of Canadian CEOs shows that 49 percent of the respondents believe it was wrong to suspend the immigration programs and companies should be allowed to hire the most skilled workers regardless of citizenship. However, 42 percent believe the suspension was right because employment of Canadians must take precedence.

44799 ■ *"CEOs With a Functional Background in Operations"* in Human Resource Management (Vol. 49, September-October 2010, No. 5)
Pub: John Wiley
Ed: Burak Koyuncu, Shainaz Firfiray, Bjorn Claes, Monika Hamori. **Description:** A study was conducted to determine whether companies that appoint chief executive officers (CEOs) with an operations background exhibit better post-succession financial performance relative to organizations that appoint CEOs with other functional backgrounds. A total of 437 CEOs from U.S. firms in eight industries were included in the study.

44800 ■ *"CEOs With Headsets"* in Harvard Business Review (Vol. 88, September 2010, No. 9, pp. 21)
Pub: Harvard Business School Publishing
Ed: Andrew Zimbalist. **Description:** Placing a salary cap on college coaches' compensation would not significantly affect coaching quality or an institution's ability to obtain talent. A salary growth rate comparison between coaches, university presidents, and full professors for the period 1986 to 2007 is also presented.

44801 ■ *"Certification Experts Germanischer Lloyd Wind Energy Assist NaiKun's Offshore Wind Project"* in Marketwired (May 14, 2007)
Pub: Comtex News Network Inc.
Description: Germanischer Lloyd Wind Energy (GL Wind) will examine, inspect, and provide quality management services for the engineering, design, and construction of the offshore wind project planned by NaiKun Wind Development Inc. in northwest British Columbia.

44802 ■ *"Challenges Await Quad in Going Public"* in Milwaukee Business Journal (Vol. 27, January 29, 2010, No. 18, pp. A1)
Pub: American City Business Journals
Ed: Rich Rovito. **Description:** Sussex, Wisconsin-based Quad/Graphics Inc.'s impending acquisition of rival Canadian World Color Press Inc. will transform it into a publicly held entity for the first time. Quad has operated as a private company for nearly 40 years and will need to adjust to changes, such as the way management shares information with Quad/Graphics' employees. Details of the merger are included.

44803 ■ *"Challenges, Responses and Available Resources"* in Journal of Small Business and Entrepreneurship (Vol. 23, Winter 2010, No. 1)
Pub: Canadian Council for Small Business and Entrepreneurship
Contact: Sandra Altner, President
Ed: Lynne Siemens. **Description:** Rural communities and their residents are exploring the potential of small business and entrepreneurship to address the

economic changes they are facing. While these rural areas present many opportunities, business people in these areas face challenges which they must navigate to operate successfully.

44804 ■ *"Chameleonic or Consistent? A Multilevel Investigation of Emotional Labor Variability and Self-Monitoring"* in Academy of Management Journal (Vol. 55, August 1, 2012, No. 4, pp. 905)
Pub: Academy of Management
Contact: Ming-Jer Chen, President
Ed: Brent A. Scott, Christopher M. Barnes, David T. Wagner. **Description:** The importance of emotional labor variability in association with job satisfaction and work withdrawal is examined. Results indicate that surface acting variability is linked to lower levels of job satisfaction and higher levels of work withdrawal and that self-monitoring influences the impact of surface acting variability on job satisfaction and work withdrawal.

44805 ■ *"Chameloeonic or Consistent? A Multilevel Investigation of Emotional Labor Variability and Self-Monitoring"* in Academy of Management Journal (Vol. 55, August 2012, No. 4, pp. 905)
Released: August 2012. **Description:** The importance of emotional labor variability in association with job satisfaction and work withdrawal is examined. Results indicate that surface acting variability is linked to lowe levels of job satisfaction and higher levels of work withdrawal and that self-monitoring influences the impact of surface acting variability on job satisfactionand work withdrawal.

44806 ■ *Change in SMEs: The New European Capitalism*
Pub: Palgrave Macmillan
Contact: Lisa Dunn, Manager
E-mail: l.dunn@palgrave.com
Ed: Katharina Bluhm, Rudi Schmidt. **Released:** September 2008. **Price:** £77, hardcover. **Description:** Effects of global change on corporate governance, management, competitive strategies and labor relations in small-to-medium sized enterprises in various European countries are discussed. **Availability:** Print; E-book; Electronic publishing.

44807 ■ *"Characteristics of Great Salespeople"* in Agency Sales Magazine (Vol. 39, November 2009, No. 10, pp. 40)
Ed: Paul Pease. **Description:** Tips for managers in order to maximize the performance of their sales personnel are presented through several vignettes. Using performance based commission that rewards success, having business systems that support sales activity, and having an organizational culture that embraces sales as a competitive edge are some suggestions.

44808 ■ *The Checklist Manifesto: How to Get Things Right*
Pub: Metropolitan Books
Contact: Sara Bershtel, Manager
Ed: Atul Gawande. **Released:** December 2009. **Price:** $27, hardcover; $9.99. **Description:** How tragic errors can be sharply reduced with a piece of paper, hand-drawn boxes, and a pencil. **Availability:** PrintE-book.

44809 ■ *Chief Culture Officer: How to Create a Living, Breathing Corporation*
Pub: Basic Books
Contact: Elizabeth Maguire, Publisher
Ed: Grant McCracken. **Price:** $16.99. **Description:** Business consultant argues that corporations need to focus on 'reading' what's happening in the culture around them. Otherwise, companies will suffer the consequences, as Levi Strauss did when it missed out on the rise of hip-hop (and the baggy pants that are part of that lifestyle). **Availability:** Print; E-book.

44810 ■ *"Chip Heath: Get Over Your Fear of Change"* in Canadian Business (Vol. 83, June 15, 2010, No. 10, pp. 38)
Pub: Rogers Media Inc.
Contact: Tony Viner, President
Ed: Michelle Magnan. **Description:** Organizational behavior professor Chip Heath says that resistance to change is based on the conflict between our

analytical, rational side and our emotional side that is in love with comfort. Heath states that businesses tend to focus on the negatives during an economic crisis while they should be focusing on what is working and ways to do more of that.

44811 ■ "Choose Your Candidate: 2012-2013 National Board of Directors" in Women in Business (Vol. 64, Summer 2012, No. 2, pp. 41)

Pub: American Business Women's Association

Contact: Lorie Burch, President

Released: Summer 2012. Description: The candidates for American Business Women's Association (ABWA) national president, vice president, secretary-treasurer and district vice presidents are presented. Each candidate's response to the question of how ABWA has helped them achieve their career goals are also provided.

44812 ■ "Choosing Strategies For Change" in Harvard Business Review (Vol. 86, July-August 2008, No. 8, pp. 130)

Pub: Harvard Business Review Press

Contact: Peter E. Walsh, Director

Ed: John P. Kotter, Leonard A. Schlesinger. Description: Methods for implementing organizational change include identifying potential areas of resistance, providing the necessary skills and information to counteract resistance, and assessing situational factors that may influence results.

44813 ■ "Chuck E. Cheese's CEO to Retire" in Dallas Business Journal (Vol. 37, March 28, 2014, No. 29, pp. 6)

Pub: American City Business Journals

Released: March 28, 2014. Description: CEC Entertainment Inc. president and CEO, Michael Magusiak, is retiring after spending almost 27 years with the parent company Chuck E. Cheese. Magusiak is confident that the future of Chuck E. Cheese's brand will continue to grow in the U.S. and globally.

44814 ■ "Cincinnati Consults Executives on Police Chief Hire" in Business Courier (Vol. 27, August 27, 2010, No. 17, pp. 1)

Pub: Business Courier

Ed: Dan Monk, Lucy May. Description: The City of Cincinnati, Ohio has begun a selection process for the new police chief by consulting the city's business executives. The city charter amendment known as Issue 5 has removed civil service protection from the chief's post and enables City Manager Milton Dohoney to hire a chief from outside the department.

44815 ■ "CISO Role Evolves Towards Balancing Business and Security Objectives: Emerging Business and Security Requirements are Demanding New Skills of the CISO Role" in Computer Weekly (January 31, 2012)

Pub: TechTarget Inc.

Contact: Kevin Beam, President

Released: January 31, 2012. Description: Balancing the demands of cyber threats and regulatory compliance along with innovation and growth need to be managed by both a chief information security officer, chief information officer, and a member of the It TEAM in order to be certain needs are being met in this ever-changing environment.

44816 ■ "Citadel Hires Three Lehman Execs" in Chicago Tribune (October 21, 2008)

Ed: James P. Miller. Description: Citadel Investment Group LLC, Chicago hedge-fund operator, has hired three former senior executives of bankrupt investment banker Lehman Brothers Holding Inc. Citadel believes that the company's hiring spree will help them to further expand the firm's capabilities in the global fixed income business.

44817 ■ "Class Management" in Canadian Business (Vol. 80, April 23, 2007, No. 9, pp. 64)

Ed: Erin Pooley. Description: The role of executive MBA programs in improving performance of employees is presented.

44818 ■ "Clearwire Struggling, Banks on Deals with Competitors" in Puget Sound Business Journal (Vol. 33, August 24, 2012, No. 18, pp. 1)

Pub: American City Business Journal

Ed: Emily Parkhurst, Alyson Raletz. Description: Clearwire Corporation's chief executive, Erik Prusch, is planning to lease the wireless spectrum of the company to major mobile providers that run out of their own supply. At issue is whether the Bellevue, Washington-based telecommunication company can manage its $4 billion debt and maximize the value of its technology while managing its partners all at the same time.

44819 ■ "The CMO of Consequence" in Business Strategy Review (Vol. 21, Autumn 2010, No. 3, pp. 42)

Pub: John Wiley & Sons Inc. Scientific, Technical, Medical, and Scholarly Div. (Wiley-Blackwell)

Contact: William J. Pesce, Manager

E-mail: wpesce@wiley.com

Ed: D. Eric Boyd, Rajesh K. Chandy, Marcus Cunha, Jr. Description: Do chief marketing officers matter? Some say that CMOs have limited effect on corporate performance and don't add significant value to the firm. The authors agree that the job in many firms is in great peril, but their research has uncovered why the contributions of some CMOs are invaluable.

44820 ■ "CMO Nicholson Exits Pepsi as Share Declines" in Advertising Age (Vol. 79, July 7, 2008, No. 26, pp. 4)

Pub: Crain Communications Inc.

Contact: Rance Crain, President

Ed: Natalie Zmuda. Description: Cie Nicholson, the chief marketing officer at Pepsi-Cola UK, is leaving the company at a time when its market share is down; the brand, which was known for its dynamic marketing, has diverted much of its attention from its core brands and shifted attention to the ailing Gatorade brand as well as Sobe Life Water and Amp.

44821 ■ "CN Profit a Boon for Top Brass" in Globe & Mail (March 23, 2007, pp. B5)

Pub: CTVglobemedia Publishing Inc.

Ed: Brent Jang. Description: Canadian National Railway Co., Montreal-based freight carrier, paid $7.3 million in compensation to its top five executives. The company has posted a record $2.1 billion profits in 2006.

44822 ■ "CN to Webcast 2007 Analyst Meeting in Toronto May 23-24" in Canadian Corporate News (May 16, 2007)

Description: Canadian National Railway Company (CN) broadcast its analyst meeting in Toronto with a webcast which focused on CN's opportunities, strategies, and financial outlook through the year 2010.

44823 ■ "Coaching Salespeople into Sales Champions: A Tactical Playbook for Managers and Executives"

Pub: John Wiley & Sons Inc.

Contact: Stephen M. Smith, President

Released: March 14, 2008. Price: , $29.95. Description: When managers train their workers around best practices, core competencies and the inner game of coaching, they will develop the champion attitude that will increase sales and profits. The author presents information to build success team of top producers.

44824 ■ "Coffee Breaks Don't Boost Productivity After All" in Harvard Business Review (Vol. 90, May 2012, No. 5, pp. 34)

Pub: Harvard Business Review Press

Contact: Peter E. Walsh, Director

Ed: Charlotte Fritz. Released: May 2012. Description: Research shows no statistical correlation between taking a short break at work and one's fatigue and vitality levels. However, a link was found between personal productivity and assisting a co-worker. Employees detach from work more successfully during long breaks rather than short ones.

44825 ■ "Cold Stone Creamery" in Ice Cream Reporter (Vol. 23, November 20, 2010, No. 12, pp. 6)

Description: Doug Ducey, former CEO of Cold Stone Creamery, was elected to the post of Arizona State Treasurer. Ducey was responsible for the firm's expansion to major brand status.

44826 ■ "The Color of Success: ELC Focuses On Making Diversity Work" in Black Enterprise (Vol. 41, December 2010, No. 5, pp. 59)

Pub: Earl G. Graves Publishing Co. Inc.

Contact: Earl G. Graves, Jr., President

Ed: Sonia Alleyne. Description: CEOs and top ELC members at the annual recognition conference held in New York in October 2010 shared their perspective on corporate inclusion and advice for C-suite aspirants.

44827 ■ "Column: Good Decisions. Bad Outcomes" in Harvard Business Review (Vol. 88, December 2010, No. 12, pp. 40)

Pub: Harvard Business School Publishing

Ed: Dan Ariely. Description: Suggestions are provided for developing and implementing improved reward systems that in turn produce better decision-making processes. These include documenting critical assumptions and changing mind sets.

44828 ■ "Column: It's Time to Take Full Responsibility" in Harvard Business Review (Vol. 88, October 2010, No. 10, pp. 42)

Pub: Harvard Business School Publishing

Ed: Rosabeth Moss Kanter. Description: A case for corporate responsibility is cited, focusing on long-term impact and the effects of public accountability.

44829 ■ "Column: Redefining Failure" in Harvard Business Review (Vol. 88, September 2010, No. 9, pp. 34)

Pub: Harvard Business School Publishing

Ed: Seth Godin. Description: Specific forms of failure, including design failure, failure of priorities, failure of opportunity, and failure to quit are examined. The negative implications of maintaining the status quo are discussed.

44830 ■ "Column: What 17th-Century Pirates Can Teach Us About Job Design" in Harvard Business Review (Vol. 88, October 2010, No. 10, pp. 44)

Pub: Harvard Business School Publishing

Ed: Hayagreeva Rao. Description: Ways in which pirates typify the importance of separating star tasks, or strategic work, from guardian tasks, or the operational work are outlined.

44831 ■ "Column: Work Pray Love" in Harvard Business Review (Vol. 88, December 2010, No. 12, pp. 38)

Pub: Harvard Business School Publishing

Ed: Rosabeth Moss Kanter. Description: It is recommended to reinvest in values in order to promote better employee-company engagement and performance.

44832 ■ "Comcast Networks" in Brandweek (Vol. 49, April 21, 2008, No. 16, pp. SR9)

Pub: Nielsen Business Media Inc.

Contact: Howard Appelbaum, President

Ed: Anthony Crupi. Description: Provides contact information for sales and marketing personnel for the Comcast networks as well as a listing of the station's top programming and an analysis of the current season and the target audience for those programs running in the current season. Experts believe Comcast will continue to acquire more stations into their portfolio.

44833 ■ "Commitment Issues: Restoring Employee Engagement" in Workforce Management (Vol. 88, November 16, 2009, No. 12, pp. 20)

Pub: Crain Communications Inc.

Contact: Rance E. Crain, President

Ed: Ed Frauenheim. Description: Employee engagement refers to how committed workers are to their company and how much extra effort they are willing to put in on the job; firms could find that they are having a more difficult time coming out of the recession if they lack this important feature in workplace relations.

44834 ■ "Competing on Talent Analytics" in Harvard Business Review (Vol. 88, October 2010, No. 10, pp. 52)
Pub: Harvard Business School Publishing
Ed: Thomas H. Davenport, Jeanne Harris, Jeremy Shapiro. **Description:** Six ways to use talent analytics to obtain the highest level of value from employees are listed. These include human-capital investment analysis, talent value models, workforce forecasts, and talent supply chains.

44835 ■ "The Competitive Imperative Of Learning" in Harvard Business Review (Vol. 86, July-August 2008, No. 8, pp. 60)
Pub: Harvard Business Review Press
Contact: Peter E. Walsh, Director
Description: Experimentation and reflection are important components for maintaining success in the business world and are the kind of character traits that can help one keep his or her competitive edge.

44836 ■ "Complaints, Workforce Composition, Productivity, Organizational Values" in HRMagazine (Vol. 54, January 2009, No. 1, pp. 29)
Pub: Society for Human Resource Management
Contact: Henry G. Jackson, President
E-mail: hjackson@shrm.org
Ed: Amy Maingault, Regan Halvorsen, Rue Dooley, Liz Petersen. **Description:** Workforce composition trends that management should monitor are outlined. A goal-development process is discussed.

44837 ■ The Complete Idiot's Guide to a Successful Family Business
Pub: Dutton Children's Books
Contact: Lauri Hornik, President
Ed: Neil Raphel. **Released:** August 04, 2009. **Price:** $18.95. **Description:** Guide to running a family business includes information for expanding beyond the original family firm and family versus hired management. **Availability:** Print.

44838 ■ "Conference Calendar" in Marketing to Women (Vol. 21, March 2008, No. 3, pp. 7)
Description: Listing of current conferences and events aimed at women entrepreneurs and leaders.

44839 ■ "Congratulations to the 2012 Top Ten Business Women of ABWA" in Women In Business (Vol. 63, Fall 2011, No. 3, pp. 14)
Pub: American Business Women's Association
Contact: Lorie Burch, President
Description: Geri Bertram, Patti Bigger, and Susan Crowther are among the top ten businesswomen of the American Business Women's Association recognized for their contribution to the group, community involvement, and career achievements. Bertram is the manager for procurement planning control in Ingalls Shipbuilding while Bigger is Specialty Screw Corporation's corporate relations manager. Also on the list are Virginia DeGiorgi and Geanna Kincanon.

44840 ■ "The Consequences of Tardiness" in Modern Machine Shop (Vol. 84, August 2011, No. 3, pp. 34)
Pub: Gardner Business Media, Inc.
Contact: Richard G. Kline, President
E-mail: rkline@gardnerweb.com
Ed: Wayne S. Chaneski. **Description:** Five point addressing motivating factors behind employees who are tardy and those who choose to be on time in the workplace are shared.

44841 ■ "Consulting Firm Goes Shopping" in Crain's Chicago Business (Vol. 31, April 28, 2008, No. 17, pp. 45)
Pub: Crain Communications Inc.
Contact: Todd Johnson, Publisher
Ed: Phuong Ly. **Description:** Clark & Wamberg LLC was created last year after the merger of Clark Inc. to a Dutch insurance conglomerate. Clark Inc. was a life insurance and benefits consultancy which had been on a downslide, returning just 5.6 percent a

year to shareholders. In contrast Clark & Wamberg posted first-year revenue of $106.8 million, fueled by business from its executive compensation and health care clients.

44842 ■ "Contextual Intelligence: Despite 30 Years of Experimentation and Study, We are Only Starting to Understand that Some Managerial Knowledge is Universal and Some is Specific to a Market or a Culture" in Harvard Business Review (Vol. 92, September 2014, No. 9, pp. 58)
Pub: Harvard Business Publishing
Released: September 2014. **Description:** Contextual intelligence is defined as the ability to adapt knowledge to circumstances different from those under which the knowledge was initially developed. Firms should observe both employees and customers to understand local variations.

44843 ■ "Contract Design as a Firm Capability: An Integration of Learning and Transaction Cost Perspectives" in Academy of Management Review (October 2007, pp. 1060)
Pub: ScholarOne Inc.
Contact: William T. Carden, Jr., President
Ed: Nicholas Argyres, Kyle J. Mayer. **Description:** A firm's capabilities for designing detailed contracts and the role of managers, engineers, and lawyers in the design of such contracts is highlighted.

44844 ■ "CoolBrands" in Canadian Business (Vol. 83, September 14, 2010, No. 15, pp. 25)
Pub: Rogers Media Inc.
Contact: Tony Viner, President
Ed: Joe Castaldo. **Description:** CoolBrands International Inc.'s merger with Swisher International Inc., a US hygiene products and services company, has formally erased the last traces of the former ice cream company. CoolBrands began as a frozen yogurt stand in 1986 and flourished across the world. How the string of acquisitions and poor corporate governance led to its demise are cited.

44845 ■ Corporate Crisis and Risk Management: Modeling, Strategies and SME Application
Ed: M. Aba-Bulgu; S.M.N. Islam. **Released:** December 2006. **Price:** , $115.00. **Description:** Methods and tools for handling corporate risk and crisis management are profiled for small to medium-sized businesses.

44846 ■ "Corporate Diversity Driving Profits" in Hispanic Business (Vol. 30, September 2008, No. 9, pp. 12)
Ed: Michael Bowker. **Description:** U.S. businesses are beginning to appreciate the importance of diversity and are developing strategies to introduce a diverse workforce that reflects the cultural composition of their customers. The realization that diversity increases profits and the use of professional networks to recruit and retain skilled minority employees are two other new trends impacting corporate diversity in the U.S.

44847 ■ "Corporate Elite Face Steep Challenges" in Hispanic Business (January-February 2008, pp. 20, 22, 24, 26, 28, 30, 32)
Pub: Hispanic Business Inc.
Contact: Jesus Chavarria, President
Ed: Jonathan Higuera. **Description:** Hispanic men and women are moving up corporate ranks at leading companies in the U.S., including Ralph de la Vega, president and CEO of AT&T Mobility. Profiles of Vega and other Hispanic business leaders are included.

44848 ■ Corporate Entrepreneurship: Top Managers and New Business Creation
Pub: Cambridge University Press
Contact: Richard Ziemacki, President
E-mail: rziemacki@cambridge.org
Ed: Vijay Sathe. **Released:** February 2007. **Price:** $54, Paperback; $45, hardback; $43. **Description:** Studies covering entrepreneurship and business growth are examined. **Availability:** PrintE-book; PDF.

44849 ■ "Corporate Governance Reforms in China and India: Challenges and Opportunities" in Business Horizons (January-February 2008)
Pub: Elsevier Advanced Technology Publications
Ed: Nandini Rajagopalan, Yan Zhang. **Description:** The evolution of corporate governance reforms and the role of privatization and globalization in India and China are studied. Shortage of qualified independent directors and lack of incentives were found to be two of the major challenges in governance. The implications of and solutions to these challenges are highlighted.

44850 ■ "Corporate Responsibility" in Professional Services Close-Up (July 2, 2010)
Description: List of firms awarded the inaugural Best Corporate Citizens in Government Contracting by the Corporate Responsibility Magazine is presented. The list is based on the methodology of the Magazine's Best Corporate Citizen's List, with 324 data points of publicly-available information in seven categories which include: environment, climate change, human rights, philanthropy, employee relations, financial performance, and governance.

44851 ■ "Corporate Social Responsibility: A Process Model of Sensemaking" in Academy of Management Review (January 2008, pp. 122)
Pub: ScholarOne Inc.
Contact: William T. Carden, Jr., President
Ed: Kunal Basu, Guido Palazzo. **Description:** A novel process model of corporate social responsibility is presented. It uses organizational sensemaking to educate managers about elements of appropriate relationships with stakeholders and others.

44852 ■ "Corporate Training" in Hawaii Business (Vol. 53, October 2007, No. 4, pp. 46)
Pub: PacificBasin Communications
Ed: Cathy S. Cruz-George. **Description:** Kalani Pa, Mike Hann, and Li Si Yang are three of the fitness trainers who have worked with some of the participants at the Hawaii's Fittest CEO contest. Pa has trained Group Pacific Inc.'s Chip Doyle while Hann was Sharon Serene's trainer. Their insights on the profession of being a fitness trainer, and on working with executives are given.

44853 ■ "The Couch in the Corner Office: Surveying the Landscape of the CEO Psyche" in Inc. (January 2008, pp. 33-34)
Pub: Gruner and Jahr USA Publishing Co.
Contact: J. Russell Denson, President
Description: Profile of Leslie G. Mayer, founder of the Leadership Group, a firm that provides assistance to CEOs of firms by offering a deep understanding of the relationships, insecurities, and blind spots that can weaken strong leadership.

44854 ■ "The Coup Is Over, the Execution Begins" in Canadian Business (Vol. 85, June 11, 2012, No. 10, pp. 9)
Pub: George Media Inc.
Ed: Matthew McClearn. **Released:** June 11, 2012. **Description:** U.S. activist investor Bill Ackman of Pershing Square Capital Management faces the challenge of satisfying the high expectations he set when he acquired Canadian Pacific (CP) Railway and all of Pershing's nominees were elected to the CP board. Ackman promises that CP would reach an operating ratio of 65 percent by 2015.

44855 ■ "Courses Make Improvement Boost Rankings" in South Florida Business Journal (Vol. 34, April 11, 2014, No. 38, pp. 9)
Pub: American City Business Journals
Released: April 11, 2014. **Description:** Golf course owners and managers across South Florida have made large investments in improving their courses facilities and appeal in recent years. The investments resulted in the increase of U.S. Golf Association rankings for some, as well as drawing new members and users. The improvements at Trump National Golf Club in Jupiter and Crandon Golf Key Biscayne are also presented.

44856 ■ *"Creating Your Personal Succession Plan"* in Black Enterprise (Vol. 38, December 2007, No. 5, pp. 86)
Pub: Earl G. Graves Publishing Co. Inc.
Contact: Earl G. Graves, Jr., President
Ed: Marcia A. Reed-Woodard. **Description:** Society for Human Resource Management's Succession Planning Survey Report shows that over 58 percent of companies surveyed use succession plans for employees preparing to transition to higher-level positions.

44857 ■ *"Creativity, Inc.: Overcoming the Unseen Forces That Stand in the Way of True Inspiration"*
Pub: Random House L.L.C.
Contact: Markus Dohle, Chief Executive Officer
Released: April 8, 2014. **Price:** , $28.00. **Description:** Ed Catmull, co-founder of Pixar Animation Studios, reaches out to managers who want to lead their employees to greater heights. Pixar has dominated the world of animated films for twenty years. Catmull addresses philosophies that protect the creative process and defy convention to inspire employees and create a successful small business.

44858 ■ *"Crisis Management"* in Black Enterprise (Vol. 38, October 1, 2007, No. 3, pp. 69)
Pub: Earl G. Graves Publishing Co. Inc.
Contact: Earl G. Graves, Jr., President
Ed: Faith Chukwudi. **Description:** Shirley W. Bridges, chief information officer for Delta Air Lines, discusses leadership skills that establish trust within an organization.

44859 ■ *"The Critical Need to Reinvent Management"* in Business Strategy Review (Vol. 21, Spring 2010, No. 1, pp. 4)
Pub: John Wiley & Sons Inc. Scientific, Technical, Medical, and Scholarly Div. (Wiley-Blackwell)
Contact: William J. Pesce, Manager
E-mail: wpesce@wiley.com
Ed: Julian Birkinshaw. **Description:** The author believes that management is undervalued today - and for good reasons. Management, he says, has failed at the big-picture level and thinks it is time to reinvent the profession.

44860 ■ *"Cross Atlantic Commodities Launches National Internet Marketing Programs"* in Manufacturing Close-Up (September 8, 2009)
Description: Profile of the Internet campaign recently launched by Cross Atlantic Commodities, Inc., a manufacturer of specialty beauty and health products.

44861 ■ *"Crucible: A New Will to Win"* in Harvard Business Review (Vol. 88, September 2010, No. 9, pp. 110)
Pub: Harvard Business School Publishing
Ed: Daniel McGinn. **Description:** Importance of succession and contingency planning are emphasized in this account of Rick Hendrick's response to business loss coupled with personal tragedy. Focus and determination in leadership are also discussed.

44862 ■ *"Crucible: Battling Back from Betrayal"* in Harvard Business Review (Vol. 88, December 2010, No. 12, pp. 130)
Pub: Harvard Business School Publishing
Ed: Daniel McGinn. **Description:** Stephen Greer's scrap metal firm, Hartwell Pacific, lost several million dollars due to a lack of efficient and appropriate inventory audits, accounting procedures, and new-hire reference checks for his foreign operations. Greer believes that balancing growth with control is a key component of success.

44863 ■ *"Crucible: Losing the Top Job - And Winning It Back"* in Harvard Business Review (Vol. 88, October 2010, No. 10, pp. 136)
Pub: Harvard Business School Publishing
Ed: Alison Beard. **Description:** Michael Mack chronicles the changes in perspectives that occurred when he was fired from Garden Fresh, a restaurant firm he co-owned. Once again at the company helm, he is now more receptive to outside input and acknowledges the importance of work-life balance.

44864 ■ *"The Cult of Ralph: Chrysler's Ralph Gilles"* in Canadian Business (Vol. 79, September 22, 2006, No. 19, pp. 90)
Pub: Rogers Media Inc.
Contact: Tony Viner, President
Ed: Thomas Watson. **Description:** The contributions of Ralph Gilles to automobile manufacturing giant Daimler Chrysler AG are discussed.

44865 ■ *"Culture Club: Effective Corporate Cultures"* in Canadian Business (Vol. 79, October 9, 2006, No. 20, pp. 115)
Pub: Rogers Media Inc.
Contact: Tony Viner, President
Ed: Calvin Leung. **Description:** Positive impacts of an effective corporate culture on the employees' productivity and the performance of the business are discussed.

44866 ■ *"Currency: I'm Outta Here"* in Entrepreneur (Vol. 35, October 2007, No. 10, pp. 72)
Pub: Entrepreneur Press
Contact: Perlman Neil, President
Ed: C.J. Prince. **Description:** Liberum Research revealed that 193 chief financial officers (CFOs) at small companies have either resigned or retired during the first half of 2007. A survey conducted by Tatum found that unreasonable expectations from the management and compliance to regulations are the main reasons why CFOs are leaving small firms. The chief executive officer's role in making CFOs stay is also discussed.

44867 ■ *"Custom Fit"* in Canadian Business (Vol. 80, November 19, 2007, No. 23, pp. 42)
Ed: Andy Holloway. **Description:** Proper employee selection will help ensure a company has the people with the skills it really needs. Employee development is integral in coping with changes in the company. The importance of hiring the right employee and developing his skills is examined.

44868 ■ *"Customer Retention is Proportionate to Employee Retention"* in Green Industry Pro (Vol. 23, September 2011)
Pub: Cygnus Business Media
Contact: Paul Mackler, Chief Executive Officer
Description: Presented in a question-answer format, information is provided to help retain customers as well as keeping workers happy.

44869 ■ *"The CW"* in Brandweek (Vol. 49, April 21, 2008, No. 16, pp. SR8)
Pub: Nielsen Business Media Inc.
Contact: Howard Appelbaum, President
Ed: John Consoli. **Description:** Provides contact information for sales and marketing personnel for the CW network as well as a listing of the station's top programming and an analysis of the current season and the target audience for those programs running in the current season. Purchases of advertising feel that Warner Bros. and CBS made a mistake merging The WB and UPN into the new CW rather than folding UPN into the more-established WB; compared to last season ratings are down more than 20 percent across the board.

44870 ■ *"The Danger from Within: The Biggest Threat to Your Cybersecurity May Be an Employee or a Vendor"* in Harvard Business Review (Vol. 92, September 2014, No. 9, pp. 94)
Pub: Harvard Business Publishing
Released: September 2014. **Description:** Corporate computer crimes involving insiders are on the rise. To reduce vulnerability, firms should incorporate employees into the watchdog process, perform regular audits of distributors and suppliers, and implement security procedures involving both management and information technology personnel.

44871 ■ *"The Darwinian Workplace: New Technology Is Helping Employers Systematically Shift More Work To Their Best Employees"* in Harvard Business Review (Vol.

90, May 2012, No. 5, pp. 25)
Pub: Harvard Business Review Press
Contact: Peter E. Walsh, Director
Ed: Serguei Netessine, Valery Yakubovich. **Released:** May 2012. **Description:** The winners-take-all model is a productivity-based system that shifts work and incentives to a firm's most productive employees. Challenges such as unpredictable pay swings, excessive competition, and unfair comparisons are addressed.

44872 ■ *"David Low"* in Hawaii Business (Vol. 53, October 2007, No. 4, pp. 38)
Pub: PacificBasin Communications
Ed: Cathy S. Cruz-George. **Description:** Hawaii Capital Management managing director David Low ranked first in the 2007 competition for fittest male executives in Hawaii. This 5-foot-9 executive, who weighed 225 lbs. in 2003, weighs 150 lbs. in 2007. The activities that improved Low's fitness, such as weight training, swimming, biking, and running, are discussed.

44873 ■ *"Davis Family Expands Cable Empire"* in St. Louis Business Journal (Vol. 32, June 15, 2012, No. 43, pp. 1)
Pub: American City Business Journal
Description: Missouri-based Fidelity Communications has become a standout in the $98 billion cable industry through low-profile management of the Davis family, with the help of John Colbert. Fidelity has made five acquisitions since 1992 and has grown its subscriber base to more than 115,000 customers or revenue generating units.

44874 ■ *"Dean Foods"* in Ice Cream Reporter (Vol. 23, September 20, 2010, No. 10, pp. 8)
Description: Dean Foods promoted Joseph Scalzo to President and Chief Operating Officer to oversee the firm's operational turnaround and near-term strategic initiatives as well as business units. Key functions will include worldwide supply chain and research and development.

44875 ■ *"Defend Your Research: It's Not "Unprofessional" to Gossip at Work"* in Harvard Business Review (Vol. 88, September 2010, No. 9, pp. 28)
Pub: Harvard Business School Publishing
Ed: Giuseppe Labianca. **Description:** Gossip can be of value to a company as an exchange of information and its use as a diagnostic tool can enable managers to address problems promptly and even head them off.

44876 ■ *"Defend Your Research: The Early Bird Really Does Get the Worm"* in Harvard Business Review (Vol. 88, July-August 2010, No. 7-8, pp. 30)
Pub: Harvard Business School Publishing
Ed: Christoph Randler. **Price:** $6. **Description:** Research indicates that those who identify themselves as 'morning people' tend to be more proactive, and thus have a career-development advantage over those who identify themselves as 'night people'. Implications of the research are also discussed. **Availability:** PDF.

44877 ■ *"Defensive Training"* in Crain's Detroit Business (Vol. 24, September 22, 2008, No. 38, pp. 11)
Pub: Crain Communications Inc.
Contact: Rance E. Crain, President
Ed: Robert Ankeny. **Description:** Rising retaliation claims in regards to discrimination complaints are creating an atmosphere in which managers must learn how to avoid or deal with these lawsuits as well as the retaliation that often follows. Examples of cases are given as well as advice for dealing with such problems that may arise in the workplace.

44878 ■ *The Definitive Drucker: Challenges for Tomorrow's Executives -- Final Advice from the Father of Modern Management*
Pub: McGraw-Hill
Ed: Elizabeth Haas Edersheim. **Released:** January 2007. **Price:** £17.99, paperback. **Availability:** Print.

44879 ■ *"Demystifying Demotion: A Look at the Psychological and Economic Consequences on the Demotee"* in *Business Horizons (November-December 2007, pp. 455)*
Pub: Elsevier Technology Publications
Ed: Paula Phillips Carson, Kerry David Carson. **Price:** $35.95. **Description:** A model of employee demotion is developed after conducting personal interviews with more than 20 demotees. The effects of demotion, such as economic harm, lower well-being, underemployment, and grief reactions and identity crises are studied. **Availability:** PDF.

44880 ■ *Design Your Own Effective Employee Handbook: How to Make the Most of Your Staff with Companion CD-ROM*
Pub: Atlantic Publishing Co.
Contact: Amanda Miller, Manager
E-mail: amiller@atlantic-pub.com
Ed: Michelle Devon. **Released:** 2007. **Price:** $39.95. **Description:** An employee handbook should include clearly written policies covering the rights and responsibilities of workers. **Availability:** CD-ROM.

44881 ■ *"Designing Events Updates Online Suite"* in *Wireless News (October 25, 2009)*
Description: Designing Events, an outsourcing and consulting firm for conferences and meetings, announced the release of an update to its Designing Events Online suite of web-based management and marketing tools; features include enhanced versions of online registration and collaboration, content management, session development, social media and conference websites.

44882 ■ *"Developing the Next Generation of Rosies"* in *Employee Benefit News (Vol. 25, November 1, 2011, No. 14, pp. 36)*
Pub: SourceMedia Inc.
Contact: James M. Malkin, Chief Executive Officer
Ed: Kathleen Koster. **Description:** According to the research group Catalyst, women made up 46.7 percent of the American workforce in 2010, however only 14.4 percent was Fortune 500 executive officers and 15.7 percent held Fortune 500 board seats. Statistical data included.

44883 ■ *"DHR Hires Carr for Sports Group"* in *Crain's Detroit Business (Vol. 25, June 8, 2009, No. 23, pp. 5)*
Pub: Crain Communications Inc. - Detroit
Contact: Keith Crain, Chairman
Ed: Sherri Begin Welch. **Description:** Lloyd Carr, former head football coach for University of Michigan, has taken a position with DHR International in order to expand its searches for collegiate and professional sports organizations, recruit athletic directors, head coaches and other executives.

44884 ■ *"Diana Bonta -- Keeping People Healthy and Thriving"* in *Hispanic Business (Vol. 30, April 2008, No. 4, pp. 30)*
Pub: Hispanic Business Inc.
Contact: Jesus Chavarria, President
Ed: Leanndra Martinez. **Description:** Diana Bonta serves as vice president of public affairs for Kaiser Permanente and is a strong advocate for health reform and improving access to health care. In order to better serve the underinsured and uninsured, she directs Kaiser's Community Benefit division that devoted $369 million last year to this cause.

44885 ■ *"Diana Sands: Vice-President of Investor Relations, Boeing Co."* in *Crain's Chicago Business (Vol. 31, May 5, 2008, No. 18, pp. 32)*
Pub: Crain Communications Inc.
Contact: Todd Johnson, Publisher
Ed: John Rosenthal. **Description:** Profile of Diana Sands who is the vice-president of investor relations at Boeing Co. which entails explaining the company's performance to securities analysts and institutional investors.

44886 ■ *"The Difference Between Management and Project Management"* in

Contractor (Vol. 57, February 2010, No. 2, pp. 30)
Pub: Penton Media, Inc.
Ed: H. Kent Craig. **Description:** There are differences when managing a two-man crew as a foreman and a 2,000 employee company as a corporate president. A project manager should have good skills in human psychology, accounting, and the knowledge of a mechanical engineer, architect, civil engineer, and also the meditative skills of a Zen master.

44887 ■ *"A Different Breed of Deal Maker is Emerging"* in *Globe & Mail (January 14, 2006, pp. B2)*
Pub: CTVglobemedia Publishing Inc.
Ed: Eric Reguly. **Description:** The managerial strategies of chief executive officers in business acquisitions of companies, such as Dofasco Inc., are presented.

44888 ■ *"Digital Marketing: Integrating Strategy and Tactics with Values, A Guidebook for Executives, Managers, and Students"*
Pub: Routledge
Contact: Kevin Bradley, President
E-mail: kbradley@taylorandfrancis.com
Released: October 22, 2014. **Price:** , $38.95 paperback. **Description:** Guidebook filled with information on the latest digital marketing tactics and strategic insights to help small businesses generate sustainable growth and achieve competitive advantage through digital integration. A five-step program: mindset, model, strategy, implementation, and sustainability is explained.

44889 ■ *"Digital-Physical Mashups: To Consumers, the Real and Virtual Worlds Are One. The Same Should Go For Your Company"* in *Harvard Business Review (Vol. 92, September 2014, No. 9, pp. 84)*
Pub: Harvard Business Publishing
Released: September 2014. **Description:** By merging their physical and virtual operations, companies can provide a seamless experience for customers, boosting competitive advantage. These include strengthening customer/engagement links, approaching innovation through complementary expertise, and ensure that chief executive officers possess adequate technological knowledge.

44890 ■ *"Discovery Networks"* in *Brandweek (Vol. 49, April 21, 2008, No. 16, pp. SR9)*
Pub: Nielsen Business Media Inc.
Contact: Howard Appelbaum, President
Ed: Anthony Crupi. **Description:** Provides contact information for sales and marketing personnel for the Discovery networks as well as a listing of the station's top programming and an analysis of the current season and the target audience for those programs running in the current season. The networks flagship station returned to the top 10 in 2007, averaging 1.28 million viewers.

44891 ■ *"Disney-ABC Domestic Television Distribution"* in *Brandweek (Vol. 49, April 21, 2008, No. 16, pp. SR13)*
Pub: Nielsen Business Media Inc.
Contact: Howard Appelbaum, President
Ed: Marc Berman. **Description:** Provides contact information for sales and marketing personnel for Disney-ABC Domestic Television Distribution as well as a listing of the station's top programming and an analysis of the current season and the target audience for those programs running in the current season.

44892 ■ *"Disrupt Yourself: Four Principles for Finding the Career Path You Really Want"* in *(Vol. 90, July-August 2012, No. 7-8, pp. 147)*
Pub: Harvard Business Review Press
Contact: Peter E. Walsh, Director
Ed: Whitney Johnson. **Released:** July-August 2012. **Description:** The four principles are: target needs that need to be met more effectively; identify one's own disruptive strengths; step down or step aside to aside to achieve growth; and allow one's strategy to emerge.

44893 ■ *The Diversity Code: Unlock the Secrets to Making Differences Work in the Real World*
Pub: AMACOM
Contact: Edward T. Reilly, Manager
Ed: Michelle T. Johnson. **Released:** September 2010. **Price:** $19.95. **Description:** The most diligent compliance with laws and regulations can't foster true work place diversity. The best organizations have become genuine cross-cultural communities that believe equality in reconciling difference and valuing them. The book promotes understanding by answering many of the toughest questions that professionals and their employers are afraid to ask. **Availability:** Print.

44894 ■ *"Do Something!"* in *Entrepreneur (Vol. 36, March 2008, No. 3, pp. 79)*
Pub: Entrepreneur Press
Contact: Perlman Neil, President
Ed: Chris Penttila. **Description:** Employers are addressing the cause of employee stress by adjusting work structure. Some of the actions taken to tackle the concern include examples such as the eCast executive having quick one-on-one talks with employees and GlaxoSmithKlline employees taking online stress assessment. Other details on reducing job/employee stress are discussed.

44895 ■ *"Do You Need to Reinvent Your Managers?"* in *Rental Product News (Vol. 33, June 2011)*
Pub: Cygnus Business Media
Contact: Paul Mackler, Chief Executive Officer
Ed: Dick Detmer. **Description:** Rental business owners need to assess their management and be sure they perform as true leaders of the organization.

44896 ■ *"Do You Really Know Your Problems: Entrepreneurs Have a Tendency To See What They Want To See"* in *Inc. (December 2007, pp. 95-96)*
Pub: Gruner and Jahr USA Publishing Co.
Contact: J. Russell Denson, President
Ed: Norm Brodsky. **Description:** Information is offered to help entrepreneurs diagnose and resolve company issues.

44897 ■ *"Does Rudeness Really Matter? The Effects of Rudeness on Task Performance and Helpfulness"* in *Academy of Management Journal (Vol. 50, No. 5, October 1, 2007, pp. 1181)*
Pub: Academy of Management
Contact: Ming-Jer Chen, President
Ed: Christine L. Porath, Amir Erez. **Description:** Study assessing the effect of impoliteness on performance and helpfulness showed rude behavior lowered performance levels and also decreased attitude of helpfulness.

44898 ■ *"Doing It Right"* in *Black Enterprise (Vol. 38, October 1, 2007, No. 3, pp. 53)*
Pub: Earl G. Graves Publishing Co. Inc.
Contact: Earl G. Graves, Jr., President
Ed: Sheiresa Ngo. **Description:** One of the hardest things for every entrepreneur to do is delegate responsibility to employees; Anthony Samuels offers tips on the art of delegating.

44899 ■ *"Don't' Hate the Cable Guy"* in *Saint Louis Business Journal (Vol. 31, August 5, 2011, No. 50, pp. 1)*
Pub: Saint Louis Business Journal
Ed: Angela Mueller. **Description:** Charter Communications named John Birrer as senior vice president of customer experience. The company experienced problems with its customer services.

44900 ■ *"Don't Leave Employees on the Outside Looking In"* in *Canadian Business (Vol. 83, July 20, 2010, No. 11-12, pp. 13)*
Ed: Richard Branson. **Description:** Managers should be careful with employee's tendencies to use the word 'they' when problems occur since this shows that employees are not associating themselves with their company. Employees should be involved in the

development of the company and improving the flow of information is important in overcoming this communication challenge.

44901 ■ *"Don't Lose That Personal Touch"* **in** *Canadian Business (Vol. 85, July 16, 2012, No. 11-12, pp. 18)*
Pub: George Media Inc.
Ed: Richard Branson. **Released:** July 16, 2012. **Description:** There are advantages to running a big company as if it were a small business which can easily adapt to changing circumstances, develop a personal level of customer service and foster a sense of community and committment among employees. These can be achieved through building up team spirit, focusing on customers and delegating tasks.

44902 ■ *"Don't Shoot the Messenger: A Wake-Up Call For Academics"* **in** *Academy of Management Journal (Vol. 50, No. 5, October 1, 2007, pp. 1020)*
Pub: Academy of Management
Contact: Ming-Jer Chen, President
Ed: David E. Guest. **Description:** Author evaluates two well-known publications: HR Magazine and People Management, to emphasize the role of U.S. academics in communicating management practice.

44903 ■ *"The Doodle Revolution: Unlock the Power to Think Differently"*
Pub: Portfolio Hardcover
Released: January 9, 2014. **Price:** , $28.95. **Description:** Powerhouse minds like Albert Einstein, John F. Kennedy, Marie Curie, Thomas Edison, and Henry Ford were all doodlers. Doodling has led to countless discoveries in science, technology, medicine, architecture, literature, and art. Brown guides us through basic doodling to the infodoodle, in other words, a higher level of thinking and empowerment for anyone, especially entrepreneurs and managers.

44904 ■ *"The Downside of Self-Management: A Longitudinal Study of the Effects tf Conflict on Trust, Autonomy, and Task Interdependence in Self-Managing Teams"* **in** *Academy of Management Journal (Vol. 50, No. 4, August 1, 2007, pp. 885)*
Pub: Academy of Management
Contact: Ming-Jer Chen, President
Ed: Claus W. Langfred. **Description:** Study reveals that self-managing teams might accidentally restructure themselves inefficiently in response to conflict, thus the possible structure-related effects are analyzed.

44905 ■ *"Downtowns Must Court Young, CEOs for Cities President Says"* **in** *Crain's Detroit Business (Vol. 24, October 6, 2008, No. 40, pp. 18)*
Ed: Amy Lane. **Description:** It is important to produce more college graduates, and keep them in Michigan, according to CEOs for Cities President Carol Coletta when she spoke to a session at the West Michigan Regional Policy Conference which was held in September in Grand Rapids. Ways in which city leaders can connect students to communities, resulting in employees who have vested interest in the region, are also discussed.

44906 ■ *"Downturn Tests HCL's Pledge to Employees"* **in** *Workforce Management (Vol. 88, November 16, 2009, No. 12, pp. 23)*
Pub: Crain Communications Inc.
Contact: Rance E. Crain, President
Ed: Ed Frauenheim. **Description:** HCL Technologies has kept its promise to keep from laying any employees off during the recession which served as a test for the tech firm's Employee First program, which seeks to give workers greater income security as well as a stronger voice in the firm.

44907 ■ *"Dramatic Results: Making Opera (Yes, Opera) Seem Young and Hip"* **in** *Inc. (October 2007, pp. 61-62)*
Pub: Mansueto Ventures L.L.C.
Contact: John Koten, Chief Executive Officer
Ed: Stephanie Clifford. **Description:** Profile of Peter Gelb, who turned New York's Metropolitan Opera into one of the most media-savvy organizations in the country, using a multifaceted marketing strategy through the media. Gelb used streaming audio and simulcasts on satellite radio and movie theaters to promote a message that opera is hip.

44908 ■ *The Dream Manager*
Pub: Hyperion
Ed: Matthew Kelly. **Released:** August 09, 2007. **Price:** $19.95; C$24.95. **Description:** A business fable about the virtues of helping those working for and with you to achieve their dreams. Managers can boost morale and control turnover by adopting this policy.

44909 ■ *Driving With No Brakes: How a Bunch of Hooligans Built the Best Travel Company in the World*
Pub: Grand Circle Corporation
Ed: Alan Lewis, Harriet Lewis. **Released:** August 20, 2010. **Price:** $6.94. **Description:** Inspirational book about how two courageous leaders built a remarkable company that can thrive in change and succeed in an unpredictable world. Important lessons for any business leader trying to create value in the 21st Century are included.

44910 ■ *"DST Turns to Banks for Credit"* **in** *The Business Journal-Serving Metropolitan Kansas City (Vol. 27, October 3, 2008, No. 3, pp. 1)*
Pub: American City Business Journals, Inc.
Contact: Whitney Shaw, President
Ed: Rob Roberts. **Description:** Kansas City, Missouri-based DST Systems Inc., a company that provides sophisticated information processing, computer software services and business solutions, has secured a new five-year, $120 million credit facility from Enterprise Bank and Bank of the West. The deal is seen to reflect that the region and community-banking model remain stable. Comments from executives are also provided.

44911 ■ *The Dynamic Small Business Manager*
Pub: Lulu.com
Ed: Frank Vickers. **Released:** October 01, 2011. **Price:** $19.95. **Description:** Practical advice is given to help small business owners successfully manage their company. **Availability:** Download; PDF.

44912 ■ *"Dynamically Integrating Knowledge in Teams: Transforming Resources Into Performance"* **in** *Academy of Management Journal (Vol. 55, August 1, 2012, No. 4, pp. 998)*
Pub: Academy of Management
Contact: Ming-Jer Chen, President
Ed: Heidi K. Gardner, Francesca Gino, Bradley R. Staats. **Description:** A method for developing a knowledge-integration capability to dynamically integrate the resources of team members into higher performance is proposed. Results suggest that the development of this capability is aided by the use of relational, structural, and experiential resources while uncertainty plays a moderating role in these relationships.

44913 ■ *E-Commerce in Regional Small to Medium Enterprises*
Pub: IGI Global
Contact: Dr. Mehdi Khosrow-Pour, President
Ed: Robert MacGregor, Lejla Vrazalic. **Released:** June 2007. **Price:** $99.95. **Description:** Strategies small to medium enterprises (SMEs) need to implement in order to compete with larger, global businesses and the role electronic commerce plays in this process are outlined. Studies of e-commerce in multiple regional areas, focusing on the role of business size, business sector, market focus, gender of CEO, and education level of the CEO are discussed. **Availability:** Print; E-book.

44914 ■ *E-Myth Mastery: The Seven Essential Disciplines for Building a World Class Company*
Pub: HarperCollins Publishers Inc.
Contact: Jane Friedman, President
E-mail: jfriedman@harpercollins.com
Ed: Michael E. Gerber. **Released:** February 20, 2007. **Price:** $18.99, paperback; $11.99. **Description:** Leadership, marketing, money, management, lead conversion, lead generation, client fulfillment are the seven keys to successful entrepreneurship. **Availability:** PrintE-book.

44915 ■ *Economic Freedom and the American Dream*
Pub: Palgrave Macmillan
Contact: Lisa Dunn, Manager
E-mail: l.dunn@palgrave.com
Ed: Joseph Shaanan. **Released:** February 2010. **Price:** £46, hardcover; $70. **Description:** An exploration into the effects of economic freedom on American in several areas such as markets, politics, and opportunities for would-be entrepreneurs. **Availability:** PrintE-book.

44916 ■ *The Economics and Management of Small Business: An International Perspective*
Pub: Routledge
Contact: Kevin Bradley, President
E-mail: kbradley@taylorandfrancis.com
Ed: Graham Bannock. **Released:** January 20, 2005. **Price:** $200, hardback. **Description:** International perspectives on the economics and management of small business, featuring case studies and empirical research. **Availability:** Print.

44917 ■ *Ecopreneuring: Putting Purpose and the Planet Before Profits*
Pub: New Society Publishers
Contact: Sue Custance, Director
Ed: John Ivanko, Lisa Kivirist. **Released:** July 01, 2008. **Price:** $17.95, paperback; $11.65. **Description:** Ecopreneurs in America are shifting profits and market share towards green living. The book provides a guideline for ecopreneurs in the areas of eco-business basics, purposeful management, marketing in the green economy, and running a lifestyle business. **Availability:** PrintE-book.

44918 ■ *"The Effect of Corporate Governance on Firm's Credit Ratings: Further Evidence Using Governance Score in the United States"* **in** *Accounting and Finance (Vol. 52, June 2012, No. 2, pp. 291)*
Pub: Blackwell Publishers Ltd.
Ed: Fatima Alali, Asokan Anandarajan, Wei Jiang. **Description:** An investigation into whether corporate governance affects a firm's credit ratings and whether improvement in corporate governance standards is associated with improvement in investing grade rating is presented.

44919 ■ *"Eight Tips For Leaders On Protecting the Team"* **in** *Puget Sound Business Journal (Vol. 35, August 22, 2014, No. 18, pp. 13)*
Pub: American City Business Journals
Released: August 22, 2014. **Description:** Advice on ways to protect corporate teams is given. Unnecessary information and processes should be filtered to avoid distraction of the team. Team action plans must be prioritized.

44920 ■ *"El Paso Firm VEMAC Rides Boom to the Top: Spotlight on This Year's Fastest-Growing Company"* **in** *Hispanic Business (Vol. 30, July-August 2008, No. 7-8, pp. 28)*
Pub: Hispanic Business Inc.
Contact: Jesus Chavarria, President
Ed: Jeremy Nisen. **Description:** VEMAC, a commercial construction management and general contracting firm that is experiencing success despite the plummeting construction market is discussed. VEMAC's success is attributed to the Pentagons' $5 billion investment in construction for the benefit of new personnel and their families to be transferred to Fort Bliss, a U.S. army base adjacent to El Paso.

44921 ■ *"The Emergence of Governance In an Open Source Community"* **in** *Academy of Management Journal (Vol. 50, No. 5, October 1, 2007, pp. 1079)*
Pub: Academy of Management
Contact: Ming-Jer Chen, President
Ed: Siobhan O'Mahony, Fabrizio Ferraro. **Description:** Study examined the method of self-governance among small communities producing collective

goods, focusing on an open source software community. Results revealed that a combination of bureaucratic and democratic practices helped its governance system.

44922 ■ "Empathy: An Entrepreneur's Killer App" in Women Entrepreneur (February 3, 2009)

Ed: Kristi Hedges. **Description:** It is just as important to treat employees with courtesy and respect during bad economic times as it is in a good economy. Employers sometimes take advantage of such bad economic times since they realize that 'employees are grateful to have a job and cannot just quit and easily find work elsewhere. The importance of empathy in a company's leadership personnel is discussed.

44923 ■ Employee Management for Small Business

Pub: Self-Counsel Press Inc.

Ed: Lin Grensing-Pophal. **Released:** October 15, 2009. **Price:** $20.95. **Description:** Management tools to help entrepreneurs maintain an effective human resources plan for a small company. **Availability:** Print.

44924 ■ "Employee Motivation: A Powerful New Model" in Harvard Business Review (Vol. 86, July-August 2008, No. 8, pp. 78)

Pub: Harvard Business Review Press

Contact: Peter E. Walsh, Director

Ed: Nitin Nohira, Boris Groysberg, Linda-Eling Lee. **Description:** Four drives underlying employee motivation are discussed as well as processes for leveraging these drives through corporate culture, job design, reward systems, and resource-allocation priorities.

44925 ■ "Empowered" in Harvard Business Review (Vol. 88, July-August 2010, No. 7-8, pp. 94)

Pub: Harvard Business School Publishing

Ed: Josh Bernoff, Ted Schadler. **Description:** HERO concept (highly empowered and resourceful operative) which builds a connection between employees, managers, and IT is outlined. The resultant additional experience and knowledge gained by employees improves customer relationship management.

44926 ■ "Enerfab Chairman Wants Results: Strategy: Hurry Up and Wait" in Business Courier (Vol. 24, January 31, 2008, No. 43, pp. 50)

Pub: American City Business Journals, Inc.

Contact: Whitney Shaw, President

Ed: Dan Monk. **Description:** It has taken years for Enerfab Inc. chairman Dave Herche to develop new product lines, form an expert management group and come up with a strategic-planning approach. However, his patience has paid off since Enerfab's revenue has grown by 93 percent since 2005. Herche's strategy for Enerfab and its impacts on the company are analyzed further.

44927 ■ "Energy Sparks Job Growth" in The Business Journal-Serving Greater Tampa Bay (Vol. 28, August 11, 2008, No. 33, pp. 1)

Pub: American City Business Journals, Inc.

Contact: Whitney Shaw, President

Ed: Margie Manning. **Description:** Energy infrastructure projects in Tampa Bay, Florida, are increasing the demand for labor in the area. Energy projects requiring an increase in labor include TECO Energy Inc.'s plan for a natural gas pipeline in the area and the installation of energy management system in Bank of America's branches in the area.

44928 ■ Enlightened Leadership: Best Practice Guidelines and Time Tools for Easily Implementing Learning Organizations

Pub: Learning House Publishing, Inc.

Ed: Ralph LoVuolo; Alan G. Thomas. **Released:** May 2006. **Price:** , $79.99. **Description:** Innovation and creativity are essential for any successful small business. The book provides owners, managers, and team leaders with the tools necessary to produce 'disciplined innovation'.

44929 ■ Enlightened Leadership: Best Practice Guidelines and Timesaving Tools for Easily Implementing Learning Organizations

Pub: Learning House Publishing, Inc.

Ed: Alan G. Thomas; Ralph L. LoVuolo; Jeanne C. Hillson. **Released:** September 2006, printable 3 times/year. **Price:** , $21.00. **Description:** Book provides the tools required to create a learning organization management model along with a step-by-step guide for team planning and learning. The strategy works as a manager's self-help guide as well as offering continuous learning and improvement for company-wide success.

44930 ■ Entrepreneurial Decision-Making: Individuals, Tasks and Cognitions

Pub: Edward Elgar Publishing Inc.

Contact: Richard Henning, Vice President

E-mail: kwight@e-elgar.com

Ed: Veronica Gustafsson. **Released:** December 2006. **Price:** $107.10, hardback. **Description:** Entrepreneurial decision-making is examined by comparing various individuals with differing levels of expertise and potential. **Availability:** Print.

44931 ■ "Entrepreneurial Orientation and Firm Performance" in Journal of Small Business and Entrepreneurship (Vol. 23, Winter 2010, No. 1)

Pub: Canadian Council for Small Business and Entrepreneurship

Contact: Sandra Altner, President

Description: The article develops a theoretical model of the relationship between firm-level entrepreneurship and firm performance. This model is intended to further clarify the consequences of an 'entrepreneurial orientation', paying particular attention to the differential relationship that exists between the three sub-dimensions of entrepreneurial orientation and firm performance. Included in the theoretical model are other important variables (such as organizational structure and environmental characteristics) that may impact the EO-performance relationship. Propositions are developed regarding the various configurations of the sub-dimensions of EO and organizational structure that would be most appropriate in a given environmental context. Future research may also benefit from considering the important role that organizational strategy and life cycle stage play in this model. The implications of this model for both researchers and managers are discussed.

44932 ■ Entrepreneurial Skills: 2nd Edition

Pub: Double Storey Books

Ed: Cecile Nieuwenhuizen. **Released:** March 1, 2009. **Price:** , $32.00. **Description:** Entrepreneurial skills are examined, showing how entrepreneurship differs from management mostly in attitude and approach.

44933 ■ The Entrepreneur's Guide to Managing Growth and Handling Crises

Pub: Greenwood Publishing Group Inc.

Contact: Janann Sherman, Manager

Ed: Theo J. Van Dijk. **Released:** December 2007. **Price:** $39.95, hardcover. **Description:** The author explains how entrepreneurs can overcome crisis by changing the way they handle customers, by putting new processes and procedures in place, and managing employees in a professional manner. The book includes appendices with tips for hiring consultants, creating job descriptions, and setting up systems to chart cash flow as well as worksheets, tables and figures and a listing of resources. **Availability:** Print.

44934 ■ The Entrepreneur's Strategy Guide: Ten Keys for Achieving Marketplace Leadership and Operational Excellence

Pub: Greenwood Publishing Group Inc.

Contact: Janann Sherman, Manager

Ed: Tom Cannon. **Released:** September 2006. **Price:** $44.95. **Description:** Ten principles of marketplace leadership are explored. The book provides a plan for small businesses, including diagnostics, checklists, and other interactive exercises to study both external and internal principles. **Availability:** Print.

44935 ■ "Everett Dowling" in Hawaii Business (Vol. 54, August 2008, No. 2, pp. 32)

Pub: PacificBasin Communications

Ed: Jason Ubay. **Description:** Real estate developer Everett Dowling, president of Dowling Company Inc., talks about the company's sustainable management and services. The company's office has been retrofitted to earn a Leadership in Energy and Environmental Design (LEED) certification. Dowling believes that real estate development can be part of the sustainable solution.

44936 ■ Everything I Know About Business I Learned at McDonald's: The 7 Leadership Principles that Drive Break Out Success

Pub: The McGraw-Hill Companies

Ed: Paul Facella, Adina Genn. **Released:** 2009. **Price:** $34. **Description:** McDonald's management philosophy is as simple as its menu, but don't underestimate the effectiveness of founder Ray Kroc's business plan.

44937 ■ "Evidence-Based Management and the Marketplace For Ideas" in Academy of Management Journal (Vol. 50, No. 5, October 2007, pp. 1009)

Pub: Academy of Management

Contact: Ming-Jer Chen, President

Ed: Wayne F. Cascio. **Description:** Study examines the relevance of material to actual usage in human resource management. Results reveal that it is important to design modules with execution in mind in seeking advice from professionals in relevant organizations.

44938 ■ "The Evolution of Carolyn Elman" in Women In Business (Vol. 62, September 2010, No. 3, pp. 11)

Pub: American Business Women's Association

Contact: Lorie Burch, President

Ed: Leigh Elmore. **Description:** Carolyn Elman, former executive director of the American Business Women's Association (ABWA), provides an overview of her career. Elman grew up with the Association, and it was part of her family's existence. She believes that the ABWA provides women the opportunity to learn and improve their skills in business.

44939 ■ "The Evolution of Corporate Social Responsibility" in Business Horizons (November-December 2007, pp. 449)

Pub: Elsevier Technology Publications

Ed: Philip L. Cochran. **Price:** $35.95. **Description:** Corporate social responsibility is now perceived as vital in enhancing the profitability of businesses while improving their reputation. It has changed business practices such as philanthropy, investment, and entrepreneurship. **Availability:** PDF.

44940 ■ Execution: The Discipline of Getting Things Done

Ed: Larry Bossidy, Ram Charan, Charles Burck. **Released:** June 15, 2002. **Price:** $27.50. **Description:** The book shows how to get things done and deliver results whether you are running an entire company or in your first management position.

44941 ■ "The Executive Brain" in Canadian Business (Vol. 80, October 22, 2007, No. 21, pp. 41)

Ed: Rachel Pulfer. **Description:** Studies by Jordan Petersen, Frank Schmidt, and John Hunter show that leaders have highly evolved capacities to think using the prefrontal cortex of the brain. Inspirational leadership ability is located in the parietal lobe. Other details of the research are discussed.

44942 ■ "Executive Decision: Just What the Doctor Ordered" in Globe & Mail (February 11, 2006, pp. B3)

Ed: Leonard Zehr. **Description:** The leadership ability of chief executive William Hunter of Angiotech Pharmaceuticals Inc., who acquired American Medical Instruments Holdings Inc. for $785 million, is discussed.

44943 ■ *"Executive Presence: The Missing Link Between Merit and Success"*
Pub: HarperBusiness
Released: June 3, 2014. **Price:** , $26.99. **Description:** Ways to find out if you possess executive presence are discussed. Executive presence is a conglomeration of qualities exuded by true leaders, a presence that shows you are in charge. Executive presences is a dynamic, collective mix of appearance, communication and gravitas and leaders must know how to use them all to their advantage.

44944 ■ *"Executive of the Year: Sullivan Led Bucyrus through Unforgettable Year"* in *Business Journal-Milwaukee (Vol. 28, December 17, 2010, No. 11, pp. A1)*
Pub: Milwaukee Business Journal
Ed: Rich Rovito. **Description:** Bucyrus International's president and CEO, Tim Sullivan, was chosen as Milwaukee, Wisconsin's Executive of the Year for 2010. Sullivan led Bucyrus through a year of dramatic change which started with the acquisition of the mining business of Terex Corporation and culminating with a deal to sell Caterpillar Inc.

44945 ■ *"Executives Exit at Wal-Mart in China"* in *Wall Street Journal Eastern Edition (October 17 , 2011, pp. B3)*
Pub: Dow Jones & Co., Inc.
Contact: Clare Hart, President
Ed: Laurie Burkitt. **Description:** Woes for Wal-Mart Inc.'s subsidiary in China are adding up as Wal-Mart China president and chief executive Ed Chan stepped down, as well as the company's senior vice president for human resources, Clara Wong. The company has been charged by regulators with mislabeling pork products, the result which has forced stores to close. Sales in China have been slow at the retail stores.

44946 ■ *"Exploring Supportive and Developmental Career Management Through Business Strategies and Coaching"* in *Human Resource Management (Vol. 51, January-February 2012, No. 1, pp. 99-120)*
Pub: John Wiley & Sons Inc.
Contact: Stephen M. Smith, President
Ed: Jesse Segers, Ilke Inceoglu. **Description:** Coaching and other career practices that are part of supportive and developmental career management are examined. Such practices are found to be most present in organizations with a prospector strategy.

44947 ■ *"Extreme Negotiations"* in *Harvard Business Review (Vol. 88, November 2010, No. 11, pp. 66)*
Pub: Harvard Business School Publishing
Ed: Jeff Weiss, Aram Donigian, Jonathan Hughes. **Description:** Examination of military negotiation skills that are applicable in business situations. Skills include soliciting others' perspectives, developing and proposing multiple solutions, and inviting others to assess them.

44948 ■ *The Facebook Era: Tapping Online Social Networks to Build Better Products, Reach New Audiences, and Sell More Stuff*
Ed: Clara Shih. **Price:** , $24.99. **Description:** The '90s were about the World Wide Web of information and the power of linking Web pages. Today it's about the World Wide Web of people and the power of the social graph. Online social networks are fundamentally changing the way we live, work, and interact. They offer businesses immense opportunities to transform customer relationships for profit: opportunities that touch virtually every business function, from sales and marketing to recruiting, collaboration to executive decision-making, product development to innovation.

44949 ■ *"Facing the Future"* in *Canadian Business (Vol. 81, March 31, 2008, No. 5, pp. 69)*
Pub: Rogers Media Inc.
Contact: Tony Viner, President
Ed: John Gray. **Description:** Discusses a web poll of 122 Canadian CEOs which shows that these leaders are convinced that the U.S. economy is slowing but are split on the impact that this will have on the Canadian economy. The aging and retiring workforce and the strong Canadian dollar are other concerns by these leaders.

44950 ■ *"Falling Local Executive Pay Could Suggest a Trend"* in *Tampa Bay Business Journal (Vol. 30, January 15, 2010, No. 4, pp. 1)*
Pub: American City Business Journals
Ed: Margie Manning. **Description:** Tampa Bay, Florida-based Raymond James Financial Inc. and MarineMax Inc.'s proxy statements have shown the decreasing compensation of the companies' highest paid executives. The falling trend in executive compensation was a result of intensified shareholder scrutiny and the economy.

44951 ■ *"Familiar Face Aims to Rebuild Distributor's Once-Strong Local Ties"* in *Crain's Cleveland Business (December 3, 2007)*
Ed: David Bennett. **Description:** Phillips Contractors Supply, a tool distributor, has a new president and co-owner, James Beckett. Beckett was once vice president of operations so he knows the company well and has plans to re-establish the firm's presence in the region.

44952 ■ *Family Business*
Pub: Cengage South-Western
Ed: Ernesto J. Poza. **Released:** 4th Edition. **Price:** $119, wholesale; $63.99. **Description:** Family-owned businesses face unique challenges in today's economy. This book provides the next generation of knowledge and skills required for profitable management and leadership in a family enterprise. **Availability:** PrintE-book.

44953 ■ *Family Business Models: Practical Solutions for the Family Business*
Pub: Palgrave Macmillan
Contact: Lisa Dunn, Manager
E-mail: l.dunn@palgrave.com
Ed: Alberto Gimeno, Gemma Baulenas, Joan Coma-Cros. **Released:** June 10, 2010. **Price:** £34. **Description:** A unique new model for understanding family businesses gives readers the potential to build better managed and more stable family firms and to plan for a success future.

44954 ■ *"Family Governance and Firm Performance: Agency, Stewardship, and Capabilities"* in *Family Business Review (Vol. 19, March 2006)*
Pub: Family Firm Institute
Contact: Judy L. Green, President
Ed: Danny Miller, Isabelle Le Breton-Miller. **Description:** Study examining the effect of governance, agency perspective, and stewardship perspective on performances of major publicly-traded family-controlled businesses in the U.S. is presented.

44955 ■ *"The Fatal Bias"* in *Business Strategy Review (Vol. 25, Summer 2014, No. 2, pp. 34)*
Pub: Blackwell Publishing Professional
Contact: Stephen M. Smith, President
Released: Summer 2014. **Description:** The prevailing managerial bias towards cost efficiency is harmful to corporate performance. Management's fatal bias is discussed.

44956 ■ *"Fearless Leaders: Sharpen Your Focus: How the New Science of Mindfulness Can Help You Reclaim Your Confidence"*
Pub: Waterfront Digital Press
Released: August 21, 2014. **Price:** , $14.95 paperback. **Description:** Executive coaches explain the principles that make managers and entrepreneurs and business leaders fearless.

44957 ■ *"Feast or Famine"* in *Entrepreneur (August 2014)*
Pub: Entrepreneur Media Inc.
Released: August 2014. **Description:** Small business owners face significant challenges when it comes to handling large changes in sales volume. The best-case scenario involves increasing the size of the company to meet a demand from a major client while the worst case is losing a major client and having to downsize. Owners need to pay attention to their business reputation no matter what stage their business is at. Managing the pricing of products and services is the easiest way to control an inconsistent sales cycle.

44958 ■ *"Feeling the Heat: Effects of Stress, Commitment, and Job Experience On Job Performance"* in *Academy of Management Journal (Vol. 50, No. 4, August 1, 2007, pp. 953)*
Pub: Academy of Management
Contact: Ming-Jer Chen, President
Ed: Larry W. Hunter, Sherry M.B. Thatcher. **Description:** Links between bank branch employees' felt job stress, organizational commitment, job experience, and performance is analyzed. Results found are uniform with the attention view of stress.

44959 ■ *"Female Hispanic Professionals by the Number"* in *Hispanic Business (Vol. 30, April 2008, No. 4, pp. 8)*
Description: More executive opportunities are presenting themselves for future generations of Hispanic women who are more frequently being found in high-level positions. Statistical data included.

44960 ■ *Fierce Leadership*
Ed: Susan Scott. **Released:** January 11, 2011. **Price:** $15. **Description:** A bold alternative to the worst 'best' practices of business in the 21st Century.

44961 ■ *"Fifth Third CEO Kabat: A World of Difference"* in *Business Courier (Vol. 26, January 1, 2010, No. 37, pp. 1)*
Pub: American City Business Journals, Inc.
Contact: Whitney Shaw, President
Ed: Steve Watkins. **Description:** CEO Kevin Kabat of Cincinnati-based Fifth Third Bancorp believes that the bank's assets of $111 billion and stock value of more than $10 indicate the recovery from the low stock prices posted in February 2009. He attributes the recovery from the federal government's stress test finding in May 2009 that Fifth Third needs to generate $1.1 billion.

44962 ■ *"Fighting the Good Fight"* in *Inc. (Vol. 33, October 2011, No. 8, pp. 8)*
Pub: Inc. Magazine
Ed: Eric Markowitz. **Description:** Rob Roy, former Navy SEAL, runs SOT-G a firm that offers an 80-hour leadership training course inspired by military combat preparations. Details of the program are outlined.

44963 ■ *Financial Times Guide to Business Start Up 2007*
Ed: Sara Williams; Jonquil Lowe. **Released:** November 2006. **Price:** , $52.50. **Description:** Guide for starting and running a new business is presented. Sections include ways to get started, direct marketing, customer relations, management and accounting.

44964 ■ *"Finding A Higher Gear"* in *Harvard Business Review (Vol. 86, July-August 2008, No. 8, pp. 68)*
Pub: Harvard Business Review Press
Contact: Peter E. Walsh, Director
Ed: Thomas A. Stewart, Anand P. Raman. **Description:** Anand G. Mahindra, the chief executive officer of Mahindra and Mahindra Ltd., discusses how his company fosters innovation, drawn from customer centricity, and how this will grow the company beyond India's domestic market.

44965 ■ *First, Break All the Rules: What the World's Greatest Managers Do Differently*
Pub: Simon and Schuster Inc.
Contact: Carolyn Reidy, President
E-mail: carolyn.reidy@simonandschuster.com
Ed: Marcus Buckingham, Curt Coffman. **Released:** May 1999. **Price:** $32. **Description:** Great managers break virtually every rule revered by conventional wisdom.

44966 ■ *"First Class All the Way"* in *Entrepreneur (July 2014)*
Pub: Entrepreneur Media Inc.
Released: July 2014. **Description:** Entrepreneurs are offered tips on dealing with problem employees and fostering diversity in business. Leaders must be

vigilant and proactive when handling an employee who has a sense of entitlement. The culture and values of the company and the reason why his me-first-and-only approach will not work must be explained to him. A healthy business environment in the 21st Century must be open to diversifying its people and ideas. Hiring women employees will help successful businesses grow.

44967 ■ The Five Dysfunctions of a Team: A Leadership Fable
Pub: John Wiley & Sons Inc.
Contact: Stephen M. Smith, President
Ed: Patrick M. Lencioni. **Released:** May 2002. **Price:** $24.95, hardcover; $16.99. **Description:** Analysis of a hypothetical tale of the CEO of a struggling, high-profile firm with a dysfunctional executive team. **Availability:** PrintE-book.

44968 ■ "Five Steps to the Corner Office" in Canadian Business (Vol. 80, March 12, 2007, No. 6, pp. 36)
Ed: Marlene Rego. **Description:** Chief executive of Rona Retail Canada Inc., Robert Dutton, and chief executive of Sysco Food Services Winnipeg, Kim Doherty explain the way they reached the top of their careers.

44969 ■ "5 Steps to an Effective Meeting" in Hawaii Business (Vol. 53, March 2008, No. 9, pp. 55)
Pub: PacificBasin Communications
Ed: Jason Ubay. **Description:** Identifying goals and writing them down can help in knowing what needs get done. Engaging everyone is a way to get cooperation in reaching the goals set. Other tips on how to have an effective meeting are discussed.

44970 ■ "5 Steps for Handling Independent Contractors" in Hawaii Business (Vol. 53, January 2008, No. 7, pp. 49)
Pub: PacificBasin Communications
Ed: Jason Ubay. **Description:** Small companies should be cautious in dealing with independent contractors. They must understand that they cannot dictate specific operational procedures, job duties, standards of conduct and performance standards to the contractors, and they cannot interfere with the evaluation and training of the contractors' employees. Tips on negotiating with independent contractors are given.

44971 ■ "Five Tips for New Managers" in Hawaii Business (Vol. 53, November 2007, No. 5, pp. 59)
Pub: PacificBasin Communications
Ed: Jason Ubay. **Description:** New managers should remember to know what their roles are, learn from others, build an infrastructure according to the customer's needs, communicate professionally and have consideration.

44972 ■ "Flurry of Activity from Restaurant Groups as Industry Strengthens" in Wichita Business Journal (Vol. 27, February 17, 2012, No. 7, pp. 1)
Pub: American City Business Journal
Description: Atlanta, Georgia-based Chick-fil-A chain is set to open two restaurants in Wichita, Kansas and those additions were highly anticipated. However, there were other local management groups and franchisees that are investing on new buildings and refurbishing stores. Insights on the increasing restaurant constructions are also given.

44973 ■ "Ford Executive Pay Could Fuel Tensions" in Globe & Mail (April 6, 2007, pp. B7)
Ed: John D. Stoll; Terry Kosdrosky; Chad Clinton. **Description:** The likely tension between workers and management over the $62 million offer of Ford Motor Co. to its top executives is discussed.

44974 ■ "Former Mayor, Paul Johnson, Driving $500M Real Estate Equity Fund" in The Business Journal - Serving Phoenix and the Valley of the Sun (Vol. 28, August 15,
2008, No. 50, pp. 1)
Pub: American City Business Journals, Inc.
Contact: Whitney Shaw, President
Ed: Jan Buchholz. **Description:** Paul John, the former mayor of Phoenix, is establishing a $500 million real estate asset management fund. The fund is dubbed Southwest Next Capital Management and has attracted three local partners, namely Joseph Meyer, Jay Michalowski, and James Mullany, who all have background in finance and construction.

44975 ■ "Former Synthes Officers Receive Prison Sentences" in Wall Street Journal Eastern Edition (November 22 , 2011, pp. B4)
Pub: Dow Jones & Co., Inc.
Contact: Clare Hart, President
Ed: Peter Loftus. **Description:** Michael D. Huggins, formerly chief operating officer of medical-device maker Synthes Ltd., and Thomas B. Higgins, formerly the president of Synthes spine unit, were given prison sentences of nine months while a third executive, John J. Walsh, formerly director of regulatory and clinical affairs in the spine division, was given a five-month sentence for their involvement in the promotion of the unauthorized use of a bone cement produced by the company.

44976 ■ "The Formula for Growth: Through a Mixture of Vision and Partnerships, Leon Richardson has ChemicoMays in Expansion Mode" in Black Enterprise (Vol. 44, June 2014, No. 10, pp. 66)
Pub: Earl G. Graves Publishing Co. Inc.
Contact: Earl G. Graves, Jr., President
Released: June 2014. **Description:** Profile of Leon Richardson, who has his family-owned business poised for growth. At the age of 13, Leon helped his family in their convenience store located in West Haven, Connecticut. He has gone from managing storefronts to overseeing a chemical management business during his entrepreneurial career.

44977 ■ "Formulating Policy With a Parallel Organization" in Strategy & Leadership (Vol. 38, September-October 2010, No. 5, pp. 33-38)
Pub: Emerald Inc.
Ed: Dale E. Zand, Thomas F. Hawk. **Description:** A study analyzes a case to examine the parallel organization concept and its successful implementation by a CEO to integrate independent divisions of a firm. Findings reveal that the implementation of the parallel organization improved the policy formulation, strategic planning profitability of the firm while also better integrating its independent divisions.

44978 ■ "Forsys Metals Corporation Goes "Live" With Q4's On-Demand Disclosure Management Software" in Canadian Corporate News (May 16, 2007)
Description: Forsys Metals Corp. selected Q4 Web Systems to automate its corporate website disclosure with Q4's software platform which also automates and simplifies many of the administrative tasks that Forsys was doing manually, allowing them to focus their internal resources on the business.

44979 ■ "Four Lessons in Adaptive Leadership" in Harvard Business Review (Vol. 88, November 2010, No. 11, pp. 86)
Pub: Harvard Business School Publishing
Ed: Michael Useem. **Description:** Four key factors to effective leadership are presented. These are establishing a personal link, making sound and timely decisions, developing a common purpose while avoiding personal gain, and ensuring that objectives are clear without micromanaging those implementing them.

44980 ■ "Four Ways to Fix Banks: a Wall Street Veteran Suggests How To Cut Through the Industry's Complexity" in (Vol. 90, June 2012, No. 6, pp. 106)
Pub: Harvard Business Review Press
Contact: Peter E. Walsh, Director
Ed: Sallie Krawcheck. **Released:** June 2012. **Description:** Despite new regulations in the post-global economic crisis of 2008, banks are sill too complex for effective management of their boards. Recommendations for improving governance include incor-

porating bank debt in executive compensation to increase their sensitivity to risk, and paying dividends as a percentage of company earnings to maintain capital.

44981 ■ "Fox" in Brandweek (Vol. 49, April 21, 2008, No. 16, pp. SR3)
Ed: John Consoli. **Description:** Provides contact information for sales and marketing personnel for the Fox network as well as a listing of the station's top programming and an analysis of the current season and the target audience for those programs running in the current season. In terms of upfront advertising dollars, it looks as if Fox will be competing against NBC for third place due to its success at courting the 18-49-year-old male demographic.

44982 ■ "Fox Cable Entertainment Networks" in Brandweek (Vol. 49, April 21, 2008, No. 16, pp. SR10)
Pub: Nielsen Business Media Inc.
Contact: Howard Appelbaum, President
Ed: Anthony Crupi. **Description:** Provides contact information for sales and marketing personnel for the Fox Cable Entertainment networks as well as a listing of the station's top programming and an analysis of the current season and the target audience for those programs running in the current season.

44983 ■ "Fraud Alleged at Norshield; Investors Out $215 Million" in Globe & Mail (March 8, 2007, pp. B1)
Ed: Paul Waldie. **Description:** The investigation of the diversion of $215 million in investors' money by the management of Norshield Asset Management (Canada) Ltd. is described.

44984 ■ "Friendly Ice Cream Corporation" in Ice Cream Reporter (Vol. 23, August 20, 2010, No. 9, pp. 8)
Description: Friendly Ice Cream Corporation appointed Andrea M. McKenna as vice president of marketing and chief marketing officer.

44985 ■ "From the Battlefield to the Boardroom" in Business Horizons (Vol. 51, March-April 2008, No. 2, pp. 79)
Pub: Elsevier Advanced Technology Publications
Ed: Catherine M. Dalton. **Description:** Effective intelligence gathering, a thorough understanding of the mission, efficient use of resources, and strategic leadership are vital to achieving success in business as well as in the battlefield. Examples of effective leadership in the battle of Gettysburg are cited.

44986 ■ "From the Editors: Plagiarism Policies and Screening at AMJ" in Academy of Management Journal (Vol. 55, August 2012, No. 4, pp. 749)
Pub: Academy of Management
Contact: Ming-Jer Chen, President
Description: The plagiarism policies and practices of the Academy of Management Journal (AMJ) based on the Committee on Publications Ethics and AOM guidelines are described. The function of the Cross-Check software tool for screening manuscripts for plagiarism is explained.

44987 ■ "Fuel for Thought" in Canadian Business (Vol. 81, April 14, 2008, No. 6, pp. 18)
Pub: Rogers Media Inc.
Contact: Tony Viner, President
Ed: John Gray. **Description:** Discusses a web poll of 133 CEOs and other business leaders that shows that they predict oil prices to increase to US $113 per barrel over the 2008 to 2010 timeframe. Most of the respondents did not favor cutting gas taxes but this group wants the government to cut taxes on fuel-efficient vehicles and increase subsidies to local transit systems.

44988 ■ "The Future of Work" in Business Strategy Review (Vol. 21, Autumn 2010, No. 3, pp. 16)
Pub: Blackwell Publishers Ltd.
Ed: Lynda Gratton. **Description:** Work is universal. But how, why, where and when we work has never been so open to individual interpretation. The certainties of the past have been replaced by ambiguity,

questions and the steady hum of technology. Now, in a groundbreaking research project covering 21 global companies and more than 200 executives, the author is making sense of the future of work.

44989 ■ "Gail Lissner: Vice-President, Appraisal Research Counselors" in Crain's Chicago Business (Vol. 31, May 5, 2008, No. 18, pp. 28)

Pub: Crain Communications Inc.

Contact: Todd Johnson, Publisher

Ed: Phuong Ly. Description: Profile of Gail Lissner who is the vice-president of the Appraisal Research Counselors, a company that puts out the quarterly 'Residential Benchmark Report,' in which Ms. Lissner co-authors and is considered a must-read in the industry. Ms. Lissner has risen to become one of the most sought-after experts on the Chicago market considering real estate.

44990 ■ "Gail Mukaihata Hannemann, Girl Scouts of Hawaii, Chief Executive Officer" in Hawaii Business (Vol. 53, January 2008, No. 7, pp. 24)

Pub: PacificBasin Communications

Ed: Cathy S. Cruz-George. Description: Discusses the Girl Scouts of Hawaii which has altered its business model to become more appealing to young girls in the 21st century. Gail Mukaihata Hanneman, the chief executive officer of the nonprofit organization, states that the Girl Scouts has consolidated some of its operations to increase efficiency. Her views on what employers must learn about the youth and on the adults' roles in developing the younger generation are given.

44991 ■ "A Gambling Man: Career Transitions that Put a Vegas Hotshot on Top" in Black Enterprise (Vol. 37, October 2006, No. 3, pp. 89)

Pub: Earl G. Graves Publishing Co. Inc.

Contact: Earl G. Graves, Jr., President

Ed: Laura Egodigwe. Description: Interview with Lorenzo Creighton, president and chief operating officer of MGM Mirage's New York-New York Hotel and Casino. Creighton talks about his history and the challenges he faced since he didn't come from the casino industry.

44992 ■ "Game Changer" in Canadian Business (Vol. 83, June 15, 2010, No. 10, pp. 52)

Pub: Rogers Media Inc.

Contact: Tony Viner, President

Ed: Jordan Timm. Description: Ubisoft chose Ontario to be the site for its new development studio and it has appointed Jade Raymond as its managing director. Raymond was born in Montreal in 1975 and studied computer science at McGill. Raymond is said to possess the understanding of the game industry's technical, art, and business components.

44993 ■ The Game-Changer: How You Can Drive Revenue and Profit Growth with Innovation

Pub: Crown Business

Ed: A.G Lafley, Ram Charan. Price: $27.50, Hardcover. Description: Management guru Charan and Proctor & Gamble CEO Lafley provide lessons to encourage innovation at all levels, including how to hire for and encourage an environment of communication and tangible work processes.

44994 ■ "Game Changing" in Business Strategy Review (Vol. 23, Spring 2012, No. 1, pp. 26)

Released: Spring 2012. Description: Barney Francis is Managing Director of Sky Sports. In a television career spanning 18 years, he has worked in the multichannel terrestrial and independent sectors. At Sky, he was executive producer for cricket, leading his team through two ICC World Cups, two Ashes Tours, England tours to nine nations, and the first Twenty20 Cup. In 2007, he became executive producer for Sky's Premier league football and in 2008 executive producer for the UEFA Champions League.

44995 ■ "Generalizing Newcomers' Relational and Organizational Identifications: Processes and Prototypicality" in Academy of Management Journal (Vol. 55, August 1, 2012, No. 4, pp. 949)

Pub: Academy of Management

Contact: Ming-Jer Chen, President

Ed: David M. Sluss, Robert E. Ployhart, M. Glenn Cobb, Blake E. Ashforth. Description: The process in which newcomers identify themselves with a supervisor and with the employing organization is examined. Results suggest that relational identification with a supervisor converges with organizational identification through effective, cognitive and behavioral mechanisms yet only when the relational other is perceived to be prototypical.

44996 ■ "Generation Y Goes To Work; Management" in The Economist (Vol. 390, January 3, 2009, No. 8612, pp. 48)

Description: Unemployment rates among people in their 20s has increased significantly and there is a lower turnover in crisis-hit firms, which has made it more difficult to simply find another job if one is unsatisfied with the management style of his or her company. Managers are adopting a more command-and-control approach which is the antithesis of the open, collaborative style that younger employees prefer.

44997 ■ "Get Back To Business Planning Fundamentals" in Entrepreneur (October 24, 2008)

Pub: Entrepreneur Press

Contact: Perlman Neil, President

Ed: Tim Berry. Description: During a recession it is important to know what adjustment to make to your business plan. Some fundamentals to remember include: watching things more closely by tracking progress on cash, sales, new projects, customer satisfaction, ad spending and expenses; looking for built-in indicators such as what drives sales or expenses; watching what drives cash flow; and do not make mistakes such as laying off experienced employees too soon.

44998 ■ Get in the Game: 8 Elements of Perseverance that Make the Difference

Pub: Gotham/Penguin Group Incorporated

Ed: Cal Ripken, Donald T. Phillips. Released: April 10, 2008. Price: $15, paperback; $12.99. Description: Guidebook written by superstar athlete Cal Ripkin to help managers and entrepreneurs achieve success. Availability: PrintElectronic publishing.

44999 ■ "Get Online Quick in the Office Or in the Field" in Contractor (Vol. 56, October 2009, No. 10, pp. 47)

Pub: Penton Media, Inc.

Ed: William Feldman, Patti Feldman. Description: Contractors can set up a web site in minutes using the www.1and1.com website. Verizon's Novatel MIFI 2372 HSPA personal hotspot device lets contractors go online in the field. The StarTech scalable business management system helps contractors manage daily operations.

45000 ■ "Get Your Mojo Working" in Small Business Opportunities (March 2011)

Pub: Harris Publications Inc.

Ed: Holly G. Green. Description: Ways to keep employees engaged and productive are discussed.

45001 ■ "Getting Drowned Out by the Brainstorm" in Canadian Business (Vol. 83, June 15, 2010, No. 10, pp. 91)

Pub: Rogers Media Inc.

Contact: Tony Viner, President

Ed: Joe Castaldo. Description: A study reveals that people generate more ideas when they do it alone rather than as part of a brainstorming group. The limited range of ideas is due to the fixation of group members on the first idea that gets offered.

45002 ■ Getting to Innovation: How Asking the Right Questions Generates the Great

Ideas Your Company Needs

Pub: AMACOM

Contact: Edward T. Reilly, Manager

Ed: Arthur B. VanGundy. Released: July 2007. Price: $29.95, hardback. Description: Guide to achieving the critical first step in formulating creative and useful ideas that lead to results for any small company. Availability: Print; E-book.

45003 ■ Getting Things Done

Ed: David Allen. Released: December 2002. Price: $16. Description: Methods for reducing stress and increasing performance are described.

45004 ■ Getting Things Done: The Art of Stress-Free Productivity

Pub: Penguin Books USA Inc.

Ed: David Allen. Released: December 31, 2002. Price: $24.95, hardcover; $12.99. Description: Coach and management consultant recommends methods for stress-free performance under the premise that productivity is directly related to our ability to relax. Availability: PrintElectronic publishing.

45005 ■ "Getting to 'Us'" in Harvard Business Review (Vol. 92, September 2014, No. 9, pp. 38)

Pub: Harvard Business Publishing

Released: September 2014. Description: Employee motivation and satisfaction can be enhanced through leadership that presents a shared goal that emphasizes kinship and relationship to others, rather than citing a common enemy.

45006 ■ Getting to Yes: Negotiating Agreement Without Giving In

Pub: Penguin Books USA Inc.

Ed: Roger Fisher, William L. Ury, Bruce Patton. Released: May 03, 2011. Price: $16, paperback; $12.99. Description: Strategies for negotiating mutually acceptable agreements in all types of conflict. Availability: PrintElectronic publishing.

45007 ■ The Girl's Guide to Being a Boss (Without Being a Bitch): Valuable Lessons, Smart Suggestions, and True Stories for Succeeding as the Chick-in-Charge

Pub: Random Housing Publishing Group

Ed: Caitlin Friedman, Kimberly Yorio. Released: May 01, 2007. Price: $13.99. Availability: Print.

45008 ■ "The Global Talent Hunt" in Business Strategy Review (Vol. 21, Spring 2010, No. 1, pp. 78)

Pub: John Wiley & Sons Inc. Scientific, Technical, Medical, and Scholarly Div. (Wiley-Blackwell)

Contact: William J. Pesce, Manager

E-mail: wpesce@wiley.com

Ed: Richard Emerton. Description: Richard Emerton explains how the new 'triple context' of economy, environment and society will have profound implications for human resource practices. He suggests that viewing talent as abundant is the right perspective for a manager.

45009 ■ "The Globe: A Cautionary Tale for Emerging Market Giants" in Harvard Business Review (Vol. 88, September 2010, No. 9, pp. 99)

Pub: Harvard Business School Publishing

Ed: J. Stewart Black, Allen J. Morrison. Description: Key factors that negatively affected Japan corporate growth and organizational effectiveness include: devotion to established path, isolated domestic markets, homogenous executive teams, and a noncontentious labor force. Solutions include leadership development programs, multicultural input, and cross-cultural training.

45010 ■ "GM Is On the Road Again" in Canadian Business (Vol. 83, September 14, 2010, No. 15, pp. 14)

Pub: Rogers Media Inc.

Contact: Tony Viner, President

Ed: Thomas Watson. Description: Former General Motors CEO Rick Wagoner has been credited for single-handedly putting the automaker back on track before he was forced to resign and GM was restructured by the government. GM earned $2.19 billion the first half of 2010 after losing more than $80 billion in the three years leading up to its failure. GM's comeback is discussed.

45011 ■ *"Go Ahead, Take That Vacation. They'll Be Fine Without You" in Canadian Business (Vol. 85, July 16, 2012, No. 11-12, pp. 69)*
Pub: George Media Inc.
Ed: Sarah Barmak. **Released:** July 16, 2012. **Description:** Managers who skip vacation time because they are anxious of leaving subordinates on their own may risk burning out. Managers are advised to assign several people in charge and try to relax because good things tend to happen when they go away.

45012 ■ *"Go East" in Canadian Business (Vol. 80, February 26, 2007, No. 5, pp. 21)*
Pub: Rogers Media Inc.
Contact: Tony Viner, President
Ed: Claire Gagne. **Description:** The managerial strategies followed by Doug Doust, who left Wal-Mart to take over the position of senior vice-president of supply chain at the struggling Seiyu of Japan are presented.

45013 ■ *Go Put Your Strengths to Work*
Pub: Free Press/Simon & Schuster Inc.
Ed: Marcus Buckingham. **Released:** December 2010. **Price:** $16. **Description:** A guide to being more productive, focused and creative at work.

45014 ■ *"Go Team! Why Building a Cohesive Organization Is a Necessary Exercise" in Black Enterprise (Vol. 38, February 2008, No. 7, pp. 66)*
Pub: Earl G. Graves Publishing Co. Inc.
Contact: Earl G. Graves, Jr., President
Ed: Angeli R. Rasbury. **Description:** Tips to help manage successful as well as productive teams are outlined for small business managers.

45015 ■ *"Going for the APEX" in Women In Business (Vol. 62, September 2010, No. 3, pp. 28)*
Pub: American Business Women's Association
Contact: Lorie Burch, President
Description: Information about the American Business Women's Association (ABWA) professional development tools, which keep members focused on personal excellence, is presented. The organization recently launched the APEX (Achieving Personal Excellence) Award to honor women who are making a commitment to themselves.

45016 ■ *"Gold Medal" in Canadian Business (Vol. 79, October 9, 2006, No. 20, pp. 57)*
Ed: Andrew Wahl. **Description:** Creativity skills and management strategies of Rob McEwen, founder and chief executive officer of Goldcorp Inc., are presented.

45017 ■ *Good to Great: Why Some Companies Make the Leap..and Others Don't*
Pub: HarperCollins Publishers Inc.
Contact: Jane Friedman, President
E-mail: jfriedman@harpercollins.com
Ed: Jim Collins. **Price:** $29.99; $19.99; C$18.99. **Description:** Management styles for growing a modern business. **Availability:** PrintE-book.

45018 ■ *"Goodbye, Locker Room: Hello, Boardroom" in Inc. (Vol. 33, October 2011, No. 8, pp. 30)*
Pub: Inc. Magazine
Ed: Issie Lapowsky, Kasey Wehrum. **Description:** In 2005, the National Football League started the NFL Business Management and Entrepreneurial Program. Since the onset of the program, 700 players have participated in the program which takes place at the business schools of Harvard, the University of Pennsylvania, Northwestern and Stanford.

45019 ■ *"Goodwill Haunts Local Companies" in Crain's Chicago Business (Apr. 28, 2008)*
Pub: Crain Communications Inc.
Contact: Todd Johnson, Publisher
Ed: Ann Saphir. **Description:** Many companies are having to face the reality that they overpaid for acquisitions made in better economic times; inves-

tors often dismiss such one-time charges as mere accounting adjustments but writeoffs related to past acquisitions can signal future problems because they mean the expected profits that justified the purchase have not materialized. Writeoffs are particularly worrisome for firms with a lot of debt and whose banks require them to have enough assets to back up their borrowings.

45020 ■ *"Gordon College Chief Explores the Secrets of Corporate Leadership" in Boston Business Journal (Vol. 34, May 23, 2014, No. 16, pp. 4)*
Pub: American City Business Journals, Inc.
Contact: Whitney Shaw, President
Released: May 23, 2014. **Description:** Gordon College president, Michael Lindsay, shares his findings on the secrets of corporate leadership in the book, 'View from the Top: An Inside Look at How People in Power See and Shape the World'. Lindsay describes the characteristics of the leaders he interviewed for the book.

45021 ■ *"Grace Puma: Senior Vice-President of Strategic Sourcing, United Airlines" in Crain's Chicago Business (May 5, 2008)*
Pub: Crain Communications Inc.
Contact: Todd Johnson, Publisher
Ed: John Rosenthal. **Description:** Profile of Grace Puma who is the senior vice-president of strategic sourcing at United Airlines and is responsible for cutting costs at the company in a number of ways including scheduling safety inspections at the same time as routine maintenance, thereby reducing the downtime of each aircraft by five days as well as replacing a third of her staff with outside talent.

45022 ■ *"Great Canadian's President Folds His Cards" in Globe & Mail (February 21, 2006, pp. B4)*
Ed: Peter Kennedy. **Description:** The reasons behind the resignation of Anthony Martin as president of Great Canadian Gaming Corp. are presented.

45023 ■ *"The Green Conversation" in Harvard Business Review (Vol. 86, September 2008, No. 9, pp. 58)*
Pub: Harvard Business Review Press
Contact: Peter E. Walsh, Director
Ed: Andrew J. Hoffman, John Woody, Judith Samuelson, Steve Bishop, Rakesh Khurana, Nitin Nohria, Sir Stuart Rose, Brian Walker. **Description:** Six guidelines are presented for addressing and benefiting from environmentally conscious corporate decision making and practices. Topics covered include marketing, supply chain, and leadership.

45024 ■ *"Grooming Your Online Persona" in Women In Business (Vol. 62, June 2010, No. 2, pp. 36)*
Pub: American Business Women's Association
Contact: Lorie Burch, President
Ed: Diane Stafford. **Description:** Employees' use of online social networks could become a basis on how their employers, clients, or business partners would judge them. Personal details, pictures and other online data should be filtered to avoid inappropriate or uncomfortable situations and distinguish personal from professional or work life.

45025 ■ *Groundswell: Winning in a World Transformed by Social Technologies*
Pub: Harvard Business Review Press
Contact: Peter E. Walsh, Director
Ed: Charlene Li, Josh Bernoff. **Released:** 2008. **Price:** $29.95. **Description:** Corporate executives are struggling with a new trend: people using online social technologies (blogs, social networking sites, YouTube, podcasts) to discuss products and companies, write their own news, and find their own deals.

45026 ■ *Group Genius: The Creative Power of Collaboration*
Pub: Basic Books/Perseus Books Group
Ed: Keith Sawyer. **Released:** March 04, 2008. **Price:** $16.95, U.S.; C$18.50, Canada; C$32.50, Canada; £11.99, UK. **Description:** Organizations can foster creativity and innovation through discussion, argumentation and group activities. **Availability:** PrintE-book.

45027 ■ *"Group Thinking" in Business Strategy Review (Vol. 23, Spring 2012, No. 1, pp. 48)*
Released: Spring 2012. **Description:** Conflicts and decision making in groups has long been a subject of fascination for Randall Peterson, Professor of Organizational Behavior at London Business School. He talks to Business Strategy Review about what ignited his interest and his latest research and thinking.

45028 ■ *Groups in Context: Leadership and Participation in Small Groups*
Pub: McGraw Hill Financial Inc.
Contact: Douglas L. Peterson, President
Ed: Gerald L. Wilson. **Released:** June 2004. **Description:** Small group communication skills for the workplace, in churches, social groups, or civic organizations.

45029 ■ *The Growing Business Handbook: Inspiration and Advice from Successful Entrepreneurs and Fast Growing UK Companies*
Pub: Kogan Page, Limited
Contact: Philip Kogan, Chairman of the Board
Ed: Adam Jolly. **Released:** April 03, 2014. **Price:** £29.99, hardback. **Description:** Tips for growing and running a successful business are covered, focusing on senior managers in middle market and SME companies. **Availability:** Print.

45030 ■ *Growing and Managing a Small Business: An Entrepreneurial Perspective*
Pub: Houghton Mifflin College Div.
Contact: June Smith, President
Ed: Kathleen R. Allen. **Released:** 2007. **Price:** A$159.95; NZ$167.95. **Description:** Introduction to business ownership and management from startup through growth. **Availability:** Print.

45031 ■ *A Guide to the Project Management Body of Knowledge*
Pub: Project Management Institute
Contact: Peter Monkhouse, Director
Released: Fifth Edition. **Price:** $49.50, Members, student; $65.95, Nonmembers. **Description:** A guide for project management using standard language, with new data flow diagrams; the Identify Stakeholders and Collect Requirements processes defined; and with greater attention placed on how knowledge areas integrate in the context of initiating, planning, executing, monitoring and controlling, and closing process groups. **Availability:** Print.

45032 ■ *"Guidelines For Family Business Boards of Directors" in Family Business Review (Vol. 19, June 2006, No. 2, pp. 147)*
Pub: Family Firm Institute
Contact: Judy L. Green, President
Ed: Suzanne Lane, Joseph Astrachan, Andrew Keyt, Kristi McMillan. **Description:** Effective corporate governance standards for boards of directors of family businesses are examined.

45033 ■ *"Guts Not Included" in Canadian Business (Vol. 81, March 31, 2008, No. 5, pp. 46)*
Pub: Rogers Media Inc.
Contact: Tony Viner, President
Ed: Andrew Wahl. **Description:** Executives need the vision to create a strategy that prepares for an uncertain future in light of growing global competition. Canadian business leaders have the right skills and education but do not have enough tolerance for risk.

45034 ■ *"Halls Give Hospital Drive $11 Million Infusion" in The Business Journal-Serving Metropolitan Kansas City (Vol. 26, July 18, 2008)*
Ed: Rob Roberts. **Description:** Don Hall, chairman of Hallmark Cards Inc., and eight family members have announced that they will give $11 million to Children's Mercy Hospitals and Clinics for its $800 million expansion plan. Hall Family Foundation president Bill Hall that contributions such as that for Children's Mercy reflect the charitable interests of the foundation's board and founders. The possible impacts of the Hall's donation are analyzed.

45035 ■ The Halo Effect: And the Eight Other Business Delusions That Deceive Managers
Pub: Free Press/Simon & Schuster Inc.
Ed: Phil Rosenzweig. **Released:** June 2014. **Price:** $17, paperback; $12.38. **Description:** Nine common business delusions, including the halo effect (which the author describes as the need to attribute positive qualities to successful individuals and companies), are illustrated using case studies of Lego, Cisco, and Nokia to show how adhering to myths can be bad for any business. **Availability:** PrintE-book.

45036 ■ "Harding Brews Success at Anheuser-Busch" in Black Enterprise (Vol. 37, February 2007, No. 7, pp. 32)
Pub: Earl G. Graves Publishing Co. Inc.
Contact: Earl G. Graves, Jr., President
Ed: Mashaun D. Simon. **Description:** Profile of Michael S. Harding, president and CEO of Anheuser-Busch packaging group. Harding oversees five business units, 15 facilities, and over 2,300 workers.

45037 ■ "Hawker Suppliers See No Issues Yet, But Are Concerned About the Future" in Wichita Business Journal (Vol. 27, February 24, 2012, No. 8, pp. 1)
Pub: American City Business Journal
Description: Hawker Beechcraft Corporation (HBC) has hired Steve Miller, a corporate restructuring specialist, as CEO and sent a positive signal to Wall Street and financial institutions. However, some of HBC's suppliers are nervous about what the future holds even though no one has yet reported any problems with the company.

45038 ■ "HBC Enlists IBM to Help Dress Up Its On-Line Shopping" in Globe & Mail (February 7, 2006, pp. B3)
Ed: Simon Avery. **Description:** The details of management contract between Hudson's Bay Co. and International Business Machines Corp. are presented.

45039 ■ "HBR Case Study: Play It Safe or Take a Stand?" in Harvard Business Review (Vol. 88, November 2010, No. 11, pp. 139)
Pub: Harvard Business School Publishing
Ed: Trish Gorman Clifford, Jay Barney. **Description:** A fictitious leadership scenario is presented, with contributors providing comments and recommendations. A female executive ponders whether to assert a point of view on a new venture. Both experts agree that after providing careful analysis of pros and cons, the executive should come to a well-informed conclusion.

45040 ■ "HBR Case Study: When the Longtime Star Fades" in Harvard Business Review (Vol. 88, September 2010, No. 9, pp. 117)
Pub: Harvard Business School Publishing
Ed: Jimmy Guterman. **Description:** A fictitious aging employee scenario is presented, with contributors offering advice. The scenarios focuses on an older employee's match with a rapidly changing industry; suggestions include consolidating a niche business around the employee, and also engaging the older employee in solving the productivity issue.

45041 ■ "He Said, She Said: Stay Clear of Gossip In the Workplace With a Mature Attitude" in Black Enterprise (February 2008)
Pub: Earl G. Graves Publishing Co. Inc.
Contact: Earl G. Graves, Jr., President
Ed: Akoto Ofori-Atta. **Description:** It is important for employees to avoid gossip in the workplace because of the negative impact; it is recommended focusing on conversations that will help an individual's professional goals.

45042 ■ "Health Nuts and Bolts" in Entrepreneur (Vol. 36, April 2008, No. 4, pp. 24)
Pub: Entrepreneur Press
Contact: Perlman Neil, President
Ed: Jacquelyn Lynn. **Description:** Encouraging employees to develop good eating habits can promote productivity at work. Ways on how to improve employee eating habits include employers setting a good example themselves and offering employees healthy options. Other details about the topic are discussed.

45043 ■ "A Heart for Software; Led by Its Upbeat CEO, Menlo Spreads Joy of Technology" in Crain's Detroit Business (Vol. 30, October 13, 2014, No. 41, pp. 1)
Pub: Crain Communications Inc. - Detroit
Contact: Keith Crain, Chairman
Released: October 13, 2014. **Description:** Profile of Rich Sheridan, one of the most prominent names in IT in Ann Arbor, Michigan. Sheridan believes in common-sense solutions and manages his workers to be empowered employees to come up with their own solutions to software coding issues, and he is a consummate salesman and marketer. He runs his company so it goes beyond understanding what the user needs, and managing a great team, to being the front man selling his goods and services.

45044 ■ "Heavy Duty: The Case Against Packing Lightly" in Crain's Chicago Business (Vol. 31, April 21, 2008, No. 16, pp. 29)
Pub: Crain Communications Inc.
Contact: Todd Johnson, Publisher
Ed: Sarah A. Klein. **Description:** Penelope Biggs, a Northern Trust executive who manages sales teams in North America, Europe and Asia gives advice on traveling abroad for business including time management skills, handling time-zone hops and avoiding jet-lag.

45045 ■ "Help, For Some" in Canadian Business (Vol. 81, December 8, 2008, No. 21, pp. 10)
Ed: Joe Castaldo. **Description:** Over 80 percent of Canadian chief executives believe that government bailouts merely reward mediocre management and encourages companies to take risks because they know the government will help prevent their bankruptcy. Respondents to a COMPAS online survey believe bailouts are unfair for properly managed companies.

45046 ■ "Help Yourself" in Entrepreneur (September 2014)
Pub: Entrepreneurial Press
Released: September 2014. **Description:** Employers can create a workplace where mutual trust is possible by expressing clearly what they expect from their employees, giving feedback that reinforces positive behavior and mentoring them to improve customer service. A leader needs to talk to a pregnant worker about her job priorities, deadlines and communicate ways to help her meet expectations. The best way to approach a company for unsolicited ideas is to find out the contact person who would be responsible for inventors or potential collaborators.

45047 ■ "Henry Mintzberg: Still the Zealous Skeptic and Scold" in Strategy and Leadership (Vol. 39, March-April 2011, No. 2, pp. 4)
Pub: Emerald Group Publishing Inc.
Ed: Robert J. Allio. **Description:** Henry Mintzberg, professor at the McGill University in Montreal, Canada, shares his thoughts on issues such as inappropriate methods in management education and on trends in leadership and management. Mintzberg believes that US businesses are facing serious management and leadership challenges.

45048 ■ "The Hidden Advantages of Quiet Bosses" in Harvard Business Review (Vol. 88, December 2010, No. 12, pp. 28)
Pub: Harvard Business School Publishing
Ed: Adam M. Grant, Francesca Gino, David A. Hofmann. **Description:** Research on organizations behavior indicates that, while extroverts most often become managers, introvert managers paired with proactive employees make a highly efficient and effective combination.

45049 ■ "High Energy: Gaurdie Banister Joins Aera As President and CEO" in Black Enterprise (Vol. 38, July 2008, No. 12, pp. 30)
Pub: Earl G. Graves Publishing Co. Inc.
Contact: Earl G. Graves, Jr., President
Ed: Brenda Porter. **Description:** Gaurdie Banister Jr. has been appointed president and CEO of Aera Energy L.L.C., becoming one of the first African Americans in the nation to run a major energy corporation. His plans for the firm include utilizing new, sophisticated technologies in order to unlock the 3-1/2 billion barrels of resources the company has on their books in a safe and environmentally friendly way. He also hopes to increase production and maintain cost leadership.

45050 ■ High Performance with High Integrity
Pub: Harvard Business Review Press
Contact: Peter E. Walsh, Director
Ed: Ben W. Heineman, Jr. **Released:** June 03, 2008. **Price:** $22, hardcover. **Description:** The dark side of today's free-market capitalist system is examined. Under intense pressure to make the numbers, executives and employees are tempted to cut corners, falsify accounts, or worse. In today's unforgiving environment that can lead to catastrophe for a small company.

45051 ■ "Higher Education" in Canadian Business (Vol. 79, October 23, 2006, No. 21, pp. 129)
Ed: Erin Pooley; Laura Bogomolny; Joe Castaldo; Michelle Magnan. **Description:** Details of some Canadian business schools, where students can simultaneously pursue a master of business administration degree and also be employed on a part time basis, are presented.

45052 ■ "Hiring: Temporary Theory" in Canadian Business (Vol. 80, November 5, 2007, No. 22, pp. 33)
Pub: Rogers Media Inc.
Contact: Tony Viner, President
Ed: Joe Castaldo. **Description:** Employing a temporary manager is ideal for companies working on a strict budget and limited time. The strategy will provide the company with the skills of an expert manager for a cost that is less than that of hiring a full-time manager. The usage of interim managers, specifically in short-term projects, is discussed.

45053 ■ "His Brother's Keeper: A Mentor Learns the True Meaning of Leadership" in Black Enterprise (Vol. 37, December 2006, No. 5, pp. 69)
Pub: Earl G. Graves Publishing Co. Inc.
Contact: Earl G. Graves, Jr., President
Ed: Laura Egodigwe. **Description:** Interview with Keith R. Wyche of Pitney Bowes Management Services, which discusses the relationship between a mentor and mentee as well as sponsorship.

45054 ■ "The Hispanic Business 100 Most Influential Hispanics" in Hispanic Business (October 2007, pp. 30)
Pub: Hispanic Business Inc.
Contact: Jesus Chavarria, President
Description: Profiles of the one hundred Hispanic business leaders are presented.

45055 ■ "Hispanic Executives Continue Their Rise to Power Amid a Shaky Economy" in Hispanic Business (January-February 2009, pp. 12-14)
Pub: Hispanic Business Inc.
Contact: Jesus Chavarria, President
Ed: Michael Bowker. **Description:** Hispanic Business Media's 2009 Corporate Elite winners defied expectations and a tough economy and rose to the top of their industries; innovation being cited as key to growth of Hispanic-owned companies.

45056 ■ "Holiday Cheer" in Business Journal-Serving Phoenix & the Valley of the Sun (Vol. 31, December 3, 2010, No. 13, pp. 1)
Pub: Phoenix Business Journal
Ed: Lynn Ducey, Mike Sunnucks. **Description:** Results of a study conducted by Challenger, Gray & Christmas Inc., shows that 68 percent of companies

are planning holiday parties in 2010, up slightly from 62 percent in 2009. About 53 percent of those having holiday parties are holding them on company premises.

45057 ■ *"Holidays Should Foster Mutual Respect" in Women In Business (Vol. 61, October-November 2009, No. 5, pp. 33)*
Pub: American Business Women's Association
Contact: Lorie Burch, President
Ed: Diane Stafford. **Description:** Workplaces have modified the way year-end holiday celebrations are held in an effort to promote mutual respect. The workers' varying religious beliefs, political affiliations, and other differences have brought about the modifications. The importance of developing mutual understanding is emphasized as a mechanism to stimulate successful business ties.

45058 ■ *"Host"*
Pub: Solutions Business Publishing
Released: October 1, 2014. **Price:** , $15.99 paperback. **Description:** Great engagement is the key to any successful business leadership. Host leadership involves six new roles in employee engagement: adopt the four positions for a Host Leader; understand how to step into and out of the six new roles of engagement; achieve greater agility, flexibility, and responsiveness; become a leader with a highly tuned sense of relationship building and engagement.

45059 ■ *"Hourly Payment and Volunteering: The Effect of Organizational Practices on Decisions About Time Use" in Academy of Management Journal (Vol. 50, No. 4, August 1, 2007, pp. 783)*
Pub: Academy of Management
Contact: Ming-Jer Chen, President
Ed: Sanford E. DeVoe, Jeffrey Pfeffer. **Description:** Brief description about theoretically important class of work, which is freely undertaken without remuneration, is presented.

45060 ■ *"How Anger Poisons Decision Making" in Harvard Business Review (Vol. 88, September 2010, No. 9, pp. 26)*
Pub: Harvard Business School Publishing
Ed: Jennifer S. Lerner, Katherine Shonk. **Description:** Importance of accountability in mitigating the negative effects of anger on the decision making process is stressed.

45061 ■ *How to Become a Great Boss: The Rules for Getting and Keeping the Best Employees*
Pub: Hyperion
Ed: Jeffrey J. Fox. **Released:** May 15, 2002. **Price:** $17, hardcover; C$19, hardcover. **Description:** The book offers valuable advice to any manager or entrepreneur to improve leadership and management skills. Topics covered include: hiring, managing, firing, partnership and competition, self and organization, employee performance, attitude, and priorities. **Availability:** Print.

45062 ■ *"How Employees' Strengths Make Your Company Stronger; Employees Who Use Their Strengths Are More Engaged, Perform Better, Are Less Likely To Leave -- and Boost Your Bottom Line" in Gallup Business Journal (February 20, 2014)*
Pub: Gallup Press
Released: February 20, 2014. **Description:** The best way for organizations to maximize their workers' strengths is through their managers. When staff members know and use their strongest skills, they are more engaged and will perform better, have a higher sense of well being, are less likely to seek employment elsewhere, while increasing the firm's bottom line.

45063 ■ *"How Fast Can This Thing Go, Anyway?" in Inc. (March 2008, pp. 94-101)*
Pub: Mansueto Ventures L.L.C.
Contact: John Koten, Chief Executive Officer
Ed: Stephanie Clifford. **Description:** Founder of Zip-car, an auto rental company, tell how he brought a new CEO into the company to boost revenue. The new CEO instituted a seven-step strategy to increase business.

45064 ■ *"How the Generation Gap Can Hurt Your Business" in Agency Sales Magazine (Vol. 39, November 2009, No. 10, pp. 16)*
Ed: Jack Foster. **Description:** Now that there are four generations of people in the workplace, there is a need to add flexibility to communications for independent manufacturers representatives. Managers can encourage the younger generations to do the research and the boomers to process information and let each side report to the other.

45065 ■ *"How Great Leaders Think: The Art of Reframing"*
Pub: Jossey-Bass
Contact: William J. Pesce, President
Released: July 8, 2014. **Price:** , $30.00. **Description:** More complex thinking is the key to better leadership. A guide to help leaders understand four major aspects of organizational life: structure, people, politics, and culture is given. The book's lessons include: how to use structural tools to organize teams and organizations for better results, how to build motivation and morale by aligning organizations and people, how to map the terrain and build a power base to navigate the political dynamics of organizations, and how to develop a leadership story that shapes culture, provides direction, and inspires commitment to excellence.

45066 ■ *"How Has Cincinnati's City Golf Privatization Played?" in Business Courier (Vol. 27, September 10, 2010, No. 19, pp. 1)*
Pub: Business Courier
Ed: Dan Monk. **Description:** It was reported that private contractors are getting more revenue from fewer golfers on city-owned courses in Cincinnati, Ohio. In 1998, the city handed over seven municipal courses to private management. However, some believe that the city has escalated a price war among the region's golf courses.

45067 ■ *"How to Heal a Broken Legg" in Barron's (Vol. 92, September 17, 2012, No. 38, pp. 18)*
Description: Legg Mason is looking for a new chief executive officer after Mark Fetting announced his resignation effective October 1, 2012. Fetting is credited with saving the company by reducing operating expenses, but had a tense relationship with the firm's affiliates. The company has limited options in finding a replacement and undertaking reorganization.

45068 ■ *"How Healthcare Managers Can Improve Outcomes and Patient Care; They Can Start With These Five Steps for Turning their Organization's Employee Engagement Results Into Clinical Improvements" in Gallup Business Journal (August 7, 2014)*
Pub: Gallup Press
Released: August 7, 2014. **Description:** Health care managers can improve outcomes and patient care by following the five steps outlined in this article.

45069 ■ *"How Healthcare Organizations Can Improve This Year; Three Strategies for 2014 That Will Help Leaders Achieve Goals Related to Patient Satisfaction Employee Onboarding Time, and Medical Supply Availability, Among Others" in Gallup Business Journal (February 13, 2014)*
Pub: Gallup Press
Released: February 13, 2014. **Description:** Three strategies to enable healthcare organizations to increase their management's success in achieving goals and visions related to patient satisfaction, employee onboarding time, and medical supply availability are outlined to help improve 2014 performance.

45070 ■ *"How Hierarchy Can Hurt Strategy Execution" in Harvard Business Review (Vol. 88, July-August 2010, No. 7-8, pp. 74)*
Pub: Harvard Business School Publishing
Description: A series of charts illustrate Harvard Business Review's Advisory Council survey results regarding perceptions of strategy development and execution identifying obstacles and key factors affecting implementation.

45071 ■ *"How I Did It: Xerox's Former CEO On Why Succession Shouldn't Be a Horse Race" in Harvard Business Review (Vol. 88, October 2010, No. 10, pp. 47)*
Pub: Harvard Business School Publishing
Ed: Anne Mulcahy. **Description:** The importance of beginning talks between chief executive officers and boards of directors as early as possible to ensure a smooth transition is stressed. This can also prevent turning successions into competitions, with the resultant loss of talent when other candidates 'lose'.

45072 ■ *"How In the World?" in Business Strategy Review (Vol. 21, Spring 2010, No. 1, pp. 12)*
Pub: John Wiley & Sons Inc. Scientific, Technical, Medical, and Scholarly Div. (Wiley-Blackwell)
Contact: William J. Pesce, Manager
E-mail: wpesce@wiley.com
Ed: Stuart Crainer. **Description:** We may think of management as a recent phenomenon, but its roots lie in the first organizing activities of our ancestors. The author looks a the emergence of management as a profession. He finds that the road to modern management leads to a paradox and questions ways to change that.

45073 ■ *"How Investors React When Women Join Boards" in Harvard Business Review (Vol. 88, July-August 2010, No. 7-8, pp. 24)*
Pub: Harvard Business School Publishing
Ed: Andrew O'Connell. **Price:** $6. **Description:** Research reveals a cognitive bias in blockholders regarding the presence of women on boards of directors despite evidence showing that diversity improves results. **Availability:** PDF.

45074 ■ *How to Make Money with Social Media: An Insider's Guide to Using New and Emerging Media to Grow Your Business*
Pub: FT Press
Contact: Timothy C. Moore, Vice President
Ed: Jamie Turner, Reshma Shah. **Released:** Second Edition. **Price:** $34.99. **Description:** Marketers, executives, entrepreneurs are shown more effective ways to utilize Internet social media to make money. This guide brings together both practical strategies and proven execution techniques for driving maximum value from social media marketing. **Availability:** E-book.

45075 ■ *"How Managers Become Leaders: The Seven Seismic Shifts of Perspective and Responsibility" in (Vol. 90, June 2012, No. 6, pp. 64)*
Pub: Harvard Business Review Press
Contact: Peter E. Walsh, Director
Ed: Michael D. Watkins. **Released:** June 2012. **Description:** The seven shifts are: from specialist to generalist, from analyst to integrator, from tactician to strategist, from bricklayer to architect, from problem solver to agenda setter, from warrior to diplomat, and from supporting cast to lead role. The specific characteristics of each transition are described.

45076 ■ *"How Many Direct Reports? Senior Leaders, Always Pressed For Time, Are Nonetheless Broadening Their Span of Control" in Harvard Business Review (Vol. 90, April 2012, No. 4, pp. 112)*
Pub: Harvard Business Review Press
Contact: Peter E. Walsh, Director
Ed: Gary L. Neilson, Julie Wulf. **Released:** April 2012. **Description:** A rise in market and geographical complexities has driven an expansion of chief executive officer control during the past 20 years. New executive development options enable CEOs to cross-collaborate, and functional leaders make up 80 percent of new positions reporting to the CEO.

45077 ■ *"How to Not Get Fired" in Entrepreneur (Vol. 37, September 2009, No. 9, pp. 62)*
Pub: Entrepreneur Press
Contact: Perlman Neil, President
Ed: Brad Feld. **Description:** Advice on how chief executive officers (CEO) of venture capital funded firms can avoid being replaced is presented. ■ A CEO

should not be defensive of the prospect of being replaced. The CEO may also work with the investors and the board for a smooth transition.

45078 ■ *"How to Protect Your Job in a Recession"* in Harvard Business Review (Vol. 86, September 2008, No. 9, pp. 113)
Pub: Harvard Business Review Press
Contact: Peter E. Walsh, Director

Ed: Janet Banks, Diane Coutu. **Description:** Strategies are presented for enhancing one's job security. These include being a team player, empathizing with management, preserving optimism, and concentrating on the customer.

45079 ■ *How to Recognize and Reward Employees: 150 Ways to Inspire Peak Performance*
Pub: American Management Association
Contact: Edward T. Reilly, President

Ed: Donna Deeprose. **Released:** 2nd Edition. **Price:** $13.95, paperback. **Availability:** PDF.

45080 ■ *How Remarkable Women Lead: A Breakthrough Model for Work and Life*
Pub: Crown Business

Ed: Joanna Barsh, Susie Cranston. **Released:** September 24, 2009. **Price:** $27.50, Hardcover. **Description:** An introduction to remarkable women, from Time Inc.'s Ann Moore to Xerox's Anne Mulcahy, who recount their inspiring struggles.

45081 ■ *"How Technology has Changed the Way People Lead"* in Pittsburgh Business Times (Vol. 33, April 25, 2014, No. 41, pp. 8)
Pub: American City Business Journals

Released: April 25, 2014. **Description:** Members of the Pittsburgh chapter of the Young Presidents' Organization (YPO) in Pennsylvania discuss how technology has influenced the way they lead their companies and organizations as part of a roundtable discussion on leadership. They note how technology has improved connection with employees, accessibility to clients, multitasking, among other things.

45082 ■ *"How To Earn Loyalty From Millenials"* in Birmingham Business Journal (Vol. 31, February 28, 2014, No. 9, pp. 16)
Pub: American City Business Journals, Inc.
Contact: Whitney Shaw, President

Released: February 28, 2014. **Description:** Advice for earning loyalty from millennial employees is offered. Management need to create an environment where mistakes are openly admitted and employees should be encouraged to give back to causes that matter most to them.

45083 ■ *"How To Help New Leaders Succeed"* in Birmingham Business Journal (Vol. 31, January 31, 2014, No. 5, pp. 9)
Pub: American City Business Journals, Inc.
Contact: Whitney Shaw, President

Released: January 31, 2014. **Description:** Advice on how new managers could attain successful careers is presented. Managers should know how their department's function fits into the organization. Reading about managerial leadership is also encouraged.

45084 ■ *"How To Help Your Organization SOAR"* in Birmingham Business Journal (Vol. 31, February 21, 2014, No. 8, pp. 8)
Pub: American City Business Journals, Inc.
Contact: Whitney Shaw, President

Released: February 21, 2014. **Description:** Ways to change disruptive behavior of an employee is examined. The SOAR Formula for feedback can help provide the necessary results to address challenging or difficult behavior before an employee can adversely affect productivity and morale in the office.

45085 ■ *"How To Identify Leadership Potential: Development and Testing of a Consensus Model"* in Human Resource Management (Vol. 51, May- June 2012, No. 3,

pp. 361-385)
Pub: John Wiley & Sons Inc.
Contact: Stephen M. Smith, President
Ed: Nicky Dries, Roland Pepermans. **Description:** A consensus model for the identification of leadership potential is proposed. This model is made up of four quadrants: analytical skills, learning agility, drive and emergent leadership.

45086 ■ *"How To Manage Your Chain of Command"* in Birmingham Business Journal (Vol. 31, June 27, 2014, No. 26, pp. 12)
Pub: American City Business Journals, Inc.
Contact: Whitney Shaw, President
Released: June 27, 2014. **Description:** Chain of command in a small business functions through junior leaders who pass information and instructions from the CEO to subordinates. The chain of command is used more effectively when CEOs work through those leaders and not around them.

45087 ■ *"How To Turn Your Efforts Into Results"* in Green Industry Pro (Vol. 23, September 2011)
Pub: Cygnus Business Media
Contact: Paul Mackler, Chief Executive Officer
Ed: Bob Coulter. **Description:** Working Smarter Training Challenge teaches that leaders are able to carry out solutions directly into their organization, develop skills and drive business results in key areas by creating a culture of energized workers who are able to take ownership of their performance as well as the performance of the company as a whole.

45088 ■ *"How To Win In Emerging Markets: Lessons From Japan"* in Harvard Business Review (Vol. 90, May 2012, No. 5, pp. 126)
Pub: Harvard Business Review Press
Contact: Peter E. Walsh, Director
Ed: Shigeki Ichii, Susumu Hattori, David Michael. **Released:** May 2012. **Description:** Corporate Japan's four challenges in engaging emerging markets are an aversion to mergers and acquisitions, an aversion to low- and middle-end segments, lack of organizational or financial commitments to emerging markets, and a shortage of executive talent placed in emerging markets. By addressing these weaknesses, Japan can succeed in global expansion.

45089 ■ *"How Tom Smith Can Help Orlando Lure 2024 Olympics"* in Orlando Business Journal (Vol. 30, January 24, 2014, No. 31, pp. 4)
Pub: American City Business Journals
Released: January 24, 2014. **Description:** Hyatt Regency Hotel Orlando general manager, Tom Smith, is working to lure the 2024 Olympics to Orlando, Florida. Smith's experience in managing hotels is useful to this effort. He aims to attract other events to the area.

45090 ■ *"How to Turn Employee Conflict Into a Positive, Productive Force"* in HR Specialist (Vol. 8, September 2010, No. 9, pp. 6)
Pub: Capitol Information Group Inc.
Description: Ways to help manage a team of workers are presented, focusing on ways to avoid conflict within the group are discussed.

45091 ■ *How We Decide*
Ed: Jonah Lehrer. **Released:** February 2009. **Price:** $25. **Description:** Insights for entrepreneurs to help with decision making; the book describes potential traps such as negative information and how it carries more weight than positive information.

45092 ■ *How to Win Friends and Influence People*
Pub: Simon and Schuster Inc.
Contact: Carolyn Reidy, President
E-mail: carolyn.reidy@simonandschuster.com
Ed: Dale Carnegie. **Released:** February 15, 1990. **Price:** $7.99, Paperback. **Description:** First published in 1937, this book helps people to understand human nature. The book teaches skills through underlying principles of dealing with people so that they feel important and appreciated.

45093 ■ *"How to Write a Great Business Plan for Your Small Business in 60 Minutes or Less*
Pub: Atlantic Publishing Co.
Contact: Amanda Miller, Manager
E-mail: amiller@atlantic-pub.com
Ed: Sharon L. Fullen. **Released:** January 2006. **Price:** $39.95, Includes CD-Rom. **Description:** A good business plan outlines goals and works as a company's resume to obtain funding, credit from suppliers, management of the operations and finances, promotion and marketing, and more. **Availability:** Print.

45094 ■ *"How Yamana CEO First Struck Gold With Desert Sun"* in Globe & Mail (February 27, 2006, pp. B3)
Ed: Andrew Willis. **Description:** The role of chief executive officer Peter Marronne of Yamana Gold Inc. in the acquisition of Desert Sun Mining Corp. is discussed.

45095 ■ *"How Young Professionals Can Position Themselves for Board Membership: 4 Quick Tips to Get You Started"* in Black Enterprise (Vol. 45, July-August 2014, No. 1, pp. 46)
Pub: Earl G. Graves Publishing Co. Inc.
Contact: Earl G. Graves, Jr., President
Released: July-August 2014. **Description:** Four tips to help young professionals secure a position on a company's board focus on: starting with nonprofits, focus on key areas of interest, continue to growth through networking and training programs, and to gain global experience.

45096 ■ *"HR Tech on the Go"* in Workforce Management (Vol. 88, November 16, 2009, No. 12, pp. 1)
Pub: Crain Communications Inc.
Contact: Rance E. Crain, President
Ed: Ed Frauenheim. **Description:** Examination of the necessity of mobile access of human resources software applications that allow managers to recruit, schedule and train employees via their mobile devices; some industry leaders believe that mobile HR applications are vital while others see this new technology as hype.

45097 ■ *"HR Technology: Meetings Go Virtual"* in HRMagazine (Vol. 54, January 2009, No. 1, pp. 74)
Pub: Society for Human Resource Management
Contact: Henry G. Jackson, President
E-mail: hjackson@shrm.org
Ed: Elizabeth Agnvall. **Description:** Microsoft Office Live Meeting conferencing software allows companies to schedule meetings from various company locations, thus saving travel costs.

45098 ■ *"Huberman Failing to Keep CTA on Track"* in Crain's Chicago Business (Vol. 31, April 21, 2008, No. 16, pp. 22)
Pub: Crain Communications Inc.
Contact: Todd Johnson, Publisher
Description: Discusses the deplorable service of CTA, the Chicago Transit Authority, as well as CTA President Ron Huberman who, up until last week had riders hoping he had the management skills necessary to fix the system's problems; Tuesday's event left hundreds of riders trapped for hours and thousands standing on train platforms along the Blue Line waiting for trains that never came.

45099 ■ *"Human Resource Management: Challenges for Graduate Education"* in Business Horizons (Vol. 51, March-April 2008, No. 2, pp. 151)
Pub: Elsevier Advanced Technology Publications
Ed: James C. Wimbush. **Description:** Human resource management education at the master's and doctoral degree levels is discussed. There is an ever-increasing need to produce human resource managers who understand the value of human resource management as a strategic business contributor. uman.

45100 ■ *"Hydronicahh - Everything in Modulation"* in Contractor (Vol. 56, December 2009, No. 12, pp. 24)
Pub: Intertec Publishing
Contact: John French, President
Ed: Mark Eatherton. **Description:** Management and the environmental impact of a home hydronic system are discussed. Radiant windows have the potential to reduce energy consumption. A variable speed delta T pump is required for the construction of a hydronic wood pit.

45101 ■ *I Can't Believe I Get Paid to Do This*
Pub: Gold Leaf Publishing
Ed: Stacey Mayo. **Price:** $16.95, plus shipping and handling. **Description:** This book is targeted to anyone unhappy in their current position. It is designed to help everyone feel good about their job.
Availability: Print; E-book.

45102 ■ *"I Just Love a Challenge"* in South Florida Business Journal (Vol. 34, July 18, 2014, No. 52, pp. 11)
Pub: American City Business Journals
Released: July 18, 2014. **Description:** Gregory Cunningham, president and CEO of Farm Credit of Florida, shares the lessons he learned from his military background that he applies to managing a company. He explains why he decided to take on the challenge of helping the agricultural credit group deal with its regulatory order.

45103 ■ *"IBM's Best-Kept Secret"* in Canadian Business (Vol. 79, September 25, 2006, No. 19, pp. 19)
Ed: Andrew Wahl. **Description:** The contribution of IBM vice-president Steve Mills in company's development is discussed.

45104 ■ *"The Idea That Saved My Company"* in Inc. (October 2007, pp. 42)
Pub: Mansueto Ventures L.L.C.
Contact: John Koten, Chief Executive Officer
Ed: Mike Hofman. **Description:** Profile of Chip Conley, founder of seventeen boutique hotels in the San Francisco, California Bay Area. Conley learned to overcome depression and regain his entrepreneurial inspiration, which in turn saved his company. Abraham Maslow, author of 'Toward of Psychology of Being' promoted Conley to write his own book, 'Peak: How Great Companies Get Their Mojo From Maslow'.

45105 ■ *"Ideas at Work: Total Communicator"* in Business Strategy Review (Vol. 21, Autumn 2010, No. 3, pp. 10)
Pub: Blackwell Publishers Ltd.
Ed: Stuart Crainer. **Description:** Vittorio Colao has been chief executive of Vodafone Group for two years. He brings to the company special experience as CEO of RCS MediaGroup in Milan, which publishes newspapers, magazines and books in Italy, Spain and France. Prior to RCS, he held other positions within Vodaphone. Colao shares his views on business, the global economy and leading Vodafone.

45106 ■ *"Ideas at Work: Total Communicator"* in Business Strategy Review (Vol. 21, Autumn 2010, No. 3, pp. 10)
Pub: John Wiley & Sons Inc. Scientific, Technical, Medical, and Scholarly Div. (Wiley-Blackwell)
Contact: William J. Pesce, Manager
E-mail: wpesce@wiley.com
Ed: Stuart Crainer. **Description:** Vittorio Colao has been chief executive of Vodafone Group for two years. He brings to the company some special experience: from 2004-2006 he was CEO of RCS MediaGroup in Milan, which publishes newspapers, magazines and books in Italy, Spain and France. Colao shares his views on business, the global economy and leading Vodafone.

45107 ■ *If Harry Potter Ran General Electric*
Pub: Doubleday Publishing Group
Contact: Stephen Rubin, President
E-mail: mpalgon@randomhouse.com
Ed: Tom Morris. **Released:** May 16, 2006. **Price:** $14.99; C$15.99. **Description:** The values and timeless truths that underlie J.K. Rowling's popular Harry

Potter books are discussed showing the lessons they offer to all individuals in their careers and daily lives.
Availability: E-book.

45108 ■ *"I'll Be Back: For Entrepreneurs, Retirement Doesn't Mean Forever"* in Inc. (February 2008, pp. 35-36)
Ed: Leigh Buchanan. **Description:** Many entrepreneurs return to business after selling their companies and retiring. Advice is given to company owners for retirement planning.

45109 ■ *"The Impact of Total Quality Management Adoption on Small and Medium Enterprises' Financial Performance"* in Accounting and Finance (Vol. 52, June 2012, No. 2, pp. 421)
Description: An examination of whether the management accounting practice of total quality management (TQM) positively impacts on the financial performance of small and medium enterprises (SMEs).

45110 ■ *"In the Hot Finance Jobs, Women Are Still Shut Out"* in (Vol. 90, July-August 2012, No. 7-8, pp. 30)
Pub: Harvard Business Review Press
Contact: Peter E. Walsh, Director
Ed: Nori Gerardo Lietz. **Released:** July-August 2012. **Description:** Although women constitute a significant proportion of business school graduates, the percentage of senior investment professionals who are female remain in a single-digit figure. Active effort will be needed to change corporate culture and industry awareness to raise this figure.

45111 ■ *"The Incentive Bubble: Outsourcing Pay Decisions To Financial Markets Has Skewed Compensation and, With It, American Capitalism"* in Harvard Business Review (Vol. 90, March 2012, No. 3, pp. 124)
Pub: Harvard Business Review Press
Contact: Peter E. Walsh, Director
Ed: Mihir Desai. **Released:** March 2012. **Description:** Basing incentive contracts and executive compensation on financial markets actually rewards luck rather than performance, and can promote dangerous risk taking. This has led to America's two main crises of capitalism: growing income inequality and governance failures. Boards of directors must focus on performance rather than stocks, and endowments and foundations must focus on incentives for long-term growth.

45112 ■ *"Increasing Building Work at Ryan Cos."* in Crain's Chicago Business (Vol. 34, May 23, 2011, No. 21, pp. 6)
Pub: Crain Communications Inc.
Contact: Todd Johnson, Publisher
Ed: Eddie Baeb. **Description:** Profile of Tim Hennelly, who is working to make Ryan Company known as a pure builder rather than a developer-builder.

45113 ■ *Influence without Authority*
Pub: John Wiley & Sons Inc.
Contact: Stephen M. Smith, President
Ed: Allan R. Cohen, David L. Bradford. **Released:** 2nd Edition. **Price:** $34.95, hardcover; $22.99. **Availability:** PrintE-book.

45114 ■ *"Information Technology Changes Roles, Highlights Hiring Needs"* in South Florida Business Journal (Vol. 34, February 14, 2014, No. 30, pp. 3)
Pub: American City Business Journals
Released: February 14, 2014. **Description:** Results of the Steven Douglas Associates survey of 218 senior and mid-level information technology executives in South Florida are presented. About 75 percent of the respondents cited cloud services, mobile technologies, big data and enterprise reporting planning as having the most profound impact on their roles. The challenges they face with the expected hiring growth are also examined.

45115 ■ *"The Innovator's Solution: Creating and Sustaining Successful Growth"*
Pub: Harvard Business Review Press
Contact: Peter E. Walsh, Director
Released: October 22, 2013. **Price:** , $30.00. **Description:** Even in today's hyper-accelerated business environment any small company can transform

their business. Advice on business decisions crucial to achieving truly disruptive growth and purpose guidelines for developing their own disruptive growth engine is given. The forces that cause managers to make bad decisions as they plan new ideas for their company are identified and new frameworks to help develop the right conditions, at the right time, for a disruption to succeed. Managers and business leaders responsible for innovation and growth will benefit their business and their teams with this information.

45116 ■ *Instant Profit: Successful Strategies to Boost Your Margin and Increase the Profitability of Your Business*
Ed: Bradley J. Sugars. **Released:** December 2005. **Price:** , $16.95 (US), $22.95 (Canadian). **Description:** Advice on management, money, marketing, and merchandising a successful small business is offered.

45117 ■ *"An Integrative Model of Experiencing and Responding to Mistreatment at Work"* in Academy of Management Review (January 2008, pp. 76)
Pub: ScholarOne Inc.
Contact: William T. Carden, Jr., President
Ed: Julie B. Olson-Buchanan, Wendy R. Boswell. **Description:** Integrative model with theoretical framework is presented to increase understanding of the effects of an individual's perceived experience of workplace mistreatment in dispute resolutions and the person's response to it.

45118 ■ *"Internationalization of Australian Family Businesses: A Managerial Capabilities Perspective"* in Family Business Review (Vol. 19, No.3, September 2006, pp. 207)
Pub: Family Firm Institute
Contact: Judy L. Green, President
Ed: Chris Graves, Jill Thomas. **Description:** Concept that managerial capabilities of family firms lag behind those of non-family counterparts as they expand is discussed.

45119 ■ *"The Interplay Between Theory and Method"* in Academy of Management Review (October 2007, pp. 1145)
Pub: ScholarOne Inc.
Contact: William T. Carden, Jr., President
Ed: John Van Maanen, Jesper B. Sorensen, Terence R. Mitchell. **Description:** Discussion about the role of theory and method in particular organization and management studies, stressing the importance of balancing primacy of theory and evidence for better research results.

45120 ■ *"Into the Wild"* in Inc. (October 2007, pp. 116-120, 122, 124, 126)
Pub: Mansueto Ventures L.L.C.
Contact: John Koten, Chief Executive Officer
Ed: Alison Stein Wellner. **Description:** Perry Klebahn, CEO of Timbuk2, manufacturer of messenger bags, tells how he took his top executives into the deep Wyoming wilderness in order to build employee team work skills. Other options for this type of team-building include cooking courses, changing a tire together, solving a kidnapping, or discussing ways to survive a nuclear winter.

45121 ■ *"Investing in the IT that Makes a Competitive Difference"* in Harvard Business Review (Vol. 86, July-August 2008, No. 8, pp. 98)
Pub: Harvard Business Review Press
Contact: Peter E. Walsh, Director
Ed: Andrew McAfee, Erik Brynjolfsson. **Description:** Components of a successful information technology management strategy are examined. These techniques are broad in spectrum, produce immediate results, are consistent and precise, facilitate monitoring, and promote enforceability.

45122 ■ *"Investment Funds: Friends with Money"* in Canadian Business (Vol. 81, May 22, 2008, No. 9, pp. 22)
Pub: Rogers Media Inc.
Contact: Tony Viner, President
Ed: Jeff Stanford. **Description:** Two of the most well connected managers in Canadian capital markets Rob Farquharson and Brian Gibson will launch

Panoply Capital Asset Management in June. The investment management company aims to raise a billion dollars from institutions and high-net worth individuals.

45123 ■ *"Investors Finding Bay Area Deals"* in Tampa Bay Business Journal (Vol. 29, November 6, 2009, No. 46, pp. 1)
Pub: American City Business Journals
Ed: Margie Manning. **Description:** Private equity investors have found dozens of privately held companies in Tampa Bay area in Florida in which to invest $84 million fresh equity. Revenue generation, growth, solid management teams are some of the factors found by the investors on these companies which span a range of sizes and industries.

45124 ■ *"Irene Rosenfeld: Chairman and CEO, Kraft Foods Inc."* in Crain's Chicago Business (Vol. 31, May 5, 2008, No. 18, pp. 31)
Pub: Crain Communications Inc.
Contact: Todd Johnson, Publisher
Ed: David Sterrett. **Description:** Profile of Irene Rosenfeld who is the chairman and CEO of Kraft Foods Inc. and is entering the second year of a three-year plan to boost sales of well-known brands such as Oreo, Velveeta and Oscar Mayer while facing soaring commodity costs and a declining market-share. Ms. Rosenfeld's turnaround strategy also entails spending more on advertising and giving managers more control over their budgets and product development.

45125 ■ *"iRobot Appoints Former BAE Systems Vice President, Frank Wilson to Lead Defense & Security Business Unit"* in News Bites US (August 9, 2012)
Pub: Financial Times Ltd.
Contact: John Ridding, Chief Executive Officer
Released: August 9, 2012. **Description:** Frank Wilson will serve as senior vice president and general manager of iRobot's Defense & Security business unit. He will focus on strategic business development and product development in order for the firm to meet military, civil defense, and security needs. Tim Trainer, previous acting interim general manager, will remain vice president of programs.

45126 ■ *"Is Business Ethics Getting Better? A Historical Perspective"* in Business Ethics Quarterly (Vol. 21, April 2011, No. 2, pp. 335)
Pub: Society for Business Ethics
Contact: Dawn Elm, Executive Director
Ed: Joanne B. Ciulla. **Description:** The question 'Is Business Ethics Getting Better?' as a heuristic for discussing the importance of history in understanding business and ethics is answered. The article uses a number of examples to illustrate how the same ethical problems in business have been around for a long time. It describes early attempts at the Harvard School of Business to use business history as a means of teaching students about moral and social values. In the end, the author suggests that history may be another way to teach ethics, enrich business ethics courses, and develop the perspective and vision in future business leaders.

45127 ■ *"Is Globalization Threatening U.S. Hispanic Progress?"* in Hispanic Business (Vol. 30, September 2008, No. 9, pp. 16)
Ed: Jessica Haro. **Description:** Talented Hispanic employees are making progress within the increasingly diverse American corporate scenario. However, while some experts believe the induction of foreign professionals through globalization will not impact this progress, others feel it could hamper opportunities for American Hispanics.

45128 ■ *"It Didn't Have To Come To This"* in Canadian Business (Vol. 85, August 13, 2012, No. 13, pp. 4)
Pub: George Media Inc.
Ed: James Cowan. Released: August 13, 2012. **Description:** The business collapse of Research in Motion (RIM) was blamed on the management's arrogance in terms of recognizing that Apple's iPhone is dominating the consumer market and that corporate

customers would remain loyal despite the emergence of better smartphones. It is speculated that the failure of RIM could lead to at least 5,000 job losses.

45129 ■ *"It's Good To Be a CEO: Top Execs Pull Millions In Raises for 2013"* in Atlanta Business Chronicle (June 20, 2014, pp. 22A)
Pub: American City Business Journals, Inc.
Contact: Whitney Shaw, President
Released: June 20, 2014. **Description:** Discussion regarding the highest paid CEOs in Georgia in 2013, with an average of 8.8 percent increase from 2012. The largest increase went to Jeffrey C. Sprecher, chairman and CEO of Intercontinental Exchange Inc., followed by John F. Brock, chairman and CEO of Coca-Cola Enterprises Inc.

45130 ■ *"It's Not the How or the What but the Who: Succeed by Surrounding Yourself with the Best"*
Pub: Harvard Business Review Press
Contact: Peter E. Walsh, Director
Released: May 13 ,2014. **Price:** , $28.00. **Description:** Surrounding yourself with the best matters in every aspect of life and can mean the difference between success and failure. The author draws upon years of experience in global executive search and talent development, as well as the latest management and psychology research, to help improve the choices management makes about employees and mentors, business partners and friends, top corporate leaders and elected officials.

45131 ■ *It's Not Just Who You Know: Transform Your Life (and Your Organization) by Turning Colleagues and Contacts into Lasting Relationships*
Ed: Tommy Spaulding. Released: August 10, 2010. Price: $23. **Description:** Tommy Spaulding teaches the reader how to reach out to others in order to create lasting relationships that go beyond superficial contacts.

45132 ■ *It's Your Ship*
Ed: Michael Abrashoff. **Released:** May 01, 2002. **Price:** $24.95. **Description:** Naval Captain D. Michael Abrashoff shares management principles he used to shape his ship, the U.S.S. Benfold, into a model of progressive leadership. Abrashoff revolutionized ways to face the challenges of excessive costs, low morale, sexual harassment, and constant turnover.

45133 ■ *"Jab, Jab, Jab, Right Hook: How to Tell Your Story in a Noisy Social World"*
Pub: HarperBusiness
Released: November 26, 2014. **Price:** , $29.99. **Description:** Author and social media expert shares advice on ways to connect with customers and beat the competition. Social media strategies for marketers and managers need to convert Internet traffic to sales. Communication is the key to online sales that are adapted to high quality social media platforms and mobile devices.

45134 ■ *"Janet Froetscher: CEO, United Way of Metropolitan Chicago"* in Crain's Chicago Business (Vol. 31, May 5, 2008, No. 18, pp. 26)
Pub: Crain Communications Inc.
Contact: Todd Johnson, Publisher
Ed: Emily Stone. **Description:** Profile of Janet Froetscher who is the CEO of United Way of Metropolitan Chicago who organized the country's largest-ever merger of non-profits with 53 smaller suburban chapters consolidating with the Chicago one. The consolidation saves $4 million a year with departments such as finance, information technology and communications which allows that money be spent funding job training, after-school programs and aid for 7,000 Hurricane Katrina evacuees living in the Chicago area.

45135 ■ *"J.C. Penney Head Shops for Shares"* in Barron's (Vol. 88, July 7, 2008, No. 27, pp. 29)
Pub: Dow Jones & Co., Inc.
Contact: Clare Hart, President
Ed: Teresa Rivas. **Description:** Myron Ullman III, chairman and chief executive officer of J.C. Penney,

purchased $1 million worth of shares of the company. He now owns 393,140 shares of the company and an additional 1,282 on his 401(k) plan.

45136 ■ *"Joanna Crangle Names MBJ Publisher"* in Sacramento Business Journal (Vol. 31, March 28, 2014, No. 5)
Pub: American City Business Journals
Released: March 28, 2014. **Description:** Joanna Crangle has been appointed the new publisher of the 'Memphis Business Journal'. She will succeed Stuart Chamblin, who is retiring as of March 31, 2014. Crangle has previously served as the newspaper's circulation director and advertising director.

45137 ■ *"Job Reviews: Annual Assessments Still the Norm"* in HR Specialist (Vol. 8, September 2010, No. 9, pp. 1)
Description: An OfficeTeam survey of 500 HR professionals asked how their organizations conduct formal performance appraisals. Responses to the questions are examined.

45138 ■ *"Job Search Made Easy"* in Black Enterprise (Vol. 38, January 2008, No. 6, pp. 54)
Pub: Earl G. Graves Publishing Co. Inc.
Contact: Earl G. Graves, Jr., President
Ed: Aisha Sylvester. **Description:** Profile of The Marquin Group's job portal called DiversityTalent.com. Marquin considered the challenges faced by corporations when recruiting senior executives; salaries, mortgage and relocation calculators for particular cities are provided.

45139 ■ *"Jobs Data Show A Slow Leak"* in Barron's (Vol. 88, July 7, 2008, No. 27, pp. 34)
Pub: Dow Jones & Co., Inc.
Contact: Clare Hart, President
Ed: Gene Epstein. **Description:** In June 2008, the United States manufacturing sector showed an expansion, with the purchasing managers' index rising to 50.2 from 49.6; the unemployment rate in the US, which stayed steady at 5.5 percent in June 2008 is also discussed. Statistical data included.

45140 ■ *"Jobs: On the Clock"* in Canadian Business (Vol. 82, April 27, 2009, No. 7, pp. 28)
Pub: Rogers Media Inc.
Contact: Tony Viner, President
Ed: Sarka Halas. **Description:** Survey of 100 Canadian executives found that senior managers can be out of a job for about nine months before their careers are adversely affected. The nine month mark can be avoided if job seekers build networks even before they lose their jobs. Job seekers should also take volunteer work and training opportunities to increase their changes of landing a job.

45141 ■ *"Joe Wikert, General Manager, O'Reilly Technology Exchange"* in Information Today (Vol. 26, February 2009, No. 2, pp. 21)
Ed: Jamie Babbitt. **Description:** Joe Wikert, general manager of O'Reilly Technology Exchange discusses his plans to develop a free content model that will evolve with future needs. O'Reilly's major competitor is Google. Wikert plans to expand the firm's publishing program to include print, online, and in-person products and services.

45142 ■ *John F. Kennedy on Leadership: The Lessons and Legacy of a President*
Pub: AMACOM
Contact: Edward T. Reilly, Manager
Ed: John A. Barnes. **Released:** May 2007. **Price:** $16, paperback/softback. **Description:** The author provides concept-based chapters on the life and presidency of John F. Kennedy and his visions. Using his inaugural address, Barnes reflects on JFKs vision and his relationship with his staff. **Availability:** Print.

45143 ■ *"John Risley"* in Canadian Business (Vol. 80, February 26, 2007, No. 5, pp. 70)
Pub: Rogers Media Inc.
Contact: Tony Viner, President
Ed: Calvin Leung. **Description:** John Risley, co-founder of Clearwater Fine Foods, shares few managerial strategies that helped him to achieve success in various businesses.

45144 ■ *"Julie Holzrichter: Managing Director of Operations, CME Group Inc."* in *Crain's Chicago Business (Vol. 31, May 5, 2008, No. 18)*
Pub: Crain Communications Inc.
Contact: Todd Johnson, Publisher
Ed: Ann Saphir. **Description:** Profile of Julie Holzrichter who works as the managing director of operations for CME Group Inc. and is known as a decisive leader able to intercept and solve problems.

45145 ■ *Jump Start Your Business Brain: Ideas, Advice and Insights for Immediate Marketing and Innovation Success*
Ed: Doug Hall. **Released:** April 2005. **Price:** , $23.99.
Description: Strategies to improve sales, marketing, and business development.

45146 ■ *"Junior Executives Need Hugs Too"* in *Canadian Business (Vol. 83, October 12, 2010, No. 17, pp. 87)*
Pub: Rogers Media Inc.
Contact: Tony Viner, President
Ed: James Cowan. **Description:** Psychology professor Mark Frame believes that sensitive men fail to meet perceptions of how a chief executive officer (CEO) should act. The results of a study show that communal qualities are highly valued in first-line and middle managers, but these qualities become less important when employees move closer to senior executive roles.

45147 ■ *"Just Be Nice: Providing Good Customer Service"* in *Canadian Business (Vol. 79, October 9, 2006, No. 20, pp. 141)*
Pub: Rogers Media Inc.
Contact: Tony Viner, President
Ed: Joe Castaldo. **Description:** The customer relationship management strategies on customer retention and satisfaction adopted by WestJet are discussed.

45148 ■ *"Justice In Self-Managing Teams: the Role of Social Networks In the Emergence of Procedural Justice Climates"* in *Academy of Management Journal (Vol. 55, June 1, 2012, No. 3, pp. 685)*
Pub: Academy of Management
Contact: Ming-Jer Chen, President
Ed: Quinetta M. Roberson, Ian O. Williamson. **Description:** The effect of social network content and structure on organizational justice in self-managing teams is studied using data from 79 project teams. Findings show that team instrumental network density has positive impact on procedural justice climate strength. Low team functional background diversity was also found to strengthen this relationship.

45149 ■ *"Karen Case: President of Commercial Real Estate Lending, Privatebancorp Inc."* in *Crain's Chicago Business (May 5, 2008)*
Pub: Crain Communications Inc.
Contact: Todd Johnson, Publisher
Ed: Dee Gill. **Description:** Profile of Karen Case who was hired by PrivateBancorp Inc. to turn its minor share of the city's commercial real estate lending market into a major one.

45150 ■ *"Kari Leong"* in *Hawaii Business (Vol. 53, October 2007, No. 4, pp. 39)*
Pub: PacificBasin Communications
Ed: Cathy S. Cruz-George. **Description:** Greater Good Inc. president Kari Leong is the number 1 fittest female executive in Hawaii for 2007. Leong exercises at the gym and at her home, and carries her two children for strength training. The physical activities she had undergone during her college life at the Gonzaga University are discussed.

45151 ■ *"Keeping Railcars 'Busy At All Times' At TTX"* in *Crain's Chicago Business (Vol. 31, April 28, 2008, No. 17, pp. 6)*
Pub: Crain Communications Inc.
Contact: Todd Johnson, Publisher
Ed: Bob Tita. **Description:** Profile of the president of Chicago railcar pool operator TTX Co. and his business plan for the company which includes improving fleet management and car purchasing through better use of data on railroad demand.

45152 ■ *"Keith Crain: Business Must Stand Up And Be Counted"* in *Crain's Detroit Business (Vol. 24, October 6, 2008, No. 40, pp. 6)*
Pub: Crain Communications Inc.
Contact: Rance E. Crain, President
Description: Discusses the challenges that the new mayor of Detroit faces concerning business, the state of the economy and the exceptionally tight budget the city is running on, which includes a lot of red ink. It is very likely that the city is going to see tax revenues fall substantially in the next few months and business leaders may find it in their favor to lend their support to the new mayor as well as provide him with the executive talent necessary to overcome some of these crucial issues.

45153 ■ *"Kelvin Taketa, President, CEO Hawaii Community Foundation"* in *Hawaii Business (Vol. 53, October 2007, No. 4, pp. 30)*
Pub: PacificBasin Communications
Ed: Scott Radway. **Description:** Hawaii Community Foundation chief executive officer Kelvin Taketa believes that the leadership shortage for nonprofit sector in Hawaii is a result of leaders retiring or switching to part-time work. Taketa adds that the duties of a nonprofit organization leader are very challenging, with the organizations being usually thinly staffed. His opinion on the prospects of young leadership in Hawaii is also given.

45154 ■ *"Key Budgeting Tips: For Your Management Team"* in *Agency Sales Magazine (Vol. 39, December 2009, No. 11, pp. 49)*
Ed: Gene Siciliano. **Description:** Constructing a budget must be the result of coordinated input and effort. Practice is also important in creating a budget and accurately predicting actual results is not the objective but giving the company a direction for course correction.

45155 ■ *"Kid Rock"* in *Canadian Business (Vol. 81, Summer 2008, No. 9, pp. 54)*
Ed: John Gray. **Description:** Damien Reynolds is the founder, chairman and chief executive officer of Vancouver-based Longview Capital Partners. The investment bank, founded in 2005, is one of the fastest-growing companies in British Columbia. The recent economic downturn has battered the stocks of the company and its portfolio of junior miners.

45156 ■ *The Kindness Revolution: The Company-Wide Culture Shift That Inspires Phenomenal Customer Service*
Pub: American Management Association
Contact: Edward T. Reilly, President
Ed: Ed Horrell. **Released:** August 2006. **Price:** $23, Hardback. **Availability:** Print.

45157 ■ *"Kinetico Exec Going Global to Increase Growth Flow"* in *Crain's Cleveland Business (Vol. 28, October 1, 2007, No. 39, pp. 5)*
Pub: Crain Communications Inc.
Ed: David Bennett. **Description:** Shamus Hurley, the new CEO and president of Kinetico Inc., a manufacturer of water filtering and softening equipment for residential, commercial and municipal use, plans to expand the company to target markets overseas.

45158 ■ *Kiss Theory Good Bye: Five Proven Ways to Get Extraordinary Results in Any Company*
Pub: Gold Pen Publishing
Ed: Bob Prosen. **Released:** August 01, 2006. **Price:** $15.62, hardcover. **Description:** Author provides wisdom from his career as a high-level executive at AT&T Global Information Solutions, Sabre, and Hitachi, as well as his consulting firm. The book focuses on business execution rather than processes or theory of business management and provides step-by-step instructions allowing organizations to maximize profitability and results.

45159 ■ *Know-How: The 8 Skills That Separate People Who Perform from Those Who Don't*
Pub: Clarkson N. Potter Publishers
Contact: Jenny Frost, President
Ed: Ram Charan. **Released:** January 02, 2007. **Price:** $13.99. **Description:** Know-how is what separates leaders who perform and deliver good results from those who don't.

45160 ■ *"Know Your Bones: Take Your Bone Health Seriously"* in *Women In Business (Vol. 62, June 2010, No. 2, pp. 40)*
Pub: American Business Women's Association
Contact: Lorie Burch, President
Description: Bone health for women with postmenopausal osteoporosis is encouraged to help create an appropriate health plan that includes exercise, diet and medication. Questions to consider when discussing possible plans with health care providers are presented.

45161 ■ *"Knowledge Workers"* in *Canadian Business (Vol. 79, October 9, 2006, No. 20, pp. 59)*
Ed: Doug Cooper. **Description:** Knowledge workers as an integral part of organizations and the need for business leaders to effectively manage and recognize the talent of knowledge workers is discussed.

45162 ■ *"Kraft Taps Cheese Head; Jordan Charged With Fixing Foodmaker's Signature Product"* in *Crain's Chicago Business (April 14, 2008)*
Pub: Crain Communications Inc.
Contact: Todd Johnson, Publisher
Ed: David Sterrett. **Description:** Kraft Foods Inc. has assigned Rhonda Jordan, a company veteran, to take charge of the cheese and dairy division which has been losing market shares to cheaper store-brand cheese among cost-sensitive shoppers as Kraft and its competitors raise prices to offset soaring dairy costs.

45163 ■ *"Labor and Management: Working Together for a Stable Future"* in *Alaska Business Monthly (Vol. 27, October 2011, No. 10, pp. 130)*
Pub: Alaska Business Publishing Company Inc.
Contact: Jim Martin, President
Ed: Nicole A. Bonham Colby. **Description:** Alaska unions and employers are working to ensure a consistent flow of skilled Alaska workers as current the current workforce reaches retirement age.

45164 ■ *"Laced Up and Ready to Run"* in *Barron's (Vol. 89, July 6, 2009, No. 27, pp. 12)*
Pub: Dow Jones & Co., Inc.
Contact: Clare Hart, President
Ed: Christopher C. Williams. **Description:** Shares of Foot Locker could raise from $10 to about $15 a share with the improvement of the economy. The company has benefited from prudent management and merchandising as well as better cost cutting, allowing it to better survive in a recession.

45165 ■ *"Lafley Gives Look At His Game Plan"* in *Business Courier (Vol. 24, March 21, 2008, No. 50, pp. 1)*
Pub: American City Business Journals, Inc.
Contact: Whitney Shaw, President
Ed: Lisa Biank Fasig. **Description:** Overview of A.G. Lafley's book entitled 'The Game-Changer', is presented. Lafley, Procter & Gamble Co.'s chief executive officer, documented his philosophy and strategy in his book. His work also includes Procter & Gamble's hands-on initiatives such as mock-up grocery stores and personal interviews with homeowners.

45166 ■ *"Land on Boardwalk"* in *Canadian Business (Vol. 82, April 27, 2009, No. 7, pp. 19)*
Ed: Calvin Leung. **Description:** Boardwalk REIT remains as one of the most attractive real estate investment trusts in Canada, with 73 percent of analysts rating the firm a Buy. Analyst Neil Downey believes that good management, as well as a good

business model, makes Boardwalk a good investment. Downey is concerned however, that a worsening of Alberta's economy could significantly impact Boardwalk.

45167 ■ "LaSalle St. Firms Cherry-Pick Talent As Wall St. Tanks" in Crain's Chicago Business (Vol. 31, November 17, 2008, No. 46)
Pub: Crain Communications Inc.
Contact: Todd Johnson, Publisher
Ed: H. Lee Murphy. **Description:** Many local businesses are taking advantage of the lay offs that many major Wall Street firms are undergoing in their workforces; these companies see the opportunity to woo talent and expand their staff with quality executives.

45168 ■ "Last Founder Standing" in Conde Nast Portfolio (Vol. 2, June 2008, No. 6, pp. 124)
Ed: Kevin Maney. **Description:** Interview with Amazon CEO Jeff Bezos in which he discusses the economy, the company's new distribution center and the hiring of employees for it, e-books, and the overall vision for the future of the firm.

45169 ■ "The Last Word Dirty Work Required" in Workforce Management (Vol. 88, November 16, 2009, No. 12, pp. 34)
Pub: Crain Communications Inc.
Contact: Rance E. Crain, President
Ed: John Hollon. **Description:** Due to salary freezes, pay cuts, layoffs, buyouts and a number of other stress factors brought about by the recession, employee engagement has been difficult to maintain by managers.

45170 ■ "Lathrop Finds Partner In LA" in The Business Journal-Serving Metropolitan Kansas City (Vol. 27, November 21, 2008, No. 11, pp. 1)
Pub: American City Business Journals, Inc.
Contact: Whitney Shaw, President
Ed: Steve Vockrodt. **Description:** Kansas, Missouri-based Lathrop and Gage LLP is planning to merge with Spillane Shaeffer Aronoff Bandlow LLP. The merging of the business law firms will add entertainment clients to Lathrop's fold. Comments from executives are also presented.

45171 ■ "Laurent Beaudoin Interview: Deja Vu" in Canadian Business (Vol. 81, July 22, 2008, No. 12-13, pp. 38)
Pub: Rogers Media Inc.
Contact: Tony Viner, President
Ed: Joe Castaldo. **Description:** Laurent Beaudoin has retired as chief executive officer for Bombardier Inc.'s, a manufacturer of regional and business aircraft, but kept a role in the firm as a non-executive chairman. Beaudoin first resigned from the company in 1999, but had to return in 2004 to address challenging situations faced by the company. Beaudoin's views on management and the company are presented.

45172 ■ "Lead Like It Matters...Because It Does: Practical Leadership Tools to Inspire and Engage Your People and Create Great Results"
Pub: McGraw-Hill
Released: September 19, 2014. **Price:** , $25.00. **Description:** The Ripple Effect method for increasing employee engagement, reducing turnover, and driving overall business success will help any manager or entrepreneur to lead his company. Important practices like eliminating wasted meetings, addressing conflict, and aligning decisions with business needs are addressed.

45173 ■ The Leader of the Future 2: Visions, Strategies, and Practices for the New Era
Pub: Jossey-Bass
Released: August 2006. **Price:** $27.95, hardcover; $18.99. **Description:** Wisdom is lent to any small business owner or leader of a nonprofit organization. **Availability:** PrintE-book.

45174 ■ "Leaders in Denial" in Harvard Business Review (Vol. 86, July-August 2008, No. 8, pp. 18)
Pub: Harvard Business Review Press
Contact: Peter E. Walsh, Director
Ed: Richard S. Tedlow. **Description:** Identifying denial in the corporate arena is discussed, along with its impact on business and how to prevent it from occurring.

45175 ■ "The Leaders Who Make M&A Work" in Harvard Business Review (Vol. 92, September 2014, No. 9, pp. 28)
Pub: Harvard Business Publishing
Released: September 2014. **Description:** Leadership capabilities for both acquiring and targeting firms are predictors of merger and acquisition success. Capabilities for acquirers include motivation, influence, adaptability, and integrity; those for targets include providing direction.

45176 ■ Leadership 101: What Every Leader Needs to Know
Pub: Nelson Business
Ed: John C. Maxwell. **Released:** September 10, 2002. **Price:** $9.99, hardcover. **Description:** Ways to enhance leadership skills focusing on following a vision and bringing others along. **Availability:** Print.

45177 ■ "Leadership Behavior and Employee Voice: Is the Door Really Open?" in Academy of Management Journal (Vol. 50, No. 4, August 1, 2007, pp. 869)
Pub: Academy of Management
Contact: Ming-Jer Chen, President
Ed: James R. Detert, Ethan R. Burris. **Description:** Relationships between two types of change-oriented leadership and subordinate improvement-oriented voice in a two-phase study are presented.

45178 ■ The Leadership Challenge: How to Make Extraordinary Things Happen in Organizations
Pub: Jossey-Bass Publishers
Contact: Matthew Hoover, Manager
E-mail: fwelsch@jbp.com
Ed: James M. Kouzes, Barry Z. Posner. **Released:** Fifth Edition. **Price:** $29.95, hardcover; $16.99. **Description:** According to research by the authors, people can make extraordinary things happen by liberating the leader within everyone around them. This handbook gives practical tips to aspire leaders in retail, manufacturing, government, community, church and school settings. **Availability:** PrintE-book.

45179 ■ "Leadership Counts" in Hispanic Business (January-February 2008, pp. 60, 62)
Pub: Hispanic Business Inc.
Contact: Jesus Chavarria, President
Ed: Frank Nelson. **Description:** Small business leaders discuss the importance of including diversity initiatives into any plan.

45180 ■ "Leadership Development In the Age of the Algorithm" in (Vol. 90, June 2012, No. 6, pp. 86)
Pub: Harvard Business Review Press
Contact: Peter E. Walsh, Director
Ed: Marcus Buckingham. **Released:** June 2012. **Description:** Guidelines to tailor leadership training to specific individuals include assessing the leadership type for each person, identifying the top leaders for each type, creating practices that are effective for each type, delivering those practices to others, and integrate user feedback to fine-tune the process.

45181 ■ "The Leadership Equation: 10 Practices That Build Trust, Spark Innovation, and Create High-Performing Organizations"
Pub: Greenleaf Book Group Press
Released: September 30, 2014. **Price:** , $18.95 paperback. **Description:** Entrepreneur and business consultant draws upon his work with corporations, government agencies, and nonprofit organizations and their human resource departments to explain the workings of high-performing organizations with his equation: Trust + Spark = Leadership Culture. He

describes the ten more important practices for building trust and spark that improves team performance, the business unit, and the entire organization.

45182 ■ Leadership in the Era of Economic Uncertainty: Managing in a Downturn
Ed: Ram Charan. **Released:** December 2008. **Price:** $22.95. **Description:** Management consultant gives advice on how to weather the economic storm, focusing on cash flow and foregoing expansion.

45183 ■ "Leadership in Flight" in Women In Business (Vol. 63, Fall 2011, No. 3, pp. 24)
Pub: American Business Women's Association
Contact: Lorie Burch, President
Ed: Leigh Elmore. **Description:** Flight attendants in major airlines are trained to keep passengers comfortable and to calmly deal with emergencies. They also have a significant role in brand image and customer loyalty as they interact with the customers directly. Examples of teamwork leadership for flight attendants are given.

45184 ■ "Leadership: Growing Pains" in Canadian Business (Vol. 80, November 19, 2007, No. 23, pp. 41)
Pub: Rogers Media Inc.
Contact: Tony Viner, President
Ed: Lauren McKeon. **Description:** Employee promotions must be done with consideration to the effects of ill-prepared leadership, which include high worker turnover, low morale, and ineffective management. Organizations must handle the transition period involved in promotion by setting clear expectations, providing guidelines on approaching different situations, and by welcoming the promoted employees; impacts are further analyzed.

45185 ■ "Leadership Is a Conversation: How To Improve Employee Engagement and Alignment In Today's Flatter, More Networked Organizations" in (Vol. 90, June 2012, No. 6, pp. 76)
Pub: Harvard Business Review Press
Contact: Peter E. Walsh, Director
Ed: Boris Groysberg, Michael Slind. **Released:** June 2012. **Description:** A two-way flow of communication is essential in promoting and maintaining employee motivation. Key points are establishing intimacy through gaining trust, interactivity via dialogue, inclusion by expanding employee roles, and intentionality through establishing an agenda.

45186 ■ "Leadership Is...: (Dot, Dot, Dot)"
Pub: CreateSpace
Contact: Daren Giles, President
Released: October 9, 2014. **Price:** , $19.95 paperback. **Description:** A leader makes others aware of the possibilities that exist and inspiring them to achieve them. The book shows through stories and personal experiences the true traits of a good leader. Managers and entrepreneurs, alike, will benefit from the information offered.

45187 ■ "Leadership: Just Shut The Hell Up" in Canadian Business (Vol. 81, July 22, 2008, No. 12-13, pp. 33)
Pub: Rogers Media Inc.
Contact: Tony Viner, President
Ed: Jane Bao. **Description:** Employees desire better communication as opposed to more communication from their managers. Advice regarding managing communication in the workplace is given including ways in which speakers can say more with fewer words.

45188 ■ The Leadership Secrets of Colin Powell
Pub: McGraw Hill Financial Inc.
Contact: Douglas L. Peterson, President
Ed: Oren Harari. **Released:** August 2003. **Price:** £11. 99, paperback. **Description:** Profile of Colin Powell, stressing his abilities as a world leader. **Availability:** Print.

45189 ■ "Leadership Training" in Black Enterprise (Vol. 37, January 2007, No. 6, pp. 56)
Pub: Earl G. Graves Publishing Co. Inc.
Contact: Earl G. Graves, Jr., President
Ed: Marcia A. Reed-Woodard. **Description:** Profile of Theopolis Holman, Group Vice-President of Duke

Energy, who discusses how he prepared for the merger between Duke Energy and Cinergy. Holman oversees a division of 9,000 service contractors and employees.

45190 ■ *Leading with Character: Stories of Valor and Virtue and the Principles They Teach*
Pub: Information Age Publishing Inc.
Contact: Justin Loeber, Director
E-mail: justin@carvertech.ne
Ed: John J. Sosik. Released: 2006. Price: $39.99, paperback; $73.99, hardcover. Description: Examination of the kind of character that leaders develop in themselves and others in order to create and sustain extraordinary organizational growth and performance.

45191 ■ *Leading the Charge: Leadership Lessons from the Battlefield to the Boardroom*
Pub: Palgrave Macmillan
Contact: Lisa Dunn, Manager
E-mail: l.dunn@palgrave.com
Ed: Tony Zinni, Tony Koltz. Released: October 2010. Price: £13.99, paperback. Description: General Anthony Zinni recalls a lifetime of competition on the battlefield and in corporate boardrooms and is leading the call to action to restore American leadership and greatness. Availability: Print.

45192 ■ *Leading at a Higher Level*
Pub: FT Press
Contact: Timothy C. Moore, Vice President
Ed: Ken Blanchard. Released: September 08, 2009. Price: $22.39, Members; $27.99, Nonmembers. Description: Tips, advice and techniques from a management consultant to help entrepreneurs create a vision for their company; includes information on manager-employee relationships. Availability: Print.

45193 ■ *"Leading the Way" in Business Strategy Review (Vol. 23, Spring 2012, No. 1, pp. 10)*
Released: Spring 2012. Description: The ability to persevere in the face of what may seem impossible odds is the story of Ursula Burns, who began her career as an engineering intern at Xerox and rose to become CEO of the company in 2009. Burns talked with Pearl Doherty about her career at Xerox.

45194 ■ *"Leading With Meaning: Beneficiary Contact, Prosocial Impact, and the Performance Effects of Transformational Leadership" in Academy of Management Journal (Vol. 55, April 1, 2012, No. 2, pp. 458)*
Pub: Academy of Management
Contact: Ming-Jer Chen, President
Ed: Adam M. Grant. Description: Transformational leadership is shown to effectively motivate followers when they interact with the beneficiaries of their work. For instance, beneficiary contact boosted the effects on call center employees' sales and revenue with these findings being extended by a survey study with government employees. How perceived prosocial impact supports a moderated mediation model is discussed.

45195 ■ *Lean Six Sigma That Works: A Powerful Action Plan for Dramatically Improving Quality, Increasing Speed, and Reducing Waste*
Pub: American Management Association
Contact: Edward T. Reilly, President
Ed: Bill Carreira, Bill Trudell. Price: $21.95, paperback. Availability: Print.

45196 ■ *"Leave Your Ego at the Door" in South Florida Business Journal (Vol. 34, June 20, 2014, No. 43, pp. 13)*
Pub: American City Business Journals
Released: June 20, 2014. Description: Doria Camaraza, senior vice president and general manager of American Express Service Centers in Fort Lauderdale, Mexico and Argentina, share advice for successfully running service centers for the credit card company. She describes ways in which she inspires creativity and drive, while promoting employee team building with her workers.

45197 ■ *"Legg's Compensation Committee Chair Defends CEO Fetting's Pay" in Boston Business Journal (Vol. 29, July 22, 2011, No. 11, pp. 1)*
Pub: American City Business Journals, Inc.
Ed: Gary Haber. Description: Legg Mason Inc. CEO Mark R. Fetting has been awarded $5.9 million pay package and he expects to receive questions regarding it in the coming shareholders meeting. However, Baltimore, Maryland-based RKTL Associates chairman emeritus Harold R. Adams believes Fetting has done a tremendous job in bringing Legg's through a tough market.

45198 ■ *"Lehman's Hail Mary Pass" in Business Week (September 22, 2008, No. 4100, pp. 28)*
Ed: Matthew Goldstein; David Henry; Ben Levison. Description: Overview of Lehman Brothers' CEO Richard Fuld's plan to keep the firm afloat and end the stock's plunge downward; Fuld's strategy calls for selling off a piece of the firm's investment management business.

45199 ■ *"Lessons I Learned in the Army: A General's Pep Talk Taught Me That a Leader Can't Lose Sight of What It Means To Be a Grunt" in Inc. (March 2008, pp. 85-86)*
Pub: Mansueto Ventures L.L.C.
Contact: John Koten, Chief Executive Officer
Ed: Joel Spolsky. Description: An Israeli general offers leadership advice to entrepreneurs.

45200 ■ *"Lessons Learned from Instructional Design Theory: An Application in Management Education" in Business Communication Quarterly (December 2007, pp. 414)*
Pub: Pine Forge Press
Contact: Blaise R. Simqu, President
Ed: Lisa A. Burke. Description: Instructors should present course information to business students in a way that enhances understanding and should use presentation techniques that students may eventually use; course materials should be kept relevant and simple.

45201 ■ *"Lessons from Turnaround Leaders" in Strategy and Leadership (Vol. 39, May-June 2011, No. 3, pp. 36-43)*
Pub: Emerald Group Publishing Inc.
Ed: David P. Boyd. Description: A study analyzes the cases of some successful turnaround leaders to present a strategic model to help firms tackle challenges such as employee inertia, competition and slow organizational renewal. It describes a change model consisting of five major steps to be followed by firms with environmental uncertainty for the purpose.

45202 ■ *"Let the Insults Fly: Want to Learn What Your Employees Really Think?" in Inc. (Vol. 33, October 2011, No. 8, pp. 36)*
Pub: Inc. Magazine
Ed: Jason Fried. Description: A company that hosts a Comedy Central-style celebrity roast of its top-selling product was able to improve their business.

45203 ■ *Liespotting: Proven Techniques to Detect Deception*
Pub: St. Martins Press/Macmillan
Ed: Pamela Meyer. Released: September 2011. Price: $14.99, paperback. Description: Liespotting links three disciplines: facial recognition training, interrogation training, and a comprehensive survey of research in the field - into a specialized body of information developed specifically to help business leaders detect deception and get the information they need to successfully conduct their most important interactions and transactions. Availability: Print.

45204 ■ *"The Life of a Builder" in Birmingham Business Journal (Vol. 31, July 4, 2014, No. 27, pp. 14)*
Pub: American City Business Journals, Inc.
Contact: Whitney Shaw, President
Released: July 4, 2014. Description: Rob Burton, CEO of Hoar Construction, one of Birmingham's largest contractors talks about his company and his

management style. According to Burton, keeping a long-term perspective helps him make better decisions and has helped him in his job. He mentions that his management style is collaborative, and his belief in his faith is the one thing that helped him overcome a serious illness and mad him realize how much he loves his job.

45205 ■ *"Lifebank Grants Stock Options" in Marketwired (May 16, 2007)*
Pub: Comtex News Network Inc.
Description: Lifebank, a biomedical service company that provides processing cryogenic storage of umbilical cord blood stem cells, announced that, under its stock option plan, it has granted incentive stock options to directors, officers, and consultants of the company.

45206 ■ *"Life's Work: Ben Bradlee" in Harvard Business Review (Vol. 88, September 2010, No. 9, pp. 128)*
Pub: Harvard Business School Publishing
Ed: Alison Beard. Price: $8.95. Description: Newspaper publisher Ben Bradlee discusses factors that lead to success, including visible supervisors, enthusiasm, appropriate expansion, and the importance in truth in reporting. Availability: PDF.

45207 ■ *"Life's Work: Oliver Sacks" in Harvard Business Review (Vol. 88, November 2010, No. 11, pp. 152)*
Pub: Harvard Business School Publishing
Ed: Lisa Burrell. Description: Neurologist and author Oliver Sacks discusses whether different types of minds tend toward certain skills, physician-patient communication, and his own perspectives from being a patient himself.

45208 ■ *"Lifetime Networks" in Brandweek (Vol. 49, April 21, 2008, No. 16, pp. SR10)*
Pub: Nielsen Business Media Inc.
Contact: Howard Appelbaum, President
Ed: Anthony Crupi. Description: Provides contact information for sales and marketing personnel for the ABC network as well as a listing of the station's top programming and an analysis of the current season and the target audience for those programs running in the current season. Lifetime will still produce its original signature movies but will now focus its emphasis more clearly on series development in order to appeal to a younger, hipper female demographic.

45209 ■ *"Like Mom, Like Son" in Washington Business Journal (Vol. 33, May 9, 2014, No. 3, pp. 6)*
Pub: American City Business Journals
Released: May 9, 2014. Description: Chef Victor Albisu convinced his mother, Rosa Susinski, to open the Taco Bamba restaurant in Falls Church, Virginia even though they are not Mexican. The taqueria is near Plaza Latina, Rose's market, so the mother and son will alternate management of the restaurant. Their goal is to open another location.

45210 ■ *Linchpin: Are you Indispensable?*
Pub: Portfolio
Ed: Seth Godin. Released: April 26, 2011. Price: $18.50, paperback; $32.50, hardcover. Description: The best way to get what you're worth, according to the author, is to exert emotional labor, to be seen as indispensable, and to produce interactions that organizations and people care about. Availability: Print.

45211 ■ *Lincoln on Leadership: Executive Strategies for Tough Times*
Pub: Grand Central Publishing
Contact: Maureen Mahon Egen, President
Ed: Donald T. Phillips. Released: 1993. Price: $16, paperback, C$18, paperback. Description: Using President Abraham Lincoln's example of leadership, the author sets out to help business leaders adopt winning strategies.

45212 ■ *"Lines of Communication" in Entrepreneur (Vol. 37, October 2009, No. 10, pp. 80)*
Pub: Entrepreneur Press
Contact: Perlman Neil, President
Ed: Brad Feld. Description: Entrepreneurial companies should establish a clear and open communica-

tion culture between their management teams and their venture capital backers. Chief executive officers should trust their leadership teams when it comes to communicating with venture capitalists.

45213 ■ "Live & Learn: Brett Wilson" in Canadian Business (Vol. 81, July 22, 2008, No. 12-13, pp. 80)
Pub: Rogers Media Inc.
Contact: Tony Viner, President
Ed: Michelle Magnan. **Description:** Interview with Brett Wilson who believes he became a 'capitalist with a heart' because he had a father who sold cars and a mother who was a social worker. He feels that being accelerated a grade was one of the biggest opportunities and challenges in his life. Brett Wilson's other views on business and on his family are presented.

45214 ■ "Clay Riddell" in Canadian Business (Vol. 80, February 12, 2007, No. 4, pp. 86)
Pub: Rogers Media Inc.
Contact: Tony Viner, President
Ed: Michelle Magnan. **Description:** Chief executive officer of Paramount Resources Clay Riddell shares his passion for oil and gas business.

45215 ■ "Live & Learn: Dick Evans" in Canadian Business (Vol. 82, April 27, 2009, No. 7, pp. 78)
Pub: Rogers Media Inc.
Contact: Tony Viner, President
Ed: Sean Silcoff. **Description:** Former Rio Tinto Alcan chief executive officer Dick Evans believes that the 1982 downturn was worse than the current recession, at least for the mining sector. He also believes that while people are anxious, there is confidence that the economy will recover in two to three years. Key information on Evans, as well as his other views on being a CEO is presented.

45216 ■ "Live & Learn: Ian Delaney" in Canadian Business (Vol. 81, Summer 2008, No. 9, pp. 168)
Pub: Rogers Media Inc.
Contact: Tony Viner, President
Ed: Joe Castaldo. **Description:** Interview with Ian Delaney who is the executive chairman of chemical company Sherritt International Corp.; Delaney previously worked as chief executive for a holding company owned by Peter Munk. Details of his beliefs, profession and family life are discussed.

45217 ■ "Live & Learn: Madeleine Paquin" in Canadian Business (Vol. 81, February 12, 2008, No. 3, pp. 92)
Pub: Rogers Media Inc.
Contact: Tony Viner, President
Ed: Regan Ray. **Description:** Madeleine Paquin, chief executive officer and president of Logistec Corp., talks about how she balanced her career and her life as a mother to two girls. Paquin thinks that working mothers need to focus on some things instead of trying to do everything. Her career in the marine cargo handling industry is also discussed.

45218 ■ "Live and Learn: Penny Chapman" in Canadian Business (Vol. 79, July 17, 2006, No. 14-15, pp. 75)
Pub: Rogers Media Inc.
Contact: Tony Viner, President
Ed: Erin Pooley. **Description:** Interview with Penny Chapman, president of Chapman's Ice Cream, who speaks about her journey from rags to riches.

45219 ■ "Live & Learn: Savvas Chamberlain" in Canadian Business (Vol. 81, February 26, 2008, No. 4, pp. 92)
Pub: Rogers Media Inc.
Contact: Tony Viner, President
Ed: Andrew Wahl. **Description:** Savvas Chamberlain says he feels cheated during his teenage years because life was not normal for him growing up in Cyprus with all the uprisings against Britain. Chamberlain says he runs Dalsa like he plays chess because all his positions are shown all the time but he keeps his strategy to himself.

45220 ■ "Live & Learn: Thomas D'Aquino" in Canadian Business (Vol. 80, November 19, 2007, No. 23, pp. 92)
Pub: Rogers Media Inc.
Contact: Tony Viner, President
Ed: Calvin Leung. **Description:** Thomas D'Aquino is the CEO and president of the Canadian Council of Chief Executives since 1981. D'Aquino thinks he has the best job in Canada because he can change the way policies are made and the way people think. Details of his career as a lawyer and CEO and his views on Canada's economy are provided.

45221 ■ "Livent Trial: Whistleblower or Manipulator?" in Canadian Business (Vol. 81, August 18, 2008, No. 12-13, pp. 11)
Pub: Rogers Media Inc.
Contact: Tony Viner, President
Ed: John Gray. **Description:** Discusses Maria Messina who is portrayed by prosecutors of the Livent Inc. trial as a whistleblower, while defense lawyers insist that she is a manipulator. Defense lawyers allege that Messina, who was Livent's chief financial officer, is a character assassin that made money out of Livent's bankruptcy. Other views on Messina, as well as information on the case, are presented.

45222 ■ Local Enterprises in the Global Economy: Issues of Governance and Upgrading
Pub: Edward Elgar Publishing Inc.
Contact: Richard Henning, Vice President
E-mail: kwight@e-elgar.com
Released: November 2004. **Price:** $54.40, paperback; $146.70, hardback. **Description:** Examination of the relationships between globalization, corporate governance, and the economic performance of small businesses and local enterprises.

45223 ■ The Logic of Life: The Rational Economics of an Irrational World
Pub: Ballantine/ Del Rey/Fawcett/Ivy Books
Contact: Gilbert Perlman, President
Ed: Tim Harford. **Released:** February 10, 2009. **Price:** $15, paperback; $11.99. **Description:** Harford excels at making economists' studies palatable for discerning but non-expert readers. The uses hard data to show why promiscuous teens are actually health-conscious, divorce hasn't gotten a fair shake, corporate bosses will always be overpaid and job prospects for minorities continue to be grim. **Availability:** PrintE-book.

45224 ■ "Looking For Financing? The Five Things You Should Know First" in Hispanic Business (Vol. 30, July-August 2008, No. 7-8, pp. 16)
Pub: Hispanic Business Inc.
Contact: Jesus Chavarria, President
Ed: Frank Nelson. **Description:** Investment firms want to know about businesses that need funding for either expansion or acquisition; companies fitting this profile are interviewed and their perceptions are discussed. Investment firms need businesses to be realistic in their expectations and business plans which show spending of funds and expected benefits, long term goals, track record and strong management teams.

45225 ■ "The Lords of Ideas" in Business Strategy Review (Vol. 21, Autumn 2010, No. 3, pp. 57)
Pub: Blackwell Publishers Ltd.
Ed: Stuart Crainer. **Description:** True originators of modern strategy are profiled.

45226 ■ "Loseley Dairy Ice Cream" in Ice Cream Reporter (Vol. 23, November 20, 2010, No. 12, pp. 8)
Pub: Ice Cream Reporter
Description: Neil Burchell has been named managing director of Loseley Dairy Ice Cream, one of the UK's largest independent producers. Burchell, with over 30 years experience in the food industry, was recently managing director of Rachel's, the leading organic dairy foods company in the UK, where he is credited with driving a sixfold increase in sales.

45227 ■ "Lots More Mr. Nice Guy" in Canadian Business (Vol. 80, October 22, 2007, No. 21, pp. 58)
Ed: Zena Olijnyk. **Description:** Galen Weston Jr., executive chairman of Loblaw and heir to the Weston family business, has his hands full running the company. Details of his turnaround strategies and ambitious plans to increase profitability of the business are discussed.

45228 ■ "Lots of Qualified Women, But Few Sit on Boards" in Globe & Mail (March 2, 2006, pp. B1)
Ed: Virginia Galt. **Description:** The findings of Catalyst Canada survey on the rise in women executives on boards of directors are presented.

45229 ■ "Macho Men" in Canadian Business (Vol. 81, November 10, 2008, No. 19, pp. 23)
Ed: Sharda Prashad. **Description:** Professors Robin Ely and Debra Meyerson found that oil rigs decreased accidents and increased productivity when they focused on improving safety and admitting errors rather than on a worker's individual strength. Professor Jennifer Berdahl shows there is pressure for men to be seen as masculine at work, which makes them avoid doing 'feminine' things such as parental leaves.

45230 ■ Made to Stick: Why Some Ideas Survive and Others Die
Pub: Doubleday Publishing Group
Contact: Stephen Rubin, President
E-mail: mpalgon@randomhouse.com
Ed: Chip Heath, Dan Heath. **Released:** January 02, 2007. **Price:** $26, hardcover; $13.99. **Description:** Entertaining, practical guide to effective business communication; information is derived form psychosocial studies on memory, emotion and motivation. **Availability:** PrintE-book.

45231 ■ "Magna Wants to Help Chrysler, but a Takeover's Not on the Cards" in Globe & Mail (March 1, 2007, pp. B1)
Ed: Greg Keenan. **Description:** The plans of Magna International Inc. to help Chrysler Corp. to overcome its financial problems are discussed. The appointment of Michael Neuman as the chief executive officer of Magna International Inc. is described.

45232 ■ "The Mailman" in Canadian Business (Vol. 80, April 9, 2007, No. 8, pp. 14)
Pub: Rogers Media Inc.
Contact: Tony Viner, President
Ed: Zena Olijnyk. **Description:** Chief executive officer of Pitney Bowes Inc. Murray Martin's entrepreneurial skills in managing the company and his personal career are discussed.

45233 ■ "The Main Ingredient of Change" in Harvard Business Review (Vol. 92, September 2014, No. 9, pp. 36)
Pub: Harvard Business Publishing
Released: September 2014. **Description:** Courage and leadership were key factors in driving organizational change at Campbell Soup Company. Leadership improved decision making processes, while courage gave the 145-year-old firm the impetus to expand the business and enter new markets.

45234 ■ "Make It Easy" in Entrepreneur (Vol. 36, May 2008, No. 5, pp. 49)
Pub: Entrepreneur Press
Contact: Perlman Neil, President
Ed: Mike Hogan. **Description:** Zoho has a Planner that keep contacts, notes and reminders and a DB & Reports feature for reports, data analysis and pricing comparisons. WebEx WebOffice Workgroup supports document management and templates for contacts lists, time sheets and sales tracking. Other online data manages are presented.

45235 ■ Making Difficult Decisions: How to Be Decisive and Get the Business Done
Pub: John Wiley & Sons Inc.
Contact: Stephen M. Smith, President
Ed: Peter Shaw. **Released:** June 2008. **Price:** $29. 95, paperback. **Description:** Experience of others can help entrepreneurs and managers make difficult

business decisions. The strategies set forth in this book have been used successfully in public, private and voluntary sectors. **Availability:** Print.

45236 ■ *"Making Diverse Teams Click" in Harvard Business Review (Vol. 86, July-August 2008, No. 8, pp. 20)*
Pub: Harvard Business Review Press
Contact: Peter E. Walsh, Director
Ed: Jeffrey T. Polzer. **Description:** 360-degree feedback to increase the efficacy of diverse-member workplace teams, which involves each member providing feedback to the others on the team is discussed.

45237 ■ *"Making the Tough Call: Great Leaders Recognize When Their Values Are On the Line" in Inc. (November 2007, pp. 36, 38)*
Pub: Mansueto Ventures L.L.C.
Contact: John Koten, Chief Executive Officer
Ed: Noel M. Tichy, Warren G. Bennis. **Description:** Good judgment by company leaders is a process involving preparation, making the call, and executing the process. Character provides a moral compass for these decision makers.

45238 ■ *Management Lessons from Mayo Clinic*
Pub: McGraw-Hill
Ed: Leonard L. Berry, Kent D. Seltman. **Released:** June 06, 2008. **Price:** $27.95. **Description:** Management practices employed by the Mayo Clinic are examined to show why it is one of the world's most successful health care facilities.

45239 ■ *"Management Matters with Mike Myatt: Are You Creating Growth in a Down Economy?" in Commercial Property News (March 17, 2008)*
Ed: Mike Myatt. **Description:** Senior executives are expected to create growth for their company regardless of recession, economic slowdown, inflation, or tight credit and capital markets.

45240 ■ *The Management Myth: Why the Experts Keep Getting It Wrong*
Pub: W.W. Norton and Company Inc.
Contact: A Malmud, President
Ed: Matthew Stewart. **Released:** August 2009. **Price:** $27.95, hardcover. **Description:** An insider's perspective on the management consulting industry, which reveals the high fees and incompetent consultants. **Availability:** Print.

45241 ■ *Management Rewired: Why Feedback Doesn't Work and Other Surprising Lessons from the Latest Brain Science*
Pub: Portfolio
Ed: Charles S. Jacobs. **Released:** 2009. **Price:** $12.99; $16, Paperback. **Description:** According to the author, human psychology works better than feedback, praise or criticism when managing employees. **Availability:** Electronic publishing.

45242 ■ *The Management of Small and Medium Enterprises*
Pub: Routledge
Contact: Kevin Bradley, President
E-mail: kbradley@taylorandfrancis.com
Released: March 16, 2011. **Price:** $54.95, paperback. **Description:** Investigation into the underlying mechanisms and practices of management within small and medium enterprises is provided. **Availability:** Print.

45243 ■ *"Managerial Rudeness: Bad Attitudes Can Demoralize Your Staff" in Black Enterprise (Vol. 37, January 2007, No. 6, pp. 58)*
Pub: Earl G. Graves Publishing Co. Inc.
Contact: Earl G. Graves, Jr., President
Ed: Chauntelle Folds. **Description:** Positive leadership in the managerial realm leads to a more productive workplace. Managers who are negative, hostile, arrogant, rude or fail to accept any responsibility for their own mistakes find that employees will not give their all on the job.

45244 ■ *"Managerial Ties with Local Firms and Governments: an Analysis of Japanese Firms In China" in International Journal of Business and Emerging Markets (Vol. 4, July 11, 2012, No. 3, pp. 181)*
Released: July 11, 2012. **Description:** This study explores how managerial ties between foreign firms and local firms and those between foreign firms and local government officials affect the performance of firms operating in transition economies. Using survey data collected from Japanese firms operating in China, this study finds that managerial ties between foreign firms and local firms and local government officials are positively associated with the performance of Japanese firms in China.

45245 ■ *The Manager's Guide to Rewards: What You Need to Know to Get the Best of-and-from-Your Employees*
Ed: Doug Jensen; Tom McMullen; Mel Stark. **Released:** 2006. **Price:** , $24.95.

45246 ■ *"Managers and Their Not-So Rational Decisions" in Business Horizons (Vol. 51, March-April 2008, No. 2, pp. 113)*
Pub: Elsevier Advanced Technology Publications
Ed: S. Trevis Certo, Brian L. Connelly, Laszlo Tihanyi. **Description:** Two cognitive systems influencing the decision making of managers are described. One is a fast, effortless, and intuitive process, while the other is slow, controlled, and rule-governed and the two systems interact with each other.

45247 ■ *"Managers as Visionaries: a Skill That Can Be Learned" in Strategy and Leadership (Vol. 39, September-October 2011, No. 5, pp. 56-58)*
Pub: Emerald Group Publishing Inc.
Ed: Stephen M. Millett. **Description:** A study uses research findings to examine whether visionary management can be learned. Results conclude that managers can learn visionary management through intuitive pattern recognition of trends and by using scenarios for anticipating and planning for likely future occurrences.

45248 ■ *Managing Business Growth: Get a Grip on the Numbers That Count*
Pub: Self-Counsel Press Inc.
Ed: Angie Mohr. **Released:** 2003. **Description:** Fourth book in the Numbers 101 for Small Business Series, teaches how small company owners can expand their businesses using sound financial planning.

45249 ■ *Managing Economies, Trade and International Business*
Pub: Palgrave Macmillan
Contact: Lisa Dunn, Manager
E-mail: l.dunn@palgrave.com
Released: January 19, 2010. **Price:** £77. **Description:** An in-depth look at the areas that affect and influence international business, exploring specific issues businesses face in terms of economic development, trade law, and international marketing and management. **Availability:** Print.

45250 ■ *"Managing the Facebookers; Business" in The Economist (Vol. 390, January 3, 2009, No. 8612, pp. 10)*
Pub: Economist Newspaper Ltd.
Description: According to a report from PricewaterhouseCoopers, a business consultancy, workers from Generation Y, also known as the Net Generation, are more difficult to recruit and integrate into companies that practice traditional business acumen. 61 percent of chief executive managers say that they have trouble with younger employees who tend to be more narcissistic and more interested in personal fulfillment with a need for frequent feedback and an over-precise set of objectives on the path to promotion which can be hard for managers who are used to a different relationship with their subordinates. Older bosses should prepare to make some concessions to their younger talent since some of the issues that make them happy include cheaper online ways to communicate and additional coaching, both of which are good for business.

45251 ■ *Managing Labour in Small Firms*
Pub: Routledge
Contact: Kevin Bradley, President
E-mail: kbradley@taylorandfrancis.com
Released: November 25, 2004. **Price:** $180, hardback. **Description:** Essays addressing conditions of workers in small business. **Availability:** Print.

45252 ■ *Managing the Older Worker: How to Prepare for the New Organizational Order*
Pub: Harvard Business Press
Ed: Peter Cappelli, Bill Novelli. **Released:** August 17, 2010. **Price:** $29.95, hardcover. **Description:** Your organization needs older workers more than ever: They transfer knowledge between generations, transmit your company's values to new hires, make excellent mentors for younger employees, and provide a 'just in time' workforce for special projects. **Availability:** Print.

45253 ■ *Managing for Results*
Pub: HarperCollins Publishers Inc.
Contact: Jane Friedman, President
E-mail: jfriedman@harpercollins.com
Ed: Peter F. Drucker. **Released:** October 03, 2006. **Price:** $16.99, paperback. **Description:** Entrepreneurs running successful small companies focus on opportunity rather than problems. **Availability:** Print.

45254 ■ *"Managing Risks: A New Framework: Smart Companies Match Their Approach to the Nature of the Threats They Face" in (Vol. 90, June 2012, No. 6, pp. 48)*
Pub: Harvard Business Review Press
Contact: Peter E. Walsh, Director
Ed: Robert S. Kaplan, Anette Mikes. **Released:** June 2012. **Description:** The importance of strategic planning in effect risk management practices is stressed. Discussion includes preventable risks, strategy risks, and external risks and provides objectives, control models, staff functions, and the business-unit interrelationships of each.

45255 ■ *Managing a Small Business Made Easy*
Pub: Entrepreneur Press
Contact: Perlman Neil, President
Ed: Martin E. Davis. **Released:** September 2005. **Description:** Examination of the essential elements for an entrepreneur running a business, including advice on leadership, customer service, financials, and more.

45256 ■ *Managing for Success: The Latest in Management Thought and Practice from Canada's Premier Business School*
Ed: Monica Fleck. **Released:** December 2000. **Description:** Canadian business school offers insight into the latest management skills of the nation's business leaders.

45257 ■ *"Managing in Times of Uncertainty; What Leaders Can Learn From the Tumultuous Past Decade" in Gallup Management Journal (June 1, 2011)*
Pub: Gallup Inc.
Contact: Jim Clifton, Chief Executive Officer
Description: Executives and managers have been facing a global financial meltdown for the past 10 years along with ongoing wars, an increase in terrorism, and epic natural disasters. The leadership lessons learned over this time are examined.

45258 ■ *"Managing Your Innovation Portfolio: People Throughout Your Organization Are Energetically Pursuing the New. But Does All That Add Up To a Strategy?" in Harvard Business Review (Vol. 90, May 2012, No. 5, pp. 66)*
Pub: Harvard Business Review Press
Contact: Peter E. Walsh, Director
Ed: Bansi Nagji, Geoff Tuff. **Released:** May 2012. **Description:** Returns on innovation are higher with transformational initiatives than with core or adjacent pursuits, but require unique management methods. These include establishing a diverse talent set, separating teams from daily operations, and obtaining funding from outside the regular budget cycle.

45259 ■ *"Managing Yourself: What Brain Science Tells Us About How to Excel"* in Harvard Business Review (Vol. 88, December 2010, No. 12, pp. 123)
Pub: Harvard Business School Publishing
Ed: Edward M. Hallowell. **Description:** Relevant discoveries in brain research as they apply to boosting employee motivation and organizational effectiveness are explained. Included is a checklist of 15 items for use in assessing the fitness of a person for a particular job, focusing on the intersection of what one likes to do, what one does best, and what increases organizational value.

45260 ■ *"M&I Execs May Get Golden Parachutes"* in Business Journal-Milwaukee (Vol. 28, December 31, 2010, No. 14, pp. A3)
Pub: Milwaukee Business Journal
Ed: Rich Kirchen. **Description:** Marshall and Isley Corporation's top executives have a chance to receive golden-parachute payments it its buyer, BMO Financial Group, repays the Troubled Asset Relief Program (TARP) loan on behalf of the company. One TARP rule prevents golden-parachute payments to them and the next five most highly paid employees of TARP recipients.

45261 ■ *"The Many Hats and Faces of NAOHSM"* in Indoor Comfort Marketing (Vol. 70, May 2011, No. 5, pp. 8)
Pub: Industry Publications Inc.
Contact: Shirleen Dorman, Editor
Description: Profile of the National Association of Oil Heating Service Managers, and its role in the industry, is presented.

45262 ■ *The Martha Rules: 10 Essentials for Achieving Success as You Start, Build, or Manage a Business*
Ed: Martha Stewart. **Released:** October 2006. **Price:** , $15.95. **Description:** Martha Stewart offers insight into starting, building and managing a successful business.

45263 ■ *The Martha Rules: 10 Essentials for Achieving Success as You Start, Grow, or Manage a Business*
Ed: Martha Stewart. **Released:** October 2005.

45264 ■ *Mastering Business Negotiation: A Working Guide to Making Deals and Resolving Conflict*
Pub: Jossey-Bass Publishers
Contact: Matthew Hoover, Manager
E-mail: fwelsch@jbp.com
Ed: Roy J. Lewicki, Alexander Hiam. **Released:** April 2010. **Price:** $31.95, paperback; $20.99. **Description:** Provides extensive insight into practical strategies and ideas for conducting business negotiations. **Availability:** PrintE-book.

45265 ■ *"MBA Guide 2008"* in Canadian Business (Vol. 81, November 10, 2008, No. 19, pp. 92)
Ed: Sharda Prashad. **Description:** Escalating tuition costs for an MBA degree means that the return on investment could take longer. One study found that MBA degree holders who graduated during recessionary times earned less than those who graduated during good economic times.

45266 ■ *MBA In A Day: What You Would Learn At Top-Tier Business Schools (If You Only Had The Time!)*
Pub: John Wiley & Sons Inc.
Contact: Stephen M. Smith, President
Ed: Steven Stralser. **Released:** September 2004. **Price:** $34.95, hardcover; $22.99. **Description:** Management professor presents important concepts, business topics and strategies that can be used by anyone to manage a small business or professional practice. Topics covered include: human resources and personal interaction, ethics and leadership skills, fair negotiation tactics, basic business accounting practices, project management, and the fundamentals of economics and marketing. **Availability:** PrintE-book.

45267 ■ *"MBAs Plus Designers Equals New Life for Business"* in Globe & Mail (April 24, 2007, pp. B1)
Ed: Gordon Pitts. **Description:** The need for Canadian companies to combine the skills of management graduates and designers to achieve corporate growth is discussed.

45268 ■ *"Meadowbrook CEO Sees 20 Percent Growth With New Acquisition"* in Crain's Detroit Business (Vol. 24, March 11, 2008, No. 10, pp. 4)
Pub: Crain Communications Inc.
Contact: Rance E. Crain, President
Ed: Jay Greene. **Description:** Discusses the major turnaround of Meadowbrook Insurance Group after Robert Cubbin became CEO and implemented a new business strategy.

45269 ■ *"MEDC: Put Venture Funds to Work"* in Crain's Detroit Business (Vol. 25, June 22, 2009, No. 25, pp. 1)
Pub: Crain Communications Inc. - Detroit
Contact: Keith Crain, Chairman
Ed: Tom Henderson. **Description:** Michigan Strategic Fund board will finalize approval for ESP Holdings II LLC, Peninsula Capital Partners LLC, Triathlon Medical Ventures LLC and Arsenal Venture Partners Inc. are expected to share $35.5 million from the fund.

45270 ■ *"Meet the 'Googlebusters'"* in Austin Business Journal (Vol. 34, February 28, 2014, No. 2, pp. 4)
Pub: American City Business Journals, Inc.
Contact: Whitney Shaw, President
Released: February 28, 2014. **Description:** Executives' views on how companies should retain employees are presented. Sailpoint Technologies CEO, Mark McClain, says companies should give employees the tools and resources they need to be successful. John Cyrier, president of Sabre Commercial Inc., says constant communication with employees is critical.

45271 ■ *"Mentoring Support"* in Black Enterprise (Vol. 38, July 2008, No. 12, pp. 64)
Pub: Earl G. Graves Publishing Co. Inc.
Contact: Earl G. Graves, Jr., President
Description: With his relocation from his multicultural team in New York to the less diverse Scripps Networks' headquarters in Knoxville, Earl Cokley has made it a top priority to push for more diversity and mentoring opportunities within the management of the media and marketing company.

45272 ■ *"Messing with Corporate Heads? Psychological Contracts and Leadership Integrity"* in Journal of Business Strategy (Vol. 35, May-June 2014, No. 3, pp. 38-46)
Pub: Emerald Group Publishing Inc.
Released: May-June 2014. **Description:** A model of leadership, i.e. the leadership psychological contract (LPC) and investigation of the contribution of psychological contract (PC) to the leadership domain is investigated. Contemporary literature on leadership and PC is reviewed and it was observed that the LPC is a predictive model consisting of three dependent variables namely trust, fairness, and fulfillment of expectations. The LPC model seeks to augment the value of ethical and effective leadership approaches.

45273 ■ *"Methodological Fit in Management Field Research"* in Academy of Management Review (October 2007, pp. 1155)
Pub: ScholarOne Inc.
Contact: William T. Carden, Jr., President
Ed: Amy C. Edmondson, Stacy E. McManus. **Description:** The importance of methodological fit in management field research is investigated in order to produce high quality results.

45274 ■ *"The Metrics of Knowledge: Mechanisms for Preserving the Value of Managerial Knowledge"* in Business Horizons (November-December 2007)
Pub: Elsevier Technology Publications
Ed: Eliezer Geisler. **Price:** $35.95. **Description:** Mechanisms to reduce the loss of managerial knowledge, such as socialization, tutoring, mentoring, and continuous reporting are proposed. These informal mechanisms should become integral components of knowledge management or organizations. **Availability:** PDF.

45275 ■ **Microfinance**
Pub: Palgrave Macmillan
Contact: Lisa Dunn, Manager
E-mail: l.dunn@palgrave.com
Ed: Mario La Torre, Gianfranco A. Vento, Philip Molyneux. **Released:** July 2006. **Price:** £84, hardcover; $120. **Description:** Microfinance involves the analysis of operational, managerial and financial aspects of a small business. **Availability:** Print; E-book.

45276 ■ *"Microsoft's Diversity Program Clicks into High Speed"* in Hispanic Business (Vol. 30, July-August 2008, No. 7-8, pp. 54)
Pub: Hispanic Business Inc.
Contact: Jesus Chavarria, President
Ed: Derek Reveron. **Description:** Microsoft's diversity hiring and vendor diversity program to capture more Hispanic consumer and business-to-business market is described. One of the main goals of these programs is to hire more Hispanic executives and managers who will help the company develop and market products and services that will appeal and benefit Hispanic consumers.

45277 ■ *"The Middle Ages"* in Hawaii Business (Vol. 53, October 2007, No. 4, pp. 42)
Pub: PacificBasin Communications
Ed: Cathy S. Cruz-George. **Description:** Starcom Builders Inc.'s Theodore 'Ted' Taketa, School Kine Cookies' Steven Gold And Sharon Serene of Sharon Serene Creative are among the participants in Hawaii's Fittest CEO competition for executives over 50 years old. Taketa takes yoga classes, and also goes to the gym while Serne has Mike Hann as her professional trainer. Eating habits of the aforementioned executives are also described.

45278 ■ *"Miller's Crossroad"* in Canadian Business (Vol. 83, September 14, 2010, No. 15, pp. 58)
Pub: Rogers Media Inc.
Contact: Tony Viner, President
Ed: Joe Castaldo. **Description:** Future Electronics founder and billionaire Robert Miller shares the secret of Future's unique operating model, which is based on inventory and market research. Miller attributes much of the company's success to its privately held status that enables quick movement against competitors.

45279 ■ *"Mini Melts"* in Ice Cream Reporter (Vol. 23, August 20, 2010, No. 9, pp. 8)
Description: Mini Melts appointed David S. Tade to position of director of sales USA in order to cultivate existing distributors and add new partners to its distribution network.

45280 ■ *"Mining Executive Telfer Pocketed Millions"* in Globe & Mail (April 5, 2007, pp. B4)
Ed: Andy Hoffman. **Description:** The issue of huge compensation for former executive of both Goldcorp Inc. and UrAsia Energy Ltd., Ian Telfer, for his efficient management of stock options is discussed.

45281 ■ *The Mirror Test: Is Your Business Really Breathing?*
Pub: Grand Central Publishing
Contact: Maureen Mahon Egen, President
Ed: Jeffrey W. Hayzlett. **Released:** May 05, 2010. **Price:** $9.99. **Description:** Consultant and author, Jeffrey Hayzlett, explains why a business is not doing well and asks the questions that most business managers are afraid to ask. **Availability:** E-book.

45282 ■ *"Mismanaging Pay and Performance"* in Business Strategy Review (Vol. 21, Summer 2010, No. 2, pp. 54)
Pub: Blackwell Publishers Ltd.
Ed: Rupert Merson. **Description:** Understanding the relationship between performance and desired behaviors is an important element of a company's talent management.

45283 ■ *"Mismanaging Pay and Performance"* in *Business Strategy Review (Vol. 21, Summer 2010, No. 2, pp. 54)*
Pub: John Wiley & Sons Inc. Scientific, Technical, Medical, and Scholarly Div. (Wiley-Blackwell)
Contact: William J. Pesce, Manager
E-mail: wpesce@wiley.com
Ed: Rupert Merson. **Description:** Understanding the relationship between performance measurement and desired behaviors is an important element of a company's talent management.

45284 ■ *"Miss Manners Minds Your Business"*
Pub: W.W. Norton and Co.
Released: October 20, 2014. **Price:** , $16.95 paperback. **Description:** Office etiquette is outlined. Practical, pertinent and correct advice is given covering office manners for anyone from convening a focus group to Human Resources management.

45285 ■ *"Modeling How to Grow: an Inductive Examination of Humble Leader Behaviors, Contingencies, and Outcomes"* in *Academy of Management Journal (Vol. 55, August 1, 2012, No. 4, pp. 787)*
Pub: Academy of Management
Contact: Ming-Jer Chen, President
Ed: Bradley P. Owens, David R. Hekman. **Description:** An inductive analysis of the behaviors, outcome and contingencies of humble leadership in relation to organizational effectiveness is presented. Results suggest that effective leadership amid market complexity and diversity requires leaders to humbly show their followers how to grow by admitting their limitations and acknowledging the contributions of the people around them.

45286 ■ *"The Moment You Can't Ignore: When Big Trouble Leads to a Great Future"*
Pub: PublicAffairs
Released: October 7, 2014. **Price:** , $25.99. **Description:** New forms of work, communication, and technology are exposing the ways in which an organization's culture conflicts with new competitive demands. Questions for small companies to ask about identity, leadership, and capacity for innovation are addressed.

45287 ■ *"Monaco Pay Cut Draws Attention"* in *The Business Journal-Portland (Vol. 25, August 8, 2008, No. 22, pp. 1)*
Pub: American City Business Journals, Inc.
Contact: Whitney Shaw, President
Ed: Erik Siemers. **Description:** Monaco Coach Corp. cut the salaries of five top executives in an effort to reduce the company's $178 million worth of inventory. The executives can earn the lost salary back if the inventory is reduced by $58 million a year after August 2008.

45288 ■ *"Monitor Work Productivity"* in *Business Owner (Vol. 35, July-August 2011, No. 4, pp. 4)*
Pub: DL Perkins Company
Description: Tips for tracking employee productivity are explained.

45289 ■ *"The Moody Blues"* in *Entrepreneur (Vol. 36, April 2008, No. 4, pp. 87)*
Pub: Entrepreneur Press
Contact: Perlman Neil, President
Ed: Mark Henricks. **Description:** Depression among employees can affect their productivity and cost the company. Businesses with a workforce that is likely to have depression should inform their employees about the health benefits covered by insurance. Other details on how to address depression concerns among employees are discussed.

45290 ■ *"More Important than Results"* in *Business Strategy Review (Vol. 21, Summer 2010, No. 2, pp. 81)*
Pub: John Wiley & Sons Inc. Scientific, Technical, Medical, and Scholarly Div. (Wiley-Blackwell)
Contact: William J. Pesce, Manager
E-mail: wpesce@wiley.com
Ed: Bert De Reyck, Zeger Degraeve. **Description:** Managing only for results leads to crises. Reward people for decisions they make, not just for the results they create.

45291 ■ *"More Leadership Changes for City's Biosciences Industry"* in *San Antonio Business Journal (Vol. 28, June 6, 2014, No. 17, pp. 8)*
Pub: American City Business Journals
Released: June 6, 2014. **Description:** Kenneth Trevett has resigned as CEO of Texas Biomedical Research Institute, but will remain until the institute searches for his successor. Trevett's resignation came after CEO Peter Sava left StemBioSys Inc. of San Antonio and returned to Boston, Massachusetts.

45292 ■ *"More Mexican Labor Needed in Oil Patch, Executives Say"* in *Globe & Mail (February 23, 2007, pp. B1)*
Ed: Steven Chase. **Description:** The plans of top North American chief executive officers to recommend the employment of temporary workers from Mexico for the development of oil sands in Alberta, Canada, are discussed.

45293 ■ *"A Motorola Spinoff Is No Panacea"* in *Barron's (Vol. 88, March 31, 2008, No. 13, pp. 19)*
Pub: Dow Jones & Co., Inc.
Contact: Clare Hart, President
Ed: Mark Veverka. **Description:** Motorola's plan to try and spinoff their handset division is bereft of details as to how or specifically when in 2009 the spinoff would occur. There's no reason to buy the shares since there's a lot of execution risk to the plan. Motorola needs to hire a proven cellphone executive and develop a compelling new cellphone platform.

45294 ■ *"Mr. Deeds"* in *Canadian Business (Vol. 81, March 31, 2008, No. 5, pp. 24)*
Pub: Rogers Media Inc.
Contact: Tony Viner, President
Ed: Thomas Watson. **Description:** Ron Sandler has the right experience to save Northern Rock PLC get through its liquidity problems. Sandler is known for saving Lloyd's of London in the mid-90's and he is not afraid to make enemies. Ron Sandler's assignment to help Northern Rock comes at a time when the health of the U.K. housing is not great.

45295 ■ *"MTV Networks"* in *Brandweek (Vol. 49, April 21, 2008, No. 16, pp. SR10)*
Pub: Nielsen Business Media Inc.
Contact: Howard Appelbaum, President
Ed: Anthony Crupi. **Description:** Provides contact information for sales and marketing personnel for the MTV networks as well as a listing of the station's top programming and an analysis of the current season and the target audience for those programs running in the current season. MTV networks include MTV, VH1, Nickelodeon and Comedy Central.

45296 ■ *"Murdoch Lifer Mans Main Street Journal"* in *Advertising Age (Vol. 79, July 7, 2008, No. 26, pp. 1)*
Pub: Crain Communications Inc.
Contact: Rance Crain, President
Ed: Nat Ives. **Description:** Profile of Les Hinton, the U.K. executive who was chosen by Rupert Murdoch to run Dow Jones and The Wall Street Journal; Hinton discusses The Wall Street Journal's unique spot in American business which has helped it survive a dwindling newspaper industry.

45297 ■ *"My Bad: Sometimes, Even CEOs Have to Say They're Sorry"* in *Inc. (October 2007, pp. 37-38)*
Pub: Mansueto Ventures L.L.C.
Contact: John Koten, Chief Executive Officer
Ed: Donna Fenn. **Description:** A leader's stature with his employees can be elevated if he can admit a mistake simply with sincerity. Unfortunately for large companies, these blunders sometimes make the news.

45298 ■ *"My Inglorious Road to Success"* in *Harvard Business Review (Vol. 88, July-August 2010, No. 7-8, pp. 38)*
Pub: Harvard Business School Publishing
Ed: Warren Bennis. **Description:** The author discusses the intersection of fortune and opportunity in his career success, and emphasizes the important role of awareness when taking advantage of both.

45299 ■ *"The Myth of the Overqualified Worker"* in *Harvard Business Review (Vol. 88, December 2010, No. 12, pp. 30)*
Pub: Harvard Business School Publishing
Ed: Andrew O'Connell. **Description:** It is recommended to seriously consider job candidates with qualifications exceeding the position being recruited because research shows these individuals work harder, but do not quit any sooner than those whose qualifications more closely match the position.

45300 ■ *"Natalie Peterson; Corporate Counsel, Steris Corp."* in *Crain's Cleveland Business (Vol. 28, November 19, 2007, No. 46, pp. F-14)*
Pub: Crain Communications Inc.
Ed: Chuck Soder. **Description:** Profile of Natalie Peterson, corporate counsel for Steris Corp., a manufacturer of sterilization products; Peterson's blue-collar background did not detour her from her collegiate goals although she hardly knew how to fill out a college application. After graduating from Stanford Law School in 1997, she opted to return to Cleveland in lieu of more lucrative job offers in San Francisco. She has joined the school board and has participated in the 3Rs program, in which lawyers visit public schools in Cleveland to get students thinking about career choices and talk about constitutional law.

45301 ■ *"Nation of Islam Businessman Who Became Manager for Muhammad Ali Dies"* in *Chicago Tribune (August 28, 2008)*
Pub: McClatchy-Tribune Information Services
Ed: Trevor Jensen. **Description:** Profile of Jabir Herbert Muhammad who died on August 25, after heart surgery; Muhammad lived nearly all his life on Chicago's South Side and ran a number of small businesses including a bakery and a dry cleaners before becoming the manager to famed boxer Mohammad Ali.

45302 ■ *"NBC"* in *Brandweek (Vol. 49, April 21, 2008, No. 16, pp. SR6)*
Pub: Nielsen Business Media Inc.
Contact: Howard Appelbaum, President
Ed: John Consoli. **Description:** Provides contact information for sales and marketing personnel for the NBC network as well as a listing of the station's top programming and an analysis of the current season and the target audience for those programs running in the current season. NBC also devised a new strategy of announcing its prime-time schedule 52 weeks in advance which was a hit for advertisers who felt this gave them a better opportunity to plan for product placement. Even with the station's creative sales programs, they could face a challenge from Fox in terms of upfront advertisement purchases.

45303 ■ *"NBC Universal Cable"* in *Brandweek (Vol. 49, April 21, 2008, No. 16, pp. SR11)*
Pub: Nielsen Business Media Inc.
Contact: Howard Appelbaum, President
Ed: Anthony Crupi. **Description:** Provides contact information for sales and marketing personnel for the NBC Universal Cable networks as well as a listing of the station's top programming and an analysis of the current season and the target audience for those programs running in the current season. The network's stations include USA, Sci Fi and Bravo. Ad revenue for the network grew 30 percent in the first quarter.

45304 ■ *"NBC Universal Domestic Television Distribution"* in *Brandweek (Vol. 49, April 21, 2008, No. 16, pp. SR13)*
Pub: Nielsen Business Media Inc.
Contact: Howard Appelbaum, President
Ed: Marc Berman. **Description:** Provides contact information for sales and marketing personnel for NBC Universal Domestic Television Distribution as well as a listing of the station's top programming and an analysis of the current season and the target audience for those programs running in the current season.

45305 ■ *"Need a Course Correction? Let ABWA Be Your Navigator"* in *Women In Business* (Vol. 62, September 2010, No. 3, pp. 6)
Pub: American Business Women's Association
Contact: Lorie Burch, President
Ed: Rene Street. **Description:** It is believed that the American Business Women's Association (ABWA) has the ability to help women in their quest for greater success. The organization also has the energy needed to move on to the next stage for women in business. ABWA's members have taken the initiative to embrace the group's potential.

45306 ■ *"Negotiating Tips"* in *Black Enterprise* (Vol. 37, December 2006, No. 5, pp. 70)
Pub: Earl G. Graves Publishing Co. Inc.
Contact: Earl G. Graves, Jr., President
Ed: Marcia A. Reed-Woodard. **Description:** Sekou Kaalund, head of strategy, mergers & acquisitions at Citigroup Securities & Fund Services, states that 'Negotiation skills are paramount to success in a business environment because of client, employee, and shareholder relationships'. He discusses how the book by George Kohlrieser, Hostage at the Table: How Leaders Can Overcome Conflict, Influence Others, and Raise Performance, has helped him negotiate more powerfully and enhance his skills at conflict-resolution.

45307 ■ *"NEMRA Announces Headquarters Move"* in *Agency Sales Magazine* (Vol. 39, September-October 2009, No. 9, pp. 53)
Description: NEMRA, the National Electrical Manufacturers' Representatives Association is moving their headquarters to 28 Deer Street, Suite 302, Portsmouth, New Hampshire. The association has also added Michelle Rivers-Jameson as their manager of operations and Kirsty Stebbins as their manager of marketing and member services.

45308 ■ *Never Eat Alone: And Other Secrets to Success, One Relationship at a Time*
Ed: Keith Ferrazzi, Tahl Raz. **Released:** February 2005. **Description:** Business networking strategies are offered.

45309 ■ *"Never Eat Alone, Expanded and Updated: And Other Secrets to Success, One Relationship at a Time"*
Pub: Crown Business
Released: June 3, 2014. **Price:** , $27.00. **Description:** The power of their relationships is what makes successful business leaders stand out from the rest. He lists specific steps to reach out and connect with colleagues, friends, and associates, along with successful ways to use social media to advance in business.

45310 ■ *"The New Arsenal of Risk Management"* in *Harvard Business Review* (Vol. 86, September 2008, No. 9, pp. 92)
Pub: Harvard Business Review Press
Contact: Peter E. Walsh, Director
Ed: Kevin Buehler, Andrew Freeman, Ron Hulme. **Description:** Goldman Sachs Group Inc. is used to illustrate methods for successful risk management. The investment bank's business principles, partnerships, and oversight practices are discussed.

45311 ■ *"New BMO Boss Set to Cut 1,000 Jobs"* in *Globe & Mail* (February 1, 2007, pp. B3)
Ed: Andrew Willis. **Description:** The decision of the new chief executive officer of the Bank of Montreal, Bill Downe, to cut down 1,000 jobs, to boost the company's performance is discussed.

45312 ■ *"New Boss at Nortel Mines GE for New Executives"* in *Globe & Mail* (February 6, 2006, pp. B1)
Ed: Catherine McLean. **Description:** Chief executive officer Mike Zafirovski of Nortel Networks Corp. appoints executives Dennis Carey, Joel Hackney and Don McKenn of GE Electric Co. The managerial abilities of Mike are discussed.

45313 ■ *"New CEO For Friendly's"* in *Ice Cream Reporter* (Vol. 23, September 20, 2010, No. 10, pp. 1)
Description: Friendly Ice Cream Corporation named Harsha V. Agadi as new chief executive officer. Agadi has 24 years experience in food service, most recently serving as CEO of Church's Chicken.

45314 ■ *The New Role of Regional Management*
Pub: Palgrave Macmillan
Contact: Lisa Dunn, Manager
E-mail: l.dunn@palgrave.com
Ed: Bjorn Ambos, Bodo B. Schlegelmilch. **Released:** December 2009. **Price:** £69, hardcover; £56.65; $110. **Description:** Regional management is becoming more important to companies as they expand globally. This book explores the challenges of European, United States and Asian companies and outlines how regional headquarters can develop into Dynamic Competence Relay centers to master these issues. **Availability:** PrintE-book; Electronic publishingE-book; PDF.

45315 ■ *"The New Schools"* in *Black Enterprise* (February 2008)
Pub: Earl G. Graves Publishing Co. Inc.
Contact: Earl G. Graves, Jr., President
Ed: Kingsley Kanu, Jr. **Description:** Ten educational programs to help top executives keep pace with the ever-changing market trends while gaining perspective on innovation and new ideas are examined.

45316 ■ *"New Sustainable Boss Seeks to Add Members"* in *Business Journal Portland* (Vol. 51, February 21, 2014, No. 51, pp. 10)
Pub: American City Business Journals
Released: February 21, 2014. **Description:** Maureen Hart, executive director of the International Society of Sustainability Professionals (ISSP), discusses her plans and goals for the ISSP. She expects the group's presence in Portland, Oregon to continue to grow and offer more networking and learning opportunities for all members.

45317 ■ *"New Work Order"* in *Black Enterprise* (Vol. 38, March 1, 2008, No. 8, pp. 60)
Pub: Earl G. Graves Publishing Co. Inc.
Contact: Earl G. Graves, Jr., President
Ed: Marcia A. Reed-Woodward. **Description:** Today's management challenges includes issues of more competition, globalization, outsourcing and technological advances. Suggestions to help create progressive leadership in small business that sustains a competitive edge are listed.

45318 ■ *"Nexstar Super Meeting Breaks Business Barriers"* in *Contractor* (Vol. 56, November 2009, No. 11, pp. 3)
Pub: Penton Media, Inc.
Ed: Candace Roulo. **Description:** Around 400 Nexstar members met to discuss the trends in the HVAC industry and the economic outlook for 2010. Former lead solo pilot John Foley for the Blue Angels made a presentation on how a business can increase overall productivity based on the culture of the Blue Angels. Some breakout sessions tackled how to optimize workflow and marketing.

45319 ■ *"Nine Paradoxes of Problem Solving"* in *Strategy and Leadership* (Vol. 39, May-June 2011, No. 3, pp. 25-31)
Pub: Emerald Group Publishing Inc.
Ed: Alex Lowy. **Description:** Nine frequently-occurring inherent paradoxes in corporate decision making for solving complex problems are identified. The methods with which these paradoxes and their influence can be recognized and dealt with for firm leaders and management team members to better understand and solve the problems are discussed.

45320 ■ *The No Asshole Rule*
Ed: Robert I. Sutton PhD. **Released:** February 22, 2007. **Price:** $22.99. **Description:** Problem employees are more than just a nuisance they are a serious and costly threat to corporate success and employee health.

45321 ■ *"No Secrets; Businesses Find It Pays to Open Books to Employees"* in *Crain's Detroit Business* (Vol. 26, January 18, 2010, No. 3)
Pub: Crain Communications Inc.
Contact: Rance E. Crain, President
Ed: Dustin Walsh. **Description:** Many businesses are finding that practicing an open-book management wherein employees share financial and decision-making duties that are usually left up to executives of firms creates a transparency within a company that eliminates the us versus them mentality between management and employees. Another benefit to this business model is that employees get to really participate in the business, learning to manage money and run a business entity.

45322 ■ *"Nobel Prize Winners Provide Insight on Outsourcing, Contract Work"* in *Workforce Management* (Vol. 88, November 16, 2009, No. 12, pp. 11)
Pub: Crain Communications Inc.
Contact: Rance E. Crain, President
Ed: Jeremy Smerd. **Description:** Insights into such workforce management issues as bonuses, employee contracts and outsourcing has been recognized by the Nobel Prize winners in economics whose research sheds a light on the way economic decisions are made outside markets.

45323 ■ *"'Nobody Knows What To Do' To Make Money on the Web"* in *Barron's* (Vol. 88, March 17, 2008, No. 11, pp. 40)
Pub: Dow Jones & Co., Inc.
Contact: Clare Hart, President
Ed: Mark Veverka. **Description:** Attendees of the South by Southwest Interactive conference failed to get an insight on how to make money on the Web from former Walt Disney CEO Michael Eisner when Eisner said there's no proven business model for financing projects. Eisner said he finances his projects with the help of his connections to get product-placement deals.

45324 ■ *Non-Standard Employment under Globalization: Flexible Work and Social Security in the Newly Industrializing Countries*
Pub: Palgrave Macmillan
Contact: Lisa Dunn, Manager
E-mail: l.dunn@palgrave.com
Ed: Koichi Usami. **Released:** December 2009. **Price:** £84, hardcover; $115. **Description:** Expansion of non-standard employment under globalization is being recognized in all of the newly industrialized countries. The book examines deregulation of labor markets, social protection for nonstandard workers, and social security reforms in accordance with the transformation of employment. **Availability:** PrintE-book.

45325 ■ *"Nortel Makes Customers Stars in New Campaign"* in *Brandweek* (Vol. 49, April 21, 2008, No. 16, pp. 8)
Pub: Nielsen Business Media Inc.
Contact: Howard Appelbaum, President
Ed: Mike Beirne. **Description:** Nortel has launched a new television advertising campaign in which the business-to-business communications technology provider cast senior executives in 30-second TV case studies that show how Nortel's technology helped their businesses innovate.

45326 ■ *"Not Just for Kids: ADHD can be Debilitating for an Employee, and Frustrating for Bosses"* in *Canadian Business* (April 14, 2008)
Pub: Rogers Media Inc.
Contact: Tony Viner, President
Ed: Andy Holloway. **Description:** Up to four percent of North American adults continue to feel the effects of Attention Deficit Hyperactivity Disorder or Attention Deficit Disorder. Explaining the value of the task at hand to people who are afflicted with these conditions is one way to keep them engaged in the workplace. Giving them opportunities to create their own working structure is another strategy to manage these people.

45327 ■ *Now, Discover Your Strengths*
Pub: Free Press/Simon & Schuster Inc.
Ed: Marcus Buckingham, Donald O. Clifton. Price: $32. Description: How to identify and develop your talents and those of your employees.

45328 ■ *Nudge: Improving Decisions About Health, Wealth, and Happiness*
Pub: Dutton Children's Books
Contact: Lauri Hornik, President
Ed: Richard H. Thaler, Cass R. Sunstein. Released: February 24, 2009. Price: $17, paperback; $13.99. Description: Advice is given to help improve the decision-making process in order to become a successful entrepreneur. Availability: PrintElectronic publishing.

45329 ■ *"The Obstacle Is the Way: The Timeless Art of Turning Trials into Triumph"*
Pub: Portfolio Hardcover
Released: May 1, 2014. Price: , $24.95. Description: The formula for success is taking any obstacle and turning it into a business opportunity. Successful leaders throughout history are profiled to show how any entrepreneur can succeed.

45330 ■ *"The Office: Do Not Disturb"* in *Inc.* (November 2007, pp. 144)
Pub: Gruner and Jahr USA Publishing Co.
Contact: J. Russell Denson, President
Ed: Leigh Buchanan. Description: The importance for any CEO to be accessible to his employees is stressed.

45331 ■ *"The Office: Good to Great"* in *Inc.* (October 2007, pp. 140)
Pub: Mansueto Ventures L.L.C.
Contact: John Koten, Chief Executive Officer
Ed: Leigh Buchanan. Description: Qualities that make a good manager great are explored. Great bosses make their employees feel smart, they know who performs what job, know when to step back, and remember things about each employee such as their families' names.

45332 ■ *"Office Pests"* in *Canadian Business* (Vol. 79, October 9, 2006, No. 20, pp. 122)
Ed: Calvin Leung. Description: Personality traits of employees and strategies for managers to effectively handle them are discussed.

45333 ■ *"The Office: The Bad and the Ugly"* in *Inc.* (January 2008, pp. 120)
Pub: Gruner and Jahr USA Publishing Co.
Contact: J. Russell Denson, President
Description: Seven signs that you are a bad boss are outlined to help managers improve their skills.

45334 ■ *The Official Guide for GMAT Verbal Review, 2nd Edition*
Ed: Graduate Management Admissions Council. Released: August 17, 2009. Price: $17.95. Description: The only official verbal review for the GMAT from the creators of the test. The guide provides questions, answers, and explanations and targets study and helps improve verbal skills by focusing on the ability to read and comprehend written material, to reason and evaluate arguments, and to correct written material to conform to Standard English.

45335 ■ *"Olympus is Urged to Revise Board"* in *Wall Street Journal Eastern Edition* (November 28, 2011, pp. B3)
Pub: Dow Jones & Co., Inc.
Contact: Clare Hart, President
Ed: Phred Dvorak. Description: Koji Miyata, once a director on the board of troubled Japanese photographic equipment company, is urging the company to reorganize its board, saying the present group should resign their board seats but keep their management positions. The company has come under scrutiny for its accounting practices and costly acquisitions.

45336 ■ *"OMERS Labors With Troubles at the Top"* in *Globe & Mail* (February 26, 2007, pp. B3)
Ed: Elizabeth Church. Description: The trouble over fund management and leadership change in the Ontario Municipal Employees Retirement System is discussed.

45337 ■ *"On the Edge: The Art of High-Impact Leadership"*
Pub: Business Plus/Warner Business Books
Released: January 7, 2014. Price: , $27.00. Description: Alison Levine provides insights into leadership garnered from her various expeditions from Mount Everest to the South Pole. Levine believes that leadership principles that apply in extreme adventure sport also apply in today's extreme business environment. She discusses your survival as well as the survival of the team.

45338 ■ *On the Make: Clerks and the Quest for Capital in Nineteenth-Century America*
Pub: New York University Press
Contact: Steve Maikowski, Director
E-mail: steve.maikowski@nyu.edu
Ed: Brian P. Luskey. Released: December 01, 2011. Price: $25, paperback; $75, cloth. Description: Through exploration into the diaries, newspapers, credit reports, census data, advice literature and fiction, the book presents the origins of the white collar culture, the antebellum clerk. Availability: Print.

45339 ■ *"On Managerial Relevance"* in *Journal of Marketing* (Vol. 75, July 2011, No. 4, pp. 211)
Pub: American Marketing Association
Contact: Lucille Pointer, President
Ed: Bernard J. Jaworski. Description: A study to define and clarify managerial relevance, in order to act as a catalyst for debate, disagreement and future scholarship, is presented. The role of chief marketing officer (CMO) is examined to identify areas of inquiry that are both novel and high managerially relevant. The analysis reveals the seven core tasks necessary to perform the CMO role.

45340 ■ *"On a Mission: Ginch Gonch Wants You to Get Rid of Your Tighty Whities"* in *Canadian Business* (Vol. 81, September 29, 2008, No. 16)
Ed: Michelle Magnan. Description: New Equity Capital acquired underwear maker Ginch Gonch in July 2008; founder Jason Sutherland kept his position as creative director of the company and will retain his title as 'director of stitches and inches'. The company is known for its products, which are reminiscent of the days when people wore underwear covered in cowboys and stars as kids. The company also claims that Nelly, Justin Timberlake, and Hilary Duff have worn their products.

45341 ■ *"On the Money"* in *San Antonio Business Journal* (Vol. 28, June 27, 2014, No. 20, pp. 4)
Pub: American City Business Journals
Released: June 27, 2014. Description: The total compensation for the top 18 highest paid public company CEOs in San Antonio, Texas has increased 11 percent in the 2013 fiscal year to $74.8 million compared to 2012 fiscal year. The average total CEO compensation in the city was $4.15 million, an 11 percent increase from the 2013 list. The trend in the 2014 highest paid CEOs list is discussed.

45342 ■ *"On a Roll"* in *Canadian Business* (Vol. 79, October 9, 2006, No. 20, pp. 51)
Ed: Joe Castaldo. Description: Corporate management strategies of Denis Turcotte, chief executive officer of Algoma Steel Inc., are presented.

45343 ■ *"On Track"* in *Canadian Business* (Vol. 79, July 17, 2006, No. 14-15, pp. 51)
Pub: Rogers Media Inc.
Contact: Tony Viner, President
Ed: John Gray. Description: Results of the annual survey conducted by CanadaEs boards, to measure the levels of corporate governance of firms in Canada, which are presented.

45344 ■ *One Foot Out the Door: How to Combat the Psychological Recession That's Alienating Employees and Hurting American Business*
Pub: AMACOM
Contact: Edward T. Reilly, Manager
Ed: Judith M. Bardwick. Released: October 31, 2007. Price: $24.95; C$32.95. Description: Drawing on research that indicates Generation X and younger

baby boomers feel disconnected from their jobs, the author explores the causes (bad management) of that disengagement. Her pragmatic suggestions about how companies can prove their commitment to employees is beneficial.

45345 ■ *"One Hundred Years of Excellence in Business Education: What Have We Learned?"* in *Business Horizons* (January-February 2008)
Pub: Elsevier Advanced Technology Publications
Ed: Frank Acito, Patricia M. McDougall, Daniel C. Smith. Description: Business schools have to be more innovative, efficient and nimble, so that the quality of the next generation of business leaders is improved. The Kelley School of Business, Indiana University ahs long been a leader in business education. The trends that influence the future of business education and useful success principles are discussed.

45346 ■ *The One Minute Manager*
Pub: William Morrow
Ed: Kenneth H. Blanchard, Spencer Johnson. Released: October 07, 2003. Price: $22.99, hardcover. Description: Managers of small businesses as well as Fortune 500 companies have been following the management techniques described in this book. Results have shown increased productivity, job satisfaction, and personal prosperity. Availability: Print.

45347 ■ *"One-Time Area Trust Executive Finds Trouble in N.H."* in *The Business Journal-Serving Metropolitan Kansas City* (September 12, 2008)
Ed: Steve Vockrodt. Description: About 200 investors, some from Missouri's Kansas City area, claim that they had conducted business with Noble Trust Co. The trust company was placed under New Hampshire Banking Department's conservatorship after $15 million was discovered to be missing from its account. It is alleged that the money was lost in a Colorado Ponzi scheme.

45348 ■ *The Opposable Mind: How Successful Leaders Win Through Integrative Thinking*
Pub: Harvard Business Review Press
Contact: Peter E. Walsh, Director
Ed: Roger L. Martin. Released: December 04, 2007. Price: $32, hardcover; $22, paperback; $22. Description: The importance of integrative thinking for successful management is discussed. Availability: PrintE-book.

45349 ■ *The Orange Revolution: How One Great Team Can Transform an Entire Organization*
Pub: Simon and Schuster Inc.
Contact: Carolyn Reidy, President
E-mail: carolyn.reidy@simonandschuster.com
Ed: Adrian Gostick, Chester Elton. Released: September 2010. Price: $25, hardcover; $16.99. Description: Based on a 350,000-person study by the Best Companies Group, as well as research into exceptional teams at leading companies, including Zappos.com, Pepsi Beverages Company, and Madison Square Garden, the authors have determined a key set of characteristics displayed by members of breakthrough teams, and have identified a set of rules great teams live by, which generate a culture of positive teamwork and led to extraordinary results. Using specific stories from the teams they studied, they reveal in detail how these teams operate and how managers can transform their own teams into such high performers by fostering: stronger clarity of goals, greater trust among team members, more open and honest dialogue, stronger accountability for all team members, and purpose-based recognition of team member contributions. Availability: PrintE-book.

45350 ■ *"Orfinger's WBJ Tenure to End"* in *Washington Business Journal* (Vol. 33, September 5, 2014, No. 20, pp. 4)
Pub: American City Business Journals
Released: September 5, 2014. Description: Alex Orfinger ended his tenure as publisher of the Washington Business Journal to serve as executive vice

president of parent company American City Business Journals. Orfinger will be responsible for the newspapers operating in 20 markets that employ more than 500 employees.

45351 ■ "The Organized Mind: Thinking Straight in the Age of Information Overload"
Pub: Penguin Group USA
Released: August 19, 2014. **Price:** , $27.95. **Description:** Leaders are expected to make more decisions faster than ever, despite the amount of information faced daily. Levitin uses the latest brain science to show how leaders are able to excel by successfully handling information flow. He shows how research into the cognitive neuroscience of attention and memory can be applied to everyday challenges, not only in managing a small business, but also in our personal lives.

45352 ■ "Organizing for Disaster: Lessons from the Military" in Business Horizons (November-December 2007, pp. 479)
Pub: Elsevier Technology Publications
Ed: Michael R. Weeks. **Price:** $35.95. **Description:** Design of resilient and robust organizational structures for disaster management is discussed. These structures must be planned before disasters in order to be more effective and efficient. **Availability:** PDF.

45353 ■ Other Essentials of Business Ownership and Management Development
Pub: PublishAmerica, Incorporated
Contact: Willem Meiners, Chief Executive Officer
Ed: Charles E. Shaw. **Price:** $24.95, Softcover. **Description:** Things a business owner, entrepreneur, or manager must be aware of in order to successfully manage a small business. **Availability:** Print.

45354 ■ Our Iceberg is Melting
Pub: St. Martin's Press
Contact: Sally Richardson, President
E-mail: sally.richardson@stmartins.com
Ed: John P. Kotter, Holger Rathgeber. **Released:** September 2006. **Price:** $19.99, Hardcover. **Description:** A fable about how to bring about change in a group.

45355 ■ Out of the Comfort Zone: Learning to Expect the Unexpected
Ed: Lisbeth Borbye. **Released:** May 10, 2010. **Price:** $35. **Description:** A collection of lectures covering technology, management and entrepreneurship.

45356 ■ "The Outcome of an Organization Overhaul" in Black Enterprise (Vol. 41, December 2010, No. 5)
Pub: Earl G. Graves Publishing Co. Inc.
Contact: Earl G. Graves, Jr., President
Ed: Tamara E. Holmes. **Description:** Savvy business owners understand the need for change in order to stay competitive and be successful. This article examines how to manage change as well as what strategies can help employees to get with the program faster.

45357 ■ Outsmart! How to Do What Your Competitors Can't
Pub: FT Press
Contact: Timothy C. Moore, Vice President
Ed: Jim Champy. **Released:** April 2008. **Price:** $22.99, hardcover. **Description:** Small business growth can be achieved through outsmarting your competition. The author identifies eight powerful ways to compete in the toughest marketplace.

45358 ■ Overcoming the Five Dysfunctions of a Team: A Field Guide for Leaders, Managers, and Facilitators
Pub: John Wiley & Sons Inc.
Contact: Stephen M. Smith, President
Ed: Patrick M. Lencioni. **Released:** February 2005. **Price:** $27.95. **Description:** Tools, exercises, assessment, and real-world examples for overcoming the five dysfunctions of a team. **Availability:** Print.

45359 ■ "Owning the Right Risks" in Harvard Business Review (Vol. 86, September 2008, No. 9, pp. 102)
Pub: Harvard Business Review Press
Contact: Peter E. Walsh, Director
Ed: Kevin Buehler, Andrew Freeman, Ron Hulme. **Description:** TXU Corp. is used to illustrate methods for successful risk management. The electric utility's

practices include determining which risks are natural, embedding risk in all processes and decisions, and organizing corporate governance around risk.

45360 ■ "Pack Mentality: Why Black Can Be Slimming" in Crain's Chicago Business (Vol. 31, April 21, 2008, No. 16, pp. 31)
Pub: Crain Communications Inc.
Contact: Todd Johnson, Publisher
Ed: Sarah A. Klein. **Description:** Jill Smart, the head of human resources for a company with 170,000 employees worldwide, frequently travels to India, London and Singapore; Ms. Smart provides advice concerning efficiency, time management and avoiding jet-lag.

45361 ■ "Part-Time Assignments" in Black Enterprise (Vol. 37, December 2006, No. 5, pp. 70)
Description: During critical change initiatives interim management, an employment model which uses senior-level executives to manage a special project or specific business function on a temporary basis, can have many benefits.

45362 ■ A Passion for Planning: Financials, Operations, Marketing, Management, and Ethics
Pub: University Press of America Inc.
Contact: Jed Lyons, President
E-mail: jlyons@nbnbooks.com
URL(s): rowman.com/ISBN/9780761818540. **Price:** $63.99, Individuals Paperback; £39.95, Individuals Paperback. **Covers:** Small business topics, including growth, manufacturing, technology, sales, distribution, services, resources, networking, and business ethics. **Entries include:** Contact details, Web sites.

45363 ■ "Passionate About Empowering Women" in Women In Business (Vol. 63, Spring 2011, No. 1, pp. 24)
Pub: American Business Women's Association
Contact: Lorie Burch, President
Ed: Leigh Elmore. **Description:** Krazy Coupon Ladies cofounder Joanie Demer shares her views about her book, 'Pick Another Checkout Lane, Honey', which she coauthored with Heather Wheeler. Demer believes using coupons is for everyone who wants to save money. She also believes that extreme couponing is not an exercise for those who lack organizational ability since it requires planning and discipline.

45364 ■ "Patience May Pay Off" in Barron's (Vol. 89, July 13, 2009, No. 28, pp. 30)
Ed: Johanna Bennett. **Description:** New CEO Craig Herkert can turn around Supervalu and their shares could double to $30 in three years from June 2009 according to one investment officer. Herkert knows how to run a lean and tight operation since he has worked for Albertsons and Wal-Mart in the past.

45365 ■ "Patricia Hemingway Hall: President, Chief Operating Officer, Health Care Service Corp." in Crain's Chicago Business (May 5, 2008)
Pub: Crain Communications Inc.
Contact: Todd Johnson, Publisher
Ed: Mike Colias. **Description:** Profile of Patricia Hemingway Hall who is the president and chief operating officer of Health Care Service Corp., a new strategy launched by Blue Cross & Blue Shield of Illinois; the new endeavor will emphasize wellness rather than just treatment across its four health plans.

45366 ■ "Pau Hana" in Hawaii Business (Vol. 53, December 2007, No. 6, pp. 118)
Pub: PacificBasin Communications
Ed: Cathy S. Cruz-George. **Description:** Presented are the hobbies of four Hawaii executives as well as the reason these hobbies are an important part of their lives and add to their ability to manage effectively. Mike Wilkins, for example, is not only Turtle Bay Resort's director of sales and marketing, but is also a glider pilot, while Aubrey Hawk Public Relations president Aubrey Hawk loves baking. The

interests of Queen Liliuokalani Trust's Thomas K. Kaulukukui Jr., Reyn Spooner's Tim McCullough, and Heide and Cook Ltd.'s Dexter S. Kekua, are discussed.

45367 ■ "Pay Fell for Many Baltimore Execs in '09" in Baltimore Business Journal (Vol. 28, July 2, 2010, No. 8, pp. 1)
Pub: Baltimore Business Journal
Ed: Gary Haber. **Description:** Compensation for the 100 highest-paid executives in the Baltimore, Maryland area decreased in 2009, compared with 2008. At least $1 million were received by 59 out of 100 executives in 2009, while 75 earned the said amount in 2008. Factors that contributed to the executives' decisions to take pay cuts are discussed.

45368 ■ Payback: Reaping the Rewards of Innovation
Pub: Harvard Business School Publishing
Ed: James P. Andrew, Harold L. Sirkin, John Butman. **Released:** January 09, 2007. **Price:** $29.95, hardcover. **Description:** Three different business innovation models are presented: integration, orchestration, and serving as licensor.

45369 ■ "Paychecks of Some Bank CEOs Have a Pre-Recession Look" in Boston Business Journal (Vol. 29, May 13, 2011, No. 1, pp. 1)
Pub: American City Business Journals, Inc.
Ed: Gary Haber. **Description:** The salaries of United States-based bank chief executive officers have increased to pre-recession levels. Wells Fargo and Company's John G. Stumpf received $17.6 million in 2010. Community bank executives, on the other hand, have seen minimal increases.

45370 ■ "Peer Power" in Business Strategy Review (Vol. 23, Spring 2012, No. 1, pp. 60)
Released: Spring 2012. **Description:** In troubled economic times, how do managers keep people engaged and motivated? Christoffer Ilehuus suggests the world of sports offers valuable inspiration.

45371 ■ "People Tools for Business: 50 Strategies for Building Success, Creating Wealth, and Finding Happiness"
Pub: Select Books
Contact: Rose Perl, Owner
Released: September 29, 2014. **Price:** , $16.95 paperback. **Description:** Tools required to enjoy success in both career and life are given. People Tools are help to develop self-confidence, improve management skills, and find constructive ways for Human Resource managers to fire workers and ways for workers to respond. Each people tool is concise and provides a straightforward strategy to produce positive results.

45372 ■ "The People Who Influence You the Most - Believe In You" in Women In Business (Vol. 62, September 2010, No. 3, pp. 9)
Pub: American Business Women's Association
Contact: Lorie Burch, President
Description: The president of the American Business Women's Association (ABWA) talks about her experiences in the organization. She believes that the dynamic women with whom she worked with helped her shape the organization into one that her predecessors believed it could become. The importance of dealing with challenges while making each experience an opportunity to learn is also discussed.

45373 ■ "Pep Talk" in Black Enterprise (Vol. 40, July 2010, No. 12, pp. 104)
Pub: Earl G. Graves Publishing Co. Inc.
Contact: Earl G. Graves, Jr., President
Ed: Tennille M. Robinson. **Description:** Advice for maintaining motivation in any small business is given.

45374 ■ "Perfecting the Process: Creating a More Efficient Organization On Your Terms" in Black Enterprise (Vol. 41, October 2010, No. 3)
Pub: Earl G. Graves Publishing Co. Inc.
Contact: Earl G. Graves, Jr., President
Ed: Tamara E. Holmes. **Description:** More than ever, entrepreneurs need to identify new ways of doing business in a cost-effective manner in order to expand their companies, while remaining true to their customer demands.

45375 ■ *"The Performer: Chess Prodigy Magnus Carlsen"* in *Canadian Business (Vol. 83, October 12, 2010, No. 17, pp. 79)*
Pub: Rogers Media Inc.
Contact: Tony Viner, President
Description: Magnus Carlsen, chess prodigy, talks about the importance of having a good feel for the game. He thinks that there are some similarities between chess and business, as both are about making good decisions in a limited amount of time. His views about motivation are also discussed.

45376 ■ *"The Performer: Soulpepper Theatre Company's Albert Shultz"* in *Canadian Business (Vol. 83, August 17, 2010, No. 13-14, pp. 71)*
Pub: Rogers Media Inc.
Contact: Tony Viner, President
Ed: Steve Maich. **Description:** Soulpepper Theater Company founder and actor/director Albert Schultz shares the key ingredient to his success both artistically and commercially. Schultz believes his success was a combination of passion and persistence, as well as team building. He believes his entrepreneurial impulse came when he began thinking of making opportunities instead of taking them.

45377 ■ *"Performing Leadership"* in *Business Strategy Review (Vol. 23, Spring 2012, No. 1, pp. 56)*
Released: Spring 2012. **Description:** Can you create a great performance in three days? Orchestra conductors do so time and time again. Bernhard Kerres investigates how they do it and what we can learn from them. Profile of Kerres in included.

45378 ■ *"Perks Still Popular: Jets May be Out, but CEO Benefits Abound"* in *Crain's Detroit Business (Vol. 25, June 22, 2009)*
Pub: Crain Communications Inc. - Detroit
Contact: Keith Crain, Chairman
Ed: Ryan Beene. **Description:** Benefits packages of local CEOs are outlined. Statistical data included.

45379 ■ *"Personal File: Esther Colwill"* in *Canadian Business (Vol. 80, April 23, 2007, No. 9, pp. 48)*
Description: A brief profile of Esther Colwill, senior manager at Deloitte & Touche LLP, including her achievements which are also presented.

45380 ■ *"Personal File: Malcolm Smillie"* in *Canadian Business (Vol. 80, April 23, 2007, No. 9, pp. 44)*
Description: A brief profile of Malcolm Smillie, marketing manager of 1-800-Got-Junk?, including his achievements which are also presented.

45381 ■ *"Pet Store Pro Adds New Curriculum"* in *Pet Product News (Vol. 66, February 2012, No. 2, pp. 2012)*
Description: Pet Store Pro, the Pet Industry Distributors Association's free online training program, is going to launch chapters of a curriculum intended to assist pet store managers learn effective approaches to motivate employees and boost profitability. Other management-level chapters to be added by Pet Store Pro throughout 2012 are listed.

45382 ■ *"Pete Carroll's Winning Rule: Protect Your Team"* in *Puget Sound Business Journal (Vol. 35, July 25, 2014, No. 14, pp. 12)*
Pub: American City Business Journals
Released: July 25, 2014. **Description:** Seattle Seahawks coach, Pete Carroll, has three simple rules for team success and the first rule is to always protect the team. The rule is also important in every workplace because it will help align the workers attention to their behavior. Seven ways to protect the team are outlined.

45383 ■ *"Peter Bynoe Trades Up"* in *Black Enterprise (Vol. 38, July 2008, No. 12, pp. 30)*
Pub: Earl G. Graves Publishing Co. Inc.
Contact: Earl G. Graves, Jr., President
Description: Chicago-based Loop Capital Markets L.L.C. has named Peter Bynoe managing director of corporate finance. Bynoe was previously a senior partner at the law firm DLA Piper U.S. L.L.P., where he worked on stadium deals.

45384 ■ *"Peter Gilgan"* in *Canadian Business (Vol. 82, April 27, 2009, No. 7, pp. 58)*
Pub: Rogers Media Inc.
Contact: Tony Viner, President
Ed: Calvin Leung. **Description:** Mattamy Homes Ltd. president and chief executive officer Peter Gilgan believes that their business model of building communities in an organized way brings advantages to the firm and for their customers. He also believes in adopting their product prices to new market realities. Gilgan considers the approvals regime in Ontario his biggest challenge in the last 20 years.

45385 ■ *"PhotoMedex Bouncing Back from Brink of Bankruptcy"* in *Philadelphia Business Journal (Vol. 30, January 6, 2012, No. 47, pp. 1)*
Pub: American City Business Journal
Description: PhotoMedex Inc. has managed to avoid bankruptcy through reorganization. The company appointed Dennis McGrath as president and chief executive. Details of the business reorganization plans are covered.

45386 ■ *Pink Slip Power!: Recover and Succeed It's Up To You!*
Pub: Infinity Publishing
Contact: Tom Gregory, President
Ed: Wade J. Wnuk. **Released:** 2004. **Price:** $9.95. **Description:** Advice is given to those facing loss of employment. The book discusses issues such as: restraining emotions before reacting to a severance package ceasing to brood on the past, focusing on the future, networking and looking for hidden job opportunities, preparing resumes, and gearing up for interviews. Four chapters cover ideas for facing reality, formulating a plan, promoting one's self, and persisting in the face of adversity.

45387 ■ *"Playing to Win: How Strategy Really Works"*
Pub: Harvard Business Review Press
Contact: Peter E. Walsh, Director
Released: February 5, 2013. **Price:** , $27.00. **Description:** A.G. Lafley outlines his business strategies used to double Proctor and Gamble's sales, quadruple its profits, and increase its market value by more than $100 billion when he led the company from 2000 to 2009. The book shows leaders in any type of business how to deal everyday actions with larger strategic business goals that are clear, essential parts that will determine the company's success. Five strategic choices are outlined.

45388 ■ *"The Play's the Thing"* in *Business Strategy Review (Vol. 21, Summer 2010, No. 2, pp. 58)*
Pub: Blackwell Publishers Ltd.
Ed: Michael G. Jacobides. **Description:** Those who study and plan strategies risk falling into the traps that maps, graphs, charts and matrices present. A better strategy might be using a playscript that can reveal the unfolding plots of business far better than traditional strategic tools as the landscapes shifts.

45389 ■ *"Political Environments and Business Strategy: Implications for Managers"* in *Business Horizons (Vol. 51, January-February 2008)*
Pub: Elsevier Advanced Technology Publications
Ed: Gerald D. Keim, Amy J. Hillman. **Description:** Various government bodies and business organizations work together in shaping new business opportunities and policies that arise from globalization. Presented is framework of public policy considerations for business managers. The framework is based on Nobel laureate Douglas North's work.

45390 ■ *The Portable MBA in Entrepreneurship*
Pub: John Wiley & Sons Inc.
Contact: Stephen M. Smith, President
Ed: William D. Bygrave, Andrew Zacharakis. **Released:** 4th Edition. **Price:** $34.95, hardcover. **Description:** An updated and revised new edition of the comprehensive guide to modern entrepreneurship that tracks the core curriculum of leading business schools.

45391 ■ *"Positive Transformational Change"* in *Indoor Comfort Marketing (Vol. 70, April 2011, No. 4, pp. 30)*
Pub: Industry Publications Inc.
Contact: Shirleen Dorman, Editor
Ed: Blaine Fox. **Description:** Management changes taking place at Shark Bites HVAC firm are discussed.

45392 ■ *"Potash Sale Must Be Blocked"* in *Canadian Business (Vol. 83, October 12, 2010, No. 17, pp. 24)*
Pub: Rogers Media Inc.
Contact: Tony Viner, President
Ed: Kasey Coholan. **Description:** Chief executive officers (CEOs) and corporate leaders in Canada are concerned about the possible sale of Potash Corporation to foreign buyers. A Compas Inc. poll recently asked CEOs whether the Canadian Government should step in to block the sale of the country's largest fertilizer firm.

45393 ■ *"The Power of ABWA"* in *Women In Business (Vol. 62, September 2010, No. 3, pp. 36)*
Pub: American Business Women's Association
Contact: Lorie Burch, President
Ed: Leigh Elmore. **Description:** Information about the internship received by Erica Rockley at American Business Women's Association (ABWA) headquarters is presented. Rockley received heartfelt professional advice the days she spent at the office. She also learned the importance of networking.

45394 ■ *Power Ambition Glory: The Stunning Parallels between Great Leaders of the Ancient World and Today... and the Lessons You Can Learn*
Pub: Crown Business
Ed: Steve Forbes, John Prevas. **Released:** June 01, 2010. **Price:** $16, paperback; $13.99. **Description:** An examination into the lives of the ancient world's greatest leaders and the lessons they have for today's business leaders. **Availability:** PrintE-book.

45395 ■ *"Power Cues: The Subtle Science of Leading Groups, Persuading Others, and Maximizing Your Personal Impact"*
Pub: Harvard Business Review Press
Contact: Peter E. Walsh, Director
Released: April 22, 2014. **Price:** , $25.00. **Description:** Renowned speaking coach and communication expert, Nick Morgan, shows how humans are programmed to respond to the nonverbal cues of others. He teaches business leaders and entrepreneurs how to take control of their communications in order to communicate more effectively while commanding influence.

45396 ■ *The Power of Full Engagement: Managing Energy, Not Time, is the Key to High Performance and Personal Renewal*
Pub: Free Press/Simon & Schuster Inc.
Ed: Jim Loehr, Tony Schwartz. **Released:** January 2005. **Price:** $15.99, paperback. **Description:** The book presents a program to help stressed individuals find more purpose in their work and ways to better handle overburdened relationships. **Availability:** Print.

45397 ■ *"Power In the Boardroom"* in *Black Enterprise (Vol. 38, February 2008, No. 7, pp. 112)*
Pub: Earl G. Graves Publishing Co. Inc.
Contact: Earl G. Graves, Jr., President
Ed: Derek T. Dingle. **Description:** Comprehensive list of Black corporate directors for 250 of the largest companies in the U.S.; these leaders play a critical role in business development.

45398 ■ *"The Power of Noticing: What the Best Leaders See"*
Pub: Simon & Schuster Adult Publishing Group
Contact: Carolyn Reidy, President
E-mail: carolyn.reidy@simonandschuster.com
Released: August 5, 2014. **Price:** , $28.00. **Description:** A guide to help entrepreneurs and managers gain the advantage in negotiations, decision making, and leadership skills. Instruction is given to see and evaluate information that others overlook.

45399 ■ "Power Play" in Harvard Business Review (Vol. 88, July-August 2010, No. 7-8, pp. 84)
Pub: Harvard Business School Publishing
Ed: Jeffrey Pfeffer. **Description:** Guidelines include in-depth understanding of resources at one's disposal, relentlessness that still provides opponents with opportunities to save face, and a determination not to be put off by the processes of politics.

45400 ■ The Power of a Positive No: How to Say No and Still Get to Yes
Pub: Random Housing Publishing Group
Ed: William Ury. **Released:** December 26, 2007. **Price:** $16; C$19.95. **Description:** According to the author, a positive no begins with yes and ends with yes. **Availability:** Print; E-book.

45401 ■ The Power of Pull: How Small Moves, Smartly Made, Can Set Big Things in Motion
Pub: Basic Books
Contact: Elizabeth Maguire, Publisher
Ed: John Hagel, III, John Seely Brown, Lang Davison. **Price:** $27.50, hardcover; C$33, hardcover. **Description:** Examination of how we can effectively address the most pressing challenges in a rapidly changing and increasingly interdependent world is addressed. New ways in which passionate thinking, creative solutions, and committed action can and will make it possible for small businesses owners to seize opportunities and remain in step with change. **Availability:** Print.

45402 ■ "Powerlessness Corrupts" in Harvard Business Review (Vol. 88, July-August 2010, No. 7-8, pp. 36)
Pub: Harvard Business School Publishing
Ed: Rosabeth Moss Kanter. **Description:** Studies show that individuals who perceive that they are being treated poorly and denied sufficient freedom for a certain level of autonomy are more likely to act negatively.

45403 ■ "PR Veteran Zeppos Sells to Laughlin" in Business Journal Milwaukee (Vol. 29, July 26, 2012, No. 41, pp. 1)
Pub: American City Business Journals, Inc.
Contact: Whitney Shaw, President
Ed: Rich Kirchen. **Released:** July 6, 2012. **Description:** Public relations firm Zeppos & Associates was sold to Milwaukee-based advertising agency Laughlin Constable. Laughlin revealed that the deal will double the size of its public relations practice. Zeppos owner, Evan Zeppos, says the move will allow him to focus on serving clients instead of doing administrative duties.

45404 ■ "Practices, Governance, and Politics: Applying MacIntyre's Ethics to Business" in Business Ethics Quarterly (Vol. 24, April 2014, No. 2, pp. 229)
Pub: Business Ethics Quarterly
Released: April 2014. **Description:** An argument to apply MacIntyre's positive moral theory to business ethics is problematic due to the cognitive closure of MacIntyre's concept of practice. The paper begins by outlining the notion of a practice, before turning Moore's attempt to provide a MacIntyrean account of corporate governance. It argues that Moore's attempt is mismatched with MacIntyre's account of moral education. Because the notion of practices resists general application it is argued that a negative application, which focuses on regulation, is more plausible. Large-scale regulation, usually thought anti-ethical to MacIntyre's advocacy of small-scale politics, has the potential to facilitate practice-based work and reveals that MacIntyre's own work can be used against his pessimism about the modern order. Furthermore, the conception of regulation can show how management is more amenable to ethical understanding than MacIntyre's work is often taken to imply.

45405 ■ Predictable Results in Unpredictable Times
Pub: RosettaBooks LLC
Contact: Marshall Sonenshine, Director
Ed: Stephen R. Covey, Bob Whitman, Breck England. **Released:** August 07, 2009. **Price:** $12.41, hard-

cover. **Description:** Four essentials for getting great performance in good times and bad are outlined for any small business. **Availability:** Print.

45406 ■ "Prevent Disasters In Design Outsourcing" in Harvard Business Review (Vol. 86, September 2008, No. 9, pp. 30)
Pub: Harvard Business Review Press
Contact: Peter E. Walsh, Director
Ed: Jason Amaral, Geoffrey Parker. **Description:** Factors that could compromise the quality and success of product platform outsourcing are examined including misaligned objectives and inadequate version control.

45407 ■ "Price War: Managerial Salaries Are Beating the National Average, But Maybe Not for Long" in Canadian Business (March 31, 2008)
Pub: Rogers Media Inc.
Contact: Tony Viner, President
Ed: Megan Harman. **Description:** Real average hourly earnings of managers increase by 20 percent in ten years as companies increase wages to avoid the risk of losing key managers to the competition and in preparation for the retirement of baby boomers. Tough market conditions affect management more since their incentives are tied to individual and corporate performance.

45408 ■ "Prichard the Third" in Canadian Business (Vol. 83, October 12, 2010, No. 17, pp. 34)
Pub: Rogers Media Inc.
Contact: Tony Viner, President
Ed: Thomas Watson. **Description:** Robert Prichard, the new chair of international business law firm Torys, talks about his current role; his job involved advising clients, representing the firm, being part of the leadership team, and recruiting talent. He considers 'Seven Days in Tibet' as the first book to have an influence on his world view.

45409 ■ "Profile: Charles Handy" in Business Strategy Review (Vol. 21, Summer 2010, No. 2, pp. 86)
Pub: Blackwell Publishers Ltd.
Ed: Stuart Crainer. **Description:** In a new series, profiles of a major thinker who has made a significant difference in how organizations are managed and how business careers are shaped are presented.

45410 ■ "Profile: Lynda Gratton" in Business Strategy Review (Vol. 21, Autumn 2010, No. 3, pp. 74)
Pub: Blackwell Publishers Ltd.
Ed: Stuart Crainer. **Description:** The early 20th Century marked the dawn of modern enterprise management and no one influenced its practice more than Frederick W. Taylor, inventor of 'scientific management'. The early 21st Century marks a radical transformation of management.

45411 ■ "Profile: Lynda Gratton" in Business Strategy Review (Vol. 21, Autumn 2010, No. 3, pp. 74)
Pub: John Wiley & Sons Inc. Scientific, Technical, Medical, and Scholarly Div. (Wiley-Blackwell)
Contact: William J. Pesce, Manager
E-mail: wpesce@wiley.com
Ed: Stuart Crainer. **Description:** The early 20th Century marked the dawn of modern enterprise management, and no one influenced its practice more than Frederick W. Taylor, inventor of 'scientific management'. This radical transformation of management and among the few thinkers most influencing this transformation is Lynda Gratton, London Business School Professor of Management Practice.

45412 ■ "The Profitability of Mobility" in Entrepreneur (Vol. 37, September 2009, No. 9, pp. 98)
Pub: Entrepreneur Press
Contact: Perlman Neil, President
Ed: John Daley. **Description:** Wireless Zone franchisee Jonah Engler says he manages the business by hiring managers that could do the job. He has given

his employees small equity ownership in the company. He also says great service and referrals have contributed to his business' growth.

45413 ■ Project Management for Small Business Made Easy
Pub: Entrepreneur Press
Contact: Perlman Neil, President
Ed: Sid Kemp. **Released:** 2006. **Description:** Strategies for implementing project management for small business are offered.

45414 ■ "Project Managers' Creed: Learn It, Live It" in Contractor (Vol. 56, November 2009, No. 11, pp. 46)
Pub: Penton Media, Inc.
Ed: H. Kent Craig. **Description:** Project managers should take the health and safety of their subordinates above all else. A manager should deal with the things that distract him from his job before starting a day on the site. The manager should maintain a comfortable and relaxed attitude with his employees.

45415 ■ "Public Opinion" in Entrepreneur (Vol. 36, April 2008, No. 4, pp. 28)
Pub: Entrepreneur Press
Contact: Perlman Neil, President
Description: According to a 2007 report from Group and Organization Management, women in top positions can lead publicly traded companies to stock price and earnings growth. Some women business owners say that going public has provided them with the capital to grow. Details on the potential of women-managed publicly traded companies are discussed.

45416 ■ "Putting an End to End-of-Year Reviews" in Inc. (December 2007, pp. 58, 61)
Pub: Gruner and Jahr USA Publishing Co.
Contact: J. Russell Denson, President
Ed: Scott Westcott. **Description:** Performance assessments can be used in place of blunt employee reviews in order to create effective annual reviews.

45417 ■ "The Puzzle of Our Productivity" in Canadian Business (Vol. 83, September 14, 2010, No. 15, pp. 22)
Pub: Rogers Media Inc.
Contact: Tony Viner, President
Ed: Rachel Madison. **Description:** Industry Canada economist Annette Ryan revealed in a presentation to the Canadian Association for Business Economics that growth in Canadian labor productivity has steadily declined since the 1980s. Ryan believes that business decisions have played an important role in the poor productivity results. Other details of the findings are presented.

45418 ■ "Q&A: Celestica's Craig Muhlhauser" in Canadian Business (Vol. 81, September 15, 2008, No. 14-15, pp. 6)
Pub: Rogers Media Inc.
Contact: Tony Viner, President
Ed: Andrew Wahl. **Description:** Interview with Craig Muhlhauser who is the CEO of Celestica, a manufacturing company that provides services for the electronics sector; Muhlhauser discusses the company's restructuring program, which he feels was the secret to their surprising first-quarter results. Muhlhauser states that the company is operating with more forward visibility and that understanding the opportunities during the current economic situation presents the biggest challenge.

45419 ■ "Q&A Patrick Pichette" in Canadian Business (Vol. 81, October 13, 2008, No. 17, pp. 6)
Ed: Andrew Wahl. **Description:** Patrick Pichette finds challenge in taking over the finances of an Internet company that has a market cap of about $140 billion. He feels, however, that serving as Google's chief financial officer is nothing compared to running Bell Canada Enterprises (BCE). Pichette's other views on Google and BCE are presented.

45420 ■ "Quality Performance of SMEs in a Developing Economy: Direct and Indirect Effects of Service Innovation and Entrepreneurial Orientation" in Journal of Business & Industrial Marketing (Vol. 29, July

2014, No. 6)
Pub: Emerald Group Publishing Inc.
Released: July 2014. **Description:** A study was conducted to investigate the effects of innovation and EO (entrepreneurial orientation) on organizational performance in Asian small enterprise context. Strategic management literature and the relationship between EO, innovation, and quality performance was tested. The results indicated that a noteworthy direct and indirect positive relationship exists between EO dimensions, innovation, and quality performance.

45421 ■ *"QuikTrip Makes Fortune 'Best' List"*
in Tulsa World (January 22, 2010)
Pub: Tulsa World
Contact: Debbie Jackson, Director, Library Services
Ed: Kyle Arnold. **Description:** According to a list released by Fortune Magazine, QuikTrip Corp. is once again ranked among the best companies in the country to work for due to the core values and culture held by the company's management.

45422 ■ *"Race and Gender Diversity: A Discussion of Recent Findings" in Business Horizons (November-December 2007, pp. 445)*
Pub: Elsevier Technology Publications
Ed: James C. Wimbush. **Price:** $35.95. **Description:** Research conducted on diversity building, employee recruitment, gender issues in management, and pay inequality from 2006 through present are discussed. Diversity conditions and attitudes toward it are slowly improving based on these findings. **Availability:** PDF.

45423 ■ *"Randy Perreira, Hawaii Government Employees Association (HGEA), Executive Director" in Hawaii Business (Vol. 53, February 2008, No. 8, pp. 28)*
Pub: PacificBasin Communications
Ed: David K. Choo. **Description:** Randy Perreira is recently named executive director of Hawaii Government Employees Association. He talks about how he was shaped growing up with a father who was a labor leader and how the challenges in 2008 compare with those in the time of his father. He also shares his thoughts about the importance of employees fighting for their rights.

45424 ■ *"The RBC Dynasty Continues" in Globe & Mail (January 30, 2006, pp. B1)*
Ed: Gordon Pitts. **Description:** The details on business growth of Royal Bank of Canada, under chief executive officer Gordon Nixon, are presented.

45425 ■ *"The Real Job of Boards" in Business Strategy Review (Vol. 21, Autumn 2010, No. 3, pp. 36)*
Pub: John Wiley & Sons Inc. Scientific, Technical, Medical, and Scholarly Div. (Wiley-Blackwell)
Contact: William J. Pesce, Manager
E-mail: wpesce@wiley.com
Ed: Harry Korine, Marcus Alexander, Pierre-Yves Gomez. **Description:** Widely seen as the key for ensuring quality in corporate governance, the board of directors has been a particular focal point for reform. The authors believe that more leadership at board level could avert many corporate crises in the future.

45426 ■ *The Real Leadership Lessons of Steve Jobs: Six Months After Jobs' Death, the Author Of His Best-Selling Biography Identifies the Practices That Every CEO Can Try to Emulate*
Pub: Harvard Business Review Press
Contact: Peter E. Walsh, Director
Ed: Walter Isaacson. **Description:** Fourteen separate leadership practices of Steve Jobs are listed. These include focus, simplify, assume end-to-end responsibility, leapfrog when behind, place products ahead of profits, engage in face-to-face, understood both the details and the big picture, blend the sciences with the humanities, push for perfection, and stay hungry.

45427 ■ *"Real-Life Coursework for Real-Life Business People" in Women In Business (Vol. 63, Summer 2011, No. 2, pp. 22)*
Pub: American Business Women's Association
Contact: Lorie Burch, President
Ed: Leigh Elmore. **Description:** American Business Women's Association National Women's Leadership Conference provides members with academic business training courses. Members can take a variety of MBA-level courses that are taught by University of Kansas School of Business professors. Courses include marketing, management, leadership and communication and decision making.

45428 ■ *Reality-Based Leadership: Ditch the Drama, Restore Sanity to the Workplace, & Turn Excuses into Results*
Pub: Jossey-Bass
Ed: Cy Wakeman. **Released:** August 2010. **Price:** $27.95, hardcover; $18.99. **Description:** Recent polls show that 71 percent of workers think about quitting their jobs every day. That number would be shocking if people actually were quitting. Worse, they go to work, punching time clocks and collecting pay checks, while checked out emotionally. Cy Wakeman reveals how to be the kind of leader who changes the way people think about and perceive their circumstances, one who deals with the facts, clarifies roles, gives clean and direct feedback, and insists that everyone do the same without drama or defensiveness. **Availability:** PrintE-book.

45429 ■ *Reality Check: The Irreverent Guide to Outsmarting, Outmanaging, and Outmarketing Your Competition*
Pub: Dutton Children's Books
Contact: Lauri Hornik, President
Ed: Guy Kawasaki. **Price:** $18, Paperback. **Description:** Marketing guru and entrepreneur, Guy Kawasaki, provides a compilation of his blog posts on all aspects of starting and operating a business.

45430 ■ *"Recession Drags Down CEO Pay: Full Impact May Not Have Played Out" in Crain's Detroit Business (Vol. 25, June 22, 2009, No. 25)*
Pub: Crain Communications Inc. - Detroit
Contact: Keith Crain, Chairman
Ed: Ryan Beene. **Description:** Median overall compensation package for Detroit's top-compensated 50 CEOs was down 10.67 percent from $2.3 million in 2007 to $2.06 million in 2008. Statistical data included.

45431 ■ *"The Recession: Problem or Opportunity" in Women In Business (Vol. 61, October-November 2009, No. 5, pp. 34)*
Pub: American Business Women's Association
Contact: Lorie Burch, President
Ed: J. Douglas Bate. **Description:** Business organizations' success during a recession is based on how management views the economic situation. The recession may be deemed as a setback or may be visualized as an opportunity that has to be grabbed for the organization. Suggestions on what management should do in the opportunity-creating or proactive approach are also highlighted.

45432 ■ *"Reduce the Risk of Failed Financial Judgments" in Harvard Business Review (Vol. 86, July-August 2008, No. 8, pp. 24)*
Pub: Harvard Business Review Press
Contact: Peter E. Walsh, Director
Ed: Robert G. Eccles, Edward J. Riedl. **Description:** Utilization of business consultants, evaluators, appraisers, and actuaries to decrease financial management risks is discussed.

45433 ■ *"Reinventing Management" in Harvard Business Review (Vol. 88, July-August 2010, No. 7-8, pp. 167)*
Ed: Roberta Fusaro. **Description:** Review of the book, 'Reinventing Management' is presented.

45434 ■ *"The Reinvention of Management" in Strategy and Leadership (Vol. 39, March-April 2011, No. 2, pp. 9)*
Pub: Emerald Group Publishing Inc.
Ed: Stephen Denning. **Description:** An examination found that critical changes in management practice involves five shifts. These shifts involve the firm's goals, model of coordination, the role of managers and values practiced. Other findings of the study are discussed.

45435 ■ *"The Relationship Between Boards and Planning In Family Businesses" in Family Business Review (Vol. 19, March 2006, No. 1, pp. 65)*
Pub: Family Firm Institute
Contact: Judy L. Green, President
Ed: Timothy Blumentritt. **Description:** Study determining the extent of control exercised by board of directors and advisory boards on business planning within family-owned businesses is covered.

45436 ■ *"Relocation, Relocation, Relocation" in Conde Nast Portfolio (Vol. 2, June 2008, No. 6, pp. 36)*
Ed: Michelle Leder. **Description:** Perks regarding executive relocation are discussed.

45437 ■ *Remarkable Leadership*
Ed: Kevin Eikenberry. **Released:** August 30, 2007. **Price:** $27.95. **Description:** Handbook for anyone wishing to be an outstanding business leader; the framework and a mechanism for learning new things and applying current knowledge in a practical to any business situation is outlined.

45438 ■ *"Remind Managers to Avoid Talk of Employee Longevity" in HR Specialist (Vol. 8, September 2010, No. 9, pp. 3)*
Description: Supervisors need to understand that casual conversations can be used against an organization in law suits.

45439 ■ *"A Renewed Sisterhood" in Women in Business (Vol. 64, Summer 2012, No. 2, pp. 6)*
Pub: American Business Women's Association
Contact: Lorie Burch, President
Ed: Rene Street. **Released:** Summer 2012. **Description:** The American Business Women's Association (ABWA) regional conference highlighted a new sense of enthusiasm and sisterhood as well as effective visioning exercise and breakout sessions. The ABWA National Women's Leadership Conference in October 2012 will feature the graduates of the Kansas University MBA Essentials Program and keynote speakers Bob Eubanks and Francine Ward.

45440 ■ *"Research Highlights Disengaged Workforce" in Workforce Management (Vol. 88, November 16, 2009, No. 12, pp. 22)*
Pub: Crain Communications Inc.
Contact: Rance E. Crain, President
Ed: Ed Frauenheim. **Description:** Most researchers have documented a drop in employee engagement during the recession due to such factors as layoffs, restructuring and less job security.

45441 ■ *"Research Note" in International Journal of Globalisation and Small Business (Vol. 4, September 21, 2010, No. 1, pp. 92)*
Pub: Publishers Communication Group
Contact: Doug Wright, Director
Ed: Alexander Bode, Tobias B. Talmon l'Armee, Simon Alig. **Description:** The cluster concept has steadily increased its importance during the past years both from practitioners' and researchers' points of view. Simultaneously, many corporate networks are established. Researchers from different areas (business management, economic social and geographical science) are trying to explain both phenomena.

45442 ■ *"Research in Personnel and Human Resources Management, Vol. 28" in Human Resource Management (Vol. 49, July-August 2010, No. 4)*
Pub: John Wiley
Ed: Mukta Kulkarni. **Description:** An overview of the book, 'Research in Personnel and Human Resources Management', Vol. 28 is presented.

45443 ■ *The Restaurant Manager's Handbook: How to Set Up, Operate, and Manage a Financially Successful Food Service Operation*
Pub: Atlantic Publishing Co.
Contact: Amanda Miller, Manager
E-mail: amiller@atlantic-pub.com
Ed: Douglas R. Brown. **Released:** September 25, 2007. **Price:** $79.95. **Description:** Insight is offered on running a successful food service business. Nine

new chapters detail restaurant layout, new equipment, principles for creating a safer work environment, and new effective techniques to interview, hire, train, and manage employees.

45444 ■ *"Rethinking the Organization" in Strategy & Leadership (Vol. 38, September-October 2010, No. 5, pp. 13-19)*
Pub: Emerald Inc.

Ed: Stephen Denning. **Description:** A study identifies the changes needed to be adopted by top managers to achieve game-changing innovation at an organization-wide level. Findings indicate that CEOs should practice pull management in order to nurture fruitful communication between employees and customers and achieve organizational involvement of customers.

45445 ■ *"Retiring Baby Boomers and Dissatisfied Gen-Xers Cause..Brain Drain" in Agency Sales Magazine (Vol. 39, November 2009, No. 10)*
Ed: Denise Kelly. **Description:** Due to the impending retirement of the baby boomers a critical loss of knowledge and experience in businesses will result. Creating a plan to address this loss of talent centered on the development of the younger generation is discussed.

45446 ■ *"Risk Management Starts at the Top" in Business Strategy Review (Vol. 21, Spring 2010, No. 1, pp. 18)*
Pub: John Wiley & Sons Inc. Scientific, Technical, Medical, and Scholarly Div. (Wiley-Blackwell)

Contact: William J. Pesce, Manager

E-mail: wpesce@wiley.com

Ed: Paul Strebel, Hongze Lu. **Description:** Authors question why, at the end of 2008, Citigroup, Merrill Lynch and UBS had well over $40 billion in sub-prime write-downs and credit losses, while some of their competitors were much less exposed. Their research into the situation revealed correlations of great import to today's firms.

45447 ■ *"The Risks and Rewards of Speaking Up: Managerial Responses to Employee Voice" in Academy of Management Journal (Vol. 55, August 1, 2012, No. 4, pp. 851)*
Pub: Academy of Management

Contact: Ming-Jer Chen, President

Ed: Ethan R. Burris. **Description:** The ways in which managers respond to suggestions made by employees is examined. Positive and negative managerial reactions to employees speaking up depend on whether the type of voice exhibited is challenging or supportive as well as on the psychological mechanisms of loyalty and threat.

45448 ■ *"Robert S. McNamara and the Evolution of Modern Management" in Harvard Business Review (Vol. 88, December 2010, No. 12, pp. 86)*
Pub: Harvard Business School Publishing

Ed: Phil Rosenzweig. **Description:** A chronicle of the emergence and development of Robert S. McNamara's management skills and perspectives, focusing on the role of his idealism. Lessons learned during the course of the Vietnam Ware are also delineated.

45449 ■ *"The Role of Human and Financial Capital in the Profitability and Growth of Women-Owned Small Firms" in Journal of Small Business Management*
Pub: Blackwell Publishing Inc.

Contact: Gordon Tibbitts, III, President

Ed: Susan Coleman. **Description:** Examines the relationship between the human and financial capital in both men and women-owned businesses and firm performance in the service and retail sectors.

45450 ■ *"The Role of Leadership In Successful International Mergers and Acquisitions: Why Renault-Nissan Succeeded and DaimlerChrysler-Mitsubishi Failed" in Human Resource Management (Vol. 51,May-*

June 2012, No. 3, pp. 433-456)
Pub: John Wiley & Sons Inc.

Contact: Stephen M. Smith, President

Ed: Carol Gill. **Description:** The effects of national and organizational culture on the performance of Nissan and Mitsubishi after their mergers with Renault and DaimlerChrysler respectively are examined. Japanese national culture was found to influence organizational culture and human resource management practices, while leadership affected the success of their turnaround efforts.

45451 ■ *The Role of the Non-Executive Director in the Small to Medium-Sized Business*
Pub: Palgrave Macmillan

Contact: Lisa Dunn, Manager

E-mail: l.dunn@palgrave.com

Ed: John Smithson. **Released:** November 2003. **Price:** $145, hardcover. **Description:** The role of the non-executive director in a small to medium-sized business is examined. **Availability:** Print.

45452 ■ *"Ron Carpenter" in Crain's Cleveland Business (Vol. 30, June 29, 2009, No. 25, pp. 12)*
Pub: Crain Communications Inc.

Ed: Dan Shingler. **Description:** Profile of Ron Carpenter, owner of Production Tool Company located in Twinsburg, Ohio. Carpenter was forced to lay off half of his staff of 14 workers after the auto business tanked. He believes it was the single most difficult decision he had to make as a manager.

45453 ■ *"The Rypple Effect; Performance Management" in The Economist (Vol. 390, January 3, 2009, No. 8612, pp. 48)*
Description: New companies such as Rypple, a new, web-based service, claim that they can satisfy the Net Generation's need for frequent assessments while easing the burden this creates for management.

45454 ■ *"Safety Managers Need to Be Safety Experts" in Indoor Comfort Marketing (Vol. 70, May 2011, No. 5, pp. 10)*
Pub: Industry Publications Inc.

Contact: Shirleen Dorman, Editor

Ed: Mike Hodge. **Description:** It is imperative to have a good safety manager in place for all heating and cooling firms.

45455 ■ *"St. Rose Professor Builds Contractors and Micro-Doctors" in Business Review, Albany New York (Vol. 34, December 31, 2007, No. 39)*
Pub: American City Business Journals, Inc.

Ed: Robin K. Cooper. **Description:** Mike Mathews is an associate professor at the College of Saint Rose School of Business and one of the founders of the Center for Micro Enterprises Development, which provides training programs on business planning and management. Details of the business school's curricula and foundations are discussed.

45456 ■ *"Salary Hike for Managers Reflects Demand" in Farmer's Weekly (March 28, 2008, No. 320)*
Description: Discusses the Institute of Agricultural Management and its survey of farm managers' pay and conditions; farm managers are getting paid 25 percent more than in 2003.

45457 ■ *Salesforce.com Secrets of Success: Best Practices for Growth and Profitability*
Pub: Prentice Hall Business Publishing

Contact: Jerome Grant, President

Ed: David Taber. **Released:** May 05, 2009. **Price:** $49.99. **Description:** Guide for using Salesforce.com; it provides insight into navigating through user groups, management, sales, marketing and IT departments in order to achieve the best results.

45458 ■ *"Sandi Jackson: Alderman, 7th Ward, City of Chicago" in Crain's Chicago Business (Vol. 31, May 5, 2008, No. 18, pp. 31)*
Pub: Crain Communications Inc.

Contact: Todd Johnson, Publisher

Ed: Sarah A. Klein. **Description:** Profile of Sandi Jackson who is an alderman of the 7th ward of the city of Chicago and is addressing issues such as

poverty and crime as well as counting on a plan to develop the former USX Corp. steel mill to revitalize the area's economic climate.

45459 ■ *Sarbanes-Oxley for Dummies*
Pub: John Wiley & Sons Inc.

Contact: Stephen M. Smith, President

Ed: Jill Gilbert Welytok. **Released:** 2nd Edition. **Price:** $21.95, paperback; $14.99. **Description:** Provides the latest Sarbanes-Oxley (SOX) legislation with procedures to safely and effectively reduce compliance costs. Topics include way to: establish SOX standards for IT professionals, minimize compliances costs for every aspect of a business, survive a Section 404 audit, avoid litigation under SOX, anticipate future rules and trends, create a post-SOX paper trail, increase a company's standing and reputation, work with SOX in a small business, meet new SOX standards, build a board that can't be bought, and to comply with all SOX management mandates. **Availability:** PrintE-book.

45460 ■ *"Save the Date" in Barron's (Vol. 90, September 13, 2010, No. 37, pp. 35)*
Pub: Barron's Editorial & Corporate Headquarters

Ed: Mark Veverka. **Description:** Mark Hurd is the new Co-President of Oracle after being forced out at Hewlett-Packard where he faced a harassment complaint. HP fired Hurd due to expense account malfeasance. Hurd is also set to speak at an Oracle trade show in San Francisco on September 20, 2010.

45461 ■ *"Scaling Up Excellence: Getting to More Without Settling for Less"*
Pub: Crown Business Books

Released: February 4, 2014. **Price:** , $26.00. **Description:** Authors have dedicated ten years to finding out what it takes to build and discover exemplary performance in businesses to help recharge organizations and help them to grow. They reveal how the best leaders and teams develop, grow, and instill the right mindsets in workers.

45462 ■ *"Scholarships for Minority Students" in Occupational Outlook Quarterly (Vol. 54, Fall 2010, No. 3, pp. 25)*
Pub: U.S. Department of Labor Bureau of Labor Statistics

Contact: Philip L. Rones, Manager

E-mail: rones.philip@bls.gov

Description: Gates Millennium Scholars scholarship is awarded to minority students with leadership skills, a good GPA, and college aspirations.

45463 ■ *Science Lessons: What the Business of Biotech Taught Me About Management*
Pub: Harvard Business Review Press

Contact: Peter E. Walsh, Director

Ed: Gordon Binder, Philip Bashe. **Released:** April 15, 2008. **Price:** $35, hardcover. **Description:** Former CFO of biotechnology startup Amgen and veteran of Ford Motor Company provides a universal guide to management based on some of the same scientific principles used to create new drugs. **Availability:** Print.

45464 ■ *"Scripps Networks" in Brandweek (Vol. 49, April 21, 2008, No. 16, pp. SR12)*
Pub: Nielsen Business Media Inc.

Contact: Howard Appelbaum, President

Ed: Anthony Crupi. **Description:** Provides contact information for sales and marketing personnel for the Scripps networks as well as a listing of the station's top programming and an analysis of the current season and the target audience for those programs running in the current season. Scripps networks include HGTV and the Food Network. HGTV boasts on of the industry's best commercial-retention averages, keeping nearly 97 percent of its viewers during advertising breaks.

45465 ■ *"Scrum: The Art of Doing Twice the Work in Half the Time"*
Pub: Crown Business

Released: September 30, 2014. **Price:** , $27.00. **Description:** Scrum is a more efficient way for getting things done, particularly when managing a company. Scrum has recorded productivity gains as high as 1200 percent and is an excellent time management tool.

45466 ■ *"SEC Doesn't Buy Biovail's Claims"* in *Barron's (Vol. 88, March 31, 2008, No. 13, pp. 20)*
Pub: Dow Jones & Co., Inc.
Contact: Clare Hart, President
Ed: Bill Alpert. **Description:** Overstatement of earnings and chronic fraudulent conduct has led the SEC to file a stock fraud suit against Biovail, Eugene Melnyk and three others present or former employees of Biovail. Melnyk had the firm file suit in 2006 that blames short-sellers and stock researchers for the company's drop in share price.

45467 ■ *"Segmenting When It Matters"* in *Business Strategy Review (Vol. 21, Spring 2010, No. 1, pp. 46)*
Pub: John Wiley & Sons Inc. Scientific, Technical, Medical, and Scholarly Div. (Wiley-Blackwell)
Contact: William J. Pesce, Manager
F-mail: wpesce@wiley.com
Ed: Andreas Birnik, Richard Moat. **Description:** Authors argue that business complexity is directly linked to the degree of segmentation implemented by a company. They propose an approach to map business activities at the segment level to make sure that complexity is only introduced when it really matters.

45468 ■ *"The Self-Destructive Habits of Good Companies"* in *Harvard Business Review (Vol. 85, July-August 2007, No. 7-8)*
Pub: Harvard Business School Publishing
Ed: John T. Landry. **Description:** Review of the book that helps companies break bad habits and develop new ones for growth and success.

45469 ■ *"Selling a Job When There's Buyer's Remorse"* in *Contractor (Vol. 56, December 2009, No. 12, pp. 37)*
Pub: Penton Media, Inc.
Ed: H. Kent Craig. **Description:** Advice on how contractors should manage low-profit jobs in the United States are presented. Efforts should be made to try and find at least one quality field foreman or superintendent. Contractors should also try to respectfully renegotiate the terms of the job.

45470 ■ *"A Set-Theoretic Approach to Organizational Configurations"* in *Academy of Management Review (October 2007, pp. 1180)*
Pub: ScholarOne Inc.
Contact: William T. Carden, Jr., President
Ed: Peer C. Fiss. **Description:** The author argues about the mismatch between theory and methods that have led to decline in research on organizational configurations. He suggests adoption of set-theoretic methods to overcome this mismatch.

45471 ■ *"Seven Things Great Employers Do (That Others Don't); Unusual, Innovative, and Proven Tactics To Create Productive and Profitable Working Environments"* in *Gallup Business Journal (April 15, 2014)*
Pub: Gallup Press
Released: April 15, 2014. **Description:** Seven unusual, innovative, and proven tactics that create productive and profitable working environments are examined through researching 32 companies. These firms represented many industries, including healthcare, financial services, hospitality, manufacturing, and retail throughout the world.

45472 ■ *"Shared Leadership In Teams: An Investigation of Antecedent Conditions and Performance"* in *Academy of Management Journal (Vol. 50, No. 5, October 1, 2007, pp. 1217)*
Pub: Academy of Management
Contact: Ming-Jer Chen, President
Ed: Jay B. Carson, Paul E. Tesluk, Jennifer A. Marrone. **Description:** Study assessed the advantages of distribution of leadership among team members rather than on a single person revealed advantages that ranged from support and shared functions along with higher ratings from clients on their performance.

45473 ■ *"Should Managers Focus on Performance or Engagement? Gallup Examined this Question and Found That the Answer Isn't as 'Either/Or' as Many Companies Might Think"* in *Gallup Business Journal (August 5, 2014)*
Pub: Gallup Press
Released: August 5, 2014. **Description:** A Gallup survey of over 8,000 employees were asked whether managers should focus on performance or engagement. High performance managers create an engaging work environment promoting peak performance in three ways.

45474 ■ *"The SI Selects Retired Air Force General Tom Sheridan to Lead National Security Space Business"* in *Entertainment Close-Up (April 21, 2012)*
Pub: Close-Up Media
Released: April 21, 2012. **Description:** SI Organization Inc. (the SI) has named retired Air Force Lt. Gen. John T. "Tom" Sheridan as vice president for National Security Space unit. Profile of Sheridan is included.

45475 ■ *"Siemens Boss on Big Scandals, Bullet-Proof Limos"* in *Globe & Mail (March 5, 2007, pp. B11)*
Description: Interview with Klaus Kleinfeld, the chief executive officer of Siemens AG, in which he shares his views on the job challenges faced by him.

45476 ■ *Silos, Politics and Turf Wars: A Leadership Fable about Destroying the Barriers That Turn Colleagues Into Competitors*
Pub: Jossey-Bass
Ed: Patrick M. Lencioni. **Released:** January 2006. **Price:** $24.95, hardcover; $16.99. **Description:** The author addresses management problems through a fable that revolves around a self-employed consultant who has to dismantle silos at an upscale hotel, a technology company and a hospital. The story explains how organizations can use a collective operational vision in order to overcome pride, greed, and tribalism and work as a team with the same goal in mind. **Availability:** PrintE-book.

45477 ■ *"Six Sears Board Members to Resign in April"* in *Globe & Mail (March 1, 2006, pp. B1)*
Ed: Marina Strauss. **Description:** The reasons behind the departure of six board members of Sears Canada Inc. are presented.

45478 ■ *"Six Ways Employees on LinkedIn Benefit the Boss"* in *South Florida Business Journal (Vol. 34, April 25, 2014, No. 40)*
Pub: American City Business Journals
Released: April 25, 2014. **Description:** LinkedIn can be a useful tool for executives. In addition to finding staff when hiring, the information service can give U.S.-based users a more global perspective. It can also be a way to share recent company accomplishment.

45479 ■ *"Size Matters"* in *Entrepreneur (Vol. 36, April 2008, No. 4, pp. 44)*
Pub: Entrepreneur Press
Contact: Perlman Neil, President
Ed: Robert Kiyosaki. **Description:** Entrepreneurs planning to expand their business face challenges when it comes to employing more people and addressing internal relationships, communications and procedures. People skills, organizational skills and leadership skills are some of the things to consider before adding employees.

45480 ■ *"A Size Smaller, But a Better Fit"* in *Business Journal (Vol. 31, May 2, 2014, No. 49, pp. 12)*
Pub: American City Business Journals
Released: May 2, 2014. **Description:** LuAnn Via, Christopher & Banks Corporation's CEO, helped improve the company's financial results. She was responsible for closing hundreds of retail women's clothing stores and overhauling the business inventory. Via completed the organization's turnaround management strategy by walking away from the firm's core customer.

45481 ■ *"Skinner's No Drive-Thru CEO"* in *Crain's Chicago Business (Vol. 31, April 28, 2008, No. 17, pp. 1)*
Pub: Crain Communications Inc.
Contact: Todd Johnson, Publisher
Ed: David Sterrett. **Description:** Profile of James Skinner who was named CEO for McDonald's Corp. in November 2004 and has proved to be a successful leader despite the number of investors who doubted him when he came to the position. Mr. Skinner has overseen three years of unprecedented sales growth and launched the biggest menu expansion in 30 years.

45482 ■ *"Small Biz Solutions: Bad Client? Make Break Cleanly, Swiftly - and Based On Numbers"* in *Crain's Detroit Business (Vol. 23, November 19, 2007, No. 47)*
Pub: Crain Communications Inc. - Detroit
Contact: Keith Crain, Chairman
Ed: Sheena Harrison. **Description:** Firing a difficult customer can be hard to do, but the best way to do it is cleanly and amicably.

45483 ■ *Small Business Clustering Technologies: Applications in Marketing, Management, IT and Economics*
Pub: IGI Global
Contact: Dr. Mehdi Khosrow-Pour, President
Ed: Robert C. MacGregor, Ann T. Hodgkinson. **Released:** September 2006. **Price:** 94.95, hardcover; $145, Institutions. **Description:** An overview of the development and role of small business clusters in disciplines that include economics, marketing, management and information systems. **Availability:** PrintE-book.

45484 ■ *Small Business for Dummies*
Pub: John Wiley & Sons Inc.
Contact: Stephen M. Smith, President
Ed: Eric Tyson, Jim Schell. **Released:** 4th Edition. **Price:** $22.95; $14.99. **Description:** Guidebook for anyone wanting to start or grow a small business; topics include information financing, budgeting, marketing, management and more. **Availability:** PrintE-book.

45485 ■ *Small Business Management in Canada*
Ed: Robert M. Knight. **Released:** June 1981. **Description:** Small business management in Canada.

45486 ■ *Small-Business Management Guide: Advice from the Brass-Tacks Entrepreneur*
Ed: Jim Schell. **Released:** October 1995. **Description:** Entrepreneurs offer advice for managing a small business.

45487 ■ *Small-Business Management Guide: Advice from the Brass-Tacks Entrepreneur*
Ed: Jim Schell. **Released:** 1995. **Description:** Collection of stories, tales and snippets from the perspective of a small business owner.

45488 ■ *The Small Business Owner's Manual: Everything You Need to Know to Start Up and Run Your Business*
Pub: Career Press Inc.
Contact: Ron Fry, President
Ed: Joe Kennedy. **Released:** June 2005. **Price:** $19.99. **Description:** Comprehensive guide for starting a small business, focusing on twelve ways to obtain financing, business plans, selling and advertising products and services, hiring and firing employees, setting up a Web site, business law, accounting issues, insurance, equipment, computers, banks, financing, customer credit and collection, leasing, and more. **Availability:** Print.

45489 ■ *The Small Business Start-Up Workbook: A Step-by-Step Guide to Starting the Business You've Dreamed Of*
Pub: How To Books
Contact: Giles Lewis, Publisher
Ed: Cheryl D. Rickman. **Released:** May 01, 2005. **Price:** £11.04; £12.99, Nonmembers. **Description:** Book provides practical exercises for starting a small business, including marketing and management strategies. **Availability:** Online.

45490 ■ *"Sobering Consequences: Chicago Rumored to be Leading MillerCoors HQ" in The Business Journal-Milwaukee (Vol. 25, July 11, 2008, No. 42, pp. A1)*
Pub: American City Business Journals, Inc.
Contact: Whitney Shaw, President
Ed: Rich Rovito. **Description:** Milwaukee Mayor Tom Barrett and Wisconsin Governor Jim Doyle met with MillerCoors management in an effort to convince the company to locate its corporate headquarters in the city. The company is expected to announce its decision by mid-July 2008. It was revealed that the decision-making process is focusing on determining an optimal location for the headquarters.

45491 ■ *"Social Intelligence and the Biology of Leadership" in Harvard Business Review (Vol. 86, September 2008, No. 9, pp. 74)*
Pub: Harvard Business Review Press
Contact: Peter E. Walsh, Director
Ed: Daniel Goleman, Richard Boyatzis. **Description:** Social intelligence within the framework of corporate leadership is defined and described. Guidelines for assessing one's own capabilities as a socially intelligent leader include empathy, teamwork, inspiration, and influence.

45492 ■ *"Social Media, E-Mail Remain Challenging for Employers" in Workforce Management (Vol. 88, December 14, 2009, No. 13, pp. 4)*
Pub: Crain Communications Inc.
Contact: Rance E. Crain, President
Ed: Ed Frauenheim. **Description:** Examining the impact of Internet social networking and the workplace; due to the power of these new technologies, it is important that companies begin to set clear policies regarding Internet use and employee privacy.

45493 ■ *"Social Networkers for Hire" in Black Enterprise (Vol. 40, December 2009, No. 5, pp. 56)*
Pub: Earl G. Graves Publishing Co., Inc.
Ed: Brittany Hutson. **Description:** Companies are utilizing social networking sites in order to market their brand and personally connect with consumers and are increasingly looking to social media specialists to help with this task. Aliya S. King is one such web strategist, working for ICED Media by managing their Twitter, Facebook, YouTube and Flickr accounts for one of their publicly traded restaurant clients.

45494 ■ *"Social Networks in the Workplace" in Strategy & Leadership (Vol. 38, July-August 2010, No. 4, pp. 50-53)*
Pub: Emerald Inc.
Ed: Daniel Burrus. **Description:** The opinions of futurist Daniel Burrus on a novel trend called 'Business 2.0', which involves the use of social networking applications as business tools, are presented. His suggestion that personal social networking technology can be used by businesses to improve collaboration, problem solving, and leadership communications to achieve continuous value innovation is discussed.

45495 ■ *"Soft Skills, Hard Success: Employers Seek Leaders Who Offer More than Just Education and Credentials" in Black Enterprise (Vol. 45, July-August 2014, No. 1, pp. 44)*
Pub: Earl G. Graves Publishing Co. Inc.
Contact: Earl G. Graves, Jr., President
Released: July-August 2014. **Description:** The top ten soft skills employer look for include: strong work ethic, dependability, positive attitude, self-motivation, team oriented, organizational skills, works well under pressure, effective communication, flexibility, and confidence.

45496 ■ *"Sometimes, Second Impressions Count Most" in Canadian Business (Vol. 83, October 12, 2010, No. 17, pp. 11)*
Ed: Richard Branson. **Description:** Developing a favorable impression at the first point of contact is imperative for businesses. Managers who want their organizations to make positive first and second impressions need to learn to balance the Web's labor-

saving efficiencies with human assistants. The importance of considering the customer relations value in company Websites is also explained.

45497 ■ *"Sony Pictures Television" in Brandweek (Vol. 49, April 21, 2008, No. 16, pp. SR13)*
Pub: Nielsen Business Media Inc.
Contact: Howard Appelbaum, President
Ed: Marc Berman. **Description:** Provides contact information for sales and marketing personnel for Sony Pictures Television Distribution as well as a listing of the station's top programming and an analysis of the current season and the target audience for those programs running in the current season.

45498 ■ *"Sophia Siskel: CEO, Chicago Botanic Garden" in Crain's Chicago Business (Vol. 31, May 5, 2008, No. 18, pp. 36)*
Pub: Crain Communications Inc.
Contact: Todd Johnson, Publisher
Ed: Christina Le Beau. **Description:** Profile of Sophia Siskel who is the CEO of the Chicago Botanic Garden and is overseeing the $100 million expansion which will put the Botanic Garden at the forefront of plant conservation science; Ms. Siskel is also an efficient marketer and researcher.

45499 ■ *"Sources" in Canadian Electronics (Vol. 23, August 2008, No. 5, pp. 12)*
Description: Directory of electronic manufacturers, distributors and representatives in Canada is provided. The list presents distributors and representatives under each manufacturer.

45500 ■ *"Spam's Biggest Fan" in Barron's (Vol. 92, August 25, 2012, No. 35, pp. 42)*
Pub: Dow Jones & Co., Inc.
Contact: Clare Hart, President
Ed: Lawrence C. Strauss. **Description:** Jeffrey Ettinger, chief executive officer of meat packing and packaged food firm Hormel Foods, is credited with expanding the company's product offerings. Ettinger, who took over in 2006, involves himself in almost every aspect of the company's business.

45501 ■ *"Spend Wisely on Managing Your Hedgerows" in Farmer's Weekly (March 28, 2008, No. 320)*
Ed: Richard Winspear. **Description:** Discusses the importance of a well-managed hedge which should gradually grow upwards and outwards where eventually it would reach the point when rejuvenation by coppicing or laying was needed to restart the cycle.

45502 ■ *"Spotlight; 'Classroom Focus' at Encyclopaedia Britannica" in Crain's Chicago Business (Vol. 34, October 24, 2011, No. 42, pp. 6)*
Pub: Crain Communications Inc.
Contact: Todd Johnson, Publisher
Ed: Paul Merrion. **Description:** Profile of Gregory Healy, product officer for Encyclopaedia Britannica is presented. Healy took the position in May 2010 and is focused on online offerings of their publication and to make them more useful to teachers.

45503 ■ *"Staffing Firm Grows by Following Own Advice-Hire a Headhunter" in Crain's Detroit Business (Vol. 24, October 6, 2008, No. 40, pp. 1)*
Pub: Crain Communications Inc.
Contact: Rance E. Crain, President
Ed: Sherri Begin. **Description:** Profile of Venator Holdings L.L.C., a staffing firm that provides searches for companies in need of financial-accounting and technical employees; the firm's revenue has increased from $1.1 million in 2003 to a projected $11.5 million this year due to a climate in which more people are exiting the workforce than are coming in with those particular specialized skills and the need for a temporary, flexible workforce for contract placements at companies that do not want to take on the legacy costs associated with permanent employees. The hiring of an external headhunter to find the right out-of-state manager for Venator is also discussed.

45504 ■ *"A Stakeholder--Human Capital Perspective On the Link Between Social Performance and Executive Compensation" in Business Ethics Quarterly (Vol. 24, January 2014, No. 1, pp. 1)*
Pub: Business Ethics Quarterly
Released: January 2014. **Description:** The link between firm corporate social performance (CSP) and executive compensation could be driven by a sorting effect (a firm's CSP is related to the initial levels of compensation of newly hired executives), or by an incentive effect (incumbent executives are rewarded for past firm CSP). An exploration of the sorting effect of firm CSP on the initial compensation of newly hired executives is discussed.

45505 ■ *"A Stalled Culture Change?" in Workforce Management (Vol. 88, December 14, 2009, No. 13, pp. 1)*
Pub: Crain Communications Inc.
Contact: Rance E. Crain, President
Ed: Jeremy Smerd. **Description:** General Motors CEO Fritz Henderson's abrupt resignation shocked employees and signaled that Henderson had not done enough to change the company's culture, especially in dealing with its top management.

45506 ■ *"Stand Out Via Service: How Volunteering Can Boost Your Professional Bottom Line" in Black Enterprise (Vol. 44, June 2014, No. 10, pp. 42)*
Pub: Earl G. Graves Publishing Co. Inc.
Contact: Earl G. Graves, Jr., President
Released: June 2014. **Description:** According to the 2013 Deloitte Volunteer IMPACT Survey, more than three of every four human resource executives volunteer. This strategy can lead to career satisfaction and help a business advance and fuel growth for individuals and the firm. Tips for finding the right volunteer opportunity are included.

45507 ■ *"Star Power" in Small Business Opportunities (September 2008)*
Pub: Entrepreneur Press
Contact: Perlman Neil, President
Description: Employee retention is an important factor for corporate executives to consider because the impact of excessive turnovers can be devastating to a company causing poor morale, unemployment claims, hiring costs, lost production and customer loss. Although there is no specific formula for retaining employees, there are several things every organization can do to keep their workers happy and increase the chances that they will stay loyal and keep working for the company for years to come; tips aimed at management regarding good employee relationships are included.

45508 ■ *The Starbucks Experience*
Ed: Joseph A. Michelli. **Released:** September 14, 2006. **Price:** $24.95. **Description:** Boardroom strategies, employee motivation tips, community involvement, and customer satisfaction are issues addressed, using Starbucks as a model.

45509 ■ *The Starfish and the Spider: The Unstoppable Power of Leaderless Organizations*
Pub: Portfolio Publishing
Contact: Adrian Zackheim, President
Ed: Ori Brafman, Rod A. Beckstrom. **Released:** July 29, 2008. **Price:** $16, Paperback; $12.99. **Description:** Through their experiences promoting peace and economic development through decentralizing networking, the authors offer insight into ways that decentralizing can change organizations. Three techniques for combating a decentralized competitor are examined. **Availability:** PrintElectronic publishing.

45510 ■ *"The Stars Align: Trail Blazers, Headline Makers on 2007 List Set Example for Others" in Hispanic Business (October 2007, pp. 22)*
Pub: Hispanic Business Inc.
Contact: Jesus Chavarria, President
Description: Top one hundred most influential Hispanic business leaders comprise of 66 percent men and 34 percent women, distributed by 27

percent in government, 42 percent corporate, 11 percent education, five percent art and entertainment, and 15 percent in other sectors. Statistical data included.

45511 ■ *"Start Filling Your Talent Gap - Now"* in *Business Strategy Review (Vol. 21, Spring 2010, No. 1, pp. 56)*
Pub: John Wiley & Sons Inc. Scientific, Technical, Medical, and Scholarly Div. (Wiley-Blackwell)
Contact: William J. Pesce, Manager
E-mail: wpesce@wiley.com
Ed: Alan Bird, Lori Flees, Paul Di Paola. **Description:** As businesses steer their way out of turbulence, they have a unique opportunity to identify their leadership supply and demand and then to close the talent gap in their organization. Authors explain how to take immediate steps to build the right team now and lay the groundwork for a long-term approach for nurturing talent within the organization.

45512 ■ *"State's Glass Ceiling Gets Higher"* in *Business Journal-Milwaukee (Vol. 25, October 5, 2007, No. 1, pp. A1)*
Pub: American City Business Journals
Ed: Jennifer Batog. **Description:** Report showed that more than a third of Wisconsin's fifty largest companies have no female executive officers, and the number of companies with at least one woman at top departments has also decreased since 2005. Companies lacking women at upper management levels risk jeopardizing their firms' vitality as diversity in executive offices leads to diverse ideas that can help in relating better to customers and clients.

45513 ■ *"Stay in School: Economy Got You Down?"* in *Canadian Business (Vol. 81, November 10, 2008, No. 19, pp. 98)*
Ed: Graham F. Scott, Jane Bao. **Description:** A guide to Canadian MBA programs is presented. The tuition and length of each program is provided along with each school. Details on whether the universities offer part-time options, diversity, and co-op/internships are also given.

45514 ■ *"Staying Engaged: Location, Location"* in *Black Enterprise (Vol. 38, February 2008, No. 7, pp. 64)*
Pub: Earl G. Graves Publishing Co. Inc.
Contact: Earl G. Graves, Jr., President
Ed: Marcia A. Reed-Woodard. **Description:** Rules to help business leaders construct networking contacts in order to maximize professional success are outlined.

45515 ■ *"A Step Up"* in *Black Enterprise (Vol. 38, January 2008, No. 6, pp. 53)*
Pub: Earl G. Graves Publishing Co. Inc.
Contact: Earl G. Graves, Jr., President
Ed: Aisha Sylvester. **Description:** Professional black women can get advice from a nonprofit program called ASCENT: Leading Multicultural Women to the Top. ASCENT's sessions last six months and are held at both Tuck School of Business at Dartmouth and UCLA Anderson School of Management.

45516 ■ *"Stone to Run Hickory Farmer's Market"* in *Charlotte Observer (January 31, 2007)*
Ed: Jen Aronoff. **Description:** Betty Stone has been hired to manage the Downtown Hickory Farmers Market. The market will run from May 5 through October 6, 2007.

45517 ■ *"Stop the Innovation Wars"* in *Harvard Business Review (Vol. 88, July-August 2010, No. 7-8, pp. 76)*
Pub: Harvard Business School Publishing
Ed: Vijay Govindarajan, Chris Trimble. **Description:** Methods for managing conflicts between partners during the innovation initiative process are highlighted. These include dividing the labor, assembling a dedicated team, and mitigating likelihood for any potential conflict.

45518 ■ *"The Story Of Diane Greene"* in *Barron's (Vol. 88, July 14, 2008, No. 28, pp. 31)*
Pub: Dow Jones & Co., Inc.
Contact: Clare Hart, President
Ed: Mark Veverka. **Description:** Discusses the ousting of Diane Greene as a chief executive of VMWare,

a developer of virtualization software, after the firm went public; in this case Greene, a brilliant engineer, should not be negatively impacted by the decision because it is common for companies to bring in new executive leadership that is more operations oriented after the company goes public.

45519 ■ *"Strategic Issue Management as Change Catalyst"* in *Strategy and Leadership (Vol. 39, September-October 2011, No. 5, pp. 20-29)*
Pub: Emerald Group Publishing Inc.
Ed: Bruce E. Perrott. **Description:** A study analyzes the case of a well-known Australian healthcare organization to examine how a company's periodic planning cycle is supplemented with a dynamic, real-time, strategic-issue-management system under high turbulence conditions. Findings highlight the eight steps that a company's management can use in its strategic issue management (SIM) process to track, monitor and manage strategic issues so as to ensure that the corporate, strategy, and capability are aligned with one another in turbulent times.

45520 ■ *"A Strategic Risk Approach to Knowledge Management"* in *Business Horizons (November-December 2007, pp. 523)*
Pub: Elsevier Technology Publications
Ed: Bruce E. Perrott. **Price:** $35.95. **Description:** Knowledge management practices of Ramsay Health Care are studied to investigate the issues facing effective knowledge management. A knowledge process model is developed and presented. **Availability:** PDF.

45521 ■ *Streetwise Motivating and Rewarding Employees: New and Better Ways to Inspire Your People*
Ed: Alexander Hiam. **Released:** March 1999. **Description:** Ways for employers and business managers to motivate difficult employees.

45522 ■ *Strengths Based Leadership*
Pub: Gallup Press
Ed: Tom Rath, Barry Conchie. **Price:** $15.99. **Description:** Three keys to being a more effective leader. **Availability:** Print.

45523 ■ *Strengthsfinder 2.0*
Pub: Gallup Press
Ed: Tom Rath. **Released:** 2007. **Description:** Author helps people uncover their talents in order to achieve their best each day.

45524 ■ *"Stress-Test Your Strategy: the 7 Questions to Ask"* in *Harvard Business Review (Vol. 88, November 2010, No. 11, pp. 92)*
Pub: Harvard Business School Publishing
Ed: Robert Simons. **Description:** Seven questions organizations should use to assess crisis management capabilities are: who is the primary customer, how do core values prioritize all parties, what performance variables are being tracked, what strategic boundaries have been set, how is creative tension being produced, how committed are workers to assisting each other, and what uncertainties are causing worry?.

45525 ■ *"Striving for Self-Verification During Organizational Entry"* in *Academy of Management Journal (Vol. 55, June 2012, No. 2, pp. 360)*
Pub: Academy of Management
Contact: Ming-Jer Chen, President
Ed: Daniel M. Cable, Virginia S. Kay. **Description:** How striving for self-verification relates with self-disclosure, self-monitoring, and core self-evaluations is explored. Striving refers to bringing others to know who a person is during the organizational entry process. Relations to the validity of interviewers' evaluations, job seekers' ability to find satisfying work, and supervisors' evaluations of newcomers' performance are given.

45526 ■ *"Stuff that Works for You: In the Mobikey of Life"* in *Canadian Business (Vol.*

81, June 11, 2008, No. 11, pp. 42)
Pub: Rogers Media Inc.
Contact: Tony Viner, President
Ed: John Gray. **Description:** Toronto-based Route1 has created a data security software system that allows employees to access files and programs stored in the head office without permanently transferring data to the actual computer being used. Mobikey technology is useful in protecting laptops of chief executive officers, which contain confidential financial and customer data.

45527 ■ *"Stymiest's RBC Compensation Triggers Shareholder Outrage"* in *Gl obe & Mail (January 28, 2006, pp. B3)*
Ed: Sinclair Stewart. **Description:** The concerns of shareholders over the issue of Royal Bank of Canada's $6.6 million pay package for chief executive officer Barbara Stymiest, in 2004, are presented.

45528 ■ *"Succeeding at Succession"* in *Harvard Business Review (Vol. 88, November 2010, No. 11, pp. 29)*
Pub: Harvard Business School Publishing
Ed: James M. Citrin, Dayton Ogden. **Description:** Analysis of various executive succession scenarios is given. The article compares insider vs. outsider performance and the effectiveness of board members assuming the CEO position.

45529 ■ *Success Built to Last: Creating a Life That Matters*
Pub: Penguin Group USA
Contact: Phyllis Grann, President
Ed: Jerry Porras, Stewart Emery, Mark Thompson. **Released:** August 28, 2007. **Price:** $17, paperback. **Description:** Interviews with successful individuals are presented to help any entrepreneur or manager. **Availability:** Print.

45530 ■ *"The Superfluous Position"* in *Entrepreneur (Vol. 37, July 2009, No. 7, pp. 62)*
Pub: Entrepreneur Press
Contact: Perlman Neil, President
Description: Profile of an anonymous editor at a multimedia company that publishes tourism guides who shares his experiences in dealing with an officemate who was promoted as creative manager of content. Everyone was irritated by this person, who would constantly do something to justify his new title. The biggest problem was the fact that this person didn't have a clear job description.

45531 ■ *"Surprise Package"* in *Business Courier (Vol. 27, June 25, 2010, No. 8, pp. 1)*
Pub: Business Courier
Ed: Dan Monk, Jon Newberry, Steve Watkins. **Description:** More than 60 percent of the chief executive officers (CEOs) in Greater Cincinnati's 35 public companies took a salary cut in 2009, but stock grants resulted in large paper gains for the CEOs. The salary cuts show efforts of boards of directors to observe austerity. Statistics on increased values of stock awards for CEOs, median pay for CEOs, and median shareholder return are also presented.

45532 ■ *"Survive the Small-to-Big Transition"* in *Entrepreneur (November 4, 2008)*
Pub: Entrepreneur Press
Contact: Perlman Neil, President
Ed: Elizabeth Wilson. **Description:** Transitioning a small company to a large company can be a challenge, especially during the time when it is too big to be considered small and too small to be considered big. Common pitfalls during this time are discussed as well as techniques business owners should implement when dealing with this transitional period.

45533 ■ *"Survivorship Policies: Planning a Policy for Two"* in *Employee Benefit News (Vol. 25, November 1, 2011, No. 14, pp. 20)*
Pub: SourceMedia Inc.
Contact: James M. Malkin, Chief Executive Officer
Ed: Marli D. Riggs. **Description:** Survivorship insurance is becoming an added benefit high net worth individuals and executives should consider when evaluating life insurance policies.

45534 ■ *"The Sustainable Organization: Blueprint for an Integrated Model"* in Journal of Business Strategy (Vol. 35, May-June 2014, No. 3, pp. 26-37)
Pub: Emerald Group Publishing Inc.

Released: May-June 2014. **Description:** For senior executives to understand the role of sustainability in their organization's future strategy and structure, a new organizational sustainability model that includes the economic dimension is presented. It is developed based on the existing Dunphy, Griffiths, and Benn model which featured only social and environmental dimensions. This integrated and comprehensive sustainability stage model can assist executives in building more sustainable organizations.

45535 ■ *"Swinging For the Fences: The Effects of Ceo Stock Options on Company Risk Taking and Performance"* in Academy of Management Journal (Vol. 50, No. 5, October 1, 2007, pp. 1055)
Pub: Academy of Management
Contact: Ming-Jer Chen, President

Ed: Gerard Sanders, Donald C. Hambrick. **Description:** Study examines managerial risk-taking vis-a-vis stock options of the company; results reveal that stock options instigate CEOs to take unwise risks that could bring huge losses to the company.

45536 ■ *Switch: How to Change Things When Change Is Hard*
Pub: Broadway Business
Contact: David Drake, Manager
E-mail: ddrake@randomhouse.com

Ed: Chip Heath, Dan Heath. **Released:** February 16, 2010. **Price:** $26, hardcover; $14.99. **Description:** Change is difficult for everyone. This book helps business leaders to motivate employees as well as to help everybody motive themselves and others. **Availability:** PrintE-book.

45537 ■ *"A System for Continuous Organization Renewal"* in Strategy & Leadership (Vol. 38, July-August 2010, No. 4, pp. 34-41)
Pub: Emerald Inc.

Ed: Oliver Sparrow, Gill Ringland. **Description:** A study presents a unique system to facilitate continuous organizational renewal. An analysis indicates that the system is effective when organizations implement all its parts to achieve organizational renewal.

45538 ■ *Take Back Your Time: How to Regain Control of Work, Information and Technology*
Pub: Palgrave Macmillan
Contact: Lisa Dunn, Manager
E-mail: l.dunn@palgrave.com

Ed: Jan Jasper. **Released:** November 1999. **Price:** $18.99, paperback; $7.99. **Description:** Strategies to become more organized and productive. **Availability:** PrintE-book.

45539 ■ *"Take Command: Lessons in Leadership: How to Be a First Responder in Business"*
Pub: Crown Business

Released: October 14, 2014. **Price:** , $25.00. **Description:** What do elite members of the military, first responders in a disaster zone, and successful business leaders have in common? Clarity of mind and purpose in the midst of chaos. Cofounder and CEO of Team Rubicon and former Marine Sniper Jake Wood, teaches the lessons in leadership and teamwork to help managers and entrepreneurs succeed in this hyper-competitive business environment today.

45540 ■ *"Taking on the World"* in Canadian Business (Vol. 79, November 22, 2006, No. 23, pp. 43)
Pub: Rogers Media Inc.
Contact: Tony Viner, President

Ed: Zena Olijnyk, Claire Gagne. **Description:** The rankings of the top Canadian business executives are presented.

45541 ■ *Talent: Making People Your Competitive Advantage*
Pub: Jossey-Bass

Ed: Edward E. Lawler, III. **Released:** March 2008. **Price:** $29.95, hardcover; $19.99. **Description:** Competitive advantage in most organizations has shifted from reliability to innovation and flexibility. Organizations must combine the right structure with the right people to make it work. **Availability:** PrintE-book.

45542 ■ *The Talent Masters: Why Smart Leaders Put People Before Numbers*
Ed: Bill Conaty, Ram Charan. **Released:** November 09, 2010. **Price:** $27.50. **Description:** This book helps leaders recognize talent in their employees, and to put that talent to work to help achieve business success.

45543 ■ *"Talk, Inc.: How Trusted Leaders Use Conversation to Power Their Organizations"* in Canadian Business (Vol. 85, August 13, 2012, No. 13, pp. 59)
Pub: George Media Inc.

Ed: Sarah Barmak. **Released:** August 13, 2012. **Description:** Review of the book entitled, *"Talk, Inc.: How Trusted Leaders Use Conversation to Power Their Organizations"*. As the title states, this book will help business leaders deliver their messages concisely and effectively.

45544 ■ *"Talk Story: Mitch D'Olier, President, CEO Kaneohe Ranch"* in Hawaii Business (Vol. 53, November 2007, No. 5, pp. 27)
Pub: PacificBasin Communications

Ed: Cathy S. Cruz-George. **Description:** Mitch D'Olier chief executive officer of Kaneohe Ranch/ Harold K.L. Castle Foundation thinks that achievement gaps are a nationwide problem and that the Knowledge is Power Program is one of the programs that focuses on achievement gaps in some communities across the US. He also provides his insights on education in Hawaii and the current shortage of teachers.

45545 ■ *"Tauri Group Partner Joining Homeland Security and Defense"* in Wireless News (December 15, 2009)
Description: Managing partner Cosmo DiMaggio III of the Tauri Group, a provider of analytic consulting for homeland security, defense and space clients, has been elected to the Board of Directors at Homeland Security and Defense Business Council.

45546 ■ *"Tax Tip: Streamlining Sales Tax Collections"* in Pet Product News (Vol. 66, September 2012, No. 9, pp. 38)
Pub: Bowtie Inc.

Ed: Mark E. Battersby. **Description:** Pointers on how pet supplies retailers and managers can streamline sales taxes are presented. Busineses are being challenge by the pressure to collect taxes on goods sold to local customers and compettiton from Internet merchants that are not required to collect sales taxes.

45547 ■ *"The Tea Bag Test"* in Canadian Business (Vol. 79, October 23, 2006, No. 21, pp. 83)
Pub: Rogers Media Inc.
Contact: Tony Viner, President

Ed: Clive Mather. **Description:** Tips for business executives, on how to manage leadership skills to attain optimal business growth, are presented.

45548 ■ *"Team Bonding for Fun and Profit"* in Women Entrepreneur (December 3, 2008)
Ed: Eve Gumpel. **Description:** Discusses the benefits that competitions such as the 2008 BG U.S. Challenge in Lake Placid, New York, can offer in terms of team building and employee motivation as well as networking and the development of a positive working relationship with partners and competitors alike.

45549 ■ *"Team Implicit Coordination Processes: A Team Knowledge-based Approach"* in Academy of Management Review (January 2008, pp. 163)
Pub: ScholarOne Inc.
Contact: William T. Carden, Jr., President

Ed: Ramon Rico, Miriam Sanchez-Manzanares, Francisco Gil, Cristina Gibson. **Description:** An integrated theoretical framework is developed to enhance understanding of the functioning of work teams and implicit coordination behaviors; the implications for team coordination theory and effective management of work teams is discussed.

45550 ■ *"Teamwork On the Fly: How To Master the New Art of Teaming"* in Harvard Business Review (Vol. 90, April 2012, No. 4, pp. 72)
Pub: Harvard Business Review Press
Contact: Peter E. Walsh, Director

Ed: Amy C. Edmondson. **Released:** April 2012. **Description:** Description of the concept of 'teaming' or flexible teamwork is given. Teaming brings together expertise from disparate fields and forms temporary groups to identify innovations and address unanticipate problems. Project management and team leadership are important components of success.

45551 ■ *"Tech Deal Couples Homegrown Firms"* in The Business Journal-Serving Greater Tampa Bay (Vol. 28, July 7, 2008, No. 28, pp. 1)
Pub: American City Business Journals, Inc.
Contact: Whitney Shaw, President

Ed: Michael Hinman. **Description:** Tampa Bay, Florida-based Administrative Partners Inc. was acquired by Tribridge Inc. resulting in the strengthening of the delivery of Microsoft products to clients. Other details of the merger of the management consulting services companies are presented.

45552 ■ *"Technology to the Rescue"* in Contractor (Vol. 56, July 2009, No. 7, pp. 22)
Pub: Intertec Publishing
Contact: John French, President

Ed: Candace Roulo. **Description:** Features of several products that will make the job of a mechanical contractor easier are discussed. These include Ridgid's line of drain and sewer inspection cameras and monitors, Motion Computing's Motion F5 tablet rugged tablet PC, the JobClock from Exaktime, and the TeleNav Track tool for mobile workforce management.

45553 ■ *"Telemundo"* in Brandweek (Vol. 49, April 21, 2008, No. 16, pp. SR8)
Pub: Nielsen Business Media Inc.
Contact: Howard Appelbaum, President

Ed: John Consoli. **Description:** Provides contact information for sales and marketing personnel for the Telemundo network as well as a listing of the station's top programming and an analysis of the current season and the target audience for those programs running in the current season.

45554 ■ *"Temp Job, Permanent Fulfillment: How the Desire To Earn a Bit of Extra Cash Opened the Door to a Long-Term Career"* in Black Enterprise (Vol. 44, June 2014, No. 10, pp. 41)
Pub: Earl G. Graves Publishing Co. Inc.
Contact: Earl G. Graves, Jr., President

Released: June 2014. **Description:** Profile of Kay Francis who started a temporary job with Darden Restaurants to earn money during her final year of college. After graduation, Francis took a permanent position with the firm and today is the Director, Concept Support and Purchasing for the company.

45555 ■ *"Tempering Urgency Within Your Shop"* in Modern Machine Shop (Vol. 84, October 2011, No. 5, pp. 16)
Pub: Gardner Business Media, Inc.
Contact: Richard G. Kline, President
E-mail: rkline@gardnerweb.com

Ed: Derek Korn. **Description:** Because machine shops operate under an environment of urgency, patience can commingle with the pressure to produce products efficiently and timely.

45556 ■ *"The Ten Commandments of Legal Risk Management"* in *Business Horizons (Vol. 51, January-February 2008, No. 1, pp. 13)*
Pub: Elsevier Advanced Technology Publications
Ed: Michael B. Metzger. Description: Effective legal risk management is tightly linked with ethical and good management, and managers' behaviors have to be professional and based on ethically defensible principles of action. Basic human tendencies cannot be used in justifying questionable decisions in court. Guidelines for legal risk management are presented.

45557 ■ *"The Ten Worst Leadership Habits"* in *Canadian Business (Vol. 81, March 31, 2008, No. 5, pp. 63)*
Pub: Rogers Media Inc.
Contact: Tony Viner, President
Ed: Michael Stern. Description: Ten leadership behaviors that aspiring leaders need to avoid are presented. These include expecting colleagues and subordinates to be like themselves, attending too many meetings, being miserly when it comes to recognition and praise, and giving an opinion often.

45558 ■ *"There's Always Something Unexpected"* in *South Florida Business Journal (Vol. 34, June 6, 2014, No. 46, pp. 13)*
Pub: American City Business Journals
Released: June 6, 2014. Description: Hannah Granade, CEO of Advantix Systems, likes how her job allows her to build the business and bring people together. The company, that provides cooling and dehumidification systems for industrial and commercial applications, encourages creative thinking by building an open culture.

45559 ■ *"Think Again: What Makes a Leader?"* in *Business Strategy Review (Vol. 21, Autumn 2010, No. 3, pp. 64)*
Pub: John Wiley & Sons Inc. Scientific, Technical, Medical, and Scholarly Div. (Wiley-Blackwell)
Contact: William J. Pesce, Manager
E-mail: wpesce@wiley.com
Ed: Rob Goffee, Gareth Jones. Description: Leadership cannot be faked and all the self-help books in the world won't make you a leader - but there are four characteristics any leader must possess and they are outlined.

45560 ■ *"Think Disruptive! How to Manage In a New Era of Innovation"* in *Strategy & Leadership (Vol. 38, July-August 2010, No. 4, pp. 5-10)*
Pub: Emerald Inc.
Ed: Brian Leavy, John Sterling. Description: The views expressed by Scott Anthony, president of an innovation consultancy Innosight, on the need for corporate leaders to apply disruptive innovation in a recessionary environment are presented. His suggestion that disruptive innovation is the only way to survive during the economic crisis is discussed.

45561 ■ *"The Thinker"* in *Canadian Business (Vol. 81, March 31, 2008, No. 5, pp. 52)*
Pub: Rogers Media Inc.
Contact: Tony Viner, President
Ed: Andrew Wahl. Description: Mihnea Moldoveanu provides much of the academic rigor that underpins Roger Martin's theories on how to improve the way business leaders think. Moldoveanu is also a classically trained pianist and founder of Redline Communications and has a mechanical engineering degree from MIT on top of his astounding knowledge on many academic fields.

45562 ■ *"Thinking Aloud"* in *Business Strategy Review (Vol. 21, Summer 2010, No. 2, pp. 47)*
Pub: John Wiley & Sons Inc. Scientific, Technical, Medical, and Scholarly Div. (Wiley-Blackwell)
Contact: William J. Pesce, Manager
E-mail: wpesce@wiley.com
Ed: Yiorgos Mylonadis. Description: In each issue we ask an academic to explain the big question on which their research hopes to shed light. Yiorgos Mylonadis looks at how people define and solve problems.

45563 ■ *"Thinking Aloud: Julian Franks"* in *Business Strategy Review (Vol. 21, Autumn 2010, No. 3, pp. 35)*
Pub: Blackwell Publishers Ltd.
Ed: Stuart Crainer. Description: Julian Franks is Academic Director of the Centre for Corporate Governance at London Business School and lead investigator for a 1.4 million (sterling pounds) grand for research into corporate governance.

45564 ■ *"Thinking Aloud: Julian Franks"* in *Business Strategy Review (Vol. 21, Autumn 2010, No. 3, pp. 35)*
Pub: John Wiley & Sons Inc. Scientific, Technical, Medical, and Scholarly Div. (Wiley-Blackwell)
Contact: William J. Pesce, Manager
E-mail: wpesce@wiley.com
Ed: Stuart Crainer. Description: Julian Franks is academic director of the Centre for Corporate Governance at London Business School and lead investigator for a (pounds sterling) 1.4 million grant for research into corporate governance.

45565 ■ *30 Reasons Employees Hate Their Managers: What Your People May Be Thinking and What You Can Do About It*
Pub: AMACOM
Contact: Edward T. Reilly, Manager
Ed: Bruce L. Katcher, Adam Snyder. Released: March 07, 2007. Price: $18.95, Paper or Softback. Description: Thirty reasons why American employees are unhappy in their jobs are outlined. Each chapter is opened with a reason, an examination of how it creates work difficulties, and makes suggestions to managers on how to best address each issue. Availability: Print.

45566 ■ *Three Moves Ahead: What Chess Can Teach You About Business*
Pub: John Wiley & Sons Inc.
Contact: Stephen M. Smith, President
Ed: Bob Rice. Released: March 30, 2008. Price: $24.95. Description: Things the game of chess can teach about business are explored.

45567 ■ *"Three Signs Your Biz Needs a COO"* in *Birmingham Business Journal (Vol. 31, April 18, 2014, No. 16, pp. 10)*
Pub: American City Business Journals, Inc.
Contact: Whitney Shaw, President
Released: April 18, 2014. Description: Business conditions that warrant the recruitment of a chief operations officer are discussed. The halting of growth results in the shifting of focus from operations to sales. Dependence on one or two employees can result in resignations.

45568 ■ *"Three Skills Every 21st Century Manager Needs"* in *Harvard Business Review (Vol. 90, January-February 2012, No.1-2, pp. 139)*
Pub: Harvard Business Review Press
Contact: Peter E. Walsh, Director
Ed: Andrew L. Molinsky, Thomas H. Davenport, Bala Iyer, Cathy Davidson. Released: January-February 2012. Description: The first skill is cultural code-switching, or the ability to adapt to one's behavior to accommodate variations in cultural norms for modern managers. The second is effective utilization of online networks. The third is maximizing the brain's natural tendency to focus on multiple items simultaneously.

45569 ■ *"Tim Armstrong"* in *Canadian Business (Vol. 81, July 21, 2008, No. 11, pp. 10)*
Ed: Calvin Leung. Description: Interview with Tim Armstrong who is the president of advertising and commerce department of Google Inc. for North America; the information technology company executive talked about the emerging trends and changes to YouTube made by the company since its acquisition in 2006.

45570 ■ *"A Timely Matter"* in *Canadian Business (Vol. 81, March 31, 2008, No. 5, pp. 12)*
Pub: Rogers Media Inc.
Contact: Tony Viner, President
Description: Discusses the committee responsible for restructuring $33 billion of asset-backed commercial paper which has moved back their implemen-

tation plan by a month citing complexities. British Columbia has surpassed the $1 billion mark in fiscal '07-'08 from their oil and gas rights. Biovail Corp. founder Eugene Melnyk said he had lost confidence in the management of the company.

45571 ■ *"To JM On Its 75th Anniversary"* in *Journal of Marketing (Vol. 75, July 2011, No. 4, pp. 129)*
Pub: American Marketing Association
Contact: Lucille Pointer, President
Ed: Ruth M. Bolton. Description: How the Journal of Marketing influenced the marketing science and practice is presented. The Marketing Science Institute's 50th anniversary coincides with the journal's 75th anniversary and both have collaborated to tackle important marketing issues identified in MSI's priorities. The mind-set of managers worldwide was also influenced by ideas in the journal's articles.

45572 ■ *"To Win With Natural Talent, Go For Additive Effects; Four Human Capital Strategies Combine to Drive Up to 59 Percent More Growth In Revenue Per Employee"* in *Gallup Business Journal (June 3, 2014)*
Pub: Gallup Press
Released: June 3, 2014. Description: Four human capital strategies, when used together, can drive growth in revenue per employee by as much as 59 percent. The strategies for selecting and implementing the right managers are explored.

45573 ■ *"Tom Gaglardi"* in *Canadian Business (Vol. 82, April 27, 2009, No. 7, pp. 56)*
Pub: Rogers Media Inc.
Contact: Tony Viner, President
Ed: Calvin Leung. Description: Northland Properties Corporation president Tom Gaglardi believes that their business model of keeping much of operations in-house allows the firm to crate assets at a lesser price while commanding higher margins than their competitors. He believes that it is an ideal time to invest in the hospitality industry because of opportunities to purchase properties at low prices.

45574 ■ *"Top Male and Female Fittest CEO"* in *Hawaii Business (Vol. 53, October 2007, No. 4, pp. 40)*
Pub: PacificBasin Communications
Ed: Cathy S. Cruz-George. Description: Discusses the outcome of the fittest chief executive officers in Hawaii competition for 2007. Hawaii Capital Management's David Low leads the list while Group Pacific (Hawaii) Inc.'s Chip Doyle and Greater Good Inc.'s Kari Leong placed second and third, respectively. The CEO's routines, eating habits, and inspirations for staying fit are provided.

45575 ■ *Tough Choices: A Memoir*
Pub: Penguin Group USA
Contact: Phyllis Grann, President
Ed: Carly Florina. Released: September 25, 2007. Price: $15, paperback; $12.99. Description: Former woman CEO at Hewlett-Packard is profiled. Availability: PrintElectronic publishing.

45576 ■ *"Tough Times for the Irving Clan"* in *Canadian Business (Vol. 83, August 17, 2010, No. 13-14, pp. 14)*
Pub: Rogers Media Inc.
Contact: Tony Viner, President
Ed: Dean Jobb. Description: The death of John E. Irving and reported health problems of his nephew Kenneth Irving was a double blow to the billionaire Irving clan. Kenneth suddenly left his job as CEO of Fort Reliance, holding company for Irving Oil and new energy ventures, wherein the explanation was for personal reasons.

45577 ■ *"Tracking Your Fleet Can Increase Bottom Line"* in *Contractor (Vol. 56, November 2009, No. 11, pp. 26)*
Pub: Penton Media, Inc.
Ed: Candace Roulo. Description: GPS fleet management system can help boost a contractor's profits, employee productivity, and efficiency. These are available as a handheld device or a cell phone that

employees carry around or as a piece of hardware installed in a vehicle. These lets managers track assets and communicate with employees about jobs.

45578 ■ "Transcendent Leadership" in Business Horizons (Vol. 51, March-April 2008, No. 2, pp. 131)
Pub: Elsevier Advanced Technology Publications
Ed: Mary Crossan, Daina Mazutis. Description: Transcendent leadership is framework integrating the leadership of self, others, and organizations. Much of the discourse regarding leadership has focused on leadership of others and the organization, while leadership of self is rarely tackled. Successful leaders are able to integrate these three levels of leadership.

45579 ■ "Trend: Tutors to Help You Pump Up the Staff" in Business Week (September 22, 2008, No. 4100, pp. 45)
Ed: Reena Janaj. Description: High-level managers are turning to innovation coaches in an attempt to obtain advice on how to better sell new concepts within their companies. Individuals as well as consulting firms are now offering this service.

45580 ■ "Trial of Enron Ex-Bosses to Begin Today" in Globe & Mail (January 30, 2006, pp. B1)
Ed: Shawn McCarthy. Description: The details of the case against former executives Kenneth L. Lay and Jeffrey Skilling of Enron Corp. are presented.

45581 ■ "Trib TV Station Switching to Fox" in Crain's Chicago Business (Vol. 31, March 31, 2008, No. 13, pp. 14)
Pub: Crain Communications Inc.
Contact: Todd Johnson, Publisher
Ed: Michelle Greppi. Description: Signaling the new Tribune owner Sam Zell's divergence from previous management is the company's shift of its KSWB-TV station in San Diego to News Corp.'s Fox from CW Television Network.

45582 ■ True to Yourself: Leading a Values-Based Business
Pub: Berrett-Koehler Communications Inc.
Contact: Steve Piersanti, President
E-mail: spiersanti@bkpub.com
Ed: Mark S. Albion. Price: $16.95, paperback, free shipping. Description: Pressures faced by entrepreneurs running small companies are discussed. Advice is offered to help grow and maintain a profitable business. Availability: Print; PDF.

45583 ■ "The Trust Edge: How Top Leaders Gain Faster Results, Deeper Relationships"
Pub: Free Press Inc.
Released: October 9, 2012. Price: , $25.99. Description: David Horsager provides the eight Pillars of Trust to business leaders, including managers and entrepreneurs. Those eight trusts are based on research and are practical for today's leaders. They include: clarity, compassion, character, competency, commitment, connection, contribution, and consistency.

45584 ■ "The Trusty Sidekick" in Canadian Business (Vol. 81, March 31, 2008, No. 5, pp. 33)
Pub: Rogers Media Inc.
Contact: Tony Viner, President
Ed: John Gray. Description: Being second-in-command is a good opportunity to be mentored by the boss and puts the executive in the position to see the whole organization and have influence to make changes. However, the chief operating officer has the unenviable task of trying to achieve unattainable goals. Executives who want to become the right hand man must go beyond their job description.

45585 ■ The Truth About Middle Managers: Who They Are, How They Work, Why They Matter
Pub: Harvard Business School Publishing
Ed: Paul Osterman. Released: 2009. Price: $35. Description: The alienation of middle managers is bad for a company.

45586 ■ "Tuesday Morning's Corporate Clearance Rack" in Dallas Business Journal (Vol. 37, February 28, 2014, No. 25, pp. 4)
Pub: American City Business Journals
Released: February 28, 2014. Description: Tuesday Morning CEO, Michael Rouleau, has been working to help the company recover from its financial problems. Rouleau has improved the shopping experience from garage sale to discount showroom. The company has also been hiring different executives in the past few years.

45587 ■ "Turner Broadcasting System" in Brandweek (Vol. 49, April 21, 2008, No. 16, pp. SR13)
Pub: Nielsen Business Media Inc.
Contact: Howard Appelbaum, President
Ed: Anthony Crupi. Description: Provides contact information for sales and marketing personnel for the Turner Broadcasting System networks as well as a listing of the station's top programming and an analysis of the current season and the target audience for those programs running in the current season. Recent acquisitions are also discussed.

45588 ■ "Twentieth Television" in Brandweek (Vol. 49, April 21, 2008, No. 16, pp. SR16)
Pub: Nielsen Business Media Inc.
Contact: Howard Appelbaum, President
Ed: Marc Berman. Description: Provides contact information for sales and marketing personnel for Twentieth Television as well as a listing of the station's top programming and an analysis of the current season and the target audience for those programs running in the current season.

45589 ■ "20 Years of Advocacy and Education" in Women Entrepreneur (January 18, 2009)
Pub: Entrepreneur Press
Contact: Perlman Neil, President
Ed: Eve Gumpel. Description: Profile of Sharon Hadary who served as executive director of the Center for Women's Business Research for two decades; Hadary discusses what she has learned about women business owners, their impact on the economy and what successful business owners share in common.

45590 ■ "2009 Boardroom Elite" in Hispanic Business (January-February 2009, pp. 24, 28)
Pub: Hispanic Business Inc.
Contact: Jesus Chavarria, President
Description: Three percent of those serving as directors of Fortune 500 companies in America are Hispanic. A listing of forty of these directors is included.

45591 ■ "TWU Offers Course in Project Management" in Bellingham Business Journal (Vol. February 2010, pp. 4)
Pub: Sound Publishing Inc.
Contact: Gloria G. Fletcher, President
Ed: Lance Henderson. Description: Trinity Western University in Bellinham, Washington is offering a new certification program in project management. Students who take and pass the certification examination of the International Project Management Institutes will lead to positions in many industries. Details of the program are provided.

45592 ■ Ubuntu!: An Aspiring Story About an African Tradition of Teamwork and Collaboration
Pub: Broadway Business
Contact: David Drake, Manager
E-mail: ddrake@randomhouse.com
Ed: Bob Nelson, Stephen Lundin. Released: March 30, 2010. Price: $19.99, hardcover; $11.99. Description: The African tradition of teamwork and collaboration is used to demonstrate these skills to small business leaders. Availability: PrintE-book.

45593 ■ "UC's Goering Center to Get New Director" in Business Courier (Vol. 24, February 14, 2008, No. 45, pp. 3)
Pub: American City Business Journals, Inc.
Contact: Whitney Shaw, President
Ed: Dan Monk. Description: Kent Lutz, director of University of Cincinnati Goering (UC) Center for Family & Private Business is to leave the resource center

in June 2008 after nine years of service. Changes in the UC-affiliated institute include the expansion of the board from three to seven members and developing new programs related to family businesses.

45594 ■ The Ultimate Competitive Advantage
Pub: Berrett-Koehler Communications Inc.
Contact: Steve Piersanti, President
E-mail: spiersanti@bkpub.com
Ed: Donald Mitchell, Carol Coles, B. Thomas Golisano. Released: March 12, 2003. Price: $36.95, hardcover. Description: Results of a ten-year study of companies that experienced fast growth over a three year period shows that while unsuccessful companies apply outdated business models, the successful ones improve their business models every two to four years. Availability: Print.

45595 ■ Ultimate Guide to Project Management
Pub: Entrepreneurial Press
Ed: Sid Kemp. Price: $29.95. Description: Project management strategies including writing a business plan and developing a good advertising campaign.

45596 ■ "The Uncompromising Leader" in Harvard Business Review (Vol. 86, July-August 2008, No. 8, pp. 50)
Pub: Harvard Business Review Press
Contact: Peter E. Walsh, Director
Ed: Russel A. Eisenstat, Michael Beer, Nathaniel Foote, Flemming Norrgren. Description: Advice regarding how to drive performance without sacrificing commitment to people is given. Topics include development of shared purpose, organizational engagement, the fostering of collective leadership capability, and maintaining perspective.

45597 ■ "Under Pressure" in Canadian Business (Vol. 81, July 21, 2008, No. 11, pp. 18)
Ed: Joe Castaldo. Description: According to a survey conducted by COMPASS Inc., meeting revenue targets is the main cause of job stress for chief executive officers. Staffing and keeping expenditures lower also contribute to the workplace stress experienced by business executives. Other results of the survey are presented.

45598 ■ "An Unfair Knock on Nokia" in Barron's (Vol. 88, March 10, 2008, No. 10, pp. 36)
Pub: Dow Jones & Co., Inc.
Contact: Clare Hart, President
Ed: Mark Veverka. Description: Discusses the decision by the brokerage house Exane to recommend a Sell on Nokia shares, presumably due to higher inventories, which is unfounded. The news that the company's inventories are rising is not an indicator of falling demand for its products. The company is also benefiting from solid management and rising market share.

45599 ■ "Unify Corp. Back in the Black, Poised to Grow" in Sacramento Business Journal (Vol. 25, August 29, 2008, No. 26, pp. 1)
Pub: American City Business Journals, Inc.
Contact: Whitney Shaw, President
Ed: Melanie Turner. Description: It was reported that Unify Corp. returned to profitability in the fiscal year ended April 30, 2008 with a net income of $1.6 million, under the guidance of Todd Wille. Wille, who took over as the company's chief executive officer in October 2000, was named as Turnaround CEO of the Year in June 2008 for his efforts.

45600 ■ "Unilever's CMO Finally Gets Down To Business" in Advertising Age (Vol. 79, July 7, 2008, No. 26, pp. 11)
Pub: Crain Communications Inc.
Contact: Rance Crain, President
Ed: Jack Neff. Description: Overview of Unilever's chief marketing officer Simon Clift's strategy for promoting its products; now that the company has restructured, Clift is able to focus all of his energy on the challenges of the new-media climate that marketers are having to face.

45601 ■ *"Univision"* in *Brandweek (Vol. 49, April 21, 2008, No. 16, pp. SR8)*
Ed: John Consoli. **Description:** Provides contact information for sales and marketing personnel for the Univision network as well as a listing of the station's top programming and an analysis of the current season and the target audience for those programs running in the current season. Univision is the No. 1 network on Friday nights in the 18-34 demographic, beating all English-language networks.

45602 ■ *"Unlimited Priorities Strengthens Executive Team"* in *Entertainment Close-Up (November 1, 2011)*
Pub: Close-Up Media
Description: Founder and president of Unlimited Priorities Corporation, Iris L. Hanney, added two executive level professionals to her team. The new employees will help increase the firm's capabilities in social media and information technology.

45603 ■ *"Unmasking Manly Men"* in *Harvard Business Review (Vol. 86, July-August 2008, No. 8, pp. 20)*
Pub: Harvard Business Review Press
Contact: Peter E. Walsh, Director
Ed: Robin J. Ely, Debra Meyerson. **Description:** Oil rig work is used to explore how focusing on job requirements and performance successfully challenged stereotypical views of masculinity and competence.

45604 ■ *"Unseen Injustice: Incivility as Modern Discrimination in Organizations"* in *Academy of Management Review (January 2008, pp. 55)*
Pub: ScholarOne Inc.
Contact: William T. Carden, Jr., President
Ed: Lilia M. Cortina. **Description:** Analysis of social psychological research on modern discrimination to explain the theory of incivility used as part of sexism and racism in organizations. The selective incivility observed is discussed, as well as its implications and efforts to eliminate it.

45605 ■ *"Unstable Atmosphere: Survey Finds State Execs Cool On Climate Change"* in *The Business Journal-Milwaukee (Vol. 25, August 8, 2008, No. 46, pp. A1)*
Pub: American City Business Journals, Inc.
Contact: Whitney Shaw, President
Ed: David Doege. **Description:** According to a survey of business executives in Wisconsin, business leaders do not see climate change as a pressing concern, but businesses are moving toward more energy-efficient operations. The survey also revealed that executives believe that financial incentives can promote energy conservation. Other survey results are provided.

45606 ■ *"Unveiling the Secrets Behind Hispanic Business' 100 Fastest-Growing Companies"* in *Hispanic Business (Vol. 30, July-August 2008, No. 7-8, pp. 22)*
Pub: Hispanic Business Inc.
Contact: Jesus Chavarria, President
Ed: Michael Bowker. **Description:** CEO's of the five fastest growing Hispanic-owned companies discuss the success of their companies; most of them attribute their success to proper investment and diversification, effective innovations and seeing growth opportunities where others see roadblocks.

45607 ■ *"USAmeriBank, Liberty Deal Spells Merger Trend"* in *The Business Journal-Serving Greater Tampa Bay (Vol. 28, September 26, 2008, No. 40, pp. 1)*
Pub: American City Business Journals, Inc.
Contact: Whitney Shaw, President
Ed: Margie Manning. **Description:** It is believed that the pending $14.9 million purchase of Liberty Bank by USAmeriBank could be at the forefront of a trend. Executives of both companies expect the deal to close by the end of 2008. USAmeriBank will have $430 million in assets and five offices in Pinellas, Florida once the deal is completed.

45608 ■ *"Used to Being Courted"* in *Business Courier (Vol. 24, March 14, 2008, No. 49, pp. 1)*
Pub: American City Business Journals, Inc.
Contact: Whitney Shaw, President
Ed: Dan Monk. **Description:** College basketball coach Sean Miller is reported to be earning up to $900,000 a year. A look into the contract at regional universities show Thad Matta makes over $2 million in a year and that UK's Billy Gillispie makes over $2.7 million.

45609 ■ *"The Value of Conversations With Employees; Talk Isn't Cheap"* in *Gallup Management Journal (June 30, 2011)*
Pub: Gallup Inc.
Contact: Jim Clifton, Chief Executive Officer
Ed: Jessica Tyler. **Description:** When managers have meaningful exchanges with their employees, they don't only show they care, they also add value to their organization's bottom line.

45610 ■ *"VC Boosts WorkForce: Livonia Software Company to Add Sales, Marketing Staff"* in *Crain's Detroit Business (March 24, 2008)*
Pub: Crain Communications Inc.
Contact: Rance E. Crain, President
Ed: Tom Henderson. **Description:** WorkForce Software Inc., a company that provides software to manage payroll processes and oversee compliance with state and federal regulations and with union rules, plans to use an investment of $5.5 million in venture capital to hire more sales and marketing staff.

45611 ■ *"Vicki Avril: Senior Vice-President of Tubular Division, Ipsco Inc."* in *Crain's Chicago Business (Vol. 31, May 5, 2008, No. 18)*
Pub: Crain Communications Inc.
Contact: Todd Johnson, Publisher
Ed: Miriam Gottfried. **Description:** Profile of Vicki Avril who is the senior vice-president of the tubular division at Ipsco Inc. where she supervises 2,800 employees and 13 mills throughout the United States and Canada.

45612 ■ *"Virginia Albanese: President and CEO"* in *Inside Business (Vol. 13, September-October 2011, No. 5, pp. NC4)*
Pub: Great Lakes Publishing Co.
Ed: Jeannie Roberts. **Description:** Profile of Virginia Albanese, CEO of FedEx's Custom Critical Division in Akron, Ohio. Albanese discusses her philosophy on business leadership.

45613 ■ *"Voices: Climategate Leads Nowhere"* in *Business Strategy Review (Vol. 21, Summer 2010, No. 2, pp. 76)*
Pub: Blackwell Publishers Ltd.
Ed: Mick Blowfield. **Description:** An examination of the recent Climategate scandal that explores the damage caused by managers who are too easily mystified or misled.

45614 ■ *"Voices: Controlled Wisdom"* in *Business Strategy Review (Vol. 23, Spring 2012, No. 1, pp. 86)*
Released: Spring 2012. **Description:** Peter Drucker observes, "Trying to predict the future is like trying to drive down a country road at night with no lights while looking out the back window." and yet, there is always a strong desire to control the uncontrollable. Management and control is discussed.

45615 ■ *"Voices: More Important than Results"* in *Business Strategy Review (Vol. 21, Summer 2010, No. 2, pp. 81)*
Pub: Blackwell Publishers Ltd.
Ed: Bert De Reyck, Zeger Degraeve. **Description:** Managing only for results leads to crises. It is important to reward people for the decisions they make, not just for the results they create.

45616 ■ *"Voices: The Strategic Innovation Cube"* in *Business Strategy Review (Vol. 23, Spring 2012, No. 1, pp. 84)*
Released: Spring 2012. **Description:** Companies that innovate tend to prosper. Yet the process used by most innovative firms remains a mystery. Is there

a way that any company can discern whether to commit resources to an innovation idea? Kiriti Rambhatla has blended the fields of science and management and offers a new way of thinking about innovation inside any company.

45617 ■ *Wake Up and Smell the Zeitgeist*
Ed: Grand McCracken. **Released:** 2010. **Price:** $26.95. **Description:** Insight is given into an element of corporate success that's often overlooked and valuable suggestions are offered for any small business to pursue.

45618 ■ *The Wall Street Journal. Complete Small Business Guidebook*
Pub: Three Rivers Press
Contact: Caroline Sincerbeaux, Editor
E-mail: csincerbeaux@randomhouse.com
Ed: Colleen DeBaise. **Released:** December 29, 2009. **Price:** $15. **Description:** The mechanics of building, running and growing a profitable business are outlined, teaching how to write a business plan, ways to finding money during lean years, how to keep stress in check, time management, investment in technology, hiring, marketing, management basics, angel investing and venture capital, as well as an exit strategy.

45619 ■ *"Wanted: African American Professional for Hire"* in *Black Enterprise (Vol. 37, November 2006, No. 4, pp. 93)*
Pub: Earl G. Graves Publishing Co. Inc.
Contact: Earl G. Graves, Jr., President
Ed: Joe Watson. **Description:** Excerpt from the book, Without Excuses: Unleash the Power of Diversity to Build Your Business, speaks to the lack of diversity in the corporate arena and why executives, recruiters, and HR professionals claim they are unable to find qualified individuals of different races when hiring.

45620 ■ *"The War for Talent"* in *Canadian Business (Vol. 80, January 29, 2007, No. 3, pp. 60)*
Ed: Erin Pooley. **Description:** The recruitment policies of Canadian businesses are described. The trends pertaining to the growth of executive salaries in Canada are discussed.

45621 ■ *"Warner Bros. Domestic Television Distribution"* in *Brandweek (Vol. 49, April 21, 2008, No. 16, pp. SR16)*
Pub: Nielsen Business Media Inc.
Contact: Howard Appelbaum, President
Ed: Marc Berman. **Description:** Provides contact information for sales and marketing personnel for Warner Bros. Domestic Television Distribution as well as a listing of the station's top programming and an analysis of the current season and the target audience for those programs running in the current season.

45622 ■ *We Are Smarter Than Me: How to Unleash the Power of Crowds in Your Business*
Pub: Wharton School Publishing
Ed: Barry Libert, Jon Spector, Don Tapscott. **Released:** September 25, 2007. **Price:** $24.99, Nonmembers; $19.99, Members; $17.59, Members; $21.99, Nonmembers. **Description:** Ways to use social networking and community in order to make decisions and plan your business, with a focus on product development, manufacturing, marketing, customer service, finance, management, and more. **Availability:** PrintE-book.

45623 ■ *"Wear More Hats"* in *Canadian Business (Vol. 80, March 12, 2007, No. 6, pp. 39)*
Ed: Michael Stern. **Description:** The need on the part of managers to volunteer to accept more responsibilities for their growth as well as that of company's is discussed.

45624 ■ *"Web-Based Solutions Streamline Operations"* in *Contractor (Vol. 56, December 2009, No. 12, pp. 28)*
Pub: Penton Media, Inc.
Ed: William Feldman, Patti Feldman. **Description:** Sage Project Lifecycle Management is a Web-based service platform for plumbing and HVAC contractors.

It enables effective workflow and document management. Projectmates, on the other hand, is a Web-based enterprise-wide solution for managing both commercial plumbing and HVAC projects.

45625 ■ "Web Site Focuses on Helping People Find Jobs, Internships with Area Businesses" in Crain's Detroit Business (Vol. 26, Jan. 4, 2010)
Pub: Crain Communications Inc.
Contact: Rance E. Crain, President
Ed: Dustin Walsh. Description: DetroitIntern.com, LLC is helping metro Detroit college students and young professionals find career-advancing internships or jobs with local businesses.

45626 ■ "A Well-Crafted Employee Handbook Can Make Work Run More Smoothly" in Idaho Business Review (September 17, 2014)
Pub: Dolan Co.
Contact: James P. Dolan, President
Released: September 17, 2014. Description: An employee handbook will provide a complaint process, provide company management flexibility and clarity and keep a company out of legal problems. Training, compensation, benefits, security, health, performance appraisals, and safety issues must be covered. Human resource managers and other mangers should cover basics to help communicate with workers.

45627 ■ "Well Done!" in Canadian Business (Vol. 80, April 23, 2007, No. 9, pp. 47)
Ed: Joe Castaldo. Description: The human resource management methods applied by different companies like Deloitte & Touche LLP are presented.

45628 ■ The Well-Timed Strategy: Managing Business Cycle for Competitive Advantage
Pub: Wharton School Publishing
Ed: Peter Navarro. Released: January 13, 2006. Price: $39.99, Nonmembers; $31.99, Members. Description: An overview of business cycles and risks is presented. Recession is a good time to find key personnel for a small business. Other issues addressed include investment, production, and marketing in order to maintain a competitive edge. Availability: Print; E-book.

45629 ■ "Wendy Turner; Vice-President and General Manager, Vocalo.org" in Crain's Chicago Business (Vol. 31, May 5, 2008, No. 18, pp. 22)
Pub: Crain Communications Inc.
Contact: Todd Johnson, Publisher
Ed: Kevin Mckeough. Description: Profile of Wendy Turner who is a leader at Vocalo, a combination of talk radio and Web site, where listeners can set up profile pages similar to those on Facebook.

45630 ■ "Werner's Legacy: 'His Word Meant Something'" in Pittsburgh Business Times (Vol. 33, June 6, 2014, No. 47, pp. 3)
Pub: American City Business Journals
Released: June 6, 2014. Description: Public relations expert, Lawrence Werner, was highly respected for his professional skills as well as his honesty and integrity. Werner's former colleague, John Verbanac, asserts 'His word meant something', as several large Pittsburgh companies and nonprofit organizations sought his advice to improve image, particularly on crisis management.

45631 ■ "WestJet Hires a New CFO After Lengthy Search" in Globe & Mail (January 23, 2007, pp. B8)
Pub: CTVglobemedia Publishing Inc.
Ed: Brent Jang. Description: Vito Culmone, formerly vice of Malson Canada, is appointed as chief financial officer.

45632 ■ "Weyerhaeuser's REIT Decision Shouldn't Scare Investors Away" in Barron's (Vol. 88, June 30, 2008, No. 26, pp. 18)
Pub: Dow Jones & Co., Inc.
Contact: Clare Hart, President
Ed: Christopher Williams. Description: Weyerhaeuser Co.'s management said that a conversion to a real estate investment trust was not likely in 2009 since the move is not tax-efficient as of the moment

and would overload its non-timber assets with debt. The company's shares have fallen by 19.5 percent. However, the company remains an asset-rich outfit and its activist shareholder is pushing for change.

45633 ■ A Whack on the Side of the Head: How You Can Be More Creative
Pub: Business Plus
Ed: Roger von Oech. Released: May 05, 2008. Price: $17, paperback; C$19, paperback. Description: The author, a consultant, shares insight into increasing entrepreneurial creativity. Availability: Print.

45634 ■ "What CEOs Will Admit Out of the Office" in Inc. (November 2007, pp. 30)
Pub: Mansueto Ventures L.L.C.
Contact: John Koten, Chief Executive Officer
Ed: Sarah Goldstein. Description: Thirty CEOs from the fastest growing companies in the U.S. answer questions about their firms.

45635 ■ "What Comes After That Job Is Cut?" in Business Review Albany (Vol. 41, August 15, 2014, No. 21, pp. 4)
Pub: The Business Journals
Released: August 15, 2014. Description: Former KeyBank regional president, Jeff Stone, has joined the list of well-known banking executives who have reinvented themselves as the financial industry transforms around the Albany, NY area. Stone, as well as other leading bank leaders, have transitioned to smaller banks or other industries. Insights into the Banking Industry's Act II are provided.

45636 ■ What Got You Here Won't Get You There
Pub: Hyperion Books
Contact: Ellen Archer, President
Ed: Marshall Goldsmith, Mark Reiter. Released: January 09, 2007. Price: $23.95; C$32.95. Description: Executive coach teaches how to climb the ladder to upper levels of management.

45637 ■ "What It Takes to Be an Effective Leader" in Black Enterprise (Vol. 41, December 2010, No. 5, pp. 62)
Pub: Earl G. Graves Publishing Co. Inc.
Contact: Earl G. Graves, Jr., President
Ed: Sonia Alleyne. Description: Redia Anderson and Lenora Billings-Harris have partnered to write the book, 'Trailblazers: How Top Business Leaders Are Accelerating Results Through Inclusion and Diversity'. The book offers insight into best practices demonstrated by some of the most influential chief diversity officers in business.

45638 ■ "What Kind of Golfer Are You?" in Baltimore Business Journal (Vol. 29, May 4, 2012, No. 53, pp. 1)
Pub: American City Business Journals, Inc.
Contact: Whitney Shaw, President
Ed: Gary Haber. Released: May 4, 2012. Description: Businesspeople playing golf are classified into different profiles according to style. These profiles also describe the behavior of businessmen during and after playing golf.

45639 ■ "What Kind of Leader Are You?" in Inc. (Vol. 36, September 2014, No. 7, pp. 76)
Pub: Mansueto Ventures L.L.C.
Contact: John Koten, Chief Executive Officer
Released: September 2014. Description: Ranking of leadership skills for entrepreneurs and managers is presented, with being a visionary leading each category.

45640 ■ What Makes People Tick: How to Understand Yourself and Others
Pub: AWC Business Solutions
Released: September 15, 2014. Price: , $29.54 paperback. Description: Management and Human Resources Development and Psychology expert offers a guide to self-discovery and personal growth. Job Compatibility Indicator is used to pinpoint the most suitable personality for each occupation.

45641 ■ "What Your Employees Need to Know; They Probably Don't Know How They're Performing" in Gallup Management

Journal (April 13, 2011)
Pub: Gallup Inc.
Contact: Jim Clifton, Chief Executive Officer
Ed: Steve Crabtree. Description: Personalized feedback and recognition aren't just extras that make workers feel good about themselves they are critical predictors of positive performance.

45642 ■ "What's More Important: Talent or Engagement? A Study With Retailer ANN INC. Seeks To Find the Essential Ingredients To High-Performing Managers and Employees" in Gallup Business Journal (April 22, 2014)
Pub: Gallup Press
Released: April 22, 2014. Description: ANN INC. is a leading women's clothing retailer that is exploring the necessary steps to achieving both high-performing managers and employees. The firm found that hiring people with the right talent and engaging them will maximize performance.

45643 ■ "What's the Ticket to a Higher-Paying Corporate Position?" in Orlando Business Journal (Vol. 29, September 14, 2012, No. 13, pp. 1)
Pub: American City Business Journal
Description: Advice on how to land higher-paying executive jobs in the US is presented. Understanding organization politics as well as compensation is encouraged. Employment alternatives for executives are also given.

45644 ■ "When Emotional Reasoning Trumps IQ" in Harvard Business Review (Vol. 88, September 2010, No. 9, pp. 27)
Pub: Harvard Business School Publishing
Ed: Rodcrick Gilkoy, Ricardo Caceda, Clinton Kilts. Description: Strategic reasoning was found to be linked more closely to areas of the brain associated with intuition and emotion, rather than the prefrontal cortex, which is typically thought to be the center of such activity. Implications for management skills are discussed.

45645 ■ When Growth Stalls: How It Happens, Why You're Stuck, and what To Do About It
Pub: John Wiley & Sons Inc.
Contact: Stephen M. Smith, President
Ed: Steve McKee. Released: February 2009. Price: $27.95, hardcover; $18.99. Description: Marketing expert presents evidence that demonstrates that slow growth experienced by a firm is usually not the cause of mismanagement or blundering, but by natural market forces and destructive internal dynamics that are often unrecognized. Availability: PrintE-book.

45646 ■ "When and How to Innovate Your Business Model" in Strategy & Leadership (Vol. 38, July-August 2010, No. 4, pp. 17-26)
Pub: Emerald Inc.
Ed: Edward Giesen, Eric Riddleberger, Richard Christner, Ragna Bell. Description: A study uses survey data to identify factors that are considered by corporate leaders regarding when and how they should innovate their business model. Findings identify a set of characteristics called the 'Three A's, Namely, Aligned, Analytical and Adaptable, which corporate leaders use consistently to successfully design and execute business-model innovation.

45647 ■ "When Key Employees Clash: How Should a Business Owner Handle a Conflict Between Two Senior Managers?" in Harvard Business Review (Vol. 90, June 2012, No. 6, pp. 135)
Pub: Harvard Business Review Press
Contact: Peter E. Walsh, Director
Ed: H. Irving Grousbeck. Released: June 2012. Description: A fictitious employee conflict scenario is presented, with contributors providing suggestions for an effective management plan. The key component is ensuring that both employees receive the coaching and support necessary to enable them to perceive their roles more clearly and to build trust.

45648 ■ *"When You Need Strong Millennials in Your Workplace"* in *Agency Sales Magazine (Vol. 39, November 2009, No. 10, pp. 22)*
Ed: Joanne G. Sujansky. **Description:** Millennials are bringing a new set of skills and a different kind of work ethics to the workplace. This generation is used to receiving a great deal of positive feedback and they expect to continue receiving this on the job. Expectations should be made clear to this generation and long-term career plans and goals should also be discussed with them.

45649 ■ *"Where Are They Now?"* in *Canadian Business (Vol. 79, October 9, 2006, No. 20, pp. 71)*
Pub: Rogers Media Inc.
Contact: Tony Viner, President
Ed: Jeff Sanford, Zena Olijnyk, Andrew Wahl, Andy Holloway, John Gray. **Description:** The profile of the top chief executive officers of Canada for the year 2005 is discussed.

45650 ■ *"Where to Buy the Right MBA"* in *Canadian Business (Vol. 79, October 23, 2006, No. 21, pp. 99)*
Ed: Erin Pooley; Laura Bogomolny; Joe Castaldo; Michelle Magnan; Claire Gagne. **Description:** Details of Canadian graduate business schools offering Master of business administration degree are presented.

45651 ■ *"Where Do Women Stand?"* in *Birmingham Business Journal (Vol. 31, April 4, 2014, No. 14, pp. 4)*
Pub: American City Business Journals, Inc.
Contact: Whitney Shaw, President
Released: April 4, 2014. **Description:** Women business executives discuss ways women are faring in the workplace. City Paper Company's Cathy Friedman says equality remains the biggest challenge for women in the workplace. Mayer Electric Supply's Nancy Goedecke, believes company's should encourage women to try new things.

45652 ■ *Where Have All the Leaders Gone?*
Pub: Simon and Schuster Inc.
Contact: Carolyn Reidy, President
E-mail: carolyn.reidy@simonandschuster.com
Ed: Lee Iacocca. **Released:** April 2008. **Price:** $15. **Description:** Lee Iacocca discusses the principles of great leadership. **Availability:** Print.

45653 ■ *"Why Bossy Is Better for Rookie Managers"* in *Harvard Business Review (Vol. 90, May 2012, No. 5, pp. 30)*
Pub: Harvard Business Review Press
Contact: Peter E. Walsh, Director
Ed: Stephen J. Sauer. **Released:** May 2012. **Description:** New managers can enhance their standing by taking control and appearing decisive and confident, especially if they may be perceived as having low status due to education, age, or experience. However, those who are already perceived as high status can be most effective by soliciting input.

45654 ■ *"Why Creating Organizational Change Is So Hard; Resistance To Change Is Entrenched In Most Companies. Here's How To Overcome Obstacles and Create Change That Lasts"* in *Gallup Business Journal (May 22, 2014)*
Pub: Gallup Press
Released: May 22, 2014. **Description:** Poorly defined objectives, politics, and unclear metrics are come of the obstacles to implementing meaningful change in any organization. Employees are motivated to change if leaders provide hope and inspiration. Ways that companies can overcome barriers to change are examined.

45655 ■ *"Why Did We Ever Go Into HR?"* in *Harvard Business Review (Vol. 86, July-August 2008, No. 8, pp. 39)*
Pub: Harvard Business Review Press
Contact: Peter E. Walsh, Director
Ed: Matthew D. Breitfelder, Daisy Wademan Dowling. **Description:** Examines the role of human resource directors and how their jobs foster new ideas and generate optimism.

45656 ■ *"Why Great Managers Are So Rare; Companies Fail To Choose the Candidate With the Right Talent For the Job 82 Percent of the Time, Gallup Finds"* in *Gallup Business Journal (March 25, 2014)*
Pub: Gallup Press
Released: March 25, 2014. **Description:** Gallup research suggests that companies hire the wrong person to manage their firm about 82 percent of the time. Many times management talent already exists within the company, but for some reason, companies look elsewhere for that talent. Bad managers cost billions of dollars to businesses annually.

45657 ■ *"Why HR Practices Are Not Evidence-Based"* in *Academy of Management Journal (Vol. 50, No. 5, October 1, 2007, pp. 1033)*
Pub: Academy of Management
Contact: Ming-Jer Chen, President
Ed: Edward E. Lawler. **Description:** A suggestion that an Evidence-Based Management Collaboration (EBMC) can be established to facilitate effective transfer of ideas between science and practice is presented.

45658 ■ *"Why I Stopped Firing Everyone and Started Being a Better Boss"* in *Inc. (Vol. 34, September 2012, No. 7, pp. 86)*
Pub: Mansueto Ventures L.L.C.
Contact: John Koten, Chief Executive Officer
Ed: April Joyner. **Released:** September 2012. **Description:** Indigo Johnson, former Marine, discusses her management style when starting her business. She fired employees regularly. Johnson enrolled in a PhD program in leadership and established a better hiring program and learned to utilize her workers' strengths.

45659 ■ *"Why It Pays to be in the Boardroom"* in *Globe & Mail (January 16, 2006, pp. B1)*
Ed: Janet McFarland. **Description:** The reasons behind higher stock compensation for board directors, in Canada, are presented. The survey is conducted by Patrick O'Callaghan & Associates and Korn/Ferry International.

45660 ■ *"Why Men Still Get More Promotions Than Women"* in *Harvard Business Review (Vol. 88, September 2010, No. 9, pp. 80)*
Pub: Harvard Business School Publishing
Ed: Herminia Ibarra, Nancy M. Carter, Christine Silva. **Description:** Sponsorship, rather than mentoring, is identified as the main difference in why men still receive more promotions than women. Active executive sponsorship is key to fostering career advancement.

45661 ■ *"Why Motivating People Doesn't Work...and What Does: The New Science of Leading, Energizing, and Engaging"*
Pub: Berrett-Koehler Communications Inc.
Contact: Steve Piersanti, President
E-mail: spiersanti@bkpub.com
Released: September 30, 2014. **Price:** , $24.95. **Description:** Leadership researcher, consultant, and business coach, Susan Fowler, shares the latest research on the nature of human motivation to present a tested model and course of action to help Human Resource leaders and managers guide workers towards motivation that will not only increase productivity and engagement but will provide employees with a sense of purpose and fulfillment.

45662 ■ *"Why Slacking Off Is Great For Business"* in *Canadian Business (Vol. 85, August 13, 2012, No. 13, pp. 60)*
Pub: George Media Inc.
Ed: Sarah Barmak. **Released:** August 13, 2012. **Description:** Procrastination can be good for busy managers to develop creative thinking which may be good for business. Ways to enhance the brain's creative engine including taking a different route to the office, reading a best seller, or playing golf.

45663 ■ *"Why Successful Entrepreneurs Are Effective Delegators; Shifting from a Do-It-Yourself Executive Style to a More Hands-Off Approach is Essential When They're Growing a Business"* in *Gallup Business Journal (August 26, 2014)*
Pub: Gallup Press
Released: August 26, 2014. **Description:** It is critical for entrepreneurs to step away from a do-it-yourself executive style to a more hands-off approach when a company begins to grow.

45664 ■ *"Why To Embrace Positive Leadership"* in *Birmingham Business Journal (Vol. 31, February 7, 2014, No. 6, pp. 14)*
Pub: American City Business Journals, Inc.
Contact: Whitney Shaw, President
Released: February 7, 2014. **Description:** The benefits achieved from managers' adoption of positive leadership are discussed. Positive leadership motivates employees to achieve higher performance levels. Tips to achieve positive leadership are listed.

45665 ■ *"Why Top Young Managers Are In a Nonstop Job Hunt"* in *(Vol. 90, July-August 2012, No. 7-8, pp. 28)*
Pub: Harvard Business Review Press
Contact: Peter E. Walsh, Director
Ed: Monika Hamori, Jie Cao, Burak Koyuncu. **Released:** July-August 2012. **Description:** Managers are moving from firm to firm in part because companies are not addressing formal training, coaching, and mentoring needs. While these are costly, companies might benefit from the investment, as managers may tend to stay longer in firms where they are provided.

45666 ■ *Why Work Sucks and How To Fix It*
Pub: Portfolio Publishing
Contact: Adrian Zackheim, President
Ed: Cali Ressler, Jody Thompson. **Released:** May 01, 2008. **Price:** $12.99; $15, Paperback. **Description:** Results-Only Work Environments (ROWE) not only make employees happier, it also delivers better results. ROWE allows employees to do whatever they want, whenever they want as long as business objectives are met. No more pointless meetings, fighting traffic to be to work on time, or asking for permission for time off. **Availability:** Electronic publishing.

45667 ■ *"Why Your Company Must Be Mission-Driven; A Clear Mission Inspires Employee Engagement, Fosters Customer Engagement, and Helps Boost Company Performance -- Among Other Benefits"* in *Gallup Business Journal (March 6, 2014)*
Pub: Gallup Press
Released: March 6, 2014. **Description:** It is stressed that executives need a clear mission in order to engage their workers, foster customer engagement, and to help boost their firm's performance.

45668 ■ *"The Wiki-Powered Workplace"* in *Workforce Management (Vol. 88, November 16, 2009, No. 12, pp. 8)*
Pub: Crain Communications Inc.
Contact: Rance E. Crain, President
Description: Many organizations are successfully using wikis inside the corporate structure for business communications and knowledge sharing. Wikis can be a very powerful tool due to the inherent transparency that comes with allowing everything to be edited with the accountability of seeing who is doing the editing. A brilliant employee may be noticed sooner because they are doing work in the wiki and the work is being judged on its own merit.

45669 ■ *"Wilderness Leadership - On the Job: Five Principles From Outdoor Exploration That Will Make You a Better Manager"* in *Harvard Business Review (Vol. 90, April 2012, No. 4, pp. 127)*
Pub: Harvard Business Review Press
Contact: Peter E. Walsh, Director
Ed: John Kanengieter, Aparna Rajagopal-Durbin. **Released:** April 2012. **Description:** Five principles of wilderness leadership are: practicing leadership, leading from everywhere, behaving well, remaining calm, and disconnecting to connect. Key points include knowing when to offer leadership to another member, and taking a break from technological devices that can distract from critical thinking.

45670 ■ *Wiley Pathways Small Business Management*
Pub: John Wiley & Sons Inc.
Contact: Stephen M. Smith, President
Ed: Richard M. Hodgetts, Donald F. Kuratko, Margaret Burlingame, Don Gulbrandsen. **Released:** March 2007. **Price:** $76.95, paperback; $42.50. **Description:** Tips for starting and running a successful small business are given, including advice on writing a business plan, financing, and the law. **Availability:** PrintE-book.

45671 ■ *"Winner: Caparo Group Plc"* in *Crain's Detroit Business (Vol. 24, March 24, 2008, No. 12, pp. 12)*
Pub: Crain Communications Inc.
Contact: Rance E. Crain, President
Ed: Brent Snavely. **Description:** London-based Caparo Group plc saw its acquisition of Voestalpine Polynorm as an opportunity to gain a foothold in the North American automotive industry. Caparo was impressed with the company's breadth of manufacturing capabilities and quality systems as well as with the management team.

45672 ■ *"The Winner's Circle: Hispanic Business Magazine's Elite Women"* in *Hispanic Business (Vol. 30, April 2008, No. 4, pp. 20)*
Pub: Hispanic Business Inc.
Contact: Jesus Chavarria, President
Ed: Hildy Medina. **Description:** Although there has been progress concerning Hispanic women professionals who are growing in numbers in the upper echelons of the corporate arena, many still find that they face discrimination when it comes to pay and promotions. Statistical data included.

45673 ■ *"Winners and Losers"* in *Crain's Detroit Business (Vol. 25, June 22, 2009, No. 25, pp. 18)*
Pub: Crain Communications Inc. - Detroit
Contact: Keith Crain, Chairman
Description: Rankings for Detroit's 50 top-compensated CEOs has changed due to the economic recession. The biggest changes are discussed.

45674 ■ *"Wisdom from the Mountaintops"* in *Canadian Business (Vol. 83, October 12, 2010, No. 17, pp. 91)*
Pub: Rogers Media Inc.
Contact: Tony Viner, President
Ed: Matthew McClearn. **Description:** Techniques used to save lives on the world's highest mountains could make companies more creative. Mountaineers have time to talk to one another, and the resulting flow of ideas help climbers reach the summit. Organizations are expected to foster communication both internally and externally.

45675 ■ *"A Woman's Advantage"* in *Black Enterprise (Vol. 38, December 2007, No. 5, pp. 86)*
Pub: Earl G. Graves Publishing Co. Inc.
Contact: Earl G. Graves, Jr., President
Ed: Marcia A. Reed-Woodard. **Description:** Leadership development is essential for any small business. Simmons College's Strategic Leadership for Women educational course offers a five-day program for professional women teaching powerful strategies to perform, compete, and win in the workplace.

45676 ■ *"Women as 21st Century Leaders"* in *Women In Business (Vol. 63, Summer 2011, No. 2, pp. 26)*
Pub: American Business Women's Association
Contact: Lorie Burch, President
Ed: Leigh Elmore. **Description:** American Business Women's Association and Park University have partnered to provide a leadership training program to attendees of the 2011 National Women's Leadership Conference. The courses will incorporate introduction to concepts, development of critical thinking skills and direct application through exercises. Comments from executives are also included.

45677 ■ *"Women Board Numbers Stagnate"* in *Boston Business Journal (Vol. 30, November 26, 2010, No. 44, pp. 1)*
Pub: Boston Business Journal
Ed: Mary Moore. **Description:** The 2010 data in 'Census of Women Directors and Executive Officers of Massachusetts Public Companies' showed little change in the number of executive officers and board members in the state's top 100 firms. The data was compiled by Bentley University, The Boston Club, and Mercer. Key information on 2010 Women on Boards is also provided.

45678 ■ *"Women Inch Forward on Corporate Boards"* in *Marketing to Women (Vol. 21, April 2008, No. 4, pp. 6)*
Description: According to the latest study by Inter-Organization Network, few huge leaps of progress and in some cases backsliding has taken place in regards to gender diversity on corporate boards. Statistical data included.

45679 ■ *"Work Force: In the Mix"* in *Entrepreneur (Vol. 35, October 2007, No. 10, pp. 109)*
Pub: Entrepreneur Press
Contact: Perlman Neil, President
Ed: Mark Henricks. **Description:** A study of 708 companies' diversity programs shows that diversity training alone is not the most effective way of increasing diversity in management. It was found that one effective way of putting minorities and women in management teams is to give a team or a person the task of improving diversity in the company. The reason why accountability succeeds in diversifying the workforce is discussed.

45680 ■ *"Working For Pennies? Huge Pay Gap Between Top Executives and Black Employees"* in *Black Enterprise (Vol. 38, March 2008, No. 8)*
Pub: Earl G. Graves Publishing Co. Inc.
Contact: Earl G. Graves, Jr., President
Ed: Cliff Hocker. **Description:** CEO pay is out of control because most board members approving high salaries and compensation packages are often executives at other firms. According to a study conducted by the Institute for Policy Studies, CEOs earn more than 1,085 times the average full-time black worker's median earnings.

45681 ■ *"The Workplace Generation Gaps"* in *Women In Business (Vol. 62, June 2010, No. 2, pp. 8)*
Pub: American Business Women's Association
Contact: Lorie Burch, President
Ed: Leigh Elmore. **Description:** Generation gaps among baby boomers, Generation X and Generation Y in the workplace are attributed to technological divides and differences in opinions. These factors could lead to workplace misunderstandings, employee turnover and communication difficulties. Details on managing such workplace gaps are discussed.

45682 ■ *"Workplace Wellness"* in *Entrepreneurs (June 2014)*
Pub: Entrepreneur Media Inc.
Released: June 2014. **Description:** Workplace wellness programs can be started by checking with insurers who may provide program and activity suggestions promotional materials or other resources. Teaming up with others is encouraged. For instance, employees from various departments or nearby companies can get flu shots or blood pressure screening. Management should also get involved in these programs, because it will then be known among employees that wellness is taken seriously. It is also important that workplace wellness programs are kept safe and legally sound.

45683 ■ *"The World Is Your Oyster"* in *Canadian Business (Vol. 80, October 22, 2007, No. 21, pp. 140)*
Ed: Regan Ray. **Description:** Business graduates are not that keen on working abroad. Fortune 500 companies are requiring executives to have a multi-country focus. The skill required for jobs abroad, as well as employment opportunities are discussed.

45684 ■ *"World's Best CEOs"* in *Barron's (Vol. 88, March 24, 2008, No. 12, pp. 33)*
Pub: Dow Jones & Co., Inc.
Contact: Clare Hart, President
Ed: Andrew Bary. **Description:** Listing of the 30 best chief executive officers worldwide which was compiled through interviews with investors and analysts, analysis of financial and stock market performance, and leadership and industry stature.

45685 ■ *The Worst-Case Scenario Business Survival Guide: How to Survive the Recession, Handle Layoffs, Raise Emergency Cash, Thwart an Employee Coup, and Avoid Other Potential Disasters*
Pub: John Wiley & Sons Inc.
Contact: Stephen M. Smith, President
Ed: David Borgenicht, Mark Joyner. **Released:** September 28, 2009. **Price:** $17.95. **Description:** Since 1999, the Worst-Case Scenario survival handbooks have provided readers with real answers for the most extreme situations. Now, in a time of economic crisis, the series returns with a new, real-world guide to avoiding the worst business cataclysms.

45686 ■ *"Worth His Salt"* in *Hawaii Business (Vol. 53, January 2008, No. 7, pp. 45)*
Pub: PacificBasin Communications
Ed: Jolyn Okimoto Rosa. **Description:** Bryan Zada owns three PretzelMaker franchises, whose total loss amounted to $40,000 in 2003. Zada believes that listening to employees was one of the key steps in turning the business around. The efforts made to improve the franchises' products are also given.

45687 ■ *"WPC Announces Executive Leadership Team Hires to Grow Business and Security & Compliance Practice"* in *Internet Wire (February 13, 2012)*
Released: February 13, 2012. **Description:** Ray Guzman was appointed senior vice president of sales and business development and Brad Hutson was named chief security officer a WPC. The firm offers full service healthcare business process consulting. The move expands WPC's security and compliance consulting team.

45688 ■ *"Wrap It Up"* in *Entrepreneur (Vol. 36, April 2008, No. 4, pp. 84)*
Pub: Entrepreneur Press
Contact: Perlman Neil, President
Ed: Barry Farber. **Description:** Tips on how to manage and get through the closing of a business sale are presented. Focus on what solutions you can bring and not on emotional attachments that can show your eagerness for the sale. Having a track of positive accomplishments can also help.

45689 ■ *"Wrigley's a Rich Meal for Mars"* in *Crain's Chicago Business (Vol. 31, May 5, 2008, No. 18, pp. 2)*
Pub: Crain Communications Inc.
Contact: Todd Johnson, Publisher
Ed: Steven R. Strahler. **Description:** Mars Inc. will have to manage wisely in order to make their acquisition of Wm. Wrigley Jr. Co. profitable due to the high selling price of Wrigley which far exceeds the industry norm. Statistical data included.

45690 ■ *"The Wrong Tune"* in *The Business Journal-Portland (Vol. 25, July 25, 2008, No. 20, pp. 1)*
Pub: American City Business Journals, Inc.
Contact: Whitney Shaw, President
Ed: Robin J. Moody. **Description:** Views and information on turnaround management and recovery plans of the Oregon Symphony, are presented. The non-profit organization has lost a total of $5.1 million between 2002 and 2008, and $400,000 annual interest payments for a $7 million bank loan. Increased ticket sales, as well as cost cutting measures, are helping improve the finance of the organization.

45691 ■ *"Yates Helps Turn Log Home Green"* in *Contractor (Vol. 56, December 2009, No. 12, pp. 40)*
Pub: Penton Media, Inc.
Description: Upgrading and greening of a log home's HVAC system in Pennsylvania is discussed.

F. W. Behler Inc. president Dave Yates was chosen to manage the project. A large coil of R-flex was used to connect the buffer tank to the garage's radiant heat system.

45692 ■ *"You Have to Lead From Everywhere" in Harvard Business Review (Vol. 88, November 2010, No. 11, pp. 76)*
Pub: Harvard Business School Publishing

Ed: Scott Berinato. **Description:** U.S. Coast Guard Admiral Thad W. Allen discusses effective leadership in successful crises management. Topics include influence of media and public perspective, the applicability of military training to the business arena, and the responsibility of a leader to set morale.

45693 ■ *"Young Executives Share Leadership Lessons" in Pittsburgh Business Times (Vol. 33, April 25, 2014, No. 41, pp. 4)*
Pub: American City Business Journals

Released: April 25, 2014. **Description:** Some members of the Pittsburgh chapter of the Young Presidents' Organization in Pennsylvania participated in a roundtable discussion exploring the different aspects of leadership. They discuss the importance of leadership, the challenges they faced and the defining moments of their careers.

45694 ■ *"Young Giants" in Canadian Business (Vol. 79, August 14, 2006, No. 16-17, pp. 47)*
Ed: Brad Purdy. **Description:** New generations of young chiefs of oil and gas companies in Canada, are featured.

45695 ■ *"Young-Kee Kim: Deputy Director, Fermi National Accelerator Laboratory" in Crain's Chicago Business (Vol. 31, May 5, 2008, No. 18)*
Pub: Crain Communications Inc.
Contact: Todd Johnson, Publisher

Ed: Phuong Ly. **Description:** Profile of Young-Kee Kim who is the deputy director of Fermilab, a physics lab where scientists study the smallest particles in the universe; Ms. Kim was a researcher at Fermilab before becoming deputy director two years ago; Fermilab is currently home to the most powerful particle accelerator in the world and is struggling to compete with other countries despite cuts in federal funding.

45696 ■ *"Your First 100 Days on Your New Job" in Women In Business (Vol. 63, Spring 2011, No. 1, pp. 28)*
Pub: American Business Women's Association
Contact: Lorie Burch, President

Ed: Diane Stafford. **Description:** The first 100 days on the job are crucial if the person's permanent hiring is conditional on surviving a probationary period. The new hire must do more than just master the job's technical details to maximize the chance of success. Details of some basic tips to fit into the corporate culture and get along with coworkers are also discussed.

45697 ■ *"Your Web Brand Counts" in Black Enterprise (Vol. 44, June 2014, No. 10, pp. 46)*
Pub: Earl G. Graves Publishing Co. Inc.
Contact: Earl G. Graves, Jr., President

Released: June 2014. **Description:** Forty-eight percent of employers use Google or other search engines to find information about job applicants and 25 percent of executives hired were originally identified or contacted through social media, thus the importance of a good Web presence is outlined.

TRADE PERIODICALS

45698 ■ *Innovative Leader*
Pub: Winston J. Brill & Associates
Contact: Winston J. Brill, Principal
E-mail: wbrill@winstonbrill.com

URL(s): www.winstonbrill.com/bril001/html/article_index/articles1_50.html. **Released:** Monthly. **Price:** Free. **Description:** Serves as a resource for managers on creativity and productivity.

45699 ■ *Journal of Economics and Management Strategy*
Pub: Blackwell Publishing Inc.
Contact: Gordon Tibbitts, III, President
URL(s): www.wiley.com/WileyCDA/WileyTitle/productCd-JEMS.htmlonlinelibrary.wiley.com/journal/10.1111/(ISSN)1530-9134. **Ed:** Daniel F. Spulber, Jeffrey L. Coles, Zhiqi Chen, Luis M.B. Cabral, Esther Gal-Or. **Released:** Quarterly **Price:** $66, Individuals print & online; €97, Individuals print & online; £65, Other countries print & online, individuals; $63, Individuals online; €93, Individuals online; £61, Other countries online, individuals; $527, Institutions print & online; €527, Institutions print & online; $811, Institutions, other countries print & online.

45700 ■ *The Journal for Quality and Participation*
Pub: American Society for Quality
Contact: Paul E. Borawski, Chief Executive Officer
URL(s): www.asq.org/pub/jqp/. **Released:** Quarterly **Price:** $58, Members domestic, individuals; $90, Members international, individuals; $83, Members includes GST individual, Canada; $99, Nonmembers domestic, individuals; $111, Nonmembers international, individuals; $111, Nonmembers Canadian, includes GST individual.

45701 ■ *Make It A Winning Life*
Pub: Wolf Rinke Associates,Inc.
URL(s): www.wolfrinke.comwww.wolfrinke.com/MIWL.html. **Ed:** Wolf J. Rinke, Ph.D., Editor, wolfrinke@aol.com. **Released:** Bimonthly **Price:** $24.95, Single issue book. **Description:** Features ideas and strategies to help individuals succeed faster and improve the quality of their life. **Remarks:** America Online, Inc.

45702 ■ *Management Report for Nonunion Organizations*
Pub: John Wiley & Sons Inc.
Contact: Stephen M. Smith, President
URL(s): www.wiley.com. **Ed:** Sarah Magee, Editor. **Released:** Monthly. **Price:** $995, U.S.; $995, Canada and Mexico; $1067, elsewhere. **Description:** Features news on current activities; employers' responses; NLRB rulings; court cases; pending legislation; government policies; and advice and opinions from Alfred T. DeMaria, "one of the country's foremost labor lawyers" representing management. Includes information on preventive tactics on how to handle human resources and labor issues without risking unionization, a campaign workshop on what the laws and regulations mean in terms of day-to-day management, white-collar organizing, and questions and answers on common problems.

45703 ■ *The Navigator*
Pub: Chart Your Course International Inc.
Contact: Gregory P. Smith, President
E-mail: greg@chartcourse.com
URL(s): www.chartcourse.com. **Released:** Quarterly. **Price:** Free. **Description:** Publishes advice, how-to tips, and trends in business, including management, TQM, leadership, customer service. Recurring features include news of research, a calendar of events, and a column titled Improving Productivity.

45704 ■ *Quality Management Journal (QMJ)*
Pub: American Society for Quality
Contact: Paul E. Borawski, Chief Executive Officer
URL(s): asq.org/pub/qmj/. **Ed:** Barbara Flynn. **Released:** Quarterly; January, April, July and October. **Price:** $69, U.S. members; $102, Canada members; $95, Other countries members; $96, U.S. nonmembers; $122, Canada non-members; $116, Other countries non-members.

45705 ■ *Quality Manager's Alert*
Pub: American Future Systems Inc.
Contact: Tom Schubert, Manager
E-mail: tschubert@pbp.com
URL(s): www.pbp.com/divisions/publishing/newsletters/regulations-compliance/quality-managers-alert/. **Ed:** Jim Giuliano, Editor. **Released:** Semimonthly **Price:** $299, Individuals. **Description:** Communicates the latest information on changing quality standards and how companies get buy-in on quality from employees. Recurring features include interviews,

news of research, a calendar of events, news of educational opportunities, and a column titled Sharpen Your Judgment.

45706 ■ *Small Business Taxes and Management*
Pub: A/N Group Inc.
Contact: Steven A. Hopfenmuller, President
URL(s): www.smbiz.com. **Released:** Semimonthly, Daily (Mon. thru Fri.). **Price:** $49.95. **Description:** Offers current tax news, reviews of recent cases, tax saving tips, and personal financial planning for small business owners. Includes articles on issues such as finance and management. **Remarks:** Available online only.

45707 ■ *Small Farm News*
Pub: University of California, Davis Agricultural and Resource Economics Department Small Farm Program
Contact: Shermain Hardesty, Leader
URL(s): www.sfc.ucdavis.edu/pubs/sfnews/news.htm. **Ed:** Susan McCue, Editor, semccue@ucdavis.edu. **Released:** Quarterly, 4/year. **Price:** Free. **Description:** Covers topics of interest to small farmers. Includes farmer profiles, government actions and crop information. Recurring features include letters to the editor, interviews, news of research, a calendar of events, notices of publications available, Directors' Column, resources section, news notes, and program news.

45708 ■ *Supervisors Legal Update*
Pub: American Future Systems Inc.
Contact: Tom Schubert, Manager
E-mail: tschubert@pbp.com
URL(s): www.pbp.com/slu.html. **Ed:** Thomas J. Gorman, IV, Editor. **Released:** Semimonthly. **Price:** $94.56, individuals. **Description:** Supplies brief updates on employment law for supervisors. Review a column titled Sharpen Your Judgment.

VIDEOCASSETTES/AUDIOCASSETTES

45709 ■ *American Business Management Series*
Instructional Video
2219 C St.
Lincoln, NE 68502-1745
Ph: (402)475-6570
Free: 800-228-0164
Fax: (402)475-6500
Co. E-mail: orders@insvideo.com
URL: http://www.insvideo.com
Contact: Kathy Damkroger, President

Released: 19??. **Description:** Management training series offers instruction on many of today's business and management issues. **Availability:** VHS.

45710 ■ *Anticipation: Rx for Crisis Management*
Aspen Publishers, Inc.
7201 McKinney Cir.
Frederick, MD 21704
Ph: (301)698-7100
Free: 800-234-1660
Fax: (800)901-9075
Co. E-mail: customerservice@aspenpublisher.com
URL: http://www.aspenpublishers.com
Contact: Robert Becker, President

Released: 1991. **Price:** $495. **Description:** A guide for supervisors on analyzing daily work situations in order to avoid trouble before it happens. **Availability:** VHS; 3/4 U.

45711 ■ *The Art of Negotiating*
Aspen Publishers, Inc.
7201 McKinney Cir.
Frederick, MD 21704
Ph: (301)698-7100
Free: 800-234-1660

Fax: (800)901-9075
Co. E-mail: customerservice@aspenpublisher.com
URL: http://www.aspenpublishers.com
Contact: Robert Becker, President
Released: 1991. **Price:** $495. **Description:** Supervisors and managers will learn how to get what they want with seven basic strategies in the fine art of negotiation. Hosted by master negotiator and world renowned counselor Gerard Nierenberg. **Availability:** VHS; 3/4 U.

45712 ■ Beyond Start-Up: Management Lessons for Growing Companies
Video Arts, Inc.
c/o Aim Learning Group
8238-40 Lehigh
Morton Grove, IL 60053-2615
Free: 877-444-2230
Fax: (416)252-2155
Co. E-mail: service@aimlearninggroup.com
URL: http://www.aimlearninggroup.com
Released: 1989. **Price:** $395. **Description:** Don't settle for being a small company—find out what it takes to expand your business. **Availability:** VHS; 3/4 U.

45713 ■ Center on Profit
International Dairy-Deli-Bakery Association (IDDBA)
636 Science Dr.
Madison, WI 53711-1073
Ph: (608)310-5000
Fax: (608)238-6330
Co. E-mail: iddba@iddba.org
URL: http://www.iddba.org
Released: 19??. **Price:** $160. **Description:** Teaches managers how to reduce unknown shrink, write effective orders and schedules, plus calculate deli items' profit and gross margin contribution to margin. **Availability:** VHS.

45714 ■ Days of Reckoning
National Safety Council, California Chapter Film Library
4553 Glencoe Ave., Ste. 150
Marina Del Rey, CA 90292
Ph: (310)827-9781
Free: 800-421-9585
Fax: (310)827-9861
Co. E-mail: california@nsc.org
URL: http://www.nsc.org/nsc_near_you/FindYourLocalChapter/Pages/California.aspx
Contact: Joseph M. Kaplan, President
Released: 198?. **Description:** This film chronicles the fables of managing a small business. **Availability:** VHS; 3/4 U.

45715 ■ Dealing with Difficult People Volume Two
RMI Media
1365 N. Winchester St.
Olathe, KS 66061-5880
Ph: (913)768-1696
Free: 800-745-5480
Fax: (800)755-6910
Co. E-mail: actmedia@act.org
URL: http://www.actmedia.org
Released: 1993. **Price:** $99. **Description:** Ed Greif explains how to handle very difficult problems with people. **Availability:** VHS.

45716 ■ Delegating Responsibility
1st Financial Training Services
1515 E. Woodfield Rd., Ste. 345
Schaumburg, IL 60173
Ph: (847)969-0900
Free: 800-442-8662
Fax: (847)969-0521
URL: http://www.1stfinancialtraining.com
Contact: Lee Marsh, Director, Operations
Released: 1987. **Price:** $150. **Description:** A primer for managers in dispersing and assigning work to employees. **Availability:** VHS; 3/4 U.

45717 ■ Discipline: A Matter of Judgment
Encyclopedia Britannica
331 N La Salle St.
Chicago, IL 60654
Ph: (312)347-7000
Free: 800-323-1229

Fax: (312)294-2104
URL: http://www.corporate.britannica.com
Contact: Jacob E. Safra
Released: 1989. **Description:** This video teaches that discipline must educate, not humiliate, and urges fair, prompt, and consistent disciplinary action. **Availability:** VHS; 3/4 U.

45718 ■ Don't Keep It To Yourself
Instructional Video
2219 C St.
Lincoln, NE 68502-1745
Ph: (402)475-6570
Free: 800-228-0164
Fax: (402)475-6500
Co. E-mail: orders@insvideo.com
URL: http://www.insvideo.com
Contact: Kathy Damkroger, President
Released: 19??. **Price:** $150. **Description:** Part of the Super Vision for the '90s management training series. Discusses the importance of communication between supervisor and employees. Also provides information on how to increase productivity and decrease tension. **Availability:** VHS.

45719 ■ Empowerment: The Attitude Opportunity
International Training Consultants, Inc.
1838 Park Oaks
Kemah, TX 77565
Free: 800-998-8764
Co. E-mail: itc@trainingitc.com
URL: http://www.trainingitc.com
Contact: Dick Leatherman, Chief Executive Officer
Released: 19??. **Price:** $495. **Description:** Part of the "Empowerment: The Employee Development Series." Teaches employees to accept responsibility for their attitude problems, seeing them as opportunities for improvement, and offers them tips on how to make the transition from attitude problem to attitude opportunity. Also provides information on how to monitor and reward their progress. Comes with leader's guide, self-study instructions, and five participant booklets. **Availability:** VHS.

45720 ■ Everything You Always Wanted to Know about Management
Provant Media
4621 121st St.
Urbandale, IA 50323-2311
Ph: (888)776-8268
Free: 888-776-8268
Fax: (515)327-2555
Co. E-mail: custsvc@ammedia.com
URL: http://www.provantmedia.com
Contact: Tiffan Yamen, Manager, Marketing
Released: 1995. **Price:** $595. **Description:** Outlines the essentials of good management, including the six steps of delegation, employee empowerment, communication, feedback, and goal achievement. Includes course guide with participant exercises and case studies. **Availability:** VHS; CC.

45721 ■ Leadership Skills by Aaron Alejandro
Films Media Group of Cos.
132 W 31st St., 17th Fl.
New York, NY 10001-3406
Ph: (609)671-1000
Free: 800-257-5126
Fax: (609)671-0266
Co. E-mail: custserv@films.com
URL: http://www.cambridgeeducational.com
Contact: David Waldherr, President
Released: 1991. **Price:** $79.95. **Description:** Fast-paced leadership workshop designed to develop and sharpen leadership skills. **Availability:** VHS.

45722 ■ Looking at It from Every Angle
American Management Association (AMA)
1601 Broadway
New York, NY 10019-7420
Ph: (212)586-8100
Free: 877-566-9441

Fax: (212)903-8168
Co. E-mail: customerservice@amanet.org
URL: http://www.amanet.org
Contact: Edward T. Reilly, President
Released: 1985. **Description:** An analysis of proper business training in terms of management decision-making, problem-solving efficiency and department use. **Availability:** VHS; 3/4 U.

45723 ■ Management Action Program
Video Arts, Inc.
c/o Aim Learning Group
8238-40 Lehigh
Morton Grove, IL 60053-2615
Free: 877-444-2230
Fax: (416)252-2155
Co. E-mail: service@aimlearninggroup.com
URL: http://www.aimlearninggroup.com
Released: 1986. **Price:** $680. **Description:** A series of videos that look at customer service, innovation and productivity. **Availability:** VHS; 8 mm; 3/4 U; Special order formats.

45724 ■ Management 1
MR Communication Consultants
5000 Yonge St., Ste. 1705
Toronto, ON, Canada M2N 7E9
Ph: (416)506-9520
Free: 800-263-8326
Fax: (416)539-9604
Co. E-mail: info@mrcomm.com
URL: http://www.mrcomm.com
Contact: Nicole Robert, Manager, Production
Released: 1980. **Description:** A course intended to teach supervisors the fundamental skills to apply to their work situation. **Availability:** VHS; 3/4 U.

45725 ■ Management Techniques That Work
Instructional Video
2219 C St.
Lincoln, NE 68502-1745
Ph: (402)475-6570
Free: 800-228-0164
Fax: (402)475-6500
Co. E-mail: orders@insvideo.com
URL: http://www.insvideo.com
Contact: Kathy Damkroger, President
Released: 19??. **Price:** $89.95. **Description:** Three management experts discuss techniques to improve productivity while also improving the workplace environment. Also looks at participative management and other techniques. **Availability:** VHS.

45726 ■ The Management of Work
Resources for Education & Management, Inc.
1804 Montreal Ct., Ste. A
Tucker, GA 30084
Released: 19??. **Description:** A series intended to show managers how to build the key skills of organizing, planning, directing, and controlling. **Availability:** VHS; 3/4 U.

45727 ■ MBA—Management Basics in Action
Phoenix Learning Group
2349 Chaffee Dr.
Saint Louis, MO 63146-3306
Ph: (314)569-0211
Free: 800-221-1274
Fax: (314)569-2834
URL: http://www.phoenixlearninggroup.com
Released: 1985. **Description:** A program library for management of business. **Availability:** VHS.

45728 ■ Nobody's Perfect: Managing the Team
Video Arts, Inc.
c/o Aim Learning Group
8238-40 Lehigh
Morton Grove, IL 60053-2615
Free: 877-444-2230
Fax: (416)252-2155
Co. E-mail: service@aimlearninggroup.com
URL: http://www.aimlearninggroup.com
Released: 1991. **Price:** $790. **Description:** How to put the right people in the right position on a team, enhancing win potential and covering weak spots. **Availability:** VHS; 8 mm; 3/4 U; Special order formats.

45729 ■ One Small Step
National Safety Council, California Chapter Film Library
4553 Glencoe Ave., Ste. 150
Marina Del Rey, CA 90292
Ph: (310)827-9781
Free: 800-421-9585
Fax: (310)827-9861
Co. E-mail: california@nsc.org
URL: http://www.nsc.org/nsc_near_you/FindYourLocalChapter/Pages/California.aspx
Contact: Joseph M. Kaplan, President
Released: 198?. **Description:** This film looks at how managers can improve their work environments through better communication with their employees. **Availability:** VHS; 3/4 U.

45730 ■ Performance Management: The Road to Excellence
Aspen Publishers, Inc.
7201 McKinney Cir.
Frederick, MD 21704
Ph: (301)698-7100
Free: 800-234-1660
Fax: (800)901-9075
Co. E-mail: customerservice@aspenpublisher.com
URL: http://www.aspenpublishers.com
Contact: Robert Becker, President
Released: 1985. **Price:** $495. **Description:** Employee work levels tend to increase when positive attributes and contributions are stressed. Learn how to implement this performance plan with these helpful tips. **Availability:** VHS; 3/4 U; Special order formats.

45731 ■ Principles of Management
RMI Media
1365 N. Winchester St.
Olathe, KS 66061-5880
Ph: (913)768-1696
Free: 800-745-5480
Fax: (800)755-6910
Co. E-mail: actmedia@act.org
URL: http://www.actmedia.com
Released: 1987. **Description:** These videos describe the basic skills needed for effective management. **Availability:** VHS; 3/4 U.

45732 ■ Problem Solving: A Process for Managers
Encyclopedia Britannica
331 N La Salle St.
Chicago, IL 60654
Ph: (312)347-7000
Free: 800-323-1229
Fax: (312)294-2104
URL: http://www.corporate.britannica.com
Contact: Jacob E. Safra
Released: 1989. **Description:** This program introduces managers to a practical, efficient six-step problem solving method applicable to most management problems. **Availability:** 3/4 U.

45733 ■ Training Needs Assessment
Aspen Publishers, Inc.
7201 McKinney Cir.
Frederick, MD 21704
Ph: (301)698-7100
Free: 800-234-1660
Fax: (800)901-9075
Co. E-mail: customerservice@aspenpublisher.com
URL: http://www.aspenpublishers.com
Contact: Robert Becker, President
Released: 1986. **Price:** $495. **Description:** Supervisor Dave Eppinger explains the process of training needs assessment and discusses the characteristics necessary for a completely efficient system. **Availability:** VHS; 3/4 U.

45734 ■ What Went Wrong?
Aspen Publishers, Inc.
7201 McKinney Cir.
Frederick, MD 21704
Ph: (301)698-7100
Free: 800-234-1660

Fax: (800)901-9075
Co. E-mail: customerservice@aspenpublisher.com
URL: http://www.aspenpublishers.com
Contact: Robert Becker, President
Released: 1985. **Price:** $495. **Description:** An instructional seminar in the art of decision-making and problem-solving in business. **Availability:** VHS; 3/4 U.

45735 ■ Where There's a Will. . .: Leadership and Motivation
Video Arts, Inc.
c/o Aim Learning Group
8238-40 Lehigh
Morton Grove, IL 60053-2615
Free: 877-444-2230
Fax: (416)252-2155
Co. E-mail: service@aimlearninggroup.com
URL: http://www.aimlearninggroup.com
Released: 1988. **Price:** $790. **Description:** Find out how you can motivate your workers to a higher productivity level. **Availability:** VHS; 8 mm; 3/4 U; Special order formats.

45736 ■ Who Does What?
Aspen Publishers, Inc.
7201 McKinney Cir.
Frederick, MD 21704
Ph: (301)698-7100
Free: 800-234-1660
Fax: (800)901-9075
Co. E-mail: customerservice@aspenpublisher.com
URL: http://www.aspenpublishers.com
Contact: Robert Becker, President
Released: 1989. **Price:** $495. **Description:** Supervisors will learn how to delegate authority and maximize employee productivity and time management by implementing a nine step checklist, demonstrated through a variety of workplace dramatizations. **Availability:** VHS; 3/4 U.

45737 ■ Winning Entrepreneurial Style
MGM Studios Inc.
245 N Beverly Dr.
Beverly Hills, CA 90210
Ph: (310)449-3000
URL: http://www.mgm.com
Released: 1986. **Description:** A bevy of nationwide entrepreneurs share their secrets for financial success. **Availability:** VHS; CC.

CONSULTANTS

45738 ■ 108 Ideaspace Inc.
108 Dundas St. W, Ste. 201
Toronto, ON, Canada M6B 2H8
Ph: (416)256-7773
Fax: (416)256-7763
Co. E-mail: request@108ideaspace.com
URL: http://www.ptadvisors.com
Contact: Randall M. Craig, President
E-mail: randall@108ideaspace.com
Scope: Organizational advisors to senior management in service- or information-based businesses: professional service firms, education and publishing and financial services. Services in management counsel (including investor/acquisition due diligence, executive coaching, risk assessment and facilitation, planning and leadership), marketing (including branding), technology and human resources. **Founded:** 1994. **Publications:** "Leaving the Mother Ship"; "The Working Resume". **Seminars:** No Job, Now What; Social Media Executive Briefing; Career Networking for Success; Development; Work-Life Balance; Integrated marketing planning workshop.

45739 ■ ABA Inc.
411-24 Wellesley St.
Toronto, ON, Canada M4Y 2X6
Ph: (416)219-8447
Fax: (416)924-4664
Contact: Ray Belanger, Vice President
E-mail: raybel2@home.com
Scope: Firm provides management consultation to emerging and growth oriented companies in the Internet, film and television and multimedia industries. Areas of expertise include planning and developing practices in strategy, finance, marketing, HR and

operations. Services range from full strategy papers to business/marketing plans and financial performance reviews. **Founded:** 1999. **Seminars:** Reduces Cycle Time; Cuts Costs; Improves Learning; Facilitates Accountability.

45740 ■ Advanced Benefits & Human Resources
9350-F Snowden River Pky., Ste. 222
Columbia, MD 21045
Ph: (410)290-9037
Contact: Linda B. Polacek, President
Scope: Provides human resource consulting to high technology businesses. Offers services in the areas of human resources, benefits and training. Creates, maintains, or updates current human resource functions. **Founded:** 1996.

45741 ■ Advisory Management Services Inc.
9600 E 129th St., Ste. B
Kansas City, MO 64149-1025
Ph: (816)765-9611
Contact: Hal Wood, Agent
Scope: A management consulting and training firm specializing in employee relations, management and staff training, organizational development, strategic planning and continuous quality improvement. **Founded:** 1979.

45742 ■ Charles J. Allen and Associates
2668 Foxglove St.
Woodridge, IL 60517
Ph: (630)963-1444
Contact: Charles J. Allen, President
Scope: Specializes in marketing, communication, advertising and promotional consulting. Also serves as business management consultants on a continuing basis. **Founded:** 1970.

45743 ■ The Alliance Management Group Inc.
38 Old Chester Rd., Ste. 300
Gladstone, NJ 07934
Ph: (908)234-2344
Fax: (908)234-0638
Co. E-mail: kathy@strategicalliance.com
URL: http://www.strategicalliance.com
Contact: Gene Slowinski, Director
E-mail: gene@strategicalliance.com
Scope: The firm enables leading companies to maximize the value of their strategic alliances, mergers and acquisitions. Offers services in partner evaluation process, a planning and negotiating program, mergers and acquisition integration, management issues, the turnaround or termination of poorly performing alliances, and a competitive strategic analysis program. **Publications:** "Effective Practices For Sourcing Innovation," Jan-Feb, 2009; "Intellectual Property Issues in Collaborative Research Agreements," Nov-Dec, 2008; "Building University Relationships in China," Sep-Oct, 2008; "Reinventing Corporate Growth: Implementing the Transformational Growth Model"; "The Strongest Link"; "Allocating Patent Rights in Collaborative Research Agreements"; "Protecting Know-how and Trade Secrets in Collaborative Research Agreements," Aug, 2006; "Sourcing External Technology for Innovation," Jun, 2006. **Special Services:** "Want, Find, Get, Manage" Model®; "Want, Find, Get, Manage" Framework®; WFGM Framework®; The Alliance Implementation Program®; WFGM Paradigm®; WFGM Model®; "Want, Find, Get, Manage" Paradigm®, Transformational Growth®; T-growth®.

45744 ■ Alliance Management International Ltd.
PO Box 470691
Cleveland, OH 44147-0691
Ph: (440)838-1922
Contact: Bob Gruss, Managing Partner
E-mail: bgruss@cox.net
Scope: A consulting company that helps to form national and international strategic alliances. Handles alliances between companies forming joint ventures. Staff specialized in small company-large company alliance, alliance assessment and analysis and alliance strategic planning. **Seminars:** Joint Business

Planning; Developing a Shared Vision; Current and New/Prospective Partner Assessment; Customer Service; Sales Training; Leader and Management Skills.

45745 ■ Allsup Inc.
300 Allsup Pl.
Belleville, IL 62223
Free: 800-854-1418
Fax: (618)236-5778
URL: http://www.allsup.com
Contact: Jim Allsup, President
Scope: Social Security disability claims services company understanding the specialized needs of those with disabilities. **Founded:** 1984. **Publications:** "The Alls up Alternative".

45746 ■ Anderson/Roethle Inc.
700 N Water St., Ste. 325
Milwaukee, WI 53202-4221
Ph: (414)276-0070
Fax: (414)276-4364
Co. E-mail: info@anderson-roethle.com
URL: http://www.anderson-roethle.com
Contact: Stanley C. Johnson, President
E-mail: scj@anderson-roethle.com
Scope: Provider of merger, acquisition and divestiture advisory services. Offers strategic planning, valuations and specialized M and A advisory services. **Founded:** 1963.

45747 ■ Apex Innovations Inc.
19951 W 162nd St.
Olathe, KS 66062
Ph: (913)254-0250
Fax: (913)254-0320
Co. E-mail: sales@apex-innovations.com
URL: http://www.apex-innovations.com
Contact: Connie Fox, Human Resources Manager
Scope: A firm of business operations and technology professionals providing solutions nationwide for business needs. Provides a bridge between operations and technology for clients in manufacturing, insurance, banking and government. Offers services in business planning, assessment, education, business performance improvement, change management and the planning and implementation management of solutions. **Founded:** 2002. **Special Services:** i-INFO. EPR™; i-INFO.WORKS™; i-INFO Classes™.

45748 ■ Aurora Management Partners Inc.
4485 Tench Rd., Ste. 340
Suwanee, GA 30024
Ph: (770)904-5209
Fax: (770)904-5226
Co. E-mail: rturcotte@auroramp.com
URL: http://www.auroramp.com
Contact: Laura C. Kendall, Director
E-mail: lkendall@auroramp.com
Scope: Specializes in turnaround management and reorganization consulting. Firm develop strategic initiatives, organize and analyze solutions, deal with creditor issues, review organizational structure and develop time frames for decision making. Turnaround services offered include Recovery plans and their implementation, Viability analysis, Crisis management, Financial restructuring, Corporate and organizational restructuring, Facilities rationalization, Liquidation management, Loan workout, Litigation support and Expert testimony, Contract renegotiation, Sourcing loan refinancing and Sourcing equity investment. **Founded:** 2005. **Publications:** "TMA Turnaround of the Year Award, Small Company, Honorable Mention," Nov, 2005; "Back From The Brink - Bland Farms," Progressive Farmer, Oct, 2004; "New Breed of Turnaround Managers," Catalyst Magazine, Aug, 2004; "Key Performance Drivers - Bland Farms," The Produce News, Apr, 2004; "Corporate Governance: Averting Crisis's Before They Happen," ABJ journal, Feb, 2004.

45749 ■ Avery, Cooper & Co.
4918-50th St.
Yellowknife, NT, Canada X1A 2P2
Ph: (867)873-3441
Free: 800-661-0787

Fax: (867)873-2353
URL: http://www.averycooper.com
Contact: Bernie H. Bauhaus, Manager
E-mail: bernieb@averyco.nt.ca
Scope: Accounting and management consulting firm. **Founded:** 1969. **Seminars:** Sage Software Training. **Special Services:** ACCPAC Plus; Sage Accpac ERP.

45750 ■ Bahr International Inc.
PO Box 795
Gainesville, TX 76241
Ph: (940)665-2344
Fax: (940)665-2359
Co. E-mail: info@bahrintl.com
URL: http://www.bahrintl.com
Contact: C. Charles Bahr, III, Chairman of the Board
Scope: Offers consulting in general management, corporate polices and culture, and strategic and long-range planning. Provides management audits and reports and profit improvement programs. High level strategic marketing, advertising strategy/tactics, turnaround consulting and management. **Founded:** 1978.

45751 ■ Melvin E. Barnette & Associates Inc.
805 Hopkins Ave.
Pendleton, SC 29670
Ph: (864)646-7622
Fax: (626)296-5113
Co. E-mail: melvin@mbarnette.com
URL: http://www.mbarnette.com
Contact: Melvin E. Barnette, President
Scope: Management consulting firm specializing in higher education and public sector consulting services. Offers services including higher education administrative, business and financial operations studies; structuring of upper-level management organizations; state government operations; legislative liaison; personnel evaluation; crisis resolution and management; and management training. **Founded:** 1986.

45752 ■ Bayer Center for Nonprofit Management (BCNM)
Robert Morris University, 6001 University Blvd.
Moon Township, PA 15219-3099
Ph: (412)397-6814
Free: 800-762-0097
Fax: (412)397-4097
Co. E-mail: bcnm@rmu.edu
URL: http://www.rmu.edu/bcnm
Contact: Peggy M. Outon, Executive Director
E-mail: outon@rmu.edu
Scope: Center offers consulting services in: Board development, business planning, collaboration and alliances, financial management, fund development, organizational effectiveness and technology planning. Also provides information and referral services, conducts applied research and serves to convene in depth discussions on the problems of society addressed by nonprofit organizations. **Founded:** 1999. **Seminars:** A Starfish Can Grow a New Arm, Why Cant I?; Carnegie Science Centers SuperFun Science Fest; Disc Driving the Electronic Mall; Steady Hand Game; Planning an Accessible World.

45753 ■ Beacon Management - Management Consultants
1000 W McNab Rd.
Pompano Beach, FL 33069
Ph: (954)782-1119
Co. E-mail: md@beaconmgmt.com
URL: http://www.beaconmgmt.com
Contact: Barbara L. Donnelly, Director
E-mail: bdonnelly@browardhealth.org
Scope: Specializes in change management, organized workplaces, multicultural negotiations and dispute resolutions and internet based decision making. **Founded:** 1985. **Publications:** "Sun-Sentinel Article," Oct, 2012.

45754 ■ Don L. Beck Associates Inc.
10050 N Foothill Blvd.
Cupertino, CA 95014-5601
Ph: (408)973-8688

Fax: (408)973-8714
Co. E-mail: dbeck@dlba.com
Contact: Don L. Beck, President
Scope: A management consulting firm specializing in building facilities planning and management worldwide. **Founded:** 1981.

45755 ■ Benchmark Consulting Group Inc. [Benchmark Advisors]
283 Franklin St., Ste. 400
Boston, MA 02110-3100
Ph: (617)482-7661
Contact: Walter E. Robb, III, President
E-mail: werobb35@aol.com
Scope: Provides financial and management services to companies. Helps companies grow through debt, equity sourcing and restructuring, business valuation, acquisition and divestiture, computer information systems and improved operation profitability. **Founded:** 1978.

45756 ■ Biomedical Management Resources (BMR)
PO Box 521125
Salt Lake City, UT 84152-1125
Ph: (801)272-4668
Fax: (801)277-3290
Co. E-mail: SeniorManagement@BiomedicalManagement.com
URL: http://www.biomedicalmanagement.com
Contact: Ping Fong, Jr., President
E-mail: pingfong@biomedicalmanagement.com
Scope: Provides business development, interim management and executive search services. Assists companies in strategic alliances, corporate partnering, business acquisition. Demonstrated success in identifying recruiting and placing key managers in difficult to hire positions. **Founded:** 1993.

45757 ■ Blackford Associates
30 George Rd.
Contoocook, NH 03229
Ph: (603)225-2228
Fax: (603)225-2228
Contact: John M. Blackford, Owner
Scope: Provider of general management consulting to smaller manufacturing companies. Counsels chief executive officers and presidents on strategy, organization, finances and operations. Areas of expertise include the following: new products, services or markets; problems of expansion or retrenchment; financing and bank relations; morale, organization and training; budgeting and business plans; factory flow and inventory control; quality control and methods; cash flow problems; and financial information and controls. **Founded:** 1984.

45758 ■ Blankinship & Associates Inc.
322 C St.
Davis, CA 95616
Ph: (530)757-0941
Fax: (530)757-0940
Co. E-mail: blankinship@envtox.com
URL: http://www.h2osci.com
Contact: Michael Blankinship, President
E-mail: mike@envtox.com
Scope: Specializes in assisting water resource and conveyance, golf and production, protection and enhancement of natural resources. **Founded:** 2000. **Publications:** "Air Blast Sprayer Calibration and Chlorpyrifos Irrigation Study," Oct, 2007; "How Green is your golf course," Prosper Magazine, 2007. **Seminars:** CDFG Wildlands IPM Seminar, Oct, 2009.

45759 ■ Blue Garnet Associates L.L.C.
8055 W Manchester Ave., Ste. 430
Los Angeles, CA 90293
Ph: (310)439-1930
Fax: (310)388-1657
Co. E-mail: hello@bluegarnet.net
URL: http://www.bluegarnet.net
Contact: Shannon Johnson, Manager
Scope: Services: Management consulting. **Founded:** 2002.

45760 ■ C. Clint Bolte & Associates
809 Philadelphia Ave.
Chambersburg, PA 17201
Ph: (717)263-5768

Fax: (717)263-8954
Co. E-mail: clint@clintbolte.com
URL: http://www.clintbolte.com
Contact: C. Clint Bolte, Principal
E-mail: cbolte3@comcast.net
Scope: Provider of management consulting services to firms involved with the printing industry. Services include outsourcing studies, graphics supply chain management studies, company and equipment valuations, plant layout services, litigation support, fulfillment warehouse consulting and product development services. **Founded:** 1989. **Seminars:** How to compete with the majors.

45761 ▪ Lisa Boyd Consulting L.L.C.
126 Clark Ave.
Ocean Grove, NJ 07756-1028
Ph: (732)774-4420
Fax: (732)774-2862
Contact: Lisa A. Boyd, Principal
E-mail: lisaboyd@earthlink.net
Scope: Provides professional housing development services. Assists with business plans, capacity building, project management and property management assessment. **Founded:** 1996.

45762 ▪ BPT Consulting Associates Ltd.
12 Parmenter Rd., Ste. B-6
Londonderry, NH 03053
Ph: (603)437-8484
Free: 888-278-0030
Fax: (603)434-5388
Contact: John Kuczynski, Managing Director
Scope: Provides management consulting expertise and resources to cross-industry clients with services for: Business Management consulting, People/Human Resources Transition and Training programs and a full cadre of multi-disciplined Technology Computer experts. Virtual consultants with expertise in e-commerce, supply chain management, organizational development and business application development consulting. **Founded:** 1991.

45763 ▪ BrightMagnet
31339 Pacific Coast Hwy.
Malibu, CA 90265
Ph: (310)457-0444
Contact: Jean Marie Bonthous, Owner
E-mail: jmb@leonardo.net
Scope: Boutique consultancy providing strategic counsel to organizations facing significant change or reputation. **Publications:** "Bibliography of Business/Competitive Intelligence and Benchmarking Literature," Aug, 1994. **Seminars:** Benchmarking; Developing Organizational Intelligence Capabilities; Coaching Skills for Managers; Effective Strategic Thinking; Competitive Analysis Techniques; Learning to Learn; Learning from Work.

45764 ▪ BroadVision Inc.
1700 Seaport Blvd., Ste. 210
Redwood City, CA 94063-5589
Ph: (650)295-0716
Free: 866-287-6669
Fax: (650)364-3425
Co. E-mail: info@broadvision.com
URL: http://www.broadvision.com
Contact: James D. Dixon, Director
Scope: Firm delivers a combination of technologies and services in to the global market that enable its customers to power mission-critical web initiatives that ultimately deliver high-value to their bottom line. Areas of expertise include strategic services, interactive services, content and creative services and client services. Services include business planning, application strategy, ROI analysis, organization and business process consulting, building and deploying applications, content management, sourcing and workflow processes. **Founded:** 1993. **Publications:** *One-to-One Financial*; *Retail Commerce Suite*; *MarketMaker*; *One-to-One Enterprise*; *One-to-One Knowledge*; *One-to-One Retail Commerce*; *One-to-One Business Commerce*; *One-To-One Command Center*; *One-To-One Publishing Center*; *One-To-One Design Center*; *Onte-To-One Instant Publisher*; *One-To-One Billing*.

45765 ▪ Business Education Associates (BEA) [Ashford Group Inc.]
4 Long Hill Rd.
Bethel, CT 06801
Ph: (203)798-6035
Contact: Robert J. Popp, President
E-mail: bob@ashfordgrp.com
Scope: Offers tailored management education programs. Has been designed to meet the business education needs of companies implementing new systems and companies to re-educate users of existing systems. **Founded:** 1984. **Publications:** "The Ashford Group and TQuist Partner to Provide High Impact Manufacturing Solutions"; "The Future of ERP"; "Winning the Implementation Game". **Special Services:** Building Manufacturing Excellence.

45766 ▪ Business Improvement Architects (BIA)
33 Riderwood Dr.
Toronto, ON, Canada M2L 2X4
Ph: (416)444-8225
Free: 866-346-3242
Fax: (416)444-6743
Co. E-mail: info@bia.ca
URL: http://www.bia.ca
Contact: Michael Stanleigh, Chief Executive Officer
E-mail: mstanleigh@bia.ca
Scope: Provider of the following services: strategic planning, leadership development, innovation and project and quality management. Specialize in strategic planning, change management, leadership assessment and development of skills. **Founded:** 1989. **Publications:** "Avoiding Pit falls to Innovation"; "Create a New Dimension of Performance with Innovation"; "The Power of Appreciation in Leadership"; "Why It Makes Sense To Have a Strategic Enterprise Office"; "Burning Rubber at the Start of Your Project"; "Accounting for Quality"; "How Pareto Charts Can Help You Improve the Quality of Business Processes"; "Managing Resistance to Change". **Seminars:** The Innovation Process From Vision to Reality, San Diego, Oct, 2007; Critical Thinking, Kuala Lump or, Sep, 2007; Critical Thinking, Brunei, Sep, 2007; Delivering Project Assurance, Auckland, Jun, 2007; From Crisis to Control: A New Era in Strategic Project Management, Prague, May, 2007; What Project Leaders Need to Know to Help Them Sleep Better At Night, London, May, 2007; Innovation Process. . .From Vision To Reality, Orlando, Apr, 2007. **Special Services:** Project Planning Tool™.

45767 ▪ Business Ventures Corp.
1650 Oakbrook Dr., Ste. 405
Norcross, GA 30093-1881
Free: 800-511-6844
Fax: (770)729-8028
URL: http://www.ontheribbon.com
Contact: Ruth A. King, Chief Executive Officer
E-mail: ruthking@bventures.com
Scope: Business development consultants specializing in construction industry. Works with HVAC, plumbing and electrical contraction who need assistance in marketing, sales and promotion, operations management or finance. Also plan, execute and monitor the marketing, sales and promotional activities for new product introductions. Firm also writes business plans, monitors financial health of businesses and performs operations management. **Founded:** 1981. **Publications:** "The Ugly Truth about Managing People," 2007; "The Ugly Truth about Small Business," 2006; "How to Write a Business Plan," Atlanta Business Chronicle; "Ask 10 Questions Before You Begin Your Business," Income Opportunities "HVAC Bookkeeping and Financial Statements"; "Service Manager's Guide to Running a Profitable Service Department"; "HVAC Career Training Manual"; "Technician's Procedures Manual"; "HVAC Residential Pricing Manual"; "21 Ways to Keep the Honest People Honest Manual"; "Keeping Score: Financial Management for Entrepreneurs"; "Keeping Score: Improving Contractor Productivity and Profitability"; "Keeping Score: Financial Management for Contractors". **Seminars:** The Seven Rules for Business Success; The Seven Greatest Lies of Small Business; Understanding the Financial Side of Business; Small Business Marketing; Strategic Business Planning.

45768 ▪ ByrneMRG Corp.
22 Isle of Pines Dr.
Hilton Head Island, SC 29928
Ph: (215)630-7411
Co. E-mail: info@byrnemrg.com
URL: http://www.byrnemrg.com
Scope: Services: Management consulting. **Founded:** 1972. **Publications:** "Implementing Solutions to Everyday Issues".

45769 ▪ Carelli & Associates
17 Reid Pl.
Delmar, NY 12054
Ph: (518)439-0233
Fax: (518)439-3006
Co. E-mail: truthaboutsupervision@yahoo.com
URL: http://www.carelli.com
Contact: Anne O Brien Carelli, Owner
E-mail: anneobriencarelli@yahoo.com
Scope: Provider of writing and editing services to industry and businesses, health care and educational institutions, and government agencies. Also provides program management in creating and disseminating publications and in implementing related training. Assists organizations in designing and implementing team-based management. Offers supervisory skills training and problem-solving work sessions for managers. Individual Consultation are provided for managers, CEOs, potential supervisors including 360 degree assessments. **Founded:** 1988. **Publications:** "The Truth About Supervision: Coaching, Teamwork, Interviewing, Appraisals, 360 degree Assessments, and Recognition". **Seminars:** Supervisory Skills Training Series; Problem-Solving Work Sessions for Managers; Effective Leadership.

45770 ▪ Cartesian Inc. [TMNG GlobalCambridge Strategic Management Group Inc.;]
7300 College Blvd., Ste. 302
Overland Park, KS 66210-1879
Ph: (913)345-9315
URL: http://www.tmng.com
Contact: Micky K. Woo, President
E-mail: micky.woo@tmng.com
Scope: A provider of strategy, management, marketing, operational and technology consulting services to the global telecommunications industry. **Founded:** 1990. **Special Services:** Lexicon™; QBC™; QSA™.

45771 ▪ Casino, Hotel & Resort Consultants L.L.C.
4825 Quality Ct., Ste. B
Las Vegas, NV 89103
Co. E-mail: john.hraba@hraba.com
URL: http://www.hraba.com
Contact: John S. Hraba, President
E-mail: jshraba@aol.com
Scope: Casino and hospitality industry consultants. Firm specializes in developing and implementing customized forecast and labor management control systems that deliver immediate, positive impact to the company's bottom line. Involved in production planning, employ surveys and communication, inventory management, business process reviews, audits, development and implementation of key management reports. **Founded:** 1989. **Seminars:** Payroll Cost Control; Effective Staff Scheduling.

45772 ▪ CBIZ Inc.
6050 Oak Tree Blvd. S, Ste. 500
Cleveland, OH 44131
Ph: (216)525-1947
Fax: (216)447-9007
URL: http://www.cbizinc.com
Contact: David J. Sibits, President
Scope: A business consulting and tax services firm providing financial, consulting, tax and business services through seven groups: Financial management, tax advisory, construction and real estate, health-care, litigation support, capital resource and CEO outsource. **Founded:** 1996. **Publications:** "FAS 154: Changes in the Way We Report Changes," 2006; "Equity-Based Compensation: How Much Does it Really Cost Your Business," 2006; "Preventing Fraud - Tips for Nonprofit Organizations"; "Today's Workforce and Nonprofit Organizations: Meeting a Critical Need"; "IRS Highlights Top Seven Form 990 Errors". **Seminars:** Health Care - What the Future

Holds; Consumer Driven Health Plans; Executive Plans; Health Savings Accounts; Healthy Wealthy and Wise; Legislative Update; Medicare Part D; Retirement Plans.

45773 ■ C.C. Comfort Consulting
3370 N Hayden Rd., Ste. 123-127
Scottsdale, AZ 85251
Ph: (480)483-8364
Contact: Clifton C. Comfort, Jr., Principal
Scope: Evaluates, develops and implements financial, operational and compliance management systems strategies, programs and practices. Has professional recognition as certified public accountant, internal auditor, cost analyst and fraud examiner plus investigatory, law enforcement and court experience ensure confidential handling of sensitive and legal matters. Works with management, audit, legal, security and outside personnel to evaluate and improve compliance, efficiency and effectiveness. **Founded:** 1983.

45774 ■ CEA Investments Corp.
301-2210 W 40th Ave.
Vancouver, BC, Canada V6M 1W6
Ph: (604)689-5547
Co. E-mail: info@ceainvestment.com
Contact: Emmanuel B. Nicolas, Principal
Scope: Specializes in strategic planning, mergers and acquisitions and operations consulting, to mid-sized corporations. Areas of expertise include corporate planning, financial engineering, joint venture structuring, international corporate networking, identifying acquisition opportunities, locating investment partners, corporate evaluations, negotiating buy/sell agreements, business planning, markets studies and products evaluation and outsourcing. **Founded:** 1988.

45775 ■ Cencir Inc.
24124 Lakeside Trl.
Crete, IL 60417
Ph: (708)672-3957
Fax: (708)672-4473
Co. E-mail: vevstad@cencir.com
URL: http://www.cencir.com
Contact: Vegard Vevstad, Chief Executive Officer
E-mail: vevstad@cencir.com
Scope: Firm seeks to transform entrepreneurial ventures into global enterprises using profitability audits and experience in highly distributed enterprises, including commercial chains selling or renting their products, services, or intellectual property through company branches, dealers, distributors, franchises, licenses, and Internet affiliates. Offers seminars and consultation with topics that include strategic decision-making, integrating entry and exit options, positioning, pricing, diversification, new ventures, vertical integration, distribution, organizational structures, and technology. Offers tools to improve recognition of key strategic issues; sell your strategy internally; identify and value core competencies; systemize and coordinate activities; select and implement dynamic IT strategy; improve asset utilization through innovation; avoid classic mistakes through continuous learning; use history of firm to affect change; apply seven forces to organization; recognize sustainable competitive advantages; predict market and competitive responses; use scenario analysis to model around uncertainty; and determine organizational requirements and adapt them. **Founded:** 1999. **Seminars:** Focus, Save Time, Learn and Ask Questions of the Preeminent Channels of Distribution Experts.

45776 ■ Center for Organizational Excellence (COE)
15204 Omega Dr., Ste. 300
Rockville, MD 20850
Ph: (301)948-1922
Free: 877-ORG-EXCEL
Fax: (301)948-2158
Co. E-mail: results@center4oe.com
URL: http://www.center4oe.com
Contact: Steve Goodrich, President
Scope: An organizational effectiveness consulting firm specializing in helping organizations achieve results through people, process and performance.

Service areas include organizational performance systems, leadership systems, customer systems and learning systems. **Founded:** 1984.

45777 ■ CFI Group USA L.L.C. [Claes Fornell International]
625 Avis Dr.
Ann Arbor, MI 48108
Ph: (734)930-9090
Free: 800-930-0933
Fax: (734)930-0911
Co. E-mail: askcfi@cfigroup.com
URL: http://www.cfigroup.com
Contact: Sheri Petras, Chief Executive Officer
E-mail: steodoru@mail.cfigroup.com
Scope: Management consulting firm that helps its clients worldwide to maximize shareholder value by optimizing customer and employee satisfaction. Clients span a variety of industries, including manufacturing, telecommunications, retail and government. **Founded:** 1988. **Publications:** "Customer Satisfaction and Stock Prices: High Returns, Low Risk," American Marketing Association, Jan, 2006; "Customer Satisfaction Index Climbs," The Wall Street Journal, Feb, 2004; "What's Next? Customer Service is Key to Post-Boom Success," The Bottom Line, Mar, 2003; "Boost Stock Performance, Nation's Economy," Quality Progress, Feb, 2003.

45778 ■ Chartered Management Co.
10 S Riverside Plz., Ste. 1800
Chicago, IL 60606
Ph: (312)214-2575
Contact: William B. Avellone, President
Scope: Operations improvement consultants. Specializes in strategic planning; feasibility studies; management audits and reports; profit enhancement; start-up businesses; mergers and acquisitions; joint ventures; divestitures; interim management; crisis management; turnarounds; business process re-engineering; venture capital; and due diligence. **Founded:** 1985.

45779 ■ Claremont Consulting Group
4525 Castle Ln.
La Canada, CA 91011-1436
Ph: (818)249-0584
Contact: Donald S. Remer, Partner
Scope: Consulting, coaching, training and litigation support in project management, engineering management, system engineering and cost estimating. **Founded:** 1979. **Publications:** "What Every Engineer Should Know About Project Management"; "100% product-oriented work breakdown structures and their importance to system engineering". **Seminars:** Project Management, System Engineering and Cost Estimating.

45780 ■ BJ Cockrell Real Estate Appraisal & Consulting
17 Tucker St.
Milton, MA 02186
Ph: (617)698-6618
Fax: (617)698-6618
Contact: Beatrice James-Cockrell, Owner
E-mail: beajcockrell@comcast.net
Scope: Consultancy performs marketability studies, market studies, asset management analyses and disposition analyses for affordable housing market interests. Focuses on housing market studies and using valuation analysis skills for acquisition and disposition advisory assignments.

45781 ■ Colmen Menard Company Inc. (CMCI)
The Woods, 994 Old Eagle School Rd., Ste. 1000
Wayne, PA 19087
Ph: (484)367-0300
Fax: (484)367-0305
Co. E-mail: cmci@colmenmenard.com
URL: http://www.colmenmenard.com
Contact: David W. Menard, President
E-mail: dmenard@colmenmenard.com
Scope: Merger and acquisition corporate finance and business advisory services for public and private companies located in North America. **Founded:** 1982. **Publications:** "Success in Selling a Troubled Company," Nov, 2002; "Savvy Dealmakers," May,

2001; "Success in Selling a Troubled Company feature article from The Technology Times bimonthly newspaper," Apr, 2002; "Truisms," M&A Today, Nov, 2000.

45782 ■ Comer & Associates L.L.C. [Energy Alliance Group]
5255 Holmes Pl.
Boulder, CO 80303
Ph: (303)786-7986
Free: 888-950-3190
Fax: (303)895-2347
Co. E-mail: jerry@comerassociates.com
URL: http://www.comerassociates.com
Contact: Jerry C. Comer, President
E-mail: jerry@comerassociates.com
Scope: Specialize in developing markets and businesses. Marketing support includes: Developing and writing strategic and tactical business plans; developing and writing focused, effective market plans; researching market potential and competition; implementing targeted marketing tactics to achieve company objectives; conducting customer surveys to determine satisfaction and attitudes toward client. Organization development support includes: Executive management training programs; executive coaching; team building; developing effective organization structures; and management of change in dynamic and competitive environments; individual coaching for management and leadership effectiveness. **Founded:** 1993. **Seminars:** Developing a Strategic Market Plan; Market Research: Defining Your Opportunity; Management and Leadership Effectiveness; Team Building; Developing a Business Plan; How to Close; Using Questions to Sell; Sales System Elements and Checklist; Working With Independent Reps; Features vs. Benefits; Overcoming Objections; Sales Force Automation.

45783 ■ Consulting & Conciliation Service (CCS)
2219 H St., Ste. 1
Sacramento, CA 95816
Ph: (916)396-0480
Free: 888-898-9780
Fax: (916)441-2828
Co. E-mail: service@azurewings.net
Contact: Jane A. McCluskey, Principal
E-mail: service@azurewings.net
Scope: Offers consulting and conciliation services. Provides pre-mediation counseling, training and research on preparing for a peaceful society, mediation and facilitation and preparation for shifts in structure, policy and personnel. Offers sliding scale business rates and free individual consultation. **Publications:** "Native America and Tracking Shifts in US Policy"; "Biogenesis: A Discussion of Basic Social Needs and the Significance of Hope". **Seminars:** Positive Approaches to Violence Prevention: Peace building in Schools and Communities.

45784 ■ The Consulting Exchange
1770 Mass Ave., Ste. 288
Cambridge, MA 02140
Ph: (617)576-2100
Free: 800-824-4828
Co. E-mail: starting@consultingexchange.com
URL: http://www.consultingexchange.com
Contact: Geoffrey Day, President
E-mail: gday@consultingexchange.com
Scope: Services: Management consultancy. **Founded:** 1982. **Publications:** "Looking for a Consultant? Success Points for Finding the Right One," Boston Business Journal, Jun, 2001; "Getting Full Value From Consulting is in Your Hands," Mass High Tech, May, 1998; "Developing Knowledge-Based Client Relationships, The Future of Professional Services"; "The Consultant's Legal Guide"; "The Business of Consulting: The Basics and Beyond".

45785 ■ The Corlund Group L.L.C. (CG)
101 Federal St., Ste. 310
Boston, MA 02110
Ph: (617)423-9364

Fax: (617)423-9371
Co. E-mail: corlund@corlundgroup.com
URL: http://www.corlundgroup.com
Contact: Wilmot J. Gravenslund, Director
E-mail: wgravenslund@corlundgroup.com
Scope: Boutique firm offering services in the areas of leadership, governance, and change with a particular focus on CEO and senior executive succession planning, including assessment, development, and orchestrating succession processes with management and Boards of Directors. Also Board governance effectiveness. **Founded:** 1996. **Publications:** "Are You Rolling the Dice on CEO Succession?" Center for Healthcare Governance, 2006; "Leadership Due Diligence: The Neglected Governance Frontier," Directorship, Sep, 2001; "Leadership Due Diligence: Managing the Risks," The Corporate Board, Aug, 2001; "Succession: The need for detailed insight," Directors and Boards, 2001; "CEO Succession: Who's Doing Due Diligence?," 2001.

45786 ■ Corporate Consulting Inc.
3333 Belcaro Dr.
Denver, CO 80209-4912
Ph: (303)698-9292
Contact: Gray Josephs, Manager
Scope: Specializes in feasibility studies, organizational development, small business management, mergers and acquisitions, joint ventures, divestitures, interim management, crisis management, turnarounds, financing, appraisals valuations and due diligence studies. **Founded:** 1983.

45787 ■ Corporate Impact
33326 Bonnieview, Ste. 200
Avon Lake, OH 44012-1230
Ph: (440)930-2477
Fax: (440)930-2525
URL: http://www.corpimpact.com
Contact: Michael G. Wachter, Principal
Scope: Provider of coaching, consultation, facilitation and training services to help you develop, a business that delivers sustained shareholder value and growth. Supports the development of the skills and implementation of the change programs learned in the workshop. Also, for small businesses, firm provides general consulting in the areas of strategic planning, marketing, and product and sales strategy. Industries served all except government and nonprofit. **Publications:** "8 Lies of Teamwork". **Seminars:** Personal Productivity Management; The Challenge of Leadership; Collaborative Problem Solving; The Creative Side of Enterprise; Teamwork and Peak Performance; Winning Customers; Conflict Resolution.

45788 ■ Morton Cotlar
700 Richards St.
Honolulu, HI 96813
Ph: (808)956-8732
Co. E-mail: morton@uhunix.bit.net
Contact: Morton Cotlar, Director
E-mail: morton@uhunix.uhcc.hawaii.edu
Scope: Provider of organizational management counsel including surveys of effectiveness in operations; training and development seminars for managers; consulting in organizational operations; development of expert systems for strategic planning and operations and assistance with implementation. Serves private industries as well as government agencies. **Founded:** 1972.

45789 ■ Crystal Clear Communications Inc.
1633 W Winslow Dr., Ste. 210
Mequon, WI 53092
Ph: (262)240-0072
Fax: (262)240-0073
Co. E-mail: barbwoods@crystalclear1.com
URL: http://www.crystalclear1.com
Contact: Barry J. Moze, Partner
E-mail: barrymoze@crystalclearl.com
Scope: Services: Management consulting and executive coaching. **Founded:** 1986. **Publications:** "Weakest Link"; "Aware Leadership"; "Integrity"; "When Your Plate is Full"; "Problem Solving"; "Strategic Thinking".

45790 ■ Dare Mighty Things
901 N Glebe Rd., Ste. 1005
Arlington, VA 22203
Ph: (703)752-4331

Fax: (703)752-4332
Co. E-mail: info@daremightythings.com
URL: http://www.daremightythings.com
Contact: David van Patten, President
Scope: Provides management consulting services that help clients implement social solutions. Specializes in the development of large scale programs that impact high risk populations. Clients are government agencies, foundations and non-profit organizations. Supports clients through the research and design of outcome-based social programs; the development of business plans and case statements; the delivery of performance-based training and technical assistance; and guidance in fund development and program sustainability. **Founded:** 1991.

45791 ■ The Decision Group (TDG)
7204 Penny Rd.
Raleigh, NC 27606
Ph: (919)851-9679
Fax: (919)851-9679
Contact: Wilfred J. Kaydos, President
E-mail: willkaydos@nc.rr.com
Scope: Provider of comprehensive consulting services to manufacturing, distribution and service companies in the areas of: productivity and quality improvement, performance measurement, information systems design and operations management. Serves private industries as well as government agencies. **Founded:** 1982. **Publications:** "Measuring, Managing, and Maximizing Performance," Productivity Press; "Operational Performance Measurement: Increasing Total Productivity," St.Lucie Press; "Implementing Manufacturing Performance Measures-a Case Study". **Seminars:** Quality Improvement Made Simple; Measuring Performance to Increase Total Productivity.

45792 ■ Del Technology Inc.
7407 E Via Estrella Ave., Ste. 10
Scottsdale, AZ 85258-1006
Ph: (480)483-7588
Fax: (480)483-7533
Contact: Georgine Donahoe, President
Scope: Provides services including management consulting, information technology and micro business. Focuses on organizational assessment, business process reengineering, quality assurance program development, hardware software evaluation and acquisition, applications software development and systems integration. **Founded:** 1990. **Publications:** "Standards for Information Systems Development and Project Administration". **Seminars:** Organization for Future Technology; Business Reengineering; Managing Successful Projects; Planning and Implementing the Information Systems Architecture; Successfully Managing the Information Resource.

45793 ■ Delohery Associates
3214 Cedar Bluff Dr. NE
Marietta, GA 30062
Ph: (770)977-3197
Fax: (770)977-9509
Contact: Pat D. Delohery, President
Scope: Offers total quality management, business process and procedure analysis and design using current contemporary quality techniques.

45794 ■ Denison Consulting
121 W Washington St., Ste. 200
Ann Arbor, MI 48104
Ph: (734)302-4002
Fax: (734)302-4023
Co. E-mail: mgillespie@denisonculture.com
URL: http://www.denisonculture.com
Contact: Bryan Adkins, Sr., President
E-mail: badkins@denisonculture.com
Scope: Organizational culture and leadership management firm. Consulting services include planning a survey program, providing feedback, linking survey results to strategic planning, leadership coaching, planning and implementing change interventions and facilitating mergers and acquisitions. **Publications:** "Executive Coaching: Does leader behavior change with feedback and coaching," 2009; "Engagement Surveys: Gallup and Best Companies Face Criticism," 2009; "Managing Expectations-of You," 2006; "Out of the Blue," 2006; "Organizational Culture: Measuring and Developing It in Your Organization," 2005;

"Riding the Tiger of Culture Change," 2004; "Like it or not, Culture Matters," 2000; "Why Mission Matters," 2000; "Ready Or Not, Here I Learn," 2000. **Seminars:** Building High Performance Organizations; Organizational Culture & Diagnosis; Managing Thought.

45795 ■ Development Resource Consultants (DRC)
PO Box 118
Rancho Cucamonga, CA 91729
Ph: (909)476-8042
Fax: (909)476-6942
Co. E-mail: drc@gotodrc.com
URL: http://www.gotodrc.com
Contact: Jerry R. Frey, Business Manager
E-mail: jfrey@gotodrc.com
Scope: Specializes in office re-organization, employee training in office organization, communication skills, sales training and career counseling. **Founded:** 1985. **Publications:** "Institute of Management Consultants Southern California Chapter," Jan, 2006.

45796 ■ Directions Ltd.
4021 Albert Dr.
Nashville, TN 37204-4009
Ph: (615)269-4043
Contact: Eddie Scheuerman, President
Scope: Works with Chief Executive Officers and companies trying to resolve problems that management and leadership have not had the time to solve due to other priorities. Areas of interest: management and leadership problems; resolving problems associated with profitability, growth, change and resources; strategic issues, under-performance issues and boards of directors issues. Experience is with publicly traded or privately owned companies in various industries. **Founded:** 1980.

45797 ■ donphin.com Inc.
1001 B Ave., Ste. 200
Coronado, CA 92118
Ph: (619)550-3533
Free: 800-234-3304
Fax: (619)600-0096
Co. E-mail: don@donphin.com
URL: http://www.donphin.com
Scope: Offers a comprehensive approach to understanding and applying a broad range of business principles: legal compliance issues, management concerns, health and safety, customer service, marketing, information management. Industries served: All developing small businesses. **Founded:** 1983. **Publications:** "Doing Business Right!"; "HR That Works!"; "Lawsuit Free! How to Prevent Employee Lawsuits"; "Building Powerful Employment Relationships!"; "Victims, Villains and Heroes: Managing Emotions in The Workplace". **Seminars:** Doing Business Right!; HR That Works!; Building Powerful Employment Relationships; Lawsuit Free!.

45798 ■ Dorn & Associates Inc.
8506 Bass Lake Rd.
Minneapolis, MN 55428-5304
Ph: (763)533-7689
Contact: John L. Dorn, President
Scope: Services include accounting, marketing, employment partnership, new doctor agreements, personnel issues and human resources assessment, practice management, practice merger acquisition sale and liquidation, practice surveys and valuation, staff development and training.

45799 ■ DRI Consulting (DRIC)
2 Otter Ln.
Saint Paul, MN 55127-6436
Ph: (651)415-1400
Free: 866-276-4600
Fax: (651)415-9968
Co. E-mail: dric@dric.com
URL: http://www.dric.com
Contact: Chelsea Berryman, Consultant
Scope: Provides high-quality, research-based services and training in leadership, team processes, supervision, and management, and organizational development, clients with direct and substantial impact on individual and team performance and on organizational success through proven processes for selecting, developing and deploying leaders. **Founded:** 1991.

45800 ■ The DuMond Group
5282 Princeton Ave.
Westminster, CA 92683-2753
Ph: (714)373-0610
Contact: Adrianne H. Geiger-Dumond, Owner
Scope: Human resources and executive search consulting firm that specializes in organizational development; small business management; employee surveys and communication; performance appraisals; and team building. **Founded:** 1992.

45801 ■ Dynamic Firm Management Inc.
4570 Campus Dr., Ste. 60
Newport Beach, CA 92660
Ph: (949)640-2220
Co. E-mail: info@dynamicfirm.com
URL: http://www.dynamicfirm.com
Contact: Dennis McCue, Principal
E-mail: mccue@dynamicfirm.com
Scope: Services: Law, accounting and other consulting. **Founded:** 1987. **Publications:** "Workflow Management," C2M: Consulting to Management - The Journal of Management Consulting, Jun, 2006; "Why Good Partnerships Go Bad," The Journal of Law Office Economics and Management, Feb, 2006; "The Wisdom of Ambulance Chasers," LACBA Update, Feb, 2005; "7 Components to Building A Successful Firm," LACBA Update, Nov, 2004; "Maximize the Productivity of Your Support Team," LACBA Update, Mar, 2004; "Perfect Union," Daily Journal, Mar, 2004; "Future Perfect," Daily Journal, Dec, 2003.

45802 ■ Effective Resources Inc. (ERI)
118 N Peters Rd., Ste. 171
Knoxville, TN 37923
Free: 800-288-6044
Fax: (800)409-2812
Co. E-mail: customerservice@effectiveresources.com
URL: http://www.effectiveresources.com
Contact: Barry L. Brown, President
E-mail: barry@effectiveresources.com
Scope: Human resource consulting firm helping clients in all aspects of planning and implementation, to assure the program meets their objectives and budget considerations. Can work with clients on an interim basis or as consultants on short term assignment. Products and services include salary and benefits surveys, employee satisfaction surveys, performance management, compensation administration, compliance assistance and personality profile testing. Specializes in compensation and incentive plans, performance appraisals, team building and personnel policies and procedures, affirmative action plan preparation. **Founded:** 1988. **Special Services:** DiSC® Personality Profile.

45803 ■ EGL Holdings Inc. [EGL Holdings]
Bldg 11, 3495 Piedmont Rd. NE, Ste. 412
Atlanta, GA 30305-1773
Ph: (404)949-8300
Fax: (404)949-8311
Co. E-mail: info@eglholdings.com
URL: http://www.eglholdings.com
Contact: Paul Terlemezian, Manager
Scope: A management consulting team that specializes in solving the financial problems of medium sized businesses and in helping the management capitalize on business opportunities. Designs and implements remedies for shortage of working capital and low profitability. Services include strategic corporate planning, cost reduction, profit improvement, acquisition analysis, divestiture and financing. Long term and short term analysis of business opportunities. **Founded:** 1988.

45804 ■ EMS Network International [EMS Consultants]
858 Longview Rd.
Burlingame, CA 94010-6974
Ph: (650)342-5259
Fax: (650)344-5005
Co. E-mail: ems@emsnetwork.com
URL: http://www.emsnetwork.com
Contact: Michael E. Shays, President
E-mail: ems@atsemsnetwork.com
Scope: Helping teams to develop and implement breakthrough solutions through purpose expansion, solution-after-next, technology fiction, people partici-

pation and change management. Serves clients in all industries. **Founded:** 1987. **Publications:** "How to Get Value from a Management Consultant"; "Code Of Professional Conduct"; "Obedience to the Unenforceable"; "Controlling the Future"; "Seven Principles of Breakthrough Thinking"; "Ethical Fitness"; "Succession Planning"; "Case Study - Old & New Management"; "Case Study - Two Sales Staffs"; "Case Study - Administration & Faculty"; "Cartoons about Consulting". **Seminars:** Facilitation skills; basic skills for internal consultants; entrepreneurs and champions; breakthrough thinking, building decision skills and ethical fitness; How to resolve conflict and manage transitions; The Purpose-Target-Results approach to solving problems and leveraging opportunities; Sponsoring and mentoring innovators and intrapreneurs in your company; Advanced practices for management consultants; Sponsoring and mentoring innovators and entrepreneurs in your company; Eliminating Waste In Management Decision Making; Bringing Out the Itrapreneurs in Your Company; The Consultant's Role in Mastering Change; Closing The Sale. **Special Services:** Ethical Fitness®; How Good People Make Tough Decisions®; How to apply Breakthrough Thinking®.

45805 ■ Espionage Research Institute International (ERII)
4445 Corporation Ln., Ste. 291C
Virginia Beach, VA 23462
Ph: (757)716-7353
Fax: (757)716-7353
Co. E-mail: membership@erii.org
URL: http://www.erii.org
Contact: J. D. LeaSure, Director
Scope: Dedicated to collect and promulgate information on hostile espionage activity. It attempts to keep all informed on hostile espionage activity that is directed against business and industry. **Founded:** 2001. **Publications:** "A Guidebook For Beginning Sweepers"; "The Ear Volume"; "The Attack on Axnan Headquarters"; "The TSCM Threat Book"; "The Russian Eavesdropping Threat As Of 1993".

45806 ■ Family Business Institute Inc.
904 Steffi Ct.
Lawrenceville, GA 30044-6933
Ph: (770)952-4085
URL: http://www.family-business-experts.com
Contact: Wayne Rivers, President
Scope: Assists families in business to achieve personal, family and organizational goals by meeting challenges that are unique to family-owned businesses. Provides coordinated and integrated assessments and solutions for family issues and needs; for company finance and for human resource and operational requirements. **Founded:** 1985. **Publications:** "Professional Intervention in the Family Owned Business"; "Building Consensus in a Family Business"; "Professionalizing Family Business Management"; "Recognizing generations - know them by their weekends"; "Succession planning tactics"; "Succession Planning Obstacles in Family Business"; "Succession: three ways to ease the transition"; "Pruning the family business tree"; "Responsibility diffusion - the most critical impediment to successfully growing any kind of business"; "Breaking Up is Hard to Do: Divorce in the Family Business".

45807 ■ FCP Consulting
500 Sutter St., Ste. 700
San Francisco, CA 94102-1114
Ph: (415)956-5558
Fax: (415)956-5722
Scope: Management consulting in Business-To-Business sales. **Founded:** 1986.

45808 ■ Firemark Investments
200 W DeVargas St., Ste. 9
Santa Fe, NM 87501
Ph: (505)989-8384
Free: 800-530-0786
Fax: (505)989-8316
Contact: Michael J. Morrissey, Chief Executive Officer
E-mail: mjm@firemarkinv.com
Scope: Firm provides management consulting, investment advice and fund management. **Founded:** 1983.

45809 ■ First Strike Management Consulting Inc. [FSMC Inc.]
4001 Loblolly Ave.
Little River, SC 29566-1188
Ph: (843)385-6338
Fax: (843)390-1004
Co. E-mail: info@fsmc.com
URL: http://www.fsmc.com
Contact: J. D. Lewis, Chief Executive Officer
E-mail: jd.lewis@fsmc.com
Scope: Offers proposal management and program management services. Specializes in enterprise systems, management systems, and staff augmentation. Serves the following industries: Nuclear/Fossil Power, Petro-Chemical, Aerospace and Defense, Telecommunications, Engineering and Construction, Information Technology, Golf Course Construction/Management, Utility Engineering/Construction, Civil Works, and Housing Development. **Founded:** 1991. **Publications:** "Project Management for Executives"; "Project Risk Management"; "Project Communications Management"; "Winning Proposals, Four Computer Based Training (CBT) courses"; "Principles of Program Management". **Seminars:** Preparing Winning Proposals in Response to Government RFPs.

45810 ■ Foresight Management Group
14 Macintosh Cres.
Saint Catharines, ON, Canada L2N 7M2
Free: 800-851-6676
Fax: (519)748-4478
Contact: Edward Brooker, Executive
E-mail: ed@foresight-management.com
Scope: Consultants in camp ground design and planning, RV park design and planning and RV resort design and planning. Assists public agencies and private entrepreneurs with feasibility studies, development strategies and marketing plans including destination branding. **Publications:** "One Canadian's Perspective on the Country's Recent Decrease in Tourism," Dec, 2007; "The Future Looks Promising But Not Guaranteed"; "Profitable Parks"; "Strategic Marketing"; "What's the value of a penny?"; "Signs of the Time"; "Effective and Efficient Campground Development"; "We need MORE foresight and innovation! FAST!"; "Effective and Efficient Campground Development"; "Inspiration From an Unlikely Source"; "Test and Measure"; "Go Figure". **Seminars:** Marketing - Big Dollars, Small Dollars; Marketing for RV Parks; Marketing for Small Business; Branding As A Key Component Of A Marketing Strategy; How to get into the campground business; Thinking Out of the Box; Developing Underutilized Campgrounds; How to determine rates; Ecotourism: A Natural Branding Strategy; Capitalizing on Ecotourism; Stress Management; US Trends in the RV Park Industry; US Trends in the RV Industry; US Trends in the Tourism Industry; Innovation in Tourist Parks.

45811 ■ The Foster Group Inc.
180 N Stetson, Ste. 3470
Chicago, IL 60601
Ph: (312)609-1009
Fax: (312)609-1109
Co. E-mail: info@thefostergroup.com
URL: http://www.thefostergroup.com
Contact: John L. Foster, Jr., Managing Partner
E-mail: rpike@thefostergroup.com
Scope: Offers information systems and data security, financial accounting services, and management consulting. **Founded:** 1986.

45812 ■ Freese & Associates Inc. [F&A Inc.]
PO Box 814
Chagrin Falls, OH 44022-0814
Ph: (440)564-9183
Fax: (440)564-7339
Co. E-mail: tfreese@freeseinc.com
URL: http://www.freeseinc.com
Contact: James H. Muir, Manager
Scope: A management consulting firm offering advice in all forms of business logistics. Consulting services are in the areas of strategic planning; network analysis, site selection, facility layout and design, outsourcing, warehousing, transportation and customer service. Typical projects include 3PL marketing surveys; third party outsourcing selection; operational audits; competitive analysis; inventory management;

due diligence; and implementation project management. **Founded:** 1987. **Publications:** "Building Relationships is Key to Motivation," Distribution Center Management, Apr, 2006; "Getting Maximum Results from Performance Reviews," WERC Sheet, Oct, 2003; "SCM: Making the Vision a Reality," Supply Chain Management Review, Oct, 2003; "Contents Under Pressure," DC Velocity, Aug, 2003; "When Considering Outsourcing, It's Really a Financial Decision," Inventory Management Report, Mar, 2003. **Seminars:** WERC/CAWS Warehousing in China Conference, Sep, 2008; CSCMP Annual Conference, Denver, Oct, 2008; Keys to Retaining and Motivating Your Associates, Dallas, Mar, 2006; The Value and Challenges of Supply Chain Management, Dubai, Feb, 2006; Best Practices in Logistics in China, Jun, 2005; Keys to Motivating Associates, Dallas, May, 2005; The Goal and the Way of International Cooperation in Logistics, Jenobuk, Apr, 2005.

45813 ■ Max Freund
246 W Green St.
Claremont, CA 91711
Ph: (909)632-1247
Co. E-mail: max.freund@cgu.edu
URL: http://www.lfleadership.com
Contact: Janice Muniz, Advisor
Scope: Consultants and coaches provide training on leadership and success for individuals and organizations. Consults with organizations, teams and communities on leadership, economic development, strategy, organizational learning and team effectiveness. Other core practice areas are coaching groups and individuals, facilitating groups, training leaders and teams in skills to communicate effectively. Consultants also speak on social leadership, community economic development, change and transition management, diversity and conflict transformation. **Seminars:** High Desert Resource Network Fundraising Academy for Grassroots Nonprofits, Aug, 2009; Developing the Next Generation of Leaders, Sep, 2008; Coaching Skills for Staff Development and Retention, Sep, 2008; Developing Funds, Transforming Leadership, San Bernardino County Grants Office, Jun, 2008; Developing Funds, Developing Leadership, High Desert Resource Network, Apr, 2008; Executive Coaching Skills; Fundraising Fundamentals for Non-profits.

45814 ■ Global Business Consultants (GBC)
200 Lake Hills Rd.
Pinehurst, NC 28374-0776
Ph: (910)295-5991
Co. E-mail: gbc@pinehurst.net
Contact: Nan S. Leaptrott, President
E-mail: nan@yourculturecoach.com
Scope: Firm specializes in human resources management; project management; software development; and international trade. Offers litigation support. **Founded:** 1987. **Publications:** "Culture to Culture: Mission Trip Do's and Don'ts," Jul, 2005; "Rules of the Game: Global Business Protocol". **Seminars:** Cross-Cultural Training.

45815 ■ Global Technology Transfer L.L.C.
1500 Dixie Hwy.
Park Hills, KY 41011-2819
Ph: (859)431-1262
Contact: Anthony Zembrodt, President
Scope: Firm specializes in product development; quality assurance; new product development; and total quality management focusing on household chemical specialties, especially air fresheners. Utilizes latest technology from global resources. Specializes in enhancement products for home and automobile. **Founded:** 1992.

45816 ■ Glynn Law Offices
49 Locust St.
Falmouth, MA 02540
Ph: (508)548-8282
Fax: (508)548-9075
Co. E-mail: pcg@glynnlawoffices.com
URL: http://www.glynnlawfirm.com
Contact: Suzanne Fay Glynn, Partner
E-mail: sfg@glynnlawoffices.com
Scope: A full service law firm specializing in affordable housing development and estate and business planning with a focus on taxation. **Founded:** 1982.

45817 ■ Arnold S. Goldin & Associates Inc.
5030 Champion Blvd., Ste. G-6231
Boca Raton, FL 33496
Ph: (561)994-5810
Fax: (561)994-5860
Co. E-mail: arnold@goldin.com
URL: http://www.goldin.com
Contact: Arnold S. Goldin, Principal
E-mail: arnold@goldin.com
Scope: An accounting and management consulting firm. Serves clients worldwide. Provides management services. Handles monthly write-ups and tax returns. **Founded:** 1978.

45818 ■ Goldore Consulting Inc.
120-5 St. NW, Ste. 1
Linden, AB, Canada T0M 1J0
Ph: (403)546-4208
Fax: (403)546-4208
Contact: Robert A. Orr, President
E-mail: orr@leadershipessentials.com
Description: Description: Publishes materials on leadership and management skills for churches and charitable organizations that provide services to developing countries. Also publishes in Spanish and Portuguese. Does not accept unsolicited manuscripts. Reaches market through direct mail and wholesalers and distributors, including Leadership Training Ministry Foundation, Inc. **Scope:** Provides consulting service in leadership and management skills. Industries served: primarily charities, non-profits; some businesses. **Founded:** 1990. **Seminars:** The Challenge Of Leadership.

45819 ■ Gordian Concepts & Solutions
16 Blueberry Ln.
Lincoln, MA 01773-2210
Ph: (617)259-8341
Contact: Stephen R. Low, President
Scope: Engineering and management consultancy offering general, financial and valuation services, civil and tax litigation support. Assists clients in entering new businesses, planning new products and services and evaluating feasibility. Targets industrial concerns engaged in manufacturing, assembly, warehousing, energy production, process systems and biotechnology, steel, paper and electronics. Serves businesses such as retailing, financial services, health care, satellite broadcasting and cable television, outdoor advertising and professional practices. **Founded:** 1990. **Publications:** "Establishing Rural Cellular Company Values," Cellular Business.

45820 ■ Great Lakes Consulting Group Inc.
54722 Little Flower Trl.
Mishawaka, IN 46545
Ph: (574)287-4500
Contact: James E. Schrager, President
Scope: Provides consulting services in the areas of strategic planning; feasibility studies; start-up businesses; small business management; mergers and acquisitions; joint ventures; divestitures; interim management; crisis management; turnarounds; business process re-engineering; venture capital; and international trade. **Founded:** 1989.

45821 ■ Great Western Association Management Inc.
7995 E Prentice Ave., Ste. 100
Greenwood Village, CO 80111
Ph: (303)770-2220
Fax: (303)770-1614
Co. E-mail: info83@gwami.com
URL: http://www.gwami.com
Contact: Karen Divincent, Manager, Marketing
Scope: Provider of clients with products and services to effectively manage existing and startup, for- and not-for-profit organizations. Clients select from a menu of services including association development and public relations, conferences and seminars, financial management, membership communications, and governance. Expertise also includes association strategic planning, compliance, lobbying, meeting planning, fundraising, marketing and communications. Serves national, regional and state organizations. **Founded:** 1983. **Seminars:** Site selection; Creative program development; Contract negotiations; On-site conference management; Trade show management; Travel and logistics.

45822 ■ Joel Greenstein & Associates (JGA)
6212 Nethercombe Ct.
McLean, VA 22101
Ph: (703)893-1888
Contact: Joel Greenstein, Principal
E-mail: jgreenstein@contractmasters.com
Scope: Provides services to minority and women-owned businesses and government agencies. Specializes in interpreting federal, agency-specific acquisition regulations and contract terms and conditions. Offers assistance with preparing technical, cost proposals and sealed bids.

45823 ■ Grimmick Consulting Services (GCS)
455 Donner Way
San Ramon, CA 94582
Ph: (925)735-1036
Fax: (925)735-1100
Co. E-mail: hank@grimmickconsulting.com
URL: http://www.grimmickconsulting.com
Contact: Henry Grimmick, President
E-mail: hank@grimmickconsulting.com
Scope: Provider of consulting services in the areas of strategic planning; organizational assessment; organizational development; leadership and management development Baldridge criteria, process improvement and balanced scorecards and team dynamics. **Founded:** 1993.

45824 ■ Harding & Co.
511 Harvard Ave.
Swarthmore, PA 19081
Ph: (610)544-9005
Co. E-mail: fharding@hardingco.com
URL: http://www.hardingco.com
Contact: Mimi Spangler, President
E-mail: mspangler@hardingco.com
Scope: Specializes in sales management, client development and employee training. **Founded:** 1993. **Publications:** "Cross-Selling Success: A Rainmakers Guide to Professional Account Development," Aug, 2002; "Rain Making: The Professional's Guide to Attracting New Clients"; "Creating Rainmakers: The Managers Guide to Training Professionals to Attract New Clients".

45825 ■ Claude Hayes & Associates
9259 Hunterboro Dr.
Brentwood, TN 37027-6118
Ph: (615)373-3179
Fax: (615)370-8106
Contact: Claude W. Hayes, Jr., Owner
Scope: Provides services in the areas of turnarounds, reengineering, restructuring, reorganization, startups, high profile growth, acquisitions, divestitures, due diligence, strategic/business (marketing/sales) plans, inventory control and management, cost pricing and control, market management, demand forecasting. **Founded:** 1994.

45826 ■ Hewitt Development Enterprises (HDE)
1717 N Bayshore Dr., Ste. 2154
Miami, FL 33132
Ph: (305)372-0941
Fax: (305)372-0941
Co. E-mail: info@hewittdevelopment.com
URL: http://www.hewittdevelopment.com
Contact: Robert G. Hewitt, Principal
E-mail: bob@hewittdevelopment.com
Scope: Specializes in strategic planning; profit enhancement; start-up businesses; interim management; crisis management; turnarounds; production planning; just-in-time inventory management; and project management. Serves senior management (CEOs, CFOs, division presidents, etc.) and acquirers of distressed businesses. **Founded:** 1985.

45827 ■ Hickey & Hill Inc.
1009 Oak Hill Rd., Ste. 201
Lafayette, CA 94549-3812
Ph: (925)283-7802
Contact: Edwin L. Hill, Chief Executive Officer
Scope: Firm provides management consulting services to companies in financial distress. Expertise area: Corporate restructuring and turnaround. **Founded:** 1984.

45828 ■ hightechbiz.com [Leahy & Associates Inc.]
4209 Santa Monica Blvd., Ste. 201
Los Angeles, CA 90029-3027
Ph: (323)913-3355
Free: 877-648-4753
URL: http://www.hightechbiz.com
Contact: Liam Leahy, Chief Executive Officer (Acting)
Scope: A full service marketing agency specializing in integrated marketing solutions. Services include: marketing surveys; positioning surveys; strategic and tactical plans; implementation plans; management consulting; product brochures; product catalos; product packaging; product data sheets; direct mail programs; media research; competitive research; complete creative; production and film; media placement; corporate identity; in-house creative; public relations. **Founded:** 1980.

45829 ■ C. W. Hines and Associates Inc. [C&W Associates Inc.]
344 Churchill Cir., Sanctuary Bay
White Stone, VA 22578
Ph: (804)435-8844
Fax: (804)435-8855
Co. E-mail: turtlecwh@aol.com
URL: http://www.cwhinesassociates.org
Contact: William A. Hines, Jr., Vice President
Scope: Management consultants with expertise in the following categories: advertising and public relations; health and human resources; management sciences; organizational development; computer sciences; financial management; behavioral sciences; environmental design; technology transfer; project management; facility management; program evaluation; and business therapy. Also included are complementary areas such as sampling procedures; job training; managerial effectiveness; corporate seminars; gender harassment; training for trainers and leadership and management skills development. **Founded:** 1979. **Publications:** "Money Muscle, 120 Exercises To Build Spiritual And Financial Strength," 2004; "Inside Track: Executives Coaching Executives"; "Money Muscle: 122 Exercises to Build Financial Strength"; "Nuts and Bolts of Work Force Diversity"; "Legal Issues, published in the Controllers Business Advisor"; "Identifying Racism: Specific Examples"; "BOSS Spelled Backwards is double SSOB! Or is it?"; "A No-Nonsense Guide to Being Stressed". **Seminars:** Career Development; Coaching and Counseling for Work Success; Communicating More Effectively in a Diverse Work Environment; Communications 600: Advanced Skills for Relationship Building; Customer Service: Building a Caring Culture.

45830 ■ Holt Capital
1916 Pike Pl., Ste. 12-344
Seattle, WA 98101
Ph: (206)484-0403
Fax: (206)789-8034
Co. E-mail: info@holtcapital.com
URL: http://www.holtcapital.com
Contact: Marilyn J. Holt, Principal
Scope: Registered investment advisory firm. Services include: Debt planning, private equity, mergers, divestitures, transaction support services. Connects companies with capital. **Founded:** 1980. **Publications:** "Early Sales Key to Early-Stage Funding"; "Financial Transactions: Who Should Be At Your Table"; "Get the Deal Done: The Four Keys to Successful Mergers and Acquisitions"; "Is Your First Paragraph a Turn-off"; "Bubble Rubble: Bridging the Price Gap for an Early-Stage Business"; "Are You Ready For The new Economy"; "Could I Get Money or Jail Time With That The Sarbanes-Oxley Act Of 2002 gives early-stage companies More Risks". **Seminars:** Attracting Private Investors; Five Proven Ways to Finance Your Company; How to Get VC Financing; Venture Packaging; How to Finance Company Expansion.

45831 ■ Human Resource Specialties Inc.
3 Monroe Pky., Ste. 900
Lake Oswego, OR 97035
Ph: (503)697-3329
Free: 800-354-3512
Fax: (503)636-1594
URL: http://www.hrspecialties.com
Contact: Sandy Henderson, President
E-mail: sandyh@hrspecialties.com
Scope: Provider of human resources assistance to organizations. Offers preparation of affirmative action plans, support documents, and adverse impact studies of personnel activities. Also offers customized consultations in small business services, diversity and discrimination, and investigations, complaints and grievances. Provides investigations, including allegations of unfair treatment, equal employment opportunity (EEO) and racial or sexual harassment. Offers customized web-based training (webinars) on a variety of HR, EEO and AAP-related topics. **Founded:** 1984.

45832 ■ I.H.R. Solutions
3333 E Bayaud Ave., Ste. 219
Denver, CO 80209
Ph: (303)588-4243
Fax: (303)978-0473
Contact: Deborah Hollands, Owner
E-mail: dhollands@ihrsolutions.com
Scope: Provides joint-venture and start-up human resource consulting services as well as advice on organization development for international human capital. Industries served: high-tech and telecommunications. **Founded:** 1997.

45833 ■ IMC Consulting & Training
901 McHenry Ave., Ste. A
Modesto, CA 95350
Ph: (209)572-2271
Fax: (209)572-2862
Co. E-mail: info@imc-1.net
URL: http://www.imc-1.net
Scope: Services: Business management and marketing programs. **Founded:** 1994. **Publications:** "Consultant Earns Advanced Certificate," Hccsc Business Review, Dec, 2004; "Adapting to Change - the New Competitive Advantage," Business Journal, Jul, 2004; "Loyalty Marketing Can Divide New Business," Jun, 2004; "Eleven Major Marketing Mistakes," Jul, 2003; "Planning to Win or Racing to Fail," Jun, 2003. **Seminars:** Negotiating High Profit Sales; How to Write Winning Proposals, Modesto Chamber of Commerce, Oct, 2007; Winning the 2nd Half: A 6-month Plan to Score New Customers and Profits.

45834 ■ The Impact Group L.L.C.
18 Stonewall Dr.
West Granby, CT 06090-1618
Ph: (860)653-0757
Fax: (928)396-2279
Co. E-mail: info@groupimpact.com
URL: http://www.groupimpact.com
Contact: Elaine A. Pullen, Principal
Scope: Firm specializes in business operations improvement and TQM consulting initiatives. **Founded:** 1997.

45835 ■ In Plain English [R.H. Wohl & Associates Inc.]
14501 Antigone Dr.
Gaithersburg, MD 20885-3300
Ph: (301)340-2821
Free: 800-274-9645
Fax: (301)279-0115
Co. E-mail: rwohl@inplainenglish.com
URL: http://www.inplainenglish.com
Contact: Ronald H. Wohl, President
E-mail: rwohl@inplainenglish.com
Scope: Management consultants helping government and businesses research, design, write and produce user oriented management information for human resources, employee benefits, business process, corporate and marketing needs. Services include: GSA mob is schedule for consulting to the government; employee benefit communications, plain English business writing workshops for print and electronic media; communicating strategy and tactics; marketing research, business planning and communications; readability testing; usability testing and monitoring strategy. **Founded:** 1977. **Publications:** "The Benefits Communication"; "The Employee Benefits Communication ToolKit," Commerce Clearinghouse; "Benefits Communication," Business and Legal Reports. **Seminars:** Plain English Writing Training; Summary Plan Description Compliance workshops; Re-Humanizing the Corporation, Human Resources and Employee Benefits Communication Workshop; 21 Writing Tips for the 21st Century; Make the Write Impression; Writing to Inform and Instruct; The Dreaded Nuts and Bolts; Writing to Persuade; Writing Policy and Procedure Manuals In Plain English; Writing for Accountants and Auditors In Plain English. **Special Services:** In Plain English®.

45836 ■ The Institute for Management Excellence
PO Box 193
Trabuco Canyon, CA 92679-0193
Ph: (949)667-1012
URL: http://www.itstime.com
Contact: Barbara Taylor, Executive Director
E-mail: btaylor@itstime.com
Scope: Management consulting and training focuses on improving productivity, using practices and creative techniques. Practices based on the company's theme: It's time for new ways of doing business. Industries served: public sector, law enforcement, finance or banking, non profit, computers or high technology, education, human resources, utilities. **Founded:** 1995. **Publications:** "Income Without a Job," 2008; "The Other Side of Midnight, 2000: An Executive Guide to the Year 2000 Problem"; "Concordance to the Michael Teachings"; "Handbook of Small Business Advertising"; "The Personality Game"; "How to Market Yourself for Success". **Seminars:** The Personality Game; Power Path Seminars; Productivity Plus; Sexual Harassment and Discrimination Prevention; Worker's Comp Cost Reduction; Americans with Disabilities Act; In Search of Identify: Clarifying Corporate Culture.

45837 ■ Interax Corp.
4524 S Michigan St.
South Bend, IN 46680-2287
Ph: (574)299-0660
Free: 800-560-4489
Fax: (574)299-0683
Co. E-mail: info@interaxcorp.com
URL: http://www.interaxcorp.com
Contact: T. Arthur Stump, President
Scope: Company provides management consulting services, including training, organizational group facilitation, total quality management, participative management, and human technology interaction management. Serves all industries worldwide. **Founded:** 1986. **Publications:** "Eye of the storm: Compaq executive turmoil traced to Pfeiffer's inner circle," May, 1999; "The Transformational Leader"; "Leading Change"; "The Human Side of Change: A practical guide to organization redesign"; "People, Performance, & Pay: Dynamic Compensation for Changing Organizations"; "Leadership is an Art"; "Managing Disagreement Constructively: Conflict Management in Organizations"; "Facilitation...From Discussion to Decision".

45838 ■ Interminds & Federer Resources Inc.
106 E 6th St., Ste. 310
Austin, TX 78701-3659
Ph: (512)476-8800
Co. E-mail: yesyoucan@interminds.com
URL: http://www.interminds.com
Contact: Frank Federer, President
E-mail: ffederer@integra100.com
Scope: Specializes in feasibility studies; startup businesses; small business management; mergers and acquisitions; joint ventures; divestitures; interim management; crisis management; turnarounds; production planning; team building; appraisals and valuations. **Founded:** 1985. **Publications:** "Yes You Can: How To Be A Success No Matter Who You Are Or Where You're From".

45839 ■ Interpersonal Coaching & Consulting (ICC)
1516 W Lake St., Ste. 2000S
Minneapolis, MN 55408
Ph: (612)381-2494
Co. E-mail: mail@interpersonal-coaching.com
URL: http://www.interpersonal-coaching.com
Contact: Richard J. Studer, Partner
E-mail: mail@interpersonal-coaching.com
Scope: Provider of coaching and consulting to businesses and organizations. Assesses the interpersonal

workplace through interviews, assessment instruments and individual group settings. Experienced as a therapist for over a decade. **Publications:** "Sexual Harassment In The Workplace For Newspapers". **Seminars:** More On Relationships; Sexual harassment and discrimination issues.

45840 ■ Johnston Co.
78 Bedford St.
Lexington, MA 02420
Ph: (781)862-7595
Fax: (781)862-9066
Co. E-mail: info@johnstoncompany.com
URL: http://www.johnstoncompany.com
Contact: Claire Sehringer, Chief Executive Officer
Scope: Services: Business consulting, financial management, strategic and advisory services. **Founded:** 1987. **Publications:** "Why are board meetings such a waste of time," Boston Business Journal, Apr, 2004.

45841 ■ K & T Training [K & T Consulting]
103 Greenville St.
Newnan, GA 30263
Ph: (770)253-5870
Contact: J. R. Tumperi, President
Scope: Specializes in strategic planning; profit enhancement; organizational development; start-up businesses; interim management; crisis management; turnarounds; business process re-engineering; team building; cost controls. **Founded:** 1983.

45842 ■ Kaiser Group Inc.
237 South St.
Waukesha, WI 53186
Ph: (262)544-4971
Fax: (262)544-6271
URL: http://www.kaisergrp.com
Contact: Terri Leisten, President
Scope: Management support consultants with an emphasis on service to capital and consumer goods manufacturers of under twenty million in sales. Current activity is concentrated on startup and turnaround management, executive and supervisory development, marketing and sales strategies and planning, development of capital and loan formation packages, modular housing and real estate development, employment and training activities, participative management implementation, product and service costing, active market research programs and employee involvement programs. Serves private industries as well as government agencies. **Founded:** 1979. **Publications:** "A Comprehensive Resource Guide for Workforce Board Staff"; "Guide to Effective Work groups and Meetings"; "From Research to Reality"; "Business Services Team Development Guide". **Seminars:** Job Readiness and Assessment Strategies; Career Advising; Understanding Motivation; Customer Service Strategies; Developing Leadership for Supervisors; Case Management Interventions; Team Development.

45843 ■ Keiei Senryaku Corp.
19191 S Vermont Ave., Ste. 530
Torrance, CA 90502-1049
Ph: (310)366-3331
Fax: (310)366-3330
Contact: Kurt Miyamoto, President
Scope: Offers consulting services in the areas of strategic planning; feasibility studies; profit enhancement; organizational development; start-up businesses; mergers and acquisitions; joint ventures; divestitures; executive searches; sales management; and competitive analysis. **Founded:** 1989.

45844 ■ KRIM M. BALLENTINE [ICOP Investigations]
5c-17/5d-4 Estate Santa Maria
Saint Thomas, VI 00803-5396
Ph: (340)776-0581
Fax: (340)776-3519
Co. E-mail: krim@thelastnegro.com
URL: http://www.thelastnegro.com
Contact: Krim M. Ballentine, Owner
E-mail: krim@thelastnegro.com
Scope: Consultant in human relations dealing with attitudes and behavior. Also consults on racism, workplace violence, domestic violence, child abuse,

sexism and philosophical attitudes to include religion. **Publications:** "The Simplistic Philosopher and Krim's Simplistic Philosophies," Vantage Press, W4, 1988.

45845 ■ William E. Kuhn & Associates
234 Cook St.
Denver, CO 80206-5305
Ph: (303)322-8233
Fax: (303)331-9032
Scope: Firm specializes in strategic planning; profit enhancement; small business management; mergers and acquisitions; joint ventures; divestitures; human resources management; performance appraisals; team building; sales management; appraisals and valuations. **Founded:** 1980. **Publications:** "Creating a High-Performance Dealership," Office SOLUTIONS and Office DEALER, Jul-Aug, 2006.

45846 ■ Leadership Development Center (LDC)
155 Edgewood Ave. S
Jacksonville, FL 32254
Ph: (904)387-0110
Free: 800-659-1720
Fax: (904)246-9270
Co. E-mail: jbleech@no-excuses.com
URL: http://www.no-excuses.com
Contact: James M. Bleech, Principal
Scope: Management consulting firm offering development of leadership skills for CEOs and senior management. Specializes in issues of corporate culture and strategic planning. Industries served: all. **Founded:** 1989. **Publications:** "Knockdown," Jul, 2002; "Let's Get Results Not Excuses," Lifetime Books; "The On Purpose Person"; "When the Other Guy's Price Is Lower," Lifetime Books. **Seminars:** Let's Get Results!; Corporate Culture and Values: Establishing the Center; The X Predicament: Maximizing Profits through Sales Department Design.

45847 ■ Liberty Business Strategies Ltd.
The Times Bldg., Ste. 400, Suburban Sq.
Ardmore, PA 19003
Ph: (610)649-3800
Fax: (610)649-0408
URL: http://www.libertystrategies.com
Contact: Emmy S. Miller, President
E-mail: emmym@libertystrategies.com
Scope: Management consulting firm working with clients to gain speed and agility in driving their business strategy. The consulting model builds the alignment of strategy, organization commitment, and technology. Provides senior leader coaching and team development coaching. **Founded:** 1980. **Seminars:** Winning with Talent, Morison Annual Conference, Jul, 2009.

45848 ■ Lupfer & Associates (L&A)
92 Glen St.
Natick, MA 01760-5646
Ph: (508)655-3950
Fax: (508)655-7826
Co. E-mail: donlupfer@aol.com
Contact: Donald Lupfer, Owner
E-mail: donlupfer@europartners.eu.com
Scope: Assists off shore hi-tech companies in entering United States markets and specializes in channel development for all sorts of products. Perform MARCOM support for hi-tech United States clients. **Founded:** 1988. **Publications:** "What's Next For Distribution-Feast or Famine"; "The Changing Global Marketplace"; "Making Global Distribution Work". **Seminars:** How to do Business in the United States.

45849 ■ Management Growth Institute (MGI)
27 Chelmsford Rd.
Rochester, NY 14618
Ph: (585)461-1353
Fax: (585)461-5266
Co. E-mail: kbalbertini@managementgrowth.com
URL: http://www.managementgrowth.com
Contact: Kathleen Barry Albertini, President
E-mail: kbalbertini@managementgrowth.com
Scope: Offers assistance in the specification, design and implementation of management development programs. Clients include individuals, small businesses, national trade associations and government agencies. **Founded:** 1961. **Publications:** "Cost Reduction Is Your Company the Target," InFocus

Magazine, Apr, 2010; "Fall-I hired this great person," The Canadian Mover, Dec, 2009; "Profit Strategies," Direction Magazine, Jul, 2009; "Customer Loyalty," InFocus Magazine, Jul, 2009; "Cash Management," The Portal Magazine, Jul, 2009; "What is Customer Loyalty," In FOCUS Magazine, Dec, 2008; "Strategies to Improve Profits," Aug, 2008; "A Question of Management," Moving World. **Seminars:** Profit Enhancement; Family-Owned Businesses; Strategic Planning; Survival and Growth in a Down Economy.

45850 ■ Management House Inc.
36422 Sidewinder Rd.
Carefree, AZ 85377-2708
Ph: (480)437-9023
Fax: (480)588-8905
Co. E-mail: info@managementhouse.com
URL: http://www.managementhouse.com
Contact: Dr. Clay Sherman, President
E-mail: drclay@managementhouse.com
Scope: Offers management consulting that emphasizes management education and human resources programming for health service, business, military, and academic organizations. This programming is based on needs analysis and can be presented as keynote addresses, half-day else full-day programs, multiple-day seminars and executive retreats. Programs is specifically developed to respond to needs analysis findings. **Founded:** 1980. **Publications:** "Raising Standards in American Healthcare"; "Creating the New American Hospital"; "Total Customer Satisfaction"; "From Losers to Winners"; "Managerial Performance & Promotability"; "Make Yourself Memorable Winning Strategies to Influence Others". **Seminars:** Offers the following in-house programs: The Uncommon Leader; The New American Organization; The New American Hospital; Productivity & Performance Improvement; Keys to Managerial Effectiveness; Creating Organizational Excellence; Managing Change & Conflict; Handling the Problem Employee; Gaining Power & Persuasion; Building a Winning Team; and Managing Stress, Strain, and Dis-Ease; Creating the New American Hospital: A Time For Greatness; Total Customer Satisfaction; Leading With Certainty in Uncertain Times; Raising Standards in American Health Care.

45851 ■ Management Methods Inc.
207 Johnston St. SE, Ste. 208
Decatur, AL 35602
Ph: (256)355-3896
Fax: (256)353-3140
Co. E-mail: davisw@managementmethods.com
URL: http://www.managementmethods.com
Contact: Davis M. Woodruff, President
E-mail: davisw@managementmethods.com
Scope: Management and manufacturing consultants who specialize in showing companies how to be the low cost, high quality producer in their industry. Services include general management consulting, total quality management, ISO-9000 or QS-9000, statistical process control, and other problem solving methods. Also a professional speaker for clients, trade associations, and professional groups. Clients include small businesses and Fortune 100 companies in the following industries: Automotive, chemicals, textiles, utilities, petroleum, plastics, and polymers, as well as government agencies. **Founded:** 1984. **Publications:** "A Manager's Guide to the 10 Essentials"; "A Manager's Guide to Tqm Success"; "Leading People and Managing Processes"; "Taking Care of the Basics, 101 Success Factors for Managers," 2005. **Seminars:** Statistical Process Control (SPC): Concepts and Applications; Advanced Statistical Methods; Team Problem Solving; Effective Management Methods; Measurement Systems SPC and ISO 9000; What To Do When Total Quality Management Isn't Working; Seven Golden Rules for the Best Customer service; How To Make Quality Management a Success; Managing Without Unions; Five Techniques for Keeping Technical People From Failing as Managers; How To Stop the War Between Sales, Engineering and Manufacturing; Reengineer Your Company with Common Sense and Compassion; Having High Values in a Low Cost, High Quality Business.

45852 ■ Management Resource Partners
181 2nd Ave., Ste. 542
San Mateo, CA 94401
Ph: (650)401-5850
Contact: John C. Roberts, Partner
Scope: Firm specializes in strategic planning; small business management; mergers and acquisitions; joint ventures; divestitures; interim management; crisis management; turn around; venture capital; appraisals and valuations. **Founded:** 1981.

45853 ■ Management Strategies
1000 S Old Woodward Ave., Ste. 105
Birmingham, MI 48009
Ph: (248)258-2756
Contact: Robert E. Hoisington, President
E-mail: bob@hois.com
Scope: Firm specializes in strategic planning; feasibility studies; profit enhancement; organizational studies; start up businesses; turnarounds; business process re engineering; industrial engineering; marketing; ecommerce. **Founded:** 1985.

45854 ■ Management Technology Associates Ltd.
2768 SW Sherwood Dr., Ste. 105
Portland, OR 97201-2251
Ph: (503)224-5220
Fax: (503)224-5334
Co. E-mail: lcuster@mta-ltd.com
Contact: Lawrence R. Custer, President
E-mail: lcuster@mta-ltd.com
Scope: Offers troubled company turn arounds, strategic business planning, productivity improvement, information systems, business mediation and business valuations. Industries served: manufacturing, wholesale distribution, forest products, transportation, construction, health care and government. **Founded:** 1982. **Publications:** "What it Takes to Manage in the '90's," Business Journal; "Bringing Management Techniques to Small Business Clients"; "How to Value and Sell Your Company". **Seminars:** Strategic Business Planning; Management Control Systems, Business Dispute Resolution; Management Techniques for Small Business Clients.

45855 ■ Market Focus
12 Maryland Rd.
Maplewood, NJ 07040
Ph: (973)378-2470
Fax: (973)378-2470
Co. E-mail: mcss66@marketfocus.com
Contact: Daniel A. Zaslow, President
E-mail: dakaslow@comcast.net
Scope: Offers advisory services to executives of corporate business units and mid-sized companies in the development and implementation of corporate and market strategies. Studies relate to business planning, new market/product entry, acquisitions and industry/competitive profiles for firms in advanced technology, business and financial services and basic industry. Projects focus on practical, effective approaches to maximizing the potential of existing operations and exploiting future growth opportunities. Practice philosophy emphasizes close client relationships, active management participation and senior consultant involvement. **Founded:** 1980. **Publications:** "Surviving in Hard Times," NJ Contractor. **Seminars:** Charting a Course for Future Company Growth; Marketing Planning; Construction Marketing in the 90's; Marketing and The CFO.

45856 ■ Stuart Matlins Associates
4 Sunset Farms, Rte. 4
Woodstock, VT 05091-0237
Ph: (802)457-4000
Free: 800-962-4544
Fax: (802)457-4004
Co. E-mail: sales@jewishlights.com
URL: http://www.jewishlights.com
Contact: Stuart M. Matlins, President
Description: Description: Publishes adult and children's books on Jewish spirituality, religion, philosophy, theology and culture for people of all faiths and backgrounds. Reaches market through commission representatives, direct mail, telephone sales, trade sales, advertising, wholesalers and distributors. Accepts unsolicited manuscripts. **Scope:** Provider of management consulting and research

services to private and public sector clients. Services include: profit improvement; growth management; planning and organization; financial, economic and market feasibility; financial management and control; negotiations for new ventures, joint ventures and licensing of products/processes; and management training. **Founded:** 1974.

45857 ■ McDonald Consulting Group Inc.
1900 W Park Dr., Ste. 280
Westborough, MA 01581
Ph: (508)366-9203
Fax: (707)276-3833
Co. E-mail: info@mcdonaldconsultinggroup.com
URL: http://www.mcdonaldconsultinggroup.com
Contact: Ron A. McDonald, President
E-mail: rmcdonald@mcdonaldconsultinggroup.com
Scope: A management consulting firm specializing in assisting insurance companies improve operations. Provides services in the areas of strategic planning; profit enhancement; organizational development; interim management; crisis management; turnarounds; business process re-engineering; benefits and compensation planning and total quality management. **Founded:** 1993. **Publications:** "Improving Customer Focus through Organizational Structure," AASCIF News; "Changing Strategies in Hard Markets," The National Underwriter; "Moving Beyond Management 101: Postgraduate Time Management for Executives," The National Underwriter; "A New Attitude: 3 Clients Improved Results Through Our Fundamental Change Process," Bests Review; "How to Organize Your Company Around Your Customers," Bests Review. **Seminars:** How to establish "expense allowable"; How to design an incentive compensation plan around a units core success measures.

45858 ■ Jerome W. McGee & Associates [Bruce W. McGee & Associates]
7826 Eastern Ave. NW, Ste. 300
Washington, DC 20012
Ph: (202)726-7272
Fax: (202)726-2946
Contact: Bruce W. McGee, President
Scope: Business consultants experienced in office automation, small business management, invention and patent counseling, technology commercialization, loan packaging and business plan development. **Founded:** 1985. **Seminars:** Marketing Research for the High-Technology Business; Introduction to Microcomputers; Marketing Technological Products to Industry; How to Evaluate Your Technical Idea; Patenting Your Own Invention.

45859 ■ MCR Capital Advisors L.L.P.
535 W 20th St., Ste. 100
Houston, TX 77028
Ph: (713)623-6778
Fax: (713)426-4601
Co. E-mail: magillp@mcrcapitaladvisors.com
URL: http://www.mcrcapitaladvisors.com
Contact: Tom A. Colvin, Founder
E-mail: colvint@mcrcapitaladvisors.com
Scope: Valuations and strategy for mergers and acquisitions, workout agreements and development of strategic partnerships, direct business advisors to senior management and board of directors utilizing industry experience and business acumen, accounting and financial consulting for debt restructuring, outsourcing of top side accounting services and preparation for significant financing or IPO and consulting for IT vendor evaluations, organizational design, human performance optimization and customer relationship management strategy. Serves the unique needs of small and mid size companies. **Founded:** 2001.

45860 ■ McShane Group L.L.C.
2345 York Rd., Ste. 102
Timonium, MD 21093
Ph: (410)560-0077
Fax: (410)560-2718
URL: http://www.mcshanegroup.com
Contact: Thomas P. McShane, President
E-mail: tmcshane@mcshanegroup.com
Scope: Turnaround consulting and crisis management firm. Specializes in due diligence services, interim management, strategic business realignments, business sale and asset depositions and debt

restructuring. Industries served: technology, financial, retail, distribution, medical, educational, manufacturing, contracting, environmental and health care. **Founded:** 1987.

45861 ■ Medema Consulting Associates L.L.C.
2342 Paris Ave., SE
Grand Rapids, MI 49507-3112
Ph: (616)235-0554
Fax: (616)988-3104
Contact: David Luke Medema, President
Scope: Firm creates and delivers customized training and consulting services in the areas of board governance and leadership development, diversity assessment and training, fund raising, human resources, meeting facilitation, performance improvement, strategic thinking, planning, evaluation, team building and workshops. **Founded:** 1999.

45862 ■ Medical Imaging Consultants Inc. (MIC)
1037 US Highway 46, Ste. G-2
Clifton, NJ 07013-2445
Ph: (973)574-8000
Free: 800-589-5685
Fax: (973)574-8001
Co. E-mail: info@micinfo.com
URL: http://www.micinfo.com
Contact: Dr. Philip A. Femano, President
E-mail: phil@micinfo.com
Scope: Provider of professional support services for radiology management and comprehensive continuing education programs for radiologic technologists. Management services include resource-critical database logistics; customer registration in educational programs; educational program development and Category A accreditation; national agency notification (e.g., ASRT, SNM-TS) of CE credits earned; meeting planning; manpower assessment; market research; expert witness; think-tank probes and executive summaries of industry issues. **Founded:** 1991. **Seminars:** Sectional Anatomy and Imaging Strategies; CT Cross-Trainer; CT Registry Review Program; MR Cross Trainer; MRI Registry Review Program; Digital Mammography Essentials for Technologists; Radiology Trends for Technologists.

45863 ■ Medical Outcomes Management Inc.
132 Central St., Ste. 215
Foxborough, MA 02035-2422
Ph: (508)543-0050
Fax: (508)543-1919
Contact: Alan F. Kaul, President
E-mail: alan@mom-inc.com
Scope: Management and technology consulting firm providing a specially focused group of services such as disease management programs and pharmacoeconomic studies. Services include clinical and educational projects, medical writing and editing, marketing and sales projects, disease registries, educational seminars, strategic planning projects, managed care organizations; and pharmaceutical and biotechnology companies. **Founded:** 1991. **Publications:** "Treatment of acute exacerbation's of chronic bronchitis in patients with chronic obstructive pulmonary disease: A retrospective cohort analysis logarithmically extended release vs. Azithromycin," 2003; "A retrospective analysis of cyclooxygenase-II inhibitor response patterns," 2002; "DUE criteria for use of regional urokinase infusion for deep vein thrombosis,"2002; "The formulary management system and decision-making process at Horizon Blue Cross Blue Shield of New Jersey," Pharmaco therapy, 2001. **Seminars:** Economic Modeling as a Disease Management Tool, Academy of Managed Care Pharmacy, Apr, 2005; Integrating Disease State Management and Economics, Academy of Managed Care Pharmacy, Oct, 2004; Clinical and economic outcomes in the treatment of peripheral occlusive diseases, Mar, 2003.

45864 ■ MHJ Associates
41 Coolidge St.
Brookline, MA 02446-2401
Ph: (617)232-7475

Fax: (617)879-1617
Co. E-mail: mhjassociates@rcn.com
Contact: Michael Jacobs, Owner
E-mail: m.jacobs@mhjassociates.com
Scope: Firm specializes in housing development and finance. Services include 40B permitting and financial analysis, project management, multifamily housing finance and feasibility analysis.

45865 ■ MIIX Healthcare Group
2 Princess Rd.
Lawrenceville, NJ 08648
Ph: (609)219-1111
Free: 800-234-6449
Fax: (609)219-6727
Contact: Daniel Goldberg, Chief Executive Officer
Scope: Firm provides comprehensive healthcare consulting services and unique products designed to assist physicians and healthcare organizations meet the challenges of a managed care environment. Consulting services range from practice management to network formation and marketing, practice valuations, practice mergers and acquisitions and compliance. **Founded:** 1996.

45866 ■ Miller/Cook & Associates Inc.
20 Marco Lake Dr., Ste. 12
Marco Island, FL 34145-3644
Ph: (239)394-5040
Free: 800-591-1141
Fax: (239)394-2652
Co. E-mail: info@millercook.com
URL: http://www.millercook.com
Contact: William B. Miller, President
Scope: Specializes in all areas of enrollment management, admissions and financial aid. Involves in institutional and enrollment analysis, strategic positioning/institutional image, enrollment integration/operation, re-recruitment, financial aid and planning, integrated communications, training and workshops and on-site management. **Founded:** 1988. **Publications:** "Capital gains: Surviving in an increasingly for profit world"; "Making steps to a brighter future". **Seminars:** Admissions: An overview of a changing profession; Admission practices: Managing the admissions office; Admission practices: Internal operations often make the difference; Effective communication and the enrollment process; Telemarketing or Tele counseling: How to use the telephone to effectively enroll and re-enroll students; Graduate and professional program recruitment: An overview Re-Recruitment: What is it? Is it necessary?; The effective use of electronic mediums in the recruitment process; The use of alumni to support and sustain your recruiting efforts.

45867 ■ Miller, Hellwig Associates
150 W End Ave.
New York, NY 10023-5713
Contact: Ernest C. Miller, President
Scope: Consulting services in the areas of start-up businesses; small business management; employee surveys and communication; performance appraisals; executive searches; team building; personnel policies and procedures; market research. Also involved in improving cross-cultural and multi-cultural relationships, particularly with Japanese clients. **Founded:** 1984. **Seminars:** Objectives and standards/recruiting for boards of directors.

45868 ■ Moats Kennedy Inc.
1155 W Madison St., Ste. 605
Chicago, IL 60607
Ph: (847)251-1661
Free: 800-728-1709
Fax: (847)251-5191
Co. E-mail: mkennedy@moatskennedy.com
URL: http://www.moatskennedy.com
Contact: Marilyn Moats Kennedy, Managing Partner
Scope: Provider of consulting services for a variety of associations and companies in the area of personnel and management. Speaks and consults on the following topics office politics, leadership skills, demographics workplace issues. Serves industry as well as government agencies in the U.S. **Founded:** 1975. **Publications:** "How to Prove Your Work Makes A Difference ," FOCUS: Journal for Respiratory Care & Sleep Medicine, 2005; "The Glamour Guide to Office Smarts"; "Salary Strategies: Everything You Need

to Know to Get the Salary You Want"; "Career Knockouts: How to Battle Back,"; "Powerbase: How to Build It/How to Keep It"; "Office Warfare: Getting Ahead in the Aggressive 80s"; "The Glamour Guide to Office Smarts"; "In the Trenches"; "Job Strategies". **Seminars:** Managing Change: Understanding the Demographics of the Evolving Workforce; The Aging Workforce; Are You Giving Satisfaction or Just Service?; Management for the Millenium: Walking your talk.

45869 ■ R.E. Moulton Inc.
50 Doaks Ln.
Marblehead, MA 1945
Ph: (781)631-1325
Fax: (781)631-2165
URL: http://www.oneamerica.com/wps/wcm/connect/REMoulton
Contact: Willard A. Knarr, Jr., President
Scope: Offers underwriting services, marketing solutions, claims administration and adjudication; policy and commission administration; and risk management solutions to clients. Supplementary service s include risk management and employee assistance. Clients include individuals, business men, employers and finance professionals. **Founded:** 1976.

45870 ■ Murray Dropkin & Associates [Dropkin Consulting]
390 George St.
New Brunswick, NJ 08901
Co. E-mail: murray@dropkin.com
URL: http://www.dropkin.com
Contact: Murray Dropkin, President
E-mail: murray@dropkin.com
Scope: Specializes in feasibility studies; business management; business process re-engineering; and team building, health care and housing. **Founded:** 1969. **Publications:** "Bookkeeping for Nonprofits," Jossey Bass, 2005; "Guide to Audits of Nonprofit Organizations," PPC; "The Nonprofit Report," Warren, Gorham & Lamont; "The Budget Building Book for Nonprofits," Jossey-Bass; "The Cash Flow Management Book for Nonprofits," Jossey-Bass.

45871 ■ Navarro, Kim & Associates
529 N Charles St., Ste. 202
Baltimore, MD 21201-5043
Ph: (410)837-6317
Fax: (410)837-6294
Contact: Beltran Navarro, Director
E-mail: bnavarro@sprynet.com
Scope: Specializes in bridging the gap between firms and non-traditional ethnic communities, especially in community development and institutional building. **Founded:** 1984.

45872 ■ New Commons
545 Pawtucket Ave., Studio 106A
Pawtucket, RI 02860
Ph: (401)351-7110
Fax: (401)351-7158
Co. E-mail: info@newcommons.com
URL: http://www.newcommons.com
Contact: Robert Leaver, Chief Executive Officer
E-mail: rleaver@newcommons.com
Scope: Builder of agile human networks to champion innovation and mobilize change; to pursue business opportunities; to custom design agile organizations and communities, to foster civic engagement. Clients include organizations on-profits, corporations, government agencies, educational institutions; networks-Trade/professional groups, IT services collaborations, service-sharing collectives; and communities- municipalities, states and statewide agencies, regional collaborations. **Founded:** 1982. **Publications:** "Plexus Imperative," Sep, 2005; "Creating 21st Century Capable Innovation Systems," Aug, 2004; "Call to Action: Building Providences Creative and Innovative Economy"; "Getting Results from Meetings"; "The Entrepreneur as Artist," Commonwealth Publications; "Leader and Agent of Change," Commonwealth Publications; "Achieving our Providence: Lessons of City-Building," Commonwealth Publications. **Seminars:** Introduction to Social Computing (Web 2.0), Jan, 2009; Every Company Counts, Jun, 2009; Facilitating for Results; Story-Making and Story-Telling.

45873 ■ Nightingale Associates
7445 Setting Sun Way
Columbia, MD 21046
Ph: (410)381-4280
Co. E-mail: fredericknightingale@nightingaleassociates.net
URL: http://www.nightingaleassociates.net
Contact: Frederick C. Nightingale, Managing Director
E-mail: fredericknightingale@nightingaleassociates.net
Scope: Management training and consulting firm offering the following skills: productivity and accomplishment; leadership skills for the experienced manager; management skills for the new manager; leadership and teambuilding; supervisory development; creative problem solving; real strategic planning; providing superior customer service; international purchasing and supply chain management; negotiation skills development and fundamentals of purchasing. **Founded:** 1984. **Seminars:** Productivity and Accomplishment Management Skills for the New Manager; Leadership and Team building; Advanced Management; Business Process Re engineering; Strategic Thinking; Creative Problem Solving; Customer Service; International Purchasing and Materials Management; Fundamentals of Purchasing; Negotiation Skills Development; Providing superior customer service; Leadership skills for the experienced manager.

45874 ■ Non-Profit Transitions L.L.C.
446 Main St.
Waltham, MA 02452
Ph: (617)501-5471
Co. E-mail: info@nptransitions.com
URL: http://www.nptransitions.com
Contact: Jeff Katz, Chief Executive Officer
Scope: Provides non-profit organizations with executive leadership and consulting during transition. Provides interim leaders, including chief executive officers, chief financial officers and human resources directors. Change leadership services include executive coaching, governance and board performance evaluation, mediation and conflict resolution, strategic planning, search process leadership and mergers and acquisitions. Other consulting services include organizational development, program performance, training and development, development and grant writing; and real estate project management. **Founded:** 2003. **Publications:** "Lessons from the Merger Culture War".

45875 ■ NOVUS L.L.C.
417 Main Ave., Ste. 209
Fargo, ND 58103
Ph: (701)280-0397
Fax: (701)298-3533
Contact: Don Blanding, Manager, Information Technology
E-mail: dblanding@novusresults.com
Scope: A full-service strategic business consulting group offering management services, including executive management, governance, human resources, operations management, financial management, information technology and medical affairs.

45876 ■ Oakdales Olde Towne Veterinary Hospital
144 S 1st Ave.
Oakdale, CA 95361-3903
Ph: (209)847-9077
Fax: (209)847-4390
URL: http://www.oakdalevet.com
Contact: Chirs Edwards, Manager
Scope: Provider of diagnostic and therapeutic services for a pet's health care needs. Offers surgical services, anesthesia, radiology services, ultrasound services, electrocardiography services, dental services and dietary and behavioral counseling. **Founded:** 1948.

45877 ■ Organizational Consulting Services Inc.
230 S Bemiston Ave., Ste. 1107
Saint Louis, MO 63105-1907
Ph: (314)863-1200

Fax: (314)863-6718
Co. E-mail: rav@ocs-oe.com
URL: http://www.ocs-oe.com
Contact: Robert A. Vecchiotti, President
E-mail: rav@ocs-oe.com
Scope: Services include business assessment, planning, and restructuring; team building, executive assessment and development; financial analysis and cost accounting; market analysis and customer surveys. Consultants also serve as facilitators of planning retreats, offering guidance in strategy development and goal setting. The firm works with CEO's and senior executives of privately held companies and major corporations. **Founded:** 1980. **Seminars:** Leadership for Entrepreneurs, Missouri, Oct, 2006; The Integrated Executive seminars; Strategic Planning and Management; Change Management; Management Transitions; Team Building.

45878 ■ P2C2 Group Inc.
4101 Denfeld Ave.
Kensington, MD 20895-1514
Ph: (301)942-7985
Fax: (301)942-7986
Co. E-mail: info@p2c2group.com
URL: http://www.p2c2group.com
Scope: Works with clients on the business side of federal program and project management. Services include program/project planning and optimization; acquisition strategy and work statements; IT Capital Planning and Investment Control (CPIC); business cases - new, revisions, critiques; budget analysis - cost benefits- alternatives; CPIC, SELC, and security documentation; research, metrics, analysis, and case studies. Consulting support helping to: Define or redefine programs; strengthen portfolio management; identify alternatives for lean budgets; improve capital planning and investment; develop better plans and documentation, and evaluate performance of existing program investments. **Founded:** 1994. **Publications:** "OMB 300s Go Online," Federal Sector Report, Mar, 2007; "Using Risk-Adjusted Costs for Projects," Federal Sector Report, Feb, 2007; "Make Better Decisions Using Case Studies," Federal Sector Report, Jan, 2007; "PMO Performance Measurement & Metrics"; "Executive Sponsors for Projects"; "ABCs of the Presidential Transition"; "Financial Systems and Enterprise Portfolio Management"; "The Future of CPIC"; "Critical Factors for Program and Project Success"; "Using Risk-Adjusted Costs for Projects"; "Tactics for a Successful Year of CPIC"; "Operational Analysis Reviews"; "Successful IT Strategic Planning"; "Information Technology Investment Management". **Seminars:** Requests For Information; Pre Solicitation Marketing; Qualifications Statement Support For The Capital Planning And Investment Control (cpic) Process; How To Hire A Management Consultant And Get The Results You Expect.

45879 ■ Papa and Associates Inc.
200 Consumers Rd., Ste. 305
Toronto, ON, Canada M2J 4R4
Ph: (416)512-7272
Fax: (416)512-2016
Co. E-mail: ppapa@papa-associates.com
Contact: Peter Papakostantinu, President
E-mail: ppapa@papa-associates.com
Scope: Provider of broad based management consulting services in the areas of quality assurance, environmental, health and safety and integrated management systems. **Founded:** 1989.

45880 ■ Parker Consultants Inc.
230 Mason St.
Greenwich, CT 06830-6633
Ph: (203)869-9400
Contact: William P. Hartl, Chief Executive Officer
Scope: Firm specializes in strategic planning; organizational development; small business management; performance appraisals; executive searches; team building; and customer service audits. **Founded:** 1988.

45881 ■ partnerTEL Inc.
5490 McGinnis Village Pl.
Alpharetta, GA 30005
Ph: (404)978-4400
Free: 800-864-8840

Fax: (404)531-0705
Co. E-mail: customersupport@partnertel.com
URL: http://www.partnertel.com
Contact: James Larsen, Chief Executive Officer
Scope: A provider of telecom consulting, procurement and managed services. Assists businesses handle the strategic, operational, support and cost-containment challenges surrounding their communications services. Services in inventory and contract management, service management, A/Optimization, tax audits and wireless services. Helps business enterprises streamline their telecom procurement, management and expenditure processes and maximize their overall telecom savings rate and return on investment (ROI). Cost management services include business process outsourcing, hosted software solutions, cost containment consulting, bill auditing and recovery, spend analysis and reporting, business process analysis and outsourcing, carrier and product benchmarking, inventory management, order management, bill management and monitoring, invoice consolidation, electronic bill presentment and payment, trouble ticket management, PBX service, support and procurement, network management and monitoring, contract negotiation and procurement, SLA and contract compliance, rate plan optimization and vendor management. **Founded:** 1996.

45882 ■ Performance Consulting Associates Inc. (PCA)
3700 Crestwood Pky., Ste. 100
Duluth, GA 30096
Ph: (770)717-2737
Fax: (770)717-7014
Co. E-mail: info@pcaconsulting.com
URL: http://www.pcaconsulting.com
Contact: Richard A. Defazio, President
E-mail: defazio@pcaconsulting.com
Scope: Maintenance consulting and engineering firm specializing in production planning, project management, team building, and re-engineering maintenance. **Founded:** 1976. **Publications:** "Does Planning Pay," Plant Services, Nov, 2000; "Asset Reliability Coordinator," Maintenance Technology, Oct, 2000; "Know What it is You Have to Maintain," Maintenance Technology, May, 2000; "Does Maintenance Planning Pay," Maintenance Technology, Nov, 2000.; "What is Asset Management?"; "Implementing Best Business Practices".

45883 ■ Performance Consulting Group Inc.
8031 SW 35th Terr.
Miami, FL 33155-3443
Ph: (305)264-5577
Fax: (305)264-9079
Contact: Jose P. Fernandez, Director
Scope: Firm provides consulting services in the areas of strategic planning; profit enhancement; product development; and production planning. **Founded:** 1980.

45884 ■ Pioneer Business Consultants
9042 Garfield Ave., Ste. 211
Huntington Beach, CA 92646
Ph: (714)964-7600
Fax: (714)962-6585
Contact: Ron von Freyman, President
Scope: Offers general management consulting specializing in business acquisitions, tax and business planning, cash flow analyses, business valuations and business sales and expert witness court testimony regarding business sales, valuations and accounting. **Founded:** 1980.

45885 ■ PYA GatesMoore
33424 Peachtree Rd. NE, Monarch Twr., Ste. 700
Atlanta, GA 30326
Ph: (404)266-9876
Fax: (404)266-2669
Co. E-mail: info@pyagatesmoore.com
URL: http://www.pyagatesmoore.com
Contact: Ed Pershing, President
E-mail: epershing@pyapc.com
Scope: Firm provides management consulting and accounting services to medical practices, hospital owned practices, staff model managed care organizations, IPAs, MSOs, PO, and PHOs. Services include comprehensive operational assessments, managed

care negotiations, practice start-ups and expansion, development of MSOs, strategic planning, mergers, cost accounting analysis, practice valuations, income division plans, medical record documentation and coding reviews, expert witness testimony, patient satisfaction surveys and corporate compliance planning. **Founded:** 1982. **Publications:** "Practicing Medicine in the 21st Century"; "Physicians, Dentists and Veterinarians"; "Insurance Portability and Accountability Act Privacy Manual"; "How To Guide for your Medical Practice and Health Insurance Portability and Accountability Act Security Manual"; "A How To Guide for your Medical Practice"; "Cost Analysis Made Simple: A Step by Step Guide to Using Cost Accounting to Ensure Practice Profitability"; "Cost Cutting Strategies for Medical Practices"; "Cost Cutting Strategies for Medical Practices"; "Getting the Jump on Year-End Tax Planning"; "New 401(k) Safe Harbor Option: Increased Opportunities for the Physician and Practice"; "Not All Tax News is Bad News"; "Shareholder Agreements: Identifying and Addressing Five Risk Areas"; "Surprise - Your Practice has a Deferred Income Tax Liability". **Seminars:** Documenting and Billing High Risk Codes, 2010; Current Challenges in Ob/Gyn Recruiting, 2010; Planning for Physician Wind-down & Retirement, 2010; HITECH "How To" - Opportunities & Risks, 2010; Pediatric Coding and Audits; Recruiting and Retaining Physicians; How to Prepare for the Recovery Audit Contractors - RAC, 2010; Meaningful Use Rule, 2010; The Revenue Stream in Practice, Apr, 2008; Improving Efficiencies in a Small Family Medicine Practice, Oct, 2007; Using Compensation Models to Improve Performance, Sep, 2007; The Financial Side of Personnel Management, Sep, 2007; Pay for Performance-Is it Really Contracting for Quality?, New York State Ophthalmological Society, Sep, 2007; Beyond the Class Action Settlement Payments- Looking Prospectively at Managed Care Companies Behavior, New York State Ophthalmological Society, Sep, 2007; Protecting your clients from Embezzlement, Jun, 2007; What P4P Means to Your Medical Practice, May, 2007; Finance for the Practicing Physician, May, 2007; Trashing, Dipping and Ghosts in Medical Practices: Protecting your clients from Embezzlement, Apr, 2006.

45886 ■ Quality Specialists (QS)
13422 215th Ave. E
Sumner, WA 98390
Ph: (253)230-2886
Fax: (253)862-4937
Co. E-mail: inquiries@qualityspecialists.com
URL: http://www.qualityspecialists.com
Contact: JoAda Wickern, Vice President
E-mail: jwickern@qualityspecialists.com
Scope: Offers services in quality control, audit configuration control and organizational culture change. **Publications:** "Audit Pigs"; "A Little Horse with Words"; "Don't Stiff Your Customers for a Measly $11"; "Grim Buck Tales"; "Health Care Reform"; "It's All How You Look At Things"; "Write to Express - Not Impress".

45887 ■ Research Applications Inc. (RAI)
414 Hungerford Dr., Ste. 220
Rockville, MD 20850-4125
Ph: (301)251-6717
Free: 888-311-6221
Fax: (301)251-6719
Contact: David H. Friedman, President
E-mail: dfriedman@resapplinc.com
Scope: A consulting firm provides specialized design, evaluation, testing and analytic services in the fields of social, computer and mathematical sciences. It brings to its customers a senior staff with strong theoretical and scientific backgrounds in areas of expertise, coupled with extensive practical knowledge and experience in contract research. The firm focuses on providing a group of interrelated services which include human resources support and improvement, computer programming support, direct mail services and MOBIS. **Founded:** 1975. **Seminars:** Gender Awareness in the Workplace; Humor in the Workplace; Understanding and Using Assessments (Validity/Reliability); Diversity in the Workplace; Structured Interviews; Leadership; Leadership and Humor.

45888 ■ Rose & Crangle Ltd.

117 N 4th St.
Lincoln, KS 67455
Ph: (785)524-5050
Fax: (785)524-3130
Co. E-mail: rcltd@nckcn.com
URL: http://www.roseandcrangle.com
Contact: Robert D. Crangle, President
E-mail: rcltd@nckcn.com
Scope: Provider of evaluation, planning and policy analyzes for universities, associations, foundations, governmental agencies and private companies engaged in scientific, technological or educational activities. Special expertise in the development of new institutions. Special skills in providing planning and related group facilitation workshops. **Founded:** 1984. **Publications:** "Preface to Bulgarian Integration Into Europe and NATO: Issues of Science Policy And research Evaluation Practice," Ios Press, 2006; "Allocating Limited National Resources for Fundamental Research," 2005.

45889 ■ Rothschild Strategies Unlimited L.L.C.

19 Thistle Rd.
Norwalk, CT 06851-1909
Ph: (203)847-5638
Fax: (203)847-1426
URL: http://www.strategyleader.com
Contact: Stephen M. Rothschild, Managing Director
Scope: Consults with senior management and business level strategy teams to develop overall strategic direction, set priorities and creates sustainable competitive advantages and differentiators. Enables organizations to enhance their own strategic thinking and leadership skills so that they can continue to develop and implement profitable growth strategies. **Founded:** 1983. **Publications:** "Putting It All Together-a guide to strategic thinking"; "Competitive Advantage"; "Ristaker, Caretaker, Surgeon & Undertaker four faces of strategic leadership"; "The Secret to GE's Success"; "Having the Right Strategic Leader and Team".

45890 ■ Sandler & Travis Trade Advisory Services Inc. (STTAS) [STTAS]

1000 NW 57th Ct., Ste. 600
Miami, FL 33126
Ph: (305)267-9200
Fax: (305)267-5155
Co. E-mail: messages@strtrade.com
URL: http://www.strtrade.com
Contact: Alfred J. D'Amico, Chief Operating Officer
E-mail: adamico@strtrade.com
Scope: An international trade and customs law firm concentrating in assisting clients with the movement of goods, personnel, and ideas across international borders. Customs and international trade consulting services include global customs modernization and compliance, customs department outsourcing and managed trade services, border security programs, tariff classification project management, valuation of merchandise, preference program project management, U.S. and Canadian customs compliance, duty drawback project management, temporary importation project management, and corporate responsibility in international sourcing. **Special Services:** STTAS™.

45891 ■ David G. Schantz

29 Wood Run Cir.
Rochester, NY 14612-2271
Ph: (716)723-8724
Fax: (716)723-8724
Co. E-mail: daveschantz@yahoo.com
URL: http://www.daveschantz.freeservers.com
Contact: David G. Schantz, Manager
Scope: Provider of industrial engineering services for photofinishing labs, including amateur-wholesale, professional, commercial, school and package. **Founded:** 1992.

45892 ■ Schneider Consulting Group Inc.

2801 E 4th Ave.
Denver, CO 80206
Ph: (303)320-4413
Fax: (303)320-5795
Co. E-mail: info@schneiderconsultinggroup.com
URL: http://www.consultscg.com
Contact: Kim Schneider Malek, Founder
Scope: Assists family-owned and privately-held business transition to the next generation and/or to a more professionally managed company, turn around consulting for small and medium size companies. **Founded:** 1987. **Seminars:** Family Business Council; Impact of the Energy Renaissance.

45893 ■ Shealy & Associates

1100 Baker Lake Rd.
Guthrie, OK 73044-8977
Ph: (405)282-5578
Contact: Lon S. Shealy, Vice President
Scope: A network of consultants whose mission is to assist small-to-mid size organizations implement successful strategic management practices. Primarily engaged in the delivery of facilitating services to implement strategic renewal and planning. **Founded:** 1993. **Publications:** "Destiny by Design"; "Metal Building Review," Industry Week; "Nation's Business and Building Systems". **Seminars:** Becoming a Leader.

45894 ■ Sklar and Associates Inc.

242 Laurel Bay Dr.
Murrells Inlet, SC 29576
Ph: (843)798-0412
Fax: (843)651-3090
Co. E-mail: sklarincdc@aol.com
URL: http://www.sklarinc.com
Contact: Tim Sklar, President
Scope: Provider of consulting services for business acquisitions, business development and project finance. Provides audit oversight services to listed corporations on Sarbanes-Oxley compliance. Services include: Due diligence analyses and corporate governance. Industries served: transportation sectors, energy sector and commercial real estate industries. **Seminars:** Financial Analysis in MBA; Emerging Company Finance; Due Diligence in Business Acquisition; Business Valuation.

45895 ■ Smart Ways to Work

1441 Franklin St., Ste. 301
Oakland, CA 94612-3219
Ph: (510)763-8482
Free: 800-599-8463
Fax: (510)763-0790
Co. E-mail: odette@smartwaystowork.com
URL: http://www.smartwaystowork.com
Contact: Odette Pollar, Owner
E-mail: odette@smartwaystowork.com
Scope: A management consulting firm specializing in the training of supervisors, managers and professional staff in the area of time management, problem solving, decision making and strategic planning. Assists businesses and corporations in developing and implementing programs for increased productivity, greater profit and improved employee morale. Serves private industries as well as government agencies. **Founded:** 1979. **Publications:** "Surviving Information Overload driving Information Overload: How to Find, Filter, and Focus on What's Important," Crisp Publications, Sep, 2003; "Take Back Your Life: Smart Ways to Simplify Daily Living," Conari Press, Apr, 1999; "365 Ways to Simplify Your Work Life," Kaplan Business, Aug, 1996; "Dynamics of Diversity: Strategic Programs for Your Organization," Crisp Publications, 1994; "Organizing Your Workspace: A Guide to Personal Productivity," Crisp Publications, May, 1992. **Seminars:** Managing Multiple Demands: Surviving Ground Zero; Defending Your Life: Balancing Work And Home; Desktop Sprawl: Conquer Your Paper Pile-Up; Getting It All Done: Breaking The Time Bind; To Give or Not To Give: The Delegation Dilemma; Information Happens: Don't Let It Happen On You; Take The Terror Out Of Talk: Secrets To Successful Speaking; To Give or Not To Give: The Delegation Dilemma; Managing Meetings.

45896 ■ Stalley Associates Inc. [Rodney E. Stalley & Associates Inc.]

10635 James Cir.
Minneapolis, MN 55431-4157
Ph: (952)888-0617
Contact: Rodney E. Stalley, President
E-mail: rstalley@stalley.com
Scope: Advises management of companies in the areas of finance, administrative and general management, corporate objectives, policies and procedures, and management and organization audits. Firm has developed a particular expertise in advising management of young and growing companies. Advises in strategic planning, capital planning and financing strategies, securing private and public investment capital, establishing strategic alliances, management and staff organizational restructuring, working with board of directors, shareholders and serving as chief financial officer and chief operations officer on a contract basis. **Founded:** 1978. **Publications:** "Knowledge: The Key to Business Success"; "The Board of Directors: A Ceo's Source for Advice, Insight and Support"; "Controlling the Audit Expense".

45897 ■ Stillman H. Publishers Inc.

21405 Woodchuck Ln.
Boca Raton, FL 33428
Ph: (561)482-6343
Contact: Herbert Stillman, President
Scope: Offers consulting services in the following areas: management, start ups, profit maximization, world wide negotiating, interim management, corporate debt resolution.

45898 ■ Straightline Services Inc.

11 Centre St., Ste. 10
Salem, CT 06420-3845
Ph: (860)889-7929
Fax: (860)885-1894
Contact: Wayne J. S. France, President
Scope: Design and implementation of organizational infrastructure, business plans and troubleshooting. Emphasizes on operations with a central and field or satellite offices. Industries served: Construction, resorts, Indian tribes, academies, small-medium sized business, mostly privately held. **Founded:** 1994.

45899 ■ Tamayo Consulting Inc.

169 Saxony Rd., Ste. 112
Encinitas, CA 92024-6779
Ph: (760)479-1352
Fax: (760)479-1465
Co. E-mail: info@tamayoconsulting.com
URL: http://www.tamayoconsulting.com
Contact: Jennifer Dreyer, President
E-mail: jdreyer@earthlink.net
Scope: It Provides training and consulting services. And also it specializes in leadership and team development. Industries served: private, non-profit, government, educational. **Founded:** 1986. **Seminars:** Presentation AdvantEdge Program; Lead point Development Program; Supervisor Development Programs.Identify Presentation Objectives; Implement 360-degree presentation assessment; conduct baseline-coaching session; Develop coaching plan; Staying connected.

45900 ■ The TEAM FOCUS Group

46 Pineridge Cres.
Saint Albert, AB, Canada T8N 4P4
Ph: (780)460-1625
Fax: (780)460-2003
Co. E-mail: mphillips@teamfocus.org
URL: http://www.teamfocus.org
Contact: Scot McClintock, Director
E-mail: smcclintock@teamfocus.org
Scope: An international consultancy group, specializing in the field of value and risk management, including project management, partnering and team alignment. Services include business program refocusing, strategy formulation, program planning, project definition, decision analysis, risk management and team building. **Publications:** "VE Using Project Performance Criteria & Measures". **Seminars:** Sharpening The Performance Edge: Project Delivery Enhancement Through Value Assurance, Nov, 2003; Results Oriented Performance Using The Project Performance Enhancement Approach, Jun, 2002; Value Is In The Eye Of The Beholder, Part 1: A Framework For Smart Project Development And Service Enhancement, May, 2002; Accredited SAVE International Module I Basic Training Seminars; Team Building and Partnering training; Advanced Project

Management training; Accredited SAVE International Module I Basic Training Seminars; Value Management Training Workshop; Risk Management Training Workshop.

45901 ■ Trendzitions Inc.
25691 Atlantic Ocean, Ste. B13
Lake Forest, CA 92630-8842
Ph: (949)727-9100
Free: 800-266-2767
Fax: (949)727-3444
Co. E-mail: ctooker@trendzitions.com
URL: http://www.trendzitions.com
Contact: Christian Tooker, President
E-mail: ctooker@trendzitions.com
Scope: Provider of services in the areas of communications consulting, project management, construction management, and furniture procurement. Offers information on spatial uses, building codes, ADA compliance and city ordinances. Also offers budget projections. **Founded:** 1986.

45902 ■ Turnaround Inc.
3415 A St. NW
Gig Harbor, WA 98335
Ph: (253)857-6730
Fax: (253)857-6344
Co. E-mail: info@turnround-inc.com
URL: http://www.turnaround-inc.com
Contact: Miles Stover, President
E-mail: mstover@turnaround-inc.com
Scope: Provider of interim executive management assistance and management advisory to small, medium and family-owned businesses that are not meeting their goals. Services include acting as an interim executive or on-site manager. Extensive practices in arena of bankruptcy management. **Founded:** 1997. **Publications:** "How to Identify Problem and Promising Management"; "How to Tell if Your Company is a Bankruptcy Candidate"; "Signs that Your Company is in Trouble"; "The Turnaround Specialist: How to File a Petition Under 11 USC 11". **Seminars:** Competitive Intelligence Gathering.

45903 ■ TWD & Associates [Thomas W. Dooley & Associates]
431 S Patton Ave.
Arlington Heights, IL 60005-2253
Ph: (847)398-6410
Fax: (847)255-5095
Contact: Larry Besterman, President
E-mail: twhdoo@yahoo.com
Scope: Consulting specialists in small business management particularly in the areas of personnel, training, marketing, franchising, sales, time management, budgeting, raising capital and long-range planning. **Founded:** 1976. **Seminars:** Alternative Methods of Financing for Franchising; Effectiveness of Organizational Development Training Programs for Hourly-Hire Workers in Manufacturing Plants. **Special Services:** ABR®.

45904 ■ Tweed-Weber Inc. (TWI)
117 N 5th St.
Reading, PA 19601
Ph: (610)376-6615
Free: 800-999-6615
Fax: (610)376-9161
Co. E-mail: mail@tweedweber.com
URL: http://www.tweedweber.com
Contact: Alfred J. Weber, President
E-mail: alweber@tweedweber.com
Scope: A consulting firm specializing in customized market research and strategic planning. Expertise in strategic planning research and conducts customer satisfaction surveys; employee satisfaction surveys; market assessment customer satisfaction surveys. **Founded:** 1979.

45905 ■ ValueNomics Value Specialists
50 W San Fernando St., Ste. 600
San Jose, CA 95113
Fax: (408)200-6401
Co. E-mail: info@amllp.com
Contact: Gary E. Jones, Chief Executive Officer
Scope: Consulting is offered in the areas of financial management, process re-engineering, growth business services; governance, risk/compliance, SOX readiness and compliance, SAS 70, enterprise risk management, system security, operational and internal audit; business advisory services; valuation services; CORE assessment; contract assurance; transaction advisory services, IT solutions and litigation support services. **Founded:** 1993. **Publications:** "Dueling Appraisers: How Differences in Input and Assumptions May Control the Value," Apr, 2005; "The Business of Business Valuation and the CPA as an expert witness"; "The Business of Business Valuation," McGraw-Hill Professional Publishers Inc.

45906 ■ VenturEdge Corp.
4711 Yonge St., Ste. 1105
Toronto, ON, Canada M2N 6K8
Ph: (416)224-2000
Fax: (416)224-2376
Contact: Mark Klingbaum, Manager
E-mail: klingbaum@venturedge.com
Scope: Provides services including strategy formulation; business planning; financial management; business coaching; performance improvement; information management; merger, acquisitions and divestitures; family succession planning; competitive intelligence. **Founded:** 1972. **Publications:** "Reputation," Harvard Business School Press, 1996; "Competing for the Future," Harvard Business School Press, 1994; "The Fifth Discipline," 1990.

45907 ■ Verbit & Co.
19 Bala Ave.
Bala Cynwyd, PA 19004-3202
Ph: (610)668-9840
Co. E-mail: verbitcompany@earthlink.net
Contact: Alan C. Verbit, President
Scope: Management consulting firm to assist executives and managers fulfill their mission and to assure that adequate planning of day-to-day operations occurs; that controls sufficient to safeguard valuable resources; and that results of decisions reviewed in sufficient time to effect continuing action. Financial planning and control-to develop accounting, budgeting, forecasting and other information systems for the management of resources and evaluation of strategies. Services also include: Evaluation of desk-top computer systems for small firms; CAD/CAM implementation plan and orderly introduction of CAD/CAM. Industries served: manufacturing, distribution, metals casting, equipment and components, professional services, health care, retail, nonprofit and government. **Founded:** 1981. **Seminars:** Integrating Manufacturing Management Systems with Business Systems; Negotiating Information Systems Agreements with Suppliers.

45908 ■ Via Nova Consulting
1228 Winburn Dr.
Atlanta, GA 30344
Ph: (404)761-7484
Scope: Consulting services in the areas of strategic planning; privatization; executive searches; market research; customer service audits; new product development; competitive intelligence; and Total Quality Management (TQM). **Founded:** 1994.

45909 ■ VIE Partners Inc. (VIE)
1973 Rte. 34, Ste. E-11
Wall, NJ 07719
Ph: (732)988-1066
Free: 888-484-3332
Fax: (732)988-4989
Co. E-mail: info@viepartners.com
URL: http://www.viepartners.com
Contact: Lisa T. Miller, President
E-mail: lmiller@viepartners.com
Scope: Expense management solutions firm specializing in expense analysis and review, procurement strategies, revenue improvement techniques, and cost reduction strategies.

45910 ■ Vision Management
149 Meadows Rd.
Lafayette, NJ 07848-3120
Ph: (973)702-1116
Fax: (973)702-8311
Contact: Norman L. Naidish, President
Scope: Firm specializes in profit enhancement; strategic planning; business process reengineering; industrial engineering; facilities planning; team building; inventory management; and total quality management (TQM). **Founded:** 1984. **Publications:** "To increase profits, improve quality," Manufacturing Engineering, May, 2000.

45911 ■ Weich & Bilotti Inc.
600 Worcester Rd., 4th Fl.
Framingham, MA 01702
Ph: (508)663-1600
Fax: (508)663-1682
Co. E-mail: info@weich-bilotti.com
Contact: Mervyn D. Weich, Director
E-mail: mweich@weich-bilotti.com
Scope: Specializes in business plans, venture capital, computer information systems, turnaround/interim management, retail consulting, start-up process, college recruiting and IS and IT personnel. **Founded:** 1995.

45912 ■ Western Business Services Ltd. (WBS)
1269 Lindsay St.
Regina, SK, Canada S4N 3B4
Ph: (306)522-1493
Fax: (306)522-9076
Co. E-mail: wbs@accesscomm.ca
URL: http://www.wbsc.ca
Contact: O'Neil Zuck, President
Scope: Provides advice and assistance to organizations on administrative management issues, such as financial planning and budgeting; equity and asset management; records management; office planning; strategic and organizational planning; site selection; new business start-up; and business process improvement. **Founded:** 1992.

45913 ■ Westlife Consultants & Counsellors
95 October Ln.
Aurora, ON, Canada L4G 7A1
Ph: (905)867-0686
Fax: (416)799-5242
Co. E-mail: westlifeconsultant@hotmail.com
URL: http://www.westlifeconsultants.com
Contact: Dr. Syed N. Hussain, President
E-mail: westlifeconsultant@hotmail.com
Scope: Provider of entrepreneurs and businesses with a highly commercial and global perspectives on the international business development ideas under consideration. **Founded:** 1990. **Publications:** "Innovative Management"; "Team Building and Leadership"; "Financial Planning"; "Estate Planning"; "Risk Management"; "Export/Import Trade Finance Mechanics"; "Marketing and Sales Management"; "What Your Banker Needs to Know"; "Building A Successful Financial Plan".

45914 ■ What Makes You Smile
3552 Vancouver Ave.
San Diego, CA 92104-3822
Ph: (619)665-1432
Free: 888-787-0419
Co. E-mail: ginalinn.espinoza@gmail.com
URL: http://www.doctoralove.com
Contact: Gina Linn Espinoza-Price, President
E-mail: gina@whatmakesyousmile.com
Scope: Personal success coaching and life skill training. One on one, group seminars, critical thinking with executives, CEO's and business owners. **Founded:** 1997. **Seminars:** What Makes You Smile?; Smile Files, Have you left your distinctive mark on the world today?; Brainstorms For Sale, Is the Customer Always Right?; Make the best of your given talent; A smile is a lifetime of balance.

45915 ■ Wheeler and Young Inc.
33 Peter St.
Markham, ON, Canada L3P 2A5
Ph: (905)471-5709
Fax: (905)471-9989
Co. E-mail: wheeler@ericwheeler.ca
URL: http://www.ericwheeler.ca
Contact: Eric S. Wheeler, Managing Partner
E-mail: ewheeler@yorku.ca
Scope: Provider of consulting services to high-tech companies on the implementation of software development processes; quality management systems (including ISO 9000 compliance) and business management systems. Offers business management and knowledge-management services to organizations. Industries served: Knowledge-based industries,

including software and hardware development, medical and legal professionals, information service providers. **Founded:** 1994.

45916 ■ Donald C. Wright CPA
3906 Lawndale Ln. N
Plymouth, MN 55446-2940
Ph: (763)478-6999
Co. E-mail: donaldwright@compuserve.com
URL: http://www.donaldwrightcpa.com
Contact: Donald C. Wright, President
E-mail: donaldwright@compuserve.com
Scope: Offers accounting, tax and small business consulting services. Services include cash flow and budgeting analysis; financial forecast and projections; financial statements; reviews and compilations; tax planning, tax preparation; IRS and state/local representation; international taxation; estate, gift and trust tax return preparation; benefit plan services; business succession planning; estate planning; financial planning; management advisory services, pension and profit sharing plans, retirement planning, expert witness services and employee benefits plans. Serves individuals, corporations, partnerships and non-profit organizations. **Founded:** 1968. **Seminars:** Qualified pension plans and employee welfare benefit plans.

45917 ■ Bruce D. Wyman Co.
6147 Poburn Landing Ct.
Burke, VA 22015-2535
Ph: (703)503-9753
Fax: (703)503-2091
Co. E-mail: bdwyman@bdwyman.com
URL: http://www.bdwyman.com
Contact: Bruce D. Wyman, President
E-mail: bdwyman@bdwyman.com
Scope: Provider of strategic business planning services to aid small and micro for-profit and nonprofit businesses and associations in identifying and handling challenges and opportunities in an environment of incomplete information. Services include business environmental scanning; mission, goal, and strategy identification and development; and development of integrated implementation plans to convert intentions into actions. Provide training in quality management tools, processes, and applications, as well as ASQ certification examination preparation. Industries served: All industries, with special emphasis on smaller firms and associations including micro businesses. **Founded:** 1988. **Publications:** "A New Acquisition Reform Culture for the Air Force," Program Manager, Feb, 1999. **Seminars:** The Best of Both Worlds: Combining Equity 3 and Integer Programming to Allocate Resources, Oct, 2004; Implementing Massive Change: Coordination, Communication, and Campaign Management, May, 2000; Strategic Business Planning for Small and Micro Businesses and Associations; quality management and processes consulting and training (CQMgr. and CQIA).

FRANCHISES AND BUSINESS OPPORTUNITIES

45918 ■ LMI Canada Inc.
205 Matheson Blvd. E, Unit 15
Mississauga, ON, Canada L4Z 3E3
Ph: (905)890-0504
Free: 877-857-4083
Co. E-mail: info@lmicanada.ca
URL: http://www.lmicanada.ca
Contact: Frank Kreze, President
Description: The franchise is a well-known personal, organizational and management development company, which enhances performance, productivity and profitability of their companies. **No. of Franchise Units:** 10. **No. of Company-Owned Units:** 1. **Founded:** 1980. **Franchised:** 1998. **Franchise Fee:** $38,000. **Training:** Initial and ongoing support provided.

COMPUTERIZED DATABASES

45919 ■ *Leadership and Management in Engineering*
Architectural Engineering Institute of ASCE
1801 Alexander Bell Dr.
Reston, VA 20191-4400

Free: 800-548-2723
Co. E-mail: aei@asce.org
URL: http://www.asce.org/aei
Contact: Mark McAfee, President
Availability: Online: Architectural Engineering Institute of ASCE. **Type:** Full-text.

45920 ■ *Stern's Management Review*
Stern & Associates
11260 Overland Ave., Ste. 16A
Culver City, CA 90230
Ph: (310)838-0551
Free: 800-773-0029
Fax: (310)838-2344
Co. E-mail: info@hrconsultant.com
URL: http://www.hrconsultant.com
Contact: Yvette Borcia, Partner
E-mail: borcia@hrconsultant.com
Availability: Online: Stern & Associates. **Type:** Full-text.

LIBRARIES

45921 ■ Boston University - Frederick S. Pardee Management Library
595 Commonwealth Ave.
Boston, MA 02215
Ph: (617)353-4301
Fax: (617)353-4307
Co. E-mail: ajac@bu.edu
URL: http://www.bu.edu/library/management
Contact: Arlyne A. Jackson, Director, Library Services
Scope: Management and management-related fields, healthcare management, public management, non-profit management. **Services:** Library open to the public. **Founded:** 1997. **Holdings:** over 25,000 e-subscriptions (journals and databases); 91,541 volumes; 333,500 microforms. **Subscriptions:** 2357 journals and other serials.

45922 ■ Business Development Bank of Canada Research & Information Centre
5 Place Ville Marie, Ste. 300
Montreal, QC, Canada H3B 5E7
Free: 877-232-2269
Fax: (877)329-9232
URL: http://www.bdc.ca
Scope: Small business; management; Canadian business and industry; banking and finance; development banking. **Services:** Interlibrary loan; library not open to the public. **Founded:** 1977. **Holdings:** 5000 books. **Subscriptions:** 100 journals and other serials; 7 newspapers.

45923 ■ Canada School of Public Service Library
Asticou Ctre.
241 de la Cite-des-Jeunes Blvd., Rm. 1359
Gatineau, QC, Canada K1N 6Z2
Ph: (819)934-7702
Free: 866-703-9598
Fax: (819)953-1702
Co. E-mail: publications@csps-efpc.gc.ca
URL: http://www.csps-efpc.gc.ca/index-eng.asp
Contact: Darlene Nadeau, Director, Information Services
Scope: Management, government, public administration, coaching, leadership, diversity, language, training. **Services:** Interlibrary loan; copying; library open to public. **Founded:** 1990. **Holdings:** 10,000 books; 450 videos. **Subscriptions:** 65 serials.

45924 ■ Carnegie Library of Pittsburgh - Downtown & Business
612 Smithfield St.
Pittsburgh, PA 15222-2506
Ph: (412)281-7141
Fax: (412)471-1724
Co. E-mail: downtown@carnegielibrary.org
URL: http://www.carnegielibrary.org/locations/downtown
Contact: Karen Rossi, Department Head
Scope: Investments, small business, entrepreneurship, management, marketing, insurance, advertising, personal finance, accounting, real estate, job and career, International business. **Services:** Library

open to the public. **Founded:** 1924. **Holdings:** 13,000 business volumes; VF materials; microfilm; looseleaf services; AV materials.

45925 ■ Chicago Public Library Central Library - Business/Science/Technology Division
Harold Washington Library Center, 4th Fl.
400 S State St.
Chicago, IL 60605
Ph: (312)747-4300
URL: http://www.chipublib.org/resources/science-technology
Contact: Linda Johnson Rice, President
Scope: Small business, marketing, technology, corporate reports, investments, management, personnel, patents, physical and biological sciences, medicine, health, computer science, careers, environmental information, gardening, cookbooks. **Services:** Interlibrary loan; copying; division open to the public. **Founded:** 1977. **Holdings:** 415,000 books; 52,100 bound periodical volumes; 33,000 reels of microfilm; Securities and Exchange Commission (SEC) reports; federal specifications and standards; American National Standards Institute standards; corporate annual reports. **Subscriptions:** 4,000 journals and other serials; 8 newspapers.

45926 ■ Comenius University - Faculty of Management Library
Odbojarov 10
820 05 Bratislava, Slovakia
Ph: 421 2 50117526
Co. E-mail: sd@fm.uniba.sk
URL: http://www.fm.uniba.sk
Contact: Zuzana Horackova, Librarian
Scope: Management. **Services:** Library open to the public. **Subscriptions:** 350 11,000 books; 350 periodic titles on the periodical ondisc; 5000 periodical titles on the pro quest direct database.

45927 ■ Lappeenranta University of Technology Library [Lappeenrannan teknillinen yliopisto]
Skinnarilankatu 34
FIN-53850 Lappeenranta, Finland
Ph: 358 5 294462111
Fax: 358 5 4117201
Co. E-mail: kirjasto@lut.fi
URL: http://www.lut.fi/web/en/library
Contact: Ulla Ohvo, Director, Library Services
Scope: Engineering, economics, management. **Founded:** 1969. **Holdings:** Books; journals. **Publications:** *WILMA*.

45928 ■ Michigan Financial Independence Agency - Office of Training and Staff Development - Resource Library
Grand Tower, Ste. 301
235 S. Grand Ave.
Lansing, MI 48909
Ph: (517)335-4698
Fax: (517)241-7041
Contact: Ron Walters
Scope: Management, supervision, self-development. **Services:** Library open to governmental units, private children's agencies and private contractors. **Founded:** 1985. **Holdings:** 350 videotapes; 150 audiocassettes; 100 book summaries.

45929 ■ Nichols College - Conant Library
124 Center Rd.
Dudley, MA 01571-6310
Ph: (508)213-2333
Free: 800-470-3379
Co. E-mail: jim.douglas@nichols.edu
URL: http://www.nichols.edu/academics/academics/Library
Contact: Jim Douglas, Director, Library Services
Scope: Management, advertising, finance and accounting, small business, marketing, taxation, economics, International trade, humanities. **Services:** Interlibrary loan; copying; information service to groups; document delivery; library open to Dudley and Webster residents. **Founded:** 1962. **Holdings:** 48,000 volumes; 1677 audio/visual titles; 3804 reels of microfilm. **Subscriptions:** 278 journals and electronic subscriptions.

45930 ■ Ontario Ministry of Economic Development and Trade - InfoSource
900 Bay St.
Hearst Block, 8th Fl.
Toronto, ON, Canada M7A 2E1
Ph: (416)325-6666
Fax: (416)325-6688
Co. E-mail: info@edt.gov.on.ca
Scope: Trade, industry, small business, management, company information, economic development. **Services:** Copying; scanning. **Founded:** 1994. **Holdings:** 200 books; microfiche; 20 CD-ROMs.

45931 ■ Southeastern University Library
501 I St., SW
Washington, DC 20024
Ph: (202)478-8225
Fax: (202)488-8093
Co. E-mail: library@seu.edu
Scope: Science, technology, humanities, health, social sciences. **Services:** Interlibrary loan; library open to the public. **Founded:** 1879. **Holdings:** 50,000 books.

45932 ■ Strategic Decisions Group Information Center
745 Emerson St.
Palo Alto, CA 94301
Ph: (650)475-4400
Fax: (650)475-4401
URL: http://www.sdg.com
Contact: Carl Spetzler, Chief Executive Officer
Scope: Business, management. **Services:** Interlibrary loan; copying; SDI; library open to the public at librarian's discretion. **Founded:** 1986. **Holdings:** 700 books. **Subscriptions:** 120 journals and other serials; 5 newspapers.

45933 ■ Touro College - Lander College for Men Library
75-31 150th St.
Kew Gardens Hills, NY 11367
Ph: (718)820-4894
Fax: (718)495-3824
URL: http://www.tourolib.org/about/libraries/kew-gardens-hills
Contact: Joan Wagner, Librarian
E-mail: joan.wagner2@touro.edu
Scope: Biology; business; computer science; management information science; political science; psychology; social sciences Judaica. **Services:** Interlibrary loan; copying; library open to college staff and students. **Holdings:** Books; diskettes; audio and video tapes; CD-ROMs; DVDs; microfiche.

45934 ■ University of Gloucestershire - Learning and Information Services - Park Learning Centre
The Park
Cheltenham GL50 2RH, United Kingdom
Ph: 44 1242 714555
Co. E-mail: nquinton@glos.ac.uk
URL: http://insight.glos.ac.uk/departments/lis/lc/Pages/pklc.aspx
Contact: Neil Quinton, Assistant Manager
Scope: Business and management, computing, hospitality and tourism management, languages, information technology law, leisure, multimedia. **Holdings:** Books; journals.

45935 ■ University of Massachusetts at Lowell - Lydon Library
North Campus
84 University Ave.
Lowell, MA 01854
Ph: (978)934-3205
Co. E-mail: margaret_manion@uml.edu
URL: http://libweb.uml.edu/Lydon.html
Contact: Margaret Manion, Librarian, Reference
Scope: Business, management, engineering, science. **Holdings:** Figures not available.

45936 ■ University of Southern Maine - Lewiston-Auburn College Library
51 Westminster St.
Lewiston, ME 04240

Ph: (207)753-6546
Co. E-mail: evelyng@usm.maine.edu
URL: http://library.usm.maine.edu/about/lac/index.php
Contact: Maureen Perry, Librarian, Reference
Scope: Social and behavioral studies, leadership, management, organizational studies, occupational therapy, nursing. **Services:** Interlibrary loan; library open to the public. **Holdings:** 16,000 volumes; 450 videocassettes. **Subscriptions:** 200 journals and other serials.

45937 ■ US West Communications - Learning Systems/Employee Development Library
2626 W. Evans Ave.
Denver, CO 80219-5506
Ph: (303)763-1252
Fax: (303)985-6496
Contact: Gaylene Pepion, Librarian
Scope: Communications, management, economics, adult education, pluralism, computer technology. **Founded:** 1976. **Holdings:** 3000 books; Bell Company Practices; Bell technical journals. **Subscriptions:** 40 journals and other serials.

45938 ■ Woodbury University Library
7500 Glenoaks Blvd.
Burbank, CA 91504-1052
Ph: (818)252-5201
Fax: (818)767-4534
Co. E-mail: jennifer.rosenfeld@woodbury.edu
URL: http://library.woodbury.edu
Contact: Nedra Peterson, Director
Scope: Business and management, International business, art, architecture, interior design, fashion marketing and design, psychology, animation. **Services:** Interlibrary loan; copying; Library open to the public for reference use only. **Founded:** 1884. **Holdings:** 65,000 books; 3070 bound periodical volumes; 17,401 slides; 2000 DVD/VHS. **Subscriptions:** 300 journals and other serials; 5 newspapers.

RESEARCH CENTERS

45939 ■ Bradley University - Center for Executive and Professional Development (CEPD)
Foster College of Business
1501 W Bradley Ave.
Peoria, IL 61625
Ph: (309)677-2253
Fax: (309)677-3374
Co. E-mail: aliberty@bradley.edu
URL: http://www.bradley.edu/fcba/community/cepd/index.shtml
Contact: Angie Liberty, Executive Director
Scope: Develops executive and management programs for business needs. **Founded:** 1991. **Educational Activities:** CEPD Customized workshops, to meet specific needs of businesses; CEPD Public seminars, on current business topics.

45940 ■ The Conference Board (TCB)
845 3rd Ave.
New York, NY 10022-6601
Ph: (212)759-0900
Fax: (212)980-7014
Co. E-mail: membership@conferenceboard.org
URL: http://www.conference-board.org
Contact: Dr. Josef Ackermann, Vice Chairman of the Board
Description: Corporations, government agencies, libraries, colleges, and universities. Fact-finding institution that conducts research and publishes studies on business economics and management experience. Holds more than 100 conferences, council meetings, and seminars per year in the U.S., Asia, and Europe where members exchange ideas and keep abreast of business trends and developments. Makes research available to secondary schools, colleges, and universities at minimum cost. Disseminates research data to the public. **Scope:** Business management practices worldwide, especially economic, and demographic in nature. Specific concerns include: corporate citizenship, including corporate contributions, diversity, environmental policy and issues, and government relations; corporate governance, including boards of directors, role of chief

executives, relations with institutional investors, and shareholder input and influence; economics, including economic and financial forecasts, consumer confidence, leading economic indicators, North American outlook and trends, and global economic environment; human resources and organizational effectiveness, including organization structure and design, compensation and benefits, training and development, and communications; and performance excellence. **Founded:** 1916. **Subscriptions:** 6000 books periodicals. **Publications:** *StraightTalk* (10/year); *The Corporate Contributions Plan: From Strategy to Budget*; *Top Executive Compensation* (Annual); *HR Executive Review* (Quarterly); *Conference Board Briefing Charts* (Quarterly); *Multinational Register & Global Business Briefing*; *The Conference Board Review* (Quarterly); *Consumer Confidence Survey, The Conference Board* (Monthly); *International Economic Scoreboard*; *Across the Board*; *Business cycle indicators* (Monthly); *Consumer Confidence Survey* (Monthly); *E-mail Express* (Monthly); *Executive Action Series*; *The Conference Board, Inc. Research reports*. **Educational Activities:** TCB The Conference Board, Inc. Conferences; TCB Forums and seminars on selected topics of business, professional, and academic interest.

45941 ■ Kansas State University - Center for Leadership
110 Calvin Hall
Department of Management
College of Business Administration
Manhattan, KS 66502
Ph: (785)532-7451
Fax: (785)532-1339
Co. E-mail: thomaswr@k-state.edu
Contact: Dr. Thomas Wright, Director
Scope: Leadership and management issues. **Founded:** 1989. **Educational Activities:** Panel discussions, workshops, conferences, and seminars.

45942 ■ Organization Development Institute - Library
11234 Walnut Ridge Rd.
Chesterland, OH 44026
Ph: (440)729-7419
Fax: (440)729-9319
Co. E-mail: don@odinstitute.org
URL: http://www.theodinstitute.org/od-library/the_od_institute.htm
Contact: Dr. Donald W. Cole, President
E-mail: DonWCole@aol.com
Description: Professionals, students, and individuals interested in organization development. Disseminates information on and promotes a better understanding of organization development worldwide. Conducts specialized education programs. Develops the International O.D. Code of Ethics and a competency test for individuals wishing to qualify as a Registered Organization Development Consultant and a statement on the knowledge and skill necessary to be competent in organization development and criteria for the accreditation of OD/OB academic programs. Maintains job and consultant information service. Sponsors International Registry of Organization Development Professionals and Research/Study Team on Nonviolent Large Systems Change. Maintains 18 committees including an International Advisory Board. **Scope:** A non-profit educational association promotes an understanding of O.D. It publishes The International Registry of O.D. Professionals and O.D. Handbook which lists names, addresses and the credentials of all registered users. It includes information on all OD/OB academic programs, O.D. Networks worldwide and the most recent edition of the International O.D. Code of Ethics. **Services:** Consulting. **Founded:** 1968. **Holdings:** 100 volumes. **Publications:** "The International Registry of O.D. Professionals and O.D. Handbook," 2003; "Conflict Resolution Technology"; "Professional Suicide or Organizational Murder"; "Improving Profits Through Organization Development"; "Organization Development: A Straight forward Reference Guide for Executives Seeking to Improve Their Organizations"; "What Is New In Organization Development; Organizations and Change"; "Organization Development Journal". **Educational Activities:** Organization Development World Congress (Annual); Organization Development Institute Annual International Congress;

What's New in Organization Development and Human Resources Development Conference, in May; Workshops for behavioral scientists and other interested parties; International, interorganizational, interdisciplinary Research/Study Team on Nonviolent Large Systems Change Meetings, in May. **Awards:** Outstanding Organizational Development Consultant of the Year Award. **Seminars:** What Is New in Organization Development and Human Resources Development.

45943 ■ University of British Columbia - Sauder School of Business - Centre for Operations Excellence (COE)
2053 Main Mall
Vancouver, BC, Canada V6T 1Z2
Ph: (604)822-1800
Fax: (604)822-1544
Co. E-mail: info@coe.ubc.ca
URL: http://www.sauder.ubc.ca/coe
Contact: Harish Krishnan, Director

Scope: Issues facing operations managers, and the development of methods, tools, and techniques to shape the business environment of the future. **Services:** Industry Partners Program: partnership with leading companies to formulate and solve operations research problems using advanced management science methods (10/year). **Founded:** 1998.

TENNESSEE VALLEY AUTHORITY

45944 ■ *"CEO Putting Rubber to Road at Lanxess Corporation" in Pittsburgh Business Times (Vol. 33, May 2, 2014, No. 42, pp. 4)*
American City Business Journals (ACBJ)

Released: May 2, 2014. **Description:** Flemming Bjoernslev, CEO for the North American operations of Germany-based Lanxess Corporation, discusses their recovery efforts following their first financial loss in 2013. He is confident that the U.S. tire manufacturing industry will help their business further in North America.

START-UP INFORMATION

45945 ■ *"Interest Soaring In 44North Business Competition" in Business First of Buffalo (Vol. 30, February 21, 2014, No. 23, pp. 3)*
Pub: American City Business Journals, Inc.
Contact: Whitney Shaw, President

Released: February 21, 2014. **Description:** The 43North business plan competition has attracted over 200 applications from entrepreneurs coming from various sectors like e-commerce, clean technology, and advanced manufacturing. The winners of the competition will qualify for the Start-Up New York program which eliminates the tax burden for qualified firms.

45946 ■ *Mommy Millionaire: How I Turned My Kitchen Table Idea Into a Million Dollars and How You Can, Too!*
Pub: Palgrave Macmillan
Contact: Lisa Dunn, Manager
E-mail: l.dunn@palgrave.com

Ed: Kim Lavine. **Released:** February 2008. **Price:** $17.99, paperback; $7.99. **Description:** Advice, secrets and lessons for making a million dollars from a mom who turned her kitchen into a successful business; tools cover developing and patenting an idea, cold calling, trade shows, QVC, big retailers, manufacturing, and raising venture capital. **Availability:** PrintE-book.

45947 ■ *"No. 27: WeVeel: Children's Art Supplies" in Inc. (Vol. 36, September 2014, No. 7, pp. 75)*
Pub: Mansueto Ventures L.L.C.
Contact: John Koten, Chief Executive Officer

Released: September 2014. **Description:** WeVeel manufactures fruity Scentos art supplies, which includes makers, pens, and stationery. Co-founders Jason Lane and Mike Pecci were former employees at Crayola. They started their company in 2009 and recently moved their headquarters to Morrisville, Pennsylvania.

45948 ■ *"Red McCombs, Partner Rolling Out New Venture Capital Fund" in San Antonio*

Business Journal (Vol. 26, April 20, 2012, No. 12, pp. 1)
Pub: American City Business Journal

Description: Entrepreneur Red McCombs has partnered with businessman Chase Fraser to create a new venture capital fund. This new fund will focus on technology startups in the automotive sector.

45949 ■ *"The Ultimate Cure" in Conde Nast Portfolio (Vol. 2, June 2008, No. 6, pp. 110)*
Ed: David Ewing Duncan. **Description:** Small upstarts as well as pharmaceutical giants are developing drugs for the neurotechnology industry; these firms are attempting to adapt groundbreaking research into the basic workings of the brain to new drugs for ailments ranging from multiple sclerosis to dementia to insomnia.

45950 ■ *"Well-Heeled Startup" in Business Journal Portland (Vol. 27, November 12, 2010, No. 37, pp. 1)*
Pub: Portland Business Journal
Ed: Erik Siemers. **Description:** Oh! Shoes LLC expects to receive about $1.5 million in funding from angel investors, while marketing a new line of high heel shoes that are comfortable, healthy, and attractive. The new line of shoes will use the technology of athletic footwear while having the look of an Italian designer. Oh! Shoes hopes to generate $35 million in sales by 2014.

45951 ■ *"Wheel Genius" in Entrepreneur (June 2014)*
Pub: Entrepreneur Media Inc.
Released: June 2014. **Description:** Electric car startup, Kenguru, has developed a hatchback that aims to improve mobility for wheelchair users, who enter the vehicle using a rear-opening tailgate and automatic ramp. The Kenguru, which is Hungarian for kangaroo, uses motorcycle-style handlebars instead of steering wheels. The 1,000-pound car has an estimated range of 60 miles and can travel up to 35 miles per hour. The Kenguru could sell for about $25,000. Founder Stacy Zoern partnered with Budapest, Hungary-based Istvan Kissaroslaki in developing the new car.

ASSOCIATIONS AND OTHER ORGANIZATIONS

45952 ■ **CAMUS International**
45738 Northport Loop W
Fremont, CA 94538
Ph: (757)766-4559
Co. E-mail: info@camus.org
URL: http://www.camus.org
Contact: Terri Glendon Lanza, President
E-mail: tlanza@camus.org
Description: Provides forum for manufacturing application users to interact with and learn from each other.

45953 ■ **Canadian Plastics Industry Association (CPIA) [Association Canadienne de l'industrie des Plastiques]**
5955 Airport Rd., Ste. 125
Mississauga, ON, Canada L4V 1R9

Ph: (905)678-7748
Fax: (905)678-0774
URL: http://www.cpia.ca
Contact: Carol Hochu, President
Description: Plastics manufacturers, distributors, importers, and exporters in Canada. Encourages research and development programs. Represents and defends members' interests. **Founded:** 1942.

45954 ■ **Canadian Tooling and Machining Association (CTMA)**
140 McGovern Dr., Unit 3
Cambridge, ON, Canada N3H 4R7
Ph: (519)653-7265
Fax: (519)653-6764
Co. E-mail: info@ctma.com
URL: http://ctma.com
Contact: David Glover, President
Description: Aims to represent Canadian tooling manufacturing at all levels of governments, their departments, and agencies. **Founded:** 1963. **Publications:** *CTMA View* (3/year).

45955 ■ *CTMA View*
140 McGovern Dr., Unit 3
Cambridge, ON, Canada N3H 4R7
Ph: (519)653-7265
Fax: (519)653-6764
Co. E-mail: info@ctma.com
URL: http://ctma.com
Contact: David Glover, President
URL(s): ctma.com/resources/magazines_newsletters. **Released:** 3/year

45956 ■ **Forest Products Association of Canada (FPAC) [Association des Produits Forestiers du Canada]**
99 Bank St., Ste. 410
Ottawa, ON, Canada K1P 6B9
Ph: (613)563-1441
Fax: (613)563-4720
Co. E-mail: ottawa@fpac.ca
URL: http://www.fpac.ca
Contact: Catherine Cobden, Executive Vice President
E-mail: ccobden@fpac.ca
Description: Forest products manufacturers. Lobbies government on legislation, taxation, and other policy matters. **Founded:** 1913. **Publications:** *Forest Products Association of Canada--Membership Directory.* **Educational Activities:** Paperweek (Annual); Paperweek.

45957 ■ **Manufacturing Jewelers and Suppliers of America (MJSA)**
57 John L. Dietsch Sq.
Attleboro Falls, MA 02763
Ph: (401)274-3840
Free: 800-444-6572
Fax: (401)274-0265
Co. E-mail: info@mjsa.org
URL: http://www.mjsa.org
Contact: Dave Meleski, Committee Chairman
Description: Represents American manufacturers and suppliers within the jewelry industry. Seeks to foster long-term stability and prosperity of the jewelry

industry. Provides leadership in government affairs and industry education. **Founded:** 1903. **Publications:** *MJSA Benchmark*; *Buyers Guide* (Biennial); *MJSA Journal* (Monthly); *Manufacturing Jewelers Buyers' Guide*. **Educational Activities:** MJSA Expo New York (Annual); MJSA Expo Providence (Biennial); Jeweler's Bench Conference and Trade Fair (Annual). **Awards:** American Vision Award (Annual); Education Foundation Scholarship Award (Annual).

45958 ■ National Association of Manufacturers (NAM)
733 10th St. NW, Ste. 700
Washington, DC 20001
Ph: (202)637-3000
Free: 800-814-8468
Fax: (202)637-3182
Co. E-mail: manufacturing@nam.org
URL: http://www.nam.org
Contact: Tiffany Adams, Vice President
E-mail: tadams@nam.org
URL(s): www.nam.org/s_nam/index.asp. **Description:** Manufacturers and cooperating non-manufacturers having a direct interest in or relationship to manufacturing. Represents industry's views on national and international problems to government. Maintains public affairs and public relations programs. Reviews current and proposed legislation, administrative rulings and interpretations, judicial decisions and legal matters affecting industry. Maintains numerous policy groups: Human Resources Policy; Small and Medium Manufacturers; Tax Policy; Resources & Environmental Policy; Regulation and Legal Reform Policy; International Economic Affairs. Affiliated with 150 local and state trade associations of manufacturers through National Industrial Council and 250 manufacturing trade associations through the Associations Council. **Founded:** 1895. **Publications:** *NAM/NIC Speakers Directory*; *NAMonline*; *National Association of Manufacturers--Congress Directory: 109th NAM Congress Directory: Second Session* (Biennial); *National Association of Manufacturers--Associations Council Membership Directory* (Annual); *NAM Member Focus* (Monthly).

45959 ■ National Council for Advanced Manufacturing (NACFAM)
2025 M St. NW, Ste. 800
Washington, DC 20036
Ph: (202)367-1178
URL: http://www.nacfam.org
Contact: Rusty Patterson, Chief Executive Officer
Description: Companies, university centers, laboratories, and manufacturing extension services, national trade associations, and national technical education associations. Seeks to "enhance the productivity, quality and competitiveness of all tiers of the U.S. domestic industrial base." Organizes public and private technology research and development projects; serves as a network linking members; conducts workforce skills standards development programs. **Founded:** 1989. **Publications:** *NACFAM Weekly* (Weekly).

EDUCATIONAL PROGRAMS

45960 ■ Advanced Electric Motor/Generator/ Actuator Design and Analysis for Automotive Applications (Onsite)
Seminar Information Service Inc.
20 Executive Park, Ste. 120
Irvine, CA 92614
Ph: (949)261-9104
Free: 877-SEM-INFO
Fax: (949)261-1963
Co. E-mail: info@seminarinformation.com
URL: http://www.seminarinformation.com
URL(s): www.seminarinformation.com. **Description:** Provide extensive details on design and analysis of electric motors/generators, actuators using state-of-the-art techniques, including the fundamentals of electromagnetism and basic electric machine equations will be presented along with examples. **Audience:** Industry professionals. **Telecommunication Services:** info@seminarinformation.com.

45961 ■ Automotive Glazing Materials (Onsite)
Seminar Information Service Inc.
20 Executive Park, Ste. 120
Irvine, CA 92614
Ph: (949)261-9104
Free: 877-SEM-INFO
Fax: (949)261-1963
Co. E-mail: info@seminarinformation.com
URL: http://www.seminarinformation.com
URL(s): www.seminarinformation.com. **Description:** An overview of the different automotive glazing materials, past, present and future, including the laws that govern their use, and manufacture, installation, usage, testing, safety aspects and how they affect automotive performance. Topics include the chemical, physical and design issues of annealed, laminated, tempered, glass-plastic and plastic glazing materials. **Audience:** Industry professionals. **Telecommunication Services:** info@seminarinformation.com.

45962 ■ Automotive Lighting (Onsite)
Seminar Information Service Inc.
20 Executive Park, Ste. 120
Irvine, CA 92614
Ph: (949)261-9104
Free: 877-SEM-INFO
Fax: (949)261-1963
Co. E-mail: info@seminarinformation.com
URL: http://www.seminarinformation.com
URL(s): www.seminarinformation.com. **Description:** Provides broad information about automotive lighting systems with emphasis on lighting functions, effectiveness, and technologies, including the legal aspects and implications related to automotive lighting and examine safety measurements used with lighting functions and human factors costs. **Audience:** Professionals. **Telecommunication Services:** info@seminarinformation.com.

45963 ■ A Familiarization of Drivetrain Components (Onsite)
Seminar Information Service Inc.
20 Executive Park, Ste. 120
Irvine, CA 92614
Ph: (949)261-9104
Free: 877-SEM-INFO
Fax: (949)261-1963
Co. E-mail: info@seminarinformation.com
URL: http://www.seminarinformation.com
URL(s): www.seminarinformation.com/qqbhnc/a-familiarization-of-drivetrain-components. **Description:** Learn to visualize both individual components and the entire drivetrain system without reference to complicated equations, with focus on the terms, functions, nomenclature, operating characteristics and effect on vehicle performance for each of the drivetrain components. **Audience:** Engineers. **Telecommunication Services:** info@seminarinformation.com.

45964 ■ OSHA Compliance and Workplace Safety
Padgett-Thompson Seminars
Rockhurst University CEC
14502 W 105th St.
Lenexa, KS 66215
Free: 800-349-1935
URL: http://www.findaseminar.com/tpd/Padgett-Thompson-Seminars.asp
URL(s): www.findaseminar.com/event1.asp?eventID=905. **Price:** $199. **Description:** This workshop offers the cost-effective solutions to keep the workplace safe and the OSHA inspectors away. **Audience:** Professionals.

DIRECTORIES OF EDUCATIONAL PROGRAMS

45965 ■ Scott's Directories: National Manufacturers (CD-ROM; +Canada)
Pub: Scott's Directories
Contact: Bruce Creighton, President
URL(s): www.scottsinfo.comwww.scottsdirectories. com. **Ed:** Barbara Peard. **Released:** Annual **Price:** $999, Individuals online; pinpointer; $1,799, Individu-

als online; profiler; $3,399, Individuals online; prospector. **Covers:** 58,000 manufacturers throughout Canada. **Entries include:** Company name, address, phone, fax, telex, names and titles of key personnel, number of employees, parent or subsidiary companies, North American Standard Industrial (NAICS) code, product, export interest, and year established.

REFERENCE WORKS

45966 ■ "$3 Million in Repairs Prep Cobo for Auto Show" in Crain's Detroit Business (Vol. 26, January 4, 2010, No. 1, pp. 1)
Pub: Crain Communications Inc.
Contact: Rance E. Crain, President
Ed: Nancy Kaffer. **Description:** Overview of the six projects priced roughly at $3 million which were needed in order to host the North American International Auto Show; show organizers stated that the work was absolutely necessary to keep the show in the city of Detroit.

45967 ■ "$49M Defense Contract Hits Austin" in Austin Business JournalInc. (Vol. 28, August 7, 2008, No. 21, pp. A1)
Pub: American City Business Journals
Ed: Laura Hipp. **Description:** BAE Systems PLC has landed a $49 million contract to build thermal cameras, which are expected to be installed on tanks in 2009 and 2010. BAE is expected to land other defense contracts and is likely to add employees in order to meet production demands.

45968 ■ "The 490 Made Chevy a Bargain Player" in Automotive News (Vol. 86, October 31, 2011, No. 6488, pp. S22)
Pub: Crain Communications Inc.
Contact: Rance E. Crain, President
Ed: David Phillips. **Description:** The first Chevrolet with the 490 engine was sold in 1913, but it was too expensive for masses. In 1914 the carmaker launched a lower-priced H-series of cars competitively priced. Nameplates such as Corvette, Bel Air, Camaro and Silverado have defined Chevrolet through the years.

45969 ■ "1914 Proved to Be Key Year for Chevy" in Automotive News (Vol. 86, October 31, 2011, No. 6488, pp. S18)
Pub: Crain Communications Inc.
Contact: Rance E. Crain, President
Ed: Jamie Lareau. **Description:** Chevy Bow Tie emblem was born in 1914, creating the brand's image that has carried through to current days.

45970 ■ "A123-Fisker Deal May Mean 540 Jobs" in Crain's Detroit Business (Vol. 26, January 18, 2010, No. 3, pp. 4)
Pub: Crain Communications Inc.
Contact: Rance E. Crain, President
Ed: Dustin Walsh. **Description:** Manufacturing plants in Livonia and Romulous may be hiring up to 540 skilled workers due to a contract that was won by A123 Systems Inc. that will result in the company supplying lithium-ion batteries to Fisker Automotive Inc. to be used in their Karma plug-in hybrid electric vehicle.

45971 ■ "AAAFCO Unveils Pet Food Resource" in Feedstuffs (Vol. 83, August 29, 2011, No. 35, pp. 15)
Pub: Miller Publishing Company
Description: The Association of American Feed Control Officials has launched a Website called The Business of Pet Food, which will address frequently asked questions about U.S. regulatory requirements for pet food. The site serves as an initial reference for anyone wishing to start a pet food business because it provides information and guidance.

45972 ■ "ABB Could Still Engineer an Upside" in Barron's (Vol. 89, July 20, 2009, No. 29, pp. M6)
Pub: Dow Jones & Co., Inc.
Contact: Clare Hart, President
Ed: Goran Mijuk. **Description:** Swiss engineering company ABB can remain profitable as its power transmission and distribution activities continue to generate earnings. The company is also benefiting from increased exposure in emerging markets.

45973 ■ *"Abraxis Bets On Biotech Hub" in Business Journal-Serving Phoenix and the Valley of the Sun (Vol. 10, November 9, 2007, No. 28)*
Ed: Angela Gonzales. **Description:** Abraxis Bio-Science Inc. purchased a 200,000 square foot manufacturing facility in Phoenix, Arizona from Watson Pharmaceuticals Inc. The company has the technology to allow chemotherapy drugs to be injected directly into tumor cell membranes. A human protein, albumin is used to deliver the chemotherapy.

45974 ■ *Achieving Planned Innovation: A Proven System for Creating Successful New Products and Services*
Pub: Simon & Schuster Higher Education Group
Contact: Larry Norton, President
Ed: Frank R. Bacon. **Released:** August 2007. **Price:** $16.95. **Description:** Planned innovation is a disciplined and practical step-by-step sequence of procedures for reaching the intended destination point: successful products. This easy-to-read book explains the system along with an action-oriented program for continuous success in new-product innovations. Five steps outlined include: a disciplined reasoning process; lasting market orientation; proper selection criteria that reflect both strategic and tactical business objectives and goals along with dynamic matching of resources to present and future opportunities, and positive and negative requirements before making major expenditures; and proper organizational staffing. The author explains what to do and evaluating the potential of any new product or service, ranging from ventures in retail distribution to the manufacture of goods as diverse as bicycles, motorcycles, aerospace communication and navigation equipment, small business computers, food packaging, and medical products. **Availability:** Print.

45975 ■ *"ACON Investments Acquires Igloo Products Corporation" in Economics & Business Week (April 19, 2014, pp. 6)*
Pub: NewsRX
Contact: Susan E. Hasty, Publisher
Released: April 19, 2014. **Description:** ACON Investments LLC has acquired Igloo Products Corporation, the top cooler manufacturer in the world. Details of the acquisition are included.

45976 ■ *"Ad Firms Stew Over Lost Car Biz: Diversifying Business Is Uphill Battle" in Crain's Detroit Business (Vol. 23, July 30, 2007, No. 31)*
Pub: Crain Communications Inc.
Contact: Rance E. Crain, President
Ed: Jean Halliday. **Description:** Struggling Detroit automakers are breaking their tradition of loyalty and moving their advertising accounts to agencies in Los Angeles, San Francisco, and Boston; This has Detroit's advertising community very worried.

45977 ■ *"Adapt or Die" in Black Enterprise (Vol. 38, July 2008, No. 12, pp. 27)*
Pub: Earl G. Graves Publishing Co. Inc.
Contact: Earl G. Graves, Jr., President
Ed: Rebecca Frances Rohan. **Description:** Turbulence in the domestic auto industry is hitting auto suppliers hard and black suppliers, the majority of whom contract with the Big Three, are just beginning to establish relationships with import car manufacturers. The more savvy CEOs are adopting new technologies in order to weather the downturn in the economy and in the industry as a whole.

45978 ■ *"AdvancePierre Heats Up" in Business Courier (Vol. 27, October 29, 2010, No. 26, pp. 1)*
Pub: Business Courier
Ed: Jon Newberry. **Description:** Bill Toler, chief executive officer of AdvancePierre Foods, is aiming for more growth and more jobs. The company was formed after the merger of Pierre Foods with two Oklahoma-based food processing companies. Toler wants to expand production and is set to start adding employees in the next 6-12 months.

45979 ■ *"Aeronautics Seeking New HQ Site" in The Business Journal-Milwaukee (Vol. 25,*

September 5, 2008, No. 50, pp. 1)
Ed: Rich Kirchen. **Description:** Milwaukee, Wisconsin-based Aeronautics Corp. of America is planning to move its headquarters to a new site. The company has started to search for a new site. It also plans to consolidate its operations under one roof.

45980 ■ *"The Great Fall of China" in Canadian Business (Vol. 85, June 11, 2012, No. 11, pp. 55)*
Pub: George Media Inc.
Ed: Bryan Borzykowski. **Released:** June 11, 2012. **Description:** Investors interested in aviation can take advantage of low company valuations amid increasing emerging-market demand for new airplanes. Some of the companies which tend to have higher margins despite a down cycle are Rockwell, Collins, United Technologies Corporation and Triumph Group.

45981 ■ *"After Price Cuts, Competition GPS Makers Lose Direction" in Brandweek (Vol. 49, April 21, 2008, No. 16, pp. 16)*
Pub: Nielsen Business Media Inc.
Contact: Howard Appelbaum, President
Ed: Steve Miller. **Description:** Garmin and TomTom, two of the leaders in portable navigation devices, have seen lowering revenues due to dramatic price cuts and unexpected competition from the broadening availability of personal navigation on mobile phones. TomTom has trimmed its sales outlook for its first quarter while Garmin's stock dropped 40 percent since February.

45982 ■ *"AgraQuest Deal Signals Growth for Biopesticide Makers" in Sacramento Business Journal (Vol. 29, July 13, 2012, No. 20, pp. 1)*
Pub: American City Business Journal
Description: Industry observes claim that biotechnology irm Bayer CropScience's upcoming acquisition of AgraQuest Inc. could signal the growth of biopesticide manufacturing chemical methods for agricultural crop protection could then be complemented with environmentally friendly approaches allowed by biopesticides.

45983 ■ *"Air Emissions Plunge in Birmingham" in Birmingham Business Journal (Vol. 29, June 15, 2012, No. 25, pp. 1)*
Pub: American City Business Journals, Inc.
Contact: Whitney Shaw, President
Ed: Nick Bowman. **Released:** June 15, 2012. **Description:** Air emissions in Birmingham, Alabama have declined in 2012. Birmingham has been struggling with air pollution owing its topography and steel production. But US Environmental Protection Agency standards have been accused of limiting industrial growth in the area.

45984 ■ *"Aircraft Maker May Land Here" in Austin Business Journal (Vol. 31, April 15, 2011, No. 6, pp. 1)*
Pub: American City Business Journals
Ed: Jacob Dirr. **Description:** Icon Aircraft Inc. is planning to build a manufacturing facility in Austin, Texas. The company needs 100,000 square feet of space in a new or renovated plant. Executive comments are included.

45985 ■ *"Airing It Out: Flanders Corp. Commits to Global Expansion" in The Business Journal-Serving Greater Tampa Bay (Vol. 28, July 14, 2008, No. 29, pp. 1)*
Pub: American City Business Journals, Inc.
Contact: Whitney Shaw, President
Ed: Jane Meinhardt. **Description:** Flanders Corp. is planning to expand its business in Europe and Southeast Asia. The St. Petersburg, Florida-based company has about 2,800 employees and manufactures air filtration products for industrial and residential applications.

45986 ■ *"Alberta's Runaway Train" in Canadian Business (Vol. 80, December 25, 2006, No. 1, pp. 17)*
Ed: Andrew Nikiforuk. **Description:** The high revenue brought about by the growth in the number of oil sand plants in Canada and the simultaneous burden on infrastructure and housing is discussed.

45987 ■ *"Alcoa: 'Going Where No Materials Scientist Has Gone Before" in Pittsburgh Business Times (Vol. 33, July 18, 2014, No. 53, pp. 5)*
Pub: American City Business Journals
Released: July 18, 2014. **Description:** Alcoa Inc. has signed a $1.1 billion supply agreement with Pratt & Whitney to build the forging for aluminum jet-engine fan blades as well as other parts made with aluminum lithium. This partnership brings together Alcoa's proprietary alloys and unique manufacturing processes with Pratt & Whitney's design, thus forging an aluminum fan blade that is lighter and enables better fuel efficiency.

45988 ■ *"Alcoa's Quebec Deal Keeps Smelters Running" in Pittsburgh Business Times (Vol. 33, February 28, 2014, No. 33, pp. 3)*
Pub: American City Business Journals
Released: February 28, 2014. **Description:** Alcoa Inc. has renewed its power supply contract with the Quebec provincial government for three of its smelters in 2014. The aluminum company is investing $250 million in the smelters over the next five years to support growth in the automotive manufacturing industry.

45989 ■ *"Algoma Shares Soar on Growing Sale Rumors" in Globe & Mail (February 13, 2007, pp. B1)*
Ed: Andrew Willis; Greg Keenan. **Description:** The stock prices of Algoma Steel Inc. have touched record high of $40 on the Toronto Stock Exchange. The growing rumors about the possible takeover bid are the major reason for the stock price growth.

45990 ■ *"All Options Open On Chrysler: Magna" in Globe & Mail (February 28, 2007, pp. B3)*
Ed: Greg Keenan. **Description:** The 65 percent drop in the profits of Magna International Inc. and the plans of its chief executive officer Don Walker to make the company more competitive are discussed.

45991 ■ *"Alstom Launches te ECO 122 ? 2.7MW Wind Turbine for Low Wind Sites" in CNW Group (September 28, 2011)*
Pub: CNW Group Ltd.
Contact: Carolyn McGill-Davidson, President
Description: Alstom is launching its new ECO 122, a 2.7MW onshore wind turbine that combines high power and high capacity factor (1) to boost energy yield in low wind regions around the world. The ECO 122 will produce about 25 percent increased wind farm yield that current turbines and fewer turbines would be installed in areas.

45992 ■ *"Alternative Energy: The Lithium Deficit" in Canadian Business (Vol. 82, April 27, 2009, No. 7, pp. 17)*
Pub: Rogers Media Inc.
Contact: Tony Viner, President
Ed: Joe Castaldo. **Description:** Experts are concerned that there may not be enough lithium available to support the expected rise in demand for the natural resource. Lithium is used in lithium ion batteries, the standard power source for electric and hybrid vehicles. Experts believe that the demand for lithium can only be measured once the technology is out in the market.

45993 ■ *"Alternative Fuels Take Center Stage at Houston Auto Show" in Houston Business Journal (Vol. 44, January 31, 2014, No. 39, pp. 8)*
Pub: American City Business Journals
Released: January 31, 2014. **Description:** An energy summit was held at the Houston Auto Show in Texas on January 22, 2014, where energy executives discussed new technology and initiatives. They considered the market for electric and natural gas-fueled vehicles as well as other options including hydrogen, fuel cells, and biofuels.

45994 ■ *"Altron" in Business Journal (Vol. 31, May 16, 2014, No. 51, pp. 10)*
Pub: American City Business Journals
Released: May 16, 2014. **Description:** Altron, Inc. makes mechanical boxes and electronic assemblies and is owned by U.S. Air Force veteran, Alan Phillips.

Marketing manager, Jim Merritt, shares that the business' veteran-owned status is important for defense contractors. One of the company's shift managers is also a veteran.

45995 ■ *"Aluminium maker Novelis Soars on Indian Takeover Talk" in Globe & Mail (January 27, 2007, pp. B5)*
Ed: Andy Hoffman. **Description:** The plans of India-based Kumar Mangalam Birla's Aditya Birla Group to bid for Atlanta-based rolled aluminum maker Novelis Inc. are discussed. The talks about the purchase have caused a rise in Novelis's share price.

45996 ■ *"American Axle Sues to Force Steelmaker to Resume Suspended Parts Shipment" in Crain's Detroit Business (Vol. 25, June 15, 2009)*
Ed: Robert Sherefkin. **Description:** American Axle & Manufacturing Holdings Inc. is facing a shutdown if a Michigan court does not force Republic Engineered Products Inc., a specialty steelmaker, to ship parts. If the parts are not shipped, it could cause assembly plants to shutdown.

45997 ■ *"Americhem to Shutter Maryland Operation" in Crain's Cleveland Business (Vol. 28, October 29, 2007, No. 43, pp. 14)*
Pub: Crain Communications Inc.
Description: Americhem Inc., a manufacturer of colors and additives for polymer products has announced plans to expand two plants in Cuyahoga Falls while phasing out its operations in Salisbury, Maryland.

45998 ■ *"Amid Recession, Companies Still Value Supplier Diversity Programs" in Hispanic Business (July-August 2009, pp. 34)*
Pub: Hispanic Business Inc.
Contact: Jesus Chavarria, President
Ed: Joshua Molina. **Description:** The decline of traditionally strong industries, from automotive manufacturing to construction, has shaken today's economy and has forced small businesses, especially suppliers and minority-owned firms, turn to diversity programs in order to make changes.

45999 ■ *"Analysts: Intel Site May Be Last Major U.S.-Built Fab" in Business Journal-Serving Phoenix and the Valley of the Sun (October 18, 2007)*
Pub: American City Business Journals, Inc.
Ed: Ty Young. **Description:** Intel's million-square-foot manufacturing facility, called Fab 32, is expected to open in 2007. The plant will mass-produce the 45-nanometer microchip. Industry analysts believe Fab 32 may be the last of its kind to be built in the U.S., as construction costs are higher in America than in other countries. Intel's future in Chandler is examined.

46000 ■ *"ANATURALCONCEPT" in Crain's Cleveland Business (Vol. 30, June 22, 2009, No. 24, pp. 1)*
Pub: Crain Communications Inc.
Ed: Dan Shingler. **Description:** Cleveland-based Bio-mimicry Institute, led by Cleveland's Entrepreneurs for Sustainability and the Cuyahoga County Planning Commission, are using biomimicry to incorporate eco-friendliness with industry. Biomimicry studies nature's best ideas then imitates these designs and processes to solve human problems.

46001 ■ *"Ann Alexander: Senior Attorney, Natural Resources Defense Council" in Crain's Chicago Business (Vol. 31, May 5, 2008, No. 18)*
Pub: Crain Communications Inc.
Contact: Todd Johnson, Publisher
Ed: Emily Stone. **Description:** Profile of Ann Alexander who is the senior attorney at the Natural Resources Defense Council and is known for her dedication to the environment and a career spent battling oil companies, steelmakers and the government to change federal regulations. One recent project aims to improve the Bush administration's fuel economy standards for SUVs. Past battles include her work to prevent permits from slipping through the cracks such as the proposal by London-based BP PLC to dump 54 percent more ammonia and 35 percent more suspended solids from its Whiting, Indiana refinery into Lake Michigan-the source of drinking water for Chicago and its surrounding communities.

46002 ■ *"Aquatic Medications Engender Good Health" in Pet Product News (Vol. 64, November 2010, No. 11, pp. 47)*
Pub: Bowtie Inc.
Ed: Madelaine Heleine. **Description:** Pet supply manufacturers and retailers have been exerting consumer education and preparedness efforts to help aquarium hobbyists in tackling ornamental fish disease problems. Aquarium hobbyists have been also assisted in choosing products that facilitate aquarium maintenance before disease attacks their pet fish.

46003 ■ *"Arizona Firms In Chicago Go For Gold With '08 Games" in The Business Journal - Serving Phoenix and the Valley of the Sun (Vol. 28, August 8, 2008, No. 49, pp. 1)*
Ed: Patrick O'Grady. **Description:** More than 20 U.S. athletes will wear Arizona-based eSoles LLC's custom-made insoles to increase their performance at the 2008 Beijing Olympics making eSoles one of the beneficiaries of the commercialization of the games. Translation software maker Auralog Inc saw a 60 percent jump in sales from its Mandarin Chinese language applications.

46004 ■ *"Around the World in a Day" in Agency Sales Magazine (Vol. 39, August 2009, No. 8, pp. 36)*
Ed: Jack Foster. **Description:** Highlights of Manufacturer's Agents National Association (MANA) member Les Rapchak one-day visit to Basra, Iraq are presented. Rapchak completed the trip via Frankfurt, Germany and Kuwait with a stop afterwards in Istanbul, Turkey. His purpose for the trip was to take part in a seminar at the State Company for Petrochemical Industries.

46005 ■ *"AT&T Wins Networking Deal from GM Worth $1 Billion" in Globe & Mail (February 22, 2007, pp. B14)*
Description: AT&T Inc., the largest telephone company in the United States, won a $1 billion contract from General Motors Corp. to provide communications services to integrate the automaker's networks.

46006 ■ *"ATK and NASA Spotlight Cost-Saving Upgrades for Solid Rocket Boosters" in Travel & Leisure Close-Up (October 8, 2012)*
Description: ATK and NASA featured the progress made in manufacturing the first ground test motor and cost-saving process upgrades for manufacturing the solid rocket booster for NASA's Space Launch System (SLS) at a event recently held. The changes made have resulted in a 46 percent time savings in assembly time, thus saving millions of dollars in projected costs of the SLS system.

46007 ■ *"ATS Secures Investment From Goldman Sachs" in The Business Journal - Serving Phoenix and the Valley of the Sun (Vol. 29, September 28, 2008, No. 4, pp. 1)*
Pub: American City Business Journals, Inc.
Contact: Whitney Shaw, President
Ed: Patrick O'Grady. **Description:** Goldman Sachs made an investment to American Traffic Solutions Inc. (ATS) which will allow it to gain two seats on the board of the red-light and speed cameras maker. The investment will help ATS maintain its rapid growth which is at 83 percent over the past 18 months leading up to September 2008.

46008 ■ *"Attorney Panel Tackles Contract Questions" in Agency Sales Magazine (Vol. 39, September-October 2009, No. 9, pp. 8)*
Ed: Jack Foster. **Description:** MANAfest conference tackled issues regarding a sales representative's contract. One attorney from the panel advised reps to go through proposed agreements with attorneys who are knowledgeable concerning rep laws. Another attorney advised reps to communicate with a company to ask about their responsibilities if that company is facing financial difficulty.

46009 ■ *"Auto Asphyxiation" in Canadian Business (Vol. 85, August 13, 2012, No. 13, pp. 38)*
Pub: George Media Inc.
Ed: Michael McCullough. **Released:** August 13, 2012. **Description:** The declining car ownership and utlization has profound business implications for oil companies and automakers and may bring substantial benefit to other sectors and the economy as a whole. The transition to the post-automotive age may happen in places where there is the will to change transportation practices but not in others.

46010 ■ *"Auto Bailout: Car Trouble" in Canadian Business (Vol. 80, April 27, 2009, No. 21, pp. 27)*
Pub: Rogers Media Inc.
Contact: Tony Viner, President
Ed: Thomas Watson. **Description:** Contract between General Motors Corporation and the United Auto Workers Union has created a competitive arm for the U.S. Big Three automakers. Data on the market and production data of car companies are presented.

46011 ■ *"Auto Bailout: Car Trouble" in Canadian Business (Vol. 82, April 27, 2009, No. 7, pp. 11)*
Pub: Rogers Media Inc.
Contact: Tony Viner, President
Ed: Thomas Watson. **Description:** The likely effects of a possible bailout of the U.S. automotive industry are examined. Some experts believe that a bailout will be good for the automotive industry and on the U.S. economy. Others argue however, that the nationalization may have a negative impact on the industry and on the economy.

46012 ■ *"Auto Bankruptcies Could Weaken Defense" in Crain's Detroit Business (Vol. 25, June 8, 2009, No. 23, pp. 1)*
Pub: Crain Communications Inc. - Detroit
Contact: Keith Crain, Chairman
Ed: Chad Halcom. **Description:** Bankruptcy and supplier consolidation of General Motors Corporation and Chrysler LLC could interfere with the supply chains of some defense contractors, particularly makers of trucks and smaller vehicles.

46013 ■ *"Auto Sector's Outlook Dims, Survey Finds" in Globe & Mail (January 4, 2006, pp. B4)*
Ed: Greg Keenan. **Description:** The findings of KPMG's survey, on the opinions of chief executives of automotive sector on the impact of higher gas prices, are presented.

46014 ■ *"Auto Show Aims to Electrify" in Crain's Detroit Business (Vol. 26, January 11, 2010, No. 2, pp. 1)*
Pub: Crain Communications Inc.
Contact: Rance E. Crain, President
Ed: Ryan Beene. **Description:** Overview of the North American International Auto show include sixteen production and concept vehicles including eight from the Detroit 3. High-tech battery suppliers as well as hybrid and electric vehicles will highlight the show.

46015 ■ *"Auto Supplier Stock Battered In Wake Of Wall Street Woes" in Crain's Detroit Business (Vol. 24, September 29, 2008, No. 39, pp. 4)*
Pub: Crain Communications Inc.
Contact: Rance E. Crain, President
Ed: Ryan Beene. **Description:** Due to the volatility of the stock market and public perception of the $700 billion banking bailout, auto suppliers are now facing a dramatic drop in their shares. Statistical data included.

46016 ■ *"Auto Suppliers Bringing Blue-Collar Jobs: US Farathane, American Tire Take Larger Sites" in Austin Business Journal (Vol.*

32, May 4, 2012, No. 9, pp. 1)
Pub: American City Business Journals, Inc.
Contact: Whitney Shaw, President
Ed: Jan Buccholz. **Released:** May 4, 2012. **Description:** Deals involving automobile suppliers have improved the industrial real estate and job markets in Austin, Texas. US Frathane Corporation is relocating to a new manufacturing facility and is hiring for manufacturing posts, customer service staff and a warehouse supervisor. The new distribution center of American Tire Distributors Inc. will open in August 2012 and will also hire workers.

46017 ■ "Autoline Goes West" in Michigan Vue (Vol. 13, July-August 2008, No. 4, pp. 6)
Ed: Dave Gibbons. **Description:** Profile of Blue Sky Productions, a Detroit-based production company that produces the nationally syndicated television series 'Autoline', which traditionally probes inside the Detroit auto industry; the company recently decided to shoot in Southern California, an area that now has an immense auto industry but has been virtually ignored by the media. Blue Sky originally slated four shows but ended up producing eleven due to the immense amount of material they discovered concerning the state of California's auto market.

46018 ■ "Automaker Foundations Run Leaner" in Crain's Detroit Business (Vol. 26, January 11, 2010, No. 2, pp. 1)
Pub: Crain Communications Inc.
Contact: Rance E. Crain, President
Ed: Sherri Welch. **Description:** Overview of the Detroit automobile industry includes restoring profitability, smarter marketing strategies and philanthropy. Each company comprising the Big 3 is examined, as is their vision for the future.

46019 ■ "AV Concept Expands Into Green Energy Storage" in Wireless News (January 25, 2010)
Description: Electronics distributor and manufacturer AV Concept Holdings Limited announced a marketing partnership with Boston-Power, a provider of lithium-ion batteries, with a focus in the Chinese and Korean markets.

46020 ■ "Backer Christmas Trade Show Preview" in Pet Product News (Vol. 66, September 2012, No. 9, pp. 12)
Description: The 46th Annual H.H. Backer Pet Industry Christmas Trade Showand Educational Conference will beheld at the Donald E. Stephens Convention Center in Rosemont, Illinois from October 12-14, 2012. More than 600 pet supply manufacturers and about 9,000 industry professionals will attend.

46021 ■ "Bad News for Canada: U.S. New-Home Starts Sink" in Globe & Mail (February 17, 2007, pp. B7)
Ed: Tavia Grant. **Description:** The new-home construction in the United States dropped by 14.3 percent in January 2007. The sinking construction activity shows significant impact on the Canadian factories and lumber companies.

46022 ■ "Baking Up a Bigger Lance" in Charlotte Business Journal (Vol. 25, December 3, 2010, No. 37, pp. 1)
Pub: Charlotte Business Journal
Ed: Ken Elkins. **Description:** Events that led to the merger between Charlotte, North Carolina-based snack food manufacturer Lance Inc. and Pennsylvania-based pretzel maker Snyder's of Hanover Inc. are discussed. The merger is expected to help Lance in posting a 70 percent increase in revenue, which reached $900 million in 2009. How the merger would affect Snyder's of Hanover is also described.

46023 ■ "Baltimore Car Dealers Have One More Shot to Get Their Franchises Back: Fighting Detroit" in Baltimore Business Journal (Vol. 27, January 22, 2010, No. 38, pp. 1)
Pub: American City Business Journals
Ed: Daniel J. Sernovitz. **Description:** Baltimore, Maryland-based car dealers could retrieve their franchises from car manufacturers, Chrysler LLC and

General Motors Corporation, through a forced arbitration. A provision in a federal budget mandates the arbitration. The revoking of franchises has been attributed to the car manufacturers' filing of bankruptcy protection.

46024 ■ "Baltimore GM Plant Moves Forward" in Baltimore Business Journal (Vol. 32, July 4, 2014, No. 9, pp. 18)
Pub: American City Business Journals, Inc.
Contact: Whitney Shaw, President
Released: July 4, 2014. **Description:** General Motors (GM) plant at White Marsh represents traditional and modern manufacturing, attracting young employees with the use of advanced technology, but still retaining its loyal, veteran workforce. Most workers at the plant's Allison Transmission facility have been with GM for 25 years or more, while the adjacent facility making electric motors for the Chevy Spark EV is primarily made up of workers in their late 20s.

46025 ■ "Baltimore's Businesses: Equipment Tax Breaks Help, But Money Still Tight: Weighing the Write-Off" in Baltimore Business Journal (Vol. 28, September 10, 2010, No. 18, pp. 1)
Pub: Baltimore Business Journal
Ed: Daniel J. Sernovitz. **Description:** President Barrack Obama has proposed to let business write off their investments in plant and equipment upgrades under a plan aimed at getting the economy going. The plan would allow a company to write off 100 percent of the depreciation for their new investments at one time instead of over several years.

46026 ■ "Bank Takes Charge: Who Gets Last Laugh?" in Barron's (Vol. 88, March 31, 2008, No. 13, pp. 17)
Pub: Dow Jones & Co., Inc.
Contact: Clare Hart, President
Ed: Leslie P. Norton. **Description:** Nord/LB will take a charge of 82.5 million euros to cover potential losses apparently related to Vatas' refusal to take the shares of Remote MDx Inc. after buying the shares. Remote MDx's main product is an ankle bracelet to monitor criminals; the firm has lost over half of its market cap due to the Nord/LB troubles and questions about its revenues.

46027 ■ "Bankruptcies" in Crain's Detroit Business (Vol. 24, September 29, 2008, No. 39, pp. 4)
Pub: Crain Communications Inc.
Contact: Rance E. Crain, President
Description: Current list of business that filed for Chapter 7 or 11 protection in U.S. Bankruptcy Court in Detroit include manufacturers, real estate companies, a printing company and a specialized staffing company.

46028 ■ "Bark and Bite" in Canadian Business (Vol. 81, March 31, 2008, No. 5, pp. 20)
Pub: Rogers Media Inc.
Contact: Tony Viner, President
Ed: Rachel Pulfer. **Description:** Hillary Clinton and Barack Obama both want to renegotiate NAFTA but the most job losses in the American manufacturing industry is caused by technological change and Asian competition than with NAFTA. The risk of protectionist trade policies has increased given the political atmosphere.

46029 ■ "Barnes Shakes Up Sara Lee Exec Suite" in Crain's Chicago Business (Vol. 31, April 21, 2008, No. 16, pp. 1)
Pub: Crain Communications Inc.
Contact: Todd Johnson, Publisher
Ed: David Sterrett. **Description:** In an attempt to cut costs and boost profits, Sara Lee Corp.'s CEO Brenda Barnes is restructuring the company's management team.

46030 ■ "Battered U.S. Auto Makers in Grip of Deeper Sales Slump" in Globe & Mail (April 4, 2007, pp. B1)
Pub: CTVglobemedia Publishing Inc.
Ed: Greg Keenan. **Description:** The fall in Canadian sales and market share of Ford Motor Co., General Motors Corp. and Chrysler Group is discussed.

46031 ■ "Bayer Job Cuts to Hit Canada" in Globe & Mail (March 3, 2007, pp. B7)
Description: Bayer AG, German drug maker, planned cut of 6,100 jobs as a part of their cost-cutting strategies. The company, which plans to save 700 million euros by the end of 2007, may eliminate some positions in Canadian branches.

46032 ■ "Because He Is Always On the Accelerator: Jay Rogers: Local Motors, Chandler, Arizona" in Inc. (Volume 32, December 2010, No. 10)
Pub: Inc. Magazine
Description: Profile of Jay Rogers, founder of Local Motors, who manufactures cars, including the Phoenix Rally Fighter made from lightweight composites rather than steel.

46033 ■ "Beer Stocks Rally on Anheuser, InBev Report" in Globe & Mail (February 16, 2007, pp. B3)
Ed: Keith McArthur. **Description:** The stock prices of beer manufacturing industries have increased considerably after impressive profit reports from Anheuser Busch Cos Inc. and InBev SA. Complete analysis in this context is presented.

46034 ■ "Behind the Scenes: Companies At the Heart of Everyday Life" in Inc. (February 2008, pp. 26-27)
Ed: Athena Schindelheim. **Description:** Profiles of companies providing services to airports, making the environment safer and more efficient, as well as more comfortable for passengers and workers. Centerpoint Manufacturing provides garbage bins that can safely contain explosions producing thousands of pounds of pressure; Infax, whose software displays arrival and departure information on 19-foot-wide screens; Lavi Industries, whose products include security barricades, hostess stands, and salad-bar sneeze guards; and SATech maker of rubber flooring that helps ease discomfort for workers having to stand for long periods of time.

46035 ■ "Bellingham Boatbuilder Norstar Yachts Maintains Family Tradition" in Bellingham Business Journal (Vol. February 2010, pp. 12)
Ed: Isaac Bonnell. **Description:** Profile of Norstar Yachts and brothers Gary and Steve Nordtvedt who started the company in 1994. The company recently moved its operations to a 12,000 square foot space in the Fairhaven Marine Industrial Park.

46036 ■ "Best Turnaround Stocks" in Canadian Business (Vol. 81, Summer 2008, No. 9, pp. 65)
Ed: Calvin Leung. **Description:** Share prices of Sierra Wireless Inc. and EXFO Electro Optical Engineering Inc. have fallen over the past year but have good chance at a rebound considering that the companies have free cash flow and no long-term debt. One-year stock performance analysis of the two companies is presented.

46037 ■ "The Best and Worst Economic Times" in Agency Sales Magazine (Vol. 39, December 2009, No. 11, pp. 22)
Ed: Mark Young. **Description:** U.S. gross domestic product grew 3.5 percent and the stock market has improved but manufacturers are cutting commissions or dropping sales representatives. Despite these challenges, it can a good time for salespeople because clients need them more than ever. Salesmen should find new ways to do business for their clients during this current challenging environment.

46038 ■ "BETC Backers Plot Future" in Business Journal Portland (Vol. 27, December 10, 2010, No. 41, pp. 1)
Pub: Portland Business Journal
Ed: Erik Siemers. **Description:** A coalition of clean energy groups and industrial manufacturers have spearheaded a campaign aimed at persuading Oregon legislators that the state's Business Energy Tax Credit (BETC) is vital in job creation. Oregon's BETC grants tax credits for 50 percent of an eligible renewable or clean energy project's cost. However, some legislators propose BETC's abolition.

46039 ■ *"Better than Advertised: Chip Plant Beats Expectations"* in *Business Review Albany (Vol. 41, June 27, 2014, No. 14, pp. 4)*
Pub: American City Business Journals, Inc.
Contact: Whitney Shaw, President
Released: June 27, 2014. Description: The $8.5 billion computer chip manufacturing plant and research center of GlobalFoundries in Malta, New York has strengthened the local economy in Saratoga County and helped the local manufacturing and construction industries recover from the recession. The Malta Plant construction project created more than 2,000 direct new construction jobs and over 10,000 indirect positions.

46040 ■ *"Better Made's Better Idea: Diversify Despite Rising Costs"* in *Crain's Detroit Business (Vol. 24, September 22, 2008, No. 38, pp. 18)*
Pub: Crain Communications Inc.
Contact: Rance E. Crain, President
Ed: Nathan Skid. Description: Better Made Snack Foods Inc. is planning to expand its product lines and market reach as well as boost manufacturing capability during a time in which the company is being buffeted by rising commodity and fuel costs. The company feels that diversification is the key to maintain sales and growth.

46041 ■ *"Betting On Volatile Materials"* in *Barron's (Vol. 88, July 14, 2008, No. 28, pp. M11)*
Pub: Dow Jones & Co., Inc.
Contact: Clare Hart, President
Ed: John Marshall. Description: Economic slowdowns in the U.S., Europe and China could cause sharp short-term declines in the materials sector. The S&P Materials sector is vulnerable to shifts in the flow of funds. Statistical data included.

46042 ■ *"Beverage Brand Vies To Be the Latest Purple Prince"* in *Brandweek (Vol. 49, April 21, 2008, No. 16, pp. 20)*
Pub: Nielsen Business Media Inc.
Contact: Howard Appelbaum, President
Ed: Becky Ebenkamp. Description: Profile on the new beverage product Purple and its founder, Ted Farnsworth; Purple is a drink that blends seven antioxidant-rich juices to create what Mr. Farnsworth calls a 'Cascade Effect' that boosts antioxidants' effectiveness. Mr. Farnsworth is marketing the brand's Oxygen Radical Absorbance Capability (ORAC) which is a value of 7,600 compared with orange juice's 1,200.

46043 ■ *"Beyond Auto; Staffing Firm Malace Grabs Revenue Jump"* in *Crain's Detroit Business (Vol. 26, January 18, 2010, No. 3, pp. 3)*
Pub: Crain Communications Inc.
Contact: Rance E. Crain, President
Ed: Sherri Welch. Description: Malace & Associates Inc., the Troy-based human resources management company, expects its diversification into nonautomotive industries to help double its revenues this year. Due to the automotive downturn, between October 2008 and March 2009 the company lost approximately 48 percent of its business.

46044 ■ *"Beyond Meat (R) Completes Largest Financing Round to Date"* in *Ecology, Environment & Conservation Business (August 16, 2014, pp. 4)*
Pub: NewsRX
Contact: Susan E. Hasty, Publisher
Released: August 16, 2014. Description: Beyond Meat (R) is the first company to recreate meat from plants and is dedicated to improving human health, positively impacting climate change, conserving natural resources and respecting animal welfare. The firm has completed its Series D financing round, which will also help the company promote consumer awareness and increase capacity at its manufacturing facility to meet demand.

46045 ■ *"Big Boys Drawn Back to Play in Oil Sands"* in *Globe & Mail (March 7, 2006, pp. B2)*
Ed: Deborah Yedlin. Description: The feasibility of companies such as Chevron Corp. in acquiring oil sands is discussed.

46046 ■ *"Birdcage Optimization"* in *Pet Product News (Vol. 64, November 2010, No. 11, pp. 54)*
Pub: Bowtie Inc.
Description: Manufacturers have been emphasizing size, security, quality construction, stylish design, and quick cleaning when guiding consumers on making birdcage options. Selecting a birdcage is gaining importance considering that cage purchases have become the highest expense associated with owning a bird. Other avian habitat trends are also examined.

46047 ■ *"Biz Assesses 'Textgate' Fallout: Conventions, Smaller Deals Affected"* in *Crain's Detroit Business (Vol. 24, March 31, 2008)*
Pub: Crain Communications Inc.
Contact: Rance E. Crain, President
Ed: Tom Henderson. Description: Businesspeople who were trying to measure the amount of economic damage is likely to be caused due to Mayor Kwame Kilpatrick's indictment on eight charges and found that: automotive and other large global deals are less likely to be affected than location decisions by smaller companies and convention site decisions. Also being affected are negotiations in which Mexican startup companies were planning a partnership with the TechTown incubator to pursue opportunities in the auto sector; those plans are being put on hold while they look at other sites.

46048 ■ *"Black Diamond Holdings Corp. Receives SEC Approval"* in *Canadian Corporate News (May 16, 2007)*
Description: Black Diamond Holdings, Corp., a British Columbia domiciled company and its two wholly owned subsidiaries are engaged in the bottling, importation, distribution, marketing, and brand creation of premium spirits and wines to worldwide consumers, announced that it has completed the SEC review process and has applied to list for trading in the United States on the OTC.BB.

46049 ■ *"Black Gold: Jobs Aplenty"* in *Canadian Business (Vol. 79, August 14, 2006, No. 16-17, pp. 57)*
Pub: Rogers Media Inc.
Contact: Tony Viner, President
Ed: Erin Pooley. Description: A list of the top ten jobs in the petroleum industry in Canada along with pay and nature of jobs, is presented.

46050 ■ *"Blast Blame: Explosion Case Set as Falk, Brennan Fault Each Other"* in *The Business Journal-Milwaukee (Vol. 25, September 5, 2008, No. 50, pp. 1)*
Pub: American City Business Journals, Inc.
Contact: Whitney Shaw, President
Ed: David Doege. Description: Rexnord Industries LLC and J.M. Brennan Inc.'s property damage trial in connection with the explosion at the Falk Corp. plant in Menomonee Valley, Wisconsin is set to begin. Lawyers for the two companies have failed to reach a settlement. A leaking propane line was seen as the cause of the blast.

46051 ■ *"Blues at the Toy Fair: Industry Reeling From Recalls, Lower Sales Volumes"* in *Crain's New York Business (February 17, 2008)*
Pub: Crain Communications Inc.
Contact: Rance Crain, President
Ed: Elisabeth Cordova. Description: Over 1,500 toy developers and vendors will attend the American International Toy Fair, expected to be low-key due to recent recalls of toys not meeting American safety standards. Toy retailers and manufacturers, as well as the Chinese government, are promoting product testing to prevent toxic metals in toys.

46052 ■ *"BMW Makes Bet on Carbon Maker"* in *Wall Street Journal Eastern Edition (November 19 , 2011, pp. B3)*
Pub: Dow Jones & Co., Inc.
Contact: Clare Hart, President
Ed: Christoph Rauwald. Description: Eight months ago, Volkswagen AG acquired a 10 percent holding in carbon-fiber maker SGL Carbon SE. Its rival BMW AG is catching up by acquiring 15.2 percent stake in SGL as it seeks alliances like the rest of the industry in order to share industrial costs of new product development.

46053 ■ *"BMW Revs Up for a Rebound"* in *Barron's (Vol. 89, July 13, 2009, No. 28, pp. M7)*
Pub: Dow Jones & Co., Inc.
Contact: Clare Hart, President
Ed: Jonathan Buck. Description: Investors may like BMW's stocks because the company has maintained its balance sheet strength and has an impressive production line of new models that should boost sales in the next few years. The company's sales are also gaining traction, although their vehicle delivery was down 1.7 percent year on year on June 2009, this was still the best monthly sales figure for 2009.

46054 ■ *"Boeing Earns Its Wings With Strong Quarter"* in *Crain's Chicago Business (Vol. 31, April 28, 2008, No. 17, pp. 4)*
Pub: Crain Communications Inc.
Contact: Todd Johnson, Publisher
Ed: Daniel Rome Levine. Description: Interview with Michael A. Crowe, the senior managing director at Mesirow Financial Investment Management, who discusses highlights from the earnings season so far, his outlook for the economy and the stock market as well as what his company is purchasing. Mr. Crowe also recommends shares of five companies.

46055 ■ *"Boeing Moving 1,000 Washington Engineering Jobs to California"* in *Business Journal Portland (Vol. 31, April 11, 2014, No. 6)*
Pub: American City Business Journals
Released: April 11, 2014. Description: Boeing plans to move 1,000 engineering jobs from Portland, Oregon to Southern California. The company says the move helps support planes in service at the company's Commercial Airplanes Engineering Center in Southern California and position the aerospace manufacturer for further growth.

46056 ■ *"Boeing Scores $21.7 Billion Order in Indonesia"* in *Wall Street Journal Eastern Edition (November 18 , 2011, pp. B6)*
Pub: Dow Jones & Co., Inc.
Contact: Clare Hart, President
Ed: David Kesmodel, Laura Meckler. Description: Boeing has garnered a large contract to deliver Boeing 737 jets to Indonesia's Lion Air. There are those who are lobbying against the US government's practice of subsidizing foreign companies that make contracts with American aerospace companies.

46057 ■ *"Boeing's Next Flight May Well Be to the South"* in *Puget Sound Business Journal (Vol. 29, November 21, 2008, No. 31, pp.)*
Ed: Steve Wilhelm. Description: Southern states in the U.S. are luring Boeing Company to locate a new plant in their region which is experiencing a growing industrial base while offering permissive labor laws as selling points.

46058 ■ *"The Book of Battery Manufacturing"*
Pub: CreateSpace
Contact: Daren Giles, President
Released: October 5, 2014. Price: , $7.86 paperback. Description: A comprehensive guide to every aspect of manufacturing batteries.

46059 ■ *"Bose Seeking Expansion Options in Framingham"* in *Boston Business Journal (Vol. 34, June 13, 2014, No. 19, pp. 15)*
Pub: American City Business Journals, Inc.
Contact: Whitney Shaw, President
Released: June 13, 2014. Description: Bose Corporation, the Framingham-based high-end audio products manufacturer, is in talks to buy a 10-acre property near its headquarters. Bose is negotiating with the owner of three buildings on Pennsylvania Avenue near the Bose headquarters. Bose already owns five buildings in Framingham, but is looking at real estate for growth and expansion.

46060 ■ "Bottler Will Regain Its Pop" in Barron's (Vol. 88, March 17, 2008, No. 11, pp. 56)

Ed: Alexander Eule. Description: Discusses he 30 percent drop in the share price of PepsiAmericas Inc. from their 2007 high which presents an opportunity to buy into the company's dependable U.S. market and fast growing Eastern European business. The bottler's Eastern European operating profits in 2007 grew to $101 million from $21 million in 2006.

46061 ■ "Branding Spree" in Pet Product News (Vol. 66, September 2012, No. 9, pp. 40)

Pub: Bowtie Inc.

Ed: Michael Ventre. Description: The extent to which pet security firm PetSafe has continued to diversify into new product categories to realize growth opportunities is explored. An arm of Radio Systems Corporation, PetSafe has been known for manufacturing products such as wireless fenses and electronic pet collars.

46062 ■ "Breaking Down Walls - 2 Kinds" in Puget Sound Business Journal (Vol. 35, August 22, 2014, No. 18, pp. 9)

Pub: American City Business Journals

Released: August 22, 2014. Description: Boeing Company's demolition of its office building in Everett, Washington along with its plan to build a new production facility may reduce jobs. Many workers at the manufacturing facility have been replaced by robots. The plant will be used to build the company's new version of the 777 twin engine.

46063 ■ "Brewing National Success" in Hawaii Business (Vol. 53, November 2007, No. 5, pp. 46)

Pub: PacificBasin Communications

Description: Kona Brewing Co. (KBC) is already selling its brews in four cities in Florida and 17 other states and Japan as well. KBC is currently forming a deal with Red Hook to produce Longboard Lager and other KBC brews at Red Hooks' brewery in New Hampshire. KBC's chief executive officer Mattson Davis shares KBC's practices for success.

46064 ■ "A Bright Spot: Industrial Space in Demand Again" in Sacramento Business Journal (Vol. 28, October 21, 2011, No. 34, pp. 1)

Pub: Sacramento Business Journal

Ed: Michael Shaw. Description: Sacramento, California's industrial sites have been eyed by potential tenants who are actively seeking space larger than 50,000 square feet.

46065 ■ "Bringing Charities More Bang for Their Buck" in Crain's Chicago Business (Vol. 34, May 23, 2011, No. 21, pp. 31)

Pub: Crain Communications Inc.

Contact: Todd Johnson, Publisher

Ed: Lisa Bertagnoli. Description: Marcy-Newberry Association connects charities with manufacturers in order to use excess items such as clothing, janitorial and office supplies.

46066 ■ "Bringing Manufacturing Concerns to Springfield" in Crain's Chicago Business (Vol. 31, March 31, 2008, No. 13, pp. 6)

Pub: Crain Communications Inc.

Contact: Todd Johnson, Publisher

Ed: Paul Merrion. Description: Profile of the new executive vice-president of Tooling & Manufacturing Assn., Paul Merrion, a man who plans to grow TMA's membership with an aggressive legislative agenda in Springfield.

46067 ■ "Brookfield Eyes 'New World'" in Globe & Mail (February 6, 2007, pp. B1)

Ed: Sinclair Stewart; Elizabeth Church. Description: The efforts of Brookfield Asset Management Inc. to acquire American paper company, Longview Fibre Co., and Australian construction company Multiplex Ltd. are discussed.

46068 ■ "Buhler Versatile Launches Next Generation of Equipment" in Farm Industry News (November 23, 2011)

Pub: Penton Business Media Inc.

Contact: David Kieselstein, Chief Executive Officer

Ed: Jodie Wehrspann. Description: Canadian owned Versatile is expanding its four-wheel drive tractor division with sprayers, tillage, and seeding equipment.

46069 ■ "Buick Prices Verano Below Rival Luxury Compacts" in Automotive News (Vol. 86, October 31, 2011, No. 6488, pp. 10)

Pub: Crain Communications Inc.

Contact: Rance E. Crain, President

Ed: Mike Colias. Description: General Motors's Verano will compete with other luxury compacts such as the Lexus IS 250 and the Acura TSX, but will be prices significantly lower coming in with a starting price of $23,470, about $6,000 to $10,000 less than those competitors.

46070 ■ "Business Briefs: Alcoholic Beverage Manufacturing Is Big Business In Idaho" in Idaho Business Review (August 19, 2014)

Pub: Dolan Co.

Contact: James P. Dolan, President

Released: August 19, 2014. Description: Idaho's alcoholic beverage manufacturing industry is growing at a steady pace, reporting an $8.7 million payroll in 2013. Breweries, as well as wineries and distilleries are also strong. Statistical data included.

46071 ■ "Business for Sale: For the Seasoned Buyer" in Inc. (Vol. 30, November 2008, No. 11, pp. 32)

Pub: Mansueto Ventures L.L.C.

Contact: John Koten, Chief Executive Officer

Ed: Darren Dahl. Description: Dominick Fimiano shares his plans to sell his ten-year-old business that manufactures and sells frozen pizza dough and crusts as well as a variety of topped pizzas. Products are purchased by schools, hospitals, bowling alleys and amusement parks. The business sale includes the buyer's taking on Fimiano's son the firm's most senior employee.

46072 ■ "Buying Chanel (All Of It)" in Conde Nast Portfolio (Vol. 2, June 2008, No. 6, pp. 34)

Ed: Willow Duttge. Description: Overview of the luxury company Chanel and an estimated guess as to what the company is worth.

46073 ■ Buyology: Truth and Lies About Why We Buy

Pub: Doubleday, a Division of Random House

Ed: Martin Lindstrom. Released: February 02, 2008. Price: $15, paperback. Description: Marketers study brain scans to determine how consumers rate Nokia, Coke, and Ford products. Availability: Print.

46074 ■ "C. Andrew McCartney; President, Owner, Bowden Manufacturing Corp., 37" in Crain's Cleveland Business (November 19, 2007)

Pub: Crain Communications Inc.

Ed: David Bennett. Description: Profile of C. Andrew McCartney who was named president of Bowden Manufacturing Corp., a company that machines and fabricates metal and plastic parts for products ranging from airplanes to medical equipment; Mr. McCartney has since purchased the company, which posted $8 million in sales last year. He feels that part of his success is due to adherence to such policies such as gaining the employees trust and to avoid making promises to customers that Bowden cannot keep.

46075 ■ "C-Class Could Boost Auto Suppliers" in Birmingham Business Journal (Vol. 31, June 27, 2014, No. 26, pp. 10)

Pub: American City Business Journals, Inc.

Contact: Whitney Shaw, President

Released: June 27, 2014. Description: The 2014 model of the Mercedes-Benz C-Class will be the first to be built at the Vance, Alabama manufacturing plant, increasing business opportunities for auto suppliers in the region. Jason Hoff, president and CEO of Mercedes-Benz US International Inc. notes that the move will impact the local economy as several companies in the area expand their operations to meet the growing demand from Mercedes.

46076 ■ "Calendar" in Crain's Detroit Business (Vol. 24, October 6, 2008, No. 40, pp. 22)

Pub: Crain Communications Inc.

Contact: Rance E. Crain, President

Description: Listing of events in the Detroit area include conferences addressing entrepreneurialism, economic development, manufacturing, marketing, the housing crisis and women business ownership.

46077 ■ "California Company Suing City's Lupin Over its Generic Diabetes Drug" in Baltimore Business Journal (Vol. 27, January 1, 2010)

Ed: Gary Haber. Description: California-based Depomed Inc. is suing Baltimore, Maryland-based Lupin Pharmaceuticals Inc. and its parent company in India over the patents to a diabetes drug. Lupin allegedly infringed on Depomed's four patents for Glumetza when it filed for permission to sell its own version of the drug with the US Food and Drug Administration. Details on generic pharmaceutical manufacturer tactics are discussed.

46078 ■ "California Water Treatment Facility Turns to Solar Power" in Chemical Business Newsbase (September 11, 2012)

Pub: Elsevier Engineering Information

Contact: Michael Hansen, Chief Executive Officer

Released: September 11, 2012. Description: Ramona, California municipal water district providing water, sewer, recycled water, fire protection, emergency medical services, and park services to the community has commissioned a 530KWp solar energy installation. Enfinity America Corporation developed and financed the solar panels and EPC services were provided by manufacturer Siliken.

46079 ■ "Can a Brazilian SUV Take On the Jeep Wrangler?" in Business Week (September 10, 2008, No. 4100, pp. 50)

Pub: Bloomberg L.P.

Contact: Matthew Winkler, Manager

Ed: Helen Walters. Description: Profile of the Brazilian company TAC as well as the flourishing Brazilian car market; TAC has launched a new urban vehicle, the Stark, which has won prizes for innovation; the company uses local technology and manufacturing expertise.

46080 ■ "Canadian Pet Charities Won't Go Hungry" in Pet Product News (Vol. 66, September 2012, No. 9, pp. 15)

Description: Premium dog and cat food manufacturer Petcurean will donate more than 42,000 pounds of Go! and Now Fresh dry foods to 25 animal rescue organizations across Canada. The donation is deemed invaluable to Petcurean's network of dog and cat foster activities.

46081 ■ "Capture New Markets" in Pet Product News (Vol. 64, December 2010, No. 12, pp. 12)

Pub: Bowtie Inc.

Ed: Ethan Mizer. Description: Flea and tick treatments are among the product categories that can be offered in order to clinch new markets. With the help of manufacturers, pet store retailers are encouraged to educate themselves about these products considering that capturing markets involves variations in customer perceptions. Retailers would then be deemed as resources and sources for these products.

46082 ■ "Car Dealer Closings: Immoral, Slow-Death" in Crain's Detroit Business (Vol. 25, June 8, 2009, No. 23)

Pub: Crain Communications Inc. - Detroit

Contact: Keith Crain, Chairman

Ed: Daniel Duggan. Description: Colleen McDonald discusses the closing of her two Chrysler dealerships located in Taylor and Livonia, Michigan, along with her Farmington Hills store, Holiday Chevrolet.

46083 ■ *"Career Transition"* in Crain's Detroit Business (Vol. 26, January 4, 2010, No. 1, pp. 14)

Pub: Crain Communications Inc.

Contact: Rance E. Crain, President

Description: Profile of Nicole Longhini-McElroy who has opted to radically change her career path from working in the manufacturing sector to becoming a self-published author of 'Charmed Adventures', a book series created to engage children in creative thought.

46084 ■ *"Catch the Wind to Hold Investor Update Conference Call on October 18, 2011"* in CNW Group (October 4, 2011)

Pub: CNW Group Ltd.

Contact: Carolyn McGill-Davidson, President

Description: Catch the Wind Ltd., providers of laser-based wind sensor products and technology, held a conference call for analysts and institutional investors. The high-growth technology firm is headquartered in Manassas, Virginia.

46085 ■ *"Caterpillar to Expand Research, Production in China"* in Chicago Tribune (August 27, 2008)

Ed: James P. Miller. Description: Caterpillar Inc., the Peoria-based heavy-equipment manufacturer, plans to establish a new research-and-development center at the site of its rapidly growing campus in Wuxi.

46086 ■ *"CAW Boss Troubled Over 'Vulnerable' Ford Plants"* in Globe & Mail (January 19, 2006, pp. B6)

Pub: CTVglobemedia Publishing Inc.

Ed: Greg Keenan. Description: The concerns of president Buzz Hargrove of Canadian Auto Workers on the impact of Ford Motor Co.'s restructuring efforts on closure of automotive plants in Canada are presented.

46087 ■ *"CAW Hopes to Beat Xstrata Deadline"* in Globe & Mail (January 30, 2007, pp. B3)

Pub: CTVglobemedia Publishing Inc.

Ed: Andy Hoffman. Description: The decision of Canadian Auto Workers to strike work at Xstrata PLC over wage increase is discussed.

46088 ■ *"Cemex Paves a Global Road to Solid Growth"* in Barron's (Vol. 88, March 10, 2008, No. 10, pp. 24)

Pub: Dow Jones & Co., Inc.

Contact: Clare Hart, President

Ed: Sandra Ward. Description: Shares of Cemex are expected to perform well with the company's expected strong performance despite fears of a US recession. The company has a diverse geographical reach and benefits from a strong worldwide demand for cement.

46089 ■ *"Cents & Sensibility"* in Playthings (Vol. 107, January 1, 2009, No. 1, pp. 19)

Pub: Reed Elsevier Group plc Reed Business Information

Contact: Mark Kelsey, Chief Executive Officer

Ed: Pamela Brill, Gary Evans. Description: Recent concerns over safety, phthalate and lead paint and other toxic materials, as well as consumers going green, are issues discussed by toy manufacturers. Doll manufacturers also face increase labor and material costs and are working to design dolls that girls will love.

46090 ■ *"Centurion Signs Egypt Deal With Shell"* in Globe & Mail (March 21, 2006, pp. B5)

Ed: Dave Ebner. Description: Centurion Energy International Inc., a Calgary-based natural gas producer in Egypt, has signed contract with Royal Dutch Shell PLC to explore about 320,000 hectares of land in Egypt. Details of the agreement are presented.

46091 ■ *"The CEO of General Electric On Sparking an American Manufacturing Renewal"* in Harvard Business Review (Vol.

90, March 2012, No. 3, pp. 43)

Pub: Harvard Business Review Press

Contact: Peter E. Walsh, Director

Ed: Jeffrey R. Immelt. Released: March 2012. Description: General Electric Company utilized human innovation and lean manufactring to improve the firm's competitiveness. By engaging the firm's entire workforce, utilizing technology and improving labor-management relations, GE boosted efficiency and reduced cost and waste.

46092 ■ *"The CEO Poll: Fuel for Thought II Canadian Business Leaders on Energy Policy"* in Canadian Business (Vol. 81, September 15, 2008, No. 14-15, pp. 12)

Pub: Rogers Media Inc.

Contact: Tony Viner, President

Ed: Joe Castaldo. Description: Most Canadian business leaders worry about the unreliability of the oil supply but feel that Canada is in a better position to benefit from the energy supply crisis than other countries. Many respondents also highlighted the need to invest in renewable energy sources.

46093 ■ *"The CEO Poll: Hot Air"* in Canadian Business (Vol. 81, July 22, 2008, No. 12-13, pp. 16)

Pub: Rogers Media Inc.

Contact: Tony Viner, President

Ed: Joe Castaldo. Description: Over half of 101 business leaders who were recently surveyed oppose Liberal leader Stephane Dion's carbon-tax proposal, saying that manufacturers in Canada are likely to suffer from the plan. Additional key results of the survey are presented.

46094 ■ *"CEOs Gone Wild"* in Canadian Business (Vol. 79, August 14, 2006, No. 16-17, pp. 15)

Ed: Thomas Watson. Description: Stock investment decisions of chief executive officers of metal companies in Canada, are discussed.

46095 ■ *"Champion Enterprises Buys UK Company"* in Crain's Detroit Business (Vol. 24, March 10, 2008, No. 11, pp. 4)

Pub: Crain Communications Inc.

Contact: Rance E. Crain, President

Ed: Daniel Duggan. Description: With the acquisition of ModularUK Building Systems Ltd., a steel-frame modular manufacturer, Champion Enterprises has continued its expansion outside the United States.

46096 ■ *"Change Is in the Air"* in Agency Sales Magazine (Vol. 39, August 2009, No. 8, pp. 30)

Ed: Jack Foster. Description: Highlights of the Power-Motion Technology Representatives Association (PTRA) 37th Annual Conference, which projected an economic upturn, are presented. Allan Bealulieu of the Institute for Trend Research gave the positive news while Manufacturer's Agents National Association (MANA) president Brain Shirley emphasized the need to take advantage of a turnaround.

46097 ■ *"A Change Would Do You Good"* in Canadian Business (Vol. 80, November 19, 2007, No. 23, pp. 15)

Ed: Geoff Kirbyson. Description: Western Glove Works will be manufacturing clothing offshore, including Sheryl Crow's jeans collection, in countries such as China and the Philippines. The company decided to operate offshore after 86 years of existence due to the high price of manufacturing jeans in Canada. Western Glove's focus on producing celebrity-endorsed goods is discussed.

46098 ■ *"Charged Up for Sales"* in Charlotte Business Journal (Vol. 25, October 15, 2010, No. 30, pp. 1)

Pub: Charlotte Business Journal

Ed: Susan Stabley. Description: Li-Ion Motors Corporation is set to expand its production lines of electric cars in Sacramento, California. The plan is seen to create up to 600 jobs. The company's total investment is seen to reach $500 million.

46099 ■ *"Cheese Spread Whips Up a Brand New Bowl"* in Brandweek (Vol. 49, April 21, 2008, No. 16, pp. 17)

Pub: Nielsen Business Media Inc.

Contact: Howard Appelbaum, President

Ed: Mike Beirne. Description: Mrs. Kinser's Pimento Cheese Spread is launching a new container for its product in order to attempt stronger brand marketing with a better bowl in order to win over the heads of households as young as in their 30s. The company also intends to begin distribution in Texas and the West Coast. Mrs. Kinser's is hoping that the new packaging will provide a more distinct branding and will help consumers distinguish what flavor they are buying.

46100 ■ *"Children's Products Maker Not the New Kid on the Block"* in Crain's Cleveland Business (Vol. 28, November 26, 2007, No. 47, pp. 3)

Pub: Crain Communications Inc.

Ed: David Bennett. Description: Discusses the business model employed by Shamrock Industries Inc., a rising star in the competitive world of children's products; the company, which does business as Foundations Quality Children's Products, has expanded into a 63,000-square-foot distribution center which has boosted its local profile significantly.

46101 ■ *"A Chinese Approach to Management: A Generation of Entrepreneurs Is Writing Its Own Rules"* in Harvard Business Review (Vol. 92, September 2014, No. 9, pp. 103)

Pub: Harvard Business Publishing

Released: September 2014. Description: The Chinese approach to management include simple structures for organizations, quick development of products, responsiveness to local values and needs, and investment in source firms and vendors. Manufacturing and engineering operations are typically co-located.

46102 ■ *"Chinese Fund Loans $33.5 Million to Prestolite"* in Crain's Detroit Business (Vol. 26, January 18, 2010, No. 3, pp. 1)

Pub: Crain Communications Inc.

Contact: Rance E. Crain, President

Ed: Ryan Beene. Description: Prestolite Electric Inc., a distributor of alternators and starter motors for commercial and heavy-duty vehicles, looked to China for fresh capital in order to fund new product launches.

46103 ■ *"Chinese Solar Panel Manufacturer Scopes Out Austin"* in Austin Business JournalInc. (Vol. 29, October 30, 2009, No. 34, pp. 1)

Pub: American City Business Journals

Ed: Jacob Dirr. Description: China's Yingli Green Energy Holding Company Ltd. is looking for a site in order to construct a $20 million photovoltaic panel plant. Both Austin and San Antonio are vying to house the manufacturing hub. The project could create about 300 jobs and give Austin a chance to become a player in the solar energy market. Other solar companies are also considering Central Texas as an option to set up shop.

46104 ■ *"Chrysler Unions Set Up Roadblocks to Private Equity"* in Globe & Mail (March 20, 2007, pp. B3)

Pub: CTVglobemedia Publishing Inc.

Ed: Greg Keenan. Description: The opposition of the Canadian Auto Workers union and the United Auto Workers to any proposal to sell Chrysler Group is discussed.

46105 ■ *"Cleanup to Polish Plating Company's Bottom Line"* in Crain's Cleveland Business (Vol. 28, October 29, 2007, No. 43, pp. 4)

Pub: Crain Communications Inc.

Ed: Jay Miller. Description: Barker Products Co, a manufacturer of nuts and bolts, is upgrading its aging facility which will allow them to operate at capacity and will save the company several hundred thousand dollars a year in operating costs. The new owners secured a construction loan from the county's new

Commercial Redevelopment Fund which will allow them to upgrade the building which was hampered by years of neglect.

46106 ■ *"Closed Minds and Open Skies"* in *Barron's (Vol. 88, March 10, 2008, No. 10, pp. 50)*
Pub: Dow Jones & Co., Inc.
Contact: Clare Hart, President
Ed: Thomas G. Donlan. **Description:** American politicians have closed minds when it comes to fair trade. The American government must not interfere with the country's manufacturing industries or worry about outsourcing defense contracts to European aerospace company Airbus.

46107 ■ *"CMO Nicholson Exits Pepsi as Share Declines"* in *Advertising Age (Vol. 79, July 7, 2008, No. 26, pp. 4)*
Pub: Crain Communications Inc.
Contact: Rance Crain, President
Ed: Natalie Zmuda. **Description:** Cie Nicholson, the chief marketing officer at Pepsi-Cola UK, is leaving the company at a time when its market share is down; the brand, which was known for its dynamic marketing, has diverted much of its attention from its core brands and shifted attention to the ailing Gatorade brand as well as Sobe Life Water and Amp.

46108 ■ *"Coca-Cola Bottler Up for Sale: CEO J. Bruce Llewellyn Seeks Retirement"* in *Black Enterprise (Vol. 37, December 2006, No. 5, pp. 31)*
Pub: Earl G. Graves Publishing Co. Inc.
Contact: Earl G. Graves, Jr., President
Ed: Marcia A. Wade. **Description:** J. Bruce Llewellyn of Brucephil Inc., the parent company of the Philadelphia Coca-Cola Bottling Co. has agreed to sell its remaining shares to Coca-Cola Co., which previously owned 31 percent of Philly Coke. Analysts believe that Coca-Cola will eventually sell its shares to another bottler.

46109 ■ *"Coca-Cola FEMSA, Family Dollar, Other Dividend Payers On a Roll"* in *Benzinga.com (June 21, 2012)*
Pub: Benzinga.com
Contact: Kyle Bazzy, President
Ed: Nelson Hem. **Description:** Dividend paying companies showing upward price trends are outlined. The firms highlighted include: Agnico-Eagle Mines, Coca-Cola FEMSA, Dean Foods, Expedia, Family Dollar Stores, Ferrellgas Partners, and InterContinental Hotels.

46110 ■ *"Coca-Cola Looks Ready to Pause"* in *Barron's (Vol. 88, March 10, 2008, No. 10, pp. 18)*
Pub: Dow Jones & Co., Inc.
Contact: Clare Hart, President
Ed: Michael Santoli. **Description:** Shares of Coca-Cola are expected to turn sideways or experience a slight drop from $59.50 each to the mid-50 level. The company has seen its shares jump 40 percent since 2006, when it was in a series of measures to improve profitability.

46111 ■ *"The Code-Cracker: Prominent Researcher at Miami Part of Federal Effort to Solve Protein Structures"* in *Business Courier (Vol. 24, January 10, 2008, No. 40, pp. 1)*
Pub: American City Business Journals, Inc.
Contact: Whitney Shaw, President
Ed: James Ritchie. **Description:** Michael Kennedy, a professor in the chemistry and biochemistry department at the Miami University, is a part of the Protein Structure Initiative, a project that is aimed at forming a catalog of three-dimensional protein structures. The initiative is a project of the Northeast Structural Genomics consortium, of which the Miami University is a member. The impacts of the research on drug development are discussed.

46112 ■ *"Cogs in R.I. Manufacturing Machine"* in *Providence Business News (Vol. 28, January 27, 2014, No. 43, pp. 1)*
Pub: American City Business Journals
Released: January 27, 2014. **Description:** Machine shops are capable of fixing or designing unique parts for manufacturing equipment and serve as a critical

link in a company's production and distribution. Rhode Island has at least 50 machine shops capable of fabricating parts for companies. The Rhode Island Manufacturers Association's efforts to close the skills gap in machining are examined.

46113 ■ *"Coming Soon: Electric Tractors"* in *Farm Industry News (November 21, 2011)*
Pub: Penton Business Media Inc.
Contact: David Kieselstein, Chief Executive Officer
Ed: Jodie Wehrspann. **Description:** The agricultural industry is taking another look at electric farm vehicles. John Deere Product Engineering Center said that farmers can expect to see more diesel-electric systems in farm tractors, sprayers, and implements.

46114 ■ *"Communications and Power Industries Awarded $6 Million to Support Apache Helicopter"* in *Defense & Aerospace Business (August 13, 2014, pp. 11)*
Pub: NewsRX
Contact: Susan E. Hasty, Publisher
Released: August 13, 2014. **Description:** Communications and Power Industries LLC procured an order totaling $6 million from Lockheed Martin Missiles and Fire Control for manufacturing tactical common data links. These links will be installed on the AH-64E Guardian variant of the Apache helicopter used to support U.S. warfighters.

46115 ■ *"Compelling Opportunities for Investors in Emerging Markets"* in *Barron's (Vol. 88, March 10, 2008, No. 10, pp. 39)*
Pub: Dow Jones & Co., Inc.
Contact: Clare Hart, President
Ed: Neil A. Martin. **Description:** Michael L. Reynal, portfolio manager of Principal International Emerging Markets Fund, is bullish on the growth prospects of stocks in emerging markets. He is investing big on energy, steel, and transportation companies.

46116 ■ *"Comtech's Winning Streak"* in *Crain's New York Business (Vol. 24, January 6, 2008, No. 1, pp. 3)*
Pub: Crain Communications Inc.
Contact: Rance Crain, President
Description: Comtech Telecommunications Corp., a designer and manufacturer of equipment that helps military track troops and vehicles on the field, has been one of the stock market's biggest winners over the past decade. Statistical data included.

46117 ■ *"Condensed Capitalism: Campbell Soup and the Pursuit of Cheap Production in the Twentieth Century"* in *Human Resource Management (Vol. 49, September-October 2010, No. 5, pp. 965-968)*
Pub: John Wiley
Ed: Matthew M. Bodah. **Description:** Review of the book, 'Condensed Capitalism: Campbell Soup and the Pursuit of Cheap Production in the Twentieth Century'.

46118 ■ *"ContiTech Celebrates 100 Years"* in *American Printer (Vol. 128, July 1, 2011, No. 7)*
Pub: Penton Media Inc.
Description: ContiTech celebrated 100 years in business. The firm started in 1911 after developing the first elastic printing blanket. Other milestones for the firm include its manufacturing process for compressible printing blankets, the Conti-Air brand and climate-neutral printing blankets.

46119 ■ *"Contract Reveals Details of ACE Jet Deals"* in *Globe & Mail (January 24, 2006, pp. B3)*
Pub: CTVglobemedia Publishing Inc.
Ed: Brent Jang. **Description:** The details of contract between Boeing Co. and Air Canada are presented.

46120 ■ *"A Conversation With: Steven Hilfinger, Foley & Lardner L.L.P."* in *Crain's Detroit Business (Vol. 24, March 24, 2008, No. 12, pp. 1)*
Pub: Crain Communications Inc.
Contact: Rance E. Crain, President
Ed: Tom Henderson. **Description:** Interview with Steven Hilfinger who is a member of Foley & Lardner L.L.P.'s mergers and acquisitions practice and is co-

chair of its automotive industry team. Hilfinger discusses such issues as the role a board of directors can play in the M&A process and the future of the auto market.

46121 ■ *"Coping With a Shrinking Planet"* in *Agency Sales Magazine (Vol. 39, December 2009, No. 11, pp. 46)*
Ed: Mark Young. **Description:** China and India are forcing big changes in the world and are posing a huge threat to U.S. manufacturers and their sales representatives. Reps may want to consider expanding into these territories. Helping sell American products out of the country presents an opportunity for economic expansion.

46122 ■ *"Copy Karachi?"* in *Barron's (Vol. 88, June 30, 2008, No. 26, pp. 5)*
Pub: Dow Jones & Co., Inc.
Contact: Clare Hart, President
Ed: Randall W. Forsyth. **Description:** Karachi bourse had a historic 8.6 percent one-day gain because the bourse banned short-selling for a month and announced a 30 billion rupee fund to stabilize the market. The shares of General Motors are trading within the same values that it had in 1974. The reasons for this decline are discussed.

46123 ■ *"Credit-Market Crisis Batters Origen Financial's Bottom Line"* in *Crain's Detroit Business (Vol. 24, March 31, 2008, No. 13, pp. 4)*
Pub: Crain Communications Inc.
Contact: Rance E. Crain, President
Ed: Tom Henderson. **Description:** Overview of the effect the credit-market crisis has had on Origen Financial Inc., a company that underwrites and services loans for manufactured housing. CEO Ronald Klein didn't think Origen would be affected by the collapse due to its sound operations but the company's share price dropped considerably causing its auditors to warn that the company's existence could be in jeopardy.

46124 ■ *"Cruising In Choppy Water"* in *The Business Journal-Portland (Vol. 25, August 22, 2008, No. 24, pp. 1)*
Pub: American City Business Journals, Inc.
Contact: Whitney Shaw, President
Ed: Erik Siemers. **Description:** Yacht builder Christensen Shipyards Inc. is experiencing robust business despite the slowing US economy, building four yachts a year as of 2008. The company expects revenues to hit $90 million and is opening a 500,000-square-foot plant in Tennessee.

46125 ■ *"The Cult of Ralph: Chrysler's Ralph Gilles"* in *Canadian Business (Vol. 79, September 22, 2006, No. 19, pp. 90)*
Pub: Rogers Media Inc.
Contact: Tony Viner, President
Ed: Thomas Watson. **Description:** The contributions of Ralph Gilles to automobile manufacturing giant Daimler Chrysler AG are discussed.

46126 ■ *"Cyclicals, Your Day Is Coming"* in *Barron's (Vol. 89, July 27, 2009, No. 30, pp. 24)*
Pub: Dow Jones & Co., Inc.
Contact: Clare Hart, President
Ed: Dimitra DeFotis. **Description:** Cyclical stocks are likely to be big winners when the economy improves and 13 stocks that have improving earnings, decent balance sheets, and dividends are presented. These candidates include U.S. Steel, Alcoa, Allegheny Tech, Dow Chemical, and Nucor.

46127 ■ *"DaimlerChrysler Bears Down on Smart"* in *Globe & Mail (March 27, 2006, pp. B11)*
Ed: Oliver Suess. **Description:** DaimlerChrysler AG, German automobile industry giant, is planning to cut down its workforce its Smart division. The Chrysler is also planning to stop the production of its four-seater models, to end losses at Smart division.

46128 ■ *"Danaher to Acquire Tectronix"* in *Canadian Electronics (Vol. 22, November-December 2007, No. 7, pp. 1)*
Description: Leading supplier of measurement, test and monitoring equipment Tektronix will be acquired by Danaher Corporation for $2.8 billion. Tektronix products are expected to complement Danaher's test equipment sector. The impacts of the deal on Tektronix shareholders and Danaher's operations are discussed.

46129 ■ *"Dealer Gets a Lift with Acquisitions at Year's End"* in *Crain's Detroit Business (Vol. 26, January 11, 2010, No. 2, pp. 3)*
Pub: Crain Communications Inc.
Contact: Rance E. Crain, President
Ed: Ryan Beene. **Description:** Alta Equipment Co., a forklift dealer, closed 2009 with a string of acquisitions expecting to double the firm's employee headcount and triple its annual revenue. Alta Lift Truck Services, Inc., as the company was known before the acquisitions, was founded in 1984 as Michigan's dealer for forklift manufacturer Yale Materials Handling Corp.

46130 ■ *"Dealing With Dangers Abroad"* in *Financial Executive (Vol. 23, December 2007, No. 10, pp. 32)*
Ed: Jeffrey Marshall. **Description:** Clear processes and responsibilities for risk management for all companies going global are essential. U.S. toy manufacturer, Matel was put into crisis mode after its Chinese-made toys were recalled due to the use of lead-based paint or tiny magnets in its products.

46131 ■ *"A Decent Proposal"* in *Hawaii Business (Vol. 53, March 2008, No. 9, pp. 52)*
Pub: PacificBasin Communications
Ed: Jacy L. Youn. **Description:** Bonnie Cooper and Brian Joy own Big Rock Manufacturing Inc., a stone manufacturing company, which sells carved rocks and bowls, lava benches, waterfalls, and Buddhas. Details about the company's growth are discussed.

46132 ■ *"Deere to Open Technology Center in Germany"* in *Chicago Tribune (September 3, 2008)*
Ed: James P. Miller. **Description:** Deere & Co. plans to open a technology and innovation center in Germany; details of the company's expansion plans are discussed.

46133 ■ *"Defense Contractor May Expand Locally: BAE Systems Ramps Up Vehicle Prototypes"* in *Crain's Detroit Business (March 24, 2008)*
Pub: Crain Communications Inc.
Contact: Rance E. Crain, President
Ed: Chad Halcom. **Description:** Profile of BAE Systems, a defense contractor, that has built a prototype in the highly competitive Joint Light Tactical Vehicle project; the company has also completed its prototype RG33L Mine Resistant Recovery Maintenance Vehicle and has plans for expansion.

46134 ■ *"Defenshield Takes Aim at New Gun-Friendly Location"* in *Orlando Business Journal (Vol. 30, June 27, 2014, No. 53, pp. 9)*
Pub: American City Business Journals
Released: June 27, 2014. **Description:** Coverage of Defenshield's move to St. Augustine, Florida, a gun-friendly location is discussed. The relocation occurred after New York's declaration of the SAFE Act, a new governmental gun control law. Defenshield manufactures military-grade bulletproof shields and barriers, which need heavy weaponry to test the products.

46135 ■ *"Delaware Diaper Maker Wanting To Expand Less Than a Year After Move"* in *Business First-Columbus (December 10, 2007, pp. A6)*
Pub: American City Business Journals, Inc.
Ed: Dan Eaton. **Description:** Duluth, Georgia-based Associated Hygienic Products LLC is planning to expand its production operations by 20 percent and hire new workers. The diaper maker was awarded state incentives to facilitate its transfer from Marion to Delaware. Details are included.

46136 ■ *"Delphi Latest In Fight Over Offshore Tax Shelters"* in *Crain's Detroit Business (Vol. 30, July 7, 2014, No. 27, pp. 1)*
Pub: Crain Communications Inc. - Detroit
Contact: Keith Crain, Chairman
Released: July 7, 2014. **Description:** Internal Revenue Service is investigating Delphi Automotive and other American companies over the use of offshore tax shelters. The latest in Delphi's dispute with the federal government over tax practices is expected to cost the supplier millions. Delphi manufactures electronics and technologies for vehicles. Apple Inc. and Google Inc. have also been targeted by the IRS for incorporating portions of the businesses offshore allowing them to avoid U.S. taxes as well as other foreign taxes.

46137 ■ *"Despite Gloom, Auto Sales Saw Gains in 2005"* in *Globe & Mail (January 5, 2006, pp. B1)*
Ed: Greg Keenan. **Description:** An overview of positive automotive sales in Canada, for 2005, is presented.

46138 ■ *"Despite Hot Toys, Holiday Sales Predicted To Be Ho-Ho-Hum"* in *Drug Store News (Vol. 29, November 12, 2007, No. 14, pp. 78)*
Ed: Doug Desjardins. **Description:** Summer toy recalls have retailers worried about holiday sales in 2007. Mattel was heavily impacted from the recall of millions of toys manufactured in China.

46139 ■ *"Detroit 3's Fall Would Be a Big One in Ohio"* in *Business First Columbus (Vol. 25, November 28, 2008, No. 14, pp. A1)*
Pub: American City Business Journals
Ed: Dan Eaton. **Description:** Ohio's economy will suffer huge negative effects in the event of a failure of one or more of the automotive companies, General Motors Corporation, Ford Motor Company, or Chrysler LLC. The state is home to 97,900 jobs in the automotive industry and is a vital link to the industry's supply network.

46140 ■ *"DeWind Delivering Turbines to Texas Wind Farm"* in *Professional Services Close-Up (September 25, 2011)*
Pub: Close-Up Media
Description: DeWind Company has begun shipment of turbines to the 20 MW Frisco Wind Farm located in Hansford County, Texas. DeWind is a subsidiary of Daewoo Shipbuilding and Marine Engineering Company. Details of the project are discussed.

46141 ■ *"Dexter Gauntlett Gauges the Wind"* in *Business Journal Portland (Vol. 30, January 31, 2014, No. 48, pp. 6)*
Pub: American City Business Journals
Released: January 31, 2014. **Description:** Navigant Research senior research analyst, Dexter Gauntlett says Vestas-American Wind Systems could boost its revenues. He added that the company has being hiring employees at its manufacturing plants. Gauntlett also said that wind energy will greatly boost state renewable portfolios.

46142 ■ *"Diana Sands: Vice-President of Investor Relations, Boeing Co."* in *Crain's Chicago Business (Vol. 31, May 5, 2008, No. 18, pp. 32)*
Pub: Crain Communications Inc.
Contact: Todd Johnson, Publisher
Ed: John Rosenthal. **Description:** Profile of Diana Sands who is the vice-president of investor relations at Boeing Co. which entails explaining the company's performance to securities analysts and institutional investors.

46143 ■ *"Digital Power Management and the PMBus"* in *Canadian Electronics (Vol. 23, June-July 2008, No. 4, pp. 8)*
Ed: Torbjorn Hohnberg. **Description:** PMBus is an interface that can be applied to a variety of devices including power management devices. Information on digital power management products using this interface are also provided.

46144 ■ *"Digital Printing Walks the Plank"* in *American Printer (Vol. 128, August 1, 2011, No. 8)*
Pub: Penton Media Inc.
Description: Digital print manufacturing is discussed.

46145 ■ *"Dipping Into a New Market: Independent Can Invests in Olive Oil Tins as Demand Grows"* in *Baltimore Business Journal (Vol. 30, May 11, 2012, No. 1, pp. 1)*
Pub: American City Business Journals, Inc.
Contact: Whitney Shaw, President
Ed: Gary Haber. **Released:** May 11, 2012. **Description:** Independent Can Company purchased a production line fro Israel which costs between $600,000 and $700,000 and reassembled it at the manufacturing plant in Belcamp, Maryland. The new production line can manufacture 9 million olive oil tins annually in sizes from 2.5 liters to 1 gallon and is expected to start operation by the end of May 2012.

46146 ■ *"Discount Beers Take Fizz Out Of Molson"* in *Globe & Mail (February 10, 2006, pp. B3)*
Ed: Omar El Akkad. **Description:** The reasons behind the decline in profits by 60 percent for Molson Coors Brewing Co., during fourth quarter 2005, are presented.

46147 ■ *"Does America Really Need Manufacturing? Yes, When Production Is Closely Tied to Innovation"* in *Harvard Business Review (Vol. 90, March 2012, No. 3, pp. 94)*
Pub: Harvard Business Review Press
Contact: Peter E. Walsh, Director
Ed: Gary P. Pisano, Willy C. Shih. **Released:** March 2012. **Description:** A framework is presented for assessing when manufacturing and research and development are crucial to innovation and therefore should be kept in close proximity to each other. The framework denotes the degree to which product design data can be separated from manufacturing, and the opportunities to improve manufacturing.

46148 ■ *"The Dominance of Doubt"* in *Barron's (Vol. 89, July 13, 2009, No. 28, pp. M3)*
Pub: Dow Jones & Co., Inc.
Contact: Clare Hart, President
Ed: Jay Palmer. **Description:** Five straight down days leading up to July 10, 2009 in the U.S. stock market reminds one strategist of 1982 when there was a feeling that things could never be the same again. One analyst is bullish on the stocks of Apple Inc. and sees the stocks rising to at least 180 in 12 months. The prospects of the shares of GM and Ford are also discussed.

46149 ■ *"The Doomsday Scenario"* in *Conde Nast Portfolio (Vol. 2, June 2008, No. 6, pp. 91)*
Ed: Jeffrey Rothfeder. **Description:** Detroit and the U.S. auto industry are discussed as well as the ramifications of the demise of this manufacturing base. Similarities and differences between the downfall of the U.S. steel business and the impact it had on Pittsburg, Pennsylvania is also discussed.

46150 ■ *"Dow Champions Innovative Energy Solutions for Auto Industry at NAIAS"* in *Business of Global Warming (January 25, 2010, pp. 7)*
Description: This year's North American International Auto Show in Detroit will host the 'Electric Avenue' exhibit sponsored by the Dow Chemical Company. The display will showcase the latest in innovative energy solutions from Dow as well as electric vehicles and the technology supporting them. This marks the first time a non-automotive manufacturer is part of the main floor of the show.

46151 ■ *"Dreyer's Grand Ice Cream"* in *Ice Cream Reporter (Vol. 23, September 20, 2010, No. 10, pp. 8)*
Description: Dreyer's Grand Ice Cream will add one hundred new manufacturing jobs at its plant in Laurel, Maryland and another 65 new hires before the end of 2010 and another 35 in 2011.

46152 ■ *"Drilling Deep and Flying High"* in *Barron's* (Vol. 88, June 30, 2008, No. 26, pp. 34)

Pub: Dow Jones & Co., Inc.

Contact: Clare Hart, President

Ed: Kenneth Rapoza. **Description:** Shares of Petrobras could rise another 25 percent if the three deepwater wells that the company has found proves as lucrative as some expect. Petrobras will become an oil giant if the reserves are proven.

46153 ■ *"Drop in the Bucket Makes a lot of Waves"* in *Globe & Mail* (March 22, 2007, pp. B1)

Pub: CTVglobemedia Publishing Inc.

Ed: Greg Keenan. **Description:** The concern of several auto makers in Canada over the impact of providing heavy rebates to customers buying energy-efficient cars is discussed.

46154 ■ *"Duro Bag to Expand, Add 130 Jobs"* in *Business Courier* (Vol. 27, August 6, 2010, No. 14, pp. 1)

Pub: Business Courier

Ed: Jon Newberry. **Description:** Duro Bag Manufacturing Company will expand capacity at its Florence, Kentucky plant and will add around 130 jobs over the next few years. The state of Kentucky has given preliminary approval for up to $1 million in tax incentives over 10 years, tied to the creation of new jobs. The company's investment will include new production and packaging equipment and building improvements.

46155 ■ *"The Dynamic DUO"* in *Canadian Electronics* (Vol. 23, February 2008, No. 1, pp. 24)

Description: Citronics Corporation not only aims to proved a good working environment for its employees, it also values the opinions of its personnel. Citronics had its employees test different workbenches before finally purchasing thirty-five of Lista's Align adjustable height workstation, which combines flexibility with aesthetics. The design of the Alin workbench is described.

46156 ■ *"Dynamic Duo: Payouts Rise at General Dynamics, Steel Dynamics"* in *Barron's* (Vol. 88, March 10, 2008, No. 10, pp. 45)

Pub: Dow Jones & Co., Inc.

Contact: Clare Hart, President

Ed: Shirley A. Lazo. **Description:** General Dynamics, the world's sixth-largest military contractor, raised its dividend payout by 20.7 percent from 29 cents to 35 cents a share. Steel Dynamics, producer of structural steel and steel bar products, declared a 2-for-1 stock split and raised its quarterly dividend by 33 percent to a split-adjusted 10 cents a share.

46157 ■ *"Early Spring Halts Drilling Season"* in *Globe & Mail* (March 14, 2007, pp. B14)

Pub: CTVglobemedia Publishing Inc.

Ed: Norval Scott. **Description:** Decreased petroleum productivity in Canadian oil drilling rigs due to early spring season in western regions is discussed.

46158 ■ *"Eclipse to Hire 50 for Airp;ort Hangar"* In *Business Review, Albany New York* (Vol. 34, November 9, 2007, No. 32, pp. 3)

Pub: American City Business Journals, Inc.

Ed: Robin K. Cooper. **Description:** Eclipse Aviation, a jet manufacturer will hire fifty workers who will operate its new maintenance hangar at Albany International Airport. The company was expected to hire around twenty-five employees after it announced its plan to open one of the seven U.S. Factory Service Centers in 2005. Denise Zieske, the airport Economic Development Manager, expects the hangar construction to be completed by December 2007.

46159 ■ *"EcoDevo Leaders Chasing More Than Repair Shops"* in *San Antonio Business Journal* (Vol. 28, April 11, 2014, No. 9, pp. 6)

Pub: American City Business Journals

Released: April 11, 2014. **Description:** San Antonio, Texas economic development officials have been trying to lure an aircraft manufacturing operation to Port

San Antonio. The city has been among the top 10 finalists in Boeing Company's search for sites to build its 777X jetliner. The impact of Texas' right-to-work rules and the port facilities in the city and the lure to attract Boeing are discussed.

46160 ■ *"Effective Use of Field Time"* in *Agency Sales Magazine* (Vol. 39, July 2009, No. 7, pp. 40)

Description: Sales representatives need to consider the value of field visits to themselves and their customers ahead of time. Several anecdotes about field visits from the perspective of manufacturers and sale representatives are presented.

46161 ■ *"Electrolux Feeding Economy: Contracts for Local Firms at $64 Million; Supplier Bids Up Next"* in *Memphis Business Journal* (Vol. 34, June 22, 2012, No. 10, pp. 1)

Pub: American City Business Journal

Ed: Michael Sheffield. **Description:** Electrolux Home Products Inc. has awarded almost $64 million of its construction contracts to local companies in Memphis, Tennessee while planning the search for suppliers for its 700,000 square foot manufacturing facility. The company aims to complete the facility by the end of 2012.

46162 ■ *"Electrolux Nears Product Testing"* in *Memphis Business Journal* (Vol. 34, September 21, 2012, No. 23, pp. 1)

Pub: American City Business Journal

Ed: Michael Sheffield. **Description:** Electrolux Home Products Inc.'s new manufacturing facility is expected to be ready for use by the end of September 2012. The company will start producing 'pilot' products once the testing of manufacturing systems is completed. Electrolux will also hire 200 employees who will assemble the first products ready for shipmenht in the first quarter of 2013.

46163 ■ *"Electronics Assembly"* in *Canadian Electronics* (Vol. 23, February 2008, No. 1, pp. 12)

Description: I&J Fisnar Inc. has launched a new system of bench top dispensing robots while Vitronics Soltec and KIC have introduced a new reflow soldering machine. Teknek, on the other hand, has announced a new product, called the CM10, which an be used in cleaning large format substrates. Other new products and their description are presented.

46164 ■ *"EnCana Axes Spending on Gas Wells"* in *Globe & Mail* (February 16, 2006, pp. B1)

Ed: Dave Ebner. **Description:** The reasons behind EnCana Corp.'s cost spending measures by $300 million on natural gas wells are presented. The company projects 2 percent cut in gas and oil sales for 2006.

46165 ■ *"Encore Container, Manufacturer of Plastic Drums and IBC Totes, Leads the Way in Environmental Sustainability"* in *Ecology, Environment & Conservation Business* (January 25, 2014, pp. 33)

Pub: NewsRX

Contact: Susan E. Hasty, Publisher

Released: January 25, 2014. **Description:** Encore Container, a leading reconditioner of IBC totes and manufacturer and reconditioner of plastic drums describes its efforts to promote environmental sustainability within the company: container reconditioning, plastic and steel recycling, water conservation and waste minimization.

46166 ■ *"The End of the Line for Line Extensions?"* in *Advertising Age* (Vol. 79, July 7, 2008, No. 26, pp. 3)

Pub: Crain Communications Inc.

Contact: Rance Crain, President

Ed: Jack Neff. **Description:** After years of double-digit growth, some of the most heavily extended personal-care products have slowed substantially or even declined in the U.S. Unilever's Dove and P&G's Pantene and Olay are two such brands that have been affected. Statistical data included.

46167 ■ *"Energy Boom Spurring Manufacturing Growth"* in *Pittsburgh Business Times* (Vol. 33, May 2, 2014, No. 42, pp. 7)

Pub: American City Business Journals

Released: May 2, 2014. **Description:** The manufacturing and energy technology sectors both showed strong growth, according to the Pittsburgh Technology Council in Pennsylvania. Data shows that the sectors added about 7,000 jobs as a result of the growth in the Marcellus Shale from 2010 to 2012.

46168 ■ *"Energy Firms Face Stricter Definitions"* in *Globe & Mail* (March 26, 2007, pp. B3)

Pub: CTVglobemedia Publishing Inc.

Ed: David Ebner. **Description:** The Alberta Securities Commission has imposed strict securities regulations on oil and gas industries. Energy industries will have to submit revenue details to stake holders.

46169 ■ *"Energy Outfitter Wings Into Houston"* in *Houston Business Journal* (Vol. 40, December 4, 2009, No. 30, pp. 2A)

Pub: American City Business Journals

Ed: Ford Gunter. **Description:** Red Wing Shoe Company Inc. has launched its personal protective equipment (PPE) line for oil and gas industry crewmen in North America by opening a 13,000 square foot distribution hub in Houston, Texas. The Houston facility was created to supply directly the oil and gas industry and to carry inventory for select distributors.

46170 ■ *"Energy Slide Slows 4th-Quarter Profits"* in *Globe & Mail* (April 13, 2007, pp. B9)

Ed: Angela Barnes. **Description:** The decrease in the fourth quarter profits of several companies across various industries in Canada, including mining and manufacturing, due to global decrease in oil prices, is discussed.

46171 ■ *"Enforcer In Fantasyland"* in *Crain's New York Business* (Vol. 24, February 25, 2008, No. 8, pp. 10)

Ed: Hilary Potkewitz. **Description:** Patent law, particularly in the toy and game industry, is recession-proof according to Barry Negrin, partner at Pryor Cashman. Negrin co-founded his patent practice group. Despite massive recalls of toys and the concern over toxic toys, legal measures are in place in this industry.

46172 ■ *"Engineering Services Supplier Launches 'Robotic Renaissance'"* in *Modern Machine Shop* (Vol. 84, September 2011, No. 4, pp. 46)

Pub: Gardner Business Media, Inc.

Contact: Richard G. Kline, President

E-mail: rkline@gardnerweb.com

Description: Profile of Applied Manufacturing Technologies (AMT) new hiring initiative that supports continuing growth in the robotics industry. AMT is located in Orion, Michigan and supplies factory automation design, engineering and process consulting services.

46173 ■ *"Eoplly Solar Modules Power Alpha Energy's 280kw Solar Project in the Silicon Valley"* in *Internet Wire* (October 1, 2012)

Released: October 1, 2012. **Description:** Eoplly New Energy Technology Company, based in California, reported the completion of a 280kW roof-top solar PV system of the Advanced Design and Manufacuring firm located in Santa Clara. Eoplly is a designer and manufacturer of solar products.

46174 ■ *"Evaluate Your Process and Do It Better"* in *Modern Machine Shop* (Vol. 84, October 2011, No. 5, pp. 34)

Pub: Gardner Business Media, Inc.

Contact: Richard G. Kline, President

E-mail: rkline@gardnerweb.com

Ed: Wayne S. Chaneski. **Description:** In order to be more competitive, many machine shops owners are continually looking at their processes and procedures in order to be more competitive.

46175 ■ *"Event Stresses Cross-Border Cooperation"* in *Crain's Detroit Business (Vol. 24, March 30, 2008, No. 13, pp. 5)*
Pub: Crain Communications Inc.
Contact: Rance E. Crain, President
Ed: Chad Halcom. **Description:** According to John Austin, a senior fellow of The Brookings Institution, open immigration policies, better transportation and trade across the border and a cleanup of the Great Lakes will bring economic resurgence to Midwestern states and Canadian provinces with manufacturing economies.

46176 ■ *"Everyone Has a Story Inspired by Chevrolet"* in *Automotive News (Vol. 86, October 31, 2011, No. 6488, pp. S003)*
Pub: Crain Communications Inc.
Contact: Rance E. Crain, President
Ed: Keith E. Crain. **Description:** Besides being a great ad slogan, 'Baseball, Hot Dogs, Apple Pie and Chevrolet', the brand conjures up memories for most everyone in our society. Louis Chevrolet had a reputation as a race car driver and lent his name to the car that has endured for 100 years.

46177 ■ *"Executive Decision: Damn the Profit Margins, Sleeman Declares War on Buck-a-Beer Foes"* in *Globe & Mail (January 28, 2006, pp. B3)*
Ed: Andy Hoffman. **Description:** The cost savings plans of chief executive officer John Sleeman of Slee-man Breweries Ltd. are presented.

46178 ■ *"Executive Decision: Just What the Doctor Ordered"* in *Globe & Mail (February 11, 2006, pp. B3)*
Ed: Leonard Zehr. **Description:** The leadership ability of chief executive William Hunter of Angiotech Pharmaceuticals Inc., who acquired American Medical Instruments Holdings Inc. for $785 million, is discussed.

46179 ■ *"Executive Decision: Lead a Double Life for Geac's Sake"* in *Globe & Mail (January 21, 2006, pp. B4)*
Ed: Simon Avery. **Description:** The details of growth of Geac Computer Corporation Ltd., under chief executive officer Charles Jones, are presented.

46180 ■ *"Executive Interview: Arturo Elias"* in *Canadian Business (Vol. 80, January 29, 2007, No. 3, pp. 16)*
Ed: Thomas Watson. **Description:** The views of Arturo Elias, the president of General Motors Canada Limited, on the prospects of the growth of the company revenues during the year 2007 are presented.

46181 ■ *"Executive Session: Mike Bergey, Bergey Windpower"* in *Journal Record (June 1, 2012)*
Pub: Dolan Media Inc.
Ed: Sarah Terry-Cobo. **Description:** Cofounder and president of Bergey Windpower located in Norman, Oklahoma, is working to keep manufacturing going in the US. His firm manufactures small wind turbines for homes and businesses. He addresses aggressive government programs in the European Union that are increasing sales in the United Kingdom and other countries in the region. California, New York, Ohio and Vermont are the strongest markets in the United States.

46182 ■ *"Executive of the Year: Sullivan Led Bucyrus through Unforgettable Year"* in *Business Journal-Milwaukee (Vol. 28, December 17, 2010, No. 11, pp. A1)*
Pub: Milwaukee Business Journal
Ed: Rich Rovito. **Description:** Bucyrus International's president and CEO, Tim Sullivan, was chosen as Milwaukee, Wisconsin's Executive of the Year for 2010. Sullivan led Bucyrus through a year of dramatic change which started with the acquisition of the mining business of Terex Corporation and culminating with a deal to sell Caterpillar Inc.

46183 ■ *"Expanding Middleby's Food Processing Biz"* in *Crain's Chicago Business (Vol. 31, April 21, 2008, No. 16, pp. 6)*
Pub: Crain Communications Inc.
Contact: Todd Johnson, Publisher
Ed: David Sterrett. **Description:** Profile of the executive vice-president of the food processing company, Middleby Corp, whose business plan is to develop new products, begin looking for acquisitions and simplify operations in order to expand the firm.

46184 ■ *"Experts Strive to Educate on Proper Pet Diets"* in *Pet Product News (Vol. 64, November 2010, No. 11, pp. 40)*
Pub: Bowtie Inc.
Ed: John Hustace Walker. **Description:** Pet supply manufacturers have been bundling small mammal food and treats with educational sources to help retailers avoid customer misinformation. This action has been motivated by the customer's quest to seek proper nutritional advice for their small mammal pets.

46185 ■ *"Extra Rehab Time Boosts M-B's Off-Lease Profits"* in *Automotive News (Vol. 86, October 31, 2011, No. 6488, pp. 22)*
Pub: Crain Communications Inc.
Contact: Rance E. Crain, President
Ed: Arlena Sawyers. **Description:** Mercedes-Benz Financial Services USA is holding on to off-lease vehicles in order to recondition them and the move is boosting profits for the company.

46186 ■ *"Exxon Braving the Danger Zones"* in *Globe & Mail (March 8, 2007, pp. B1)*
Ed: Shawn McCarthy. **Description:** The plans of Exxon Mobil Corp. to increase its revenues through the expansion of its operations in Asia, Africa, and the Middle East are discussed.

46187 ■ *"Factory Girls: From Village to City in a Changing China"*
Pub: Spiegel & Grau
Ed: Leslie T. Chang. **Released:** August 04, 2009. **Price:** $16, paperback. **Description:** Young women who flee the rural villages in China find exhausting work and social mobility working in factories. **Availability:** Print.

46188 ■ *"Fair Play? China Cheats, Carney Talks and Rankin Walks; Here's the Latest"* in *Canadian Business (Vol. 81, March 17, 2008, No. 4)*
Pub: Rogers Media Inc.
Contact: Tony Viner, President
Description: Discusses the World Trade Organization which says that China is breaking trade rules by taxing imports of auto parts at the same rate as foreign-made finished cars. Mark Carney first speech as the governor of the Bank of Canada made economists suspect a rate cut on overnight loans. Andre Rankin was ordered by the Ontario Securities Commission to pay $250,000 in investigation costs.

46189 ■ *"Familiar Fun"* in *Crain's Cleveland Business (Vol. 28, October 22, 2007, No. 42, pp. 3)*
Ed: John Booth. **Description:** Marketing for the 2007 holiday season has toy retailers focusing on American-made products because of recent recalls of toys produced in China that do not meet U.S. safety standards.

46190 ■ *"Feet on the Street: Reps Are Ready to Hit the Ground Running"* in *Agency Sales Magazine (Vol. 39, July 2009, No. 7, pp. 12)*
Ed: Jack Foster. **Description:** One of the major benefits to manufacturers in working with sales representatives is the concept of synergistic selling where the rep shows his mettle. The rep of today is a solution provider that anticipates and meets the customer's needs.

46191 ■ *"Fight Against Fake"* in *The Business Journal-Portland (Vol. 25, July 18, 2008, No. 19, pp. 1)*
Ed: Erik Siemers. **Description:** Companies, such as Columbia Sportswear Co. and Nike Inc., are fighting the counterfeiting of their sportswear and footwear products through the legal process of coordinating

with law enforcement agencies to raid factories. Most of the counterfeiting factories are in China and India. Other details on the issue are discussed.

46192 ■ *"Finalist: BlackEagle Partners L.L.C."* in *Crain's Detroit Business (Vol. 24, March 24, 2008, No. 12, pp. 12)*
Pub: Crain Communications Inc.
Contact: Rance E. Crain, President
Ed: Brent Snavely. **Description:** Overview of private-equity firm, BlackEagle Partners L.L.C., an upstart that acquired Rockford Products Corp. in order to improve the performance of the company who does business with several major tier-one automotive suppliers; Rockford manufactures highly engineered chassis and suspension components for automakers and the automotive aftermarket.

46193 ■ *"Finalist: Private Company, $100M-$1B"* in *Crain's Detroit Business (Vol. 25, June 22, 2009, No. 25)*
Pub: Crain Communications Inc. - Detroit
Contact: Keith Crain, Chairman
Ed: Chad Halcom. **Description:** Profile of U.S. Far-athane Corporation, the Sterling Heights, Michigan-based automotive plastic components maker. The company's CFO discusses ways they are coping with the cutbacks at major automobile factories.

46194 ■ *"Financing for NNSA Plant Is a Work in Progress"* in *The Business Journal-Serving Metropolitan Kansas City (October 24, 2008)*
Ed: Rob Roberts. **Description:** The Kansas City Council approved a development plan for a $500 million nuclear weapons parts plant in south Kansas City. The US Congress approved a $59 million annual lease payment to the plant's developer. Financing for the construction of the plant remains in question as the plant's developers have to shoulder construction costs.

46195 ■ *"Firms Upbeat About Future, Survey Shows"* in *Globe & Mail (January 17, 2006, pp. B4)*
Ed: Heather Scoffield. **Description:** The issue of labor shortage for manufacturing sector, in Canada, is discussed. The survey results of Bank of Canada are presented.

46196 ■ *"First Impressions of Robotic Farming Systems"* in *Farm Industry News (September 30, 2011)*
Pub: Penton Business Media Inc.
Contact: David Kieselstein, Chief Executive Officer
Ed: Jodie Wehrspann. **Description:** Farm Science Review featured tillage tools and land rollers, including John Deere's GPS system where a cart tractor is automatically controlled as well as a new line of Kinze's carts and a video of their robotic system for a driver-less cart tractor.

46197 ■ *"First Sustainability Standard for Household Portable and Floor Care Appliances Developed to Identify Environmentally Responsible Products"* in *Ecology, Environment & Conservation Business (September 13, 2014, pp. 39)*
Pub: NewsRX
Contact: Susan E. Hasty, Publisher
Released: September 13, 2014. **Description:** the Association of Home Appliance Manufacturers (AHAM), CSA Group, and the UL Environment released the AHAM 7002-2014/CSA SPE-7002-14/UL 7002, Sustainability Standard for Household Portable and Floor Care Appliances. This is the first voluntary sustainability standards for these appliances and is the third in a unit of product sustainability standards under development by the group. These standards are intended for use by manufacturers, governments, retailers, and others to identify products conforming to these standards in six key areas: materials, manufacturing and operations, energy consumption during use, end-of-life, consumables, and innovation.

46198 ■ *"First Suzlon S97 Turbines Arrive in North America for Installation"* in *PR*

Newswire (September 28, 2011)
Pub: UBM L.L.C.
Contact: Kate Spellman, President
E-mail: kspellman@cmp.com
Description: Suzlon Energy Ltd., the world's fifth largest manufacturer of wind turbines, will install its first S97 turbine at the Amherst Wind Farm Project. These turbines will be installed on 90-meter hub height towers and at full capacity, will generate enough electricity to power over 10,000 Canadian homes.

46199 ■ *"Five Reasons Why the Gap Fell Out of Fashion" in Globe & Mail (January 27, 2007, pp. B4)*
Ed: Keith McArthur. **Description:** The five major market trends that have caused the decline of fashion clothing retailer Gap Inc.'s sales are discussed. The shift in brand, workplace fashion culture, competition, demographics, and consumer preferences have lead to the Gap's brand identity.

46200 ■ *"Flying High?" in Canadian Business (Vol. 80, April 9, 2007, No. 8, pp. 42)*
Ed: Thomas Watson. **Description:** The increase in Bombardier Inc.'s income by 30 percent to $112 million and increase in its share prices are discussed. The caution of analysts about its accounting methods that may adversely hit the company in future, too is discussed.

46201 ■ *"Foods for Thought" in Pet Product News (Vol. 64, December 2010, No. 12, pp. 16)*
Pub: Bowtie Inc.
Ed: Maddy Heleine. **Description:** Manufacturers have been focused at developing species-specific fish foods due to consumer tendency to assess the benefits of the food they feed their fish. As retailers stock species-specific fish foods, manufacturers have provided in-store items and strategies to assist in efficiently selling these food products. Trends in fish food packaging and ingredients are also discussed.

46202 ■ *"For Baxter, A Lingering PR Problem" in Crain's Chicago Business (April 21, 2008)*
Pub: Crain Communications Inc.
Contact: Todd Johnson, Publisher
Ed: Mike Colias. **Description:** Baxter International Inc.'s recall of the blood-thinning medication heparin has exposed the company to costly litigation and put the perils of overseas drug manufacturing in the spotlight. Wall Street investors predict that an indefinite halt in production of the drug should not hurt the company's bottom line since heparin represents a tiny sliver of the business. Since Baxter began recalling the drug in January its shares have continued to outpace most other medical stocks.

46203 ■ *"Ford Canada's Edsel of a Year: Revenue Plummets 24 Percent in '05" in Globe & Mail (February 2, 2006, pp. B1)*
Ed: Greg Keenan. **Description:** Ford Motor Company of Canada Ltd. posted 24% decline in revenues for 2005. The drop in earnings is attributed to plant shutdown in Oaksville, Canada.

46204 ■ *"Ford, Chrysler Dinged as Little Cars Rule Road" in Globe & Mail (March 2, 2007, pp. B3)*
Ed: Greg Keenan. **Description:** The Ford Motor Co. and the Chrysler Group posted a decline in automobile sales in the first two months of 2007. The sales statistics of other automobile companies in Canada are also presented.

46205 ■ *"Ford: Down, Not Out, and Still a Buy" in Barron's (Vol. 92, July 23, 2012, No. 30, pp. 14)*
Pub: Dow Jones & Co., Inc.
Contact: Clare Hart, President
Ed: Vito J. Racanelli. **Released:** July 23, 2012. **Description:** Stocks of Ford Motor Company could gain value as the company continues to improve its finances despite fears of slower global economic growth. The company's stock prices could double from $9.35 per share within three years.

46206 ■ *"Ford Fix Requires 'Painful' Remedy" in Globe & Mail (January 9, 2006, pp. B1)*
Pub: CTVglobemedia Publishing Inc.
Ed: Greg Keenan. **Description:** The plans of Ford Motor Co. to streamline Canadian operations are presented.

46207 ■ *"Ford's $12.7 Billion Loss Signals End of an Era" in Globe & Mail (January 26, 2007, pp. B1)*
Ed: Greg Keenan. **Description:** The loss of $12.7 billion incurred by Ford Motors Co., and its decision to close down several of its plants, cut thousands of jobs and focus on passenger cars, is discussed.

46208 ■ *"Formaspace Finds a Bigger Home" in Austin Business JournalInc. (Vol. 29, December 4, 2009, No. 39, pp. 1)*
Pub: American City Business Journals
Ed: Kate Harrington. **Description:** Formaspace Technical Furniture has signed a lease for 56,700 square feet in Harris Ridge Business Center at Northeast Austin, Texas, which represents one of the area's largest leases for 2009. The new lease enables Formaspace to hire new employees, invest in new equipment, and take advantage of a taxing designation created for manufacturers.

46209 ■ *"Former Chrysler Dealers Build New Business Model" in Crain's Detroit Business (Vol. 25, June 22, 2009, No. 25, pp. 3)*
Pub: Crain Communications Inc. - Detroit
Contact: Keith Crain, Chairman
Ed: Daniel Fuggan. **Description:** Joe Ricci is one of 14 Detroit area dealerships whose franchises have been terminated. Ricci and other Chrysler dealers in the area are starting new businesses or switching to new franchices. Ricci's All American Buyer's Service will be located in Dearborn and will sell only used cars.

46210 ■ *"Former P&G Soap Plant Looks to Clean Up" in Business Courier (Vol. 26, January 15, 2010, No. 39, pp. 1)*
Pub: American City Business Journals, Inc.
Contact: Whitney Shaw, President
Ed: Jon Newberry. **Description:** Cincinnati-based St. Bernard Soap Company plans to focus on new services such as product development and logistics and to continue growth and put excess capacity to work. The unit of Ontario, Canada-based Trillium Health Care Products Inc. is the largest contract manufacturer of bar soap in North America.

46211 ■ *"Fraser and Neave Acquires King's Creameries" in Ice Cream Reporter (Vol. 23, November 20, 2010, No. 12, pp. 1)*
Description: Fraser and Neave Ltd., a Singapore-based consumer products marketer, has entered a conditional agreement to acquire all outstanding shares of King's Creameries, the leading manufacturer and distributor of frozen desserts.

46212 ■ *"Frito Lay Plans to Spice Up Life With New Chips" in Globe & Mail (February 21, 2006, pp. B3)*
Ed: Andy Hoffman. **Description:** The reasons behind the launch of potato chips by Frito Lay Canada Inc., a subsidiary of PepsiCo. Inc., are presented.

46213 ■ *"From American Icon to Global Juggernaut" in Automotive News (Vol. 86, October 31, 2011, No. 6488, pp. S003)*
Pub: Crain Communications Inc.
Contact: Rance E. Crain, President
Ed: Peter Brown. **Description:** Chevrolet celebrates its 100th Anniversary. The brand revolutionized its market with affordable cars that bring technology to the masses. Chevys have been sold in 140 countries and the company is responding to a broader market.

46214 ■ *"Fromm Family Foods Converts Old Feed Mill Into Factory for Gourmet Pet Food" in Wisconsin State Journal (August 3, 2011)*
Pub: Capital Newspapers
Ed: Barry Adams. **Description:** Fromm Family Foods, a gourmet cat and dog food company spent $10 million to convert an old feed mill into a pet food

manufacturing facility. The owner forecasts doubling or tripling its production of 600 tons of feed per week in about five years.

46215 ■ *"Fuel King: The Most Fuel-Efficient Tractor of the Decade is the John Deere 8295R" in Farm Industry News (November 10, 2011)*
Pub: Penton Business Media Inc.
Contact: David Kieselstein, Chief Executive Officer
Description: Farm Industry News compiled a list of the most fuel-efficient tractors with help from the Nebraska Tractor Test Lab, with the John Deere 8295R PTO winner of the most fuel-efficient tractor of the decade.

46216 ■ *"Fuel for Thought" in Canadian Business (Vol. 81, April 14, 2008, No. 6, pp. 18)*
Pub: Rogers Media Inc.
Contact: Tony Viner, President
Ed: John Gray. **Description:** Discusses a web poll of 133 CEOs and other business leaders that shows that they predict oil prices to increase to US $113 per barrel over the 2008 to 2010 timeframe. Most of the respondents did not favor cutting gas taxes but this group wants the government to cut taxes on fuel-efficient vehicles and increase subsidies to local transit systems.

46217 ■ *"Full-Court Press for Apple" in Barron's (Vol. 88, March 24, 2008, No. 12, pp. 47)*
Pub: Dow Jones & Co., Inc.
Contact: Clare Hart, President
Ed: Mark Veverka. **Description:** Apple Inc. is facing more intellectual property lawsuits in 2008, with 30 patent lawsuits filed compared to 15 in 2007 and nine in 2006. The lawsuits, which involve products such as the iPod and the iPhone, present some concern for Apple's shareholders.

46218 ■ *"Funky Footwear: Walk This Way" in Barron's (Vol. 90, August 23, 2010, No. 34, pp. 13)*
Pub: Barron's Editorial & Corporate Headquarters
Ed: Christopher C. Williams. **Description:** Crocs and Skechers are selling very popular shoes and sales show no signs of winding down. The shares of both companies are attractively prices.

46219 ■ *"Furniture Making May Come Back--Literally" in Business North Carolina (Vol. 28, March 2008, No. 3, pp. 32)*
Pub: Business North Carolina
Description: Due to the weak U.S. dollar and the fact that lumber processors never left the country, foreign furniture manufacturers are becoming interested in moving manufacturing plants to the U.S.

46220 ■ *"Future Autoworkers will Need Broader Skills" in Crain's Detroit Business (Vol. 25, June 8, 2009, No. 23, pp. 13)*
Pub: Crain Communications Inc. - Detroit
Contact: Keith Crain, Chairman
Ed: Ryan Beene. **Description:** Auto industry observers report that new workers in the industry will need advanced skills and educational backgrounds in engineering and technical fields because jobs in the factories will become more technology-based and multidisciplinary.

46221 ■ *"The Game of Operation" in Crain's Chicago Business (Vol. 31, April 28, 2008, No. 17, pp. 26)*
Pub: Crain Communications Inc.
Contact: Todd Johnson, Publisher
Ed: Samantha Stainburn. **Description:** Revenue at Medline Industries Inc., a manufacturer of medical products, has risen 12 percent a year since 1976, reaching $2.81 billion last year. Growth at the company is due to new and increasingly sophisticated operations by surgeons which brings about the need for more specialized tools.

46222 ■ *"Gamesa Office Closing Part of Political Reality" in Pittsburgh Business*

Times (Vol. 33, February 7, 2014, No. 30, pp. 6)

Pub: American City Business Journals

Released: February 7, 2014. **Description:** Due to political uncertainty surrounding the production tax credit for wind energy and changes in the supply chain needs in the North America wind market, a Spanish wind blade maker Gamesa will be shutting down its manufacturing unit in Ebesnburg March 31, 2014. The general counsel for Gamesa, Frank Fuselier, stated that optimizing the company's supply chain will help them survive in a market devoid of a production tax credit.

46223 ■ *"Gaming Infrastructure Paves Ready Path for Manufacturing" in Memphis Business Journal (No. 35, February 14, 2014, No. 45, pp. 4)*

Pub: American City Business Journals

Released: February 14, 2014. **Description:** The city of Tunica, Mississippi is trying to expand its reputation as a gaming destination into manufacturing in an effort seek new opportunities for economic development and revenue. German crankshaft manufacturer, Feurer Powertrain, is building a $140 million manufacturing facility that will open in late 2014.

46224 ■ *"Gas Supplies Low Heading Into Summer Season" in Globe & Mail (April 13, 2007, pp. B6)*

Ed: Shawn McCarthy. **Description:** The decrease in the supply of gas due to maintenance problems at refineries in the United States and Canada is discussed.

46225 ■ *"Gatorade Loses Its Competitive Edge" in Crain's Chicago Business (April 28, 2008)*

Pub: Crain Communications Inc.

Contact: Todd Johnson, Publisher

Ed: Natalie Zmuda. **Description:** According to beverage-marketing experts, Gatorade is losing some of its market share to aggressive new rivals who are appealing to younger consumers.

46226 ■ *"GE Looking to Extend Hot Streak" in Business Courier (Vol. 24, January 24, 2008, No. 42, pp. 1)*

Pub: American City Business Journals, Inc.

Contact: Whitney Shaw, President

Ed: Jon Newberry. **Description:** GE Aviation has enjoyed strong revenues and sales due to increase aircraft engine orders. It has an engine backlog order of $19 million as of the end of 2007. Data on the aviation company's revenues, operating profit and total engine orders for the year 2004 to 2007 are presented.

46227 ■ *"GE Milestone: 1,000th Wind Turbine Installed in Canada" in CNW Group (October 4, 2011)*

Pub: CNW Group Ltd.

Contact: Carolyn McGill-Davidson, President

Description: GE installed its 1,000th wind turbine in Canada at Cartier Wind Energy's Gros Morne project in the Gaspesie Region of Quebec, Canada. As Canada continues to expand its use of wind energy, GE plans to have over 1,100 wind turbines installed in the nation by the end of 2011.

46228 ■ *"General Electric Touts Going Green for Business Fleet Services" in America's Intelligence Wire (June 1, 2012)*

Pub: Financial Times Ltd.

Contact: John Ridding, Chief Executive Officer

Released: June 1, 2012. **Description:** General Capital Fleet Services if featuring alternative-fuel vehicles in Eden Prairie for its corporate customers. GE Capital is the world's largest fleet management service and is offering its customers the first of its kind service that allows corporate lease customers to test drive alternative fuel cars from 20 different manufacturers.

46229 ■ *"General Motors Can't Kick Incentives-But They Work" in Advertising Age (Vol. 79, July 7, 2008, No. 26, pp. 3)*

Pub: Crain Communications Inc.

Contact: Rance Crain, President

Ed: Jean Halliday. **Description:** General Motors Corp. was able to maintain their market share just as Toyota Motor Corp. was beginning to pass the manufacturer; GM lured in customers with a sales incentive that they heavily advertised and subsequently helped build demand; investors, however, were not impressed and GM shares were hammered to their lowest point in 50 years after analysts speculated the company might go bankrupt.

46230 ■ *"German Firm Ifm Electronic to Open Second Local Unit" in Philadelphia Business Journal (Vol. 28, July 20, 2012, No. 23, pp. 1)*

Pub: American City Business Journal

Description: German electronic control and sensor manufacturer, ifm electronic gmbh, has established ifm provor USA in January 2012, its second subsidiary in Exton, Pennsylvania after ifm efector Inc. Ifm prover will relocate in July 2012 to a new 36,000 square foot building that features a product development area and multiple laboraties for testing and quality control.

46231 ■ *"Getting Inventive With..Ed Spellman" in Crain's Cleveland Business (Vol. 28, October 22, 2007, No. 42, pp. 18)*

Pub: Crain Communications Inc.

Ed: Kimberly Bonvissuto. **Description:** Profile featuring Ed Spellman, a mechanical engineer who decided to quit his job at Invacare Corp., a medical equipment manufacturer and distributor, in order to devote his full attention to promoting his numerous inventions, including the DV-Grip, a vehicle mount for portable DVD players.

46232 ■ *"Getting the Word Out" in Modern Machine Shop (Vol. 84, September 2011, No. 4, pp. 16)*

Pub: Gardner Business Media, Inc.

Contact: Richard G. Kline, President

E-mail: rkline@gardnerweb.com

Ed: Derek Korn. **Description:** Many times machine shops create devices to streamline their own machining processes and find these devices can be used by other shops, thus developing a marketable product. Tips for this process are outlined.

46233 ■ *"Give 'Em a Boost" in Entrepreneur (Vol. 36, April 2008, No. 4, pp. 120)*

Pub: Entrepreneur Press

Contact: Perlman Neil, President

Ed: Kristen Henning. **Description:** Amir Levin of Kaboost Corp. markets a plastic booster system that attaches to the bottom of a regular chair and raises it. He thought of the idea of creating the product after seeing his young cousins refusing to sit in their booster seats. Levin started his company in 2006.

46234 ■ *"Global Pain: Alberta's Gain" in Canadian Business (Vol. 79, August 14, 2006, No. 16-17, pp. 60)*

Ed: Jeff Sanford. **Description:** Political problems and conflicts in oil-rich countries like Iran, Venezuela, and Russia among others, which have benefited the petroleum industry in Alberta, is discussed.

46235 ■ *"Global Steel Makers Circle Stelco" in Globe & Mail (April 19, 2007, pp. B3)*

Ed: Greg Keenan. **Description:** The details of the take over bids offered to Stelco Inc. are presented. Due to these bids the shares of Stelco Inc rose up to 70 percent.

46236 ■ *"The Globe Goes Birmingham" in Birmingham Business Journal (Vol. 31, July 4, 2014, No. 27, pp. 4)*

Pub: American City Business Journals, Inc.

Contact: Whitney Shaw, President

Released: July 4, 2014. **Description:** Foreign-owned firms are investing heavily in the city of Birmingham, Alabama and are creating jobs. The number of employees in Birmingham at foreign-owned firms continues to rise and it is a trend not expected to slow in the near future. This is helping the area economy that has struggled with job creation during the low economic times. Low taxes, lower wage

requirements and labor laws, and Birmingham's location and proximity to key manufacturers are factors attracting multi-million dollar investments in the city.

46237 ■ *"GM Axing Prices; Kerkorian Calls for Crisis Plan" in Globe & Mail (January 11, 2006, pp. B1)*

Ed: Greg Keenan. **Description:** The financial restructuring proposal of investor Kirk Kerkorian for General Motors Corp. is presented.

46238 ■ *"GM Canada Revved Up Over Camaro" in Globe & Mail (February 17, 2006, pp. B4)*

Ed: Greg Keenan. **Description:** General Manager of General Motors Canada is planning to start the production of company's muscle car Camaro in Canadian facility. The car was exhibited at Canadian International Auto Show held in Toronto.

46239 ■ *"GM-Chrysler Merger Could Cull Dealerships From Coast to Coast" in Globe & Mail (February 20, 2007, pp. B17)*

Ed: Greg Keenan. **Description:** General Motors Corp. is planning to acquire Chrysler Group. The challenges before the possible merger are presented.

46240 ■ *"GM-Chrysler Merger: Just a Bigger Mess?" in Globe & Mail (February 17, 2007, pp. B3)*

Ed: Barrie McKenna; Greg Keenan. **Description:** The General Motors Corp. is negotiating talks to acquire DaimlerChrysler AG's Chrysler Group. The five reasons for the possible merger of the companies are presented.

46241 ■ *"GM Flexes Muscles With New Camaro Concept" in Globe & Mail (January 10, 2006, pp. B15)*

Ed: Greg Keenan. **Description:** General Motors Corp. has displayed the new concept car Chevrolet Camaro at the North American International Auto Show in Detroit. The features of this automobile manufactured at the company's assembly plant in Quebec are discussed.

46242 ■ *"GM Is On the Road Again" in Canadian Business (Vol. 83, September 14, 2010, No. 15, pp. 14)*

Pub: Rogers Media Inc.

Contact: Tony Viner, President

Ed: Thomas Watson. **Description:** Former General Motors CEO Rick Wagoner has been credited for single-handedly putting the automaker back on track before he was forced to resign and GM was restructured by the government. GM earned $2.19 billion the first half of 2010 after losing more than $80 billion in the three years leading up to its failure. GM's comeback is discussed.

46243 ■ *"GM Releases 2010 Product Guide, Ends Production of Medium-Duty Trucks" in Contractor (Vol. 56, July 2009, No. 7, pp. 5)*

Pub: Intertec Publishing

Contact: John French, President

Ed: Candace Roulo. **Description:** General Motors will cease production of the Chevrolet Kodiak and GMC Topkick by July 31, 2009. Their 2010 Product Guide for the U.S. still has four remaining brands including the Buick, Cadillac, Chevrolet, and GMC.

46244 ■ *"GM Scores High Marks For Its Use of Solar Power" in Blade (September 13, 2012)*

Pub: McClatchy Tribune Information Services

Ed: Tyrel Linkhorn. **Description:** General Motors scores high among top corporate generators of solar power in the United States. The Solar Energy Industries Assocation ranked GM's on-site solar power generation capacity at number 13, making GM the first in the automotive sector. Details of GM's solar projects are outlined.

46245 ■ *"GM's Decision to Boot Dealer Prompts Sale" in Baltimore Business Journal (Vol. 27, November 6, 2009, No. 26, pp. 1)*

Pub: American City Business Journals

Ed: Daniel J. Sernovitz. **Description:** General Motors Corporation's (GM) decision to strip Baltimore's Anderson Automotive Group Inc. of its GM franchise has prompted the owner, Bruce Mortimer, to close the automotive dealership and sell the land to a developer. The new project could make way for new homes, a shopping center and supermarket.

46246 ■ "GM's Volt Woes Cast Shadow on E-Cars" in Wall Street Journal Eastern Edition (November 28, 2011, pp. B1)
Pub: Dow Jones & Co., Inc.
Contact: Clare Hart, President
Ed: Sharon Terlep. **Description:** The future of electric cars is darkened with the government investigation by the National Highway Traffic Safety Administration into General Motor Company's Chevy Volt after two instances of the car's battery packs catching fire during crash tests conducted by the Agency.

46247 ■ "Got Skills? Think Manufacturing" in Occupational Outlook Quarterly (Vol. 58, Summer 2014, No. 2, pp. 28)
Pub: Government Printing Office
Released: Summer 2014. **Description:** According to the U.S. Bureau of Labor Statistics, 264,000 job openings in manufacturing were reported in March 2014. Employers are finding it difficult to fill jobs for machinists and maintenance technicians, among other skilled trades. Manufacturers are also looking for welders, but also for workers outside of production, including biomedical engineers, dispatchers, and truck drivers. An overview of current manufacturing issues and statistics is included.

46248 ■ "Great Expectations" in Canadian Business (Vol. 81, April 14, 2008, No. 6, pp. 34)
Pub: Rogers Media Inc.
Contact: Tony Viner, President
Ed: Andy Holloway. **Description:** Therma Blades Inc. says that the reports that say their Therma Blade ice skates were not working properly were inaccurate. The major mistake of the company was to fail to manage the public's expectation when they touted the blades as revolutionary. Therma Blades Inc. has since tested the product with the help of 120 players and physiological testing done on elite level players show that there was a 10 percent improvement in energy efficiency.

46249 ■ "Green Acres" in Hawaii Business (Vol. 54, September 2008, No. 3, pp. 48)
Pub: PacificBasin Communications
Ed: Jan Tenbruggencate. **Description:** Bill Cowern's Hawaiian Mahogany is a forestry business that processes low-value trees to be sold as wood chips, which can be burned to create biodiesel. Cowern is planning to obtain certification to market carbon credits and is also working with Green Energy Hawaii for the permit of a biomass-fueled power plant. Other details about Cowern's business are discussed.

46250 ■ "Green Energy Exec Hits State Policy" in Boston Business Journal (Vol. 30, December 3, 2010, No. 45, pp. 1)
Pub: Boston Business Journal
Ed: Kyle Alspach. **Description:** American Superconductor Corporation President Dan McGahn believes that the state government of Massachusetts is not proactive enough to develop the state into a manufacturing hub for wind power technology. McGahn believes that while Governor Deval Patrick campaigned for wind turbines in the state, his administration does not have the focus required to build the turbines in the state.

46251 ■ "Green Manufacturer Scouts Sites in Greater Cincinnati" in Business Courier (Vol. 27, July 23, 2010, No. 12, pp. 1)
Pub: Business Courier
Ed: Dan Monk. **Description:** CresaPartners is searching for a manufacturing facility in Cincinnati, Ohio. The company is set to tour about ten sites in the area.

46252 ■ "Green Shift Sees Red" in Canadian Business (Vol. 81, September 29, 2008, No. 16)
Ed: Jeff Sanford. **Description:** Green Shift Inc. is suing the Liberal Party of Canada in an $8.5 million lawsuit for using the phrase 'green shift' when they

rolled out their carbon tax and climate change policy. The company has come to be recognized as a consultant and provider of green products such as non-toxic, biodegradable cups, plates, and utensils for events.

46253 ■ "Greening the Auto Industry" in Business Journal-Serving Phoenix & the Valley of the Sun (Vol. 30, July 23, 2010, No. 46, pp. 1)
Pub: Phoenix Business Journal
Ed: Patrick O'Grady. **Description:** Thermo Fluids Inc. has been recycling used oil products since 1993 and could become Arizona's first home for oil filter recycling after retrofitting its Phoenix facility to include a compaction machine. The new service could help establish Thermo Fluids as a recycling hub for nearby states.

46254 ■ "GreenTech Gears Up for Production" in Memphis Business Journal (Vol. 33, April 6, 2012, No. 52, pp. 1)
Pub: American City Business Journal
Description: GreenTech Automotive has broken ground for construction of a new production facility in Tunica, Tennessee. The company will focus its manufacturing operations in the new facility.

46255 ■ "Grote Company Puts Final Wrap on Sandwich-Making Line" in Business First-Columbus (October 29, 2007, pp. A1)
Pub: American City Business Journals, Inc.
Ed: Dan Eaton. **Description:** Grote Company acquired Oxfordshire, England-based Advanced Food Technology Ltd., giving the Ohio-based food cutting equipment company a manufacturing base in Europe. This is the company's second deal in four months. Details on Grote Company's plan to tap into the prepared fresh sandwich market are discussed.

46256 ■ "Growth in Fits and Starts" in Canadian Business (Vol. 83, July 20, 2010, No. 11-12, pp. 18)
Ed: James Cowan. **Description:** US home sales and manufacturing indicators have dropped and fears of a double-dip recession are widespread. However, a chief economist says that this is endemic to what can be seen after a recession caused by a financial crisis. In Canada, consumer optimism is rising and anxiety over losing one's job is waning.

46257 ■ "GTI Licenses TMC to Cannon Boiler Works" in Contractor (Vol. 56, December 2009, No. 12, pp. 6)
Pub: Penton Media, Inc.
Description: Gas Technology Institute has licensed Cannon Boiler Works Inc. to use its transport membrane condenser technology. The technology can be applied to elevated-temperature industrial processes such as boilers. It allows the capture and beneficial use of latent waste heat and water vapor from exhaust/flue gas.

46258 ■ "Halls Give Hospital Drive $11 Million Infusion" in The Business Journal-Serving Metropolitan Kansas City (Vol. 26, July 18, 2008)
Ed: Rob Roberts. **Description:** Don Hall, chairman of Hallmark Cards Inc., and eight family members have announced that they will give $11 million to Children's Mercy Hospitals and Clinics for its $800 million expansion plan. Hall Family Foundation president Bill Hall that contributions such as that for Children's Mercy reflect the charitable interests of the foundation's board and founders. The possible impacts of the Hall's donation are analyzed.

46259 ■ "H&M Offers a Dress for Less" in Canadian Business (Vol. 83, September 14, 2010, No. 15, pp. 20)
Pub: Rogers Media Inc.
Contact: Tony Viner, President
Ed: Laura Cameron. **Description:** Swedish clothing company H&M has implemented loss leader strategy by pricing some dresses at extremely low prices. The economy has forced retailers to keep prices down despite the increasing cost of manufacturing, partly due to Chinese labor becoming more expensive. How the trend will affect apparel companies is discussed.

46260 ■ "Happy New Year, Celestica?" in Canadian Business (Vol. 80, January 15, 2007, No. 2, pp. 25)
Ed: Andrew Wahl. **Description:** Speculations on the performance of the electronics manufacturing company Celestica Inc. in 2007, which has been labelled as a 'sick' company in recent times, are presented.

46261 ■ "Hardware Stores Get Some Love" in Business Journal Portland (Vol. 31, May 9, 2014, No. 10, pp. 8)
Pub: American City Business Journals
Released: May 9, 2014. **Description:** Contract manufacturer Axiom Electronics launched an incubator called Electr0n. Axioum believes the incubator will help deliver innovation and insight. Axiom president, Robert Toppel, thinks that open hardware is coming and it will affect the company and its customers. Axiom delivers mission critical flight hardware, spacecraft components, medical devices, test systems, and other high performance systems.

46262 ■ "Harvesting the Royal Oak" in Barron's (Vol. 92, September 17, 2012, No. 38, pp. 18)
Description: The Royal Oak wrist watch made by Audemars Piguet of Switzerland was considered revolutionary during its creation in the 1970s, but enjoys wide popularity 40 years later. The all-steel sports watch pays attention to detail and has enabled its manufacturer to survive.

46263 ■ "Have I Got a Deal For You" in Canadian Business (Vol. 83, October 12, 2010, No. 17, pp. 65)
Pub: Rogers Media Inc.
Contact: Tony Viner, President
Ed: Bryan Borzykowski. **Description:** U.S. automobile market currently has more than three players, providing investors with a number of investment options. The sector is still mired in uncertainty, but people believe that these companies can only grow from this point forward. However, investors should use due diligence before jumping into the market.

46264 ■ "Hayes Lemmerz Reports Some Good News Despite Losses" in Crain's Detroit Business (Vol. 24, April 14, 2008, No. 15, pp. 4)
Pub: Crain Communications Inc.
Contact: Rance E. Crain, President
Ed: Nancy Kaffer. **Description:** Hayes Lemmerz International Inc., a wheel manufacturer from Northville that has reported a positive free cash flow for the first time in years, a narrowed net loss in the fourth quarter and significant restructuring of the company's debt.

46265 ■ "Heart Test No Boom for BG Medical" in Boston Business Journal (Vol. 31, June 17, 2011, No. 21, pp. 1)
Pub: Boston Business Journal
Ed: Julie M. Donnelly. **Description:** The Galectin-3 test failed to boost stock prices of its manufacturer, BG Medicine, which has fallen to $6.06/share. The company hopes that its revenue will be boosted by widespread adoption of an automated and faster version of the test, which diagnoses for heart failure.

46266 ■ "Heavy Industry" in Business North Carolina (Vol. 28, February 2008, No. 2, pp. 54)
Ed: Arthur O. Murray. **Description:** Volvo Construction Equipment factory in Asheville, North Carolina expanded its factory that builds road-construction machinery.

46267 ■ "Help in Wings for Aviation, Defense" in Globe & Mail (March 12, 2007, pp. B1)
Ed: Simon Tuck. **Description:** The creation of a corporate subsidy fund by the Canadian government, to facilitate the growth of the aerospace and defense industries, is described.

46268 ■ "Helping Customers Fight Pet Waste" in Pet Product News (Vol. 64, November 2010, No. 11, pp. 52)
Pub: Bowtie Inc.
Ed: Sandy Robins. **Description:** Pet cleaning products manufacturers have been enjoying high sales figures by paying attention to changing pet ownership

trends and environmental awareness. Meanwhile, the inclusion of user-friendly features in these products has also been boosted by the social role of pets and the media attention to pet waste. How manufacturers have been responding to this demand is explored.

46269 ■ *"Hey, You Can't Do That" in Green Industry Pro (Vol. 23, September 2011)*
Pub: Cygnus Business Media
Contact: Paul Mackler, Chief Executive Officer
Ed: Rod Dickens. **Description:** Manufacturers of landscape equipment are making better use of energy resources, such as the use of fuel-injection systems instead of carburetors, lightweight materials, better lubricants, advanced battery technology, and innovative engine designs.

46270 ■ *"High Marks; Parker Hannifin's Stock Lauded by Wall Street Journal" in Crain's Cleveland Business (Vol. 28, November 5, 2007, No. 44, pp. 5)*
Pub: Crain Communications Inc.
Ed: Shannon Mortland. **Description:** According to The Wall Street Journal, Parker Hannifin Corp., a manufacturer of motion and control equipment, is one of eight stocks that are attractively priced and continuously showing growth.

46271 ■ *"High-Yield Turns Into Road Kill" in Barron's (Vol. 88, July 7, 2008, No. 27, pp. M7)*
Pub: Dow Jones & Co., Inc.
Contact: Clare Hart, President
Ed: Emily Barrett. **Description:** High-yield bonds have returned to the brink of collapse after profits have recovered from the shock brought about by the collapse of Bear Stearns. The high-yield bond market could decline again due to weakness in the automotive sector, particularly in Ford and General Motors.

46272 ■ *"HispanTelligence Report" in Hispanic Business (July-August 2007, pp. 18)*
Description: Presentation of the Hispanic Business Stock Index shows the current value of fifteen Hispanic companies from January 3 through July 6, 2007. Results of a survey covering Hispanic household spending on new automobiles are also included. Statistical data included.

46273 ■ *A History of Small Business in America*
Pub: University of North Carolina Press
Contact: Kate Douglas Torrey, Director
E-mail: kate_torrey@unc.edu
Ed: Mansel G. Blackford. **Released:** Second Edition. **Price:** $32.50. **Description:** History of American small business from the colonial era to present, showing how it has played a role in the nation's economic, political, and cultural development across manufacturing, sales, services and farming. **Availability:** Print.

46274 ■ *"Hoping To Make a Big Splash" in Austin Business Journal (Vol. 34, June 20, 2014, No. 18, pp. 14)*
Pub: American City Business Journals, Inc.
Contact: Whitney Shaw, President
Released: June 20, 2014. **Description:** Austin-based Hydro Toys LLC launched ZORBZ in May 2014, a self-sealing balloon made out of Goodyear latex. ZORBZ balloons are manufactured in specially designed molds made from aircraft-quality aluminum, while a proprietary, natural, non-toxic and biodegradable material is used to make the valve system.

46275 ■ *"How CoolBrands' Thrills Turned to Chills" in Globe & Mail (January 25, 2007, pp. B1)*
Pub: CTVglobemedia Publishing Inc.
Ed: Keith McArthur. **Description:** The key reasons behind the sudden share price fall of ice cream giant CoolBrands International Inc. are discussed.

46276 ■ *"How the Generation Gap Can Hurt Your Business" in Agency Sales Magazine (Vol. 39, November 2009, No. 10, pp. 16)*
Ed: Jack Foster. **Description:** Now that there are four generations of people in the workplace, there is a need to add flexibility to communications for independent manufacturers representatives. Manag-

ers can encourage the younger generations to do the research and the boomers to process information and let each side report to the other.

46277 ■ *"How Much Profit is Enough?" in Automotive News (Vol. 86, October 31, 2011, No. 6488, pp. 12)*
Pub: Crain Communications Inc.
Contact: Rance E. Crain, President
Ed: Keith Crain. **Description:** Workers at the big three automobile companies are unhappy about the issues of class wealth, like the high compensations offered to CEOs.

46278 ■ *"How Our Picks Beat The Bear" in Barron's (Vol. 88, July 14, 2008, No. 28, pp. 18)*
Pub: Dow Jones & Co., Inc.
Contact: Clare Hart, President
Ed: Andrew Bary. **Description:** Performance of the stocks that Barron's covered in the first half of 2008 is discussed; some of the worst picks and most rewarding pans have been in the financial sector while the best plays were in the energy, materials, and the transportation sectors.

46279 ■ *"How to Plan and Execute Effective Sales Meetings" in Agency Sales Magazine (Vol. 39, August 2009, No. 8, pp. 8)*
Pub: Manufacturers' Agents National Association
Contact: Charles Cohon, President
Ed: Jack Foster. **Description:** Basic guide to successful representative-manufacturer sales meetings based on effective planning is presented. The representative and the manufacturer will reap the benefits of a productive meeting only when they both focus on what's going to transpire before, during and after the event. Insights from industry players are also presented.

46280 ■ *"How To Freshen Up a 107-Year-Old Caramel" in Canadian Business (Vol. 87, October 2014, No. 10, pp. 45)*
Pub: American City Business Journals
Released: October 2014. **Description:** Purdys Chocolatier merchandising and marketing vice president, Kriston Dean, discusses the evolution of the company's best-selling Himalayan Pink Salt Caramels. Dean explains how important it is to manufacture the products in Vancouver, British Columbia, Canada.

46281 ■ *"HP Eats Into Rival Dell Sales as Profits Soar" in Globe & Mail (February 21, 2007, pp. B15)*
Ed: Connie Guglielmo. **Description:** The world's largest personal computer maker Hewlett Packard Co. has reported increased profits by 26 percent to $1.55 billion during the first quarter. The company has outpaced its competitor Dell Inc. by offering low priced personal computers during this period.

46282 ■ *"'Huge Contract' Means 299 New Jobs, $96M Expansion for ZF Steering Systems" in Business Courier (Vol. 26, November 6, 2009, No. 28, pp. 1)*
Pub: American City Business Journals, Inc.
Contact: Whitney Shaw, President
Ed: Jon Newberry. **Description:** Proposed $96 million expansion of German-owned automotive supplier ZF Steering systems LLC is anticipated to generate 299 jobs in Boone County, Kentucky. ZF might invest $90 million in equipment, while the rest will go to building and improvements.

46283 ■ *"Husky Proceeds on Heavy-Oil Expansion" in Globe & Mail (March 21, 2006, pp. B1)*
Ed: Patrick Brethour. **Description:** Canadian energy giant Husky Energy Inc. has started its $90 million engineering effort to determine the cost of the $2.3 billion heavy-oil up gradation expansion plan. Details of the project are elaborated upon.

46284 ■ *"Hybrid Popularity Pushes Automakers to Add to Offerings" in Crain's Cleveland Business (Vol. 28, November 12,*

2007, No. 45, pp. 30)
Ed: David Sedgwick. **Description:** Due in part to Toyota's innovative marketing, automotive hybrids have caught on with consumers thus forcing other automakers to add hybrids to their product plans.

46285 ■ *"Hyundai Enters Minivan Market" in Globe & Mail (February 15, 2006, pp. B7)*
Ed: Greg Keenan. **Description:** The reasons behind the launch of minivan by Hyundai Auto Canada Inc. are presented.

46286 ■ *"Hyundai's Hitting Its Stride" in Barron's (Vol. 89, July 20, 2009, No. 29, pp. M7)*
Pub: Dow Jones & Co., Inc.
Contact: Clare Hart, President
Ed: Assif Shameen. **Description:** Hyundai Motors has kept growing by producing better products, enabling it to increase its sales and market share despite the weaker automotive market. The shares of Hyundai and Kia are poised to rise due to their improved finances.

46287 ■ *"Idea-Generation Program Creates Winning Programs" in Business Journal-Serving Metropolitan Kansas City (October 19, 2007)*
Ed: James Dombrook. **Description:** Eureka Ranch has developed 'Eureka! Winning Ways', a program that helps companies create new ideas for their business. Brunson Instruments is the first Missouri manufacturer to engage in the program. The procedures in the new product idea generation program are supplied.

46288 ■ *"Idea Nation" in Canadian Business (Vol. 80, December 25, 2006, No. 1, pp. 57)*
Pub: Rogers Media Inc.
Contact: Tony Viner, President
Ed: Andy Holloway. **Description:** The potential of manufacturing companies and their innovations in the progress of the Canadian economy is discussed.

46289 ■ *"Importers Share Safety Liability" in Feedstuffs (Vol. 80, January 21, 2008, No. 3, pp. 19)*
Description: Pet food and toys containing lead paint are among products from China being recalled due to safety concerns. American Society for Quality's list of measures that outsourcing companies can take to help ensure safer products being imported to the U.S.

46290 ■ *"Imports Frothing Up Beer Market" in Globe & Mail (February 16, 2006, pp. B4)*
Ed: Andy Hoffman. **Description:** The reasons behind the rise in market share of beer imports, in Canada, are presented.

46291 ■ *"IMRA's Ultrafast Lasers Bring Precision, profits; Ann Arbor Company Eyes Expansion" in Crain's Detroit Business (March 10, 2008)*
Pub: Crain Communications Inc.
Contact: Rance E. Crain, President
Ed: Tom Henderson. **Description:** IMRA America Inc. plans to expand its headquarters and has applied for permits to build a fourth building that will house research and development facilities and allow the company more room for manufacturing; the company plans to add about 20 more employees that would include research scientists, manufacturing and assembly workers, engineers and salespeople. The growth is due mainly to a new technology of ultrafast fiber lasers that reduce side effects for those getting eye surgeries and help manufacturers of computer chips to reduce their size and cost.

46292 ■ *"In the Bag?" in Canadian Business (Vol. 81, March 3, 2008, No. 3, pp. 57)*
Ed: Calvin Leung. **Description:** American stocks are beginning to appear cheap amidst the threat of a worldwide economic slowdown, United States economic crisis and declining stock portfolios. Investors looking for bargain stocks should study the shares of Apple and Oshkosh Corp. Evaluation of other cheap-looking stocks such as the shares of Coach and 3M is also given.

46293 ■ *"In Search of a Job Revival"* in *Providence Business News (Vol. 29, June 2, 2014, No. 9, pp. 1)*
Pub: American City Business Journals
Released: June 2, 2014. **Description:** A Rhode Island 2014 gubernatorial candidate plans to boost the state's economy by creating new jobs. Her economic plan is based on five elements she believes are vital for growth: manufacturing, tourism, regulatory reform, workforce development and infrastructure.

46294 ■ *"Industrial Vacancies Hit High"* in *Crain's Chicago Business (Apr. 21, 2008)*
Pub: Crain Communications Inc.
Contact: Todd Johnson, Publisher
Ed: Alby Gallun. **Description:** Hitting its highest level in four years in the first quarter is the Chicago-area industrial vacancy rate, a sign that the slumping economy is depressing demand for warehouse and manufacturing space.

46295 ■ *"Innovation Adoption and Diffusion in Business-to-Business Marketing"* in *Journal of Business & Industrial Marketing (Vol. 29, May 2014, No. 4, pp. 324-331)*
Pub: Emerald Group Publishing Inc.
Released: May 2014. **Description:** Evaluation of the innovation adoption and diffusion approach that links it with the key theoretical fields within business-to-business marketing is explored. A conceptual discussion is presented with the aim to develop an integrative conceptual framework and concludes that the proposed theoretical approaches could provide support in establishing a more matter-of-fact view of adoption and diffusion in the industrial sector.

46296 ■ *"Insert Grade Coating Improves Tool Live"* in *Modern Machine Shop (Vol. 84, October 2011, No. 5, pp. 124)*
Pub: Gardner Business Media, Inc.
Contact: Richard G. Kline, President
E-mail: rkline@gardnerweb.com
Ed: Emily K. Tudor. **Description:** Profile of Sumitomo Electric Carbide's AC420K insert that is a CVD-coated carbide grade that features layers of TiCN and Al.sub.2 O.sub.3 for wear, chipping and heat resistance.

46297 ■ *"Intel Forges New Strategy With Chinese Fabrication Plant"* in *Globe & Mail (March 26, 2007, pp. B6)*
Ed: Don Clark. **Description:** World's largest semiconductor manufacturing giant Intel Corp. is planning to construct a new chip fabrication plant in China. It will be investing an estimated $2.5 billion for this purpose.

46298 ■ *"Intel: Tax Breaks Key"* in *Business Journal Portland (Vol. 27, October 22, 2010, No. 34, pp. 1)*
Pub: Portland Business Journal
Ed: Erik Siemers. **Description:** Intel Corporation believes that state tax incentives will be critical, especially in the purchase of manufacturing equipment, as they build a new chip factory in Hillsboro, Oregon. The tax breaks would help Intel avoid paying 10 times more in property taxes compared to average Washington County firms. Critics argue that Intel has about $15 billion in cash assets, and can afford the factory without the tax breaks.

46299 ■ *"Intermodal Makes Suppliers Look to Rack Up Big Sales to Distributors"* in *The Business Journal-Serving Metropolitan Kansas City (August 15, 2008)*
Pub: American City Business Journals, Inc.
Contact: Whitney Shaw, President
Ed: James Dornbrook. **Description:** Suppliers of shelving units, conveyor systems and other equipment used in distribution facilities are expecting new business opportunities along with the planned intermodal projects in the Kansas City area. Suppliers have already observed that small distributors have started to relocate to the city because of the intermodal projects. Demand for shelves and lifts have also increased.

46300 ■ *"Into the Wild"* in *Inc. (October 2007, pp. 116-120, 122, 124, 126)*
Pub: Mansueto Ventures L.L.C.
Contact: John Koten, Chief Executive Officer
Ed: Alison Stein Wellner. **Description:** Perry Klebahn, CEO of Timbuk2, manufacturer of messenger bags, tells how he took his top executives into the deep Wyoming wilderness in order to build employee team work skills. Other options for this type of team-building include cooking courses, changing a tire together, solving a kidnapping, or discussing ways to survive a nuclear winter.

46301 ■ *"Iogen in Talks to Build Ethanol Plant in Canada"* in *Globe & Mail (March 21, 2007, pp. B7)*
Pub: CTVglobemedia Publishing Inc.
Ed: Shawn McCarthy. **Description:** Ottawa based Iogen Corp. is planning to construct a cellulosic ethanol plant in Saskatchewan region. The company will be investing an estimated $500 million for this purpose.

46302 ■ *"Iogen, VW Look to Build Ethanol Plant"* in *Globe & Mail (January 9, 2006, pp. B3)*
Pub: CTVglobemedia Publishing Inc.
Ed: Simon Tuck. **Description:** Iogen Corp. and Volkswagen AG plan cellulose ethanol plant in Germany. The details of the project are presented.

46303 ■ *"Irene Rosenfeld: Chairman and CEO, Kraft Foods Inc."* in *Crain's Chicago Business (Vol. 31, May 5, 2008, No. 18, pp. 31)*
Pub: Crain Communications Inc.
Contact: Todd Johnson, Publisher
Ed: David Sterrett. **Description:** Profile of Irene Rosenfeld who is the chairman and CEO of Kraft Foods Inc. and is entering the second year of a three-year plan to boost sales of well-known brands such as Oreo, Velveeta and Oscar Mayer while facing soaring commodity costs and a declining marketshare. Ms. Rosenfeld's turnaround strategy also entails spending more on advertising and giving managers more control over their budgets and product development.

46304 ■ *"It May Be Cheaper to Manufacture At Home"* in *Harvard Business Review (Vol. 88, October 2010, No. 10, pp. 84)*
Pub: Harvard Business School Publishing
Ed: Suzanne de Treville, Lenos Trigeorgis. **Description:** Using a real options framework rather than a discounted cash flow model to assess and value supply chain processes is examined. This enables companies to assess costs for a variety of situations, not just ideal or normal circumstances, which can make the difference between domestic and foreign manufacturing decisions.

46305 ■ *"It's In the Bag"* in *Entrepreneur (Vol. 36, April 2008, No. 4, pp. 122)*
Pub: Entrepreneur Press
Contact: Perlman Neil, President
Ed: Celeste Hoang. **Description:** Sandy Stein launched Alexx Inc in 2004, which markets keychains, called Finders Key Purse, with unique designs to help find keys easier inside the purse. Some of the key ring designs are hearts, sandals, and crowns. The company has approximately $6 million worth of sales in 2007.

46306 ■ *"It's Time To Swim"* in *Canadian Business (Vol. 81, March 3, 2008, No. 3, pp. 37)*
Ed: Megan Harman. **Description:** Canadian manufacturers should consider Asian markets such as India and the United Arab Emirates as the U.S. economic downturn continues. Canada's shortage in skilled labor is also expected to negatively affect manufacturing industries. Ontario's plans to assist manufacturers are also presented.

46307 ■ *"ITT Places Its Bet With Defense Buy: Selling Equipment to Army Pays Off"* in

Crain's New York Business (Vol. 24, January 6, 2008)
Pub: Crain Communications Inc.
Contact: Rance Crain, President
Description: ITT Corp.'s revenue has jumped by 20 percent in each of the past three years due to demand for the company's radio sets and night-vision goggles. The firm has acquired EDO Corp., which specializes in battlefield communications systems, in an attempt to expand its defense-industry division.

46308 ■ *"Jacksonville Doing Well In Growing Economy"* in *Orlando Business Journal (Vol. 30, June 27, 2014, No. 53, pp. 8)*
Pub: American City Business Journals
Released: June 27, 2014. **Description:** Jerry Mallot is the president of JaxUSA Partnership, the economic development arm of the Jax Chambers. According to Mallot, Northeast Florida's strongest selling points for business site or relocation there include advanced manufacturing, financial services, aviation and aerospace technology, life sciences, logistics and information technology.

46309 ■ *"Japan-Brand Shortages Will Linger Into '12"* in *Automotive News (Vol. 86, October 31, 2011, No. 6488, pp. 1)*
Pub: Crain Communications Inc.
Contact: Rance E. Crain, President
Ed: Amy Wilson, Mark Rechtin. **Description:** Floods in Thailand and the tsunami in Japan have caused shortages of Japanese-brand vehicle parts. These shortages are expected to linger into 2012.

46310 ■ *"Jeans Draw a Global Following"* in *Marketing to Women (Vol. 21, April 2008, No. 4, pp. 6)*
Description: According to a global study by Synovate of jeans and the women who wear them uncovered trends such as brand loyalty and if given a choice 45 percent of all respondents say that if given a choice, they would wear jeans every day.

46311 ■ *"Jet Sales Put Bombardier Back in Black"* in *Globe & Mail (March 30, 2006, pp. B1)*
Ed: Bertrand Morotte. **Description:** The details on Bombardier Inc., which posted 20 percent rise in shares following $86 million profit for fourth quarter 2005, are presented.

46312 ■ *"Jobs Data Show A Slow Leak"* in *Barron's (Vol. 88, July 7, 2008, No. 27, pp. 34)*
Pub: Dow Jones & Co., Inc.
Contact: Clare Hart, President
Ed: Gene Epstein. **Description:** In June 2008, the United States manufacturing sector showed an expansion, with the purchasing managers' index rising to 50.2 from 49.6; the unemployment rate in the US, which stayed steady at 5.5 percent in June 2008 is also discussed. Statistical data included.

46313 ■ *"Johnson's Taps Online Animation"* in *Marketing to Women (Vol. 21, April 2008, No. 4, pp. 3)*
Description: Johnson's has launched a new integrated campaign for its baby lotion in an effort to appeal to the growing number of moms online.

46314 ■ *"Just Add Water and Lily Pads"* in *Crain's Chicago Business (Vol. 31, April 28, 2008, No. 17, pp. 50)*
Pub: Crain Communications Inc.
Contact: Todd Johnson, Publisher
Ed: Phuong Ly. **Description:** Aquascape Inc., a major manufacturer of pond-building supplies, is using the recent drought in the South which hurt its business significantly to create a new product: an upscale, decorative version of the rain barrel which will collect rainwater to circulate through a pond or a fountain.

46315 ■ *"Kawasaki's New Top Gun"* in *Brandweek (Vol. 49, April 21, 2008, No. 16, pp. 18)*
Pub: Nielsen Business Media Inc.
Contact: Howard Appelbaum, President
Description: Discusses Kawasaki's marketing plan which included designing an online brochure in which visitors could create a video by building their own

test track on a grid and then selecting visual special effects and musical overlay. This engaging and innovative marketing technique generated more than 166,000 unique users within the first three months of being launched.

46316 ■ *"KC-Area Ford, GM Plants Downshift" in The Business Journal-Serving Metropolitan Kansas City (Vol. 27, November 7, 2008, No. 9, pp. 1)*
Pub: American City Business Journals, Inc.
Contact: Whitney Shaw, President

Ed: James Dornbrook. **Description:** Discusses Ford Motor Co. and General Motors' factories in the region; Ford Motor Co. removed the second shift on the F-150 line at the Kansas City Assembly Plant but added a shift to the production of the Ford Escape and Mercury Mariner in an attempt to avoid layoffs. One spokesman for General Motors, however, states that they cannot guarantee that they won't make any production cuts and layoffs in the future.

46317 ■ *"Keeping the Vehicle On the Road -- a Survey On On-Road Lane Detection Systems" in ACM Computing Surveys (Vol. 46, Spring 2014, No. 1, pp. 2)*
Pub: Association for Computing Machinery - High Plains Chapter
Contact: Stewart Jenkins, Chairman

Released: Spring 2014. **Description:** The development of wireless sensor networks, such as researchers Advanced Driver Assistance Systems (ADAS) requires the ability to analyze the road scene in the same as a human. Road scene analysis is an essential, complex, and challenging task and it consists of: road detection and obstacle detection. The detection of the road borders, the estimation of the road geometry, and the localization of the vehicle are essential tasks in this context since they are required for the lateral and longitudinal control of the vehicle. A comprehensive review of vision-based road detection systems vision in automobiles and trucks is examined.

46318 ■ *"Keltic Gets Nod to Build N.S. Petrochemical Plant" in Globe & Mail (March 15, 2007, pp. B9)*
Pub: CTVglobemedia Publishing Inc.

Ed: Shawn McCarthy. **Description:** The government of Nova Scotia has awarded clearance to Keltic Inc. for the construction of new petrochemical plant in Goldboro region. Complete details in this context are discussed.

46319 ■ *"Kerkorian Shakes Up Chrysler Race" in Globe & Mail (April 6, 2007, pp. B1)*
Ed: Greg Keenan. **Description:** The bid of Kirk Kerkorian's Tracinda Corp. to acquire Daimler-Chrysler AG for $4.5 billion is discussed.

46320 ■ *"Kerry Steel to Sell Inventory, Close Business After 30 Years" in Crain's Detroit Business (Vol. 24, March 30, 2008, No. 11, pp. 26)*
Pub: Crain Communications Inc.
Contact: Rance E. Crain, President

Ed: Brent Snavely. **Description:** Kerry Steel Inc. has confirmed that it is selling all of its inventory and equipment and is going out of business; the company, which was once one of the largest steel service centers in the Midwest, has sustained financial losses and is in violation of its loan agreements.

46321 ■ *"Key FDA Approval Yanked for Avastin" in Wall Street Journal Eastern Edition (November 19 , 2011, pp. B1)*
Pub: Dow Jones & Co., Inc.
Contact: Clare Hart, President

Ed: Thomas M. Burton, Jennifer Corbett Dooren. **Description:** Avastin, a drug manufactured by Genetech Inc. and used in the treatment of metastatic breast cancer in women, has had its approval by the US Food and Drug Administration withdrawn by the agency, which says there is no evidence the widely-used drug is successful in increasing the longevity of breast cancer patients.

46322 ■ *"Kinetico Exec Going Global to Increase Growth Flow" in Crain's Cleveland Business (Vol. 28, October 1, 2007, No. 39, pp. 5)*
Pub: Crain Communications Inc.

Ed: David Bennett. **Description:** Shamus Hurley, the new CEO and president of Kinetico Inc., a manufacturer of water filtering and softening equipment for residential, commercial and municipal use, plans to expand the company to target markets overseas.

46323 ■ *The King of Vodka: The Story of Pyotr Smirnov and the Upheaval of an Empire*
Pub: HarperCollins Publishers Inc.
Contact: Jane Friedman, President
E-mail: jfriedman@harpercollins.com

Ed: Linda Himelstein. **Released:** 2009. **Price:** $15.99, Paperback. **Description:** Biography of Pyotr Smirnov and how his determination took him from serf to the head of Smirnov Vodka. Smirnov's marketing techniques are defined and show how he expanded the drink worldwide.

46324 ■ *"Kohler Building Earns LEED Silver Certification" in Contractor (Vol. 56, September 2009, No. 9, pp. 12)*
Pub: Penton Media, Inc.

Description: United States Green Building Council has awarded Kohler Co. with the Silver Leadership in Energy and Environmental Design Status. The award has highlighted the company's work to transform its building into a more environmentally efficient structure. A description of the facility is also provided.

46325 ■ *"Kraft Taps Cheese Head; Jordan Charged With Fixing Foodmaker's Signature Product" in Crain's Chicago Business (April 14, 2008)*
Pub: Crain Communications Inc.
Contact: Todd Johnson, Publisher

Ed: David Sterrett. **Description:** Kraft Foods Inc. has assigned Rhonda Jordan, a company veteran, to take charge of the cheese and dairy division which has been losing market shares to cheaper store-brand cheese among cost-sensitive shoppers as Kraft and its competitors raise prices to offset soaring dairy costs.

46326 ■ *"Lancaster Firm Helps Tidy Navy Aircraft Carriers" in Business First of Buffalol> (Vol. 30, February 7, 2014, No. 21, pp. 4)*
Pub: American City Business Journals, Inc.
Contact: Whitney Shaw, President

Released: February 7, 2014. **Description:** Performance Advantage Company sells aluminum took racking systems for use by fire trucks, SWAT teams and departments of public works. The Lancaster, New York-based firm also manufactures clamps and racks for the U.S. Navy, which uses them in aircraft carriers.

46327 ■ *"Late to Minivan Party, VW Hitches Ride With Daimler" in Globe & Mail (January 6, 2006, pp. B1)*
Ed: Greg Keenan. **Description:** DaimlerChrysler AG and Volkswagen AG plans to manufacture minivan. The details of joint venture are presented.

46328 ■ *"Laurent Beaudoin Interview: Deja Vu" in Canadian Business (Vol. 81, July 22, 2008, No. 12-13, pp. 38)*
Pub: Rogers Media Inc.
Contact: Tony Viner, President

Ed: Joe Castaldo. **Description:** Laurent Beaudoin has retired as chief executive officer for Bombardier Inc.'s, a manufacturer of regional and business aircraft, but kept a role in the firm as a non-executive chairman. Beaudoin first resigned from the company in 1999, but had to return in 2004 to address challenging situations faced by the company. Beaudoin's views on management and the company are presented.

46329 ■ *"A Lawsuit That Seemed Like a Lifetime" in Puget Sound Business Journal*

(Vol. 34, April 11, 2014, No. 52, pp. 4)
Pub: American City Business Journals

Released: April 11, 2014. **Description:** Fife, Washington-based Continuant has won a court ruling along with a $20 million verdict against Santa Clara, California-based Avaya Inc. after eight years in court. Avaya sued Continuant claiming the company did not have the right to service Avaya manufactured products. Insights into the lawsuit are given.

46330 ■ *"Lawyers Sued Over Lapsed Lacrosse Patent" in Crain's Detroit Business (Vol. 25, June 8, 2009, No. 23, pp. 5)*
Pub: Crain Communications Inc. - Detroit
Contact: Keith Crain, Chairman

Ed: Chad Halcom. **Description:** Warrior Sports Inc., a manufacturer of lacrosse equipment located in Warren, Michigan is suing the law firm Dickinson Wright PLLC and two of its intellectual property lawyers over patent rights to lacrosse equipment.

46331 ■ *"Lead-Free Products must Meet Requirements" in Contractor (Vol. 56, September 2009, No. 9, pp. 30)*
Pub: Penton Media, Inc.

Ed: Robert Gottermeier. **Description:** United States Environmental Protection Agency's adoption of the Safe Drinking Water Act is aimed at lowering lead extraction levels from plumbing products. Manufacturers have since deleaded brass and bronze potable water products. Meanwhile, California and Vermont have passed a law limiting lead content for potable water conveying plumbing products.

46332 ■ *The Leadership Challenge: How to Make Extraordinary Things Happen in Organizations*
Pub: Jossey-Bass Publishers
Contact: Matthew Hoover, Manager
E-mail: fwelsch@jbp.com

Ed: James M. Kouzes, Barry Z. Posner. **Released:** Fifth Edition. **Price:** $29.95, hardcover; $16.99. **Description:** According to research by the authors, people can make extraordinary things happen by liberating the leader within everyone around them. This handbook gives practical tips to aspire leaders in retail, manufacturing, government, community, church and school settings. **Availability:** PrintE-book.

46333 ■ *"Lean Machine: Health Care Follows Auto's Lead, Gears Up for Efficiency" in Crain's Detroit Business (Vol. 26, Jan. 11, 2010)*
Pub: Crain Communications Inc.
Contact: Rance E. Crain, President

Ed: Jay Greene. **Description:** Reducing waste and becoming more efficient is a goal of many businesses involved in the health care industry. These firms are looking to the local manufacturing sector, comparing themselves in specifically to the auto industry, for ways in which to become more efficient.

46334 ■ *"Lean Machine; Health Care Follows Auto's Lead, Gears Up for Efficiency" in Crain's Detroit Business (Vol. 26, January 11, 2010)*
Pub: Crain Communications Inc.
Contact: Rance E. Crain, President

Ed: Jay Greene. **Description:** Reducing waste and becoming more efficient is a goal of many businesses involved in the health care industry. These firms are looking to the local manufacturing sector, comparing themselves in specifically to the auto industry, for ways in which to become more efficient.

46335 ■ *"Leapin' Lizards, Does SoBe Have Some Work To Do On Life Water" in Brandweek (Vol. 49, April 21, 2008, No. 16, pp. 32)*
Pub: Nielsen Business Media Inc.
Contact: Howard Appelbaum, President

Ed: Amy Shea. **Description:** Discusses the competing marketing campaigns of both Vitaminwater, now owned by Coca-Cola, and SoBe Life Water which is owned by Pepsi; also looks at the repositioning of Life Water as a thirst-quencher, rather than a green product as well as the company's newest advertising campaign.

46336 ■ *"Learn New Ideas from Experienced Menu Makers"* in *Nation's Restaurant News (Vol. 45, June 27, 2011, No. 13, pp. 82)*
Pub: Intertec Publishing
Contact: John French, President
Ed: Nancy Kruse. **Description:** National Restaurant Association Restaurant, Hotel-Motel Show featured the Food Truck Spot, a firm committed to all aspects of mobile catering, foodtruck manufacturers, leasers of fully equipped truck and a food-truck franchising group.

46337 ■ *Lethal Logic: Exploding the Myths that Paralyze American Gun Policy*
Pub: Potomac Books
Ed: Dennis A, Henigan. **Released:** 2009. **Price:** $23.96. **Description:** Marketing tactics being used by gun manufacturers regarding possible new gun control laws are examined.

46338 ■ *"Li'l Guy Rolls Up Into Bigger Company"* in *The Business Journal-Serving Metropolitan Kansas City (Vol. 26, September 12, 2008)*
Pub: American City Business Journals, Inc.
Contact: Whitney Shaw, President
Ed: Suzanna Stagemeyer. **Description:** Li'l Guy Foods, a Mexican food company in Kansas City, Missouri, has merged with Tortilla King Inc. Li'l Guy's revenue in 2007 was $3.3 million, while a newspaper report said that Tortilla King's revenue in 2001 was $7.5 million. Growth opportunities for the combined companies and Li'l Guy's testing of the Wichita market are discussed.

46339 ■ *"Linens 'N Things, Dyson in Dust-Up"* in *Crain's Chicago Business (Vol. 31, March 24, 2008, No. 12, pp. 12)*
Pub: Crain Communications Inc.
Contact: Todd Johnson, Publisher
Description: Linens 'N Things is being sued by vacuum-cleaner manufacturer Dyson who is alleging that it hasn't been paid some of the $1.3 million it says it is owed for merchandise.

46340 ■ *"Lining Up at the Ethanol Trough (Ethanol Production in Canada)"* in *Globe & Mail (January 25, 2007, pp. B2)*
Pub: CTVglobemedia Publishing Inc.
Ed: Eric Reguly. **Description:** The future of ethanol production in Canada is discussed; alternate fuel market is expected to reach 35 billion gallons by 2017.

46341 ■ *"Linking Human Capital to Competitive Advantages: Flexibility in a Manufacturing Firm's Supply Chain"* in *Human Resource Management (Vol. 49, September-October 2010, No. 5)*
Pub: John Wiley
Ed: Yan Jin, Margaret M. Hopkins, Jenell L.S. Wittmer. **Description:** A study was conducted to confirm the links among human capital, firm flexibility, and firm performance. The study also examines the emerging role of flexibility for a company's performance. A total of 201 senior supply chain management professionals from several manufacturing companies were included in the study.

46342 ■ *"The Little Insect"* in *Canadian Electronics (Vol. 23, June-July 2008, No. 4, pp. 6)*
Ed: Tim Gouldson. **Description:** Electronics designers should not be underestimated because they can manufacture technologies vital to saving lives and bringing peace. They have designed robots and other electronic equipment that are as small as insects.

46343 ■ *"Clay Riddell"* in *Canadian Business (Vol. 80, February 12, 2007, No. 4, pp. 86)*
Pub: Rogers Media Inc.
Contact: Tony Viner, President
Ed: Michelle Magnan. **Description:** Chief executive officer of Paramount Resources Clay Riddell shares his passion for oil and gas business.

46344 ■ *"Live & Learn: Ian Delaney"* in *Canadian Business (Vol. 81, Summer 2008, No. 9, pp. 168)*
Pub: Rogers Media Inc.
Contact: Tony Viner, President
Ed: Joe Castaldo. **Description:** Interview with Ian Delaney who is the executive chairman of chemical company Sherritt International Corp.; Delaney previously worked as chief executive for a holding company owned by Peter Munk. Details of his beliefs, profession and family life are discussed.

46345 ■ *"Local Auto Suppliers Upbeat as Detroit 3's Prospects Trend Up"* in *Crain's Cleveland Business (Vol. 30, June 8, 2009, No. 22, pp. 1)*
Pub: Crain Communications Inc.
Ed: Dan Shingler. **Description:** According to the Center for Automotive Research located in Ann Arbor, Michigan, if Detroit automakers can hold their market share, they will end up producing more vehicles as the market recovers.

46346 ■ *"Local Green Technology on Display"* in *Crain's Detroit Business (Vol. 26, January 18, 2010, No. 3, pp. 1)*
Pub: Crain Communications Inc.
Contact: Rance E. Crain, President
Ed: Ryan Beene. **Description:** Detroit's 2010 North American International Auto Show put the newest, most innovative green technologies on display showing that the Southeast Michigan automobile industry is gaining traction with its burgeoning e-vehicle infrastructure. Think, a Norwegian electric city-car manufacturer is eyeing sites in Southeast Michigan in which to locate its corporate headquarters and technical center for its North American branch.

46347 ■ *"Local Industrial Vacancies Climb"* in *Crain's Chicago Business (Vol. 31, November 17, 2008, No. 46, pp. 18)*
Pub: Crain Communications Inc.
Contact: Todd Johnson, Publisher
Ed: Eddie Baeb. **Description:** Demand for local industrial real estate has declined dramatically as companies that use warehouse and factory space struggle to survive in an ailing economy. According to a report by Colliers Bennett & Kahnweiler Inc., a commercial real estate brokerage, the regional vacancy rate has risen to 9.86 percent in the third quarter, the fourth straight increase and the highest in the past 14 years.

46348 ■ *"Local Manufacturers See Tax Proposal Hurting Global Operations"* in *Crain's Cleveland Business (Vol. 30, May 18, 2009, No. 20)*
Pub: Crain Communications Inc.
Ed: Dan Shingler. **Description:** New tax laws proposed by the Obama Administration could hinder the efforts of some Northeast Ohio industrial companies from expanding their overseas markets. The law is designed to prevent companies from moving jobs overseas.

46349 ■ *"Local Shops' Wares Sound Good To Boomers Needing Some Fun"* in *Crain's Cleveland Business (Vol. 30, May 18, 2009, No. 20, pp. 5)*
Pub: Crain Communications Inc.
Ed: Dan Shingler. **Description:** Dr. Z Amplification, who makes amplifiers for guitars and SuperTrapp Performance Exhausts, producer of tunable exhausts for motorcycles, are seeing increased sales as baby boomers look to add enjoyment to their lives.

46350 ■ *"LoJack Shows It's Not Just for Tracking Stolen Cars Anymore"* in *Boston Business Journal (Vol. 34, February 28, 2014, No. 4, pp. 3)*
Pub: American City Business Journals, Inc.
Contact: Whitney Shaw, President
Released: February 28, 2014. **Description:** LoJack Corporation's revenues have increased in 2013 by offering clients the opportunity to install LoJack devices on their entire fleets ahead of time. The company manufactures devices that can track down stolen vehicles. LoJack's stock prices have risen by 21 percent in February 2014.

46351 ■ *"A Look Ahead Into 2007"* in *Canadian Business (Vol. 80, December 25, 2006, No. 1, pp. 40)*
Description: The 2007 forecasts for various industrial sectors like telecom, information technology, manufacturing, retail, financial and energy among others is discussed.

46352 ■ *"The Lost Opportunity for a Canadian Steel Giant"* in *Globe & Mail (April 23, 2007, pp. B1)*
Ed: Greg Keenan. **Description:** The efforts of Algoma Steel Inc. to create a Canadian steel manufacturer that could survive the global trends of consolidation in the steel industry are described. The company's efforts to acquire Stelco Inc., Ivaco Inc. and Slater Steel Inc. are discussed.

46353 ■ *"Lynn Johnson, President: Dowland-Bach"* in *Alaska Business Monthly (Vol. 27, October 2011, No. 10, pp. 11)*
Pub: Alaska Business Publishing Company Inc.
Contact: Jim Martin, President
Ed: Peg Stomierowski. **Description:** Profile of Lynn C. Johnson cofounder of Dowland-Bach Corporation, a manufacturing and distribution company is presented. The firms primary products are wellhead control and chemical injection systems for corrosion control, UL industrial control panels, and specialty stainless steel sheet metal fabrication.

46354 ■ *"Made In Canada"* in *Canadian Business (Vol. 80, March 12, 2007, No. 6, pp. 11)*
Ed: Ian Harvey. **Description:** The devision of Christie Digital Systems Canada Inc. to increase production of its DLP projectors, in view of high demand from the United States, is discussed.

46355 ■ *"Magna Nears Top of Auto Parts Heap"* in *Globe & Mail (May 1, 2007, pp. B4)*
Ed: Greg Keenan. **Description:** Magna International Inc. is poised to become the largest automobile parts supplier in North America. The state of the automobile parts industry in Canada is also discussed.

46356 ■ *"Magna in Talks on Building Cars for DaimlerChrysler"* in *Globe & Mail (February 27, 2007, pp. B1)*
Ed: Greg Keenan. **Description:** The plans of Magna International Inc. to purchase securities of Chrysler Corp. are discussed. The possibility of the manufacture of cars by Magna International Inc. for DaimlerChrysler AG is discussed.

46357 ■ *"Magna Wants to Help Chrysler, but a Takeover's Not on the Cards"* in *Globe & Mail (March 1, 2007, pp. B1)*
Ed: Greg Keenan. **Description:** The plans of Magna International Inc. to help Chrysler Corp. to overcome its financial problems are discussed. The appointment of Michael Neuman as the chief executive officer of Magna International Inc. is described.

46358 ■ *"Major Auto Makers Take Aim at Toyota in Battle for Green Market Shares"* in *Hispanic Business (Vol. 30, September 2008, No. 9, pp. 90)*
Pub: Hispanic Business Inc.
Contact: Jesus Chavarria, President
Ed: Daniel Soussa. **Description:** Three major car manufacturers, Chevrolet, BMW, and Honda, are giving market leader Toyota competition for the next generation of eco-friendly car. The latest and most advanced of the gasoline-less cars designed by the three firms, namely, the Chevrolet Volt, BMW's Hydrogen 7, and the Honda FCX Clarity, are reviewed.

46359 ■ *"Major Tech Employers Pulling Out"* in *Sacramento Business Journal (Vol. 25, August 1, 2008, No. 22, pp. 1)*
Pub: American City Business Journals, Inc.
Contact: Whitney Shaw, President
Ed: Celia Lamb. **Description:** Biotechnology company Affymetrix Inc. is planning to close its West Sacramento, California plant and lay off 110 employ-

ees. The company said it will expand a corporate restructuring plan. Affymetrix also plans to lease out or sell its building at Riverside Parkway.

46360 ■ *"Making Factory Tours Count" in Playthings (Vol. 107, January 1, 2009, No. 1, pp. 14)*

Pub: Reed Elsevier Group plc Reed Business Information

Contact: Mark Kelsey, Chief Executive Officer

Ed: Malcolm Denniss. **Description:** The importance of touring an overseas toy supplier's manufacturing facility is stressed. Strategies for general factory visits are outlined in order to determine safety-related quality assurance issues in production.

46361 ■ *Managing Complexity and Change in SMEs: Frontiers in European Research*

Pub: Edward Elgar Publishing Inc.

Contact: Richard Henning, Vice President

E-mail: kwight@e-elgar.com

Ed: Poul Rind Christensen, Flemming Poulfelt. **Released:** 2006. **Price:** £72. **Description:** Complexities faced by entrepreneurs in an expanding marketplace are discussed. **Availability:** Print.

46362 ■ *"Manufacturers Become Part of Coalition" in Contractor (Vol. 56, July 2009, No. 7, pp. 40)*

Pub: Penton Media, Inc.

Description: Bradford White Water Heaters, Rheem Water Heating, Rinnai America Corp., and A.O. Smith Water Heaters have joined the Consortium for Energy Efficiency in the Coalition for Energy Star Water Heaters. The coalition seeks to increase the awareness of Energy Star water heaters.

46363 ■ *"Manufacturers Urged to Adapt to Defense" in Crain's Cleveland Business (Vol. 30, June 22, 2009, No. 24, pp. 3)*

Pub: Crain Communications Inc.

Ed: Dan Shingler. **Description:** Manufacturers in Northeast Ohio are making products for the military from steel, polymers or composite materials. The U.S. Department of Defense is teaching companies to work with titanium and other advanced metals in order to further manufacture for the military.

46364 ■ *"Manufacturing Behind the Great Wall: What Works, What Doesn't" in Canadian Electronics (Vol. 23, February 2008, No. 1, pp. 6)*

Ed: Michel Jullian. **Description:** Electronic component producers are increasingly transitioning their manufacturing operations to China in order to take advantage of the growing Chinese manufacturing industry. It is believed that manufacturers have to carefully consider whether their run sizes are appropriate for Chinese manufacturing before moving their operations.

46365 ■ *"Manufacturing Boom Leads to Local Warehouse Leasing Fury" in Houston Business Journal (Vol. 44, April 11, 2014, No. 49, pp. 10A)*

Pub: American City Business Journals

Released: April 11, 2014. **Description:** The growth of Houston, Texas manufacturing sector has resulted in companies' investment in local warehouse space. Siemens AG and Emerson Electric Company have leased new warehouse space in the area. Meanwhile, other energy companies have also contributed to the decline of industrial vacancy rates.

46366 ■ *"Manufacturing a Comeback" in San Francisco Business Times (Vol. 28, February 14, 2014, No. 30, pp. 4)*

Pub: American City Business Journals

Released: February 14, 2014. **Description:** Reports show that San Francisco, California's manufacturing industry is making a comeback due to the rise in new entrepreneurs. However, some observers believe that the increasing costs of production could limit the sector's growth. San Francisco currently supports more than 4,000 manufacturing jobs.

46367 ■ *"Manufacturing in the Middle Kingdom" in Inc. (December 2007, pp. 54-57)*

Pub: Gruner and Jahr USA Publishing Co.

Contact: J. Russell Denson, President

Ed: Alex Salkever. **Description:** Tips for manufacturing any new product in China as well as marketing said product is examined; five key steps for successfully managing Chinese contractors are listed.

46368 ■ *"A Manufacturing Revival" in Boston Business Journal (Vol. 31, May 27, 2011, No. 18, pp. 1)*

Pub: Boston Business Journal

Ed: Kyle Alspach. **Description:** Massachusetts' manufacturing sector has grown despite the high cost of labor, real estate and electricity. Manufacturing jobs in the state have increased to 2,800 in April 2011.

46369 ■ *"Manufacturing Skills Fading Away" in Memphis Business Journal (Vol. 34, July 20, 2012, No. 14, pp. 1)*

Pub: American City Business Journal

Ed: Michael Sheffield. **Description:** Chemical manufacturers in Memphis, Tennessee are seen to face a shortage of skilled workers. A large portion of employees are nearing retirement age.

46370 ■ *"Many Procter Products To Get Price Increase" in Business Courier (Vol. 24, November 14, 2007, No. 31, pp. 1)*

Pub: American City Business Journals, Inc.

Contact: Whitney Shaw, President

Ed: Lisa Biank Fasig. **Description:** Procter & Gamble Co. is increasing the prices of its products as a means to offset the rising costs of gas, plastics and raw materials. The price increase will be somewhere between 3 to 12 percent, depending on the product.

46371 ■ *"Market Takes Shape for Emissions Credits" in Globe & Mail (April 16, 2007, pp. B3)*

Ed: Shawn McCarthy. **Description:** The effort of Canadian companies to prepare for emissions trading after the government imposes climate change regulations is discussed.

46372 ■ *"Marketer Bets Big on U.S.'s Growing Canine Obsession" in Advertising Age (Vol. 79, April 14, 2008, No. 15, pp. 14)*

Pub: Crain Communications Inc.

Contact: Rance Crain, President

Ed: Emily Bryson York. **Description:** Overview of FreshPet, a New Jersey company that began marketing two brands of refrigerated dog food-Deli Fresh and FreshPet Select-which are made from fresh ingredients such as beef, rice and carrots. The company projects continued success due to the amount of money consumers spend on their pets as well as fears derived from the 2007 recalls that inspired consumers to look for smaller, independent manufacturers that are less likely to source ingredients from China.

46373 ■ *"Markets Defy the Doomsayers" in Barron's (Vol. 88, March 24, 2008, No. 12, pp. M5)*

Pub: Dow Jones & Co., Inc.

Contact: Clare Hart, President

Ed: Leslie P. Norton. **Description:** US stock markets registered strong gains, with the Dow Jones Industrial Average rising 3.43 percent on the week to close at 12,361.32, in a rally that may be seen as short-covering. Shares of Hansen Natural are poised for further drops with a slowdown in the energy drink market.

46374 ■ *"The Markets' Tender Spring Shoots, But a Swift Rebound Is Unlikely" in Barron's (Vol. 88, March 31, 2008, No. 13, pp. M3)*

Pub: Dow Jones & Co., Inc.

Contact: Clare Hart, President

Ed: Kopin Tan. **Description:** Expansion in price-earnings multiples and a lower credit-default risk index has encouraged fans of the spring-awakening theory. Shares of industrial truckers have gone up 32 percent in 2008 and some shares are pushing five-

year highs brought on by higher efficiency and earnings from more load carried. The prospects of the shares of Foot Locker are also discussed.

46375 ■ *"Massive Ford Restructuring to Cut 1,200 More Canadian Jobs" in Globe & Mail (January 24, 2006, pp. B1)*

Ed: Greg Keenan. **Description:** The details on streamlining of operations of Ford Motor Co., in Canada, are presented.

46376 ■ *"Maternity Wear Goes Green" in Marketing to Women (Vol. 21, March 2008, No. 3, pp. 3)*

Description: Mother's Work Inc. has launched a series of environmentally-friendly products made from such sustainable fibers as organic cotton and bamboo.

46377 ■ *"Medical Connectors: Meeting the Demands of Reliability, Portability, Size and Cost" in Canadian Electronics (February 2008)*

Ed: Murtaza Fidaali, Ted Worroll. **Description:** Component manufacturers who serve the medical industry need to ensure component reliability in order to maintain patient safety. Because of this, connectors in medical equipment are becoming more versatile. It is concluded that these manufacturers are facing challenges meeting the medical industry standards or reliability, miniaturization, portability, and cost.

46378 ■ *"Medical Device Makers Brace for Excise Tax" in Memphis Business Journal (Vol. 34, July 20, 2012, No. 14, pp. 1)*

Pub: American City Business Journal

Ed: Michael Sheffield. **Description:** The US Government's plan to increase excise tax is seen to impact medical device manufacturers. The tax is expected to raise as much as $60 billion over the next 10 years.

46379 ■ *"Medical Market a Healthy Alternative" in Crain's Cleveland Business (Vol. 30, June 1, 2009, No. 21, pp. 3)*

Pub: Crain Communications Inc.

Ed: Dan Shingler. **Description:** Manufacturing for the Medical Market: Requirements for Supply Chain Entry, was an event held in Northeast Ohio. Representatives from various health systems addressed 250 area manufacturers about their future medical supply needs.

46380 ■ *"Memphis Area Manufacturing Companies" in Memphis Business Journal (No. 35, March 14, 2014, No. 49, pp. 10)*

Pub: American City Business Journals

Released: March 14, 2014. **Description:** The top 25 manufacturing firms in Memphis, Tennessee are ranked by local full-time employees. Smith and Nephew Inc. got the top spot, while UTC-Carrier Corporation ranked second.

46381 ■ *"Mentor Medical Device Maker's Partnerships Open New Opportunities" in Crain's Cleveland Business (Vol. 30, June 22, 2009, No. 24)*

Pub: Crain Communications Inc.

Ed: Chuck Soder. **Description:** Frantz Medical Development Ltd. develops medical devices based on ideas from outside inventors. The company wants to manufacture the innovations at its Mentor campus.

46382 ■ *"Menu Foods Seeks Answers in Death of Ten Pets" in Globe & Mail (March 19, 2007, pp. B2)*

Ed: Thomas M. Burton. **Description:** The failure of Menu Foods Inc. to ascertain the cause of ten deaths of house pets, which were fed its food products, prompting the government to recall the products from the market, is discussed.

46383 ■ *"Mercury (1939-2010)" in Canadian Business (Vol. 83, June 15, 2010, No. 10, pp. 27)*

Pub: Rogers Media Inc.

Contact: Tony Viner, President

Ed: Steve Maich. **Description:** Ford's Mercury brand of cars began in 1939 and it was designed by Ford to attract a wealthier clientele. Mercury was mentioned in a 1949 song by K.C. Douglas and was driven in the movie, 'Rebel Without a Cause'. However, the brand was too expensive for the mass market and not exclusive enough through the years, so Ford Motor Company decided to discontinue the brand in 2010.

46384 ■ "Michael Medline" in Canadian Business (Vol. 87, October 2014, No. 10, pp. 58)
Pub: George Media Inc.
Released: October 2014. Description: "Canadian Tire president, Michael Medline, discusses his upcoming role as a CEO, the firm's digital and acquisition strategies and its relationship with tire dealers. He describes how the business maintains the things that consumers love about Canadian Tire while trying to reinvent the manufacturers operations vision for a modern age.

46385 ■ "MicroPort Wasting No Time To Raise Manufacturing Capacity" in Memphis Business Journal (Vol. 35, January 24, 2014, No. 42, pp. 7)
Pub: American City Business Journals
Released: January 24, 2014. Description: MicroPort Orthopedics has occupied the 250,000-square-foot manufacturing, distribution and office space in Arlington, Tennessee since its acquisition from Wright Medical Group Inc. MicroPort CEO, Ted Davis, plans to add a surgical training facility and increase manufacturing capacity.

46386 ■ "Minimizing Import Risks" in Canadian Sailings (July 7, 2008)
Ed: Jack Kohane. Description: New food and product safety laws may be enacted by Canada's Parliament; importers, retailers and manufacturers could face huge fines if the new laws are passed.

46387 ■ "Minority Auto Suppliers Get Help Diversifying" in Crain's Detroit Business (Vol. 26, January 11, 2010, No. 2, pp. 3)
Pub: Crain Communications Inc.
Contact: Rance E. Crain, President
Ed: Sherri Welch. Description: Displaced minority auto suppliers are being given assistance by the Kauffman's Foundation Urban Entrepreneur Partnership Detroit program, a three-year effort to assist 150 of the region's suppliers into more diversified businesses.

46388 ■ "A Model Machine for Titanium" in Modern Machine Shop (Vol. 84, October 2011, No. 5, pp. 84)
Pub: Gardner Business Media, Inc.
Contact: Richard G. Kline, President
E-mail: rkline@gardnerweb.com
Ed: Peter Zelinski. Description: Researchers have developed a machine tool that controls vibration in order to mill titanium more productively. In-depth information on the machine tool as well as understanding the processes involved in milling titanium is covered.

46389 ■ "Modular Home Center Opens in Arcadia" in Charlotte Observer (February 1, 2007)
Ed: John Lawhorne. Description: Arcadia Home Center features modular homes constructed on a steel frame; regulations regarding the manufacture and moving of these homes are included.

46390 ■ "Monaco Pay Cut Draws Attention" in The Business Journal-Portland (Vol. 25, August 8, 2008, No. 22, pp. 1)
Pub: American City Business Journals, Inc.
Contact: Whitney Shaw, President
Ed: Erik Siemers. Description: Monaco Coach Corp. cut the salaries of five top executives in an effort to reduce the company's $178 million worth of inventory. The executives can earn the lost salary back if the inventory is reduced by $58 million a year after August 2008.

46391 ■ "Monogram Foods Eyes Acquisition: Midwest Manufacturer Target of Latest Expansion" in Memphis Business Journal
(Vol. 34, August 10, 2012, No. 17, pp. 1)
Pub: American City Business Journal
Description: Monogram Food Solutions, a Memphis-based food company is raising $12.5 million for the acquisition of an undisclosed company or companies. The acquistion is expected to generate $50 million revenue, add 200 new employees for Monogram, and strengthen its manufacturing arm.

46392 ■ "Monogram Foods Lands Another Acquisition In Quest for Growth Goals" in Memphis Business Journal (Vol. 34, September 14, 2012, No. 22, pp. 1)
Pub: American City Business Journal
Ed: Michael Sheffield. Description: Memphis, Tennessee-based Monogram Food Solutions has announced a deal to acquire Enjoy and Hickory Best Beef Jerky brands from Colton, California-based Enjoy Foods International. The move follows the acquisition of Bristol, Indiana-based Hinsdale Farms, which manufactures corn dogs.

46393 ■ "Montana's Manufacturing Industry" in Montana Business Quarterly (Vol. 49, Spring 2011, No. 1, pp. 29)
Pub: University of Montana Bureau of Business and Economic Research
Contact: Patrick Barkey, Director
E-mail: patrick.barkey@business.umt.edu
Ed: Todd A. Morgan, Charles E. Keegan III, Colin B. Sorenson. Description: Manufacturing remains a vital part of Montana's economy despite the recession and decline in the production of wood products. Statistical data included.

46394 ■ "The Mood of a Nation" in Canadian Business (Vol. 81, April 14, 2008, No. 6, pp. 56)
Pub: Rogers Media Inc.
Contact: Tony Viner, President
Ed: Joe Castaldo. Description: Independent Fish Harvesters Inc. processes more kilograms a year and has had to hire more workers but its managers worry about how a slowdown in the U.S. economy will affect his business. A planned shopping complex in Mirabel Quebec, the manufacturing industry in Kitchener, Ontario, and a cattle farming business in Sarnia, Ontario are discussed to provide a snapshot of the challenges that business in Canada are facing as recession looms.

46395 ■ "The More Incredible Egg" in Entrepreneur (June 2014)
Pub: Entrepreneur Media Inc.
Released: June 2014. Description: San Francisco, California-based startup Hampton Creek has developed a plant-based alternative to eggs. The startup touts it as a healthier, more humane and environment-friendly egg alternative. The company used several varieties of the yellow pea and discovered that its properties mimic egg emulsion. Hampton Creek's first food product was Beyond Eggs, a powder that allows food manufacturers to eliminate eggs from food products. It also developed Just Mayo, an egg-free mayonnaise substitute, and is developing Eat the Dough, an egg-free substitute for cookie dough.

46396 ■ "More Manufacturers Scout Military Contracts As Auto Industry Lags" in Crain's Detroit Business (Vol. 24, September 29, 2008, No. 39, pp. 37)
Pub: Crain Communications Inc.
Contact: Rance E. Crain, President
Ed: Chad Halcom. Description: Many Michigan manufacturers are looking to grow with new military contracts now that the reality of the auto industry is becoming more clear; these companies see that the government contracts may be the only way in which they will be able to stay in business through these rough economic times.

46397 ■ "More Pain" in Canadian Business (Vol. 81, December 24, 2007, No. 1, pp. 12)
Ed: Lauren McKeon. Description: Manufacturing sector in Canada is sinking with a forecast by as much as 23 percent for 2008, which can be offset as manufacturers say they plan to increase productivity by 25 percent. Details on the sector's competitive-

ness, workforce, importing of machinery from the U.S. and financial needs for research and development are examined.

46398 ■ "Morgan Hill Attracts Manufacturing to South County" in Silicon Valley/San Jose Business Journal (Vol. 30, September 21, 2012, No. 26, pp. 1)
Pub: American City Business Journal
Description: The Grow Morgan Hill Fund offers $2 million in loans to qualifying businesses off of an initial $500,000 city investment. The fund is a way for the city of Morgan Hill, California to help local businesses expand int he absence of redevelopment agencies.

46399 ■ "Mosaid Grants First Wireless Parent License To Matsushita" in Canadian Electronics (Vol. 23, June-July 2008, No. 5, pp. 1)
Description: Matsushita Electric Industrial Co. Ltd. has been granted a six-and-a-half-year license by Mosaid Technologies Inc. to manufacture the latter's products. The patent portfolio license agreement covers Mosaid's Wi-Fi, Wi-Max, CDMA-enabled notebook computers and other products.

46400 ■ "Motorola's New Cell Phone Lineup Includes Green Effort" in Chicago Tribune (January 14, 2009)
Pub: McClatchy-Tribune Information Services
Ed: Eric Benderoff. Description: Motorola Inc. introduced a new line of mobile phones at the Consumer Electronics Show in Las Vegas; the phones are made using recycled water bottles for the plastic housing.

46401 ■ "Motors and Motion Control" in Canadian Electronics (Vol. 23, February 2008, No. 1, pp. 23)
Description: A new version of MicroMo Electronics Inc.'s Smoovy Series 0303..B has been added to MicroMo's DC motor product line. United Electronic Industries, on the other hand, has introduced the new UEIPAC series of programmable automation controllers that can offer solutions to various applications such as unmanned vehicle controllers. Features and functions of other new motors and motion control devices are given.

46402 ■ "Move South Could Bring Big Benefits" in Business Journal-Portland (Vol. 24, November 9, 2007, No. 36, pp. 1)
Pub: American City Business Journals, Inc.
Ed: Matthew Kish. Description: Freightliner LLC has announced that it would move around one-tenth of its jobs to Fort Mill, South Carolina, but stated that immediate plans for headquarters relocation have not been made. The relocation of its headquarters is expected to earn $100 million in economic incentives. The benefits of moving to the area, aside from the economic incentives, are discussed.

46403 ■ "Mover and Sheika" in Conde Nast Portfolio (Vol. 2, June 2008, No. 6, pp. 104)
Ed: John Arlidge. Description: Profile of Princess Sheika Lubna who is the first female foreign trade minister in the Middle East, the United Arab Emirates biggest business envoy, paving the way for billions in new investment, and also a manufacturer of her own perfume line.

46404 ■ "Myths of Deleveraging" in Barron's (Vol. 90, August 23, 2010, No. 34, pp. M14)
Pub: Barron's Editorial & Corporate Headquarters
Ed: Gene Epstein. Description: The opposite is true against reports about deleveraging or the decrease in credit since inflation-adjusted-investment factories and equipment rose 7.8 percent in the first quarter of 2010. On consumer deleveraging, sales of homes through credit is weak but there is a trend towards more realistic homeownership and consumer spending on durable goods rose 8.8 percent.

46405 ■ "Natalie Peterson; Corporate Counsel, Steris Corp." in Crain's Cleveland Business (Vol. 28, November 19, 2007, No. 46, pp. F-14)
Pub: Crain Communications Inc.
Ed: Chuck Soder. Description: Profile of Natalie Peterson, corporate counsel for Steris Corp., a manufacturer of sterilization products; Peterson's

blue-collar background did not detour her from her collegiate goals although she hardly knew how to fill out a college application. After graduating from Stanford Law School in 1997, she opted to return to Cleveland in lieu of more lucrative job offers in San Francisco. She has joined the school board and has participated in the 3Rs program, in which lawyers visit public schools in Cleveland to get students thinking about career choices and talk about constitutional law.

46406 ■ *"Natural Attraction: Bath and Body Products Maker Delivers Wholesome Goodness" in Black Enterprise (Vol. 38, November 2007, No. 4)*
Pub: Earl G. Graves Publishing Co. Inc.
Contact: Earl G. Graves, Jr., President
Ed: Kaylyn Kendall Dines. **Description:** Profile of Dawn Fitch, creator of Pooka Inc., manufacturer of handmade bath and body products that contain no preservatives. Sales are expected to reach $750,000 for 2007.

46407 ■ *"Navistar, Cat Talk Truck Deal" in Crain's Chicago Business (Vol. 31, March 24, 2008, No. 12, pp. 1)*
Pub: Crain Communications Inc.
Contact: Todd Johnson, Publisher
Ed: Bob Tita. **Description:** Caterpillar Inc. and Navistar International Corp. are negotiating a partnership in which Navistar would build Cat-branded trucks with engines supplied by the Peoria-based equipment manufacturer, Caterpillar.

46408 ■ *"NEMRA Announces Headquarters Move" in Agency Sales Magazine (Vol. 39, September-October 2009, No. 9, pp. 53)*
Description: NEMRA, the National Electrical Manufacturers' Representatives Association is moving their headquarters to 28 Deer Street, Suite 302, Portsmouth, New Hampshire. The association has also added Michelle Rivers-Jameson as their manager of operations and Kirsty Stebbins as their manager of marketing and member services.

46409 ■ *Nevada Manufacturers Register*
Pub: Harris InfoSource
Contact: Dennis Abrahams, President
E-mail: dennisa@harrisinfo.com
URL(s): www.harrisinfo.com. **Released:** Annual; latest edition 2010. **Covers:** Approximately 2,800 manufacturers in Nevada plus names and titles of key executives. **Entries include:** Company name, address, parent name/location, telephone, fax and 800 numbers, Web site address (on CD-ROM only), number of employees, year established, annual revenue, plant size, business description, Standard Industrial Classification (SIC) codes, executive names/titles, public ownership, legal structure, import/export designators, female/minority ownership. **Arrangement:** Classified by product/service, line of business. **Indexes:** Product/service, alphabetical, geographical, international trade.

46410 ■ *"New Battle of Alberta: Pipelines" in Globe & Mail (February 3, 2006, pp. B1)*
Ed: Dave Ebner. **Description:** The details on stiffening competition between Enbridge Inc. and TransCanada Corp., to build petroleum pipeline from Alberta to Wisconsin, are presented.

46411 ■ *"New Developments in Cat's Play" in Pet Product News (Vol. 66, September 2012, No. 9, pp. 1)*
Description: Developments in toys for cats have been characterized by items that bring out a cat's natural instincts, toxin-free composition, and durability, among other trends. Meanwhile, consumers are encouraged to try these toys so follow-up purchases can be made. Ways in which manufacturers have addressed the demand for these toys is also discussed.

46412 ■ *"New Drug Could Revitalize Amgen" in Barron's (Vol. 88, July 7, 2008, No. 27, pp. 23)*
Ed: Johanna Bennett. **Description:** Shares of the biotechnology company Amgen could receive a boost from the release of the anti-osteoporosis drug denos-

umab. The shares, priced at $48.84 each, are trading at 11 times expected earnings for 2008 and could also be boosted by cost cutting measures.

46413 ■ *"New Ethanol Plant, Planned for Nevada, IA, Will Use Corn Stover" in Farm Industry News (June 27, 2011)*
Pub: Penton Business Media Inc.
Contact: David Kieselstein, Chief Executive Officer
Ed: Lynn Grooms. **Description:** DuPont Danisco Cellulosic Ethanol (DDCE) will buy land next to the Lincolnway Energy corn-based ethanol plant in Nevada, Iowa in order to produce ethanol from corn stover at the location.

46414 ■ *"The New Frontier" in Crain's Detroit Business (Vol. 26, January 18, 2010, No. 3, pp. S025)*
Ed: Richard Truett; Bradford Wernle. **Description:** Due to the changing consumer preference resulting from new fuel-efficiency standards, concern about climate change and higher gasoline prices, Detroit car designers are beginning to shift focus onto smaller vehicles.

46415 ■ *"New Life for Porsche's VW Dreams" in Barron's (Vol. 89, July 6, 2009, No. 27, pp. 9)*
Pub: Dow Jones & Co., Inc.
Contact: Clare Hart, President
Ed: Vito J. Racanelli. **Description:** Porsche and Volkswagen moved closer to a merger after the Qatar Investment Authority offered to take a stake in Porsche. The QIA could take up to a 30 percent stake in Porsche and purchase all Volkswagen calls for up to $6 billion.

46416 ■ *"New Race Suit at Local Coke Plant" in Business Courier (Vol. 24, January 31, 2008, No. 43, pp. 1)*
Pub: American City Business Journals, Inc.
Contact: Whitney Shaw, President
Ed: Jon Newberry. **Description:** Another racial harassment lawsuit has been filed against the Coca-Cola Enterprises Inc. plant in Madisonville by its 23 black workers. The lawsuit alleges that the working environment at the plant continues to be offensive, abusive, intimidating and hostile. Details of the class-action suit are provided.

46417 ■ *"Nexen, OPTI Boost Oil Sands Spending" in Globe & Mail (February 18, 2006, pp. B5)*
Ed: Dave Ebner. **Description:** The reasons behind the decision of Nexen Inc. and OPTI Canada Inc., to allocate 10 percent more funding on oil sands, are presented.

46418 ■ *"Nike's Next Splash" in The Business Journal-Portland (Vol. 25, August 22, 2008, No. 24, pp. 1)*
Pub: American City Business Journals, Inc.
Contact: Whitney Shaw, President
Ed: Erik Siemers. **Description:** Business analysts expect Nike to bid for the endorsement services of swimmer Michael Phelps after the swimmer's contract with Speedo expires. The company, however, is a lightweight in the swimming apparel market and is not focusing on swimming as a growth sector.

46419 ■ *"Nissan Unveils Family Concept Car" in Marketing to Women (Vol. 21, February 2008, No. 2, pp. 3)*
Description: Nissan displayed its latest design for the ultimate family vehicle at the 2008 North American International Auto Show in Detroit. The Nissan Forum targets families with older children.

46420 ■ *"NKC Keeps Pace with Auto Industry" in Memphis Business Journal (Vol. 34, September 14, 2012, No. 22, pp. 1)*
Pub: American City Business Journal
Ed: Michael Sheffield. **Description:** Memphis, Tennessee-based NKC of American Inc. has been expecting sales to increase to about $60 million for 2012 after its revenue dropped to about $20 million during the peak of the recession in 2008-2009. NKC's growth is being driven by new contracts with automotive manufacturers.

46421 ■ *"No End to the Nightmare; America's Car Industry" in The Economist (Vol. 390, January 3, 2009, No. 8612, pp. 46)*
Description: Detroit's struggling auto industry and the government loan package is discussed as well as the United Auto Worker union, which is loathed by Senate Republicans.

46422 ■ *"No Fluff: My Pillow Soars After Infomercial" in Business Journal (Vol. 30, June 22, 2012, No. 4, pp. 1)*
Pub: American City Business Journals, Inc.
Contact: Whitney Shaw, President
Ed: John Vomhof Jr. **Released:** June 22, 2012. **Description:** The growth of Chanhassen, Minnesota-based open-cell, poly-foam pillow manufacturer My Pillow Inc. in terms of sales and workforce happened following the launch of a 30-minute infomercial in October 2011. Aside from increasing its workforce from 40 to more than 400 since then, sales could reach $150 million in 2012.

46423 ■ *"No Frills - And No Dodge" in Crain's Detroit Business (Vol. 24, September 22, 2008, No. 38, pp. 3)*
Pub: Crain Communications Inc.
Contact: Rance E. Crain, President
Ed: Bradford Wernle. **Description:** Chrysler LLC is in the middle of a business plan known as Project Genesis, a five-year strategy in which the company will reduce the dealer count by combining its Jeep, Chrysler and Dodge brands under one rooftop wherever possible. Not every dealer will be able to arrange this deal because of the investment required to expand stores in which have low-overhead; many of these stores feel that low-overhead structures are more likely to survive difficult times than the larger stores in which the Genesis consolidation plan intends to implement.

46424 ■ *"Nonstop Round Baler Earns Top International Award for Krone" in Farm Industry News (November 18, 2011)*
Pub: Penton Business Media Inc.
Contact: David Kieselstein, Chief Executive Officer
Ed: Karen McMahon. **Description:** The new Ultima baler from Krone can make and net a bale in 40 seconds without stopping, thus producing 90 bales an hour. The new baler, still in test stage, won top honors at the Agritechnica farm equipment show in Hannover, Germany.

46425 ■ *"Not All Contracts a Good Fit for Fashion Reps" in Agency Sales Magazine (Vol. 39, September-October 2009, No. 9, pp. 10)*
Ed: Jack Foster. **Description:** Difficult situations regarding the relationship between sales representatives and their principals in the fashion industry are presented and suggestions on how to create contracts that seek to prevent potential problems are provided. Sales reps should make sure that manufacturer has a viable business that is well thought-out and adequately financed.

46426 ■ *"Now See This" in Entrepreneur (Vol. 36, April 2008, No. 4, pp. 53)*
Pub: Entrepreneur Press
Contact: Perlman Neil, President
Ed: Mike Hogan. **Description:** New high definition (HD) products are to be introduced in 2008 at the Consumer Electronics Show and the Macworld Conference & Expo. HD lineup from companies such as Dell Inc. and Hewlett-Packard Co. are discussed.

46427 ■ *"Nuclear Plans May Stall on Uranium Shortage" in Globe & Mail (March 22, 2007, pp. B4)*
Pub: CTVglobemedia Publishing Inc.
Ed: Shawn McCarthy. **Description:** The poor investments in uranium production and enrichment despite growing demand for it for nuclear energy is discussed.

46428 ■ *"No. 300: My Job Is To Solve Every Kind of Crisis" in Inc. (Vol. 36, September 2014, No. 7, pp. 72)*
Pub: Mansueto Ventures L.L.C.
Contact: John Koten, Chief Executive Officer
Released: September 2014. **Description:** Saima Chowdhury started her integrated sourcing company in New York City after receiving an MBA from Whar-

ton School. Noi Solutions helps retailers manufacture goods in Bangladesh while helping Bangladeshi factories market their capabilities to retailers. Chowdhury discusses the challenges and has learned to remain calm during any crisis.

46429 ■ "Nvidia Shares Clobbered After Gloomy Warning" in Barron's (Vol. 88, July 7, 2008, No. 27, pp. 25)
Pub: Dow Jones & Co., Inc.
Contact: Clare Hart, President
Ed: Eric J. Savitz. Description: Shares of graphics chip manufacturer Nvidia suffered a 30 percent drop in its share price after the company warned that revenue and gross margin forecasts for the quarter ending July 27, 2008 will be below expectations. Stan Glasgow, chief operating officer of Sony Electronics, believes the US economic slowdown will not affect demand for the company's products. Statistical data included.

46430 ■ "Nvidia's Picture Brighter Than Stock Price Indicates" in Barron's (Vol. 88, March 24, 2008, No. 12, pp. 46)
Pub: Dow Jones & Co., Inc.
Contact: Clare Hart, President
Ed: Eric J. Savitz. Description: Shares of graphics chip maker Nvidia, priced at $18.52 each, do not indicate the company's strong position in the graphics chip market. The company's shares have dropped due to fears of slower demand for PCs, but the company is not as exposed to broader economic forces.

46431 ■ "NYPA Grants Aid Area Companies" in Business First of Buffalo (Vol. 30, January 10, 2014, No. 17, pp. 6)
Pub: American City Business Journals, Inc.
Contact: Whitney Shaw, President
Released: January 10, 2014. Description: New York Power Authority (NYPA) trustees have approved more than $3.5 million in financial aid to Western New York enterprises. The NYPA and Empire State Development have also funded a package that includes low cost hydropower and $7 million in capital grants and tax credits. The Western New York area manufacturers that were granted aid are also presented.

46432 ■ "Oakland County Hopes Auto Suppliers Can Drive Medical Industry Growth" in Crain's Detroit Business (March 10, 2008)
Pub: Crain Communications Inc.
Contact: Rance E. Crain, President
Ed: Chad Haloom. Description: Oakland County officials are hoping to create further economic development for the region by pairing health care companies and medical device makers with automotive suppliers in an attempt to discover additional crossover technology.

46433 ■ "Ocean of Opportunity" in Hawaii Business (Vol. 53, October 2007, No. 4, pp. 61)
Pub: PacificBasin Communications
Ed: Mike Markrich. Description: Brew Moon owner Marcus Bender and former Coca-Cola Enterprises Inc. executive Jim Stevens have introduced Kai Vodka in June 2007. The new drink is being marketed to professional women, the number of which is increasing based on a research by the Queens College Department of Sociology. The development process of the new product is also discussed.

46434 ■ "Old Ford Plant to Sign New Tenants" in Business Courier (Vol. 27, August 13, 2010, No. 15, pp. 1)
Pub: Business Courier
Ed: Dan Monk. Description: Ohio Realty Advisors LLC, a company handling the marketing of the 1.9 million-square-foot former Ford Batavia plant is on the brink of landing one distribution and three manufacturing firms as tenants. These tenants are slated to occupy about 20 percent of the facility and generate as many as 250 jobs in Ohio.

46435 ■ "On a Mission: Ginch Gonch Wants You to Get Rid of Your Tighty Whities" in Canadian Business (Vol. 81, September 29,
2008, No. 16)
Ed: Michelle Magnan. Description: New Equity Capital acquired underwear maker Ginch Gonch in July 2008; founder Jason Sutherland kept his position as creative director of the company and will retain his title as 'director of stitches and inches'. The company is known for its products, which are reminiscent of the days when people wore underwear covered in cowboys and stars as kids. The company also claims that Nelly, Justin Timberlake, and Hilary Duff have worn their products.

46436 ■ "Ontario Keeps Bleeding Jobs as Michelin Closes Tire Plant" in Globe & Mail (February 3, 2006, pp. B1)
Ed: Greg Keenan; Heather Scoffield. Description: The reasons behind facility shutdown and workforce reduction by Michelin SA, in Ontario, are presented.

46437 ■ "Optimum Nutrition, Maximum Profit" in Pet Product News (Vol. 66, September 2012, No. 9, pp. S1)
Description: How pet food manufacturers have expanded brand lines to address pet owners' demand for fresh, balanced superfood diets that provide optimum pet nutrtion and foster rapid digestion among pets is explored. Retailers have been maximizing profits by guiding pet owners in selecting he appropriate superfood brands for their pets.

46438 ■ "Options Abound in Winter Wares" in Pet Product News (Vol. 64, November 2010, No. 11, pp. 1)
Pub: Bowtie Inc.
Ed: Maggie M. Shein. Description: Pet supply manufacturers emphasize creating top-notch construction and functional design in creating winter clothing for pets. Meanwhile, retailers and pet owners seek human-Inspired style, quality, and versatility for pets' winter clothing. How retailers generate successful sales of pets' winter clothing outside of traditional brand marketing is also examined.

46439 ■ "The Oracle's Endgame" in Crain's Chicago Business (May 5, 2008)
Pub: Crain Communications Inc.
Contact: Todd Johnson, Publisher
Ed: Ann Saphir. Description: Discusses Warren Buffett's deal with Mars Inc. to buy Wm. Wrigley Jr. Co., a move which would make Mr. Buffett a minority shareholder in a privately held company, a departure from his typical investment strategy. Mr. Buffett's Berkshire Hathaway Inc. agreed to provide $4.4 billion to help finance the $23 billion deal to pay another $2.1 billion for an equity stake in the company once it became a subsidiary of Mars.

46440 ■ "O'Reilly Automotive Will Soup Up KC Warehouse" in The Business Journal-Serving Metropolitan Kansas City (Vol. 26, August 15, 2008, No. 49)
Pub: American City Business Journals, Inc.
Contact: Whitney Shaw, President
Ed: Rob Roberts. Description: O'Reilly Automotive Inc. plans to construct a 215,000-square foot warehouse in Kansas City. The move is expected to triple the size of the company's distribution center. Other views and information on the planned warehouse construction, are presented.

46441 ■ "Our Gadget of the Week: Screen Star" in Barron's (Vol. 88, March 10, 2008, No. 10, pp. 36)
Pub: Dow Jones & Co., Inc.
Contact: Clare Hart, President
Ed: Jay Palmer. Description: Review of the $1,599 Fujitsu Lifebook T2010 tablet notebook which is a lightweight notebook offering a comfortable keyboard and a 12-inch screen illuminated by light emitting diodes. The notebook, however, also offers limited capability with its low-end processor and the lack of a built-in optical drive and a touchpad.

46442 ■ "Outlook 2008 (9 Sectors to Watch): Automotive" in Canadian Business (Vol. 81, December 19, 2007, No. 1, pp. 47)
Pub: Rogers Media Inc.
Contact: Tony Viner, President
Ed: Thomas Watson. Description: Forecasts on the Canadian automotive sector for 2008 are presented. Details on contract concessions made by American

unions, the industry's Big Three (General Motors, Chrysler, and Ford) operations in Canada, and Canadian Auto Workers demand for higher wages are also discussed.

46443 ■ "Outlook 2008 (9 Sectors to Watch): Metals" in Canadian Business (Vol. 81, December 19, 2007, No. 1, pp. 46)
Pub: Rogers Media Inc.
Contact: Tony Viner, President
Ed: John Gray. Description: Forecasts on the Canadian metal industries for 2008 are discussed. Details on mine production and the rise in prices are also presented.

46444 ■ Outsourcing: Information Technology, Original Equipment Manufacturer, Leo, Oursourcing, Offshoring Research Network, Crowdsourcing
Released: May 01, 2010. Price: $14.14. Description: Chapters include information for outsourcing firms and how to maintain an outsourcing business.

46445 ■ "Packaging Firm Wraps Up Remake: Overseas Plants Help Firm Fatten Margins" in Crain's New York Business (January 6, 2008)
Pub: Crain Communications Inc.
Contact: Rance Crain, President
Description: Sealed Air Corp., a packaging manufacturer, has seen its share price fall nearly 20 percent over the past two years, making it one of the worst performers in the packaging sector.

46446 ■ "Pain Ahead as Profit Pressure Increases" in Crain's Chicago Business (Vol. 31, May 5, 2008, No. 18, pp. 4)
Pub: Crain Communications Inc.
Contact: Todd Johnson, Publisher
Ed: Daniel Rome Levine. Description: Interview with David Klaskin, the chairman and chief investment officer at Oak Ridge Investments LLC, who discusses the outlook for the economy and corporate earnings, particularly in the housing and auto industries, the impact of economic stimulus checks, the weakness of the dollar and recommendations of stocks that individual investors may find helpful.

46447 ■ "Paradise Lost" in Inc. (February 2008, pp. 102-109)
Ed: Bo Burlingham. Description: Profile of Bo Burlingham, founder of Precision Manufacturing, a firm cited in books, magazines and newspaper articles for its people-centered culture and success.

46448 ■ "Parent Firm's Global Reach, Stricter Air Quality Rules Have Stock Smiling" in Crain's Cleveland Business (October 15, 2007)
Pub: Crain Communications Inc.
Ed: David Bennett. Description: Since Stock Equipment Co., a firm that makes industrial pollution control equipment, was acquired by Schenck Process Group, a diversified global manufacturer based in Germany, the company's orders from abroad have been on the rise. The purchase has opened the doors to regions such as Eastern and Central Europe, Latin America and Australia.

46449 ■ "A Parts Maker Primed for Takeoff" in Barron's (Vol. 92, August 25, 2012, No. 35, pp. 39)
Pub: Dow Jones & Co., Inc.
Contact: Clare Hart, President
Ed: David Englander. Description: The stocks of machinery maker Curtiss-Wright could gain value due to the manufacturing company's healthy commercial business. The company's stock prices have fallen to $29.27/share due to concerns about reductions in defense spending, but could be worth $40/share.

46450 ■ "Parts, Tooling Manufacturer Machinists Inc. Opts to Expand in South Park" in Puget Sound Business Journal (Vol. 34, February 21, 2014, No. 45, pp. 6)
Pub: American City Business Journals
Released: February 21, 2014. Description: Seattle, Washington-based Machinists Inc. announced an expansion with a seventh building in South Park. The new 20,000-square-foot building will increase the

company's footprint to 115,000-square-feet when fully outfitted. The machine manufacturer shares insight into its decision to stay in Seattle rather than relocate is offered.

46451 ■ *"Patchy Oil Profits" in Canadian Business (Vol. 80, February 12, 2007, No. 4, pp. 89)*
Ed: Michelle Magnan. **Description:** The fall in fourth-quarter earnings of several oil and gas companies in Canada, in view of rise in their expenditure, is discussed.

46452 ■ *"PCI Express Powers Machine Vision" in Canadian Electronics (Vol. 23, February 2008, No. 1, pp. 8)*
Ed: Inder Kohli. **Description:** PCI Express is an innovative peripheral bus that can be used in industrial computing. The peripheral bus delivers a high-bandwidth, scaleable, point-to-point path from peripheral cards to the computing core. Features and functions of PCI Express are described in detail.

46453 ■ *"Pepsi Co. Breaches the Walls of Coke Fortress McDonald's" in Globe & Mail (March 13, 2007, pp. B1)*
Pub: CTVglobemedia Publishing Inc.
Ed: Keith McArthur. **Description:** Soft drinks giant Pepsi Co. has entered an agreement with fast food chain McDonald's for offering its products in outlets across Canada. Earlier Coca-Cola Co. used to offer its exclusive products in these outlets.

46454 ■ *The Perfect Scent: A Year Inside the Perfume Industry in Paris and New York*
Pub: Henry Holt and Co.
Contact: Michael Naumann, President
Ed: Chandler Burr. **Released:** January 2009. **Price:** $17, paperback. **Description:** An insider's glimpse at the development of two new fragrances from Hermes and Coty. **Availability:** Print.

46455 ■ *"Perry Ellis and G-III Apparel -- Out of Fashion, But Still in Style" in Barron's (Vol. 88, March 17, 2008, No. 11, pp. 48)*
Pub: Dow Jones & Co., Inc.
Contact: Clare Hart, President
Ed: Robin Goldwyn Blumenthal. **Description:** Shares of Perry Ellis International and G-III Apparel Group have taken some beating in the market despite good growth earnings prospects. Perry Ellis sees earnings growth of 8 to 11 percent for fiscal 2009, while G-III Apparel expects earnings growth of 25 percent.

46456 ■ *"Pet Food Bank 'Shares the Love" in Pet Product News (Vol. 64, December 2010, No. 12, pp. 6)*
Pub: Bowtie Inc.
Description: Winston-Salem, North Carolina-based nonprofit Share the Love Pet Food Bank has donated 60,000 pounds of pet food since its establishment in 2009. It has been linking pet food manufacturers and rescue groups to supply unsold pet food to needy animals. The nonprofit intends to reach out to more animal welfare groups by building more warehouses.

46457 ■ *"Pet-Food Industry Too Slow: Crisis-PR Gurus" in Advertising Age (Vol. 78, March 23, 2007, No. 13, pp. 29)*
Pub: Crain Communications Inc.
Contact: Rance Crain, President
Ed: Jack Neff. **Description:** Many crisis-communications experts believe that the pet-food industry mishandled the problem by waiting almost a month to recall the 60 million 'wet-food' products after numerous consumer complaints. Experts site that the first 24 to 49 hours are the most important in dealing with a crisis of this nature.

46458 ■ *"Pet Waste Products Pick Up Sales" in Pet Product News (Vol. 66, September 2012, No. 9, pp. 58)*
Pub: Bowtie Inc.
Ed: Sandi Cain. **Description:** Pet supplies manufacturers are developing dog waste pickup bags and other convenient cleanup tools characterized by environment-friendliness and fashion. The demand for these cleanup tools has been motivated by dog owners' desire to minimize their and their dogs' environmental footprints.

46459 ■ *"PG&E Buys New Employee-Designed Gas Trucks" in Travel & Leisure Close-Up (October 8, 2012)*
Description: Pacific Gas and Electric Company has ordered trucks designed by a crew of their gas workers in Stockton, California. A truck assembly plant in Tracy, California has added 50 new workers to help assemble the utility's next-generation of gas maintenance and construction trucks. These trucks will be built to exact specifications and will help the economic vitality of the communities PG&E serve.

46460 ■ *"Phoenix Company, Dreambrands Inc., Realizing Dream of Global Growth" in The Business Journal - Serving Phoenix and the Valley of the Sun (Vol. 28, July 18, 2008, No. 46, pp. 1)*
Pub: American City Business Journals, Inc.
Contact: Whitney Shaw, President
Ed: Chris Casaccia. **Description:** Phoenix, Arizona-based lubricant maker DreamBrands Inc. is realizing global growth. The company, which has been generating interest from institutional investors, is seeking a second round of funding. Details of the company's products and marketing plans are also discussed.

46461 ■ *"Pierre's Ice Cream" in Ice Cream Reporter (Vol. 23, October 20, 2010, No. 11, pp. 8)*
Description: Pierre's Ice Cream has started work on its new $8 million manufacturing facility in Cleveland, Ohio.

46462 ■ *"Pilates Manufacturer Moves to New Space" in Sacramento Business Journal (Vol. 31, August 29, 2014, No. 27, pp. 6)*
Pub: American City Business Journals
Released: August 29, 2014. **Description:** Balanced Body Inc. is moving its headquarters from Depot Park to 5909 88th Street in Sacramento, California. The Pilates equipment manufacturer will have nearly 23,000-square-feet in the new location and spaces will be devoted to filming instructional fitness videos and conducting Pilates training sessions for instructors.

46463 ■ *"A Pioneer of Paying With Plastic" in Crain's Chicago Business (Vol. 31, April 28, 2008, No. 17, pp. 39)*
Pub: Crain Communications Inc.
Contact: Todd Johnson, Publisher
Ed: Phuong Ly. **Description:** Profile of Perfect Plastic Printing Corp., a family-owned company which manufactures credit cards, bank cards and gift cards and whose sales hit $50.1 million last year, a 16 percent jump from 2006.

46464 ■ *"Pitch for SPX Expansion was Full of Energy" in Charlotte Business Journal (Vol. 25, November 19, 2010, No. 35, pp. 1)*
Pub: Charlotte Business Journal
Ed: John Downey. **Description:** SPX Corporation announced that it will expand their headquarters in Ballantyne after Charlotte and North Carolina leaders made an aggressive push to retain the company. SPX Corporation is expected to invest $70 million for the expansion, which would mean 180 new jobs in Charlotte.

46465 ■ *"The Plane Truth" in Pittsburgh Business Times (Vol. 33, July 11, 2014, No. 52, pp. 8)*
Pub: American City Business Journals
Released: July 11, 2014. **Description:** Large U.S. aerospace manufacturers such as Boeing Company, Airbus SAS, Alcoa and other local companies have seen a boost in their sales, which shows the overall strength of the aerospace industry. With backlogs stretching well into the next decade and strong economic and leisure and business passenger growth, the industry seems bullish on the future of aerospace.

46466 ■ *"Playing Defense" in Crain's Chicago Business (Vol. 31, November 10, 2008, No. 45, pp. 4)*
Pub: Crain Communications Inc.
Contact: Todd Johnson, Publisher
Ed: Monee Fields-White. **Description:** Chicago's money managers are increasingly investing in local companies such as Caterpillar Inc., a maker of construction and mining equipment, Kraft Foods Inc. and Baxter International Inc., a manufacturer of medical products, in an attempt to bolster their portfolios. These companies have a history of surviving tough economic times.

46467 ■ *"Porsche Raises VW Stake, Makes Bid for Firm" in Globe & Mail (March 26, 2007, pp. B5)*
Pub: CTVglobemedia Publishing Inc.
Ed: Chad Thomas, Jeremy Van Loon. **Description:** Automobile giant Porsche AG has increased its stake in Volkswagen AG to $54 billion recently. The company is planning a merger by claiming 30% stake under German law.

46468 ■ *"Portability and Durability Are Key When It Comes to Pet Containment" in Pet Product News (Vol. 66, September 2012, No. 9, pp. 64)*
Pub: Bowtie Inc.
Ed: Wendy Bedwell-Wilson. **Description:** Containment products that have been offered by pet supply manufacturers are marked by features such as portability and durability. Some of these products include crates, partitions, and adjustable pens to cordon off dog and ensure their safety within the household premises.

46469 ■ *"Powder River Reports First Quarter Revenues Over 5 Million" in Canadian Corporate News (May 16, 2007)*
Description: Financial report for Powder River Basin Gas Corp., a revenue generating producer, marketer, and acquirer of crude oil and natural gas properties. Statistical data included.

46470 ■ *"Precision Fertilizer Spreading Shown at Agritechnica" in Farm Industry News (November 23, 2011)*
Pub: Penton Business Media Inc.
Contact: David Kieselstein, Chief Executive Officer
Ed: Karen McMahon. **Description:** Rauch, the German firm, introduced a new system that precisely spreads fertilizer on crops. The new product was shown at Agritechnica.

46471 ■ *"Predictions 2014; 7. New Model Launches to Challenge Suppliers" in Crain's Detroit Business (Vol. 30, January 6, 2014, No. 1, pp. 9)*
Pub: Crain Communications Inc. - Detroit
Contact: Keith Crain, Chairman
Released: January 6, 2014. **Description:** Ford Motor Company is introducing 37 new vehicles into its lineup for 2014, 23 globally and 16 in North America. Keeping pace with the new models and their changes creates a challenge for local automotive suppliers. Statistical data included.

46472 ■ *"Press Release: Revolver Grain Auger End from Mauer Manufacturing" in Farm Industry News (December 17, 2010)*
Description: Profile of the Revolver Grain Auger End from Mauer Manufacturing is presented. The new design eliminates grain loss/dribble, reduces grain in the next year's crop, and has a greater clearance for combine including auger.

46473 ■ *"Pricey Oil, High Dollar Wipe Out Jobs" in Globe & Mail (February 11, 2006, pp. B6)*
Ed: Heather Scoffield. **Description:** The impact of higher oil prices and dollar value, on manufacturing jobs in Canada, is discussed.

46474 ■ *"Priority: In Memoriam" in Inc. (December 2007, pp. 25-26, 28, 30)*
Pub: Gruner and Jahr USA Publishing Co.
Contact: J. Russell Denson, President
Ed: Ryan McCarthy. **Description:** Profiles of entrepreneurs who died in 2007; these individuals helped to create some major business trends in the last fifty years, from the advent of socially responsible business to development of quality manufacturing.

46475 ■ "Products and Services" in Canadian Electronics (Vol. 23, August 2008, No. 5, pp. 46)
Description: Directory of companies under the alphabetical listing of electronic equipment and allied components that they offer is presented.

46476 ■ "Proof Is In the Purse Strings: Katie Kalsi Line Expects to Hit $4.8 Million In Sales" in Memphis Business Journal (Vol. 34, August 31, 2012, No. 20, pp. 1)
Pub: American City Business Journal
Description: The company Katie Kalsi continues to grow with the strength of its custom-made handbags which are manufactured in El Paso, Texas. The hand-painted purses with removable straps have brought the company big department store contracts in 13 states. The owner predicts sales from retail increasing to $4.8million 2012.

46477 ■ "Providing Expertise Required to Develop Microsystems" in Canadian Electronics (Vol. 23, February 2008, No. 1, pp. 6)
Ed: Ian McWalter. **Description:** CMC Microsystems, formerly Canadian Microelectronics Corporation, is focused on empowering microelectronics and Micro-systems research in Canada. Microsystems offers the basis for innovations in the fields of science, environment, technology, automotives, energy, aerospace and communications technology. CMC's strategy in developing Microsystems in Canada is described.

46478 ■ "PRWT Service Acquires Pharmaceutical Plant: Firm Wins Multimillion-Dollar Contract with Merck" in Black Enterprise (March 1, 2008)
Pub: Earl G. Graves Publishing Co. Inc.
Contact: Earl G. Graves, Jr., President
Ed: Tamara E. Holmes. **Description:** PRWT Services Inc. expanded through its acquisition of a chemical manufacturing plant in New Jersey. The Whitehouse Station, part of Merck & Co. Inc. produces active pharmaceutical ingredients for antibiotics, making PRWT the first minority-owned company in the U.S. to manufacture active pharmaceutical ingredients.

46479 ■ "PSC Decision Could Help Bolster a Solar Market Supernova" in Tampa Bay Business Journal (Vol. 29, November 6, 2009, No. 46, pp. 1)
Pub: American City Business Journals
Ed: Michael Hinman. **Description:** Florida's Public Service Commission (PSC) decision on a power purchase agreement that could add 25 megawatts of solar energy on Tampa Electric Company's offerings is presented. The decision could support the growing market for suppliers and marketers of renewable energy such as Jabil Circuit Inc., which manufactures photovoltaic modules. Details of the agreement are discussed.

46480 ■ "Pulp Friction: Spin Off Mills to Boost Wood Products" in Globe & Mail (February 18, 2006, pp. B3)
Ed: Peter Kennedy. **Description:** The reasons behind the decision of chief executive officer Jim Shepherd of Canfor Corp. to sell pulp mills are presented.

46481 ■ "Put It In Drive" in Entrepreneur (Vol. 36, April 2008, No. 4, pp. 31)
Pub: Entrepreneur Press
Contact: Perlman Neil, President
Ed: Jill Amadio. **Description:** Commercial vehicle models for 2008 are presented. These new models are more user- and environment-friendly. Features and prices of car models and tips to consider before purchasing are presented.

46482 ■ "Putting 'Extra' in Extra-Silky Shampoo" in Crain's Chicago Business (Vol. 31, April 28, 2008, No. 17, pp. 37)
Pub: Crain Communications Inc.
Contact: Todd Johnson, Publisher
Ed: Phuong Ly. **Description:** Profile of HallStar Co., a Chicago-based company which develops and manufactures specialty chemicals to upgrade existing

products such as hair dye, lotion and deodorant. Hall-Star has seen its annual earnings rise more than 30 percent since 2002.

46483 ■ "Q&A: Celestica's Craig Muhlhauser" in Canadian Business (Vol. 81, September 15, 2008, No. 14-15, pp. 6)
Pub: Rogers Media Inc.
Contact: Tony Viner, President
Ed: Andrew Wahl. **Description:** Interview with Craig Muhlhauser who is the CEO of Celestica, a manufacturing company that provides services for the electronics sector; Muhlhauser discusses the company's restructuring program, which he feels was the secret to their surprising first-quarter results. Muhlhauser states that the company is operating with more forward visibility and that understanding the opportunities during the current economic situation presents the biggest challenge.

46484 ■ "Q&A: David Labistour" in Canadian Business (Vol. 81, March 17, 2008, No. 4, pp. 10)
Pub: Rogers Media Inc.
Contact: Tony Viner, President
Ed: Lauren McKeon. **Description:** David Labistour says that the difference between being a co-op retailer and a corporate-owned retailer in the case of Mountain Equipment Co-op (MEC) is that the company is owned by their customers and not by share-holders. Labistour also says that MEC works with their factories to ensure that these maintain ethical standards in the manufacturing process.

46485 ■ "Q&A Interview With Perrin Beatty" in Canadian Business (Vol. 80, October 8, 2007, No. 20, pp. 13)
Description: Perrin Beatty, president and chief executive officer of the Canadian Chamber of Commerce, talks about his move from the Canadian Manufacturers and Exporters to his current organization. He also discusses the state of Canada's economy, as well as the need for leadership.

46486 ■ "Q&A: Joseph Ribkoff" in Canadian Business (Vol. 81, March 31, 2008, No. 5, pp. 4)
Pub: Rogers Media Inc.
Contact: Tony Viner, President
Ed: Zena Olijnyk. **Description:** Joseph Ribkoff started his career in the garment trade by sweeping floors and running deliveries for a dress manufacturer called Town & Country and earned $16 a week. Ribkoff says that the key to controlling costs in Canada is to invest in the latest equipment and technology to stay competitive.

46487 ■ "Q&A: The CAPP's Greg Stringham" in Canadian Business (Vol. 81, February 12, 2008, No. 3, pp. 8)
Pub: Rogers Media Inc.
Contact: Tony Viner, President
Ed: Michelle Magnan. **Description:** Canadian Association of Petroleum Producers' Greg Stringham thinks that the new royalty plan will result in companies pulling out their investments for Alberta's conventional oil and gas sector. Stringham adds that Alberta is losing its competitive advantage and companies must study their cost profiles to retrieve that advantage. The effects of the royalty system on Alberta's economy are examined further.

46488 ■ "Qualcomm Could Win Big as the IPhone 3G Calls" in Barron's (Vol. 88, July 4, 2008, No. 28, pp. 30)
Pub: Dow Jones & Co., Inc.
Contact: Clare Hart, President
Ed: Eric J. Savitz. **Description:** Apple iPhone 3G's introduction could widen the smartphone market thereby benefiting handset chipmaker Qualcomm in the process. Qualcomm Senior V.P., Bill Davidson sees huge potential for his company's future beyond phones with their Snapdragon processor. The prospects of Sun Microsystems' shares are also discussed.

46489 ■ "The Quest for the Smart Prosthetic" in Canadian Business (Vol. 83, October 12,

2010, No. 17, pp. 26)
Pub: Rogers Media Inc.
Contact: Tony Viner, President
Ed: Jacqueline Nelson. **Description:** Information about a two-year research project led by Southern Methodist University (SMU) and funded by the Defense Advance Research Projects Agency (DARPA) is provided. The agency aims to create a 'smart prosthetic' which will improve the lives of military amputees. The planned prosthetic will use a sensor that can carry nerve signals through synthetic channels.

46490 ■ "The Question: Who Do You Think Is the Most Genuine?" in Advertising Age (Vol. 79, July 7, 2008, No. 26, pp. 4)
Pub: Crain Communications Inc.
Contact: Rance Crain, President
Ed: Ken Wheaton. **Description:** According to a survey conducted by Harris Interactive Reputation Quotient, Johnson & Johnson was deemed the most genuine brand. Google came in second followed by UPS.

46491 ■ "A Questionable Chemical Romance" in Barron's (Vol. 88, July 14, 2008, No. 28, pp. 28)
Pub: Dow Jones & Co., Inc.
Contact: Clare Hart, President
Ed: Andrew Bary. **Description:** Dow Chemical paid $78-a-share for the surprise takeover of Rohm & Haas. The acquisition is reducing Dow Chemical's financial flexibility at a time when chemical companies are being affected by high costs and a weak U.S. economy.

46492 ■ "R&R Ice Cream" in Ice Cream Reporter (Vol. 23, November 20, 2010, No. 12, pp. 8)
Pub: Ice Cream Reporter
Description: R&R Ice Cream, the United Kingdom's largest ice cream manufacturer, has completed a private offering of senior secured notes that has raised 298 million (pounds sterling) to fund expansion and acquisitions.

46493 ■ "R&R Launches Upscale Spoony's and Low Fat Dragon's Den" in Ice Cream Reporter (Vol. 23, August 20, 2010, No. 9, pp. 3)
Description: European ice cream manufacturer R&R has acquired French ice cream maker Rolland and will position itself as an upscale challenger to brands like Ben & Jerry's.

46494 ■ "RavenBrick Ready to Manufacture Its High-Tech Windows" in Denver Business Journal (Vol. 64, September 7, 2012, No. 16, pp. 1)
Pub: American City Business Journal
Description: RavenBrick LLC is set to build a new manufacturing plant in Denver, Colorado. The company manufactures auto-darkening window films. RavenBrick has raised a total of $13.5 million in new investment capital.

46495 ■ "Rebuffed, BAE Systems Fights Army Contract Decision" in Business Courier (Vol. 26, September 25, 2009)
Pub: American City Business Journals, Inc.
Contact: Whitney Shaw, President
Ed: Jon Newberry. **Description:** BAE Systems filed a complaint with the US Government Accountability Office after the US Army issued an order to BAE's competitor for armoured trucks which is potentially worth over $3 billion. Hundreds of jobs in Butler County, Ohio hinge on the success of the contract protest.

46496 ■ "Recession Management" in Canadian Business (Vol. 81, March 3, 2008, No. 3, pp. 62)
Ed: Joe Castaldo. **Description:** Some companies such as Capital One Financial Corp. are managing their finances as if a recession has already taken place to prepare themselves for the looming economic downturn. Intel Corp., meanwhile shows how

increasing its investments during a recession could be advantageous. Tips on how companies can survive a recession are provided.

46497 ■ *"Recovery on Tap for 2010?"* in *Orlando Business Journal (Vol. 26, January 1, 2010, No. 31, pp. 1)*
Pub: American City Business Journals
Ed: Melanie Stawicki Azam, Richard Bilbao, Christopher Boyd, Anjali Fluker. **Description:** Economic forecasts for Central Florida's leading business sectors in 2010 are presented. These sectors include housing, film and TV, sports business, law, restaurants, aviation, tourism and hospitality, banking and finance, commercial real estate, retail, health care, insurance, higher education, and manufacturing. According to some local executives, Central Florida's economy will slowly recover in 2010.

46498 ■ *"Red Diesel Cost Sparks a Move to Home-Grown Fuel"* in *Farmer's Weekly (March 28, 2008, No. 320)*
Description: Due to the rising cost of red diesel, the idea of growing one's own tractor fuel has an undeniable attraction for many farmers. A growing pressure is weighing on engine manufacturers to produce designs that can run on both SVO as well as biodiesel.

46499 ■ *"Redcorp Ventures Ltd.: Tulsequah Camp Construction Begins"* in *Canadian Corporate News (May 16, 2007)*
Description: Redfern Reources Ltd., a subsidiary of Redcorp Ventures Ltd., announced that Modular Transportable Solutions LLC was selected to design and manufacture its prefabricated, modular construction camp, cookhouse, administration buildings, and mine dry at the Tulsequah Mine location in northwest British Columbia due to the virtually indestructible design of the units that withstand extreme weather conditions.

46500 ■ *"Region to Be Named Innovation Hub"* in *Business Courier (Vol. 27, July 2, 2010, No. 9, pp. 1)*
Pub: Business Courier
Ed: Dan Monk. **Description:** The selection of Cincinnati's consumer-marketing cluster as a 'Hub of Innovation' by the Ohio Department of Development could boost Cincinnati's chances of receiving $100 million in grants from Ohio's Third Frontier program and other funding sources. Implications of the University of Cincinnati's designation as a Center of Excellence in Advanced Transportation and Aerospace are also discussed.

46501 ■ *"Region Wins as GE Puts Plants Close to R&D"* in *Business Review Albany (Vol. 41, July 4, 2014, No. 15, pp. 8)*
Pub: American City Business Journals, Inc.
Contact: Whitney Shaw, President
Released: July 4, 2014. **Description:** General Electric Company (GE) invested over $400 million into the expansion of its health care, battery and renewable energy businesses in the Albany, New York region. The company's local growth secured about 7,000 private-sector jobs in the area and strengthened the relationship between GE research and manufacturing.

46502 ■ *"Reinventing Your Rep Training Program"* in *Agency Sales Magazine (Vol. 39, August 2009, No. 8, pp. 40)*
Description: Tips on how to encourage manufacturer's representatives to attend scheduled training sessions are given. Manufacturers should learn the value of keeping the training program up-to-date and communicate with the sales team to know what needs to be revamped. Problems faced by representatives with inside sales staff should also be addressed by the manufacturer.

46503 ■ *"Relationship "Farming" Tools"* in *Agency Sales Magazine (Vol. 39, August 2009, No. 8, pp. 46)*
Ed: Terry L. Brock. **Description:** Manufacturer's representatives should spend time, money and effort in establishing and maintaining relationships; one tool to help is the new Fujitsu S1500 scanner. The

scanner can accomplish critical tasks, quickly, easily and at low cost. Other suggestions to help build better business relationships are given.

46504 ■ *"Remington Has Scouted Region"* in *Charlotte Business Journal (Vol. 27, May 25, 2012, No. 10, pp. 1)*
Pub: American City Business Journals, Inc.
Contact: Whitney Shaw, President
Ed: Ken Elkins. **Released:** May 25, 2012. **Description:** Remington Arms Company has been searching Charlotte, North Carolina for an industrial site. The company will use the site for its corporate headquarters. The firm has selected Lincoln Harris as site-selection consultant.

46505 ■ *"Rental Demand Boosts Revenue for Sun Communities Inc."* in *Crain's Detroit Business (Vol. 24, March 24, 2008, No. 12, pp. 4)*
Pub: Crain Communications Inc.
Contact: Rance E. Crain, President
Ed: Daniel Duggan. **Description:** Despite the decline in sales of manufactured homes, demand for rental units and rent-to-own programs have brought Sun Communities Inc. increased revenue. The real estate investment trust, based in Southfield, owns, operates, finances and develops manufactured home communities in the Midwest and Southeast. Statistical data included.

46506 ■ *"Rep Contracts: Simple, Clear, Fair"* in *Agency Sales Magazine (Vol. 39, September-October 2009, No. 9, pp. 3)*
Ed: Bryan C. Shirley. **Description:** Things that a manufacturer and a sales representative needs to strive for when creating an Agreement for Representation includes an agreement that is simple and complete, one that covers all the needs of both parties and is fair, equitable, and balanced. Sales representatives need to make more sales calls and find new opportunities during this recession.

46507 ■ *"Rep Vs. Direct: Always an Interesting Story"* in *Agency Sales Magazine (Vol. 39, July 2009, No. 7, pp. 3)*
Ed: Bryan C. Shirley. **Description:** Manufacturers benefit from outsourcing their field sales to professional sales representatives in the areas of multi-line selling and customer knowledge and relationship. Some misperceptions about sales reps include the belief that they are an additional 'channel' in sales.

46508 ■ *"Rep Vs. Direct: Inside the Mind of One Manufacturer"* in *Agency Sales Magazine (Vol. 39, July 2009, No. 7, pp. 8)*
Ed: Jack Foster. **Description:** Fantech President Glenn Thompson believes that a commissioned representative sales force is the most effective means of going to market. Thompson also discusses the pros and cons of working with reps and the qualities to look for in a rep.

46509 ■ *"Report: McD's Pepsi Score Best With Young Hispanics"* in *Brandweek (Vol. 49, April 21, 2008, No. 16, pp. 8)*
Pub: Nielsen Business Media Inc.
Contact: Howard Appelbaum, President
Ed: Della de Lafuente. **Description:** According to a new report, in order to reach Hispanic Gen Yers, marketing strategists need to understand this demographic's 'bi-dentity,' something which has proved an elusive task to many marketers. Another trend is the emergence of Latinas who have careers, as opposed to just jobs. There is an opportunity to tap this new, young and empowered female market with innovative messaging. Statistical data included.

46510 ■ *"Reports of Banks' Revival were Greatly Exaggerated"* in *Barron's (Vol. 88, July 7, 2008, No. 27, pp. L14)*
Pub: Dow Jones & Co., Inc.
Contact: Clare Hart, President
Ed: Jack Willoughby. **Description:** Performance of mutual funds improved for the second quarter of 2008 compared to the previous quarter, registering an average gain of 0.13 percent; funds focusing on natural resources rose the highest, their value rising by an average of 24.50 percent.

46511 ■ *"Reps Have Needs Too!"* in *Agency Sales Magazine (Vol. 39, December 2009, No. 11, pp. 16)*
Ed: Bill Heyden. **Description:** There is common information that a sales representatives needs to know prior to choosing a manufacturer to represent. Both parties must keep promises made to customers and prospects. Reps also need the support from the manufacturers and to clear matters regarding their commission. Interviewing tips for representatives to get this vital information are presented.

46512 ■ *"Reps Vs. Factory Direct Sales Force..Which Way to Go?"* in *Agency Sales Magazine (Vol. 39, September-October 2009, No. 9, pp. 28)*
Ed: Eric P. Johnson. **Description:** Hiring independent manufacturers' sales representative is a cost-effective alternative to a direct sales force. Sales reps have predictable sales costs that go up and down with sales, stronger local relationships and better market intelligence.

46513 ■ *"Reps Vs. Factory Direct Sales Force..Which Way to Go?"* in *Agency Sales Magazine (Vol. 39, September-October 2009, No. 9, pp. 28)*
Ed: Eric P. Johnson. **Description:** Hiring independent manufacturers' sales representative is a cost-effective alternative to a direct sales force. Sales reps have predictable sales costs that go up and down with sales, stronger local relationships and better market intelligence.

46514 ■ *"Research Reports: How Analysts Size Up Companies"* in *Barron's (Vol. 88, July 14, 2008, No. 28, pp. M13)*
Pub: Dow Jones & Co., Inc.
Contact: Clare Hart, President
Ed: Anita Peltonen. **Description:** Shares of Bankrate and AutoZone both get a 'Buy' rating from analysts while Zions Bancorporation's shares are downgraded from 'Outperform' to 'Neutral'. The shares of Jet Blue Airline and Deckers Outdoor, a manufacturer of innovative footwear, are also rated and discussed. Statistical data included.

46515 ■ *"A Reverse-Innovation Playbook: Insights From a Company That Developed Products For Emerging Markets and Then Brought Them Back Home"* in *Harvard Business Review (Vol. 90, April 2012, No. 4, pp. 120)*
Pub: Harvard Business Review Press
Contact: Peter E. Walsh, Director
Ed: Vijay Govindarajan. **Released:** April 2012. **Description:** An overview is presented on the organizational change implemented by Harman International Industries Inc. to create products for emerging markets and ensure that they would be accepted in already established middle markets. Components include setting radical goals, selecting team leaders with no competing interests, and leveraging global resources.

46516 ■ *"Revisiting Rep Coping Strategies"* in *Agency Sales Magazine (Vol. 39, December 2009, No. 11, pp. 32)*
Ed: Jack Foster. **Description:** Independent manufacturers representatives should become a well-rounded and complete businessman with continued education. The new type of representative is a problem solver and the resource for answering questions. Employing the concept of synergistic selling is also important to salespeople.

46517 ■ *"ReWalk Robotics Aims for IPO"* in *Boston Business Journal (Vol. 34, July 18, 2014, No. 24, pp. 7)*
Pub: American City Business Journals, Inc.
Contact: Whitney Shaw, President
Released: July 18, 2014. **Description:** ReWalk Robotics, an Israeli firm that manufactures wearable robotics exoskeletons for paraplegics, wants to launch an initial public offering (IPO) to raise US$57.5 million. In a July 2014 filing, ReWalk cited an accumulated debt of US$27 million at the end of 2013, justifying the need to go public and raise additional funds.

46518 ■ "RipCode Founder Starts Private Equity Firm Vspeed Capital" in Dallas Business Journal (Vol. 35, September 9, 2012, No. 51, pp. 1)
Pub: American City Business Journal
Ed: Jeff Bounds. **Description:** Brendon Mills, founder of Genband Inc., cofounds Vspeed Capital LLC, a new private equity firm. The company has joined forces with Galatyn Private Equity to make its first purchase, that of Fortress Solutions Ltd. Vspeed plans to acquire companies in the manufacturing and distribution sectors, and double its revenue in the next 24 months.

46519 ■ Risk-Free Entrepreneur
Ed: Don Debelak. **Released:** June 2006. **Price:** , $14.95. **Description:** Information is offered to help entrepreneurs to develop an idea for a product or service and have other companies provide the marketing, manufacturing and staff.

46520 ■ "River Plan in Disarray" in Business Journal Portland (Vol. 26, December 4, 2009, No. 39, pp. 1)
Pub: American City Business Journals, Inc.
Ed: Andy Giegerich. **Description:** Portland's proposed rules on a waterfront development plan for the Willamette River calls for fees intended for river bank preservation, a move that could drive industrial manufacturers away. The manufacturers, under the Working Waterfront Coalition, claim that the proposals could increase riverfront building costs by 15 percent.

46521 ■ "Robai Aims To Sell Robot Arm for Manufacturers" in Boston Business Journal (Vol. 34, July 4, 2014, No. 22, pp. 5)
Pub: American City Business Journals, Inc.
Contact: Whitney Shaw, President
Released: July 4, 2014. **Description:** Robai aims to raise $5 million in funding to help commercialize a lightweight and easy to use robot arm, called Cyton. The robot arm operates much like a human arm with multiple ranges of motion. It weighs under five pounds, can be programmed in 15 minutes, has the ability to reach around obstacles, and is meant to do repetitive, mundane tasks for contract manufacturing companies.

46522 ■ "The Role of Leadership In Successful International Mergers and Acquisitions: Why Renault-Nissan Succeeded and DaimlerChrysler-Mitsubishi Failed" in Human Resource Management (Vol. 51, May-June 2012, No. 3, pp. 433-456)
Pub: John Wiley & Sons Inc.
Contact: Stephen M. Smith, President
Ed: Carol Gill. **Description:** The effects of national and organizational culture on the performance of Nissan and Mitsubishi after their mergers with Renault and DaimlerChrysler respectively are examined. Japanese national culture was found to influence organizational culture and human resource management practices, while leadership affected the success of their turnaround efforts.

46523 ■ "Ron Carpenter" in Crain's Cleveland Business (Vol. 30, June 29, 2009, No. 25, pp. 12)
Pub: Crain Communications Inc.
Ed: Dan Shingler. **Description:** Profile of Ron Carpenter, owner of Production Tool Company located in Twinsburg, Ohio. Carpenter was forced to lay off half of his staff of 14 workers after the auto business tanked. He believes it was the single most difficult decision he had to make as a manager.

46524 ■ "Room For the Boom?" in Dallas Business Journal (Vol. 37, May 9, 2014, No. 35, pp. 4)
Pub: American City Business Journals
Released: May 9, 2014. **Description:** North Texas needs more housing and better transportation systems to sustain its economic growth. It also lacks residential land for new development construction projects. Meanwhile, Toyota Motor Company is set to move 4,000 manufacturing jobs to the region.

46525 ■ "Ross: There's Still Money In the Auto Industry" in Crain's Detroit Business (Vol. 24, January 28, 2008, No. 4, pp. 12)
Pub: Crain Communications Inc. - Detroit
Contact: Keith Crain, Chairman
Ed: Brent Snavely. **Description:** Wilbur Ross, chairman and CEO of WL Ross and Company LLC, a private equity firm, predicts U.S. vehicle sales will fall by about 750,000 in 2008, but continues to look for supplier bargains.

46526 ■ "Rough Q1 Begs Question: Is the Crocs Craze Over?" in Brandweek (Vol. 49, April 21, 2008, No. 16, pp. 16)
Pub: Nielsen Business Media Inc.
Contact: Howard Appelbaum, President
Ed: Eric Newman. **Description:** Crocs, a rubber shoemaker, announced last week that it missed its expected first quarter revenues by 15 percent. The popular rubber sandals are suffering in sales due to a number of factors including a tougher economic environment, less expensive, knock-off brands, the cold weather delay of the spring season and fading consumer interest in plastic shoes.

46527 ■ "Roundtable: Natural Sourcing Trends" in Pet Product News (Vol. 66, September 2012, No. 9, pp. S12)
Description: Business owners and executives from the manufacturing and retail sectors of pet supplies industry share how their companies have been sourcing proteins for natural foods for dogs and cats. They also share views about trends in the market for these foods.

46528 ■ "Roundtable: The Auto Sector Shifts Gears" in Mergers & Acquisitions: The Dealmaker's Journal (March 1, 2008)
Pub: SourceMedia Inc.
Contact: James M. Malkin, Chief Executive Officer
Description: Industry professionals discuss the current state of the automotive sector as well as what they predict for the future of the industry; also provides information for investors about opportunities in the sector.

46529 ■ "Royal Dutch's Grip Firm on Shell" in Globe & Mail (March 19, 2007, pp. B1)
Pub: CTVglobemedia Publishing Inc.
Ed: David Ebner. **Description:** The proposed acquisition of Shell Canada Ltd. by Royal Dutch Shell PLC for $8.7 billion is discussed.

46530 ■ "Rumors Kill Algoma Takeover Talks" in Globe & Mail (March 14, 2007, pp. B14)
Ed: Tara Perkins. **Description:** Canada-based steel manufacturing giant Salzgitter AG has dropped its acquisition negotiations with Algoma Steel Inc. The decision comes after the secret price quotation was leaked to competitors.

46531 ■ "Russia: Uncle Volodya's Flagging Christmas Spirit" in The Economist (Vol. 390, January 3, 2009, No. 8612, pp. 22)
Description: Overview of Russia's struggling economy as well as unpopular government decisions such as raising import duties on used foreign vehicles so as to protect Russian carmakers.

46532 ■ "Russian Renaissance" in Chicago Tribune (September 22, 2008)
Pub: McClatchy-Tribune Information Services
Ed: Alex Rodriguez. **Description:** Winemakers from Russia are returning to the craft and quality of winemaking now that they are free from Soviet restraints.

46533 ■ "Rust Belt No More: The Demise of Manufacturing" in Crain's Chicago Business (Vol. 31, March 31, 2008, No. 13, pp. 52)
Pub: Crain Communications Inc.
Contact: Todd Johnson, Publisher
Ed: Sarah A. Klein. **Description:** Discusses the history of manufacturing in the Chicago area as well as the history of manufacturer International Harvester Co.

46534 ■ "S.A. Chasing Tesla, Other Auto-Industry Firms" in San Antonio Business Journal (Vol. 28, April 4, 2014, No. 8, pp. 7)
Pub: American City Business Journals
Released: April 4, 2014. **Description:** San Antonio, Texas has joined cities trying to land the $5 billion battery plant of Tesla Motors that could employ 6,500 workers. San Antonio's drive to establish a major auto-industry cluster in the region would be boosted by Tesla's choosing the city as the site for manufacturing batteries. The benefits from the Texas-Mexico Automotive SuperCluster initiative are also explored.

46535 ■ "St. Crispin's Legacy: Shoemaking in Perth, Ontario 1834-2004"
Pub: Epic Press
Released: September 29, 2014. **Price:** , $24.95 paperback. **Description:** Historical presentation that traces the surprising evolution of shoemaking in a small Ontario, Canada town. A profile of the Brown Shoe Company, the manufacturer that rose from traditional craft to a major industry and how it impacted the sector, the town and its local citizens is chronicled.

46536 ■ "Sale of Solo Cup Plant Pending" in Boston Business Journal (Vol. 29, June 17, 2011, No. 6, pp. 1)
Pub: American City Business Journals, Inc.
Ed: Daniel J. Sernovitz. **Description:** Baltimore developers Vanguard Equities Inc. and Greenberg Gibbons Commercial have contracted to buy the Solo Cup Company facility in Owing Mills and are now considering several plans for the property. Sale should be completed by September 2011 but no proposed sale terms are disclosed.

46537 ■ "Sales Reps: How Manufacturers and Reps Can Better Work with Each Other for Mutual Gain"
Pub: R & R Publishing
Released: November 19, 2012. **Price:** , $4.99 Kindle. **Description:** Advice is given to help manufacturers and sales representatives can create a positive partnership that will increase revenue, while extending their working relationship. Topics include: reasons to work with a representative, who becomes a rep, reps domain, finding and selecting a rep's services, commission, manufacturer complaints about reps, sales representative training, advice for both parties, and the future of these relationships.

46538 ■ "Sales of What's Under Feet Add Up Fast" in Pet Product News (Vol. 66, September 2012, No. 9, pp. S8)
Description: Pet supplies retailers and manufacturers have been emphasizing the type of substances in creating new approaches to developing environment-friendly natural litters and beddings for small mammals and cats. Some of these approaches are highlighted, along with marketing strategies retailers have implemented.

46539 ■ "San Jose Hopes to Build on Uptick in Manufacturing" in Silicon Valley/San Jose Business Journal (Vol. 30, July 13, 2012, No. 16, pp. 1)
Pub: American City Business Journal
Description: San Jose, California-based manufacturing companies that cater to high-technology companies and startups have been experiencing an uptick in business. The San Jose metropolitan area is the country's second-largest specialized manufacturing market and the city has rolled out its efforts to help support this growth.

46540 ■ "Sandi Jackson: Alderman, 7th Ward, City of Chicago" in Crain's Chicago Business (Vol. 31, May 5, 2008, No. 18, pp. 31)
Pub: Crain Communications Inc.
Contact: Todd Johnson, Publisher
Ed: Sarah A. Klein. **Description:** Profile of Sandi Jackson who is an alderman of the 7th ward of the city of Chicago and is addressing issues such as poverty and crime as well as counting on a plan to develop the former USX Corp. steel mill to revitalize the area's economic climate.

46541 ■ *"Sandvik Expands Energy-Saving Program"* in *Modern Machine Shop* (Vol. 84, September 2011, No. 4, pp. 48)
Pub: Gardner Business Media, Inc.
Contact: Richard G. Kline, President
E-mail: rkline@gardnerweb.com
Description: Sandvik Coromant, based in Fair Lawn, New Jersey, expanded its Sustainable Manufacturing Program that originally was developed to help Japanese-based firms reduce electricity consumption by 15 percent after the recent earthquake that cause loss of electrical power. The program now provides energy reduction through the Sandvick cutting tool technology, application techniques and productivity increases.

46542 ■ *"Saratoga Eagle Project Quenches Thirst To Grow"* in *Business Review, Albany New York* (Vol. 34, November 29, 2007, No. 35, pp. 3)
Pub: American City Business Journals, Inc.
Ed: Robin K. Cooper. **Description:** Saratoga Eagle Sales and Service will be searching for contractors for the construction of its new beverage distribution center at the WJ Grande Industrial Park in Saratoga Springs, New York. The $8 million, 107,000 square foot facility is part of Saratoga Eagle's expansion plan. The company's growth in the Capital Region market and $1.3 million tax break are discussed.

46543 ■ *"Search Engine: GE Looks Around"* in *Business Courier* (Vol. 24, March 7, 2008, No. 48, pp. 1)
Pub: American City Business Journals, Inc.
Contact: Whitney Shaw, President
Ed: Laura Baverman. **Description:** GE Aviation, an aircraft engine company, could move about 1,500 Tri-employees to its new office in West Chester, Liberty Township, Northern Kentucky, as its leases are set to expire in 2009 and 2010. The company revealed that developers are prompting the firm to send out a request-for-proposal to choose development companies in 2008.

46544 ■ *"The Second Most Fuel-Efficient Tractor of the Decade: John Deere 8320R"* in *Farm Industry News* (November 10, 2011)
Pub: Penton Business Media Inc.
Contact: David Kieselstein, Chief Executive Officer
Description: John Deere's 8320R Tractor was ranked second in the Farm Industry News listing of the top 40 most fuel-efficient tractors of the decade, following the winner, John Deere's 8295R PTO tractor.

46545 ■ *"SECO's Second Incite Brand Prism, A Front Locking Prism Assembly"* in *Point of Beginning* (Vol. , 2008, No. , pp.)
Pub: BNP Media
Contact: Tagg Henderson, Chief Executive Officer
Description: Seco Manufacturing's 3015-Series lock features an all-metal tilting holder with an improved brass front locking lever for improved security for any building.

46546 ■ *"Sellers Shift Gears"* in *Crain's Detroit Business* (Vol. 25, June 22, 2009, No. 25, pp. 3)
Pub: Crain Communications Inc. - Detroit
Contact: Keith Crain, Chairman
Description: Of the 14 new car Chrysler dealerships in the Detroit area who had franchises terminated, Joe Ricci of Dearborn will sell used cars at his new business called All American Buyer's Service; Lochmoor Automotive Group in Detroit will focus on Mahindra & Mahindra trucks; Mt. Clemens Dodge, Clinton Township is also selling Mahindra & Mahindra trucks; and Monicatti Chrysler Jeep, Sterling Heights, will offer service along with selling used cars.

46547 ■ *"Selling Michigan; R&D Pushed as Reason For Chinese To Locate In State"* in *Crain's Detroit Business* (Vol. 24, January 14, 2008)
Pub: Crain Communications Inc. - Detroit
Contact: Keith Crain, Chairman
Ed: Marti Benedetti. **Description:** Southeast Michigan Economic Development organizations are working to develop relationships with Chinese manufacturers so they will locate their automotive research and development operations in the state.

46548 ■ *"Seven Things Great Employers Do (That Others Don't); Unusual, Innovative, and Proven Tactics To Create Productive and Profitable Working Environments"* in *Gallup Business Journal* (April 15, 2014)
Pub: Gallup Press
Released: April 15, 2014. **Description:** Seven unusual, innovative, and proven tactics that create productive and profitable working environments are examined through researching 32 companies. These firms represented many industries, including healthcare, financial services, hospitality, manufacturing, and retail throughout the world.

46549 ■ *"Seven Tips for Continuous Improvement"* in *American Printer* (Vol. 128, July 1, 2011, No. 7)
Pub: Penton Media Inc.
Description: Seven tips are given to help any graphic arts or printing company improve by integrating lean manufacturing into operations.

46550 ■ *"Sharp Restarts Toner Manufacturing: Production Moved from Japan to Serve China Market"* in *Memphis Business Journal* (Vol. 34, May 11, 2012, No. 4, pp. 1)
Pub: American City Business Journal
Ed: Michael Sheffield. **Description:** Sharp Manufacturing Company of America has decided to reopen its ink toner production plant in Memphis, Tennessee because of cheaper material, labor and freight costs. The company's move was also attributed to local economic growth and the government support they received after a 2008 tornado hit the area surrounding the area.

46551 ■ *"Sharp To Halt Panel Production In Face of Foreign Competition"* in *Memphis Business Journal* (Vol. 35, January 31, 2014, No. 43, pp. 7)
Pub: American City Business Journals
Released: January 31, 2014. **Description:** Sharp Manufacturing Company of America will no longer produce solar panels in Memphis, Tennessee because of increased competition in the solar industry. The company, which benefited from the Solar Investment Tax Credit, reveals that its solar business is changing with new technology.

46552 ■ *"Shedding Light on Innovation"* in *Rental Product News* (Vol. 33, June 2011)
Pub: Cygnus Business Media
Contact: Paul Mackler, Chief Executive Officer
Ed: Rod Dickens. **Description:** Light tower manufacturers have introduced numerous new products that feature alternative power sources, LED lighting and a second generation of performance and value.

46553 ■ *"Shell Profit Top $2 Billion as Oil Sands Output Surges"* in *Globe & Mail* (January 26, 2006, pp. B6)
Ed: Patrick Brethour. **Description:** The reasons behind posting of $2 billion profits for 2005, by Shell Canada Ltd. are presented.

46554 ■ *"Shermag Plans Two Shutdowns, 300 More Layoffs"* in *Globe & Mail* (February 13, 2007, pp. B5)
Ed: Bertrand Marotte. **Description:** Shermag Inc., Canada's largest publicly traded furniture company, is permanently closing two plants and eliminating 300 jobs. The mounting losses and deteriorating stock prices are stated as main reasons for plant shutdowns.

46555 ■ *"Sherwin-Williams Workers Forgo Travel for Virtual Trade Show"* in *Crain's Cleveland Business* (Vol. 28, October 15, 2007, No. 41, pp. 4)
Pub: Crain Communications Inc.
Ed: John Booth. **Description:** Overview of Cyber-Coating 2007, a cutting-edge virtual three-dimensional trade show that exhibitors such as Sherwin-Williams Co.'s Chemical Coatings Division will take part in by chatting verbally or via text messages in order to exchange information and listen to pitches just like they would on an actual trade show floor.

46556 ■ *"Shipbuilding & Defence"* in *Canadian Sailings* (July 7, 2008)
Ed: Sharon Hobson. **Description:** Overview of the Joint Support Ship Project whose initial budget was set at $2.1 billion for the acquisition of the ships required for the Canadian navy; another $800 million was allotted for 20 years of in-service support. Four teams of competitors bid for the contract and the Department of National Defence decided to fund two teams for the project definition phase of the competition.

46557 ■ *"Shoe's On Other Foot"* in *Business Courier* (Vol. 24, November 29, 2007, No. 33, pp. 1)
Pub: American City Business Journals, Inc.
Contact: Whitney Shaw, President
Ed: Lucy May. **Description:** Ronald Hummons was fresh out of prison for felony in 2000, and through the help of spiritual non-profit group the Lord's Gym he was able to turn his life around and start his own company Grapevine Ltd. LLC, which makes C-town athletic shoes.

46558 ■ *The Six Sigma Manual for Small and Medium Businesses: What You Need to Know Explained Simply*
Pub: Atlantic Publishing Co.
Contact: Amanda Miller, Manager
E-mail: amiller@atlantic-pub.com
Ed: Marsha R. Ford. **Price:** $24.95. **Description:** The Six Sigma set of practices used to systematically improve business practices by eliminating defects. To be Six Sigma compliant, a company must produce no more than 3.4 defects per one million products, and if achieved will save the firm millions of dollars. The two main methodologies of Six Sigma are outlined.

46559 ■ *"Size Does Matter"* in *International Journal of Globalisation and Small Business* (Vol. 4, September 21, 2010, No. 1, pp. 61)
Pub: Publishers Communication Group
Contact: Doug Wright, Director
Ed: Julia Cornnell, Ranjit Voola. **Description:** Examination of how members of an Australian-based manufacturing and engineering cluster share knowledge through networking as a means to improve competitive advantage.

46560 ■ *"Sizing Up Bentley"* in *Barron's* (Vol. 92, September 17, 2012, No. 38, pp. 16)
Description: The energy efficiencies of cars produced by Bentley Motors have shown little improvement over time. The company needs to invest in improving the fuel efficiencies of its vehicles to attract new customers and remain competitive.

46561 ■ *"Slimmed-Down Supplier TI Automotive Relaunches"* in *Crain's Detroit Business* (Vol. 26, January 11, 2010, No. 2, pp. 14)
Pub: Crain Communications Inc.
Contact: Rance E. Crain, President
Ed: Robert Sherefkin. **Description:** TI Automotive Ltd., one of the world's largest suppliers of fuel storage and delivery systems, has reorganized the company by splitting it into five global divisions and is relaunching its brand which is now more focused on new technology.

46562 ■ *"Slimmer Interiros Make Small Cars Seem Big"* in *Automotive News* (Vol. 86, October 31, 2011, No. 6488, pp. 16)
Pub: Crain Communications Inc.
Contact: Rance E. Crain, President
Ed: David Sedgwick. **Description:** Cost-conscious buyers want luxury car amenities in their smaller vehicles, so automakers are rethinking interiors. Style, efficiency and value could be the next trend in vehicles.

46563 ■ *"Slots Contractors: Maryland Minority Goal a Test"* in *Baltimore Business Journal* (Vol. 27, November 20, 2009, No. 28, pp. 1)
Pub: American City Business Journals
Ed: Scott Dance. **Description:** Slot machine manufacturers in Maryland have been searching minority

business enterprises (MBEs) that will provide maintenance and delivery services to the machines. MBEs will also build the stands where the machines will be mounted.

46564 ■ *"S.M. Whitney Co. (1868-2010)" in Canadian Business (Vol. 83, October 12, 2010, No. 17, pp. 27)*
Pub: Rogers Media Inc.
Contact: Tony Viner, President

Ed: Angelina Chapin. **Description:** A history of S.M. Whitney Company is presented. The cotton company was opened in 1868. The cotton is sold to textile manufacturers after crops have been picked, ginned and baled. The company closed down in 2010 after chief executive officer Barry Whitney decided to sell his last bale of cotton.

46565 ■ *"Small is the New Big in Autos" in Globe & Mail (February 16, 2006, pp. B3)*
Ed: Greg Keenan. **Description:** The reasons behind the introduction of subcompact cars by companies such as Ford Motor Co. are presented. The automobiles were unveiled at Canadian International Auto Show in Toronto.

46566 ■ *"Smart Car Sales Take Big Hit in Recession" in Business Journal-Milwaukee (Vol. 28, December 10, 2010, No. 10, pp. A1)*
Pub: Milwaukee Business Journal

Ed: Stacy Vogel Davis. **Description:** Sales of smart cars in Milwaukee declined in 2010. Smart Center Milwaukee sold only 52 new cars through October 2010. Increased competition is seen as a reason for the decline in sales.

46567 ■ *Sneaker Wars: The Enemy Brothers Who Founded Adidas and Puma and the Family Feud that Forever Changed the Business of Sports*
Pub: HarperCollins Ecco

Ed: Barbara Smit. **Released:** March 17, 2009. **Price:** $15.99, paperback. **Description:** A history of Puma and Adidas shoes and the two German brothers who built the empires. **Availability:** Print.

46568 ■ *"Sobering Consequences: Chicago Rumored to be Leading MillerCoors HQ" in The Business Journal-Milwaukee (Vol. 25, July 11, 2008, No. 42, pp. A1)*
Pub: American City Business Journals, Inc.
Contact: Whitney Shaw, President

Ed: Rich Rovito. **Description:** Milwaukee Mayor Tom Barrett and Wisconsin Governor Jim Doyle met with MillerCoors management in an effort to convince the company to locate its corporate headquarters in the city. The company is expected to announce its decision by mid-July 2008. It was revealed that the decision-making process is focusing on determining an optimal location for the headquarters.

46569 ■ *"Solar Credit Lapse Spur Late Demand" in The Business Journal - Serving Phoenix and the Valley of the Sun (Vol. 28, July 18, 2008)*
Pub: American City Business Journals, Inc.
Contact: Whitney Shaw, President

Ed: Patrick O'Grady. **Description:** Businesses looking to engage in the solar energy industry are facing the problems of taxation and limited solar panel supply. Solar panels manufacturers are focusing more on the European market. Political issues surrounding the federal tax credit policy on solar energy users are also discussed.

46570 ■ *"Solar Gaining Power in Tennessee" in Memphis Business Journal (Vol. 34, June 15, 2012, No. 9, pp. 1)*
Pub: American City Business Journal

Ed: Michael Sheffield. **Description:** Tennessee's solar energy industry has grown, the Tennessee Solar Institute has reported. Solar energy use, manufacture and employment in the state have increase in the past four years.

46571 ■ *"Solectria Renewables Supplies Solar Stations for Solar Farm in New*

England" in Professional Close-Up (October 2, 2012)
Description: Solectria Renewables LLC reported that its Megawatt Solar Stations (MSS) will be used for the 5MW True North solar farm in Salisbury, Massachusetts. Solectria is an American PV inverter manufacturer. Details of the project are given.

46572 ■ *"Solidarity UAW Forever" in Crain's Detroit Business (Vol. 25, June 1, 2009, No. 22, pp. M001)*
Pub: Crain Communications Inc. - Detroit
Contact: Keith Crain, Chairman

Ed: Ryan Beene. **Description:** United Auto Workers union has made it difficult for certain businesses to move to Michigan. Discussion is made about the issues involved and changes that need to be made in the way labor and management do business.

46573 ■ *"Solon Wire to Ramp Up Plant" in Memphis Business Journal (Vol. 33, March 23, 2012, No. 50, pp. 1)*
Pub: American City Business Journal
Description: Solon Wire Company is set to reopen a production facility, following its acquisition of Bluff City Steel Industries. Solon will begin manufacturing steel wires again by the end of March 2012.

46574 ■ *"The Solution" in Entrepreneur (Vol. 37, October 2009, No. 10, pp. 71)*
Pub: Entrepreneur Press
Contact: Perlman Neil, President

Ed: Jennifer Wang. **Description:** Ford's 2010 Transit Connect is a compact commercial van developed specifically for small business owners. The compact van offers an integrated in-dash computer system providing a cellular broadband connection.

46575 ■ *"Somanetics to Buy Back Up to $15 Million of Common Shares" in Crain's Detroit Business (Vol. 24, April 7, 2008, No. 14, pp. 4)*
Pub: Crain Communications Inc.
Contact: Rance E. Crain, President

Ed: Tom Henderson. **Description:** Somanetics Corp., a company that manufactures and markets noninvasive devices for monitoring blood oxygen levels in the brain and elsewhere in the body during surgery, plans to buy back up to $15 million worth of its common shares. Statistical data included on the company's current and past earnings and stock prices as well as its plans to increase revenue.

46576 ■ *"Some Relief Possible Following Painful Week" in Barron's (Vol. 88, July 14, 2008, No. 28, pp. M3)*
Pub: Dow Jones & Co., Inc.
Contact: Clare Hart, President

Ed: Kopin Tan. **Description:** Dow Chemical is offering a 74 percent premium to acquire Rohm & Haas' coatings and electronics materials operations. Frontline amassed a 5.6 percent stake in rival Overseas Shipholding Group and a merger between the two would create a giant global fleet with pricing power. Highlights of the U.S. stock market during the week that ended in July 11, 2008 are discussed. Statistical data included.

46577 ■ *"Sources" in Canadian Electronics (Vol. 23, August 2008, No. 5, pp. 12)*
Description: Directory of electronic manufacturers, distributors and representatives in Canada is provided. The list presents distributors and representatives under each manufacturer.

46578 ■ *"Spam's Biggest Fan" in Barron's (Vol. 92, August 25, 2012, No. 35, pp. 42)*
Pub: Dow Jones & Co., Inc.
Contact: Clare Hart, President

Ed: Lawrence C. Strauss. **Description:** Jeffrey Ettinger, chief executive officer of meat packing and packaged food firm Hormel Foods, is credited with expanding the company's product offerings. Ettinger, who took over in 2006, involves himself in almost every aspect of the company's business.

46579 ■ *"The Spark's Back in Sanyo" in Barron's (Vol. 88, March 31, 2008, No. 13, pp. M9)*
Pub: Dow Jones & Co., Inc.
Contact: Clare Hart, President

Ed: Jay Alabaster. **Description:** Things are looking up for Sanyo Electric after its string of calamities that

range from major losses brought on by earthquake damage to its semiconductor operations and its near collapse and bailout. The company looks poised for a rebound as they are on track for their first net profit since 2003 and could beat its earnings forecast for 2008.

46580 ■ *"Special Sector" in Crain's Cleveland Business (Vol. 28, November 5, 2007, No. 44, pp. 3)*
Pub: Crain Communications Inc.

Ed: David Bennett. **Description:** Specialty Metals Processing Inc. is investing more than $6 million to amp up productions; the company believes this big investment will pay off due to the company's ability to process complex metal alloys, such as titanium, in a region where there is a small number of competitors.

46581 ■ *"Spectre of Iran War Spooks Oil Markets" in Globe & Mail (March 28, 2007, pp. B1)*
Pub: CTVglobemedia Publishing Inc.

Ed: Shawn McCarthy. **Description:** The increase in the price of crude oil by $5 a barrel to reach $68 in the United States following speculation over war against Iran, is discussed.

46582 ■ *"Spell It Out" in Entrepreneur (Vol. 36, April 2008, No. 4, pp. 123)*
Pub: Entrepreneur Press
Contact: Perlman Neil, President

Ed: Emily Weisberg. **Description:** IM:It is an apparel and accessories company that markets products with instant messaging (IM) acronyms and emoticons. Examples of these are 'LOL' and 'GTG'. Other details on IM:It products are discussed.

46583 ■ *"Spending the Stimulus" in Crain's Cleveland Business (Vol. 30, June 29, 2009, No. 25, pp. 3)*
Pub: Crain Communications Inc.

Ed: Dan Shingler. **Description:** Three of northeast Ohio's industrial firms will receive funding from the President's economic stimulus package. Eaton Corporation, Cleveland, Ohio; Parker Hannifin Corporation and Timken Company are expected to see higher revenues from the government spending plans.

46584 ■ *"A Stalled Culture Change?" in Workforce Management (Vol. 88, December 14, 2009, No. 13, pp. 1)*
Pub: Crain Communications Inc.
Contact: Rance E. Crain, President

Ed: Jeremy Smerd. **Description:** General Motors CEO Fritz Henderson's abrupt resignation shocked employees and signaled that Henderson had not done enough to change the company's culture, especially in dealing with its top management.

46585 ■ *"STAR TEC Incubator's Latest Resident Shows Promise" in The Business Journal-Serving Greater Tampa Bay (August 11, 2008)*
Pub: American City Business Journals, Inc.
Contact: Whitney Shaw, President

Ed: Jane Meinhardt. **Description:** Field Forensics Inc., a resident of the STAR Technology Enterprise Center, has grown after being admitted into the business accelerator. The producer of defense and security devices and equipment has doubled 2007 sales as of 2008.

46586 ■ *"State Democrats Push for Changes to Plant Security Law" in Chemical Week (Vol. 172, July 19, 2010, No. 17, pp. 8)*
Pub: Access Intelligence L.L.C.
Contact: Donald Pazour, President

Ed: Kara Sissell. **Description:** Legislation has been introduced to revise the existing U.S. Chemical Facility Anti-Terrorism Standards (CFATS) that would include a requirement for facilities to use inherently safer technology (IST). The bill would eliminate the current law's exemption of water treatment plants and certain port facilities and preserve the states' authority to establish stronger security standards.

46587 ■ *"Steeling for Battle"* in *Crain's Chicago Business* (Vol. 31, April 21, 2008, No. 16, pp. 3)
Pub: Crain Communications Inc.
Contact: Todd Johnson, Publisher
Ed: Bob Tita. **Description:** Discusses contract negotiations between the United Steelworkers union and ArcelorMittal USA Inc., the nation's largest steelmaker, and U.S. Steel Corp., the third-largest; the union sees these negotiations as the best chance in two decades to regain lost ground but industry experts predict the companies will try to reduce benefits, demand a separate, lower wage scale for new hires and look for relief from the rising costs for retirees' health insurance coverage.

46588 ■ *"Steeling Themselves"* in *Baltimore Business Journal* (Vol. 30, July 6, 2012, No. 9, pp. 1)
Pub: American City Business Journals, Inc.
Contact: Whitney Shaw, President
Ed: James Bach. **Released:** July 6, 2012. **Description:** Members of Maryland's steel sector have been seeking to revive the Sparrows Point steel plant. The plan also involves saving 2,000 jobs. Comments from executives included.

46589 ■ *"Steering Toward Profitability"* in *Black Enterprise* (Vol. 41, December 2010, No. 5, pp. 72)
Pub: Earl G. Graves Publishing Co. Inc.
Contact: Earl G. Graves, Jr., President
Ed: Alan Hughes. **Description:** Systems Electro Coating LLC had to make quick adjustments when auto manufacturers were in a slump. The minority father-daughter team discuss their strategies during the auto industry collapse.

46590 ■ *"Steve Meginniss Helped Reinvent the Toothbrush. Can He Do the Same Thing for Wheels?"* in *Inc.* (February 2008, pp. 32)
Ed: Dalia Fahmy. **Description:** Profile of Steve Meginniss, co-inventor of Sonicare Toothbrush and inventor of a two-gear wheel for wheelchairs. Mgeinniss discusses his need to raid $1 million to promote and cut manufacturing costs for this new product that helps reduce pain for users.

46591 ■ *"Stimulus 'Loser' Won't Build Plant in Mass."* in *Boston Business Journal* (Vol. 30, November 5, 2010, No. 41, pp. 1)
Pub: Boston Business Journal
Ed: Kyle Alspach. **Description:** Boston-Power Inc. no longer plans to build an electric vehicle battery plant in Massachusetts after it failed to obtain stimulus funds from the federal government. The company is instead looking to build a lithium-ion battery plant in China and possibly Europe.

46592 ■ *"Stock Car Racing"* in *Canadian Business* (Vol. 81, September 15, 2008, No. 14-15, pp. 29)
Ed: Thomas Watson. **Description:** Some analysts predict a Chapter 11-style tune-up making GM and Ford a speculative turnaround stock. However, the price of oil could make or break the shares of the Big Three U.S. automobile manufacturers and if oil goes up too high then a speculative stock to watch is an electric car company called Zenn Motor Co.

46593 ■ *"A Stock Worth Trading Down To"* in *Barron's* (Vol. 88, July 14, 2008, No. 28, pp. 36)
Pub: Dow Jones & Co., Inc.
Contact: Clare Hart, President
Ed: Alexander Eule. **Description:** Shares of Ralcorp Holdings are cheap at around $49.95 after slipping 20 percent prior to their acquisition of Post cereals from Kraft. Some analysts believe its shares could climb over 60 percent to $80 as value-seeking consumers buy more private label products.

46594 ■ *"The Story of a Complex Project, Seen From a Bridge"* in *Business Review Albany* (Vol. 41, June 27, 2014, No. 14, pp. 7)
Pub: American City Business Journals, Inc.
Contact: Whitney Shaw, President
Released: June 27, 2014. **Description:** The bridge connecting the manufacturing and technology development buildings at GlobalFoundries in Malta, NY

allows employees to transport computer chip-containing wafers without the risk of contamination. The connector is a cleanroom and has its own air conditioning system and foundation vibration control.

46595 ■ *"Stronach Confirms Magna Eyeing Chrysler"* in *Globe & Mail* (March 9, 2007, pp. B1)
Ed: Greg Keenan. **Description:** The decision of auto parts manufacturing firm Magna International Inc. to participate in the take-over bid for Chrysler Group, as announced by its founder Frank Stronach, is discussed.

46596 ■ *"Succeed With the Right Equipment"* in *Pet Product News* (Vol. 64, November 2010, No. 11, pp. 42)
Pub: Bowtie Inc.
Ed: Sandi Cain. **Description:** Grooming shop owners have been focusing on obtaining ergonomic, durable, and efficient products such as restraints, tables, and tubs. These products enhance the way grooming tasks are conducted. Ways pet supply manufacturers have responded to this trend are examined.

46597 ■ *"Suitors Circling Chrysler as Sale Likely"* in *Globe & Mail* (February 19, 2007, pp. B1)
Ed: Jason Singer. **Description:** DaimlerChrysler AG is planning to sell or spin-off the Chrysler Group, as a cost cutting strategy. Chrysler reported a 40 percent drop in fourth quarter profit because of the $1.5 billion operating loss.

46598 ■ *"Supplements Mix Nutrition With Convenience"* in *Pet Product News* (Vol. 64, November 2010, No. 11, pp. 44)
Pub: Bowtie Inc.
Ed: Karen Shugart. **Description:** Pet supply manufacturers have been making supplements and enhanced foods that improve mineral consumption, boost bone density, and sharpen appetite in herps. Customers seem to enjoy the convenience as particular herps demands are being addressed by these offerings. Features of other supplements and enhanced foods for herps are described.

46599 ■ *"Suppliers May Follow Fiat: Local Group Says Italian Firms are Inquiring"* in *Crain's Detroit Business* (Vol. 25, June 15, 2009, No. 24, pp. 1)
Pub: Crain Communications Inc. - Detroit
Contact: Keith Crain, Chairman
Ed: Ryan Beene. **Description:** Italian suppliers to Fiat SpA are looking toward Detroit after the formation of Chrysler Group LLC, the Chrysler-Fiat partnership created from Chrysler's bankruptcy. The Italian American Alliance for Business and Technology is aware of two Italy-based powertrain component suppliers that are considering a move to Detroit.

46600 ■ *"Supply-Chain Collaboration, Image of Industry are OESA Chief's Top Tasks; Q&A Julie Fream, Original Equipment Suppliers Association"* in *Crain's Detroit Business* (Vol. 30, January 6, 2014, No. 1, pp. 4)
Pub: Crain Communications Inc. - Detroit
Contact: Keith Crain, Chairman
Released: January 6, 2014. **Description:** Julie Fream is the new CEO of the Original Equipment Suppliers Assocation. Fream is a former Visteon Corporation executive and has held numerous positions in automotive manufacturing, sales and marketing. She is committed to holding transparency and collaboration within the industry.

46601 ■ *"The 'Supply Side' of the Auto Industry"* in *Montly Labor Review* (Vol. 133, September 2010, No. 9, pp. 72)
Pub: U.S. Department of Labor Bureau of Labor Statistics
Contact: Philip L. Rones, Manager
E-mail: rones.philip@bls.gov
Description: Restructuring and geographic change in the automobile industry is discussed.

46602 ■ *"Surfing's Next Safari"* in *Entrepreneur* (Vol. 37, July 2009, No. 7, pp. 24)
Pub: Entrepreneur Press
Contact: Perlman Neil, President
Ed: Dennis Romero. **Description:** Profile of Firewire Surfboards, a San Diego-based maker of lightweight surfboards, aims to capture surfing enthusiasts' attention with its use of unusual and high-tech materials. Firewire's biggest challenge is the preference for old-school surfboards, but the company is determined to revolutionize how surfboards should be made. The company's various innovations and experiences are also discussed.

46603 ■ *"Survey: Confident Parts Makers Plan to Expand, Hire"* in *Crain's Detroit Business* (Vol. 30, August 18, 2014, No. 33, pp. 5)
Pub: Crain Communications Inc. - Detroit
Contact: Keith Crain, Chairman
Released: August 18, 2014. **Description:** North American automotive suppliers are increasing capital expenditure, hiring new workers, and raising funds for possible mergers and acquisitions. Automotive manufacturing suppliers are forecasting a rebound in new vehicle sales. Statistical data included.

46604 ■ *"Suzlon S88-Powered Wind Farm in Minnesota Secures Long-Term Financing"* in *PR Newswire* (September 21, 2011)
Pub: UBM L.L.C.
Contact: Kate Spellman, President
E-mail: kspellman@cmp.com
Description: Suzlon Energy Limited is the world's fifth largest manufacturer of wind turbines. Owners of the Grant County Wind Farm in Minnesota have secured a long-term financing deal for the ten Suzlon S88 2.1 MW wind turbines that generate enough electricity to power 7,000 homes.

46605 ■ *"Swagelok Boss Doesn't Follow Conventional Path"* in *Crain's Cleveland Business* (Vol. 30, June 29, 2009, No. 25, pp. 4)
Pub: Crain Communications Inc.
Ed: Dan Shingler. **Description:** Swagelok Company president and CEO has not laid off an employee in its 65 years of existence and said at a recent convention that he plans to keep his 4,000 employees working and inventories at normal levels despite the recession.

46606 ■ *"Syracuse Gear Manufacturer Buys Buffalo Company"* in *Business First of Buffalo* (Vol. 30, January 24, 2014, No. 19, pp. 3)
Pub: American City Business Journals, Inc.
Contact: Whitney Shaw, President
Released: January 24, 2014. **Description:** Niagara Gear Corporation of Buffalo, New York was acquired by Gear Motions Inc., in a deal that could make Gear Motions the largest precision gear manufacturer for the commercial and industrial compressor market. Niagara Gear will supply larger ground and cut spur and helical gears to existing customers as part of the sale.

46607 ■ *"Taiwan Technology Initiatives Foster Growth"* in *Canadian Electronics* (Vol. 23, February 2008, No. 1, pp. 28)
Description: A study conducted by the Market Intelligence Center shows that currently, Taiwan is the world's larges producer of information technology products such as motherboards, servers, and LCD monitors. In 2006, Taiwan's LED industry reached a production value of NTD 21 billion. This push into the LED sector shows the Ministry of Economic Affairs' plan to target industries that are environmentally friendly.

46608 ■ *"Takeover Frenzy Stokes Steel Stocks"* in *Globe & Mail* (February 7, 2006, pp. B1)
Description: The impact of merger speculations, on shares of steel companies such as Ipsco Inc., is discussed.

46609 ■ *"Taking on Intel: AMD Faces Off"* in *Canadian Business (Vol. 79, October 23, 2006, No. 21, pp. 27)*
Pub: Rogers Media Inc.
Contact: Tony Viner, President
Ed: Andrew Wahl. **Description:** The decision of ATI Technologies Inc., a Canadian computer peripherals company to acquire cash and stocks worth US$5.4-billion from American microprocessor maker Advanced Micro Devices Inc., is discussed.

46610 ■ *"The Tata Way"* in *Business Strategy Review (Vol. 21, Summer 2010, No. 2, pp. 14)*
Pub: John Wiley & Sons Inc. Scientific, Technical, Medical, and Scholarly Div. (Wiley-Blackwell)
Contact: William J. Pesce, Manager
E-mail: wpesce@wiley.com
Ed: Stuart Crainer. **Description:** Tata Motors is one of the world's most talked-about companies. Its new ultra-low-cost Nano car is being heralded as the people's car. Vice chairman, Ravi Kant, talks about India and its emerging markets.

46611 ■ *"Tate & Lyle to Sell Redpath Division to American Sugar"* in *Globe & Mail (February 15, 2007, pp. B15)*
Description: American Sugar Refining has agreed to acquire the Canadian sugar unit of Tate & Lyle PLC for $301.9 million. Tate & Lyle PLC has been selling off businesses and closing plants in order to focus on starches and Splenda.

46612 ■ *"Taylor Tests Land Grant Program"* in *Austin Business Journal (Vol. 31, June 3, 2011, No. 13, pp. 1)*
Pub: American City Business Journals
Ed: Vicky Garza. **Description:** Taylor Economic Development Corporation implemented a land grant program called Build On Our Lot to lure businesses to Taylor City, Austin, Texas. They are targeting small businesses, especially those in the renewable energy, advanced manufacturing, technical services and food products. Program details are included.

46613 ■ *"Tech Investing: March's Long Road"* in *Canadian Business (Vol. 80, January 29, 2007, No. 3, pp. 67)*
Ed: Calvin Leung. **Description:** The efforts of March Networks, a manufacturer of digital surveillance equipment, from the decline in the price of its shares at the beginning of the year 2007 are described.

46614 ■ *"Tecumseh Products to Begin Moving HQ"* in *Crain's Detroit Business (Vol. 24, March 31, 2008, No. 13, pp. 35)*
Pub: Crain Communications Inc.
Contact: Rance E. Crain, President
Ed: Chad Halcom. **Description:** Tecumseh Products Co., a manufacturer of compressor products, will transfer its headquarters to Pittsfield Township near Ann Arbor.

46615 ■ *"Ted Stahl: Executive Chairman"* in *Inside Business (Vol. 13, September-October 2011, No. 5, pp. NC6)*
Pub: Great Lakes Publishing Co.
Ed: Miranda S. Miller. **Description:** Profile of Ted Stahl, who started working in his family's business when he was ten years old is presented. The firm makes dies for numbers and letters used on team uniforms. Another of the family firms manufactures stock and custom heat-printing products, equipment and supplies. It also educates customers on ways to decorate garments with heat printing products and offers graphics and software for customers to create their own artwork.

46616 ■ *"Teeling and Gallagher: A Textbook for Success"* in *Agency Sales Magazine (Vol. 39, September-October 2009, No. 9, pp. 20)*
Pub: Manufacturers' Agents National Association
Contact: Charles Cohon, President
Ed: Jack Foster. **Description:** Profile of Teeling & Gallagher, a manufacturing firm that was founded in 1946 as the D.G. Teeling Company and continued as a one-person agency until 1960 when Tom Gallagher joined the company. Tom Gallagher talks about how things have changed and his work with his son Bob in the agency.

46617 ■ *"Tempel Steel To Expand Its Chicago Plant"* in *Chicago Tribune (August 22, 2008)*
Pub: McClatchy-Tribune Information Services
Ed: James P. Miller. **Description:** Tempel Steel Co. is no longer considering transferring a Libertyville factory's production to Mexico; the company has responded to government incentives and will instead shift that work to its plant on Chicago's North Side.

46618 ■ *"Terrafugia's Flying Cars On the Radar for 2016"* in *Boston Business Journal (Vol. 34, June 13, 2014, No. 19, pp. 17)*
Pub: American City Business Journals, Inc.
Contact: Whitney Shaw, President
Released: June 13, 2014. **Description:** Terrafugia, a Woburn, Massachusetts manufacturer of flying cars, is seeking to launch its first flying car, the Transition, in mid-2016. The vehicle can fly at speeds up to 100 miles per hour at up to 10,000 feet in the air. Terrafugia has been developing the concept of a flying car over the past eight years and is seeking $30M in funding. The firm is also working on TF-X, a semi-autonomous plug-in hybrid vehicle that can fly at speeds up to 200 miles per hour.

46619 ■ *"Tesla Eyes Two Sites for New Battery-Pack Plant"* in *San Antonio Business Journal (Vol. 28, May 16, 2014, No. 14, pp. 8)*
Pub: American City Business Journals
Released: May 16, 2014. **Description:** The City of San Antonio, Texas is competing with other cities in five states to land the contract for the $5 million battery-pack plant of Texla Motors. Bill Avila of Bracewell & Giuliani LLPO law firm believes that San Antonio has an edge over some of the cities competing for the Tesla manufacturing plant because of its successful recruitment of Toyota in 2003.

46620 ■ *"Thai Ice Cream Cremo Expanding to Middle East"* in *Ice Cream Reporter (Vol. 23, September 20, 2010, No. 10, pp. 3)*
Description: Thai-based frozen dessert manufacturer Chomthana, maker of Cremo brand ice cream, is expanding into the Middle East.

46621 ■ *"There's More Upside in Germany"* in *Barron's (Vol. 90, September 6, 2010, No. 36, pp. M7)*
Pub: Barron's Editorial & Corporate Headquarters
Ed: Jonathan Buck. **Description:** Germany's stocks have gone up since the beginning of 2010, and investors can still benefit. These stocks will benefit from Germany's stellar economic performance and the relative weakness of the Euro. The prospects of the shares of Daimler and Hochtief are discussed.

46622 ■ *"They Like It Cold"* in *Business Journal Portland (Vol. 27, October 15, 2010, No. 33, pp. 1)*
Pub: Portland Business Journal
Ed: Erik Siemers. **Description:** Ajinomoto Frozen Foods USA Inc. has been investing in its Portland, Oregon facility. The company has completed a new rice production line. It has also spent $1.2 million on a new packaging technology.

46623 ■ *"This Just In"* in *Crain's Detroit Business (Vol. 25, June 1, 2009, No. 22, pp. 1)*
Pub: Crain Communications Inc. - Detroit
Contact: Keith Crain, Chairman
Ed: Daniel Duggan. **Description:** Three veterans of the auto industry have partnered to create, Revitalizing Michigan, a nonprofit dedicated to help manufacturers improve their processes. The firm is seeking federal, state and private grants to fund the mission.

46624 ■ *"Thomas and His Washington Friends"* in *CFO (Vol. 23, October 2007, No. 10, pp. 18)*
Ed: Alix Stuart. **Description:** Reliance on Chinese suppliers to America's toymakers may become quite costly as Congress considers legislation that would increase fines to as high as $50 million for companies selling tainted products. The legislation would also require independent mandatory testing for makers of products for children.

46625 ■ *"Thomas Industrial Network Unveils Custom SPEC"* in *Entertainment Close-Up (March 3, 2011)*
Pub: Close-Up Media
Description: Thomas Industrial Network assists custom manufacturers and industrial service providers a complete online program called Custom SPEC which includes Website development and Internet exposure.

46626 ■ *"Ticket Tiff Erupts Over Fund Ads"* in *Globe & Mail (January 31, 2007, pp. B1)*
Ed: Keith McArthur. **Description:** The opposition of Cineplex Entertainment LP to Mackenzie Financial Corp.'s advertisement about high cost of movie ticket is discussed.

46627 ■ *"A Timely Matter"* in *Canadian Business (Vol. 81, March 31, 2008, No. 5, pp. 12)*
Pub: Rogers Media Inc.
Contact: Tony Viner, President
Description: Discusses the committee responsible for restructuring $33 billion of asset-backed commercial paper which has moved back their implementation plan by a month citing complexities. British Columbia has surpassed the $1 billion mark in fiscal '07-'08 from their oil and gas rights. Biovail Corp. founder Eugene Melnyk said he had lost confidence in the management of the company.

46628 ■ *"Timken's Bearings Rolling in China, India"* in *Crain's Cleveland Business (Vol. 28, October 29, 2007, No. 43, pp. 14)*
Pub: Crain Communications Inc.
Ed: David Bennett. **Description:** Canton-based Timken Co., a manufacturer of bearings and specialty metals, is seeing growing demand for its line of tapered roller bearings, which allow rail users to carry heavy car loads. The company is finding significant growth in China and India due to their rapidly growing rail markets.

46629 ■ *"To Be or Not To Be an S Corporation"* in *Modern Machine Shop (Vol. 84, September 2011, No. 4, pp. 38)*
Pub: Gardner Business Media, Inc.
Contact: Richard G. Kline, President
E-mail: rkline@gardnerweb.com
Ed: Irving L. Blackman. **Description:** The definitions of both C corporations and S corporations are defined to help any machine shop discover which best suits the owner's business plan.

46630 ■ *"To Offshore Or Not To Offshore?"* in *Converting (Vol. 25, October 1, 2007, No. 10, pp. 10)*
Ed: Mark Spaulding. **Description:** Offshore manufacturing and the issue of buying raw materials from foreign suppliers by American companies is discussed. Results of a study conducted by Cap Gemini and Pro Logis regarding offshore manufacturing, especially to China, are presented.

46631 ■ *"Tony Armand, Shock Doctor CEO"* in *Business Journal (Vol. 31, March 21, 2014, No. 43, pp. 6)*
Pub: American City Business Journals
Released: March 21, 2014. **Description:** Tony Armand, CEO of Shock Doctor Inc., discusses the company's acquisition by private equity firm Bregal Partners. Armand believes the deal will give the sports protective equipment manufacturer a strong financial partner that will help with the executive strategy.

46632 ■ *"Toolmakers' New Tack: Firms' Goal -- Advance Wind-Turbine Technology"* in *Crain's Detroit Business (Vol. 25, June 8, 2009,)*
Pub: Crain Communications Inc. - Detroit
Contact: Keith Crain, Chairman
Ed: Ryan Beene, Amy Lane. **Description:** MAG Industrial Automation Systems LLC and Dowding Machining Inc. have partnered to advance wind-turbine technology. The goal is to cut costs of wind energy to the same level as carbon-based fuel.

46633 ■ *"Top 50 Exporters: In Volatile Market, Food and Green Companies Lead the List"* in *Hispanic Business (Vol. 30, July-August 2008, No. 7-8, pp. 42)*
Pub: Hispanic Business Inc.
Contact: Jesus Chavarria, President
Ed: Hildy Medina. Description: Increases in exports revenues reported by food exporters and green companies in a time of economic slowdown in the U.S are described. Food exporters have benefited from the growth of high-volume grocery stores in underdeveloped countries and the German governments' promotion of solar energy has benefited the U.S. solar heating equipment and solar panel manufactures.

46634 ■ *"Top Design Award for Massey Ferguson 7624 Dyna-VT"* in *Farm Industry News (November 14, 2011)*
Pub: Penton Business Media Inc.
Contact: David Kieselstein, Chief Executive Officer
Description: Massey Ferguson won top honors for its MF 7624 Dyna-VT as the Golden Tractor for Design award in the 2012 Tractor of the Year competition. The award is presented annually by journalists from 22 leading farming magazines in Europe and manufacturers have to be nominated to enter.

46635 ■ *"Tory Green?"* in *Canadian Business (Vol. 80, January 15, 2007, No. 2, pp. 72)*
Ed: Joe Chidley. Description: The need for the government to participate actively in protecting the environment through proper enforcement of the Tories Clean Air Act, is discussed.

46636 ■ *The Towering World of Jimmy Choo: A Story of Power, Profits, and the Pursuit of the Perfect Shoe*
Pub: Bloomsbury USA
Ed: Lauren Goldstein Crowe, Sagra Maceira de Rosen. Released: 2009. Price: £11.69, Paperback. Description: Profile of Jimmy Choo and his pursuit to manufacture the perfect shoe.

46637 ■ *"Toy Scares Drive Business"* in *Boston Business Journal (Vol. 27, November 23, 2007, No. 43, pp. 1)*
Ed: Joan Goodchild. Description: Several Boston businesses have tapped into the lead content scare in toys and other products manufactured in China. ConRoy Corporation LLC launched Toy Recall Alert!, an online tool to alert consumers about new recalls while Hybrivet Systems introduced screening test kit, LeadCheck. Other new products pertaining to toy safety are discussed.

46638 ■ *"Toy Story"* in *Forbes (Vol. 180, October 15, 2007, No. 8, pp. 102)*
Pub: Forbes Inc.
Contact: Malcolm S. Forbes, Jr., President
Ed: Tatiana Serafin. Description: Three voluntary recalls of Chinese-made toys were announced by American toymakers, sending Mattel stocks plummeting.

46639 ■ *"Toy Story: U.S.-Made a Hot Seller"* in *Crain's Detroit Business (Vol. 23, December 17, 2007, No. 51, pp. 3)*
Ed: Chad Halcom. Description: American Plastic Toys, located in Walled Lake, Michigan reports all its toys are made in the U.S. and have passed all U.S. safety standards. Revenue for American Plastic Toys reached nearly $33 million in 2005, and the company expects to exceed that because of recent toy safety recalls of products produced in China.

46640 ■ *"Toyota Expected to Construct Two N.A. Plants"* in *Globe & Mail (February 14, 2007, pp. B4)*
Description: Toyota Motor Corp. is planning to construct two vehicle assembly plants in North America and one more plant in Canada. The company is also planning to sell 208,000 vehicles in 2007.

46641 ■ *"Toyota Marks Record Profit Sales"* in *Globe & Mail (February 7, 2007, pp. B10)*
Ed: Martin Fackler. Description: The record quarterly sales and earnings reported by Japanese automaker Toyota Motor Corp. are discussed. The company sold 2.16 million vehicles during the quarter while registering 426.8 billion yen in profits.

46642 ■ *"Toyota Revs Up Plans for Ontario Plant"* in *Globe & Mail (February 7, 2006, pp. B1)*
Ed: Greg Keenan. Description: The production output and workforce addition proposals of Toyota Motor Corp., at Ontario plant, are presented.

46643 ■ *"Toyota Tops GM in Global Sales"* in *Globe & Mail (April 24, 2007, pp. B1)*
Ed: Greg Keenan. Description: The success of Toyota Motor Corp. in surpassing General Motors Corp. in its global sales is discussed.

46644 ■ *"Training the Troops: Battlefield Simulations Bring Growth to UNITECH"* in *Black Enterprise (Vol. 38, February 2008, No. 7, pp. 30)*
Pub: Earl G. Graves Publishing Co. Inc.
Contact: Earl G. Graves, Jr., President
Ed: Cliff Hocker. Description: Universal Systems and Technology (UNITECH) received a total of over $45 million U.S. Department of Defense orders during September and October 2007. UNITECH designs and manufactures battlefield simulation devices used to train troops in the Army and Marine Corps.

46645 ■ *"Trillium Turmoil"* in *Canadian Business (Vol. 81, December 8, 2008, No. 21, pp. 16)*
Pub: Rogers Media Inc.
Contact: Tony Viner, President
Ed: Jeff Sanford. Description: Ontario's manufacturing success in the past was believed to have been built by the 1965 Canada-U.S. automotive pact and by advantages such as low-cost energy. The loss of these advantages along with the challenging economic times has hurt Ontario's manufacturing industry.

46646 ■ *"The Trouble With $150,000 Wine"* in *Barron's (Vol. 88, July 7, 2008, No. 27, pp. 33)*
Pub: Dow Jones & Co., Inc.
Contact: Clare Hart, President
Ed: Jay Palmer. Description: Review of the book, 'The Billionaire's Vinegar: The Mystery of the World's Most Expensive Bottle of Wine,' which discusses vintners along with the marketing and distribution of wine as well as the winemaking industry as a whole.

46647 ■ *"Turnaround Plays: The Return of Wi-LAN"* in *Canadian Business (Vol. 80, January 29, 2007, No. 3, pp. 68)*
Ed: Joe Castaldo. Description: The recovery of the wireless equipment manufacturing firm Wi-LAN from near-bankruptcy, under the leadership of Jim Skippen, is described.

46648 ■ *"Turning Drivers Into Geeks; Auto Dealers Debate Need for Technology Specialists to Bring Buyers Up to Speed"* in *Crain's Detroit Business (Vol. 30, January 6, 2014, No. 1, pp. 3)*
Pub: Crain Communications Inc. - Detroit
Contact: Keith Crain, Chairman
Released: January 6, 2014. Description: Dealers at the 2014 North American International Auto Show discuss the need for technology specialists to educate sales staff as well as customers on the new high-tech items manufactured on today's automobiles and trucks.

46649 ■ *"Turning Green Ink to Black"* in *The Business Journal-Serving Metropolitan Kansas City (Vol. 26, August 8, 2008, No. 48, pp. 1)*
Ed: James Dornbrook. Description: InkCycle has introduced grenk, a line of environmentally-friendly printer toner and ink cartridges. The cartridges are collected and recycled after use by the company, which separates them into their metal, cardboard, and plastic components.

46650 ■ *"Twice the Innovation, Half the Tears"* in *Business Courier (Vol. 24, March 7, 2008, No. 48, pp. 1)*
Pub: American City Business Journals, Inc.
Contact: Whitney Shaw, President
Ed: Lisa Biank Fasig. Description: Procter & Gamble was able to develop a pant-style diaper called Pampers First Pants by creating a virtual, three-dimensional baby. The company was able to reduce the number of real mock-ups that it had to make by putting the diapers on the virtual baby first. Specifics about product designs were not revealed by the company.

46651 ■ *"UC May Expand into Old Ford Plant"* in *Business Courier (Vol. 26, December 25, 2009, No. 35, pp. 1)*
Pub: American City Business Journals, Inc.
Contact: Whitney Shaw, President
Ed: Dan Monk. Description: Developer Stuart Lichter is planning to acquire University of Cincinnati (UC) as a tenant at a two-story office building on a 132-acre site where a vacant Ford transmission plant is located. Details of the transaction are outlined.

46652 ■ *"Unexpected Guest: Caterpillar-Bucyrus Deal Came Out of Nowhere"* in *Business Journal-Milwaukee (Vol. 28, November 19, 2010, No. 7, pp. A1)*
Pub: Milwaukee Business Journal
Ed: Rich Rovito. Description: Caterpillar has agreed to purchase Bucyrus for $92 per share. The deal, which is subjected to a $200 million termination fee, is expected to close in mid-2011.

46653 ■ *"An Unfair Knock on Nokia"* in *Barron's (Vol. 88, March 10, 2008, No. 10, pp. 36)*
Pub: Dow Jones & Co., Inc.
Contact: Clare Hart, President
Ed: Mark Veverka. Description: Discusses the decision by the brokerage house Exane to recommend a Sell on Nokia shares, presumably due to higher inventories, which is unfounded. The news that the company's inventories are rising is not an indicator of falling demand for its products. The company is also benefiting from solid management and rising market share.

46654 ■ *"Unilever Acquiring EVGA's Ice Cream Brands in Greece"* in *Ice Cream Reporter (Vol. 23, October 20, 2010, No. 11, pp. 1)*
Pub: Ice Cream Reporter
Description: Unilever will acquire the ice cream brands and distribution network of the Greek frozen dessert manufacturer EVGA.

46655 ■ *"Unilever's CMO Finally Gets Down To Business"* in *Advertising Age (Vol. 79, July 7, 2008, No. 26, pp. 11)*
Pub: Crain Communications Inc.
Contact: Rance Crain, President
Ed: Jack Neff. Description: Overview of Unilever's chief marketing officer Simon Clift's strategy for promoting its products; now that the company has restructured, Clift is able to focus all of his energy on the challenges of the new-media climate that marketers are having to face.

46656 ■ *"Union, Heal Thyself"* in *Canadian Business (Vol. 81, July 21, 2008, No. 11, pp. 9)*
Description: General Motors Corp. was offered by the federal government a $250 million fund after the company declared plans to close its facility in Ontario. The government move is geared towards supporting the workers who have refused to support the automotive company. Details of the labor contract between General Motors and the Canadian Auto Workers are presented.

46657 ■ *"U.S. Enters BlackBerry Dispute Compromise Sought Over Security Issues"* in *Houston Chronicle (August 6, 2010)*
Pub: Houston Chronicle
Contact: Sherry Adams, Director, Library Services
Ed: Matthew Lee. Description: U.S. State Department is working for a compromise with Research in Motion, manufacturer of the BlackBerry, over security issues. The Canadian company makes the smartphones and foreign governments believe they pose a security risk.

46658 ■ *"U.S. Firm to Acquire Manufacturer GSW"* in *Globe & Mail (January 21, 2006, pp. B4)*
Ed: Gordon Pitts. **Description:** The details on A.O. Smith Corp.'s acquisition of GSW Inc. are presented.

46659 ■ *"U.S. Playing Card Might Shuffle HQ"* in *Business Courier (Vol. 24, March 21, 2008, No. 50, pp. 1)*
Pub: American City Business Journals, Inc.
Contact: Whitney Shaw, President
Ed: Jon Newberry. **Description:** United States Playing Card Co. is considering the possibility of relocating. It is expected that the company will finalize its decision by June 2008. According to Phil Dolci, the company's president, the firm is looking at certain locations in Ohio, Kentucky, and Indiana. He also revealed that the plan to relocate was prompted by the desire to improve the company's manufacturing facilities.

46660 ■ *"U.S. Widens Rocket Field"* in *Wall Street Journal Eastern Edition (October 17, 2011, pp. B4)*
Pub: Dow Jones & Co., Inc.
Contact: Clare Hart, President
Ed: Andy Pasztor. **Description:** An agreement has been reached between National Aeronautics and Space Administration, the Department of Defense and the Air Force that will assist small commercial space ventures in bidding for profitable contracts for government launching. The program will give those companies a chance to compete against larger corporations.

46661 ■ *"Upsurge"* in *Puget Sound Business Journal (Vol. 33, July 13, 2012, No. 12, pp. 1)*
Description: Kent, Washington-based Flow International Corporation posted a record of $254 million in annual sales for fiscal 2012 and it is expected to reach about $300 million by 2014. Flow is being lifted by a global manufacturing revival and by its machines' ability to handle the carbon-fiber composites used in aerospace. Insights on Flow's water jet cutting tools are also given.

46662 ■ *Utah Manufacturers Register*
Pub: Harris InfoSource
Contact: Dennis Abrahams, President
E-mail: dennisa@harrisinfo.com
URL(s): www.harrisinfo.com. **Released:** Annual; latest edition 2010. **Covers:** Approximately 4,600 manufacturers in Utah, plus names of key executives. **Entries include:** Company name, address, parent name/location, telephone, fax and 800 numbers, Web site address (on CD-ROM only), number of employees, year established, annual revenue, plant size, business description, Standard Industrial Classification (SIC) codes, executive names/titles, public ownership, legal structure, import/export designators, female/minority ownership. **Arrangement:** Classified by product/service, line of business. **Indexes:** Product/service, alphabetical, geographical, international trade.

46663 ■ *"VASCO DIGIPASS GO3 in Combination With IDENTIKEY Enhances the Security of Business Intelligence Solution Developed by CDS for General Motors Brazil"* in *News Bites US (March 29, 2012)*
Pub: Financial Times Ltd.
Contact: John Ridding, Chief Executive Officer
Released: March 29, 2012. **Description:** VASCO Data Security International Inc. will provide Condominio de Corporativas, a vendor and business solutions integrator, its DIGIPASS GO 3 authentication solution along with IDENTIKEY Authentacation Server to provide security to the BI Retail Program developed for General Motors Brazil. VASCO is a leading software security firm specializing in authentication products.

46664 ■ *"Versatile's Back"* in *Farm Industry News (Vol. 42, January 1, 2009, No. 1)*
Pub: Intertec Publishing
Contact: John French, President
Ed: Jodie Wehrspann. **Description:** Overview of Winnipeg, Manitoba's tractor manufacturer Versatile's strategy to rebrand its tractor segment; the strategy

comes a year after Russian Combine Factory Rostselmash Ltd. bought the majority share of common stock from the Canadian business.

46665 ■ *"Veteran-Owned Business 3E Services Gains Recognition in 2011 and Welcomes 2012 With New Offerings"* in *Marketwired (January 10, 2012)*
Pub: COMTEX
Contact: Chip Brian, President
Description: 3E Services Inc. specializes in the selling, repairing, and remanufacturing of electrical components. It is a veteran-owned busiens located in Tucker, Georgia near Atlanta.The Washington Post recognized 3E as an exemplary veteran-owned business. David Loftin, president and founder, learned his skills as a US Navy nuclear electrician and attributes that training to his firm's growth and success.

46666 ■ *"Vicki Avril: Senior Vice-President of Tubular Division, Ipsco Inc."* in *Crain's Chicago Business (Vol. 31, May 5, 2008, No. 18)*
Pub: Crain Communications Inc.
Contact: Todd Johnson, Publisher
Ed: Miriam Gottfried. **Description:** Profile of Vicki Avril who is the senior vice-president of the tubular division at Ipsco Inc. where she supervises 2,800 employees and 13 mills throughout the United States and Canada.

46667 ■ *"A Virtual Jog Mode for CAM"* in *Modern Machine Shop (Vol. 84, November 2011, No. 6, pp. 22)*
Pub: Gardner Business Media, Inc.
Contact: Richard G. Kline, President
E-mail: rkline@gardnerweb.com
Ed: Edwin Gasparraj. **Description:** In many cases, CAM programming required a specific, user-defined path. Siemens PLMs Generic Motion Controller is an alternative that defines the tool path within CAM. The program is a virtual 'teach' mode that enables the user to capture cutter locations by jogging machines axes within CAM.

46668 ■ *"Volvo: Logistics Agreement to Reduce Environmental Impact"* in *Ecology, Environment & Conservation Business (July 19, 2014, pp. 28)*
Pub: NewsRX
Contact: Susan E. Hasty, Publisher
Released: July 19, 2014. **Description:** Scandinavian Logistics Partners AB (Scanlog) will sell surplus capacity in rail transport from Belgium to Sweden to the Volvo Group. The partnership benefits both costs and environmental impact. The Volvo group is committed to optimizing transport of their manufactured cars and trucks.

46669 ■ *"Washington Manufacturing Jobs Go Begging in Downturn"* in *Puget Sound Business Journal (Vol. 29, December 26, 2008, No. 36, pp. 1)*
Pub: American City Business Journals
Ed: Steve Wilhelm. **Description:** Trends show that skilled jobs in aerospace and other technology manufacturing industries are in a state of decline as layoffs hit broad sectors of the economy. Too few people are entering the field, prompting companies to try to maintain these skilled workers, thus creating problems that could affect the sector's vitality.

46670 ■ *"We All Scream for Ice Cream"* in *Crain's Chicago Business (Vol. 31, April 28, 2008, No. 17, pp. 48)*
Pub: Crain Communications Inc.
Contact: Todd Johnson, Publisher
Ed: Phuong Ly. **Description:** Profile of Oberweis' ice cream shops which has expanded its business by delivering dairy products to grocery stores.

46671 ■ *We Are Smarter Than Me: How to Unleash the Power of Crowds in Your Business*
Pub: Wharton School Publishing
Ed: Barry Libert, Jon Spector, Don Tapscott. **Released:** September 25, 2007. **Price:** $24.99, Nonmembers; $19.99, Members; $17.59, Members; $21. 99, Nonmembers. **Description:** Ways to use social

networking and community in order to make decisions and plan your business, with a focus on product development, manufacturing, marketing, customer service, finance, management, and more. **Availability:** PrintE-book.

46672 ■ *"Weaving a Stronger Fabric: Organizing a Global Sweat-Free Apparel Production Agreement"* in *WorkingUSA (Vol. 11, June 2008, No. 2)*
Ed: Eric Dirnbach. **Description:** Tens of millions of workers working under terrible sweatshop conditions in the global apparel industry. Workers are employed at apparel contractors and have been largely unsuccessful in organizing and improving their working conditions. The major apparel manufacturers and retailers have the most power in this industry, and they have adopted corporate social responsibility programs as a false solution to the sweatshop problem. The major North American apparel unions dealt with similar sweatshop conditions a century ago by organizing the contractors and brands into joint association contracts that significantly raised standards. Taking inspiration from their example, workers and their anti-sweatshop allies need to work together to coordinate a global organizing effort that builds worker power and establishes a global production agreement that negotiates with both contractors and the brands for improved wages, benefits, and working conditions.

46673 ■ *"WEDC Credits Could Create 400 Area Jobs"* in *Business Journal Milwaukee (Vol. 29, July 27, 2012, No. 44, pp. 1)*
Pub: American City Business Journals, Inc.
Contact: Whitney Shaw, President
Ed: Rich Kirchen. **Released:** July 27, 2012. **Description:** Wisconsin Development Corporation (WEDC) has provided $2.2 million in tax credits to six southeastern Wisconsin employers that are expected to add nearly 400 jobs. The companies are Unico Inc., Spee-Dee Packaging Machinery, All Tool Sales Inc., Echo Lake Foods Inc., Novation Companies Inc., and Trico Corporation.

46674 ■ *"A Week of the Worst Kind of Selling"* in *Barron's (Vol. 88, June 30, 2008, No. 26, pp. M3)*
Pub: Dow Jones & Co., Inc.
Contact: Clare Hart, President
Ed: Kopin Tan. **Description:** In the week that ended in June 27, 2008 the selloff in the U.S. stock market was brought on by mounting bank losses and the spread of economic slowdown on top of high oil prices. The 31 percent decrease in the share price of Ingersoll-Rand since October 2007 may have factored in most of its risks. The company has completed its acquisition of Trane to morph into a refrigeration-equipment company.

46675 ■ *"Wenzel Downhole Tools Ltd. Announces First Quarter Results for 2007"* in *Marketwired (May 14, 2007)*
Pub: Comtex News Network Inc.
Description: Wenzel Downhole Tools Ltd., a manufacturer, renter, and seller of drilling tools used in gas and oil exploration, announced its financial results for the first quarter ended March 31, 2007 which includes achieved revenues of $14.5 million. Statistical data included. ■

46676 ■ *"What Do Your ISO Procedures Say?"* in *Modern Machine Shop (Vol. 84, September 2011, No. 4, pp. 34)*
Pub: Gardner Business Media, Inc.
Contact: Richard G. Kline, President
E-mail: rkline@gardnerweb.com
Ed: Wayne S. Chaneski. **Description:** ISO 9000 certification can be time-consuming and costly, but it is a necessary step in developing a quality management system that meets both current and potential customer needs.

46677 ■ *"What Is In Your Company Library?"* in *Modern Machine Shop (Vol. 84, October 2011, No. 5, pp. 60)*
Pub: Gardner Business Media, Inc.
Contact: Richard G. Kline, President
E-mail: rkline@gardnerweb.com
Ed: Mike Lynch. **Description:** A good company library in any machine shop can help keep employees

productive. Safety as well as information are critical to complete any task in a shop.

46678 ■ *"What Makes for an Effective, Production-Oriented VMC?"* in *Modern Machine Shop (Vol. 84, November 2011, No. 6, pp. 24)*
Pub: Gardner Business Media, Inc.
Contact: Richard G. Kline, President
E-mail: rkline@gardnerweb.com
Ed: Derek Korn. **Description:** When a machine shop's existing VMC only offers a modest spindle performance and slow, non-cutting functions, the latest VMC technology for high-volume production that minimizes cycle times and maximizes competitiveness could be helpful. Makino's new Production Standard (PS) series of VMCs provides not only a number of standard features to shrink cycle times, but also design elements that can effectively support a shops production elements are defined.

46679 ■ *"What's New"* in *Crain's Cleveland Business (Vol. 30, June 8, 2009, No. 22, pp. 23)*
Pub: Crain Communications Inc.
Description: Air Technical Industries in Ohio has launched a new product called the Scorpion Aircraft Tug that includes a built-in crane lift and auxiliary power unit that enables a fixed-base operator aircraft mechanic to move and precisely position aircraft weight up to 15,000 pounds.

46680 ■ *"What's New"* in *Crain's Cleveland Business (Vol. 30, June 1, 2009, No. 21, pp. 19)*
Pub: Crain Communications Inc.
Description: Profile of Precision Polymer Casting, a manufacturer located in Northeast Ohio. Precision has launched its new product, Castinite HCR polymer composite pump base castings that are base plates that are used to mount a pump and electric motor for various chemical pumping operations. Details of the pump are included.

46681 ■ *"What's Working Now: In Providing Jobs for North Carolinians"* in *Business North Carolina (Vol. 28, February 2008, No. 2, pp. 16)*
Pub: Business North Carolina
Ed: Edward Martin, Frank Maley. **Description:** Individuals previously employed in the furniture, tobacco, or textile manufacturing sectors have gone back to school to be trained in new sectors in the area such as life sciences, finances and other emerging sectors.

46682 ■ *"Wheatfield First Choice for Canadian Manufacturer"* in *Business First Buffalo (November 26, 2007, pp. 1)*
Pub: American City Business Journals, Inc.
Ed: James Fink. **Description:** Niagara County Industrial Development Agency is preparing an enticement program that would lure automotive parts manufacturer Pop & Lock Corporation to shift manufacturing operations to Wheatfield, Niagara County, New York. The package includes job-training grants and assistance for acquiring new machinery. Details of the plan are included.

46683 ■ *"When R&D Spending Is Not Enough: The Critical Role of Culture When You Really Want to Innovate"* in *Human Resource Management (Vol. 49, July-August 2010, No. 4, pp. 767-792)*
Pub: John Wiley
Ed: Sheng Wang, Rebecca M. Guidice, Judith W. Tansky, Zhong-Ming Wang. **Description:** A study was conducted to examine the effect of contextual contingencies on innovation. Findings indicate that Chinese manufacturers with cultures emphasizing innovation and teamwork more effectively utilize financial resources in the innovation process. Results also show that a culture emphasizing outcomes and stability leads to lower levels innovation irrespective of investments.

46684 ■ *"When Worlds Collide"* in *Entrepreneur (September 2014)*
Pub: Entrepreneur Media Inc.
Released: September 2014. **Description:** A growing number of startups are connecting the real world with its digital counterpart by leveraging next-generation

software, robotics and artificial intelligence to revolutionize traditional entertainment. Anki introduces toy race cars with virtual steering wheels that can be controlled by human gamers or an artificial intelligence. Tiggly, creator of learning games and products for toddlers, manufactured thermoplastic rubber toys with silicon touch points that interact with a tablet screen.

46685 ■ *"Where the Money Is"* in *Conde Nast Portfolio (Vol. 2, June 2008, No. 6, pp. 113)*
Description: Revenue generated from treatments for common brain disorders that are currently on the market are listed.

46686 ■ *"Where Nutrition Meets Love"* in *Pet Product News (Vol. 66, September 2012, No. 9, pp. S14)*
Description: Michael Landa, coowner of Nulo Pet Products, discusses the role of his company in reducing pet obesity through the manufacture of high-protein foods. Aside from explaining his interest in pet obesity, Landa also describes how the company differentiates itself from competitors.

46687 ■ *"Where Rubber Meets Road"* in *Canadian Business (Vol. 80, March 13, 2007, No. 6, pp. 15)*
Pub: Rogers Media Inc.
Contact: Tony Viner, President
Ed: Michelle Magnan. **Description:** The partnership between Engineered Drilling Solutions Inc. and EnCana Corp. to build road from rubber wastes and follow environment-friendly methods in work is discussed.

46688 ■ *"The Whole Package"* in *Entrepreneur (Vol. 36, February 2008, No. 2, pp. 24)*
Pub: Entrepreneur Press
Contact: Perlman Neil, President
Ed: Laura Tiffany. **Description:** Holy Bohn, owner of The Honest Statuto, developed an environmentally-friendly packaging for her pet food products. The company hired a packaging consultant and spent $175,000. Big corporations also spend money and plunge into the latest trends in packaging ranging from lighter and flexible to temperature-sensitive labels.

46689 ■ *"Why Change?"* in *Canadian Business (Vol. 80, October 8, 2007, No. 20, pp. 9)*
Ed: Joe Chidley. **Description:** The need for economic change in Canada is discussed. Despite the country's economic growth and low unemployment rate, economic reform is needed in order to maximize its economic potential in the future. Other reasons for the need to further develop its economy, such as the rise of manufacturing and service industries in Asia and the emergence of regional trade pacts in South America are also tackled.

46690 ■ *"Why the Ethanol King Loves Driving his SUV"* in *Globe & Mail (January 29, 2007, pp. B17)*
Ed: Gordon Pitts. **Description:** Ken Field, chairman of Canada's leading ethanol manufacturer GreenField Ethanol, talks about the cars he drives, the commercial use of cellulose, ethanol's performance as an alternative to gasoline and about the plans of his firm to go public.

46691 ■ *Why GM Matters: Inside the Race to Transform an American Icon*
Pub: Walker Publishing Company Inc.
Contact: Peter Miller, Manager
E-mail: pmiller@walkerbooks.com
Ed: William Holstein. **Released:** 2009. **Price:** $20.99; $26, Hardback. **Description:** A timely examination of General Motors Corporation and the problems it is facing. **Availability:** Electronic publishing.

46692 ■ *"Why Intel Should Dump Its Flash-Memory Business"* in *Barron's (Vol. 88, March 10, 2008, No. 10, pp. 35)*
Pub: Dow Jones & Co., Inc.
Contact: Clare Hart, President
Ed: Eric J. Savitz. **Description:** Intel Corp. must sell its NAND flash-memory business as soon as it possibly can to the highest bidder to focus on its PC

processor business and take advantage of other business opportunities. Apple should consider a buyback of 10 percent of the company's shares to lift its stock.

46693 ■ *"Why Nestle Should Sell Alcon"* in *Barron's (Vol. 88, March 17, 2008, No. 11, pp. M12)*
Pub: Dow Jones & Co., Inc.
Contact: Clare Hart, President
Ed: Sean Walters. **Description:** Nestle should sell Alcon because Nestle can't afford to be complacent as its peers have made changes to their portfolios to boost competitiveness. Nestle's stake in Alcon and L'Oreal have been ignored by investors and Nestle could realize better value by strengthening its nutrition division through acquisitions.

46694 ■ *"Will Workers Be Left To Build It Here?"* in *Boston Business Journal (Vol. 31, June 3, 2011, No. 19, pp. 1)*
Pub: Boston Business Journal
Ed: Kyle Alspach. **Description:** Lack of skilled workers has resulted in delayed expansion of local manufacturing operations in Massachusetts. Acme Packet Inc. expects to add only 10 jobs by the end of 2011.

46695 ■ *"William Barr III; President, Co-Founder, Universal Windows Direct, 33"* in *Crain's Cleveland Business (November 19, 2007)*
Pub: Crain Communications Inc.
Ed: David Bennett. **Description:** Profile of William Barr III, the president and co-founder of Universal Windows Direct, a manufacturer of vinyl windows and siding, whose successful salesmanship and leadership has propelled his company forward.

46696 ■ *"Wing and a Prayer"* in *Canadian Business (Vol. 81, November 10, 2008, No. 19, pp. 70)*
Pub: Rogers Media Inc.
Contact: Tony Viner, President
Ed: Sean Silcoff. **Description:** The 61st Annual National Business Aviation Association convention in Orlando, Florida saw unabashed display of wealth and privilege, but the U.S. market meltdown and possible economic crash has raised questions on the industry's future. Statistical details included.

46697 ■ *"Winner: Caparo Group Plc"* in *Crain's Detroit Business (Vol. 24, March 24, 2008, No. 12, pp. 12)*
Pub: Crain Communications Inc.
Contact: Rance E. Crain, President
Ed: Brent Snavely. **Description:** London-based Caparo Group plc saw its acquisition of Voestalpine Polynorm as an opportunity to gain a foothold in the North American automotive industry. Caparo was impressed with the company's breadth of manufacturing capabilities and quality systems as well as with the management team.

46698 ■ *"With Algoma Steel Gone, Is Stelco Next?"* in *Globe & Mail (April 16, 2007, pp. B1)*
Ed: Greg Keenan. **Description:** Speculation in Canadian steel industry over possible sale of Stelco Inc. too after the sale of Algoma Steel Inc. to Essar Global Ltd. is discussed.

46699 ■ *"Worry No. 1 at Auto Show: Recession"* in *Crain's Detroit Business (Vol. 24, January 21, 2008, No. 3, pp. 1)*
Pub: Crain Communications Inc. - Detroit
Contact: Keith Crain, Chairman
Ed: Brent Snavely. **Description:** Recession fears clouded activity at the 2008 Annual North American International Auto Show. Automakers are expecting to see a drop in sales due to slow holiday retail spending as well as fallout from the subprime lending crisis.

46700 ■ *"Wrigley's Juicy Feud"* in *Crain's Chicago Business (Vol. 31, May 5, 2008, No. 18, pp. 1)*
Pub: Crain Communications Inc.
Contact: Todd Johnson, Publisher
Ed: David Sterrett. **Description:** Discusses the sale of Wm. Wrigley Jr. Co. to Mars Inc. and Warren Buffett for $23 billion as well as the intra-family feuding

which has existed for nearly a decade since William Wrigley Jr. took over as CEO of the company following his father's death.

46701 ■ "Wrigley's a Rich Meal for Mars" in Crain's Chicago Business (Vol. 31, May 5, 2008, No. 18, pp. 2)
Pub: Crain Communications Inc.
Contact: Todd Johnson, Publisher
Ed: Steven R. Strahler. Description: Mars Inc. will have to manage wisely in order to make their acquisition of Wm. Wrigley Jr. Co. profitable due to the high selling price of Wrigley which far exceeds the industry norm. Statistical data included.

46702 ■ "Xerox Diverts Waste from Landfills" in Canadian Electronics (Vol. 23, February 2008, No. 1, pp. 1)
Description: Xerox Corporation revealed that it was able to divert more than two billion pounds of electronic waste from landfills through waste-free initiatives. The company's program, which was launched in 1991, covers waste avoidance in imaging supplies and parts reuse. Environmental priorities are also integrated into manufacturing operations.

46703 ■ "Xstrata and CAW Get Tentative Deal' in Globe & Mail (February 2, 2007, pp. B3)
Ed: Andy Hoffman. Description: The agreement between Xstrata PLC and Canadian Auto Workers union over wage hike is discussed.

46704 ■ "Young Giants" in Canadian Business (Vol. 79, August 14, 2006, No. 16-17, pp. 47)
Ed: Brad Purdy. Description: New generations of young chiefs of oil and gas companies in Canada, are featured.

46705 ■ "Zakkamono Taps Growing Market for Collectibles" in Hawaii Business (Vol. 54, September 2008, No. 3, pp. 68)
Ed: Casey Chin. Description: Profile of Zakkamono, a business that designs and sells designer toys, shirts and other collectibles; the first toys being Mousubi and Miao figurines. Owners Zakka and Rae Huo say that one of the business' challenges is finding manufacturing resources. Other details about Zakkamono are discussed.

46706 ■ "Zebra's Changing Stripes" in Crain's Chicago Business (Vol. 31, November 17, 2008, No. 46, pp. 4)
Pub: Crain Communications Inc.
Contact: Todd Johnson, Publisher
Ed: John Pletz. Description: Zebra Technologies Corp., the world's largest manufacturer of bar-code printers is profiled; the company's stock has plunged with shares declining 40 percent in the past three months grinding the firm's growth to a halt. Zebra's plans to regain revenue growth are also discussed.

STATISTICAL SOURCES

46707 ■ RMA Annual Statement Studies
Pub: Risk Management Association
Contact: Kevin M. Blakey, President
Released: Annual. Price: $105; $175. Description: Contains composite balance sheets and income statements for more than 360 industries, including the accounting, auditing, and bookkeeping industries. Also contains five years of comparative historical data for discerning trends. Includes 16 commonly used ratios, computed for most of the size groupings for nearly every industry.

TRADE PERIODICALS

46708 ■ CAMM News
Pub: Canadian Association of Moldmakers
Contact: David Palmer, Chairman
E-mail: david.palmer@applasman.ca
URL(s): www.camm.ca/resources.asp. Ed: Patricia Papp, Editor. Released: Quarterly, 5-6/year. Description: Contains items of interest to members of the moldmaking industry. Recurring features include editorials, information on education and shows, letters

to the editor, a calendar of events, reports of meetings, news of educational opportunities, and columns titled Technical Corner and Members in the News.

46709 ■ Composites in Manufacturing
Pub: Society of Manufacturing Engineers
Contact: Mark C. Tomlinson, Executive Director
URL(s): www.sme.org. Released: Quarterly. Price: $108, U.S. nonmembers; $120, Canada and Mexico nonmembers. Description: Covers composites and advanced composite materials from development through application. Recurring features include a calendar of events, news of educational opportunities, industry news, and notices of publications available.

46710 ■ Compoundings
Pub: Independent Lubricant Manufacturers Association
Contact: Brenda Gillinson, Manager, Corporate Communications
E-mail: bgillinson@ilma.org
URL(s): www.ilma.org; www.compoundings.org. Ed: Michael Cannizzaro, Editor, editor@ilma.org. Released: Monthly. Price: Included in membership; $150, nonmembers in the U.S. Description: Presents timely technical and marketing news about the lubricant manufacturing industry. Covers trends, new products, legislative, and regulatory information. Also focuses on Association members and events.

46711 ■ Electrical Product News
Pub: Business Marketing & Publishing Inc.
URL(s): www.epnweb.com/index.html. Ed: George B. Young, Editor, editor@epnweb.com. Released: Monthly. Description: Covers electrical products and distributor services. Provides information on new products, product applications, manufacturer programs supporting product sales, features added to existing products, special promotions and incentive programs, and marketing/sales news. Recurring features include letters to the editor, news of research, reports of meetings, and columns titled Telemarketing and Taxes.

46712 ■ Industrial Laser Solutions
Pub: PennWell Publishing Co.
URL(s): www.industrial-lasers.comwww.omeda.com/ils/. Ed: Laureen Belleville, Editor, laureenb@pennwell.com. Released: Bimonthly. Price: Free. Description: Devoted exclusively to the increased productivity and profitability of industrial lasers. Offers current information on the application of lasers in material processing, lasers on the production line, new systems and products, technical and economic analyses, company information, business news and more.

46713 ■ Manufacturer's Mart
Pub: Manufacturers' Mart Publications
URL(s): www.manufacturersmart.com. Released: Monthly

46714 ■ Manufacturing and Technology News
Pub: Publishers & Producers
URL(s): www.manufacturingnews.com. Ed: Richard McCormack, Editor, richard@manufacturingnews.com. Released: 20 issues /year. Price: $495, Individuals /year. Description: Relates breaking news on manufacturing programs and policies, electronic commerce, new manufacturing technologies, and techniques. Carries guest editorials. Recurring features include letters to the editor, interviews, news of research, reports of meetings, book reviews, and notices of publications available.

46715 ■ The MFP Report
Pub: Bissett Communications Corp.
Contact: Brian Bissett, Editor
E-mail: bbissett@ix.netcom.com
URL(s): www.mfpreport.com. Released: Monthly Price: $699, Individuals; $739, Other countries. Description: Offers business intelligence on the latest multifunction peripherals business, market and technology issues, and their impact. Features standards, products, trade shows, and company features. Recurring features include interviews, news of research, and a collection.

46716 ■ SEMA News
Pub: Specialty Equipment Market Association
Contact: Chris Kersting, President
E-mail: chrisk@sema.org
URL(s): www.sema.org/Main/SemaOrgHome.aspx?ID=50435. Released: Monthly Price: free access for members. Description: Covers the automotive specialty, performance equipment, and accessory sectors. Recurring features include news of government and legislative actions, new products, international markets, and member and Association activities.

46717 ■ Teamwork
Pub: Dartnell Publications
URL(s): www.dartnellcorp.com/newsletters/teamwork.php. Released: Monthly. Price: $179, online only.; $249, print and online. Description: Focuses on successful teamwork in manufacturing and corporate businesses. Recurring features include columns titled What Would You Do?, Test Yourself and See, and Teamwork in Action.

VIDEOCASSETTES/ AUDIOCASSETTES

46718 ■ Competing Through Manufacturing
Video Arts, Inc.
c/o Aim Learning Group
8238-40 Lehigh
Morton Grove, IL 60053-2615
Free: 877-444-2230
Fax: (416)252-2155
Co. E-mail: service@aimlearninggroup.com
URL: http://www.aimlearninggroup.com
Released: 1989. Price: $2,890. Description: These three 50-minute videos will help you make your company competitive through innovative manufacturing. Availability: VHS; 8 mm; 3/4 U; Special order formats.

46719 ■ Concerns Quarterly with Footage from CBS News: General Business
Harcourt Brace College Publishers
301 Commerce St., Ste. 3700
Fort Worth, TX 76102
Ph: (817)334-7500
Free: 800-237-2665
Fax: (817)334-0947
Co. E-mail: info@harcourt.com
URL: http://www.hmhco.com
Released: 1995. Price: $80. Description: Video newsletter containing footage from such CBS programs as CBS Evening News, 48 Hours, Street Stories, and CBS This Morning. Provides information on such topics as ethical responsibilities in business, people in business, competition, manufacturing, and marketing. Comes with instructor's guide. Available at an annual subscription rate of $300.00. Availability: VHS.

46720 ■ Manufacturing Control in the Small Plant
SkillSoft
107 Northeastern Blvd.
Nashua, NH 03062
Ph: (603)324-3000
Free: 877-545-5763
Fax: (603)324-3009
Co. E-mail: information@skillsoft.com
URL: http://www.skillsoft.com
Contact: Chuck Moran, President
Released: 19??. Description: Part of an integrated course for anyone involved in the management and operation of a small company, or a small division of a large company. Availability: 3/4 U.

TRADE SHOWS AND CONVENTIONS

46721 ■ Design & Manufacturing Midwest
UBM Canon
2901 28th St., Ste. 100
Santa Monica, CA 90405-2975
Ph: (310)445-4200

Fax: (310)445-4299
URL: http://www.ubmcanon.com
URL(s): dmmidwest.designnews.com. **Frequency:** Annual. **Audience:** Trade professionals and industry professionals. **Principal Exhibits:** Process control/automation, compressors and air equipment, computers in manufacturing, fluid power, general manufacturing, lubrication, heat treatment, lasers in manufacturing, machine tools, weighing sensors and instrumentation, drives and controls, pumps and valves, safety equipment, welding equipment, design in engineering, engineering products and materials, assembly, automation and robotics.

46722 ■ Plant Maintenance and Design Engineering Show/Montreal (PMDS)
Canadian Fluid Power Association
1250 Marlborough Ct.
Oakville, ON, Canada L6H 2W7
Ph: (905)844-6822
URL: http://www.cfpa.ca
Contact: John Lamb, Chairman
URL(s): www.pmds.ca/. **Audience:** Managers, engineers, operations and practitioners. **Principal Exhibits:** Original equipment manufacturing, and the aftermarket of maintenance, repair/overhaul and operating of industrial machinery and equipment.

46723 ■ Wisconsin Manufacturing & Technology Show
Expo Productions Inc.
510 Hartbrook Dr.
Hartland, WI 53029
Ph: (262)367-5500
Free: 800-367-5520
Fax: (262)367-9956
Co. E-mail: expo@execpc.com
URL: http://www.expoproductionsinc.com
URL(s): www.epishows.com/wmts/. **Frequency:** Biennial. **Audience:** Manufacturing and technology industry professionals. **Principal Exhibits:** Metal working machinery and related manufacturing equipment, supplies, and services machine tools. **Dates and Locations:** 2015 Oct 06-08, Wisconsin State Fair Park, West Allis, WI. **Telecommunication Services:** carrie@epishows.com.

CONSULTANTS

46724 ■ AGH & Associates
69 E Alden Ln.
Lake Forest, IL 60045-1297
Ph: (847)295-9220
Contact: Arthur Helt, Jr., President
E-mail: aghelt@aol.com
Scope: Industrial consultants specializing in plant layout and design for warehouse, packing systems, cranes specifications, office layouts and material handling and material flow systems. Additional equipment selection and appraisal, manpower assessment, order processing and production scheduling and time motion studies. Industries served: steel service centers and manufacturing plants. **Founded:** 1983.

46725 ■ Anderson/Roethle Inc.
700 N Water St., Ste. 325
Milwaukee, WI 53202-4221
Ph: (414)276-0070
Fax: (414)276-4364
Co. E-mail: info@anderson-roethle.com
URL: http://www.anderson-roethle.com
Contact: Stanley C. Johnson, President
E-mail: scj@anderson-roethle.com
Scope: Provider of merger, acquisition and divestiture advisory services. Offers strategic planning, valuations and specialized M and A advisory services. **Founded:** 1963.

46726 ■ Blackford Associates
30 George Rd.
Contoocook, NH 03229
Ph: (603)225-2228
Fax: (603)225-2228
Contact: John M. Blackford, Owner
Scope: Provider of general management consulting to smaller manufacturing companies. Counsels chief executive officers and presidents on strategy, organization, finances and operations. Areas of expertise

include the following: new products, services or markets; problems of expansion or retrenchment; financing and bank relations; morale, organization and training; budgeting and business plans; factory flow and inventory control; quality control and methods; cash flow problems; and financial information and controls. **Founded:** 1984.

46727 ■ Distribution Assistance
PO Box 1418
East Dennis, MA 02641-1418
Ph: (508)385-9802
Fax: (508)385-9802
Co. E-mail: atsilk@gis.net
Contact: Mildred T. Silk, Secretary Treasurer
Scope: Developer of management logistics consultant solutions. It serves the banking, consumer products, financial services, insurance, non-profit, paper and public warehousing industries. **Founded:** 1985. **Publications:** "Improving Warehouse Operations"; "Fundamentals of Traffic Management"; "Advanced Transportation Management"; "Cost Effective Worldwide Product Delivery"; "Supply Chain Management". **Seminars:** Professional development Logistics and Supply Chain Operations Seminars; ECR/Quick Response High Efficiency Supply Chain Management and Supply Chain Management in the Nineties.

46728 ■ Obie Good & Associates [SEM Obie Good & Associates]
122 Lake Lure Dr.
Alma, GA 31510
Ph: (912)632-6208
Fax: (912)632-6208
Contact: Obie Good, President
Scope: Manufacturing consultant in metal working field for commercial and military products, manufacturing management and engineering.

46729 ■ Hewitt Development Enterprises (HDE)
1717 N Bayshore Dr., Ste. 2154
Miami, FL 33132
Ph: (305)372-0941
Fax: (305)372-0941
Co. E-mail: info@hewittdevelopment.com
URL: http://www.hewittdevelopment.com
Contact: Robert G. Hewitt, Principal
E-mail: bob@hewittdevelopment.com
Scope: Specializes in strategic planning; profit enhancement; start-up businesses; interim management; crisis management; turnarounds; production planning; just-in-time inventory management; and project management. Serves senior management (CEOs, CFOs, division presidents, etc.) and acquirers of distressed businesses. **Founded:** 1985.

46730 ■ Industrial Management Services
103 Woodmancy Ln.
Fayetteville, NY 13066-1534
Ph: (315)637-8966
Contact: Lawrence H. Wishart, Owner
Scope: Assists manufacturers in minimizing their manufacturing costs by maximizing the return on investments in and expenditures for facilities and labor. This is accomplished by determining where improvements can be made, evaluating the potentials in each selected area and developing ways of causing the potential improvement to be accomplished. Specific areas include: Economic feasibility studies, labor utilization studies, work measurement, expense reduction studies, facilities planning, long range planning, management controls, profit improvement surveys, incentive systems, design of manufacturing systems, plant layout, cost improvement programs and assistance with safety programs. **Founded:** 1954.

46731 ■ The Institute for Management Excellence
PO Box 193
Trabuco Canyon, CA 92679-0193
Ph: (949)667-1012
URL: http://www.itstime.com
Contact: Barbara Taylor, Executive Director
E-mail: btaylor@itstime.com
Scope: Management consulting and training focuses on improving productivity, using practices and creative techniques. Practices based on the compa-

ny's theme: It's time for new ways of doing business. Industries served: public sector, law enforcement, finance or banking, non profit, computers or high technology, education, human resources, utilities. **Founded:** 1995. **Publications:** "Income Without a Job," 2008; "The Other Side of Midnight, 2000: An Executive Guide to the Year 2000 Problem"; "Concordance to the Michael Teachings"; "Handbook of Small Business Advertising"; "The Personality Game"; "How to Market Yourself for Success". **Seminars:** The Personality Game; Power Path Seminars; Productivity Plus; Sexual Harassment and Discrimination Prevention; Worker's Comp Cost Reduction; Americans with Disabilities Act; In Search of Identify: Clarifying Corporate Culture.

46732 ■ The Manhattan Consulting Group Inc.
214 E 54th St., Ste. 600
New York, NY 10022-6207
Ph: (212)751-3000
Contact: Thomas H. Kieren, President
Scope: Specializes in industry and corporate performance studies. It serves the pharmaceuticals, food, fabricated products, government and other related industrial, commercial and process industries. **Founded:** 1983. **Publications:** "Customer Satisfaction in the Electronics and Electrical Industries," Connector Technology Magazine; "Customer Satisfaction in the Chemical Industry," Chemical Week Magazine; "Customer Satisfaction in the Food Industry," Part 1, Food Processing Magazine; "Organization Change Issues for the 90s," Business Age Magazine; "Assessing the Viability of the Manufacturing Company," Commercial Lending Review.

46733 ■ Northwest Trade Adjustment Assistance Center
1200 Westlake Ave. N, Ste. 802
Seattle, WA 98109
Ph: (206)622-2730
Free: 800-667-8087
Fax: (206)622-1105
Co. E-mail: nwtaac@nwtaac.org
URL: http://www.nwtaac.org
Contact: Gary Kuhar, Executive Director
Scope: Provider of up to 75 percent cost paid technical assistance to help manufacturers improve their competitive position relative to imported products. areas of expertise include website design, ISO 9000 certification, new market identification, new product introduction, business plans, marketing plans, upgrading of product design and packaging, improvement of distribution, use of new technology, inventory cost reduction, production cost reduction, development of employee incentive plans and preparation of loan applications, industries served, manufacturers and food processors. **Founded:** 1979.

46734 ■ The Walden Group
968 Main St., Ste. 8
Wakefield, MA 01880-3979
Ph: (781)246-7599
Fax: (781)245-7598
URL: http://www.thewaldengroup.com
Contact: Don Harnson, Senior Partner
Scope: Provider of solutions for firms in the distribution and manufacturing arenas. Specializes in small to medium sized enterprises. Services include distribution and manufacturing operations, information system selection and implementation and self managing team implementation. Industries served: all. **Seminars:** New Age Warehousing; How to Control Manufacturing Without Acronyms; Information Technology in Manufacturing Today; 7 Steps to a Successful Manufacturing System.

FRANCHISES AND BUSINESS OPPORTUNITIES

46735 ■ The Gutter Guys
The Gutter Guys Franchisor, Inc.
2547 Fire Rd., Ste. E-5
Egg Harbor Township, NJ 08234

Ph: (609)646-1400
URL: http://www.thegutterguys.com
Description: Seamless gutter manufacturing, installation and maintenance. **No. of Franchise Units:** 10. **No. of Company-Owned Units:** 4. **Founded:** 1988. **Franchised:** 2000. **Equity Capital Needed:** $36,500 liquid; $90,000 total investment range. **Franchise Fee:** $15,000. **Training:** Yes.

46736 ■ Old Hippy Wood Products Inc.
2415 80 Ave.
Edmonton, AB, Canada T6P 1N3
Ph: (780)448-1163
Free: 888-464-9700
Co. E-mail: jo@oldhippy.com
URL: http://www.oldhippy.com
Description: Manufacturers high quality solid wood furniture in Pine, Birch, Cherry, Maple and Oak. From the manufacturing centre in Edmonton, Old Hippy supplies Canadian franchise-store outlets and is proud to be an experienced exporter to Japan. Old Hippy furniture is destined to become a cherished antique. **No. of Franchise Units:** 8. **No. of Company-Owned Units:** 1. **Founded:** 1990. **Franchised:** 1992. **Equity Capital Needed:** $125,000 required investment; $25,000 start-up capital required. **Franchise Fee:** $15,000. **Training:** Initial training and ongoing support provided.

RESEARCH CENTERS

46737 ■ California State Polytechnic University, Pomona - Apparel Technology and Research Center (ATRC)
College of Agriculture
3801 W Temple Ave., Rm. 45-123
Pomona, CA 91768
Ph: (909)869-2082
Fax: (909)869-4454
Co. E-mail: pkilduff@csupomona.edu
URL: http://www.csupomona.edu/~atrc
Contact: Prof. Peter Kilduff, Director
Scope: Apparel and textile market research, strategic analysis and apparel technology transfer. **Services:** Consulting and technical assistance. **Founded:** 1992. **Educational Activities:** ATRC Seminars (Monthly).

46738 ■ Grand Valley State University - Michigan Small Business and Technology Development Center (MI-SBTDC)
1020-L William Seidman Center
50 Front Ave. SW
Grand Rapids, MI 49504
Ph: (616)331-7480
Fax: (616)331-7485
Co. E-mail: sbtdchq@gvsu.edu
URL: http://misbtdc.org
Contact: Carol Lopucki, Director
E-mail: lopuckic@gvsu.edu
Description: Provides a full-range of services for a variety of small businesses including: counseling; training; programs for a variety of needs, from how to get started, to financing; effective selling and e-commerce as well as how to develop business plans. Also provides research help and advocacy. **Scope:** Manufacturing, financing, and international business information (particularly the export process) for small businesses. Resources for the export

process includes determining and detailing international feasibility, foreign market entry plans, and responding to international inquiries. Foreign market information includes business etiquette and negotiating, country demographics, detailed tax information, financing sources, industry specific information, intellectual property rights, market contracts, rules and regulations, specific market information, and tariff reduction schedules. **Services:** Business management consulting. **Founded:** 1983. **Publications:** *Changing the Face of the American Economy--A Resource Guide for the Michigan Woman Business Owner* (Biennial).

46739 ■ National Center for Manufacturing Sciences (NCMS)
3025 Boardwalk
Ann Arbor, MI 48108-3230
Ph: (734)995-0300
Free: 800-222-6267
Fax: (734)995-1150
Co. E-mail: info@ncms.org
Contact: John A. Decaire, President
Scope: Fundamental manufacturing sciences, process technology and capabilities, behavior of materials during manufacturing, machine mechanics and components, precision manufacturing, sensor and control techniques, test and evaluation methods, quality assurance and reliability techniques, equipment and component standards, manufacturing systems design, electronic manufacturing. Technology, and environmental manufacturing (prevention, minimization, treatment, remediation and monitor control). **Founded:** 1986. **Publications:** *SOLV-DB® - Solvents Database*; *NCMS at a Glance.* **Educational Activities:** NCMS Annual meetings with exhibits.

46740 ■ North American Manufacturing Research Institution of SME
1 SME Dr.
Dearborn, MI 48128-2408
Ph: (313)425-3000
Free: 800-733-4763
Fax: (313)425-3400
Co. E-mail: membership@sme.org
URL: http://www.sme.org/namri
Contact: Dennis S. Bray, President
Description: A division of the Society of Manufacturing Engineers. Represents individuals engaged in manufacturing research and technology development. Works to promote and stimulate research, writing, publication, and dissemination of new manufacturing technology; works to coordinate efforts and cooperate with counterpart organizations worldwide; works to provide a forum for the active community of researchers whose work contributes in furthering manufacturing technology and productivity. **Scope:** Manufacturing research and technology development. Provides researchers and industry practitioners with a means of exchanging ideas and sharing findings with leading researchers in the field of manufacturing. **Founded:** 1932. **Subscriptions:** archival material books clippings periodicals. **Publications:** *Proceedings of the North American Manufacturing Research Institution of the Society of Manufacturing Engineers* (Annual). **Educational Activities:** NAMRI/SME Annual meeting and conference; NAMRI/SME International Forum; North American Manufacturing

Research Conference (Annual), in June, collocated with ASME Manufacturing Science and Engineering Conference. **Awards:** NAMRI/SME Outstanding Paper Award (Annual); NAMRI/SME S.M. Wu Research Implementation Award (Annual).

46741 ■ Ohio State University - Engineering Research Center for Net Shape Manufacturing (ERC/NSM)
339 Baker Systems
1971 Neil Ave.
Columbus, OH 43210-1271
Ph: (614)292-9267
Fax: (614)292-7219
Co. E-mail: altan.1@osu.edu
URL: http://nsmwww.eng.ohio-state.edu
Contact: Dr. Taylan Altan, Director
URL(s): nsm.eng.ohio-state.edu. **Scope:** Manufacturing processes, specifically the manufacture of discrete parts to net or near-net dimensions, sheet forming, precision forging, tube/sheet hydroforming, machining, die/mold manufacturing. **Services:** Continuing education courses. **Founded:** 1986. **Publications:** *Technical papers and presentations.*

46742 ■ Rochester Institute of Technology - Center for Integrated Manufacturing Studies (CIMS)
Louise M. Slaughter Hall, Bldg. 78
111 Lomb Memorial Dr.
Rochester, NY 14623-5608
Ph: (585)475-5385
Fax: (585)475-5250
Co. E-mail: info@sustainability.rit.edu
URL: http://www.rit.edu/gis/research-centers/cims
Contact: Dr. Nabil Nasr, Director
Scope: Electronics, imaging, supplier integration, remanufacturing, ergonomics and simulation. Areas of study include total quality management, cycle time reduction, life cycle costs, product and process development, concurrent engineering, and integration theory. Special emphasis is on serving groups of companies to understand common requirements such as training and ISO 9000. process development, concurrent engineering, and integration theory. Special emphasis is on serving groups of companies to understand common requirements such as training and ISO 9000. **Services:** Extension services: for small businesses. **Founded:** 1992. **Educational Activities:** CIMS Training programs.

46743 ■ Tennessee Technological University - Center for Manufacturing Research (CMR)
PO Box 5077
Cookeville, TN 38505-0001
Ph: (931)372-3362
Fax: (931)372-6345
Co. E-mail: kcurrie@tntech.edu
URL: http://www.tntech.edu/cmr/home
Contact: Prof. Kenneth R. Currie, Director
Scope: Control of processes and equipment; next generation materials and manufacturing processes; integrated product/process realization; and pervasive simulation and modeling. **Services:** Material testing, seminars, workshops, and short courses. **Founded:** 1984. **Publications:** *CMR Annual report* (Annual); *Executive Summary* (Annual); *CMR Research reports.* **Educational Activities:** Center for Manufacturing Research Conferences; Industrial Study-Work Program.

CPSIA information can be obtained
at www.ICGtesting.com
Printed in the USA
FFOW04n0047120315
11752FF

9 781573 025850